Bruce Rat

Checked Out To:

Mike ADAMS

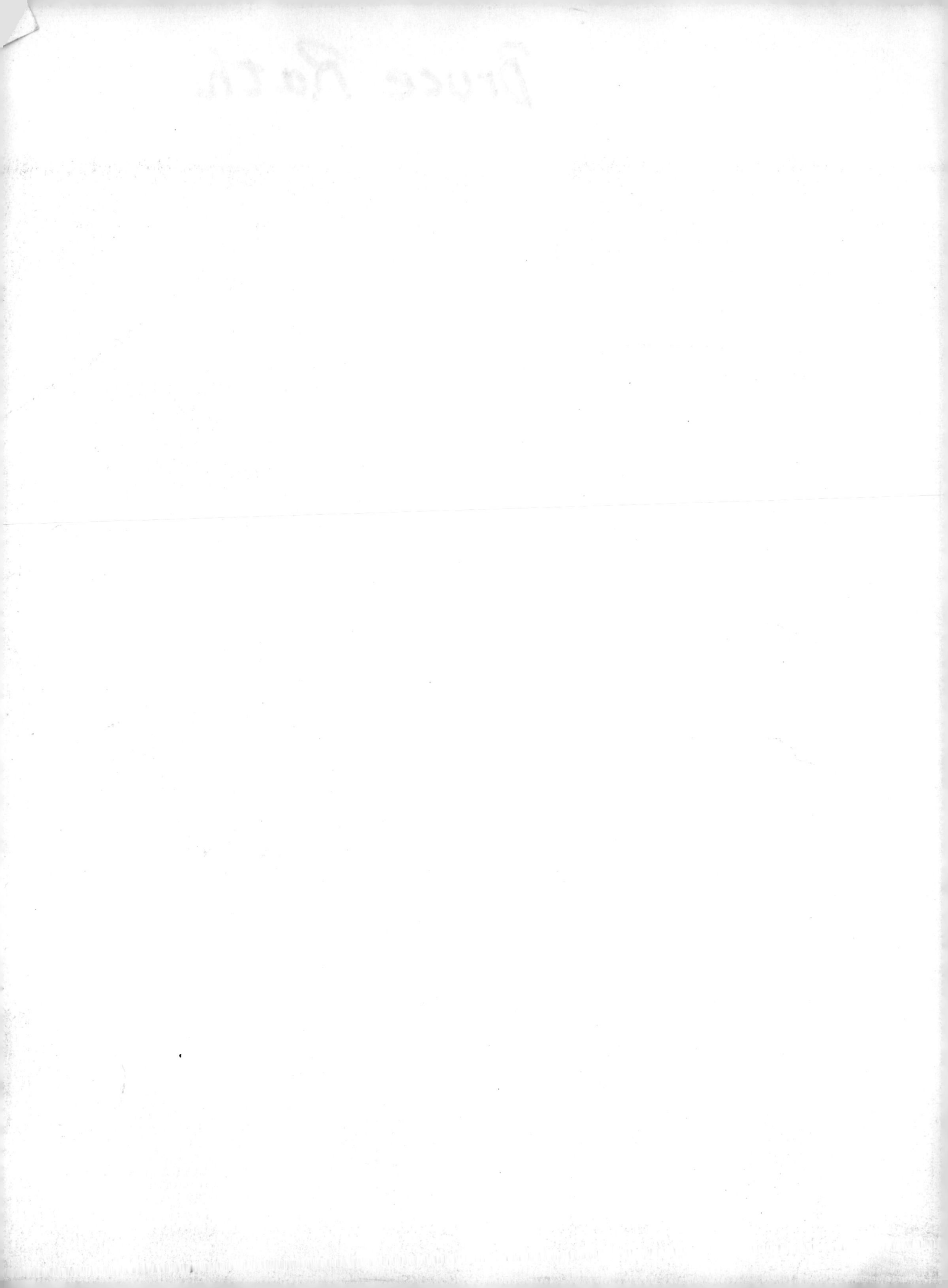

JONES & BARTLETT LEARNING

CDX Automotive

Fundamentals of

Medium/Heavy Duty Commercial Vehicle Systems

Owen C. Duffy
Professor, Centennial College

Gus Wright
Professor, Centennial College

JONES & BARTLETT
LEARNING

World Headquarters
Jones & Bartlett Learning
5 Wall Street
Burlington, MA 01803
978-443-5000
info@jblearning.com
www.jblearning.com

Jones & Bartlett Learning books and products are available through most bookstores and online booksellers. To contact Jones & Bartlett Learning directly, call 800-832-0034, fax 978-443-8000, or visit our website, www.jblearning.com.

Substantial discounts on bulk quantities of Jones & Bartlett Learning publications are available to corporations, professional associations, and other qualified organizations. For details and specific discount information, contact the special sales department at Jones & Bartlett Learning via the above contact information or send an email to specialsales@jblearning.com.

For every task, the following safety requirements must be strictly enforced: Comply with personal and environmental safety practices associated with clothing and eye protection; hand tools; power equipment; proper ventilation; and the handling, storage, and disposal of chemicals/materials in accordance with local, state, and federal safety and environmental regulations.

Production Credits
Chief Executive Officer: Ty Field
President: James Homer
Chief Product Officer: Eduardo Moura
Executive Publisher: Vernon Anthony
Acquisitions Editor—CDX Automotive: Ian Andrew
Managing Editor—CDX Automotive: Amanda J. Mitchell
Editorial Assistant: Jamie Dinh
VP of Marketing: Alisha Weisman
Associate Director of Production: Julie C. Bolduc
Production Manager: Tina Chen
Senior Marketing Manager: Brian Rooney
VP, Manufacturing and Inventory Control: Therese Connell
Composition: B-books, Ltd.
Cover Design: Kristin E. Parker
Rights & Media Manager: Joanna Lundeen
Rights & Media Research Assistant: Robert Boder
Cover Image: © Max Popov/123RF.com
Printing and Binding: RR Donnelley
Cover Printing: RR Donnelley

ISBN: 978-1-284-04116-3

Library of Congress Cataloging-in-Publication Data
Unavailable at time of printing.

6048

Printed in the United States of America
20 19 18 17 16   10 9 8 7 6 5 4

BRIEF CONTENTS

SECTION I **Foundation and Safety** 2

CHAPTER 1 Introduction to Heavy-Duty Commercial Vehicles 4
CHAPTER 2 Careers, Employability Skills, and Workplace Practices 34
CHAPTER 3 Safety, Personal Protection Equipment, and First Aid 68
CHAPTER 4 Basic Tools and Lubricants 106
CHAPTER 5 Fasteners, Locking Devices, and Lifting Equipment 162

SECTION II **Electrical and Electronic Systems** 202

CHAPTER 6 Principles of Electricity 204
CHAPTER 7 Generating Electricity 226
CHAPTER 8 Electric Circuits and Circuit Protection 248
CHAPTER 9 Circuit Control Devices 274
CHAPTER 10 Electrical Test Instruments 304
CHAPTER 11 Commercial Vehicle Batteries 328
CHAPTER 12 Advanced Battery Technologies 350
CHAPTER 13 Servicing Commercial Vehicle Batteries 370
CHAPTER 14 Heavy-Duty Starting Systems and Circuits 392
CHAPTER 15 Charging Systems 428
CHAPTER 16 Electrical Wiring and Circuit Diagrams 460
CHAPTER 17 Body Electrical Systems—Lighting Systems 488
CHAPTER 18 Body Electrical Systems—Instrumentation 510
CHAPTER 19 Electronic Signal Processing Principles 532
CHAPTER 20 Sensors 556
CHAPTER 21 On-Board Vehicle Networks 596
CHAPTER 22 On-Board Diagnostics 626

SECTION III **Suspension, Steering, and Brakes** 658

CHAPTER 23 Commercial Vehicle Tires 660
CHAPTER 24 Wheel Rims and Hubs 704
CHAPTER 25 Front Axles and Vehicle Alignment Factors 728
CHAPTER 26 Truck Frames 762
CHAPTER 27 Suspension Systems 792
CHAPTER 28 Steering Systems and Integral Steering Gears 840
CHAPTER 29 Braking Fundamentals 880
CHAPTER 30 Air Brake Foundation Systems and Air Brake Circuits 924
CHAPTER 31 Servicing Air Brake Systems 968

CHAPTER 32 Anti-Lock Braking, Vehicle Stability, and Collision Avoidance Systems 1036

CHAPTER 33 Fundamentals of Hydraulic and Air-Over-Hydraulic Braking Systems 1066

CHAPTER 34 Fifth Wheels and Hitching Devices 1102

SECTION IV **Drive Trains 1136**

CHAPTER 35 Heavy-Duty Clutches 1138

CHAPTER 36 Servicing Heavy-Duty Clutches 1166

CHAPTER 37 Basic Gearing Concepts 1192

CHAPTER 38 Standard Transmissions 1210

CHAPTER 39 Servicing Standard Transmissions 1260

CHAPTER 40 Automated Manual Transmissions 1298

CHAPTER 41 Torque Converters 1340

CHAPTER 42 Planetary Gear Concepts 1370

CHAPTER 43 Hydraulically Controlled Automatic Transmissions 1392

CHAPTER 44 Maintaining Automatic Transmissions 1420

CHAPTER 45 Electronically Controlled Automatic Transmissions 1444

CHAPTER 46 Driveshaft Systems 1530

CHAPTER 47 Heavy-Duty Truck Drive Axles 1570

CHAPTER 48 Servicing and Maintaining Drive Axles 1604

CHAPTER 49 Hybrid Drive Systems and Series-Type Hybrid Drives 1642

CHAPTER 50 Allison EV Drive Hybrid Systems 1668

SECTION V **Heating, Ventilation, and Air Conditioning 1690**

CHAPTER 51 Principles of Heating and Air-Conditioning Systems 1692

CHAPTER 52 Servicing Heating and Air-Conditioning Systems 1730

CHAPTER 53 Trailer Refrigeration 1768

SECTION VI **Hydraulics 1786**

CHAPTER 54 Hydraulics 1788

SECTION VII **Preventative Maintenance and Inspection 1836**

CHAPTER 55 Preventative Maintenance and Inspection 1838

Appendix A 2014 NATEF Medium/Heavy-Duty Truck Accreditation Task List Correlation Guide 1886

Glossary 1902

Index 1932

CONTENTS

SECTION I **Foundation and Safety** 2

CHAPTER 1 Introduction to Heavy-Duty Commercial Vehicles 4
Introduction 6
Classification by Operational Characteristics 6
Vocational Applications of Commercial Vehicles 8
Design Factors for Vocational Applications 13
Classification of Heavy Vehicles by Weight and Length 18
Classification of Heavy Vehicles by Combination 21
Common Terms and Conventions 25

CHAPTER 2 Careers, Employability Skills, and Workplace Practices 34
Introduction 36
Careers in the Commercial Vehicle Industry 36
Employability Skills 40
Professional Workplace Habits 52
Vehicle and Service Resources 55

CHAPTER 3 Safety, Personal Protection Equipment, and First Aid 68
Introduction 70
Safety Overview 70
Standard Safety Measures 74
Hazardous Materials Safety 80
Shop Safety Inspections 89
Personal Protective Equipment 90
Injury Protection Practices 95
First Aid Principles 97

CHAPTER 4 Basic Tools and Lubricants 106
Introduction 108
Basic Tool Preparation and Safety 108
Tools and Equipment Fundamentals 109
Precision Measuring Tools 110
Power Tools 117
Air Tools 119
Hand Tools 120
Additional Tools 134
Diagnostic Equipment 136
Servicing Equipment 138
Oxyacetylene 139
Cleaning Equipment 140
Electrical Equipment 141
Fluids and Lubricants 145
Metals 151
Materials 152

CHAPTER 5 Fasteners, Locking Devices, and Lifting Equipment 162
Introduction 164
Locking Devices and Tools 164
Fasteners and Torque 170
Locking Device Measuring Tools 172
Helical Inserts 175
Locking Pins and Keys 175
Gaskets and Seals 177
Lifting in the Shop 185
Types of Lifting and Moving Equipment 186
Using Lifting Equipment 193

SECTION II **Electrical and Electronic Systems** 202

CHAPTER 6 Principles of Electricity 204
Introduction 206
Electrical Fundamentals 207
Basic Electricity 208
Understanding Current 210
Electrical Versus Electronic Circuits 220

CHAPTER 7 Generating Electricity 226
Introduction 228
Sources of Electricity 228
Electricity from Friction 228
Electricity from Light 230
Electricity from Heat 230
Electricity from Pressure 232
Electricity from Magnetism 232
Electricity from Chemistry 241
Fuel Cells 242

CHAPTER 8 Electric Circuits and Circuit Protection 248
Introduction 250
Current Flow in Circuits 250
Circuit Classification 252
Circuit Protection Devices 263
Inspecting and Testing Circuit Protection Devices 267

CHAPTER 9 Circuit Control Devices 274
Introduction 276
Simple Control Devices 276
Complex Electronic Controls 289

CHAPTER 10 Electrical Test Instruments 304
Introduction 306
Test Lights 306
Multimeters 308
Electrical Measurement with Multimeters 312
Circuit Tracers 319
Graphing Meters and Oscilloscopes 319
Vibration Analyzers 321
Electronic Service Tools—Scanners 321

CHAPTER 11 Commercial Vehicle Batteries 328
Introduction 330
What Is a Battery? 330
Types and Classification of Batteries 333
Battery Construction and Operation 335

CHAPTER 12 Advanced Battery Technologies 350
Introduction 352
Types of Advanced Batteries 352
Battery Management Systems 359

CHAPTER 13 Servicing Commercial Vehicle Batteries 370
Introduction 372
Battery Service Precautions 373
Causes of Battery Failure 374
Battery Inspecting, Testing, and Maintenance 375
Jump-Starting Vehicles 383
Measuring Parasitic Draw 384
Identify and Test Low-Voltage Disconnect (LVD) Systems 385
Battery Recycling 386

CHAPTER 14 Heavy-Duty Starting Systems and Circuits 392
Introduction 394
Fundamentals of Starting Systems and Circuits 394
Types of DC Motors 399
Components of Starters 403
Starter Control Circuits 408
Starting System Testing 414

CHAPTER 15 Charging Systems 428
Introduction 430
Alternator Functions 431
Alternator Advantages 431
Alternator Principles 432
Alternator Components 433
Dual Alternators—Paralleling 446
Alternator Wiring Connections 446
Charging System Diagnosis 449
Overhauling an Alternator 454

CHAPTER 16 Electrical Wiring and Circuit Diagrams 460
Introduction 462
Electric Wiring 462
Wiring Failure and Repair 468
Wiring Diagrams 471

CHAPTER 17 Body Electrical Systems—Lighting Systems 488
Introduction 490
Fundamentals of the Body Electrical System 490
Lighting Systems 491
Trailer Cords and Plug 501

CHAPTER 18 Body Electrical Systems—Instrumentation 510
Introduction 512
Warning Lights 512
Gauge Operating Systems 515
Sending Units 519
Speedometers 522
Driver Information Screens 524
Troubleshooting Instrument Gauge Problems 526

CHAPTER 19 Electronic Signal Processing Principles.......... 532
Introduction.......... 534
Benefits of Electronic Control.......... 534
Elements of Electronic Signal Processing Systems.......... 538
Types of Electrical Signals.......... 539
Processing Function.......... 548

CHAPTER 20 Sensors.......... 556
Introduction.......... 558
Types of Sensors.......... 558
Sensors and Position Calculations.......... 575
Sensor Fault Detection Principles.......... 577
Maintenance of Sensors.......... 588

CHAPTER 21 On-Board Vehicle Networks.......... 596
Introduction.......... 598
Overview of On-Board Networks.......... 598
Network Classification.......... 599
Time Division Multiplexing.......... 603
Controlled Area Networks (CAN).......... 611
Wireless Network Communication.......... 617
Power Line Carrier (PLC) Communication.......... 618

CHAPTER 22 On-Board Diagnostics.......... 626
Introduction.......... 628
Fundamentals of HD-OBD.......... 628
Types of HD-OBD Monitors.......... 631
Maintaining HD-OBD.......... 641

SECTION III Suspension, Steering, and Brakes.......... 658

CHAPTER 23 Commercial Vehicle Tires.......... 660
Introduction.......... 662
Fundamentals of Commercial Vehicle Tires.......... 662
Tire Safety.......... 664
Types of Commercial Vehicle Tires.......... 667
Construction of Commercial Vehicle Tires.......... 673
Maintenance and Service of Commercial Tires.......... 683
Tire Diagnosis.......... 694

CHAPTER 24 Wheel Rims and Hubs.......... 704
Introduction.......... 706
Fundamentals of Wheels and Rims.......... 707
Wheel Types.......... 709
Types of Wheel Hubs.......... 716
Maintaining and Servicing Wheels and Hubs.......... 721

CHAPTER 25 Front Axles and Vehicle Alignment Factors.......... 728
Introduction.......... 730
Types and Functions of Non-Drive Axles.......... 730
Fundamentals of Vehicle Alignment.......... 736
Types of Wheel Alignment.......... 747
Performing Vehicle Alignments.......... 748

CHAPTER 26 Truck Frames.......... 762
Introduction.......... 764
Fundamentals of Frame Design.......... 764
Design and Construction of Frames.......... 769
Frame-Supported Attachments.......... 772
Maintenance and Service of Truck Frames.......... 777

CHAPTER 27 Suspension Systems.......... 792
Introduction.......... 794
Fundamentals of Suspension Systems.......... 794
Components of a Suspension System.......... 798
Types of Suspension Systems Found on Heavy-Duty Trucks.......... 802
Leaf Spring Systems.......... 802
Equalizing Beam Suspensions.......... 808
Air Spring Suspension Systems.......... 813
Electronically Controlled Air Suspension Systems.......... 817
Suspension System Inspection and Maintenance.......... 819

CHAPTER 28 Steering Systems and Integral Steering Gears.......... 840
Introduction.......... 842
Fundamentals of Steering Systems.......... 842
Steering System Classifications.......... 843
Components of Basic Steering Systems.......... 844
Hydraulic Components of Power Steering Systems.......... 857

Maintenance and Service of the Steering System 863
Maintenance and Service of the Hydraulic System 867

CHAPTER 29 Braking Fundamentals 880
Introduction 882
How Brakes Work 884
Types of Braking Systems 887
Air Brake Foundation Systems 890

CHAPTER 30 Air Brake Foundation Systems and Air Brake Circuits 924
Introduction 926
Advantages of Air Systems 926
Disadvantages of Air Systems 928
Air Brake Subsystems and Control Circuits 928
Components of the Air Supply System 930
Components of Air Delivery and Control Systems 944
Park/Emergency Brake Circuit 955
Trailer Air Circuits 957

CHAPTER 31 Servicing Air Brake Systems 968
Introduction 972
Safety During Brake System Service 972
Diagnosing Brake System Malfunctions 974
Conducting Preliminary Testing on Brake Systems 980
Servicing the Air Supply System 1006
Servicing Foundation Brakes 1010
Adjusting Air Brakes 1021
Maintaining Air Disc 1029

CHAPTER 32 Anti-Lock Braking, Vehicle Stability, and Collision Avoidance Systems 1036
Introduction 1038
Fundamentals of Anti-Lock Braking Systems 1038
Anti-Lock Braking System Components 1042
Enhancements to Anti-Lock Braking Systems 1052
Maintaining Anti-Lock Braking Systems 1060

CHAPTER 33 Fundamentals of Hydraulic and Air-Over-Hydraulic Braking Systems 1066
Introduction 1069
Fundamental Configurations for Hydraulic Braking Systems 1069
Foundation Components of Hydraulic Braking Systems 1071
Emergency/Hand Brakes 1074
Hydraulic Components of Hydraulic Brake Systems 1075
Hydraulic Brake Power-Assist Systems 1080
Air-Over-Hydraulic Braking Systems 1082
Park Brake and Emergency Circuits 1086
Hydraulic Brake Anti-Lock Braking System (ABS) 1088
Maintenance of Hydraulic Brake Systems 1090

CHAPTER 34 Fifth Wheels and Hitching Devices 1102
Introduction 1104
Fundamentals of Fifth Wheels and Hitching Devices 1105
Types of Fifth Wheels and Coupling Devices 1109
Construction of Fifth Wheels 1116
Troubleshooting Fifth Wheel Locking Complaints 1122
Maintenance and Service of Fifth Wheels and Upper Couplers 1122

SECTION IV Drive Trains 1136

CHAPTER 35 Heavy-Duty Clutches 1138
Introduction 1140
Fundamentals of Heavy-Duty Clutches 1140
Types and Design of Clutches 1142
Components of Clutches 1147

CHAPTER 36 Servicing Heavy-Duty Clutches 1166
Introduction 1168
Preventative Maintenance of Clutches 1168

Troubleshooting Clutch Problems..... 1172
Maintenance and Repair of a Clutch..... 1172

CHAPTER 37 Basic Gearing Concepts... 1192
Introduction..... 1194
Fundamentals of Gears..... 1195
Types of Gears..... 1201

CHAPTER 38 Standard Transmissions... 1210
Introduction..... 1212
Fundamentals of Transmissions..... 1212
Types of Sliding-Gear and Constant-Mesh Transmissions..... 1217
Single Countershaft Transmissions.. 1221
Multiple Countershaft Transmissions and Auxiliary Transmissions..... 1227
Auxiliary Sections..... 1231
Auxiliary Section Air Control..... 1243
Transfer Cases..... 1251
Power Take-Off Devices..... 1252

CHAPTER 39 Servicing Standard Transmissions..... 1260
Introduction..... 1262
Fundamentals of Standard Transmission Servicing..... 1262
Preventative Maintenance of Transmissions..... 1265
Troubleshooting Transmission System Problems..... 1268
Repair and Maintenance of Transmissions..... 1277
Analysis of Transmission Failure..... 1289

CHAPTER 40 Automated Manual Transmissions..... 1298
Introduction..... 1300
Types of Electronically Automated Manual Transmissions..... 1302
Operation of Automated Manual Transmissions..... 1306
Troubleshooting Automated Manual Transmissions..... 1329

CHAPTER 41 Torque Converters..... 1340
Introduction..... 1342
Fundamentals of Torque Converters..... 1342
Components of Torque Converters..... 1344
Operation of Torque Converters..... 1346
Troubleshooting Torque Converter Failure..... 1355
Servicing Torque Converters..... 1362

CHAPTER 42 Planetary Gear Concepts..... 1370
Introduction..... 1372
Fundamentals of Planetary Gearing..... 1372
Planetary Gear Power Flows..... 1374
Ratio Calculations for Planetary Gears..... 1377
Power Train Control Devices..... 1378
Planetary Gear Set Combinations.... 1380
Compound Planetary Gear Set Power Flows..... 1382

CHAPTER 43 Hydraulically Controlled Automatic Transmissions..... 1392
Introduction..... 1394
The History of Transmissions in the North American Truck and Coach Market..... 1394
Fundamentals of Hydraulically Controlled Automatic Transmissions..... 1395
Transmission Hydraulic Control System Components..... 1401
Operation of a Hydraulically Controlled Automatic Transmission..... 1412

CHAPTER 44 Maintaining Automatic Transmissions..... 1420
Introduction..... 1422
Fundamentals of Transmission Fluid..... 1422
Types of Transmission Fluids..... 1426
Troubleshooting Problems with Automatic Transmissions..... 1427
Maintenance of Automatic Transmissions..... 1428

CHAPTER 45 Electronically Controlled Automatic Transmissions..... 1444
Introduction..... 1446
Basics of Electronic Control—ATEC and CEC..... 1446
World Transmission..... 1462
World Transmissions—3000, 4000, and B Series..... 1462

Electro-Hydraulic Control—
WTEC II and WTEC III 1471
Allison Fourth Generation Electro-Hydraulic Control Valve Body 1488
Allison Fifth Generation Electronic Control 1497
TC-10-TS 1504
Voith DIWA Transmissions 1514
ZF Friedrichshafen AG EcoMat and EcoLife Transmissions 1521
Caterpillar Automatic Transmissions 1521

CHAPTER 46 Driveshaft Systems 1530
Introduction.................................... 1532
Fundamentals of Driveshaft Systems 1533
Components of Driveshafts/ Drive Lines 1535
Operation of Driveshafts................ 1539
Troubleshooting Vibrations and Failures 1551
Inspection and Maintenance of Driveshafts.................................. 1555

CHAPTER 47 Heavy-Duty Truck Drive Axles..................................... 1570
Introduction.................................... 1572
Fundamentals of Axles.................... 1572
Types of Drive Axle Gearing and Housings............................... 1575
Functions of Differential Gear Sets 1578
Types of Differential Gear Sets 1581
Types of Axle Shafts 1597
Lubricating Drive Axles.................... 1597

CHAPTER 48 Servicing and Maintaining Drive Axles 1604
Introduction.................................... 1606
Fundamentals of Servicing Drive Axles................................... 1606
Drive Axle Overhaul—Removal and Inspection 1608
Drive Axle Overhaul—Reassembly ... 1617
Overhauling the Inter-Axle Differential (Power Divider) 1627
Diagnosing Component Failures in Drive Axle Systems.................. 1631

CHAPTER 49 Hybrid Drive Systems and Series-Type Hybrid Drives 1642
Introduction.................................... 1644
Fundamentals of Hybrid Drives 1644
Types of Hybrid Drives 1645
Hybrid Drive Electrical Safety 1649
Series-Type Hybrid Drive Systems 1652
Major System Components of Series HybriDrive 1654
Maintenance and Service 1663

CHAPTER 50 Allison EV Drive Hybrid Systems............................. 1668
Introduction.................................... 1670
Overview of Allison EV Drive Hybrid System 1670
System Components....................... 1673
Operating Modes 1683
EP System Maintenance.................. 1684

SECTION V **Heating, Ventilation, and Air Conditioning 1690**

CHAPTER 51 Principles of Heating and Air-Conditioning Systems 1692
Introduction.................................... 1694
Brief History of Air Conditioning 1694
Fundamentals of Air-Conditioning Systems 1695
Air-Conditioning Operating Principles 1697
The Refrigeration System 1703
Air-Conditioning Controls............... 1721
Air-Conditioning Protection and Diagnostic System (APADS) 1722

CHAPTER 52 Servicing Heating and Air-Conditioning Systems 1730
Introduction.................................... 1734
The Air-Conditioning Service Process 1735
Air Conditioner Capacity................. 1736
Diagnosis.. 1737
Maintenance and Repair 1741

CHAPTER 53 Trailer Refrigeration 1768
Introduction 1770
Fundamentals of Trailer Refrigeration 1770
Heating Principles in Transportation Refrigeration 1773
Types of Transport Refrigeration Systems 1773
Heating, Cooling, and Defrost Cycles 1774
Components of Trailer Refrigeration Systems 1778
Unique Refrigeration Fluids 1781
Refrigeration System Maintenance 1782

SECTION VI Hydraulics 1786

CHAPTER 54 Hydraulics 1788
Introduction 1791
Fundamentals of Hydraulic Systems 1791
Hydraulic Operating Principles 1794
Common Components of Hydraulic Systems 1796
Lines 1798
Fittings 1804
Hydraulic Pumps 1806
Hydraulic Actuators 1815
Valves 1819
Hydraulic Accumulators 1824
Hydraulic System Preventative Maintenance 1827

SECTION VII Preventative Maintenance and Inspection 1836

CHAPTER 55 Preventative Maintenance and Inspection 1838
Introduction—What Is Preventative Maintenance? 1846
Schedules and Types of Preventative Maintenance Inspection (PMI) 1847
Effective PM Program Development 1851
Shop and Vehicle Rules for PM and PMI 1856
PMI Process 1856

Appendix A 2014 NATEF Medium/Heavy-Duty Truck Accreditation Task List Correlation Guide 1886
Glossary 1902
Index 1932

ACKNOWLEDGMENTS

Writing a textbook to put the best possible information in the hands of technicians about the latest technology in commercial vehicle chassis systems could not take place without the practical support, critical feedback, and assistance of many individuals. We're grateful for those who have allowed us to gain knowledge and skills from their vast experiences and expertise. As industry contacts patiently fielded our questions during the preparation of this textbook it's been a privilege to meet many remarkable people working in this industry who have an infectious excitement for education in skilled trades and a genuine passion for service excellence. Our colleagues at Centennial College in Toronto, Canada have been extremely helpful and supportive. To Professors David Morgan and Gino Tamburro, whose insights helped us at many stages of the project, we extend our heartfelt thanks. We also want to thank Ian Andrew, whose input was essential.

In addition, along with the CDX editorial team, we'd like to thank the following individuals for their contributions to and feedback about this textbook:

Abraham P. Arispe
Tidewater Community College

Jim Baird
Jones Technical Institute

Larry Baker
Aims Community College

Ron Beaumont
Brisbane, Queensland, Australia

Westin A. Blidy
Orleans Niagara BOCES

Gary Bronson
Laurel Oaks Career Development Campus

Les Brown
UAW LETC

Pete Carpentier Jr.
Delmar College

Jerry Clemons
Elizabethtown Community and Technical College

Tim Dunn
Sydney, New South Wales, Australia

Casey Eglinton, M.Ed.
Western Technical College

Mike Erny
Ivy Tech Community College

Mike Hagan
Cherokee High School

Justin Carpenter
Pikes Peak Community College

Brent Newville
Dakota County Tech College

Curtis Happe
Richland Community College

Scott Heard
Fleming College

Kevin Heimbach
Berks Career and Technology Center

Doyle Howard
West Kentucky Community
and Technical College

Jim Hunnicutt
Jacksonville, Florida

Ron Iocandro
Chisholm Institute

Jack Ireland
Johnson County Community College

Edward Jackson
ASE Certified Instructor

Kevin Jesser
Member of Institute of Automotive
Mechanical Engineers

Bob Johnson
Fred W. Eberle Technical Center

Dr. John F. Kershaw
Harrisburg Area Community College

Brian King
Boone County Area Technology Center

Aaron A. Lemoine
South Louisiana Community College
T.H. Harris Campus

Robbie Lindhorst
Southeastern Illinois College

Stefan Liszka
Chisholm Institute

Ron Locandro
Chisholm Institute

James Mack
Berks Career and Technology Center

Hugh M. Mann
Houston Community College

Michael Mauntel
Ivy Tech Community College

Jim McEwen
UAW-LETC

Jonathon Merritt
James Sprunt Community College

Jed Metzler
South Branch Career and Technical Center

John Miller
Valley Career and Technical Center

James Mitchell
Tampa Bay Technical High School

John Murphy
Centennial College

Chad M. Parsons
Wyotech

Brian L. Particka
Huron Area Technology Center

Billy Phillips
Johnston Community College

Adam Prusakiewicz
University of Northwestern Ohio

James D. Scott
Crowder College

Larry Seibel
Miami Valley Career Technology Center

Tyler Slettedahl
North Dakota State College of Science

David Stone
High Plains Technology Center

Claude Townsend
Oakland Schools

J.W. Turnpaugh
Mid America Technology Center

Larry Wehunt
Gwinnett Technical College

John Yinger
Ozarks Technical Community College

Lamar Zorn
Florida Panhandle Technical College

We've also been challenged by the exceptional students who have attended Centennial College. They are an extraordinary class of technicians who daily compel us to pursue teaching excellence and keep us from succumbing to the occupational hazard of falling behind in our comprehension of the industry's technological advancements.

We particularly want to thank Vern Anthony who saw the potential of this project, gave it a home at CDX, and pushed hard to see this work reach fruition.

And finally for our families—thank you Vivian and Ingrid for the immeasurable and unconditional support that you offered and the countless week-ends, evenings, and vacations you gave up to allow us to finish this work. Without your steadfast patience and inspiration, the task would have been impossible.

SECTION I

Foundation and Safety

CHAPTER 1	Introduction to Heavy-Duty Commercial Vehicles
CHAPTER 2	Careers, Employability Skills, and Workplace Practices
CHAPTER 3	Safety, Personal Protection Equipment, and First Aid
CHAPTER 4	Basic Tools and Lubricants
CHAPTER 5	Fasteners, Locking Devices, and Lifting Equipment

CHAPTER 1

NATEF Tasks

There are no NATEF tasks for this chapter.

Knowledge Objectives

After reading this chapter, you will be able to:

1. Define and describe classification of medium and heavy-duty vehicles according to application, weight, length, and axle configuration. (pp 6–21)
2. Identify and explain classifications of vehicles according to type of articulation. (pp 21–24)
3. Identify and explain terminology associated with measurements of vehicle dimensions, lengths, weight, and axle configuration. (pp 25–28)

Introduction to Heavy-Duty Commercial Vehicles

Skills Objectives

After reading this chapter, you will be able to:

1. Decode a North American VIN. (p 28) **SKILL DRILL 1-1**

Introduction

Globally, commercial vehicles perform an endless variety of revenue-generating tasks having unique and even unusual functions. When you think about the types of commercial vehicles seen every day, you begin to understand how vast the categories and configurations are—medium-sized delivery vehicles used almost exclusively in cities; ambulances; fire and rescue vehicles; highway semi-trailers; gravel haulers; fuel tankers; utility trucks; highway coaches; urban transit buses; and more. FIGURE 1-1 illustrates a number of different commercial vehicles separated into their classifications. In this chapter we will show you a range of commercial vehicles that are from different parts of the globe and their application. The one common thing that you will see from these examples is that, no matter where you are a technician, the same set of fundamental skills are required for working on them. In this chapter we will predominantly use US classifications as examples. If you are a technician in another country, you should refer to the regulations for the correct classifications in your location.

No matter where you are in the world, within each of those various larger vehicle classification categories, there are an enormous number of subtypes based upon the vehicle's application. For example, buses transporting children to school every day are very different from the ones moving people on urban transit systems or luxury highway coaches. Each application will be built according to its own specialized requirements, such as carrying people, products or performing services. Those specialized requirements can include factors such as: where they travel, what they carry, how much they carry, how far they travel, maneuverability, safety, capacity, stability, and speed. These are just a few design considerations determining the unique ways a vehicle is built and operates.

To properly maintain and service commercial vehicles, it is important to understand the variety of ways commercial vehicles are classified and configured. The reason is that a vehicle's application, operating condition, and design will determine its service practices and recommendations for its maintenance.

Classification by Operational Characteristics

A helpful way to classify commercial vehicles is by considering where a commercial vehicle performs its primary job. For example, trucking or even bus operations can be classified as regional or long haul. Regional operations will return more than 90% of vehicles back to a terminal in a single day. Long-haul operations dispatch vehicles on trips lasting days—and even weeks—before returning them to a dispatch or maintenance facility.

Operating conditions also shape the classification of vehicles. That is, vehicles can be classified according to their suitability for travel on various road surfaces or grades. As shown in FIGURE 1-2, road grade is expressed

You Are the Technician

A tractor-trailer combination vehicle comes to your repair shop. The vehicle has a tractor and two trailers combined. Your supervisor asks you to check it out and let him know what type of combination vehicle it is, its gross combined weight rating, and the general law maximum weight rating for this vehicle.

The combination has a tractor with three axles:

- a front axle and a tandem rear axle,
- a trailer with two axles at the rear
- an attached frame with a fifth wheel at the back of the trailer and a second trailer coupled to the fifth wheel of the front trailer.

You check the vehicle decals for the GVWR for the axles on the tractor. They indicate a GVWR of 12,000 lbs (5,454 kg) for the front axle, and 20,000 lb (9,090 kg) for each of the tandem axles.

1. What class of vehicle is the tractor?
2. What type of trailer combination is this A, B, or C?
3. What is the general allowable GCVW for this combination vehicle?

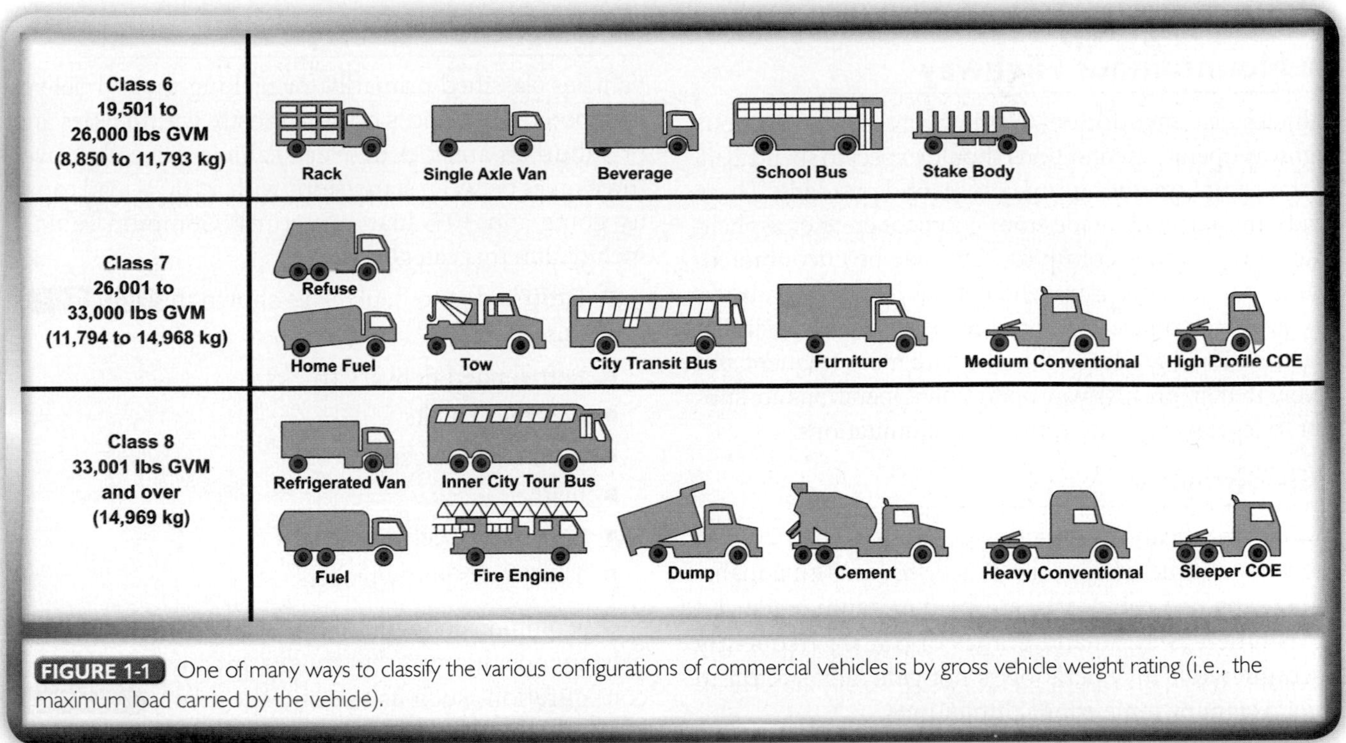

FIGURE 1-1 One of many ways to classify the various configurations of commercial vehicles is by gross vehicle weight rating (i.e., the maximum load carried by the vehicle).

as a percentage and refers to the steepness of a hill. For example, a 15% grade means the road drops or increases 15 feet (4.6 m) for every 100 feet (30.5 m) travelled.

Similarly, heavy-duty commercial vehicles can be classified according to how frequently they start and stop or even by their speed of travel. When classifying commercial vehicles by operating conditions, five broad categories are used: turnpike or interstate; on-highway; on-off-highway or mountainous highway; off-highway; and urban.

FIGURE 1-2 Road grade indicates steepness.

Turnpike or Interstate

Major highways are constructed differently than secondary highways. The road materials, vehicle speeds, amount of stop-and-go driving, and degree of road crown are all factors that determine a vehicle's suitability for turnpike or interstate applications. Those factors also influence the design, equipment, and accessories an interstate vehicle will use. Vehicles classified for operation on interstates, highways, or turnpikes are designed to run on limited-access, well-maintained, multi-lane highways made of excellent concrete or asphalt with maximum adverse grades not in excess of 3%.

On-Highway

Vehicles classified for use in on-highway operating conditions will operate exclusively on well-maintained major highways of excellent concrete or asphalt construction. Roads are typically level to rolling with occasional maximum grades to 8%. These vehicles must operate within legal weight and dimensional limitations and be able to handle the steeper grades that may be encountered.

On-/Off-Highway or Mountainous Highway

Vehicles classified for on-/off-highway or mountainous highway operating conditions should expect to spend 20% of their total operating time on secondary roads. These roads are normally made from good concrete or asphalt. Intermittent grades of up to 12% may be encountered. The remaining time is travelled on off-highway roadways that are based on well-maintained crushed rock or similar material. Road grades in this class are more frequent and severe than in on-highway operation. Operations are subject to legal weight and dimensional limitations.

Off-Highway

In this classification, vehicles spend more than 20% of their travel time on gravel roads or roads with a maintained crushed rock surface. The maximum grade can be as much as 12%, and grades of 8% are frequently encountered. This operation is not generally subject to legal weight or dimensional limitations.

Urban

Vehicles in this classification face operating conditions that are primarily within cities and suburban areas. That means these vehicles are subject to frequent stops and starts. Operation occurs on concrete, asphalt, and maintained gravel road surfaces. Because of the urban environment, vehicles in this class must have greater levels of maneuverability than is required of other classes. Vehicles in this class often use engines with a lower power output.

Vocational Applications of Commercial Vehicles

A second way to classify commercial vehicles is by the job (vocation) the vehicle performs. Common vocational applications include:

- Pick-up and delivery
- Construction
- Fire service
- Heavy haul
- Intercity coach
- Line haul
- Logging
- Mining
- Refuse collection
- Rescue vehicles
- School bus
- Urban transit coach

The following sections discuss these classifications in greater detail.

Pick-up and Delivery

Vehicles classified primarily for picking-up and delivering goods and services operate mostly within cities and/or suburban areas. A delivery vehicle typically travels three miles between starts/stops with a 100% load capacity going and 40% load on return. Common vehicles included in this category are:

- Drop bed auto haulers, as shown in FIGURE 1-3
- Moving vans
- Refrigerated delivery trucks
- Beverage trucks
- Municipal trucks
- Flatbed trucks
- Newspaper delivery trucks
- Tow trucks and wreckers

A common configuration of vehicle for pick-up and delivery operations is the straight or conventional truck configuration, such as the one shown in FIGURE 1-4. A straight truck used in the city will typically have a single axle because weight limits on city streets are much lower than those on major highways. In addition, a single axle will help the vehicle to be maneuverable.

FIGURE 1-3 Drop bed auto hauler.

FIGURE 1-4 A straight truck.

Construction

Vehicles used in construction are primarily engaged in moving material to and from a job site. Operating conditions are generally 90% of loaded operation on road surfaces made of concrete, asphalt, gravel, crushed rock, or hard packed dirt and up to 10% of loaded operation in loose sand or on muddy job sites. Maximum grades encountered are 12%. As a result, construction vehicles tend to use short-step, deep-reduction transmissions. Loads are distributed equally from side to side.

Common vehicles included in this category are:

- Asphalt and gravel trucks, sometimes referred to as dump trucks, as shown in FIGURE 1-5
- Flatbed trucks hauling lumber and building supplies
- Tank trucks, as shown in FIGURE 1-6
- Landscape trucks, often referred to as tipper trucks in some locations, as shown in FIGURE 1-7
- Concrete mixers
- Snowplows

Fire Service

These vehicles are used to transport people and equipment to extinguish fires, paramedics, or for ambulance services. Annual distances travelled are typically less than 20,000 miles (32,187 km) per year. Typical vehicle routes are three miles between start and stop. High deceleration stops are frequent.

Common vehicles in this category are:

- Aerial ladders and fire trucks, as shown in FIGURE 1-8
- Pumpers tankers
- Aerial platforms and special applications, as shown in FIGURE 1-9
- Ambulance/paramedic

FIGURE 1-5 Dump truck.

FIGURE 1-6 Tanker.

FIGURE 1-7 Tipper truck.

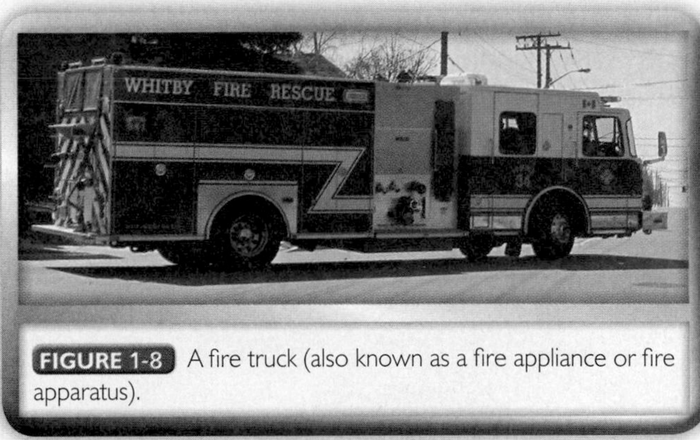

FIGURE 1-8 A fire truck (also known as a fire appliance or fire apparatus).

FIGURE 1-9 Specialist applications.

Heavy Haul

Vehicles in the heavy haul category move heavy equipment or materials at legal maximums for length, width, and weight. They may actually exceed those limits with special loading permits. Operation is mostly on road surfaces made of concrete, asphalt, and maintained gravel. Load weights are 100% of vehicle capacity going and empty on return. Vehicles in this classification require high horsepower engines with the ability to pull the heaviest loads. FIGURE 1-10 illustrates a typical heavy-haul configuration.

Typical vehicle types in this category are:

- Equipment hauling flatbed trailers
- Steel haulers using high or low trailers

Intercity Coach

This category of vehicles transports people, and occasionally light freight, between cities and/or suburban areas. Intercity coaches will travel on highway and in urban conditions accumulating high mileage on routes exceeding 30 miles (48.3 km) between start and stop.

Typical vehicle types in this category are:

- Tour coaches
- Cross country coaches

Line-Haul

Line-haul trucks move freight over long distances—generally over 60,000 miles/year (96,561 km/year). More than 30 miles (48.3 km) of distance between starting and stopping are typical for line-haul service. Straight trucks (trucks with only a box) use either single or tandem axles. Tractor-trailer combinations are most common.

Typical line-haul vehicles include:

- General freight trucks in either straight or tractor-trailer configurations such as shown in FIGURE 1-11
- Refrigerated food trucks
- Livestock tractor trailers
- Flatbed trailers such as the one in FIGURE 1-12
- Side curtains, as shown in FIGURE 1-13, that enable fast pallet unloading and loading with forklift trucks

Line-haul trucks travel long distances with heavy loads and at high speeds. As a result, line-haul trucks have unique vehicle specifications on their engines, tires, suspensions, cab configurations, and so on.

Logging

Logging trucks move shipments of wood logs, chips, and pulp between logging sites or to and from logging or

FIGURE 1-11 General freight truck.

FIGURE 1-10 A heavy-haul configuration.

FIGURE 1-12 Flatbed truck.

paper mills. Logging trucks travel distances of 3 to 30 miles (4.8 to 48.3 km) between starts and stops. Mostly, they travel on road surfaces of concrete, asphalt, maintained gravel, crushed rock, or hard packed dirt, but up to 10% of their loaded operation can occur on sandy or muddy job sites. Trucks will be loaded to 100% capacity when delivering loads and empty when returning.

Typical logging vehicles are:

- Wood chip haulers—either a straight truck or tractor and trailer
- Log hauling tractor trailer combinations, as shown in FIGURE 1-14

Logging trucks that operate in off-road conditions have unique requirements for specialized traction capabilities provided by tires and drive axles. Heavy frames are also needed to resist damage from twisting and bending. Suspensions are designed to better handle severe off-road terrains while carrying the heaviest possible loads.

FIGURE 1-13 Side curtains.

FIGURE 1-14 A logging truck.

Mining

Mining operation trucks move rock, ore, gravel, and other minerals. Average trip distances are 30 miles (48.3 km) between starting and stopping. While most operations are on-highway, up to 10% of distances travelled are over sandy or muddy job sites. The trucks are typically 100% loaded while delivering and empty on return trips.

Typical mining vehicle types are:

- Belly dump trailers
- Semi-end dump hopper trailer combinations

The gravel hauler in FIGURE 1-15 is an example of a mining application. The tilting dump box requires a power take-off to operate a hydraulic pump called a wet-line.

Refuse Collection

Refuse vehicles, better known as garbage trucks, are used for pick-up and transportation of residential garbage or recycling materials. These vehicles encounter steep grades of up to 20% when they travel into landfill, transfer, or recycling sites. Refuse trucks typically have a high proportion of starts and stops for every mile travelled.

Typical refuse vehicles are:

- Front-/rear-/side-loading garbage trucks, as shown in FIGURE 1-16
- Sewer/septic/vacuum trucks
- Liquid waste haulers

To enable the greatest level of maneuverability and highest load capacity, refuse vehicles are typically built on low-entry, cab-over-engine (COE) chassis.

FIGURE 1-15 A gravel hauler.

FIGURE 1-16 Garbage truck.

Rescue Vehicles

Rescue vehicles are specialized vehicles designed for rapid acceleration to crash sites on highways or airport tarmacs away from hydrant hookups. They are low mileage operation vehicles with high horsepower engines and automatic transmissions.

Typical rescue vehicle types are:

- Airport Rescue Fire (ARF)
- Crash Rescue Fire (CRF)
- Rapid Intervention Vehicle (RIV) Emergency Service

Some of the most powerful trucks with the fastest acceleration rates are crash-and-rescue trucks, as shown in FIGURE 1-17. These trucks are used to quickly extinguish fires at airports or on the highway. As a result, crash-and-rescue trucks require high-speed capabilities while carrying heavy loads.

FIGURE 1-17 Crash-and-rescue truck.

School Bus

School buses are familiar people haulers that transport students to and from school or school-related events. Two stops per mile over mixed road surfaces are typical. School buses frequently operate under fully loaded capacity.

Typical school bus configurations are:

- Front-engine commercial chassis
- Front- or rear-engine integral coach, as shown in FIGURE 1-18

Urban Transit Coach

As the name indicates, urban transit coaches are the city buses that transport people in and around cities or suburban areas. City buses operate on well-maintained highways and residential streets made of asphalt or concrete. These units have a high frequency of starts and stops per mile—nine is considered typical!

Typical urban transit vehicles are:

- Airport shuttle buses
- City transit buses, such as the one in FIGURE 1-19

FIGURE 1-18 School bus with rear engine.

FIGURE 1-19 City transit bus.

These can come in a range of configurations as shown in FIGURE 1-20A and FIGURE 1-20B, including double deckers and articulated or "bendy buses," as they are known in some countries.

Design Factors for Vocational Applications

A commercial vehicle's design features are strongly influenced by its application. Depending on the operating conditions and job performed by the vehicle, a commercial vehicle will have a particular chassis, engine, powertrain, cab, suspension, and other specific chasis equipment, as discussed in the following sections.

Chassis Frames

Frame rails of a truck or bus are the vehicle's backbone. All equipment ultimately must mount or attach to the frame. A frame must be sized and built appropriately to be capable of supporting the loads applied to it while adapting to the forces that bend and twist the frame.

Many trucks are built on a ladder-type frame such as the one shown in FIGURE 1-21.

FIGURE 1-20 **A.** Double decker bus. **B.** Articulated bus.

Engines

Engines must have sufficient power to move heavy loads and accelerate up grades while providing good fuel economy. Torque is the twisting force applied to the crankshaft. Torque is a function of cylinder pressure and it is the force that moves a load.

Horsepower is a function of engine speed and torque. **Horsepower** describes how fast the engine can turn while producing torque. A high-horsepower, high-torque engine can produce lots of power at high engine speeds. In contrast, a high-torque, low-horsepower engine cannot turn as fast while it produces torque. The following is an equation for horsepower:

$$\text{Horsepower} = \text{RPM} \times \frac{\text{Torque}}{5252}$$

Torque rise is the difference between engine torque produced at rated speed (maximum engine RPM under load) and **peak torque**, or maximum torque an engine can produce. Torque rise is expressed as a percentage of torque at the rated speed.

To calculate torque rise, use the following equation:

$$\%\ \text{Torque} = \frac{\text{Peak torque} - \text{Rated torque}}{\text{Rated torque}} \times 100$$

For example, consider a vehicle with a peak torque rise of 1,800 ft/lb (248.9 m/kg) and a torque at rated speed of 1,200 ft/lb (166 m/kg). The percent torque rise would be calculated as follows:

$$\%\ \text{Torque rise} = \frac{1800\text{–}1200}{1200} \times 100$$

$$\text{Torque rise} = 20\%$$

FIGURE 1-21 A ladder-type frame/chassis.

High-torque-rise engines are used for line haul applications and have a steep increase in torque. City trucks will use low-torque-rise engines, which have less peak torque but more torque is available over a wider engine operating range. FIGURE 1-22 graphically illustrates the difference between low torque rise and high torque rise.

High-torque-rise engines allow the vehicle's driver to keep the vehicle in a higher gear range longer under load. As such, that type of engine is used in only line-haul, on-highway trucks and buses. Torque is available in high-torque-rise engines though only over a narrow speed range. Its peak torque occurs at 10 to 15 mph (16.1 to 24.1 km/hr) or so below its cruising speed.

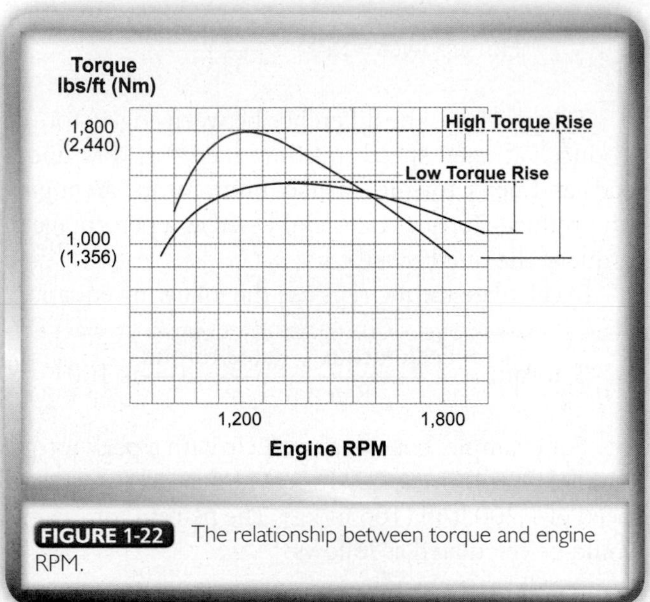

FIGURE 1-22 The relationship between torque and engine RPM.

Low-torque-rise engines produce torque over a wider engine RPM operating range. That makes them ideal for stop-start traffic and varying speed/load conditions. Torque output is not as high but more widely available.

Another difference between high-torque-rise and low-torque-rise engines is in their gearing. High-torque-rise vehicles generally use transmissions with fewer gears and wider ratio steps between gears. Low-torque-rise engines use transmissions with smaller ratio steps but need more gears.

Power Trains

Commercial vehicles require powertrains designed specifically for their particular vocations. FIGURE 1-23 illustrates the powertrain in a conventional configuration of heavy truck. Transmissions and rear axles provide the mechanical advantage through gear ratios to efficiently use engine power while moving the vehicle at the road speeds and grades required by its operation. Gear ratios should be numerically fast enough to achieve desired highway speeds for the particular operation. In addition, gears must be available which are also numerically slow enough to provide maximum hill-climbing ability with the lowest gear combinations and maximum startability under all operating conditions.

Startability is an important feature or specification factor for some trucks. **Startability** refers to the capability to commence moving forward on a specified grade. An engine's torque output and powertrain gear ratios will determine the steepest grade a truck can begin to climb from a standing stop. A similar term, **gradability**,

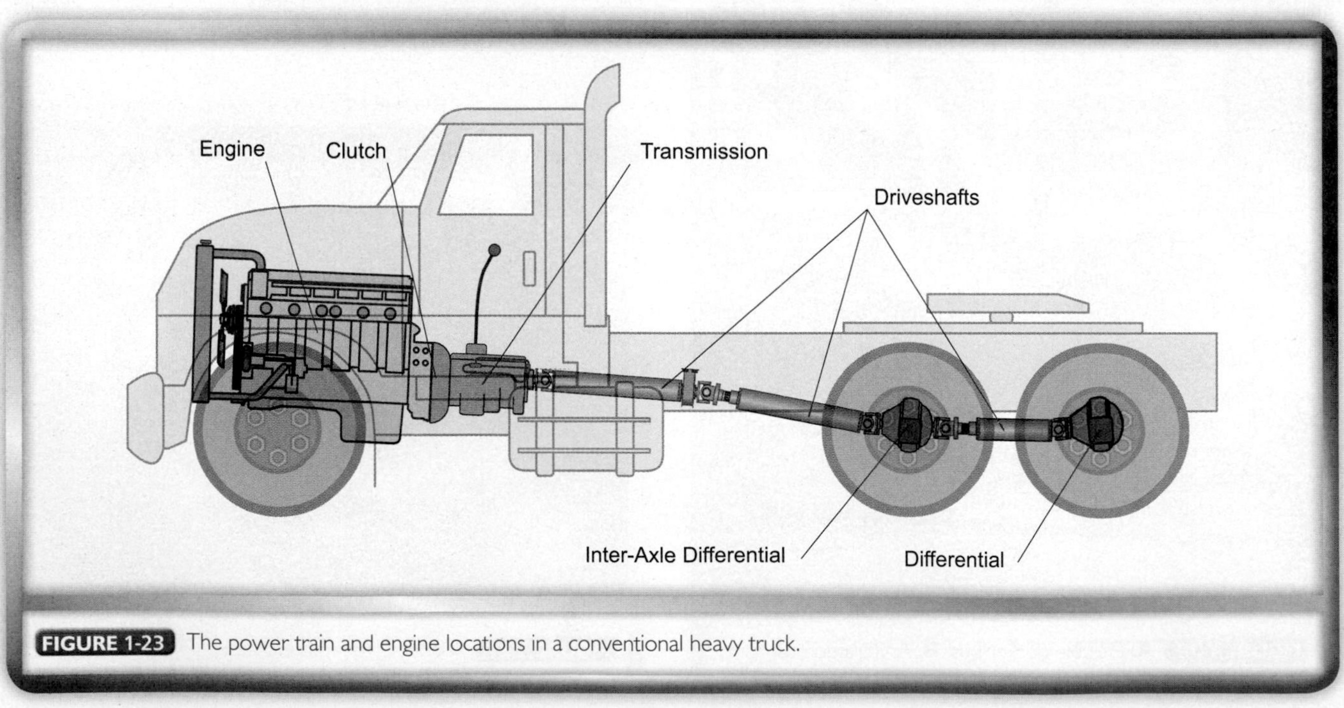

FIGURE 1-23 The power train and engine locations in a conventional heavy truck.

refers to the capability to maintain forward motion on specified grade while sustaining a minimum speed.

Tractors and trucks can also be classified according to their drive and non-drive axle configurations. Trailers may be classified similarly but by non-drive axle configurations. Single-unit, or straight, trucks can have two, three, four, or sometimes more axles. Typically these include closed (van-type) trailers, dump trucks, tankers, and heavy concrete mixers.

Another element of the powertrain that varies depending on vehicle vocation is the rear axle. Factors influencing rear axle selection include:

- Gross combination vehicle weight (GCVW)
- Type of terrain
- Road speed
- Tire size
- Axle ratio required
- Transmission ratios
- Engine torque
- Engine speed

Trucks are categorized by the number of wheel positions and drive axles they have. TABLE 1-1 charts classification by wheel ends and drive axles. For example, a 4×2 vehicle has four wheel positions with one drive axle having two wheels driven. This would be a single rear axle truck or bus. FIGURE 1-24 illustrates a typical tire-and-wheel configuration of an 18-wheeler. White tires are on non-driving axles. Tires 3 to 10 are drive tires, which are a part of a tandem drive axle configuration. FIGURE 1-25A depicts an 8 × 4 configuration, and FIGURE 1-25B depicts a 6 × 4 configuration.

A common configuration is the tandem axle combination. It uses two drive axles and has the following advantages:

- Greater ability to carry legal loads
- Better traction
- Better weight distribution over road surfaces
- Better braking capability for improved safety
- Improved load distribution over axles, tires, and frame
- Reduced road shock to chassis components

TABLE 1-1: Truck Classification by Drive Wheels

Chassis Type	Total Wheel Ends	Driven Wheels	Driven Axles	Total Axles
4×2	4	2	1	2
4×4	4	4	2	2
6×2	6	2	1	3
6×4	6	4	2	3
6×6	6	6	3	3
8×8	8	4	2	4
8×8	8	8	4	4

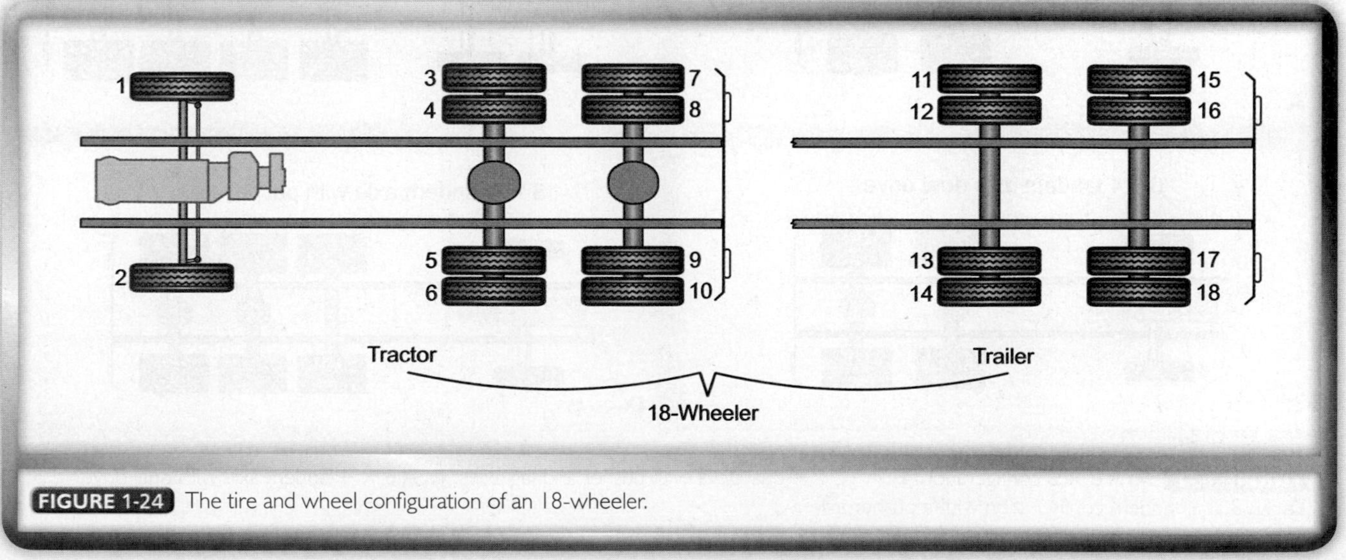

FIGURE 1-24 The tire and wheel configuration of an 18-wheeler.

FIGURE 1-26A and FIGURE 1-26B show different configurations using tandem axles.

Two other types of axles used on heavy-duty commercial vehicles are the pusher axle and tag axle. A pusher axle is non-driving and is located in front of a drive axle. A tag axle is located behind the drive axles. Both pusher and tag axles help increase maximum gross vehicle weight ratings. FIGURE 1-27A-D shows various axle configurations using pusher and tag axles.

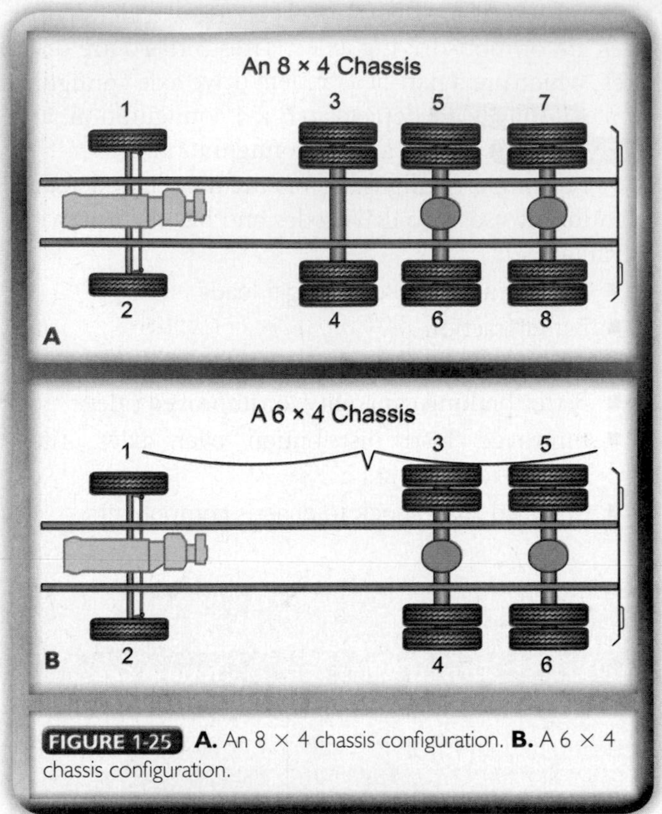

FIGURE 1-25 **A.** An 8 × 4 chassis configuration. **B.** A 6 × 4 chassis configuration.

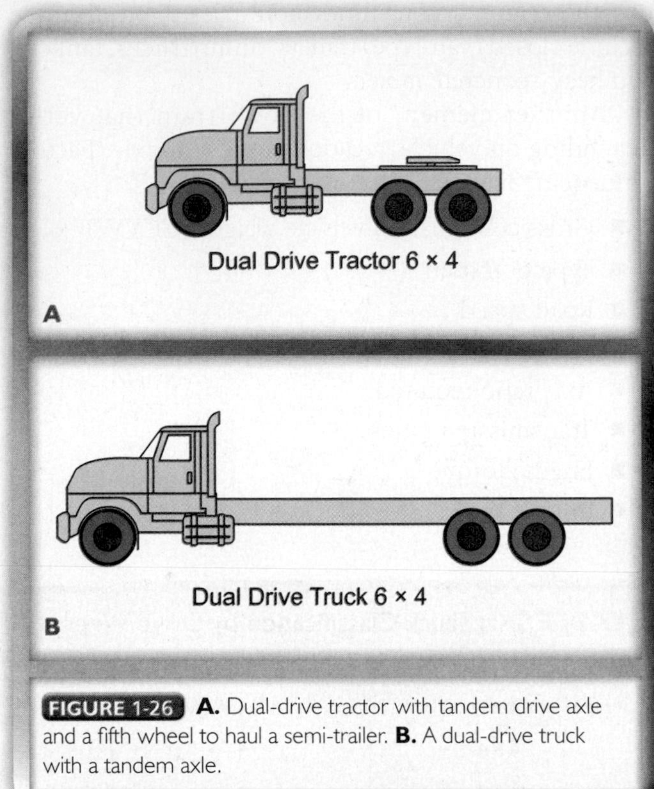

FIGURE 1-26 **A.** Dual-drive tractor with tandem drive axle and a fifth wheel to haul a semi-trailer. **B.** A dual-drive truck with a tandem axle.

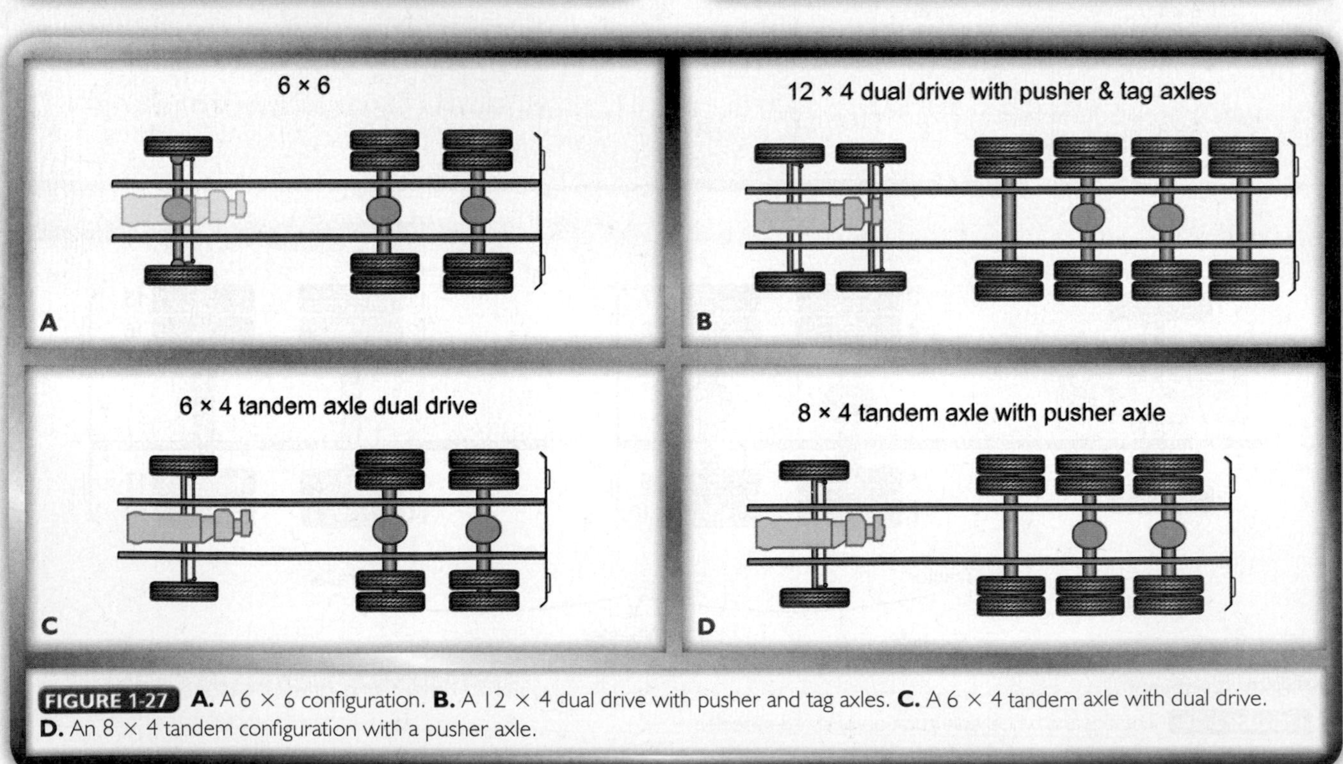

FIGURE 1-27 **A.** A 6 × 6 configuration. **B.** A 12 × 4 dual drive with pusher and tag axles. **C.** A 6 × 4 tandem axle with dual drive. **D.** An 8 × 4 tandem configuration with a pusher axle.

Cabs

Just as different vocations of trucks use specific engines and powertrains, they also use cabs designed for specific types of usage. FIGURE 1-28 shows three conventional tractors, each using an identical engine and powertrain. The cabs, however, are different and bring different enhancements to the vehicle. The cab shown in FIGURE 1-28A has a high-rise bunk integrated into the cab and also has aerodynamic fairings or skirts around the chassis. The cab shown in FIGURE 1-28B has no bunk and for that reason sometimes called a "day cab." The cab shown in FIGURE 1-28C has an integral bunk with grab handles for improved access to the back of the cab.

Regardless of design, most cabs include some type of aerodynamic fairings and wind deflectors to improve fuel economy. Aerodynamic enhancements are, therefore, another consideration when developing vehicle specifications. FIGURE 1-29 shows how various aerodynamic enhancements are integrated into a cab's design.

A common configuration of cab is the conventional cab in which the engine is placed in front of the cab. The ride in a conventional cab is smoother than in the common cab-over-engine (COE) configuration, which is illustrated in FIGURE 1-30. The COE configuration enables the use of a longer trailer, however, and the design also allows for greater maneuverability than a conventional cab when a small turning radius is needed.

The location of the front axle can also influence the turning radius of a vehicle and affect ride quality. A set-back axle moves the axle closer to the cab to shorten the

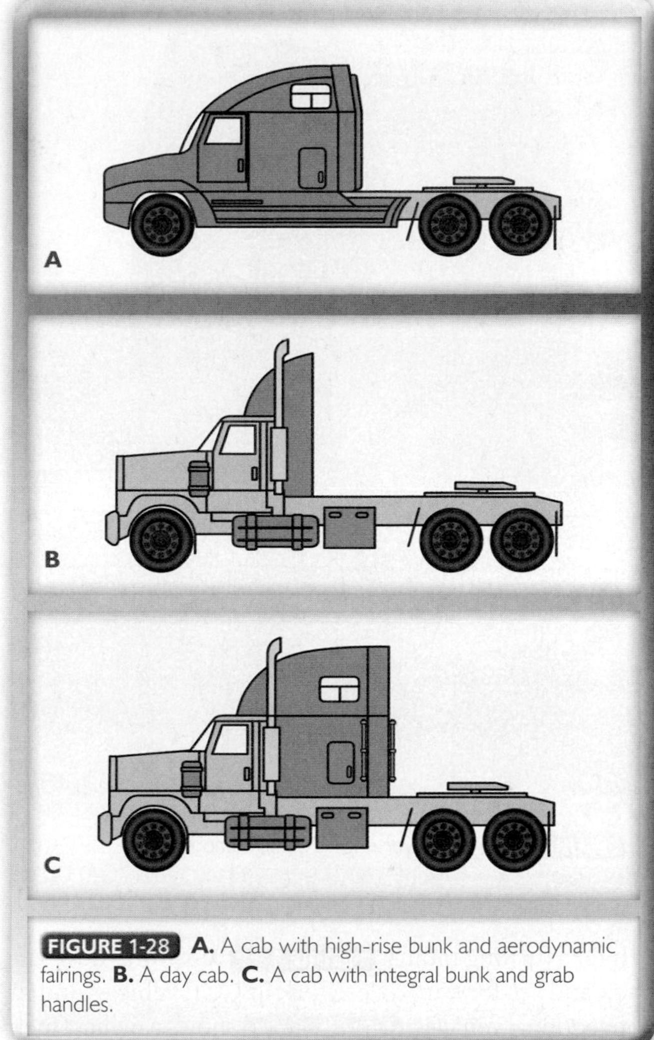

FIGURE 1-28 **A.** A cab with high-rise bunk and aerodynamic fairings. **B.** A day cab. **C.** A cab with integral bunk and grab handles.

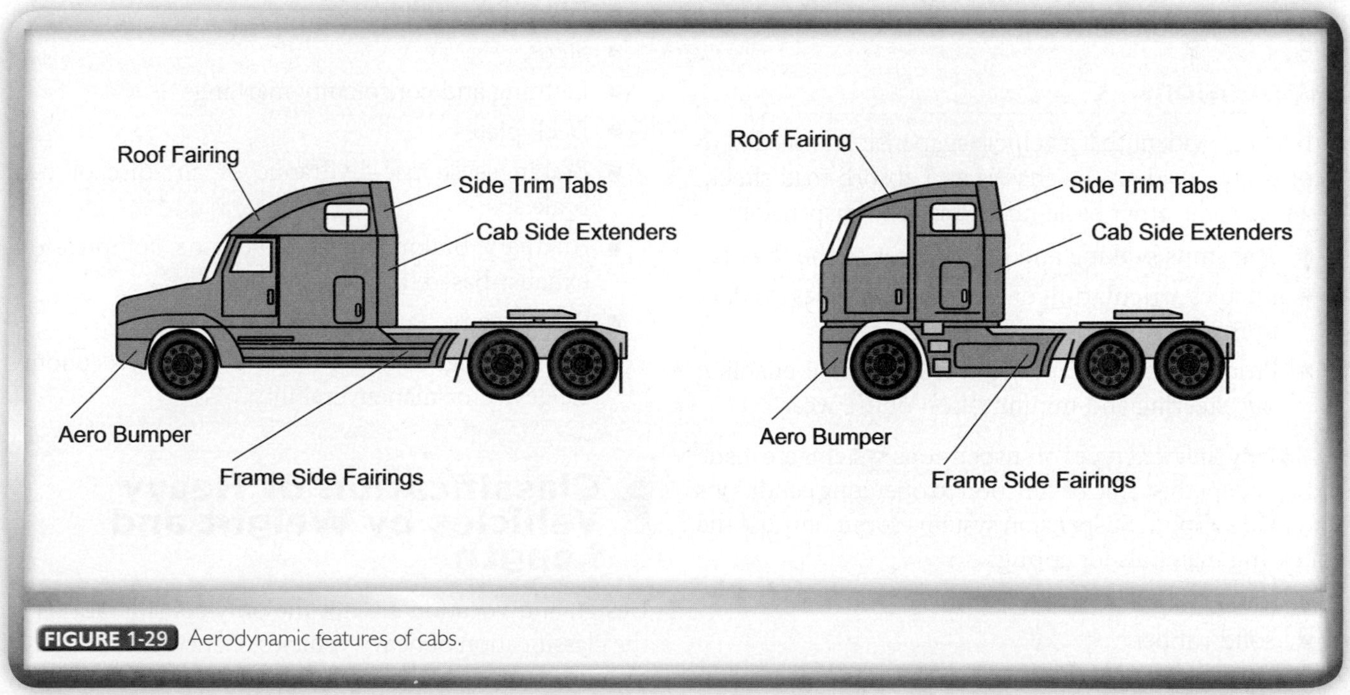

FIGURE 1-29 Aerodynamic features of cabs.

FIGURE 1-30 Cab-over-engine configuration.

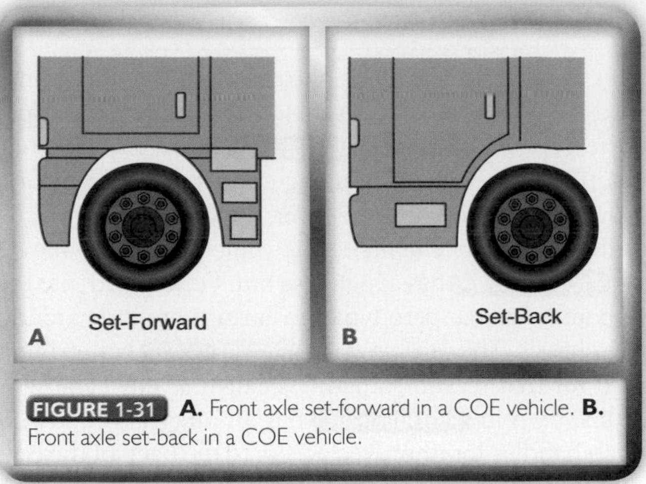

FIGURE 1-31 **A.** Front axle set-forward in a COE vehicle. **B.** Front axle set-back in a COE vehicle.

vehicle's turning radius. FIGURE 1-31 illustrates how set-back and set-forward axles work in COE vehicles and in conventional vehicles. FIGURE 1-31A shows a higher truck with a higher COE and a set-forward axle. FIGURE 1-31B shows a lower truck with a set-back front axle. One is a high COE and the other is a low COE.

Suspensions

While it is evident that a vehicle suspension is needed to support the load on the chassis and absorb road shock, it serves some other basic functions. The suspension:

- Transmits braking and drive forces to the chassis
- Enables **articulation** or movement of axles to adapt to road conditions
- Promotes proper vehicle tracking while enabling safe steering and minimization of tire wear

Many different types of suspensions systems are made to best adapt the vehicle's function to operating conditions and load support. Suspension systems commonly use the following materials for springs:

- Air
- Solid rubber
- Leaf spring

Other Chassis Equipment

Chassis equipment used on a vehicle largely depends on what the vehicle does and where and how far the vehicle will travel. The following is a list of special equipment options that vary by application:

- Fuel tanks—number and size
- Exhaust—vertical or horizontal
- Hitching devices and fifth wheels
- Batteries—type and number
- Auxiliary power supplies
- Auxiliary heaters
- Back of cab access
- Day cab or sleeper cab
- Seating—air ride, bench or fixed seat
- Power take-off's
- Steps
- Lighting and conspicuity markings
- Deck plates
- Braking systems—hydraulic or air; disc or cam brakes
- Auxiliary braking devices—engine compression, exhaust-based, or driveline retarders
- Aerodynamic fairings
- Tires—designed for off-road traction, fuel economy, longevity, or maneuverability

Classification of Heavy Vehicles by Weight and Length

Design and vocation are not the only considerations in the classification of heavy vehicles. Considerations must also be given to their configurations based on weight and length. Combination vehicles that use hitching devices, for example, are configurations that have specific characteristics.

Federal Bridge Gross Weight Formula

In the early 20th century, vehicle weight limits were legislated to protect dirt and gravel roads from damage caused by the heavy wheel weights of commercial vehicles. As truck traffic and load weights increased continually, truck weight limits began to focus primarily on gross weight limits to protect bridges from damaging truck weights. **Gross weight limits** are the maximum legal weight of a vehicle that can travel on roads and bridges.

By the mid-1970s, a law was passed to limit the weight-to-length ratio of heavy trucks to protect roads and bridges from the damage caused by the concentrated weight of shorter trucks. The law created the **Federal Bridge Gross Weight Formula** (also known as **Bridge Formula B** and the **Federal Bridge Formula**). Those formulas established the maximum weights for a commercial motor vehicle (CMV) based on the number of axles the vehicle had and the spacing between those axles.

The formula is part of US/Canadian weight and length regulations regarding interstate/interprovincial commercial traffic. Axle spacing is as important as axle weight in bridge design. Consider a vehicle with two axles carrying significant weight. If not spaced far enough apart, those two axles act like a single axle in terms of loading road surfaces. The longer the axle spread—a distance measured from axle center to axle center—the better weight distribution is achieved to prevent road and bridge damage. FIGURE 1-32 illustrates the impact of vehicle weight on bridges.

The bridge formula, therefore, allows motor vehicles to be loaded to maximum weight only if each group of axles and their spacing also satisfy the requirements of the formula. In North America, the weight limit is typically 20,000 lb (9,072 kg) for a single-axle vehicle with a total weight on one or more axles which are not more than 40" (101.6 cm) apart. For tandem axles, the total weight limit is typically 34,000 lb (15,422 kg) for a vehicle with its full weight on two or more consecutive axles that are between 40 and 96 inches (101.6 and 243.8 cm) apart. Because the bridge formula defines the maximum weight allowed on each axle according to the distances between each axle, the vehicle illustrated in FIGURE 1-33 would have a gross vehicle weight (GVW) of 80,000 lb (36,287 kg).

Axle spacing is, therefore, a critical consideration. The vehicle illustrated in FIGURE 1-34 has two axle groups. The distance between each group is identical, but there is a critical difference. The three-axle group carries only minimal amount of extra load compared to the tandem group since the axles are close together.

To increase a vehicle's potential load rating, vehicle designers may specify certain features. For example, according to the Federal Bridge Formula, no more than 600 lb per square inch (42.18 kg/cm2) are allowed on a tire's contact patch. Designers may specify super-single

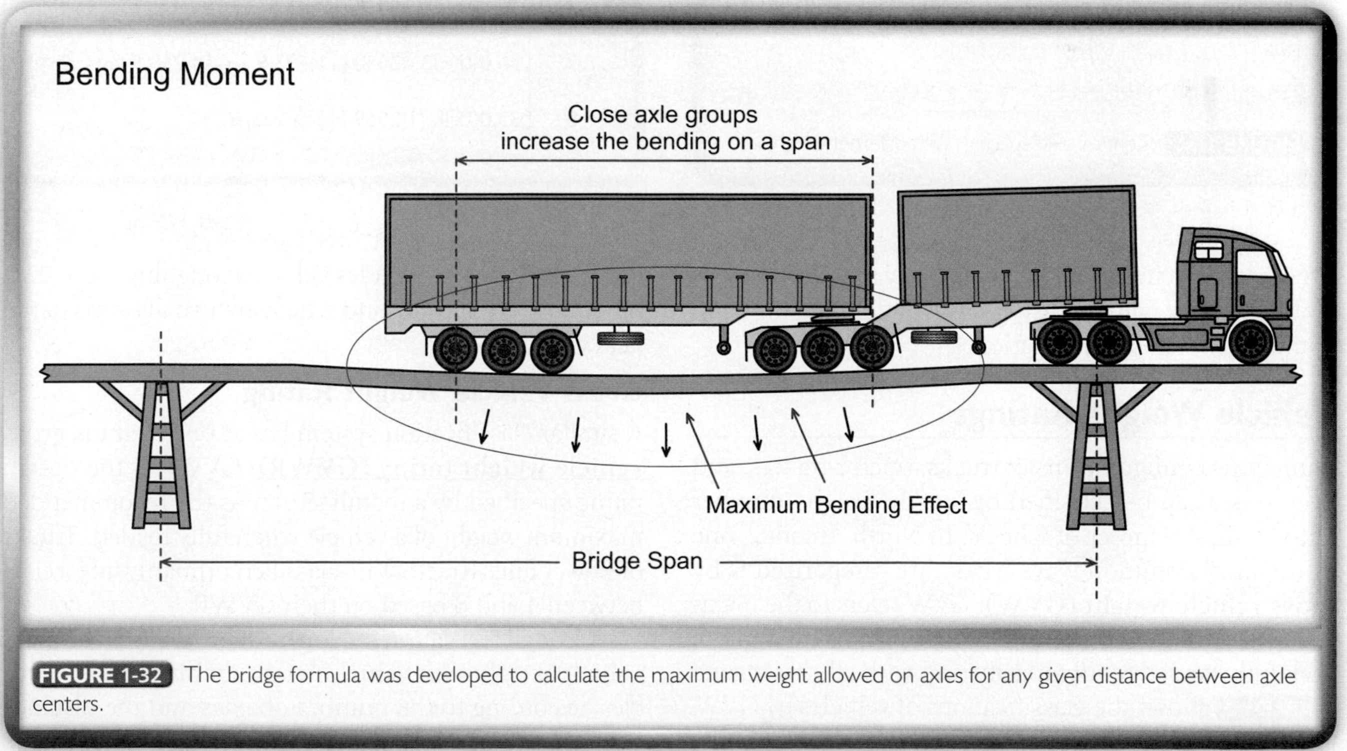

FIGURE 1-32 The bridge formula was developed to calculate the maximum weight allowed on axles for any given distance between axle centers.

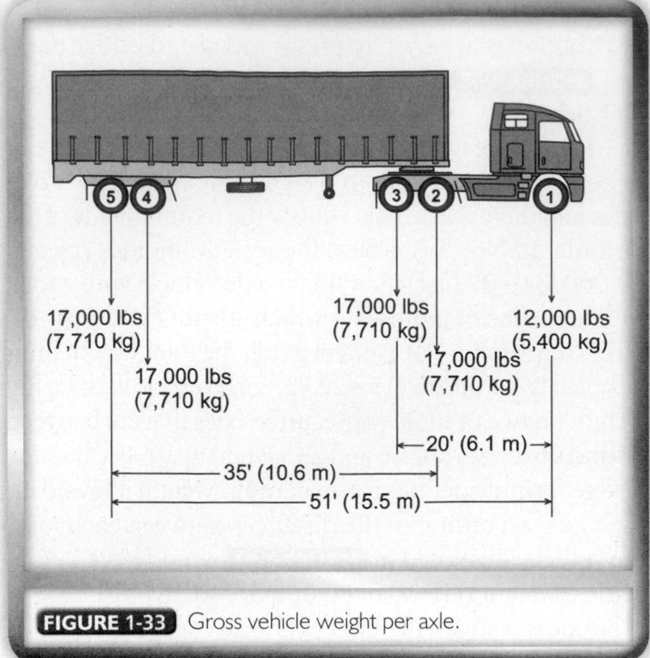

FIGURE 1-33 Gross vehicle weight per axle.

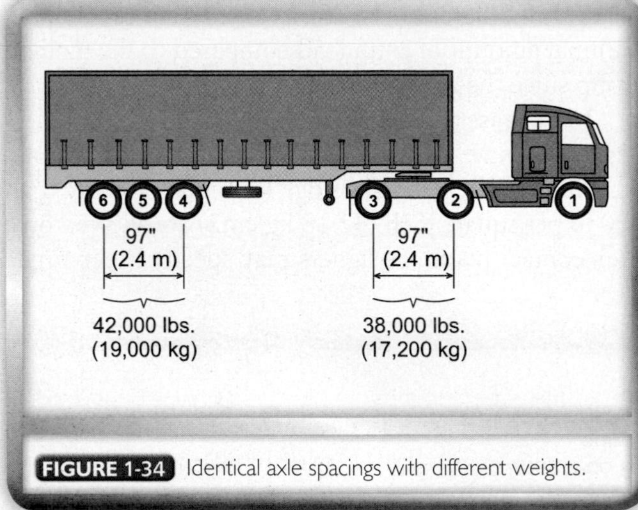

FIGURE 1-34 Identical axle spacings with different weights.

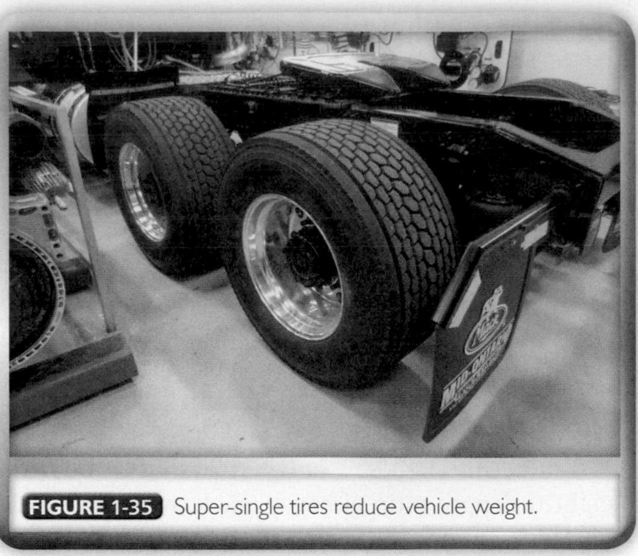

FIGURE 1-35 Super-single tires reduce vehicle weight.

TABLE 1-2: Classification of Chassis by Gross Vehicle Weight (GVW)

Class	Gross Vehicle Weight (GVW) lb (kg)
1	6,000 lb (2,721.6 kg) or less
2	6,001–10,000 lb (2,722–4,535.9 kg)
3	10,001–14,000 lb (4,536.4–6,350.3 kg)
4	14,001–16,000 lb (6,350.7–7,257.5 kg)
5	16,001–19,500 lb (7,257.9–8,845.1 kg)
6	19,501–26,000 lb (8,845.5–11,793.4 kg)
7	26,001–33,000 lb (11,793.9 kg–14,968.5 kg)
8	33,001 lb (14,969 kg) or more

tires, as shown in FIGURE 1-35, as a way to reduce a vehicle's overall weight (by using fewer tires) but still be in compliance with the regulation.

Vehicle Weight Ratings

Numerous configurations of trucks, tractor-trailers, and even buses can be classified by length, weight, number of axles, and number of wheels. In North America, one of the most common ways trucks are categorized is by **gross vehicle weight (GVW)**. GVW refers to the maximum design weight of a vehicle including a full tank of fuel, fully loaded to its capacity, and with all passengers. TABLE 1-2 shows the classifications of vehicles by GVW. The heaviest classification using this method is GVW class 8 vehicles. Class 8 includes vehicles weighing more than 33,001 lb (14,969 kg) and which are usually considered heavy trucks.

Gross Vehicle Weight Rating

A similar classification system based on weight is **gross vehicle weight rating (GVWR)**. GVWR is the design rating specified by a manufacturer as the recommended maximum weight of a vehicle when fully loaded. Trucks or power units (tractor) are classified primarily into a class between 4 and 8 based on their GVWR.

General legislation in North America limits the gross vehicle weight of a vehicle, or a combination of vehicles, according to the number of axles and the distance between the axles. Those limits are listed in TABLE 1-3.

TABLE 1-3: General Law Gross Weight Limits

Number of Axles	Weight Limit
2 Axles	34,000 pounds (15,422.1 kg)
3 Axles	54,000 pounds (24,494 kg)
4 Axles	69,000 pounds (31, 297.9 kg)
5 Axles	80,000 pounds (36,287.4 kg)
6 or More Axles	100,000 pounds (45,359.2 kg)

Many exceptions and variations are made to the general rule. As an example of how axle spacing affects maximum load, consider that vehicles with multiple axles whose centers are less than 4 feet (1.2 m) apart are classified as a single axle unit. The situation is even more complex for triaxle combinations. When a vehicle has a single axle with center-to-center distances closer than 10 feet (3.0 m) (or a steering axle closer than 9 feet (2.7 m) to a triaxle unit, the single axle is considered part of that triaxle. The presence of the additional axle does not increase the allowable legal load capacity of that triaxle unit.

FIGURE 1-36A shows a manufacturer's decal with GVWR for a tandem axle tractor; **FIGURE 1-36B** shows a decal with GVWR of a single-axle straight truck.

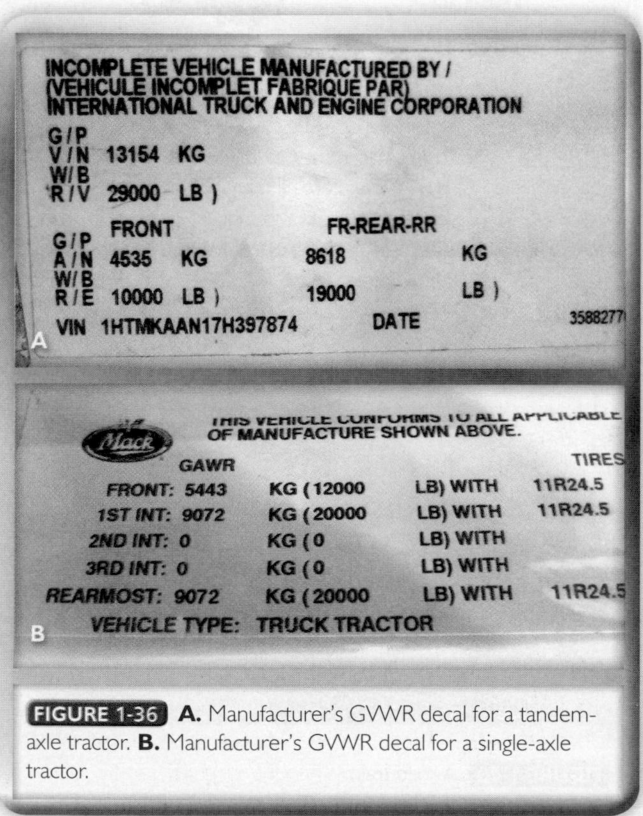

FIGURE 1-36 **A.** Manufacturer's GVWR decal for a tandem-axle tractor. **B.** Manufacturer's GVWR decal for a single-axle tractor.

Gross Combined Weight Rating

The **gross combined weight rating (GCWR)** is a specific maximum weight limit determined by the vehicle manufacturer. Unlike other weight ratings, the GCWR takes into account two individual (yet attached) vehicles—the tow vehicle, or tractor, and the trailer.

Classification of Heavy Vehicles by Combination

Combination vehicles are two or more combined or coupled vehicle units. Combined vehicles can be divided into tractor/semi-trailers, truck/full trailers, and truck/pole trailers. A **full trailer** is a trailer that is supported at both ends with an axle and does not rest on a fifth wheel. The name **semi-trailer** comes from the coupling method where some of the trailer's load is actually carried by the tractor through a connection known as a fifth wheel, which is a hitching device located above its drive wheels. (We will cover hitching devices in greater detail in the chapter Fifth Wheels and Hitching Devices.)

In contrast to a semi-trailer, a full trailer has axles at the front and rear of the trailer, which carry the entire load. That allows the trailer to be pulled by any vehicle with an appropriate hitching system. Combinations may also have multiple trailers, referred to as A-trains, B-trains, and C-trains, which are differentiated by the hitching mechanism connecting the trailers.

A-Trains

An **A-train's** second trailer is a full trailer unit connected by a draw bar to a single hitch point on the lead (first) trailer. An A-train consists of a tractor pulling a semi-trailer and a second, full trailer, behind the semitrailer. The shape of the articulation point—the "A" shape of the draw bar on the converter dolly—lends the name to the tractor trailer combination. **FIGURE 1-37A** shows an A-train configuration and **FIGURE 1-37B** shows how the dolly connects the trailer to the semitrailer.

B-Trains

A **B-train** consists of a tractor pulling a semi-trailer and a second, semi-trailer behind the first semi-trailer. This combination gets its name from the shape of the articulation points that connect the trailers which are shaped like a letter "B", as shown in **FIGURE 1-38A**. The B-train does not use a converter dolly. Instead, the lead trailer has a sliding section of frame to which a fifth wheel is attached. A B-train's second trailer is simply another semi-trailer connected to a fifth wheel on the rear of the first trailer. In some locations this is referred to as a "B Double" or an

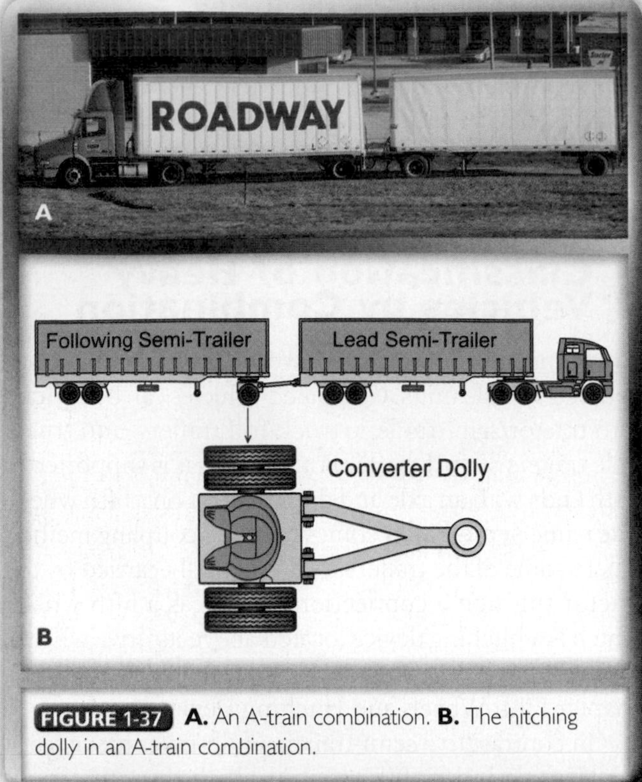

FIGURE 1-37 **A.** An A-train combination. **B.** The hitching dolly in an A-train combination.

FIGURE 1-38 **A.** A B-train combination. **B.** The articulation points on a typical B-train configuration.

"Interlink" arrangement. The B-train is the most stable of the three combinations (A, B, C) because it uses a fifth-wheel connection between trailers. The fifth-wheel connection is the best at resisting the rollover of the second trailer. **FIGURE 1-38B** shows the articulation points of a B-train configuration.

C-Trains

A **C-train** is similar to the A-train except that it has two drawbars and is therefore somewhat more stable. The different dolly types are shown in **FIGURE 1-39**. Depending on the location where C-trains are used, they often have different names. Western doubles, Rocky Mountain doubles, or Road Trains (if more than two trailers are used) are names given to combination vehicles with multiple trailers of different lengths and hitching mechanisms. **FIGURE 1-40** shows a road train.

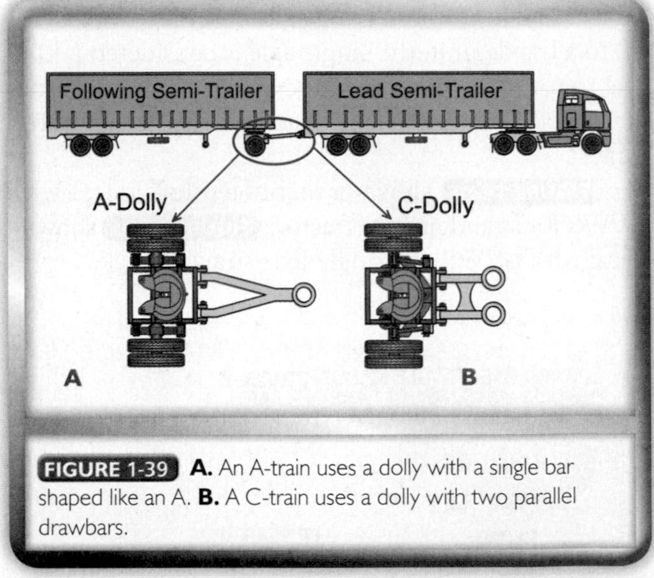

FIGURE 1-39 **A.** An A-train uses a dolly with a single bar shaped like an A. **B.** A C-train uses a dolly with two parallel drawbars.

FIGURE 1-40 A road train.

Hitching Devices

While a variety of vehicle factors and operating conditions can change the general rules for maximum axle weight, the best solution to enable transportation of heavier and larger loads is to add more axles to the vehicle configuration in order to minimize damage to road surfaces. However, adding more axles to a rigid chassis would make steering and maneuvering a vehicle almost impossible—particularly with the addition of tens of thousands of pounds of cargo. Therefore, trailers must be attached in such a way to enable improved steering and maneuverability and to allow the vehicle to articulate or bend when turning.

A variety of coupling devices are used to connect or hitch trailers to tractors while allowing articulation between tractor and towed units. Which type of device is used in a given situation depends on the size and type of trailer and the product being transported. Fifth wheels, pintle hooks, couplers, and ball hitches are some of the hitching devices that have been developed to tow trailers and specialized equipment. These are described in greater detail in the following sections.

Fifth Wheels

Fifth wheels are a plate-type coupling device designed to support the weight of a semi-trailer. As illustrated in FIGURE 1-41, the fifth wheel is mounted on the rear frame of a tractor and has locking jaws that fasten the trailer kingpin to the plate. The fifth wheel is the point of articulation between the trailer and the tractor. That means the fifth wheel enables the trailer and tractor to turn effectively, for example, when cornering or changing direction.

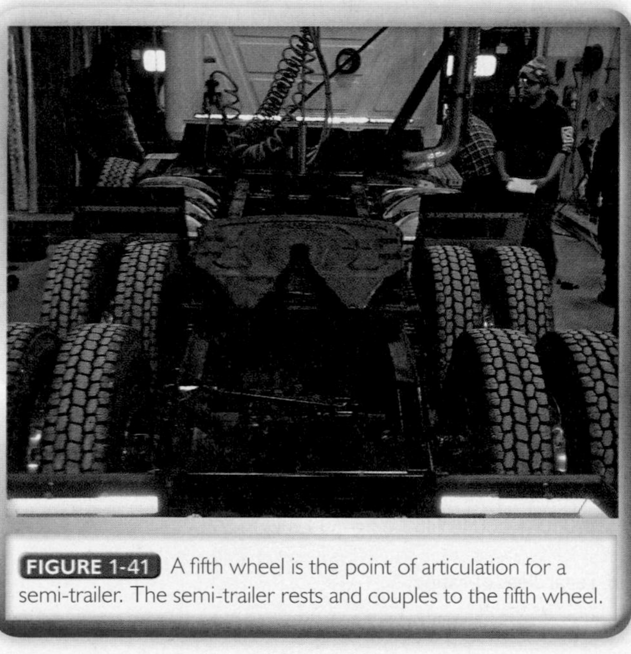

FIGURE 1-41 A fifth wheel is the point of articulation for a semi-trailer. The semi-trailer rests and couples to the fifth wheel.

Resting on the fifth wheel is the **upper coupler**. As illustrated in FIGURE 1-42A and FIGURE 1-42B, upper couplers consist of a steel plate and a kingpin fastened to the underside of the forward portion of a semi-trailer frame. The upper coupler is designed to tow and support the weight of the trailer. The upper coupler is attached to the underside of the trailer frame. The coupler contains a kingpin that is coupled to the tractor's fifth wheel.

Pintle Hooks and Couplers

Draw bars are used to connect tow vehicles to a tractor or lead towing unit. A lunette is the round attachment to a drawbar that attaches with a pintle hook or coupler. **Pintle hooks** are trailer hitching devices that use a fixed towing horn that connects with a drawbar eye attached to the towed vehicle. As illustrated in FIGURE 1-43, pintle hooks are coupled by raising the drawbar eye over the pintle horn and locking it closed with a pivoting latch. An air-cushioned pintle hook is a rigid pintle hook equipped with an air chamber connected to a plunger, which removes the slack between the pintle horn and the drawbar.

FIGURE 1-42 **A.** The top plate (lower coupler) of a fifth wheel. **B.** The upper coupler of a fifth wheel with the kingpin showing.

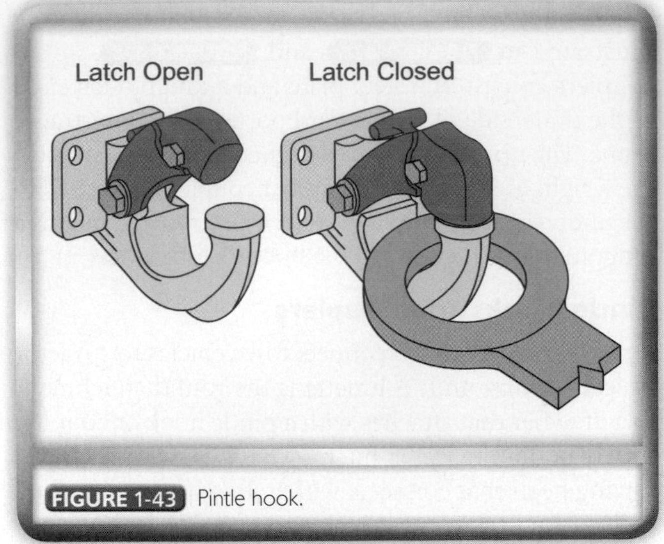

FIGURE 1-43 Pintle hook.

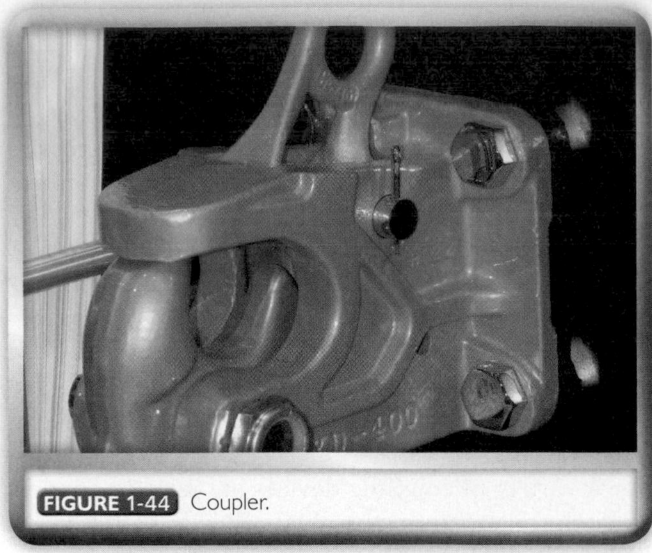

FIGURE 1-44 Coupler.

Couplers are hitching devices that look similar to pintle hooks with one exception. As illustrated in FIGURE 1-44, the towing horn pivots and is not fixed. Since the wider opening coupler connects easier than a pintle hook, couplers are especially useful in applications with frequent trailer coupling and uncoupling.

Pintle hooks and couplers are selected by towing and vertical weight. To minimize shock loads when initially moving a trailer or during braking, a snubber or load dampener can be used. Rubber cushions or heavy springs are integrated into the device to permit some movement along the centerline and some side to side strain relief.

Ball Hitches

Ball hitches are used with tongue-trailer draw bars. Ball hitches are used on light- and medium-duty vehicles using a tongue type tow bar, which loops over a ball. The tow-ball allows swiveling and articulation of a trailer with a trailer tongue. Ball hitches have the advantage of providing a positive no-slack fit.

Ball hitches are classified in two ways. They are classified by the weight supported by the ball or **tongue weight (TW)** and by the **gross trailer weight (GTW)**, which is the weight of the trailer and cargo. Different sizes of balls are used depending on the category of hitch. A 2-5/16" (5.9 cm) diameter ball coupler is the largest size for a Class 4 hitch. Goose neck trailers, such as those used for hauling large motor homes, can use ball hitches mounted to a pick-up truck bed. The ball is fastened to the vehicle at a frame section called a receiver.

As a general rule, the vertical load on the trailer tongue should be at least 10% of the gross trailer weight. When loaded properly, the weight of the load will assist stabilizing the drawbar for improved directional control when cornering. When loaded properly, the weight of the load will also reduce the wear caused by surging speed changes. Excessive vertical load results in accelerated wear on the tongue and tow bar.

Trailer hitches are classified according to the weights listed in TABLE 1-4.

TABLE 1-4: Trailer Hitch Classifications

Class	Weight-Carrying Rating in Gross Trailer Weight (GTW)	Weight-Carrying Rating in Tongue Weight (TW)
Class 1	Up to 2,000 lb (907.2 kg) GTW	Up to 200 lb (90.7 kg) TW
Class 2	Up to 3,500 lb (1,587.6 kg) GTW	300–350 lb (136.1–158.8 kg) TW
Class 3*	Up to 5,000 lb (2,268 kg) GTW	Up to 500 lb (226.8 kg) TW
Class 4	Up to 10,000 lb (4,535.9 kg) GTW	1,000–1,200 lb (453.6 kg–544.3 kg) TW

* Also sometimes used to refer to a hitch with any 2" (5.1 cm) receiver, regardless of rating.

Common Terms and Conventions

Becoming a successful heavy-duty commercial vehicle technician requires an understanding of common terminology and acronyms. TABLE 1-5 lists common truck terms, their definitions, and their abbreviations, along with some illustrations to clarify exactly what each term and abbreviation refers to on a heavy-duty vehicle.

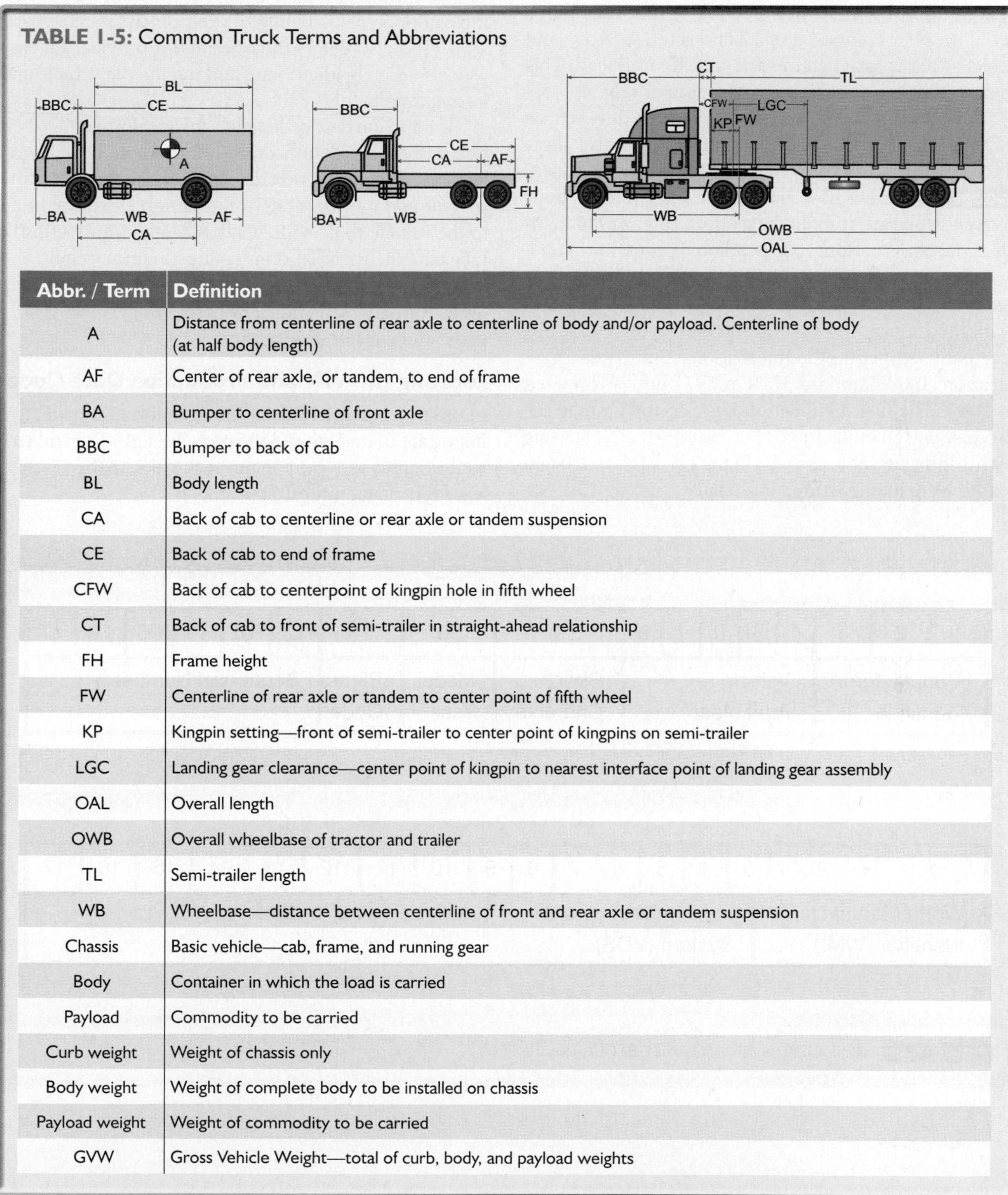

TABLE 1-5: Common Truck Terms and Abbreviations

Abbr. / Term	Definition
A	Distance from centerline of rear axle to centerline of body and/or payload. Centerline of body (at half body length)
AF	Center of rear axle, or tandem, to end of frame
BA	Bumper to centerline of front axle
BBC	Bumper to back of cab
BL	Body length
CA	Back of cab to centerline or rear axle or tandem suspension
CE	Back of cab to end of frame
CFW	Back of cab to centerpoint of kingpin hole in fifth wheel
CT	Back of cab to front of semi-trailer in straight-ahead relationship
FH	Frame height
FW	Centerline of rear axle or tandem to center point of fifth wheel
KP	Kingpin setting—front of semi-trailer to center point of kingpins on semi-trailer
LGC	Landing gear clearance—center point of kingpin to nearest interface point of landing gear assembly
OAL	Overall length
OWB	Overall wheelbase of tractor and trailer
TL	Semi-trailer length
WB	Wheelbase—distance between centerline of front and rear axle or tandem suspension
Chassis	Basic vehicle—cab, frame, and running gear
Body	Container in which the load is carried
Payload	Commodity to be carried
Curb weight	Weight of chassis only
Body weight	Weight of complete body to be installed on chassis
Payload weight	Weight of commodity to be carried
GVW	Gross Vehicle Weight—total of curb, body, and payload weights

Vehicle Identification Numbers

Large numbers of vehicles with many variations of makes and models with different equipment levels are produced every day across the world. Vehicle information labels have become very important because they help to uniquely identify the vehicle. Those labels contain a **vehicle identification number (VIN)** that is a unique serial number composed of 17 characters—letters and digits—that is assigned to each vehicle produced. This means that no two vehicles have the same VIN.

As with other vehicle types, every heavy-duty vehicle has a unique identification number. These VINs allow the equipment on a truck or bus to be clearly identified. **FIGURE 1-45** shows how the number and letter positions convey information about the manufacturer, make, vehicle type, chassis, front-axle position, brakes, and more.

Since 1981, the VIN has been made up of 17 characters. The VIN is designed to identify motor vehicles of all kinds: cars, trucks, buses, motorcycles, etc. It was originally defined in the International Standards Organization (ISO) Standard 3779 in 1977 and was revised in 1983. The first digit identifies the country where the product was manufactured. For example, VINs starting with 1 indicate vehicles made in the US. VINs that begin with 2 were manufactured in Canada.

The second digit designates the original equipment manufacturer (OEM). For example, an "H" in the second position indicates the vehicle was manufactured by Navistar. A "V" would be Volvo and "F" would be a Freightliner vehicle.

VINs can be used to check the service history of a vehicle and also are used to identify the vehicle for ordering components. Labeling the vehicle and vehicle parts with VINs also deters theft because it provides an easy way of uniquely identifying and tracing the vehicle and its major parts.

Production date codes and vehicle information labels also add to the identification information available on vehicles. The production date is the date of manufacture by year and month. Other information labels are fitted to the vehicle to provide ready access to information—for example, tire inflation pressures, vehicle weight, and load-carrying capacity. All of these information labels are used regularly by technicians to identify vehicles, order parts, and check service history.

Locating the VIN and Production Date Code

In order to locate a VIN and production date code, it is important to understand the principles of VINs and correctly identify the components that make up the 17-character vehicle identification number.

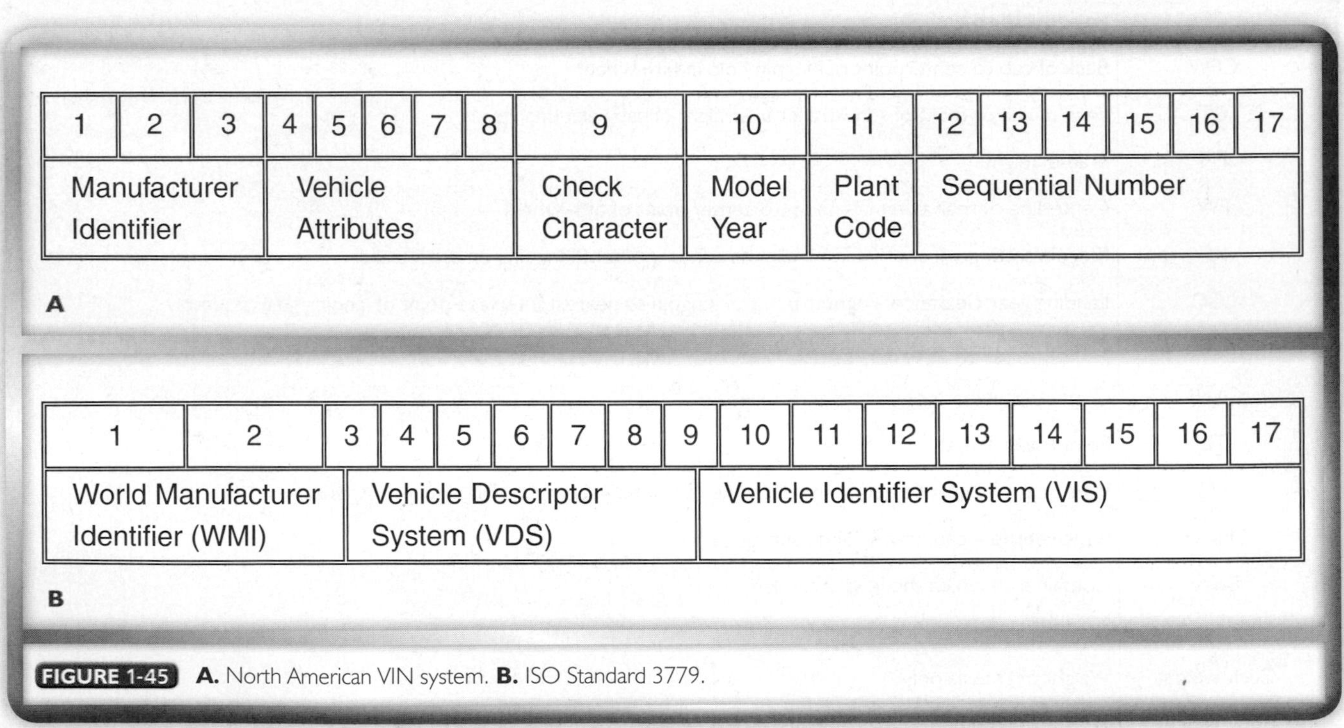

FIGURE 1-45 **A.** North American VIN system. **B.** ISO Standard 3779.

The VIN is usually located on the frame, engine, inside the driver's door on an information sticker, and even on some components and in the vehicle's computer modules. The VIN is unique worldwide, identifying the country of manufacture, manufacturer's name, division name, model, and other important information. Since 1981, all worldwide vehicle manufacturers use this numbering system. By learning to interpret the system, the identity of a vehicle or a component can be determined and verified.

Whenever a vehicle is registered or a registered vehicle is sold, a record of the VIN is kept. From this registry, information about the vehicle can be accessed, including the title history, which can tell you who has owned the vehicle. The registry may reveal a salvage title, which tells you that the vehicle has been wrecked and suffered irreparable damage. The registry can also indicate if the vehicle has had an odometer rollback (mileage reduction), which is evidence of odometer tampering.

Decoding a VIN

There are two different, but essentially compatible, 17-character VIN standards shown in FIGURE 1-45: the North American VIN system and the ISO Standard 3779, which is used in most of the rest of the world. FIGURE 1-46 shows how the numbers are structured.

To decode a North American VIN, follow the steps in SKILL DRILL 1-1.

Seventeen-Character Vehicle Identification Number (VIN)									
Typical VIN	**1HT**	**M**	**K**	**AA**	**N**	**1**	**7**	**H**	**397874**
Character Position	**1, 2, 3**	**4**	**5**	**6, 7**	**8**	**9**	**10**	**11**	**12 thru 17**
Code Description									
Manufacturer, Make, Vehicle Type									
Chassis, Front Axle Position, Brakes									
Vehicle Model Series, Cab									
Engine Model, Horsepower Range									
Gross Vehicle Weight Rating (GVWR)									
Check Digit									
Vehicle Model Year									
Plant of Manufacture									
Production Number									

FIGURE 1-46 Vehicle Identification Number and what each digit or character indicates.

SKILL DRILL 1-1 Decoding the VIN number

Seventeen-Character Vehicle Identification Number (VIN)									
Typical VIN	**1HT**	**M**	**K**	**AA**	**N**	**1**	**7**	**H**	**397874**
Character Position	**1, 2, 3**	**4**	**5**	**6, 7**	**8**	**9**	**10**	**11**	**12 thru 17**
Code Description									

1. The VIN is 1HTMKAAN17H397874. The first character is the country of origin. This number or letter indicates the company that manufactured the vehicle and the country of origin.
2. The second character is usually a letter; it tells you the name of the manufacturer, which is International in this case..
3. The third character tells you the vehicle type; in this case, "truck".
4. The fourth character indicates the type of chassis
5. The fifth character describes the model series and cab. This is a Durastar 4400.
6. The sixth and seventh characters tell you the engine model and horsepower range. In this case, it's a DT 466.
7. The eighth character provides details , such as vehicle recommended gross vehicle weight rating (GVWR), which is in this case 26,001 to 33,000 lb (11,818 to 15,000 kg).
8. The ninth character is the check character. It is used internally by the manufacturer.
9. The tenth character tells you the year of manufacture. You can decode this character according to a model year identification chart, which in this example shows us that the vehicle was assembled for the 2007 model year.
10. The eleventh character tells you the assembly plant or factory where the vehicle was put together.
11. The final six numbers make up the sequential number of the vehicle as it comes off the assembly line, starting at a base number, which is usually one hundred thousand (100000). So the first vehicle to be produced will usually, but not always, have the number 100001.

Wrap-up

Ready for Review

- Commercial vehicles perform an endless variety of revenue-generating tasks having unique and even unusual functions.
- To properly maintain and service commercial vehicles, it is important to understand the variety of ways commercial vehicles are classified and configured.
- A helpful way to classify commercial vehicles is by considering where a commercial vehicle performs its primary job.
- When classifying commercial vehicles by operating conditions, five broad categories are used: turnpike or interstate; on-highway; on-off-highway or mountainous highway; off-highway; and urban.
- Vehicles are also classified by their vocation, or the work they perform, such as transit, hauling, delivery, fire service, rescue, and so on.
- Depending on the operating conditions and job performed by the vehicle, a commercial vehicle will have a particular chassis, engine, powertrain, cab, and suspension.
- The frame of every heavy vehicle must be sized and built appropriately to be capable of supporting the loads applied to it while adapting to the forces that bend and twist the frame.
- Heavy-vehicle engines must have sufficient power to move heavy loads and accelerate up grades while providing good fuel economy.
- Commercial vehicles require powertrains designed specifically for their particular vocations.
- Tractors and trucks can also be classified according to their drive and non-drive axle configurations. Trailers may be classified similarly but by non-drive axle configurations.
- A common configuration is the tandem axle combination, which uses use two drive axles. Pusher and tag axles are other common types of axles on heavy-duty vehicles.
- Commercial vehicles are commonly classified by their weight and length.
- The Federal Bridge Gross Weight Formula is a legal calculation that establishes the maximum allowable weight of a commercial vehicle traveling on roads and bridges. Axle spacing is a critical consideration in this calculation.
- A common classification system for heavy vehicles uses their gross vehicle weight (GVW). There are eight classes in this system, with the heaviest vehicles having GVW of 33,000 lb (1360.8 kg) or more.
- In addition to regulating the overall weight of vehicle, in North America, a vehicle's weight per axle is also regulated.
- Heavy vehicles can also be classified by combination, such as tractor/semi-trailer, truck/full trailer, and truck/pole trailer.
- Combinations may also have multiple trailers, referred to as A-trains, B-trains, and C-trains, which are differentiated by the hitching mechanism connecting the trailers.
- The best solution to enable transportation of heavier and larger loads is to add more axles to the vehicle configuration in order to minimize damage to road surfaces. Trailers must also be attached in such a way to enable improved steering and maneuverability and to allow the vehicle to articulate or bend when turning.
- The fifth wheel is the point of articulation between the trailer and the tractor and as such enables the trailer and tractor to turn effectively, for example, when cornering or changing direction.
- Vehicle classifications by hitching device rely on the gross trailer rate and the tongue weight.

Vocabulary Builder

articulation The movement of the suspension system in reaction to road bumps or terrain.

A-train A combination vehicle in which the second trailer is a full trailer unit connected by a draw bar to a single hitch point on the lead (first) trailer.

ball hitch A single-point connection configuration for a hitch that uses a tongue shaped draw bar, which loops over a ball connected to the tow vehicle.

Bridge Formula B *See* Federal Bridge Gross Weight Formula

B-train A combination vehicle in which the tractor pulls a semi-trailer and a third, full trailer behind the semi-trailer.

combination vehicles Two or more combined or coupled vehicle units.

coupler Trailer hitching device, similar to pintle hooks, but in which the towing horn pivots and is not fixed.

C-train A combination vehicle similar to an A-train but using a dolly that has two parallel drawbars.

draw bars Bars used to connect tow vehicles to a tractor or lead towing unit.

Federal Bridge Formula *See* Federal Bridge Gross Weight Formula

Federal Bridge Gross Weight Formula Laws that limit the weight-to-length ratio of heavy trucks with the goal of protecting roads and bridges from the damage caused by the concentrated weight of shorter trucks. Also known as *Bridge Formula B* or *Federal Bridge Formula.*

fifth wheel A plate-type coupling device designed to support the weight of a semi-trailer.

full trailer A trailer that is supported at both ends with an axle and does not rest on a fifth wheel.

gradability The capability of a vehicle to maintain forward motion on a specified grade while sustaining a minimum speed.

gross combined weight rating (GCWR) A specific maximum weight limit determined by the vehicle manufacturer and which takes into account two individual (yet attached) vehicles—the tow vehicle, or tractor, and the trailer.

gross trailer weight (GTW) The maximum carrying capacity of a trailer calculated by measuring the trailer weight and load.

gross vehicle weight (GVW) The maximum design weight of a vehicle including a full tank of fuel, fully loaded to its capacity, and with all passengers.

gross vehicle weight rating (GVWR) The design rating specified by a manufacturer as the recommended maximum weight of a vehicle when fully loaded to capacity, including all passengers and a full tank of fuel.

gross weight limit The maximum legal weight of a vehicle that can travel on roads and bridges.

horsepower A unit of measure of power that conveys how fast the engine can turn while producing torque.

peak torque The maximum torque an engine can produce.

pintle hook Trailer hitching device that uses a fixed towing horn that connects with a drawbar eye attached to the towed vehicle.

semi-trailer A trailer that has some of its load carried by the tractor through a hitching device.

startability The capability of a vehicle to commence moving forward on a specified grade.

tongue weight (TW) The weight supported by the ball (tongue) in a ball hitch.

torque rise The difference between engine torque produced at rated speed (maximum engine RPM under load) and peak torque. Torque rise is expressed as a percentage of torque at the rated speed.

upper coupler A steel plate and a kingpin fastened to the underside of the forward portion of a semi-trailer frame and designed to tow and support the weight of the trailer.

vehicle identification number (VIN) A unique serial number composed of 17 characters—letters and digits—that is assigned to each vehicle produced.

Review Questions

1. An example of an operating condition for commercial vehicles includes:
   a. road surfaces.
   b. grades.
   c. speed of travel.
   d. All of the choices are correct.
2. Commercial vehicles operate on on-highway conditions where the roads are typically level to rolling with occasional maximum grades up to:
   a. 3%.
   b. 8%.
   c. 12%.
   d. 14%.
3. Common vehicles in the pick-up and delivery application include:
   a. tow trucks and wreckers.
   b. flatbed trucks.
   c. auto haulers.
   d. All of the choices are correct.
4. The following are common examples of fire service vehicles, EXCEPT:
   a. tractor-trailers.
   b. aerial platforms.
   c. aerial ladders.
   d. pumpers tankers.
5. A typical logging vehicle is a:
   a. wood chip hauler: straight truck.
   b. wood chip hauler: tractor and trailer.
   c. log hauling tractor trailer combination.
   d. All of the choices are correct.
6. A typical school bus configurations is a:
   a. front engine commercial chassis.
   b. front engine integral coach.
   c. rear engine integral coach.
   d. All of the choices are correct.
7. Engines provide which of the following features?
   a. Power to move loads
   b. Power to accelerate up grades
   c. Good fuel economy
   d. All of the choices are correct.
8. Suspension systems commonly use which of the following materials for springs?
   a. Air
   b. Solid rubber
   c. Leaf springs
   d. All of the choices are correct.
9. For tandem axles spread more than 40", the total weight on two or more consecutive axles is typically:
   a. 20,000 lb.
   b. 34,000 lb.
   c. 36,000 lb.
   d. 40,000 lb.
10. What is the General Law Gross Weight Limit for a vehicle with four axles?
    a. 54,000 lb
    b. 69,000 lb
    c. 75,000 lb
    d. 80,000 lb

ASE-Type Questions

1. Technician A says each application of commercial vehicles will be purpose built according its own specialized requirements. Technician B says each application's vehicle being purpose built includes the ability to carry people, products, or perform services. Who is correct?
   a. Technician A
   b. Technician B
   c. Both Technician A and Technician B
   d. Neither Technician A nor Technician B

2. Technician A says the operating condition of off-highway includes 20% of the total operating time on secondary roads made from good concrete or asphalt. Technician B says the operating condition of off-highway includes intermittent grades of up to 12%. Who is correct?
   a. Technician A
   b. Technician B
   c. Both Technician A and Technician B
   d. Neither Technician A nor Technician B

3. While discussing construction vehicles, technician A says operation is primarily movement of material to and from a job site. Technician B says operating conditions are 90% of loaded operation on road surfaces made of concrete, asphalt, gravel, crushed rock, or hard packed dirt. Who is correct?
   a. Technician A
   b. Technician B
   c. Both Technician A and Technician B
   d. Neither Technician A nor Technician B

4. 4. Technician A says the intercity coach is a category of vehicles that transports people and occasionally light freight between cities and/or suburban areas. Technician B says typical vehicle types in this category are tour coaches and cross country coaches. Who is correct?
   a. Technician A
   b. Technician B
   c. Both Technician A and Technician B
   d. Neither Technician A nor Technician B

5. Technician A says refuse vehicles encounter steep grades of up to 20% when travelling into landfill, transfer, or recycling sites. Technician B says refuse vehicles typically have a high frequency of accelerations and stops for every mile travelled. Who is correct?
   a. Technician A
   b. Technician B
   c. Both Technician A and Technician B
   d. Neither Technician A nor Technician B

6. Technician A says a frame must be sized and built appropriately to be capable of supporting the loads applied to it. Technician B says the frame has the additional task of adapting to the forces that bend and twist the frame. Who is correct?
   a. Technician A
   b. Technician B
   c. Both Technician A and Technician B
   d. Neither Technician A nor Technician B

7. Technician A says start-ability refers to the capability to commence forward motion on a specified grade. Technician B says an engine's torque output and powertrain gear ratios will determine the steepest grade a truck can begin to climb from a standing stop. Who is correct?
   a. Technician A
   b. Technician B
   c. Both Technician A and Technician B
   d. Neither Technician A nor Technician B

8. Technician A says auxiliary braking devices: compression release, exhaust-based, or driveline retarders are not considered to be in the category of special equipment. Technician B says aerodynamic fairings are considered special equipment. Who is correct?
   a. Technician A
   b. Technician B
   c. Both Technician A and Technician B
   d. Neither Technician A nor Technician B

9. Technician A says GVW class 8 vehicles are usually considered heavy trucks. Technician B says trucks or power units (tractors) are classified primarily into a class between 2 and 8 based on their GVW. Who is correct?
   a. Technician A
   b. Technician B
   c. Both Technician A and Technician B
   d. Neither Technician A nor Technician B

10. Technician A says the gross combination weight rating is a specific maximum weight limit determined by the manufacturer. Technician B says tractors and trucks can also be classified according to their drive and non-drive axle configurations. Who is correct?
   a. Technician A
   b. Technician B
   c. Both Technician A and Technician B
   d. Neither Technician A nor Technician B

CHAPTER 2

NATEF Tasks

Required Supplemental Tasks

Preparing Vehicle for Service	Page
■ Identify information needed and the service requested on a repair order.	49, 61
■ Complete work order to include customer information, vehicle identifying information, customer concern, related service history, cause, and correction.	49–50, 61
■ Demonstrate use of the three Cs (concern, cause, and correction).	49
■ Identify purpose and demonstrate proper use of fender covers, mats.	55
■ Review vehicle service history.	61
Preparing Vehicle for Customer	
■ Ensure vehicle is prepared to return to customer per school/company policy (floor mats, steering wheel cover, etc.).	55

Workplace Employability Skills

Chapter 2 covers all NATEF tasks under Workplace Employability Skills—Personal Standards and Workplace Employability Skills—Work Habits/Ethic.

Knowledge Objectives

After reading this chapter, you will be able to:

1. Identify career paths in a commercial vehicle shop. (pp 38–39)
2. Explain trade certification processes and meaning of various certification levels. (pp 40–41)
3. Describe the barriers to effective listening. (pp 40–41)
4. Describe the components of active listening. (pp 42–43)
5. Explain the elements of effective speaking, including asking constructive questions and proper phone etiquette. (pp 42–43)

Careers, Employability Skills, and Workplace Practices

Knowledge Objectives, continued

6. Explain the purpose of people skills and self-presentation, including appearance, body language, and tone of voice. (pp 42–43)
7. Explain effective reading and researching techniques. (pp 45–46)
8. Describe the purpose and use of owner's manuals and shop manuals/service information. (pp 46–48)
9. Describe effective writing or documentation techniques. (pp. 48–49)
10. Describe the information and its use within a repair/work order. (pp 49, 61)
11. Describe the elements of good customer service. (pp 53–54)
12. Explain how TSBs, service campaigns, and recall information are used. (pp 57–58)
13. Describe the purpose and use of labor guides. (pp 58–59)
14. Identify the purpose and use of a parts program. (p 59)
15. Describe the purpose and use of service history. (pp 61–62)

Skills Objectives

After reading this chapter, you will be able to:

1. Use effective strategies for listening. (pp 42–43)
2. Use effective strategies for speaking. (pp 42–43)
3. Use effective strategies for reading. (pp 45–46)
4. Use a service information program while conducting a service or repair. (pp 46–48)
5. Use effective strategies for writing, including completing a repair order, a shop or equipment inspection sheet, an accident report, and a vehicle inspection form. (pp 48–49)
6. Use a shop/repair manual while conducting a service or repair. (pp 47–48)
7. Use a labor guide to estimate the cost or charge of conducting a service or repair. (p 60) **SKILL DRILL 2-1**
8. Use a parts program to identify and order the correct replacement parts for a service or repair. (p 60) **SKILL DRILL 2-2**
9. Use a repair/work order to identify the information needed and the service requested. (p 61) **SKILL DRILL 2-3**
10. Use service history in the repair and service of vehicles. (p 62) **SKILL DRILL 2-4**
11. Use an owner's manual to obtain vehicle information. (pp 62–63)

Introduction

The saying "if you've got it, a truck brought it" is a catchy summary underlining the importance of the trucking industry. Whether it is moving groups of people from place to place, transporting raw materials to factories, or manufactured goods to retail centers, commercial vehicles perform a wide variety of essential functions needed to keep people and economies operating productively and efficiently.

These vehicles do not maintain themselves though. Skilled technicians are vital to ensure commercial vehicles stay on the road, operating efficiently, safely, and reliably. So, if you are a person who values results-oriented work and is interested in a vocational pathway that allows you to use your strong, hands-on technical abilities, a career as a heavy-duty commercial vehicle technician offers meaningful and satisfying work that few other occupations can boast.

This chapter will cover basic information about careers available in the heavy-duty commercial trucking industry, including the various classifications of jobs and the skills and certifications required to hold them. The chapter will also discuss several critical communication skills and workplace habits that contribute to a successful career servicing heavy-duty commercial vehicles.

Careers in the Commercial Vehicle Industry

Careers in the commercial vehicle industry are numerous and range from basic technicians to technicians that hold specialty certifications. This section will describe the duties of heavy-duty vehicle (HDV) technicians, the job classifications for different career pathways, and the workplace conditions common in the industry.

Technician Duties

Commercial vehicle technicians, are the people who inspect, repair, and diagnose mechanical, electrical, and electronic control systems in heavy-duty trucks, buses, trailers, and medium-duty commercial transportation trucks. They are employed by new truck and trailer dealerships, garages of commercial fleets, specialty repair shops, transit and bus companies, plus other service centers, which may include service shops. Technicians are also employed by vehicle manufacturers to perform diagnostic work and major repairs or replacement of components on new vehicles.

On any typical workday a truck-coach and trailer technician will be involved in any of the following:

- Road testing vehicles, performing diagnostic testing of vehicle systems and components using specialized

You Are the Technician

During your second week on the job, your supervisor has pulled you off the shop floor and into the service department office. You will be shadowing the service manager, Bob, to gain firsthand experience communicating effectively with customers in person. The first customer has an appointment with the service department for a safety recall issue. Bob asks questions to gather all the necessary information from the customer while making eye contact with him. As a new service technician, you will practice writing up your own work orders for Bob to critique after the customer has been taken care of. After the customer has answered all the questions, Bob reviews and reiterates to the customer his understanding of the concern to be sure it is accurate. Bob writes up a work order, reviews the concern and agreed upon course of action with the customer, and then guides the customer to the service department lounge to wait for his vehicle.

1. What are the three types of "right questions" to ask when gathering information?
2. What are the three Cs all work orders should contain?
3. Explain why empathy is an important skill to have when dealing with upset customers.

equipment and diagnostic software to identify and pinpoint faults or validate their proper operation.

- Adjusting, repairing, or replacing parts and components of engine and chassis systems including the frame cab, body, air brakes, steering, transmissions, drive axles, fuel injection systems, hydraulic, exhaust after treatment, air conditioning, electrical, and electronic systems. **FIGURE 2-1** shows the parts department of a truck service center in a typical heavy-duty vehicle dealership.
- Testing and adjusting repaired systems to manufacturer's performance specifications.
- Performing inspections and preventative maintenance service, such as chassis lubrication, oil changes, and tire repairs.
- Making operating and service recommendations to customers about vehicle repairs.
- Completing reports, reviewing work orders, and discussing work with a supervisor.

While many technicians become skilled in diagnosing, servicing, and repairing most vehicle systems, specialization of skills can take place in the areas of engine and fuel systems, transmission and driveline, air conditioning, refrigeration and heating systems, brakes, steering, vehicle alignment, trailer repair, or diagnostic services.

Job Classifications

The commercial vehicle industry offers a range of employment opportunities. One need not be an experienced technician to enter this field. A variety of entry level jobs in service facilities provide a helpful starting point to get exposure to the trade. Cleaning vehicles, pick-up and delivery of vehicles, equipment, and/or parts, assisting other technicians performing chassis lubrication and oil change services, and washing parts are common activities that can provide useful experience when making a decision about whether to begin a career in the industry. The training and exposure provided by working and learning in a service facility or vocational college, such as that shown in **FIGURE 2-2**, can also lead to positions in management, sales, technical support, or teaching. Service managers, service writers, and technical advisors are typically recruited after they have demonstrated skill and expertise in the trade as technicians.

Service Technicians

Joining the commercial vehicle service industry in its repair and service sector as a service technician is the most popular trade pathway. This position allows for maximum exposure to the most recent technological developments and advancements in the industry. Becoming a service technician may require the completion of a college program. Many of these programs are run in partnership with truck manufacturers who provide prospective technicians with an in-depth education and some practical experience in the operation and service of all commercial vehicle systems. The experience gained working on the job provides students with the necessary skills to handle troubleshooting in service facilities while using the classroom instruction provided by the vocational school or manufacturer. Technicians are expected to be knowledgeable in machine shop processes, pneumatics, hydraulics, electronics, as well as in computer skills required to perform many diagnostic and service procedures. **FIGURE 2-3** shows a technician performing repairs on a heavy-duty on-highway truck.

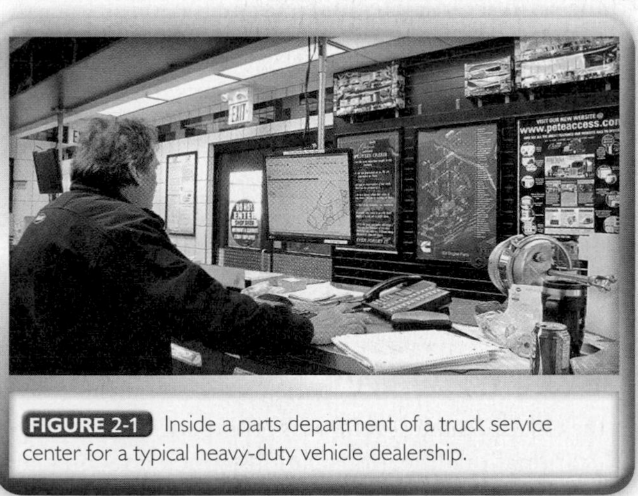

FIGURE 2-1 Inside a parts department of a truck service center for a typical heavy-duty vehicle dealership.

FIGURE 2-2 A typical vocational college lab where students learn to apply theory about hydraulic and pneumatic systems used in commercial vehicles.

FIGURE 2-3 A technician performing repairs on a heavy-duty on-highway truck.

FIGURE 2-4 Apprenticeship students at a vocational college learning to perform electrical diagnostic work on a school bus.

Job opportunities are currently predicted to grow at an annual rate of 15% percent between 2010 and 2020. Retirement by many older workers is also expected to increase demand for more technicians equipped with newer information about the latest technologically advanced equipment. Entry level positions in the industry include tire service, performing service maintenance, or simply assisting experienced technicians in the capacity of a trainee or apprentice, as they are correctly referred to.

Educational Requirements

Although not always compulsory, depending on your country of residence, service technicians are normally required to successfully complete trade related courses or a program at a college or vocational school in addition to having a high school diploma or completion certificate. In most countries, employers prefer technicians who have completed an apprenticeship or received certification from a vocational training program. Most employers only recruit technicians with educational qualifications from an accredited college certificate or associate degree program. For instance, in Canada, trade qualifications are mandatory to work on motor vehicles operated on public roads. A formal apprenticeship period must be served with an employer, as the students in FIGURE 2-4 are doing, before applying for a final general certificate of qualification. After registering the apprenticeship contract with the provincial governing body, apprentices are required to meet performance-based learning outcomes and complete in-school trade-related classes before taking the final exam for a certificate of qualification. An interprovincial red seal is granted to technicians with qualifying exam results to work in all provinces in Canada.

ASE Certification

In the United States, while certification is not a mandatory requirement to work in the trade, the National Institute for Automotive Service Excellence (ASE) offers credentialing to truck-coach and medium-duty truck technicians. Possessing ASE certification leads to better employment opportunities. To gain the ASE qualifications, candidates need a minimum of two year's working experience before taking an exam for each area of specialization. The National Institute for Automotive Service Excellence (ASE) administers certification procedures throughout the United States. Certification tests are scheduled throughout the year and taken at secure testing centers nationwide.The certification areas needed for heavy-duty truck technicians are the following:

- T-series for medium-/heavy-duty truck technicians
- S-series for school bus technicians
- H-series for transit bus technicians (as shown in FIGURE 2-5)

For those aspiring to be a master technician in medium- and heavy-duty trucks, successful completion in the following T-series certification areas is required: T2, T3, T4, T5, T6, and T7.

Master Technicians

In the United States, several years of experience and proper educational qualifications can fast-track a technician's

FIGURE 2-5 Inside a transit bus garage where repair and maintenance are performed on a fleet of urban transit buses.

FIGURE 2-6 A recently overhauled engine connected to a dynamometer in a test cell.

career to that of a master technician status. To be certified as a T-, H-, or S-series ASE Master Technician, the following certification tests must be taken and passed:

- T-Series Master Tech: T2 through T7 inclusive
- S-Series Master Tech: S1 through S6 inclusive
- H-Series Master Tech: H2 through H7 inclusive

Specialty Technicians

Electronics, engines, brakes, hybrid vehicle, and alternate fuels are just a few of the areas in commercial vehicle service and repair on which a technician can specialize. A specialized technician is engaged in an in-depth, continuous education to develop and refine skills to diagnose, service, and maintain the latest vehicle technologies. **FIGURE 2-6** shows a recently overhauled S-50 Detroit engine. The engine is connected to a dynamometer in a test cell to validate its operation and performance. The overhaul and testing of diesel engines is generally performed by a specialist technician with advanced qualifications often obtained from the original equipment manufacturer.

S- and H-Series Certification

There are two certification series under Automotive Service Excellence (ASE) specifically for transit operations: the S-series (school bus) and the H-series (transit bus) certification. All ASE's heavy-duty certifications are designed in such a way that the number represents the subject matter and the letter represents the classification of the vehicle type. Examples of specific S- and H-tests are the following:

- H1 certification for compressed natural gas (CNG)–fueled bus engines
- H8 certification for preventive maintenance
- S1 certification for school bus body systems

Other Countries' Qualifications

Just as outlined above for the United States and Canada, many other countries also have qualifications and formal training specific to those locations. For example, countries like Australia, New Zealand, South Africa, and the UK also have their own formal qualification standards. If you are a budding technician in those countries, and indeed any other geographic location, you should seek information from the appropriate regulatory authorities about the specific requirements and training packages relevant to that country.

Working Conditions

Bus and truck technicians normally work in well-lit, well-ventilated shops, such as the one shown in **FIGURE 2-7**. Shop cleanliness, order, plus care and protection of customer/fleet vehicles are important to a successful and respected business. Health and safety legislation demand strict adherence by employers to regulations in the use of certified personal and shop safety equipment for all workers. Today, working conditions minimize exposure to any working conditions that have the potential to harm shop workers. Professional looking uniforms and or coveralls are always worn to protect clothing from grime, which

FIGURE 2-7 This chassis inspection pit used by a fleet operation is typical of a clean, well-ventilated and well-lit service facility.

FIGURE 2-8 Mobile repair truck.

can be picked up during some work operations. Work is occasionally performed outside a shop environment if a vehicle cannot be towed or moved inside for repairs. Some businesses even specialize in mobile service work where technicians will travel to a customer's work place with tools and basic supplies to perform minor repair work. A mobile repair vehicle is shown in FIGURE 2-8.

If you prefer hands-on work, like problem solving, and enjoy working with tools, repair technician is an ideal career. Having one's own tools and skills enables a technician amazing mobility to work anywhere there are trucks, buses, and trailers needing repair and maintenance.

Employability Skills

Although we have been communicating all of our lives, most of us are not aware of the importance of the communication skills of listening, reading, writing, and speaking. In fact, they are critical skills in the workplace. Learning and applying good communication skills will save you time in the workplace and help you avoid or get through tricky situations. These skills will build over time, and you will find that you learn something new every day when you encounter new situations or meet new people. It is a lifelong learning process to perfect your communication skills.

Since communication is an essential workplace skill needed to function successfully in the commercial-vehicle service facility, this entire section is dedicated to communication. This chapter describes the steps to becoming an effective communicator, offers tips on how to be a good listener—the first step in good communication—and explains how to speak to both customers and your coworkers. Along the way, we will discuss the requirement for writing and preparing documentation used in the workplace.

Effective Listening

Effective listening is an essential skill. We may hear what someone is saying, but are we truly understanding what the person is trying to communicate? The listening process can be difficult to perfect, but is one of the most important skills to possess when gathering information from a customer or any other person. The active listener, like the technician shown in FIGURE 2-9, focuses all of his or her attention on the speaker, including verbal and nonverbal messages. When appropriate, the active listener encourages the speaker to further communicate details that may have otherwise been left out.

The Listening Process

To be a good listener, we need to be aware of barriers that can disrupt the listening process. These barriers can be mental and physical.

Mental barriers are thoughts and feelings that interfere with our listening, such as our own assumptions, emotions, and prejudices. To fully absorb what someone is telling us, we need to learn to set these feelings aside. It takes effort and is not always easy, but it is important to keep an open mind throughout the listening process. For example, when listening to a customer who is describing his or her vehicle concern, it is good practice to allow the customer to fully complete what he or she is saying, even if you believe you have all the information you need.

FIGURE 2-9 The active listener focuses all of his or her attention on the speaker.

Keeping an open mind is also an important first step in practicing empathy, discussed later.

As a listener and active participant, we can encourage the flow of communication by welcoming the speaker, letting him or her know that we care enough to want to understand the message, and acknowledging the speaker's feelings and concerns. To accomplish that, give the speaker your undivided attention by focusing on him or her. This means removing as many distractions as possible. Stop what you are doing, clear your mind of distractions, and look the speaker in the eye.

As the person is speaking, you will also need to provide listening feedback, which indicates to the speaker that you are engaged in what he or she is saying. Feedback can be nonverbal (e.g., facial expressions, body posture) and verbal. Nonverbal language, such as nodding while listening and gesturing while speaking, is used to reinforce or add emphasis. If, while speaking, you send a conflicting message, such as looking annoyed while stating that you value the customer's opinion, the person may tend to believe the nonverbal message over the verbal one, even though it is only half of the total message. For example, consider a customer who contacts you because of a vehicle that will not start and who has his vehicle towed into your shop. The customer complains that the cause is a "bad headlight." Regardless of your personal opinion, you must, as a professional, maintain a sincere and attentive attitude toward the customer. Because nonverbal communication is perceived to be more spontaneous and less conscious, most people tend to believe the nonverbal message more than the actual words expressed.

Empathy

Empathy can help us to avoid selective hearing. To empathize with someone is to attempt to see the situation from his or her point of view. It requires good listening skills, which include an effective use of verbal and nonverbal listening feedback, in order to take in and consider the message without applying our own biases. True empathy means breaking down or putting aside existing mental barriers. For example, when a customer brings a vehicle in with a fault requiring an expensive repair that is not in his or her budget, we risk coming across as uncaring with a "take it or leave it" attitude if we expect the customer to do the repair regardless of the expense. Expressing your understanding of the customer's situation and seeking to explore valid options to resolve the issue will go a long way in building trust with the customer. Remember, we can empathize with people even if we do not agree with them. Also, we do not have to take responsibility for their problem. But we can at least attempt to help them find the best possible solution that will work for them. You will know that you have demonstrated empathy when no valid options were found but the customer thanks you deeply for your assistance.

Empathy not only helps you understand the message better, but also helps you to be less reactive in a negative way as you realize you could feel the same way in that person's position. It may also help to motivate you to find a better resolution of the situation, knowing that it could be you in the very same situation.

Nonverbal Feedback

Nonverbal feedback can be a very useful tool when listening. Your body position, eye contact, and facial expression can all set the direction of a conversation.

We use body language to help emphasize our message, and when listening, we can use it to provide listening feedback. When listening to a speaker, try to sit or stand upright, while making eye contact. Try to avoid folding your arms, as this can be perceived as either an aggressive stance or defensive. At the same time, do not act too casual, such as standing with your hands in your pockets. It may seem harmless, but a customer or supervisor would likely see such a posture as a sign of disrespect or disinterest. Imagine that you are talking to a service manager during a job interview and the manager leans back and puts his or her feet up on the desk. That one gesture would send you a message about the manager's level of professionalism and his or her respect for you and overall interest in the conversation, and in turn would have an effect on the way you viewed the meeting.

Maintaining some eye contact during the conversation, and not looking at something or someone else, will also let your speaker know you are paying attention. If you are taking notes, be sure to look up periodically and make eye contact with the person.

Just as our own facial expressions are being noted by the speaker, remember to pay attention to the speaker's facial expressions to get a clearer sense of his or her message. If, for example, a customer scrunches up her face while talking about the squealing noise the brakes are making, you can probably assume the customer would be happy if you could make that noise go away.

Verbal Feedback

Verbal feedback includes very simple signals that can enhance the conversation and let the person know you comprehend. Some examples are the use of validating statements and supporting statements.

A **validating statement** shows common interest in the topic being discussed. A phrase such as "I see" or "Tell me more" indicates that you are paying attention. A validating statement also helps show empathy for the person speaking and can be a simple "I understand" or "That must be frustrating for you."

A **supporting statement** can urge the speaker to elaborate on a particular topic. Statements like "Go on" and "Give me an example" let the speaker know you would like more detail because you are genuinely interested in finding a solution. This is a necessary part of communication when you are gathering information from the customer—by asking for more details, you are likely to obtain more thorough information, giving you a better starting point for solving the problem. For example, imagine you are talking with a customer about a noise his dump truck made while going over a bump. If you were to say "Tell me more," the customer would know that you understood but wanted a little more information.

Effective Speaking

Speaking is often referred to as an art. That is because there are so many facets to effectively communicate and/or gather information. Whether you are asking a customer about a vehicle or your boss for a raise, knowing how to "artfully speak" will benefit you.

Speaking is a three-step process:

1. Think about the message.
2. Accurately present the message.
3. Check whether the message is correctly understood. If it is not, we have to respond by rethinking and reiterating the message and rechecking with our listener. This process continues until we are satisfied that the listener correctly understands our message.

Think before you speak is easier said than done, but it is not impossible. In some situations, we have time to think and plan beforehand. Others require us to think on our feet. Thinking on your feet simply means you may be called upon to answer or handle a difficult situation quickly. Having to get things right in a fast-paced setting can result in rash decisions, but there are a few tactics you can use to make these situations easier:

1. **Relax.** It is not easy to do in an urgent situation, but attempting to remain calm is extremely beneficial, keeping your mind clear and helping you to embody the confidence needed in such a situation.
2. **Listen.** If the situation requires you to answer a tough question, make sure you fully understand the question before answering. You can always ask the questioner to repeat or, better yet, rephrase the question. This gives you more time to think about your answer and also another chance to read into the intent of the question. Remember that if someone is asking a question of you, then he or she is showing interest. Interest is a good thing!
3. **Pause.** Silence is golden—when used properly. Most people are uncomfortable with silence, but it is perfectly acceptable to take slight pauses before speaking to organize your thoughts. This will also give you the advantage of controlling the pace of the conversation. If a situation that you have been put in charge of is slipping out of control, regain control with slight pauses and thoughtful answers. It may be beneficial to say something like, "Let me think about that for a second." Or you may take a few seconds to restate your understanding of the problem and the person's question. Doing so can help the other person understand that you are devoting effort to the question while giving you a bit of time to decide on an answer.

Before speaking, take a moment to consider that your tone of voice reveals a lot about your feelings and adds significant meaning to your message. The tone of voice includes how high or low the pitch of our voice is, how fast or slow we speak, how soft or loud, and most importantly, what our voice characteristics or emotional indications are.

After thinking about what we want to say, and how to say it, we can then use the second step of the process by presenting a message using verbal and nonverbal language. Remember that when we say "verbal language," we mean the actual words that are being spoken. Nonverbal language includes how we speak those words—our tone of voice, body language, and appearance—and takes into consideration the environment. Imagine you are with a friend in a quiet café, drinking coffee, and she is telling you how much she values your opinion. Now imagine that she is clenching her fists, scowling, and screaming those same words to you. It would change the message a little, wouldn't it?

The last step of the speaking process is to make sure our message is correctly understood by the listener. Look to see that the listener is making eye contact with you. If you perceive a lack of understanding or confusion, be prepared to repeat yourself while trying to explain it in another way or by using an example. Make sure you suppress any outward irritation you may feel at needing to do so. In stressful situations, the parties involved are often not as open minded as in calmer moments and are therefore not as receptive to your words. This can also end with misunderstandings and expectations that go unmet. So take the extra step and ask clarifying questions or summarize the message.

Caring for the Customer

A calm and happy customer or coworker is normally easy to communicate with. Most people struggle with how to handle the angry one. In almost all cases, keeping a calm and steady tone of voice and overall demeanor is the best bet. Never lose your temper; doing so will only escalate the situation and lead to an unwanted outcome.

Asking Questions

Questioning is an important speaking skill that helps keep us out of a lot of trouble. We speak to deliver a message, but many times we need more information or we need to confirm the details of an agreement. Asking questions to gather more information can provide us with enough information to make good decisions. Or, once we come to an agreement with another person, we can use questions to confirm those details. In either of these situations, we have avoided trouble. In the first case, we gathered enough information to avoid a bad decision. And in the second, we confirmed the expectations that each person had regarding the agreement, helping to avoid disappointment and loss of trust.

To use questions effectively, we need to know how to ask the right questions. We can ask three types of questions:

- Open questions
- Closed questions
- Yes or no questions

Each type of question is beneficial when used appropriately. Good communicators know when and how to use the appropriate type. In dealing with customers, we usually start with open questions to gather general information about the issue. Then we use closed questions to find out specific details. We use yes/no questions to further check or confirm the listener's responses or to gain the customer's agreement to authorize a repair or diagnostic procedure.

Open Questions

An open question encourages people to speak freely so we can gather facts, insights, and opinions from them. It is a good way to start a conversation with a new acquaintance or even a customer. Open questions usually begin with the words:

- What
- How
- Why
- Could you tell me

For example, if you were questioning a customer about their visit to a repair facility, you could ask, "What type of service did you receive from the XYZ repair center?" This question opens the topic up for discussion and allows the customer to give details about his or her visit.

Closed Questions

If we want to know more information, we can use closed questions to establish facts and details. Closed questions usually begin with the words:

- When
- Where
- Which
- Who
- How many
- How much

This type of question requires a specific answer, and there is usually only one answer. For example, you could ask a customer, "How many times have you visited the XYZ repair center?" or, "When did you start going to them?" These closed questions allow for only one answer, without much room for discussion. These questions help you to narrow the topic and guide the discussion in the direction you would like it to go, which is helpful when talking with a customer.

Yes/No Questions

Yes/no questions allow individuals to answer with a simple yes or no. This type of question is useful for checking or confirming a person's responses. For example, "Would you recommend them?" gets to the point and helps clarify information. We should generally not start out with yes/no questions because they discourage further explanation or discussion. However, ending with yes/no questions is a good way to get confirmation. For example, after explaining the need for replacing the customer's water pump and answering the customer's questions about the job, it would be very appropriate to ask, "Can we go ahead and replace the faulty water pump for you?"

Telephone Skills

We have learned about the important aspects of the speaking process. A phone conversation presents some different challenges. Since we cannot see each other, we can rely only upon verbal messages and some nonverbal cues, such as the tone of voice. Other nonverbal cues that we miss are body language, appearance, and the environment.

On the phone, we are limited in how we present our messages, so we need to think about our words and tone more carefully perhaps than in person. It is a good idea to plan and even write down each of the points you want to say before even picking up the phone.

Phone communication consists of three parts: greeting, exchanging messages, and finishing the call.

We should always answer a phone call by first saying hello, identifying ourselves, and identifying our place of business, succinctly and clearly. An example could be, "Hello, this is John with the XYZ repair center. How may I help you?" Try to keep your greeting friendly and short.

The second part of the phone conversation is exchanging messages. This requires concise, clear communication followed by clarifying questions and summarizing any main points. At all times, we should be polite and considerate, and remember that the most important nonverbal clue we send out over the phone is our tone of voice, since it reveals a lot about our feelings. Here are a few tips to create a good impression:

- Do not sound bored. Try to keep some inflection in your voice; do not speak in a monotone.
- Sound calm and in control, even if you were caught at a busy moment.
- No matter what, never lose your temper or patience.
- If there is a need to keep someone on hold for an extended time, offer to call him or her back, and do it.

Finish a call by confirming actions both you and the caller will take to ensure that the messages on both sides were accurately received, and end, as shown in FIGURE 2-10, with a pleasant and friendly goodbye. Remember to thank all customers for their business, and invite them to come back. When taking a phone message for someone else, make sure you have the caller's name and organization, contact details, the date and time of the call, and a summary of the caller's message.

When making a phone call, use these same skills and always have necessary information available to give to the person you are calling. For example, if you need to order parts, relevant vehicle information should be shared with your parts supplier. You usually need to have vehicle make, model, year, engine size, and transmission type, and many times you will need the vehicle identification number (VIN).

Giving and Receiving Instructions

A critical aspect of an efficient and well-run workshop is the ability to give clear, logical instructions and to receive instructions. Usually, instructions should contain information about who, what, when, where, why, and directions for how a task should be completed. What is the job that needs to be done? Who should do it? When should the job be done? Apart from knowing what information we should include in our instructions, we should also know how to present them.

When receiving instructions, we should make sure we can understand and follow the instructions successfully. For example, the instruction "Use the tire machine to change a tubeless tire" indicates what to do. Asking follow-up questions such as, "Should I install new valve stems?" or "Should I use a new tire or retread replacement" helps ensure we understood correctly what needs to be done. Such questions may not be needed every time

FIGURE 2-10 Always end calls with a friendly goodbye.

an instruction is given, but by clarifying, the quality of work will be closer to the person's expectations and will save time in the long run.

Communication in a Team

Being part of a team can make working an enjoyable experience or a horrible experience, depending on the team. In large part, the ability of each team member to communicate effectively will determine the success of the team. A high-performing team can accomplish much. As the saying goes, the sum is greater than its parts. We can achieve more when we effectively work together. Being part of a team allows us to:

- Learn new things from other team members
- Share ideas, knowledge, and resources
- Complement each other's strengths and weaknesses
- Feel a sense of belonging

A poorly functioning team spends a lot of time and energy bickering and blaming, and not enough time and energy being productive. Transitioning from a poorly functioning team to a high-performing team requires commitment to the team along with self-discipline. When all team members are committed to a set of common goals, they can contribute in positive ways to the success of the team.

Developing such a team requires good leadership skills as well as good followership skills. Good leadership skills involve setting a clear vision of the goals, empowering each team member to contribute his or her best efforts, and recognizing each team member's strengths and weaknesses. Good leadership also provides training or mentoring to address any weaknesses in the team. Followership is just as important as leadership. Not much would get done if everyone were a leader. Good followership skills involve being fully engaged in the team and its goals, stepping in and performing the work that needs to be done, participating fully in all decision making, and giving honest feedback.

We need to be committed to the team and team goals to make teamwork successful. Each team member should have a defined role and responsibilities that go with that role. Each member is then able to rely on the others to do their part. Think of a team as a chain; one broken link can break the whole chain. A good team player is someone who commits to being a part of that team and contributes to its success by fulfilling his or her role. Each member is then able to rely on the others to do their part. Think of a team as a chain; one broken link can break the whole chain. A good team player is someone who commits to being a part of that team and contributes to its success by fulfilling his or her role.

> **TECHNICIAN TIP**
>
> To be able to fulfill the team commitment, we need to know what our roles and responsibilities are and what is expected of us. Leaders help facilitate that. Good communication is required for the team to come together and work efficiently.

Effective Reading

Every day we are faced with interpreting service information, emails, voicemails, and work orders with customer concerns. Understanding these messages without the verbal and nonverbal clues that come with face-to-face communication can be more difficult.

Reading Comprehension

Technicians are required to read a lot of information, including repair orders, service information, technical service bulletins (TSBs), and training materials. Many of these reading materials can be written at high grade levels. For example, many service manuals and TSBs are written at grade level 14 and higher. Technicians need to be proficient readers to be able to comprehend this information. Before we start reading, we need to know the purpose of the particular material and what we intend to do with the information once we understand it. In reading, the objective may be to:

- Access information quickly, such as a particular specification
- Understand the information, such as how to perform a particular series of tests on a system you are diagnosing
- Remember the information, such as learning about new technology that a manufacturer is introducing to its vehicles, how it works, and what kind of tests are used during diagnosis

Once we know our reading purpose, we can choose the suitable reading method, which can be selective, comprehending, or absorbing. Selective reading is reading only the parts we need to know. This method is useful when looking for a particular piece of information. The quickest way to use selective reading is to read through the table of contents, introduction, conclusion, headings, and index until we find what we are looking for. When we use comprehending reading, we need to interpret and understand the information. Understanding what is being communicated requires careful attention to the structure of the sentences and paragraphs. To use an absorbing reading method, we need to:

- Interpret and understand the information
- Absorb it into our memory
- Review the information regularly

When we talk about reading, we are not concerned only about how fast we can read but also how well we understand and retain what we have read. Unfortunately, the faster we try to read, the less we are likely to concentrate on the meaning, so these two objectives (speed and comprehension) work against each other. Reading is about practice, and the more we practice, the faster, more efficiently, and more accurately we can read.

All of these reading strategies can be used when researching a particular problem with a vehicle. For example, if you have a vehicle that is hard to start only when it is cold outside, you might first check the service information to see if there are any related TSBs. A TSB is released when there are many of the same vehicles having the same symptoms and causes, so you can quickly skim through hundreds of TSBs looking for specific symptoms. When one is found, read it and interpret the information. Then if the TSB addressing the fault is found, absorb the information presented, including the symptoms, cause, test procedures, and corrective actions, into your memory.

> **TECHNICIAN TIP**
>
> Charts, tables, and graphs help you to find information in a timely manner. An example would be torque specifications listed in an easy-to-use format. This information is usually presented as a chart showing the component and the required torque, usually listed in newton-meters (Nm) as well as foot-pounds (ft-lb).

> **TECHNICIAN TIP**
>
> The Society of Automotive Engineers (SAE) has a well-known list of industry agreed upon terms, which are abbreviations used by the manufacturers. In addition, manufacturers may have additional abbreviations that differ from the SAE terms. For example, the term GEN (generator) is used by the SAE, and the term ALT (alternator) is used by several vehicle manufacturers.

Researching and Using Information Sources

Technicians spend a lot of time researching information. This could be looking for a specification needed to perform a specific step in a task, or it could be researching how a manufacturer designed the system to operate in order to determine if it is operating correctly or not. In some cases, research is needed to see what work has been performed on the vehicle in previous shop visits so you will know what has and has not been performed previously.

Researching, like the technician shown in **FIGURE 2-11** is doing, is like conducting an investigation. It can be done in three steps.

1. When we first come across a problem, we have to define what the real issue is; that requires us to know how the system or part is meant to work.
2. We look for information or clues that can help us solve the problem.
3. Finally, we put the pieces together to determine the best solution.

It can be tempting to dive directly into research, but it is important not to jump ahead. It is important that you first define the problem. As you are defining the problem, make sure you narrow it down as accurately as possible. For example, if the truck will not start, does it not crank over at all, or does it crank over but not start? Narrowing the problem down in this way will help you to filter out irrelevant information. If the problem is very broad, it is better to break it into smaller chunks and conduct a separate research activity on each one. Once the research is complete, you will have a better idea of how to proceed with determining the cause of the problem.

FIGURE 2-11 Research is like conducting an investigation.

Once you have defined the problem, the next step is to look for the information that may help solve the problem. That means you must do some research into root causes. There is plenty of information readily available, but to determine how useful and reliable the information is, we need to know the sources of that information. We can obtain information from two sources: primary and secondary. The **primary sources** of information are people who have direct experience with the same or a similar problem. We can obtain information by interviewing those primary sources directly.

However, sometimes information from primary sources can be subjective. Therefore, it is not always reliable. Generally, information from **secondary sources**, or secondhand information, is compiled from a variety of sources. As such secondary information tends to be more reliable since it is more generic and objective. This secondhand information is available in various formats, including print, audiovisual, and computerized, as shown in **FIGURE 2-12**.

We can divide this information into different content categories, including:

- Vehicle service information
- Heavy-duty commercial vehicle educational sources
- Troubleshooting

If using a book for reference, start at the table of contents to help find the section you are looking for. If you come across a word you do not understand, look up the definition. Most books will have a dictionary or glossary of terms toward the rear of the text. When using an online resource or database, try to familiarize yourself with the site's/database's navigation first. Take note of all drop-down menus, shortcut options, and search features.

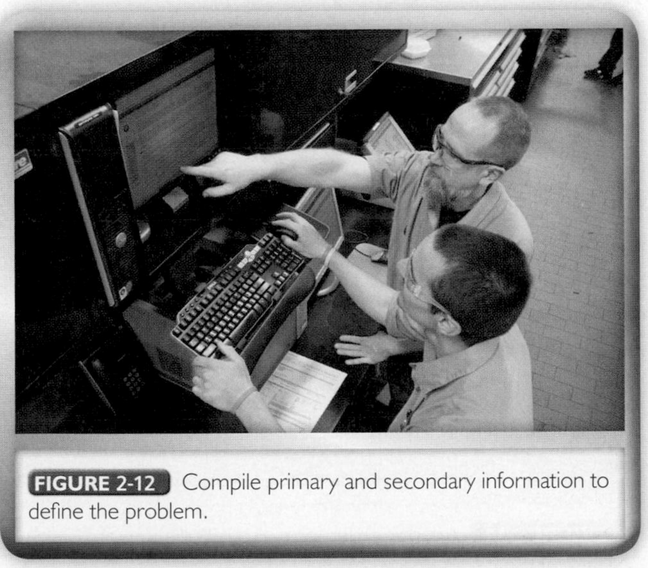

FIGURE 2-12 Compile primary and secondary information to define the problem.

While using these types of resources, you can use the skimming technique discussed earlier to find information quickly. Try skimming for key words. For example, if you are looking for information on oil specifications for a particular vehicle, you could just skim through the resource's text looking for the words oil, lubrication, or specifications. Charts, tables, and graphs, if included in the reference material, are usually easy to scan.

Most manufacturer-supported resources will include diagnostic trouble charts. These provide a great way to narrow down faults without missing any steps in the procedure. Trouble trees also use the cause-and-effect approach to diagnosis. For example, if a fuse is blown, you can use the trouble tree to help you, step-by-step, find the cause of what made the fuse blow, rather than simply replace the fuse. As you gather symptoms and perform the diagnostic tests, you should take notes on your results to aid you in diagnosing and solving the problem as well as to complete the repair order when finished.

Always save the manuals for shop equipment and tools, and organize them in one place for future reference. Refer to these documents to maintain the equipment and tools. For example, most air tools require a drop or two of hydraulic oil every day, along with the use of a water separator in the air line.

When encountering problems with a new or unique system, it is often helpful to look up a definition or description of that system. This information can typically be found in either the front or the back of a book, or you may be able to search for it on computer-based information systems.

As you gain experience in the heavy-duty commercial vehicle industry, you will find that many vehicles have similar faults. Do not hesitate to use your prior knowledge to assist you in a new diagnostic situation. Just do not assume that all similar problems are caused by the same fault. You will want to test and verify your assumptions before suggesting a course of action to the customer.

Vehicle Information

The first place to look for information about a vehicle is in the shop. Computer databases, shop manuals, aftermarket manuals, and owner manuals are good resources for basic service information, including vehicle systems and how to operate them, the locations of major components and lifting points, and vehicle care and maintenance information. Manufacturers usually provide training videos covering specific information about a vehicle of a particular make and model. Similarly, aftermarket and components suppliers will provide specific information about their products. This information is also available from their DVDs and websites.

The manufacturer's service information will guide the technician in the correct sequence of procedures to correct a given problem. The basic idea is to check the simple things first. In most cases, this will involve a visual inspection for obvious issues such as a vacuum line or electrical connector that is loose or disconnected. If no problem is found, then the technician will go to the next step in the service procedure, which will likely involve test equipment. **FIGURE 2-13** shows results from a brake test. The service information will continue to guide the technician in other steps as necessary.

Educational Sources

Publishers provide extensive materials covering the basic theory of operation of vehicle systems and components. These materials come in a variety of forms. Textbooks and workbooks come as paper-based materials. Then there are computer-based materials, which provide more options for interactivity and visual engagement of the student. While there is free information available, most of these sources require a subscription to enroll in their courses.

Technical Assistance Services

For troubleshooting, there is help available on the phone and on the Internet. To use either resource, you must subscribe as a member, which normally involves paying a fee. Technical assistance hotlines put you in contact with professionals who can assist you in diagnosing a particularly difficult problem over the phone. The technical assistant has access to a variety of technical service information. Some of this information is gathered while helping other technicians with their issues. Thus, a large database of information can be accumulated, which can save a technician a lot of time.

For free information, there are chat rooms and bulletin boards where questions can be posted to other technicians online, although there is no guarantee of the accuracy and availability of the resources.

> **TECHNICIAN TIP**
>
> If you are ever working on a vehicle and seem to have hit a dead end in diagnosis, do not be afraid to discuss the symptoms with other technicians or supervisors around you. Sometimes others have seen the same issue or have a bit more experience and will be able to help. Or maybe they will look at the problem from a slightly different perspective and can suggest something new to try.

Effective Writing

Technicians need to document their findings, conclusions, and any repairs on the repair order, like that shown in **FIGURE 2-14**. This requires an accurate, short, but complete summary of the work you completed. In fact, the shop and ultimately the technicians get paid based on the quality of the write-up of the repair order. If there is ever a problem in the future, such as a customer filing a lawsuit against the shop over the repair, the repair order becomes a legal document that will be used by the court to determine if the shop has any liability in the situation. Thus, if the repair order is poorly written, incomplete, or inaccurate, the shop will be much more likely to lose the court case, putting it at risk of having to pay thousands of dollars—or more in the case of an injury accident. So writing is one of the most important tasks a technician does on a daily basis. **FIGURE 2-15** shows a wall organizer for all the written communication in a workshop.

FIGURE 2-13 Detailed results from a brake test.

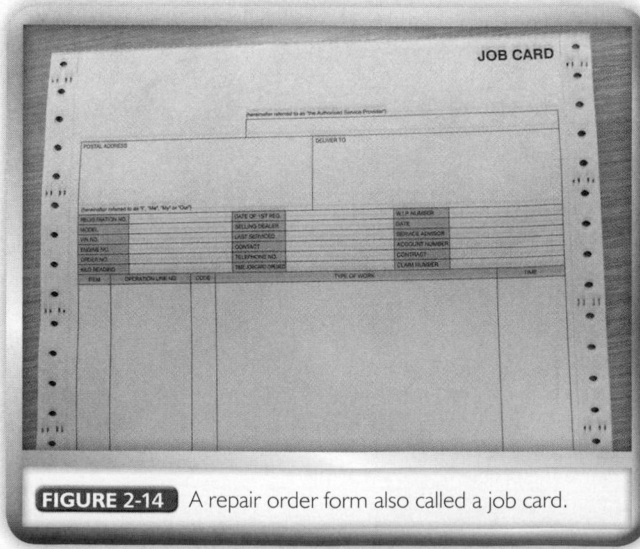

FIGURE 2-14 A repair order form also called a job card.

Writing Business Correspondence

Writing for technicians generally involves completing a write-up of diagnosis and repair conclusions on repair orders and filling out parts requests. However, they may sometimes need to undertake a more formal business correspondence using complete paragraphs. As with any type of writing, first think about what you want to say and draft your message, then refine and finalize your message. Just as it is important to think before we speak, we also need to think about what we want to say, and what we want to achieve, before we compose our written message.

Using your notes, sketch out a short outline of major topics; this is a great place to start when writing. Then use the outline to assist you in the writing. Use complete sentences. Remember to carefully proofread your writing so that you catch and fix any spelling or grammatical errors. You should use spell-check, but do not rely on it to catch everything; spell-checkers cannot tell you when you have used "two" and "to" incorrectly, or "there" and "their," or when you meant to use "they" and only typed "the"—to mention a few examples. Once you have completed the draft, it may be necessary to create a revised, final version of the write-up.

When writing a business letter, after creating an outline of the main points, you must then organize and put them together. Here are a few tips:

- Structure your letter logically so readers can follow your flow of thoughts; check the content by reading it out loud.
- Use plain English when addressing a customer, avoiding complicated words or technical jargon.
- On the other hand, when addressing a manufacturer or warranty clerk, be very specific.

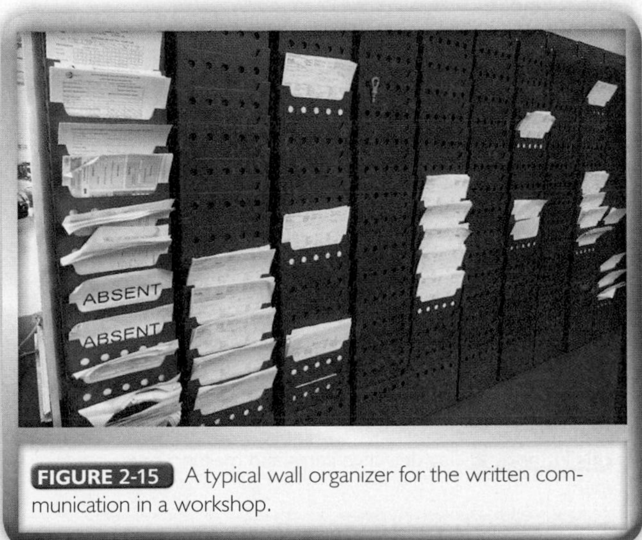

FIGURE 2-15 A typical wall organizer for the written communication in a workshop.

- Check your spelling and punctuation. This is easily done using spell-check or by looking up the term(s). Be aware that spell-check can misinterpret your words, so you need to double-check spelling corrections.
- Be courteous and empathize with the readers, especially when writing a complaint letter or delivering bad news.
- Be precise, direct, and to the point. Repetition or unnecessary words waste time and can confuse readers.

There is a simple but necessary format to follow when creating a business letter. The letter should have your company name and address at the top. Most business letterheads have these details preprinted. Next include the date, followed by the recipient's name and address. Usually, you should start a letter with a greeting like "Dear Sir or Madam," or when we know the receiver's name, "Dear Mr. Mortenson." "Re:" or "Reference" is followed by the subject or purpose of the letter. The next part is the content that you composed in your outline. A business letter usually concludes with a complimentary closing, such as "Sincerely." Finally, a letter needs to be signed and followed by the sender's typewritten name and position.

Completing a Repair Order

If you are writing up your findings, conclusions, and repairs performed on a repair order, one thing to remember is that the information needs to be concise, yet complete. This is a difficult skill to develop, but will improve with practice.

A repair order should contain:

- The customer's concern: Describe the concern and how you verified the concern and any related issues found.
- The cause of the concern: Describe what specifically is the root cause of the concern.
- The action taken, or needed to be taken, to correct the concern: Describe specifically how the concern was, or could be, resolved.

These elements constitute what is called the **three Cs**: Concern, Cause, and Correction. Remember that each of these sections needs to be written up as concisely yet completely as possible. For example:

Concern: The vehicle overheats within about 10 minutes of vehicle operation from a cold start, no matter whether it is hot or cold outside. Coolant is full and protected to −30°F (−35.6°C). Started vehicle, monitored engine temperature with temp gun. Temperature exceeded specified 195°F (90.6°C) thermostat opening temperature, and still not open at 205°F (96.1°C).

Cause: Thermostat faulty, not opening at specified temperature. Removed; no external damage noted.

Correction: Replaced thermostat with new OE thermostat. Retested; thermostat starts to open at 193°F (89.4°C), which is within specifications.

While in school, you will document tasks performed in the shop on forms referred to as job sheets or task sheets. You can use these forms to develop your ability to accurately complete the three Cs. Doing so will prepare you for the repair orders you will complete when working out in the industry.

A repair order should also contain the customer's contact information, vehicle information (e.g., make/model/VIN), parts, prices, labor time, taxes, and any recommended service that is found while repairing the vehicle.

Completing a Shop Safety Inspection Form

Most shops should have a safety inspection form that needs to be completed on a regular basis, typically weekly or monthly, although some tasks may need to be performed daily. This form will guide you to visually inspect critical items in the shop such as lifts, overhead doors, hydraulic equipment, pneumatic equipment, hoses and cords, fire extinguishers, and emergency exits. The importance of these inspections should not be taken lightly, as neglect of these items can cause safety issues and cause premature product failure. These pieces of equipment are used often and will require frequent inspection.

Safety inspection forms are also a way of keeping up on routine maintenance tasks, such as changing the oil or replacing the belt of an air compressor, refilling the tire machine automatic oiler, and draining any water traps in the compressed air system. If you are the person completing the inspection, make sure you are trained to evaluate the safety and condition of the items you are inspecting. Inspect the items carefully and thoroughly so you do not miss any issues.

Completing a Defective Equipment Report

One way to help ensure safety in the workshop is to inspect equipment regularly and arrange for repair or replacement whenever it does not meet safety standards. Keeping equipment well maintained will help avoid equipment downtime to provide a safer work environment. Whenever you come across any defective equipment, you should do the following:

- Tag the defective items and either place them in a secured area or secure them so no one else can use them by mistake, as illustrated in FIGURE 2-16.
- Complete a defective equipment report.
- Notify your supervisor.

Your immediate actions can help protect coworkers from accidents and injuries. If there is an accident resulting from defective equipment, you will need to complete both an accident report and a defective equipment report. On the report, you will record the date when the defect was detected, the location of the defective equipment, the name of the equipment, the serial number (if possible), and a description of the defect and the action you have taken. Then sign your name as the reporter. Finally, notify your supervisor.

Completing an Accident Report

Safety is the most important issue in the workplace. We must make a conscious decision to work safely and act responsibly to protect others and ourselves. Unfortunately, accidents do happen. When one occurs, an accident report should be completed by those involved, both the victim and witnesses, if possible. The information in the report is used to protect both employees and employers. It protects the employer and employee against false claims. And it protects future employees by calling attention to a situation that caused an accident, so hopefully measures can be taken to prevent it in the future. To ensure that the information is accurate, the accident report should be completed as soon as practically possible while the facts of the accident are still fresh in everyone's memory.

A typical accident report includes the date and time when the accident happened, the location where the accident happened, the name of the person who was injured, the name of any witnesses, the details of the accident, any first aid treatment provided, and any medical assistance rendered. It is also important to note if the accident will be subject to, or covered by, any insurance claims. Finally,

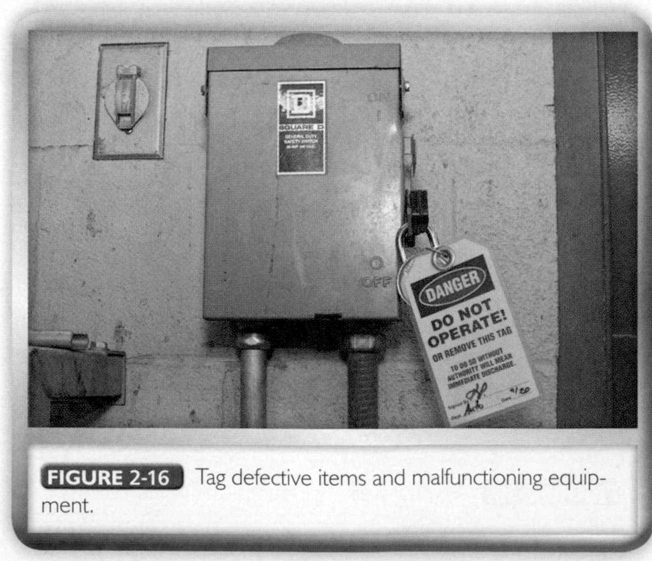

FIGURE 2-16 Tag defective items and malfunctioning equipment.

the form needs to be signed by the person reporting the accident and turned in to the supervisor.

Completing a Vehicle Inspection Form

We provide customers with a very beneficial service when we perform a thorough inspection of their vehicles. When performing an inspection, we need to check that all major components and systems are operational, secured, and safe in accordance with the vehicle manufacturer's recommendations.

This means testing the operation of the electrical and mechanical systems, such as lights and brakes, and visual inspections of the components, such as tires and glass.

An inspection form is a useful guide when conducting a vehicle inspection. By following the checklist, a technician can test all the components in a systematic way and ensure that they are operational or serviceable. It also becomes a record for the shop to bring a customer's attention to needed service, or in the event that a customer declines repairs, shows that the repair shop made the customer aware of them. Many repair shops use their own inspection form that lists every item tested, which are known as points. Depending on the number of points covered, the inspection may be called by a particular name, these names are generally associated with either a time or distance travelled specification.

To complete the inspection form, you must inspect all the components and systems on the checklist, such as:

- Fluids, belts, and hoses
- Steering and suspension system
- Brakes
- Drive line
- Fuel system
- Exhaust system
- Tires
- Lighting system
- Electrical system
- Visibility
- Seat belts

General Components

Once the inspection is completed, the results should be presented to the customer so he or she can decide if any repairs are to be made. This is where verbal communication comes back into play, as it is important to accurately communicate with the customer so he or she has a good understanding of what the vehicle needs, why it is important to have it repaired, and the consequences of not repairing it. All of this conversation should be based on trust and the relationship you have built with the customer during his or her experience with you and the shop. And as you can see, successful communication includes good verbal, nonverbal, listening, clarifying, writing, and presentation skills.

Lockout/Tagout

There are many dangers in the repair facility that may need to be properly documented and tagged. One example could be a defective vehicle lift. If a problem is noticed with a piece of equipment, a lockout/tagout procedure should be followed. Lockout/tagout procedures have been developed to prevent avoidable and unnecessary workshop accidents. Most workshops have a defined process and steps to be followed which should be adhered to at all times. These procedures have many functions:

- The tag notifies other users that the tool or component is dangerous to use, as shown in **FIGURE 2-17**. Any equipment that is found to be faulty needs to be identified so that other users are not put at risk. Write the fault, the date, and your name on the tag. Attach the tag to the tool. Smaller equipment should also be tagged and placed in a location where it is not forgotten. Notify your supervisor so that repairs or a replacement can be arranged.
- If a machine is faulty, the lockout procedure is used. Most large workshop equipment is permanently wired to the electrical supply and usually will have an isolation switch that will disconnect the electrical power. A lockout tag should be placed on the isolation switch as well as the equipment. Turn the machine off at the power and master switches, attaching the lockout tag in a manner that prevents the switches from being turned on. Once again, notify your supervisor so repairs can be arranged.

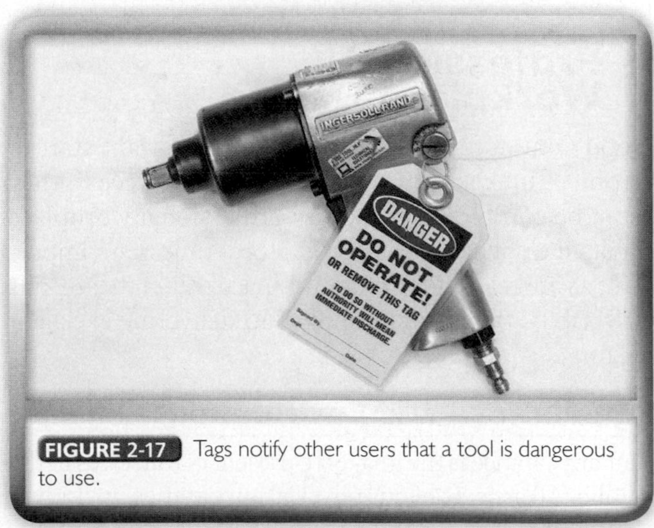

FIGURE 2-17 Tags notify other users that a tool is dangerous to use.

- The lockout/tagout procedure is also used to notify other technicians that a vehicle is not drivable.

Your workshop will have a procedure for vehicle lockout/tagout. Most workshops have a defined process and steps to be followed, which should be adhered to at all times. It may involve the technician filling out a "defective vehicle" label listing the nature of the defect, name of the technician, and date and time of the defect.

If you remove the vehicle keys, do not keep them in your pocket or on your workbench. Attach a label or tag to the keys that identify the vehicle they belong to and store them in a secure key organizer.

If a vehicle is going through a relearn process (i.e., the vehicle's computer communicating with another computer), it may be necessary to leave the ignition on for many hours. In this case, tag the vehicle with instructions to leave the ignition on; otherwise a passing technician may turn it off in an effort to be helpful. If a vital component has been removed for service, it may not be obvious to a casual observer, so it is necessary to tag the vehicle. The best place to tag the vehicle is in on the steering wheel or driver's window where others trying to operate the vehicle will see it. Also, remove the ignition key and store it in a safe place. Ask your supervisor to demonstrate the lockout/tagout process used in your workshop and to show you the location of the key organizer.

In conclusion, communication is a critical component of a successful business and an efficient workplace. Often overlooked in our current digital world, where face-to-face contact is getting less and less common, it is increasingly important to familiarize yourself with a wide variety of communication skills. From listening to simply filling out an inspection report, using and practicing these skills can be a big determining factor in how far you can go and how much money you make in the industry. And the good news is that it does not even require expensive tools!

Professional Workplace Habits

Good communication skills are an important start to strong employability skills, but for true success, they must be combined with other professional workplace habits. Personal appearance and orderliness are important, as are respect for time and space. All of those skills and habits, then, can be applied to delivering excellent customer service.

Appearance and Environment

Our appearance is the image we present of ourselves to the public. All aspects of our physical appearance, including our clothes, jewelry, hairstyle, posture, and outward demeanor, culminate to create the first impression made in any encounter. That first impression often informs the judgment others make about us, which in turn affects the level of respect and trust you achieve. It is much harder to convey your message effectively if your audience is distracted by some aspect of your appearance or does not take you seriously. When working in a professional environment, always do your best to look professional. Remember that, while you are at work, you embody the image of your company. Shorts, improper footwear, or untucked or filthy clothes can all send negative signals to a customer. A customer will be much more willing to have his or her vehicle serviced by someone who looks well put together, such as the person shown in **FIGURE 2-18**, than someone who does not.

The surrounding environment is also worth consideration, as it can affect the outcome of our communication. A disorganized, cluttered, and dirty area leaves a negative impression with most customers, leading them to believe that you do not care about appearances or quality. Look around you and evaluate the housekeeping. Is it clean, organized, and inviting? Or is it neglected, dirty, and gross? A little housekeeping goes a long way toward making customers feel comfortable. You will also want to avoid distractions such as excessive background noise, a blaring radio, or inappropriate coworker conversations. **FIGURE 2-19** shows a professional, orderly environment.

FIGURE 2-18 When working in a professional environment, always do your best to look presentable.

Interruptions by both coworkers and phone calls can hinder communication. Whenever it is in your power to do so, work to keep these distractions at a minimum.

Be aware of dangers around you as well. While most insurance policies prohibit customers in the work area, there may be occasional times when they need to see a particular issue. If you have to take customers into the shop, always escort them, and be sure to keep them safe. Do they need safety glasses on? Escort them back out of the shop as soon as possible and continue the conversation in the customer write-up area.

Time and Space

We know that in the work environment, time is money. This is especially true in most repair shop environments, where every minute is costing somebody something—the customer, the shop owner, and/or the technician. Punctuality is an important nonverbal message in a business environment. When you are punctual, clocking in on time, for example, as shown in FIGURE 2-20, you demonstrate a good work attitude and professionalism. Punctual means showing up on time (typically 5–10 minutes early to get ready to start work at the appointed time). If you have an unexpected delay, such as finding a flat tire when you get into your car to go to work, make sure you call your supervisor and let him or her know what happened and when you will be in. The same applies if you need to call in sick; do so as soon as you can so that other arrangements can be made.

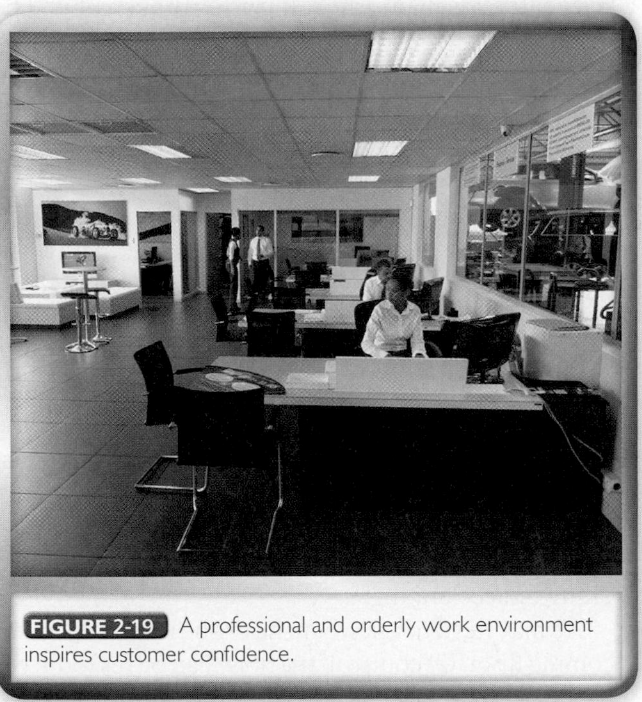

FIGURE 2-19 A professional and orderly work environment inspires customer confidence.

Punctuality also means you will complete the job when you say you will. If you tell a customer his vehicle will be finished at 3:00, you should plan on finishing it prior to that just in case something goes wrong. Occasionally, there will be unforeseen events that keep you from completing a job on time, but those should be rare exceptions. If there is a delay, then you need to communicate that to your customers as quickly as possible so that they can make other arrangements.

Lastly, you should be giving a full measure of work for the time you are being paid. Routinely texting your friends or taking personal calls during work hours is stealing from your employer. Use your work time efficiently, just as you would want your own employees to do.

When we say that space is a part of nonverbal language, we are referring to the physical space between ourselves and the people with whom we are communicating, commonly known as "personal space" (generally 3 feet (0.9 m)). How we use personal space depends on how we feel about others; it is also a consideration for another person's comfort level. Familiarity, gender, status, and culture will determine the use of our personal space. Be aware of space as a nonverbal message and adjust accordingly.

Customer Service

Good customer service is vital in today's competitive business environment. As illustrated by FIGURE 2-21, the quality of our customer service influences people to choose us over our competitors; good service makes people feel good about continuing to buy our products or services, which is how the business gets the money to pay your wages. So, customer service has a direct impact on

FIGURE 2-20 Punctuality sends an important nonverbal message about professionalism.

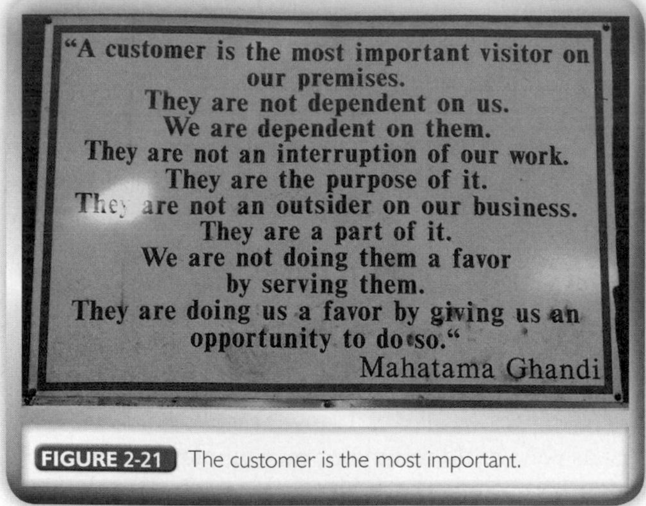

"A customer is the most important visitor on our premises.
They are not dependent on us.
We are dependent on them.
They are not an interruption of our work.
They are the purpose of it.
They are not an outsider on our business.
They are a part of it.
We are not doing them a favor by serving them.
They are doing us a favor by giving us an opportunity to do so."
Mahatama Ghandi

FIGURE 2-21 The customer is the most important.

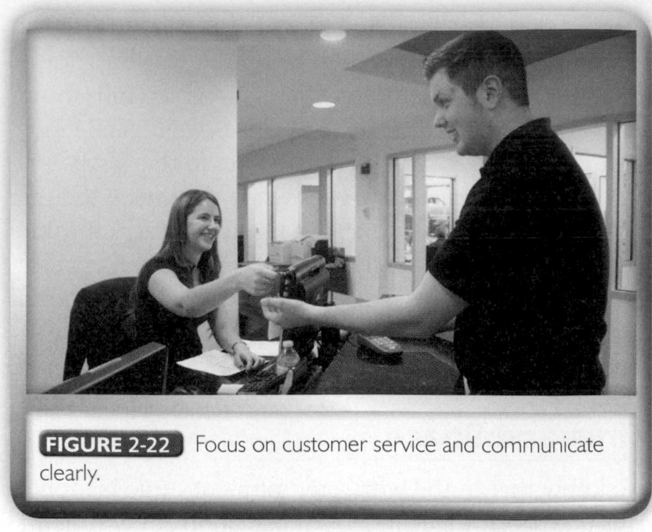

FIGURE 2-22 Focus on customer service and communicate clearly.

the ability of employers to hire employees, provide wages, and offer promotions. In fact, most vehicle manufacturers place great importance on the customer satisfaction index (CSI) rating at their dealerships. The CSI rating is gathered from virtually all of the customers who have service work completed. The CSI rating is reported each month and used to evaluate individual technicians and the entire service facility. If the CSI rating is high, bonuses can be paid to everyone who contributed to that success. If the CSI rating slips, bonuses can be withheld, and new processes can be implemented to help restore the CSI rating.

To be able to provide good customer service, we must first understand who our customers are and then identify their needs. Internal customers, such as parts suppliers, are as important as external customers. By helping our coworkers with their jobs, it will ultimately help our external customers and our organization. It is helpful to remember that it is almost always external customers who bring resources into your organization when they trade their money for your service or product.

Being focused on customer service, as shown in **FIGURE 2-22**, means you are fully engaged in providing the highest level of service that you can. This includes clear, friendly communication to help prevent misunderstandings and helping to establish achievable expectations. It also includes simple things like not getting grease on the vehicle's steering wheel, upholstery, or paint. And it means taking extra steps such as washing the vehicle when the work is completed or vacuuming it out so it is cleaner than when you started working on it. Keep in mind, one of the most important parts of customer service is repairing the vehicle correctly the first time. This goes a long way toward maintaining customer satisfaction.

In most cases, we can divide our customers into three categories: those who are more concerned about getting things right; those who want to get things done; and those who just want to get along with people. Each of these customers is motivated by different factors. The person who wants the job done right will usually not be interested in lesser quality parts and will want you to take the time to make sure the job is not rushed. If the diagnosis was rushed and was incorrect, this person will likely not be happy.

People who are most interested getting things done will probably be very keen to have the repairs finished on schedule. If the vehicle is not finished on schedule, this person will likely not be happy. For the person who just wants to get along with people, it will be important that a level of trust is maintained. If trust is broken, it will be hard to regain. We have to identify what our customers' needs are, so we can serve them properly.

If you are the one in charge of questioning the customer about symptoms, be sure to get specific information from the customer about what happens, when it happens, and how often it happens. Take notes that will help to diagnose the problem. Then be sure that, when relaying this information to someone else, the other person understands the symptoms with the same level of detail that you do. For example, a customer is concerned about a particular noise in a vehicle. If the noise does not happen all the time, then we would ask when the noise happens or under what conditions the noise happens. We may need to prompt the customer with follow-up questions like, "Does it happen when it is cold or hot, or when going around a corner or over bumps, or when braking or accelerating?"

We may need to ask where he or she thinks the noise is coming from. Of course, if the noise can be reproduced, we may need to drive or ride with the customer so that he or she can identify the noise for us.

Protecting the Customer's Vehicle

Care should always be taken to protect the customer's vehicle during servicing by using fender covers and floor mats. Since the purpose of fender covers and floor mats is to protect the vehicle, you should always inspect them for damage prior to use. Ensure that fender covers and floor mats are clean on both sides and do not have any metal or hard objects stuck to them. Ensure that they fit securely and provide adequate protection.

Fender covers cannot generally be used on heavy vehicles because the fenders are attached to the hood. The covers would fall off upon raising the hood. On cab-over-engine (COE) tractors the hood folds forward for servicing, so there is no provision for using fender covers. If fender covers can be fitted to the vehicle you are servicing, then you should use them.

Some fender covers are made with a magnetic strip in them, which is designed to help hold the fender cover in place. Unfortunately, the magnet attracts metal particles, which can be held between the cover and the fender and scratch the paint. Always check these types of covers very thoroughly for metal particles.

Preparing the Vehicle for Customer Pickup

To ensure that the vehicle is prepared to return to the customer per school/company policy:

- Identify shop policy or procedures for returning a customer's vehicle.
- Check the vehicle for cleanliness.
- Clean the vehicle according to shop policy.
- Remove all vehicle protection prior to customer pickup.
- Dispose of any waste products in an environmentally safe manner, and clean and return fender covers, seat covers, and floor mats to the appropriate storage area.

Make sure all vehicle protection is removed prior to releasing the vehicle to the customer. After removing the vehicle protection, such as fender covers, floor mats, and steering and seat covers, ensure that no damage to the vehicle has been sustained during repair. Check the vehicle for cleanliness by ensuring that all trash has been removed and no oil or grease marks are on the vehicle prior to returning it to the customer. Check that all of the windows are crystal clear, that the dashboard, knobs, steering wheel, and center console are spotless and clean, that floor mats have no dirt, and that there are no fingerprints on the door latches, fenders, or the backs of the mirrors. Now go back through the vehicle and look for tools. Wear appropriate personal protective gear such as safety glasses and gloves when working with cleaning materials.

Vehicle and Service Resources

Vehicle and customer information from various sources provides the fundamental knowledge required to conduct repairs and servicing. Today, the ability to properly perform maintenance and repair activities is increasingly dependent on the technician's ability to research and apply technical information. Vehicle information can come from a number of sources, including vehicle identification plates, operator's manuals, shop manuals, repair orders, service and parts programs, and technical service bulletins. The various sources of information can be published in books or manuals or made available through software packages or the Internet. It is important that you know how to research and apply this information correctly so you can properly repair and service vehicles.

Vehicle Operators' Manual

Manufacturers supply a vehicle operator's manual, which comes with every new vehicle purchased. The operator's manual is usually kept in the vehicle's glove compartment. Secondhand vehicles may or may not have the operator's manual in the glove compartment. The **operator's manual**, like that shown in FIGURE 2-23, contains information about the vehicle and is a valuable source of information for both the owner and the technician.

The information contained in the operator's manual will vary for each manufacturer. In general, it contains basic information on the safe operation and specifications of the vehicle. A typical operator's manual includes an overview of the controls and features of the vehicle; the proper operation, care, and maintenance of the vehicle; operator service procedures; and specifications or technical data The operator's manual also details such

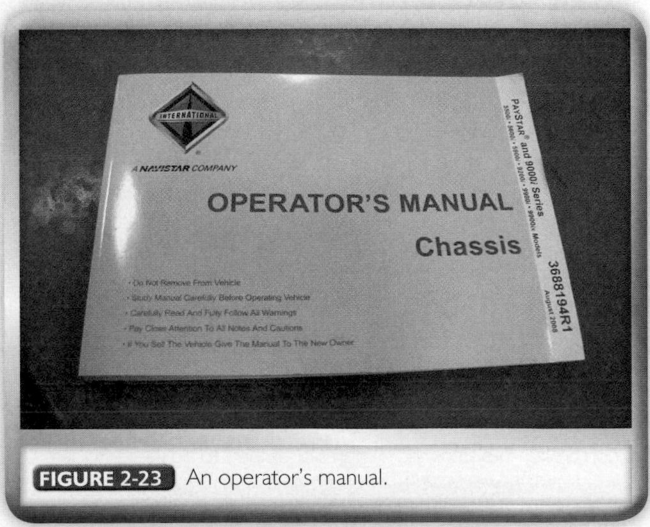

FIGURE 2-23 An operator's manual.

elements as vehicle security PIN codes; warranty and service information; fuel, lubricant, and coolant capacities; tire changing specifications; jacking and towing information; and a list of service facilities. In addition, most include information about warning light identification, how to reset maintenance minder functions, and fuse circuit breaker locations.

The layout and amount of detail in an operator's manual will vary according to the manufacturer and age of the vehicle.

Shop Manual

Shop or service manuals are available for just about every make and model of every vehicle made. Service manuals come in two types—factory and after-market. Factory manuals are produced by vehicle manufacturers and specify the procedures to maintain, repair, and diagnose their vehicles. Usually a factory service manual is specific to one year and make/ model of a particular vehicle.

Most manufacturers shop manuals are now available online. These services are usually provided through a daily, monthly, or yearly subscription. Electronic versions are becoming very popular because they allow shops to access the information they need without having to pay for and store large numbers of shop manuals. Also, it is easier for the publisher to update information as changes or corrections are needed, so the information is generally more accurate than printed materials, which require supplemental printed updates on a periodic basis.

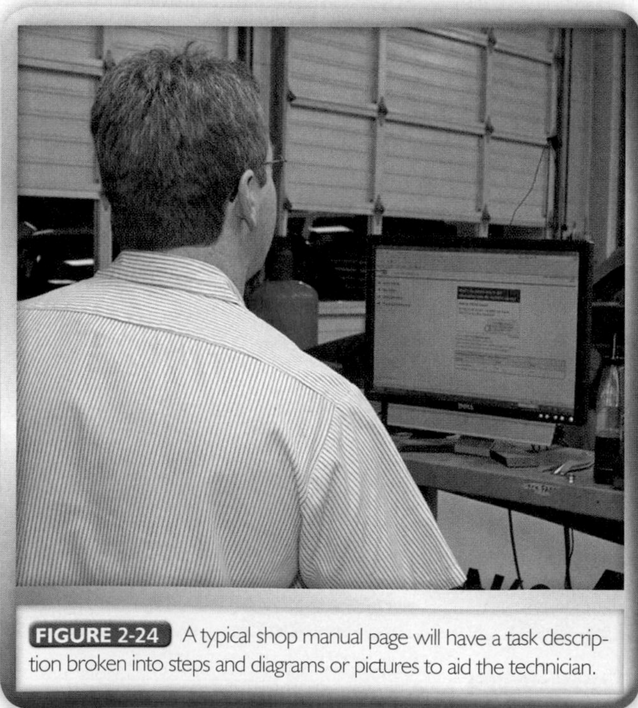

FIGURE 2-24 A typical shop manual page will have a task description broken into steps and diagrams or pictures to aid the technician.

TECHNICIAN TIP

In many heavy-vehicle applications (generally over one ton and due to the many engine options available) some additional information on engines cannot be normally sourced or generally found in the vehicle service manual. This information can be found in specific (engine) manufacturer manuals or databases such as the Cummins Quickserve system.

Typical shop manuals will be broken into a number of sections that relate to systems within the vehicle—for example, engine, transmission, drivetrain, suspension, and electrical. The sections of the shop manuals will be further divided into topics or subject areas; for example, in the engine section, topics could be general description, engine diagnosis, and on-vehicle service. A typical shop manual page, like that shown in FIGURE 2-24, will have a task description broken into steps and diagrams or pictures to aid the technician. It is important to know that all service manuals arrange the content in their own way, so using a variety of different manuals will help you become familiar with finding the information you are looking for.

Service Information Programs

Service information programs are computer applications used to provide technical information for the repair and maintenance of vehicles. The software, as shown in FIGURE 2-25, can be installed on the computer, accessed via the Internet using a browser, or run from a CD or DVD.

1.8hr	1.9hr	1.0hr
1.1hr	1.7hr	1.0hr
1.6hr	2.7hr	1.6hr
2.0hr	2.7hr	1.1hr
1.5hr	1.5hr	1.0hr
2.0hr	2.7hr	1.5hr
1.2hr	1.9hr	1.2hr

FIGURE 2-25 Computer databases provide information on procedures, parts, and service problems.

Using a Service Information Program

To use a service information program, you need to have a basic understanding of how to start and use a computer. Usernames and passwords may be required to log in to the computer and the service information program, so make sure you have these available before you start. A printer is also helpful to print copies of the information so that you can use it when conducting service and repairs; alternatively, you may need to take notes.

To obtain the correct information, you will need vehicle identification information, such as the date of manufacture, model, engine and VIN numbers, and an understanding of the type of repair or scheduled service that is being performed. The repair order may provide you with this information, or you may have to research vehicle identification information from the vehicle. You may need to perform some initial diagnosis of the fault to further continue the search for information.

Information can usually be obtained by searching for the vehicle and then selecting from the list of systems such as brakes or maintenance, followed by subsystems such as disc brakes or fluid capacities. A keyword search may also be available; for example, use the keyword "service interval" to obtain a list of scheduled service intervals. Using a generic word like "engine" may return a very large list. If this occurs, the search can be narrowed further by entering more specific criteria such as "engine oil," "water pump," or "camshaft."

The information will be displayed on pages that will have a mixture of text and diagrams with explanations. Some of the diagrams may have detailed views so you can see how parts fit together, while links may be provided to other relevant information such as a schematic diagram. Most systems will contain help menus or training guides with examples to assist you in using the software, if required.

Technical Service Bulletins

Technical service bulletins (TSBs) are issued by manufacturers to provide information to technicians on unexpected problems, updated parts, or changes to repair procedures that may occur with a particular vehicle system, part, or component. The typical TSB contains step-by-step procedures and diagrams on how to identify if there is a fault and perform an effective repair.

At the time of production, manufacturers prepare service and technical information and attempt to anticipate the information the technicians will require to undertake service and repairs. Once the vehicle is in use, situations can arise when particular components or repair procedures may need either additional information or changes. This is where TSBs are most useful. For example, a TSB may provide details about a change to the procedure that bleeds air from the cooling system. In this situation, the manufacturer would issue a service bulletin explaining the problem and the changes to the current procedure performed to bleed air from the cooling system.

Using TSBs

To use a TSB, follow these guidelines. Locate where the TSBs are kept in your shop or look them up with your electronic service information system. Prior to performing repairs, look through the TSBs and get to know the type of information contained in them. Before working on a vehicle, it is good practice to check if a TSB has been issued for that vehicle and the type of fault or repair. This can save a lot of wasted time.

Compare the information contained in the TSB to that found in the shop manual. Note the differences, and if necessary, copy the TSB and take it with you to perform the repair. Perform the repair following the TSB where appropriate while also referring to the shop manual. If required in your shop policy, note the details of the service bulletin in the appropriate area on the repair order.

TECHNICIAN TIP

Follow these guidelines when using a technical service bulletin (TSB):

- Locate where the TSBs are kept in your shop or look them up with your electronic service information system.
- Prior to performing repairs, look through the TSBs and become familiar with the type of information contained in them.
- Before working on a vehicle, check whether a TSB has been issued for that vehicle and the type of fault or repair.
- Compare the information contained in the TSB to the shop manual information and note the differences. You may copy the TSB and take it with you to perform the repair.
- Perform the repair following the TSB where appropriate while also referring to the shop manual.
- If required by your shop policy, note the details of the service bulletin in the appropriate area on the repair order.

Service Campaigns and Recalls

Service campaigns and recalls are usually conducted by manufacturers when a safety issue is discovered with a particular vehicle. Recalls are costly to manufacturers because they can require the repair of an entire model or production run of vehicles. Potentially, this could involve many thousands of vehicles. Depending on the nature of the problem, recalls can be mandatory and enforced by law, or manufacturers may choose to voluntarily conduct a recall to ensure the safe operation of the vehicle or minimize damage to their business and product image.

Safety

Each country has specific laws regarding product recalls. Find out the laws in your jurisdiction.

An example of a mandatory recall is a fault within the locking mechanism of a seatbelt fitted to a vehicle that results in the seatbelt operating not as a restraint when it should. In this case, the manufacturer would need to identify the problem, its cause, the vehicles affected, and the recertification requirements. A recall would then be issued and advertised in popular media. Letters would be sent from the manufacturer to known owners of the particular vehicle indicating that the vehicles should be returned for repair. Usually all costs associated with the recall are paid by the manufacturer.

Using Service Campaign Information

To utilize service campaigns or recall information, follow these guidelines. Locate where the special service messages, service campaigns/recalls, vehicle/service warranty applications, and service interval recommendations can be accessed in your shop. Look through the TSBs, service recalls, service warranty applications, and service interval recommendations, and get to know the type of information that is contained in them. Identify how they could be used in your daily tasks.

When working on vehicles, check to see if a TSB has been issued for that vehicle and type of repair. Perform service and repairs following the special service messages, service campaigns/recalls, vehicle/service warranty applications, and service interval recommendations. Fill in the required documentation as required in your shop policies. Note the details of the special service messages, service campaigns/recalls, vehicle/service warranty applications, and service interval recommendations in the appropriate area on the repair order.

Labor Guide

Labor guides list how much time will be involved in performing a standard or warranty-related service or repair. They are regularly updated as new models are released into the market and provide a basis for making job estimates and standard charges for the customer. Flat rate servicing costs are usually derived from a labor guide. For example, if a customer wants to know how much it will cost to replace a leaking intake manifold gasket on a particular vehicle, a technician can look up this procedure in a labor guide and find the information on the time and parts required for that particular repair on the specific vehicle.

With the advent of technology and the Internet, many providers of labor guides have started making them available online as well as in print. The online versions are paid for by subscription, which is usually a monthly or annual fee to access the information. Having access to online labor guides means the shop does not have to wait for a new version of the print publication to become available. Online versions of labor guides also can be updated as new models of vehicles are released or updates are made by the manufacturer.

Using a Labor Guide

The labor guide, like that shown in FIGURE 2-26, indicates how quickly an average technician can complete the task. Experienced technicians who have performed the task many times and who are working efficiently can usually perform the job quicker than the labor guide specifies. But since each task and vehicle has its small

TECHNICIAN TIP

Dealership technicians have one advantage over most independent technicians: they have an onsite parts department that stocks many of the parts needed for repairs. Many independent shops maintain a relatively small inventory of high-demand parts such as filters, belts, and light bulbs and use a local parts house to supply the less common parts. This can result in delays waiting for parts to arrive.

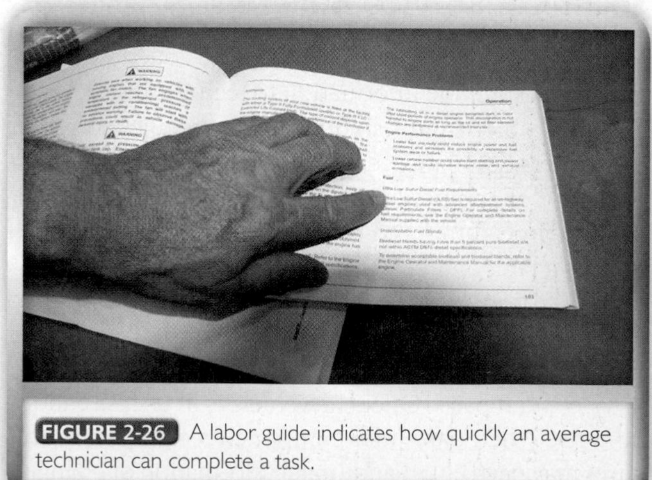

FIGURE 2-26 A labor guide indicates how quickly an average technician can complete a task.

differences, the time is not always completely accurate. The information contained within a labor guide is referenced in a similar manner as a repair manual or online service information system.

To use a labor guide, follow the steps in SKILL DRILL 2-1.

Parts Program

Parts programs are the modern-day version of parts manuals. They are essentially an electronic version of a parts manual. Parts programs may be available via a CD/DVD, a computer network, or the Internet. Technicians and **parts specialists**, the individuals working at the parts counter, use these programs to identify parts and find order numbers.

Parts manuals are produced for all makes and models of vehicles and are essentially a catalogue of all the parts that make up a vehicle. The parts are catalogued by systems—for example, brake, engine, and transmission. Diagrams of each part are shown along with a part number, which is a unique identifying number for that particular part.

Using a Parts Program

To use a parts program, you need to have a basic understanding of how to start and use a computer. Usernames and passwords may be required to log in to the computer and the parts program, so make sure you have those available before you start. A printer is also helpful to print out copies of the information so that you can use it when ordering parts; alternatively, you may need to take notes.

To identify the correct part, you will need to know where on the vehicle the part is installed, what system or subsystem it comes from, and vehicle identification information, such as date of manufacture, model, and engine and VIN numbers. Make sure you have this information on hand before you use the system. Searches can be conducted by keywords. If the part is for the brake system, in the search criteria box, enter "brake." Using a generic word like "brake" may return a very large list. If this occurs, the search can be narrowed further by entering more specific criteria such as "disc brake."

The parts will be displayed in diagrams that are labeled and show individual parts in exploded view, making it easier to identify parts. The diagrams may number the parts and have a key on the page for reference to part numbers, or arrows may point to listed part numbers on the page. Most systems will contain help menus or training guides with examples to assist you in using the software, if required.

To locate parts information on the computer, follow the steps in SKILL DRILL 2-2.

Repair Order Information [Driver Vehicle Inspection Report (DVIR)]

A Driver Vehicle Inspection Report (DVIR) is a daily log filled out by the driver prior to operating a commercial vehicle. These are required by federal motor carrier standards to be filled out daily. One copy must be filed in the maintenance office and another copy kept in the vehicle. A driver notes any problems found on this form and decides whether or not a vehicle is safe to operate. If it is not safe, the driver should not operate the vehicle and the problem should be reported immediately. If the vehicle is safe to operate, the driver will turn the completed form in at the end of the day. The DVIR is a vital tool in communicating vehicle condition to the maintenance department. From that, a repair order can be generated to ensure that the required repairs are carried out.

A **repair order**, or work order, like that shown in FIGURE 2-27, is a form used by shops to collect information regarding a vehicle coming in for repair. Initial information for the repair order includes customer and vehicle details, along with a brief description of the

DRIVER'S INSPECTION REPORT

Date: ______________

TRACTOR/TRUCK NO.: ______________ TRAILER(S) NO.(S): ______________

TRACTOR/TRUCK	Defective?	Remarks	TRACTOR/TRUCK	Defective?	Remarks
Air compressor			Brake connections		
Air lines			Brakes		
Battery			Coupling chains		
Brake accessories			Coupling (kingpin)		
Brakes			Doors		
Carburetor			Hitch		
Clutch			Landing gear		
Defroster			Lights—all		
Drive line			Roof		
Engine			Springs		
Fifth wheel			Tarpaulin		
Front axle			Tires		
Fuel tank			Wheels		
Heater			OTHER		
Horn			Condition of vehicle is satisfactory? ○ Yes ○ No		
Lights					
Mirrors			Defects corrected? ○ Yes ○ No		
Muffler					
Oil pressure			Defects need not be corrected for vehicle safety. ○ Yes ○ No		
On-board recorder					
Radiator			DRIVER'S Signature:		
Reflectors					
Safety equipment			MECHANIC Signature:		
Springs					
Starter					
Steering					
Tachograph					
Tires					
Transmission					
Wheels					
Windows					
Windshield wipers					
OTHER					

FIGURE 2-27 A Driver Vehicle Inspection Report (DVIR).

SKILL DRILL 2-1 Using a Labor Guide

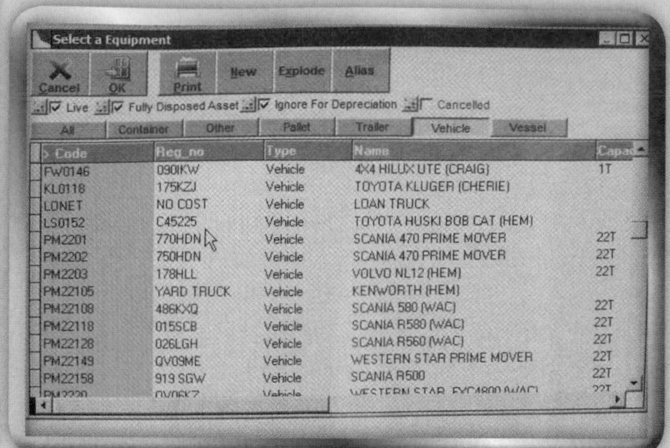

1. Decide what specific labor operations you need to locate. Make sure you know the year, make, model, engine, and any other pertinent details of the vehicle.
2. Log in to the labor estimating system.
3. Enter the vehicle information into the system.
4. Find the labor operation either by working your way through the menu tree or by typing a keyword into the search bar.
5. Once you locate the labor operation, there are usually two columns that list the time. The first one is "warranty time." It is the amount of time the manufacturer would pay the shop for the operation under a customer warranty. The second time listed is the "customer pay" time. That is the amount of time a customer would be billed for and is usually 20–40% longer than warranty time. The length of time is usually listed in tenths of an hour. So 0.6 hours represents 36 minutes. Every tenth of an hour equals 6 minutes.
6. Check for any "combination" time that would need to be added to the base job when a related job is also being completed. Combination time recognizes that combined tasks in many cases save a lot of time over individual tasks because the customer is already being charged for part of the job in the first task. This could be time needed to flush the brakes while the main operation is to replace the brake pads.
7. Check for an "additional" time. This is extra time needed to deal with situations that occur on a relatively common basis, such as vehicle-installed options that are not common to all vehicles, like wheel locks. If you are replacing an engine, swap with or without transfer of associated parts. Obviously transfer of parts would require additional time that would need to be factored in.

   The customer should be charged for the extra time it takes to remove and replace the various additional components Thus, "additional" time needs to be added to the base operation time if the vehicle meets the criteria for the particular "additional" situation.
8. Calculate the total time and multiply it by the shop's hourly labor rate. You now have the correct figure to estimate the charge for the particular service.

SKILL DRILL 2-2 Locating Parts Information on the Computer

1. Log in to the application using the appropriate username and password.
2. Enter the year, make, model, and engine and VIN number information into the system in the appropriate places.
3. Search for the parts you require to conduct the service or repair.
4. The search engine will provide a list of possible matches for you to select from. If the initial search does not produce what you are looking for, try changing the search criteria. Keep searching until you find the information.
5. Gather information on the identified parts, including part numbers, location, availability, and cost.
6. Print, write down, or directly place an order for the desired parts.

customer's complaint(s). The repair order is used by the technician to guide him or her to the problem, and by the customer service staff to create the invoice when the work is completed.

Detailed information that will be on the repair order includes customer details such as name and address; the vehicle make, model, and year; the odometer reading; the date; customer concern information; the cause of the problem(s); the correction for the problem(s); the hours of labor; and the parts used for the repair. The repair order should always include all of the information pertaining to the customer, vehicle, and cost of repair. Repair orders are legal documents that can be used as evidence in the event of a lawsuit. Make sure the information is complete and accurate whenever filling out a repair order, and store it in an organized safe place, such as in a file cabinet or electronically on a secure computer network.

To identify the information needed and the service requested on a repair order, follow the steps in SKILL DRILL 2-3.

Accounting

The accounting section contains information about the methods of payment, which can be cash, credit card, or account. An account system can be set up to handle all payments related to a customer or to a company that uses your service for a number of vehicles. When a vehicle on an account system comes in, you need to record both the account number and the order number.

To work out the total cost of the service, you need to know:

- The labor cost
- The cost of parts
- The tax amounts
- The cost of gas and consumables you used to service the vehicle

You also need to have the customer's authorization to carry out the service. Remember, before making any changes to this service invoice or work order after the authorization, you will need to receive the customer's approval.

> **TECHNICIAN TIP**
>
> A vehicle's service history is valuable for several reasons:
>
> - It can provide helpful information to the technician when performing repairs.
> - It allows potential new owners of the vehicle to know how well the vehicle and its systems were maintained.
> - Manufacturers use the history to evaluate warranty claims.

SKILL DRILL 2-3 Identifying Information Needed and Service Requested

1. Locate a repair order used in your shop.
2. Familiarize yourself with the repair order, and identify the following information on the repair order:
   a. Date
   b. Customer details: name and address, daytime phone number
   c. Vehicle details: year, make, model, color, odometer reading, VIN
   d. Customer concern details: Note any additional information that is required on your shop's repair order.
3. Following the shop procedures, determine the workflow for the tasks that are listed.
4. Use the repair order to carry out the requested service or repair. Fill in the repair order with details of the cause of the customer concern(s) and the correction(s) conducted.

> **TECHNICIAN TIP**
>
> Always obtain the customer's authorization before servicing his or her vehicle, and also make sure you have the customer's approval before making any changes to the service invoice or the work order.

> **TECHNICIAN TIP**
>
> Repair orders are used also to inform the customer of needed repairs or service. This usually results in the customer agreeing to the needed repair, in which case all is well. But if he or she does not agree to the repair and the vehicle is involved in an accident because of the faulty components, having the customer's initials on the repair order signifying that he or she understands the safety issues can help prevent the shop from being held liable for the accident.

Service History

Service history is a complete list of all the servicing and repairs that have been performed on a vehicle. The scheduled service history is often recorded in a service booklet or owner's manual, like that shown in **FIGURE 2-28**, that is kept in the glove compartment. The service history can provide valuable information to technicians when conducting repairs. It also can provide potential new owners of used vehicles an indication of how well the vehicle was maintained.

A vehicle with a regular service history is a good indication that all of the vehicle's systems have been well maintained and the vehicle will often be worth more during resale. Most manufacturers store all service history performed in their dealerships (based on the VIN) on a corporate server that is accessible from any of their dealerships. They will also use this vehicle service history when it comes to evaluating warranty claims. A vehicle that does not have a complete service history may not be eligible for warranty claims. Independent shops generally keep records of the repairs they perform. However, if a vehicle is repaired at multiple shops, repair history is much more difficult to track and, again, may result in a denial of warranty claims.

To review the vehicle service history, follow the steps in **SKILL DRILL 2-4**.

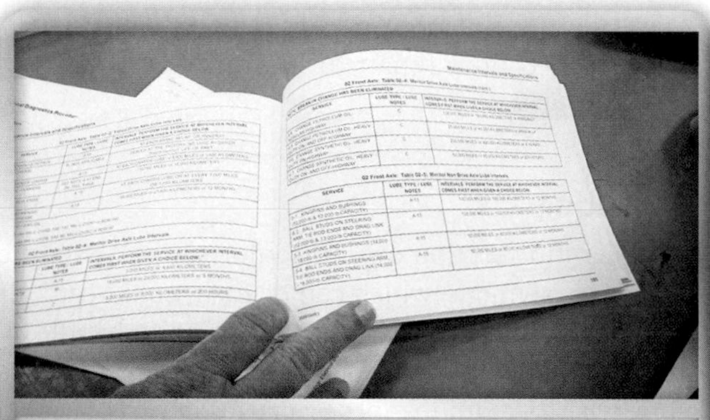

FIGURE 2-28 The scheduled service history is often recorded in a service booklet that is kept in the glove compartment.

SKILL DRILL 2-4 Reviewing Vehicle Service History

1. Locate the service history for the vehicle. This may be in shop records or in the service history booklet within the vehicle glove compartment. Some shops may keep the vehicle's service history on a computer.
2. Familiarize yourself with the service history of the vehicle.
   a. On what date was the vehicle first serviced?
   b. On what date was the vehicle last serviced?
   c. What was the most major service performed?
   d. Was the vehicle ever serviced for the same problem more than once?
3. Compare the vehicle service history to the manufacturer's scheduled maintenance requirements and list any discrepancies.
   a. Have all the services been performed?
   b. Have all the items been checked?
   c. Are there any outstanding items?

Vehicle Information Labels

The **Vehicle Emission Control Information (VECI) label**, like the one shown in FIGURE 2-29, is used by technicians to identify engine and emission control information for the vehicle. It is usually located in the engine compartment on either the hood or radiator support or attached to the engine. It typically includes the following information:

- Engine family and displacement
- Model year the vehicle conforms to
- Spark plug part number and gap
- Evaporative emission system family
- Emission control system schematic
- Certification application

The **Vehicle Safety Certification (VSC) label**, like the one shown in FIGURE 2-30, certifies that the vehicle meets the Federal Motor Vehicle Safety, Bumper, and Theft Prevention Standards in effect at the time of manufacture. It is used by technicians to identify some basic types of information about the vehicle such as month and year of manufacture, Gross Vehicle Weight Rating (GVWR), and tire information. It is usually affixed to the driver's side door pillar or on the side of the door next to the pillar. It typically includes the following information:

- Month and year of manufacture
- GVWR and Gross Axle Weight Rating (GAWR)
- VIN
- Recommended tire sizes

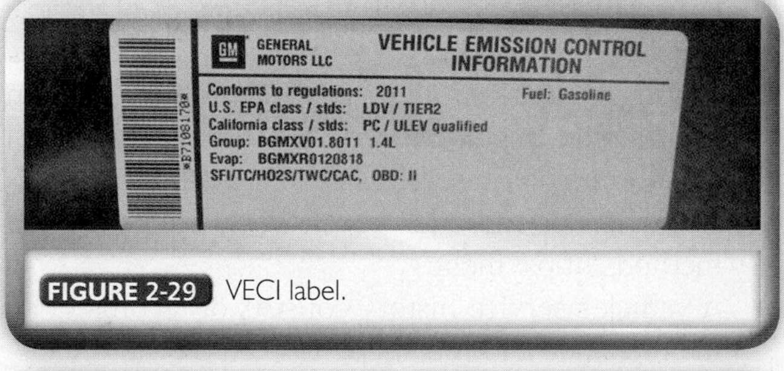

FIGURE 2-29 VECI label.

FIGURE 2-30 VSC label.

- Recommended tire inflation pressures
- Paint and trim codes

Other labels include the refrigerant label, the coolant label, and the belt routing label. The **refrigerant label**, like that shown in FIGURE 2-31, lists the type and total capacity of refrigerant that is installed in the A/C system. The **coolant label**, as shown in FIGURE 2-32, lists the type of coolant installed in the cooling system. The **belt routing label**, like that shown in FIGURE 2-33, lists a diagram of the serpentine belt routing for the engine accessories.

FIGURE 2-31 Refrigerant label.

FIGURE 2-32 Coolant label.

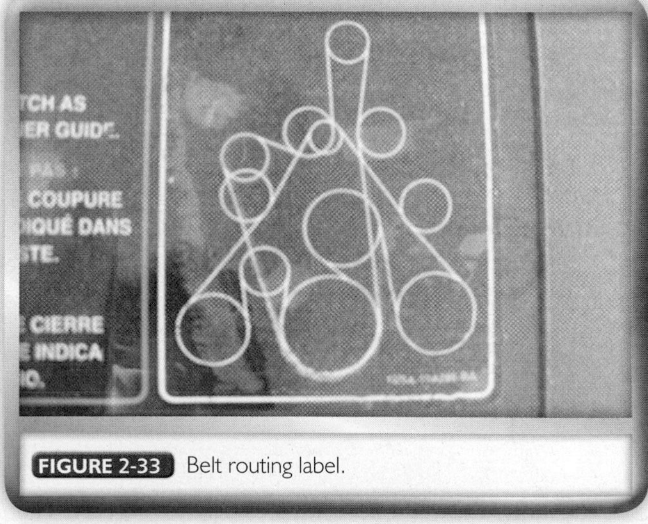

FIGURE 2-33 Belt routing label.

Wrap-up

Ready for Review

- Careers in the commercial vehicle industry are numerous and range from basic technicians to technicians that hold specialty certifications.
- Communication includes listening, reading, writing, and speaking skills—soft skills that every good heavy-duty commercial vehicle technician needs to master over time.
- To empathize with someone is to attempt to see the situation from his or her point of view.
- Nonverbal feedback helps to emphasize our message.
- When listening, information gained can be used to provide feedback.
- Verbal feedback includes very simple signals that can enhance the conversation and let the person know you comprehend.
- A supporting statement can urge the speaker to elaborate on a particular topic.
- Speaking is often referred to as an art because there are so many facets involved in effectively communicating and/or information gathering.
- Speaking is a three-step process: think about the message, present it, and check that it was understood.
- When encountering an upset customer, empathize, de-escalate, do not argue, and stay calm.
- There are three types of questions: open, closed, and yes/no.
- A critical aspect of an efficient and well-run workshop is the ability to give clear, logical instruction and to receive instruction.
- Your appearance makes the first impression and informs others' judgment of who you are.
- In the work environment, time is money. Always strive to be on time, ready to do your part by being present, both physically and mentally.
- Good customer service is vital in today's competitive business environment.
- Every day we are faced with interpreting service information, emails, voicemails, and work orders with customer concerns.
- Researching is an important part of troubleshooting a vehicle. First define the problem, then gather clues, and then put all the pieces together to get the conclusion.
- When a technician is writing a repair order, the three Cs need to be included: concern, cause, and correction. The customer and vehicle information should also be included.
- The operator's manual provides information on how to operate the vehicle and basic maintenance to be performed.
- Manufacturers provide shop (or service) manuals for each make and model of truck; these manuals provide vehicle-specific instructions on service and repair.
- Service information programs allow users to access maintenance and repair information via computer.
- After-market repair manuals are not produced by manufacturers and provide less detailed information for specific makes and models.
- Manufacturers provide technical service bulletins (TSBs) as updates to shop manuals when new problems or maintenance concerns arise for certain vehicle makes or models.
- If a safety issue is discovered on a certain make of vehicle, the manufacturer may issue a service campaign or recall.
- Labor guides provide up-to-date information on service repair times and cost estimates.
- Parts programs are electronic catalogues of vehicle parts.
- Repair or work orders detail customer concern information to guide the service technician, as well as information on services as they are performed.
- Account systems track repair costs and customer methods of payment.
- A vehicle's service history consists of records of all maintenance and repairs performed on the vehicle.
- Manufacturers also provide vehicle information labels to provide further specifications for each model of vehicle.

Vocabulary Builder

belt routing label A label that lists a diagram of the serpentine belt routing for the engine accessories.

coolant label A label that lists the type of coolant installed in the cooling system.

labor guide A guide that provides information to make estimates for repairs.

operator's manual A document that contains information about a vehicle, which is a valuable source of information for both the owner and the technician.

parts program A computer software program for identifying and ordering replacement vehicle parts.

parts specialist The person who serves customers at the parts counters.

primary sources People who have direct experience with the same or a similar problem.

refrigerant label A label that lists the type and total capacity of refrigerant that is installed in the A/C system.

repair order A form used by shops to collect information regarding a vehicle coming in for repair, also referred to as a work order.

secondary sources Secondhand information compiled from a variety of sources.

service campaign and recall A corrective measure conducted by manufacturers when a safety issue is discovered with a particular vehicle.

service history A complete list of all the servicing and repairs that have been performed on a vehicle.

shop or service manual Manufacturer's or after-market information on the repair and service of vehicles.

supporting statement A statement that urges the speaker to elaborate on a particular topic.

technical service bulletin (TSB) Information issued by manufacturers to alert technicians of unexpected problems or changes to repair procedures.

three Cs Concern (the concern, or problem, with the vehicle); cause (the cause of the concern); and correction (fixing the problem).

validating statement A statement that shows common interest in the topic being discussed.

vehicle emission control information (VECI) label A label used by technicians to identify engine and emission control information for the vehicle.

vehicle safety certification (VSC) label A label certifying that the vehicle meets the Federal Motor Vehicle Safety, Bumper, and Theft Prevention Standards in effect at the time of manufacture.

Review Questions

1. What type of technician has the responsibility for inspecting, repairing, and diagnosing mechanical, electrical, and electronic control systems in heavy-duty trucks, buses, trailers, and medium-duty commercial transportation trucks?
   a. Powertrain technician
   b. Commercial vehicle technician
   c. Specialized technician
   d. Chassis technician
2. Employers prefer technicians who have completed an apprenticeship or received certification from a:
   a. business school.
   b. vocational school.
   c. secondary school.
   d. private school.
3. To gain the ASE qualifications, candidates need a minimum of _____ years of working experience before taking an exam for each area of specialization.
   a. 2
   b. 3
   c. 4
   d. 5
4. Which of the following are important to a successful and respected equipment repair business?
   a. Shop cleanliness
   b. Order
   c. Care and protection of customer/fleet vehicles
   d. All of these are important.
5. As a listener and active participant, what should you do to give the speaker your undivided attention?
   a. Stop what you are doing and give your attention to the speaker.
   b. Smile at the speaker periodically.
   c. Continue to speak to others as you try and listen to the speaker.
   d. Continue listening to the speaker while answering the phone.
6. The lockout/tagout tag notifies other users that the tool or component:
   a. is in working order.
   b. is dangerous to use.
   c. should be lubricated.
   d. None of the answers listed
7. Asking a knowledgeable colleague to share his experiences with repairs similar to the one you are working on is an example of collecting which type of information?
   a. Secondhand
   b. Primary
   c. Manufacturer
   d. Technical
8. The proper way to listen to a customer involves which of the following?
   a. Crossing your arms and making a concentrated face to show you care
   b. Talking to the customer while flipping through the manufacturer's manual
   c. Interrupting often to make sure you understand
   d. Maintaining eye contact with the customer in between taking notes
9. To become a master technician in medium- and heavy-duty trucks, a technician should ideally complete which level of certification?
   a. H-series
   b. M-series
   c. T-series
   d. H-, M-, and T-series
10. To become a certified transit bus technician, a technician should complete which type of certification?
   a. H-series
   b. M-series
   c. T-series
   d. S-series

ASE-Type Questions

1. Technician A says that maintaining an appearance of neatness is important as it conveys to the customer the idea of careful, professional technicians. Technician B says that a dirty and cluttered shop indicates that the shop gets a lot of quality work done. Who is correct?
   a. Technician A
   b. Technician B
   c. Both Technician A and Technician B
   d. Neither Technician A nor Technician B
2. Technician A says researching the service information is a waste of time. Technician B says that researching the service information saves time. Who is correct?
   a. Technician A
   b. Technician B
   c. Both Technician A and Technician B
   d. Neither Technician A nor Technician B
3. Technician A says that an example of an open question is: "What are the conditions like when your A/C is not working?" Technician B says that an example of an open question is: "Does your A/C work at all?" Who is correct?
   a. Technician A
   b. Technician B
   c. Both Technician A and Technician B
   d. Neither Technician A nor Technician B
4. Technician A says that labor guides are necessary for the service writer to quote prices for a customer on the repair bill. Technician B says that labor guides are what the customer pays and that warranty pays more for labor using a different labor guide. Who is correct?
   a. Technician A
   b. Technician B
   c. Both Technician A and Technician B
   d. Neither Technician A nor Technician B
5. Technician A says joining the commercial vehicle service industry in its repair and service sector as a service technician is the most popular trade pathway. Technician B says the position of a service technician allows for maximum exposure to the most recent technological developments and advancements in the industry. Who is correct?
   a. Technician A
   b. Technician B
   c. Both Technician A and Technician B
   d. Neither Technician A nor Technician B
6. Technician A says that hybrid vehicle is a specialized area in commercial vehicle service and repair on which a technician can specialize. Technician B says that the manufacturing of parts is a specialized area in commercial vehicle service and repair on which a technician can specialize. Who is correct?
   a. Technician A
   b. Technician B
   c. Both Technician A and Technician B
   d. Neither Technician A nor Technician B
7. Technician A states that it is a lifelong learning process to perfect your communication skills. Technician B states that learning and applying good communication skills will not save you time but it will help you avoid or get through tricky situations. Who is correct?
   a. Technician A
   b. Technician B
   c. Both Technician A and Technician B
   d. Neither Technician A nor Technician B
8. While discussing effective writing, technician A says a repair order can never be considered a legal document. Technician B says writing is one of the most important tasks a technician does on a daily basis. Who is correct?
   a. Technician A
   b. Technician B
   c. Both Technician A and Technician B
   d. Neither Technician A nor Technician B
9. Technician A says you should always escort customers in the shop to keep them safe and continue any conversation in the customer write-up area as soon as possible. Technician B says customers should be given safety glasses to enter a shop, and the shortest amount of time possible should be spent with the customer in the shop. Who is correct?
   a. Technician A
   b. Technician B
   c. Both Technician A and Technician B
   d. Neither Technician A nor Technician B
10. Technician A says being focused on customer service means you are fully engaged in providing the highest level of service that you can. Technician B says one of the most important parts of customer service is repairing the vehicle correctly the first time. Who is correct?
    a. Technician A
    b. Technician B
    c. Both Technician A and Technician B
    d. Neither Technician A nor Technician B

CHAPTER 3

NATEF Tasks

Required Supplemental Tasks

Shop and Personal Safety

	Page
■ Identify the location of the posted evacuation routes.	71
■ Identify general shop safety rules and procedures.	72–74
■ Identify marked safety areas.	74
■ Identify the location and the types of fire extinguishers and other fire safety equipment; demonstrate knowledge of the procedures for using fire extinguishers and other fire safety equipment.	78–80
■ Identify the location and use of eye wash stations.	80
■ Locate and demonstrate knowledge of material safety data sheets (MSDS).	80–87
■ Comply with the required use of safety glasses, ear protection, gloves, and shoes during lab/shop activities.	90–95
■ Identify and wear appropriate clothing for lab/shop activities.	90–95
■ Secure hair and jewelry for lab/shop activities.	95
■ Utilize proper ventilation procedures for working within the lab/shop area.	96
■ Workplace Employability Skills Tasks	

Safety, Personal Protection Equipment, and First Aid

Knowledge Objectives

After reading this chapter, you will be able to:

1. Describe how to follow safe practices in the workplace. (pp 72–74)
2. Describe how the Occupational Safety and Health Administration (OSHA) and the Environmental Protection Agency (EPA) impact the workplace. (pp 72–73)
3. Describe the difference between a shop policy and a shop procedure. (pp 72–73)
4. Explain how shop policies, procedures, and safety inspections make the workplace safer. (pp 72–73)
5. Describe how to identify hazardous environments and the safety precautions that should be undertaken in hazardous environments. (pp 72–73)
6. Explain how the shop layout contributes to efficiency and safety. (pp 72–73)
7. Identify workplace safety signs and their meanings. (p 74)
8. Describe the standard safety equipment that should be in the workplace. (p 74)
9. Describe how to maintain a safe level of air quality in the workplace. (pp 75–76)
10. Describe the safety precautions to be taken when working with electrical tools and equipment. (p 76)
11. Describe how to reduce the risk of fires in the shop. (pp 77–78)

Skills Objectives

After reading this chapter, you will be able to:

1. Identify hazardous environments and apply appropriate risk prevention strategies. (p 73) **SKILL DRILL 3-1**
2. Locate information on an SDS and apply appropriate safety measures. (p 87) **SKILL DRILL 3-2**
3. Safely clean and dispose of brake dust. (p 88) **SKILL DRILL 3-3**

Introduction

Occupational safety and health is very important to ensure that everyone can work without being injured. Governments will normally have legislation in place with significant penalties for those who do not follow safe practices in the workplace. Potential hazards are in most workplaces, especially repair shops. It is important to learn about hazards so you can identify them and take action to protect yourself and your coworkers. Some hazards are obvious, such as vehicles falling from hoists or jacks or tires exploding during inflation. Other hazards are less obvious, such as the long-term effects of fumes from solvents. There are many things to learn about safety in the automotive shop, but it is impossible to cover every situation you will encounter. One of the most important skills to learn is the ability to recognize unsafe practices or equipment and put in place measures to prevent injuries from happening.

Occupational safety and health is everyone's responsibility. You have a responsibility to ensure that you work safely and take care not to put others at risk by acting in an unsafe manner. Your employer also has a responsibility to provide a safe working environment. To ensure the safety of yourself and others, make sure you are aware of the correct safety procedures at your workplace. This means listening very carefully to safety information provided by your employer and asking for clarification, help, or instructions if you are unsure how to perform a task safely. Always think about how you are performing shop tasks, be on the lookout for unsafe equipment and work practices, and wear the correct **personal protective equipment (PPE)**. PPE refers to items of safety equipment like safety footwear, gloves, clothing, protective eyewear, and hearing protection FIGURE 3-1.

Safety Overview

Commercial vehicle servicing is one of the most common vocations worldwide. Hundreds of thousands of shops service millions of vehicles every day. That means many people are conducting servicing and there is a great potential for things to go wrong. It is up to you and your workplace to make sure work activities are conducted safely. Accidents are not caused by properly maintained tools; accidents are caused by people.

FIGURE 3-1 Personal protective equipment (PPE) refers to items of safety equipment like safety footwear, gloves, clothing, protective eyewear, and hearing protection.

You Are the Technician

You are changing the oil on a new type of vehicle for the first time. The oil pan has the drain plug on the side of the oil pan, instead of the bottom of the pan. You place the drain pain directly under the drain plug like you normally do. Unfortunately, when the plug comes out, the oil shoots sideways right over the side of the drain pan. You reposition it quickly, but not before a large puddle is on the floor.

1. Why is it important to review the SDS before cleaning up a spill?
2. What is the minimum PPE that should be worn to manage this spill?
3. What are some of the health hazards of coming into frequent or prolonged contact with used engine oil?

Don't Underestimate the Dangers

Because vehicle servicing and repair are so commonplace, it is easy to overlook the many potential risks relating to this field. Think carefully about what you are doing and how you are doing it. Think through the steps, trying to anticipate things that may go wrong and taking steps to prevent them. Also be wary of taking shortcuts. In most cases, the time saved by taking a shortcut is nothing compared to the time spent recovering from an accident.

Accidents and Injuries Can Happen at Any Time

There is the possibility of an accident occurring whenever work is undertaken. For example, fires and explosions are a constant hazard wherever there are flammable fuels. Electricity can kill quickly, as well as cause painful shocks and burns. Heavy equipment and machinery can easily cause broken bones or crush fingers and toes. Hazardous solvents and other chemicals can burn or blind as well as contribute to many kinds of illness. Trips and falls can be caused by things such as oil spills and tools left lying around. Poor lifting and handling techniques can cause chronic strain injuries, particularly to your back FIGURE 3-2.

Accidents and Injuries are Avoidable

Almost all accidents are avoidable or preventable by taking a few precautions. Think of nearly every accident you have witnessed or heard about. In most cases someone made a mistake. Whether involved in horse play or neglecting maintenance on tools or equipment, these instances lead to injury. Most of these accidents can be prevented if people follow policies and develop a "safety first" attitude.

By following regulations and safety procedures, you can make your workplace safe. Learn and follow all of the correct safety procedures for your workplace. Always wear the right PPE and stay alert and aware of what is happening around you. Think about what you are doing, how you are doing it, and its effect on others. You will also need to know what to do in case of an emergency. Document and report all accidents and injuries whenever they happen, and take the proper steps to make sure they never happen again.

Evacuation Routes

Evacuation routes are a safe way of escaping danger and gathering in a safe place where everyone can be accounted for in the event of an emergency. It is important to have more than one evacuation route in case any single route is blocked during the emergency. Your shop may have an evacuation procedure that clearly identifies the evacuation routes FIGURE 3-3.

Often the evacuation routes will be marked with colored lines painted on the floors. Exits should be highlighted with signs that may be illuminated. Always make sure you are familiar with the evacuation routes for the shop. Before conducting any task, identify which route you will take if an emergency occurs.

> **TECHNICIAN TIP**
>
> Never place anything in the way of evacuation routes, including equipment, tools, parts, or vehicles.

FIGURE 3-2 Poor lifting and handling techniques can cause chronic strain injuries, particularly to your back.

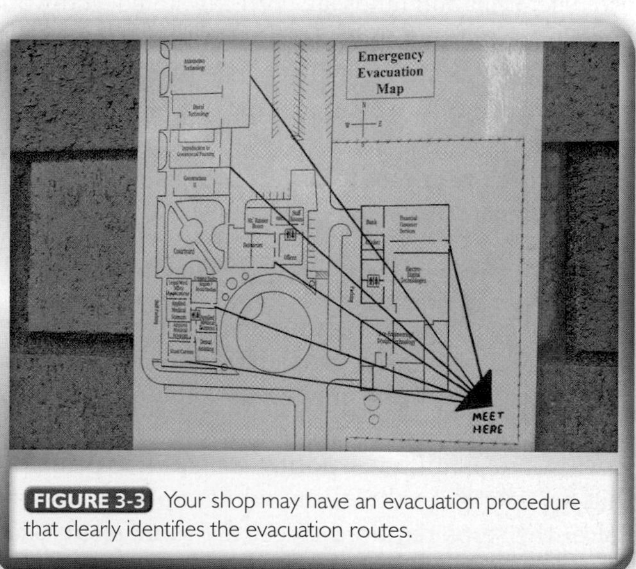

FIGURE 3-3 Your shop may have an evacuation procedure that clearly identifies the evacuation routes.

Work Environment

The work environment can be described as anywhere you work. The condition of the work environment plays an important role in making the workplace safer. A safe work environment goes a long way toward preventing accidents, injuries, and illnesses. There are many ways to describe a safe work environment, but generally it would contain a well-organized shop layout, use of shop policies and procedures, safe equipment, safety equipment, safety training, employees who work safely, a workplace orientation, good supervision, and a workplace culture that supports safe work practices.

OSHA and EPA

OSHA stands for the **Occupational Safety and Health Administration (OSHA)**. It is a U.S. government agency that was created to provide national leadership in occupational safety and health. It finds the most effective ways to help prevent worker fatalities and workplace injuries and illnesses. It has the authority to conduct workplace inspections and, if required, fine employers and workplaces if they violate OSHA regulations and procedures. For example, a fine may be imposed on the employer or workplace if a worker is electrocuted by a piece of faulty machinery that has not been regularly tested and maintained.

EPA stands for the **Environmental Protection Agency**. This federal government agency deals with issues related to environmental safety. The EPA conducts research and monitoring, sets standards, and can hold employees and companies legally accountable in order to keep the environment protected. Shop activities will need to comply with EPA laws and regulations by ensuring that waste products are disposed of in an environmentally responsible way, chemicals and fluids are correctly stored, and work practices do not contribute to damaging the environment.

While the examples in this chapter refer to OSHA and EPA, most countries have equivalent organizations. If you are in a different geographic region to North America, you should check with your local government authorities for the appropriate regulations that apply to your location.

Shop Policies and Procedures

Shop policies and procedures are a set of documents that outline how tasks and activities in the shop are to be conducted and managed. They also ensure that the shop operates according to OSHA and EPA laws and regulations. A **policy** is a guiding principle that sets the shop direction, while a **procedure** is a list of the steps required to get the same result each time a task or activity is performed. An example of a policy would be an OSHA document for the shop that describes how the shop complies with legislation. A procedure would be a document that describes the steps required to safely use a commercial vehicle hoist.

Each shop will have its own set of policies and procedures and a system in place to make sure the policies and procedures are regularly reviewed and updated. Regular reviews ensure that new policies and procedures are developed and old ones are modified in case something has changed. For example, if the shop moves to a new building, then a review of policies and procedures will ensure that they relate to the new shop, its layout, and equipment. In general, the policies and procedures are written to guide shop practice; help ensure compliance with laws, statutes, and regulations; and reduce the risk of injury. Always follow your shop policies and procedures to reduce the risk of injury to your coworkers and yourself and to prevent damage to property.

It is everyone's responsibility to know and follow the rules. Locate the general shop rules and procedures for your workplace. Look through the contents or index pages to familiarize yourself with the contents. Discuss the policy and the shop rules and procedures with your supervisor. Ask questions to ensure that you understand how the rules and procedures should be applied and your role in making sure they are followed.

Identifying Hazardous Environments

A **hazardous environment** is a place where hazards exist. A **hazard** is anything that could hurt you or someone else, and most workplaces have them. It is almost impossible to remove all hazards, but it is important to identify hazards and work to reduce their potential for causing harm by putting specific measures in place. For example, operating a bench grinder poses a number of hazards. While it is not possible to eliminate the hazards of using the bench grinder, by putting specific measures in place, the risk of those hazards can be reduced.

A risk analysis of a bench grinder would identify the following hazards and risks: a high-velocity particle that could damage your eyesight or that of someone working nearby; the grinding wheel breaking apart, damaging eyesight or causing cuts and abrasion; electrocution if electrical parts are faulty; a risk to your hands from heat or high-velocity particles; a risk to your hearing due to excessive noise; and a risk of entrapment of clothing or body parts through rotating machinery. To reduce the risk of these hazards, the following measures are taken: position the bench grinder in a safe area away from where others work; make sure electrical items are regularly checked for electrical and mechanical safety; when operating the equipment, wear PPE such as protective eyewear, gloves, hearing protection, hairnets, or caps; and do not wear loose clothing that can be caught in the bench grinder.

An important first step in identifying hazardous environments is to familiarize yourself with the shop layout. There are special work areas that are defined by painted lines. These lines show the hazardous zone around certain machines and areas. If you are not working on the machines, you should stay outside the marked area.

Study the various warning signs around your shop. Understand the meaning of the signal word, the colors, the text, and the symbols or pictures on each sign. Ask your supervisor if you do not fully understand any part of the sign.

To identify hazardous environments, follow the steps in **SKILL DRILL 3-1**.

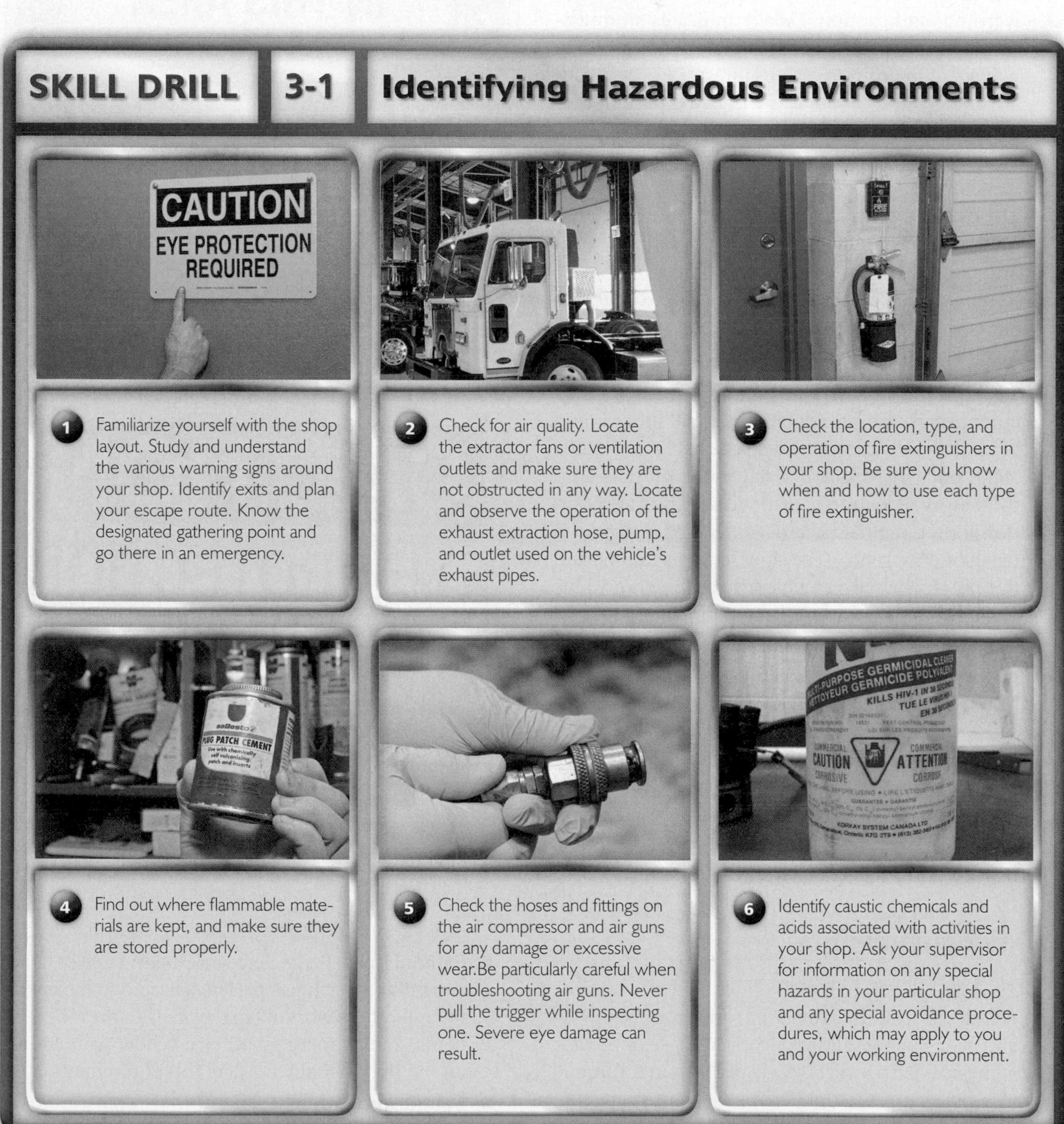

SKILL DRILL 3-1 Identifying Hazardous Environments

1. Familiarize yourself with the shop layout. Study and understand the various warning signs around your shop. Identify exits and plan your escape route. Know the designated gathering point and go there in an emergency.
2. Check for air quality. Locate the extractor fans or ventilation outlets and make sure they are not obstructed in any way. Locate and observe the operation of the exhaust extraction hose, pump, and outlet used on the vehicle's exhaust pipes.
3. Check the location, type, and operation of fire extinguishers in your shop. Be sure you know when and how to use each type of fire extinguisher.
4. Find out where flammable materials are kept, and make sure they are stored properly.
5. Check the hoses and fittings on the air compressor and air guns for any damage or excessive wear.Be particularly careful when troubleshooting air guns. Never pull the trigger while inspecting one. Severe eye damage can result.
6. Identify caustic chemicals and acids associated with activities in your shop. Ask your supervisor for information on any special hazards in your particular shop and any special avoidance procedures, which may apply to you and your working environment.

Standard Safety Measures

Signs

Always remember that a shop is a hazardous environment. To make people more aware of specific shop hazards, legislative bodies have developed a series of safety signs. These signs are designed to give adequate warning of an unsafe situation. Each sign has four components:

- **Signal word:** There are three signal words—danger, warning, and caution. *Danger* indicates an immediately hazardous situation, which, if not avoided, will result in death or serious injury. Danger is usually indicated by white text with a red background FIGURE 3-4 A. *Warning* indicates a potentially hazardous situation, which, if not avoided, could result in death or serious injury. The sign is usually in black text with a yellow or orange background FIGURE 3-4 B. *Caution* indicates a potentially hazardous situation, which, if not avoided, may result in minor or moderate injury. It may also be used to alert against unsafe practices. This sign is usually in black text with a yellow background FIGURE 3-4 C.
- **Background color:** The choice of background color also draws attention to potential hazards and is used to provide contrast so the letters or images stand out. For example, a red background is used to identify a definite hazard; yellow indicates caution for a potential hazard. A green background is used for emergency-type signs, such as for first aid, fire protection, and emergency equipment. A blue background is used for general information signs.
- **Text:** The sign will sometimes include explanatory text intended to provide additional safety information. Some signs are designed to convey a personal safety message.
- **Pictorial message:** In symbol signs, a pictorial message appears alone or is combined with explanatory text. This type of sign allows the safety message to be conveyed to people who are illiterate or who do not speak the local language.

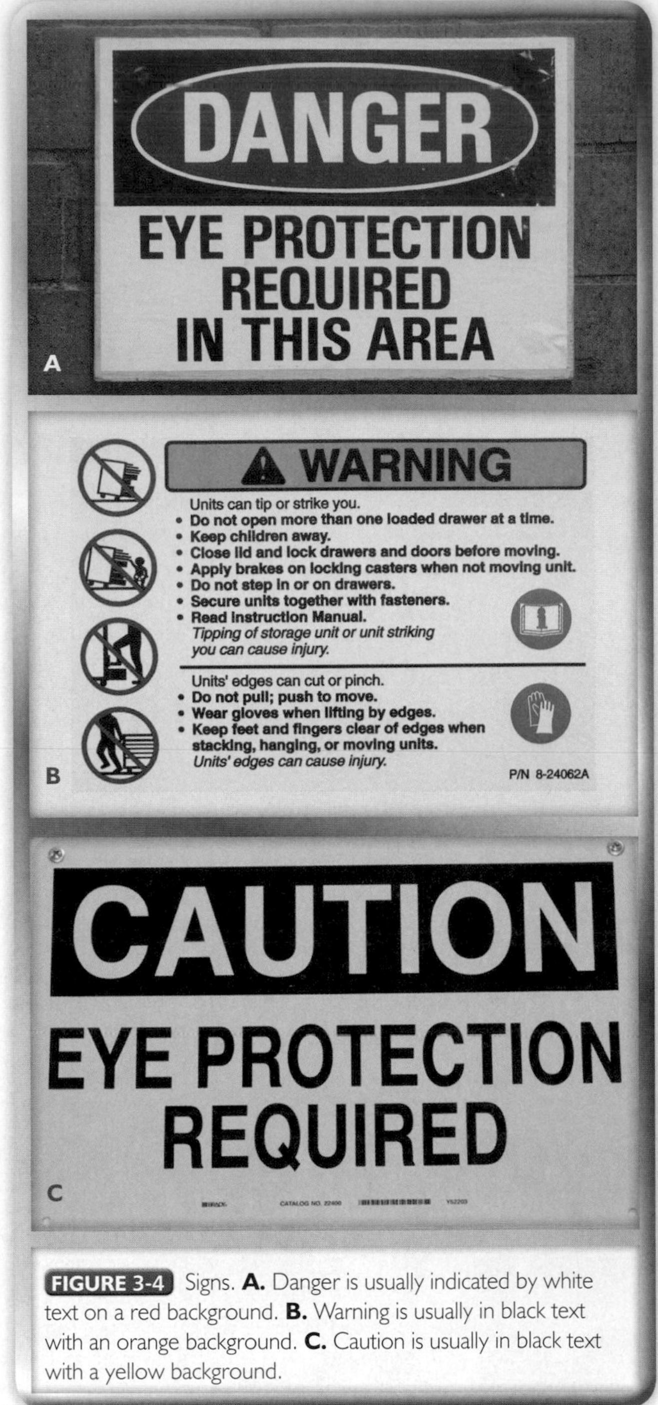

FIGURE 3-4 Signs. **A.** Danger is usually indicated by white text on a red background. **B.** Warning is usually in black text with an orange background. **C.** Caution is usually in black text with a yellow background.

Safety Equipment

Shop safety equipment includes items such as:

- **Handrails:** Handrails are used to separate walkways and pedestrian traffic from work areas. They provide a physical barrier that directs pedestrian traffic and also provide protection from vehicle movements.
- **Machinery guards:** Machinery guards and yellow lines prevent people from accidentally walking into the operating equipment or indicate that a safe distance should be kept from the equipment.
- **Painted lines:** Large, fixed machinery such as lathes and milling machines present a hazard to the operator and others working in the area. To prevent accidents, a machinery guard or a yellow painted line on the floor usually borders this equipment.
- **Soundproof rooms:** Soundproof rooms are usually used when a lot of noise is made by operating equipment. An example is the use of a chassis

dynamometer. A vehicle operating on a dynamometer produces a lot of noise from its tires, exhaust, and engine. To protect other shop users from the noise, the dynamometer is usually placed in a soundproof room, keeping shop noise to a minimum.

- **Adequate ventilation:** Exhaust gases in shops are a serious health hazard. Whenever a vehicle's engine is running, toxic gases are emitted from its exhaust. To prevent an excess of toxic gas buildup, a well-ventilated work area is needed as well as a method of directly venting the vehicle's exhaust to the outside.
- **Gas extraction hoses:** The best way to get rid of these gases is with a suction hose that fits over the vehicle's exhaust pipe. The hose is attached to an extraction pump that vents the gas to the outside.
- **Doors and gates:** Doors and gates are used for the same reason as machinery guards and painted lines. A doorway is a physical barrier that can be locked and sealed to separate a hazardous environment from the rest of the shop or a general work area from an office or specialist work area.
- **Temporary barriers:** In the day-to-day operation of a shop, there is often a reason to temporarily separate one work bay from others. If a welding machine or an oxyacetylene cutting torch is in use, it may be necessary to place a temporary screen or barrier around the work area to protect other shop users from welding flash or injury.

> **TECHNICIAN TIP**
>
> Stay alert for hazards or anything that might be dangerous. If you see, hear, or smell anything odd, take steps to fix it or tell your supervisor about the problem.

> **TECHNICIAN TIP**
>
> Whenever you perform a task in the shop, you must use personal protective clothing and equipment that are appropriate for the task and that conform to your local safety regulations and policies. Among other items, these may include:
>
> - Work clothing, such as coveralls and steel-capped footwear
> - Eye protection, such as safety glasses and face masks
> - Ear protection, such as earmuffs and earplugs
> - Hand protection, such as gloves and barrier cream
> - Respiratory equipment, such as face masks and valved respirators
>
> If you are not certain what is appropriate or required, ask your supervisor.

Air Quality

Managing air quality in shops helps protect you from potential harm and also protects the environment. There are many shop activities and stored liquids that can reduce the quality of air in shops. Some of these are dangerous fumes from running engines, welding (gas and electric), painting, liquid storage areas, air-conditioning servicing, and dust particles from brake servicing.

Running Engines

Running engines produce dangerous exhaust gases including carbon monoxide and carbon dioxide. Carbon monoxide in small concentrations can kill or cause serious injuries. Carbon dioxide is a greenhouse gas, and vehicles are a major source of carbon dioxide in the atmosphere. Exhaust gases also contain hydrocarbons and oxides of nitrogen. These gases can form smog and also cause breathing problems for some people.

Carbon monoxide in particular is extremely dangerous, as it is odorless and colorless and can build up to toxic levels very quickly in confined spaces. In fact, it doesn't take very much carbon monoxide to pose a danger. The maximum OSHA permissible exposure limit (PEL) is 50 parts per million (ppm) of air for an 8-hour period. The National Institute for Occupational Safety and Health has established a recommended exposure limit of 35 ppm for an 8-hour period. The reason the PEL is so low is because carbon monoxide attaches itself to red blood cells much more easily than oxygen does, and it never leaves the blood cell. This prevents the blood cells from carrying as much oxygen, and if enough carbon monoxide has been inhaled, it effectively asphyxiates the person. Always follow the correct safety precautions when running engines indoors or in a confined space, including over service pits since gases can accumulate there.

The best solution when running engines in an enclosed space is to directly couple the vehicle's exhaust pipe to an exhaust extraction system hose that will ventilate the fumes away from the enclosed space to the outside air. The extraction hose should be vented to where the fumes will not be drawn back indoors, to a place well away from other people and other premises FIGURE 3-5.

Do not assume that a gasoline engine fitted with a catalytic converter can be run safely indoors; it cannot. Catalytic converters are fitted into the exhaust system in a similar way as mufflers and have a ceramic core with a catalyst that when in operation controls exhaust emissions through chemical reaction. Diesel trucks equipped with

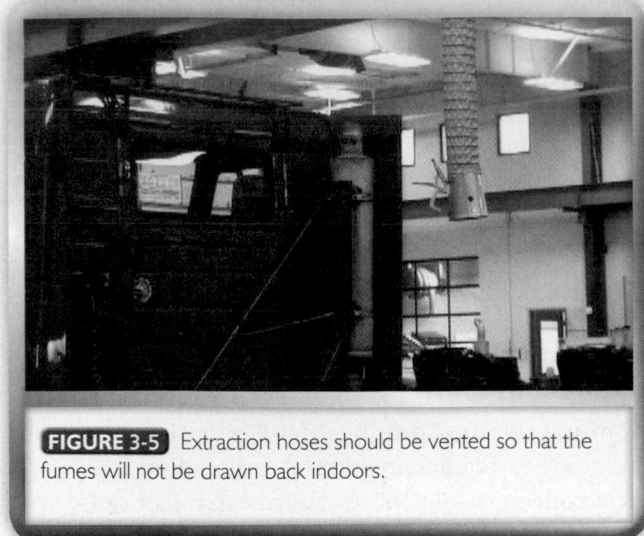

FIGURE 3-5 Extraction hoses should be vented so that the fumes will not be drawn back indoors.

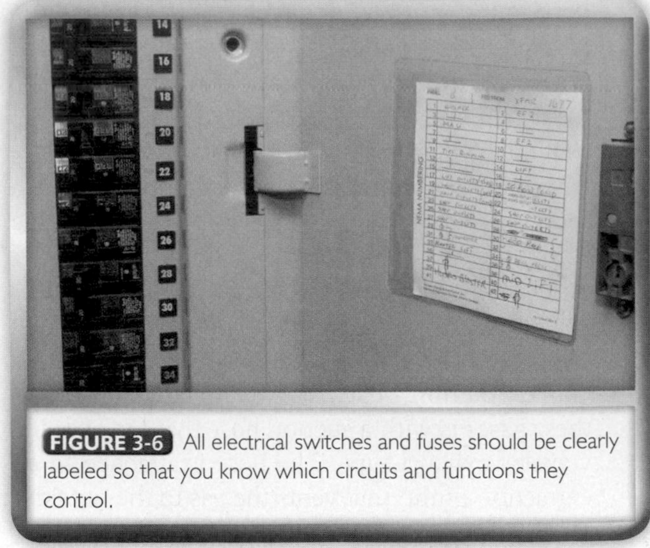

FIGURE 3-6 All electrical switches and fuses should be clearly labeled so that you know which circuits and functions they control.

after-treatment exhaust systems operate in much the same manner, and the same safety precautions should be taken with a running diesel truck. They require high temperatures to operate efficiently and are less effective when the exhaust gases are relatively cool, such as when the engine is only idling or being run intermittently. A catalytic convertor can never substitute for adequate ventilation or exhaust extraction equipment. In fact, even if the catalytic converter were working at 100% efficiency, the exhaust would contain large amounts of carbon dioxide and very low amounts of oxygen, neither of which conditions can sustain life.

Electrical Safety

Many people are injured by electricity in shops. Poor electrical safety practices can cause shocks and burns, as well as fires and explosions. Make sure you know where the electrical panels for your shop are located. All circuit breakers and fuses should be clearly labeled so that you know which circuits and functions they control FIGURE 3-6. In the case of an emergency, you may need to know how to shut off the electricity supply to a work area or to your entire shop.

Keep the circuit breaker and/or electrical panel covers closed to keep them in good condition, prevent unauthorized access, and prevent accidental contact with the electricity supply. It is important that you do not block or obstruct access to this electrical panel; keep equipment and tools well away so emergency access is not hindered. In some localities, 3 feet (0.91 m) of unobstructed space must be maintained around the panel at all times.

There should be a sufficient number of electrical receptacles in your work area for all your needs. Do not connect multiple appliances to a single receptacle with a simple double adapter. If necessary, use a multi-outlet safety strip that has a built-in overload cutout feature. Electric receptacles should be at least 3 feet (0.91 m) above floor level to reduce the risk of igniting spilled fuel vapors or other flammable liquids.

Portable Electrical Equipment

If you need to use an extension cord, make sure it is made of flexible wiring—not the stiffer type of house wiring—and that it is fitted with a ground wire. The cord should be neoprene-covered, as this material resists oil damage FIGURE 3-7. Always check it for cuts, abrasions, or other damage. Be careful how you place the extension cord so it does not cause a tripping hazard. Also avoid rolling equipment or vehicles over it, as doing so can damage the cord. Never use an extension cord in wet conditions or around flammable liquids.

Portable electric tools that operate at 240 volts are often sources of serious shock and burn accidents. Be particularly careful when using these items. Always inspect the cord for damage and check the security of the attached plug before connecting the item to the power supply. Use 110-volt or lower voltage tools if they are available.

All electric tools must be equipped with a ground prong or double-insulated. If they are not, do *not* use them. Never use any high-voltage tool in a wet environment. Air-operated tools cannot give you an electric shock, because they operate on air pressure instead of electricity; so they are safer to use in a wet environment.

Portable Shop Lights

Portable shop lights/droplights can be very useful tools to add light to a particular area or spot on the vehicle you are working on. Always make sure you follow the safety

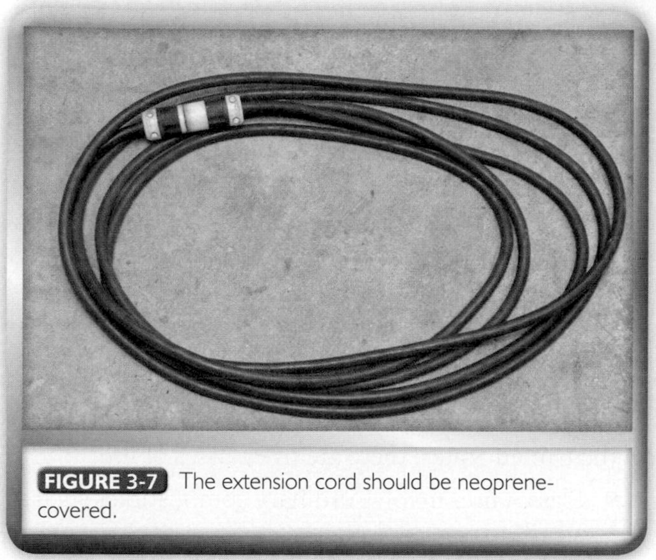
FIGURE 3-7 The extension cord should be neoprene-covered.

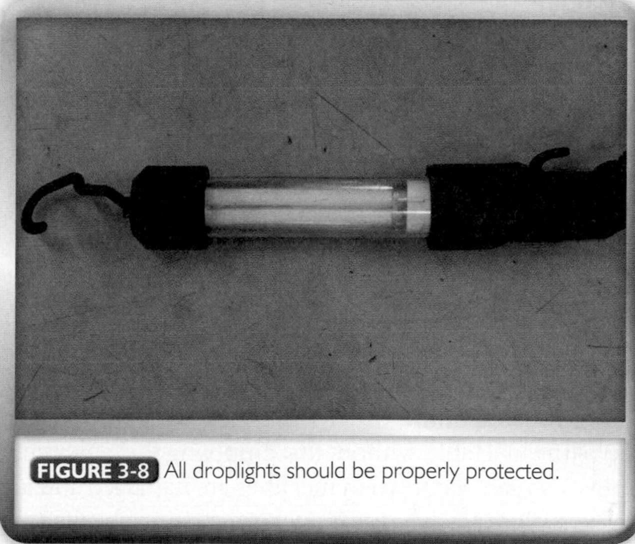
FIGURE 3-8 All droplights should be properly protected.

directions when using shop lights. Shop lights should have protective covers fitted to them to prevent accidentally breaking the lamp. If a lamp breaks, it can be an electrical hazard, particularly if a metal object comes in contact with exposed live electricity. For this reason, often low-voltage lamps or lamps with safety switches fitted are used to prevent accidental electrocution. Some shop lights are now cordless, particularly those with LEDs fitted as the light source. Cordless lights are a very safe option because they isolate you from the high voltage.

Electric droplights are a common source of shocks, especially if they are the wrong type for the purpose or if they are poorly constructed or maintained. All droplights should be designed in such a way that the electrical parts can never come into contact with the outer casing of the device. Such lights are called **double-insulated**. The bulb should be completely enclosed in a transparent insulating case or protected within a robust insulating cage FIGURE 3-8.

The bulbs used in electric droplights are very vulnerable to impact and must not be used without insulating cage protection. Incandescent bulbs present an extreme fire hazard if broken in the presence of flammable vapors or liquids and should not be used in repair shops. LED and fluorescent bulbs, while still hazardous, are much safer.

> **TECHNICIAN TIP**
>
> Always inspect the wiring for damage and check the security of the attached plug before connecting a droplight to the power supply. Always switch off and unplug a droplight before changing the bulb.

Shop Layout

The shop should have a layout that is efficient and safe with clearly defined working areas and walkways. Customers should not be allowed to wander through work areas unescorted. A good shop layout can be achieved by thinking about how the work is to be done, how equipment is used, and what traffic movements, both pedestrian and vehicular, occur within the shop. A well-planned shop should have clearly defined areas for various activities, like parts cleaning, parts storage, tool storage, flammable liquid storage, jacking or lifting, tire fitting, and painting. All flammable items should be kept in an approved fireproof storage container or cabinet, with firefighting equipment close at hand.

> **TECHNICIAN TIP**
>
> The danger of a fire is always present in shops, particularly because of the amount of flammable liquids and materials used in shops and vehicles. Always be aware of the potential for a fire, and plan ahead by thinking through the task you are about to undertake. Know where firefighting equipment is kept and how it works.

Preventing Fires

The danger of a fuel fire is always present in an repair shop. Most vehicles carry a fuel tank, often with large quantities of fuel on board, which is more than sufficient to cause a large, very destructive, and potentially explosive fire. Take precautions to make sure you have the correct type and size of extinguishers on hand for a potential fuel fire. Make sure you clean up spills immediately and avoid ignition sources, like sparks, in the presence of flammable liquids or gases.

Fuel Vapor

Liquid fuel vaporizes to different degrees, especially when spilled, and the vapor is generally easy to ignite.

Because fuel vapor is invisible and heavier than air, it can spread unseen across a wide area, and a source of ignition can be quite some distance from the original spill. Fuel can even vaporize from the cloths or rags used to wipe up liquid spills. These materials should be allowed to dry in the open air, not held in front of a heater element. Any spark or naked flame, even a lit cigarette, can start an explosive fire.

Spillage Risks

Spills frequently occur when technicians remove and replace fuel filters. They also occur during removal of a fuel tank sender unit, which can be located on the side or top of the fuel tank, without first emptying the tank safely. Spills also can occur when fuel lines are damaged and are being replaced, when fuel systems are being checked, or when fuel is being drained into unsuitable containers. Avoid spills by following the manufacturer's specified procedure when removing fuel system components. Also, keep a spill response kit nearby to deal with any spills quickly. Spill kits should contain absorbent material and barrier dams to contain moderate-sized spills.

Draining Fuel

If there is a possibility of fuel spillage while working on a vehicle, then you should first remove the fuel safely. Do this only in a well-ventilated, level space, preferably outside in the open air. Make sure all potential sources of ignition have been removed from the area, and disconnect the battery on the vehicle. Do not drain fuel from a vehicle over an inspection pit. Make sure the container you are draining into is an approved fuel storage container (fuel retriever) and that it is large enough to contain all of the fuel in the system being drained.

Using a Fuel Retriever

Always use a fuel retriever, preferably removing the fuel through the filler neck. A fuel retriever will minimize the chance of sudden large spills occurring. You may need to use narrow-diameter hoses or adapters to drain fuel lines or to bypass anti-spillage devices. Check the service manual for details on how best to drain the fuel from the vehicle you are working on.

Safety

Never weld anywhere near a gas tank or any kind of fuel line. Welding work on a tank is a job for specialists. An empty fuel tank can still contain vapor and therefore can be even more dangerous than one full of liquid fuel. Do not attempt to repair a tank yourself.

Extinguishing Fires

Three elements must be present at the same time for a fire to occur: fuel, oxygen, and heat. The secret of firefighting involves the removal of at least one of these elements, usually the oxygen or the heat, to extinguish the fire. For example, a fire blanket when applied correctly removes the oxygen, while a water extinguisher removes heat from the fire. In the shop, fire extinguishers are used to extinguish the majority of small fires. Never hesitate to call the fire department if you cannot extinguish a fire safely.

Fire Classifications

In the United States, there are five classes of fire:

- Class A fires involve ordinary combustibles such as wood, paper, or cloth.
- Class B fires involve flammable liquids or gaseous fuels.
- Class C fires involve electrical equipment.
- Class D fires involve combustible metals such as sodium, titanium, and magnesium.
- Class K fires involve cooking oil or fat.

Fire Extinguisher Types

Fire extinguishers are marked with pictograms depicting the types of fires that the extinguisher is approved to fight **FIGURE 3-9**:

- Class A: Green triangle
- Class B: Red square
- Class C: Blue circle
- Class D: Yellow pentagram
- Class K: Black hexagon

Fire Extinguisher Operation

Always sound the alarm before attempting to fight a fire. If you cannot fight the fire safely, leave the area while you wait for backup. You will need to size up the fire before you make the decision to fight it with a fire extinguisher by identifying what sort of material is burning, the extent of the fire, and the likelihood of it spreading.

To operate a fire extinguisher, follow the acronym for fire extinguisher use: PASS (Pull, Aim, Squeeze, Sweep). *Pull* out the pin that locks the handle at the top of the fire extinguisher to prevent accidental use **FIGURE 3-10 A**. Carry the fire extinguisher in one hand, and use your other hand to *aim* the nozzle at the base of the fire **FIGURE 3-10 B**. Stand about 8–12' (2.4–3.7 m) away from the fire and *squeeze* the handle to discharge

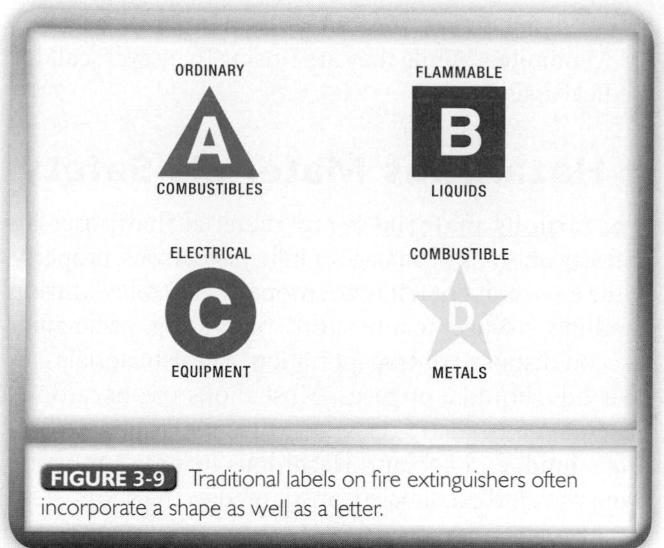

FIGURE 3-9 Traditional labels on fire extinguishers often incorporate a shape as well as a letter.

the fire extinguisher **FIGURE 3-10 C**. Remember that if you release the handle on the fire extinguisher, it will stop discharging. *Sweep* the nozzle from side to side at the base of the fire **FIGURE 3-10 D**. Continue to watch the fire. Although it may appear to be extinguished, it may suddenly reignite.

If the fire is indoors, you should be standing between the fire and the nearest safe exit. If the fire is outside, you should stand facing the fire with the wind on your back, so that the smoke and heat are being blown away from you. If possible, get an assistant to guide you and inform you of the fire's progress. Again, make sure you have a means of escape, should the fire get out of control. When you are certain that the fire is out, report it to your supervisor. Also report what actions you took to put out the fire. Once the circumstances of the fire have been investigated, and your supervisor or the fire department has given you the all clear, clean up the debris and submit the used fire extinguisher for inspection.

Fire Blankets

Fire blankets are designed to smother a small fire and are very useful in putting out a fire on a person. They are also used in situations where a fire extinguisher could cause damage. For example, if there is a small fire under

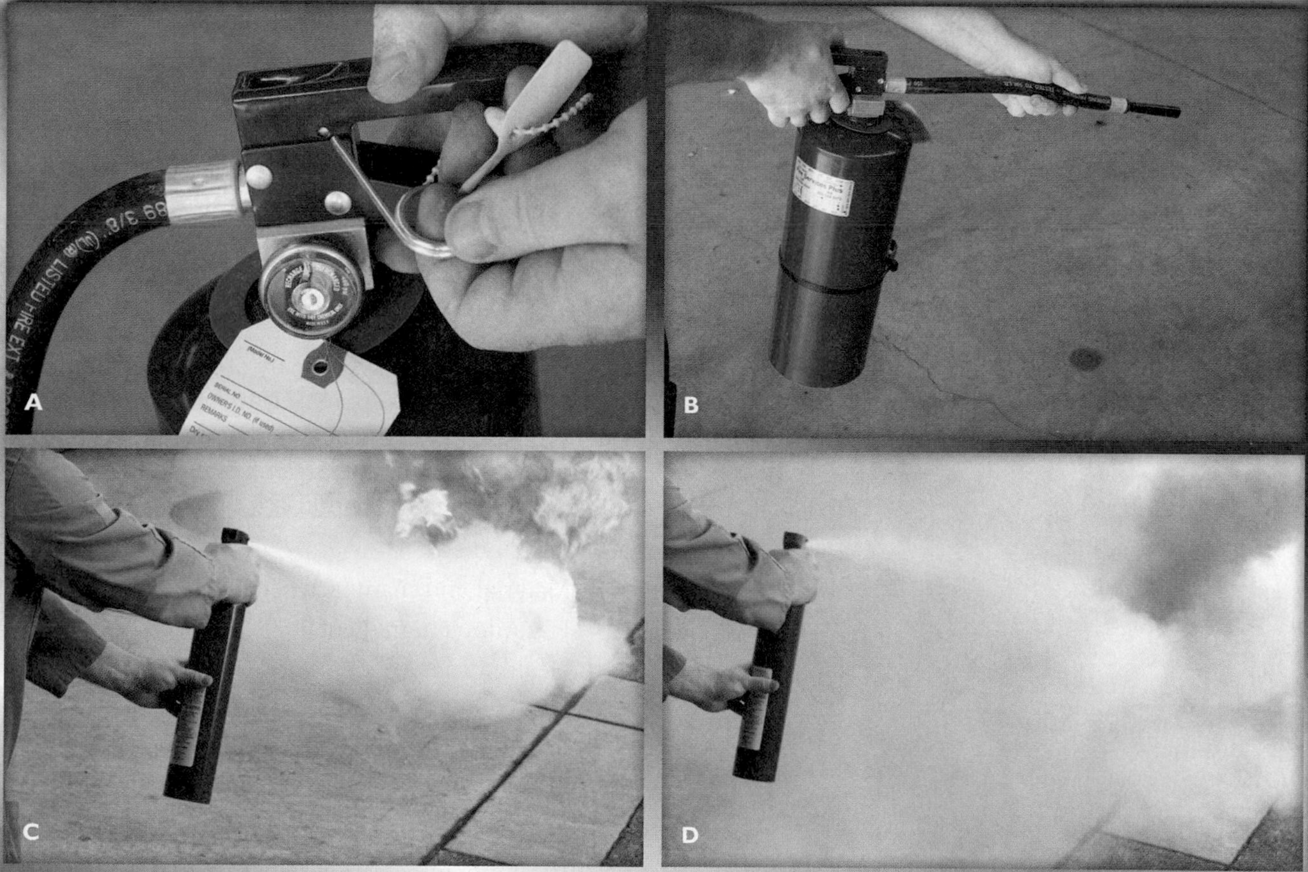

FIGURE 3-10 To operate a fire extinguisher, follow PASS. **A.** Pull. **B.** Aim. **C.** Squeeze. **D.** Sweep.

the hood of a vehicle, a fire blanket might be able to smother the fire without running the risk of getting fire extinguisher powder down the intake system. Obtain a fire blanket and study the how-to-use instructions on the packaging. If instructions are not provided, research how to use a fire blanket or ask your supervisor. You may require instruction from an authorized person in using the fire blanket. If you do use a fire blanket, make sure you return the blanket for use or, if necessary, replace it with a new one.

Eyewash Stations and Emergency Showers

Hopefully you will never need to use an eye wash station or emergency shower. The best treatment is prevention, so make sure you wear all the PPE required for each specific task to avoid injury. Eye wash stations are used to flush the eye with clean water or sterile liquid in the event that you get foreign liquid or particles in your eye. There are different types of eye washers; the main ones are disposable eye wash packs and eye wash stations. Some emergency or deluge showers also have an eye wash station built in FIGURE 3-11.

When individuals get chemicals in their eyes, they typically need assistance in reaching the eye wash station. Take their arm and lead them to it. They may not want to open their eyes even in the water, so encourage them to use their fingers to pull their eyelids open. If a chemical splashed in their eyes, encourage them to rinse their eyes for 15 minutes. While they are rinsing their eyes, call for medical assistance.

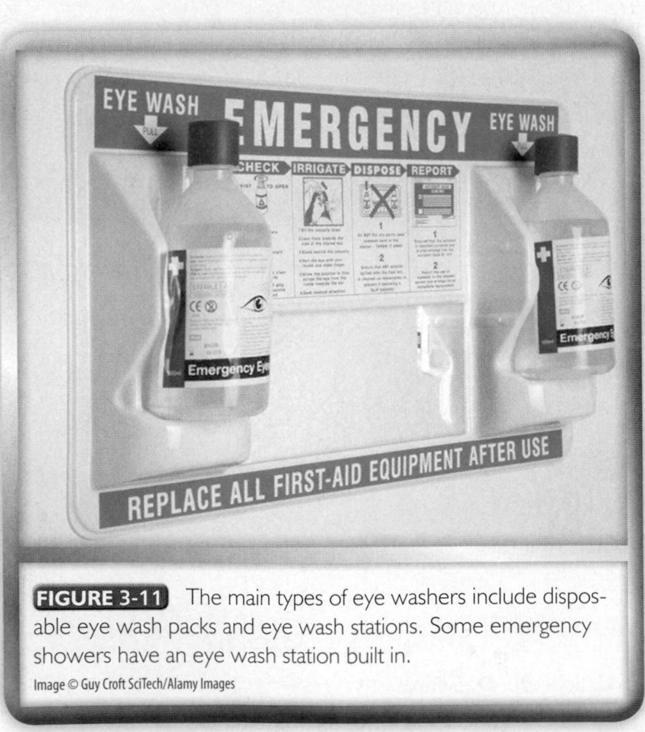

FIGURE 3-11 The main types of eye washers include disposable eye wash packs and eye wash stations. Some emergency showers have an eye wash station built in.

Image © Guy Croft SciTech/Alamy Images

Hazardous Materials Safety

A **hazardous material** is any material that poses an unreasonable risk of damage or injury to persons, property, or the environment if it is not properly controlled during handling, storage, manufacture, processing, packaging, use and disposal, or transportation. These materials can be solids, liquids, or gases. Most shops use hazardous materials daily, such as cleaning solvents, gasket cement, brake fluid, and coolant. Hazardous materials must be properly handled, labeled, and stored in the shop.

Safety Data Sheets

Hazardous materials are used daily and may make you very sick if they are not used properly. **Safety data sheets (SDS)** contain detailed information about hazardous materials to help you understand how they should be safely used, any health effects relating to them, how to treat a person who has been exposed to them, and how to deal with them in a fire situation. An SDS can be obtained from the manufacturer of the material. The shop should have an SDS for each hazardous substance or dangerous product. In the United States it is required that workplaces have an SDS for every chemical that is on site.

Whenever you deal with a potentially hazardous product, you should consult the SDS to learn how to use that product safely. If you are using more than one product, make sure you consult all the SDS for those products. Be aware that certain combinations of products can be more dangerous than any of them separately.

SDS are usually kept in a clearly marked binder and should be regularly updated as chemicals come into the workplace. Generally the SDS must contain at least the following information FIGURE 3-12:

- Revision date
- Material and manufacturer ID
- Hazardous ingredients
- Health hazard data
- Fire and explosion data
- Details about the material mixing or reacting with other materials
- Special precautions

To identify information found on an SDS, follow the steps in SKILL DRILL 3-2.

SAFETY DATA SHEET

1. Identification

Product identifier **Brakleen® Brake Parts Cleaner**

Other means of identification

Product code 05089, 05089T, 85089, 85089AZ

Recommended use Brake cleaner

Recommended restrictions None known.

Manufacturer/Importer/Supplier/Distributor information

Manufactured or sold by:

Company name CRC Industries, Inc.

Address 885 Louis Dr.
Warminster, PA 18974 US

Telephone

General Information 215-674-4300

Technical Assistance 800-521-3168

Customer Service 800-272-4620

24-Hour Emergency (CHEMTREC) 800-424-9300 (US)
703-527-3887 (International)

Website www.crcindustries.com

2. Hazard(s) identification

Physical hazards	Gases under pressure	Compressed gas
Health hazards	Skin corrosion/irritation	Category 2
	Carcinogenicity	Category 1B
	Specific target organ toxicity, single exposure	Category 3 narcotic effects
Environmental hazards	Hazardous to the aquatic environment, long-term hazard	Category 2
OSHA defined hazards	Not classified.	

Label elements

Signal word Danger

Hazard statement Contains gas under pressure; may explode if heated. Causes skin irritation. May cause drowsiness or dizziness. May cause cancer. Toxic to aquatic life with long lasting effects.

Precautionary statement

Prevention Obtain special instructions before use. Do not handle until all safety precautions have been read and understood. Do not puncture or incinerate container. Do not expose to heat or store at temperatures above 49°C/120°F. Use with adequate ventilation. Open doors and windows or use other means to ensure a fresh air supply during use and while product is drying. If you experience any symptoms listed on this label, increase ventilation or leave the area. Avoid breathing mist or vapor. Avoid breathing gas. Wash thoroughly after handling. Wear protective gloves/protective clothing/eye protection/face protection. Avoid release to the environment.

Response If on skin: Wash with plenty of water. If skin irritation occurs: Get medical attention. Take off contaminated clothing and wash before reuse. If inhaled: Remove person to fresh air and keep comfortable for breathing. Call a poison center/doctor if you feel unwell. If exposed or concerned: Get medical attention. Collect spillage.

Storage Store locked up. Protect from sunlight. Store in a well-ventilated place. Exposure to high temperature may cause can to burst.

Disposal Dispose of contents/container in accordance with local/regional/national regulations.

3. Composition/information on ingredients

Mixtures

Chemical name	Common name and synonyms	CAS number	%
Tetrachloroethylene	Perchloroethylene	127-18-4	90 - 100
Carbon dioxide		124-38-9	1 - 5

Specific chemical identity and/or percentage of composition has been withheld as a trade secret.

Material name: Brakleen® Brake Parts Cleaner
05089, 05089T, 85089, 85089AZ Version #: 02 Revision date: 08-07-2014 Issue date: 12-20-2013 SDS US 1 / 9

FIGURE 3-12 An example of an SDS. Image Courtesy of CRC Industries, Inc.

Continued on next page

4. First-aid measures

Inhalation	Remove victim to fresh air and keep at rest in a position comfortable for breathing. Call a POISON CENTER or doctor/physician if you feel unwell.
Skin contact	Remove contaminated clothing. Rinse skin with water/shower. If skin irritation occurs: Get medical advice/attention. Wash contaminated clothing before reuse.
Eye contact	Rinse with water. Get medical attention if irritation develops and persists.
Ingestion	In the unlikely event of swallowing contact a physician or poison control center. Rinse mouth.
Most important symptoms/effects, acute and delayed	May cause drowsiness and dizziness. Headache. Nausea, vomiting. Irritation of eyes and mucous membranes. Irritation of nose and throat. Skin irritation. May cause redness and pain.
Indication of immediate medical attention and special treatment needed	Provide general supportive measures and treat symptomatically. Keep victim under observation. Symptoms may be delayed.
General information	IF exposed or concerned: Get medical advice/attention. Ensure that medical personnel are aware of the material(s) involved, and take precautions to protect themselves.

5. Fire-fighting measures

Suitable extinguishing media	Dry chemical, CO2, or water spray.
Unsuitable extinguishing media	Do not use water jet as an extinguisher, as this will spread the fire.
Specific hazards arising from the chemical	Contents under pressure. Exposure to high temperature may cause can to burst. When exposed to extreme heat or hot surfaces, vapors may decompose to harmful or fatal corrosive gases such as hydrogen chloride and possibly phosgene.
Special protective equipment and precautions for firefighters	Firefighters must use standard protective equipment including flame retardant coat, helmet with face shield, gloves, rubber boots, and in enclosed spaces, SCBA.
Fire-fighting equipment/instructions	In case of fire: Stop leak if safe to do so. Move containers from fire area if you can do so without risk. Containers should be cooled with water to prevent vapor pressure build up.

6. Accidental release measures

Personal precautions, protective equipment and emergency procedures	Keep unnecessary personnel away. Keep people away from and upwind of spill/leak. Keep out of low areas. Wear appropriate protective equipment and clothing during clean-up. Avoid breathing mist or vapor. Avoid breathing gas. Do not touch damaged containers or spilled material unless wearing appropriate protective clothing. Ensure adequate ventilation. Local authorities should be advised if significant spillages cannot be contained. For personal protection, see section 8 of the SDS.
Methods and materials for containment and cleaning up	Eliminate all ignition sources (no smoking, flares, sparks, or flames in immediate area). Keep combustibles (wood, paper, oil, etc.) away from spilled material. This material is classified as a water pollutant under the Clean Water Act and should be prevented from contaminating soil or from entering sewage and drainage systems which lead to waterways. Stop the flow of material, if this is without risk. Collect spillage. Wipe up with absorbent material (e.g. cloth, fleece). Clean surface thoroughly to remove residual contamination. For waste disposal, see section 13 of the SDS.
Environmental precautions	Avoid release to the environment. Contact local authorities in case of spillage to drain/aquatic environment. Prevent further leakage or spillage if safe to do so. Do not contaminate water. Avoid discharge into drains, water courses or onto the ground.

7. Handling and storage

Precautions for safe handling	Obtain special instructions before use. Do not handle until all safety precautions have been read and understood. Pressurized container: Do not pierce or burn, even after use. Do not use if spray button is missing or defective. Do not spray on a naked flame or any other incandescent material. Do not smoke while using or until sprayed surface is thoroughly dry. Use with adequate ventilation. Open doors and windows or use other means to ensure a fresh air supply during use and while product is drying. If you experience any symptoms listed on this label, increase ventilation or leave the area. Do not cut, weld, solder, drill, grind, or expose containers to heat, flame, sparks, or other sources of ignition. Use caution around energized equipment. The metal container will conduct electricity if it contacts a live source. This may result in injury to the user from electrical shock and/or flash fire. Avoid breathing mist or vapor. Avoid breathing gas. Avoid contact with eyes, skin, and clothing. Avoid prolonged exposure. Use only in well-ventilated areas. Should be handled in closed systems, if possible. Wear appropriate personal protective equipment. Observe good industrial hygiene practices. Avoid release to the environment. Do not empty into drains. For product usage instructions, please see the product label.
Conditions for safe storage, including any incompatibilities	Level 1 Aerosol. Contents under pressure. Do not puncture or incinerate container. Do not expose to heat or store at temperatures above 49 °C/120 °F. Do not handle or store near an open flame, heat or other sources of ignition. Exposure to high temperature may cause can to burst. Store in a well-ventilated place. Store away from incompatible materials (see Section 10 of the SDS).

8. Exposure controls/personal protection

Occupational exposure limits

US. OSHA Table Z-1 Limits for Air Contaminants (29 CFR 1910.1000)

Components	Type	Value
Carbon dioxide (CAS 124-38-9)	PEL	9000 mg/m3

Continued on next page

		5000 ppm

US. OSHA Table Z-2 (29 CFR 1910.1000)

Components	Type	Value
Tetrachloroethylene (CAS 127-18-4)	Ceiling	200 ppm
	TWA	100 ppm

US. ACGIH Threshold Limit Values

Components	Type	Value
Carbon dioxide (CAS 124-38-9)	STEL	30000 ppm
	TWA	5000 ppm
Tetrachloroethylene (CAS 127-18-4)	STEL	100 ppm
	TWA	25 ppm

US. NIOSH: Pocket Guide to Chemical Hazards

Components	Type	Value
Carbon dioxide (CAS 124-38-9)	STEL	54000 mg/m3
		30000 ppm
	TWA	9000 mg/m3
		5000 ppm

Exposure guidelines

US - Minnesota Haz Subs: Skin designation applies

Tetrachloroethylene (CAS 127-18-4) Skin designation applies.

Appropriate engineering controls Good general ventilation (typically 10 air changes per hour) should be used. Ventilation rates should be matched to conditions. If applicable, use process enclosures, local exhaust ventilation, or other engineering controls to maintain airborne levels below recommended exposure limits. If exposure limits have not been established, maintain airborne levels to an acceptable level. Eye wash facilities and emergency shower must be available when handling this product.

Individual protection measures, such as personal protective equipment

Eye/face protection Wear safety glasses with side shields (or goggles).

Skin protection

Hand protection Wear protective gloves such as: Viton®. Polyvinyl alcohol (PVA). Nitrile. Silver Shield®

Other Wear appropriate chemical resistant clothing.

Respiratory protection If engineering controls are not feasible or if exposure exceeds the applicable exposure limits, use a NIOSH-approved cartridge respirator with an organic vapor cartridge. Use a self-contained breathing apparatus in confined spaces and for emergencies. Air monitoring is needed to determine actual employee exposure levels.

Thermal hazards Wear appropriate thermal protective clothing, when necessary.

General hygiene considerations When using do not smoke. Always observe good personal hygiene measures, such as washing after handling the material and before eating, drinking, and/or smoking. Routinely wash work clothing and protective equipment to remove contaminants.

9. Physical and chemical properties

Appearance

Physical state Liquid.

Form Aerosol.

Color Colorless.

Odor Irritating.

Odor threshold 50 ppm

pH Not available.

Melting point/freezing point -8.1 °F (-22.3 °C) estimated

Initial boiling point and boiling range 250.3 °F (121.3 °C) estimated

Flash point None (Tag Closed Cup)

Evaporation rate Very fast.

Flammability (solid, gas) Not available.

Upper/lower flammability or explosive limits

Flammability limit - lower (%) Not available.

Flammability limit - upper (%) Not available.

Vapor pressure 1352.4 hPa estimated

Vapor density 5.76 (air = 1)

Relative density 1.62

Continued on next page

10. Stability and reactivity

Reactivity The product is stable and non-reactive under normal conditions of use, storage and transport.

Chemical stability Material is stable under normal conditions.

Possibility of hazardous reactions No dangerous reaction known under conditions of normal use.

Conditions to avoid Heat, flames and sparks. Contact with incompatible materials. When exposed to extreme heat or hot surfaces, vapors may decompose to harmful or fatal corrosive gases such as hydrogen chloride and possibly phosgene.

Incompatible materials Strong oxidizing agents. Strong acids. Strong bases.

Hazardous decomposition products Hydrogen chloride. Trace amounts of chlorine and phosgene. Carbon oxides. Halogenated materials. Carbonyl halides.

11. Toxicological information

Information on likely routes of exposure

Inhalation Prolonged inhalation may be harmful. May cause drowsiness and dizziness. Headache. Nausea, vomiting.

Skin contact Causes skin irritation.

Eye contact Direct contact with eyes may cause temporary irritation.

Ingestion Ingestion of large amounts may produce gastrointestinal disturbances including irritation, nausea, and diarrhea.

Symptoms related to the physical, chemical and toxicological characteristics May cause drowsiness and dizziness. Headache. Nausea, vomiting. Irritation of nose and throat. Irritation of eyes and mucous membranes. Skin irritation. May cause redness and pain.

Information on toxicological effects

Acute toxicity Narcotic effects.

Product	Species	Test Results
Brakleen® Brake Parts Cleaner		
Acute		
Dermal		
LD50	Rabbit	3305.1284 mg/kg estimated
Inhalation		
LC50	Rat	20.4779 mg/l, 4 Hours estimated
Oral		
LD50	Rat	2691.8162 mg/kg estimated

* Estimates for product may be based on additional component data not shown.

Skin corrosion/irritation Causes skin irritation.

Serious eye damage/eye irritation Direct contact with eyes may cause temporary irritation.

Respiratory sensitization Not available.

Skin sensitization This product is not expected to cause skin sensitization.

Germ cell mutagenicity No data available to indicate product or any components present at greater than 0.1% are mutagenic or genotoxic.

Carcinogenicity May cause cancer.

IARC Monographs. Overall Evaluation of Carcinogenicity

Tetrachloroethylene (CAS 127-18-4) 2A Probably carcinogenic to humans.

US. National Toxicology Program (NTP) Report on Carcinogens

Tetrachloroethylene (CAS 127-18-4) Reasonably Anticipated to be a Human Carcinogen.

Reproductive toxicity This product is not expected to cause reproductive or developmental effects.

Specific target organ toxicity - single exposure May cause drowsiness and dizziness.

Specific target organ toxicity - repeated exposure Not classified.

Aspiration hazard May be an aspiration hazard.

Chronic effects Prolonged inhalation may be harmful. Prolonged exposure may cause chronic effects.

12. Ecological information

Ecotoxicity Toxic to aquatic life with long lasting effects. Accumulation in aquatic organisms is expected.

Product		Species	Test Results
Brakleen® Brake Parts Cleaner			
Aquatic			
Fish	LC50	Fish	19.1805 mg/l, 96 hours estimated
Components		**Species**	**Test Results**
Tetrachloroethylene (CAS 127-18-4)			

Continued on next page

13. Disposal considerations

Disposal of waste from residues / unused products This material and its container must be disposed of as hazardous waste. Consult authorities before disposal. Contents under pressure. Do not puncture, incinerate or crush. Do not allow this material to drain into sewers/water supplies. Do not contaminate ponds, waterways or ditches with chemical or used container. Dispose in accordance with all applicable regulations.

Hazardous waste code D039: Waste Tetrachloroethylene
F001: Waste Halogenated Solvent - Spent Halogenated Solvent Used in Degreasing
F002: Waste Halogenated Solvent - Spent Halogenated Solvent

US RCRA Hazardous Waste U List: Reference

Tetrachloroethylene (CAS 127-18-4) U210

Contaminated packaging Empty containers should be taken to an approved waste handling site for recycling or disposal. Since emptied containers may retain product residue, follow label warnings even after container is emptied.

14. Transport information

DOT

UN number UN1950
UN proper shipping name Aerosols, poison, Packing Group III, Limited Quantity, MARINE POLLUTANT
Transport hazard class(es)
Class 2.2
Subsidiary risk 6.1(PGIII)
Label(s) 2.2, 6.1
Packing group Not applicable.
Environmental hazards
Marine pollutant Yes
Special precautions for user Read safety instructions, SDS and emergency procedures before handling.
Special provisions Not available.
Packaging exceptions 306
Packaging non bulk None
Packaging bulk None

IATA

UN number UN1950
UN proper shipping name Aerosols, non-flammable, containing substances in Division 6.1, Packing Group III, Limited Quantity

15. Regulatory information

US federal regulations This product is a "Hazardous Chemical" as defined by the OSHA Hazard Communication Standard, 29 CFR 1910.1200.

TSCA Section 12(b) Export Notification (40 CFR 707, Subpt. D)

Not regulated.

SARA 304 Emergency release notification

Not regulated.

US. OSHA Specifically Regulated Substances (29 CFR 1910.1001-1050)

Not listed.

US EPCRA (SARA Title III) Section 313 - Toxic Chemical: Listed substance

Tetrachloroethylene (CAS 127-18-4)

CERCLA Hazardous Substance List (40 CFR 302.4)

Tetrachloroethylene (CAS 127-18-4)

CERCLA Hazardous Substances: Reportable quantity

Tetrachloroethylene (CAS 127-18-4) 100 LBS

Spills or releases resulting in the loss of any ingredient at or above its RQ require immediate notification to the National Response Center (800-424-8802) and to your Local Emergency Planning Committee.

Clean Air Act (CAA) Section 112 Hazardous Air Pollutants (HAPs) List

Tetrachloroethylene (CAS 127-18-4)

Clean Air Act (CAA) Section 112(r) Accidental Release Prevention (40 CFR 68.130)

Not regulated.

Safe Drinking Water Act (SDWA) Not regulated.

Food and Drug Administration (FDA) Not regulated.

Superfund Amendments and Reauthorization Act of 1986 (SARA)

Section 311/312 Hazard categories Immediate Hazard - Yes
Delayed Hazard - Yes
Fire Hazard - No
Pressure Hazard - Yes
Reactivity Hazard - No

SARA 302 Extremely hazardous substance No

Continued on next page

US state regulations

US. California Controlled Substances. CA Department of Justice (California Health and Safety Code Section 11100)

Not listed.

US. New Jersey Worker and Community Right-to-Know Act

Carbon dioxide (CAS 124-38-9)
Tetrachloroethylene (CAS 127-18-4)

US. Massachusetts RTK - Substance List

Carbon dioxide (CAS 124-38-9)
Tetrachloroethylene (CAS 127-18-4)

US. Pennsylvania Worker and Community Right-to-Know Law

Tetrachloroethylene (CAS 127-18-4)
Carbon dioxide (CAS 124-38-9)

US. Rhode Island RTK

Tetrachloroethylene (CAS 127-18-4)

US. California Proposition 65

WARNING: This product contains a chemical known to the State of California to cause cancer.

US - California Proposition 65 - CRT: Listed date/Carcinogenic substance

Tetrachloroethylene (CAS 127-18-4) Listed: April 1, 1988

Volatile organic compounds (VOC) regulations

EPA

VOC content (40 CFR 51.100(s))	0 %
Consumer products (40 CFR 59, Subpt. C)	Not regulated

State

Consumer products	This product is regulated as a Brake Cleaner. This product is not compliant to be sold for use in California and New Jersey. This product is compliant in all other states.
VOC content (CA)	0 %
VOC content (OTC)	0 %

International Inventories

Country(s) or region	Inventory name	On inventory (yes/no)*
Australia	Australian Inventory of Chemical Substances (AICS)	Yes
Canada	Domestic Substances List (DSL)	Yes
Canada	Non-Domestic Substances List (NDSL)	No
China	Inventory of Existing Chemical Substances in China (IECSC)	Yes
Europe	European Inventory of Existing Commercial Chemical Substances (EINECS)	Yes
Europe	European List of Notified Chemical Substances (ELINCS)	No
Japan	Inventory of Existing and New Chemical Substances (ENCS)	Yes
Korea	Existing Chemicals List (ECL)	Yes
New Zealand	New Zealand Inventory	Yes
Philippines	Philippine Inventory of Chemicals and Chemical Substances (PICCS)	Yes
United States & Puerto Rico	Toxic Substances Control Act (TSCA) Inventory	Yes

*A "Yes" indicates that all components of this product comply with the inventory requirements administered by the governing country(s)
A "No" indicates that one or more components of the product are not listed or exempt from listing on the inventory administered by the governing country(s).

16. Other information, including date of preparation or last revision

Issue date	12-20-2013
Revision date	08-07-2014
Prepared by	Allison Cho
Version #	02
Further information	CRC # 491G
HMIS® ratings	Health: 2* Flammability: 0 Physical hazard: 0 Personal protection: B
NFPA ratings	Health: 2 Flammability: 0 Instability: 0

Continued on next page

NFPA ratings

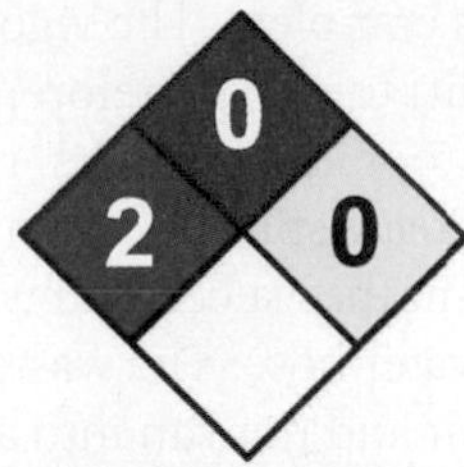

Disclaimer

CRC cannot anticipate all conditions under which this information and its product, or the products of other manufacturers in combination with its product, may be used. It is the user's responsibility to ensure safe conditions for handling, storage and disposal of the product, and to assume liability for loss, injury, damage or expense due to improper use. The information contained in this document applies to this specific material as supplied. It may not be valid for this material if it is used in combination with any other materials. This information is accurate to the best of CRC Industries' knowledge or obtained from sources believed by CRC to be accurate. Before using any product, read all warnings and directions on the label. For further clarification of any information contained on this (M)SDS consult your supervisor, a health & safety professional, or CRC Industries.

SKILL DRILL 3-2 Identifying Information on a Safety Data Sheet

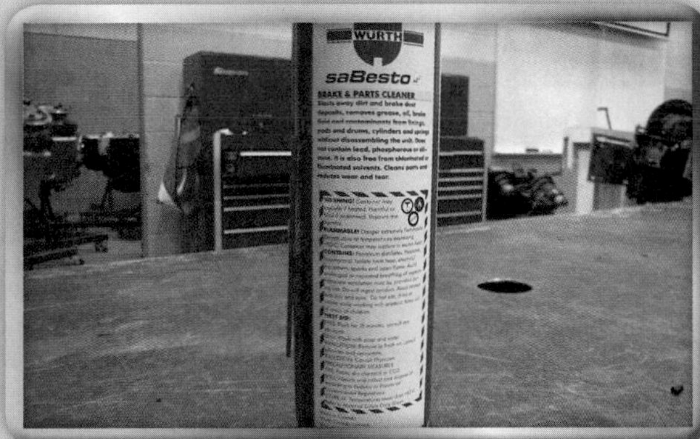

1. Once you have studied the information on the container label, find the SDS for that particular material. Always check the revision date to ensure that you are reading the most recent update.
2. Note the chemical and trade names for the material, its manufacturer, and the emergency telephone number to call.
3. Find out why this material is potentially hazardous. It may be flammable, it may explode, or it may be poisonous if inhaled or touched with your bare skin. Check the threshold limit values (TLVs). The concentration of this material in the air you breathe in your shop must not exceed these figures.

There could be physical symptoms associated with breathing harmful chemicals. Find out what will happen to you if you suffer overexposure to the material, either through breathing it or by coming into physical contact with it. This will help you take safety precautions, such as eye, face, or skin protection, wearing a mask or respirator while using the material, or washing your skin afterwards.

4. Note the flash point for this material so that you know at what temperature it may catch fire. Also note what kind of fire extinguisher you would use to fight a fire involving this material. The wrong fire extinguisher could make the emergency even worse.
5. Study the reactivity for this material to identify the physical conditions or other materials that you should avoid when using this material. It could be heat, moisture, or some other chemical.
6. Find out what special precautions you should take when working with this material. This will include personal protection for your skin, eyes, or lungs and storage and use of the material.
7. Be sure to refresh your knowledge of your SDS from time to time. Be confident that you know how to handle and use the material and what action to take in an emergency, should one occur.

Cleaning Toxic Dust Safely

Toxic dust is any dust that may contain fine particles that could be harmful to humans or the environment. If you are unsure as to the toxicity of dust, then you should always treat it as toxic and take the precautions identified in the SDS or shop procedures. Brake and clutch dust are potential toxic dusts that repair shops must manage. The dust is made up of very fine particles that can easily spread and contaminate an area. One of the more common sources of toxic dust is inside drum brakes and manual transmission bell housings.

It is a good idea to avoid all dust if possible, whether it is classified as toxic or not. If you do have to work with dust, never use compressed air to blow it from components or parts and always use PPE such as face masks, eye protection, and gloves. If you are cleaning up your area after a repair, do not dry sweep dust; instead, use a low-pressure wet cleaning method. Such methods include a soap and water solution used in a dedicated portable wash station, a low-pressure aerosol brake cleaning solution, or a pump spray bottle filled with water. You may also use a HEPA vacuum cleaner to collect dust and clean equipment. HEPA stands for high-efficiency particulate absorbing. HEPA filters can trap very small particles and prevent them from being redistributed into the surrounding air.

After completing a servicing or repair task on a vehicle, there is often dirt left behind. The chemicals present in this dirt usually contain toxic chemicals that can build up and cause health problems. To keep the levels of dirt to a minimum, clean up dirt immediately after the task is complete. The vigorous action of sweeping causes the dirt to rise; therefore, when sweeping the floor, use a soft broom that pushes, rather than flicks, the dirt forward. Create smaller dirt piles and dispose of them frequently. Another successful way of cleaning shop dirt is to use a water hose. The waste water must be caught in a settling pit and not run into a storm water drain.

Various tools have been developed to clean toxic dust from vehicle components. The most common one is the brake wash station. It uses an aqueous solution to wet down and wash the dust into a collection basin. The basin needs periodic maintenance to properly dispose of the accumulated sludge. This tool is probably the simplest way to effectively deal with hazardous dust because it is easy to set up, use, and store.

Another such tool uses a vacuum cleaner that has a large cone attachment at the nozzle end. The base of the cone is open so the brake assembly can fit into the cone. A compressed air nozzle, which is also attached to the inside of the cone, is used to loosen dirt particles. The particles are drawn into the cleaner via a very fine filter. Domestic vacuum cleaners are not suitable for this application because their filters are not fine enough to capture very small dust particles.

To safely clean brake dust, follow the steps in **SKILL DRILL 3-3**.

SKILL DRILL 3-3 Safely Cleaning Brake Dust

1. When performing any cleaning tasks on brake or clutch components, always wear a face mask, gloves, and eye protection.
2. Position the brake wash station under the bottom of the backing plate. When cleaning brakes, remove the brake drum and check for the presence of dust and brake fluid. When cleaning a clutch, position the wash station underneath the bell housing.
3. Turn on the wash station pump and paint the solution over the components to wet and clean the components and remove the dust. Any toxic dust will be washed down and caught in the wash station.
4. Periodically dispose of the residue in an approved manner.

Used Engine Oil and Fluids

Used engine oil and fluids are liquids that have been drained from the vehicle, usually during servicing operations. Used oil and fluids will often contain dangerous chemicals and impurities and need to be safely recycled or disposed of in an environmentally friendly way FIGURE 3-13. There are laws and regulations that control the way in which they are to be handled and disposed. The shop will have policies and procedures that describe how you should handle and dispose of used engine oil and fluids. Be careful not to mix incompatible fluids such as used engine oil and used coolant. Generally speaking, petroleum products can be mixed together. Follow your local, state, and federal regulations when disposing of waste fluids.

Used engine oil is a hazardous material containing many impurities that can damage your skin. Coming into frequent or prolonged contact with used engine oil can cause dermatitis and other skin disorders, including some forms of cancer. Avoid direct contact as much as possible by always using gloves and other protective clothing, which should be cleaned or replaced regularly. Using a barrier-type hand lotion will also help protect your hands as well as make cleaning them much easier. Also follow safe work practices, which minimize the possibility of accidental spills. Keeping a high standard of personal hygiene and cleanliness is important so that you get into the habit of washing off harmful materials as soon as possible after contact. If you have been in contact with used engine oil, you should regularly inspect your skin for signs of damage or deterioration. If you have any concerns, see your doctor.

TECHNICIAN TIP

- Some vehicle components, including brake and clutch linings, contain asbestos, which, despite having very good heat properties, is toxic. Asbestos dust causes lung cancer. Complications from breathing the dust may not show until decades after exposure.
- Airborne dust in the shop can also cause breathing problems such as asthma and throat infections.
- Never cause dust from vehicle components to be blown into the air. It can stay floating for many hours, meaning that other people will breathe the dust unknowingly.
- Wear protective gloves whenever using solvents.
- If you are unfamiliar with a solvent or a cleaner, refer to the SDS for information about its correct use and applicable hazards.
- Always wash your hands thoroughly with soap and water after performing repair tasks on brake and clutch components.
- Always wash work clothes separately from other clothes so that toxic dust does not transfer from one garment to another.
- Always wear protective clothing and the appropriate safety equipment.

TECHNICIAN TIP

Whenever using an atomizer with solvents and cleaners, make sure there is adequate exhaust ventilation. Wear appropriate breathing apparatus and eye protection.

Shop Safety Inspections

Shop safety inspections are valuable ways of identifying unsafe equipment, materials, or activities so they can be corrected to prevent accidents or injuries. The inspection can be formalized by using inspection sheets to check specific items, or they can be general walk-arounds where you consciously look for problems that can be corrected. Some of the commons things to look for would be items blocking emergency exits or walkways, poor safety signage, unsafe storage of flammable goods, tripping hazards, faulty or unsafe equipment or tools, missing fire extinguishers, clutter, spills, unsafe shop practices, and people not wearing the correct PPE. Formal and informal safety inspections should be held regularly. For example, an inspection sheet might be used weekly or monthly to formally evaluate the shop, while informal inspections might be held daily to catch issues that are of a more immediate nature.

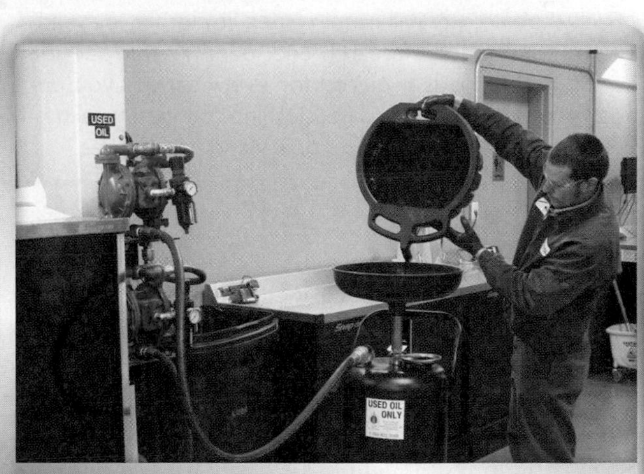

FIGURE 3-13 Used oil and fluids will often contain dangerous chemicals and need to be safely recycled or disposed of in an environmentally friendly way.

Personal Protective Equipment

Personal protective equipment (PPE) is equipment used to block the entry of hazardous materials into the body or to protect the body from injury. PPE includes clothing, shoes, safety glasses, hearing protection, masks, and respirators FIGURE 3-14. Before you undertake any activity, think about all potential hazards and select the correct PPE based on the risk associated with the activity. For example, if you are going to change hydraulic brake fluid, put on some gloves to protect your skin from chemicals.

As you go through this chapter, you will learn how to identify the correct PPE for a given activity and how to wear it safely. It is important that the PPE you use fits correctly and is appropriate for the task you are undertaking. For example, if the task requires you to wear eye protection and specifies that you should use a full face shield, do not try to cut corners and only wear safety glasses. You also need to make sure the PPE you are using is worn correctly. For example, a hairnet that does not capture all of your hair is not protecting you adequately.

Protective Clothing

Protective clothing includes items like shirts, pants, shoes, and gloves. These items are your first line of defense against injuries and accidents and must be worn when performing any work. Always make sure protective clothing is kept clean and in good condition. You should replace any clothing that is not in good condition, since it is no longer able to fully protect you.

> **TECHNICIAN TIP**
>
> Each shop activity will require specific clothing depending on its nature. Research and identify what specific type of clothing is required for every activity you undertake. Wear appropriate clothing for various activities according to the shop's policy and procedures.

Work Clothing

Always wear appropriate work clothing. Whether this is a one-piece coverall/overall or a separate shirt and pants, the clothes you work in should be comfortable enough to allow you to move, without being loose enough to catch on machinery. The material must be flame retardant and strong enough that it cannot be easily torn. A flap must cover buttons or snaps. If you wear a long sleeve shirt, the cuffs must be close fitting, without being tight. Pants should not have cuffs, so that hot debris cannot become trapped in the fabric.

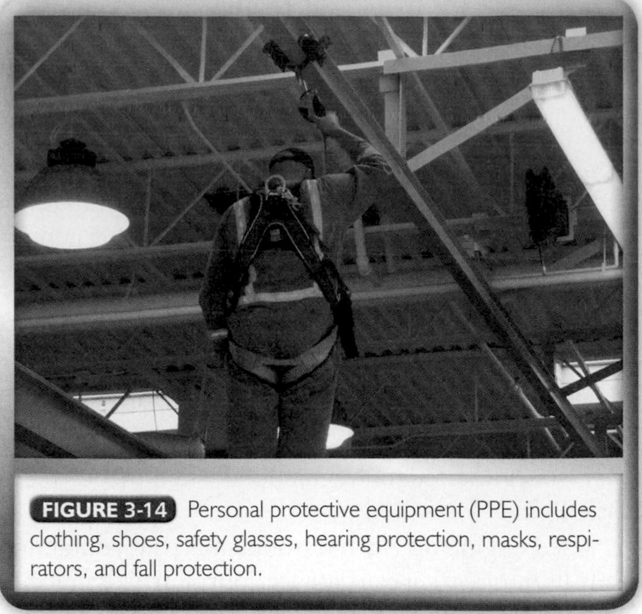

FIGURE 3-14 Personal protective equipment (PPE) includes clothing, shoes, safety glasses, hearing protection, masks, respirators, and fall protection.

Care of Clothing

Always wash your work clothes separately from your other clothes. Start a new working day with clean work clothes and change out of contaminated clothing as soon as possible. It is a good idea to keep a spare set of work clothes in the shop in case a toxic or corrosive fluid is spilled on the clothes you are wearing.

Footwear

The proper footwear provides protection against items falling on your feet, chemicals, cuts, abrasions, and slips. The soles of your shoes must be acid and slip resistant, and the uppers must be made from a puncture-proof material such as leather. Some shops and technicians prefer safety shoes with a steel cap to protect the toes FIGURE 3-15. Always wear shoes that comply with your local shop standards.

Headgear

Headgear includes items like hairnets, caps, and hard hats. They help protect you from getting your hair caught in rotating machinery and protect your head from knocks or bumps. For example, your hard hat can protect you from bumping your head on a vehicle when the vehicle is raised on a hoist. It is also good practice to wear a cap to hold longer hair in place and to keep it clean when working under a vehicle. Some caps are designed specifically with additional padding on the top to provide extra protection against bumps.

Hand Protection

Hands are a very complex and sensitive part of the body with many nerves, tendons, and blood vessels. They are

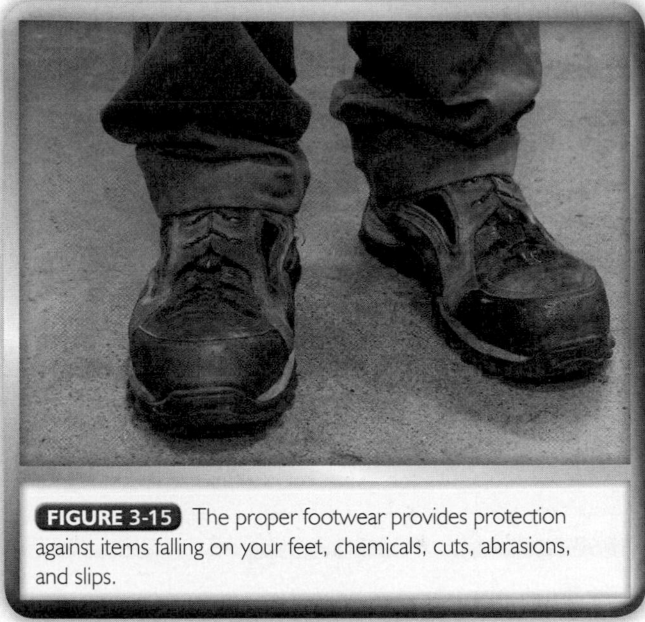

FIGURE 3-15 The proper footwear provides protection against items falling on your feet, chemicals, cuts, abrasions, and slips.

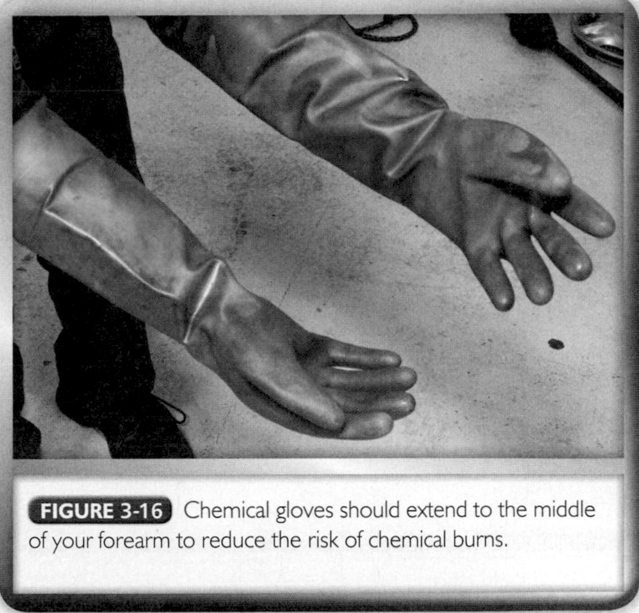

FIGURE 3-16 Chemical gloves should extend to the middle of your forearm to reduce the risk of chemical burns.

susceptible to injury and damage. Nearly every activity performed on vehicles requires the use of your hands, which provides many opportunities for injury. Whenever possible, wear gloves to protect your hands. There are many types of gloves available and their applications vary greatly. It is important to wear the correct type of glove for the various activities you perform.

Chemical Gloves

Heavy-duty and impenetrable chemical gloves should always be worn when using solvents and cleaners. They should also be worn when working on batteries. Chemical gloves should extend to the middle of your forearm to reduce the risk of chemicals splashing onto your skin FIGURE 3-16. Always inspect chemical gloves for holes or cracks before using them, and replace them when they become worn.

Some chemical gloves are also slightly heat resistant. This type of chemical glove is suitable for use when removing radiator caps and mixing coolant.

Leather Gloves

Leather gloves will protect your hands from burns when welding or handling hot components FIGURE 3-17. You should also use them when removing steel from a storage rack and when handling sharp objects. When using leather gloves for handling hot components, be aware of the potential for **heat buildup**. Heat buildup occurs when the leather glove can no longer absorb or reflect heat, and heat is transferred to the inside of the leather glove. At this point, the leather gloves' ability to protect you from the heat is reduced and you will need to stop work, remove the leather gloves, and allow them to cool

FIGURE 3-17 Leather gloves will protect your hands from burns when welding or handling hot components.

down before continuing to work. Also, avoid picking up very hot metal with leather gloves because it causes the leather to harden, making it less flexible during use. If very hot metal must be moved, it would be better to use an appropriate pair of pliers.

Light-Duty Gloves

Light-duty gloves should be used to protect your hands from exposure to greases and oils FIGURE 3-18. Light-duty gloves are typically disposable and can be made from a few different materials, such as nitrile, latex, and even plastic. Some people have allergies to these materials. If you have an allergic reaction when wearing these gloves, try using a glove made from a different material.

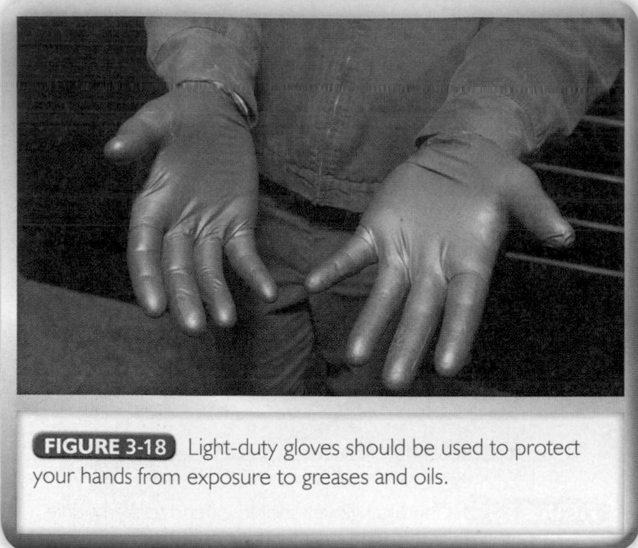

FIGURE 3-18 Light-duty gloves should be used to protect your hands from exposure to greases and oils.

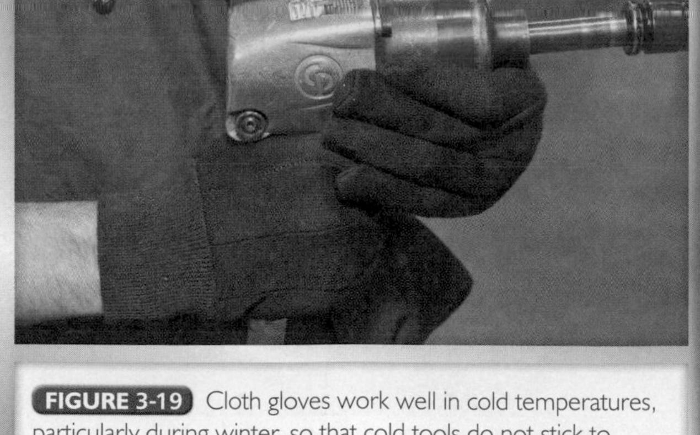

FIGURE 3-19 Cloth gloves work well in cold temperatures, particularly during winter, so that cold tools do not stick to your skin.

General-Purpose Cloth Gloves

Cloth gloves are designed to be worn in cold temperatures, particularly during winter, so that cold tools do not stick to your skin **FIGURE 3-19**. Over time, cloth gloves will accumulate dirt and grime so you will need to wash them regularly. Regularly inspect cloth gloves for damage and wear, and replace them when required. Cloth gloves are not an effective barrier against chemicals or oils, so never use them for that purpose.

Barrier Cream

Barrier cream looks and feels like a moisturizing cream, but it has a specific formula to provide extra protection from chemicals and oils. Barrier cream prevents chemicals from being absorbed into your skin and should be applied to your hands before you begin work **FIGURE 3-20**. Even the slightest exposure to certain chemicals can lead to dermatitis, a painful skin irritation. Never use a standard moisturizer as a replacement for proper barrier cream. Barrier cream also makes it easier to clean your hands because it can prevent fine particles from adhering to your skin.

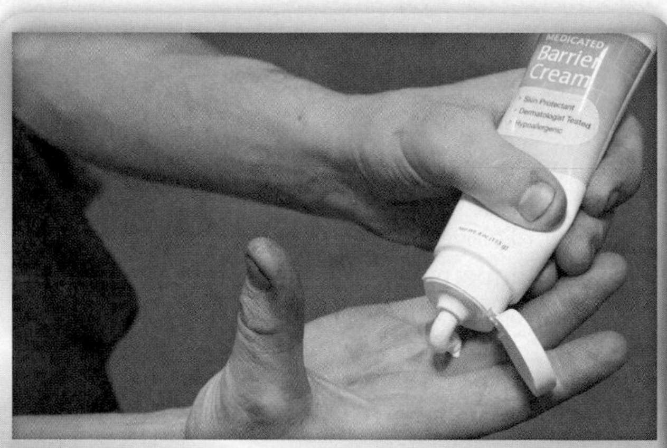

FIGURE 3-20 Barrier cream helps prevent chemicals from being absorbed into your skin and should be applied to your hands before you begin work.

Cleaning Your Hands

When cleaning your hands, use only specialized hand cleaners, which protect your skin **FIGURE 3-21**. Your hands are porous and easily absorb liquids on contact. Never use solvents such as gasoline or kerosene to clean your hands, because they can be absorbed into the bloodstream and remove the skin's natural protective oils.

FIGURE 3-21 When cleaning your hands, use only specialized hand cleaners, which protect your skin.

Ear Protection

Ear protection should be worn when sound levels exceed 85 decibels, when you are working around operating machinery for any period of time, or when the equipment you are using produces loud noise. If you have to raise your voice to be heard by a person who is 2' (0.6 m) away from you, then the sound level is about 85 decibels or more. Ear protection comes in two forms: One type covers the entire outer ear, and the other is fitted into the ear canal FIGURE 3-22. Generally speaking, the in-the-ear style has higher noise-reduction ratings. If the noise is not excessively loud, either type of protection will work. If you are in an extremely loud environment, you will want to verify that the option you choose is rated high enough.

Breathing Devices

Dust and chemicals from your workspace can be absorbed into the body when you breathe. When working in an environment where dust is present or where the task you are performing will produce dust, you should always wear some form of breathing device. There are two types of breathing devices: disposable dust masks and respirators.

Disposable Dust Mask

A disposable dust mask is made from paper with a wire-reinforced edge that is held to your face with an elastic strip. It covers your mouth and nose and is disposed of at the completion of the task FIGURE 3-23. This type of mask should only be used as a dust mask and should not be used if chemicals, such as paint solvents, are present in the atmosphere.

Respirator

A **respirator** has removable cartridges that can be changed according to the type of contaminant being filtered. Always make sure the cartridge is the correct type for the contaminant in the atmosphere. For example, when chemicals are present, use the appropriate chemical filter in your respirator. The cartridges should be replaced according to the manufacturer's recommendation to ensure their effectiveness. To be completely effective, the respirator mask must make a good seal onto your face FIGURE 3-24.

Eye Protection

Eyes are very sensitive organs and they need to be protected against damage and injury. There are many things in the shop environment that can damage or injure eyes, such as high-velocity particles coming from a grinder or high-intensity light coming from a welder. In fact, the American National Standards Institute (ANSI) reports that 2000 workers per day suffer on-the-job eye

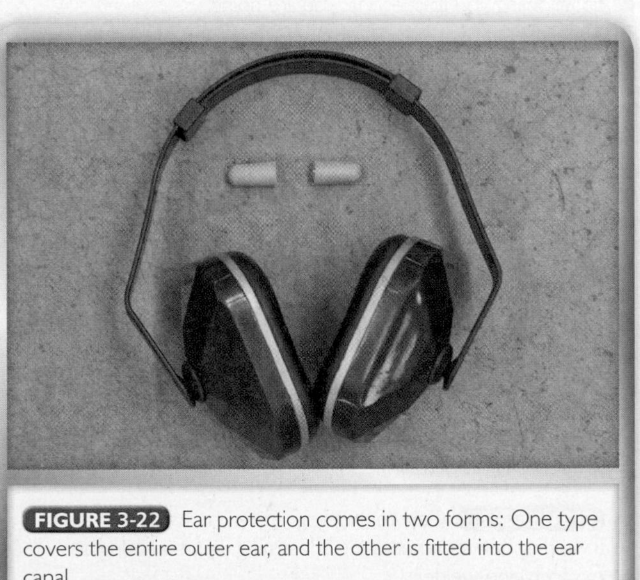

FIGURE 3-22 Ear protection comes in two forms: One type covers the entire outer ear, and the other is fitted into the ear canal.

FIGURE 3-23 A disposable dust mask covers your mouth and nose and is disposed of at the completion of the task.

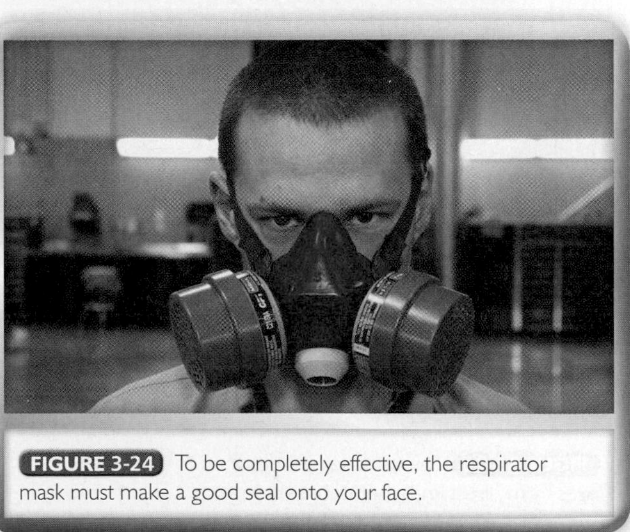

FIGURE 3-24 To be completely effective, the respirator mask must make a good seal onto your face.

injuries. Always select the appropriate eye protection for the work you are undertaking. Sometimes this may mean that more than one type of protection is required. For example, when grinding, you should wear a pair of safety glasses underneath your face shield for added protection.

Safety Glasses

The most common type of eye protection is a pair of safety glasses, which must be marked with "Z87" on the lens and frame. Safety glasses have built-in side shields to help protect your eyes from the side. Approved safety glasses should be worn whenever you are in a shop. They are designed to help protect your eyes from direct impact or debris damage **FIGURE 3-25**. The only time they should be removed is when you are using other eye protection equipment. Prescription and tinted safety glasses are also available. Tinted safety glasses are designed to be worn outside in bright sunlight conditions. Never wear them indoors or in low light conditions because they reduce your ability to see.

Welding Helmet

Wear a **welding helmet** when using or assisting a person using an electric welder. The light from a welding arc is very bright and contains high levels of ultraviolet radiation. The lens on a welding helmet has heavily tinted glass to reduce the intensity of the light from the welding tip, allowing you to see the task you are performing more clearly **FIGURE 3-26**. Lenses come in a variety of ratings depending on the type of welding you are doing; always make sure you are using a properly rated lens.

The remainder of the helmet is made from a durable material that blocks any other light from reaching your face. Welding helmets that tint automatically when an arc is struck are also available. Their big advantage is that you do not have to lift and lower the lens by hand.

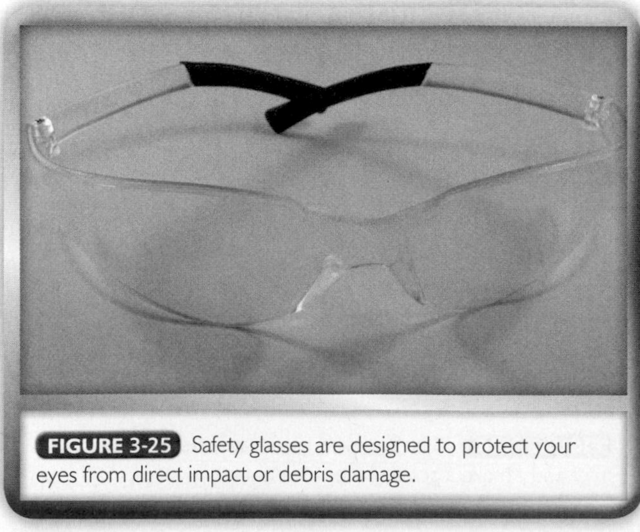

FIGURE 3-25 Safety glasses are designed to protect your eyes from direct impact or debris damage.

Safety

Be aware that the ultraviolet radiation can burn your skin like a sunburn, so wear the appropriate welding apparel to protect yourself from this hazard.

Gas Welding Goggles

Gas welding goggles can be worn instead of a welding mask when using or assisting a person using an oxyacetylene welder **FIGURE 3-27**. The eyepieces are available in heavily tinted versions, but not as tinted as those used in an electric welding helmet. There is no ultraviolet radiation from an oxyacetylene flame, so the welding helmet is not required. However, the flame is bright enough to damage your eyes, so always use goggles of the correct rating.

Full Face Shield

It is necessary to use a full face shield when using solvents and cleaners, epoxies, and resins or when working on a

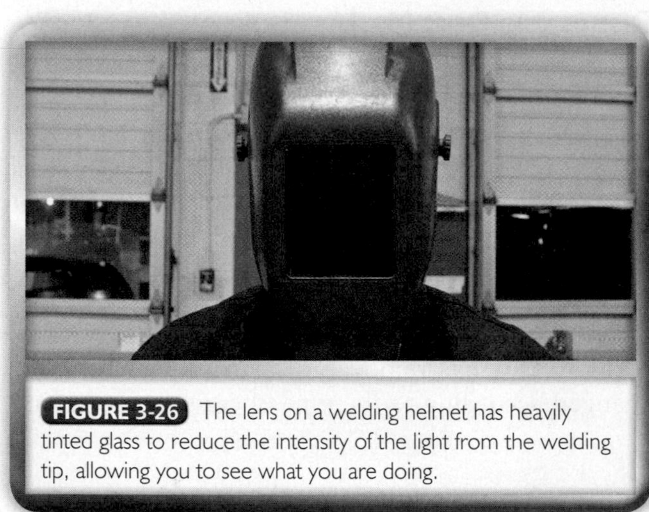

FIGURE 3-26 The lens on a welding helmet has heavily tinted glass to reduce the intensity of the light from the welding tip, allowing you to see what you are doing.

FIGURE 3-27 Gas welding goggles can be worn instead of a welding helmet when using or assisting a person using an oxyacetylene welder.

battery FIGURE 3-28. The clear mask of the face shield allows you to see all that you are doing, but will protect your entire face from chemical burns should there be any splashes or battery explosions. It is also recommended that you use a full face shield combined with safety goggles when using a bench or angle grinder.

Safety Goggles

Safety goggles provide much the same eye protection as safety glasses but with added protection against harmful chemicals that may splash up behind the lenses of glasses FIGURE 3-29. Goggles also provide additional protection from foreign particles. Safety goggles must be worn when servicing air-conditioning systems or any other system that contains pressurized gas. Goggles can sometimes fog up when in use; if this occurs, use one of the special anti-fog cleaning fluids or cloths to clean them.

FIGURE 3-28 It is necessary to use a full face shield when using a grinder, solvents and cleaners, epoxies, and resins or when working on a battery.

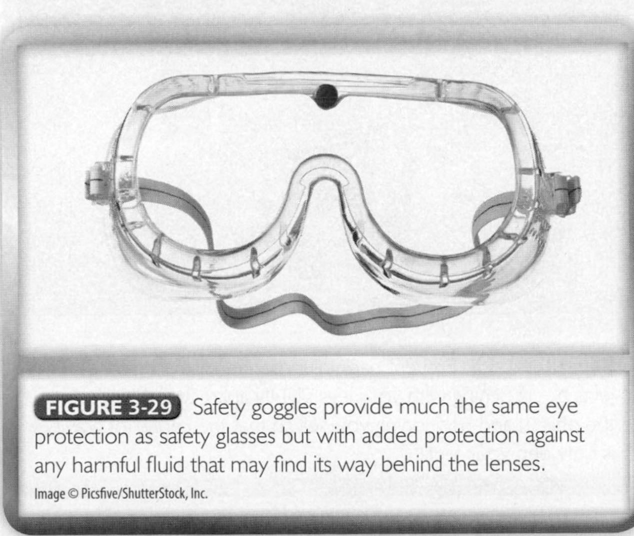

FIGURE 3-29 Safety goggles provide much the same eye protection as safety glasses but with added protection against any harmful fluid that may find its way behind the lenses.

> **TECHNICIAN TIP**
>
> Each lab/shop activity will require at least the safe use of safety glasses, clothing, and shoes depending on its nature. Research and identify whether any additional safety devices are required for every activity you undertake.

Hair Containment

It is easy to get hair caught in rotating machinery, such as drill presses or running engines, and it can happen very quickly. If your hair gets caught in the machinery, you can be pulled into the machinery and injured or killed. Hair should always be tied back and contained within a hairnet or cap.

Your shop will have policies and procedures relating to appropriate hairstyles for shop activities. Research the policy and procedures to determine appropriate hairstyles for activities. Always wear your hair according to the policy and procedures. Use hairnets, caps, or elastic bands as required for each activity.

Watches and Jewelry

When in a shop environment, watches, rings, and jewelry present a number of hazards. They can get caught in rotating machinery, and because they are mainly constructed from metal, they can conduct electricity. Imagine leaning over a running engine with a dangling necklace; it could get caught in the fan belt and be ripped from your neck; not only will it get destroyed, but it could seriously injure you. A ring or watch could inadvertently short out an electrical circuit, heat up quickly and severely burn you, or cause a spark that may make the battery explode. A ring can also get caught on moving parts, breaking the finger bone or even ripping the finger out of the hand. To be safe, always remove watches, rings, and jewelry before starting work. Not only is it safer to remove these items, but your valuables will not get damaged or lost.

Injury Protection Practices

Safe Attitude

Develop a safe attitude toward your work. You should always think "safety first" and then act safely. Think ahead about what you are doing, and put in place specific measures to protect yourself and those around you. For example, you could ask yourself the following questions:

- What could go wrong?
- What measures can I take to ensure that nothing goes wrong?
- What PPE should I use?
- Have I been trained to use this piece of equipment?
- Is the equipment I'm using safe?

Answering these questions and taking appropriate action before you begin will help you work safely.

Proper Ventilation

Proper ventilation is required for working in the shop area. The key to proper ventilation is to ensure that any task or procedure that may produce dangerous or toxic fumes is recognized so that measures can be put in place to provide adequate ventilation. Ventilation can be provided by natural means, such as by opening doors and windows to provide air flow for low-exposure situations. However, in high-exposure situations, such as vehicles running in the shop, a mechanical means of ventilation is required; an example is an exhaust extraction system.

Parts cleaning areas or areas where solvents and chemicals are used should also have good general ventilation, and if required, additional exhaust hoods or fans should be installed to remove dangerous fumes. In some cases, such as when spraying paint, it may be necessary to use a personal respirator in addition to proper ventilation.

> **TECHNICIAN TIP**
>
> Before beginning a task, research the proper ventilation procedure for working within the shop area. Use the correct ventilation equipment and procedures for the activities you are working on within the shop area.

Lifting

Whenever you lift something, there is always the possibility of injury; however, by lifting correctly, you reduce the chance of something going wrong. Before lifting anything, you can reduce the risk of injury by breaking down the load into smaller quantities, asking for assistance if required, or possibly using a mechanical device to assist the lift. If you have to bend down to lift something, you should bend your knees to lower your body; do not bend over with straight legs because this can damage your back **FIGURE 3-30**. Place your feet about shoulder width apart and lift the item by straightening your legs while keeping your back as straight as possible.

Housekeeping and Orderliness

Good housekeeping is about always making sure the shop and your work surroundings are neat and kept in good order. Trash and liquid spills should be quickly cleaned up, tools need to be cleaned and put away after use, spare parts need to be stored correctly, and generally everything needs to have a safe place to be kept. You should carry out good housekeeping practices while working, not just after a job is completed. For example, get rid of trash as it accumulates, clean up spills when they happen, and put tools away when you are finished working with them. It is also good practice to periodically perform a deep clean of the shop so that any neglected areas are taken care of.

Slip, Trip, and Fall Hazards

Slip, trip, and fall hazards are ever present in the shop, and they can be caused by trash, tools and equipment, or liquid spills being left lying around. Always be on the lookout for hazards that can cause slips, trips, or falls. Floors and steps can become slippery so they should be kept clean and have anti-slip coatings applied to them. High-visibility strips with anti-slip coatings can be applied to the edge of step treads to reduce the hazard.

Clean up liquid spills immediately and mark the area with wet floor signs until the floor is dry. Make sure the shop has good lighting so hazards are easy to spot, and keep walkways clear from obstruction. Think about what you are doing and make sure the work area is free of slip, trip, and fall hazards as you work.

FIGURE 3-30 Prevent back injuries when lifting heavy objects by crouching with your legs slightly apart, standing close to the object, and positioning yourself so that the center of gravity is between your feet.

Safety

Never lift anything that is too heavy for you to comfortably lift, and always seek assistance if you need help.

First Aid Principles

The following information is designed to provide you with an awareness of basic first aid principles and the importance of first aid training courses. You will find general information about how to take care of someone who is injured. However, this information is only a guide. It is not a substitute for training or professional medical assistance. Always seek professional advice when tending to an injured person.

First aid is the immediate care given to an injured or suddenly ill person. Learning first aid skills is valuable in the workplace in case an accident or medical emergency arises. First aid courses are available through many organizations, such as the Emergency Care and Safety Institute (ECSI). It is strongly advised that you seek out a certified first aid course and become certified in first aid. The following information highlights some of the principles of first aid.

In the event of an accident, the possibility of injury to the rescuer or further injury to the victim must be assessed. The first step is to survey the scene. While doing this, try to determine what happened, what dangers may still be present, and the best actions to take. Remove the injured person from a dangerous area only if it is safe for you to do so. When dealing with electrocution or electrical burns, make sure the electrical supply is switched off before attempting any assistance.

Always perform first aid techniques as quickly as is safely possible after an injury. When breathing or the heart has stopped, brain damage can occur within 4 to 6 minutes. The degree of brain damage will increase with each passing minute, so make sure you know what to do, and do it quickly.

TECHNICIAN TIP

Three important rules of first aid are:

1. Know what you must not do.
2. Know what you must do.
3. If you are not sure what procedures to follow, send for trained medical assistance.

First Aid Concepts

Prompt care and treatment prior to the arrival of emergency medical assistance can sometimes mean the difference between life and death. The goals of first aid are to make the immediate environment as safe as possible, preserve the life of the patient, prevent the injury from worsening, prevent additional injuries from occurring, protect the unconscious, promote recovery, comfort the injured, prevent any delay in treatment, and provide the best possible care for the injured person.

When attending to an injured victim, always send for assistance. Make sure the person who stays with the injured victim is more experienced in first aid than the messenger. If you are the only person available, request medical assistance as soon as reasonably possible. When you approach the scene of an accident or emergency, do the following:

1. **Danger:** Make sure there are no other dangers, and assist only if it is safe to do so.
2. **Response:** Check to see if the victim is responsive and breathing. If responsive, ask the victim if he or she needs help. If the victim does not respond, he or she is unresponsive.
3. Have a bystander call 9-1-1. If alone, call 9-1-1 yourself (or, if in another country, the relevant emergency assistance phone number).
4. If the victim is unresponsive and not breathing, place your hands in the center of the victim's chest and provide 30 chest compressions hard and fast FIGURE 3-31.

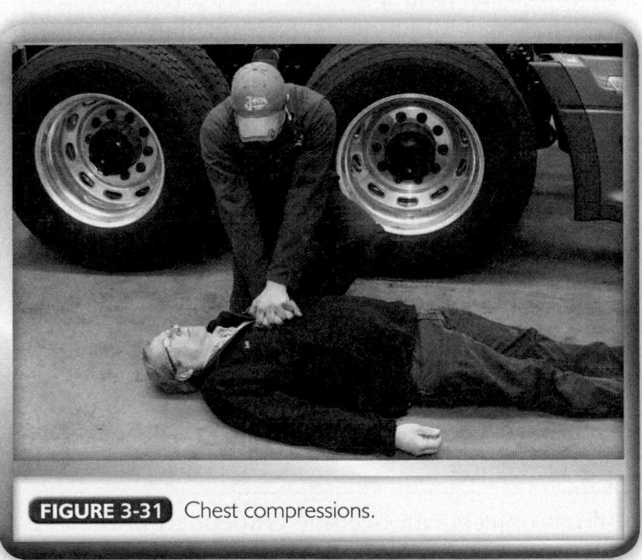

FIGURE 3-31 Chest compressions.

5. Tilt the victim's head back and lift the chin to open the airway. Give one rescue breath lasting 1 second, take a normal breath for yourself, and then give the victim another breath lasting 1 second. Each rescue breath should make the victim's chest rise.
6. Repeat the compression and breath cycles until an AED is available or EMS personnel arrive.
7. Once an automated external defibrillator (AED) arrives, expose the victim's chest and turn on the AED. Attach the AED pads. Ensure that no one touches the victim. Follow the audio and visual prompts from the AED. If no shock is advised, resume CPR immediately (five sets of 30 compressions and two breaths). If a shock is advised, do not touch the victim and give one shock. Or, shock as advised by AED. Resume immediately 30 compressions and two breaths.

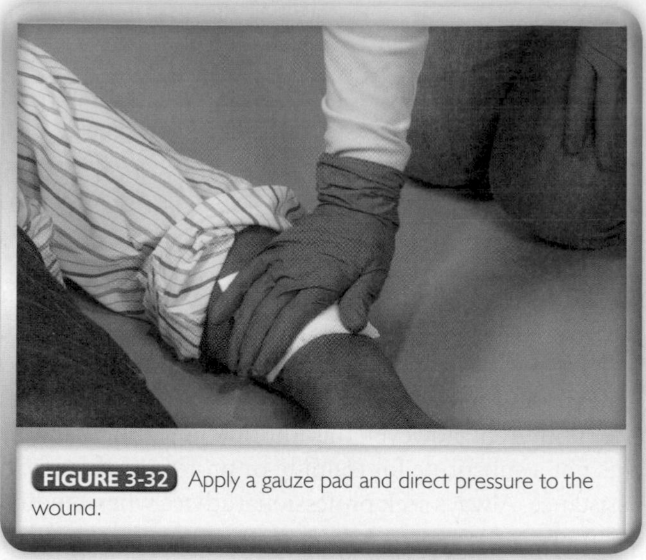

FIGURE 3-32 Apply a gauze pad and direct pressure to the wound.

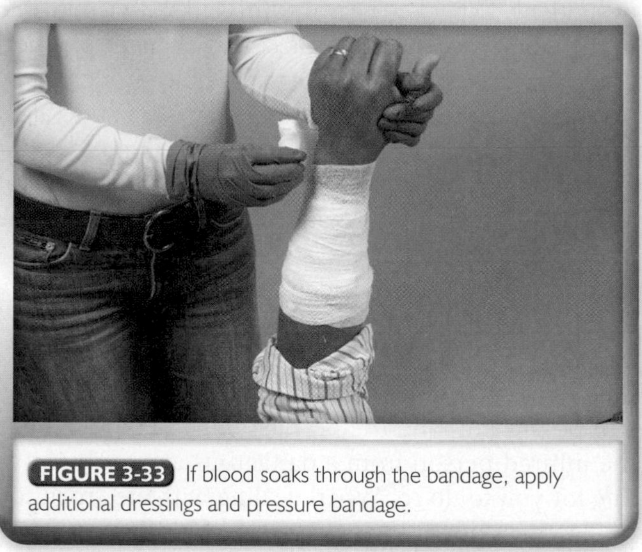

FIGURE 3-33 If blood soaks through the bandage, apply additional dressings and pressure bandage.

Bleeding

A wound that is severely bleeding is serious. If the bleeding is allowed to continue, the victim may collapse or die. Bleeding is divided into two categories: external and internal. **External bleeding** is the loss of blood from an external wound where blood can be seen escaping. **Internal bleeding** is the loss of blood into a body cavity from a wound with no obvious sign of blood.

Before providing first aid, make sure you are not exposed to blood. Wear latex gloves or an artificial barrier. Lay the victim down, then apply a gauze pad and direct pressure to the wound FIGURE 3-32. Apply a pressure bandage over the gauze. If blood soaks through the bandage, apply additional dressings and pressure bandage FIGURE 3-33. Call 9-1-1 if bleeding cannot be controlled. Give nothing by mouth and seek medical aid immediately.

If an object punctures the victim's skin and becomes embedded in the victim's body, do not attempt to remove the object. Stabilize the object with a bulky dressing. Seek medical care immediately.

If the injured person has internal bleeding, it may not be immediately obvious. Symptoms of internal bleeding are bruising, a painful or tender area, coughing frothy blood, vomiting blood, stool that is black or contains bright red blood, and passing blood with urine. To assist an injured victim with internal bleeding, lay the victim down, loosen tight clothing, give nothing by mouth, and seek medical aid immediately.

Eye Injuries

Foreign objects can become embedded in the eye or chemicals can splash into the eye. If an object penetrates and becomes embedded in the eye, do not attempt to remove it. Lay the victim down, stabilize the object with a bulky dressing or clean cloths, ask the victim to close the other eye, and call 9-1-1 (or relevant emergency assistance phone number) FIGURE 3-34.

If an object is loose on the surface of the eye, pull the upper lid over the lower lid. Hold the eyelid open and gently rinse with water. Examine the lower lid by pulling it down gently. If you can see the object, remove it with a moistened sterile gauze, a clean cloth, or a moistened cotton swab. Examine the underside of the upper lid by grasping the lashes of the upper lid and rolling the lid upward over a cotton swab. If you can see the object, remove it with a moistened sterile gauze or a clean cloth FIGURE 3-35.

If a chemical splashes into the eyes, you may be able to flush it out using an eye wash station FIGURE 3-36. Hold the eye wide open and flush with warm water for at

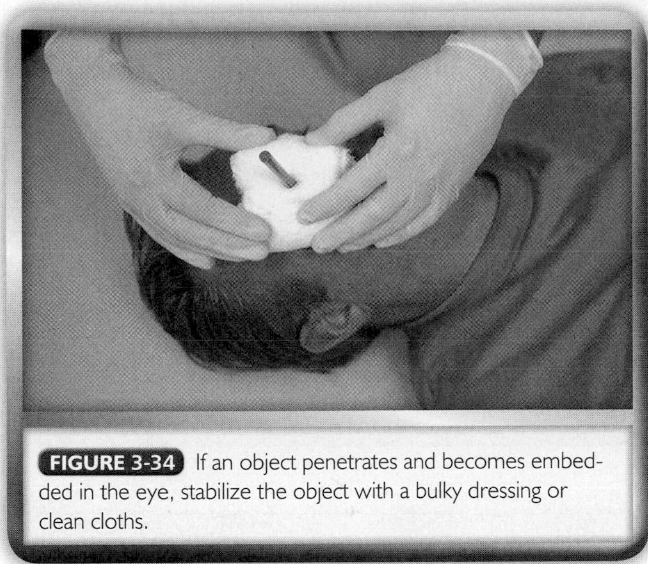

FIGURE 3-34 If an object penetrates and becomes embedded in the eye, stabilize the object with a bulky dressing or clean cloths.

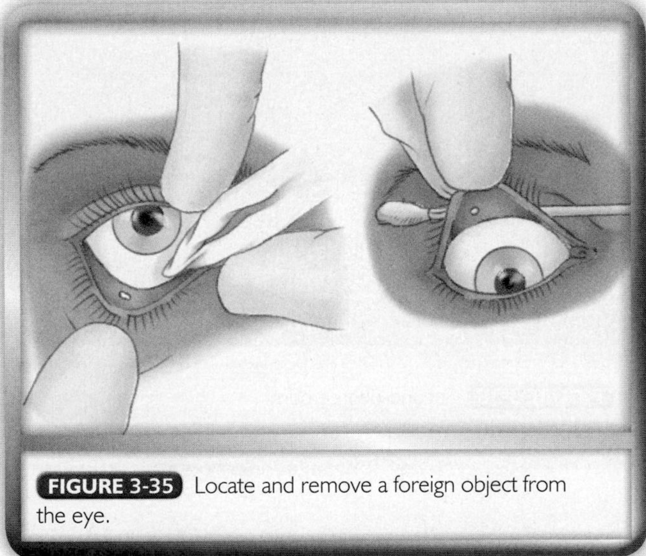

FIGURE 3-35 Locate and remove a foreign object from the eye.

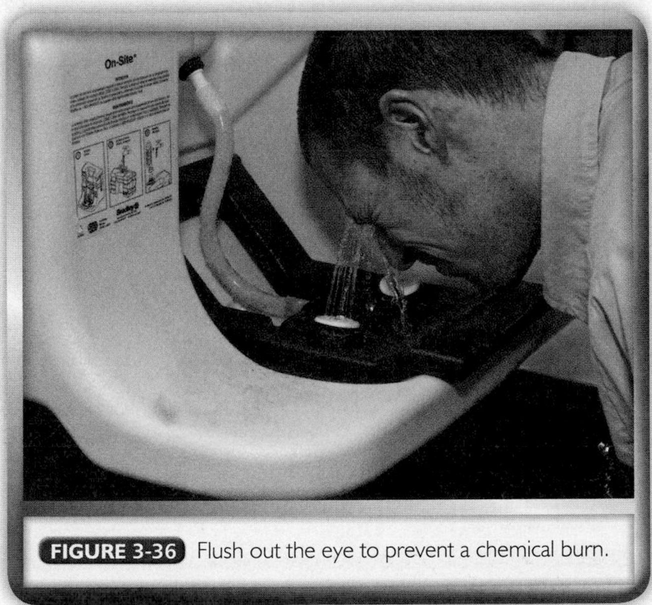

FIGURE 3-36 Flush out the eye to prevent a chemical burn.

least 20 minutes, continuously and gently. Irrigate from the nose side of the eye toward the outside to avoid flushing material into the other eye. Loosely bandage the eyes with wet dressings. Call 9-1-1 (or the relevant emergency assistance phone number).

Fractures

A fracture is a broken or cracked bone. Always seek medical care for all fractures. There may be symptoms you are not aware of that may make the injury more complex than first thought. There are three types of bone fractures: A **simple fracture** involves no wound or internal or external bleeding, an **open fracture** involves bleeding or the protrusion of bone through the skin, and a **complicated fracture** involves penetration of a bone into a vital organ.

The symptoms of a fracture include hearing a snapping noise when the injury occurred, pain or tenderness at or near the injury, inability to move the limb, loss of strength in the limb, shortening of the limb or an abnormally shaped limb, swelling and/or bruising around the area, and a grinding noise if the limb is moved. Allow the victim to support the injured area in the most comfortable position. Stabilize the injured part with your hands or a splint to prevent movement. If the injury is an open fracture, do not push on any protruding bone. Cover the wound and exposed bone with a dressing. Apply ice or a cold pack if possible to help reduce swelling or pain. Call 9-1-1 (or the relevant emergency assistance phone number) for any open fractures or large bone fractures. Do not move the victim unless there is an immediate danger. Be aware of the onset of **shock**, which may present as the victim vomiting or fainting. Shock is when the body's tissues do not receive enough oxygenated blood.

Sprains, Strains, and Dislocations

When a joint has been forced past its natural range of movement, or a muscle or ligament has been overstressed or torn, a sprain, strain, or dislocation may occur. A **sprain** occurs when a joint is forced beyond its natural movement limit. This causes stretching or tearing in the ligaments that hold the bones together. The symptoms of a sprain include pain and loss of limb function, with swelling and bruising present. When a sprain occurs, apply covered ice packs every 20 minutes, elevate the injured limb, and apply an elastic compression bandage to the area and beyond the affected area. You should always treat a sprain as a fracture until medical opinion says otherwise.

A **strain** is an injury caused by the overstretching of muscles and tendons. Symptoms of a strain are sharp pain in the area immediately after the injury occurs, increased pain when using the limb, or tenderness over the entire muscle. The muscle may also have an indentation at the strain location. When a strain occurs, have the victim rest, elevate the injured limb, apply covered ice packs every 20 minutes, and apply an elastic compression bandage.

A **dislocation** is the displacement of a joint from its normal position; it is caused by an external force stretching the ligaments beyond their elastic limit. Symptoms of a dislocation are pain or tenderness around the area, inability to move the joint, deformity of the joint, and swelling and discoloration over the joint. If a dislocation occurs, try to immobilize the limb and seek medical attention. Do not try to put the joint back in place.

FIGURE 3-37 First-degree burn.

Burns and Scalds

Burns are injuries to body tissues, including skin, that are caused by exposure to heat, chemicals, and radiation. Burns are classified as either superficial, partial thickness, or full thickness. Superficial burns, or **first-degree burns**, show reddening of the skin and damage to the outer layer of skin only FIGURE 3-37. Partial-thickness burns, or **second-degree burns**, involve blistering and damage to the outer layer of skin FIGURE 3-38. Full-thickness burns, or **third-degree burns**, involve white or blackened areas and include damage to all skin layers and underlying structures and tissues FIGURE 3-39.

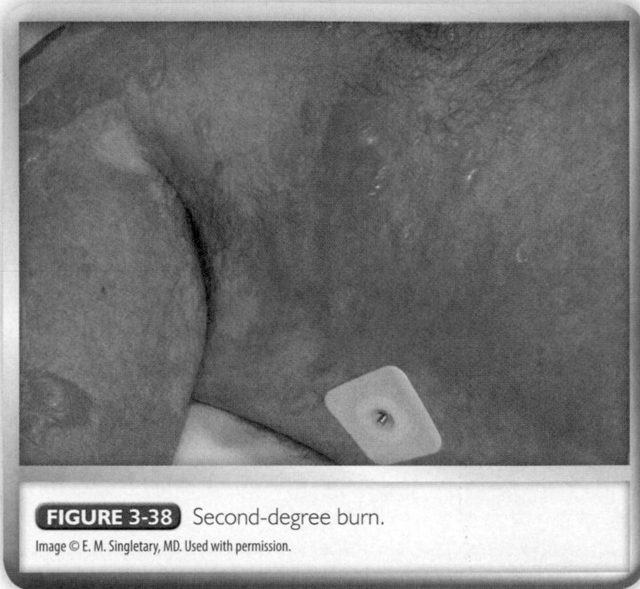

FIGURE 3-38 Second-degree burn.
Image © E. M. Singletary, MD. Used with permission.

Burns can be caused by excessive heat, such as from fire; friction, such as from a rope burn; radiation, such as from a welding flash or a sunburn; chemicals, including acids and bases; or electricity, such as from faulty appliances. Scalds are injuries to the skin caused by exposure to hot liquids and gases. The effects of burns and scalds can include permanent skin and tissue damage, blisters caused by damage to surface blood vessels, severe pain, and shock.

Remove the victim from any danger. If clothing is burning, have the victim roll on the ground using the "stop, drop, and roll" method. Smother the flames with a fire blanket or douse the victim with water. For minor burns, cool the burn with cool water until the body part is pain free. After the burn has cooled, apply antibiotic ointment. Do not apply lotions or aloe vera. Cover the burn loosely with a dry, nonstick, sterile or clean dressing. Do not break any blisters. Give an over-the-counter pain medication such as ibuprofen. Seek medical care. Any large or third-degree burn must be treated by a qualified medical practitioner. Serious burns include skin that is blackened, whitened, or charred; a burn that is larger than .75" (2 cm) in diameter; or a burn that is in the airway or on the face, hands, or genitals. When presented with such burns, call 9-1-1 immediately.

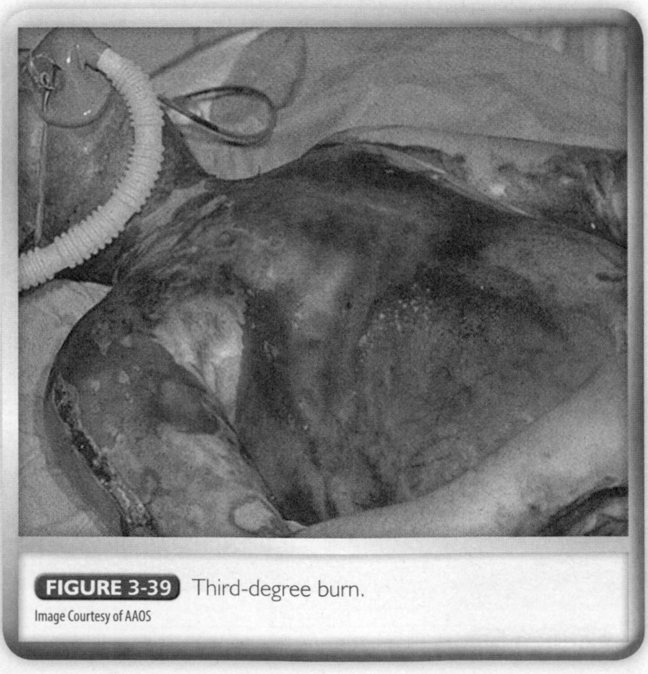

FIGURE 3-39 Third-degree burn.
Image Courtesy of AAOS

Wrap-up

Ready for Review

- Your employer is responsible for maintaining a safe work environment; you are responsible for working safely.
- Always wear the correct personal protective equipment, such as gloves or hearing protection. Personal protective equipment (PPE) protects the body from injury but must fit correctly and be task appropriate.
- Accidents and injuries can be avoided by safe work practices.
- Every shop should mark evacuation routes; always know the evacuation route for your shop.
- OSHA is a federal agency that oversees safe workplace environments and practices.
- The EPA monitors and enforces issues related to environmental safety.
- Shop policies and procedures are designed to ensure compliance with laws and regulations, create a safe working environment, and guide shop practice.
- Identify hazards and hazardous materials in your work environment.
- Safety signs include a signal word, background color, text, and a pictorial message.
- Shop safety equipment includes handrails, machinery guards, painted lines, soundproof rooms, adequate ventilation, gas extraction hoses, doors and gates, and temporary barriers.
- Air quality is an important safety concern. Carbon monoxide and carbon dioxide from running engines can create a hazardous work environment.
- Electrical safety in a shop is important to prevent shocks, burns, fires, and explosions.
- Portable electrical equipment should be the proper voltage and should always be inspected for damage.
- Shop layouts should be well planned to maximize safety.
- Fuels and fuel vapors are potential fire hazards.
- Use fuel retrievers when draining fuel and have a spill response kit nearby.
- Types of fires are classified as A, B, C, D, or K, and fire extinguishers match them accordingly.
- Do not fight a fire unless you can do so safely.
- Eyewash stations and emergency showers allow flushing of chemicals or other irritants.
- Safety data sheets contain important information on each hazardous material in the shop.
- Vacuuming and using water are the safest methods of cleaning dust or dirt that may be toxic.
- Used engine oil and fluids must be handled and disposed of properly.
- Shop safety inspections ensure that safety policies and procedures are being followed.
- Hazardous chemicals and oils can be absorbed into your skin.
- Breathing devices include disposable dust masks and respirators.
- Forms of eye protection are safety glasses, welding helmet, gas welding goggles, full face shield, and safety goggles.
- Before starting work, remove all jewelry and watches, and make sure your hair is contained.
- Thinking "safety first" will lead to acting safely.
- All shops require proper ventilation.
- Lifting correctly or seeking assistance will prevent back injuries.
- First aid involves providing immediate care to an ill or injured person.
- Do not perform first aid if it is unsafe to do so.

Vocabulary Builder

barrier cream A cream that looks and feels like a moisturizing cream but has a specific formula to provide extra protection from chemicals and oils.

complicated fracture A fracture in which the bone has penetrated a vital organ.

dislocation The displacement of a joint from its nor- mal position; it is caused by an external force stretching the ligaments beyond their elastic limit.

double-insulated Tools or appliances that are designed in such a way that no single failure can result in a dangerous voltage coming into contact with the outer casing of the device.

ear protection Protective gear worn when the sound levels exceed 85 decibels, when working around operating machinery for any period of time, or when the equipment you are using produces loud noise.

Environmental Protection Agency (EPA) Federal government agency that deals with issues related to environmental safety.

external bleeding The loss of blood from an external wound; blood can be seen escaping.

first aid The immediate care given to an injured or suddenly ill person.

first-degree burns Burns that show reddening of the skin and damage to the outer layer of skin only.

gas welding goggles Protective gear designed for gas welding; they provide protection against foreign particles entering the eye and are tinted to reduce the glare of the welding flame.

hazard Anything that could hurt you or someone else.

hazardous environment A place where hazards exist.

hazardous material Any material that poses an unreasonable risk of damage or injury to persons, property, or the environment if it is not properly controlled during handling, storage, manufacture, processing, packaging, use and disposal, or transportation.

headgear Protective gear that includes items like hairnets, caps, or hard hats.

heat buildup A dangerous condition that occurs when the glove can no longer absorb or reflect heat and heat is transferred to the inside of the glove.

internal bleeding The loss of blood into the body cavity from a wound; there is no obvious sign of blood.

Occupational Safety and Health Administration (OSHA) Government agency created to provide national leadership in occupational safety and health.

open fracture A fracture in which the bone is protruding through the skin or there is severe bleeding.

personal protective equipment (PPE) Safety equipment designed to protect the technician, such as safety boots, gloves, clothing, protective eyewear, and hearing protection.

policy A guiding principle that sets the shop direction.

procedure A list of the steps required to get the same result each time a task or activity is performed.

respirator Protective gear used to protect the wearer from inhaling harmful dusts or gases. Respirators range from single-use disposable masks to types that have replaceable cartridges. The correct types of cartridge must be used for the type of contaminant encountered.

safety data sheet (SDS) A sheet that pro- vides information about handling, use, and storage of a material that may be hazardous.

second-degree burns Burns that involve blistering and damage to the outer layer of skin.

shock Inadequate tissue oxygenation resulting from serious injury or illness.

simple fracture A fracture that involves no open wound or internal or external bleeding.

sprain An injury in which a joint is forced beyond its natural movement limit.

strain An injury caused by the overstretching of muscles and tendons.

third-degree burns Burns that involve white or blackened areas and damage to all skin layers and underlying structures and tissues.

threshold limit value (TLV) The maximum allowable concentration of a given material in the surrounding air.

toxic dust Any dust that may contain fine particles that could be harmful to humans or the environment.

welding helmet Protective gear designed for arc welding; it provides protection against foreign articles entering the eye, and the lens is tinted to reduce the glare of the welding arc.

Review Questions

1. Who is responsible for providing a safe work environment?
   a. The customer
   b. The coworkers
   c. The technician
   d. The employer
2. Your shop should have a(n) ______ that clearly identifies the evacuation routes.
   a. safety procedure
   b. safety first manual
   c. emergency manual
   d. evacuation procedure
3. All automotive shop activities need to comply with EPA laws and regulations by:
   a. ensuring that waste products are disposed of in an environmentally responsible way.
   b. storing chemicals and fluids correctly.
   c. ensuring that work practices do not contribute to damaging the environment.
   d. All of the choices are correct.
4. A ______ is a list of the steps required to get the same result each time a task or activity is performed.
   a. theory
   b. measure
   c. policy
   d. procedure
5. Which of the following is a typical component found in safety signage?
   a. Background color
   b. Text
   c. A signal word
   d. All of the choices are correct.
6. There are three signal words: ______, ______, and ______.
   a. stop; warning; danger
   b. warning; general; danger
   c. danger; warning; caution
   d. caution; stop; danger
7. The maximum OSHA permissible exposure limit (PEL) for carbon monoxide is ______ parts per million (ppm) of air for an 8-hour period.
   a. 20
   b. 30
   c. 40
   d. 50
8. Typically, there should be ______ of unobstructed space around an electrical panel.
   a. 1'
   b. 2'
   c. 3'
   d. None of the choices is correct.
9. Which of the following bulb types presents an extreme fire hazard if broken in the presence of flammable vapors or liquids?
   a. Incandescent
   b. LED
   c. Fluorescent
   d. None of the choices is correct.
10. Class C fires involve:
    a. electrical equipment.
    b. paper and wood.
    c. flammable liquids.
    d. None of the choices is correct.

ASE-Type Questions

1. Technician A says that exposure to solvents may have long-term effects. Technician B says that accidents are almost always avoidable. Who is correct?
   a. Technician A
   b. Technician B
   c. Both Technician A and Technician B
   d. Neither Technician A nor Technician B
2. Technician A says that both OSHA and the EPA can inspect facilities for violations. Technician B says that a shop safety rule does not have to be reviewed once put in place. Who is correct?
   a. Technician A
   b. Technician B
   c. Both Technician A and Technician B
   d. Neither Technician A nor Technician B
3. Technician A says that both caution and danger indicate a potentially hazardous situation. Technician B says that an exhaust extraction hose is not needed if the vehicle is only going to run for a few minutes. Who is correct?
   a. Technician A
   b. Technician B
   c. Both Technician A and Technician B
   d. Neither Technician A nor Technician B
4. Technician A says that firefighting equipment includes safety glasses. Technician B says that a class A fire extinguisher can be used to fight an electrical fire only. Who is correct?
   a. Technician A
   b. Technician B
   c. Both Technician A and Technician B
   d. Neither Technician A nor Technician B
5. Technician A says that a good way to clean dust off brakes is with compressed air. Technician B says that asbestos may be in current auto parts. Who is correct?
   a. Technician A
   b. Technician B
   c. Both Technician A and Technician B
   d. Neither Technician A nor Technician B
6. Technician A says that personal protective equipment (PPE) does not include clothing. Technician B says that the PPE used should be based on the task you are performing. Who is correct?
   a. Technician A
   b. Technician B
   c. Both Technician A and Technician B
   d. Neither Technician A nor Technician B
7. Technician A says that appropriate work clothes include loose-fitting clothing. Technician B says that you should always wear cuffed pants when working in a shop. Who is correct?
   a. Technician A
   b. Technician B
   c. Both Technician A and Technician B
   d. Neither Technician A nor Technician B
8. Technician A says that a hat can help keep your hair clean when working on a vehicle. Technician B says that chemical gloves may be used when working with solvent. Who is correct?
   a. Technician A
   b. Technician B
   c. Both Technician A and Technician B
   d. Neither Technician A nor Technician B
9. Technician A says that barrier creams are used to make cleaning your hands easier. Technician B says that hearing protection only needs to be worn by people operating loud equipment. Who is correct?
   a. Technician A
   b. Technician B
   c. Both Technician A and Technician B
   d. Neither Technician A nor Technician B
10. Technician A says that tinted safety glasses can be worn when working outside. Technician B says that welding can cause a sunburn. Who is correct?
   a. Technician A
   b. Technician B
   c. Both Technician A and Technician B
   d. Neither Technician A nor Technician B

CHAPTER 4

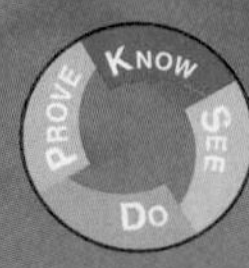

NATEF Tasks

Required Supplemental Tasks

Shop and Personal Safety	Page
■ Utilize safe procedures for handling of tools and equipment.	108–109
Tools and Equipment	
■ Identify tools and their usage in automotive applications.	109–142
■ Identify standard and metric designation.	109
■ Demonstrate safe handling and use of appropriate tools.	108–142
■ Demonstrate proper cleaning, storage, and maintenance of tools and equipment.	109–142
■ Demonstrate proper use of precision measuring tools (i.e., micrometer, dial-indicator, dial-caliper).	110–118

Basic Tools and Lubricants

Knowledge Objectives

After reading this chapter, you will be able to:

1. Discuss basic tool preparation and safety. (pp 108–109)
2. Discuss tools and equipment fundamentals. (p 109)
3. Discuss tool location. (pp 108–109)
4. List and describe precision measuring tools. (pp 110–118)
5. List and describe power tools. (pp 117–119)
6. List and describe air tools. (pp 119–120)
7. List and describe common shop tools. (pp 136–144)
8. List and describe diagnostic equipment. (pp 137–138)
9. List and describe servicing equipment. (pp 138–139)
10. Discuss the use of oxyacetylene torches. (pp 139–140)
11. List and describe cleaning equipment. (pp 140–141)
12. List and describe electrical equipment. (pp 141–145)
13. Identify fluids and lubricants commonly used in the industry. (pp 145–150)
14. Identify metals commonly used in the industry. (pp 151–152)
15. Identify materials commonly used in the industry. (pp 152–154)

Skills Objectives

After reading this chapter, you will be able to:

1. Measure using an outside micrometer. (pp 113–114) SKILL DRILL 4-1
2. Measure using a dial bore gauge. (pp 113–114) SKILL DRILL 4-2
3. Measure using vernier calipers. (p 114–115) SKILL DRILL 4-3
4. Measure using a dial indicator. (pp 115–116) SKILL DRILL 4-4
5. Select and use feeler gauge sets. (pp 116–117) SKILL DRILL 4-5

Introduction

Heavy vehicles are the result of a number of engineering sciences. Not only are they structurally complex, but they also combine a number of unique characteristics that unite together to provide passenger comfort in sometimes harsh environments.

Engine blocks and components are made of metals that are able to withstand very high temperatures and stresses. Lubricants keep the engine and its cooling systems functioning smoothly by reducing friction on moving parts and allowing the engine to perform reliably. The vehicle body is made of materials that are durable and strong enough to withstand harsh conditions and repeated use.

In addition to understanding the basic materials used in heavy-duty vehicle construction and the fluids used to keep them operating safely and efficiently, technicians must know which tools to use for different types of service applications. Tools and equipment are vital components of an efficient and effective shop operation. Nearly all shop tasks involve the use of some sort of tool or piece of equipment.

In this chapter, you will learn about the basic tools found in a shop and how to identify the correct tool for a particular application, how to use the tool correctly, and how to clean, inspect, and store it properly after using it. You will also learn about the fluids, lubricants, materials, and metals that make a vehicle what it is.

Basic Tool Preparation and Safety

Although it is important to be trained on the safe use of tools and equipment, it is even more critical to have a safe attitude. A safe attitude will help you avoid being involved in an accident. Students who think they will never be involved in an accident will not be as aware of unsafe situations as they should be, and such an attitude could lead to accidents. Therefore, as we discuss the various tools and equipment you will encounter in the shop, pay close attention to the safety and operation procedures. Tools are a technician's best friend, but if used improperly, they can injure or kill.

Work Safe and Stay Safe

Always think "safety first" whenever you use tools. There is nothing more important than your personal safety. If you use tools (both hand and power) incorrectly, you could potentially injure yourself and others. Always follow equipment and shop instructions, including the use of recommended personal protective equipment (PPE). Accidents take only a moment to occur, but can take a lifetime to recover from. You are ultimately responsible for your own safety, so remember to work safe and stay safe.

Handling and Using Tools Safely

Tools must be safely handled and used to prevent injury and damage. Always inspect tools prior to use and never

You Are the Technician

After finishing work on the last vehicle of the day, you are required to return your workstation back to order. You clean, inspect, and return tools and equipment to their designated place. You wipe up any spills according to the shop procedure and clear the floor of any debris to avoid slips and falls. During your workspace inspection, you determine that the insulation on the drop light cord is frayed, there are some tools that need to be cleaned, and air-powered tools to be put away.

1. What needs to happen with the drop light?
2. What should you do to air tools before using them each day?
3. What are the steps you take in cleaning electric power tools?

use damaged tools or any replacement tool. Check the manufacturer documentation and the shop procedures, or ask your supervisor if you are uncertain about how to use any tool. Inspect and clean tools when you have finished using them. Always return tools to their correct storage location. Some tools are heavy or awkward to use, so seek assistance if necessary, and use correct manual handling techniques.

Tools and Equipment Fundamentals

Why Proper Tool Usage Is Critical

Every tool is designed to be used in a certain way to do the job safely. It is critical to use a tool in the way it is designed to be used and to do so safely. For example, a screwdriver is designed to tighten and loosen screws, not to be used as a chisel. **Ratchets** are designed to turn **sockets**, and are not to be used as a hammer. Think about the task you are undertaking, select the correct tools for the task, and use each tool for what it was designed.

> **TECHNICIAN TIP**
>
> The correct tools make you much more efficient and effective in performing your job. Without tools, it would be very difficult to carry out vehicle repairs and servicing. This is the reason many technicians invest thousands of dollars in their personal tools. If purchased wisely, tools will help you perform more work in a shorter amount of time, thereby making you more productive. Therefore, think of your tools as an investment that pays for itself over time.

Lockout/Tagout

Lockout/tagout is an umbrella term that describes a set of safety practices and procedures. These practices and procedures are intended to reduce the risk of technicians inadvertently using tools, equipment, or materials that have been determined to be unsafe or potentially unsafe, or that are in the process of being serviced. An example of lockout is physically securing a broken, unsafe, or out-of-service tool so that it cannot be used by a technician FIGURE 4-1A. In many cases, the item is also tagged out so it is not inadvertently placed back into service or operated. An example of tagout is affixing a clear and unavoidable label to a piece of equipment that describes the fault found, the name of the person who found the fault, and the date that the fault was found, and that warns not to use the equipment FIGURE 4-1B.

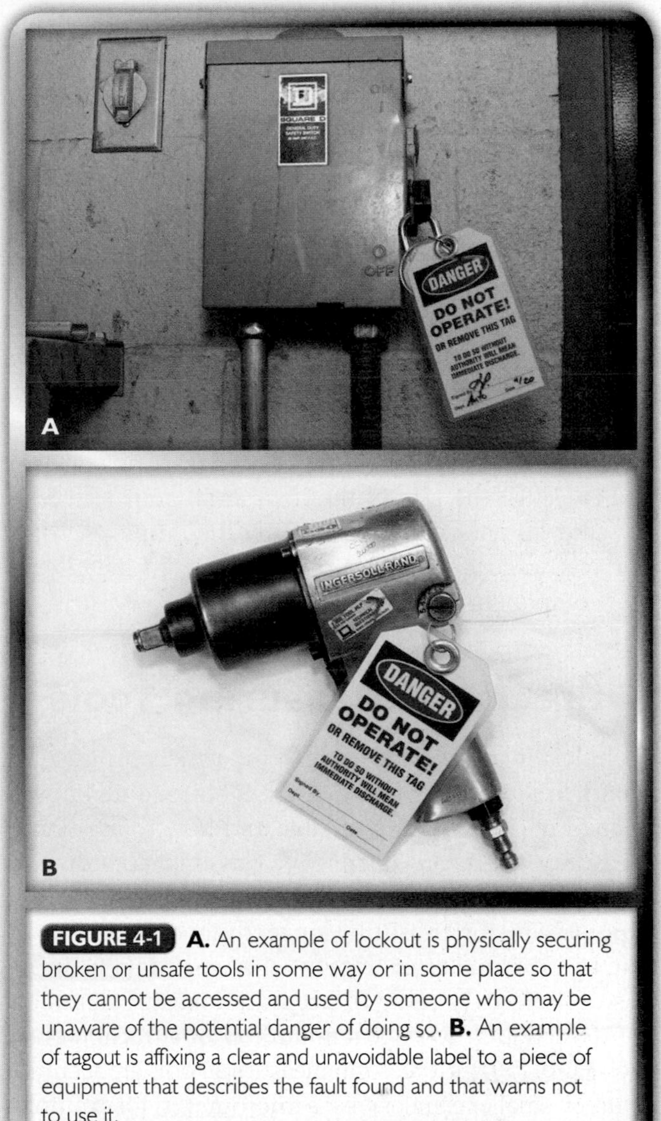

FIGURE 4-1 **A.** An example of lockout is physically securing broken or unsafe tools in some way or in some place so that they cannot be accessed and used by someone who may be unaware of the potential danger of doing so. **B.** An example of tagout is affixing a clear and unavoidable label to a piece of equipment that describes the fault found and that warns not to use it.

> **TECHNICIAN TIP**
>
> Standardized lockout/tagout procedures are a mandatory part of workplace safety regulations in most countries. Familiarize yourself with your local legislation and with the specific lockout/tagout practices that apply in your workplace.

Identifying Metric and Imperial Designation

Many tools, measuring instruments, and fasteners come in metric and imperial sizes. Tools are identified as metric or imperial by markings identifying their sizes, or by the increments on measuring instruments. Fasteners bought new will have their designation identified on the packaging. Other fasteners may have to be measured by a ruler or **vernier caliper** to identify their designation. Manufacturers' charts showing thread and fastener sizing will assist in identifying standard or metric sizing.

To identify metric or imperial designation, follow these steps:

1. Examine the component, tool, or fastener to see whether any marking identifies it as metric or imperial. Manufacturer specifications and shop manuals may be referred to and may identify components as metric or imperial.
2. If no markings are available, use measuring devices to gauge the size of the item and compare thread and fastener charts to identify the sizing. Inch-to-metric conversion charts will assist in identifying component designation.

Precision Measuring Tools

Technicians are required to perform a variety of measurements while carrying out their job. This requires knowledge of what tools are available and how to use them. Measuring tools can generally be classified according to what type of measurements they can make. A **measuring tape** is useful for measuring longer distances and is accurate to a millimeter or fraction of an inch FIGURE 4-2A. A steel rule is capable of accurate measurements on shorter lengths, down to a millimeter or a fraction of an inch FIGURE 4-2B. Precision measuring tools are accurate to much smaller dimensions: a **micrometer**, for example, can accurately measure down to 1/1000 of a millimeter (0.001 mm) in some cases.

> **TECHNICIAN TIP**
>
> The metric and imperial systems are two sets of standards for quantifying weights and measurements. Each system has defined units. For example, the metric system uses millimeters, centimeters, and meters; whereas the imperial system uses inches, feet, and yards. Conversions can be undertaken from one system to the other. For example, 25.4 mm is equal to 1 inch, and 304.8 mm is equal to 1 foot.
>
> Tools that make use of a measuring system, such as wrenches, sockets, drill bits, micrometers, rulers, and many others, come in both metric and imperial measurements. In many countries, metric measurements are the standard. However, conversion tables can be used to convert from one system to the other if needed.

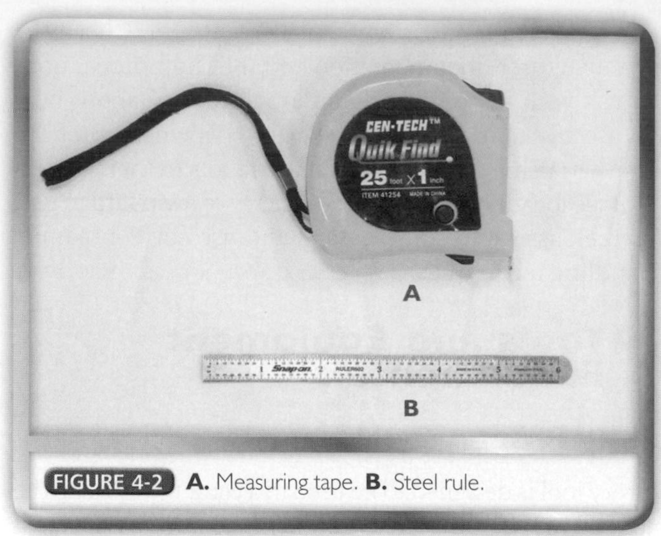

FIGURE 4-2 **A.** Measuring tape. **B.** Steel rule.

Measuring Tape

Measuring tapes are a flexible type of ruler and are a common measuring tool. The most common type found in shops is a thin metal strip about .5" to 1" (13 to 25 mm) wide that is rolled up inside a housing with a spring return mechanism. Measuring tapes can be of various lengths, 16 to 25 feet (5 or 8 meters) and longer being very common. The measuring tape is pulled from the housing to measure items, and a spring return winds it back into the housing. The housing will usually have a built-in locking mechanism to hold the extended measuring tape against the spring return mechanism.

Stainless Steel Rulers

As the name suggests, a stainless **steel ruler** is a ruler that is made from stainless steel. Stainless steel rulers commonly come in 12", 24", and 36" (30 cm, 61 cm, and 1 meter) lengths. They are used like any ruler to measure and mark out items. They are very strong, have precise markings, and resist damage. When using a stainless steel ruler, you can rest it on its edge so the markings are closer to the material being measured, which helps to mark the work precisely. Always protect the steel ruler from damage by storing it carefully; a damaged ruler will not give an accurate measurement. Never take measurements from the very end of a damaged steel ruler, as damaged ends may affect the accuracy of your measurements.

> **TECHNICIAN TIP**
>
> If the end of a ruler is damaged, you may be able to measure from the 25-mm mark and subtract 25 mm from the measurement.

Outside, Inside, and Depth Micrometers

Micrometers are precise measuring tools designed to measure small distances, and are available in both millimeter (mm) and inch (") calibrations. Typically, they can measure down to a resolution of 1/1000 of an inch (0.001") for a standard micrometer or 1/100 of a millimeter (0.01 mm) for a metric micrometer. Vernier micrometers equipped with the addition of a vernier scale can measure down to 1/10,000 of an inch (0.0001") or 1/1000 of a millimeter (0.001 mm).

The most common types of micrometers are the outside, inside, and depth micrometers. As the name suggests, an **outside micrometer** FIGURE 4-3A measures the outside dimensions of an item. For example, it could measure the diameter of a valve stem. The **inside micrometer** measures inside dimensions. For example, the inside micrometer could measure an engine cylinder bore FIGURE 4-3B. **Depth micrometers** measure the depth of an item, such as how far a piston is below the surface of the block FIGURE 4-3C.

The most common micrometer is an outside micrometer. The horseshoe-shaped part is the frame. It is built to make sure the micrometer holds its shape. Some frames have plastic finger pads so that body heat is not transferred to the metal frame as easily because heat can cause the metal to expand slightly and affect the reading. On one end of the frame is the anvil, which contacts one side of the part being measured. The other contact point is the spindle. The micrometer measures the distance between the anvil and spindle, so that is where the part being measured fits.

The measurement is read on the sleeve/barrel and thimble. The sleeve/barrel is stationary and has linear markings on it. The thimble fits over the sleeve and has graduated

TECHNICIAN TIP

Micrometers are precision measuring instruments and must be handled and stored with care. They should always be stored with a gap between the spindle and anvil so metal expansion does not interfere with their calibration.

TECHNICIAN TIP

All micrometers need to be checked for calibration (also called "zeroing") before each use. A 0-1" or 0—25 mm outside micrometer can be lightly closed all of the way. If the anvil and spindle are clean, the micrometer should read 0.000, indicating the micrometer is calibrated correctly. If the micrometer is bigger than 1" or 25 mm, then a "standard" is used to verify the calibration. A standard is a hardened machined rod of a precise length, such as 2" or 50 mm. When inserted in the same-sized micrometer, the reading should be exactly the same as listed on the standard. If a micrometer is not properly calibrated, it should not be used until it is recalibrated. See the tool's instruction manual for the calibration procedure.

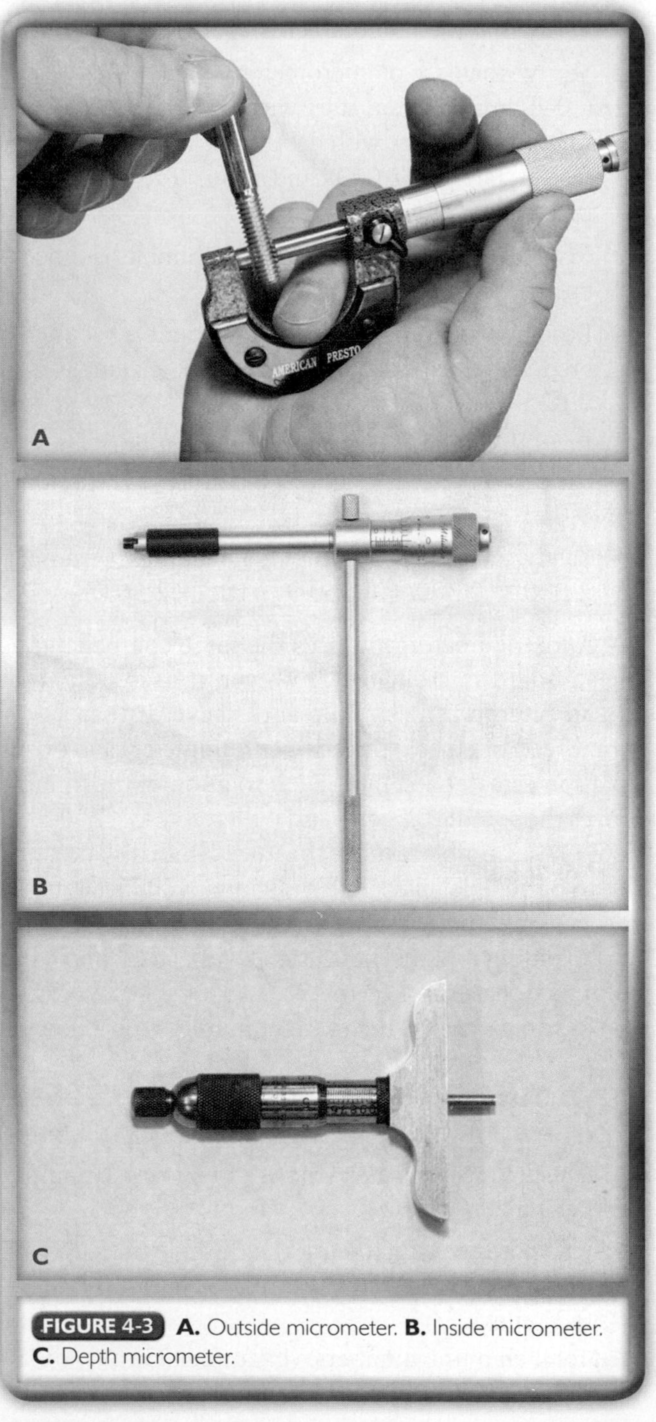

FIGURE 4-3 **A.** Outside micrometer. **B.** Inside micrometer. **C.** Depth micrometer.

markings on it. The thimble is connected directly to the spindle, and both turn as a unit. Because the spindle and sleeve/barrel have matching threads, the thimble rotates the spindle inside of the sleeve/barrel, and the thread moves the spindle inwards and outwards. The thimble usually incorporates either a ratchet or a clutch mechanism, which prevents overtightening of the micrometer thimble when taking a reading. A lock nut, lock ring, or lock screw is used on most micrometers and locks the thimble in place while you read the micrometer.

To read a standard micrometer, perform the following steps:

1. Verify that the micrometer is properly calibrated.
2. Verify what size of micrometer you are using. If it is a 0–1" micrometer, start with 0.000. If it is a 1–2" micrometer, start with 1.000". A 2–3" micrometer would start with 2.000", and so on. (To give an example, let's say it is 2.000".)
3. Read how many 0.100" marks the thimble has uncovered. (Example: 0.300")
4. Read how many 0.025" marks the thimble has uncovered past the 0.100" mark in step 3. (Example: 2 × 0.025 = 0.050")
5. Read the number on the thimble that lines up with the zero line on the sleeve. (Example: 13 × 0.001 = 0.013")
6. Lastly, total all of the individual readings. (Example: 2.000 + 0.300 + 0.050 + 0.013 = 2.363")

A metric micrometer uses the same components as the standard micrometer. However, it uses a different thread pitch on the spindle and sleeve. It uses a 0.5-mm thread pitch (2.0 threads per millimeter) and opens up approximately 25 mm. Each rotation of the thimble moves the spindle 0.5 mm, and it therefore takes 50 rotations of the thimble to move the full 25-mm distance. The sleeve/barrel is labelled with individual millimeter marks and half-millimeter marks, from the starting millimeter to the ending millimeter, 25 mm away. The thimble has graduated marks from 0 to 49.

Reading a metric micrometer involves the following steps:

1. Read the number of full millimeters the thimble has passed. (To give an example, let's say it is 23 mm.)
2. Check to see if it passed the 0.5-mm mark. (Example: 0.50 mm)
3. Check to see which mark the thimble lines up with or has just passed. (Example: 37 × 0.01 mm = 0.37 mm)
4. Total all of the numbers. (Example: 23 mm + 0.50 mm + 0.37 mm = 23.87 mm)

If the micrometer is equipped with a vernier gauge, meaning it can read down to 1/1000 of a millimeter (0.001 mm), you need to complete one more step. Identify which of the vernier lines is closest to one of the lines on the thimble. Sometimes it is hard to determine which is the closest, so decide which three are the closest and then use the center line. At the frame side of the sleeve will be a number that corresponds to the vernier line. It will be numbered 1 to 0. Take the vernier number and add it to the end of your reading. For example: 23.77 + 0.007 = 23.777 mm.

For inside measurements, the inside micrometer works on the same principles as the outside micrometer, and so does the depth micrometer. The only difference is that the scale on the sleeve of the depth micrometer is backward, so be careful when reading it.

Using a Micrometer

To maintain accuracy of measurements, it is important that both the micrometer and the items to be measured are clean and free of any dirt or debris. Also make sure the micrometer is zeroed before taking any measurements. Never overtighten a micrometer or store it with its measuring surfaces touching, as this may damage the tool and affect its accuracy. When measuring, make sure the item can pass through the micrometer surfaces snugly and squarely. This is best accomplished by using the ratchet to tighten the micrometer. Always take the measurement a number of times and compare results to ensure you have measured accurately.

To correctly measure using an outside micrometer, follow the guidelines in **SKILL DRILL 4-1**.

Telescoping Gauge

For measuring distances in awkward spots, such as the bottom of a deep cylinder, the **telescoping gauge** has spring-loaded plungers that can be unlocked with a screw on the handle so they slide out and touch the walls of the cylinder **FIGURE 4-4**. The screw then locks them in that position, the gauge can be withdrawn, and the distance across the plungers can be measured with an outside micrometer or calipers to convey the diameter of the cylinder at that point. Telescoping gauges come in a variety of sizes to fit various sizes of holes and bores.

Split Ball Gauge

A **split ball gauge (small hole gauge)** is good for measuring small holes where telescoping gauges cannot fit. They use a similar principle to the telescoping gauge, but the measuring head uses a split ball mechanism that allows it to fit into very small holes. Split ball gauges are ideal for measuring valve guides on a cylinder head for wear.

SKILL DRILL 4-1 Measuring Using an Outside Micrometer

1. Select the correct size of micrometer. Verify that the anvil and spindle are clean and that it is calibrated properly.
2. Clean the surface of the part you are measuring.
3. In your right hand, hold the frame of the micrometer between your little finger, ring finger, and palm of your hand, with the thimble between your thumb and forefinger.
4. With your left hand, hold the part you are measuring and place the micrometer over it.
5. Using your thumb and forefinger, lightly tighten the ratchet. It is important that the correct amount of force is applied to the spindle when taking a measurement. The spindle and anvil should just touch the component, with a slight amount of drag when the micrometer is removed from the measured piece. Be careful that the part is square in the micrometer so the reading is correct. Try rocking the micrometer in all directions to make sure it is square.
6. Once the micrometer is properly snug, tighten the lock mechanism so the spindle will not turn.
7. Read the micrometer and record your reading.
8. When all readings are finished, clean the micrometer, position the spindle so it is backed off from the anvil and return it to its protective case.

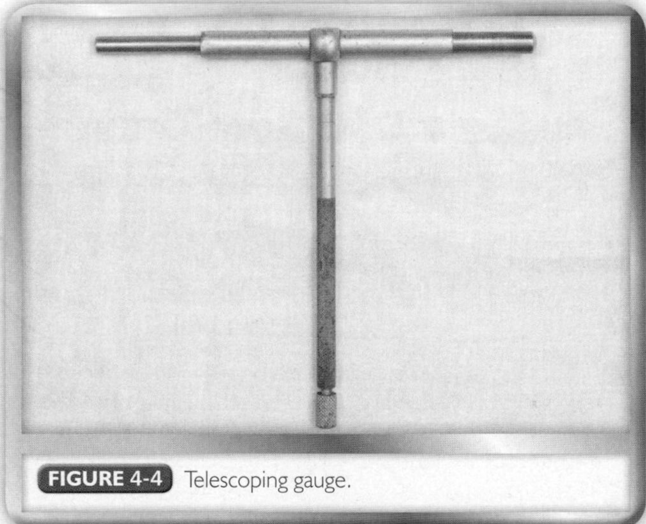

FIGURE 4-4 Telescoping gauge.

A split ball gauge can be fitted in the bore and expanded until there is a slight drag. Then it can be retracted and measured with an outside micrometer. Like some of the other measuring instruments discussed, the split ball gauge may have a dial or digital measurement scale fitted for direct reading purposes.

Dial Bore Gauge

A **dial bore gauge** is used to measure the inside diameter of bores with a high degree of accuracy and speed FIGURE 4-5. The dial bore gauge can measure a bore directly by using telescoping pistons on a T-handle with a dial mounted on the handle. The dial bore gauge combines a telescoping gauge and dial indicator in one instrument. A dial bore gauge determines whether the diameter is worn, tapered, or out-of-round according to the manufacturer's specifications. The resolution of a dial bore gauge is typically accurate to 5-10,000 of an inch (0.0005") or 1/100 of a millimeter (0.01 mm).

Using a Dial Bore Gauge

To use a dial bore gauge, select an appropriately sized adapter to fit the internal diameter of the bore, and install it to the measuring head. Many dial bore gauges also have a fixture to calibrate the tool to the size you desire. The fixture is set to the size desired, and the dial bore gauge is placed in it. The dial bore gauge is then adjusted to the proper reading. Once it is calibrated, the dial bore gauge can be inserted inside the bore to be measured. Hold the

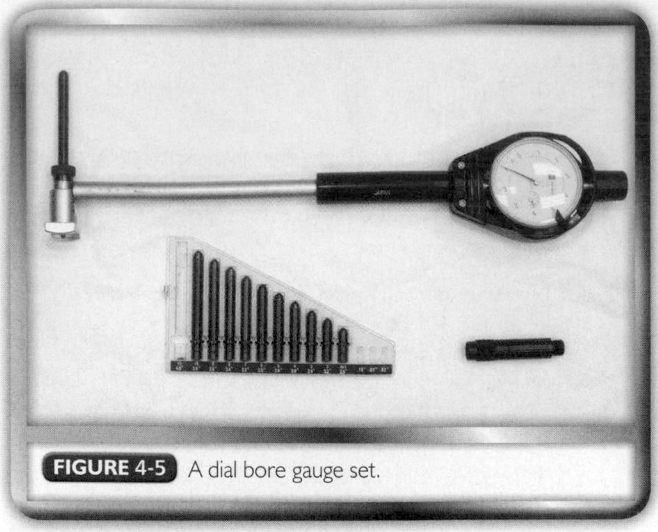

FIGURE 4-5 A dial bore gauge set.

gauge in line with the bore and slightly rock it to ensure it is centered. Read the dial when it is fully centered and square to the bore to determine the correct measurement.

Store a bore gauge carefully in its storage box and ensure the locking mechanism is released while in storage. Bore gauges are available in different ranges of size. It is important to select a gauge with the correct range for the bore you are measuring. When measuring, make sure the gauge is at a 90-degree angle to the bore and read the dial. Always take the measurement a number of times and compare results to ensure you have measured accurately.

To correctly measure using a dial bore gauge, follow the guidelines in **SKILL DRILL 4-2**.

Vernier Calipers

Vernier calipers are a precision instrument used for measuring outside dimensions, inside dimensions, and depth measurements, all in one tool. They have a graduated bar with markings like a ruler. On the bar, a sliding sleeve with jaws is mounted for taking inside or outside measurements. Measurements on older versions of vernier calipers are taken by reading the graduated bar scales, while fractional measurements are read by comparing the scales between the sliding sleeve and the graduated bar. Technicians will often use vernier calipers to measure length and diameters of bolts and pins or the depth of blind holes in housings.

Newer versions of vernier calipers have dial and digital scales. The dial vernier has the main scale on the graduated bar, while fractional measurements are taken from a dial with a rotating needle. These tend to be easier to read than the older versions. More recently, digital scales on vernier calipers have become commonplace. The principle of their use is the same as any vernier caliper; however, they have a digital scale that reads the measurement directly.

Using Vernier Calipers

Always store vernier calipers in a storage box to protect them and ensure the measuring surfaces are kept clean for accurate measurement. If making an internal or external measurement, make sure the caliper is at right angles to the surfaces to be measured. You should always repeat

SKILL DRILL 4-2 Measuring Using a Dial Bore Gauge

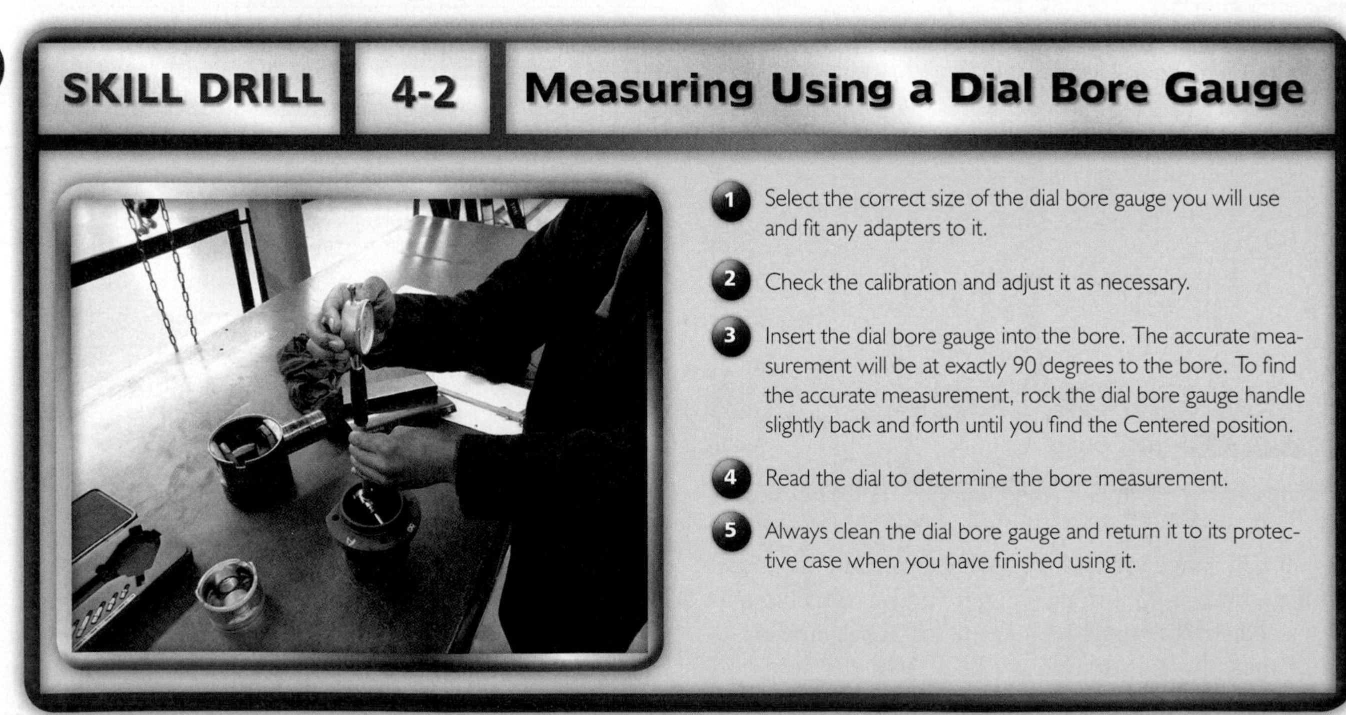

1. Select the correct size of the dial bore gauge you will use and fit any adapters to it.
2. Check the calibration and adjust it as necessary.
3. Insert the dial bore gauge into the bore. The accurate measurement will be at exactly 90 degrees to the bore. To find the accurate measurement, rock the dial bore gauge handle slightly back and forth until you find the Centered position.
4. Read the dial to determine the bore measurement.
5. Always clean the dial bore gauge and return it to its protective case when you have finished using it.

the measurement a number of times and compare results to ensure you have measured accurately.

To correctly measure using vernier calipers, follow the guidelines in SKILL DRILL 4-3.

Dial Indicators

Dial indicators can also be known as dial gauges, and, as the name suggests, they have a dial and needle where measurements are read. They have a measuring plunger with a pointed contact end that is spring-loaded and connected via the housing to the dial needle. The dial accurately measures movement of the plunger in and out as it rests against an object. For example, they can be used to measure the trueness of a rotating disc brake rotor.

A dial indicator can also measure how round something is. A **crankshaft** can be rotated in a set of **V blocks**. If the crankshaft is bent, it will show as movement on the dial indicator as the crankshaft is rotated. The dial indicator senses slight movement at its tip and magnifies it into a measurable swing on the dial.

Dial indicators typically measure ranges from 0.010" to 12" or 0.25 mm to 300 mm and have graduation marks of 0.0005" to 0.01" or 0.001 mm to 0.01 mm. The large needle is able to move numerous times around the outer scale. One full turn may represent 1 mm or 0.1″. The small inner scale indicates how many times the outer needle has moved around its scale. In this way, the dial indicator is able to read movement of up to 1" or 2 cm.

Dial indicators can measure with an accuracy of 0.001" or 0.01 mm. The type of dial indicator you use will be determined by the amount of movement you expect from the component you are measuring. The indicator must be set up so that there is no gap between the dial indicator and the component to be measured. Most dial indicator sets contain various attachments and support arms so they can be configured specifically for the measuring task.

Using a Dial Indicator

Dial indicators are used in many types of service jobs. They are particularly useful in determining run-out on rotating shafts and surfaces. Run-out is the side-to-side variation of movement when a component is turned.

When attaching a dial indicator, keep support arms as short as possible. Make sure all attachments are tightened to prevent unnecessary movement between the indicator and the component. Make sure the dial indicator pointer is positioned at 90 degrees to the face of the component to be measured. Always read the dial face straight on, as a view from the side can give a considerable parallax error. The outer face of the dial indicator is designed so it can be rotated so that the zero mark can be positioned directly over the pointer. This is how a dial indicator is zeroed.

To correctly measure using a dial indicator, follow the guidelines in SKILL DRILL 4-4.

SKILL DRILL 4-3 Measuring Using Vernier Calipers

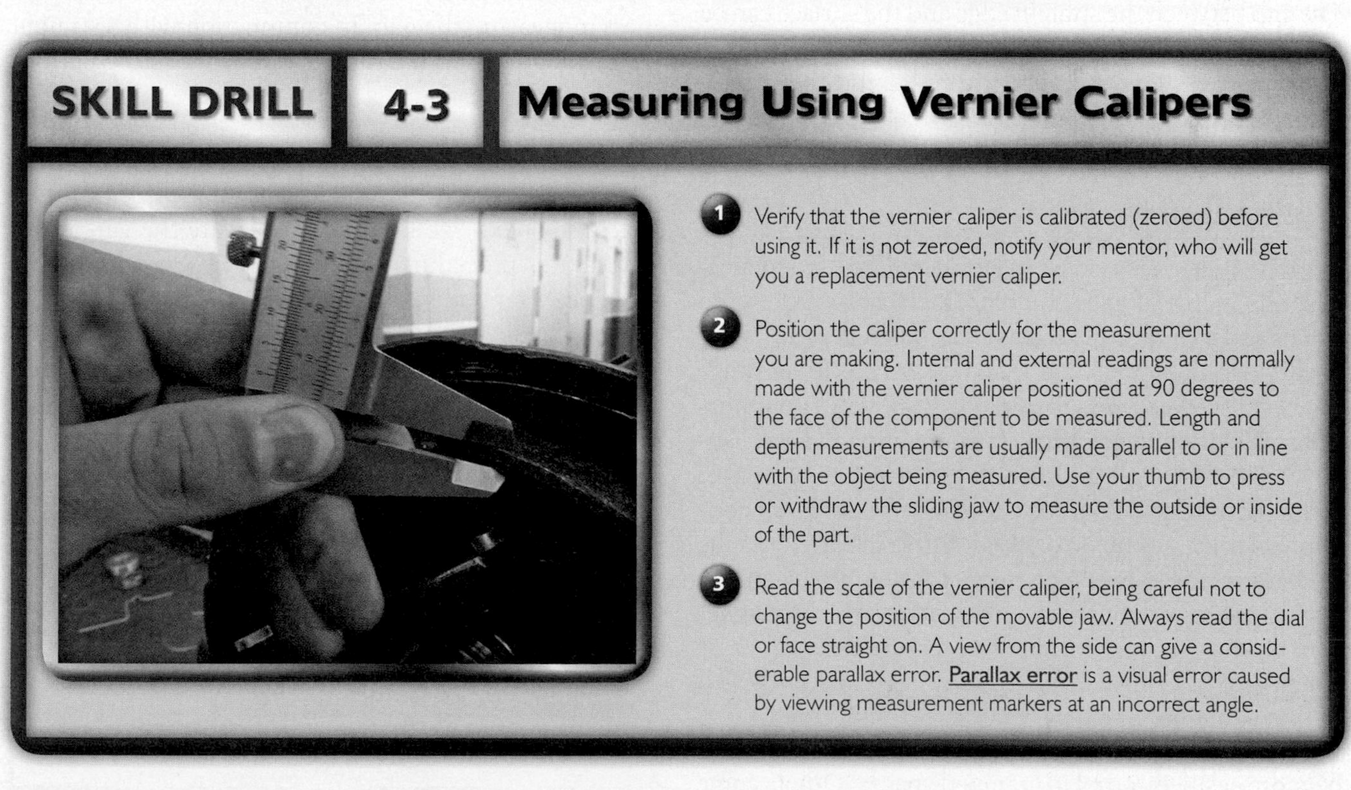

1. Verify that the vernier caliper is calibrated (zeroed) before using it. If it is not zeroed, notify your mentor, who will get you a replacement vernier caliper.
2. Position the caliper correctly for the measurement you are making. Internal and external readings are normally made with the vernier caliper positioned at 90 degrees to the face of the component to be measured. Length and depth measurements are usually made parallel to or in line with the object being measured. Use your thumb to press or withdraw the sliding jaw to measure the outside or inside of the part.
3. Read the scale of the vernier caliper, being careful not to change the position of the movable jaw. Always read the dial or face straight on. A view from the side can give a considerable parallax error. **Parallax error** is a visual error caused by viewing measurement markers at an incorrect angle.

SKILL DRILL 4-4 Measuring Using a Dial Indicator

1. Select the gauge type, size, attachment, and bracket that fit the part you are measuring. Mount the dial indicator firmly to keep it stationary.
2. Adjust the indicator so that the plunger is at 90 degrees to the part you are measuring and lock it in place.
3. Rotate the part one complete turn and locate the low spot. Zero the indicator.
4. Find the point of maximum height and note the reading. This will indicate the run-out value.
5. Continue the rotation and make sure the needle does not go below zero. If it does, reverse the indicator and remeasure the point of maximum variation.
6. Check your readings against the manufacturer's specifications. If the deviation is greater than the specifications allow, consult your supervisor.

Straight Edge

Straight edges are usually made from hardened steel and are machined so that the edge is perfectly straight. A straight edge is used to check the flatness of a surface. It is placed on its edge against the surface to be checked. The gap between the straight edge and the surface can be measured by using feeler gauges. Sometimes the gap can be seen easily if light is shone from behind the surface being checked. Straight edges are often used to measure the amount of warpage the surface of a cylinder head has.

Feeler Gauges

Feeler gauges (also called *feeler blades*) are used to measure the width of gaps, such as the clearance between valves and rocker arms. Feeler gauges are flat metal strips of varying thicknesses. The thickness of each feeler gauge is clearly marked on each one. They are sized from fractions of a millimeter or fractions of an inch. They usually come in sets with different sizes and are available in metric and imperial measurements. Some sets contain feeler gauges made of brass. These are used to take measurements between components that are magnetic. If steel gauges were used, the drag caused by the magnetism would mimic the drag of a proper clearance. Brass gauges are not subject to magnetism, so they work well in that situation.

Some feeler gauges come in a bent arrangement to be more easily inserted in cramped spaces. Others come in a stepped version. Two or more feeler gauges can be stacked together to make up a desired thickness. Alternatively, if you want to measure an unknown gap, you can interchange feeler gauges until you find the one or more that fit snugly into the gap, and total their thickness to measure the gap. In conjunction with a straight edge, they can be used to measure surface irregularities in a cylinder head.

Using Feeler Gauges

If the feeler gauge feels too loose when measuring a gap, select the next size larger and measure the gap again. Repeat this procedure until the feeler gauge has a slight drag between both parts. If the feeler gauge is too tight, select a smaller size until the feeler gauge fits properly. When measuring a spark plug gap, feeler gauges should not be used because the surfaces are not perfectly parallel, so it is preferable to use wire feeler gauges. Wire feeler gauges use accurately machined pieces of wire instead of metal strips.

To select and use feeler gauge sets, follow the guidelines in SKILL DRILL 4-5.

> **TECHNICIAN TIP**
>
> Never use feeler gauges on operating machinery.

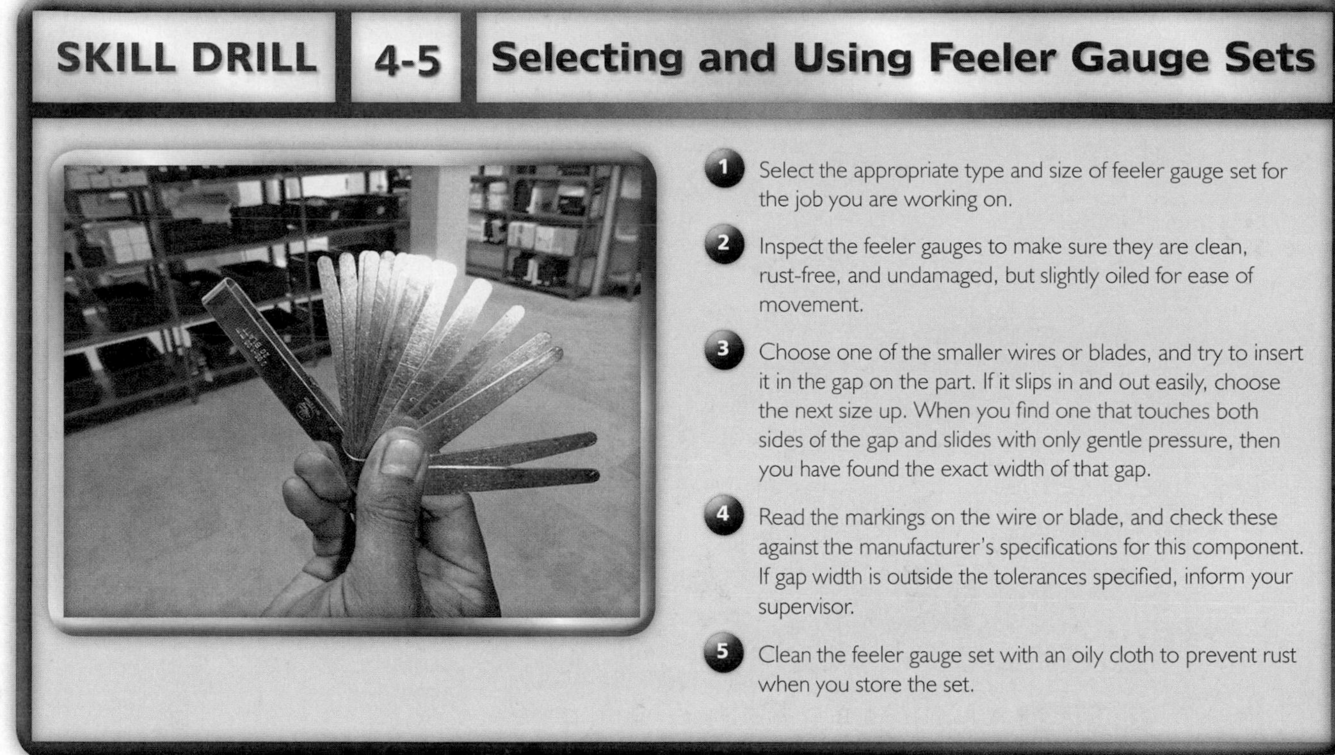

SKILL DRILL 4-5 Selecting and Using Feeler Gauge Sets

1. Select the appropriate type and size of feeler gauge set for the job you are working on.
2. Inspect the feeler gauges to make sure they are clean, rust-free, and undamaged, but slightly oiled for ease of movement.
3. Choose one of the smaller wires or blades, and try to insert it in the gap on the part. If it slips in and out easily, choose the next size up. When you find one that touches both sides of the gap and slides with only gentle pressure, then you have found the exact width of that gap.
4. Read the markings on the wire or blade, and check these against the manufacturer's specifications for this component. If gap width is outside the tolerances specified, inform your supervisor.
5. Clean the feeler gauge set with an oily cloth to prevent rust when you store the set.

Safety

Feeler gauges are strips of hardened metal that have been ground or rolled to a precise thickness. They can be very thin and will cut through skin if not handled correctly.

Power Tools

Power tools are typically powered by an electric motor or compressed air. They may also be powered by burning of propellant, as in the case of a nail gun, or by a petroleum engine, as in the case of a portable compressor. A power tool may be stationary, such as a bench grinder, or portable, such as a portable electric drill. There are many different power tools designed to perform specific tasks. Some are corded and have to be plugged in, and others are cordless and have batteries. Power tools make many tasks quicker and easier to perform, and they can save many hours of work when used and maintained correctly.

Drills and Drill Bits

A portable drill may be corded or cordless FIGURE 4-6A. A corded drill has a lead that has to be plugged into an electrical supply. The operating voltage of a drill depends on the country's supply. Corded drills are a good choice when moderate power is needed or when extended drilling is required. Cordless drills use their own internal batteries FIGURE 4-6B. Use a cordless drill when you cannot bring the work to the drill; instead take the drill to the work. However, do not expect a cordless drill to be able to drill large holes through hard metal. Although they are very versatile, the amount of work they can do is limited by their power rating. The biggest drill bit that will fit into the chuck of these drills is usually marked on the body of the drill or chuck, along with the speeds at which it will turn. Some portable drills have two operating speeds, but most have a variable speed rating that is determined by how much pressure is placed on the trigger and which may be set to any speed within the drill's range.

Drill bits come in many closely spaced sizes and types FIGURE 4-6C. The most common is the **twist drill**. It has a point with cutting flutes that form a common angle of 118 degrees. Its body, which usually has two spiral grooves, and its shank, are gripped in the jaws of the **drill chuck**. A drill chuck is a device for gripping drill bits securely in a drill. The twist drill is a good all-purpose bit for drilling metals.

A **drill press** allows for accurate drilling and has more control than is offered by a portable drill—which, although convenient, can be difficult to guide accurately FIGURE 4-6D. A mounted drill can feed the drill bit at a controlled rate, and the worktable on the drill typically has a vice to secure the job at a constant angle to the drill bit. This type of drill can also be set to run at different

FIGURE 4-6 **A.** Portable drill. **B.** Cordless drill. **C.** Drill bits. **D.** Drill press.

drilling speeds. Most drill presses have a drill chuck that takes bits up to 0.5" (13 mm) or more in diameter.

Morse taper is a system for securing drill bits to drills. The Morse taper size changes according to drill size. The shank of the drill bit is tapered and looks like the tang of a file. It fits snugly into the drill spindle, which has a similar taper on its inside. The tang on the drill bit is located in the spindle, and it drives the drill. It is a quick way to change drills without constantly adjusting the chuck.

When there is a hole already drilled in sheet metal that needs enlarging, a multi-fluted tapered-hole drill will do the job in practically the same time it takes to say the name of this tool. A drilling speed chart is usually supplied with the drill press and should be kept nearby for handy reference. It compares drill sizes and metals to show the proper speed. For example, to drill a 0.5" (10-mm) hole through a piece of aluminum, the drill speed should be 1800 rpm. Note also that drilling metals is best performed with the aid of a lubricant. The lubricant helps cool the cutting edges of the drill bit as well as lubricate it. Each metal requires its own type of lubricant, so check a drilling guide to identify the correct lubricant for the metal you are working on.

> **TECHNICIAN TIP**
>
> Drills are also used to drive other accessories, such as rotary files, screwdriver bits, and sockets.

Bench and Angle Grinders

Power grinders are available in a range of sizes and speeds. The size of a power grinder is usually determined by the diameter of the largest grinding wheel or disc that can be fitted to it. Some grinders are fixed to a bench or pedestal and the work is brought to the grinder; others are portable devices that may be taken to the work. Bench or pedestal grinders are generally powered by electricity, whereas portable grinders may be electric or air powered.

Grinding wheels and discs usually have a maximum safe operating speed printed on them. This maximum speed must never be exceeded, or the wheel or disc could disintegrate. Every well-equipped shop has a solidly mounted grinder, either on a pedestal bolted to the shop floor or securely attached to the workbench. Appropriate eye protection must be worn when grinders are being used, and the wheel guards, tool rests, and shields must be correctly and firmly in place.

A **bench grinder (pedestal grinder)** usually has a rating specifying the size of the grinding wheel it can take FIGURE 4-7A. Do not attempt to install a grinding wheel larger or smaller than the grinder's rating. Grinding wheels come in grades from coarse to very fine, depending on the size of the abrasive grains that are bonded together to make the wheel. They also range in hardness, depending on the abrasive used and the material used to bond the particles together. When a particular grinding application is required, a check should be done to verify the most suitable grinding wheel for the application.

An **angle grinder** is usually needed when the bench grinder is not appropriate FIGURE 4-7B. The angle grinder uses discs rather than wheels. During grinding, the face of the disc is used instead of the edge. An angle grinder can emit sparks to a distance of a few meters, so direct the sparks in a safe direction or set up a guard to catch them. Use hearing protection whenever grinding, as it is very noisy and can damage your ears.

FIGURE 4-7 **A.** Bench grinder. **B.** Angle grinder.

Although not as common in an automotive shop, the **straight grinder** accepts conventional grinding wheels, just as stationary grinders do. However, the grinding wheel diameter is limited to about 126 mm. In many cases, the grinder has a long shaft that moves the grinding wheel away from the motor. This makes it useful for getting into recessed areas.

Hand-held cut-off wheels are powered either by electricity or air. They use a special thin grinding disk to enable them to cut. They use the edge of the wheel for cutting and are useful for jobs that cannot be reached with a hacksaw.

Air Tools

Air tools operate by using compressed air at high pressure. Air compressors in automotive shops typically run at greater than 90 psi (621 kPa), so exercise caution around them. Compressed air is transported through pipes and hoses. Air tools have quick-connect fittings so that various air tools can easily be used on the same air hose. There are several styles of quick-connect fittings; a shop usually uses one style throughout the entire shop.

An **air ratchet** uses the force of compressed air to turn a ratchet drive FIGURE 4-8A. It is used on smaller nuts and bolts. Once the nut is loosened, the air ratchet spins it off in a fraction of the time it would take by hand. The air ratchet also works well when there is not much room to swing a ratchet handle.

An **air nozzle** is probably the simplest air tool FIGURE 4-8B. It simply controls the flow of compressed air. It is controlled by a lever or valve and is used to blast debris and dirt out of confined spaces. Blasting debris and dirt can be dangerous, so eye protection must be worn whenever this tool is used. Noise levels are usually high, so ear protection should also be worn. It is dangerous to use an air nozzle to clean yourself off. Its blast should always be directed away from the user and anyone else working nearby.

An **air hammer**, sometimes called an *air chisel*, is useful for driving and cutting FIGURE 4-8C. The extra force that is generated by the compressed air makes it more efficient than a hand chisel and hammer. Just as there are many chisels, there are many bits that fit into the air hammer. Their selection depends on the job at hand.

An **air drill** has some important advantages over the more common electric power drill FIGURE 4-8D. With the right attachment, an air drill can drill holes, grind, polish, and clean parts. Unlike the electric drill, it does not carry the risk of producing sparks, which is an important

FIGURE 4-8 **A.** Air ratchet. **B.** Air nozzle. **C.** Air hammer. **D.** Air drill. **E.** Air-impact wrench.

consideration around flammable liquids or petroleum tanks. An air drill does not trail a live electric lead behind it that could be cut and possibly cause shock and burns. Neither does it become hot with heavy use.

The most common air tool in an automotive shop is the **air-impact wrench** FIGURE 4-8E. It is also called an *impact gun* or **rattle gun**, and it is easy to understand why when you hear one. Taking the wheels off a vehicle to replace the tires is a typical application for this air tool. Removing lug nuts often requires a lot of torque to twist the nuts free, and air-impact wrenches work well for that.

The air-impact wrench may be set to spin in either direction, and a valve controls roughly how much torque it applies. It should never be used for final tightening of wheel nuts. There is a danger in overtightening the wheel nuts, as this could cause the bolts to fail and the wheel to separate from the vehicle while it is moving. Another rule to remember about the air-impact wrench is that you have to use special hardened impact sockets, extensions, and joints. The sockets are special heavy-duty, six-point types, and the flats can withstand the hammering force that the impact wrench subjects them to.

Grease Gun

Air can also be used to power a grease gun, which is used to lubricate components with grease fittings. The air power forces the grease through the aperture.

Creeper

To work underneath a vehicle, technicians use creepers, which are platforms on rollers that allow the technician to roll under the vehicle while on his or her back.

Hand Tools

A large percentage of your personal tools will be hand tools. These are available in a variety of shapes, sizes, and functions and, like all tools, they extend your ability to do work. Over the years, manufacturers have introduced new fasteners, wire harness terminals, quick-connect fittings for fuel and other lines, and additional technologies that require their own specific types of hand tools. This means that technicians need to add tools to their toolboxes all of the time.

TECHNICIAN TIP

Invest in quality tools. Because tools extend your abilities, poor-quality tools will affect the quality and quantity of your work. Price is not always the best indicator of quality, but it plays a role. As you learn the purpose and function of the tools in this section, you should be able to identify high-quality tools versus poor-quality tools by looking at them, handling them, and putting them to work.

Wrenches

Wrenches (often referred to as spanners in some countries) are used to tighten and loosen nuts and bolts, which are two types of fasteners. There are three commonly used wrenches: the **closed-end wrench**, the **open-end wrench**, and the **combination wrench.** The *closed-end wrench* fits fully around the head of the bolt or nut and grips each of the six points at the corners, just as a socket does. This is precisely the kind of grip needed if a nut or bolt is very tight, and it gives you a better chance of loosening very tight fasteners. Its grip also makes the closed-end wrench less likely than the open-end wrench to round off the points on the head of the bolt FIGURE 4-9A. The ends of closed-wrenches are bent or offset so they are easier to grip, and have different-sized heads at each end. One disadvantage of the closed-end wrench is that it can be awkward to use once the nut or bolt has been loosened a little because you have to lift it off the head of the fastener and move it to each new position.

The *open-end wrench* is open on the end, and the two parallel flats grip only two points of the fastener FIGURE 4-9B. Open-end wrenches usually have either different-sized heads on each end of the wrench, or heads the same size but with different angles. The head is at an angle to the handle, and is not bent or offset, so it can be flipped over and used on both sides. This is a good wrench to use in very tight spaces as you can flip it over at the end of its travel and get a new angle, so the head can catch new points on the fastener. Although an open-end wrench often gives the best access to a fastener, it should not be used if the fastener is extremely tight, as this type of wrench grips only two points. If the jaws flex slightly or the flats do not fit tightly around them, the wrench could suddenly slip when force is applied. This slippage can round off the points of the fastener. The best way to tackle a tight fastener is to use a closed-end wrench to break the bolt or nut free; then use the open-end wrench to finish the job. The open-end wrench should be used only on fasteners that are no more than firmly tightened.

The *combination wrench* has an open-end head on one end and a closed-end head on the other FIGURE 4-9C. Both ends are usually the same size, so the closed end may be used to break the bolt loose and the open end to turn the bolt. Because of its versatility, this is probably the most popular wrench for technicians.

A variation on the open-end wrench is the **flare-nut wrench**, also called a flare-tubing wrench FIGURE 4-9D. This type of wrench gives a better grip than the open-end wrench because it grabs all six points of the fastener, instead of two. However, because it is open on the end, it is not as strong as a closed-end wrench. The partially open sixth side allows the wrench to be placed over tubing or pipes so it can be used to turn the tube fittings. Do not use the flare-nut wrench on extremely tight fasteners as the jaws may spread, damaging the nut.

Another open-end wrench is the *open-end adjustable wrench,* or *crescent wrench*. This wrench has a movable jaw that, by turning an adjusting screw, can be adjusted to fit any fastener within its range. It should be used only if other wrenches are not available because it is not as strong as a fixed wrench, and could slip off of and damage the heads of tight bolts or nuts. Still, it is a handy tool to have because it can be adjusted to fit most fastener sizes.

A *ratcheting closed-end wrench* is a useful tool for some applications because it can be repositioned without having to be removed FIGURE 4-9E. It has an inner piece that fits over and grabs the fastener points and is able to rotate within the outer housing. A ratcheting mechanism allows it to rotate in one direction and lock in the other direction. In some cases, the wrench needs simply to be flipped over to be used in the opposite direction. In other cases, it has a lever that changes the direction from clockwise to counterclockwise. Be careful to not overstress this tool by using it to tighten or loosen very tight fasteners, as the outer housing is not very strong.

There is also a *ratcheting open-end wrench,* but it uses no moving parts. One of the sides is partially removed so that only the bottom one-third remains to catch a point on the bolt. The normal side works just like a standard open-end wrench. The shorter side of the

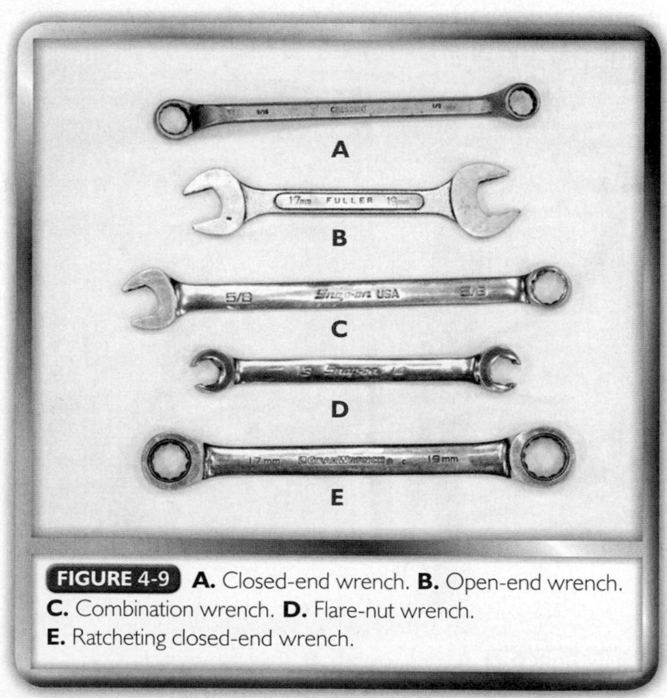

FIGURE 4-9 **A.** Closed-end wrench. **B.** Open-end wrench. **C.** Combination wrench. **D.** Flare-nut wrench. **E.** Ratcheting closed-end wrench.

open-end wrench catches the point on the fastener so it can be turned. When moving the wrench to get a new bite, the wrench is pulled slightly outwards, disengaging the short side while leaving the long side to slide along the faces of the bolt. The wrench is then rotated to the new position and pushed back in so the short side engages the next point. This wrench, like other open-end wrenches, is not designed to tighten or loosen tight fasteners, but it does work well in blind places where a socket or ratcheting closed-end wrench cannot be used.

> **TECHNICIAN TIP**
>
> Wrenchs do a job properly only if they are the right size for the given nut or bolt head. The size used to describe a wrench is the distance across the flats of the nut or bolt. There are two systems in common use—metric (in millimeters) and imperial (in inches). Each system provides a range of sizes, which are identified either by a number, which indicates millimeters for the metric system, or by a fraction, which indicates fractions of an inch for the imperial system.

The *pipe wrench* grips pipes and can exert a lot of force to turn them FIGURE 4-10A. Because the handle pivots slightly, the more pressure put on the handle to turn the wrench, the more the grip tightens. The jaws are hardened and serrated, so increasing the pressure increases the risk of marking or even gouging the metal of the pipe. The jaw is adjustable so it can be threaded in or out to fit different pipe sizes. Pipe wrenches are also available in different lengths, allowing increased leverage to be applied to the pipe.

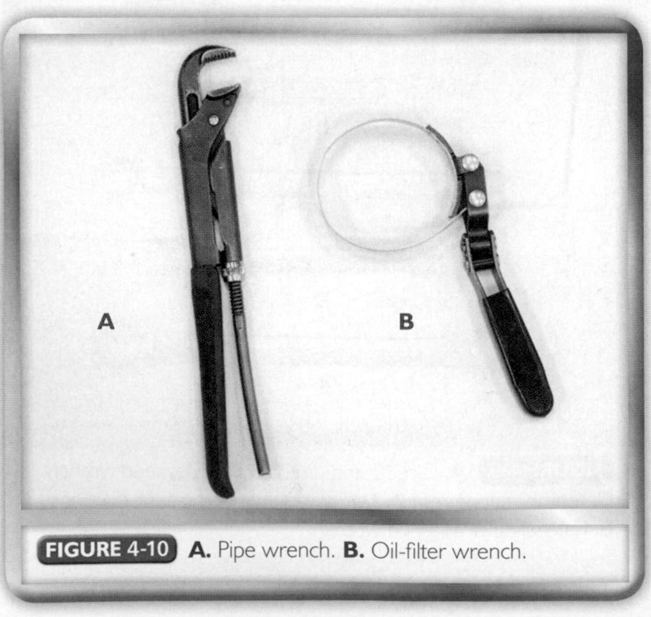

FIGURE 4-10 **A.** Pipe wrench. **B.** Oil-filter wrench.

A specialized tool called an *oil-filter wrench* grabs the filter and gives you extra leverage to remove an oil filter when it is tight FIGURE 4-10B. These are available in various designs and sizes. Some oil-filter wrenches are adjustable to fit many filter sizes. Note also that an oil-filter wrench should be used *only* to remove an oil filter, never to install it. Almost all oil filters should be installed by hand.

Sockets

Sockets are very popular because of their adaptability and ease of use FIGURE 4-11. Sockets are a good choice when the top of the fastener is reasonably easily accessible. The socket fits onto the fastener snugly and grips it on all six corners, providing the type of grip needed on any nut or bolt that is extremely tight. They are available in a variety of configurations, and technicians usually have a lot of sockets so they can access a multitude of tight places. Individual sockets fit a particular size of nut or bolt, so they are usually purchased in sets.

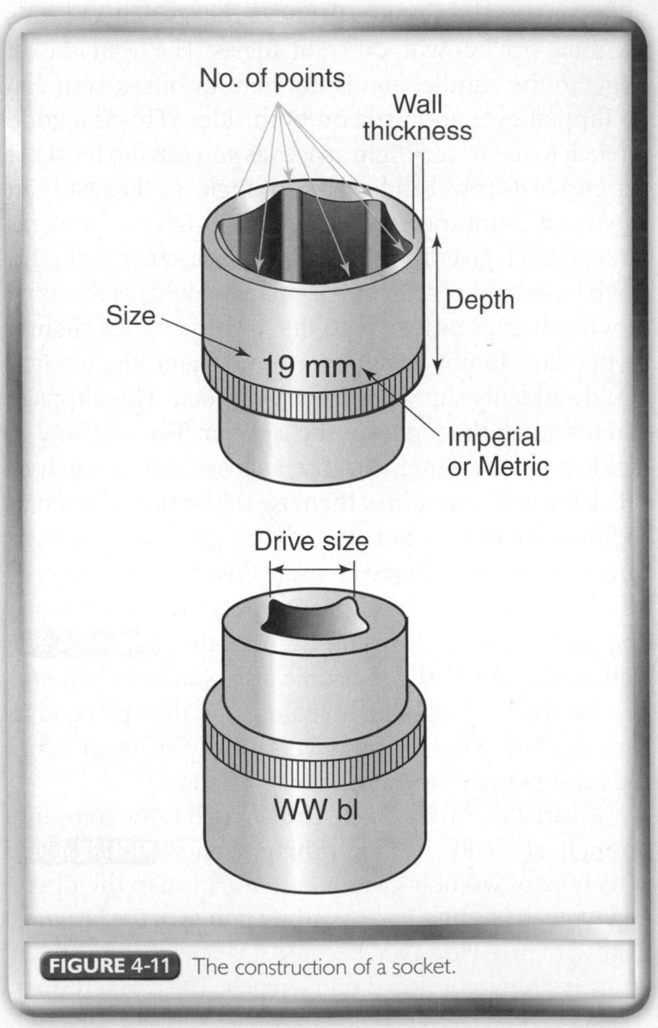

FIGURE 4-11 The construction of a socket.

Sockets are classified by the following characteristics:

- Metric or imperial depending on the vehicle manufacturer.
- Size of drive used to turn them: 1/2", 3/8", and 1/4" are most common; 1" and 3/4" are less common.
- Number of points: 6 and 12 are most common; 4 and 8 are less common.
- Depth of socket: Standard and deep are most common; shallow is less common.
- Thickness of wall: Standard and impact are most common; thin wall is less common.

Sockets are built with a recessed square drive that fits over the square drive of the ratchet or other driver. The size of the drive determines how much twisting force can be applied to the socket. The larger the drive, the larger the twisting force. Small fasteners usually need only a small torque, so do not use a drive larger than you need because too large a drive may impede the socket's access to the bolt. For fasteners that are really tight, an impact wrench exerts a lot more torque on a socket than turning it by hand. Impact sockets are usually thicker walled than standard wall sockets and have six points so they can withstand the forces generated by the impact wrench as well as grip the fastener securely.

Six- and 12-point sockets fit the heads of hexagonal-shaped fasteners. Four- and 8-point sockets fit the heads of square-shaped fasteners. Because 6-point and 4-point sockets fit the exact shape of the fastener, they have the strongest grip on the fastener, but they fit on the fastener in only half as many positions as a 12-point or 8-point socket.

> **TECHNICIAN TIP**
>
> Because sockets are usually purchased in sets, with each set providing a slightly different capability, you can see why technicians could easily have several hundred sockets in their toolbox.

Another factor in accessing a fastener is the depth of the socket. If a nut is threaded quite a distance down a stud, then a standard-length socket will not fit far enough over the stud to reach the nut. In this case, a deep socket will usually reach the nut FIGURE 4-12A.

Turning a socket requires a handle. The most common socket handle, the *ratchet*, makes easy work of tightening or loosening a nut when not a lot of pressure is involved FIGURE 4-12B. A ratchet may be set to turn in either direction and does not need much room to swing. It is built to be convenient, not super strong, so too much pressure could damage it. For heavier tightening or loosening, a breaker bar gives the most leverage FIGURE 4-12C. When that is not available, a **sliding T-handle** may be more useful. With this tool, both hands may be used, and the position of the tee piece is adjustable to clear any obstructions when turning it FIGURE 4-12D.

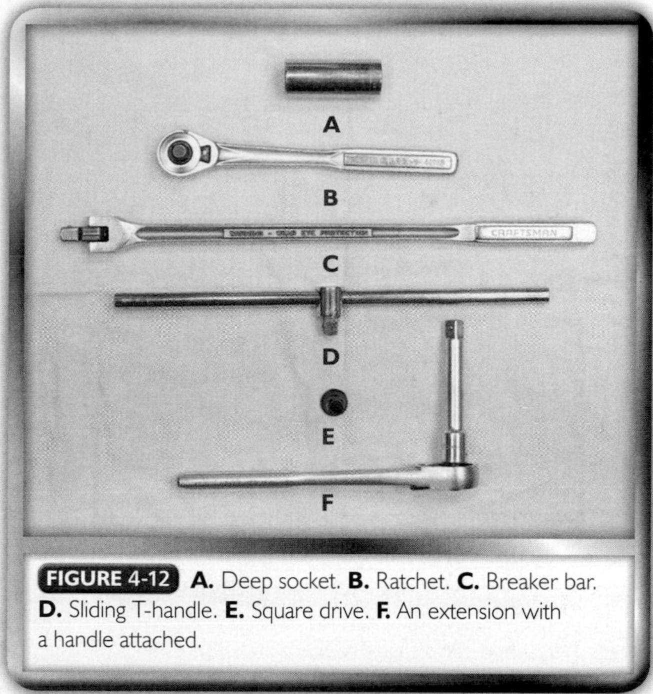

FIGURE 4-12 **A.** Deep socket. **B.** Ratchet. **C.** Breaker bar. **D.** Sliding T-handle. **E.** Square drive. **F.** An extension with a handle attached.

The connection between the socket and the accessory is made by a square drive FIGURE 4-12E. The larger the drive, the heavier and bulkier the socket. The 1/4 inch drive is for small work in difficult areas. The 3/8 inch drive accessories handle a lot of general work where torque requirements are not too high. The 1/2 inch drive is required for all-round service. The 3/4 inch and 1 inch are required for large work with high-torque settings. Many fasteners are located in positions where access can be difficult. There are many different lengths of extensions available to allow the socket to be on the fastener while extending the drive point out to where a handle can be attached FIGURE 4-12F.

A **speed brace** or speeder handle is the fastest way to spin a fastener on or off a thread by hand, but it cannot apply much torque to the fastener; therefore, it is used mainly to remove a fastener that has already been loosened, or to run the fastener onto the thread until it begins to tighten FIGURE 4-13A. A universal joint takes the turning force that needs to be applied to the socket through an angle FIGURE 4-13B.

Pliers

Pliers are a hand tool designed to hold, cut, or compress materials FIGURE 4-14. They are usually made out of two

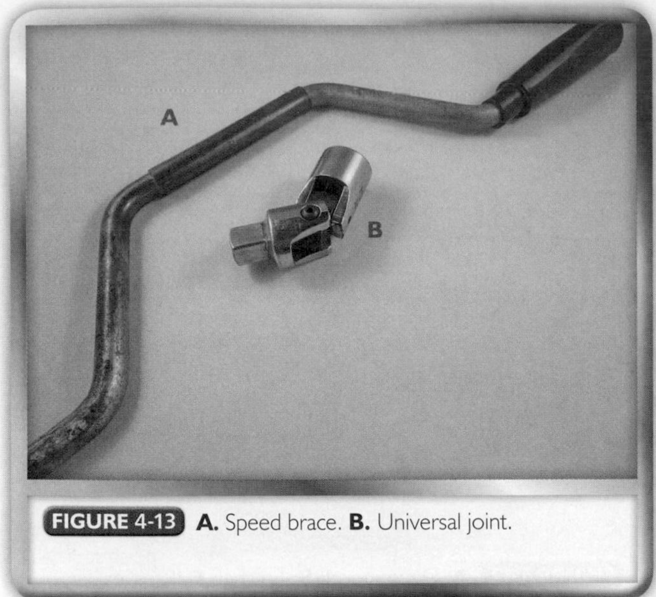

FIGURE 4-13 **A.** Speed brace. **B.** Universal joint.

FIGURE 4-14 Pliers are used for grasping and cutting.

pieces of strong steel joined at a fulcrum point, with jaws and cutting surfaces at one end and handles designed to provide leverage at the other. There are many types of pliers, including slip-joint, combination, arc joint, needle-nosed, and flat-nosed.

Quality **combination pliers** FIGURE 4-15A are the most commonly used pliers in a shop. They are made from two pieces of high-carbon or alloy steel. They pivot together so that any force applied to the handles is multiplied in the strong jaws. Some pliers provide a powerful grip on objects, whereas others are designed to cut. Combination pliers can do both, which is why they are the most commonly used (please note that pliers are job specific).

Combination pliers offer two surfaces, one for gripping flat surfaces and one for gripping rounded objects, and two pairs of cutters. The cutters in the jaws should be used for softer materials that will not damage the blades. The cutters next to the pivot can shear through hard, thin materials, such as steel wire or pins.

Most pliers are limited by their size in what they can grip. Beyond a certain point, the handles are spread too wide, or the jaws cannot open wide enough, but **water-pump pliers** overcome that limitation with a movable pivot. These are often called Channellocks, after the company that first made them. These pliers have parallel jaws that allow you to increase or decrease the size of the jaws by selecting a different set of channels. They are useful for a wider grip and a tighter squeeze on parts too big for conventional pliers.

There are a few specialized pliers in most shops. **Needle-nosed pliers**, which have long, pointed jaws, can reach tight spots or hold small items that other pliers cannot. For example, they can pick up a small bolt that has fallen into a tight spot FIGURE 4-15B. **Flat-nosed pliers** have an end or nose that is flat and square; in contrast, combination pliers have a rounded end. A flat nose makes it possible to bend wire or even a thin piece of sheet steel accurately along a straight edge FIGURE 4-15C. **Diagonal-cutting pliers** FIGURE 4-15D are used for cutting wire or cotter pins. Diagonal cutters are the most common cutters in the toolbox, but they should not be used on hard or heavy-gauge materials because the cutting surfaces will be damaged. End cutting pliers, also called **nippers**, have a cutting edge at right angle to their length FIGURE 4-15E. They are designed to cut through soft metal objects sticking out from a surface.

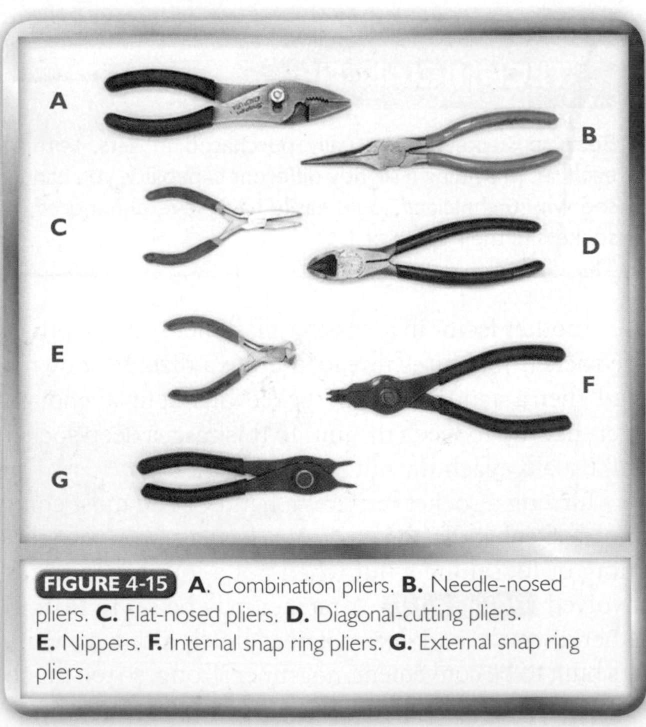

FIGURE 4-15 **A.** Combination pliers. **B.** Needle-nosed pliers. **C.** Flat-nosed pliers. **D.** Diagonal-cutting pliers. **E.** Nippers. **F.** Internal snap ring pliers. **G.** External snap ring pliers.

Snap ring pliers have metal pins that fit in the holes of a snap ring. Snap rings can be of the internal or external type. If internal, then internal snap ring pliers compress the snap ring so it can be removed from and installed in its internal groove FIGURE 4-15F. If external, then external snap ring pliers are used to remove and install the snap ring in its external groove FIGURE 4-15G. Always wear safety glasses when working with snap rings, as the rings can easily slip off the snap-ring pliers and fly off at tremendous speeds, possibly causing severe eye injuries.

> **TECHNICIAN TIP**
>
> When applying pressure to pliers, make sure your hands are not greasy, or they might slip. Select the right type and size of pliers for the job. As with most tools, if you have to exert almost all your strength to get something done, then you are using either the wrong tool or the wrong technique. If the pliers slip, you will get hurt. At the very least, you will damage the tool and what you are working on. Pliers get a lot of hard use in the shop, so they do get worn and damaged. If they are worn or damaged, they will be inefficient and can be dangerous. Always check the condition of all shop tools on a regular basis.

Locking pliers, also called *vice grips*, are general-purpose pliers used to clamp and hold one or more objects FIGURE 4-16. Locking pliers are helpful because they free up one or more of your hands when working; they clamp something and lock themselves in place to hold it. They are also adjustable, so they can be used for a variety of tasks. To clamp an object with locking pliers, put the object between the jaws, turn the screw until the handles are almost closed, then squeeze them together to lock them shut. You can increase or decrease the gripping force with the adjustment screw. To release them, squeeze the release lever and they should open up.

Cutting Tools

Bolt cutters cut heavy wire, non-hardened rods, and bolts FIGURE 4-17A. Their compound joints and long handles give the leverage and cutting pressure needed for heavy-gauge materials. **Tin snips** are the nearest thing in the toolbox to a pair of scissors FIGURE 4-17B. They cut thin sheet metal, and lighter versions make it easy to follow the outline of gaskets. Most snips come with straight blades, but if there is an unusual shape to cut, there is a pair with left- or right-hand curved blades. **Aviation snips** are designed to cut soft metals FIGURE 4-17C. They are easy to use because the handles are spring-loaded open and double-pivoted for extra leverage.

Allen Wrenches

Allen wrenches, sometimes called Allen keys or *hex keys,* are tools designed to tighten and loosen fasteners with Allen heads FIGURE 4-18. The Allen head has an internal hexagonal recess that the Allen wrench fits into. Allen wrenches come in sets, and there is a correct wrench size for every Allen head. They give the best grip on a screw or bolt of all the drivers, and their shape makes them good at getting into tight spots. Care must be utilized to make sure the correct size of Allen wrench is used, or the wrench and/or socket head will be rounded off. The traditional Allen wrench is a hexagonal bar with a right-angle bend at one end. They are made in various sizes in both metric and imperial. As their popularity has increased, so too has the number of tool variations. Now Allen sockets are available, as are T-handle Allen wrenches.

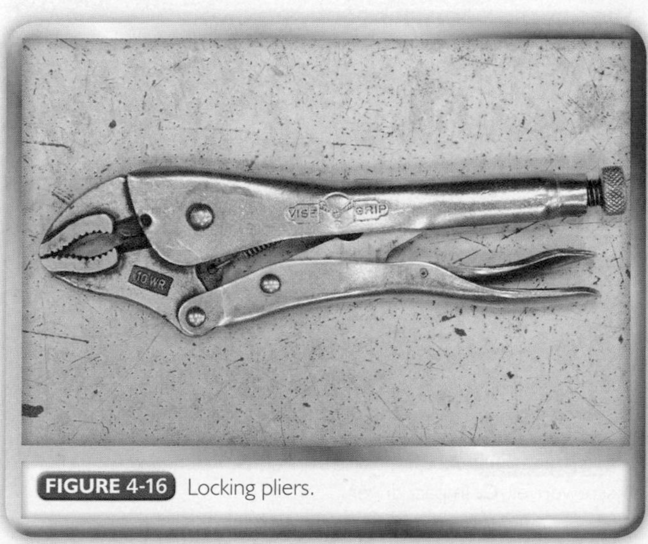

FIGURE 4-16 Locking pliers.

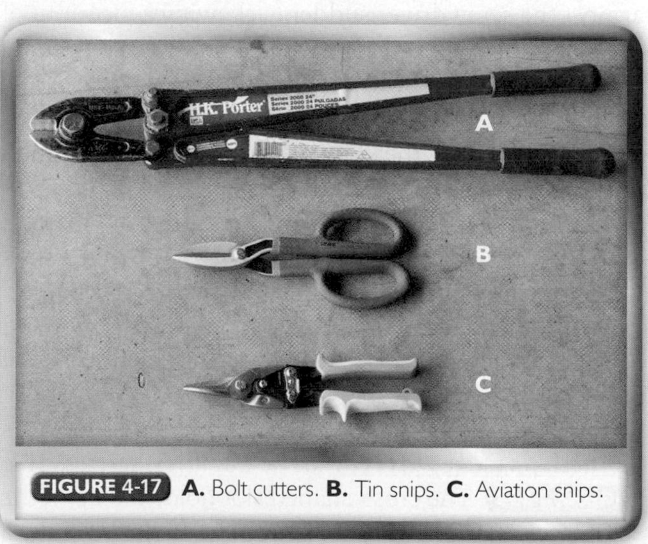

FIGURE 4-17 **A.** Bolt cutters. **B.** Tin snips. **C.** Aviation snips.

FIGURE 4-18 Allen wrench.

Screwdrivers

The correct screwdriver to use depends on the type of slot or recess in the head of the screw or bolt, and how accessible it is. Most screwdrivers cannot grip as securely as wrenches, so it is very important to match the tip of the screwdriver exactly with the slot or recess in the head of a fastener; otherwise the tool might slip, damaging the fastener or the tool and possibly injuring you. When using a screwdriver, always check where the screwdriver tip could end up if it slipped off the head of the screw. Many technicians who have not taken this precaution have stabbed a screwdriver into or through their hand.

The most common screwdriver has a flat tip, or blade, which gives it the name **flat-tip screwdriver** FIGURE 4-19A. The tip should be almost as wide and thick as the slot in the fastener, so that twisting force applied to the screwdriver is transferred right out to the edges of the head where it has the most effect. The tip should be a snug fit in the slot of the screw head. Then the twisting force is applied evenly along the sides of the slot. This will guard against the screwdriver suddenly chewing a piece out of the slot and slipping just when the most force is being exerted. Flat-tip screwdrivers are available in a variety of sizes and lengths, so find the right one for the job.

If viewed from the side, the tip should taper slightly until the very end where the tip fits into the slot. If the tip is not clean and square, it should be reshaped or replaced.

When you use a flat-tip screwdriver, support the shaft with your free hand as you turn it (but keep it behind the tip). This helps keep the tip square on the slot and centered. Screwdrivers that slip are a common source of damage and injury in shops.

A screw or bolt with a cross-shaped recess requires a **Phillips screwdriver** or a *Pozidriv screwdriver* FIGURE 4-19B. The cross-shaped slot holds the tip of the screwdriver securely on the head. The Phillips tip fits a tapered recess, whereas the Pozidriv fits into slots with parallel sides in the head of the screw FIGURE 4-19C. Both a Phillips and a Pozidriv screwdriver are less likely to slip sideways because the point is centered in the screw, but again, the screwdriver must be the right size. The fitting process is simplified for these two types of screwdrivers because four sizes are enough to fit almost all fasteners with this type of screw head.

The **offset screwdriver** fits into spaces where a straight screwdriver cannot and is useful where there is not much room to turn it FIGURE 4-20A. The two tips look identical, but one is set at 90 degrees to the other. This is because sometimes there is room to make only a quarter turn of the driver. Thus the driver has two tips on opposite ends, so that offset ends of the screwdriver can be used alternately.

The **ratcheting screwdriver** is a popular screwdriver handle that usually comes with a selection of flat and Phillips tips FIGURE 4-20B. It has a ratchet inside the handle

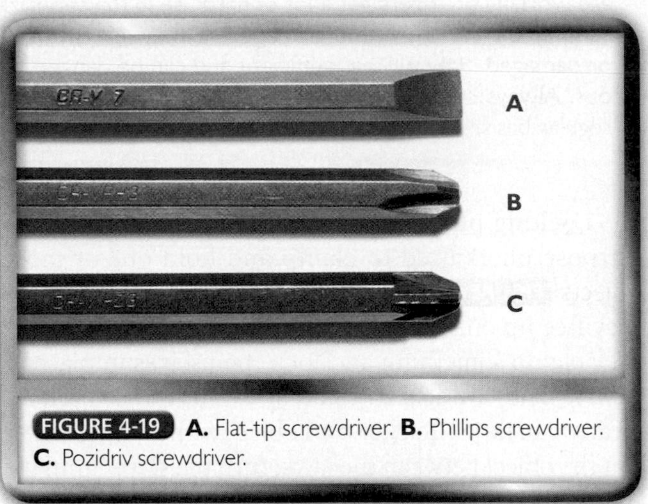

FIGURE 4-19 **A.** Flat-tip screwdriver. **B.** Phillips screwdriver. **C.** Pozidriv screwdriver.

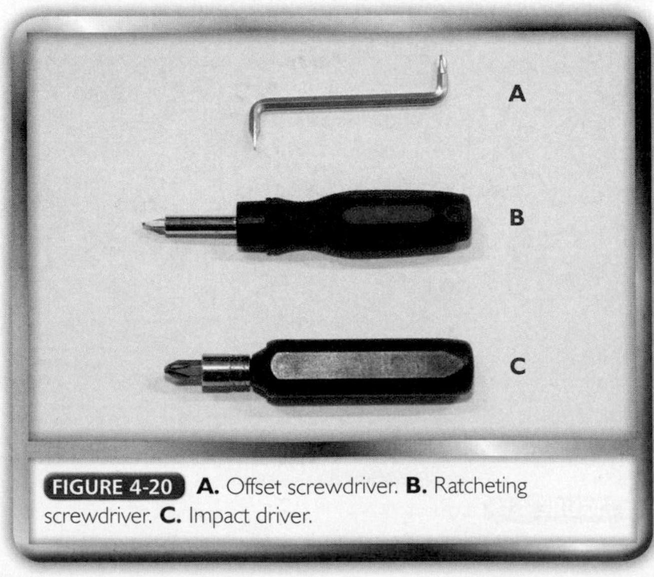

FIGURE 4-20 **A.** Offset screwdriver. **B.** Ratcheting screwdriver. **C.** Impact driver.

that turns the tip in only one direction depending on how the slider is set. When set for loosening, a screw can be undone without removing the tip from the head of the screw. When set for tightening, a screw can be inserted just as easily.

An **impact driver** is used when a screw or a bolt is rusted/corroded in place, or overtightened, and needs a tool that can apply more force than the other members of this family FIGURE 4-20C. Screw slots could easily be stripped with the use of a standard screwdriver. The force of the hammer pushing the bit into the screw, and at the same time turning it, makes it more likely the screw will break loose. The impact driver accepts a variety of special, impact tips. Choose the right one for the screw head, fit the tip in place, and then tension it in the direction it has to turn. A sharp blow with the hammer breaks the screw free, and then it can be unscrewed.

Magnetic Pickup Tools and Mechanical Fingers

Magnetic pickup tools and **mechanical fingers** are very useful for grabbing items in tight spaces. A magnetic pickup tool is typically a telescoping stick that has a magnet attached to the end on a swivel joint FIGURE 4-21A. The magnet is strong enough to pick up screws, bolts, and sockets. For example, if a screw is dropped into a tight crevice where your fingers cannot reach, a magnetic pickup tool can be used to extract it.

Mechanical fingers are also designed to extract or insert objects in tight spaces FIGURE 4-21B. Because they actually grab the object, they can pick up non-magnetic items, which makes them handy for picking up rubber or plastic parts. They use a flexible body and come in different lengths, but are typically about 12-18" (305 to 457 mm) long. They have expanding grappling fingers on one end to grab items, and the other end has a push mechanism to expand the fingers and a retracting spring to contract the fingers.

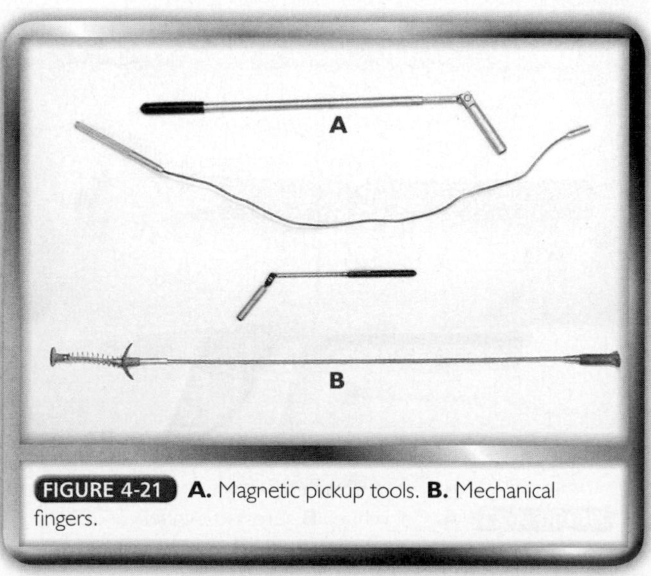

FIGURE 4-21 **A.** Magnetic pickup tools. **B.** Mechanical fingers.

> **TECHNICIAN TIP**
>
> The challenge is to get the magnet down inside some areas because the magnet wants to keep sticking to the sides. One trick in this situation is to roll up a piece of paper so that a tube is created. Stick that down into the area of the dropped part, then slide the magnet down the tube, which will help it get past magnetic objects. Once the magnet is down, you may want to remove the roll of paper. Just remember two things: First, patience is important when using this tool; and second, don't drop anything in the first place!

Hammers

Hammers are a vital part of the shop tool collection, and a variety are commonly used. The most common hammer in an automotive shop is the **ball-peen (engineer's) hammer** FIGURE 4-22A. Like most hammers, its head is hardened steel. A punch or a chisel can be driven with the flat face. Its name comes from the ball peen or rounded face. It is usually used for flattening and **peening** a rivet. The hammer should always match the size of the job, and it is better to use one that is too big than too small.

> **TECHNICIAN TIP**
>
> The hammer you use depends on the part you are striking. Hammers with a metal face should almost always be harder than the part you are hammering. Never strike two hardened tools together, as this can cause the hardened parts to shatter.

Hitting chisels with a steel hammer is fine, but sometimes you need only to tap a component to position it FIGURE 4-22B. A steel hammer might mark or damage the part, especially if it is made of a softer metal such as aluminum. In such cases, a soft-faced hammer should be used for the job. Soft-faced hammers range from very soft, with rubber or plastic heads, to slightly harder, with brass or copper heads.

When a large chisel needs a really strong blow, it is time to use a **club hammer** FIGURE 4-22C. The club hammer is like a small mallet, with two square faces made of high-carbon steel. It is the heaviest type of hammer that can be used one-handed. The club hammer is used in conjunction with a chisel to cut off a bolt where corrosion has made it impossible to remove the nut.

The most common small-headed mallet in the shop has a head made of hard nylon FIGURE 4-22D. It is a special-purpose tool and is often used for moving things into place where it is important not to damage the item being moved. For example, it can be used to tap a crankshaft, to measure end play, or to break a gasket seal on an aluminum casing.

A **dead-blow hammer** is designed not to bounce back when it hits something FIGURE 4-22E. A rebounding hammer can be dangerous or destructive. A dead-blow hammer may be made with a lead head or, more commonly, a hollow polyurethane head filled with lead shot or sand. The head absorbs the blow when the hammer makes contact, reducing any bounce-back or rebounding. This hammer can be used when working on the vehicle chassis or when dislodging stuck parts.

Safety

When using hammers and chisels, safety goggles must always be worn.

Chisels

The most common kind of chisel is a cold chisel FIGURE 4-23A. It gets its name from the fact that it is used to cut cold metals, rather than heated metals. It has a flat blade made of high-quality steel and a cutting angle of approximately 70 degrees. The cutting end is tempered and hardened because it has to be harder than the metals to be cut. The head of the chisel needs to be softer so it will not chip when it is hit with a hammer. Technicians sometimes use a cold chisel to remove bolts whose heads have rounded off.

A **cross-cut chisel** is so named because the sharpened edge is across the blade width. This chisel narrows down along the stock, so it is good for getting in grooves FIGURE 4-23B. It is used for cleaning out or even making key ways. The flying chips of metal should always be directed away from the user.

TECHNICIAN TIP

Chisels and punches are designed with a softer striking end than hammers. Over time, this softer metal "mushrooms," and small fragments are prone to breaking off when hammered. These fragments could cause eye or other penetrative injuries to people in the area. Always inspect chisels and punches for mushrooming and dress them on a grinder when necessary.

Pry Bars

Pry bars (also known as **crowbars**) are composed of a strong metal and are used as levers to move, adjust or pry. Pry bars are available in a variety of shapes and sizes. Many have a tapered end that is slightly bent, with a plastic handle on the other end FIGURE 4-24A. This design works well for applying force to tension belts or for moving parts into alignment. Another type of pry bar is the roll bar FIGURE 4-24B. One end is sharply curved and tapered and is used for prying. The other end is tapered to a dull point and is used to align larger holes, such

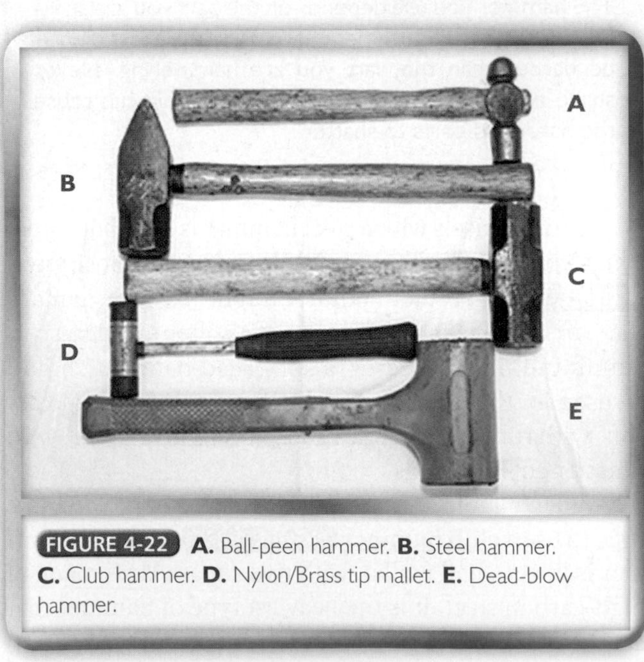

FIGURE 4-22 **A.** Ball-peen hammer. **B.** Steel hammer. **C.** Club hammer. **D.** Nylon/Brass tip mallet. **E.** Dead-blow hammer.

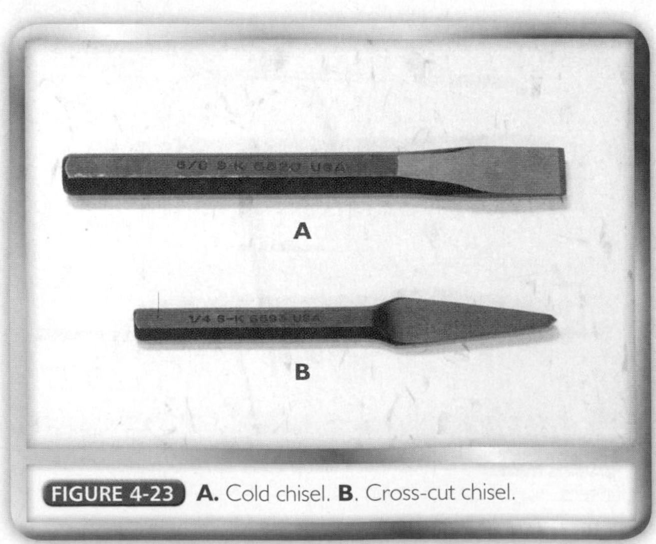

FIGURE 4-23 **A.** Cold chisel. **B.** Cross-cut chisel.

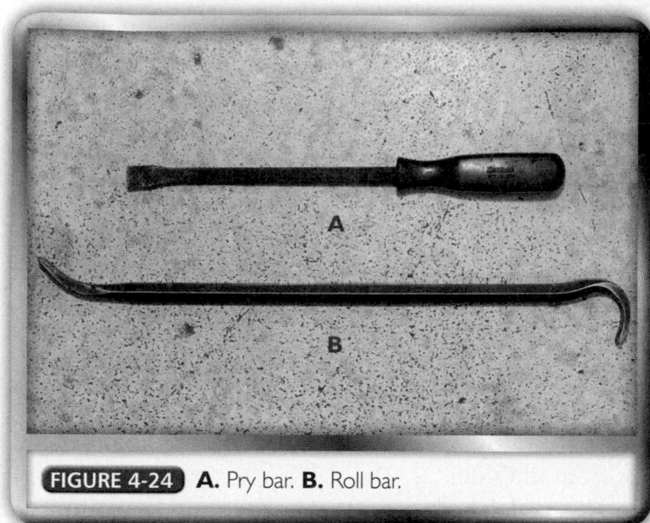

FIGURE 4-24 **A.** Pry bar. **B.** Roll bar.

as transmission bell housings or engine motor mounts. Because pry bars are made of hardened steel, care should be taken when using them on softer materials to avoid any damage.

Gasket Scrapers

A **gasket scraper** has a hardened, sharpened blade. It is designed to remove a gasket without damaging the sealing face of the component, when used properly FIGURE 4-25. On one end, it has a comfortable handle to grip like a screwdriver handle; on the other end, a blade is fitted with a sharp edge to assist in the removal of gaskets. The gasket scraper should be kept sharp to make it easy to remove all traces of the old gasket and sealing compound. The blades come in different sizes, with a typical size being 1" (25 mm) wide. Whenever you use a gasket scraper, be very careful not to nick or damage the surface being cleaned.

> **TECHNICIAN TIP**
>
> Many engine components are made of aluminum. Because aluminum is quite soft, it is critical that you use the gasket scraper very carefully so as not to damage an aluminum surface. This can be accomplished by keeping the gasket scraper at a fairly flat angle to the surface. The gasket scraper should also be used only by hand, not with a hammer.

Files

Files are cutting devices designed to remove small amounts of material from the surface of a workpiece. Files are available in a variety of shapes, sizes, and coarseness,

FIGURE 4-25 A gasket scraper.

depending on the material being worked on and the size of the job. Files have a pointed tang on one end that is fitted to a handle. Files are often sold without handles, but they should not be used until a handle of the right size has been fitted. A correctly sized handle fits snugly without working loose when the file is in use. Always check the handle before using the file. If the handle is loose, give it a sharp rap to tighten it up, or if it is the threaded type, screw it on tighter. If it fails to fit snugly, you must use a different-sized handle.

> **Safety**
>
> Hands should always be kept away from the surface of the file and the metal that is being worked on. Filing can produce small slivers of metal that can be difficult to remove from a finger or hand. Clean hands will help avoid slipping and lessen the corrosion caused by acids and moisture from the skin.

What makes one file different from another is not just the shape but also how much material it is designed to remove with each stroke. The teeth on the file determine how much material will be removed FIGURE 4-26. Since the teeth face in one direction only, the file cuts in only one direction. Dragging the file backwards over the surface of the metal only dulls the teeth and wears them out quickly.

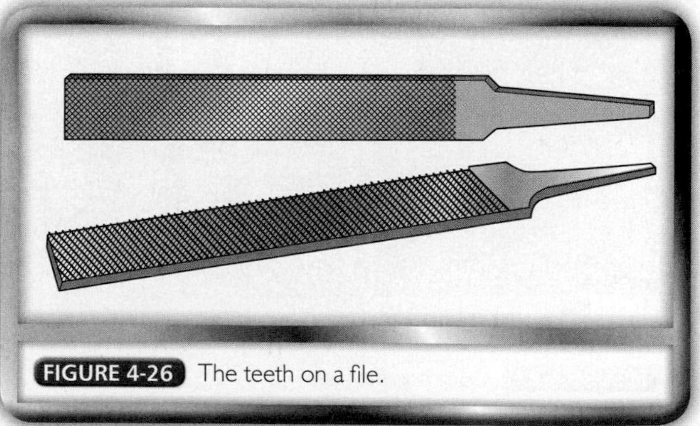
FIGURE 4-26 The teeth on a file.

Teeth on a coarse-grade file are longer, with a greater space between them. A coarse-grade file working on a piece of mild steel will remove a lot of material with each stroke, but it leaves a rough finish. A smooth-grade file has shorter teeth cut more closely together. It removes much less material on each stroke, and the finish is much smoother. The coarse file is used first to remove material quickly, then a smoother file gently removes the last of it and leaves a clean finish to the work.

The full list of grades in flat files, from rough to smooth, follows FIGURE 4-27:

- *Rough files* have the coarsest teeth, with approximately 20 teeth per 1 inch (25 mm). They are used when a lot of material must be removed quickly. They leave a very rough finish and have to be followed by finer files to produce a smooth final finish.
- *Coarse bastard files* are still coarse files, with approximately 30 teeth per 1 inch (25 mm), but they are not as coarse as the rough file. They are also used to rough out or remove material quickly from a job.
- *Second-cut files* have approximately 40 teeth per 1 inch (25 mm), and provide a smoother finish than the rough or coarse bastard file. They are good all-round intermediary files and leave a reasonably smooth finish.
- *Smooth files* have approximately 60 teeth per 1 inch (25 mm), and are a finishing file used to provide a smooth final finish.
- *Dead-smooth files* have 100 teeth per 1 inch (25 mm), or more, and are used where a very fine finish is required.

Some flat files are available with one smooth edge and are called *safe-edge files*. They allow filing up to an edge without damaging it.

Flat files are fine on straightforward jobs, but you need files that work in some awkward spots as well. A **warding file** is thinner than other files and comes to a point; it is used for working in narrow slots FIGURE 4-28A. A **square file** has teeth on all four sides, so you can use it in a square or rectangular hole FIGURE 4-28B. A square file can make the right shape for a squared metal key to fit in a slot. A triangular file has three sides FIGURE 4-28C. Because it is triangular, it can get into internal corners; it is able to cut right into a corner without removing material from the sides.

Curved files are either half-round or round. A half-round file has a shallow convex surface that can file in a concave hollow or in an acute internal corner FIGURE 4-29A. The fully round file, sometimes called a *rat-tail file*, can make holes bigger. It can also file inside a concave surface with a tight radius.

The thread file cleans clogged or distorted threads on bolts and studs FIGURE 4-29B. Thread files are available in either metric or imperial configurations, so make sure you use the correct file. Each file has eight different surfaces that match different thread dimensions, so the right face must be used.

Files should be cleaned after each use. If they are clogged, they can be cleaned by using a file card or file brush FIGURE 4-29C. This tool has short steel bristles that clean out the small particles that clog the teeth of the file. Rubbing a piece of chalk over the surface of the file prior to filing will make it easier to clean.

FIGURE 4-27 Common flat files.

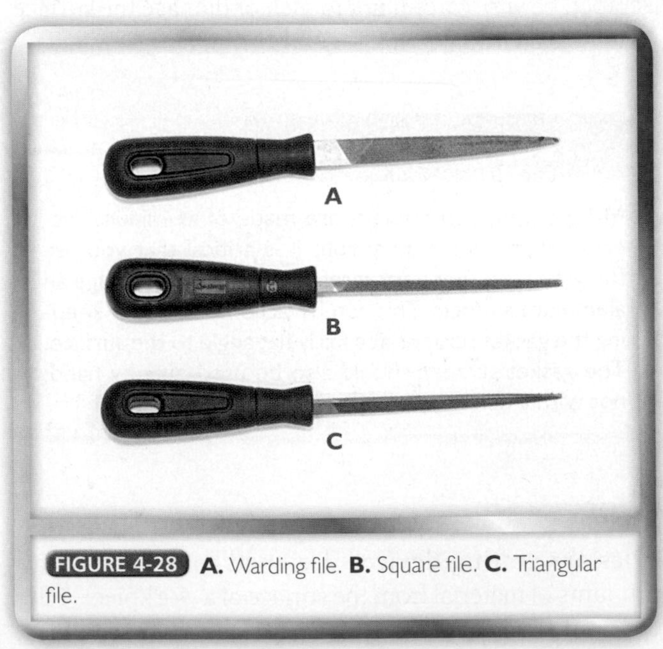

FIGURE 4-28 **A.** Warding file. **B.** Square file. **C.** Triangular file.

Hacksaw

The hacksaw is used for the general cutting of metals for a crude cut FIGURE 4-30. The frames and blades are adjustable and rated according the number of teeth and hardness of the saw.

Clamps

The **bench vice** is a useful tool for holding anything that can fit into its jaws FIGURE 4-31A. Some common uses include sawing, filing, or chiselling. The jaws are serrated to give extra grip. They are also very hard, which means that when the vice is tightened, the jaws can mar whatever they grip. To prevent this, a pair of soft jaws may be fitted whenever the danger of damage arises. These are usually made of aluminum or some other soft metal, or can have a rubber-type surface applied to them.

When materials are too awkward to grip vertically in a plain vice, it may be easier to use an **offset vice**. The offset vice has its jaws set to one side to allow long components to be held vertically. For example, a long threaded bar can be held vertically in an offset vice to cut a thread with a die.

A **drill vice** is designed to hold material on a drill worktable. The drill worktable has slots cut into it to allow the vice to be bolted down on the table to hold material securely FIGURE 4-31B. To hold something firmly and drill it accurately, the object must be secured in the jaws of the vice. The vice can be moved on the bed until the precise drilling point is located, and then tightened down by bolts to hold the drill vice in place during drilling.

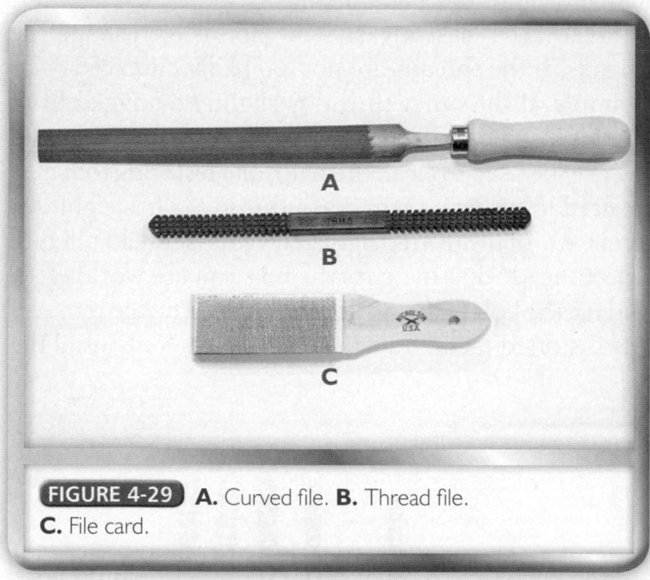

FIGURE 4-29 **A.** Curved file. **B.** Thread file. **C.** File card.

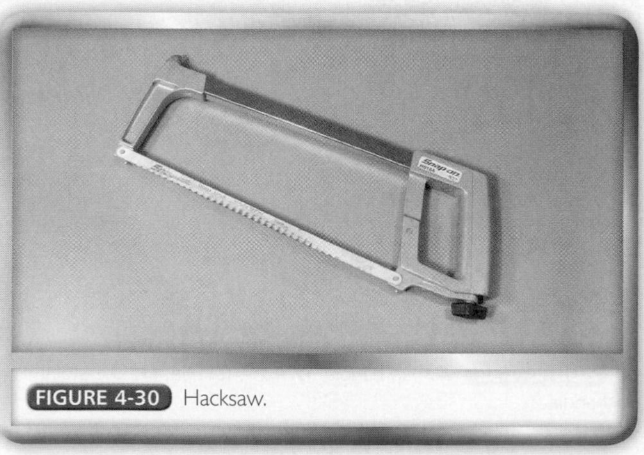

FIGURE 4-30 Hacksaw.

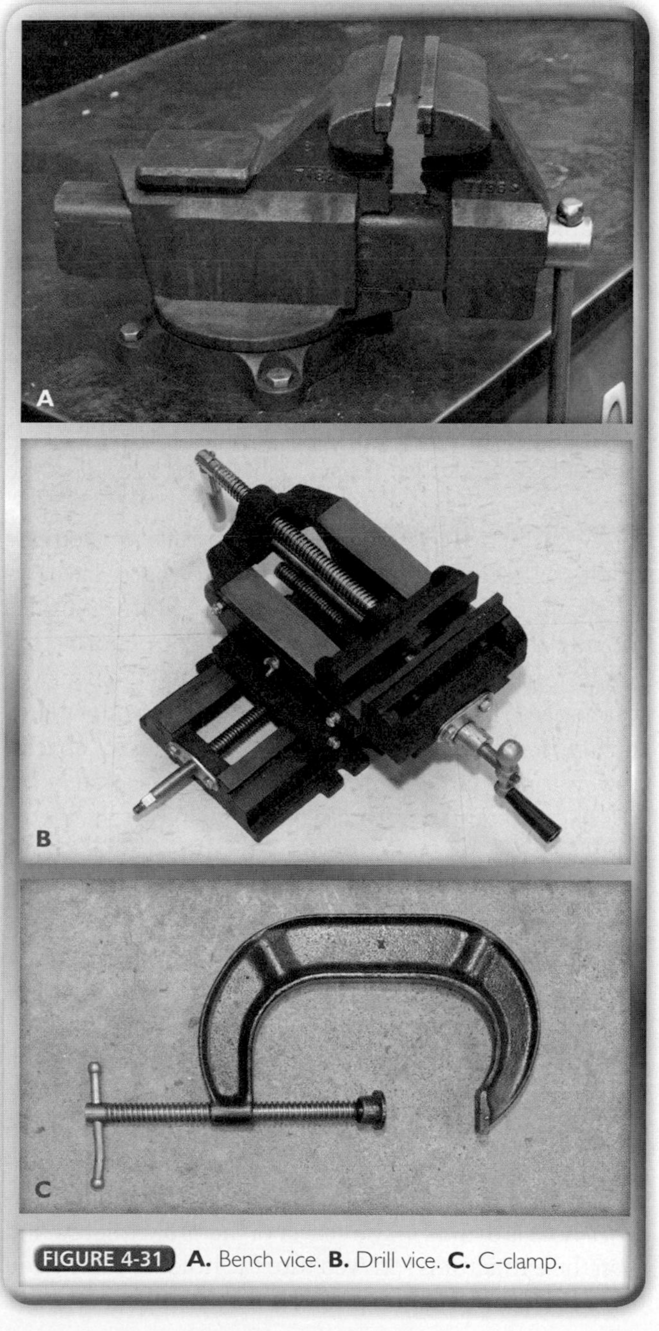

FIGURE 4-31 **A.** Bench vice. **B.** Drill vice. **C.** C-clamp.

The name for the C-clamp comes from its shape FIGURE 4-31C. It holds parts together while they are being assembled, drilled, or welded. It can reach around awkwardly shaped pieces that will not fit in a vice. It is also commonly used to retract disc brake caliper pistons. This clamp is portable, so it can be taken to the work.

Taps and Dies

Taps cut threads inside holes or nuts FIGURE 4-32A. They usually are available in three different types. The first is known as a taper tap. It narrows at the tip to give it a good start in the hole where the thread is to be cut. The diameter of the hole is determined by a tap drill chart, which can be obtained from engineering suppliers. This chart shows what hole size has to be drilled and what tap size is needed to cut the right thread for any given bolt size. Remember that if you are drilling a 0.250" (6 mm) or larger hole, you should use a smaller pilot drill first. Once the properly sized hole has been drilled, the taper tap can tap a thread right through a piece of steel to enable a bolt to be screwed into it.

The second type of tap is an intermediate tap, also known as a *plug tap*, and the third is a bottoming tap. They are used to tap a thread into a hole that does not come out the other side of the material, called a blind hole. A taper tap is used to start the thread in the hole and then the intermediate tap is used, followed by a bottoming tap to take the thread right to the bottom of the blind hole.

A tap handle FIGURE 4-32B has a right-angled jaw that matches the squared end that all taps have. The jaws are designed to hold the tap securely, and the handles provide the leverage for the operator to rotate the tap comfortably to cut the thread. To cut a thread in an awkward space, a T-shaped tap handle is very convenient. Its handles are not as long, so it fits into tighter spaces; however, it is harder to turn and to guide accurately.

To cut a brand-new thread on a blank rod or shaft, a die FIGURE 4-32C held in a die stock handle, FIGURE 4-32D is used. The die may be split so that it can be adjusted more tightly onto the work with each pass of the die, as the thread is cut deeper and deeper, until the nut fits properly. The thread chaser is also common in the shop. It is hexagonal-shaped to fit a wrench, and it is commonly used to clean up threads that are rusty or have been damaged.

Screw extractors are devices designed to remove screws, studs, or bolts that have broken off in threaded holes. A common type of extractor uses a coarse, left-hand tapered thread formed on its hardened body. Usually, a hole is drilled in the center of the broken screw and then the extractor is screwed into the hole. The left-hand thread grips the broken part of the bolt and unscrews it. The extractor is marked with the sizes of the screw it is designed to remove and the hole that needs to be drilled. It is important to drill the hole carefully in the center of the bolt or stud in case you end up having to drill the bolt out. If you drill the hole off-center, you will not be able to drill it out all the way to the inside diameter of the threads, and removal will be nearly impossible.

Thread Repair

Thread repair is used in situations where it is not possible to replace a damaged component. This may be because the thread is located in a large, expensive component, such as the engine block or cylinder head, or because parts are not available. The aim of thread repair is to restore the thread to a condition that restores the fastening integrity. It can be performed on internal threads, such as in a housing, engine block, or cylinder head, or on external threads, such as on a bolt.

Types of Thread Repair

Many different tools and methods can be used to repair a thread. The least invasive method is to reshape the threads. If the threads are not too badly damaged—for example, if the outer thread is slightly damaged from being started crooked (cross-threaded)—then a thread file may be used to clean them up, or a restoring tool may be used to reshape them. Each thread file has eight different sets of file teeth that match various thread pitches. Select the set that matches the bolt you are working on and file the bolt in line with the threads. The file removes any distorted metal from the threads. File only until the

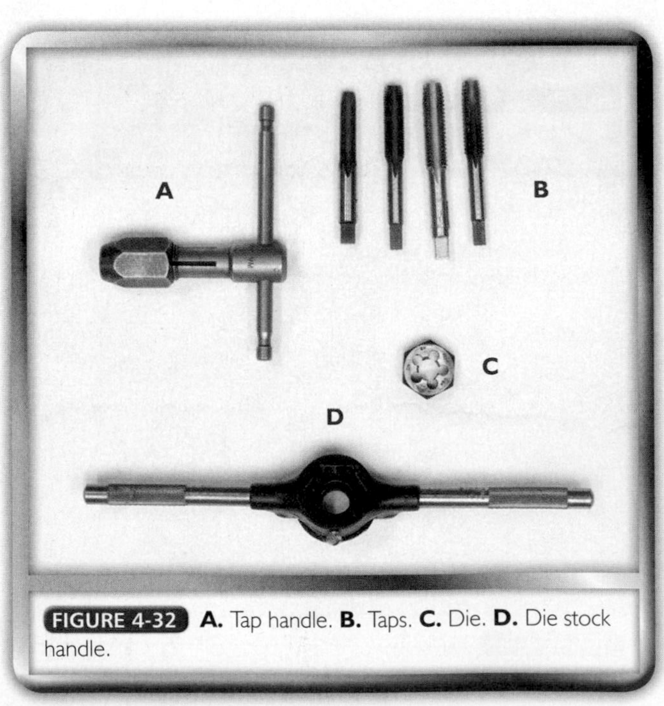

FIGURE 4-32 **A.** Tap handle. **B.** Taps. **C.** Die. **D.** Die stock handle.

bad spot is reshaped. The thread-restoring tool looks like an ordinary tap and die set, but instead of cutting the threads, it reshapes the damaged portion of the thread.

Threads that have substantial damage require other methods of repair. A common method for repairing damaged internal threads is a thread insert. A number of manufacturers make thread inserts, and they all work in a similar fashion. The thread insert is a sleeve that has both an internal and external thread. The internal thread on the insert matches the original damaged thread size. The hole with the damaged thread is made larger and a fresh, larger-diameter thread is cut. This thread matches the external thread on the insert. The thread insert can then be screwed and secured into the prepared hole. The insert provides a brand-new threaded inside thread that matches the original size.

Pullers

Pullers are a very common, universal tool that are used for removing bearings, bushings, pulleys, and gears FIGURE 4-33A. Specialized pullers are also available for specific tasks where a standard puller is not as effective.

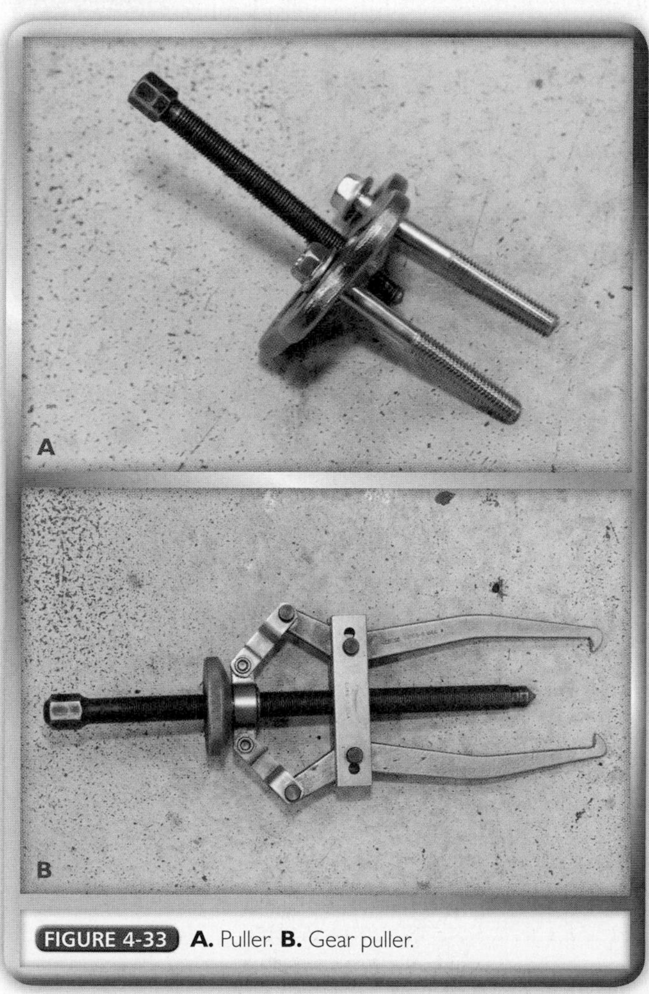

FIGURE 4-33 **A.** Puller. **B.** Gear puller.

The most common pullers have two or three legs that grip the part to be removed. A center bolt, called a forcing screw or jacking bolt, is then screwed in, producing a jacking or pulling action, which extracts the part.

Gear pullers come in a range of sizes and shapes, all designed for particular applications FIGURE 4-33B. They consist of three main parts: jaws, a **cross-arm**, and a forcing screw. There are generally two or three jaws on a puller. They are designed to work either externally around a pulley or internally. The **forcing screw** is a long, fine-threaded bolt that is applied to the center of the cross-arm. When the forcing screw is turned, it applies many tons of force through the component you are removing. The cross-arm attaches the jaws to the forcing screw. There may be two, three, or four arms. If the cross-arm has four arms, three of the arms are spaced 120 degrees apart. The fourth arm is positioned 180 degrees apart from one arm. This allows the cross-arm to be used as either a two- or a three-arm puller.

Flaring Tools

A **tube-flaring tool** is used to flare the end of a tube so it can be connected to another tube or component. One example of this is where the brake line screws into a wheel cylinder. The flared end is compressed between two threaded parts so that it will seal the joint and withstand high pressures. The three most common shapes of flares are the **single flare**, for tubing carrying low pressures, such as a fuel line; the **double flare**, for higher pressures, such as in a brake system; and the ISO flare (sometimes called a bubble flare), which is the metric version used in brake systems FIGURE 4-34A.

Flaring tools have two parts: a set of bars with holes that match the diameter of the tube end that is being shaped; and a yoke that drives a cone into the mouth of the tube FIGURE 4-34B. To make a single flare, the end of the tube is placed level with the surface of the top of the flaring bars. With the clamp screw firmly tightened, the feed screw flares the end of the tube.

Making a double flare is similar, but an extra step is added and more of the tube is exposed to allow for the folding over into a double flare. A double-flaring button is placed into the end of the tube, and when it is removed after tightening, the pipe looks like a bubble. Placing the cone and yoke over the bubble allows you to turn the feed screw and force the bubble to fold in on itself, forming the double flare.

An ISO flare uses a flaring tool made specifically for that type of flare. It is similar to the double-flare process but stops with the use of the button. It does not get doubled back on itself. It should resemble a bubble shape when you are finished.

A **tubing cutter** is more convenient and neater than a saw when cutting pipes and metal tubing FIGURE 4-34C. The sharpened wheel does the cutting. As the tool turns around the pipe, the screw increases the pressure, driving the wheel deeper and deeper through the pipe until it finally cuts through. There is a larger version that is used for cutting exhaust pipes.

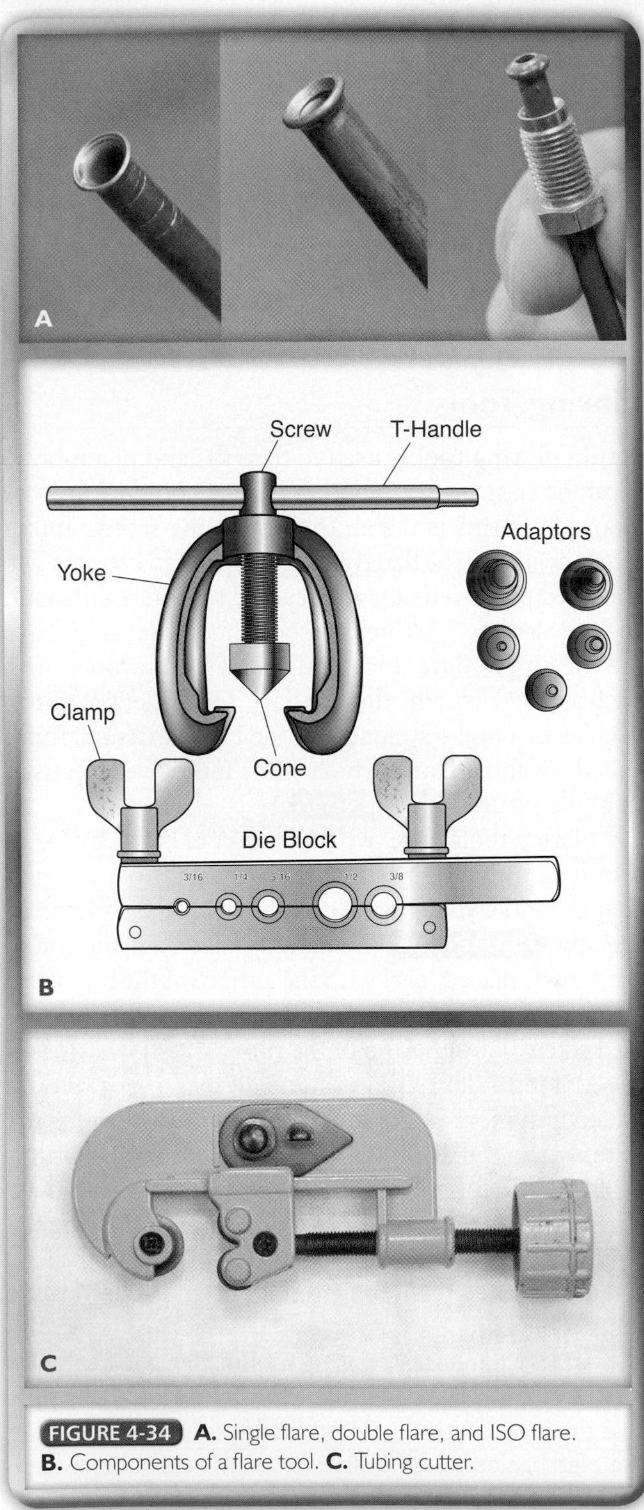

FIGURE 4-34 **A.** Single flare, double flare, and ISO flare. **B.** Components of a flare tool. **C.** Tubing cutter.

> **TECHNICIAN TIP**
>
> A flaring tool is used to produce a pressure seal for sealing brake lines and fuel system tubing. Make sure you test the flared joint for leaks before completing the repair; otherwise the brakes could fail or the fuel could catch on fire.

Additional Tools

Punches

Punches are used when the head of the hammer is too large to strike the object being hit without causing damage to adjacent parts. A punch transmits the hammer's striking power from the soft upper end down to the tip that is made of hardened high-carbon steel. A punch transmits an accurate blow from the hammer at exactly one point, something that cannot be guaranteed using a hammer on its own.

When marks need to be drawn on an object such as a steel plate to help locate a hole to be drilled, a **prick punch** is used to mark the points so they will not rub off FIGURE 4-35A. They can also be used to scribe intersecting lines between given points. The prick punch's point is very sharp, so a gentle tap leaves a clear indentation. The center punch is not as sharp as a prick punch and is usually bigger FIGURE 4-35B. It makes a bigger indentation that centers a drill bit at the point where a hole needs to be drilled.

A **drift punch** is also named a starter punch because you should always use it first to get a pin moving FIGURE 4-35C. It has a tapered shank, and the tip is slightly hollow so it does not spread the end of the pin and make it an even

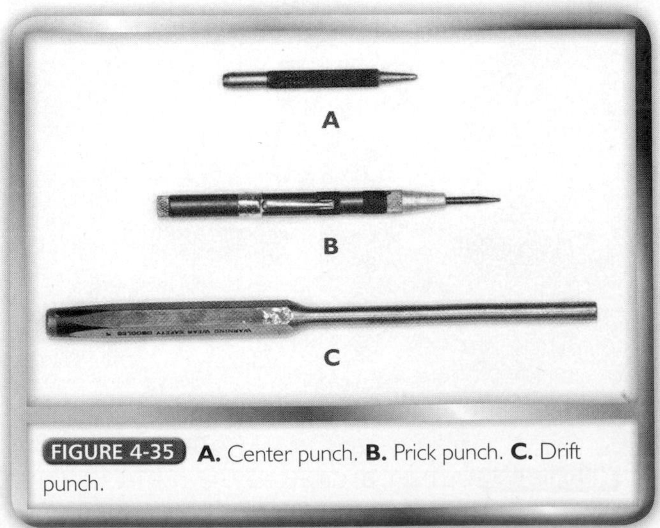

FIGURE 4-35 **A.** Center punch. **B.** Prick punch. **C.** Drift punch.

tighter fit. Once the starter drift has got the pin moving, a suitable pin punch will drive the pin out or in. A drift punch also works well for aligning holes on two mating objects, such as a valve cover and cylinder head. Forcing the drift punch in the hole will align both components for easier installation of the remaining bolts.

Pin punches are available in various diameters. A pin punch has a long, slender shaft with straight sides. It is used to drive out rivets or pins FIGURE 4-36A. A lot of components are either held together or accurately located by pins. Pins can be pretty tight, and a group of pin punches is specially designed to deal with them.

Special punches with hollow ends are called **wad punches** or **hollow punches** FIGURE 4-36B. They are the most efficient tool to make a hole in soft sheet material, such as shim steel, plastic and leather or, most commonly, in a gasket. When they are used, there should always be a soft surface under the work, ideally the end grain of a wooden block. If a hollow punch loses its sharpness or has nicks around its edge, it will make a mess instead of a hole.

Numbers and letters, like the engine numbers on some cylinder blocks, are usually made with number and letter punches that come in boxed sets FIGURE 4-36C. The rules for using these punches are the same as for all punches. The punch must be square with the surface being worked on, not on an angle, and the hammer must hit the top squarely.

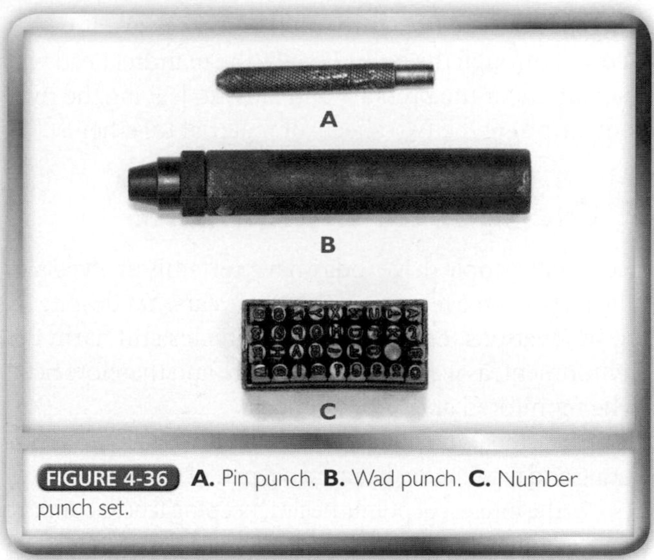

FIGURE 4-36 **A.** Pin punch. **B.** Wad punch. **C.** Number punch set.

Riveting Tools

There are many applications for blind rivets, and various rivet types and tools may be used to do the riveting. **Pop-rivet guns** are convenient for occasional riveting of light materials FIGURE 4-37. A typical pop or **blind rivet** has a body, which forms the **finished rivet**, and a **mandrel**, which is discarded when the riveting is completed FIGURE 4-38. It is called a blind rivet because there is no need to see or reach the other side of the hole in which the rivet goes to do the work. In some types, the rivet is plugged shut so that it is waterproof or pressure-proof.

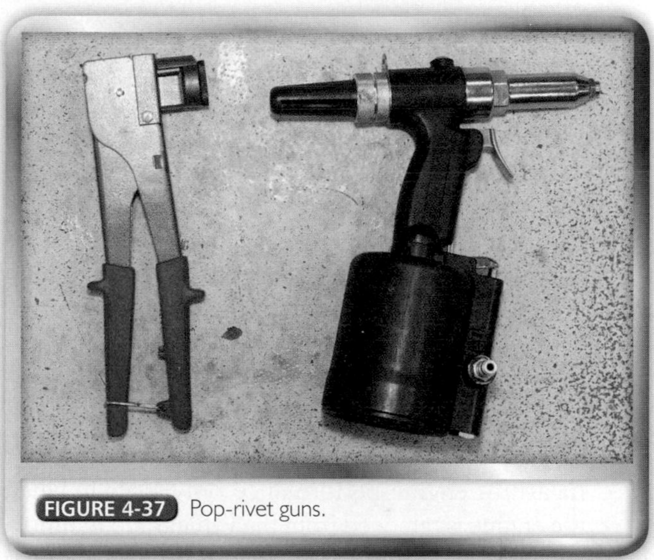

FIGURE 4-37 Pop-rivet guns.

> **TECHNICIAN TIP**
>
> A rivet is a one-time-use fastener. Unlike a nut and bolt, which can generally be disassembled and reused, a rivet cannot. The metal shell that makes up a pop rivet is crushed into place so that it holds the parts firmly together. If it ever needs to be removed, it must be drilled out.

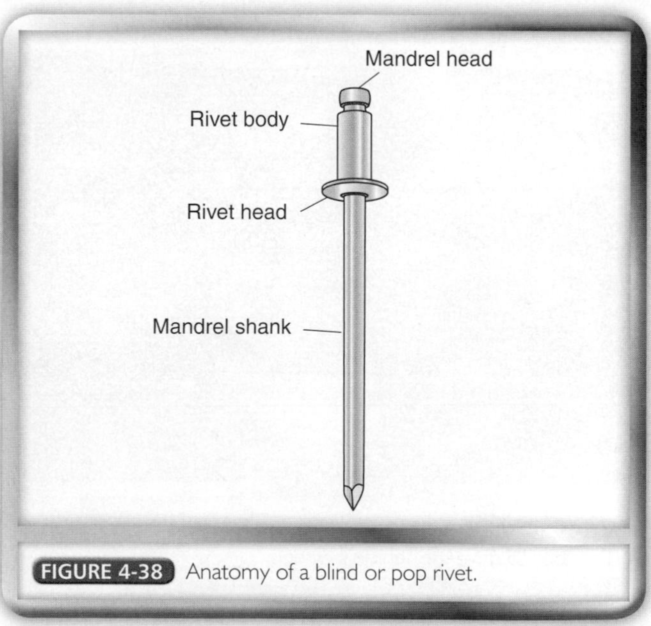

FIGURE 4-38 Anatomy of a blind or pop rivet.

The rivet is inserted into the riveting tool, which, when squeezed, pulls the end of the mandrel back through the body of the rivet. Because the **mandrel head** is bigger than the hole through the body, it swells out as it comes through the body. Finally, the mandrel head will snap off under the pressure and fall out, leaving the rivet body gripping the two sheets of material together.

Diagnostic Equipment

The trucks people drive today have certainly evolved significantly, even over just the last few years. Yet despite all the innovations, emissions from vehicles still harm the environment, as well as human health, and therefore need to be monitored and kept in check.

Truck repair technicians know that vehicle emissions testing and repair remedies are a big part of day-to-day business. In the interest of public health, keeping trucks running clean is a mandate. Low tailpipe emissions also mean a truck is running efficiently, which helps to conserve energy.

Dynamometer

A dynamometer is a machine that measures the torque and power produced by an engine FIGURE 4-39. It applies various loads to an engine and is usually connected to a computer that can analyze and calculate all the aspects of engine operation measured.

Dynamometers are particularly useful in designing and refining engine technology. They can help identify how an engine or its drivetrain needs to be modified or tuned to achieve more efficient power transfer.

There are two types of dynamometer:

- **Engine dynamometer.** The engine dynamometer measures engine performance only, usually when the engine is removed from the vehicle and mounted onto a special frame. It is coupled directly to the engine flywheel and measures performance independent of the vehicle's drivetrain, such as its gearbox, transmission, or differential.
- **Chassis dynamometer.** The chassis dynamometer measures the power from the engine through a vehicle's driven wheels. The whole vehicle is mounted on rollers and fixed to the ground to prevent it jumping when it is driven during testing. The vehicle is driven in gear, and turns the rollers without moving, while its power output is measured.

FIGURE 4-39 A chassis dynamometer. Notice the rollers on the floor to drive the vehicle's wheels.

Safety

In many cases, the vehicle is being operated at full throttle and making maximum horsepower. Always make sure the vehicle is secured effectively and the area is clear of tools, equipment, and people before using a chassis dynamometer. If the vehicle were ever to break free, the resulting accident would be catastrophic.

Pressure Testers/Tire Inflators

There is a range of pressure testers, or gauges, used in the automotive industry. All are used to provide information about the potential condition of various systems and components.

All gauges consist of a measurement scale, from which a reading is taken. Depending on its type of fitting, the gauge is normally fitted to the vehicle component via a pipe or tube. Instructions provided with the gauge describe how to take a correct reading. These should include the specific operational circumstances under which the reading should be taken, to enable correct interpretation of the condition of the item being tested.

Most gauges are designed to read "zero" at atmospheric pressure (1 bar at sea level or 14.7 psi) as a base measurement.

Here are some common types and applications:

- **Tire pressure gauge with attached inflation device.** This type of gauge is the one familiar to most people. Tire pressure gauges are normally part of a tire inflation device and are used to ensure that the air pressure inside a vehicle's tires is maintained at the recommended setting.
- **Tire pressure gauge with no inflation device.** Gauges that only measure—that is, they just check the pressure without being able to inflate as well—are also quite common. FIGURE 4-40 is an example of this type, known as a "pencil-type" pressure gauge.

- **Pressure vacuum gauge.** Pressure vacuum gauges are a particular type of pressure gauge that measures "negative" pressure below atmospheric pressure FIGURE 4-41. They are normally used to determine an engine's general operational condition. Depending on the reading, a number of engine faults can be identified.
- **Pressure compression gauge.** Pressure compression gauges are used to measure the compression pressures inside an engine cylinder and can identify overall condition and pressure leakage situations that could be caused by a range of engine faults FIGURE 4-42.
- **Cooling system pressure gauge.** Cooling system pressure gauges are used to identify faults in cooling systems and components such as pressure caps FIGURE 4-43.

Scan Tools

Essentially, a scan tool ("scanner") is a device able to communicate electronically with and extract data from the vehicle's one or more on-board computers. On-board computer modules include the power control module (PCM), electronic brake control module (EBCM), body control module (BCM), the transmission control module (TCM), and perhaps numerous others. Simple scan tools from the 1980s could read and erase fault codes and little more. Today, such scanners are sold to consumers. But as on-board systems have become more complex, so too have professional-grade scan tools used in the service bay.

Cost and complexity increase commensurate with the bells and whistles desired in a scanner. Technicians today are finding that they must use faster and more accurate diagnostic instruments—like graphing scan tools—

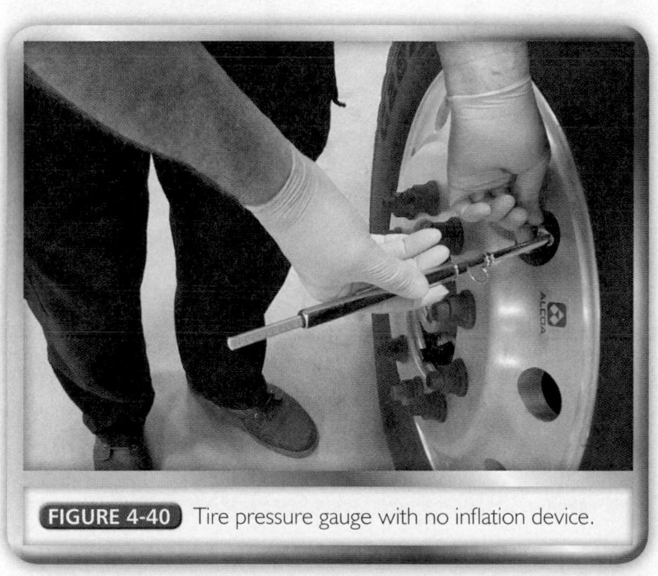

FIGURE 4-40 Tire pressure gauge with no inflation device.

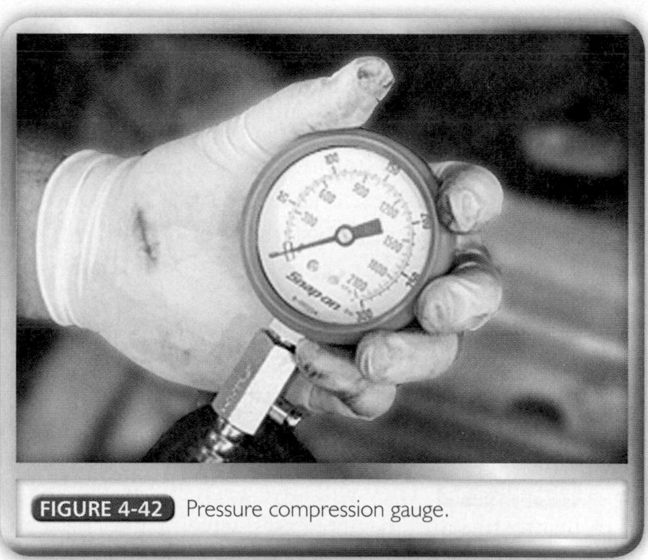

FIGURE 4-42 Pressure compression gauge.

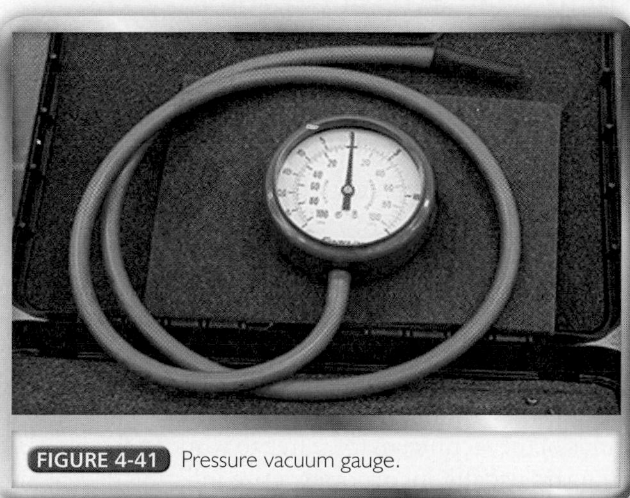

FIGURE 4-41 Pressure vacuum gauge.

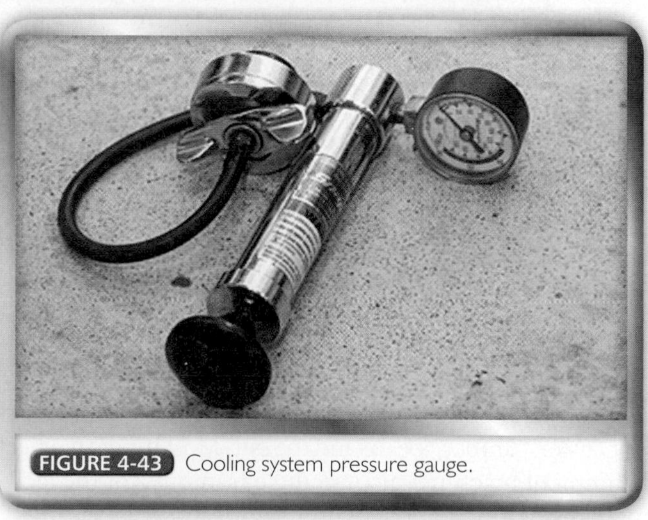

FIGURE 4-43 Cooling system pressure gauge.

to see hidden faults in component or system waveforms. Scanners are now used to monitor engine compression, vacuum, internal engine anomalies, and so forth. They are used to "drive" various components and systems to test for their proper function. Scanners are used—along with digital storage oscilloscopes, portable emissions analyzers, and much more—for effective time-saving diagnostic routines.

Training and experience play a major role in using these modern information-gathering tools effectively. Understanding the principles of combustion theory, internal combustion engine operation, and emissions are essential ingredients for success. Indeed, the field demands extensive training—and also a sizeable investment! As one tool manufacturer has said, "It takes a lot to be a technician!" Opportunities abound for the technician who understands the theory and masters the use of the scanner to quickly and efficiently analyze, diagnose, and solve problems on today's advanced vehicle engine systems.

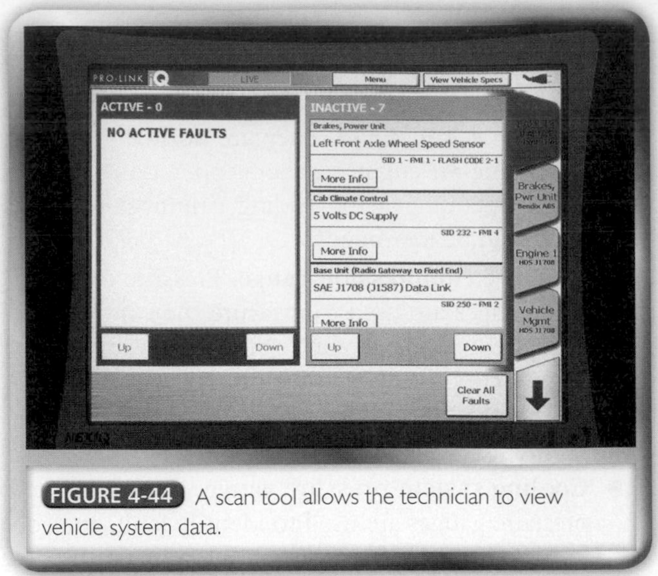

FIGURE 4-44 A scan tool allows the technician to view vehicle system data.

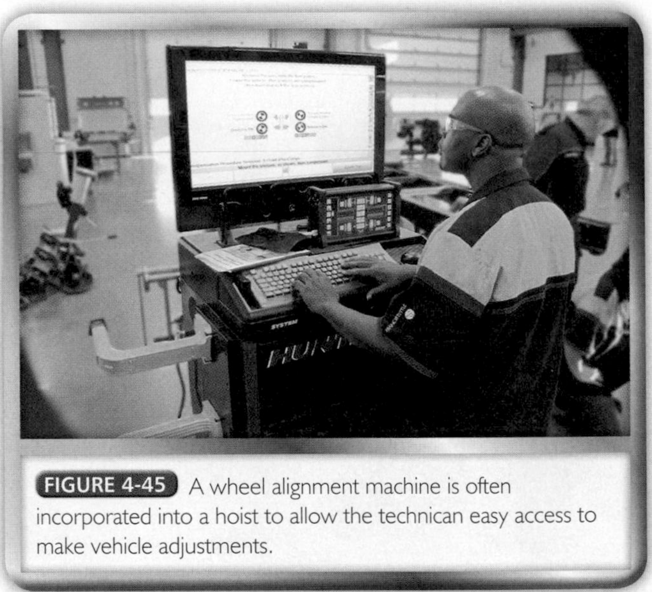

FIGURE 4-45 A wheel alignment machine is often incorporated into a hoist to allow the technican easy access to make vehicle adjustments.

Servicing Equipment

Shops are equipped with machines that help technicians carry out servicing procedures. Those machines include computerized wheel alignment machines, pneumatic tire changing machines, and engine analyzers, which pinpoint faults in engine systems. For disc skimming, there is an on-vehicle lathe, but other skimming jobs are outsourced.

Engine Scanner

An engine scanner is a diagnostic or service tool that is used to view data from the vehicle electronic control systems FIGURE 4-44. They will have a screen for displaying data, test results and in some cases waveforms. The scanner will have a lead that is connected to the vehicle's diagnostic plug. They are used to check the performance of a vehicle's electrical and electronic systems. Some systems will also allow data to be stored on a computer and printed for later analysis or added to vehicle service history.

Wheel Alignment Machine

Wheel alignment systems are often incorporated into a special-purpose vehicle hoist and use light beams with calibration equipment to check vehicle wheel alignment FIGURE 4-45. The hoist allows easy access for the technician to adjust under body components where necessary. The wheel aligner enables technicians to check and adjust for caster, camber, toe in, and toe out. Most modern wheel alignment machines also produce printouts for the technician and customer showing before and after settings.

On-Vehicle Wheel Balancer

On-vehicle wheel balancers do not require the wheel to be removed from the vehicle. The balancer uses an electric motor to run the wheel at speed, and analyzes the wheel's balance, providing a report to the technician on the amount of weights required and their position on the wheel FIGURE 4-46.

Pneumatic Tire Changer

Tire changers are designed to break the bead of the tire and remove and reinstall it on the rim. Pneumatic foot controls are usually used on the tire changer to allow both hands of the technician to be free to work on the tire. Tire changers usually incorporate a tire inflating device and pressure gauge FIGURE 4-47.

FIGURE 4-46 An on-vehicle wheel balancer spins the wheel at speed. The safety shield should always be lowered while the wheel is spinning.

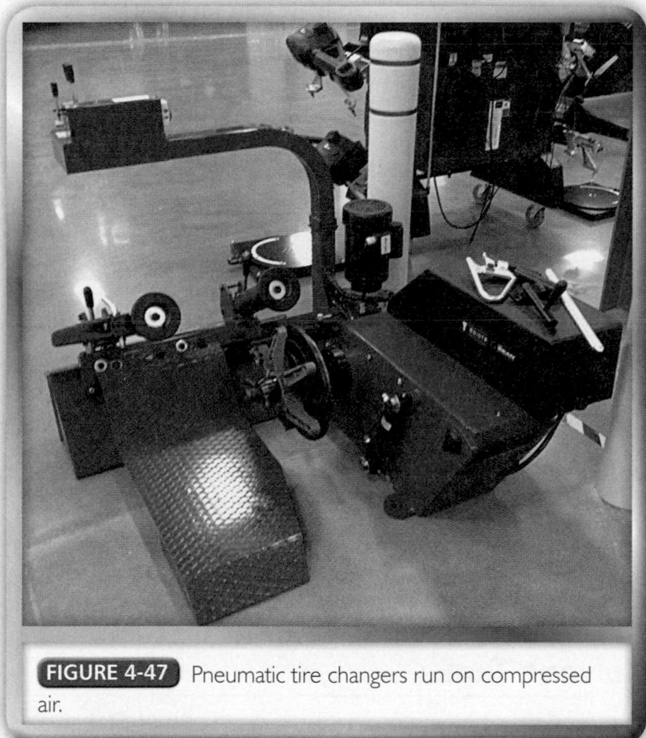

FIGURE 4-47 Pneumatic tire changers run on compressed air.

Drum Disc Lathe

Drum and disc lathes are special purpose lathes designed specifically to machine brake drums and discs FIGURE 4-48. They remove small amounts of metal to refinish the drum or disc surface. It's important not to remove too much material from the drum or disc. Always check manufacturers' specifications for minimum allowable thicknesses of drum and disc.

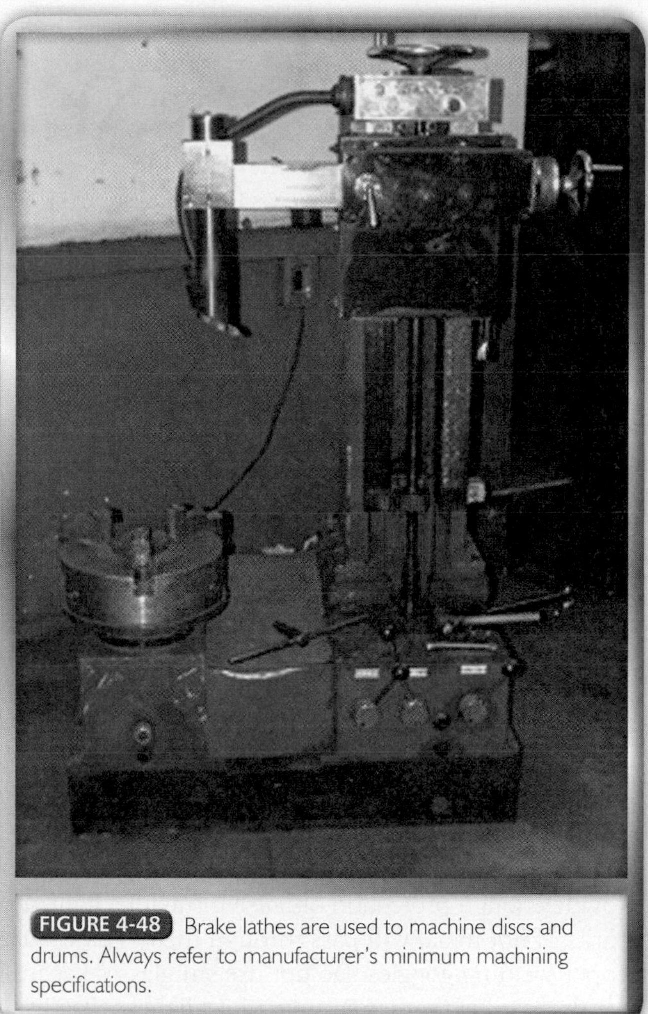

FIGURE 4-48 Brake lathes are used to machine discs and drums. Always refer to manufacturer's minimum machining specifications.

Oxyacetylene

Oxyacetylene torches are occasionally used by technicians to heat, braze, weld, and cut metal. Acetylene is a highly combustible gas, and when combined with oxygen, it produces a very hot temperature of 6300°F to 6800°F (3480°C to 3760°C). Heating is used to loosen rusted fasteners to help remove them. Brazing uses brass filler rod, which is melted by the torch to join or patch metals.

The torch consists of an acetylene cylinder, an oxygen cylinder, a pressure regulator for each cylinder, hoses, a flashback arrestor for each hose, the torch handle, and the tip. The cylinders hold the gases. Each pressure regulator has two pressure gauges. One gauge shows how much pressure is in the cylinder, and the other gauge shows how much pressure is in the line. The line (hose) pressure is adjusted on the pressure regulator by the operator. The hoses run from each regulator to the flashback arrestors on the torch handle. The acetylene hose is red, and the oxygen hose is blue. The **flashback arrestors** are spring-loaded check valves that allow flow through the hoses in one direction only—from the cylinders to the torch handle. They prevent flame from travelling back up the hose in the case of a flashback, which is when the oxygen and acetylene ignite inside the torch handle. Flashback happens if the torch valves are set lower than they should be for a particular tip, which produces low gas flow out of the tip; if a welding spark jumps up into the tip; or if the torch is set with too much oxygen flowing. The torch handle usually has the flashback arrestors screwed into it. The gas flow valves are also near the base of the handle. The top of the handle is threaded so that different tips can be installed.

Oxyacetylene Torch Safety

Safety needs to be first and foremost when working with an oxyacetylene torch. Oxyacetylene cylinders carry very high pressures. The acetylene pressure in a full cylinder is approximately 250 psi (1724 kPa), and the oxygen cylinder is approximately 2200 psi (15,168 kPa). If an oxygen cylinder falls over and breaks the main valve off, the cylinder will become a missile and can even go through concrete block walls, so always secure the cylinders properly to the wall or an approved welding cart.

Wear a leather apron or similar protective clothing and welding gloves when using an oxyacetylene torch. T-shirts or nylon- and polyester-blend clothing will not provide enough protection because ultraviolet light and sparks of hot metal will pass through them. Always use proper welding goggles. Do not use sunglasses because they do not filter the extreme ultraviolet light as effectively and the plastic used in the lenses of sunglasses will not protect your eyes from sparks.

Never point the lighted flame towards another person or any flammable material. Always light the oxyacetylene torch with the striker. A cigarette lighter could explode, and a match would put your hand too close to the igniting tip. Wherever possible, use a heat shield behind the component you are heating. This will prevent nearby objects from becoming hot. After heating a piece of metal, label it as "HOT" with a piece of chalk so that others will not attempt to pick it up.

 Cleaning Equipment

Pressure Washers and Cleaners

Pressure washers/cleaners are a valuable tool in the shop for cleaning vehicles, engine compartments, and components. They can be powered by an electric motor or a petroleum engine fitted to a high-pressure pump. The pressure washer takes water at normal pressure and boosts it through the high-pressure pump to exit through a cleaning gun, which has a control trigger. The **cleaning gun** has a high-pressure nozzle that focuses high pressure water (possibly over 2,000 psi or 13 790 kPa) to clean accumulated dirt and grease from components quickly. Some pressure washers have a provision for detergent to be injected into the high-pressure output to clean more effectively. Others have the ability to heat the water, in some cases hot enough to turn it to steam. Hot water and steam help loosen oil and grease buildup.

Pressure washers are dangerous because of their high pressure and possibly high temperature. Always wear appropriate PPE when working with pressure cleaners—for example, goggles or face shield, protective gloves, close-fitting clothes with long sleeves, full-length trousers, and leather-type boots or shoes.

Because pressure washers spray water at very high pressures, it is important that the water jet is directed properly. It can peel the paint off painted surfaces if the nozzle is brought too close to the surface. It can also damage soft parts such as labels and rubber hoses. Some components can be harmed by water, such as paper filters and some electronic components, including electronic control units, and ignition coils. You may need to cover those devices with plastic bags.

Spray-Wash Cabinets

Spray-wash cabinets spray high-temperature, high-pressure cleaning solutions onto parts inside a sealed cabinet. They are automated and act like a dishwasher for parts. This significantly reduces the labor required to clean parts because once the door is closed and they are turned on, the technician is free to move on to other tasks. They are available in a variety of sizes to cater to different-sized parts, and provide a high level of cleaning performance. The cleaning solution is designed to clean effectively without leaving residue on the parts, and most spray cabinets are fitted with a filtering system to reduce the frequency of cleaning solution changes.

Solvent Tanks

A **solvent tank** is a cleaning tank that is filled with a suitable solvent to clean parts by removing oil, grease, dirt, and grime. Solvent tanks are available in different sizes. Many solvent tanks have a pump that pushes solvent out of a nozzle into a sink, where it can be directed to the parts being cleaned. A brush either on the nozzle or separate from it can be used to loosen the grease and grime. The solvent falls back into the bottom of the solvent tank, where the heavier residue settles to the bottom. Other solvent tanks are designed so that parts can be immersed into the tank on racks or suspended on pieces of wire, and slowly lowered and soaked in the tank for a period of time. Some solvent tanks may have an agitation system or use a heated cleaning fluid to speed up the process. They may also have a circulation system and filters to remove debris and residue in the solvent to extend its life between changes.

Brake Washers

Brake washers are used to wash brake dust from wheel brake units and their components. Because it is possible that the brake dust may contain asbestos, which is a cancer-causing agent, and because dust in general is a lung irritant, brake washers are designed to capture the brake dust before it enters the shop environment. It does so by wetting down the dust on the brake parts and then washing it into the cleaning tray. Brake washers incorporate a built-in waste recovery system where the contaminated washer fluids can be captured to enable disposal in an environmentally friendly manner.

Brake washers are normally designed to operate at low pressure and use a range of cleaning agents. The most popular agent is an aqueous solution made up of water and a water-soluble detergent. A low-pressure air blower may be provided to remove the fluid from the component into the tray area and then back to the tank by gravity.

Avoid using solvent when cleaning brake components, as it contaminates friction materials and may cause seals to swell. Never use paraffin oil as a general cleaning agent to clean brake components, as it does not clean away brake fluid, can be absorbed into lining materials, and can cause seals to swell. Water is a good cleaning agent for brake components.

Sand or Bead Blasters

<u>Sand or bead blasters</u> use high pressure to blast small abrasive particles to clean the surface of parts. The most common method of propelling the sand or glass beads is with compressed air. In shops, sand or bead blasting can occur in a specially designed cabinet, or there are portable models that are available for use in open-air situations. The cabinets contain the blasting operation in a controlled, safe environment and are best for smaller parts that can fit into the cabinet. Portable systems that do not operate within a cabinet can blast larger parts but do require more protection for the operator and surrounding environment.

The sand or bead blaster cabinet is fitted with a hand-operated blasting nozzle, a viewing port, and an on/off switch (often this may be a foot-operated switch), and it has openings with tough rubber gloves sealed into them to allow a technician's hands to be inside the cabinet while being protected from the abrasive sand or beads. Wet sand or bead blasters are also available, and have the additional advantage of reducing the amount of dust and providing additional cleaning to the part being cleaned.

Electrical Equipment

Multimeters **FIGURE 4-49**, which are also known as digital volt-ohmmeters (DVOMs), and oscilloscopes **FIGURE 4-50** are electrical measuring tools frequently used to diagnose and repair electrical faults. Like many diagnostic tools, practice is required to understand how the multimeter and oscilloscope are used to take

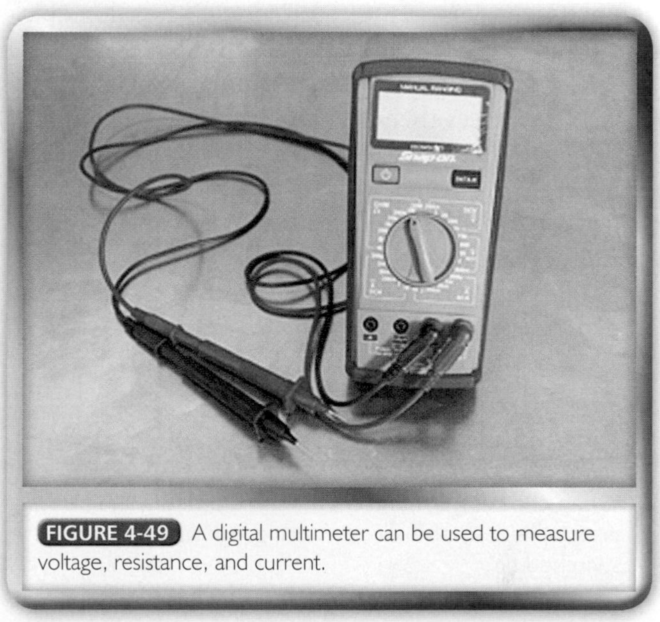

FIGURE 4-49 A digital multimeter can be used to measure voltage, resistance, and current.

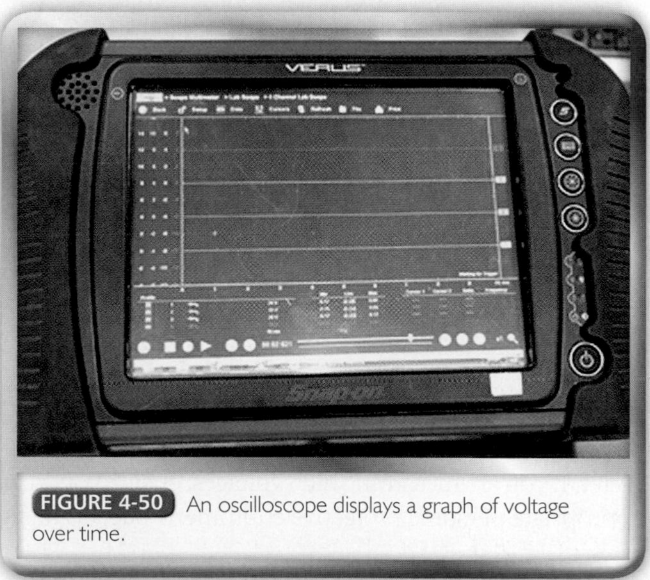

FIGURE 4-50 An oscilloscope displays a graph of voltage over time.

electrical measurements, and how to connect them into electrical circuits to ensure correct readings are obtained. Once a reading is obtained, it needs to be interpreted and applied to diagnose the circuit under test. This section provides an explanation of how to use and set up a multimeter for measuring voltage, current, and resistance.

Using Ohm's Law to Diagnose Circuits

Ohm's law is used to calculate electrical quantities in an electrical circuit and is valuable as a way of cross-checking actual measured results within a circuit. For example, if the resistance and voltage of a circuit is known, then the theoretical current can be calculated using Ohm's law. The calculated result can then be compared to the measured results from an ammeter to determine whether the circuit is functioning correctly. Technicians will often do a quick calculation, in their heads, to obtain an approximate value of an electrical quantity before they take actual measurements. This gives them a good indication of what they will be measuring and allows them to set the measuring tool to the correct range. Always remember that a calculation may be only an approximate value because, in actual circuits, variation or tolerances exist in components, causing some variation between calculated values and actual measurements.

> **TECHNICIAN TIP**
>
> When checking continuity with a multimeter, the power supplied to the circuit during operation must be switched *off*.

Electrical Testing Equipment

Using a Multimeter to Measure Voltage

The electrical system is becoming increasingly complex on modern vehicles, and measuring voltages with a multimeter is a very common task when diagnosing electrical faults. For most measurements, set the multimeter to auto range for ease of use. Select multimeter leads and probe ends to match the task at hand; for example, if you need to take a measurement but require both hands to be free, use probe ends with crocodile clips. Ensure that you do not exceed the maximum allowable voltage or current for the multimeter. If you are measuring high voltages, ensure you wear appropriate personal protective equipment, such as high-voltage safety gloves, long-sleeved shirts, long trousers and protective eyewear, and remove any personal jewelry, or items that may cause an accidental short circuit.

Checking a Circuit with a Test Light

Non-powered test lights are useful in determining the live part of a circuit; however, make sure that the circuit voltage you are testing is not higher than the test light is rated for, otherwise the test light could be damaged. Most test lights are rated for 6- or 12-volt systems, and using them in a 24-volt system will usually blow out the bulb. You should never use a test light to test SRS (Supplemental Restraint Systems), as unintended deployment of the airbags could result—a very dangerous and costly mistake. In addition, using a test light on a computer circuit designed for very small amounts of current flow can damage the circuit.

Checking a Circuit with Fused Jump Leads

Jump leads may be used in a number of ways to assist in checking circuits. They can be created by the technician or purchased in a range of sizes, lengths, and fittings, or connectors. They are used to extend connections to allow circuit readings or tests to be undertaken with a multimeter, scope, current clamps on fuses, relays, and connector plugs on components. In some circumstances, jump leads may provide an alternative current or ground source for components under test. Regardless of their application, it is important that the circuit remain protected by a fuse of the correct size. To determine the correct size of fuse required for any particular application, refer to the manufacturer's information.

Locating Opens, Shorts, Grounds, and High Resistance

Multimeters, test lights, and simulated loads tend to be the tools used most often for locating opens, shorts, grounds, and high-resistance faults. An **open circuit** is a break in the electrical circuit where either the power supply or ground circuit has been interrupted. Most open circuits can be located by testing along the circuit at various points to test for power, and at the ground point to check for an effective ground. Perform a systematic check of the circuit by first checking the voltages at the component, if possible. Analysis of the readings will usually dictate the next point to be checked.

Shorts or **short circuits** may occur anywhere in the circuit and can be difficult to locate, especially if they are intermittent. A short is a circuit fault where current travels along an accidental or unintended route. The short may occur to ground or to supply voltage. A short to ground causes low circuit resistance. The low-resistance fault would cause an abnormally high current flow in the circuit and could cause the circuit-protection devices, such as fuses or circuit breakers, to open circuit. A short to supply voltage may cause the circuit to remain live even after the switch is turned off. For example, a short between a fuse with power on all the time and a fuse switched by the ignition switch would cause the circuit controlled by the ignition switch to remain on after the switch is turned off. Shorts may be caused by faulty components or damaged wiring.

Grounds is a term often used in conjunction with shorts and is usually a reference to a short to ground. An initial test may be conducted by carrying out resistance checks or by disconnecting the load. To test the blower motor, for example, disconnect the blower motor and, if the short is still in place, then the wiring between the fuse or circuit breaker and the load must be at fault. To further narrow down the site of the short to ground, inspect the wiring harness, looking for obvious signs of damage. Another test may be conducted by connecting a test lamp or buzzer in place of a fuse: current will flow through the test lamp or buzzer and find a ground through the short; parts of the circuit may then be disconnected along the wiring harness to narrow down the location of the short. Specialized short-circuit detection tools are also available. They work by injecting a signal into the wiring where a short is suspected. A receiving device is then moved along the wiring loom and indicates where a short is located. This type of device is very useful in situations where it is difficult to access the wiring; for example, under guards or vehicle trim.

High resistance refers to a circuit where there is unintended resistance, which then causes a fault. It can be caused by a number of problems; for example, corroded or loose harness connectors, incorrectly sized cable for the circuit current flow, incorrectly fitted terminals, and poorly soldered joints. The high resistance causes an unintended voltage drop in a circuit when the current flows. The high-resistance fault reduces the current flow in the circuit, affecting its performance. It can be located by conducting a resistance check with a multimeter, or by checking for voltage drop in the power and ground circuits. Resistance checks are initial tests undertaken on components—for example, testing the resistance of a fuel injector or ignition coil—but should always be followed up with working tests, using a multimeter or oscilloscope. Due to the relatively low resistance of wires, it is usually more effective to conduct voltage-drop tests while the load current is flowing through the circuits.

To locate opens, shorts, grounds, and high resistance, follow these steps:

1. Identify the circuit to be checked and conduct a visual inspection.
2. Select and set up appropriate test equipment, and determine the type and location of the fault: opens, shorts, grounds, or high resistance.
3. Determine and perform the necessary actions.

Using an Alternator Test Bench

An alternator test bench is normally compact and should be easy to use for fast and accurate testing of a wide range of alternators and starter motors. The test bench can be operated at two speeds, ensuring thorough testing both at higher and lower speeds. It can also include vacuum testing.

A good test bench should have many of the specific features, such as a built-in power source, thus eliminating the need for external batteries. It must be capable of testing 12-volt and 24-volt systems with a digital ammeter/voltmeter FIGURE 4-51.

Battery Chargers

There are many different types of **battery chargers**, and each is designed for a particular purpose and application. **Fast chargers** have high current output to charge a **battery** quickly. **Slow chargers** take longer to charge a battery and have lower current outputs; they put less stress on the battery, which is ideal if time is not a consideration. **Smart chargers** incorporate microprocessors to monitor

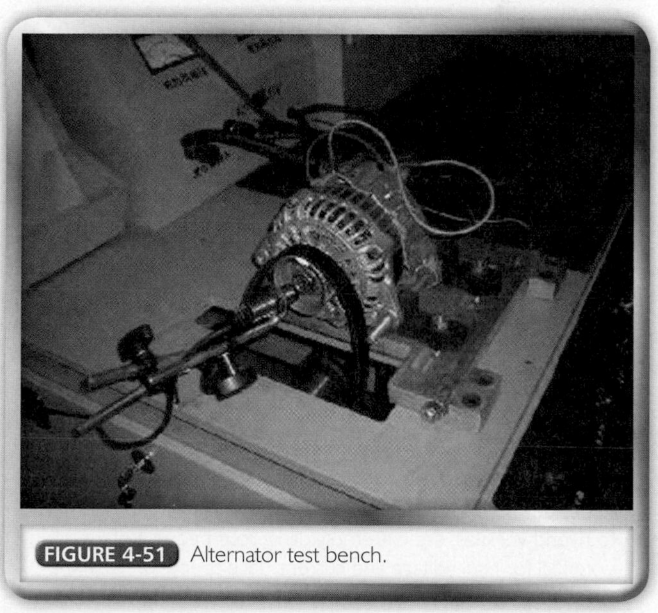

FIGURE 4-51 Alternator test bench.

and control the charge rate so that the battery receives the correct amount of charge according to its state of charge. These types of chargers are becoming more popular; they ensure that the battery receives the optimal charge, thus promoting longer battery life.

Even though a motor vehicle battery is typically 12 volts, it stores a lot of energy. The high-current supply from a battery can be very dangerous. Remember, batteries have to deliver enough power to crank over a cold engine. They also produce enough power to melt a metal rod resting across the terminals. High-voltage battery packs, like those fitted to hybrid vehicles, are even more dangerous because of the potential for high voltage and current, so special precautions for dealing with high-voltage systems must be taken FIGURE 4-52. Always treat batteries with care and respect.

Safety

High voltages used in a hybrid vehicle are extremely dangerous. The voltage and current flow is several times greater than that needed to kill a person. Most hybrid manufacturers require technicians to undergo special factory training before they will allow them to service a hybrid vehicle. They usually allow only very experienced technicians to undergo the training, not novices. In fact, one of the tools that Toyota requires of their shops for working on a hybrid vehicle is a non-conductive shepherd's hook. This can be used to drag a technician away from high voltage if the technician is electrocuted while working on the vehicle.

Battery Safety

Batteries give off hydrogen gas while they are being charged, and for some time afterwards. Hydrogen is a light and highly explosive gas that is easily ignited by a simple spark. Batteries are filled with **sulfuric acid**, so if the hydrogen does explode, the battery case can then rupture and spray everything and everyone nearby with this dangerous and corrosive liquid.

TECHNICIAN TIP

Always remove your hand, wrist, and neck jewelry before working with batteries and electrical systems. If jewelery comes into contact with the battery terminals or power wire, it can cause a short circuit. You will receive painful skin burns from the very rapid heating of the metal you are wearing, or even flash burns from an arcing current. A wristwatch or ring is much harder to take off when it is red- or white-hot and burned onto your skin!

Be very careful not to create a spark when you are connecting or disconnecting battery cables or hooking up a charger to the battery terminals. Switch off the charger before connecting and disconnecting them from the battery FIGURE 4-53.

Do not try to charge a battery faster than the battery manufacturer recommends, and never use a battery load tester immediately after charging a battery. This is because

FIGURE 4-52 High-voltage battery packs, like those fitted to hybrid vehicles, are extremely dangerous because of the potential for high voltage and current. Take special precautions when dealing with high-voltage systems.

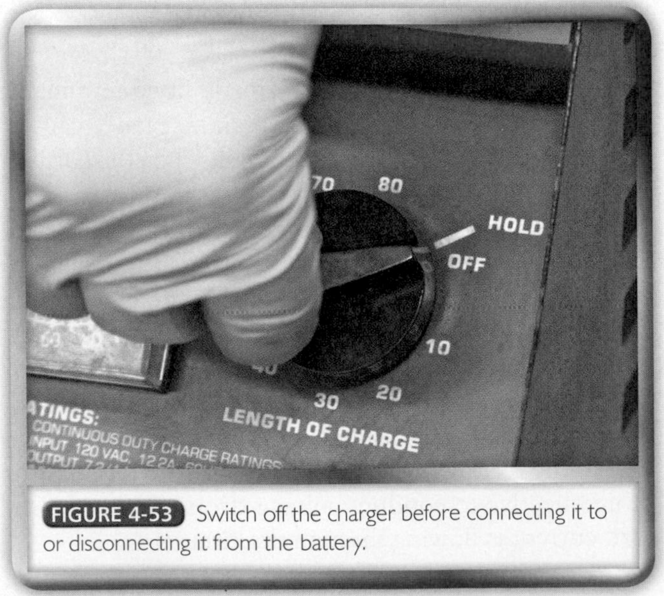

FIGURE 4-53 Switch off the charger before connecting it to or disconnecting it from the battery.

both charging and rapidly discharging a battery generate heat and hydrogen. If you load-test a battery after charging it without waiting for it to cool down, you will increase the risk of distorting the plates inside the battery, as well as increase the risk of explosion.

Fluids and Lubricants

Reducing friction and cooling are the primary functions of fluids and lubricants. This section outlines the key fluids used to keep vehicles running smoothly and introduces the use of alternative fuels.

Anti-Freeze

All truck engines currently on the market are liquid-cooled engines. A liquid-cooled system uses **coolant**, a fluid that contains special anti-freezing and anti-corrosion chemicals mixed with water FIGURE 4-54.

Water alone is by far the best coolant there is because it can absorb a larger amount of heat than most other liquids. But water has some drawbacks. It freezes if its temperature drops to 0°C (the temperature at which water becomes a solid). As water freezes, it expands into a solid. If it expands in the coolant passages inside the engine, these passages—typically made of cast aluminum or cast iron—will not flex to allow expansion and will break. This renders the engine inoperative and unrepairable in most cases.

Another thing to realize about using water alone as a coolant is that water is corrosive and causes metal to rust. Anti-freeze prevents corrosion and rusting through anti-corrosion additives (called corrosion inhibitors) mixed into the solution. Another important note on water is that water contains minerals and will potentially lead to excessive deposits, even when added to anti-freeze. Because of this, most manufacturers recommend using distilled water for cooling systems.

Anti-freeze is mixed with water to lower the freezing point of water and reduce the chances of cracking the engine block, cylinder heads, and other cooling system components. Anti-freeze is made from one of two base chemicals—ethylene glycol or propylene glycol—plus a mixture of additives to protect against corrosion and foaming. Ethylene and propylene glycol may achieve a maximum very low freezing point of -71°F (-57°C) when mixed with the appropriate amount of water. **Ethylene glycol** is a chemical that resists freezing but is very toxic to people and animals. **Propylene glycol** is another chemical that resists freezing but is not toxic and is used in nontoxic anti-freezes. Either of these anti-freezes will actually freeze at around -0.4°F (-18°C) if not mixed with water, so water is a necessary part of coolant. The freezing point of coolant will vary depending upon how much water is added to the anti-freeze. Because anti-freeze does not absorb heat as effectively as water, it should not be mixed at a ratio higher than 65% anti-freeze and 35% water. Using a higher proportion of anti-freeze will actually reduce the cooling quality of the mixture and raise the operating temperature of the engine FIGURE 4-55.

The best coolant is a 50/50 balance of water and anti-freeze, making it an ideal coolant for both hot and cold climates and providing adequate corrosion protection. In addition, when anti-freeze is added at a 50% mixture,

FIGURE 4-54 Coolant is a fluid that contains special anti-freezing and anti-corrosion chemicals mixed with water.

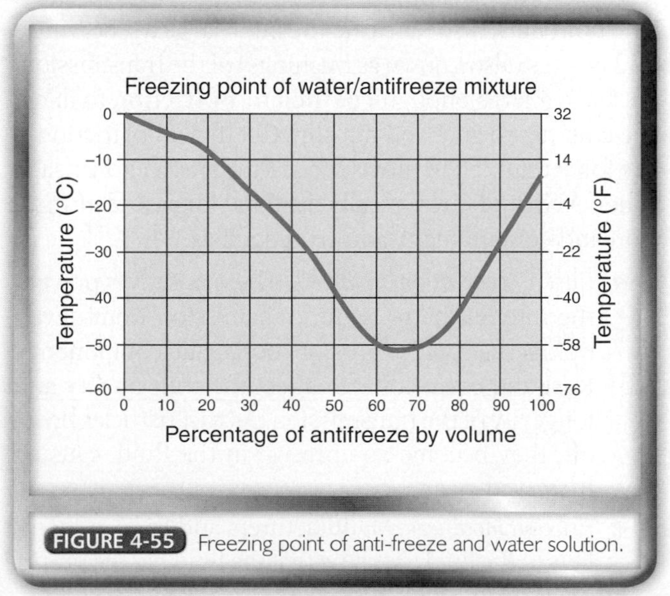

FIGURE 4-55 Freezing point of anti-freeze and water solution.

the boiling point increases to around 228°F (109°C). As you can see, this is an extremely beneficial characteristic of anti-freeze as manufacturers continue to build engines that are more powerful, create more heat, and operate at higher temperatures.

Anti-freeze can be purchased as straight anti-freeze (100%) or as a 50/50 premix with water. Straight anti-freeze that you buy from the dealer or parts store consists of three parts: glycol (around 96%), corrosion inhibitors and additives (around 2–3%), and water (around 2%). Glycol, as discussed previously, keeps the freezing point low and the boiling point high. Corrosion inhibitors and additives prevent corrosion and erosion, resist foaming, ensure coolant is compatible with cooling system component materials and hard water, resist sedimentation, and balance the acid-to-alkaline content of the anti-freeze. Water is added to blend the inhibitors with the glycol.

Anti-freeze is an amazing chemical that performs a monumental task in the operation of our vehicles. It works so well that it is often overlooked for maintenance by the customer. However, because the additives wear out and become less effective over time, coolant does need to be changed at recommended intervals. Doing so reduces the possibility of engine damage and failure over time. Similarly, lubrication enhancers, which keep the water pump and seals functioning properly, wear out and need to be replaced.

Automatic Transmission Fluid (ATF)

Automatic transmission fluid (ATF) is a specialized fluid that has been designed for a specific job. The ATF must be able to transfer heat from the internal components of the transmission to the transmission cooler to prevent damaging the internal seals of the transmission **FIGURE 4-56**. The fluid must also lubricate the internal gears, bearings, and bushes (also known as bushings) of the transmission, yet have a large enough **coefficient of friction** to allow the clutches to grab and not slip. Coefficient of friction is the force required to move two sliding surfaces over each other. ATF fluids are typically dyed red for easy identification and contain many additives such as:

- *Rust and corrosion inhibitors:* These additives prevent the internal parts of the transmission from developing rust and corrosion on metal components. Rust and corrosion can affect the shift quality and longevity of the transmission. As rust particles break off, they become an abrasive in the fluid, causing increased wear.
- *Friction modifiers:* Manufacturers add friction modifiers to the fluid to ensure that the fluid has the proper coefficient of friction to produce the desired shift quality. A fluid with a lower coefficient of friction will produce softer, longer shifts, causing an increase in clutch slippage. A fluid with a higher coefficient of friction will cause shorter, harsher shifts, reducing clutch slippage but increasing driveline shock.
- *Seal conditioners:* These additives are designed to help protect the seals inside a transmission and cause the seals to swell slightly to help prevent leaks and clutch slippage.
- *Detergents:* ATF has a large amount of detergent to prevent dirt and other foreign particles from becoming trapped inside the transmission. The detergent causes the dirt and other particles to be attracted to the fluid so they transfer with the fluid. When the fluid passes through the filter, the large particles become trapped in the filter; the small particles are removed during the next transmission fluid change.
- *Anti-foam:* These additives help to prevent foaming of the transmission fluid. When moving parts spin through a fluid, they tend to produce air bubbles. These air bubbles can quickly multiply and become foam. Foam is compressible and can cause

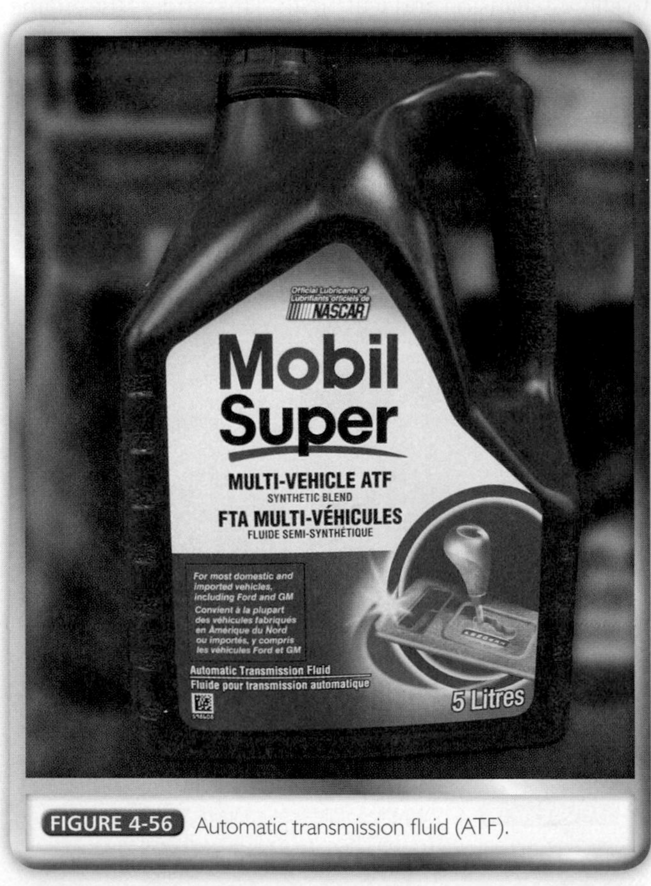

FIGURE 4-56 Automatic transmission fluid (ATF).

a transmission to slip because insufficient pressure is applied to the clutches.

- *Viscosity modifiers:* These additives are similar to the engine oil additives that allow us to have multiviscosity engine oils such as 5W-30. These additives allow the fluid to remain thin when the temperature is cold and prevent the fluid from becoming too thin as the transmission fluid warms up.

ATFs can be mineral oil-based or a synthetic lubricant. Many late-model trucks recommend a specific synthetic ATF. In the past few decades, most vehicle manufacturers have developed their own fluids for use in their transmissions. This practice has required repair facilities to carry many different types of fluids. Some shops carry a few major types of fluids and use those in every vehicle, but that is not recommended as it may cause undesirable transmission operation and may void the transmission warranty. Several vehicle manufacturers have published technical service bulletins (TSBs) related to incorrect fluid use and the negative effects on the transmission.

ATF needs to be changed periodically to remove dirt and contaminants from the transmission. Technicians used to tell whether the transmission fluid needed to be changed by looking at and smelling the fluid. If the fluid was dark or smelled burnt, it needed to be changed. You cannot determine the condition of modern ATF by looks and smell. Some newer synthetic fluids will have a burnt smell when they are brand new and are often darker than mineral-based ATF. To check ATF for contaminants, drop a few drops of transmission fluid onto a white paper towel. The fluid will spread out on the paper towel, but the contaminants will remain where the fluid was dropped.

Acid and Alkali

The main use of sulfuric acid in the industry is in the construction of batteries. Sulfuric acid is mixed with distilled water to create an electrolyte, which is used in a lead-acid battery to store electrical energy. Batteries were developed in the early 1800s, and since that time many varieties and designs have been developed. The battery is part of everyday life and is widely used in modern electrical and electronic devices. Batteries store electricity in chemical form, which is possible because electricity causes a chemical reaction within the battery. In other words, the electrical energy is transformed into chemical energy **FIGURE 4-57**.

The traditional vehicle battery type is the lead-acid battery. Although it is available in many types, all types have the same basic components as shown in **FIGURE 4-58** including two dissimilar metals, an insulator material separating the metals, and an electrolyte.

Lead-Acid Flooded Cell Battery

The wet cell lead-acid battery is the main storage device in use. It is called a *flooded cell battery* because the lead plates are immersed in a water-acid electrolyte solution. A typical battery can supply very high discharge currents while maintaining a high voltage, which is useful when cold starting. It gives a high power output for its compact size, and it is rechargeable.

The standard 12-volt battery consists of six cells connected in series. Each cell has a nominal 2.1 volts, for a total of 12.6 volts for a fully charged "12-volt" battery. Each cell contains two sets of electrodes (called plates), one set of lead (Pb) and the other set of lead dioxide (PbO_2), in an electrolyte solution of diluted sulfuric acid (H_2SO_4). As the battery discharges, the sulfuric acid is

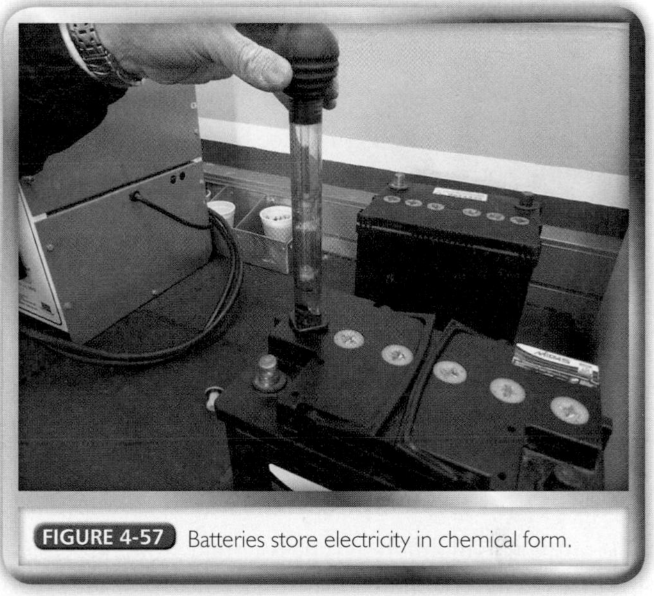

FIGURE 4-57 Batteries store electricity in chemical form.

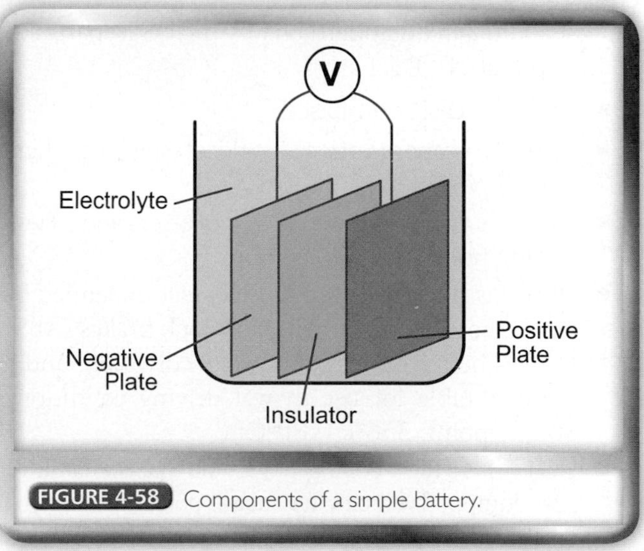

FIGURE 4-58 Components of a simple battery.

absorbed into the lead plates and both of the plates slowly turn into lead sulphate. At the same time, the strength of the electrolyte becomes less acidic as the acid is absorbed into the plates. Recharging the battery reverses this process.

Alkalis are a chemical compound—bi-carb of soda is an example—which are used to neutralise acidic compounds. For example, bi-carb is used to clean battery terminals. A substance is rated acidic or alkaline on a pH scale. Alkalis have a pH value greater than 7.

Brake Fluid

Hydraulic and air-over-hydraulic brakes use a special brake fluid, which is a special-purpose high-boiling-point fluid. It transmits the hydraulic pressure generated by the master cylinder to the brake units FIGURE 4-59.

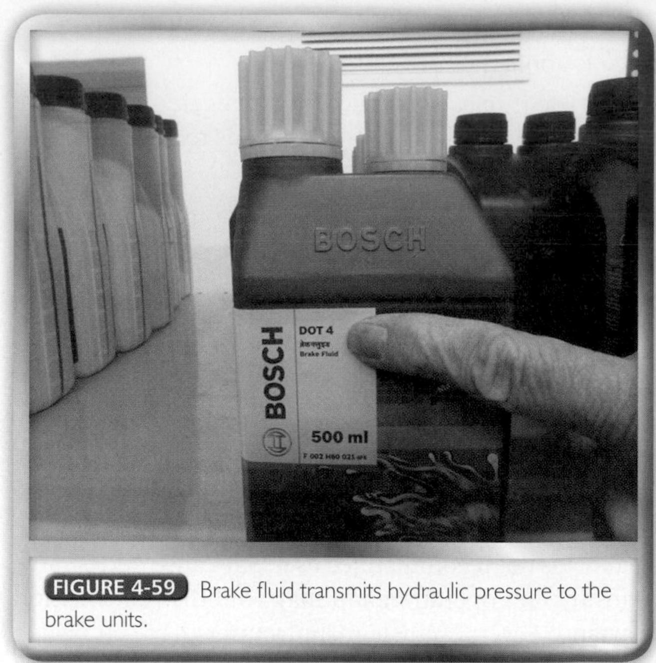

FIGURE 4-59 Brake fluid transmits hydraulic pressure to the brake units.

Brake fluid is hydraulic fluid that has specific properties. The fluid is used to transfer force while under pressure through hydraulic lines to the wheel braking system.

Braking applications produce heat, so the fluid used must have both a high boiling point to remain effective and a low freezing point so as not to freeze or thicken in cold conditions.

Brake fluid is **hygroscopic**, which means it absorbs water from the atmosphere. This will gradually reduce its boiling point, so the fluid should be changed periodically to remove water and other contaminants and to ensure the continued effectiveness of the braking system FIGURE 4-60.

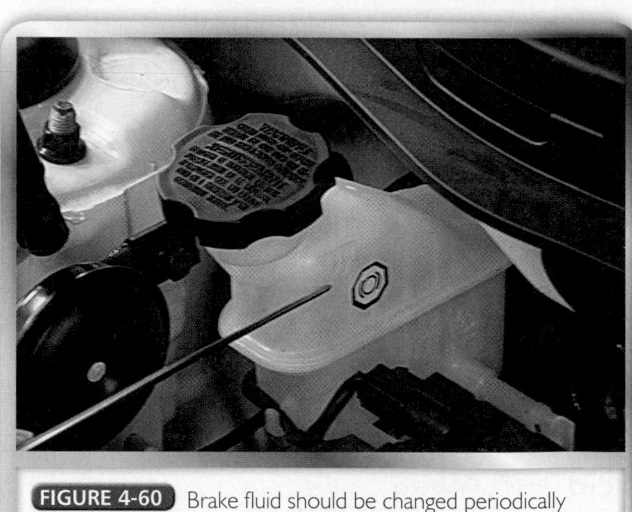
FIGURE 4-60 Brake fluid should be changed periodically to remove water and other contaminants and to ensure the continued effectiveness of the braking system.

Brake Fluid DOT Specifications

The properties of different types of brake fluids are tested for many different characteristics, such as pH value, viscosity, resistance to oxidation, and stability, and graded against compliance standards set by the US Department of Transportation (DOT):

- DOT 2 is castor oil-based.
- DOT 3 is composed of various glycol esters and ethers. Boiling point: 284°F (140°C)
- DOT 4 is also composed of glycol esters and ethers. Boiling point: 311°F (155°C)
- DOT 5 is silicone-based. It is *not* recommended for any vehicle equipped with anti-lock brakes (ABS). It gives better protection against corrosion, and is more suitable for use in wet driving conditions. Boiling point: 356°F (180°C)
- DOT 5.1 is a high-boiling-point fluid that is suitable for ABS-equipped vehicles. It contains polyalkylene glycol ether, but is more expensive than other brake fluids. Boiling point: 375°F (190.6°C).

> **TECHNICIAN TIP**
>
> Even if they have similar base composition, fluids with different DOT ratings must not be mixed.

Diesel Oil

Diesel fuel oil is a derivative of **crude** oil that is used to power diesel engines, also known as compression ignition or CI engines FIGURE 4-61. Diesel fuel is produced as a fractional distillate of crude oil between 392°F and 662°F (200°C and 350°C). Ultra-low sulfur diesel (ULSD) is commonly used in passenger vehicles in Europe, the USA, and Canada. The principal measure of diesel fuel quality is its cetane number. A higher cetane number indicates that the fuel ignites more readily when sprayed into hot compressed air. European (EN 590 standard) road diesel has a minimum cetane number of 51. Fuels with higher cetane numbers, normally "premium" diesel fuels with additional cleaning agents and some synthetic content, are available in some markets.

Biodiesel

Biodiesel is renewable fuel made by chemically combining natural oils from soybeans (or cottonseeds, canola, etc.; animal fats; or even recycled cooking oil) with an alcohol such as methanol (or ethanol).

Biodiesel fuels are usually more expensive than petrodiesel, but biodiesel burns with less particulate and with no sulfur or aldehydes, producing less harmful and irritating tailpipe emissions. NO_X sometimes increases with biodiesel, but after-treatment devices benefit from the lack of sulfur in biodiesel. The improved lubricity and zero sulfur content of biodiesel result in longer maintenance intervals, longer engine, and fuel system life and lower emissions.

Biodiesel fuel is compatible with petrodiesel and may be used 100% (B100) in place of petrodiesel, or may be blended with petrodiesel. A typical blend would be 20% biodiesel with 80% petrodiesel fuel (B20).

Biodiesel tends to clean petrodiesel residues from the fuel system, so fuel filters may require frequent servicing for the first few tank fills. Alcohol-based alternative fuels are used extensively in light duty passenger vehicles but have not found widespread acceptance in the heavy vehicle industry. In some countries, the trucking industry instead is more reliant on biodiesel blends, such as B20.

In South Africa, heavy vehicles run only on diesel.

Engine Oil

Engine oil reduces unwanted friction. It reduces wear on moving parts, and helps cool an engine. It also absorbs shock loads and acts as a cleaning agent **FIGURE 4-62**:

- Clearances fill with oil so that engine parts move or float on layers of oil instead of directly on each other. Much less power is needed to move them.
- Oil helps cool an engine. It collects heat from the engine, and then returns to the sump, where it cools.
- It helps absorb shock loads. A diesel engine's power stroke can suddenly put as much as 15 tons of force on main bearings. Layers of oil cushion this loading.
- Oil is also a cleaning agent. It collects particles of metal and carbon and carries them back to the oil filter to be suspended until the filter is replaced.

FIGURE 4-61 Diesel oil is a derivative of crude oil that is used to power diesel engines.

FIGURE 4-62 Engine oil reduces unwanted friction, reduces wear on moving parts, helps cool an engine, and acts as a cleaning agent.

For oil to do all of the work that is expected of it, it must have special properties. Its viscosity is crucial. *Viscosity* is a measure of how easily a liquid flows. Low-viscosity liquid is thin and flows easily. High-viscosity liquid is thick and flows slowly. Lubricating oil must be thin enough to circulate easily between moving parts, but not so thin that it will be forced out from between them. If it is forced out, parts will be left in direct contact and they will be damaged.

Synthetic Oils

Synthetic lubricating oils are more costly to manufacture and to use but they have a number of advantages over conventional mineral oils.

They offer better protection against engine wear and can operate at the higher temperatures needed by performance engines; they have better low-temperature viscosity, without the wax impurities that coagulate at low temperatures; they are chemically more stable; and they are generally thinner, so they allow for closer tolerances in engine components without loss of lubrication. They also last considerably longer, extending oil change intervals out to 20,000 miles (30,000 km) or more, which benefits the environment by reducing the used oil stream.

True synthetic oils are based on man-made hydrocarbons, commonly polyalphaolefin, or PAO, but very few of the synthetic oils on the market are full PAO oils. Many of the oils allowed to be labelled as synthetic are in fact blends of processed mineral oil and PAO, or even just heavily processed natural crude oil.

Gear Oil

Gear oil is the lubricant used in transmissions, transfer cases, and differentials **FIGURE 4-63**. It is of a higher viscosity than engine oil because it needs to protect meshing gears, which are in enclosed cases without the benefit of pumps. Most lubricants for manual gearboxes and differentials contain extreme pressure and anti-wear additives to cope with the sliding action of bevel gears.

Paint

Paint is used to cover metal parts of vehicles to provide protection and an attractive color. Once applied, a clear coat is often applied to the surface of the paint to protect the paint from damage **FIGURE 4-64**.

Paraffin

Paraffin, also known as mineral oil, is used mainly as a cleaning agent in the automotive industry. It is a liquid by-product of the petroleum distillation process of crude oil. It is a transparent, colorless oil, which is produced in light and heavy grade.

Solvents

A **solvent** is a highly flammable liquid that can dissolve other substances. Examples of solvents are turpentine, methylated spirits, and lacquer thinners used as an additive to paints.

Water

Water is the universal solvent. Given a long enough time, water will dissolve any material. In this industry, distilled water is often used to top off batteries. Water is also used in windshield washers and radiators and to wash vehicles.

FIGURE 4-63 Gear oil is of a higher viscosity than engine oil because it needs to protect meshing gears.

FIGURE 4-64 Paint covers metal parts to provide protection and add color.

Metals

Metals play an integral role in the construction of major vehicle components, particularly engine components and the vehicle body itself. Metals can roughly be divided into ferrous and non-ferrous categories. **Ferrous metals** use iron as an alloying agent. Cast iron, steel, and stainless steel are the main categories of iron alloys used in the industry. **Non-ferrous metals**, such as copper, are pure metals that can be used in alloys as well.

Cast Iron

Cast iron is an alloy, or combination, of materials. There are many different kinds of cast iron, depending on the particular materials they contain.

Grey iron, for example, is a cast iron that contains carbon in the form of graphite, plus silicon, manganese, and phosphorus. The fractured surface of a cast iron with graphite appears grey, hence the name. It is brittle and cannot absorb shocks. It resists heat and corrosion, and can be cast into many different shapes. It is used for many components, such as engine cylinder blocks and crankcases.

Steel

When carbon and other materials are alloyed with iron they form steel. The amount of carbon is very small; it can be less than 1%. Changing the amount of carbon, even by small amounts, will dramatically change properties, such as hardness, ductility, and toughness.

Different properties mean different uses. Generally, low-carbon steels, also known as mild steels, are used where toughness is needed, such as in the frame, body, bolts, nuts, and washers. Increasing the amount of carbon increases hardness, so high-carbon steels are used where hardness is needed, such as in engine parts, springs, dies, and punches.

Stainless steels are also used in vehicle applications for their resistance to corrosion and toughness FIGURE 4-65. Stainless steel has a shiny appearance and can be polished to a bright, mirror-like finish. Stainless steel is used in the construction of valves, pipes, bolts, and screws.

FIGURE 4-65 Stainless steel is resistant to corrosion and tough.

FIGURE 4-66 Copper is often combined with brass or bronze for bearings and bushes.

Copper

Copper is a non-ferrous, pure metal that can be alloyed (combined) with other metals but is not combined with iron. Copper is often alloyed with brass or bronze for bearings and bushes FIGURE 4-66. It is also used in vehicle wiring because of its electrical conducting properties.

Lead

Lead is used in the construction of vehicle batteries. The wet cell lead-acid battery is the main storage device in vehicle use FIGURE 4-67. A vehicle battery can supply very high discharge currents while maintaining a high voltage—which is useful for cold starting. It gives a high power output for its compact size, and it is rechargeable.

The most common standard 12-volt truck batteries consist of six cells, each of a nominal 2 volts. Each cell contains two electrodes, one of lead (Pb) and the other of lead peroxide (PbO_2), in an electrolyte of dilute sulfuric acid (H_2SO_4). As the battery discharges, both electrodes turn into lead sulphate and the acid turns into water. Recharging the battery reverses this process.

Brass

Brass is an alloy of zinc and copper and is used in the automotive field for hose connections and fittings.

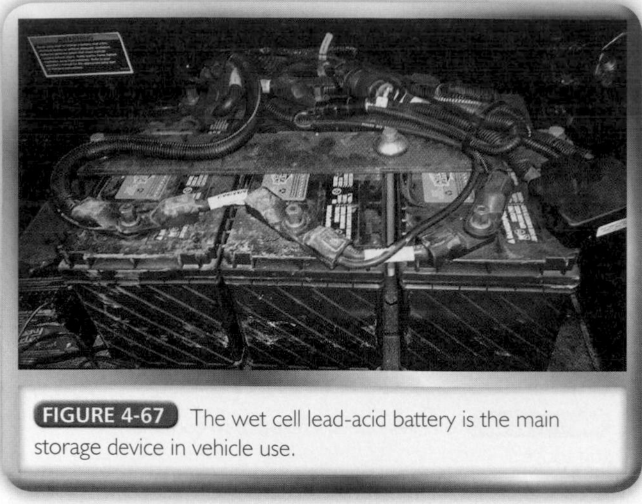

FIGURE 4-67 The wet cell lead-acid battery is the main storage device in vehicle use.

FIGURE 4-68 Brass is an alloy of zinc and copper and is used to make fuel line fittings and connectors.

Low-pressure fuel-line connections are commonly made from brass FIGURE 4-68. In the past, brass was used extensively in cooling system radiators because of its excellent heat dissipation properties. Today radiators are constructed primarily from aluminum because of the high cost and heavy weight of brass.

Chrome

Chrome may be confused with stainless steel. Like stainless, it is a bright, shiny corrosion-resistant metal and is used mostly for decorative purposes, such as on hubcaps.

Aluminum

As more manufacturers try to make vehicles lighter and more fuel-efficient, more and more components are being cast from aluminum such as fuel tanks, wheels, and some suspension components.

Tin

Tin is most often used as a corrosion-resistant coating in vehicle applications. Fuel tanks, for example, are made of tinned sheet steel that has been pressed into shape. Tin is also used as a coating. Solder used in vehicle electrical applications is an alloy typically made up of 60% tin and 40% lead. Fuel lines in light diesel systems are usually made of stainless steel tubing coated with tin to prevent rust.

Materials

Materials used in the commercial vehicle industry are used in everything from dashboard coverings to interior trim. They often determine the look of the vehicle but also have important structural elements that can be applied to vehicle components TABLE 4-1.

Safety

Asbestos is a name used to describe a number of naturally occurring non-combustible fibrous mineral compounds, mostly iron or magnesium silicates.

Because of its heat- and fire-resistant qualities, asbestos was used in brake shoes, silencer systems, and some gaskets for many years. Asbestos fiber or powder inhalation is now known to cause some very serious respiratory diseases, such as a lung fibrosis called "asbestosis," and a very aggressive form of cancer called "mesothelioma." As a result, the use of asbestos has been banned in many countries.

Manufacturers of vehicle brake components now use a range of alternative materials in the manufacturing process depending on the particular braking application. These can be various ceramic compounds; semi-metallic, low-metallic, synthetic fibers such as Kevlar; and non-asbestos organic compounds.

TECHNICIAN TIP

PVC, or polyvinyl chloride, is in the top three worldwide-produced plastics.

TABLE 4-1: Materials Used in the Vehicle Industry

Material	Definition
Bakelite	A synthetic resin that was used primarily in the construction of distributor caps and rotors. It is easily moulded and machined.
Cloth	A fabric used as internal trimming on some vehicles.
Cork	Often used in combination with rubber to form gaskets for engine blocks. It is lightweight and prevents oil and water from leaking into cylinders, which makes it ideal for use as a gasket material.
Felt	A woven material that is used as an underlay in floor mats.
Fiberglass	A metal glass that is used in some timing belts. Fiberglass is a lightweight, extremely strong, and robust material.
Formica	Often used in public transport vehicles as a decorative, laminated board.
Glass	Used for windshields, windows, and headlight coverings. Glass technology has resulted in shatter-proof windshields that help protect drivers and passengers.
Graphite	Used as a lubricant in vehicle applications. It is a black substance that is often used as an additive to grease or it can be sprayed on.
Leather	Expensive vehicles use leather, which is a tanned animal hide, for seat covers and other vehicle trim.
Melamine	A compound used to make synthetic resins and used for moulding some lightweight vehicle body parts.
Nylon	A synthetic plastic material that is used in the construction of some bushings.
Perspex	A tough, clear plastic used as partitions on instrument panels. It resembles glass by its transparency.
Polish	A wax liquid that is spread onto a vehicle body surface after washing. It is buffed to a high-gloss polish.

Continued on next page

TABLE 4-1: Materials Used in the Vehicle Industry, continued

Material	Definition
Polyurethane	A fire-resistant plastic resin that is used in the manufacture of vehicle seats.
Polyvinyl chloride (PVC) 	Lightweight, strong, and flexible with acid-resistant properties. You can find PVC used as piping in plumbing applications such as water distribution. In vehicle applications, it is used for oil seals and other flexible gaskets. It can also be found incorporated into floor mats because of its toughness and wear resistance.
Rubber  	A versatile, elastic material that has dozens of applications in the motor trade industry. It is used in the manufacture of tires, for example. The rubber is mostly synthetic, with carbon black added to increase strength and toughness. When used in the tread, this combination gives a long life: ■ Natural rubber is weaker than the synthetic version. It is used mainly in sidewalls. ■ The plies are made from cords of fabric, coated with rubber. ■ Early tires used cords of cotton, but with increased vehicle speeds and loads, rayon and nylon cords are now common. ■ Cords of synthetic fabric have high tensile strength. They resist stretching, but are flexible under load. ■ The cords are placed in parallel and impregnated with rubber to form sheets called plies. Plies have high strength in one direction, and are flexible in other directions. ■ Steel reinforced rubber is also used in the manufacture of radiator hoses.
Silicone rubber	A synthetic rubber that is used for spark plug high-tension leads, seals, and gaskets.
Vinyl	A synthetic plastic material used for interior vehicle upholstery. Because it resembles leather, it is a cheaper alternative to the animal hide product.
Wax	The base substance used for polish.
Wood	Often used as an interior trim material. In super-luxury vehicles, such as the Rolls Royce or Bentley, highly polished, rare wood is used throughout the interior.

Wrap-up

Ready for Review

- Tools and equipment should be used only for the task they were designed to do.
- Always have a safe attitude when using tools and equipment and wear necessary personal protection equipment.
- Do not use damaged tools; inspect before using, then clean and inspect again before putting them away.
- Lockouts and tagouts are meant to prevent technicians from using tools and equipment that are potentially unsafe.
- Many tools and measuring instruments have USCS or metric system markings to identify their size.
- Micrometers can be outside, inside, or depth.
- Gauges are used to measure distances and diameters; types include telescoping, split ball, and dial bore.
- Vernier calipers measure outside, inside, and depth dimensions; newer versions have dial and digital scales.
- Dial indicators are used to measure movement.
- A straight edge is designed to assess the flatness of a surface.
- Feeler blades are flat metal strips that are used to measure the width of gaps.
- Power tools can be stationary or portable, corded, or cordless and are powered by electricity, batteries, compressed air, a propellant, or a gasoline engine.
- Drills are designed to drive a drill bit into metal (or other material) to create a hole; check drilling speed charts for proper drilling speed.
- Portable grinders are designed to grind down metals, but can also be fitted with a cutting disc to cut sheets of metal.
- Air tools use compressed, pressurized air for power; types include the air impact wrench, air ratchet, air hammer, air drill, and blowgun/air nozzle.
- Common wrenches include box end, open end, combination (most popular), flare nut (or flare tubing), open-end adjustable, and ratcheting box end.
- Use the correct wrench for the situation, so as not to damage the bolt or nut.
- Sockets grip fasteners tightly on all six corners are classified as follows: standard or metric, size of drive used to turn them, number of points, depth of socket, and thickness of wall.
- Fasteners can be spun off or on (but not tightened) by a speed brace or speeder handle.
- Pliers hold, cut, or compress materials; types include slip-joint, combination, arc joint, needle nose, flat, diagonal cutting, snap ring, and locking.
- Cutting tools include bolt cutters, tin snips, and aviation snips.
- Allen wrenches are designed to fit into fasteners with recessed hexagonal heads.
- Screwdriver types include flat blade (most common), Phillips, Pozidriv, offset, ratcheting, and impact.
- The tip of the screwdriver must be matched exactly to the slot or recess on the head of a fastener.
- Types of hammers include ball peen (most common), sledge, mallet, and dead blow.
- Chisels are used to cut metals when hit with a hammer.
- Punches are used to mark metals when hit with a hammer and come in different diameters and different points for different tasks; types of punches include prick, center, drift, pin, ward, and hollow.
- Pry bars can be used to move, adjust, or pry parts. Gasket scrapers are designed to remove gaskets without damaging surrounding materials.
- Files are used to remove material from the surface of a truck part.
- Types of files include flat, warding, square, triangular, curved, and thread.
- Bench vices, offset vices, drill vices, and G-clamps all hold materials in place while they are worked on.
- Taps are designed to cut threads in holes or nuts; types include taper, intermediate, and bottoming.
- Gear and bearing pullers are designed to remove components from a shaft when considerable force is needed.
- Flaring tools create flares at the end of tubes to connect them to other components; types include single, double, and ISO.
- Rivet tools join together two pieces of metal; each rivet can be used only once.
- Most shops will have diagnostic equipment such dynamometers, scanning tools and various pressure testing equipment.
- Other shop equipment may be wheel alignment machines, tire changers and or brake drum/disc lathes.
- Oxyacetylene torches are designed to heat, braze, weld, and cut metal by combining acetylene with oxygen at a high temperature.

- Pressure washers/cleaners use focused, pressurized water to clean accumulated dirt and grease from vehicle components; water must be directed properly so as not to damage other parts.
- Spray wash cabinets are designed to clean automotive parts in a sealed cabinet, much like a dishwasher.
- Solvent tanks are designed for immersion of vehicle parts to remove oil, dirt, grease, and grime.
- Brake washers are designed to remove brake dust from wheel brake units and their components.
- Sand or bead blasters are designed to clean paint, corrosion, or dirt from metal parts by blasting small abrasive particles onto the surface.
- Electrical testing equipment used in the shop include multi-meters, oscilloscopes, and graphing meters.
- Battery chargers can be fast chargers, slow chargers, or smart chargers that analyze the battery and select the best charging method.
- Vehicle batteries can be dangerous due to their high voltage; hybrid vehicle batteries have extremely high voltage and current flows.
- Many fluids are used in vehicles as coolants and lubricants.
- Engine coolants prevent freezing in the winter and increase the engine coolant's boiling point in the summer.
- ATF automatic transmission fluid can be specific to the vehicle, so always check and use the OEM recommended fluid.
- Brake fluid is hygroscopic meaning that it readily absorbs water.
- Diesel fuel is a crude oil distillate used in CI engines.
- Biodiesel is made from either soybeans or canola an or animal fats.
- Engine oil and gear oil can be petroleum or synthetic based.
- Many different metals and substances are used in vehicle manufacture technicians should work on being able to identify these materials.

Vocabulary Builder

air drill A compressed air-powered drill.

air hammer A tool powered by compressed air with various hammer, cutting, punching, or chisel attachments. Also called an air chisel.

air-impact wrench An impact tool powered by compressed air designed to undo tight fasteners.

air nozzle A compressed-air device that emits a fine stream of compressed air for drying or cleaning parts.

air ratchet A ratchet tool for use with sockets powered by compressed air.

alkalis Chemical compounds that have a pH value greater than 7. They are commonly used in toy batteries and bleaches.

Allen wrench A type of hexagonal drive mechanism for fasteners.

angle grinder A portable grinder for grinding or cutting metal.

aviation snips A scissor-like tool for cutting sheet metal.

ball-peen (engineer's) hammer A hammer that has a head that is rounded on one end and flat on the other; designed to work with metal items.

battery A device that converts and stores electrical energy through chemical reactions.

battery charger A device that charges a battery, reversing the discharge process.

bench grinder (pedestal grinder) A grinder that is fixed to a bench or pedestal.

bench vice A device that securely holds material in jaws while it is being worked on.

biodiesel A renewable fuel made by chemically combining natural oils from soybeans (or cottonseeds, canola, etc.; animal fats; or even recycled cooking oil) with an alcohol such as methanol (or ethanol).

blind rivet A rivet that can be installed from its insertion side.

bolt cutters Strong cutters available in different sizes, designed to cut through non-hardened bolts and other small-stock material.

bottoming tap A thread-cutting tap designed to cut threads to the bottom of a blind hole.

C-clamp A clamp shaped like the letter C; it comes in various sizes and can clamp various items.

chassis dynamometer A machine with rollers that allows a vehicle to attain road speed and load while sitting still in the shop.

chrome A bright, shiny corrosion-resistant metal; it is mostly used for decorative purposes, such as on hubcaps.

cleaning gun A device with a nozzle controlled by a trigger fitted to the outlet of pressure cleaners.

closed-end wrench A wrench with a closed or ring end to grip bolts and nuts.

club hammer The club hammer is like a small mallet, with two square faces made of high-carbon steel. It is the heaviest type of hammer that can be used one-handed.

coefficient of friction (CoF) The amount of friction between two particular objects in contact; calculated by dividing the force required to move the object by the weight of the object.

combination pliers A type of pliers for cutting, gripping, and bending.

combination wrench A type of wrench that has an open end on one end and a closed-end wrench on the other.

coolant A fluid that contains special anti-freezing and anti-corrosion chemicals mixed with water.

copper A non-ferrous, pure metal that can be alloyed (combined) with other metals but is not combined with iron.

crankshaft A vehicle engine component that transfers the reciprocating movement of pistons into rotary motion.

cross-arm A description for an arm that is set at right angles or 90 degrees to another component.

cross-cut chisel A type of chisel for metal work that cleans out or cuts key ways.

curved file A type of file that has a curved surface for filing holes.

dead-blow hammer A type of hammer that has a cushioned head to reduce the amount of head bounce.

depth micrometers A micrometer that measures the depth of an item such as how far a piston is below the surface of the block.

diagonal-cutting pliers Cutting pliers for small wire or cable.

dial bore gauge A gauge that is used to measure the inside diameter of bores with a high degree of accuracy and speed.

dial indicators A dial that can also be known as a dial gauge, and as the name suggests, has a dial and needle where measurements are read.

die A device used to cut threads on a bolt or shaft.

die stock handle A handle for securely holding dies to cut threads.

double flare A seal that is made at the end of metal tubing or pipe.

drift punch A type of punch used to start pushing roll pins to prevent them from spreading.

drill chuck A device for securely gripping drill bits in a drill.

drill press A device that incorporates a fixed drill with multiple speeds and an adjustable worktable. It can be free-standing or fixed to a bench.

drill vice A tool with jaws that can be attached to a drill press table for holding material that is to be drilled.

ethylene glycol A chemical that resists freezing but is very toxic to people and animals.

fast chargers A type of battery charger that charges batteries quickly.

feeler gauges Also called feeler blades; flat metal strips used to measure the width of gaps, such as the clearance between valves and rocker arms.

ferrous metals Metals that use iron as an alloying agent. Cast iron, steel, and stainless steel are the main categories of iron alloys used in the automotive industry.

finished rivet A rivet after the completion of the riveting process.

flare-nut wrench A type of closed-end wrench that has a slot in the box section to allow the wrench to slip through a tube or pipe. Also called a flare tubing wrench.

flashback arrestor A spring-loaded valve installed on oxyacetylene torches as a safety device to prevent flame from entering the torch hoses.

flat-nosed pliers Pliers that are flat and square at the end of the nose.

flat-tip screwdriver A type of screwdriver that fits a straight slot in screws.

forcing screw The center screw on a gear, bearing, or pulley puller. Also called a jacking screw.

fuel (gasoline, diesel) A derivative of crude oil.

gasket scraper A broad, sharp, flat blade to assist in removing gaskets and glue.

gear pullers A tool with two or more legs and a cross-bar with a center forcing screw to remove gears.

grinding wheels and discs Abrasive wheels or flat discs fitted to bench, pedestal, and portable grinders.

ground The return path for electrical current in a vehicle chassis, other metal of the vehicle, or dedicated wire.

high resistance Describes a circuit or components with more resistance than designed.

hygroscopic When brake fluid absorbs water from the atmosphere.

hollow punch A punch with a center hollow for cutting circles in thin materials such as gaskets.

impact driver A tool that is struck with a blow to provide an impact turning force to remove tight fasteners.

inside micrometer Micrometer that measures inside dimensions.

intermediate tap One of a series of taps designed to cut an internal thread. Also called a plug tap.

locking pliers A type of plier where the jaws can be set and locked into position.

lockout/tagout A safety tag system to ensure that faulty equipment or equipment in the middle of repair is not used.

magnetic pickup tools An extending shaft, often flexible, with a magnet fitted to the end for picking up metal objects.

mandrel The shaft of a pop rivet.

mandrel head The head of the pop rivet that connects to the shaft.

measuring tapes A flexible type of ruler and a common measuring tool.

mechanical fingers Spring-loaded fingers at the end of a flexible shaft that pick up items in tight spaces.

micrometers Precise measuring tools designed to measure small distances and are available in both millimeter (mm) and inch calibrations.

Morse taper A tapered mounting shaft for drill bits and chucks in larger drills and lathes.

needle-nosed pliers Pliers with long tapered jaws for gripping small items and getting into tight spaces.

nippers Pliers designed to cut protruding items level with the surface.

non-ferrous metals Pure metals such as copper; can also be used in alloys.

offset screwdriver A screwdriver with a 90-degree bend in the shaft for working in tight spaces.

offset vice A vice that allows long objects to be gripped vertically.

open circuits Describes a circuit that has a break and no current can flow.

open-end wrench A wrench with open jaws to allow side entry to a nut or bolt.

outside micrometer Measures the outside dimensions of an item.

oxyacetylene torch A gas welding system that combines oxygen and acetylene.

paraffin (mineral oil) Used mainly as a cleaning agent in the commercial vehicle industry.

parallax error A visual error caused by viewing measurement markers at an incorrect angle.

peening A term used to describe the action of flattening a rivet through a hammering action.

Phillips screwdriver A type of screwdriver that fits a head shaped like a cross in screws; also called Phillips head screwdriver.

pin punch A type of punch in various sizes with a straight or parallel shaft.

pliers A hand tool with gripping jaws.

pop-rivet gun A hand tool for installing pop rivets.

power tools Tools powered by electricity or compressed air.

pressure washer/cleaner A cleaning machine that boosts low-pressure tap water to a high-pressure output.

prick punch A punch with a sharp point for accurately marking a point on metal.

Propylene glycol An organic based chemical that resists freezing and, unlike ethylene glycol, is non-toxic.

pry bars (crowbars) A high-strength carbon-steel rod with offsets for levering and prying.

pullers A generic term to describe hand tools that mechanically assist the removal of bearings, gears, pulleys, and other parts.

punches A generic term to describe a high-strength carbon-steel shaft with a blunt point for driving. Center and prick punches are exceptions and have a sharp point for marking or making an indentation.

ratchet A generic term to describe a handle for sockets that allows the user to select direction of rotation. It can turn sockets in restricted areas without the user having to remove the socket from the fastener.

ratcheting screwdriver A screwdriver with a selectable ratchet mechanism built into the handle that allows the screwdriver tip to ratchet as it is being used.

rattle gun The most common air tool in a shop; also called the air-impact wrench or impact gun.

sand or bead blasters A cleaning system that uses high-pressure fine particles of glass bead or sand.

screw extractor A tool for removing broken screws or bolts.

short circuits Describe a condition in which the current flows along an unintended route.

single flare A sealing system made on the end of metal tubing.

sliding T-handle A handle fitted at 90 degrees to the main body that can be slid from side to side.

slow charger A battery charger that charges at low current.

smart charger A battery charger with microprocessor-controlled charging rates and times.

snap ring pliers A pair of pliers for installing and removing internal or external snap rings.

socket An enclosed metal tube commonly with 6 or 12 points to remove and install bolts and nuts.

solvent A highly flammable liquid that can dissolve other substances.

solvent tank A tank containing solvents to clean vehicle parts.

speed brace A U-shaped socket wrench that allows high-speed operation. Also called a speeder handle.

split ball gauge (small hole gauge) A gauge that is good for measuring small holes where telescoping gauges cannot fit.

spray-wash cabinet A cleaning cabinet that sprays solvent under pressure to clean vehicle parts.

square file A type of file with a square cross-section.

steel ruler A ruler that is made from stainless steel. Stainless steel rulers commonly come in various lengths.

straight edges A measuring device generally made of steel to check how flat a surface is.

straight grinder A powered grinder with the wheel set at 90 degrees to the shaft.

sulfuric acid A type of acid that when mixed with pure water forms the basis of battery acid or electrolyte.

tap A term used to generically describe an internal thread-cutting tool.

tap handle A tool designed to securely hold taps for cutting internal threads.

taper tap A tap with a tapper; it is usually the first of three taps used when cutting internal threads.

telescoping gauge Gauge used for measuring distances in awkward spots such as the bottom of a deep cylinder.

thread repair A generic term to describe a number of processes that can be used to repair threads.

thread chaser A device similar to a die that cleans up rusty or damaged threads.

tin A metal most often used as a corrosion-resistant coating in automotive applications.

tin snips Cutting device for sheet metal; works in a similar fashion to scissors.

tube-flaring tool A tool that makes a sealing flare on the end of metal tubing.

tubing cutter A hand tool for cutting pipe or tubing squarely.

twist drill A hardened steel drill bit for making holes in metals, plastics, and wood.

V blocks Metal blocks with a V-shaped cutout for holding shafts while working on them. Also referred to as vee blocks.

vernier caliper An accurate measuring device for internal, external, and depth measurements that incorporates fixed and adjustable jaws.

volatile organic compounds (VOCs) Evaporative emissions that vehicles emit.

wad punch A type of punch that is hollow for cutting circular shapes in soft materials, such as gaskets.

warding file A type of thin, flat file with a tapered end.

water-pump pliers Adjustable pliers with parallel jaws that allow you to increase or decrease the size of the jaws by selecting a different set of channels.

wrench A generic term to describe tools that tighten and loosen fasteners with hexagonal heads.

Review Questions

1. When carbon is alloyed with iron it forms
   a. Aluminum
   b. Lead
   c. Steel
   d. Copper
2. Brake fluid absorbs water from the atmosphere. This water absorption is called:
   a. Hydrophilic
   b. Hyperhydro
   c. Heteroscopic
   d. Hygroscopic
3. First and foremost, _______ will help you avoid being involved in an accident.
   a. a clean tool
   b. a regularly inspected tool
   c. using the correct tool
   d. a safe attitude
4. Lockout/tagout is an umbrella term that describes a set of safety practices and procedures that are intended to reduce the risk of technicians inadvertently using _______ that have been determined to be unsafe or potentially unsafe or that are in the process of being serviced.
   a. tools
   b. equipment
   c. materials
   d. All of the choices are correct.
5. Manufacturer's charts showing _______ will assist in identifying standard or metric sizing.
   a. thread zoning
   b. fastener sizing
   c. Both A and B
   d. Neither A nor B
6. The fumes from cleaning chemicals can be toxic, so wear _______ wherever you are using these products.
   a. appropriate hearing protection
   b. an appropriate respirator
   c. Both A and B
   d. Neither A nor B
7. A(n) _______ is capable of accurate measurements on shorter lengths, down to a millimeter or a fraction of an inch.
   a. steel rule
   b. measuring tape
   c. inside micrometer
   d. depth micrometer
8. The _______ micrometer measures the distance between the anvil and spindle, so that is where the part being measured fits.
   a. inside
   b. outside
   c. depth
   d. standard
9. When measuring spark plug gap, feeler gauges should not be used because the surfaces are not perfectly _______, so it is preferable to use wire feeler gauges.
   a. parallel
   b. perpendicular
   c. flat
   d. curved
10. _______ pliers, also called vice grips, are general purpose pliers used to clamp and hold one or more objects.
    a. Arc joint
    b. Locking
    c. Needle-nosed
    d. Flat-nosed

ASE-Type Questions

1. Technician A says that you would use an outside micrometer to measure the bottom of a cylinder. Technician B says that you would use a telescoping gauge to measure the bottom of a cylinder. Who is correct?
   a. Technician A
   b. Technician B
   c. Both Technician A and Technician B
   d. Neither Technician A nor Technician B
2. Technician A says to use nippers to cut through soft metal. Technician B says to use an Allen wrench. Who is correct?
   a. Technician A
   b. Technician B
   c. Both Technician A and Technician B
   d. Neither Technician A nor Technician B
3. Technician A says pressure compression gauges are used to measure the compression pressures inside an engine cylinder. Technician B says pressure compression gauges can identify overall condition and pressure leakage situations that could be caused by a range of engine faults. Who is correct?
   a. Technician A
   b. Technician B
   c. Both Technician A and Technician B
   d. Neither Technician A nor Technician B
4. Technician A says the most commonly used pair of pliers in the shop is the needle-nosed plier. Technician B says the most common is the snap ring plier. Who is correct?
   a. Technician A
   b. Technician B
   c. Both Technician A and Technician B
   d. Neither Technician A nor Technician B
5. Technician A says bolt cutters cut hardened rods. Technician B says tin snips can cut thin sheet metal. Who is correct?
   a. Technician A
   b. Technician B
   c. Both Technician A and Technician B
   d. Neither Technician A nor Technician B
6. Technician A says that a drift punch is also named a starter punch because you should always use it first to get a pin moving. Technician B says a center punch centers a drill bit at the point where a hole is required to be drilled. Who is correct?
   a. Technician A
   b. Technician B
   c. Both Technician A and Technician B
   d. Neither Technician A nor Technician B
7. Technician A states that a tap handle has a right-angled jaw that matches the squared end that all taps have. Technician B states that to cut a thread in an awkward space, a T-shaped tap handle is very convenient. Who is correct?
   a. Technician A
   b. Technician B
   c. Both Technician A and Technician B
   d. Neither Technician A nor Technician B
8. Technician A states that there are many applications for blind rivets, and various rivet types and tools may be used to do the riveting. Technician B states that a typical pop or blind rivet has a body, which will form the finished rivet, and a mandrel, which is discarded when the riveting is complete. Who is correct?
   a. Technician A
   b. Technician B
   c. Both Technician A and Technician B
   d. Neither Technician A nor Technician B
9. Technician A says a battery could discharge if the vehicle is not started for as little as one month due to normal vehicle drains. Technician B says slow charging a battery is less stressful on a battery than fast charging. Who is correct?
   a. Technician A
   b. Technician B
   c. Both Technician A and Technician B
   d. Neither Technician A nor Technician B
10. Technician A says engine oil reduces wear on moving parts. Technician B says engine oil absorbs shock loads. Who is correct?
    a. Technician A
    b. Technician B
    c. Both Technician A and Technician B
    d. Neither Technician A nor Technician B

CHAPTER 5

NATEF Tasks

Supplemental Task List

Shop and Personal Safety

	Page
■ Identify and use proper placement of floor jacks and jack stands.	188–190
■ Identify and use proper procedures for safe lift operation.	190–192

Knowledge Objectives

After reading this chapter, you will be able to:

1. Identify locking devices and tools. (pp 164–172)
2. Describe fasteners and torque. (pp 172–175)
3. Identify locking device measuring tools. (172–175)
4. Describe helical inserts. (p 175)
5. Identify locking pins and keys. (pp 176–177)
6. Discuss the design and function of head gaskets. (pp 177–178)
7. Discuss the design and function of lip-type seals. (pp 181–182)
8. Discuss the design and function of ring seals. (p 181)
9. Discuss the design and function of crankshaft seals. (pp 181–182)
10. Discuss the design and function of mechanical seals. (pp 183–184)
11. Discuss the use of adhesives and sealants. (pp 184–185)
12. Describe the correct procedure for manual lifting. (p 185)
13. Describe the application and purpose of lifting equipment. (pp 185–186)
14. Describe the safe use of lifting equipment. (p 186)
15. Identify types of lifting and moving equipment. (pp 186–187)
16. Know how to use lifting equipment. (pp 186–188)

Fasteners, Locking Devices, and Lifting Equipment

Skills Objectives

After reading this chapter, you will be able to:

1. Use a torque wrench and torque angle gauge. (p 175) SKILL DRILL 5-1
2. Remove and install split pins. (p 176) SKILL DRILL 5-2
3. Fit a formed head gasket. (p 179) SKILL DRILL 5-3
4. Assemble and make a user-formed gasket. (p 179) SKILL DRILL 5-4
5. Assemble and make a user-formed gasket—tap method. (p 180) SKILL DRILL 5-5
6. Remove and replace lip-type seals. (p 182) SKILL DRILL 5-6
7. Remove and replace ring seals. (p 183) SKILL DRILL 5-7
8. Lift and secure a vehicle with a vehicle floor jack and stands. (p 191) SKILL DRILL 5-8
9. Lift a vehicle using a hydraulic hoist. (p 194) SKILL DRILL 5-9
10. Use engine hoists and stands. (p 196) SKILL DRILL 5-10

Introduction

Locking devices used in this industry are primarily designed to hold things in a particular location or to hold things together. These devices come in many forms, and depending on the particular application, one or more types of locking devices may be used. They can be in the form of a physical fastener and/or chemical adhesive. This chapter provides a description of the types of locking devices and fasteners found in automotive design vehicle applications. We will also discuss the safe use of lifting equipment.

Locking Devices and Tools

Fasteners

There are many different **fasteners** used in vehicle applications, including screws, bolts, studs and nuts. Washers and chemical compounds can be used to help secure these fasteners.

Screws

Screws are generally smaller than bolts and are sometimes referred to as metal threads FIGURE 5-1. They can have a variety of heads, they're used on smaller components, and often their thread extends right from the tip to the head so they can hold together components of different thickness.

FIGURE 5-1 Screws are generally smaller than bolts and are sometimes referred to as metal threads.

Different screws can be tightened with a range of tools. An **Allen head screw** has a recess for an **Allen wrench** FIGURE 5-2A AND 2B. An Allen head screw is sometimes called a cap screw. It usually screws into a hole rather than a nut, and it needs tightening with an Allen wrench.

A **machine screw** has a slot for a screwdriver FIGURE 5-3. Screwdrivers come in many sizes and you should always use the correct size blade for the particular machine screw slot.

There are a number of special screws that cut their own threads as they go. This is called *tapping a thread.* Pictured in FIGURE 5-4A is a **self-tapping screw**. It is made of hard material that cuts a mirror image of itself into the hole as you turn it. The screw in FIGURE 5-4B is

You Are the Technician

After finishing work on the last vehicle of the day, you are required to return your workstation back to order. You must replace all the tools and fasteners to their designated place. You wipe up any spills according to the shop procedure and clear the floor of any debris to avoid slips and falls. During your workspace inspection, you find a numbers of fasteners of various sizes lying on the floor beside an air drill and the electric hand held drill that need to be cleaned and stored.

1. What needs to happen with the fasteners?
2. What should you do to air tools before using them each day?
3. What are the steps you take in cleaning electric power tools?

FIGURE 5-2 **A.** An Allen head screw. **B.** An Allen wrench set.

FIGURE 5-3 A machine screw.

also known as a self-tapping screw, but it is designed for cutting and holding thin sheet metal, so it is often used on car bodies.

Bolts, Studs, and Nuts

Bolts, studs, and nuts are fasteners designed for heavier jobs than screws and tend to be made of metal or metal alloys. **Bolts** are cylindrical pieces of metal with a hexagonal head on one end and a thread cut into the shaft at the other end FIGURE 5-6. They are often bigger than screws and are used for heavier jobs. Bolts are always threaded into a nut or hole that has an identical thread cut inside. The thread acts as an inclined plane; as the bolt is turned, it is drawn into or out of the matching thread.

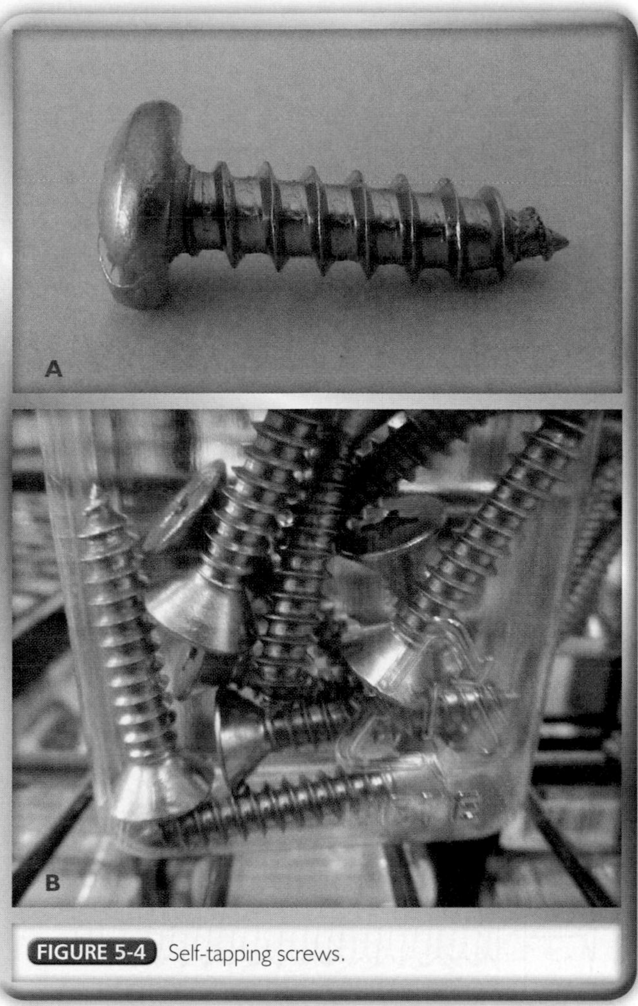
FIGURE 5-4 Self-tapping screws.

TECHNICIAN TIP

Threads are cut on screws, bolts, nuts and studs, and inside holes to allow components to be attached and assembled. There was a time when there were many different thread designs used throughout the world. Modern vehicles still use a range of thread patterns, but due to standardization, it is getting much simpler FIGURE 5-5. Nearly all the nuts, bolts, screws, and studs on a vehicle have a V-thread cut into them.

A screw jack or a clamp has square threads cut into it. The square thread is more difficult to machine and is used mainly in situations where rotational movement needs to be transferred into lateral movement—for example, the screw in a vice where the rotary movement of turning the handle is translated into the lateral movement of the jaws closing.

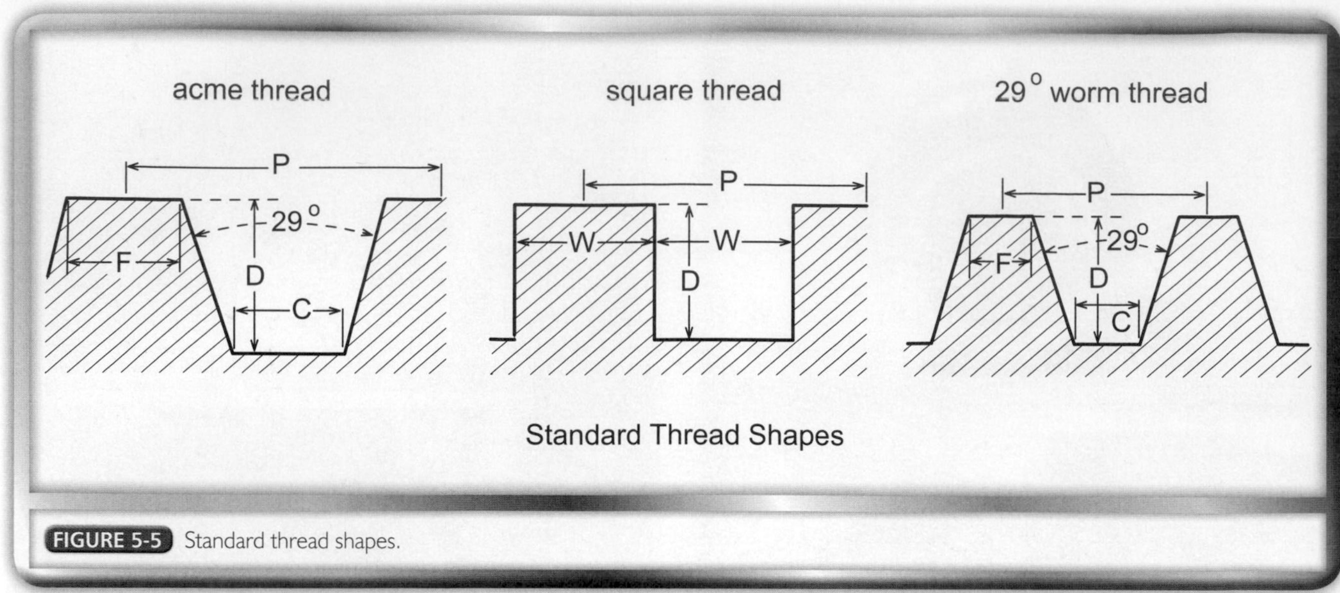

FIGURE 5-5 Standard thread shapes.

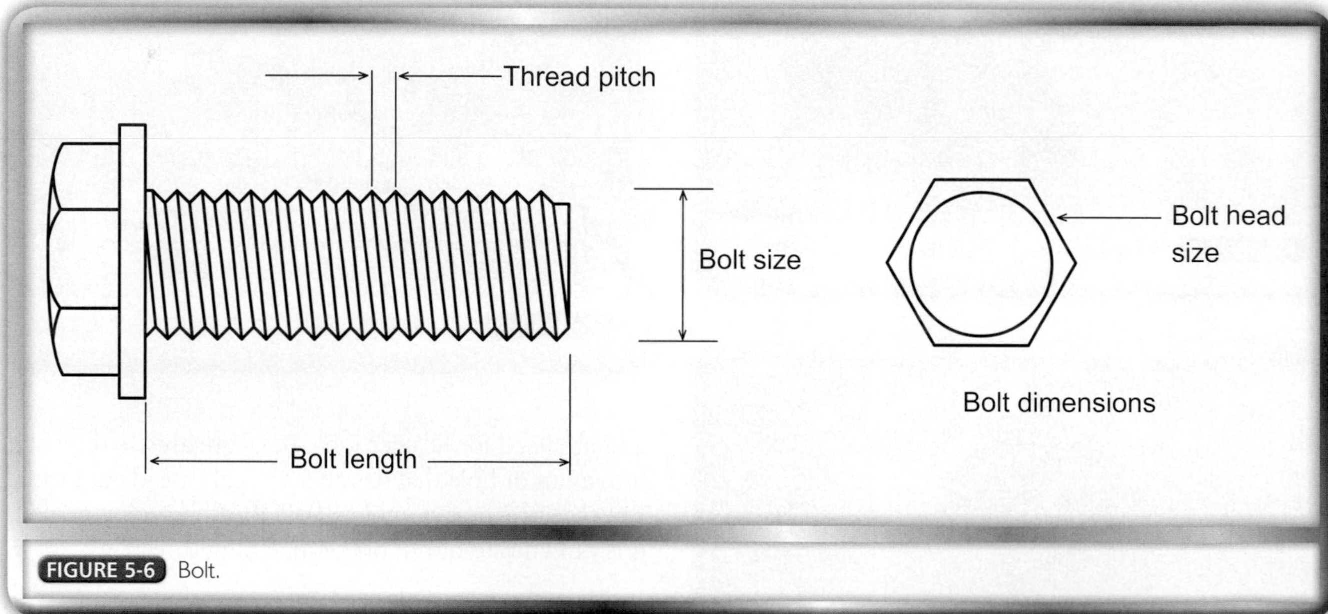

FIGURE 5-6 Bolt.

Nuts are often used with bolts. A nut is a piece of metal, usually hexagonal, with a thread cut through it to fit the bolt thread. The hexagonal heads for the bolt and nut are designed to fit tools such as combination wrenchs and sockets FIGURE 5-7.

Torx drivers are used for **torx bolts** and are often found in vehicle engines; they may be found in places such as cylinder heads to blocks, where particular tightening sequences are required FIGURE 5-8.

There are many different ways to keep the nut and bolt done up tightly. A self-locking or **Nylock nut** can have a plastic or nylon insert. Tightening the bolt squeezes it into the insert, where it resists any movement. The self-locker is highly resistant to being loosened by the kind of vibration that engines and vehicles experience FIGURE 5-9.

FIGURE 5-7 Bolts usually have hexagonal heads.

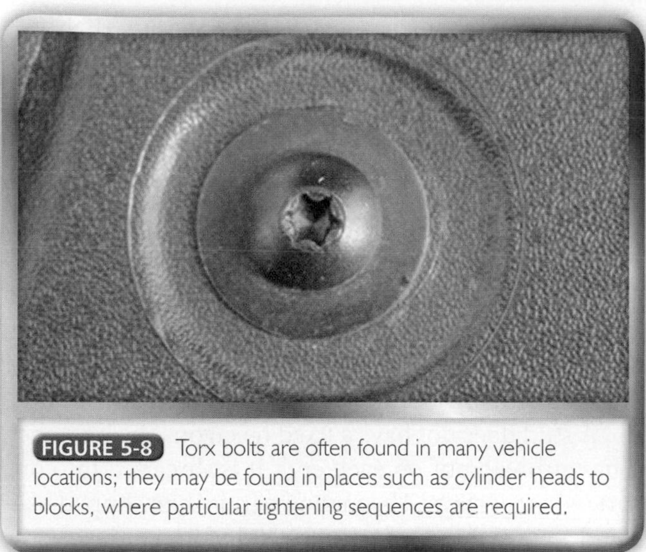

FIGURE 5-8 Torx bolts are often found in many vehicle locations; they may be found in places such as cylinder heads to blocks, where particular tightening sequences are required.

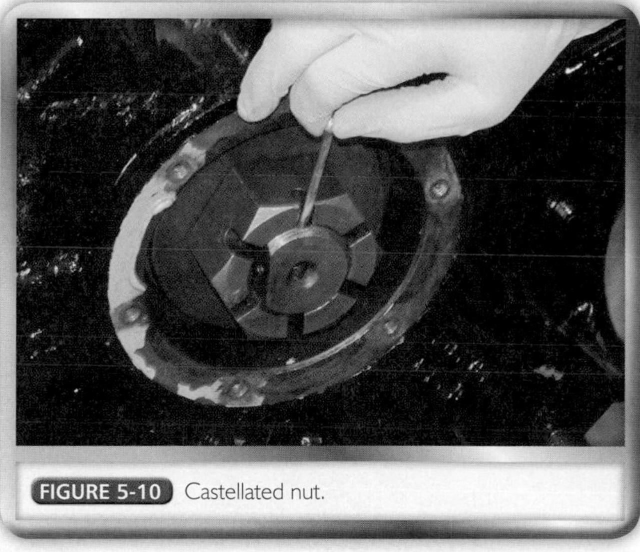

FIGURE 5-10 Castellated nut.

FIGURE 5-9 A self-locking nut is highly resistant to being loosened by engine vibrations.

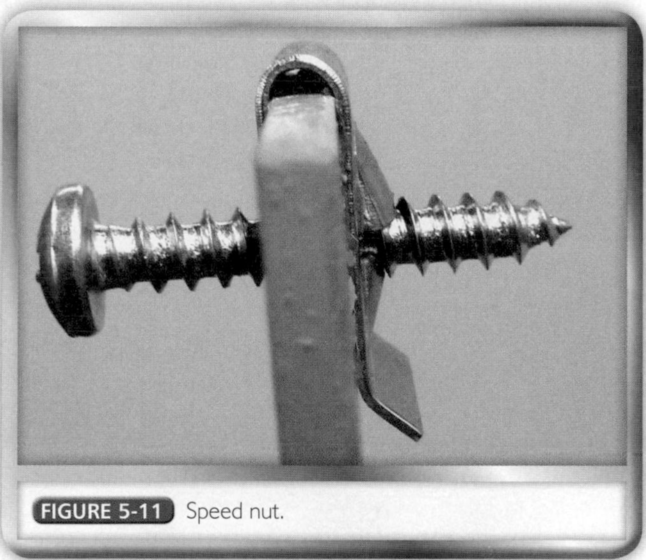

FIGURE 5-11 Speed nut.

Tightening this style of nut distorts the insert, so it provides its locking effect only the first time you use it. If you remove the nut, it should be replaced with a new one.

A **castellated nut** has slots like towers on a castle FIGURE 5-10. When it is screwed onto a bolt that has been drilled in the right spot, a split pin can be passed through them both and then spread open to lock the nut in place. Castellated nuts are used where scheduled maintenance requires inspection and adjustments to take place for items such as front wheel bearings.

A **speed nut** is not as strong as the other types, but it can be a fast and convenient way to secure a screw FIGURE 5-11. Once the speed nut is started, it does not need to be held. These are often used in places like body component fixings.

Some bolts and nuts need washers. Washers can be made from a number of materials depending on their application, including aluminum, copper, fiber, and steel. Here are some brief descriptions of the more common washers:

- **Flat washers** spread the load of a bolt head or a nut as it is tightened and distribute it over a greater area FIGURE 5-12A. This protects the surface underneath from being marked by the nut or head as it turns and tightens down. Flat washers should always be used to protect aluminum alloy.
- A **spring (lock) washer** compresses as the nut tightens, and the nut is spring loaded against this surface, which makes it unlikely to work loose FIGURE 5-12B. The ends of the spring washer also bite into the metal. Spring washers are used more for bolts and nuts.
- Screws mostly rely on smaller **serrated edge shakeproof washers** FIGURE 5-12C. The external ones

FIGURE 5-12 Types of washers. **A.** Flat washer. **B.** Spring washer. **C.** Serrated edge shake-proof washers. **D.** Spindle washer.

have teeth on the outside, and the internal ones have teeth on the inside; one type has both.

- **Spindle washers** are used behind a wheel bearing. The key or tab on the washer FIGURE 5-12D prevents the washer from spinning due to bearing rotation.

Often, the thread on a stud is only as long as it needs to be to tighten onto the nut or into the threaded hole. Some special versions have both a left- and right-hand thread on them. A **stud** FIGURE 5-13 is like two bolts in one; for instance, an exhaust manifold on the cylinder head is normally located and held by studs and nuts.

A stud does not have a fixed hexagonal head; rather, it has a thread cut on each end. It is threaded into one part, where it stays. The mating part is then slipped over it and a nut is threaded onto the end of the stud to secure the part. Studs are commonly used to attach a throttle body to the intake manifold. Studs can have different threads on each end.

Bolts, nuts, and studs can have either standard or metric threads. They are designated by their thread diameter, thread pitch, length, and grade. The diameter is measured across the outside of the threads; it is measured in fractions of an inch for standard-type fasteners and millimeters for metric-type fasteners. A 3/8" (9.5 mm) bolt has a thread diameter of 3/8" (9.5 mm); 3/8" (9.5 mm) is not the size of the bolt head.

The **standard (imperial) system** also uses a marking system to indicate tensile strength, as shown in FIGURE 5-14. This is a grade 5 bolt, and can be tightened to specific torque as specified by the manufacturer. **Torque** is a way of defining how much a fastener should be tightened.

The metric system uses numbers stamped on the heads of metric bolts and on the face of metric nuts FIGURE 5-15. Even studs have a marking system to make sure they are not over-stressed when you tighten them.

FIGURE 5-13 A stud has threads on both ends.

The numbers indicate the *tensile strength* of the bolt. The number does *not* mean the size of the bolt. NOTE: The distance between flats on the bolt or nut heads generally indicates wrench size to be used.

The coarseness of any thread is called its **thread pitch** FIGURE 5-16A. In the standard system, the thread pitch is measured in threads per inch (tpi) which is the distance between the peaks of the threads in inches FIGURE 5-16B. Each bolt diameter in the metric system can have up to four thread pitches. Metric threads, designated with a capital M, are rated according to their outer diameter and their pitch FIGURE 5-16C.

The length of a bolt is fairly straightforward. It is measured from the end of the bolt to the bottom of the head and is listed in inches or millimeters. The grade of a fastener relates to its strength. The higher the grade

TECHNICIAN TIP

The global version of metric is called the International System of Units, or SI. The standard system of inch-pounds is still used by some manufacturers, particularly in the US.

The metric system, however, has produced some competing classifications for fasteners. For example, metric hex cap screws may have three different standards:

1. DIN 931 (DIN 933 fully threaded)
2. ISO 4014 (ISO 4017 fully threaded)
3. ANSI/ASME B18.2.3.1M

These three standards are interchangeable, differing primarily in the width across the flat dimensions.

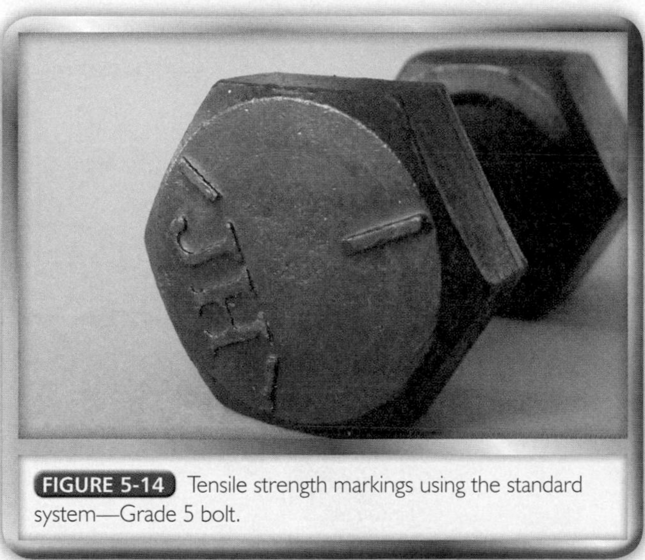

FIGURE 5-14 Tensile strength markings using the standard system—Grade 5 bolt.

FIGURE 5-15 Bolts and nuts are often marked to indicate how much torque can be safely applied to them. Markings using the metric system are shown here.

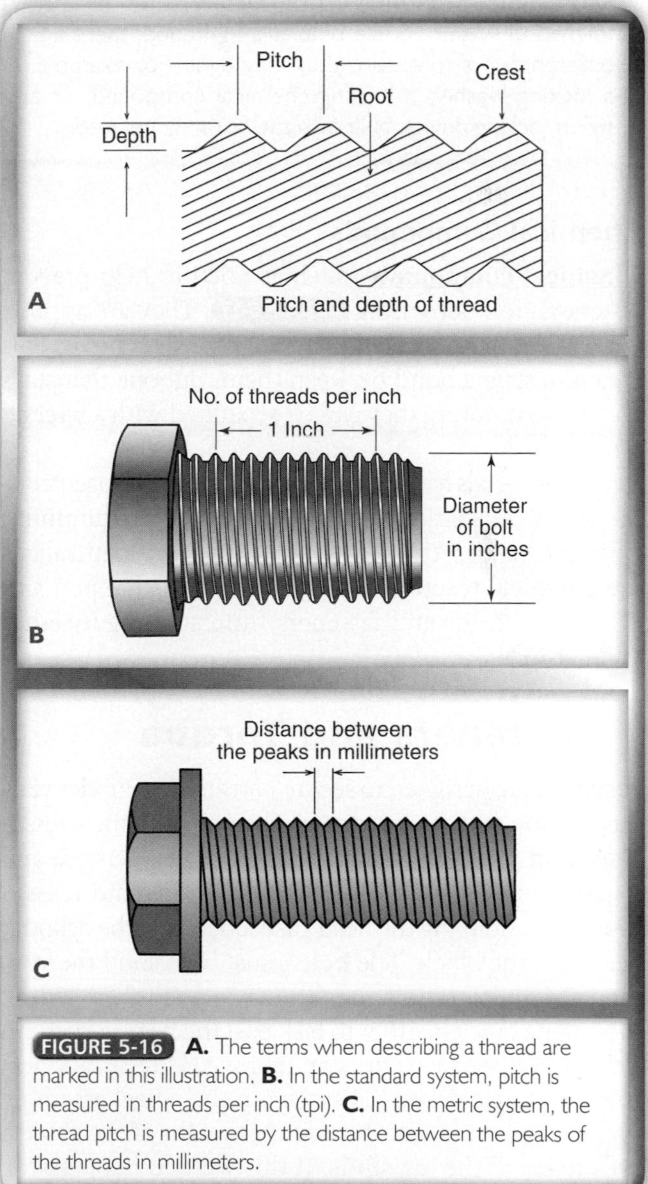

FIGURE 5-16 **A.** The terms when describing a thread are marked in this illustration. **B.** In the standard system, pitch is measured in threads per inch (tpi). **C.** In the metric system, the thread pitch is measured by the distance between the peaks of the threads in millimeters.

number, the higher the **tensile strength**, which refers to how much tension it can withstand before it breaks. Tensile strength for fasteners is generally listed in pounds per square inch (megapascals, or MPa), of bolt shaft area.

> **TECHNICIAN TIP**
>
> Many automotive bolts and nuts need to be tightened to a specified level—tight enough to hold components together but not so tight that the component or the fastener could fail. This level of tightness is called the torque specification. Bolts and nuts are often marked with grades to tell you their strength, which determines how much torque can safely be applied to them. For example, a grade 8 bolt is stronger than a grade 5 bolt and can be tightened to a higher torque. The specific torque required for every bolt on the vehicle should always be obtained from the manufacturer's technical information system. Once bolts are tightened, there are different ways to ensure they stay tight. For example, a locking washer, a locking chemical compound, or a nylon locking device built into the nut may be used.

FIGURE 5-17 Applying a chemical compound such as Loctite to the threads helps prevent fasteners from loosening.

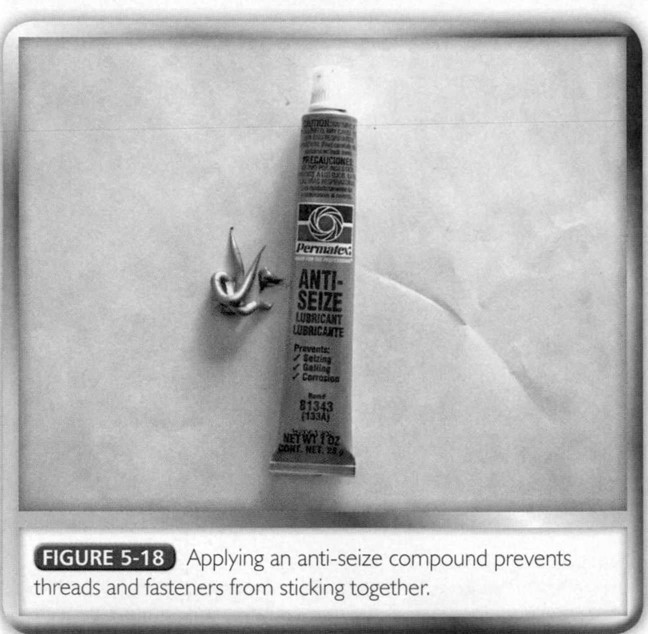

FIGURE 5-18 Applying an anti-seize compound prevents threads and fasteners from sticking together.

Chemical Compounds

Chemical compounds (such as Loctite) help prevent fasteners from loosening FIGURE 5-17. They are applied to one thread, and then the other is screwed onto it. This creates a strong bond between them, but one that stays plastic, so in future they can be separated with a wrench if necessary.

Some metals react with each other and bind together—for instance, spark plugs when they are in aluminum cylinder heads. An **anti-seize compound** neutralizes the chemical reaction that can make this happen and prevents threads and fasteners from sticking together FIGURE 5-18.

Fasteners and Torque

Fasteners are designed to secure parts that are under various tension and shear stresses. The nature of the stresses placed on parts and fasteners depends on their use and location. For example, head bolts withstand *tension stresses* by clamping the head gasket between the cylinder head and the block. The bolts must withstand the very high combustion pressures trying to push the head off the engine block in order to leak past the head gasket. An example of fasteners withstanding *shear stresses* is wheel studs and wheel nuts. They clamp the wheel assembly to the suspension system, and the weight of the vehicle tries to shear the lug studs. If this were to happen, the wheel would fall off the vehicle, leading to an accident.

To accomplish their job, fasteners come in a variety of diameters and hardnesses, which are defined in tensile strength grades. Fasteners with screw threads are designed to be tightened to a specific torque depending on the job at hand, the tensile strength or hardness of the material they are made from, their size, and the thread pitch. If a fastener is overtightened, it could become damaged or could break. If it is undertightened, it could work loose over time.

Torque Charts

Torque specifications for bolts and nuts in vehicles will usually be contained within shop manuals. Bolt, nut, and stud manufacturers also produce torque charts, which contain all the information you need to determine the maximum torque of bolts or nuts FIGURE 5-19. For example, most charts include the bolt diameter, threads per inch (mm), grade, and maximum torque setting for both dry and lubricated bolts and nuts TABLE 5-1. A lubricated bolt and nut will reach maximum torque value at a lower setting. In practice, most torque specifications call for the nuts and bolts to have dry threads prior to tightening. There are some exceptions, so close examination of the torque specification chart is critical.

In the absence of torque specifications the values below can be used as a guide to the maximum safe torque for a specific diameter/grade of fastener. The torque specification is for clean dry threads, if the threads are oiled reduce the torque by 10%.

Bolt Diameter	Bolt Grade Marking									
	4.6		4.8		8.8		10.9		12.9	
	Maximum Torque		Maximum Torque		Maximum Torque		Maximum Torque		Maximum Torque	
	lb ft	Nm	lb ft	Nm	lb ft	Nm	lb ft	Nm	lb ft	Nm
M4	0.8	1.1	1	1.5	2	3	3	4.5	4	5
M5	1.5	2.5	2	3	4.5	6	6.5	9	7.5	10
M6	3	4	4	5.5	7.5	10	1.1	15	13	18
M8	7	9.5	10	13	18	25	26	35	33	45
M10	14	19	18	25	37	50	55	75	63	85
M12	26	35	33	45	63	85	97	130	111	150
M14	37	50	55	75	103	140	151	205	177	240
M16	59	80	85	115	159	215	232	315	273	370
M18	81	110	118	160	225	305	321	435	376	510
M20	118	160	166	225	321	435	457	620	535	725
M22	159	215	225	305	435	590	620	840	726	985

FIGURE 5-19 Torque specification chart.

TABLE 5-1: U.S. Bolt Torque Specifications

	SAE Grade	5 (Dry)	7 (Dry)	8 (Dry)
Bolt Diameter	Threads per inch	Torque (lb-ft)	Torque (lb-ft)	Torque (lb-ft)
1/4"	20	8	10	12
1/4"	28	10	12	14
5/16"	18	17	21	25
5/16"	24	19	24	29
3/8"	16	30	40	45
3/8"	24	35	45	50
7/16"	14	50	60	70
7/16"	20	55	70	80

Continued on next page

TABLE 5-1: U.S. Bolt Torque Specifications, continued

	SAE Grade	5 (Dry)	7 (Dry)	8 (Dry)
Bolt Diameter	Threads per inch	Torque (lb-ft)	Torque (lb-ft)	Torque (lb-ft)
1/2"	13	75	95	110
1/2"	20	90	100	120
9/16"	12	110	135	150
9/16"	18	120	150	170
5/8"	11	150	140	220
5/8"	18	180	210	240
3/4"	10	260	320	380
3/4"	16	300	360	420
7/8"	9	430	520	600
7/8"	14	470	580	660
1"	8	640	800	900
1"	12	710	860	990

Locking Device Measuring Tools

Torque Wrenches

A **torque wrench** is also known as a tension wrench FIGURE 5-20. It is used to tighten fasteners to a predetermined torque. It is designed to tighten bolts and nuts using the drive on the end, which fits with any socket and accessory of the same drive size found in an ordinary socket set. Although manufacturers do not specify torque settings for every nut and bolt, it is important to follow the specifications when they do. For example, manufacturers specify a torque for cylinder head bolts. The torque specified will ensure that the bolt provides the proper clamping pressure and will not come loose, but will not be so tight as to risk breaking the bolt or stripping the threads FIGURE 5-21.

The torque value will be specified in foot pounds (ft lbs) or newton meters (Nm). The torque value is the amount of twisting force applied to a fastener by the torque wrench. For example, foot-pound (newton meter) is described as the amount of twisting force applied to a shaft by a perpendicular lever 1 foot (meter) long with a force of 1 pound (newton) applied to the outer end. A torque value of 100 ft-lb will be the same as applying a 100-pound force to the end of a 1-foot-long lever. *(One ft-lb is equal to 1.35 Nm.)*

Torque wrenches come in various types: beam style, clicker, dial, and electronic FIGURE 5-22. The simplest and least expensive is the *beam-style* torque wrench. It uses a spring steel beam that flexes under tension. A smaller fixed rod then indicates the amount of torque on a scale mounted to the bar. The amount of deflection of the bar coincides with the amount of torque on the scale. One drawback of this design is that you have to be positioned directly above the scale so you can read it accurately. That can be a problem when working under the hood of a vehicle.

The *clicker-style* torque wrench uses an adjustable clutch inside that slips (clicks) when the preset torque is reached. You can set it for a particular torque on the

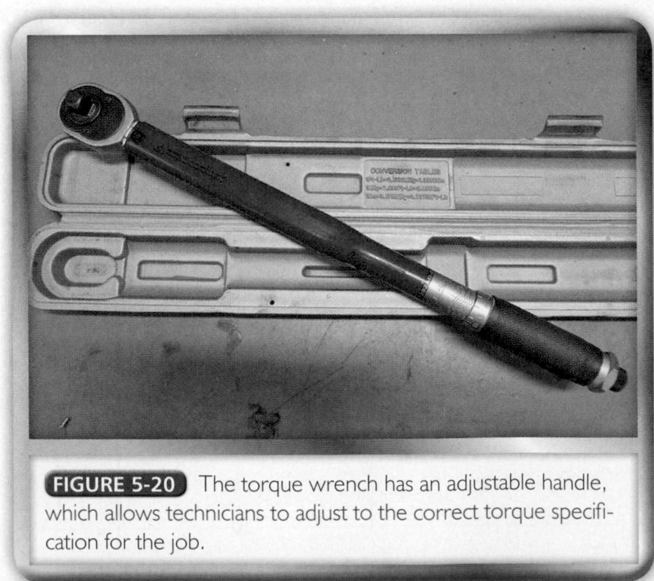

FIGURE 5-20 The torque wrench has an adjustable handle, which allows technicians to adjust to the correct torque specification for the job.

handle. As the bolt is tightened, once the preset torque is reached, the torque wrench will click. This makes it especially handy in situations where the scale of a beam-style torque wrench cannot be read. The higher the torque, the louder the click; the lower the torque, the quieter the click. Be careful when using this style of torque wrench, especially at lower torque settings. It is easy to miss the click and overtighten, break, or strip the bolt. Once the torque wrench clicks, stop turning it, as it will continue to tighten the fastener if you turn it past the click point.

The *dial* torque wrench turns a dial that indicates the torque based on the torque being applied. Like the beam-style torque wrench, you have to be able to see the dial to know how much torque is being applied. Many dial torque wrenches have a movable indicator that is moved by the dial and stays at the highest reading. That way, you can double-check the torque achieved once the torque wrench is released. Once the proper torque is reached, the indicator can be moved back to zero for the next fastener being torqued.

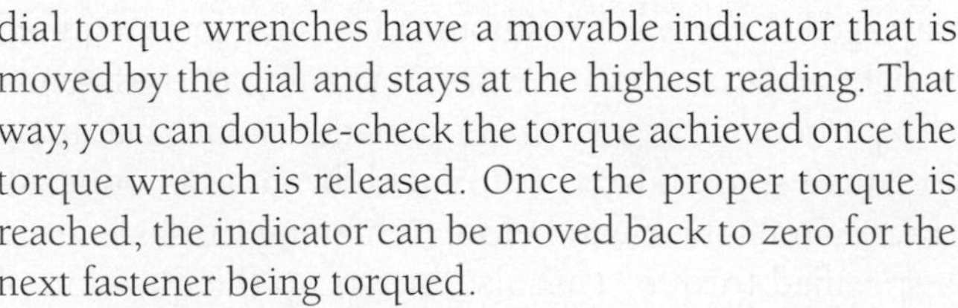

The *digital* torque wrench usually uses a spring steel bar with an electronic strain gauge to measure the amount of torque being applied. The torque wrench can be preset to the desired torque. It will then display the torque as the fastener is being tightened. When it reaches the preset torque, it will usually give an audible signal, such as a beep. This makes it useful in situations where a scale or dial cannot be read.

Torque wrenches fall out of calibration over time or if they are not used properly, so they should be checked and calibrated annually. This can be performed in the shop if the proper calibration equipment is available, or the torque wrench can be sent to a qualified service center. Most quality torque wrench manufacturers provide a recalibration service for their customers.

FIGURE 5-21 The torque wrench is fitted over the wheel locking nuts and tightened to the specified torque.

Using a Torque Wrench and a Torque Angle Gauge

To help ensure that the proper amount of torque gets from the torque wrench to the bolt, support the head of the torque wrench with one hand FIGURE 5-23. When using a torque wrench, it is best not to use extensions. Extensions make it harder to support the head, which can end up absorbing some of the torque. If possible, use a deep socket instead.

Torque is not always the best method of ensuring that a bolt is tightened enough to give the proper amount of clamping force. If the threads are rusty, rough, or

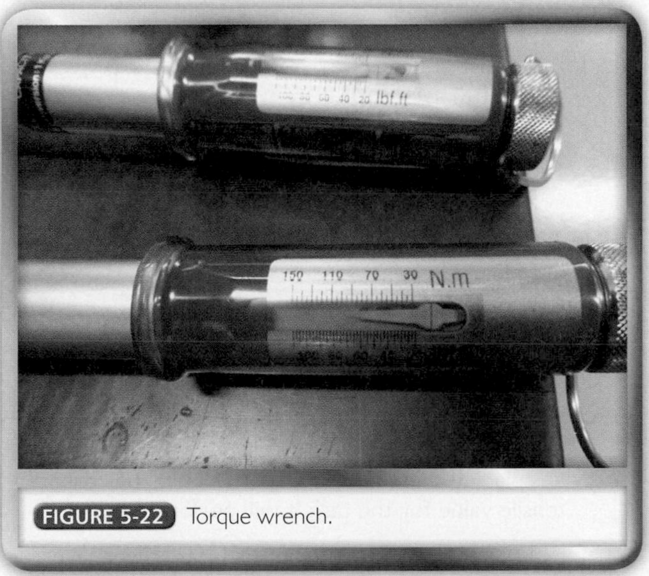

FIGURE 5-22 Torque wrench.

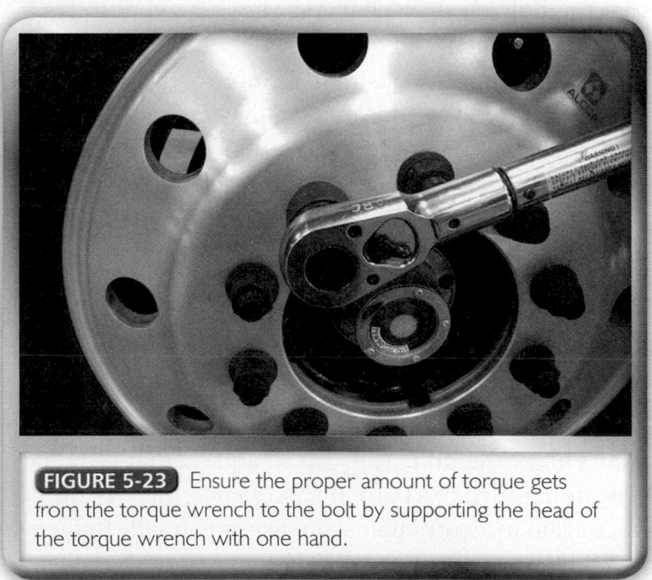

FIGURE 5-23 Ensure the proper amount of torque gets from the torque wrench to the bolt by supporting the head of the torque wrench with one hand.

damaged in any way, the amount of twisting force required to tighten the fastener increases. Tightening a rusty fastener to a particular torque will not provide as much clamping force as a smooth fastener torqued the same amount. All threads must be clean before tightening the fastener to a specified torque. This also brings up the question of whether threads should be lubricated. In most cases, the torque values specified are for dry, non-lubricated threads, but always check the manufacturer's specifications.

When bolts are tightened, they are also stretched. As long as they are not tightened too much, they will return to their original length when loosened. This is called **elasticity**. If they continue to be tightened and stretch beyond their point of elasticity, they will not return to their original length when loosened. This is called the **yield point**. **Torque-to-yield (TTY)** means that a fastener is torqued to, or just beyond, its yield point.

With the changes in engine metallurgy that manufacturers are using in modern vehicles, bolt technology has had to change as well. To help prevent bolts from loosening over time and to maintain an adequate clamping force when the engine is both cold and hot, manufacturers have adopted "stretch" or **torque-to-yield (TTY) bolts**. TTY bolts are designed to provide a consistent clamping force when torqued to their yield point or just beyond. The challenge is that the torque does not increase very much, or at all, once yield is reached, so using a torque wrench by itself will not indicate the point at which the manufacturer wants the bolt tightened. Consequently, TTY bolts generally require a new torqueing procedure called **torque angle**. It is important to note that, in virtually all cases, TTY bolts cannot be reused because they have been stretched into their yield zone and would very likely fail if re-torqued. Always check the manufacturer's specifications when doing this as some manufacturers say that the bolt must be changed once a maximum length has been reached.

Torque angle is considered a more precise method to tighten TTY bolts and is essentially a multistep process. Bolts are first torqued in the required pattern using a standard torque wrench to a required moderate torque setting FIGURE 5-24. They are then further tightened an additional specified angle (torque angle) using an angle gauge, thus providing further tightening to tighten the bolt to, or beyond, its yield point. In some cases, after torqueing, the manufacturer first wants all of the bolts to be turned to an initial angle, and then turned an additional angle FIGURE 5-25. In other cases, the manufacturer wants all of the bolts torqued in a particular sequence, then de-torqued in a particular sequence, then re-torqued once again in a particular sequence, and finally tightened an additional specified angle. You must therefore always check the manufacturer's specifications and procedure before torqueing TTY bolts.

FIGURE 5-24 Torque sequence.

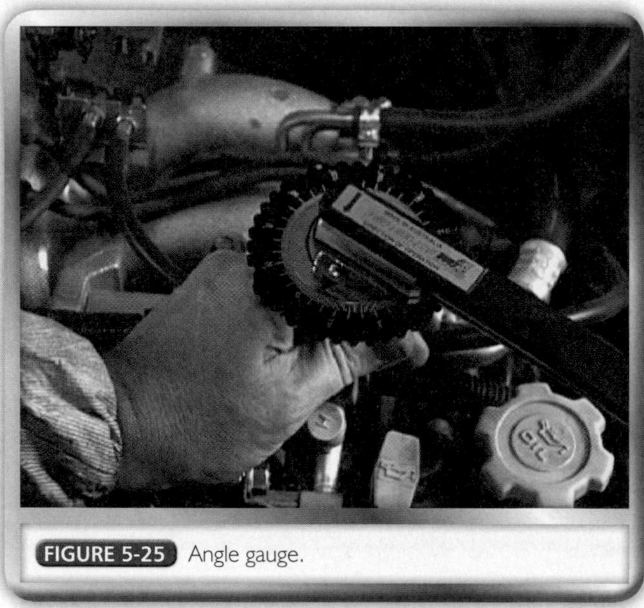

FIGURE 5-25 Angle gauge.

To use a torque wrench and torque angle gauge, follow the guidelines in SKILL DRILL 5-1.

Safety

For your safety:

- Refer to the manufacturer's specifications when tightening fasteners.
- Return the torque wrench to its lowest setting when finished.
- If replacing a fastener, make sure it has the correct tensile value for the task it will perform.

Helical Inserts

No matter how strong a bolt is, it can break. There are a number of techniques used to remove broken bolts and repair threads. Those techniques will be demonstrated in later chapters. One of the tools used to repair damaged bolt holes is the helical insert, more commonly known by its trademark *Heli-coil* FIGURE 5-26. Heli-coils are made of coiled wire and are inserted into a tapped hole that is larger than the desired hole. Heli-coils are self-anchoring, and special tools are required to install them. Once in place, a new bolt or spark plug is threaded into the heli-coil insert.

Locking Pins and Keys

A split pin is used to secure other fasteners, typically castellated nuts FIGURE 5-27. Split pins are often made of soft metal, making them easy to install or remove. They

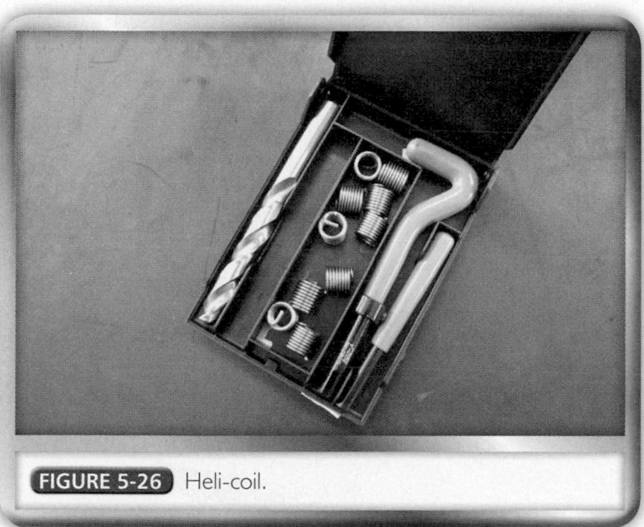

FIGURE 5-26 Heli-coil.

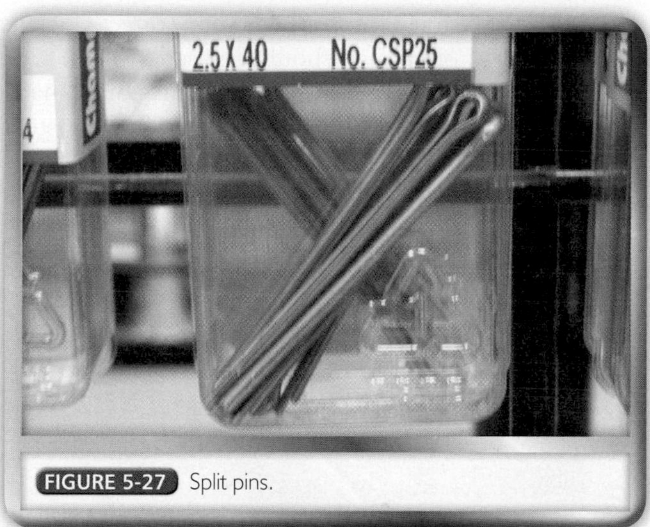

FIGURE 5-27 Split pins.

SKILL DRILL 5-1 Using a Torque Wrench and Torque Angle Gauge

1. Identify the stretch bolt either through the manufacturer's specifications. (In some cases, stretch bolts themselves have a specific marking on the head of the bolt.) In addition, the diameter of the shank of the bolt is thinner than the threaded diameter.

2. Check the specifications. Determine the correct torque value and sequence for the bolts or fastener you are using. This will be in foot-pounds (ft-lb). Also check the torque angle specifications for the bolt or fastener, and whether the procedure is one step or more than one step.

3. Tighten the bolt to the specified torque. If the component requires multiple bolts or fasteners, make sure to tighten them all to the same torque value in the sequence and follow the steps that are specified by the manufacturer. Some torqueing procedures could call for four or more steps to complete the torqueing process.

   For example, vehicle specifications as follows:

   a. Step 1: Torque bolts to 30 foot pounds (40 newton meters).

   b. Step 2: Torque bolts to 44 foot pounds (60 newton meters)

   c. Step 3: Finally, tighten the bolt a further 90 degrees.

should never be used more than once, and they should not be used in applications where there are strong shearing forces at play. Split pins are also used to keep other components, such as nuts, from coming off shafts. To remove and install split pins, follow the guidelines in SKILL DRILL 5-2.

Locking Pins

Dowel pins are used to keep components in place where shearing forces are high FIGURE 5-28. For example, they are used in high-pressure pumps to keep valve plates anchored in position. Pins should never be directly struck by a hammer; a pin punch should be used instead.

Taper pins are used to position parts on a shaft, for example gears, pulleys, and collars. They are steel rods with one end having a slightly larger diameter than the other.

Rawl pins are often used to hold components on rotating shafts. They are a type of shear pin, used when excessive force is applied to avoid further damage to a component. They are normally made from a spring-type steel.

Locking Keys

Locking keys are used to prevent the free rotation of gears or pulleys on a shaft FIGURE 5-29. Keys come in various shapes depending on their use:

- **Parallel keys**, for example, can be used to secure a gear wheel on its shaft FIGURE 5-30.
- **Taper keys** are used to anchor a pulley to a shaft or a disc to a driving shaft FIGURE 5-31.

FIGURE 5-28 Dowel pins.

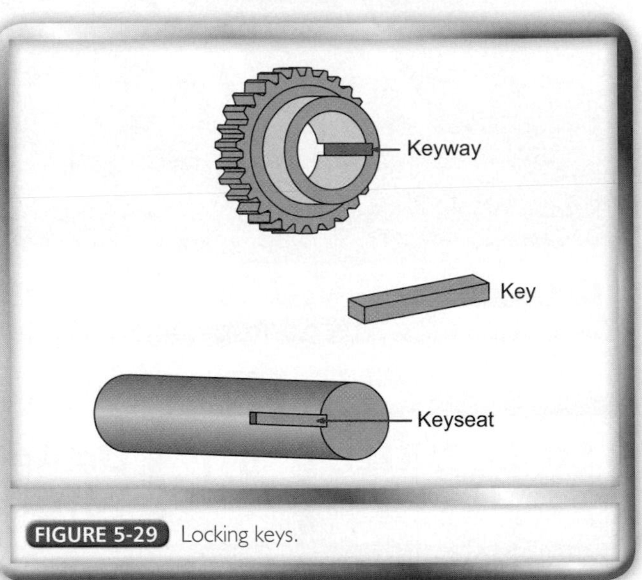

FIGURE 5-29 Locking keys.

SKILL DRILL 5-2 Removing and Installing Split Pins

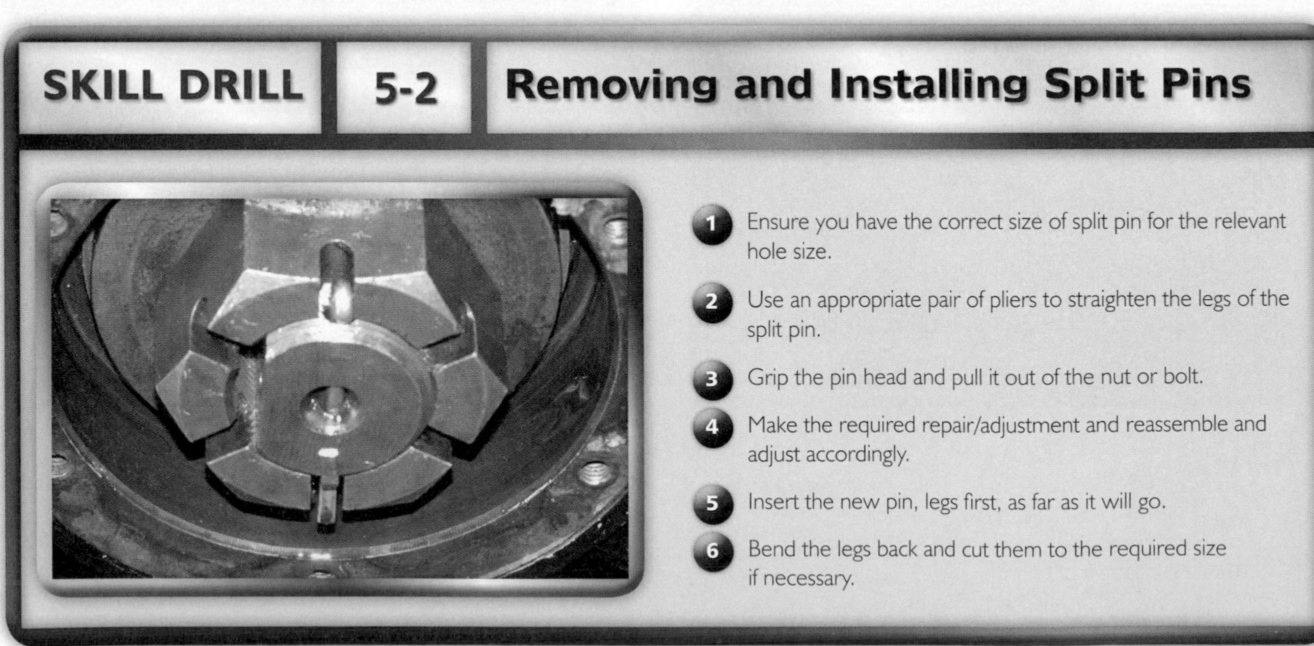

1. Ensure you have the correct size of split pin for the relevant hole size.
2. Use an appropriate pair of pliers to straighten the legs of the split pin.
3. Grip the pin head and pull it out of the nut or bolt.
4. Make the required repair/adjustment and reassemble and adjust accordingly.
5. Insert the new pin, legs first, as far as it will go.
6. Bend the legs back and cut them to the required size if necessary.

- A **feather key** is usually attached to levers that have to slide along a shaft to allow engagement of a part FIGURE 5-32. A feather key is an extra component used with a shaft-to-collar connection. The connection is positive fitting and serves to transmit torques and revs, for example, on the drive shaft of a belt pulley.
- **Gibb-head keys** are designed to be pulled out easily and are used when a gear or a pulley has to be attached to a shaft FIGURE 5-33.

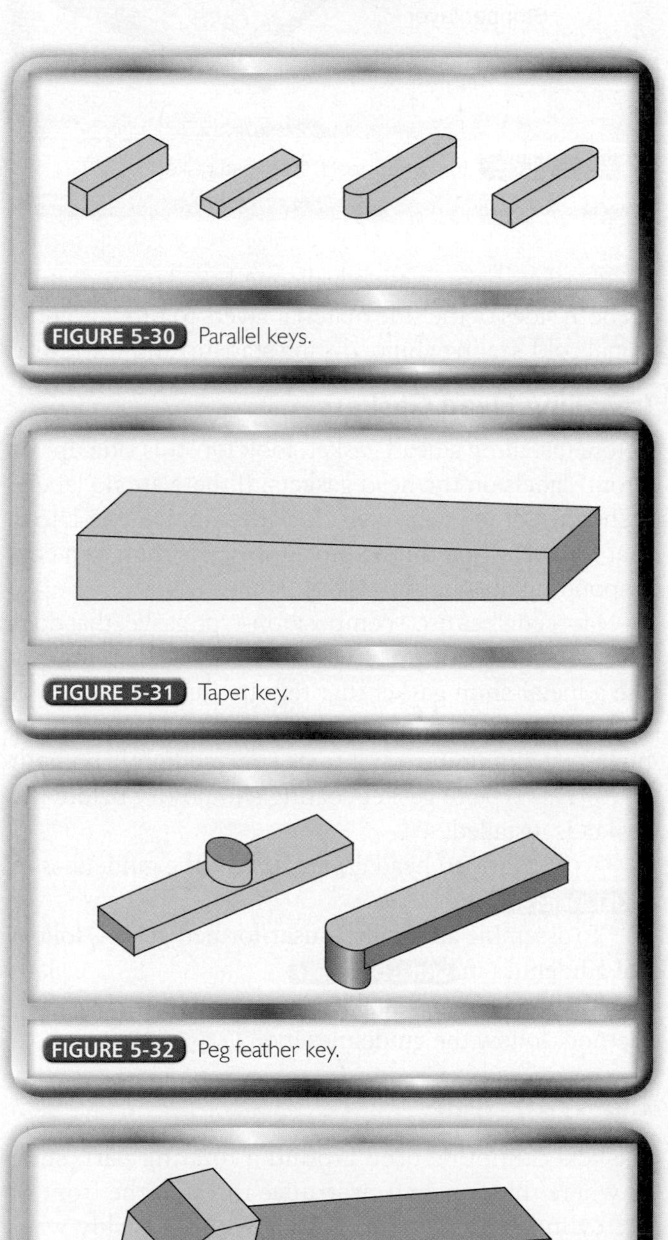

FIGURE 5-30 Parallel keys.

FIGURE 5-31 Taper key.

FIGURE 5-32 Peg feather key.

FIGURE 5-33 Gibb-head key.

Gaskets and Seals

Gaskets and seals are critical in stopping leaks of critical fluids and lubricants in all mechanical systems that often operate under extremely high temperatures and pressures. So they have to be durable and made of materials that withstand extreme conditions. Gaskets are generally used in static conditions where components need to be sealed. Seals are used in dynamic operations where there are moving parts such as shafts. Both gaskets and seals operate on the same principle: keep critical fluids in and contaminants out.

Machinery vibration, heat, and expanding metal would make it virtually impossible to stop leaks if it were not for the critical performance of gaskets and seals.

Gaskets form a seal by being compressed between stationary parts where liquid or gas could pass. Most gaskets are made to be used only once. They can be made of soft materials such as cork, rubber, nitrile, paper, heat-resistant materials, or graphite; or they can be made of soft alloys and metals such as brass, copper, aluminum, or soft-steel sheet metal. Such materials may be used individually or, in some cases, as blends, to produce the required functional material.

Choosing which material and design to use depends on the substance to be sealed, the pressures and temperatures involved and the materials and mating surfaces to be sealed.

Gaskets are often purchased pre-manufactured, or they can be made by hand, a procedure that will be demonstrated in this chapter FIGURE 5-34.

Head Gaskets

One of the most critical gaskets in automotive applications is the head gasket. Head gaskets seal and contain the pressures of combustion within the engine, between the cylinder head and the engine block. They also seal oil

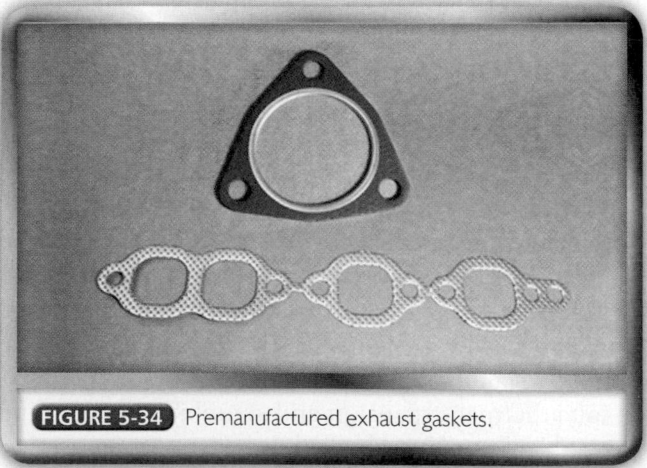

FIGURE 5-34 Premanufactured exhaust gaskets.

passages between the engine block and the cylinder head. Finally, head gaskets control the flow of coolant between the engine block and the cylinder head. Modern head gaskets have to be constructed to resist high temperatures and engine detonation.

With the increasing emphasis on environmental considerations and the reduced use of asbestos, a known carcinogen, replacement materials have been developed. Some of these modern special materials that are now used for the side layers of head gaskets are designed to withstand temperatures up to 2100°F (1150°C). Such materials are also designed to allow the cylinder head and block, some of which have considerable distortion rates, to move slightly on the head gasket as they expand during engine warm-up. This feature is vital for preventing head gasket failure.

Some high-temperature head gaskets are called **anisotropic** in nature. *Anisotropic* means that the gasket is designed to conduct heat laterally to transfer heat from the combustion chamber to the coolant faster. These gaskets are normally constructed with a steel core. Special facing materials are added to both sides of the gasket core to provide a comprehensive seal under varying expansion conditions.

On some engines, the head gasket provides or adjusts the proper clearances between the piston and the cylinder head by the thickness of the gasket. The service information (or repair information) for a vehicle will specify how to select the proper thickness of gasket and why that thickness is needed. Sometimes, it is as simple as looking for a mark denoting the thickness of the old gasket and using that to order the new gasket.

Other head gaskets incorporate stainless steel **fire rings** to help contain heat and pressure within the cylinder. Fire rings are steel rings built into the cylinder head gasket. The rings provide extra sealing on the top of the cylinder to help seal in the high-combustion pressures (hence the name "fire ring"). For high-performance use, such as in racing cars, some engine builders use soft metal O-rings, which fit in shallow grooves cut in the head around the cylinders and passageways to seal the compression and fluids. The O-rings are crushed in place when the head bolts are torqued into place. This is a very effective but expensive way to seal the heads.

For many late-model vehicles, the preferred head gasket is a **multilayer steel (MLS) head gasket** FIGURE 5-35. These gaskets offer a wide range of benefits, such as strategically placed sealing beads that help eliminate leak paths; extra-strong layers that provide superior combustion sealing; and a stainless steel material that maintains its shape despite thermal expansion and scrubbing between the engine block and the cylinder head. Many MLS and other

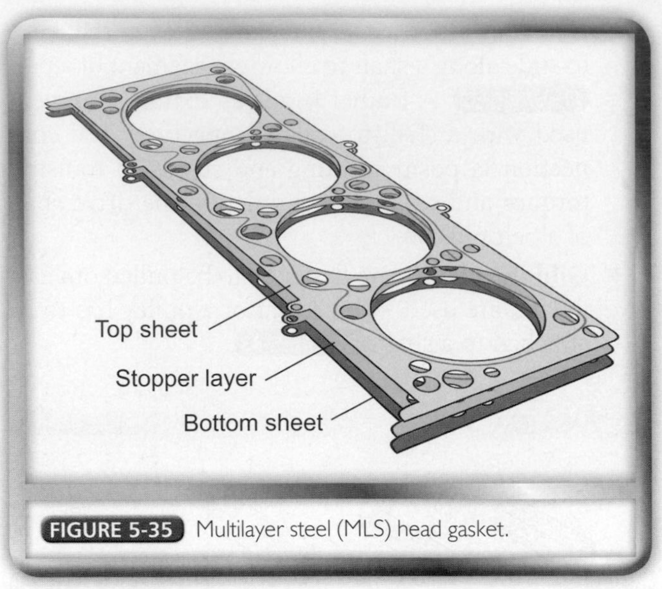

FIGURE 5-35 Multilayer steel (MLS) head gasket.

head gaskets have an added silicone-based outer coating on both sides of the side material layers to provide additional cold-sealing ability during start-up and warm-up.

Installing Head Gaskets

Before installing a head gasket, look for "this side up" or "front" labels on the head gaskets. If there are no labels, it should not matter which side goes up. Double-check that for every hole in the block or heads there is a corresponding hole in the gasket.

Most engines use a composition-type gasket that does not require sealant on either side. Some older engines use a metal-shim gasket that requires an even coat of a high-tack gasket sealant to be sprayed on both sides, or high-heat aluminum paint to be sprayed lightly on both sides. This type of gasket coating should dry before the gasket is installed.

To fit a formed head gasket, follow the guidelines in SKILL DRILL 5-3.

To assemble and make a user-formed gasket, follow the guidelines in SKILL DRILL 5-4.

To assemble and make a user-formed gasket—tap method, follow the guidelines in SKILL DRILL 5-5.

Lip-Type Seals

Gaskets cannot be used around a rotating part, such as where the camshaft protrudes through the front of the cylinder head, because they would quickly wear out and leak. To seal the rotating parts of an engine, **oil seals** are needed. Oil seals are round seals made of rubber or rubber-type compounds of silicone, ethylene propylene diene monomer (M-class), rubber (EPDM)—a type of synthetic rubber—or another durable, flexible material, placed in a metal housing TABLE 5-2. These

SKILL DRILL 5-3 Fitting a Formed Head Gasket

1. Obtain an assembly that will need a gasket replaced, in this case the head gasket.
2. Remove the head cover and keep track of the head bolts.
3. Remove the old gasket.
4. Clean the mating surfaces with the proper cleaning fluid.
5. Select a gasket according to the manufacturer's specifications.
6. Inspect the gasket for cracks or other deformities.
7. Select a sealant that is manufacturer recommended.
8. Spread the sealant on the mating surfaces according to the manufacturer's specifications.
9. Align the gasket with the mating surface.
10. Assemble the components and tighten the bolts to their torque specification and tightening sequence.

SKILL DRILL 5-4 Assembling and Making a User-Formed Gasket

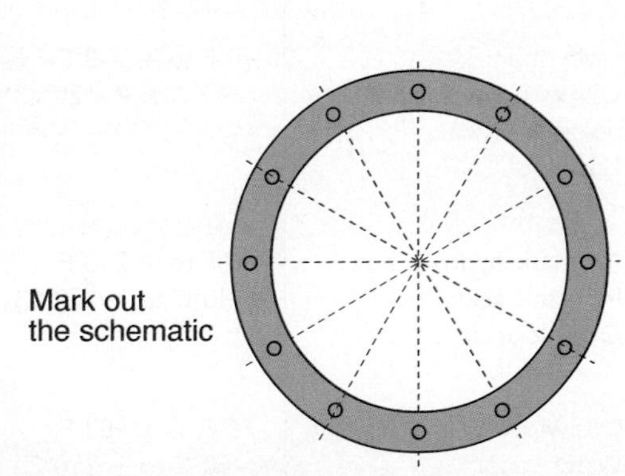

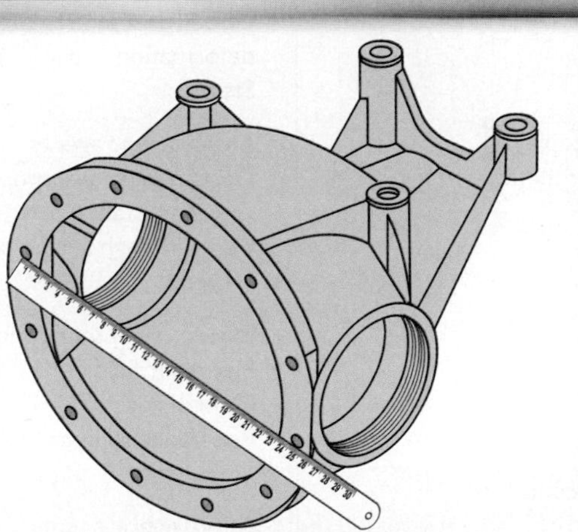

1. Use the object that the gasket is being made for as the die for forming the new gasket.
2. Select a suitable gasket material. (In this case, paper is being used as an example.)
3. Inspect and clean the mating surfaces.
4. Measure the sealing surface to assure coverage of your gasket material.
5. Use tin snips to cut the gasket shape and a punch to open the gasket holes.

SKILL DRILL 5-5 Assembling and Making a User-Formed Gasket—Tap Method

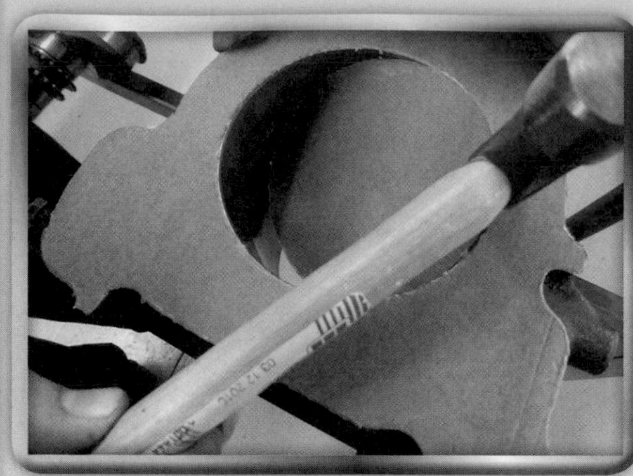

1. Select the correct gasket material.
2. Clean the component mating surfaces.
3. Place the gasket over the face of the component and use your fingers to rub along the outer profiles of the component. Use tin snips to cut along the profile.
4. Once you have the general shape of the gasket, use your thumb to make small indentations in the component holes.
5. Using the round end of the ball-peen hammer, tap along the surfaces of the holes and lift the gasket often to make sure it matches the mating surfaces and holes.
6. Continue this process of tapping and inspecting until the gasket is made.

TABLE 5-2: Common Materials for Manufacturing Seals

Material	Material suitable for:	Material not suitable for:	Operating Temperature
Ethylene Propylene	• Atmospheric agents • Diluted acids • Good resistance to heat • Good resistance to permanent deformation • Steam	• Oils • Gasoline	–40°F to + 320°F (–40°C to + 160°C)
Neoprene (synthetic rubber)	• Atmospheric agents • Good mechanical properties • Good resistance to acid • Oils with high aniline point • Oxygen	• Hot water • Oils with low aniline point • Gasoline	–40°F to + 248°F (–40°C to + 120°C)
Nitrile	• Extreme weather conditions • Hydraulic fluids • Mineral oils • Resistance to permanent deformation	• Aromatic hydrocarbons • Inorganic acids • Organic acids	–40°F to + 248°F (–40°C to + 120°C)
Silicone	• Air • Atmospheric agents • Gas • Good resistance to very high temperature • Good resistance to very low temperature	• Oils with low aniline point • Water vapor	–76°F to + 482°F (–60°C to + 250°C)
Viton	• Acids • Good resistance to high temperatures in the presence of oils and lubricants • Oxygen	• Dynamic uses	–22°F to + 446°F (–30°C to + 230°C)

seals are typically driven into a machined bore around a rotating part FIGURE 5-36. A metal spring, called a **garter spring**, is wrapped circularly around the inside of the seal and applies a small, constant pressure to keep the lip in contact with the rotating part it is sealing. The most widely used seal for rotating parts is the **lip-type dynamic oil seal**. This seal is a precisely shaped, dynamic rubber lip. Like other oil seals, the lip-type dynamic oil seal also uses a garter spring to help keep the lip of the seal in contact with the shaft FIGURE 5-37.

> **TECHNICIAN TIP**
>
> As a general rule, oil seals must be replaced with new ones when they are removed or when a component is overhauled or replaced.

A similar sealing principle is used to seal the valve stem to prevent oil from entering the engine combustion chamber. Like the oil seals, the valve stem seal is pressed onto the valve guide. It allows the valve to be wiped almost clean of oil on its opening trip, keeping a minimum amount of oil pulled down between the valve stem and the guide for lubrication purposes.

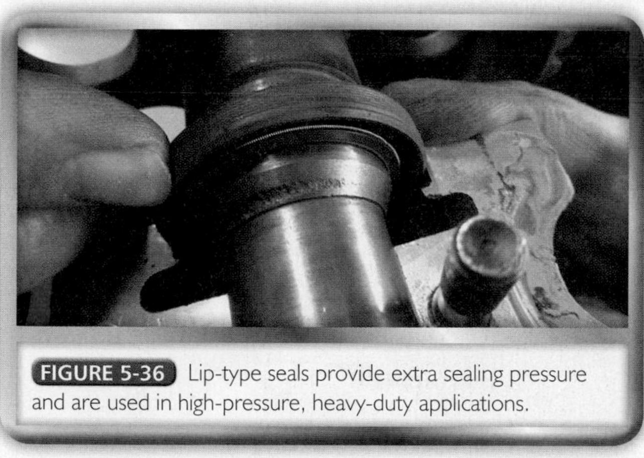

FIGURE 5-36 Lip-type seals provide extra sealing pressure and are used in high-pressure, heavy-duty applications.

FIGURE 5-37 A garter spring.

To remove and replace lip-type seals, follow the guidelines in SKILL DRILL 5-6.

> **TECHNICIAN TIP**
>
> Like the oil seals, the valve stem seal is pressed onto the valve guide. It allows the valve to be wiped almost clean of oil on its opening trip, keeping a minimum amount of oil pulled down between the valve stem and the guide for lubrication purposes.

Ring Seals

Stationary and slowly rotating or sliding shafts can also be sealed by using an O-ring, a simple sealing device consisting of a rounded ring of rubber or plastic. O-rings are typically used to seal a joint against high pressure or the circumference of a rotating shaft from high- or low-pressure fluid leakage. O-rings come in a wide variety of sizes with reference numbers giving the internal and external diameter. Their selection depends on the speed of moving parts, the type of lubricant and fluid being used, working pressures (minimum and maximum), and the size and finish of working components.

The O-ring is inserted around the part to be sealed and held in place by an external housing. The O-ring seals the two surfaces FIGURE 5-38. In many cases, the housing supplies the force to keep the ring in direct contact with the shaft. O-rings are generally effective at sealing high pressures where the differential speed between the opposing surfaces is minimal. In contrast, a lip seal is effective at sealing low pressures, but the differential speed of the opposing surfaces can be substantial. As the lip-type seal wears, the garter spring holds tension on the seal, keeping it against the part it is sealing. The O-ring seal has no mechanism for self-adjustment. Once worn, its sealing ability is compromised.

Two other types of ring seals are the D-ring and square ring. The square ring seal in FIGURE 5-39 is being removed from an oil filter cartridge.

To remove and replace ring seals, follow the guidelines in SKILL DRILL 5-7.

Crankshaft Seals

Crankshaft seals are located at each end of the crankshaft assembly where it projects through the crankcase. The seals help contain the lubricating oils inside the lower part of the crankcase and prevent them from leaking out. A rear main seal is located just after the rear main bearing FIGURE 5-40. In engines that use a **timing chain** or **timing gears**, the front main seal is located in the

SKILL DRILL 5-6 Removing and Replacing Lip-Type Seals

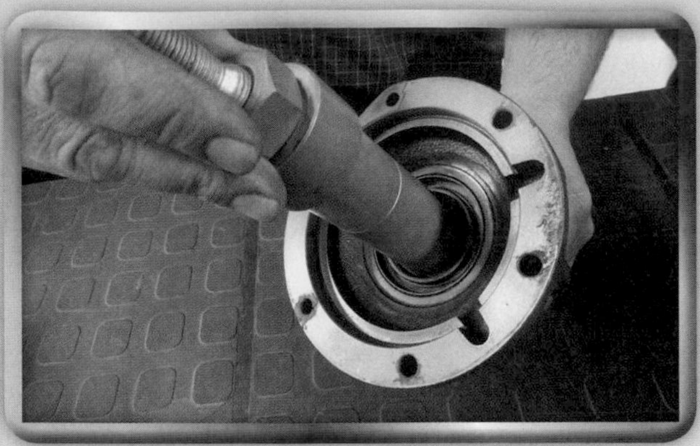

1. Use a component that requires a lip-type seal, usually a shaft.
2. Inspect the assembly for leaks, sharp edges, or burrs.
3. Clean the assembly and assess seal failure.
4. Seal failure can include a broken garter spring or a damaged component at the sealing surface.
5. Remove the seal with an oil seal puller.
6. Measure and record the housing bore diameter, the shaft diameter, and depth of the seal landing.
7. Select the recommended replacement seal.
8. Compare the new seal with the old to make sure they are the same size.
9. Lubricate the shaft and the seal with clean grease before fitting the new seal over the shaft, making sure that the seal spring faces into the housing.
10. Locate the seal in the housing according to the manufacturer's specifications.
11. Press the seal into the housing with the sealing lip towards the fluid being sealed.
12. Use a hammer to make sure the seal is snugly fit.
13. Check the installation and make sure the fluid level is correct.

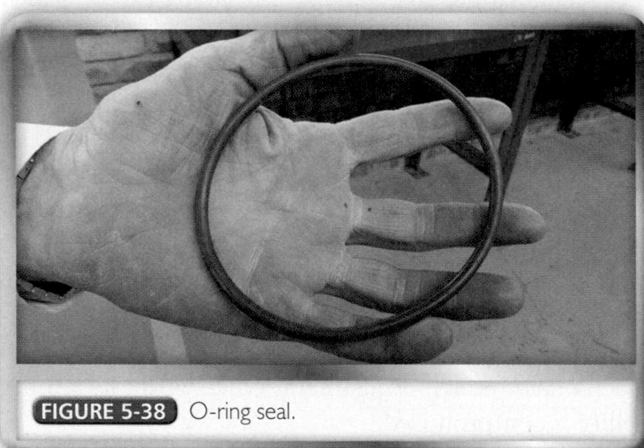

FIGURE 5-38 O-ring seal.

FIGURE 5-39 Square ring seal from an oil filter.

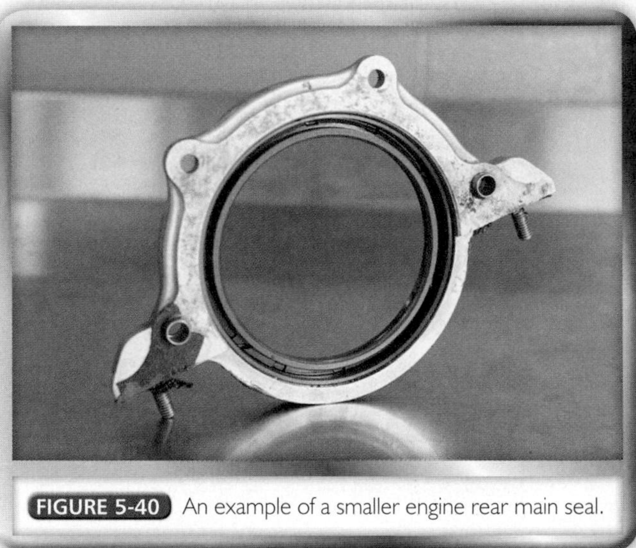

FIGURE 5-40 An example of a smaller engine rear main seal.

front timing cover. In engines equipped with a timing belt, the front main seal is located in a housing bolted to the front of the engine block FIGURE 5-41 and sits between the block and the timing belt. Most modern crankshaft seals are of a circular one-piece style with a sealing lip. Some seals use a small spring, called a *garter spring*, around the inside of the sealing lip to tension the lip against the sealing surface of the crankshaft or harmonic balancer.

SKILL DRILL 5-7 Removing and Replacing Ring Seals

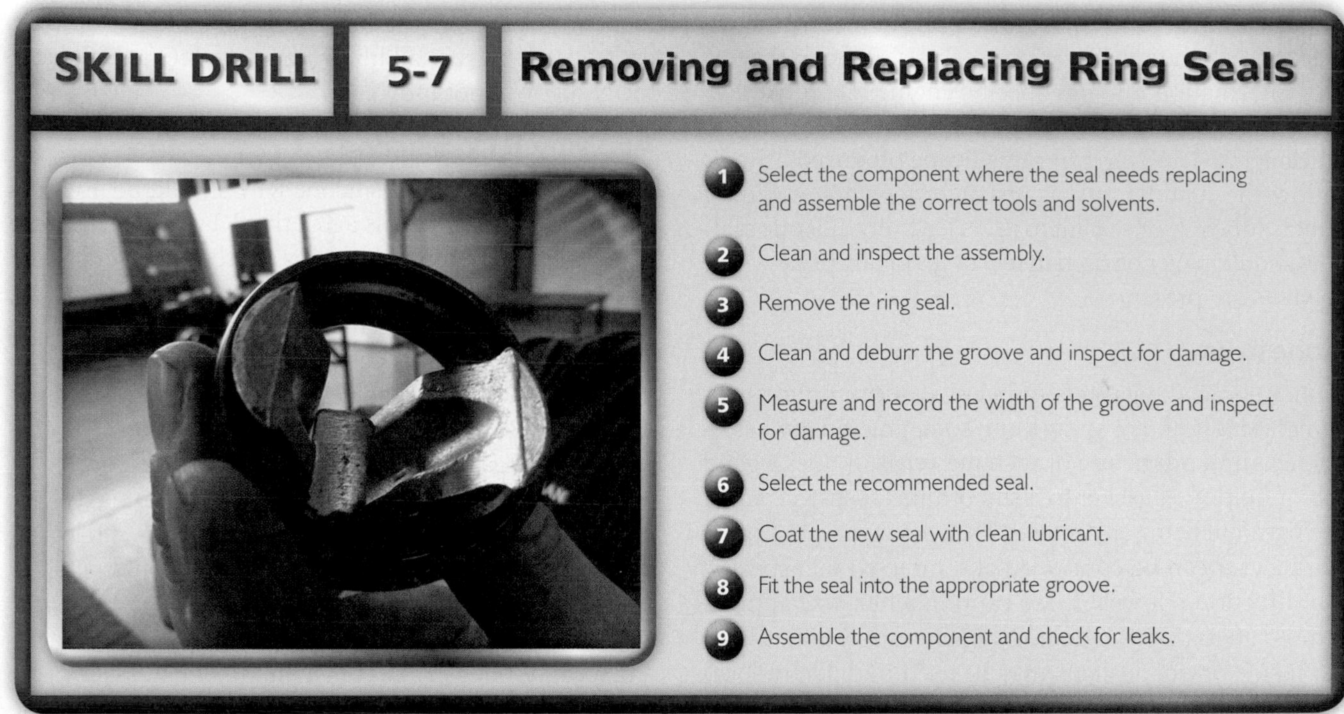

1. Select the component where the seal needs replacing and assemble the correct tools and solvents.
2. Clean and inspect the assembly.
3. Remove the ring seal.
4. Clean and deburr the groove and inspect for damage.
5. Measure and record the width of the groove and inspect for damage.
6. Select the recommended seal.
7. Coat the new seal with clean lubricant.
8. Fit the seal into the appropriate groove.
9. Assemble the component and check for leaks.

Mechanical Seals

Mechanical seals are used to seal between two working fluids or to prevent leakage of working fluids to the atmosphere past a rotating shaft. This rotary motion is a feature of mechanical seals. Mechanical seals are capable of sealing pressures of up to 7,250 psi (500 bar). The core parts of the seal are the rotating "floating" seal ring and the stationary seat.

The rotating floating seal ring and the stationary seat are made of wear-resistant materials. The floating ring is kept under force from a spring or bellows to force it into contact with the seat face. This "face seal" is commonly used in vehicle applications such as water pumps and automatic transmission gearboxes.

Welch plugs, also known as *core plugs*, are used to seal holes in the engine block that were left during original manufacture to remove the sand core during the casting process. Made from brass and steel, welch plugs are designed to prevent water and oil leaks during use **FIGURE 5-42**.

Adhesives and Sealants

When installing engine covers, manifolds, and oil sumps, sealants are often used to ensure there are no leaks.

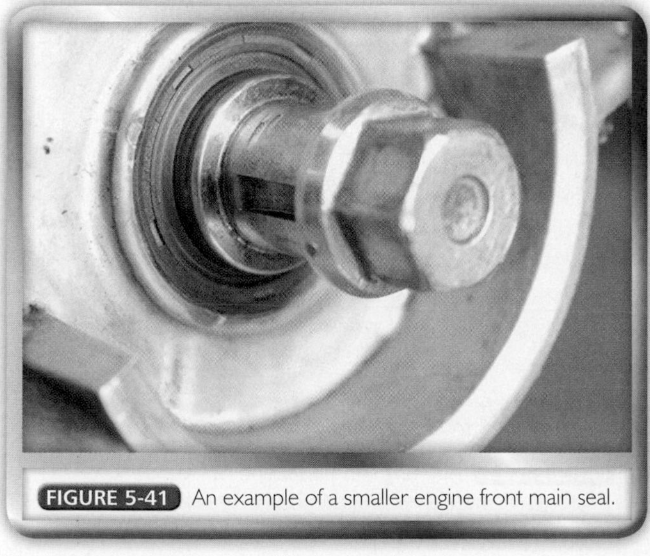

FIGURE 5-41 An example of a smaller engine front main seal.

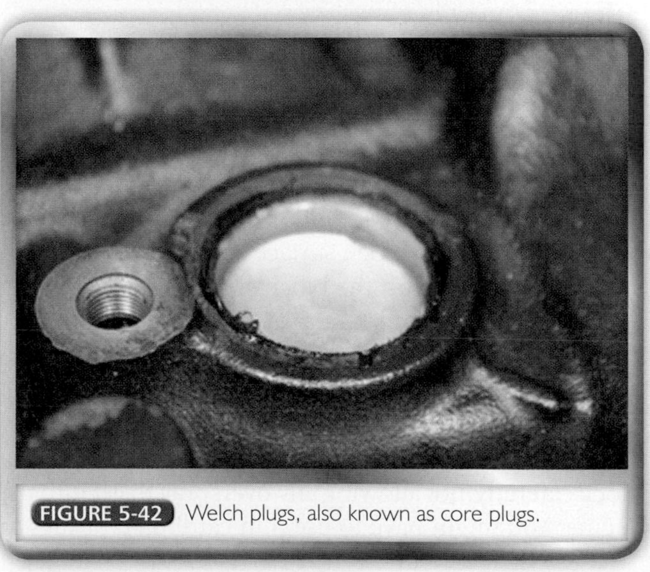

FIGURE 5-42 Welch plugs, also known as core plugs.

There are many different engine applications and engine designs, which require various sealants. Refer to the service information for your specific engine. There are also many types of adhesives and brands of room temperature vulcanizing (RTV) oxygen-safe silicone produced. Always follow the manufacturer's instructions when deciding which adhesive or sealant to use. Generally, silicone sealants should never be used in fuel tanks or any place where solvents are present.

Adhesives

To help hold the gaskets in place, you can use contact cement in a liquid or spray form; sometimes manufacturers recommend the use of such materials. It does a good job of holding a gasket to a smooth metal surface while the parts are being assembled. The spray type has a spray nozzle that can be controlled and directed in a specific fan direction. However, use caution when you apply it around areas that you do not want any spray adhesive to get inside or on. Sealants may be used in different locations dependent on use. Always be sure to use only such materials that the manufacturer specifies, as damage can occur if used incorrectly and in the wrong location.

Silicone Sealants

There are many different silicone sealants, with variants based on the temperature range the silicone can withstand or the type of fluid it is designed to seal. RTV is used to help seal fiber gaskets and gasket joints, and sometimes on surfaces designed to be assembled with no gasket. Make sure the RTV is labelled oxygen-sensor safe. Otherwise, it could harm the sensors on the engine by coating them with a silicone film, which, after a short time of engine operation, would negatively affect the operation of the sensor. Be sure to use the appropriate product and follow its instructions.

Applying Gaskets with Adhesive

For cork, felt or neoprene gaskets, a light coat of adhesive spray is used on each surface of the block and the gasket. Be sure no overspray gets into the engine—that can be done in two different ways. One way is to spray the gasket only with a heavy coat and then put the sprayed side of the gasket on the block surface and slide it around to smear the adhesive on the block surface. Then pull the gasket off, making sure there is adhesive on both surfaces. Let both the gasket and the block area dry. Position the gasket and make sure it is aligned, because you will not be able to move the gasket after you set it in place. The other way is to spray the gasket and then spray the block carefully, not allowing any overspray to get into the engine. You might have to use thin cardboard or rags to block any overspray. Let the adhesive dry and position the gasket, making sure all holes are aligned. Once in place, the gasket will not move.

Applying RTV Silicone

It is debatable whether silicone RTV should be used on gaskets. Most technicians agree that RTV can be used on paper gaskets. Some technicians say that cork and cork/rubber gaskets should be installed dry. Other technicians say that neoprene gaskets should use an adhesive other than RTV because RTV can make the neoprene slippery and cause the gasket to slip out of place during assembly. Do not use RTV on neoprene gaskets with multi-sealing edges. These gaskets are designed so that when one edge fails another edge will seal. If you use RTV on this style of gasket, the RTV fills up the multi-sealing edges and leaves only one sealing edge. In addition, RTV should be used in appropriate amounts. Using too much RTV will cause excess RTV to be squeezed out from between the surfaces and form ribbons inside the engine. This excess RTV can then tear away and be carried by oil or coolant throughout the system and clog up the oil pickup screen or passages in the lubrication or cooling system FIGURE 5-43.

Applying RTV Where the Manufacturer Specifies No Gaskets

On some engines, the manufacturer has designed some sealing surfaces that do not require a gasket, only RTV. When using only RTV and no gasket, a moderately larger bead of RTV is required to seal between the two surfaces. An example of this application is an oil sump; the manufacturer may have designed the engine to use no gasket. This is another reason that checking the manufacturer's specifications is so important.

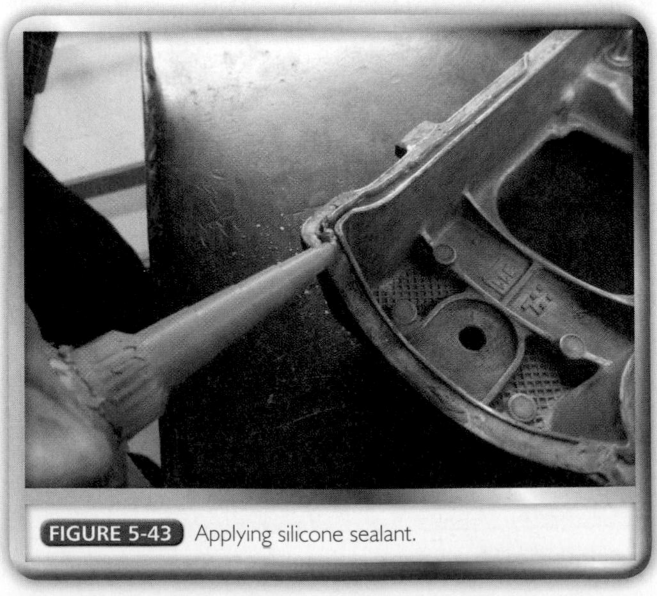

FIGURE 5-43 Applying silicone sealant.

Lifting in the Shop

Technicians do a lot of lifting in a shop. While they do some lifting with raw muscle power, they do the remainder with the aid of lifting equipment. Lifting equipment is an essential tool in any heavy vehicle shop. It allows technicians to more easily access a vehicle's difficult-to-reach areas for repairs. To use lifting equipment properly ensures technicians' physical safety as well as preventing damage to a customer's vehicle. This section focuses on the types of lifting equipment you will use in a shop and their proper use.

A professional shop always takes precautions to guarantee that all work is conducted safely and efficiently, as well as making certain that a customer's vehicle is treated with respect to protect it against accidental damage. Therefore, before you start repairs, pause for a moment to identify good work practices. This will prevent injury to yourself and co-workers as well as accidental damage to a customer's vehicle.

For your personal safety, it is important that lifting equipment such as vehicle lifts, jack stands (also known as jack stands), engine hoists, slings, and chains be inspected before each use and be well maintained. Most countries require annual certification inspections of all lifting equipment such as vehicle lifts and hydraulic jacks to help ensure their safety.

The Correct Procedure for Manual Lifting

The most elementary piece of lifting equipment is the muscle. But human muscles can be easily injured, affecting your ability to work. You can prevent many debilitating back and knee injuries by using proper lifting techniques. When bending down to lift an object, for example, always bend at the knees before attempting to lift. Never bend from the waist FIGURE 5-44, which is the surest way to strain your back or, in a worst-case scenario, rupture a disc in your back. Place your feet on either side of the object you want to lift and point them in the direction you wish to travel. If an item is too awkward or large for you to lift on your own, ask someone to help you lift it FIGURE 5-45.

> **TECHNICIAN TIP**
>
> Never attempt to lift heavy objects that may damage your body. Use the proper lifting equipment instead.

FIGURE 5-44 Do not lift something without bending your knees.

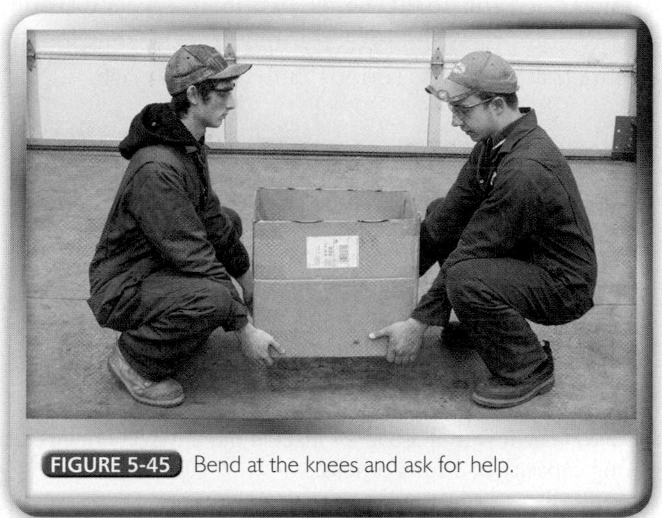

FIGURE 5-45 Bend at the knees and ask for help.

Selecting Appropriate Lifting Equipment

You may end up using many different types of lifting equipment in a shop. Lifting equipment is designed to lift and securely hold loads. Some examples of lifting equipment include vehicle hoists, floor jacks, jack or jack stands, engine and component hoists, mobile gantries, chains, slings, and shackles FIGURE 5-46.

Each piece of lifting equipment has a maximum weight it can support. The maximum operating capacity is usually expressed as the **safe working load (SWL)**. For example, if the SWL is 1 ton, the equipment can safely lift up to 2,000 pounds (907 kilograms). When using lifting equipment, never exceed its capacity and always maintain some reserve capacity as an extra safety margin.

In addition, you should use each piece of lifting equipment for its designed purpose only. For example, use a

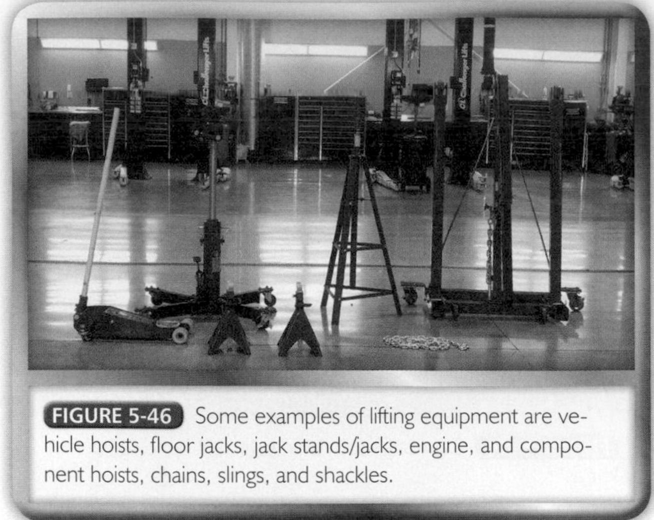

FIGURE 5-46 Some examples of lifting equipment are vehicle hoists, floor jacks, jack stands/jacks, engine, and component hoists, chains, slings, and shackles.

vehicle hoist only to lift vehicles within its capacity. Using lifting equipment incorrectly may lead to equipment failure that can cause serious injury and damage.

> **TECHNICIAN TIP**
>
> When using multiple pieces of lifting equipment, the SWL is limited to the lowest rated piece of equipment. Remember that "a chain is only as strong as its weakest link." Whatever fittings you are using on a piece of lifting equipment, the lifting equipment's capacity is limited by the strength of any single component. For example, a 5-ton chain with a 3-ton D-shackle has a maximum lifting capacity of 3 tons or less.

> **TECHNICIAN TIP**
>
> Manufacturers supply operating information for lifting equipment, including the equipment's SWL. Check the lifting equipment's SWL and compare it with the weight of the object/vehicle you intend to lift. Never exceed the SWL.

The Safe Use of Lifting Equipment

In addition to double-checking safe working loads and using equipment only for its intended purpose, technicians can take a number of other steps to ensure a safe operating environment. These include testing and test certification. Requirements can vary by country and your local area so be sure to check with your supervisor if you have any questions.

Testing Lifting Equipment

Lifting equipment should be periodically checked and tested to make sure it is safe, in accordance with local regulatory requirements. The testing should be recorded for each piece of lifting equipment and clearly labeled with a sticker affixed to the equipment with its inspection date and SWL. Inspections should identify any damage, such as cracks, dents, marks, cuts, and abrasions, that could prevent the lifting equipment from performing as designed.

Refer to the manufacturer's manual to find out how often maintenance inspections are recommended. The time frame is usually every 12 months in the case of hoists and lifts, but may be longer for lifting equipment such as chains and slings. Always check local regulations to determine the requirements for periodic testing of lifting equipment.

Checking the Test Certificate

In most countries, lifting equipment is subject to statutory testing and certification. If this is the case where you work, the **test certificate** should be attached to or displayed near the lifting equipment FIGURE 5-47. Before using a piece of lifting equipment, make sure the most recent inspection recorded on the test certificate is within the prescribed time limit. If it is not, the test certificate has expired and you should notify your supervisor.

Types of Lifting and Moving Equipment

Once you have verified that a piece of equipment is safe to use, you can get to work. You will use your shop's lifting equipment not only to raise heavy components but to move and lower pieces into place as well. Which

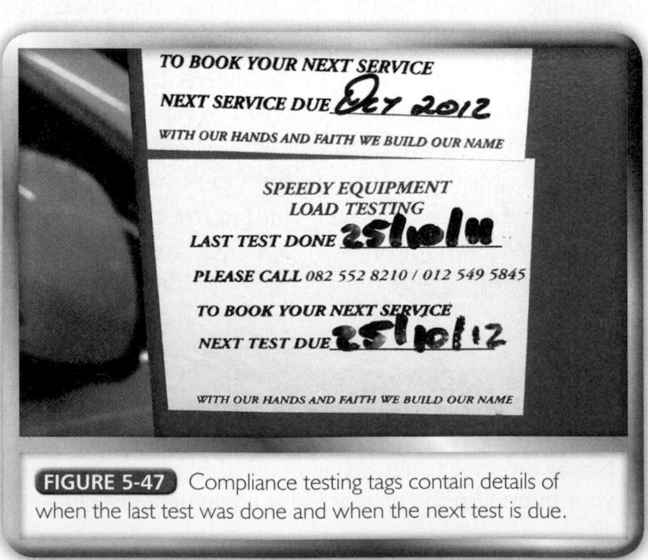

FIGURE 5-47 Compliance testing tags contain details of when the last test was done and when the next test is due.

equipment you use depends on a part's size, weight, and type as well as the job you intend to perform. This section looks at a number of different types of lifting and moving equipment.

Chain Blocks and Mobile Gantries

Chain blocks and mobile gantries are often used together to lift larger components inside heavy vehicle shops. Chain blocks can be attached to and hang from mobile gantries. Chain blocks lift parts and mobile gantries move wherever the work needs to be done.

Chain blocks have a safety latch and hook fittings that attach to lifting points on a component. Once attached to a load, the chain block lifts large components when the technician pulls the chain through a rotating wheel.

Mobile gantries can either be wheeled into place on a floor or are mounted on tracks near the roof of the shop and operated with hand controls that move the gantry into position and lower the chain block with a hook FIGURE 5-48.

Both of these lifting devices relieve the technician of having to exert a lot of effort to remove heavy components and lower them into an area where they can be serviced or replaced. Carefully check the lifting hooks on these devices before use to make sure the end of the hook hasn't opened beyond the standard limit. Inspect chains for any mud or grit, and examine safety latches to be sure they are working properly.

Slings and Shackles

Slings are another type of lifting equipment. Technicians use them to lift and lower many things in the shop, for example, transmissions FIGURE 5-49, engines, and differentials. They can be made from strong webbing material, wire rope, or chain.

Webbed slings have an eye at each end for the connection of shackles (discussed later in this section) to attach loads. Wire rope and chain slings may have any number of different fittings for different applications. Regardless of the sling type and its fittings, each will have a maximum working load that you cannot exceed. As with all lifting equipment, you must test slings regularly to ensure they are safe to use. If you suspect that any piece of lifting equipment is damaged, *do not use it*. Have it tested before placing it into service.

Webbed slings are usually flat in appearance and made from strong synthetic materials such as polyester. Synthetic slings can be more susceptible to cutting or abrasive damage than harder materials, such as chains or wire, and should be checked before each use to ensure they are not damaged. Web slings are available in a variety of lifting capacities for different lifting tasks. When using synthetic slings, always ensure they are protected from sharp corners, which may damage the slings and reduce lifting capacity.

Wire rope slings are made from many strands of fine wire and a core. The size, number, and arrangement of the wires determine the sling's lifting capacity. Wire rope slings are less susceptible to abrasion and cutting than synthetic slings but always check them for any damage, such as kinks and broken or cut wires, as these will reduce their lifting capacity.

Chains are made from hardened steel and are not as susceptible to damage as synthetic or wire rope slings. Chains can have a number of different types of fittings attached to the ends, such as eyes, shackles, and hooks

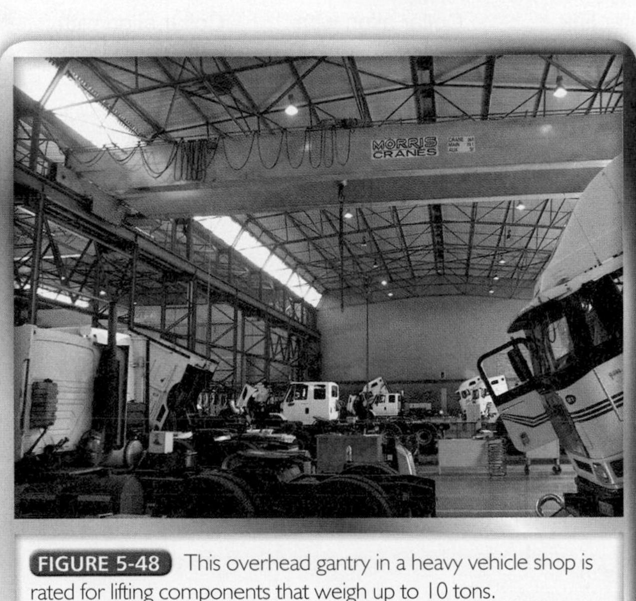

FIGURE 5-48 This overhead gantry in a heavy vehicle shop is rated for lifting components that weigh up to 10 tons.

FIGURE 5-49 Chains and an overhead gantry can be used to lift a transmission.

FIGURE 5-50. Chains, like all lifting equipment, should be checked for damage before being used and regularly tested and tagged.

Shackles are attached to slings and chains to use as connectors between a component and various applications, such as lifting equipment FIGURE 5-51. In lifting equipment, shackles are secured with a pin through the bottom of the shackle. Secure D-shackles, a common type of shackle, with a piece of wire through the shackle's eye to lock the pin and prevent it from working loose. The same applies to bow shackles. As with all lifting equipment, inspect shackles to make sure they are in good condition and free from dirt and grime.

Jacks and Jack Stands

Jacks and **jack stands** are used every day in heavy vehicle shops to safely lift and secure vehicles. As with other shop equipment, it's important to check jacks and jack stands for safety reasons before use. If you suspect that they are faulty, *do not use them*. Take them out of service and have them tested and serviced.

Jacks

A vehicle jack is a lifting tool that can raise part of a vehicle from the ground prior to removing or replacing components or raise heavy components into position. While you can use a vehicle's emergency jack to raise and support a vehicle to change a wheel on the side of the road, you must not use a vehicle jack to support a vehicle's weight during any task that requires you to get underneath any part of the vehicle. For any shop tasks that call for you to crawl under a vehicle, only use the vehicle jack to raise the vehicle so that it can then be lowered onto suitably rated and carefully positioned stable jack stands FIGURE 5-52.

The three main types of vehicle jacks are the **hydraulic jack**, **pneumatic jack** and **mechanical jack**. Hydraulic and pneumatic jacks are the most common types. They can be mounted on slides or on a wheeled floor. In hydraulic jacks, pressurized oil acts on a piston to provide the lifting action; in pneumatic jacks, compressed air lifts the vehicle; in mechanical jacks, a

FIGURE 5-51 D-shackles can be used to connect pieces of lifting equipment.

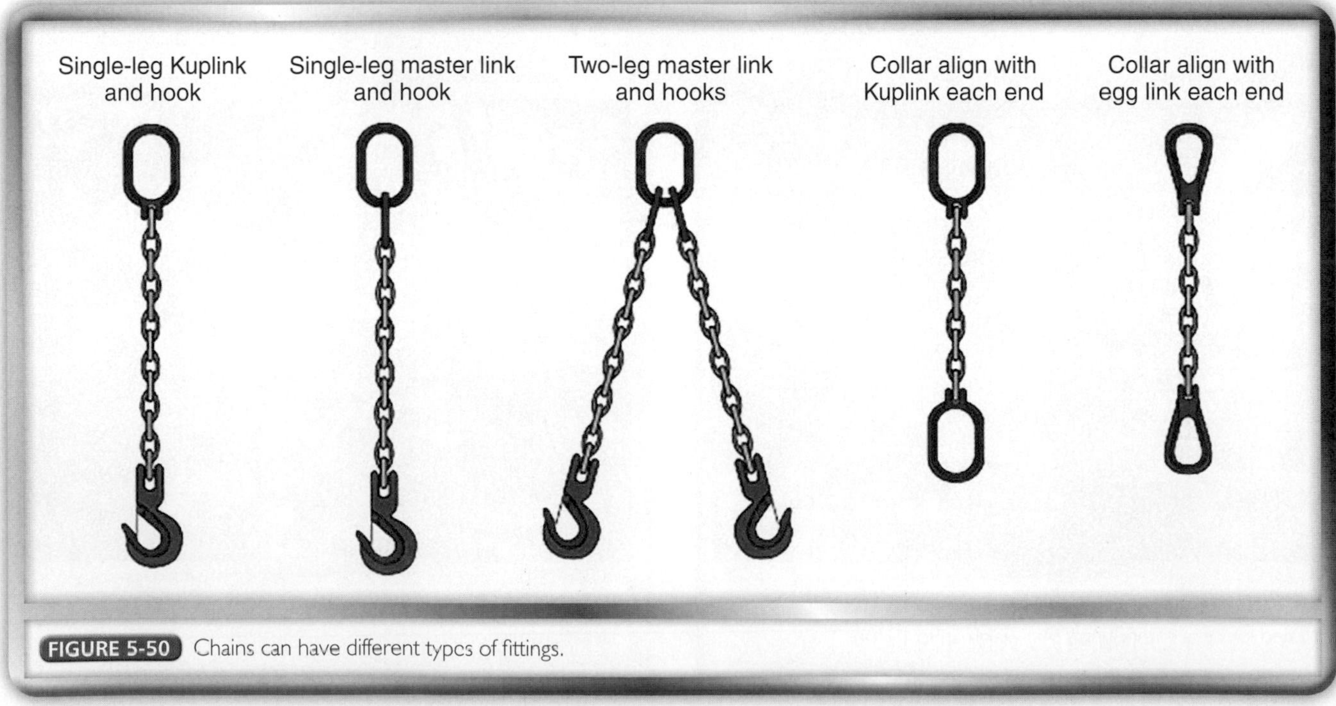

FIGURE 5-50 Chains can have different types of fittings.

screw or gears provide the mechanical leverage required for lifting.

Different jacks are available for different purposes, including FIGURE 5-53:

- *Floor jacks* are a common type of hydraulic jack that is mounted on four wheels, two of which swivel to provide a steering mechanism. The floor jack has a long handle that is used both to operate the jacking mechanism and to move and position the jack. Floor jacks have a low profile, making them suitable to position under vehicles.

FIGURE 5-52 A vehicle jack should be used only to raise the vehicle so that it can then be lowered onto suitably rated and carefully positioned stable jack stands.

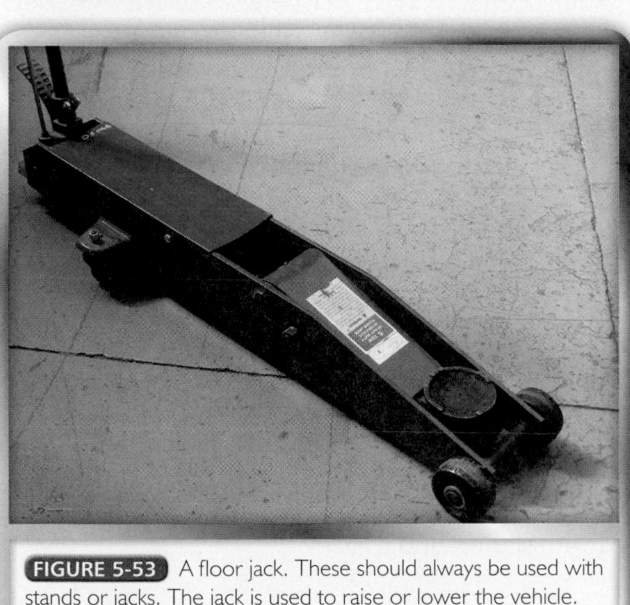

FIGURE 5-53 A floor jack. These should always be used with stands or jacks. The jack is used to raise or lower the vehicle. The stands, or jacks, are designed to support the vehicle.

- *Bottle jacks* are portable jacks that usually have either a mechanical screw or a hydraulic ram mechanism that rises vertically from the jack's center as you operate the handle. They are relatively inexpensive and may be provided with vehicles for the purpose of changing flat tires.
- *Air jacks* use compressed air either to operate a large ram or to inflate an expandable air bag to lift the vehicle. Often the air jack is fitted to a movable platform with a long handle. You use air jacks to lift vehicles as an alternative to floor jacks. Because they require a compressed air supply, air jacks are usually used in the shop rather than for mobile operations.
- *Sliding-bridge jacks* are usually fitted in pairs to four-post hoists as an accessory to allow the vehicle to be lifted off the drive-on hoist runways. Operated by a hydraulic mechanism or compressed air, they use a platform mounted to a scissor-action jack to lift the vehicle along the length of the runway, thus making it more convenient to work on wheels and brakes.
- *Transmission jacks* are specialized jacks for lifting and lowering transmissions during removal and installation. Transmission jacks are usually mounted on a floor with wheels and have a large flat plate area on which the transmission rests securely. They are usually operated by a hydraulic mechanism but can also be powered by compressed air.

Jack Stands

Jack stands, also known as just *stands*, are adjustable supports used with vehicle jacks. They are designed to support a vehicle's weight once a vehicle has been raised by a vehicle jack. They normally come in matched pairs and should always be used as a pair FIGURE 5-54.

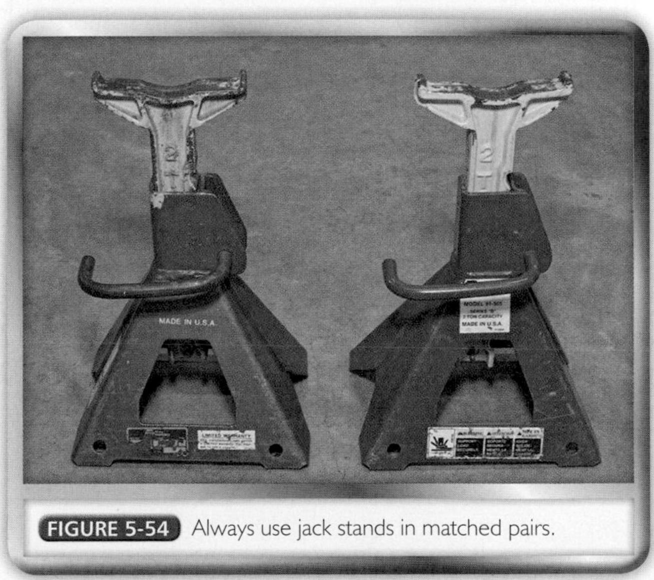

FIGURE 5-54 Always use jack stands in matched pairs.

Jack stands are mechanical devices, meaning they mechanically lock in place at the height selected. Stands are load rated, so you should only use them for loads less than the rating indicated on the jack stand. They are very dependable, if you use them properly.

Always grip jack stands by the sides to move them. Never grip them by the top or the bottom to move them, as they can slip and pinch or injure you. Check that a stand's base is flat on the ground before lowering a vehicle onto it; otherwise, the stand might tip over, causing the vehicle to slip off. Once you have the jack stands positioned correctly, you can lower the vehicle onto the stands and move the vehicle jack out of the way.

TECHNICIAN TIP

For safety's sake, always place the jack stand locking pins into the aligned holes of the jack stand frame and the movable support platform.

Vehicle stands provide a stable support for a raised vehicle that is safer than the jack because the vehicle cannot be accidentally lowered while the stands are in place. Once you are ready to lower a vehicle that is on stands, you first raise it again with a vehicle jack so you can remove the stands. Since lifting devices are also lowering devices, remember that it's unsafe to work underneath a vehicle that is supported only by a vehicle jack because it could give way or be accidentally lowered. Never use stands for a job for which they are not recommended.

TECHNICIAN TIP

Never support a vehicle on anything other than jack stands. Do not use wood or steel blocks to support a vehicle; the blocks might slide or split under the vehicle's weight. Do not use bricks or concrete blocks to support a vehicle either; they will crumble under the weight.

Some shops have tall stands that are used along with a vehicle hoist; they are much taller than standard stands. Shops use tall stands to stabilize a vehicle up on a hoist that is having a heavy component, such as a transmission, removed or installed. Do not try to lower the vehicle with the tall stands still in place; doing so can cause the vehicle to slip off the hoist.

Using Vehicle Jacks and Jack Stands

The weight of the vehicle you want to lift will determine the size of the vehicle jack you use. Always check the capacity of the jack before lifting a vehicle. If the end of the vehicle is heavier than usual, or if the vehicle is loaded, you will need to use a vehicle jack with a larger lifting capacity.

Make sure the stands are in good condition and that their size and capacity are adequate before you use them to support the vehicle. If they are cracked or bent, they will not support the vehicle safely. Always use matched pairs of jack stands. To lift and secure a vehicle with a vehicle floor jack and stands, follow the guidelines in SKILL DRILL 5-8.

Safety

Air bags, shocks and other suspension components can be damaged if a vehicle is lifted incorrectly. Make sure you always use the specified lift points to lift the vehicle.

Vehicle Hoists

A **vehicle hoist** raises a whole vehicle off the ground so that a technician can easily work on the vehicle's underside. The vehicle hoist is also useful for raising a vehicle to a height that removes the need for the technician to bend down. For example, when changing wheels, you can raise the vehicle to waist height to avoid excessive bending.

Vehicle hoists are available in a number of different designs. They also come in a range of sizes and configurations to meet a shop's particular needs. For instance, some vehicle hoists are mobile and others are designed for use where the ceiling height is limited. You can electronically link together some vehicle hoists to use on longer vehicles, such as trucks and buses.

Hydraulic Hoist

One type of vehicle hoist, the **hydraulic hoist**, is very easy to use with most vehicles. You drive a vehicle onto a platform so that the wheels rest on two long, narrow platforms, one on each side of the vehicle FIGURE 5-55. The platforms are then raised, taking the vehicle with them. The vehicle's underside is then accessible to the technician. Since the vehicle rests on its wheels on the hoist, you can't remove the wheels unless the hoist is fitted with sliding-bridge jacks.

SKILL DRILL 5-8 Lifting and Securing a Vehicle with a Vehicle Floor Jack and Stands

1. Position the vehicle on a flat, solid surface. Put the vehicle into neutral or park and set the emergency or hand brake. Place wheel chocks in front of and behind the wheels that are not going to be raised off the ground.
2. Select two stands of the same type, suitable for the vehicle's weight. Place one stand on each side of the vehicle at the same point, and adjust them so that they are both the same height.
3. Roll the vehicle jack under the vehicle, and position the lifting pad correctly under the frame, cross member, or specified jacking point. Turn the jack handle clockwise, and begin pumping the handle up and down until the lifting pad touches and begins to lift the vehicle. If jacking on the truck frame, always use a wooden block or similar device between the jack and the frame to protect the frame from gouges.
4. Once the wheels lift off the floor, stop and check the placement of the lifting pad under the vehicle to make sure there is no danger of slipping. Double-check the position of the wheel chocks to make sure they have not moved. If the vehicle is stable, continue lifting it until it is at the height at which you can safely work under it.
5. Slide the two stands underneath the vehicle and position them to support the vehicle's weight. Slowly turn the jack handle counterclockwise to open the release valve and gently lower the vehicle onto the stands. When the vehicle has settled onto the stands, lower the vehicle jack completely and remove it from under the vehicle. Gently push the vehicle sideways to make sure it is secure. Repeat this process to lift the other end of the vehicle.
6. When the repairs are complete, use the jack to raise the vehicle off the stands. Slide the stands from under the vehicle. Make sure no one goes under the vehicle or puts any body parts under the vehicle, since the jack could fail or slip.
7. Slowly turn the jack handle counterclockwise to gently lower the vehicle to the ground. Return the jack, stands, and wheel chocks to their storage area before you continue working on the vehicle.

FIGURE 5-55 A hydraulic hoist.

Portable Lifting Hoists

Another type of vehicle hoists is **portable lifting hoists**—or *Portalift mobile hoists* as they are sometimes referred to—which offer an economical and flexible solution to shop servicing and maintenance requirements. They offer a lifting system that is simple to operate and allow complete underbody access for maintenance and repair. Portable lifting hoists provide shop flexibility as they are fully portable and can be easily moved to any area of a standard shop floor.

You can raise or lower the hoist posts individually, in pairs, or all together. When used as a group, they are coupled together FIGURE 5-56 with cables to ensure that they operate in sync with each other and the vehicle is raised equally on each leg of the hoist. Many types have

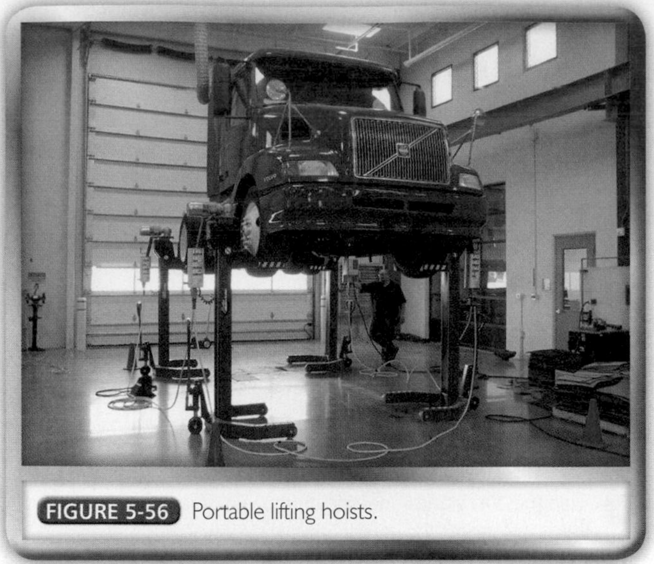

FIGURE 5-56 Portable lifting hoists.

cable hangers allowing you to keep your cables off the shop floor.

The vehicle being worked on can always be put in the best possible position to suit the type of work being done. This can save time and provides the correct working condition for the technician. The vehicle can be set at the best height for the task being performed and for the individual technician doing the job.

Some types of portable lifting hoists have the controller on one of the pedestal legs, and others have a mobile controller that gives the operator complete lifting control away from the lifting zone. Both types of hoists have a remote pendant that allows the operator to safely inspect the lifting operation from any point around the vehicle.

Safety Locks

Every vehicle hoist in the shop must have a built-in mechanical locking device so the vehicle hoist can be secured at the chosen height after the vehicle is raised. This locking device prevents the vehicle from being accidentally lowered and holds the vehicle in place, even if the lifting mechanism fails. You should never physically go under a raised vehicle for any reason unless the safety locking mechanism has been activated.

Ratings and Inspections

All vehicle hoists are rated for a particular weight and type of vehicle. Never use them for any task other than that recommended by the manufacturer. In particular, never use a vehicle hoist to lift a vehicle that is heavier than its rated limit. Most countries have regulations that require hoists to be periodically inspected, typically annually, and certified as fit for use. Before you use a vehicle hoist, check the identification plate for its rating, and make sure it has a current registration or certification label.

Inspection Pits

An alternative to vehicle hoists is a pit. These are very common in purpose-built heavy-duty vehicle servicing facilities. Pit walls often have lubrication and air tool outlets. Once you drive the vehicle over the pit, you can inspect and service the underside without fear of the vehicle toppling over. Beware some hazards associated with pits, however, as they require special attention. Pits must be appropriately marked FIGURE 5-57 to prevent a falling hazard for staff. Pits must also be well ventilated as chemical vapors can cause a fire or pose health hazards to those working in the pit, where harmful vapors can gather.

Safety

Fuel, paints, and solvents can all give off flammable vapors that are heavier than air. Like water, these vapors tend to flow down and accumulate in places such as vehicle-inspection pits, increasing the risk of explosion and polluting the breathable air. Unless bulkier and more expensive explosion-protected power tools are available in your shop, the only safe power tools to use in a vehicle-inspection pit are air-powered. These are less likely to cause sparks that could ignite flammable gases.

Engine Hoists

Engine hoists, or mobile floor cranes, are capable of lifting very heavy objects, such as engines, while the engines are being removed from a vehicle or refitted. The engine hoist's lifting arm is moved by a hydraulic cylinder and is adjustable for length. However, extending the lifting arm reduces its lifting capacity, because it moves the load farther away from the supporting frame. You can extend the supporting legs for stability, but the more you extend the arm and the legs, the lower the engine hoist's lifting capacity. The safe lifting capacity at various extensions is normally marked on the lifting arm.

The engine or component to be lifted is attached to the lifting arm by a sling or a lifting chain. The sling and lifting chain must be rated as capable of lifting weights in excess of the engine or component being lifted and must be firmly attached before the engine hoist is raised. When the engine or other component has been lifted and slowly and carefully moved away from the vehicle, it should be lowered onto an engine stand or onto the floor FIGURE 5-58. The farther off the ground an engine is lifted, the less stable the engine hoist becomes.

FIGURE 5-57 Inspection pits have safety lines clearly marking their position.

FIGURE 5-59 Make sure that all chains and fixtures are in good condition.

FIGURE 5-58 A folded engine hoist.

FIGURE 5-60 Overhead cranes are commonplace in heavy vehicle shops.

When using these types of hoists or cranes, always make sure that the slings and rope, cables, and chains that are used are compliant with relevant regulations and do not exceed the load ratings FIGURE 5-59.

Overhead Cranes

Many heavy vehicle shops are equipped with overhead cranes FIGURE 5-60. These must be used in accordance with local regulations and with the correct slings, ropes and chains. The crane is only as good as the slings connecting it to the equipment to be moved. Operate the crane smoothly, slowly, and with caution. Don't rush. Always ask for assistance, if required. In many cases, two people will be required to operate an overhead crane—one to operate the crane, the other as a lookout—to watch the load and guide it if necessary.

Safety

Never use a hoist to lift any weight greater than the lifting capacity of the hoist, sling, chains, or bolts.

Using Lifting Equipment

Like many shop activities, using lifting equipment involves managing risks. Think carefully about what you are going to do, plan your activities, and check the equipment to make sure it is safe to use.

Using a Hydraulic Hoist

Four-post hoists are often used to lift a vehicle for wheel alignment services. Make sure you know how to operate the hydraulic hoist, taking particular care to know where the stop control is so you can use it quickly in an emergency. Always refer to the operations manual for the correct procedure for stopping the hoist. To lift a vehicle using a hydraulic hoist, follow the guidelines in SKILL DRILL 5-9.

Using Engine Hoists and Stands

Engine hoists are capable of lifting very heavy objects, which make them suitable for lifting engines. Make sure the lifting attachment at the end of the lifting arm is strong enough to lift the engine and is not damaged or cracked. When attaching the lifting chain or sling to an engine, make sure it is firmly attached and that the engine hoist is configured to lift that weight. Make sure the fasteners attaching the lifting chain, or sling, have a tensile strength that is in excess of the engine's weight. To keep from overstressing the sling, leave enough length in the sling so that when the engine is hanging, the angle at the top of the sling is close to 45 degrees and not exceeding 90 degrees.

In areas where space is limited for lifting, you should use a spreader bar to aid the lifting operation FIGURE 5-61. The bar is a straight piece of reinforced steel that bridges

SKILL DRILL 5-9 Lifting a Vehicle Using a Hydraulic Hoist

1. Read and follow the safety instructions that are provided with the hoist. They should be displayed near the lift operating controls. Also verify the vehicle's weight and compare it against the hoist's safe load capacity. Check the hydraulic system for any leaks and the steel cables for any sign of damage. Make sure there are no oil spills around or under the hoist. The hoist should be completely down before you attempt to drive the vehicle onto it.

2. The platform may have built-in wheel restraints or attachments for wheel alignment equipment. A set of bars is normally mounted at the front of each ramp to prevent the vehicle from being driven off the front of the hoist. At the back will be ramps that allow the vehicle to be driven onto the hoist. The back of the ramps will pivot upwards when the hoist is raised and prevent the vehicle from rolling off the back.

3. Prepare to use the vehicle hoist safely. With the aid of an assistant guiding the driver, or a large mirror in front of the hoist, drive the vehicle slowly and carefully onto the fhoist and position it centrally. If the vehicle has front wheel restraints, drive the vehicle forward until the wheels lock into the brackets.

4. Get out of the vehicle and check that it is correctly positioned on the platform. If it is, apply the emergency brake.

5. Make sure the hydraulic hoist area is clear. Move to the controls and lift the vehicle until it reaches the appropriate work height. If the hoist has a manual safety mechanism, lock it in place to engage whatever safety device is used.

6. Before the hoist is lowered, remove all tools and equipment from the area and wipe up any spilled fluids. Remove the safety device or unlock the lift before lowering it. Make sure no one is near the area. Once the hoist is fully lowered, carefully back the vehicle off the hoist with the help of a guide.

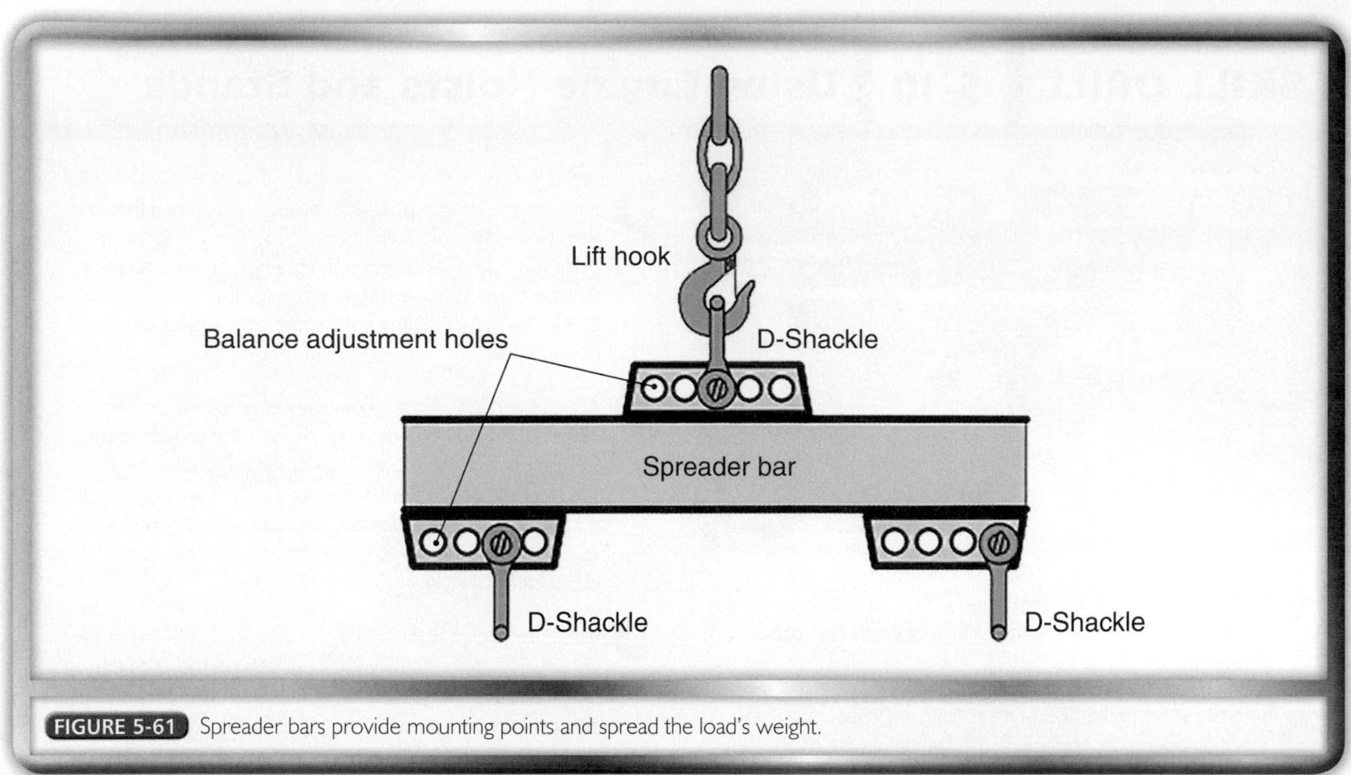

FIGURE 5-61 Spreader bars provide mounting points and spread the load's weight.

across the lifting eyes and is connected by D-shackles. The bar's center has a ring or D-shackle that is attached to the crane for lifting.

If removing an engine from an engine bay, lower the engine so that it is close to the ground after removal. If the engine is lifted high in the air, the engine hoist will be unstable. When moving a suspended engine, move the engine hoist slowly. Do not change direction quickly because the engine will swing and may cause the whole apparatus to tumble. To use engine hoists and stands, follow the guidelines in SKILL DRILL 5-10.

TECHNICIAN TIP

- The engine hoist's load rating must be greater than the weight of the object to be lifted.
- Never leave an unsupported engine hanging on an engine hoist. Secure the engine on an engine stand, or on the ground, before starting to work on it.
- If using an engine stand, make sure it is designed to support the weight of the engine and that you have the correct number of bolts to hold the engine to the stand.
- Always extend the engine hoist's legs in relation to the lifting arm to ensure adequate stability.

SKILL DRILL 5-10 Using Engine Hoists and Stands

1. Prepare to use the engine hoist. Lower the lifting arm and position the lifting end and chain over the center of the engine.

2. Wear appropriate PPE, such as leather gloves, during the entire operation, beginning with inspecting the chain, steel cable, or sling, and bolts to make sure they are in good condition. Before you use the crane, make sure the chain/sling is rated higher than the weight of the item to be lifted. Also ensure that the lifting arm is only extended to the length of its lifting capacity applicable to the weight of the item to be lifted. Only use approved lifting equipment, nothing homemade. Look carefully around the component, which is about to be lifted, to determine if it has lifting eyes or other anchor points.

3. If the engine or component has lifting eyes, attach the sling with D-shackles or chain hooks. If you need to screw in bolts and spacer washers to lift the engine, make sure you use the correct bolt and spacer size for the chain or cable. Screw the bolts until the sling is held tight against the component.

4. Attach the hoist's hook under the center of the sling and raise the engine hoist just enough to lift the engine to take the slack up on the cable, chain or sling. Double-check the sling and attachment points for safety. The engine's or component's center of gravity should be directly under the engine hoist's hook, and there should be no twists or kinks in the chain or sling.

5. Raise the engine hoist until the engine is clear of the ground and any obstacles. Slowly and gently move the engine hoist and lifted component to the new location with minimum ground clearance to prevent swinging and potential tilting of the whole crane.

6. Make sure the engine is positioned correctly. You may need to place blocks under the engine to stabilize it. Once you are sure the engine is stable, lower the engine hoist and remove the sling and any securing fasteners. Finally, return the equipment to its storage area.

Wrap-up

Ready for Review

- Threaded fasteners include bolts, studs, and nuts, and are designed to secure vehicle parts under stress.
- Torque defines how much a fastener should be tightened.
- Bolts, nuts, and studs use threads to secure each part; these threads can be in standard or metric measures.
- Flat washer spread the load on a bolt or nut.
- Spring, (or Lock washers) and, serrated edge washers are designed to prevent the bolt or nut from loosening.
- Metric bolts have a numbering system stamped on the bolt head that indicates the tensile strength of the bolt.
- The Imperial system uses symbols to indicate the tensile strength or grade of a bolt.
- Metric bolts are sized and classified by millimeters in diameter and the distance in millimeters between the thread peaks.
- Imperial system bolts are sized and classified by the diameter and the number of threads per inch.
- Torque wrenches and torque angle gauges are used to ensure the bolts torque.
- Torque to yield bolts are usually not reusable as they stretch when they are tightened correctly.
- Keys and lock pins are used to prevent bolts or components from turning after assembly.
- Gaskets and seals are used to prevent fluid or gas escape and to prevent contamination from entering.
- Gasket and or seal may or may not require adhesives or RTV sealant during replacement check OEM literature.
- Always use the proper lifting techniques when moving heavy objects.
- The safe working load indicates the operating capacity for lifting equipment.
- Lifting equipment includes vehicle hoists, floor jacks, jack stands, engine and component hoists, chains, slings, and shackles.
- Periodically check and test lifting equipment; consult the test certificate if available.
- Vehicle jacks can be classified by the type of lifting mechanism they use: hydraulic, pneumatic, or mechanical.
- Jack types include floor jacks, high-lift (farm) jacks, bottle jacks, air jacks, scissor jacks, sliding bridge jacks, and transmission jacks.
- Choose vehicle jacks according to size and lifting capacity.
- Jack stands support a vehicle's weight when it has been raised; always use jack stands in pairs.
- Vehicle hoists raise the vehicle to allow technicians underside access.
- Never use a vehicle hoist without activating the safety lock or for lifting a vehicle heavier than the rated limit.
- Make sure a vehicle has enough clearance over the lifting mechanism.
- Engine hoists can lift heavy objects out of a vehicle and onto an engine stand.
- Vehicle inspection pits allow access to the vehicle's underside without using a hoist or jack.
- Cover or fence inspection pits when not in use to prevent others from falling in.
- Check for damage before using an engine hoist, and make sure all components have the lifting capacity needed for the task.

Vocabulary Builder

Allen head screw Sometimes called a cap screw, it has a hexagonal recess in the head which fits an Allen key. This type of screw usually anchors components in a predrilled hole.

Allen wrench A type of hexagonal drive mechanism for fasteners.

anisotropic An object that has unequal physical properties along its various axes. Used in head gaskets to pull heat laterally from the edge surrounding the combustion chamber to the water jacket.

anti-seize compound Neutralizes a chemical reaction that can prevent threads and fasteners from sticking together and freeze spark plugs in place in aluminum cylinder blocks.

bolt A type of threaded fastener with a thread on one end and a hexagonal head on the other.

castellated nut A nut with slots, similar to towers on a castle, that is used with split pins; it is used primarily to secure wheel bearings.

chemical compound Helps prevent fasteners from loosening; it is applied to one thread, then the other fastener is screwed onto it. This creates a strong bond between them, but one that stays plastic, so they can be separated by a wrench.

dowel pins Used to keep components in place where shearing forces are high, such as valve plates on high-pressure pumps.

elasticity The amount of stretch or give a material has.

engine hoist A small crane used to lift engines.

fasteners Devices that securely hold items together, such as screws, cotter pins, rivets, and bolts.

feather key Used to prevent the free rotation of gears or pulleys on a shaft; usually attached to levers that have to slide along a shaft to allow engagement of a part. The connection is a positive fitting and serves to transmit torques and revs, for example, on the drive shaft of a belt pulley.

fire rings Steel rings integrated into the cylinder head gasket nearest the combustion chambers that provide extra sealing to seal in the high combustion pressures.

flat washers Spread the load of bolt heads or nuts as they are tightened and distribute it over a greater area. They are particularly useful in protecting aluminum alloy

garter spring A metal spring wrapped circularly around the inside of a lip seal to keep it in constant contact with the moving shaft.

Gibb-head key Used to prevent the free rotation of gears or pulleys on a shaft; designed to be pulled out easily and are used when a gear or a pulley has to be attached to a shaft.

hydraulic hoist A type of hoist that the vehicle is driven onto that uses two long, narrow platforms to lift the vehicle.

hydraulic jack A type of vehicle jack that uses oil under pressure to lift vehicles.

jack stands Metal stands with adjustable height to hold a vehicle once it has been jacked up.

lip-type dynamic oil seal A seal with a precisely shaped dynamic rubber lip that is held in contact with a moving shaft by a garter spring. An example would be a valve seal or camshaft seal.

machine screw A screw with a slot for screwdrivers.

mechanical jacks A type of vehicle jack that uses mechanical leverage to lift a vehicle.

multilayer steel (MLS) head gasket A gasket composed of multiple layers of steel and coated with a rubberlike substance that adheres to metal surfaces. They are typically used between the cylinder head and the cylinder block.

nut A fastener with a hexagonal head and internal threads for screwing on bolts.

Nylock nut Keeps the nut and bolt done up tightly; can have a plastic or nylon insert. Tightening the bolt squeezes it into the insert, where it resists any movement. The self-locker is highly resistant to being loosened.

oil seal Any seal used to seal oil in and dirt, moisture, and debris out.

parallel keys Used to prevent the free rotation of gears or pulleys on a shaft and can be used to secure a gear wheel on its shaft.

pneumatic jacks A type of vehicle jack that uses compressed gas or air to lift a vehicle.

portable lifting hoists A type of vehicle hoist that is portable and can be moved from one location to another.

rawl pins Often used to hold components on rotating shafts. They are a type of shear pin, used when excessive force is used to avoid further damage to a component.

safe working load (SWL) The maximum safe lifting load for lifting equipment.

screws Usually smaller than bolts and are sometimes referred to as metal threads. They can have a variety of heads and are used on smaller components. The thread often extends from the tip to the head so they can hold together components of variable thickness.

self-tapping screw A screw that cuts down its own thread as it goes. It is made of hard material that cuts a mirror image of itself into the hole as you turn it.

serrated edge shake-proof washer A washer that is used to anchor smaller screws.

speed nut A nut usually made of thin metal; it does not need to be held when started but it is not as strong as a conventional nut. A fast and convenient way to secure a screw.

spring washer A washer that compresses as the nut tightens; the nut is spring loaded against this surface, which makes it unlikely to work loose. The ends of the spring washer also bite into the metal.

square thread A thread type with square shoulders used to translate rotational to lateral movement.

standard (imperial) system Bolts, nuts, and studs can have either metric or imperial threads. They are designated by their thread diameter, thread pitch, length, and grade. Imperial measures are in feet, inches, and fractions of inches. Most countries use metric.

stud A type of threaded fastener with a thread cut on each end, as opposed to having a bolt head on one end.

tab washer A washer that gets its name from the small tabs that are folded back to secure the washer. After the nut or bolt has been tightened, the washer remains exposed and is folded up to grip the flats and prevent movement.

taper key Used to prevent the free rotation of gears or pulleys on a shaft; used to anchor a pulley to a shaft or a disc to a driving shaft.

taper pins Used to position parts on a shaft; for example, gears, pulleys, and collars.

tensile strength The amount of force required before a material deforms or breaks.

test certificate A certificate issued when lifting equipment has been checked and deemed safe.

thread pitch The coarseness or fineness of a thread as measured by the distance from the peak of one thread to the next, in threads per inch.

timing chain A steel chain connecting the crankshaft assembly to the camshaft assembly.

timing gear A sprocket attached to the crankshaft assembly and the camshaft assembly.

torque The twisting force applied to a shaft that may or may not result in motion.

torque angle A method of tightening bolts or nuts based on angles of rotation.

torque specification Describes the amount of twisting force allowable for a fastener or a specification showing the twisting force from an engine crankshaft; supplied by manufacturers.

torque-to-yield (TTY) A method of tightening bolts close to their yield point or the point at which they will not return to their original length.

torque-to-yield (TTY) bolts Bolts that are tightened using the torque-to-yield method.

torque wrench A tool used to measure the rotational or twisting force applied to fasteners.

torx bolt Often found in vehicle engines in places such as cylinder heads to blocks, where particular tightening sequences are require

vehicle hoist A type of vehicle lifting tool designed to lift the entire vehicle.

yield point The point at which a bolt is stretched so hard that it fails; it is measured in pounds per square inch (psi) or kilopascals (kPa) of bolt cross-section.

Review Questions

1. A ______ ______ is usually used in conjunction with a ______ nut.
   a. hex bolt; flat
   b. feather key; dome
   c. torque wrench; castellated
   d. split pin; castellated
2. Studs are commonly used to attach a throttle body to the ______ manifold.
   a. exhaust
   b. injector
   c. intake
   d. None of the choices is correct.
3. Torque values are measured in ______ meters.
   a. mega
   b. kilo
   c. pascal
   d. newton
4. ______ strength refers to the amount of force a bolt can take before it breaks.
   a. Shaft
   b. Thread
   c. Tensile
   d. Turning
5. Washers can be made from ______ .
   a. aluminum
   b. copper
   c. steel
   d. All of the choices are correct.
6. Some head gaskets incorporate stainless steel ______ to help contain heat and pressure within the cylinder.
   a. pressure rings
   b. fire rings
   c. expansion rings
   d. None of the choices is correct.
7. Most torque charts include all of the following EXCEPT the:
   a. bolt circumference
   b. grade
   c. threads per inch/threads per millimeter
   d. maximum torque setting for both dry and lubricated bolts and nuts
8. The selection of gasket material depends upon the:
   a. substance to be sealed.
   b. pressures and temperatures involved.
   c. materials and mating surfaces.
   d. All of the choices are correct.
9. Which of the following are among the many different fasteners used in heavy vehicle applications?
   a. Screws
   b. Bolts
   c. Nuts
   d. All of the choices are correct.
10. Most modern crankshaft seals are of a circular ______ style with a sealing lip.
    a. one-piece
    b. two-piece
    c. three-piece
    d. None of the choices is correct.

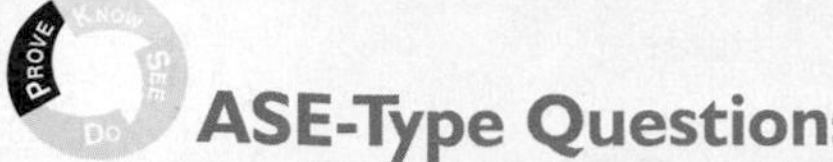

ASE-Type Questions

1. Technician A says seals are usually used on stationary components and gaskets are used on rotating parts. Technician B says seals are usually used on rotating parts whereas gaskets are used for stationary components. Who is correct?
   a. Technician A
   b. Technician B
   c. Both Technician A and Technician B
   d. Neither Technician A nor Technician B
2. Technician A says the purpose of gaskets and seals is to keep critical fluids from leaking and to keep contaminants out. Technician B disagrees. Who is correct?
   a. Technician A
   b. Technician B
   c. Both Technician A and Technician B
   d. Neither Technician A nor Technician B
3. Technician A says a garter spring is used in lip-type seals. Technician B says it is used to maintain high pressure without fluid leaking. Who is correct?
   a. Technician A
   b. Technician B
   c. Both Technician A and Technician B
   d. Neither Technician A nor Technician B
4. Technician A says that hoists should be inspected and certified periodically. Technician B says that safety locks do not need to be applied before working under a vehicle, unless you will be working for more than 10 minutes. Who is correct?
   a. Technician A
   b. Technician B
   c. Both Technician A and Technician B
   d. Neither Technician A nor Technician B
5. Technician A says that an engine sling should have an angle greater than 90 degrees. Technician B says that all slings and lifting chains should be inspected for damage prior to use. Who is correct?
   a. Technician A
   b. Technician B
   c. Both Technician A and Technician B
   d. Neither Technician A nor Technician B
6. Technician A says that you should have a co-worker help guide you onto an inspection pit. Technician B says that all lights should be on in the pit before driving over it. Who is correct?
   a. Technician A
   b. Technician B
   c. Both Technician A and Technician B
   d. Neither Technician A nor Technician B
7. Technician A says if a fastener is overtightened, it could become damaged or could break. Technician B says if a fastener is undertightened, it is likely to be satisfactory. Who is correct?
   a. Technician A
   b. Technician B
   c. Both Technician A and Technician B
   d. Neither Technician A nor Technician B
8. Technician A says torque specifications for bolts and nuts in vehicles will usually be contained within workshop manuals. Technician B says that in practice, most torque specifications call for the nuts and bolts to have oiled threads prior to tightening. Who is correct?
   a. Technician A
   b. Technician B
   c. Both Technician A and Technician B
   d. Neither Technician A nor Technician B
9. Technician A says one of the tools used to repair damaged bolt holes is the helical insert, more commonly known by its trademark, Heli-coil. Technician B says Heli-coils are made of coiled wire and are inserted into a tapped hole that is larger than the desired hole. Who is correct?
   a. Technician A
   b. Technician B
   c. Both Technician A and Technician B
   d. Neither Technician A nor Technician B
10. Technician A says a MLS head gasket has multiple layers that provide superior combustion sealing. Technician B says one of the most critical gaskets in automotive applications is the head gasket. Who is correct?
    a. Technician A
    b. Technician B
    c. Both Technician A and Technician B
    d. Neither Technician A nor Technician B

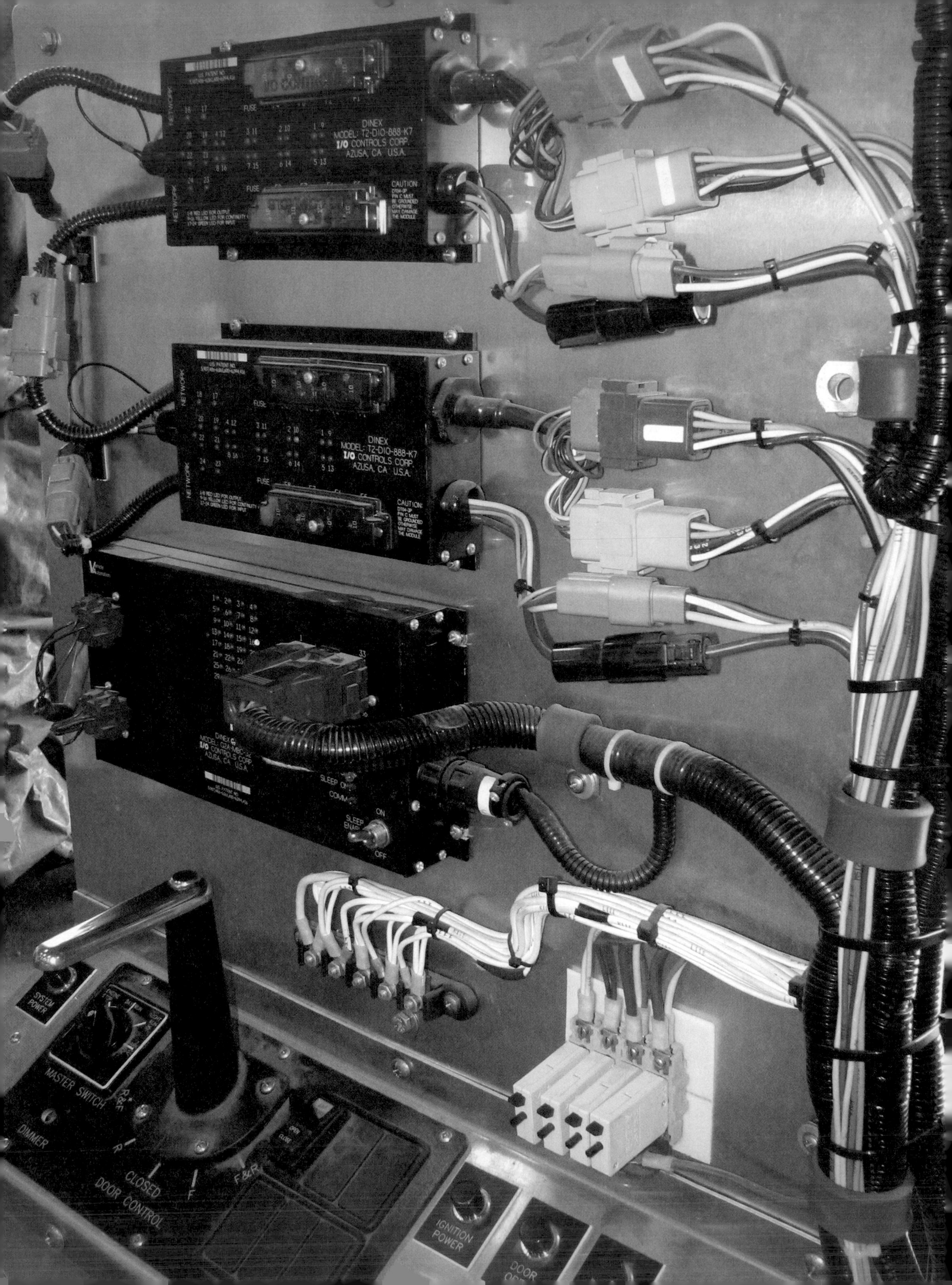

DINEX
MODEL: T2-DIO-888-K7
I/O CONTROLS CORP.
AZUSA, CA U.S.A.
NETWORK
FUSE
CAUTION:
DINEX
MODEL: T2-DIO-888-K7
I/O CONTROLS CORP.
AZUSA, CA U.S.A.
SLEEP
ON
OFF
SYSTEM POWER
MASTER SWITCH
DIMMER
CLOSED
DOOR CONTROL
R
F
F&R
IGNITION POWER

SECTION II

Electrical and Electronic Systems

CHAPTER 6	Principles of Electricity
CHAPTER 7	Generating Electricity
CHAPTER 8	Electric Circuits and Circuit Protection
CHAPTER 9	Circuit Control Devices
CHAPTER 10	Electrical Test Instruments
CHAPTER 11	Commercial Vehicle Batteries
CHAPTER 12	Advanced Battery Technologies
CHAPTER 13	Servicing Commercial Vehicle Batteries
CHAPTER 14	Heavy-Duty Starting Systems and Circuits
CHAPTER 15	Charging Systems
CHAPTER 16	Electrical Wiring and Circuit Diagrams
CHAPTER 17	Body Electrical Systems—Lighting Systems
CHAPTER 18	Body Electrical Systems—Instrumentation
CHAPTER 19	Electronic Signal Processing
CHAPTER 20	Sensors
CHAPTER 21	On-Board Vehicle Networks
CHAPTER 22	On-Board Diagnostics

CHAPTER 6

NATEF Tasks

There are no NATEF tasks for this chapter.

Knowledge Objectives

After reading this chapter, you will be able to:

1. Identify and explain the functions of the electrical elements of the atom. (pp 208–209)
2. Identify and describe conductors, insulators, and semiconductors. (pp 209–210)
3. Define and explain concepts of voltage amperage and resistance. (pp 210–215)
4. Calculate the energy used in a heating circuit. (p 214)
5. Predict the effect of resistance on voltage and amperage in a circuit. (p 214)
6. Predict the effects of increasing voltage and amperage in a circuit. (p 214)
7. Explain the relationship between voltage amperage and resistance. (pp 214–216)
8. Describe the differences between alternating and direct current. (pp 217–219)
9. Calculate power consumption in an electric circuit. (pp 219–220)

Principles of Electricity

Skills Objectives

After reading this chapter, you will be able to:

1. Differentiate between electrical units of measurement for voltage, amperage, and resistance. (pp 214–216)
2. Calculate power consumption in an electric circuit. (pp 219–220)
3. Calculate energy consumption in a heating circuit. (pp 219–220)

Introduction

Not long ago, a typical heavy-duty truck had fewer than 200 electrical circuits. Lighting, starting, and charging were the most significant electrical systems along with a few other electrical accessories like the horn and wipers. Today, the number of electrical circuits has increased into the thousands, and not a single truck and bus system is without electronic control FIGURE 6-1. Where the radio was once the most sophisticated electrical device, microprocessors containing millions of transistors not only control the traditional electrical systems, such as lighting and accessories, but the software contained in the control modules operates braking, transmissions, engine operation, and on-board entertainment (infotainment) systems.

FIGURE 6-1 Electronic controls extend to every vehicle system.

Increasing sophistication of heavy-duty electrical systems include radar-based collision-avoidance systems, hybrid electric powertrain and telematics which is monitoring and control of vehicles using satellite, cell phone, and internet-based vehicle communication.

Today's electrical system components are no longer separated into distinct systems. Electronic control modules (ECMs) provide electrical signals to operate individual electrical components. The modules are then connected together by on-board networks enabling the control of the electrical system to be distributed over many electronic control modules FIGURE 6-2. Networking electrical system components adds new vehicle features that can enhance safety, performance, and passenger comfort simply by adding only software and a twisted pair of wires to connect all the vehicle ECMs. For example, receiving a hands-free cell phone call today will automatically mute the radio volume; using the wipers will simultaneously turn-on the headlights; a wheel slip event detected by the antilock brake system will disable engine brakes or reduce engine power and apply brakes to the slipping wheel, enabling torque transfer to non-slipping wheels. Information from the low-fuel warning is integrated with intelligent vehicle controls, which can inform the driver through the on-board navigation system of nearby fuelling stations. A GPS tracking system used to locate goods

You Are the Technician

When measuring the amount of amperage drawn by a starting motor cranking a 15L Detroit Diesel DD15 engine, a technician observed close to 900 amps of current was needed. The engine cranking speed was normal and close to 200-rpm, but the technician observed light smoke rising from some of the battery cable connections. After replacing all three batteries and making sure all batteries were fully charged, only 500 amps of current was needed to start the engine. The engine then cranked at close to the same speed before replacing the batteries.

1. Explain why more amperage was used by the starting motor before replacing the truck's batteries than after replacing the batteries.
2. If it were possible for the 12-volt starting motor to be used in a 24-volt circuit, what would you predict would happen to the amount of amperage drawn by the starting motor?
3. Explain why smoke was rising from the battery cable connections when the cranking amperage was high. Include the name of the applicable electrical law in your explanation.

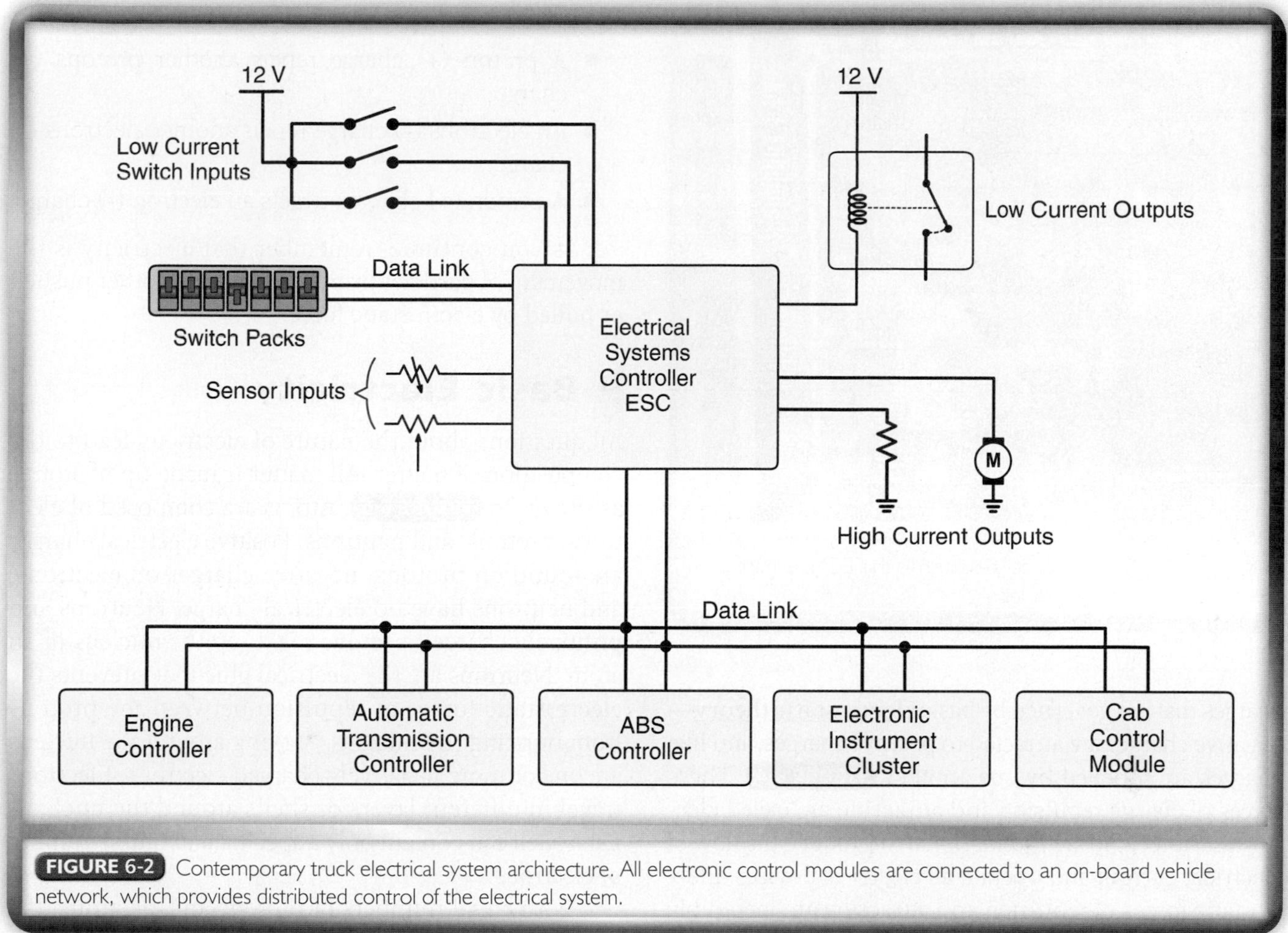

FIGURE 6-2 Contemporary truck electrical system architecture. All electronic control modules are connected to an on-board vehicle network, which provides distributed control of the electrical system.

or people in a truck, trailer, or bus will reroute—without prompting—a vehicle around traffic jams based on information automatically transmitted to the vehicle.

What is the point being made? The technology in today's heavy-duty (HD) vehicles is both complex and sophisticated. A successful and valued technician needs more than ever to have a sound understanding of electrical principles underlying HD vehicle electrical technology. Arguably, the technician's most essential skills are to understand principles of electricity, analyzing electrical problems, comprehending electrical system and component operation, plus knowing how to use test equipment to diagnose electrical problems.

Electrical Fundamentals

Understanding the behavior of electricity can be more difficult than understanding mechanical concepts such as four-stroke cycle engine operation or braking fundamentals since electricity itself cannot be seen, but only its effects. At the same time, electricity is governed by the laws of science, so learning how electricity behaves can be approached in a logical manner, as with any other subject. By applying yourself, over time it will make more and more sense. This chapter explores basic principles about the nature of electricity and how it behaves.

To get started, it is useful to know there are good analogies for how electricity behaves, which are helpful to understand different aspects of electricity's properties. Visualizing electrical concepts using these comparisons helps many learners to more easily understand electrical principles. In fact one analogy is to think of electricity as nothing more than the movement of particles from one point to another. For example, imagine a line of marbles rolling through a tube or the flow of water through a pipe. The moving marbles or flow of water has energy that can be harnessed and made to perform work or some specialized function. Electrical devices can extract the energy from moving particles FIGURE 6-3. The energy can be converted into a variety of others forms such as light, heat, sound, electrical signals, or magnetic fields, which are then used to operate motors, solenoids, or relays. That is where some of electricity's magic comes in. Moving these electrical particles involves using positive and negative

FIGURE 6-3 Electrical devices, such as this ECM, extract energy from moving particles.

charges that are governed by basic **electrostatic theory**—negative charges are attracted to positive charges, and like charges are repelled by one another FIGURE 6-4. These forces of charge repulsion and attraction are called electrostatic force and are foundational to produce the flow of electrical current and operate all electrical devices. Electrostatic forces of repulsion and attraction are incredibly powerful and the energy they contain can be harnessed by electrical devices to perform work.

Electrostatic Law Summary:

- A proton (+) charge repels another protons (+) charge.
- An electrons (-) charge repels another electrons (-) charge.
- A proton (+) charge attracts an electron (-) charge.

As you continue, remember that electricity is the movement of particles from one place to another pushed or pulled by electrostatic force.

Basic Electricity

All questions about the nature of electricity lead to the composition of matter. All matter is made up of atoms, as shown in FIGURE 6-5. Atoms are composed of electrons, protons, and neutrons. Positive electrical charges are found on protons, negative charges on electrons, and neutrons have no electrical charge. Neutrons and positively charged protons make-up the nucleus of an atom. Neutrons are the electrical glue that prevents the electrostatic forces of repulsion between the protons from bursting the nucleus. Moving around the nucleus are one or more negatively charged electrons. Electrons travel in different layers or shells around the nucleus. Each shell can contain only a specific maximum number of electrons.

With equal numbers of protons and electrons, the charges within an atom balance each other, leaving the atom with no overall charge. It is the goal of every atom

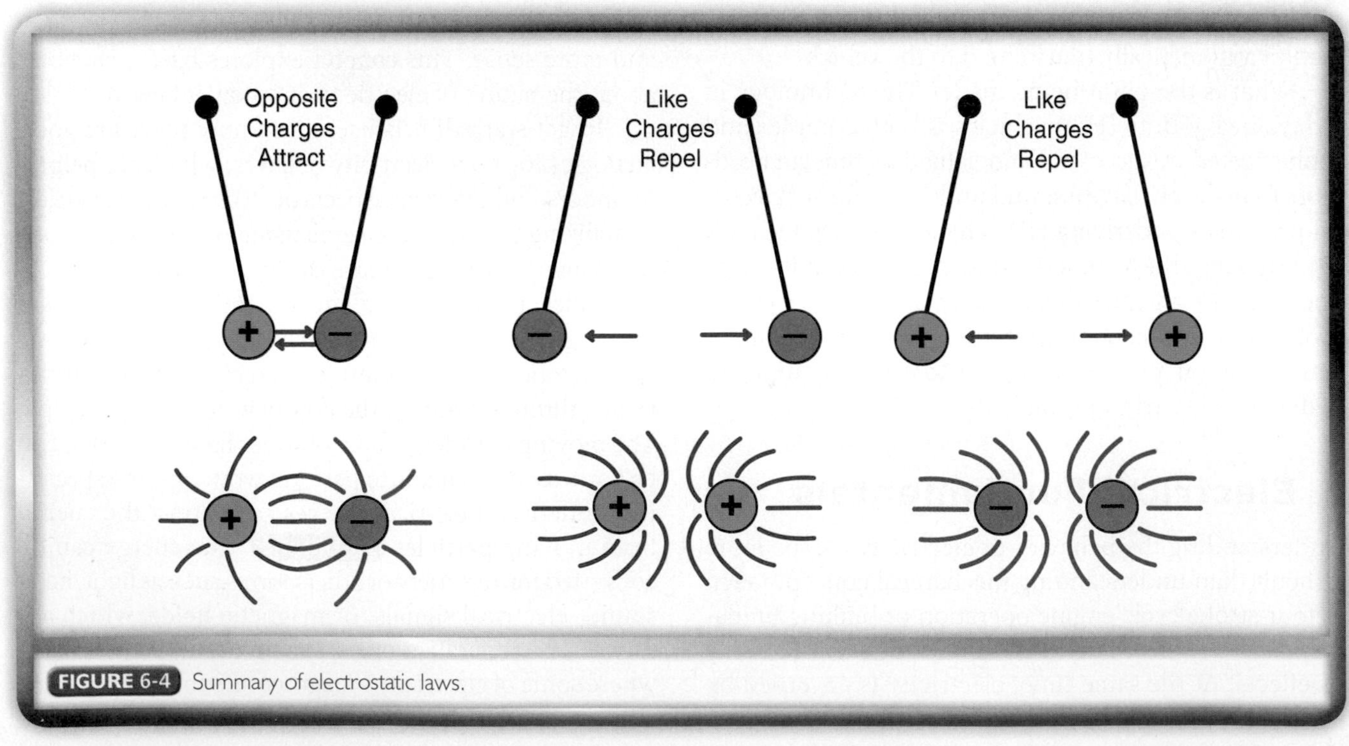

FIGURE 6-4 Summary of electrostatic laws.

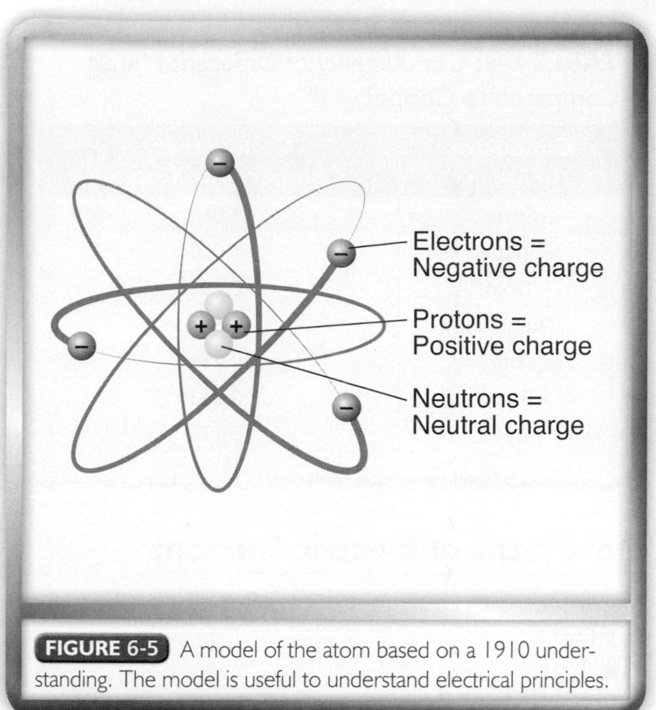

FIGURE 6-5 A model of the atom based on a 1910 understanding. The model is useful to understand electrical principles.

to achieve this state of balance between the electrical charges. Only electrons can be removed or added to an atom and not protons. If an atom loses or gains an electron, it is called an ion. An atom with more electrons than protons has an overall negative charge and is called a negative ion. The term ion simply means the atom has an imbalance of electrical charges due to the gain or loss of electrons. Ions are unstable and the atom will want to return to a state where the electrical charges are balanced or neutral. In the case of a negatively charged ion, the presence of an extra electron will cause the forces of repulsion to try and push the electron away from the atom, as illustrated in FIGURE 6-6.

A deficiency of electrons gives the atom an overall positive charge and is called a positive ion. It is also not balanced and will try to achieve a state of balance between the positive and negative charges and become neutral. In this case, the positively charged protons will pull on any available electron to return the atom to a state of balance between electrical charges.

If a negative ion and positive ion are close enough, the negative charge on the negative exerts a repelling force on the extra electron, causing it to be pushed away from its atom; at the same time, the positive ion exerts an attracting force on the extra electron. These forces of repulsion and attraction cause the electron to be pushed from one atom and pulled towards the positive atom, balancing the charges on both atoms. It is this movement of electrons from one atom to another that is called electricity.

Conductivity

Not all atoms can give up or accept electrons easily. Materials that hold electrons loosely enable electrons in its outer shell to easily move. These materials are categorized as **conductors**, while materials that hold electrons tightly and prevent electron movement are called **insulators**. The electrons that are only loosely held by the positive charges in the nucleus can move when another force

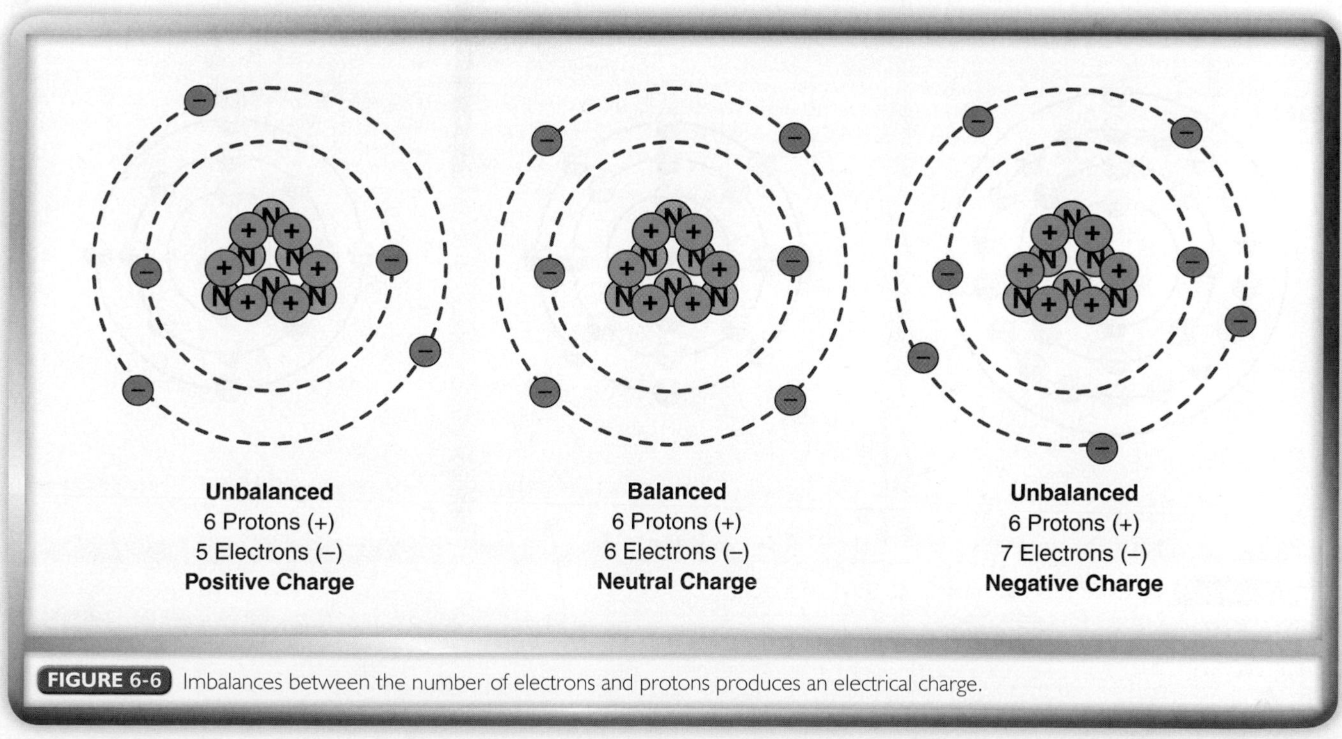

FIGURE 6-6 Imbalances between the number of electrons and protons produces an electrical charge.

strong enough to overcome the forces of attraction holding an electron in the atom.

In fact, atoms with the fewest electrons in its outer shell are the best conductors. Copper (Cu) is an example of a metal with only one electron in the atom's outer shell FIGURE 6-7A. Because a single electron is held loosely by the nucleus, copper makes an excellent conductor. By contrast, argon (Ar) is a noble gas, meaning that it generally does not form molecules and so is an insulator FIGURE 6-7B. Semiconductors such as Silicon (Si) FIGURE 6-7C will be discussed in greater detail in the section Semiconductors. TABLE 6-1 shows how the conductivity of other metals compares to the conductivity of copper.

Metals typically have lots of easily moved electrons, which make them good conductors. But it's not just metals that conduct electricity; liquids can too. Electrolytes are liquids which conduct electric current. The liquid inside a lead acid battery is an example of where electrolyte is used. Under some circumstances, air and other gases can conduct electricity, which is seen when a spark crosses an air gap.

Understanding Current

Understanding conductivity is the foundation of understanding currents. This section will discuss the basics of current movement, how quickly electrical currents move, and in what direction.

TABLE 6-1: Conductivity of Different Metals Compared to Copper

Conductor	Conductivity Compared to Copper
Silver	1.064
Copper	1.000
Gold	0.707
Aluminum	0.659
Zinc	0.288
Brass	0.243
Iron	0.178

Movement of Electric Current

The forces that can move electrons on or off an atom include:

- light
- heat
- pressure
- friction
- magnetic fields
- chemical energy

The force applied by each of these energy sources against an electron will determine how fast an electron is moved from one atom to the next. This is like hitting a

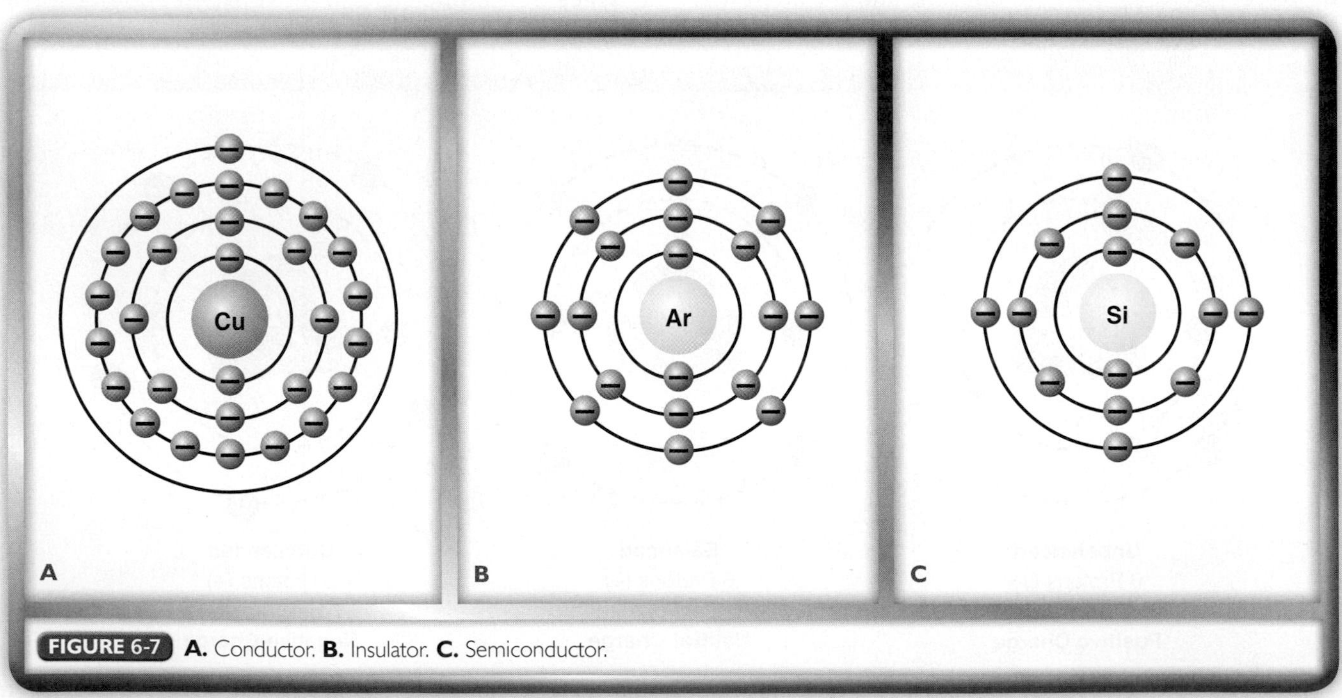

FIGURE 6-7 **A.** Conductor. **B.** Insulator. **C.** Semiconductor.

baseball FIGURE 6-8. The harder the ball is hit, the faster it travels. As an electrical concept, the speed of electron travel from atom to atom is voltage FIGURE 6-9. Higher electron **voltage** means the electrostatic forces pushing or pulling an electron are stronger. When using an analogy of electricity represented as water in a pipe, the concept of voltage is like pressure FIGURE 6-10. Just as higher pressure in a pipe moves water faster, high voltage means electrons move with greater speed from atom to atom.

Amperage is another electrical term used to describe the movement of electrons or electrical current. The unit of measurement for amperage is the **ampere**.While voltage can describe the average speed of one or many electrons, amperage measures how many electrons are in movement at one time. When using the analogy of water in a pipe to describe the movement of electrons, amperage is like the number of gallons or liters moving past a point in the pipe per second of time. In a sense, amperage really describes the volume of electron flow

When describing the flow of electricity, a circuit's voltage and amperage together is called electric current. Without either of these two electrical properties operating, there can be no electric current. No voltage means no pressure is available to push or pull electrons. No amperage means there are no electrons to move in a circuit. Please note, often the term "current" is used in

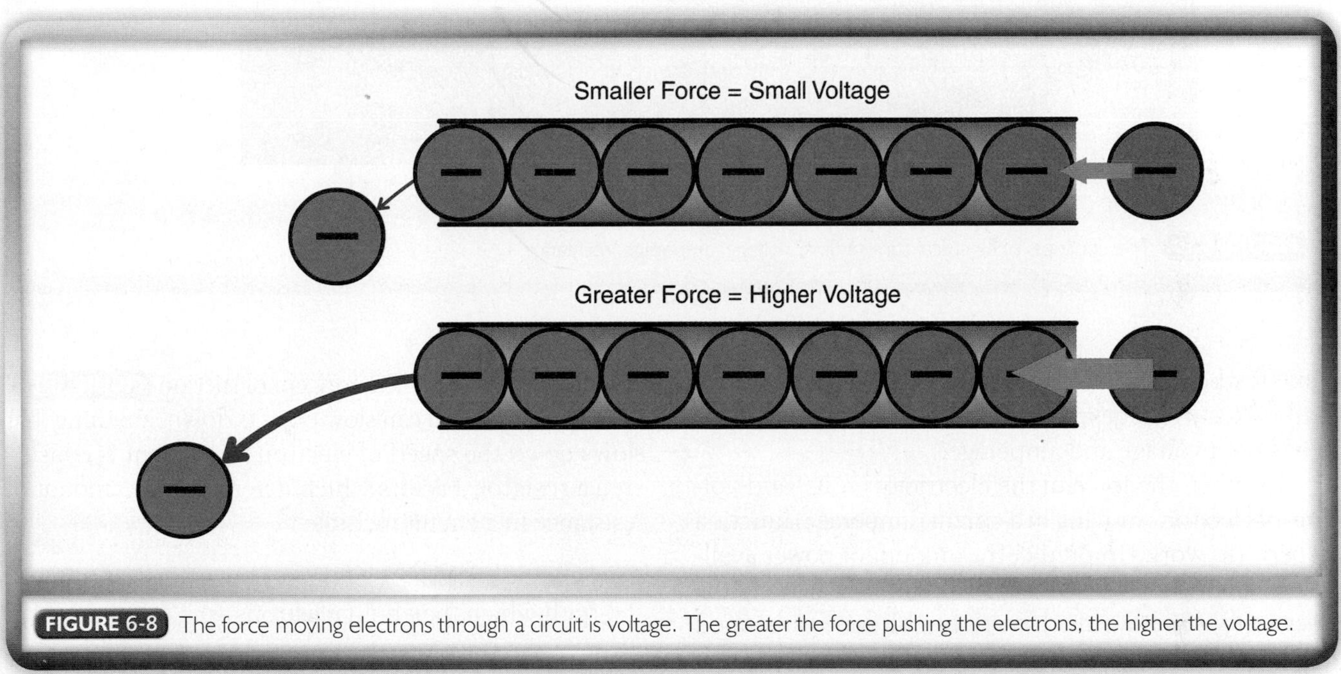

FIGURE 6-8 The force moving electrons through a circuit is voltage. The greater the force pushing the electrons, the higher the voltage.

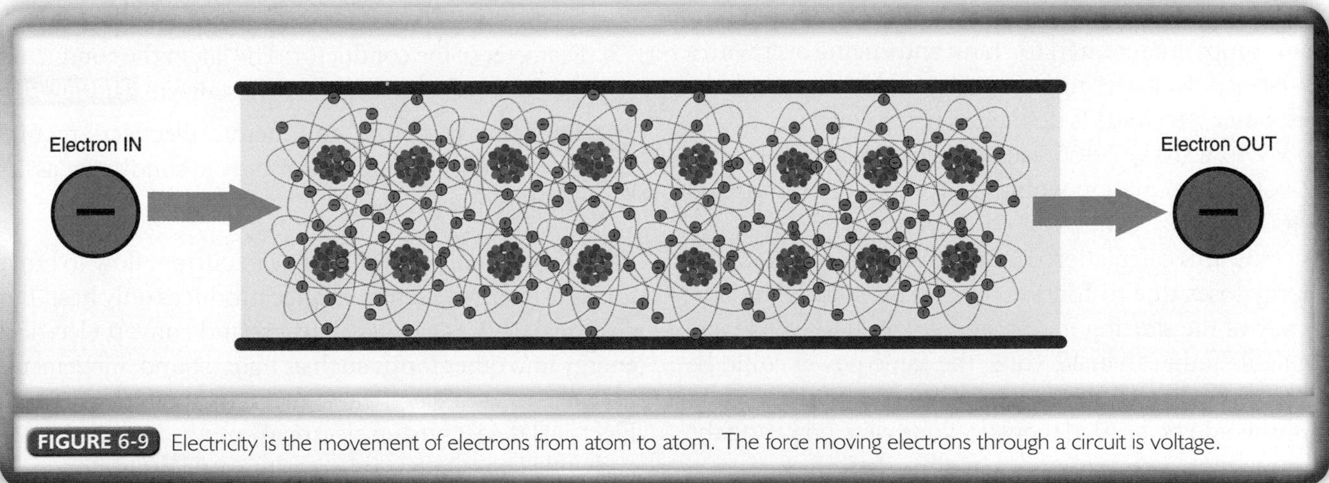

FIGURE 6-9 Electricity is the movement of electrons from atom to atom. The force moving electrons through a circuit is voltage.

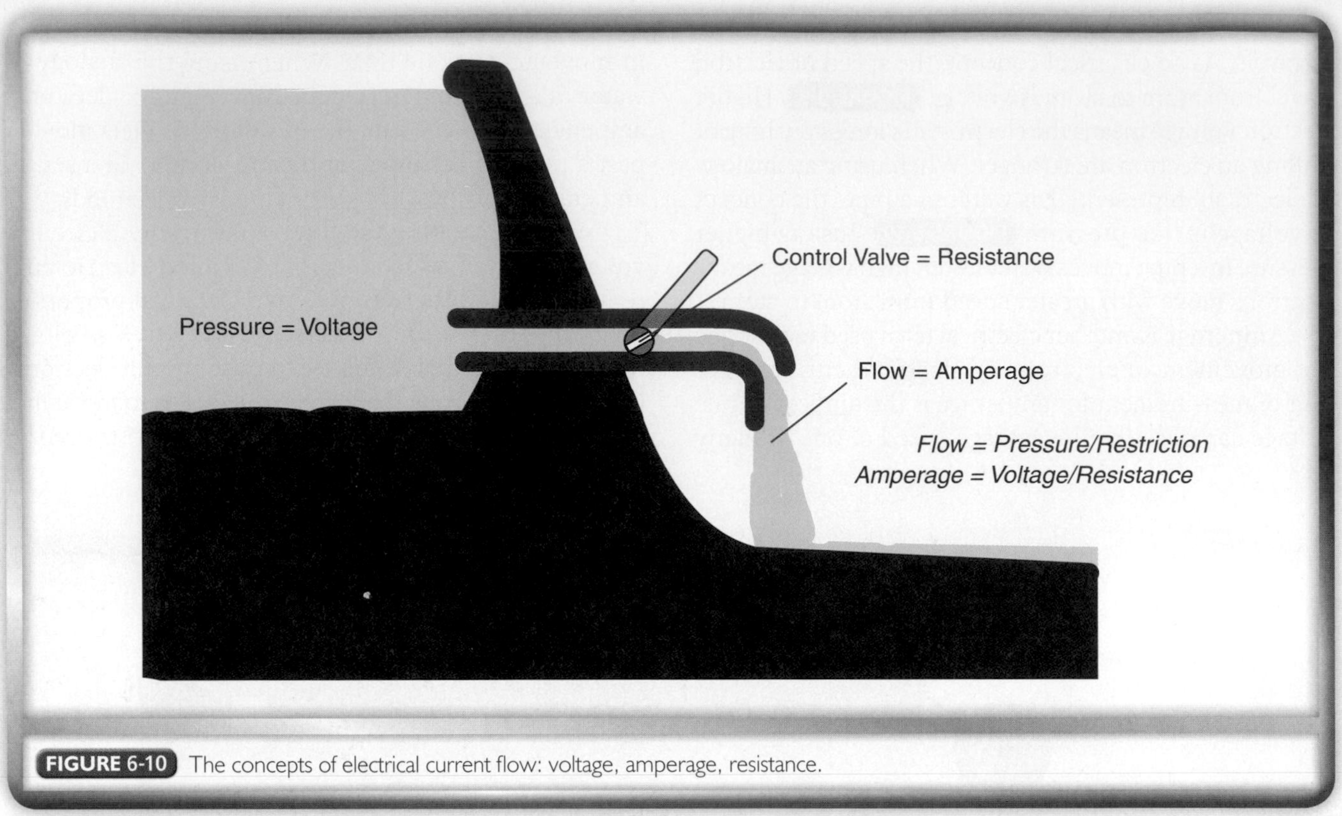

FIGURE 6-10 The concepts of electrical current flow: voltage, amperage, resistance.

some textbooks to describe amperage. Throughout this textbook, current describes the flow of electricity, which needs both voltage and amperage.

Together, the force of the electricity (volts) and volume of electrons moving in a circuit (amperage) function to perform work. To predict the amount of power available to perform work, a simple calculation answers the question about how much work can be done per second of time. Watts or wattage is the unit for measuring power. Wattage is a function of Voltage × Amperage, or Power = Volts × Amps. For example, if one wanted to find out how many amps are required to crank and engine over with a 10-horsepower starting motor, the calculation would be this: Since 746 watts is defined as being equal to 1 hp. 10 hp × 746 watts = 7,460 watts. If the available voltage is 12 volts, the equation would be 7,460 = 12 × amps and 7,460/12 = 621.6 amps

Now this calculation does not take into consideration energy loses due to friction, circuit resistance, the efficiency of the starting motor, and so on. If 24 volts were available rather than 12 volts, the same power could be produced with half the amperage, or 311 amps. 1,243 amps would be needed if only 6-volts were powering the starting motor.

Another important electrical concept is resistance. **Electrical resistance** is a material's property that reduces voltage and amperage in an electrical current. Electrical resistance is similar to the concept of friction FIGURE 6-11. Like friction, which can slow objects down, anything that slows down the speed of electron movement is considered a **resistor**. Factors which determine the amount of resistance in a circuit include:

1. Type of material: Conductors vary in the strength with which they hold electrons.
2. Length of the conductor: As length of a circuit or conductor increases, electrons travel farther and loose some energy.
3. Diameter of the conductor: The larger the conductor, the greater the capacity to carry current FIGURE 6-12
4. Temperature of the conductor: Electrons require more energy to move through a conductor as its temperature increases.

Resistors convert the energy in current flow to other forms of energy. Often resistance produces only heat. But electrical devices can also harness and convert electrical energy into other forms such as light, sound, movement, magnetism, and electrical signals carrying information. Electrical devices using electrical energy are called loads and will always have some resistance FIGURE 6-13.

The electrical unit for measuring the amount of resistance in a DC circuit is **ohms**. The term is named after the person who discovered that one **volt** of electrical pressure

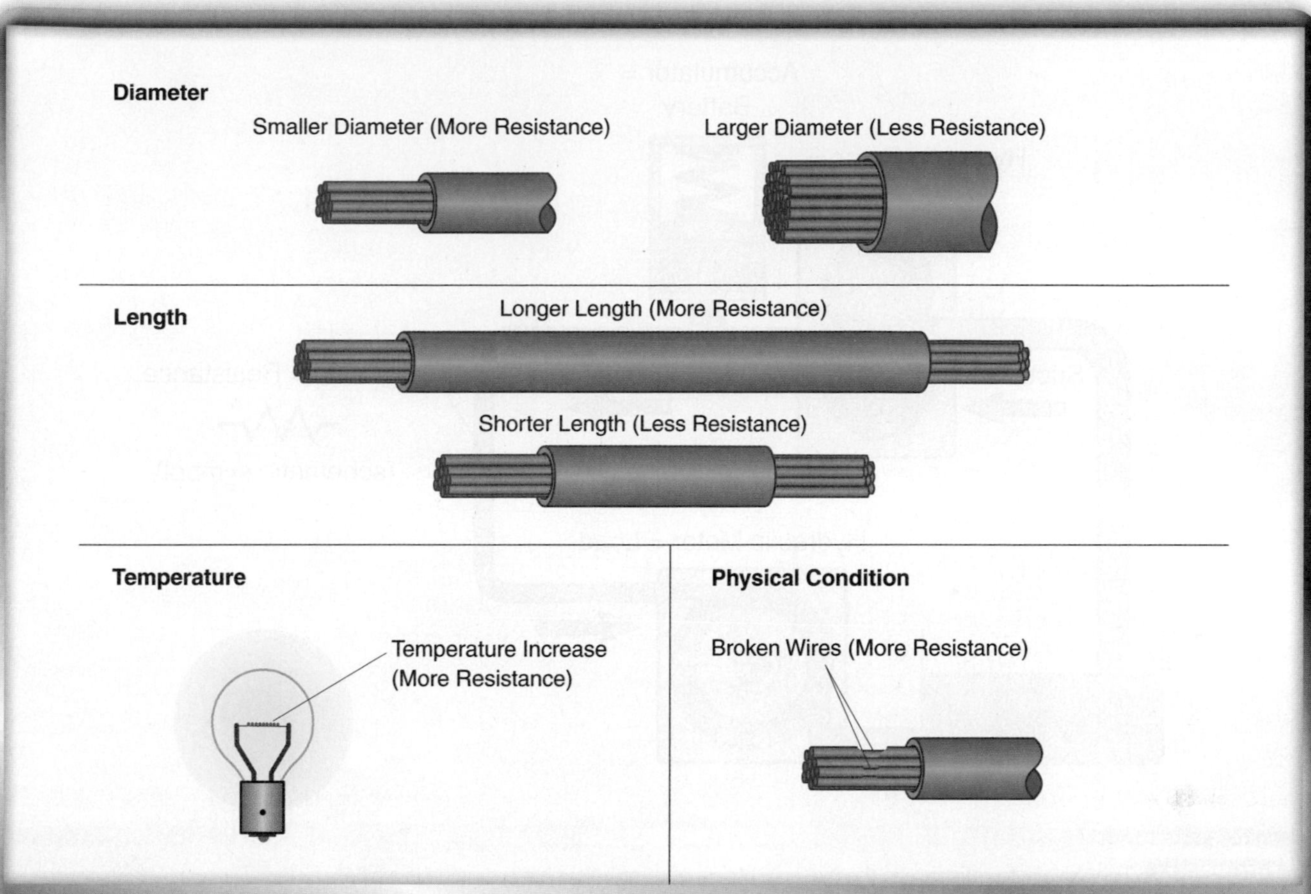

FIGURE 6-11 Factors affecting resistance in a circuit.

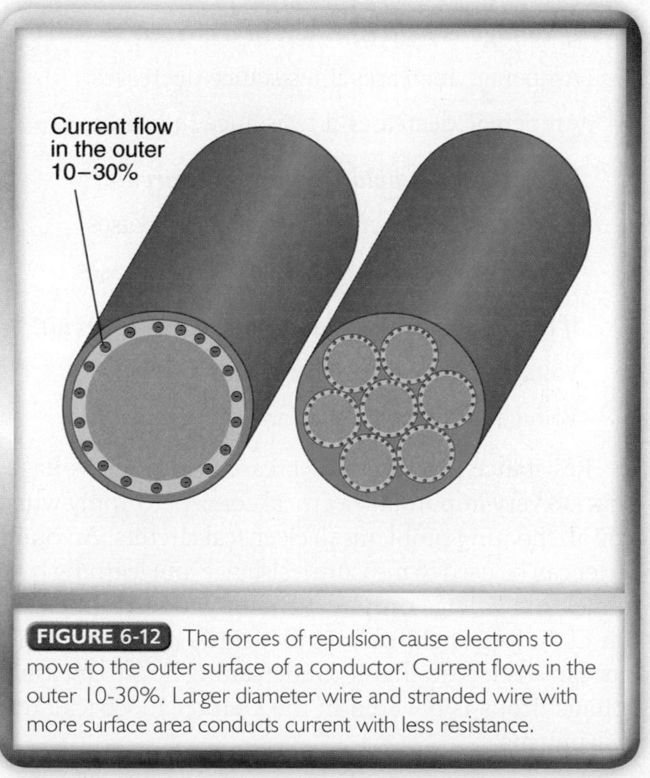

FIGURE 6-12 The forces of repulsion cause electrons to move to the outer surface of a conductor. Current flows in the outer 10-30%. Larger diameter wire and stranded wire with more surface area conducts current with less resistance.

is required to push one amp of current through a circuit if the circuit has a resistance of one ohm **FIGURE 6-14**.

This relationship is known as **Ohm's law**. Stated mathematically, Ohm's law is:

$$\text{Voltage} = \text{Resistance} \times \text{Amperage}$$

Restating Ohm's law using a hydraulic analogy, 1 psi of water pressure is needed to push one gallon of water through a pipe in one second having a diameter of one inch.

Although the hydraulic analogy is not perfect, it provides a good visual image for remembering that, according to Ohm's law, increasing voltage in a circuit is like increasing water pressure. Just as more water will flow through a pipe when water pressure is higher, more amperage flows through a circuit with higher voltage if the resistance or restrictions remain the same. Likewise, making a smaller restriction in a pipe is like increasing a circuit's resistance. Just as water pressure and volume will drop in a narrower or restricted pipe, voltage and amperage are reduced with increased circuit resistance. The Greek letter omega (Ω) represents Ohms, which is the unit used to measure resistance.

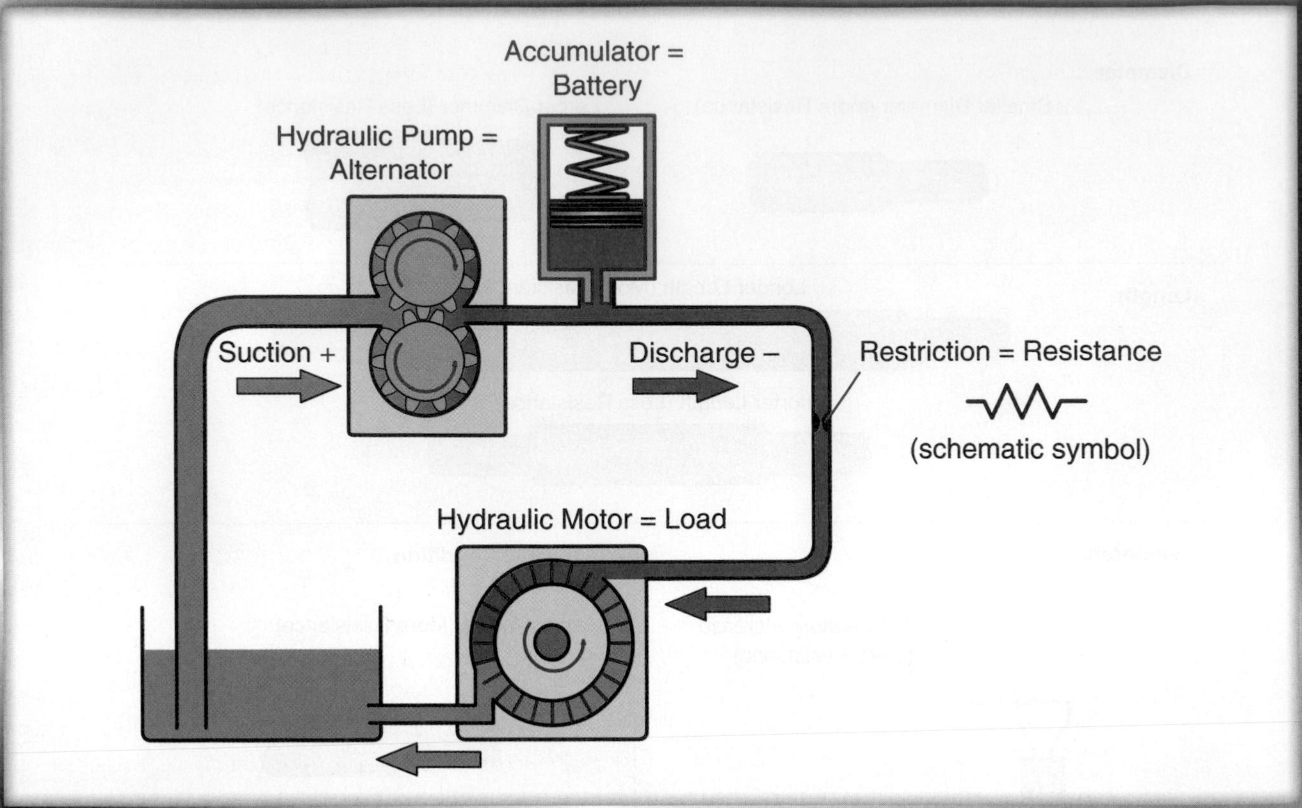

FIGURE 6-13 The analogy to resistance in the hydraulic model of current flow is a restriction in a pipe.

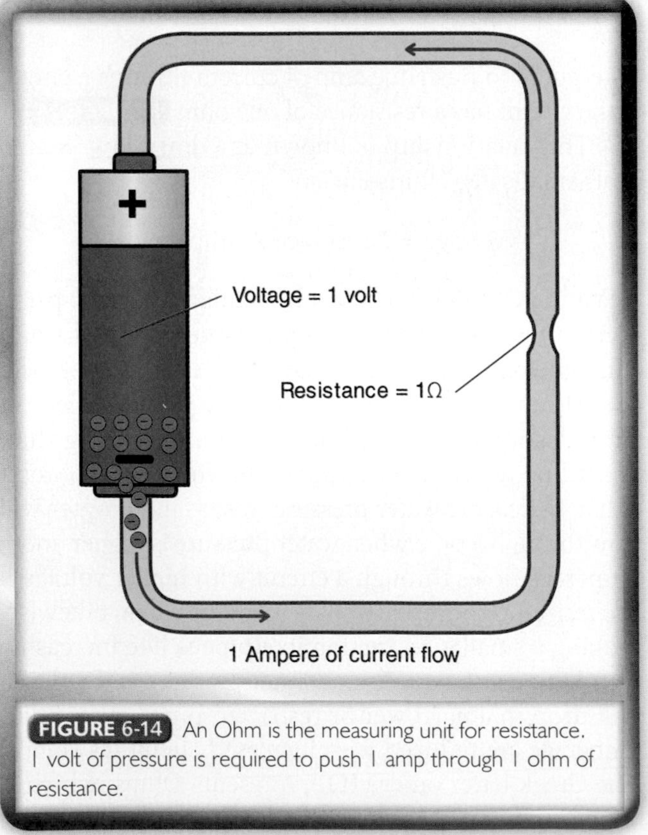

FIGURE 6-14 An Ohm is the measuring unit for resistance. 1 volt of pressure is required to push 1 amp through 1 ohm of resistance.

Observing the relationship between the three factors of Ohm's law leads to the following conclusions:

If voltage is held constant in a circuit:

Amperage increases if resistance decreases.

Amperage decreases if resistance increases.

If resistance is held constant in a circuit:

Amperage will increase if voltage increases.

Amperage will decrease if voltage decreases.

If amperage is to remain the same in a circuit:

Voltage must increase if resistance increases.

Voltage decreases if resistance decreases.

Resistance produces a decrease or drop in voltage. That is a very important electrical concept to apply when troubleshooting problems in electrical circuits. An ohmmeter can be used to measure resistance, but learning how to measure voltage drop in a circuit with a voltmeter is one of the most helpful ways to identify unwanted resistance in an electric circuit. Understating how to measure voltage drops is covered in the chapter Electrical Test Instruments.

Direction of Current Flow

Only electrons can be moved on and off an atom to create either a negative or positive electric charge. A charge is created when source of energy, such as a moving magnetic field, moves electrons from outer shell of an atom. That movement changes the charge balance. Movement of electrons through a conductor continues to take place by using the electrostatic forces of either repulsion or attraction. For example, electrons on a negatively charged atom will want to push the extra electron away. Positively charged atoms will want to pull electrons onto the atom to balance the number of protons with electrons.

When areas of positive or negative charges are created, a pole or polarity is established. **Polarity** is simply the state of charge. Polarity produces current flow FIGURE 6-15. Electrons will always move towards a positive pole and not the other way around. In FIGURE 6-16, areas of unbalanced electrical charges create positive or negative poles. Polarity differences, also called a potential difference, produce current flow.

The movement of negatively charged electrons to a positive charge is called the **electron theory of current movement**. It is actually not a theory but a fact. The idea that electric current movement takes place when positive charges move to a negative pole is called **conventional current theory**. Conventional current theory of electric charge movement was based on a 1910 model of the atom, which was incomplete. Later investigation found this idea was incorrect and only negatively charged electrons moved in a circuit – in a negative to positive direction.

There are still many textbooks and training aids used in trade occupations using conventional theory to explain electrical behavior. Trying to separate electron and conventional theory in practice can become confusing. However, the acceptance and use of either idea is generally not important for the technician. It is only important to remember that current flow is described by both concepts.

Technicians should be aware that some test instruments such as Amp/Volt/Resistance (AVR) machines are designed presuming current flow is conventional FIGURE 6-17. By contrast, **digital multimeter,** as shown in FIGURE 6-18, use electron theory and the direction of current flow is generally provided by polarity indicators. Connecting the black or common lead of a meter to a positive voltage and the positive meter lead to a negative will cause the meter to display a negative symbol beside the number in the digital display. Diagnosing an unin-

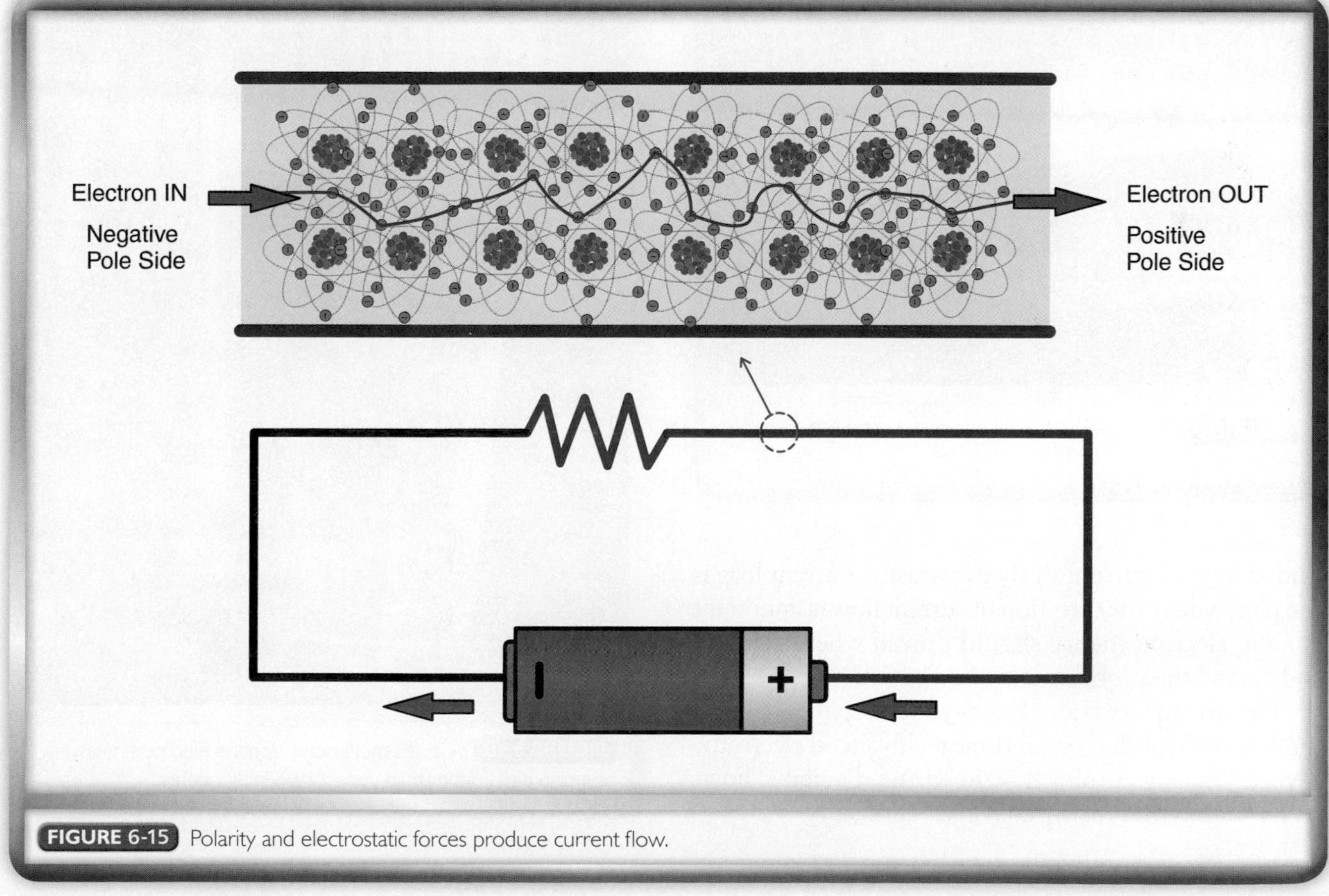

FIGURE 6-15 Polarity and electrostatic forces produce current flow.

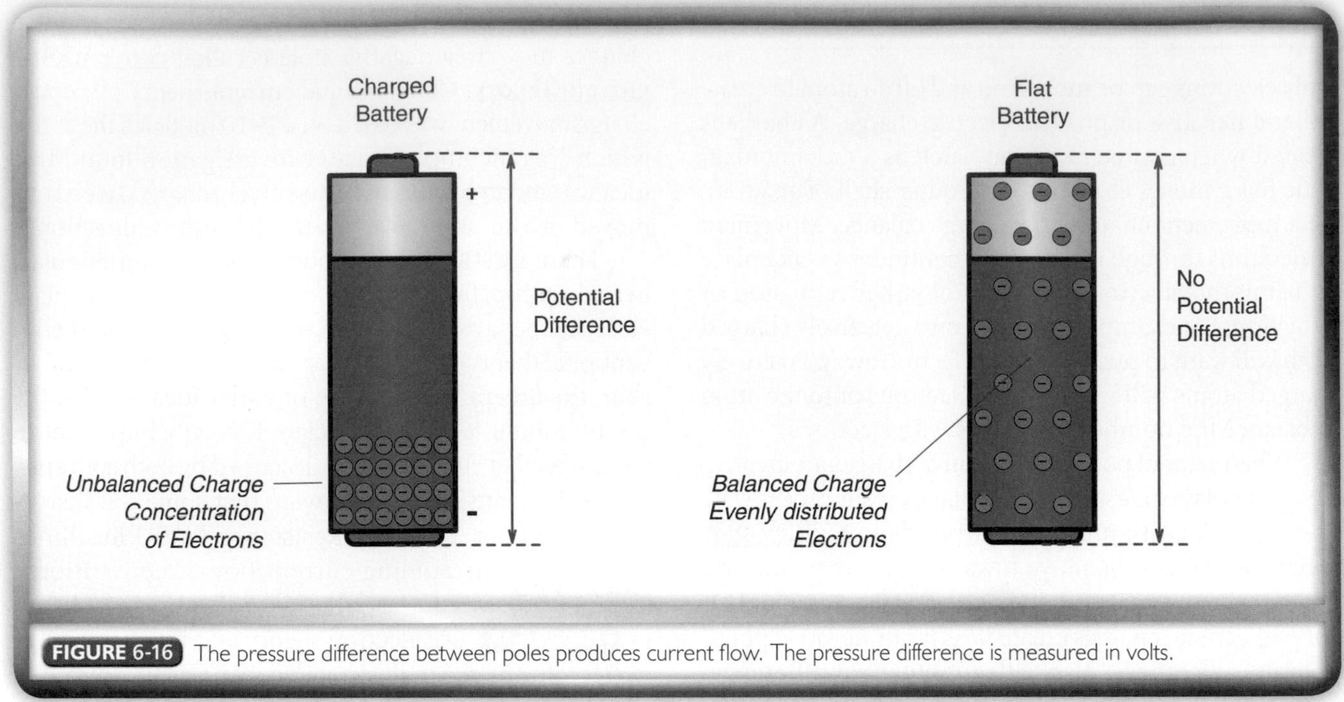

FIGURE 6-16 The pressure difference between poles produces current flow. The pressure difference is measured in volts.

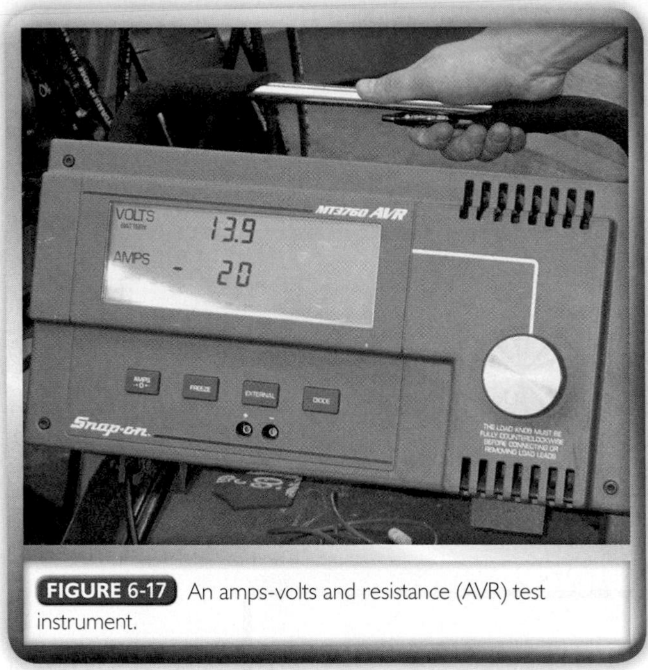

FIGURE 6-17 An amps-volts and resistance (AVR) test instrument.

FIGURE 6-18 A digital multimeter displays electrical measurements in digits rather than using a sweeping needle.

tended key-off current draw or parasitic current loss is one place where the direction of current flow is important to note; electron theory should prevail when trying to understand the problem.

Electron theory is also best used to describe the operation of semiconductors and more advanced electronic devices. Tracing current flow in wiring diagrams, however, is often easier using conventional theory.

Direct Current and Alternating Current

When electrons move only in one direction in a circuit, the current is described as being **direct current (DC)**. In a DC circuit, electrons move continuously from positive to negative **FIGURE 6-19**. When electrons are alternately pulled and pushed, it regularly changes the direction of current flow. That type of current flow is described as **alternating current (AC)** **FIGURE 6-20**. Alternating current is measured by how frequently the alternating current changes direction each section. That frequency (direction changes per second) is called **Hertz (HZ)**, which is another term for cycles per second. Plotting DC voltage on a graph produces as straight line, as shown in **FIGURE 6-21A**. Plotting AC voltage on a graph produces what is called a **sine wave** shape, illustrated in **FIGURE 6-21B**.

DC current flows only in one direction—from a negative to positive pole. A truck or bus battery and chassis are an example where DC current flow takes place **FIGURE 6-22** High concentrations of extra electrons at the negative polarity battery post will travel through negative vehicle **ground** circuits and electrical devices to reach the positive polarity post, which is deficient of electrons. Battery voltage is determined by the difference in the over-concentration of electrons at the negative post and electron deficiency at the positive post. The greater the difference in electron concentration between the

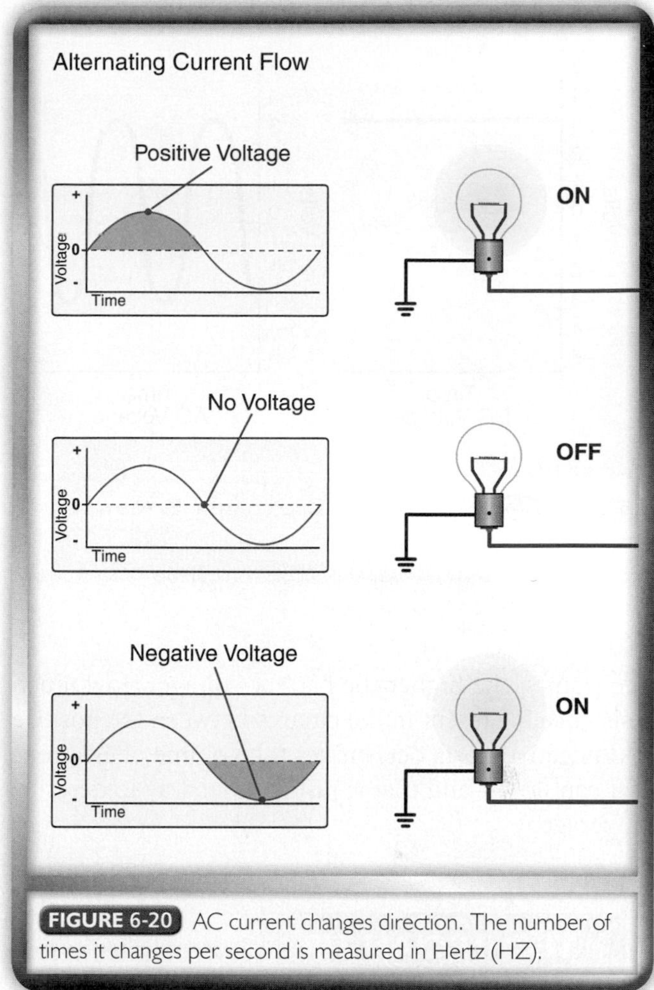

FIGURE 6-20 AC current changes direction. The number of times it changes per second is measured in Hertz (HZ).

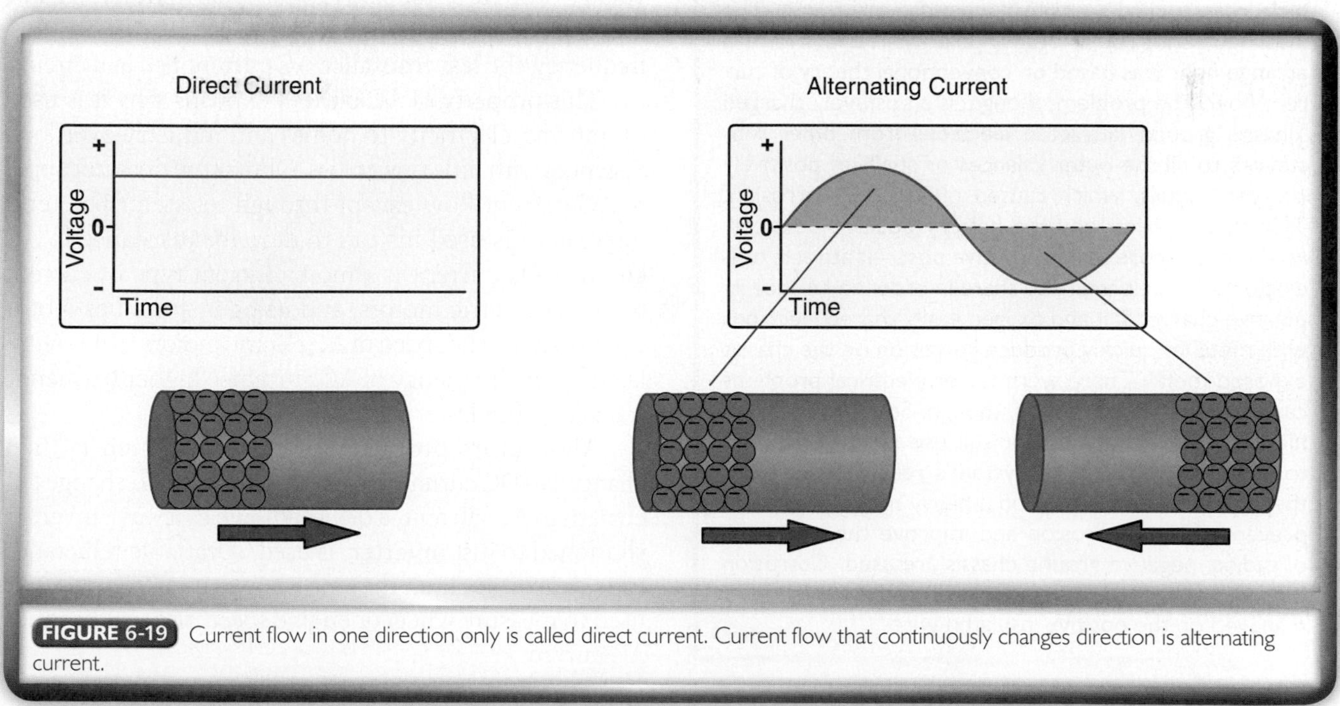

FIGURE 6-19 Current flow in one direction only is called direct current. Current flow that continuously changes direction is alternating current.

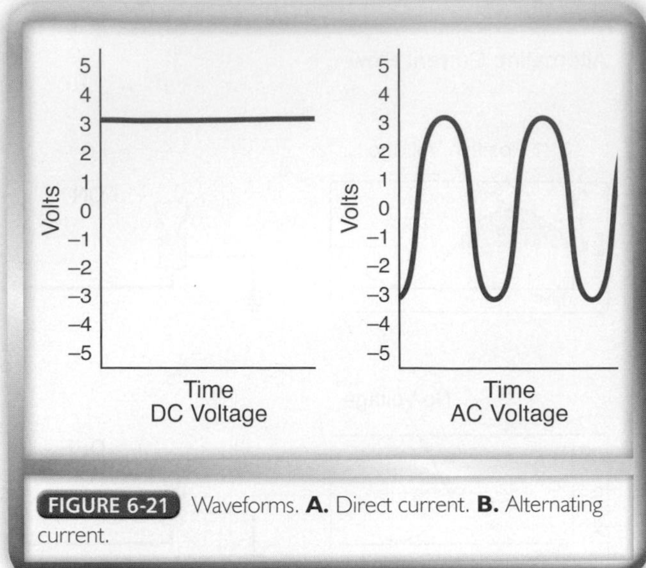

FIGURE 6-21 Waveforms. **A.** Direct current. **B.** Alternating current.

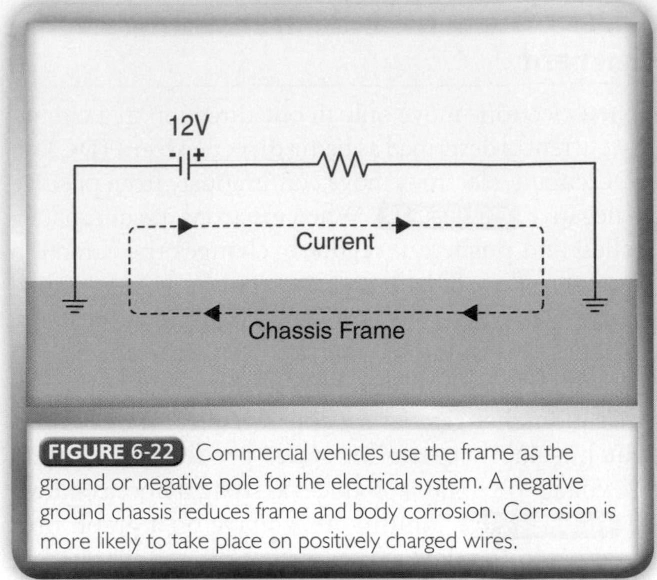

FIGURE 6-22 Commercial vehicles use the frame as the ground or negative pole for the electrical system. A negative ground chassis reduces frame and body corrosion. Corrosion is more likely to take place on positively charged wires.

two points, the higher the battery voltage. How much resistance is present in the circuits between the positive and negative posts determines the volume of electrons that can flow—and that is just another way to describe amperage.

TECHNICIAN TIP

During the first half of the twentieth century, many vehicle chassis used a positive ground metal frame. The insulated wiring had a negative polarity. The idea for this arrangement was based on conventional theory of current flow. The problem, though, is a positively charged "chassis ground" attracted electrons from other substances to fill the outer valances or shells of positively charged metals. which caused rapid body corrosion. This also explains why the battery positive post corrodes much more than a negative post—it attracts other atoms with electrons to share in order to balance its positive charge. Salt and oxygen easily shared electrons with metal to quickly produce corrosion on the chassis exposed metal. There were fewer electrical problems caused by corroded wiring, though. Some military vehicles and heavy-equipment still use positive grounds to increase the electrical system's reliability—even at the expense of corrosion on a heavy metal chassis. To prevent chassis corrosion and improve the operation of radios, negative ground chassis are used. Corrosion caused by exposed positive voltage potentials is better managed on the positive insulated wires.

DC circuits are used in virtually all chassis circuits because a battery can easily store and supply DC current. But DC current has one major disadvantage: The farther it travels, the more resistance is present in the circuit. If circuit amperage is high and correct size of wiring is not used, battery voltage can drop from 12.6 volts at a truck battery to just over 9 volts at the rear of a trailer.

AC current is used to power hybrid drive electric motors. AC current's main advantage is that it can be transmitted farther distances with less resistance and little voltage drop. Resistance is proportional to the frequency of AC polarity change. That is, the higher AC current's frequency, the less resistance AC current has in a circuit.

This property of AC current explains why it is used to transmit electricity to homes and industry over long distances with little power loss. Ohm's Law does not apply to AC current flow except through resisters. The term impedance is used instead to describe resistance in AC circuits. AC current is a more efficient type of current to power electric motors, and using it simplifies motor construction. The speed of AC electric motors is also regulated by the frequency of AC current—higher frequency translates into faster motor speed.

Alternators produce AC current, which is then changed to DC current inside the alternator. To change DC current to AC current, a device known as a wave inverter, shortened to just **inverter**, is used. A variable reluctance type sensor such as the one shown in FIGURE 6-23 is used to measure wheel or engine speed also can produce AC current.

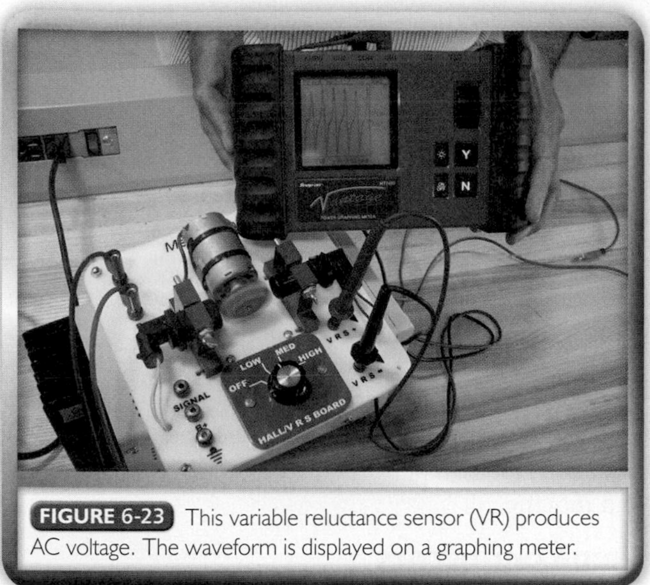

FIGURE 6-23 This variable reluctance sensor (VR) produces AC voltage. The waveform is displayed on a graphing meter.

Heating Effect of Current

When an electric current travels through a bulb filament or electric heating element, the filament or resistive element heats. Resistance in the elements converts electrical energy into heat energy. This observation is referred to as the "heating effect of current." As amperage and resistance increase, so does the heat produced, as shown in FIGURE 6-24.

So, why does the bulb filament heat and glow but the wires connecting the bulb do not? The simple answer is that the narrowing of the circuit conductor causes collisions to take place between the electrons as they funnel into the circuit's restriction. Electrons, which are three times the size of protons, release kinetic energy produced by current voltage and convert it to heat and light.

To understand this effect, think of a busy highway as traffic merges from six lanes to a single lane. The single lane cannot accommodate all the vehicles, so traffic must slow. Applying brakes reduces vehicle speed, much like voltage drop, and kinetic energy converts to heat due to friction between the brake drums, rotors, and friction material.

Fuses take advantage of this heating effect by using a narrow metal strip made of highly conductive material. When the amount of amperage exceeds a wire's ability to conduct the current without heating up, the strip melts to protect circuit wiring from burning. The amount of heat

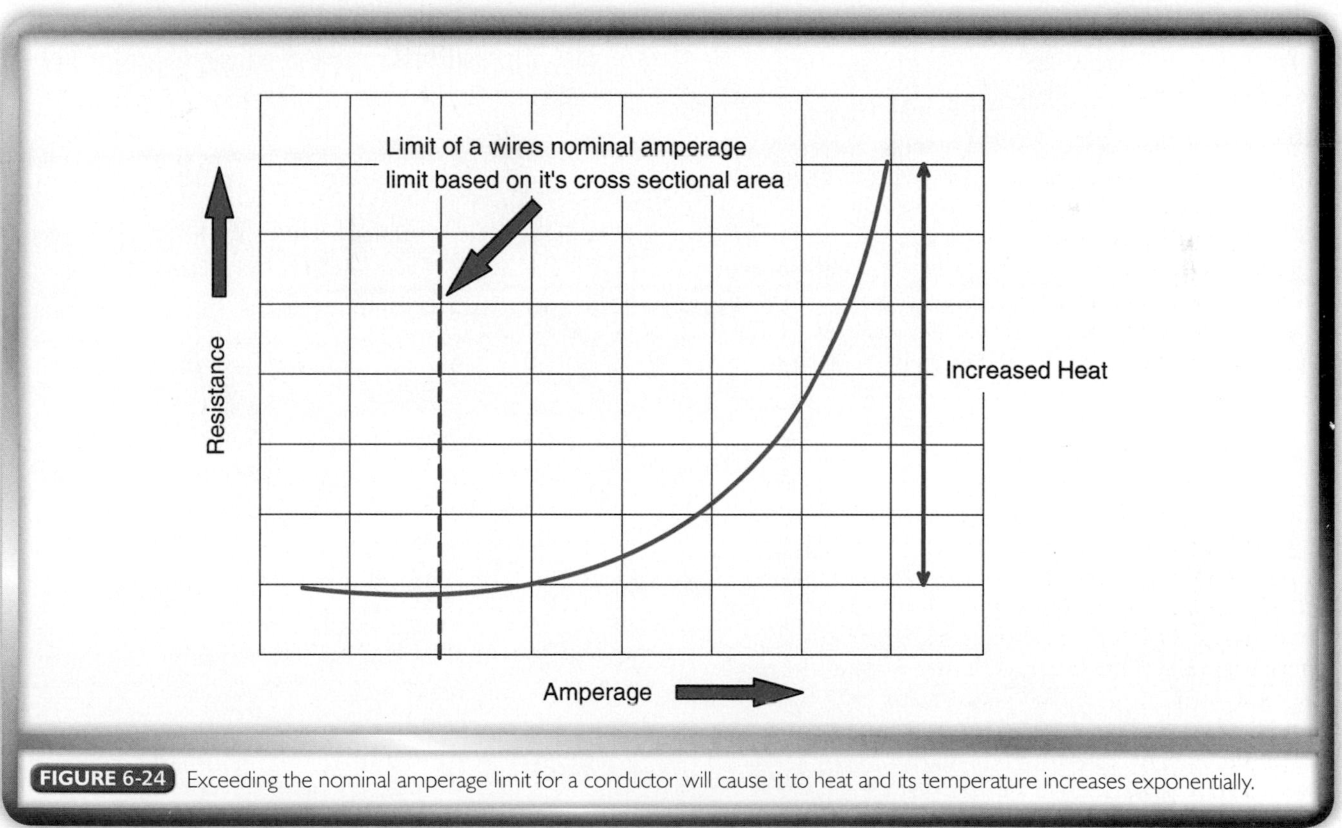

FIGURE 6-24 Exceeding the nominal amperage limit for a conductor will cause it to heat and its temperature increases exponentially.

produced is directly proportional to the fuse's resistance, the time current flows, and the amount of amperage in the current. The transformation during heating is measured in Joules. Mathematically, the relationship is described as:

$$H = I2Rt$$

where H is the heat output, I is the current (amps), R is the resistance in the circuit (ohms), and t is the time (seconds). So, if 2 amps pass through a wire with 25 ohms of resistance over the course of one minute (60 seconds), then the heat output is 6,000 Joules:

$$H = (22) \times (25) \times (60)$$

$$H = 6{,}000 \text{ Joules}$$

Joule's law refers to the heating effect of electric current. It also helps explain why the seemingly small resistance of narrow wire or a 00 gauge battery cable terminal having 0.01 ohms will drop voltage by only one-tenth with one amp of current but will completely burn if 750 amps of current pass through the connection. The heating effect of increased amperage would cause the terminal to quickly become overheated and burn.

Electrical Versus Electronic Circuits

Even though electricity is used to operate electrical and electronic circuits, the two types of circuit are not identical. What are the differences between electrical and electronic circuits? Electrical circuits usually conduct higher amounts of current through heavier conductors and commonly operate devices such as solenoids, relays motors, lights, and more. Electronic circuits use electricity to operate semiconductors such as transistors, integrated circuits, microprocessors, or micro-controllers. Electronic circuits use less amperage and often process signals rather than perform the work of lighting, heating, and moving.

Semiconductors

Semiconductors are the most important type of material used to construct electronic devices. This material can have properties of both conductors and insulators and can switch back and forth between either state using small electrostatic charges. Early semiconductors were made from alloyed materials such as silicon or germanium. The very small quantity of another material making up the silicon or germanium alloy gives the semiconductor its unique electrical properties.

Most semiconductors today are made from metal oxides. Metal oxide semiconductors are used in MOS-type transistors and microprocessors. MOS types have less resistance and conduct more current than the older semiconductor materials. Field effect transistors made from metal oxides are abbreviated **MOSFET** and are one of the most common types of transistors used in circuit boards by electronic control modules. **FIGURE 6-25** shows a MOSFET transistor.

Transistors can be used to switch current flow on and off and amplify electrical signals. They are also used to construct logic gates in integrated circuits. Logic gates enable integrated circuits and larger microcontrollers and processors to perform mathematical calculations essential for the proper functioning of an ECM.

Two types of materials make up a basic semiconductor. One is a **P-type material**, which is made from material that can accept electrons. The P stands for positive because of its ability to accept and transport electrons. **N-type material** contains loosely held electrons, which explain why it's called N, or negative, material. Both P and N materials are useless on their own, but when placed together, they can form diodes and transistors. Using MOS semiconductors, the material can be arranged in a chip to function both as a resistor and capacitor.

FIGURE 6-25 MOSFETs and other MOS semiconductor devices are used in ECM circuit boards. This is an ECM from a Mercedes MB900 diesel engine and the MOSFETs are output drivers.

Wrap-up

Ready for Review

- Today, the number of electrical circuits has increased into the thousands, and not a single truck and bus system is without electronic control.
- Electrical system components on heavy-duty vehicles are no longer separated into distinct systems. Electrical control is distributed over multiple electronic control modules (ECMs). ECMs are connected together to form on-board networks.
- It may be helpful to think of electricity as nothing more than the movement of specific particles from one point to another. The analogy of electric current flow using the hydraulic model is helpful to understand concepts of voltage, amperage, and resistance.
- The concept of voltage indicates the speed of electron movement from atom to atom. It is equivalent to the measurement of pressure in a pipe in pounds per square inch (psi).
- Amperage is a measurement of the number of electrons flowing past one point in a circuit during one second. It is equivalent to the measurement of flow or volume in a pipe in gallons or liters per second.
- Electrical resistance is similar to the idea of friction. Resistance slows down electron speed, which in turn reduces voltage and amperage.
- Forces of repulsion and attraction between electrons and protons are termed electrostatic force and are the primary type of energy contained in electricity used to perform work.
- Atoms are made of three fundamental particles: electrons, protons, and neutrons. Positive electrical charges are found on protons, negative charges on electrons, and neutrons have no electrical charge.
- Poles are areas of concentrated positive and negative electrical charges. Polarity is needed to produce electron flow.
- Ions are atoms with an imbalance of electrical charges due to the gain or loss of electrons.
- The flow of electrons from atom to atom is the basic concept of electricity.
- Current can be described as a function of voltage and amperage in a circuit—in other words, the speed and quantity of electron flow. Without either property, there is no flow of electricity in a circuit.
- The number of free electrons in an atom's valence ring determines how conductive the atom is. Fewer outer shell electrons are associated with greater conductivity.
- Electron theory states that electrons move from negative to positive. Conventional theory states that electrons move from positive to negative. Both theories convey the idea of current flow and each may in some instances be helpful when performing electrical diagnostic work.
- Electrical circuits usually conduct higher amounts of current through heavier conductors, and electronic circuits use electricity to operate semiconductors.
- The two fundamental types of current flow are direct current (DC) and alternating current (AC).
- Direct current has a constant polarity; alternating current has continuously changing polarity that produces a sine wave.
- Resistance is measured in ohms and depends on the type of material, its length, diameter, and temperature of the conductor.
- Good conductors have low resistance, and insulators have high resistance. Electrical energy lost through resistance is converted into heat.
- Semiconductors combine P-type and N-type materials.
- Semiconductors are very versatile materials and are used to make various electronic components. Their conductivity can be manipulated and precisely controlled using small electrostatic charges.

Vocabulary Builder

alternating current (AC) A type of current flow that continuously changes direction and polarity.

amperage The measurement of the quantity of electrons in electric current movement.

ampere (amp) The unit for measuring the quantity of electron flow past one point in a circuit per unit of time.

conductor A material that easily allows electricity to flow through it. It is made up of atoms with very few outer shell electrons, which are loosely held by the nucleus.

conventional current theory The theory that the direction of current flow is positive to negative.

direct current (DC) Movement of current that flows in one direction only.

electrical resistance A material's property that reduces voltage and amperage in an electrical current.

electron theory of current movement The movement of negatively charged electrons to a positive charge.

electrostatic theory The idea that like charges repel one another and unlike electrical charges attract.

ground The return path for electrical current in a vehicle chassis, other metal of the vehicle, or dedicated wire.

hertz (Hz) The unit for electrical frequency measurement, in cycles per second.

insulator A material that holds electrons tightly and prevents electron movement.

inverter A device that changes direct current into alternating current. Also called a *wave inverter*.

MOSFET A field effect transistor made from metal-oxide semiconductor material.

N-type material Semiconductor material with a small amount of extra electrons.

ohm The unit for measuring electrical resistance.

Ohm's law A law that defines the relationship between amperage, resistance, and voltage.

polarity The state of charge, positive or negative.

P-type material Semiconductor material having electron deficiency or a place to hold additional electrons.

resistor A component designed to produce electrical resistance.

semiconductor A material that can have properties of both conductors and insulators and that can switch back and forth between either state using small electrostatic charges.

sine wave A mathematical function that describes a repetitive waveform, such as an alternating current signal.

volt The unit used to measure potential difference or electrical pressure.

voltage The speed at which electrons travel from atom to atom.

Review Questions

1. Which of the following statements is correct concerning conductivity?
   a. Copper makes an excellent conductor.
   b. Electrolytes are liquids which conduct electric current.
   c. The liquid inside a lead acid battery is an example of where electrolyte is used.
   d. All of these are correct.
2. Which of the following is correct concerning electrostatic law?
   a. A proton (+) charge repels another proton (+) charge.
   b. An electron (-) charge repels another electron (-) charge.
   c. A proton (+) charge attracts an electron (-) charge.
   d. All of these are correct.
3. Which of the following is NOT correct concerning basic electricity?
   a. All matter is made up of atoms.
   b. Atoms are composed of electrons, protons, and neutrons.
   c. Positive electrical charges are found on protons.
   d. Negative electrical charges are found on neutrons.
4. Which of the following is NOT a factor that determines the level of electrical resistance?
   a. Type of material
   b. Length of the conductor
   c. Diameter of the conductor
   d. Weight of the conductor
5. Which of the following is NOT correct concerning movement of electric current?
   a. Watts or wattage is the unit for measuring power.
   b. Resistance produces a decrease or drop in voltage.
   c. Wattage is a function of Voltage × Amperage.
   d. Resistance is measured in amps.
6. Which of the following statements about Ohm's law is correct?
   a. If voltage is held constant in a circuit: amperage increases if resistance decreases; amperage decreases if resistance increases.
   b. If resistance is held constant in a circuit: amperage increases if voltage increases; amperage decreases if voltage decreases.
   c. If amperage is to remain the same in a circuit: voltage must increase if resistance increases; voltage decreases if resistance decreases.
   d. All of these are correct.
7. Which of the following statements is correct concerning semiconductors?
   a. Transistors can be used to switch current flow on and off and amplify electrical signals.
   b. Transistors are used to construct logic gates in integrated circuits.
   c. Logic gates enable integrated circuits and larger microcontrollers and processors to perform mathematical calculations essential for the proper functioning of an ECM.
   d. All of these are correct.
8. Which of the following is NOT correct concerning semiconductors?
   a. Semiconductors are the most important type of material used to construct electronic devices.
   b. Semiconductors can have properties of both conductors and insulators and can switch back and forth between either state using small electrostatic charges.
   c. Early semiconductors were made from alloyed materials such as silicon or germanium.
   d. Most semiconductors today are made from platinum or a silicone blend.
9. All of the following statements about the heating effect of current and fuses are true EXCEPT:
   a. Fuses use a narrow metal strip made of highly conductive material.
   b. When the amount of amperage exceeds a wire's ability to conduct the current without heating up, the strip melts to protect circuit wiring from burning.
   c. Boyle's law refers to the heating effect of electric current.
   d. The amount of heat produced is directly proportional to the fuse's resistance, the time current flows, and the amount of amperage in the current.
10. Which of the following statements is correct concerning direct current and alternating current?
    a. When electrons move only in one direction in a circuit, the current is described as being direct current (DC).
    b. Plotting DC voltage on a graph produces a straight line.
    c. Plotting AC voltage on a graph produces what is called a sine wave.
    d. All of these are correct.

ASE-Type Questions

1. Technician A says there are two theories of current flow: the electron theory and the conventional theory. Technician B says it is only important to remember that current flow is described by both concepts. Who is correct?
   a. Technician A
   b. Technician B
   c. Both Technician A and Technician B
   d. Neither Technician A nor Technician B

2. Technician A says AC circuits are used in virtually all chassis circuits because a battery can easily store and supply AC current. Technician B says DC current is used to power hybrid drive electric motors. Who is correct?
   a. Technician A
   b. Technician B
   c. Both Technician A and Technician B
   d. Neither Technician A nor Technician B

3. Technician A says AC current's main advantage is that it can be transmitted farther distances with less resistance and little voltage drop. Technician B says the term resistance is used with AC circuits as well as DC circuits. Who is correct?
   a. Technician A
   b. Technician B
   c. Both Technician A and Technician B
   d. Neither Technician A nor Technician B

4. Technician A says when an electric current travels through a bulb filament or electric heating element, the filament or resistive element heats. Technician B says resistance in the elements converts electrical energy into heat energy. Who is correct?
   a. Technician A
   b. Technician B
   c. Both Technician A and Technician B
   d. Neither Technician A nor Technician B

5. Technician A says electronic circuits use less amperage and often process signals rather than perform the work of lighting, heating, and moving. Technician B says electrical circuits usually conduct higher amounts of current through heavier conductors and commonly operate devices such as solenoids, relays, motors, lights, and more. Who is correct?
   a. Technician A
   b. Technician B
   c. Both Technician A and Technician B
   d. Neither Technician A nor Technician B

6. Technician A says metal oxide semiconductors are used in MOS-type transistors and microprocessors. Technician B says MOS types have less resistance and conduct more current than the older semiconductor materials. Who is correct?
   a. Technician A
   b. Technician B
   c. Both Technician A and Technician B
   d. Neither Technician A nor Technician B

7. Technician A says two types of materials make up a basic semiconductor. Technician B says the two types are R- type and M- type. Who is correct?
   a. Technician A
   b. Technician B
   c. Both Technician A and Technician B
   d. Neither Technician A nor Technician B

8. Technician A says today's electrical system components are no longer separated into distinct systems. Technician B says networking electrical system components add new vehicle features that can enhance safety, performance, and passenger comfort. Who is correct?
   a. Technician A
   b. Technician B
   c. Both Technician A and Technician B
   d. Neither Technician A nor Technician B

9. Technician A says all questions about the nature of electricity lead to the composition of matter. Technician B says the movement of electrons from one atom to another is called electricity. Who is correct?
   a. Technician A
   b. Technician B
   c. Both Technician A and Technician B
   d. Neither Technician A nor Technician B

10. Technician A says metals typically have lots of easily moved electrons which make them good conductors. Technician B says liquids cannot function as a conductor. Who is correct?
    a. Technician A
    b. Technician B
    c. Both Technician A and Technician B
    d. Neither Technician A nor Technician B

CHAPTER 7

NATEF Tasks

There are no NATEF tasks for this chapter.

Knowledge Objectives

After reading this chapter, you will be able to:

1. Identify and describe the types of energy that are the sources of electricity. (p 228)
2. Describe how each type of energy is used to create electricity in heavy-duty vehicles. (pp 228–242)
3. Determine the direction of induced current flow. (pp 228–242)
4. Explain how electromagnetic induction produces electricity. (pp 237–238)
5. Identify the components of a fuel cell and describe their function. (pp 242–243)

Generating Electricity

Skills Objectives

There are no skills objectives in this chapter.

Introduction

When thinking about how electricity is produced, batteries and generators quickly come to mind. But there are a surprising number of other ways electrical current is produced on commercial vehicle chassis. The importance of those other methods of generating electricity is easily overlooked. Some methods to move electrons in circuits are obvious, but other not-so-evident sources of current are just as significant, with implications for safety, maintenance practices, and service procedures.

Sources of Electricity

Seven methods to produce electron flow are generally recognized. These include:

- Friction
- Light
- Heat
- Pressure
- Magnetism
- Chemical reactions
- Fuel cells

This chapter will explore all of those methods in greater detail.

Electricity from Friction

Electric charges can be produced when two materials rub together. Electron transfer using friction leaves one material with more electrons than the other. Producing electricity using friction is known as triboelectricity (tribo means friction). The zap of an electric shock after walking across a carpet and then touching a metal handle is a common way to experience triboelectricity. Static electricity is another name given to triboelectricity, but more accurately refers to objects with stationary high voltage charges.

Triboelectricity is produced because different materials have different capacities to retain electrons. Contact between different materials in what is called the triboelectric series causes some materials to easily give up electrons, while others will attract electrons. The same effect is observed when materials in close contact are separated. Consider separating plastic wrap from paper, as in FIGURE 7-1. The large difference in positive and negative charges between the materials causes them to cling to one another to balance the charges.

The triboelectric series is a name for the list that indicates the tendency of materials to become either positively or negatively charged when separated, or during frictional contact with one another TABLE 7-1.

Understanding that electricity is produced through friction is important to the technician trying to solve electrical problems.

For example, grounding protocol must be observed when handling components with sensitive microelectronic circuits, as they may be damaged by electrostatic discharge (ESD) FIGURE 7-2. Grounding oneself by touching a metal workbench or door handle draws-off any electric charge. Using a

You Are the Technician

While performing some tire work on a number of tractors, the hub-piloted outer aluminum disc wheels were very hard to remove, even after removing all the wheel nuts. After the first few wheel rims were removed using a purpose built puller, it was discovered that the rims were very badly corroded around the wheel studs, and likely all needed to be discarded. The inner steel disc wheels were unaffected by the corrosion but needed to be cleaned and repainted. The wheel nuts were in acceptable condition for reuse, but all the bolt holes around the nuts were corroded as well.

1. What was the likely cause of the aluminum wheel disc corrosion?
2. What service practice would have prevented the destruction of the aluminum rims?
3. What service recommendations would you make to prevent this situation from happening again, either to the tractors or others in the fleet?

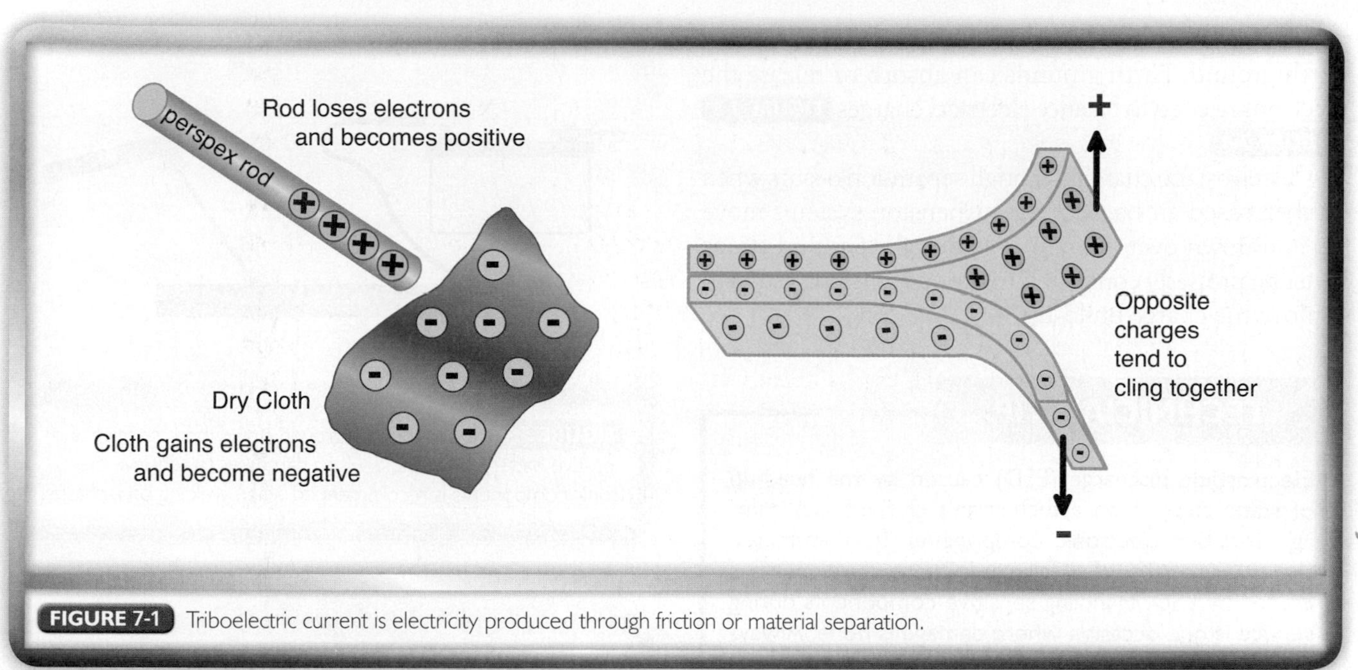

FIGURE 7-1 Triboelectric current is electricity produced through friction or material separation.

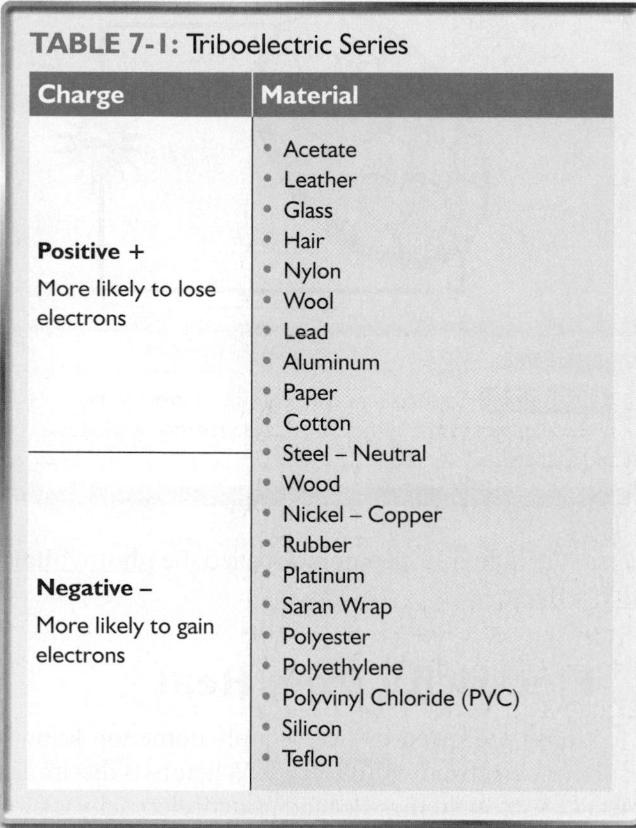

TABLE 7-1: Triboelectric Series

Charge	Material
Positive + More likely to lose electrons	• Acetate
	• Leather
	• Glass
	• Hair
	• Nylon
	• Wool
	• Lead
	• Aluminum
	• Paper
	• Cotton
	• Steel – Neutral
Negative – More likely to gain electrons	• Wood
	• Nickel – Copper
	• Rubber
	• Platinum
	• Saran Wrap
	• Polyester
	• Polyethylene
	• Polyvinyl Chloride (PVC)
	• Silicon
	• Teflon

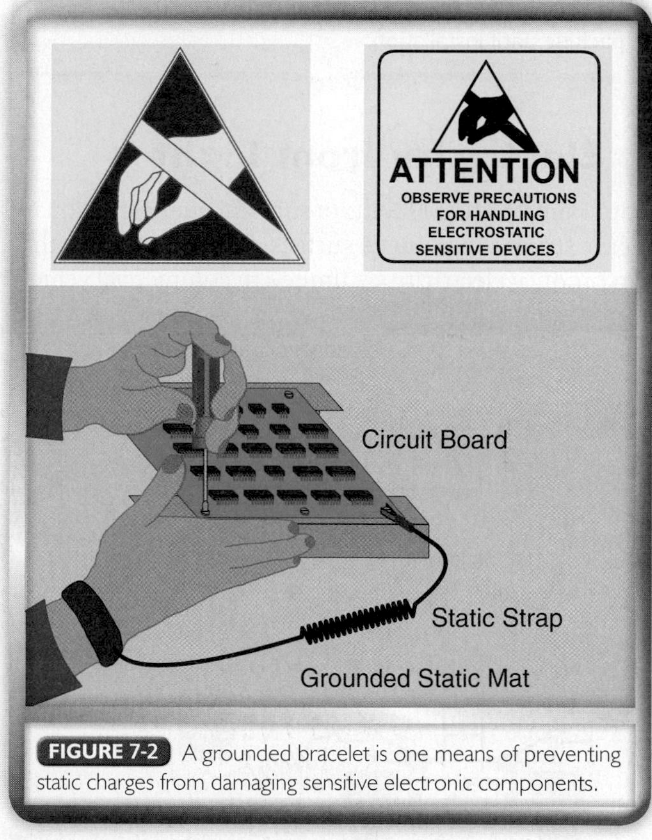

FIGURE 7-2 A grounded bracelet is one means of preventing static charges from damaging sensitive electronic components.

special bracelet or anklet is a standard practice while handling unconnected integrated circuits. Electronic components are usually wrapped in electrically conductive Mylar packaging for protection against high voltage static electricity.

Electrons are removed from the bodies of trucks, buses, and trailers by wind friction. Some buses are equipped with static wicks, conductive cables that drag along the road to prevent small electric shocks to exiting passengers. When fuel and powdered products such as flour or cement are removed from a tanker trailer, the separation of the materials produces a build-up of high voltage static charges. To minimize the likelihood of an explosion caused by a high voltage spark, a grounding clamp is connected between the chassis and an earth ground. Earth grounds can absorb or release the electrons needed to balance electrical charges FIGURE 7-3 FIGURE 7-4.

Electrostatic charging though separation occurs when rubber-based air bags for air suspension systems move up and down over aluminum pedestals. Ground straps must be properly connected to the suspension system to remove the charge build-up.

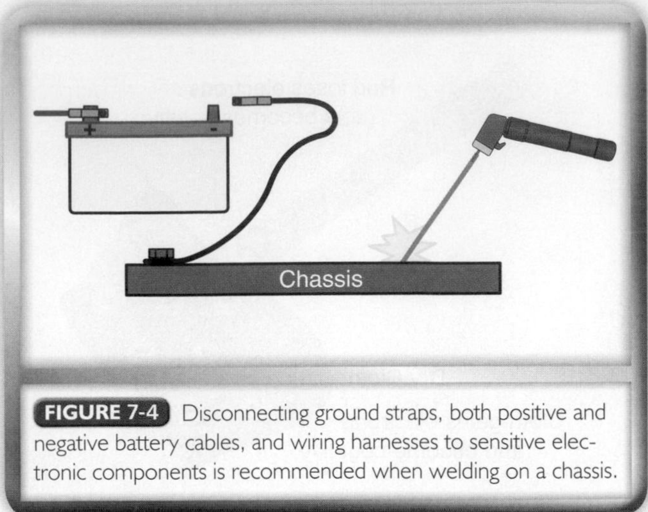

FIGURE 7-4 Disconnecting ground straps, both positive and negative battery cables, and wiring harnesses to sensitive electronic components is recommended when welding on a chassis.

> **TECHNICIAN TIP**
>
> Electrostatic discharge (ESD) caused by the build-up of static charges on a technician's clothing can damage sensitive electronic components. It is estimated that 30% to 70% of all failures in these components is caused by ESD. Handling sensitive components during service is one occasion where damage is done. Always remove charges by wearing a ground bracelet or making contact with a metal part of the chassis, such as the door handle. Leave components in conductive foam packing until installation.

Electricity from Light

Approximately 1,000 watts of sunlight energy per square meter strike the planet's surface daily. Solar cells that can produce electricity are limited in commercial vehicle applications FIGURE 7-5. However, commercially available cells are used as trickle chargers for batteries. The conversion of light into electricity is called the **photovoltaic (PV) effect**.

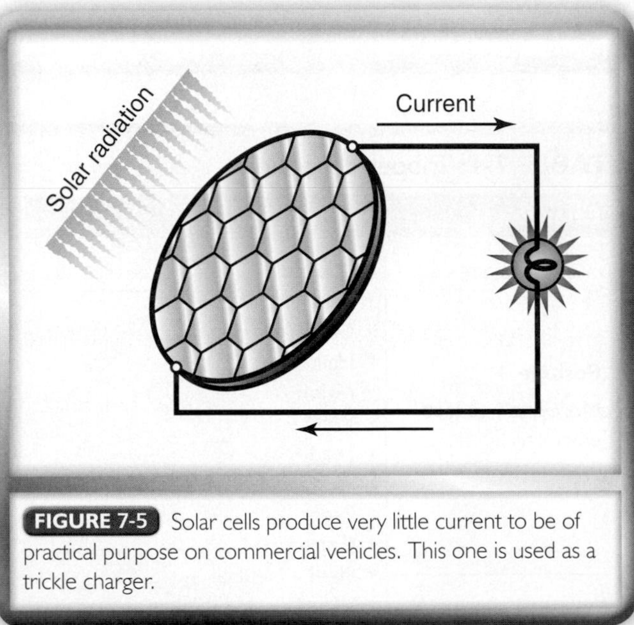

FIGURE 7-5 Solar cells produce very little current to be of practical purpose on commercial vehicles. This one is used as a trickle charger.

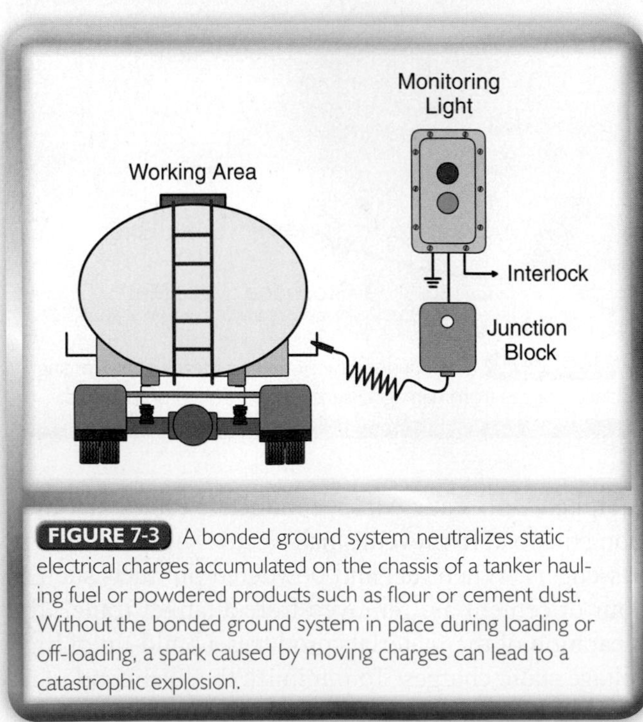

FIGURE 7-3 A bonded ground system neutralizes static electrical charges accumulated on the chassis of a tanker hauling fuel or powdered products such as flour or cement dust. Without the bonded ground system in place during loading or off-loading, a spark caused by moving charges can lead to a catastrophic explosion.

Electricity from Heat

Electricity produced by heat is a phenomenon known as thermoelectricity FIGURE 7-6. When two dissimilar metals are brought together and heated, electricity is produced at the junction points. Coupling and heating two dissimilar metals to produce electricity is called thermocoupling, and the device that is used is a **thermocouple**. The engine pyrometer uses a thermocoupler to measure exhaust temperature FIGURE 7-7. This device works to measure the incremental increase in exhaust temperature through voltage changes produced by the pyrometer. The hotter the device becomes, the greater the output voltage.

Cup holders combining heating and cooling, and small portable electric cooler-heaters can produce temperature differences using these thermocouple principles.

Thermoelectric Device (TED)

A cooling effect is observed when electricity passes through the thermocouple's junction. One of the metals becomes hot and the other cold. Thermoelectric devices (TED) are solid-state heat pumps formed from several layers of semiconductor materials **FIGURE 7-8**. When voltage is applied in one direction through the material, heat is created on one side and a cooling effect is observed on the opposite side. Changing polarity reverses the direc-

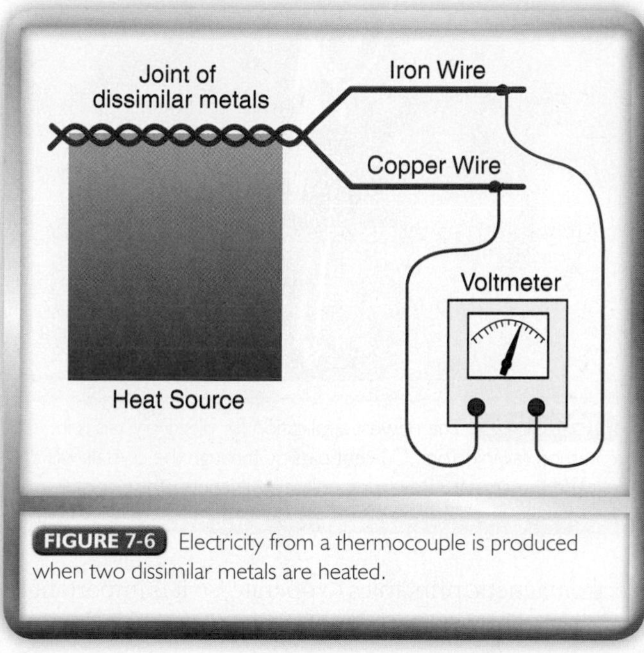

FIGURE 7-6 Electricity from a thermocouple is produced when two dissimilar metals are heated.

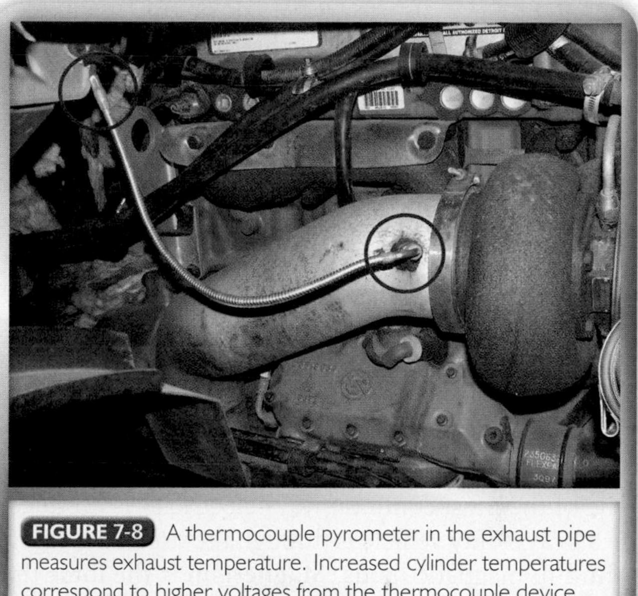

FIGURE 7-8 A thermocouple pyrometer in the exhaust pipe measures exhaust temperature. Increased cylinder temperatures correspond to higher voltages from the thermocouple device.

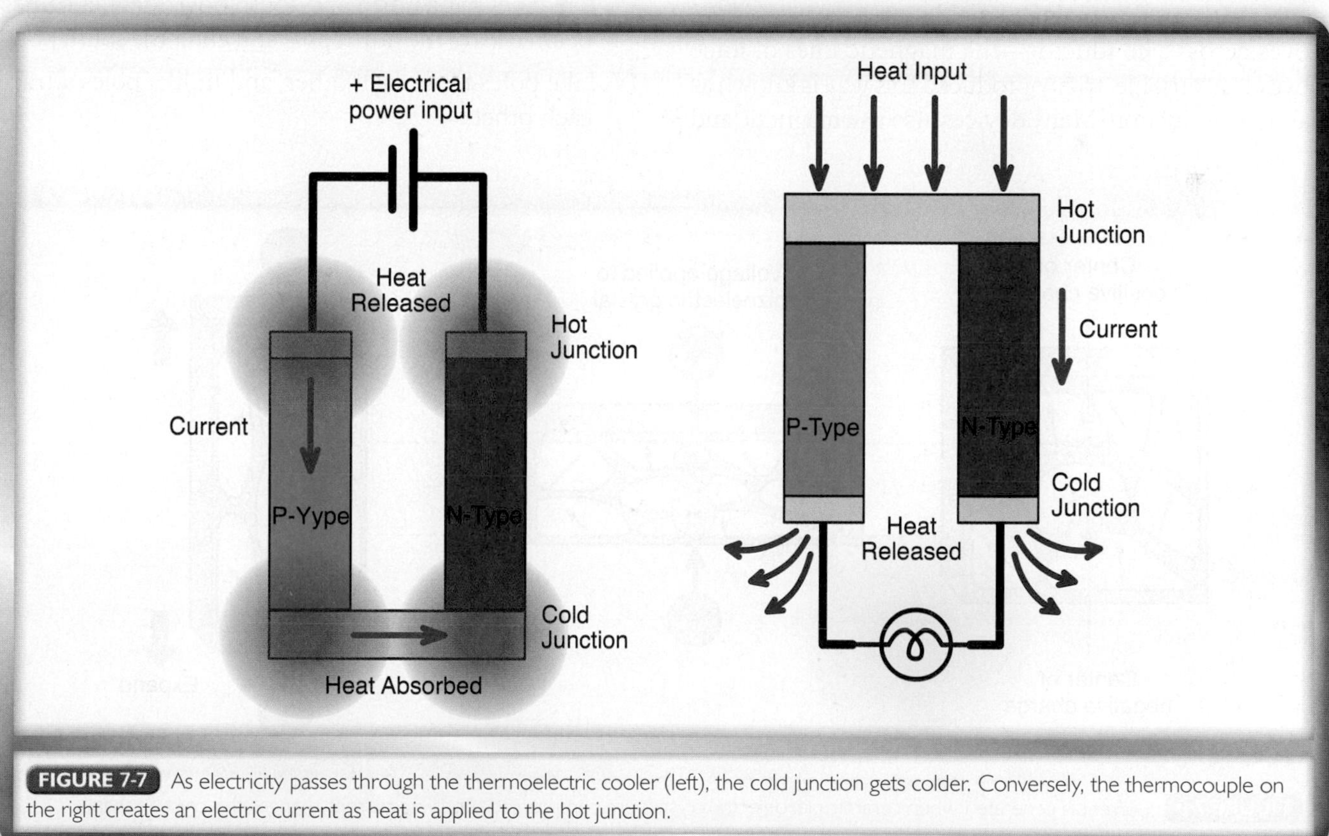

FIGURE 7-7 As electricity passes through the thermoelectric cooler (left), the cold junction gets colder. Conversely, the thermocouple on the right creates an electric current as heat is applied to the hot junction.

tion of heating and cooling. TEDs are used for cooling or heating small areas, including seats, steering wheels, cup holders, or beverage storage compartments.

Electricity from Pressure

When certain types of mineral crystals are squeezed or bent, electron flow is created according to the **Piezoelectric effect**. Piezoelectric crystals are commonly used to generate the electric current in a variety of devices ranging from pressure sensors, microphones, and speaker tweeters, to knock sensors and YAW sensors for stability control systems FIGURE 7-9. Piezoelectric crystals are even found in barbecue grill lighters. Just as squeezing the crystal produces current, passing current through the crystal also produces movement. When used in common rail injectors, piezo crystals produce the fastest rate of injector response when switching the injection event on and off FIGURE 7-10.

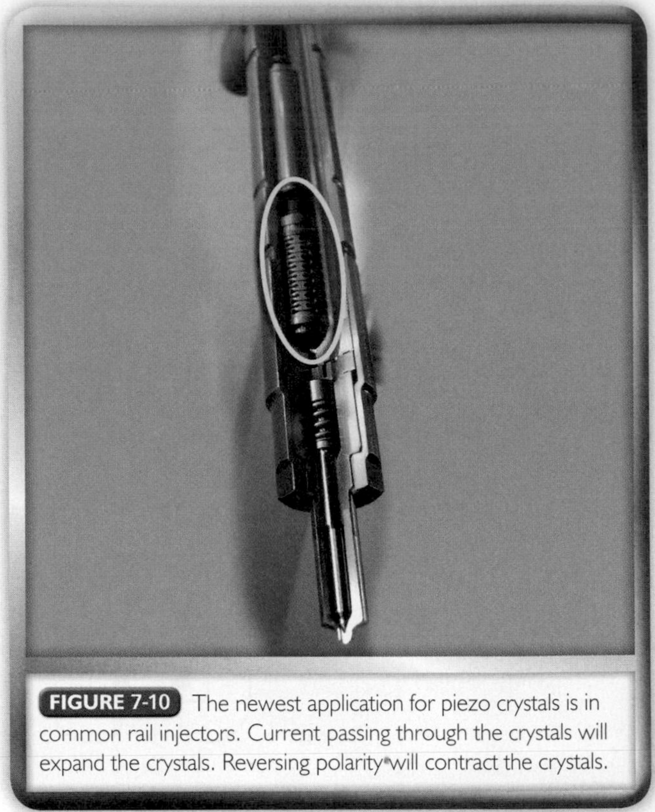

FIGURE 7-10 The newest application for piezo crystals is in common rail injectors. Current passing through the crystals will expand the crystals. Reversing polarity will contract the crystals.

Electricity from Magnetism

One of the most common ways electricity is produced on a heavy-duty vehicle is through the use of the energy found in magnetic fields. **Magnetism** is the force that attracts or repels magnetic charges; or the property of a material to respond to a magnetic field. When a conductor is moved through a magnetic field—or a magnetic field moves across a conductor—the magnetic lines of force move electrons. Electricity produced this way is known as magnetic induction. Many devices also use magnetic and electromagnetic principles to operate, so it is important to understand basic principles of magnetism and induction:

1. A magnet has a north and south pole. Magnetic lines of force leave the north pole and enter the south pole.
2. Like poles repel each other, and unlike poles attract each other.

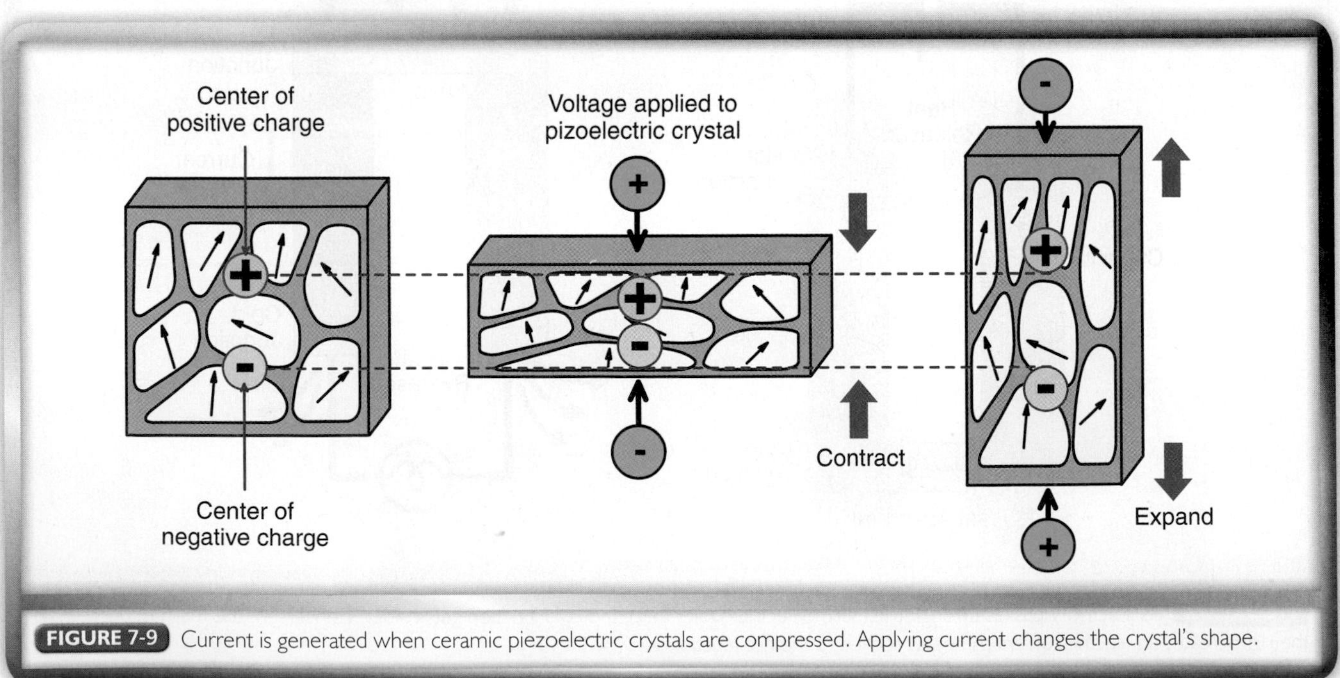

FIGURE 7-9 Current is generated when ceramic piezoelectric crystals are compressed. Applying current changes the crystal's shape.

3. If you divide a permanent magnet, the result is two shorter magnets, each with its own north and south poles.
4. There is no known insulation against magnetic lines of force. Magnetic lines of force can only be redirected through more permeable soft iron material. Laminated soft iron is the best conductor of lines of force FIGURE 7-11.

Important terms associated with magnetism include:

- **reluctance**—opposition or resistance to magnetic lines of force. Reluctance is to magnetism as resistance is to electricity FIGURE 7-12.
- **flux**—the number of lines of magnetic force. Stronger magnets have more flux FIGURE 7-13.

FIGURE 7-11 A soft iron laminated core used by starter motor field coils to intensify magnetic field strength.

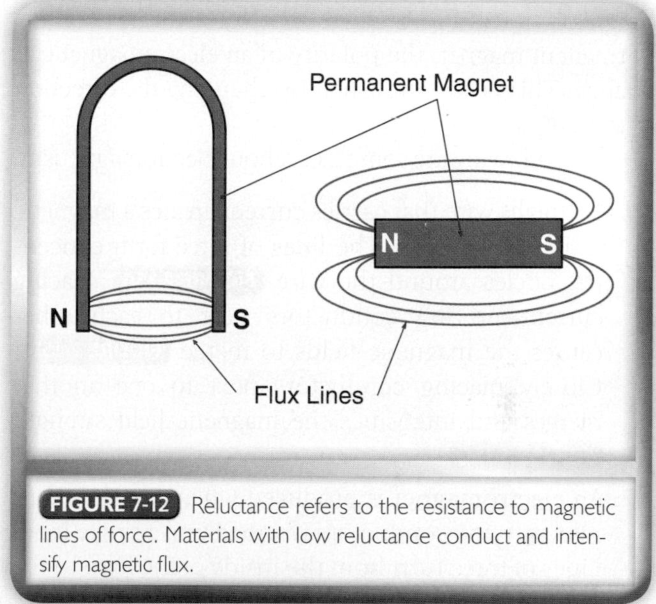

FIGURE 7-12 Reluctance refers to the resistance to magnetic lines of force. Materials with low reluctance conduct and intensify magnetic flux.

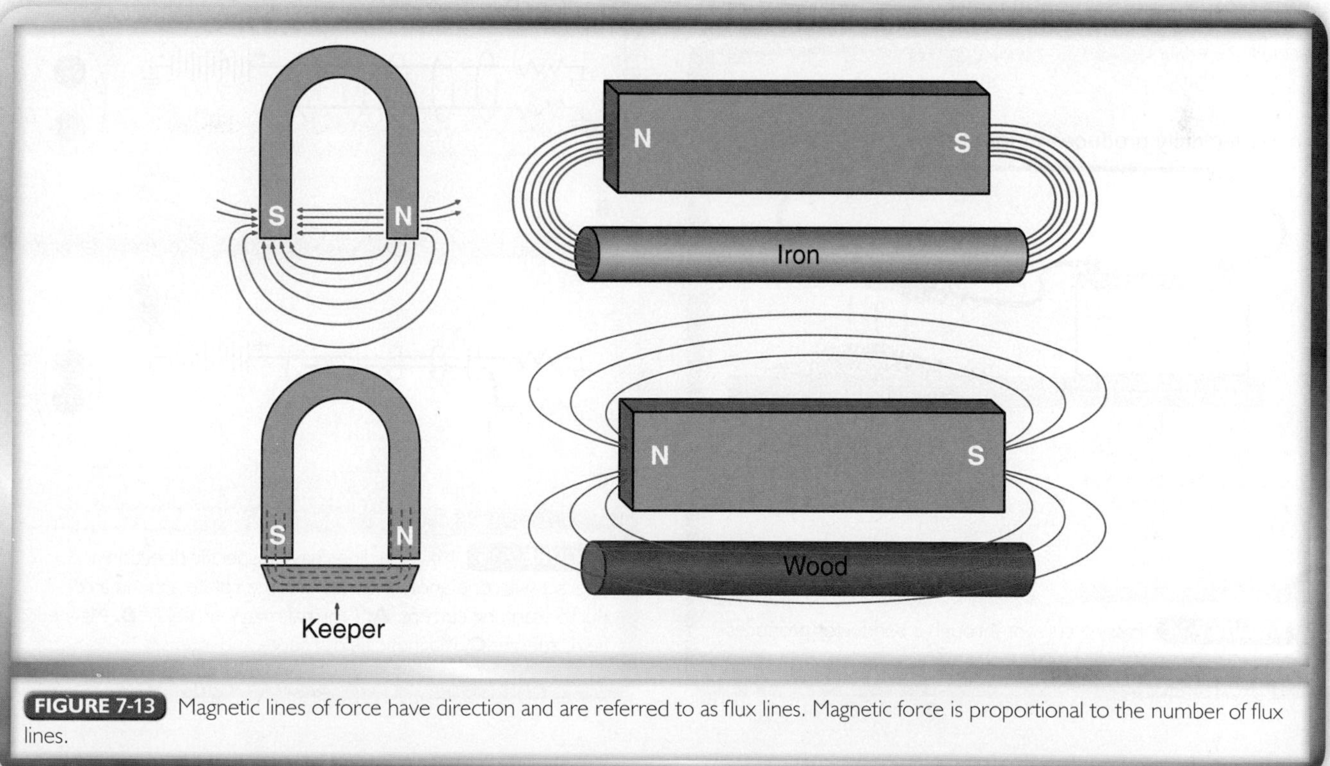

FIGURE 7-13 Magnetic lines of force have direction and are referred to as flux lines. Magnetic force is proportional to the number of flux lines.

- **flux density**—the number of magnetic lines of force per square inch. More lines of force mean a stronger magnetic field.

Electromagnetism

A corresponding relationship exists between electricity and magnetism—magnetism can produce electricity, and electricity can produce magnetism **FIGURE 7-14**. Electric current moving through a conductor produces a magnetic field that behaves nearly the same as a permanent magnet. As electrical current flows from negative to positive, magnetic lines of force travel north to south. Unlike a permanent magnet, the polarity of an electromagnet can change. This is accomplished by changing the direction of current flow.

The following are some facts about electromagnetism.

1. A straight wire that carries current creates a magnetic field around itself. The lines of force form concentric circles around the wire **FIGURE 7-15A**. Placing current-carrying conductors near to each other causes the magnetic fields to merge **FIGURE 7-15B**. Closely placing conductors next to one another merges and intensifies the magnetic field strength **FIGURE 7-15C**.
2. An **electromagnet** is produced when a straight current-carrying conductor is formed into a single loop. Lines of force turn from the inside of the loop to the outside.
3. Increasing the number of wire loops increases the magnetic field strength.
4. Air has a high reluctance to magnetic lines of force. For example, the smaller the air gap between a variable reluctance sensor and the iron reluctor wheel, the greater the number of lines of force **FIGURE 7-16**.
5. When a soft iron core is inserted into the coil of an electromagnet, lines of force easily travel through it. The magnetic field flux (lines of force) will increase as much as several hundred times because the permeability of rough iron is close to 2500 times that of air **FIGURE 7-17**.
6. Amperage through a coil or conductor and magnetic field strength are proportional. For example, if amperage is increased five times from 10 to 50 amps, the magnetic lines of force also increase in the ratio of 1:5 **FIGURE 7-18**.

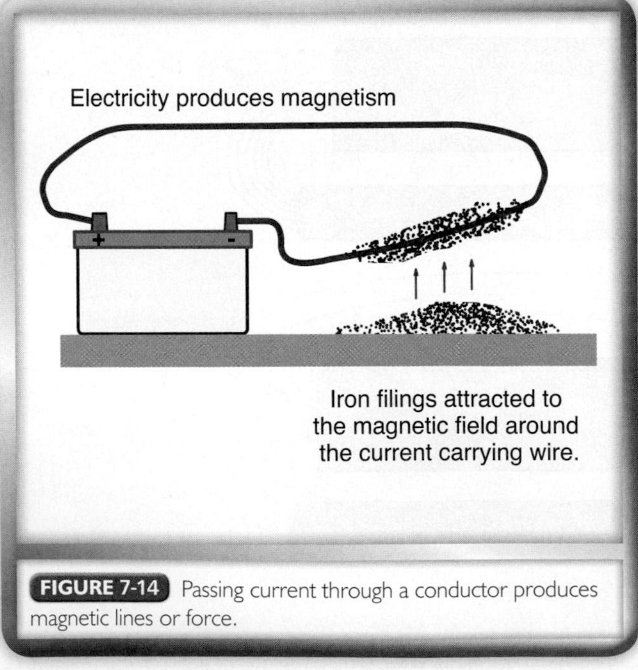
Electricity produces magnetism
+
-
Iron filings attracted to the magnetic field around the current carrying wire.

FIGURE 7-14 Passing current through a conductor produces magnetic lines or force.

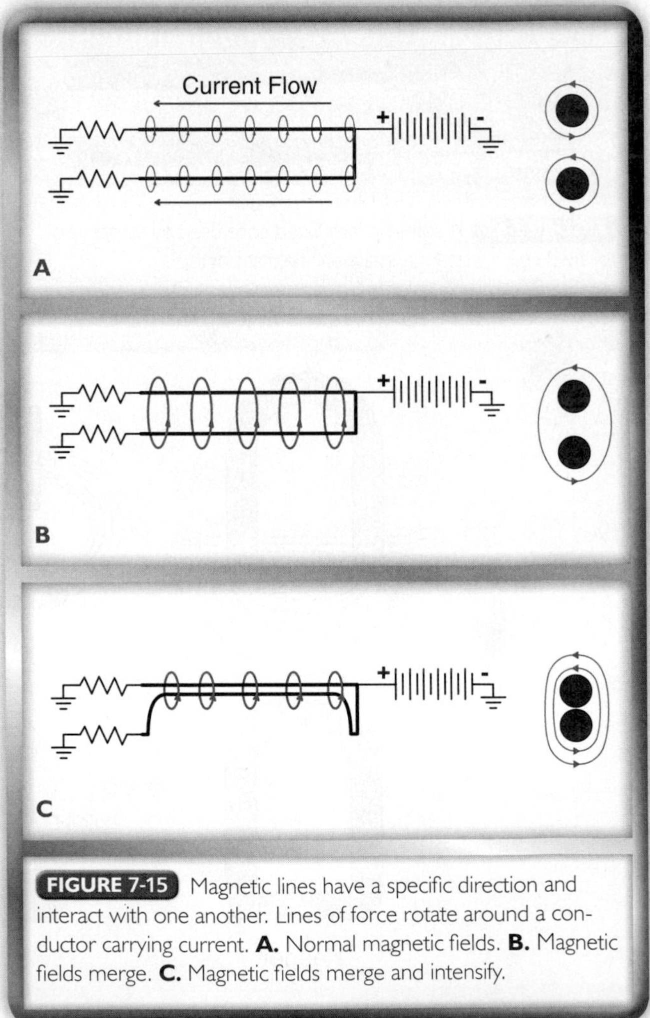
Current Flow
A
B
C

FIGURE 7-15 Magnetic lines have a specific direction and interact with one another. Lines of force rotate around a conductor carrying current. **A.** Normal magnetic fields. **B.** Magnetic fields merge. **C.** Magnetic fields merge and intensify.

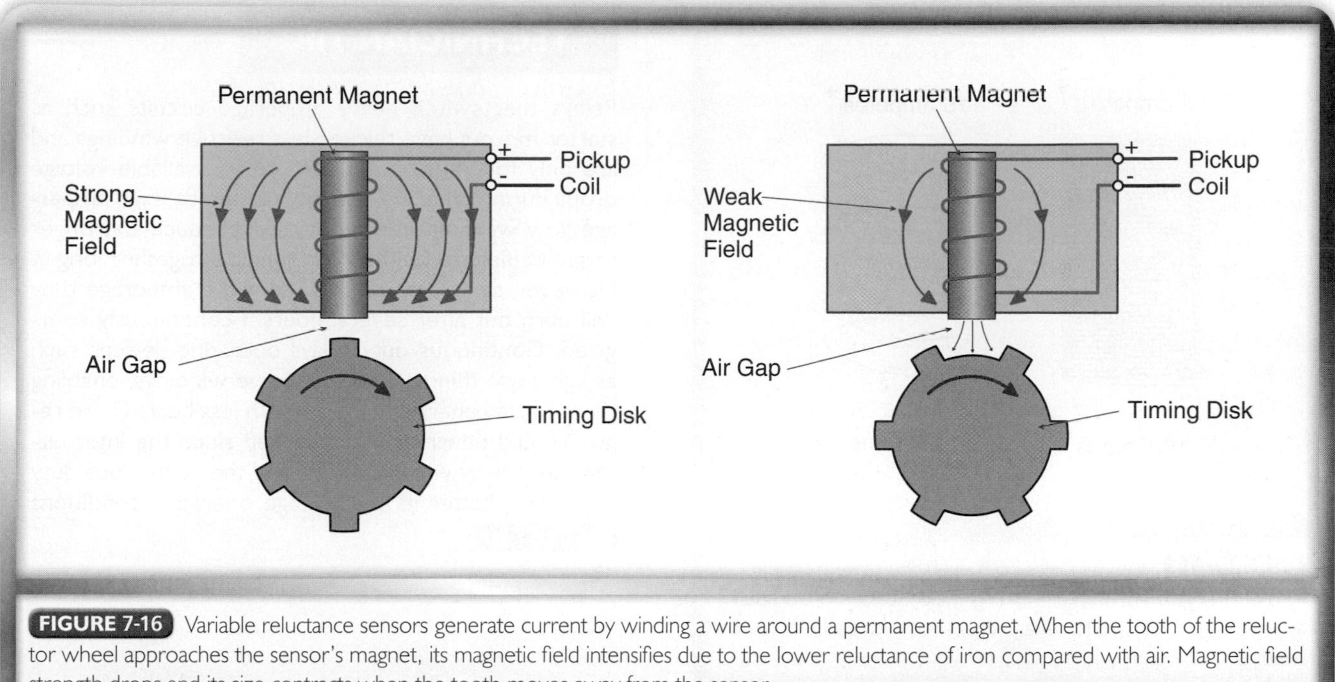

FIGURE 7-16 Variable reluctance sensors generate current by winding a wire around a permanent magnet. When the tooth of the reluctor wheel approaches the sensor's magnet, its magnetic field intensifies due to the lower reluctance of iron compared with air. Magnetic field strength drops and its size contracts when the tooth moves away from the sensor.

FIGURE 7-17 The pole pieces of this rotor found inside an alternator intensifies the magnetic field created by the electro magnet. **A.** Iron pole pieces. **B.** Electromagnetic coil.

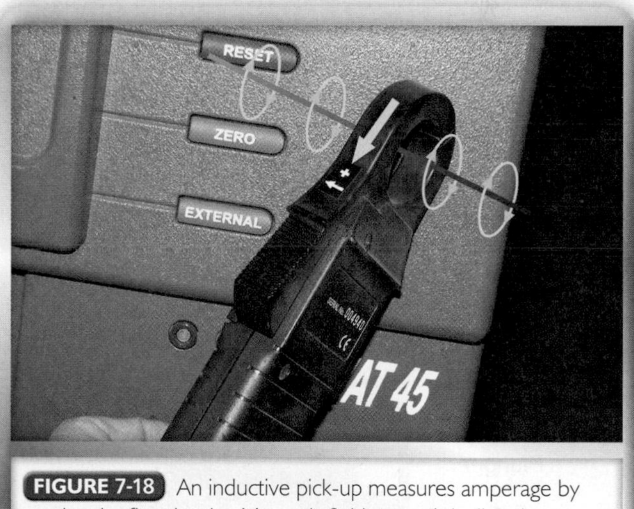

FIGURE 7-18 An inductive pick-up measures amperage by sensing the flux density. Magnetic field strength is directly proportional to amperage. A Hall effect sensor that is influenced by magnetic flux is used to sense the field strength.

7. The same magnetic force will be produced by an electromagnet having 1,000 turns of wire carrying 10 A as that of an electromagnet having 200 turns of wire carrying 50 A. In this case, the number of turns times the amperes equals 10,000 ampere-turns in either case **FIGURE 7-19**.
8. The left hand rule is used to determine the direction of magnetic lines of force when the electron theory is applied. When your hand is wrapped around a conductor with the thumb pointed in the direction of current flow, magnetic lines of force follow the direction of your fingers. The magnetic field of a current-carrying conductor behaves in the same manner as the magnetic field of a permanent magnet as long as current is flowing through it. When the direction of current flow is changed, the direction of the lines of force also changes.

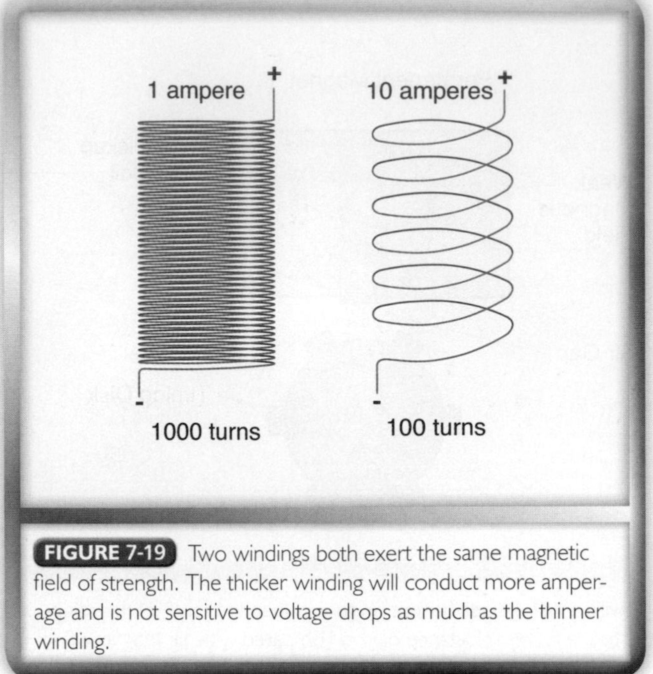

FIGURE 7-19 Two windings both exert the same magnetic field of strength. The thicker winding will conduct more amperage and is not sensitive to voltage drops as much as the thinner winding.

TECHNICIAN TIP

Relays that switch heavy amperage circuits such as starter motors have thicker, less resistive windings and are only for intermittent use. When available voltage drops during cranking, the low resistance, high amperage flow windings in the relay will produce a stronger magnetic field to hold switch contacts together longer. However, since these relays use more amperage they will burn out after several hours if continuously energized. Continuous duty relays operating devices such as lights use thinner, more resistive windings, enabling them to stay energized longer with less heat. These relays should never be interchanged since the intermittent duty relay will fail quickly and the continuous duty relay will chatter in low voltage operating conditions FIGURE 7-20.

9. When two conductors carrying equal currents flowing in opposite directions are placed side by side, the lines of force are also in opposite directions and are more concentrated between the conductors than on the outside of the two conductors. The current-carrying conductors are pushed apart until the fields are concentric.
10. If there is an equal current flow in the same direction through two or more parallel conductors, each conductor alone creates a circular field of magnetic force that joins with the other to move in the same direction.

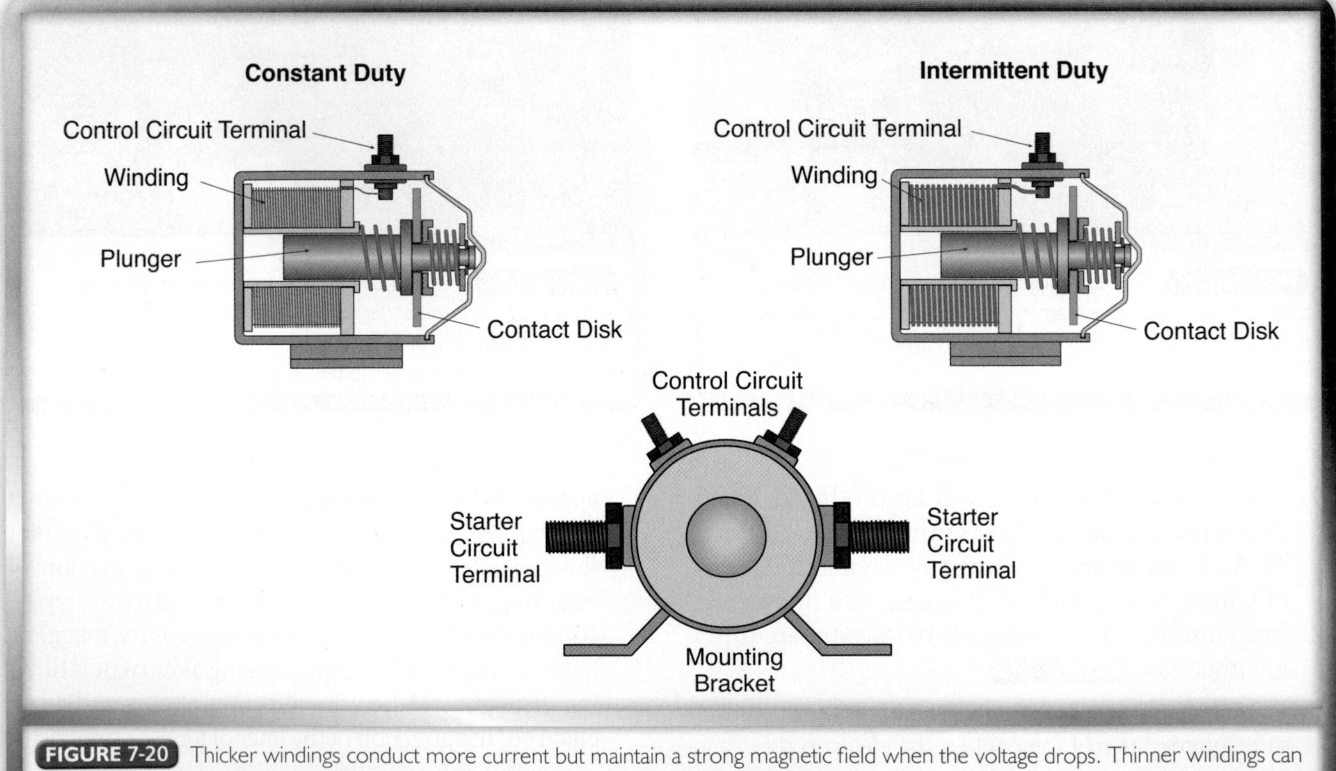

FIGURE 7-20 Thicker windings conduct more current but maintain a strong magnetic field when the voltage drops. Thinner windings can be used for continuous operation but lose magnetic field strength when voltage drops.

Electron flow can be created using magnetic fields in one of three ways:

- Magnetic induction or electromagnetic induction
- Self-induction
- Mutual induction

Electromagnetic Induction

The principle of producing electrical current flow using electromagnets is known as **electromagnetic induction**. Alternators, generators, and speed sensors use this electrical principle to produce electrical current. Lines of force leaving the north pole of the magnet will push electrons. The south pole, with lines of force moving inward, will pull electrons FIGURE 7-21. For example, a magnetic field cutting across a wire will move electrons, producing a positive and negative charge at each end of the wire. Charge polarity depends upon the angle of wire movement relative to the magnetic field and the direction of movement relative to the magnetic field FIGURE 7-22.

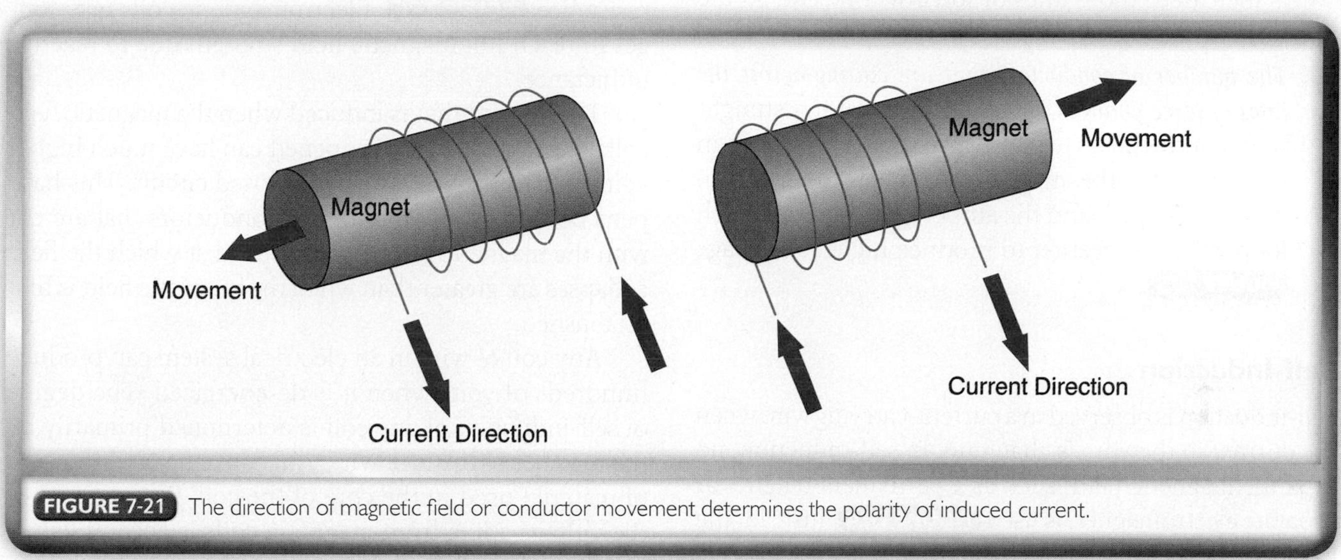

FIGURE 7-21 The direction of magnetic field or conductor movement determines the polarity of induced current.

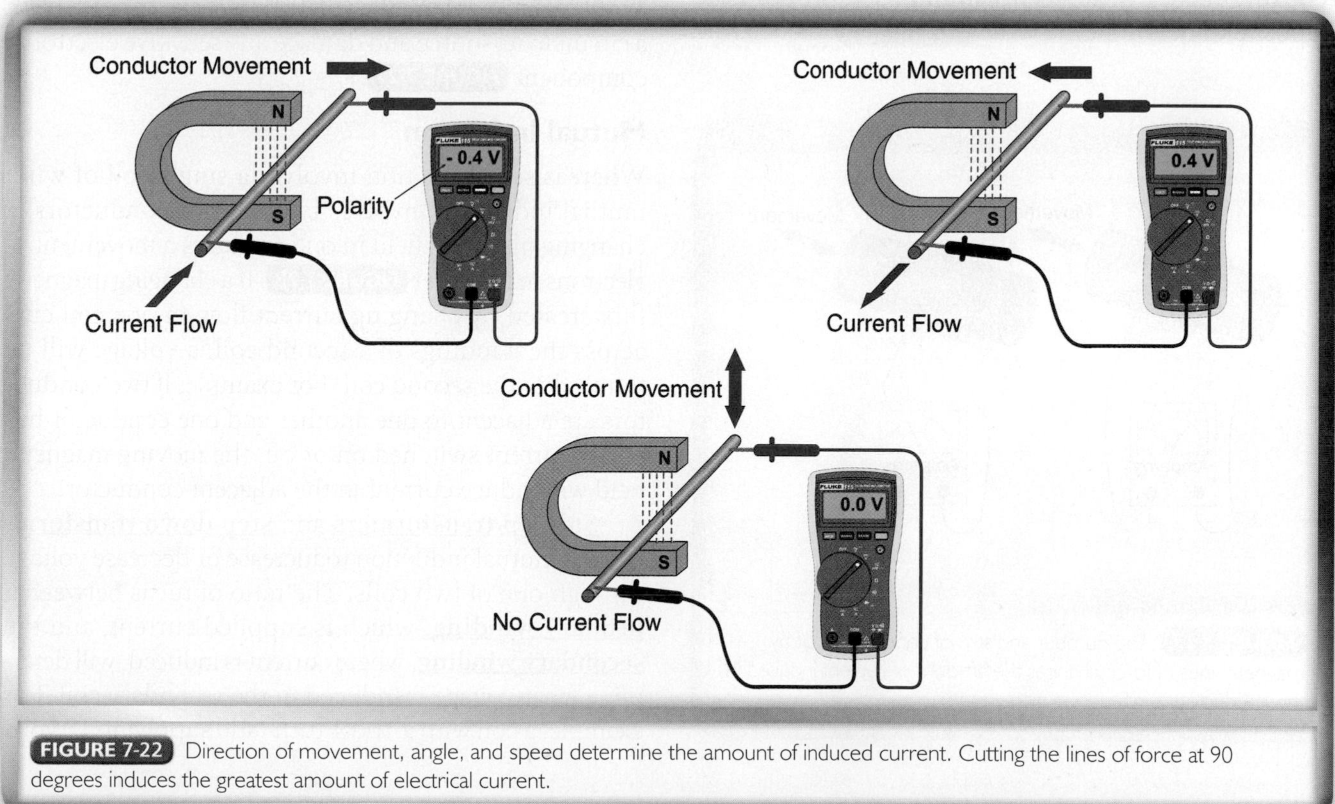

FIGURE 7-22 Direction of movement, angle, and speed determine the amount of induced current. Cutting the lines of force at 90 degrees induces the greatest amount of electrical current.

Some important facts to remember about electromagnetic induction are:

1. *The strength of the magnetic field changes induced voltage.* If the magnetic field is made stronger—for example, by using a more powerful magnet—the conductor will cut more lines of force and induce higher voltage.
2. *The speed at which lines of force are cutting across the conductor changes induced voltage.* If the relative motion between the conductor and magnetic field is increased, more lines of force will be cut, so the induced voltage will be higher.
3. *The number of conductors that are cutting across the lines of force changes induced amperage.* If a straight wire conductor is wound into a coil that is then moved across the magnetic field, all the loops of wire are merged, and the amperage induced in each loop will add together to produce higher amperage **FIGURE 7-23**.

Self-Induction

Self-induction is observed in a current-carrying wire when the current in the wire is changing. In self-induction, no separate magnetic field, such as a permanent magnet or separate electromagnet, is used **FIGURE 7-24**. Instead, the magnetic field created by an increasing or decreasing current through the wire itself will induce current in the opposite direction in the wire **FIGURE 7-25**. Hence, the current is self-induced. The cause of self-induction is the changing size and strength of the magnetic field. Changing current flow expands or contracts the field. Because there is relative motion between the field and conductor, the conditions necessary for inducing current are met.

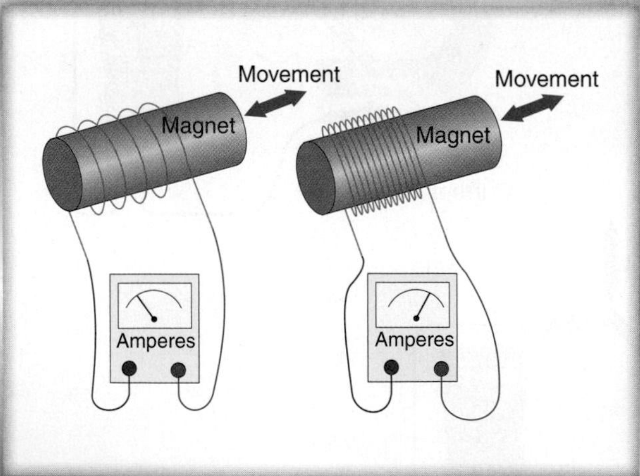

It is important for technicians to know that the polarity of the induced current flow is the opposite that of the current that induced the original magnetic field. This means the polarity of an induced current will oppose a change in the current that produced it. Another term describing this effect is inductive reactance or inductive resistance **FIGURE 7-26**. Electromagnetic coils take longer to reach full magnetic field strength due to reactive inductance.

The current that is induced when the magnetic field collapses after a circuit is opened can have much higher voltage than the voltage in the closed circuit. This happens because of the number of conductors that are cut with the magnetic field and the speed at which the field collapses are greater than when the magnetic field is first established.

Any coil of wire in an electrical system can produce hundreds of volts when it is de-energized. The degree of self-induction of any coil is determined primarily by the number of turns of wire, their spacing, and the type of material used in the core of the coil. Suppression of the voltage spike from magnetic coils is accomplished using diodes, capacitors, resistors, or induction coils. Without suppression, the voltage spike can travel back in a circuit to its source and damage any sensitive electronic component **FIGURE 7-27**.

Mutual Induction

Whereas self-induction involves a single coil of wire, mutual induction involves two coils or conductors; a changing magnetic field in one produces a movement of electrons in the other **FIGURE 7-28**. If a changing magnetic flux created by changing current flow in one coil cuts across the windings of a second coil, a voltage will be induced in the second coil. For example, if two conductors are adjacent to one another and one conductor has either current switched on or off, the moving magnetic field will induce current in the adjacent conductor.

Step-up transformers and **step-down transformers** use mutual induction to increase or decrease voltage through one of two coils. The ratio of turns between a **primary winding**, which is supplied current, and the **secondary winding**, where current is induced, will determine what voltage is induced in the secondary coil. For example, a coil with a 100:1 turn ratio supplying 12 volts

FIGURE 7-23 The number and size of conductors cut by magnetic lines of force changes the amount of current induced in the conductors.

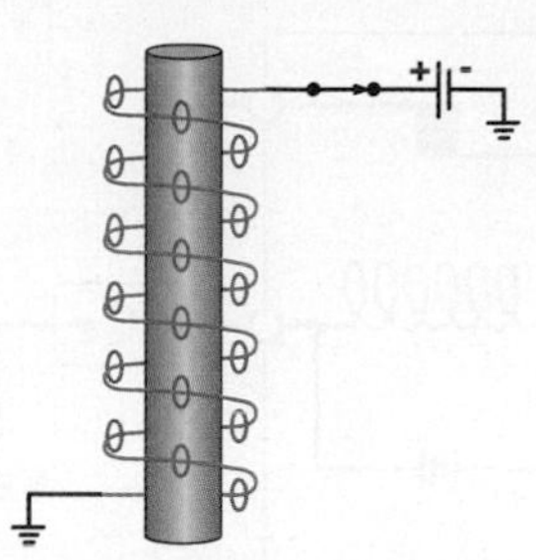
Stage 1
A weak magnetic field is established.

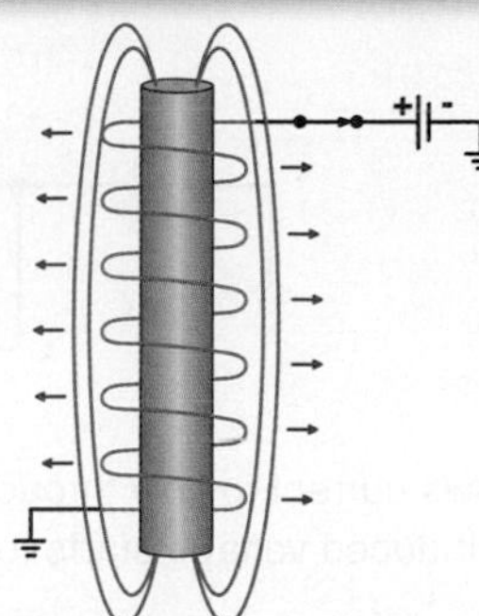
Stage 2
The magnetic field expands and gets stronger.

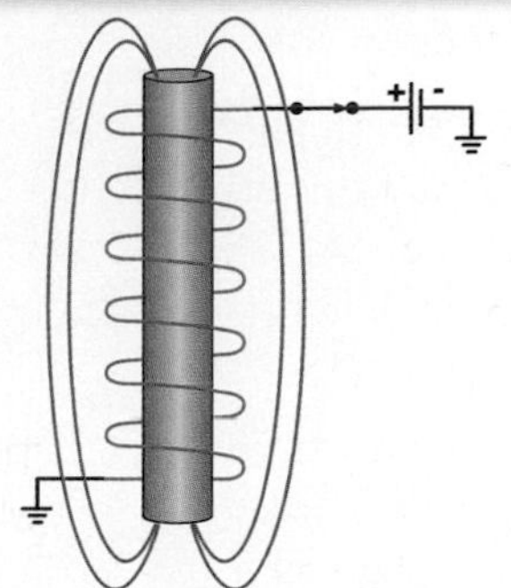
Stage 3
The magnetic field is stationary.

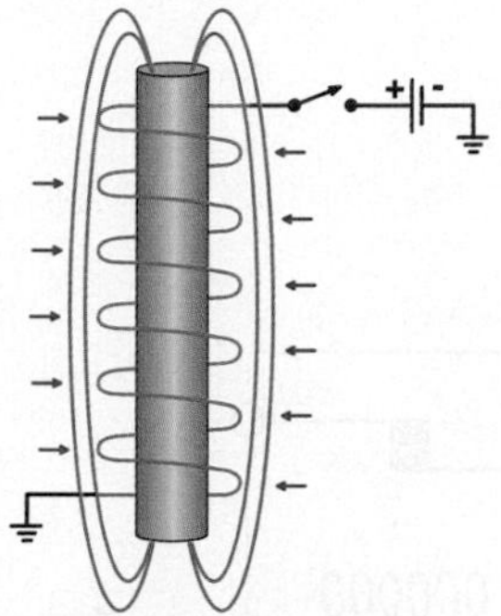
Stage 4
The switch is opened and the magnetic field begins to collapse.

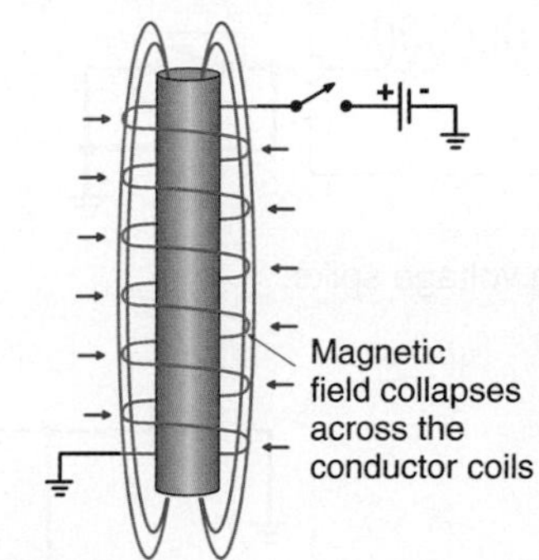

Stage 5
The magnetic field collapses rapidly.

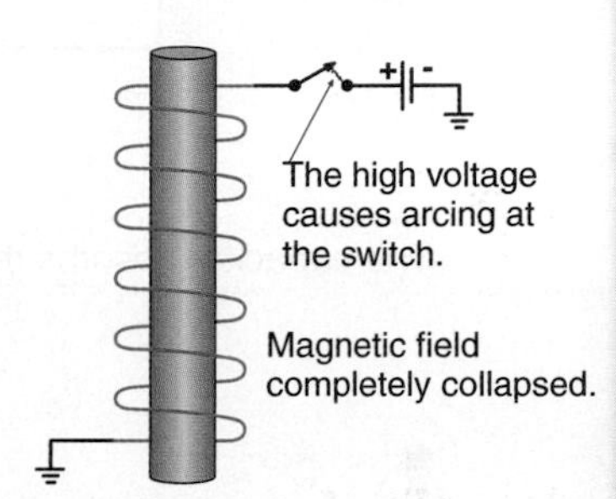

Stage 6
The current induced by the collapsing magnetic field causes arcing across the switch contacts.

FIGURE 7-24 Self-induction is caused by the changing size of magnetic field in a coil of wire. Lines of force from contracting magnetic field move rapidly across the conductors. When current to a coil is turned-off, a large spark is observed at the switch due to induced voltage.

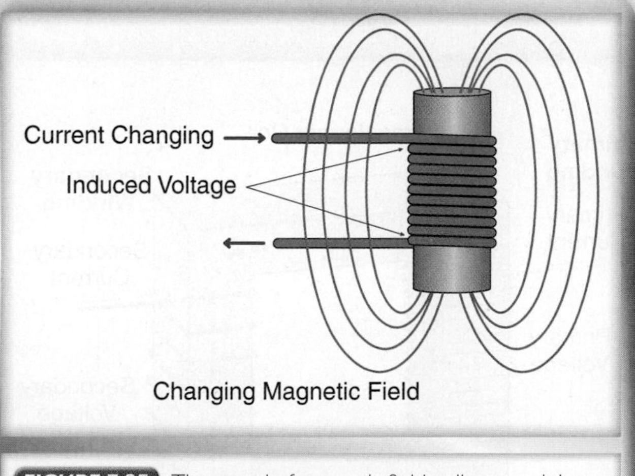

FIGURE 7-25 The speed of magnetic field collapse and the number or mass of conductors determine self-induced voltage. Induced voltage is always much higher than the voltage initially producing the magnetic field.

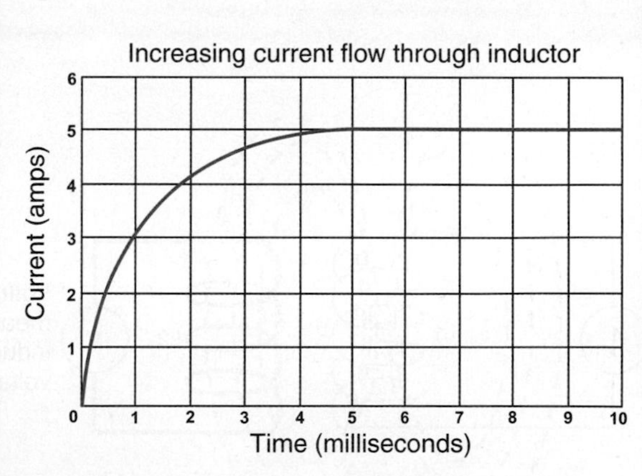

FIGURE 7-26 Increasing current flow through an inductor. Initially, the current rises dramatically, but over time levels off.

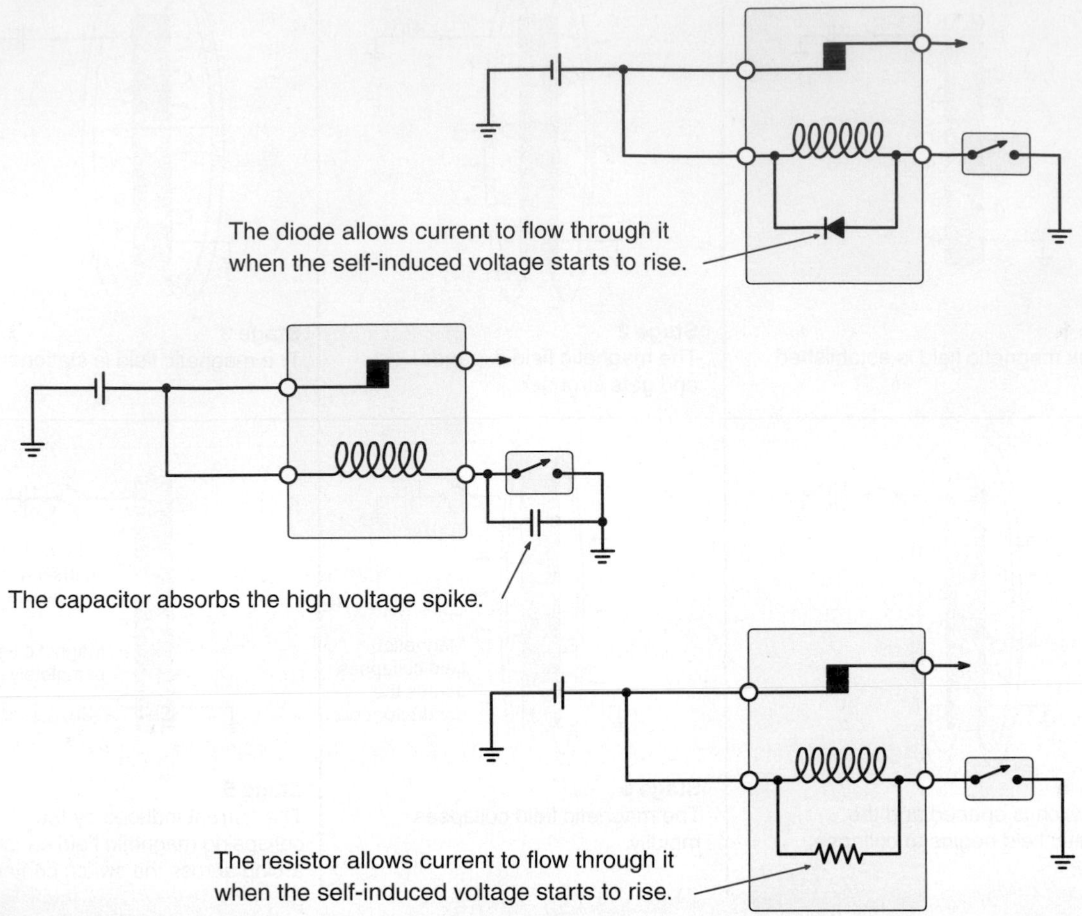

The diode allows current to flow through it when the self-induced voltage starts to rise.

The capacitor absorbs the high voltage spike.

The resistor allows current to flow through it when the self-induced voltage starts to rise.

FIGURE 7-27 Self-induction produces a voltage spike, which can damage sensitive electrical components connected to the same circuit. Resistors, diodes, and capacitors are used to suppress voltage spikes.

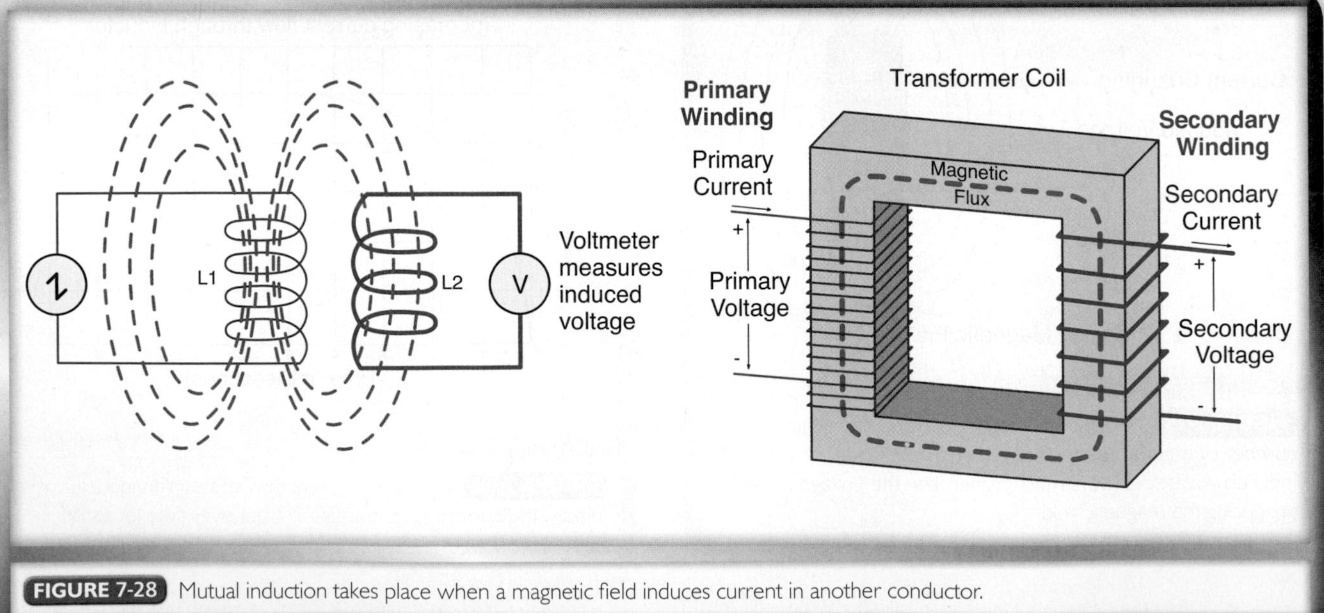

FIGURE 7-28 Mutual induction takes place when a magnetic field induces current in another conductor.

in the primary coil will increase that voltage to 1,200 volts in the secondary coil. Injector drive modules will often use step-up transformers to increase the voltage in a 12-volt system to between 75 and 110 volts FIGURE 7-29.

Induction and Twisted Pair Wires

The phenomenon of mutual induction explains why network data bus wires use a twisted pair of wires to carry low-voltage serial data. Twisting the lines helps to reduce the signal noise. Serial data is the digital language electronic modules use to talk and listen to one another. The wire pair is like the telephone line carrying the information. Any voltage induced in these wires can interfere with communication and potentially be processed as valid data.

By twisting the wires, any current induced by a magnetic field is reversed in every loop or twist of the next. So, if the same current is induced by a magnetic field along the length of the twisted pair, each loop area will get the same current induced in it. Because the wires have an opposite polarity of one another, the same voltage is induced in both, and that voltage is effectively cancelled by the loop or twist in front or behind it.

Enclosing the twisted wire pair in a metal foil further helps reduce signal interference. Magnetic fields and low-frequency radio waves that can also induce current are stopped by the low reluctance of the metal foil. The magnetic field will induce current flow in the foil and then drain that current to chassis ground. This happens because magnetic lines of force and electromagnetic waves find an easier pathway through the foil than air. A ground wire connected to the foil will conduct induced voltage away from the wire pair FIGURE 7-30.

FIGURE 7-29 The injector drive module powering HEUI injectors uses step-up transformers to energize injectors. **A.** Injector current storage capaciter (2). **B.** Inductors – step-up transformers (2).

Electricity from Chemistry

Producing electricity from chemical reactions is commonly done with galvanic reactions. Galvanic reactions take place when two dissimilar metals are placed in an electrolyte FIGURE 7-31. An electrolyte is any liquid that conducts electric current. For example, pure water will not conduct current. Tap water, however, often contains minerals and chlorine, and those impurities enable the conduction of current. Water containing salt, acids, or alkaline solutions are even better conductors of electricity.

Dissimilar metals form electrodes, which are the elements of a galvanic cell forming the positive and negative poles. Chemical action between the electrolyte and electrodes strips electrons from one metal electrode and adds electrons to another electrode, which produces galvanic cell polarity.

Galvanic reactions are observed in many places. Corrosion is an example of a galvanic reaction. The cooling system of an engine contains water, an electrolyte, and dissimilar metals such as copper injector tubes, cast iron blocks, aluminum water pump housings, and so on form potential electrodes. Some metals losing electrons will

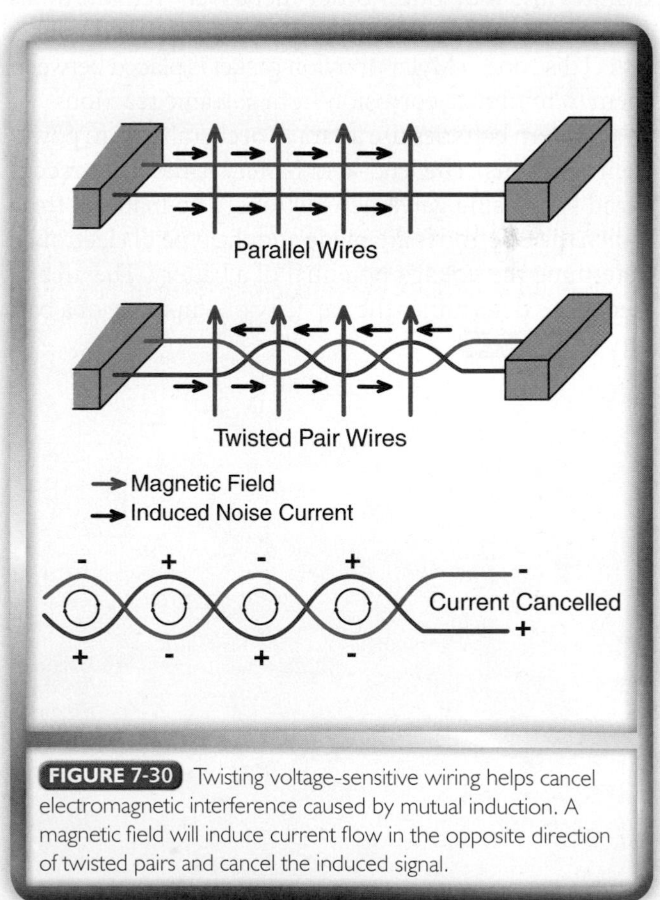

FIGURE 7-30 Twisting voltage-sensitive wiring helps cancel electromagnetic interference caused by mutual induction. A magnetic field will induce current flow in the opposite direction of twisted pairs and cancel the induced signal.

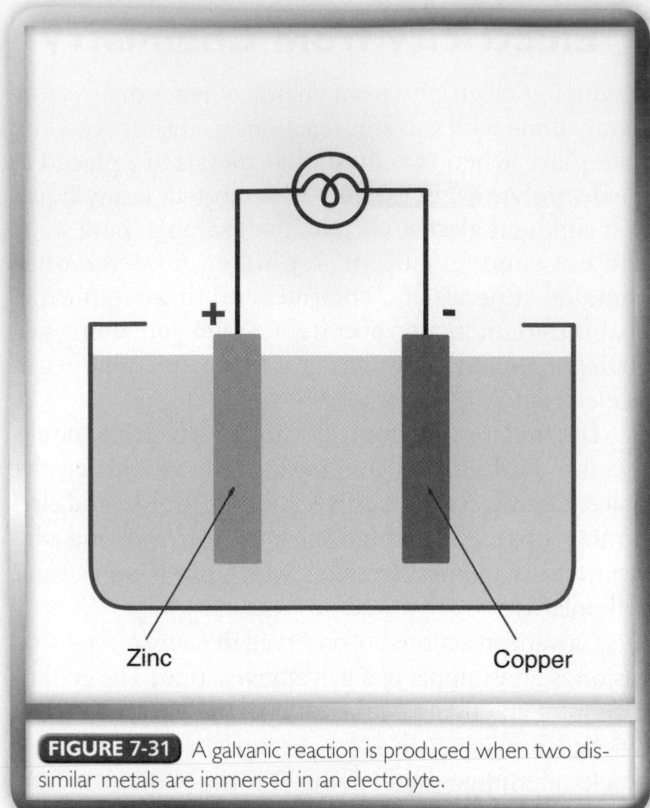

FIGURE 7-31 A galvanic reaction is produced when two dissimilar metals are immersed in an electrolyte.

disintegrate (corrode); other metals can remain unaffected. When an aluminum disc wheel is installed against a steel disc one, a Mylar or nylon gasket is placed between them to minimize corrosion from galvanic reactions.

Modern batteries use a variety of chemistries to power their reactions. The lead-acid battery is the most recognized type using galvanic reactions. The material from which the electrodes are made and the type of electrolyte determine the voltage potential of a battery. The area of electrodes determines the capacity or amperage of a battery **FIGURE 7-32**.

Fuel Cells

Another type of electrochemical device producing electricity is a **fuel cell**, which combines hydrogen and oxygen to produce electricity and water. Unlike a battery, a fuel cell does not require recharging but produces energy in the form of electricity and heat as long as fuel is supplied **FIGURE 7-33**.

Dozens of varieties of fuel cells exist, but they all fundamentally work in the same manner. Like batteries, fuel cells consist of three sections—the positive and negative plates and an electrolytic membrane. Two chemical reactions occur between three different plates—the negative, positive, and fuel cell membrane—creating water, heat, and electricity.

As hydrogen and oxygen combine, an electron exchange must take place between the gases. The electron

FIGURE 7-32 The area of electrodes determines the capacity of a battery.

essentially travels through the electrical device connected to the fuel cell to reach the plate deficient in electrons. Fuel cells require hydrogen as a fuel to operate. Together with oxygen, these gases pass over the plates, producing the current flow.

A fuel reformer operates along with a fuel cell to remove hydrogen from diesel fuel, natural gas, methanol, or gasoline. Because fuel cells use chemistry and not combustion to produce energy, there are zero noxious emissions from these devices.

Voltage from a single cell is approximately 0.7 volts, so cells are connected in a series to increase output voltage. In a few commercial vehicles, fuel cells currently have limited use as auxiliary power units that are used to supply electrical power when the engine is not operating. The high cost of fuel cells removes them from practical consideration as a viable auxiliary power supply.

Hydrogen Gas
Oxidant (Oxygen)
Excess Hydrogen
Excess Oxidant and Water
Anode (Platinum catalyst)
Cathode
Polymer Electrolyte Membrane

FIGURE 7-33 Process of converting hydrogen and oxygen in a fuel cell into electricity, heat, CO2, heat, and water.

TECHNICIAN TIP

When repairing wire terminals and conductors exposed to outside elements, it is not a good practice to use terminals made of different materials or even join wiring made from different metals. Always solder connections and use shrink tube to protect the joint from water intrusion. Covering a wiring splice with tape after soldering and using shrink tube also helps protect the connection from abrasion. Exposed wire terminals should always be covered with a dielectric grease (electrically non-conduction silicone grease) or suitable corrosion inhibitor **FIGURE 7-34**. Keeping water away from these connections will prevent galvanic reactions from quickly corroding connections.

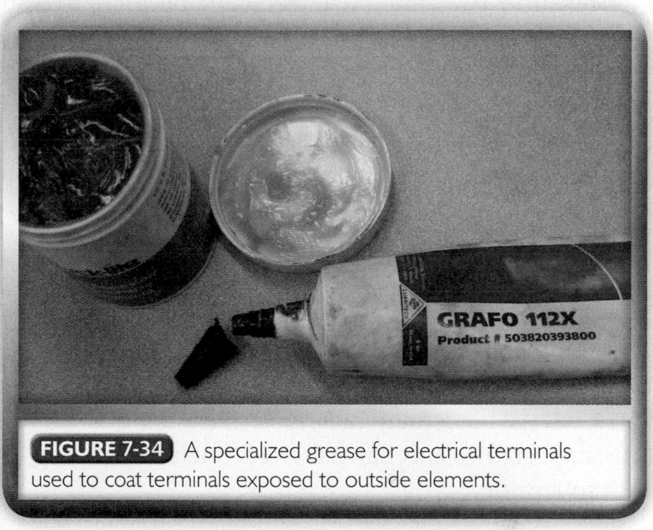

FIGURE 7-34 A specialized grease for electrical terminals used to coat terminals exposed to outside elements.

Wrap-up

Ready for Review

- Friction, heat, chemicals, light, pressure, and magnetic induction are all sources of electricity. That is, each type of energy can move electrons so they can do work.
- Static electricity can be induced by rubbing or separating two materials on opposite sides of the triboelectric series. During this process, one material loses electrons to the other.
- If two different metals are joined and heated, a small electrical current can be generated. This system is a thermoelectric source of energy.
- Galvanic reactions producing electricity are the result of two dissimilar metals being immersed in an electrical conductive liquid called an electrolyte.
- Fuel cells are a type of electrochemical device that combines hydrogen and oxygen to produce water and in the process it produces electricity and heat. They operate without combustion. The three basic elements to a fuel cell are the anode, the cathode, and the electrolytic membrane.
- Photovoltaic energy is produced from converting light to electricity. Solar cells are an example of photovoltaic energy.
- The Piezoelectric effect creates electricity when crystals of certain materials, such as quartz, are subjected to mechanical stress such as bending or squeezing.
- Magnetic induction involves moving a wire inside a magnetic field to induce current flow. Similarly, magnetic induction can take place by moving a magnet inside a stationary coil of wire.
- Mutual induction involves two coils or conductors with a changing magnetic field in one producing a movement of electrons in the other. Step up and step down transformers use mutual induction plus a turn ratio difference between the primary and secondary coil windings.
- Self-induction is observed in a current-carrying coil when the current in the wire is changing. Expanding or collapsing a magnetic field will self-induce current flow in the coil. In self-induction, no separate magnetic field such as a permanent magnet or separate electromagnet is used.
- Twisting the data bus wire lines helps to reduce the signal noise. Electromagnetic interference, which could induce current in the network wires, is cancelled by loops in front or behind the loop with induced current.
- Electromagnetic induction requires three things: a winding, a magnet, and relative movement (that is, movement of one past the other).
- Electricity can also create magnetic effects, referred to as electromagnetism. These magnetic forces can be used to create mechanical movement, such as in a relay or electric motor.

Vocabulary Builder

electromagnet A conductor wound in a coil that produces a magnetic field when current flows through it.

electromagnetic induction The production of an electrical current in a conductor when it moves through a magnetic field or a magnetic field moves past it.

fuel cell An electrochemical device that combines hydrogen and oxygen to produce electricity and water.

magnetism The force that attracts or repels magnetic charges; or the property of a material to respond to a magnetic field.

photovoltaic (PV) effect The conversion of light into electricity.

Piezoelectric effect A type of electricity produced by bending or squeezing a unique type of quartz crystal.

primary winding The coil of wire in the low-voltage circuit, which creates the magnetic field in a step-up transformer.

secondary winding The coil of wire in which high voltage is induced in a step-up transformer.

step-down transformer A transformer used to reduce voltage in the secondary coil. A battery charger would use a step-down transformer to change 120 volts into 12 to charge a 12-volt battery.

step-up transformer A transformer used to increase the voltage from a lower input voltage to a higher output, such as an ignition coil.

thermocouple A thermoelectric device consisting of two dissimilar metals that produce voltage when heated.

Review Questions

1. Which of the following statements is correct concerning frictional electricity?
   a. Frictional electricity is significant to the technician for a number of electrical issues.
   b. Grounding protocol must be observed when handling components with sensitive microelectronic circuits, as they may be damaged by electro-static discharge (ESD).
   c. Grounding yourself by touching a metal workbench or door handle draws-off any electric charge.
   d. All of the choices are correct.
2. Which of the following statements is NOT correct concerning electricity produced by heat?
   a. Electricity produced by heat is a phenomenon known as thermoelectricity.
   b. When two dissimilar metals are brought together and heated, electricity is produced at the junction points.
   c. The engine pyrometer uses a thermocouple to measure exhaust temperature.
   d. As the thermocouple becomes hotter, less output voltage is produced.
3. _______ uses a single coil of wire.
   a. Mutual induction
   b. Self-induction
   c. A step-up transformer
   d. A step-down transformer
4. Which of the following is/are correct concerning electricity from magnetism?
   a. A magnet has a north and south pole. Magnetic lines of force leave the north pole and enter the south pole.
   b. Like poles repel each other, and unlike poles attract each other.
   c. If you divide a permanent magnet, the result is two shorter magnets, each with its own north and south poles.
   d. All of the choices are correct.
5. Which of the following is NOT correct concerning electromagnetism?
   a. A straight wire that carries current creates a magnetic field around itself.
   b. An electromagnet is produced when a straight current-carrying conductor is formed into a single loop.
   c. Increasing the number of wire loops increases the magnetic field strength.
   d. When a soft iron core is inserted into the coil of an electromagnet, lines of force find it difficult to travel through it.
6. Which of the following is/are correct concerning electromagnetic induction?
   a. The strength of the magnetic field changes induced voltage.
   b. The speed at which lines of force are cutting across the conductor changes induced voltage.
   c. The number of conductors that are cutting across the lines of force changes induced amperage.
   d. All of the choices are correct.
7. Which of the following is/are correct concerning self-induction?
   a. Self-induction is observed in a current-carrying wire when the current in the wire is changing.
   b. In self-induction, no separate magnetic field, such as a permanent magnet or separate electromagnet, is used.
   c. The cause of self-induction is the changing size and strength of the magnetic field.
   d. All of the choices are correct.
8. Which of the following is/are correct concerning induction and twisted pair wires?
   a. The phenomenon of mutual induction explains why network data bus wires use a twisted pair of wires to carry low-voltage serial data. Twisting the lines helps to reduce the signal noise.
   b. Serial data is the digital language electronic modules use to talk and listen to one another.
   c. Enclosing the twisted wire pair in a metal foil further helps reduce signal interference.
   d. All of the choices are correct.
9. Which of the following is NOT correct concerning electricity from chemistry?
   a. An electrolyte is any liquid that conducts electric current.
   b. Pure water will conduct current.
   c. Corrosion is an example of a galvanic reaction.
   d. The lead-acid battery is the most recognized type using galvanic reactions.
10. A fuel cell consists of three parts: a positive plate, a negative plate, and a(n):
   a. glass mat
   b. Piezoelectric plate
   c. electrolytic membrane
   d. step-up transformer

ASE-Type Questions

1. Technician A says electric charges are produced when two materials rub together. Technician B says static electricity is another name given to tribo-electricity, because objects can develop stationary high voltage charges. Who is correct?
   a. Technician A
   b. Technician B
   c. Both Technician A and Technician B
   d. Neither Technician A nor Technician B
2. Technician A says solar cells that can produce electricity are widely used in commercial vehicle applications. Technician B says commercially available cells are used as trickle chargers for batteries. Who is correct?
   a. Technician A
   b. Technician B
   c. Both Technician A and Technician B
   d. Neither Technician A nor Technician B
3. Technician A says thermoelectric devices (TED) are solid-state heat pumps formed from several layers of semiconductor materials. Technician B says TEDs are used for cooling or heating small areas, including seats, steering wheels, cup-holders, or beverage storage compartments. Who is correct?
   a. Technician A
   b. Technician B
   c. Both Technician A and Technician B
   d. Neither Technician A nor Technician B
4. Technician A says one of the most common ways electricity is produced in a heavy-duty vehicle is through the use of the energy found in magnetic fields. Technician B says magnetism is the force that attracts or repels magnetic charges, or the property of a material to respond to a magnetic field. Who is correct?
   a. Technician A
   b. Technician B
   c. Both Technician A and Technician B
   d. Neither Technician A nor Technician B
5. Technician A says magnetism can produce electricity. Technician B says electricity cannot produce magnetism. Who is correct?
   a. Technician A
   b. Technician B
   c. Both Technician A and Technician B
   d. Neither Technician A nor Technician B
6. Technician A says the principle of producing electrical current flow using electromagnets is known as electromagnetic induction. Technician B says alternators, generators, and speed sensors use this electrical principle to produce electrical current. Who is correct?
   a. Technician A
   b. Technician B
   c. Both Technician A and Technician B
   d. Neither Technician A nor Technician B
7. Technician A says the current that is induced when the magnetic field collapses after a circuit is opened can have much lower voltage than the voltage in the closed circuit. Technician B says any coil of wire in an electrical system can produce hundreds of volts when it is de-energized. Who is correct?
   a. Technician A
   b. Technician B
   c. Both Technician A and Technician B
   d. Neither Technician A nor Technician B
8. Technician A says suppression of the voltage spike from magnetic coils is accomplished using diodes, capacitors, resistors, or induction coils. Technician B says without suppression, the voltage spike can travel back in a circuit to its source and damage any sensitive electronic component. Who is correct?
   a. Technician A
   b. Technician B
   c. Both Technician A and Technician B
   d. Neither Technician A nor Technician B
9. Technician A says the primary winding is where current is induced. Technician B says the secondary winding is supplied current. Who is correct?
   a. Technician A
   b. Technician B
   c. Both Technician A and Technician B
   d. Neither Technician A nor Technician B
10. Technician A says dozens of varieties of fuel cells exist, but they all fundamentally work in the same manner. Technician B says like a battery, a fuel cell requires recharging. Who is correct?
    a. Technician A
    b. Technician B
    c. Both Technician A and Technician B
    d. Neither Technician A nor Technician B

CHAPTER 8

NATEF Tasks

Electrical/Electronic Systems

General Electrical Systems

	Page
■ Inspect and test fusible links, circuit breakers, relays, solenoids, and fuses; replace as needed.	260
■ Locate shorts, grounds, and opens in electrical/electronic circuits.	261

Knowledge Objectives

After reading this chapter, you will be able to:

1. Define and describe types of electric circuits. (pp 244–247)
2. Describe the behavior of current flow in each type of electric circuit. (pp 244–247)
3. Identify factors causing voltage drop in electrical circuits. (pp 244–248)
4. Describe the relationship between voltage amperage power and resistance in electrical circuits. (pp 248–250)
5. Mathematically predict and describe the relationship between voltage amperage power and resistance in electrical circuits. (pp 248–250)
6. Recommend wire gauge size for use in DC circuits. (p 250)
7. Identify and describe electrical circuit failures. (pp 252–254)
8. Identify and describe types of circuit protection devices. (pp 255–259)
9. Recommend circuit protection requirement based on amperage and conductor diameter. (p 257)
10. Describe virtual circuit protection and e-fuses. (p 259)

Electric Circuits and Circuit Protection

Skills Objectives

After reading this chapter, you will be able to:

1. Inspect and test circuit protection devices. (p 260) SKILL DRILL 8-1
2. Identify a resistive ground connection. (p 261) SKILL DRILL 8-2

Introduction

Circuits are pathways made by electrical conductors that enable the flow of electrons. A variety of classifications are used to describe circuit configurations and failures. Most important for technicians to understand is how circuits are constructed. With that knowledge, a technician can properly analyze electrical problems, use correct diagnostic procedures with test instruments, and, of course, make accurate recommendations for repair rather than guess at what may be wrong.

As shown in **FIGURE 8-1**, circuits consist of the following basic parts:

- Power source—in the form of a battery or alternator
- Conductors—paths for electricity (e.g., wiring, printed circuits, chassis frame, etc.)
- Loads—the working devices that turn electrical energy into some other form of energy, such as lamps, motors, radio, microcontrollers, and more. Loads are considered the resistance of a circuit.
- Control—a device, such as a switch, that directs the flow of electrons though the circuit
- Safety/circuit protection devices—fuses, circuit breakers, and virtual fuses, which protect the electrical system by interrupting the flow of current if the current flow becomes excessive

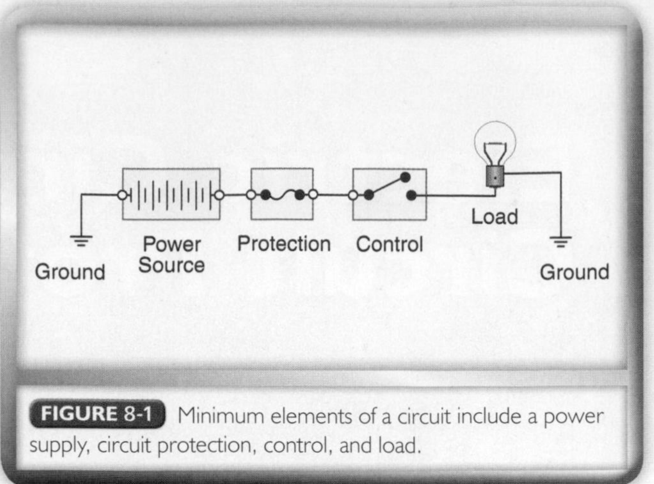

FIGURE 8-1 Minimum elements of a circuit include a power supply, circuit protection, control, and load.

Current Flow in Circuits

Electrons making up current flow are not magically created by the circuit or power source. Only the electrons found in the conductors of a circuit move in a circuit. That means only the electrons already present in conductors, electrolyte, or devices of the circuit are put in motion. An analogy using a closed hydraulic system using a water pump shows that only electrons already present in the circuit are flowing **FIGURE 8-2**. Consider water that is pulled from a reservoir and put into motion. Water pressure

You Are the Technician

An intercity bus has arrived at your shop with the request to install several wave inverters to enable bus passengers to charge cell phones and tablets and use laptop computers. The bus company wants you to supply 120-volts AC to a receptacle with one receptacle for each of the 36 rows of seats. Upon inspection, you find that the bus is equipped with a split voltage electrical system with a 24-volt alternator used to charge the batteries and supply the starter motor. An isolated ground is used on the rest of the bus, which uses 12 volts for all lights and accessories outside the engine compartment. When you ask the bus company representative what amount of amperage the company wants to supply each receptacle, the representative asks you to make a recommendation.

After researching the problem, you learn that the heaviest power users would be laptops consuming 3–5 amps to charge a dead battery. As you prepare quotes and recommendations for supplying DC-AC converters, wiring them, and providing circuit protection to the inverters, you will need to consider the following:

1. What would be the maximum wattage required for the inverter if one inverter is supplying power to two rows of seats? Assume there is no heat or other losses of electrical energy.
2. What would be the minimum fuse rating for each of the inverters using a single positive conductor if they were supplied either 12 or 24 volts?
3. What would be the minimum size of the conductors required if the inverters were connected to either 12- or 24-volt power supply?

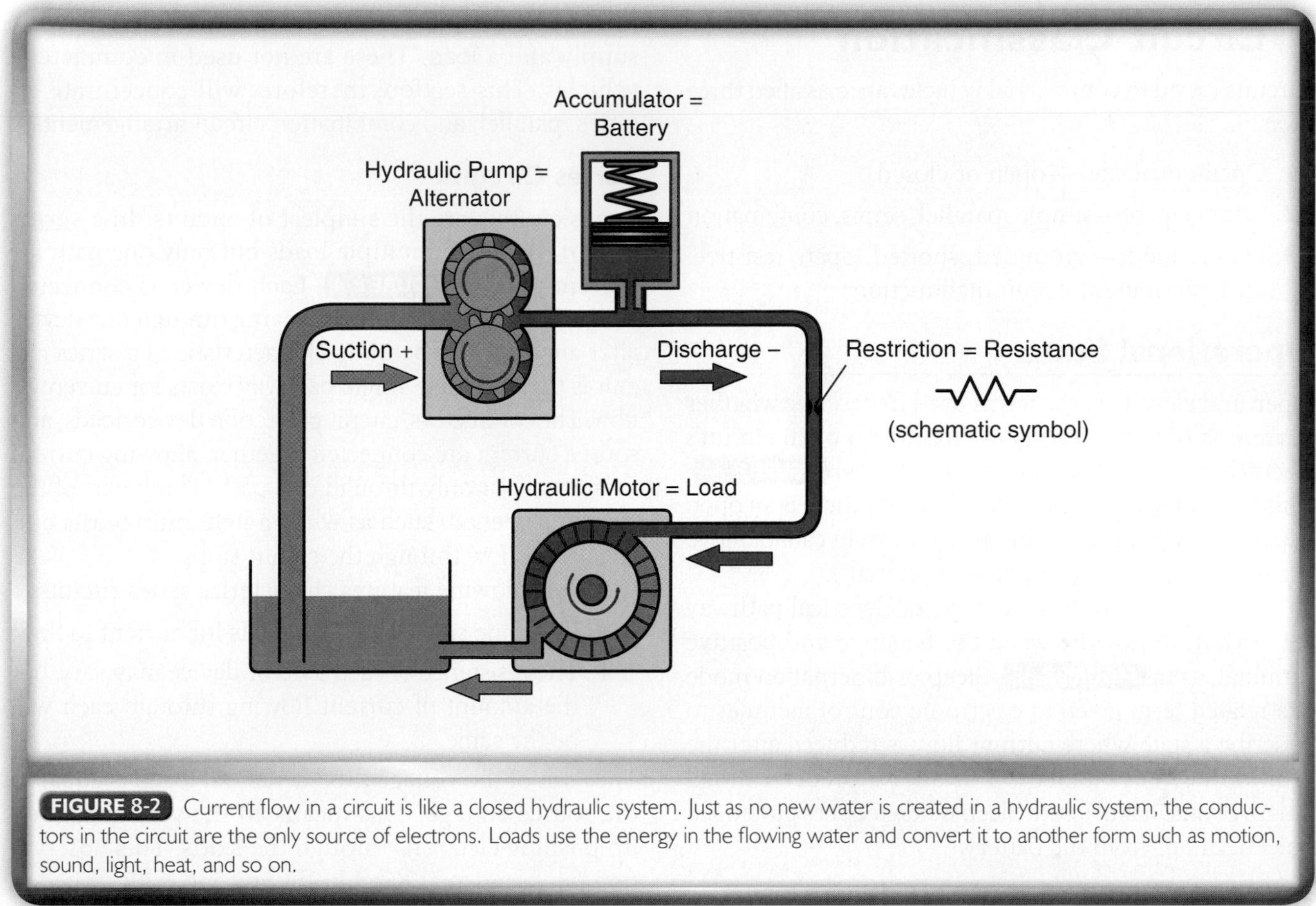

FIGURE 8-2 Current flow in a circuit is like a closed hydraulic system. Just as no new water is created in a hydraulic system, the conductors in the circuit are the only source of electrons. Loads use the energy in the flowing water and convert it to another form such as motion, sound, light, heat, and so on.

and volume determine how much power the system has. Eventually the water pushed out the water pump outlet returns to its inlet to keep the flow going. In the same way, electrons are pulled and pushed though conductors and loads in electric devices. The negative terminal pushes electrons using electrostatic forces of repulsion, and the positive terminal pulls electrons by forces of electrostatic attraction. The battery and alternator are the devices corresponding to the water pump.

Resistance

Resistance refers to the force in a circuit that impedes or slows the transfer of electrons from one atom to the next. Explained another way, resistance is electrical friction. Resistance will lower both voltage and amperage in a circuit in proportion to the amount of resistance. Ohm's law mathematically describes the electrical relationship between voltage amperage and resistance. Ohm's law will be discussed in greater detail in the section Ohm's Law.

> **TECHNICIAN TIP**
>
> Technicians will rarely ever need to use an electrical formula to diagnose and repair a problem on the shop floor. And most instructors would need to agree that it is rare ever to perform mathematical calculations in the average repair facility. So, the question that naturally follows this observation is: What is the point of learning formulas or performing calculations while learning about electrical systems? It's simply this—mathematics is another language that is effective in describing the behavior of electricity. Many learners who have struggled understanding electrical concepts have quickly grasped important insights while doing calculations using formulas based on electrical laws. Math is very often a shortcut to better comprehension of electrical subject matter.

Circuit Classification

Circuits found in commercial vehicles are classified three ways:

1. Operational state—open or closed
2. Arrangement—simple, parallel, series, combination
3. Failure mode—grounded, shorted, open, resistive, and intermittent circuit malfunctions

Operational State

Open and closed are the terms used to describe whether current is flowing through a circuit. An open circuit's electrical pathway is broken or unconnected FIGURE 8-3A. This means current cannot flow because there is an open gap between two ends of the circuit. Current cannot move across the gap until the opening is closed.

A closed circuit has a complete electrical pathway for current to flow between the negative and positive terminal, as in FIGURE 8-3B. Sleep or hibernation mode is a related term given to electronic control modules to describe a state where current flow is reduced after the ignition key is switched off or after a predetermined length of time has elapsed. Sleep mode reduces prolonged current drains from the battery.

Circuit Arrangement

Electric circuits are also classified according to the way electric components and loads are connected. Circuits on commercial vehicles are made from these types of arrangements:

- Simple
- Series
- Parallel
- Series-parallel, also called combination circuits

Simple circuits are circuits that have only a power supply and a load. These are not used in commercial vehicles. This section, therefore, will concentrate on series, parallel, and combination circuit arrangements.

Series Circuits

Series circuits are the simplest of circuits. In a **series circuit**, there are multiple loads but only one path for current to flow FIGURE 8-4. Each device is connected like a chain, with all current flowing through one device after another. The defining characteristic of a series circuit is that only one single pathway exists for current to flow. The conductors, circuit protection device, loads, and source current are connected together, allowing current to move—but only through one path. If any part of the circuit is opened, such as when a light bulb burns out, all current flow through the circuit stops.

The following features characterize series circuits:

- Only one single pathway exists for current to flow.
- The resistance of each load or device may vary, but the amount of current flowing through each will be the same.

The sum of the voltage drop across all loads is equal to the source voltage. This means all the voltage is used up pushing electrons through the loads. This observation is referred to as **Kirchhoff's law** and is illustrated in FIGURE 8-5. The voltage drops across each of the loads will change if the resistance of the device or load is different from the others.

- At any given point in the circuit, the amperage is the same.
- The total circuit resistance is equal to the sum of each individual resistance.

Many vehicle circuits are series circuits. Switches, terminals, circuit protection, cables, and so on are common

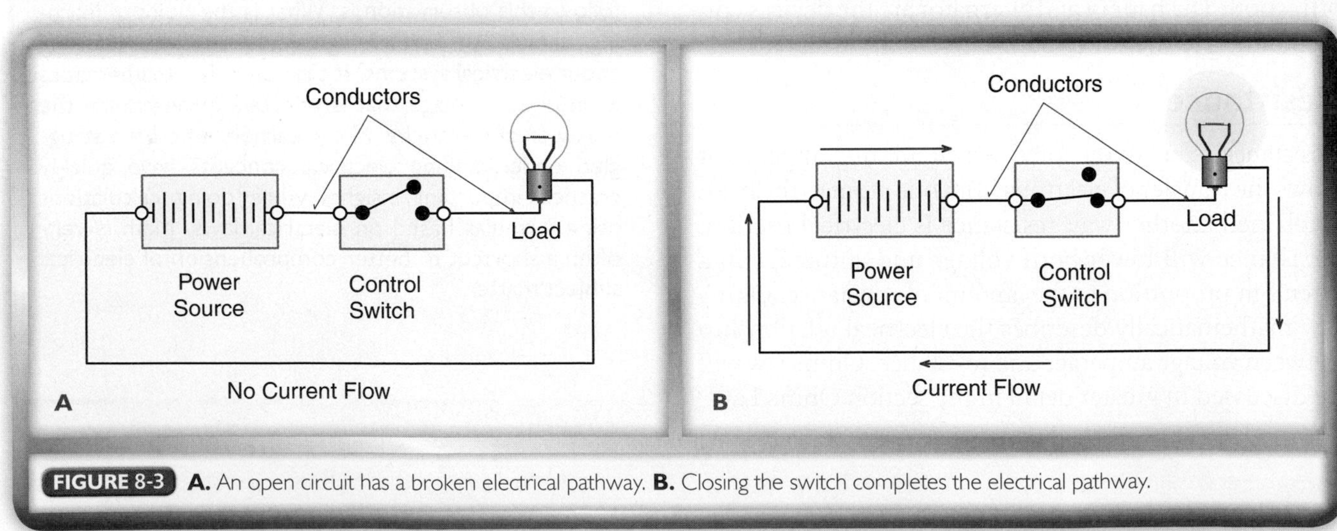

FIGURE 8-3 **A.** An open circuit has a broken electrical pathway. **B.** Closing the switch completes the electrical pathway.

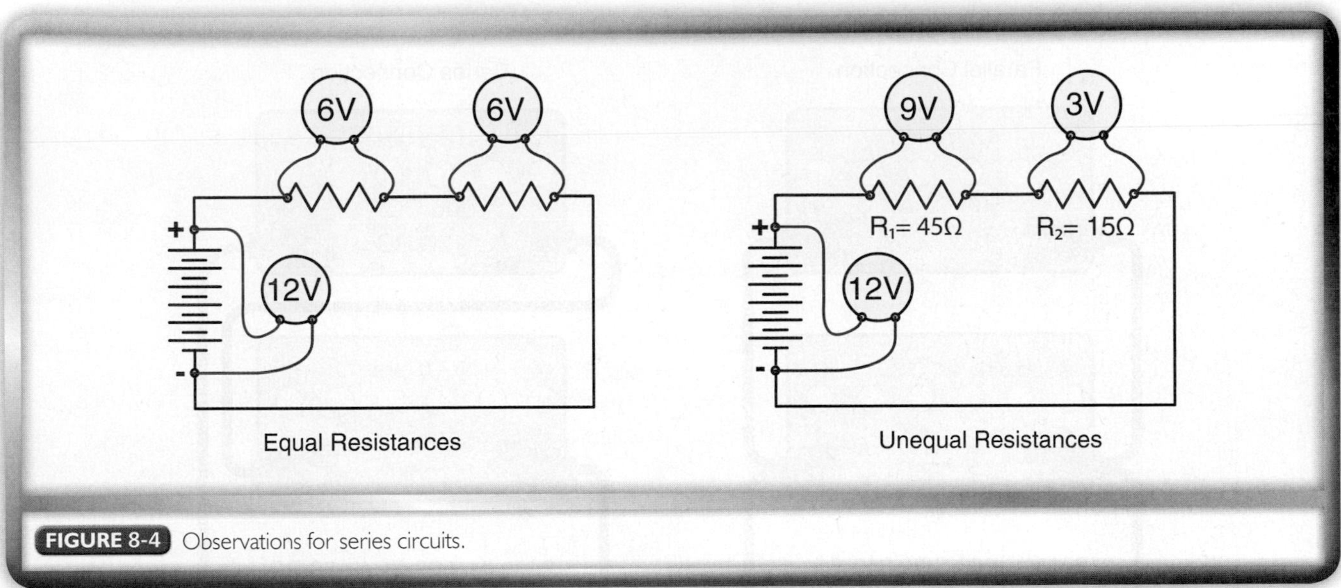

FIGURE 8-4 Observations for series circuits.

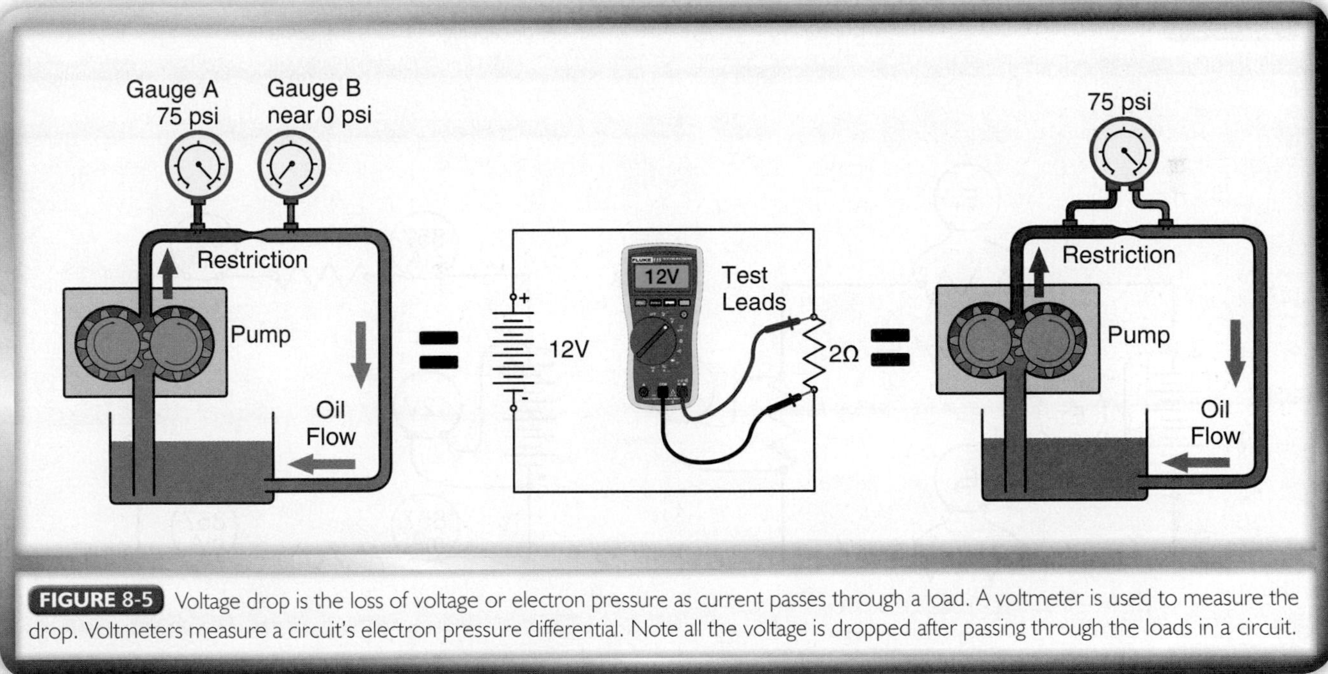

FIGURE 8-5 Voltage drop is the loss of voltage or electron pressure as current passes through a load. A voltmeter is used to measure the drop. Voltmeters measure a circuit's electron pressure differential. Note all the voltage is dropped after passing through the loads in a circuit.

circuit components arranged in series FIGURE 8-6. Identifying problems in series circuits often becomes a matter of measuring voltage drops to locate poor connections and deteriorated or defective components FIGURE 8-7. A starter cable voltage loss test is one example of a test procedure using series circuit electrical principles to locate problems causing hard starting. A starter motor circuit is a more complex example of a series circuit. Current passes from chassis ground, the brushes, and field coils of the motor before entering the solenoid and then back to the battery. An open brush or coil will prevent the starter motor from turning because it is a series circuit.

Parallel Circuits

A more complex circuit than a series circuit arrangement is a **parallel circuit**. In a parallel circuit, there are multiple pathways for current flow, and all components are connected directly to the voltage supply. On paper, the schematic diagram of a parallel circuit resembles a ladder. The sides are sources of voltage—one is positive and the other negative. The ladder rungs are called branches. Because all branches connect to the same positive and negative current source, amperage in each branch can be different, depending on the branches' resistance. Adding the amperage in each branch will equal the total amperage

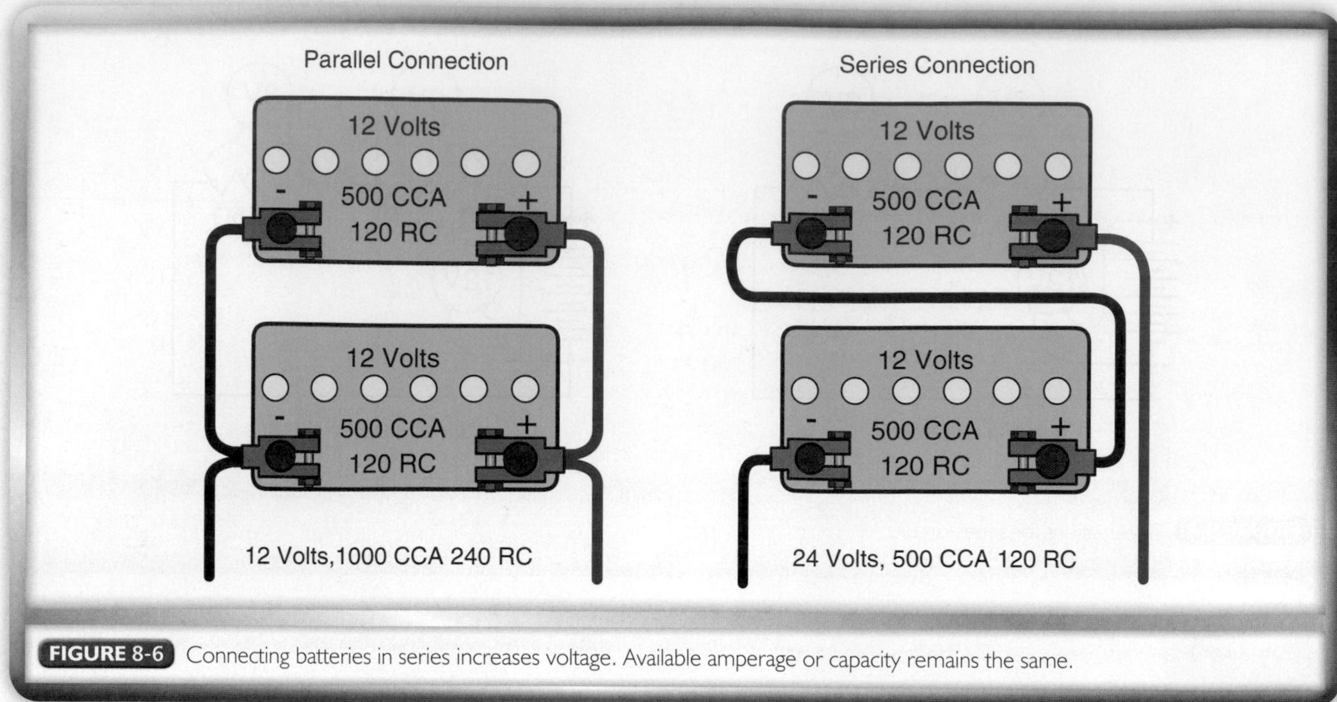

FIGURE 8-6 Connecting batteries in series increases voltage. Available amperage or capacity remains the same.

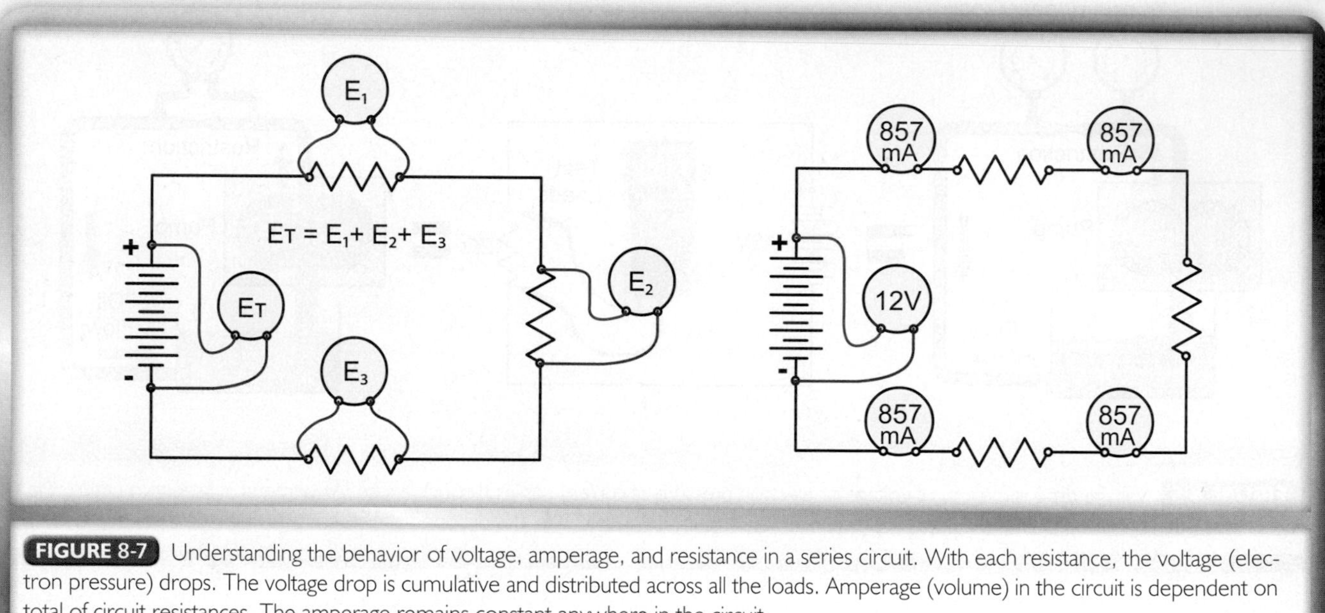

FIGURE 8-7 Understanding the behavior of voltage, amperage, and resistance in a series circuit. With each resistance, the voltage (electron pressure) drops. The voltage drop is cumulative and distributed across all the loads. Amperage (volume) in the circuit is dependent on total of circuit resistances. The amperage remains constant anywhere in the circuit.

in the circuit **FIGURE 8-8**. Adding loads, however, lowers circuit resistance; the total resistance is always less than the smallest resistance in any branch.

In summary, a parallel circuit is characterized by:

- Two or more pathways for the current **FIGURE 8-9**
- The voltage applied to each branch being the same throughout the circuit **FIGURE 8-10**
- Amperage flow through each branch depends on its resistance. If the resistances in each branch are the same, the amperage will be the same.
- If one branch of the circuit is broken, current will continue to flow in the other branches.
- Total circuit resistance is always less than the resistance of the smallest resister **FIGURE 8-11**.

FIGURE 8-8 Connecting batteries together in parallel increases available cranking amperage, but voltage stays the same.

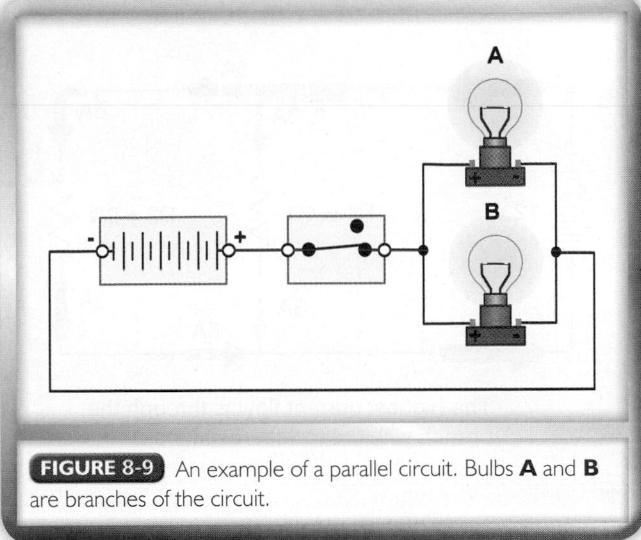

FIGURE 8-9 An example of a parallel circuit. Bulbs **A** and **B** are branches of the circuit.

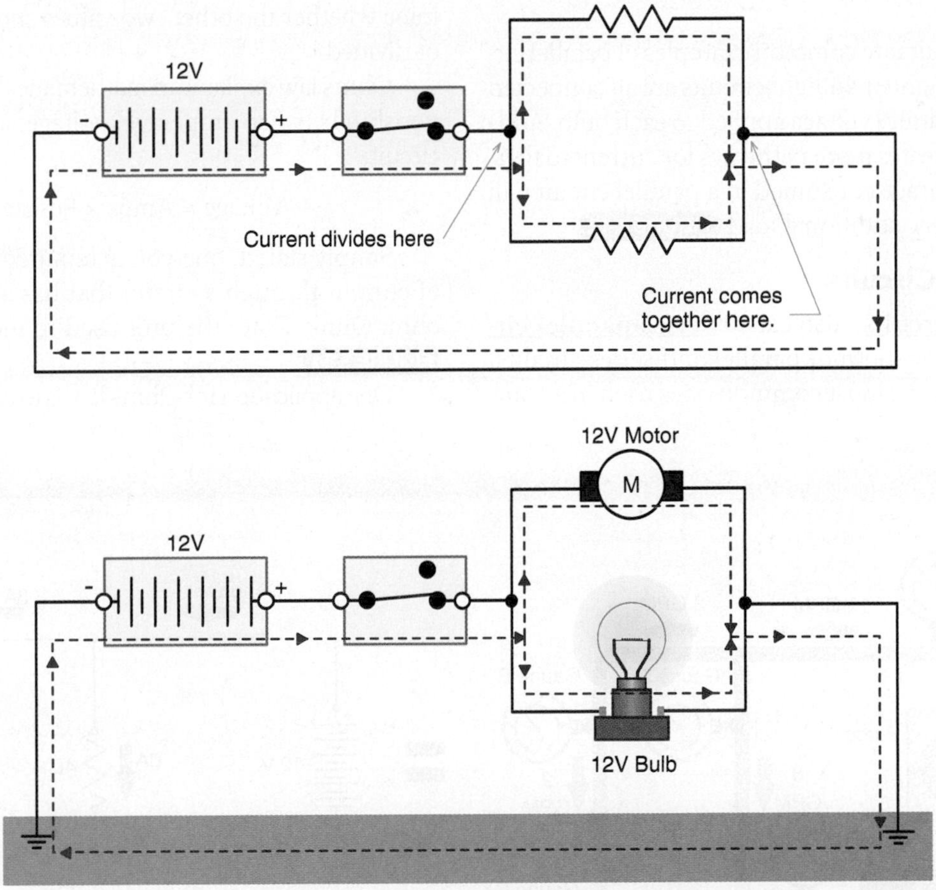

12V
Current divides here
Current comes together here.
12V Motor
M
12V
12V Bulb

FIGURE 8-10 All loads in a parallel circuit receive the same voltage. The amperage used by each branch will vary with the resistance in each branch.

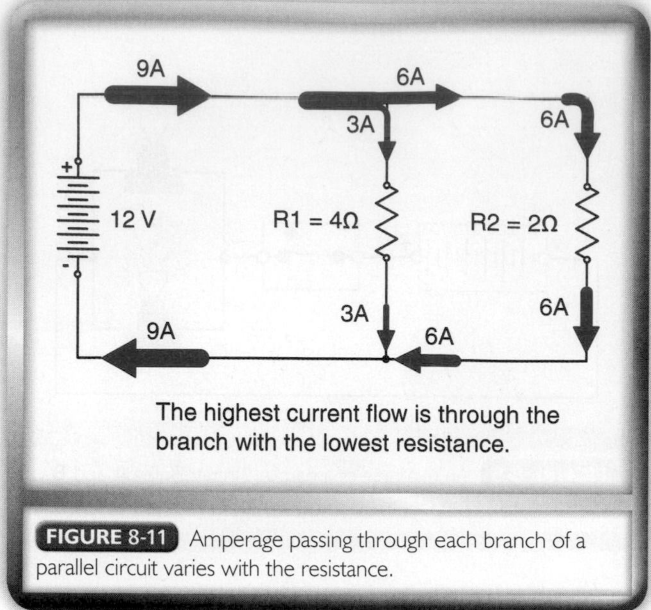

FIGURE 8-11 Amperage passing through each branch of a parallel circuit varies with the resistance.

Lighting circuits are common examples of parallel circuits. Clearance light or taillight circuits are all connected in parallel with battery voltage applied to each bulb. Adding more lights creates more pathways for current to flow. This means amperage consumed in a parallel circuit will increase with every additional load FIGURE 8-12.

Combination Circuits

Combination circuits, also called **series-parallel circuits**, use elements both of parallel and series circuits. These circuits are the most common ones used in a commercial vehicle chassis. Typically, the power and control circuits are in series, but the loads are in parallel. When calculating or measuring voltage, amperage, and resistance, the rules for parallel and series circuits apply to each part of the circuit. That means the circuit must be subdivided into series and parallel circuits, and then calculations can be performed for each type of circuit.

Ohm's Law

Ohm's law defines the relationship between current, resistance, and voltage. Ohm's law calculations are seldom used by a technician, but comprehending its principles can help you better understand how electricity behaves. Working through calculations using Ohm's formula also enhances your intuitive understanding of electricity, which is invaluable when troubleshooting electrical circuits. The tradeperson's triangle in FIGURE 8-13 is used to help calculate the values of either voltage, amperage, or power. Placing your finger over the unknown value will help you determine whether the other two values should be multiplied or divided.

Ohm's law explains in mathematical language the relationship between amperage, voltage, and resistance in a circuit.

Voltage = Amps × Resistance.

Simply stated, one volt is required to push one amp of current through a circuit that has a resistance of one ohm. Ohms Ω are the unit used to measure resistance. FIGURE 8-14.

One application for Ohm's law is to calculate the voltage

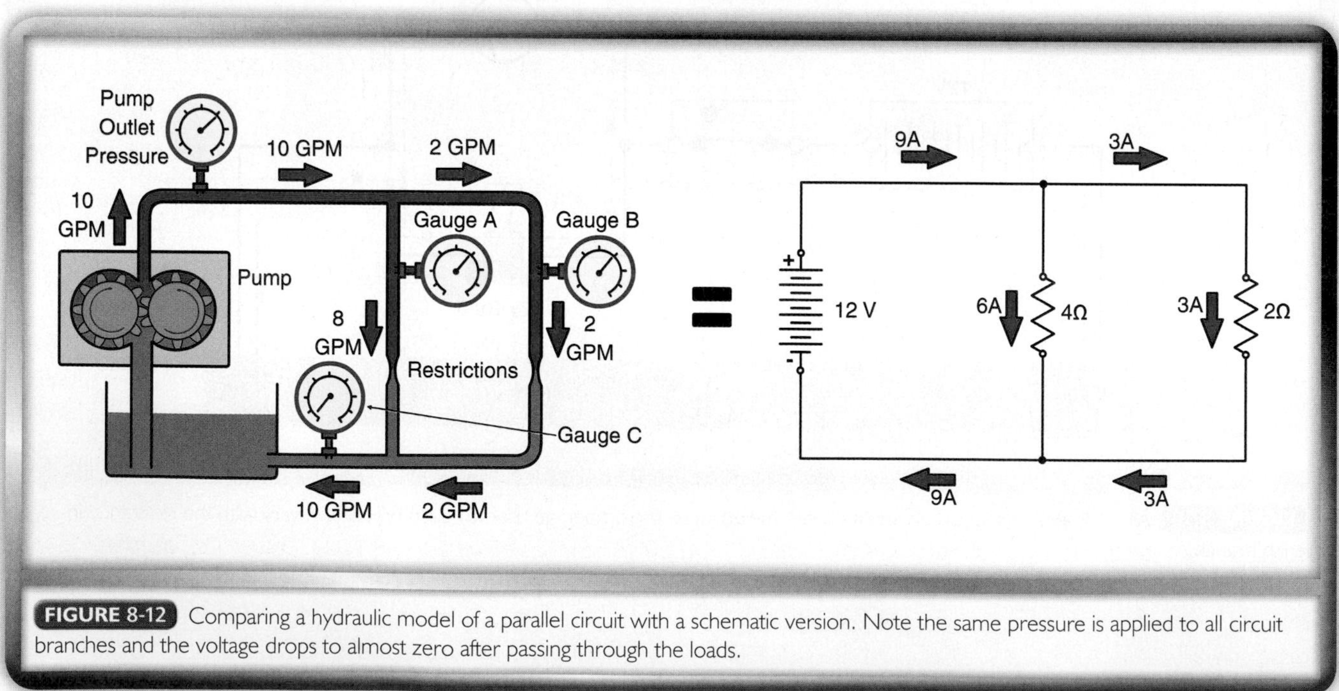

FIGURE 8-12 Comparing a hydraulic model of a parallel circuit with a schematic version. Note the same pressure is applied to all circuit branches and the voltage drops to almost zero after passing through the loads.

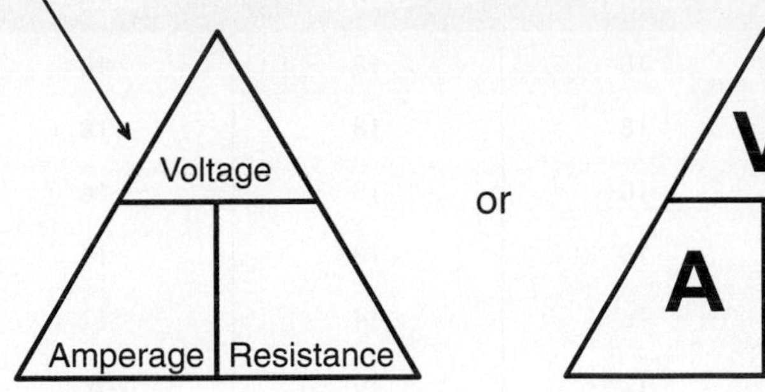

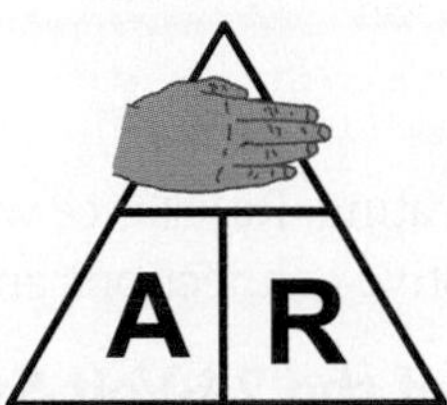

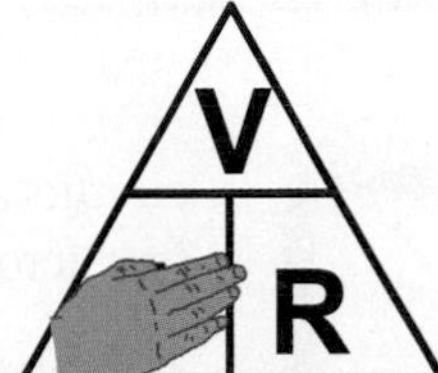

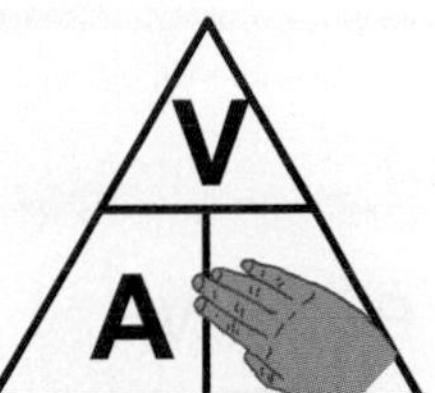

FIGURE 8-13 The tradesperson's triangle for calculating power.

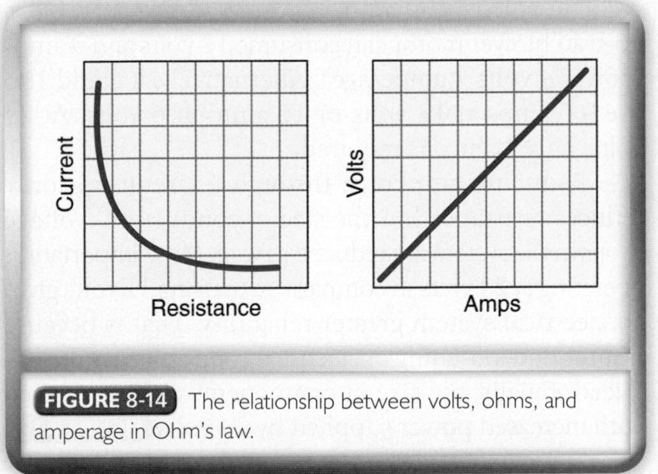

FIGURE 8-14 The relationship between volts, ohms, and amperage in Ohm's law.

drop in a conductor for trailer wiring. All conductors have some resistance, so there will be a voltage drop going to the lights at the rear of the trailer. The amount of the drop depends on the amperage carried by the circuit and the resistance of the wiring. TABLE 8-1 summarizes recommended wire gauge size required to minimize voltage drop.

Watt's Law

Watt's law, which is related to Ohm's law, explains the relationship between resistance and amperage FIGURE 8-15. Mathematically described, Watt's law is

$$\text{Power (Watts)} = \text{Voltage} \times \text{Amperage}.$$

Increasing amperage through a circuit produces proportionally more resistance. Heat is generally an unwanted by-product of resistance. Heat is produced as electron energy is lost due to resistance. Collisions occurring between electrons as they converge at "choke points" or resistive parts of a circuit produce heat. Increasing the amperage in a circuit is something like increasing the number of cars on the highway during rush hour—the greater the number of cars, the slower the traffic. More collisions between electrons take place in a crowded conductor, and electron energy is converted to heat.

This relationship between amperage and resistance explains why a thin wire can carry low amperage current but would burn-up (or at least overheat) if it were carrying excessive amperage. Excessive amperage through

TABLE 8-1: Recommended Wire Gauges to Minimize Voltage Drop

Amperage	10 – Feet Gauge	20 – Feet Gauge	30 – Feet Gauge	50 – Feet Gauge	100 – Feet Gauge
1	18	18	18	18	18
2	18	18	18	18	16
3	18	18	18	16	16
5	18	18	18	14	12
10	18	16	14	12	10
25	16	12	10	8	6
50	12	10	8	6	2

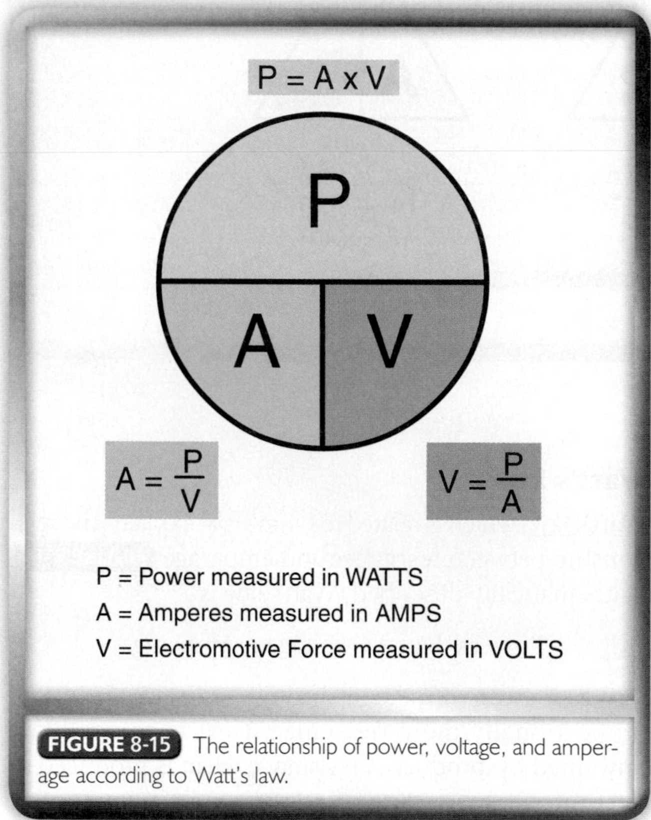

FIGURE 8-15 The relationship of power, voltage, and amperage according to Watt's law.

terminals and connectors will produce heat, which in turn loosens electrical connections due to temperature cycling. Resistance in connections at the battery or in a starter motor circuit, and which are undetectable with an ohmmeter, will show up as heat when a starter is cranking or when heavy loads are switched on in a vehicle. The most effective way to measure resistances in these circuits is to perform a voltage drop test when the high amperage circuits are operating. Resistance will show up as voltage loss across resistive connections and components.

Advantages of the 24-Volt System

The 24-volt electrical systems used by transit buses, military vehicles, and heavy equipment have several advantages. First, by using higher voltage, less amperage passes through a circuit to produce the same amount of power as a 12-volt circuit. For example, a device needing 120 watts of power would use 10 amps at 12 volts (Power = Amperage X Voltage). Electric motors are examples of constant power devices **FIGURE 8-16**. This means the number of watts they use to maintain speed is the same if circuit voltage and amperage change. For example, a 96-watt blower motor can consume 12 volts and 9 amps (power = volts × amperage). Alternatively, it could also use 9.6 amps at 12 volts or 16 amps at 6 volts. At 24 volts, only 5 amps is required.

Reducing amperage through a circuit not only reduces resistance but the size of conductors. Voltage drops in the system are reduced as well. More importantly, operating at 24 volts in comparison to using 12 volts gives an electrical system greater reliability. That is because heating and loosening of electrical connections are minimized. Finally, the size of components can be reduced with increased power supplied by 24 volts **FIGURE 8-17**.

Power Calculations for 12- and 24-Volt DC Systems

It can be useful for a technician to be able to perform quick estimates of the DC amps required to operate a DC-AC inverter. The following examples use a "rule of thumb" guideline for estimating. A safety factor should be

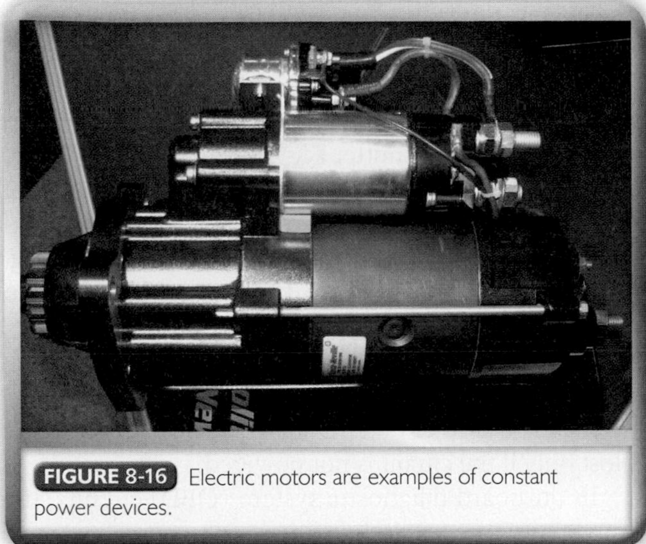

FIGURE 8-16 Electric motors are examples of constant power devices.

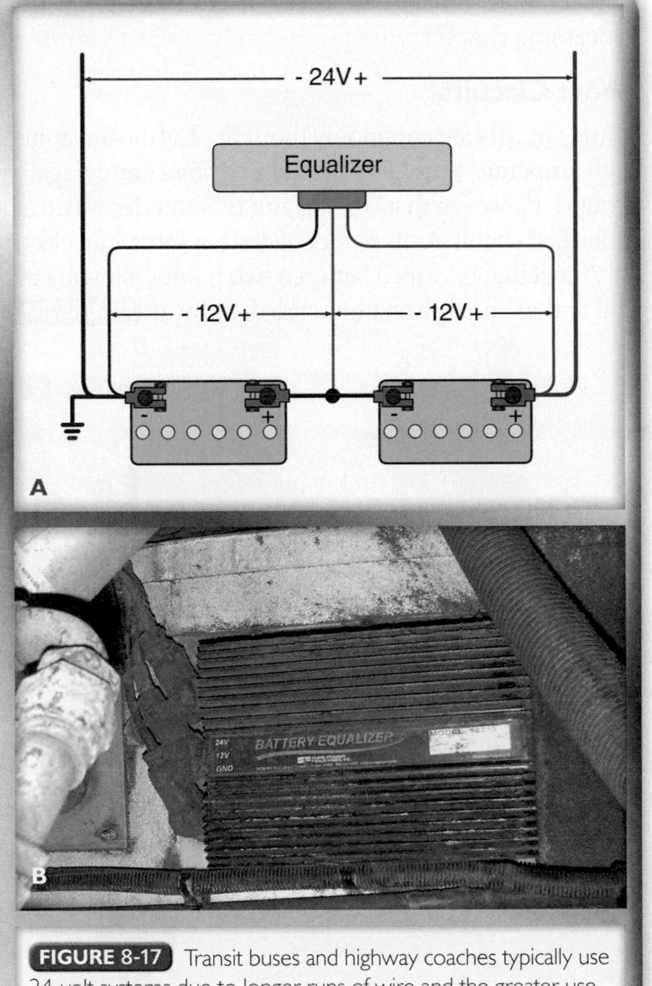

FIGURE 8-17 Transit buses and highway coaches typically use 24-volt systems due to longer runs of wire and the greater use of electrical accessories such as lighting and ventilation. Voltage drops and electrical system problems due to high current flow are minimized. **A.** A battery equalizer allows voltage to split between 24-volt and 12-volt devices. **B.** A battery equalizer.

included when selecting wire sizes, inverter capabilities, and circuit protection.

Consider supplying current to a small bunk refrigerator that is rated for 5 amps of power consumption at 120 volts AC. You need to know how many watts of power you need your 12-volt DC-AC inverter to supply:

$$\text{Power} = \text{Voltage} \times \text{Amperage}$$

$$\text{Wattage} = 120 \times 5 \text{ amps} = 600 \text{ watts}$$

A 600-watt minimum inverter rating is required.

The same formula can be used to make basic calculations, such as determining how many DC amps a 12-volt inverter will require to operate a 600-watt electrical load.

$$\text{Power} = \text{Voltage} \times \text{Amperage}$$

$$12 \text{ watts} = 12 \text{ volts} \times 1 \text{ amp}$$

600watts/12watts per amp = 50-amps DC at 12-volts.

50-amps DC per hour is needed to operate a 120-volt, 600-watt appliance using an inverter.

OR

5 amps at 120 volts = 10 × 5 amps at 12 volts.

$$\frac{\text{5-amps}}{\text{120-volts AC}} = \frac{X\text{-amps}}{\text{12-volts}} \qquad X = \text{50-amps}$$

Finally, depending on the voltage of your system, you will need a completely different circuit amperage. To figure out the difference between circuit amperage of a 60-watt light operating at 12 or 24 volts, use this formula:

$$\text{Amperage} = \frac{\text{Watts}}{\text{Volts}}$$

At 12 volts, the calculation looks like this:

$$\frac{60}{12} = 5 \text{ amps}$$

At 24 volts, the calculation looks like this:

$$\frac{60}{24} = 2.5 \text{ amps}$$

The 24-volt system will use half the amperage required by a 12-volt system.

Circuit Malfunctions

Just as there are categories for operational circuits, defective circuits have names based on failure mode. Classification of circuit malfunction can include:

- Opened
- Shorted
- Grounded
- High resistance
- Intermittent

Open Circuit Faults

When a circuit defect is caused by an opening in the electrical pathway, no current can flow. Opened circuits can be caused by a variety of problems, including poor ground or terminal connections, defective switches, and broken wiring FIGURE 8-18. An open circuit will not burn the fuse, but the fuse may be open if the circuit was overloaded by a short to ground. Where the open in the circuit occurs determines how the failure presents itself. For example, a broken wire to a single clearance light in a parallel circuit will have a different effect than a blown fuse.

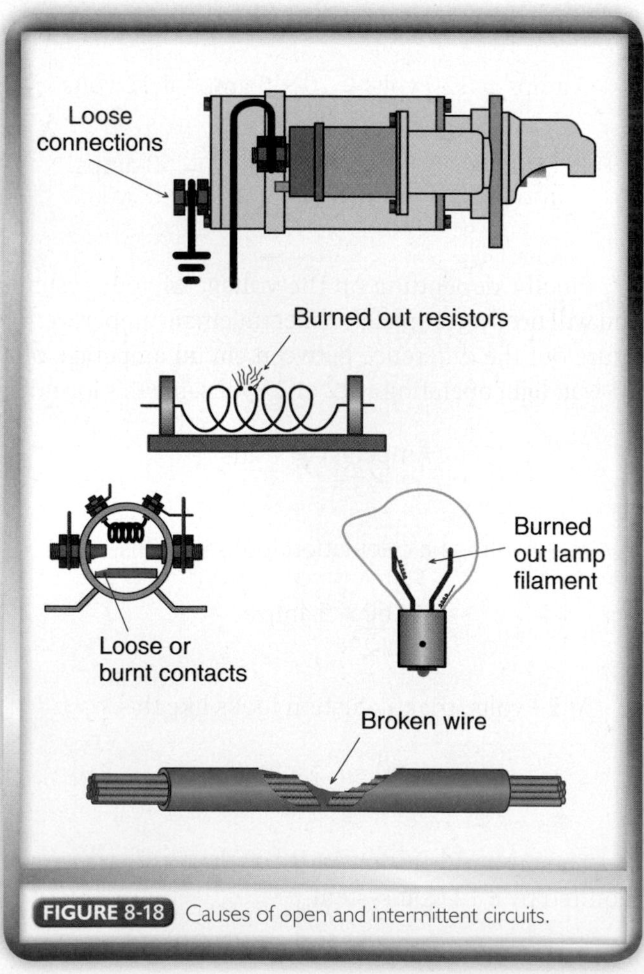

FIGURE 8-18 Causes of open and intermittent circuits.

Depending on the type of fault, open circuits are typically detected using test lights and multimeters FIGURE 8-19. Radio waves are also used to identify faults in bundles of wiring or in long runs of wiring hidden behind panels. A radio transmitter FIGURE 8-20 installed in the fuse of an open or shorted circuit will emit short bursts of radio signals or low-voltage current into the defective circuit. The signal is not powerful enough to damage wiring, but open and shorts are located using a hand-held radio receiver. A schematic diagram is useful when identifying open circuits to locate strategic points where circuit voltage can be measured using a test light or multimeter. An ohmmeter can be used to find points where circuit continuity is lost only if the circuit is not powered.

In on-board diagnostic system (OBD) circuits, the continuous component monitor constantly checks for open circuits by comparing signal out and return voltages. This strategy is fully explained in the Electrical Signal Processing chapter.

Short Circuits

<u>Short circuits</u> are commonly thought of as the unwanted, high amperage flow between battery power and negative ground. However, that type of fault is better described as a grounded circuit. As its name suggests, a short is an electrical circuit that is formed between two points, allowing current to flow through an unintended pathway FIGURE 8-21.

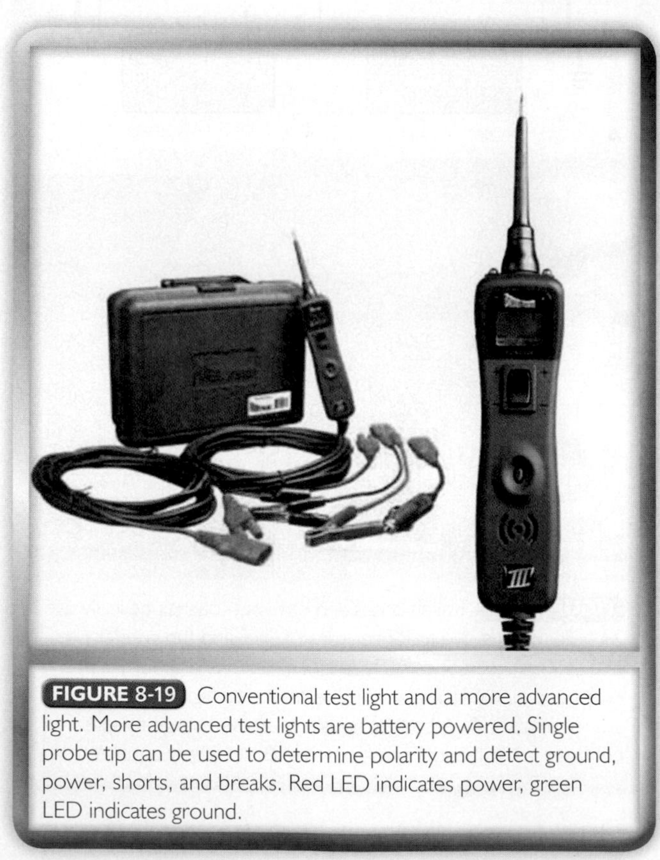

FIGURE 8-19 Conventional test light and a more advanced light. More advanced test lights are battery powered. Single probe tip can be used to determine polarity and detect ground, power, shorts, and breaks. Red LED indicates power, green LED indicates ground.

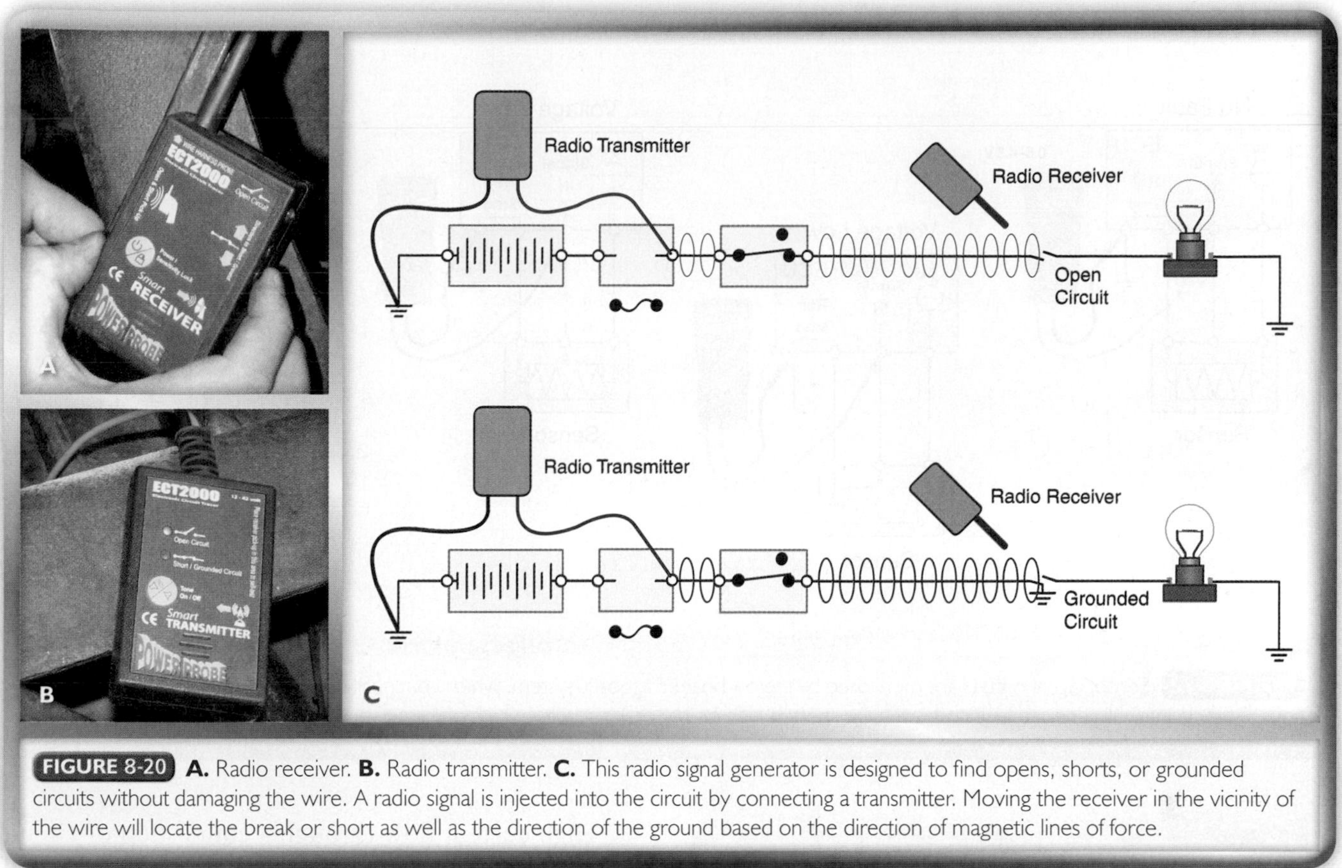

FIGURE 8-20 **A.** Radio receiver. **B.** Radio transmitter. **C.** This radio signal generator is designed to find opens, shorts, or grounded circuits without damaging the wire. A radio signal is injected into the circuit by connecting a transmitter. Moving the receiver in the vicinity of the wire will locate the break or short as well as the direction of the ground based on the direction of magnetic lines of force.

A short may draw a higher or lower than normal amperage and simply be an unintended connection between two wires or circuits. A coil of wire is considered shorted if current does not pass through all the intended loops but instead takes a shorter path. Another simple example of a short to power is a short between the brake light and clearance lights circuits. Stepping on the brakes would cause the clearance lights to illuminate and vice versa. Some may call this a problem with current "back-feed," but it is more accurate to call it a short.

12V
Normal Operation
12V
Short Circuit

FIGURE 8-21 When current bypasses its intended load, it is referred to as a short circuit.

On-board diagnostic systems that continuously monitor electrical signals from sensors and output devices will detect shorted conditions, too. For example, if a three-wire sensor signal circuit is shorted to +5 volt reference voltage, it meets conditions required to generate the fault code "Sensor Input Voltage High" **FIGURE 8-22**. The fault description "Sensor Input Voltage Low" is produced if either the sensor +5 volt supply is shorted to the sensor return circuit or the sensor signal wire is shorted to the sensor return circuit or to ground.

Grounded Circuits

A **grounded circuit**, sometime called "dead short," is characterized by an unwanted low resistance connection between battery positive power and chassis ground. Unlike the short-to-power malfunction, in all cases the short-to-ground will draw higher than expected current. A common example of a grounded circuit would be a battery or power cable insulation rubbing through against the negative ground chassis frame **FIGURE 8-23**. The direct, low-resistance connection would cause high current flow resulting in blown fuse links and activation of other circuit protection devices.

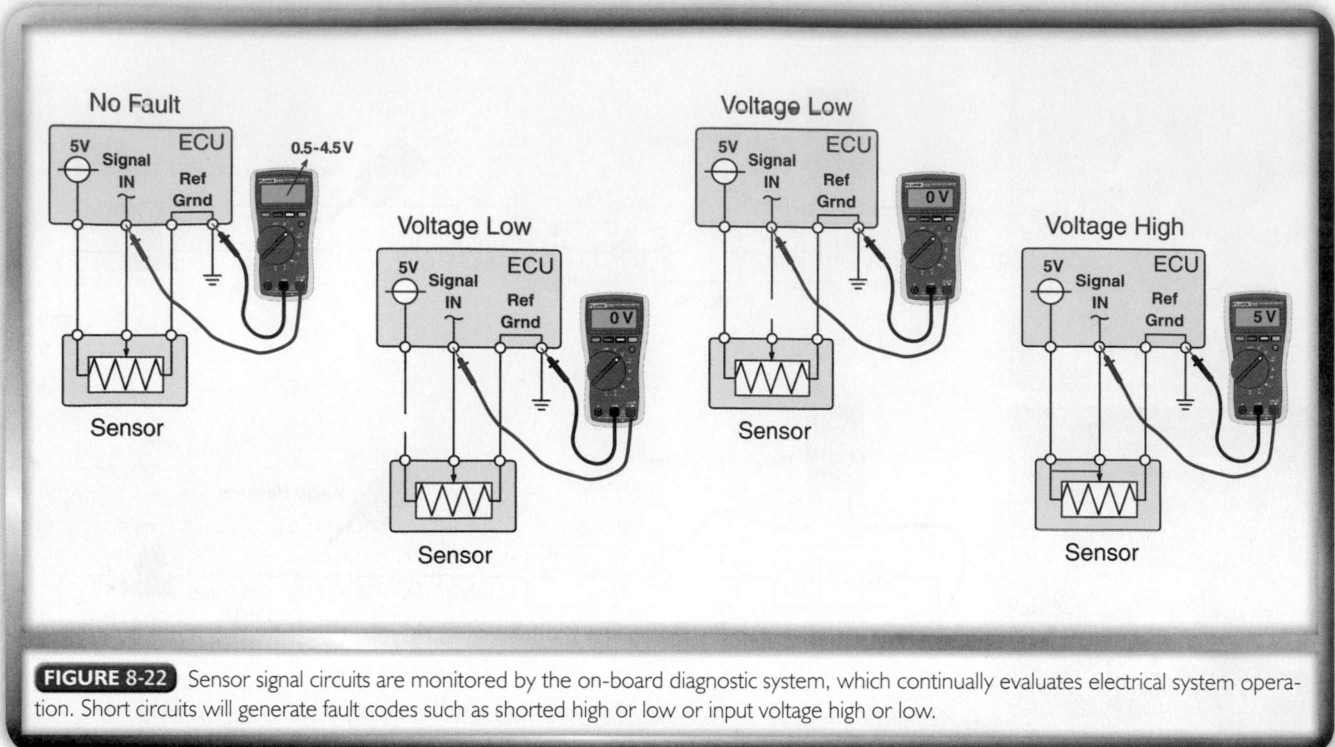

FIGURE 8-22 Sensor signal circuits are monitored by the on-board diagnostic system, which continually evaluates electrical system operation. Short circuits will generate fault codes such as shorted high or low or input voltage high or low.

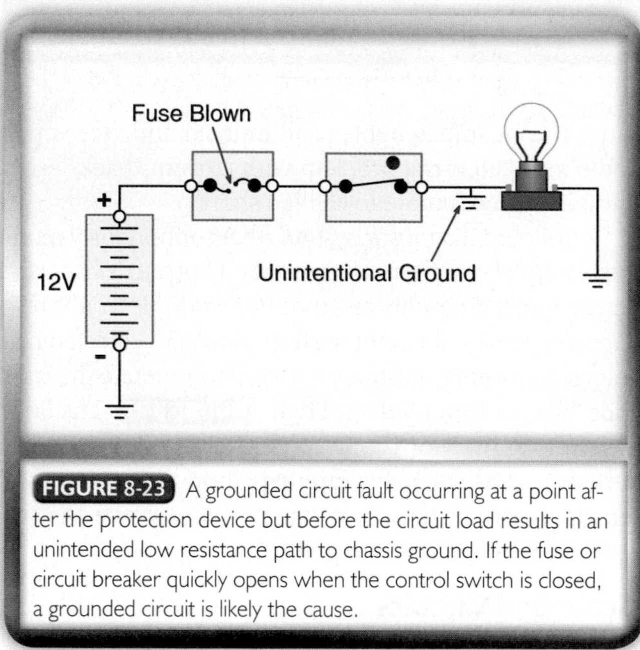

FIGURE 8-23 A grounded circuit fault occurring at a point after the protection device but before the circuit load results in an unintended low resistance path to chassis ground. If the fuse or circuit breaker quickly opens when the control switch is closed, a grounded circuit is likely the cause.

High-Resistance Circuits

When grounds or power connections in circuits become resistive, circuits cannot properly function, either. Neither can they operate properly if components become excessively resistive. Dirty, corroded, or loose connections result in **resistive circuits** that do not allow components to properly operate. Battery terminals, light bulb sockets, and connector sockets are common points for resistances to develop.

High current flow through a connection or circuit that has almost no resistance can turn highly resistive if high amperage passes through the connection. Resistive ground connections can often be difficult to troubleshoot because circuits will find alternate grounds or components will operate in very unusual ways. Double filament combined stop/tail bulbs are one common example of what is sometimes called a "back-feed" due to resistive grounds FIGURE 8-24. A poor ground in the bulb socket of one lamp will cause the current to find a ground through the bulb on the opposite side of a vehicle. The taillights will flash alternately when the turn signal is on, and other bulb filaments will glow dimly even when they should not FIGURE 8-25.

Intermittent Circuits

Intermittent circuits are characterized by uneven current flow. Intermittent current flow through circuits is often attributed to vibration from a moving vehicle. An example is the connectors on the engine ECM, which receives a lot of vibration and has the strain of heavy wiring harnesses. Heat at terminal connections can cause continuous thermal cycling, and engine vibration can contribute to a momentary loss of continuity through a pin connection. ECM connections are packed with dielectric grease to help prevent this condition from taking place FIGURE 8-26.

Terminals on the J-560 trailer cord have split pins to help prevent loosening of the electrical pin connection

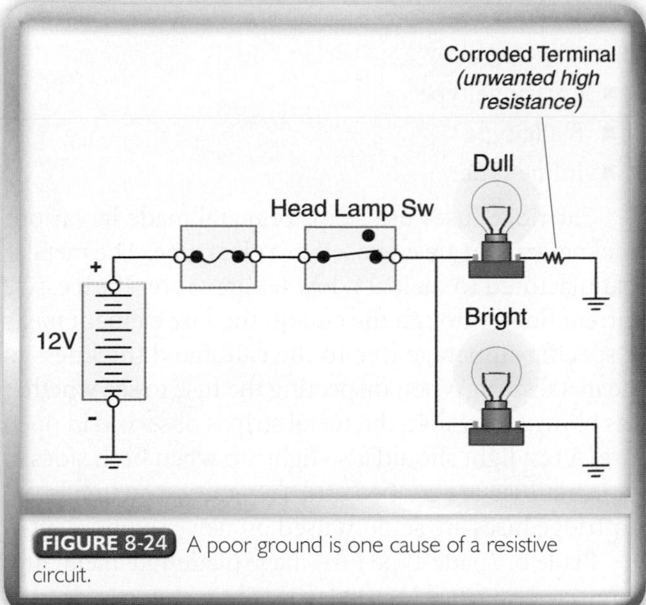

FIGURE 8-24 A poor ground is one cause of a resistive circuit.

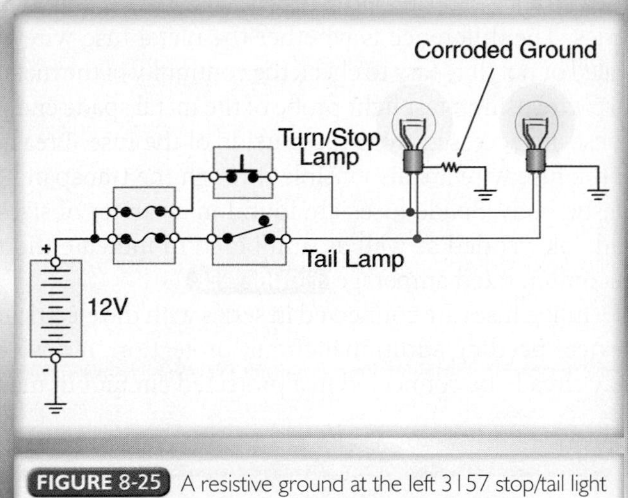

FIGURE 8-25 A resistive ground at the left 3157 stop/tail light bulb will cause a current to flow through the right bulb filaments as the circuit seeks a ground. The right bulb filaments will glow dimly because it becomes a series circuit.

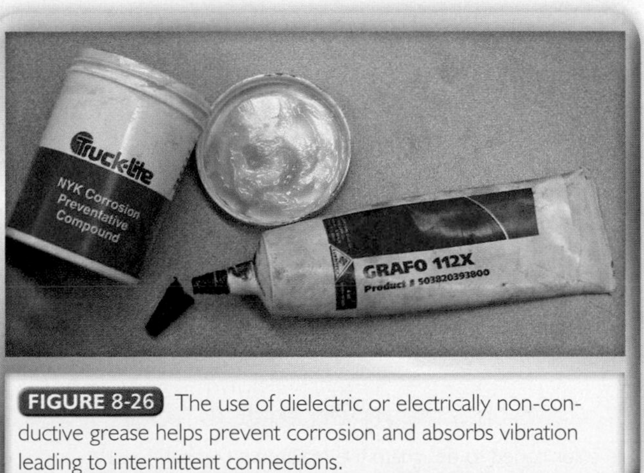

FIGURE 8-26 The use of dielectric or electrically non-conductive grease helps prevent corrosion and absorbs vibration leading to intermittent connections.

from heat and vibration. The split pin will possess spring-like capabilities to keep the trailer cord socket in contact with the receptacle pins.

Overheated modules and coils are often another source of intermittent circuit problems. Heat causes resistance to climb in semiconductor devices as well as magnetic coils in solenoids or relays. If, after allowing modules or coils to cool, the devices or circuits operate, these heat-sensitive resistive components should be replaced.

TECHNICIAN TIP

Electrical connectors should be packed with dielectric grease wherever possible during assembly. Unlike chassis grease, dielectric grease is electrically non-conductive and will prevent corrosion of terminal pins. The grease will also help absorb mechanical vibration to prevent terminal pins from loosening or breaking electrical contact for a split second.

TECHNICIAN TIP

In spite of the advanced electrical technology today, the trailer cord plug has the same configuration it did fifty years ago. Split pins in the receptacle are used to help maintain a good electrical connection using the pin's spring-like capabilities. Over time, the pin's diameter becomes smaller. To maintain a good connection, the pins occasionally need to be spread open again using a flat-blade screwdriver.

Circuit Protection Devices

High amperage flow through circuits produces resistance induced heat. If excess amperage is allowed to pass through conductors they can become overheated to the point where the insulation melts, and a fire can result. Circuits overloaded with current-hungry components or grounded circuits are the quickest way to cause damage to wiring and even start fires. So to protect wiring harnesses and the safety of vehicle occupants, circuit protection devices are used. A second reason for circuit protection is because damage to sensitive electronic components can also be caused by unintended reversal of battery polarity such as when using booster cables. Third, excessive charging system voltage can also push more current through these devices and destroy them.

Traditional fuses, fuse links, and circuit breakers are connected in series and use heat produced from excessive current flow in overloaded circuits to open the circuits.

Fuses and circuit breakers will blow and open overloaded circuits when amperage typically exceeds 10%–15% of the fuse rating. This means a 20-amp fuse will open at 22 to 23 amps of current. Recently, network control of the electrical system in late-model equipment has enabled software control of current flow through circuits, introducing what is called the virtual fuse—circuit protection without a fuse.

Thermal Fuses

Thermal fuses come in many configurations FIGURE 8-27. There are three basic types of fuses currently in use which are opened by heat produced from resistance caused by high amperage flow:

- Cartridge type
- Blade type
- Inline type

Cartridge fuses use strips of metal made in various thicknesses that are enclosed in a glass tube. The metal is manufactured to melt at a low temperature. If excessive current flows through the circuit, the fuse element melts at specific amperage due to the calibrated thickness of the metal strip. When inspecting the fuse to see whether it is blown, a break in the metal strip is observed in open fuse. A test light should also light-up when both sides of an intact fuse are probed and the ignition switch is on. Cartridge fuses are seldom used on newer equipment.

Blade or spade-type fuses have blade-like metal lugs connected by a fusible metal wire. The compact, transparent, plastic body allows more fuses to be inserted into a fuse carrier. There are two categories used: ATO and ATC series. The difference is whether the metal fuse wire is sealed or not. It is easy to check the continuity of the metal fuse wire using a test light probe of the metal spade ends. These are accessed from the outside of the fuse. Breaks in the fuse wire are also visible through the transparent plastic body. Spade fuses are found in a variety of sizes and color coded as well as numbered to indicate their maximum rated amperage FIGURE 8-28.

Inline fuses are connected in series with the electrical devices needing additional circuit protection. A device may already be connected in a protected circuit but may

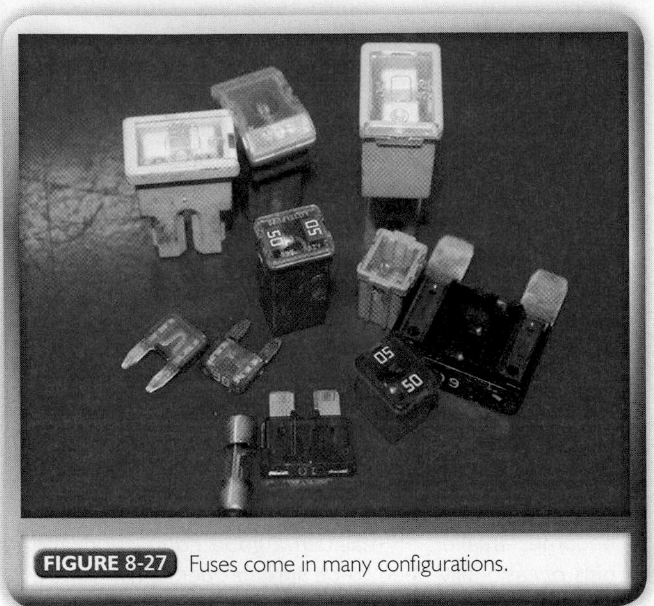

FIGURE 8-27 Fuses come in many configurations.

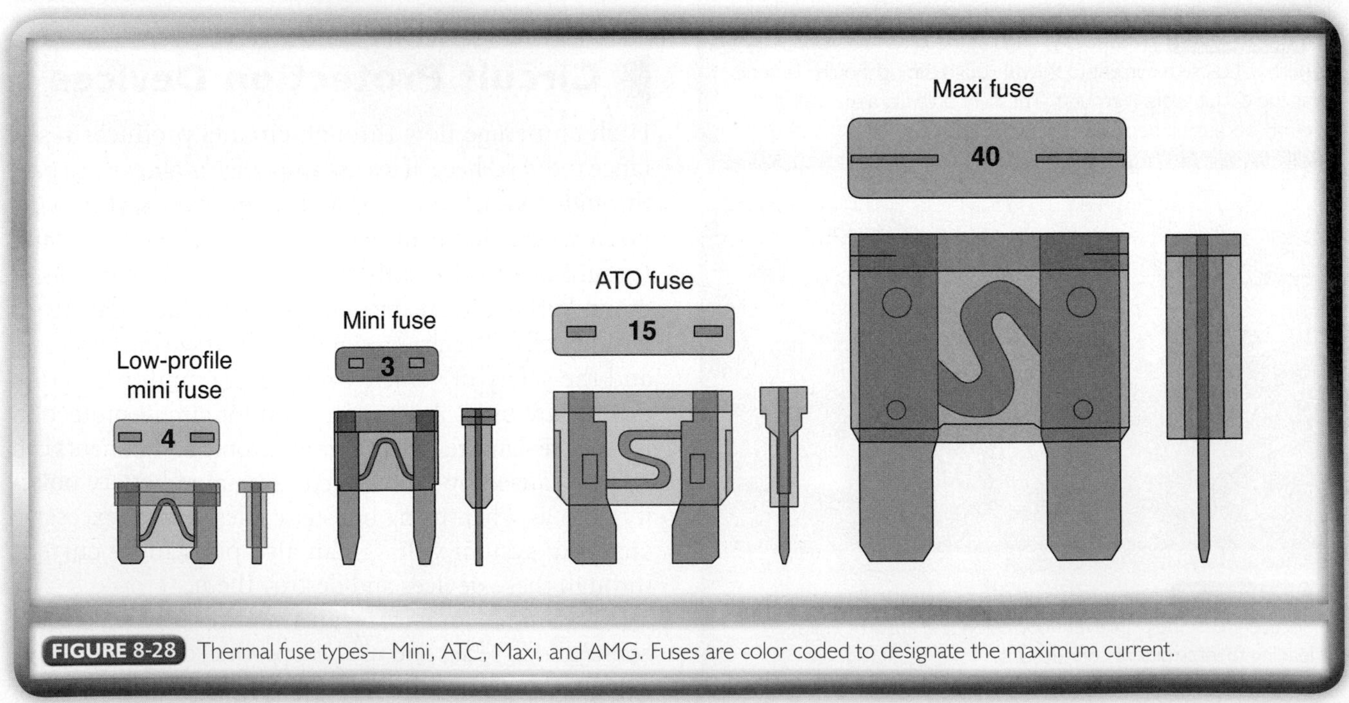

FIGURE 8-28 Thermal fuse types—Mini, ATC, Maxi, and AMG. Fuses are color coded to designate the maximum current.

have a lower tolerance for over-current or reverse polarity conditions. Electronic control modules (ECMs) are a common example of devices with inline fuses protecting the constant battery voltage supply line and supply of current from the ignition switch FIGURE 8-29.

Low-amperage fuses are easily blown in over-current and reverse polarity conditions due to internal circuits using Zener diodes. These diodes allow supply current to go ground under abuse conditions. Inline fuse are also used when adding electrical accessories to a circuit. Locating the fuses as close to the devices as possible shortens the time needed to blow the fuse. TABLE 8-2 provides the recommended maximum fuse ratings for the corresponding wire size (per the American Wire Gauge system).

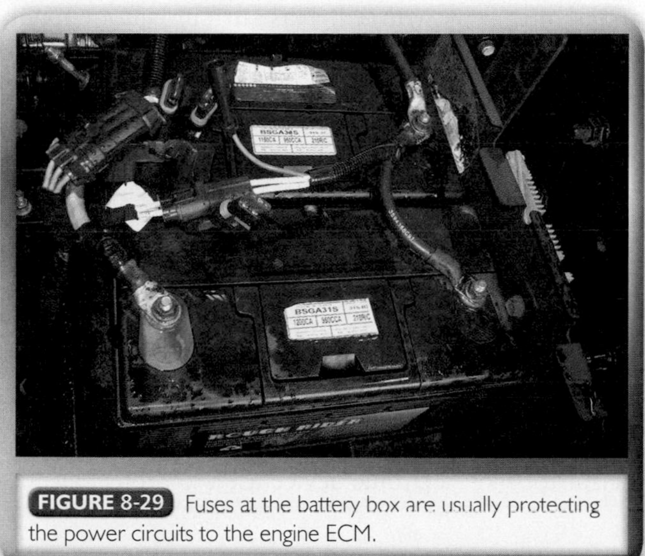

FIGURE 8-29 Fuses at the battery box are usually protecting the power circuits to the engine ECM.

TABLE 8-2: Recommended Maximum Fuse Ratings by Wire Gauge

Wire Gauge (AWG)	Recommended Maximum Fuse Rating
00	400 amps
0	325 amps
1	250 amps
2	200 amps
4	125 amps
6	80 amps
8	50 amps
10	30 amps
12	20 amps
14	15 amps
16	7.5 amps

Major Harness Protection

Fuses are used to protect individual circuits but not necessarily major wiring harnesses. For those, fusible links are used. Fuse links are short sections of wire installed in series with larger diameter conductors. At one quarter of the gauge of the main conductor, the fuse link will overheat and melt instead of the larger conductor when excessive amperage passes through the wire. This means brief overloads are possible with fuse links without causing current disruptions. Special plastic covers the link and will bubble when the link melts. Fuse links are effective protection in major harnesses because limiting amperage in harnesses is not as critical as protecting them from overheating and burning.

Glow plug circuits, alternator battery cables, and major cab harness cables are a few examples where fuse links were once used. Fuse links are checked with test lights or by simply pulling the conductor where it usually attaches to a major battery terminal or starter cable connection. A link that stretches excessively like a rubber band is likely melted. Current should be found on both sides of an intact link if checked with a test light.

Maxi fuses have replaced fuse links as circuit protection devices. The use of power distribution boxes, usually located under the hood, has broken down commercial vehicle electrical systems into smaller and more numerous sections using shorter runs of wiring FIGURE 8-30. Easier to replace maxi fuses found inside distribution boxes, typically in sizes from 20–80 amps, will protect several circuits. Larger specialized ratings are available from OEMs.

Safety

When replacing blown fuses and circuit breakers, never install one with a higher amp rating. This could cause a wire or component to overheat and possibly cause an electrical fire. If a breaker or fuse is operating in an overloaded circuit, replace the wiring with a larger diameter and then increase the rating of the circuit protection device.

Circuit Breakers

Circuit breakers are used in circuits where intermittent current overloads are common and where power must be rapidly restored, such as with wipers, headlights, and other lighting circuits. Unlike fuses, circuit breakers do not require replacement when they trip. Instead, they may either automatically reset or require a manual reset.

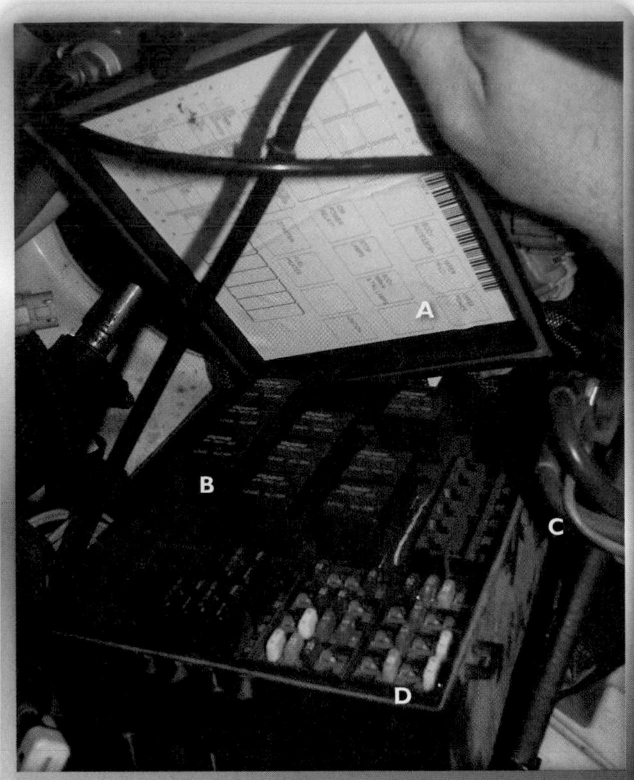

FIGURE 8-30 Power distribution boxes are the main location for circuit protection. The boxes break the electrical system into smaller and more numerous sections. Large electrical conductors do not pass through the occupant compartment, where potential fires can occur. **A.** Cover with component locator. **B.** Relays. **C.** Insulated positive cables. **D.** Blade-type fuses.

Typically, circuit breakers are made from bi-metallic contacts connected in series with a circuit. These are strips of metal made from two different materials with different rates of expansion. When heated, the bimetallic strip bends and opens the contacts, disconnecting current flow from the circuit. Heat is produced when too much current flows through the bimetallic strip in the circuit breaker. In **Type 1 circuit breakers**, or automatically resetting breakers, current is restored when the bimetallic strip cools FIGURE 8-31.

A circuit breaker can be a non-cycling type too. Typically, those are **Type 2 circuit breakers**. One type is reset by removing the power from the circuit. A heating coil connected in parallel with the contacts is wrapped around a bimetal arm, keeping the arm hot and contacts disconnected after it has tripped. This current is not enough to operate a load, but the coil does continue heating the bimetal arm until power is removed. Another non-cycling breaker is the **Type 3 circuit breaker**, which must be reset by depressing a reset button. The reset button pushes a spring back into position. That spring force holds the bimetal contacts open after the breaker has tripped. TABLE 8-3 shows this classification for circuit breakers.

PPT Coefficient Fuses

A **polymeric positive temperature coefficient device (PPTC)**, commonly known as a **resettable fuse**, is a thermistor-like electronic device used to protect against

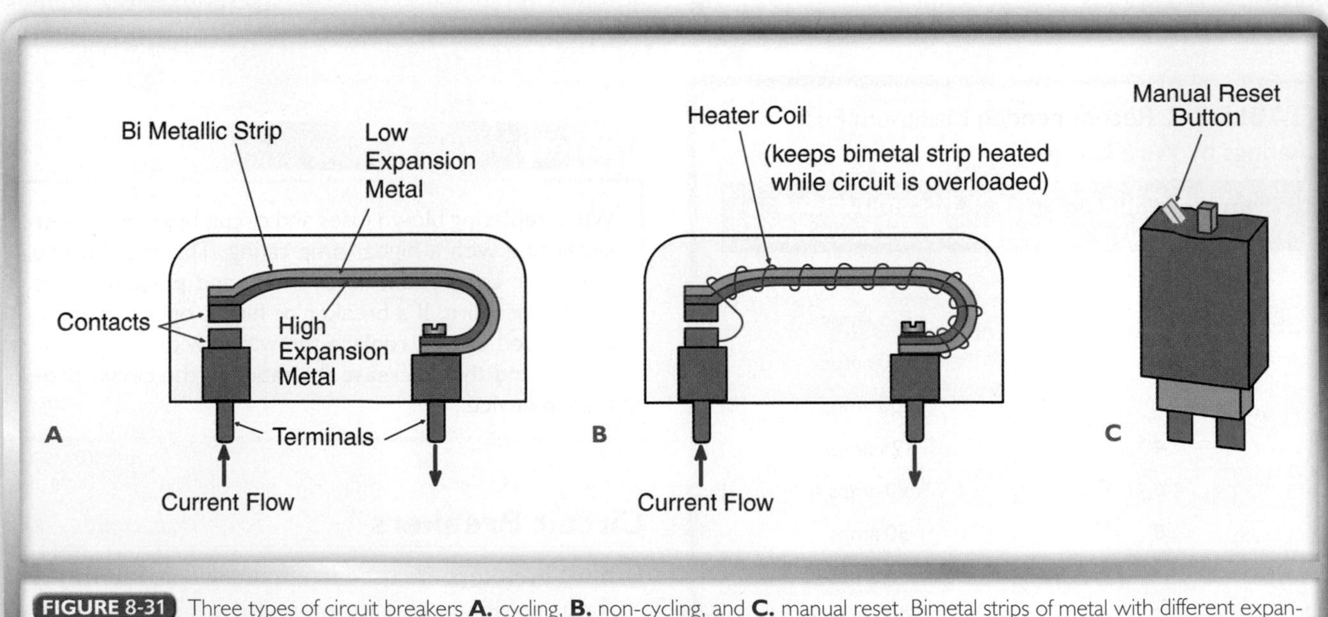

FIGURE 8-31 Three types of circuit breakers **A.** cycling, **B.** non-cycling, and **C.** manual reset. Bimetal strips of metal with different expansion rates bend when heated. Heat produced during high current flow causes contacts inside the breaker to open to protect the circuit wiring from overheating.

TABLE 8-3: Classification of Circuit Breakers

Type 1	Automatically resetting—Will cycle the circuit breaker on and off until the overload condition is removed.
Type 2	Modified Type 1—Keeps the circuit breaker open until the overload condition is removed.
Type 3	A manual resetting thermal non-cycling circuit breaker—Remains tripped until the operator manually resets it by pushing a button located on the breaker.

circuit overloads. These devices are similar to non-linear PTC thermistors. When heated while conducting excessive current, however, they will quickly cycle between a conductive and non-conductive state until after current is removed or the device has cooled FIGURE 8-32. Resistance in the device will suddenly increase to thousands of ohms.

Current trip ratings for PPTCs range from 20 mA to 100 A. Dozens of these devices are used in a single electrical control module to harden them against damage from shorts to power or ground as well as other electrical faults in the external circuits they control.

Virtual Fuses

E-fuses are a more recent innovation in circuit protection. **E-fuses**, or **virtual fuses** as they are sometimes called, are software-controlled fuses that use **field effect transistors** (FET) for the circuit control device. The development of virtual fuses is important because it saves not only the cost of the fuse but the fuse holder and the largest cost associated with using a traditional fuse—the wiring to and from the fuse. Relays and most other fuses are expected to be replaced by virtual fuses.

Virtual fuses are now used in most power distribution modules in multiplexed electrical systems to enable programmable limits of amperage to body-builder-installed circuits and any other vehicle circuits. Combinations of two FETs are used along with a signal from a microcontroller to establish a threshold for current transmission FIGURE 8-33. These fuses are reset when the ignition switch is either turned off or when the FETs have sensed the overcurrent condition has ended.

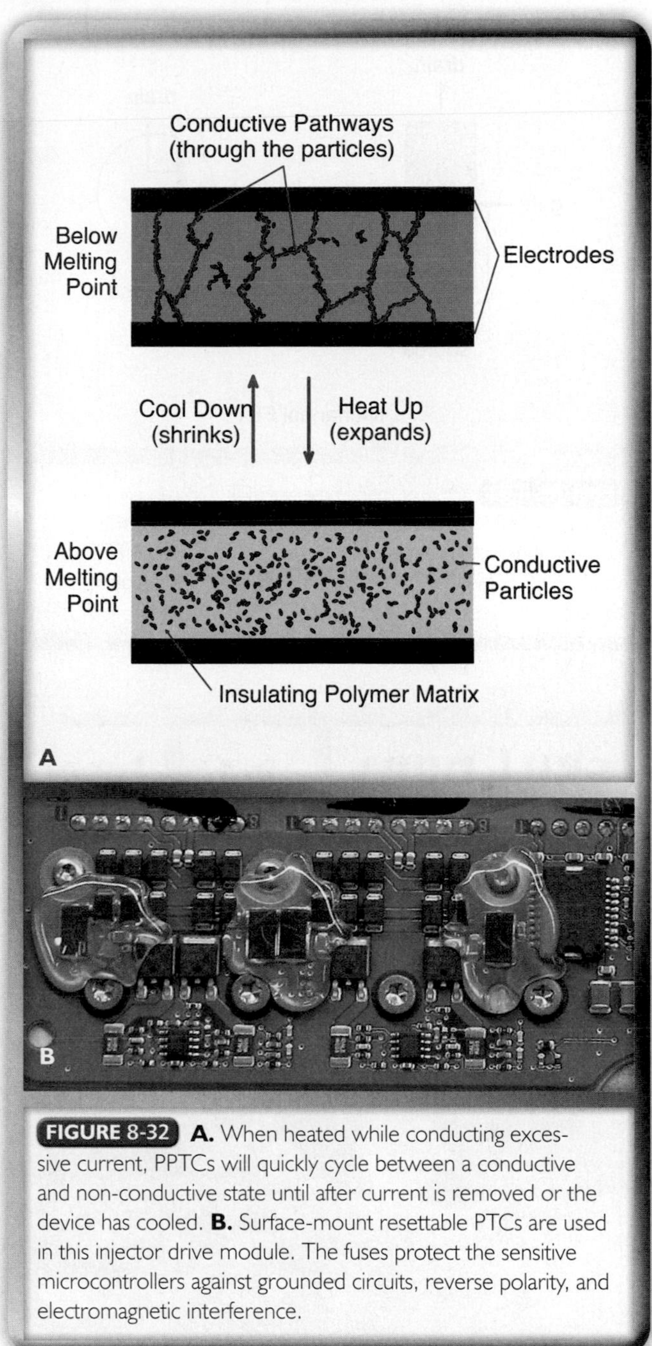

FIGURE 8-32 **A.** When heated while conducting excessive current, PPTCs will quickly cycle between a conductive and non-conductive state until after current is removed or the device has cooled. **B.** Surface-mount resettable PTCs are used in this injector drive module. The fuses protect the sensitive microcontrollers against grounded circuits, reverse polarity, and electromagnetic interference.

Inspecting and Testing Circuit Protection Devices

Protection devices are designed to prevent excessive current from flowing in the circuit. Protection devices such as fuses and fusible links are sacrificial, meaning that if excessive current flows, they will blow or trip and have to be replaced. Circuit breakers can be reset. Once they trip, they either reset automatically or require a manual reset by pushing a button or moving a lever.

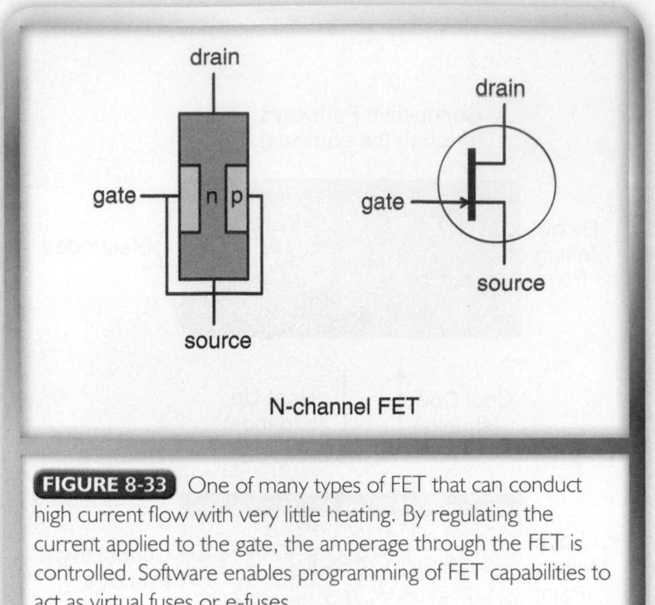

FIGURE 8-33 One of many types of FET that can conduct high current flow with very little heating. By regulating the current applied to the gate, the amperage through the FET is controlled. Software enables programming of FET capabilities to act as virtual fuses or e-fuses.

Fuses, fusible links, and circuit breakers are available in various ratings, types, and sizes, and must always be replaced with the same rating and type. In most vehicles, protection devices are located in the power battery positive side of the circuit. A blown or faulty fuse can be tested using a DVOM or test lamp. A good fuse will have virtually the same voltage on both sides. A blown fuse will typically have battery voltage on one side of the fuse and 0 volts on the other side. They can also sometimes be visually inspected. This may require the removal of the fuse from the fuse holder. The fusible metal strip should be intact and, if measured by an ohm-meter, should have no, or very low resistance. The contacts on both the fuse and the fuse holder should be clean and free of corrosion and should fit snugly together. To inspect and test circuit protection devices, follow the guidelines in SKILL DRILL 8-1. To identify a resistive ground connection, follow the steps in SKILL DRILL 8-2.

SKILL DRILL 8-1 Inspecting and Testing Circuit Protection Devices

1. Identify the protection device to be inspected and tested. A fuse or circuit breaker are most commonly checked at a power distribution box or fuse panel.
2. Turn the ignition switch to the run or on position to supply power to the fuse.
3. Using a test light, probe the fuse or circuit breaker on each side (supply and load) to determine whether current is supplied to the device and whether current is available to the loads in the circuit.
4. If there is only power available to the circuit protection device and not to the load, the device is open. This requires replacement if it is a fuse or resetting the circuit breaker if possible. Fuse replacement is performed after identifying the cause for the overloaded circuit.

SKILL DRILL 8-2 Identifying a Resistive Ground Connection

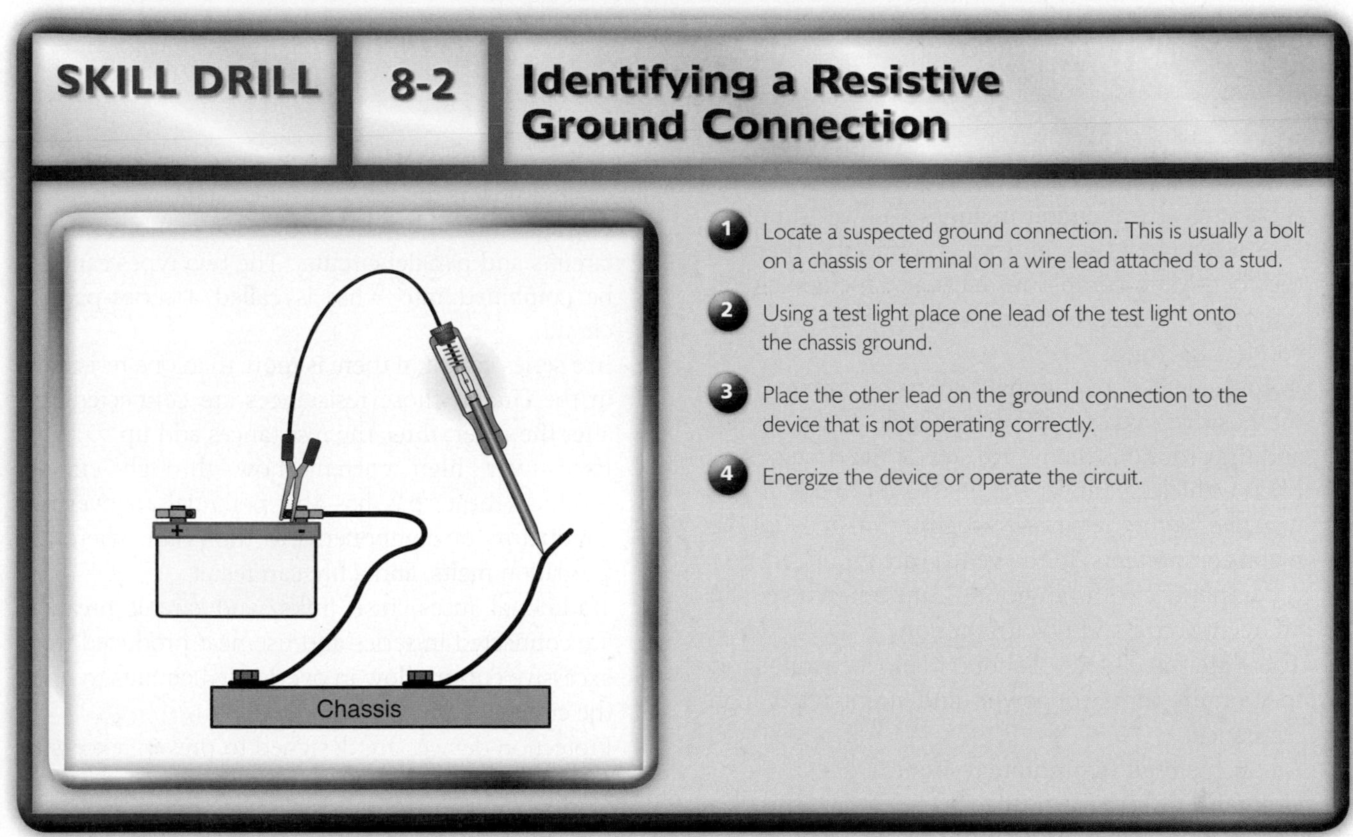

1. Locate a suspected ground connection. This is usually a bolt on a chassis or terminal on a wire lead attached to a stud.
2. Using a test light place one lead of the test light onto the chassis ground.
3. Place the other lead on the ground connection to the device that is not operating correctly.
4. Energize the device or operate the circuit.

Wrap-up

Ready for Review

- A basic electrical circuit includes a power supply, a fuse, a switch, a load, and wires connecting them all together. More complex circuits also include circuit protection devices, control device, and load and connecting wires.
- According to conventional theory of current flow, the positive power is the supply side of the circuit, and the ground is the return side of the circuit.
- Many vehicles connect the chassis and body to the negative battery terminal, which means most of the metal components on the vehicle are grounded.
- A component with no ground connection results in an open circuit and no current flow.
- There are three types of short circuit: a circuit, short to ground, short to power, and unintended high resistance.
- An open circuit has infinite resistance.
- Unintended high resistance in a circuit causes a reduction in amperage in the circuit as well as a drop in voltage at the resistance.
- Volts, amps, and ohms are three basic units of electrical measurement.
- The higher the resistance, the less amperage that will flow in the circuit for any particular voltage.
- The lower the resistance, the higher the current flow in the circuit.
- Ohm's law is an mathematical formula that expresses the relationship among volts (V), amps (A), and ohms (R)—A = V×R.
- Most of the time, when circuits fail, it is because the current flow is too low or non-existent.
- Circuits come in two basic configurations—series circuits and parallel circuits. The two types can also be combined into what is called a series-parallel circuit.
- In a series circuit, if there is more than one resistance in the circuit, those resistances are connected one after the other; thus, the resistances add up.
- Excessively high current flow through circuits produces heat that has the potential to overheat conductors or components to the point where the insulation melts, and a fire can result.
- Traditional fuses, fuse links, and circuit breakers are connected in series and use heat produced from excessive current flow in overloaded circuits to open the circuits.
- Protection devices are designed to prevent excessive current from flowing in the circuit.
- Protection devices such as fuses and fusible links are sacrificial, meaning that if excessive current flows, they will burn out and need replacement.
- Circuit breakers are resettable. A fuse or circuit breaker should be overrated by about 10%–15% to prevent accidental tripping.
- Virtual fuses save not only the cost of the fuse but the fuse holder and the largest cost associated with using a traditional fuse—the wiring to and from the fuse.

Vocabulary Builder

circuit breaker A device that trips and opens a circuit, preventing excessive current flow in a circuit. It is resettable to allow for reuse.

combination (series-parallel) circuit A circuit that uses elements both of series and parallel circuits.

e-fuse A software-controlled fuse that uses field effect transistors for the circuit control device. Also called *virtual fuses*.

field effect transistor (FET) A unipolar transistor that uses an electric field to control the conductivity of a semiconductor material.

grounded circuit A circuit characterized by an unwanted low resistance connection between battery positive power and chassis ground.

intermittent circuit A circuit characterized by uneven current flow.

Kirchhoff's law A law that states that the sum of the current flowing into a junction is the same as the current flowing out of the junction.

Ohm's law A law that defines the relationship between amperage, resistance, and voltage.

parallel circuit A circuit in which all components are connected directly to the voltage supply.

polymeric positive temperature coefficient (PPTC) device (resettable fuse) A thermistor-like electronic device used to protect against circuit overloads. Also called *resettable fuse*.

resistive circuit A circuit in which grounds and power connections cannot properly function due to overly high resistance.

series circuit The simplest type of electrical circuit with multiple loads but only one path for current to flow.

short circuit An electrical circuit that is formed between two points, allowing current to flow through an unintended pathway.

thermal fuse A type of fuse opened by heat produced from resistance caused by high amperage flow.

Type 1 circuit breaker A cycling circuit breaker that automatically resets.

Type 2 circuit breaker A non-cycling circuit breaker.

Type 3 circuit breaker A circuit breaker that requires manual reset.

virtual fuse A software-controlled fuse that uses field effect transistors for the circuit control device A circuit protection strategy that monitors circuit amperage with software and shuts off the circuit when amperage exceeds a predetermined threshold. Also called *e-fuses*.

Watt's law A law that defines the relationship between power, amperage, and voltage.

Review Questions

1. Which of the following are basic parts of an electrical circuit?
   a. Power source
   b. Conductors
   c. Loads
   d. All of the choices are correct.
2. Which of the following statements is/are correct concerning the term operational state?
   a. Open and closed are the terms used to describe whether current is flowing through a circuit.
   b. An open circuit's electrical pathway is broken or unconnected.
   c. An open circuit means current cannot flow because there is an open gap between two ends of the circuit.
   d. All of the choices are correct.
3. Which of the following is NOT correct concerning parallel circuits?
   a. There are two or more pathways for the current.
   b. The voltage applied to each branch is the same through-out the circuit.
   c. If one branch of the circuit is broken current will continue to flow in the other branches.
   d. Total circuit resistance is always more than the resistance of the smallest resister.
4. Which of the following is/are correct concerning combination circuits?
   a. Combination circuits use elements both parallel and series circuits.
   b. Combination circuits are the most common types used in a commercial vehicle chassis.
   c. Typically, the power and control circuits are in series, but the loads are in parallel.
   d. All of the choices are correct.
5. Which of the following is NOT correct concerning Ohm's law?
   a. Ohm's law is often used by a technician.
   b. An understanding of Ohm's law can help you better understand how electricity behaves.
   c. Ohm's law defines the relationship between current, resistance, and voltage.
   d. Simply stated, Ohm's law requires one volt to push one amp of current through a circuit that has a resistance of one ohm.
6. Why do heavy vehicles often use a 24 volt system?
   a. Reducing amperage not only reduces resistance but the size of conductors.
   b. Voltage drops in the system are reduced.
   c. Both A and B
   d. Neither A nor B
7. Which of the following is/are common points for resistances to develop?
   a. Battery terminals
   b. Light bulb sockets
   c. Connector sockets
   d. All of the choices are correct.
8. Which of the following is NOT a type of thermal fuse?
   a. Cartridge type
   b. Modular type
   c. Blade type
   d. In line type
9. Which type of circuit breaker must be reset by depressing a reset button?
   a. Type 1
   b. Type 2
   c. Type 3
   d. Type 4
10. Which of the following is/ are correct concerning inspecting and testing circuit protection devices?
    a. Protection devices such as fuses and fusible links are sacrificial, meaning that if excessive current flows, they will blow or trip and have to be replaced.
    b. Circuit breakers can be reset.
    c. Fuses, fusible links and circuit breakers are available in various ratings, types and sizes, and must always be replaced with the same rating and type.
    d. All of the choices are correct.

ASE-Type Questions

1. Technician A says circuits are pathways made by electrical conductors that enable the flow of electrons. Technician B says a variety of classifications are used to describe circuit configurations and failures. Who is correct?
   a. Technician A
   b. Technician B
   c. Both Technician A and Technician B
   d. Neither Technician A nor Technician B
2. Technician A says resistance is electrical friction. Technician B says resistance will lower voltage, but in a circuit, will not proportionately lower amperage to the amount of resistance. Who is correct?
   a. Technician A
   b. Technician B
   c. Both Technician A and Technician B
   d. Neither Technician A nor Technician B
3. Technician A says circuits found in commercial vehicles are classified in an operational state of open and closed. Technician B says circuits found in commercial vehicles are classified in the failure mode of blocked as well as shorted or open. Who is correct?
   a. Technician A
   b. Technician B
   c. Both Technician A and Technician B
   d. Neither Technician A nor Technician B
4. Technician A says a series circuit is a circuit with multiple loads and only one path for current to flow. Technician B says in a series circuit total circuit resistance is equal to the sum of the individual resistances. Who is correct?
   a. Technician A
   b. Technician B
   c. Both Technician A and Technician B
   d. Neither Technician A nor Technician B
5. Technician A says Watt's Law, which is related to Ohm's law, explains the relationship between resistance and amperage. Technician B says increasing amperage through a circuit produces proportionally more resistance. Who is correct?
   a. Technician A
   b. Technician B
   c. Both Technician A and Technician B
   d. Neither Technician A nor Technician B
6. Technician A says a grounded circuit should not be confused with a "dead short," which is a different condition. Technician B says a common example of a grounded circuit would be a battery or power cable insulation rubbing against the negative ground chassis frame. Who is correct?
   a. Technician A
   b. Technician B
   c. Both Technician A and Technician B
   d. Neither Technician A nor Technician B
7. Technician A says when circuits are overloaded with current, hungry components, or grounded circuits, it is the quickest way to cause damage to wiring, or even start fires. Technician B says a 20-amp fuse will open at 32 to 33 amps of current. Who is correct?
   a. Technician A
   b. Technician B
   c. Both Technician A and Technician B
   d. Neither Technician A nor Technician B
8. Technician A says fuse links are short sections of wire installed in series with larger diameter conductors. Technician B says when the gauge on the main conductor is at halfway, the fuse link will overheat and melt as excessive amperage passes through the wire. Who is correct?
   a. Technician A
   b. Technician B
   c. Both Technician A and Technician B
   d. Neither Technician A nor Technician B
9. Technician A says a polymeric positive temperature coefficient device (PPTC) is a thermistor-like electronic device used to protect against circuit overloads. Technician B says PPTCs are commonly known as resettable fuses. Who is correct?
   a. Technician A
   b. Technician B
   c. Both Technician A and Technician B
   d. Neither Technician A nor Technician B
10. Technician A says virtual fuses, or e-fuses, are a recent innovation in circuit protection. Technician B says virtual fuses are software-controlled fuses that use Field Effect Transistors (FET) as the circuit control device. Who is correct?
    a. Technician A
    b. Technician B
    c. Both Technician A and Technician B
    d. Neither Technician A nor Technician B

CHAPTER 9

NATEF Tasks

Electrical/Electronic Systems

General Electrical Systems	Page
■ Inspect and test spike suppression devices; replace as needed.	287

Knowledge Objectives

After reading this chapter, you will be able to:

1. Classify and describe switches. (pp 276–279)
2. Define and describe common types of circuit control devices. (pp 277–297)
3. Identify and describe fixed and variable types of resistors. (pp 279–281)
4. Identify and describe the operation of solenoids, capacitors, and relays. (pp 282–289)
5. Identify standardized pin numbers of electrical relays. (p 283)
6. Recommend techniques used to test circuit control devices. (p 288)
7. Describe and explain the operation and construction of semiconductors. (p 290)
8. Classify diodes and transistors according to function. (pp 293–297)
9. Identify and describe the operation of diodes and transistors. (pp 293–297)
10. Identify and describe types of integrated circuit components. (pp 297–298)

Circuit Control Devices

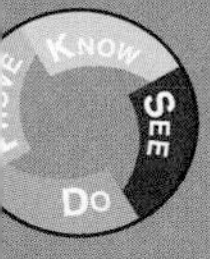

Skills Objectives

There are no skills objectives in this chapter.

Introduction

Electric circuits use control devices to direct the flow of current. Current may be started, stopped, slowed, amplified, or simply redirected. In more sophisticated electronic devices, electrical current can be conditioned to carry information in either digital or analog form. Controls can be as simple as a switch, resistor, electromagnetic relay, solenoid, or capacitor. They can also be more complex electronic devices such as diodes, transistors, integrated circuits, microprocessors, and microcontrollers. This chapter will cover all of those topics in detail.

Simple Control Devices

Switches

Switches are the simplest circuit control device **FIGURE 9-1**. Opening and closing switches completes or breaks a circuit's electrical pathway. Simple switches are categorized by the number of input and output terminals they have. Input terminals are called poles, and output terminals called throws as described in **TABLE 9-1**. The simplest switch is a single pole single throw (SPST). A double pole double throw switch is called DPDT. Other switches are SPDT (used as a headlight dimmer switch), DPST, and multi-pole multi-throw (MPMT), such as a transmission selector switch on a hydra-mechanical automatic transmission.

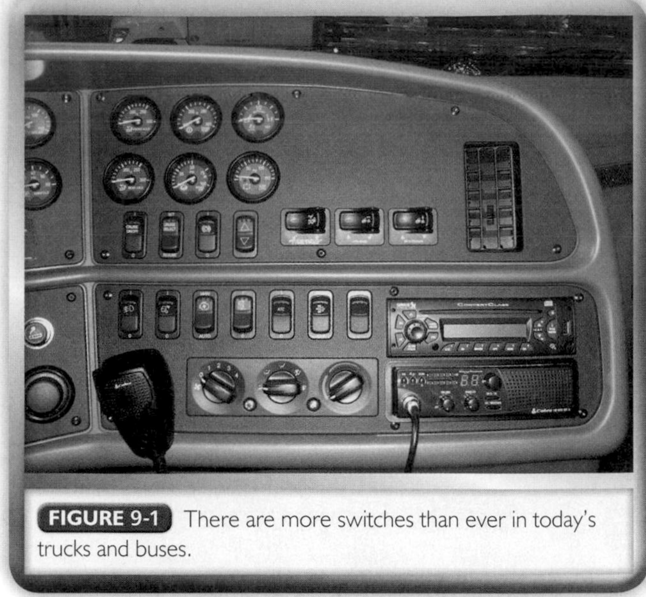

FIGURE 9-1 There are more switches than ever in today's trucks and buses.

Switches are also categorized by operation. If the switch closes a circuit in its resting position (without any energizing), it is called normally closed (NC). If its resting position is open, it is called normally open (NO)

Types of Switches

Switches can be toggle, momentary contact, pressure, temperature sensitive, or proximity. **TABLE 9-2** shows and describes several types of switches.

You Are the Technician

A 26' straight truck arrives at your shop with the request to install 20 additional clearance lights on the box, 5 additional lights on the top and bottom of each side in addition to the 6 lights on each side currently in place. After calculating the current load for the additional lights using 0.6amps/light, you find that an additional load will be 12 amps plus 8 amps for the other lights in place. Deciding the truck's stock headlamp switch cannot handle the additional current, you wire a relay to the clearance light circuit to switch the higher amperage. The headlight switch opens and closes the relay's control circuit. After successfully installing the lights and relay, the customer returns the next day complaining the clearance lights no longer work. When investigating, you discover the relay has developed an internal open circuit and smells burned. After replacing the relay with a different one, you discover the relay "buzzes" and the lights flicker unless the engine is running.

1. What is a likely cause for the first relay to have burned-up so quickly?
2. What is a likely cause for the second relay to buzz and cause the lights to flicker unless the charging system is supplying current?
3. Suggest a practical solution for correcting the problem of buzzing, chattering relays and flickering lights.

TABLE 9-1: Common Contact Arrangements

Term	Abbreviation	Description	Contact Diagram
Single Pole Single Throw	SPST	Simple on/off set of contacts.	
Single Pole Double Throw	SPDT	Also called changeover contacts. Often used in the description of a relay type, "Changeover Relay."	
Double Pole Single Throw	DPST	The same as having two SPST sets of contacts controlled by a single mechanism.	
Double Pole Double Throw	DPDT	Equivalent to two SPDT sets of contacts controlled by a single mechanism.	

1. *Toggle switches* use an angled lever having an internal spring loaded mechanism to keep the switch in its latch position.
2. *Momentary contact* types may be toggled or pushbutton type and may also be either NC or NO. Horn contact or starter button are examples of momentary contact switches.
3. *Pressure switches* are used for gas or liquids. Pressure is applied to a piston, diaphragm, or bellows to close or open contacts. Low pressure oil, air, or the refrigerant sensors in the air-conditioning systems are examples of pressure switches **FIGURE 9-2**.
4. *Temperature-sensitive switches* use a bimetal arm that bends when heated. Internal contacts complete or open a circuit.
5. *Proximity switches* sense the approach of components. Simple proximity switches use a permanent magnet to toggle a sealed switch mechanism as two parts approach one another. More complex proximity switches use a coil of wire energized with high-frequency AC current. As the strength of the magnetic field changes with the approach of another metal part, induced current in the coil intensifies with a change in magnetic reluctance. Proximity sensors are used in hydraulic systems using lifting rams and other power components to sense position.

Rotary, pushbutton, rocker, magnetic, and even voice-activated and touch-sensitive switches are other types of switches found on commercial vehicles.

Smart Switches

Smart switches can function as digital inputs to electronic control systems. Because switches can be in only one of two states, switch inputs are binary inputs. This means a switch can provide data such as whether a device or system is on or off, high or low, open or closed, up or down, and so on.

When switches are arranged in electronic control system, they are categorized as either pull-up or pull-down

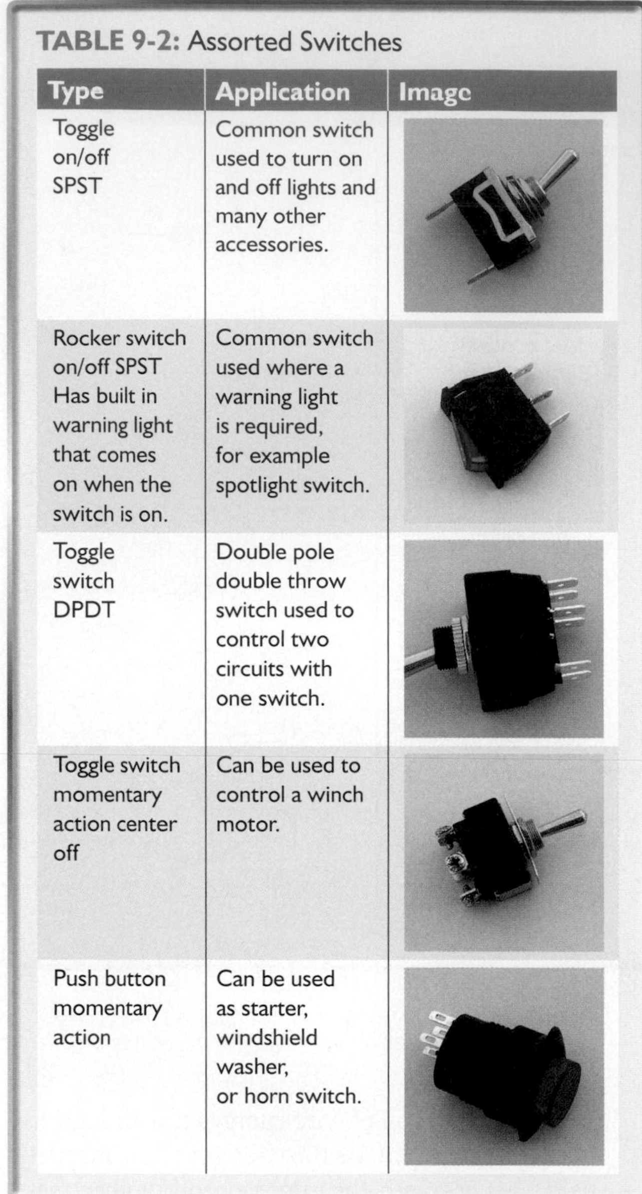

TABLE 9-2: Assorted Switches

Type	Application	Image
Toggle on/off SPST	Common switch used to turn on and off lights and many other accessories.	
Rocker switch on/off SPST Has built in warning light that comes on when the switch is on.	Common switch used where a warning light is required, for example spotlight switch.	
Toggle switch DPDT	Double pole double throw switch used to control two circuits with one switch.	
Toggle switch momentary action center off	Can be used to control a winch motor.	
Push button momentary action	Can be used as starter, windshield washer, or horn switch.	

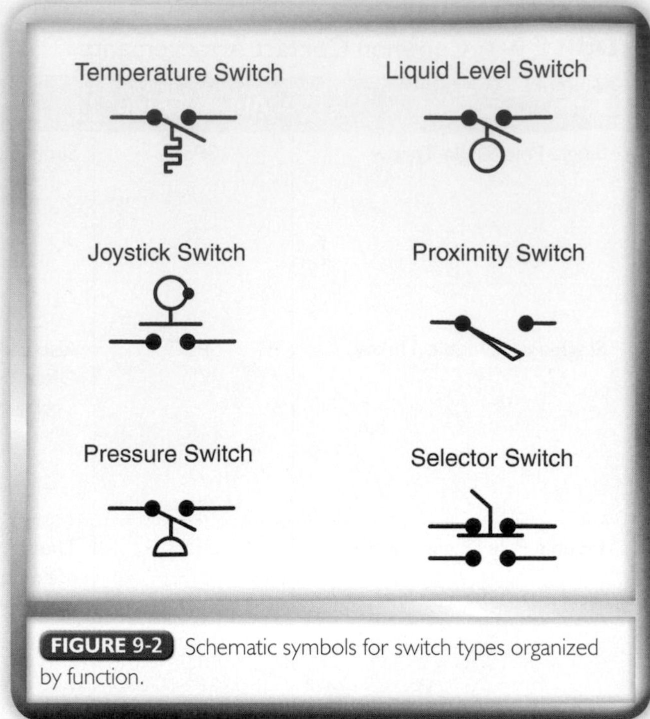

FIGURE 9-2 Schematic symbols for switch types organized by function.

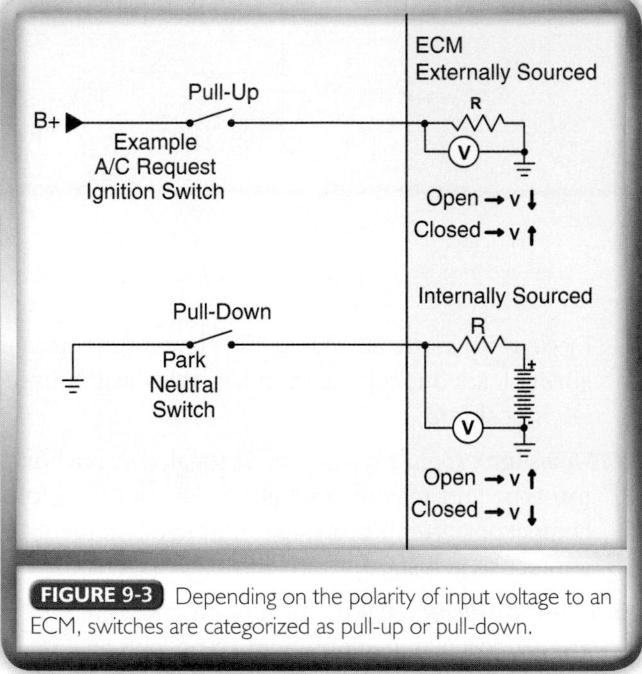

FIGURE 9-3 Depending on the polarity of input voltage to an ECM, switches are categorized as pull-up or pull-down.

depending on the type of voltage supplied to an ECM. A switch connecting a positive voltage to the ECM is a pull-up; switching a negative voltage input is considered a pull-down switch **FIGURE 9-3**.

One of the first types of smart switches is used not only to supply a pull-up or pull-down voltage input to the ECM but also to incorporate one or two resistors to differentiate a closed or open switch from a circuit problem **FIGURE 9-4**. For example, a high- or low-pressure refrigerant switch used by the air-conditioning system could become disconnected, shorted, or grounded, causing the system to malfunction and become severely damaged.

By installing a resistor in parallel across the switch contacts, the control module could detect one of several conditions. If the switch is open, the resistance value of the resistor is measured **FIGURE 9-5**. If the wire to the switch is disconnected or broken, the ECM would measure infinite resistance and identify a fault in the circuit.

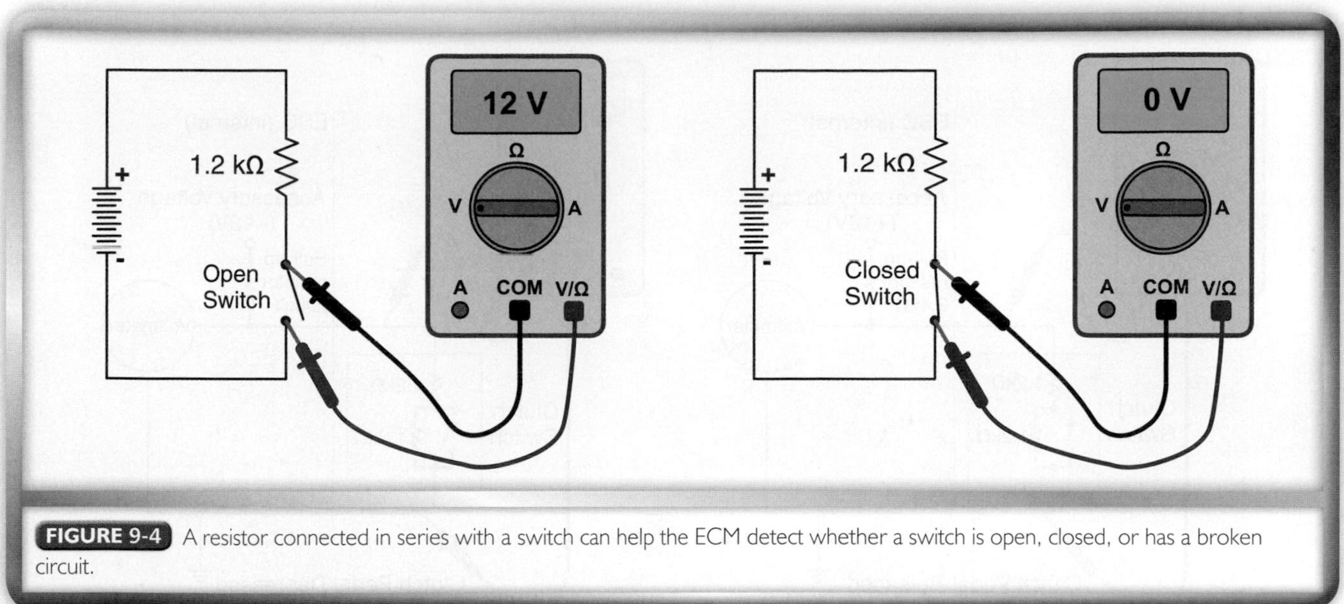

FIGURE 9-4 A resistor connected in series with a switch can help the ECM detect whether a switch is open, closed, or has a broken circuit.

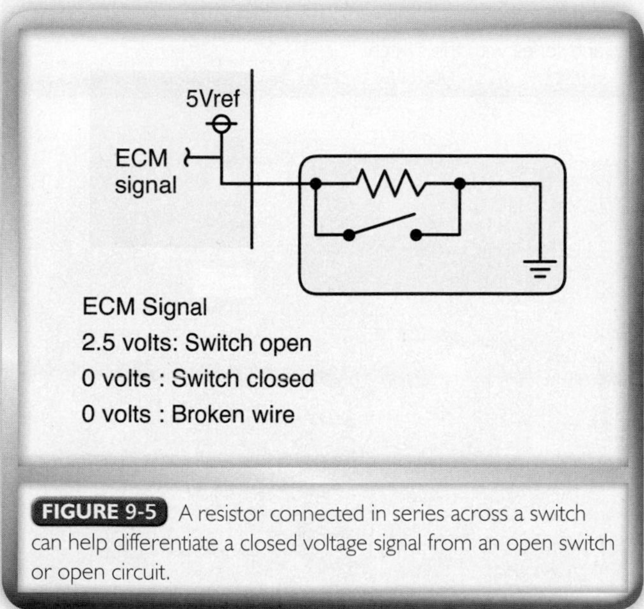

FIGURE 9-5 A resistor connected in series across a switch can help differentiate a closed voltage signal from an open switch or open circuit.

A closed switch would have no resistance. Two resistors are used to differentiate between a shorted, grounded, or open circuit. One resistor is connected in parallel across the switch contacts and another is in series with the switch **FIGURE 9-6**. An open switch would supply a voltage proportional to the voltage drop across the parallel and series resistor. A closed switch would provide a voltage drop across only the series resistor.

In either the open or closed state, then, some resistance is always measured by the ECM across the switch when the circuit is properly functioning. A wire shorted to ground, or to a positive voltage source or simply disconnected, would supply an out-of-expected-range voltage to the ECM and a fault would be identified. Even more elaborate fault detection methods can be built into switch inputs using Zener diodes, more resistors, and by using field effect transistors (FETs), which are discussed later in this chapter.

When several switches are connected together in switch packs, such as those used by the cruise control or in dash-mounted switch clusters, the same arrangement of either a series, parallel, or series-parallel arrangement of resistors helps identify a unique voltage value for a specific switch while using a single wire input to the ECM for multiple switches **FIGURE 9-7**.

Resistors

Three types of resistors are commonly found in commercial vehicles:

1. Fixed
2. Stepped
3. Variable

Fixed Resistors

Fixed-type resistors are designed to conduct either heavy or light amounts of current. Wire-wound (power) resistors are made from resistive nickel/chrome wire. These function as current limiters because they become more resistive when connected in series and amperage increases. Carbon resistors are commonly found in electronic circuit

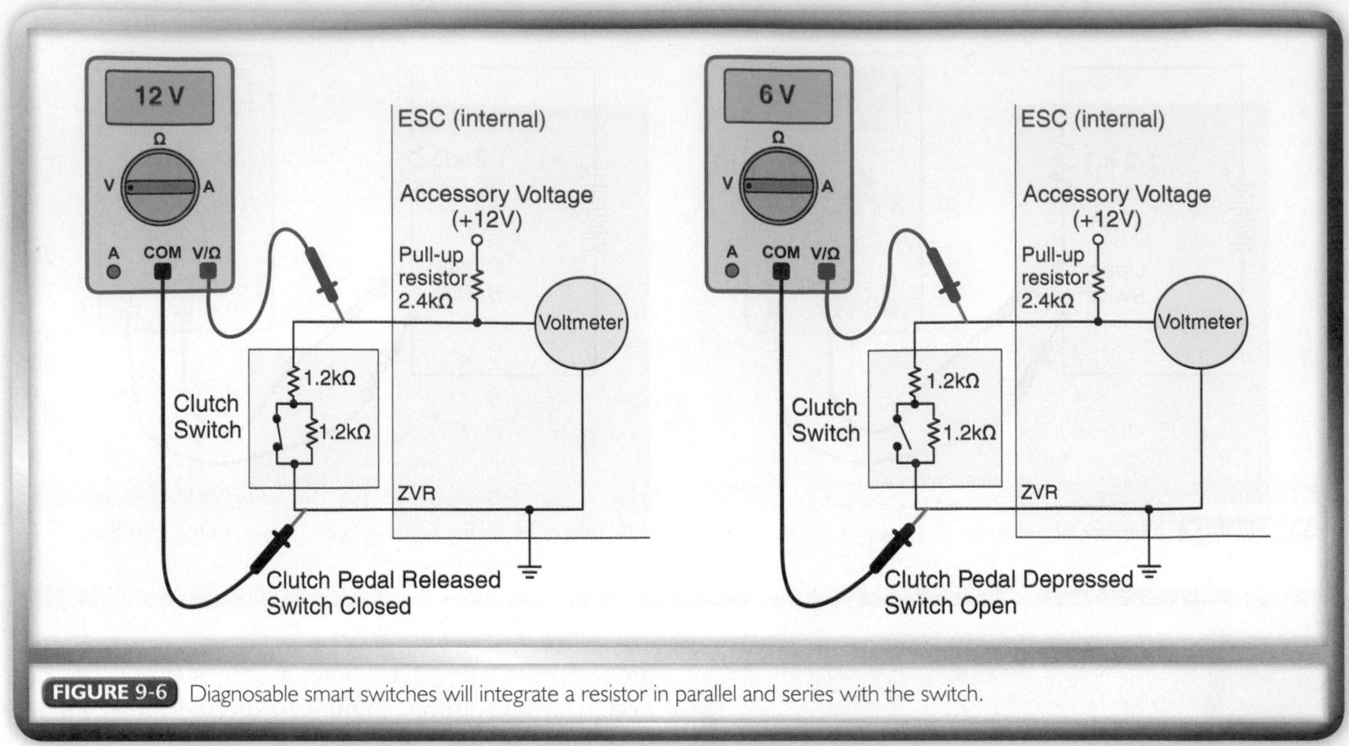

FIGURE 9-6 Diagnosable smart switches will integrate a resistor in parallel and series with the switch.

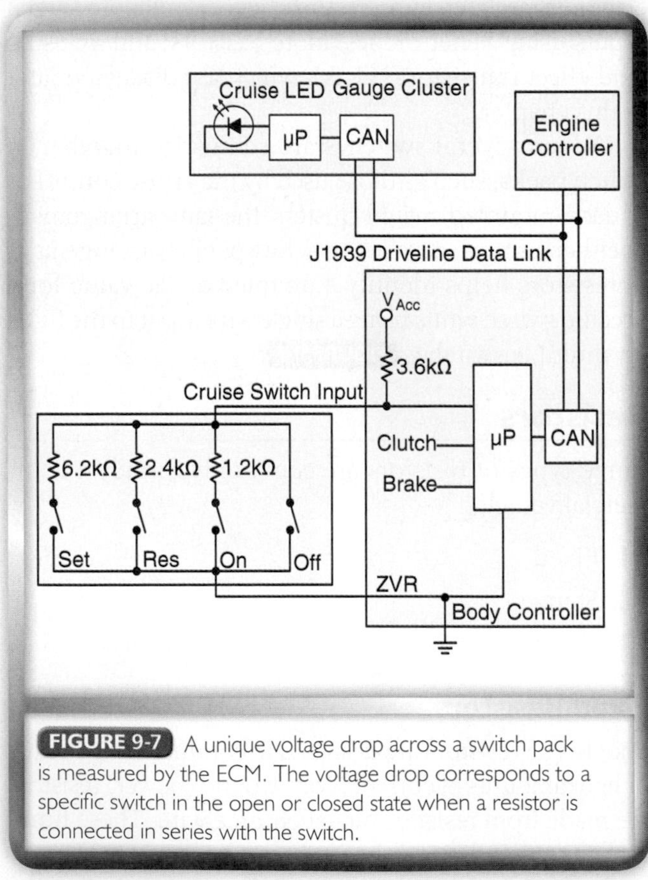

FIGURE 9-7 A unique voltage drop across a switch pack is measured by the ECM. The voltage drop corresponds to a specific switch in the open or closed state when a resistor is connected in series with the switch.

boards. These change the direction or supply of current to other components on circuit boards. Colored bands around the resistor identify its numerical resistance in ohms **FIGURE 9-8**.

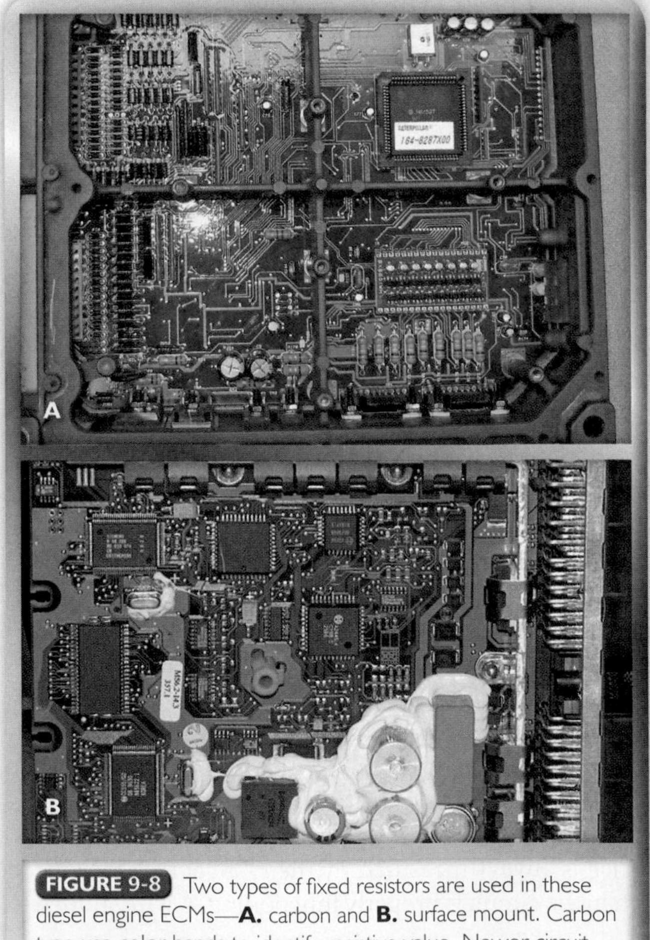

FIGURE 9-8 Two types of fixed resistors are used in these diesel engine ECMs—**A.** carbon and **B.** surface mount. Carbon type use color bands to identify resistive value. Newer circuit boards use surface mount resistors.

Stepped Resistors

Stepped resistors are made from two or more wire-wound resistors. A common application for this type of resistor is in a blower motor speed control circuit FIGURE 9-9. Each of these resistors connected in series is also connected to a terminal on the blower switch. The output of the resistor is connected to a blower motor. Varying the switch position changes the current available to the blower motor. Locating the resistor in the blower motor housing where it is cooled helps prevent premature burn-out of the resistor.

Variable Resistors

Four types of variable resistors are used today in commercial vehicles:

1. Rheostat
2. Potentiometer
3. Thermistor
4. Photoresistor

Rheostats vary current flow by passing current through a long, resistive, tightly coiled wire FIGURE 9-10. A wiper-like contact sliding over the coil supplies a variable current output. This happens as the wiper contact changes the length of the resistive pathway. Moving the wiper closer to the powered input reduces resistance. Moving the wiper farther from the input increases resistance. Instrument cluster dimmer switches and fuel tank sending units are examples of applications for rheostats. Rheostats have only two terminals—a fixed input and a variable output.

Similar to the rheostat, **potentiometers** are variable resistors but with three connections—one at each end of a resistive path. A third connection is a sliding contact

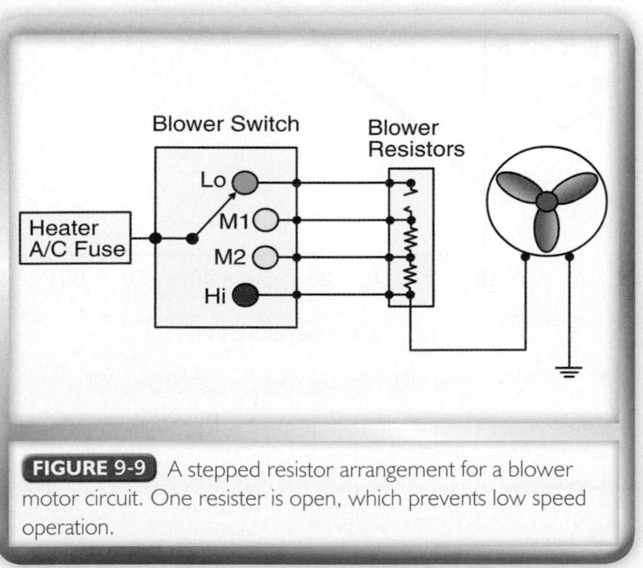

FIGURE 9-9 A stepped resistor arrangement for a blower motor circuit. One resister is open, which prevents low speed operation.

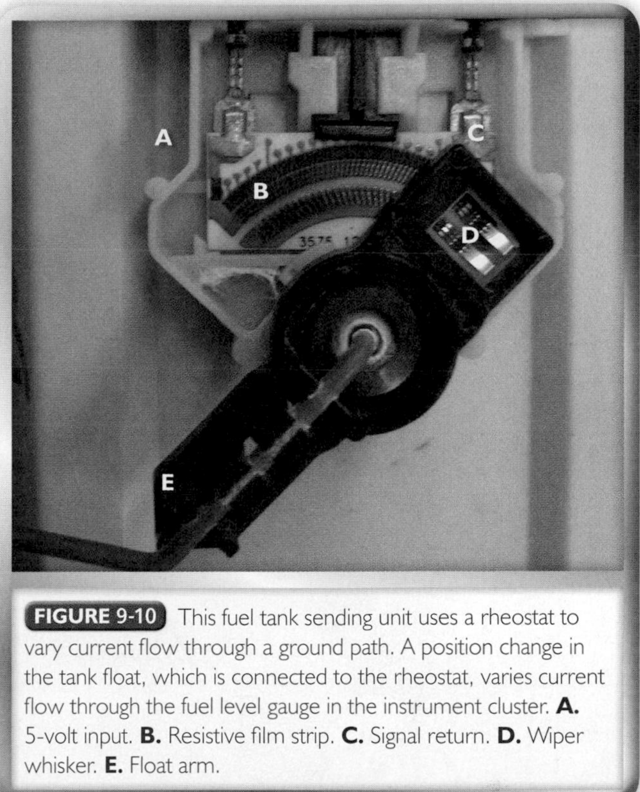

FIGURE 9-10 This fuel tank sending unit uses a rheostat to vary current flow through a ground path. A position change in the tank float, which is connected to the rheostat, varies current flow through the fuel level gauge in the instrument cluster. **A.** 5-volt input. **B.** Resistive film strip. **C.** Signal return. **D.** Wiper whisker. **E.** Float arm.

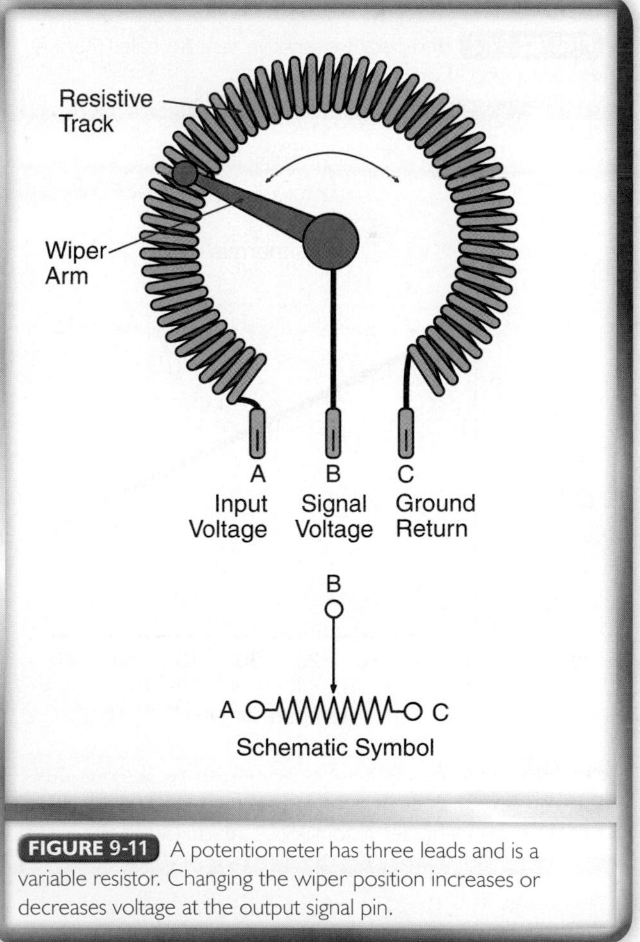

FIGURE 9-11 A potentiometer has three leads and is a variable resistor. Changing the wiper position increases or decreases voltage at the output signal pin.

that moves along the resistive pathway FIGURE 9-11. The pathway may have a little or a lot of resistance depending on the position of the potentiometer along the pathway. Throttle pedal position sensors are a common application for potentiometers.

Thermistor is a combination of the word resistor and temperature. And as the name suggests, it is a temperature-sensitive variable resistor FIGURE 9-12. Made from semiconductor materials, thermistors are found anywhere where temperature sensing is needed—fuel, air inlet, oil, coolant, and so on. They are even used in electronic voltage regulators for temperature-sensitive charging voltage correction. **Negative temperature coefficient (NTC) thermistors** are the most common type. An NTC thermistor's resistance decreases as the temperature increases. **Positive temperature coefficient (PTC) thermistors** are used in higher heat or amperage applications such as in electric motors for power windows or exhaust aftertreatment systems. Their resistance increases as the temperature increases FIGURE 9-13.

FIGURE 9-12 Temperature sensitive resistors called thermistors are a type of variable resistor.

Photoresistors are a semiconductor-type of resistor in which resistance decreases as light intensity increases FIGURE 9-14. Made from cadmium sulfide (CdS), these devices are used to control some lighting circuits, such as some instrument clusters or auto-dimming headlights, and rear view mirrors. For a failsafe feature, some auxiliary coolant heaters use photoresistors to detect light from the combustion of fuel. If no combustion is sensed by the photoresistors, the unit will shut-down.

Relays

A relay is a switch that uses a small amount of current to switch a larger amount of current. Locating a relay closer to a load requiring large amounts of current eliminates voltage drop caused by resistance from long runs of wires. Relays also eliminate the use of heavy conductors inside the cab of a vehicle, and that allows for safer operation.

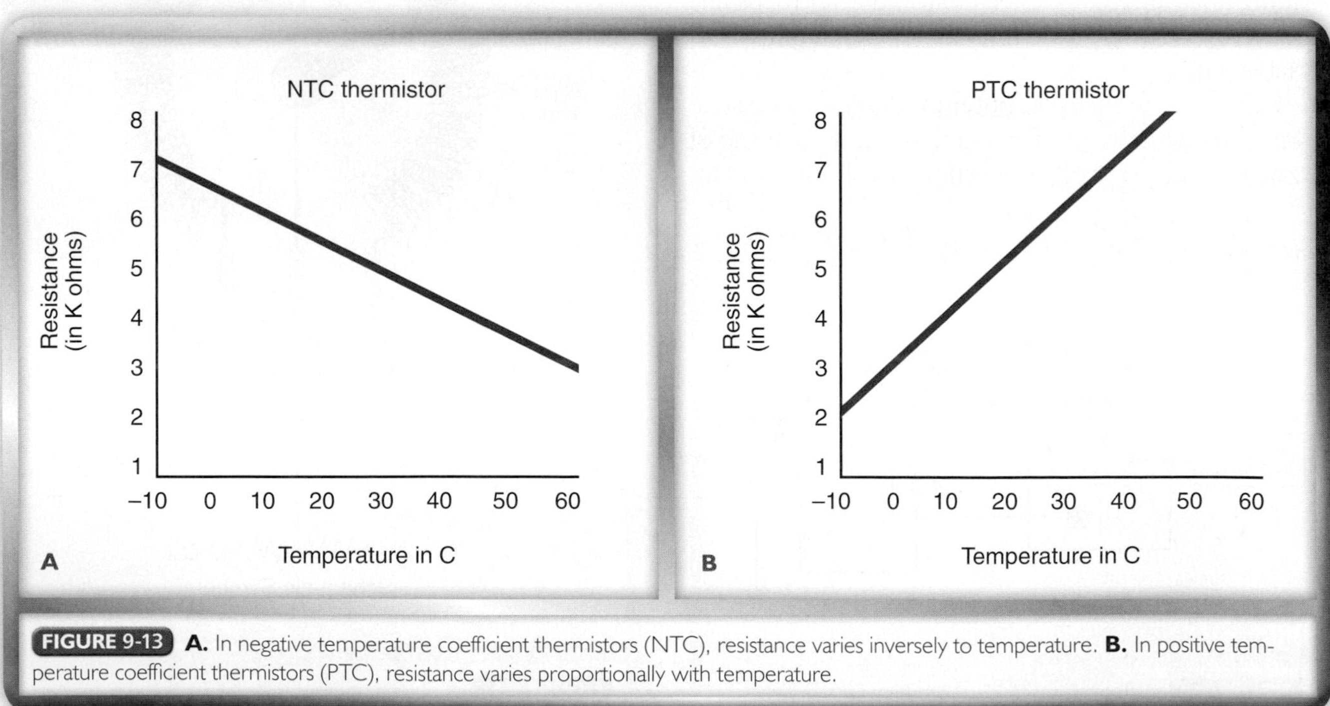

FIGURE 9-13 **A.** In negative temperature coefficient thermistors (NTC), resistance varies inversely to temperature. **B.** In positive temperature coefficient thermistors (PTC), resistance varies proportionally with temperature.

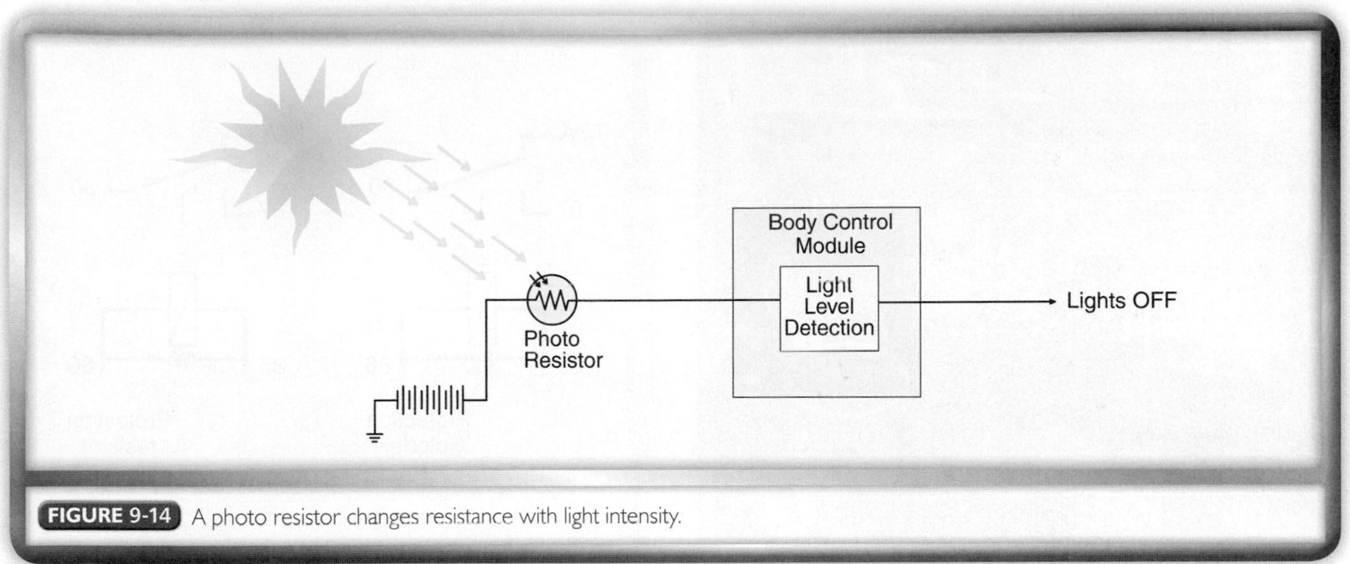

FIGURE 9-14 A photo resistor changes resistance with light intensity.

A typical relay has a control circuit and a load circuit. The control circuit is supplied current through a switch, which often is opened or closed by an electronic control module or the vehicle operator. Inside the relay, an electromagnetic coil will pull a set of contacts closed. It is across these contacts that a larger amount of current is switched. The relay's control circuit can be switched by supplying a power or ground to the relay. If an ECM supplies a positive voltage to control the relay, it is termed a pull-up circuit. If it supplies a ground, it is called a pull-down circuit.

International Standards Organization (ISO) relays, also called mini-cube relays, are the most common relays used today. See FIGURE 9-15 and FIGURE 9-16. The relay is standardized to be used across all vehicle manufacturers, having standard pin numbers, functions, and dimensions to fit into a power distribution box. These can switch as much as 35 amps in a 12-volt system.

Because relays use electromagnetic coils, a large voltage spike is produced when the coils are de-energized. See FIGURE 9-17 and FIGURE 9-18. The rapidly collapsing magnetic field will move across the coil conductors,

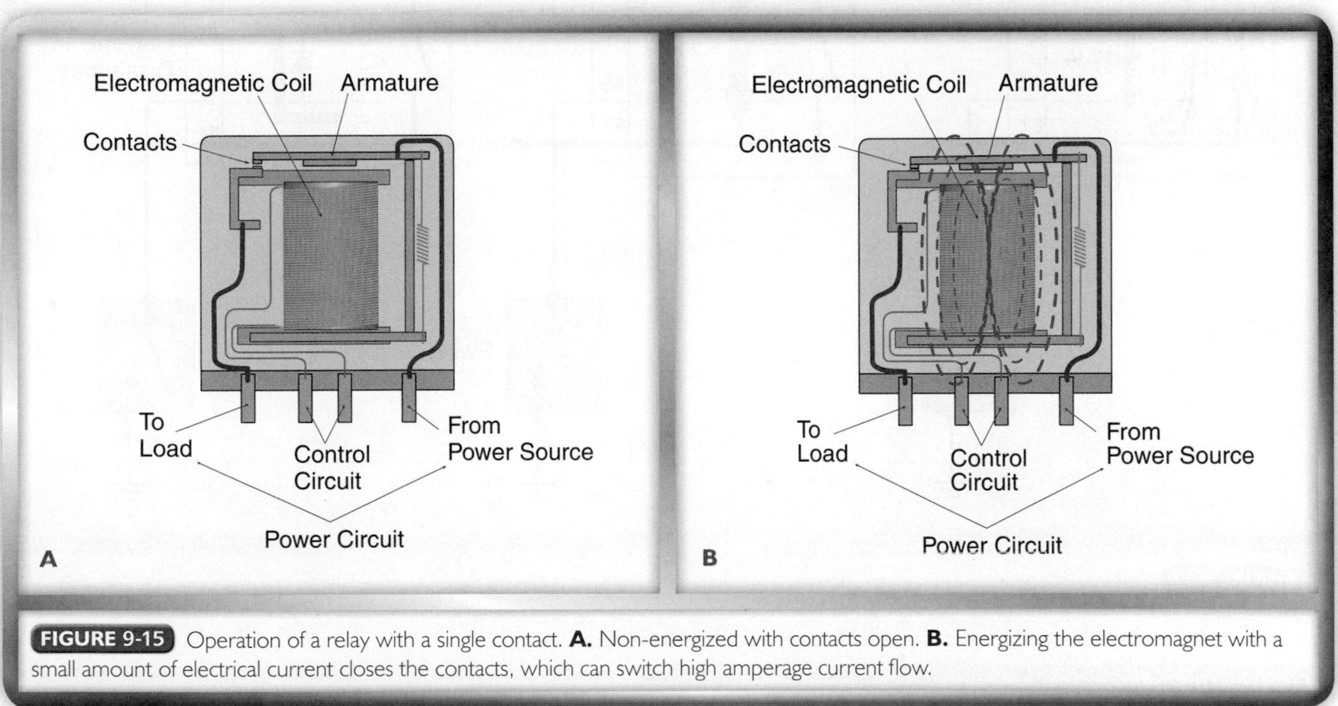

FIGURE 9-15 Operation of a relay with a single contact. **A.** Non-energized with contacts open. **B.** Energizing the electromagnet with a small amount of electrical current closes the contacts, which can switch high amperage current flow.

FIGURE 9-16 Mini ISO relays in a power distribution box. Current suppressed relays use a diode, resistor, and sometimes a capacitor to minimize a voltage spike produced through self-induction.

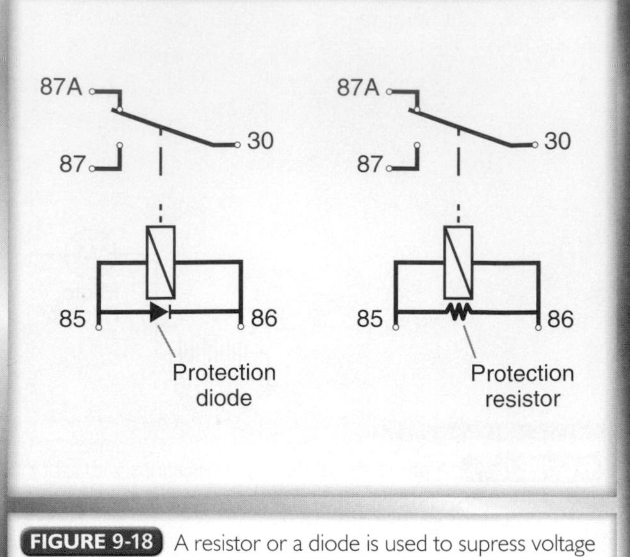

FIGURE 9-18 A resistor or a diode is used to supress voltage spike produced through self-induction.

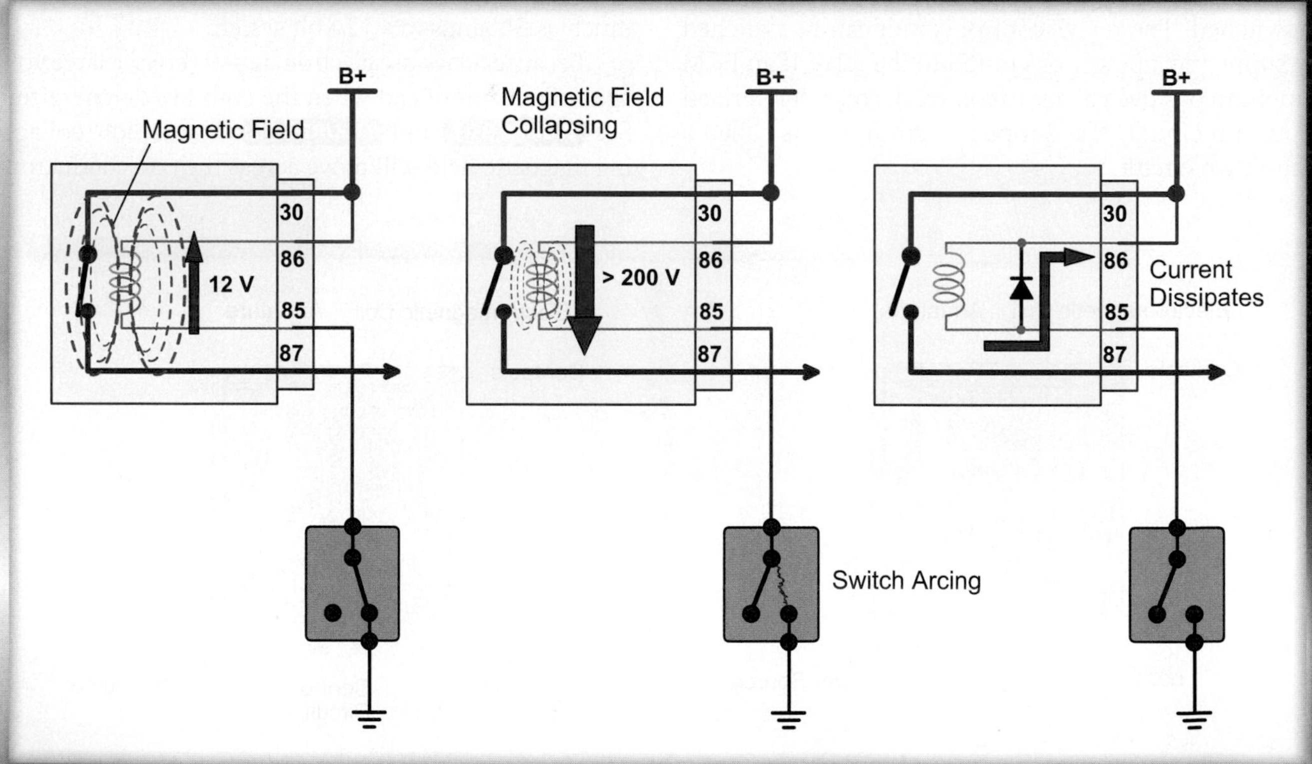

FIGURE 9-17 Self-induction inside a relay can supply a large voltage spike, which can damage sensitive electronic components. No conduction takes place through the diode during normal operation. High voltage current moving in the opposite direction of the original current will forward bias the diode, and current dissipates through resistance in the circuit.

inducing over 200 volts. If the relay control circuit shares a voltage supply with the ignition switch or sensitive electronic component, electrical damage can occur. To prevent this, a diode or resistor connected in parallel across the coil will provide an alternate pathway for the voltage spike to dissipate when the magnetic field collapses.

Magnetic Switches

Magnetic or "mag" switches are identical in function to relays except that they switch even larger amounts of current and have atypical dimensions. See FIGURE 9-19. Magnetic switches are also classified as continuous or intermittent duty service. When switching heavy amounts of current, such as to the starter motor solenoid, available battery voltage can drop. See FIGURE 9-20. Low available voltage will reduce the magnetic field strength in the switch, causing the relay to "chatter" as it rapidly engages and disengages when the electrical system voltage drops.

To counter this effect, the electromagnetic coil windings are wound from heavier gauge wire. The result is fewer coils but more amperage through the low resistance coil, which helps maintains magnetic field strength , as shown in FIGURE 9-21. High amperage flow through the winding will cause the coil to quickly burn out after just a few hours of continuous operation. To prevent that, continuous duty relays are made from thinner wire with higher resistance. Although they can remain energized for longer periods of time, continuous duty relays are sensitive to voltage drop, leading to relay chatter.

TECHNICIAN TIP

Continuous and intermittent duty magnetic switches can look identical but will cause problems if not used in the correct application. Continuous duty relays when used to operate glow plug or starter motor solenoids will chatter during cranking. Intermittent duty relays will burn out if left energized for a few hours. Always verify the mag switch is meant for its intended applications.

FIGURE 9-20 **A.** A magnetic switch used to switch high current flow to the **B.** starter solenoid. The chassis ECM supplies a ground to energize the control circuit.

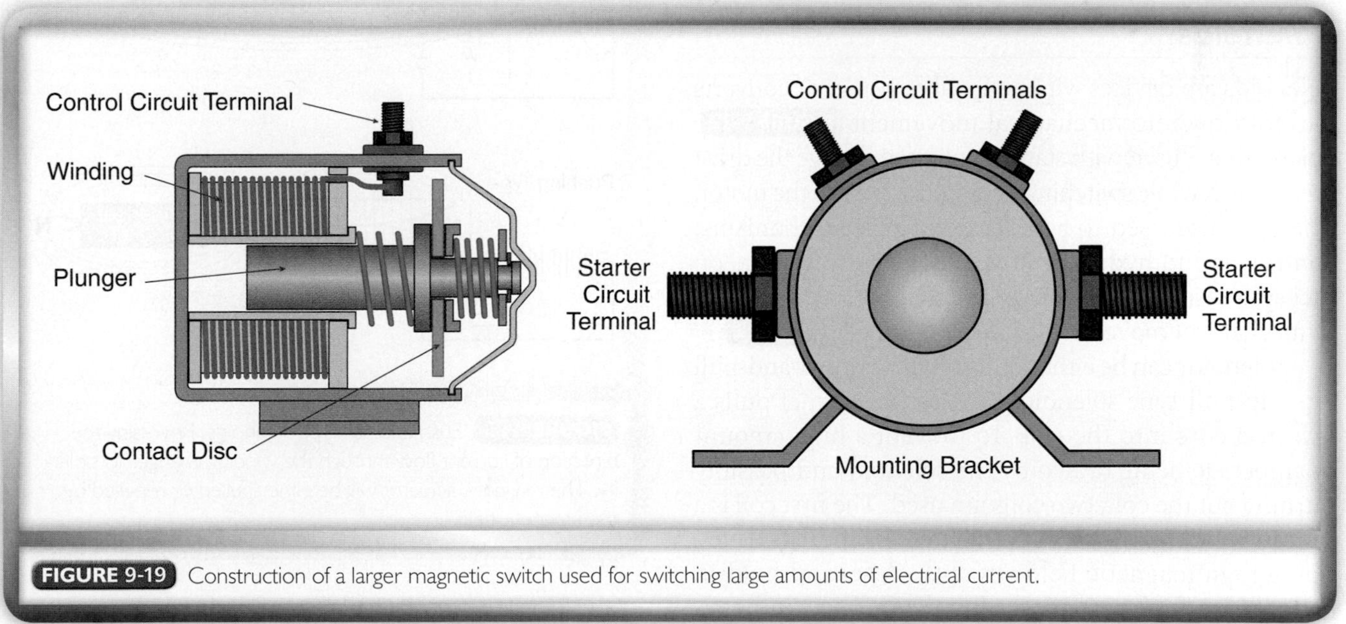

FIGURE 9-19 Construction of a larger magnetic switch used for switching large amounts of electrical current.

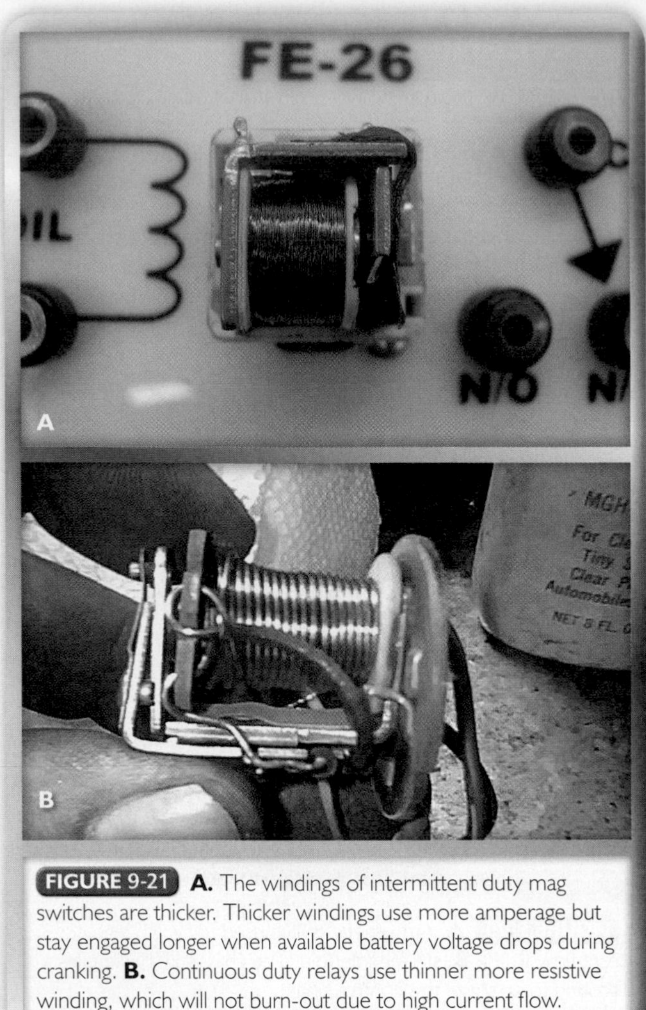

FIGURE 9-21 **A.** The windings of intermittent duty mag switches are thicker. Thicker windings use more amperage but stay engaged longer when available battery voltage drops during cranking. **B.** Continuous duty relays use thinner more resistive winding, which will not burn-out due to high current flow.

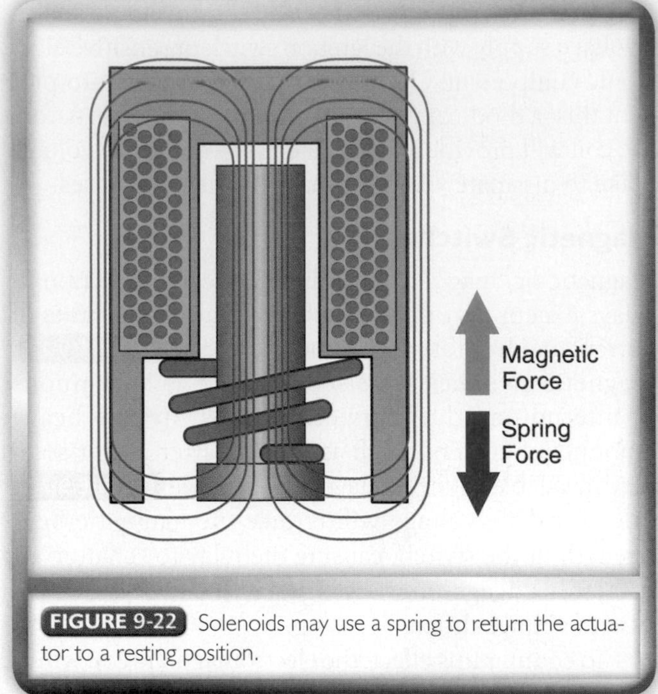

FIGURE 9-22 Solenoids may use a spring to return the actuator to a resting position.

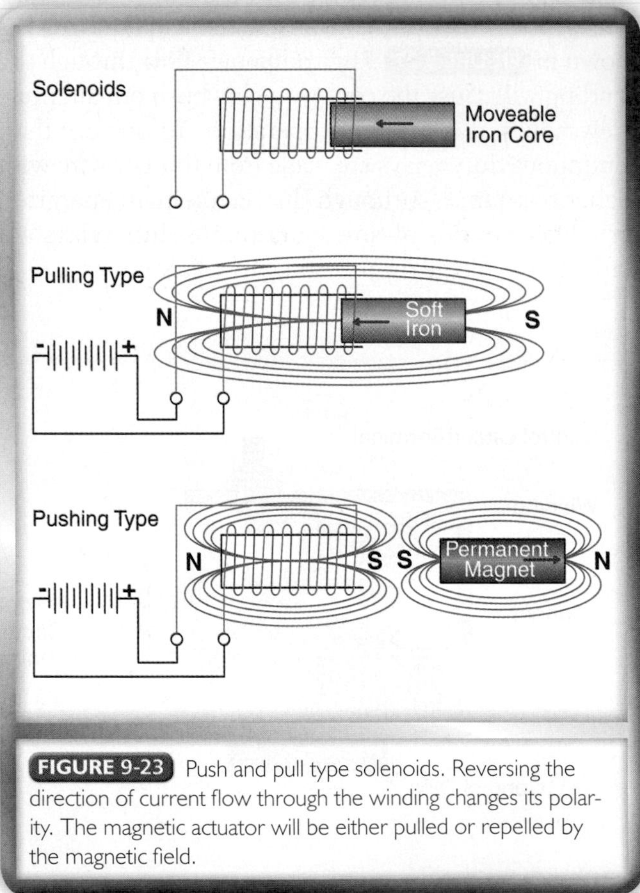

FIGURE 9-23 Push and pull type solenoids. Reversing the direction of current flow through the winding changes its polarity. The magnetic actuator will be either pulled or repelled by the magnetic field.

Solenoids

Solenoids are devices with a movable core that converts current flow into mechanical movement FIGURE 9-22. Solenoids are used with starter motors to engage the drive mechanism while switching heavy current into the motor. They are also used to actuate door lock mechanisms, control air and hydraulic flow, move shut-off levers on fuel systems, and any other place where electric control of mechanical movement is needed. See FIGURE 9-23.

Solenoids can be either pull-in type or push-and-pull type. In pull-type solenoids, an electro magnet pulls a soft iron core into the coil. To prevent a high amount of amperage being drawn by the solenoid and possibly burning out the coil, two coils are used. The first coil is a pull-in winding, which uses thick wire windings developing high magnetic field strength. A second hold-in coil "holds" the core in place after the pull-in winding is electrically disconnected.

Push-pull type solenoids use a permanent magnet instead of an iron core to produce bi-directional movement. By changing the polarity of the coil, the magnetic field around the permanent magnet core can either repel or attract the coil. Push-pull solenoids are commonly used to actuate electric door locks.

> **TECHNICIAN TIP**
>
> It is important for the pull-in winding of a solenoid to be electrically disconnected after a solenoid is initially engaged. The thinner, more resistive windings of the hold-in winding will take over from the pull-in windings and keep the core engaged. If the solenoid remained engaged, the pull-in windings would burn-out due to excessive current flow. Adjustment of solenoid travel is crucial to prevent this from happening by ensuring that the winding is not disconnected internally. Adjustable linkage on the solenoid plunger should be checked against manufacturer's specifications FIGURE 9-24.

FIGURE 9-24 This injection pump shut-off solenoid has a high amperage pull-in and low amperage hold-in winding to move the control rack from no-fuel position.

Capacitors

Capacitors are devices that act like electric shock absorbers and are capable of storing and discharging current much like a battery or hydraulic accumulator. Capacitors are simple devices made up of three components—two plates and an insulating material separating the plates FIGURE 9-25. The insulation is called a dielectric. The plates are not connected but each has a lead FIGURE 9-26. The dielectric material, an electrical insulator, separates the plates and is made from a variety of materials such as air, paper, plastic, ceramic, mica, and so on. When the lead of either plate is connected to a positive or negative of a power source, electrostatic induction occurs. This involves removing an electron from one plate, thereby creating a positive charge, which draws an electron to the opposite plate FIGURE 9-27. Alternatively, when an electron is added to one plate, an electron is driven away from the opposite plate.

The capacitor can hold the charge indefinitely because of the electrostatic attraction of the charges located on opposite plates. The area of the plates and properties of the dielectric determine the charge-holding capacity of the capacitor, which is measured in Farads. Maximum charge voltage will be the same as the power supply connected to the capacitor. A capacitor's voltage rating is based on the ability of the dielectric material to prevent internal arcing.

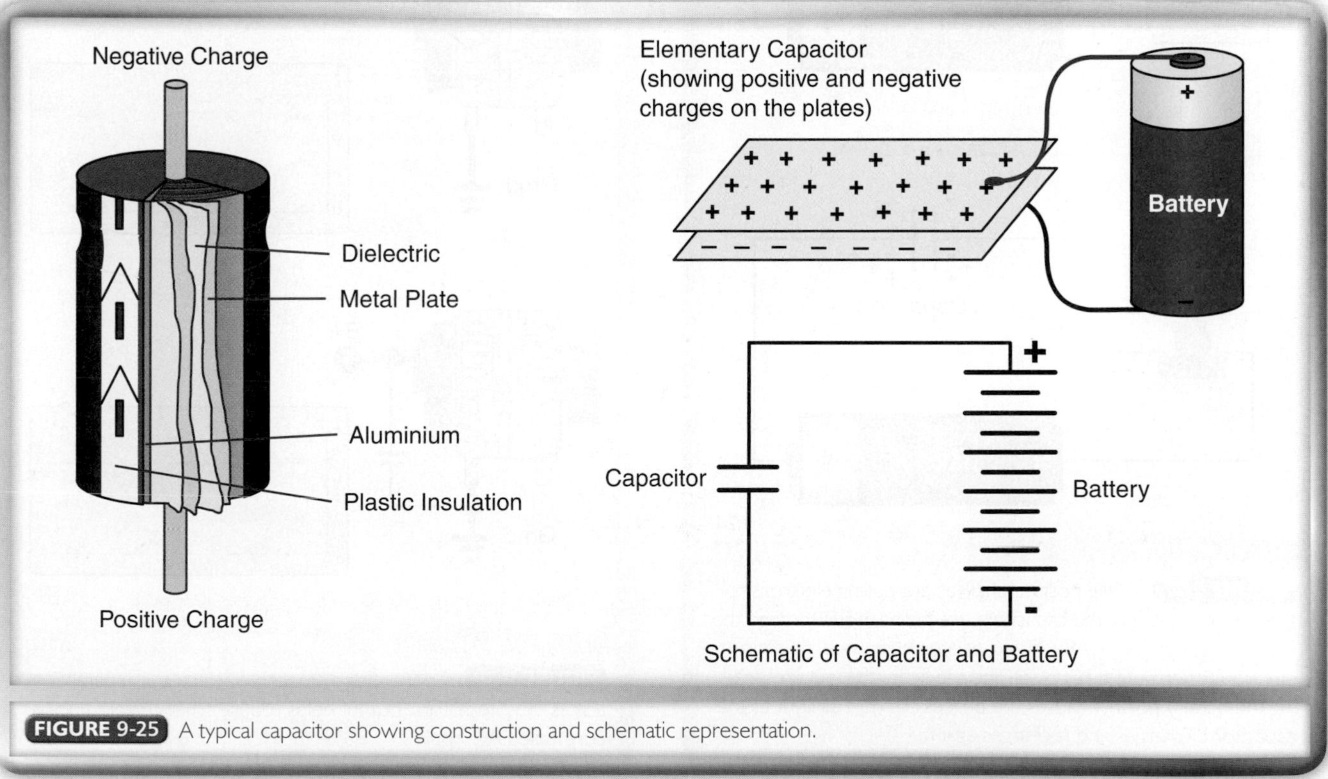

FIGURE 9-25 A typical capacitor showing construction and schematic representation.

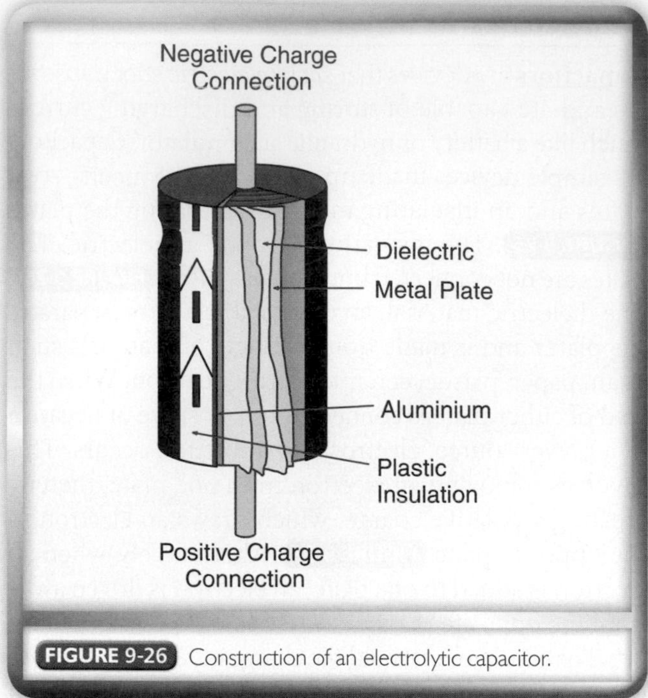

FIGURE 9-26 Construction of an electrolytic capacitor.

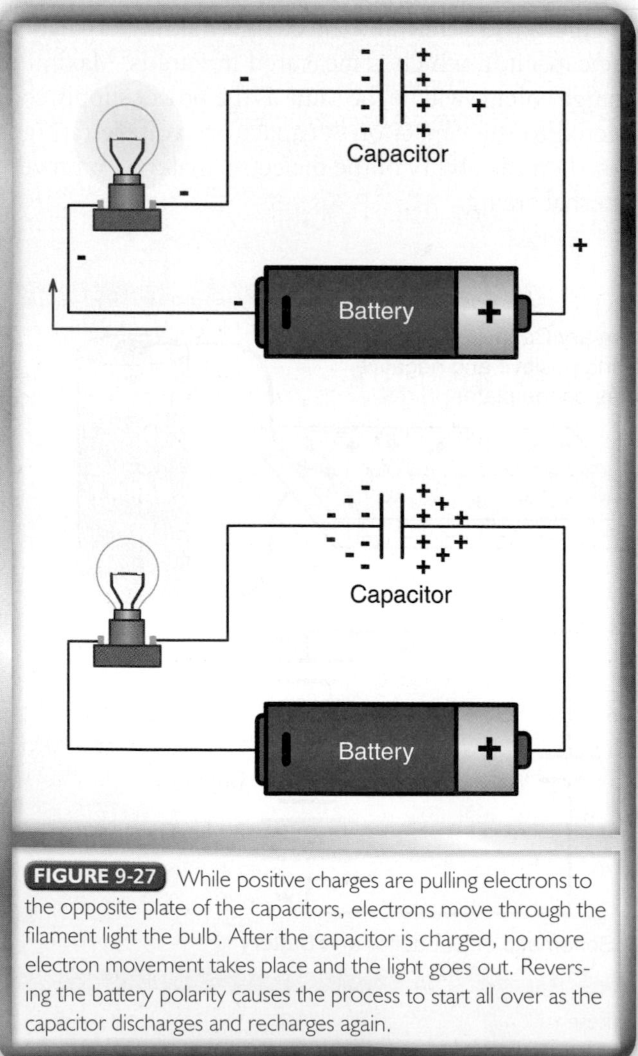

FIGURE 9-27 While positive charges are pulling electrons to the opposite plate of the capacitors, electrons move through the filament light the bulb. After the capacitor is charged, no more electron movement takes place and the light goes out. Reversing the battery polarity causes the process to start all over as the capacitor discharges and recharges again.

> **TECHNICIAN TIP**
>
> When checking for parasitic draws, remember that capacitor will pull current until they are charged and then stop. Test lights and meter connected between the battery and vehicle electrical system will light up momentarily until any on-board capacitors are charged. The alternator is one point where a large capacitor will draw current until charged. Connecting battery cables will often produce some sparking due to current draw from capacitors.

Applications

Capacitors can be discharged more rapidly than batteries, making them ideal for energizing injectors operating above battery voltage. They are also useful for smoothing out or "stiffening" voltage fluctuations that interfere with the operation of sensitive electronic components FIGURE 9-28. Connected across a power supply positive and negative terminal, the capacitor will absorb momentary increases in voltage and discharge the current when voltage drops for devices such as alternators and radios.

Capacitors can also absorb voltage spikes caused by inductive reactance when a magnetic field of a coil

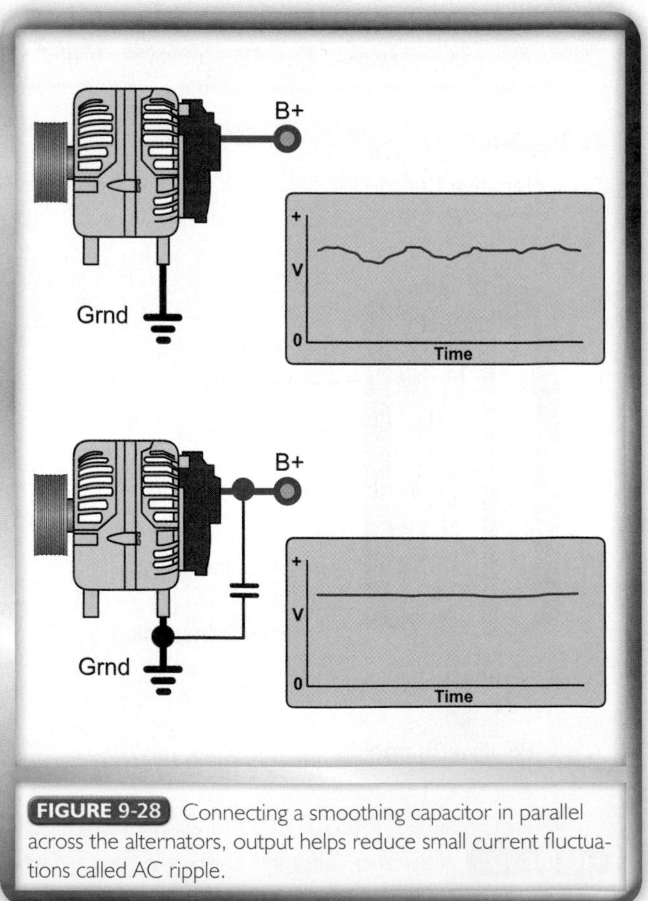

FIGURE 9-28 Connecting a smoothing capacitor in parallel across the alternators, output helps reduce small current fluctuations called AC ripple.

collapses. Ignition systems need capacitors connected in parallel to ignition coil switching devices to prevent damage that is caused during the build-up and collapse of magnetic fields.

Capacitors are also used as timers in circuits, such as wiper delay modules or dimming of dome lights. When connected to the base of a transistor, a charged capacitor can **forward bias** the transistor to modulate, or vary current flow through the emitter collector circuit. (This process is explained later in the section Forward Bias). By using a fixed- or variable-type resistor connected in series with the capacitor, the speed of the capacitors charge rate is controlled, as is how much current passes through the emitter collector circuit.

Testing Capacitors

Capacitors never wear out, but they can short out. An ohmmeter connected to each lead of the capacitor should show no continuity. It may briefly show some continuity as current from the meter charges the capacitor, but that should quickly diminish. Shorted plates will allow continuity. A meter will measure the time it takes to charge a capacitor with a small amount of voltage FIGURE 9-29.

Complex Electronic Controls

Complex electronic controls differ from the simple electric controls that regulate large amounts of current flow. A foundational component of electronic controls is the semiconductor. Common electronic semiconductor controls include diodes, transistors, integrated circuits (IC), microprocessors, and microcontrollers.

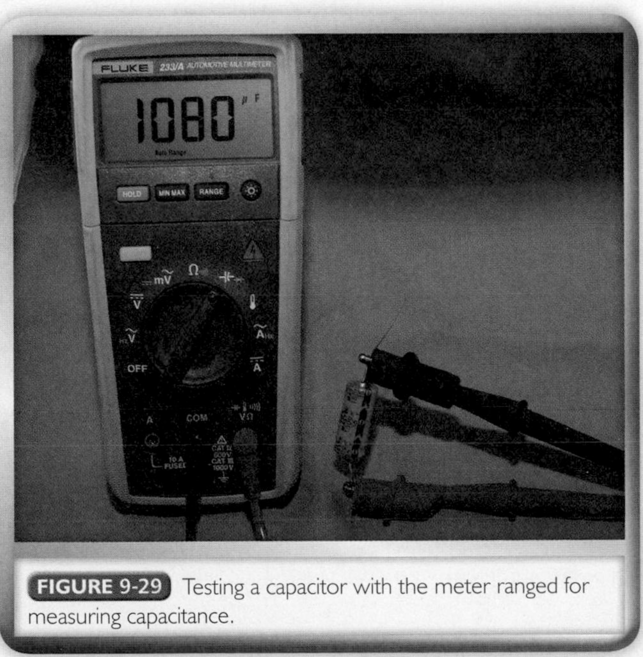

FIGURE 9-29 Testing a capacitor with the meter ranged for measuring capacitance.

Electronic Versus Electrical Control

In contrast to electrical and electromechanical devices, which conduct large amounts of current to produce heat, magnetism, motion, light, or sound, electronic circuit control operates invisibly using lower current flow. Electronic devices use semiconductor materials to control current flow rather than switches or resistors. Electrical signals, rather than large movements of current, pass through electronic circuits. Low-voltage signals are amplified, modulated, or digitized rather than switched or resisted.

What Are Semiconductors?

Semiconductors are the most important material used to construct electronic devices. This material can have properties of both conductors and insulators and can switch back and forth between either state using small electrostatic charges. By combining conductor and insulating materials to form semiconductors, the new material is changed to behave as either a conductor or insulator when under the influence of electric charges.

Silicon is an example of a material that is commonly transformed into a semiconductor. In its pure state, there are no free electrons in silicon crystals. Instead, the electrons are all arranged in tight bonds with adjacent atoms. By adding a small amount of impurity to the crystal when it's heated into a liquid state, silicon can become a conductor—but a poor one, which is why it is called a semiconductor.

Introducing impurities into the silicon is called doping. Two types of impurities introduced, or doped, with the silicon can create either a shifting positive or negative charge. Either free, unbound electrons are available in the silicon, or a shortage of bound electrons in the material can make the material unstable and needing electrons.

Phosphorous- and arsenic-doped silicon will leave free unbound electrons in silicon, making silicon a good conductor. Because the material has unbound electrons, it will have a movable negative charge, which explains why it is called **N material**. Doping silicon with boron or gallium leaves a deficit of electrons in the silicon, creating a movable positive charge or a **P material**. By themselves, P- and N-type semiconductors are not of much use. When sandwiched together, however, they form some of the most useful electronic components created FIGURE 9-30.

Diodes

Sandwiching a P- and N- semiconductor material produces a diode. Diodes are electronic devices that operate as one-way electrical check valves. Current can flow in only one direction through a diode and is blocked in

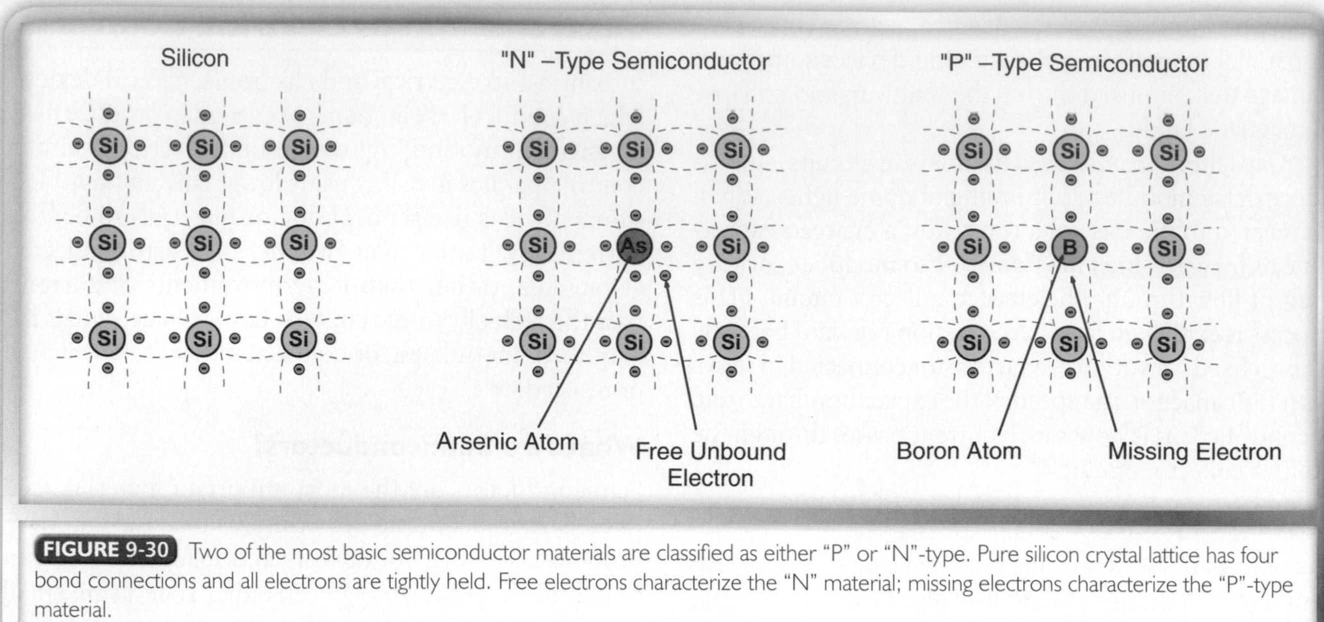

FIGURE 9-30 Two of the most basic semiconductor materials are classified as either "P" or "N"-type. Pure silicon crystal lattice has four bond connections and all electrons are tightly held. Free electrons characterize the "N" material; missing electrons characterize the "P"-type material.

another. Diodes have this ability because of the way P and N material behaves. When the N material is connected to a positive potential of a battery and the P material to the negative terminal, the extra negative electrons in the N material are attracted to the positive terminal of the battery. Likewise, the positive holes in the P material are attracted to the negative terminal of the battery. At the junction point between the N and P material, no current flows. That is because only insulating material remains in this area—there are no holes or electrons FIGURE 9-31. Therefore, at the junction, the positive holes and the free electrons are each moving away from one another.

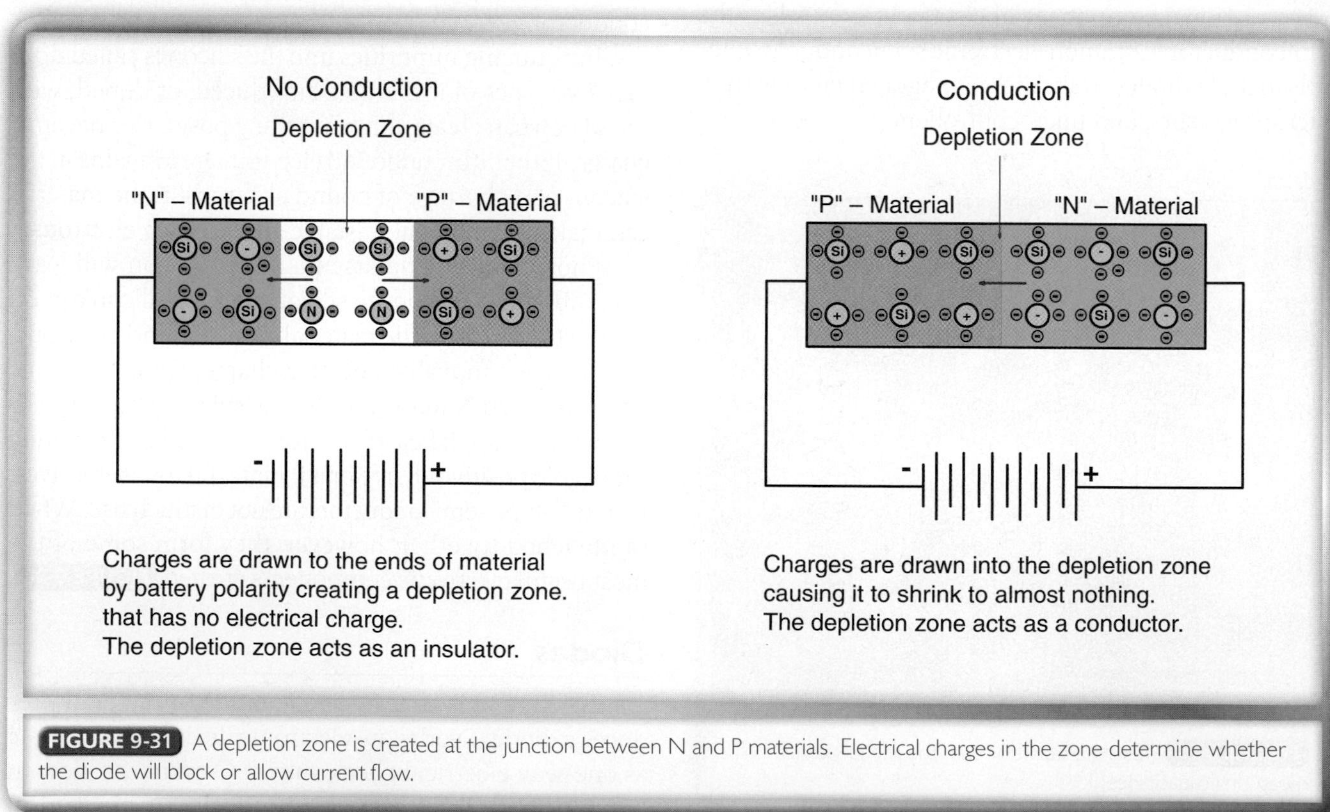

FIGURE 9-31 A depletion zone is created at the junction between N and P materials. Electrical charges in the zone determine whether the diode will block or allow current flow.

Forward Bias

If the battery polarity is reversed, connecting the positive terminal with P material and negative with N material, the diode readily conducts current FIGURE 9-32. That is because free electrons in the N material are driven towards the junction area by the excess electrons at the negative terminal of the battery FIGURE 9-33. The holes in the P material are also repelled by the positively charged battery terminal. At the junction between the N and P material, holes and free electrons join and all the material becomes conductive. Movement of the electrons into the positive holes and onto the battery positive terminal depletes the N material of electrons. More electrons are drawn into the N material, causing current to continuously flow through the diode. The voltage differential required for electron flow across the junction, also called barrier voltage, is between 0.3 and 0.7-volts FIGURE 9-34.

When a diode conducts current, it is said to be in **forward bias**. When the diode blocks flow, it is in **reverse bias**. Diodes will block current in reverse bias until the

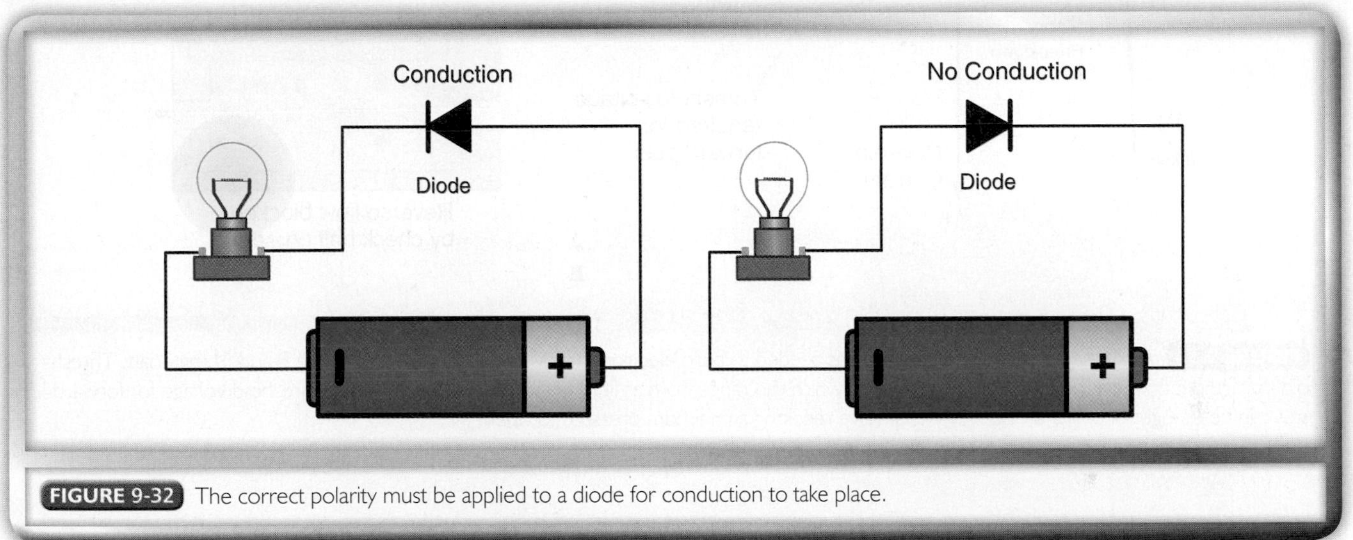

FIGURE 9-32 The correct polarity must be applied to a diode for conduction to take place.

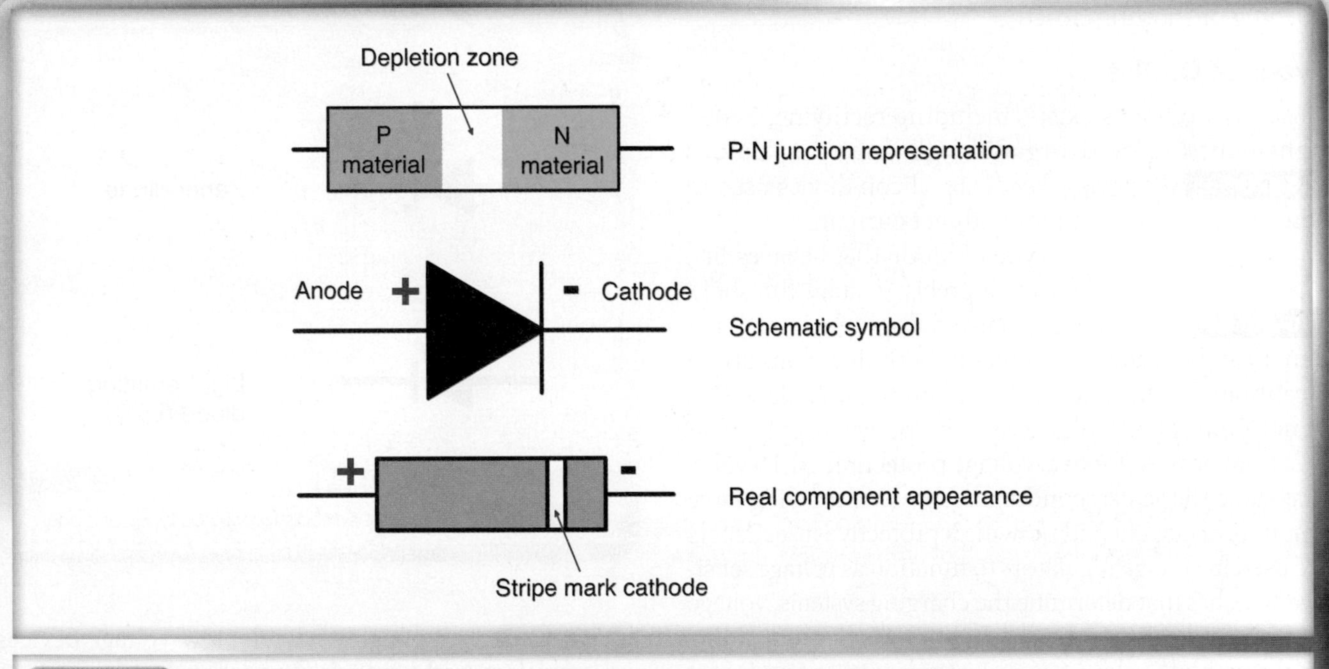

FIGURE 9-33 Symbol for a diode. Remember the negative side as having a negative line turned 90 degrees. The arrow points the direction of flow using conventional theory. Electron flow is in the opposite direction of the arrow. The arrowhead can also be thought of as a loudspeaker indicating the direction of current flow. A line on a diode body designates the negative or cathode side.

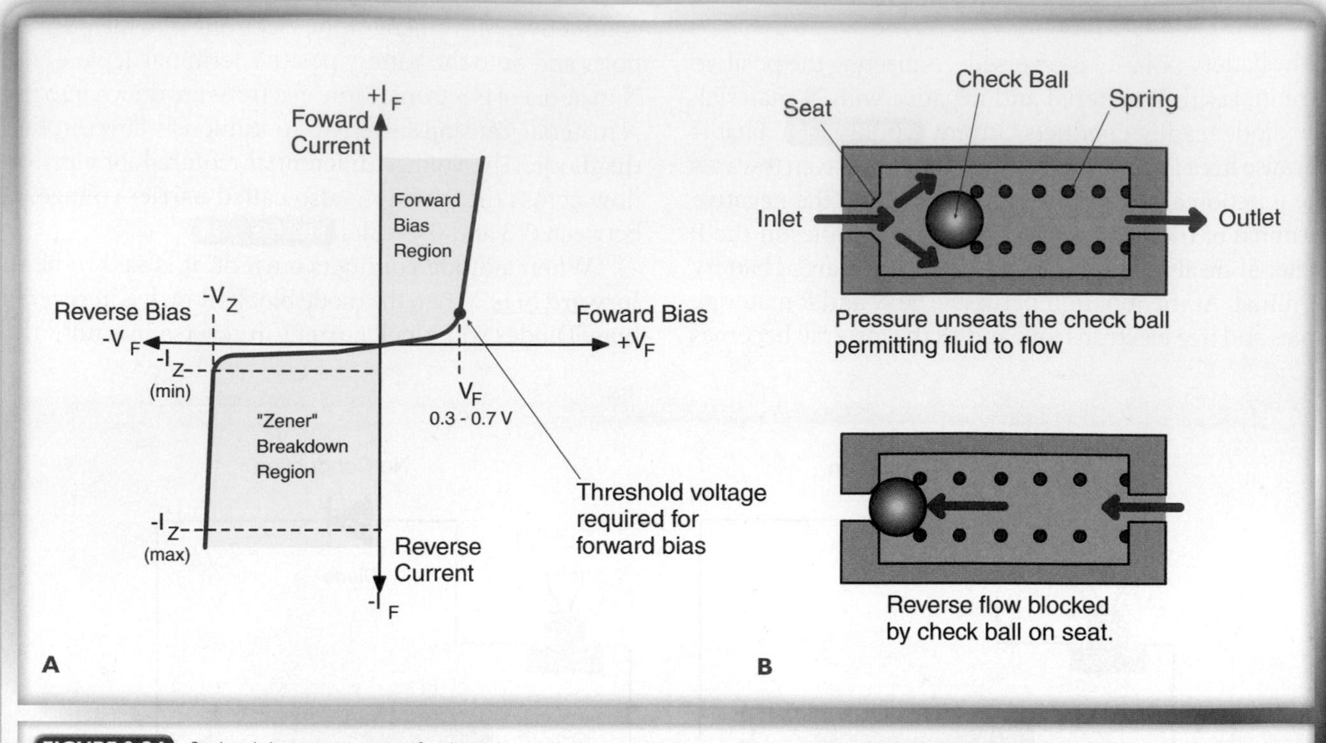

FIGURE 9-34 **A.** A minimum amount of voltage is needed to push electrons across the junction between the P and N materials. Threshold voltage depends on the type of materials used, which can range from as little as 0.3 volts to 0.7 volts. **B.** Threshold voltage for forward bias can be thought of as like a one way check valve requiring a minimum pressure to open.

voltage reaches the diodes' **Zener point**. The Zener point for a silicon diode is anywhere from 20 to 70 volts. At that point, the diode will be destroyed by either permanently opening or shorting closed.

Types of Diodes

A variety of diodes exists, including rectifying, Zener, light-emitting, and organic light-emitting diodes FIGURE 9-35. *Rectifying diodes* are silicon diodes used to convert alternating current to direct current.

Zener diodes are a type of diode that behaves like a typical silicon diode up to a precise voltage threshold FIGURE 9-36. By using specialized doping material, the Zener can be made to conduct in both directions above a calibrated voltage level. For example, a diode with a Zener point of 15 volts across the power supply of an ECM can be used for overvoltage protection. At 15 volts, that same diode can conduct both ways, drawing large amounts of current and blowing a protective fuse. Zeners are used in voltage regulators to function as voltage sensitive switches that determine the charging systems, voltage set point. The Zener diode symbol has a Z-shaped line on the cathode side.

Light-emitting diodes (LEDs) are used in a large variety of digital displays and lighting applications and are replacing incandescent lighting in most applications FIGURE 9-37. These highly reliable, low-voltage devices are manufactured using different doping materials to produce different colors. Recent LED doping materials produce white light diodes. **Photodiodes** will forward bias when light strikes the diode FIGURE 9-38.

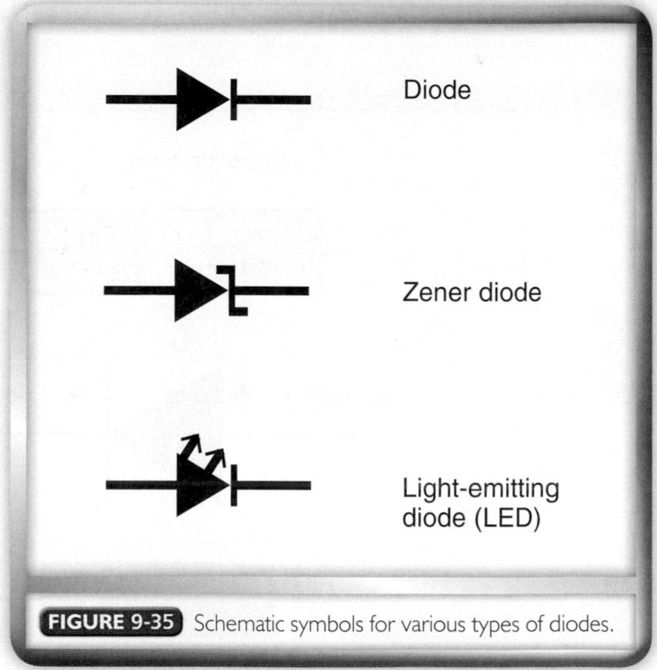

FIGURE 9-35 Schematic symbols for various types of diodes.

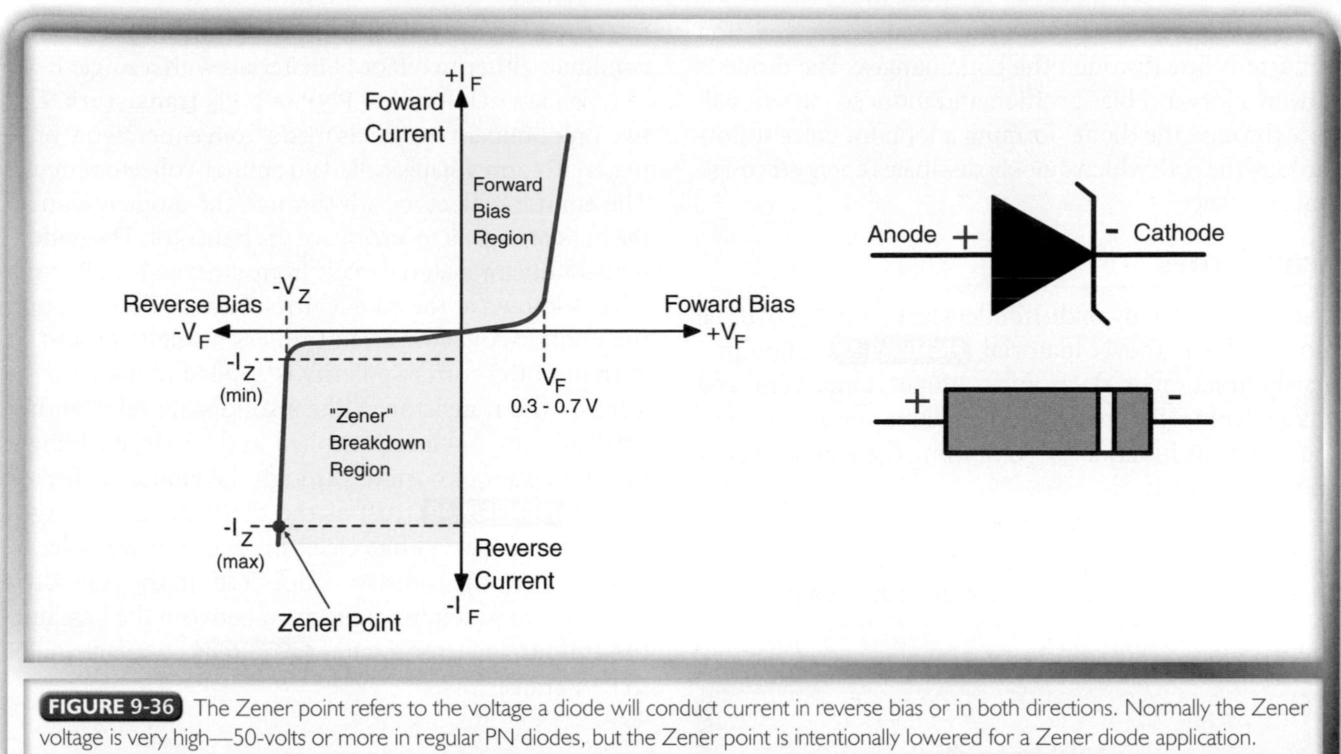

FIGURE 9-36 The Zener point refers to the voltage a diode will conduct current in reverse bias or in both directions. Normally the Zener voltage is very high—50-volts or more in regular PN diodes, but the Zener point is intentionally lowered for a Zener diode application.

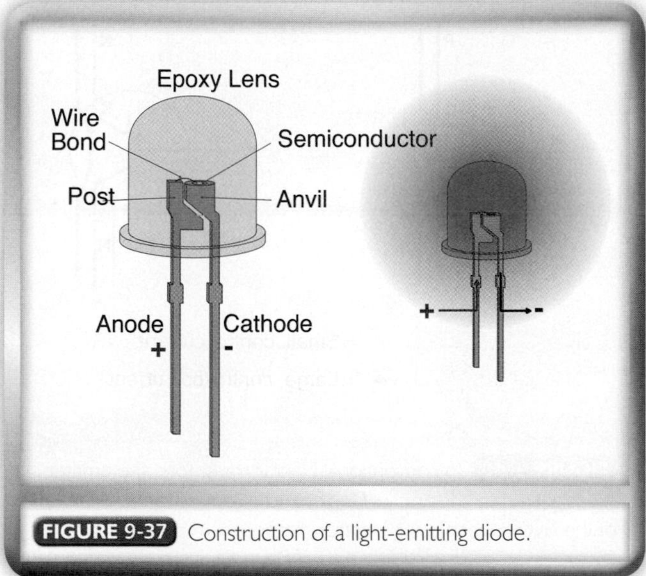

FIGURE 9-37 Construction of a light-emitting diode.

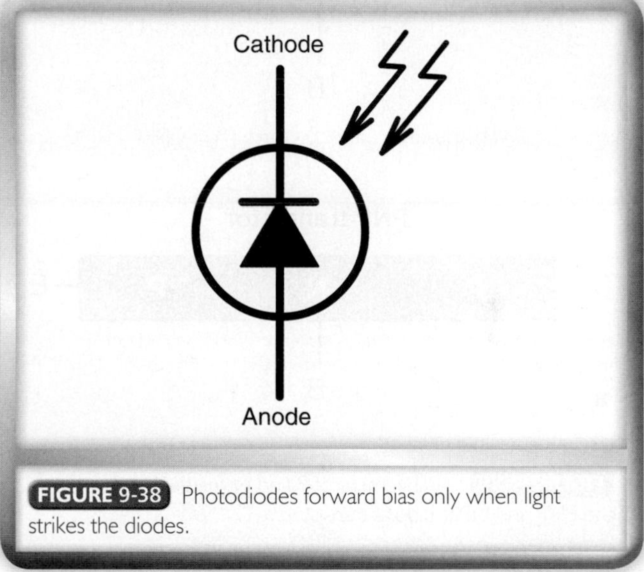

FIGURE 9-38 Photodiodes forward bias only when light strikes the diodes.

<u>**Organic light-emitting diodes (OLEDs)**</u> are the latest LED technology. Rather than using minerals, the silicon or germanium material is replaced with carbon-based semiconductors. Currently OLEDs are used for display screens, but OLEDs do not yet have the efficiency or lifespan of LEDs.

Clamping Application of Diodes

One important application of diodes is to suppress high-voltage spikes caused by self-induction in coils. The rapid collapse of a coil's magnetic field induces high-voltage current in the opposite direction of the flowing current that originally produced the magnetic field. Induced voltage can be hundreds of volts, and so can damage any sensitive components connected to the circuit. Arcing of switch contacts will also take place.

To prevent this from occurring, a diode can be connected in parallel with a coil, such as one found in a relay or AC clutch. When the coil is energized, the diode is connected to be in reverse bias, so all current flows through the coil. When the circuit is open, however, the direction of current flow through the coil changes. The diode is now in a forward bias position and induced current will flow through the diode, forming a loop for current flow through the coil, which quickly dissipates energy through coil resistance.

Transistors

Transistors are semiconductor devices composed of three blocks of a P and N material FIGURE 9-39. They primarily function as electronic switches, amplifiers, and voltage-controlled resistors. The name transistor communicates its function by combining the words resistor and transformer.

Since their appearance in commercial applications in the 1950s, transistors have proliferated, and a very large variety of transistors is available today. A representative type of transistor is the **bipolar transistor** type that combines either two P or N materials with a single P- or N-type material, forming **PNP** or **NPN transistors**. The two predominant materials made from either two P or N materials form what is called an emitter-collector circuit. The emitter-collector path through the diode conducts the bulk of current in and out of the transistor. The middle semiconductor material made from either an N or P forms what is known as the base. Current cannot flow through the emitter-collector circuit unless a small amount of current of the correct polarity is applied to the base. In a sense, the transistor is like a solid state relay with a small amount of current applied to the base, enabling a larger amount of current through the emitter-collector circuit FIGURE 9-40. Just as the diode needed charges on each end to send free electrons and positive holes to the junction, the transistors does too. In the transistor though, two junctions are formed between the base and the emitter-collector circuit. TABLE 9-3 compares NPN to PNP transistors.

A
NPN transistor
C N P N E
B

B
PNP transistor
C P N P E
B

FIGURE 9-39 Arrangement of P and N materials comprising the PNP and NPN bipolar transistors.

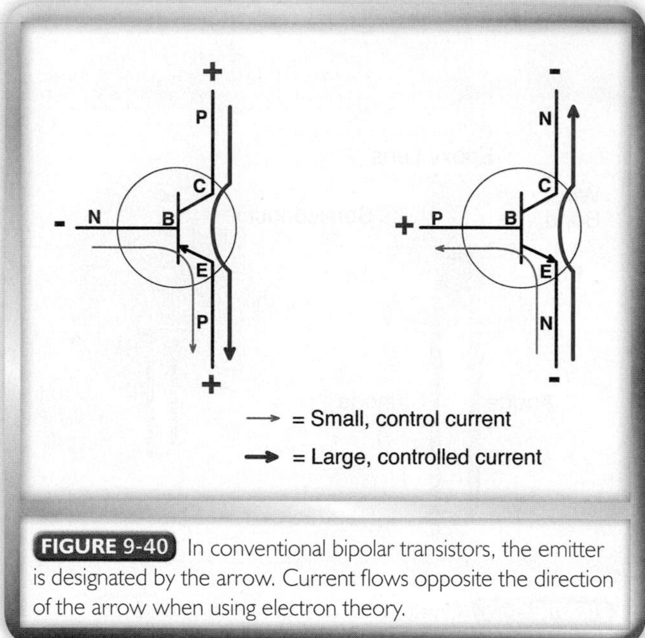

FIGURE 9-40 In conventional bipolar transistors, the emitter is designated by the arrow. Current flows opposite the direction of the arrow when using electron theory.

TABLE 9-3: NPN-Type and PNP-Type Transistors

NPN Type	Forward Bias – Conduction	PNP Type	Forward Bias – Conduction
Emitter–N	Negative polarity	Emitter–P	Positive polarity
Base–P	Positive polarity	Base–N	Negative polarity
Collector–N	Positive polarity	Collector–P	Positive polarity

Transistor Bias

To conduct current, the NPN transistor requires the base to have a positive voltage applied to it to allow current to pass across the emitter-collector circuit. When current flows through the emitter-collector circuit, the transistor is said to forward bias. In a PNP transistor, the base must be negative to forward bias the transistor.

To achieve the greatest current flow across the emitter-collector circuit (rather than the emitter base or collector base), the P and N materials are doped differently FIGURE 9-41. The emitter of a transistor is the most heavily doped, producing the greatest number of free electrons or holes depending on the material. Slightly less doping is used in the collector circuit; the base is relatively thin, and has the least amount of doping with impurities.

In the transistor symbols, the arrow that designates the emitter points in the direction of current flow (according to conventional theory). The collector is opposite the emitter, and the base is located at the bottom of the "T." Electron flow will take place in the opposite direction of the arrows in both transistors.

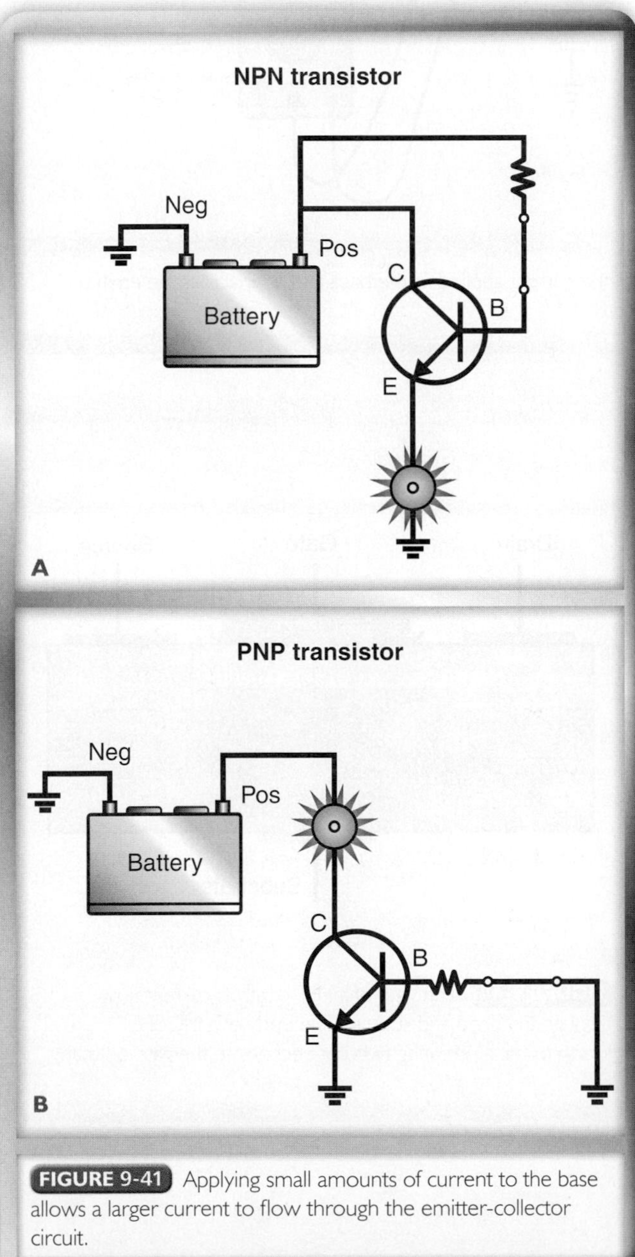

FIGURE 9-41 Applying small amounts of current to the base allows a larger current to flow through the emitter-collector circuit.

Transistor Applications

A small amount of current applied to the base will produce a much larger flow of current through the emitter-collector circuit. The proportion of increase in current flow is referred to as gain FIGURE 9-42. When a transistor can control its gain proportional to the base current, it can be used as an amplifier. Alternatively, a transistor can be used as a relay in locations where a small amount of base current can switch a larger amount of current either on or off. Injector drivers in an ECM are a common application for switching transistors.

MOSFET Field Effect Transistor

Field effect transistors (FETs) FIGURE 9-43 are built and operate very differently in many ways, but they generally have similar applications to bipolar transistors. Instead of an emitter-collector circuit, the P- and N-type substrate equivalents are labelled gate, source, and drain FIGURE 9-44. The gate controls current flow between source and drain—similar to the base control of the emitter-collector circuit of a bipolar transistor. MOSFETs are FETs made from metal-oxide semiconductor material. MOSFETS are discussed in detail in the Principles of Electricity chapter. MOSFETs are universally considered to have an insulated gate separate from the body of the transistor. What is unique about a FET is the body can also operate as a gate. That means two separate circuits can connect to a FET and open the gate. In a sense, the gate is like a fourth terminal on the FET, and electric charges applied to the body can influence electrical conduction between the source and drain.

FETs are the most common transistor used in digital and analog circuits today. They also have more features and better operating characteristics than bipolar transistors. Not only can they operate as switches and amplifiers, FETs:

- *Increase current flow exponentially through the source and drain circuit compared with the gate voltage.*
- *Operate as voltage controlled resistors.* Varying the voltage between the gate and body changes the conductivity between the drain and source. This feature, called the body effect or body-gate, allows FETs to be programmed to operate as virtual fuses and cut

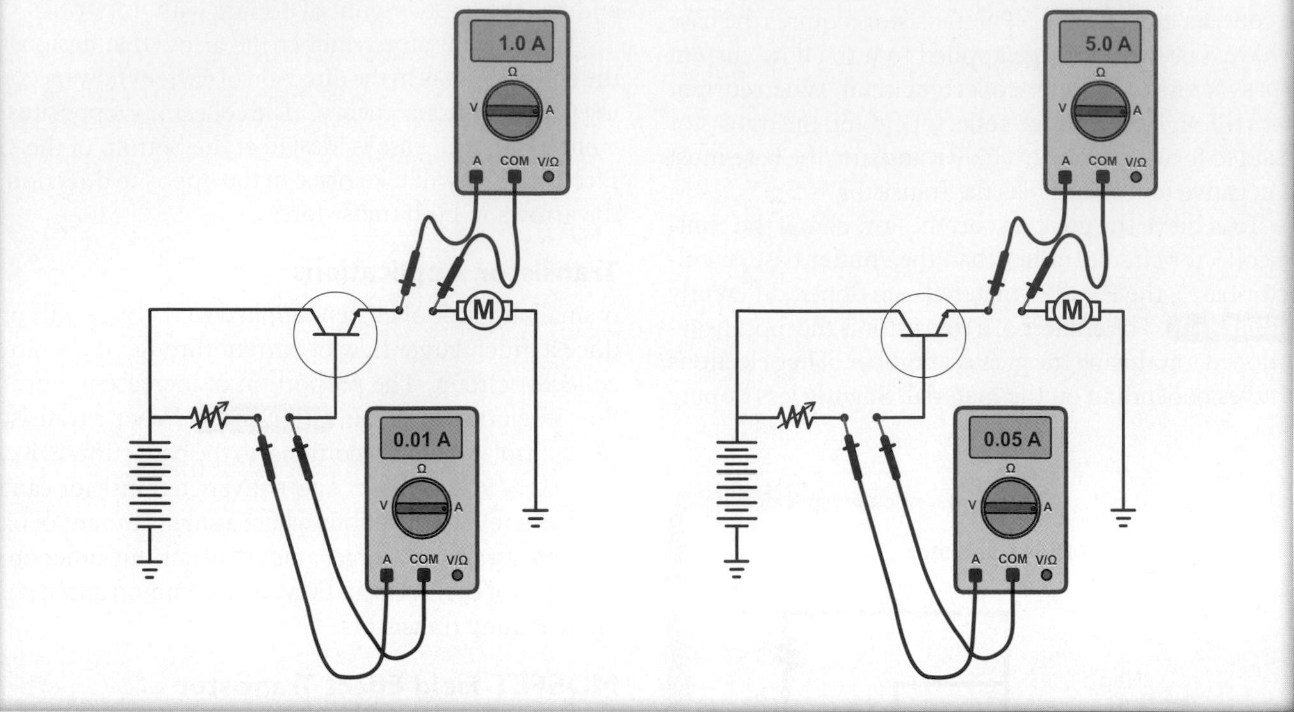

FIGURE 9-42 Transistor gain is observed by observing the ratio between the current applied to the base and flow across the emitter-collector circuit.

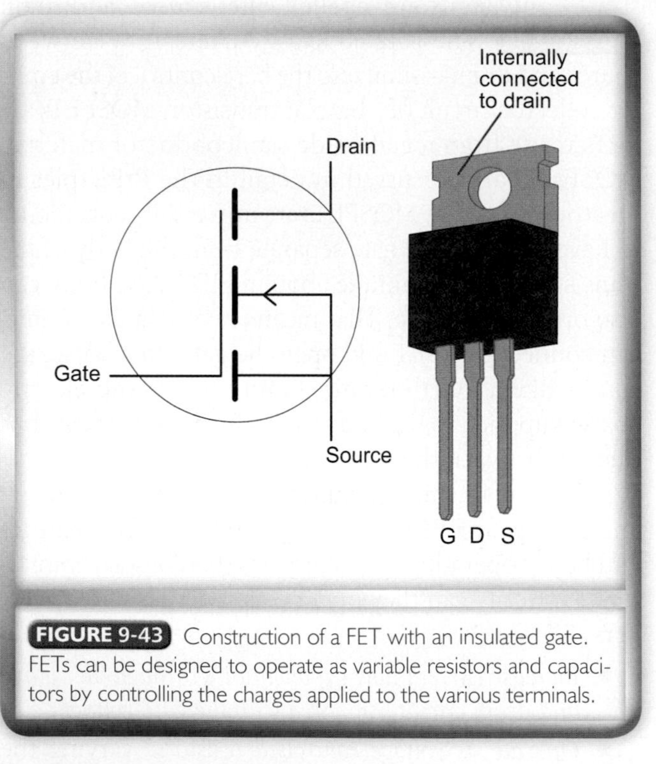

FIGURE 9-43 Construction of a FET with an insulated gate. FETs can be designed to operate as variable resistors and capacitors by controlling the charges applied to the various terminals.

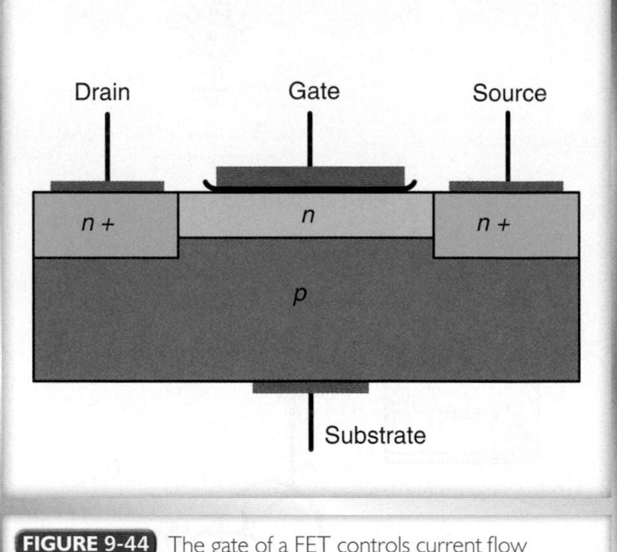

FIGURE 9-44 The gate of a FET controls current flow through the drain and source. The body of a MOSFET is like a fourth terminal, creating two connections to the gate on many FETs.

current flow to output devices drawing excessive current. Only voltage is affected, not amperage.

- *Have voltage blocking capabilities superior to bipolar transistors.* FETs can therefore operate as switches, blocking voltage of 120 volts in the OFF state.
- *Conduct large amounts of current without damage.* A single FET found as an output driver in an ECM can continuously conduct 30 amps in its ON state FIGURE 9-45. While controlling over 2,000 watts (12.5 volts at 160 amps) of power, they will emit only 100 watts of heat. This happens because there is virtually no voltage drop through an FET across a junction point (bipolar transistors have that drop). The output circuits of all multiplexed electrical devices—whether they are lighting, body accessories, or auxiliary electrical devices—will use FETs.

Virtual Fusing

FETs can be configured into pairs that are capable of measuring the amount of current being conducted by the FET. This information is sent back to the microcontroller enabling the FET to be switched-off if the FET is conducting too much current for its rating. Grounded circuits or simply circuits with too many loads would trigger this event.

Virtual fusing is the description given to the use of FETs that replace a fuse or circuit breaker in the individual high-side controlled circuits. Virtual fusing is also designed to imitate the characteristics of SAE Type I and II circuit breakers. SAE Type I circuit breakers reset automatically, typically trying to reset every ½-second. If the current flow is still excessive, the cycle time becomes even longer with every successive reset. SAE Type II circuit

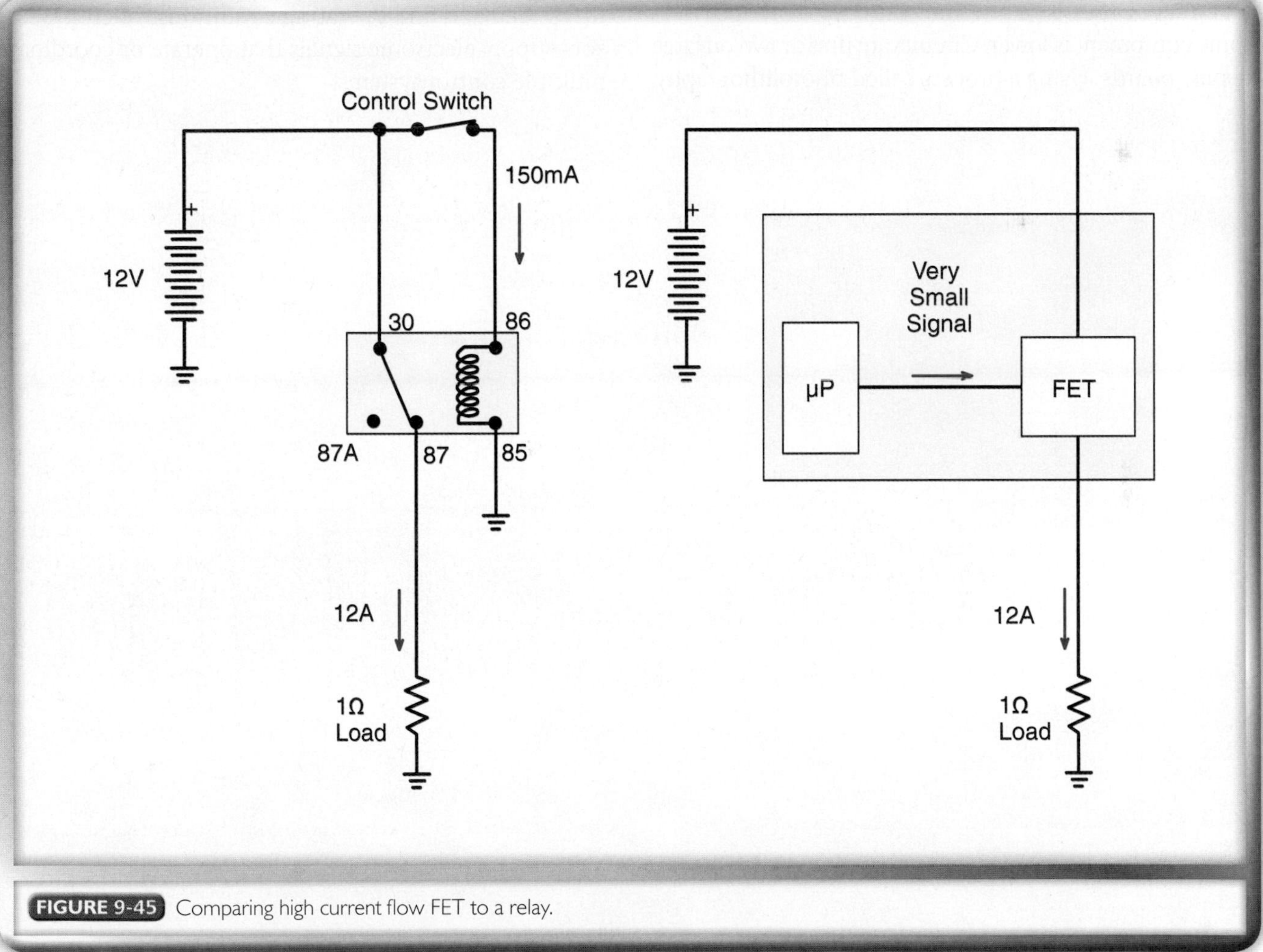

FIGURE 9-45 Comparing high current flow FET to a relay.

breakers reset when the load is disconnected and reapplied or, in this case, the key is cycled on and off. Software instructions are used to calculate a combination of time amperage flows through the circuit to determine whether the load is excessive. A diagnostic fault code can be set and stored even after the FET is cycled back on. Virtual fusing is also discussed in the Electric Circuits and Circuit Protection chapter.

Integrated Circuits (IC)

Integrated circuits (IC) are semiconductor devices having anywhere from a hundred to over a billion transistors embedded into a single silicon wafer. Diodes, resistors, and capacitors are also embedded into the chip, packaged in a ceramic or plastic body with multiple pins forming input and output connection points. ICs are capable of processing digital on/off signals or analog signals that vary continuously with time. Because integrated circuits are not built one transistor at a time, the cost to produce electronic equipment is lower. Circuits are first drawn on large display boards. Using a process called photolithography, the circuits are photographically reduced from dozens of square feet to nanometers and then etched onto silicon wafers. Miniaturization of IC circuitry makes devices smaller and faster while consuming less power. Two common applications of integrated circuits are microprocessors and microcontrollers **FIGURE 9-46**.

Microprocessors

Microprocessors use integrated circuitry but are formed from vast numbers of transistors, resistors, and capacitors in multiple layers. They contain memory and logic circuits that enable them to operate using sophisticated programmed sets of stored instructions. Sensors supply processors with data, and an arithmetic unit performs calculations using algorithms based on programmed instructions. Algorithms are simply mathematical formulas used to solve problems, such as when to fire an injector or how long to energize an injector coil based on driver demand and operating conditions. Microprocessors supply electronic signals that operate or coordinate multiple control systems.

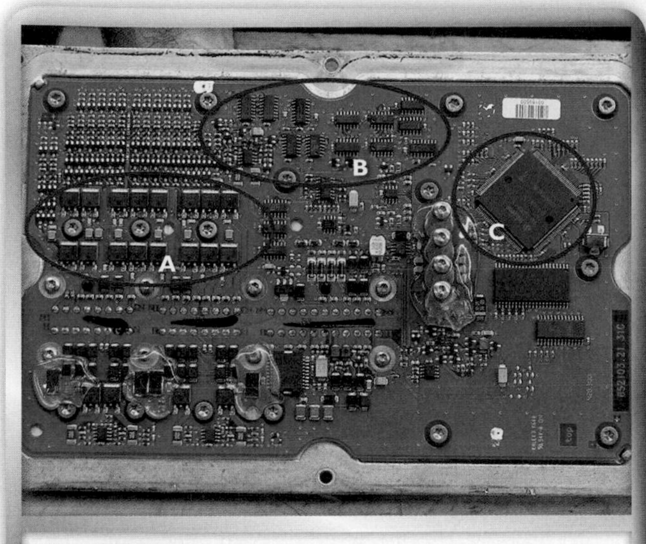

FIGURE 9-46 The microprocessor execute software code. The operation of microcontrollers on this board is coordinated by the microprocessor. FETs are used to conduct high current to output devices are called drivers. **A.** FET drivers. **B.** 2-bit microcontrollers. **C.** 32-bit microprocessors.

Microcontrollers

A microcontroller is an integrated circuit containing an arithmetic logic core, limited memory, and programmable input and output pins. Microcontrollers are embedded devices used inside sensor controllers for electric motors and stepper motors, control modules for injector drivers, instrument clusters, body controls, and other vehicle systems. Microcontrollers differ from microprocessors in that they have minimal requirements for memory and software and use no operating system. Typical input and output devices operated by microcontrollers include sensors and stepper motors. Microcontrollers often operate more like digital signal processors (DSPs). For example, a microcontroller's output may be a pulse-width-modulated electrical signal, making it possible for it to control resistive loads, motors, ABS solenoids, and engine controls.

Wrap-up

Ready to Review

- Electric circuits use control devices to direct the flow of current. Controls can be simple electrical or complex electronic devices.
- Switches are the simplest circuit control device. Opening and closing switches completes or breaks a circuit's electrical pathway.
- Simple switches are categorized by the number of input and output terminals they have and by their operation.
- Smart switches can function as digital inputs to electronic control systems.
- Resistors in commercial vehicles are typically fixed, stepped, or variable.
- Fixed-type resistors are designed to conduct either heavy or light amounts of current.
- Stepped resistors are made from two or more wire-wound resistors.
- Common variable resistors include rheostats, potentiometers, thermistors, and photoresistors.
- Relays use a small amount of current to switch a larger amount of current. As such, they eliminate voltage drop caused by resistance and eliminate the use of heavy conductors inside the cab.
- A typical relay has a control circuit and a load circuit.
- Magnetic switches are identical in function to relays except that they switch even larger amounts of current and have atypical dimensions.
- Solenoids are devices with a movable core that converts current flow into mechanical movement.
- Solenoids can be either pull-in type or push-and-pull type. In pull-type solenoids, an electro magnet pulls a soft iron core into the coil. Push-pull type solenoids use a permanent magnet instead of an iron core to produce bi-directional movement.
- Capacitors act like electric shock absorbers and are capable of storing and discharging current. Capacitors are made up of three components—two plates and an insulating material separating the plates.
- In contrast to electrical and electromechanical devices, which conduct large amounts of current, electronic circuit control operates invisibly using lower current flow.
- Semiconductors are the most important material used to construct electronic devices. This material can have properties of both conductors and insulators and can switch back and forth between either state using small electrostatic charges.
- Semiconductors are created by introducing impurities into silicon in a process called doping. The impurities introduced can be of several materials, and the material used creates a shifting positive P or negative N charge.
- Sandwiching a P- and N- semiconductor material produces a diode, which is an electronic device through which current can flow in only one direction.
- When a diode conducts current, it is said to be in forward bias. When the diode blocks flow, it is in reverse bias.
- Types of diodes include rectifying, Zener, light-emitting, and organic light-emitting diodes.
- A critical function of diodes is to suppress high-voltage spikes caused by self-induction in coils.
- Transistors are semiconductor devices composed of three blocks of a P and N material. They primarily function as electronic switches, amplifiers, and voltage-controlled resistors.
- Transistors can be used as relays and as current amplifiers.
- Field effect transistors (FETs) are the most common transistor used in digital and analog circuits today. FETs can also be configured to perform as virtual fuses.
- Integrated circuits (IC) are semiconductor devices having anywhere from a hundred to over a billion transistors embedded into a single silicon wafer.
- Two common applications of integrated circuits are microprocessors and microcontrollers.
- Microprocessors contain memory and logic circuits that enable them to operate using sophisticated programmed sets of stored instructions. By contrast, microcontrollers have minimal requirements for memory and software and contain no operating system.

Vocabulary Builder

bipolar transistor A transistor that combines either two P or N materials with a single P or N-type material forming PNP or NPN transistors.

capacitor A circuit-control device made up of two plates separated by an insulating material.

forward bias A situation in which a diode conducts current.

light-emitting diode (LED) A diode that produces light in different colors depending on the doping material used in its manufacture.

N material A material with a movable negative charge.

negative temperature coefficient (NTC) thermistor A thermistor in which resistance decreases as the temperature increases.

NPN transistor A type of bipolar transistor with two blocks of N material and one block of P material.

organic light-emitting diode (OLED) A light-emitting diode that uses carbon-based semiconductor material.

P material A material with a movable positive charge.

photodiode A diode that will forward bias only when light strikes it.

photoresistor A semiconductor-type of resistor in which resistance decreases as light intensity increases.

PNP transistor A type of bipolar transistor with two blocks of P material and one block of N material.

positive temperature coefficient (PTC) thermistor A thermistor in which resistance increases as the temperature increases.

potentiometer A variable resistor with three connections—one at each end of a resistive path, and a third sliding contact that moves along the resistive pathway.

reverse bias A situation in which a diode blocks current flow.

rheostat A variable resistor constructed of a fixed input terminal and a variable output terminal, which vary current flow by passing current through a long resistive tightly coiled wire.

Zener diode A type of diode that behaves like a typical silicon diode up to a precise voltage threshold called the Zener point. After it reaches the Zener point voltage, the diode conducts in both directions.

Zener point The voltage at which a diode will conduct current in both directions instead of just one.

Review Questions

1. Which of the following statements is correct concerning electrical control devices?
   a. By means of electrical control devices, current may be started, stopped, slowed amplified, or simply redirected.
   b. Circuit controls can be as simple as a switch, resister, electromagnetic relay, solenoid, and timing circuit using a capacitor.
   c. They can also be more complex electronic devices such as diodes, transistors, integrated circuits, microcontrollers, and microprocessors.
   d. All of the choices are correct.
2. Which of the following is NOT a type of switch?
   a. Toggle
   b. Slider
   c. Momentary contact
   d. Temperature sensitive
3. Which type of resistor is commonly found in commercial vehicles?
   a. Fixed
   b. Stepped
   c. Variable
   d. All of the choices are correct.
4. Which of the following is correct concerning stepped resistors?
   a. Stepped resistors are made from two or more wire-wound resistors.
   b. A common application for this type of resistor is in a blower motor speed control circuit.
   c. Locating the resistor in the blower motor housing prevents premature burn-out of the resistor.
   d. All of the choices are correct.
5. Which of the following is correct concerning solenoids?
   a. Solenoids are devices with a movable core that converts current flow into mechanical movement.
   b. Solenoids are used with starter motors to engage the drive mechanism while switching heavy current into the motor.
   c. They are also used to actuate door lock mechanisms, control air and hydraulic flow, move shut-off levers on fuel systems, and any other place where electric control of mechanical movement is needed.
   d. All of the choices are correct.
6. Which of the following is NOT a type of variable resistor?
   a. Rheostat
   b. Modulator
   c. Potentiometer
   d. Thermistor
7. Which of the following statements about the applications of capacitors is correct?
   a. Capacitors are ideal for energizing injectors operating above battery voltage.
   b. Capacitors are also useful for smoothing out voltage fluctuations that interfere with the operation of sensitive electronic components.
   c. Both A and B
   d. Neither A nor B
8. Which of the following is NOT correct concerning semiconductors?
   a. Semiconductors are the most important material used to construct electronic devices.
   b. Silicon is an example of a material which is commonly transformed into a semiconductor.
   c. Introducing impurities into the silicon is called doping.
   d. Doping silicon with boron or gallium leaves a deficit of electrons in the silicon, creating a movable negative charge.
9. Which of the following statements about integrated circuits (IC) is NOT correct?
   a. Integrated circuits (IC) are semiconductor devices having anywhere from a dozen to over a hundred transistors embedded into a single silicon wafer.
   b. Diodes, resistors and capacitors are also embedded into the chip packaged in a ceramic or plastic body with multiple pins forming input and output connection points.
   c. Circuits are first drawn on large display boards.
   d. Using a process called photo-lithography, the circuits are photographically reduced from dozens of square feet to nanometers and etched onto silicon wafers.
10. A microcontroller contains a(n):
    a. arithmetic logic core.
    b. programmable input pins.
    c. programmable output pins.
    d. All of the choices are correct.

ASE-Type Questions

1. Technician A says simple switches are categorized by the number of input terminals they have. Technician B says input terminals are called throws, and output terminals called poles. Who is correct?
   a. Technician A
   b. Technician B
   c. Both Technician A and Technician B
   d. Neither Technician A nor Technician B
2. Technician A says smart switches can function as digital inputs to electronic control systems. Technician B says because switches can be in only one of two states, switch inputs are binary inputs. Who is correct?
   a. Technician A
   b. Technician B
   c. Both Technician A and Technician B
   d. Neither Technician A nor Technician B
3. Technician A says fixed-type resistors are designed to conduct either heavy or light amount of current. Technician B says colored bands around the resistor identify its numerical resistance in amps. Who is correct?
   a. Technician A
   b. Technician B
   c. Both Technician A and Technician B
   d. Neither Technician A nor Technician B
4. Technician A says a relay is a switch which uses a small amount of current to switch a larger amount of current. Technician B says locating a relay closer to a load requiring large amounts of current eliminates voltage drop caused by resistance from long runs of wires. Who is correct?
   a. Technician A
   b. Technician B
   c. Both Technician A and Technician B
   d. Neither Technician A nor Technician B
5. Technician A says magnetic switches have a different function as compared to a relay. Technician B says magnetic switches can be classified as continuous or intermittent duty service. Who is correct?
   a. Technician A
   b. Technician B
   c. Both Technician A and Technician B
   d. Neither Technician A nor Technician B
6. Technician A says capacitors are devices that act like electric shock absorbers and are capable of storing and discharging current much like a battery or hydraulic accumulator. Technician B says capacitors are simple devices made up of three components—two plates and an insulating material. Who is correct?
   a. Technician A
   b. Technician B
   c. Both Technician A and Technician B
   d. Neither Technician A nor Technician B
7. Technician A says capacitors never wear out, but they can short out. Technician B says an ohmmeter connected to each lead of the capacitor should show continuity. Who is correct?
   a. Technician A
   b. Technician B
   c. Both Technician A and Technician B
   d. Neither Technician A nor Technician B
8. Technician A says sandwiching a P- and N- semiconductor material produces a diode. Technician B says diodes are electronic devices which operate as one way electrical check valves. Who is correct?
   a. Technician A
   b. Technician B
   c. Both Technician A and Technician B
   d. Neither Technician A nor Technician B
9. Technician A says "virtual fusing" is the description given to the use of FETs which replace a fuse or circuit breaker in the individual high-side controlled circuits. Technician B says virtual fusing is also designed to imitate the characteristics of SAE type 2 and 3 circuit breakers. Who is correct?
   a. Technician A
   b. Technician B
   c. Both Technician A and Technician B
   d. Neither Technician A nor Technician B
10. Technician A says microprocessors contain memory and logic circuits that enable them to operate using sophisticated programmed sets of stored instructions. Technician B says actuators supply processors with data, and an arithmetic unit performs calculations using algorithms based on programmed instructions. Who is correct?
    a. Technician A
    b. Technician B
    c. Both Technician A and Technician B
    d. Neither Technician A nor Technician B

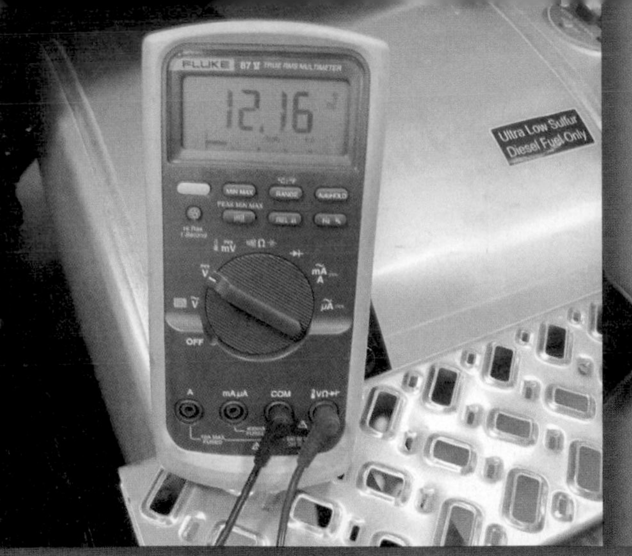

CHAPTER 10

NATEF Tasks

Electrical/Electronic Systems

General Electrical Systems	Page
■ Check resistance in electrical/electronic circuits and components using appropriate test equipment.	312
■ Check applied voltages, circuit voltages, and voltage drops in electrical/electronic circuits using appropriate test equipment.	314–316
■ Check continuity in electrical/electronic circuits using appropriate test equipment.	316–319
■ Check current flow in electrical/electronic circuits and components using appropriate test equipment.	316–319

Knowledge Objectives

After reading this chapter, you will be able to:

1. Classify and identify the applications of electrical test instruments used in commercial vehicle service. (pp 306–323)
2. Identify and describe the operation of handheld electronic test equipment and accessories used to perform basic electrical measurements. (pp 306–323)
3. Identify and explain safe work practices used during measurement and testing of electrical circuits. (pp 307, 315)
4. Describe the set-up of a digital multimeter (DMM) and procedures for performing basic electrical measurements. (pp 309–310)
5. Describe safety procedures used to operate handheld test equipment in a safe manner. (pp 315–316)

Electrical Test Instruments

Skills Objectives

After reading this chapter, you will be able to:

1. Check meter shunts. (p 311) SKILL DRILL 10-1

Introduction

Diagnosing and repairing electrical problems requires not only logic and deductive reasoning, but electrical test tools, too. A variety of electrical test instruments are needed, which range from the simple test lights and electrical multimeters to more elaborate instrumentation for checking fault codes and viewing electrical signal wave forms.

Test Lights

A **test light** is the simplest piece of electrical test equipment used to determine the presence or absence of current. It consists of either a 12- or 24-volt incandescent light bulb connected to an insulated lead and a sharpened metal probe. The insulated lead is a long wire with an alligator clip used to connect to chassis ground or insulated positive. The sharpened metal probe is used to pierce insulation and surface corrosion at test points. Taking the shape of a screwdriver, the internal lamp will light whenever current can flow between the lead and test light probe. Test lights are used by connecting the alligator clip to chassis ground or current at the insulated positive side of a circuit. A blown fuse, for example, will light up a test light when probed on only one side with the key-on. Both sides should light up if the fuse is good. Electrical connections to switches, motors, relays, and power distribution blocks are easily checked with test lights. Current in insulated positive wire is traced by probing the wire with the sharpened metal end FIGURE 10-1.

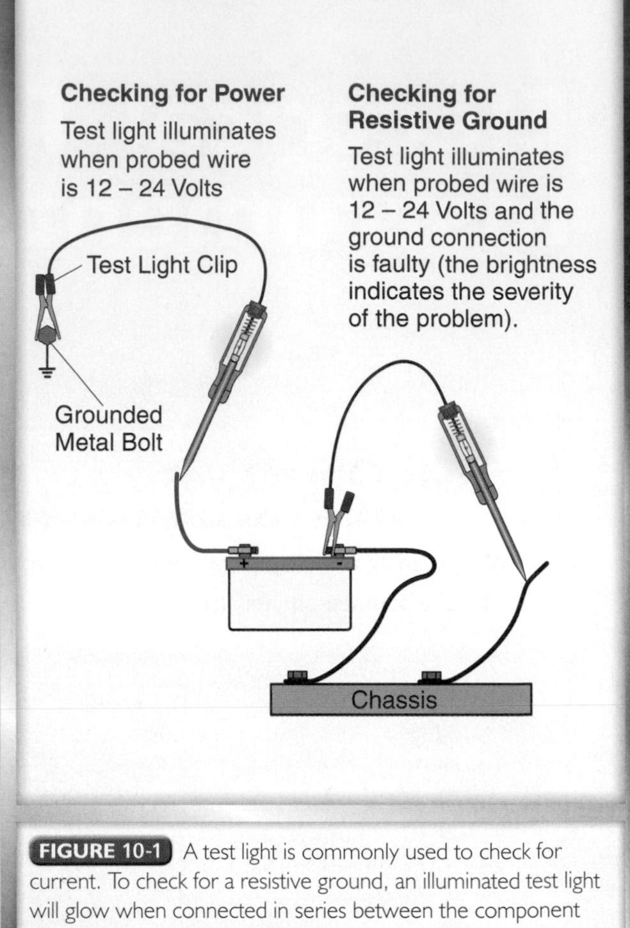
Checking for Power
Test light illuminates when probed wire is 12 – 24 Volts
Checking for Resistive Ground
Test light illuminates when probed wire is 12 – 24 Volts and the ground connection is faulty (the brightness indicates the severity of the problem).
Test Light Clip
Grounded Metal Bolt
Chassis

FIGURE 10-1 A test light is commonly used to check for current. To check for a resistive ground, an illuminated test light will glow when connected in series between the component ground and chassis ground.

You Are the Technician

In the school bus fleet that you help maintain, quite a high number of buses are developing electrical short circuits, grounded circuits, and open circuits in the wiring connecting the driver's console to the rear lights. Many of the problems are likely the result of wiring being improperly secured, insulated, and tied at the factory. Repairing the wiring problem has become very time consuming, as several wiring circuits pass through the cavity between the inner and outer sheet metal. Often, the panels need removing to replace or repair the wiring. Even after replacing large sections of wiring between the body panels, many of these same buses need further repairs. Later repairs need to be made to the wiring that connects the signal and clearance lights, as corrosion has taken place due to punctures from test lights. While reviewing maintenance strategies and procedures, consider the following:

1. What electrical test instrument would you recommend using to find shorts, grounded circuits, and open circuits behind the bus body panels?
2. What electrical test instrument would you recommend for finding grounded circuits in the wiring between the lights and the grounded wire that is routed through an open channel beneath the bus?
3. What maintenance recommendations would you make to prevent further repeat repairs of wiring after technicians have performed initial repairs?

> **TECHNICIAN TIP**
>
> The metal probe of a test light is designed to pierce electrical insulation and penetrate the surface of lightly corroded terminals and metal surfaces. Piercing wire can allow water and oxygen into the wiring, causing corrosion and oxidation. Avoid piercing a wire with a test light probe. In instances where this is not practical, always reseal pierced points on an electrical wire with adhesive sealant FIGURE 10-2. This is especially necessary with conductors outside the cab/body where wiring is exposed to the elements.

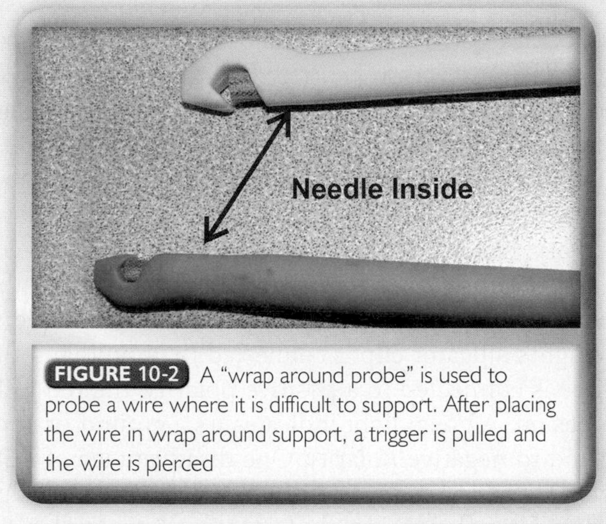

FIGURE 10-2 A "wrap around probe" is used to probe a wire where it is difficult to support. After placing the wire in wrap around support, a trigger is pulled and the wire is pierced

When connected in series with a circuit, test lights can indicate bad grounds or parasitic current drawn from a battery. FIGURE 10-3. If the test light illuminates when connected between chassis ground and component ground, it indicates a resistive or missing ground connection.

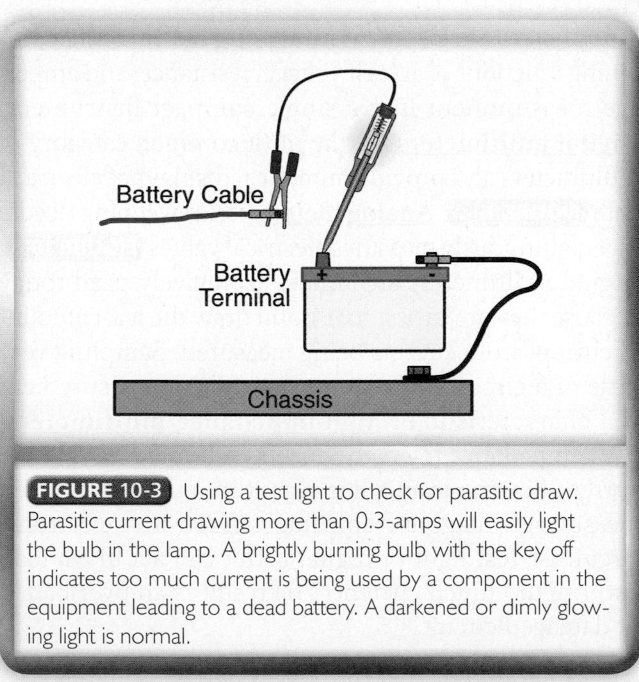

FIGURE 10-3 Using a test light to check for parasitic draw. Parasitic current drawing more than 0.3-amps will easily light the bulb in the lamp. A brightly burning bulb with the key off indicates too much current is being used by a component in the equipment leading to a dead battery. A darkened or dimly glowing light is normal.

> **Safety**
>
> High voltage from hybrid drives, the latest common rail injectors, and other electric systems can easily kill or cause serious physical harm if pierced by a technician. Always ensure appropriate power disconnect switches are removed when working around these circuits. Also, never pierce wiring covered in heavy protective loom or brightly coloured insulation without first determining what voltage the conductors are carrying. The bright color and insulation often designate high voltage or sensitive circuits FIGURE 10-4.

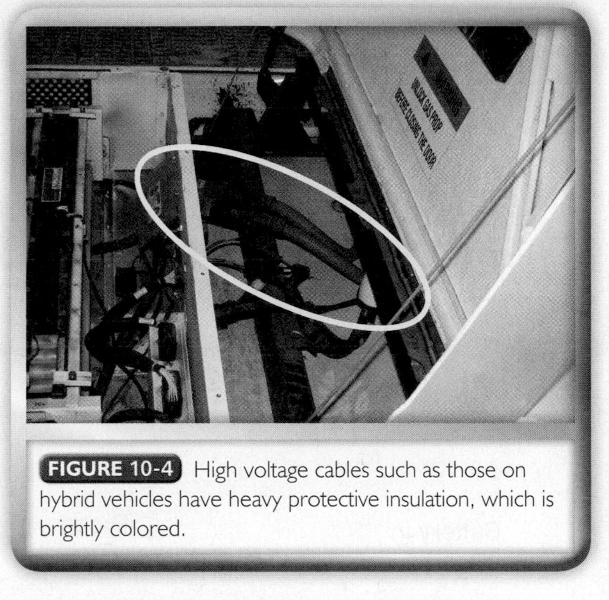

FIGURE 10-4 High voltage cables such as those on hybrid vehicles have heavy protective insulation, which is brightly colored.

Self-Powered Test Light

Self-powered test lights are like regular test lights except that they contain a 1.5-volt battery FIGURE 10-5. Self-powered lights can be used to check for both open circuits and grounded circuits when either chassis power or ground is removed from the circuit FIGURE 10-6. The internal battery can supply current needed to illuminate the light. To check for an opening in a circuit, the vehicle battery is first disconnected. The light's alligator clip is connected to ground and the circuit is probed sequentially from the switch or power supply to the load. Where the test light glows, the circuit is closed from chassis ground to power. An open circuit prevents current from traveling from the ground to an insulated positive. For example, a broken wire between a heater blower motor and fuse will illuminate between the blower motor and break in the wire, but not after the break and before the fuse.

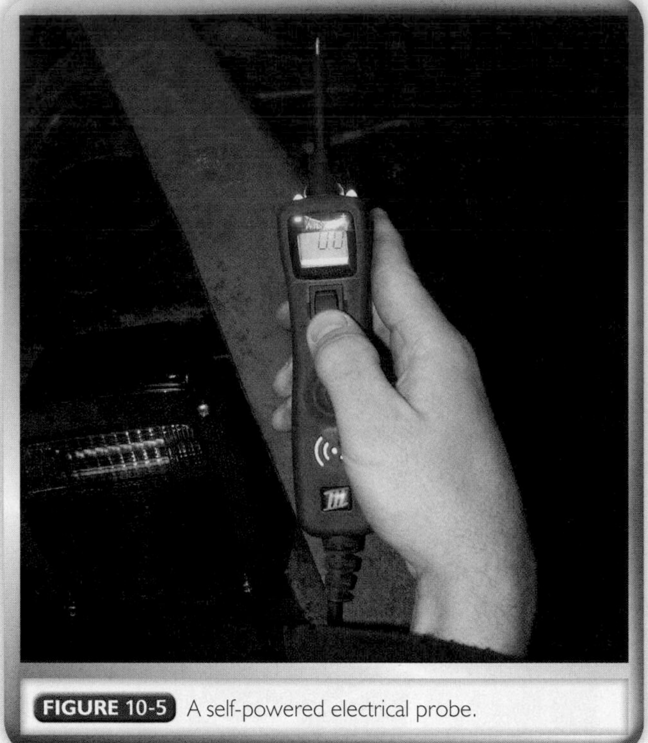

FIGURE 10-5 A self-powered electrical probe.

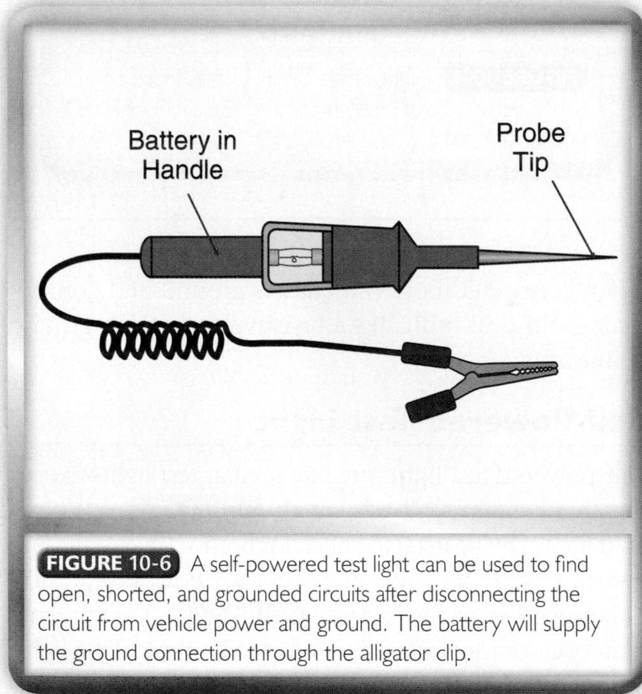

FIGURE 10-6 A self-powered test light can be used to find open, shorted, and grounded circuits after disconnecting the circuit from vehicle power and ground. The battery will supply the ground connection through the alligator clip.

Grounded circuits are checked in a similar manner. While probing the circuit, its switches and connectors are opened. The light will stay illuminated in the section that is grounded. However, the light will go out after the section of circuit with an unintentional ground is disconnected. Self-powered voltmeters with probes are also useful for close-quarter probing of electrical circuits.

> **TECHNICIAN TIP**
>
> A 12- or 24-volt battery current will easily blow the bulb out of self-powered test lights, so battery current should always be removed when using these lights. Although 1.5 volts is relatively low, it is still enough to damage computer circuits. They should never be used in electronic circuits using semiconductors—that includes sensors.

Self-Powered LED Test lights

One of the disadvantages of incandescent test lights is that they can draw excessive current from a circuit to operate the bulb. In some cases, the additional load may damage a circuit. Using light emitting diodes (LEDs) instead of a bulb overcomes this difficulty and adds capabilities to a test light. A popular type of LED test light is battery powered and has two LEDs—one red, and the other green. With two LEDs, the technician can find out what the polarity of a circuit is as it's being tested. For example, if the light's alligator clip is connected to ground and the probe is connected to a positive polarity, the red LED comes on. A green light indicates it's a ground or connected to negative polarity. One disadvantage of LED lights is they provide no indication of a circuit voltage and will be relatively bright between 1.5 to 3 volts. An incandescent light will change brightness depending on the circuit's voltage.

Multimeters

Multimeters are electrical measuring instruments combining functions of at least voltage, resistance, and amperage measurement into a single compact instrument. **Digital multimeters** are the most common category of multimeters and provide numerical displays of electrical data  FIGURE 10-7. **Analog meters** use a sweeping needle that continuously measures electrical values FIGURE 10-8. Digital multimeters are almost exclusively used today because they are easiest to use and draw the least amount of current from circuits being measured. Sampling very little of a circuit's own current to take a measurement is a characteristic of **high-impedance multimeters**. High impedance refers to a meter's internal resistance to current flowing from a live circuit into the meter when measuring voltage and amperage. In sensitive electronic circuits, a test light or digital meter can act like a load and use too much current. The result is an overloaded or damaged circuit.

FIGURE 10-7 A digital multimeter with typical basic features.

FIGURE 10-8 An analog meter uses a needle and sweeping scale to measure properties of electrical current.

Basic Multimeter Electrical Measurements

Before using a multimeter, it is important to understand the basic measurements that it can produce. A multimeter measures resistance, continuity, voltage, and amperage:

1. **Resistance** – Measures circuit resistance in Ohms to determine whether it is within specifications. Wire coils and heating elements are examples of common devices where a measure of resistance determines serviceability. Open and short circuits are easily detected using the ohmmeter to measure resistance **FIGURE 10-9**.

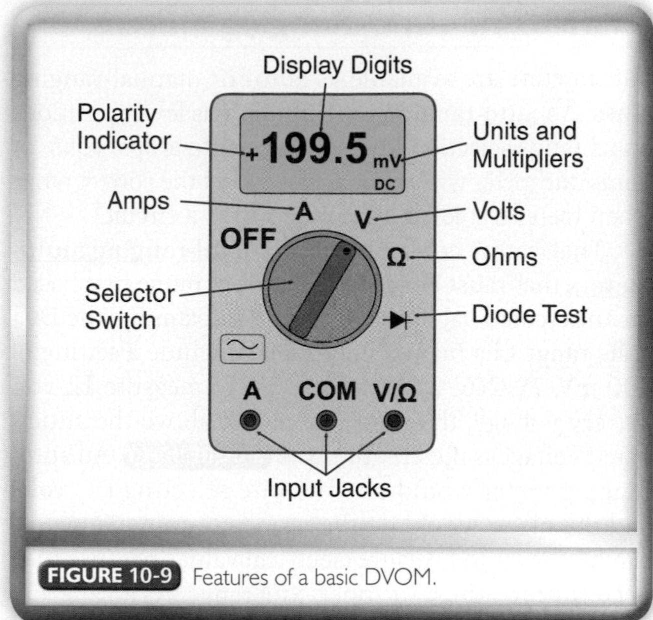

FIGURE 10-9 Features of a basic DVOM.

2. **Continuity** – Determines whether two points are electrically connected. Continuity is also valuable when checking for opens and shorts.
3. **Voltage** – Measurements are used to determine whether a component or circuit has the correct amount of available power. Measuring voltage drops in a circuit can help evaluate resistance in high amperage circuits such as the starting circuit. A voltmeter behaves like a pressure differential gauge by measuring the difference in electron pressure between two points in a circuit.
4. **Amperage** – Most measurements of amperage are performed at levels higher than multimeters can typically handle, so an inductance amp clamp is used instead. However, meters are usually capable of measuring up to 10-amps of current flow. Starter draw and alternator output are two common measurements of amperage regularly made using multimeters with an inductance clamp meter accessory.

Multimeters may also perform additional electrical measures including:

- Diode testing
- Frequency
- Capacitance
- Temperature
- Duty cycle
- Transistor testing
- Continuity tester with beeper
- Waveform display
- Engine RPM

Manual and Auto-Ranging Meters

Multimeters are available as auto- or manual-ranging types. An **auto-ranging multimeter** has fewer positions on its range selection knob. When set to amps, volts, or ohms, the meter will automatically select the correct range when meter test leads are connected to a circuit.

This feature contrasts with **manual-ranging multimeters** that must be set to the correct range first based on anticipated values measured. For example, the DC-volts range of a manual meter may include a setting of 200 mV, 2V, 20V, 200V, and 500V. To measure 12-volt battery voltage, the range value just above the anticipated voltage is the 20-volt scale FIGURE 10-10. An auto-ranging meter would only require selecting DC volts and the meter would do the rest. Auto-ranging meters can be slower to measure electrical values because they need time to adjust the operating range. As an alternative, auto-ranging meters can usually be set to operate as manual-ranging units.

TECHNICIAN TIP

When making measurements and performing diagnostic tests with auto-ranging meters, the display may change continuously for some time until the correct range is established. If the measured value changes or test lead probes move too much, the meter may begin to auto-range once again. The process can lead to incorrect results if measurements are taken too quickly. Using the peak and hold feature or auto-hold will help to produce more accurate values. Otherwise, more patience and care is required when using these meters.

With either automatic or manual-ranging meters, it is important to learn the electrical symbols and units of measurement listed in TABLE 10-1.

TABLE 10-1: Symbols and Meanings for Electrical Units of Measurement

Symbol	Meaning
M	Mega or million
K	Kilo or thousand
m	Milli or one thousandth
µ	Micro or one millionth
V̄	V dc
Ṽ	V ac
mV	Millivolts (0.001 V or 1/1,000 V)
A	Amperage (amps)
mA	Milliamps (0.001A or 1/1,000 A)
µA	Microamps (0.000001 A or 1/1,000,000 A)
Ω	Resistance (ohms)
kΩ	Kilo-ohms (1,000 ohms)
MΩ	Megohms (1,000,000 ohms)
)))	Continuity beeper
Diode →⊢	Diode testing
Hz	Frequency (hertz, which is cycles/sec)
dB	Sound (decibels)
F	Capacitance (farad)
µF	Microfarads
nF	Nanofarads
Touch Hold & Auto HOLD	The last recorded stable reading
MIN MAX	Highest, lowest recorded readings
OL	Out of range

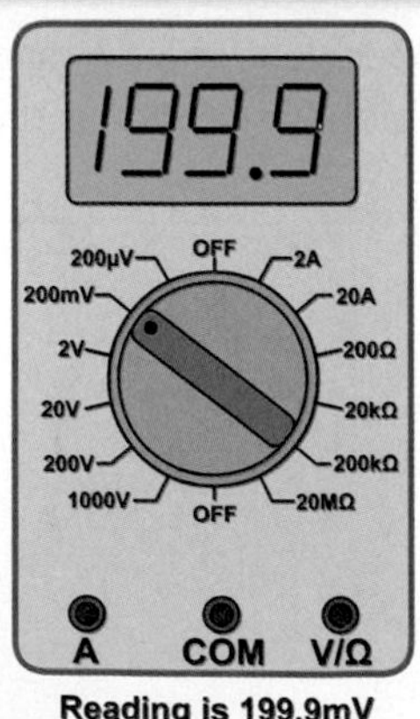

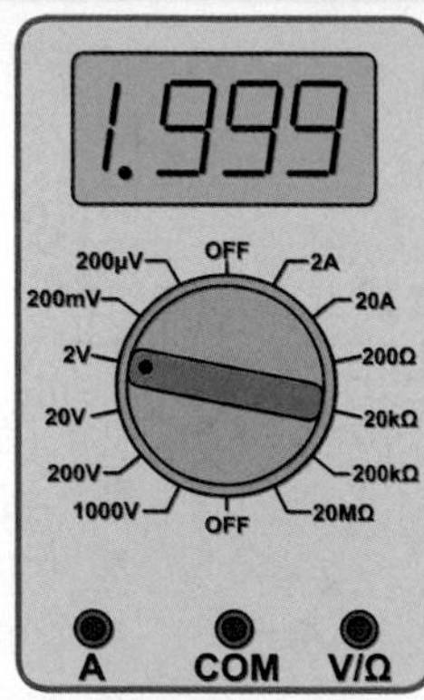

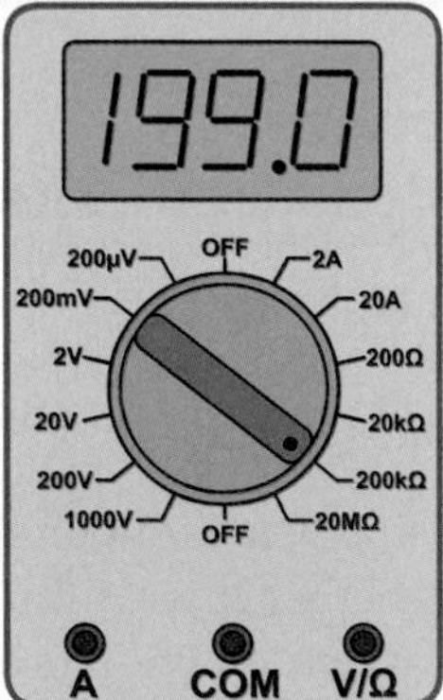

FIGURE 10-10 A manual-ranging meter will move the decimal point for many electrical measurements.

Meter Shunts

Before using a digital meter, one of the first things to check is whether its shunts or fuses are in place and functioning. Shunts are internal conductors with a small calibrated resistance, which directs some current flow into the meter when measuring amperage **FIGURE 10-11**. Almost all circuit current will pass through meter shunt, but some resistance is needed to send current into the measuring circuits of the meter. Shunts operate like fuses and have a maximum rating. A shunt should blow in an extremely short time if current exceeds the meter's capacity. If an ordinary fuse is used to replace a fast-blowing shunt, current will enter and damage the meter in the time it takes to open the ordinary fuse.

Shunts are checked by touching inserting the positive lead probe while in the volt/ohm port, into the amperage probe port **FIGURE 10-12**. A meter set to check continuity or resistance should display continuity and some resistance. If two amperage ports are used on a meter, the larger amperage shunt will have a higher resistance than the low amperage shunt. To check meter shunts, follow the steps in **SKILL DRILL 10-1**.

20A fuse
200mA fuse
Shunt

FIGURE 10-11 An ammeter shunt allows most of the current to pass through the shunt while allowing some small amount of current into the meter's measurement mechanism.

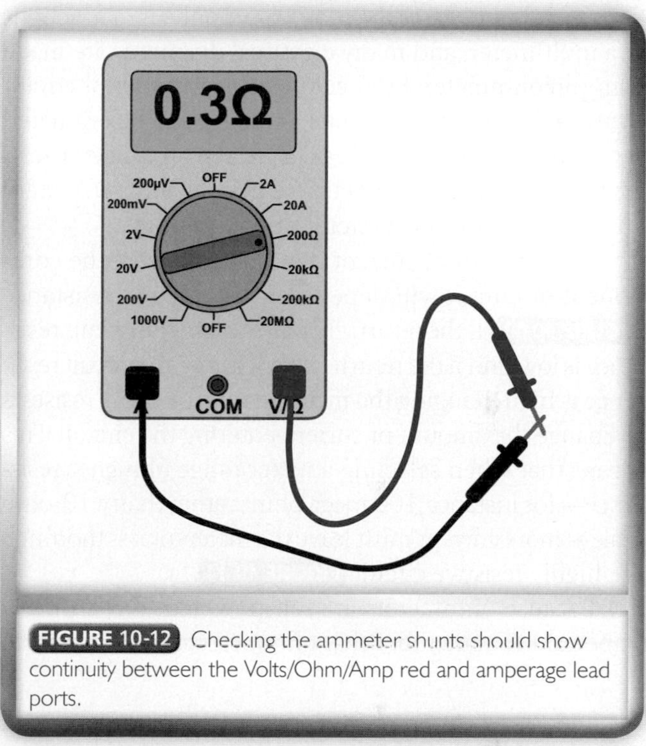

FIGURE 10-12 Checking the ammeter shunts should show continuity between the Volts/Ohm/Amp red and amperage lead ports.

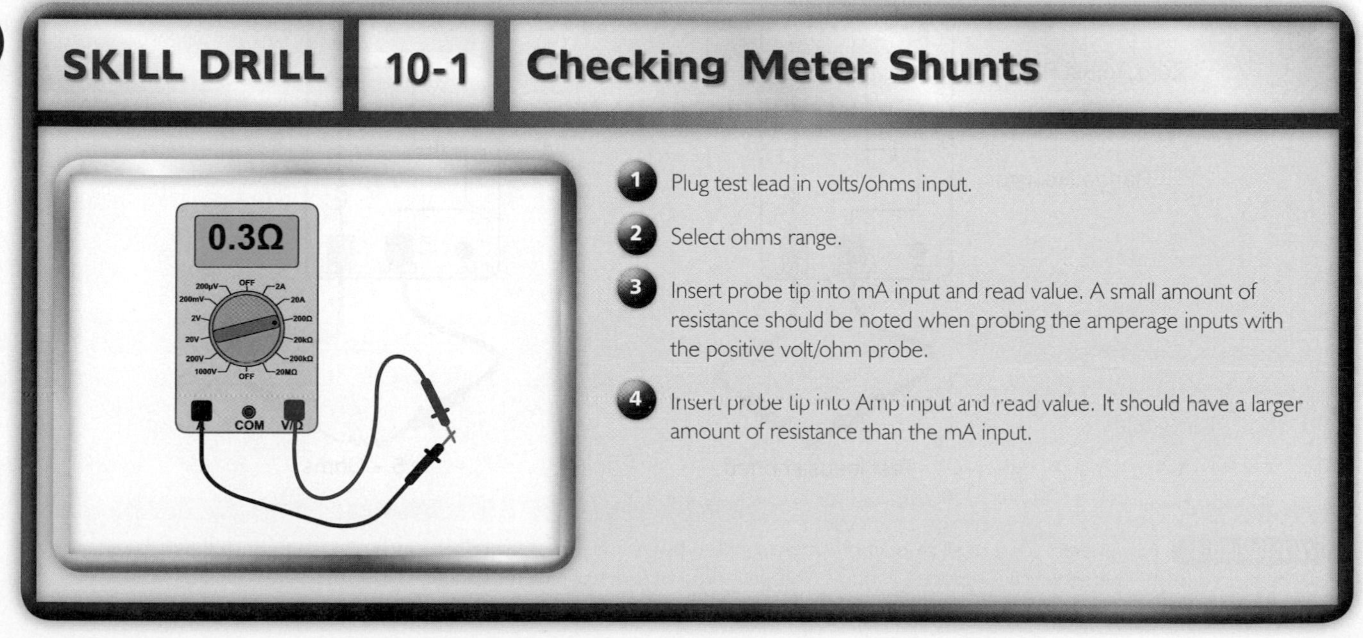

SKILL DRILL 10-1 Checking Meter Shunts

1. Plug test lead in volts/ohms input.
2. Select ohms range.
3. Insert probe tip into mA input and read value. A small amount of resistance should be noted when probing the amperage inputs with the positive volt/ohm probe.
4. Insert probe tip into Amp input and read value. It should have a larger amount of resistance than the mA input.

Electrical Measurement with Multimeters

Multimeters are versatile instruments that allow the technician to take a variety of measurements.

Three types of measurements—voltage, resistance, and amperage—can be taken from circuits in three different ways. Understanding them is necessary to prevent meter damage and ensure accurate measurements.

Measuring Resistance—Ohmmeters

Ohmmeters are one of the most commonly used functions of a multimeter, and many electrical diagnoses are made using an ohmmeter. By checking the resistance or circuit continuity with an ohmmeter, a circuit can be evaluated for shorts, opens, or high resistance. An ohmmeter uses a small amount of electrical current from an internal battery and sends it through a circuit or component.

The amount of current that flows through the component or circuit will depend on the circuit's resistance FIGURE 10-13. If the return current is high, the circuit resistance is low, and if the return current is low, the circuit resistance is high. Ranging the meter is done by using resistors to change the amount of current entering the circuit. This means that when selecting a meter range of higher resistance—for instance, 100 mega ohms rather than a 10-ohm scale—more current must leave the meter to pass thorough the highly resistive circuit FIGURE 10-14.

Because ohmmeters are self-powered, it is critically important to remember that ohmmeters should never be connected to a powered circuit. Connecting an ohmmeter into a powered circuit will blow the fuse or battery in the meter or otherwise damage the meter. Semiconductor circuits and sensors should not be checked with an ohmmeter, as the meter current may damage the device FIGURE 10-15.

Ohmmeters are ineffective when checking for resistances in high-amperage, low-resistance circuits, such as when measuring battery cable voltage loss. Measuring voltage drop with a voltmeter when a circuit is operating is a more effective way of measuring resistances FIGURE 10-16.

When measuring with an ohmmeter, it is important to observe how a meter displays infinite resistance or an

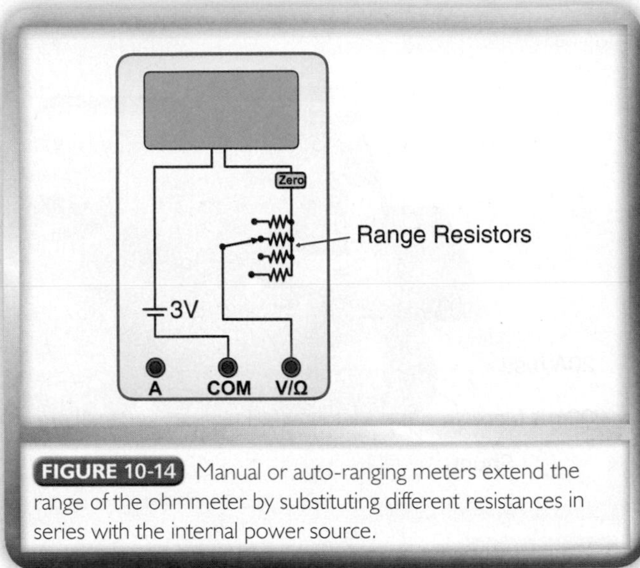

FIGURE 10-14 Manual or auto-ranging meters extend the range of the ohmmeter by substituting different resistances in series with the internal power source.

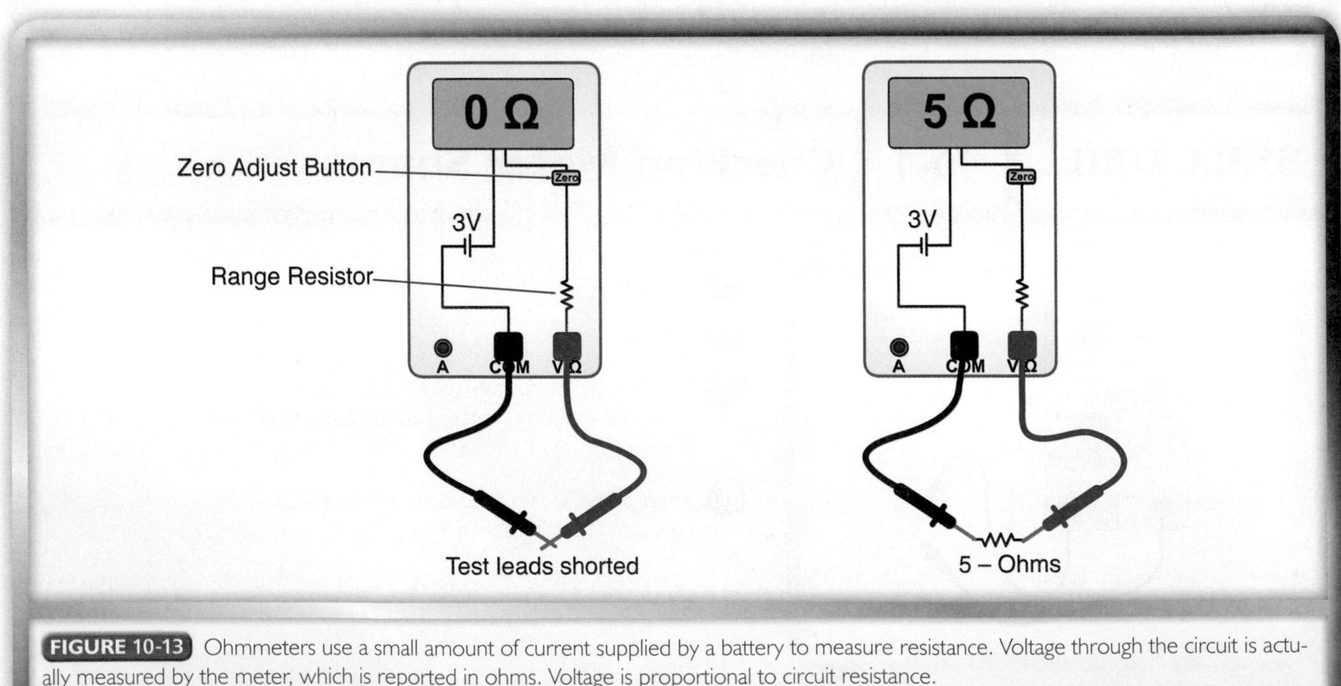

FIGURE 10-13 Ohmmeters use a small amount of current supplied by a battery to measure resistance. Voltage through the circuit is actually measured by the meter, which is reported in ohms. Voltage is proportional to circuit resistance.

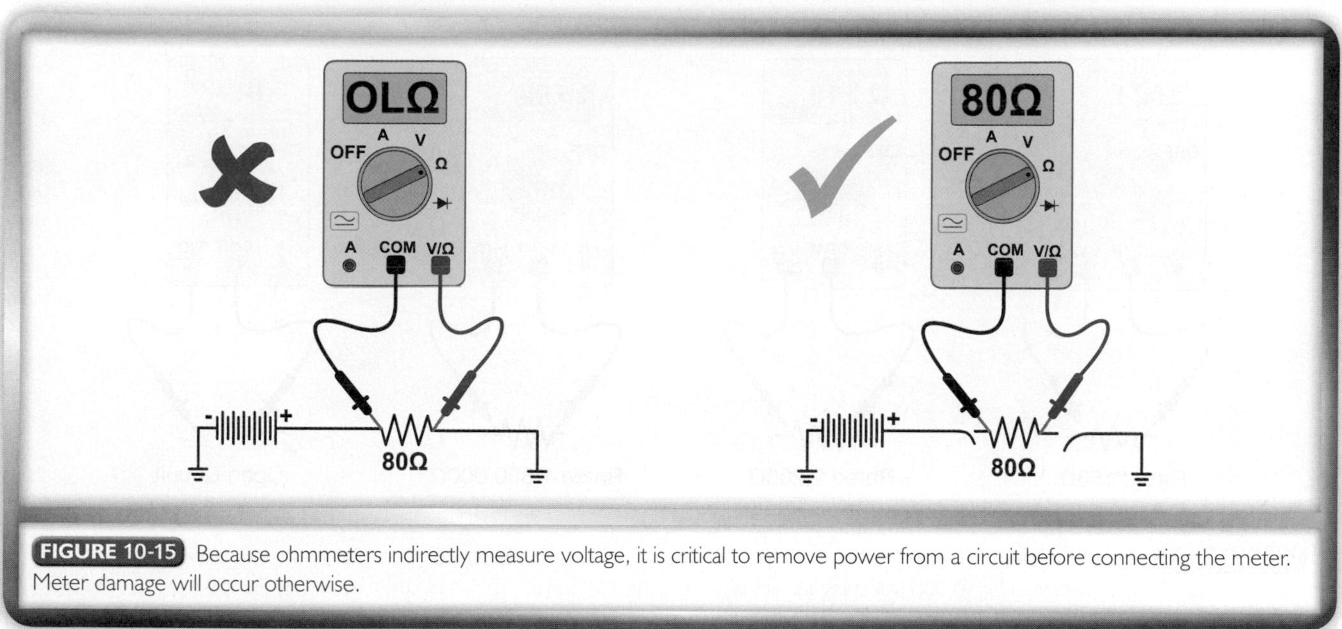

FIGURE 10-15 Because ohmmeters indirectly measure voltage, it is critical to remove power from a circuit before connecting the meter. Meter damage will occur otherwise.

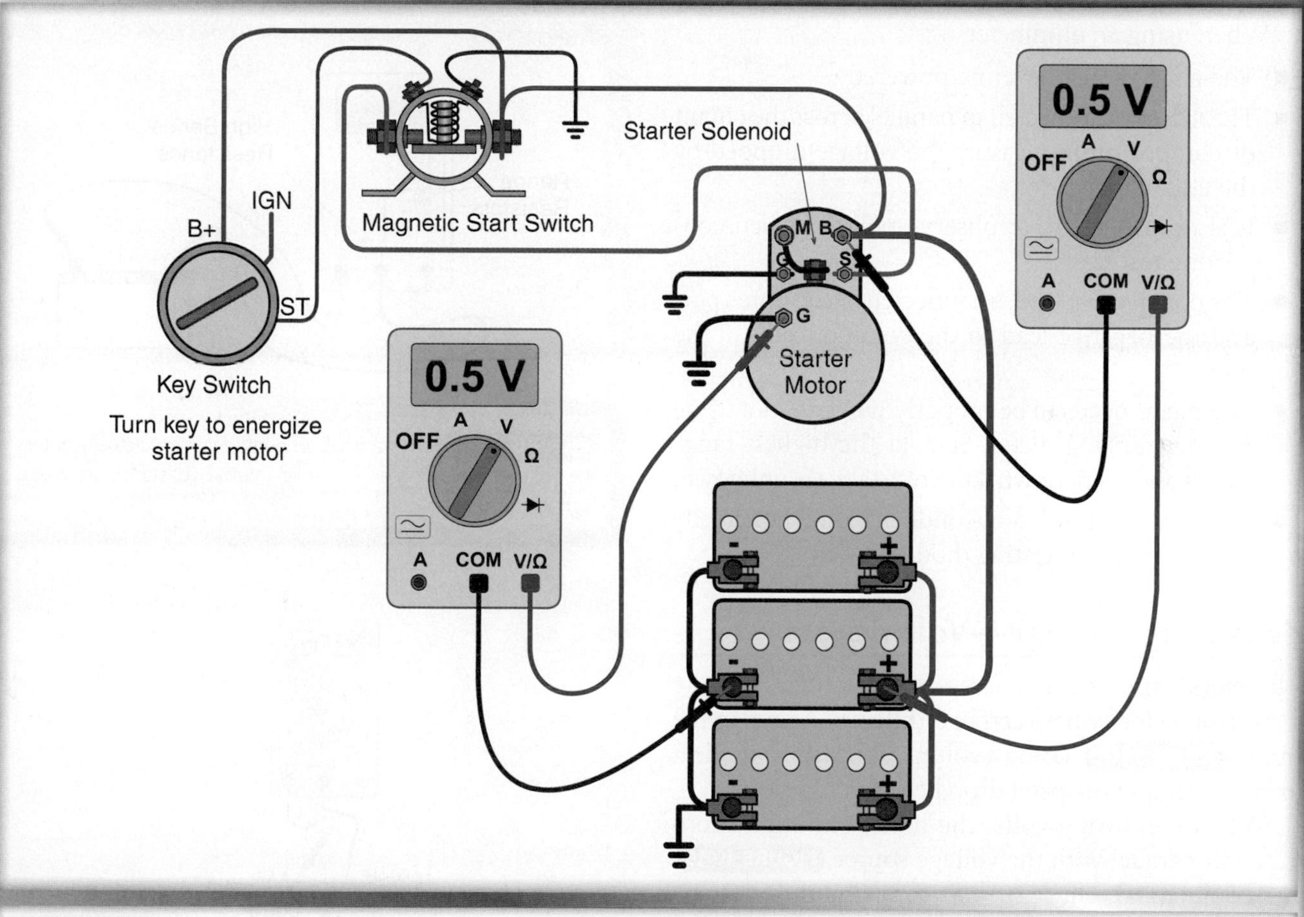

FIGURE 10-16 A voltmeter is best used to check for resistance in high amperage circuits. Voltage drop means the circuit has resistance.

open circuit. Some meters will display either a 1 or 0 to indicate an open circuit. **FIGURE 10-17**. It is important to understand also the range that the display is reporting. Million, thousand, and hundred are common ranges for an ohmmeter, and the displayed value may need to be multiplied by multimeter range.

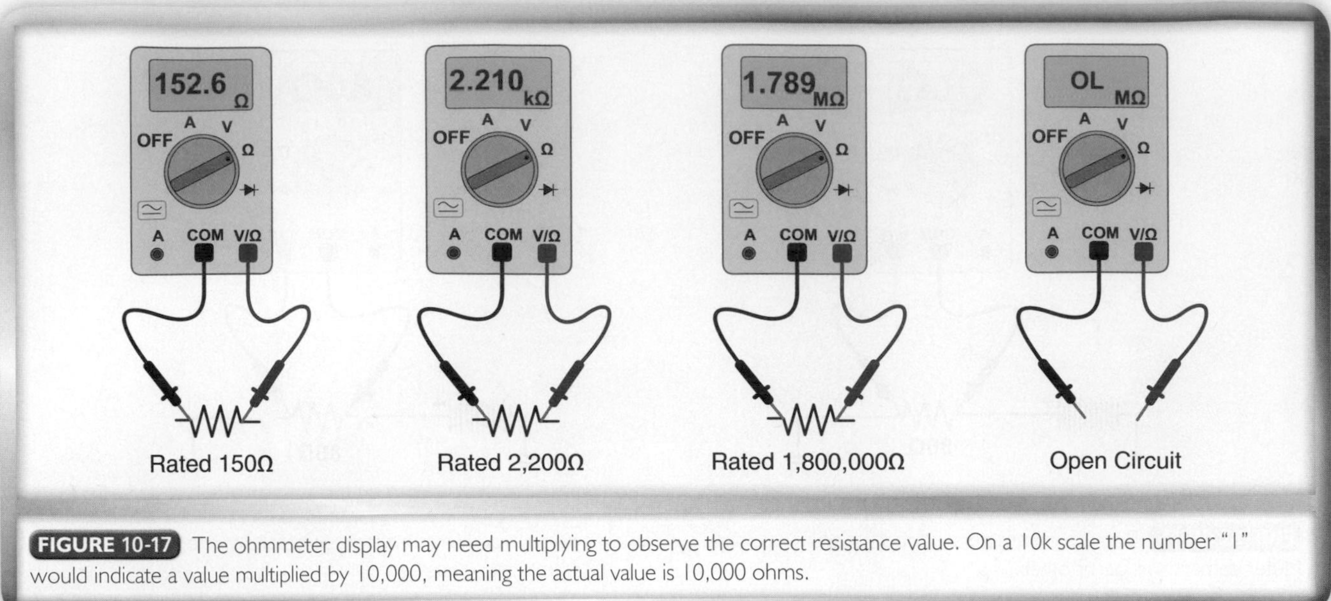

FIGURE 10-17 The ohmmeter display may need multiplying to observe the correct resistance value. On a 10k scale the number "1" would indicate a value multiplied by 10,000, meaning the actual value is 10,000 ohms.

When using an ohmmeter:

- The circuit must never be powered.
- The meter is connected in parallel across the circuit or component to measure the voltage dropped by the circuit resistance.
- It is not necessary to observe polarity when connecting test leads.
- The positive test lead is connected to the ohms port and the negative lead to the common port of the meter.
- The meter needs to be properly ranged if not using an auto-ranging meter. Start at the highest range values and work down if the resistance is unknown.
- Not to be used with semiconductors and potentially inaccurate when testing diodes.

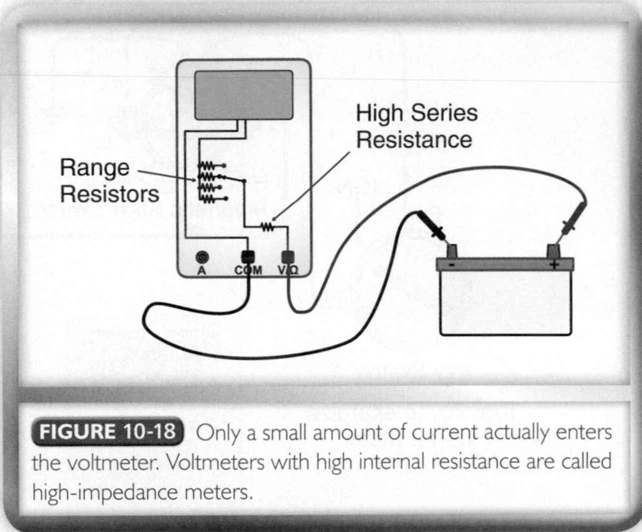

FIGURE 10-18 Only a small amount of current actually enters the voltmeter. Voltmeters with high internal resistance are called high-impedance meters.

Measuring Voltage—Voltmeters

Voltmeters measure the difference in electrical pressure or electron velocity between two different points in the circuit FIGURE 10-18. Using a voltmeter is similar to measuring a pressure or speed drop between two points.

When measuring volts, the meter should be connected in parallel with the voltage source FIGURE 10-19. On a commercial vehicle, you would commonly be measuring voltage drops across loads, determining whether there is sufficient power to a component, or measuring sensor voltages. In any of these cases, the meter would be set to its 20 volts for 12-volt systems or 40 volts for 24-volt systems. Auto-ranging meters are set to the DC volts scale.

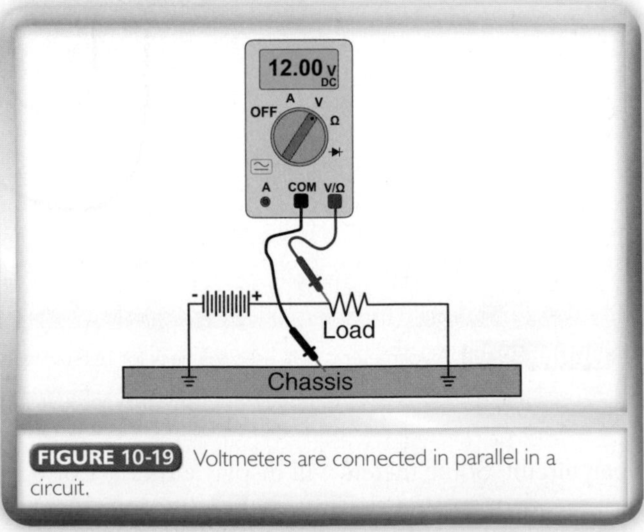

FIGURE 10-19 Voltmeters are connected in parallel in a circuit.

The positive meter lead probe is inserted into the volt-ohms port and the negative to the common port FIGURE 10-20. If the circuit polarity is not correctly observed (i.e., the negative probe is connected to the positive side of the circuit and vice versa), digital meters will show a negative volts symbol.

Practices to observe when measuring voltage include:

- Connecting the voltmeter in parallel with the circuit
- Observing polarity when measuring DC volts but not AC voltage FIGURE 10-21
- Ranging AC and DC volts separately
- When not using an auto-range meter, selecting the first voltage scale that is higher than the anticipated voltage; if unknown, starting at the highest scale
- Connecting the positive lead to volts/ohms port and the negative lead to common port
- Ensuring that the circuit is powered

Voltmeters commonly include several protections against damage and safety risks TABLE 10-2.

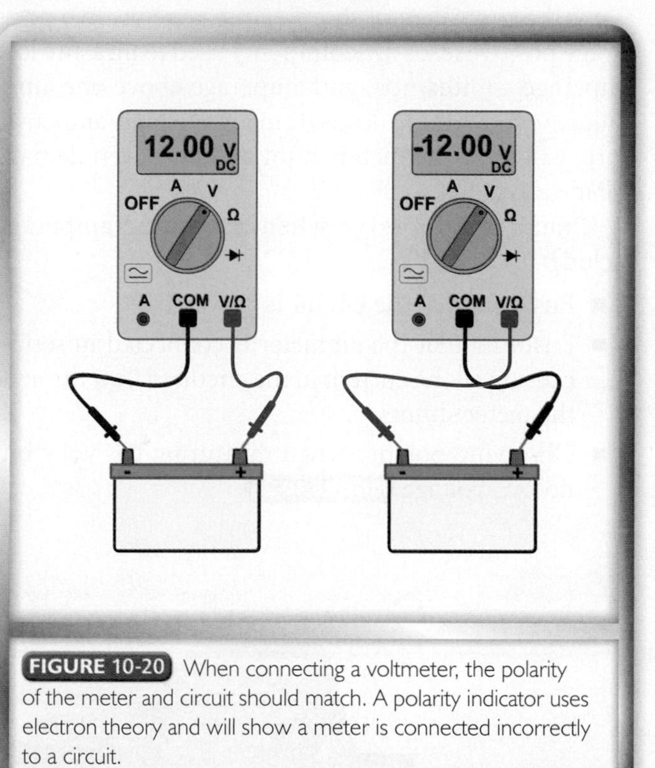

FIGURE 10-20 When connecting a voltmeter, the polarity of the meter and circuit should match. A polarity indicator uses electron theory and will show a meter is connected incorrectly to a circuit.

Safety

Multimeters can and do blow up, causing personal injury and equipment damage. Safety features—such as using PTC thermistors in the ohmmeter, which become highly resistive when heated—are built into meters to limit damage to the meter. Voltage circuits are capacitive coupled, eliminating a direct connection to meter circuits. Low-impedance ammeters use shunts that blow when overloaded. Double insulation of meters, shrouded connectors, and the use of finger guards are other safety features. Check meters before using to see that insulation is not melted, cut, or cracked. Connectors and leads should not show any damage, such as insulation pulled away from end connectors. Probe tips should not be loose or broken off. Make sure the meter is safe for the application in which it is being used. IEC 61010 is a safety standard that establishes safety limits for meters. A Cat I meter in this standard, which is satisfactory for most technicians, should not be used to check voltages above 600 volts continuous, or 2,500 volts at peak. The top rated CAT III meter can operate with 1,000 volts continuous and 8,000 volts transient peak FIGURE 10-22.

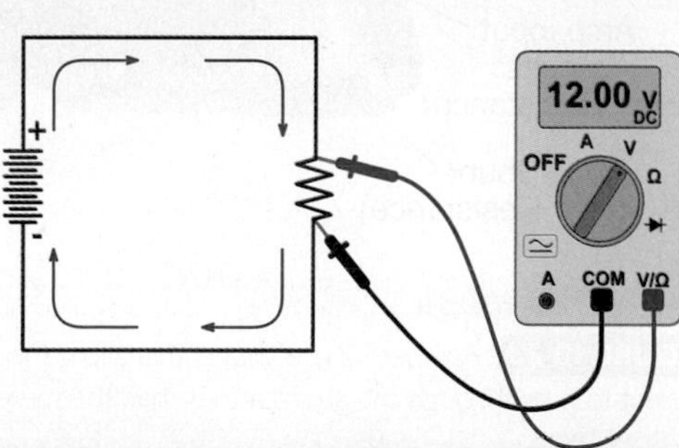

When measuring DC volts, the meter must be connected to the circuit with the correct polarity or the meter reading will be incorrect.

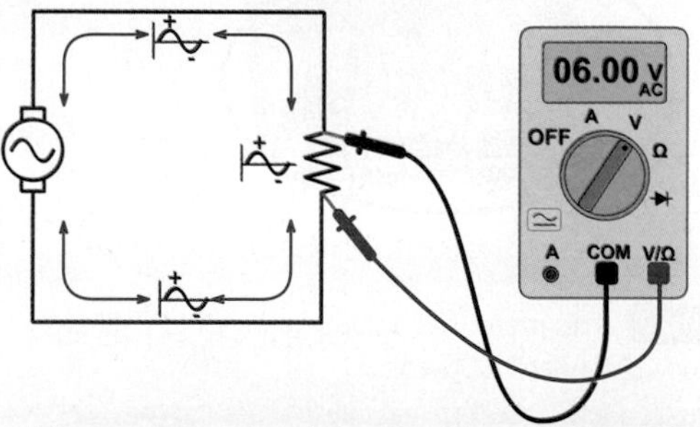

When measuring AC volts, the polarity of the meter to the circuit is unimportant and will not affect the meter reading.

FIGURE 10-21 Polarity does not need to be observed when measuring AC voltage.

TABLE 10-2: Multimeter Features to Protect Meter and User

Risk	Protection
Electrical arcing from transients high voltage sources (lightning, load switching)	Independent certification to meet CAT III-1000 V and CAT IV-600 V or higher
Voltage damage to meter while in continuity or resistance ranges	Overload protection in ohms up to the meter's volt rating.
Measuring voltage with test leads in amperage inputs	Fast blowing, high energy fuses rated to the meter's voltage rating. Use induction clamps to measure amperage
Shock from accidental contact with live components	Double insulated test leads, recessed and/or shrouded with finger guards

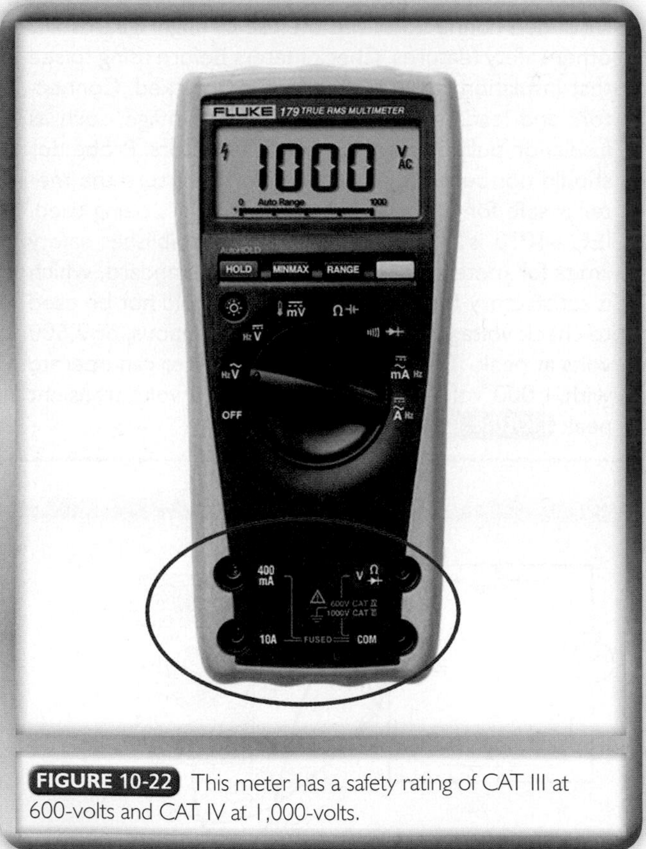

FIGURE 10-22 This meter has a safety rating of CAT III at 600-volts and CAT IV at 1,000-volts.

Measuring Amperage—Ammeters

Ammeters measure the quantity of electrons flowing through a circuit per second of time. Amperage is the volume aspect of current flow, and voltage is the speed or pressure of electrical flow. Measuring amperage requires that the circuit be broken and the meter placed in series with the circuit so that all the current flows through the meter shunts. See FIGURE 10-23 and FIGURE 10-24. Because all circuit current flows through the meter, the meter should never be connected to a current source in parallel, as it is the equivalent of shorting out a circuit. Two ports for the positive leads are commonly used to measure low amperage—milliamps, and amperage above one amp. Failure to move meter leads from low- to high-amperage ports will blow the meter shunt and may even damage the meter.

Practices to observe when measuring amperage include:

- Ensuring that the circuit is powered
- Ensuring that the ammeter is connected in series, causing all the current in the circuit to flow through the meter shunts
- Observing polarity when measuring DC volts but not AC voltage FIGURE 10-25

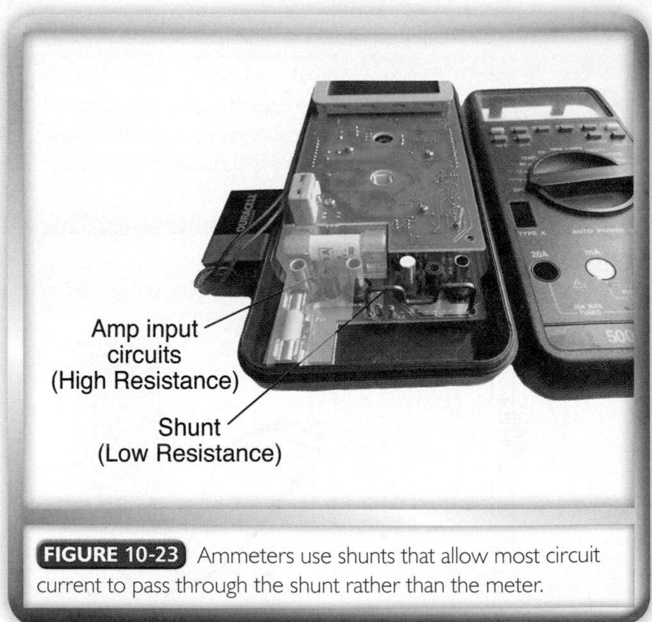

FIGURE 10-23 Ammeters use shunts that allow most circuit current to pass through the shunt rather than the meter.

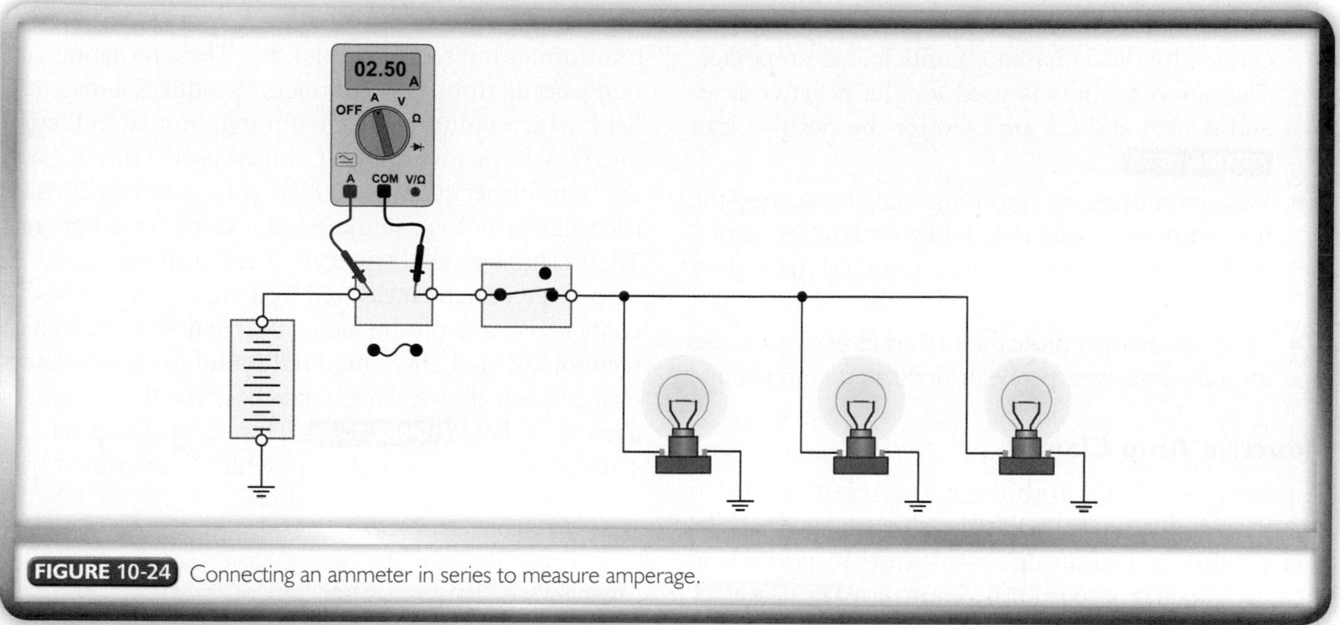

FIGURE 10-24 Connecting an ammeter in series to measure amperage.

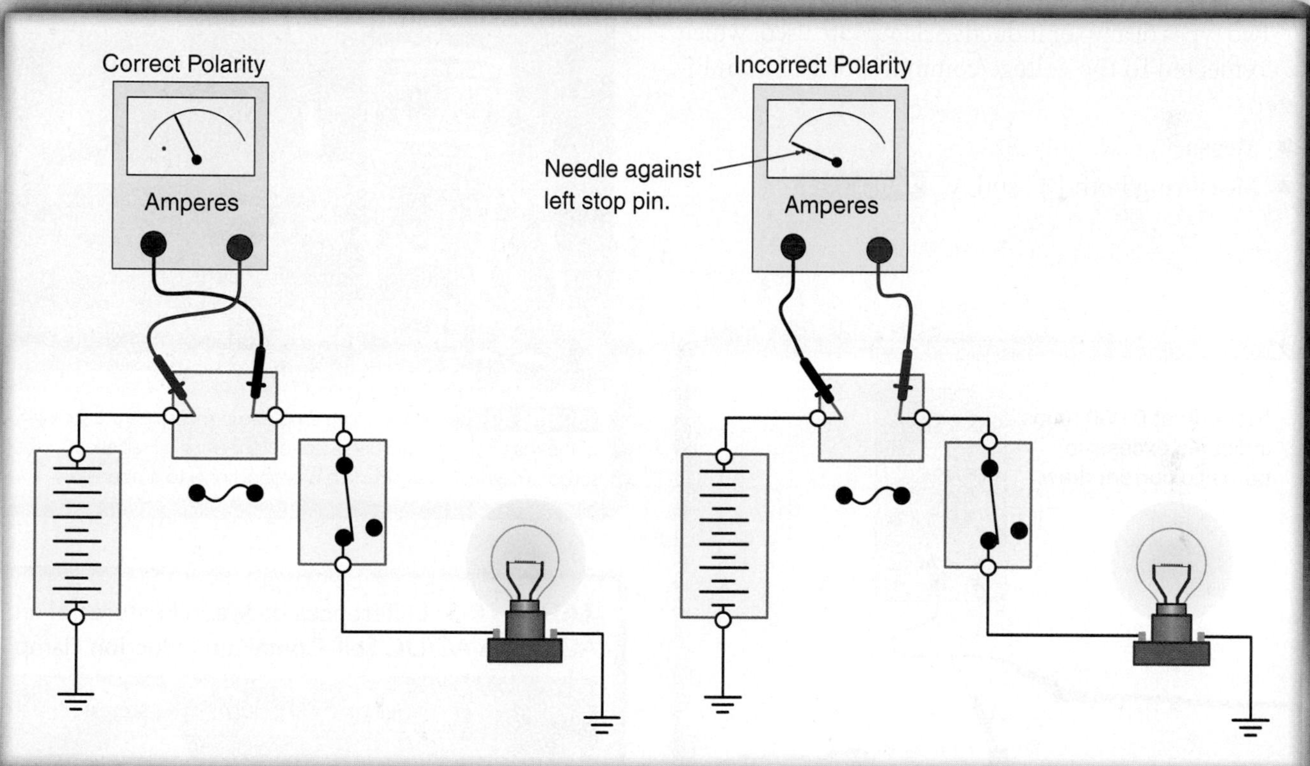

FIGURE 10-25 Ammeters require connection using correct polarity as noted using this analog ammeter. Digital meters will indicate the polarity is incorrect.

- Choosing the correct shunt or port in the meter for connecting leads based on anticipated amperage. The common port is used for the negative lead, and A, mA and uA are used for the positive lead FIGURE 10-26
- When not using an auto-range meter, selecting the first amperage scale that is higher than the anticipated amperage; if unknown, starting at the highest scale
- When measuring more than 10 amps of current, use an inductive-type probe or dedicated amp clamp

Inductive Amp Clamps

In powered circuits, **inductive amp clamps** placed around a conductor are used to measure amperage. These devices work by measuring a conductor's magnetic field strength, which is proportional to amperage FIGURE 10-27. While using an amp clamp, an electrical circuit does not need to be disturbed by connecting a meter in series.

Two types of amp or inductive clamps are used, which are connected to the voltage/common ports of a multimeter.

- Measuring AC only
- Measuring both DC and AC TABLE 10-3

Clamps that measure AC current use a current transformer built into the pick-up. The alternating current passing through a conductor produces a magnetic field, which induces voltage through mutual induction into transformer windings. Using a specific turn ratio in the transformer such as 1000:1, voltage induced inside the transformer is calculated as a value for amperage. These clamps generate typically 1-millivolt per measured amp, which can be measured by a multimeter, or is self-contained in a clamp-on meter. DC clamps use Hall effect technology. Hall effect material found in these sensors changes their electrical resistance based on the strength of a magnetic field FIGURE 10-28. This clamp also produces 1 millivolt per measured amp, which is measured by a

FIGURE 10-27 An inductive amp clamp measures the strength of the magnetic field around a conductor using a Hall effect sensor. Magnetic field strength is proportional to amperage.

TABLE 10-3: Differences between Features of an AC and an AC/DC Self-Contained Induction clamp

Feature	AC	AC/DC
Output current	Current	Voltage
Scale factor	1 milliAmp per Amp	1 milliVolt per Amp
Sensor	Current transfer	Hall effect
Battery	No	Yes

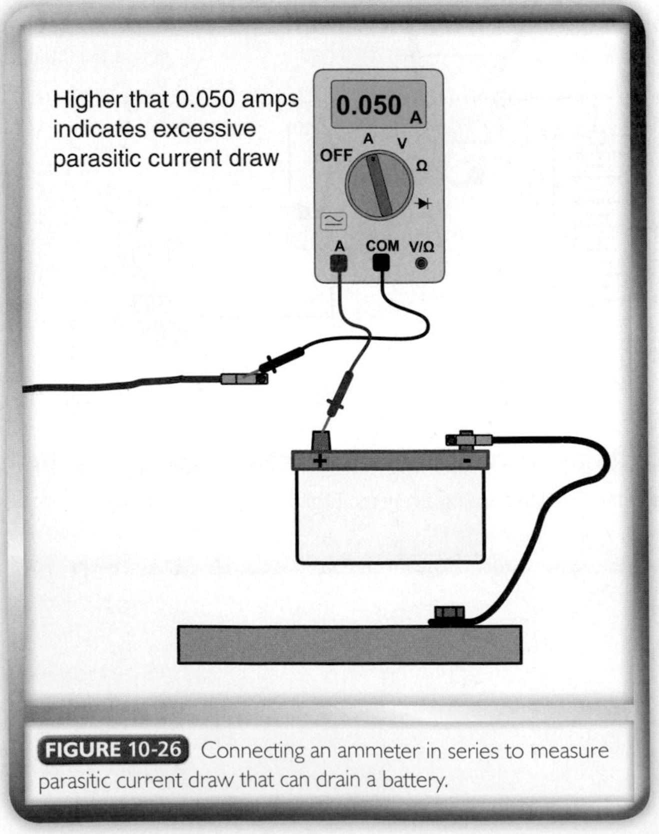

FIGURE 10-26 Connecting an ammeter in series to measure parasitic current draw that can drain a battery.

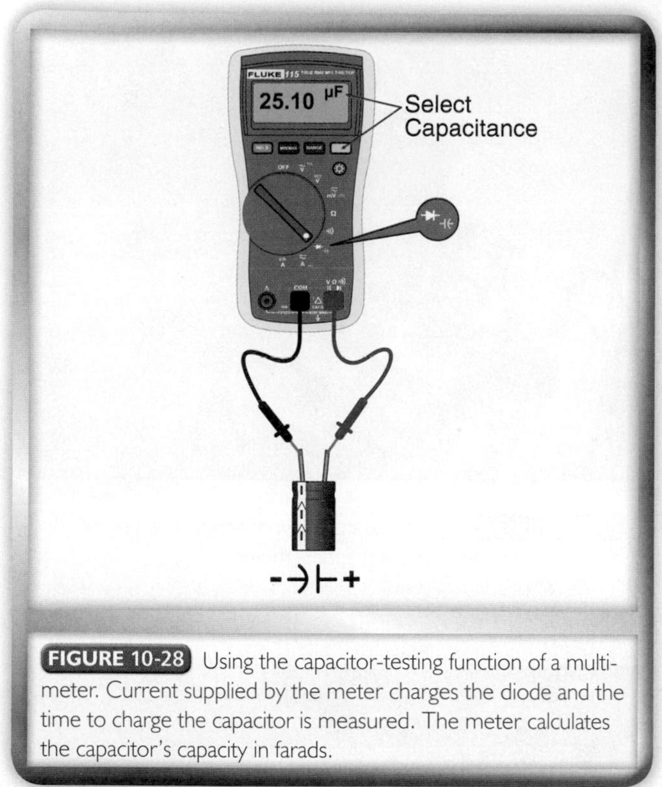

FIGURE 10-28 Using the capacitor-testing function of a multimeter. Current supplied by the meter charges the diode and the time to charge the capacitor is measured. The meter calculates the capacitor's capacity in farads.

FIGURE 10-29 A polarity indicator on a DC amp clamp points to the most positive side of the circuit due to the direction of magnetic fields.

voltmeter. Batteries in either the clamp or test instrument are needed to power inductive clamps using Hall effect sensors.

Measuring Temperature

Multimeters use a thermocouple accessory to measure temperature by contact. Heating the thermocouple produces voltage proportional to temperature. **Type K thermocouples** are low-cost, general-purpose, temperature-sensing elements, and are connected to the same meter terminals for measuring DC millivolts. Internal meter circuits convert the voltage measurements into a temperature reading.

Diode Scale

The low-voltage settings of an ohmmeter may not properly evaluate a diode, as a good silicon diode requires approximately 0.5–0.7 volts to forward bias or conduct current. Below this voltage, the diode may appear to block current in both directions. When placed in the diode range, a meter will put out higher voltage than barrier voltage of 0.7 volts to cause the diode to reverse and forward bias FIGURE 10-29.

Circuit Tracers

Circuit tracers, also called **wire tracers**, are electronic service tools used to trace a single wire over a distance where multiple wires are bundled, shorted, or open. Telephone companies once commonly used these to help field technicians locate problematic phone circuits. These units can identify wires deeply buried behind walls or in tightly bundled harness.

Several methods are used to identify circuit problems. Commonly though, one part of the signal tracing unit is clipped to a suspect wire and ground. When switched on, the unit injects a strong, two-tone square wave radio signal into the wire. The receivers consist of a sensitive radio with an audio amplifier and speaker. Slowly waving this device over a group of wires will detect where a conductor is located and ends. See FIGURE 10-30 and FIGURE 10-31. The intensity of the sound produced by the signal or the flickering of an LED light varies with proximity to the wire. The probe's tip is insulated for safety purposes.

Graphing Meters and Oscilloscopes

One of the latest diagnostic tools is a digital **graphing meter** used to analyze electrical waveforms produced by sensors, motors, actuators, and alternators. These test instruments plot an electrical value of a signal over time, displaying an easy-to-read graph with time on the *x* axis and the signal value on the *y* axis FIGURE 10-32.

Component serviceability can be determined by analyzing the waveform or comparing it to known signals of good quality FIGURE 10-33. For example, a Hall effect sensor may have intermittent problems that may not be detected by the vehicle's on-board diagnostic system.

FIGURE 10-30 Using the circuit tracers after connecting the signal generator to a defective circuit.

FIGURE 10-32 A graph of a pulse-width-modulated signal waveform obtained using a graphing meter.

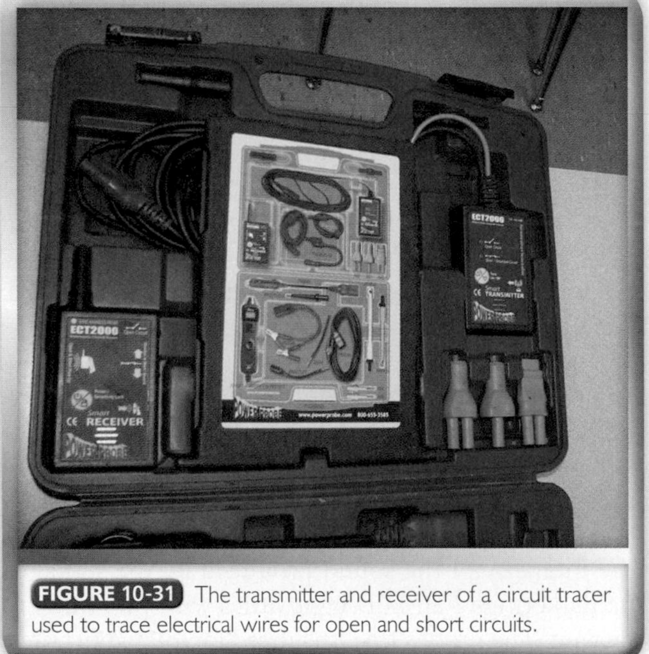

FIGURE 10-31 The transmitter and receiver of a circuit tracer used to trace electrical wires for open and short circuits.

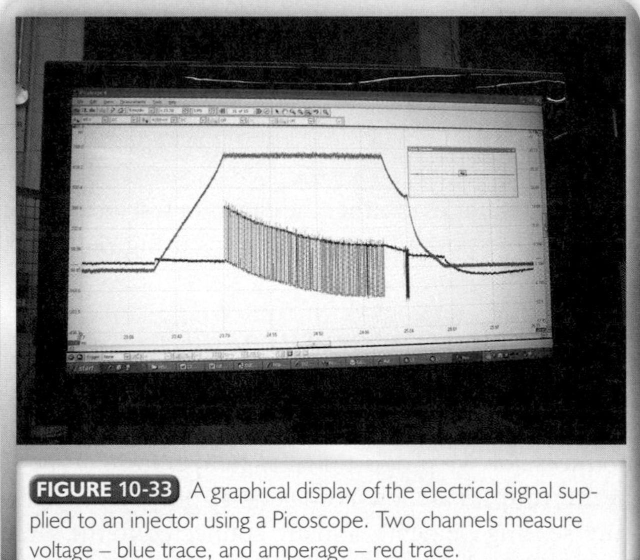

FIGURE 10-33 A graphical display of the electrical signal supplied to an injector using a Picoscope. Two channels measure voltage – blue trace, and amperage – red trace.

A faster-sampling graphing meter is better suited to detect a problem like this.

The life expectancy of an electric motor is another example of a component that can be evaluated by examining the small changes in current and voltage spikes caused by worn brushes. Scanners and OEM diagnostic software can also graph values captured by the ECM associated with a vehicle system such as engine, ABS, or body control through the diagnostic connector. Dedicated graphing meters will connect directly to a sensor, circuit, or component needing testing. Whereas a single-channel graphing meter will have only one input, two-, three-, and four-channel units will have as many inputs and can graph the values together or on separate screens for comparative purposes. Oscilloscopes have more elaborate display modes to capture one-off signal glitches or jitter. Selectable signal triggers, sources, display rulers, slope measurement, and a wider variety of display options are also used by oscilloscopes.

When performing electrical circuit diagnostics, purpose-made jumper wires, fused jumper wires, and break-out boxes are helpful for quickly and effectively diagnosing problems without damaging wiring or connectors by back-probing or piercing wires FIGURE 10-34. A break-out box is connected in series with a major component or wiring harness to an ECM. Signals on each wire in the harness will correspond to a pin on the break-out box FIGURE 10-35. OEM templates, which are thin plastic sheets with printed numbers or letters, can be obtained to lay over the pins, helping to identify specific pin functions or circuit numbers. Smaller break-out harnesses, which connect to sensors or special wiring harnesses, are also useful to make pin-point tests of circuits required by diagnostic procedures FIGURE 10-36.

FIGURE 10-34 Purpose-made jumper wires with terminal ends matching specific types of connector terminals are used to perform pin-point tests of volts, amperage, and resistance.

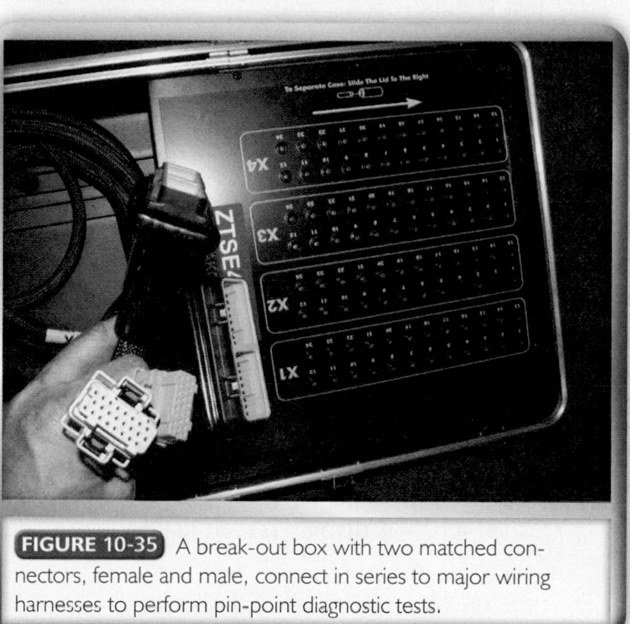

FIGURE 10-35 A break-out box with two matched connectors, female and male, connect in series to major wiring harnesses to perform pin-point diagnostic tests.

Vibration Analyzers

Vibration analyzers are used to identify the root cause of vehicle vibration. Typically, flywheel speed and road speed sensors are used along with data collected from a three-axis accelerometer placed under the driver's seat using a magnet. Data are collected from the sensors into a signal-conditioning module that stores the information for analysis by a computer.

Electronic Service Tools—Scanners

A variety of scanner types are used to read serial data from a vehicle data link connector. The scanner uses software to translate the serial data into a format that can be read by the technician. See FIGURE 10-37 and FIGURE 10-38. More sophisticated scanners use bi-directional communication between the tool and the ECM to send commands that can actuate output devices, or cause the ECM to enter diagnostic routines such as performing cylinder cut-out tests.

FIGURE 10-36 Break-out harnesses are used to connect to sensors, smaller wiring harnesses, and other components to perform pin-point tests.

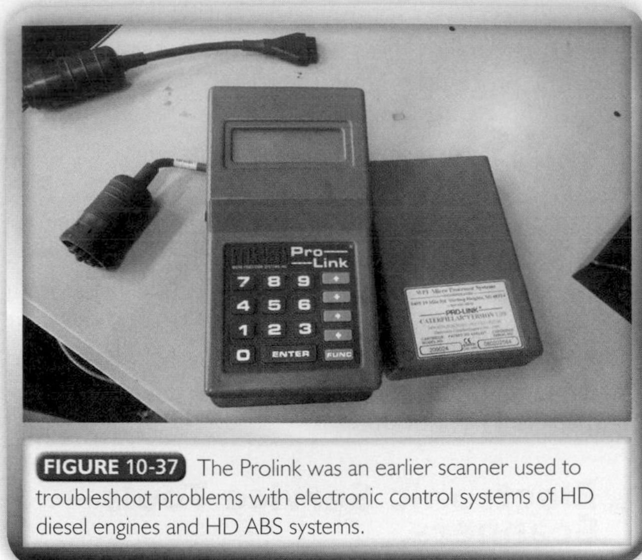

FIGURE 10-37 The Prolink was an earlier scanner used to troubleshoot problems with electronic control systems of HD diesel engines and HD ABS systems.

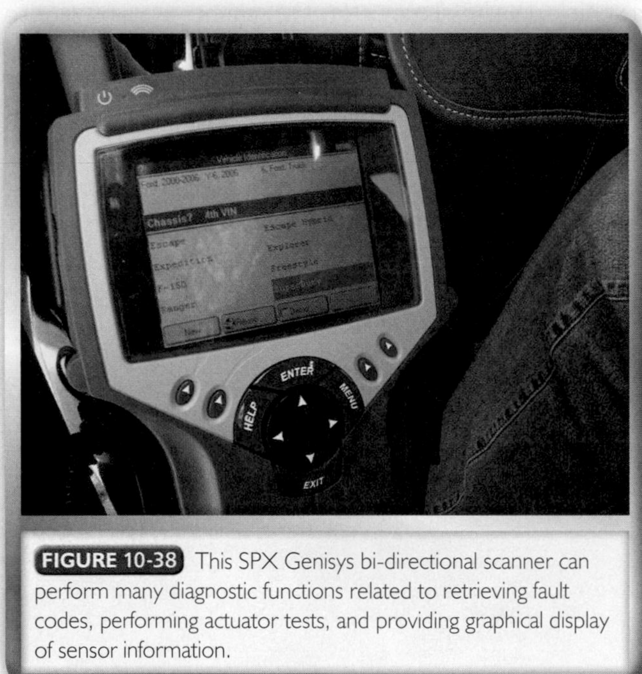

FIGURE 10-38 This SPX Genisys bi-directional scanner can perform many diagnostic functions related to retrieving fault codes, performing actuator tests, and providing graphical display of sensor information.

SAE Requirements for On-Board Diagnostic Scan Tools

The SAE has developed on-board diagnostic (OBD) standards for hand-held scan tools. These standards include the following:

1. Standards for 6- and 9-pin DLC connectors
2. J1978 – Describes the basic functions that an OBD scanner must support, including::
   - Automatic hands-off determination of the communication protocol
   - Obtaining and displaying the status of OBD evaluations such as supported and completed readiness or monitor tests and lamp MIL lamp status
   - Obtaining and displaying Diagnostic Trouble Codes (DTCs)
   - Obtaining and displaying emissions-related data from engine parameters
   - Obtaining and displaying emissions-related freeze frame data
   - Clearing stored emissions-related DTCs, freeze frame data, and diagnostic test results
3. J1979 – Describes diagnostic test modes for emission-related diagnostic data that can be displayed by scan tools, including:
   - Mode #1 – Request for current powertrain diagnostic data including: engine parameters, MIL status, and readiness codes
   - Mode #2 – Request for powertrain freeze frame data
   - Mode #3 – Request emission-related powertrain diagnostic trouble codes (DTCs)
   - Mode #4 – Clear/Reset emission-related diagnostic information including MIL status, DTCs, freeze frame and readiness codes
   - Mode #5 – Request exhaust gas sensor monitor test results
   - Mode #6 – Request latest on-board monitoring test results for non-continuous monitor systems (i.e., aftertreatment catalysts, exhaust gas recirculation [EGR], missfire, etc.)
   - Mode #7 – Request latest on-board monitoring test results for continuous monitor systems (i.e., comprehensive component monitor)
   - Mode #8 – This mode can be used to request control of an on-board system and is manufacturer defined
   - Mode #9 – This optional mode is used to report vehicle information such as the VIN number, and possibly calibration information stored in the vehicle ECM
   - Mode #10 – A display screen listing fault codes

Additional Scan Tool Functions

Scan tools are versatile instruments that can perform a variety of additional functions:

- *Bi-directional control* – Scan tools can control selected vehicle components or initiate systems actuator or diagnostic tests on command.
- *Graphical display* – Scan tools can display real-time engine parameters or recorded data in a graphing format.
- *Help menu/trouble code library* – Scan tools can guide a technician through certain procedures or has a built-in library of all the SAE generic trouble codes.
- *Printer/Computer output* – Scan tools connect to a printer or computer and prints or displays information from the vehicle.
- *Record/playback or snapshot mode* – Scan tools can record a block of real-time engine data and replay that information in order to root cause a malfunction.
- *Reprogramming of vehicle ECM* – Scan tools can perform off-board or on-board reprogramming of a vehicle's computer modules, specifically the powertrain (ECM).
- *Scopes and meters* – Scan tools can operate as a multimeter (measuring voltage, resistance, amperage, etc.).

Code Readers

The most basic diagnostic scanner is a code reader. Code readers can access, interpret, and display on-board diagnostic (OBD) codes from the vehicle's ECM. Inexpensive models may only display a numerical OBD code. Enhanced readers may provide an alphabetic explanation of the code. Code readers may also clear codes, turn off the MIL, and display the "ready" status of various OBD monitors. However, a code reader does not display any sensor data or other operating information needed for advanced diagnostic work.

Code readers can become outdated as new OBD codes are added every year. Updating a code reader's capabilities is usually not possible.

Data Link Adapters

Data link adapters are used to translate serial data from the DLC into a format readable by a desktop or laptop computer. The adapter may connect to the PC using a cable connected to a serial port, USB port, or wirelessly over the internet or Bluetooth communication **FIGURE 10-39**.

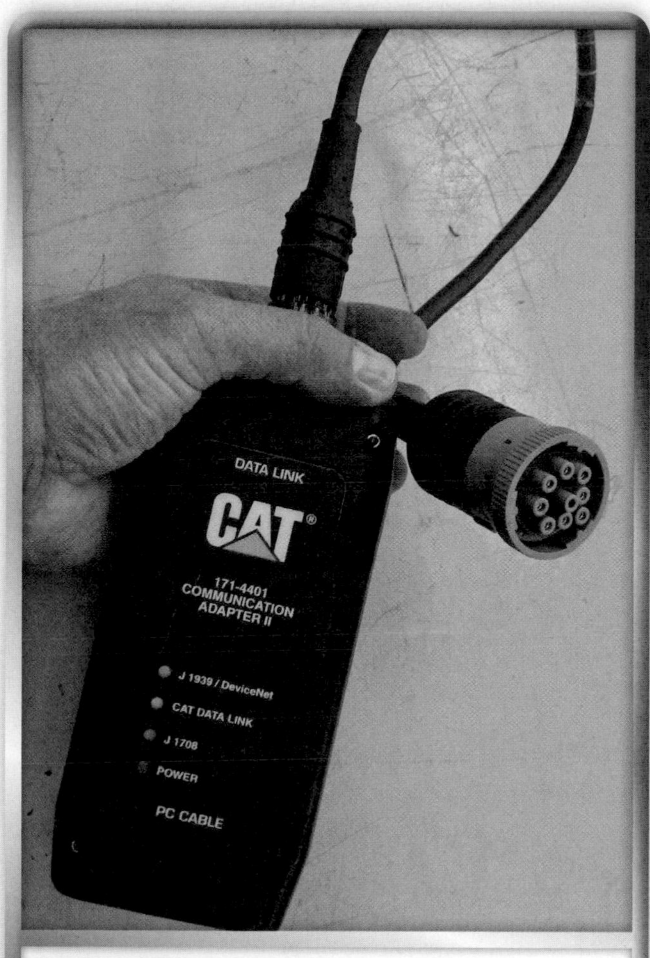

FIGURE 10-39 This data link adapter connected to the vehicle data link can translate DLC serial data into serial data readable by PCs or laptops. The adapter can communicate using a cable or with another adapter wirelessly over the same radio frequency as wireless internet, or by using Bluetooth radio frequencies.

Wrap-up

Ready for Review

- A variety of electrical test instruments are needed to diagnose and repair electrical problems.
- The simplest piece of electrical test equipment used to determine the presence or absence of current is a test light.
- Self-powered test lights are like regular test lights except that they contain a 1.5-volt battery.
- Multimeters are electrical measuring instruments combining functions of at least voltage, resistance, and amperage measurement into a single compact instrument.
- Multimeters can be analog, digital, or high-impedance and come in auto-ranging and manual-ranging types.
- Before using a digital meter, one of the first things to check is whether its shunts or fuses are in place and functioning. Shunts are internal conductors with a small calibrated resistance, which directs some current flow into the meter when measuring amperage.
- By checking the resistance or circuit continuity with an ohmmeter, a circuit can be evaluated for shorts, opens, or high resistance.
- Ohmmeters are ineffective when checking for resistances in high-amperage, low-resistance circuits, such as when measuring battery cable voltage loss.
- Voltmeters measure the difference in electrical pressure or electron velocity between two different points in the circuit.
- Measuring amperage requires that the powered circuit is opened, and the meter placed in series with the circuit so that all the current flows through the meter shunts.
- Inductive amp clamps are useful tools for measuring amperage without disturbing the circuit.
- Multimeters use a thermocouple accessory to measure temperature by contact. Heating the thermocouple produces voltage proportional to temperature.
- Circuit tracers are useful for identifying circuit problems in wires deeply buried behind walls or in tightly bundled harness.
- Graphing meters allow technicians to assess component serviceability by analyzing the waveforms.
- When performing electrical circuit diagnostics, purpose-made jumper wires, fused jumper wires, and break-out boxes are helpful for quickly and effectively diagnosing problems without damaging wiring or connectors by back-probing or piercing wires.
- A variety of scanner types are used to read serial data from a vehicle data link connector.
- The most basic diagnostic scanner is a code reader. Code readers can access, interpret, and display on-board diagnostic (OBD) codes from the vehicle's ECM.

Vocabulary Builder

analog meter A meter that uses a sweeping needle that continuously measures electrical values.

auto-ranging multimeter A multimeter that has fewer positions on its range selection knob and will automatically select the correct range when meter test leads are connected to a circuit.

circuit (wire) tracer An electronic service tool used to trace a single wire over a distance where multiple wires are bundled, shorted, or open.

data link adapter A device used to translate serial data from the DLC into a format readable by a desktop or laptop computer.

digital multimeter A type of multimeter that provides numerical displays of electrical data.

graphing meter An electrical test instrument used to analyze waveforms and graphically plot an electrical value of a signal over time.

high-impedance multimeter A meter that samples very little of a circuit's own current to take a measurement.

inductive amp clamp A device that measures amperage by measuring a conductor's magnetic field strength, which is proportional to amperage.

manual-ranging multimeter A multimeter that must be set to the correct range first based on anticipated values measured.

shunts Internal conductors with small calibrated resistance and that direct current flow into the meter while measuring amperage.

test light The simplest piece of electrical test equipment, which consists of either a 12- or 24-volt incandescent light bulb connected to an insulated lead and a sharpened metal probe.

Type K thermocouple A low-cost, general-purpose, temperature-sensing element connected to the same meter terminals for measuring DC millivolts.

vibration analyzer A device used to identify the root cause of vehicle vibration.

Review Questions

1. Which of the following statements about self-powered test lights is correct?
   a. Self-powered test lights are like regular test lights except that they contain a 1.5-volt battery.
   b. Self-powered lights can be used to check for both open circuits and grounded circuits when either chassis power or ground
   c. The internal battery can supply current needed to illuminate the light.
   d. All of the choices are correct.
2. What is the usual capability of a multimeter to measure current flow in amps?
   a. 5 amps
   b. 10 amps
   c. 15 amps
   d. 20 amps
3. Which of the following is NOT correct concerning electrical measurement with multimeters?
   a. Three types of measurements—voltage, resistance, and amperage—can be taken from circuits in three different ways.
   b. An ohmmeter uses a small amount of electrical current from an internal battery and sends it through a circuit or component.
   c. The circuit must never be powered when connected to an ohmmeter.
   d. When using an ohmmeter, it is necessary to observe polarity when connecting test leads.
4. When using a manual-ranging multimeter, what range setting should be selected to measure 12 volts?
   a. 12 volt
   b. 18 volt
   c. 20 volt
   d. 24 volt
5. Which of the following statements about inductive amp clamps is correct?
   a. In powered circuits, inductive amp clamps placed around a conductor are used to measure amperage.
   b. These devices work by measuring a conductor's magnetic field strength, which is proportional to amperage.
   c. Both A and B
   d. Neither A nor B
6. Type K thermocouples are a(n) ________ temperature-sensing element.
   a. high-cost
   b. inefficient
   c. general-purpose
   d. rudimentary
7. Which of the following statements about the diode scale is correct?
   a. The low-voltage settings of an ohmmeter may not properly evaluate a diode, as a good silicon diode requires approximately 0.5–0.7 volts to forward bias or conduct current.
   b. Below 0.5–0.7 volts, the diode may appear to block current in both directions; when placed in the diode range, a meter will put out higher voltage than barrier voltage of 0.7 volts to cause the diode to reverse and forward bias.
   c. Both A and B
   d. Neither A nor B
8. Which of the following statements about graphing meters is NOT correct?
   a. One of the latest diagnostic tools is a digital graphing meter used to analyze electrical waveforms produced by sensors, motors, actuators, and alternators.
   b. Graphing meters plot an electrical value of a signal over time, displaying an easy-to-read graph with signal value on the x-axis and the time on the y-axis.
   c. Component serviceability can be determined by analyzing the waveform or comparing it to known signals of good quality.
   d. A Hall effect sensor may have intermittent problems that may not be detected by the vehicle's on-board diagnostic system.
9. Which of the following statements about scanners is correct?
   a. A variety of scanner types are used to read serial data from a vehicle data link connector.
   b. The scanner uses software to translate the serial data into a format that can be read by the technician.
   c. More sophisticated scanners use bi-directional communication between the tool and the ECM to send commands that can actuate output devices, or cause the ECM to enter diagnostic routines such as performing cylinder cut-out tests.
   d. All of the choices are correct
10. Which of the following is included in the SAE J1978 requirements?
    a. Obtaining and displaying Diagnostic Trouble Codes (DTCs)
    b. Obtaining and displaying emissions-related data from engine parameters.
    c. Both A and B
    d. Neither A nor B

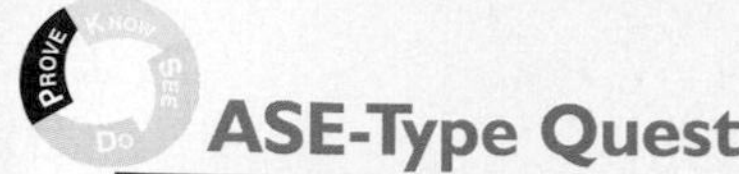

ASE-Type Questions

1. Technician A says that a test light is the simplest piece of electrical test equipment used to determine the presence or absence of current. Technician B says that a test light consists of either an 18- or 36-volt incandescent light bulb connected to an insulated lead and a sharpened metal probe. Who is correct?
   a. Technician A
   b. Technician B
   c. Both Technician A and Technician B
   d. Neither Technician A nor Technician B
2. Technician A says that a popular type of LED test light is battery powered and has two LEDs—one red and the other green. Technician B says that the LED light will change brightness depending on the circuit's voltage. Who is correct?
   a. Technician A
   b. Technician B
   c. Both Technician A and Technician B
   d. Neither Technician A nor Technician B
3. Technician A says that multimeters are electrical measuring instruments combining functions of at least voltage, resistance, and amperage measurement into a single compact instrument. Technician B says that digital multimeters are the most common category of multimeters and provide numerical displays of electrical data. Who is correct?
   a. Technician A
   b. Technician B
   c. Both Technician A and Technician B
   d. Neither Technician A nor Technician B
4. Technician A says that a multimeter measures resistance, continuity, voltage, and amperage. Technician B says that the multimeter can be used to measure circuit resistance in amps to determine whether amperage is within specifications. Who is correct?
   a. Technician A
   b. Technician B
   c. Both Technician A and Technician B
   d. Neither Technician A nor Technician B
5. Technician A says that before using a digital multimeter, the first task is to check that its shunts and fuses are in place and functioning. Technician B says that shunts do not operate like fuses and do not have a maximum rating. Who is correct?
   a. Technician A
   b. Technician B
   c. Both Technician A and Technician B
   d. Neither Technician A nor Technician B
6. Technician A says that the multimeter is connected in series with the circuit or component to measure the voltage dropped by the circuit resistance. Technician B says that the ohmmeter works well in testing semiconductors. Who is correct?
   a. Technician A
   b. Technician B
   c. Both Technician A and Technician B
   d. Neither Technician A nor Technician B
7. Technician A says that ammeters measure the quantity of electrons flowing through a circuit per second of time. Technician B says that measuring amperage requires that the circuit be broken and the meter placed in series with the circuit so that all the current flows through the meter shunts. Who is correct?
   a. Technician A
   b. Technician B
   c. Both Technician A and Technician B
   d. Neither Technician A nor Technician B
8. Technician A says that multimeters use a thermocouple accessory to measure temperature by contact. Technician B says that heating the thermocouple produces amperage proportional to temperature. Who is correct?
   a. Technician A
   b. Technician B
   c. Both Technician A and Technician B
   d. Neither Technician A nor Technician B
9. Technician A says that circuit tracers, also called wire tracers, are electronic service tools used to trace a single wire over a distance where multiple wires are bundled, shorted, or open. Technician B says that circuit tracers can identify wires deeply buried behind walls or in tightly bundled harness. Who is correct?
   a. Technician A
   b. Technician B
   c. Both Technician A and Technician B
   d. Neither Technician A nor Technician B
10. Technician A says that vibration analyzers are used to identify the root cause of vehicle vibration. Technician B says that, typically, flywheel speed and road speed sensors are used along with data collected from a three-axis accelerometer placed under the driver's seat using a magnet. Who is correct?
    a. Technician A
    b. Technician B
    c. Both Technician A and Technician B
    d. Neither Technician A nor Technician B

CHAPTER 11

NATEF Tasks

There are no NATEF tasks for this chapter.

Knowledge Objectives

After reading this chapter, you will be able to:

1. Describe the purpose and applications of batteries. (pp 330–333)
2. Identify and describe the construction and types of lead–acid batteries. (pp 333–339)
3. Identify and describe the features of lithium, nickel-cadmium, and nickel-metal hydride batteries as well as ultra capacitors. (pp 333–334)
4. Identify and describe the purpose, operation, and application of battery types. (pp 333–334)
5. Define battery terminology and explain battery ratings. (pp 339–341)
6. Recommend the correct size, type, and rating of replacement batteries. (pp 341–342)
7. Identify and explain chemical reactions in lead–acid batteries during charging and discharging. (pp 343–344)

Commercial Vehicle Batteries

Skills Objectives

There are no skills objectives for this chapter.

Introduction

Batteries are the most essential component in a vehicle's, electrical system. Not only do batteries provide starting power for engines and operating electrical accessories, they play a critical role in proper operation and longevity of many other electrical components. The recent development of medium- and heavy-duty hybrid drive vehicles has added to the battery's list of jobs. In addition to their traditional functions, batteries must now supply energy to electric drive motors and help recover energy during braking. Today's technicians need to know a lot more about the various types of batteries they will encounter, how those batteries work, as well as what should be done to maintain, test, and work safely with them.

What Is a Battery?

Batteries are not devices that store electricity. In reality, they just convert chemical energy into electrical energy and vice versa. When connected to an electrical load, such as a light or electric motor, chemical reactions taking place inside the battery force electrons from the negative to the positive terminal of the battery though the load. Flow of electricity will end when the battery's chemical energy is depleted by the electrical loads in the circuit. The single direction electrons flow during discharge means a battery is a source of direct current (DC).

Battery Classifications

Batteries can be classified into two basic categories: primary and secondary. In a **primary battery**, chemical reactions are not reversible, and the battery cannot be recharged. In contrast, **secondary batteries** are rechargeable **FIGURE 11-1**. By reversing the direction of current and pushing electricity back into the battery, the chemical reactions that originally produced electrical current

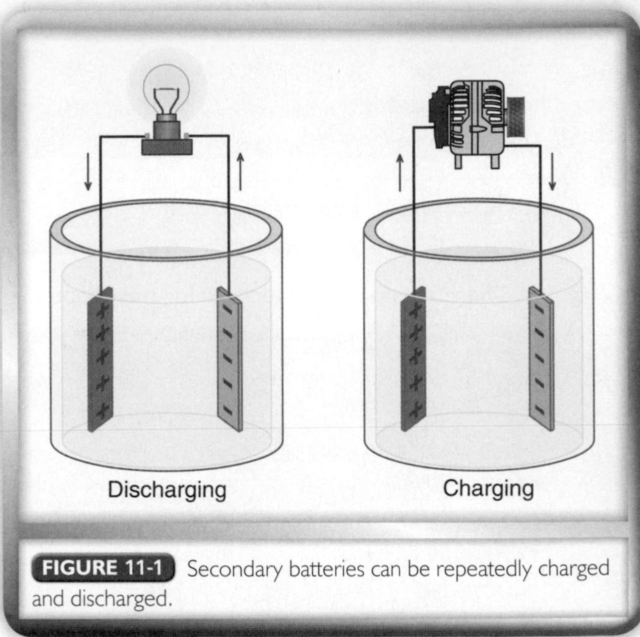

FIGURE 11-1 Secondary batteries can be repeatedly charged and discharged.

You Are the Technician

As a technician with many years of service in your truck and heavy equipment dealership, you've been asked to join the health and safety committee. Your experience working in a shop environment has made you conscious of the importance of using safe working practices and making workplace safety a top priority. One of the initiatives of the health and safety committee is implementing the best safety practices to use while working with batteries. In fact, development of an in-house policy in addition to OSHA requirements originates from a recent incident where one worker was injured by an exploding battery while jump-starting a vehicle. As you are considering the various procedures that should be rigorously followed in the shop to avoid any accidents, injuries, or damage to customer vehicles and property.

1. What are the major safety issues related to working with batteries?
2. What protective equipment should you use when filling batteries or checking cell electrolyte with a hydrometer?
3. Outline a sequence of actions a technician should follow while jump-starting a vehicle.

are renewed, allowing the secondary battery to be used over and over again. For this reason, secondary batteries based on the principles of galvanic reaction are the most practical for use in automotive applications. A **galvanic reaction** is a chemical reaction in which electricity is generated when two dissimilar metals are placed in an electrolyte.

Galvanic Batteries

The term *battery* more accurately refers to a collection of electrochemical cells connected together. A discovery made more than two hundred years ago by a medical experimenter named Galvani found that electricity is produced when two dissimilar metals are placed in an electrolyte. **Electrolyte** refers to any liquid that conducts electric current. For example, pure water will not conduct current. Tap water, however, will. That's because tap water often contains minerals and chlorine, so tap water is an electrolyte. Water containing salt, acids, or alkaline solutions are even better conductors of electricity. The dissimilar metals placed in an electrolyte form electrodes—which are the points of the battery forming the positive and negative electrical poles. Chemical action between the electrolyte and electrodes strips electrons from one metal electrode and adds electrons to another electrode. That process develops the battery's polarity. After Galvani, another experimenter named Volta built the first battery by alternately stacking copper and zinc plates separated with a piece of saltwater-soaked cardboard. Volta named it a "voltaic pile" after demonstrating its electrical properties.

TECHNICIAN TIP

Galvanic reactions are observed in many places. Corrosion is one example of a galvanic reaction. The cooling system of an engine contains water (an electrolyte) and dissimilar metals like copper injector tubes, cast iron blocks, aluminum water pump housings, and so on. Metals losing electrons disintegrate while other metals remain unaffected. However, the electron transfer between the metals through coolant is easily observed by placing a voltmeter with one lead in the coolant and the other on the engine block or other metal part. (Corrosion inhibitors in the cooling system work by minimizing the loss of electrons from metals.) On trailers, aluminum side plates are insulated with a piece of nonconductive Mylar or insulating tape to electrically isolate the plate from steel I-beams supporting the floor. For the same reason, when aluminum and steel disc wheels are placed together on the same wheel end, they are separated with a plastic or nylon gasket to minimize corrosion caused by galvanic reactions.

A battery consists of two dissimilar metals: an insulator material separating the metals and an electrolyte, which is an electrically conductive solution. The material from which the electrodes are made and the type of electrolyte determine the voltage potential of a battery. The area of the plates making up each positive and negative electrode determines the capacity or amperage of a battery.

The traditional commercial vehicle battery type is the lead-acid battery. It is available in a variety of sizes and designs to meet the requirements for various applications. For example, the battery used for starting a vehicle's engine is different from the battery used for a boat, golf cart, or bulldozer. Each requires unique design characteristics based on its applications. Batteries for commercial vehicles using diesel engines are designed to supply high amperage to the starting motor for short periods of time. In contrast, a deep cycle battery is intended for use where its current is almost completely depleted, supplying smaller, continuous loads over longer periods of time.

TECHNICIAN TIP

Maintaining a strong negative ground on a vehicle will minimize chassis corrosion caused by galvanic reaction. You may notice most corrosion takes place at positive battery posts and at the end of non-insulated, positively charged wires. This happens because positively charged wire ends and battery posts are deficient of electrons. Oxygen and molecules in road salt are examples of substances that easily provide those electrons to electron-depleted metal and then are electrically bound to positive terminals and wire ends. Some military equipment and off-road heavy equipment from Europe use a positive ground system to protect the exposed wiring on starters, alternators, and wiring harnesses from the effects of corrosion. Electrical system reliability is enhanced at the expense of chassis corrosion, which instead attacks large heavy steel chassis components.

Battery Functions

Batteries similar to those shown in FIGURE 11-2 have traditionally been used in heavy vehicles to provide starting current and operate electrical accessories if the engine is not running.

And, although supplying electric current for starting is the most obvious function for a battery, it's important to consider the other jobs the battery performs that are critical to proper electrical system operation. Battery

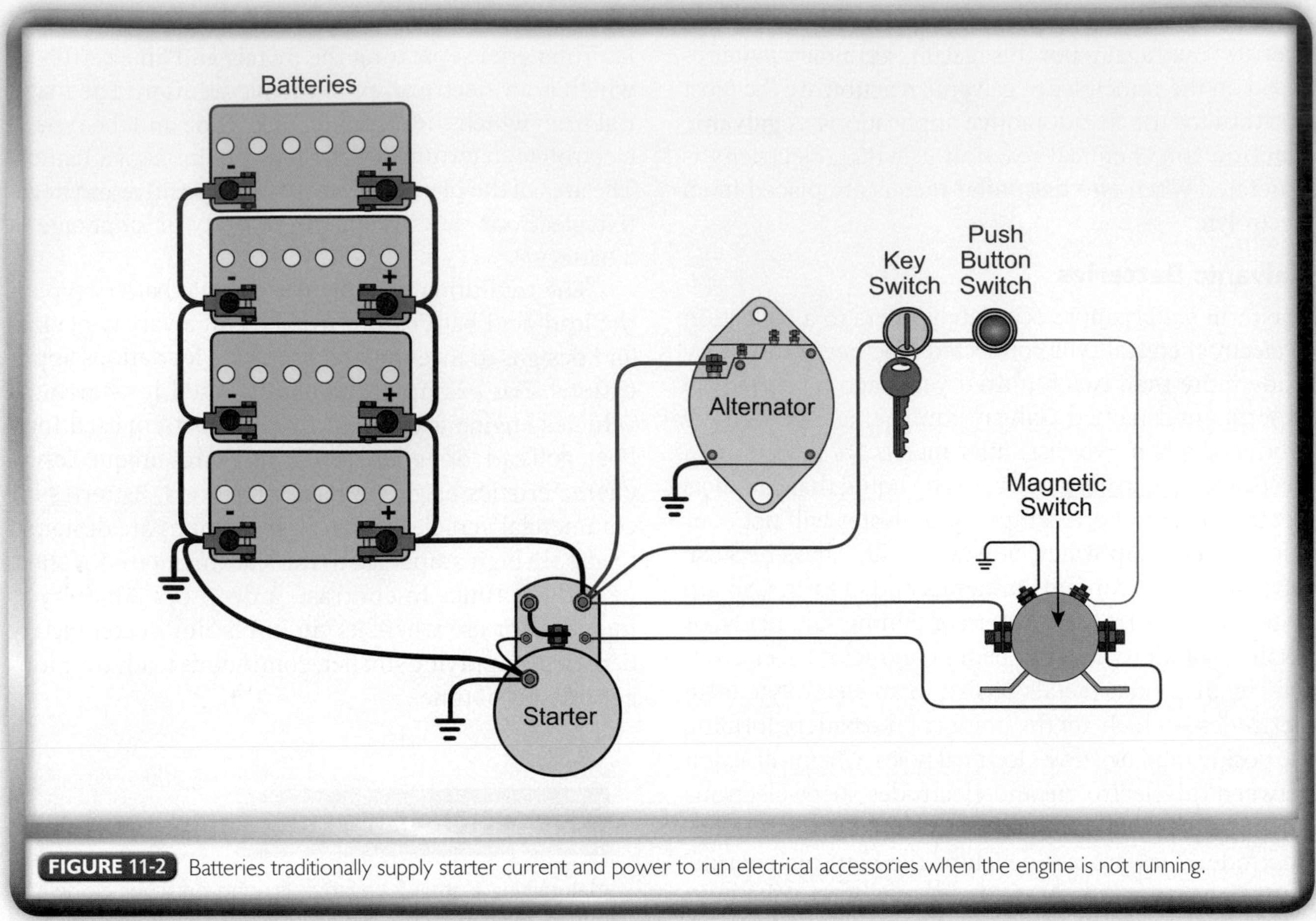

FIGURE 11-2 Batteries traditionally supply starter current and power to run electrical accessories when the engine is not running.

functions on medium- and heavy-duty commercial vehicles include:

1. **Providing electrical energy to the vehicle whenever the engine is not running.** When the engine is running, a properly designed and operational charging system will supply electrical current to meet most electrical demands and charge the battery. For today's heavy vehicles and equipment, the limitation on or, even elimination of, engine idle means batteries need to supply electrical current for prolonged periods to devices such as electro-hydraulic pumps for hydraulic brakes, power steering, coolant pumps, and air conditioning compressors. Hybrid electric vehicles are now commonplace in urban transit. Hybrid electric transit buses are dependent on battery-supplied electrical current to operate all electrical devices, including electric drive motors and all electrical accessories, for much longer periods than conventional vehicles using accessories driven by an internal combustion engine.
2. **Providing electrical energy to operate the starter motor, ignition, and other electrical systems during cranking.** Other devices, such as hydraulic or air starter motors, could be used to start engines. However, even electronically controlled diesel injection systems require current to operate during cranking. When electric starter motors are used, batteries must be capable of delivering high current flow for short periods of time. Batteries used for cranking purposes have unique construction features and are commonly termed **starting, lighting, and ignition (SLI) batteries**. Commercial equipment, particularly diesel-powered equipment, will use multiple batteries, called a bank of batteries, connected in series or parallel to produce adequate starting current.
3. **Providing extra electrical power whenever power requirements exceed the output of the charging system.** High current demands are occasionally placed on the electrical system. For example, when an engine is idling, the charging system current output is low. Current flow to blower motors operating at high speed for heating or air conditioning systems, lighting circuits, and other electrical devices can exceed the output of the charging system. To maintain proper operation of these circuits, the batteries should be sized to provide adequate current.

4. **Storing energy over long periods of time. Even when vehicles are not in use for extended periods of time, the battery is still expected to deliver current to start a vehicle.** Today, heavy vehicles and equipment have numerous **key-off electrical loads**. These are current draws on the battery when the ignition is switched off. Also called **parasitic draw**, this battery current is required to continually operate vehicle security systems, GPS devices, and computer memory for multiple electronic control modules, entertainment systems, and other electrical accessories requiring constant power.
5. **Acting as an electric shock absorber for the vehicle's electrical systems.** The use of microprocessors and microcontrollers in almost every vehicle system makes today's heavy equipment sensitive to fluctuations in voltage. Operating on current in the millivolt range, stray and uneven electrical current can interfere with and even damage the operation of these sensitive electronic devices. The operation of common components such as alternators, switches, and electrical devices with inductive coils regularly produce this type of electrical interference. Batteries help minimize fluctuations in a vehicle electrical system by absorbing and smoothing variations in electrical current.
6. **Operating electric drive traction motors.** The development of hybrid electric vehicles (HEVs) has created new functions in addition to the traditional purposes of batteries. In HEVs, batteries must provide even higher amounts of current for longer periods of time to operate electric traction motors used to propel the vehicle, as illustrated in FIGURE 11-3. The same battery is also used to store energy recovered by the drive motors during braking. HEVs require new battery chemistry and construction to extend battery life, reduce weight, increase energy density, charge more quickly, and discharge and charge more frequently while delivering higher amounts of current flow for extended periods of time. Batteries must accomplish these goals in the harsh operating environment and duty cycle of commercial vehicles. At the same time, batteries must perform with greater and more consistent reliability than ever before. New types of batteries and battery-management systems are used to help meet these operational demands.

Types and Classification of Batteries

Batteries are generally classified by application. In other words, batteries are classified according to what they are used for and how they are made. Batteries are also classified according to the type of plate materials and chemistry used to produce current. Until recently, lead–acid batteries have been the only battery technology used

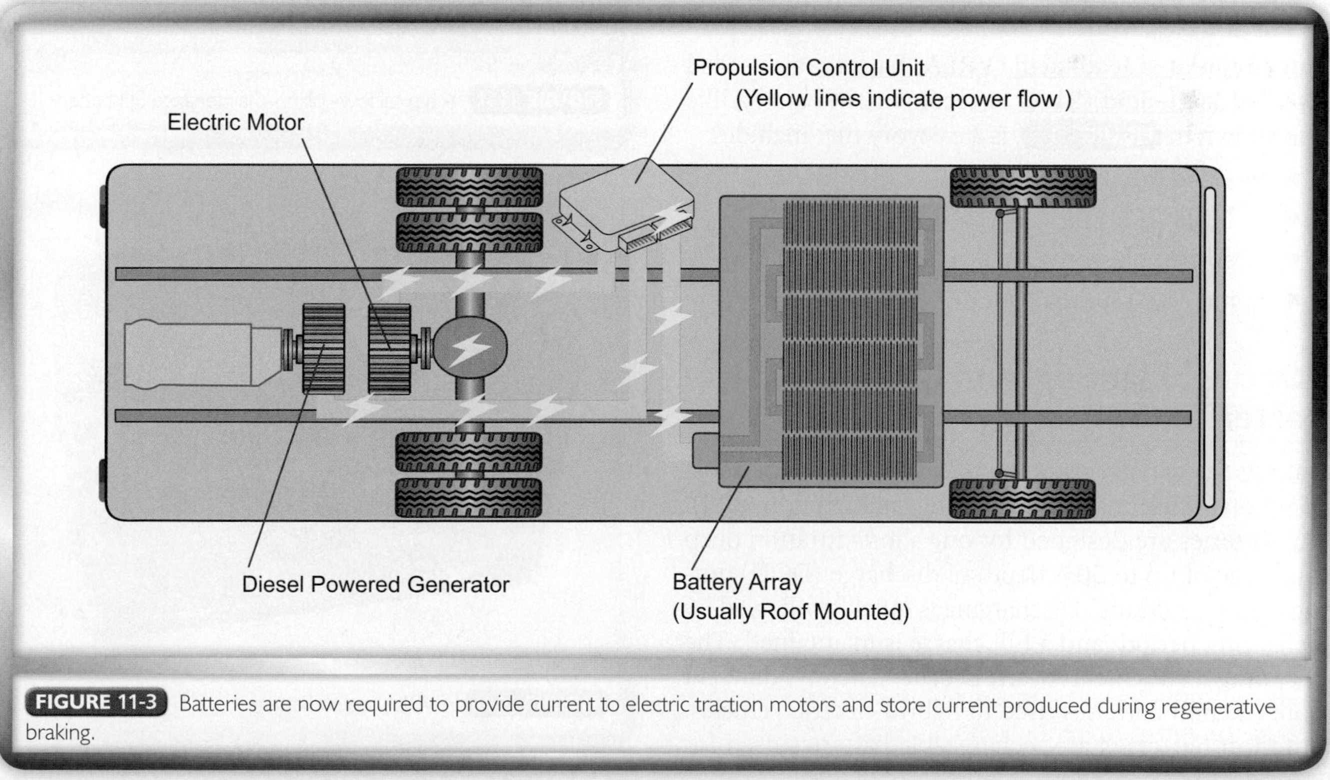

FIGURE 11-3 Batteries are now required to provide current to electric traction motors and store current produced during regenerative braking.

in commercial vehicles. While the search for more durable and reliable lead–acid batteries has brought innovation to that category of batteries, the development of hybrid drive vehicles has resulted in the introductions of different types of battery technology such as nickel–metal hydride and lithium batteries. Other chemistries will be further discussed in the Advanced Battery Technologies chapter.

Lead–Acid Batteries

Lead–acid batteries have been developed commercially for over 130 years and are a mature, reliable, and well-understood technology. They are also the most common battery used in the transportation industry. Lead–acid batteries deliver high rates of current with a higher tolerance for physical and electrical abuse compared to other battery technology. These batteries hold a charge well and when stored dry—without electrolyte—the shelf life is indefinite. Relatively simple compared to other battery technologies, lead–acid batteries are also the least expensive to manufacture in terms of cost per watt of power.

Contributing to the popularity of lead–acid batteries is the fact that they are available in a wide range of sizes and capacities from many suppliers worldwide. Lead–acid batteries can be classified by their construction and application. Six types of construction are found in on-highway commercial vehicles, but the basic chemical action is identical in all, including:

- Flooded cell, including low maintenance (like that shown in FIGURE 11-4) or maintenance free.
- Deep cycle flooded cell.

Valve-regulated lead–acid (VRLA) battery, also called a **sealed lead–acid (SLA)** or recombinant battery, like that shown in FIGURE 11-5, is a category that includes:

- Flooded
- Gel cell
- Absorbed glass mat (AGM)
- Spiral cell (Optima batteries)

Starting, Lighting, and Ignition Batteries (SLI)

Among the categories of lead-acid batteries, the most common use is for starting, lighting, and ignition, (SLI). SLI batteries are designed for one short-duration deep discharge of up to 50% depth of discharge (DOD) during engine cranking. Discharging is quickly followed by a charging period, and a full charge is maintained. The operating requirements of an SLI battery are very different from traction batteries used in hybrid electric vehicles. **Traction batteries** are rechargeable batteries used for propulsion in hybrid electric vehicles. Though identical in appearance, SLI batteries are also constructed differently than deep cycle batteries.

Deep Cycle—Deep Discharge

Deep cycle batteries are used to deliver a lower, steady level of power for a much longer period of time than an SLI type battery. Furthermore, battery plate construction and charging and discharging characteristics of deep cycle batteries are different from SLI type batteries. In heavy vehicles, deep cycle batteries are used to supply current to constantly powered accessories like driver and vehicle communication devices. Deep cycle batteries also supply power to wave inverters, which in turn supply alternating current (AC) to appliances such as

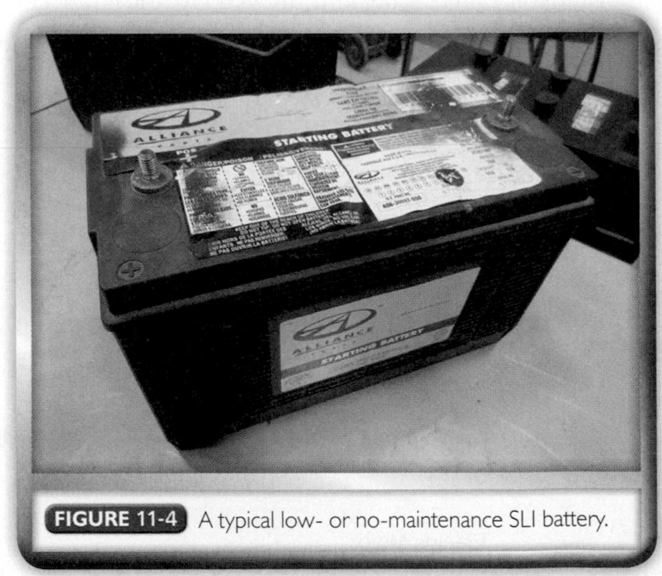

FIGURE 11-4 A typical low- or no-maintenance SLI battery.

FIGURE 11-5 A VRLA sealed battery.

refrigerators, TVs, or laptop chargers. In addition, deep cycle batteries are also used to power accessory lighting, electric winches, and tailgates. This type of battery will typically use a battery isolator system that separates the main vehicle electrical system from the deep cycled battery circuit. The charging system will replenish the deep cycle battery charge but cannot be accessed by the main vehicle electrical circuits.

Battery Construction and Operation

The basic components of a battery are its case, terminals, plates, and electrolyte. Even though the construction of batteries can vary depending on their type and application, these basic components remain the same. It is important that the correct size, type, and construction are selected for the application. Before selecting a battery for a particular application, the technician needs to answer a number of questions. For example, is the requirement for a starting battery or a deep cycle battery used to supply electrical accessories? Is the battery working in extremes of temperature? Is it a high vibration environment? What electrical load does the battery need to supply and for how long? What case and terminal configuration is required?

This section examines battery construction and discusses how those questions and their answers aid in the selection of the correct battery for an application. This section will also explain the charge and discharge cycle of a battery.

Flooded Lead–Acid Batteries

Flooded lead-acid batteries refer to battery cell construction where the electrodes are made from thin lead (Pb) plates submersed in liquid electrolyte. Two dissimilar compositions of lead form the positive and negative electrodes FIGURE 11-6. Sponge lead, which is lead made porous with air bubbles, forms the negative plate. Lead dioxide (PBO_2) is the active material of the positive plate.

The electrodes and electrolyte of a lead-acid battery cell produce 2.1 volts. Connecting cells together in series allows batteries to be produced in a variety of output voltage. This means a fully charged 12-volt battery, in fact, will produce 12.6 volts with no electrical loads by connecting six cells together. 24-volt systems are commonly used in heavy-duty off-road equipment, urban transit buses, highway coaches, and by the military. These are combinations of 12-volt batteries connected in series to produce 24 volts.

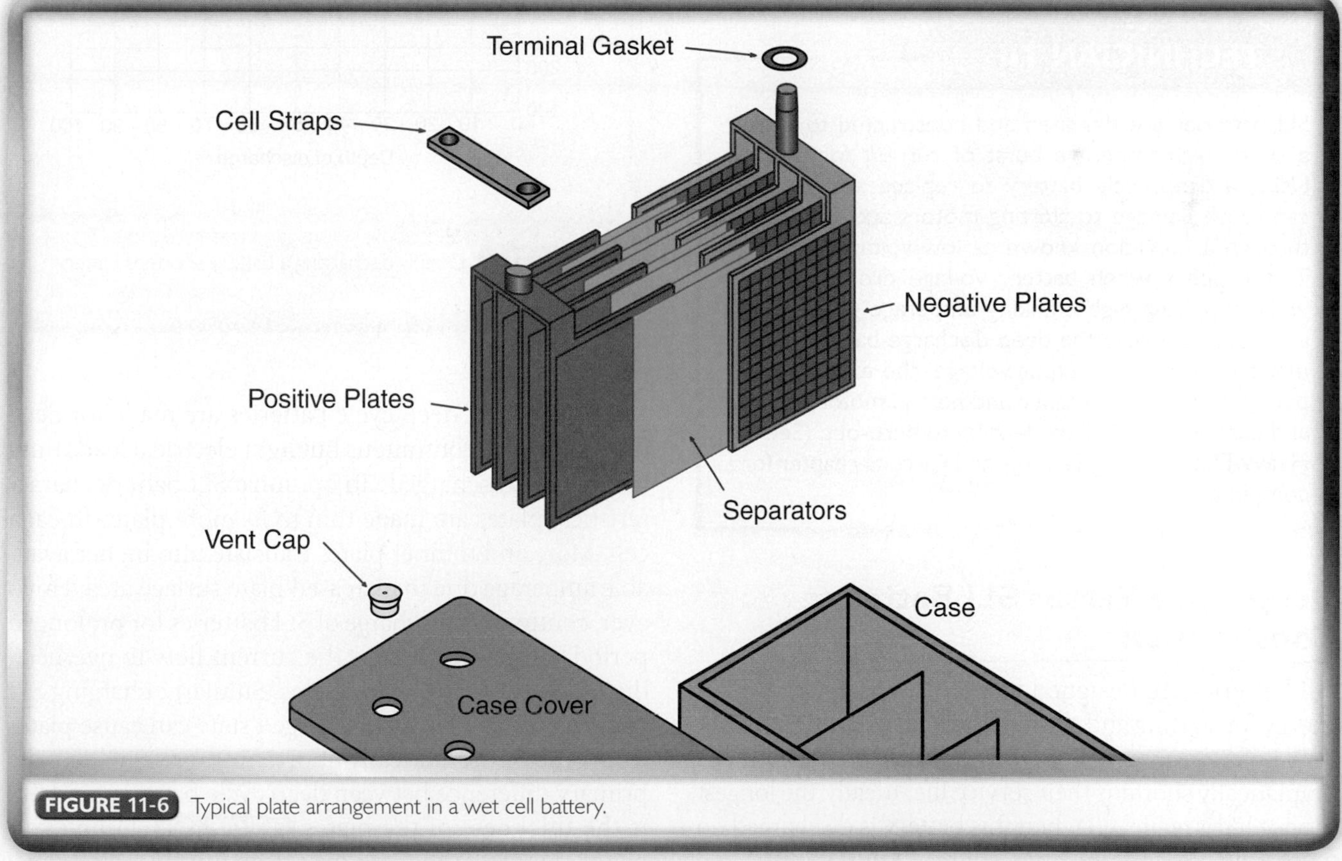

FIGURE 11-6 Typical plate arrangement in a wet cell battery.

Adding Amperage and Voltage

The amount of amperage a battery supplies is a function of the surface area of the plates. To increase the amperage deliverable from a battery, the surface area or number of plates needs to increase. Plates are connected together in parallel within each cell to increase the amperage or capacity of a battery. Positive plates are connected only to other positive plates within each cell and likewise with negative plates. Plate straps for each cell set of positive and negative plates are joined through a connector to another strap in adjacent cells. There are two rows of these inter-cell straps and connectors. In a 12-volt battery, six positive plate straps are linked in series to six negative plate straps, alternating a positive strap to negative strap as each cell is connected FIGURE 11-7. The last cell in the series circuit will contain one of the battery posts, either positive or negative. Strap connections between the cells are made either through the cell partitions in the case or over the top of the partition.

FIGURE 11-7 Interconnections between all six cells in a battery, showing the most negative and positive points of the battery.

Separator Plates

To prevent the battery positive and negative plate from touching and short circuiting, separator plates are placed between each plate in every cell. Separator plates are very thin, porous, glass-fiber materials allowing electrolyte to diffuse freely throughout the cell and at the same time prevent plate contact.

> **TECHNICIAN TIP**
>
> SLI batteries are designed and constructed to deliver a short, high-amperage burst of current for starting. Using a deep cycle battery to replace a SLI battery can cause damage to starting motors and conductors through a condition known as low-voltage burn-out. This happens when battery voltage drops very low while supplying high cranking amperage to the starting motor. Because the deep discharge battery cannot maintain as high an output voltage, the excessive amperage produces resistance and heat in motors, cables, and connection windings, leading to burn-out. (See the Heavy-Duty Starting Systems and Circuits chapter for a complete explanation.)

Deep Cycle Versus SLI Battery Construction

SLI batteries are designed to produce a quick burst of energy for starting and should not be discharged less than 50% before recharging. Deeply discharging SLI batteries dramatically shortens their service life. Ideally, the longest service life is achieved when this battery is discharged no more than 5% and quickly recharged FIGURE 11-8.

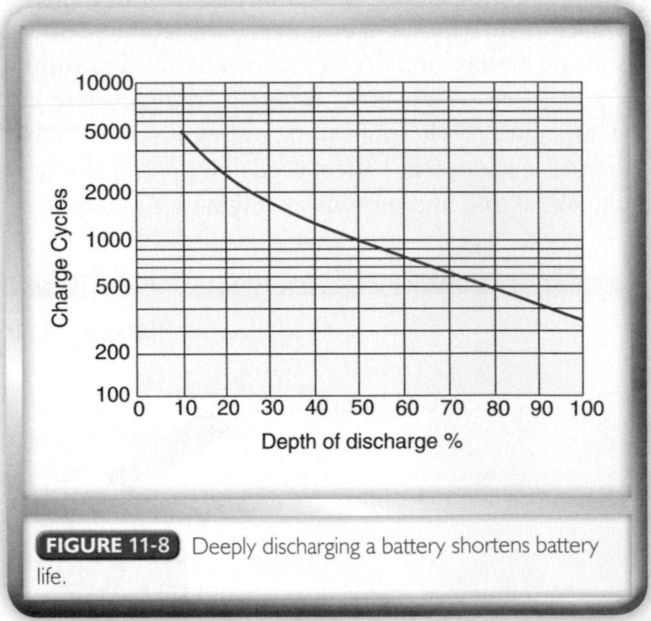

FIGURE 11-8 Deeply discharging a battery shortens battery life.

In contrast, deep cycle batteries are made for deep discharging by continuous but light electrical loads until completely discharged. To optimize SLI battery characteristics, plates are made thin to fit more plates in each cell. More and thinner plates translate into higher available amperage due to increased plate surface area. However, continuous discharge of SLI batteries for prolonged periods of time will cause the current flow to overheat, distort, and warp the thin plates. Similarly, charging SLI batteries from a deeply discharged state can cause plates to overheat, dramatically shortening battery life. The primary difference between deep cycle batteries and SLI is the thickness of the plates FIGURE 11-9. Deep cycle plates are thicker to resist distortion during a discharge/

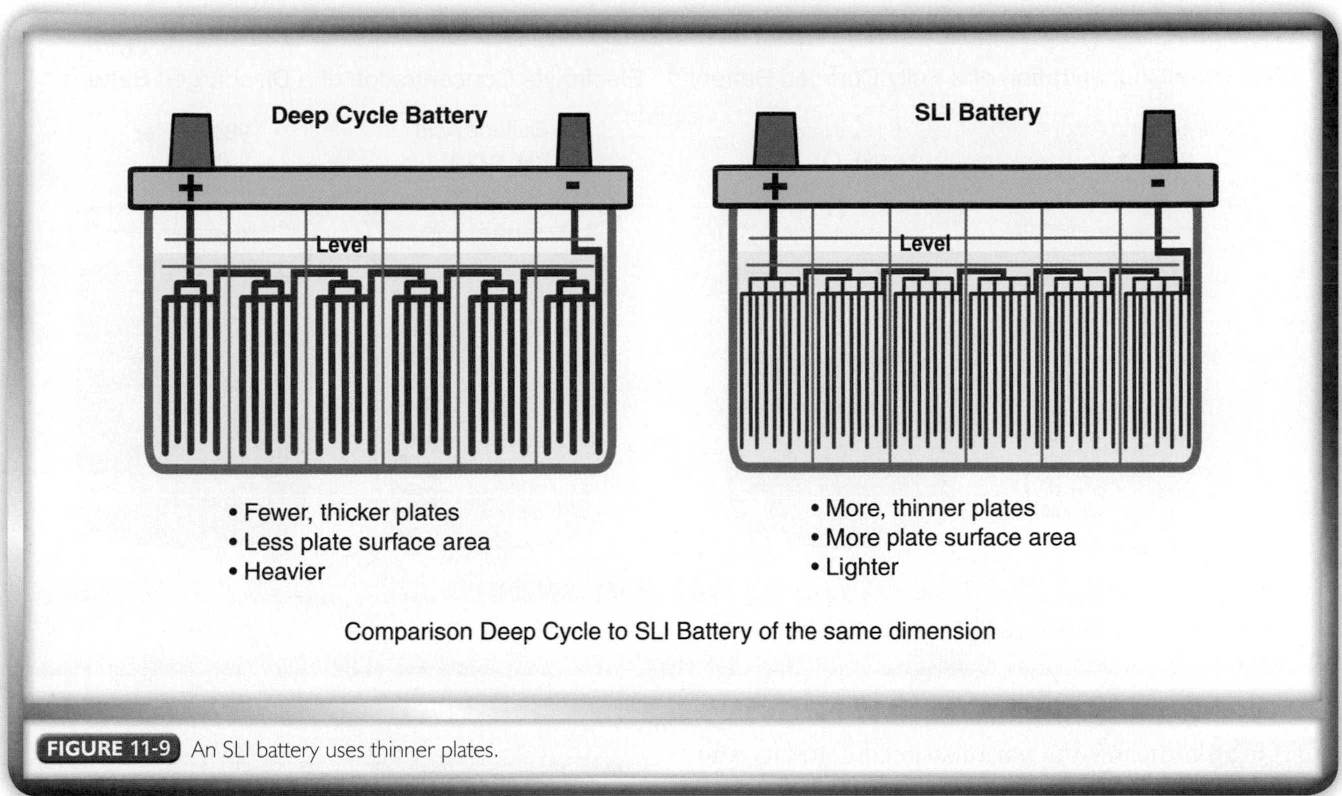

FIGURE 11-9 An SLI battery uses thinner plates.

charge cycle. However, thicker plates mean fewer plates compared to a SLI battery with identical dimensions. Thicker plate batteries also have higher resistance during high amperage charging and discharging in comparison to SLI batteries.

Electrolyte

Lead–acid battery electrolyte is a mixture of 36% sulfuric acid and 64% water. The specific gravity of water is 1.000. (**Specific gravity** is a measure of density.) Sulfuric acid has a specific gravity of 1.835, which means it is much heavier than water. Combined, the sulfuric acid and water solution has a specific gravity of 1.265. This makes it an electrolyte 1.265 times heavier than plain water. During charging and discharging, the specific gravity of the electrolyte changes. When discharging occurs, sulfate from the sulfuric acid enters both positive and negative plates. Oxygen also leaves the positive plate and combines with hydrogen left around in the electrolyte by the departing sulfate. This means the electrolyte has increasingly more water content and less acid during discharge, as illustrated in FIGURE 11-10. The process reverses during charging when sulfate is electrically driven from the plates and renters the electrolyte. Measuring the specific gravity or density of an electrolyte, therefore, is a good measure of battery state of charge (SOC).

Flooded cell batteries can be manufactured with or without an electrolyte. Dry batteries (without electrolyte) can be stored on the shelf for extended periods without the fear of sulfation and are lighter to transport. For this reason electrolyte is often only added to the battery at the point of sale.

When the specific gravity of battery acid is too low, such as when a battery is discharged, it may freeze in colder climates. An electrolyte that has lost water and is, therefore, over concentrated with acid can accelerate corrosion of battery grids to which lead plate material is bonded.

It is important to note that sodium bicarbonate (baking soda, not baking powder) is an effective way to neutralize electrolyte spills. Using a power washer, for example, will reduce the concentration of acid but not neutralize it. Squirting a mixed solution of ammonia and water on spilled battery acid will also neutralize the acid. Water and ammonia will also evaporate, leaving no mess to clean up.

A squeeze bulb and float type **hydrometer**, like the one shown in FIGURE 11-11A, is an instrument used to measure the density or the specific gravity of liquids. It also can be used to measure the specific gravity of batteries. A refractometer is an optical device that measures the density of coolant and battery electrolyte. When a drop of liquid is placed beneath the lens of the device, and then held up against a bright light source, a graduated scale in the view finder indicates the battery's specific gravity. A refractometer is shown in FIGURE 11-11B.

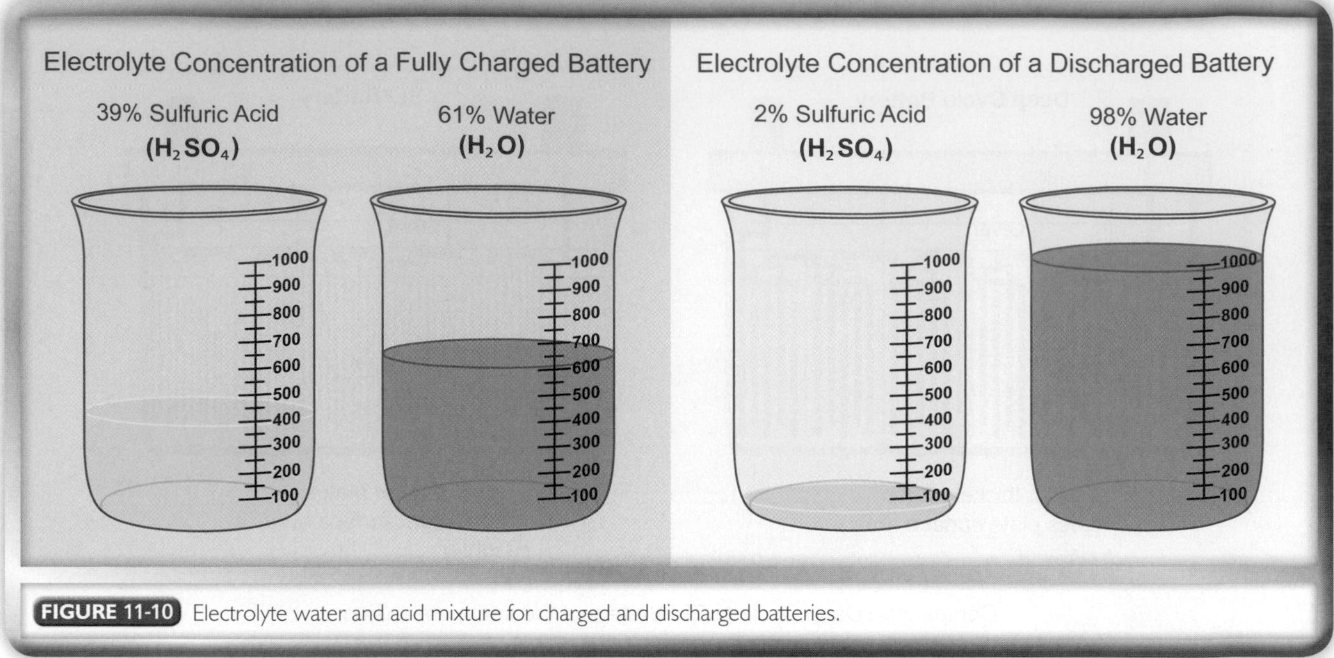

FIGURE 11-10 Electrolyte water and acid mixture for charged and discharged batteries.

TABLE 11-1 indicates the various specific gravity and voltage readings for flooded lead-acid batteries. Electronic hydrometers enable faster, temperature-compensated measurement of the battery's state of charge. Remember that battery acid is highly corrosive, so when using these devices, properly protect yourself by wearing eye protection, a rubber apron, and acid-resistant gloves, particularly when handling electrolyte.

Battery Cases

The battery case is usually made of polypropylene. Ribbing and irregular features on the outside of the case are designed to increase the length of resistive electrical

TABLE 11-1: State of Charge as Indicated by Specific Gravity and Voltage Reading for Flooded Cell Batteries*

Open Circuit Voltage	Specific Gravity	Percentage of Charge
12.65 or greater	1.265 (minimum)	100%
12.45	1.225	75%
12.24	1.190	50 %
12.06	1.155	25%
11.89	1.120	0%

*AGM voltages will differ.

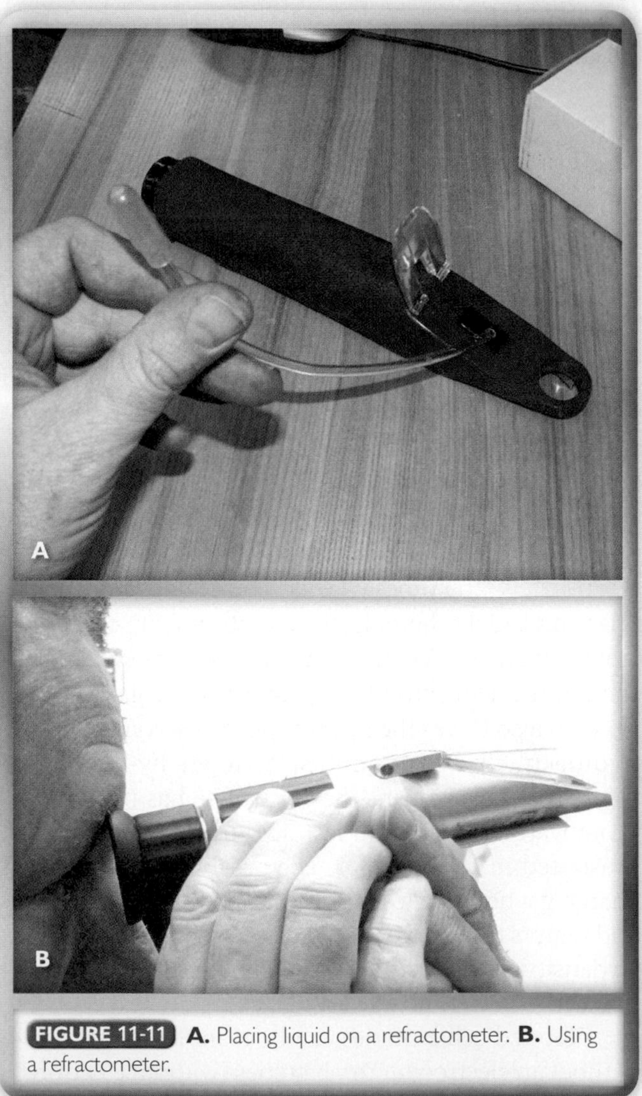

FIGURE 11-11 **A.** Placing liquid on a refractometer. **B.** Using a refractometer.

conductive pathways made when dirt and water accumulate on the case. These accumulations can allow current to drain from the battery posts. Each of the six cells in a 12-volt battery is sealed and electrolytes cannot move between cells. A gap between the plates and the bottom of each cell forms a sediment trap, as illustrated in FIGURE 11-12. The trap collects battery plate material that sheds during operation. Vibration and deeply discharging a battery accelerate the loss of plate material and reduce the battery's capacity. Without the trap, plate material would accumulate and potentially short circuit the plates, leading to rapid self-discharge of the battery.

During charging and discharging, batteries produce hydrogen and oxygen gas caused by the break-down of water through a process called hydrolysis. These gases require venting and are an explosion hazard. In older flooded batteries, each cell used a cap to vent gases, add water to the electrolyte level, and permit inspection of the electrolyte with a hydrometer. Low-maintenance batteries use a small, single vent near the top of the battery. Extra electrolyte is added to these batteries to compensate for water loss over the expected lifetime of the battery. Low-maintenance batteries have advanced plate material that result in less water loss than conventional flooded batteries. Nonetheless, a removable plug is often still used to allow access to the electrolyte during testing and servicing.

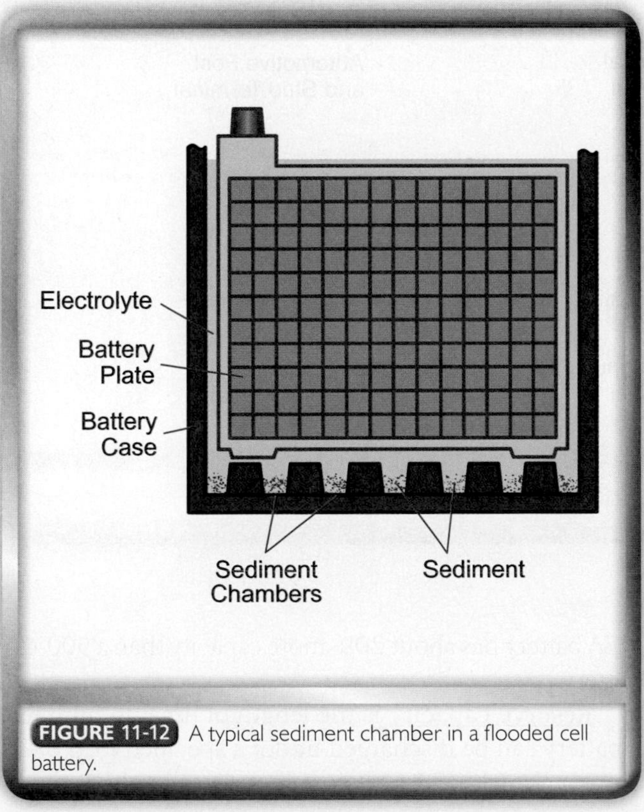

FIGURE 11-12 A typical sediment chamber in a flooded cell battery.

Sizing and Terminal Configuration

Batteries for commercial vehicles are available in a wide variety of sizes. Manufacturers build their batteries to an internationally adopted Battery Council International (BCI) group number. BCI group numbers are established according to the physical case size, terminal placement, terminal type, and polarity. For example, battery terminals used in medium- and heavy-duty commercial applications use a top post, threaded stud, or "L" terminal, with combinations of each of these types. TABLE 11-2 classifies various heavy-duty commercial battery groups.

Other designations relate to the battery terminal configuration, which refers to the shape and location of the positive and negative terminals on the battery, as illustrated in FIGURE 11-13. Different types of battery posts are also available for batteries, including top post, threaded stud, side terminal, or "L" terminal, as well as combinations of each of these types.

> **TECHNICIAN TIP**
>
> To help identification and prevent incorrect connection to post-type batteries, the positive terminal is 1/16" (1.6 mm) larger than the negative terminal. Because terminals are only soldered to the cell straps and anchored by the polyethylene case, they are vulnerable to damage if abused. Prying and hammering on posts are common types of abuse that will break the seal between the post and case and damage the connection to the plate strap.

Battery Ratings

The **electrical capacity** of a battery is the amount of electrical current a lead-acid battery can supply. Common battery capacity ratings used by North American manufacturers are established by the BCI and the Society of Automotive Engineers (SAE). Technicians will encounter other rating systems depending on the origin of the vehicle and while using some testing equipment, including:

- Japanese Industrial Standard (JIS)
- EN (European Norms) Standard
- DIN (Deutsches Institut für Normung)
- IEC (International Electrotechnical Commission) Standard

There are several methods used to rate lead-acid battery capacity. The three most common are cold cranking amps (CCA), cranking amps (CA), and reserve capacity. **Cold cranking amps (CCA)** is a measurement of

TABLE 11-2: Heavy-Duty Commercial Batteries Groups (12-VOLT)

BCI Group Size	Length (mm)	Width (mm)	Height (mm)	Length (inches)	Width (inches)	Height (inches)
4D	527	222	250	20 3/4	8 3/4	9 7/8
6D	527	254	260	20 3/4	10	10 1/4
8D	527	283	250	20 3/4	11 1/8	9 7/8
28	261	173	240	10 5/16	6 13/16	9 7/16
29H	334	171	232	13 1/8	6 3/4	9 1/8 10
30H	343	173	235	13 1/2	6 13/16	9 1/4 10
31	330	173	240	13	6 13/18	9 7/16

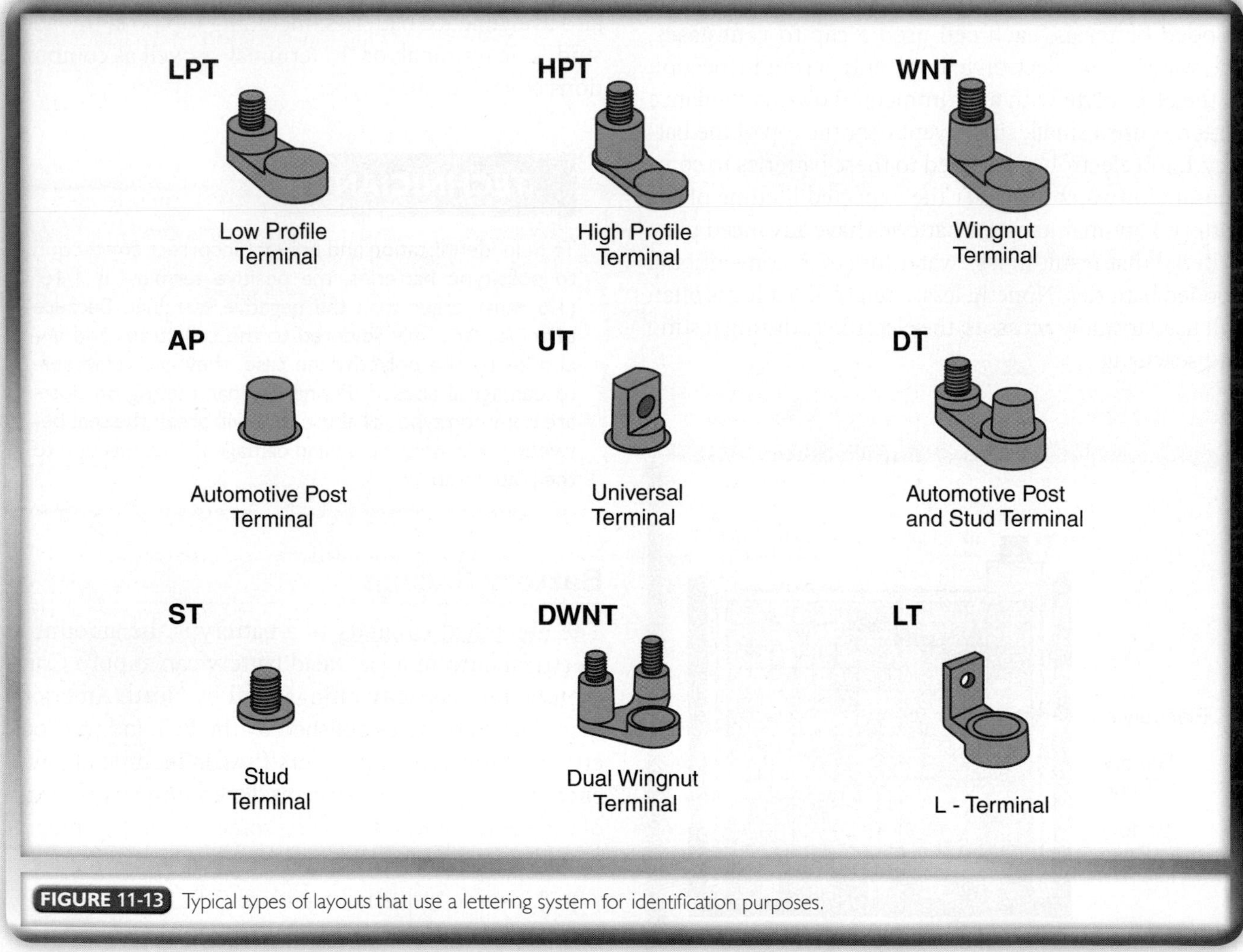

FIGURE 11-13 Typical types of layouts that use a lettering system for identification purposes.

battery capacity, in amps, that a battery can deliver for 30 seconds while maintaining a voltage of 1.2 volts per cell (7.2 volts for a 12-volt battery) or higher at 0°F (−18°C) **FIGURE 11-14**. **Cranking amps (CA)** measure the same thing, but at a higher temperature: 32°F (– 0°C). A 500-CCA battery has about 20% more capacity than a 500-CA battery.

Reserve capacity is the length of time, in minutes, a battery can be discharged under a specified load of 25 amps at 26.6°C (80°F) before battery cell voltage drops

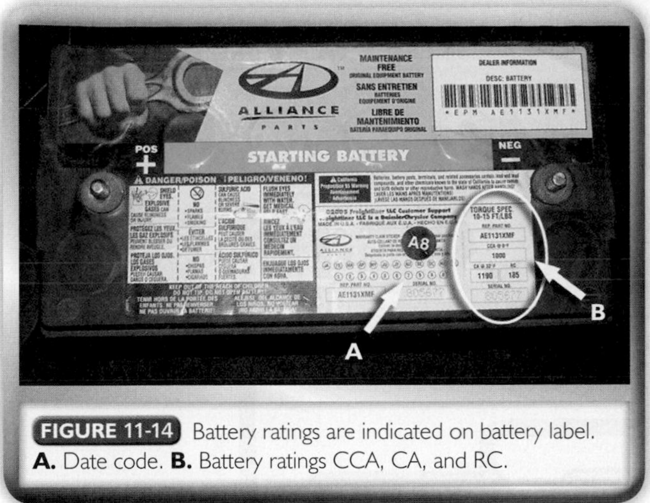

FIGURE 11-14 Battery ratings are indicated on battery label. **A.** Date code. **B.** Battery ratings CCA, CA, and RC.

below 1.75 volts per cell (10.5 volts for a 12-volt battery). This measure is modeled on estimates of how long an automobile could be driven after an alternator fails with electrical loads from headlights and other loads before the ignition system fails.

> **TECHNICIAN TIP**
>
> Early commercial vehicles with minimal electrical loads used 6-volt batteries for a 6-volt electrical system. In the 1950s, 12-volt systems and batteries became widely used. 24-volt systems are made from combinations of 12-volt batteries connected in series to produce 24 volts. Operating with higher voltages means less amperage will flow through electrical circuits and connections yet maintain the same power levels. With less amperage travelling through conductors, the reliability of the vehicle's electrical system improves because connections and cables do not heat nearly as much from high amperage flow. The size of components and wire diameters are reduced as well.

Amp-hour is a measure of a battery's capacity. Specifically, it is a measure of how much amperage a battery can continually supply over a 20-hour period without the battery voltage falling below 10.5 volts. Amp-hour is measured at 80°F (26.7°C)—the temperature at which lead–acid batteries perform best. A battery with a 200 amp-hour rating would deliver 10 amps continually for 20 hours (20 hours × 10 amps). This is an important rating when selecting a deep cycle battery.

Multiple-Battery Configurations

Batteries can be connected together to supply either more amperage or more voltage. Diesel engines, which require more cranking torque, will either connect batteries in parallel, like those illustrated in FIGURE 11-15 to supply more cranking amperage, or in series to supply higher voltage. For example, if two 600-CCA 12-volt batteries were connected in parallel, the batteries' potential output would be 1,200 CCA at 12 volts. If the batteries are connected in series, the batteries' voltage output is added together even though the cranking amperage remains the same. That means, if two 600-CCA 12-volt batteries were connected in series, the batteries' potential output would be 600 CCA at 24 volts.

Battery Selection

Factors that determine the battery rating required for a vehicle include the current needed for key-off loads, operating electrical accessories, the engine type (diesel or spark ignited), the engine size, and climate conditions under which equipment must operate.

In cold weather, battery power drops drastically because the electrolyte thickens and cold temperatures slow chemical activity inside the battery. In colder weather, engines are also harder to crank due to increased resistance from oil thickening. It is calculated that engine resistance increases between 50% to 250% in the winter compared to the summer, as illustrated in FIGURE 11-16. Simultaneously, available battery current can drop as much as 75%. As batteries age, their capacity drops too.

> **TECHNICIAN TIP**
>
> Equipment with excessive battery capacity (too many CCAs) can lead to premature failure of the starter motor and starter drive due to excessively high torque. Excessive battery CCA increases the amperage through cables, connections, and starter circuit components, causing damage from resistance heating. However, inadequate battery capacity will shorten battery life from deep discharging. Equipment may even fail to start in cold weather or as batteries age. Starter motors, cables, and circuits can be damaged from low-voltage burn-out caused by undersized batteries.

BCI estimates diesel engines require 220% to 300% more battery power than a similar gasoline engine. A typical 15L diesel engine today uses approximately 10,000 watts of current (or close to 12 horsepower) during cranking and initially needs 15,000 watts, or 20 horsepower. Vehicle manufacturers make recommendations about the capacity of batteries. The CCA rating of the battery is the most important rating considered when selecting batteries. Although selecting a

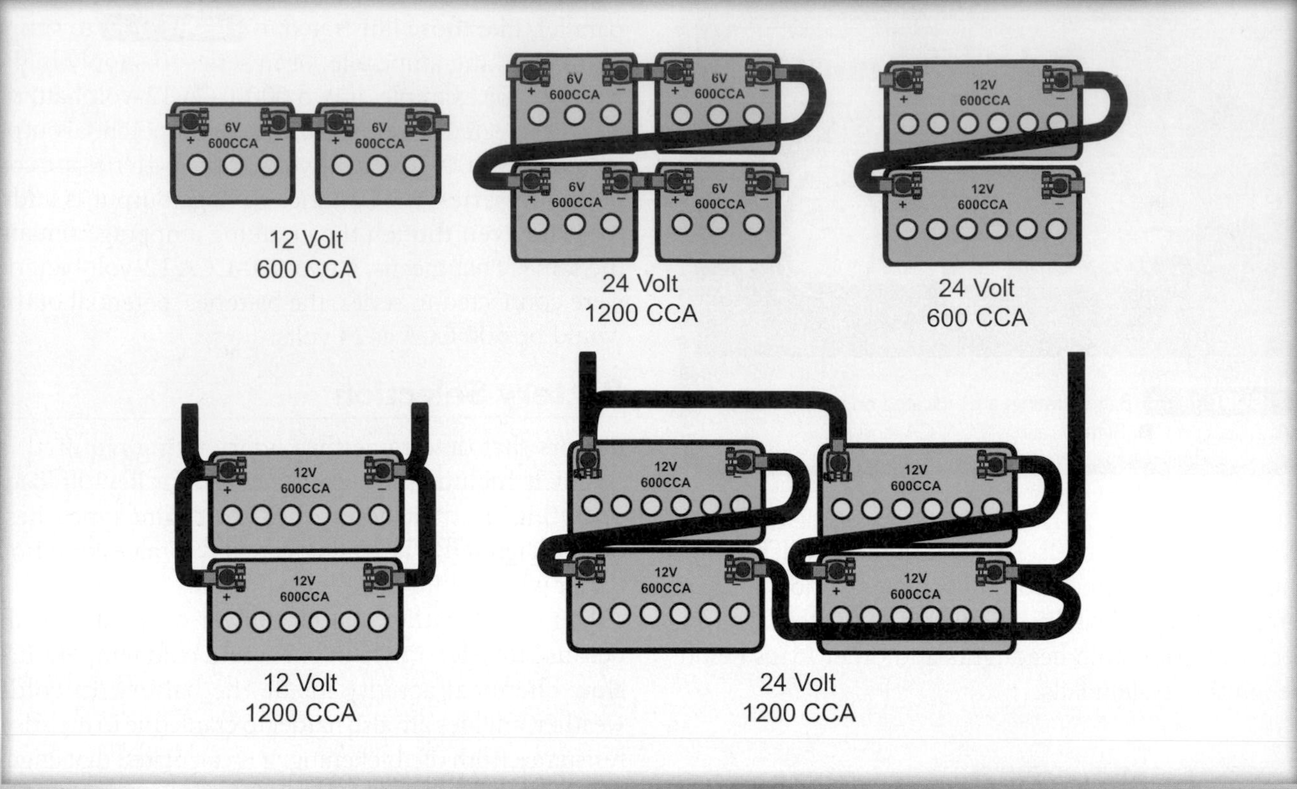

FIGURE 11-15 Typical battery bank configurations.

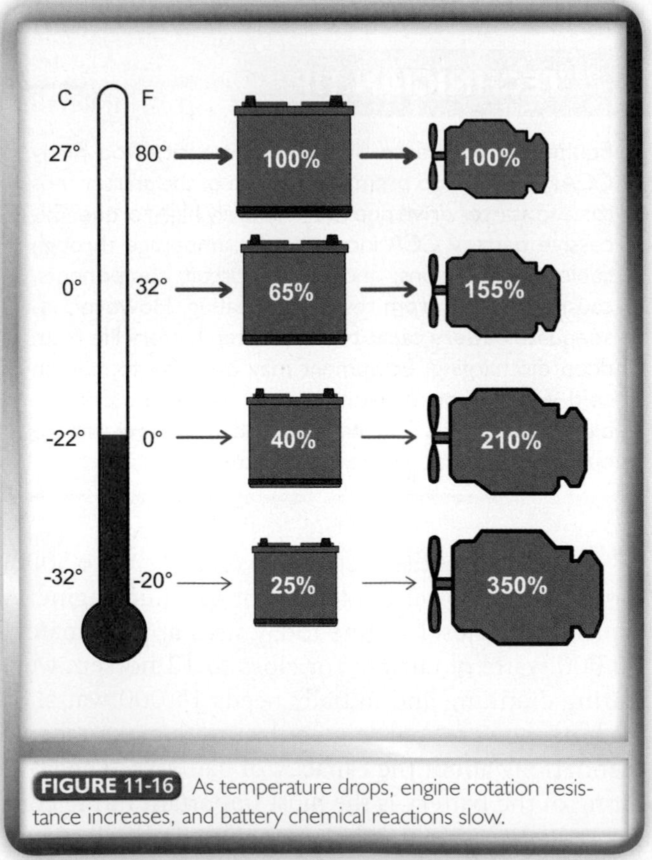

FIGURE 11-16 As temperature drops, engine rotation resistance increases, and battery chemical reactions slow.

battery with excessive current capacity might seem like a good idea, it is not. Extra capacity is expensive and high amperage capacity available from batteries can lead to premature starter drive failure from excessive torque and damage from excessive amperage through starting circuit connections.

Equipment manufacturers use a number of variables when calculating battery capacity, but the most significant one is battery voltage at the end of engine cranking. Generally batteries are sized to ensure a minimum cranking voltage of no less than 10.5 volts after three consecutive cranking periods of 30 seconds with a 2-minute cool-down period between each cranking period.

Internal Resistance of Batteries

All electrical devices have internal resistance—even batteries. Not all battery types have the same internal resistance, however. A battery's internal resistance depends on the types of materials used to make the plates and the chemical composition of the electrolyte. A battery's internal resistance determines how quickly a battery can be charged or discharged.

Batteries with a relatively low internal resistance, such as a standard lead–acid battery, can be charged quickly, and they can also be discharged quickly to supply a lot of current over a short period of time. This makes them ideal for use in vehicles as starter batteries because they can supply the high discharge current required by the starter motor to start the vehicle. Batteries are available with a lower internal resistance than that of a lead–acid battery, such as the newer lithium batteries now being used in battery banks for electric and hybrid vehicles. These types of batteries are more expensive than the standard lead–acid battery, and their lower internal resistance is generally not needed for everyday starter motor applications.

Battery Charging and Discharging Cycle

Battery plates are made of two different compositions of lead fabricated from paste bonded to lead alloy grids. The negative plate uses lead (Pb) and the positive plate uses lead peroxide (PbO_2). Antimony, calcium, or other metals are alloyed with the lead grid material to minimize corrosion of the lead by acidic electrolyte. Because the plates are made of dissimilar metals, the addition of electrolyte will cause galvanic reactions in each cell.

In a fully charged condition, the positive plate material is predominantly lead peroxide (PbO_2), and the negative plate is sponge lead. The composition of the electrolyte is 64% water and 36% sulfuric acid. Chemical interactions between the plates and electrolyte strip electrons from the positive plate and add electrons to the negative plate. That produces a 12.6-volt difference between the battery terminals. A lead-acid battery will remain in this condition without a load applied. However, due to activity of chemical reactions, a slow rate of self-discharge occurs, which will eventually discharge the battery. This self-discharge rate is dependent on temperature and the selection of materials used during manufacturing. In hot climates, complete self-discharge is measured in weeks. Cold slows down chemical reactions, so the self-discharge rate can take almost two years in colder climates.

When a load is applied across the battery, electrons moving from the negative to the positive terminal accelerate galvanic reactions. This process is illustrated in **FIGURE 11-17A**. Both plates and the electrolyte composition change as a result of electron movement. Oxygen atoms in the positive plate move into the electrolyte while the sulfate part of the acid moves into the positive plate, changing the cell from lead peroxide (PbO_2) to lead sulfate ($PbSO_4$). On the negative plate, sulfate also moves into the plate material, forming lead sulfate ($PbSO_4$). The electrolyte becomes less acidic and turns to water, as sulfate leaves and hydrogen in the electrolyte combines with oxygen driven from the positive plate.

Galvanic reaction in a battery will stop under two circumstances. One is if the battery has the electrical load removed. This halts chemical reactions caused by movement of electrons from one battery terminal to the other. Electron movement also stops when the positive and negative plates become saturated with sulfate in a process called **sulfation**.

When charging a lead-acid battery, the chemical reactions used to produce current are reversed, restoring the plate and electrolyte to its charged condition **FIGURE 11-17B** While charging, sulfate is driven from both plates back into the electrolyte. Oxygen in the electrolyte recombines with the lead in the positive plate.

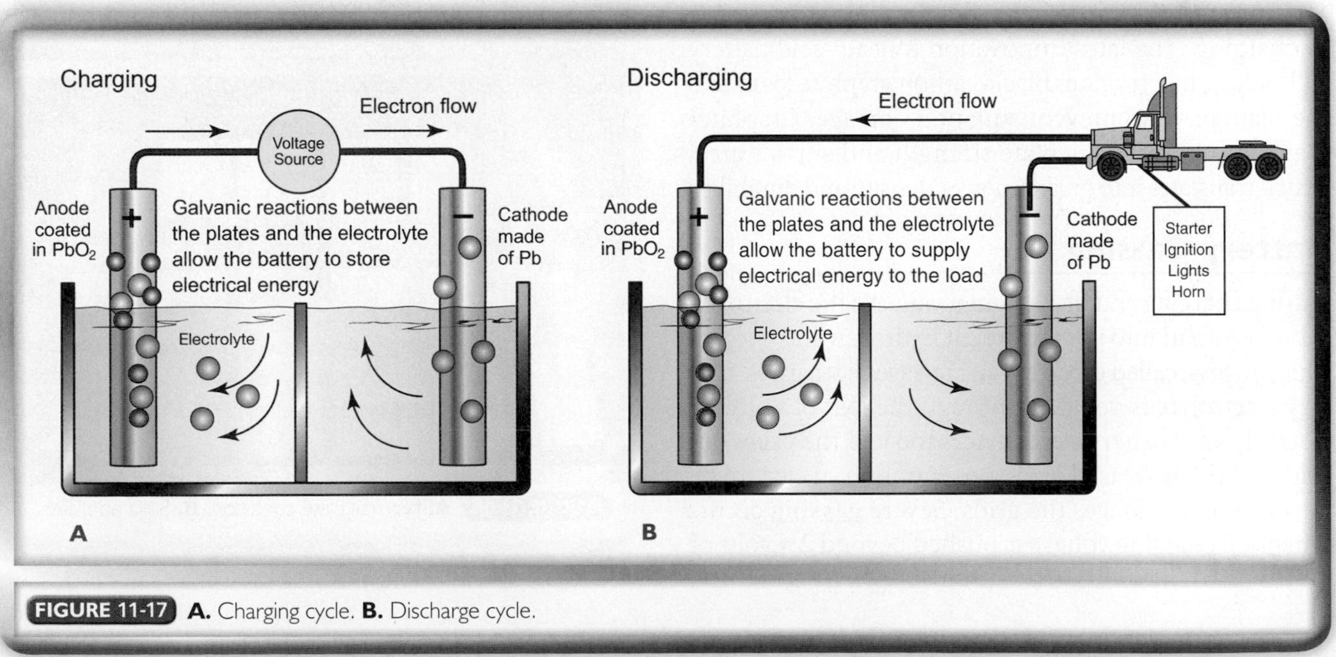

FIGURE 11-17 **A.** Charging cycle. **B.** Discharge cycle.

The chemical action is accomplished by connecting a charger or an alternator (DC current), stripping the positive post of electrons and forcing them back into the negative terminal. Charging voltage needs to be sufficiently high enough to overcome a battery's natural resistance to current flow. Most charging systems maintain a maximum charging voltage of approximately 0.5-volts above battery voltage. This explains why the charging system set point for most 12.65-volt batteries is around 14.2-volts. Higher voltages used by battery chargers push more current into the battery at a higher amperage.

> **TECHNICIAN TIP**
>
> If a battery is completely discharged, the similar chemical composition of both plates permits the battery polarity to be reversed if connected incorrectly to a charger or charging system. The battery will charge up with reverse polarity. If a battery with reverse polarity is reconnected to a vehicle, the results are disastrous. Burnt wiring, blown fuses, and alternator damage will quickly result, leading to a potential vehicle fire.

Plate Sulfation

Sulfate is driven off battery plates when charging, as shown in FIGURE 11-18A. However, if a battery is left in a discharged state for a long period of time, continually undercharged, or left partially charged, the soft sulfate turns to a hardened crystalline form, as shown in FIGURE 11-18B. Hard sulfate cannot be driven from the plates.

This means the battery cannot be recharged and the remaining active plate material develops a high resistance to charging. The latest innovation to lead–acid battery technology incorporates black-carbon graphite foam into the plate paste to prevent sulfation damage. Graphite-foam carbon increases plate strength and surface area, which translates into greater power density and durability.

Battery Gassing

During charging and discharging, water in the electrolyte is broken apart into its constituent hydrogen and oxygen. This process, called **electrolysis**, releases both gases. Battery electrolyte is depleted through the loss of water by electrolysis. If battery electrolyte is too low, the plates dry out, and the increased acid concentration of electrolyte permanently damages the grids. Severe **gassing** occurs when cell charging voltage is pushed beyond 2.4 volts or severe discharge takes place, such as when a wrench or piece of metal is laid across battery terminals.

Low- and No-Maintenance Batteries

The use of antimony alloy in the plate grids of conventional flooded battery technology minimizes grid corrosion and allows these batteries to accept up to 10 times more overcharging than newer low- or no-maintenance batteries. Unfortunately, antimony alloyed grids cause excessive gassing, resulting in substantial water loss. No- or low-maintenance battery technology solves that problem.

Introduced in the middle 1970s, no- and low-maintenance batteries reduce or eliminate the antimony content in grids. Calcium is used primarily now to replace antimony but barium, cadmium, or strontium is also used. No-maintenance batteries eliminate all the antimony, whereas low-maintenance batteries contain a reduced level of antimony content (approximately 2%). No- and low-maintenance batteries still require venting and need

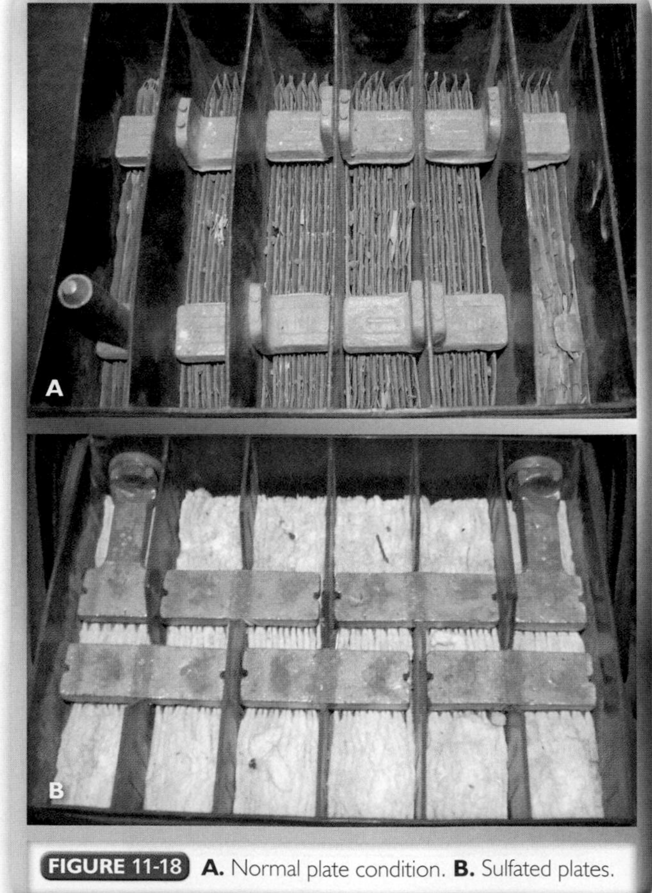

FIGURE 11-18 **A.** Normal plate condition. **B.** Sulfated plates.

a large electrolyte reserve area above the plates to compensate for some water loss.

Another recent advance in grid composition involves the addition of silver into the calcium-lead alloy. Silver alloy has demonstrated a very high resistance to grid growth and corrosion. Thus, silver alloy significantly lengthens battery life in high heat and severe service conditions.

The advantages of low- or no-maintenance batteries include:

- Less water usage
- Less grid corrosion
- Less gassing
- Lower self-discharge rate
- Less terminal corrosion because less corrosive gas is emitted from the vents

The disadvantages of low- and no-maintenance batteries include:

- A lower electrical reserve capacity
- Often a shorter life expectancy
- Grid growth/expansion when exposed to high temperatures
- More quickly discharged by parasitic losses
- Difficulty accepting a boost when completely discharged

Although no-maintenance batteries contain a vent located beneath the top cover, the battery tops are completely sealed. Delco, which introduced the first no-maintenance battery, uses a built-in hydrometer that has colored balls. These balls will rise or fall in the electrolyte depending on the electrolyte density, thereby providing an indication of the state of charge. To boost these batteries from a completely discharged state, a small charge is recommended for about ten minutes to begin the hydrolytic process of breaking water into hydrogen and oxygen. After that, the batteries are capable of receiving a higher rate of charge.

Low-maintenance batteries may look completely sealed, but they will usually have a means of adding water if required. Often the caps are concealed under a plastic cover that is removed to reveal cell caps that can be unscrewed FIGURE 11-19.

The latest and most advanced commercial vehicle battery technology are **absorbed glass mat (AGM) batteries**. AGMs provide improved safety, efficiency, and durability over existing battery types. The electrolyte is absorbed into a fine glass mat, as shown in FIGURE 11-20, preventing it from sloshing or separating into layers of heavier acid and water. The fiber first helps by enhancing gas recombination rather than simply venting gas to the atmosphere and lowering electrolyte levels. AGM material also possesses low electrical resistance. As a result, it can deliver more cranking amperage and absorb up to 40% more charging current than conventional lead–acid, leading to faster charging. Higher cell voltage and sensitivity to overcharging requires special service consideration. Those topics will be covered in the Advanced Battery Technologies and Servicing Commercial Vehicle Batteries chapters.

FIGURE 11-19 The spiral cell Optima battery is an example of an AGM-type battery.

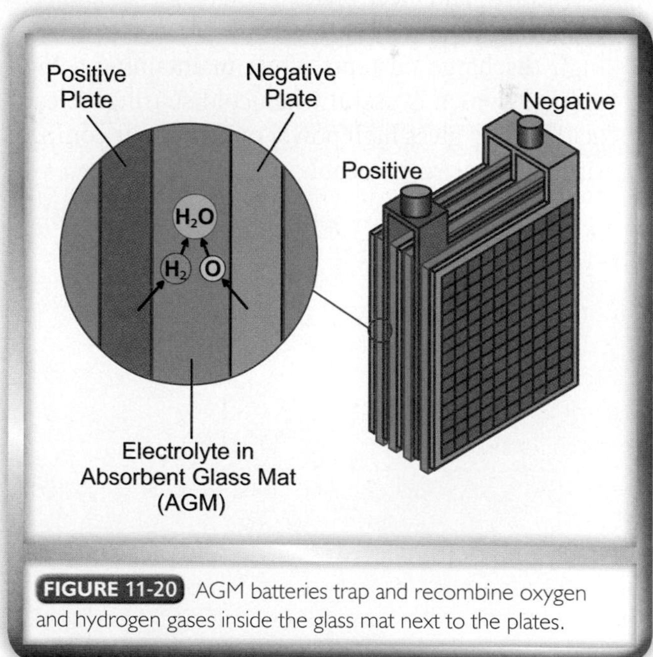

FIGURE 11-20 AGM batteries trap and recombine oxygen and hydrogen gases inside the glass mat next to the plates.

Wrap-up

Ready for Review

- There are two types of batteries. Primary batteries cannot be recharged; secondary batteries are rechargeable.
- Secondary batteries operate using the principles of galvanic reaction and are the most practical for use in commercial vehicle applications.
- Through a galvanic reaction, electricity is produced when two dissimilar metals are placed in an electrolyte.
- Batteries have traditionally been used in heavy vehicles to provide starting current and operate electrical accessories if the engine is not running.
- Batteries are classified by use, application, and chemistry used within the battery. Although lead–acid batteries are most prevalent, hybrid-drive vehicles also make use of nickel-metal hydride and lithium batteries.
- Lead–acid batteries deliver high rates of current with a higher tolerance for physical and electrical abuse compared to other battery technology. These batteries hold a charge well and when stored dry—without electrolyte—the shelf life is indefinite.
- Regardless of battery construction, all batteries have the same basic components: case, terminals, plates, cell straps, and electrolyte.
- A starting-lighting-ignition battery can supply very high discharge currents while maintaining a high voltage, which is useful when cold starting. A lead-acid battery gives high power output for its compact size, and it is rechargeable.
- Starting, lighting, and ignition batteries (SLI) are designed for a single short-duration deep discharge during engine cranking. Deep cycle batteries provide lower amperage current continually for electrical devices and accessories.
- Lead-acid batteries can be manufactured with electrolyte or dry. Dry batteries can be stored on the shelf for extended periods without the fear of sulfation and are lighter to transport.
- During charging and discharging, batteries produce hydrogen and oxygen gas caused by the break-down of water through a process called hydrolysis. These gases require venting and are an explosion hazard.
- Batteries can be configured into battery banks in cases where larger current or higher-voltage batteries are required.
- Battery temperature plays an important role in the performance of a battery and lead-acid batteries have ideal operating temperature range. A battery's internal resistance depends on the types of materials used to make the plates and the chemical composition of the electrolyte. A battery's internal resistance determines how quickly a battery can be charged or discharged.

Vocabulary Builder

absorbed glass mat (AGM) battery A battery in which electrolyte is absorbed in a fine glass mat that prevents prevent the solution from sloshing or separating into layers of heavier acid and water.

amp-hour A measure of how much amperage a battery can continually supply over a 20-hour period without the battery voltage falling below 10.5 volts.

cold cranking amps (CCA) A measurement of the load, in amps, that a battery can deliver for 30 seconds while maintaining a voltage of 1.2 volts per cell (7.2 volts for a 12-volt battery) or higher at 0°F (–18°C).

cranking amps (CA) A measurement of the load, in amps, that a battery can deliver for 30 seconds while maintaining a voltage of 1.2 volts per cell (7.2 volts for a 12-volt battery) or higher at 32°F (– 0°C).

deep cycle battery A battery used to deliver a lower, steady level of power for a much longer time.

electrical capacity The amount of electrical current a lead-acid battery can supply.

electrolysis The use of electricity to break down water into hydrogen and oxygen gases.

electrolyte An electrically conductive solution.

flooded lead-acid battery A lead–acid battery in which the plates are immersed in a water–acid electrolyte solution.

galvanic reaction A chemical reaction that produces electricity when two dissimilar metals are placed in an electrolyte.

gassing A situation that occurs when overcharging or rapid charging causes some gas to escape from the battery.

hydrometer An instrument used to measure the specific gravity of liquids.

key-off electrical loads Unwanted drain on the vehicle battery when the vehicle is off. Also called *parasitic draw*.

parasitic draw Unwanted drain on the vehicle battery when the vehicle is off. Also called *key-off electrical load*.

primary battery A battery in which chemical reactions are not reversible and the battery cannot be recharged.

reserve capacity The time, in minutes, that a new, fully charged battery at 80°F (26.7°C) will supply a constant load of 25 amps without its voltage dropping below 10.5 volts for a 12-volt battery.

sealed lead–acid battery A battery that does not have a liquid electrolyte nor requires the addition of water. Also called a *valve-regulated lead–acid battery (VRLA)* or *recombinant battery*.

secondary battery A rechargeable battery.

specific gravity A measurement of the density of a substance.

starting, lighting, and ignition (SLI) battery A battery designed for one, short-duration, deep discharge of up to 50% depth of discharge (DOD) during engine cranking.

sulfation A chemical reaction that results in the soft sulfate turning to a hardened crystalline form that cannot be driven from the plates in the battery.

traction battery A rechargeable battery used for propulsion in hybrid electric vehicles.

valve-regulated lead–acid (VRLA) battery A type of sealed lead–acid battery used in heavy-duty equipment. It does not require the addition of water. Also called a *sealed lead–acid battery (SLA) or recombinant battery*.

Review Questions

1. Which of the following is correct concerning battery classifications?
   a. Primary battery: chemical reactions are not reversible, and the battery cannot be recharged.
   b. Secondary battery: rechargeable
   c. Both A and B
   d. Neither A nor B
2. Which of the following is correct concerning types and classification of batteries?
   a. Batteries are classified according to what they are used for and how they are made.
   b. Batteries are classified by the type of plate material and chemistry used to produce current.
   c. Both A and B
   d. Neither A nor B
3. Which of the following statements is correct concerning deep cycle-deep discharge batteries?
   a. Deep cycle batteries are used to deliver a lower, steady level of power for a much longer period of time than an SLI type battery.
   b. Battery plate construction and charging and discharging characteristics of deep cycle batteries are different from SLI type batteries.
   c. In heavy vehicles, deep cycle batteries are used to supply current to constantly powered accessories, such as driver and vehicle communication devices.
   d. All of the choices are correct.
4. Which of the following is NOT a basic component of a battery?
   a. Case
   b. Terminals
   c. Plates
   d. Gasket
5. Which of the following statements is correct concerning separator plates?
   a. To prevent the battery positive and negative plate from touching and short circuiting, separator plates are placed between each plate in every cell.
   b. Separator plates are very thin, porous, glass-fiber plates allowing electrolyte to diffuse freely throughout the cell and at the same time prevent plate contact.
   c. Both A and B
   d. Neither A nor B
6. One of the characteristics of low- or no-maintenance batteries is:
   a. greater corrosion.
   b. higher electrical reserve capacity.
   c. lower water usage.
   d. slow discharge rate due to parasitic loss.
7. Which of the following is correct concerning multiple-battery configurations?
   a. Batteries can be connected together to supply either more amperage or more voltage.
   b. Diesel engines, which require more cranking torque, will either connect batteries in parallel, to supply more cranking amperage, or in series to supply higher voltage.
   c. Both A and B
   d. Neither A nor B
8. Which of the following statements is correct concerning battery selection?
   a. The CCA rating of the battery is the most important rating considered when selecting batteries.
   b. In colder weather, engines are also harder to crank due to increased resistance from oil thickening.
   c. BCI estimates diesel engines require 220% to 300% more battery power than a similar gasoline engine.
   d. All of the choices are correct.
9. Which of the following is NOT correct concerning the internal resistance of batteries?
   a. All electrical devices have internal resistance—even batteries.
   b. A battery's internal resistance determines how quickly a battery can be charged or discharged.
   c. Newer lithium batteries have a lower internal resistance than that of a lead-acid battery.
   d. Newer lithium batteries cost about the same as the standard lead-acid battery.
10. As ________ drops, engine rotation resistance ________, and battery chemical reactions ________.
    a. The low- or no-maintenance battery uses less water.
    b. The low- or no-maintenance battery has a longer life expectancy.
    c. The low- or no-maintenance battery has less grid corrosion.
    d. The low- or no-maintenance battery is more quickly discharged by parasitic losses.

ASE-Type Questions

1. Technician A says that hybrid electric vehicles are not commonplace in urban transit but are likely to be in the future. Technician B says that commercial equipment, particularly diesel-powered equipment, will use multiple batteries connected in series or parallel to produce adequate starting current. Who is correct?
   a. Technician A
   b. Technician B
   c. Both Technician A and Technician B
   d. Neither Technician A nor Technician B
2. Technician A says that a spiral cell (Optima battery) is not considered a sealed lead-acid (SLA) battery. Technician B says that an absorbed glass mat (AGM) battery is not considered a sealed lead-acid (SLA) battery. Who is correct?
   a. Technician A
   b. Technician B
   c. Both Technician A and Technician B
   d. Neither Technician A nor Technician B
3. Technician A says that a fully charged 12-volt battery is 12.00 volts. Technician B says that connecting cells together in series allows batteries to be produced in a variety of output voltage. Who is correct?
   a. Technician A
   b. Technician B
   c. Both Technician A and Technician B
   d. Neither Technician A nor Technician B
4. Technician A says that the primary difference between deep cycle batteries and SLI is the thickness of the plates. Technician B says that deeply discharging SLI batteries dramatically shortens their service life. Who is correct?
   a. Technician A
   b. Technician B
   c. Both Technician A and Technician B
   d. Neither Technician A nor Technician B
5. Technician A says that lead-acid battery electrolyte is a mixture of 64% sulfuric acid and 36% water. Technician B says that sulfuric acid has a specific gravity of 1.835 which means it is much heavier than water. Who is correct?
   a. Technician A
   b. Technician B
   c. Both Technician A and Technician B
   d. Neither Technician A nor Technician B
6. Technician A says that the battery case is usually made of polypropylene. Technician B says that ribbing and irregular features on the outside of the case add to the appearance of the battery and make it sturdy. Who is correct?
   a. Technician A
   b. Technician B
   c. Both Technician A and Technician B
   d. Neither Technician A nor Technician B
7. Technician A says that battery plates are made of two different compositions of lead that is fabricated from paste and bonded to lead-alloy grids. Technician B says that the negative plate uses lead peroxide ($PbO2$) and the positive plate uses lead (Pb). Who is correct?
   a. Technician A
   b. Technician B
   c. Both Technician A and Technician B
   d. Neither Technician A nor Technician B
8. Technician A says that both soft and hard sulfate can be driven from the plates, bringing the battery back into service. Technician B says that the latest innovation to lead-acid battery technology incorporates black-carbon graphite foam into the plate paste to prevent sulfation damage. Who is correct?
   a. Technician A
   b. Technician B
   c. Both Technician A and Technician B
   d. Neither Technician A nor Technician B
9. Technician A says that during charging and discharging, water in the electrolyte is broken apart into its constituent hydrogen and oxygen in a process called electrolysis. Technician B says if battery electrolyte is too low, the plates dry out, and the increased acid concentration of electrolyte permanently damages the grids. Who is correct?
   a. Technician A
   b. Technician B
   c. Both Technician A and Technician B
   d. Neither Technician A nor Technician B
10. Technician A says that the latest and most advanced commercial vehicle battery technology are absorbed glass mat (AGM) batteries. Technician B says that the AGM battery can deliver more cranking amperage and absorb up to 10% more charging current than conventional lead acid. Who is correct?
   a. Technician A
   b. Technician B
   c. Both Technician A and Technician B
   d. Neither Technician A nor Technician B

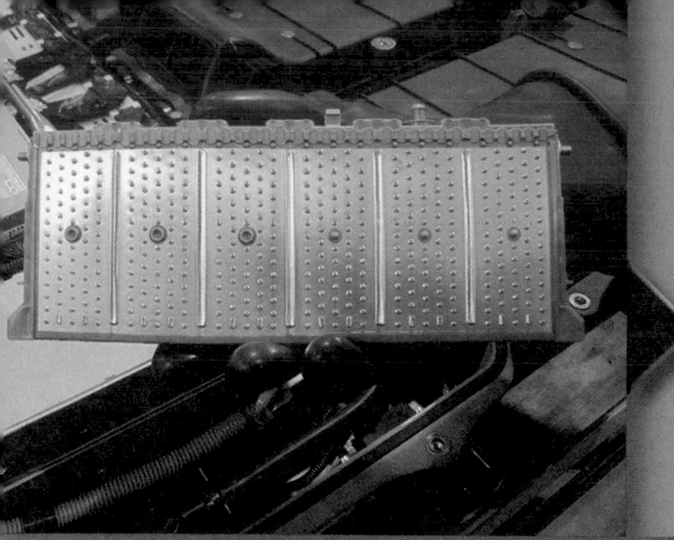

CHAPTER 12

NATEF Tasks

There are no NATEF tasks for this chapter.

Knowledge Objectives

After reading this chapter, you will be able to:

1. Identify and describe the features of lithium and nickel-metal hydride batteries, and ultra capacitors. (pp 352–359)
2. Identify and describe common battery failures. (p 360)
3. Identify and explain the operation of battery isolators, low voltage disconnect, charge equalizers, and battery management systems. (pp 360–364)

Advanced Battery Technologies

Skills Objectives

There are no skills objectives for this chapter.

Introduction

The demand for advanced battery technology in commercial vehicles is growing. Not only do the increasingly popular hybrid electric vehicles require advanced batteries, heavy-duty commercial vehicles also have a greater need for electrical storage capacity to run accessories. Several key factors are at play in determining which application of a variety of battery technologies to use on commercial vehicles, including:

- Energy density—FIGURE 12-1—expressed in Watt-hour per kilogram (Wh/kg) and Watt-hour per liter (Wh/l)
- Energy efficiency—the ability to convert charging current into storage capacity
- Life span—measured by the number of charge/discharge cycles as a function of depth of discharge
- The state of charge window—the availability of usable battery voltage
- Cost in dollars per kWh

Types of Advanced Batteries

The major battery technologies used in heavy-duty commercial vehicles are nickel–metal hydride (NiMH), lithium, and lead-acid. Each technology has distinct capabilities, which we will discuss in this section. TABLE 12-1 compares the capacities of different battery types.

Nickel–Metal Hydride Battery (NiMH)

Nickel–metal hydride (NiMH) batteries are used not only in consumer electronics but are also a preferred battery chemistry for hybrid drive vehicles. That is because NiMH batteries are relatively lightweight and have high

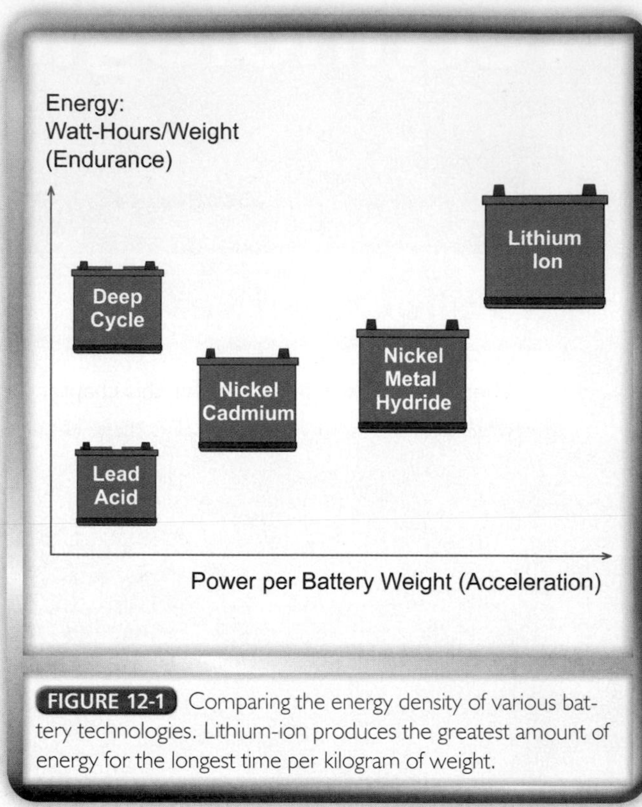

FIGURE 12-1 Comparing the energy density of various battery technologies. Lithium-ion produces the greatest amount of energy for the longest time per kilogram of weight.

You Are the Technician

Maintaining a fleet of trucks, buses, and other diesel powered machinery in extreme winter climate has its own unique challenges. One of the problems you are encountering is hard starting of engines on cold winter mornings and nights, when even hot engines drop to ambient temperature in just a couple of hours. A significant amount of downtime, labor, and associated expenses is lost to jump-starting vehicles and equipment—not to mention the cost of battery replacements.

One solution you've tried is the use of electric battery warmers. You have also insulated battery boxes with high density polyurethane foam to try and keep battery temperature warmer during the shutdown periods. Your reasoning is that since battery temperatures increase when batteries are charging, retaining some of that heat will improve starting capabilities after several hours. Consider other strategies to reduce the aggravation level and cost of service for no-start conditions due to cold.

1. What is the purpose of keeping batteries warm?
2. List and explain several ways an ultra-capacitor battery would help promote faster starter start-up.
3. Explain how switching batteries to AGM type might help promote better cold starting capabilities.

TABLE 12-1: Comparison of Properties for Different Battery Chemistries

Range			Energy Density		
Battery Type	**Voltage/cell**	**Cost Watt/hour**	**Watt-hour/kg**	**Joules/kg**	**Watt-hour/liter**
Lead–acid	2.1 volts	Lowest = 1	41	146,000	100
NiMH	1.2 volts	6 times lead-acid	95	340,000	300
Li–Ion	~ 4.0 volts	25 times lead-acid	128	460,000	230
Ultra Capacitors	~ 2-3 volts	4–5 times lead-acid	30 - 60	–	–
Diesel Fuel	–	–	–	–	10,942

power output and long life expectancy. Allison Ev heavy-duty hybrids use these as well as many automotive electric hybrid systems. NiMH batteries provide twice the energy storage of lead-acid by weight, but only half the power output—at 1.2 volts/cell compared to 2.1 volts/cell for lead-acid batteries. As illustrated in FIGURE 12-2, a unique alloy of rare earth metal, which has an unusual ability to absorb hydrogen, forms the metal hydroxide negative electrode. The positive electrode is made of nickel oxide ($NiOH_2$). The electrolyte is composed of potassium-hydroxide, which is an alkaline.

Lithium-Ion Battery

Lithium-ion batteries were developed for commercial use in the early 1990s. Since then, they have been used in laptops, cell phones, and other consumer electronic devices. Lithium-ion (Li-ion) batteries are secondary batteries and are not the same as disposable, primary-type lithium batteries, which contain metallic lithium.

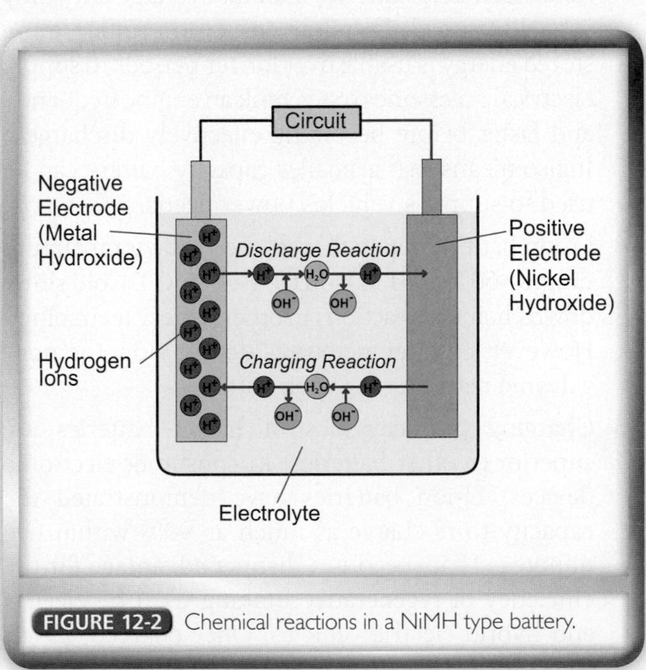

FIGURE 12-2 Chemical reactions in a NiMH type battery.

Like conventional batteries, Li-ion batteries have electrodes and use an electrolyte. Unlike conventional batteries, the chemical reactions in Li-ion batteries are not galvanic, and the material separating the electrodes is a gel, salt, or solid material. With no liquid electrolyte, Li-ion batteries are immune to leaking. Currently there are dozens of different cell chemistries used to produce lithium-ion batteries. The voltage, capacity, life cycle, and safety characteristics of a lithium-ion battery can change dramatically depending on the choice of material for the anode, cathode, and electrolyte. Regardless of their specific chemistry, lithium batteries have a higher energy density than other battery types such as lead-acid, nickel–cadmium, and NiMH, as shown in FIGURE 12-3.

Popular Li-ion chemistries incorporate electrodes made from lithium combined with phosphate, cobalt, carbon, nickel, and manganese oxide. Lithium–phosphate chemistry demonstrates the most promising attributes for electric and hybrid-electric vehicle batteries in transportation applications. For example, FIGURE 12-4 shows a transit bus with battery tubs containing lithium batteries. The tubs and the battery management system are both located on the roof of the vehicle. Note that the stairs used to access the rooftop battery tubs have been specially designed for this purpose. A123 Systems produces lithium–phosphate batteries ($LiFePO_4$ chemistry) for use in heavy-duty hybrid and electric vehicles produced by BAE Systems, Navistar, Eaton, and Magna Steyr.

There are several advantages to using lithium-ion batteries in on-highway vehicles, including:

1. The best power-to-weight ratio compared to other battery technology. For example, the replacement of lead-acid batteries on a BAE-Orion Hybrid transit bus with equivalent lithium-ion, reduces battery pack weight from 4,100 lb (1,865 kg) to 1,000 lb (455 kg).

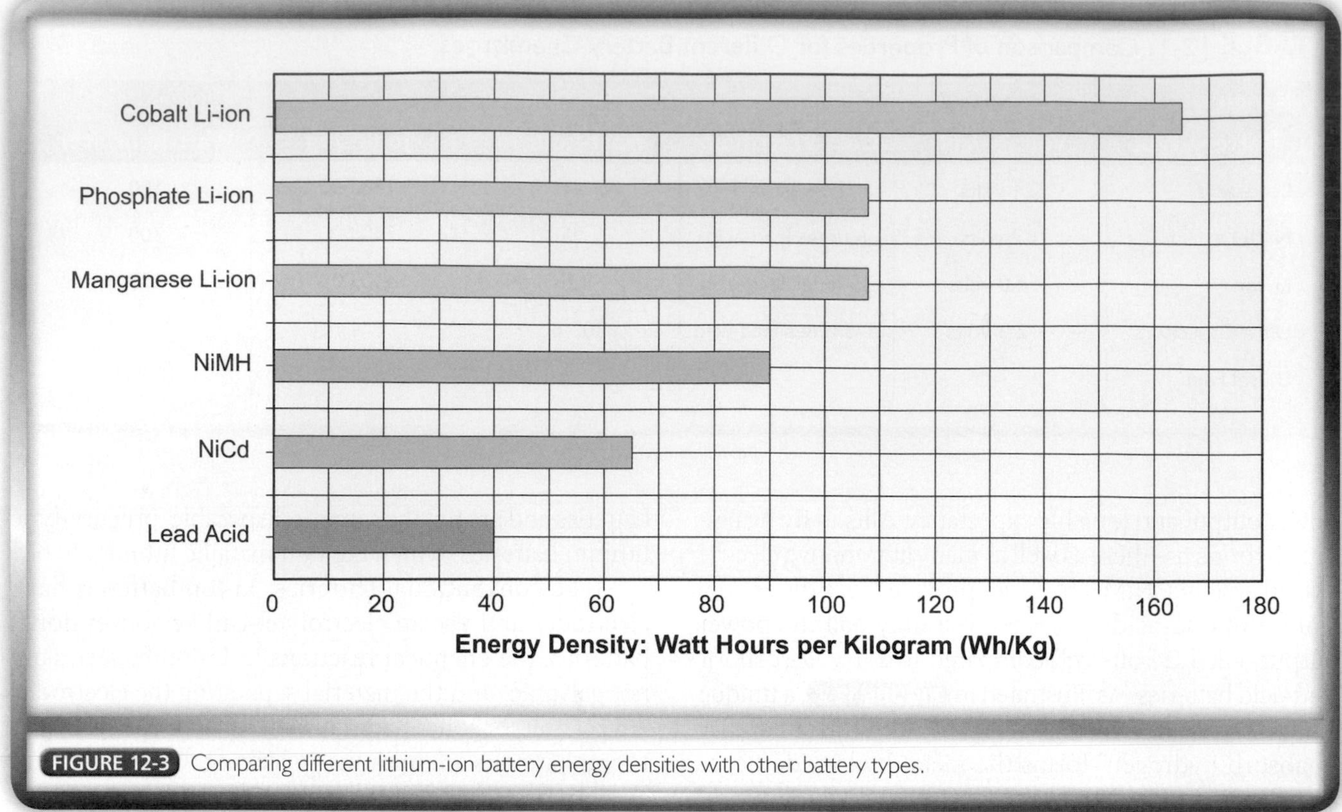

FIGURE 12-3 Comparing different lithium-ion battery energy densities with other battery types.

FIGURE 12-4 Transit bus with rooftop battery tubs and battery management system.

Li-ion batteries have twice the power density per kilogram of weight compared to NiMH chemistry (Bulletin from the Toronto Transit Commission).

2. Li-ion batteries have higher cell voltages—with as much as 5 volts in some designs. A typical cell voltage averages between 3.3 and 4.2 volts, which means fewer Li-ion cells are required to form high voltage batteries. It also translates into fewer vulnerable and resistive cell connections and reduced electronics in the battery management system. One lithium cell can replace three nickel–cadmium (NiCad) or NiMH cells, which have a cell voltage of only 1.2 volts.
3. Li-ion cells maintain a constant voltage for over 80% of their discharge curve. In comparison, conventional lead-acid batteries maintain voltage until only 50% discharged. Therefore, in a Li-ion battery, more stored energy is usable over longer periods to supply electrical accessories or to crank an engine frequently and faster before becoming effectively discharged. It also means that a smaller capacity battery can be used to supply a vehicle's power needs.
4. Li-ion batteries operate well over wide temperature ranges –60°F (–51°C) to 167°F (+75°C). Cold slows down chemical reactions in other battery technology. However, cold temperatures do not slow the non-galvanic reactions in Li-ion batteries.
5. Charging characteristics of Li-ion batteries are superior to other batteries. In consumer electronic devices, Li-ion batteries have demonstrated the capacity to re-charge as much as 90% within five minutes. That speed is a distinct advantage for the efficiency of regenerative braking used by electric and hybrid electric vehicles. Once charged, Li-ion batteries self-discharge at a very low rate.

6. Li-ion batteries have low internal resistance and can discharge their current four times faster when compared to lead-acid batteries. In addition, high discharge and charge rates do not wear out a Li-ion battery to the extent that charge and discharge cycles reduce the lifespan of other types of batteries. Currently, typical Li-ion batteries can withstand 1,200 charge–discharge cycles in comparison to 500–800 cycles for lead-acid and 1,500 for NiMH, as illustrated in the chart shown in FIGURE 12-5. Li-ion batteries last for millions of micro-discharge cycles. A micro-discharge cycle occurs when the charge is maintained between 40 and 80%. In contrast, lead-acid batteries last the longest only when discharged less than 5%.

While Li-ion technology appears to have every advantage over other battery technology, use of Li-on technology is restricted by a number of limitations. Extensive investment and research are currently aimed at correcting serious limitations to the use of Li-ion technology in automotive applications. As a result, a variety Li-ion chemistries are now competing for widespread use, each with unique advantages and disadvantages.

One disadvantage of current Li-ion battery technology is cost. Li-ion batteries cost eight times more than conventional lead-acid batteries for each kilowatt of power produced per hour. However, continuous innovation and increasing production are steadily dropping the price differential.

Chemical stability of Li-ion batteries is also a concern. Some batteries are destroyed at high temperatures and are known to overheat and even catch fire when overcharged or damaged. Other Li-ion batteries are ruined if completely discharged. The highly reactive chemistry of the Li-ion cell requires special safety precautions to prevent physical or electrical abuse of the battery. To maintain the cells within design operating limits, a microprocessor-controlled battery management system is required for Li-ion batteries to prevent damage and extend life cycle. Electronic controls add costs to production.

Valve-Regulated Lead-acid Batteries (VRLA)

Recall from the Commercial Vehicle Batteries chapter that valve-regulated lead-acid batteries (VRLA) are sealed lead-acid batteries that do not have a liquid electrolyte

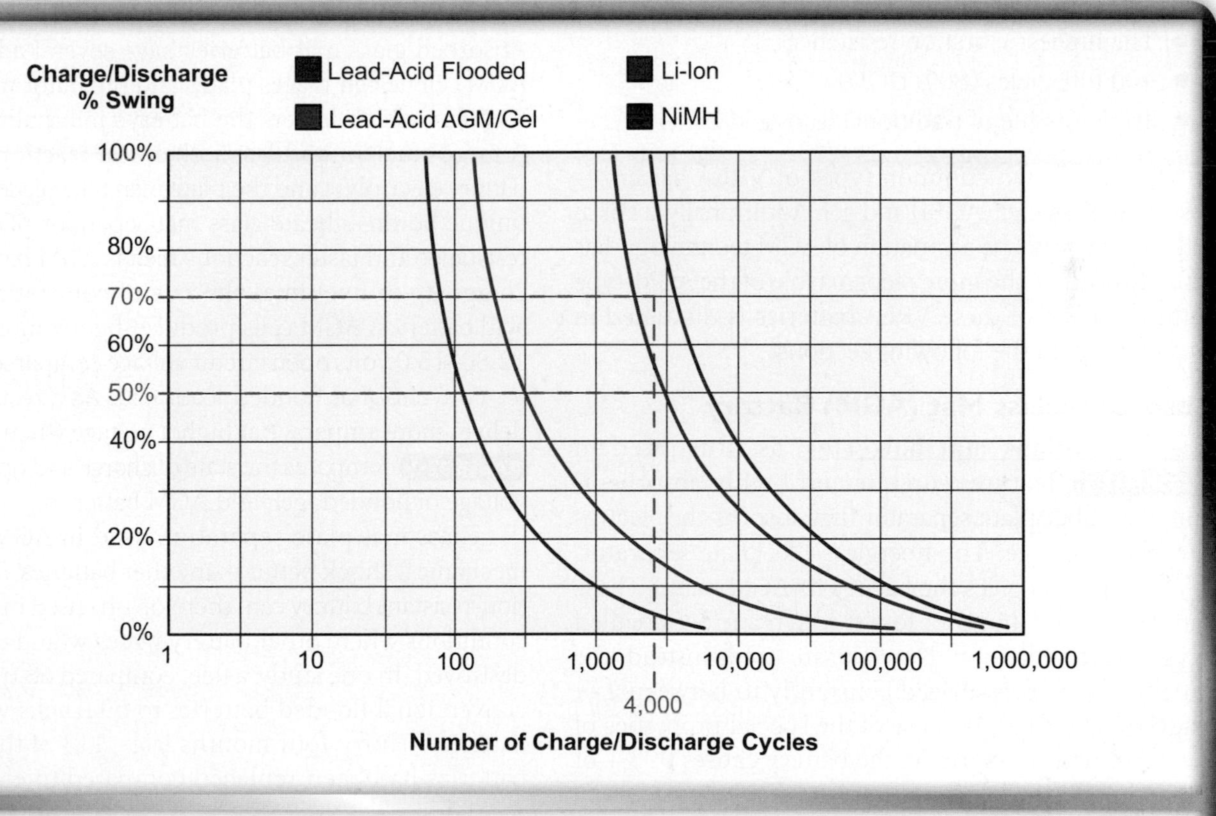

FIGURE 12-5 The extent to which a battery is discharged has a significant impact on battery life. The chart compares the service life compared to the depth of discharge for four common commercial vehicle battery technologies. Minimizing the depth of discharge dramatically improves battery life.

and do not require the addition of water. That design has numerous advantages. Plate and electrolyte technology used in VRLAs result in lower self-discharge rates because VRLAs typically lose only 1% to 3% of their charge per month. This compares to lead antimony grid batteries having a self-discharge rate of 2% to 10% per week and with 1% to 5% per month for batteries using lead calcium grids.

Since VRLA batteries are completely sealed, they can be installed in any position without leaking—even under water. Sealing the battery eliminates the need to replenish the electrolyte or to check specific gravity. Battery state of charge is determined through voltage checks.

Other advantages of VRLA batteries include:

- No required specific gravity readings or adjustments
- No need to add distilled water
- No acid or lead to deal with in wash water
- No cable corrosion
- No tray corrosion
- No corrosive gas in battery compartment to damage electronics
- The longest service life of all battery types
- The highest cranking amps, even at low temperature
- The fastest recharge possible
- The highest vibration resistance
- 400 full cycles (80% DOD)
- Triple the life of traditional lead-acid batteries

There are two common types of VRLA battery—absorbed glass mat (AGM) and gel. Additionally, a spiral cell battery, which is a variation of AGM technology, has actually become the more recognizable of the AGM-type batteries. Each of these VRLA batteries is discussed in greater detail in the following sections.

Absorbed Glass Mat (AGM) Battery

Absorbed glass mat batteries, as illustrated in FIGURE 12-6, feature a unique and highly absorbent, thin glass fiber plate separator that absorbs the electrolyte like a sponge. The fiberglass-like plate separator, or mat, material gives the battery its AGM name. These batteries eliminate water loss through a process called oxygen recombination. No vents are used. Instead, the battery case is pressurized constantly to between 1–4 psi (6.9–27.6 kPa). Because of the special properties of the glass mat, pressurizing the battery causes 99%+ of the hydrogen and oxygen gases to recombine back into water when recharging. A piece of foil in place of a traditional vent cap allows the battery gases to vent only under severe conditions such as during overcharging when voltage is greater than 15 volts. If venting occurs, the battery is likely damaged, and the cell will dry out like any other cell. Charging above 2.7 volts per cell, the battery is severely damaged.

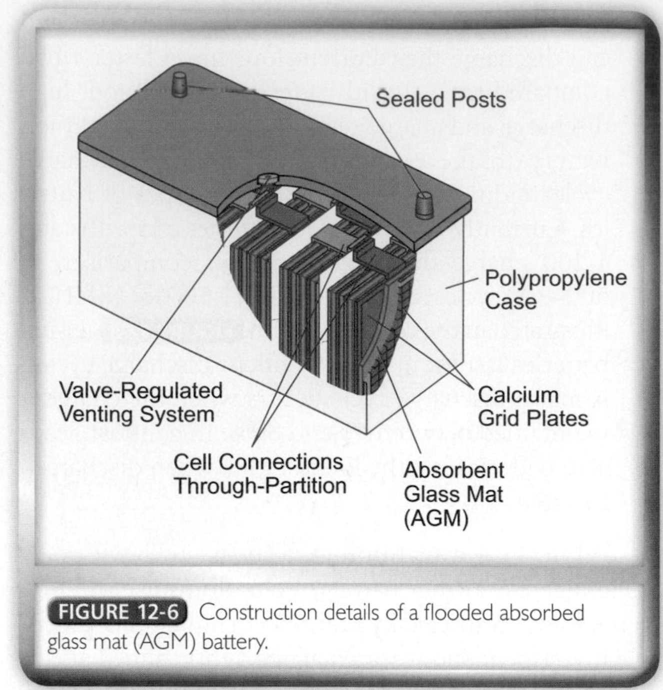

FIGURE 12-6 Construction details of a flooded absorbed glass mat (AGM) battery.

Advantages to AGM Batteries

Absorbed glass mat batteries have several advantages. AGM cell design places plates and separator mats closer together, which lowers the battery's internal resistance. A more efficient and faster chemical reaction between battery electrolyte and the plates can take place using the unique boron–silicate glass mat separator plate. Lower resistance and faster reactions means AGM batteries can charge up to five times the rate of conventional lead-acid batteries. AGM cells produce slightly more voltage: 12.80–13.0 volts open circuit voltage compared to 12.65 for conventional flooded lead-acid. As a result, AGMs deliver more amperage at higher voltage when cranking. TABLE 12-2 compares the state of charge and open-circuit voltage of flooded, gel, and AGM batteries.

Glass mat plate separators used in AGMs absorb mechanical shock better than other batteries. The vibration-resistant battery can, therefore, be used in operating conditions where other battery plates would quickly be destroyed. In one study, a fleet compared 68 trucks with conventional flooded batteries to 69 trucks with AGM batteries. Thirty-four months later, 113 of the flooded batteries had been replaced compared to eight of the AGM designs.

Service Precautions with AGM Batteries

AGM cells are extremely sensitive to damage from overcharging and require chargers that will limit charging

TABLE 12-2: State of Charge versus Open Circuit Voltage

Charge	Open Circuit Voltage		
	Flooded	Gel	AGM
100%	12.65	12.85	12.80
75%	12.40	12.65	12.60
50%	12.20	12.35	12.30
25%	12.00	12.00	12.00
0%	11.80	11.80	11.80

voltage to between 14.4 and 14.6 volts maximum at 68°F (20°C). Using conventional shop taper chargers, which can charge at up to 18 volts, will destroy an AGM battery. Sustained charging at 15 volts will also cause the battery to overheat and gas excessively due to electrolysis. Instead, a smart charger, such as the one shown in FIGURE 12-7, should be used. A **smart charger** is a battery charger with an internal microcontroller used to regulate charging rates and times. It is an intelligent, temperature-compensated charger with an "AGM" setting. Because cell voltage is slightly higher for AGM batteries, a vehicle's charging system voltage may need adjustment to keep it in range between 13.8 and 14.4 volts maximum at 68°F (20°C) for optimum performance and service life. Voltage regulator settings on some vehicles are too high for AGM batteries and may require adjustment. The higher open-circuit voltage also means that AGM batteries cannot be mixed with other battery types to prevent unequal charging and shortened battery life. Without access to the electrolyte, AGM state of charge can only be determined by measuring battery voltage.

FIGURE 12-7 Only microprocessor-controlled, or "smart," chargers should be used to charge AGM batteries.

The depth of discharge also affects the life cycle of batteries. In general, the deeper the discharge between charges, the shorter the life cycle of batteries. TABLE 12-3 compares the depth of discharge against the number of charge/discharge cycles that can be expected from different battery chemistry types.

Safety

AGM batteries are very sensitive to overcharging, as they will gas excessively and burst cell vents. Intelligent chargers that limit maximum charging voltage to 14.6 volts are required. Traditional taper chargers (used by most shops) that have an adjustable charging amperage setting should not be used to charge AGM batteries because taper chargers increase charging amperage to batteries by raising voltage to over 15 volts—and as much as 18 volts in some conditions.

TABLE 12-3: Comparison of Depth of Discharge Cycle to Battery Life for Different Battery Chemistries

Depth of Discharge	Gel: Cycle Life	AGM: Cycle Life	Flooded Lead-acid: Cycle Life	Li-ion	NiMH
100%	450	200	30–150	Potentially ruined/ damaged with some Li-ion chemistries	500–3,000 (demonstrated only)
80%	600	250			
50%	1,000	500	500	2,000	
25%	2,100	1,200			
10%	5,700	3,200	2,000	Millions +	300,000+ (demonstrated only)

Spiral Cell Optima Batteries

In the late 1980s, AGM battery technology advanced further with the introduction of spiral-wound plate technology. A typical spiral-wound cell battery is shown in FIGURE 12-8. **Spiral-wound cell batteries** are AGM batteries in every way except that the electrodes for each cell are not made of rectangular plates. Instead, two long, thin, lead plates—the positive and negative electrodes—are coiled into a tight spiral cell with an absorbent micro-glass mat placed between the plates absorbing the electrolytes, as illustrated in FIGURE 12-9. Replacing multiple plates with two coiled electrodes reduces internal battery resistance even further, thus enabling higher charging absorption rates for faster charging and higher discharge rates. These batteries also use higher internal gas pressures than other AGM batteries.

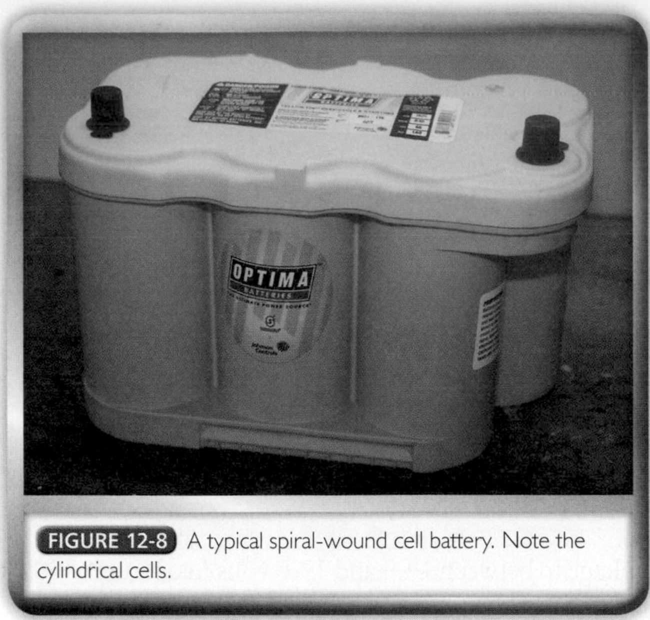

FIGURE 12-8 A typical spiral-wound cell battery. Note the cylindrical cells.

> **TECHNICIAN TIP**
>
> Many commercial vehicles use several batteries connected in parallel, or series and parallel, to supply adequate current for starting and operating electrical accessories. It is not a good practice to mix battery types or old and new batteries within battery banks for several reasons. First, slight open-circuit voltage differences exist between battery types caused by variations in plate and electrolyte composition. Similarly, variations exist in the internal resistances of different types of batteries. All these changes produce different discharge and charging characteristics. In a mixed set of batteries, some batteries will discharge quicker at higher rates of current. Others will not accept a charge easily. Those differences quickly lead to shorter battery life, undercharged, and eventually dead batteries in a set of batteries.

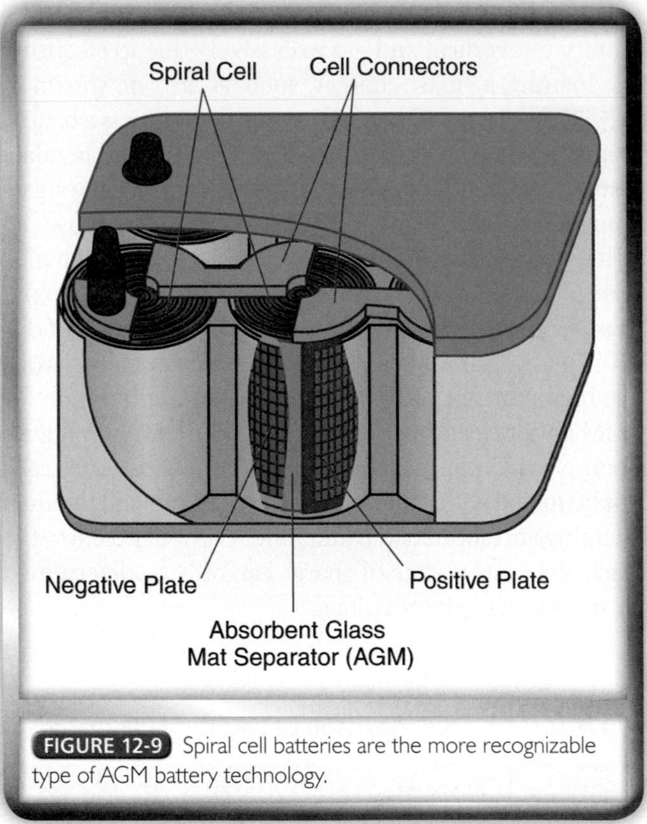

FIGURE 12-9 Spiral cell batteries are the more recognizable type of AGM battery technology.

Spiral cell batteries are produced in three categories, designated by the color of the battery's top cover.

- Red top—a 12-volt SLI battery
- Blue top—a deep cycle battery
- Yellow top—a combination deep cycle and SLI or leisure battery

Gel Cell

Just as battery plate and grid materials technologies have advanced to allow more powerful, lighter, and longer-lasting lead-acid batteries, electrolyte technology has also evolved. In the mid-1960s, spill-proof batteries were introduced using gel cells. **Gel cell batteries** are created by adding silica powder to the electrolyte, which turns the liquid into the consistency of petroleum jelly, hence the name "gel cells." A fully charged gel cell battery will have an open-circuit voltage of at least 12.85 volts and, like AGM cells, gel batteries are sensitive to overcharging and can be ruined by overcharging.

Ultra Capacitors

Compared to more traditional capacitors, **ultra capacitors** are a new generation of high-capacity and high-energy density capacitors. Capacitors are electrical devices well known for their ability to temporarily store short bursts of electrical energy. For example, capacitors suppress and smooth voltage fluctuations, or ripple, from alternators. Capacitors also suppress radio static when connected across the power line-in. Ultra capacitors are capable of supplying large bursts of energy and quickly recharging themselves, which make them ideal for use in modern vehicles. Ultra capacitors are particularly advantageous in situations requiring regenerative braking and in frequent stop-start systems, such as in electric and hybrid vehicles.

Ultra capacitors have a very low internal resistance when compared to lead-acid batteries. Consequently, ultra capacitors deliver and absorb high-energy currents much more readily. In hybrid vehicles, using regenerative braking applications, typical batteries are slow to absorb a charge, thus limiting the maximum recovery of energy. Ultra capacitors do not have this problem and are quickly recharged when depleted. This also makes them ideal for plug-in hybrid technology because they would allow vehicles to recharge in seconds—not hours! Furthermore, unlike other battery technologies, ultra capacitors are not worn out by continuous charge and discharge cycles. Whereas other battery technologies can be cycled between 200 and several thousand times, ultra capacitors can be cycled literally millions of times!

An ultra capacitor is constructed using two electrodes (plates), an electrolyte, and a separator plate, as illustrated in FIGURE 12-10A. The dielectric material is double layered—not single as in conventional capacitors—and is made from a porous carbon. While the construction features are similar to a cell of a galvanic-type battery, the method by which it stores electrical energy is different. Ultra capacitors store electrical energy within electrostatic fields (electrostatically) and do not produce electricity through electrochemical reactions. Like any capacitor, the main factors that determine how much electrical energy an ultra capacitor can store are as follows:

- Plate/electrode surface area—the greater the plate area, the higher the capacity.
- Distance between the plates—the closer the plates are, the higher the capacity.
- Electrical properties of the dielectric insulating layer separating the electrodes—some materials have better storage properties within capacitors than others.

A popular Ultra capacitor type battery is the Maxwell ESM Ultra series FIGURE 12-10B. Having the same dimensions as a group 31 battery, it can also produce 1,800 CCA for 3 seconds and is unaffected by the cold. Three terminals are used. Two are for charging the battery, and a third connects directly to the starter motor. An internal battery control module regulates the charging rate to each cell and performs diagnostic tests.

Ultra capacitors are currently used to assist batteries for the first 1.5 seconds during cranking where they can supply an additional 2,000 amps of current to supplement the starter batteries, as illustrated in FIGURE 12-11. That supplement increases starter torque and speed. when cranking amperage is highest during the initial starter engagement.

Battery Management Systems

Battery failure is a costly service issue for commercial vehicles. Weak batteries can lead to premature failure of starting and charging system components and loss of service caused by no-start conditions. The severe operating conditions and use of multiple batteries in many

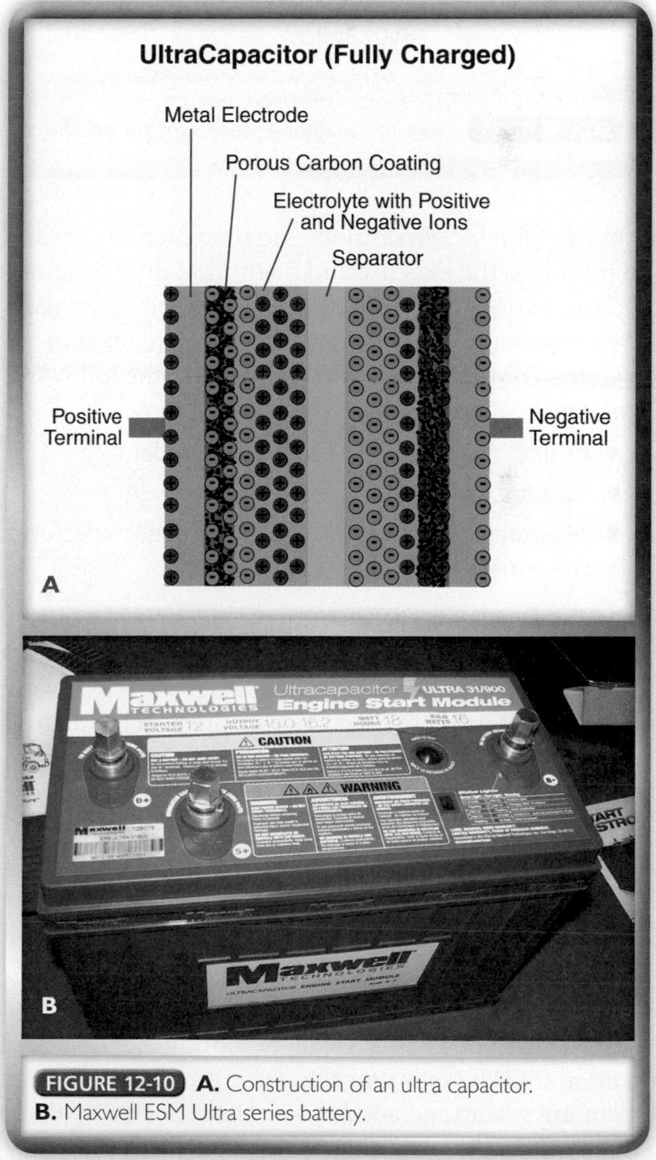

FIGURE 12-10 **A.** Construction of an ultra capacitor. **B.** Maxwell ESM Ultra series battery.

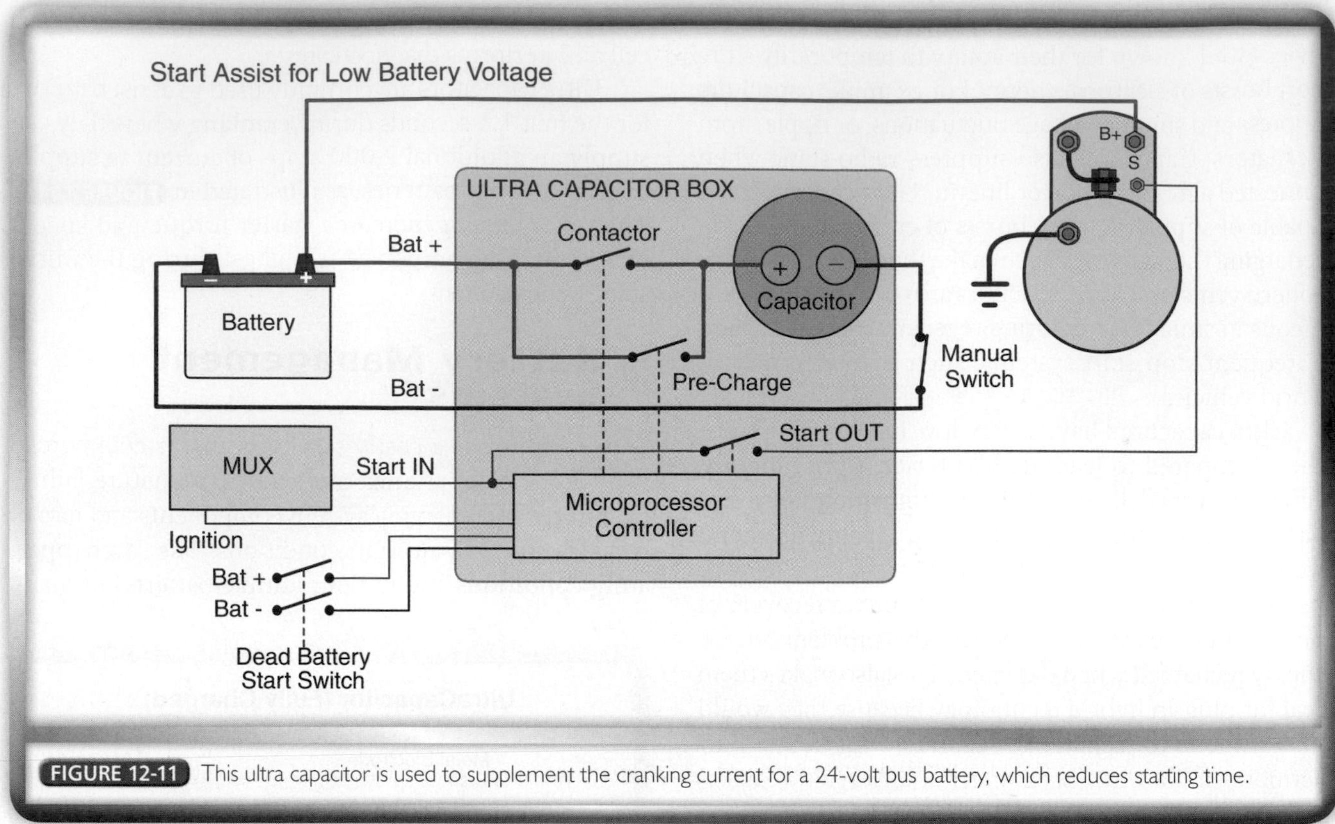

FIGURE 12-11 This ultra capacitor is used to supplement the cranking current for a 24-volt bus battery, which reduces starting time.

commercial vehicles contributes to shortened battery life. To minimize the expense and disruption due to battery failures, various electrical devices and systems are used to manage battery performance. **Battery management systems (BMS)** are designed to perform the following functions:

- Protect the cells or the battery from damage
- Prolong the life of the battery
- Maintain the battery in a state of charge to perform the work for which it was specified

The development of commercial hybrid-vehicle applications places more demands on batteries and requires sophisticated battery management systems for sensitive battery technology. Components of the battery management system include battery isolators, low-voltage disconnects, battery balancers and equalizers, and battery monitors. Each of these components is discussed in the following sections.

Battery Isolators

Many commercial vehicles use multiple batteries that can be separated according to function. For example, consider a vehicle with one battery bank of starting, lighting, and ignition (SLI) batteries for the starting and main vehicle operating system and another set of batteries for auxiliary deep cycle batteries for accessories or systems that may be required to operate after the engine is shut down. Permanently connecting all the battery banks in parallel could cause the SLI battery to become discharged if a continual electrical load is placed on the auxiliary deep cycle batteries for extended periods. This would prevent the vehicle from starting.

Battery isolator systems, or **split charge relays**, as illustrated in FIGURE 12-12, enable charging of an auxiliary battery by the vehicle charging system and electrical separation of the auxiliary battery from the starting circuit when the engine shuts down. Separation of the main starting and auxiliary batteries can take place automatically during charging and discharging. Battery isolation systems range from simple, isolating solenoids, or relays, to complex battery management systems that monitor charge rates and voltages for both the SLI and auxiliary batteries.

Low-Voltage Disconnect (LVD)

Low-voltage disconnects (LVD) are devices that monitor battery voltage and disconnect non-critical electrical loads when the battery voltage level falls below a preset threshold value. LVD devices preserve battery current to a level adequate to start the vehicle's engine when key-off loads or other parasitic draws are draining the battery. LVD devices then reconnect the electrical loads when the battery level is restored to a high enough voltage—for example, when the alternator begins charging above 12.6

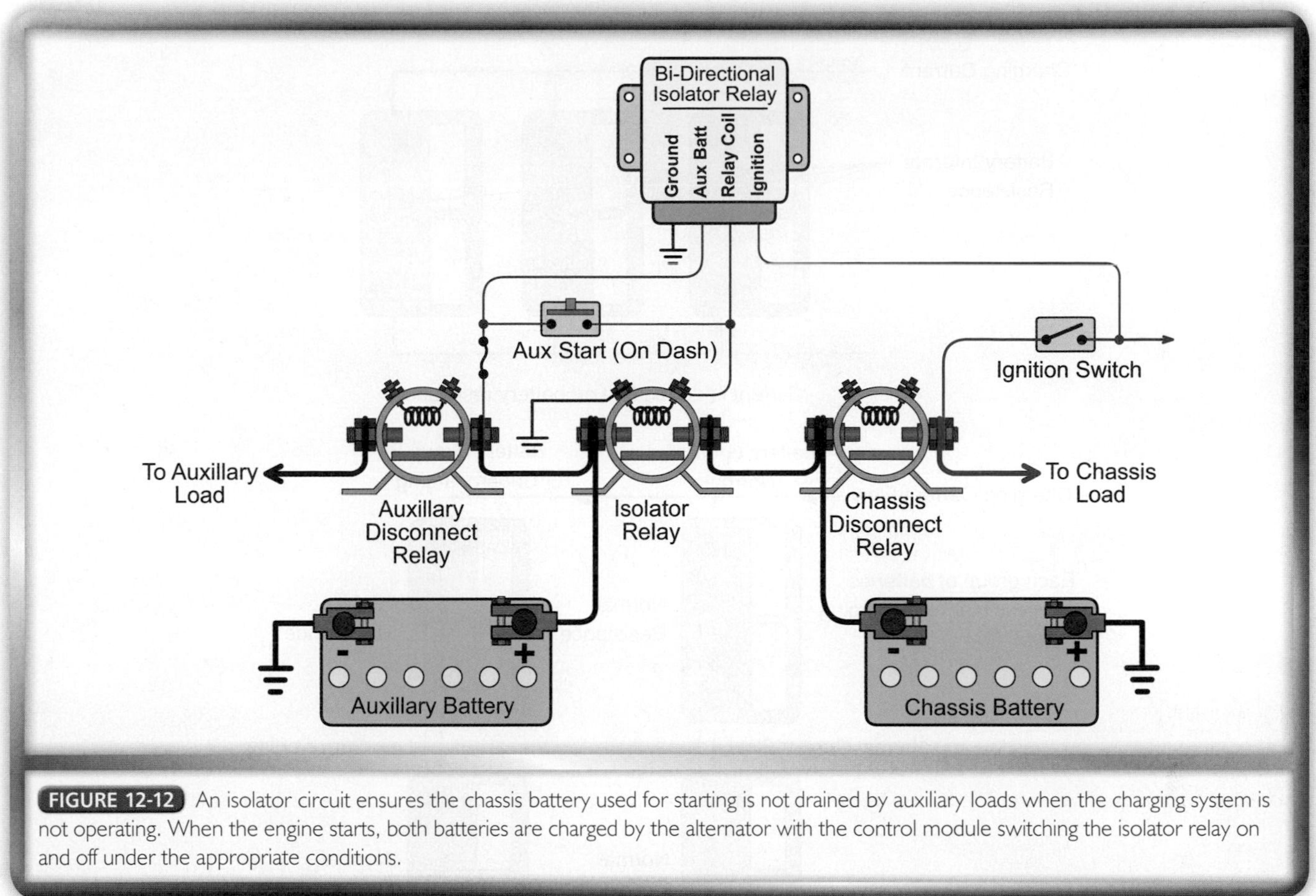

FIGURE 12-12 An isolator circuit ensures the chassis battery used for starting is not drained by auxiliary loads when the charging system is not operating. When the engine starts, both batteries are charged by the alternator with the control module switching the isolator relay on and off under the appropriate conditions.

volts. No intervention is required by the vehicle operator to protect the batteries, as the LVD automatically disconnects and reconnects the load. An audible warning typically alerts the operator before a disconnect event occurs, which is generally between 12.0 and 12.2-volts. LVDs can be integrated with the vehicle's power distribution system and will progressively shed loads as battery voltage drops.

Battery Balancers and Equalizers

Higher cranking amperage and greater electrical loads in commercial equipment require two or more batteries connected either in series, for 24-volt electrical systems, or in parallel, in 12-volt systems. Charging and discharging resistance changes with battery use and the electrical distance from the alternator. For example, longer battery cables and more electrical connections are almost unavoidable in many vehicles. This means one or more batteries in a bank gets undercharged, which in turn leads to undercharging and progressive plate sulfation. Sulfation, in turn, increases battery resistance, causing the battery to become weaker **FIGURE 12-13**.

Balancers (sometimes called **battery equalizers**), illustrated in **FIGURE 12-14**, attempt to adjust battery voltage to compensate for unequal charges in multiple batteries. Equalizers are found in many commercial applications using 24-volt charging systems, including transit and tour buses, private coaches, off-highway equipment, yachts, and alternative energy systems.

In multiple battery configurations, whether connected in series or in parallel, batteries will eventually charge and discharge unevenly, shortening battery life. For example, you may often discover that while testing two 12-volt batteries connected in parallel, one battery will become completely dead while the other stays in good condition. When testing three batteries, one will be good, another fair, and the third defective. The defective battery is always the farthest from the alternator in terms of electrical distance.

There are two methods of correcting this common condition of unequal charge and discharge rates. One is to regularly rotate the batteries and exchange their positions in the configuration. Another method is to use a battery equalizer. Also, remember to check the equipment manufacturer's recommendation for connecting battery cables. Properly connecting cables is one way to minimize the charge and discharge imbalances between batteries.

Various configurations of charge equalizers enable:

- Charging 12-volt batteries from a 24-volt charging system

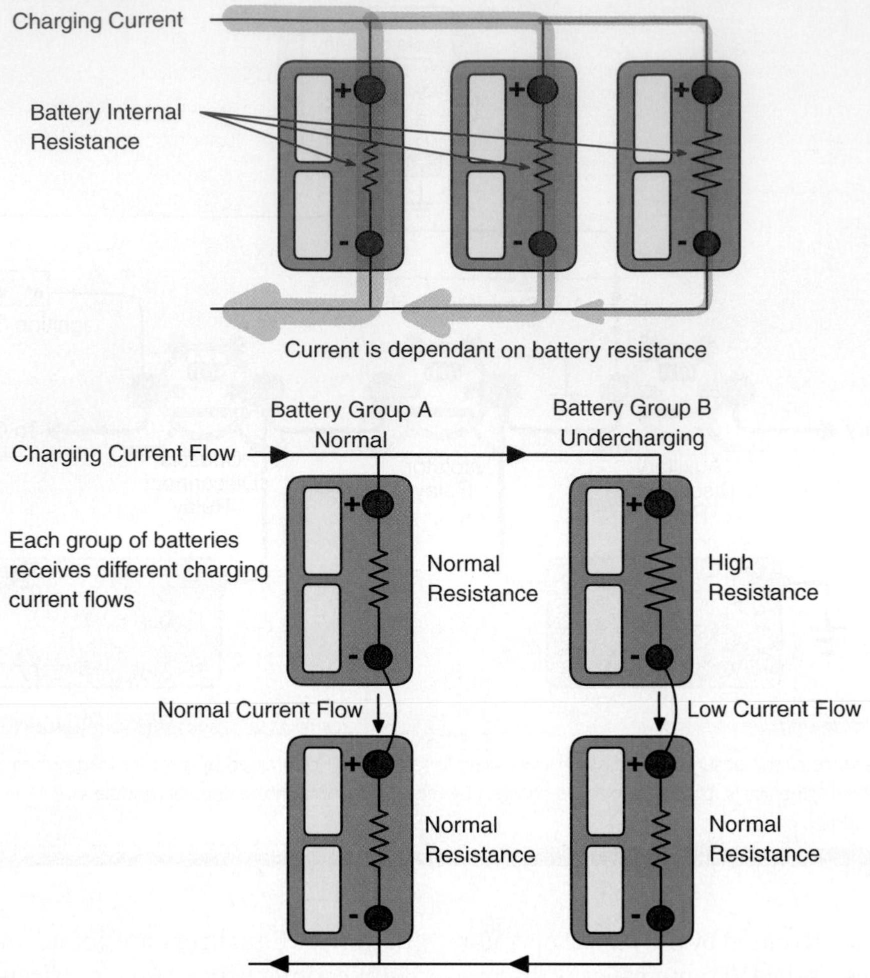

FIGURE 12-13 Batteries can develop unequal resistances with use.

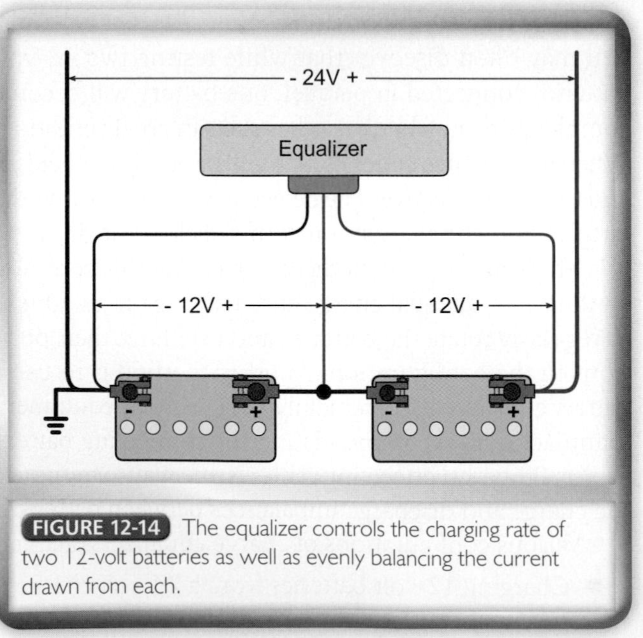

FIGURE 12-14 The equalizer controls the charging rate of two 12-volt batteries as well as evenly balancing the current drawn from each.

- Charging 24-volt batteries from a 12-volt charging system
- Charging series-connected 12-volt batteries at 24 volts and providing a 12-volt output for 12-volt chassis electrical loads
- Balanced battery charging of 12-volt batteries from 24 volts to within a difference of 0.1 volts
- Balanced draining of batteries to supply a 12-volt load so that each battery is depleted to within a difference of 0.1 volts

A common bus configuration has 12-volt batteries connected to the equalizer that interfaces the batteries with the 24-volt alternators, as illustrated in **FIGURE 12-15**. The equalizer will sense battery voltage and drive a higher charge rate into weaker batteries and less current into stronger batteries. The voltage balance and charge acceptance rate of each battery is kept to within 0.1 volts under

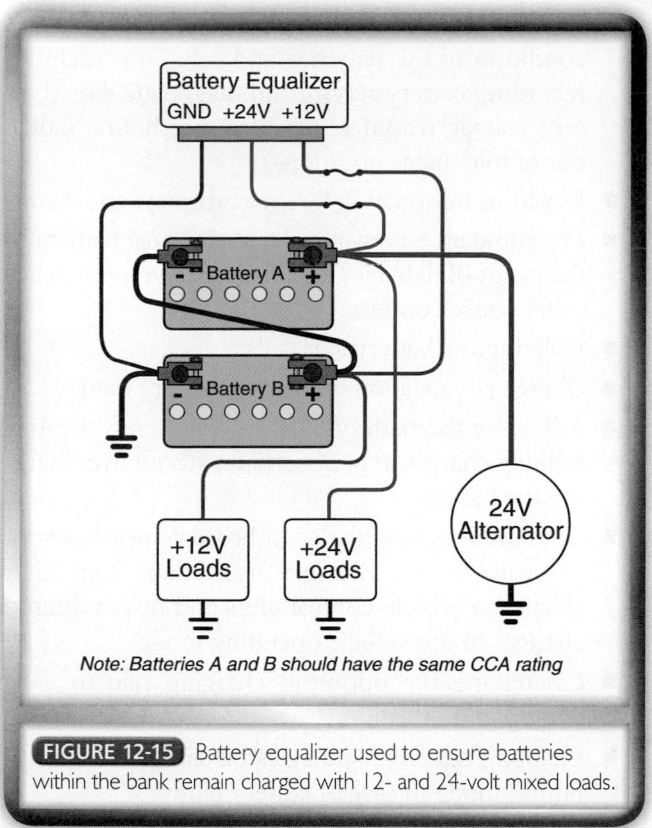

FIGURE 12-15 Battery equalizer used to ensure batteries within the bank remain charged with 12- and 24-volt mixed loads.

light loads and within 0.5 volts at full loads. When the voltage of Battery A is higher than that of Battery B, the battery equalizer switches to standby mode. This means no power is transferred from its 24-volt alternator input to its 12-volt output. If a 12-volt load is present, and Battery A's voltage decreases to just below the voltage of Battery B, the battery equalizer activates and transfers sufficient current from Battery B to Battery A, satisfying the load and maintaining an equal voltage and charge in both batteries.

More complex systems, like that illustrated in FIGURE 12-16, can have both battery isolation and battery equalization across multiple banks. For example, auxiliary or house batteries used in motor homes and chassis batteries are isolated from each other when the alternator is not charging, but are connected together so both banks charge when the alternator is charging—along with battery equalization for each bank.

Charge equalization is critical for series-connected battery cells in hybrid vehicle applications. The higher voltage in hybrid-drive systems requires very long, series strings of batteries pushing battery performance to extremes. Without battery management systems incorporating charge equalization, batteries banks would quickly fail.

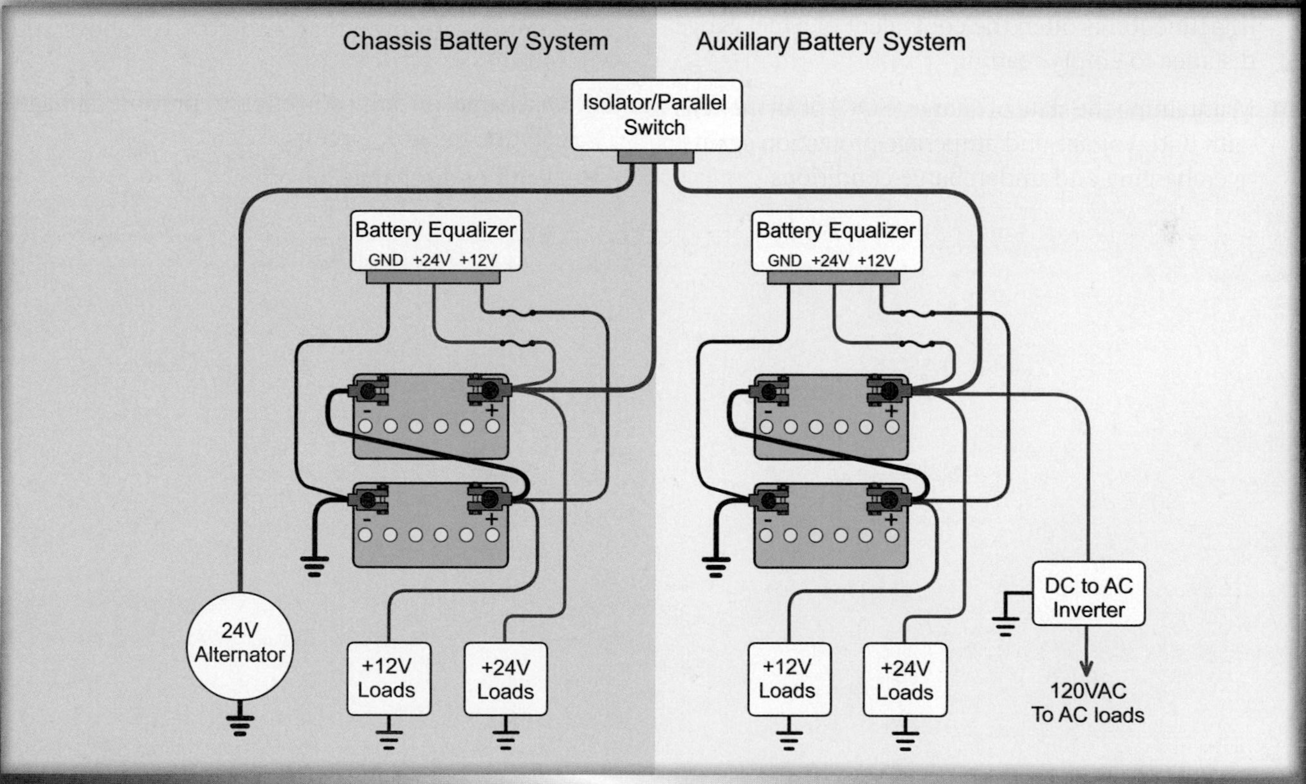

FIGURE 12-16 Schematic diagram of a battery equalizer combined with a battery isolator. The chassis system provides current to supply the starting motor batteries.

Battery Monitors

Hybrid commercial vehicles use battery monitors to collect battery data for display to the operator and service technician. The data that is typically collected includes:

- Temperature of each battery or pack
- Voltage of the pack
- Rate of charge or discharge

Hybrid Battery Management Systems

Hybrid-drive battery management is much more demanding than the previously described battery management devices. Batteries in these applications work in a demanding and harsh environment because of rapidly changing charging and discharging conditions, such as when the vehicle accelerates using electric motors and charges during regenerative braking. Li-ion and NiMH batteries are best charged to between 40% and 70% of full capacity to allow absorption of current generated during braking and to extend their lifecycle. An on-board battery management system, like that illustrated in FIGURE 12-17, will perform some, but not necessarily all, of the following functions:

- Monitoring the state of charge (SOC) of the battery and battery cells that compose the battery banks; this function is often the equivalent of a fuel gauge distance to empty reading
- Maintaining the state of charge (SOC) of all the cells with both voltage and amperage protection against overcharging and undercharge conditions
- Providing service and diagnostic information on the condition of the batteries and cells; this includes recording battery service and diagnostic data (battery voltage readings, temperature, hours, faults, out of tolerance conditions)
- Providing information for driver displays and alarms
- Providing an emergency protection mechanism in the event of damage, uncontrolled overheating, or other abuse condition
- Isolating the batteries or cells
- Charge equalization within the battery bank
- Adjusting the battery SOC to enable regenerative braking charges to be absorbed without overcharging the battery
- Communicating with the on-board vehicle network to receive information and instructions from other electronic vehicle-control units and responding to changes in the vehicle operating mode
- Calculating the optimum charging rate to each battery and or cell
- Enabling adaptive strategies or emergency "limp-home" mode in case of battery failure
- Provide reverse polarity protection
- Control temperature-dependent charging; some batteries can be damaged by charging when temperatures are lower than 32°F (0°C) or above 100°F (45°C)
- Discharge current protection to prevent damage to cell due to short circuits
- Depth of discharge cut-off

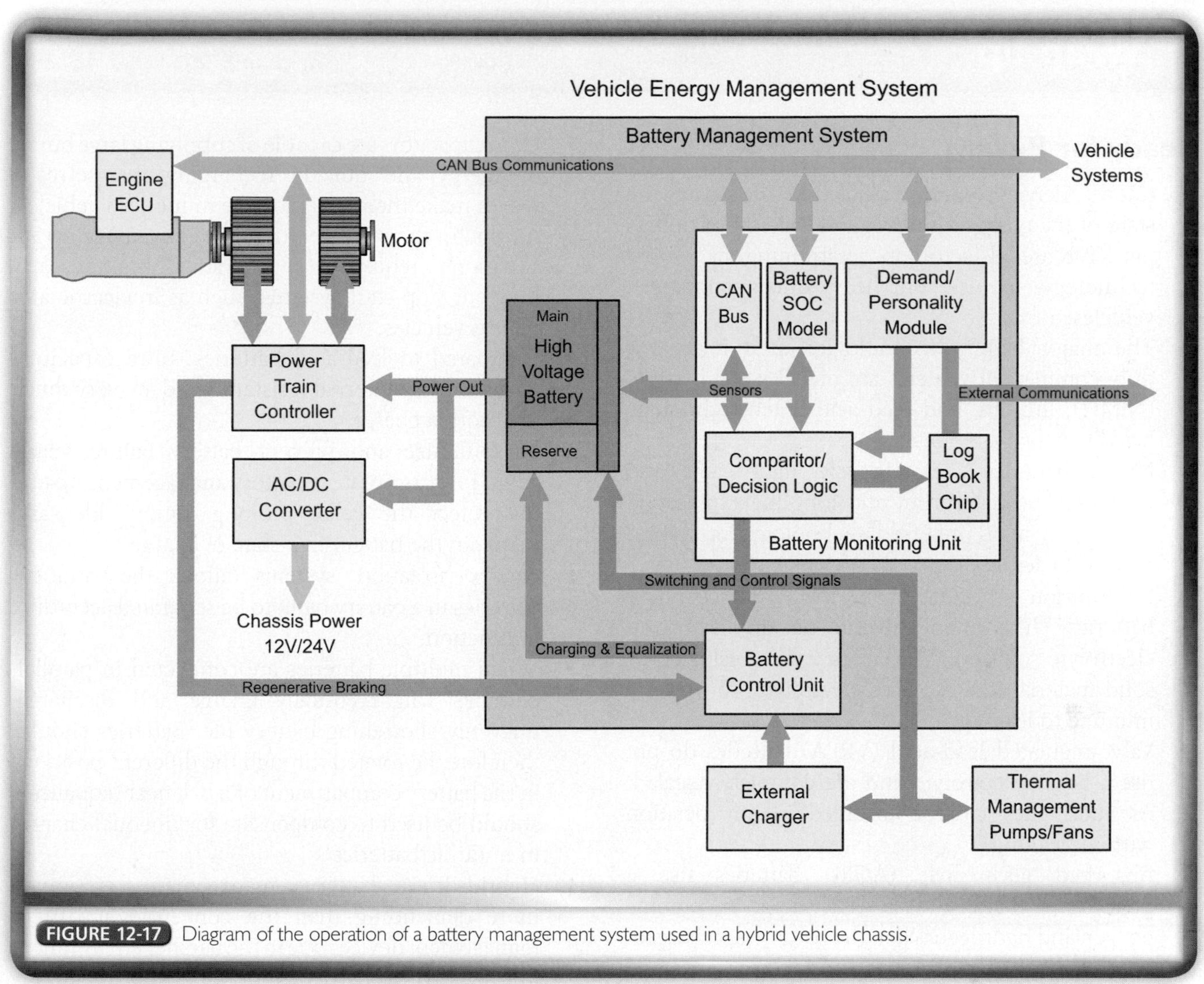

FIGURE 12-17 Diagram of the operation of a battery management system used in a hybrid vehicle chassis.

Wrap-up

Ready for Review

- Energy density, energy efficiency, life span, the state of the charge window, and the cost in dollars per kWh are all factors in determining the battery technology to use on heavy-duty commercial vehicles.
- The major battery technologies used in heavy-duty commercial vehicles are nickel-metal hydride (NiMH), lithium, and lead-acid. Each technology has distinct capabilities.
- NiMH batteries are relatively lightweight and have high power output and long life expectancy, making them a preferred technology for hybrid drive vehicles.
- Lithium-ion (Li-ion) batteries are secondary batteries. They are not galvanic, nor do they use an electrolyte solution. Rather, they use a gel, salt, or solid material that replaces electrolyte, so they are immune to leaking.
- Valve-regulated lead-acid (VRLA) batteries do not use a liquid electrolyte and are completely sealed. As such, they can be installed in any position without leaking.
- Absorbed glass mat (AGM) batteries use a pressurized battery case that helps recombine oxygen and hydrogen when the battery is recharged. These batteries have a lower internal resistance and a more efficient and faster chemical reaction.
- A spiral-wound cell battery is a special type of AGM battery that reduces internal resistance even further.
- Ultra capacitors are capable of supplying large bursts of energy and quickly recharging themselves—which make them ideal for use in modern vehicles. As such, they are particularly advantageous in situations requiring regenerative braking and frequent stop-start systems, such as in electric and hybrid vehicles.
- Compared to lead-acid batteries, ultra capacitors have very low internal resistance and are very quick to absorb a charge.
- To minimize and prevent battery failure, many vehicles incorporate a battery management system to protect the cells, prolong battery life, and maintain the battery in a state of charge.
- Battery isolation systems allow the multiple batteries in a battery bank to be separated according to function.
- When multiple batteries are connected in parallel, batteries will eventually charge and discharge, unevenly shortening battery life. Batteries should, therefore, be rotated through the different positions in the battery compartment or a balancer (equalizer) should be used to compensate for unequal charges in multiple batteries.
- Hybrid-drive battery management is much more demanding than the conventional battery management devices due to the harsher environment in which hybrid-drive batteries operate (e.g., rapidly changing charging and discharging conditions).

Vocabulary Builder

absorbed glass mat (AGM) battery A type of lead acid battery that uses a thin fiberglass plate to absorb the electrolyte; prevents the solution from sloshing or separating into layers of heavier acid and water.

balancers A device designed to adjust battery voltage to compensate for unequal charges in multiple batteries. Also called *battery equalizers*.

battery equalizers A device designed to adjust battery voltage to compensate for unequal charges in multiple batteries. Also called *balancers*.

battery isolator systems A system designed to separate the main starting battery and the auxiliary battery. Also called a *split charge relay*.

battery management system (BMS) A system of electrical devices used to manage battery performance.

gel cell battery A type of battery to which silica has been added to the electrolyte solution to turn the solution to a gel-like consistency.

lithium-ion (Li-ion) battery A type of battery that does not use a galvanic reaction and in which a gel, salt, or solid material replaces the electrolyte solution.

low-voltage disconnect (LVD) A device that monitors battery voltage and disconnects non-critical electrical loads when battery voltage level falls below a preset threshold value.

nickel–metal hydride (NiMH) battery A battery in which metal hydroxide forms the negative electrode and nickel oxide forms the positive electrode.

smart charger A battery charger with microprocessor-controlled charging rates and times.

spiral-wound cell battery A type of AGM battery in which the positive and negative electrodes are coiled into a tight spiral cell with an absorbent micro-glass mat placed between the plates.

split charge relay A system designed to separate the main starting battery and the auxiliary battery. Also called a *battery isolator system*.

ultra capacitor A new generation of high-capacity and high-energy density capacitors

Review Questions

1. Which of the following is correct concerning the nickel–metal hydride battery?
   a. NiMH batteries are relatively light weight.
   b. NiMH batteries have good power output.
   c. NiMH batteries have a long life expectancy.
   d. All of the choices are correct.
2. Which of the following is NOT correct concerning lithium-ion batteries?
   a. Lithium-ion batteries have liquid electrolyte similar to lead-acid batteries.
   b. Currently there are dozens of different cell chemistries used to produce lithium-ion batteries.
   c. Regardless of their specific chemistry, lithium batteries have a higher energy density than other battery types, such as lead–acid, nickel–cadmium, and NiMH.
   d. Popular Li-ion chemistries incorporate electrodes made from lithium combined with phosphate, cobalt, carbon, nickel, and manganese oxide.
3. Which of the following is NOT correct concerning absorbed glass mat batteries?
   a. Lower resistance and faster reactions means AGM batteries can charge up to two times the rate of conventional lead–acid batteries.
   b. AGM cells produce slightly more voltage, 12.80–13.0 open circuit voltage compared to 12.65 V for conventional flooded lead–acid batteries.
   c. Glass-mat plate separators used in AGMs absorb mechanical shock better than other batteries.
   d. The vibration-resistant battery can be used in operating conditions where other battery plates would quickly be destroyed.
4. Which of the following is NOT correct concerning gel cell batteries?
   a. Gel cell batteries can be considered spill-proof batteries.
   b. A fully charged gel cell battery will have an open-circuit voltage of at least 12.55 volts.
   c. Gel cell batteries are created by adding silica powder to the electrolyte, which turns the liquid into the consistency of petroleum jelly, hence the name “gel cells.”
   d. Gel cell batteries are sensitive to overcharging and can be ruined by overcharging.
5. Which of the following is correct concerning valve regulated lead–acid batteries (VRLA)?
   a. With a VRLA battery there is no need to add distilled water.
   b. With a VRLA battery there is no cable corrosion.
   c. With a VRLA battery there is the longest service life of all battery types.
   d. All of the choices are correct.
6. Which of the following is correct concerning ultra capacitors?
   a. Ultra capacitors are capable of supplying large bursts of energy and quickly recharging themselves, which make them ideal for use in modern vehicles.
   b. Ultra capacitors are particularly advantageous in situations requiring regenerative braking and in frequent stop-start systems, such as those used in electric and hybrid vehicles.
   c. Unlike other battery technologies, ultra capacitors are not worn out by continuous charge and discharge cycles.
   d. All of the choices are correct.
7. Which of the following is NOT a component of the battery management system?
   a. Battery isolator
   b. Battery modulator
   c. Low-voltage disconnect
   d. Battery balancer and equalizers
8. In heavy-duty vehicles, battery isolators are used to:
   a. keep all the electrical functions in a single battery unit.
   b. permanently connect all battery banks in parallel.
   c. power auxiliary systems.
   d. separate the main starting and auxiliary batteries.
9. At what threshold would an operator typically hear a warning from a low-voltage disconnect that a disconnect event is about to occur?
   a. 6 volts
   b. 12 volts
   c. 18 volts
   d. 24 volts
10. Li-ion and NiMH batteries are best charged to between ________ % and ________ % of full capacity to allow absorption of current generated during braking and to extend their lifecycle.
    a. 50; 100
    b. 40; 70
    c. 80; 100
    d. 70; 90

ASE-Type Questions

1. Technician A says that the demand for advanced battery technology in commercial vehicles is growing. Technician B says that, not only do the increasingly popular hybrid electric vehicles require advanced batteries, heavy-duty commercial vehicles also have a greater need for electrical storage capacity to run accessories. Who is correct?
   a. Technician A
   b. Technician B
   c. Both Technician A and Technician B
   d. Neither Technician A nor Technician B
2. Technician A says that nickel–metal hydride (NiMH) is one type of battery used in commercial vehicles. Technician B says that lithium and lead-acid batteries are also used in commercial vehicles. Who is correct?
   a. Technician A
   b. Technician B
   c. Both Technician A and Technician B
   d. Neither Technician A nor Technician B
3. Technician A says that Li-ion cells maintain a constant voltage for over 90% of their discharge curve as compared to conventional lead–acid batteries maintaining voltage until only 60% discharged. Technician B says that once charged, Li-ion batteries self-discharge at very low rate. Who is correct?Technician A
   a. Technician B
   b. Both Technician A and Technician B
   c. Neither Technician A nor Technician B
4. Technician A says that one disadvantage of current Li-ion battery technology is cost. Technician B says that Li-ion batteries cost four times more than conventional lead–acid batteries for each kilowatt of power produced per hour. Who is correct?
   a. Technician A
   b. Technician B
   c. Both Technician A and Technician B
   d. Neither Technician A nor Technician B
5. Technician A says that a VRLA battery has the highest cranking amps—even at low temperature. Technician B says that a VRLA battery has triple the life of traditional lead–acid batteries. Who is correct?
   a. Technician A
   b. Technician B
   c. Both Technician A and Technician B
   d. Neither Technician A nor Technician B
6. Technician A says that no vents are used on AGM batteries. Technician B says that AGM batteries will be damaged if charged at greater than 13.2 volts. Who is correct?
   a. Technician A
   b. Technician B
   c. Both Technician A and Technician B
   d. Neither Technician A nor Technician B
7. Technician A says that a smart charger is a battery charger in which microprocessors control charging rates and times. Technician B says that AGM state of charge can be tested with a battery hydrometer. Who is correct?
   a. Technician A
   b. Technician B
   c. Both Technician A and Technician B
   d. Neither Technician A nor Technician B
8. Technician A says that ultra capacitors supplement increases to starter torque and speed. Technician B says that ultra capacitors are currently used to assist batteries for the first 3.5 seconds during cranking, during which time they can supply an additional 1,000 amps of current to supplement the starter batteries. Who is correct?
   a. Technician A
   b. Technician B
   c. Both Technician A and Technician B
   d. Neither Technician A nor Technician B
9. Technician A says that battery management systems (BMS) are designed to protect the cells or the battery from damage. Technician B says that battery management systems (BMS) are designed to prolong the life of the battery. Who is correct?
   a. Technician A
   b. Technician B
   c. Both Technician A and Technician B
   d. Neither Technician A nor Technician B
10. Technician A says that battery balancers attempt to adjust battery voltage to compensate for unequal charges in multiple batteries. Technician B says that equalizers are found in many commercial applications using 24-volt charging systems, including transit and tour buses, private coaches, and off-highway equipment. Who is correct?
    a. Technician A
    b. Technician B
    c. Both Technician A and Technician B
    d. Neither Technician A nor Technician B

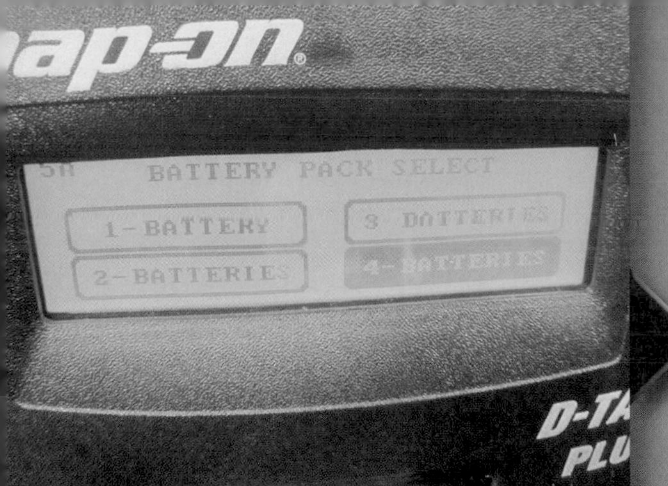

CHAPTER 13

NATEF Tasks

Electrical/Electronic Systems

General Electric Systems	Page
■ Identify parasitic (key-off) battery drain problems; perform tests; determine needed action.	385
Battery	
■ Inspect, clean, and service battery; replace as needed.	377
■ Inspect and clean battery boxes, mounts, and hold downs; repair or replace as needed.	377
■ Inspect, test, and clean battery cables and connectors; repair or replace as needed.	377
■ Determine battery state of charge using an open circuit voltage test.	379
■ Perform battery capacitance test; determine needed action.	380
■ Identify battery type; perform appropriate battery load test; determine needed action.	381
■ Charge battery using appropriate method for battery type.	383
■ Jump start a vehicle using jumper cables and a booster battery or appropriate auxiliary power supply using proper safety procedures.	384
■ Identify and test low-voltage disconnect (LVD) systems; determine needed repair.	387

Servicing Commercial Vehicle Batteries

Knowledge Objectives

After reading this chapter, you will be able to:

1. Identify safety equipment and safe work practices for servicing batteries. (pp 373–374)
2. Identify and describe failure modes of batteries. (p 374)
3. Recommend battery replacement based on battery testing procedures. (pp 375–381)
4. Identify and describe procedures and equipment used to test lead-acid batteries. (pp 375–381)

Skills Objectives

After reading this chapter, you will be able to:

1. Inspect, clean, fill, or replace the battery, battery cables, clamps, connectors, hold-downs, and battery boxes. (p 377) **SKILL DRILL 13-1**
2. Perform a battery state of charge test. (p 379) **SKILL DRILL 13-2**
3. Perform a conductance test on a battery. (p 380) **SKILL DRILL 13-3**
4. Perform a load test on a battery. (p 381) **SKILL DRILL 13-4**
5. Charge a commercial battery. (p 383) **SKILL DRILL 13-5**
6. Jump-start a commercial vehicle. (p 384) **SKILL DRILL 13-6**
7. Measure parasitic draw on a battery. (p 385) **SKILL DRILL 13-7**
8. Identify and test a low-voltage disconnect. (p 387) **SKILL DRILL 13-8**

Introduction

Batteries should be the starting point when diagnosing complaints such as hard starting, slow cranking, or no-start complaints FIGURE 13-1. Battery testing is also indicated when lights dim when an engine idles or when other electrical problems occur. Battery testing is also recommended whenever an alternator is replaced. A variety of instruments and tools are used to evaluate the condition of vehicle batteries, and a number of procedures are commonly used to service batteries during maintenance checks. These techniques are covered in this chapter.

Traditional comprehensive maintenance and testing of batteries includes the following evaluation methods:

- Visual inspection, cleaning, filling, and battery replacement
- State of charge testing using a voltmeter
- Cell voltage checks
- Load or capacity testing
- Conductance or impedance testing
- Charging batteries
- Jump-starting vehicles
- Measuring parasitic draw

Batteries should be evaluated visually first before proceeding with any other significant tests. Visual checks include checking the electrolyte level if it is possible. Most batteries today are sealed, low- or no-maintenance type, which prevents this procedure.

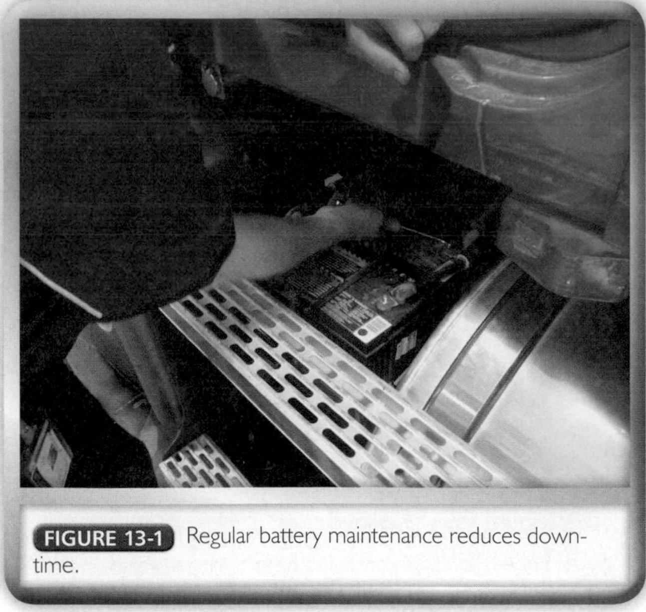

FIGURE 13-1 Regular battery maintenance reduces downtime.

Another basic maintenance task is to make sure the exterior case is dry and free of dirt. Dirt on top of the battery can actually cause premature self-discharge of the battery as current “leaks” across the path of dirt or grime. Grime and vapors from a battery can become conductive and drain the battery over time. To tell if the surface of the battery is leaking current, use a digital volt-ohm meter (DVOM), like the one shown in FIGURE 13-2, set to “volts” to measure the voltage on the surface of the top of the battery. You can do this by placing the black

You Are the Technician

Maintaining a fleet of trucks, buses, and other diesel-powered machinery in hot climates presents unique challenges. One of the problems you are frequently encountering is hard starting of engines due to dead batteries. Within a few months, many of the batteries have become defective, usually just one out of two batteries or two out of three batteries in a multiple-battery configuration. One battery is usually in good condition. A significant amount of downtime, labor, and associated expenses is lost to jump-starting vehicles and equipment in addition to the cost of battery replacements. From your experience working in other areas and even during cooler months, you associate hot weather with more frequent battery failures. Even if the batteries do not fail during hot weather, the first cold morning after a long season of heat often produces many no-start conditions. Consider strategies to reduce the aggravation level and cost of service for no-start conditions due to the effects of high temperatures on batteries.

1. Why do batteries fail more quickly in hot climates?
2. How can you determine if batteries are sulfated?
3. Identify several maintenance procedures used to minimize battery failure due to sulfation.

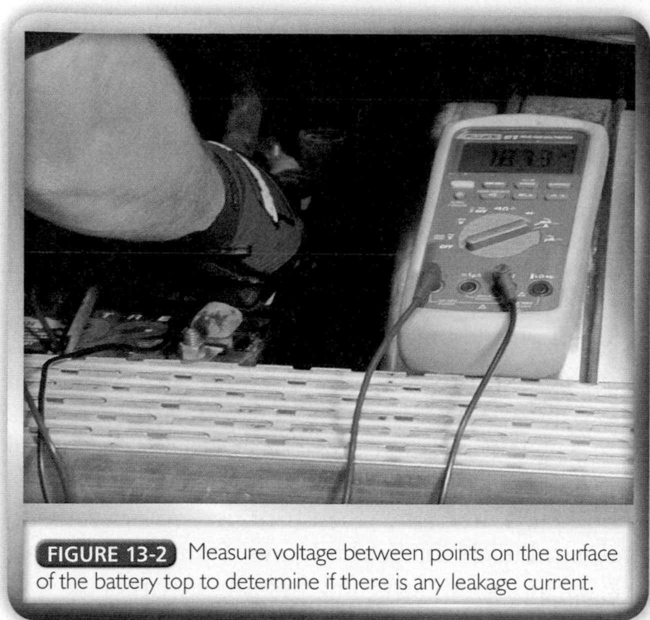

FIGURE 13-2 Measure voltage between points on the surface of the battery top to determine if there is any leakage current.

lead on the negative battery post and rubbing the red lead around the top of the battery, measuring the voltage present there. Any voltage exceeding 0.5 volts means the battery should be washed down with water. Do not use mixtures of diluted ammonia or baking soda, as they can enter the battery cells and contaminate electrolyte.

Batteries should be fully charged to perform properly and prolong their service life. A weakened battery causes the alternator to work harder charging batteries and shortening its life. Lower current level available to the starter will lead to low-voltage burn-out of the starter, too. State of charge will be covered in detail in the section Testing Battery State of Charge and Specific Gravity.

> **TECHNICIAN TIP**
>
> Treatments specifically designed to coat battery terminals should be applied to battery terminals to prevent corrosion and resistance from developing at battery connections. These treatments are not electrically conductive and will not attack cable insulating materials. Many other types of grease, such as chassis grease, are electrically conductive and will lead to battery self-discharge and even corrosion of battery terminals.

Electrolyte level and condition are also important factors in battery service life. Electrolyte condition is checked at the same time specific gravity is evaluated. Electrolyte level and condition will be discussed further in the section Electrolyte Level and Condition.

The section Battery Inspecting, Testing, and Maintenance covers several tests can be used to determine battery service life and identify reasons for battery failure. Load or capacity tests determine the ability of a battery to deliver cranking amperage and will be discussed in detail in the section Testing Battery Capacity. Conductance testing, or impedance testing, has replaced this method for evaluating battery capacity and will be covered in the section Testing Battery Conductance. Testing for sulfation is not performed as part of a regular battery evaluation but only to validate a diagnosis of sulfation. The procedure is discussed in the section Performing a Sulfation (Three-Minute Charge) Test.

Parasitic draw testing and case drain or leakage testing are other means to detect conditions that cause batteries to lose their charge. A parasitic drain of battery current should be no more than 0.5 amps of current. An inductive ammeter placed on either battery cable with all vehicle accessories off will easily measure and detect excessive draw. Wet and dirty batteries will leak voltage, too. Placing one voltmeter lead on a battery post and the other lead on the case will identify voltage leaks exceeding 0.5 volts. Battery cases should be cleaned and dried to remove electrically conductive grime from the case. Parasitic draw will be discussed in greater detail in the section Measuring Parasitic Draw.

Battery Service Precautions

Nearly 6,000 people in the United States are recently reported to have suffered eye injuries from batteries, according to Prevent Blindness America organization. Safety should be the first priority when working around and servicing batteries. Batteries are dangerous for a couple of reasons. First, electrolyte inside lead-acid batteries is corrosive. Acid on skin, in eyes, on clothing, or on paint will burn, causing bodily harm and vehicle damage. Also, an explosive gas mixture consisting of hydrogen and oxygen is produced during charging and discharging of the battery. Ensure the following precautions are followed to reduce the risk when working with batteries:

- Always wear protective clothing such as rubber gloves and goggles or full-face shields when handling batteries. When handling a battery or checking electrolyte levels, wear a rubber apron to protect clothing from splashed battery acid. If acid contacts your skin or eyes, flush with water immediately.
- Never wear any conductive jewelry (neck chains, watches, or rings) when working on or near batteries, as they may provide an accidental short-circuit path for high currents.

- Do not smoke, weld, or grind metal near batteries since sparks may ignite the explosive gas mixture.
- Never create a low-resistance connection or short across the battery terminals.
- Never disconnect a battery charger, jumper cables, or power booster from a battery when charging or jump-starting. Sparks will occur when disconnected and can result in battery explosions. Shut the power booster off. Disconnect the chassis ground clamp which is away from the battery first. Connect the ground clamp last when boosting.
- Charge batteries in a well-ventilated area.

Always remove the negative or ground terminal first when disconnecting battery cables, because this procedure reduces the possibility of a wrench creating a short circuit between any positive voltage wiring and the chassis ground.

- All battery cable connections to the battery terminals need to be properly tightened. Loose connections are resistive and may cause sparks.
- Never set a wrench or other tool on a battery, as doing so can cause short battery terminals, leading to gassing, overheating, and an explosion in an alarmingly short period.

TECHNICIAN TIP

Always connect and disconnect the main battery ground first. If there are other ground cables connected to the battery for the engine and other electronic control modules, connect these grounds last. When additional grounds are either connected or disconnected and the main battery ground is NOT connected, voltage spikes could occur and may damage electronic control modules.

Safety

Never allow a spark or flame around a battery, and never try to jump-start a frozen, faulty, or open-circuit battery; doing so could cause the battery to explode, causing injury.

Causes of Battery Failure

According to several studies, 52% of vehicle break-downs or failures to provide service are caused by batteries. Battery failures are by far the leading cause for service break-downs, with tires being the next most common (15%), followed by engines (8%). The two most common complaints concerning batteries are that they will either not charge or not hold a charge. Batteries may suddenly fail through the loss of a cell or open circuits within the internal connections. Batteries may also slowly fail over time through the gradual loss of capacity caused by plate deterioration.

Sulfation

According to a study, of all lead-acid batteries returned to the manufacturer under warranty, close to half were found to have no defect. Of those found defective, close to 80% were caused by sulfation. Sulfation can be observed when a white colored substance coats and swells, as shown in FIGURE 13-3. It occurs when batteries are subjected to prolonged undercharge conditions. During normal use, soft sulfate crystals form and dissipate as part of the normal charge and discharge cycle. During periods of prolonged undercharge, the sulfate converts to hard crystals and deposit on the negative plates. During subsequent charging, the hardened sulfate cannot be driven from the plate and reduces the active area of plate material. Sulfation also increases the internal resistance of a battery. This means higher charging voltage is needed to regenerate active plate material when charging. Pulse-type battery chargers have a setting for potentially reconditioning batteries that may have been sitting for periods of time in an undercharged state.

Common reasons for sulfation include:

1. *Leaving batteries too long in a state of discharge*—Soft sulfation occurring during normal discharge turns to hard sulfate crystals over time. Batteries should be recharged as soon as possible after discharging. Key-off loads, also called parasitic drains, contribute to sulfation caused by prolonged discharge.
2. *Undercharging of a battery*—High resistance at battery connections, particularly in batteries connected in series or parallel, leads to undercharging of cells. Incorrect charging system voltage can also cause undercharging.

FIGURE 13-3 Sulfate on the top of the plates of a lead acid battery.

3. *High ambient temperatures*—Temperatures in excess of 100°F (39°C) speeds-up chemical activity inside a battery, accelerating the self-discharge of a battery. It is calculated that a new, fully charged, flooded battery would most likely not start an engine if continuously exposed to 110°F (47°C) in as little as 30 days. Significantly higher rates of battery failures occur in warm regions of North America than in cold areas. To minimize self-discharge, batteries are best stored in cool, dry places.
4. *Low electrolyte level*—Battery plates exposed to air will dry out and prevent transfer of sulfate from the plate material back into electrolyte during charging. Adding acid to a battery will not recover a dead battery. Instead, it will increase the concentration of sulfate in the battery.

Performing a Sulfation (Three-Minute Charge) Test

Sulfation is indicated using a three-minute battery charge test. This test is not performed as part of a regular battery evaluation but only to validate a diagnosis of sulfation. This battery test requires charging the battery at 30–40 amps for three minutes, while measuring the battery voltage with the charger on. If the voltage rises above 15.5 volts, the battery is excessively resistive and is likely sulfated.

Vibration

Excessive vibration can cause open circuits in the internal battery connections and "shed" or shake loose plate material, which settles to the bottom of the battery case. **Shedding** reduces the plate surface area and therefore reduces capacity. Shedding may also produce short circuits between the bottom of positive and negative plates.

Electrolyte Level and Condition

Low electrolyte level exposes the plates to air, preventing the transfer of sulfate from the plate material back into the electrolyte during charging. It is critical to maintain the correct acid-water mix of electrolyte. If electrolyte level is lost through evaporation, then distilled water should be added. If electrolyte is lost due to spillage, then the battery should be topped up with electrolyte.

Plates and grids that are damaged are often detected by examining the electrolyte. Gray or dirty electrolyte in any cell renders a battery defective. Although voltage and electrolyte readings may be satisfactory, contaminants even in one cell will cause the battery to self-discharge quickly. Series connections between cells will cause even one dead or defective cell to discharge all other cells in the battery. Electrolyte condition is checked at the same time specific gravity is evaluated.

Grid Corrosion

Grid corrosion, like that illustrated in FIGURE 13-4, takes place primarily in the positive grid and is accelerated by overcharging and high temperatures. When corrosion takes place, grid resistance increases during charging and discharging. Grids are the foundation and the electrical conducting layer for the battery plate. Although grids are alloyed with antimony, calcium, or sometimes barium to minimize the corrosive effects of the electrolyte, grids do disintegrate. The mud-like lead paste attached to grids also falls apart when grids corrode.

Battery Inspecting, Testing, and Maintenance

As noted earlier, batteries last longer if they are properly maintained. In fact, one of the most common causes of vehicle no-starts is dirty or corroded battery cables. Inspecting, cleaning, and filling (if not maintenance free) are common tasks that should be performed every six months to one year on top-post batteries, and one to two years on side-post batteries. During periodic maintenance, batteries should be checked for proper ventilation. All slide mechanisms on battery trays should work properly. Battery cables should be inspected for rubbing

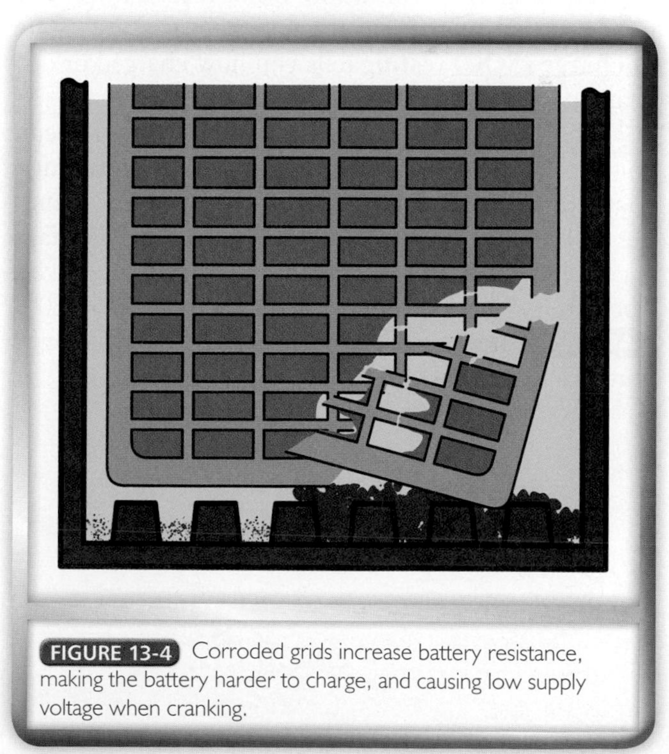

FIGURE 13-4 Corroded grids increase battery resistance, making the battery harder to charge, and causing low supply voltage when cranking.

or binding. Battery terminals should be tight and show no evidence of overheating. Always coat battery terminals with a dielectric sealer to prevent corrosion.

Batteries should be evaluated visually first before proceeding with any other significant tests. Visual checks include:

- Cracks
- Bulges—Indicate batteries have either overheated or been frozen
- Cable connections—Connections should be clean, tight, acid resistant, and show no signs of heat damage
- Battery hold-downs—Loose or missing hold downs cause plate shedding
- Dirty case—Causes current to leak out of batteries
- Leaks
- Electrolyte level—Level should be above the plates
- Electrolyte appearance—Liquid should be clear; a brownish color indicates the plates maybe damaged or the electrolyte contaminated

To inspect, clean, fill, or replace the battery, battery cables, clamps, connectors, and hold-downs, follow the guidelines in SKILL DRILL 13-1.

Testing Battery State of Charge and Specific Gravity

Although the capacitance test is the industry standard to evaluate battery condition, other tests may still be used. One of those tests is the state of charge test. **State of charge (SOC) testing** tells you how charged or discharged a battery is, not how much capacity it has.

A fully charged battery should have an open-circuit voltage of 12.65 volts. If the battery has been recently charged, a light load applied to the battery for a minute will remove a surface charge. Open-circuit voltage is consequently affected by the battery specific gravity. About 1/10-volt change occurs for every 10°F below 80°F. TABLE 13-1 shows state of charge as indicated by specific gravity and voltage reading.

Voltage reading can also identify defective cells. Using a multi-meter, place one meter lead on either terminal of the battery, and dip the other lead into battery electrolyte (if accessible). The meter should record a change of 2.1 volts for each cell when moving across the battery.

The state of charge is best evaluated by measuring the density of electrolyte in each cell using either a bulb-type hydrometer or refractometer. The specific gravity (SG) of electrolyte indicates the state cell charge. Cells should not have wide variations. If the SG reading between the highest and lowest cell is more than 0.050 points, the battery is defective. For example if the highest SG is 1.265 points in one cell and only 1.210 in the lowest, the battery is scrap. FIGURE 13-5A and FIGURE 13-5B show two different tools used to measure battery specific gravity. A refractometer is shown in Figure 13-5B.

TECHNICIAN TIP

When performing a state of charge test, keep these tips in mind:

- When filling a battery that is not fully charged, never fill it to the top of the full line, as charging the battery will raise the electrolyte level.
- Small amounts of electrolyte in the hydrometer may leak out, potentially damage and corrode parts and battery terminals.
- Do not inadvertently remove electrolyte from one cell or add it to another cell when testing; doing so will cause incorrect readings.

Unlike the reading from a refractometer, the hydrometer's reading must be corrected for electrolyte temperature. The density of battery electrolyte changes with temperature and 1.265 is only the density of electrolyte at 80°F (27°C). To correct for temperature effects on specific gravity, add or subtract 4 points to the reading either above or below 80°F (27°C) for every 10°F (6°C) temperature change. (For example add 0.004 for

SKILL DRILL 13-1 Inspecting, Cleaning, Filling, or Replacing the Battery, Battery Cables, Clamps, Connectors, Hold-Downs, and Battery Boxes

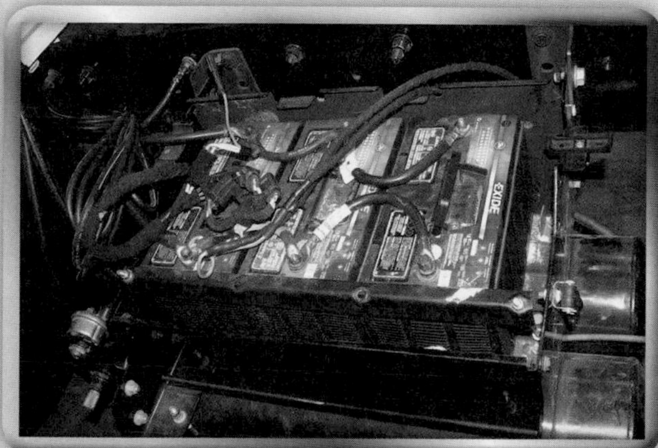

1. Always remove the cable clamp from the negative terminal first. Then remove the positive terminal clamp. While they are disconnected, bend the cables back, or if necessary, tie them out of the way so that they cannot fall back and touch the battery terminals accidentally.
2. Remove the battery hold-downs or other hardware securing the battery. Depending on the type of vehicle, you will need to unbolt, unscrew, or unclip the restraint and move it away from the battery.
3. Keeping it upright, remove the battery from its tray and place it on a clean, level work surface. Visually inspect the battery for damage, cracks, bulges, loose or leaking posts, and so on. If any are found, the battery will need to be replaced.
4. Measure the voltage on the top of the battery with a DVOM. Place the black lead on the negative post and move the red lead across the top of the battery until you find the highest reading. The higher the voltage reading, the larger the potential drain.
5. Check the electrolyte level and its appearance.
6. Carefully clean the case of the battery, hold-downs, and battery tray and box either by (a) washing them or by (b) wiping them down with damp paper towels if the battery and tray are not very dirty. It is best to wear rubber gloves while doing this in case any corrosive electrolyte has leaked from the battery. Safely dispose of the paper towels.
7. Clean the battery posts or screw terminals with a battery terminal tool. On lead posts and terminals, the preferred tool is a scraper style, since it is designed to produce smooth surfaces that are more airtight when clamped together. Do not use the wire-brush style of battery terminal tool, which leaves rougher surfaces that are more likely to corrode.
8. Clean the cable terminals with the same battery terminal tool or wire brush. Examine the battery cables for fraying or corrosion. If the damage looks extensive, the cables and terminals should be replaced.
9. Reinstall the cleaned and serviced battery. Reinstall the hold-downs and make sure the battery is securely held in position. If a new battery needs to be installed, be sure to compare the outside dimensions as well as the type of terminals and their locations prior to installation. These must meet the original manufacturer's specifications.
10. Reconnect the positive battery terminal and tighten it in place. Once the positive terminal is finished, reconnect the negative terminal and tighten it.
11. Coat the terminal connections with anti-corrosive paste or spray to keep oxygen from the terminal connections. Verify that you have a good electrical connection by starting the vehicle.

TABLE 13-1: State of Charge as Indicated by Specific Gravity and Voltage Reading.

Open Circuit Voltage	Specific Gravity	Percentage of Charge
12.65 or greater	1.265 (minimum)	100
12.45	1.225	75%
12.24	1.190	50%
12.06	1.155	25%
11.89	1.120	0%

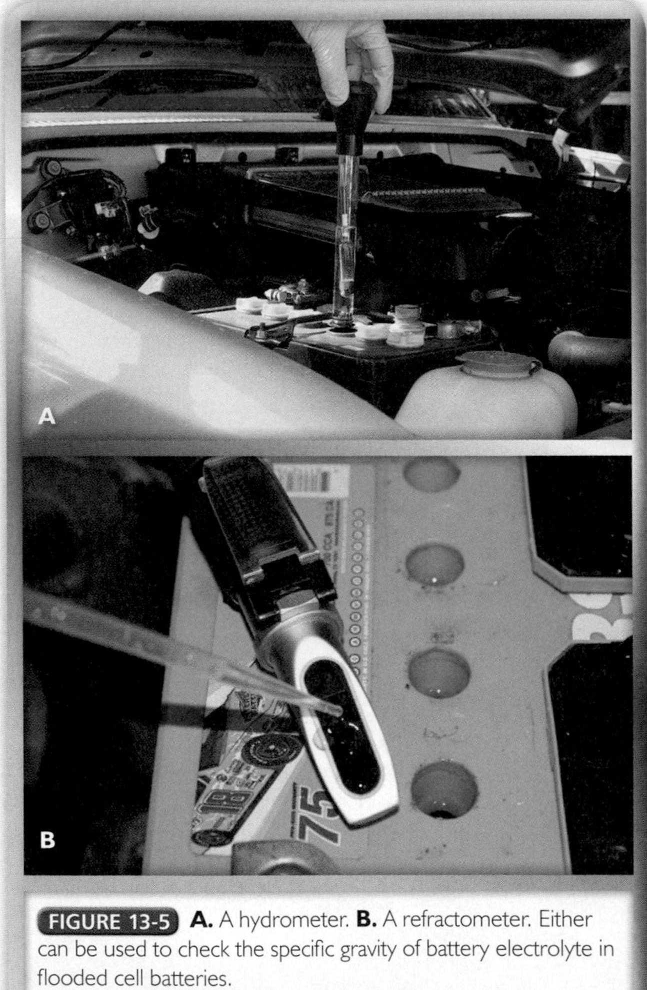

FIGURE 13-5 **A.** A hydrometer. **B.** A refractometer. Either can be used to check the specific gravity of battery electrolyte in flooded cell batteries.

temperatures at 70°F or at 21°C.) Because the hydrometer draws electrolyte into it to raise a float, the electrolyte level must be at least slightly above the top of the plates. If it is not, then distilled water will need to be added and the battery fully charged. To perform a battery state of charge test, follow the guidelines in SKILL DRILL 13-2.

Testing Battery Conductance

Evaluating a battery's condition using hydrometers, refractometers, and load testers provides reasonably accurate results if the instruments are used correctly and the battery is tested under proper conditions. In the field, however, batteries often need charging for hours before they can be tested, and SOC testing is time consuming.

In cold weather, testing on equipment outside presents other problems, too. In the last 15 years, several rapid-test battery testers have emerged that eliminate the need for SOC and discharge-type testing. Referred to collectively as conductance testers, this equipment performs a measurement of the amount of active plate surface area available for chemical reaction. Active plate surface, as measured by conductivity, is a reliable indication of a healthy battery, as it corresponds directly to battery capacity. Also referred to as impedance testing, the AC equivalent to resistance, battery plate conductance declines as the battery fails.

All manufacturers are now requiring the use of a conductance test instead of a high-amperage load test in order for warranty coverage to be considered. A **conductance test** determines the battery's ability to produce current. Many of the testers have integrated printers and, for the battery to be warranted, a printout of the test result has to accompany the returned battery. Advantages of conductance testing are as follows:

- It does not require any battery discharge activity
- It requires only minimal technician involvement, as only two clip-on connectors are attached to the battery terminals during the test
- It is fast—the testing can usually be performed in under two minutes
- Low-frequency AC does not affect battery
- Conductance testing does not prematurely age the battery
- It is safe—no heat or gassing is produced
- Conductance testing can be repeated immediately to verify result
- Batteries can be evaluated in a state of discharge; some testers only require as little as 2 volts of battery voltage to qualify the battery
- The testing method is endorsed by all electrical standards testing organizations including Battery Council International (BCI)
- Printed read-outs can be supplied to the customer or accompany warranty claims FIGURE 13-6

The most common type of conductance tester works by applying an AC voltage of a known frequency and amplitude across the battery. The battery's response to

SKILL DRILL 13-2 Performing a Battery State of Charge Test

1. If the battery is not a sealed unit, it will have individual or combined removable caps on top. Remove them and look inside to check the level of the electrolyte. If the level is below the tops of the plates and their separators inside, add distilled water or water with a low mineral content until it covers them. Be careful not to overfill the cells; they could "boil" over when charging. If water is added, the battery will need to be charged to ensure the newly added water mixes with the electrolyte before measuring the specific gravity.

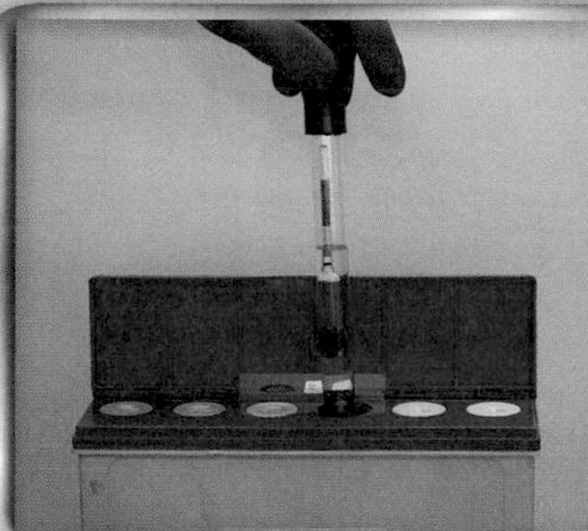

2. Using a hydrometer designed for battery testing, draw some of the electrolyte into the tester and look at the float inside it. A scale indicates the battery's relative state of charge by measuring how high the float sits in relation to the fluid level. A very low overall reading (1.150 or below) indicates a low state of charge. A high overall reading (about 1.280) indicates a high state of charge. The reading from each cell should be the same. If the variation between the higest and lowest cell exceed 0.050, the battery is defective and should be replaced. Be sure to consult temperature correction tables if the battery electrolyte temperature is not at or around 80°F (27°C).

3. Using the refractometer, place one or two drops of electrolyte on the specimen window and lower the cover plate. Make sure the liquid completely covers the specimen window. If not, add another drop of electrolyte:
   - Look into the eyepiece with the refractometer under a bright light.
   - Read the scale for battery acid. The point where the dark area meets the light area is the reading. Compare the readings with the values given in step 2.

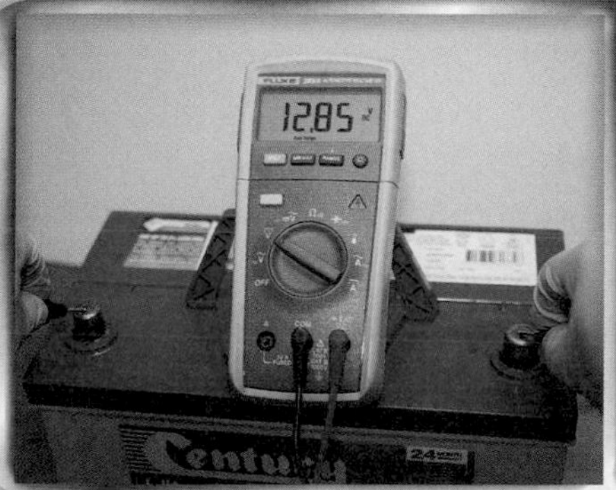

4. For open circuit voltage testing with a DVOM, perform the following actions: (a) With the engine not running, select the "volts DC" position on your DVOM and attach the probes to the battery terminals (red to positive, black to negative). (b) With all vehicle accessories switched off and the battery near 80°F (27°C), the voltage reading should be 12.65 volts if the battery is fully charged. This may be slightly lower at cooler temperatures.

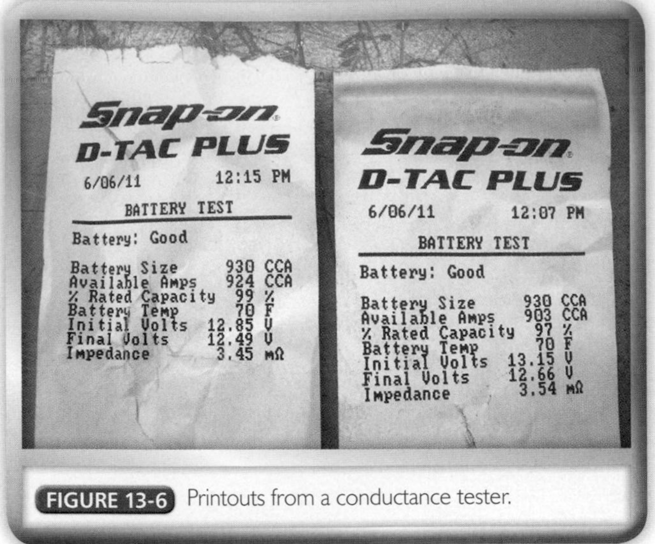

FIGURE 13-6 Printouts from a conductance tester.

the signal is interpreted by a microprocessor inside the test unit. Conductance, or acceptance of the AC voltage, is measured by comparing the shape of the AC waveform exiting the battery to the waveform sent into the battery. The closer the waveforms match, the better the conductivity of the battery.

The most sophisticated testers today analyze, lead acid, Li-ion, and NiMH batteries using a microprocessor containing algorithms that match waveforms from known battery configurations. These analyzers can identify not only the type and condition of a battery, but also the manufacturer and other battery details.

To conductance test a battery, follow the guidelines in **SKILL DRILL 13-3**.

> **TECHNICIAN TIP**
>
> Never use steel bolts, nuts, washers, etc. on battery terminals when using conductance testers. Instead, only use the lead adapters supplied with the conductance tester. The materials and any coatings on other hardware will interfere with the signals sent through the battery and affect the tester's accuracy. Conductance testing is best suited for SLI batteries and may not provide accurate results for deep cycle batteries using thicker plate.

Testing Battery Capacity

Traditionally, the load test was used to evaluate a battery's capacity, but the test has become less popular due to the overwhelming advantages of conductance testing.

The **load test** determines the ability of a battery to deliver cranking amperage and is based on the battery CCA rating. For example, a 1,000 CCA battery can deliver 1,000 amps at –18°C, or 0°F for 30 seconds, while maintaining a voltage of 7.2 volts. During a load test, only half the CCA rating is applied as an electrical load for 15 seconds.

A battery must be at least 75% charged to perform a capacity test, so SOC must be first evaluated before proceeding. A carbon pile is used to simulate the high amperage electrical load on the battery. At the end of 15 seconds, after one-half the CCA rating has been applied, battery voltage must not fall below 9.6 volts. If it does, the battery is scrap. Because temperature affects battery

PROVE KNOW SEE DO

SKILL DRILL 13-3 Conductance Testing a Battery

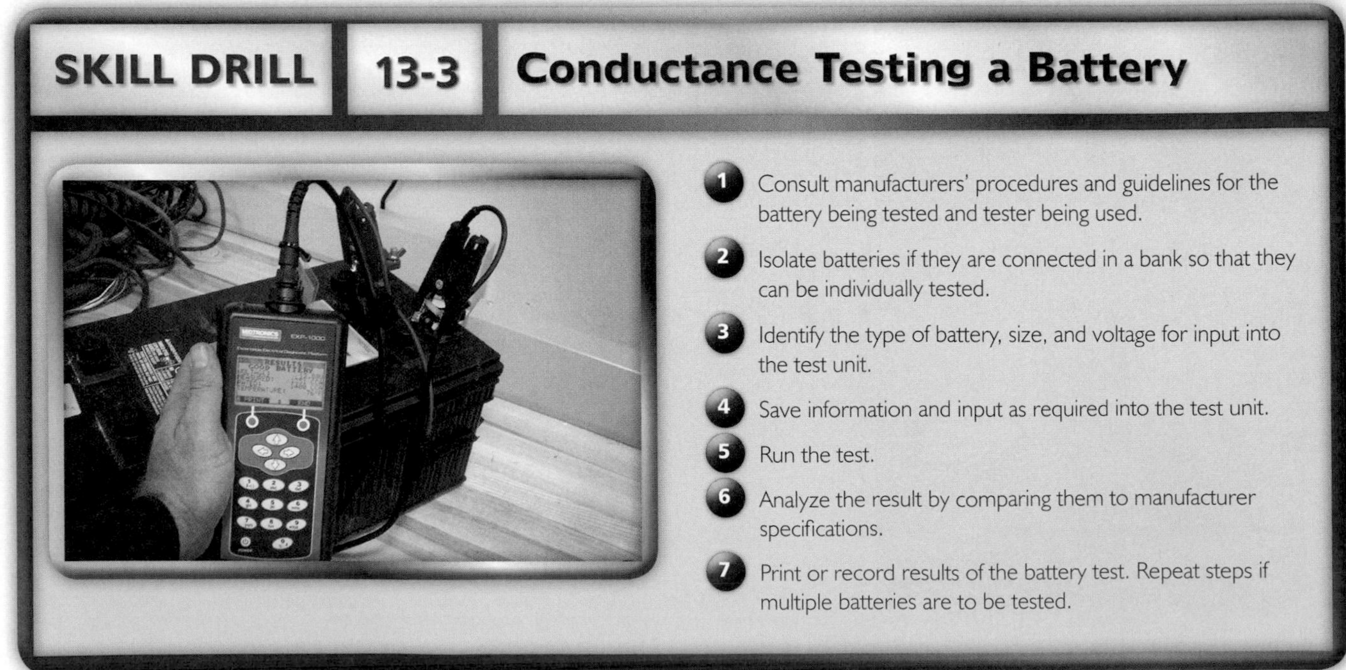

1. Consult manufacturers' procedures and guidelines for the battery being tested and tester being used.
2. Isolate batteries if they are connected in a bank so that they can be individually tested.
3. Identify the type of battery, size, and voltage for input into the test unit.
4. Save information and input as required into the test unit.
5. Run the test.
6. Analyze the result by comparing them to manufacturer specifications.
7. Print or record results of the battery test. Repeat steps if multiple batteries are to be tested.

voltage, 0.1 volts is subtracted from the failure threshold voltage level of 9.6 volts for every 10°F below 70°F.

Another way to think of a load test is that you are testing the battery's ability to produce the high starting current, while maintaining enough voltage to operate the engine's electronic control systems.

If the battery fails the load test after its has had its state of charge properly qualified, the battery should be discarded. No attempt should be made to recharge and re-load test after it has failed the first time. To load test a battery, follow the guidelines in SKILL DRILL 13-4.

Charging Batteries

Batteries go dead for a variety of reasons. Parasitic drains, self-discharge, or battery leakage are common reasons a battery may quickly lose its charge. A number of different chargers are available to recharge dead batteries, each with its own advantages and disadvantages.

Battery Charger Types

Differentiating between the types of battery chargers is useful for determining the best method for recharging a battery, given its condition and other operating variables. The most common types of chargers include constant-voltage chargers, constant-current chargers, taper-current chargers, pulsed chargers, and intelligent chargers.

- **Constant-voltage chargers**, like the one shown in FIGURE 13-7, are direct current (DC) power supplies that use a step-down transformer and a rectifier to convert AC voltage to DC voltage for charging. As the name suggest, output voltage is constant between 13 and 14 volts. A manual switch may allow the voltage setting to increase or decrease to change the charge rate. These designs are found in inexpensive chargers and must be used with care because they can cause overcharging of batteries. **Trickle chargers**, which charge a battery at a low amperage rate, are made following this design. Slow charging or trickle charging a battery is less stressful on a battery than fast charging because a low amperage charge does not excessively heat and gas a battery.
- **Constant-current chargers** automatically vary the voltage applied to the battery to maintain a constant amperage flow into the battery. These vary the voltage to maintain the constant current into the battery as its resistance changes. Also called

SKILL DRILL 13-4 Load Testing a Battery

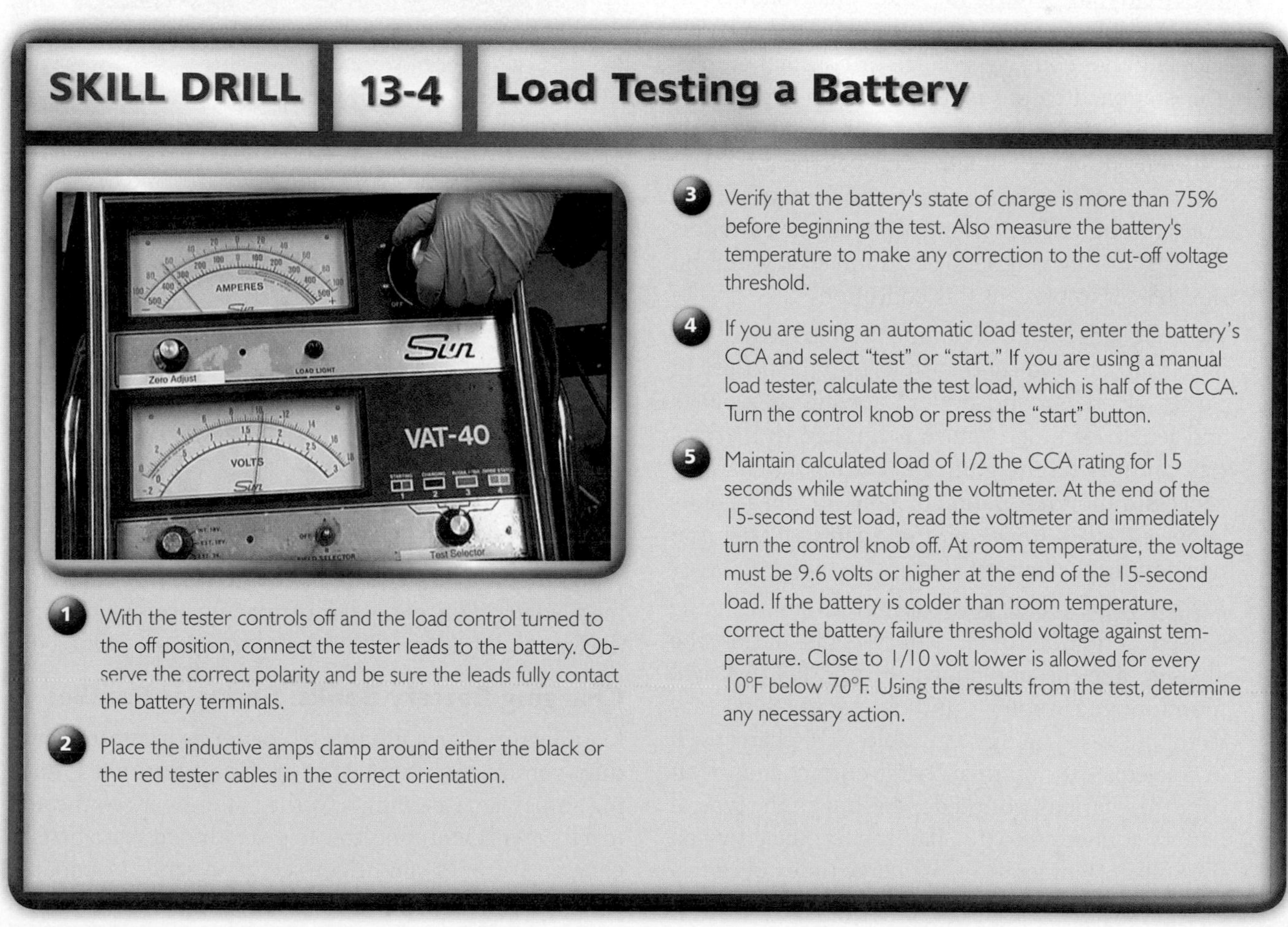

1. With the tester controls off and the load control turned to the off position, connect the tester leads to the battery. Observe the correct polarity and be sure the leads fully contact the battery terminals.
2. Place the inductive amps clamp around either the black or the red tester cables in the correct orientation.
3. Verify that the battery's state of charge is more than 75% before beginning the test. Also measure the battery's temperature to make any correction to the cut-off voltage threshold.
4. If you are using an automatic load tester, enter the battery's CCA and select "test" or "start." If you are using a manual load tester, calculate the test load, which is half of the CCA. Turn the control knob or press the "start" button.
5. Maintain calculated load of 1/2 the CCA rating for 15 seconds while watching the voltmeter. At the end of the 15-second test load, read the voltmeter and immediately turn the control knob off. At room temperature, the voltage must be 9.6 volts or higher at the end of the 15-second load. If the battery is colder than room temperature, correct the battery failure threshold voltage against temperature. Close to 1/10 volt lower is allowed for every 10°F below 70°F. Using the results from the test, determine any necessary action.

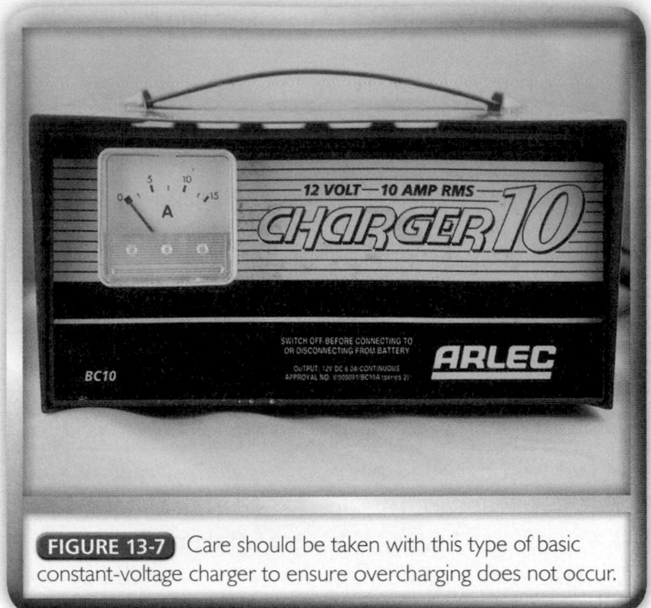

FIGURE 13-7 Care should be taken with this type of basic constant-voltage charger to ensure overcharging does not occur.

series chargers, several batteries can be connected together in series and charged together. These are premium, high-end chargers not commonly found in service facilities.

- **Taper-current chargers**, like that shown in FIGURE 13-8, are the most common found in repair shops. Either constant voltage or constant amperage is applied to the battery through a manually adjusted current selection switch. Charger current only diminishes as the cell voltage increases. These chargers can cause serious damage to batteries through overcharging if the charge current is adjusted too high. Timers can automatically shut-off the charger to prevent this condition.
- **Pulsed chargers** are recommended to recover sulfated batteries and send current into the battery in pulses of one-second cycles. Varying the voltage and length of time a pulse is applied to the battery controls the charging rate. During the charging process, a short rest period of 20 to 30 milliseconds between pulses improves the quality of chemical reactions in the battery.
- An **intelligent charger's** output varies with the sensed condition of a battery. This means the charger, like the one shown in FIGURE 13-9, will monitor battery voltage and temperature and vary its output based on these variables. The charger will also calculate the optimal charge current and vary it over the charging period depending on the type of battery connected to it. Charging terminates when the voltage, temperature, or charge time indicates a full charge. VRLA batteries are best suited to these types of chargers. These chargers can be left connected indefinitely without overcharging since they can maintain a float charge. This means the charging voltage floats at zero or a very minimal charge voltage until it senses that the battery voltage has fallen and then resumes charging.

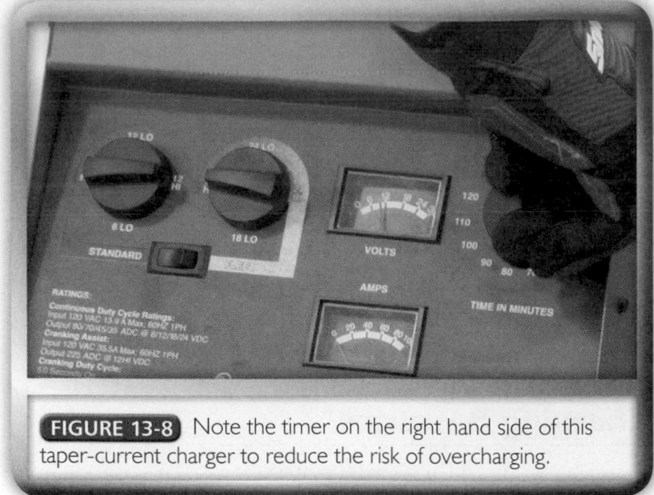

FIGURE 13-8 Note the timer on the right hand side of this taper-current charger to reduce the risk of overcharging.

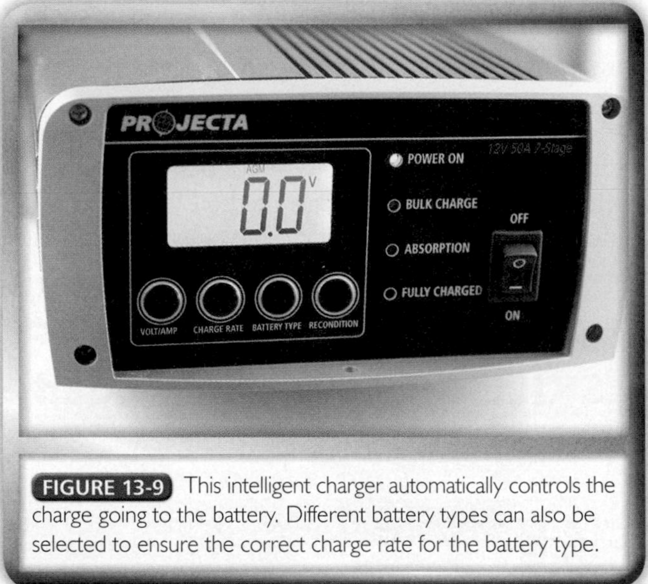

FIGURE 13-9 This intelligent charger automatically controls the charge going to the battery. Different battery types can also be selected to ensure the correct charge rate for the battery type.

Removing the negative battery terminal while charging a battery reduces the risk of burning up any electronic devices on the vehicle if the ignition key is switched on.

Charging Battery Banks: Series or Parallel

Manufacturers install multiple batteries in most heavy-duty commercial vehicles to provide additional cranking amperage. Knowing how the batteries are connected together will determine how to properly connect a battery charger. Batteries can be connected in series or parallel. Batteries connected in series are connected in line with each other, with the positive of one connected to the negative of the other. Batteries connected in parallel are connected side by side, with positive connected to positive and negative to negative.

To charge a 24-volt set of batteries, a 24-volt charger is needed to charge all the batteries at the same time. If you only have a 12-volt charger, you will have two options: either charge one battery at a time, or reconnect the batteries so they are connected in parallel. To charge batteries, follow the guidelines in SKILL DRILL 13-5.

Jump-Starting Vehicles

Jump-starting a vehicle is the process of using one vehicle with a charged battery to provide electrical energy to start another vehicle that has a discharged battery. Because starting a vehicle requires a high amount of electrical energy, jump-starting a vehicle can put stresses on both vehicles.

To jump-start commercial vehicles, follow the guidelines in SKILL DRILL 13-6.

SKILL DRILL 13-5 Charging Commercial Batteries

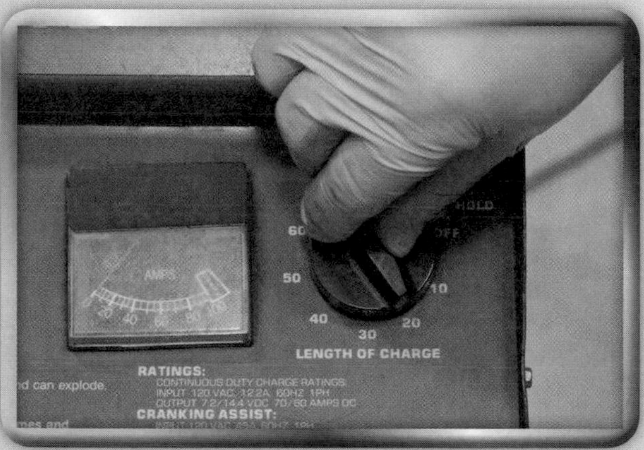

1. Determine the voltage of the system that needs charging. If you are charging a 12-volt battery, use the 12-volt setting on the charger. If you are charging a 24-volt battery, or two 12-volt batteries connected in series, use the 24-volt setting on the charger, if it has one.
2. Identify the positive and negative terminals. Never simply use the color of the cables to determine the positive or negative terminals; use the + and – or the Pos and Neg marks.
3. Visually inspect the battery to ensure there are no cracks, holes, or damage to the casing.
4. Verify that the charger is unplugged from the wall and turned off. Connect the red lead from the charger to the positive battery terminal. Connect the black lead from the charger to the negative battery terminal.
5. Check the settings on the charger and verify that they are correct for what you are charging.
6. Turn the charger on and select the automatic setting, if equipped. Select the rate of charge. A slow charger usually charges at a rate of less than 5 amperes. A fast charger charges at a much higher ampere rate depending on the original battery state of charge; a fast charge should be carried out only under constant supervision.
7. Verify that the voltage and amperage the charger is putting out is proper.
8. Once the battery is charged, turn the charger off. Disconnect the black lead from the negative battery terminal and then the red lead from the positive battery terminal.
9. Allow the battery to stand for at least five minutes before testing the battery. Using a load tester or hydrometer, test the charged state of the battery.

Safety

When connecting jumper cables, a spark will almost always occur on the last connection you make. That is why it is critical that you make the last connection on the chassis away from the battery and any other flammables. A spark also occurs when you disconnect the first jumper cable connection, so that also needs to be the connection somewhere on the chassis.

- Keep your face and body as far back as you can while connecting jumper leads.
- Do not connect the negative cable to the discharged battery because the spark may blow up the battery.
- Use only specially designed heavy-duty jumper cables to start a vehicle with a dead battery. Do not try to connect the batteries with any other type of cable.
- Always make sure you wear the appropriate personal protective equipment (PPE) before starting the job. Remember, batteries contain sulfuric acid, and it is very easy to injure yourself.
- Always follow any manufacturer's personal safety instructions to prevent damage to the vehicle you are servicing.

SKILL DRILL 13-6 Jump-Starting Commercial Vehicles

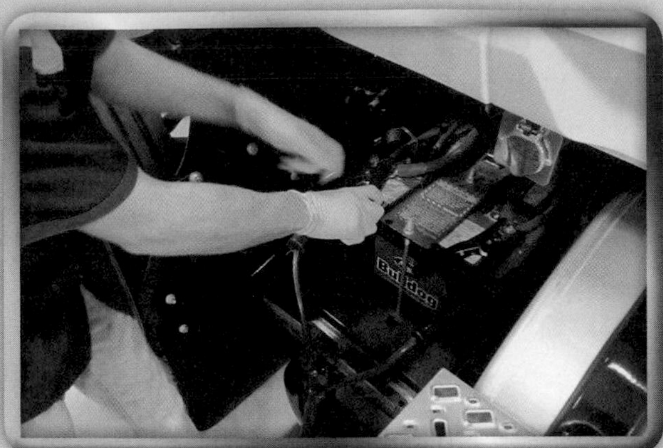

1. Position the charged battery close enough to the discharged battery that it is within comfortable range of your jumper cables. If the charged battery is in another vehicle, make sure the two vehicles are not touching.

2. Always connect the leads in this order:
   - First, connect the red jumper lead to the positive terminal of the discharged battery in the vehicle you are trying to start. The positive terminal is the one with the plus sign.
   - Next, connect the other end of this lead to the positive terminal of the charged battery.
   - Then connect the black jumper lead to the negative terminal of the charged battery. The negative terminal is the one with the minus sign.
   - Connect the other end of the negative lead to a good ground on the chassis of the vehicle with the discharged battery, and as far away as possible from the battery.
   - DO NOT connect the lead to the negative terminal of the discharged battery itself; doing so may cause a dangerous spark.

3. Try to start the vehicle with the discharged battery. If the booster battery does not have enough charge or the jumper cables are too small in diameter to do this, start the engine in the booster vehicle and allow it to partially charge the discharged battery for several minutes. Try starting the first vehicle again with the booster vehicle's engine running.

4. Disconnect the leads in the reverse order of connecting them. Remove the negative lead from the chassis ground away from the battery. Then disconnect the negative lead from the booster battery. Next remove the positive lead from the booster battery, and lastly, disconnect the other positive end from the battery in the vehicle you have just started. If the charging system is working correctly and the battery is in good condition, the battery will be recharging while the engine is running. Note, a deeply discharged set of batteries can cause the alternator to charge at an excessively high rate for too long and damage the alternator.

Measuring Parasitic Draw

All modern vehicles have a small amount of current draw when the ignition is turned off. This charge is used to run some of the vehicle systems, such as various modules making up the onboard vehicle network. The vehicle computer systems also require a small amount of power to maintain the computer memory while the vehicle is off. The parasitic current draw should be a relatively small amount of current, since excessive draw will discharge the battery over a short amount of time.

Parasitic current draw does not necessarily immediately drop to its lowest level the instant the ignition is turned off. This usually occurs over a period of time as various systems go into hibernation or sleep mode, which can take up to a few hours. Consult the manufacturer's service information to determine the maximum allowable parasitic current draw and the time period, after the ignition is turned off, that it takes the modules to go to sleep.

Parasitic current draw can be measured in several ways, the most common being the process of using an ammeter capable of measuring milliamps and inserting it in series between the battery post and the battery terminal. The ammeter is usually put in series with the negative battery lead. If the vehicle is equipped with systems or modules that will require electronic memory to be maintained, follow the procedure for identifying modules that lose their initialization during battery removal and maintain or restore electronic memory functions. Note that the timers may reset during the process of disconnecting the battery terminal and connecting the ammeter in series, so you may have to wait for the timers to go back to sleep. If excessive parasitic draw is measured, disconnect fuses or systems one at a time while monitoring parasitic current draw to determine the systems causing excessive draw.

Disconnecting the battery can be avoided if a sensitive low-current (that is, milliamps) clamp is available. The low-amp **current clamp** measures the magnetic field generated by a very small current flow through a wire or cable. Placing the low-amp current clamp around the negative battery cable will allow you to measure the parasitic draw. If excessive parasitic draw is measured, disconnect fuses or systems one at a time while monitoring parasitic current draw to determine the systems causing the excessive draw. To measure parasitic draw with a parasitic load test, follow the guidelines in SKILL DRILL 13-7.

Identify and Test Low-Voltage Disconnect (LVD) Systems

Low-Voltage Disconnect (LVD) systems disconnect a battery load when the voltage of the battery falls below a preset threshold. By doing this, they protect the battery from being excessively discharged and the vehicle from starting. The voltage threshold is normally set between 12.2 and 12.4 volts. Once the battery voltage rises above the set threshold, as it does when the vehicle starts and the alternator commences charging, the load is reconnected automatically. In many cases LVDs will also incorporate an audible alarm and visual warning light to alert the operator before disconnection occurs.

LVDs are connected in series with the load. They are tested by varying the amount of input voltage around the threshold settings and checking the switching of the output or load to determine if the device switches on and off at the correct voltages. Testing can be conducted on the vehicle or off the vehicle on a test bench. The LVD is tested on the vehicle by monitoring the input and output, or load voltage, with a DVOM while placing a load across the battery to reduce battery voltage. At the

SKILL DRILL 13-7 Measuring Parasitic Draw on a Battery

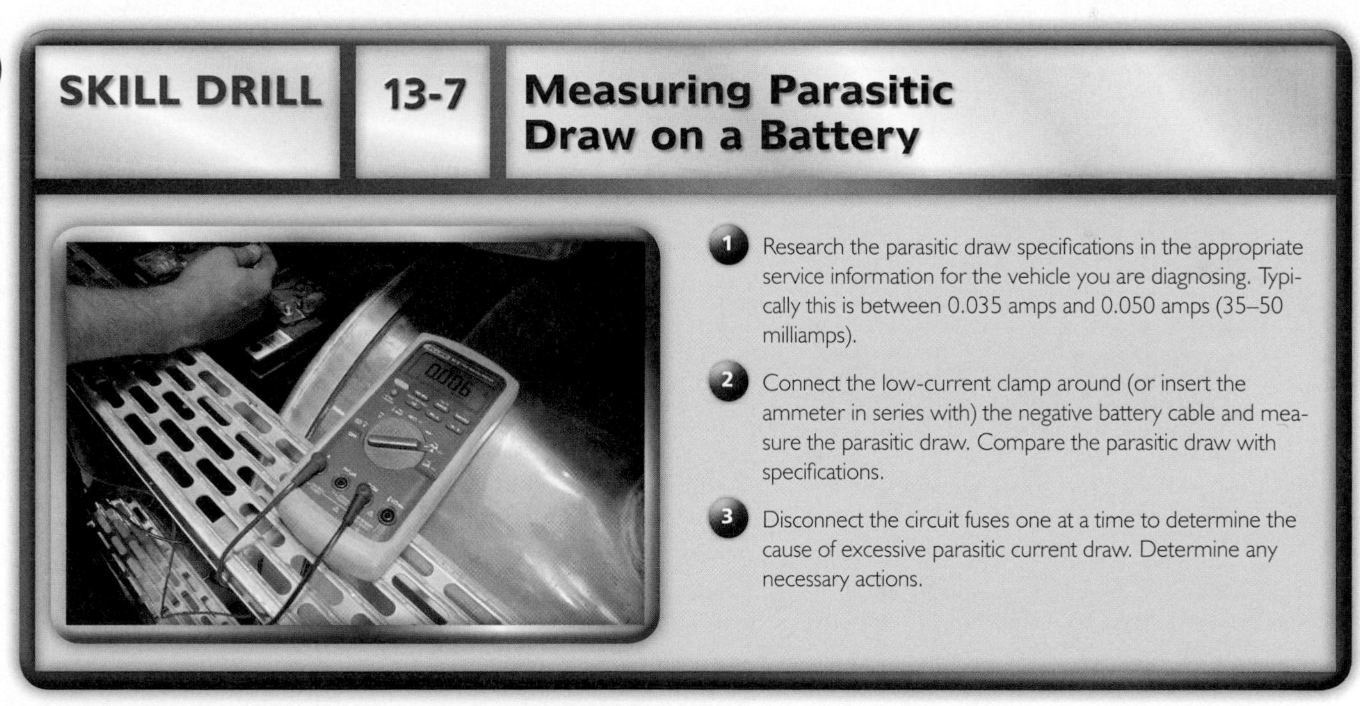

1. Research the parasitic draw specifications in the appropriate service information for the vehicle you are diagnosing. Typically this is between 0.035 amps and 0.050 amps (35–50 milliamps).
2. Connect the low-current clamp around (or insert the ammeter in series with) the negative battery cable and measure the parasitic draw. Compare the parasitic draw with specifications.
3. Disconnect the circuit fuses one at a time to determine the cause of excessive parasitic current draw. Determine any necessary actions.

threshold point, the device should turn the power off to the output or load. If two DVOMs are not available, a test lamp may be used to indicate when the output or load voltage drops away as the device switches off, although you should also check the output voltage at some point to ensure the load is receiving full battery voltage when the LVD has the load turned on. Compare the threshold voltages for turn on and off with the manufacturer's specifications. The units are usually sealed and are not serviceable, although some units may provide a means for adjusting threshold voltages.

The LVD can also be tested off vehicle using a variable voltage power supply. When using a variable voltage power supply to test an LVD, you duplicate the connections made on the vehicle with the power supply taking the place of the battery. You must ensure that the power supply is capable of supplying enough current to operate the LVD and any load you connect to it on the bench. Once the unit is connected to the power supply and load, as per manufacturer requirements, you can slowly increase and decrease the power supply voltage to test the threshold voltages at which the LVD switches on and off the output or load. To identify and test a low voltage disconnect system, follow the guidelines in SKILL DRILL 13-8.

Battery Recycling

Disposal is a critical issue at the end of every battery's service life. Batteries contain many environmentally damaging chemicals and neurotoxic lead. If they find their way into a landfill, the lead can contaminate the soil and groundwater. For this reason, recycling of batteries is mandatory. Many municipalities require battery recycling and levy a "core charge" on every new lead-acid battery sold. The core charge is refunded if an old battery is brought in and exchanged for the new one. This process helps prevent batteries from being discarded in landfills. Check local laws and regulations to ensure that batteries are disposed of correctly.

SKILL DRILL 13-8 Identifying and Testing a Low-Voltage Disconnect (LVD)

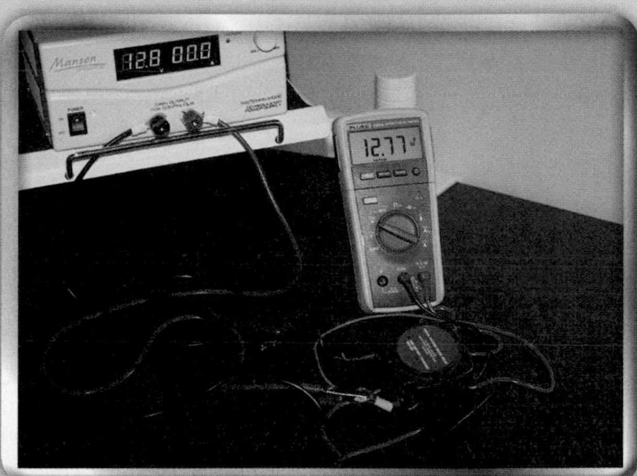

1. Research the LVD specifications such as the wiring schematic, device operation, and threshold voltages in the appropriate manufacturer's information.

2. Check the unit on the vehicle for appropriate power and grounds as per the manufacturer's specifications. If no battery voltage is present on the input side of the LVD, check fuses or circuit breakers for correct operation. Rectify any power or ground issues before proceeding to check LVD threshold voltages.

3. If you are testing the unit on a test bench, remove the unit from the vehicle and connect both power and grounds to the unit as per manufacturer's specifications.

4. Connect a DVOM to the input or battery side connection of the LVD and a second DVOM or test lamp to the output or load side connection. Note the voltage readings on both the input and output of the LVD.

5. Vary the battery voltage by connecting a variable load to the vehicle battery if testing in the vehicle or adjust the voltage if using a variable voltage power supply for bench testing.

6. Note the DVOM readings of the threshold voltages from the input of the LVD as the unit turns the load or output on and off. Compare the voltage readings with manufacturer's specifications. If the unit does not meet specifications, adjust the threshold voltage if adjustment is possible. If the unit is not adjustable or cannot be adjusted to manufacturer's specifications, then the unit will need to be replaced.

7. Connect an appropriate load to the output or load side of the LVD and recheck the threshold voltages to ensure the unit is capable of supplying the current with minimal voltage drop between the input and output or load.

8. Check the operation of any warning lights or bulbs fitted to the unit, ensuring they turn and off as the output or load of the LVD is turned on and off. Report any recommendations and return the unit to normal operation.

Wrap-up

Ready for Review

- Testing the batteries should be the starting point when diagnosing complaints such as: hard starting, slow cranking, or no start; when lights dim when an engine idles or other electrical problems occur; and whenever an alternator is replaced.
- Keeping the battery and terminals clean is one of the best maintenance practices for batteries.
- Safety should be the first priority when working around and servicing batteries. The electrolyte inside lead-acid batteries is corrosive and can cause injury to skin and eyes and can cause damage to clothing and the vehicle's parts.
- Batteries also produce an explosive gas mixture of hydrogen and oxygen during charging and discharging of the battery.
- Batteries fail suddenly due to the loss of a cell or open circuits within the internal connections. Batteries also fail gradually through loss of capacity caused by age, sulfation, extremes in operating temperature, vibration, low electrolyte levels, and grid corrosion.
- Inspecting, cleaning, and filling (if not maintenance free) are common tasks that should be performed every six months to one year on top-post batteries and one to two years on side-post batteries.
- The reverse current flow can damage some or all of the electronic control units (ECUs) throughout the vehicle, so it is critical to connect the battery correctly to prevent sending the current in the reverse direction through the electrical system.
- The capacitance test is the preferred test of battery condition.
- State of charge testing indicates how charged or discharged a battery is. Low-maintenance or no-maintenance type batteries may not provide access to the electrolyte in the cells for state of charge testing.
- Technicians use hydrometers and refractometers to measure the specific gravity of the electrolyte in the battery during a state of charge test.
- Load testing has long been used to test a battery's capacity and internal condition, but is no longer used. Manufacturers now insist on conductance testing for batteries, particularly any battery returned under warranty.
- There are a number of different battery charger types available for charging batteries: constant-voltage, constant-current, taper-current, pulsed charger, and intelligent chargers.
- Even with the ignition turned off, all modern vehicles have a small amount of current draw used to run some of the vehicle systems, such as the on-board network modules.
- The parasitic current draw should be a relatively small amount of current, since excessive draw will discharge the battery over a short amount of time.
- Correct disposal of batteries by recycling them is good for the environment and the precious metals can be reclaimed for reuse.

Vocabulary Builder

conductance test A type of battery test that determines the battery's ability to conduct current.

constant-current charger A battery charger that automatically varies the voltage applied to the battery to maintain a constant amperage flow into the battery.

constant-voltage charger A direct current (DC) power that is a step-down transformer with a rectifier to provide the DC voltage to charge.

current clamp A device that claps around a conductor to measure current flow. It is often used in conjunction with a digital volt-ohm meter (DVOM).

intelligent charger A battery charger that varies its output according to the sensed condition of the battery it is charging.

load test A battery test that subjects the battery to a high rate of discharge, and the voltage is then measured after a set time to see how well the battery creates that current flow.

pulse charger A battery charger that sends current into the battery in pulses of one-second cycles; used to recover sulfated batteries.

shedding A process that reduces the plate surface area and therefore reduces capacity. Shedding may also produce short circuits between the bottom of positive and negative plates.

state of charge test A test that indicates how charged or discharged a battery is, not how much capacity it has.

taper-current charger A battery charger that applies either constant voltage or constant amperage to the battery through a manually adjusted current selection switch.

trickle charger A battery charger that charges at a low amperage rate.

Review Questions

1. Which of the following is NOT correct concerning battery service precautions?
   - **a.** Safety should be the first priority when working around and servicing batteries.
   - **b.** Electrolyte inside lead–acid batteries is corrosive.
   - **c.** An explosive gas mixture consisting of hydrogen and oxygen is produced during charging and discharging of the battery.
   - **d.** Always remove the positive terminal first when disconnecting battery cables.
2. Which of the following statements about sulfation is correct?
   - **a.** Sulfation occurs when batteries are subjected to prolonged undercharge conditions.
   - **b.** Sulfation also increases the internal resistance of a battery.
   - **c.** During periods of prolonged undercharge, the sulfate converts to hard crystals and deposits on the negative plates.
   - **d.** All of the choices are correct.
3. Which of the following statements about battery vibration and shedding is correct?
   - **a.** Excessive vibration can cause open circuits in the internal battery connections and "shed," or shake loose, plate material, which settles to the bottom of the battery case.
   - **b.** Shedding reduces the plate surface area and therefore reduces capacity.
   - **c.** Shedding may also produce short circuits between the bottom of positive and negative plates.
   - **d.** All of the choices are correct.
4. Grid corrosion normally takes place on the ______ grid.
   - **a.** primary
   - **b.** secondary
   - **c.** positive
   - **d.** negative
5. Which of the following statements about battery inspection is correct?
   - **a.** Bulges indicate batteries have either overheated or been frozen.
   - **b.** Cable connections should be clean, tight, acid resistant, and show no signs of heat damage.
   - **c.** Electrolyte should be clear; a brownish color indicates the plates maybe damaged.
   - **d.** All of the choices are correct.
6. Which of the following statements about battery testing is NOT correct?
   - **a.** Although the capacitance test is the preferred test of battery condition, other tests may still be used.
   - **b.** The state of charge is best evaluated by measuring the density of electrolyte in each cell using either a bulb-type hydrometer or refractometer.
   - **c.** During a hydrometer test, if the specific gravity reading between the highest and lowest cell is more than 0.150 points, a battery is defective.
   - **d.** Unlike the reading from a temperature-compensated refractometer, the hydrometer's reading must be corrected for electrolyte temperature.
7. A(n) ______ charger is not a type of battery charger.
   - **a.** intelligent
   - **b.** pulsed
   - **c.** taper-current
   - **d.** modulated
8. Which of the following statements about charging battery banks is correct?
   - **a.** Batteries can be connected in series or parallel.
   - **b.** Batteries connected in series are connected in line with each other, with the positive of one connected to the negative of the other.
   - **c.** Batteries connected in parallel are connected side by side, with positive connected to positive.
   - **d.** All of the choices are correct.
9. Low-Voltage Disconnect (LVD) systems:
   - **a.** disconnect a battery load when the voltage of the battery falls below a preset threshold.
   - **b.** protect the battery from being excessively discharged.
   - **c.** Both A and B
   - **d.** Neither A nor B
10. Which of the following statements about battery recycling is correct?
    - **a.** Batteries contain many environmentally damaging chemicals and metals.
    - **b.** Disposing of batteries in a landfill can contaminate the soil and waterways.
    - **c.** Many municipalities require battery recycling and levy a "core charge" on every new automotive battery sold.
    - **d.** All of the choices are correct.

ASE-Type Questions

1. Technician A says that batteries should be the starting point when diagnosing complaints such as hard starting, slow cranking, or no start. Technician B says that dirt on top of the battery does not cause premature self-discharge of the battery. Who is correct?
   a. Technician A
   b. Technician B
   c. Both Technician A and Technician B
   d. Neither Technician A nor Technician B
2. Technician A says you should never create a low-resistance connection or short across the battery terminals. Technician B says to always wear protective clothing such as rubber gloves and goggles or full-face shields when handling batteries. Who is correct?
   a. Technician A
   b. Technician B
   c. Both Technician A and Technician B
   d. Neither Technician A nor Technician B
3. Technician A says that a low electrolyte level is a common reason for sulfation. Technician B says that high ambient temperature is a common reason for sulfation. Who is correct?
   a. Technician A
   b. Technician B
   c. Both Technician A and Technician B
   d. Neither Technician A nor Technician B
4. Technician A says that batteries may slowly fail over time through due to the loss of a cell or open circuits within the internal connections. Technician B says that batteries may slowly fail over time through the gradual loss of capacity caused by plate deterioration. Who is correct?
   a. Technician A
   b. Technician B
   c. Both Technician A and Technician B
   d. Neither Technician A nor Technician B
5. Technician A says that, if electrolyte is lost due to spillage, then the battery should be topped up with electrolyte. Technician B says that, if electrolyte level is lost through evaporation, then tap water should be added. Who is correct?
   a. Technician A
   b. Technician B
   c. Both Technician A and Technician B
   d. Neither Technician A nor Technician B
6. Technician A says to always coat battery terminals with chassis grease to prevent corrosion. Technician B says that all slide mechanisms on battery trays should work properly. Who is correct?
   a. Technician A
   b. Technician B
   c. Both Technician A and Technician B
   d. Neither Technician A nor Technician B
7. Technician A says that a fully charged battery should have an open-circuit voltage of 12.25 volts. Technician B says that, if the battery has been recently charged, a light load applied to the battery for a few minutes will remove a surface charge.
   a. Technician A
   b. Technician B
   c. Both Technician A and Technician B
   d. Neither Technician A nor Technician B
8. Technician A says that a conductance test determines the battery's ability to conduct current. Technician B says that batteries must be fully charged to test battery conductance. Who is correct?
   a. Technician A
   b. Technician B
   c. Both Technician A and Technician B
   d. Neither Technician A nor Technician B
9. Technician A says that the load test determines the ability of a battery to deliver cranking amperage and is based on the battery CCA rating. Technician B says that a battery must be at least 95% charged to perform a capacity test, so SOC must be first evaluated before proceeding. Who is correct?
   a. Technician A
   b. Technician B
   c. Both Technician A and Technician B
   d. Neither Technician A nor Technician B
10. Technician A says that all modern vehicles have a small amount of current draw when the ignition is turned off. Technician B says that this charge is used to run some of the vehicle systems, such as various modules making up the onboard vehicle network. Who is correct?
    a. Technician A
    b. Technician B
    c. Both Technician A and Technician B
    d. Neither Technician A nor Technician B

CHAPTER 14

NATEF Tasks

Electrical/Electronic Systems

Starting Systems

	Page
■ Perform starter circuit cranking voltage and voltage drop tests; determine needed action.	419
■ Inspect and test components (key switch, push button, and/or magnetic switch) and wires and harnesses in the starter control circuit; replace as needed.	420
■ Inspect and test starter relays and solenoids/switches; replace as needed.	421
■ Remove and replace starter; inspect flywheel ring gear or flex plate.	420–422

Heavy-Duty Starting Systems and Circuits

Knowledge Objectives

After reading this chapter, you will be able to:

1. Identify and describe the various classification and construction features of heavy-duty starting motors and circuits. (pp 394–398)
2. Explain operating principles of DC motors. (pp 398–401)
3. Identify and describe the major components of a starting system. (pp 403–408)
4. Identify and explain the purpose and function of starting system control components. (pp 408–414)
5. Identify and describe the procedures for performing an on-vehicle starting system test. (p 415)
6. Identify and describe test procedures for starting system components. (pp 415–420)
7. Identify and explain the causes of starter system failures. (p 416)
8. List and explain maintenance procedures for starting systems and circuits. (pp 420–423)

Skills Objectives

After reading this chapter, you will be able to:

1. Measure starter draw. (p 418) SKILL DRILL 14-1
2. Measure the voltage drop in a starter circuit. (p 419) SKILL DRILL 14-2
3. Inspect and test the starter control circuit. (p 420) SKILL DRILL 14-3
4. Inspect and test relays and solenoids. (p 421) SKILL DRILL 14-4
5. Remove and replace a starter motor and inspect the ring gear or flex plate. (422) SKILL DRILL 14-5
6. Overhaul a starter motor. (p 423) SKILL DRILL 14-6

Introduction

Dozens of electric motors are found in heavy vehicles operating a variety of devices from electric seats, fuel and coolant pumps, fan blower motors, and even instrument gauges. The largest of all these electric motors is the starter motor, like the one shown in **FIGURE 14-1**. The starting system provides a method of rotating (cranking) the heavy vehicles, internal combustion engine (ICE) to begin the combustion cycle. The starter is designed to work for short periods of time and must crank the engine at sufficient speed for it to start. Modern starting systems are very effective provided that they are well-maintained.

Understanding and maintaining starting systems is important since diagnosing "no-start" conditions are costly in terms of vehicle downtime and component costs if they are "over-repaired" or haphazardly investigated. In fact, various manufacturers have noted that between 55% and 80% of all starters returned for warranty were not defective. Vehicle and passenger safety can be jeopardized if the starting system is not properly repaired and maintained. Interlocked circuits, which prevent the engine from starting under various operating conditions, and the high current supplied by multiple starting batteries are just a few of the safety concerns with this system.

FIGURE 14-1 Typical starter motor cross section.

Fundamentals of Starting Systems and Circuits

The starting/cranking system consists of the battery, high- and low-amperage cables, a solenoid, a starter motor assembly ring gear, and the ignition switch. On ECM-controlled starting systems, the ECM enables the operation of a relay to energize the starter circuit. Data supplied by other on-board network modules, along with control algorithms in the module, determine when and for how long the starter will crank. A control circuit determines when and if the cranking circuit will function.

During the cranking process, two actions occur. The pinion of the starter motor engages with the flywheel ring

You Are the Technician

The cost of a no-start condition in the fleet of diesel-powered equipment you maintain is extraordinarily high. Equipment productivity, labor hours, and driver and operator time are all lost. In addition, customer aggravation increases, as does the expense of resolving no-start conditions. At the specific direction from management to end or dramatically reduce the number of no-start complaints, you begin to analyze some of the common root cause of the starting system failures. Reviewing service records for the repaired equipment, you discover that the starting motors are frequently burned-out and cable terminals are loose and often burned as well. You also notice that there doesn't seem to be a specific preventative maintenance schedule in place to evaluate the condition of the starting system. It is only when the equipment does not start that the problems are identified, but that occurs too late to prevent disruption of operations. As you consider what steps to take to prevent the no-start complaints, answer the following questions.

1. Explain how the conditions that cause low-voltage burn-out actually damage starting motors and starting-motor connections.
2. What maintenance practices would you recommend to prevent low-voltage burn-out of starting motors and connections?
3. What trend would you observe regarding the voltage and amperage measurements made during a starter draw test if a starter were beginning to fail due to burnt brushes, armature, and field windings?

gear, and the starter motor then rotates to turn over, or crank, the engine. The starter motor is an electric motor mounted on the engine block or transmission. It is typically powered by a 12- or 24-volt battery and is designed to have high rotational torque at low speeds. The starter cables are the heaviest conductors in the vehicle because they carry the high current needed by the starter motor. The starter motor causes the engine flywheel and crankshaft to rotate from a resting position and keeps them turning until the engine fires and runs on its own.

High-compression-ratio diesel engines with large displacements require high amounts of electrical current, so multiple batteries are connected together to supply more amperage or voltage. To supply more cranking amperage in a 12-volt system, batteries are connected in parallel. Adding more batteries increases the amount of amperage available for cranking, but the system voltage remains the same. Connecting batteries in series increases available voltage, but amperage supplied to the starter remains the same.

Demands on Today's Starting Systems

Today's heavy-vehicle engines demand the most from starter motors since emission reduction strategies have increased engine cylinder pressures during cranking. Anti-idling laws, which require drivers to reduce the amount of time their engine idles, require modern starter motors to crank warm and more mechanically resistive engines many more times than before. Start-stop energy reducing drive systems and hybrid drive vehicles place even more strain on starter motors.

In spite of the increasing demands, new designs of starter motors and systems controls are enabling starters to last longer and increase output torque while substantially reducing motor weight. A typical example of this is the improvements and changes that have occurred to Delco Remy™ starter motors in recent times. The Delco Remy™ 40MT **FIGURE 14-2A** weighs 66 lb (30 kg), and the 39MT weighs only 30 lb (14 kg) yet produces more cranking torque with much greater reliability **FIGURE 14-2B**. The 37MT is the latest, third-generation starter using a gear reduction drive system to multiply torque output. The 37 MT weighs approximately 50 lb (23 kg). All three starters are used on engines from 10 to 15L displacement **FIGURE 14-2C**. Minimum life expectancy for a starter now is 4 years with 7,000 start cycles.

Most starting systems have only a single starter motor to crank the engine. In large displacement engines, where the starting demands are higher, two starter motors may be required to crank the engine over.

Starter Motor Classification

Electric starter motors were first installed in the 1912 Cadillac cars to replace hand-operated engine cranks. While electric motors were invented decades before this, the concept that made electric starters practical was the idea of building motors to operate at high amperage levels for a few seconds and not burn out. The Dayton Electric

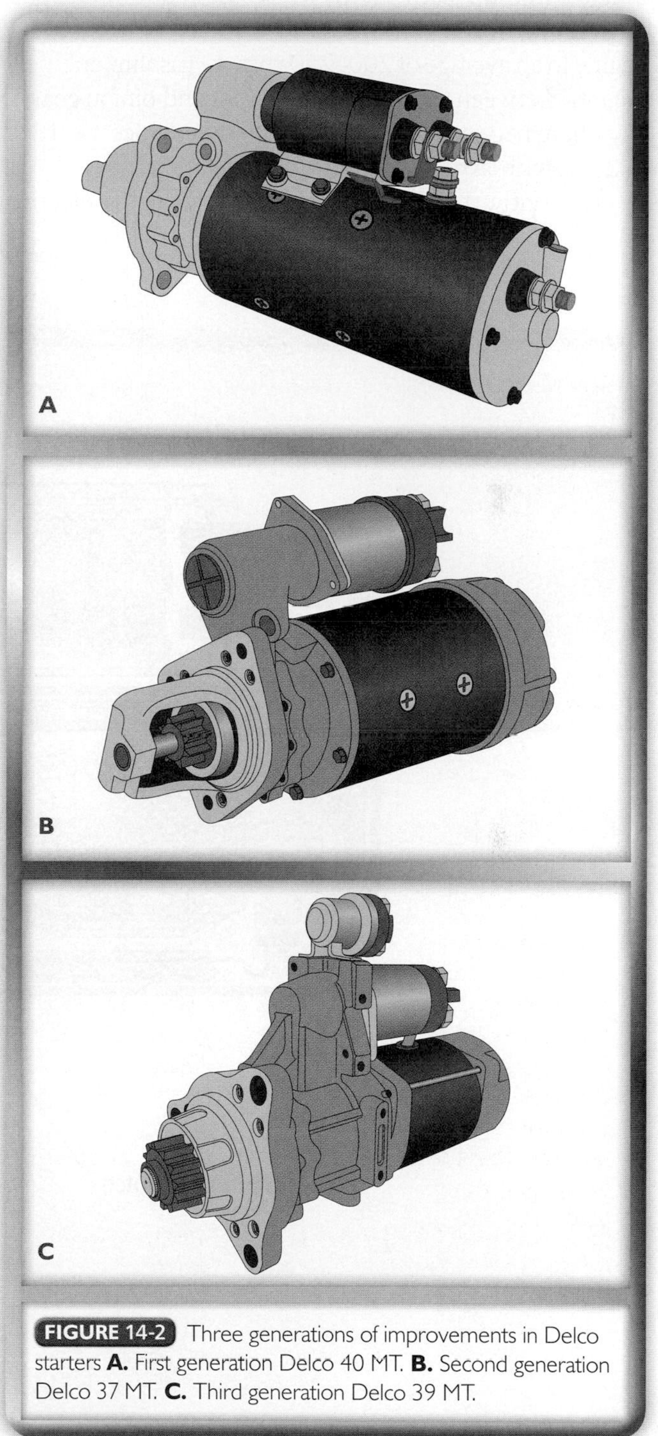

FIGURE 14-2 Three generations of improvements in Delco starters **A.** First generation Delco 40 MT. **B.** Second generation Delco 37 MT. **C.** Third generation Delco 39 MT.

Company, later shortened and called DELCO™, pioneered the use of high-current-draw motors that enabled the starter to develop a tremendous amount of torque. The motors were unlike any compact electric motors of the day, which were all designed for continuous operation.

Using a small pinion gear, the starter motor rotates the engine through a ring gear attached to the flywheel. When the starter motor begins to turn, the pinion teeth quickly line up with the flywheel teeth and rotate the engine at a minimum of 125 rpm for a 4-stroke diesel engine to an average of 200–250 rpm. In gasoline engines, the ratio between the flywheel ring gear and pinion gear is anywhere between 10 and 15:1. Diesel engines use 18:1 to 25:1, with 20:1 being most common.

Currently, there are three major categories of electric starters used in heavy vehicles.

- **Direct drive**—The motor armature directly engages the flywheel through a pinion gear. In this arrangement, as illustrated in **FIGURE 14-3**, the only gear torque multiplication is between the pinion gear and the ring gear.
- **Reduction gear drive**—The motor multiplies torque to the starter pinion gear by using an extra gear between the armature and the starter drive mechanism. The gear reduction allows the starter to spin at a higher speed with lower current, while still creating the required torque through the reduction gear to crank the engine. The reduction drive of this type of starter motor is approximately between 3.3:1 and 5.7:1. These types of starters, like that illustrated in **FIGURE 14-4**, can be identified by an offset drive housing to the motor housing.

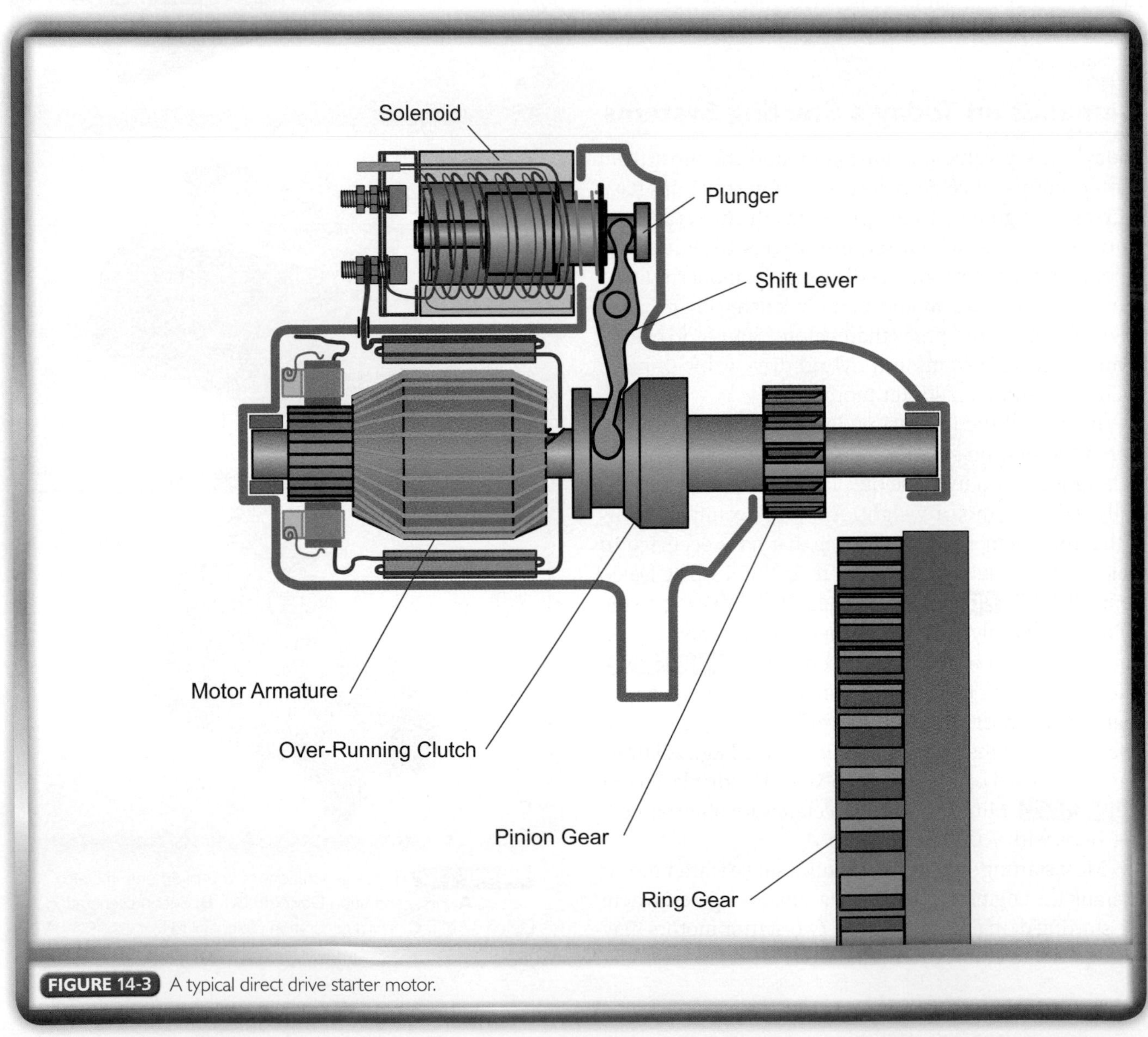

FIGURE 14-3 A typical direct drive starter motor.

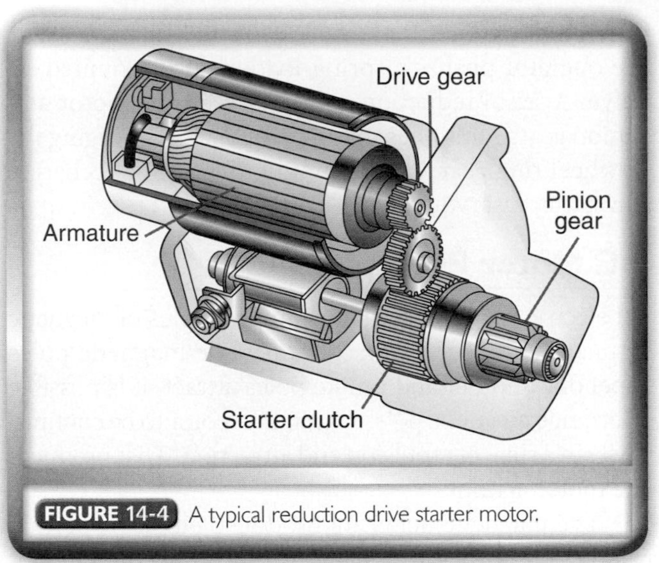

FIGURE 14-4 A typical reduction drive starter motor.

- **Planetary gear reduction drive**—Another type of gear reduction system, the planetary gear system, illustrated in **FIGURE 14-5**, reduces the starter profile using a planetary gear set rather than a spur type gear to multiply motor torque to the pinion gear. Gear reduction starters can reduce starter weight by more than 50%.

Direct drive starters are becoming less common due to their larger size, heavier weight, and higher current requirements. The use of gear reduction and planetary gear reduction starter designs means the motor will require less current, is more compact, and is lighter—while increasing cranking torque. Higher motor speeds used in these units result in potentially less motor damage than direct drive units because less current is needed to produce torque The disadvantage of the smaller starter

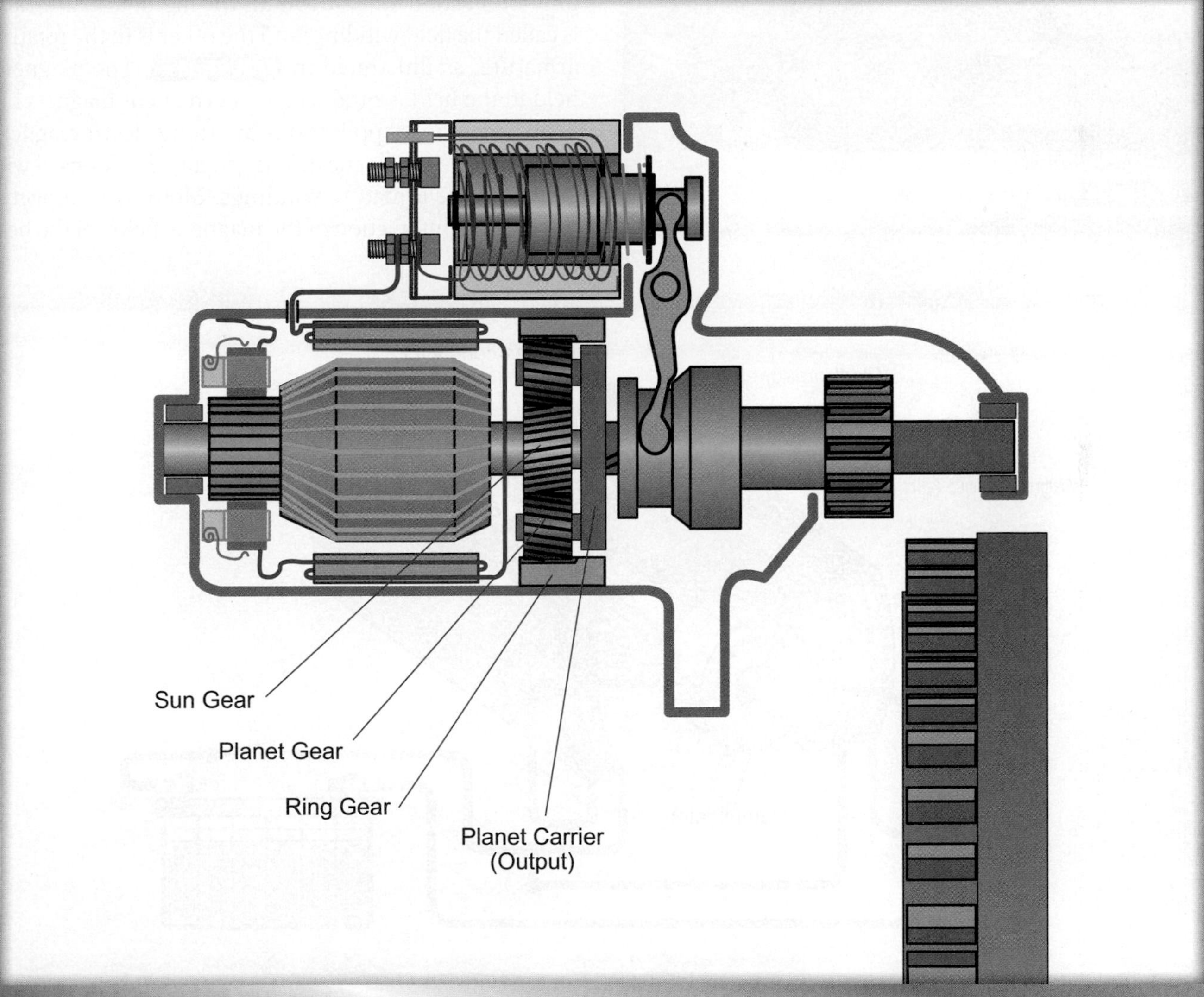

Sun Gear
Planet Gear
Ring Gear
Planet Carrier (Output)

FIGURE 14-5 A typical planetary gear reduction drive starter motor

profile in comparison to direct drive starters is the inability to tolerate high heat loads caused by prolonged engine cranking.

Pneumatic, or air starters, like that shown in FIGURE 14-6, are another type of starter motor used on some older diesel engines, particularly two-stroke Detroits, which need a minimum of 200 cranking rpm to start. The system consists of a geared air motor, starting valve, and a pressure tank. Compressed air from a dedicated reservoir tank is used to spin the motor after the operator pushes a spring-loaded dash mounted air valve. A set of reduction gears between the motor and pinion gears multiplies motor torque while engaging the flywheel ring gear. Once running, the engine recharges the starter reservoir tank.

FIGURE 14-6 A typical air-starter.

DC Motor Principles

All electric motors operate using principles of magnetic attraction and repulsion. Because like magnetic poles repel one another and unlike poles attract, it is possible to arrange magnetic poles within the motor to be continuously in a state of repulsion and attraction. That produces the motor action.

The magnetic fields are produced either by permanent magnets or electromagnets, which use coils or loops of conductors with electric current flowing through them to create magnetic fields. Two magnetic fields are required for motor action: one surrounds the motor armature and is called the field winding, and the other is in the rotating armature, as illustrated in FIGURE 14-7. The magnetic field in the field is produced by permanent magnets but in all heavy-duty applications by strong electromagnets. The armature's magnetic field is generated in loops of wire that form the armature windings. Motor action occurs through the interaction of the magnetic fields of the field

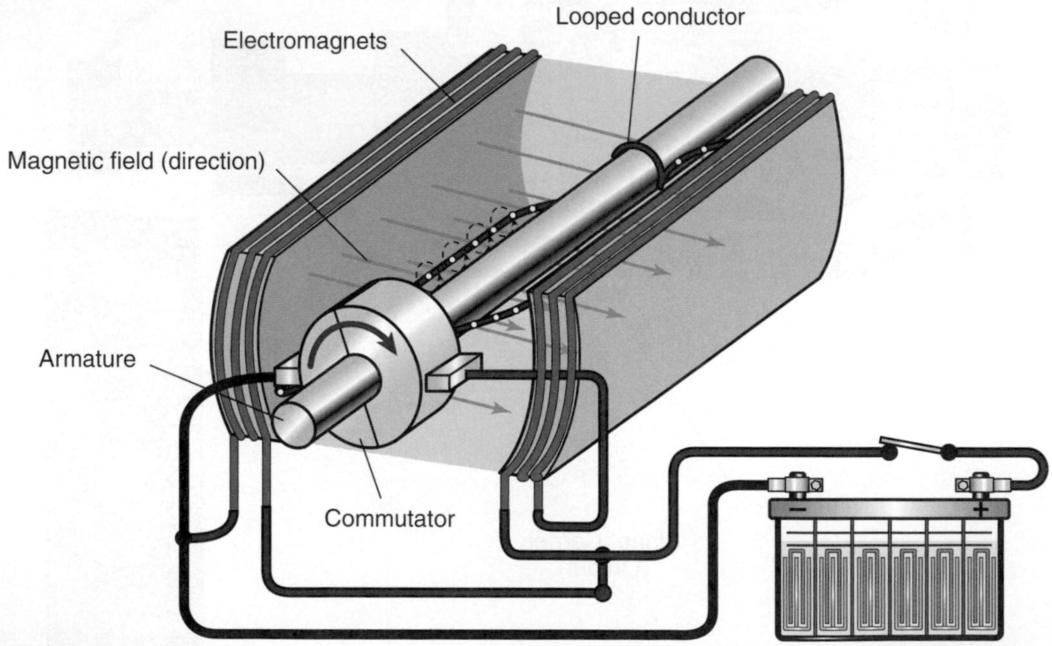

FIGURE 14-7 Basic direct-current electric motor operation. Two magnetic fields are required for motor action, one in the field and the other in the armature.

coils and the armature, which causes a rotational force to act on the armature, producing the turning motion.

Heavy-duty starter motors use electromagnets in the field and armature windings, which are intensified by the low reluctance laminated iron armature shaft and soft iron starter case. Motors used for smaller applications, such as blower and wiper motors, may use permanent magnets for the field and electromagnets for the armature. Permanent magnet field starter motors are not used in medium or heavy-duty starter applications.

Regardless of its design, a starter motor consists of housing, field coils, an armature, a commutator and brushes, end frames, and a solenoid-operated shift mechanism. Major variations between starters are in the starter drive mechanism, with most starters using a gear-reduction drive rather than a direct-drive configuration.

Types of DC Motors

Direct current motors are categorized by the arrangement of electromagnetic circuits producing magnetic forces of repulsion and attraction. Common electric motor classification used in heavy vehicles includes:

- Series—Field and armature windings are connected in series. These motors develop the highest torque and are used as starting motors.
- Shunt (parallel wound)—Field and armature windings are connected in parallel. These motors develop less torque but maintain a constant speed. They are often used as blower motors.
- Compound—Field and armature windings have both series and parallel connections. The motor has good starting torque and stable operating speed. These motors are commonly used in wipers and power seats.
- Stepper—The field is made from an electromagnet and the armature has two or more coils that are energized by a micro controller. These motors are used in instrument clusters gauges, turbochargers, and EGR actuators where high precision movement is required.

Series Motors

The series and shunt motor are the two most common types found in the automotive industry. FIGURE 14-8 shows the current flow circuits through a series and shunt motor. Note the difference in the way the current flows through the fields. Series motors are called "series" because the field and armature windings are connected in series. So, current will flow through the field windings first and then to the armature windings before leaving the armature through the positive brush. This means current first passes from the negative chassis ground, through a brush, and into the armature. Current leaves from another brush and passes into the field coils before returning to the battery positive. Because it is a series circuit, any unwanted resistance inside the motor, whether it is a burnt contact or loose brush, will reduce current flow throughout the entire motor circuit.

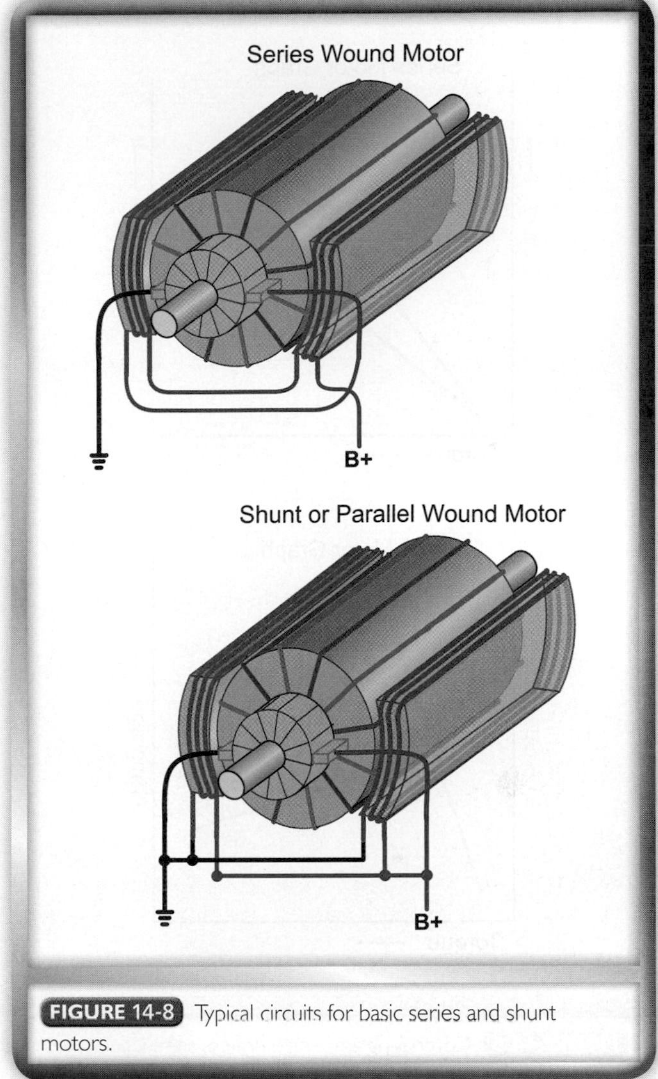

FIGURE 14-8 Typical circuits for basic series and shunt motors.

Series-wound motors are primarily used in starter motors because they develop the greatest amount of torque at zero rpm, which is ideal for developing break-away torque needed to crank a stopped engine. As magnetic field strength is always proportional to amperage and not voltage, the initial amperage drawn by a series motor produces the most torque. In comparison, as illustrated in FIGURE 14-9, shunt motors produce less torque than series motors but do not drop as much speed as torque diminishes. This makes them ideal for applications like blower motors.

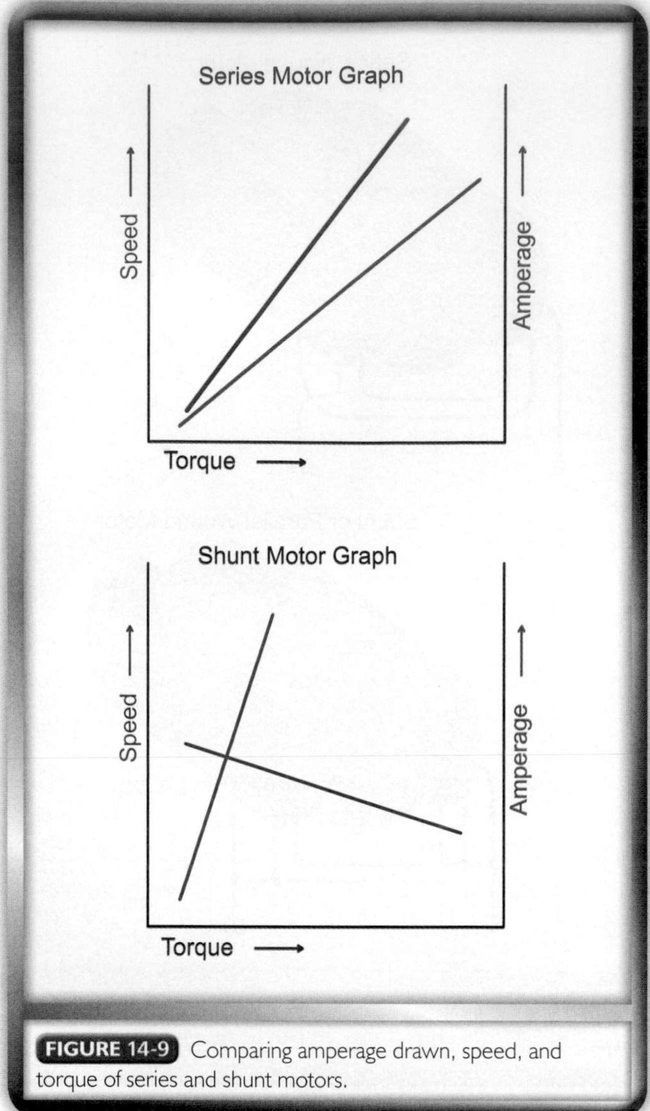

FIGURE 14-9 Comparing amperage drawn, speed, and torque of series and shunt motors.

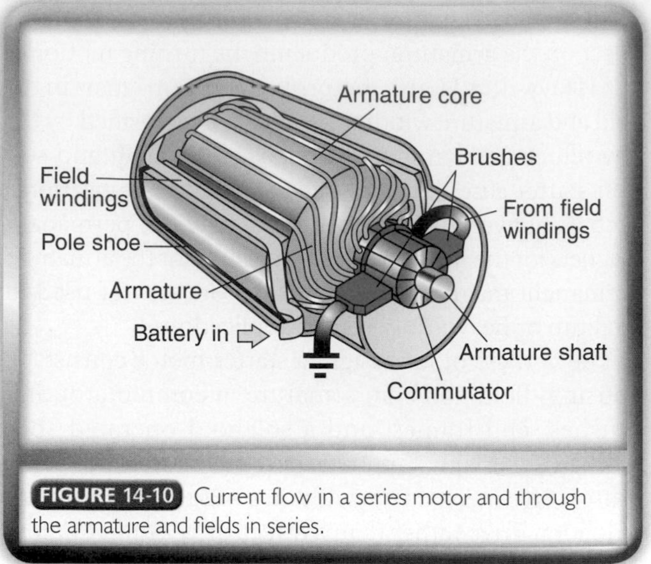

FIGURE 14-10 Current flow in a series motor and through the armature and fields in series.

Series Motor Current Flow

The current flow for a series motor, such as the one illustrated in FIGURE 14-10, are as follows:

1. Current first enters the motor through the brush connected to negative chassis ground. Current passes through the armature via the commutator and leaves through the second brush connected to the field winding. A magnetic field is created in the armature.
2. Current passes through the windings of the field coils. The laminated iron making up the pole shoes intensifies the magnetic field strength. The direction the winding is wound around the pole shoe establishes the polarity of the pole shoe. The field windings are wound in directions opposite to one another to produce a like pole to the armatures, which always opposes the magnetic pole produced in the armature.
3. The forces of repulsion between the field coil and armature cause the armature to turn.
4. Each armature winding is connected to a pair of segments on the commutator. The commutator turns with the armature, causing the stationary brushes to continuously connect with a new armature winding as the armature rotates. This arrangement enables the forces of repulsion to constantly reposition to maintain starter motor rotation.

Series Motor Operational Characteristics

Series wound motors also are self-limiting in speed due to the development of a **counter-electromotive force (CEMF)**. CEMF is produced by the spinning magnetic field of the armature, which induces current in the opposite direction of battery current through the motor. Battery current and CEMF current both flow through a motor at the same time but in opposite directions. The faster the motor turns, the higher the CEMF, and the less current is drawn from the battery. Higher voltage from cranking batteries produces greater motor speed and more CEMF. FIGURE 14-11 illustrates the relationship between motor speed, torque, and amperage draw.

Consider the following relationship between armature speed, CEMF, amperage, and torque for a series starter motor:

- The faster the armature spins, the greater the CEMF current induced in the opposite polarity of battery voltage.
- The starter draws less current from the battery as it spins faster due to CEMF resistance.
- Since less current is used at higher speeds, magnetic fields will weaken and starter torque drops off.

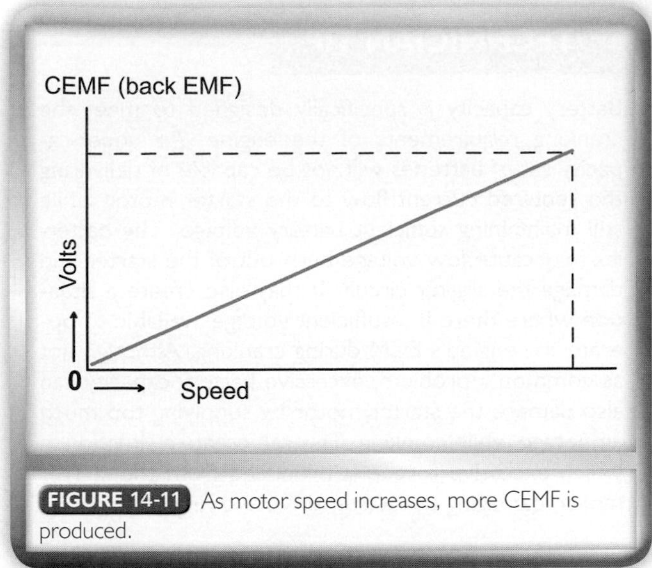

FIGURE 14-11 As motor speed increases, more CEMF is produced.

- Slower motor speeds mean less CEMF resistance to current flow through the starter and higher battery amperage drawn by the starter.
- Greatest torque is produced at low speed since the motor will draw the highest amperage.

> **TECHNICIAN TIP**
>
> Weak and discharged batteries are a starting motor's worst enemy because they can cause low-voltage burn-out. Low battery voltage will prevent the starter from spinning as fast as it should, which reduces CEMF—a starter's internal resistance when operating. With lower internal resistance, the starter will draw more amperage than it should, which leads to heat damage to starter windings, solenoids, and external circuits.

Amperage drawn by a starter at normal room temperature with a fully charged battery will range from an average of 350 amps for a 7-liter engine to 800 or 900 amps for a 15-liter engine. Initial starting amperage is much higher because the engine is stopped and needs more torque from the starting motor to accelerate the engine from 0 rpm to cranking speed. Because of the high amperage drawn during cranking, the starter can only operate for short periods of time before cooling. Heat produced by continuous operation for any length of time will cause serious damage to the motor. Connections become loose and burnt. Some will even melt. Brushes and insulation will become burned as well as motor windings. To prevent heat damage, armature windings are brazed rather than soldered to the commutator. The starter must never operate for more than 30 seconds at a time and should rest for 2 minutes between extended crank cycles. This permits the heat to dissipate without damage to the unit.

Low-Voltage Burn-Out

Cranking an engine with low battery voltage causes one of the most damaging conditions for a starter. **Low-voltage burn-out** occurs when excess amperage flows through the starter, causing the motor to burn out prematurely. When battery voltage is low the starter will use even more amperage to rotate. This happens because starters are constant power devices. That is, starters will use any combination of voltage and amperage to produce the necessary output power, rated in watts. For example, if 7,200 watts of power is needed to operate a starter at 12 volts, 600 amps is needed. If available battery voltage fell to 10 volts, then 720 amps would be needed according to Watts Law (watts = volts × amperage). Increasing amperage drawn from batteries, in turn, increases batteries' internal resistance. Increased resistance causes available voltage to drop even further, which in turn increases the amperage needed to rotate the starter. Slower starter rotation means less CEMF is developed. Consequently, amperage through the starter climbs even more. To prevent damage to the starter, cables, solenoid, and switches from low voltage, several design and maintenance practices are required.

- Correct battery sizing. Batteries must be sized according to their CCA to maintain a cranking voltage of no less than 10.5 volts after three consecutive cranking periods lasting 30 seconds. The appropriate two-minute cooling period is included in this estimation.
- Correct sizing of battery cables. Dedicated battery negative and positive cables are needed for heavier starting systems. Cable diameters should be sized for maximum amperage capacity using OEM recommendations. Double cables are needed when using four or more starting batteries.
- Using overcrank protection switches. Thermal protection switches may be located in the starter housing and connected in series with the starter solenoid ground circuit. When hot, the switch opens and prevents the starter solenoid from operating until the starter is sufficiently cooled.
- Using voltage sensitive starter control circuit relays. Starter relays are produced that will disengage when battery voltage falls below a predetermined level, thus disconnecting the starter circuit. Alternatively, an electronic control module (ECM), which supplies current to energize the starter, can monitor

battery voltage, enabling the ECM to disconnect the starter relay when battery current falls too low during cranking. Disconnect voltage is approximately 7.2 volts.

- Using ultra-capacitors. Ultra-capacitors are a recent application of organic capacitors used to provide cranking assist to HD starters. Up to 1,800 amps of current can rapidly discharge for a brief moment to provide battery assist to the starting motor. As illustrated in FIGURE 14-12, ultra-capacitors connected in parallel to the battery provide a high initial current to the starter to speed up the armature rotation. Supplementing the available amperage to the starter during the initial cranking period reduces the likelihood of a low-voltage burn-out due to low CEMF when armature speed is reduced

> **TECHNICIAN TIP**
>
> Battery capacity is specifically designed to meet the cranking requirements of the engine. An under-capacity set of batteries will not be capable of delivering the required current flow to the starter motor while still maintaining sufficient battery voltage. The batteries may cause low-voltage burn-out of the starter and damage the starter circuit. It may also create a situation where there is insufficient voltage available to operate the engine's ECM during cranking. Although not as common a problem, excessive battery capacity can also damage the starter motor by supplying too much amperage while cranking. This can create a situation in which excessive torque is produced from the starter motor, damaging the starter drive and ring gear.

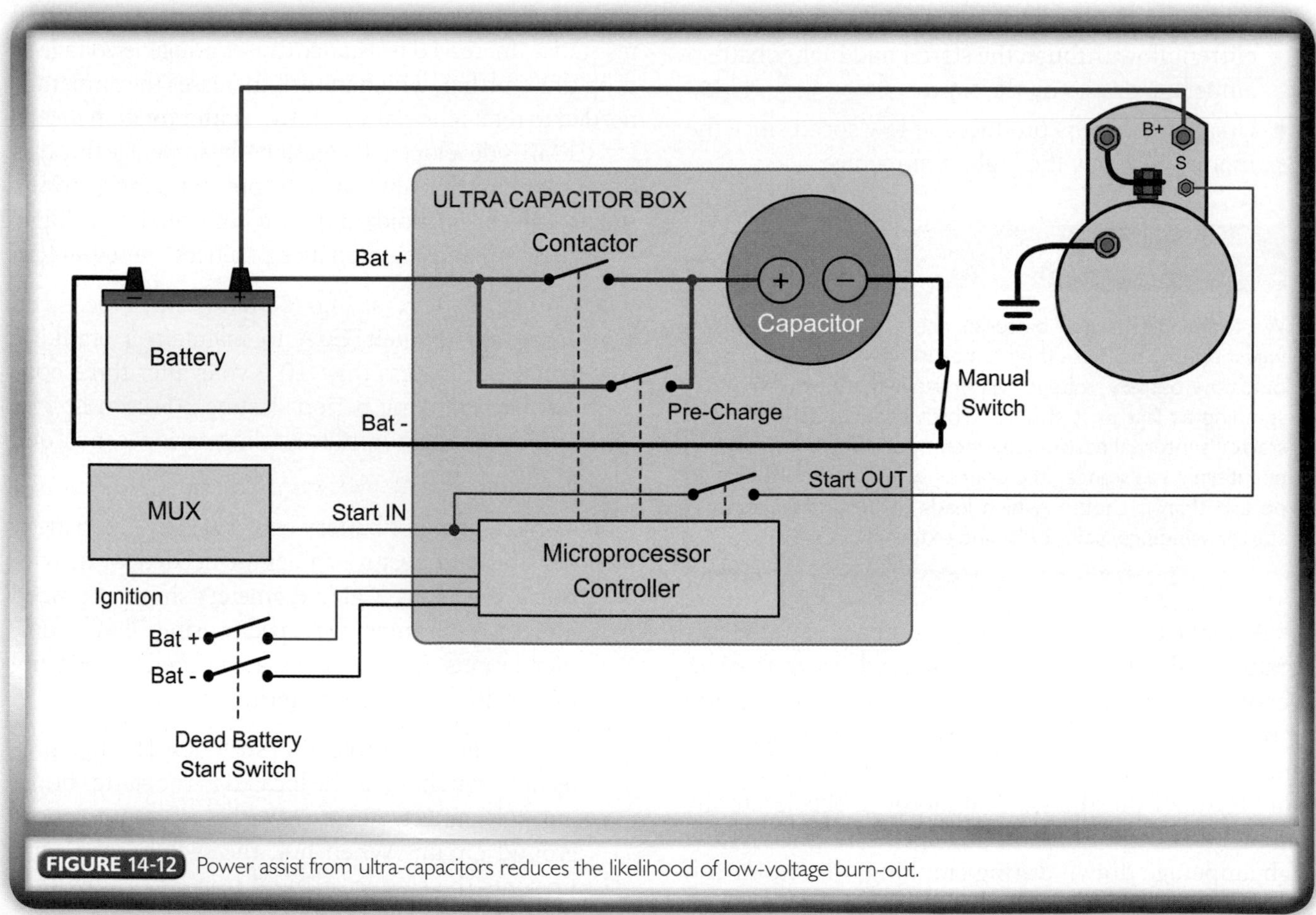

FIGURE 14-12 Power assist from ultra-capacitors reduces the likelihood of low-voltage burn-out.

Components of Starters

Regardless of the motor design, a starter motor consists of housing, field coils, an armature, a commutator, brushes, end frames, and a solenoid-operated shift mechanism. Major variations between starters are in the starter drive mechanism. Some starters use a gear-reduction drive, while others use a direct drive configuration. Still other starter motors, called axial starter motors, are a type of direct drive starter. Axial starter motors use an axial sliding armature to engage the pinion with the flywheel. This type of starter will be discussed later in this chapter.

Starter Housing and Field Coils

The starter housing, or frame, encloses and supports the internal starter components, protecting them and intensifying the magnetic fields produced in the field coils. Housings and pole shoes are made from soft iron, which conduct magnetic fields with less resistance than air or other materials, which concentrates the magnetic field produced in the fields, making a more powerful magnet. In the starter housing shown in FIGURE 14-13, field coils and their pole shoes are securely attached to the inside of the iron housing. The field coils are insulated from the housing and are connected to a terminal, called the motor terminal, which protrudes through to the housing. Fields will have a "North" or "South" magnetic polarity facing inward or outward depending on the direction of current flow. The magnetic flux of the pole shoes is illustrated in FIGURE 14-14.

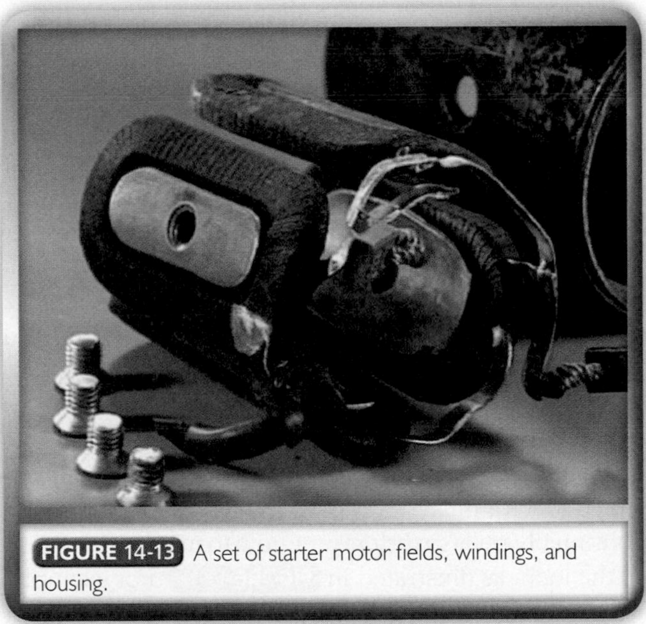

FIGURE 14-13 A set of starter motor fields, windings, and housing.

Field coils are connected in series with the armature windings through the starter brushes. In a four-brush starter motor, two brushes are used to connect the field coils to the armature and the other two brushes connect to ground to complete the series circuit.

Armature

The **armature** is the only rotating component of the starter. Armatures, like that shown in FIGURE 14-15, have three main components: the shaft, windings, and the commutator.

Armature Shaft and Windings

Different from the thin wire used in shunt motors, armature windings are made of heavy, flat, copper strips that can handle the heavy current flow of the series motor. The windings are made of numerous coils of a single loop each. The sides of these loops fit into slots in the armature core or shaft, but they are insulated from it with insulating strips and varnish applied to the winding before placement. Each slot contains the side of one half of a coil and a commutator segment. In a four-brush motor, each half of a coil is wound at 90-degrees to each other. The coils connect to each other at the commutator so that current flows through all of the armature windings at the same time. This arrangement generates a magnetic field around each armature winding. The interaction between the armature and field windings' magnetic fields produces a torque or twisting force that turns the armature.

Commutator and Commutation

The commutator assembly presses onto the armature shaft. It is made up of heavy copper segments separated from each other and the armature shaft by insulation. The commutator segments connect to the ends of the armature windings. Starter motors have four or more brushes that ride on the commutator segments and carry the heavy current flow from the stationary field coils to the rotating armature windings via the commutator segments. A brush holder holds the brushes in position.

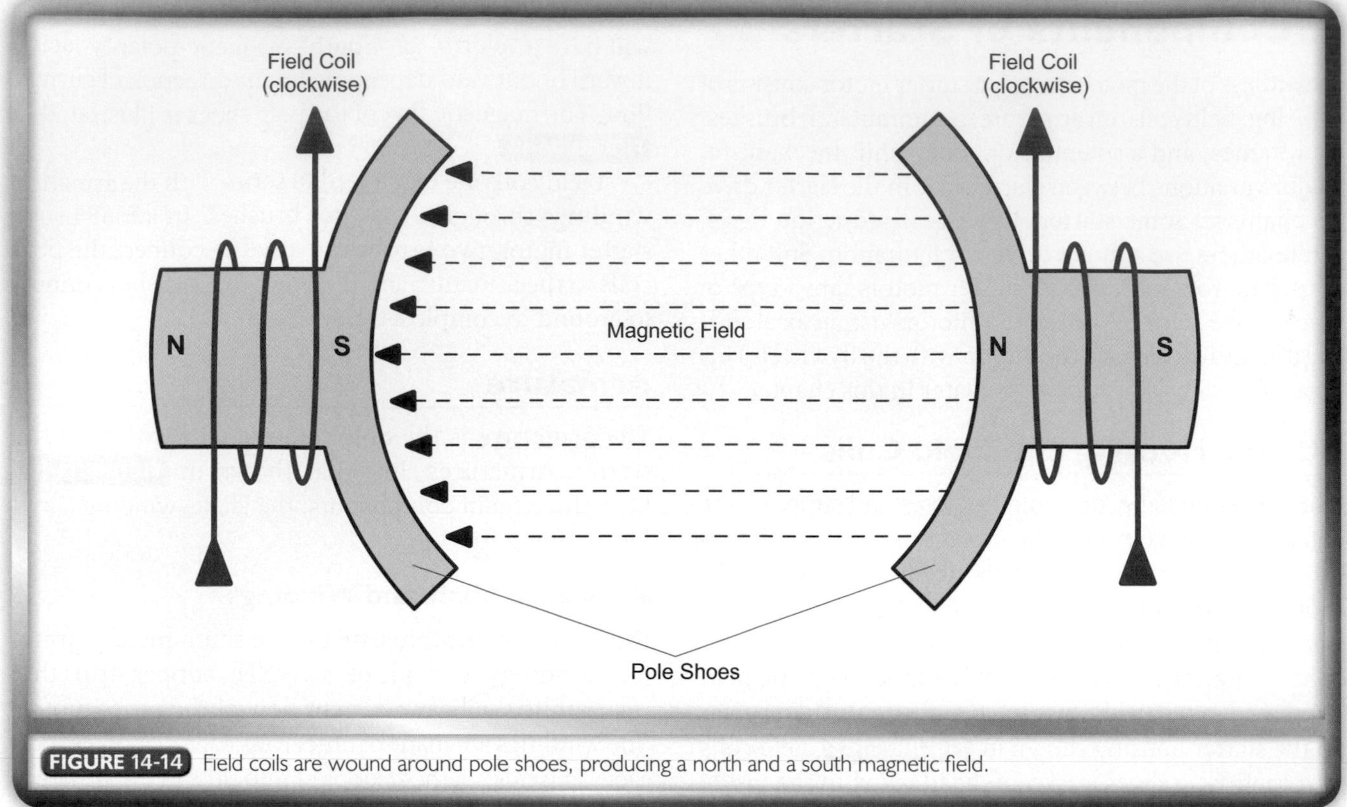

FIGURE 14-14 Field coils are wound around pole shoes, producing a north and a south magnetic field.

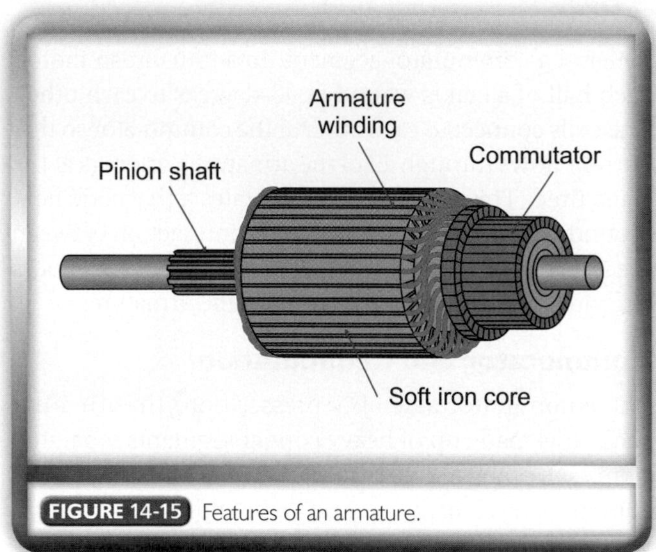

FIGURE 14-15 Features of an armature.

The commutator's role is to switch the direction of current flow through each armature coil as the armature rotates, thereby maintaining the rotary movement by ensuring the magnetic pole in the field winding is always the same as the pole in the armature winding opposite it. For a simple explanation of how a commutator works, consider a basic motor with a single loop of wire. When current flows in a conductor, an electromagnetic field is generated around it. If the conductor is placed in a stationary electromagnetic field with current flowing through the field in the opposite direction, the two magnetic fields will oppose one another, and the conductor will be repelled or pushed away from the stationary field. Reversing the direction of current flow in the conductor will cause the conductor to move in the opposite direction. This is known as the motor effect and is greatest when the current-carrying conductor and the stationary magnetic field are at right angles to each other.

By switching the direction of current flow through the conductor at the right time, the conductor can be continuously pushed away from one field winding and pulled towards another, as illustrated in FIGURE 14-16. The turning motion is called the motor effect and causes the loop to rotate until it is at 90 degrees to the magnetic field. To continue rotation, the direction of current flow in the conductor must be reversed. A commutator is used to continually reverse the current flow to maintain rotation of the loop, as illustrated in FIGURE 14-17. For example, a commutator consists of two semicircular segments that are connected to the two ends of the loop and are insulated from each other. Carbon brushes provide a sliding connection to the commutator to complete the circuit and allow current to flow through the loop.

This continuously changing direction of current through the loop maintains a consistent direction of rotation of the loop. To achieve a uniform motion and torque

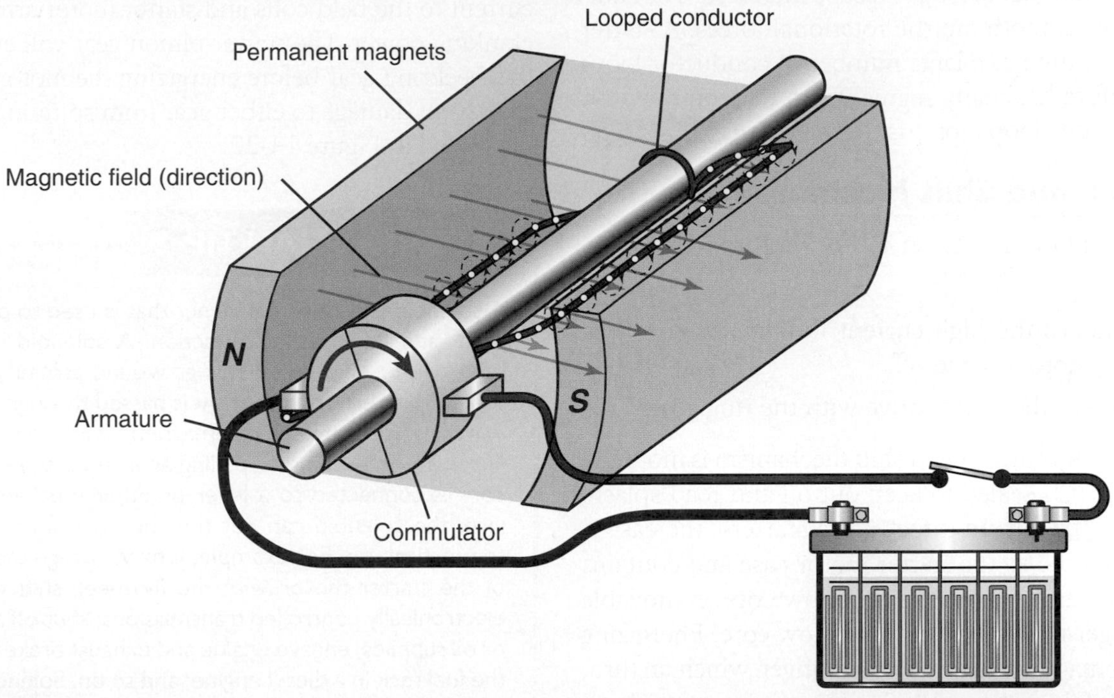

FIGURE 14-16 Simple single-loop motor and electromagnetic fields—with commutator and brushes.

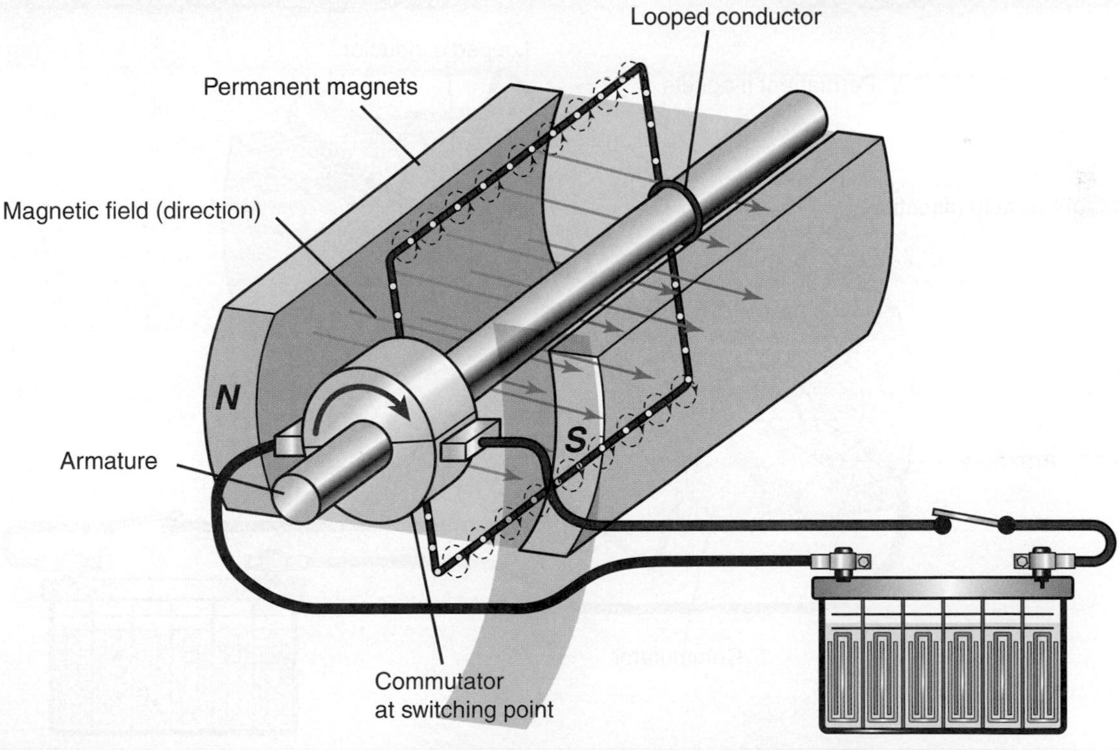

FIGURE 14-17 Simple single-loop motor and electromagnetic fields at the switching point of the commutator.

output, the number of loops must be increased. The additional loops smooth out the rotational forces. A starter motor armature has a large number of conductor loops and therefore has many segments on the commutator. A simple multi-loop motor is depicted in FIGURE 14-18.

Solenoid and Shift Mechanism

The solenoid on the starter motor performs two main functions:

1. It switches the high current flow required by the starter motor on and off.
2. It engages the starter drive with the ring gear.

The solenoid-operated shift mechanism is mounted in a case that is sealed to keep out oil and road splash, as in FIGURE 14-19. In direct-drive starters, the case is flange mounted to the starter motor case and contains two electromagnets around a hollow core. A movable iron plunger is installed in the hollow core. Energizing the electromagnets pulls the iron plunger, which, in turn, moves a shift lever, engaging the drive pinion gear. This is illustrated in FIGURE 14-20. At the same time, moving the iron core also closes a set of contacts to connect battery current with the motor terminal, directing full battery current to the field coils and starter motor armature for cranking power. The starter pinion gear will engage the flywheel ring gear before energizing the motor terminal to prevent damage to either gear from spinning teeth, as illustrated in Figure 14-20.

TECHNICIAN TIP

A solenoid is an electromagnet that is used to perform work and has mechanical action. A solenoid is made with one or two coil windings wound around an iron tube. When electrical current is passed through the coil windings, it creates electromagnetic force that creates linear action pushing or pulling an iron core. When the core is connected to a lever or other mechanical device, the solenoid can put this mechanical movement to practical use. For example, it may: engage the pinion of the starter motor with the flywheel; shift gears in electronically controlled transmissions; shut off air, fuel, or oil supplies; engage engine and exhaust brakes; move the fuel rack in a diesel engine; and so on. Solenoids can also close contacts, such as the solenoid contact in a starter motor solenoid.

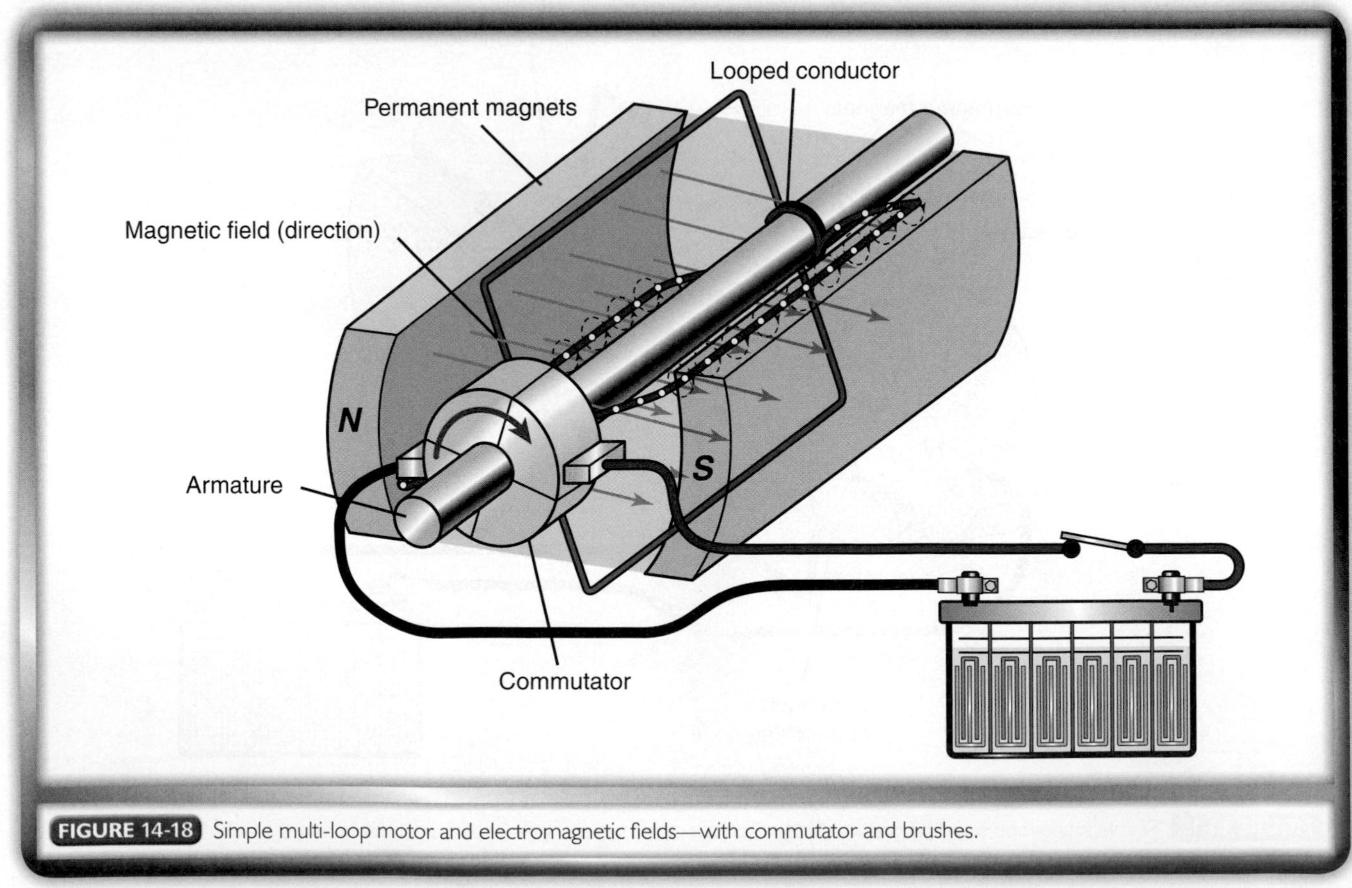

FIGURE 14-18 Simple multi-loop motor and electromagnetic fields—with commutator and brushes.

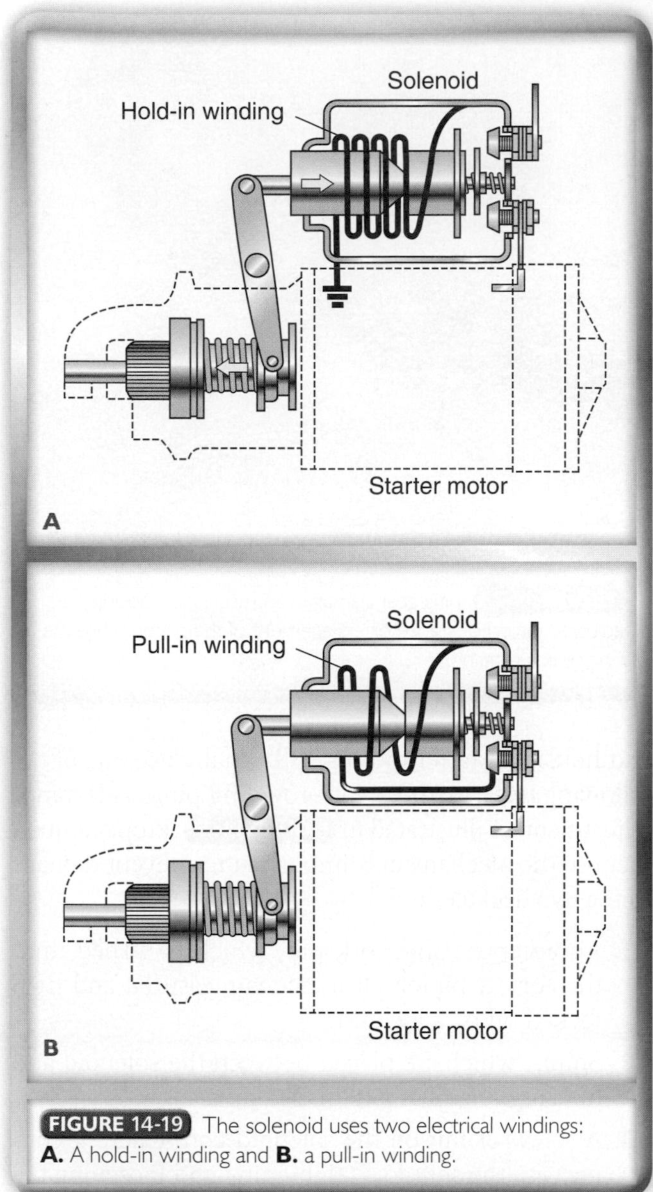

FIGURE 14-19 The solenoid uses two electrical windings: **A.** A hold-in winding and **B.** a pull-in winding.

> **TECHNICIAN TIP**
>
> Low battery voltage produces starter chatter—the rapid cycling of the solenoid plunger in and out of engagement. This happens because the thinner windings of the hold-in circuit are more sensitive to voltage drop than pull-in windings. When the solenoid closes the connection between the battery and motor terminal, the available voltage also drops due to the increased amperage flow from the battery.

Starter Drive Mechanisms

The starter drive transmits the rotational force from the starter armature to the engine via the ring gear that is mounted on the engine flywheel or torque converter.

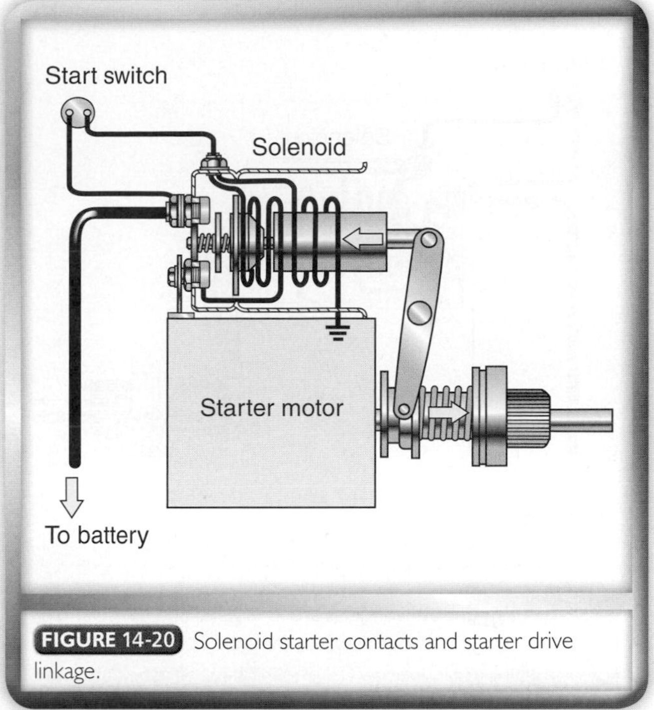

FIGURE 14-20 Solenoid starter contacts and starter drive linkage.

Armature rotation is transferred to the pinion gear through a variety of mechanisms.

Direct-drive starters, which diesel engines used exclusively for many decades, transferred torque directly to the pinion gear. Today, gear reduction starters using both planetary and spur-gear mechanisms have replaced direct drives.

With a solenoid-actuated, direct-drive starting system, teeth on the pinion gear do not immediately mesh with the flywheel ring gear. If this occurs, a spring located behind the pinion gear compresses so that the solenoid plunger can complete its stroke. When the starter motor armature begins to turn, the pinion teeth will quickly line up with the flywheel teeth and the spring pressure will help them to mesh **FIGURE 14-21**.

The pinion drive gear is attached to a roller-type, one-way or, overrunning clutch that is splined to the starter armature as in **FIGURE 14-22**. A one-way clutch is in all pinion gears and operates like a ratchet to protect the starter motor. It will drive when turned in one direction and slip when turned in the opposite direction.

When the engine starts and runs, the starter motor would be damaged if it remained connected to the engine through the flywheel. The ring gear-to-pinion gear ratio, which multiplies starter torque, also multiplies the starter's speed when driven by the engine. At idle, with a 20:1 gear ratio, the starter's armature will turn 14,000 rpm or more, which will destroy the armature windings. To prevent this, the one-way overrunning clutch allows the pinion gear to spin—but not turn the armature if

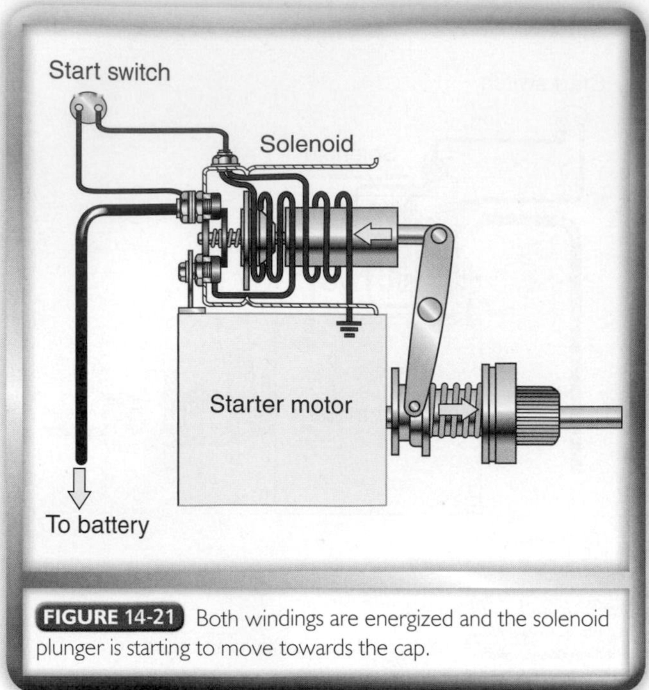

FIGURE 14-21 Both windings are energized and the solenoid plunger is starting to move towards the cap.

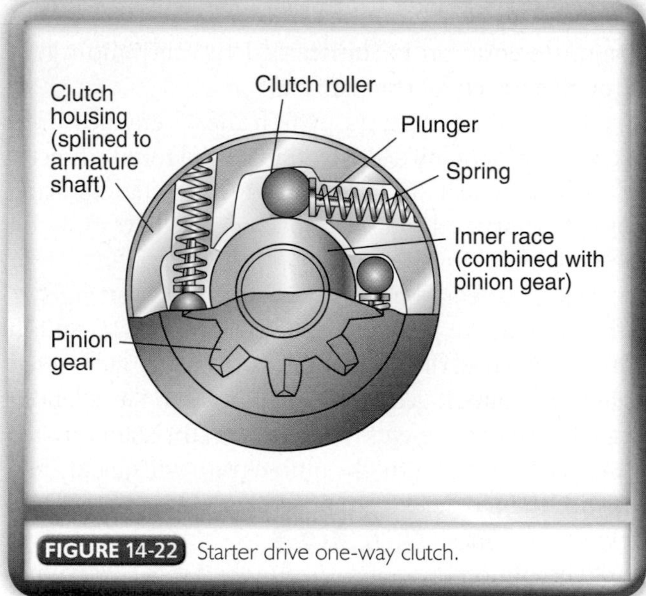

FIGURE 14-22 Starter drive one-way clutch.

it remains or is accidentally engaged with the flywheel. When the solenoid is de-energized, the shift assembly is pulled away from the flywheel through spring pressure FIGURE 14-23.

Most heavy-vehicle starters will have a pinion clearance adjustment to ensure the pinion engages fully with the flywheel while maintaining a clearance from the drive end housing. Starter motors will usually use one of the following three methods for providing pinion clearance adjustment, as illustrated in FIGURE 14-24. Proper adjustment of the mechanism is important to prevent damage to the flywheel teeth.

FIGURE 14-23 Ring gear damage can result from poorly adjusted pinion clearance or engagement of the pinion while the ring gear is rotating.

1. An eccentric shift fork pin, which is turned until the correct pinion clearance is measured and then locked off by a lock nut
2. Shims, which are placed between the solenoid and housing to adjust pinion clearance
3. A screw or nut on the solenoid core where it connects to the shift fork; tightening and loosening the screw or nut adjusts pinion clearance

Starter Control Circuits

The starter control circuit, in its most basic form, would have an ignition switch directly controlling the starter solenoid to operate the starter motor. In modern heavy vehicles, the circuits are more complex, as relays and control circuits such as transmission neutral and clutch switches are added to improve reliability and the safety of vehicles. The latest models of vehicles use an electrical system control module, which interfaces with the

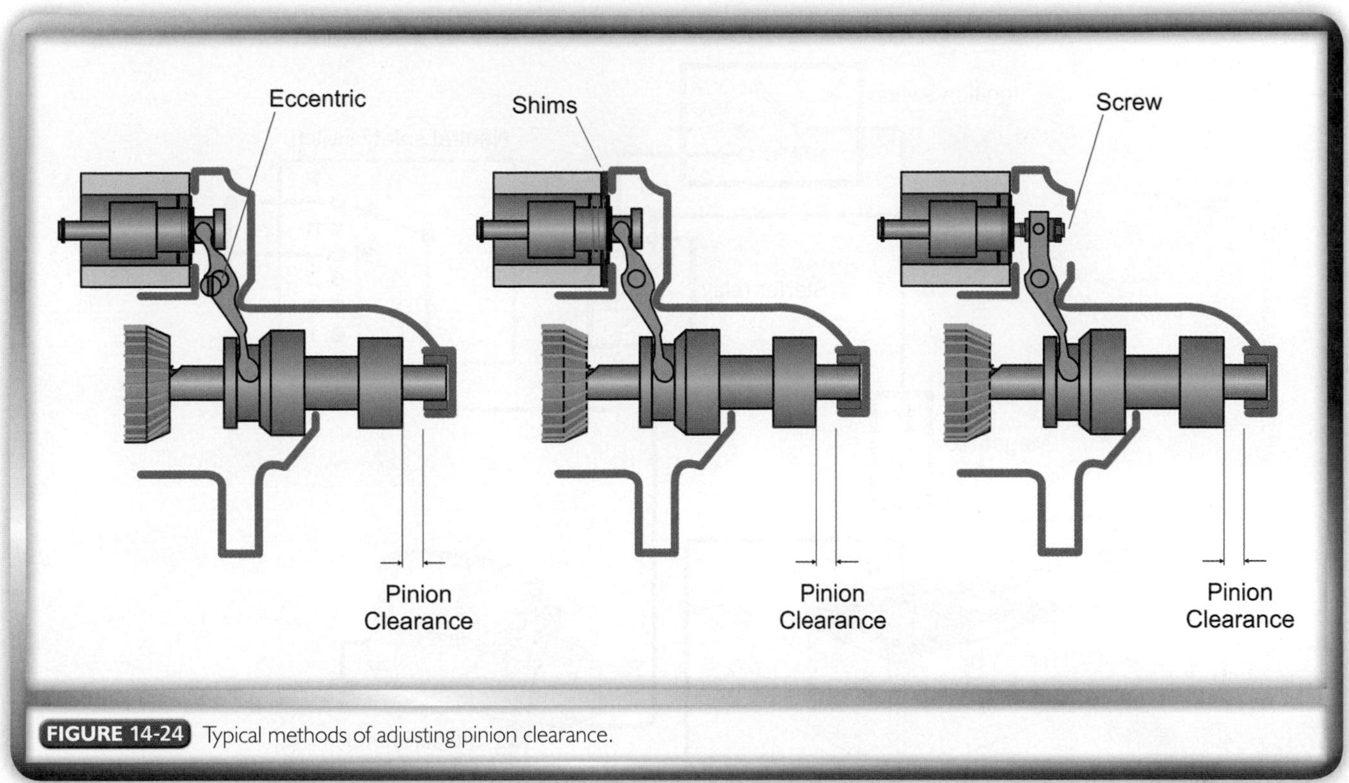

FIGURE 14-24 Typical methods of adjusting pinion clearance.

on-board vehicle network that receives data from various sensors, and various sensors to control the operation of the starter control circuit.

Solenoid Control Relay

Since it is neither practical nor safe to have large battery and starter cables routed in the cab of a vehicle, the starter control circuit allows the operator to use a small amount of battery current provided by the ignition switch to control the flow of a large amount of current in the starting circuit. The control circuit may also have a provision for locking out the starter engagement if the engine is running or the starter has overheated. Safety switches, also called neutral safety switches FIGURE 14-25A, can be located in either of two places in the control circuit—interrupting either the ground or battery positive of the starter relay FIGURE 14-25B. Placing the transmission in PARK or NEUTRAL or depressing the clutch will close the starter control circuit so current can flow to the relay switch. The safety switch can also be connected between the relay switch and its ground so that the switch must be closed before current can flow from the magnetic switch to ground.

ECM controlled circuits use the ignition key as an input device and control the starter operation by supplying a ground to the starter relay. The starter relay is the point in the starting system where the control circuit and starter solenoid circuit join. Because starter solenoids can consume between 30 and 60 amps, relays are needed to switch low current from the ignition switch or starter button to energize the starter solenoid circuit. Starter relays are a type of intermittent duty relay. This means they are not intended for continuous operation or operation longer than a minute. The intermittent duty relay has heavy, large-gauge windings in the control circuit capable of producing strong magnetic fields, which are less sensitive to voltage drop during cranking.

As there is a relatively high amount of amperage drawn by the starter solenoid itself, solenoid circuits have a minimum of one relay to switch current flow to the solenoid circuit. The relay may be controlled by a separate push button located in the dash or by an ignition key switch. On electronically controlled engines, it is more common to have the circuit controlled by a start button than the key switch. Having a start button

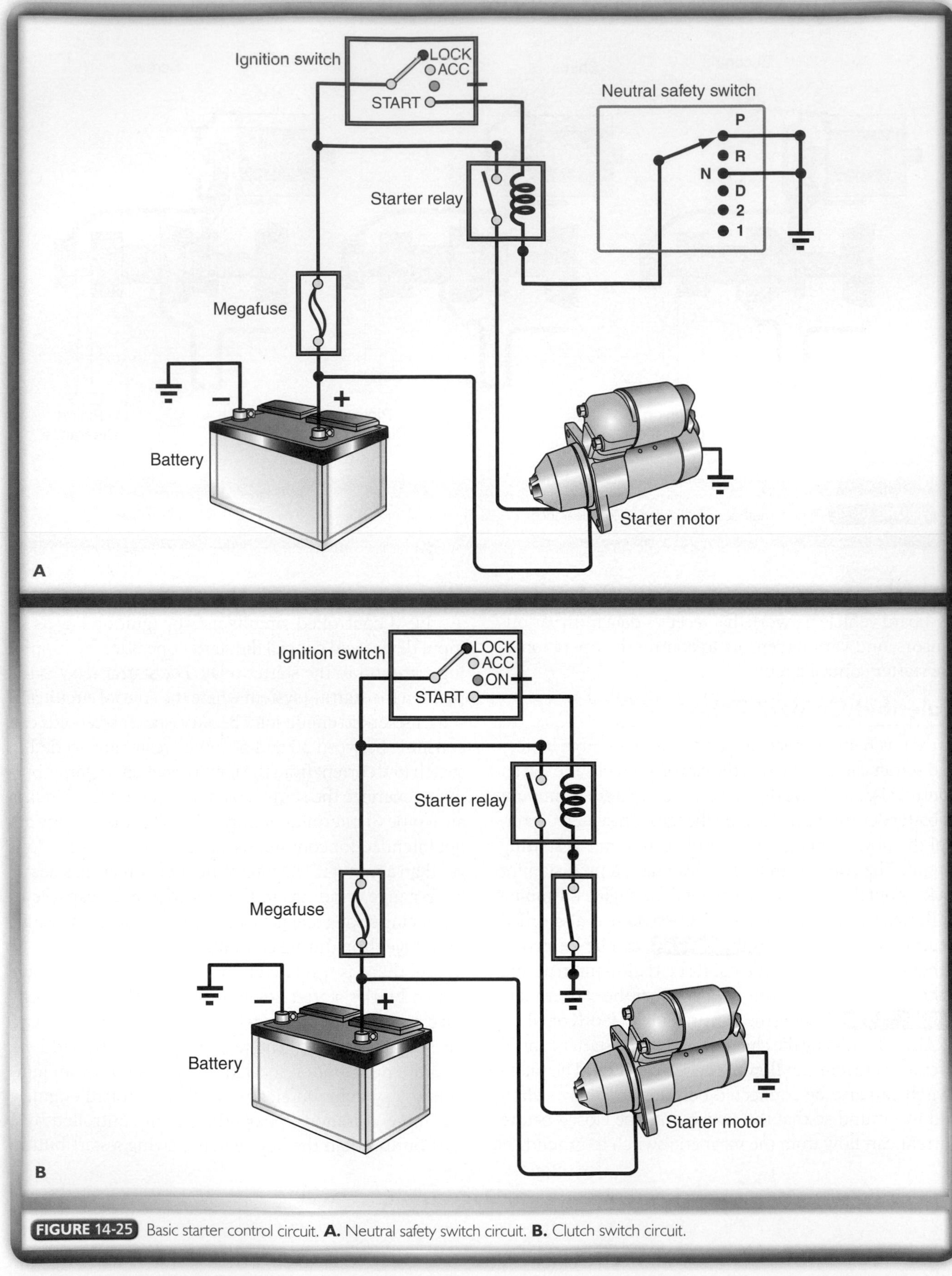

FIGURE 14-25 Basic starter control circuit. **A.** Neutral safety switch circuit. **B.** Clutch switch circuit.

prevents voltage drops through the switch. Likewise, a start button also prevents voltage spikes from the magnetic field collapse of the relay's coil that could travel back to other ignition circuits through the key FIGURE 14-26.

The ignition switch has other jobs besides controlling the starting circuit. The ignition switch normally has at least four separate positions: Accessory, Off, On (Run), and Start. There may be a separate position for "proving-out," which test illuminates on-dash lights and gauges. When a vehicle has a pushbutton starter switch, battery voltage is available to the button switch only when the ignition switch is in the ON position. When the starter pushbutton is pushed, current flows through the control circuit to the starter relay.

Relays use electromagnets to close contacts and act like a switch. Larger relays are sometimes referred to as "mag" switches.

Overcrank Protection (OCP)

Some starter motors are equipped with an **overcrank protection (OCP) thermostat**. The thermostat, as illustrated in FIGURE 14-27, monitors the temperature of the motor. If prolonged cranking causes the motor temperature to exceed a safe threshold, the thermostat will open the relay circuit and the current to the solenoid is interrupted.

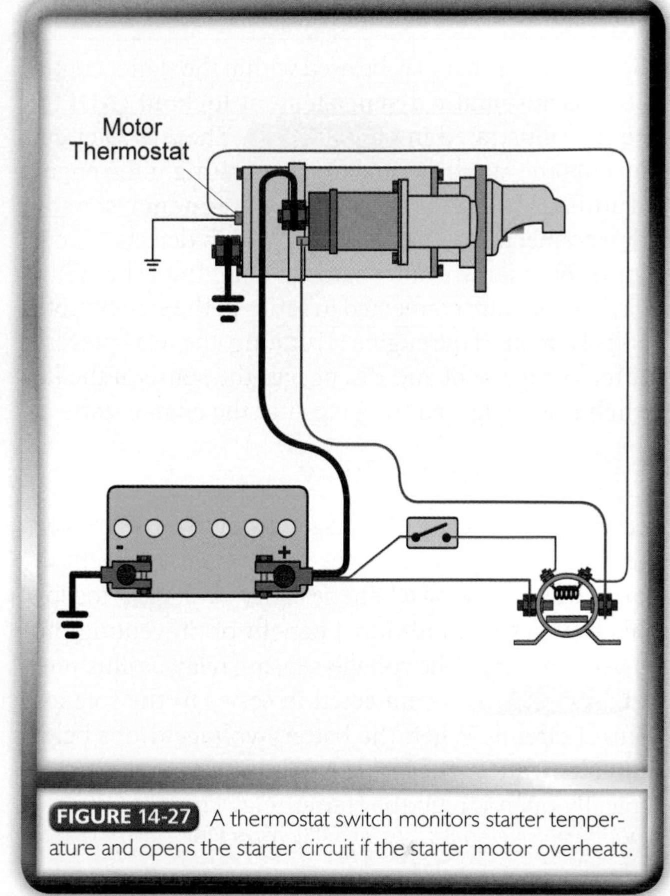

FIGURE 14-27 A thermostat switch monitors starter temperature and opens the starter circuit if the starter motor overheats.

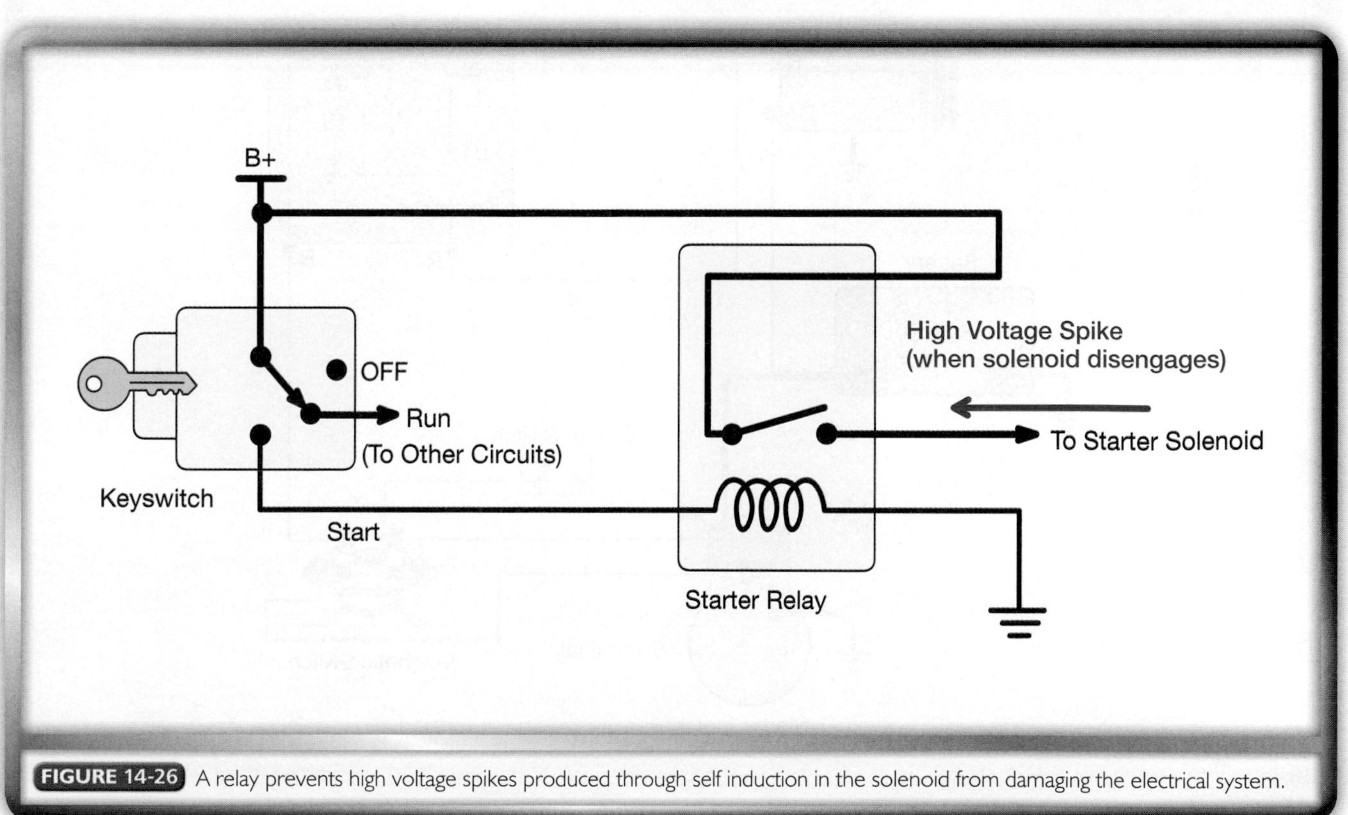

FIGURE 14-26 A relay prevents high voltage spikes produced through self induction in the solenoid from damaging the electrical system.

ADLO Lockout

Another device that may be used within the starter control circuit is **automatic disengagement lockout (ADLO)**, like that illustrated in FIGURE 14-28. The ADLO circuit prevents the starter motor from operating if the engine is running. It does this by using a **frequency-sensing relay** connected to the alternator, which detects AC current only when the alternator is charging. The ADLO relay contacts are connected in series in the starter motor control circuit. If the engine is running, the relay prevents starter engagement and disengages the starter if the key switch is left engaged too long after the engine starts.

Voltage-Sensing Relay

Because starters can be damaged from low battery voltage, some companies find the solution is to prevent the starter from cranking when the battery voltage is too low. This also has the additional benefit of preventing prolonged cranking. The voltage-sensing relay, as illustrated in FIGURE 14-29, is connected in series to the solenoid control circuit. When the battery voltage drops below 7.2 volts while cranking, the voltage-sensing relay will typically open-circuit the starter relay circuit.

Series-Parallel Electrical Systems—Split Load

Series Parallel Electrical Systems, or spilt load as it is generally called, use two, four, or six 12-volt batteries connected in series through an equalizer to supply most of the vehicle's electrical systems. Buses and heavy equipment are common examples of vehicles using split loads for several reasons. Large engines with high starter torque requirements will use 24-volt starters. Other electrical devices using large amounts of power benefit from 24 volts, as their size and the gauge of electrical wire supplying current is smaller.

Conducting less amperage also means resistance in circuits is reduced, with less damage and loosening of electrical connections. On buses, the 24-volt supply powers the majority of the vehicle's electrical components, while on other vehicles, 12 volts may supply the exterior lighting or other 12-volt accessories. Batteries are recharged by a 24-volt alternator, and current is redistributed by a battery equalizer to ensure the batteries charge at an equal rate FIGURE 14-30.

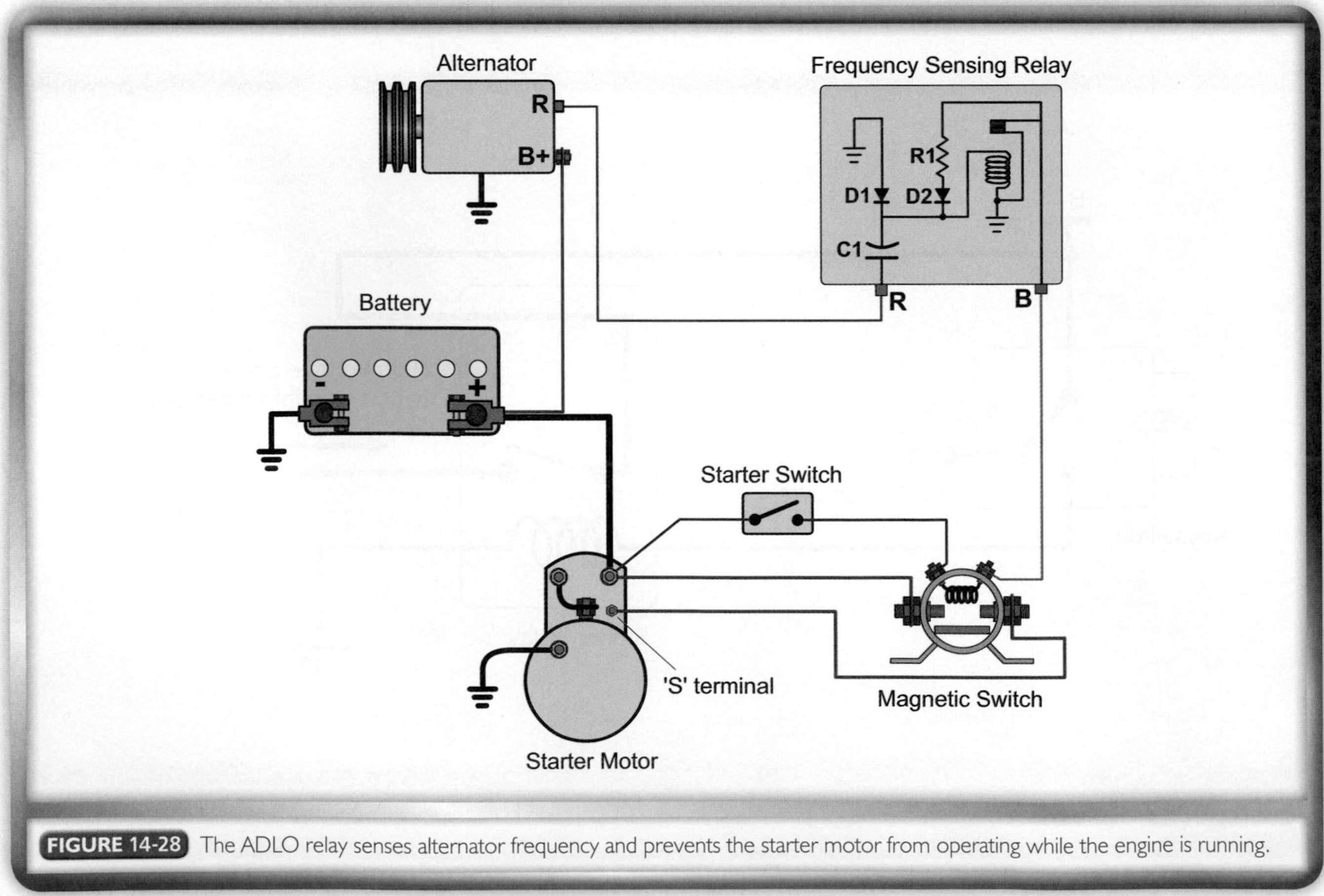

FIGURE 14-28 The ADLO relay senses alternator frequency and prevents the starter motor from operating while the engine is running.

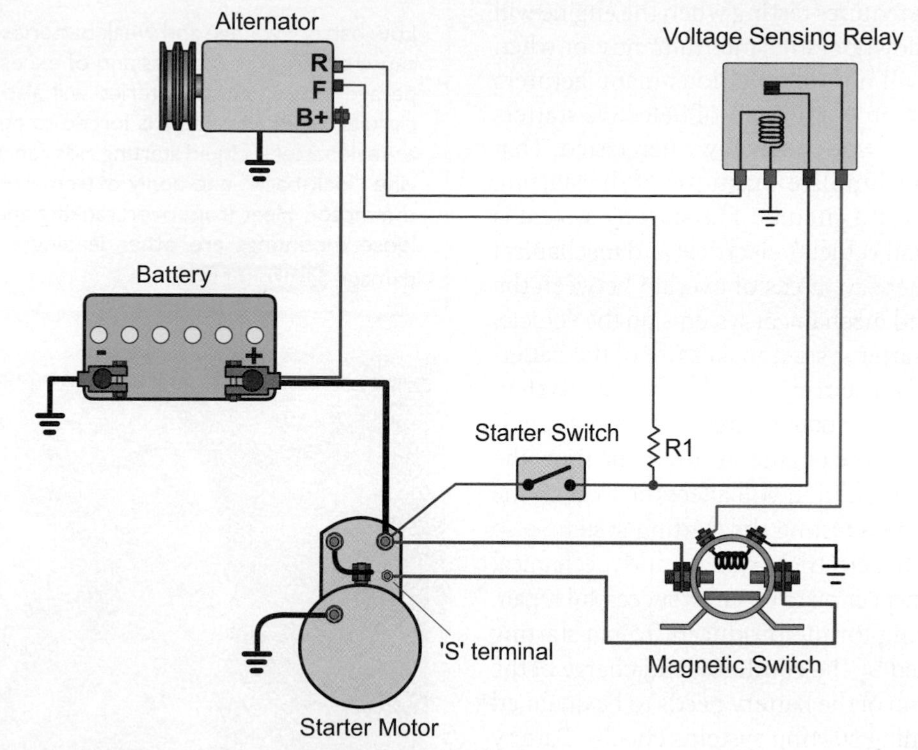

FIGURE 14-29 A low voltage-sensing relay can be connected in series with the starter control circuit to prevent the starter motor from operating if a low battery voltage condition occurs.

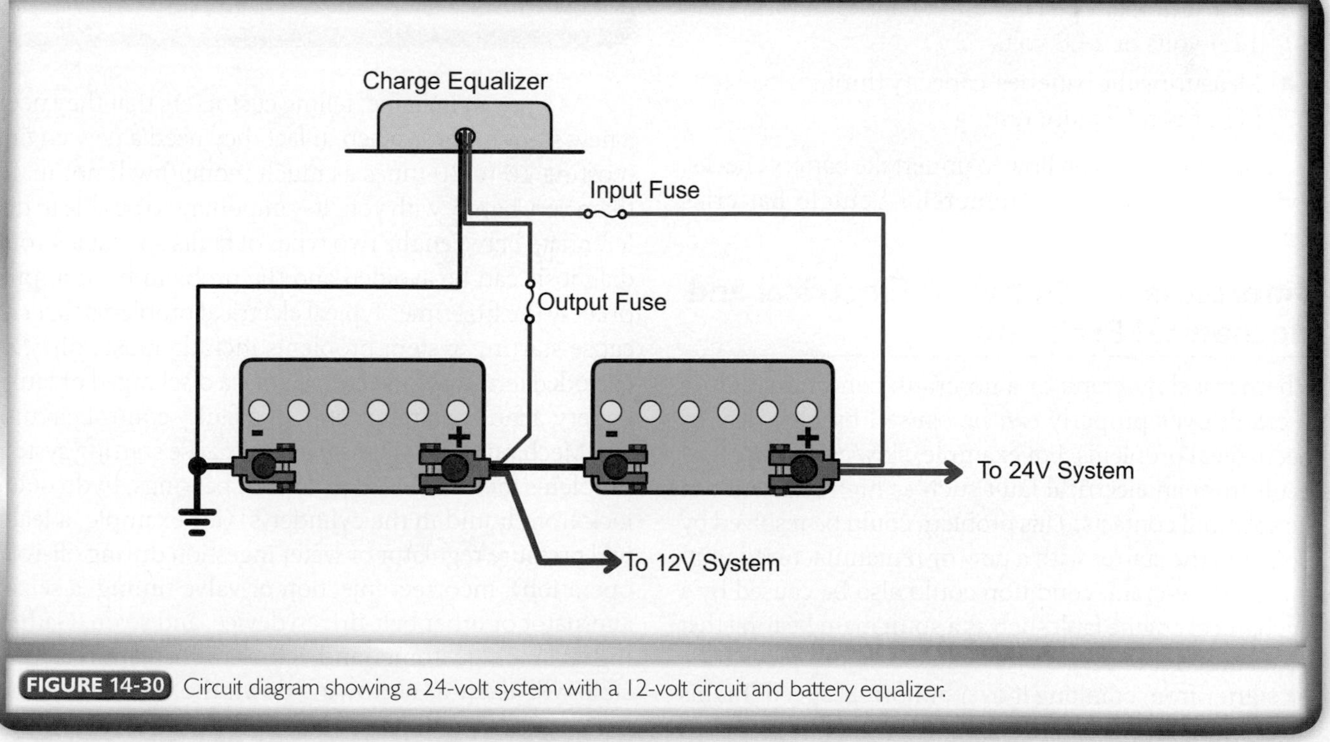

FIGURE 14-30 Circuit diagram showing a 24-volt system with a 12-volt circuit and battery equalizer.

Starting System Testing

The starting system requires testing when the engine will not crank, cranks slowly, cranks intermittently, or when the starter motor will not turn. Various manufacturers report that between 55% and 80% of defective starters returned for warranty work normally when tested. That points to poor or incomplete diagnosis of the starting and related systems and circuits. The starting system is just part of the overall vehicle's electrical and mechanical system. As such, there are areas of overlap between the various electrical and mechanical systems on the vehicle. For example, the starter system makes use of the batteries to supply power for starting, but the charging system needs to provide an adequate charge to ensure there is enough power to start the engine. At the same time, the engine's mechanical condition will affect the load on the starter motor. So, when testing the starting system, also bear in mind that other electrical systems and mechanical items may require inspection to ensure a successful repair.

Because cranking torque produced from a starting motor is also affected by the condition and charge of the battery, the condition of the battery needs to be qualified first before performing starting systems checks. Battery checks include:

- Verifying the battery voltage matches the voltage rating of the starter motor
- Ensuring that cranking amperage (CA or CCA) of the batteries meet or exceed OEM recommendations
- Verifying that the state of charge is not lower than 50% and that open circuit voltage is not less than 12.4 volts or 24.8 volts
- Measuring the batteries' capacity through load testing or conductance testing

For information on how to undertake battery checks, review the Servicing Commercial Vehicle Batteries chapter.

Differentiating Between Electrical and Mechanical Problems

Whether a slow-crank or a no-crank condition, failure to crank over properly can be caused by electrical or mechanical problems. For example, slow cranking could result from an electrical fault such as high resistance in the solenoid contacts. This problem could be resolved by replacing the starter with a new or remanufactured unit. But the slow-crank condition could also be caused by a mechanical engine fault such as a spun main bearing that is causing a lot of drag on the crankshaft and preventing the starter from cranking it over at normal speed. In this case, the entire engine will need to be rebuilt.

> **TECHNICIAN TIP**
>
> Low battery voltage and weak batteries are the primary cause of stress to starters and of excessive starter amperage draw. Faulty batteries will also stress charging circuits, as an alternator is forced to continually charge a weak battery. Liquid starting aids can also produce engine "kick-back" and apply extreme twisting forces to the motor. Heat from overcranking and vibration from loose mountings are other leading causes of starter damage FIGURE 14-31.

FIGURE 14-31 A burned solenoid contact disc caused by low available voltage.

As you can imagine, telling customers that they need a new starter motor when in fact they need a new engine (costing 10 to 20 times as much money) will not make them very happy with you. It is important to be able to differentiate between the two types of faults so that a wrong diagnosis can be avoided and the problem fixed appropriately the first time. Typical electrical problems that can cause starting system problems include loose, dirty, or corroded terminals and connectors, a discharged or faulty battery, a faulty starter motor, or a faulty control circuit.

Mechanical problems that may cause starting system problems include seized pistons or bearings, hydrostatic lock from liquid in the cylinder(s) (for example, a leaky fuel pressure regulator or water ingestion during off-road operation), incorrect injection or valve timing, a seized alternator or other belt-driven device, and so on. Gathering as much customer and vehicle information as possible will assist in narrowing down the options of what is causing the fault.

A slow-crank condition accompanied by a high draw could be due to a fault in the starter or to engine mechanical fault. If a mechanical fault is suspected, check the oil and coolant for signs of contamination. If the coolant and oil are mixing, suspect a head gasket or cracked head/block issue. If the oil and coolant are not contaminated, turn the engine over by hand to see if it is tight compared with a similar engine that is known to be good. If it is harder to turn than it should be, remove the accessory drive belt, spin each of the accessories, and try to turn the engine over again. If it is still hard to turn over, you will have to go deeper in your visual inspection and start disassembling components based on the information you have gathered along the way. For example, if the crankshaft cannot be turned a complete revolution, remove the injectors and see if liquid is ejected out of one or more cylinders. If so, the engine was hydrolocked and you will need to determine the cause. If no liquids are ejected, then you will need to disassemble the engine further until you determine the cause of the mechanical resistance.

The important thing to remember is that slow-crank and no-crank conditions can be caused by both electrical and mechanical faults, so do not jump to conclusions. You need to identify the root cause of the fault through tests so that you can advise the customer on what is needed to repair the vehicle.

Starter Motor Tests

The inspection and measurement procedures used to diagnose starting system complaints should be symptom based. That is, a flow chart should be used to begin a proper sequence of pinpoint checks recommended by the OEM. Symptoms include intermittent and no start, slow cranking, prolonged cranking, starter chatter, or starter noise. Any diagnostic procedure should begin with qualifying the condition of the batteries and inspecting all battery cables, grounds, and connections. Information on how to undertake battery checks can be found in the Servicing Commercial Vehicle Batteries chapter.

Faults within the starter motor may include:

- Worn brushes—Intermittent starter operation or starter operation that resumes after it is tapped with a hammer indicates brushes with poor commutator contact. Poor contact could be due to weak spring tension after a brush wears out. Poor brush contact with the commutator can also be caused by loss of brush spring tension due to heating from excessively high amperage flow—often due to prolonged cranking or low battery voltage. It can be evidenced by blued or even charred brush springs.
- Damaged field coils—Insulation can break down, causing shorts between coils or shorts to ground. This can be caused by age, by contaminants breaking down the insulation, or by excessive current flow. Excessive heat may also cause connections to be melted, creating additional resistance in the circuit.
- Damaged armature—An armature may have the commutator excessively worn or unevenly worn. The armature may also develop shorts between the windings, shorts to ground, and opens between windings and the commutator. A test instrument called a growler is used to test an armature.
- Worn bushings or bearings—Sintered brass bushings or, in some cases, bearings are used to suspend the armature in the starter case. Because motor efficiency is dependent on having the smallest clearance between the armature and field coils, any wear of bushing or bearings will cause contact between the armature and field coils. Worn bushing or bearings will cause excessive current draw that can be observed during a starter draw test.

Use TABLE 14-1 below to assist in diagnosing starting system problems. Always consult manufacturers' information before commencing any work.

The tests explained in the following sections include:

- Available voltage test
- Measuring starter current draw
- Measuring starter circuit voltage drop
- Inspecting and testing the starter control circuit
- Inspecting and testing relays and solenoids

Available Voltage Test

If the starting system complaint is slow cranking, the available voltage test is recommended. This test measures the amount of voltage at the starter battery positive cable and ground stud on the starter, if equipped. Minimum available voltage to the starter must not fall below 10.5 volts after three consecutive cranking periods of 30 seconds, with a 2-minute cooling period between each cranking period. If the voltage falls below 10.5 volts, the electrical system may not have adequate current to energize injectors or operate ECMs even though cranking speed is adequate.

To measure available voltage, first disable the engine from starting by removing a fuse for the ECM, disabling the shut-off solenoid, or alternative method. Then, connect a voltmeter between the starter ground stud and battery positive terminal on the solenoid. While cranking the engine, measure and record the amperage and voltage and evaluate the results.

TABLE 14-1: Starting System Diagnosis Chart

Concern	Possible Cause	Remedy
Engine cranks slowly, does not start	Discharged battery	Charge; test and replace if necessary
	Very low temperature	Allow battery to warm up; check circuits and battery
	Battery cables too small or poor connections	Install correct battery cables or clean and replace connections
	Defective starter motor	Test; repair or replace as needed
	Engine malfunction	Check engine for low oil or mechanical problems
Solenoid clicks, chatters	Loose or corroded battery terminals	Remove, clean, reinstall
	Battery discharged	Charge; test and replace if necessary
	Wiring problem inside solenoid	Replace solenoid
Lights stay bright, vehicle does not crank	Open circuit in starter	Disassemble and repair or replace starter
	Open circuit or high resistance in circuit	Check solenoid, relays, and neutral start switch or clutch switch; repair or replace if needed
	Open circuit in safety switch	Check; repair or replace switch
Lights dim greatly, vehicle does not crank	Discharged or malfunctioning battery	Charge and test battery; replace if necessary
	High resistance at battery connection	Clean and tighten terminal connections
	Loose or corroded battery terminals	Remove, clean, reinstall
	Very low temperature	Allow battery to warm up; check circuits and battery
	Pinion not engaging ring gear	Check for damaged parts and alignment of starter
	Solenoid engaged but not cranking	Check starter motor and connections
	Pinion jammed—starter and flywheel out of alignment	Check pinion and gear teeth
	Stuck armature in starter	Replace or repair starter
	Short in starter	Check engine for low oil or mechanical problem
	Engine malfunction	Charge and test battery; replace if necessary
Lights out, vehicle does not crank	Poor connection (probably at battery or earth)	Clean cable clamp and terminal; tighten clamp
	Open circuit	Clean and tighten connections; replace wiring if necessary
	Discharged or faulty battery	Charge and test battery; replace battery if necessary
Whine or siren sound just after starting	Overrunning clutch defective	Repair or replace as needed
	Solenoid plunger sticking	Repair or replace solenoid
	Weak return spring	Replace spring
	Damaged flywheel ring gear teeth	Remove and replace
	Pinion jammed, too tight – starter and flywheel out of alignment	Check pinion alignment with gear teeth; shim if necessary
Starter turns, engine does not	Pinion not engaging – starter and flywheel out of alignment	Check pinion alignment with gear teeth; shim if necessary
	Pinion slipping	Replace or repair starter
	Damaged flywheel ring gear teeth	Remove and replace
Pinion disengages slowly when engine starts	Solenoid plunger sticking	Repair or replace solenoid
	Overrunning clutch defective	Repair or replace as needed
	Weak return spring	Replace spring
	Pinion jammed, too tight – starter and flywheel out of alignment	Check pinion alignment with gear teeth; shim if necessary

Starter Current Draw Testing

Testing starter motor current draw is the best indicator of overall cranking system performance. Manufacturers will specify the current draw for starter motors, and any tests must be performed with a fully charged and correct capacity battery for the vehicle. Starter motors can be tested in two ways: on vehicle or off vehicle. The on-vehicle test is usually called a starter draw test, while the off-vehicle test is called a no-load test. Manufacturers will provide specifications for one or both of the tests.

If the starting system complaint is slow cranking, a starter draw and available voltage test is recommended using the following steps:

1. The engine is disabled from starting by removing a fuse for the ECM, disabling the shut-off solenoid or alternative method.
2. A voltmeter is connected between the starter ground stud and battery positive terminal on the solenoid.
3. An inductive type amp clamp is placed over the either battery cable to the starter.
4. While cranking, the amperage and voltage are measured and recorded.

Results are compared with the manufacturer's specifications found in a shop manual. Properly charged batteries with adequate capacity should not allow available voltage to fall below 10.5 volts during cranking FIGURE 14-32.

If cranking speed is low, and amperage measured is below normal but available voltage is high, the starting motor or starting circuit has high resistance. Worn brushes or loose or burnt internal connections could cause this condition.

If amperage drawn by the starting motor is high and available voltage low, the starter may be defective internally, the engine seizing or resistive, or the battery voltage low. Shorted field coils caused by the armature contacting the coils are a likely cause of an internal defect. Low available voltage to the starter may also be the cause. Undersized cables, loose connections, or a corroded and highly resistive connection will reduce available voltage to the starter, causing excessive amperage draw. Each electrical connection and cable in the starter circuit needs to be measured for voltage loss due to excessive resistance in this situation. Small resistances will become larger as amperage increases predicted by Joule's Heating Law. Resistive wire or connections will drop voltage and heat

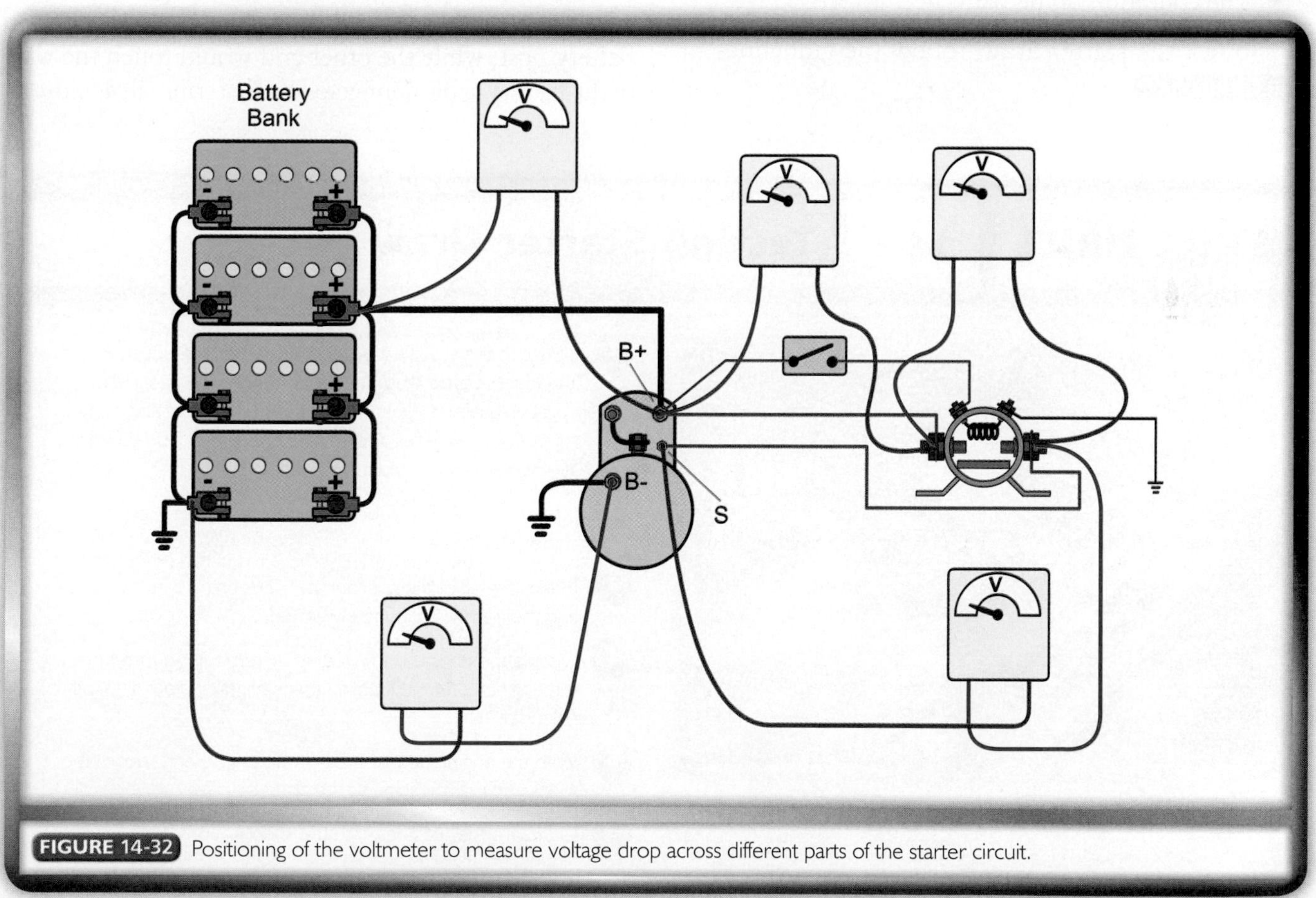

FIGURE 14-32 Positioning of the voltmeter to measure voltage drop across different parts of the starter circuit.

up at the same time. By using a carbon pile to load cables and circuits to 500 amps, voltage loss should not total more than 5% in a 12-volt circuit (0.5 volts), with no more than 2% loss in any single cable.

There is no "fixed" amount of amperage draw for each and every engine. However, no more than one amp per cubic inch of engine displacement should be observed. Manufactures will publish some guidelines for an engine or starter configuration. The amount of amperage will vary, however, due to the following reasons:

- Engine displacement—larger engines require more torque to turn and consequently more cranking amperage
- The compression ratio may change the amount of cranking torque
- The type of starter—direct drive or gear reduction will change the amount of amperage used
- Mechanical condition of engine—loose or tight due to varying mechanical conditions such as temperature, amount of lubrication, wear, bearing or piston seizure, ring condition, combustion chamber deposits, and so on
- The starter drive-to-flywheel ratio
- The condition of the battery

To test the starter draw, follow the guidelines in SKILL DRILL 14-1.

Testing Starter Circuit Voltage Drop

The electrical circuit of the starter motor consists of a high-current circuit and a control circuit. The high-current circuit consists of the battery, main battery cables to the starter motor solenoid, solenoid contacts, and heavy ground cables back to the battery from the engine and chassis. The control circuit activates the solenoid and can ECM controlled. Voltage drop can occur across both the high-current and control circuits.

A voltmeter is used to measure voltage drop across all parts of the circuit. A voltmeter with a minimum/maximum range setting is very useful when measuring voltage drop because it will record and hold the maximum voltage drop that occurs for a particular operation cycle. Small resistance and poor connections are magnified when high amperage passes through the circuit—resistances that will not be observable when low amperage current passes through a circuit.

Voltage drop is tested while the circuit is under load. The voltmeter is connected in parallel across the component or part of the circuit that is to be tested for voltage drop. This means the voltmeter would be connected on either side of a terminal connection or either end of a cable. For example, to measure the voltage drop across a battery terminal, one voltmeter lead would touch the battery post, while the other end would touch the wire of the battery cable connected to the terminal, as close as

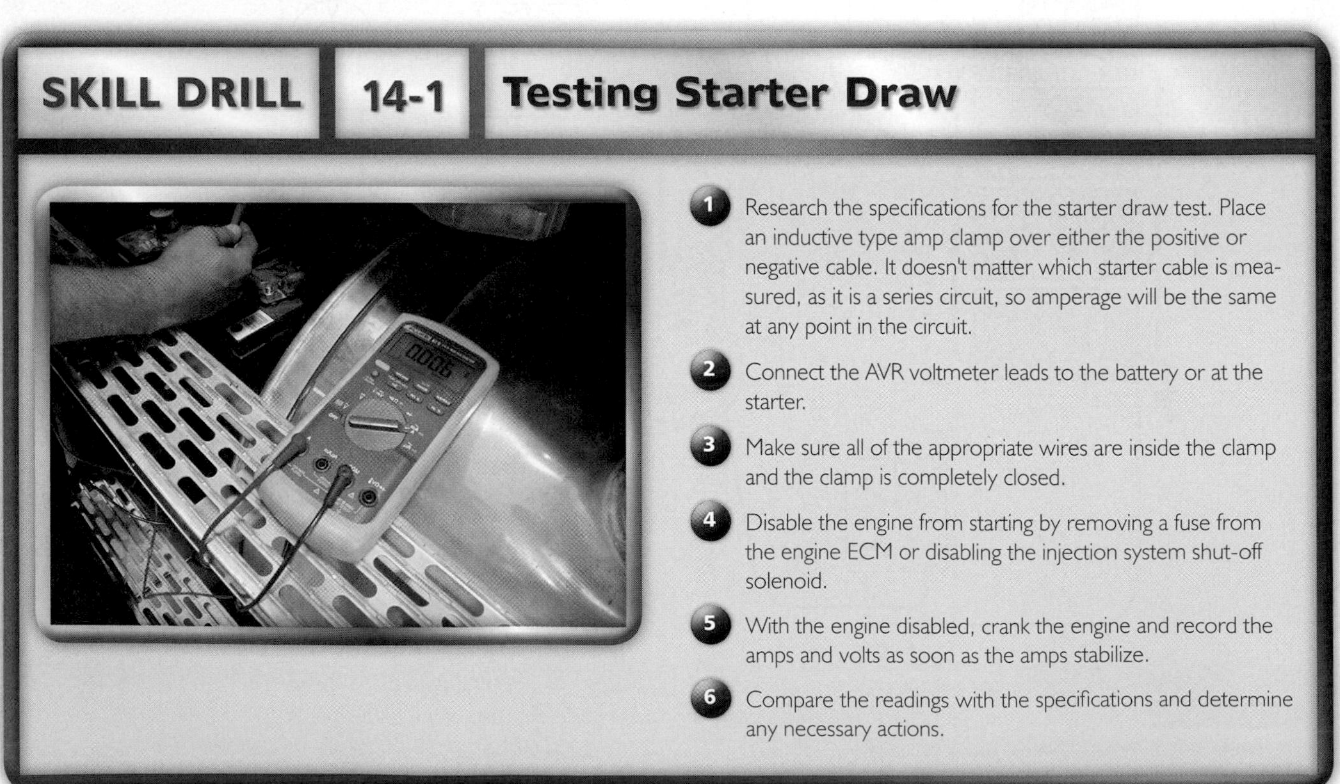

1. Research the specifications for the starter draw test. Place an inductive type amp clamp over either the positive or negative cable. It doesn't matter which starter cable is measured, as it is a series circuit, so amperage will be the same at any point in the circuit.
2. Connect the AVR voltmeter leads to the battery or at the starter.
3. Make sure all of the appropriate wires are inside the clamp and the clamp is completely closed.
4. Disable the engine from starting by removing a fuse from the engine ECM or disabling the injection system shut-off solenoid.
5. With the engine disabled, crank the engine and record the amps and volts as soon as the amps stabilize.
6. Compare the readings with the specifications and determine any necessary actions.

possible to the post. When the starter is cranked, or a load applied through a carbon pile load tester, any resistance will be observed as a voltage reading. A high voltage reading indicates excessive resistance. Similarly, a voltmeter with long leads can be connected to each end of a battery cable. When the starter is cranked, cable resistance is observed with a voltmeter reading. In both cases, the voltmeter is simply measuring the voltage or pressure differential between two points.

To test starter circuit voltage drop, follow the guidelines in SKILL DRILL 14-2.

> **TECHNICIAN TIP**
>
> A faulty battery will affect voltage drop tests, so always ensure that the battery is fully charged and in good condition before performing tests.

Inspecting and Testing the Starter Control Circuit

The starter control circuit activates the starter solenoid, and the starter solenoid activates the starter motor. If there is a problem in the starter control circuit, the vehicle will likely not crank over at all, or maybe intermittently. The control circuit is made up of the battery, ignition switch, neutral safety switch (automatic vehicles), clutch switch (manual vehicles), starter relay, and solenoid windings. If the starter is controlled by the ECM, then you must be aware of all of the circuits, such as the immobilizer circuit and the ECM itself.

To inspect and test the starter control circuit, follow the guidelines in SKILL DRILL 14-3.

> **TECHNICIAN TIP**
>
> The starter relay bypass test is a quick method of determining if the relay is operational. This test should be performed when the starter motor does not crank when the ignition is in the start position (or when the starter button is depressed). Connect a jumper wire between the battery and starter terminal on the relay. This connection bypasses the control circuit of the relay, so the engine should crank. If the engine cranks with the jumper installed, check to see whether current is supplied to the relay when the ignition key or starter button is in the crank position. If current is available to the relay, check the ground supplying the control circuit to determine whether it is properly connected or resistive. If the control circuit is properly energized, and the starter cranks when the jumper wire is used, the starter relay is defective. If the starter motor still does not crank, check the cables and other circuits to the starter.

Inspecting and Testing Relays and Solenoids

The starting system typically contains solenoids and relays that activate the control circuit. The solenoid is mounted on the starter motor, while one or more of the starter circuit relays are found on the starter, or firewall.

SKILL DRILL 14-2 Testing Starter Circuit Voltage Drop

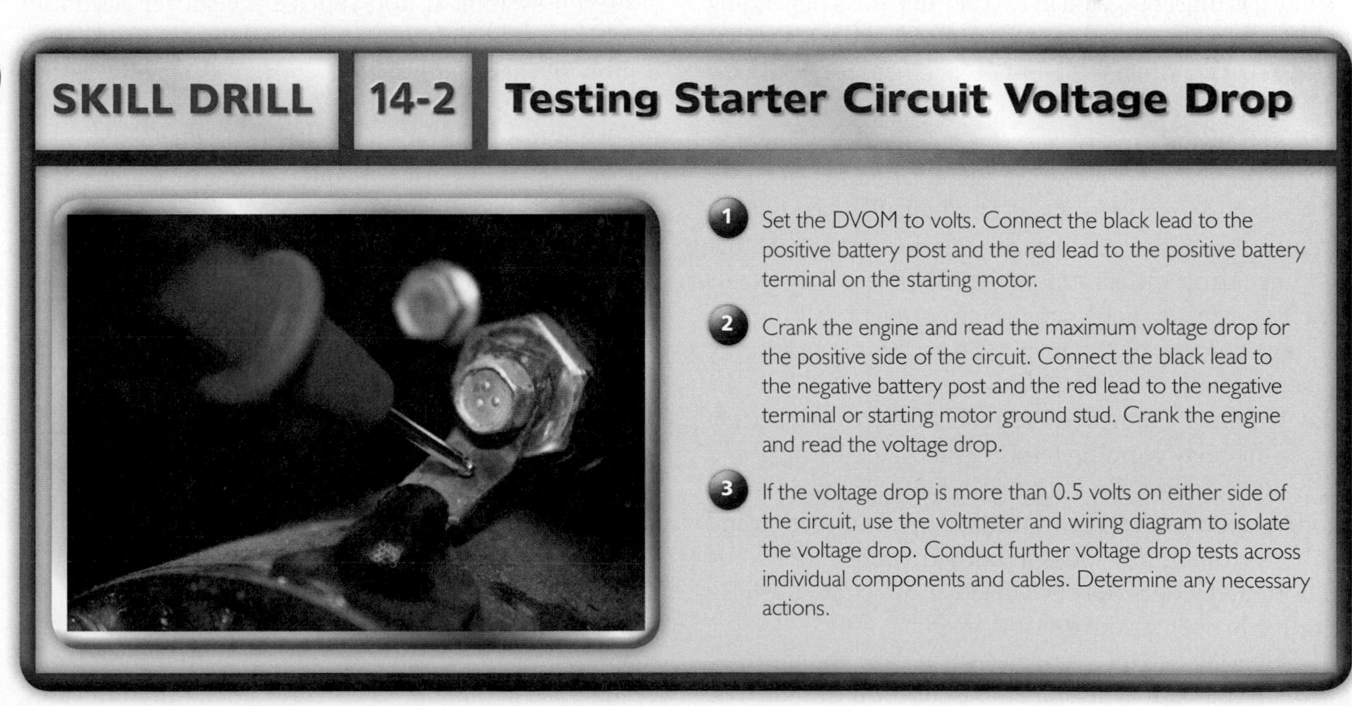

1. Set the DVOM to volts. Connect the black lead to the positive battery post and the red lead to the positive battery terminal on the starting motor.
2. Crank the engine and read the maximum voltage drop for the positive side of the circuit. Connect the black lead to the negative battery post and the red lead to the negative terminal or starting motor ground stud. Crank the engine and read the voltage drop.
3. If the voltage drop is more than 0.5 volts on either side of the circuit, use the voltmeter and wiring diagram to isolate the voltage drop. Conduct further voltage drop tests across individual components and cables. Determine any necessary actions.

SKILL DRILL 14-3 Inspecting and Testing the Starter Control Circuit

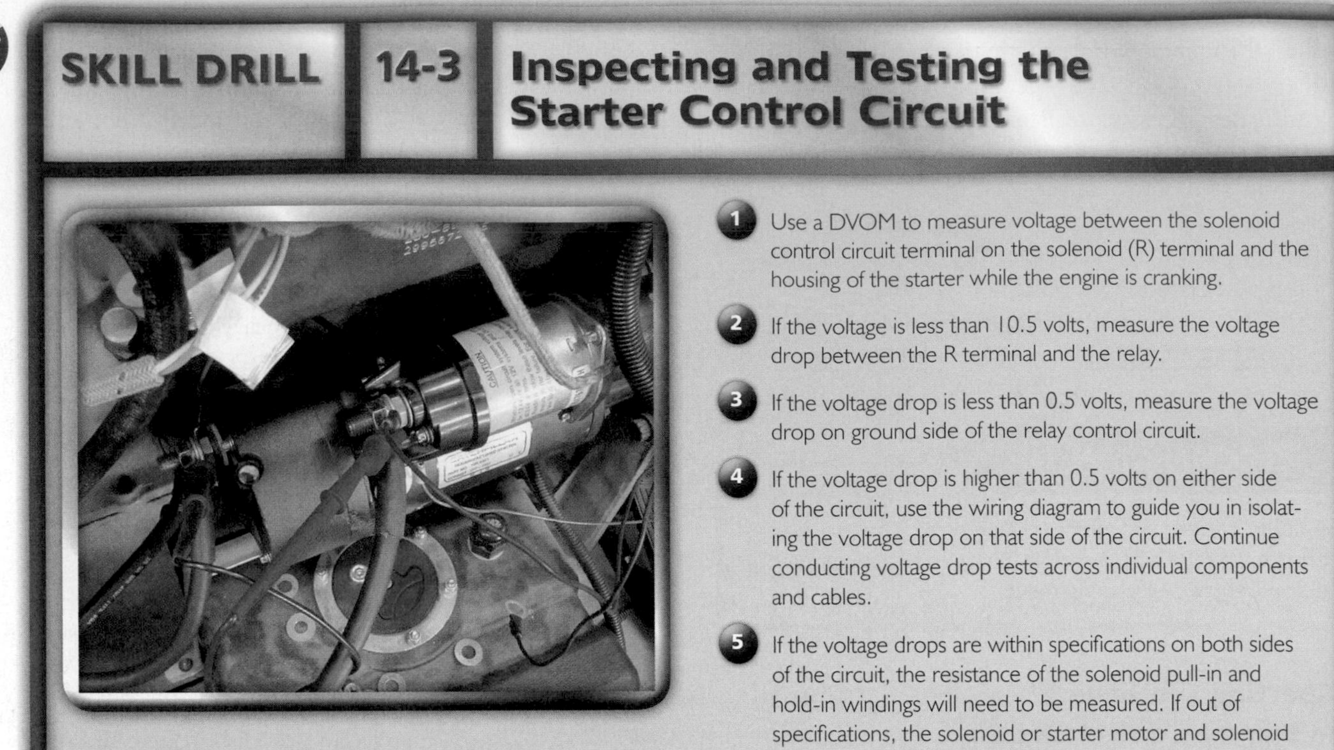

1. Use a DVOM to measure voltage between the solenoid control circuit terminal on the solenoid (R) terminal and the housing of the starter while the engine is cranking.
2. If the voltage is less than 10.5 volts, measure the voltage drop between the R terminal and the relay.
3. If the voltage drop is less than 0.5 volts, measure the voltage drop on ground side of the relay control circuit.
4. If the voltage drop is higher than 0.5 volts on either side of the circuit, use the wiring diagram to guide you in isolating the voltage drop on that side of the circuit. Continue conducting voltage drop tests across individual components and cables.
5. If the voltage drops are within specifications on both sides of the circuit, the resistance of the solenoid pull-in and hold-in windings will need to be measured. If out of specifications, the solenoid or starter motor and solenoid will need to be replaced.

Before performing any tests, ensure that the vehicle battery is charged and in good condition. The manufacturer's wiring diagrams should be checked to determine the circuit operation, identification, and location of all components in the starter circuit.

Relays must be tested in two or three ways depending on the relay. The simplest test is to measure the resistance of the relay winding. If it is out of specifications, the relay will need to be replaced. If it is OK, the contacts will need to be tested for an excessive voltage drop. The best way to do this is by using an adapter that fits between the relay and the relay socket. This will allow the normal circuit current flow to flow through the contacts so that a voltage drop measurement can be taken. Any excessive voltage drop across the relay contacts will require the replacement of the relay. The last test is used only on relays with a suppression diode in parallel with the relay winding. Connect a reasonably fresh 9-volt battery across the relay winding terminals in one direction, and then switch polarity by turning the battery around. If the diode is good, the relay should click in one direction and not in the other. If it clicks in both directions, the diode is shorted. If it does not click in either direction, the relay winding is open or the diode is open.

Solenoids are tested by measuring the voltage drop between the battery terminal and motor terminal. The first test to perform is a voltage drop test across the solenoid contacts. Place the red lead on the solenoid B-positive input and the black lead on the solenoid B-positive output. The voltage drop should be less than 0.5 volts for a 12-volt system and less than 1.0 volts for a 24-volt system. If not, replace the starter assembly. Testing of the solenoid winding requires partial disassembly of the solenoid. Therefore, it is usually best to disconnect the control circuit connector from the solenoid and use a jumper wire to activate the solenoid. If the solenoid and starter operate, there is probably a fault in the vehicle's control circuit that needs further testing. If the solenoid or starter does not work (and the circuit is grounded), then the starter is likely faulty and will need to be replaced.

To inspect and test relays and solenoids, follow the guidelines in SKILL DRILL 14-4.

Removing and Replacing a Starter, and Inspecting the Ring Gear or Flex Plate

The starter motor will need to be removed to check for on-bench testing, poor drive engagement, or starter motor overhaul or replacement. The starter motor may be mounted in difficult-to-access locations. In some cases,

SKILL DRILL 14-4 Inspecting and Testing Relays and Solenoids

1. To test a relay, measure the resistance of the relay winding and compare with specifications. If the relay is out of specifications, replace it.
2. Use a relay adapter to mount the relay on top of the relay socket so you can check the control circuit wiring and perform voltage drop tests on the contacts.
3. Activate the relay while measuring the voltage across the relay winding. If it is near battery voltage, the control circuit wiring is OK.
4. Measure the voltage across the contacts with the relay not activated. This should read near battery voltage if both sides of the switched circuit are OK. If not, perform voltage drop tests on each side of the switch circuit.
5. Activate the relay while measuring the voltage drop across the contacts. If it is more than 0.5 volts, the relay will need to be replaced.
6. To test a starter solenoid, measure the voltage drop across the solenoid contact terminals with the key in the crank position. If it is more than 0.5 volts, replace the solenoid or starter assembly.
7. If the solenoid does not click with the key in the crank position, remove the electrical connection for the control circuit at the solenoid.
8. Use a jumper wire to apply battery voltage to the control circuit terminal on the solenoid and see if the solenoid clicks. If it does, then there is likely a fault in the control circuit wiring. If the solenoid still does not click (and the circuit is grounded), then the solenoid windings or starter brushes are likely worn (sometimes tapping on the starter while the key is turned to the crank position will free up the brushes enough that the pull-in winding can operate). Determine any necessary actions.

other vehicle parts may need to be removed before the starter itself can be removed. Access to both the topside and underside of the vehicle may be required to remove mounting bolts. It may also be necessary to have another technician assist you to remove the heavy starter motor from vehicle.

To remove and replace a starter motor and inspect the ring gear or flex plate, follow the guidelines in SKILL DRILL 14-5.

Overhauling a Starter Motor

Overhauling a starter motor requires the disassembly and checking of all component parts. The starter motor component parts should also be cleaned and replaced or repaired and lubricated as necessary. Always mark the position of the housings in relation to each other before commencing disassembly. This ensures that the housings are correctly aligned when reassembled. Each starter motor is unique and may require slightly different disassembly and overhaul procedures. Always consult the manufacturer's procedures for the specific starter motor on which you are working.

Note that the assembly procedure is the reverse of disassembly. When assembling, be sure to correctly lubricate all lubrication points. Check the manufacturer's procedure for the lubrication points and type of lubricant.

Once the starter motor has been disassembled into its component parts, conduct the following tests for each component as follows:

- Solenoid:
  - Test the resistance and current draw of the pull-in and hold-in windings.
  - Check for the free movement of the iron core.
  - Check contacts and terminal end cap for wear and cracks. Make replacements if necessary.
- Drive and yoke:
  - Visually inspect the drive engagement yoke for wear and damage. Replace if there is excessive wear.

SKILL DRILL 14-5 Removing and Replacing a Starter Motor and Inspecting the Ring Gear or Flex Plate

1. Locate and follow the appropriate procedure in the service manual.
2. Disconnect the battery ground and electrical connections to the starter motor.
3. Loosen the mounting bolts, leaving them in place until you are ready to remove the starter motor.
4. Remove the starter motor by supporting its weight while the mounting bolts are removed. You may need assistance to support the weight of the starter while this step is being conducted.
5. Examine the starter drive for any wear to the drive teeth.
6. Using a work light, inspect the ring gear or flex plate teeth for damage. Slowly turn the engine over while checking the ring gear or flex plate, ensuring the circumference is inspected. In difficult-to-see locations, an engine borescope may provide assistance. Report and report any damage to the ring gear.
7. Reinstall the starter motor by reversing the steps used in steps 1 through 4 above.

- Check the drive clutch for slippage. If there is excessive slippage, replace the drive.

- Brushes:
  - Check the length of the brushes with the manufacturer's specifications and replace if necessary.
  - Check the brush springs for tension, brush movement in the brush holder, and the insulation of the brush holder.
- Field windings:
  - Visually check the insulation for cracks or damage. Check for short circuits through the field insulation and case by connecting a 110-volt test lamp between the field coil and case. If the lamp lights, there is a short circuit. If the field insulation fails, the field will need to be replaced or reinsulated.
- Armature:
  - Check the armature on a growler for shorts between windings. Using a thin metal strip, rotate the armature. A vibrating strip means the armature is shorted and requires replacement. However, before condemning it, check to ensure there are no shorts between the commutator segments. Retest if you find any.
  - Also check the armature insulation to ground using an insulation tester or the insulation tester fitted to the growler. Use an insulation test no higher than 110 volts for a 12- or 24-volt armature. Note that to pass an insulation test, the armature needs to be dry and free of contaminants.
  - If the armature fails either test, it must be replaced.
  - Machine the commutator in a lathe if it is worn.
  - Check the armature shaft for wear or damage to the bearing surfaces. Also check the drive splines for wear or damage. Check the laminations for damage. Check the shaft to ensure it is not bent. Check the windings to ensure they are not damaged or bent. Any damage to the above items will mean the armature needs to be replaced.
- Housings:
  - Check the housings for damage or wear. Replace if they are cracked or broken.

- Bushes:
  - Check the bushings for wear using the armature bearing surfaces. Replace the bushings if they are worn.
  - When replacing bushings, use soft bush drifts to drive or press the bushes into and out of the housing.
  - Oil-sintered bushings before fitting them into housing.
  - Some bushings may require machining to size once they are fitted into the housing.

Once the starter motor has been overhauled, it should be tested on a starter test bench with a full load if possible. If a full load test is not possible, conduct a no-load bench test as per the procedure in this chapter. To overhaul a starter motor, follow the guidelines in SKILL DRILL 14-6.

Engine and Starter Rotation

When observing engine rotation, many technicians often note the front engine pulley/harmonic balancer turns clockwise. However, not all engines are mounted in-line with the driveline (e.g., "V" drives). Some engines are mounted sideways in a vehicle and some are mounted at the rear and sideways. Since there is an abundance of configurations including engines in heavy-duty stationary applications, the SAE references engine rotation from the flywheel end of the engine. Most automotive engines are LEFT-HAND or CCW counter clockwise rotation.

The location and position of the starter on the engine can determine which direction the engine is cranked. Starter drive mechanism and the cut of the teeth will be changed along with helix features of the armature that may move the drive.

SKILL DRILL 14-6 Overhauling a Starter Motor

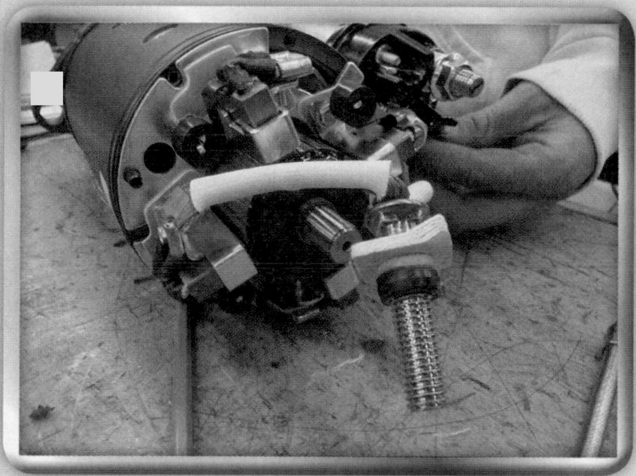

1. Locate and follow the appropriate procedure in the service manual.
2. Remove the solenoid and the yoke securing pin.
3. Remove the bearing end cap and circlip from the brush end of the starter motor if it is fitted.
4. Remove the through bolts holding the starter motor together.
5. Prize the starter motor apart while checking for any remaining screws or bolts.
6. Remove the brushes from the brush holder if necessary.
7. Slide the armature out of the main casing.
8. Remove the drive circlip and remove the drive assembly.
9. Clean, test, and inspect all component parts. Use specialized testers where necessary; for example, growler to test the armature, insulation tester to test fields and armature, and DVOM to check resistances of solenoid windings.
10. Replace any faulty components. You may need to arrange for the commutator to be machined to make it true.
11. Remove and replace the bushings into the end housing. Ensure bushes are pre-oiled if they are the sintered type. Bushings will need to be driven or pressed out and in using a bushings drift.
12. If the brushes require replacement, disconnect or de-solder them, and replace them.
13. Reassemble the drive to the armature, ensuring it is appropriately lubricated.
14. Reassemble the armature into the main case and locate the brushes. At this stage, the drive yoke and securing pin may need to be fitted. In some cases, the securing pin is not fitted until after the armature is in place.
15. Assemble the main case and end housing securing with the through bolts.
16. Reassemble the solenoid, its connections, and the brush end armature circlip. Ensure the appropriate lubrication if fitted.
17. Check to ensure that all components are fitted and the drive and armature are free to move.
18. Test the starter motor in the test bench.
19. Clean the work area and return tools and materials to proper storage.

Wrap-up

Ready for Review

- The starting system provides a method of rotating (cranking) the vehicle's engine to begin the combustion cycle.
- Diesel engines require large starter current draw, so several batteries are often connected in parallel of series to increase available cranking amperage or voltage.
- New designs of starter motors and systems controls are enabling starters to last longer and increase output torque while substantially reducing motor weight.
- There are three major categories of electric starters used in heavy vehicles: direct drive, reduction, and planetary gear reduction.
- The three most common types of DC motors found in commercial vehicles are series, shunt, and compound motors.
- Series motors are called "series" because the current pathway through various components inside the motor is in series. Because it is a series circuit, any unwanted resistance inside the motor, whether it is a burnt contact or loose brush, will reduce current flow throughout the entire motor circuit.
- Series wound motors also are self-limiting in speed due to the development of a counter-electromotive force (CEMF) that induces current in the opposite direction of battery current through the motor.
- Cranking an engine with low battery voltage is destructive to a starter motor.
- Regardless of the motor design, a starter motor consists of housing, fields, an armature, a commutator, brushes, end frames, and a solenoid-operated shift mechanism.
- Some starter motors are equipped with overcrank protection thermostats that will open the relay circuit and interrupt the current to the solenoid if prolonged cranking causes the motor temperature to exceed a safe threshold.
- Another protection device for the starter control circuit is the automatic disengagement lockout, which prevents the starter motor from operating if the engine is running.
- Dual-voltage systems allow the vehicle to be started on 24 volts for improved electrical efficiency, while the other electrical loads operate on the more common 12 volts.
- The starting system is just part of the overall vehicle's electrical and mechanical system. As such, there are areas of overlap between the various electrical and mechanical systems on the vehicle.
- Whether a slow-crank or a no-crank condition, failure to crank over properly can be caused by electrical or mechanical problems. It is important to be able to differentiate between the two types of faults so that a wrong diagnosis can be avoided and the problem fixed appropriately the first time.

Vocabulary Builder

armature The only rotating component of the starter; has three main components: the shaft, windings, and the commutator.

automatic disengagement lockout (ADLO) A device that prevents the starter motor from operating if the engine is running.

counter-electromotive force (CEMF) An electromagnetic force produced by the spinning magnetic field of the armature, which induces current in the opposite direction of battery current through the motor.

direct drive A starter motor drive system in which the motor armature directly engages the flywheel through a pinion gear.

frequency-sensing relay A relay connected to the alternator that detects alternating current only when the alternator is charging.

low-voltage burn-out A damaging condition for starter motors in which excess current flows through the starter, causing the motor to burn out prematurely.

overcrank protection (OCP) thermostat A thermostat that monitors the temperature of the motor and opens a relay circuit to interrupt the current to the solenoid if prolonged cranking causes the motor temperature to exceed a safe threshold.

planetary gear reduction drive A type of gear reduction system in which a planetary gear set reduces the starter profile to multiply motor torque to the pinion gear.

reduction gear drive A starter motor drive system in which the motor multiplies torque to the starter pinion gear by using an extra gear between the armature and the starter drive mechanism.

Review Questions

1. Which of the following statements about the starting/cranking system is correct?
   a. On ECM starting systems, the ECM controls the operation of a relay to energize the starter circuit.
   b. Data supplied by other onboard network modules, along with control algorithms in the module, determine when and for how long the starter will crank.
   c. A control circuit determines when and if the cranking circuit will function.
   d. All of the choices are correct.
2. In diesel engines, what is the most common ratio between the flywheel ring gear and pinion gear?
   a. 10:1
   b. 15:1
   c. 17:1
   d. 20:1
3. What is the minimum life expectancy for a modern starter?
   a. 2 years with 4,000 start cycles
   b. 3 years with 5,000 start cycles
   c. 4 years with 7,000 start cycles
   d. 5 years with 9,000 start cycles
4. Which of the following common electric motors develop the highest torque and are used as starter motors?
   a. Stepper
   b. Compound
   c. Shunt (parallel wound)
   d. Series
5. Which of the following statements concerning current flow for a series motor is correct?
   a. Current passes through the armature via the commutator and leaves through the second brush connected to the field winding.
   b. A magnetic field is created in the armature.
   c. Current passes through the windings of the field coils.
   d. All of the choices are correct.
6. Which of the following is NOT a component of a starter?
   a. Field coils
   b. Rotor
   c. End frames
   d. A solenoid-operated shift mechanism
7. Which of the following is NOT a main component of the armature?
   a. Shaft
   b. Body
   c. Windings
   d. Commutator
8. Which of the following statements about the commutator is correct?
   a. The commutator assembly presses onto the armature shaft.
   b. The commutator is made up of heavy copper segments separated from each other and the armature shaft by insulation.
   c. The commutator segments connect to the ends of the armature windings.
   d. All of the choices are correct.
9. Which of the following statements about starter control circuits is correct?
   a. In its most basic form, the starter control circuit has an ignition switch directly controlling the starter solenoid to operate the starter motor.
   b. In modern heavy vehicles, the circuits are more complex, as relays and control circuits, such as transmission neutral and clutch switches, are added to improve reliability and the safety of vehicles.
   c. The latest models of vehicles use an electrical system control module, which interfaces with the on-board vehicle network that receives data from various sensors, and various sensors to control the operation of the starter control circuit.
   d. All of the choices are correct.
10. A possible cause of a solenoid clicking and chattering is:
    a. loose or corroded battery terminals.
    b. short in the starter.
    c. an open circuit.
    d. a slipping pinion.

ASE-Type Questions

1. Technician A says that dozens of electric motors are found in heavy vehicles operating a variety of devices from electric seats, fuel and coolant pumps, fan blower motors, and even instrument gauges. Technician B says that the largest of all these electric motors is the starter motor. Who is correct?
   a. Technician A
   b. Technician B
   c. Both Technician A and Technician B
   d. Neither Technician A nor Technician B
2. Technician A says that all electric motors operate using principles of magnetic attraction and repulsion. Technician B says that, because like magnetic poles attract one another and unlike poles repel, it is possible to arrange magnetic poles within the motor to be continuously in a state of repulsion and attraction. Who is correct?
   a. Technician A
   b. Technician B
   c. Both Technician A and Technician B
   d. Neither Technician A nor Technician B
3. Technician A says that the series and shunt motor are the two most common types of motor found in the automotive industry. Technician B says that series motors are called "series" because the field and armature windings are connected in series. Who is correct?
   a. Technician A
   b. Technician B
   c. Both Technician A and Technician B
   d. Neither Technician A nor Technician B
4. Technician A says that series-wound motors also are self-limiting in speed due to the development of a counter-electromotive force (CEMF). Technician B says that CEMF is produced by the spinning magnetic field of the armature, which induces current in the same direction of battery current through the motor. Who is correct?
   a. Technician A
   b. Technician B
   c. Both Technician A and Technician B
   d. Neither Technician A nor Technician B
5. Technician A says that cranking an engine with low battery voltage causes one of the most damaging conditions for a starter. Technician B says that low-voltage burn-out occurs when excess amperage flows through the starter, causing the motor to burn out prematurely. Who is correct?
   a. Technician A
   b. Technician B
   c. Both Technician A and Technician B
   d. Neither Technician A nor Technician B
6. Technician A says that the starter housing, or frame, encloses and supports the internal starter components, protecting them and intensifying the magnetic fields produced in the field coils. Technician B says that in the starter housing field coils and their pole shoes are securely attached to the inside of the iron housing. Who is correct?
   a. Technician A
   b. Technician B
   c. Both Technician A and Technician B
   d. Neither Technician A nor Technician B
7. Technician A says that different from the thin wire used in shunt motors, armature windings are made of heavy, flat, copper strips that can handle the heavy current flow of the series motor. Technician B says that in a four-brush motor, each half of a coil is wound at 60 degrees to each other. Who is correct?
   a. Technician A
   b. Technician B
   c. Both Technician A and Technician B
   d. Neither Technician A nor Technician B
8. Technician A says that the solenoid on the starter motor generates the high current flow required by the starter motor on and off. Technician B says that the solenoid on the starter motor engages the starter drive with the pinion gear. Who is correct?
   a. Technician A
   b. Technician B
   c. Both Technician A and Technician B
   d. Neither Technician A nor Technician B
9. Technician A says that the starter drive transmits the rotational force from the starter armature to the engine via the ring gear that is mounted on the engine flywheel or torque converter. Technician B says that in the past gear reduction starters were used but that today, direct-drive starters have replaced them. Who is correct?
   a. Technician A
   b. Technician B
   c. Both Technician A and Technician B
   d. Neither Technician A nor Technician B
10. Technician A says that some starter motors are equipped with an over-crank protection (OCP) thermostat. Technician B says that the thermostat monitors the temperature of the motor. Who is correct?
    a. Technician A
    b. Technician B
    c. Both Technician A and Technician B
    d. Neither Technician A nor Technician B

CHAPTER 15

NATEF Tasks

Electrical/Electronic Systems

Charging System Diagnosis and Repair

Task	Page
■ Test instrument panel mounted volt meters and/or indicator lamps; determine needed action.	447–449
■ Identify causes of no charge, low charge, or overcharge problems; determine needed action.	449–451
■ Inspect and replace alternator drive belts, pulleys, fans, tensioners, and mounting brackets; adjust drive belts and check alignment.	450
■ Perform charging system voltage and amperage output tests; perform AC ripple test; determine needed action.	450–451
■ Perform charging circuit voltage drop tests; determine needed action.	452
■ Remove and replace alternator.	453–454
■ Inspect, repair, or replace cables, wires, and connectors in the charging circuit.	453

Charging Systems

Knowledge Objectives

After reading this chapter, you will be able to:

1. Identify and explain principles of electromagnetic induction. (pp 432–433)
2. Describe principles of current rectification. (pp 437–441)
3. Describe the operation of voltage regulators. (pp 441–444)
4. Describe techniques for electrical balancing of multiple alternators. (pp 446–449)
5. Identify and explain recommended procedures for diagnosing charging system complaints. (pp 449–453)
6. Identify tools and test instruments for evaluating charging systems. (pp 449–454)

Skills Objectives

After reading this chapter, you will be able to:

1. Replace a serpentine belt. (p 450) SKILL DRILL 15-1
2. Perform a charging system output test. (p 451) SKILL DRILL 15-2
3. Test charge a circuit voltage drop. (p 452) SKILL DRILL 15-3
4. Inspect, repair, or replace connectors and wires of charging circuits. (p 453) SKILL DRILL 15-4
5. Remove, inspect, and replace an alternator. (p 454) SKILL DRILL 15-5
6. Overhaul an alternator. (p 455) SKILL DRILL 15-6

Introduction

Compared with older heavy vehicles, modern heavy-duty vehicles are increasingly dependent on electronic and electrical systems that require a constant and reliable supply of electrical power. As heavy-duty vehicles become more sophisticated and add more comfort and convenience items, alternators are working harder than ever to meet the demands of the electrical system. For example, years ago, a DC generator supplying 8 to 45 amps of current was all that was needed to operate lights, wipers, and horn and to charge the batteries. Today, the average 12-volt electrical system loads for a late model highway tractor add up to 150 amps at peak with an 84-amp average. School buses have a 102-amp average load, and highway coaches will use as much as 160 amps at 24 volts just to power the heating, ventilation, and air conditioning system. It is now normal for vehicles to use 200- to 300-amp alternators, like that in FIGURE 15-1, to supply adequate electrical system amperage at idle and charge depleted batteries. Lighting, electronic powertrain controls, power accessories, communication, telematic systems, and many smaller electrical accessories add to the load carried by contemporary alternators.

FIGURE 15-1 A typical heavy-vehicle alternator.

Both DC generators and alternators produce electricity by relative movement of conductors in a magnetic field. That movement induces an electrical potential or voltage within the conductors. The key difference between an alternator and a DC generator is which component rotates or moves to generate electricity. In the DC generator, the conductors that generate power rotate as part of the armature, and the armature rotates within a magnetic field created by the stationary pole shoes. In the alternator, the magnetic field is created by the rotor, which rotates within the stationary stator windings to generate electricity there. In both cases, there is relative movement between the magnetic field and the conductors.

You Are the Technician

There is a bus that has had numerous service calls for jump-starting because the batteries often go dead. Service calls are taking place almost every day, causing a high level of aggravation to the customer and the service center where you work. On previous occasions, the batteries have been replaced. In addition, the charging system output has been measured and found to be OK. Furthermore, the presence of parasitic draws has been checked, and none were found.

The bus drivers have often been blamed for the problems, assuming that they have left lights or other accessories on, draining the battery. Out of frustration, the service manager has asked you to accompany the bus driver for a day to find out when the bus batteries drain and whether electrical loads are left on. After the bus has stopped for a 45-minute break, you find the batteries are dead. Checking the alternator, you discover that the back of the alternator where the rectifier bridge is located has become excessively hot to touch. Finally, the cause has been found. Before explaining the fault to the customer, you'll need to have answers to the following questions.

1. Why has the rectifier bridge of the alternator become hot to touch while the engine was shut down?
2. During previous checks of the charging system, what inspection procedure would have identified that fault?
3. What component has failed in the rectifier bridge? Be specific.

Alternator Functions

The charging system provides electrical energy for all of the electrical components on the vehicle. The main parts of the charging system, as illustrated in FIGURE 15-2, include the battery, the alternator, the voltage regulator (which may be integrated into the alternator), a charge warning light or voltmeter, and wiring that completes the circuits.

The battery stores an electrical charge in chemical form, acts as an electrical dampening device for variations in voltage or voltage spikes, and provides the electrical energy for cranking the engine. Once the engine is running, the alternator—which is connected to the engine and driven by a drive belt—converts some of the mechanical energy of the engine into electrical energy to supply energy to all the electrical components of the vehicle. The alternator also charges the battery to replace the energy used to start the engine. The voltage regulator circuit maintains optimal battery state of charge by sensing and maintaining a required charging system output voltage.

Older vehicles have separate (discrete) regulators mounted on the firewall. The next generation of charging systems included regulators that were incorporated inside the alternator. More recently, electrical system control modules have been used to regulate the charging system more efficiently by controlling alternator output based on a number of parameters such as electrical load, engine load and rpm, alternator capability, battery type and temperature, fuel economy benefits, and more.

Battery technology is also altering the charging requirements of alternators. For example, more OEMs are using absorbed glass mat (AGM) batteries now because AGMs are capable of absorbing an electrical charge of up to five times faster than older flooded-type lead acid batteries. Different battery types and variations to cell chemistry also result in differences to required charging voltages, the charging voltage profile or the charge rate over time, and the state of charge voltage readings. Modern charging systems need to adapt to these various challenges, and in many cases this is achieved through the use of ECM control over the charging system.

Alternator Advantages

Alternators have not always been used on commercial vehicles. Until the 1960s, DC generators were used to supply direct current to the electrical system and charge batteries. The current produced by DC generators became inadequate as vehicle electrical loads increased. Generators were especially inefficient at low speeds, leading to a discharged battery condition after a few short trips. The development of low-cost solid-state rectifiers in the 1950s made the use of alternating current "generators" (alternators) possible. Alternators are much more efficient at producing current than DC generators. Alternating current—not DC

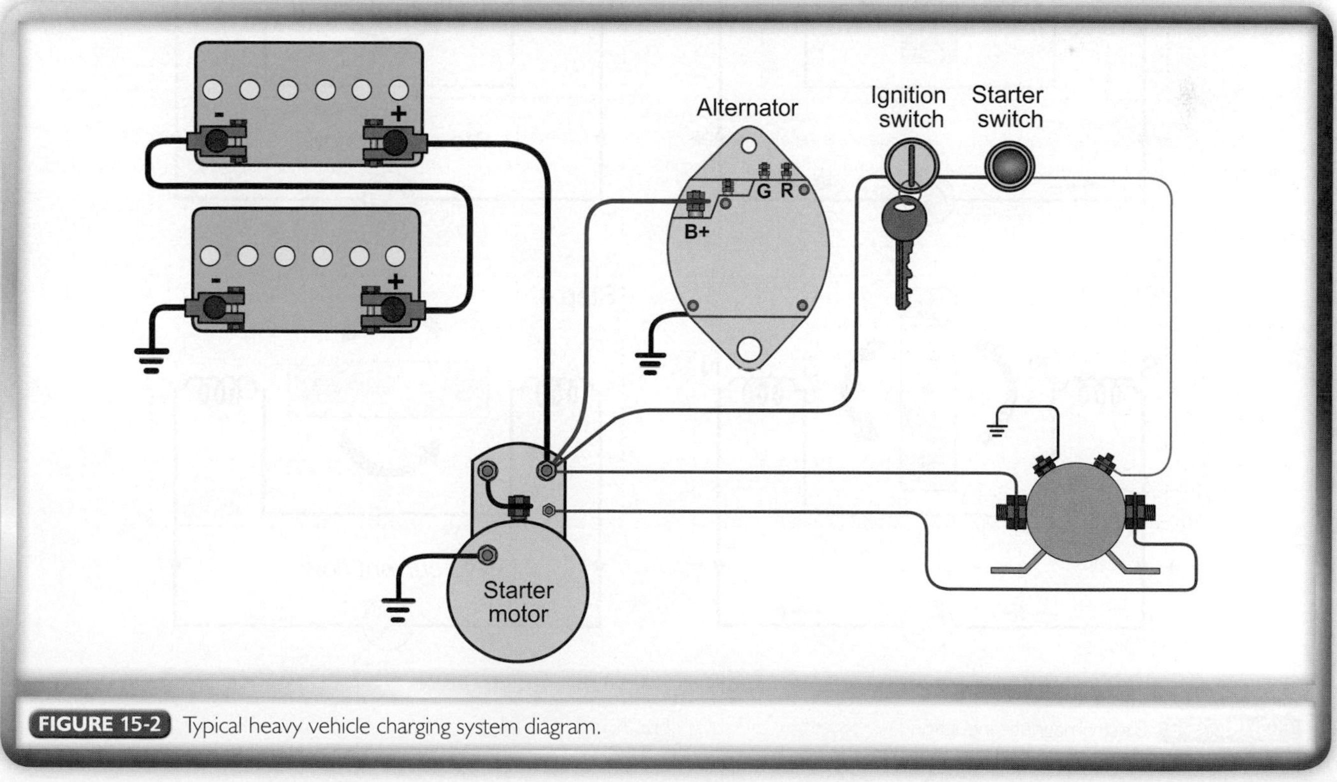

FIGURE 15-2 Typical heavy vehicle charging system diagram.

current—is produced inside an alternator. Several pairs of diodes, referred to as the rectifier bridge, have the job of converting AC current to usable DC current.

Thanks to solid state electronics and circuitry, alternators have become the dominant design due to their superior operating characteristics compared to generators. For example:

- Alternators weigh less per ampere of output.
- Alternators have fewer moving parts.
- Alternators can produce power at engine idle speeds; generators cannot.
- Alternators can be operated at much higher speeds. Alternators use a lighter rotor compared with a heavy armature in generators.
- Alternators conduct less current through the brushes, if equipped, thus reducing wear.
- Alternators do not require current regulators; they control their own maximum amperage output.
- Alternators will produce current when rotated in either direction. Polarity from generators will change when rotated in the opposite direction. Note that cooling fans in alternators can turn only in one direction.
- Alternators allow the reduction of battery capacity due to faster recharging rate.

Alternator Principles

The alternator converts mechanical energy into electrical energy by electromagnetic induction, as illustrated in FIGURE 15-3. In a simplified version, a bar magnet rotates in an iron yoke, which concentrates the magnetic field. A coil of wire is wound around each end of the yoke. As the magnet turns, voltage is induced in the coil, producing a current flow. When the north pole is up and the south pole is down, voltage is induced in the coil, producing current flow in one direction. As the magnet rotates and the positions of the poles reverse, the polarity of the voltage reverses as well. As a result, the direction of current flow also reverses. Current that changes direction in this way is called alternating current (AC). In this example, the change in direction occurs once for every complete revolution of the magnet.

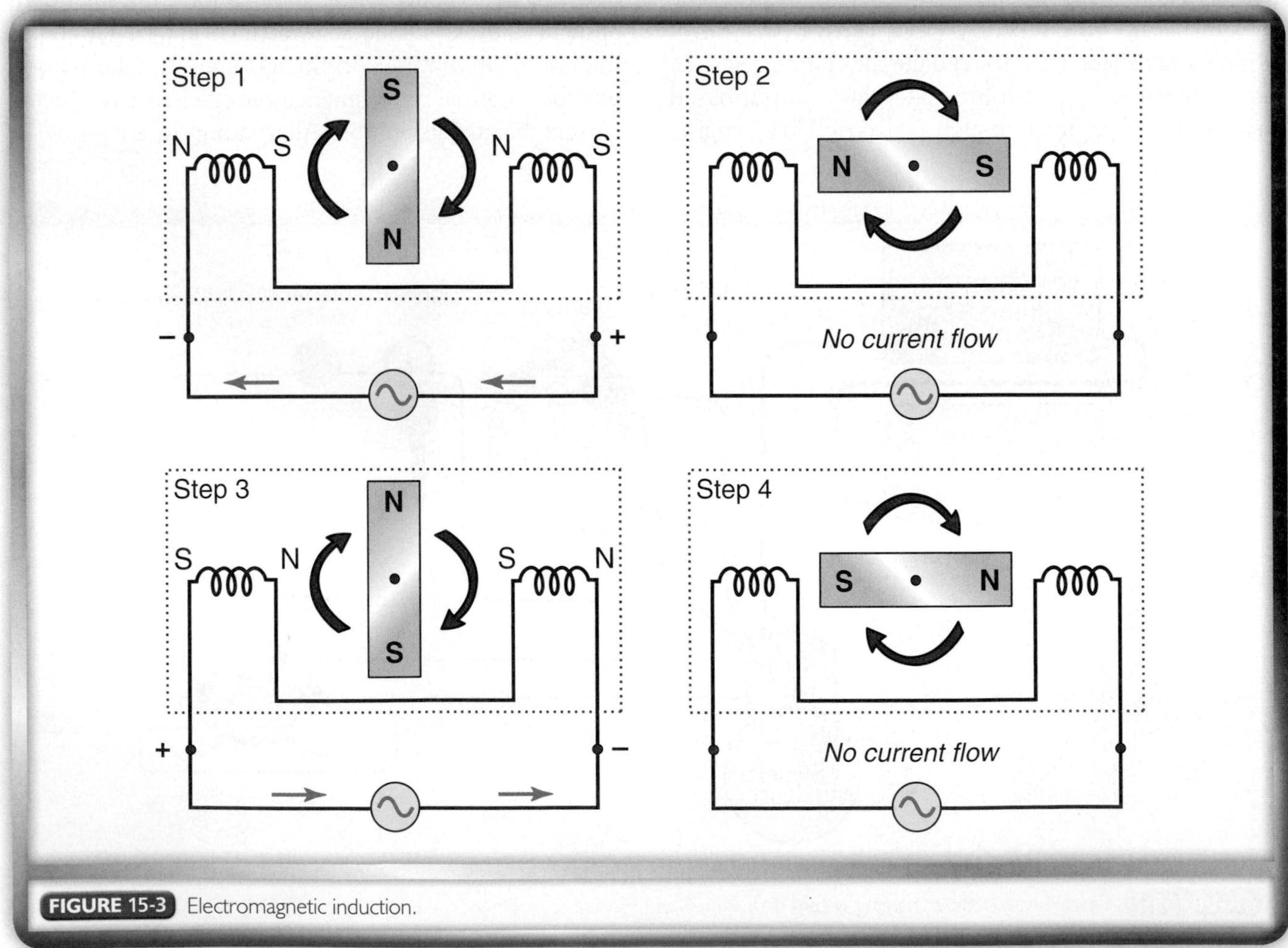

FIGURE 15-3 Electromagnetic induction.

Alternating Current

The two most important parts in an alternator used to produce electrical current are the rotor and stator winding. The rotor contains a spinning electromagnet that induces current flow in the stator winding, which is made up of numerous coils of wire. By varying the current supplied to the rotor's electromagnetic coil, the strength of its magnetic field changes. The parts of the alternator are illustrated in FIGURE 15-4 and will be discussed in detail in the section Alternator Components. The amount of current produced from an alternator is proportional to the following four factors. The first is the strength of the magnetic field in the rotor. Increasing the strength of the magnetic field increases the force pushing and pulling on electrons in a stator winding. Stronger magnetic fields in the rotor translate directly into higher output voltage and amperage. The second factor is the speed at which the magnetic field rotates. The third factor is the angle between the magnetic field and conductors in the stator. The last factor is the number and/or size of conductors cutting magnetic lines of force.

Maximum amperage output of an alternator is limited by the speed at which an alternator rotates. As the alternator spins faster, a counter electrical current is induced in the stator by the continuously changing polarity of AC current in the stator windings. This induced current, called the counter electromotive force (CEMF), opposes any increase in current induced in the stator by the spinning rotor. At high alternator speeds, the CEMF, which is induced in the opposite direction of output current by changing AC current polarity, will be begin to equal any increase to induced stator current. The result is CEMF. CEMF acts to reduce the output current of the alternator. The faster the alternator turns, the higher the CEMF produced in the stator, as shown in FIGURE 15-5.

Alternator Classification

Alternators can be categorized by a number of variables including whether voltage regulation is internal or external; the diameter of the housing; whether the alternator is sealed, oil cooled, or externally air cooled; amperage output; charging voltage; manufacturer; and many other factors. The SAE classifies alternator automotive mounting configurations into standards to enable the adaptation of alternators from all manufacturers to fit engines. Two common mounting types for alternators are a pad-mount alternator FIGURE 15-6A and a hinge-mount type FIGURE 15-6B.

Alternator Components

Regardless of the alternator's classification, all alternators share common components. Major components of the alternator are illustrated in Figure 15-4. These include:

- Rotor—A rotating electromagnet that provides the magnetic field to induce voltage and current in the stator.
- Brushes/slip rings—Make an electrical connection to the rotor field coil to supply current from the voltage regulator.

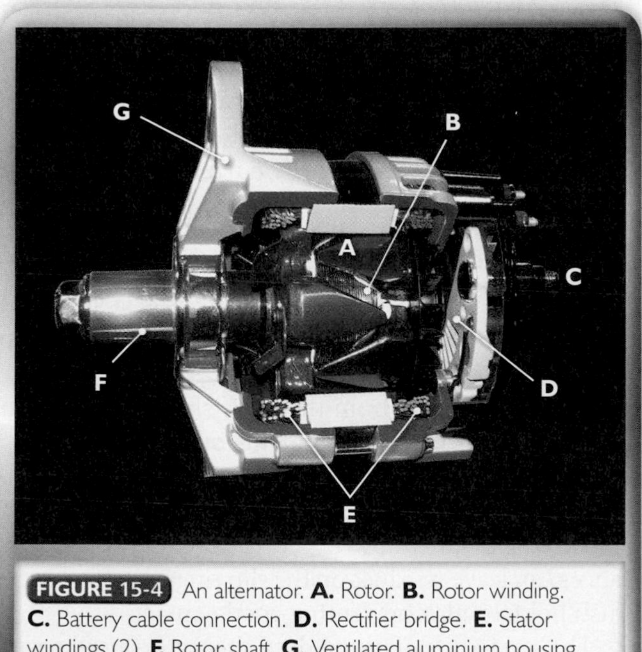

FIGURE 15-4 An alternator. **A.** Rotor. **B.** Rotor winding. **C.** Battery cable connection. **D.** Rectifier bridge. **E.** Stator windings (2). **F.** Rotor shaft. **G.** Ventilated aluminium housing.

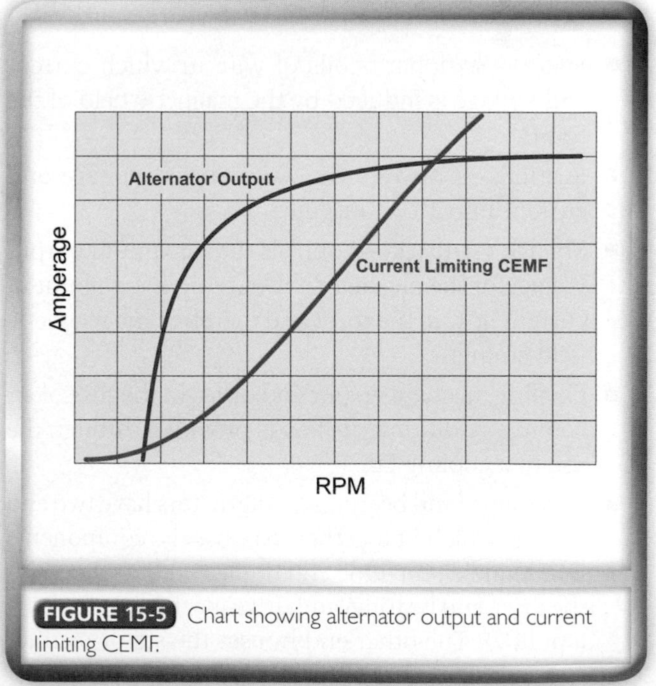

FIGURE 15-5 Chart showing alternator output and current limiting CEMF.

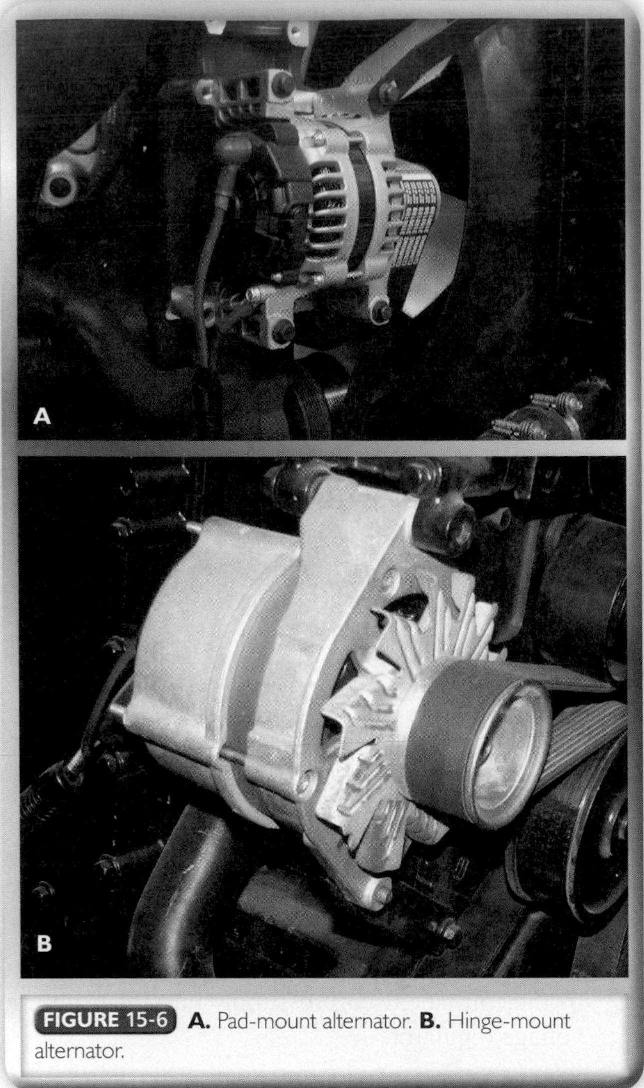

FIGURE 15-6 **A.** Pad-mount alternator. **B.** Hinge-mount alternator.

- Stator—Stationary coils of wire in which current and voltage is induced by the magnetic field of the rotor.
- Rectifier—Converts the AC induced voltage and current into a DC output.
- Voltage regulator—Controls the maximum output voltage of the alternator by varying the amount of current flow in the rotor and therefore the magnetic field strength.
- Cooling mechanism (air and oil)—In the case of air cooling, additional airflow is provided through the use of a cooling fan.
- End frames and bearings—Alternators have two end frames, which fit together to house the components into a single unit. One end frame contains the rotor, the drive end bearing, and drive mechanism (usually a pulley). The other end houses the stator rectifier regulator and brush assembly.
- Drive mechanism—In most cases, a pulley drive is used, but direct-gear drive mechanisms may also be employed.

Rotor

The rotor provides the rotating magnetic field that cuts the wire coils within the stator to induce the flow of electrical current in the stator. The rotor consists of an iron core that encloses a coil of many turns of wire. Each end of the wire coil is connected to one of two conductive slip rings on the rotor shaft. The wire coil and slip rings are electrically insulated from the rotor shaft. Energizing the rotor's wire coil with typically 2 to 5 amps produces an electromagnetic field beneath two halves of the soft iron core. These two halves are arranged into claws or pole pieces.

The pole pieces have two purposes. One is to intensify the electromagnetic field, and the other is to arrange magnetic lines of flux produced in the coil into poles on each claw of the rotor. Each of the claws or pole pieces will have a stationary pole that alternates in sequence with each pole piece as north and south. A heavy alternator has more pole pieces or "claws"—typically between 12 and 16. Fourteen is a common number of claws for heavy-duty alternators. Passing current through the rotor coil magnetizes the rotor claws. Alternating poles of magnetism are formed north-south-north-south on the rotor.

The output of the alternator is determined by a couple of the alternator's physical features. The first is the size and number of windings in the stator that is cut by the magnetic lines of force. The second is the strength of the magnetic field of the rotor. Increasing or decreasing the current flow through the rotor winding will change the magnetic field strength. Usually the maximum possible amperage is 5 amps or less. Controlling the strength of the magnetic field is the job of the voltage regulator. FIGURE 15-7 illustrates how the current flows through the rotor.

Brushes and Brushless Alternators

Regulated current to the alternator rotor is supplied through a pair of graphite brushes sliding against slip rings on the rotor shaft. The slip rings and the coil are electrically insulated from the rotor shaft. Lightweight springs help the brushes maintain contact with the slip rings. Brushes are designed to have a minimum of 95,000 miles (150,000 km) service life but eventually wear out. Dirt, fluids, engine blow-by, corrosion, and other substances can leave residues on the slip rings or gum up the brush holders, also preventing good contact.

The service life of heavy-duty alternators used needs to be extended in chassis accumulating travel distances

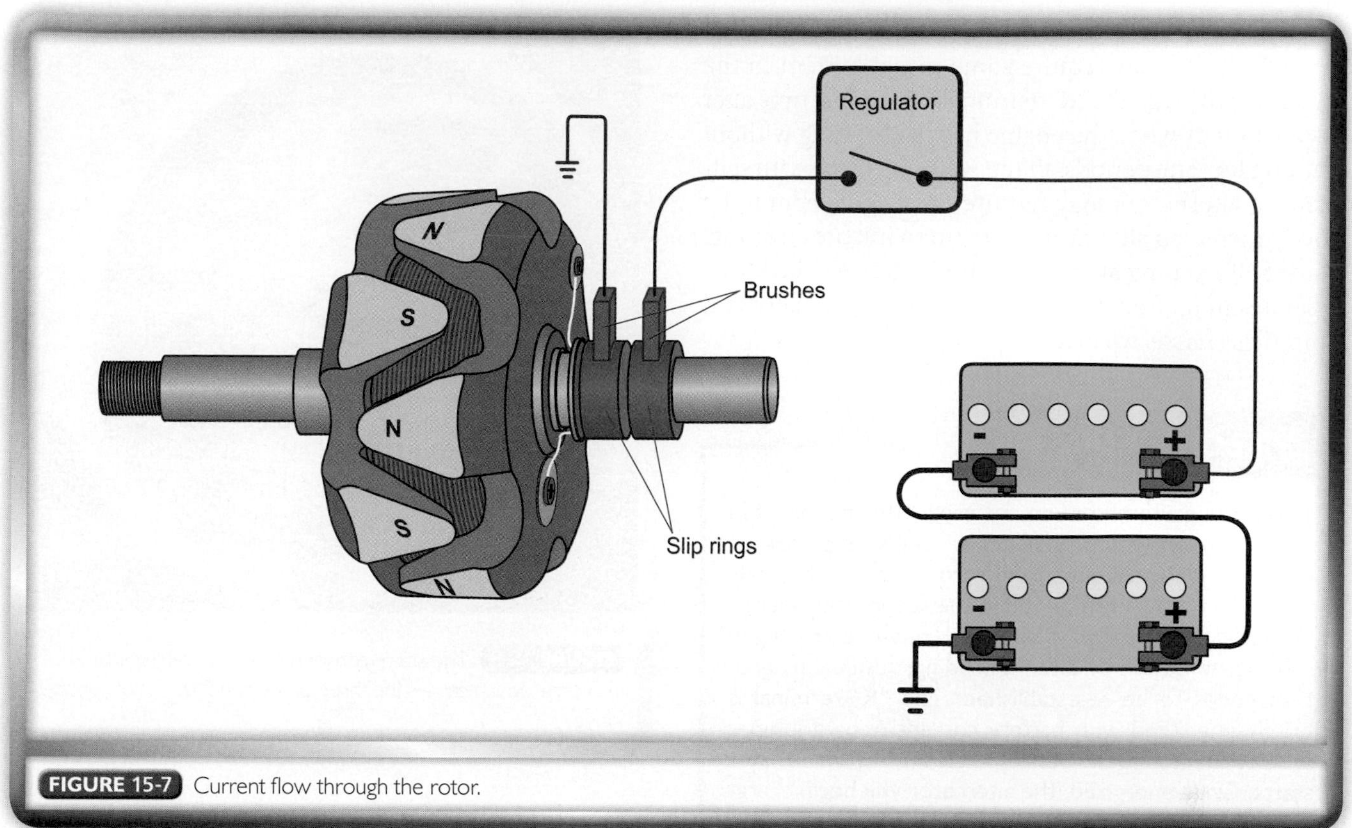

FIGURE 15-7 Current flow through the rotor.

in excess of 620,000 miles (one million kilometers). One way to extend the service life is by using brushless alternator designs such as the one illustrated in FIGURE 15-8 to bypass the problems of using brushes. Instead of locating the magnetic field coil inside a rotating rotor, these alternators use a stationary field winding bolted to the alternator end frame. The rotor's pole pieces rotate around the stationary coil. Brushes, therefore, are not required to deliver the current to the rotor. As a result, there is no need to service the brushes and slip rings.

FIGURE 15-8 A brushless alternator has rotating pole pieces around a stationary field winding. **A.** Rotor. **B.** Pole pieces (2). **C.** Stator windings. **D.** Stationary field coil.

Exciting the Alternator

While the voltage regulator will supply current to the rotor, some alternators require some residual magnetism on the rotor before current is generated. **Residual magnetism** refers to the small amount of magnetism left on the rotor after it is initially magnetized by the coil's magnetic field. Residually magnetized rotors will begin to induce current in the stator windings when the alternator starts rotating without any current passing through the rotor coil. The stator, in turn, supplies current to the voltage regulator through exciter diodes. Normal alternator operation using a regulator will resume once current is supplied to the regulator. This category of self-exciting alternators generally features a single, heavy-gauge battery cable connecting the alternator to the vehicle batteries.

Self-exciting alternators do not require the use of a circuit but may require some initial current in the rotor's coil through the "R" terminal for the first time after installation or when the engine has been sitting without running for long periods. Often, vehicles fitted with self-exciting alternators may require the engine rpm to be briefly increased after every start-up to initiate charging. Using self-exciting alternators eliminates the need for a separate circuit from the key switch to the alternator and simplifies chassis wiring.

> **TECHNICIAN TIP**
>
> Self-exciting alternators do not use a circuit connected to the ignition switch to switch on the voltage regulator and supply current to the rotor. Instead, they rely on residual magnetism found in the rotor after operating. If the alternator stays unexcited due to a prolonged shut-down period or after rebuilding, residual magnetism needs to be re-established. The "R" terminal is briefly energized with battery current using a jumper wire connected to the battery cable after the alternator starts. Once energized, the alternator will begin charging and should not need initializing with current again. Many alternators are regularly returned as defective because technicians are unaware of the procedure to excite the rotor initially.

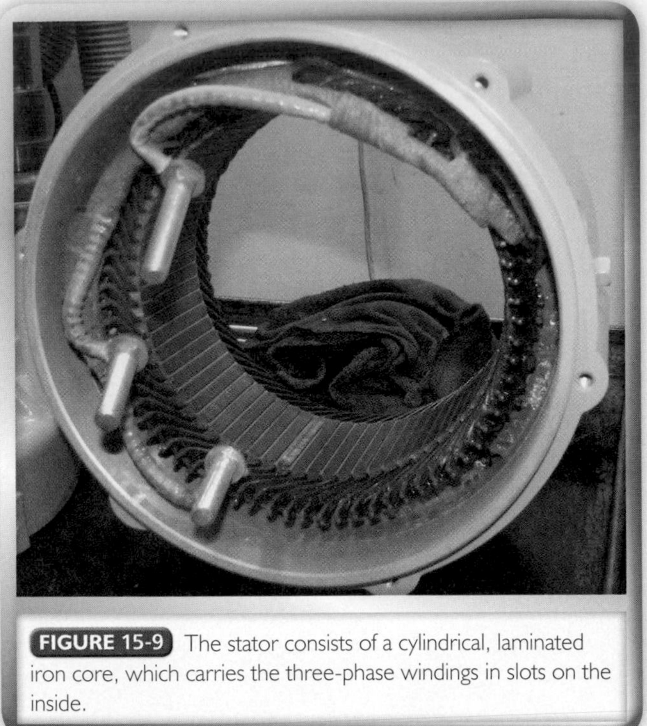

FIGURE 15-9 The stator consists of a cylindrical, laminated iron core, which carries the three-phase windings in slots on the inside.

Stator

The stator is made of loops of coiled wire wrapped around a slotted metal alternator frame. The laminated-iron stator frame channels magnetic lines of force through the conductors where current is induced by the spinning rotor. Because the wires are looped, with alternating magnetic N-S poles passing beneath the loops, alternating current is produced from the stator FIGURE 15-9. The windings are insulated from each other and also from the iron core. They form a large number of conductor loops, which are each subjected to the rotating magnetic fields of the rotor. The stator is mounted between two end housings, and it holds the stator windings stationary so that the rotating magnetic field cuts through the stator windings, inducing an electric current in the windings. To smooth the pulsating current flow, there are three distinct layers of windings offset 120 degrees in each layer from one another. This arrangement produces a more even flow of current from the alternator. The number of loops in each winding corresponds to the number of rotor poles. So, if the rotor has 14 poles, there will be 14 loops of wire in each of the three windings. Ultimately, the amount of amperage the alternator is capable of producing depends on the mass of wire in the stator. A larger stator having more loops, more turns of wire in each loop, and/or thicker wire will have higher maximum output amperage than one with fewer loops, less wire, and thinner wire. FIGURE 15-10 provides a side-by-side comparison of low- and high-output stators.

Phase Winding Connections

Two methods of connection can be used for the stator or phase windings: the Wye and Delta configurations. Both types of windings produce three-phase AC current, but voltage and amperage outputs differ. Windings connected in a Wye-type configuration have four connection points. As the name suggests, **Wye windings** resemble the letter "Y" FIGURE 15-11A. Three ends of each of the windings are connected together to a point called the neutral junction. The other three free ends are connected to a pair of diodes in the rectifier bridge. The advantage of Wye windings is that they produce higher voltage at comparably lower rotor speeds. This means the alternator can begin charging a battery at lower engine speeds.

Delta windings, shaped like the symbol "delta," are more popular in alternators for diesel engines FIGURE 15-11B. These windings have only three connection points. The three junction points between the windings are connected to a pair of diodes found in the rectifier bridge. Because stator windings are connected in parallel, the resistance of Delta windings is one third less than Wye windings. Although Delta windings do not

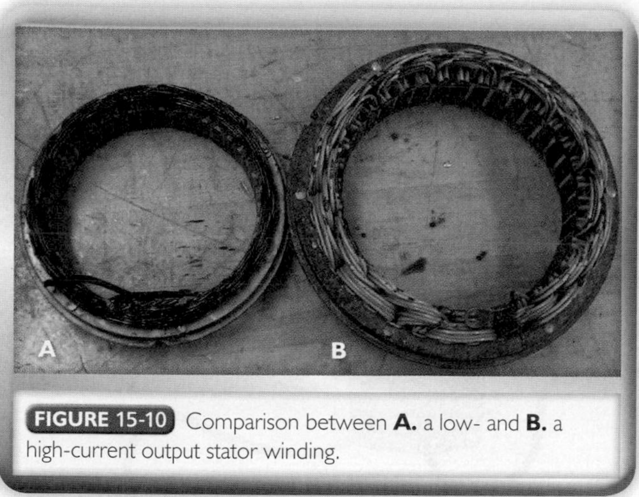

FIGURE 15-10 Comparison between **A.** a low- and **B.** a high-current output stator winding.

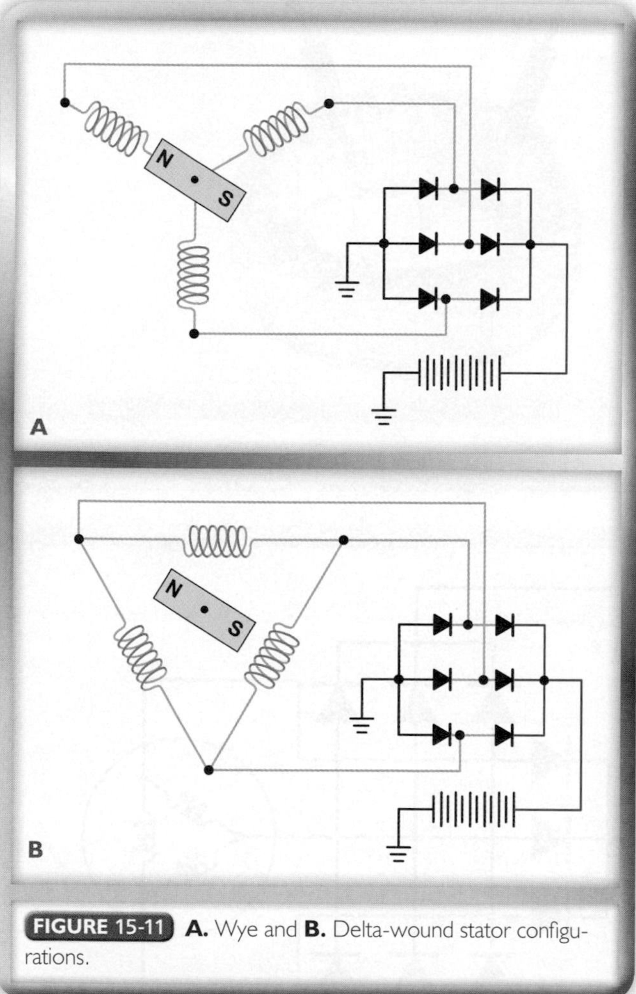

FIGURE 15-11 **A.** Wye and **B.** Delta-wound stator configurations.

produce as much voltage as Wye windings at same low rotor speeds, they do, however, produce substantially more amperage. Delta-wound alternators are best adapted to supply higher amperage output to charge multiple batteries and the heavy electrical loads found in trucks and buses. Combination Wye and Delta stators are rarely found in HD alternators.

Testing Stators

Stators, like rotors, are not normally serviced in a repair facility. However, when rebuilding, stators can be visually checked for burnt, cut, or nicked winding laminations. Winding junction points are checked to ensure they are solid. Continuity should exist between all junction points of the stator. An amperage draw test of each winding can be performed to check the resistance and balance of each section of winding. No continuity should exist between the windings and alternator frame. As illustrated in FIGURE 15-12, a stator can be tested for short circuits and open circuits. A leakage to ground test evaluates winding insulation and is also known as an insulation stress test. Stress testing involves passing high voltage, low amperage current through the windings. Any breakdown in insulation is detected when continuity exists between the windings and frame.

Rectifier

Alternators produce alternating current, which is acceptable for operating many electrical devices. However, not all AC-operated devices are cost effective to produce or efficient to operate. AC current cannot charge a battery either. Converting the AC current to usable DC current is referred to as **rectification**.

AC current is produced in the stator due to the influence of the rotors, magnetic fields. Alternating north–south poles passing over windings will alternately push and pull electrons. Moving the electrons in two different directions gives stator current flow its AC characteristic. The speed at which the lines of force cut the conductors, the angle the magnetic field cuts the stator conductors, the number of conductors, and the wire gauge will determine the amount of amperage induced in the stator.

Two diodes are connected to each wire end of either Delta- or Wye-wound stators. Each stator winding will produce one of three phases of AC current FIGURE 15-13. So, a minimum of six diodes is required to completely rectify all three phases of alternating current into DC current. The silicon diodes making up the rectifier behave like a one-way electrical check valve. The two diodes connected to each winding will allow either a positive or negative current potential to appear at the output of the rectifier. If only a single diode is used at the end of the windings, only half the AC sine wave will be rectified. Two diodes enable full wave rectification FIGURE 15-14.

The top of the waveform is called the **alternator ripple**. A ripple that is consistent across each winding indicates that the stator windings and diodes are each creating current flow and voltage consistently. Inconsistent ripple indicates a fault in either the diodes or the stator windings. Study the illustrations carefully so that

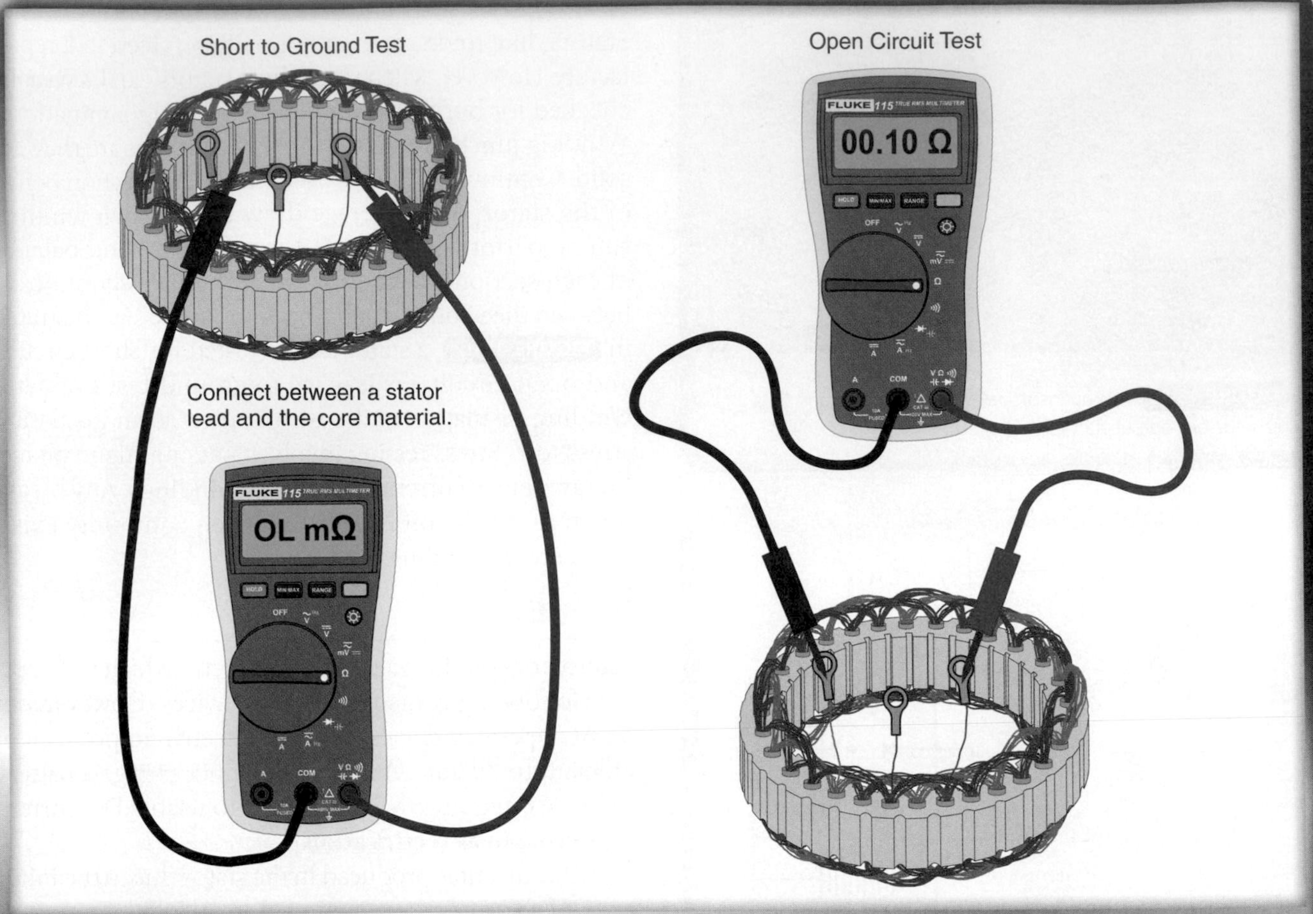

Short to Ground Test

Connect between a stator lead and the core material.

OL mΩ

Open Circuit Test

00.10 Ω

FIGURE 15-12 A stator can be tested for short and open circuits.

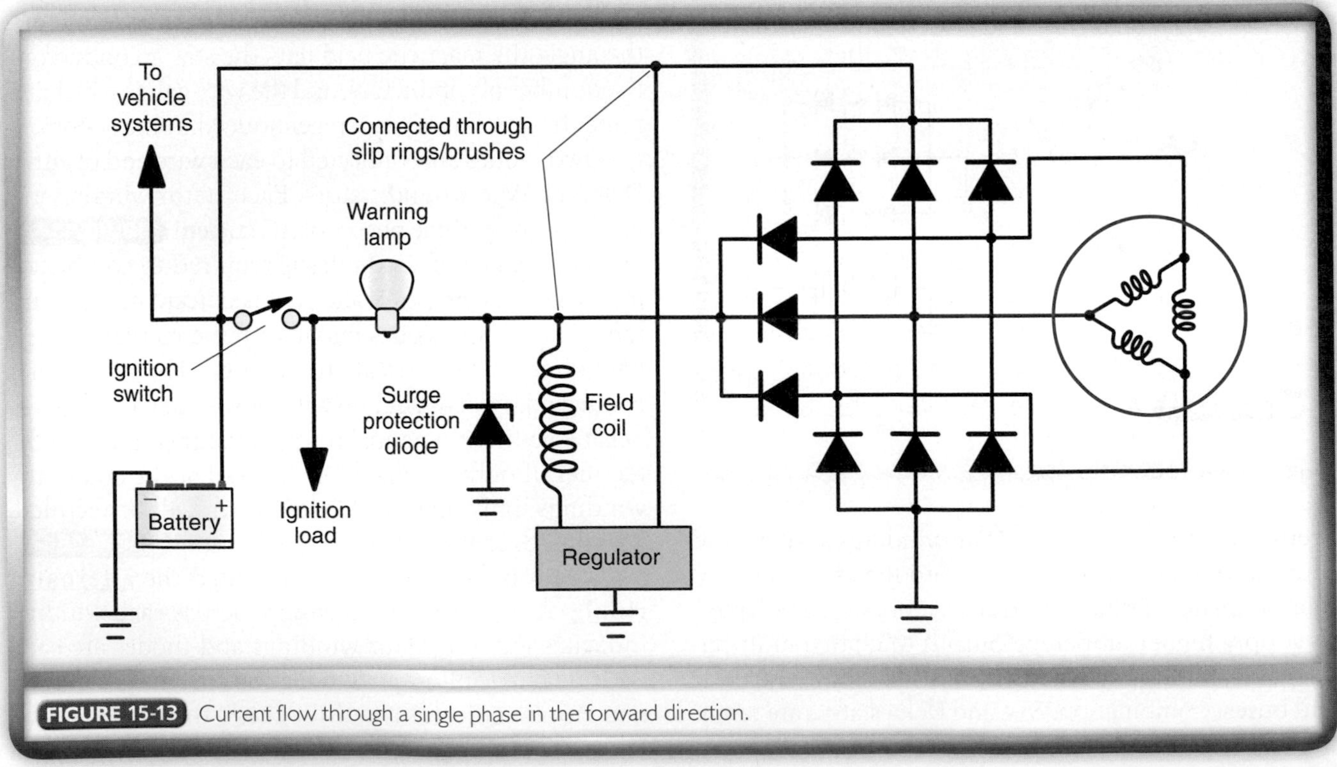

FIGURE 15-13 Current flow through a single phase in the forward direction.

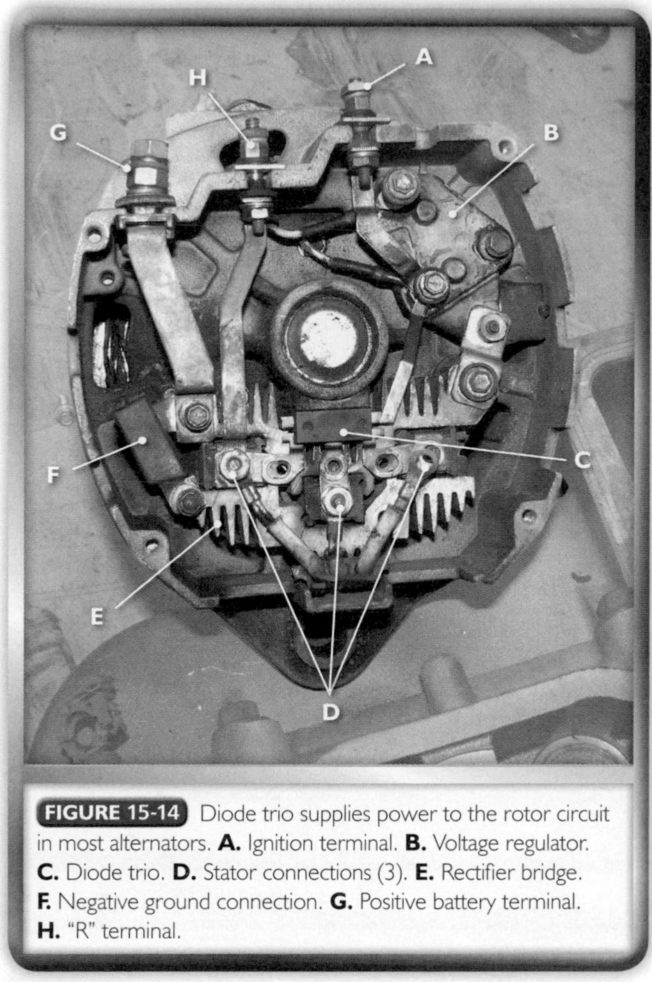

FIGURE 15-14 Diode trio supplies power to the rotor circuit in most alternators. **A.** Ignition terminal. **B.** Voltage regulator. **C.** Diode trio. **D.** Stator connections (3). **E.** Rectifier bridge. **F.** Negative ground connection. **G.** Positive battery terminal. **H.** "R" terminal.

FIGURE 15-15 Rectifier in an alternator housing. Note the fins on the heat sink to remove heat.

you understand the role the diode bridge plays in providing the relatively smooth DC output required by the vehicle's systems.

Rectifier Diode Problems

Heat can cause premature failures of diodes FIGURE 15-15. Additional cooling of rectifier bridges can be accomplished with heavier diodes and heat sinks or by connecting diodes in parallel so that six rather than three pairs accomplish the work. Another problem facing an alternator occurs when the diodes become open or shorted. An internally shorted positive diode will cause a parasitic loss of battery current through the alternator when the engine is not running. This condition will also cause a loss of up to 67% of alternator output because it interferes with the rectification of current from two winding phases. Shorted diodes can be detected with an AC voltmeter measurement of alternator output. Generally, any more than 0.4–0.7 volts of AC current superimposed over the DC output indicate that AC current is passing through a shorted diode. Many AVRs have a diode ripple feature that detects this large AC waveform and illuminates a diagnostic light on the machine. Graphing the alternator output with a graphing meter or oscilloscope and carefully observing the pattern also indicates the condition of the diodes. An open diode will not cause as much of a loss of output as a shorted diode—only up to 33% of output—but will cause increased fluctuations or pulsing of DC output current.

When measuring alternator output using an AC (not DC) voltmeter, AC current can normally be measured. An alternator with output voltage fluctuations between 13.9 to 14.2 volts DC, for example, will produce a 0.3-volt AC current. When graphed, the waveform looks like a ripple of a wave, hence the term **AC ripple** FIGURE 15-16. The voltage fluctuations are produced by the differences between the peak voltage of an AC sine wave and the minimum voltage found in the trough between sine waves FIGURE 15-17. AC ripple is suppressed by a capacitor inside the alternator and is absorbed by the battery. If AC ripple is too great, it leads to radio noise and electromagnetic interference (EMI) in many electronic control devices FIGURE 15-18. For example, an engine ECM may fail to function correctly, causing the engine to run rough. An ABS module may even generate fault codes.

Smoothing Capacitors

Capacitors can be used to smooth alternator AC ripple and prevent EMI. In the alternator, one is connected across the output to act like an electric shock absorber. When the output voltage increases slightly, the capacitor will charge and absorb the new increase. When voltage drops, the capacitor will drain, topping up the output voltage and is then ready for a new charge.

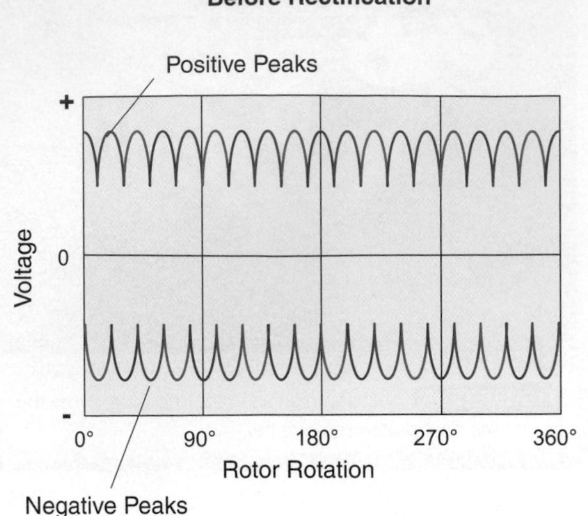

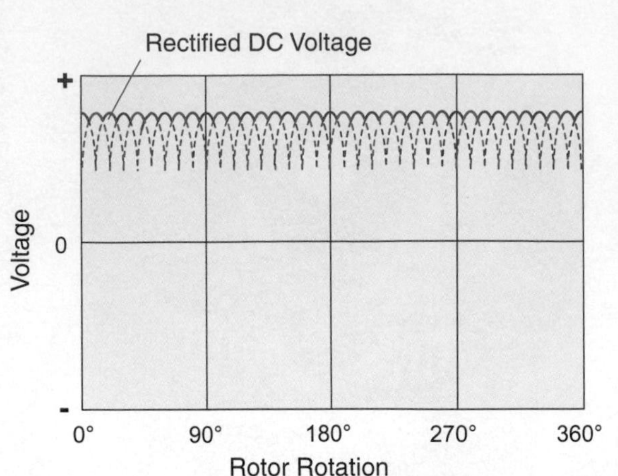

FIGURE 15-16 Typical alternator oscilloscope pattern showing AC ripple.

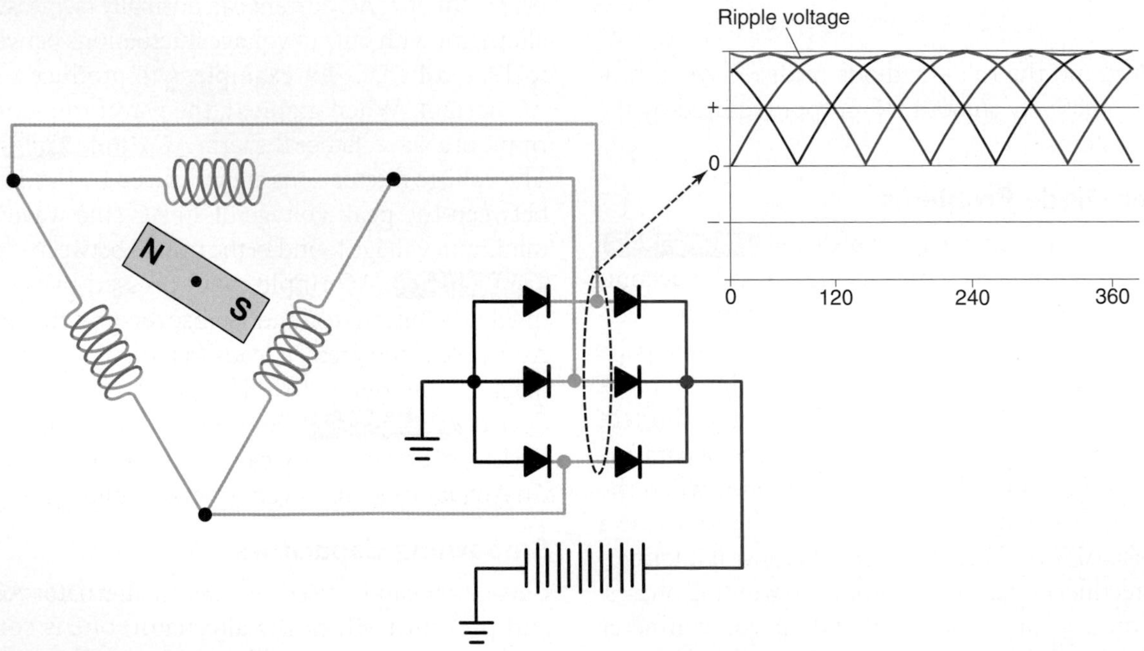

FIGURE 15-17 Three phases rectified.

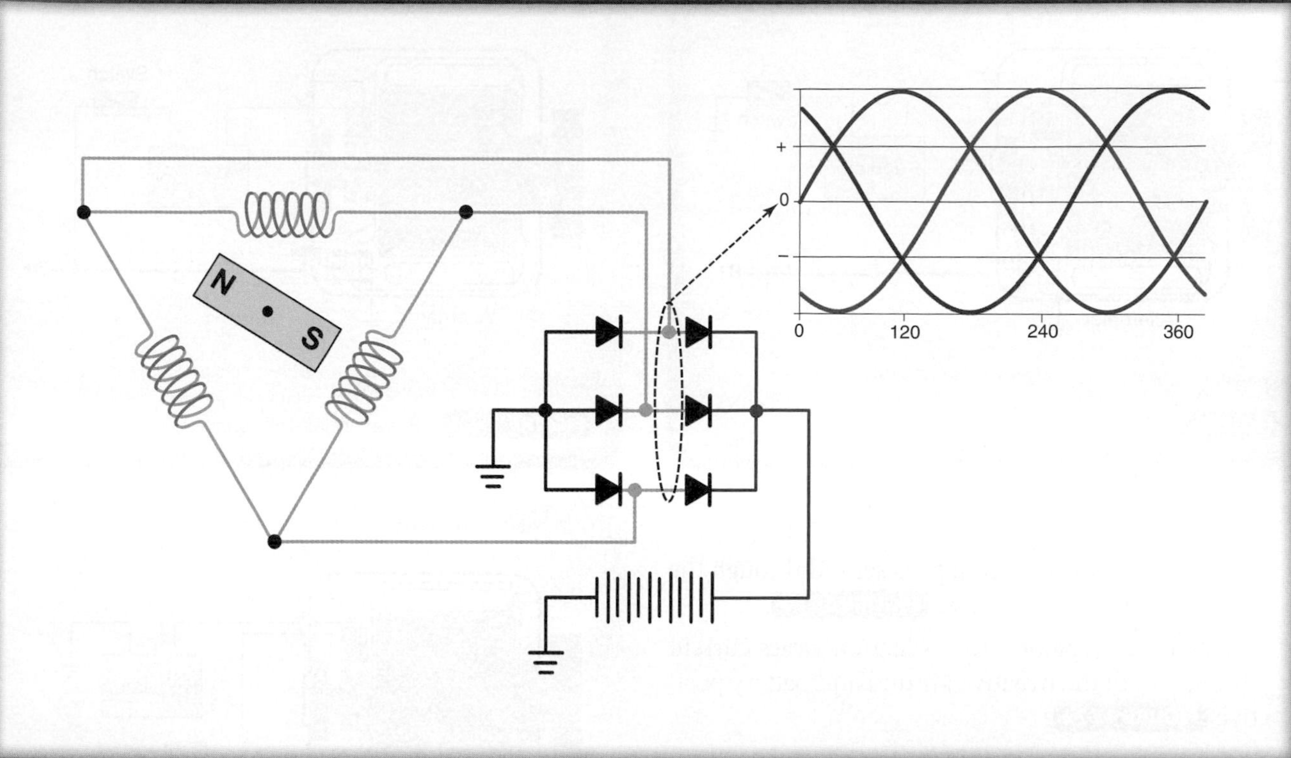

FIGURE 15-18 Three phases—not rectified.

> **TECHNICIAN TIP**
>
> A missing or defective alternator capacitor can cause radio noise and EMI interference with chassis electronic modules. When checking for parasitic draws, the capacitor may give a false indication of current draw as it charges for a few seconds after the battery is disconnected. If batteries are disconnected for even a short time, they will spark when connected while the capacitor charges.

Voltage Regulator

Voltage regulators are first classified as either external FIGURE 15-19 or internal. The majority of late-model alternators have internal regulators. Regulators can also be categorized by circuit connections used to supply current to the rotor used to induce "field excitation." Knowing the type of field excitation circuit used is helpful when developing diagnostic strategies for testing alternators:

1. "A" type regulators regulate the field current by controlling the resistance through to ground. One rotor brush is connected to the alternator output or B+, and the other is connected to ground through the regulator FIGURE 15-20.

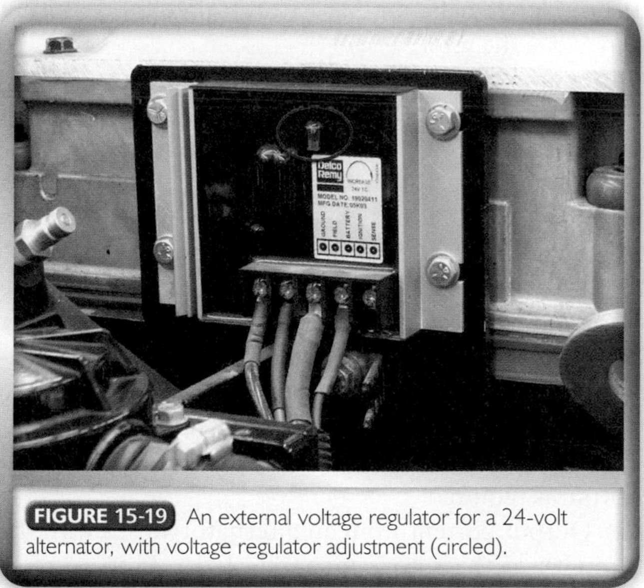

FIGURE 15-19 An external voltage regulator for a 24-volt alternator, with voltage regulator adjustment (circled).

2. "B" type regulators control the battery positive supply to the rotor. One brush is connected directly to negative ground and the regulator varies battery positive voltage supplied to the other brush. B-type circuits are used only by external regulators. If the electronic regulator fails or develops a resistive ground due to corrosion, it commonly causes the alternator to

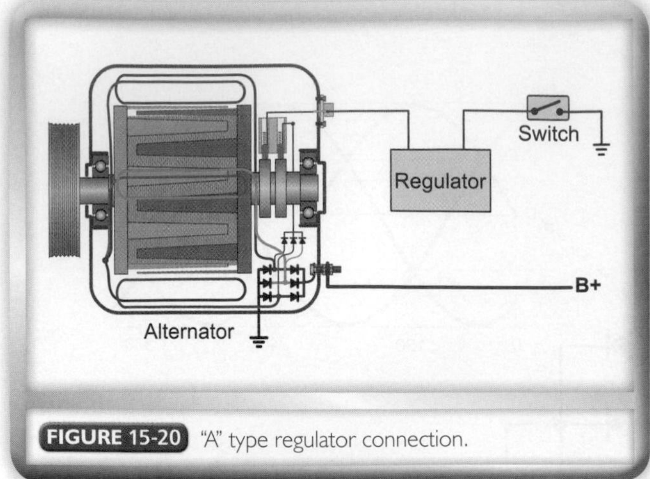

FIGURE 15-20 "A" type regulator connection.

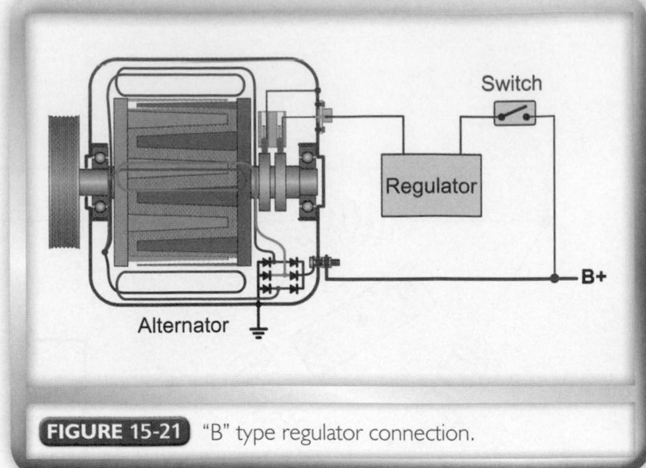

FIGURE 15-21 "B" type regulator connection.

overcharge, as system voltage is sensed through the ground and battery positive FIGURE 15-21.

3. Isolated field-type of rotor excitation varies current through both the negative ground and battery positive FIGURE 15-22.

In SI series Delco alternators, current supplied to the regulator is provided by the diode trio. These three diodes will perform single wave rectification of each phase of the alternators, windings. Single phase rectification means only a maximum of half the alternators, output can excite the rotor.

Some voltage regulators use an analog voltage signal to modulate the strength of the magnetic field. This means that the current to the rotor continuously varies. As the alternator reaches its set point, the field current gradually diminishes. Digital regulators will use a pulse-width-modulated signal to control the magnetic field strength. These alternators will have a duty cycle frequency interval of between 10 and 7,000 times per second. Within that frequency interval, the voltage regulator changes the length of "on-time" current applied to the rotor. Current is cycled on and off hundreds of times each second, the length of on-time increasing as higher output is required.

Output current from an alternator varies with the strength of the rotor's magnetic field. Increasing or decreasing current flow through the rotor will change output. Low current through the rotor produces low output and vice versa with high current flow. Changing electrical demands, varying engine speeds, and changing the battery all require rapid, continuous adjustments to output voltage.

Current or amperage regulation is a function of voltage regulation. To understand this, consider that an alternator's output depends on two factors. One is the regulator set-point, and the other is the vehicle's electrical system total circuit resistance. So, an electrical system with a low battery charge, and many other electrical loads switched on, has low resistance. Multiple current pathways exist, which lowers total circuit resistance. Low resistance permits high amounts of amperage to flow out of the alternator. (Remember Ohm's law: Voltage = Amperage × Resistance.) Because the alternator is connected to all these circuits, the voltage regulator will supply the highest possible current flow to the rotor for maximum magnetic field strength. As the batteries charge and some loads are turned off, less amperage is needed, as electrical system resistance increases. Because electrical system resistance increases, the system voltage will rise as amperage is reduced. When the system voltage reaches the alternator's set-point, it will turn off current to the rotor until the voltage falls again.

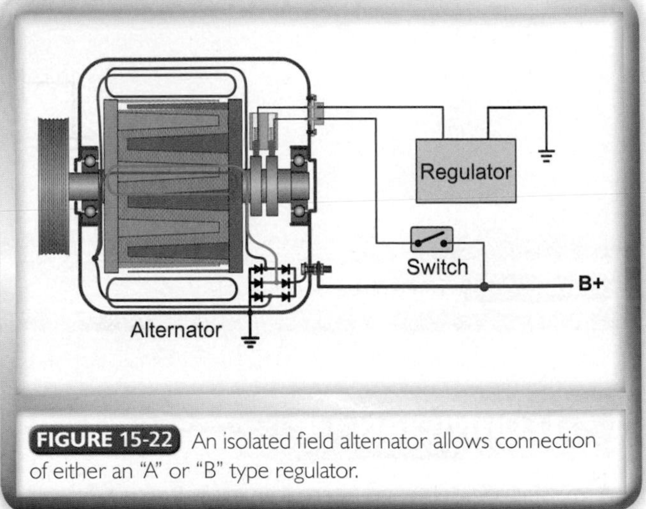

FIGURE 15-22 An isolated field alternator allows connection of either an "A" or "B" type regulator.

Stated another way, using power and Ohm's law (Power = Volts × Amps)—if 1,200 watts of power are needed to supply the electrical system, the voltage-amperage combination could be 85 amps at 14.0 volts or 100 amps at 12.0 volts.

Voltage regulators controlled by the electrical system control module (ECM) are commonplace. Using engine speed, air intake temperature, coolant temperature, and other variables, the ECM will adjust charging voltage to match battery temperature. To reduce drag when cranking, no field excitation takes place until after the engine starts. Once the engine is started, current output is slowly raised to minimize rough engine operation. If battery voltage is too low, engine idle speed can be increased. Communication between the PCM and voltage regulator takes place over the CAN network **FIGURE 15-23**.

Charging System Set Point

Alternators must be capable of controlling the output of the DC current. There must be enough current to adequately charge the batteries but not so much current that it causes damage to the vehicle's electrical system. Voltage regulation for 12-volt systems will establish a maximum charging voltage, known as the set point. Charging voltage set point averages between 13.5 volts and 14.6 volts. This is 1.5 to 2.0 volts above 12.6-volt open-circuit voltage for a typical 12-volt battery. 24-volt systems use 27 and 28.4 volts for a typical set point. Lower charging voltages may be encountered, however, particularly on vehicles that are doing long-haul runs. It is always advisable to check manufacturer specifications for correct charging voltage ranges for the vehicle and operating conditions. Charging at voltages above 15 volts (12-volt system) and 31 volts (24-volt system) causes:

- Batteries to gas excessively
- Batteries to overheat and lose electrolyte through electrolysis
- Battery plates to shed grid material, buckle, and generally become heat damaged as the temperature rises above 125°F (52°C)
- Vehicle electrical systems, control modules, and so on, to be damaged by high voltage
- Premature and extensive bulb failure and LED light failure

Undercharging leads to battery plate sulfation and grid corrosion. This is a condition where sulfate deposited on the plates during discharge is left too long. If left long enough, sulfate turns to a hard crystalline structure

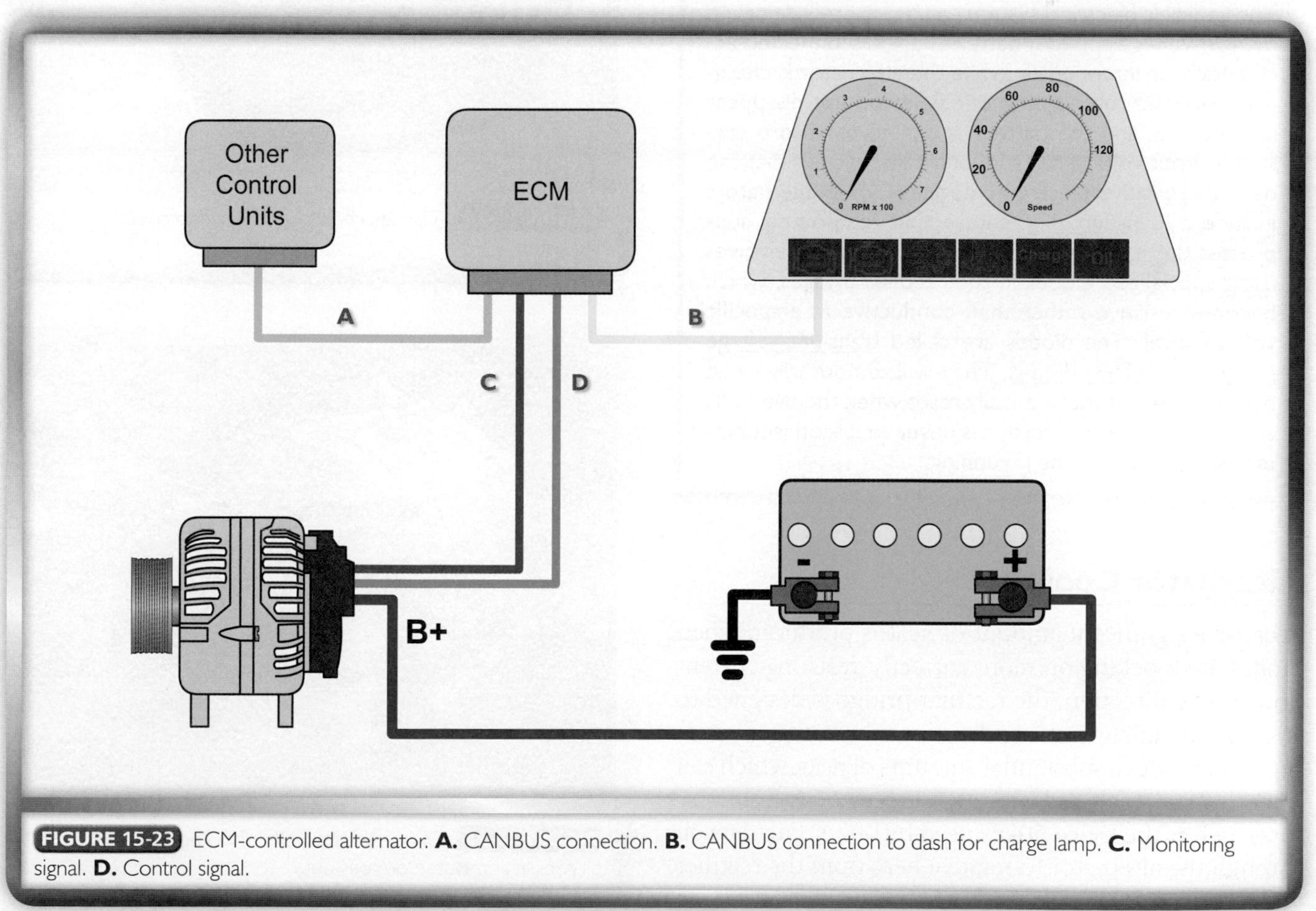

FIGURE 15-23 ECM-controlled alternator. **A.** CANBUS connection. **B.** CANBUS connection to dash for charge lamp. **C.** Monitoring signal. **D.** Control signal.

and cannot be driven off by charging. Multiple battery installations are especially vulnerable to the problems of uneven charge rates causing plate sulfation.

Factors affecting the precise set point include:

- Type of batteries—Flooded batteries (standard lead acid) charge at lower voltages than no-maintenance or AGM batteries. AGM batteries are more easily damaged by overcharging.
- States of battery charge—Discharged batteries have low resistance to current compared to charged batteries. AGM batteries can absorb 40% more current than flooded and low-maintenance batteries.
- Temperature—Battery resistance to charging increases as temperatures decrease. Temperature sensors in voltage regulators can adjust set points. To warm-up the battery, Delco CS alternators charge at 16.5 volts for the first few minutes after start-up when the weather is cold.
- Drive cycle—Low-speed operation requires higher set points to keep batteries charged.

TECHNICIAN TIP

The vehicle's electrical system can be severely damaged by high-voltage spikes if batteries are disconnected accidentally or intentionally while the alternator is charging. Since the rotor's magnetic fields do not disappear immediately and the battery is unable to absorb current, output voltage can suddenly rise to levels that can damage sensitive electronic devices. Some alternators include a load-dumping feature that temporarily suppresses these high voltage spikes. This usually involves using specialized diodes in the rectifier bridges, which become resistive rather than conductive at a specific voltage level. The diodes are called transient voltage suppression (TVS) diodes. They will temporarily resist high voltage and automatically reset when the overvoltage goes away. Best practice is never to disconnect batteries when the engine is running.

Alternator Cooling

Because a significant amount of heat is produced when diodes are blocking or, more correctly, resisting current flow in one direction, the rectifier bridge is designed to absorb and radiate heat it to the atmosphere. Stator windings also produce substantial amounts of heat, which can burn the insulation and windings. Larger 24-volt alternators, such as the Delco 50DN used by buses, circulate oil through the alternator to remove heat from the rectifier and stator windings.

When operating in environments where a spark from an alternators, brush could trigger an explosion or cause a fire, the alternator is sealed, and heat is radiated through the housing. Most alternators, however, rely on air to internally cool internal components FIGURE 15-24. If equipped with a cooling fan, the alternator must rotate in a direction that will push air through the unit. Today most cooling fans will push air through the alternator regardless of rotational direction.

Large alternators used by buses producing as much as 300 amps at 24 volts require superior cooling. In these situations, oil-cooled alternators, such as the one in FIGURE 15-25, may be used. A minimum of 2 gallons (7.6 liters) flow per minute is required. The engine oil

FIGURE 15-24 A fan attached to rotor used to cool the alternator.

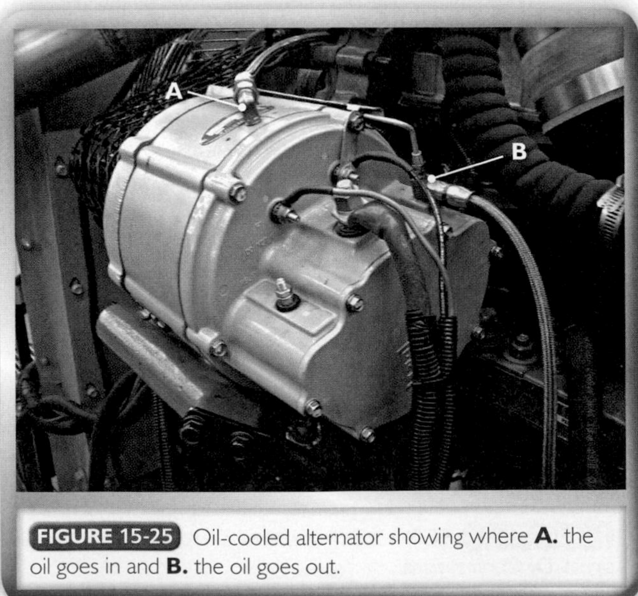

FIGURE 15-25 Oil-cooled alternator showing where **A.** the oil goes in and **B.** the oil goes out.

cooling system keeps internal engine oil temperatures below 250°F (121°C), and this can be used to cool the alternator. Alternators using oil cooling do need to be sealed well and serviced to prevent any internal shorts or sparks, which may lead to a crankcase explosion caused by ignition of volatile oil vapors inside the alternator case.

Alternator End Frames and Bearings

The alternator housings support and enclose all of the alternator components and are typically constructed from aluminum, as shown in FIGURE 15-26. Vents within the frames provide for a large amount of airflow to assist in dissipating heat. The housings accept the bearing assemblies, which support the rotor at the drive and slip ring ends. A pulley that is driven by a belt is mounted at the end of the rotor shaft. Most slip ring end frames also house the rectifier assembly. In some cases, the negative diodes are pressed into holes in the frame to provide a ground, while the positive diodes are mounted on insulated plates.

Drive Mechanism

A drive gear, rather than a pulley, is used to couple the alternator to the engine. It requires the alternator to be bolted directly to the engine in a location where a driving gear is available. This arrangement eliminates maintenance issues around belt tension and replacement but does require the alternator to be well sealed to prevent any oil leakage.

The correct gearing or pulley size needs to be selected for the alternator to ensure that the alternator does not over speed at higher engine rpm but also produces enough output at idle to cater for electrical demand. Since a highway diesel operates typically between 650 rpm and 2,100 rpm, a mechanical advantage between the alternator pulley and engine speed is needed to spin the alternator fast enough. Most larger alternators are limited to 8,000 rpm, which means the alternator drive ratio is precisely chosen to produce high output at idle yet stay below maximum speeds. This is particularly true as output curves tend to flatten out and brush and bearing wear increase with increasing speed.

For large-bore diesel engines found in trucks and busses, the driven ratio is approximately 2.7:1, which means that every engine rpm produces 2.7 rotor shaft revolutions. In recent years a ratio of 3:1 or even 3.1:1 is becoming common. At 2,000 rpm the alternator will turn 6,000 rpm. Some slow rpm diesels may use a ratio as high as 5:1 in comparison to smaller capacity, higher revving engines that use a ratio as low as 2:1.

V-type belts and pulleys have been the traditional method of driving alternators. However, to extend belt maintenance intervals, manufacturers have moved completely away from using V-type pulleys in favor of serpentine belts, like that shown in FIGURE 15-27, equipped with automatic tensioners. A serpentine belt is a type of multi-rib belt that is long enough to drive multiple accessories. Due to the length of the serpentine belt and the number of accessories it drives, idler pulley are required to ensure

FIGURE 15-26 Alternator end frames enclose and support all components and allow for maximum airflow through the alternator to remove excess heat.

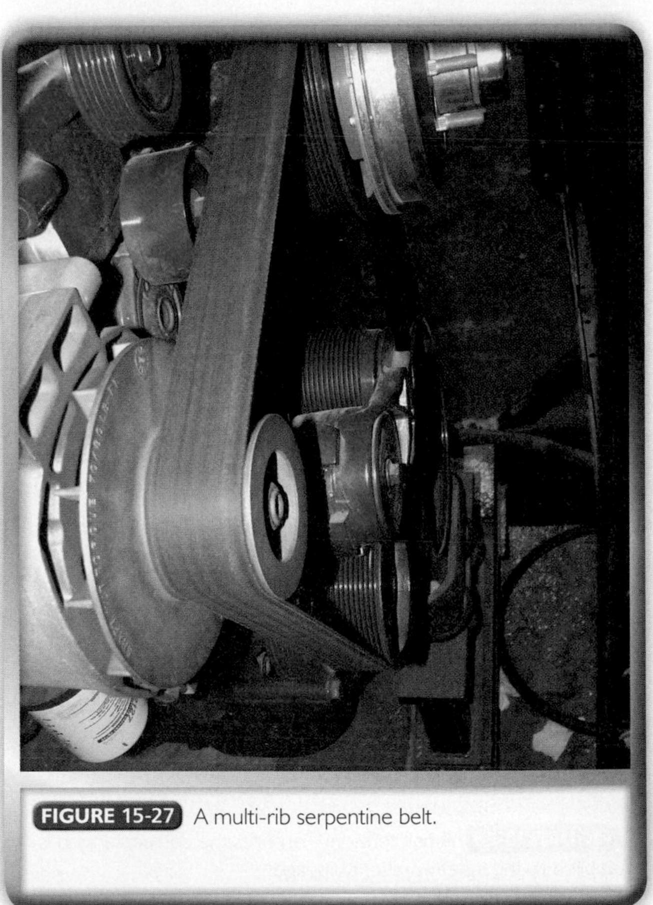

FIGURE 15-27 A multi-rib serpentine belt.

each pulley has enough wrap or surface contact with the belt. Serpentine belt systems reduce belt wear while improving the coupling force with multiple accessories.

Belt tensioners, like that shown in FIGURE 15-28, can be spring-loaded or hydraulic can absorb some of the torsional vibration found in diesels as the crankshaft accelerates and decelerates with each cylinder power and compression event. The alternator drive belt bears the brunt of this damaging force occurring as the engine acceleration rate changes and the alternators, mass resists the speed change. When the belt and alternator speed are out of phase, the belt is snapped and slips. This force is magnified by the 3:1 drive ratio between the crankshaft and alternator pulley. To improve belt life and mechanical efficiency, it is becoming common to use **overrunning alternator decoupler (OAD)** pulleys rather than a conventional solid pulley and tensioner. An OAD pulley uses an internal spring and clutch system that allows it to rotate freely in one direction and provide limited, spring-like movement in the other direction. The pulley acts like a shock absorber, absorbing the force associated with belt accelerations and speed reversals, enabling the alternator to free-wheel when the belt suddenly decelerates.

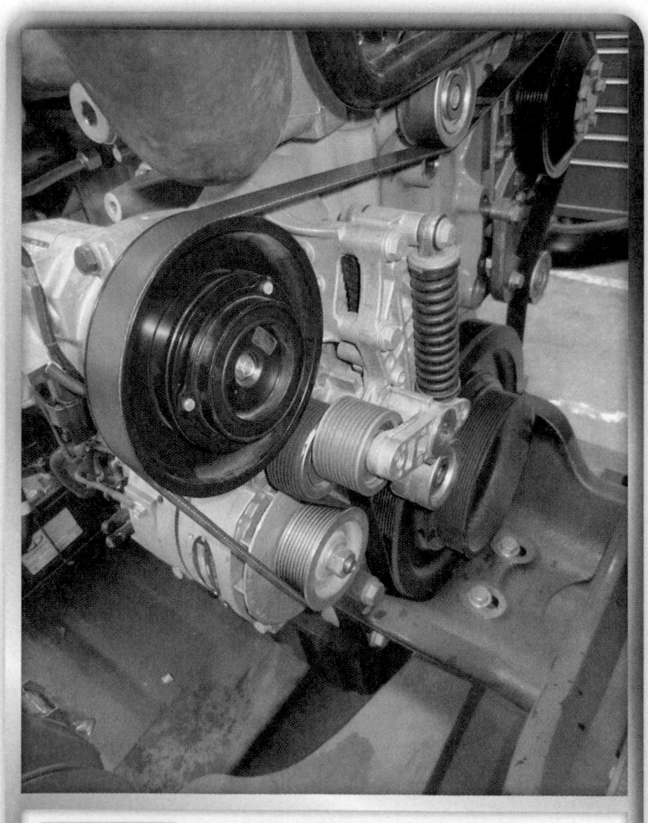

FIGURE 15-28 A belt tensioner ensures the correct tension is applied to the belt to prevent slippage.

Dual Alternators—Paralleling

Vehicles needing extra high current output at idle or those with extra electrical loads can use two or more alternators. Fire trucks, ambulances, RVs, buses, and highway tractors running extra accessories are examples where using **parallel alternators** provides a higher charging voltage at idle with more available amperage. Connecting alternators in parallel requires the output of each to be properly balanced so one will not work harder than the other and wear out. This can happen unless the alternators are exactly identical and sense the same system voltage. In practice this is difficult to achieve because even slight differences using the same regulators and alternators will cause one alternator to charge at a slightly higher voltage than the other. The second alternator will not charge as much, and the first alternator will wear or burn out prematurely.

Several strategies can be used to prevent that from happening:

- Use engineered systems with alternators and regulators designed to work in dual alternator systems.
- While using an amp-clamp to measure output, the alternators, if equipped with adjustable voltage regulators, are adjusted to produce the same amperage output with the lights and accessories switched-on.
- When using identical alternators matched by model and output and having the same regulators, a shunt or cable is connected between the battery positive terminals on the alternators. This helps both alternators to sense the same output current.
- A single regulator for both alternators can be used so the current supplied to the rotor is identical and should produce similar output amperage and set point.
- ECM-controlled alternators may be configured to support two alternators. In this arrangement, the ECM ensures that each alternator produces just the right amount of output for the given requirements.

Alternator Wiring Connections

The terms and connections used in this section are ones commonly used for heavy vehicles. Different manufacturers may use different socket arrangements, color codes, and naming conventions for the various terminals and connectors on alternators, so it is always important to check manufacturer's wiring diagrams and naming conventions for information. The wiring requirements for alternators are relatively simple. This is particularly true for internal regulator self-exciting alternators, like that shown in FIGURE 15-29, as they only use a single battery cable. The battery positive cable is large, red, gauge wire (4AWG or larger). It connects to the battery terminal on the starter and has voltage present at all times. Some alternators, particularly high output ones, will also have a ground or negative cable. A large-gauge wire (4AWG or larger) is connected to battery or chassis ground, as illustrated in FIGURE 15-30. This prevents the engine block from conducting hundreds of amps the alternator may produce and minimizes voltage loss.

A remote sensing connection, as illustrated in FIGURE 15-31, will also be used on some alternators and will usually be marked on the back of the alternator with an "S." The term **sensing** refers to the voltage reference point the alternator uses for regulation of the output. Many alternators reference the battery positive connection from within the alternator. Those alternators using **remote sensing** provide direct reading battery input terminal that is used for the regulator reference voltage. This allows the remote sensing terminal to be connected directly to the batteries, providing the regulator with an accurate battery reference voltage for alternator output and reducing the effect on alternator output of any voltage drop in the battery connection to the alternator.

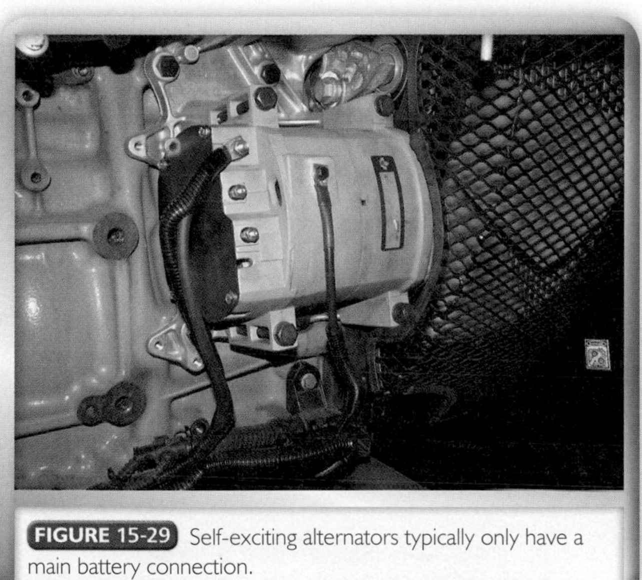

FIGURE 15-29 Self-exciting alternators typically only have a main battery connection.

External regulator alternators will have additional connections to allow for field connections from the regulator to the alternator, as was shown in Figure 15-19. Provision for the connection of alternator warning lights may also be fitted to both internal and external regulator alternators.

Alternators that require external excitation will have an ignition excite or "I" connection. This small gauge wire has voltage present only when the ignition switch is in the run position. Current through this wire switches the voltage regulator on. In light-duty vehicles without voltmeters in the dash and equipped with an instrument cluster warning light, current will pass from the switch and to the light into the alternator regulator to provide initial excitation of the rotors, magnetic field. In heavy-duty vehicles, however, voltmeters are used FIGURE 15-32. When the alternator starts charging, charging voltage appears at the "I" terminal, which provides battery positive to both sides of the light and extinguishes the charging system warning light. In situations where a charge warning light is not required, an ignition feed may be directly connected to the "I" terminal.

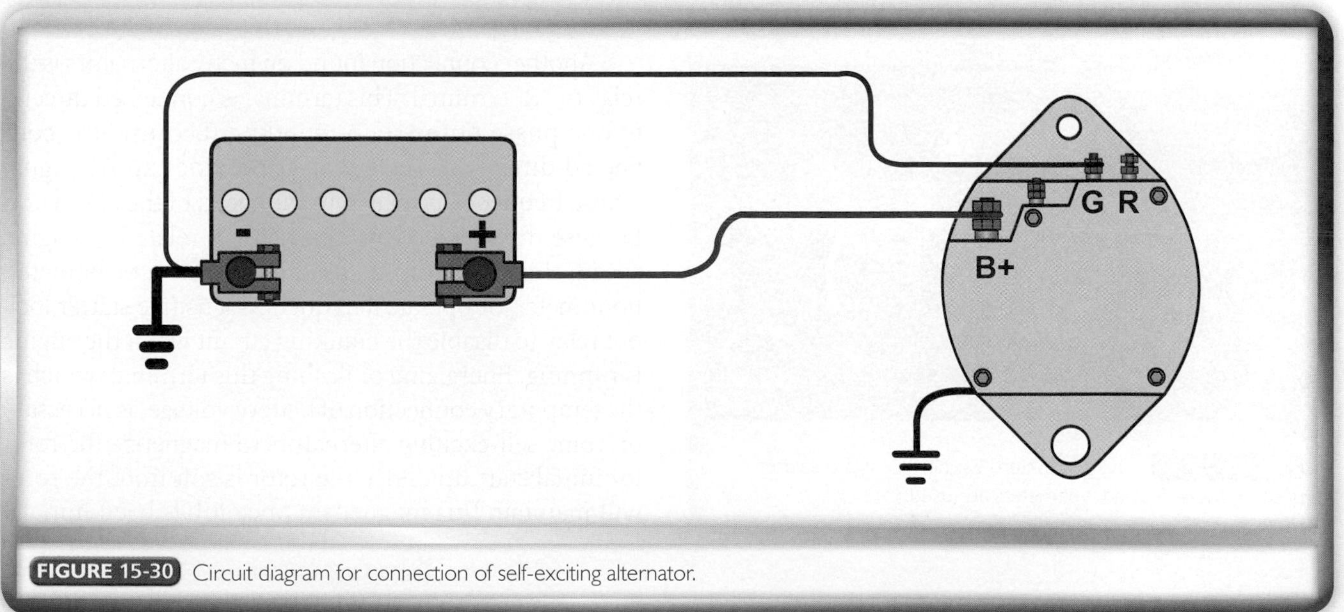

FIGURE 15-30 Circuit diagram for connection of self-exciting alternator.

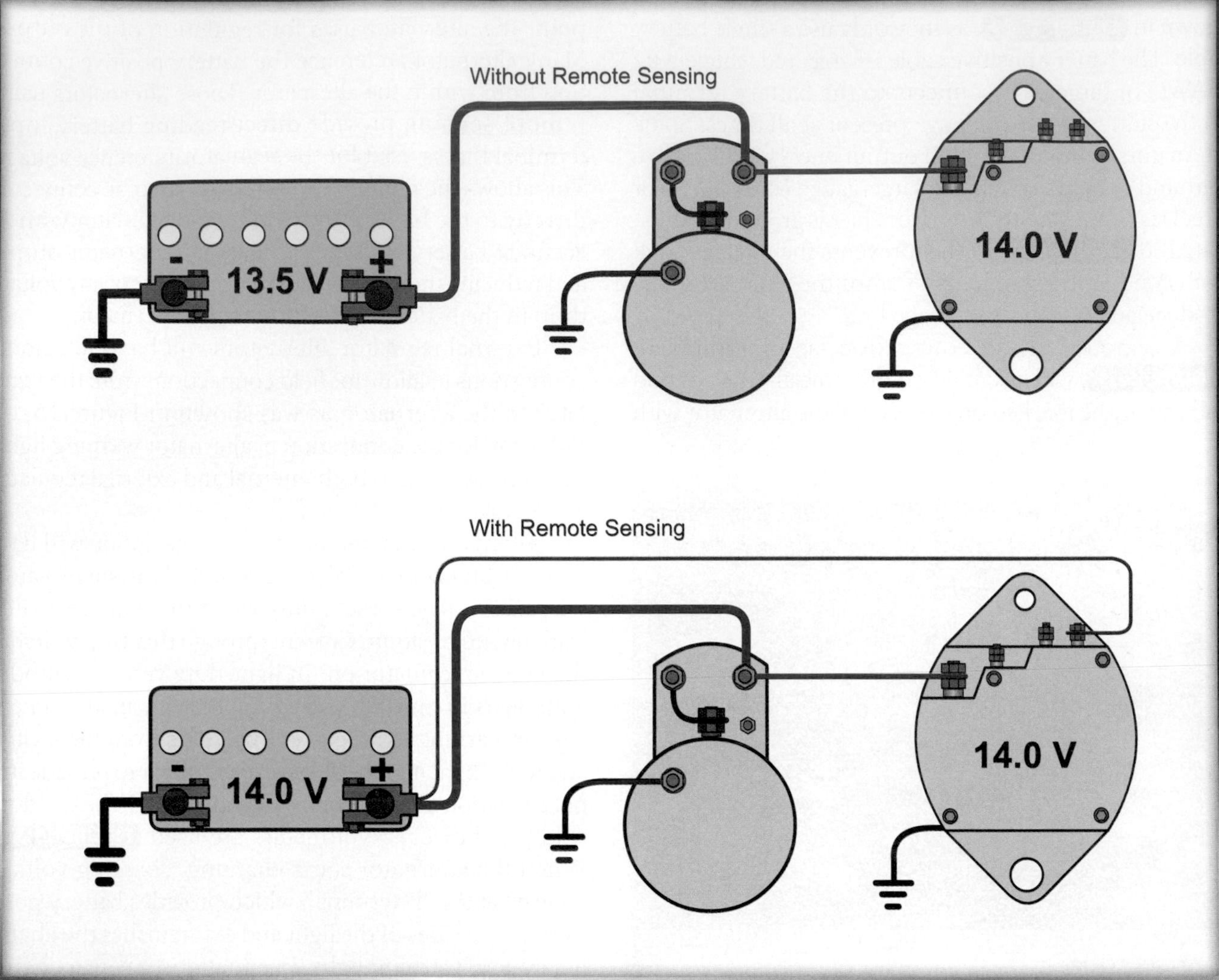

Without Remote Sensing

13.5 V

14.0 V

With Remote Sensing

14.0 V

14.0 V

FIGURE 15-31 Remote sensing allows the voltage regulator to use battery voltage as a reference for alternator output voltage.

FIGURE 15-32 Charging system warning lights are seldom used in trucks. Instead, voltmeters are used.

Another connection found on many alternators is the relay or "R" terminal. This terminal is connected directly to one phase of the stator winding. Because it is connected directly to the stator, it provides an AC signal whose frequency is related to the speed of the alternator. Because the speed of the alternator is related to engine speed, this signal can be used to operate a tachometer, hour meter, or operate a frequency-sensitive starter lock out relay to disable the cranking circuit when the engine is running. Energizing or flashing this terminal, which is the temporary connection of battery voltage, is necessary on some self-exciting alternators to magnetize the rotor for initial start up. Since the rotor is soft iron, the rotor will maintain this magnetism once it has been initially excited. However, after rebuilding or through prolonged inactivity, the rotor may lose the residual magnetism. For this reason, the relay terminal is needed on self-exciting single wire alternators. This feature is common to some Bosch and Delco SI series alternators.

Charging System Diagnosis

When diagnosing charging system problems, always start with the battery. A weak or dead battery, corroded battery cable connections, and/or damaged or worn components may cause a no-crank or slow-crank problem. Check for dirt build-up on the battery top, case damage, loose or corroded connections, or any other trouble that could drain the battery charge. Charging system malfunctions are often identified by battery condition Use TABLE 15-1 to assist in diagnosing charging system problems. Always consult manufacturers' information before commencing any work.

Inspecting, Adjusting, and Replacing Alternator Drive Belts, Pulleys, and Tensioners

If a problem arises with an alternator, perform a visual inspection of its drive belts, pulleys, and tensioners. An index mark on a belt tension indicates whether the belt is too loose or too tight. The tensioner arm should ideally be centered between the two stop points on the tensioner bracket.

Preventive Maintenance Practices

When performing preventative maintenance, the following areas require attention.

1. *Cleaning cable terminals, wiring, and alternator connection points or corrosion*. Alternator surfaces should be cleaned until they are free of accumulations of dirt, grease, and dust. Air passages need to be unobstructed to allow air to easily pass through. All

TABLE 15-1: Charging System Diagnosis Chart

Concern	Cause	Remedy
Overcharged batteries	Resistive voltage sensing lead contact at alternator or electrical system	Repair
	Open voltage sensing circuit	Repair circuit
	Defective voltage regulator	Replace regulator
	Improperly adjusted voltage regulator	Adjust regulator
	One shorted battery in a battery bank	Replace battery
Low voltage or no-charge condition	Loose drive belts	Tighten or replace belt as necessary
	Corroded, broken, burnt, or loose wiring connections	Repair connections
	Undersize battery cables	Install proper gauge cables
	Defective batteries	Replace batteries as required
	Batteries too far from sensing lead contact	Reposition
	Missing sensing lead contact	Repair contact
	Defective voltage regulator	Replace regulator
	Improperly adjusted voltage regulator	Adjust regulator
	Defective rectifier bridge; shorted or open diodes	Replace or overhaul alternator
No magnetic field at alternator	Poor contact between brushes and slip rings	Overhaul alternator / replace brushes
	Damaged or worn brushes/slip rings	Overhaul alternator / replace brushes
	No residual magnetism present in the rotor	Overhaul / replace alternator
	Defective or improperly adjusted regulator	Adjust or replace regulator as required
	Open, shorted, or grounded rotor winding	Overhaul alternator / replace rotor
	No ignition excitation of regulator	Check and repair connection
	No current feed to internal regulator	Check and repair connection

connection points must be clean and free from corrosion since voltage is sensed from between ground and battery positive.

2. *Mounting brackets should be inspected for loose bolts and to allow correct belt alignment*. Broken and loose mounting may indicate damage from engine torsional vibration. If other accessory drive system components are functioning correctly, a sturdier model of alternator may be required.
3. *Condition of belts and belt tension*. A loose belt will slip and cause undercharging. Tensioners must be correctly aligned operating perpendicular to the belt. Multi-grooved belts should be check for cracks, which may extend completely across the belt. The back side of the belt should not be worn and glazed.

Belts can have several issues, as shown in **FIGURE 15-33**. To replace a serpentine belt, follow the guidelines in **SKILL DRILL 15-1**.

Charging System Output Test

Vehicle charging systems are voltage regulated, which means that the alternator will try to maintain a set voltage across the electrical systems. As electrical load current increases in the vehicle systems, voltage starts to drop. The voltage regulator senses this voltage drop and increases the current output of the alternator, which in turn increases system voltage to try to maintain the correct voltage in the system. The testing of an alternator output initially involves the testing of the system's regulated voltage using a voltmeter. Regulated voltage is the voltage at

FIGURE 15-33 Failure conditions for serpentine belts.

SKILL DRILL 15-1 Replacing a Serpentine Belt

1. For safety reasons, disconnect the battery and set the park brake. Inspect the belt for failure. Repair any condition causing belt contamination or failure due to misalignment.
2. Familiarize yourself with the belt routing. Draw a sketch, take a picture of the belt routing, or locate the belt routing diagram in a shop manual or on the radiator module.
3. Release the belt tension to remove the belt. To release belt tension, the automatic belt tensioner is retracted away from the belt using a wrench, socket wrench, 1/2" drive or 3/8" drive ratchet.
4. Inspect the drive belt pulley system for wear. Make sure the tensioner and the pulleys operate freely, without noise or looseness, and are in perfect condition. The tensioner pulley should contact the belt squarely; if not, the tensioner should be replaced. The installation of a belt kit containing a new tensioner and drive pulleys is recommended when replacing a belt at high accumulated mileage.
5. Before installing the new belt, inspect the alignment of the pulleys to prevent severe belt wear, damage, and belt noise.
6. Route and install the new belt according to the belt routing diagram. Align the belt ribs with the pulley grooves and ensure that the belt fits squarely on each pulley and all the belt grooves fit into the pulley grooves.
7. Release the belt tensioner once again to install the belt over the tensioner pulley. The automatic tensioner will apply the correct tension to the belt. When the installation tension is correct, start the engine and observe if the belt drive and tensioning system is properly functioning.

which the regulator is allowing the alternator to create only a small charge due to the battery being relatively charged, as evidenced by the greatly reduced current output.

Unless the batteries are deeply discharged, the vehicle headlights should not dim at idle when the alternator is operating satisfactorily. To performance test the charging system, also called a set-point test, alternator voltage and amperage is measured with the engine running at 1,000–1,500 rpm. With all the vehicle loads switched off and the batteries fully charged, alternator output should be 20 amps or less, and voltage should be 13.8–14.4 volts for a 12-volt system. 24-volt systems should charge between 27.8 and 28.4 volts. If the voltage is not within this range and the regulator not adjustable, the alternator is likely defective.

An alternator's performance is tested under load and measured while the engine is at 1,500 rpm. A carbon pile tester is connected to the batteries, and the system is loaded until it drops to 12.5 volts. At 12.5 volts, the amperage output from the alternator is also measured. Output should generally be within 10% of the alternator's maximum rating. This means that a 200-amp alternator should deliver at least 180 amps.

To differentiate between a defective regulator and the current generating section of an alternator, a full field test of the alternator is performed. This means that the voltage regulator is by-passed, and full battery voltage is supplied briefly to the rotor slip rings. The type of alternator circuit must be identified before performing this test.

"A" circuit alternators will ground one brush. In Delco alternators, ground is done by passing a screwdriver through the "D" tab at the back of the alternator. With the screwdriver against the alternator frame and the other end on a tab of the voltage regulator, a working alternator will begin to generate current. A voltmeter is used to measure output. If voltage rises, the regulator is defective and may be replaced instead of replacing the entire alternator.

"B" circuits will use a jumper wire connected to battery positive to full-field. Isolated circuits will use two jumper wires. CAN-controlled alternators will provide diagnostic information needed to diagnose alternator problems. If current output does not rise after **full fielding**, it may indicate one of the following conditions:

- A shorted, open, or grounded rotor coil
- Stator windings shorted, open, or grounded
- Rectifier bridge shorted, open, or grounded

To perform a charging system output test, follow the guidelines in **SKILL DRILL 15-2**.

SKILL DRILL 15-2 Performing a Charging System Output Test

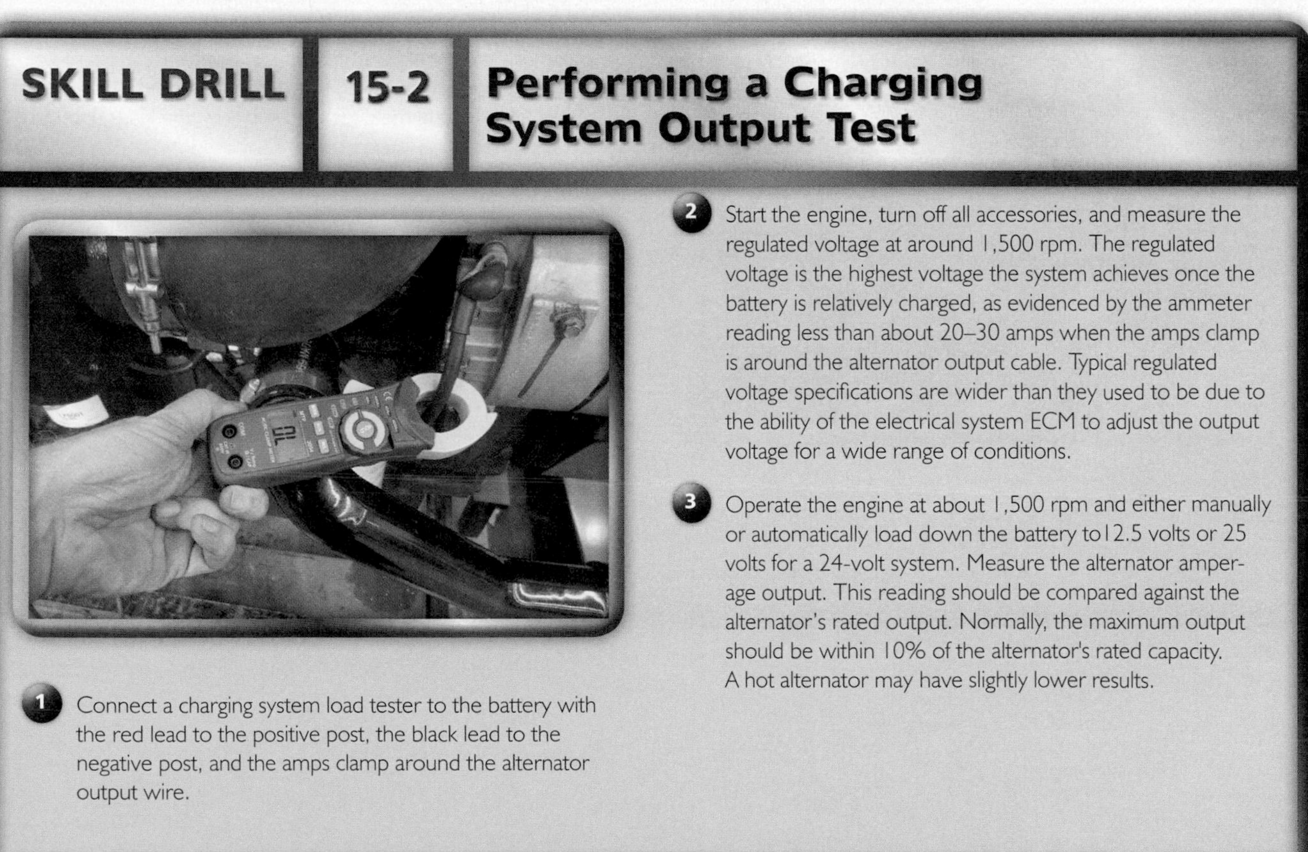

1. Connect a charging system load tester to the battery with the red lead to the positive post, the black lead to the negative post, and the amps clamp around the alternator output wire.

2. Start the engine, turn off all accessories, and measure the regulated voltage at around 1,500 rpm. The regulated voltage is the highest voltage the system achieves once the battery is relatively charged, as evidenced by the ammeter reading less than about 20–30 amps when the amps clamp is around the alternator output cable. Typical regulated voltage specifications are wider than they used to be due to the ability of the electrical system ECM to adjust the output voltage for a wide range of conditions.

3. Operate the engine at about 1,500 rpm and either manually or automatically load down the battery to 12.5 volts or 25 volts for a 24-volt system. Measure the alternator amperage output. This reading should be compared against the alternator's rated output. Normally, the maximum output should be within 10% of the alternator's rated capacity. A hot alternator may have slightly lower results.

> **TECHNICIAN TIP**
>
> The battery, or battery terminals, should never be removed when the engine is running. Removing battery terminals on alternator-equipped vehicle may damage the alternator and sensitive electronic equipment fitted to the vehicle.

Testing Charging System Circuit Voltage Drop

An excessive voltage drop in the charging system output and ground circuit tends to cause one of two problems: (1) The battery is not able to be fully charged because, although the alternator is producing the specified voltage, the voltage drop is reducing the amount of voltage to the battery, or (2) the battery is fully charged, but the alternator is working at a higher voltage to do so, potentially overheating it. Which of the two issues is occurring depends on where the voltage is sensed. If it is sensed at the alternator, then the battery will generally be undercharged. If the voltage is sensed at the battery, then the alternator will work at the higher voltage. Knowing the system will help you diagnose voltage drop issues in the output and ground circuits of the charging system.

The alternator cable voltage drop test is performed to test the positive cable for excessive resistance between the alternator and the batteries. With the engine running at 1,500 rpm and the alternator loaded to 75% of its output capacity, voltage is measured at the alternator and batteries. If the voltage difference is greater than 0.25 volts in a 12-volt circuit or 0.50 volts in a 24-volt circuit, all positive and ground wire cable connections should be checked. Acceptable cable voltage drop readings are less than 0.25 volts in 12-volt system and 0.50 volts in a 24-volt system. To test charging circuit voltage drop, follow the guidelines in **SKILL DRILL 15-3**.

SKILL DRILL 15-3 Testing Charging Circuit Voltage Drop

1. Set the DVOM up to measure voltage, and select min/max if available. Connect the red probe of the DVOM to the output terminal of the alternator and the black probe to the positive post of the battery. The red probe goes on the positive battery post because, in this case, the alternator output terminal is higher voltage than the positive battery terminal. For the meter to read correctly, the leads need to be connected as listed.
2. Start the engine and turn on as many electrical loads as possible or use an external load bank to load the battery. Read the maximum voltage drop for the output circuit.
3. Move the leads to measure the voltage drop on the ground circuit by placing the black probe on the alternator case and the red probe on the negative terminal of the battery. With the engine running and the circuit still loaded, read the maximum voltage drop for the ground circuit.
4. If the measurements are excessive, check each part of the circuit for excessive voltage drops by slowly bringing the probes closer together on each section of the circuit. Determine any necessary actions.

Inspecting, Repairing, or Replacing Connectors and Wires of Charging Circuits

When you are diagnosing charging system problems, you should always make sure you visually inspect connectors and wires of charging circuits for tightness, wear, or damage. Check the connection on the voltage regulator and the alternator for loose electrical connections or shorted wires. Move the wires around while running the engine. If the warning lamp flickers or the ammeter instrument indicates incorrect charging, the problem is in the wire being jarred. You may need to perform a voltage drop test to check wiring along the charging system path. When replacing connectors and/or wires, always refer to the appropriate manufacturer's service manual for the exact procedure. To inspect, repair, or replace connectors and wires of charging circuits, follow the guidelines in SKILL DRILL 15-4.

Removing, Inspecting, and Replacing an Alternator

During charging system tests, low voltage and current output problems may indicate a defective alternator. If you find that the alternator is defective, it will need to be replaced. It is the rotors, brushes, stators, rectifier bridges, and cooling fans of the alternator that work together to create magnetic fields, produce current, and charge the system.

Alternators all operate on the same principle. There are, however, differences in their construction and style. Different manufacturers will usually favor different types of alternators. Always refer to the appropriate manufacturer's service manual for the specific type and style of alternator. Follow the manufacturer's instructions when installing a new alternator. To remove, inspect, and replace an alternator, follow the guidelines in SKILL DRILL 15-5.

SKILL DRILL 15-4 Inspecting, Repairing, or Replacing Connectors and Wires of Charging Circuits

1. Locate and follow the appropriate procedure and wiring diagram in the service manual.
2. Move the vehicle into the shop, apply the parking brakes, and chock the vehicle wheels. Observe lockout and tagout procedures.
3. If the vehicle has a manual transmission, place it in "neutral." If it has an automatic transmission, place it in "park" or "neutral."
4. Trace the wiring harness from the alternator to the battery and around the engine bay.
5. Check the harness and connectors for wear, damage, or corrosion.
6. Disconnect the battery negative cable if repairs are necessary.
7. Repair damaged areas with replacement cables or connectors. Ensure all harnesses are secured to prevent abrasion or damage from vibration.
8. Reconnect all harness plugs and secure all connections.
9. Reconnect the battery negative cable.
10. Check repair by visual inspection and running the vehicle.
11. Clean the work area and return tools and materials to their proper storage.

Overhauling an Alternator

Overhauling an alternator requires the disassembly and checking of all component parts. The alternator component parts should also be cleaned and replaced or repaired as necessary. The alternator is relatively simple to disassemble. You should always mark the position of the housings in relation to each other before commencing disassembly. This ensures that the housings are correctly aligned when reassembled.

Most alternators have the brushes inside the alternator, and they cannot be removed until the alternator is disassembled. However, some alternators have a brush box, which should be removed before the alternator is disassembled. Before commencing disassembly, check to see if the brushes can be removed while the alternator is in one piece. If so, undo the brush box and remove it. To disassemble the alternator, remove the through bolts with a suitable wrench or socket. Pry the housings apart; this may require a screwdriver to lever apart the housings, as they are usually a tight fit. When prying the housings apart, be careful not to damage any of the stator windings. The rotor will usually be attached to the pulley end housing. Once the alternator is separated into its two housings, further disassemble the alternator into its component parts. This may require the use of a soldering iron to remove the rectifier diodes and the brushes. The rectifier and main battery terminals will have a number of insulating bushings fitted to them. Be sure to note how the insulators are fitted for later replacement.

Once the alternator has been disassembled into its component parts, conduct the following tests for each component:

- **Housings**: Clean and check housings for cracks. If they are damaged, replace them.
- **Rotor**:
  - Check the resistance of the winding against the manufacturer's specifications. In some cases, it is also useful to check the current draw of the winding. Remember, the winding is inductive. This means it will produce a spark when power is connected or disconnected.

SKILL DRILL 15-5 Removing, Inspecting, and Replacing an Alternator

1. Locate and follow the appropriate procedure in the service manual.
2. Move the vehicle into the workshop, apply the parking brakes, and chock the vehicle wheels. Observe lockout and tagout procedures.
3. If the vehicle has a manual transmission, place it in "neutral." If it has an automatic transmission, place it in "park" or "neutral."
4. Disconnect the battery from the vehicle.
5. Disconnect wires at the connector on the alternator. Make a note of the location and any special insulating washers.
6. Loosen bolts.
7. Slide the belt off the alternator.
8. Lift the alternator out of vehicle.
9. Place a new alternator onto the engine.
10. Hand screw the bolts without tightening; connect wires first if needed.
11. After checking the condition of the belt and replacing it if needed, slip the belt on each pulley and align properly.
12. If required, adjust belt tension using belt tension gauge.
13. Tighten the bolts.
14. Reconnect the battery.
15. Start the vehicle and verify that the alternator is charging.
16. Clean the work area and return tools and materials to their proper storage.

- If the alternator has slip rings, check them for mechanical wear. If they are excessively worn, the slip ring assembly will need to be replaced. To do this, remove the coil wires and press off the old slip ring. Press on a new slip ring and reconnect the coil wires. You may need to machine a new slip ring in the lathe to produce a clean, round finish.
- Check bearing surfaces and pulley retaining thread for wear. Replace the rotor if they are excessively worn.

- **Diode rectifier**: Check the diode rectifier with a diode checker. You can use a DVOM, however, a specialized alternator diode tester is recommended as it places a load on the diodes. Replace diodes if they fail the test. In some cases, individual diodes can be replaced. In others, the whole rectifier must be replaced as a unit.
- **Regulator**: Use a regulator tester to check the regulator. Each regulator tester is slightly different, although they perform the same job. Always check the manufacturer's specifications for the correct hookup and procedure. Modern regulators are electronic and generally cannot be repaired. Replace the regulator if required.
- **Brushes**: If fitted, brushes should be replaced whenever the alternator is overhauled. Take care when reassembling the alternator to ensure the brushes are not damaged. Many alternators require the insertion of a pin to hold the brushes away from the slip rings as the alternator is reassembled.
- **Bearings**: Bearings should be replaced whenever the alternator is overhauled.
- **Pulley and fan**: Check the pulley and fan for wear and replace if necessary. When replacing the fan, ensure that it is replaced with one that operates in the same direction as the one removed.

Once the alternator has been overhauled, you will need to test it in an alternator test bench. Clamp the alternator securely in the test bench and make the electrical connections. Pay particular attention to the battery, regulator, and warning light to ensure they are connected as per the manufacturer's specifications. Run the alternator up to speed and make sure the warning light operates correctly, the alternator can generate its specified maximum current output, and the regulated voltage is according to specifications. To overhaul an alternator, follow the guidelines in SKILL DRILL 15-6.

SKILL DRILL 15-6 Overhauling an Alternator

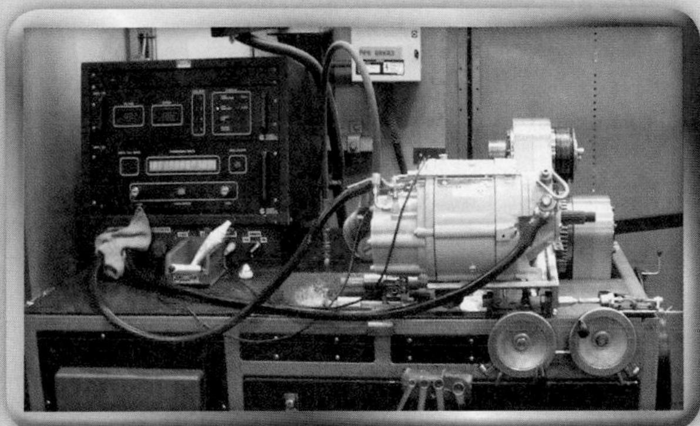

1. Locate and follow the appropriate procedure in the service manual.
2. Check to see if the brushes need to be removed first. If so, remove the brush box or regulator.
3. Remove the through bolts holding the alternator together.
4. Pry the alternator apart.
5. Disassemble the component parts from the housing. Take note of the placement of insulator bushes.
6. Clean, test, and inspect all component parts. Use specialized testers where necessary; for example, regulator tester, diode tester, and DVOM.
7. Replace any faulty components. If the slip ring assembly requires replacement, ensure the new slip ring is machined on the lathe.
8. Reassemble component parts into the housings.
9. Reassemble the alternator housings. Ensure the brushes are retained using a retaining pin to prevent damage to them.
10. Test the alternator in the alternator test bench. Ensure the warning light circuit is working and test for maximum current output and voltage regulation.
11. Clean the work area and return tools and materials to their proper storage.

Wrap-up

Ready for Review

- Both DC generators and alternators produce electricity by relative movement of conductors in a magnetic field. The key difference between an alternator and a DC generator is which component rotates or moves to generate electricity.
- The charging system provides electrical energy for all of the electrical components on the vehicle. The main parts of the charging system include the battery, the alternator, the voltage regulator (which may be integrated into the alternator), a charge warning light or voltmeter, and wiring that completes the circuits.
- The alternator converts mechanical energy into electrical energy by electromagnetic induction.
- A single-phase stator has a single winding, which creates a single sine wave. In a typical vehicle alternator, there are three seprate coils of wire composing the stator.
- Alternators have a built in maximum current limitation due to the counter electromotive force (CEMF) in the stator coils.
- Brushless alternators have greater longevity than alternators with brushes.
- Alternators require an initial magnetic field to be produced within the rotor to initiate the process of generating electricity. Initial excitation can be either internal or external.
- Wye and Delta windings produce three-phase AC current, but voltage and amperage outputs differ. The Wye configuration produces higher voltage at lower rotor speeds.
- Alternators are much more efficient at producing current than DC generators. Alternating current—not direct current—is produced inside an alternator.
- To change AC to DC, automotive alternators use a rectifier assembly consisting of two diodes for every phase of the stator winding.
- Alternators' voltage output is controlled by a voltage regulator. The voltage regulator regulates current output and limits maximum charging system voltage.
- A significant amount of heat is produced within the alternator from the rectifier, stator, and rotor windings. The two main types of cooling systems used on heavy-duty vehicle alternators are air and oil cooling.
- Alternators can be driven by a pulley or direct drive through a gear.
- Vehicles needing extra high current output at idle or those with extra electrical loads can use two or more alternators.
- When diagnosing charging system problems, always start with the battery. A weak or dead battery, corroded battery cable connections, and/or damaged or worn components may cause a no-crank or slow-crank problem.

Vocabulary Builder

AC ripple A pattern produced by voltage fluctuations from the alternator that create differences between the peak voltage of an AC sine wave and the minimum voltage found in the trough between sine waves.

alternator ripple The top of the waveform.

Delta windings Stator windings in which the windings are connected in the shape of a triangle.

full fielding Making the alternator produce maximum amperage output.

load-dumping A feature that allows temporary suppression of high-voltage spikes.

overrunning alternator decoupler (OAD) A pulley that uses an internal spring and clutch system that allows it to rotate freely in one direction and provide limited, spring-like movement in the other direction.

parallel alternators The practice of connecting alternators in parallel to provide higher charging voltage at idle with more available amperage.

rectification A process of converting alternating current (AC) into direct current (DC).

remote sensing Referencing the battery positive connection through an input terminal that is used for the regulator reference voltage.

residual magnetism The small amount of magnetism left on the rotor after it is initially magnetized by the coil windings' magnetic field.

self-exciting alternator An alternator that relies on the residual magnetism found in the rotor after operating as a way to switch on the voltage regulator and supply current to the rotor.

sensing The voltage reference point the alternator uses for regulation of the output.

transient voltage suppression (TVS) diodes Specialized diodes in the rectifier bridge that become resistive rather than conductive at a specific voltage level.

Wye windings Stator windings in which one end of each phase winding is taken to a central point where the ends are connected together.

Review Questions

1. Which of the following are functions of the battery?
   a. Stores an electrical charge in chemical form.
   b. Acts as an electrical dampening device for variations in voltage or voltage spikes
   c. Provides the electrical energy for cranking the engine.
   d. All of the choices are correct.
2. Which of the following are correct concerning alternator principles?
   a. The alternator converts mechanical energy into electrical energy by electromagnetic induction.
   b. In a simplified version, a bar magnet rotates in an iron yoke, which concentrates the magnetic field.
   c. A coil of wire is wound around each end of the yoke; as the magnet turns, voltage is induced in the coil, producing a current flow.
   d. All of the choices are correct.
3. Which of the following is NOT an alternator classification?
   a. Externally air cooled
   b. Oil cooled
   c. Water cooled
   d. Sealed
4. Between ________ and ________ pole pieces or "claws" are found in the rotor of heavy vehicle alternators.
   a. 4; 8
   b. 8; 12
   c. 12; 16
   d. 18 ; 22
5. Which of the following is correct concerning phase winding connections?
   a. As the name suggests, Wye windings resemble the letter "Y."
   b. The advantage of Wye windings is that they produce higher voltage at comparably lower rotor speeds.
   c. This means the alternator can begin charging a battery at lower engine speeds.
   d. All of the choices are correct.
6. Which of the following is correct concerning rectifier diode problems?
   a. Heat can cause premature failures of diodes.
   b. Additional cooling of rectifier bridges can be accomplished with heavier diodes and heat sinks or by connecting diodes in parallel so that six rather than three pairs accomplish the work.
   c. Both A and B
   d. Neither A nor B
7. Which of the following is correct concerning smoothing capacitors?
   a. Capacitors can be used to smooth alternator AC ripple and prevent EMI.
   b. In the alternator, one is connected across the output to act like an electric shock absorber.
   c. When the output voltage increases slightly, the capacitor will charge and absorb the new increase.
   d. All of the choices are correct.
8. Which of the following charging system set points is accurate 12.6 to 12.9 volts?
   a. 13.0 to 13.4 volts
   b. 13.5 to 14.6 volts
   c. 14.1 to 15.1 volts
9. What is the minimum oil flow to cool a large, oil-cooled alternator used on a bus?
   a. 1 gallon (3.8 liters) flow per minute
   b. 2 gallons (7.6 liters) flow per minute
   c. 3 gallons (11.4 liters) flow per minute
   d. 4 gallons (15.2 liters) flow per minute
10. Vents within the frames provide for a ________ amount of airflow to assist in dissipating heat.
    a. large
    b. steady
    c. small
    d. barely perceptible

ASE-Type Questions

1. Technician A says that today, the average 12-volt electrical system loads for a late-model highway tractor add up to 150 amps at peak with an 84-amp average. Technician B says that both DC generators and alternators produce electricity by relative movement of conductors in a magnetic field. Who is correct?
   a. Technician A
   b. Technician B
   c. Both Technician A and Technician B
   d. Neither Technician A nor Technician B
2. Technician A says that alternators have more moving parts as compared to generators. Technician B says that alternators can produce power at engine idle speeds; generators cannot. Who is correct?
   a. Technician A
   b. Technician B
   c. Both Technician A and Technician B
   d. Neither Technician A nor Technician B
3. Technician A says that the two most important parts in an alternator used to produce electrical current are the rotor and stator winding. Technician B says that the rotor contains a spinning electromagnet that induces current flow in the stator winding, which is made up of numerous coils of wire. Who is correct?
   a. Technician A
   b. Technician B
   c. Both Technician A and Technician B
   d. Neither Technician A nor Technician B
4. Technician A says that the rotor is a rotating electromagnet that provides the magnetic field to induce voltage and current in the stator. Technician B says that the direct-gear drive mechanism is used in most cases but that a pulley drive may also be employed. Who is correct?
   a. Technician A
   b. Technician B
   c. Both Technician A and Technician B
   d. Neither Technician A nor Technician B
5. Technician A says that regulated current to the alternator rotor is supplied through a pair of graphite brushes sliding against slip rings on the rotor shaft. Technician B says that heavy duty springs help the brushes maintain contact with the slip rings. Who is correct?
   a. Technician A
   b. Technician B
   c. Both Technician A and Technician B
   d. Neither Technician A nor Technician B
6. Technician A says that vehicles fitted with self-exciting alternators may require the engine rpm to be briefly increased after every start-up to initiate charging. Technician B says that using self-exciting alternators eliminates the need for a separate circuit from the key switch to the alternator and simplifies chassis wiring. Who is correct?
   a. Technician A
   b. Technician B
   c. Both Technician A and Technician B
   d. Neither Technician A nor Technician B
7. Technician A says that the stator is mounted between two end housings, and it holds the stator windings stationary so that the rotating magnetic field cuts through the stator windings, inducing an electric current in the windings. Technician B says that to smooth the pulsating current flow, there are three distinct layers of windings offset 60 degrees in each layer from one another. Who is correct?
   a. Technician A
   b. Technician B
   c. Both Technician A and Technician B
   d. Neither Technician A nor Technician B
8. Technician A says that stators are normally serviced in a repair facility. Technician B says that stators can be visually checked during rebuilding for burnt, cut, or nicked winding laminations. Who is correct?
   a. Technician A
   b. Technician B
   c. Both Technician A and Technician B
   d. Neither Technician A nor Technician B
9. Technician A says that alternators produce alternating current, which is acceptable for operating many electrical devices. Technician B says that converting the AC current to usable DC current is referred to as modulation. Who is correct?
   a. Technician A
   b. Technician B
   c. Both Technician A and Technician B
   d. Neither Technician A nor Technician B
10. Technician A says that voltage regulators are first classified as either external or internal. Technician B says that the majority of late-model alternators have external regulators. Who is correct?
    a. Technician A
    b. Technician B
    c. Both Technician A and Technician B
    d. Neither Technician A nor Technician B

CHAPTER 16

NATEF Tasks

Electrical/Electronic Systems

General Electrical Systems | Page

- Read and interpret electrical/electronic circuits using wiring diagrams. **471–483**

Knowledge Objectives

After reading this chapter, you will be able to:

1. Describe the elements that make up a wiring schematic (i.e., wire markings, wire size, symbols of components, grounds, relationship between components and circuits, power distribution). (pp 462–463)
2. Identify types and applications of electrical wiring. (pp 462–465)
3. Identify and describe wiring repair procedures. (pp 468–470)
4. Identify schematic diagram electrical symbols SAE, DIN, and Valley Forge. (pp 471–482)
5. Describe how to read wiring schematics. (pp 471–482)
6. 6. Recommend diagnostic strategies using electrical schematics and test equipment. (pp 471–482)
7. Describe various uses of electrical schematics. (pp 474–481)
8. Identify differences between various types of electrical schematics—pictorial, isometric, block, schematic, and wiring diagrams—and power and ground distribution. (pp 474–481)

Electrical Wiring and Circuit Diagrams

Skills Objectives

After reading this chapter, you will be able to:

1. Strip wire insulation. (p 469)
2. Install a solderless terminal. (p 470)
3. Solder wires and connectors. (p 470)
4. Use wiring diagrams to diagnose electrical circuits. (p 471–483)

Introduction

Wires and wiring harnesses connect components in the vehicle's electrical system, and as such they need to be kept in good condition, free of any damage or corrosion. They carry the electrical power and signals through the vehicle to control virtually all of the systems on a vehicle. As technology in vehicles has increased, so, too, has the number of wires and cables installed on these vehicles. Although wireless communication is being used in some vehicle security, entertainment, and tire pressure monitoring systems, wires are still the dominant signal carriers in a vehicle. This chapter will cover basics about wiring, including wiring requirements, how wires are sized and coded, basic wiring repair, and types of wiring diagrams.

Electric Wiring

Electrical wiring has numerous requirements specific to heavy-duty vehicles. Wiring is sized and color- and number-coded to ensure the proper wire is used for the specific application.

Wiring Requirements

Because conductors carry electron flow through the electrical system, wiring is a critical component in the electrical system. When selecting wires or cables for applications, consideration needs to be given to the following factors:

- *The amount of amperage flowing through a circuit*. Smaller wires become more resistant and heat up as amperage increases. Larger wiring increases cost and weight.
- *The operating environment*. The type of wire will differ depending on whether it is used in the engine compartment, inside the engine, inside or outside the cab, or along the chassis. Exposure to oil, grease, fuel, abrasion, and the elements change the requirements for electrical wiring.
- *Circuit identification*. The complexities of chassis wiring necessitates the use of color coding and numbering of circuits for assembling and connecting harnesses as well as to simplify repairs.

Wire Sizing

Increasing amperage through a circuit increases resistance, as predicted by Joule's law. Circuits carrying too much current will heat to the point where they can even cause a fire. Using wires that are too small in diameter may also cause a fire. Ohm's law predicts voltage drop using the formula:

$$V_{drop} = \text{Amperage} \times \text{Resistance}$$

You Are the Technician

After a positive battery cable grounded out near the alternator, high-amperage current melted the cable and burned though a number of other nearby wiring harnesses, damaging them. Several of the other harnesses also grounded through the battery cable when they were melting. Because the vehicle was relatively new, the insurance adjuster has requested the vehicle be repaired by replacing or repairing the harness as necessary.

After inspecting the damage, you've determined there are two possible directions for the repairs to take. One approach is to replace the harnesses, as the vehicle has a modular harnesses system. Several major harnesses would have to be disconnected and removed and a new one reinstalled. The other approach is to replace only damaged sections of the harnesses. This second approach would be less labor intensive, and the material cost would be substantially lower. There are a number of other factors that will also guide your final decisions, but as you weigh them, consider the following:

1. Outline the various factors that will guide the selection of materials for replacing sections of the harnesses. Include information about the features of the wiring, connectors, splices, and so on.
2. Outline in the correct sequence the steps you should take to properly make multiple splices to replace wiring in a major wiring harness.
3. Identify and list the tools and any other resources you will need to make proper repairs of the wiring harness.

This means a conductor 100' long with 0.5 ohms of resistance required to carry 10 amps of current in a 12-volt circuit will see a voltage drop of 5 volts FIGURE 16-1. Available voltage at the end of the conductor is:

$$12 - 5 = 7 \text{ volts}$$

The same circuit carrying only 5 amps of current will drop only 2.5 volts, resulting in 9.5 available volts. Therefore, the diameter of wire for a circuit is based on the amount of amperage and the length of the circuit. Longer circuits and higher amperage require larger diameter of wire. As shown in TABLE 16-1, as wire diameter increases, less voltage is dropped.

Two major classification systems for measuring wire diameter the American Wire Gage (AWG) and the Metric Gauge system. See FIGURE 16-2. Both systems measure the wire size only and not the wire and insulator. The AWG system is more than a hundred years old and measures wire gauge in numbers from 0000 to 50. As the gauge number increases, the diameter of the wire decreases. A 0000 wire is approximately 0.5" diameter while a 10 gauge is 0.102" in diameter. Using the AWG system, the wire diameter doubles for every 6-gauge decrease. The gauges 00, 000, and 0000 are often used to measure battery cables and can also be written 2/0, 3/0, and 4/0, respectively.

The Metric Gauge scale measures the cross sectional surface area of the wire and not its diameter. Sizes are rounded up to provide an even number for the wire size. For example, a 1 mm^2 wire is 0.823 mm^2, and a 2.080 mm^2 is 2.5 mm^2. In most wiring diagrams, metric-sized

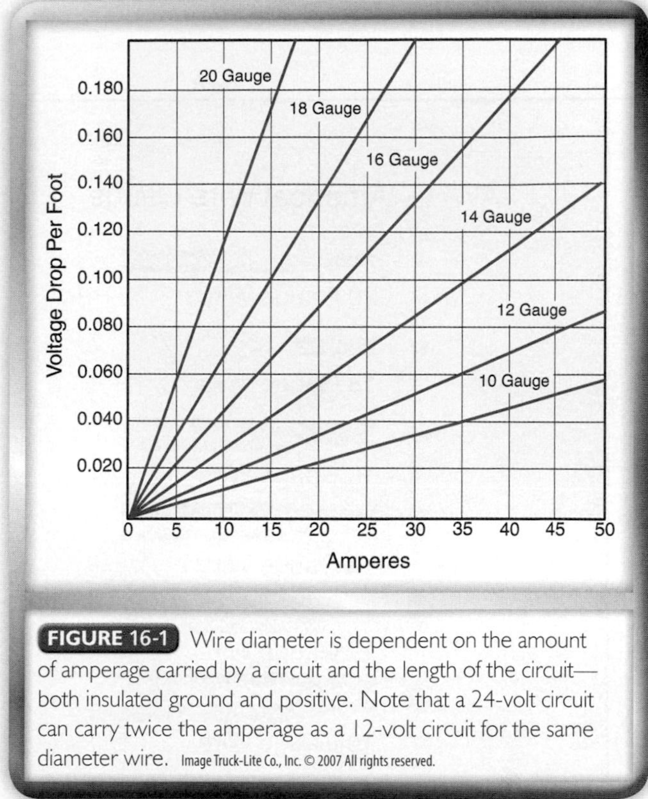

FIGURE 16-1 Wire diameter is dependent on the amount of amperage carried by a circuit and the length of the circuit—both insulated ground and positive. Note that a 24-volt circuit can carry twice the amperage as a 12-volt circuit for the same diameter wire.

TABLE 16-1: Total Footage of Wire from Power Source to the Most Distant Electric Lamp

Amperage Required

24v System	12v System	10'	20'	30'	40'	50'	60'	70'	80'	90'	100'
2.0	1.0	18	18	18	18	18	18	18	18	18	18
3.0	1.5	18	18	18	18	18	18	18	18	18	18
4.0	2.0	18	18	18	18	18	18	18	16	16	16
6.0	3.0	18	18	18	18	18	16	16	16	14	14
8.0	4.0	18	18	18	16	16	16	14	14	14	12
10.0	5.0	18	18	18	16	14	14	14	12	12	12
12.0	6.0	18	18	16	16	14	14	12	12	12	12
14.0	7.0	18	18	16	14	14	12	12	12	10	10
16.0	8.0	18	18	16	14	12	12	12	10	10	10
20.0	10.0	18	16	14	12	12	12	10	10	10	10
22.0	11.0	18	16	14	12	12	10	10	10	10	8
24.0	12.0	18	16	14	12	12	10	10	10	8	8
30.0	15.0	18	16	12	12	10	10	10	8	8	8
36.0	18.0	16	14	12	10	10	8	8	8	8	8
40.0	20.0	16	14	12	10	10	8	8	8	8	6

Source: Truck-Lite Co., Inc. © 2007 All rights reserved.

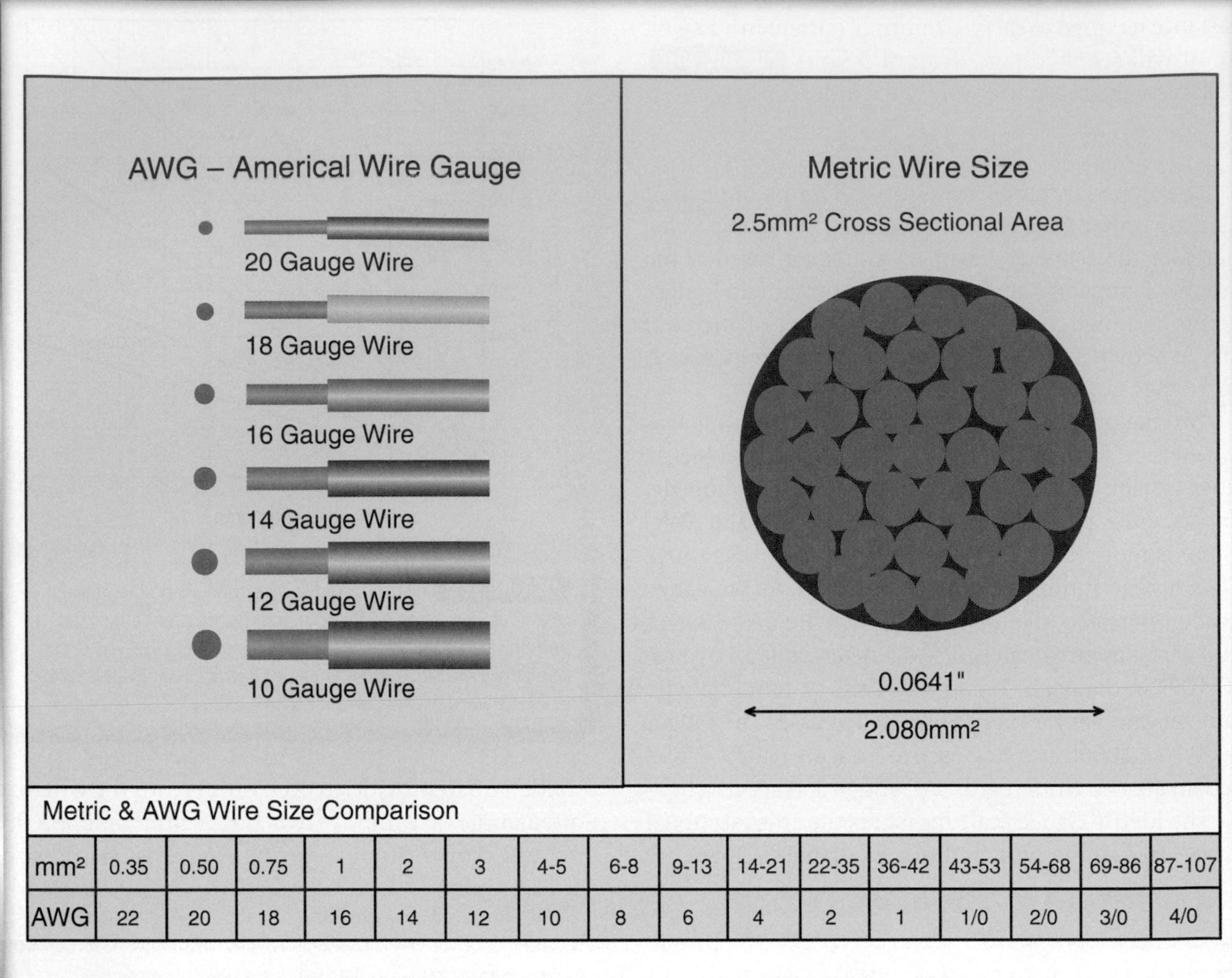

Metric & AWG Wire Size Comparison

mm²	0.35	0.50	0.75	1	2	3	4-5	6-8	9-13	14-21	22-35	36-42	43-53	54-68	69-86	87-107
AWG	22	20	18	16	14	12	10	8	6	4	2	1	1/0	2/0	3/0	4/0

FIGURE 16-2 Comparing American wire gauge system with metric. AWG represents the diameter of a wire while metric measures the cross sectional area in mm^2.

wire is specified in millimeters rather than metric gauge diameter. As the diameter of the wire increases in the metric standard, the gauge will also increase. This is opposite to the AWG standard, which uses a smaller gauge to indicate a larger diameter wire.

Wire Color Coding

Wire-coding systems are another useful feature of wiring to aid troubleshooting and service of electrical systems. Both colors and numbering systems designate wiring circuits, application, and even the routing of wires. The SAE also recommends color coding for circuits. For example, the J560 trailer plug connector identifies seven colors used for each lighting circuit. Wire color codes recommended by International Organization for Standardization (ISO) are partially listed in **TABLE 16-2**. Note, these are only recommendations and manufacturers will often use their own color codes.

SAE J1128 Standard

The **SAE J1128 standard** and newer ISO 6722 standard specify the dimensions, test methods, and performance requirements for single-core primary wire intended for use in road vehicle applications. Primary wire is used in low-voltage applications under 60 volts. The number of strands a wire should have, its temperature rating, and its resistance to chemicals and resistance to oxidation are just a few standards specified. Five common types of wire for use in bus, truck, and trailer applications are classified by their insulation. These include:

- **GPT (General Purpose Thermoplastic Wire)**—Has a PVC insulation jacket and is used for general connection wiring inside a cab. Temperature rating is 176°F (80°C).
- **SXL**—Has extra-thick insulation using cross-linked polyethylene insulation to withstand operating conditions in the engine compartment where the highest heat is possible. Temperature rating is 275°F (135°C). Heat sources will cause the wire to blister like popcorn but insulation will not "melt" off wire.
- **GXL**—Uses cross-linked polyethylene insulation and, like SXL, is also used where heat, flame, and abrasion resistance is a requirement. The insulation is thinner that SXL and is used typically inside a cab or passenger compartment. Temperature rating is 275°F (130°C).
- **TXL**—Extra thin primary wire that has a cross-linked polyethylene jacket that is resistant to oil, grease, gasoline, and acids. It is used where small diameter and minimal weight are desirable. Temperature rating is 275°F (130°C).

TABLE 16-2: Partial Listing of Wire Color Designations by ISO

ISO Wire Color	Abbreviation	Function
Black	bk	• Ground and general purpose
Black-red	bk-r	• Battery power • Ignition • Run
Blue-dk	dkbl	• Back up light • Windshield wipers • Trailer auxiliary
Brown	br	• Tail, marker, and panel lights
Green-dk	dkg	• Right turn signal • Driver's display • Data recording • J1587 positive • J1939 negative
Orange	o	• ABS or EBS • J1587 negative
Pink	pk	• Starter control • Charging, voltmeter, or ammeter • J1922 negative
Pink-white	pk-w	• Fuel control • Indicators for speed and shut-down
Yellow	y	• Left turn signal • J1939 positive • GXL insulated wire
White	w	• Transmission • SXL insulated wire

SGR-type wire refers to starting, ground, and battery cable and is required to meet a different SAE standard than regular primary wiring. These cables use a chlorinated polyethylene (CPE) insulation, which provides the highest heat resistance of any primary wiring. Temperature rating is 194°F (90°C). **Parallel wiring** refers to a type of custom-made wiring harness that encloses multiple conductors into a single vinyl insulator covering. Parallel wiring harness is often used for a rear taillight wiring harness that includes a separate wire for stop, turn, reverse, and tail lights. The harness is typically flat, and even though wires are insulated from one another, the wiring insulation is fused together to form a single harness.

TECHNICIAN TIP

Multi-stranded wire is better at conducting higher amounts of current with less resistance because it has more surface area to conduct electron flow. It is also more flexible for routing through a chassis and cab. Multi-stranded wire can break down more quickly, however, with each smaller strand being less resistant to physical damage than a larger single strand. Under the valve cover or inside the harsh operating environment of an engine, single-stranded wire is better.

Wire Number Coding

Chassis wiring often uses numerical codes to identify which circuit the wire belongs to, where the wire is in the circuit, which harness it belongs in, and the wire gauge and color. An SAE standard J-2191 designates standard numbers for wiring circuits for power and signal distribution systems of Class 8 trucks and tractors. TABLE 16-3 contains examples of these circuit designations. A proprietary corporate wire identification number together with an SAE number may also be printed on the wire every six to eight inches apart. The SAE system will supplement the manufacturer's system. FIGURE 16-3 contains an example of SAE wiring code.

Wiring Connectors

To join electrical wires to components or other circuits, terminal connections are used. The simplest connector is a terminal block that uses small studs to which ring or spade type connectors are attached and secured with machine screws. The ideal electrical connector would offer a low contact resistance, a body with high insulation value, and resistance to vibration, water, fuel, and oil.

Connectors need also to be connected and disconnected easily and repeatedly. Servicing connectors must also require only simple tooling, such as what is shown in FIGURE 16-4, that maintains the connectors' shape to preserve the orientation of the connectors with components. Each application requires an emphasis on connector characteristics, so there are a large variety used. Many

TABLE 16-3: Examples of SAE Circuit Designations to Supplement OEM Wire Identification

Circuit Number	Circuit Description
1	Battery cable, ground
6	Battery cable, 12-volt positive
15	Starter, engine
82	Starter magnetic switch, power supply
117	Speed sensor "+", vehicle, mph (km/h)
118	Speed sensor "–", vehicle, mph(km/h)
295	Radio, AM/FM/CB
305	Ignition switch, accessory
306	Ignition switch, run position
468	Obstacle detection system (ODS), vehicle on-board radar (VORAD)
1102	Ignition buss feed
1504	Cruise control on/off
1515	Air management
1939	Data link, controls, SAE J1939

FIGURE 16-3 An example of a wire code using SAE J-2191 wire numbering standard.

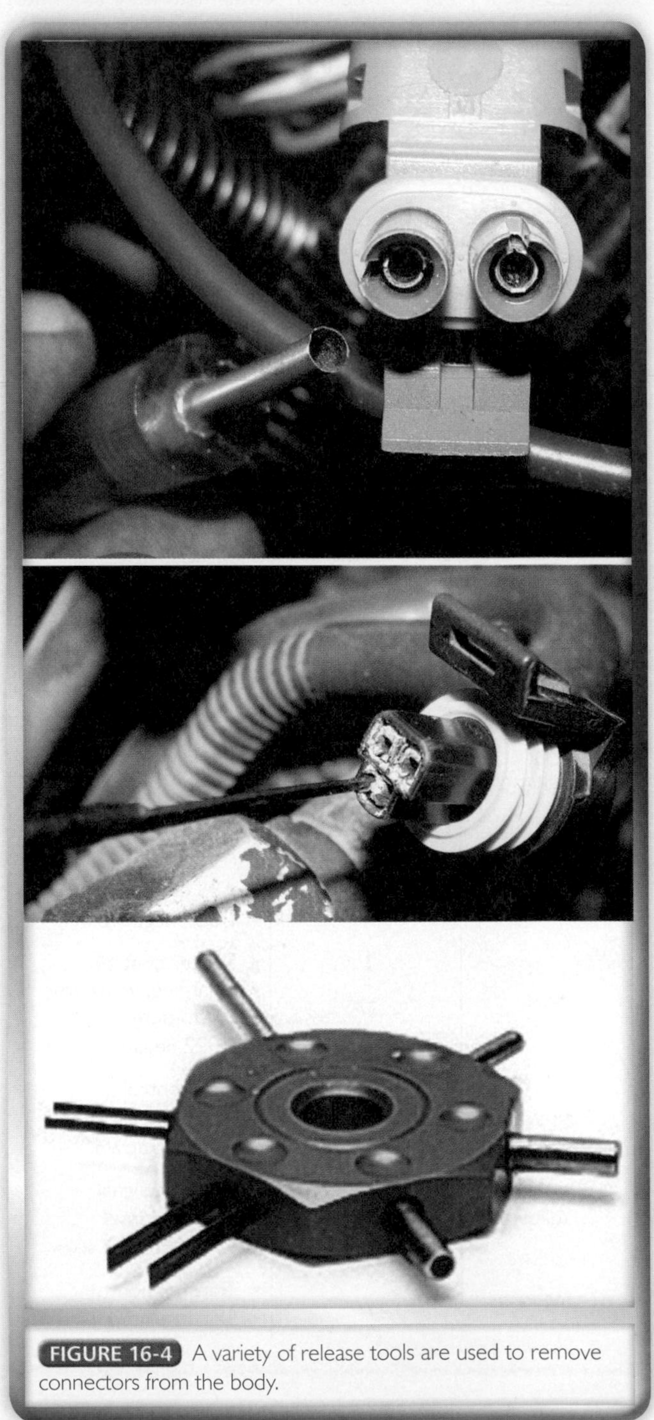

FIGURE 16-4 A variety of release tools are used to remove connectors from the body.

connectors are keyed or have indexing slots to prevent mis-mating, which damages connectors and pins from forcing connectors together at the wrong angle or fitting into incorrectly connected connections. The connector generally has three parts: a body or housing, silicone seals to prevent water intrusion, and the terminal. Terminals are the metal part that is crimped to a wire and housed inside a connector. There are two main types of terminals used in harness connectors—pull-to-seat and push-to-seat terminals. **Pull-to-seat terminals** are terminals that are installed by inserting the wire through the connector cavity, crimping on a terminal, and then pulling the terminal back into the connector cavity to seat it. **Push-to-seat terminals** are inserted into the back of the connector cavity to seat after the terminal is crimped to the wire.

Connector housings have male and female sides and are usually shaped so that they can be connected in only one way. Some connectors also use a connector position assurance clip (CPA) or secondary lock. This is a plastic part of the connector that assures that two connector halves will stay locked together and not work loose. FIGURE 16-5 shows typical harness connectors. Many of these connectors are weatherproofed to keep moisture out. Special tools are usually needed to insert and remove the terminals from the connector housing.

A **Weather-Pack connector** from Delphi is an environmentally sealed push-to-seat electrical connection system supplied in one- to six-pin configurations. As illustrated in FIGURE 16-6, this system uses only round pin terminals and round socket terminals. The male pin end of the connector is called the tower while the female socket end is the shroud. Terminals (pin and sleeve) are tin plated and have special core wings that allow crimp-only wire attachment, eliminating the need for solder. The self-lubricating silicone connector and cavity seals are triple-ribbed. Connectors are rated at 20 amps per pin at 16 volts DC.

A **Metri-Pack connector** from Delphi is a family of electrical connection systems similar to the Weather Pack connectors except that the terminals are flat rather than round and it is a pull-to-seat connector. FIGURE 16-7 shows a Metri-Pack connector. Standardized male blade sizes and box-like female terminals designate the five different series of these connectors. Each series has a different current-carrying capacity. Terminals are tin plated and have special core wings that allow crimp-only connections,

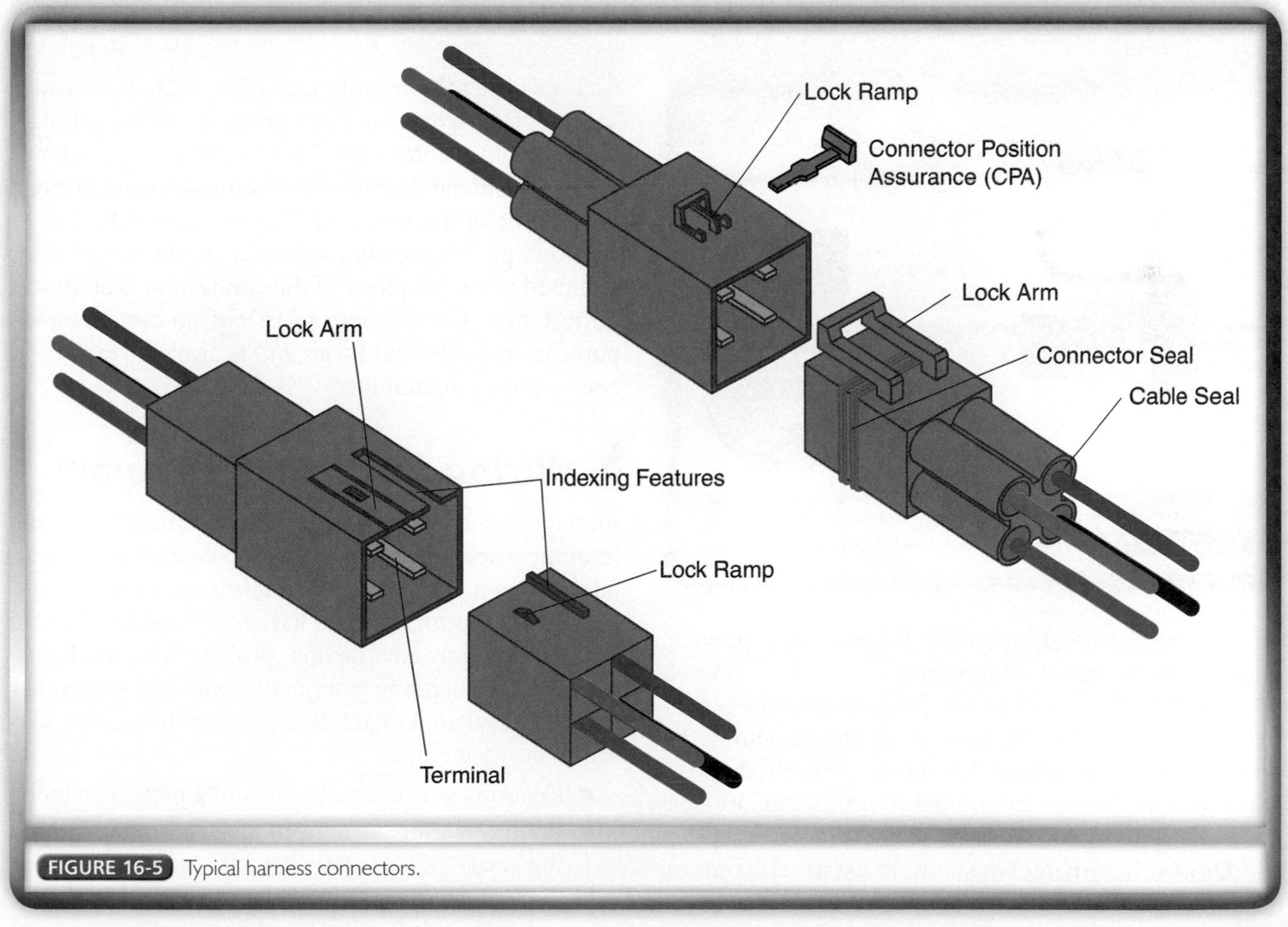

FIGURE 16-5 Typical harness connectors.

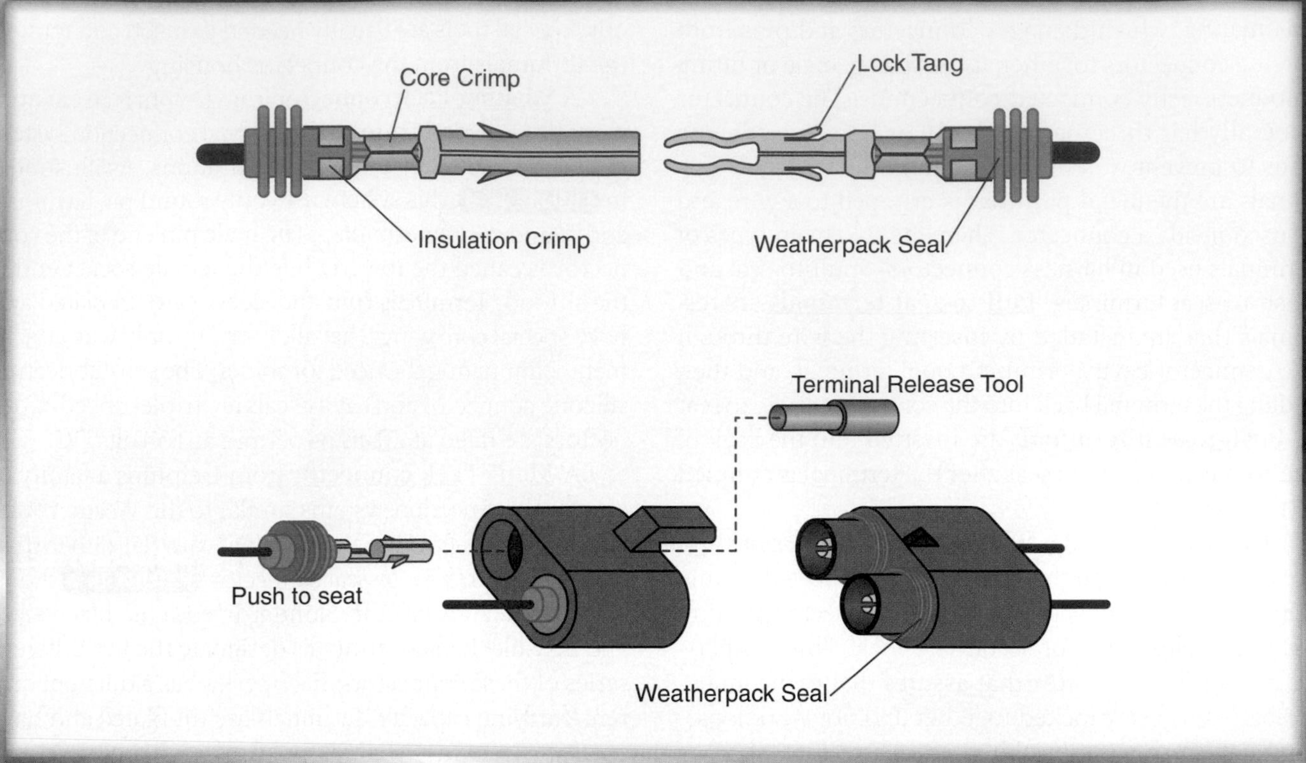

FIGURE 16-6 Weather Pack is a push-to-seat connector.

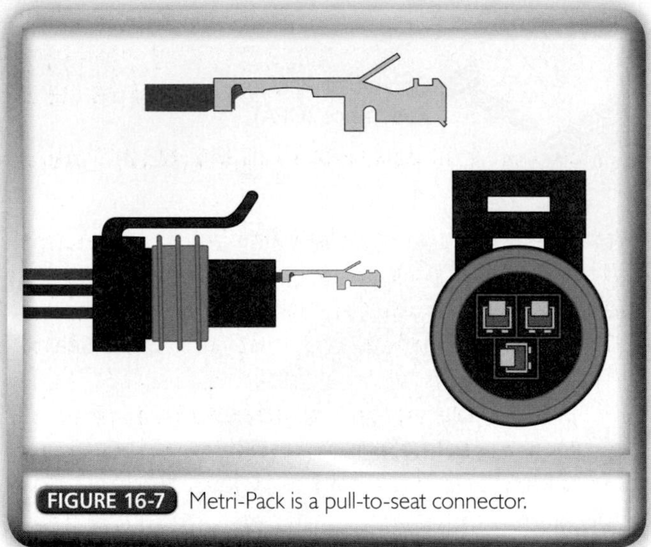

FIGURE 16-7 Metri-Pack is a pull-to-seat connector.

eliminating the need for solder. Silicone seals prevent water intrusion into the connector.

Bosch/AMP connectors use push-to-seat-type terminals. They are available in two- to six-pin configurations and rated at 9 amps per pin. Like other terminals, they use wings to crimp the wire to terminal. A metal secondary lock easily helps distinguish this connector from other types.

Deutsch connectors, such as illustrated in **FIGURE 16-8**, are also an environmentally sealed connector. Using solid round metal pins and hollow female sockets, Deutsch connectors are much more compact than any other connector. They occupy one quarter of the volume of the Weather-Pack connectors and one half the volume of the Bosch/AMP connectors. Rated at 15 amps per pin, they are considered a premium connector and used when reliability of the connection is of utmost importance. The DT Series of Deutsch connectors is popular on trucks and buses and is available in two- to twelve-pin configurations.

Wiring Failure and Repair

After component failures, wiring and connectors are the leading causes of electrical problems. Wire chaffing, heat, oil and fuel damage, and road debris are common preventable causes for wire and harness failure. Mechanical damage from repeated flexing, probing with test lights, stretching, or bending can break a wire and sometimes leave the insulation intact. Best practices to increase wiring longevity include:

- Covering wiring and harness in a protective loom
- Routing wiring away from heat sources and moving parts
- Securing wire with clips and plastic ties

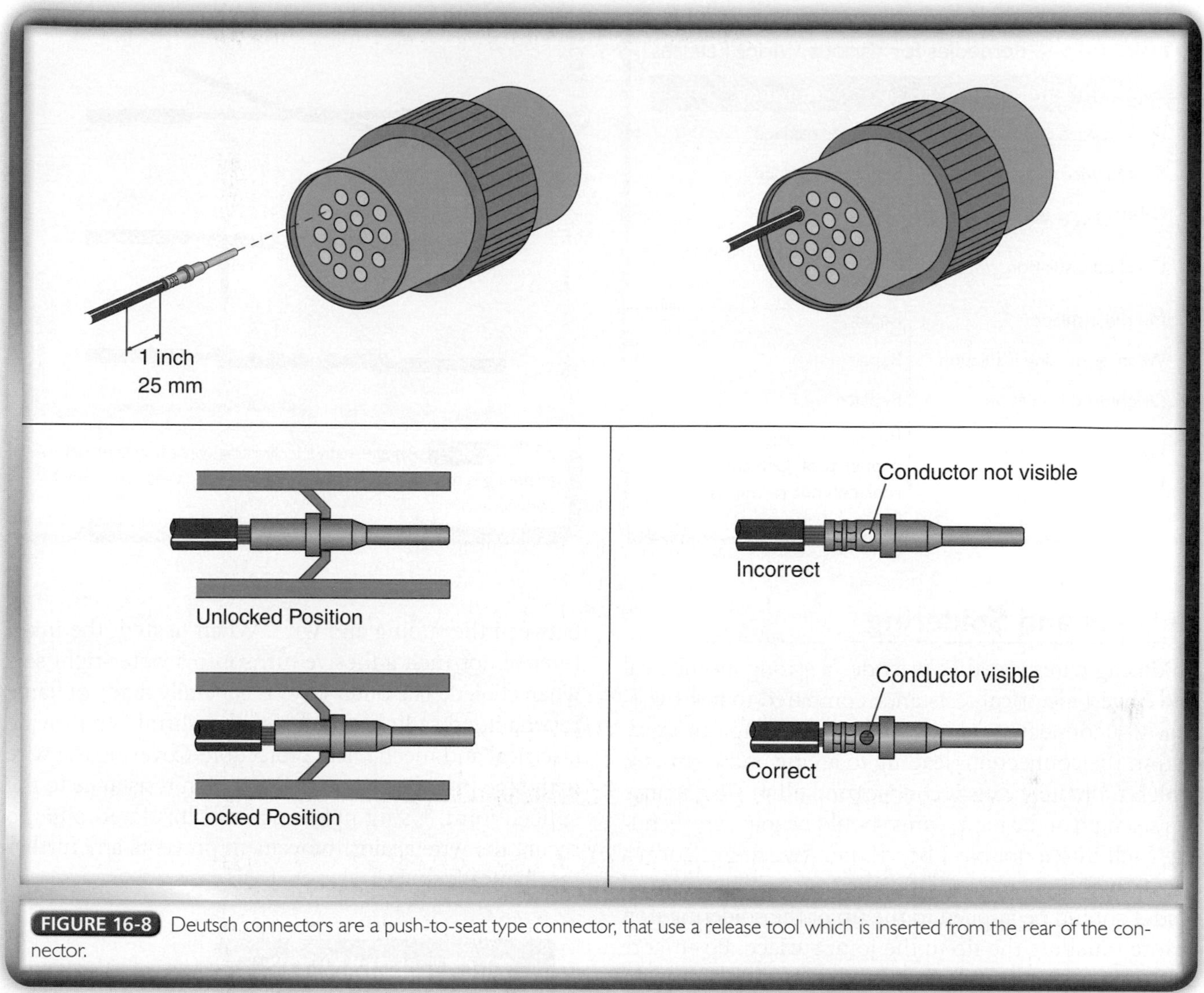

FIGURE 16-8 Deutsch connectors are a push-to-seat type connector, that use a release tool which is inserted from the rear of the connector.

One of the greatest enemies to wiring is water. Water with dissolved road salt is particularly aggressive at damaging wiring. The tendency of water to "wick" inside insulation is what makes it so destructive. **Water wicking** is the movement of water through wiring due to its adhesive and cohesive properties. This essentially means water is sticky. It will easily attach itself to copper wire and has a high surface tension. That means water stays together or beads-up. Once inside a wire, water will move into the smallest openings and spaces through adhesion. More water gets dragged along inside a wire because the water sticks so well to itself. Because of the effect of wicking, water can travel far along a wire to the point where an entire length of wire is corroded.

Wicking failures often happen close to connectors due to a defective or missing seal. Punctures from test lights also lead to damage of the entire harness. A powder-like substance inside connectors or wire insulation indicates a wicking-related failure. Wiring may actually appear swollen or cracked from corrosion pressure. TABLE 16-4 shows possible remedies for various wiring and terminal faults.

Cutting and Stripping Wires

The amount of wire cut out of a damaged portion of wire will depend on the amount needed to produce ends that are clean and free of any corrosion. After stripping the insulation from the remaining wire ends, the wires should appear clean and bright. Wire-stripping tools remove only the insulation and do not nick or cut wire. Dull or dirty wiring can be cleaned with fine emery-cloth sand paper. Tin-plated copper wiring used to add corrosion resistance to wiring in marine applications is commonly used in truck and bus repair, too. This wire has a dull grey appearance that cannot be cleaned. The section of wire to replace must be slightly longer than the original section removed to provide some slack.

TABLE 16-4: Remedies for Various Wiring Failures

Fault	Remedy
Broken wire conductor	Repair or replace
Kinked wire conductor	Repair or replace
Oil-damaged insulation	Replace
Cracked insulation	Repair if minor; otherwise replace
Melted insulation	Repair
Worn or missing insulation	Repair
Discolored insulation	Replace
Damaged connectors or terminals	Repair or replace with proper tool. Use correct replacement terminals.

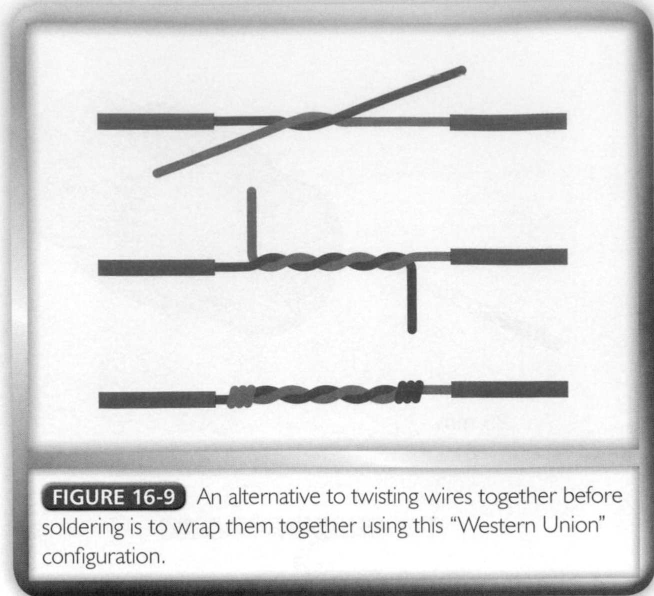

FIGURE 16-9 An alternative to twisting wires together before soldering is to wrap them together using this "Western Union" configuration.

Splicing and Soldering

Soldering wires together provides a strong mechanical and lowest electrical resistance compared to just twisting. If a connection is not soldered, wiring can move within the connection, leading to arcing and resistance which ultimately causes connection failure. To enhance the strength of the joint, wires should be joined by bending each into a double-J bend, then twisting to form a Western Union splice FIGURE 16-9. A small amount of solder should be applied to the tip of the soldering iron before touching the tip to the joint surface. Rosin-core solder wire is then applied to the joint but is not brought into contact with the iron. Heat from the joint should melt the solder into the wire. This procedure avoids a cold solder joint that could cause a poor electrical connection.

Safety

Although soldering is generally thought of as a simple process, it can be very dangerous. The solder, soldering iron, and wires are very hot and can cause severe burns. Be careful what you grab or where you set hot items. Molten solder can be flicked by springy wire up into your eyes, so always wear safety glasses or goggles.

Sealing and Securing

Spliced connections need protection against water wicking. Heat-shrink tubing provides the best seal for a spliced electrical connection. Heat shrink is available in two types—double and single wall. Double-walled tubing is recommended because it has an adhesive layer between the tubing and wire. When heated, the inner layer of hot-melt adhesive turns into a water-tight seal when cooled. The outer layer is generally made of flame retardant, cross-linked polyolefin. It shrinks to provide electrical and mechanical protection. Covering the wire with tape provides additional abrasion resistance to the spliced joint. Using nylon ties and insulated clips to secure the wire against movement prevents any further mechanical damage.

TECHNICIAN TIP

Heat is required to contract and seal shrink tube. Heat from a hair dryer is not adequate. Rather, a similar-looking heat gun is needed. Heat from the gun provides enough heat to melt the inner adhesive and shrink the outer layer. Propane torches and lighters will actually burn char and split shrink tube, so they are not recommended tools for activating heat-shrink tubing.

Crimp-Type Connectors

Faster splice repairs are made with crimp-type connectors FIGURE 16-10 Stripped wire ends placed inside aluminum metal tubes are squeezed together with barrel-type crimping pliers.

Crimp connectors can provide mechanical strength similar to solder but must be used with double-walled shrink tube to make the repair permanent. Color codes are used to designate wire gauge to use for shrink crimp connectors. An incorrectly sized crimp connector can become loose, leak, and fail.

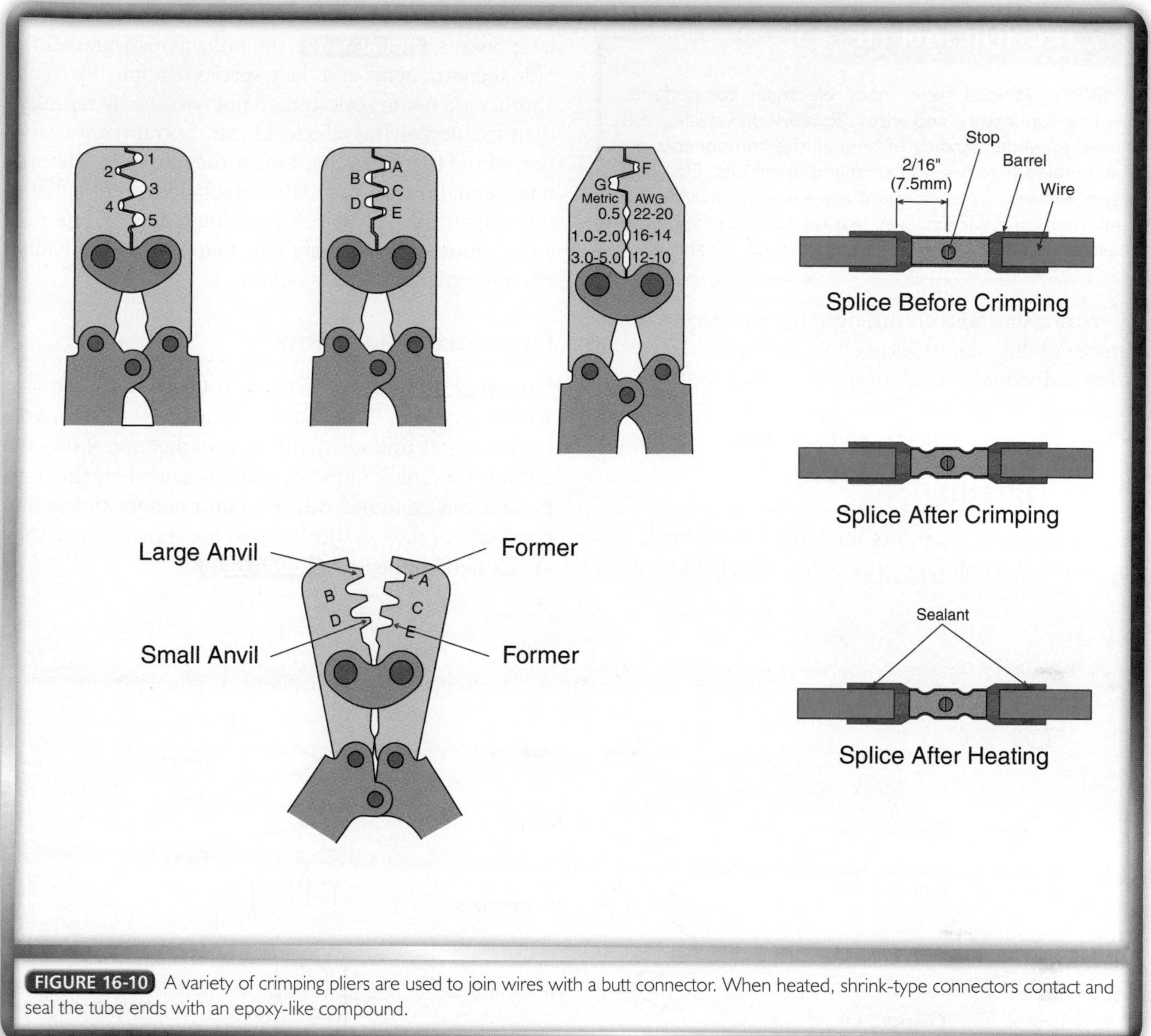

FIGURE 16-10 A variety of crimping pliers are used to join wires with a butt connector. When heated, shrink-type connectors contact and seal the tube ends with an epoxy-like compound.

Wiring Diagrams

Magneto ignition systems used at the beginning of the 1900s were the first electrical systems. With only four major components—the high-voltage magnetic, a distributor, spark plugs, and coil—identifying and connecting these components was simple. By 1911, the electrical system expanded to include a DC generator, headlamps, a battery, voltage regulator, and switches. In 1950, the main interests were the starting, ignition, and lighting circuits. Today the types of electrical components number into the thousands—over 3,000 circuits are commonly found in HD commercial vehicles!

Modern electronic controls applied to every vehicle system and networked electrical systems have increased the complexity of today's vehicles. Added to traditional vehicle systems are convenience devices, such as navigational and multimedia devices, vehicle safety and security systems, custom electrical circuits for body builders, and so on.

The complexity of the electrical circuits and their interconnections requires electrical road maps that allow a technician to trace circuits from power supplies, through switches, components, circuit protection devices, harnesses, splices, junction blocks, connectors, and finally to ground. Technicians must be able to correctly understand and interpret a wiring diagram in order to reduce diagnostic time for electrical problems and eliminate guesswork.

> **TECHNICIAN TIP**
>
> Modern vehicles have many electrical components, wiring connectors, and wires. To work on vehicles, you need an understanding of how all the components are assembled together and arranged in circuits. Electrical symbols and circuit diagrams are a way to provide this information in a logical way that represents the physical wiring harness and components attached to vehicles.

Wiring diagrams are arranged by manufacturers in a number of different styles to show with a high degree of clarity individual circuit components, connections, and their locations. The three main types of wiring diagrams include are map, isometric, and schematic diagrams.

Map Diagrams

Map or **pictorial diagrams** show the entire vehicle wiring circuit. Symbols for components are usually pictorial FIGURE 16-11. That is, the symbol looks like a component it represents. FIGURE 16-12 contains a map diagram. Individual components and their spatial relationship to one another are not to scale and do not necessarily represent their location on the vehicle. Linear diagrams are a variation of the map diagram. Linear diagrams use pictorial representations with a mixture of schematic symbols and internal wiring. A linear diagram may start on one page and continue onto several more, mapping out individual circuits with a separate diagram.

Isometric Diagrams

Isometric diagrams are used to locate a component within a system. If the location of a component or wiring harness is unknown, this type of diagram shows the outline of a vehicle or piece of equipment where the component can be found. Various components and wiring harnesses of the electrical system are shown where they are located on the unit FIGURE 16-13.

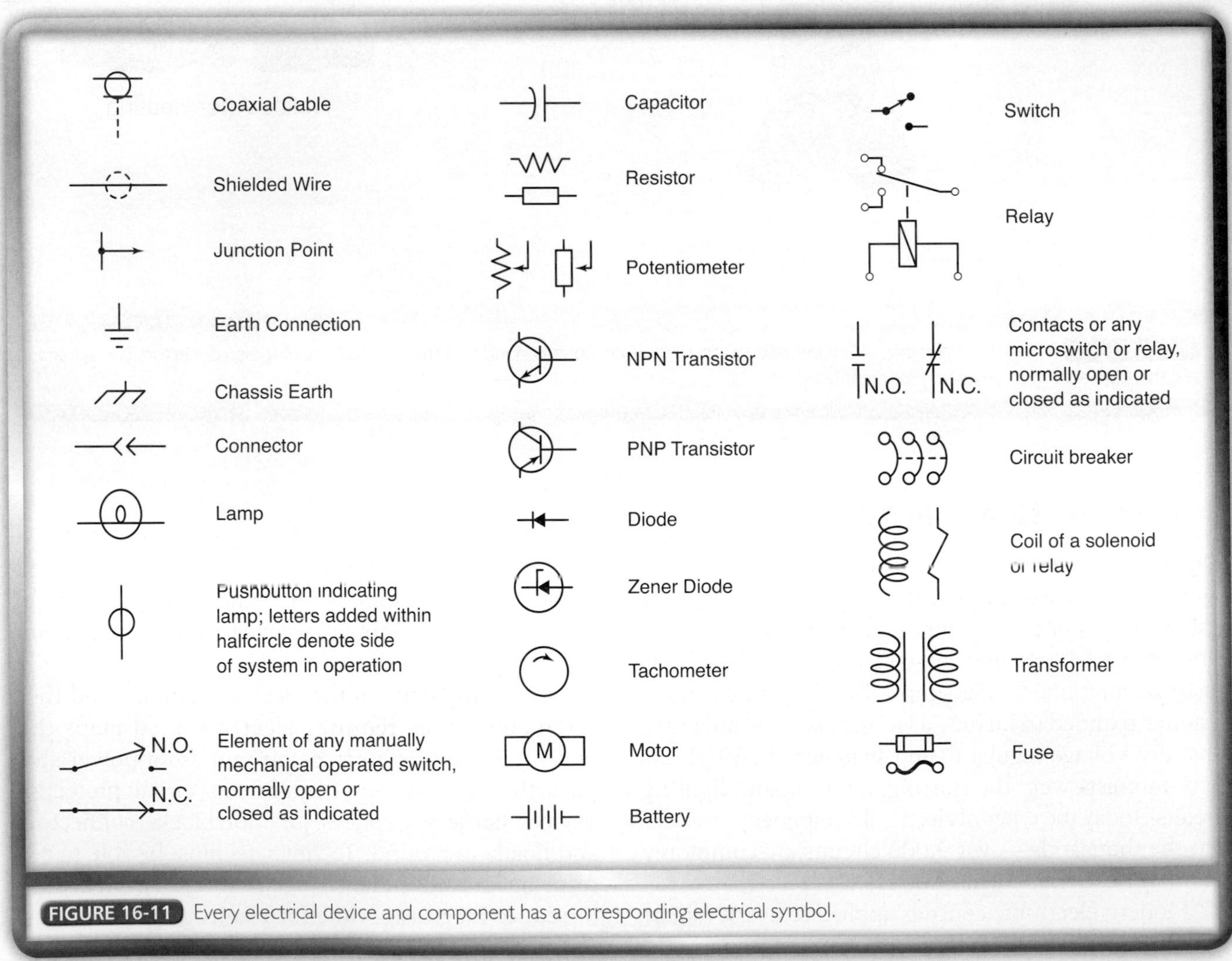

FIGURE 16-11 Every electrical device and component has a corresponding electrical symbol.

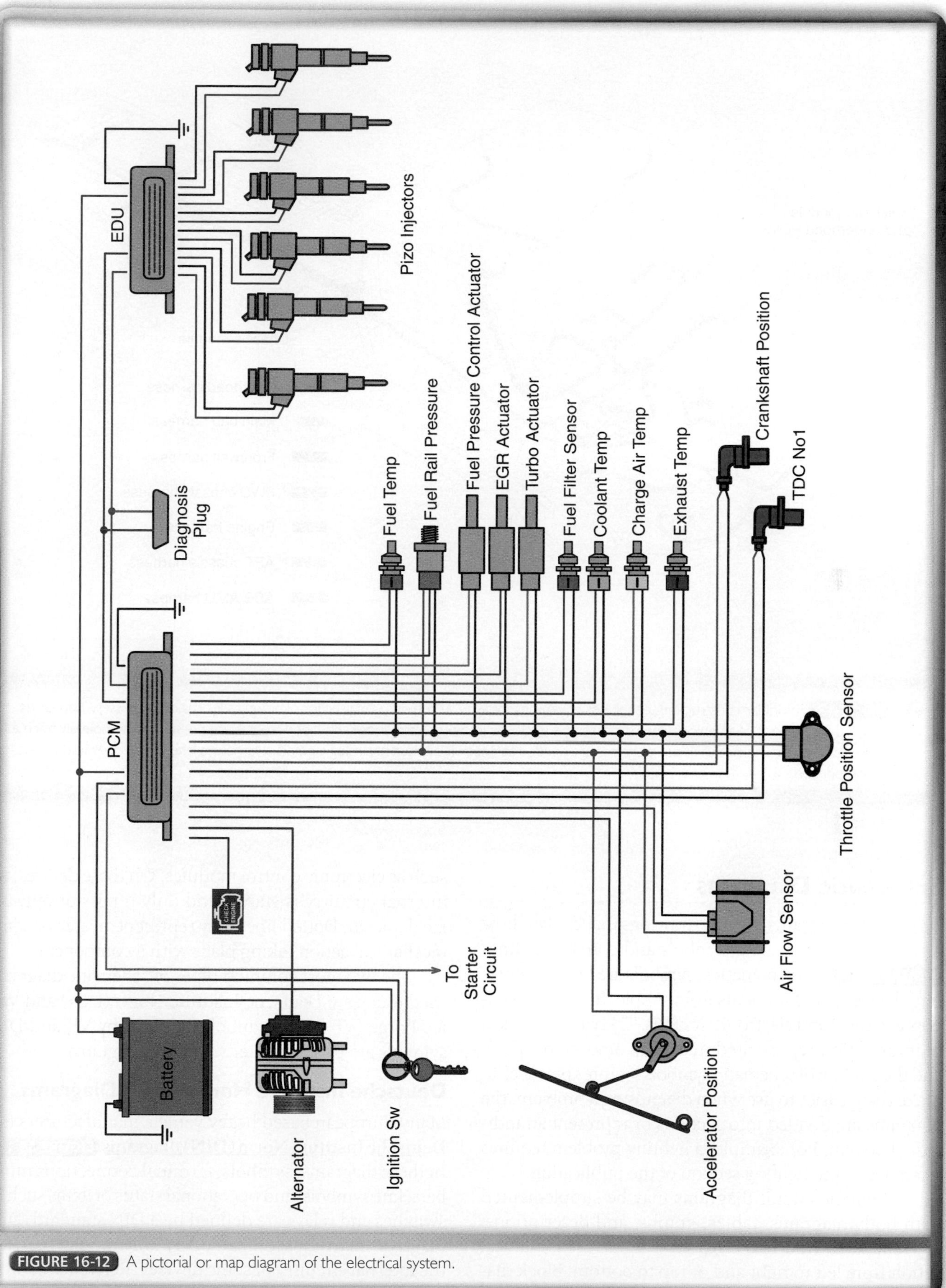

FIGURE 16-12 A pictorial or map diagram of the electrical system.

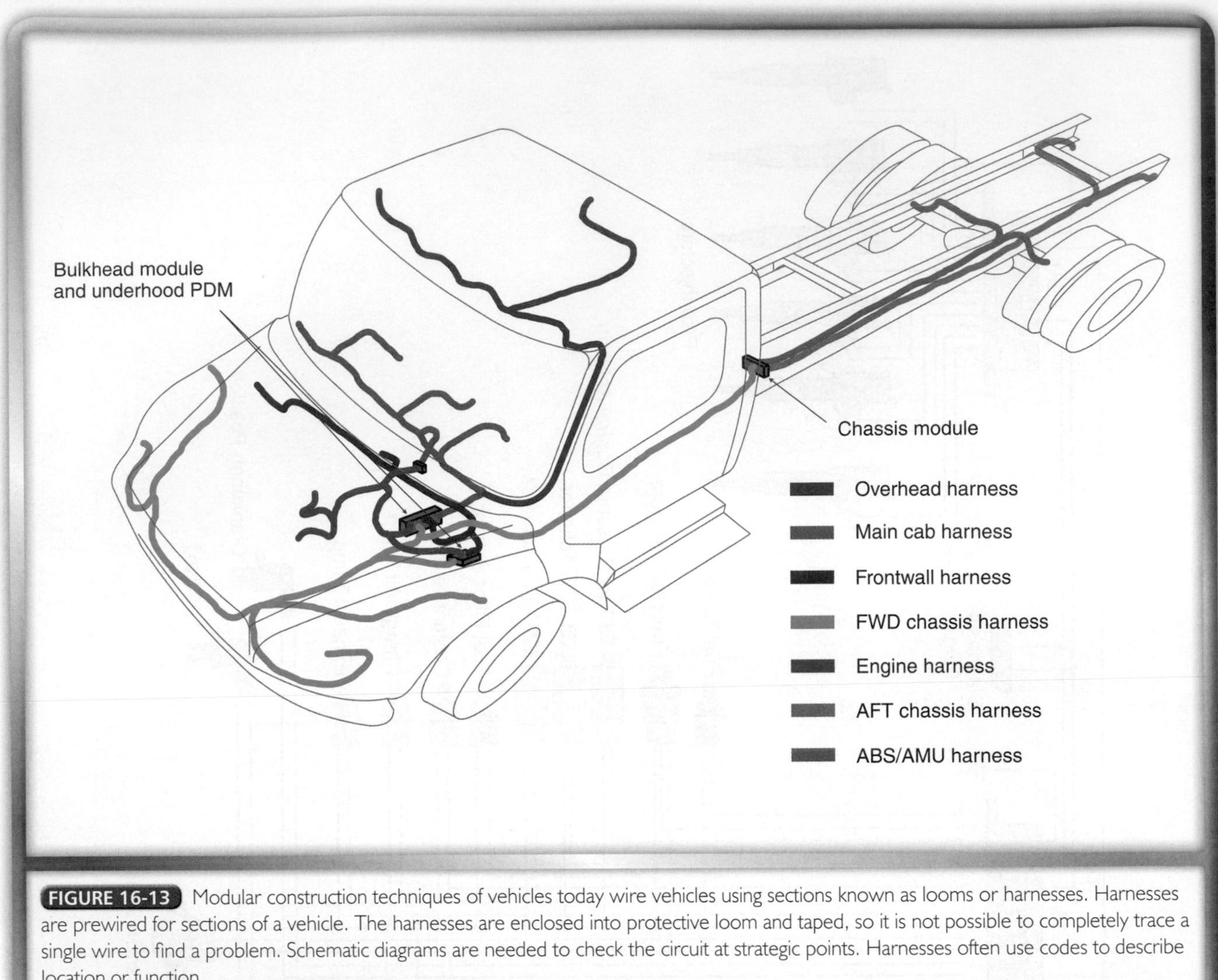

FIGURE 16-13 Modular construction techniques of vehicles today wire vehicles using sections known as looms or harnesses. Harnesses are prewired for sections of a vehicle. The harnesses are enclosed into protective loom and taped, so it is not possible to completely trace a single wire to find a problem. Schematic diagrams are needed to check the circuit at strategic points. Harnesses often use codes to describe location or function.

Schematic Diagrams

Schematic diagrams are line drawings that explain how a system works by using symbols and connecting lines FIGURE 16-14. On schematics, symbols are used to represent devices or components from simple through to complex electrical and electronic systems. There is a great deal of information represented in a small amount of space, and the reading of schematic symbols requires practice. To make them easier to use when diagnosing a problem, the diagrams are divided into sections or represent an individual system. For example, a lighting problem requires reference to the lighting section of the publication.

Schematic circuit diagrams may be supplemented with body diagrams, tables, graphs, and descriptions. Current paths are arranged to show signal or mechanical action from left to right and or top to bottom. Block diagrams are used to represent complex electronic circuitry such as electronic control modules. On these devices, no internal circuitry is shown and only inputs or outputs are depicted. Dotted lines may represent an area or some mechanical action taking place with a component.

The two most common types of schematic diagrams used today are Deutsche Institute Norm (DIN) and Valley Forge (VF). SAE symbols are used by VF, and DIN symbols are used together with DIN diagrams.

Deutsche Institute Norm (DIN) Diagrams

Many European based heavy vehicle manufacturers use **Deutsche Institute Norm (DIN) diagrams** FIGURE 16-15. In these diagrams, symbols, terminal connections numbers, line symbols, and operational status of items such as switches and relays are defined by a DIN standard. DIN diagrams may be accompanied by illustrations showing the internal circuitry of some devices. Reference coordinates are often supplied to assist in locating components.

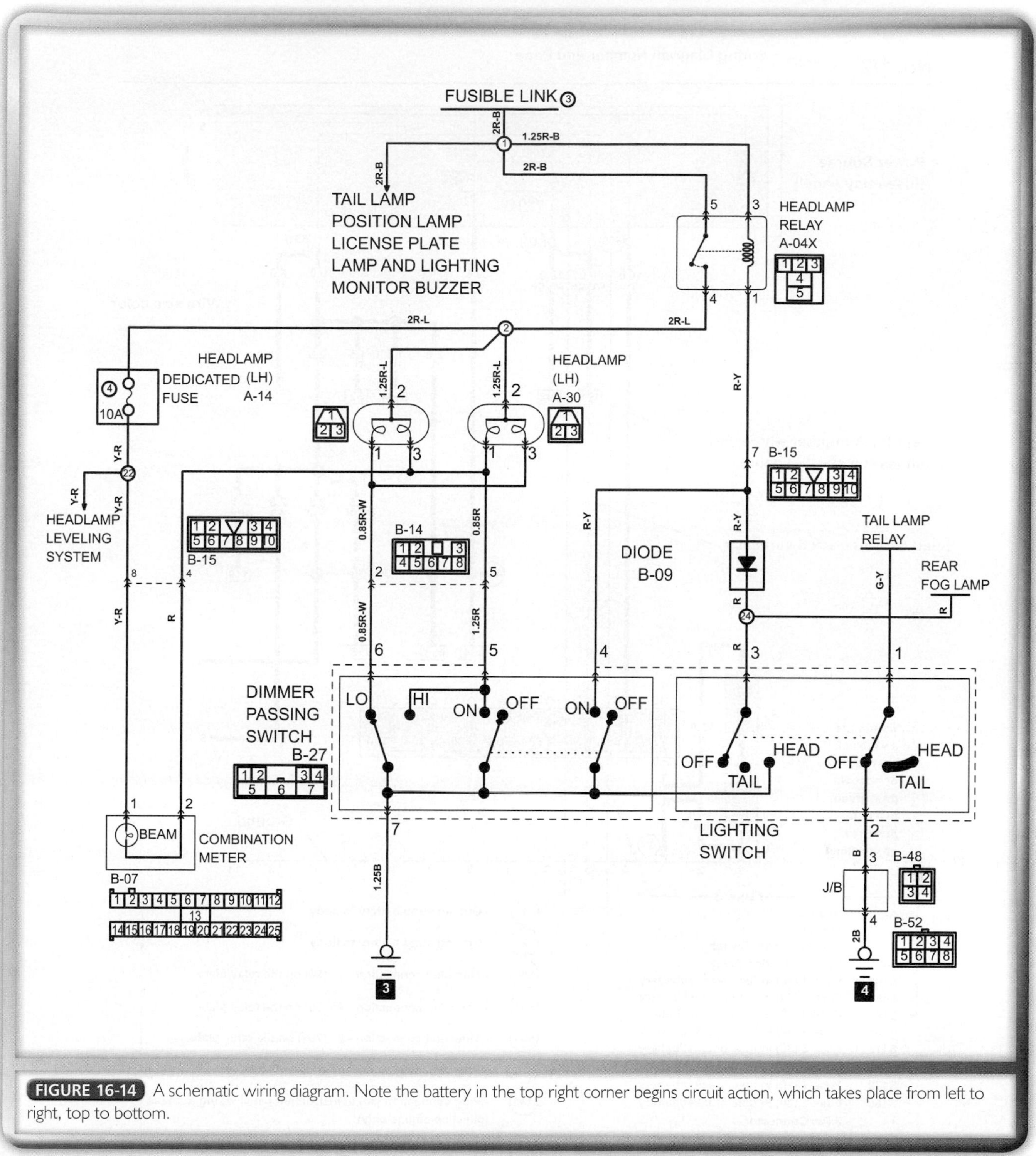

FIGURE 16-14 A schematic wiring diagram. Note the battery in the top right corner begins circuit action, which takes place from left to right, top to bottom.

DIN schematic diagrams are also called **current track** wiring diagrams because they show the power source at the top of the page and the ground points at the bottom. This format simplifies the wiring diagram and minimizes conductor and symbol overlap where they do not connect. Situated between power and ground are current tracks that contain electrical components and conductors. Symbols are used to represent components and conductors in the wiring diagrams. Arrangement of the components and circuit paths on the diagram do not usually correspond to their physical locations on the vehicle. However, newer DIN standards do indicate on which side of the vehicle a component may be located. For example, an R or L suffix after a component will designate a right- or left-side location.

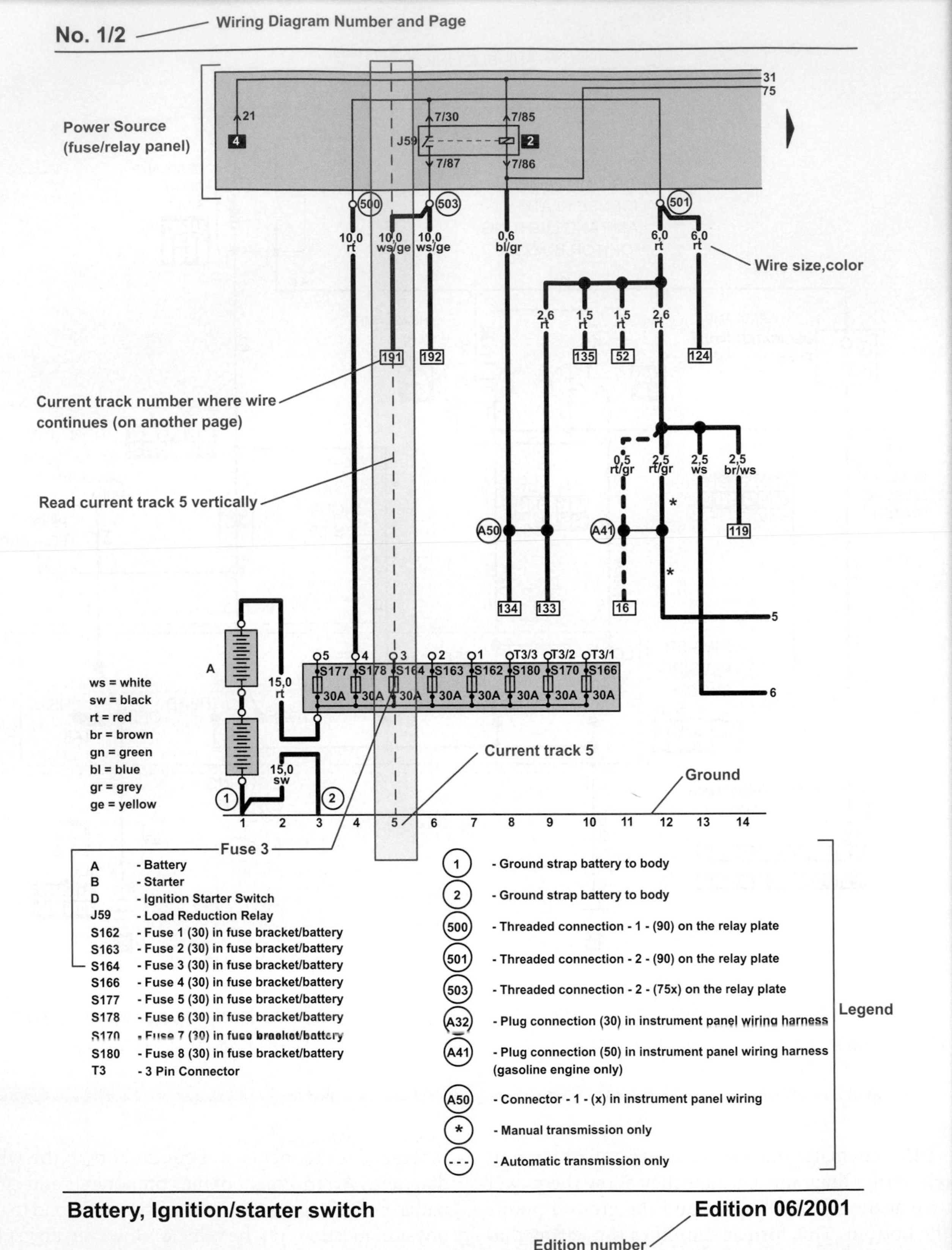

FIGURE 16-15 A typical Deutsche Institute Norm (DIN) diagram. Image Modified from ©2001 Volkswagen of America, Self-Study Program, Course Number 873003

Elements of a DIN Wiring Diagram

DIN diagrams are representative of all wiring diagrams in use today. They contain elements that every electrical circuit needs at a minimum to operate:

- Power supply
- Load
- Ground
- Conductors (usually wire)
- Circuit protection (fuse, virtual fuse)

If any of these are missing, a complete circuit is broken, and the load will not function. The ability to break down a circuit into its individual parts is the key to being able to diagnose failures in the circuit. Wiring diagrams also incorporate many standardized DIN symbols and codes used to illustrate a complete circuit **FIGURE 16-16**. These DIN unique symbols and codes can include:

- Current track numbers
- Components and devices (DIN standard 40 719 and 42 400)
- Terminal designations (DIN standard 72552)
- Conductors
- Connectors

FIGURE 16-17 Identifies many of the features of a DIN schematic diagram:

1. Relay location number on a relay panel.
2. Arrow. Indicates wiring circuit is continued on another page.
3. Connector designation for the relay terminal and connector panel. For example: 17/30 equals terminal 30 of relay would connect to terminal 17 of central relay panel.
4. Threaded pin on relay panel. The white circle indicates the connection is threaded.
5. Fuse indicating location and amperage. For example: S228 means fuse 28 is rated for 15 amps,
6. Reference of wire for continuing current track number.
7. Wire connection designation in wiring harness. The location of wire connections are indicated in the accompanying legend.

8a. Terminal designation on a multi-point connector.

8b. Terminal designation on a component. This number will appear on the component and/or terminal number of a multi-point connector.

9. Ground connection designation in wire harness. The locations of ground connections provided in legend.
10. Component designation, which follows a standardized coding. The legend at bottom of page identifies the component in this diagram.
11. Component symbols. A schematic symbol of component type.
12. Wire cross section size in mm^2 and wire colors.
13. Component symbol with an open side indicates the component is continued on another wiring diagram.
14. Internal connections (thin lines) and are not wires. Internal connections allow technicians to trace current flow inside a component or wiring harness.
    a. Internal Harness Splice (Welded connection)
    b. Physical Contact (Mounted to engine)
15. Reference of continuation of wire to component
16. Central Relay panel connectors, which depicts wiring of multi-point or single connectors on the central relay panel. For example: S3/3 equals Multi-point connector S3, terminal 3.
17. Reference of internal connection continuation. Letters indicate where connection continues on previous and/or next page.
18. Central Relay Panel
19. Ground Path. In this example, the welded harness connection 135 connects to welded harness connection 81 to welded harness connection 42.

In addition to the above general symbols and codes, individual manufacturers will include specialized codes for:

- Harness naming codes
- System identifying codes—Indicates a system to which a circuit belongs. For example, trailer, driveline, or braking electrical circuits will have a code associated
- Splice naming standards
- Inline connector naming standards

Together these elements make up a complete and accurate wiring diagram. The key to reading wiring diagrams is in understanding the symbols. These symbols are standardized, allowing quick recognition of various components.

Power Distribution Flow

Since power flow begins at the top of a DIN diagram, a central power, fuse link, or relay panel is typically located at the top of the wiring diagram page. Circuit grounds, ground studs, and splices are located at the bottom of the diagram or the diagram will indicate the circuit ground

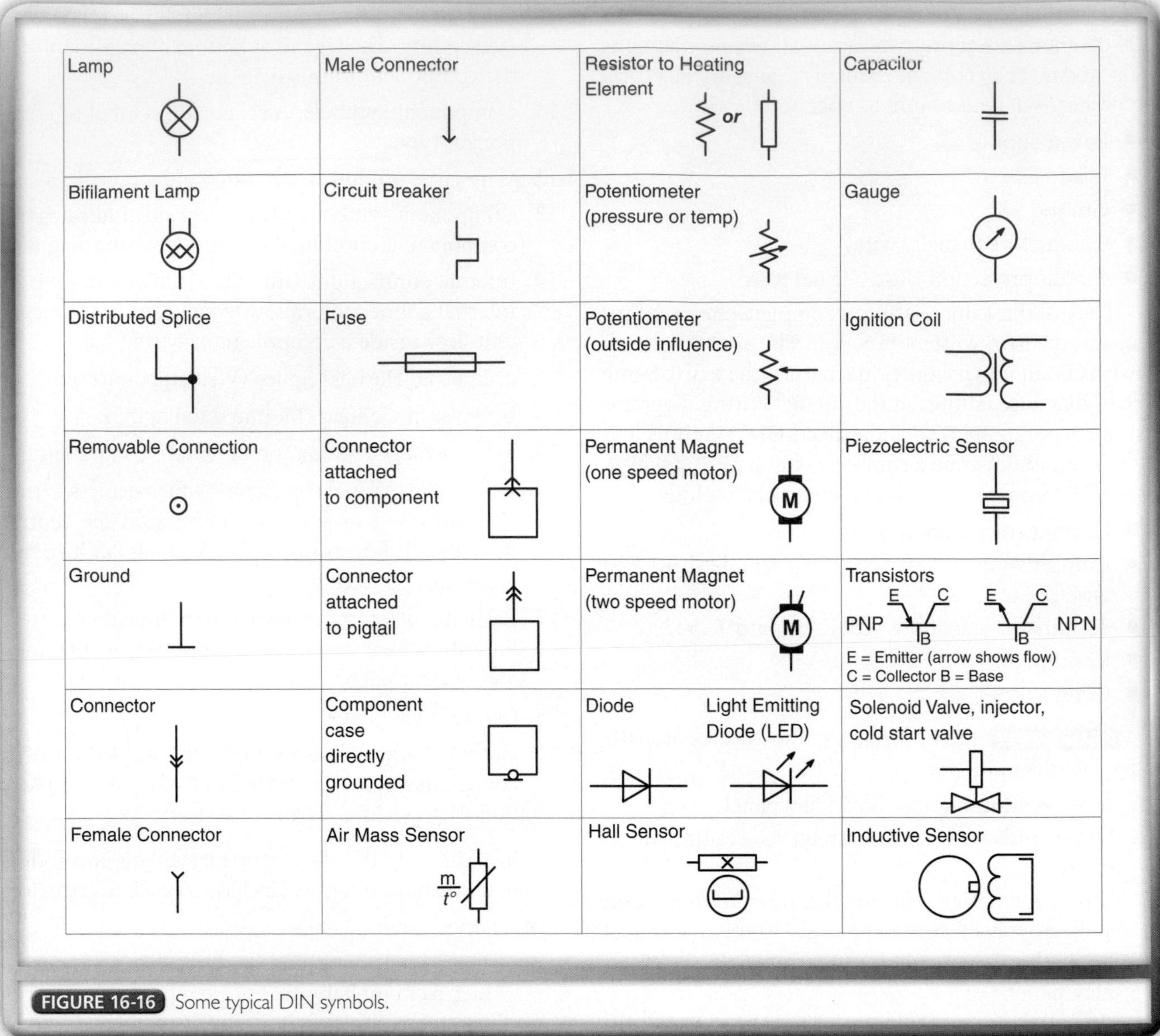

FIGURE 16-16 Some typical DIN symbols.

on another page. All ground connections, whether they occur as a splice in a harness or the final ground source, are numbered and identified in the wiring diagram.

Component and Device Codes

Between the central relay panel and the vehicle ground at the bottom of the diagram are located the component symbols and conductors. Components are marked with a component code listed in the legend. Conductors are marked with wire color and size. Components in wiring diagrams are given a DIN standardized alphanumeric designation for identification (DIN Standard 40717). The first letter portion of the code separates the component into basic groups. The letters A to Z are used with the exception of Q and O. The letter G, for example, will designate a device that supplies current that includes alternators, batteries, or even battery chargers. Switches receive an S designation; motors, M.

The next code is a number that differentiates between the various sub-types of electrical devices. A prefix R, for example, is a resistor, which could mean it's a glow-plug, heater element, potentiometer thermistor, and so on. The number 3 in the designation R3 will indicate sub-type of resistor. The final number in a DIN code indicates a terminal or designation.

Terminal Designation

DIN Standard 72552 applies to the terminal designations for circuits. The purpose of the terminal designation system is to enable connection verification of wiring to various components when diagnosis and repair is necessary. For example, B+ indicates a battery positive terminal.

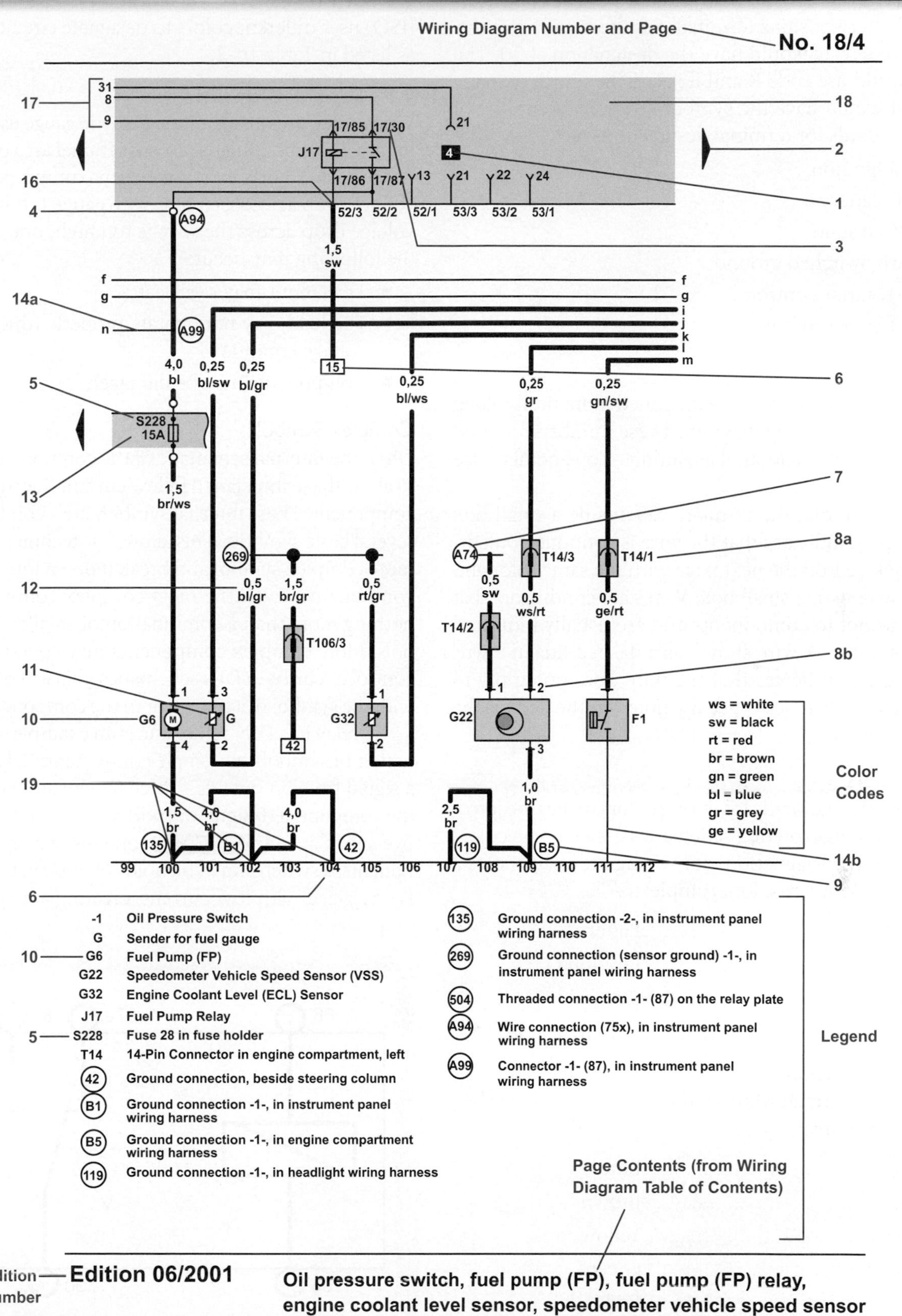
Wiring Diagram Number and Page
No. 18/4
J17
17/85 17/30
17/86 17/87
52/3 52/2 52/1 53/3 53/2 53/1
A94
1,5
sw
A99
15
S228
15A
4,0 bl
0,25 bl/sw
0,25 bl/gr
0,25 bl/ws
0,25 gr
0,25 gn/sw
1,5 br/ws
269
0,5 bl/gr
1,5 br/gr
0,5 rt/gr
T106/3
A74
T14/3
T14/1
T14/2
0,5 sw
0,5 ws/rt
0,5 ge/rt
G6
G
G32
G22
F1
42
1,0 br
1,5 br
4,0 br
4,0 br
2,5 br
135 B1 42 119 B5
99 100 101 102 103 104 105 106 107 108 109 110 111 112
ws = white
sw = black
rt = red
br = brown
gn = green
bl = blue
gr = grey
ge = yellow
Color Codes
-1 Oil Pressure Switch
G Sender for fuel gauge
G6 Fuel Pump (FP)
G22 Speedometer Vehicle Speed Sensor (VSS)
G32 Engine Coolant Level (ECL) Sensor
J17 Fuel Pump Relay
S228 Fuse 28 in fuse holder
T14 14-Pin Connector in engine compartment, left
42 Ground connection, beside steering column
B1 Ground connection -1-, in instrument panel wiring harness
B5 Ground connection -1-, in engine compartment wiring harness
119 Ground connection -1-, in headlight wiring harness
135 Ground connection -2-, in instrument panel wiring harness
269 Ground connection (sensor ground) -1-, in instrument panel wiring harness
504 Threaded connection -1- (87) on the relay plate
A94 Wire connection (75x), in instrument panel wiring harness
A99 Connector -1- (87), in instrument panel wiring harness
Legend
Page Contents (from Wiring Diagram Table of Contents)
Edition number
Edition 06/2001
Oil pressure switch, fuel pump (FP), fuel pump (FP) relay, engine coolant level sensor, speedometer vehicle speed sensor

FIGURE 16-17 Elements of a DIN diagram highlighted. Image Modified from ©2001 Volkswagen of America, Self-Study Program, Course Number 873003

The number 30 indicates the circuit is a wire conductor to the battery positive terminal. So, the battery positive circuit to a relay would have the designation of 30. The relay would use code K and if it was the fourth of many relays it would have the symbol K4. Some examples of DIN standards for terminal designations are:

- 15 Ignition
- 30 Battery +
- 31 Ground
- 31b Switched ground
- 50 Starter control
- 53 Wiper motor +

Current Tracks

Individual current tracks are identified numerically along the base of the wiring diagram. These numbers are used to find the continuation of a conductor on another page or diagram.

For example, the number 221 inside a small box on one page indicates that the wire is continued on current track 221 on the next page with the same color and size of wire with a small box. Wires are conductors that carry current to components and are usually indicated by a solid line. A wire shown as a dashed line in a wiring diagram indicates that the wire does not apply to all vehicles. That fact is usually noted in the key for the wiring diagram.

Wire Colors

Knowing the standards for wiring colors makes the job of reading and interpreting schematics easier. Some colors and terminal designations for wiring are used across a number of standards, for example:

Red .... Battery +
Green .... Ignition (1)
Brown .... Ground (31)
Yellow .... Headlights (58)

In DIN diagrams, wire colors are shown as abbreviations of the German word for the color (DIN standard 47 002) for example:

bl .... Blue
br .... Brown
ge .... Yellow
gn.. Green
ro .... Red
sw .... Black
li .... Violet
ws .... White

The International Organization for Standardization (ISO) uses different colors to designate circuit functions as listed in Table 16-2.

Wire Sizes on Diagrams

Wiring diagrams also indicate the wire gauge used (shown in mm^2), designating the cross sectional area of the wire. Because standards exist for the maximum permissible voltage drop across a circuit, wire gauge is critical. If the voltage drop across the wire is too high, one or more of the following may occur:

- The circuit may overheat
- The load may not operate properly (due to low voltage condition)
- Components may be damaged

Complex Symbols

Often the internal schematic of the component is shown to allow the technician to follow current flow through the component. These internal symbols are a combination of several basic symbols. This allows the technician to take a more complex symbol and break it down into its smaller components. Even the most complex components are nothing more than a combination of smaller basic symbols. More complex components may contain complex control circuitry. In DIN schematics, this will be indicated with the symbol of a transistor in the component symbol.

A relay in a DIN schematic is an example of a combination of symbols in a single component. Relays require a signal from an outside source to activate. Relays share the component designator J with control units. The basic five-pin relay in FIGURE 16-18 contains two separate components: a switch and a solenoid. The coil in the solenoid is energized with low current, creating a magnetic pull

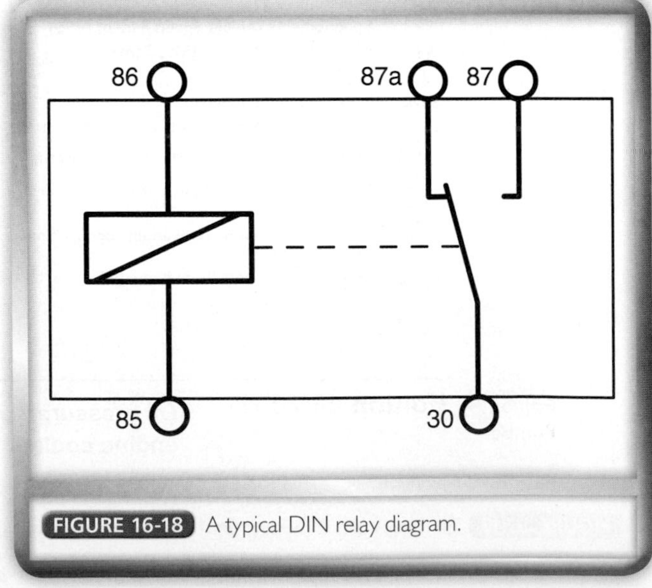

FIGURE 16-18 A typical DIN relay diagram.

that closes or opens the switch. Terminal designation for a standard 5 pin relay is:

- 30 Receives + battery current
- 87 Normally open contact to load
- 86 Control circuit receives a switched battery positive
- 85 Receives a switched ground to activate the solenoid winding in the relay
- 87a Normally closed contact to load

Note: All switches and relays are shown in a non-operated state.

Valley Forge Diagrams

Valley Forge (VF) wiring diagrams are used by many North American based OEMs. VF diagrams share many commonalities with DIN standards. For example, VF diagrams also show power flow from top to bottom and circuit operation from left to right, with inputs on the left and outputs on the right. VF diagrams use standards for wiring colors, circuit codes, and symbols.

A primary difference between the two types of schematic diagrams is that VF diagrams use SAE-type symbols . Conductor sizes, symbol representations, component, and terminal designations are different from DIN standards. Some of the common features shown in the Valley Forge diagram in FIGURE 16-19 are:

1. Battery positive. Begins at top right of diagram, indicating a location to check for power.
2. Dotted line indicates the fuse location in a fuse block, but the dotted line means the component is not completely shown.

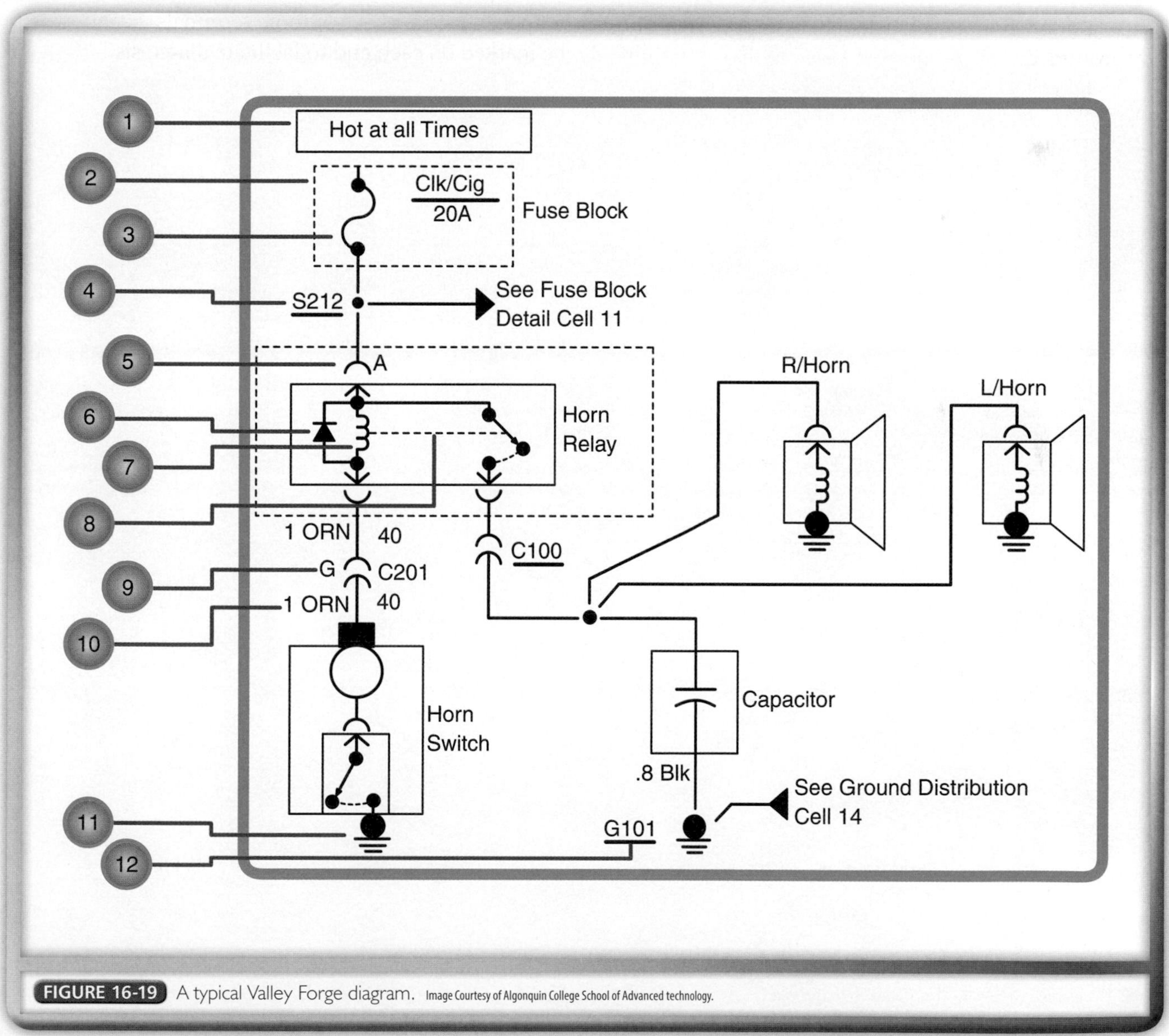

FIGURE 16-19 A typical Valley Forge diagram. Image Courtesy of Algonquin College School of Advanced technology.

3. Thermal fuse. Circuit protection fuse size, circuit name, and location.
4. Wiring splice number indicates wires are joined. 121 indicated the splice number and "S" designate a splice.
5. Terminal location designated A. It shows a connection point on the horn relay.
6. A diode for suppression of voltage spike produced when the magnetic field of the relays, coil collapses.
7. Control circuit of the relay.
8. Dotted line represents mechanical action.
9. G indicates the wire position in the connector. 201 is the circuit number. C designates it as a connector.
10. Identification of wire color, circuit number, and size. 1 indicates the wires, cross sectional area is $1 mm^2$. ORN indicates an orange wire. The wire circuit number is 40.
11. A ground symbol indicates the component itself is grounded.
12. G indicates a ground source. 101 indicates the number and location of the ground.

Module Connector Pin Assignments

Wiring diagrams tell the user at which pin numbers the wires terminate. Knowing where the wires terminate simplifies diagnosis. There are four main types of terminal designations:

- Push-on/multi-point connections
- Component/multi-point
- Central/relay panel
- Relay

Generally, pin assignments are labelled on the plastic hard-shell connector housing and/or the corresponding component. On larger connectors, pin assignments are labelled at either end of a row **FIGURE 16-20**. For example, the Engine Control Module (ECM) plug often has four to ten rows, each with 12 or more terminals. Each row will be marked on each end to facilitate diagnosis.

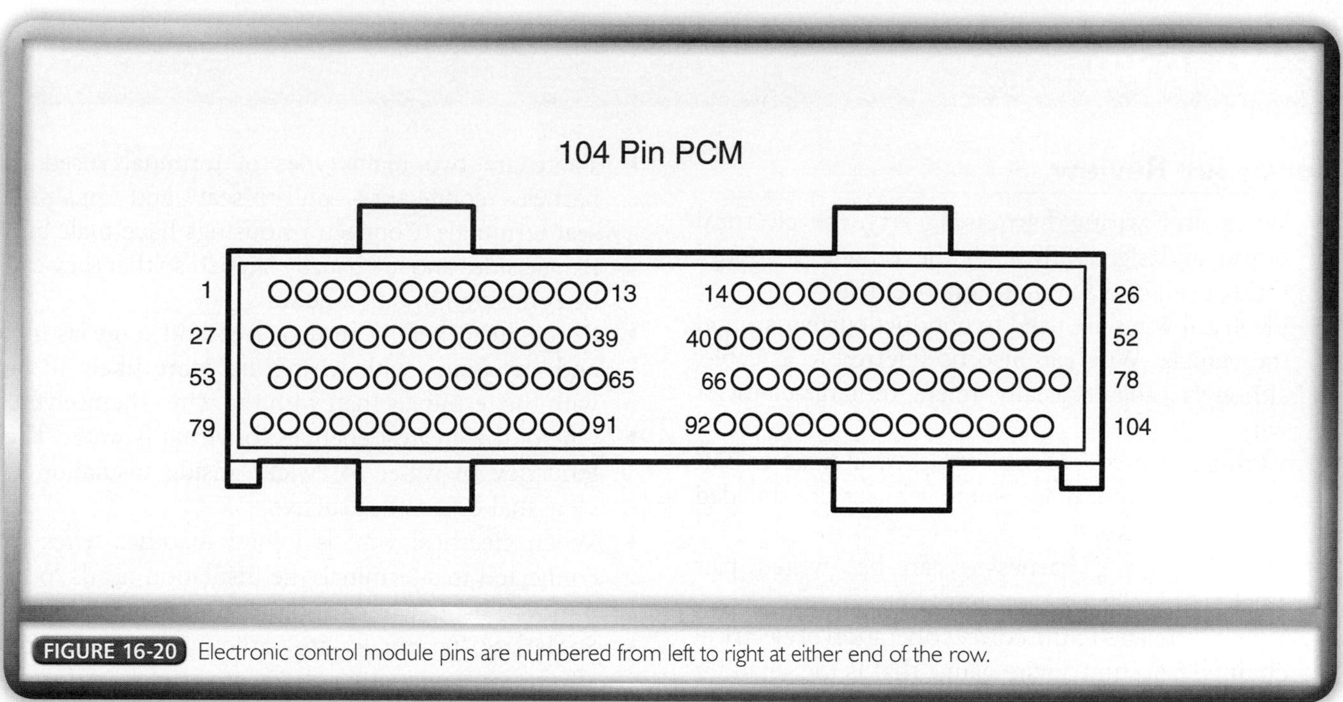

FIGURE 16-20 Electronic control module pins are numbered from left to right at either end of the row.

Wrap-up

Ready for Review

- Wires and wiring harnesses carry the electrical power and signals through the vehicle to control virtually all of the systems on a vehicle.
- Electrical wires are used to conduct current around the vehicle. Wire can also be referred to as cable, although cable typically refers to large-diameter wire.
- Wiring harnesses are subject electrical noise or EMI noise. To prevent noise, some vehicles use shielded wiring harnesses.
- Shielded wiring harnesses can be twisted pair shielding, Mylar tape, or drain lines.
- Wire size relates to the correct operation of electrical circuits. Selecting a wire gauge that is too small for an application will have an adverse effect on the operation of the circuit. Selecting a wire gauge that is too large increases costs and the weight and size of wiring harnesses.
- The resistance of a wire affects how much current it can carry.
- There are two scales used to measure the sizes of wires: the metric wire gauge and the American wire gauge (AWG).
- Wire-coding systems are another useful feature of wiring to aid troubleshooting and service of electrical systems. Both colors and numbering systems designate wiring circuits, application, and even the routing of wires.
- SAE and ISO standards specify the dimensions, test methods, and requirements for single-core primary wire intended for use in road vehicle applications.
- Chassis wiring often uses numerical codes to identify which circuit the wire belongs to, where the wire is in the circuit, which harness it belongs in, and the wire gauge and color.
- Terminals installed to the wire ends provide low-resistance termination to wires. Terminals allow electricity to be conducted from the end of one wire to the end of another wire.
- There are two main types of terminals used in harness connectors—pull-to-seat and push-to-seat terminals. Connector housings have male and female sides and are usually shaped so that they can be connected in only one way.
- Wires are generally trouble free and long lasting, and any issues with wiring are more likely to be with the terminals than with the wires themselves.
- One of the greatest enemies to wiring is water. The tendency of water to "wick" inside insulation is what makes it so destructive.
- When electrical wire is joined to other wires or connected to a terminal, the insulation needs to be removed using wire-stripping tools.
- Solderless terminals are quick to install and effective at conducting electricity across joints that are designed to be disconnected. Connectors can also be soldered.
- Wiring diagrams use abstract graphical symbols to represent electrical circuits and their connection or relationship to other components in the system. They are essentially a map of all of the electrical components and their connections.
- Three main types of wiring diagrams are map, isometric, and schematic diagrams.
- The two most common types of schematic diagrams are the Deutsche Institute Norm (DIN) and the Valley Forge (VF).
- Schematic wiring diagrams show power supply, load, ground, conductors (wires), and circuit protection.
- Schematic wiring diagrams show power flow from top to bottom and circuit operation from left to right, with inputs on the left and outputs on the right.
- Reading a wiring diagram is like reading a road map. There are a lot of interconnected circuits, wires, and components to decipher.

Vocabulary Builder

current track Another name for a DIN diagram.

Deutsch connector A compact, environmentally sealed electrical connector that uses solid, round metal pins and hollow female sockets.

Deutsche Institute Norm (DIN) diagram A schematic wiring diagram on which symbols, terminal connection numbers, line symbols, and operational status of items such as switches and relays are defined by a DIN standard. Also called *current track*.

isometric diagram A wiring diagram used to locate a component within a system and which shows the outline of a vehicle or piece of equipment where the component can be found.

map (pictorial) diagram A wiring diagram that shows the entire vehicle wiring circuit using pictorial symbols.

Metri-Pack connector A pull-to-seat electrical connector with flat terminals instead of round.

parallel wiring A type of custom-made wiring harness that encloses multiple conductors into a single vinyl insulator covering.

pull-to-seat terminal A terminal installed by inserting the wire through the connector cavity, crimping on a terminal, and then pulling the terminal back into the connector cavity to seat it.

push-to-seat terminal A terminal inserted into the back of the connector cavity to seat after the terminal is crimped to the wire.

SAE J1128 standard A standard that specifies the dimensions, test methods, and requirements for single-core primary wire intended for use in road vehicle applications.

schematic diagram A line drawing that explains how a system works by using symbols and connecting lines.

Valley Forge (VF) diagram A schematic wiring diagram that uses SAE-type symbols.

water wicking The movement of water through wiring due to its adhesive and cohesive properties.

Weather-Pack connector An environmentally sealed push-to-seat electrical connection system supplied in one- to six-pin configurations.

Review Questions

1. Fuses prevent circuit damage by:
   a. stopping excessive current flow.
   b. reducing wiring length.
   c. limiting voltage increases.
   d. decreasing circuit resistance.
2. Wiring diagrams enable technicians to:
   a. trace the location of wiring circuit connections and color codes when a system is faulty.
   b. trace the voltage applied through a particular circuit.
   c. work out the current flow to components.
   d. work out the component circuit resistance.
3. When selecting wires or cables for applications, consideration needs to be given to all of the following except:
   a. the amount of current flowing through the circuit.
   b. the components and mounting environment.
   c. the amount of voltage flowing through the circuit.
   d. the ambient environment.
4. To enhance the strength of the joint, wires should be joined by bending each into a double J bend then twisting to form a:
   a. Northern Union splice.
   b. Southern Union splice.
   c. Eastern Union splice.
   d. Western Union splice.
5. Which of the following is another name for wiring diagrams?
   a. Electrical schematics
   b. Electrical diagrams
   c. Abstract graphical symbols representation
   d. Electrical graphical representations
6. The three main types of wiring diagrams include:
   a. map, spatial, and schematic diagrams.
   b. spatial, isometric, and schematic diagrams.
   c. map, isometric, and linear diagrams.
   d. map, isometric, and schematic diagrams.
7. Which type of diagram is used to locate a component in a system?
   a. Linear diagram
   b. DIN diagram
   c. Isometric diagram
   d. Valley Forge diagram
8. What is the purpose of current tracks?
   a. To find the continuation of a conductor on another page
   b. To match the wiring to the vehicle
   c. To assist in locating a battery terminal
   d. To conduct electricity in the system
9. Wire gauge is a measurement of:
   a. wire size.
   b. diameter of wire plus its insulator.
   c. length of wire.
   d. wire material.
10. Whiich of the following is a pull-to-seat type connector?
    a. Metri-Pak
    b. Deutsch
    c. Weather-Pak
    d. All of the choices are pull-to-seat connectors.

ASE-Type Questions

1. Technician A says that wires and wiring harnesses are the arteries of the vehicle's electrical system, and as such they need to be kept in good condition, free of any damage or corrosion. Technician B says that they carry the electrical power and signals through the vehicle to control virtually all of the systems on a vehicle. Who is correct?
   a. Technician A
   b. Technician B
   c. Both Technician A and Technician B
   d. Neither Technician A nor Technician B
2. Technician A says the insulation is designed to protect the wire and prevent leakage of the current flow so that it can get to its intended destination. Technician B says aluminum is typically used because it offers low electrical resistance and remains flexible even after years of use. Who is correct?
   a. Technician A
   b. Technician B
   c. Both Technician A and Technician B
   d. Neither Technician A nor Technician B
3. Technician A says selecting a wire gauge that is too large increases the amount of current flowing into the wiring harnesses. Technician B says the resistance of a wire affects how much current it can carry. Who is correct?
   a. Technician A
   b. Technician B
   c. Both Technician A and Technician B
   d. Neither Technician A nor Technician B
4. Technician A says that terminals installed to wire ends provide low-current termination to wires. Technician B says that terminals allow voltage to be conducted from the end of one wire to the end of another wire. Who is correct?
   a. Technician A
   b. Technician B
   c. Both Technician A and Technician B
   d. Neither Technician A nor Technician B
5. Technician A says a common mistake while soldering is trying to apply the solder directly to the tip of the soldering iron while the iron is heating up the wires. Technician B says it will not melt the solder leading to a cold joint. Who is correct?
   a. Technician A
   b. Technician B
   c. Both Technician A and Technician B
   d. Neither Technician A nor Technician B
6. Technician A says linear diagrams are a variation of the map diagram. Technician B says symbols for components are always pictorial. Who is correct?
   a. Technician A
   b. Technician B
   c. Both Technician A and Technician B
   d. Neither Technician A nor Technician B
7. Technician A says DIN schematic diagrams are also called power source track wiring diagrams because they show the power source at the top of the page and the ground points at the bottom. Technician B says newer DIN standards do indicate on which side of the vehicle a component may be located. Who is correct?
   a. Technician A
   b. Technician B
   c. Both Technician A and Technician B
   d. Neither Technician A nor Technician B
8. Technician A says knowing the standards for wiring colors makes the job of reading and interpreting schematics easier. Technician B says some colors and terminal designations for wiring are used across a number of standards. Who is correct?
   a. Technician A
   b. Technician B
   c. Both Technician A and Technician B
   d. Neither Technician A nor Technician B
9. Technician A says DIN wiring diagrams also indicate the wire gauge used (shown in mm^2), designating the cross sectional area of the wire. Technician B says because standards exist for the maximum permissible voltage drop across a circuit, wire gauge is critical. Who is correct?
   a. Technician A
   b. Technician B
   c. Both Technician A and Technician B
   d. Neither Technician A nor Technician B
10. Technician A says wiring diagrams tell the user where pin numbers for wires could terminate. Technician B says knowing where the wires terminate intensifies the diagnostic procedure. Who is correct?
   a. Technician A
   b. Technician B
   c. Both Technician A and Technician B
   d. Neither Technician A nor Technician B

CHAPTER 17

NATEF Tasks

Required Supplemental Tasks Shop and Personal Safety	Page
■ Demonstrate awareness of the safety aspects of high-voltage circuits (such as high intensity discharge (HID) lamps, ignition systems, injection systems, etc.).	497

Electrical/Electronic Systems Lighting Systems	
■ Interface with vehicle's on-board computer; perform diagnostic procedures using recommended electronic service tool(s) (including PC-based software and/or data scan tools); determine needed action.	488–489
■ Identify causes of brighter than normal, intermittent, dim, or no headlight and daytime running light (DRL) operation.	490–498
■ Inspect and test switches, bulbs/LEDs, sockets, connectors, terminals, relays, wires, and control components/modules of parking, clearance, and taillight circuits; repair or replace as needed.	490–496
■ Inspect and test interior cab light circuit switches, bulbs/LEDs, sockets, low voltage disconnect (LVD), connectors, terminals, wires, and control components/modules; repair or replace as needed.	492–493
■ Inspect and test instrument panel light circuit switches, relays, bulbs/LEDs, sockets, connectors, terminals, wires, and printed circuits/control modules; repair or replace as needed.	492–493
■ Test, aim, and replace headlights.	496–497
■ Test headlight and dimmer circuit switches, relays, wires, terminals, connectors, sockets, and control components/modules; repair or replace as needed.	496–497
■ Inspect and test tractor-to-trailer multi-wire connector(s); repair or replace as needed.	499–500

Body Electrical Systems—Lighting Systems

NATEF Tasks, continued

Electrical/Electronic Systems Lighting Systems, continued	Page
■ Inspect, test, and adjust stoplight circuit switches, bulbs/LEDs, sockets, connectors, terminals, wires, and control components/modules; repair or replace as needed.	500–503
■ Inspect and test reverse lights and warning device circuit switches, bulbs/LEDs, sockets, horns, buzzers, connectors, terminals, wires, and control components/modules; repair or replace as needed.	500–503
■ Inspect and test turn signal and hazard circuit flasher(s), switches, relays, bulbs/LEDs, sockets, connectors, terminals, wires, and control components/modules; repair or replace as needed.	500–503

Knowledge Objectives

After reading this chapter, you will be able to:

1. Identify a vehicle's optional and accessory electrical systems. (p 490–492)
2. Describe and explain network control of lighting circuits. (p 490–491)
3. Recommend service and maintenance practices for lighting circuits. (p 490–502)
4. Identify and describe various types of lighting technology used in commercial vehicles. (p 492–500)
5. Identify and describe commercial vehicle interior and exterior lighting circuits. (p 492–493)
6. Identify lighting standards for commercial vehicles. (p 492–493)
7. Categorize and describe failures in bulbs and lighting circuits. (p 494–495)

Skills Objectives

There are no skills objectives for this chapter.

Introduction

A traditional body electrical system consists of basic functional electrical systems found in all vehicles. This chapter will cover the body electrical systems related to lighting, but before diving into those details, we will discuss how the electrical systems are organized, as well as how they are classified by category according to whether they are conventional or use network control.

Fundamentals of the Body Electrical System

Body Electrical Sections

A traditional body electrical system consists of two parts. The first section is the standard electrical circuitry found in all vehicles, such as lighting, wipers, horn, directional signal indicators, heater blower motors, instrumentation, and so on. Optional accessories make up the other section of the body electrical system. Power windows, seats, supplemental restraint systems (SRS), on-board entertainment systems, vehicle security, and collision avoidance systems are just a few examples of the hundreds of electrical accessories available today.

Conventional and Network Control

Body electrical systems are now also divided into two major categories. Conventional systems, which are quickly disappearing, use electrical components operating in isolation. Point-to-point wiring will connect the dome light, horn, or power windows to a switch operated by the driver. Other devices such as the wipers, head lights, or power door locks operate independently of one another. However, most body electrical systems today use a networked or distributed control of the electrical system. Switching on the wipers will typically illuminate the headlights. Locking the doors with a remote transmitter will beep the horn while momentarily switching on the dome and headlights circuits. Adding weight to the rear axles may cause the headlights to automatically level.

Just as an electronic control module is used to operate the engine or ABS systems, an electronic control module now controls large sections of the electrical system by switching current on or off to devices. Decisions are based on inputs received from a variety of sources, including the driver and logic circuits, or OEM software **FIGURE 17-1**. Electronic control modules not only control electrical circuit operation but also serve as a power distribution point for the electrical system. Instead of fuses, circuits are protected using electronic switches. Adding accessories more likely involves changing electrical system control software instructions and less likely adding wiring and switches.

Ladder Logic

Body electrical equipment will vary by application. For example, the wipers and heating system in a transit bus

You Are the Technician

As a technician working in a fleet operation where you are responsible for safety compliance of hundreds of trucks and trailers crossing many jurisdictional boundaries, lighting system safety is a major concern. The use of particular lighting configurations in one area is not necessarily tolerated in another area. There have been several high-profile nighttime accidents in which cars have collided with trucks and trailers parked or broken down on the side of the road. Drivers are often adding additional lights or installing different colored light lenses for decorative reasons on trucks they regularly drive. On top of that, there is a steady amount of maintenance work related to replacing broken lights and burned-out light bulbs, problems with resistance in trailer electrical cords, loose trailer cord electrical pins—not to mention damage to wiring harnesses that often takes place due to improper repair procedures. In order to enhance vehicle safety and reduce the costs of maintenance and fines for non-compliance as well as blemishes on the company's safety record, you are considering a number of strategies. As you contemplate next steps, consider the following:

1. What legal standard or reference can you use to determine the minimum safety requirements for vehicle lighting and reflective markers?
2. List the advantages of using LED lighting for all marker, tail, and clearance lights for vehicles in your fleet.
3. How could a charging system voltage test reduce maintenance costs for vehicle lighting?

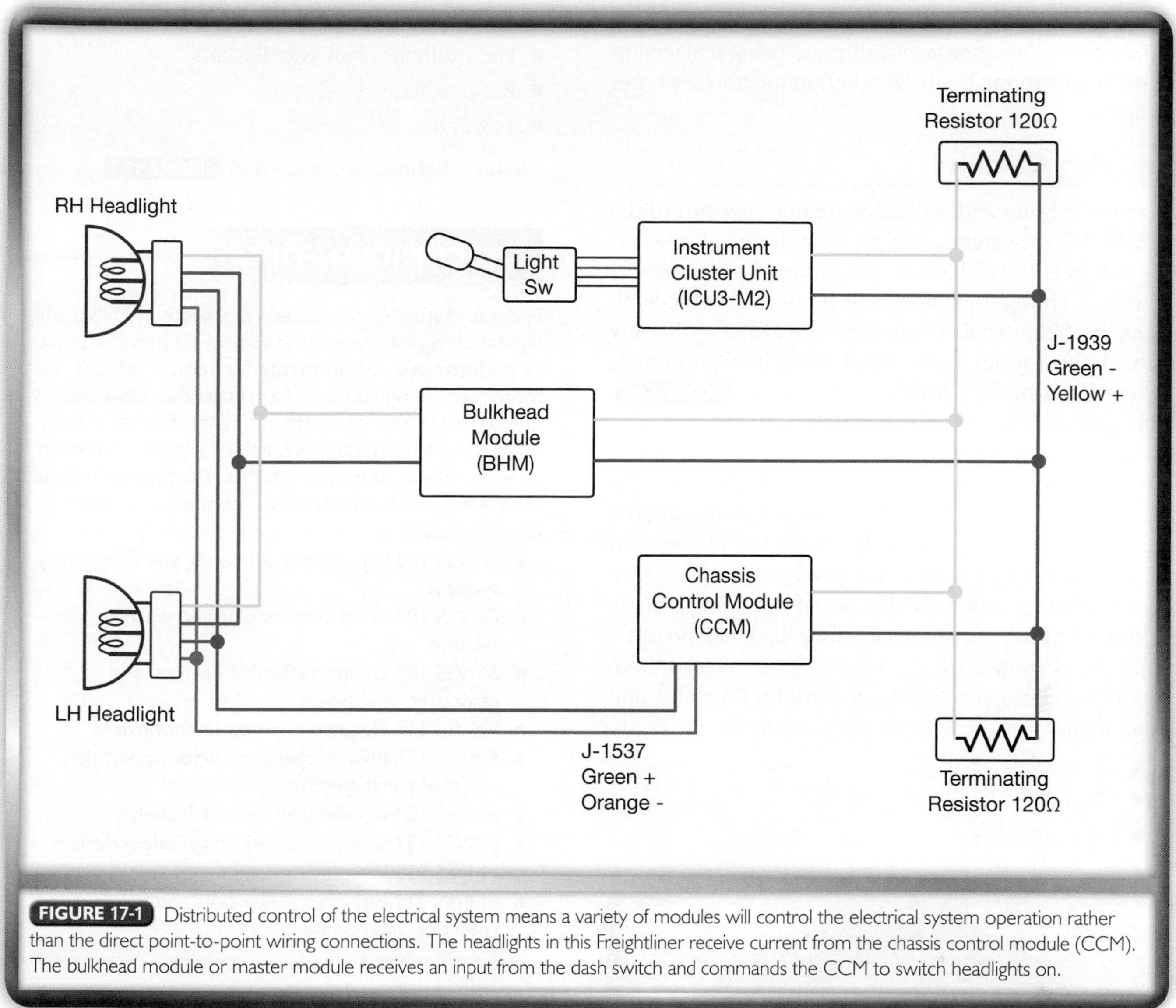

FIGURE 17-1 Distributed control of the electrical system means a variety of modules will control the electrical system operation rather than the direct point-to-point wiring connections. The headlights in this Freightliner receive current from the chassis control module (CCM). The bulkhead module or master module receives an input from the dash switch and commands the CCM to switch headlights on.

are very different than those found in an ambulance or highway tractor. So, too, will the electrical door locking mechanisms. In addition to the variety of electrical accessories, the sophistication of these systems makes it almost impossible to solve electrical problems without the ability to access, read, and interpret electrical schematic diagrams. A few systems even require an understanding of how circuit logic operates. For example, in a networked system, a technician needs to know what conditions are necessary to activate a specific electrical circuit. The simple action of extending a signal arm from a school bus requires a number of other actions to occur before it can take place. In other systems, park brakes may not release if outriggers are still extended, wheel chocks are not stowed away, or a bus door is open. The designed-in logic of a circuit that determines what activates a specific circuit is referred to as **ladder logic**.

Lighting Systems

There are many different styles and types of lights. Each style and type is designed to perform specific roles. For example, warning lamps, indicators, stop lights, taillights, courtesy lamps, and headlamps all perform different roles. In addition, modern vehicles use many different kinds and sizes of bulbs. There are several bulb types available, including standard incandescent bulbs, fluorescent bulbs, halogen bulbs, high-intensity discharge (HID) lamps, daytime running lights, and LEDs. Conventional incandescent bulbs are being replaced in many applications by these other, more efficient types of lights.

Lighting Circuits

Exterior lighting and reflectors are not only part of the vehicle safety systems, but are also designed to identify the length, width, and orientation of a commercial vehicle. Lighting standards are legislated by the Federal/ Canadian Motor Vehicle Standard 108 (FMVSS 105). Any light on the exterior of the vehicle must have **photometric certification** for FMVSS 105 standards FIGURE 17-2. This means lamps are submitted to testing labs to evaluate factors such as light color, brightness, the angle at which the light is effectively observed, and so on. Light lenses carry SAE identification numbers indicating the standard they meet. Generally, lamps facing rearward must emit red light, lamps facing sideways and all turn signals must emit either amber or red light, lamps facing frontward must emit white or yellow light, and no other colors are permitted except on emergency vehicles. Bulb numbers indicate they meet standards for durability and light intensity. Major exterior lighting circuits include:

- Headlights
- Clearance identification lights
- Park-taillights

FIGURE 17-2 The SAE code found on every exterior light indicates the position where it can be used and the photometric standard it meets.

- Turn signals
- Hazard lights (four-way flashers)
- Reverse lights
- Fog lights

Vehicle lighting is depicted in FIGURE 17-3.

> **TECHNICIAN TIP**
>
> Federal Motor Vehicle Safety Standards (FMVSS) are legislated regulations written to provide minimum safety performance requirements for motor vehicles and motor vehicle equipment. To protect the public against unreasonable risk of death or injury due to crashes, FMVSS legislates standards for the design, construction, or performance of motor vehicles. Commercial vehicle body electrical is affected by a number of these standards including:
>
> - FMVSS 103 Windshield defrosting and defogging systems
> - FMVSS 104 Windshield wiping and washing systems
> - FMVSS 108 Lamps, reflective devices, and associated equipment
> - FMVSS 112 Headlamp concealment devices
> - FMVSS 118 Power-operated window, partition, and roof panel systems
> - FMVSS 124 Accelerator control Systems
> - FMVSS 131 School bus pedestrian safety devices
> - FMVSS 125 Warning devices
> - FMVSS 217 Bus emergency exits and window retention and release

Lighting Technologies

What is light? Light is produced by atoms whenever an electron moves from a higher orbital ring (farther from the nucleus) to a lower orbital requiring less energy. Energy given up by the electron is released in the form of a photon. **Photons** are particles of energy and are the basic unit of light FIGURE 17-4.

To produce light and illuminate interiors and instrument clusters, lighting technology has evolved rapidly in recent years beyond the use of incandescent bulbs. These include:

- Fluorescent
- Halogen
- Light-emitting diodes (LEDs)

Incandescent Bulbs

Incandescent bulbs are the conventional bulb technology first invented by Thomas Edison. A filament of metal,

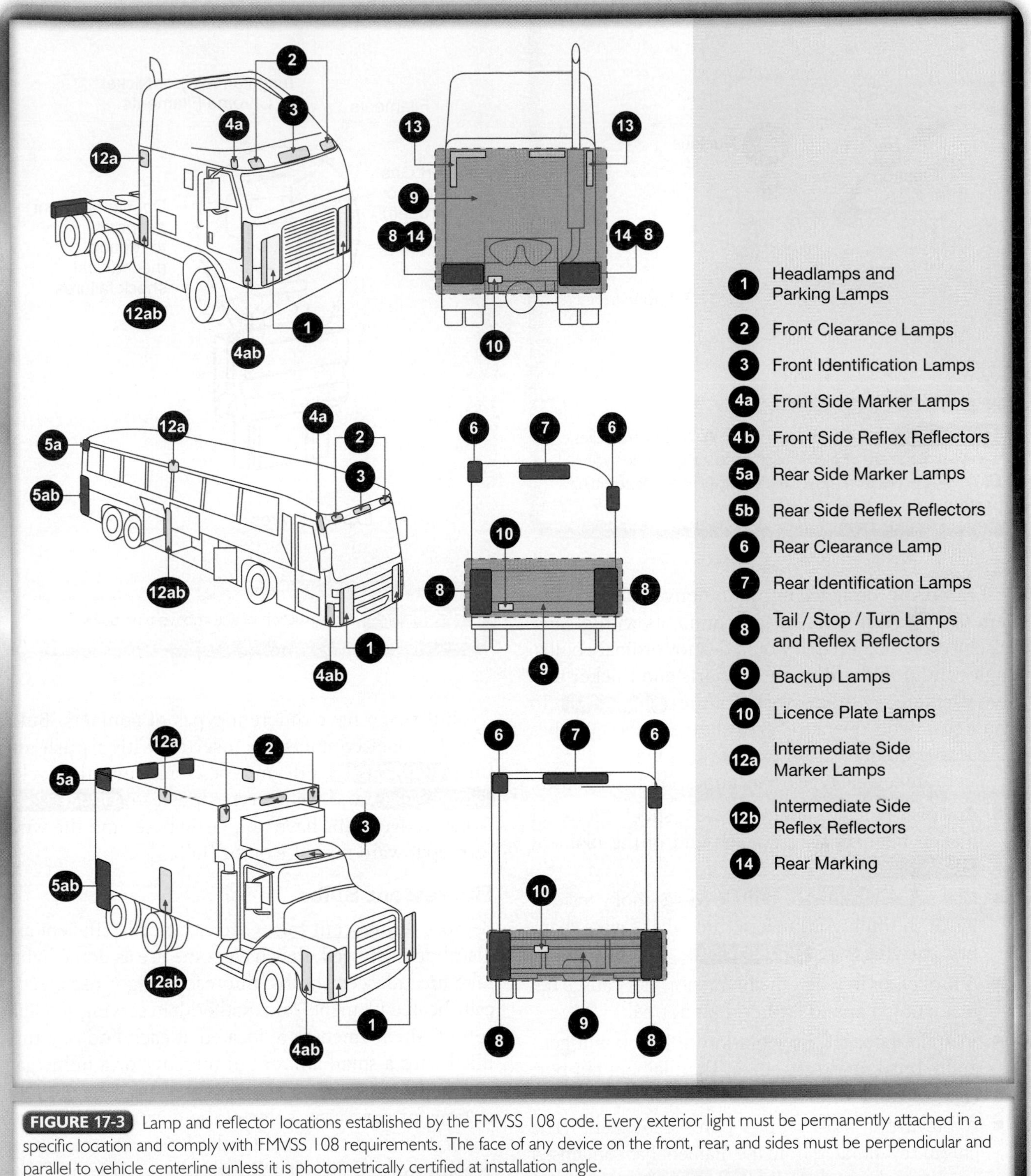

FIGURE 17-3 Lamp and reflector locations established by the FMVSS 108 code. Every exterior light must be permanently attached in a specific location and comply with FMVSS 108 requirements. The face of any device on the front, rear, and sides must be perpendicular and parallel to vehicle centerline unless it is photometrically certified at installation angle.

which is essentially a resistor, is electrically heated to the temperature at which it produces light. The energy lost by colliding electrons trying to squeeze through the filament is converted into light energy. Incandescent bulbs were originally manufactured with a vacuum inside a glass enclosure. That was because air rapidly oxidizes the filament at high temperatures, so the filament burns up. Even inside a vacuum, the filament will eventually boil away, depositing metal on the cooler walls of the bulb. Filling the bulb with an inert gas, such as argon or an argon-nitrogen mixture, slows evaporation of the filament.

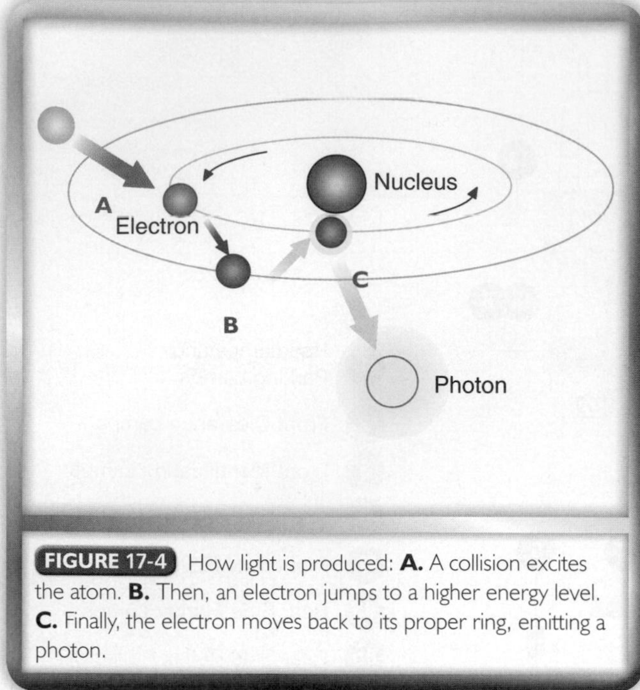

FIGURE 17-4 How light is produced: **A.** A collision excites the atom. **B.** Then, an electron jumps to a higher energy level. **C.** Finally, the electron moves back to its proper ring, emitting a photon.

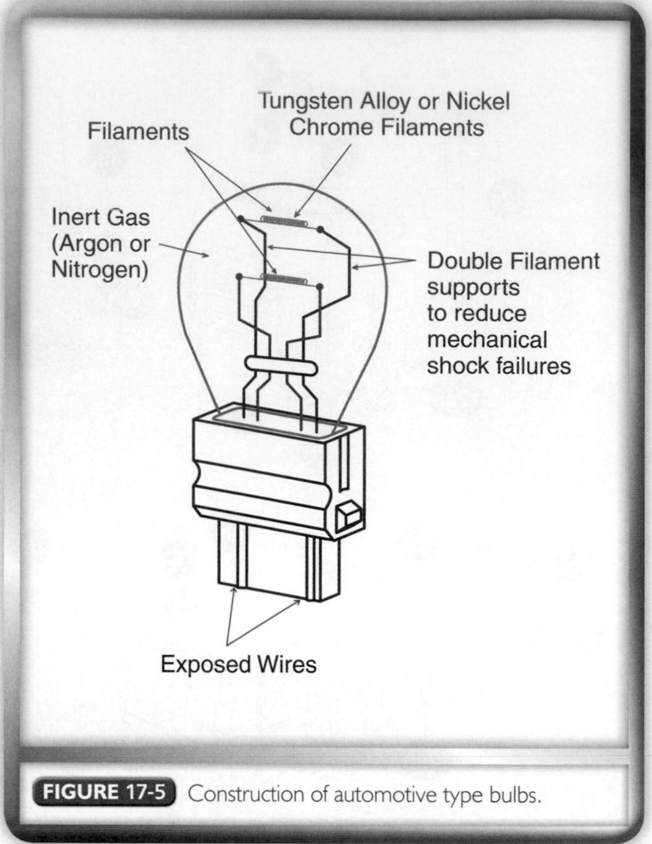

FIGURE 17-5 Construction of automotive type bulbs.

Features are designed into automotive bulbs to allow them to operate in harsher environments with greater resistance to vibration that would destroy ordinary bulbs. Single- and double-filament supports and thicker filament wires are a couple of these features FIGURE 17-5. To ensure that lights operate effectively, the SAE establishes standards and numbers for exterior lighting.

There are several types of incandescent light failures:

- An over-voltage failure leaves small blobs of melted filament wire at each end of the filament FIGURE 17-6A.
- Leakage of air into the bulb leaves a smoky residue inside the bulb. Air can leak through the glass channels carrying wire FIGURE 17-6B.
- A broken bulb when the filament is hot causes the filament to expand farther than normal.
- A bulb damaged by vibration or shock will generally break and separate at the filament support FIGURE 17-6C.
- A burnt-out bulb with a chrome filament. The chrome evaporated from the filament has condensed on the cooler bulb wall FIGURE 17-6D.
- A burnt out tungsten bulb has a brown bulb coating.

Over-voltage conditions cause 60% of all lighting failures. For every 1 volt above designed limits, the life expectancy of the bulb drops by 50% FIGURE 17-7.

Bulbs can have different types of contacts. Bulbs with bayonet contacts are inserted with a push and turn FIGURE 17-8A, Edison types screw into the socket FIGURE 17-8B, and wedge types push in FIGURE 17-8C. Some wedge bulbs have no plastic base, and the wires turn up toward the sides of the bulb.

Fluorescent Bulbs

Because **fluorescent bulbs** are electrically efficient and distribute light well, they have some use as dome lights. Like incandescent bulbs, fluorescent light use electrically heated filaments, too. Rather than serving as a light source, the filaments are located at each end of a tube filled with a small amount of mercury or a noble gas, such as neon, argon, or xenon. A step-up voltage circuit or transformer causes some of the mercury to turn to a vapor, which in turn enables the gas inside the tube to become ionized. In others words, the gas becomes electrically conductive.

Electrons emitted from the filament will move through the gas and hit mercury atoms, which momentarily knocks their electrons into higher orbits. When the electrons fall back to their normal energy levels, the

FIGURE 17-6 **A.** Voltage failure melts bulb filaments. **B.** Air leakage. **C.** Mechanical shock breaks filaments. **D.** Condensed chrome vapor on the bulb walls causes filament evaporation.

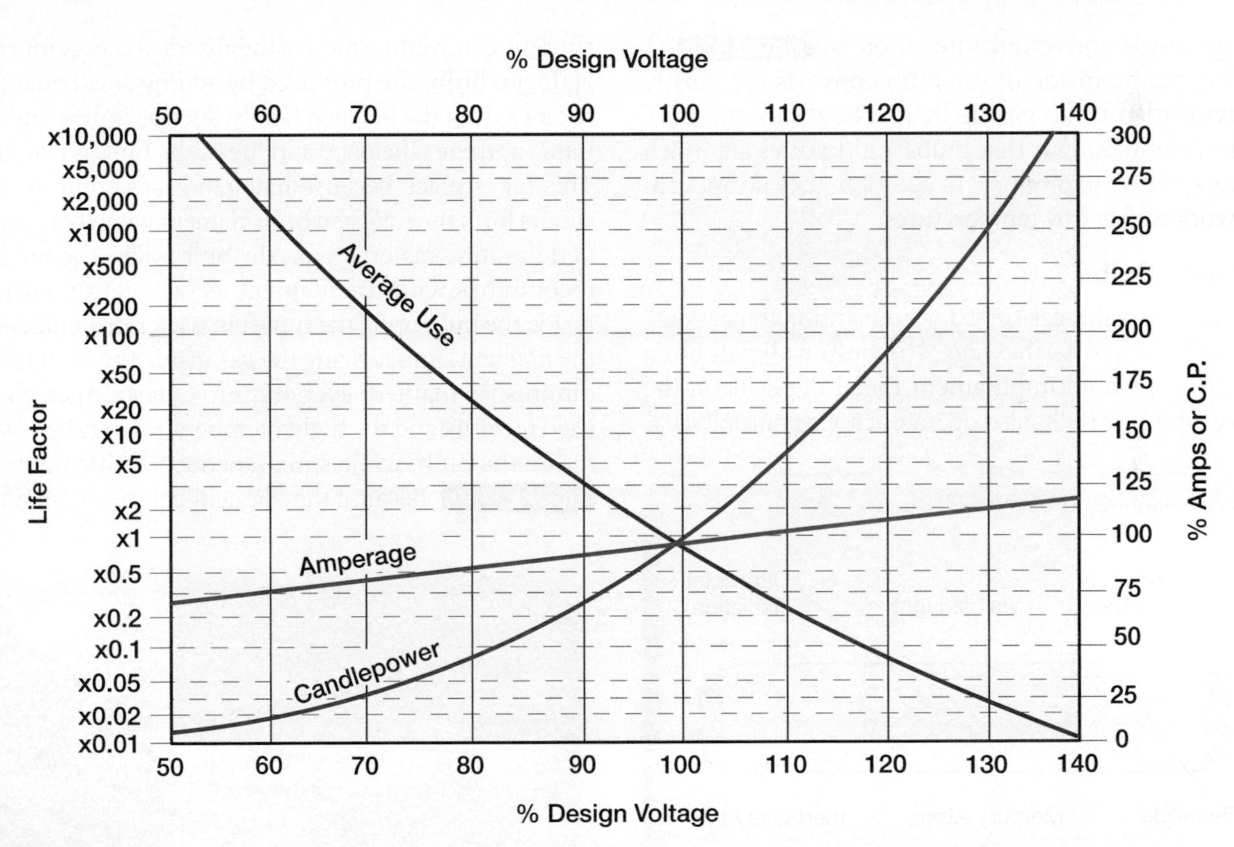

FIGURE 17-7 Increasing voltage supplied to a bulb causes it to become brighter but shortens its service life.

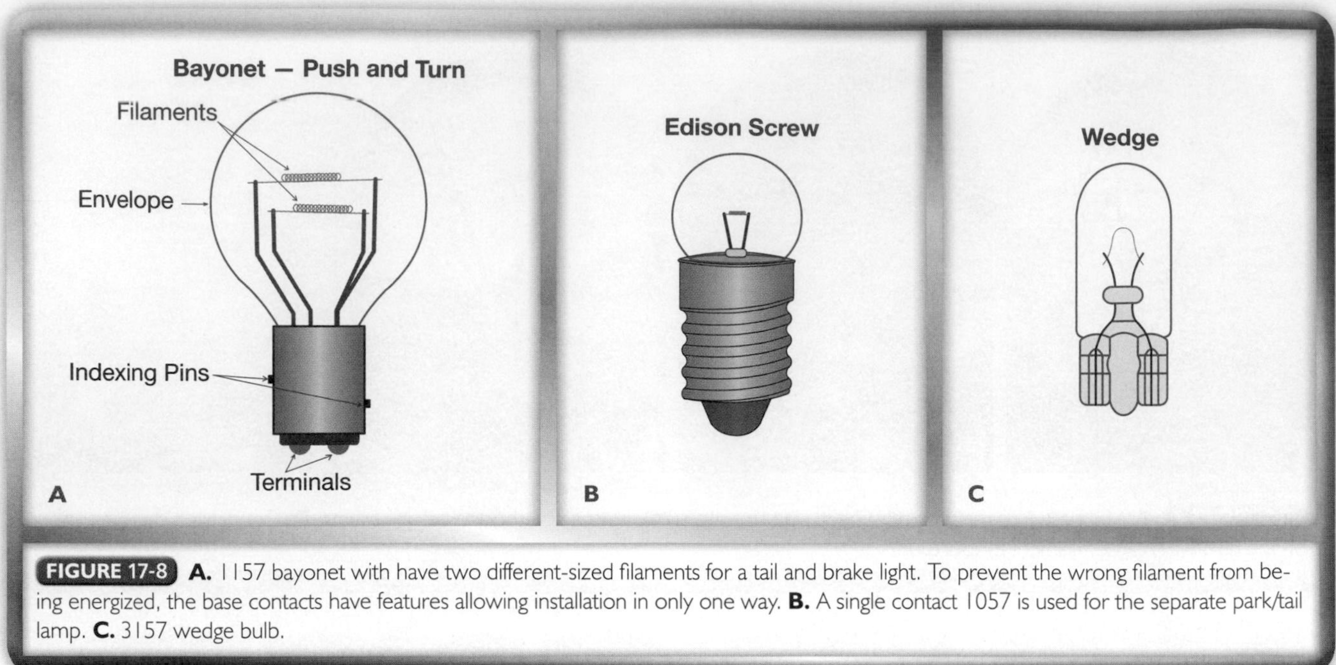

FIGURE 17-8 **A.** 1157 bayonet with have two different-sized filaments for a tail and brake light. To prevent the wrong filament from being energized, the base contacts have features allowing installation in only one way. **B.** A single contact 1057 is used for the separate park/tail lamp. **C.** 3157 wedge bulb.

energy lost is converted into photons FIGURE 17-9. A coating on the inside of the bulb converts the mostly ultraviolet light into visible light. The disadvantage of fluorescent lighting is that bulbs and fixtures are much more expensive to produce. In addition, they do not usually work well at low temperatures.

Halogen Bulbs

Several disadvantages exist for conventional incandescent technology. As they age, the bulb wall will often darken as evaporating filament metal deposits on the bulb wall. These bulbs also operate at approximately 10% efficiency, converting most of the electrical energy into heat. **Halogen bulbs** are produced by adding small quantities of gases from the halogen family, such as iodine and bromine, and the efficiency and life of the bulb is extended. This takes place because halogen gases combine with vapors from the tungsten bulb filament when hot. Instead of depositing material onto the bulb walls, the tungsten recombines with the filament as convection currents inside the bulb bring the tungsten back into contact with the filament. Pressurizing the gas inside the bulb further diminishes filament evaporation. Quartz silica glass is used to withstand the higher temperatures and pressures inside the bulb, while simultaneously reducing its size FIGURE 17-10. Because the filament can be operated at a

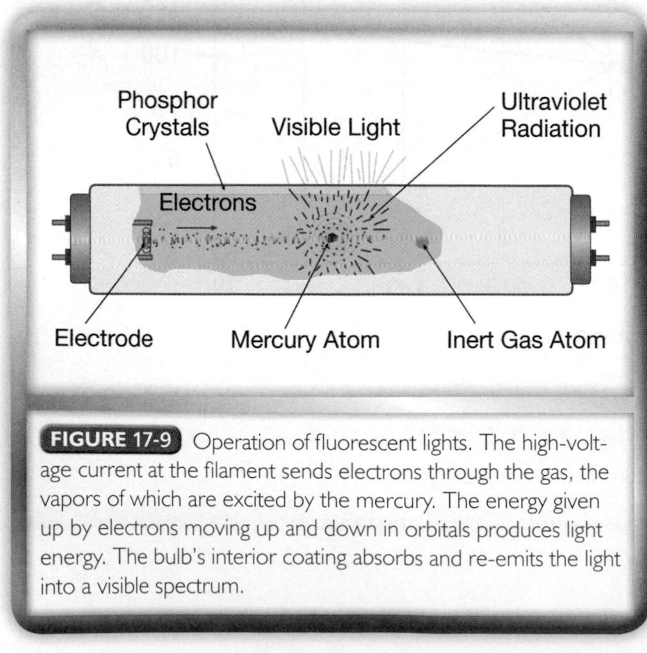

FIGURE 17-9 Operation of fluorescent lights. The high-voltage current at the filament sends electrons through the gas, the vapors of which are excited by the mercury. The energy given up by electrons moving up and down in orbitals produces light energy. The bulb's interior coating absorbs and re-emits the light into a visible spectrum.

FIGURE 17-10 Halogen bulbs use thicker quartz glass, and contain some halogen gas combined with other gases under pressure. The Halogen cycle recirculates tungsten back onto the filament instead of depositing it onto cooler bulb walls.

higher temperature without burning up, more energy is converted to light, the light is whiter, and the bulb's life is extended FIGURE 17-11.

Halogen Infrared Discharge (HID)

Halogen infrared discharge (HID) bulbs should not be confused with high-intensity discharge bulbs. Halogen infrared discharge bulbs use a special coating on an inside portion of the bulb wall. The coating reflects infrared heat back onto the filament, causing it to burn hotter. Increased filament heat produces more light with the same energy. These bulbs are used only in headlight applications FIGURE 17-12.

TECHNICIAN TIP

Any surface contamination, such as from greasy fingerprints, can damage the halogen bulb's quartz glass after it is heated. Hot spots on the bulb surface are created during operation, as the bulb cannot release heat at that point. In extreme cases, the localized heating changes the composition of the quartz, allowing pressurized bulb gases to leak out. A weakened bulb may also explode or form a bubble, distorting the glass envelope. Manufacturers recommend that halogen bulbs be handled without touching the envelope. Using a clean paper towel while handling, or handling the bulb only by its base, will lengthen bulb life. If the quartz is contaminated, it can be cleaned with alcohol before use.

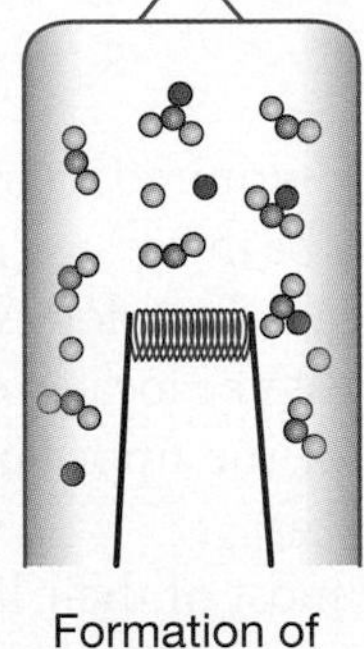
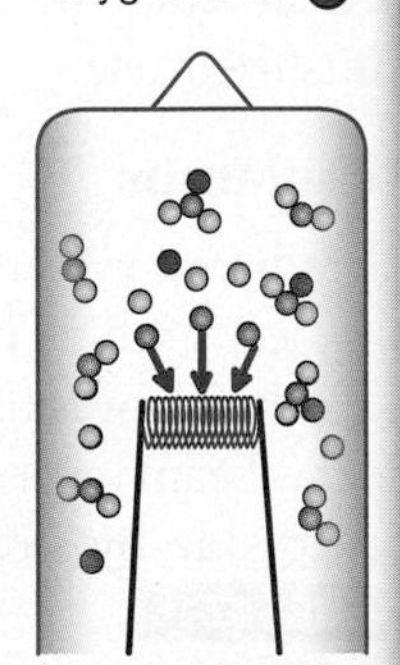
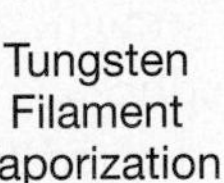

FIGURE 17-11 The halogen cycle recirculates tungsten back onto the filament instead of depositing it onto cooler bulb walls.

FIGURE 17-12 Halogen infrared discharge bulbs use a reflective coating inside the bulb causing it to glow brighter.

Safety

Halogen bulbs pose a number of safety hazards. First, halogen bulbs operate hot enough to severely burn anyone touching them while illuminated and can even cause fires. Touching the bulb walls or contaminating the bulb surfaces in any way will lead to bulb walls weakening, and even exploding. Pressurized gas inside the bulbs will spread shards of quartz glass a considerable distance.

High-Intensity Discharge Lamps (HID)

High-intensity discharge (HID) lamps used for headlight systems employ an electric arc to produce the light. Another name for these lamps is xenon lamps, which use the gas to initially activate the bulb's electric arc FIGURE 17-13. Their higher light output of between 2,800 and 3,800 lumens is brighter than the 700 to 2,100 lumens put out by halogen lights. A **lumen** is a measure of light intensity. In general, small automotive lamps produce between 50 and 400 lumens. For reference,

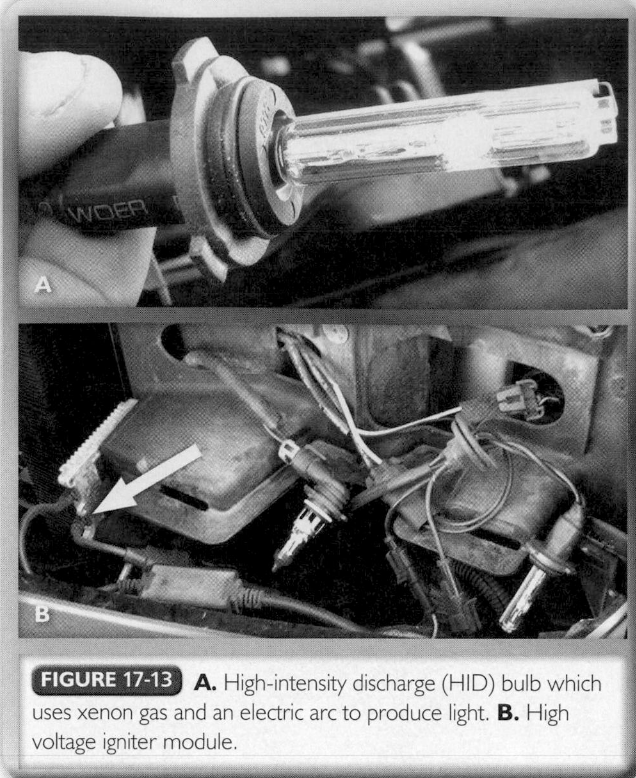

FIGURE 17-13 **A.** High-intensity discharge (HID) bulb which uses xenon gas and an electric arc to produce light. **B.** High voltage igniter module.

FIGURE 17-14 A high-intenisity discharge (HID) lamp xenon headlight uses dangerously high voltage, which can injure technicians if wiring is probed while illuminated.

a standard 23-Watt automotive stop light produces about 400 lumens of light output. The intensity of light from high-intensity discharge bulbs is produced using close to half the current consumed by halogen bulbs, and yet the bulbs last twice as long, with a life cycle of 2,000 hours.

In high-intensity discharge bulbs, light is produced by using a high-voltage electric arc of between 2,000 and 2,500 volts inside a chamber containing gasified metal, which requires a ballast to step up battery voltage **FIGURE 17-14**. Approximately 3 amps of current are used to excite the electrons of the metal atoms into producing a bright white light. When in use, the bright light can produce excessive glare for oncoming drivers. A headlamp lens cleaning system and automatic beam leveling control are recommended but not required in North America. A headlamp self-leveling system will sense the change in vehicle inclination produced by a cargo load or road grade to automatically adjust the headlamps' vertical aim. The high cost of these systems currently limits their use.

> **TECHNICIAN TIP**
>
> An intensive study by a major manufacture has estimated the cost of producing power from a truck alternator is four times the cost to power a household. The cost of on-board electricity at 0.13 kW/hour assumes a fuel cost of $4/gallon and an alternator efficiency of approximately 60%. Broken down another way, the cost to produce a single amp per hour is $0.015. Assuming a lights-on only current load of 20-amps, the cost to light a vehicle is $0.31 for a single hour, or 60 miles at highway speed. This also works out to $5.16 for a thousand miles.

Headlamps

A headlamp system is required to produce a low and a high beam, which may be integrated into a single lamp or individual lamps for each function. When used in pairs, the low beam must always be located on the outside when placed side-by-side, or the upper beam when stacked **FIGURE 17-15**.

High beams cast most of their light straight ahead, maximizing seeing distance, but will produce excessive glare for oncoming drivers. High beams also reduce visibility due to light reflection when driving in fog, snow, or rain. This effect, called back-dazzle, is minimized by the use of lights with bluer spectrum and the use of fog lights. To alert the driver when high beams are operating, a high-beam indicator is placed in the instrument cluster. Low

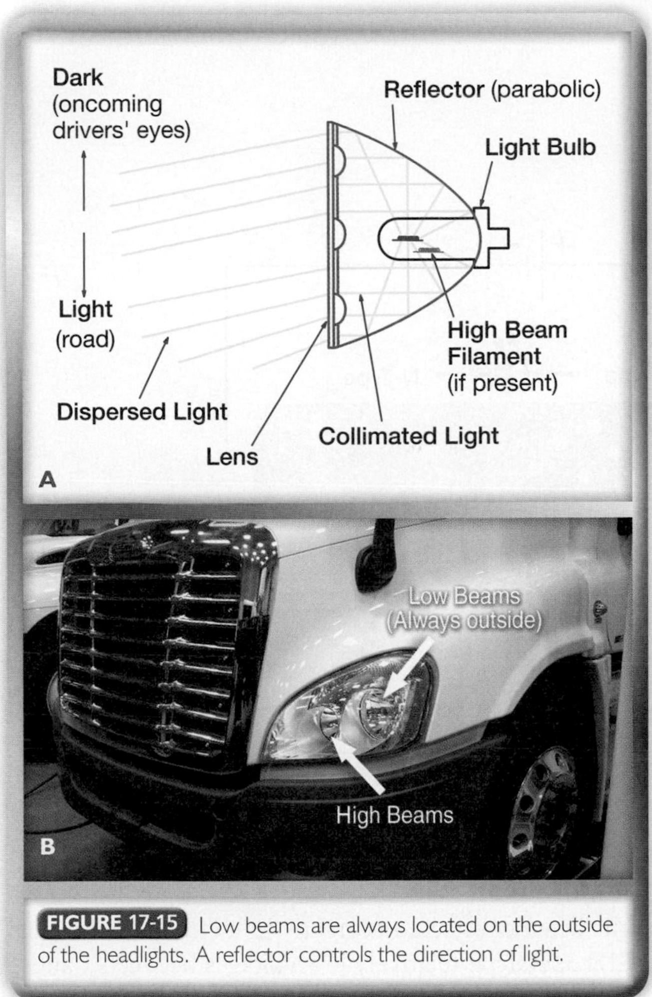

FIGURE 17-15 Low beams are always located on the outside of the headlights. A reflector controls the direction of light.

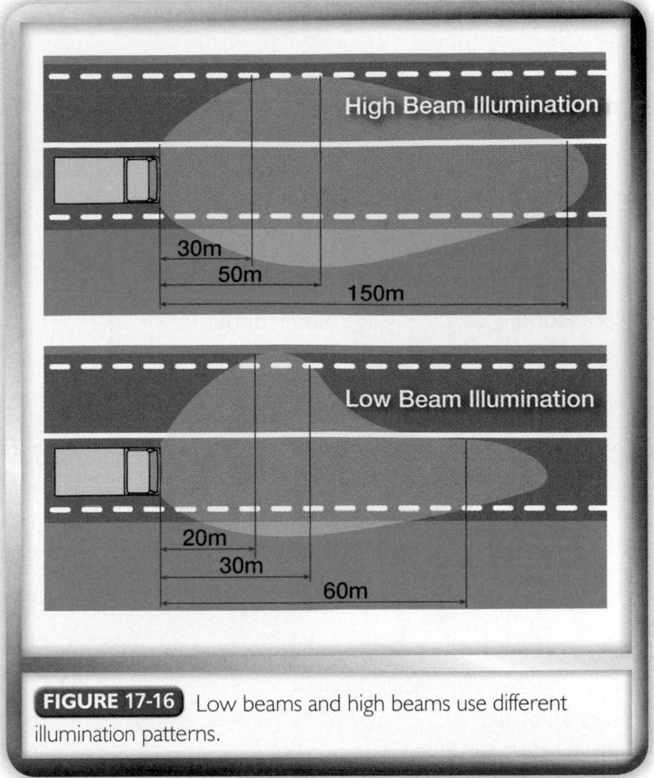

FIGURE 17-16 Low beams and high beams use different illumination patterns.

beam lights direct their light downward and rightward to provide safe forward visibility without causing excessive glare to oncoming drivers or back-dazzle FIGURE 17-16.

Low beams and high beams may operate together when the high beams are illuminated. A dimmer switch is used to switch current between the two circuits. Composite lamps using nonstandard shapes and an internal reflector enable the use of replaceable bulbs.

> **TECHNICIAN TIP**
>
> Because vehicle lighting is photometrically certified and meets FMVSS 108 standards when built, any change to lighting may change conformity to safety standards. Adding additional taillights, for example, might seem like a good policy, but it is frowned upon in some jurisdictions and can earn the driver a ticket. Using blue light lenses, replacing headlight bulbs with all-weather bulbs, adding additional clearance lights, and placing additional lighting around license plates are also changes that are considered to alter or interfere with FMVSS-108 conformity.

Daytime Running Lights (DRL)

Daytime running lights (DRL) are designed to improve vehicle visibility in the daytime. Either the low- or high-beam circuits are powered at a reduced voltage of approximately 80% system voltage. This is accomplished using a DRL module containing a resistor connected in series with the headlight beam filaments. When the headlamp switch is engaged, the DRL module resister is disconnected and the light filaments receive 100% system voltage.

Light-Emitting Diodes

Light-emitting diodes (LEDs) are another unique type of diode that emits light when forward biased. Each time an electron fills a positively charged hole, some energy is released as a photon FIGURE 17-17. The light frequency that determines the color is related to the semiconductor material used. To provide different colors, diodes use a wide combination of semiconductor materials, such as gallium, indium, arsenic, aluminum, phosphorus, and many others. The first LED was red and made from a gallium insulator doped with arsenic and phosphorous. Green, yellow, blue, and almost any other color can be produced from LEDs. To produce the impression of white light, red, green, and blue are mixed FIGURE 17-18. High-intensity white lights, such as spotlights and headlights, use a phosphor material to convert a blue or ultraviolet LED to broad-spectrum white light. This is similar to the way a fluorescent light bulb works.

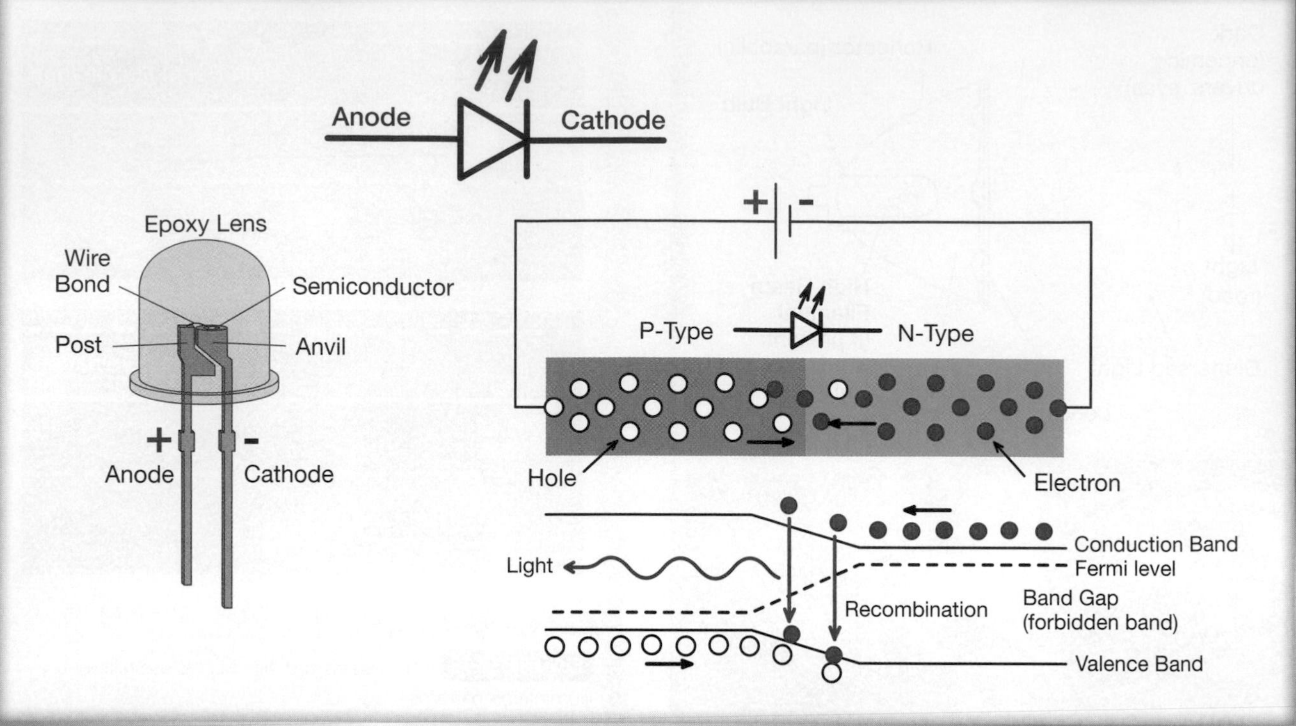

FIGURE 17-17 Construction and operating principles of LED lamps.

FIGURE 17-18 A white light LED bulb combines red, green, and blue LED semiconductors.

Organic LEDs (OLEDs) use a flexible carbon material for the substrate, rather than inorganic crystal semiconductors. These devices, while using even less current, have short life spans, but may have future use in instrument panels or other sources of light.

LEDs have several advantages. Because an LED operates like a conventional diode, polarity must be observed when connecting an LED. Like other diodes, LEDs emit light when connected correctly in a circuit. Individual LEDs operate at relatively low voltages between 1 and 4 volts, and draw currents between 10 and 40 milliamperes. Current above these levels can melt an LED chip. The main advantages of LEDs include the following:

- **Long life.** The life of an LED is roughly 100,000 hours, which means it can often last the life of the vehicle. Incandescent bulbs will last anywhere between 1,000 to 5,000 hours. LEDs are shock-resistant, so they will dim rather than abruptly fail. This extended durability translates into reduced maintenance expenses for fleets.
- **Safety.** Because LEDs light up instantly—0.5 seconds faster following vehicles have more time to brake. Incandescent lamps need 0.25 seconds to heat and turn on. This shortened time translates into about 80' (24 m) more stopping distance at 60 mph (40 kph).
- **Low current consumption.** Using LEDs not only reduces power consumption and the need for larger wires, but can also help maintain sufficient voltage for the trailer ABS system to function when all the lights are on. An 85% drop in current takes place when lights are converted to LEDs.

Despite those many advantages, LEDs do have some disadvantages, including:

- LEDs are voltage sensitive—and will quickly fail in even moderate over-voltage conditions.
- LEDs have a high initial cost compared to other lighting.
- LED output is temperature dependent—meaning that LEDs do not produce enough heat to melt snow and ice covering exterior lighting. However, their light output actually rises at colder temperatures. Their efficiency drops with increased temperature.

Trailer Cords and Plug

The **J-560 trailer connector** is an SAE standard set for connecting the trailer cord to the tractor and trailer electrical system together and has existed since the late 1950s. This seven-pin connector bears the stamp SAE J560, indicating compliance with physical and performance standards of the SAE. Plugs may be plastic or a die-cast zinc metal material. With the mandatory introduction of trailer ABS in 2001, constant battery power to the module could be supplied through the #7-pin blue color-coded wire of the J-560 plug. However, if auxiliary equipment, such as electrically operated solenoids for lift axles, on the trailer is controlled by a dedicated cab, tractors and trailers connecting two circuits through the #7 pin will not supply enough current. FIGURE 17-19 shows the color code for a J-560 trailer plug.

A tractor and trailer may use either a 13-pin Euro style connector, which provides room for as many as six additional circuits, or an ISO 3731connector in tandem with the J-560 FIGURE 17-20. The ISO 3731 connector resembles a J-560, with the exception of an inverted female ground terminal to prevent a connection with a J-560 plug. The connecting cable has a recessed male pin for a ground connection. A tractor using a J-560 in combination with an ISO 3731 plug allows it to hook up with older non-ABS trailers, trailers with ABS and no other electrical accessories, or trailers with ABS and other switched circuits.

An index lug on the cord and spring-loaded door, plus highly polished surfaces, improve latching force to prevent light flickering. Split pins with radial spring tension ensure a good connection between the plug and cable terminals in spite of regular thermal cycling caused by current flow through the connectors. Solid or split pins are acceptable, and male split pins can be spread with a small screwdriver if the connection becomes loose.

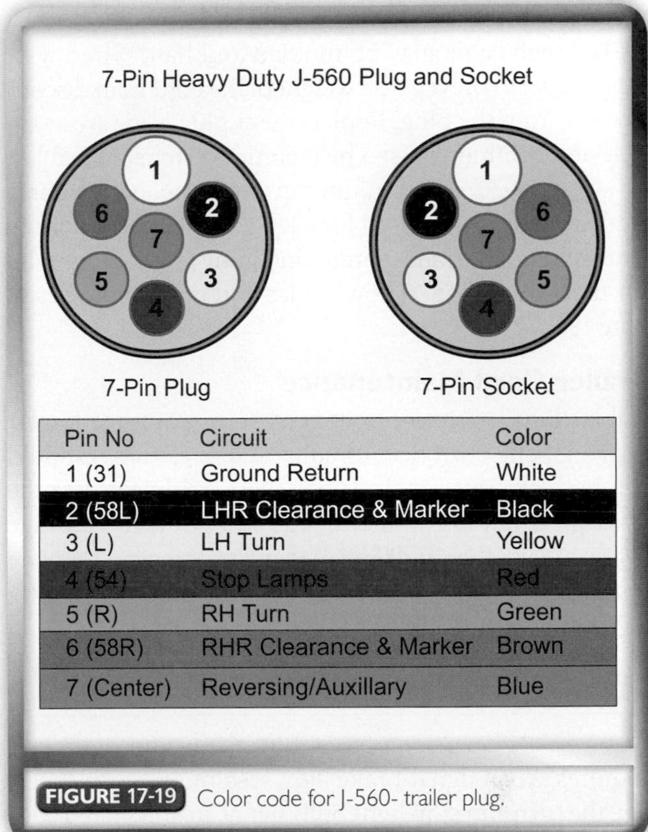

Pin No	Circuit	Color
1 (31)	Ground Return	White
2 (58L)	LHR Clearance & Marker	Black
3 (L)	LH Turn	Yellow
4 (54)	Stop Lamps	Red
5 (R)	RH Turn	Green
6 (58R)	RHR Clearance & Marker	Brown
7 (Center)	Reversing/Auxillary	Blue

FIGURE 17-19 Color code for J-560- trailer plug.

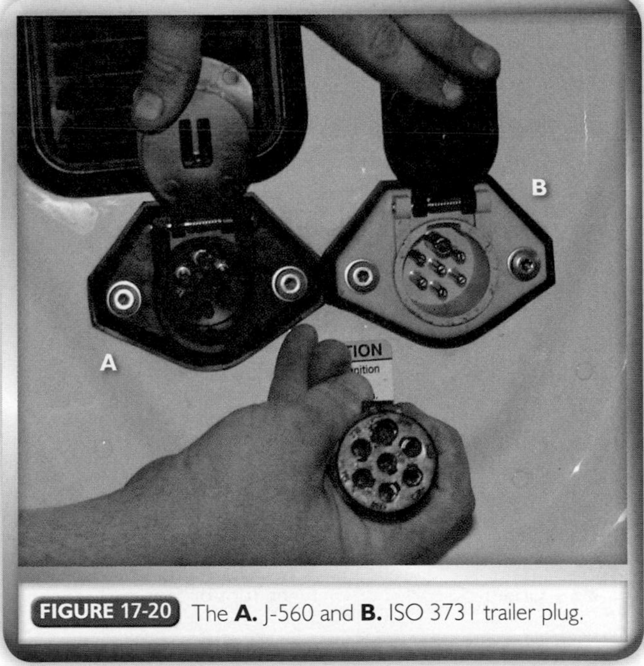

FIGURE 17-20 The **A.** J-560 and **B.** ISO 3731 trailer plug.

Trailer Cords

Trailer cords connecting the trailer and tractor are between 60 inches and 100 inches in working length. When coiled, the 60-inch cable is approximately 12 feet in length, while the 100-inch cable is 20 feet. Plugs at the end of each cable may be molded and hard-wired with strain relief to prevent the weight of the cord from disconnecting from the plug. Replacement plug leads are available and commonly used by technicians to repair cables.

TABLE 17-1 shows minimum wire sizes and standardized SAE color code used for each circuit. Green-colored cables designate trailer cords containing larger-gauge wire for the ABS circuit. Yellow cables and connectors designate ISO 3731.

Trailer Cord Maintenance

Cable plugs and connectors need periodic inspection for broken, bent, corroded, or collapsed pins. Cords should not have any cuts or abrasions that could penetrate the wiring. When not in use, cords should have a storage place where they will not be easily damaged. Wiring should be checked for pull-out from plugs caused by cable strain FIGURE 17-21.

Turn Signal Circuits

Any vehicle operating on public roads and highways requires a turn signal-brake light system. In North America, the turn and stop light bulb signal are integrated with the major bulb filament of a double-filament bulb. The bulb's brighter element then operates as the red-colored lens covering the stop-turn signal. The smaller, minor filament of a double-filament bulb is the taillight. In European systems, the stop-turn signal is not integrated and uses a separate bulb and circuit. In those non-integrated systems, the stop signals are red, while the turn signals are amber.

The directional signal switch in mechanical directional signal systems is supplied current from two sources FIGURE 17-22. One is the service brake light switch; the other is through the turn signal flasher relay. Internal switch contacts within the directional signal switch supply current to the stop-turn bulb filaments. Current is always supplied to the directional signal switch and either stops in the switch or is directed to the left or right turn-signal lights as well as the indicator lights in the instrument cluster. Power then flows through the switch, to the light bulb filaments of the stop-turn lights and then to chassis ground. When the brakes are applied, current will be supplied by the brake light switch through the directional switch to the bulb that is not illuminated FIGURE 17-23. If a four-way hazard flasher switch is integrated into the directional signal switch, the four-ways will supply power to both turn signals. This means applying the brakes causes the lights to remain on constantly since power is no longer being supplied by the flasher relay.

Power for the integrated stop-turn is often constantly supplied in commercial vehicles integrating a four-way

TABLE 17-1: Minimum Wire Sizes and Colors Based on Type of Circuit

Plug Pin Number	Circuit Function	Gauge – w/ABS	< 52 feet (<15.85 metrers)	>52 feet (>15.85 meters)
#1 – White	Ground	10	10	10
#2 – Black	Clearance ID Lights License Light (Circuit balanced with brown #6)	14	14	12
#3 – Yellow	Left Turn or Stop	14	14	12
#4 – Red	Stop Intermittent ABS Power	12	12	8
#5 – Green	Right Turn or Stop	14	14	12
#6 – Brown	Taillight Clearance Lights (Circuit balanced with black #2)	14	14	12
#7 – Blue	Constant ABS Power or Auxiliary	12	14	12

Conductor No.	Color	Key	Lamp and Signal Circuits
1	White	⏚	Ground return to towing vehicle
2	Black	✖	Side marker and identification lamps
3	Yellow	■	Left-hand turn signal and hazard signal
4	Red	▲	Stop lamps and antilock devices
5	Green	⬢	Right-hand turn signal and hazard signal
6	Brown	●	Tail, combined rear clearance, and license plate
7	Blue	AUX	Auxillary, optional lamps, dome, etc.

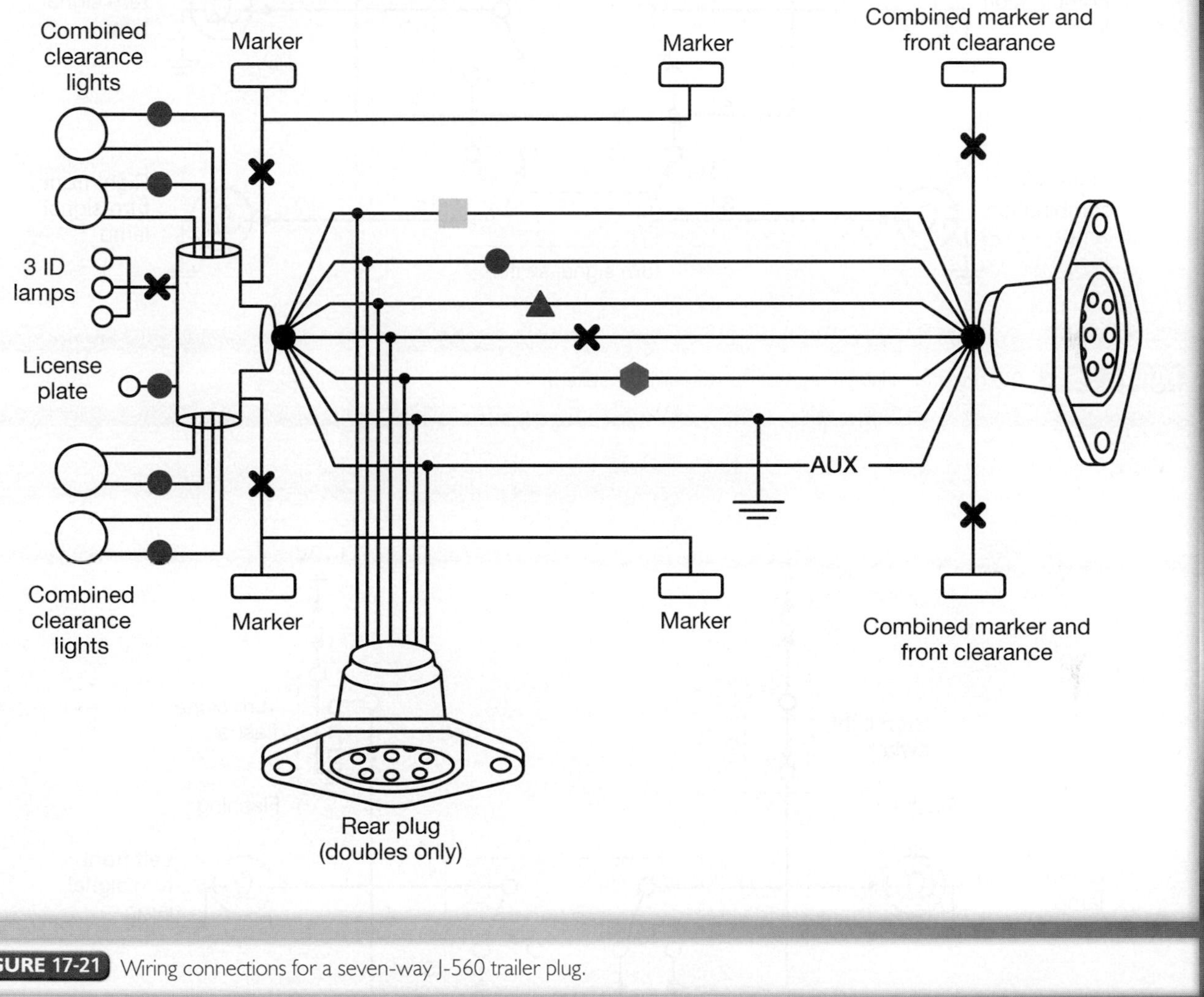

FIGURE 17-21 Wiring connections for a seven-way J-560 trailer plug.

hazard signal switch, so leaving the turn signal stalk switched left or right will cause the light to remain flashing with the ignition off. This configuration prevents excessive battery use through other ignition-on loads when the turn signals or the frequently used four way hazard flashers only are used. The additional number of turns the steering wheel a truck or bus will rotate through also means there is no cancelling mechanism for many medium and heavy-duty vehicles.

The flasher relay is uniquely designed to interrupt power at a fixed frequency. Older flasher relays with few lamp loads used a bimetallic contact that heated and

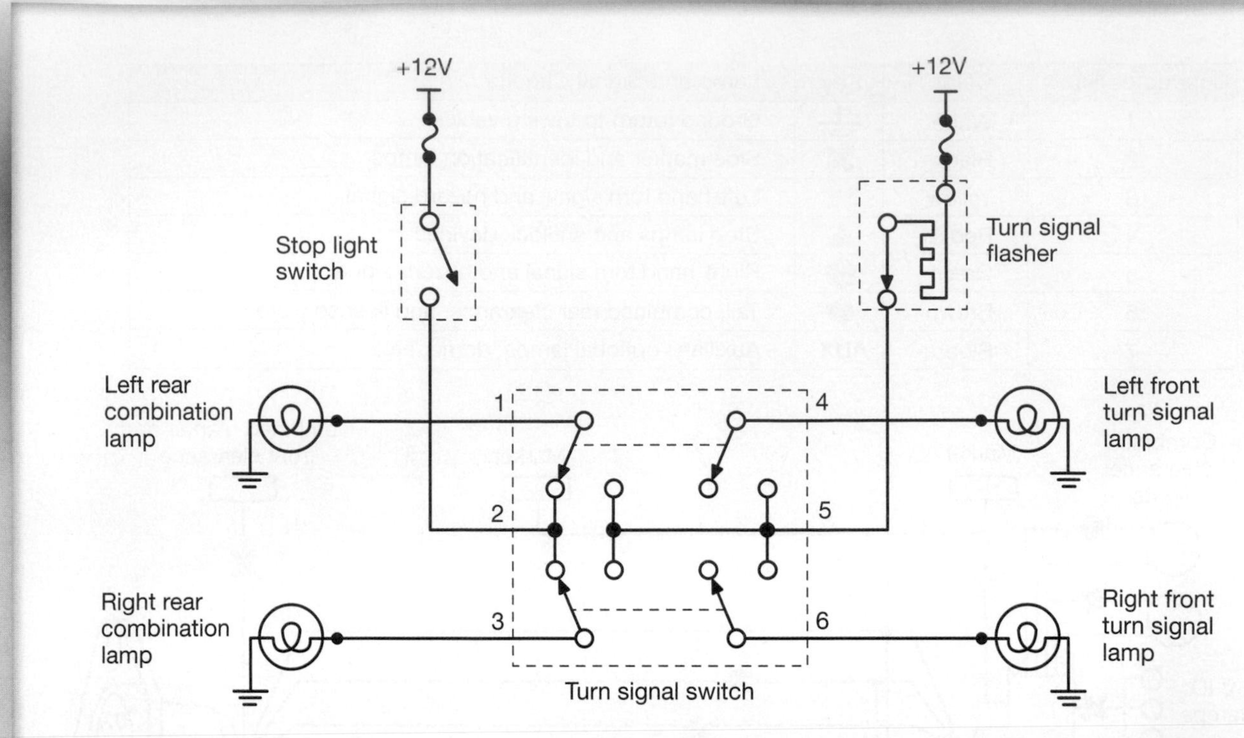

FIGURE 17-22 The circuit for a integrated stop-turn signal lamp system.

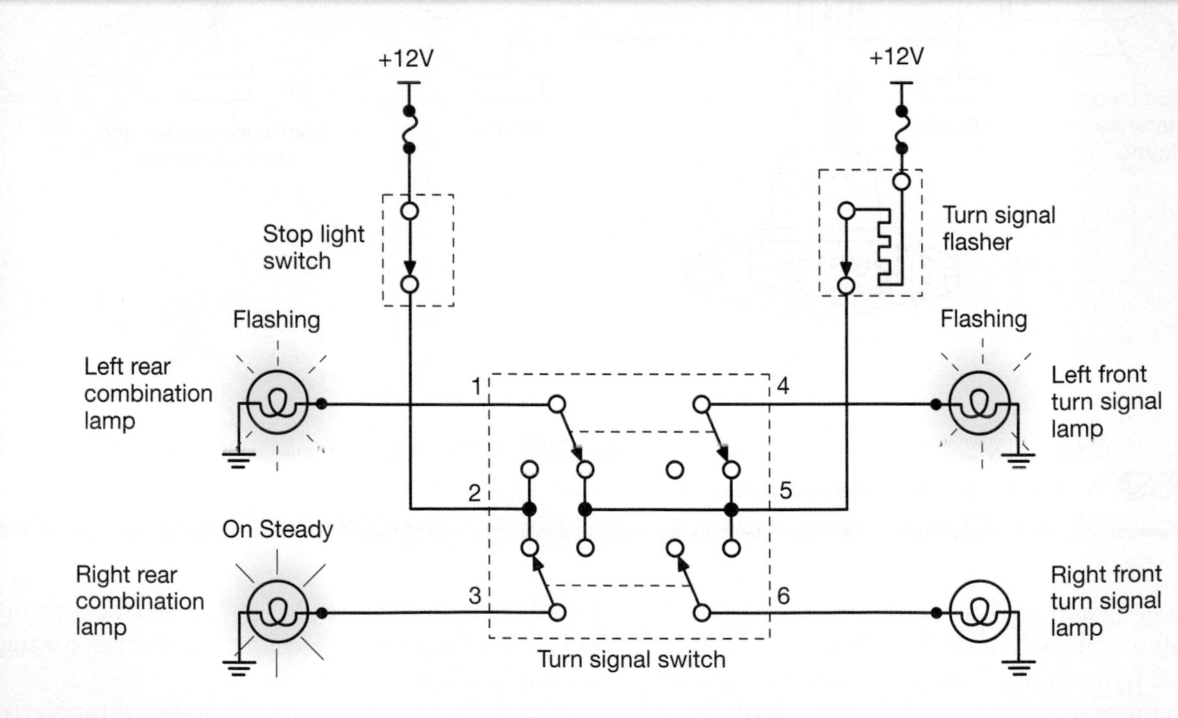

FIGURE 17-23 Current flow through the stop turn-signal light system with the brakes applied.

opened switch contacts when current flowed through the relay. Opening the contacts allowed a bimetal switch to cool and close the light circuit again. More recent flasher relays, which do not control directional signals through an ECM used for body electrical control, use timer circuits with a relay and even completely transistorized designs for high numbers of lamp loads.

Interrupter Switch

Flash to pass or interrupter lights are integrated into most HD tractors. This switch interrupts only the top clearance light circuit on the tractor and trailer to signal other drivers it is safe to pass FIGURE 17-24. An interrupter switch is generally located in the turn signal switch FIGURE 17-25.

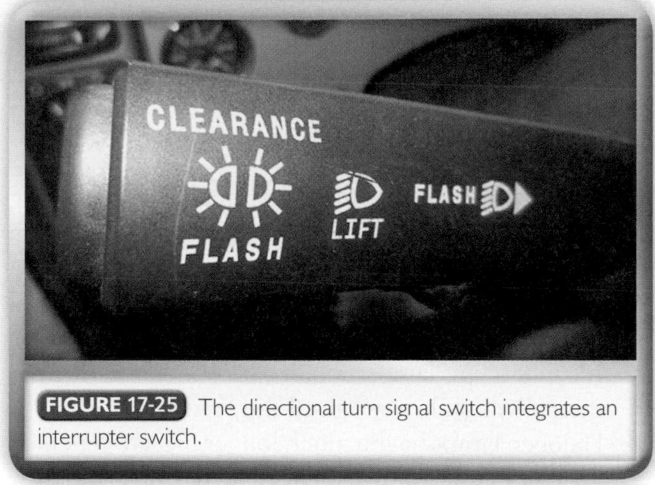

FIGURE 17-25 The directional turn signal switch integrates an interrupter switch.

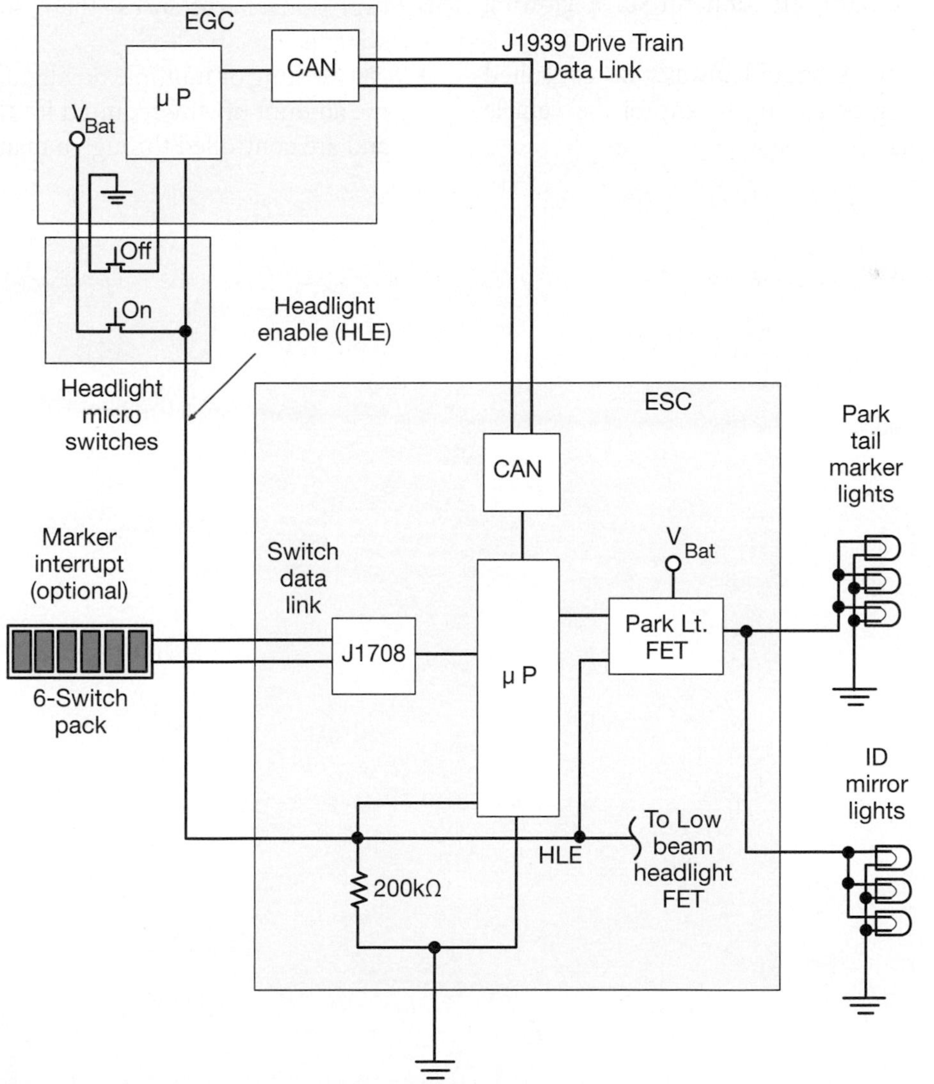

FIGURE 17-24 The lighting control module uses high current flow Field Effect Transistors (FET).

Wrap-up

Ready for Review

- Electrical systems on modern vehicles are becoming increasingly complex with the addition of a range of electronic and accessory systems. Many of these systems are controlled by elecrical system control modules.
- Incandescent lamps consist of one or more filaments, which heat up until they glow.
- Halogen lamps have a much longer life, are generally brighter, and produce more light per unit of power consumed, but they become very hot during use.
- High-intensity discharge (HID) headlamps produce light with an electric arc rather than a glowing filament.
- Lighting regulations should always be consulted before modifying or adding to any of the vehicle lighting systems.
- Hazard lights can warn other road users that a hazardous condition exists or that the vehicle is standing or parked in a dangerous position on the side of the road; they normally use the same bulbs as the turn signal indicators.
- Park, tail, and marker lamps are all photometric certified lamps used to mark the outline or width of the vehicle.
- The low beam is always set to the outside of the front, and the high beams are closer to the front center of the vehicle.
- The driving lights are installed on the front of the vehicle and provide higher intensity illumination over longer distances than standard headlight systems.
- Networking or multiplexing light systems eliminate the amount of wire required for the lighting system and are controlled through a main computer.

Vocabulary Builder

daytime running lights (DRL) Lights designed to improve vehicle visibility in the daytime.

fluorescent bulb A light bulb that uses electrically heated filaments located at each end of a tube filled with a small amount of mercury or a noble gas, such as neon, argon, or xenon.

halogen bulb A light bulb produced by adding small quantities of gases from the halogen family, such as iodine or bromine.

halogen infrared discharge (HID) bulb A light bulb that has a special coating on an inside portion of the bulb wall which reflects infrared heat back onto the filament, causing it to burn hotter.

high-intensity discharge (HID) lamps Lamps that use an electric arc to produce higher light outputs of between 2,800 and 3,800 lumens.

incandescent bulb A conventional bulb that electrically heats a filament of metal to the temperature at which it produces light.

J-560 trailer connector A trailer cord plug and receptacle located at the rear of the tractor.

ladder logic The designed-in logic of a circuit that determines what activates a specific circuit.

light-emitting diode (LED) A diode that produces light in different colors depending on the doping material used in its manufacture.

lumen The units used to measure light intensity.

photometric certification A certification based on testing lamps to evaluate factors such as light color, brightness, and the angle at which the light is effectively observed.

photon A particle of energy and the basic unit of light.

Review Questions

1. Which of the following statements about conventional and network control is correct?
   a. Body electrical systems are now also divided into two major categories.
   b. Conventional systems, which are quickly disappearing, use electrical components operating in isolation.
   c. Most body electrical systems today use a networked or distributed control of the electrical system.
   d. All of the choices are correct.

2. Which of the following is correct concerning lighting systems?
   a. There are many different styles and types of lights.
   b. Warning lamps, indicators, stop lights, tail lights, courtesy lamps, and headlamps all perform different roles.
   c. Both A and B
   d. Neither A nor B

3. Which of the following is NOT correct concerning lighting technologies?
   a. Light is produced by atoms whenever an electron moves from a lower orbital ring to a higher orbital (farther from the nucleus) requiring less energy.
   b. Energy given up by the electron is released in the form of a photon.
   c. Photons are particles of energy and are the basic unit of light.
   d. To produce light and illuminate interiors and instrument clusters, lighting technology has evolved rapidly in recent years beyond the use of incandescent bulbs.

4. A fluorescent bulb would work best as a:
   a. marker light.
   b. dome light.
   c. backup light.
   d. license plate lamp.

5. Halogen infrared discharge (HID) bulbs are __________ high-intensity discharge bulbs.
   a. the same as
   b. nearly identical to
   c. interchangeable with
   d. not to be confused with

6. Which of the following is correct concerning headlamps?
   a. A headlamp system is required to produce a low and a high beam, which may be integrated into a single lamp or individual lamps for each function.
   b. When used in pairs, the low beam must always be located on the outside when placed side-by-side, or the upper beam when stacked.
   c. High beams cast most of their light straight ahead, maximizing seeing distance, but will produce excessive glare for oncoming drivers.
   d. All of the choices are correct.

7. Individual LEDs operate at relatively low voltages between __________ volts.
   a. 0.5 and 3
   b. 1 and 4
   c. 4 and 6
   d. 7 and 10

8. Which of the following statements about trailer cord maintenance is correct?
   a. Cable plugs and connectors need periodic inspection for broken, bent, corroded, or collapsed pins.
   b. Cords should not have any cuts or abrasions that could penetrate the wiring.
   c. When not in use, cords should have a storage place where they will not be easily damaged.
   d. All of the choices are correct.

9. Which of the following is NOT correct concerning turn signal circuits?
   a. Any vehicle operating on public roads and highways requires a turn signal brake light system.
   b. In North America, the turn and stop light bulb signal are integrated with the major bulb filament of a double-filament bulb.
   c. The bulb's brighter element then operates as the red colored lens covering the stop-turn signal.
   d. The smaller, minor filament of a double-filament bulb is the turn signal light.

10. Which of the following is correct concerning the interrupter switch?
    a. Flash to pass, or interrupter, lights are integrated into most HD tractors.
    b. The interrupter switch interrupts only the top clearance light circuit on the tractor and trailer to signal other drivers it is safe to pass.
    c. An interrupter switch is generally located in the turn signal switch.
    d. All of the choices are correct.

ASE-Type Questions

1. Technician A says that a traditional body electrical system consists of two parts. Technician B says that the first section is the standard electrical circuitry found in all vehicles and that optional accessories make up the other section of the body electrical system. Who is correct?
   a. Technician A
   b. Technician B
   c. Both Technician A and Technician B
   d. Neither Technician A nor Technician B
2. Technician A says that the designed-in logic of a circuit that determines what activates a specific circuit is referred to as ladder logic. Technician B says that it is not necessary to have the ability to access, read, and interpret electrical schematic diagrams to repair electrical circuits. Who is correct?
   a. Technician A
   b. Technician B
   c. Both Technician A and Technician B
   d. Neither Technician A nor Technician B
3. Technician A says that lighting standards are legislated by the Federal/ Canadian Motor Vehicle Standard 108 (FMVSS 105). Technician B says that it is not necessary for light lenses to carry SAE identification numbers indicating the standard they meet. Who is correct?
   a. Technician A
   b. Technician B
   c. Both Technician A and Technician B
   d. Neither Technician A nor Technician B
4. Technician A says that incandescent bulbs are the conventional bulb technology first invented by Thomas Edison. Technician B says that for every 1 volt above designed limits, the life expectancy of the bulb drops by 25%. Who is correct?
   a. Technician A
   b. Technician B
   c. Both Technician A and Technician B
   d. Neither Technician A nor Technician B
5. Technician A says that halogen bulbs are produced by adding small quantities of gases from the halogen family, such as iodine and bromine, which extends the efficiency and life of the bulb. Technician B says that because the filament can be operated at a higher temperature without burning up, more energy is converted to light, the light is whiter, and the bulb's life is extended. Who is correct?
   a. Technician A
   b. Technician B
   c. Both Technician A and Technician B
   d. Neither Technician A nor Technician B
6. Technician A says that high-intensity discharge (HID) lamps used for headlight systems employ an electric arc to produce the light. Technician B says that the intensity of light from high-intensity discharge bulbs is produced using close to half the current consumed by halogen bulbs, and the bulbs last half as long. Who is correct?
   a. Technician A
   b. Technician B
   c. Both Technician A and Technician B
   d. Neither Technician A nor Technician B
7. Technician A says that daytime running lights are designed to improve vehicle visibility in the daytime. Technician B says that either the low or high beam circuits are powered at a reduced voltage of approximately 50% system voltage. Who is correct?
   a. Technician A
   b. Technician B
   c. Both Technician A and Technician B
   d. Neither Technician A nor Technician B
8. Technician A says that the J-560 electrical connector is an SAE standard set for connecting the trailer cord to the tractor and trailer electrical system together and has existed since the late 1950s. Technician B says that this five-pin connector bears the stamp SAE J560, indicating compliance with physical and performance standards of the SAE. Who is correct?
   a. Technician A
   b. Technician B
   c. Both Technician A and Technician B
   d. Neither Technician A nor Technician B
9. Technician A says that plugs at the end of each cable may be molded and hard-wired with strain relief to prevent the weight of the cord from disconnecting from the plug. Technician B says that replacement plug leads are available and commonly used by technicians to repair cables. Who is correct?
   a. Technician A
   b. Technician B
   c. Both Technician A and Technician B
   d. Neither Technician A nor Technician B
10. Technician A says that the directional signal switch in mechanical directional signal systems is supplied current from two sources. Technician B says that power is supplied by the service brake light switch; the other is through the turn signal flasher relay. Who is correct?
    a. Technician A
    b. Technician B
    c. Both Technician A and Technician B
    d. Neither Technician A nor Technician B

CHAPTER 18

NATEF Tasks

Electrical/Electronic Systems Gauges and Warning Devices	Page
■ Inspect and test warning devices (lights and audible), circuit sensor/sending units, bulbs/LEDs, sockets, connectors, wires, and control components/modules; repair or replace as needed.	512–515
■ Interface with vehicle's on-board computer; perform diagnostic procedure, verify instrument cluster operations using recommended electronic service tool(s) (including PC-based software and/or data scan tools); determine needed action.	515
■ Inspect, test, replace, and calibrate (if applicable) electronic speedometer, odometer, and tachometer systems.	522–523
■ Identify causes of intermittent, high, low, or no gauge readings; determine needed action.	527
■ Identify causes of data bus-driven gauge malfunctions; determine needed action.	527
■ Inspect and test gauge circuit sensor/sending units, gauges, connectors, terminals, and wires; repair or replace as needed.	527
Related Electrical Systems	
■ Interface with vehicle's on-board computer; perform diagnostic procedures, verify instrument cluster operations using recommended electronic service tool(s) (including PC-based software and/or data scan tools); determine needed action.	515

Body Electrical Systems—Instrumentation

Knowledge Objectives

After reading this chapter, you will be able to:

1. Describe the operation of data bus-driven gauges and warning devices. (p 515–519)
2. Describe the operation of stepper motors and stepper motor type gauges. (p 517–527)
3. Identify and describe procedures to inspect and verify electronic speedometer and odometer systems. (p 522–524)
4. Identify and describe procedures to inspect and test electronic gauge systems. (p 524–525)
5. Describe the operation of capacitance and resistive touch driver information screens. (p 525–526)
6. Describe procedures to inspect, test, and adjust gauge sending units and circuits. (p 527)

Skills Objectives

There are no skills objectives for this chapter.

Introduction

Instrument gauges, warning lamps, and driver information centers enable the operator to monitor the vehicle's operating condition, status of equipment, and safety systems. The types of displays, warning lights, and gauges differ widely among vehicles and manufacturers but break down into common gauge groups, sensing, and input systems. For example, monitoring engine operation involves measuring pressure and temperature of parameters of the lubrication, cooling, and air induction system. Charging voltage and amperage of the electrical system, fuel level, air pressure, engine, and vehicle speed are other common gauge systems. Warning lights for systems ranging from supplemental restraint, antilock braking, traction control, low air pressure, body doors, parking brakes, and so on are used in situations where limited but simplified information is useful. Newer digital instrumentation has superior accuracy plus built-in self-diagnostic capabilities offering the driver confidence that gauges and warning systems are operational. Driver display and input systems connected to the vehicle network provide informational capabilities far beyond previous instrumentation design.

Warning Lights

Warning lights provide easily understood information to alert the equipment operator to potentially dangerous operating conditions **FIGURE 18-1**. Low air pressure, antilock brake faults, low diesel exhaust fluid, door ajar lights, and so on are activated a number of ways and include:

- Mechanical ground switches
- Electronic switches
- Voltage drop circuits

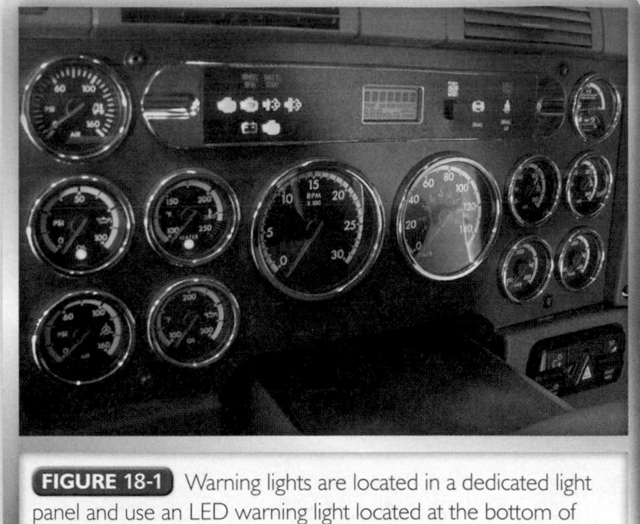

FIGURE 18-1 Warning lights are located in a dedicated light panel and use an LED warning light located at the bottom of each critical gauge.

The charging system indicator light is an example of a light operated through voltage drop **FIGURE 18-2**. After the engine starts and the alternator begins charging, battery voltage and charging system voltage are applied to

You Are the Technician

A late-model vehicle has arrived at your shop with several complaints related to the electrical system. One complaint is about the yellow check engine light being continuously illuminated. Another is about the instrument gauges going to zero and sweeping from zero to full scale and then back again to a correct reading while driving down the road. Other times the instrument gauge cluster does not move at all when the vehicle is started and running. In addition to asking that the electrical problems are corrected, the driver expresses concern about running out of fuel if the gauges are not reading accurately. Having time-sensitive loads, an incorrect fuel reading for a fuel tank that is empty would be financially disastrous to the company.

As you proceed to diagnose the problem, you discover that lightly pulling on the wiring harness going to the gauge cluster duplicates the complaint about the gauges sweeping from zero to full scale and back again to a correct reading again. Consider the following questions to predict what you think the technician will write on the work order.

1. Explain why the gauges complete a full-scale sweep when electrical power is interrupted.
2. What is potentially the simplest procedure the technician could use to identify the problem illuminating the yellow check engine light?
3. Outline a procedure the technician could use to validate the correct gauge readings for the fuel level.

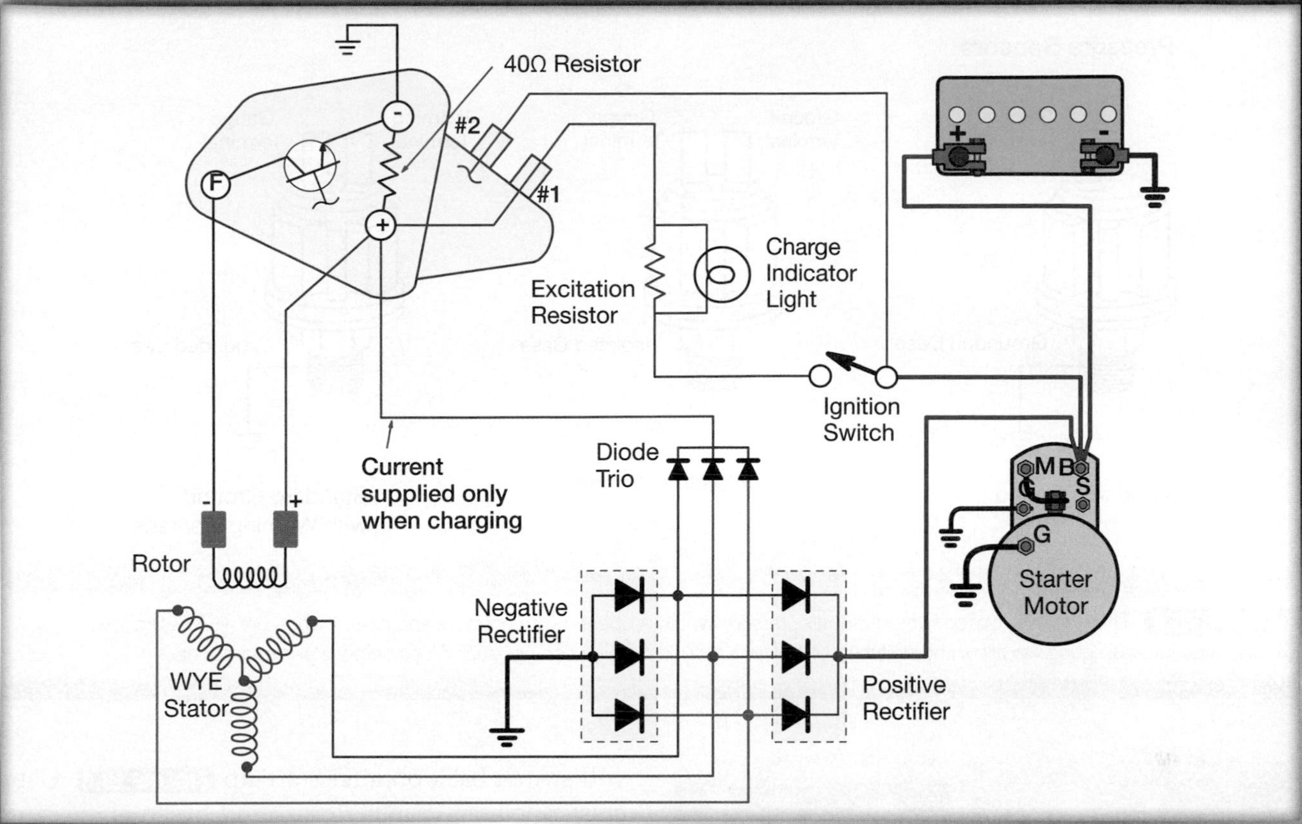

FIGURE 18-2 Alternator voltage regulators provide a ground path for a bulb when not charging and supply battery + current when charging to the warning light bulb terminal to extinguish the light.

both terminals of a bulb. If battery voltage is equal to or becomes higher than charging system voltage, the voltage differential will cause the light to illuminate.

Mechanical ground switches are used to indicate low fluid levels, low air pressure warning systems, or power divider engagement locks **FIGURE 18-3**. Normally closed pressure switches opened with air or oil pressure provide a path to ground to illuminate a bulb **FIGURE 18-4**.

Electronic switches found in electronic control modules are the most common way warning lights are illuminated in today's vehicles. If a condition is sensed to which the driver needs to be alerted, the module has control logic to supply a ground or battery voltage to the light.

Prove-Out Sequence

In order to validate the correct operation of a warning light, the instrument cluster is designed to illuminate a bulb for several brief seconds with the key on and engine off or during key-on engine cranking **FIGURE 18-5**. If the engine starts, the bulb may remain lit until proper operating conditions are met, such as correct oil pressure is reached, the supplementary restraint system is

FIGURE 18-3 A water in fuel sensor is a mechanical float-type switch in this Duramax diesel fuel filter. Denser water will raise the float fluid level sensor and ground the signal wire. **A.** Fuel filter. **B.** Internal electric float. **C.** Water in fuel sensor signal wire.

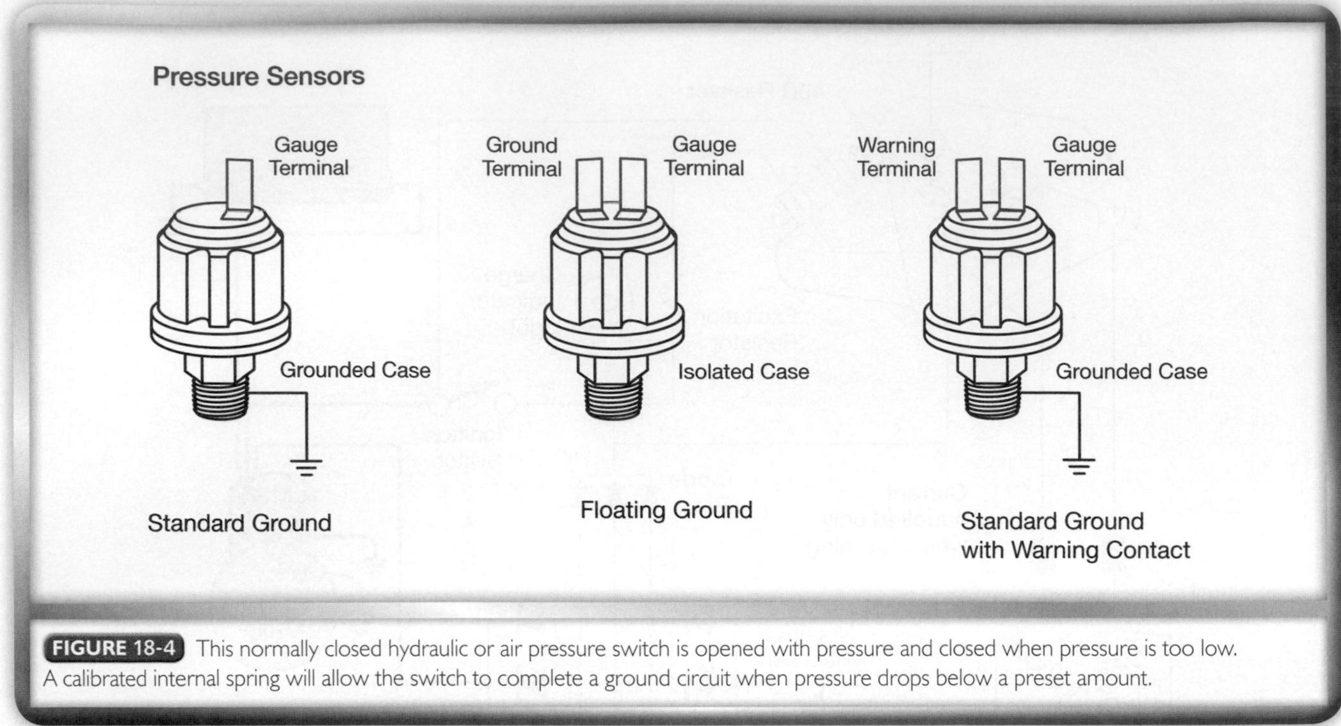

FIGURE 18-4 This normally closed hydraulic or air pressure switch is opened with pressure and closed when pressure is too low. A calibrated internal spring will allow the switch to complete a ground circuit when pressure drops below a preset amount.

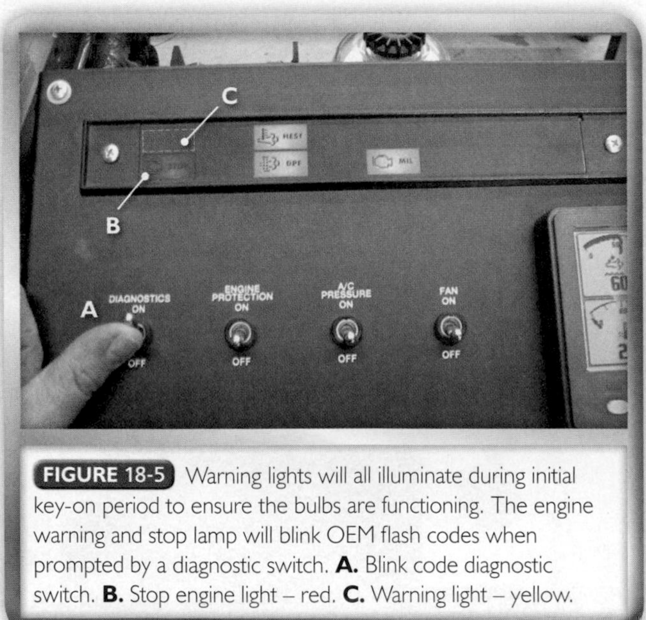

FIGURE 18-5 Warning lights will all illuminate during initial key-on period to ensure the bulbs are functioning. The engine warning and stop lamp will blink OEM flash codes when prompted by a diagnostic switch. **A.** Blink code diagnostic switch. **B.** Stop engine light – red. **C.** Warning light – yellow.

operational, or coolant level is satisfactory. That sequence is called a **prove-out sequence**.

In older vehicles the ignition key will supply a circuit to provide a ground and/or positive battery voltage path to illuminate instrument warning lights. Control modules will perform the same function during key-on events. The malfunction indicator lamp (MIL) and check engine lamp (CEL) will illuminate for approximately three to five seconds during engine start-up and then extinguish. If there are active fault codes, the lights will switch back on after start-up **FIGURE 18-6**. Gauge cluster pointers may perform a full sweep of the gauge, from minimum to maximum, back to minimum, and then to received value. This prove-out sequence enables the driver to have confidence in the correct operation of the gauge unit.

Blink codes are often used by some manufacturers to provide fault code data for a specific system. These codes are derived by counting the number of flashes from a warning lamp and observing longer pauses between the light blink. For example, OEM-specific ABS codes, or engine fault codes, may be either two or three digits in length. The fault code of 32 is displayed by three light blinks in quick succession, followed by a short pause and two more blinks. A longer pause will separate multiple codes when available for display.

TECHNICIAN TIP

Urban transit buses may have a brake and accelerator interlock system with a warning light. The interlock applies the rear brakes and holds the throttle in idle position when a passenger door is open. The interlock releases when the door is closed. For security reasons, this warning light may remain illuminated even after the key is off until the door is closed. The exterior rear brake light may even illuminate after the ignition is switched off and the door remains open.

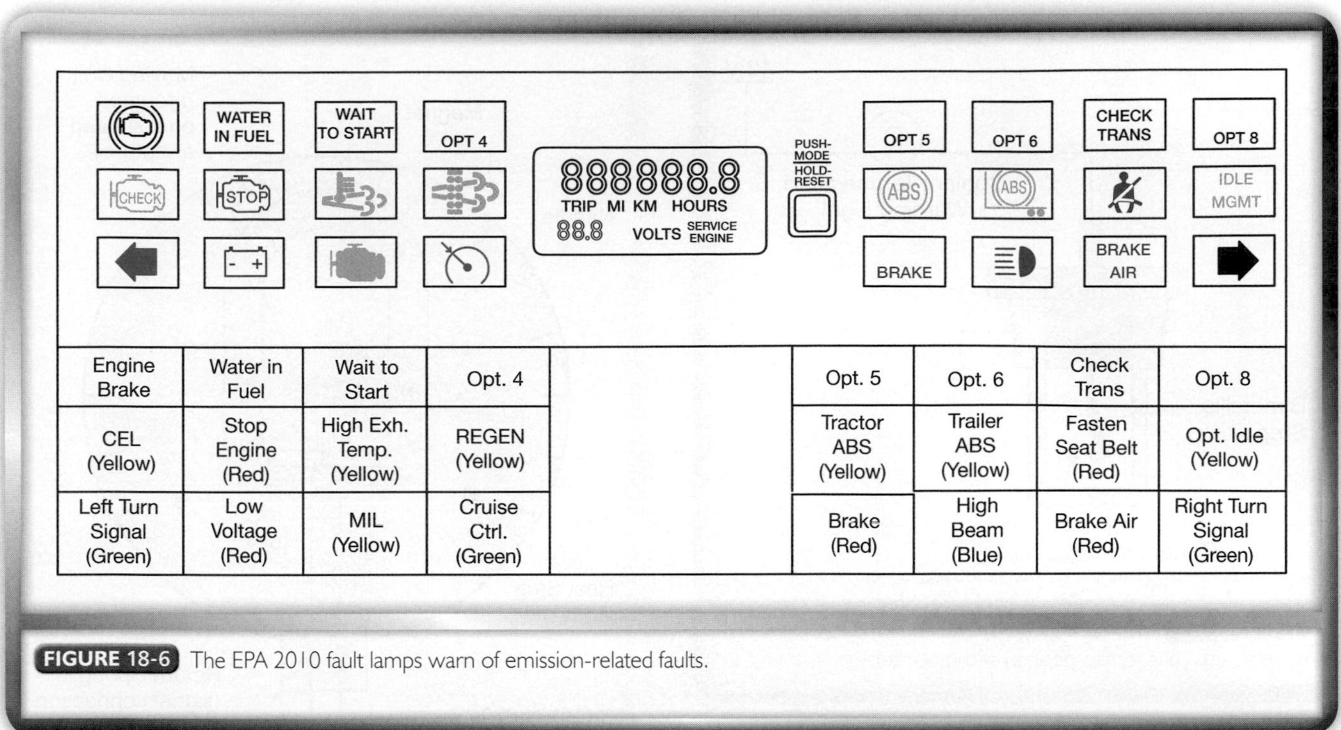

Engine Brake	Water in Fuel	Wait to Start	Opt. 4		Opt. 5	Opt. 6	Check Trans	Opt. 8
CEL (Yellow)	Stop Engine (Red)	High Exh. Temp. (Yellow)	REGEN (Yellow)		Tractor ABS (Yellow)	Trailer ABS (Yellow)	Fasten Seat Belt (Red)	Opt. Idle (Yellow)
Left Turn Signal (Green)	Low Voltage (Red)	MIL (Yellow)	Cruise Ctrl. (Green)		Brake (Red)	High Beam (Blue)	Brake Air (Red)	Right Turn Signal (Green)

FIGURE 18-6 The EPA 2010 fault lamps warn of emission-related faults.

> **TECHNICIAN TIP**
>
> In the absence of a readily available electronic service tool used to obtain fault codes, warning lights can often blink-out fault codes. Supplemental restraint systems, antilock brakes, and engine fault information are often provided by blinking warning lamps. Consult the owner's or shop manual to determine the procedure for obtaining blink codes. In newer vehicles, the driver's information display system is a network device capable of supplying fault codes and information about the vehicle.

Gauge Operating Systems

Common gauge systems use the following technologies:

- Mechanical (direct reading)
- Bimetallic
- Electromagentic
- Stepper motor
- Digital display

Mechanical Gauges

Mechanical direct reading gauges are not electrical since they depend on cables, air, or fluid pressure to operate. Speedometers operated by cables and oil pressure read by bourdon tube gauges are examples of direct-reading mechanical gauges.

Sending units are used in electrical instrumentation to convert pressure and temperature into analog signals used by instrument gauges. Sending units differ from sensors in that they are electromechanical devices, whereas sensors are nonmechanical electronic devices. Pressure and temperature switches will often operate warning lights.

Bimetallic Gauges

Bimetallic gauges work by heating metal strips, which bend and move a gauge pointing needle **FIGURE 18-7**. Two dissimilar pieces of metal are bonded together into a strip, much like a circuit breaker, and expand at different rates as when heated. Heat produced through resistance of a wire coil wrapped around the bimetal strip is proportional to current flow **FIGURE 18-8**. Current supplied by a sending unit changes the position of the pointing needle attached to the bimetal strip. Because vehicle voltage fluctuates with changes to electrical loads and charging system output, a voltage regulator is required to maintain consistent gauge readings. Commonly, another bimetallic type device will hold voltage supplied to gauges and sending units to between approximately 5 and 10 volts. The instrument voltage regulator (IVR) will use a bimetal arm with a set of breaker points that open and close rapidly when heating and cooling to maintain instrument gauge voltage.

D'Arsonval Gauges

D'Arsonval gauges are a type of electromagnetic gauge that moves a pointing needle directly proportional to

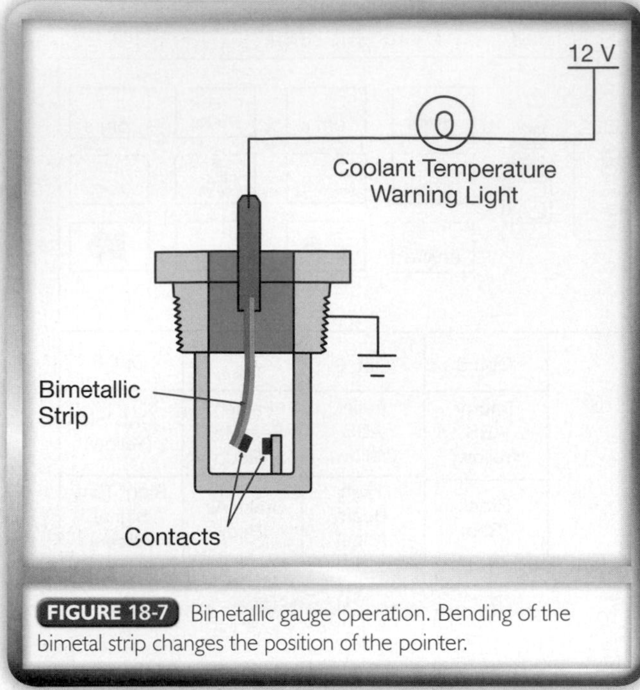

FIGURE 18-7 Bimetallic gauge operation. Bending of the bimetal strip changes the position of the pointer.

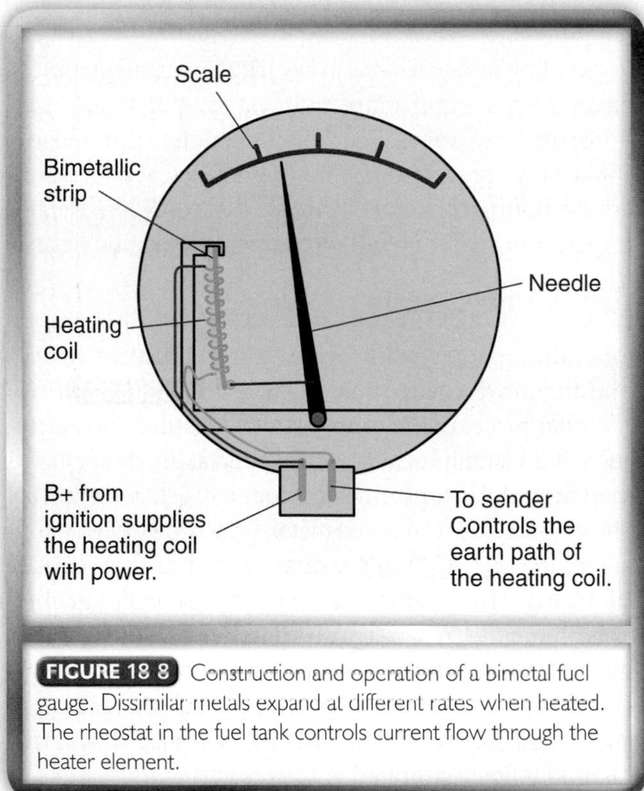

FIGURE 18-8 Construction and operation of a bimetal fuel gauge. Dissimilar metals expand at different rates when heated. The rheostat in the fuel tank controls current flow through the heater element.

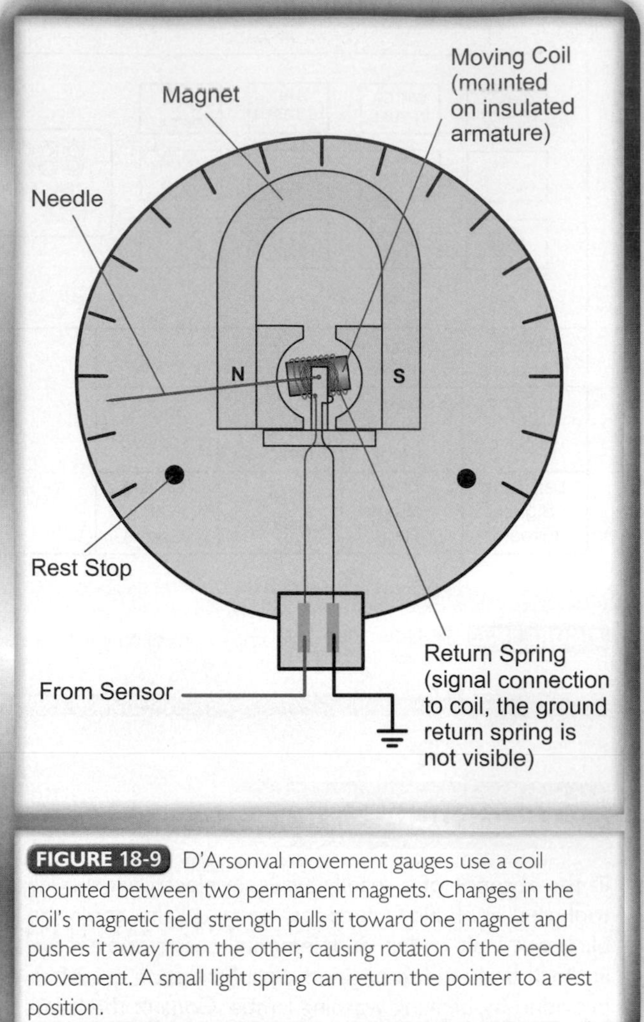

FIGURE 18-9 D'Arsonval movement gauges use a coil mounted between two permanent magnets. Changes in the coil's magnetic field strength pulls it toward one magnet and pushes it away from the other, causing rotation of the needle movement. A small light spring can return the pointer to a rest position.

current flow through an electromagnet attached to the pointer FIGURE 18-9. Needle deflection is controlled by current in the coil, which changes magnetic field strength interacting with the fields of two permanent magnets fixed on either side of the coil. A larger flow of current produces a magnetic field that opposes one of the permanent magnet's fields and is attracted to another. Voltmeters are an example of a gauge that can use D'Arsonval movement. Other gauges using a D'Arsonval movement require a voltage regulator to maintain consistent readings.

Two- and Three-Coil Movements

Variations of the D'Arsonval movement use a pointer with a permanent magnet rather than an electromagnet. Two or three electromagnetic coils surround the pointer to rotate the gauge. Two-coil designs require a voltage regulator to maintain consistent readings, as charging voltage varies, while three-coil designs generally do not FIGURE 18-10. Both these gauges are more accurate than D'Arsonval movement gauges and are unaffected by temperature. In the two-coil gauge design, the field coils are wound in series but in opposite directions. This places a north and south pole on maximum and minimum reading sides of the pointer's magnet.

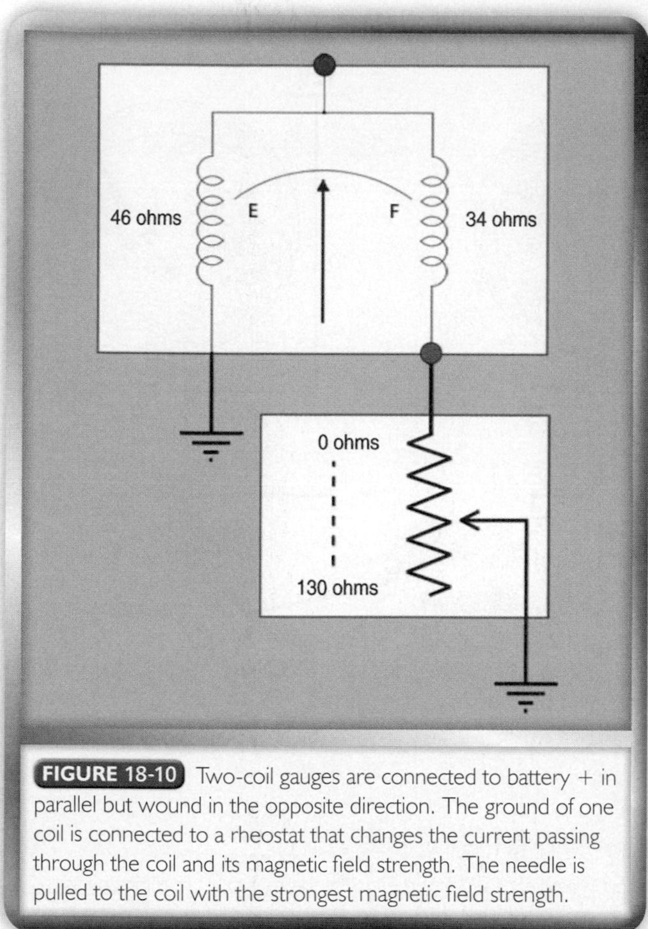

FIGURE 18-10 Two-coil gauges are connected to battery + in parallel but wound in the opposite direction. The ground of one coil is connected to a rheostat that changes the current passing through the coil and its magnetic field strength. The needle is pulled to the coil with the strongest magnetic field strength.

Regulated ignition current is supplied to one end of the series coil, and the ground pathway is through a sending unit. Increasing current flow through the coil will intensify the forces of repulsion in one coil and attraction in the other. Pointer rotation takes place as magnetic field strength increases or decreases proportional to current flow in the coils.

In the **three-coil gauge** design, a coil is placed at the minimum and maximum reading ends of the pointer's, rotation FIGURE 18-11. A third coil called a bucking coil is placed between the minimum and maximum gauge reading. Ignition current passes through all three coils, which are wound in series. Two ground connections are supplied to the coil. One is at the end of the maximum coil, allowing all current to pass through all three coils. The other is a ground supplied through a sending unit. This ground connects to the gauge at a point between the minimum and bucking coil. Current flow passes through all three coils when resistance through the sending unit ground path is high.

The maximum reading coil exerts the greatest force to pull the pointer magnet in that direction, as the minimum reading and bucking coil are wound in opposite directions to cancel each other's magnetic field. However, decreasing resistance through the sending unit permits more current to pass through the minimum reading coil, which progressively cancels out the effect of the bucking and maximum reading coil with decreasing sending unit resistance.

Stepper Motor Design

By far, **stepper motor gauges** are the most commonly used gauge technology in late-model instrument gauge clusters. The use of stepper motors to rotate pointers for analog displays bypasses the problem of inaccurate readings from bimetallic and electromagnetic coil gauges caused by voltage fluctuations, temperature changes, and oil leaks from fluid dampened gauge clusters.

This inexpensive and unique category of electric motors can precisely control the pointer rotation by dividing full motor rotation into a large number of fine resolution steps. Most gauges have 3,060 possible steps of positions between zero and full-scale deflection. Speedometers, odometers, pressure, and temperature gauges will use stepper motors to accurately display data. Stepper motors are brushless, DC electromechanical devices that generally use a permanent magnet shaft surrounded by two or more pairs of electromagnetic coils. Energizing one or more of these field coils will cause the shaft to align with the coil, pulling and holding the shaft in a stationary position. To continue rotating the shaft, another field coil next to the first is energized, causing the shaft's magnet to realign with the energized coil while the first coil is de-energized.

Alternately energizing and de-energizing coils in a particular sequence moves the shaft in the desired direction in incremental steps. A large number of steps make the gauge appear to move in a smooth motion. The speed of rotation can be precisely controlled by changing the rate at which coils are switched on and off. A particular sequence of energizing and re-energizing of coils will pull and/or push the shaft in a full 360 degrees of rotation, but full rotation is unnecessary because the gauge only sweeps through 270 degrees for its minimum and maximum range. During start-up, gauge calibration and operation are checked by having the gauge sweep though its entire range, returning to zero, and then rotating to the correctly sensed position. A Hall effect sensor and magnet built into the gauge are sometimes used to identify the full range of needle sweep.

Unipolar Stepper Motor

Two common types of stepper motors are used for instrument gauges: unipolar and bipolar motors. The unipolar

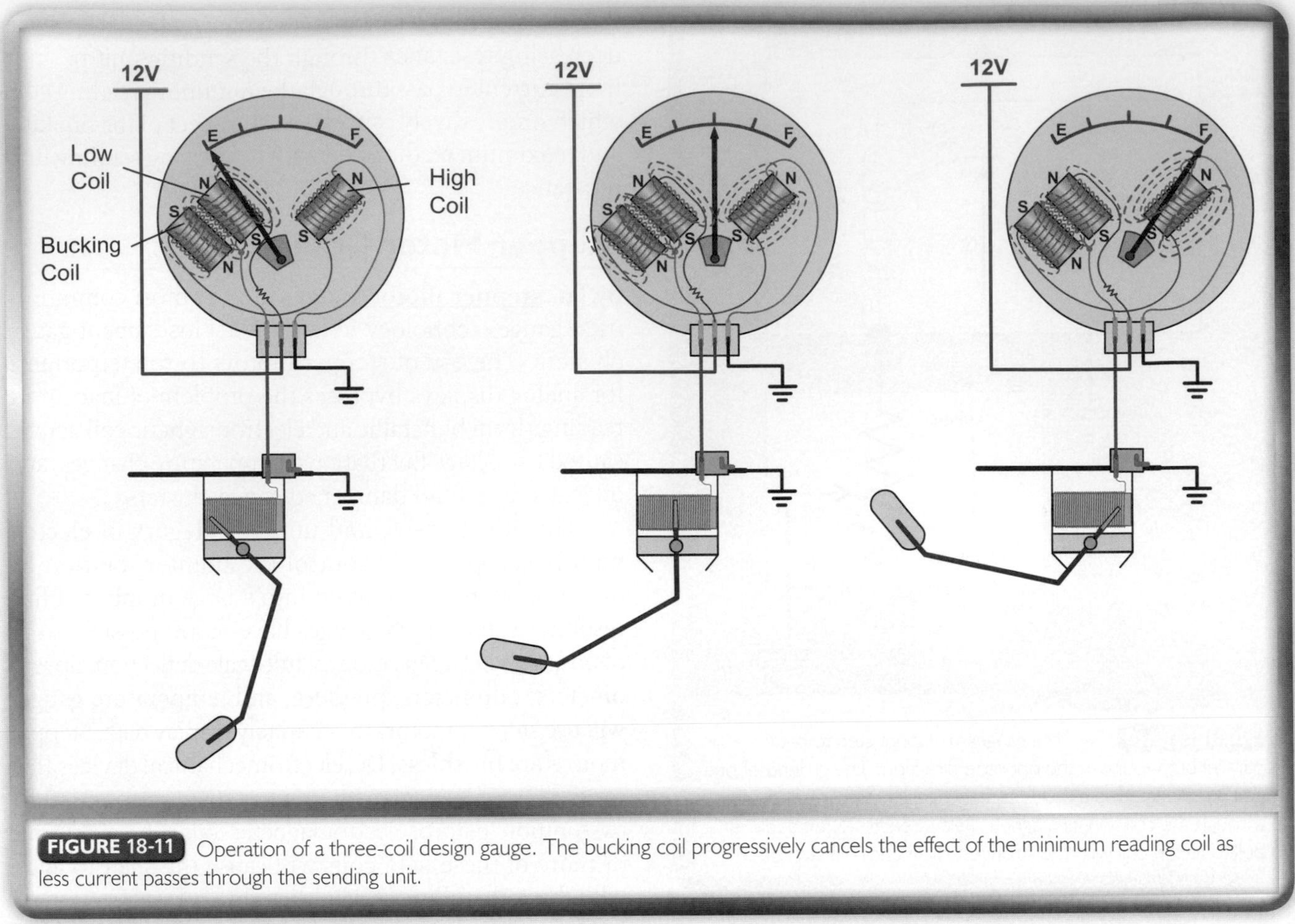

FIGURE 18-11 Operation of a three-coil design gauge. The bucking coil progressively cancels the effect of the minimum reading coil as less current passes through the sending unit.

stepper motor is identified by its five or six wires that connect four field coils. The ends of all the coils have one common connection that is supplied power, giving the motor the name unipolar stepper because power always is supplied to this single point to form magnetic poles in the field coils. The other coil ends are connected to driver circuits of a microcontroller. Using digital logic and microcontrollers, the field coils are switched on and off to rotate the motor forward, backward, or to hold the shaft FIGURE 18-12.

TABLE 18-1 shows the steps used to rotate a 4-pole unipolar stepper motor. A constant battery positive or ground is supplied to the coils while a ground or positive current source is switched on and off to rotate the motor.

Bipolar Stepper Motor

Unlike unipolar steppers, bipolar stepper motors have no common connection between the motor stator. Instead, coils used in the stator are independent sets of coils that enable a change in current polarity FIGURE 18-13. By measuring the resistance between the lead wires, bipolar steppers are distinguished from unipolar motors since any two pairs of wires will have equal resistance and no continuity between the coils in the stator FIGURE 18-14. Like unipolar motors, digital logic will energize the motors to produce desired motor travel characteristics. Torque is increased in bipolar motors at the expense of finer steps to produce rotation. Adding a second wire to each pair of coils in a unipolar motor allows half the coil to be energized, producing even finer steps of rotation. Directional changes are capable in both unipolar and bipolar stepper motors.

Digital CAN Gauges

Digitally driven, networked gauges, or intelligent gauges are designed to display information broadcast over the SAE J1939 communications. These gauges, which can use stepper motors or LCD/LED displays, are wired directly to the J1939 CAN bus. Circuits inside the gauges eliminate the need for a graphic label, interface module, or other device to drive them. Custom programming of the gauge at the manufacturer level is required to translate the PGM

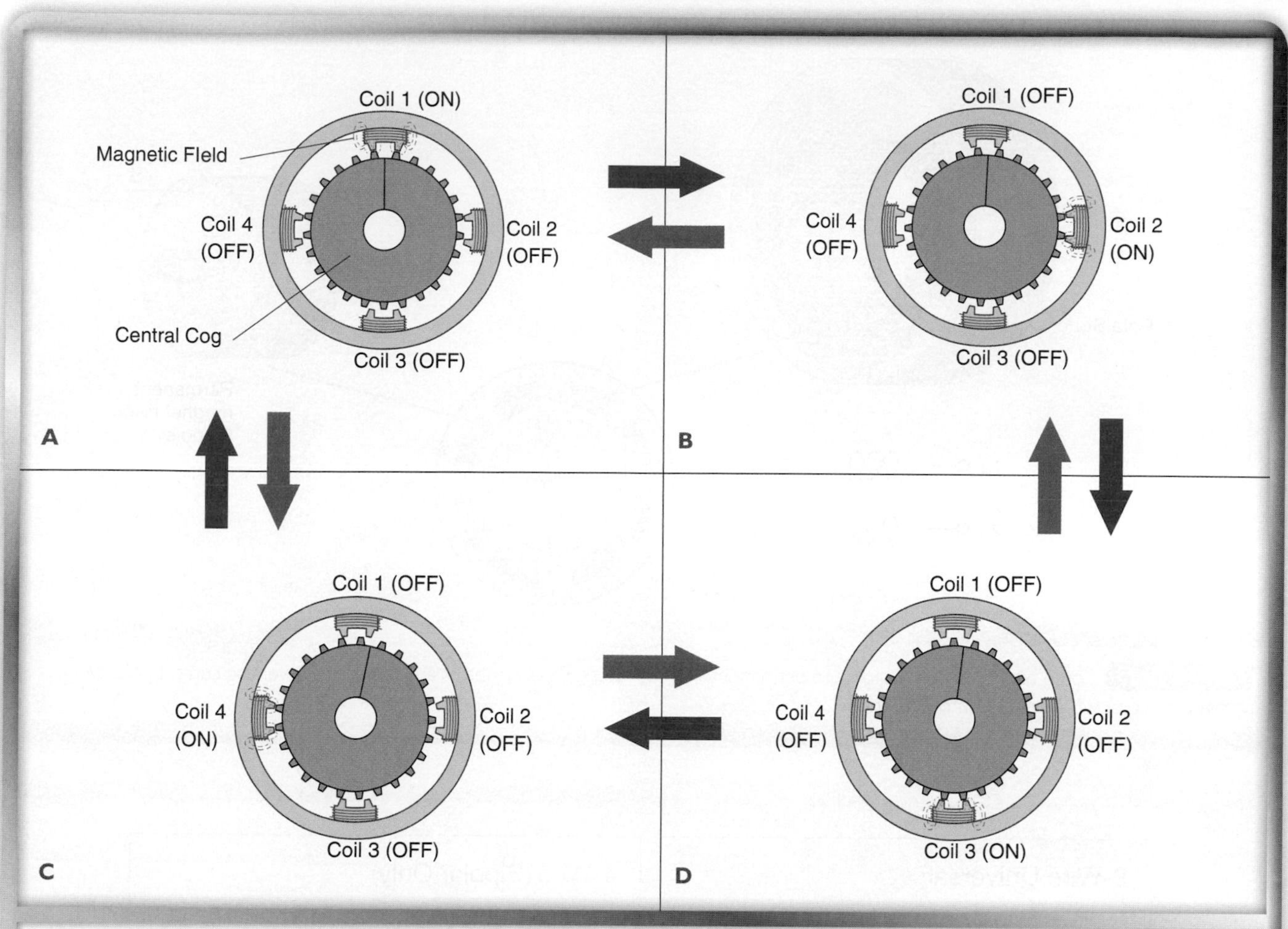

FIGURE 18-12 Unipolar motor operation. **A.** The upper electromagnet (1) is activated and the teeth of the central cog line up accordingly. **B.** The upper electromagnet (1) is deactivated and the right one (2) is turned on. The closest cog teeth then jump to line up with this new magnetic field. This causes a step turn of 1.8 degrees if there are 200 step turns. **C.** The right electromagnet (2) is deactivated and the lower one (3) is turned on. The cog teeth then jump to line up with the bottom electromagnet. This causes another step. **D.** The lower electromagnet (3) is switched off and the left (4) electromagnet is switched on. The cog teeth then jump to line up with the left electromagnet, producing another step.

TABLE 18-1: Steps Used to Rotate a 4-Pole Unipolar Stepper Motor

Step number	Coil A	Coil B	Coil C	Coil D
1	5-volts	0	0	0
2	0	0	5-volts	0
3	0	5-volts	0	0
4	0	0	0	5-volts
5	5-volts	0	0	0

message for proper interpretation or user-defined values FIGURE 18-15. Entire instrument clusters rich with data are operated now using CAN-driven data generated by control modules throughout the vehicle. Just two wires connecting the instrument panel gauge clusters to the CAN network are all that is necessary to display vehicle data and trip information, provide fault codes, and display warning lamps.

Sending Units

Sending units are electromechanical devices that convert pressure or fluid level into a variable voltage signal. Sending units are different from sensors, which are low-voltage electronic devices with no moving parts. Most sending units are a variable resistive type FIGURE 18-16.

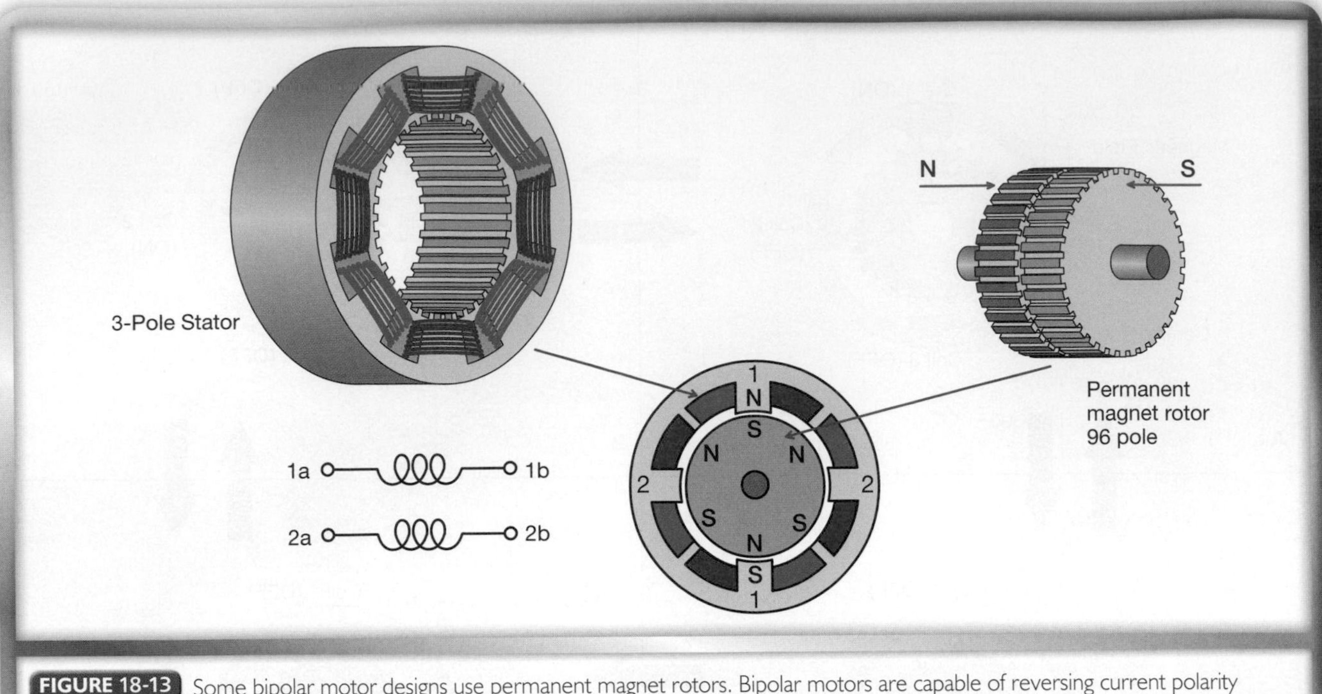

FIGURE 18-13 Some bipolar motor designs use permanent magnet rotors. Bipolar motors are capable of reversing current polarity across their coils, while unipolar motors cannot.

8-Wire Universal

4-Wire (Bipolar Only)

Typical 5-Wire Unipolar/Bipolar

Typical 6-Wire Unipolar/Bipolar

FIGURE 18-14 A variety of wiring combinations exist for various stepper motors. Stepper motor coils are energized one at a time or in pairs to increase torque output. EGR motors are another application on diesel engines for stepper motors.

FIGURE 18-15 A CAN-driven gauge will display data available on the vehicle network. CAN displays are both input and output devices. Menu buttons allow the driver or technicians to access a variety of data sets.

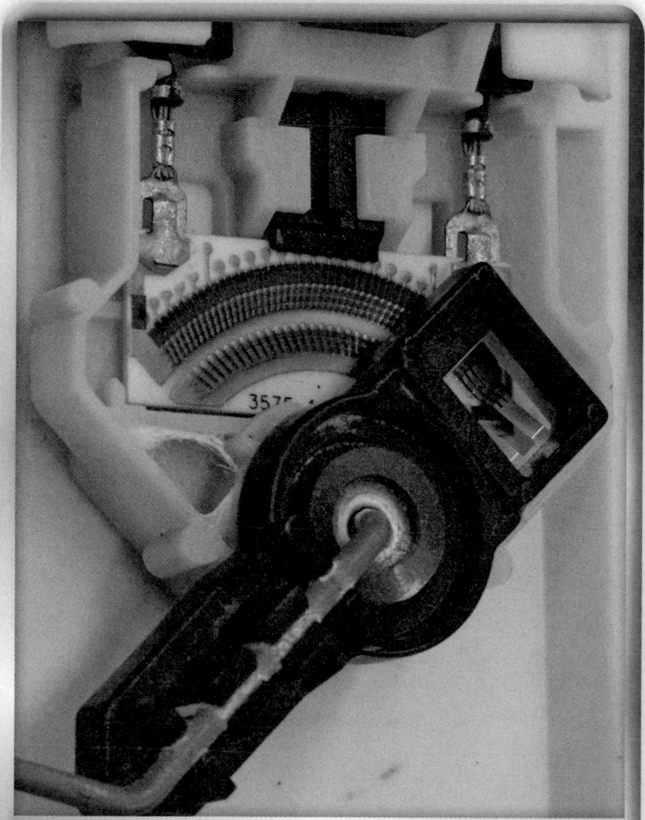

FIGURE 18-16 A rheostat used for the sending unit of a fuel tank.

The fuel tank sending unit, for example, uses a resistive wiper mechanism. An electrical whisker or brush moves along a resistor track depending on fuel level. Low-voltage current originating through the instrument panel fuel gauge passes through the resistor track and then through to ground via the whisker.

Oil pressure sending units use a flexible bellow also containing a whisker that passes along a resistor track. Pressure below the bellows moves the whisker along the resistive track to supply a ground FIGURE 18-17. Current to the sending unit is also supplied by the gauge. With less resistance in the sending unit, more current passes through the gauge to deflect the pointer between minimum and maximum readings.

Temperature sending units use a wax pellet similar to the design of a coolant thermostat. As temperature changes, the wax pellet will expand or contract. A disc over the wax pellet acts like a whisker to change the resistance of the current pathway through an internal resistive track. Electronic modules are available to convert variable voltage values into digital signals for use by digital gauges.

Diagnosing Sending Units and Gauges

Resistive type gauges are quickly checked by opening the circuit to the sending unit or grounding the sending unit lead. When a circuit is opened, circuit resistance becomes infinite and will move a gauge to either its minimum or maximum reading. If that does not happen, the circuit to the gauge or the gauge itself is defective. Grounding the lead wire to the sending unit should move the gauge to a maximum or minimum value, too. The type of gauge construction—D'Arsonval, two-, or three-wire—will determine which direction the gauge will move when opened or grounded. A gauge testing unit can evaluate gauge accuracy by supplying a resistance of known value to the circuit and observing whether the gauge pointer is positioned where expected. The accuracy of a fuel gauge

TECHNICIAN TIP

Low or no resistance of a sending unit to ground through the engine block, transmission, or axle case is critical for accurate gauge operation. Undiagnosed resistive grounds can often lead to unnecessary replacement of sending units and gauges. Always check the continuity of a major component case or block-to-chassis ground as part of a diagnostic pinpoint test. The use of Teflon tape can also interfere with sending unit continuity. Use liquid thread sealer rather than tape to prevent thread leakage. Because gauges often operate at low voltage, never touch the sender lead to ignition + 12 volt.

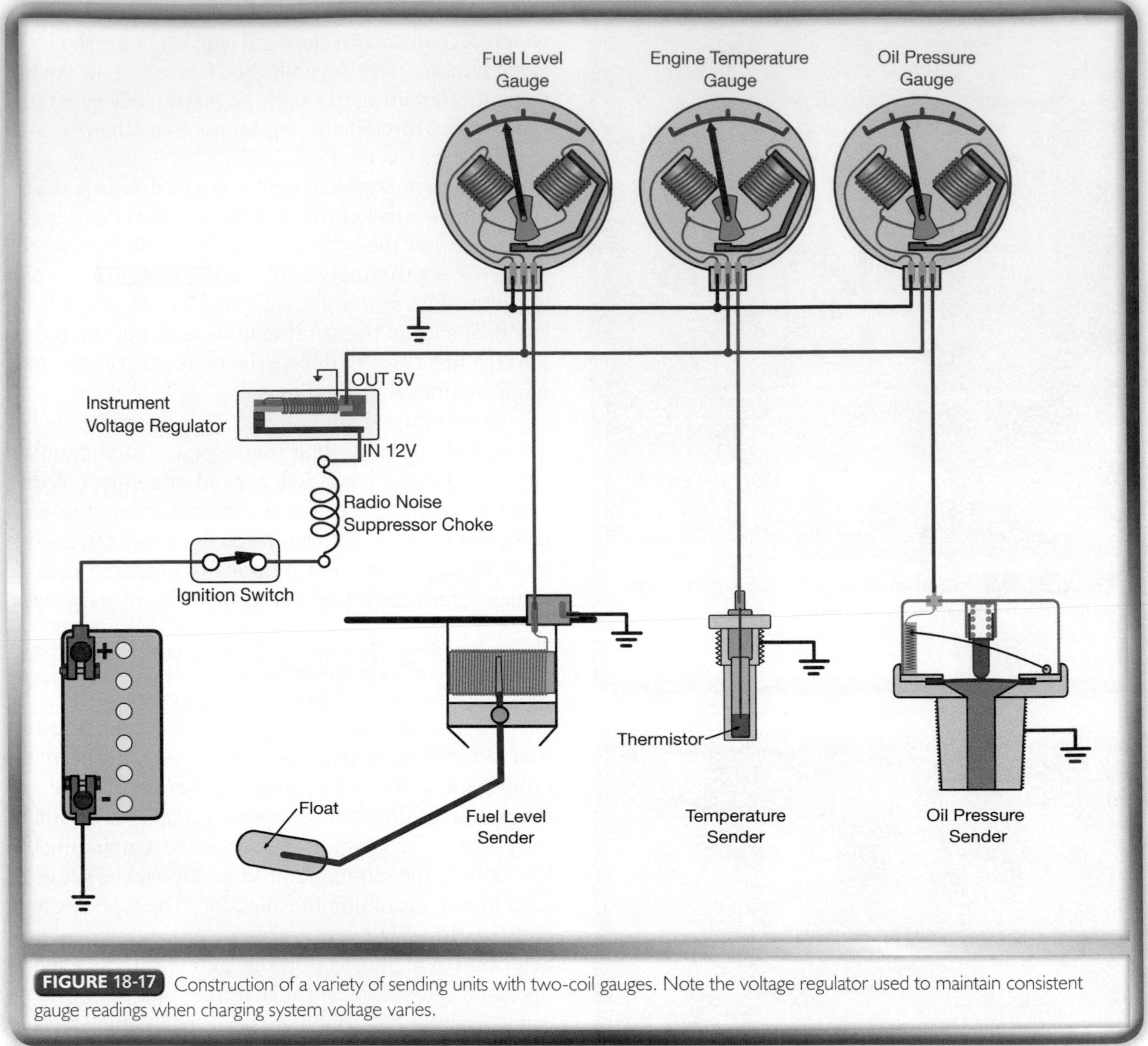

FIGURE 18-17 Construction of a variety of sending units with two-coil gauges. Note the voltage regulator used to maintain consistent gauge readings when charging system voltage varies.

is ideally evaluated using this method. The resistance of a sending unit measured with an ohmmeter can determine if its resistance is within the range expected for a given pressure temperature or liquid level FIGURE 18-18. It's important to verify the ground supplied to the sending unit is good, as this will interfere with sending unit resistance values. Some sending units are designed with two terminals, one of which provides a dedicated ground for the gauge circuit.

Speedometers

Speedometers electronically measure the driveshaft speed by counting a series of electrical pulses produced per mile or kilometer of distance travelled. A variable reluctance sensor is a toothed metal wheel typically placed at the transmission output shaft to measure drive line speed, which corresponds to road speed. An alternative method uses an average speed of ABS wheel speed sensors to produce a calculated road speed. As heavy-duty commercial vehicles are sold with customized tire sizes, rear axle ratios, and transmission ratios, a calibration method is used to adapt the speedometer to the pulse count from the vehicle drive line speed sensor.

Earlier equipment enables customized calibrations for the various chassis pulse counts using **DIP switches**. These are small slide switches located at the rear of the speedometer head, placed in either the on or off, (1 or 0) position. Circuits inside the speedometer convert the number of received speed sensor pulses

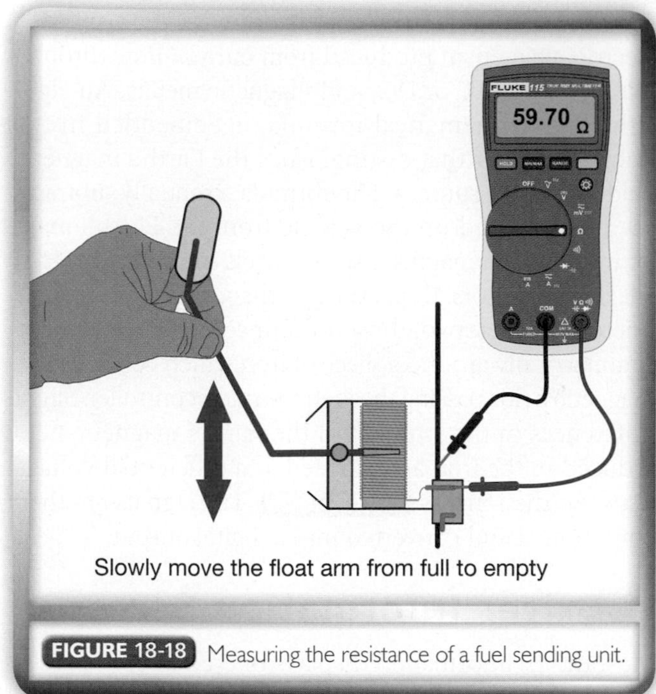

FIGURE 18-18 Measuring the resistance of a fuel sending unit.

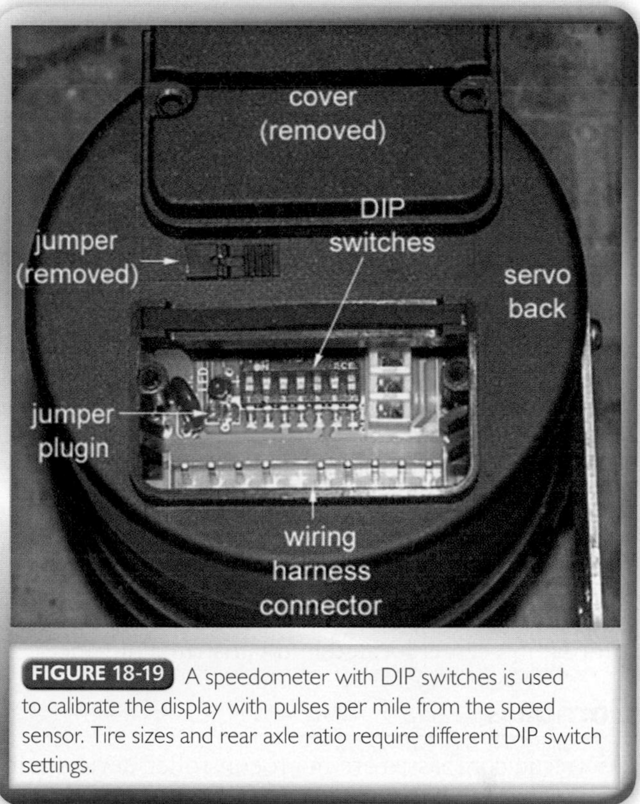

FIGURE 18-19 A speedometer with DIP switches is used to calibrate the display with pulses per mile from the speed sensor. Tire sizes and rear axle ratio require different DIP switch settings.

to a pulse count per mile that varies with wheel speed. While DIP switches are set at the factory for an original equipment pulse count, switches may need to be reset if the drive line components, such as tire size or rear axle ratios, have changed from those originally installed on the chassis. Procedures to adjust the DIP switches are outlined in service manuals and usually involve plugging variables for tire size or rolling radius and rear axle into a formula to determine the settings FIGURE 18-19. Inaccurate or fluctuating speedometer readings can be caused by other systems associated with the speedometer signal. Interference can originate from the cruise controls, ABS module, engine/transmission signals and controllers, the alternator, and other charging system components. Alternating current ripple from the alternator can also induce electrical interference with speedometer signals.

> **TECHNICIAN TIP**
>
> Most speedometers have tolerances of ±10% due primarily to variations in tire diameter. Sources of error due to tire diameter variations are wear, temperature, pressure, vehicle load, and nominal tire size. Vehicle manufacturers usually calibrate speedometers to read slightly higher than actual road speed by an amount equal to the average error. This practice eliminates potential liability caused by speedometers displaying a lower speed than the actual road speed of the vehicle. Dynamometers and even GPSs can be used to validate the calibration of a speedometer. Failures or interference with signals from the variable reluctance speed sensor are best analyzed using a wave-form meter. Comparing the observed signal pattern with known good quality wave forms can identify potential problems with the speed signal.

Manufacturers currently use unique, proprietary software and diagnostic and maintenance tools that enable access to the vehicle speed settings within certain limits to accommodate changes in tire size or rear axle ratio and to adjust the speedometer calibration. Speed limiters required by many jurisdictions are associated with speedometer settings. Typically, access to the speed limit settings and related calibration parameters are protected by a customer password.

Tachometers and Odometers

Tachometers used to observe engine speed are constructed and operate almost identically to speedometers. Variable reluctance or Hall effect sensors are used to generate signals to the tachometer head. The engine ECM counts all of the pulses from both the speedometer and tachometer to track overall distance traveled by vehicle and engine. Several times per second in networked vehicles, the engine ECM sends out a packet of information consisting of a header and speed-distance data. The header is identifying the packet as a distance or speed reading can be read by the tachometer or odometer. Distance travelled may also be stored in an instrument cluster control module. In networked vehicles trip values stored in the engine ECM are compared with an instrument cluster control. This means that if an attempt is made to roll back the odometer, the value stored in the engine ECM will not correspond and will generate a fault code.

Tachographs

Tachographs are devices used to record a vehicle's speed over time. Data can determine whether the vehicle is stopped or moving and at what speed. Older mechanical tachographs used a pen and ink to plot speed on a rotating paper disk that completed one revolution in 24 hours. As this type was vulnerable to tampering, electronic tachographs are now used to record data on removable smart cards. Trip information and accumulated vehicle totals can also be extracted from the engine ECM using proprietary software or even accessed through the drive information center located in the instrument panel.

Compass

Electronic compasses are microcontroller devices constructed to sense and measure any source of magnetic fields. Sources of magnetic fields in commercial vehicles include permanent magnets in audio speakers, motors, electric magnetism produced from current flow through wiring, either AC or DC, and magnetic metals. An algorithm or, mathematical formula, is embedded in the microcontroller that distinguishes the Earth's magnetic field from these sources. This formula essentially subtracts the fields sensed on the vehicle from the Earth's magnetic field. The magnetic sensor itself is made from Hall effect-type sensors. Depending on the sophistication of the microcontroller, two, three, or four sensors are arranged symmetrically around a piece of iron which concentrates magnetic fields passing through the microcontroller. Slight differences in the strength of the Earth's magnetic field induced in the iron are detected as a differential voltage between the sensors FIGURE 18-20. The signals are then conditioned and converted into a digital output.

Driver Information Screens

Most driver information displays offered in commercial vehicles today display vehicle speed, fluid levels, fluid temperatures, warning lights, trip information, and some basic diagnostic information or codes on liquid crystal displays (LCD). Enormous amounts of other information systems can be added to the list, including tire pressure,

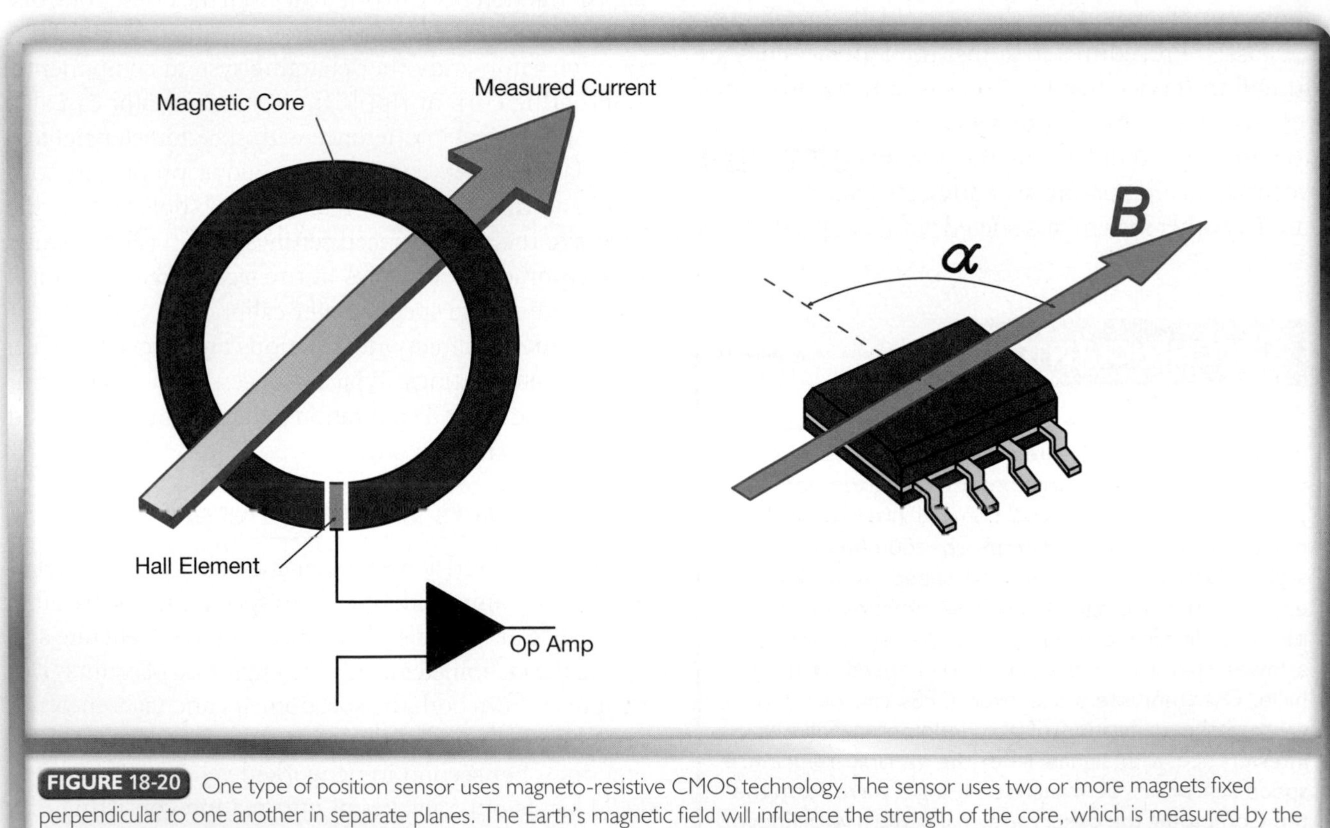

FIGURE 18-20 One type of position sensor uses magneto-resistive CMOS technology. The sensor uses two or more magnets fixed perpendicular to one another in separate planes. The Earth's magnetic field will influence the strength of the core, which is measured by the Hall-effect sensor. The difference in strength between the two cores is measured, and an output signal of varying voltage is provided, which is relative to the North Pole.

fuel consumption, compass headings, outside temperature, telematics, and freight information. To navigate the drivers's information display menu, a variety of options are available: odometer buttons, the turn-signal wiper stalk, or a touch screen.

Liquid Crystal Display (LCD)

Liquid crystal displays (LCDs) use a compact passive display technology and consume little current to operate. Passive display means that LCDs do not emit light but instead use ambient light around the display to reflect images. The displays are made of several layers. An important one contains the liquid crystal (LC), which is an organic substance having a liquid form with a crystal molecular structure FIGURE 18-21. The liquid is made of rod-shaped molecules that are arranged in a parallel lattice-like structure—a property that makes crystals transparent. However, an electric field can be used to control arrangement of the molecules.

To do this, LCD glass has transparent electrical conductors embedded into each side of the glass, which are in contact with the liquid crystal fluid. Made of indium-tin oxide (ITO), the liquid crystal molecules will rotate in the direction of the electric current when it passes through the glass. When this happens, incoming light can pass through the glass and is reflected off a silver, gray, or black reflector surface called the rear analyzer. What is observed is a black or gray character on a silver background taking the shape of the LCD cell. When the current is switched off, the molecules revert back to a twisted, light-blocking structure that reflects ambient light back to the observer, resembling a light gray or silvery image. Using multiple selectable current pathways through the glass and selectively applying voltage to the current paths, a variety of patterns can be achieved.

Resistive Touch Screens

All touch screen devices digitize the input from finger contact using an *x*/*y* coordinate. This means that there is a unique input determined by how far the contact is from the horizontal screen bottom or vertical side FIGURE 18-22. Two types of technology used to sense the coordinates are capacitance and resistive touch screens.

Resistive touch screens are composed of two flexible transparent sheets lightly coated with an electrically conductive yet slightly resistive material. The sheets are separated by an air gap or microdot that closes like a switch when finger, object, or other pressure is applied to

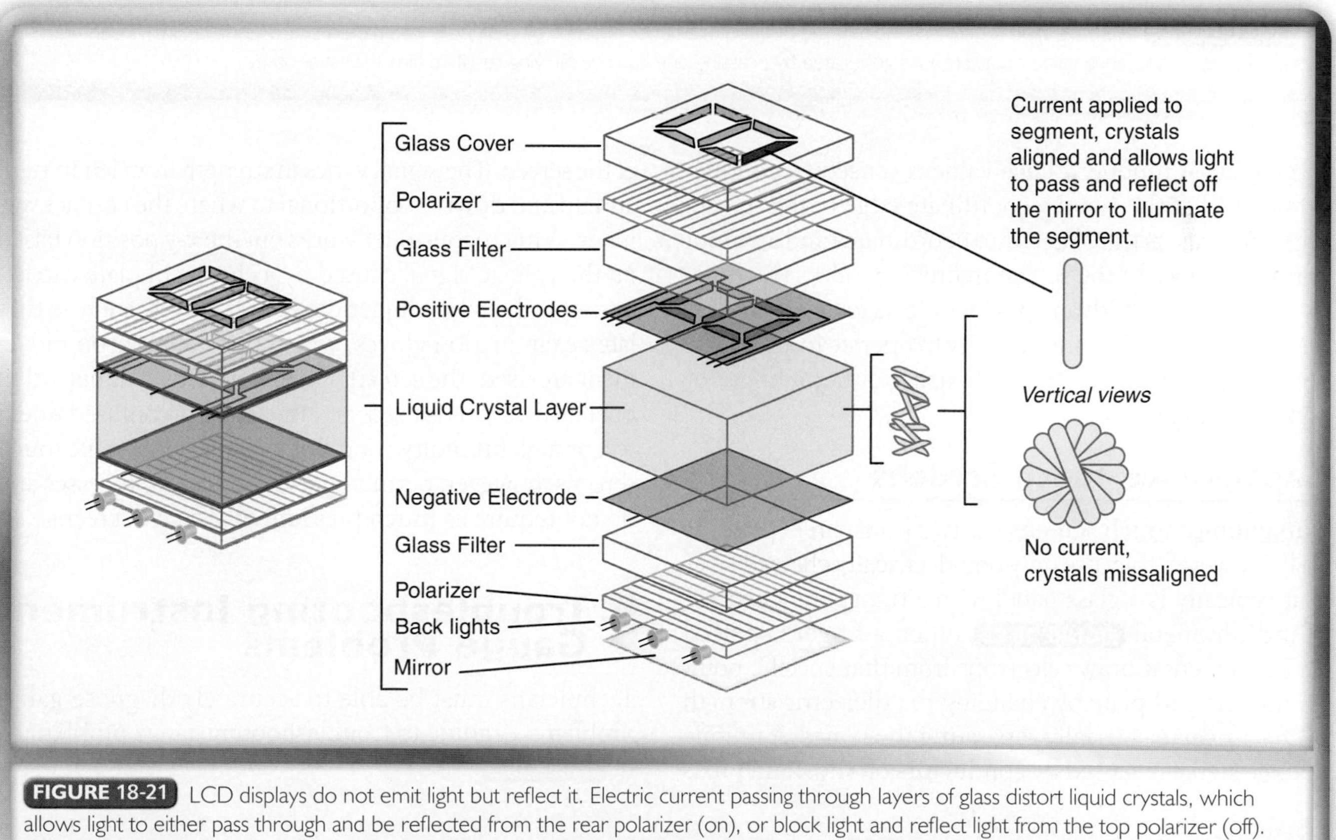

FIGURE 18-21 LCD displays do not emit light but reflect it. Electric current passing through layers of glass distort liquid crystals, which allows light to either pass through and be reflected from the rear polarizer (on), or block light and reflect light from the top polarizer (off). Light reflected from the rear polarizer hits a dark gray or black surface. Light reflected from the top polarizer layer is silver or light gray.

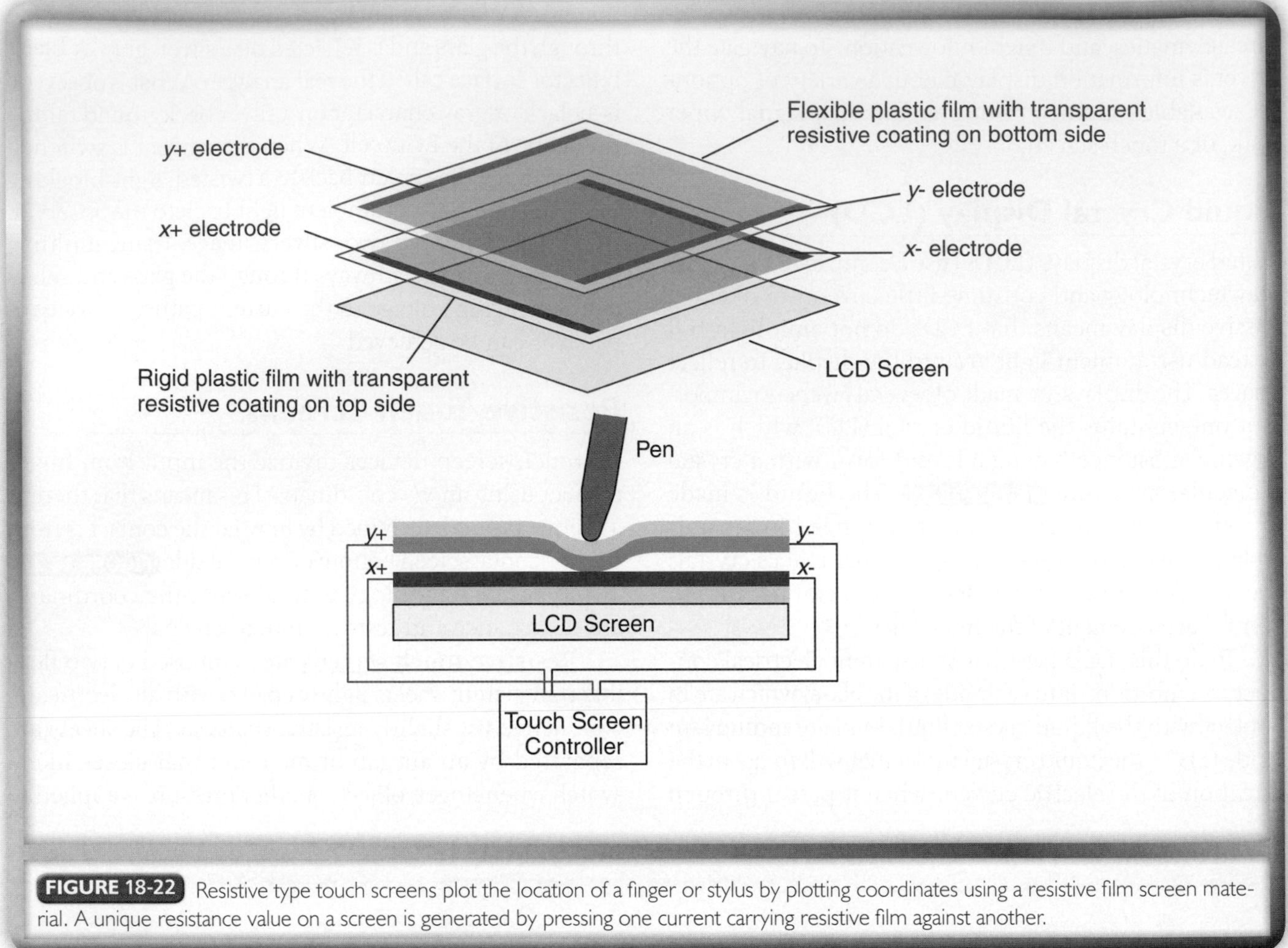

FIGURE 18-22 Resistive type touch screens plot the location of a finger or stylus by plotting coordinates using a resistive film screen material. A unique resistance value on a screen is generated by pressing one current carrying resistive film against another.

the screen. A unique voltage value is sensed by conductors placed at the *x* and *y* coordinate edge of the screen. Signal voltage is translated into coordinates and an input command goes to the screen microcontroller. The resistive touch screen's advantages include its low cost, scratch resistance, durability, and capacity to operate in all climate conditions. Input can be made using either a finger or stylus or finger.

Capacitance Touch Screens

Capacitance touch screens use two transparent plates as well. However, they use only one electrically charged layer that typically is a glass panel with a transparent coating of indium metal FIGURE 18-23. When a finger is placed on the screen, it draws electrons from that specific point on the charged plate by changing the dielectric strength of the air gap electrically separating the plates. A unique voltage signal is sensed by conductors on the *x* and *y* axis of the screen. The signal varies in strength from left to right and up and down, proportional to where the contact was made. A microcontroller works out the *x*-*y* position based on the voltage signal caused by a change of plate capacitance produced by finger contact. If gloves, such as thin latex examination gloves, which prevent electron movement are used, the screen will not operate. Neither will it operate if a stylus is used, and the screen is confused under wet or high humidity conditions. Capacitance-type touch screens, however, permit dual-finger touch processes and do not require as much pressure as resistive screens.

Troubleshooting Instrument Gauge Problems

Technicians must be able to accurately diagnose gauge problems. A guide to troubleshooting gauge problems is in TABLE 18-2.

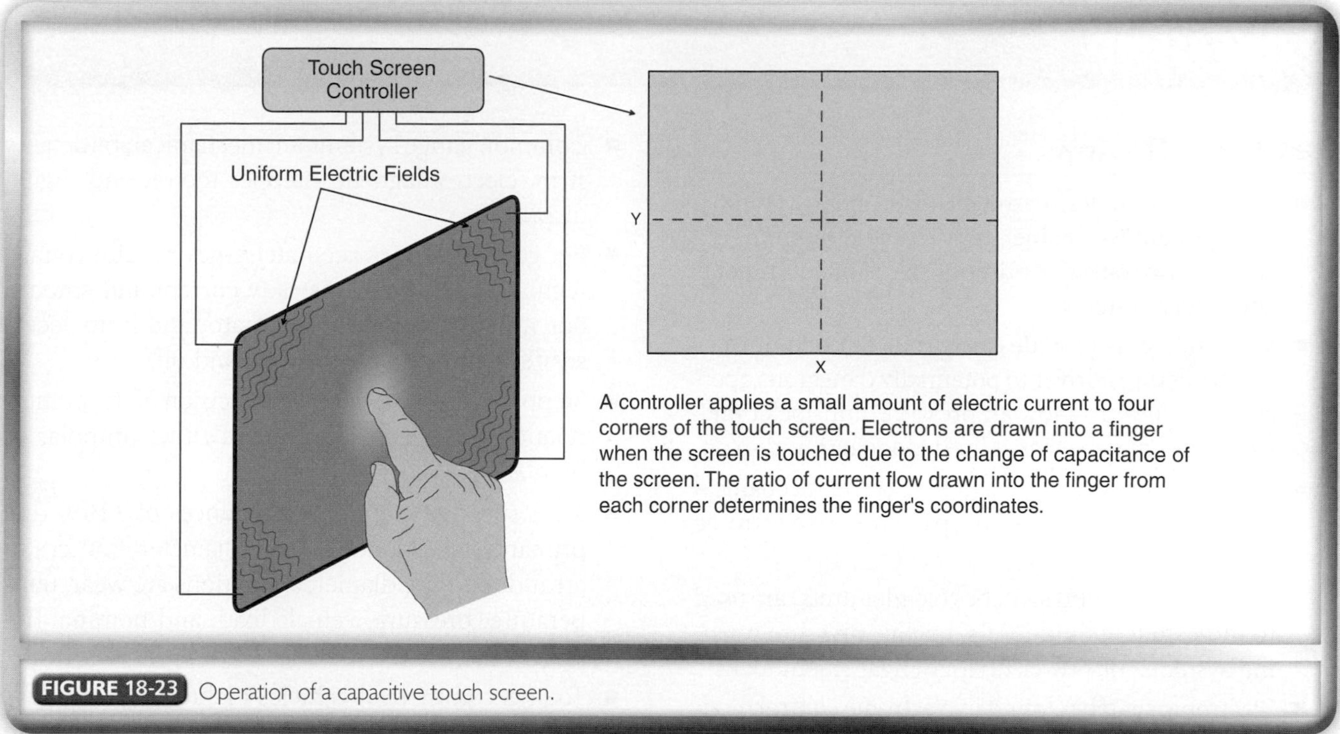

Touch Screen Controller
Uniform Electric Fields
Y
X
A controller applies a small amount of electric current to four corners of the touch screen. Electrons are drawn into a finger when the screen is touched due to the change of capacitance of the screen. The ratio of current flow drawn into the finger from each corner determines the finger's coordinates.

FIGURE 18-23 Operation of a capacitive touch screen.

TABLE 18-2: Troubleshooting Instrument Gauge Problems

Symptom	Possible Cause	Diagnostic Strategy
Gauges do not repond with a prove-out sequence when ignition is switched on.	Missing or broken ignition or ground wire	Check for power and grounds to instrument cluster.
	Blown fuse	Check fuses and breakers.
	Defective stepper motor	Continuity checks of stepper motor.
Erratic gauge readings	Loose connections at sender unit and/or gauge	Verify connections.
	Poor, loose, or resistive grounds	Measure resistance of sending unit and compare with specifications.
	Defective sending unit or gauge	Evaluate gauge during prove-out. Stepper motor gauges should smoothly sweep from min to max values then to minimum before moving to sensed value.
Gauge stays at minimum or maximum value all the time (i.e., fuel empty, no oil pressure, low coolant temperature)	Sender unit wire disconnected or open circuited	Verify oil pressure with master mechanical gauge. Visually check fuel tank level. Verify engine temperature using an infrared thermometer.
	Sender unit wires shorted to ground	Remove sender wire. Check harness isolate shorts to ground and repair.
	Sender unit defective, (i.e., broken unit, missing or leaking float, internally shorted to ground)	Measure resistance of sending unit over its full range. Check float.
	Defective gauge	Supply a calibrated resistance to sending unit lead to evaluate gauge. Ground out sending unit wire to observe whether gauge moves. Disconnect sending unit wire to observe whether gauge moves.
No data on CAN instrument gauge display	Pinched, shorted, or open CAN bus to instrument cluster	Check CAN signal to clusters using oscilloscope. Measure CAN power and ground with voltmeter.
	Missing terminating resistors	Measure CAN signals using a voltmeter. Measure resistance of CAN line batteries disconnected.

Wrap-up

Ready for Review

- Instrument gauges, warning lamps, and driver information centers enable the driver to monitor the vehicle's operating condition, status of equipment, and safety systems.
- Warning lights provide easily understood information to alert the driver to potentially dangerous operating conditions—low air pressure, anti-lock brake faults, low diesel exhaust fluid, door ajar, and so on.
- Warning lights can be switched on by mechanical ground switches, voltage drop circuits, or electronic modules.
- Mechanical ground switches (sender units) are used to indicate low fluid levels, low air pressure warning systems, or power divider engagement locks.
- Electronic switches found in electronic control modules are the most common way warning lights are illuminated in today's vehicles.
- To test the correct operation of a warning light, vehicles use a prove-out sequence in which the instrument cluster illuminates the warning lights for several brief seconds with the key on and engine off or during key-on engine cranking.
- Manufacturers use blink codes to provide fault code data.
- Gauge systems are designed to inform the driver about a developing problem by displaying a representation of a physical measure of system conditions (pressure, temperature, or fluid level).
- Common gauge systems are mechanical, bimetallic strip, electromagnetic, stepper motor, and digital display.
- For gauges to work accurately, they require voltage regulators to supply a steady current and smooth out variations from the alternator and from accessory systems being turned on and off.
- Stepper motors increase the precision of the pointer rotation on a gauge and can be either unipolar or bipolar.
- Most speedometers have tolerances of ±10% due primarily to variations in tire diameter. Sources of error due to tire diameter variations are wear, temperature, pressure, vehicle load, and nominal tire size.
- Today's commercial vehicles include data displays that allow the driver to view information about tire pressure, fuel consumption, compass headings, outside temperature, telematics, freight information, and more. Many of these displays use liquid crystal technology.
- Touch screens can use resistive or capacitance touch technologies.
- Vehicles use a number of different types of gauge sending units, including thermistors and variable resistors.
- Electrical problems such as blown fuse, faulty wiring, gauges, or sender units can result in faulty gauge readings.

Vocabulary Builder

bimetallic gauge A gauge in which two dissimilar pieces of metal are bonded together and expand at different rates when heated, thereby converting the heating effect of electricity into mechanical movement.

blink code A method of providing fault code data for a specific system that involves counting the number of flashes from a warning lamp and observing longer pauses between the light blinks.

capacitance touch screen A display screen that uses two transparent plates, one of which is electrically charged.

D'Arsonval gauge A type of electromagnetic gauge that moves a pointing needle directly proportional to current flow through an electromagnet attached to the pointer.

DIP switches A small slide switch located at the rear of the speedometer head placed in either an on or off (1 or 0) position.

prove-out sequence A sequence in which the warning lights for several brief seconds with the key on and engine off or during key-on engine cranking.

resistive touch screen A display screen composed of two flexible, transparent sheets lightly coated with an electrically conductive yet slightly resistive material.

tachograph A device fitted to a vehicle to record various pieces of information, such as time, speed, rest periods, and distance travelled by each of the vehicle's drivers.

three-coil gauge A gauge in which three field coils are wound in series, with a coil at minimum reading, one at maximum reading, and one between the two.

Review Questions

1. Which of the following statements about instrumentation is correct?
   a. The type of displays, warning lights, and gauges differ widely among vehicles and manufacturers but break down into common gauge groups, sensing, and input systems.
   b. Monitoring engine operation involves measuring pressure and temperature of parameters of the lubrication, cooling, and air induction system.
   c. Charging voltage and amperage of the electrical system, fuel level, air pressure, engine, and vehicle speed are other common gauge systems.
   d. All of the choices are correct.
2. Which of the following is the most common method of illuminating warning lights in today's vehicles?
   a. Voltage drop circuits
   b. Pneumatic switches
   c. Mechanical ground switches
   d. Electronic switches
3. Which of the following statements about the prove-out sequence is correct?
   a. In older vehicles, the ignition key will supply a circuit to provide a ground and/or positive battery voltage path to illuminate instrument warning lights.
   b. In order to validate the correct operation of a warning light, the instrument cluster is designed to illuminate a bulb for several brief seconds with the key on and engine off or during key-on engine cranking.
   c. If the engine starts, the bulb may remain lit until proper operating conditions are met, such as correct oil pressure is reached.
   d. All of the choices are correct.
4. Which of the following is NOT a technology used with common gauge systems?
   a. Electromagnetic
   b. Stepper motor
   c. Bi-electrical
   d. Digital display
5. Mechanical gauges depend upon ________ to operate.
   a. cables
   b. air pressure
   c. fluid pressure
   d. All of the choices are correct.
6. How much voltage is supplied to gauges and sending units?
   a. Between .5 and 1 volts
   b. Between 1.5 and 2 volts
   c. Between 3 and 4 volts
   d. Between 5 and 10 volts
   e. All of the choices are correct.
7. What is an example of a gauge that can use D'Arsonval movement?
   a. Ammeter
   b. Voltmeter
   c. Fuel pressure
   d. Water temperature
8. Which of the following statements about two- and three-coil movements is correct?
   a. Variations of the D'Arsonval movement use a pointer with a permanent magnet rather than an electromagnet.
   b. Two or three electromagnetic coils surround the pointer to rotate the gauge.
   c. Two-coil designs require a voltage regulator to maintain consistent readings, as charging voltage varies, but three-coil designs generally do not.
   d. All of the choices are correct.
9. How many possible steps of positions do most stepper gauges have?
   a. 1,530
   b. 2,400
   c. 2,800
   d. 3,060
10. The unipolar stepper motor can be identified by its ________ wires that connect ________ field coils.
    a. 2 or 3; 2
    b. 4; 4
    c. 5 or 6; 4
    d. 7 or 8; 4

ASE-Type Questions

1. Technician A says warning lights can be built into gauges or mounted in a dedicated panel in the instrument panel. Technician B says warning lights require a power feed and ground for the light to illuminate. Who is correct?
   a. Technician A
   b. Technician B
   c. Both Technician A and Technician B
   d. Neither Technician A nor Technician B
2. Technician A says normally closed pressure switches opened with air or oil pressure provide a path to ground to illuminate a bulb. Technician B says normally-opened pressure switches opened with air or oil pressure provide a path to ground to illuminate a bulb. Who is correct?
   a. Technician A
   b. Technician B
   c. Both Technician A and Technician B
   d. Neither Technician A nor Technician B
3. Technician A says after the engine starts and the alternator begins charging, charging system voltage is applied to both terminals of a bulb. Technician B says the charging system indicator light is an example of a light operated through voltage drop. Who is correct?
   a. Technician A
   b. Technician B
   c. Both Technician A and Technician B
   d. Neither Technician A nor Technician B
4. Technician A says the malfunction indicator lamp (MIL) and check engine lamp (CEL) will illuminate for approximately three to five seconds during engine start-up and then extinguish. Technician B says if there are active fault codes, the lights will switch back on after start-up. Who is correct?
   a. Technician A
   b. Technician B
   c. Both Technician A and Technician B
   d. Neither Technician A nor Technician B
5. Technician A says stepper motor gauges are reduce the problems associated with inaccurate readings from bimetallic and electromagnetic coil gauges caused by voltage fluctuations. Technician B says stepper motors are brush-type DC electromechanical devices that generally use a permanent magnet shaft surrounded by more than two pair of electromagnetic coils. Who is correct?
   a. Technician A
   b. Technician B
   c. Both Technician A and Technician B
   d. Neither Technician A nor Technician B
6. Technician A says speedometers electronically measure the driveshaft speed by counting a series of electrical pulses produced per mile or kilometer of distance traveled. Technician B says two wires connecting the instrument panel gauge clusters to the CAN network are all that is necessary to supply the data necessary to display vehicle data and trip information, provide fault codes, and display warning lamps. Who is correct?
   a. Technician A
   b. Technician B
   c. Both Technician A and Technician B
   d. Neither Technician A nor Technician B
7. Technician A says gauge senders output an electronic signal based on an electrical input. Technician B says electronic modules are available to convert variable voltage values into digital signals for use by digital gauges. Who is correct?
   a. Technician A
   b. Technician B
   c. Both Technician A and Technician B
   d. Neither Technician A nor Technician B
8. Technician A says gauge faults will range from not working at all, to erratic gauge operation or inaccurate readings and you must refer to the manufacturer's information for the correct test procedures. Technician B says gauge faults will range from not working at all, to erratic gauge operation or inaccurate readings can be repaired in-house. Who is correct?
   a. Technician A
   b. Technician B
   c. Both Technician A and Technician B
   d. Neither Technician A nor Technician B
9. Technician A says digital tachographs are calibrated by accessing the tachograph's electronic memory. Technician B says calibration adjustments within the tachograph are located in a sealed area of the unit to prevent tampering by unauthorized personnel. Who is correct?
   a. Technician A
   b. Technician B
   c. Both Technician A and Technician B
   d. Neither Technician A nor Technician B
10. Technician A says you should use a DVOM when checking for smooth operation of a fuel sender unit. Technician B says the fuel sender unit should be reconnected to the fuel gauge to check for full-range operation while it is out of the tank. Who is correct?
    a. Technician A
    b. Technician B
    c. Both Technician A and Technician B
    d. Neither Technician A nor Technician B

CHAPTER 19

NATEF Tasks

Electrical/Electronic Systems

General Electrical Systems

	Page
■ Check frequency and pulse width signal in electrical/electronic circuits using appropriate test equipment.	538, 548–550

Knowledge Objectives

After reading this chapter, you will be able to:

1. Identify and explain the advantages of electronic signal processing over mechanical system control. (pp 538–548)
2. Identify and describe the types of electrical signals and associated terminology. (pp 539–541)
3. Identify and describe the operating principles of electronic signal processing systems used in electrical system control on commercial vehicles. (pp 538–539)
4. Identify and describe the functions, construction, and application of electronic control modules. (pp 535–536)

Electronic Signal Processing Principles

Skills Objectives

There are no skills objectives for this chapter.

Introduction

Today's commercial vehicles are often described as computers on wheels, and technicians are just as likely to use a computer as they will a wrench to service them. Not a single vehicle system operates without complete or at least some degree of electronic control. This has not always been the case. Until recent years, mechanical devices such as levers, springs, linkage, gears, cables, or bellows-controlled system operation. Electronic systems using microcontroller- and microprocessor-based control now provide operational capabilities far exceeding any mechanical system capabilities and can do this with greater precision, efficiency, and reliability. The dominance and sophistication of electronic control makes skill development related to servicing this technology one of the most important priorities for successful technicians. Understanding the operating principles of electronic control systems is foundational for choosing diagnostic strategies, using service tools effectively, and making sound repair recommendations.

Benefits of Electronic Control

Electronic control offers many benefits to today's commercial vehicles, including increased power and efficiency, enhanced reporting capabilities, telematics, increased safety, programmable features, and self-diagnostic capabilities.

Increased Power and Efficiency

Diesel engines were the first commercial vehicle systems transformed by electronic controls FIGURE 19-1. Engines had reached their limit of efficiency and the next logical step was to apply electronic controls already used on gasoline engines. The immediate benefits of these refinements to engine operation are lower engine emissions, improved fuel economy, increased reliability, and enhanced performance. Smarter engines continue to deliver ever-increasing power from smaller displacements, quieter operation, and longer service intervals in addition to needing less maintenance. The increased costs of some of these features are offset through improved engine efficiency. Many of the electronic control systems have in fact lowered the cost of vehicle production while adding more features with the improved operating benefits. In comparison to mechanical controls, electronic controls enable far greater flexibility to adjust fuel injection metering, injection rate, and timing over a large number of operating conditions. When engine operational problems leading to excess emissions do occur, self-monitoring and self-diagnostic capabilities of electronic controls can identify the problem, alert the operator, and revert to operating modes that minimize noxious emission production.

You Are the Technician

A number of vehicles have arrived at your shop with a list of apparently unrelated complaints: speedometer needles that begin to bounce at 55 mph (90 kph) cruise controls that do not work, automatic transmissions that shift erratically, dozens of ABS codes for components and circuits that have no faults, and rough running engines. On one of the vehicles, when performing some pinpoint tests with a digital multimeter, you accidentally set the meter to read AC and not DC voltage. You are surprised to discover close to 4 volts of AC current are superimposed on the system's 12-volt DC current. Realizing that the only component that could produce AC current is the alternator, you disconnect the alternator and find the AC voltage has disappeared along with the unusual electrical system complaints. To repair the problem, the alternator is replaced and so are the vehicle's batteries, which all tested defective. As you prepare to document the diagnosis and justify the parts replacement on the work orders, consider the following questions:

1. What shop equipment could be used to capture and record the AC voltage signal frequency and waveform to document the problem?
2. Would the ECM be processing the correct data from some sensor inputs if AC voltage accompanies the DC voltage inputs? Explain your answer.
3. After gaining the experience repairing these vehicles, what checks would you recommend in future for diagnosing electrical problems that may be related to electrical signal interference?

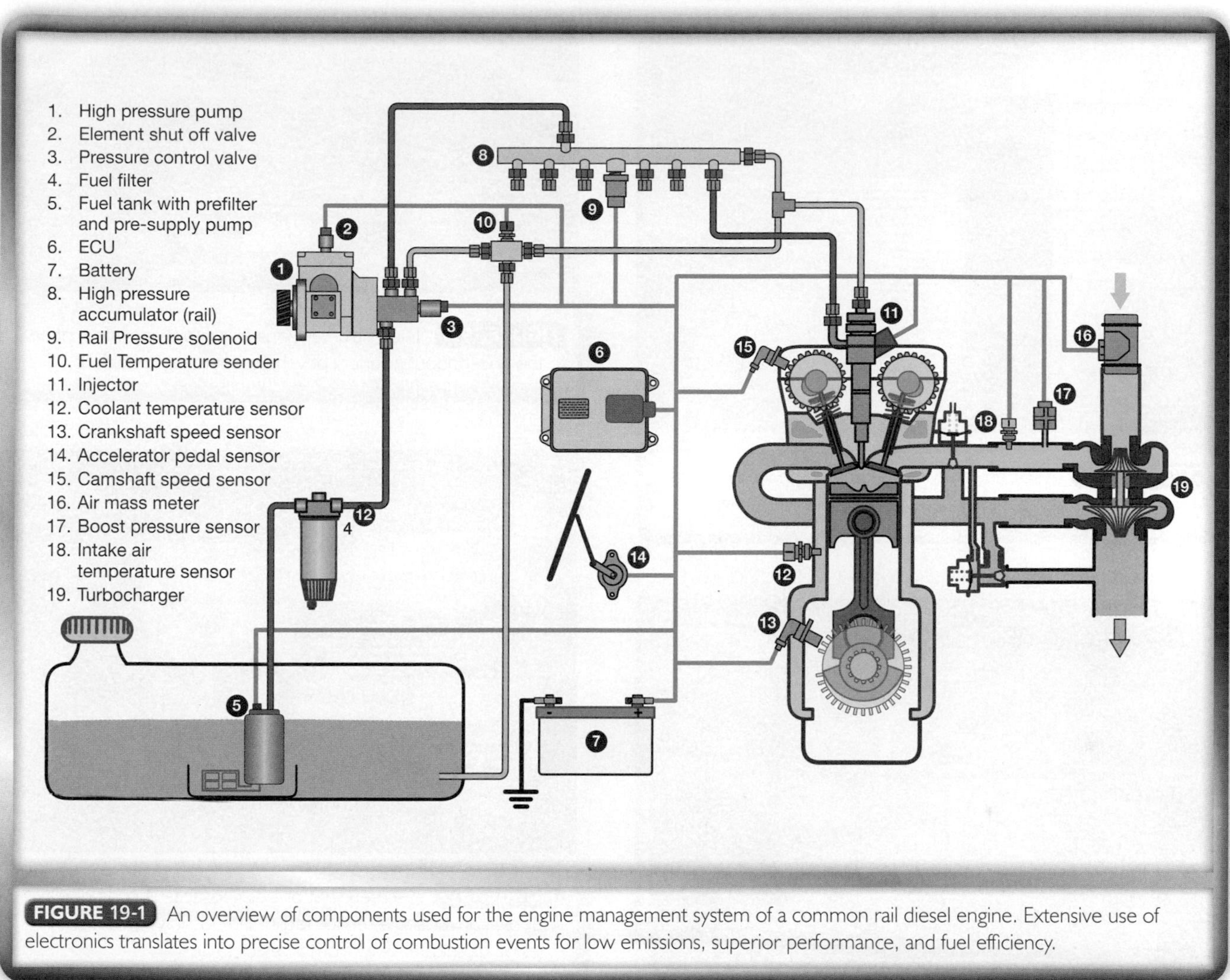

FIGURE 19-1 An overview of components used for the engine management system of a common rail diesel engine. Extensive use of electronics translates into precise control of combustion events for low emissions, superior performance, and fuel efficiency.

TABLE 19-1 shows the increase in power output per cubic inch of displacement and lowering of emissions achieved through advanced technology and electronic control of the fuel system.

Information Reporting Capabilities

Life cycle costs of operating vehicles with these engines is further reduced through the ability of the engine control systems to interface with tablets and Windows-based diagnostic and service software. Service technicians, particularly in fleet operations, can access a wealth of diagnostic and service data much faster and with more precise detail than before FIGURE 19-2. Trip reports from the vehicle ECM (electronic control module) extracted during scheduled maintenance intervals report details such as diagnostic fault codes, fuel consumption, idle time, emission system performance, and vehicle abuse statistics FIGURE 19-3.

TABLE 19-1: Increase in Power Output per Cubic Feet of Displacement

Engine Model	1988 – 7.3L IDI Diesel	2015 – 6.7L Powerstroke
Horsepower	180 hp	440 hp
Torque	338 ft/lb @ 1,600 rpm	860 ft/lb @ 1,600 rpm
NO_x emissions	2.5 grams/bhp	0.07grams/bhp
Intake air flow @ 3,330 rpm	360 cubic feet/minute	732 cubic feet/minute
Exhaust flow @ 3,300 rpm	1,080 cubic feet/minute	1,499 cubic feet/minute
Fuel system	Mechanical distributor pump	Bosch piezoelectric injectors CP4.2 Common Rail Pump Electronic

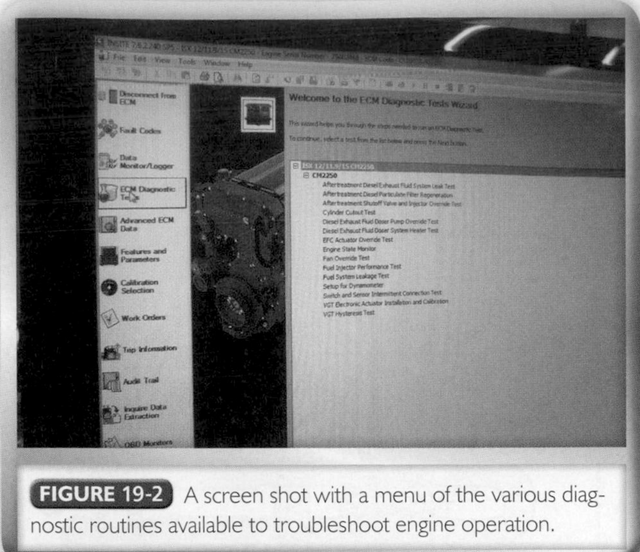

FIGURE 19-2 A screen shot with a menu of the various diagnostic routines available to troubleshoot engine operation.

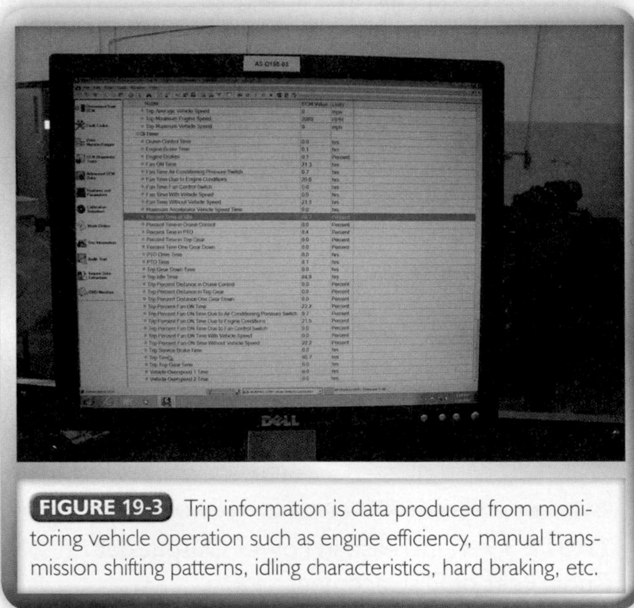

FIGURE 19-3 Trip information is data produced from monitoring vehicle operation such as engine efficiency, manual transmission shifting patterns, idling characteristics, hard braking, etc.

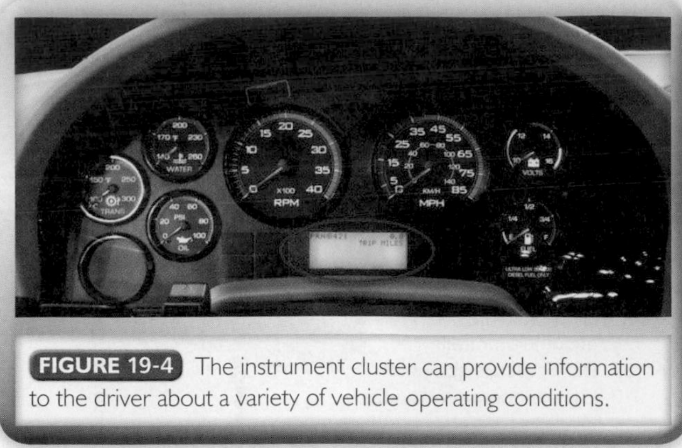

FIGURE 19-4 The instrument cluster can provide information to the driver about a variety of vehicle operating conditions.

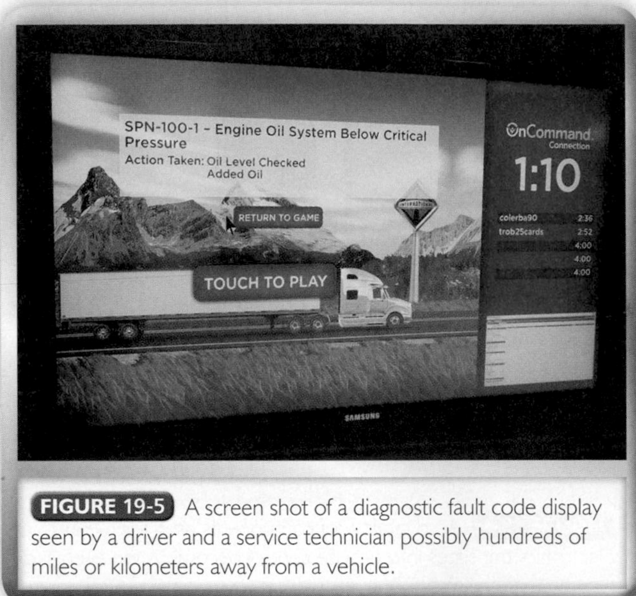

FIGURE 19-5 A screen shot of a diagnostic fault code display seen by a driver and a service technician possibly hundreds of miles or kilometers away from a vehicle.

Telematics

In addition to the obtaining vehicle and trip information downloaded at scheduled maintenance intervals, ECM data can be collected and modified by other means FIGURE 19-4. When equipped with the correct vehicle interface devices, vehicle and engine diagnostics can be performed from distant locations FIGURE 19-5. **Telematics**, a branch of information technology, uses specialized telecommunication applications for long-distance transmission of information to and from a vehicle FIGURE 19-6. For example, when vehicles are equipped with radio-satellite or cellular-based vehicle communications, a technician or equipment manager can remotely monitor any information about the vehicle, engine, or product the vehicle is carrying that is available from the vehicle network data link connector. Messages can be sent back and forth between the vehicle and a central dispatch location. For example, if low on fuel, a list of nearby fuel stops can be generated with the least interference or delay to a trip. A GPS can report vehicle location to a dispatcher as well as display fuel stop locations. A fault code can be evaluated to determine if immediate repairs are needed. For large fleet operations, short-range wireless technology allows diagnostics and programming of vehicles when they are in the vicinity of a maintenance or equipment facility for increased productivity.

Safety

The use of electronic engine and vehicle management provides for enhanced vehicle and occupant safety and security. If a vehicle is involved in a collision, a call can be made to an emergency dispatch. Engine systems can be monitored for operating conditions having destructive potential. Low oil pressure, high intake, or coolant temperatures are commonly monitored conditions that

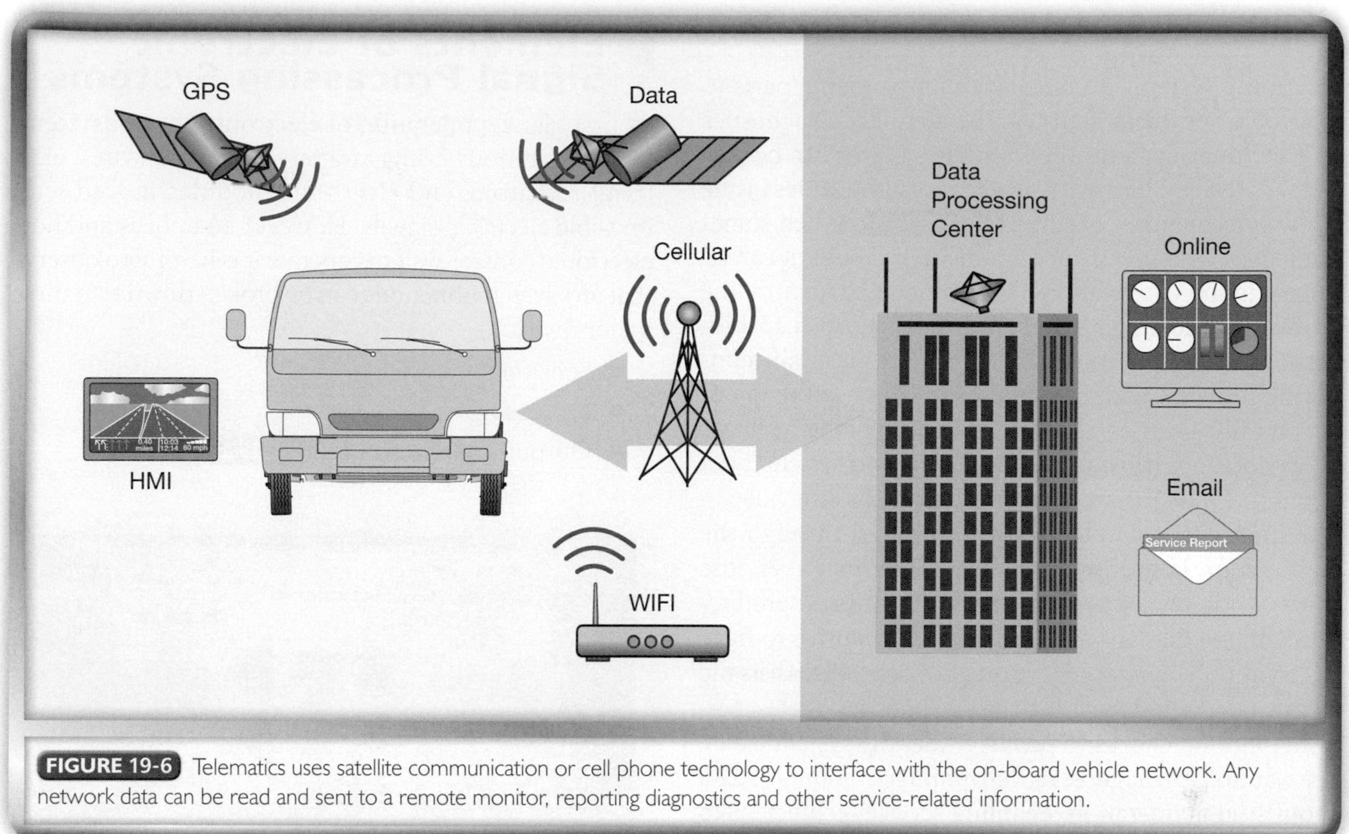

FIGURE 19-6 Telematics uses satellite communication or cell phone technology to interface with the on-board vehicle network. Any network data can be read and sent to a remote monitor, reporting diagnostics and other service-related information.

can initiate an adaptive response to prevent catastrophic failure or damage. Dangerous operating conditions can trigger the engine to shut down, de-rate power, or simply warn the operator. The microprocessor power train control makes it possible to build in features that will protect the power train from damage due to excessive torque or speed as well. Hard braking and speeding are other measurable conditions monitored by management systems to ensure road safety.

Programmable Vehicle Features

Service technicians and operators can take advantage of programmable electronic controls. Programmable software provides flexibility to engines, transmissions, and body accessories for adaptation to specific job applications, enhancing vehicle productivity, longevity, and driver comfort. Programmable changes may include things as simple as idle shut-down timers, cruise control, or maximum vehicle speed limits to adding safety interlocks preventing the vehicle from moving if a door is open, a boom is raised, or outriggers are extended FIGURE 19-7.

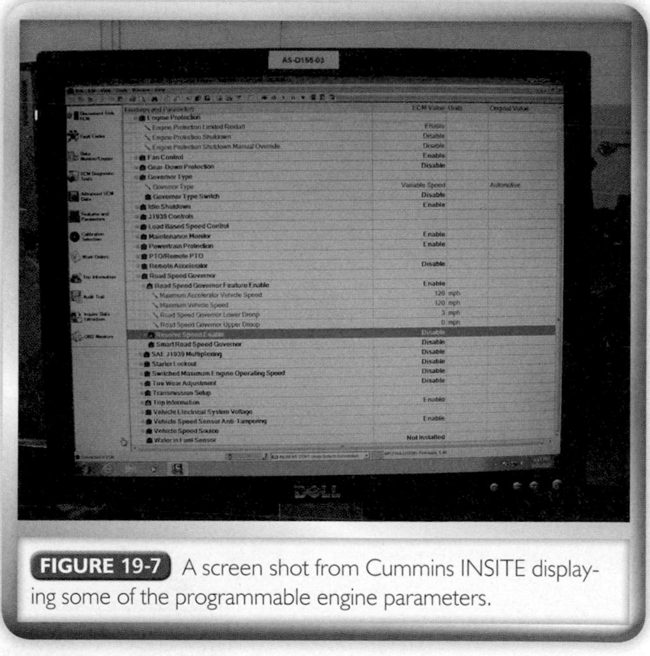

FIGURE 19-7 A screen shot from Cummins INSITE displaying some of the programmable engine parameters.

Power and torque rise profiles are easily altered electronically. Depending on the application, it is beneficial to performance and fuel economy to have maximum torque appear over different rpm ranges. Instead of replacing an injection pump and turbocharger to change engine power characteristics, electronically controlled engines are recalibrated with new software instructions. In a few minutes with some keystrokes, a stock vehicle chassis can be reprogrammed to operate as an ambulance, an on-highway tractor, dump truck, bus, rental truck, or recreational vehicle.

Self-Diagnostic Capabilities

Electronic systems do not have many moving parts to wear out, but the systems can be complex. Diagnostics on electronically controlled vehicle systems can be performed easily, often with fewer tools and in less time than on mechanical systems FIGURE 19-8. When something goes wrong with a component or circuit, it can be extremely time consuming and difficult to identify the problem without some built-in self-diagnostic capabilities. Built into electronic control systems is a self-monitoring function with capabilities to check operation of circuits and electrical devices, evaluate whether voltages are out of range, the rationality of data, and system functionality. Problems are quickly identified as they occur. The presence of faults is communicated through the malfunction indicator lamps. An engine may even lose power or de-rate to prevent excessive emission production, engine damage and provide an incentive to have the condition repaired. Electronic service tools assists the technicians to perform off-board diagnostics, that is, perform pinpoint checks to precisely identify system faults. Software-based diagnostics deliver huge amounts of data about system operation, enabling service technicians to identify problems more quickly than with mechanical systems. Since modules, sensors and actuators are more compact, they are replaced quickly with minimal training and experience required FIGURE 19-9.

Elements of Electronic Signal Processing Systems

At first glance, operation of electronic control systems looks mysterious, using a variety of sensors, wires, electrical actuators, and electronic modules moved with invisible electrical signals. However, to understand how electronic control systems operate it is helpful to observe that any system functions can be broken down into three major divisions:

- Sensing
- Processing
- Output or actuation FIGURE 19-10

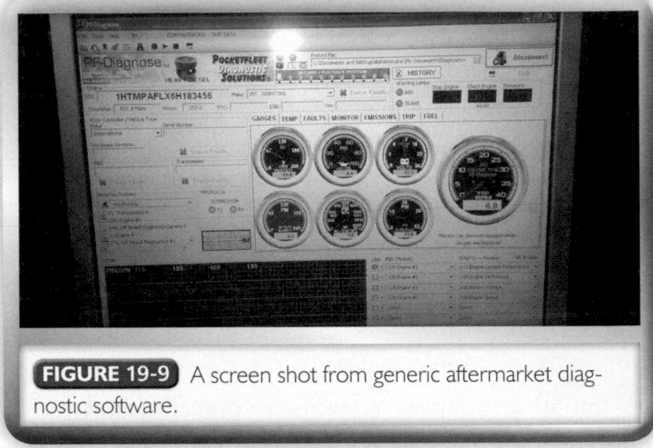

FIGURE 19-9 A screen shot from generic aftermarket diagnostic software.

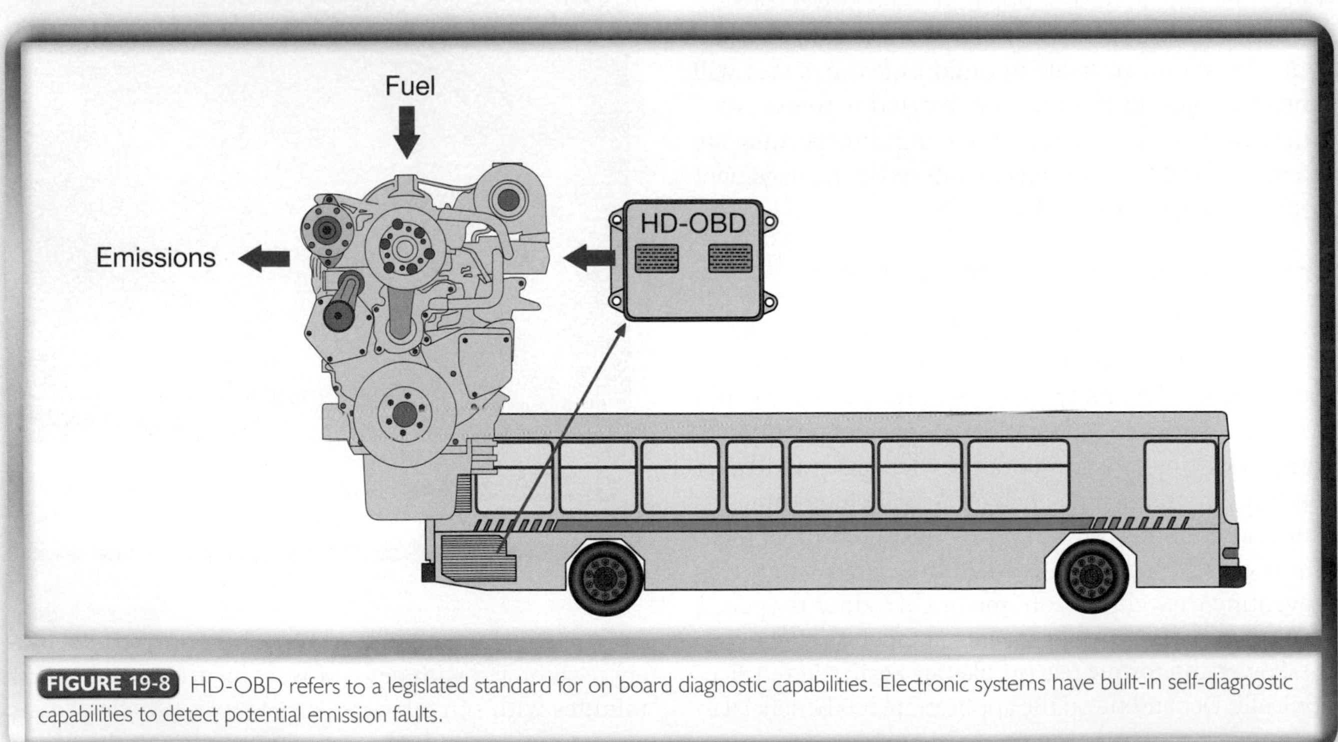

FIGURE 19-8 HD-OBD refers to a legislated standard for on board diagnostic capabilities. Electronic systems have built-in self-diagnostic capabilities to detect potential emission faults.

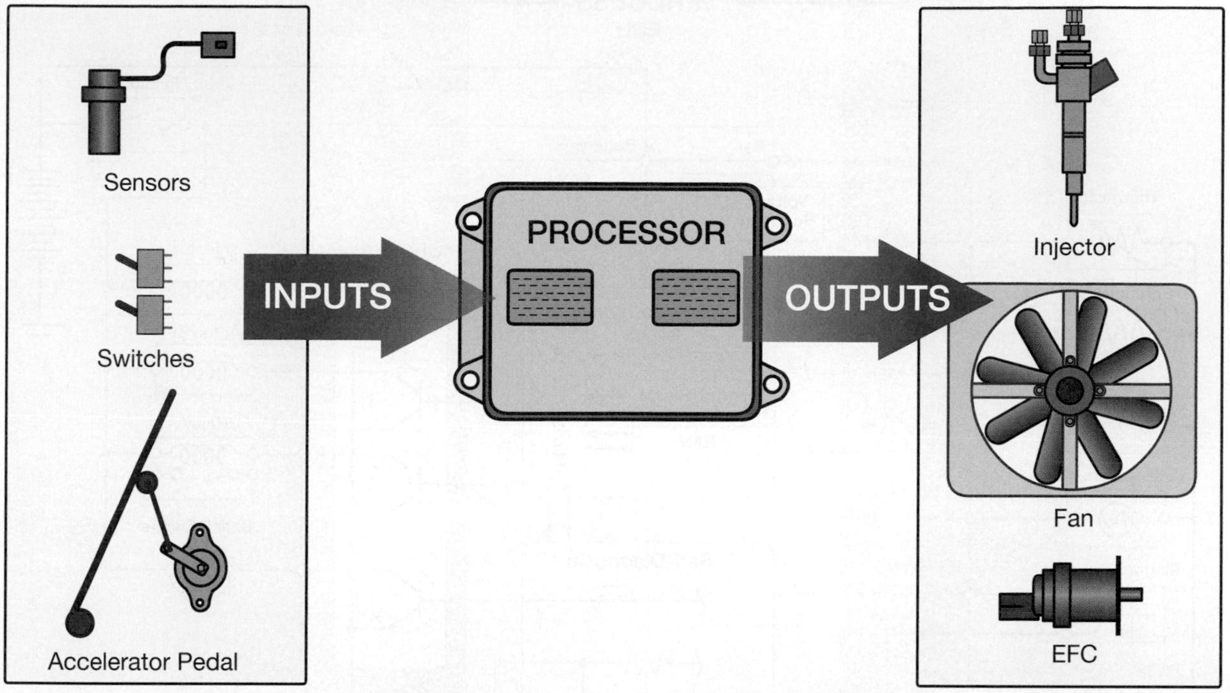

FIGURE 19-10 All engine management systems process electrical signals in three distinct stages: data collection from sensor inputs; data processing inside an electronic control module; and output devices; which are electrically operated.

Sensing Functions

Sensing functions collect data about operational conditions or the state of a device by measuring some value such as temperature, position, speed, pressure, flow, angle, etc. Sensors are devices designed to collect specific data in an electronic format.

Processing

Processing refers to the control system element that collects sensor data and determines outputs based on a set of instructions or program software. Operational algorithms, which are simply mathematical formulas used to solve problems, are included in the software that determines the steps taken when processing electrical data.

Outputs

The outputs of a system are functions performed by electrical signals produced by the processor. These may be signals to operate anything from a digital display of numeric or alphabetic information, current to operate solenoids or injectors, actuators, motors, lights, or other electromechanical devices **FIGURE 19-11**.

Types of Electrical Signals

Before looking at the elements of the electronic management system, it is first important to look at types of electrical signals used in information processing systems **FIGURE 19-12**.

Three types of electrical signals commonly used as either inputs and or outputs in electronic engine control applications are:

- Analog
- Digital
- Pulse Width Modulation (PWM)

Analog Signals

An **analog signal** is electric current that is proportional to a continuously changing variable. Analog signals then will have a changing value of voltage, amperage frequency, or amplitude. For example, temperature changes continuously. A thermometer measuring temperature change can represent every possible temperature with the movement of liquid in a glass or a hand on a dial. An analog electrical signal would represent the smallest change in

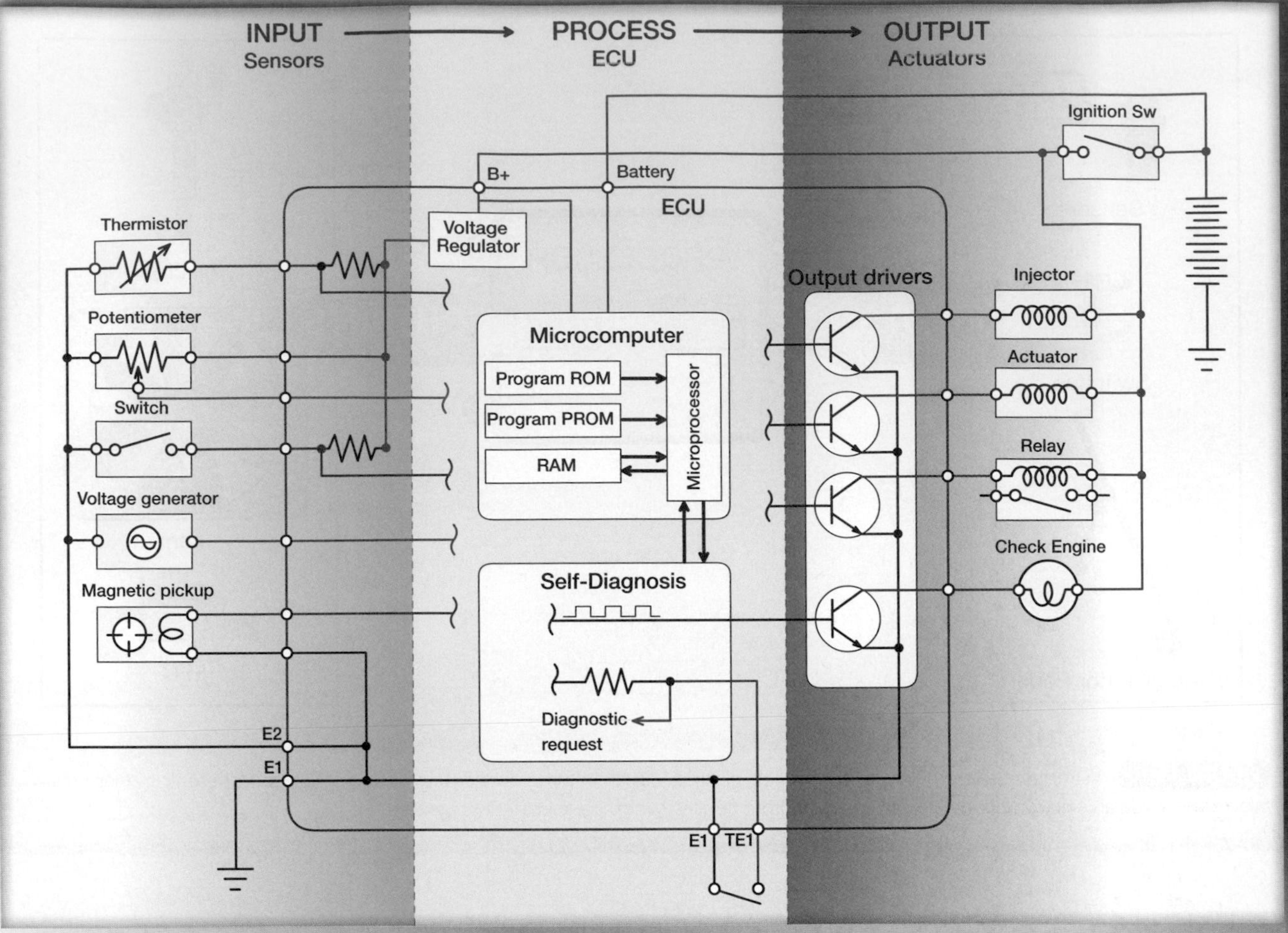

FIGURE 19-11 Three stages of signal processing. Sensors form input signals, software-controlled microprocessors are used to manipulate data, while electrically operated output devices carry out instructions of the processor.

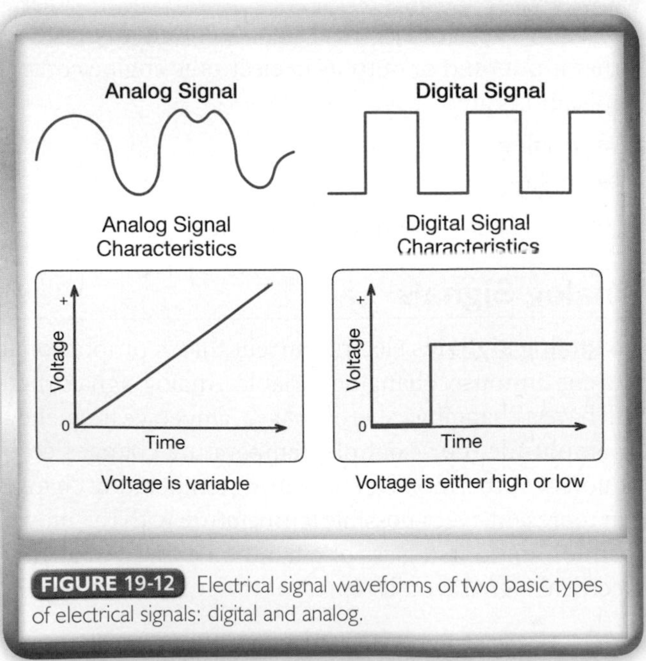

FIGURE 19-12 Electrical signal waveforms of two basic types of electrical signals: digital and analog.

temperature proportional to the movement of liquid or hand on the dial.

Measurement of alternating electrical current is another example of an analog signal. Variable reluctance–type sensors such as wheel speed or some engine position sensors will produce an alternating current. Changing wheel or engine speeds will continuously alter the frequency of current polarity change leaving the sensor. The intensity of the voltage will further continuously vary with speed.

A throttle position sensor is another example where analog data can be collected. The electrical signal produced by the sensor varies proportionally to pedal angle. A continuously changing voltage output from the sensor will vary with the driver input **FIGURE 19-13**.

Outputs can be analog as well. The intensity of a light or sound in an output device such as a lamp or speaker can be produced by varying voltage and frequency of an electrical signal. A light is dimmed or brightened by

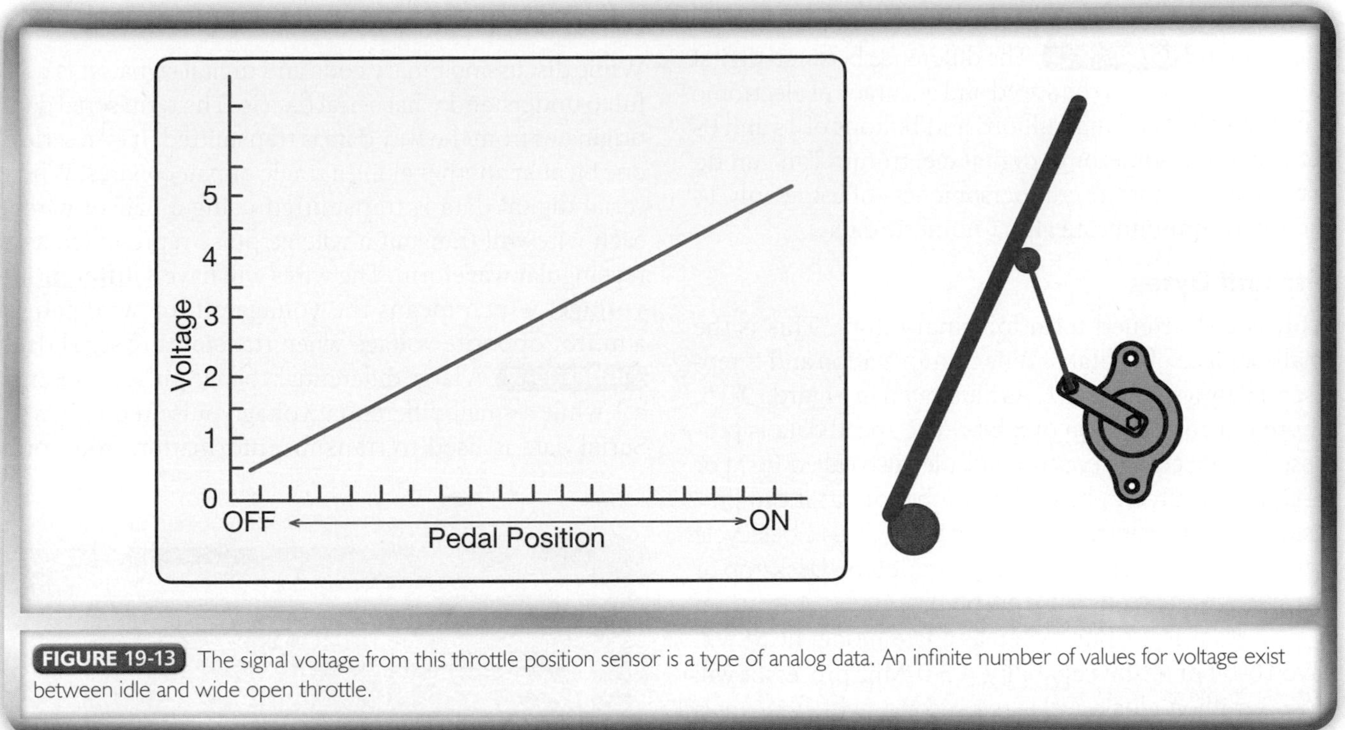

FIGURE 19-13 The signal voltage from this throttle position sensor is a type of analog data. An infinite number of values for voltage exist between idle and wide open throttle.

increasing or decreasing current to a bulb. An analog signal representing sound produces loudness and pitch by varying the voltage and frequency current to a speaker.

Digital Signals

In contrast to analog signals, **digital signals** do not vary in voltage, frequency, or amplitude. Instead, they are electrical signals that represent data in discrete, finite values. This means the data is broken down into separate or smaller meaningful values. For example, the movement of hands on an analog clock will represent time in every possible value. However, a digital watch represents time in finite values such as seconds. A digital multimeter represents data the same way. The numerical display for an electrical measurement is represented as a fixed number **FIGURE 19-14**. In contrast, an analog meter would measure the same electrical value using a sweeping needle on a scale.

A more common understanding of digital signals describes them representing data using only two conditions or values. This can beon or off, yes or no, 1 or 0, open or closed, up or down, etc. Binary code is an example of a digital signal. Every number from 0 to infinity and the letters of the alphabet letters are represented by a combination of 0s and 1s. Binary code easily lends itself to use in microprocessor circuits where processing large amounts of alphabetic or numerical data, represented in strings of 0s or 1s is performed.

Computerized power train management systems process information electronically using digital signals and binary code. This means that all information, whether analog or alphabetic is converted into 1s and 0s. Using long strings of 1s and 0s may seem cumbersome, but just as the Morse code tapped out on telegraphs could send information using only dots and dashes, the 1s and

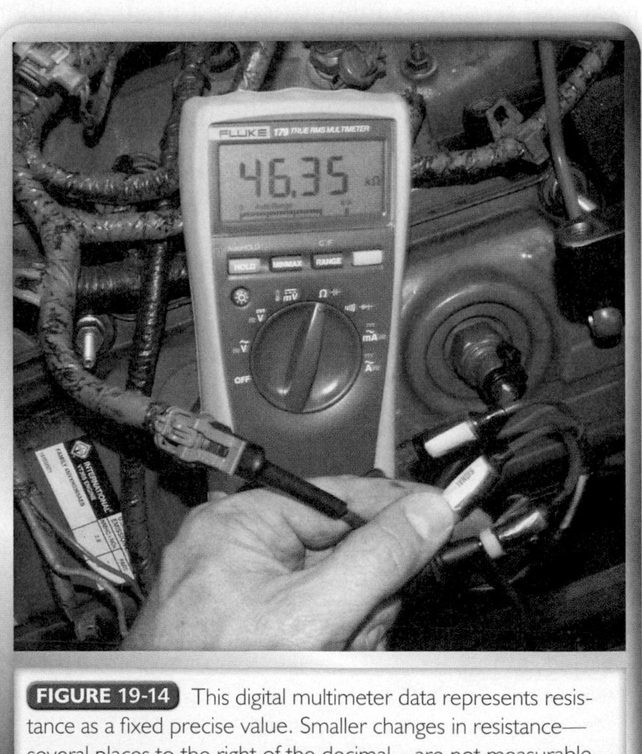

FIGURE 19-14 This digital multimeter data represents resistance as a fixed precise value. Smaller changes in resistance—several places to the right of the decimal—are not measurable.

0s of binary code can satisfactorily convey all kinds of information **FIGURE 19-15**. The difference between digital and Morse code is in the speed and accuracy of electronic processing. Processing millions and billions of 1s and 0s per second is something digital electronics can can do to compensate for the cumbersomeness of using only 1's and 0's to communicate alpha-numeric data.

Bits and Bytes

A **bit** is a shortened term for binary digit. This is the smallest piece of digital or binary information and is represented by a single 0 or 1. As illustrated in Figure 19-15, a **byte** is a combination of 8 bits. The speed data is processed in the engine control module, also called ECM or ECU, is measured in bits. The number of bits it can process during one central processing unit (CPU) clock cycle classifies power train ECMs and computers. Desk-top or laptop computers often use 64-bit processors. A Pentium IV processor is 32-bits, whereas a late model ECM will have 16-bit or 32-bit capability. A 3.0-Mhz processor will have 3 million clock cycles per second, which means a 32-bit processor processes 96 million bits of data per second. While the clock speeds and bit size of the processors in an engine ECM are smaller than an average desktop, so is the programming code. The capabilities of an engine ECM may appear to lag a personal computer, but the PC operates using hundreds of complex software programs. An engine or power train control microprocessor that operates using only one program with much simpler software code to process information and produce output signals has enormous processing capability **FIGURE 19-16**. Today's vehicle processors have many times the digital processing capabilities of the on-board computers used send Apollo rockets to the moon.

Digital Signal
Binary Translation 1 0 0 1 1 0 1 0
One Word

FIGURE 19-15 A bit is the smallest piece of digital information that is either a 1 or a 0. A byte is a unit of 8 bits. Binary code represents letters and numbers in strings of 1s and 0s. Digital data can be represented as 0s and 1s.

Serial Data

While discussing binary code and digital signals it is useful to understand what serial data is. The term serial data originates from the way data is transmitted. It is in series, one bit after another along a single or pair of wires. When serial digital data is transmitted using a pair of wires, each wire will transmit a voltage pulse represented as a rectangular waveform. The wires will have a **differential voltage**, which means the voltage on the wire pair is a mirror opposite voltage when transmitting serial data **FIGURE 19-17**. A large differential voltage pulse represents a 1 while a small differential voltage pulse represents 0. Serial data is used to transmit information from one

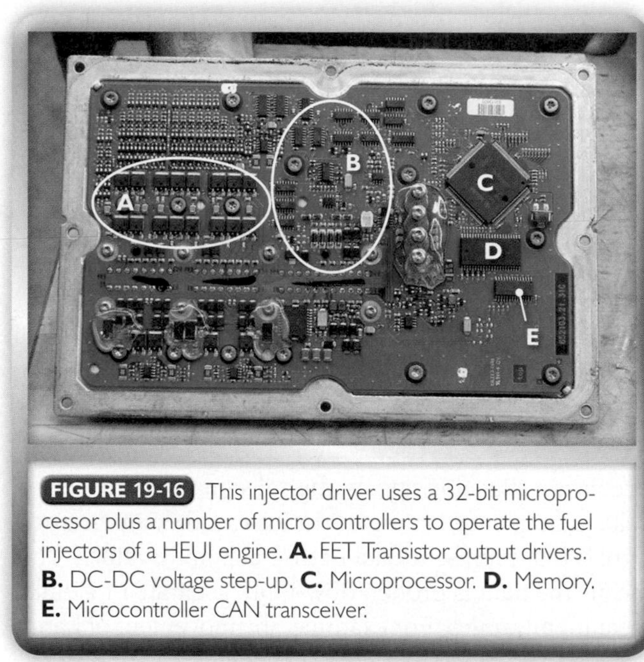

FIGURE 19-16 This injector driver uses a 32-bit microprocessor plus a number of micro controllers to operate the fuel injectors of a HEUI engine. **A.** FET Transistor output drivers. **B.** DC-DC voltage step-up. **C.** Microprocessor. **D.** Memory. **E.** Microcontroller CAN transceiver.

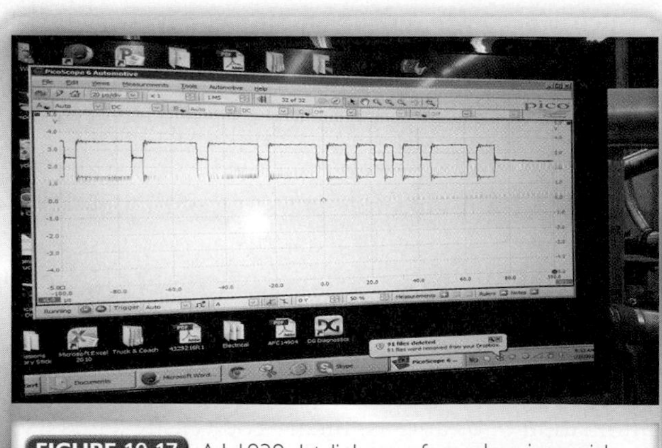

FIGURE 19-17 A J-1939 datalink waveform showing serial data. Serial data transmits a series of 1s and 0s and has a digital form. The wide part of the waveform represents 1 or a string of 1s while the narrow part of the wave from represents 0 or a string of 0s.

electronic module to another. On-board data networks share information and control vehicle operation using serial data. More important to the technician, electronic service tools will use serial data to receive and send data. The rate at which serial data is transmitted is referred to as the baud rate. **Baud rate** refers to the number of data bits transmitted per second.

Analog to Digital Conversion

Because electronic processing units can only handle binary digital data, analog signals are converted to digital signals in a process called **analog to digital conversion** FIGURE 19-18. To convert analog signals to digital binary information, special circuits, known as buffers or analog to digital (AD) converters, are used FIGURE 19-19. To convert an analog signal, the electronics do a couple of things. First, the changing analog signal is sampled or divided up into segments like a loaf of bread. In one second of time the varying analog signal could be sampled 10, 100, or even 1,000 times FIGURE 19-20. Each of these segments will represent a specific voltage value. The finer or more accurate the processor wants the data to be, the more frequent the sampling rate, resulting in better signal resolution or fidelity. Each of the segments will be assigned a digital value that is translated into a binary number. MP3 files are an example of an analog (wave file) to digital conversion. A digital wave file could be sampled 64K times a second or 128K times a second or more. The higher fidelity—the faithfulness to the original analog signal—is achieved at the more frequent sample rate.

TECHNICIAN TIP

The current used in the electronic control systems system is generally DC voltage. Radio frequency interference (RFI) induced into the system by magnetic fields of high-voltage power lines, radio transmitters, and even a microwave would be AC voltage. The signal processing systems of ECM input conditioning circuits generally recognize and ignore these types of signals. This does not mean all electromagnetic interference goes unnoticed. Magnetic fields can induce voltage in signal wires and cause confusion for signal processing units producing numerous types of unintended consequences.

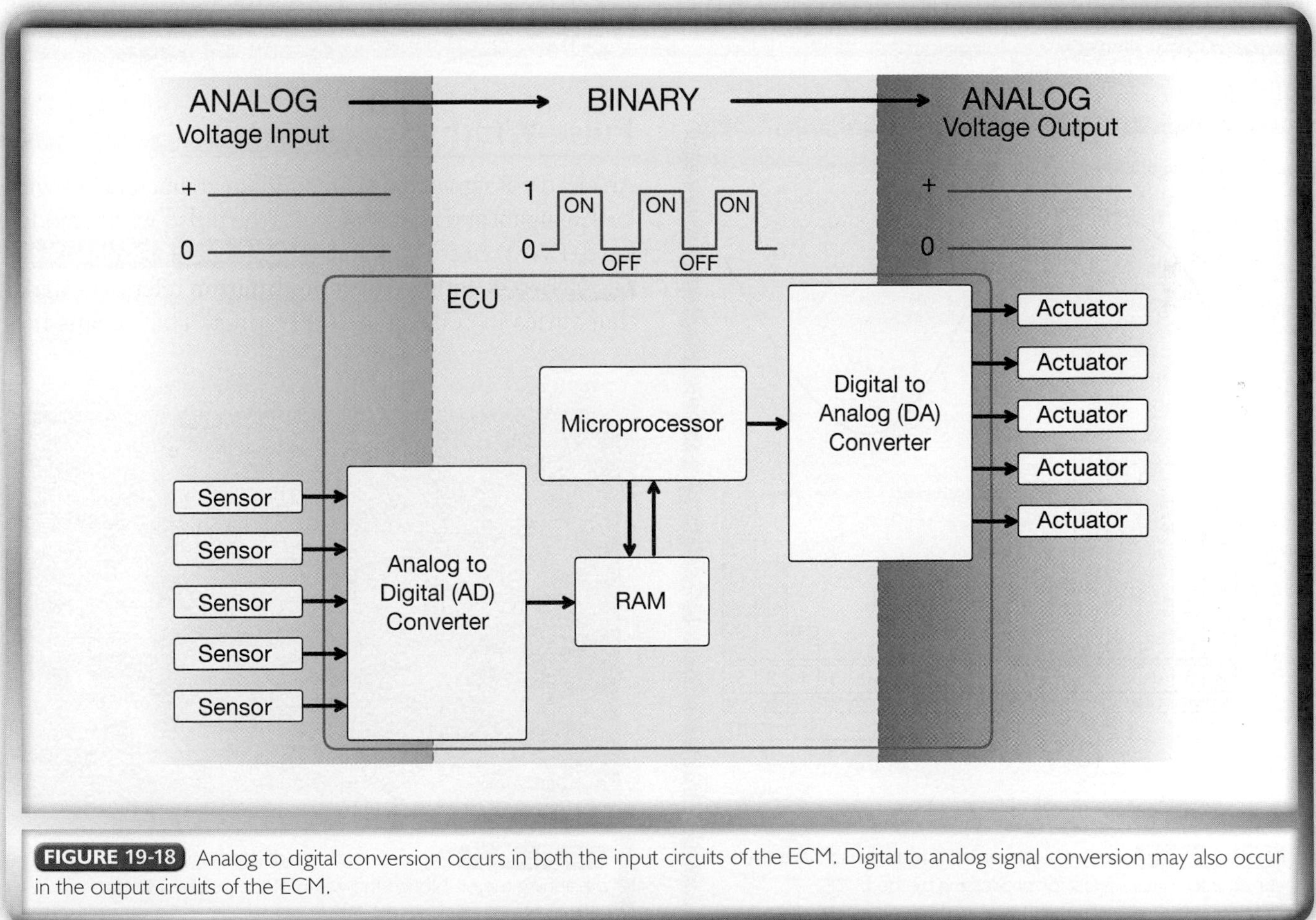

FIGURE 19-18 Analog to digital conversion occurs in both the input circuits of the ECM. Digital to analog signal conversion may also occur in the output circuits of the ECM.

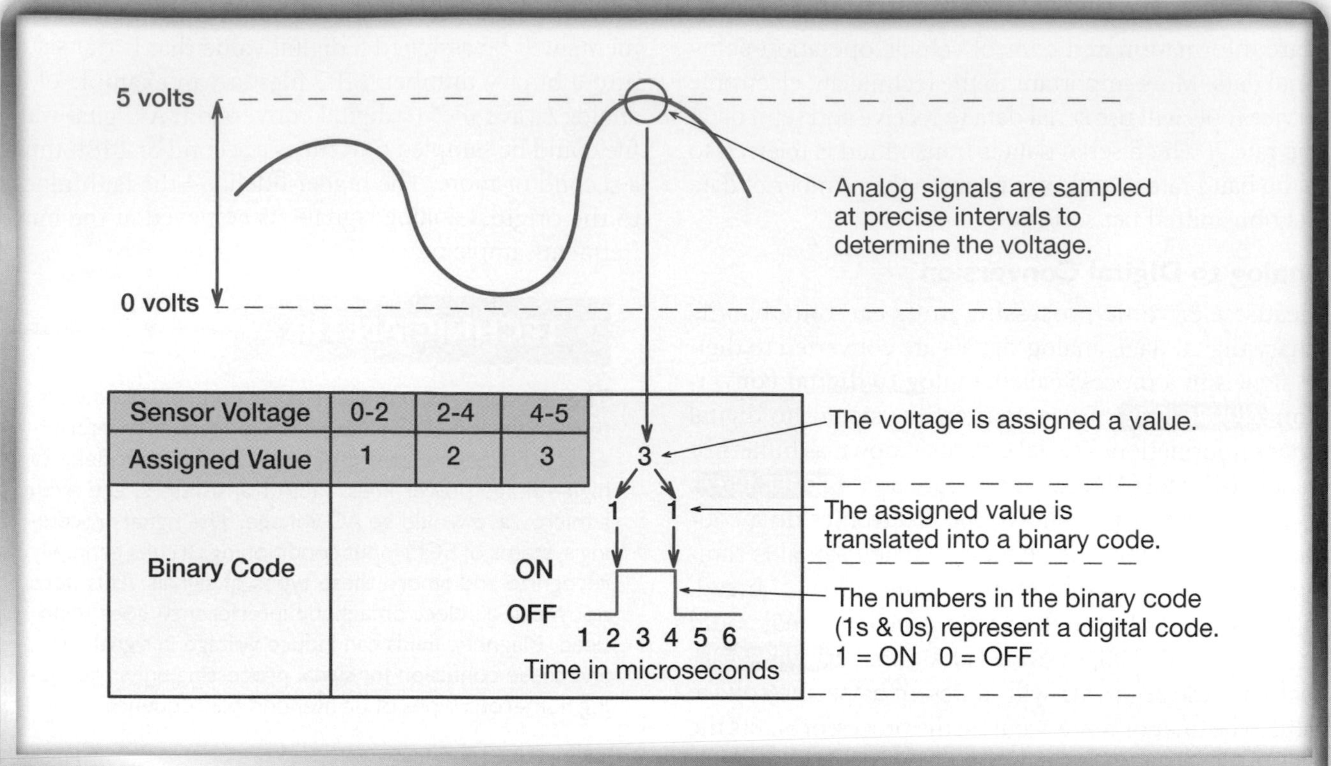

FIGURE 19-19 An analog to digital conversion. An analog waveform is sampled and measured many times a second to generate a digital representation of the waveform. This process is identical to forming an MP3 files. The more frequently the signal is sampled—128K, 256K, or more—the higher the signal quality.

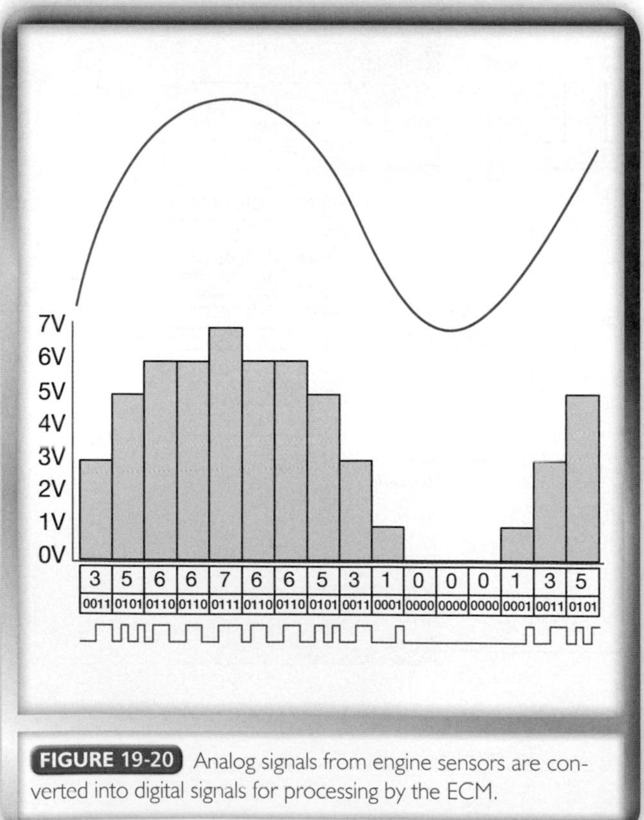

FIGURE 19-20 Analog signals from engine sensors are converted into digital signals for processing by the ECM.

Pulse-Width Modulation

An electrical signal that shares similar characteristics with both a digital and analog signal is the pulse-width-modulated (PWM) electrical signal **FIGURE 19-21**, **FIGURE 19-22**, **FIGURE 19-23**. **Pulse-width modulation** refers to a signal that varies in "ON" and "OFF" time. That means it is

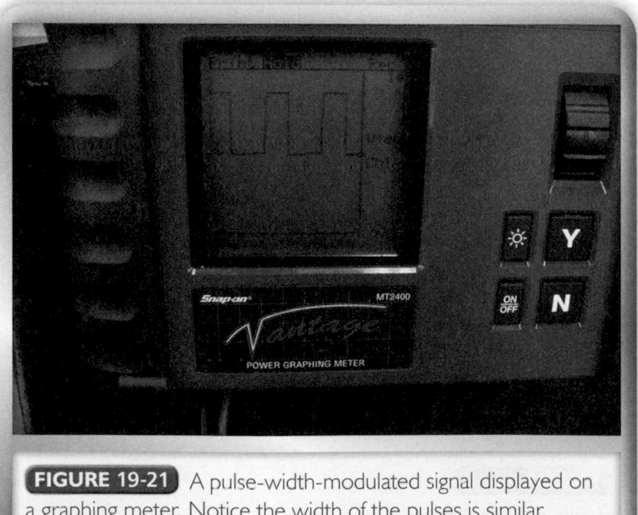

FIGURE 19-21 A pulse-width-modulated signal displayed on a graphing meter. Notice the width of the pulses is similar.

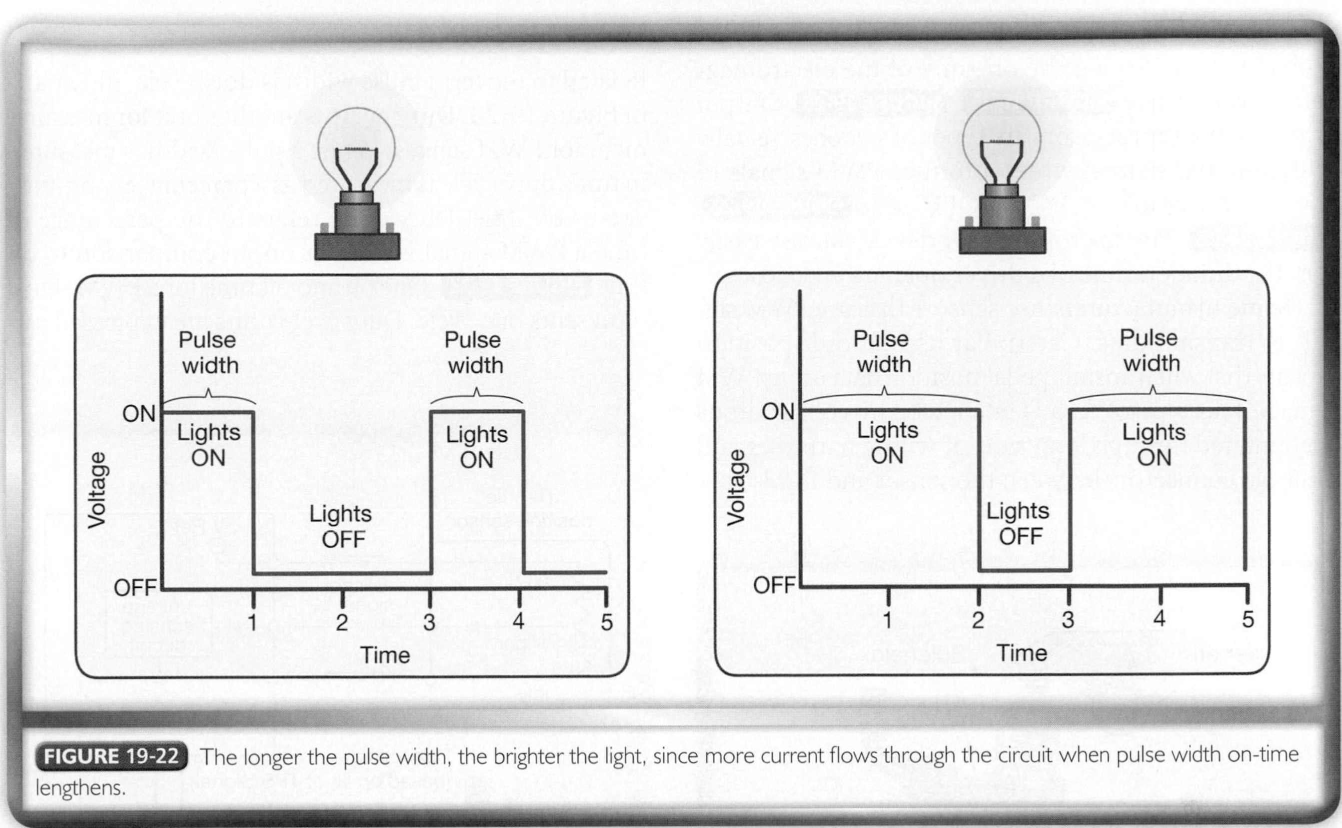

FIGURE 19-22 The longer the pulse width, the brighter the light, since more current flows through the circuit when pulse width on-time lengthens.

digital in one aspect because it represents data in two states only—either on or off, or high or low. However, information is also conveyed by the amount of time the signal stays on or off. Time on or off is variable, which gives it an analog characteristic. The units for measuring pulse width are always expressed in units of time. Time is the measure of how long the signal is high or on.

FIGURE 19-23 Duty cycle is a comparison of on time to off time in one cycle. A cycle can be 1 second, 500 msec, or any length of time, but the cycle time is fixed when measuring pulse width.

To understand PWM, consider a light illuminated by a PWM signal. In one second of time the light may be cycled on and off once. If the signal is applied for one-quarter of the second, the pulse width would be 0.25 seconds wide FIGURE 19-24.

Common examples of devices using PWM signals are solenoids, injectors, and light circuits. A PWM signal units of measurement are typically milliseconds. PWM signals are commonly used as an output signal of an ECM. For example, the current supplied to a fuel injector or

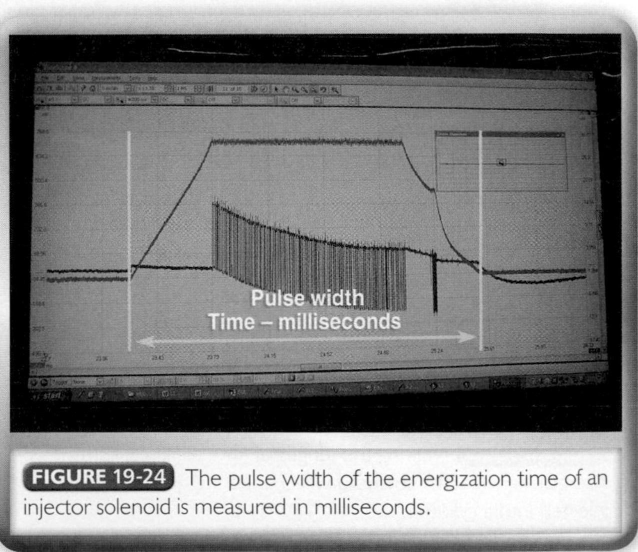

FIGURE 19-24 The pulse width of the energization time of an injector solenoid is measured in milliseconds.

the pressure regulator of a HEUI or common rail pump is changed by varying the on-time of the electromagnetic control valve FIGURE 19-25, FIGURE 19-26. Output drivers of microprocessors are types of switches, usually switching transistors, which produce PWM signals to operate devices in an "ON" or "OFF" state FIGURE 19-27, FIGURE 19-28. The microprocessor device can also easily vary the duration time of a driver opening and closing.

Some manufacturers use sensors that use PWM signals to transmit data. Caterpillar uses throttle position sensors that will transmit pedal position data using PWM signals. This type of data is unaffected by voltage drops encountered through long runs of wiring harnesses and multiple connectors between the sensor and ECM.

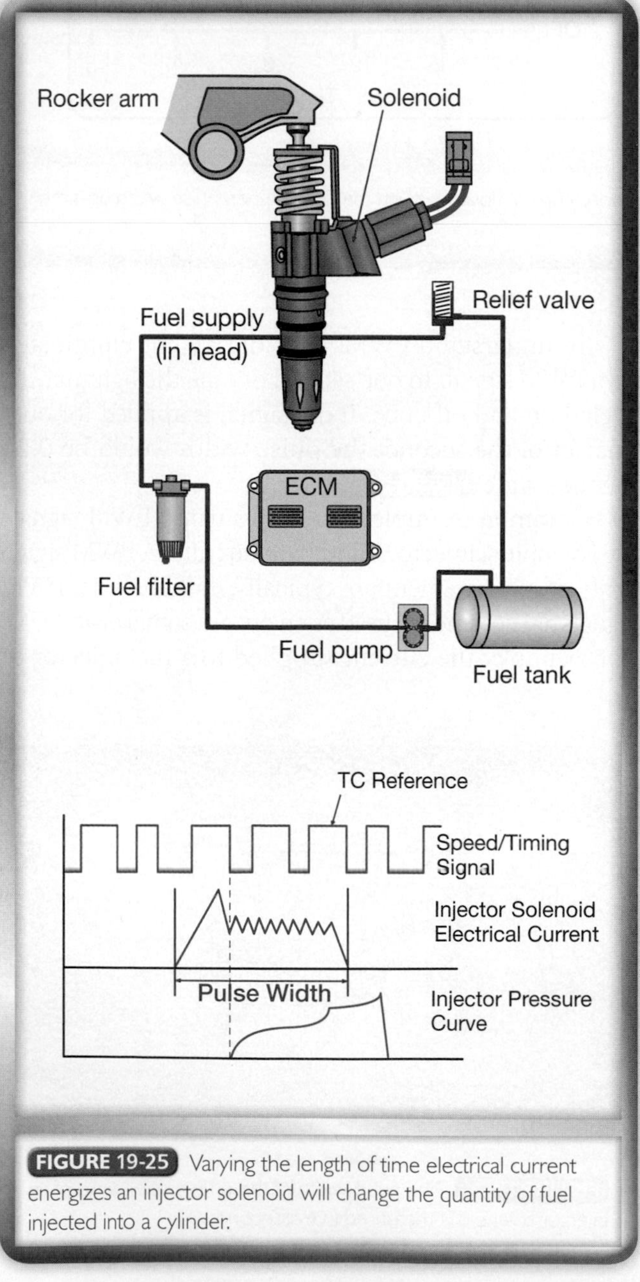

FIGURE 19-25 Varying the length of time electrical current energizes an injector solenoid will change the quantity of fuel injected into a cylinder.

Duty Cycle

Related to the term pulse width is duty cycle, illustrated in Figure 19-23. **Duty cycle** is another unit for measurement for PWM signals. While a pulse width is measured in time, duty cycle is measured as a percentage—on-time versus off time. Duty cycle refers to the percentage of time a PWM signal is high or on, in comparison to off time FIGURE 19-29. One on and off time for a PWM signal represents one cycle. Duty cycle units are expressed as a

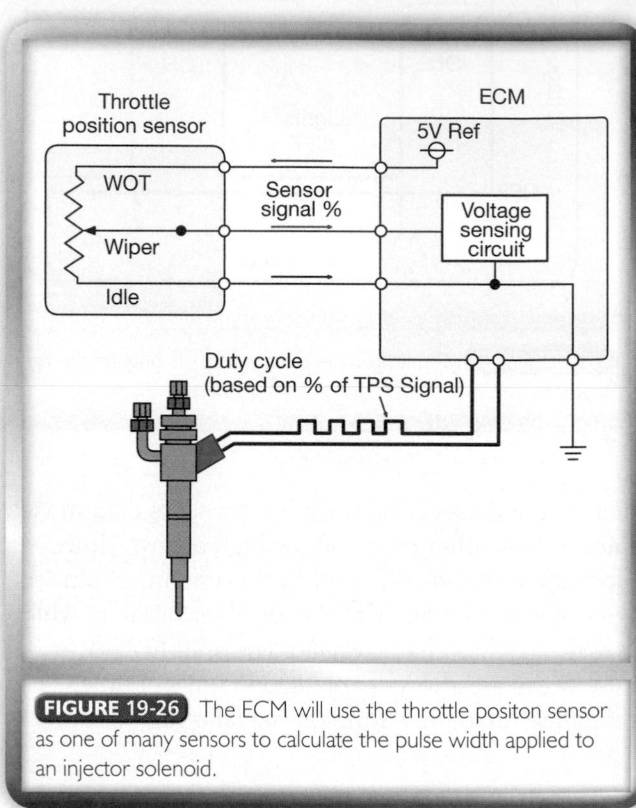

FIGURE 19-26 The ECM will use the throttle positon sensor as one of many sensors to calculate the pulse width applied to an injector solenoid.

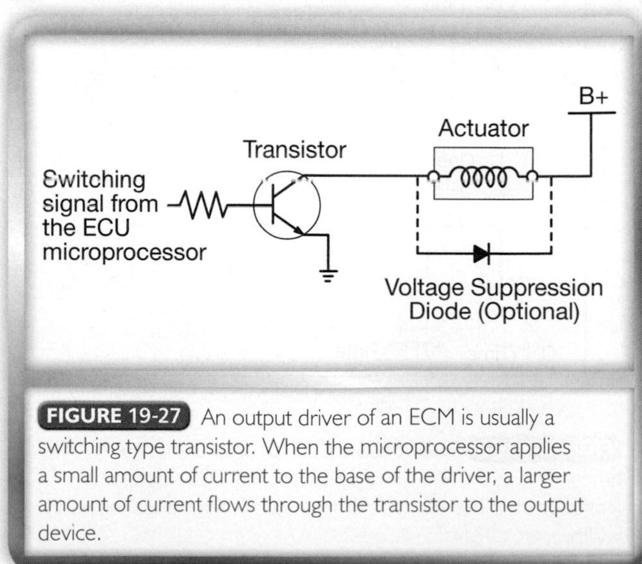

FIGURE 19-27 An output driver of an ECM is usually a switching type transistor. When the microprocessor applies a small amount of current to the base of the driver, a larger amount of current flows through the transistor to the output device.

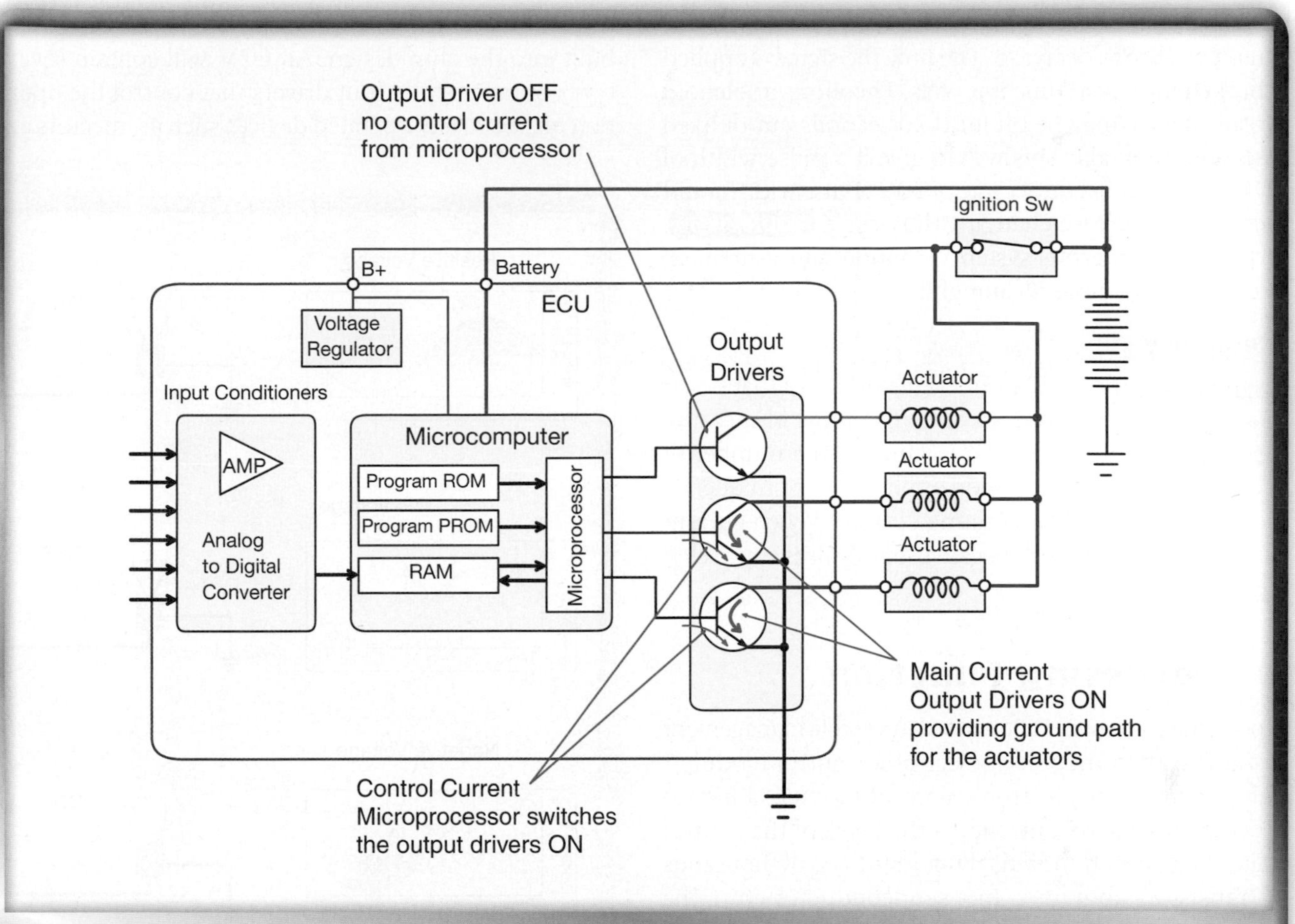

FIGURE 19-28 The microprocessor controls the operation of the output drivers, which switch current flow on and off to electrical devices.

percentage of cycle time. For example, if the pulse width is 0.8 seconds and the off time is 0.2 seconds, a cycle is 1 second in length. This means the duty cycle is 80%. A 100% duty cycle means the signal is on all the time, while a 0% duty cycle is off. Another way of expressing this relationship is signal off time versus on time. A signal that is applied for three-quarters of a cycle is 75% duty cycle.

What is different about duty cycle in comparison with PWM is where the signal is used. Duty cycle is commonly used to measure the time a signal is applied to an output device operating at a fixed frequency, whereas pulse width measures a signal applied to devices operating at a varying frequency interval. For example, an engine may speed up and slow down, so the pulse width or time an injector is energized will vary with speed. It is practical to measure actuation time only, since it is difficult to always know the frequency of a cycle—rpm, in this instance. Depending on engine speed, 10 or 20 injections may take place in 1 second, making it practical to only measure pulse width.

Consider however, an electrohydraulic pressure regulator. This device will have a PWM signal applied to close

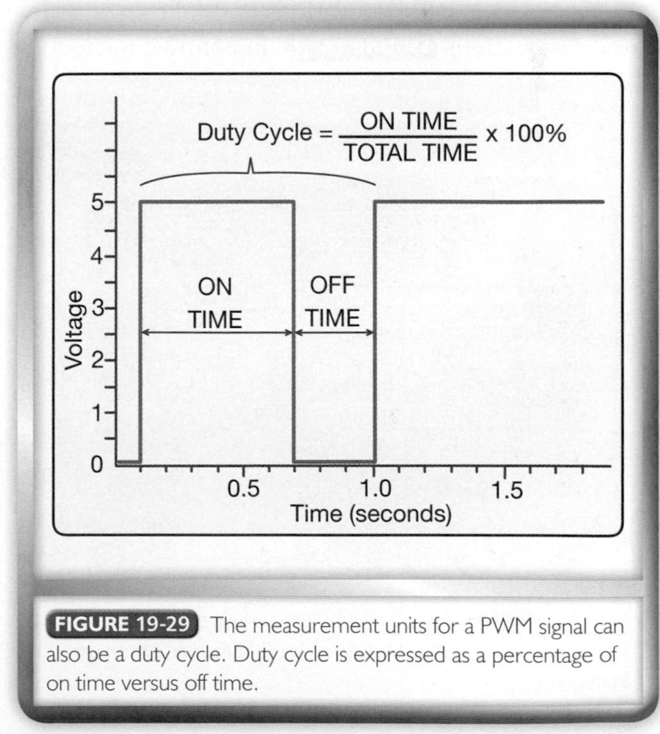

FIGURE 19-29 The measurement units for a PWM signal can also be a duty cycle. Duty cycle is expressed as a percentage of on time versus off time.

a valve and increase pressure. Removing the signal will cause pressure to decrease. The time the signal is applied is broken into fixed time intervals. Therefore, a solenoid for this device may be on for 0.20 seconds out of fixed 1 second intervals. This would give it a pulse width of 0.20 seconds but a duty cycle of 20%. Pulse width could increase or decrease changing duty cycle FIGURE 19-30. To practically interpret system operation, a measurement of duty cycle is more meaningful.

Frequency

Frequency is the number of events or cycles that occur in a period, usually one second. The units of measure for frequency are **hertz (Hz)**, which is the number of cycles per second. A common application for frequency measurements is for alternating current. When current switches from positive to negative, one cycle is completed FIGURE 19-31.

Processing Function

Processing electronic signals used in vehicle management systems is the function of electronic control modules. Referred to as the electronic control module, a microprocessor or microcontroller is the heart of the control unit. Made from hundreds if not hundreds of thousands of transistors contained in a semiconductor chip, the integrated circuit chips making up microprocessors and various controllers will contain a minimal amount of memory plus input and output circuits. Microprocessors have more memory, which gives them the capability to perform advanced calculations and follow software-based instructions FIGURE 19-32. In contrast microcontrollers are less capable, and carry out specific functions built into the chip design. An ECM will contain several types of memory, output drivers that control the operation of electrically operated devices such as injectors and

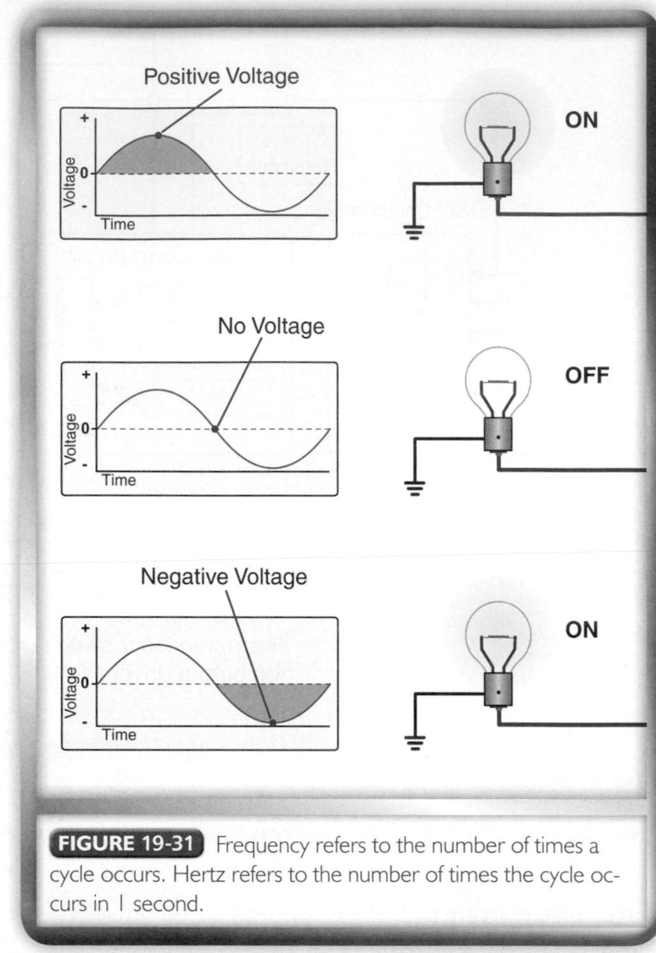

FIGURE 19-31 Frequency refers to the number of times a cycle occurs. Hertz refers to the number of times the cycle occurs in 1 second.

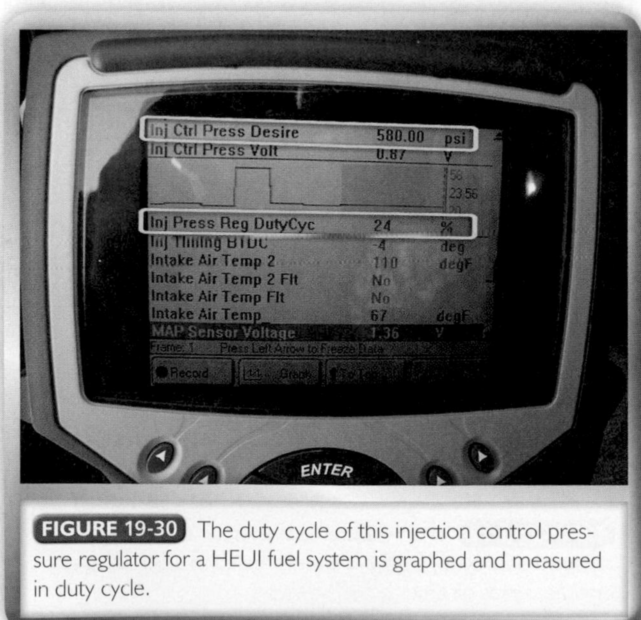

FIGURE 19-30 The duty cycle of this injection control pressure regulator for a HEUI fuel system is graphed and measured in duty cycle.

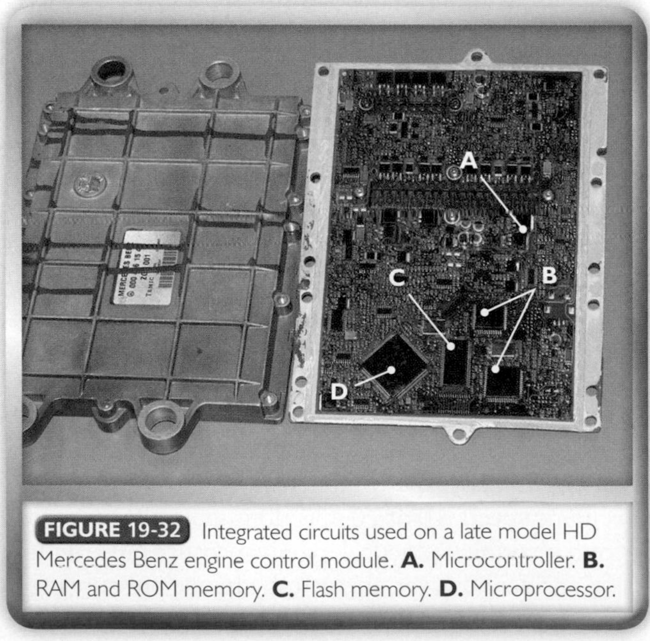

FIGURE 19-32 Integrated circuits used on a late model HD Mercedes Benz engine control module. **A.** Microcontroller. **B.** RAM and ROM memory. **C.** Flash memory. **D.** Microprocessor.

relays as well as complex signal conditioning circuits for information processing functions. An ECM will contain a transceiver which enables it to receive and send communication signals to an on-board vehicle network.

Several types of integrated circuit devices or "chips" are on-board a typical ECM, which are essential to processing and ECM operation:

- The clock
- Microprocessor
- Microcontrollers
- A-D converter
- Memory

CPU Clock

The clock is an oscillator inside the microprocessor that controls how fast instruction stored in memory are processed FIGURE 19-33. It is like the drum beat that controls the pace of the work in the microprocessor. The clock speed is measured in hertz (or megahertz, or gigahertz). With each cycle of the clock, the microprocessor will perform a set of tasks. Obviously, the faster the clock speed, the greater number of instructions processed per second.

Computer Memory

Several types of memory are used in an ECM depending on its application. Some memory is used to store data from sensors since the ECM cannot process all sensor data simultaneously FIGURE 19-34. Other types of memory are required to store the instructions for operating the microprocessor. This memory would store software code to give the ECM its unique operational characteristics. Common categories of memory include:

- Read only memory (ROM)
- Random access memory (RAM)
- **Programmable read only memory (PROM)**
- Electrically erasable programmable read only memory (EEPROM)
- Flash memory or nonvolatile RAM (NVRAM), which is a ROM/RAM hybrid that can be written to but which does not require power to maintain its contents

Read Only Memory (ROM)

Read only memory (ROM) is used for permanent storage of instructions and fixed values used by the ECM that control the microprocessor. Information stored in the

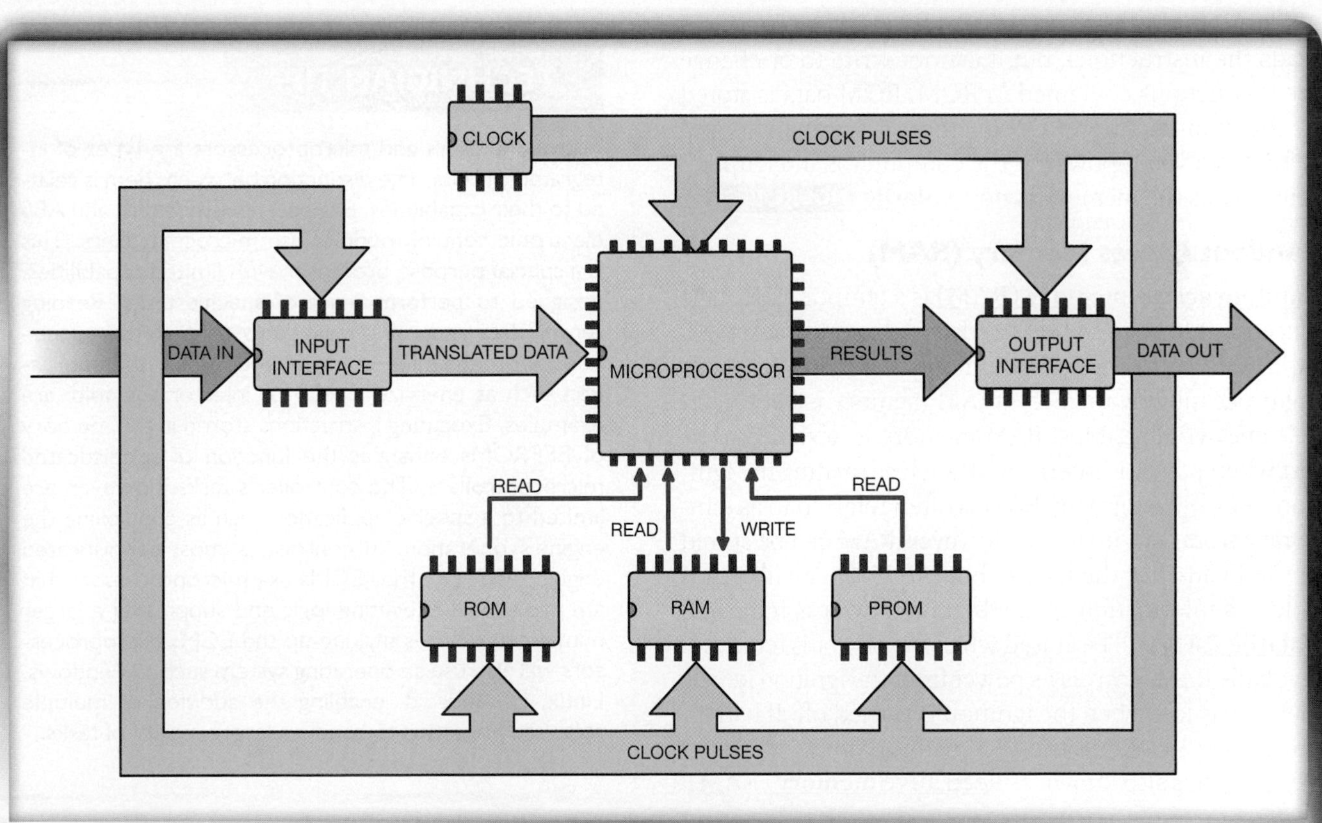

FIGURE 19-33 The CPU clock controls the pace of calculations inside the microprocessor. Each device inside the microprocessor waits for the clock to signal the executions of a particular instruction.

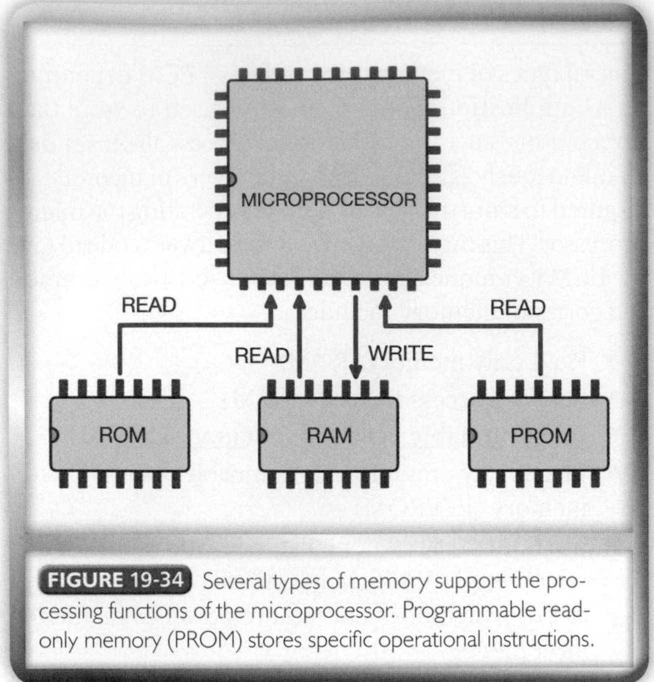

FIGURE 19-34 Several types of memory support the processing functions of the microprocessor. Programmable read-only memory (PROM) stores specific operational instructions.

ROM would include algorithms such as how to calculate the pulse width for the injectors or the horsepower ratings for the vehicle. Other fixed values would identify a maximum engine rpm, the temperature value for an engine overheat condition, or the type of transmission. The ECM reads the instructions, but it cannot write to or change the instructions contained in ROM. ROM data is stored by the manufacturer. ROM memory is permanent and is not lost even if power to the computer is interrupted. This means the memory is **non-volatile** **FIGURE 19-35**.

Random Access Memory (RAM)

Random access memory (RAM) is a temporary storage place for information that needs to be quickly accessed. Input data from sensors is commonly stored in RAM waiting processing by the ECM. RAM memory is both readable and writable. Most RAM memory is designed to be lost when power is interrupted, such as turning the ignition key off. That is why RAM is often referred to as temporary storage of memory. However, RAM can be stored in the ECM after the key is shut off. Non-volatile RAM holds its information even when the power is removed. **Volatile RAM** will be erased when the power is removed. If volatile RAM receives its power from the ignition key, its memory is lost when the ignition is turned off. If battery power is used to keep the RAM memory intact when the key is off, it is also known as **keep alive memory (KAM)**.

EEPROM and Flash Memory

Electrically erasable programmable read only memory (EEPROM) was developed to allow manufacturers to change the software operating the ECM electronically rather than physically fix it into the ECM during its design and construction.

In recent years flash memory, which is non-volatile, is EEPROM memory. This is almost identical to the type used on a USB memory stick. It has enormous shock resistance and durability and is able to withstand intense pressure, extremes of temperature, and immersion in water, which are conditions found in commercial vehicles. It also offers the convenience of easily reprogramming or recalibrating the ECM, also known as **flashing** or flash programming. Flash programming involves the installation of look-up tables in the ECM. Look-up tables are used by the ECM to solve mathematical problems called algorithms. An example of a simple algorithm would solve the problem of how fast is the vehicle traveling. The mathematical formal for speed would be distance/time. More complex algorithms involve calculating how much fuel to inject, when to inject fuel, or how long the injector should be energized. The look-up table provides specific data to help solve the problems for a specific engine.

TECHNICIAN TIP

Microcontrollers and microprocessors are types of integrated circuits. The distinction between them is related to their capabilities. Engines, transmissions, and ABS electronic control modules use microcontrollers. This is a special purpose processor with limited capabilities, designed to perform a set of specific tasks. Reading sensor data and using logic gates to perform calculations and determine outputs required for the application such as energize a relay or injector solenoid, are examples. Executing instructions stored in the memory of EEPROMs enhances the function of sophisticated microcontrollers. The controller's tasks, however, are limited to a specific application such as controlling the engine's operation. In contrast, a most sophisticated engine, ABS, or other ECMs use microprocessors that are capable of executing logic and supporting a larger number of devices making-up the ECM. Microprocessors will also use an operating system such as Windows, Linux, or Android, enabling the addition of multiple software programs to handle a larger variety of tasks.

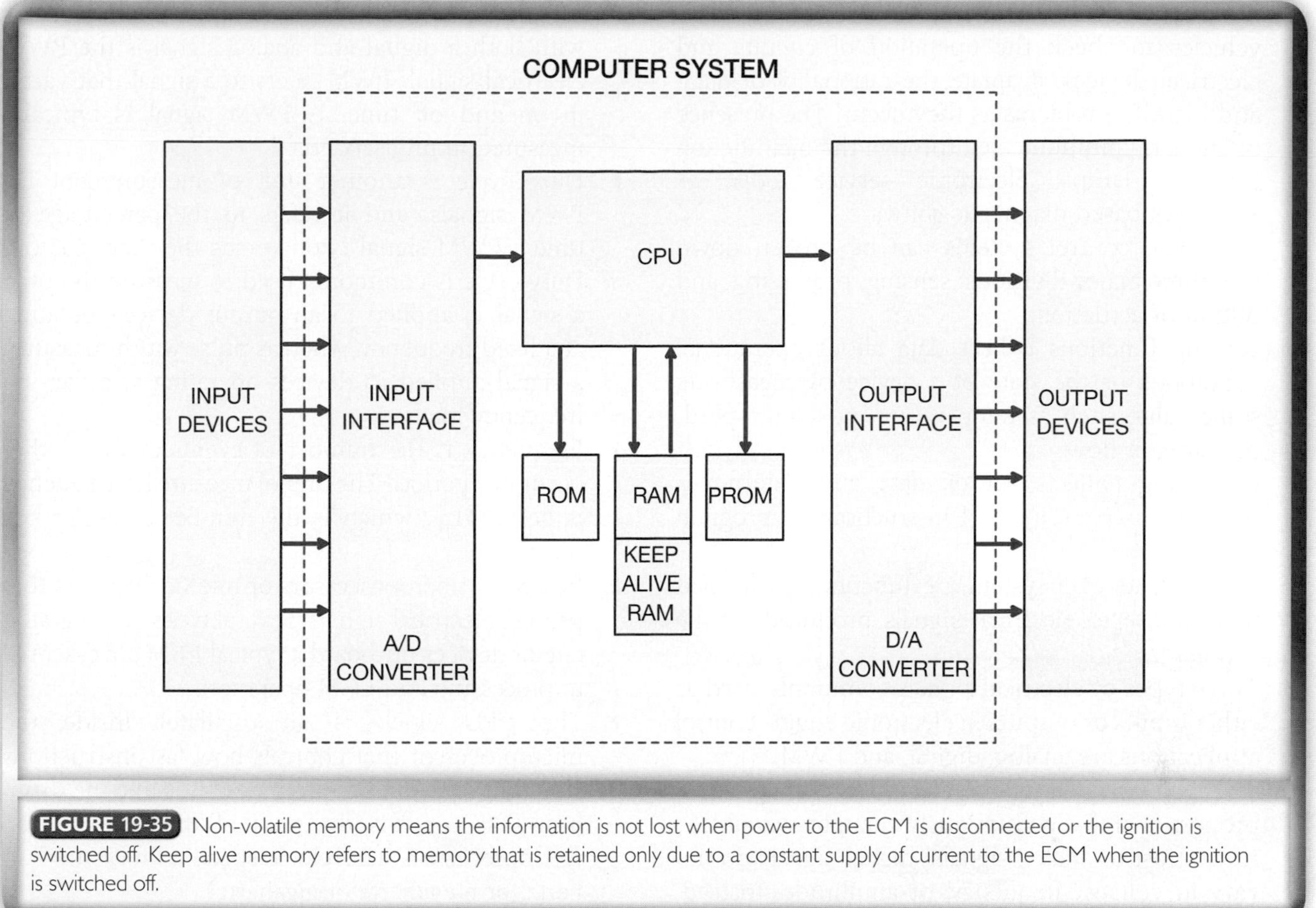

FIGURE 19-35 Non-volatile memory means the information is not lost when power to the ECM is disconnected or the ignition is switched off. Keep alive memory refers to memory that is retained only due to a constant supply of current to the ECM when the ignition is switched off.

Wrap-up

Ready for Review

- Electronic systems using microprocessor- and microcontroller-based control provide operational capabilities far exceeding any mechanical system. The dominance and sophistication of electronic control makes skill development related to servicing this technology one of the most important priorities for successful technicians.
- Diesel engines were the first commercial vehicle systems transformed by electronic controls. The immediate benefits of these refinements to power train control include lower engine emissions, improved fuel economy, increased reliability, and enhanced performance.
- Service technicians, particularly in fleet operations using medium-duty engines, can access a wealth of diagnostic and service information much faster and with more precise detail than before.
- Telematics, a branch of information technology, uses specialized applications for long-distance transmission of information to and from a vehicle. Messages can be sent back and forth between the vehicle and a central dispatch location.
- The use of electronic engine and vehicle management provides for enhanced vehicle and occupant safety and security.
- Programmable software provides flexibility to engines, transmissions, and body accessories to adapt to; adaptation to specific job applications; and enhanced vehicle productivity, longevity, and driver comfort. Programmable features include idle shut-down timers, cruise control, maximum vehicle speed limits, and safety interlocks that prevent the vehicle from moving if a door is open, a boom is raised, or outriggers are extended.

- Built-in electronic management systems allow vehicles to check the operation of circuits and electrical devices, evaluate the rationality of data, and identify problems as they occur. The presence of faults is communicated through the malfunction indicator lamps, electronic service tools, or Windows-based diagnostic software.
- Electronic control systems can be broken down into three major divisions: sensing, processing, and output or actuation.
- Sensing functions collect data about operational conditions or the state of a device by measuring some value such as temperature, position, speed, pressure, or flow.
- Processing collects sensor data and determines outputs based on a set of instructions or program software.
- The outputs of a system are functions performed in response to electrical signals produced by the processor.
- Three types of electrical signals commonly used as either inputs or outputs in electronic engine control applications are analog, digital, and PWM.
- An analog signal is an electric current that is proportional to a continuously changing variable.
- In contrast to analog signals, digital signals do not vary in voltage, frequency, or amplitude. Instead, they are electrical signals that represent data as binary values, such as on-off, 0 or 1, yes-no, up-down, open-closed, and so on.
- Binary code is an example of a digital signal. "Bit" is a shortened term for binary digit. This is the smallest piece of digital or binary information and is represented by a single 0 or 1. A byte is a combination of 8 bits.
- Serial data is used to transmit information from one electronic module to another. On-board data networks share information and control vehicle operation using serial data.
- Because electronic processing units can only handle binary digital data, analog signals are converted to digital signals by special circuits known as buffers or AD converters.
- An electrical signal that shares similar characteristics with both a digital and analog signal is the PWM electrical signal. PWM refers to a signal that varies in on and off time. A PWM signal is typically measured in milliseconds.
- Duty cycle is another unit of measurement for PWM signals, and it refers to the percentage of time a PWM signal is on versus the time it is off. Duty cycle is commonly used to measure the time a signal is applied to an output device operating at a fixed frequency, whereas pulse width measures a signal applied to devices operating at a varying frequency interval.
- Frequency is the number of events or cycles that occur in a period. The unit of measure for frequency is hertz (Hz), which is the number of cycles per second.
- ECMs are microprocessors or microcontrollers that process electrical signals. Several types of integrated circuit devices on-board a typical ECM are essential to processing and ECM operation.
- The CPU clock is an oscillator inside the microprocessor that controls how fast instructions stored in memory are processed. It is like the drum beat that controls the pace of the work in the microprocessor. The clock speed is measured in hertz (or megahertz or gigahertz).
- Several types of memory are used in an ECM, depending on its application. Some memory is used to store data from sensors because the ECM cannot process all sensor data simultaneously. Other types of memory are required to store the instructions for operating the microprocessor.
- Common categories of memory include ROM, RAM, PROM, EEPROM, and flash memory (a ROM/RAM hybrid that can be written to but does not require power to maintain its contents).

Vocabulary Builder

analog signal An electric current that is proportional to a continuously changing variable.

analog to digital conversion The process when an analog waveform is sampled and measured many times a second to generate a digital representation of the waveform.

baud rate The rate at which serial data is transmitted.

bit The smallest piece of digital information that is either a 1 or 0.

byte A unit of 8 bits.

differential voltage Refers to the voltage difference on a wire pair when one wires voltage is the mirror opposite voltage. A wide separation between the voltage pulses represents a 1 and a narrow separation represents a 0.

digital signals Electrical signals that represent data in discrete, finite values. Digital signals are considered as binary meaning it is either on or off, yes or no, high or low, 0 or 1.

duty cycle The percentage of time a PWM signal is ON in comparison to OFF time.

electrically erasable read only memory (EEPROM) Non-volatile memory technology that is used to store operating instructions or programming for an ECM.

flashing Reprogramming or recalibrating the ECM. Information is stored in the ECMs memory.

frequency The number of events or cycles that occur in a period, usually 1 second.

hertz (Hz) The unit for electrical frequency measurement, in cycles per second.

keep alive memory (KAM) Memory that is retained by the ECM when the key is off.

microcontroller A special-purpose processor with limited capabilities, designed to perform a set of specific tasks.

non-volatile memory Memory that is not lost when power is removed or lost.

programmable read only memory (PROM) Memory that stores programming information and cannot be easily written over.

pulse-width modulation (PWM) An electrical signal that varies in on and off time.

random access memory (RAM) A temporary storage place for information that needs to be quickly accessed.

read only memory (ROM) Memory used for permanent storage of instructions and fixed values used by the ECM that control the microprocessor.

telematics A branch of information technology that uses specialized applications for long-distance transmission of information to and from a vehicle.

volatile memory A type of data storage that is lost or erased when the ignition power is switched off.

Review Questions

1. Which of the following is a benefit of electronic control?
   a. Increased power and efficiency
   b. Programmable features
   c. Self-diagnostic capabilities
   d. All of the choices are correct.

2. Which of the following statements about information reporting capabilities is correct?
   a. Life cycle cost of operating vehicles with these engines is further reduced through the ability of the engine control systems to interface with tablets and diagnostic and service software.
   b. Service technicians can access a wealth of diagnostic and service data much faster and with precise detail than before.
   c. Trip reports from the vehicle ECM extracted during scheduled maintenance intervals report details such as diagnostic fault codes, fuel consumption, idle time, emission system performance, and vehicle abuse.
   d. All of the choices are correct.

3. Which of the following statements about safety is correct?
   a. If a vehicle is involved in a collision, a call can be made to an emergency dispatch.
   b. Engine systems can be monitored for operating conditions having destructive potential.
   c. Hard braking and speeding are other measurable conditions monitored by management systems to ensure road safety.
   d. All of the choices are correct.

4. Which of the following is NOT correct concerning self-diagnostic capabilities?
   a. Diagnostics on electronically controlled vehicle systems can be performed easily, often with fewer tools and in less time than on mechanical systems.
   b. The presence of faults is unable to be communicated through the malfunction indicator lamps.
   c. Electronic service tools assist the technicians in performing off-board diagnostics, that is, performing pinpoint checks to precisely identify system faults.
   d. As modules, sensors, and actuators are more compact, they can be replaced quickly with minimal training and experience required.

5. What type of data is collected by the sensing functions of the electronic control system?
   a. Temperature
   b. Pressure
   c. Both A and B
   d. Neither A nor B

6. What are some examples of outputs of the electronic control assembly?
   a. Current to operate solenoids or injectors
   b. Current to operate actuators
   c. Current to operate lights
   d. All of the choices are correct.

7. Analog signals will have a changing value of:
   a. voltage.
   b. amperage frequency.
   c. amplitude.
   d. All of the choices are correct.

8. A bit, is a shortened term for binary digit; a byte is a combination of ________ bits.
   a. 2
   b. 4
   c. 6
   d. 8

9. Which of the following statements about analog to digital conversion is correct?
   a. Because electronic processing units can only handle binary digital data, analog signals are converted to digital signals.
   b. To convert analog signals to digital binary information, special circuits, known as buffers, or analog to digital (AD) converters, are used.
   c. Both A and B
   d. Neither A nor B

10. Which of the following is NOT correct concerning duty cycle?
    a. Duty cycle is another unit for measurement for PWM signals.
    b. Duty cycle units are expressed as a percentage of cycle time.
    c. A 100% duty cycle means the signal is off.
    d. Duty cycle refers to the percentage of time a PWM signal is high or on in comparison to off time.

ASE-Type Questions

1. Technician A says that not a single vehicle system operates without at least some degree of electronic control. Technician B says that understanding the operating principles of electronic control systems is fundamental for choosing diagnostic strategies. Who is correct?
   a. Technician A
   b. Technician B
   c. Both Technician A and Technician B
   d. Neither Technician A nor Technician B
2. Technician A says that diesel engines were the first commercial vehicle systems transformed by electronic controls. Technician B says that smarter engines deliver ever-increasing power from smaller displacements. Who is correct?
   a. Technician A
   b. Technician B
   c. Both Technician A and Technician B
   d. Neither Technician A nor Technician B
3. Technician A says that telematics uses specialized telecommunication applications for long-distance transmission of information to and from a vehicle. Technician B says that telematics is not capable of transmitting information on fault codes. Who is correct?
   a. Technician A
   b. Technician B
   c. Both Technician A and Technician B
   d. Neither Technician A nor Technician B
4. Technician A says that technicians can take advantage of programmable electronic controls. Technician B says that power and torque rise profiles are easily altered electronically. Who is correct?
   a. Technician A
   b. Technician B
   c. Both Technician A and Technician B
   d. Neither Technician A nor Technician B
5. Technician A says that electronic control systems use a variety of sensors, wires, electrical actuators, and electronic modules moved with invisible electrical signals. Technician B says that the three major divisions of electronic control systems are sensing, processing, and output. Who is correct?
   a. Technician A
   b. Technician B
   c. Both Technician A and Technician B
   d. Neither Technician A nor Technician B
6. Technician A says that processing refers to the control system element that collects sensor data and determines outputs based on a set of instructions or program software. Technician B says that operational algorithms are included in the software that determines the steps taken when processing electrical data. Who is correct?
   a. Technician A
   b. Technician B
   c. Both Technician A and Technician B
   d. Neither Technician A nor Technician B
7. Technician A says that an analog signal is one type of electrical signal commonly used in electronic engine control applications. Technician B says that a tandem signal is one type of electrical signal commonly used in electronic engine control applications. Who is correct?
   a. Technician A
   b. Technician B
   c. Both Technician A and Technician B
   d. Neither Technician A nor Technician B
8. Technician A says that, in contrast to analog signals, digital signals do not vary in voltage, frequency, or amplitude. Technician B says that the binary code does not lend itself to use in microprocessor circuits where processing large amounts of alphabetic or numerical data, represented in strings of 0s or 1s, is performed. Who is correct?
   a. Technician A
   b. Technician B
   c. Both Technician A and Technician B
   d. Neither Technician A nor Technician B
9. Technician A says that serial data is used to transmit information from one electronic module to another. Technician B says that baud rate refers to the number of data bits transmitted per minute. Who is correct?
   a. Technician A
   b. Technician B
   c. Both Technician A and Technician B
   d. Neither Technician A nor Technician B
10. Technician A says that a pulse-width-modulated electrical signal is an electrical signal that shares similar characteristics with both a digital and analog signal. Technician B says that common examples of devices using PWM signals are solenoids, injectors, and light circuits. Who is correct?
    a. Technician A
    b. Technician B
    c. Both Technician A and Technician B
    d. Neither Technician A nor Technician B

CHAPTER 20

NATEF Tasks

Diesel Engines

General

	Page
■ Check and record electronic diagnostic codes.	588

Fuel System—Electronic Fuel Management System

■ Inspect and test switches, sensors, controls, actuator components, and circuits; adjust or replace as needed.	583–587

Electrical/Electronic Systems

General Electrical Systems

■ Check applied voltages, circuit voltages, and voltage drops in electrical/electronic circuits using appropriate test equipment.	586
■ Check continuity in electrical/electronic circuits using appropriate test equipment.	591

Sensors

Knowledge Objectives

After reading this chapter, you will be able to:

1. Identify and describe the operating strategies of electronic signal processing systems used in electrical system control on commercial vehicles. (pp 560–577)
2. Identify and describe the functions, construction, and application of electronic sensors used to produce electrical signals for electronic control systems. (pp 560–577)
3. Recommend and describe diagnostic procedures for sensors used in electronic control systems. (pp 579–590)

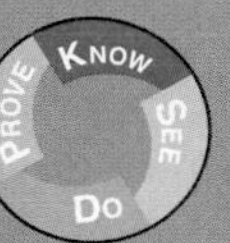

Skills Objectives

There are no skills objectives for this chapter.

Introduction

Devices that convert one form of energy into another are called transducers. Sensors are a type of transducer that convert physical conditions or states into electrical data. Pressure, temperature, angle, speed, mass, etc. are just a few of the changing physical variables about which sensors supply electrical data to processors. A distinction is made between sending units and sensors. Sensors provide information to electronic control units, whereas sending units provide information to instrument gauges.

Types of Sensors

An enormous number of sensor types exist to measure diverse types of data required by increasingly sophisticated vehicle management systems.

- Accelerometers for vehicle dynamic control and airbags
- Pressure sensors for engine oil, fuel, crankcase, and intake boost
- Position sensors for wheel speed, camshafts, crankshafts, and pedal position
- Humidity sensors for adjusting air–fuel ratio control and cabin comfort control
- Sunlight and rain/moisture sensors
- Distance sensors for near obstacle detection and collision avoidance
- Magnetoresistive (MR) sensors that use the earth's magnetic field to operate vehicle electronic compasses and navigation systems
- Torque sensors
- Fuel level sensors
- Oil quality sensors
- Temperature sensors
- Coolant level sensors
- Barometric pressure sensors
- Mass airflow sensors
- Engine knock sensors
- Exhaust gas – NO_X, ammonia, and oxygen sensors
- Yaw sensors using the Coriolis effect to sense yaw rates
- Global positioning sensors for GPS

Active Versus Passive Sensors

All the types of sensors listed above are more simply classified other ways. For example, a sensor is considered active or passive depending on whether they use power supplied by the electronic control module (ECM) to operate. **Active sensors** use a current supplied by the ECM to operate while **passive sensors** do not FIGURE 20-1.

You Are the Technician

A customer has brought a truck to your shop complaining that the engine will occasionally not accelerate. Sometimes, after the throttle pedal is pushed multiple times, the engine will only idle. Other times the engine drops to idle while the vehicle is moving in traffic. Sometimes the problem corrects itself after the ignition key is cycled; other times the throttle starts operating correctly on its own. After checking for fault codes, you learn the truck has had codes erased at another shop. You suspect the problem is in the accelerator position sensor (APS), but you wonder if the problem could be in the wiring or the fuel system, or if it's a power derate condition caused by some other fault. After carefully inspecting the wiring harness and connectors to the APS, you believe they are in good condition. You connect a software-based vehicle diagnostic program to the vehicle data link to monitor the APS. There are three APS signals displayed with different voltages on each sensor. Consider the following as you proceed:

1. Does this APS use an idle validation switch?
2. What complaint would the driver have if one, two, or three of the APS voltages were incorrect?
3. How will you determine if the APS has a fault?

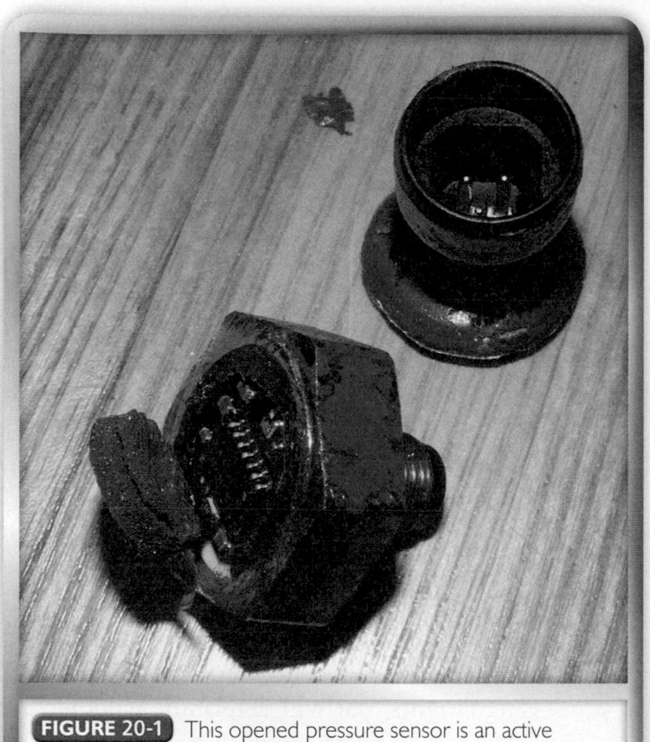

FIGURE 20-1 This opened pressure sensor is an active sensor. Note the integrated circuit used to change the sensed physical data into an electrical signal used by the ECM.

Other classifications of sensors include:

- Resistive sensors: rheostats, potentiometers, thermistors, piezoresistive sensors, Wheatstone bridge pressure sensors
- Voltage generators: oxygen sensors, NO_X sensors, ammonia sensors, variable reluctance sensors, piezoelectric sensors
- Switches
- Variable capacitance pressure sensors

Reference Voltage

Reference voltage (Vref) refers to a precisely regulated voltage supplied by the ECM to sensors. Reference voltage value is typically 5 volts direct current (VDC), but some manufacturers use 8 or 12 volts. The use of a reference voltage is important in processor operation, because the value of the variable resistor can be calculated by measuring voltage drop when another resistor with a known voltage input is connected in series with it. In **FIGURE 20-2**, +5Vref is used in the calculations performed by an ECM. Reference voltage also supplies active sensors with current to operate integrated circuits contained inside the sensor. Switches will also use +5Vref to signal the ECM.

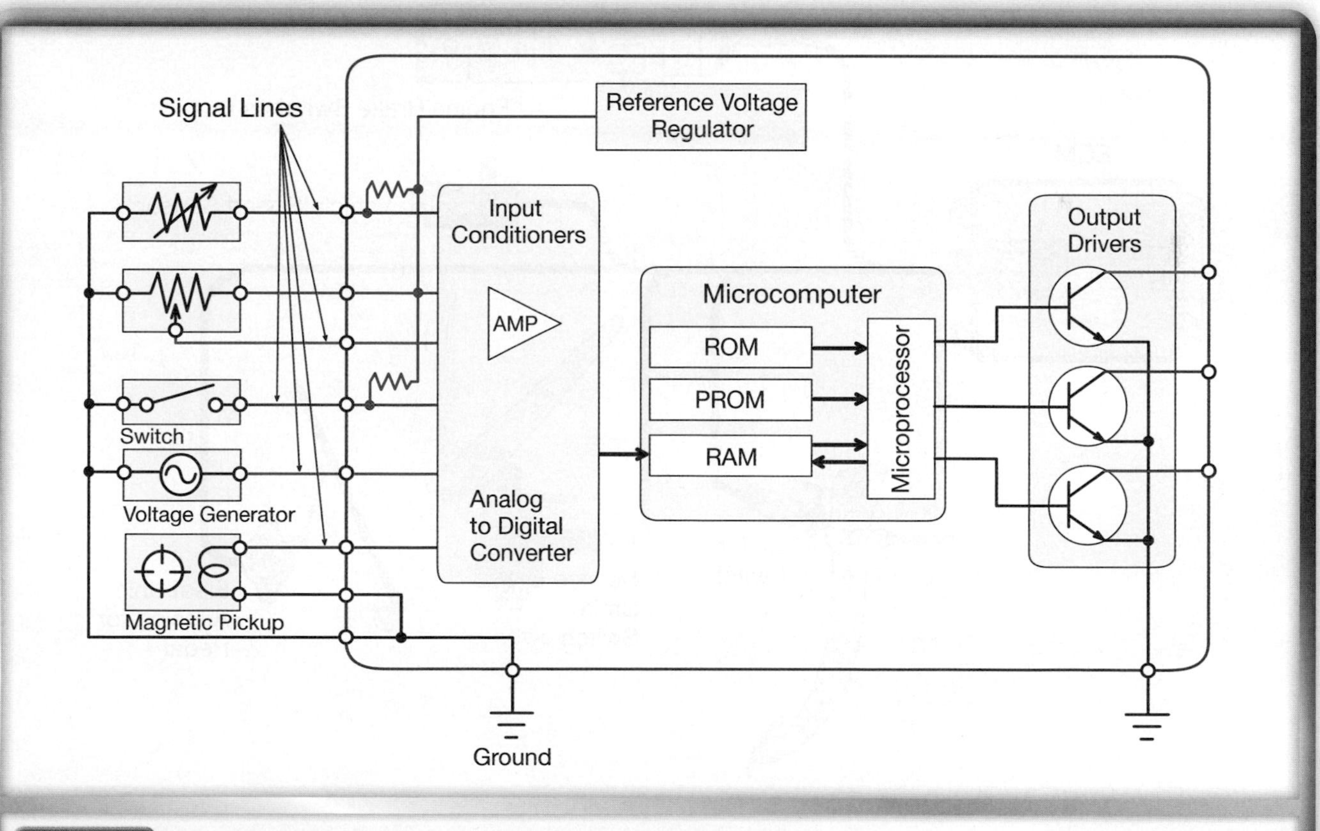

FIGURE 20-2 Reference voltage is supplied to power active sensors and to accurately calculate voltage drop across the sensor. The resistor in series with the reference voltage also limits current to the sensors.

Switches as Sensors

Switches are the simplest sensors of all, because they have no resistance in the closed position and infinite resistance in the open position. Switches are categorized as sensors whenever they provide information to an electronic control system. The data may indicate a physical value such as open or closed, up or down, high or low (e.g., a coolant level sensor or oil pressure switch), or it may indicate on and off (e.g., a brake light switch).

Switches as Digital Signals

The simplest digital signal is a single pole single throw (SPST) switch. It is found in either an open or closed state. The on/off, open/closed state data provided by this switch can provide input information to an ECM required for decision making. For example, the decision to start an engine based on whether a transmission is in neutral or the clutch is disengaged depends on the signal from a switch FIGURE 20-3. A zero-volt signal would present as an open switch, while twelve volts would present as a closed switch. Ignition, brake, or door switches provide similar data to ECMs to answer simple yes or no, open or closed, on or off questions posed by operating software.

Pull-Up and Pull-Down Switches

Switches are further categorized by their connection to a current source and the ECM. When the switch is connected between the ECM and a battery positive, the switch it is known as a **pull-up switch** FIGURE 20-4. A circuit inside the module monitoring the switch connection will measure the voltage drop across a fixed resistor inside the ECM. The voltage data will provide information to processing circuits that will determine whether the circuit or switch is open, closed, out of range, or shorted to ground.

A **pull-down switch** is connected between the ECM and a negative ground current potential FIGURE 20-5. When the switch is closed, ground current will flow into the ECM. A circuit inside the ECM monitoring the switch connection will also measure voltage drop across a fixed resistor. Once again, voltage data will provide information to processing circuits that will determine whether the

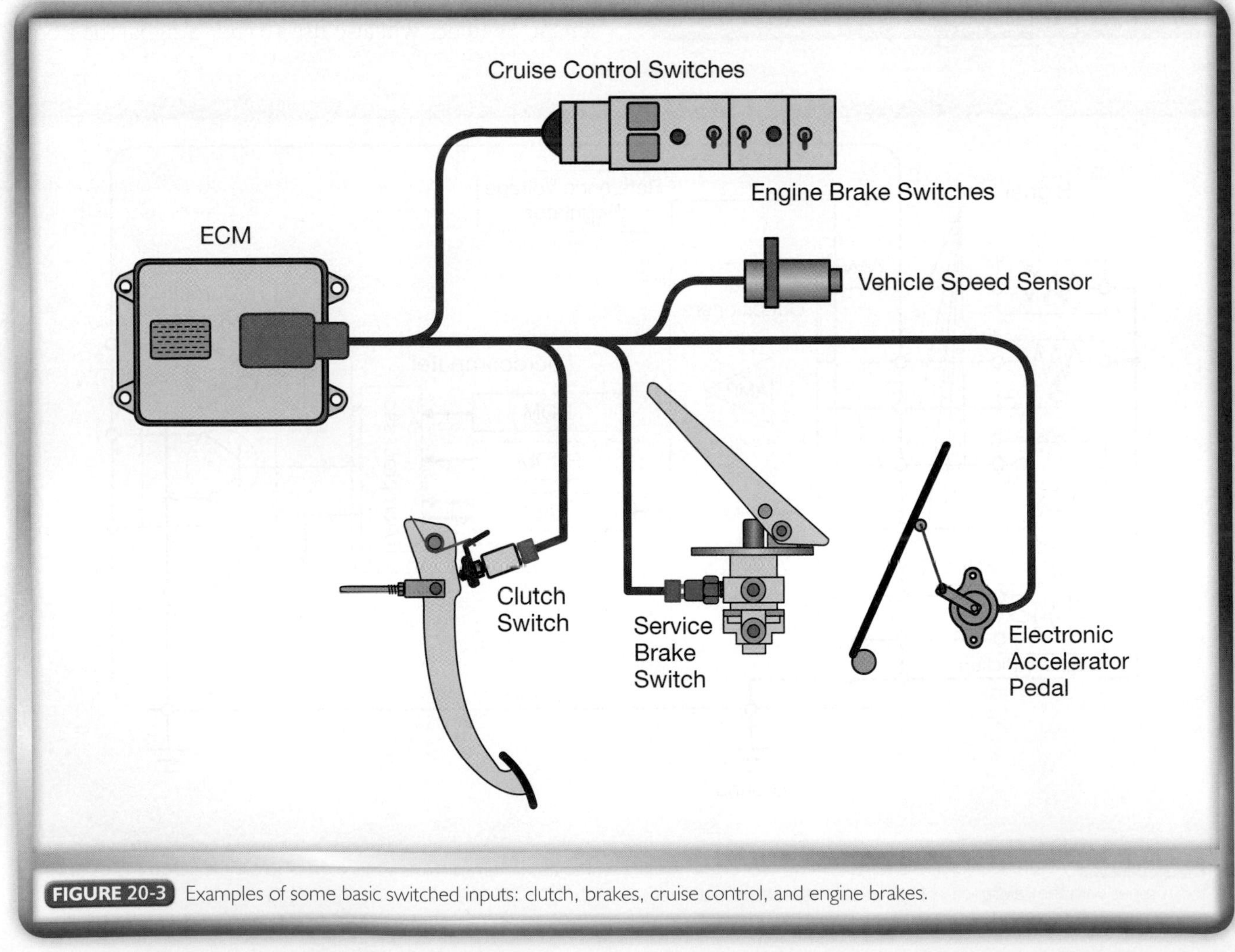

FIGURE 20-3 Examples of some basic switched inputs: clutch, brakes, cruise control, and engine brakes.

circuit or switch is open, closed, out of range, or shorted to a positive current potential.

Resistive Sensors

Resistive sensors are a class of sensors that will condition or change a voltage signal applied to the sensor. Many types of resistive sensors exist, and pressure, temperature, and position sensors are the most common. Some of these sensors are three-wire active sensors.

Thermistors

A **thermistor** is a temperature-sensitive variable resistor commonly used to measure coolant, oil, fuel, and air temperatures. The name itself combines the words thermal and resistor. Thermistors are two-wire sensors that change resistance in proportion to temperature. This means thermistors provide analog data to processing circuits. When the sensor is measuring air temperature such as in an intake manifold, the sensor is often constructed with a plastic body to minimize heat transfer from surrounding metal. When used to measure coolant or oil temperature, the sensor element is enclosed in a brass case to make it more responsive to temperature change FIGURE 20-6.

Thermistors are semiconductor devices with no moving parts. Two types of thermistors exist: negative and positive temperature coefficient. In a negative temperature coefficient (NTC) thermistor, the resistance decreases as the temperature increases FIGURE 20-7. In a positive temperature coefficient (PTC) thermistor, the resistance increases as the temperature increases FIGURE 20-8.

The most common type of thermistor is an NTC, in which the sensor's resistance goes down as the temperature goes up. So, when the sensor is cold, the sensor resistance is high, and the ECM measures a lower return signal voltage in comparison to reference voltage. The voltage drop across the sensor is interpreted as a temperature value. Likewise, when the engine warms, the internal resistance of the sensor decreases and causes a proportional increase in the return signal voltage.

Rheostats

Rheostats are also two-wire variable resistance sensors. They are not commonly used as input devices to an ECM but are instead used to signal sending units such as for fuel level and oil pressure FIGURE 20-9 and FIGURE 20-10. Rheostats use a variable sliding contact moving along a resistive wire. When current passes through the resistive wire, the sliding contact will conduct current flow from the wire. Current intensity at the sliding contact will vary depending on its position along the resistive wire.

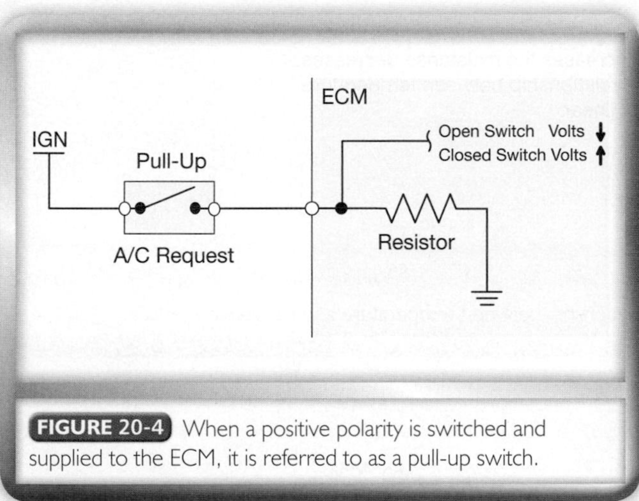

FIGURE 20-4 When a positive polarity is switched and supplied to the ECM, it is referred to as a pull-up switch.

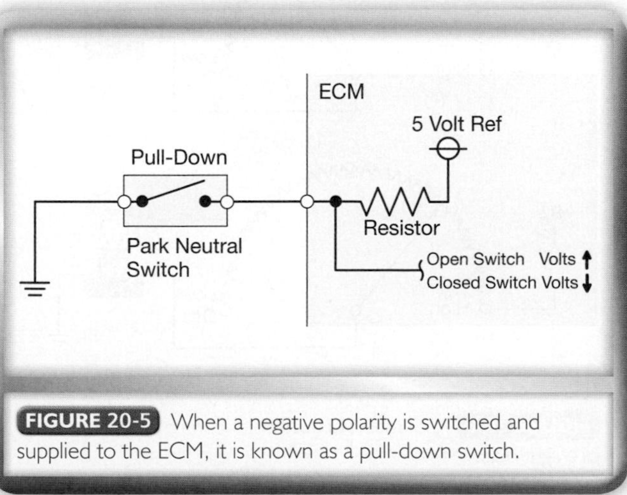

FIGURE 20-5 When a negative polarity is switched and supplied to the ECM, it is known as a pull-down switch.

FIGURE 20-6 Three thermistor applications. **A.** For intake manifold temperature. **B.** For coolant temperature. **C.** For intake manifold temperature. Note the semiconductor material in the fast response, air-intake thermistor.

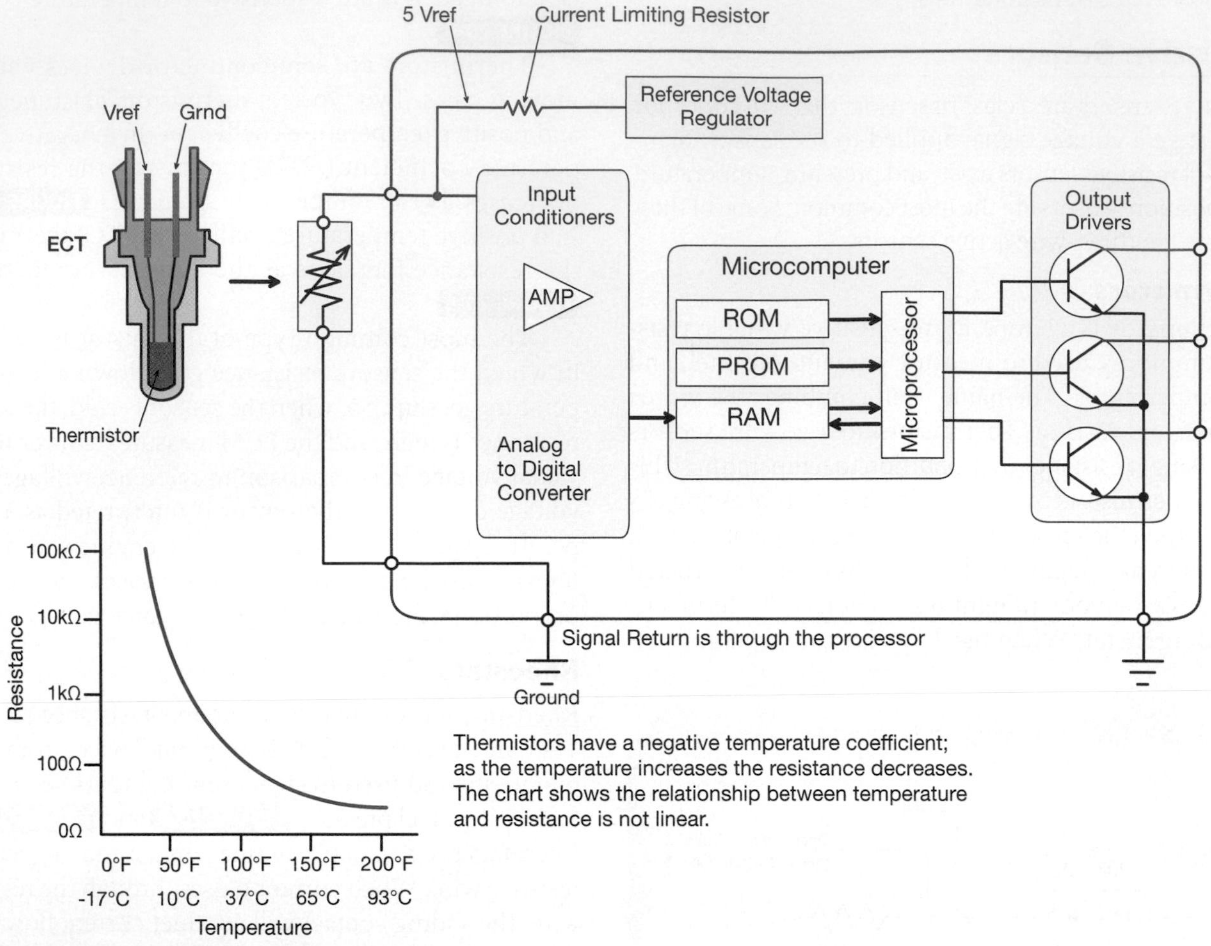

FIGURE 20-7 A thermistor circuit. Note the graph that illustrates the relationship between temperature and resistance.

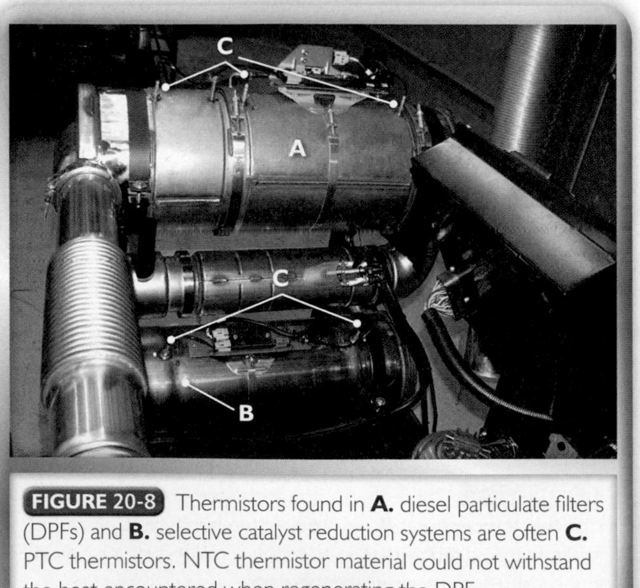

FIGURE 20-8 Thermistors found in **A.** diesel particulate filters (DPFs) and **B.** selective catalyst reduction systems are often **C.** PTC thermistors. NTC thermistor material could not withstand the heat encountered when regenerating the DPF.

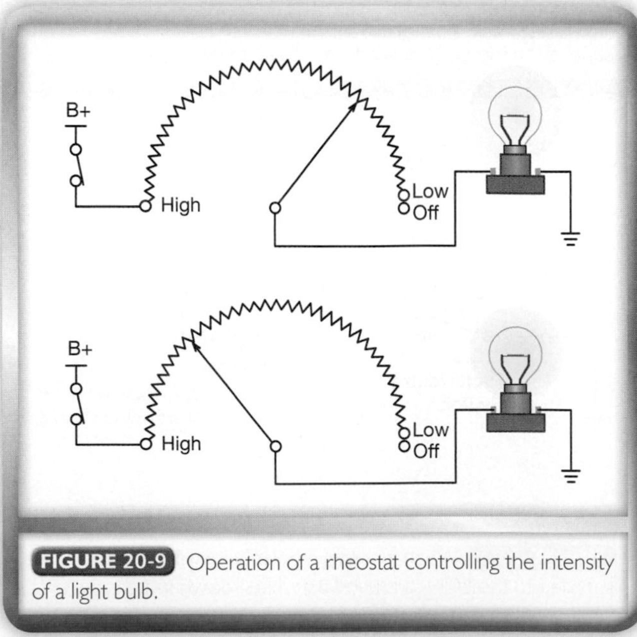

FIGURE 20-9 Operation of a rheostat controlling the intensity of a light bulb.

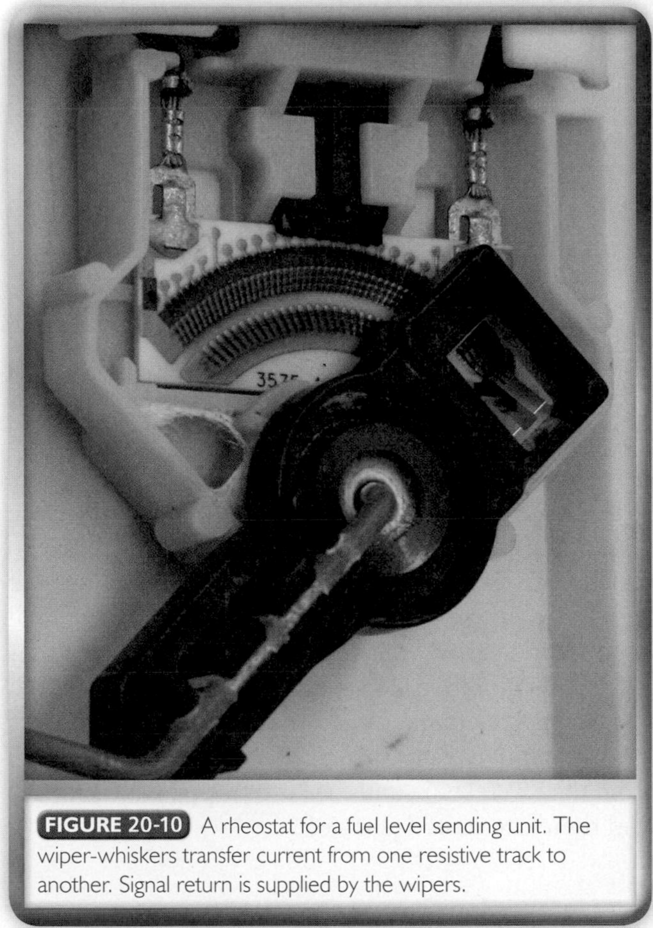

FIGURE 20-10 A rheostat for a fuel level sending unit. The wiper-whiskers transfer current from one resistive track to another. Signal return is supplied by the wipers.

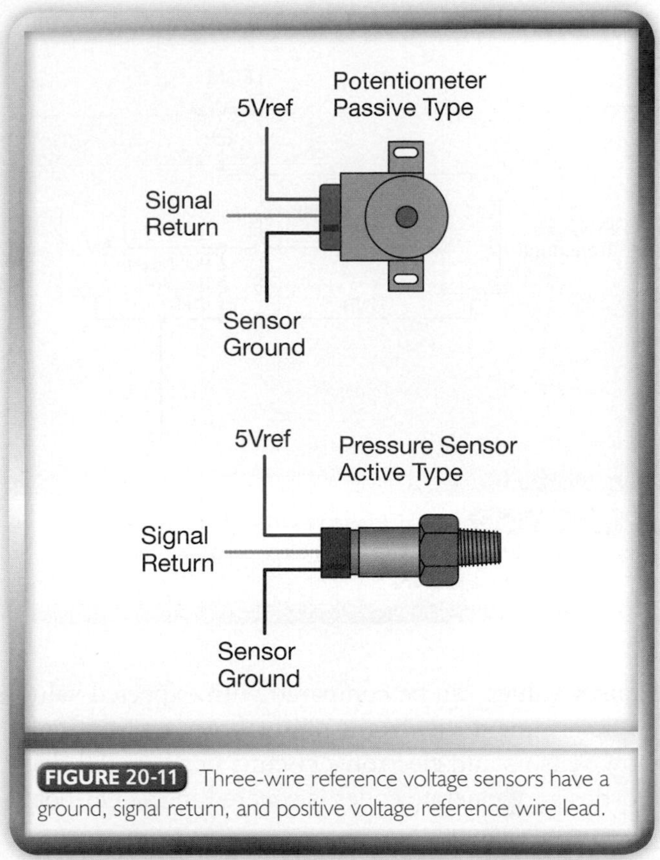

FIGURE 20-11 Three-wire reference voltage sensors have a ground, signal return, and positive voltage reference wire lead.

Reference Voltage Sensors—Three-Wire Sensors

Three wire sensors, regardless of how they appear or what function they perform, have a common wiring configuration: they all have ground, signal return, and positive voltage reference wire leads FIGURE 20-11.

One wire provides reference voltage to the sensor. If it is an active sensor, reference voltage will supply current to operate an integrated chip inside the device. Reference voltage is also produced by the ECM as a comparison point for voltage calculations associated with sensor data.

The second sensor wire provides a negative ground signal through the ECM and not to engine ground. This ECM return or ground is also called zero volt return (ZVR) and is identical to engine ground except it is free of any type of electrical interference. Active sensors will use the ZVR or negative ground for the other source of current to operate the sensor. In resistive sensors, the ZVR acts as a reference point to measure voltage drop across the sensor.

The third wire is a signal return from the sensor. This circuit provides a positive voltage proportional to the physical value measured by the sensor. If pressure is the physical input measured, the signal wire data will carry an analog voltage signal proportional to pressure. Typically, low voltage of, for example, 0.8 volts will represent little to no pressure, while 3.9 volts will represent high pressure depending on the range of the sensor.

The advantage of using three-wire sensors is that they provide comprehensive diagnostic information about the sensor and its circuit operation. Sending units can be constructed with reduced complexity and expense and yet still provide the ECM with data to operate an engine, transmission, or other device. However, sending units lack the capability to self-monitor circuit operation. Consider an open or shorted to ground signal wire from a single-wire sensor. In this case there is no means by which the ECM could accurately evaluate the situation. The wire could be broken or rubbed though, and still the unit voltage data received by the ECM would not be different from normal. It is very labor intensive to find an electrical fault based on only an operational symptom—no fault codes or malfunction indicator lights are available to identify a circuit problem.

The ECM does have capabilities to monitor and diagnose two- and three-wire sensor circuits to an extent not possible with single-wire sensors. By monitoring the voltage range of the ground return path, signal voltage, and reference voltage, the ECM can determine if the sensor and circuit are functioning correctly FIGURE 20-12.

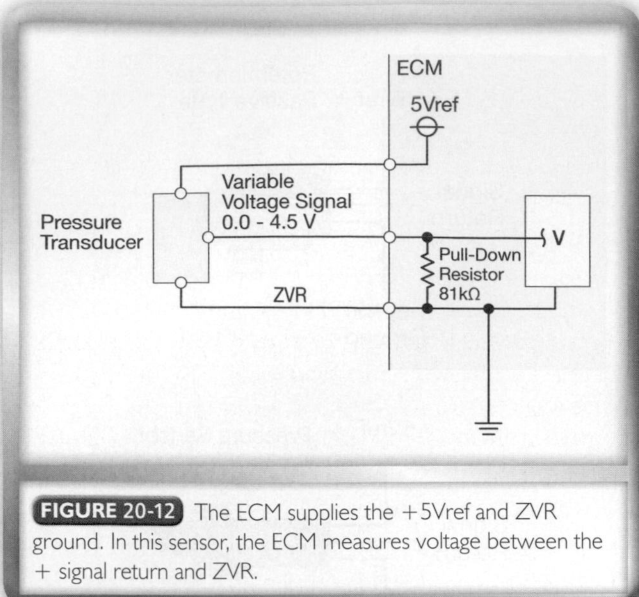

FIGURE 20-12 The ECM supplies the +5Vref and ZVR ground. In this sensor, the ECM measures voltage between the + signal return and ZVR.

Sensor values can be compared with expected values to determine if the data is rational. An explanation of how sensors and electronic circuits perform self-diagnostics and generate codes is covered in the On-Board Diagnostics chapter.

Potentiometers

Potentiometers are similar to rheostats in that they vary signal voltage depending on the position of a sliding contact or wiper moving across a resistive material. They are three-wire sensors with the signal wire connected to the internal wiper. Potentiometers supply analog data to processing circuits.

A common application of a potentiometer is a position sensor such as the throttle position sensor (TPS) FIGURE 20-13. This sensor is connected to a throttle pedal and provides data regarding the driver's desired engine speed or power output by measuring pedal angle or travel. The ECM will measure the voltage drop between the ground return circuit and the signal wire to calculate pedal position. Voltage produced from the signal wire will be proportional to the pedal travel. This means that at idle or part throttle, the voltage at the signal wire will be low. Increasing pedal travel will produce increasing voltage to the signal wire as the sensor's internal wiper moves closer to the +5Vref end of the resistive element. When the pedal returns to idle, the wiper will have less voltage because it is farther way from the +5Vref wire and the current pathway is longer and therefore more resistive.

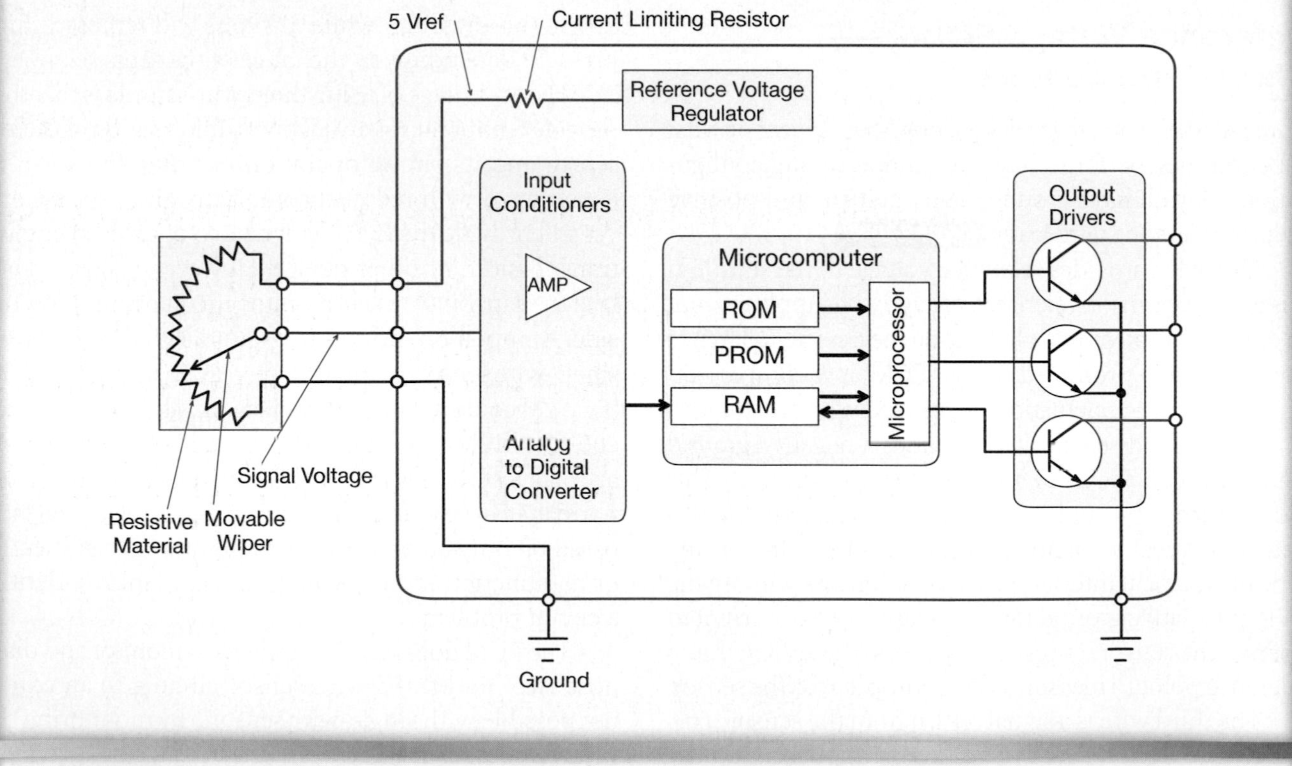

FIGURE 20-13 The TPS circuit commonly uses a potentiometer to measure throttle angle.

Idle Validation Switches and Throttle Position Sensors

A short circuit or incorrect data from the TPS, also called the accelerator position sensor (APS), can potentially cause uncontrolled acceleration of an engine. For safety reasons, manufacturers will build an additional safety system to verify throttle position. One common throttle safety system is the **idle validation switch (IVS)**. This circuit uses two switches: at idle, one switch will be open and the other closed. Off idle, the switches change state, which means the normally open switch closes, and the normally closed switch opens FIGURE 20-14. This data is used by the ECM to verify the driver has in fact moved the accelerator pedal and the circuit is not malfunctioning. At idle, the state of the switch must correspond to the TPS voltage sensed by the ECM. If the expected position sensor voltage and IVS position do not match, the ECM will revert engine speed to idle or not allow the engine rpm to increase beyond idle speed.

Dual- and Multiple-Path Throttle Position Sensors

To improve reliability of an TPS and validate accelerator position signals, some manufacturers are replacing the single TPS sensor track with a dual-track or even three-path TPS. The voltage of one sensor pathway is compared with another to verify that the sensor is operating at expected values FIGURE 20-15. If there is an unexpected difference between the voltage signals, the engine will only operate at idle speed. If one or even two of the resistive tracks wears out, the engine may still accelerate normally, but an APS fault is logged and the yellow fault warning indicator lamp will illuminate. Dual-path TPSs are potentiometers. Hall effect TPSs are even more reliable, because they have no moving parts. This throttle position sensor uses an AC magnetic field to induce current in a rotor moved by the throttle pedal. A circuit is used to convert the rotor's position into pedal position. This type of noncontact TPS sensor has no sliding friction parts to wear out FIGURE 20-16.

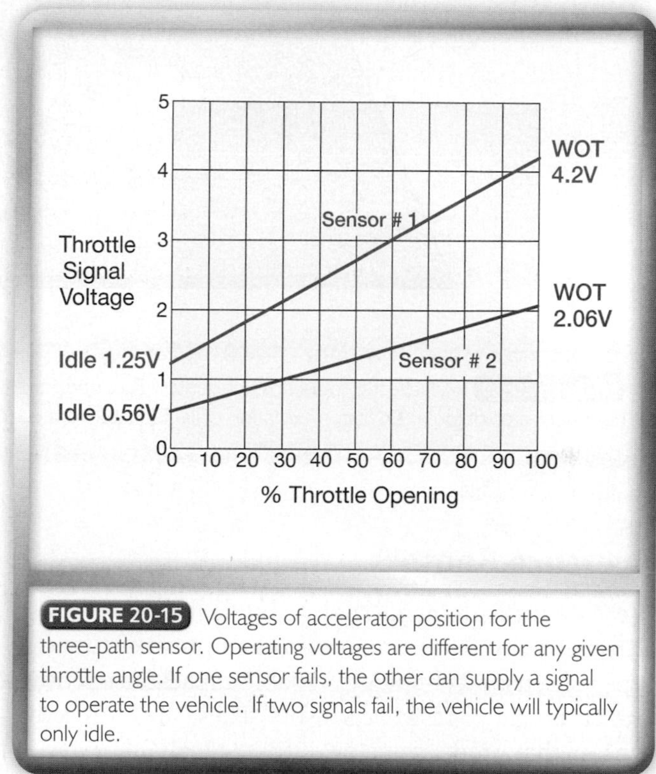

FIGURE 20-15 Voltages of accelerator position for the three-path sensor. Operating voltages are different for any given throttle angle. If one sensor fails, the other can supply a signal to operate the vehicle. If two signals fail, the vehicle will typically only idle.

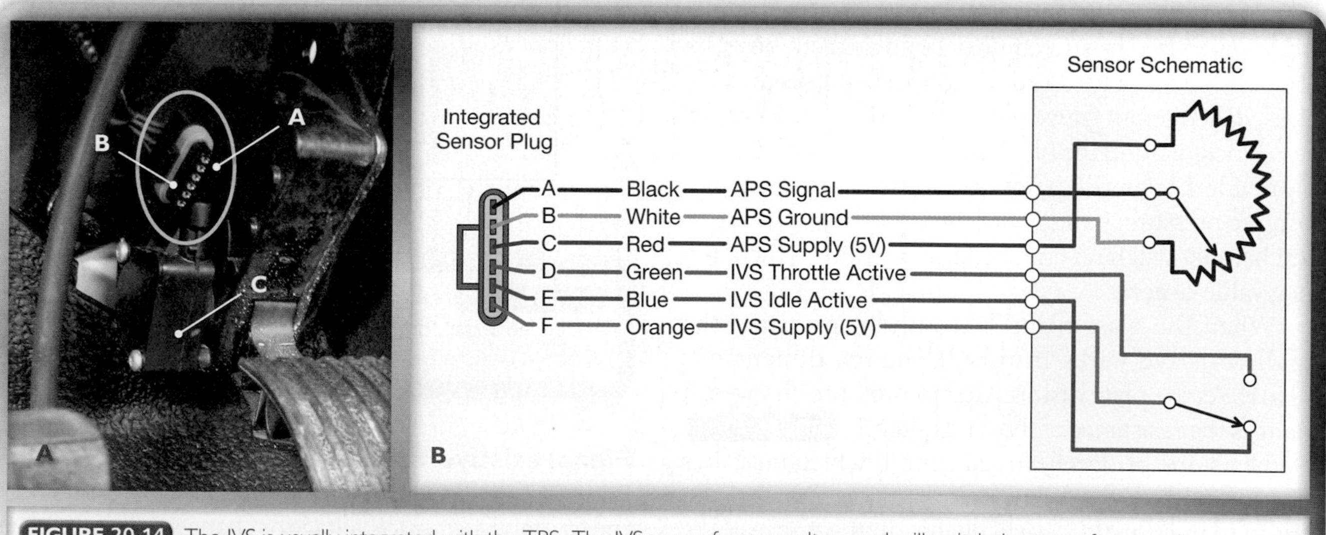

FIGURE 20-14 The IVS is usually integrated with the TPS. The IVS uses reference voltage and will switch the state of a normally open and a normally closed switch when moved off idle. **A.** Three sensor wires (A), three IVS wires (B), and the throttle position sensor (C). **B.** Color coding for integrated sensor plug.

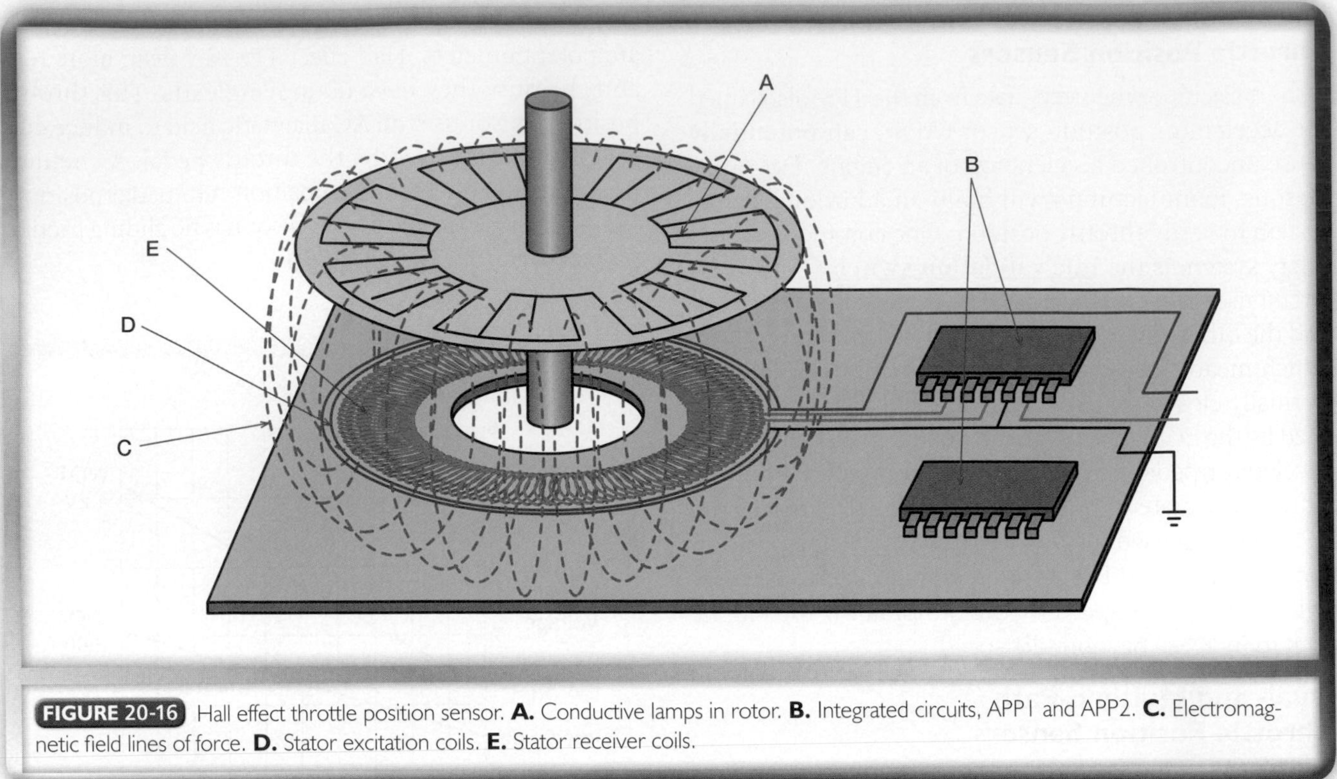

FIGURE 20-16 Hall effect throttle position sensor. **A.** Conductive lamps in rotor. **B.** Integrated circuits, APP1 and APP2. **C.** Electromagnetic field lines of force. **D.** Stator excitation coils. **E.** Stator receiver coils.

Pressure Sensors

Pressure measurements such as intake manifold boost, barometric pressure, and oil and fuel pressure, use two types of sensor technology: variable capacitance sensors and strain gauge resistive sensors. These are both active sensors that produce analog output signals.

Strain Gauge

A strain gauge measures small changes in the resistance of tiny wires caused by stretching or contraction. Construction of this type of pressure-sensing device uses resistive wires, called strain gauge wires, embedded in a flexible glass block. Behind the block may be a vacuum chamber to provide a reference point of zero for measurement of absolute pressure. If the device measures gauge pressure, the chamber will have atmospheric pressure as the reference value of zero.

When the glass plate flexes under pressure, the small resistive wires in it will change dimensions slightly. As the plate distorts due to pressure changes, it changes the resistance of the wires slightly FIGURE 20-17. A Wheatstone bridge electrical circuit, which measures changes in resistance of an unknown variable resistor, is used to measure this small change in resistance of the strain gauge wires FIGURE 20-18. By measuring this small change in the wires' resistance, the pressure applied to the plate is determined.

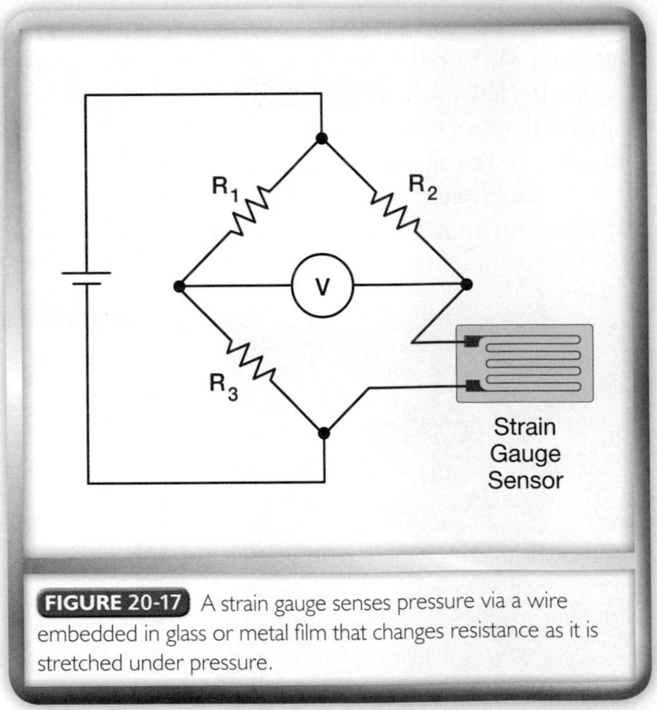

FIGURE 20-17 A strain gauge senses pressure via a wire embedded in glass or metal film that changes resistance as it is stretched under pressure.

Piezoresistive Sensors

Piezoresistive sensors rely on the ability of certain mineral crystals to produce voltage or change resistance when compressed FIGURE 20-19. Rather than using a strain gauge wire construction, these sensors have a piezoresistive crystal arranged with a Wheatstone bridge to measure

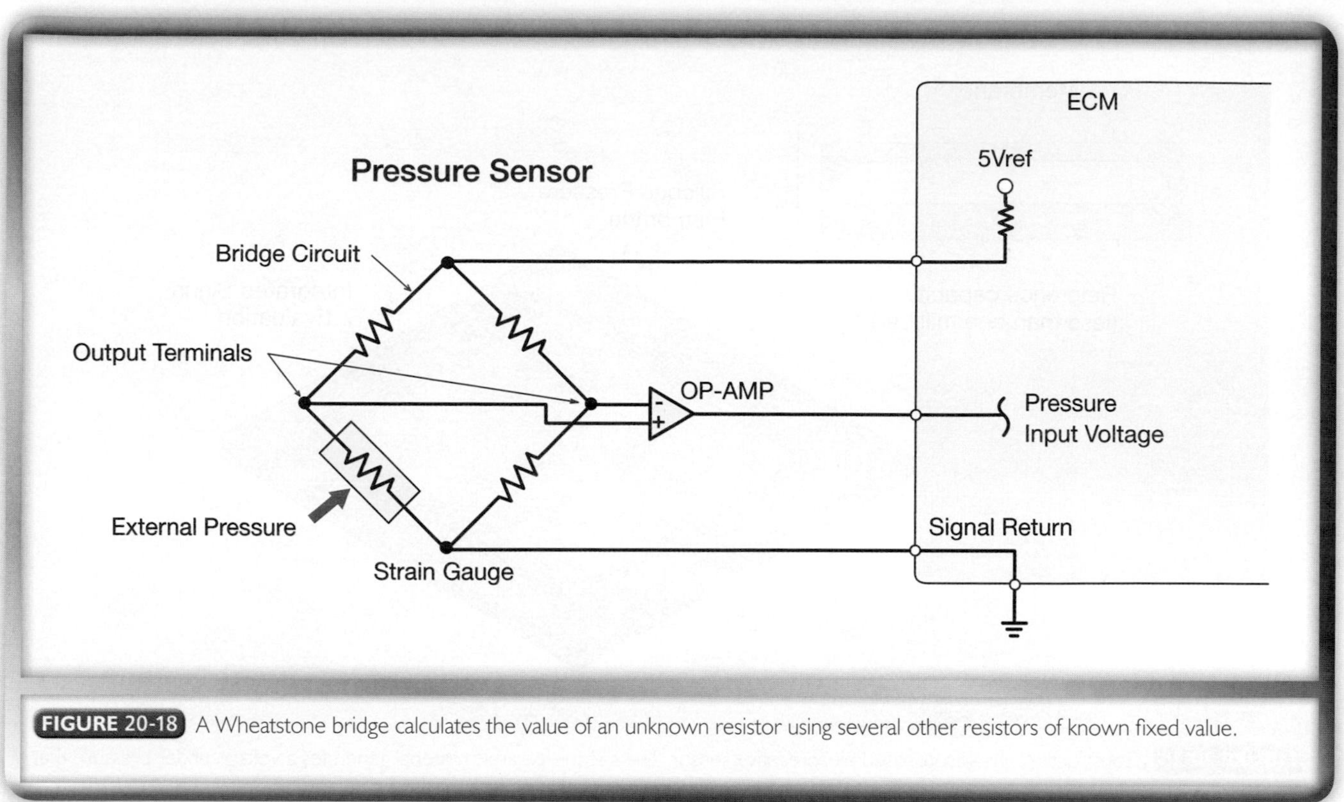

FIGURE 20-18 A Wheatstone bridge calculates the value of an unknown resistor using several other resistors of known fixed value.

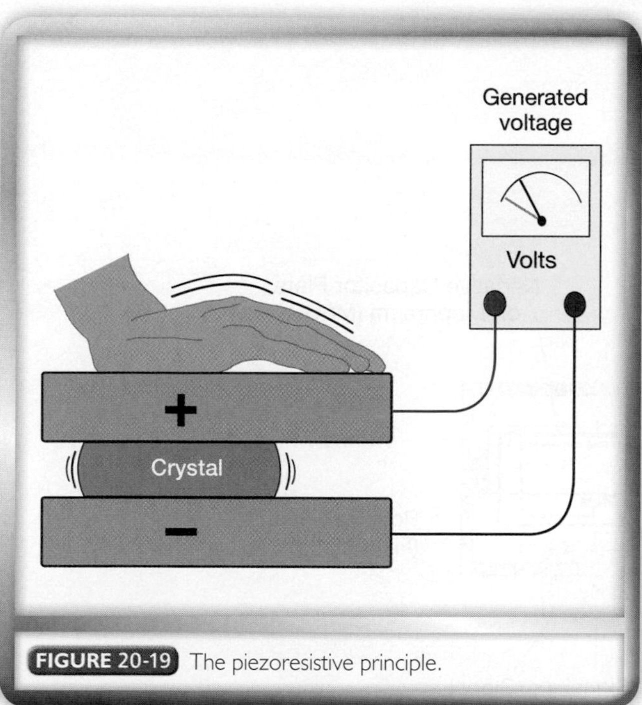

FIGURE 20-19 The piezoresistive principle.

the change in resistance of the piezo crystal. These sensors produce analog electrical signals.

The advantage of these sensors is their ability to measure very high pressures. Because of the sturdiness of the crystal, piezo sensors are better adapted to measuring vibration and dynamic or continuous pressure changes. Knock sensors measuring abnormal combustion signals are a common application of piezoresistive sensors. Another type of piezoresistive sensor uses mineral crystals arranged on a substrate of silicon FIGURE 20-20. The crystals behave as a semiconductor to produce electrical signals that are amplified and conditioned by internal circuits. Silicon-based piezoresistive sensors are very sensitive to slight pressure changes.

Variable Capacitance Pressure Sensor

A **variable capacitance pressure sensor** is an active sensor that measures both dynamic and static pressure. Though they are more expensive to manufacturer than a piezoresistive or strain gauge sensor, the variable capacitance pressure sensor offers a greater range of measurement flexibility and more accurate readings. Because it is an active sensor, the stronger circuit signals to the ECM are not as vulnerable to voltage drop or electromagnetic interference.

Variable capacitance sensors use the distance between two plates, or dielectric strength, inside the sensor to measure pressure FIGURE 20-21. One plate diaphragm will move in response to intake manifold, oil, fuel, or some other physical pressure being measured. The other plate is fixed and has on one side a reference vacuum or pressure chamber to calibrate it for accurate pressure readings. As pressure increases or decreases, the distance between the two plates will change. An electrical charge is

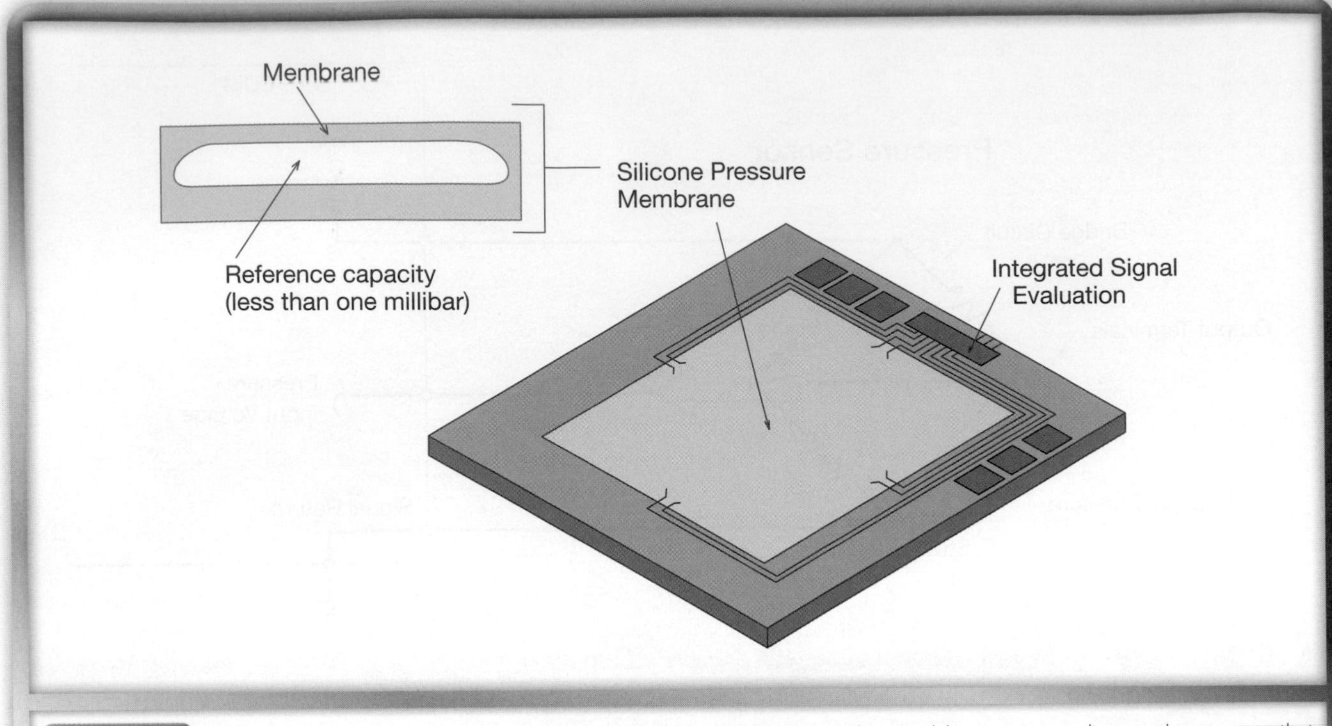

FIGURE 20-20 Construction of a silicon-based piezoresistive sensor. The silicone-ceramic material generates a voltage under pressure that is converted to an analog signal.

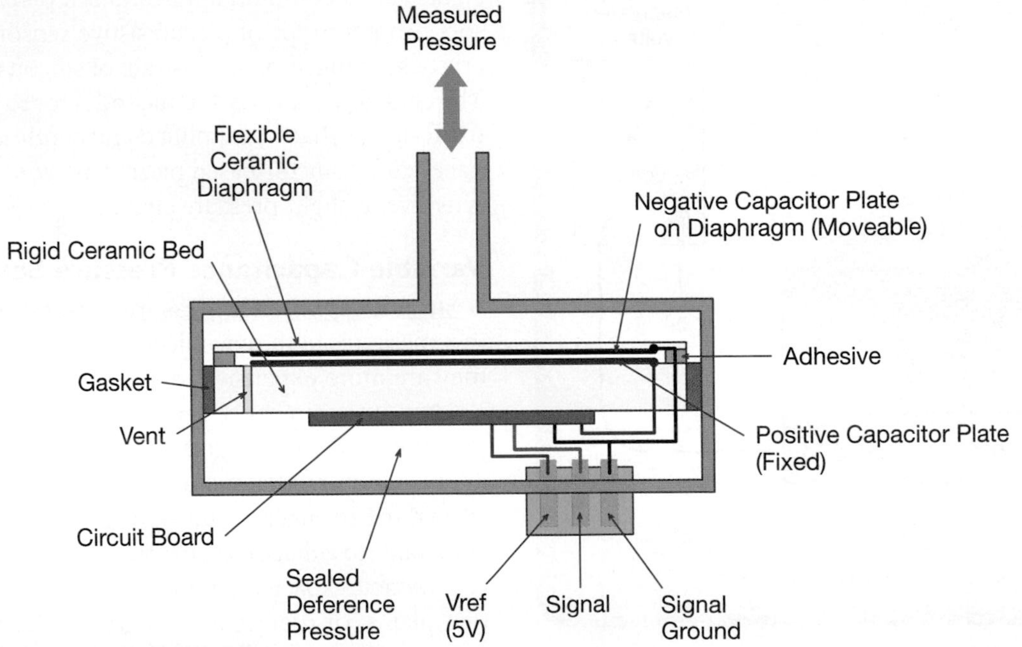

FIGURE 20-21 Cross section of a variable capacitance sensor.

applied to the fixed plate, and the time it takes to charge the plate is measured. Charging time will change proportionally to the dielectric strength between the plates. An electronic circuit in the chip integrated inside the sensor measures the changing voltage/time value produced by the flexing plate and outputs an analog electrical signal of less than 5 volts.

Voltage Generators

This category of sensors is passive and produces an analog signal of varying voltage or AC frequency. Variable reluctance and galvanic sensors are two examples of voltage-generating sensors. While the gas sensors used on today's diesel engines are active sensors with modules that produce and condition signals, the operating principle is still a galvanic reaction that produces voltage. Exhaust stream gas sensors are used to measure oxygen, NO_X, or ammonia gases in the exhaust stream. On diesel engines, data from oxygen sensors is commonly used to adjust exhaust gas recirculation (EGR) rates and sometimes to adjust the intake throttle plate position to control the operation of exhaust aftertreatment systems. Ammonia and NO_X sensors are used to identify faults in the exhaust aftertreatment systems on most diesels from 2010 and later. Ammonia sensors are more frequently used on diesel engines from 2015 and later.

Variable Reluctance Sensors

Variable reluctance sensors are two-wire sensors used to measure rotational speed. Wheel speed, vehicle speed, engine speed, and camshaft and crankshaft position sensors are their most common applications FIGURE 20-22. Signals from the camshaft and crankshaft position sensors are used to calculate engine position for determining the beginning of engine firing order and injection timing. The camshaft gear has raised lugs that generate waveform signals to identify top dead center (TDC) for each cylinder. When graphed against time, the AC waveform produced by the sensor data is used to precisely calculate not only engine speed but also degrees of crankshaft rotation FIGURE 20-23.

The ability of a material to conduct or resist magnetic lines of force is known as reluctance. Variable reluctance sensors use changing sensor reluctance to induce current flow by changing magnetic field strengths inside

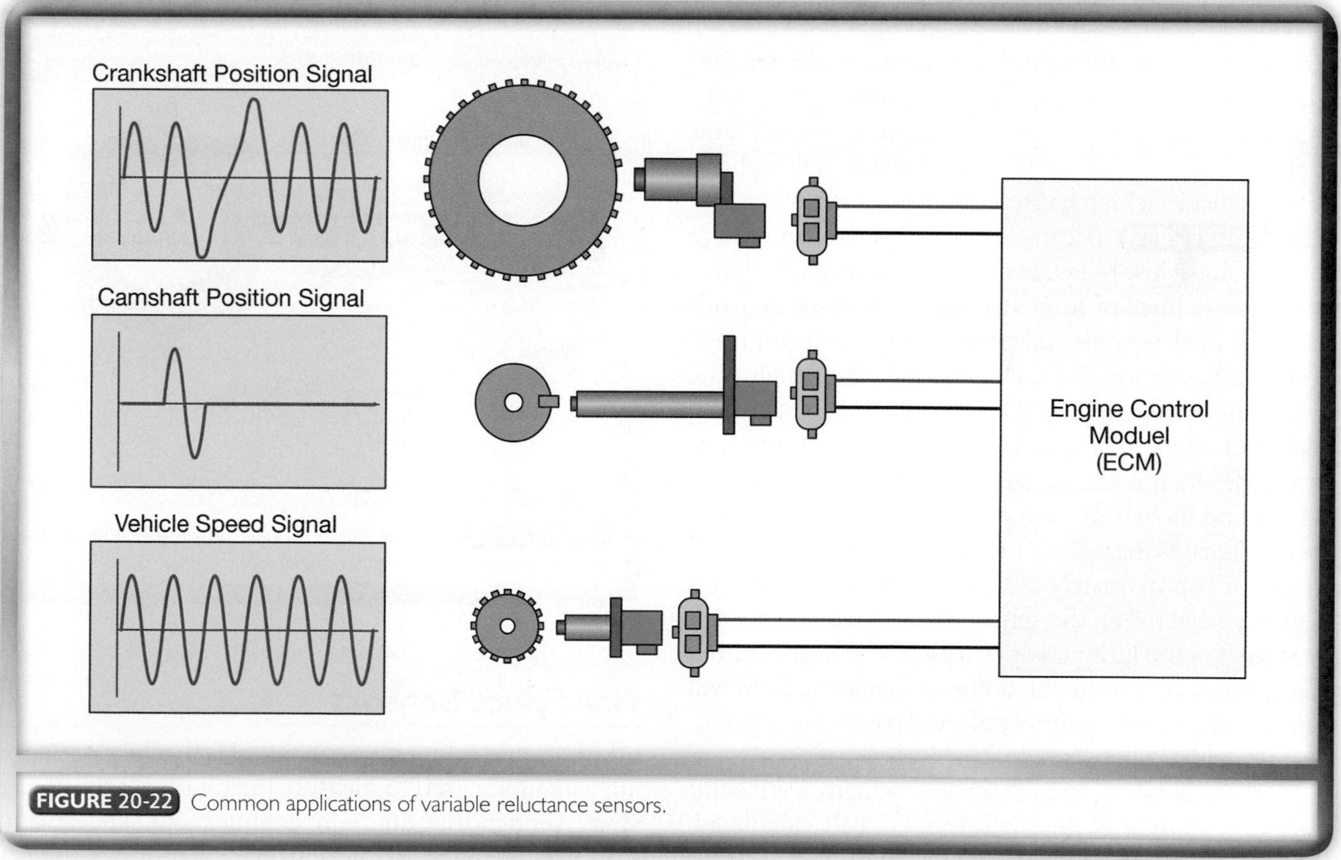

FIGURE 20-22 Common applications of variable reluctance sensors.

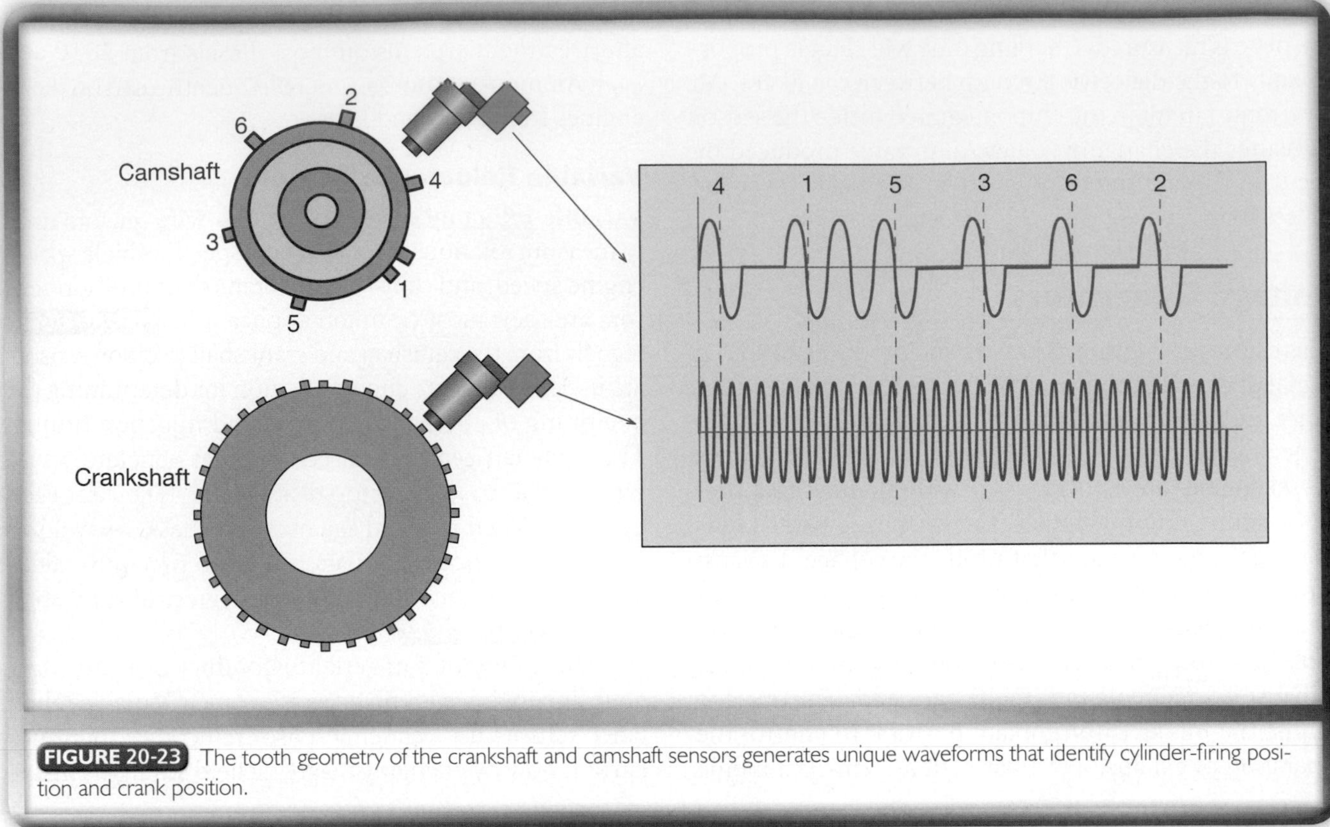

FIGURE 20-23 The tooth geometry of the crankshaft and camshaft sensors generates unique waveforms that identify cylinder-firing position and crank position.

the sensor. A variable reluctance sensor is constructed with two main elements: a coil of narrow-gauge wire wrapped many times around a permanent magnet, and a reluctor ring (also called the sensor wheel, pulse wheel, or tone wheel), which has soft iron teeth and rotates on a shaft FIGURE 20-24. Because ferrous metals, particularly soft iron, have low reluctance and air has high reluctance to magnetic lines of force, the strength of the sensor's magnetic field expands and collapses as the reluctor ring's iron teeth pass across the sensor's magnet. By changing the density of magnetic lines of force, alternately expanding and contracting the magnetic field when a gear tooth or gap passes by the sensor, current is induced in the wire coil around the sensor magnet. Increasing reluctor wheel speed increases the voltage induced in the sensor. A small air gap of approximately 0.02–0.03" (0.51–0.76 mm) is maintained between the sensor and the reluctor wheel. Too much or too little air gap will prevent the sensor from detecting tooth movement. Software inside the ECM will detect and count the number of teeth passing by the sensor to calculate shaft speed.

If the processing circuits track how many teeth complete one rotation of the shaft, rpm is easily calculated. If the engine software can divide the number of teeth passing by the sensor per unit of time, it can precisely calculate the number of degrees of crankshaft rotation.

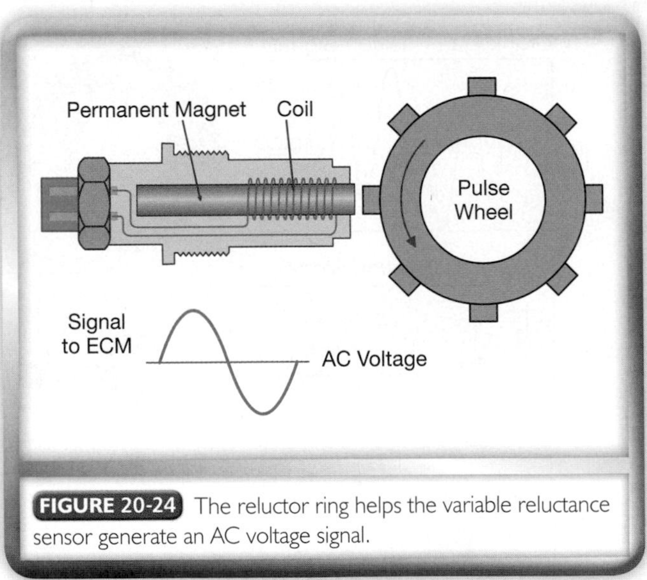

FIGURE 20-24 The reluctor ring helps the variable reluctance sensor generate an AC voltage signal.

Hall Effect Sensors

Like variable reluctance sensors, **Hall effect sensors** are commonly used to measure the rotational speed of a shaft. Though they are more complex and expensive to manufacture than variable reluctance sensors, Hall effect sensors have the advantage of producing a digital signal square waveform and have strong signal strength at low shaft rotational speeds. This is especially useful when cranking an engine when engine rpm is slow. The durability and accuracy of the digital signal is preferred when more precise injection event timing is necessary, which is why most engines today use Hall effect sensors.

The operation principle of a Hall effect sensor is simple: current flow through a Hall effect material is made from semiconductive material that changes resistance in the presence of a magnetic field FIGURE 20-25. When current is applied to a Hall effect material, no conduction occurs. However, in the presence of a magnetic field, the material will conduct current. The electrical signal output from the sensor material is analog, but circuits within the sensor will convert and amplify the rising and falling voltage into a square-shaped electrical waveform FIGURE 20-26.

To produce the signal from the Hall effect sensor, two configurations are used. The most common arrangement is the use of a metal interrupter ring or shutter and a permanent magnet positioned across from the sensor. Because ferrous metals have a lower magnetic reluctance than air, magnetic lines of force from a magnet placed opposite the sensor will flow through the metal shield rather than the sensor. Gaps in the interrupter ring will allow magnetism to penetrate the sensor, changing current flow through the Hall effect material. Attaching the interrupter ring to a moving shaft provides rotational speed information to the control module.

Another configuration for the Hall effect sensor incorporates the magnet into the sensor itself. When a gear tooth or other ferrous metal trigger is present near the sensor, the magnetic field expands. Movement of the ferrous trigger or tooth away from the magnet causes magnetic field contraction. This pulsing magnetic field generates the signal within the sensor FIGURE 20-27.

Oxygen Sensors

Oxygen sensors are used to measure air–fuel ratio in order to calibrate EGR flow rates and air–fuel ratios for exhaust aftertreatment devices. Diesel engines use a heated planar, wide-band, zirconium-dioxide (ZrO_2) dual-cell oxygen sensor. This sensor technology is different from the narrow-band oxygen sensor technology used commonly on gasoline engines operating at stoichiometric air–fuel ratios. Wide-band oxygen sensors are used in diesel engines because they use lean-burn combustion systems, which normally leaves an excess of air in the exhaust. Rather than producing a sharply falling and rising voltage near 0.5 volts, with 2% exhaust oxygen content found in gasoline engines, wide-band sensors produce a voltage proportional to a widely varying oxygen level FIGURE 20-28. The type of ceramic sensing element commonly used by wide-band sensors is a platinum-coated oxide of zirconium (Zr). An important property of this ceramic is that it conducts oxygen ions when voltage is applied at high temperatures.

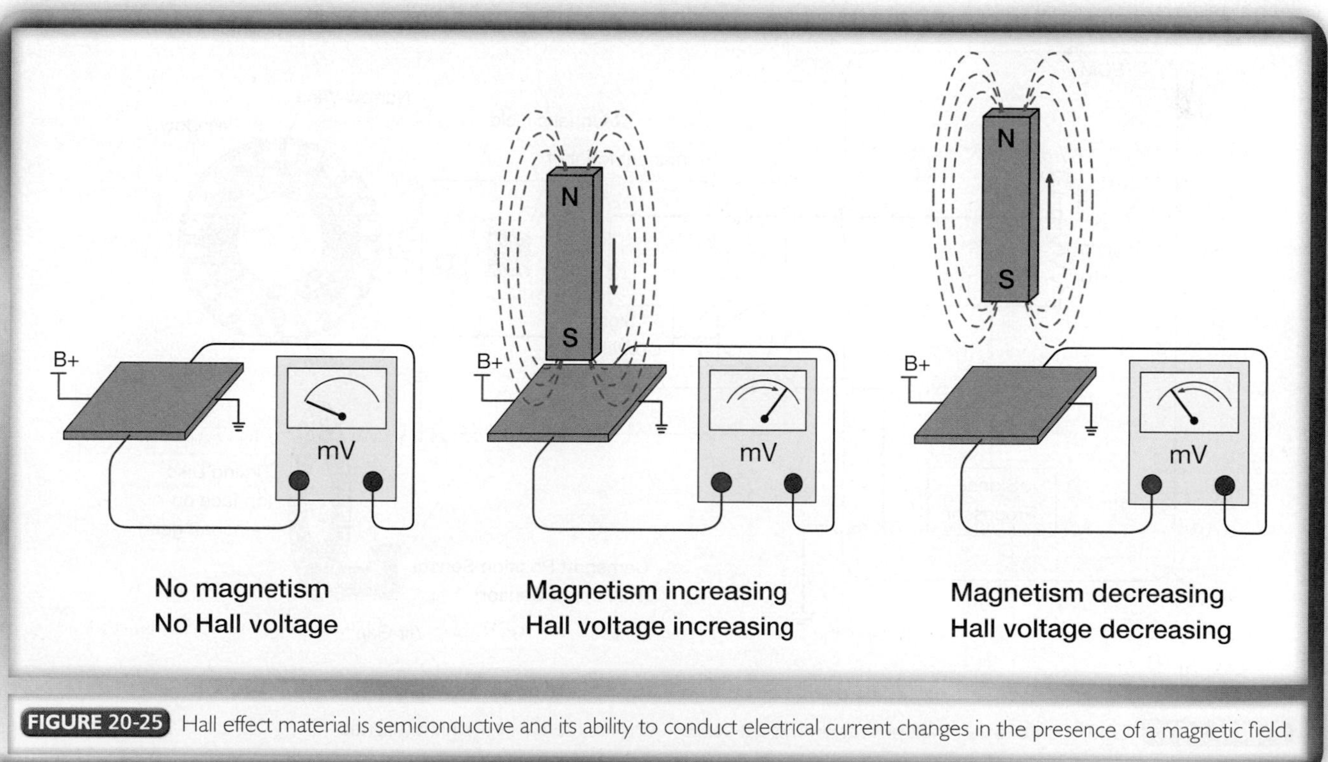

FIGURE 20-25 Hall effect material is semiconductive and its ability to conduct electrical current changes in the presence of a magnetic field.

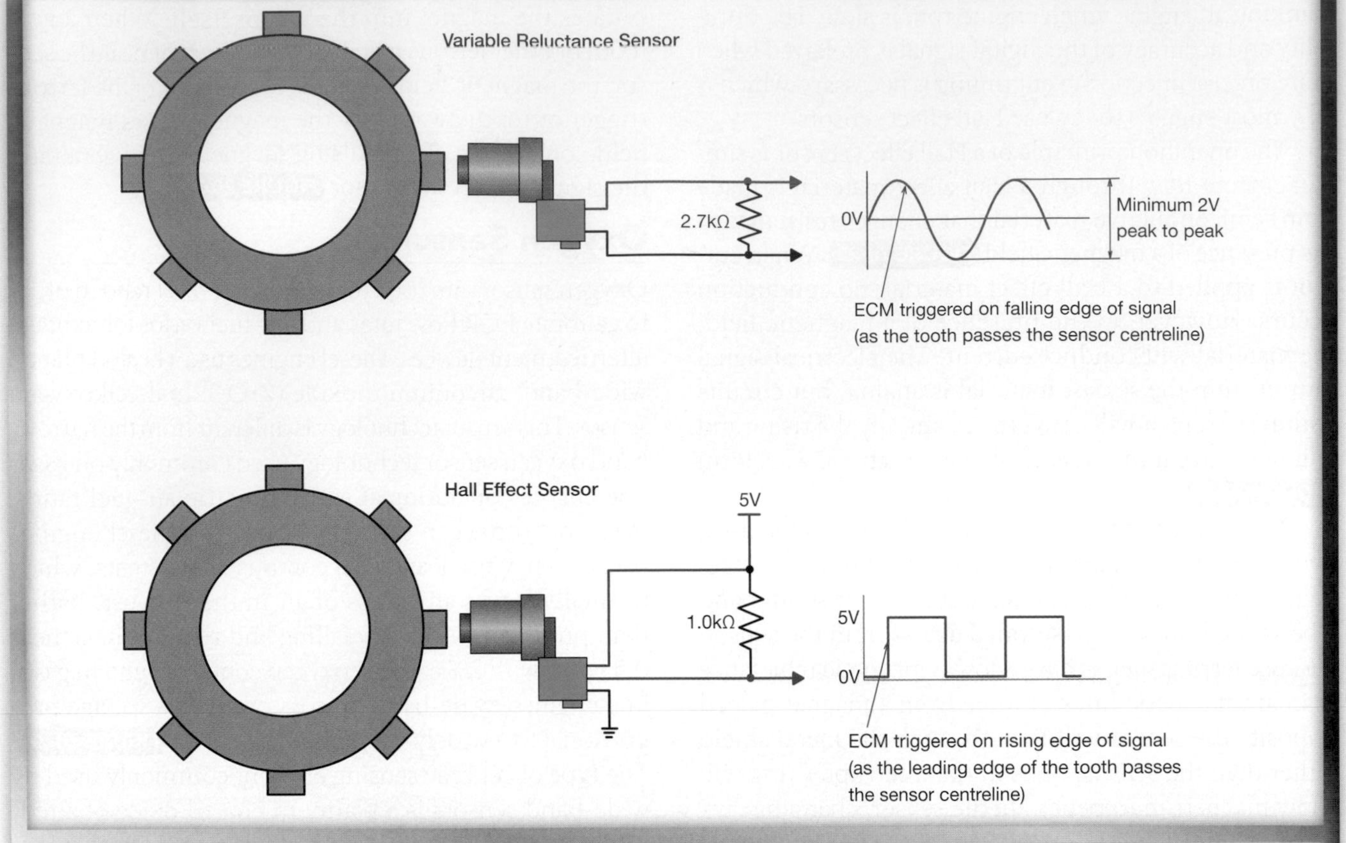

Variable Reluctance Sensor

2.7kΩ

0V

Minimum 2V peak to peak

ECM triggered on falling edge of signal (as the tooth passes the sensor centreline)

Hall Effect Sensor

5V

1.0kΩ

5V

0V

ECM triggered on rising edge of signal (as the leading edge of the tooth passes the sensor centreline)

FIGURE 20-26 Comparing the signals of a Hall effect sensor and variable reluctance sensor.

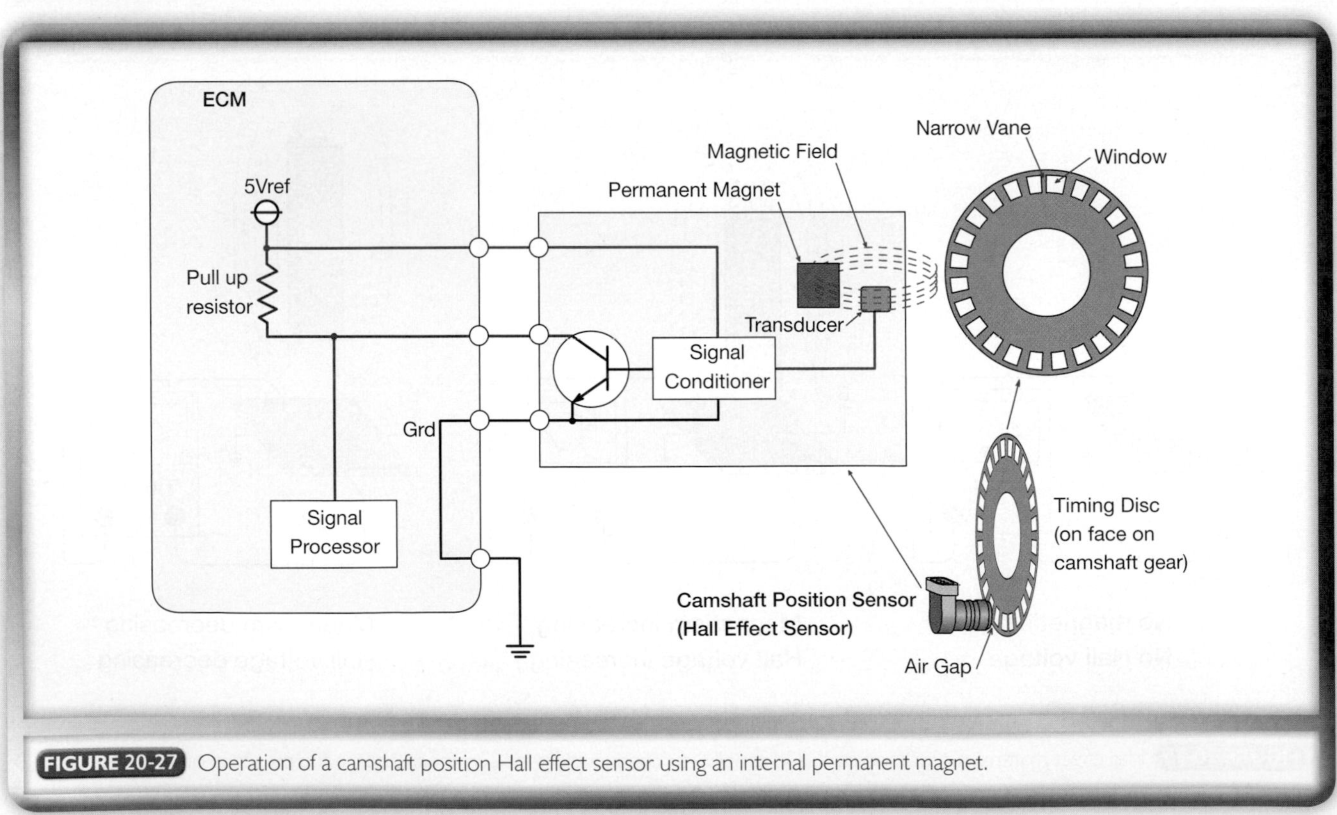

FIGURE 20-27 Operation of a camshaft position Hall effect sensor using an internal permanent magnet.

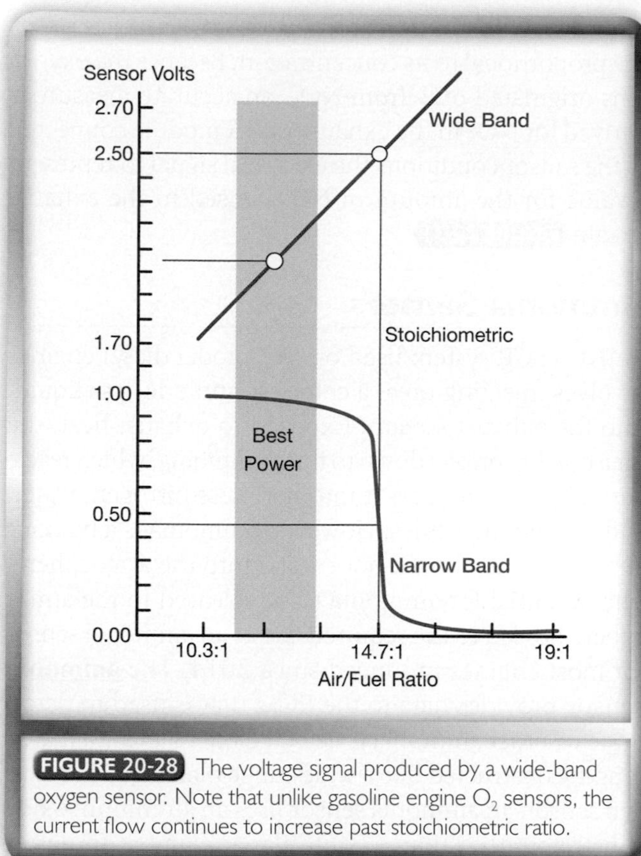

FIGURE 20-28 The voltage signal produced by a wide-band oxygen sensor. Note that unlike gasoline engine O_2 sensors, the current flow continues to increase past stoichiometric ratio.

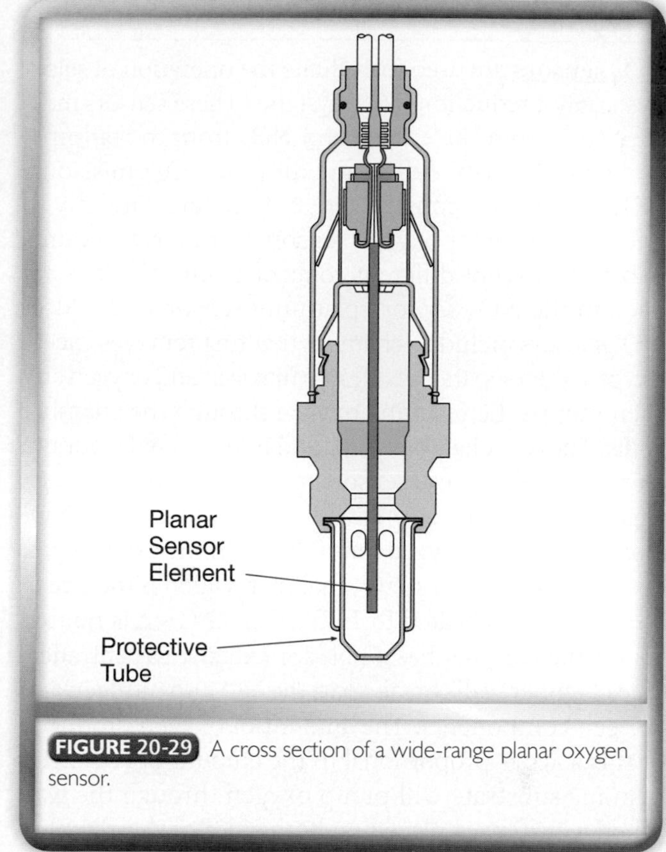

FIGURE 20-29 A cross section of a wide-range planar oxygen sensor.

Diesel oxygen sensors are **wide-range planar sensors**, which means they are flat rather than thimble-shaped like the sensors used on older gasoline-fueled engines **FIGURE 20-29**. They are also wide-band, which means they generate a signal with a wide air–fuel ratio between 0.7:1 and infinity. When heated to over 1,200°F (700°C), the sensor becomes electrically conductive to oxygen ions. Because the oxygen content in the exhaust sample chamber is less than the oxygen concentration in the atmosphere, the oxygen content absorbed by the platinum coating on the ZrO_2 ceramic that contacts the exhaust and the coating that contacts the air will be slightly different **FIGURE 20-30**. This chemical difference in the sensor ceramic generates a voltage proportional to the oxygen content in the exhaust stream. The greater the difference in oxygen content, the higher the voltage. This voltage is produced because of the galvanic effect in which dissimilar metals in the presence of an electrolyte will produce electric current. Using the voltage produced across the two coatings, an amplifier circuit, called an oxygen pump cell circuit, will transfer excess electrons from the coating in the exhaust gas chamber to an electron-depleted electrode in the atmospheric reference chamber. The amount of current used to transfer these electrons is proportional to air–fuel ratio, and a circuit will precisely calculate air–fuel ratios based on the amount of current required to balance the voltage differential.

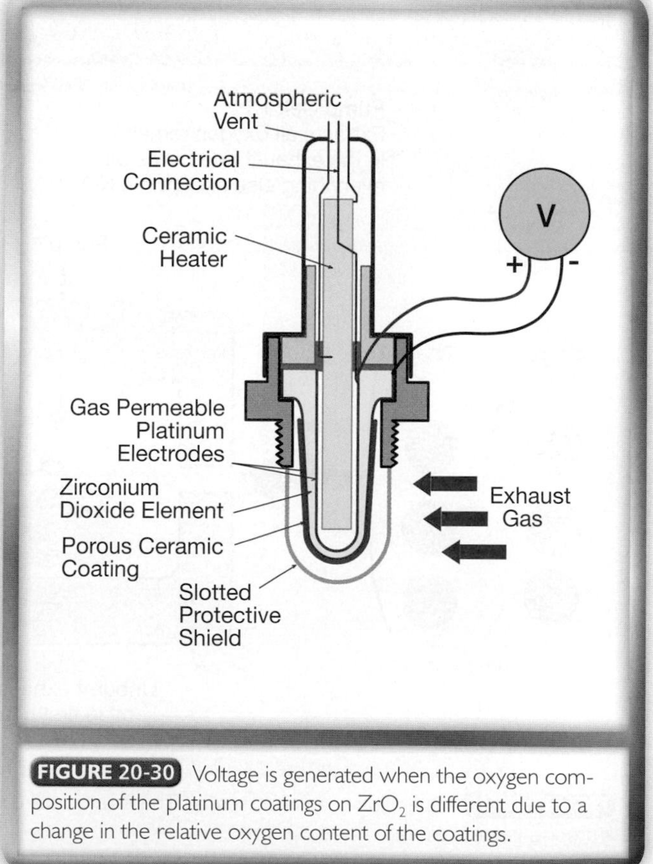

FIGURE 20-30 Voltage is generated when the oxygen composition of the platinum coatings on ZrO_2 is different due to a change in the relative oxygen content of the coatings.

NO_X Sensors

NO_X sensors are used to evaluate the operation of selective catalyst reduction (SCR) systems. These sensors measure NO_X from the engine and NO_X from the tailpipe, and should verify a dramatic drop in NO_X emissions. NO_X sensors are constructed and operate similarly to wide-range planar oxygen sensors using ZrO_2 ceramic substrate, except different concentrations of alloys are used in the NO_X sensor's platinum sensor walls. Also, NO_X sensors include a chamber that first removes excess oxygen, then separates NO_X into nitrogen and oxygen and then pumps the resulting oxygen through the chamber walls. The two-chamber shape and multilayered platinum element enable these sensors to differentiate with high precision oxygen ions originating from nitric oxide (NO) from among the oxygen ions present in the exhaust gas.

The NO_X sensor's ZrO_2 chamber, which is the size of a thumbnail, is heated to 1,200°F (700°C). It is housed in a metal can that has a hole for exhaust gas entrance. The chamber walls break apart the NO into nitrogen and oxygen components. The amount of oxygen produced at this stage is proportional to the amount of NO. ZrO_2 ceramic substrate will pump oxygen through the wall when a current is placed on both sides of the chamber wall. As oxygen is pumped from the first chamber, the amount of oxygen can be measured as it passes through the wall of the second chamber because it generates a voltage proportional to its concentration. Because the oxygen ions originated only from NO_X, an accurate measure is derived for NO_X in the exhaust gas. A module connected to the sensor conditions the electrical signal to represent a value for the amount of NO_X sensed in the exhaust stream FIGURE 20-31.

Ammonia Sensors

An NO_X SCR system used on late-model diesel engines involves injecting urea, a colorless and odorless liquid, into the exhaust stream. Exposed to exhaust heat, the urea quickly breaks down to form ammonia, which reacts with NO_X and renders it into harmless nitrogen, water, and oxygen molecules. However, ammonia is a noxious substance and should not escape into the atmosphere. The potential for ammonia to be released to the atmosphere has led to the required use of an ammonia sensor for most engines produced since 2014. The **ammonia sensor** provides data to the ECM that is used to determine whether ammonia is detected out of an anticipated range. Constructed like a wide-range planar NO_X or oxygen sensor, an ammonia sensor uses an aluminum oxide substrate rather than a ZrO_2 planar element to detect and generate a voltage for ammonia in a range from 0 to 100 ppm.

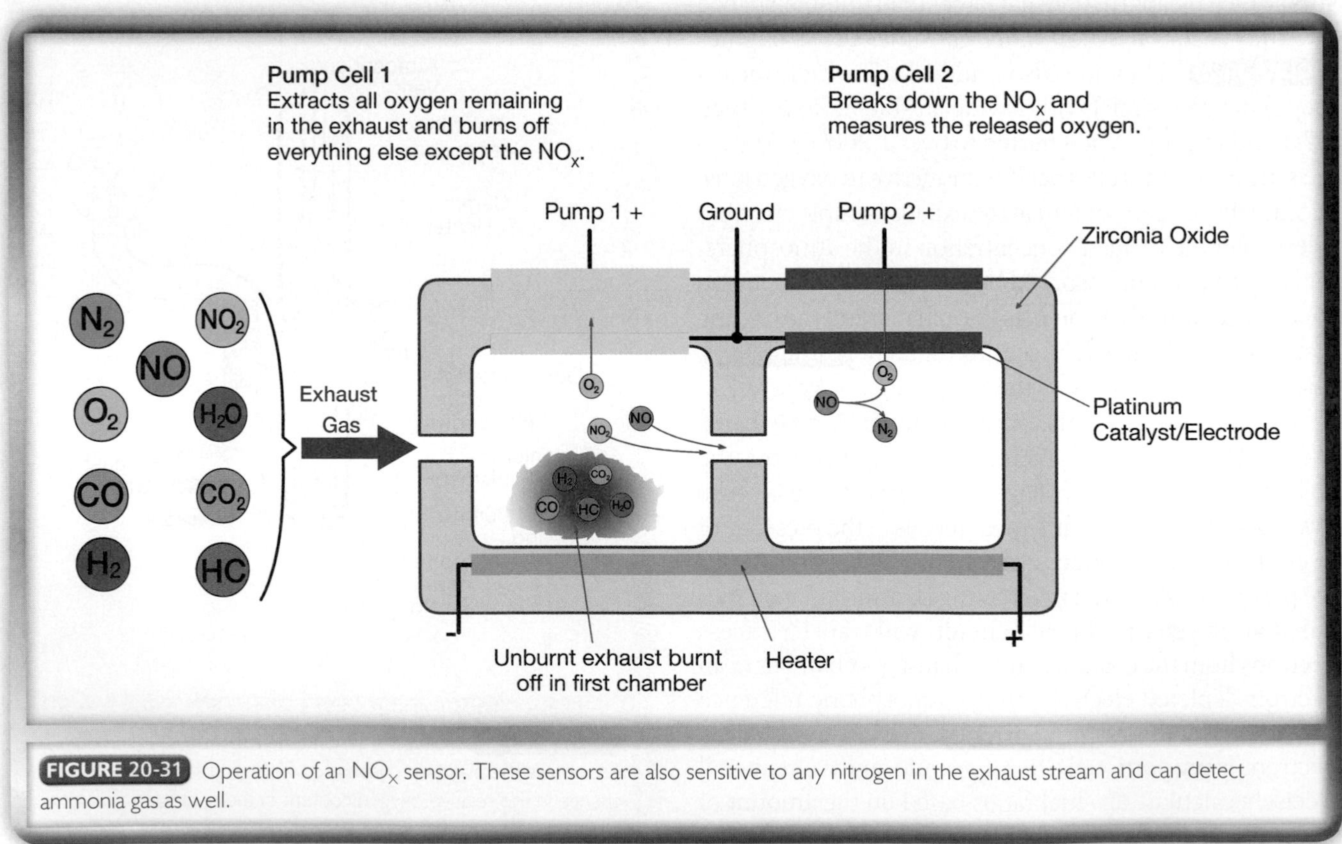

FIGURE 20-31 Operation of an NO_X sensor. These sensors are also sensitive to any nitrogen in the exhaust stream and can detect ammonia gas as well.

Soot Sensors

Another new sensor introduced in 2014 is a particulate sensor that measures any soot present in the exhaust. This sensor is a type of variable capacitance sensor that uses soot to change the dielectric strength between two charged plates. Increasing amounts of soot or particulate matter will reduce the dielectric strength and the electric charge the plates can store.

Mass Airflow Sensors

The mass airflow (MAF) sensor is a device that measures the weight of air entering the engine intake. Its unique design also reports data about air density and, to some extent, the vapor content.

MAF sensors are common on engines operating at stoichiometric air–fuel ratios. However, on the diesel engines operating with an excess air ratio, the MAF is used as part of the heavy-duty onboard diagnostics (HD-OBD) component monitor for the EGR. A variety of electrical signals originate from MAF sensors, but all work using a hot wire operating principle. Heated platinum wires or a thin film of silicon nitride embedded with several heated platinum wires are located in the intake air stream. A heating circuit maintains a fixed voltage drop across the wires, maintaining a constant resistance and temperature of the wires regardless of the airflow in the intake system. This means that if a voltage drop of 5 volts is maintained across the heated wire, more current needs to flow through the wire if it cools faster due to increased airflow. Similarly, if airflow drops, less current is needed to maintain the same voltage drop across the wire FIGURE 20-32. Circuits internal to the MAF measure the variation in current flow proportional to the cooling effect of air mass. Due to the large valve overlap characteristic of diesel engines, some intake air may be forced back out in pulses from the intake system. MAF sensors on some engines use a reverse airflow detection circuit. Because colder air is denser than warmer air, manufacturers will also use an air temperature sensor to provide additional data for calculations to compensate for the change in air mass FIGURE 20-33.

Output Circuits

Output circuits, or output control devices, consist of display devices, serial data for network communication, and electromagnetic operator devices. The two basic types of operators are solenoids and relays. Injectors will use solenoids to meter fuel and adjust the timing of injection events.

Transistors inside the ECM are most often used to open or close circuits controlling these operators. A small amount of current flowing from the microprocessor through the transistor base will control the output devices by supplying either a ground or battery current to complete a circuit FIGURE 20-34. Output drivers use field effect transistors (FETs) that are switched either on or off with very small voltages and produce little heat, which makes them ideal for output drivers.

Sensors and Position Calculations

Engine control systems need to determine the correct cylinder and point in the combustion cycle for injection.

FIGURE 20-32 Heated wires that change resistance as airflow across the sensor increases or decreases. Air mass is calculated based how much electrical current is required to cancel the cooling effect of airflow across a heated wire.

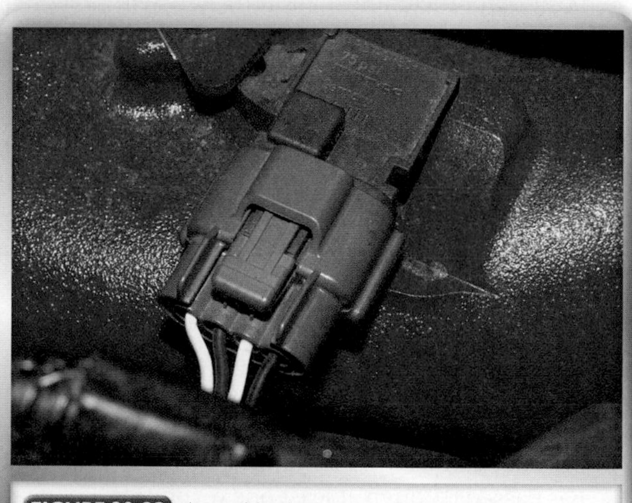

FIGURE 20-33 A combination pressure and temperature sensor is used to calculate air mass entering an engine using a speed density algorithm. Note the two white signal wires.

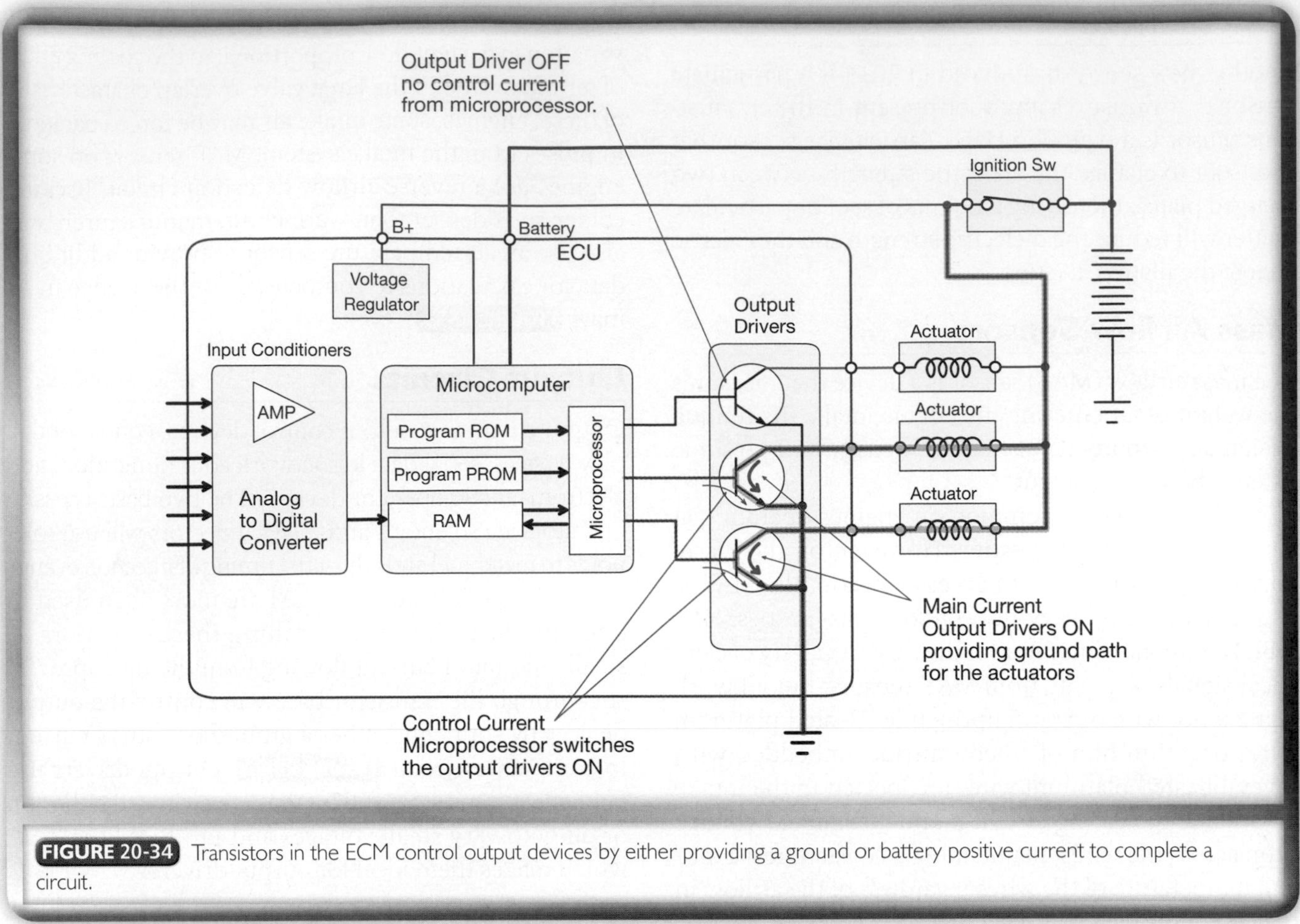

FIGURE 20-34 Transistors in the ECM control output devices by either providing a ground or battery positive current to complete a circuit.

In order to send an electrical signal to fire the injectors, the ECM needs to know two things:

1. *Crankshaft position*. The ECM must know the exact position of the crankshaft in reference to TDC, that is, the number of degrees the crankshaft has rotated since it turned past TDC.
2. *Cylinder identification*. This information is necessary to determine in which cylinder the injection event should take place, based on cylinder stroke position. Once the ECM can determine when the first cylinder has reached TDC compression stroke, it can use the engine firing order stored in memory to fire the remaining cylinders in the correct sequence. However, because the crankshaft rotates through 720 degrees of a four-stroke operating cycle, or two rotations of the crankshaft, cylinder stroke for any given cylinder can only be determined after the camshaft has passed through at least one revolution. To measure crankshaft position and identify cylinder stroke to begin a firing sequence, manufacturers have developed a number of strategies using either variable reluctance or Hall effect sensors.

Single Engine Position Sensor

Teeth or raised lugs on a cam gear that turns at one-half engine speed can generate signals using a Hall effect or variable reluctance sensor. A number of evenly spaced reluctor teeth, corresponding to the number of cylinders an engine has, will produce a waveform or pattern that can be used to calculate the rotational velocity and engine position. This means that for every tooth that passes over the sensor, the ECM can calculate a specific number of degrees of crank or camshaft rotation has occurred. Counting the signals produced by reluctor wheel teeth and measuring the time elapsed between signals generated by the sensor allows the ECM to precisely calculate engine rotation in fractions of degrees.

Evenly spaced reluctor ring teeth or lugs, however, will not identify the cylinder stroke position. To identify TDC of the first cylinder's compression stroke, the cam gear may use an additional tooth or lug to identify the stroke position of each cylinder. A seventh tooth or lug on the cam gear of a six-cylinder engine could correspond to TDC of the first cylinder's compression stroke. Alternatively, a manufacturer may remove a tooth from a reluctor wheel. The longer time between two teeth is detected by the ECM's analysis of the sensor's waveform and will identify cylinder stroke as, say, TDC of the first cylinder FIGURE 20-35. Variations of this basic strategy include using one or two narrower teeth or an odd arrangement of teeth that corresponds to a particular engine position for a given waveform. It should be noted that the additional or missing tooth strategy may require as many as three crankshaft revolutions before the ECM can determine what the cylinder stroke position is.

Using Two Sensors

A better strategy than using a single sensor on the camshaft is to use both camshaft and crankshaft position sensors. The advantage that two sensors provides is improved precision in calculating crankshaft position. Using only the camshaft sensor, error is introduced due to backlash between the crankshaft and camshaft gears. Worn gears can result in a significant amount of gear train backlash, producing unacceptable error in reporting crankshaft position. Using the crank sensor, the ECM can determine exactly where the position of the piston is FIGURE 20-36.

Cylinder Misfire and Contribution Detection

The crankshaft of a diesel engine will speed up and slow down with each power and compression stroke in the engine. The waveform that is generated from the engine position sensor(s) can determine the rotational velocity of the crank. A cylinder that is misfiring or producing little power in comparison to the other cylinders will turn more slowly, resulting in fewer teeth passing the position sensor per unit of time. Analyzing sensor waveforms using edge detection software algorithms, the ECM can determine how much power each cylinder is contributing to overall performance. Similarly, a loss of compression in a cylinder results in less crankshaft deceleration during an operating cycle. The ECM may change injection quantities to even out cylinder contribution based on data from the crankshaft and camshaft position sensors.

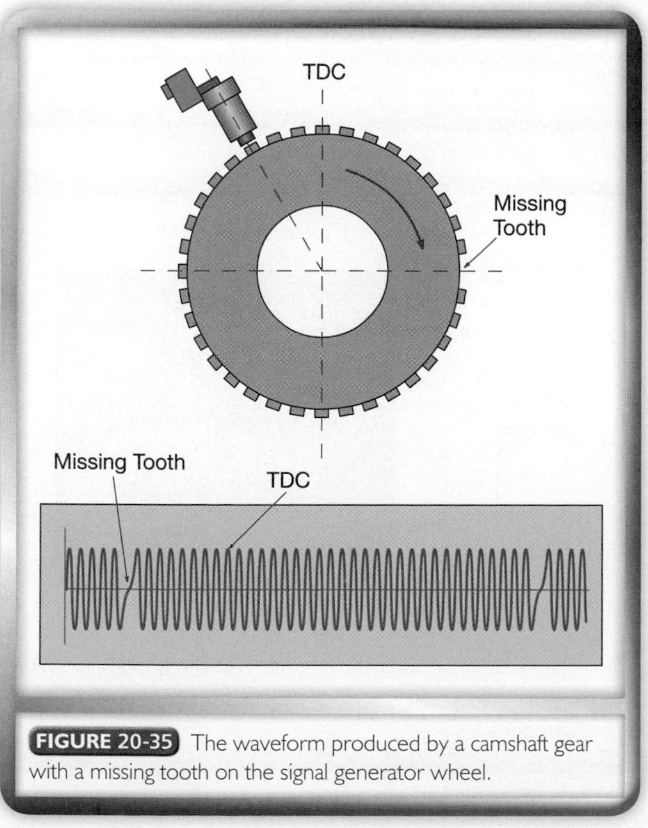

FIGURE 20-35 The waveform produced by a camshaft gear with a missing tooth on the signal generator wheel.

Sensor Fault Detection Principles

Technicians are often called upon to diagnose fault codes associated with sensors or sensor circuits. Understanding how sensor-related faults are detected and the diagnostic strategies used by an ECM will help you stay focused when performing pinpoint checks.

Sensors and Onboard Diagnostics

Electronic control systems have self-diagnostic capabilities to identify faults in circuits and sensors. Without the ability of an ECM to monitor circuit operation, diagnosing faults would become an extraordinarily difficult task, requiring the technician to manually perform voltage, resistance, and current measurements for every circuit with the potential to produce a particular symptom of system malfunction. Waveforms from sensors producing varying frequencies, pulse width modulation, digital, or sine wave would also require a staggering amount of time and resources to analyze.

Because all vehicles are required by emission legislation to monitor engine and other system operations for faults that could produce excessive emissions, evaluating sensor operation is a critical function of the HD-OBD system. Three major categories of fault codes identified by engine manufacturer diagnostics (EMD) and HD-OBD are:

1. *Out of range faults*. These faults primarily check sensor voltages, and in a few cases, they also check current draw to determine whether the sensor or associated circuits are open or have shorts. Voltages should be within 85% of reference voltage. That means for most sensors operating with a 5 Vref, signal voltages should not fall below 0.5 volts or above 4.5 volts FIGURE 20-37.
2. *Rationality, plausibility, or logical faults*. Manu-facturers use different terms to describe the same fault

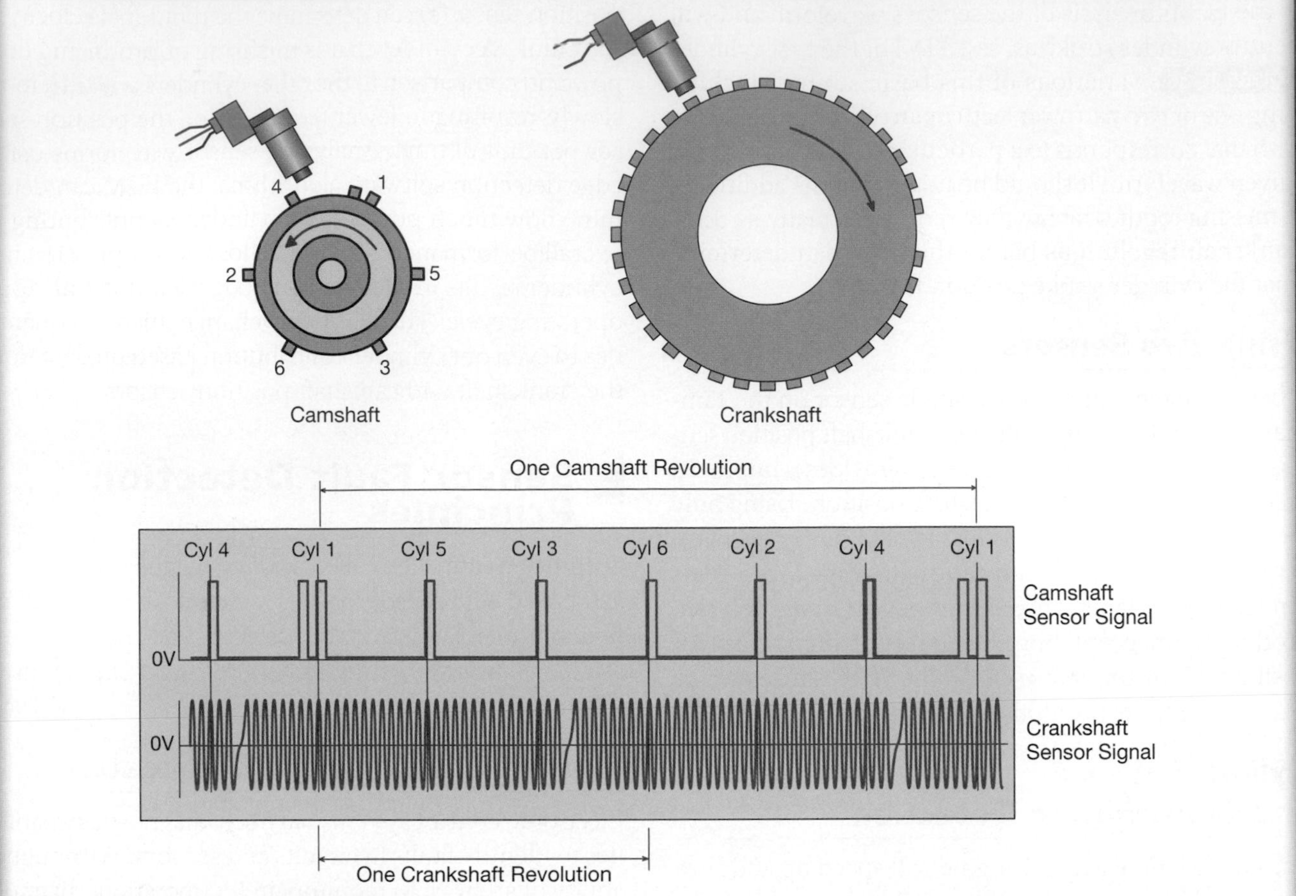

FIGURE 20-36 Two sensors produce crankshaft and engine position data with little error in comparison to a single sensor on the camshaft. The camshaft reluctor wheel of a Hall effect sensor produced the top waveform. A variable reluctance sensor generated the crankshaft waveform.

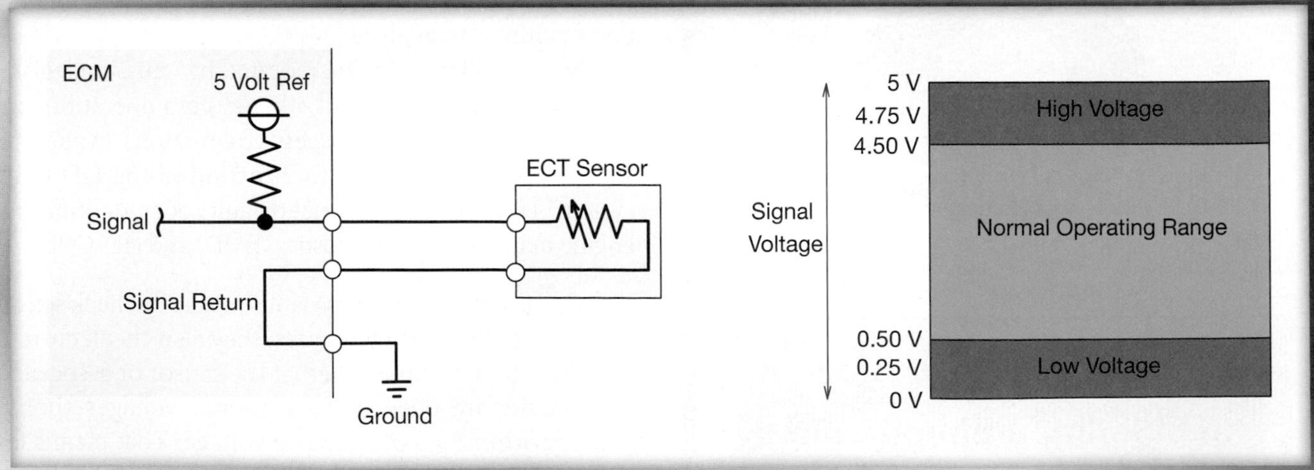

FIGURE 20-37 Out of range voltage codes on sensors are produced when the signal voltage falls outside 85% of reference voltage. This means signal voltages below 0.5 and above 4.5 typically trigger out of range voltage codes.

detection strategy whereby the validity or accuracy of sensor data is evaluated by comparing sensor voltages with expected values. Most often, sensor data from several more sensors or measurement systems is compared with data from a particular sensor to see if the data makes sense (that is, that it's logical or rational). Another name given to these types of faults is in-range faults, because the sensor could produce signal voltages that are not above or below a fault threshold voltage but the sensor may have failed and is supplying incorrect data.

3. *Functionality faults*. HD-OBD systems are required to evaluate the operation of at least 12 to 14 other major emission systems, such as the exhaust aftertreatment, boost pressure, EGR, and so on. Simple or elaborate fault detection strategies are used to check whether a particular emission system is functioning correctly. The major system monitors, as they are called, depend on sensor data to function, but they do not specifically check the sensor except to analyze the influence of sensor data on a system. For example, if a system could not enter closed loop operation because the sensor data was out of range, irrational, or had some problem with its operation such as abnormal operating frequency or switching time or defective waveform, the sensor would be identified as having a fault. NO_X sensor faults are a common example in which the sensor is working properly but, due to some other incorrect system function, and the sensor is producing higher NO_X levels, the sensor is identified as defective. In many cases, the NO_X sensor is identified as being faulty but problems with a catalytic converter, EGR valve, or restricted air intake systems will produce what appears to be an in-range fault but the problem actually lies outside the sensor.

Comprehensive Component Monitor

The comprehensive component monitor (CCM) is one of the system monitors required for EMD and HD-OBD systems. It is a continuous monitor that constantly checks for malfunctions in any engine or emission-related electrical circuit or component providing input or output signals to an ECM. Electrical inputs and outputs are evaluated for circuit continuity and shorts by measuring voltage drops in a circuit. The monitor is also responsible for performing rationality checks of sensors. For example, if an oil pressure sensor indicated the engine had 40 psi (276 kPa) of oil pressure and the engine was stopped, the data would not make sense and therefore a rationality fault would be stored. Another example would be that of a coolant temperature sensor that indicated the coolant was warm, say 140°F (60°C), but all other sensors such as oil, fuel, air inlet, and transmission temperatures were at –20°F (-29°C) and the engine had just started after cold soaking for 20 hours. Such a code could be triggered by plugging in a block heater, or it might indicate a defective sensor. Rationality codes need careful pinpoint diagnostic tests to determine if a sensor is defective or some outside influence is affecting sensor data.

Outputs such as injector solenoids, relays, and dosing valves are evaluated by the CCM for opens and shorts by monitoring a feedback circuit from the field effect transistor (FET), or "smart driver" associated with the output circuit. Smart FETs, as they are called, are FETs designed to supply data about the amount of amperage passing through the transistor gate **FIGURE 20-38**. These same gates can operate as virtual fuses that can disconnect power to the circuit if current flow is excessive. CCM codes use fault mode indicators (FMIs) developed by the Society of Automotive Engineers (SAE)that indicate how an electrical circuit has failed **TABLE 20-1**. Out of range voltage codes that are the most common when sensors and circuits are open or shorted include FMI 3 and 4. J1587 and J1939 SAE rationality codes are 0, 1, and 2. J1939 also adds FMI codes 15–18, 20, and 21 for rationality-related faults. Codes 8–10 are used to report problems with waveforms from sensors or systems. Codes 5 and 6 are used by smart drivers detecting excessive or insufficient amperage in a circuit. Only FMI codes 11–14, 19, and 31 are not used by the CCM.

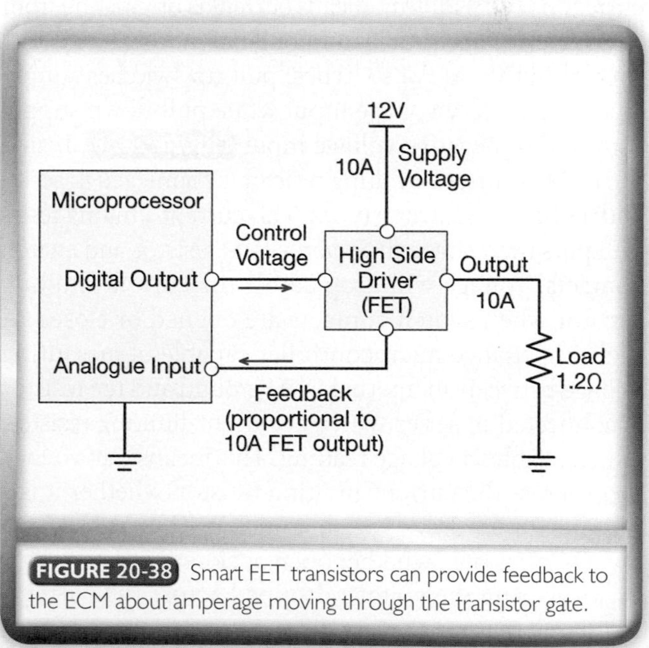

FIGURE 20-38 Smart FET transistors can provide feedback to the ECM about amperage moving through the transistor gate.

TABLE 20-1: Society of Automotive Engineers (SAE) J1939 Failure Mode Identifier (FMI)

FMI	SAE Text
0	Data valid but above normal operational range—most severe level
1	Data valid but below normal operational range—most severe level
2	Data erratic, intermittent, or incorrect
3	Voltage above normal or shorted to high source
4	Voltage below normal or shorted to low source
5	Current below normal or open circuit
6	Current above normal or grounded circuit
7	Mechanical system not responding or out of adjustment
8	Abnormal frequency or pulse width or period
9	Abnormal update rate
10	Abnormal rate of change
11	Root cause not known
12	Bad intelligent device or component
13	Out of calibration
14	Special instructions
15	Data valid but above normal operating range—least severe level
16	Data valid but above normal operating range—moderately severe level
17	Data valid but below normal operating range—least severe level
18	Data valid but below normal operating range—moderately severe level
19	Received network data in error
20–30	Reserved for SAE assignment
31	Condition exists

Circuit Monitoring—Voltage Drop Measurement

The way in which switch operation is monitored inside helps provide a foundation for other circuits to monitor sensors. Two basic types of switch inputs to the ECM are pull-up and pull-down switches. The terms pull-up and pull-down are often used to describe whether current through a circuit is supplied by the positive or negative current polarity. Pull-up means current is originating from a positive voltage source, and pull down from a negative source. In the case of switches, pull-up switches supply a positive battery voltage input while pull-down supply a ground or negative voltage input **FIGURE 20-39**. Inside the ECM, a current-limiting resistor is connected in series with either of the switch types. This current-limiting resistor splits the voltage drop across the resistor and switch contacts. Voltage will drop across the current-limiting resistor when switch contacts are opened or closed. A high-impedance microcontroller capable of measuring voltage between an internal ECM ground and the resistor is connected in series with the current-limiting resistor, which enables a voltage reading. This means that voltage drop across the current-limiting resistor, whether it is a pull-up or pull-down switch, is measured by a voltmeter. Switch status (i.e., whether open or closed) is determined by measuring the voltage dropped across the current-limiting resistor.

Pull-Up Resistors

When two resistors are connected in series, the greatest voltage drop takes place across the resistor with the highest resistance. The remaining resistor will drop the remaining voltage in a circuit. This is predicted by Kirchhoff's law, which states the sum of the voltage drops in a circuit equals source voltage **FIGURE 20-40**. Because the microcontroller inside the ECM that measures voltage has very high resistance, it behaves like the largest of the resistors in a circuit. A pull-up resistor will have most voltage drop measured after the current-limiting resistor when the switch is open, because it places the microcontroller in series with the resistor. In this case, only a small amount of voltage is dropped by the current-limiting resistor and the most voltage through the highly resistive microcontroller to an internal ground. When the switch is closed, the very low resistance across the contacts will cause the most current to flow through the switch contacts and the series connected current-limiting resistor. Almost no current flows through the highly resistive microcontroller, because the microcontroller has much higher resistance compared to the pull-up resistor and switch, which are connected in series.

Smart-Diagnosable Switches

Disconnected switches, shorted switch wiring, and resistive switch contacts cannot be diagnosed using open or closed diagnostic logic. To differentiate a disconnected

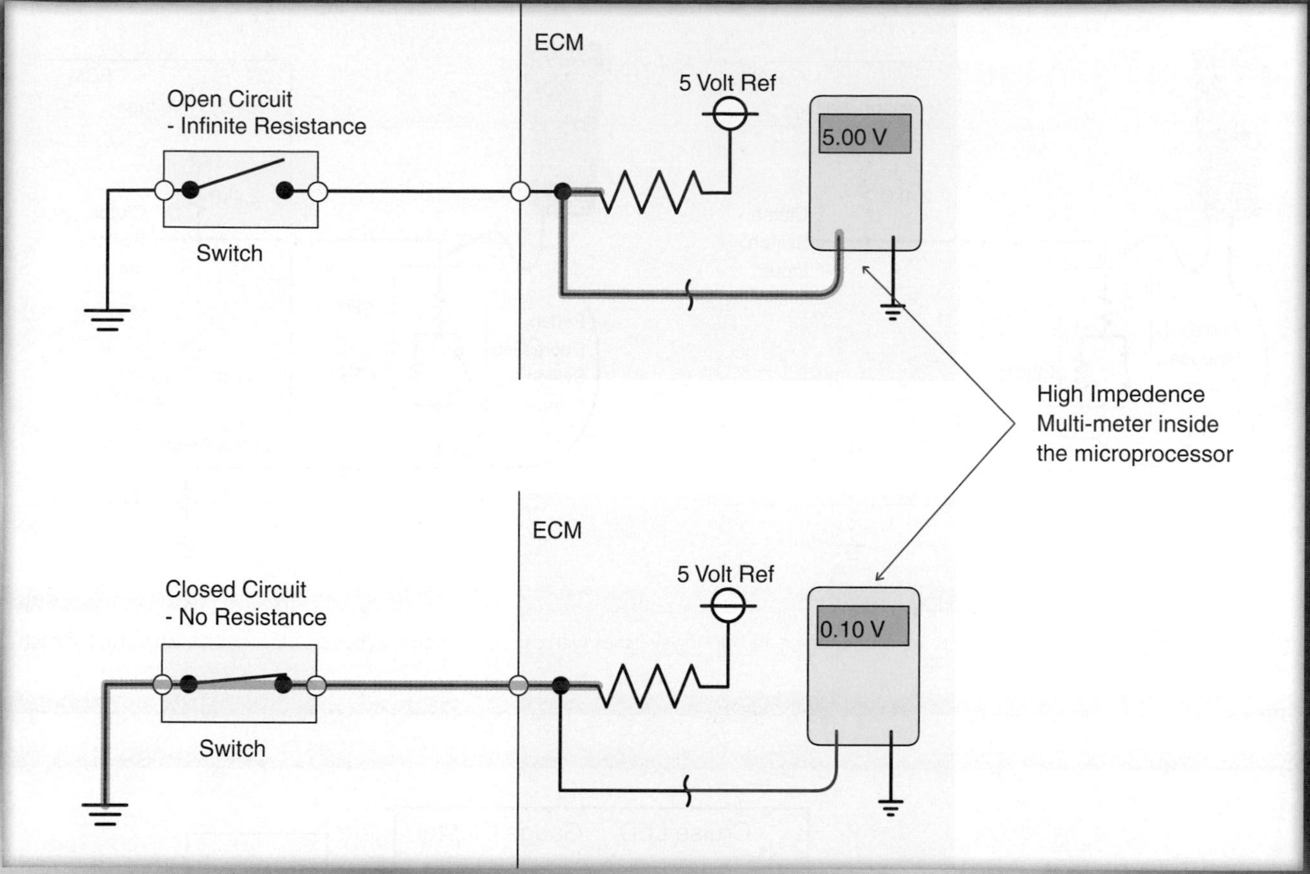

FIGURE 20-39 Pull-up switches supply a positive voltage to the ECM while pull-down switches supply negative or ground.

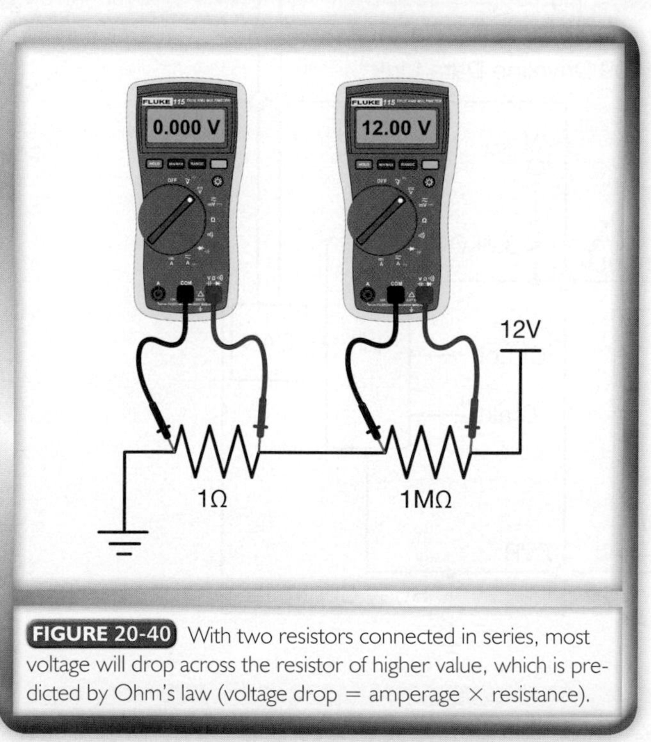

FIGURE 20-40 With two resistors connected in series, most voltage will drop across the resistor of higher value, which is predicted by Ohm's law (voltage drop = amperage × resistance).

switch from an open switch, resistors are placed in series or in parallel with the switch **FIGURE 20-41**. This enables the microcontroller to identify problems in the wiring between the switch and ECM for failures such as shorted to ground or open circuited wiring. When properly connected in a functioning circuit, the resistor incorporated into the switch in series will have a calibrated resistance sensed by the microcontroller and measured as a specific voltage drop. If a switch has a resistor connected in parallel across its contacts, opening the switch provides a specific voltage drop measured by the microcontroller. If the switch wiring is shorted to ground, to battery positive, or simply disconnected, programmed logic within the microcontroller will identify the voltage reading as different from the switch resistance when opened or closed and log the appropriate fault code **FIGURE 20-42**. Pull-up resistors can be connected in series with the switches to further enhance the diagnostic capabilities of the microcontroller. Clutch, brake light, or AC pressure switches often use these arrangements because of their critical functions.

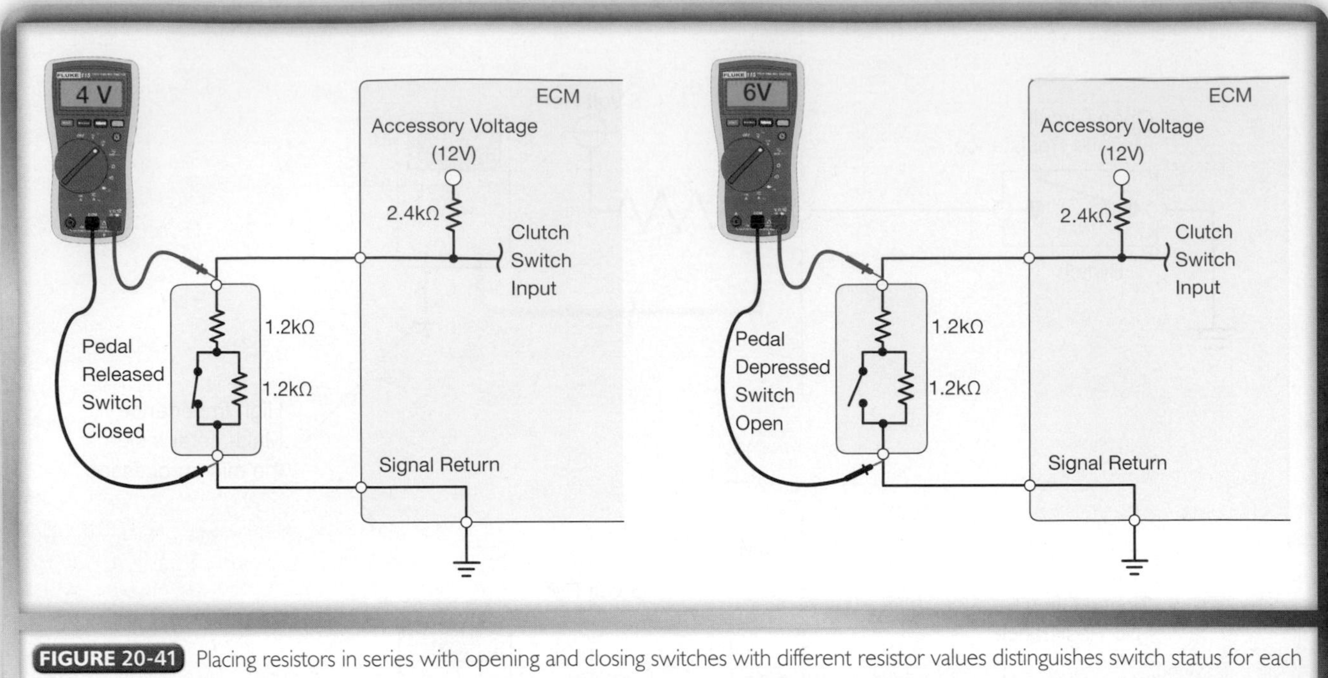

FIGURE 20-41 Placing resistors in series with opening and closing switches with different resistor values distinguishes switch status for each of these "smart switches."

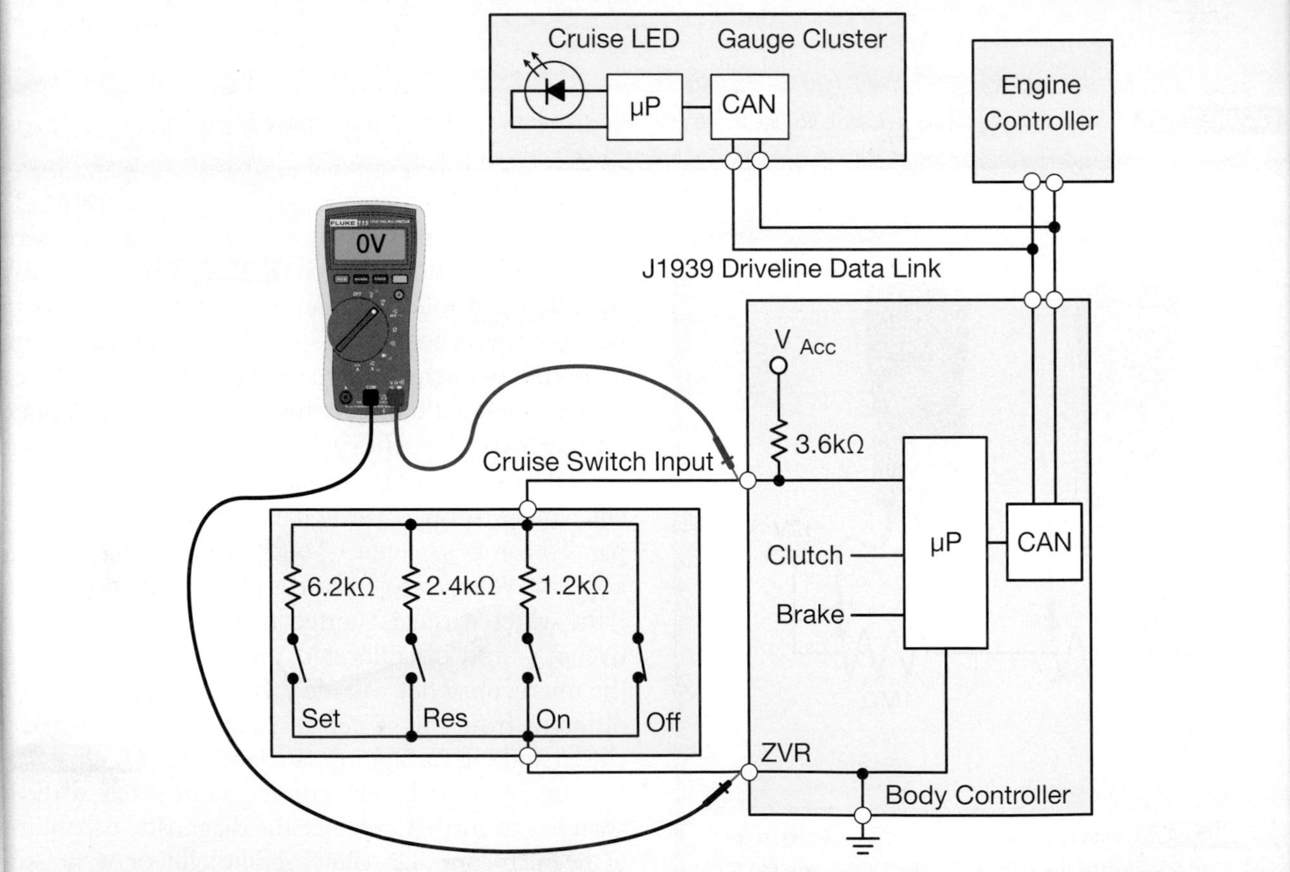

FIGURE 20-42 Resistors internal to the microcontroller are used to identify the different switches in a vehicle for proper control logic.

> **TECHNICIAN TIP**
>
> It is a very important and fundamental principle of electrical troubleshooting that when an ECM stores a diagnostic code, the code generally points to a problem somewhere in the circuit and not necessarily to the device connected to the circuit. If a code for a sensor is logged, further pinpoint testing using a diagnostic flowchart is required to properly diagnose the circuit.

Regulated Reference Voltage (Vref)

Regulated voltage supplied to sensor circuits is called reference voltage (Vref) and is important for several reasons. First, a stable and precise voltage is necessary for accurate voltage drop calculations used to determine the unknown resistance value of a sensor. Without the regulated voltage supply, changes in system voltage would produce sensor error. Current-limiting resistors are supplied a voltage lower than battery Vref to prevent excessive current flow through the microcontroller circuit if wiring becomes shorted. Vref values are typically 5 volts. (There are some exceptions: Caterpillar uses 8 volts on some control systems.) An internal ground called zero-volt reference (ZVR) is just as important. All sensors using reference voltage return current through the control module and not to chassis ground. Variations in voltage at chassis ground would produce error in voltage drop calculations, resulting in incorrect signal voltages. The internal ground is also filtered and "cleaned," meaning it is free from electromagnetic interference.

> **TECHNICIAN TIP**
>
> Just as Vref to sensors and switch circuits is regulated to typically +5 volts, a regulated ground circuit is provided through control modules. All sensors using reference voltage need a regulated ground return circuit through the control module and never to chassis ground to prevent electrical interference and variations to voltage measurements. The control module in turn is connected to chassis ground, which is the only way the electronic control system can function effectively.

Two-Wire Pull-Up Circuit Monitoring

To identify faults and measure signal voltage, thermistors are often connected to internal pull-up resistors. Thermistors are variable resistors that change resistance with temperature. These temperature-sensing devices are monitored for:

- Resistance to validate normal signal voltage and detect out of range faults
- Opens, either internal or in the circuit wiring
- Shorts to power
- Shorts to ground

Like switches, the control module will measure voltage drop across an internal current-limiting resistor to calculate voltage drop across a thermistor. NTC thermistors increase resistance when they become colder and decrease resistance when they become warmer. Measuring temperature is performed by calculating the voltage drop across the thermistor connected in series with the current-limiting resistor. As the resistance of the thermistor increases, less voltage is dropped across the pull-up resistor and more across the thermistor. The microcontroller will measure more voltage drop across the pull-up resistor when the thermistor becomes less resistive. Unwanted extra resistance in the circuit will produce a higher voltage drop across the sensor, generating colder temperatures. An open circuit (high resistance) will read the coldest temperature possible. Circuit monitoring fault detection is typically designed to recognize sensor resistance values within approximately 85% of the voltage supplied from the pull-up resistor to be within normal range, and voltage readings outside of that range are recognized as abnormal **FIGURE 20-43**. Normal signal range used to diagnose most sensor circuits covers the entire operating range of the sensor signal, and the circuit should always have some resistance whether hot or cold. A disconnected sensor will have infinite resistance,

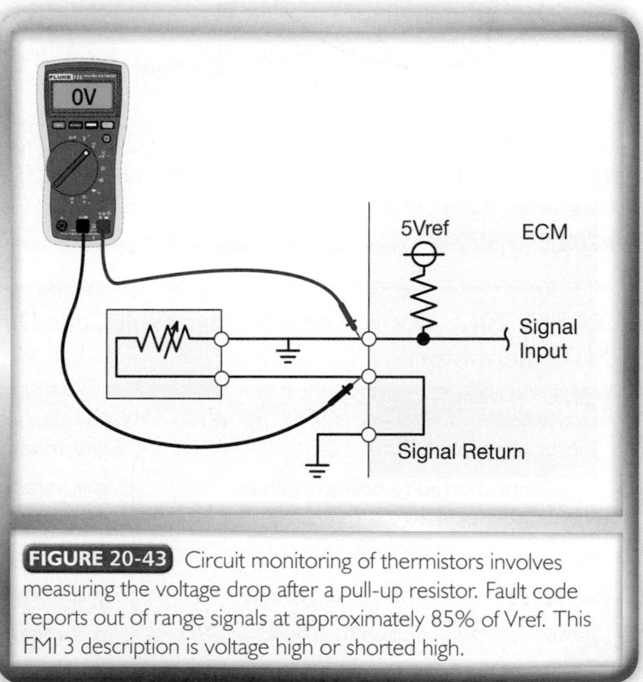

FIGURE 20-43 Circuit monitoring of thermistors involves measuring the voltage drop after a pull-up resistor. Fault code reports out of range signals at approximately 85% of Vref. This FMI 3 description is voltage high or shorted high.

and no voltage is dropped across the thermistor. In these circumstances, the voltage reading by the circuit's microcontroller will see maximum voltage between its internal ground and the current-limiting resistor. An open sensor or disconnected open wiring will produce an SAE fault code description of "out of range high or shorted high" (FMI 3) FIGURE 20-44.

The manufacturing and SAE FMI code descriptions point to the higher voltage sensed by the microcontroller because no voltage is dropped by the disconnected or open thermistor circuit and all voltage is now dropped by the microcontroller. Note that the sensor signal wire that is shorted to positive battery voltage or another +5-volt supply will generate an identical fault code as an open circuited signal wire FIGURE 20-45. The logic used by the microcontroller that senses no or little voltage drop across the pull-up resistor could be caused by a positive voltage supply shorted to the signal wire. The ZVR could also be open and produce the same voltage readings by the microcontroller. Both conditions require appropriate pinpoint testing to isolate the fault.

If a thermistor signal wire is rubbed through and making contact to chassis ground, more current will flow through the signal circuit and the fault code description typically includes:

- Out of range low or shorted low (FMI 4)
- Signal wire shorted to sensor return or battery negative (OEM code)
- Signal source shorted to ground (OEM code)

Excessive current flow across the pull-up resistor connected in series with the grounded circuit means low or no voltage is measured between the pull-up resistor and the signal wire. Because most current will flow through the short to ground, little current will flow through the microcontroller, and the voltage drop will be less than 0.5 volts. This explains why the code description given is out of range low or shorted low (FMI 4). Diagnostic logic programmed into the microcontroller points to a short to ground, causing excessive voltage drop across the current-limiting resistor of more than 85% of the voltage supplied to the resistor TABLE 20-2.

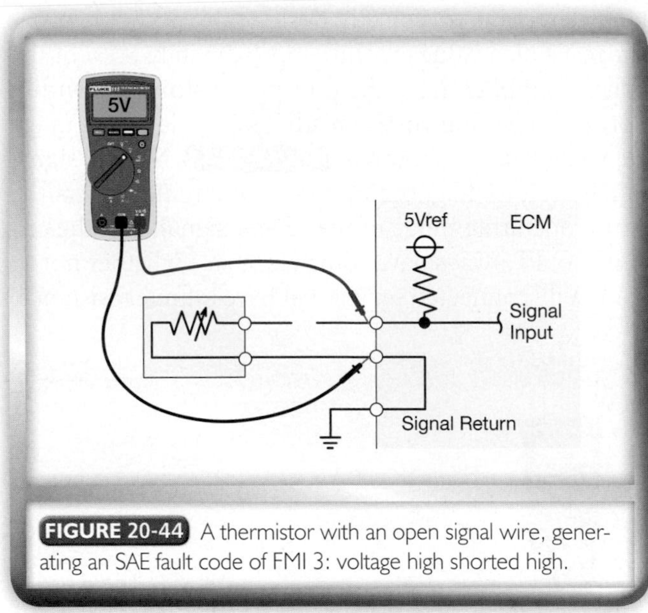

FIGURE 20-44 A thermistor with an open signal wire, generating an SAE fault code of FMI 3: voltage high shorted high.

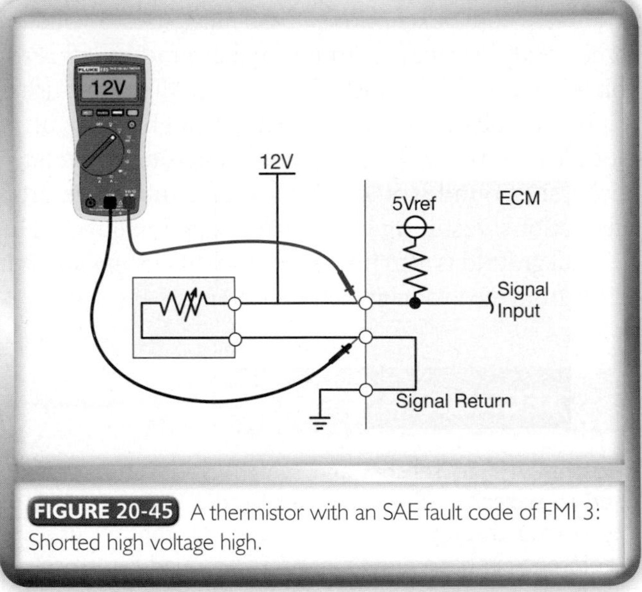

FIGURE 20-45 A thermistor with an SAE fault code of FMI 3: Shorted high voltage high.

TABLE 20-2: Out-of-Range Voltage Fault Code Descriptions Using a Pull-Up Resistor (i.e., two-wire NTC thermistor)

Condition	Observation	Code Description
Sensor disconnected	Signal voltage higher than 4.5 volts	FMI 3: Out of range high, shorted high
Signal wire shorted to positive voltage (12v battery or +5 volts reference)	Signal voltage higher than 4.5 volts	FMI 3: Out of range high, shorted high
Sensor open	Signal voltage higher than 4.5 volts	FMI 3: Out of range high, shorted high
Sensor signal wire shorted to ground	Signal voltage lower than 0.5 volts	FMI 4: Out of range low, shorted low
Sensor internally shorted to ground or ZVR	Signal voltage lower than 0.5 volts	FMI 4: Out of range low, shorted low

Manufacturers can go beyond SAE minimum standards for reporting faults using J1939 protocols and add additional fault code descriptions using their own coding system. In the case of the disconnected thermistor, an enhanced code could carry a code description such as "signal wire shorted to sensor supply" or "short to battery volt," "signal source shorted to voltage source," "open return," or "signal circuit."

TECHNICIAN TIP

Pressure, temperature position, and other sensors can share a +5 Vref or ZVR wire. Return is the equivalent to chassis ground through the control module, which is free of electromagnetic interference and is regulated to provide the cleanest signal path. Problems in the reference voltage or signal return path can cause unusual problems and multiple fault codes from all the sensors. "Shorted high or low" and "voltage high or low" are typical fault code descriptions produced if sensors share common Vref and ZVR pathways. This happens because the voltage supplied to the sensors has changed. Less than +5 volts or the absence of a ZVR distorts the ECM's ability to properly sense correct signal voltages. If the return is connected to chassis ground, voltage fluctuations and electromagnetic interference can sometimes distort electrical signals and measurement of voltage drops across the sensor circuits. A single defective sensor may have an internal short circuit to ground and +5 volts, which can interfere with the operation of all sensors. Disconnecting a defective sensor can sometimes cause the multiple fault codes to disappear. The use of an LED diode installed in series with the ZVR circuit at each sensor can detect a malfunctioning circuit or device because the polarity-sensitive LED will light in both directions when connected to the defective sensor.

TECHNICIAN TIP

Just because a control module does not log a fault code does not mean that no problems exist in the electronic control system. Because the normal signal range (within 85%) used to diagnose most sensor circuits spans the entire operating range of the sensor, it is possible for the sensor to produce a signal that does not measure the actual operating condition and therefore will not be identified with a fault code. A good strategy to identify problems is to monitor signal voltage using a scanner or software data list while comparing observed values with expected values reported in a shop manual.

TECHNICIAN TIP

Quick-testing to determine whether a fault code is generated by defective wiring, pin connectors, or sensor can be performed using jumper wires. While monitoring sensor signal voltage using an electronic service tool, the signal voltage values should change when either disconnecting the sensor or jumping sensor signal wires to ZVR or +5 Vref. If no change is observed when momentarily grounding the signal wire or supplying the signal wire with +5 Vref, the wiring or pin connections in the circuit are suspect. Some manufacturers recommend using a calibrated resistor in series with the jumper wire when performing these tests to prevent damage to sensitive control modules.

Three-Wire Sensor Circuit Monitoring

Three-wire circuits, whether digital or analog, passive or active, use a reference voltage, signal, and ZVR wire, also referred to as ground return by some manufacturers. Voltage out of range faults (FMI 3 and 4) are detected when the signal voltage from a sensor typically exceeds 0.5–4.5 volts out-of-range fault threshold TABLE 20-3. The majority of three-wire sensors typically measure signal voltage between the positive voltage on the signal wire and the

TABLE 20-3: Out-of-Range Voltage Fault Code Descriptions Using a Pull-Down Resistor (i.e., three-wire potentiometer)

Condition	Observation	Code Description
Sensor disconnected	Signal voltage lower than 0.5 volts	FMI 4: Out of range low, shorted low
Signal wire shorted to positive voltage (12v battery or +5 Vref)	Signal voltage higher than 4.5 volts	FMI 3: Out of range high, shorted high
Sensor open	Signal voltage lower than 0.5 volts	FMI 4: Out of range low, shorted low
Sensor signal wire shorted to ground	Signal voltage lower than 0.5 volts	FMI 4: Out of range low, shorted low
Sensor internally shorted to ground or ZVR	Signal voltage lower than 0.5 volts	FMI 4: Out of range low, shorted low

ZVR wire across a pull-down resistor FIGURE 20-46. However, some active three-wire sensors such as Hall effect sensors and several manufacturers of pressure sensors supply variable resistance ground path for a +5-Vref from the ECM through the sensor's ZVR FIGURE 20-47.

In this case, measuring signal voltage with three-wire sensors involves using a pull-up or pull down resistor located in the ECM. In the case of a circuit using a pull-down resistor, a voltage-measuring microcontroller connected in parallel across the pull-down resistor measures voltage drop across the resistor between the positive signal wire and the negative ZVR. Because there is only one pull-down resistor, all the voltage supplied by the signal wire will be dropped across the pull-down resistor. This means that a defective active type sensor will have a fault code of FMI 4 for low voltage or shorted low if the +5 Vref and ZVR circuits are open FIGURE 20-48. Because no current is supplied to the active sensor with either an open Vref or ZVR, internal sensor circuits cannot operate and supply a varying signal voltage. Voltage in this case would be 0, which is below the 0.5-volt fault threshold for low voltage. A short to ground signal wire will produce an identical shorted low, voltage low FMI fault code.

If the sensor supplies a ground path for a signal circuit from the ECM containing a pull-up resistor carrying +5 volts, a disconnected sensor will produce a voltage high, shorted high FMI fault code. In this instance, the active sensor cannot work and provide an electronically variable resistance to ZVR for the current supplied through the pull-up resistor. This means the microcontroller will see +5 volts on the signal wire and produce a fault code of FMI 3: voltage high, shorted high, as illustrated in Figure 20-47.

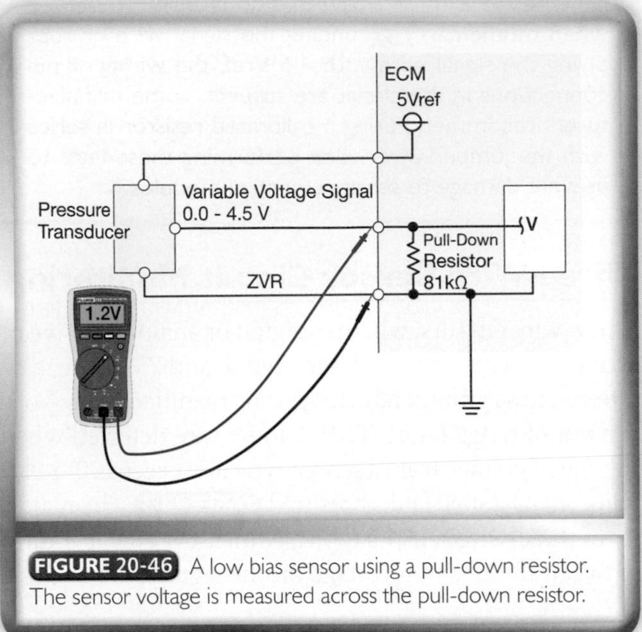

FIGURE 20-46 A low bias sensor using a pull-down resistor. The sensor voltage is measured across the pull-down resistor.

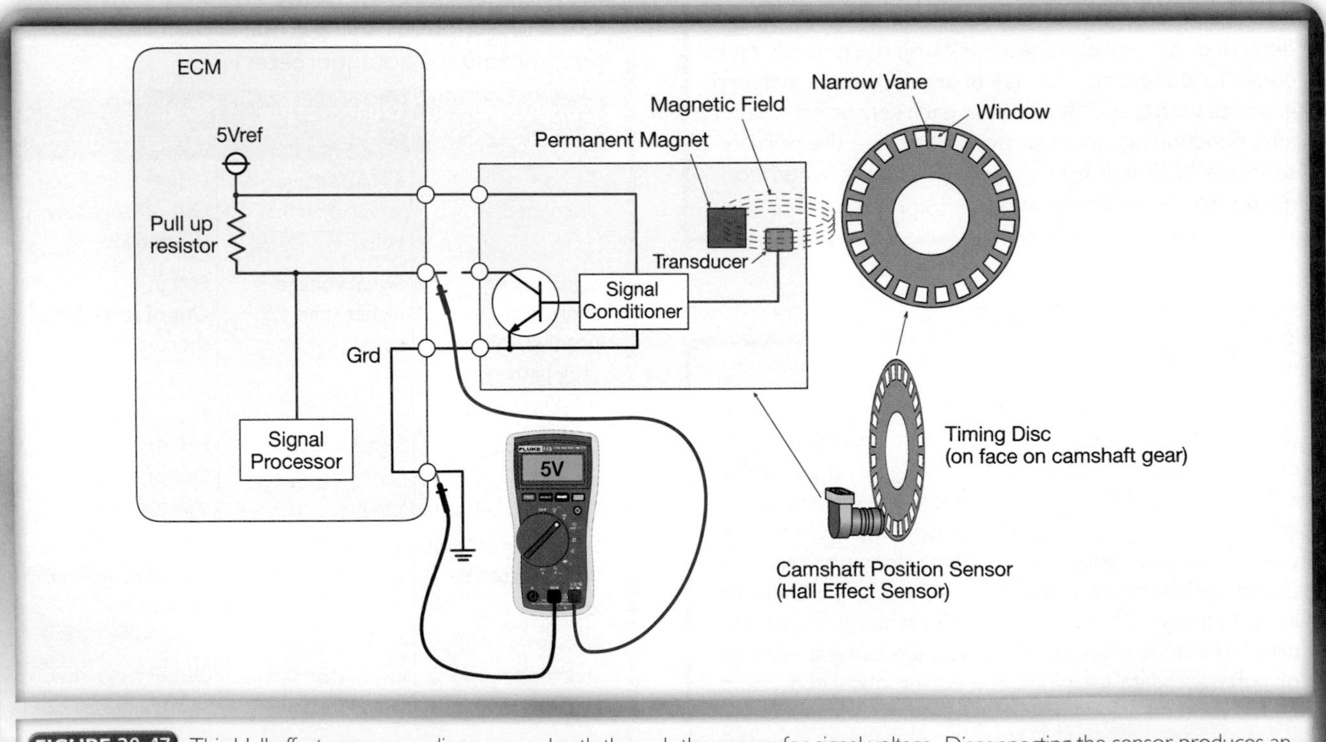

FIGURE 20-47 This Hall effect sensor supplies a ground path through the sensor for signal voltage. Disconnecting the sensor produces an out of range +5 volts signal, which makes it a high-bias three-wire active sensor. Grounding the signal wire produces a 0-volts signal.

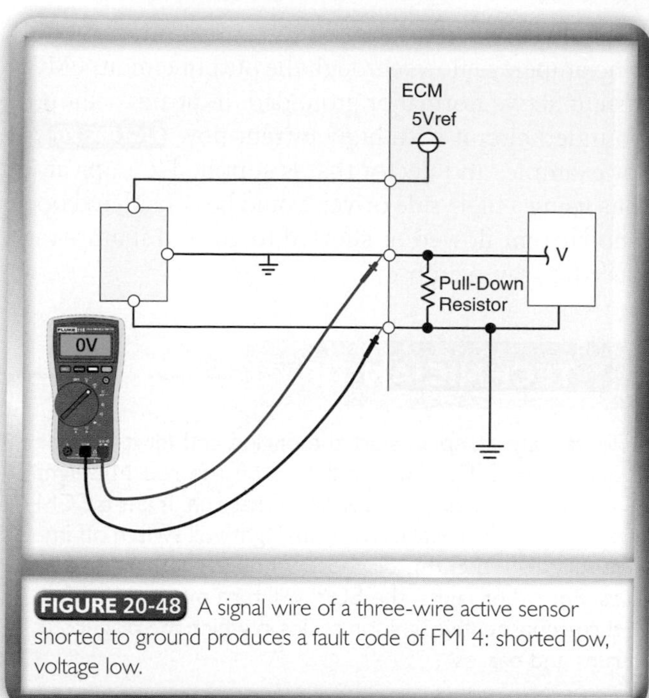

FIGURE 20-48 A signal wire of a three-wire active sensor shorted to ground produces a fault code of FMI 4: shorted low, voltage low.

High- and Low-Bias Sensors

Whenever a sensor is disconnected or open, the out of range voltage code will either be out of range high or low. If the arrangement of the pull-up resistor causes signal voltage to go high when disconnected, it is considered a high-bias resistor. That is, it has a bias or tendency to produce a fault code of out-of-range high, voltage high, or FMI 3. If the tendency for a sensor circuit is to produce a voltage low code when disconnected, it is considered a low-bias sensor. Generally, high-bias sensors use a pull-up resistor and low-bias sensors monitor signal voltage with a pull-down resistor.

Circuits using pull-up and pull-down resistors have the added advantage of limiting excessive current flow to a sensor to protect the wiring, sensor, or control module if a short to ground or battery positive takes place. Excessive current flow would be reduced by the resistor when a fault condition exists. By limiting excessive current flow during shorted conditions in sensor circuits, Vref and ZVR circuits are protected as well.

More comprehensive circuit monitoring also takes place between the Vref and ZVR in some but not all control systems. Open, shorted to ground, or shorted to voltage source or resistive circuit pathways result in fault codes for these circuits. Because ZVR is common to the sensors, problems with the reference voltage to a specific sensor circuit may only be detected.

TECHNICIAN TIP

After performing a repair to an electronic control system, the repair should be validated before returning a vehicle to service to confirm the fault code does not reappear. In HD-OBD systems, repair validation requires operating the circuit or device under the enabling conditions for a major system monitor to run and obtain a system readiness code. Make sure the conditions to operate the device or run the monitor are met during the testing procedure. These procedures are outlined in the service manual. Double check that no codes are pending or waiting to illuminate a malfunction indicator lamp (MIL). Occasionally, diagnostic codes can be set during routine service procedures or by problems outside the electronic control system. Always clear codes and confirm that they reset prior to circuit troubleshooting. Comprehensive monitor codes on HD-OBD vehicles often only require cycling the ignition switch on and off after a repair is completed to extinguish the MIL light.

TECHNICIAN TIP

Tools required for fault isolation pinpoint testing include a Digital Volt Ohm Meter (DVOM) and some test leads or jumper wires. Proper break-out harness or pin connectors are needed to access the various connectors and components to be tested. Using improper tools can result in damage to pins and connectors and faulty meter reading, causing misleading diagnosis and produce even more diagnostic codes.

TECHNICIAN TIP

If an intermittent fault is suspected, a physical check of the suspect circuit can be performed by flexing connectors and harnesses at likely failure points while monitoring the circuit with a multimeter or oscilloscope. Graphing meters with glitch testing capabilities can identify and record the circuit fault in microseconds. If the problem is related to temperature, vibration, or moisture, the circuit or control module can be heated, lightly tapped, or even sprayed with water to simulate the failure conditions. Some testing software features pull test capabilities, which can provide an audible alert when brief interruption in circuit voltages takes place when pulling or bending wiring harnesses.

Low- and High-Side Driver Faults

A large variety of electrical devices such as relays, motors, and injectors depend on current supplied from a control module to operate. When supplying a negative polarity or ground to a device, current is switched through a transistor called a low-side driver. Similarly, switching transistors supplying positive DC voltage are referred to as high-side drivers. Two techniques are used to detect opens, shorts, high resistance, and excessive current draw in these circuits. Current-limiting resistors used to measure voltage drop in the output circuit much like in sensor circuits are used to evaluate circuit performance. Another method involves direct measurement of output current using smart FETs **FIGURE 20-49**. In these circuts, the drain-to-source current flows are measured through a special feedback circuit to the microcontroller. Time on and amperage are used to set fault codes. FMIs 5 and 6 are produced when amperage exceeds out of range thresholds.

FMI 5, current below normal or open, is produced if little or no amperage flows through the output circuit. FMI 6, current above normal or grounded, indicates a short to grounded circuit with high current flow **FIGURE 20-50**. For example, an injector that is supplied 2 amps at 70 volts using a high-side driver would be considered open if no current flowed or shorted to ground if amperage exceeded, say, 5 amps.

> **TECHNICIAN TIP**
>
> To validate a repair, start the engine and let it idle for one minute. The ECM will turn off the red MIL light whenever the diagnostic monitor has run. If it is a CCM evaluating electrical circuits, the light will switch off immediately when this diagnostic monitor runs and passes. For other faults, the ECM will turn off the MIL after three consecutive ignition cycles in which the diagnostic runs and passes.

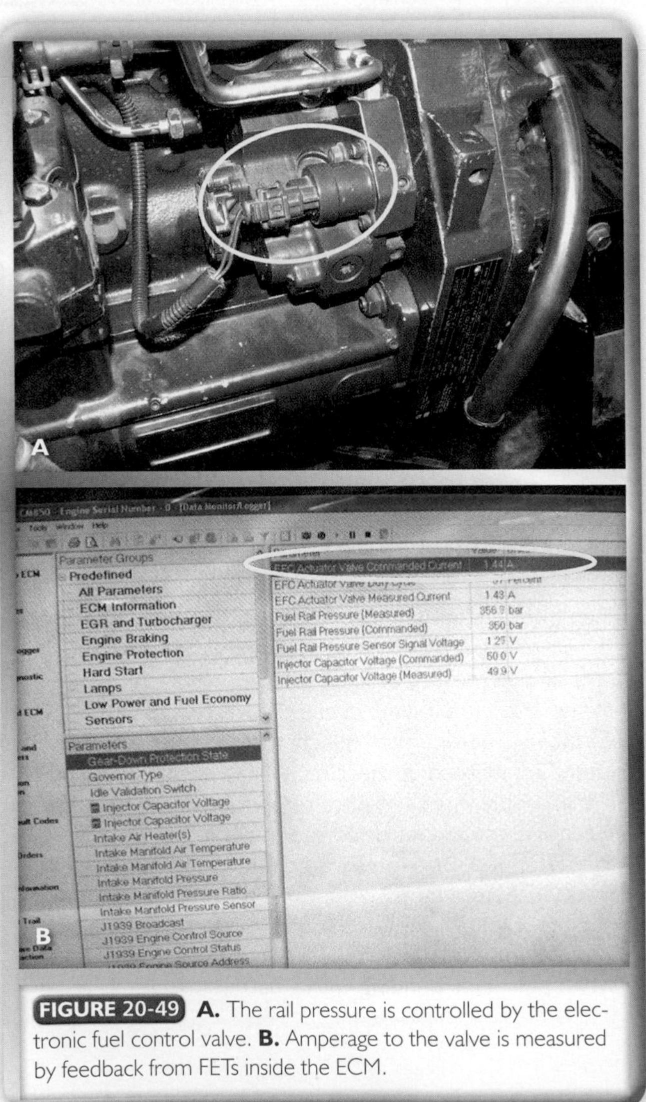

FIGURE 20-49 **A.** The rail pressure is controlled by the electronic fuel control valve. **B.** Amperage to the valve is measured by feedback from FETs inside the ECM.

Maintenance of Sensors

The on-board diagnostic system capabilities are limited and can only narrow a fault to a circuit or system. After that, the technician must identify what the nature of the problem is that produced the diagnostic fault code. Servicing of sensor faults involves performing pinpoint electrical tests and making other observations to identify

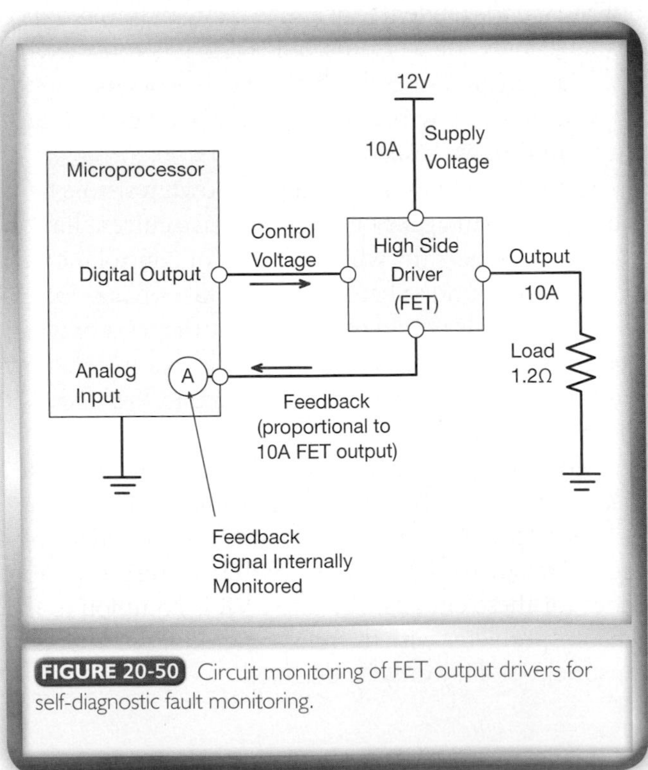

FIGURE 20-50 Circuit monitoring of FET output drivers for self-diagnostic fault monitoring.

precisely where and what caused the fault. This stage of diagnostic testing is called off-board diagnostics.

Diagnostic Testing of Pressure Sensors

Diagnostic tests of pressure sensors are similar to other strategies for evaluating three-wire sensors. Onboard diagnostic systems will identify problems in the circuits. Scan tools can then measure real-time data to observe abnormal but in-range functional problems and retrieve fault codes associated with the circuits TABLE 20-4. Pinpoint tests using break-out harnesses are performed on live circuits, too. Resistance tests are used to identify shorted or open wires in harnesses to these sensors. However, because these are active sensors with sensitive electronic circuits, it is not possible to perform resistance tests on the sensors themselves.

Safety

Never use a 12-volt jumper wire connected to battery positive to quick-check sensor harnesses. The ECM can easily be damaged by this method.

Diagnostic Testing of Thermistors

The range of resistance values of a thermistor varies by manufacturer and what temperature range the sensor measures. The change in resistance is not linear or directly proportional to temperature, either TABLE 20-5. At the low and high ends of temperature range, small changes in temperature produce large changes in resistance while changes in midrange temperature values produce smaller changes to sensor resistance. Several temperature and resistance values are supplied by the manufacturer to properly evaluate a thermistor when testing using an ohmmeter.

Diagnostic Testing of Variable Reluctance Sensors

Variable reluctance sensors are two-wire passive sensors. The coil of wire surrounding a magnet should be tested for continuity and its resistance measured. Resistance is high because there are hundreds of wire winding turns and the wire diameter is very small. The output of the sensor can be measured with an alternating-current voltmeter. As the reluctor speed increases, the voltage produced by the sensor will rise proportionately.

A broken magnet will cause a low voltage reading. Likewise, an improper air gap between the sensor and reluctor will cause sensor output failure. Iron filings at the magnet of the sensor will also cause an inadequate change in sensor reluctance, generating insufficient voltage. Simply removing, cleaning, and reinstalling the sensor can sometimes correct inadequate or erratic sensor signals.

Variable reluctance sensor operation can often be evaluated from a scan tool or waveform graphing meter. For example, if an engine speed sensor is defective, engine speed data cannot be observed from a scanner. Graphing meters can compare known good sensor waveforms with observed waveforms to detect sensor faults.

TABLE 20-4: Fault Code Descriptions for a Two- or Three-Wire Sensor

Condition	Observation	Code Description
In-range voltage but signal not valid	No rationality or plausibility when data compared with normal system behavior or other sensor inputs	In-range fault

TABLE 20-5: The Inverse and Non-Linear Relationship Between Temperature and Resistance of a Thermistor

Temperature		Resistance
°Celsius	°Fahrenheit	Ohms
100	210	185
70	160	450
38	100	1,600
20	70	3,400
–4	40	7,500
–7	20	13,500
–18	0	250,000
–40	–40	100,700

Diagnostic Testing of Hall Effect Sensors

Diagnostic testing of Hall effect sensors will follow similar diagnostic strategies for any other three-wire active sensor FIGURE 20-51. Out of range faults on the sensor can be pinpoint tested with a voltmeter by first verifying +5 Vref and ZVR are available to the sensor FIGURE 20-52. After disconnecting the sensor and harness plug, a quick check to differentiate between a defective sensor and defective wiring harness is to short the +5 Vref to the signal return circuit. While monitoring sensor voltage using software or a scanner connected to the diagnostic data link connector, the signal voltage will show 5 volts or an "on" state. If there is no change in the voltage, the wiring harness or connector plugs are likely defective. Shorts of any of the circuit wires to ground, battery voltage, or to one another are checked using either an ohmmeter when the vehicle battery is disconnected or measuring voltages in the sensor harness when the circuit is live.

Another important check of Hall effect sensors is made using a graphing meter. Sometimes the circuit-board within the sensor can fail and produce a waveform unrecognizable to the ECM, such as when the edges of a normally square waveform are not sharp and well defined. This often happens during hot soak period, and the vehicle will not start until the engine cools. A graphing meter allows examination of the waveform for comparison between known good waveforms.

Diagnostics of Mass Airflow Sensors

MAF sensors produce waveforms or data that can be observed by using a graphing meter. Sensor operation can also be monitored using a scanner, OEM software, or a multimeter with a break-out harness. Diagnostics of MAF sensors will follow those of any three-wire active sensor. It is also important to remember turbulence and airflow velocity variations can give false signals. For example, dirty heater wires or hot film or film wires can cause incorrect readings. Screens placed within the sensor to reduce turbulence can catch debris. These parts will require cleaning or replacement to restore proper operation. If the heater wire is intermittently breaking open, tapping the sensor to disconnect the wire will reveal the glitch if the sensor output is observed on a graphing meter or scanner.

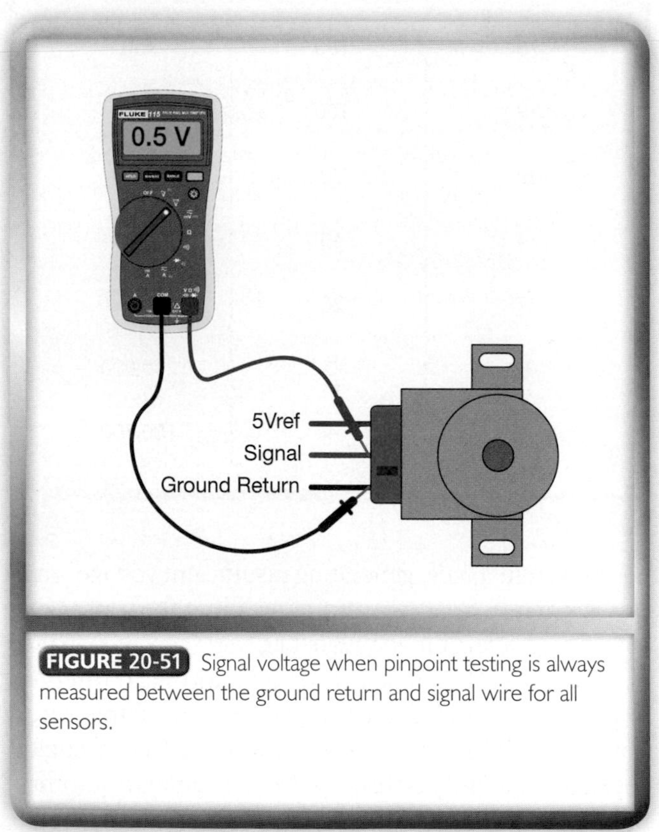

FIGURE 20-51 Signal voltage when pinpoint testing is always measured between the ground return and signal wire for all sensors.

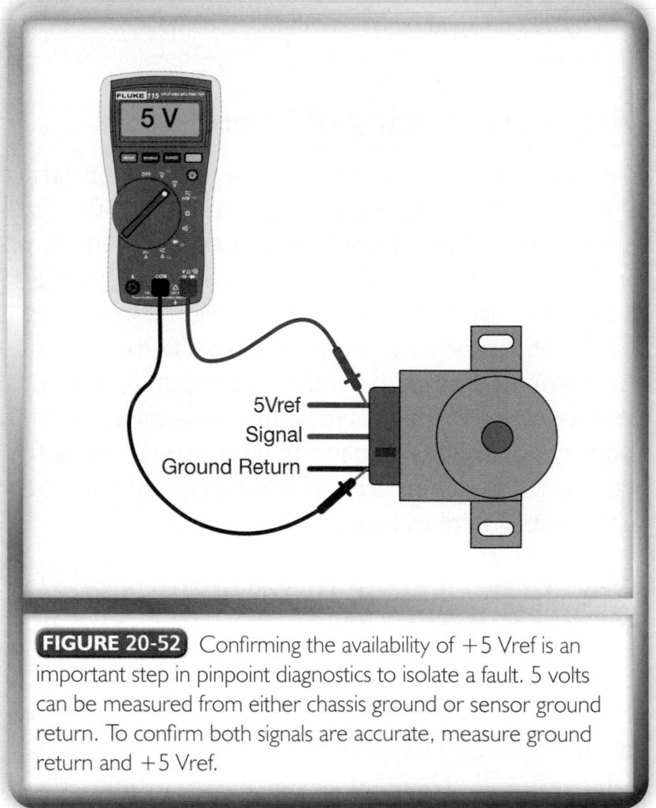

FIGURE 20-52 Confirming the availability of +5 Vref is an important step in pinpoint diagnostics to isolate a fault. 5 volts can be measured from either chassis ground or sensor ground return. To confirm both signals are accurate, measure ground return and +5 Vref.

Wrap-up

Ready for Review

- Devices that convert one form of energy into another are called transducers. Sensors are a type of transducer because they convert physical conditions or states into electrical data. Pressure, temperature, angle, speed, and mass are just a few of the physical variables about which sensors supply electrical data to processors.
- A sensor is considered active or passive depending on whether it uses power supplied by the ECM to operate.
- Reference voltage refers to a precisely regulated voltage supplied by the ECM to sensors. It is significant to processor operation because the value of the variable resistor can be calculated by measuring voltage drop across the resistor with a known input voltage.
- Other classifications of sensors include resistive sensors, voltage generators, switch sensors, variable capacitance pressure sensors, and piezo-pressure and piezoresistive sensors.
- Switches are the simplest sensors of all because they have no resistance in the closed position and infinite resistance in the open position. Switches are categorized as sensors whenever they provide information to an electronic control system.
- The simplest digital signal is a single pole single throw (SPST) switch. It is found in either an open or closed state.
- When a switch is connected between the ECM and a battery positive, it is known as a pull-up circuit. A pull-down circuit is constructed when current to the switch is connected between the ECM and a negative ground current potential.
- Resistive sensors belong to the class of sensors that condition or change a voltage signal applied to the sensor. Many types of resistive sensors exist.
- A thermistor is a temperature-sensitive variable resistor commonly used to measure coolant, oil, fuel, or air temperature. The most common type of thermistor is a negative temperature coefficient (NTC) thermistor.
- Rheostats are two-wire variable resistance sensors. They are not commonly used as input devices to an ECM but instead are used for sending units such as fuel level, oil pressure, and some temperature gauges.
- Three-wire sensors, regardless of how they appear or what function they perform, have a common wiring configuration. The first wire provides reference voltage to the sensor. The second wire provides a negative ground signal to the ECM. The third wire is a signal return from the sensor. The advantage of using three-wire sensors is that they provide comprehensive diagnostic information about the sensor and its circuit operation.
- Potentiometers are similar to rheostats in that they vary signal voltage depending on the position of a sliding contact or wiper moving across a resistive material. However, they are three-wire sensors with the signal wire connected to the internal wiper. Potentiometers supply analog data to processing circuits.
- Pressure measurements such as intake manifold boost, barometric pressure, and oil and fuel pressure use two types of sensor technology. One is a variable capacitance sensor and the other uses strain gauge resistive sensors. These are both active sensors that produce analog output signals.
- Strain gage measurements record small changes in the resistance of tiny wires caused by stretching or contraction of the wires.
- Piezoresistive sensors rely on the ability of certain mineral crystals to produce voltage or change resistance when compressed. Rather than using a strain gauge resistor wire construction, these sensors use a piezoresistive crystal arranged with a Wheatstone bridge to measure the change in resistance of the piezo crystal. The advantage of these sensors is their ability to measure very high pressures.
- A variable capacitance sensor is an active pressure sensor used to measure both dynamic and static pressure.
- Voltage generators are passive and produce an analog signal of varying voltage or AC frequency.
- Variable reluctance sensors are used to measure rotational speed. Wheel speed, vehicle speed, engine speed, and camshaft and crankshaft position sensors are common applications of these sensors.
- The ability of a material to conduct or resist magnetic lines of force is known as reluctance. Variable reluctance sensors use changing sensor reluctance to induce current flow by changing magnetic field strengths inside the sensor.

- Like variable reluctance sensors, Hall effect sensors are commonly used to measure rotational speed of a shaft. Though they are more complex and expensive to manufacture than variable reluctance sensors, they produce a digital signal square waveform and have strong signal strength at low shaft rotational speeds.
- Oxygen sensors are used adjust EGR flow on diesels and exhaust oxygen content for exhaust aftertreatment devices.
- NO_X sensors are constructed and operate similarly to wide-range planar oxygen sensors, except that different concentrations of alloys are used in the sensor walls.
- Constructed like a wide-range planar NO_X or oxygen sensor, an ammonia sensor uses an aluminum oxide substrate rather than a ZrO_2 element to detect and generate a voltage for ammonia in a range from 0 to 100 ppm.
- The mass airflow (MAF) sensor measures the weight of air entering the engine intake. Its unique design also reports data about air density, and to some extent, the vapor content.
- MAF sensors are common on engines operating at stoichiometric air–fuel ratios. However, on diesel engines operating with an excess air ratio, the MAF is used as part of the HD-OBD component monitor for the EGR. A variety of electrical signals originate from MAF sensors, but all work using a hot-wire operating principle.
- Output control devices consist of display devices, serial data for network communication, and operators—electromagnetic devices that transform electrical current into movement. Two basic types of operators are solenoids and relays.
- ECMs need to determine the correct cylinder and point in the combustion cycle for injection. To send an electrical signal for firing the injectors, the ECM needs to know two things: crankshaft position and the stroke a cylinder is on.
- Using teeth or raised lugs on a cam gear that turns at one-half engine speed can generate engine position data using a Hall effect or variable reluctance sensor.
- A better strategy than using a single sensor on the camshaft is to use both a camshaft and crankshaft position sensor. The advantage that using two sensors provides is improved precision in calculating crankshaft position.
- The crankshaft of a diesel engine will speed up and slow down with each power and compression stroke in the engine. The waveform generated from the engine position sensor(s) can determine the rotational velocity of the crank. Analyzing sensor waveforms using edge detection software algorithms, the ECM can determine how much power each cylinder is contributing to overall performance.
- A thermistor's resistance value varies by manufacturer and the substance being measured.
- Variable reluctance sensors are two-wire passive sensors. The output of the sensor can be measured using an alternating-current voltmeter. As the reluctor speed increases, the voltage produced by the sensor will rise proportionately.
- Hall effect sensors can be tested and diagnosed in a similar way to any three-wire active sensor.
- MAF sensors produce waveforms that can be observed by using a graphing meter. Sensor operation can also be monitored using a scanner or a multimeter. Diagnostics of MAF sensor follow those of any three-wire active sensor.

Vocabulary Builder

active sensor A sensor that uses a current supplied by the ECM to operate.

ammonia sensor A sensor used in selective catalyst reduction (SCR) that provides data to the ECM that is used to determine if ammonia values are out of anticipated range.

Hall effect sensor A sensor commonly used to measure the rotational speed of a shaft; they have the advantage of producing a digital signal square waveform and have strong signal strength at low shaft rotational speeds.

idle validation switch (IVS) A circuit used for safety reasons that is used to verify throttle position.

NO_X sensor A sensor that detects oxygen ions originating from nitric oxide (NO_X) from among the other oxygen ions present in the exhaust gas.

passive sensor A sensor that does not use a current supplied by the ECM to operate.

piezoresistive sensor A sensor that uses a piezoresistive crystal arranged with a Wheatstone bridge to measure the change in resistance of the piezo crystal; these sensors are adapted to measuring vibration and dynamic or continuous pressure changes.

potentiometer A variable resistor with three connections—one at each end of a resistive path, and a third sliding contact that moves along the resistive pathway.

pull-down switch A switch connected between the ECM and a negative ground current potential.

pull-up switch A switch connected between the ECM and a battery positive.

reference voltage (Vref) A precisely regulated voltage supplied by the ECM to sensors; the value is typically 5 VDC, but some manufacturers use 8 or 12 volts.

rheostat A variable resistor constructed of a fixed input terminal and a variable output terminal, which vary current flow by passing current through a long resistive tightly coiled wire.

thermistor A temperature-sensitive variable resistor commonly used to measure coolant, oil, fuel, and air temperatures.

variable capacitance pressure sensor An active sensor that measures both dynamic and static pressure.

variable reluctance sensor A sensor used to measure rotational speed, including wheel speed, vehicle speed, engine speed, and camshaft and crankshaft position.

wide-range planar sensor A type of sensor technology that uses a current pump to calculate relative concentrations of oxygen, nitric oxide, and ammonia in exhaust gases.

Review Questions

1. Which type of input sensor is used by the truck engine management system and uses power supplied by the truck's ECM?
   a. Active
   b. Passive
   c. Inactive
   d. Delta
2. The use of a reference voltage is important in engine computer processor operation, because the value of the variable resistor can be calculated by measuring which of these values when another resistor with a known voltage input is connected in series with the variable resistor?
   a. Increase in voltage
   b. Voltage drop
   c. Amperage drop
   d. Decrease in resistance
3. To make sure that an engine fuel system drivability malfunction is identified and repaired correctly, always refer to:
   a. aftermarket service manuals.
   b. diagnostic trouble code(DTC) diagnosis.
   c. aftermarket training manuals.
   d. OEM owners' manuals.
4. Which of these is LEAST LIKELY to be used as a potentiometer in a diesel engine management system?
   a. Throttle position (TP) sensor
   b. Accelerator pedal position (APP) sensor
   c. Accelerator position sensor (APS)
   d. Mass air flow (MAF) sensor
5. Which of these devices measures small changes in the resistance of tiny wires caused by stretching or contraction?
   a. Strain gauge
   b. Wire gauge
   c. Potentiometer
   d. Thermometer
6. ________ voltage is a precisely regulated voltage supplied by the ECM to sensors.
   a. Supply
   b. Reference
   c. System
   d. Control
7. A ________ switch is connected between the ECM and a negative ground current potential.
   a. pull-down
   b. pull-up
   c. resistive
   d. conductive
8. A two-wire sensor that changes resistance in proportion to temperature is called a:
   a. variable resistor.
   b. thermistor.
   c. capacitor.
   d. transistor.
9. On a pressure sensor, which wire provides the signal return from the sensor to the electronic control module (ECM)?
   a. First
   b. Second
   c. Third
   d. Fourth
10. Which of these sensor designs has the advantage of producing a digital signal square waveform and has strong signal strength at low shaft rotational speeds?
    a. Variable reluctance
    b. Voltage generating
    c. Variable capacitance
    d. Hall effect

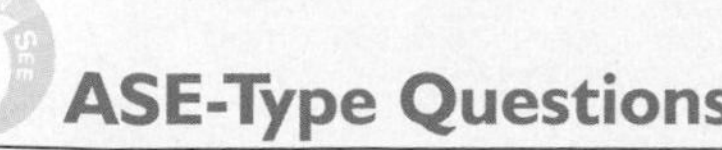

ASE-Type Questions

1. All of the following are examples of a terminal connector, EXCEPT:
   a. split-bolt.
   b. butt.
   c. eye ring.
   d. push-on spade.
2. Two technicians are discussing engine management input sensors. Technician A says that switches are the simplest sensors of all, because they have no resistance in the closed position and infinite resistance in the open position. Technician B says that a zero-volt signal would present as an closed switch, while twelve volts would present as an open switch Who is correct?
   a. Technician A
   b. Technician B
   c. Both Technician A and Technician B
   d. Neither Technician A nor Technician B
3. Technician A says that a knock sensor measuring abnormal combustion signals is a common application of piezoresistive sensors. Technician B says that silicon-based piezoresistive sensors are very sensitive to slight pressure changes. Who is correct?
   a. Technician A
   b. Technician B
   c. Both Technician A and Technician B
   d. Neither Technician A nor Technician B
4. A mass air flow (MAF) Hall effect sensor is being diagnosed using a graphing multimeter. Sometimes the circuit within the sensor can fail and produce a waveform unrecognizable to the ECM. Which of these is LEAST LIKELY resulting waveform?
   a. Not sharp and well defined
   b. Sharp and look square
   c. Sawtooth shaped
   d. Wavy shaped square wave
5. If the problem is related to temperature, vibration, or moisture, the circuit or control module can be heated, lightly tapped, or even sprayed with water to simulate the failure conditions. What measuring tool with glitch testing capabilities can identify and record the circuit fault in microseconds?
   a. Scan tool
   b. ProLink 9000
   c. Digital multimeter
   d. Graphic multimeter
6. Technician A says that switches are categorized as sensors whenever they provide information to an electronic control system. Technician B says that switch data may indicate a physical value such as open or closed, up or down, high or low, or it may indicate on and off. Who is correct?
   a. Technician A
   b. Technician B
   c. Both Technician A and Technician B
   d. Neither Technician A nor Technician B
7. All of these are examples of variable reluctance sensors EXCEPT:
   a. CKP (crankshaft position)
   b. CMP (camshaft position)
   c. VSS (vehicle speed sensor)
   d. ECT (engine coolant temperature)
8. Technician A says that wide-band oxygen sensors produce a voltage proportional to a narrow oxygen level. Technician B says that oxygen sensors are used to measure air–fuel ratio in order to calibrate EGR flow rates and air–fuel ratios for exhaust after-treatment devices. Who is correct?
   a. Technician A
   b. Technician B
   c. Both Technician A and Technician B
   d. Neither Technician A nor Technician B
9. At which of these locations is diesel exhaust fuel (DEF) added on a light-duty vehicle diesel equipped vehicle?
   a. Fitting near fuel door
   b. Fitting near the SCR (selective catalyst reduction)
   c. Directly into the fuel tank
   d. Special tank next to the fuel pump
10. What type of engine fault checks sensor voltages and, in a few cases, current draw to determine whether the sensor or associated circuits are open or have shorts?
    a. Plausibility
    b. Out of range
    c. Functionality
    d. Rationality

CHAPTER 21

NATEF Tasks

There are no NATEF tasks for this chapter.

Knowledge Objectives

After reading this chapter, you will be able to:

1. Identify and describe classifications of on-board vehicle networks. (pp 599–602)
2. Identify and explain the purpose and advantages of vehicle networks and multiplex technology. (pp 602–605)
3. Identify and explain basic principles of multiplex communication technology. (pp 602–619)
4. Describe the function, construction, and operating principles of vehicle networks. (pp 599–618)
5. Describe and explain common diagnostic and service procedures for on-board vehicle networks. (pp 619–621)

On-Board Vehicle Networks

Skills Objectives

After reading this chapter, you will be able to:

1. Check for completion of HD-OBD monitors for an engine. (p 606)
2. Diagnose an HD-OBD-related fault code using diagnostic trees, appropriate code priority, appropriate flow charts, and pinpoint tests. (p 618)
3. Perform a terminating resistor check. (pp 614–615)
4. Measure resistance of terminating resistors. (p 615) SKILL DRILL 21-1
5. Perform pinpoint voltage tests on a DLC connector. (p 620) SKILL DRILL 21-2
6. Check for shorts in the controlled area network (CAN). (p 621) SKILL DRILL 21-3

Introduction

Today's commercial vehicles are often described as computers on wheels, and technicians are just as likely to use a computer as they will a wrench to service them. Nowhere is this more evident than in the electrical system, where its evolution has reached a new level of sophistication and capability in recent years with the introduction of on-board vehicle networks. TABLE 21-1 traces the evolution of on-board networks.

This chapter will cover advances in networks and multiplexing, controlled area networks, and wireless and power line carrier (PLC) communication.

Overview of On-Board Networks

The architecture of the modern electrical system is shown in FIGURE 21-1. On-board vehicle networks are formed by connecting vehicle electronic control modules to one another to communicate and exchange information FIGURE 21-2. In concept, a vehicle network is somewhat similar to a social network, in which people are connected through websites or organizations that allow them to exchange information and collaborate to accomplish tasks or reach goals otherwise unachievable when unconnected. The idea of the "whole being greater than the sum of its parts" applies to vehicle networks, too. Extensive use of microprocessor-based controls applied to nearly

TABLE 21-1: Progression of the Use of Commercial Vehicle Electronics

Generation	Development
First Generation— Simple electronics	The addition of simple electronics to improve the efficiency of vehicle operation. Examples: electronic voltage regulators, electronic instrument gauges, two-speed axle shift module, and LED lights.
Second Generation— Control modules	Incorporating electronics into control modules used to operate engines, transmissions, climate control, and anti-lock braking system.
Third Generation— On-board integration of control modules into networks	Development of control module networks used to provide greater safety, efficiencies, and capabilities than any control module can perform on its own. Information and processing capabilities are shared between modules. An ABS module will sense wheel speed lock-up and deactivate the engine brake. A traction control module will reduce engine power output when wheel slip is detected.
Telematics— Two-way vehicle communication over distances	On-board network communication with remote facilities, allowing the vehicle to operate even more efficiently in a larger control environment. Examples: uploading vehicle and trip data to a dispatch center or sending route information to vehicle to avoid traffic or pick up freight.

You Are the Technician

After arriving at a customer's yard for a service call, you are asked to diagnose the problem with a brand-new Class 8 highway tractor. The vehicle will start and run, but the engine will not accelerate above idle speed. After the engine is started, a red warning light immediately flashes for 30 seconds before the engine shuts down. You perform typical visual inspections of the vehicle, inspecting the exhaust systems and wiring harnesses and checking for fuel coolant air and oil leaks. According to the dash gauge and visual verification, the SCR tank is three-quarters full. Nothing seems amiss, but you realize that certain emission-related faults and engine protection system-related faults will produce these symptoms. Without being able to easily return to the shop with the vehicle to access diagnostic software and service information, finding the fault that is specifically causing the severe engine power de-rate conditions and shutdown is challenging. Before calling for a tow truck to bring the tractor to the shop, consider the following questions:

1. What are two procedures that can be used to retrieve fault codes other than using OEM or other types of diagnostic software?
2. Explain why the red engine warning lamp—the stop engine lamp—is flashing before the engine shuts down.
3. Are SAE J-1939 fault codes retrievable from this vehicle without OEM software? Explain your answer.

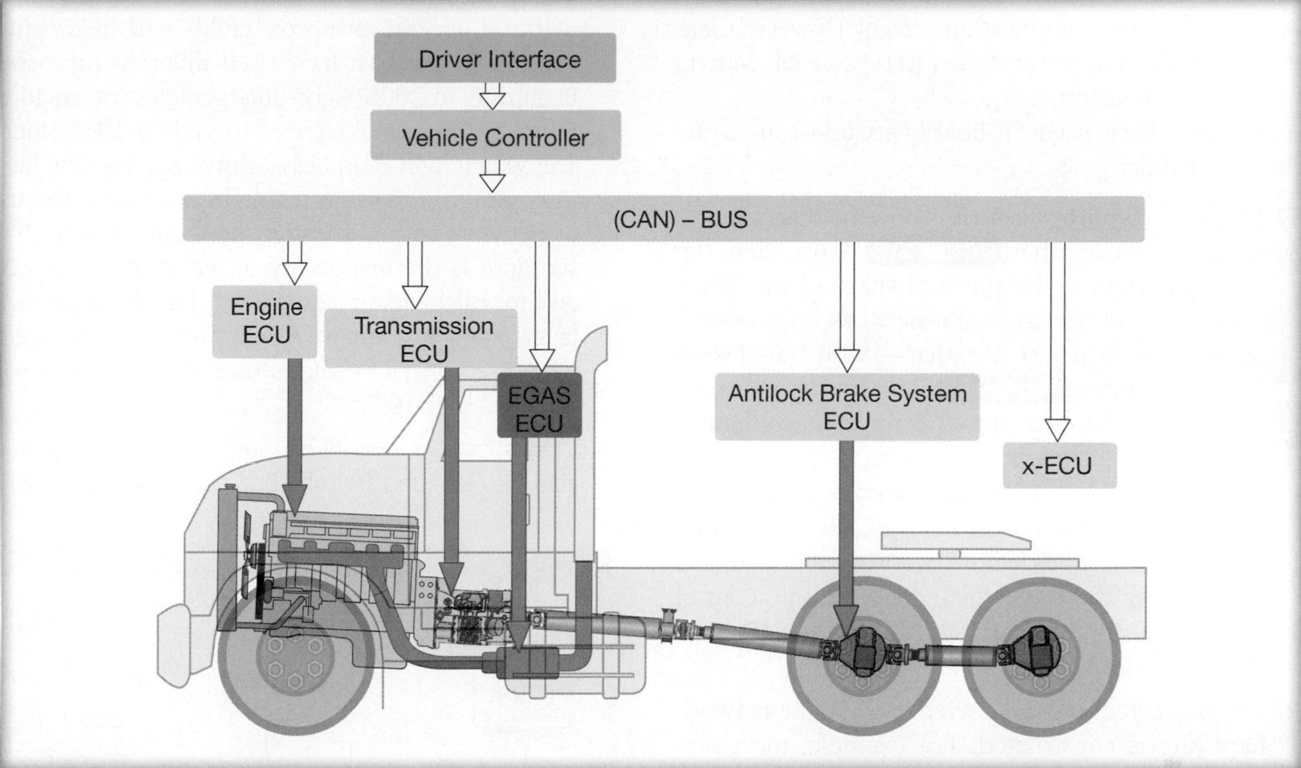

FIGURE 21-1 Architecture of modern electrical system.

every vehicle system can also be leveraged with network communication to provide a huge number of benefits not possible with modules and devices left unconnected.

Communication takes place between all the modules and devices connected to the network using an electrical signal-processing strategy called multiplexing. **Multiplexing** simply refers to a concept where transmission of more than one electrical signal or message takes place over a single wire or pair of wires. In modern vehicles, thousands of messages are exchanged every second over on-board networks. Originally devised as a way to eliminate bulky wiring harnesses, multiplex communication across modules and other network devices has made on-board networks practical. Networking modules enables customization of a vehicle's electrical system, providing new operating features, enhanced diagnostic capabilities, and simplified repair procedures. A good understanding of vehicle network construction, operation, and diagnostic techniques is critical for technician success.

Network Classification

All networks have in common the concepts of interconnected modules, the use of serial data to enable digital

FIGURE 21-2 Today's electrical systems are much more advanced than those of even a few years ago. **A.** Monitor: Telematics module. **B.** Monitor: Engine for timing and injection quantity. **C.** Monitor: ABS and traction control. **D.** Monitor: Stability control. **E.** CAN Bus. **F.** Monitor: Transmission shift points. **G.** Monitor: Body control module: Lock doors, power train and suspension interlocks, infotainment system. **H.** Measure: Road speed. **I.** Monitor: Speedometer and instrument cluster. **J.** Monitor: Collision avoidance system module.

communication between each module, and time division multiplexing as a communication strategy. However, there are a multitude of different networks types, each with its own unique characteristics.

The most basic ways on-board networks can be categorized include:

1. *Typology*—**Typology** describes how modules are connected to one another FIGURE 21-3. Most often, the typology refers to the physical shape of the way a network is connected. A star network interconnections are shaped just like that— with star-shaped interconnections FIGURE 21-4. Ring and bus networks are other common layouts of connection configurations for the channels exchanging data. The word "bus," when used in network typology, describe a network connection that looks just like a bus route. These configurations feature two-way traffic and "bus stops" along the way, which are electronic control modules. The J-1939 network used by all HD commercial vehicles uses a bus-type typology.
2. *The physical layer*—This refers to how the network hardware is constructed. For example, most networks use twisted wire pairs, but some use single wires, connect wirelessly, or even communicate using fiber optics. Standards exist for each type of network, such as how many nodes (number of modules) can connect, the type of connectors used, the lengths of the network wires, and so on.
3. *Network protocol*—This refers to the rules or standards used to communicate over the networks. Communication standards, device naming, definitions, fault code structure, and the physical layer are examples of network elements governed by rules within a specific protocol. Light- and heavy-duty vehicles in the past have used different protocols. Beginning in 2008, light-duty vehicles use an additional SAE protocol referred to as the J-1939 standard, which light- and heavy-duty vehicles now have in common. Emission regulations legislate the use of network communication protocols. The J-1939 standard is the mandatory on heavy-duty vehicles and for off-highway equipment. J-1708, a physical layer protocol, and J-1587, a fault code protocol, were used on HD vehicles until 2001 when it was replaced by J-1939
4. *Centralized or distributed control*—Networks may also be classified by whether network operation is

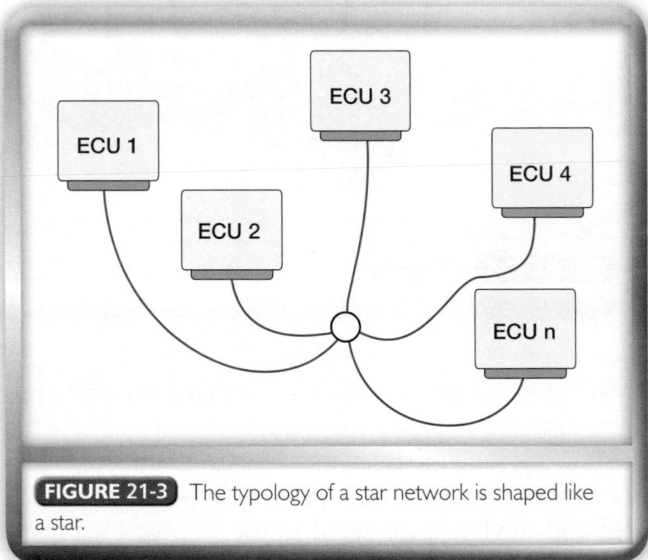

FIGURE 21-3 The typology of a star network is shaped like a star.

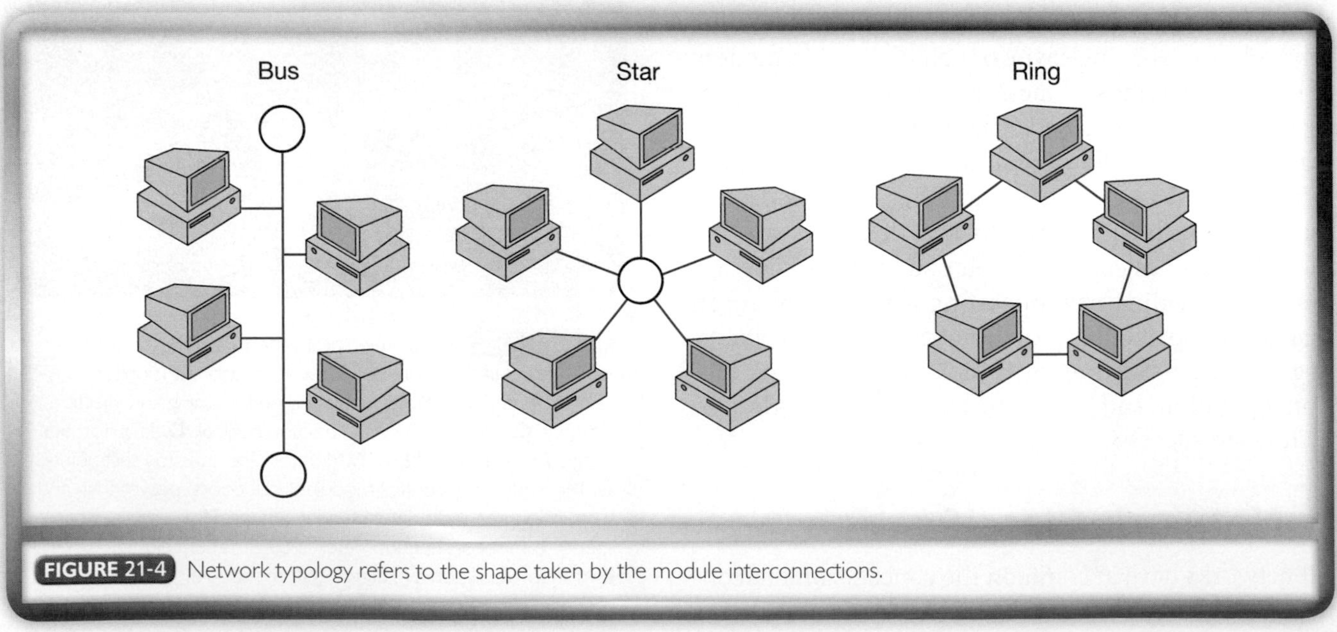

FIGURE 21-4 Network typology refers to the shape taken by the module interconnections.

(a) dependent on one master module directing the operation of several other slave modules, or (b) if control of the vehicle's electrical system is shared among the vehicle's ECMs.. Master-slave networks are referred to as centralized network control. The master module will send **serial data** to various other less sophisticated control modules, which contain only microcontrollers, to carry out instructions. The master module will make requests for information and sends commands to be executed by a slave module. A slave module responds only to requests by the master or central control module **FIGURE 21-5**. Distributed networks control vehicle operation and the electrical system using several to dozens of modules, all sharing information and sending output signals to electrical devices **FIGURE 21-6**. Most late model vehicles and equipment have, in

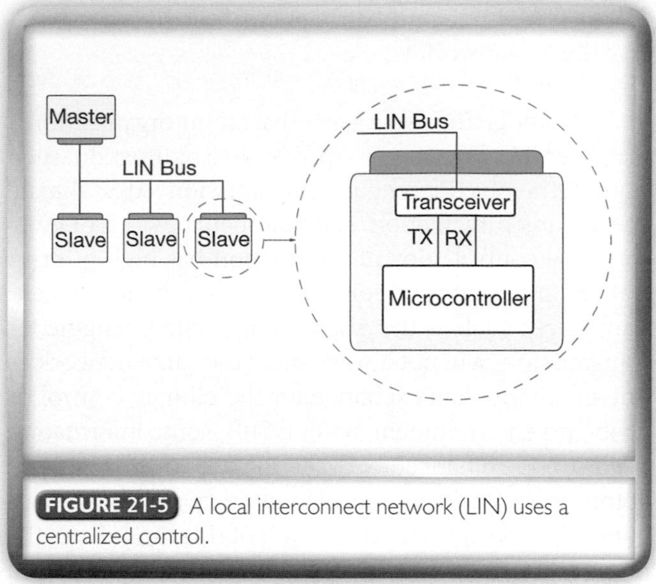

FIGURE 21-5 A local interconnect network (LIN) uses a centralized control.

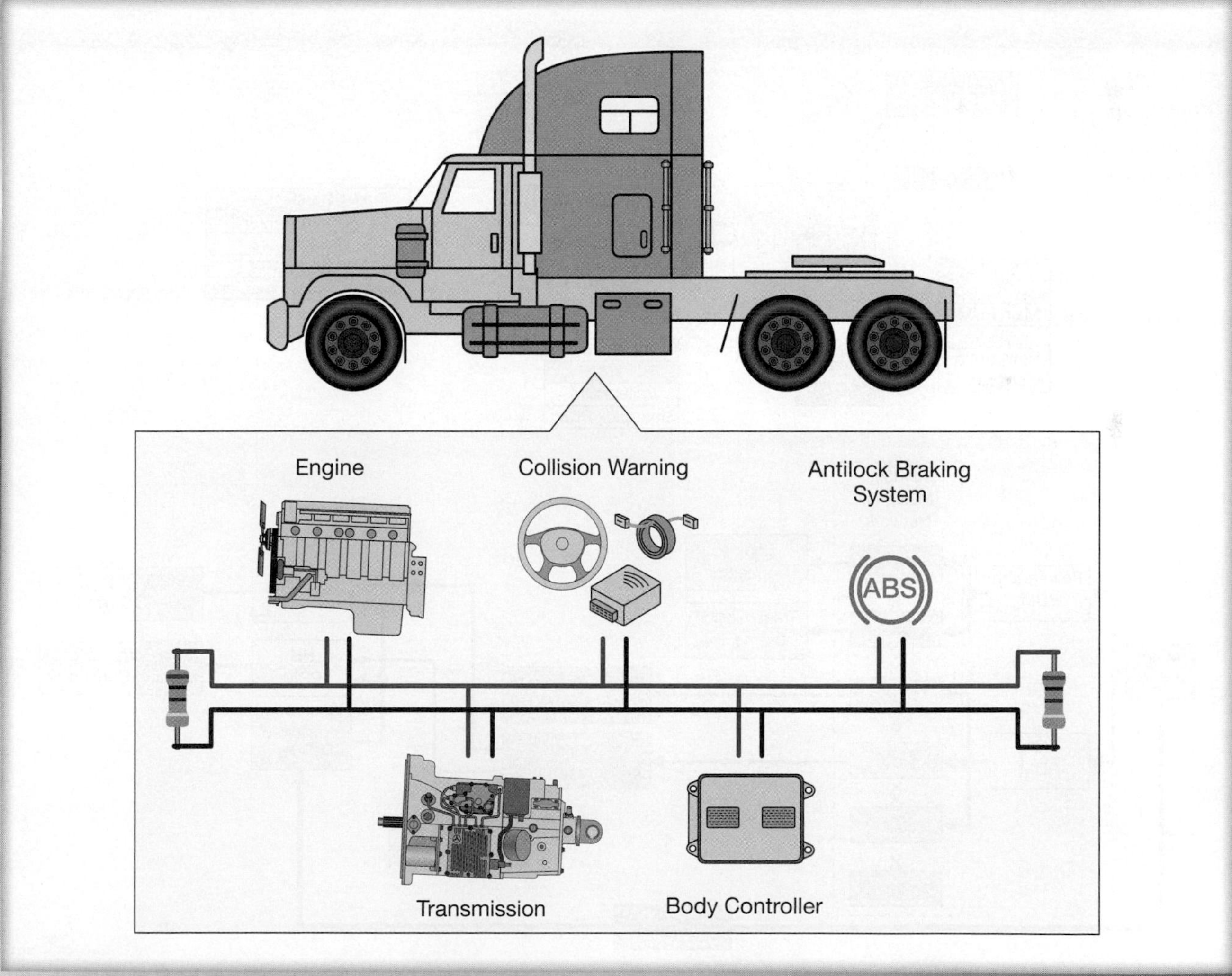

FIGURE 21-6 A J-1939 network uses distributed control of the vehicle's electrical system.

fact, multiple on-board networks using a combination of network types.

Networks are also formed based on organizational priorities. Modules are grouped by area or function, such as those involved in engine, transmission, ABS, climate control, instrumentation, entertainment devices, or body electrical control. Not all information has high priority. For example, information that affects vehicle or occupant safety, such as the ABS braking system, engine, or transmission, will not always share the same network as one involving data exchange for the climate control or on-board entertainment system. Still, some information needs to be exchanged between the networks. To enable communication between different on-board networks, a **gateway module** is used. The job of this module, as the name suggests, is to translate communication between different networks operating using different protocols or speeds. Without the gateway module, access to networks through the data link connector using electronic service tools would not be possible.

Late-model Freightliner heavy-duty vehicles use multiple on-board networks having inter-network communication **FIGURE 21-7**. In Freightliner's Signals Detect and Acquisition Module (SAM), output signals to electrical system devices in the cab and those on the chassis are controlled separately by two modules to prevent congestion from excessive amounts of data using only one network: One SAM module controls chassis electrical system devices such as lighting or air system, while another operates devices inside the cab. These networks are connected using Freight's own proprietary network protocol operating at a different speed than the J-1939 backbone network used by the engine and other power train systems. To communicate, a gateway module translates information for each network to use. Another advantage of this arrangement is cost effectiveness. Slower modules that are not J-1939 compliant are generally more cost-effective to use.

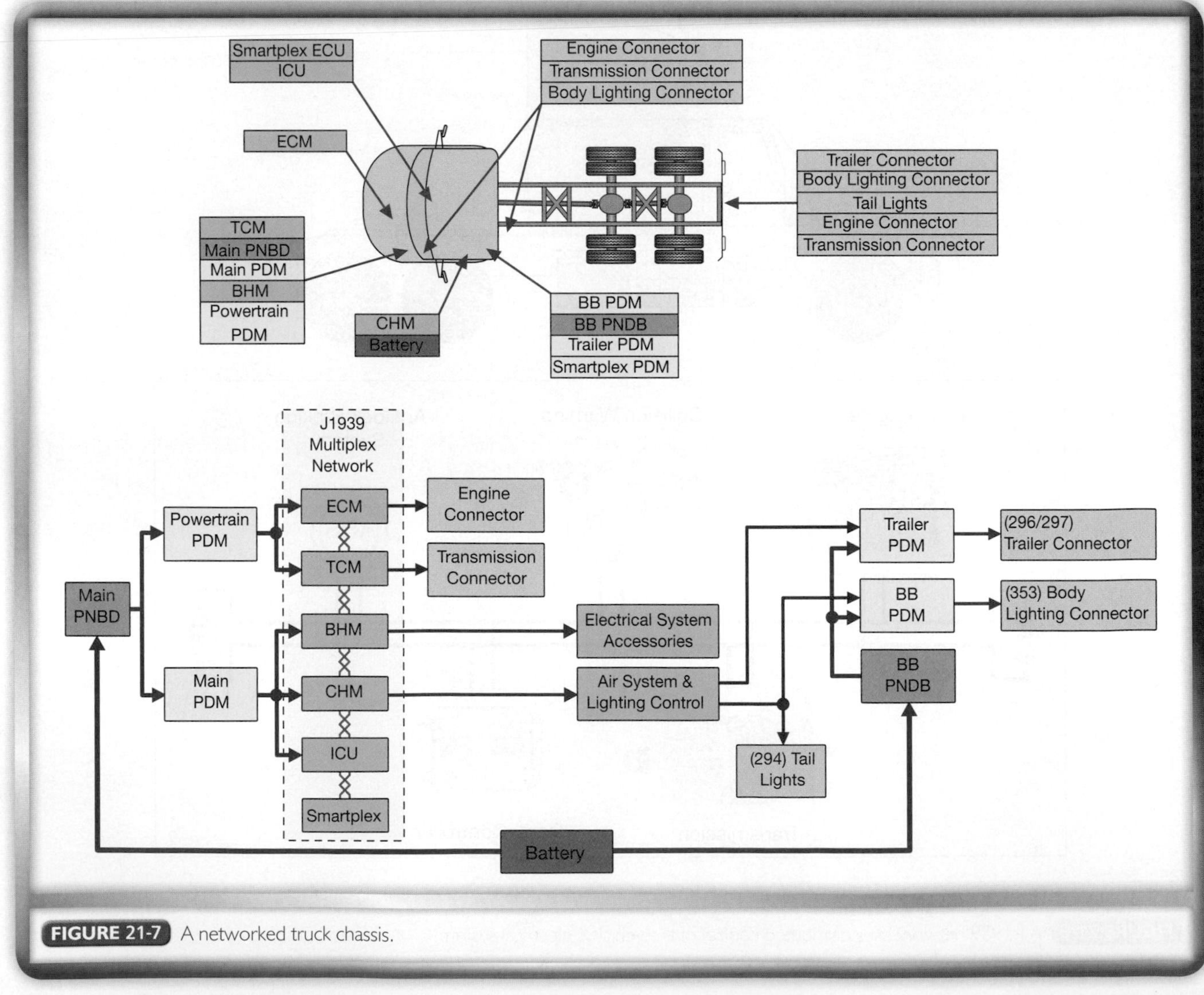

FIGURE 21-7 A networked truck chassis.

Time Division Multiplexing

Communication between modules and network devices typically takes place over a single wire or pair of wires connected to each module. When paired together and connected in parallel to all modules in the network, the typology forming the communication pathway is called a **data bus**. Information is communicated digitally using a series of 1s and 0s representing numbers and letters. The digital communication used by on-board networks is similar to the electrical language of Morse code. Under this system, communication took place over a pair of telegraph wires using a series of dots and dashes. Both Morse code and on-board networks use what is called binary code, which means there are only two choices or types of information—0 or 1, dot or dash.. The biggest difference is the speed at which the data is exchanged. Digital modules communicate much faster than Morse code; the increased speed is made possible through the use of digital electronics.

It may be puzzling to understand how only the same two wires connected to each module can send and receive information, apparently simultaneously, especially considering the enormous volume of data passing over the networks. If communication took place simultaneously, the positive and negative voltage pulses representing 0s and 1s would collide, canceling one another or generally becoming garbled, a lot like a noisy classroom when everyone is speaking at once and no one is understood.

However, using an electrical signal communication strategy called multiplexing overcomes the problem. The type of multiplexing used in on-board networks works by dividing the time available to each network module or device to transmit and listen to information. **Time division multiplexing (TDM)** requires the modules and other devices to take turns, sharing the data bus communication pathway FIGURE 21-8. Only one module is allowed to talk, and all other modules must listen until it is their turn to talk. This should remind you of a well-ordered classroom where there is cooperation around communication and no one interrupts anyone else until they are finished speaking. Data transfer back and forth along the data bus does not take place simultaneously, but each device transmits and receives data by cooperating to time-share a common signal path FIGURE 21-9.

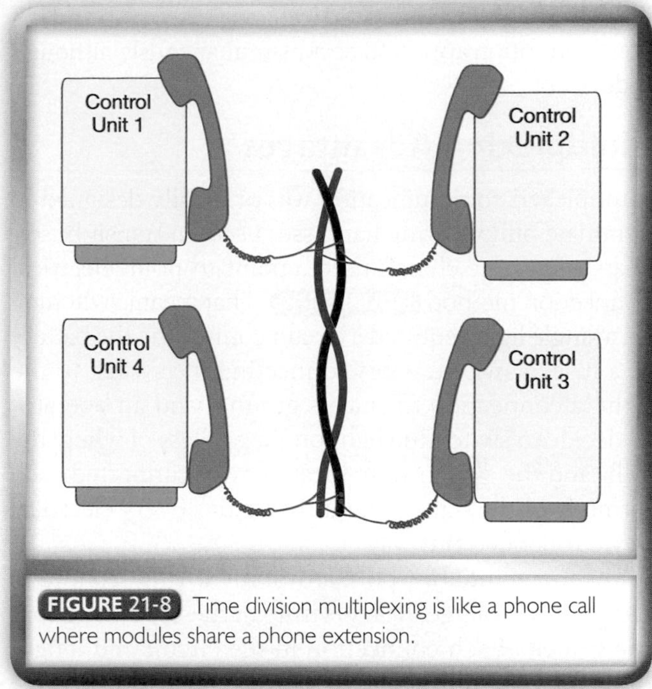

FIGURE 21-8 Time division multiplexing is like a phone call where modules share a phone extension.

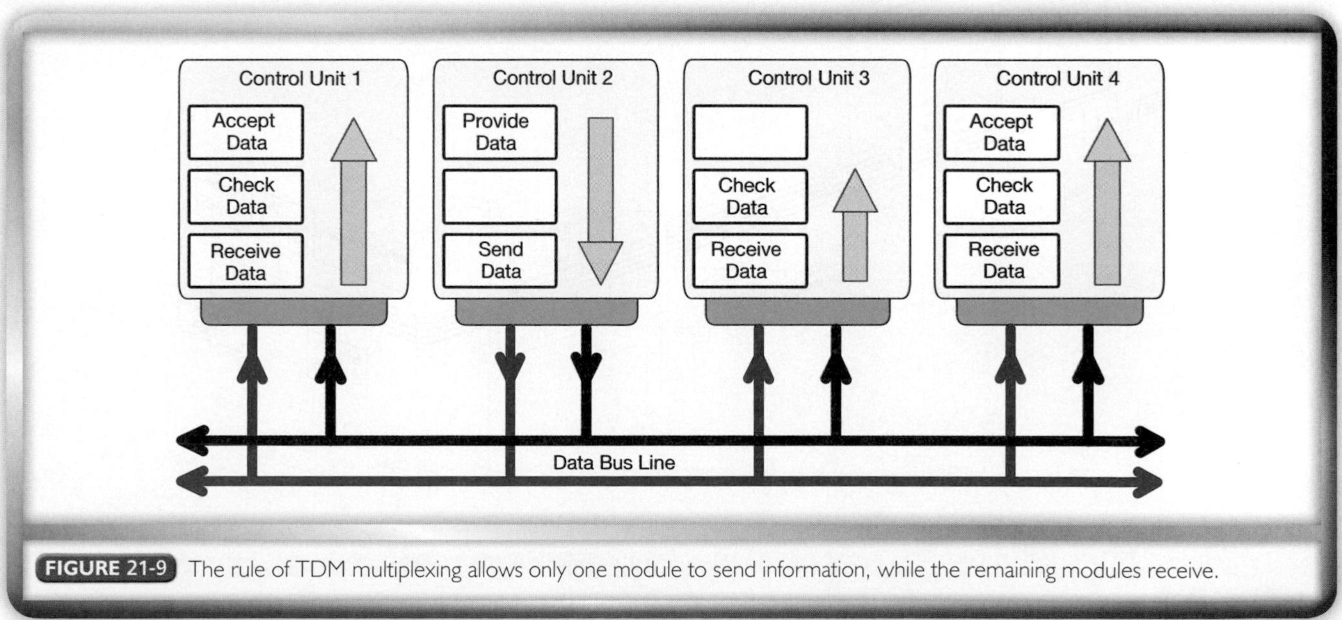

FIGURE 21-9 The rule of TDM multiplexing allows only one module to send information, while the remaining modules receive.

The speed at which the data exchange takes place makes communication appear to occur simultaneously, although it does not.

Multiplexing Advantages

Multiplexed communication was originally designed to eliminate bulky wiring harnesses used on transit buses. Years ago, those chassis used a point-to-point electrical connection method FIGURE 21-10. That meant switching on a single light required a circuit connecting the battery to a fuse, a switch, wires connecting the switch to the light, a connection to chassis ground, and an operator to decide to switch the light on. Regardless of where the light and the switch were located, wire connected each terminal of the light or lighting circuit. Every electrical device operated this way.

Understandably, point-to-point wiring technique results in very large, heavy wiring harnesses throughout the vehicle. Each connection in the circuit and length of wire also produce electrical resistance and a source of potential failure. Corrosion, loose connections, and chafed wiring were common electrical system failures, and the technique created a notoriously unreliable system that was difficult to troubleshoot.

Point-to-point wiring construction created unique problems for urban transit and highway coach buses where the driver is at the front of the vehicle, and engines and transmissions are located at the rear. Many miles of electrical wire were needed to control the electrical systems. Adding electrical relays to operate other simple 12/24-volt circuits built further complexity into the electrical system, which accounted for as much one-half of engineering time and 15% of vehicle assembly cost, according to one transit bus manufacturer FIGURE 21-11.

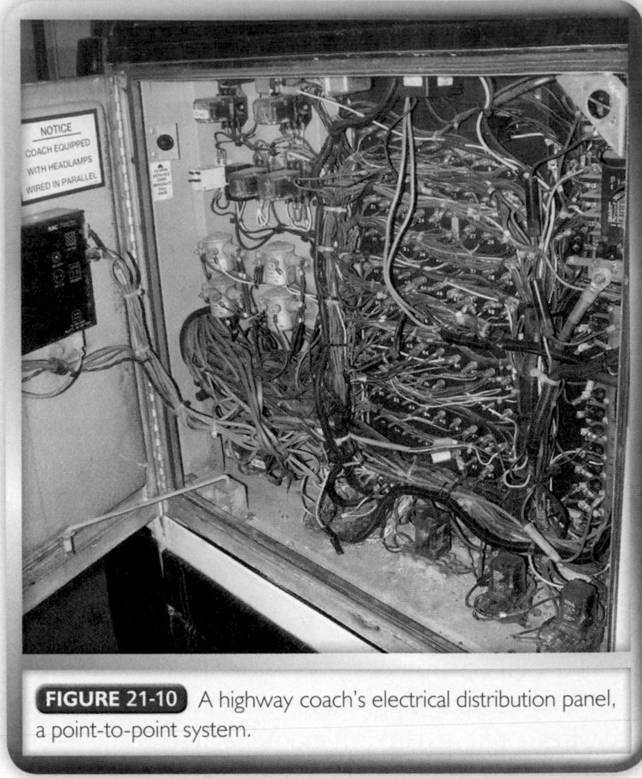

FIGURE 21-10 A highway coach's electrical distribution panel, a point-to-point system.

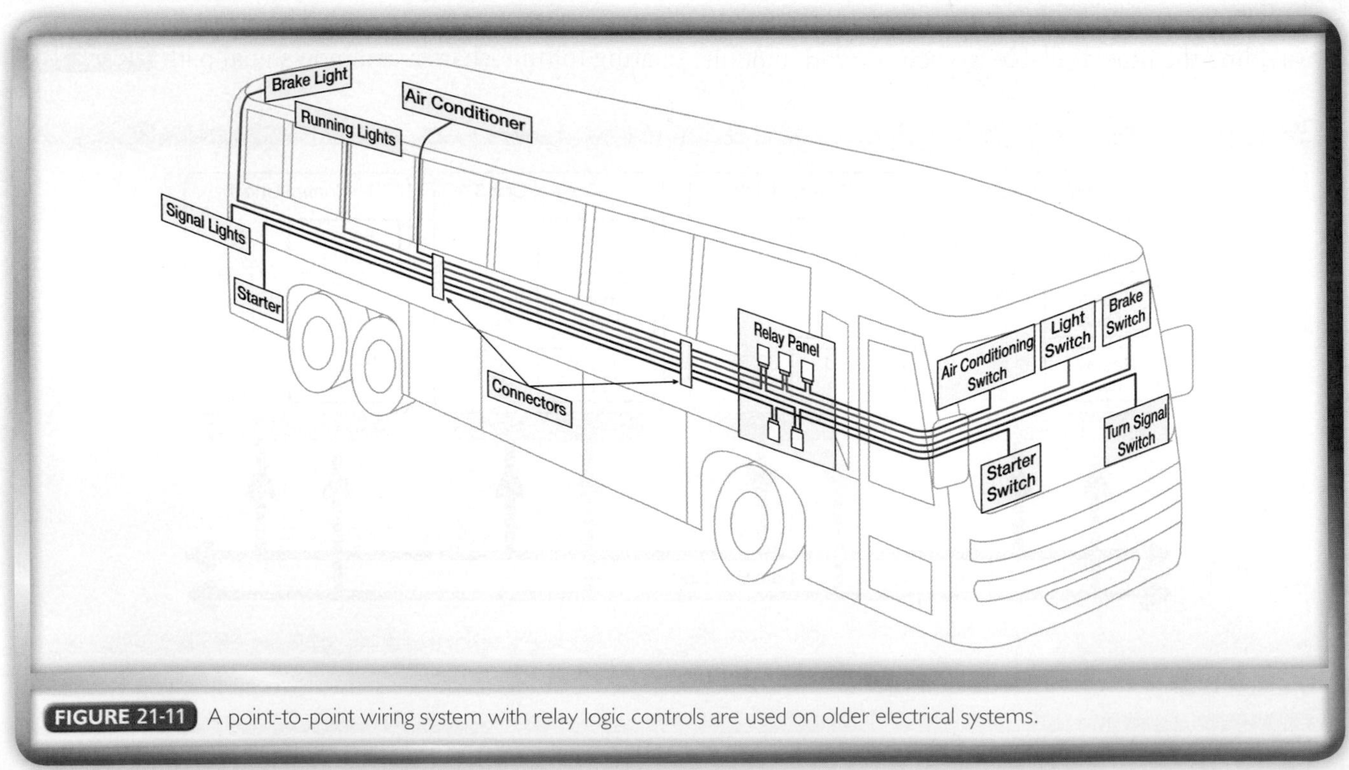

FIGURE 21-11 A point-to-point wiring system with relay logic controls are used on older electrical systems.

To eliminate the problems created by point-to-point wiring and relay logic systems, bus chassis were the first commercial vehicles to use multiplex communication to operate on-board networks. Bulky wiring harnesses were replaced with electronic, microprocessor-controlled lighting modules strategically positioned near the light circuits or other electrical devices FIGURE 21-12. An input processor module near the driver collected input data from switches and other devices. The input module then sent low-voltage multiplexed electrical signals to the output module controlling lighting FIGURE 21-13.

Additional multiplexing advantages include:

- Software control of the electrical system
- Enabled on-board diagnostics
- Ease of connecting electronically controlled accessories and features
- Reduction in number of sensors

Software Control of Electrical System

When using networks, electrical system complexity is absorbed by software instead of a huge array of hard-wired components and circuit boards. The electrical system occupies less space, is lighter in weight, easier to design, install, troubleshoot, and repair. On a transit bus, the use of network communication represents a reduction of approximately 500 lbs (227 kg) of wire alone. An estimated two-thirds reduction in manufacturing cost and assembly time is achieved through the use of multiplexed

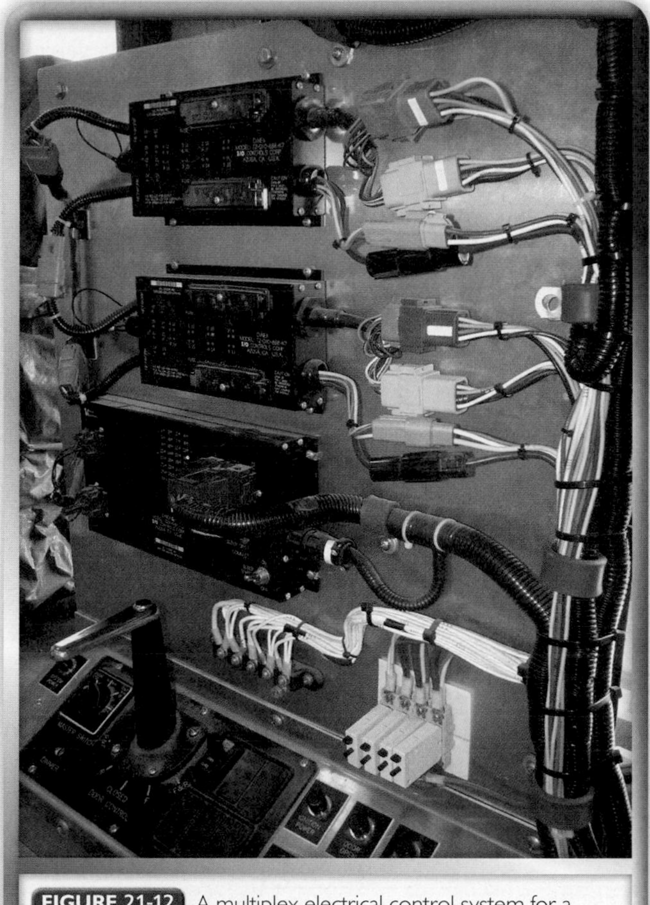

FIGURE 21-12 A multiplex electrical control system for a transit bus consolidates thousands of wires and relays into a few input-output control modules.

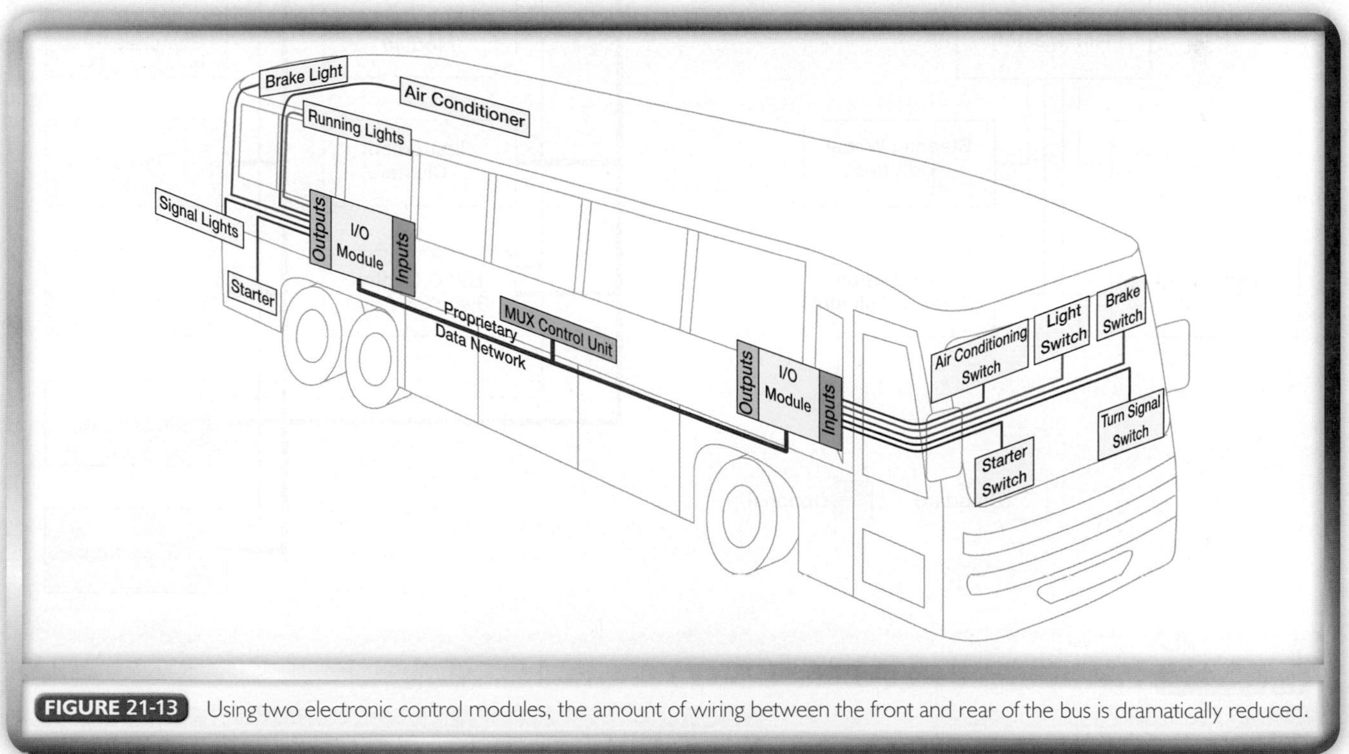

FIGURE 21-13 Using two electronic control modules, the amount of wiring between the front and rear of the bus is dramatically reduced.

network communication. GM claims it realizes over a 70% reduction in wiring needed in some of its light-duty vehicles using network communication. The newest vehicle communication networks permit enhanced features and control of every electrical subsystem from vehicle lighting and body controls (e.g., wipers, door locks, windows) to every chassis electrical accessory. Multiplexed networks also allow precise electrical control of ABS, ATC, instrument gauges, air and hydraulic-operated accessories, climate control, inter-axle differentials, and engine and transmission operations FIGURE 21-14.

Enabling On-Board Diagnostics

Legislation setting ever-lower limits on exhaust emissions required a greater level of precision of diesel fuel injection system operation. Those lower limits are only attainable through the extensive use of electronics. The problem with diagnosing and repairing electronic systems in comparison to mechanical ones is the relatively invisible and silent operation of electricity. Broken mechanical systems are often diagnosed visually or with mechanical tools such as pressure gauges, dial indicators, and so on.

However, a defective engine sensor or broken wire in a harness is not so easily detected, and it can be a time-consuming operation to diagnose based on only symptoms and a multimeter. Self-monitoring or self-diagnostic capabilities are, therefore, built into electronic control systems to help technicians perform faster diagnostic checks and repairs. Electronic control modules can easily evaluate the voltage and current levels of circuits to which they are connected and determine whether the data makes sense and is in the correct operational

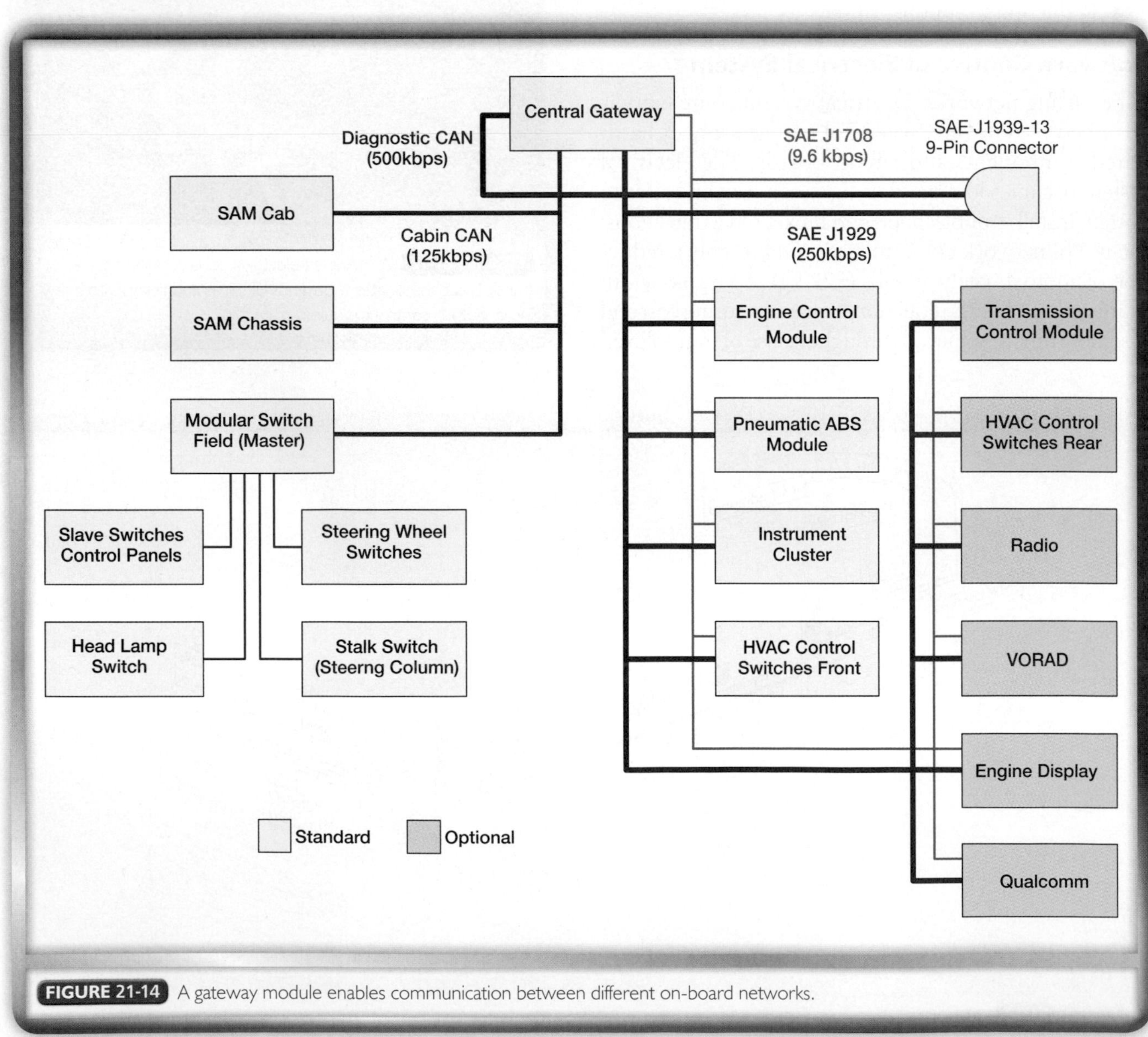

FIGURE 21-14 A gateway module enables communication between different on-board networks.

range. These self-diagnostic capabilities are referred to as **on-board diagnostics (OBD)** systems.

All electronically controlled engines and power train components have built-in self-diagnostic capabilities. To communicate this data to an electronic service tool from even a single module requires the use of duplex or **bidirectional communications**, meaning two-way multiplex communication. As modules for transmissions, anti-lock braking, and other electronic controls are added, network communication allowed these modules to communicate fault codes and data to a single diagnostic data link connector (DLC) FIGURE 21-15.

Because a variety of modules can impact the vehicle's emissions, network communication enables easy identification of specific faults using electronic service tools connected to the DLC. For example, incorrect or missing vehicle speed data supplied by the ABS control module can interfere with correct injection timing and injection quantities, leading to excessive emission production. When a malfunction is detected, diagnostic information is stored in the vehicle's control module, which identifies the fault to assist in diagnosis and repair of the malfunction. The legislative standard developed by the Society of Automotive Engineers (SAE) is referred to as heavy-duty on-board diagnostics (HD-OBD). This same legislation regulates the construction of a mandatory on-board network to access emission-related information. The OBD standard has many network-related requirements, all intended to reduce the cost and difficulties of repairing emission-related failures by independent repair facilities. Consequently, fault code reporting, the configuration of the DLC, communication language, and other network characteristics associated with emission control systems are standardized.

Ease of Connecting Electronically Controlled Accessories and Features

Vehicle accessories can be added at the factory or during aftermarket installation without any complex programming or vehicle modification using on-board networks. Connecting the device to the vehicle can occur automatically, or through the use of service programming software. When a network-compatible accessory connects to a network, its presence is recognized and the network will provide access to information it needs to perform its job. This is much like plug-and-play hardware for personal computers. Remote power modules or other modules can be programmed to function according to customized specifications, allowing body builders to easily connect to the electrical system FIGURE 21-16.

The ease of vehicle customization afforded by network communication has resulted in a long list of special

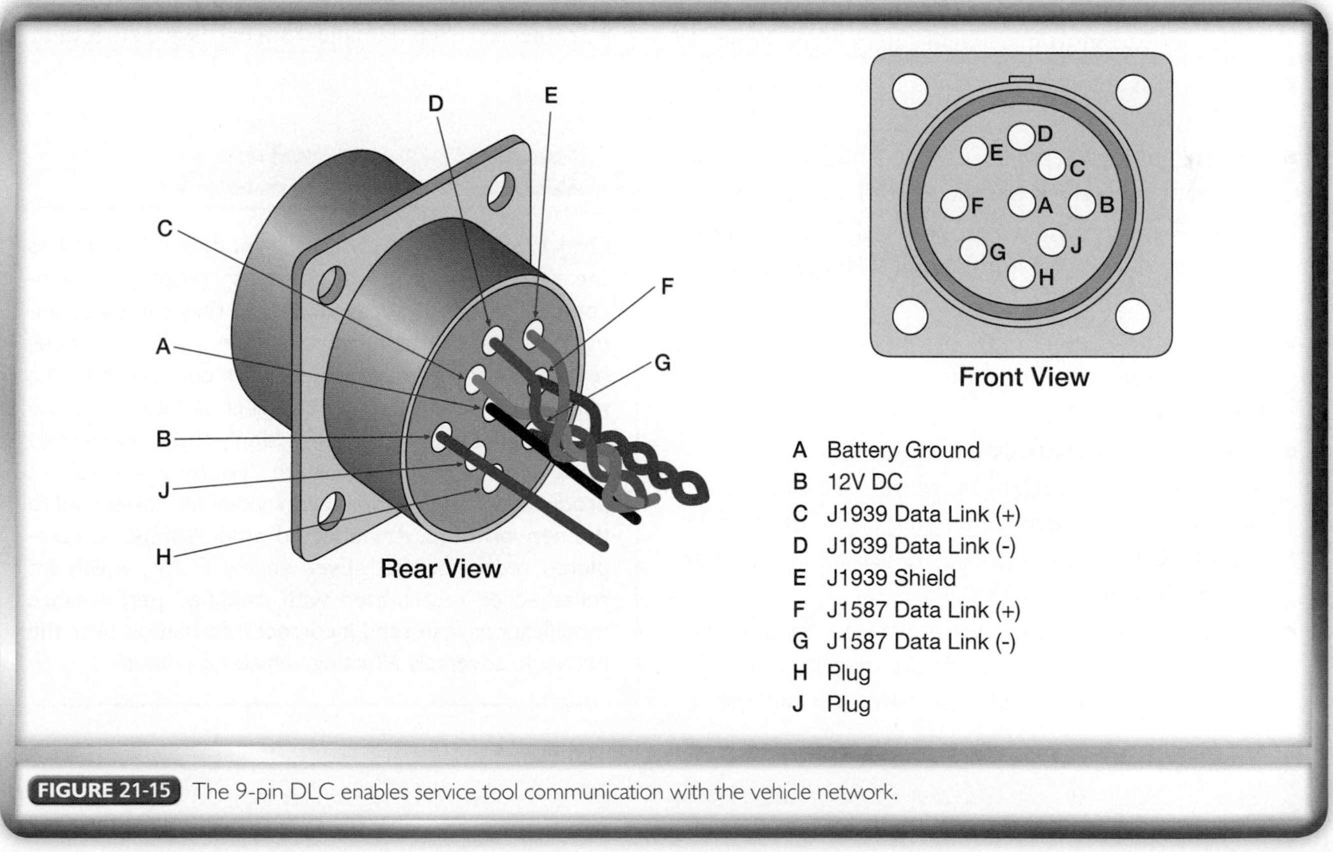

FIGURE 21-15 The 9-pin DLC enables service tool communication with the vehicle network.

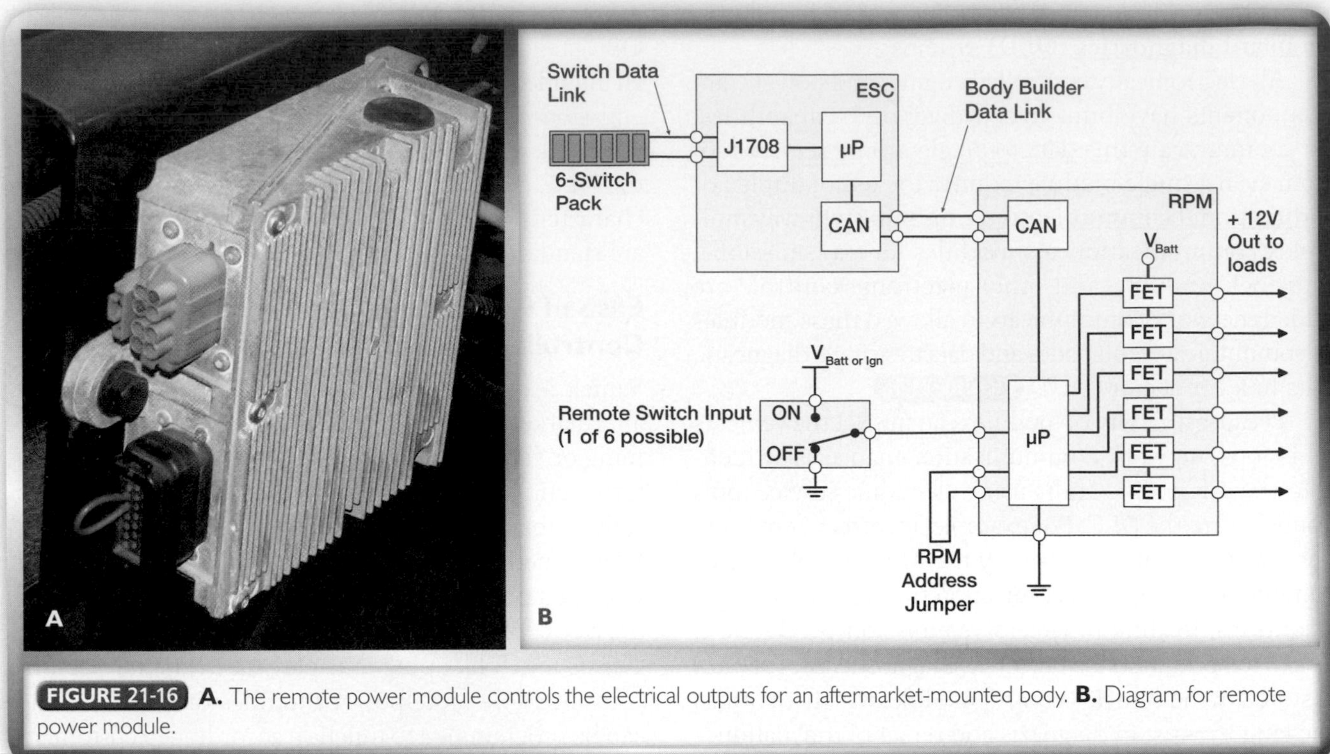

FIGURE 21-16 **A.** The remote power module controls the electrical outputs for an aftermarket-mounted body. **B.** Diagram for remote power module.

features used to enhance vehicle productivity, safety, and comfort. A few examples of hundreds of new safety features made possible by network communication include:

- Headlights that are automatically switched on with wiper activation to meet road safety regulations
- Interior bus lighting that dims to minimize windshield glare
- Power door lock activation above 5 mph (8 kph) for occupant protection in the event of a crash
- A dome or work light that shuts off after 10 minutes with door open and key off to protect against battery run-down
- Air solenoids controlling air-operated accessories shutoff under certain faults for truck and driver protection
- Interlocking of controls for equipment and operator protection. Transfer case gears, for example, are programmed to prevent changing unless the vehicle is parked. Bus passenger doors cannot be opened unless the vehicle is stopped.
- Air suspensions, which cannot be dumped above 10 mph, or power divider locks that limit vehicle speed protect the vehicle against costly damage
- Virtual fusing of electrical circuits. Special field effect transistors (FET) in output modules can be programmed to open at programmable current limits. Wiring and current-sensitive devices are thus protected from damage from excessive current flow.

Safety

On J-1939 CAN networks, any module connected to the network must be certified as compatible. Noncompatible modules may work, but they can cause unusual, and even catastrophic, problems. For example, security systems or remote starters connected to the network or networked devices, such as door locks and starting/ignition circuits, can suddenly and unexpectedly cause a vehicle to stop operation. "Footprint errors" are produced when incompatible devices are connected to the network, too. Any affected module must be completely reprogrammed. Even engine ECMs, which are reflashed or recalibrated with modified performance modifications, can send incorrect information over the network, adversely affecting vehicle operation.

TECHNICIAN TIP

The use of electronic service tools such as scanners, PCs, and other devices to communicate with modules connected to the vehicle network is critical to the diagnosis and repair of emission-related faults. Fault codes, communication language, and other features of the on-board network are standardized by EPA legislation to make it easier for technicians to repair a wide variety of vehicles with a minimum amount of electronic service tools. The right to repair aspects of the EPA legislation enabled aftermarket tool manufacturers—not just the OEMs—to supply service tools to communicate with the network.

Reduction in Number of Sensors

Sensor data can be shared across a large number of devices connected into a network. This network feature eliminates duplication of sensors needed for a module. A simple example is the use of a vehicle speed sensor. This data is required in many places by various devices. The instrument gauge cluster, transmission, engine, and anti-lock braking system (ABS) all require vehicle speed data, as does the entertainment system, which might lower or raise the radio volume depending on road speed. Using one electronic module to sense and process speed sensor data, then distribute the information over the network, reduces the construction cost and associated wiring required to connect a sensor to each device needing road speed data. Note, too, that the information-processing capabilities are distributed over many modules, which enhances the power of the total network. Instead of numerous modules performing the same task—such as processing speed data—only one module does it, which frees the processors in other ECMs to perform different work.

Other Network Outputs and Inputs

Multiplexed components on networks also include:

- Instrument panel and gauge clusters
- Odometers, now with digital LCD displays that can serve as a numeric fault code reader FIGURE 21-17
- Driver displays
- Voice synthesizers
- Global positioning systems (GPS)
- Collision avoidance systems

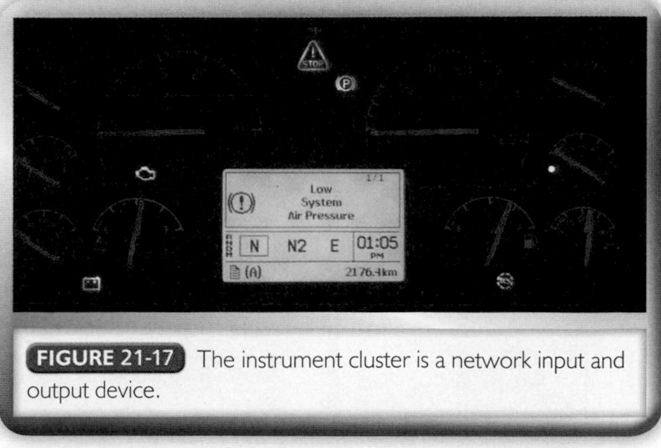

FIGURE 21-17 The instrument cluster is a network input and output device.

Air control modules that control air pressure through electrically controlled solenoid valves provide general-purpose control of air-operated body equipment accessories. Not only do these modules minimize the number of air lines, but they also eliminate the need for air lines to connect to switches located in the dash FIGURE 21-18.

Multiplex switch packs permit dash switches to connect to the network with a twisted pair data bus. A variety of resistors and diodes within switch packs, such as those used by Freightliner, create a unique identifier for each switch, allowing them to be mapped to a unique function on the network FIGURE 21-19. This means that when accessories are installed, holes do not need to be cut into the dash, nor do new circuits need to be made. Outputs will originate from chassis or cab modules.

Power distribution modules incorporating inputs and power outputs with 20 amps or more of current-carrying capacity are useful programmable output devices for body builders. Modules containing **field effect transistors (FETs)**, which operate like a combined solid-state relay and a circuit breaker, also have virtual fusing for circuit protection. When current is applied to the gate, an FET can switch current flow like a regular switching transistor. However, a fourth leg or terminal on an FET allows monitoring of current levels through the FET. This means that, if the programmed maximum current is exceeded, the current flow will switch off the FET.

Navistar's electrical system controllers (ESCs) are an example of this networked power distribution arrangement. An external module to the cab provides connection points for body builders and other electrical system accessories. These remote power modules are supplied network data and can switch multiple outputs up to 30 amps each using programmable virtual fuses. Outputs

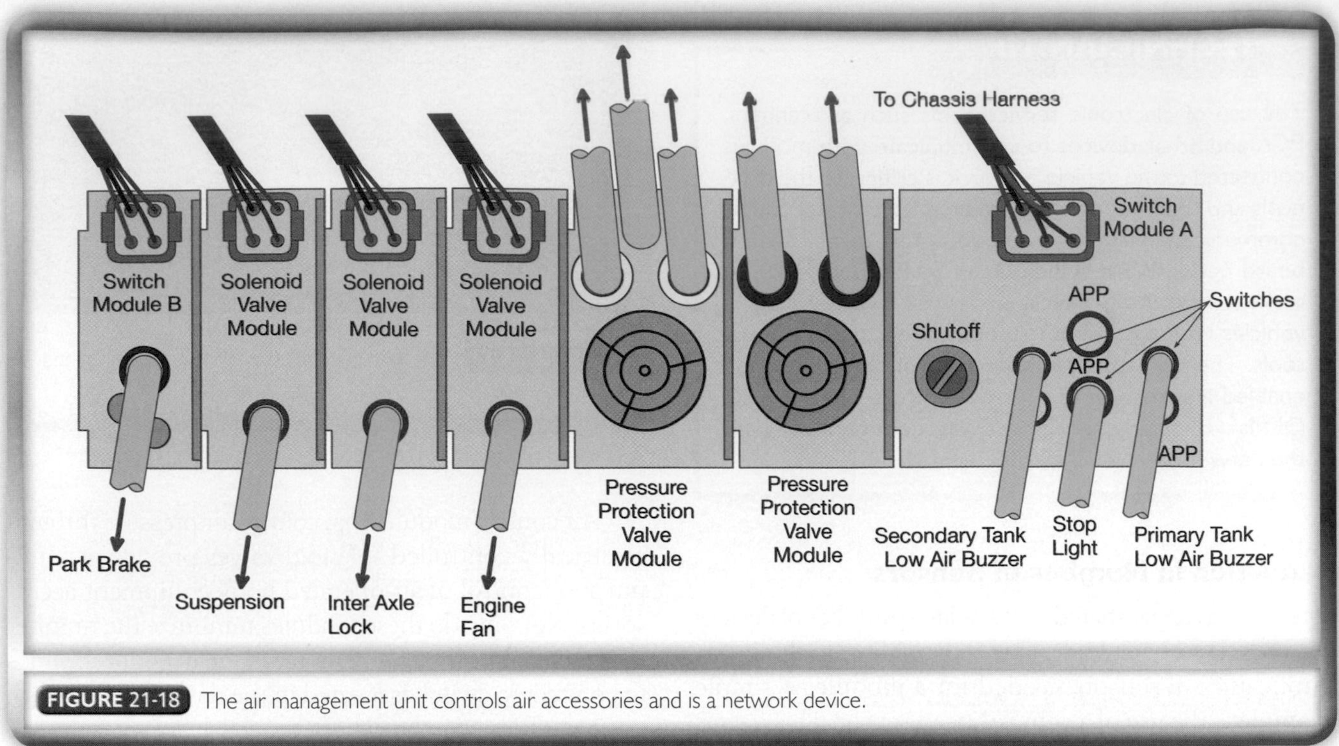

FIGURE 21-18 The air management unit controls air accessories and is a network device.

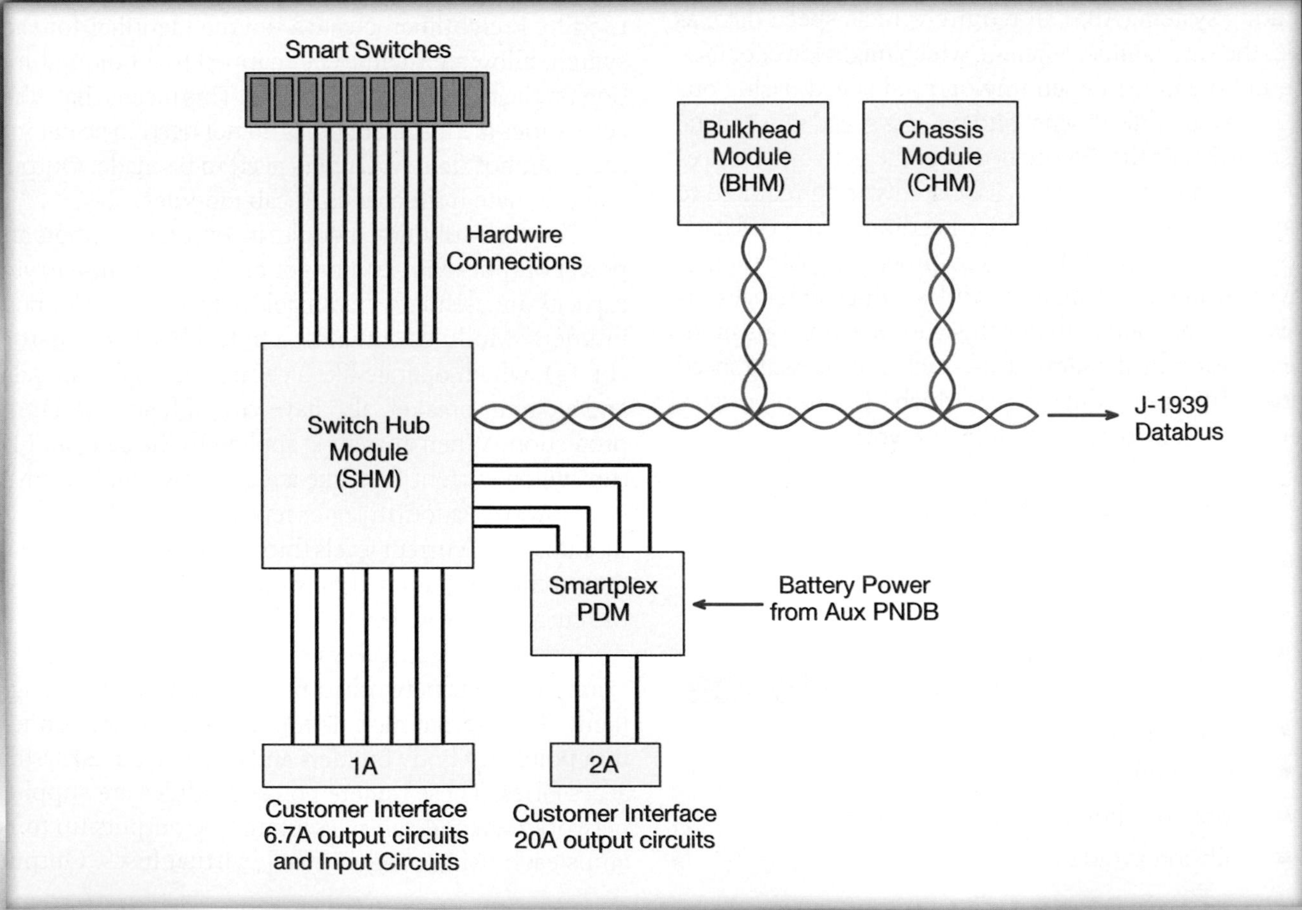

FIGURE 21-19 Programmable switch packs enable customization of switch functions.

operating devices such as lights, hydraulic and air controls, relays, and so on can be programmed to fit the unique application of the vehicle FIGURE 21-20.

Controlled Area Networks (CAN)

The term controlled area networks (CAN) describes a distributed network control system. This means no single central control module is used. Instead, each module or node on the network has processing capabilities that can initiate electrical control for faster response and also synchronize their operation with other network modules. Therefore, each module on the network has memorized the rules of what it has to do and what the rules are for doing it. Because the network has no central control, the connected components will still operate in the event that parts of it are severed.

Controlled area networks are the most widely used type of network for integrating power train operation of all the latest vehicles. Since 2002, heavy-duty on-highway vehicles have used CAN. These networks are often integrated in local area networks (LANs), which are vehicles using multiple types of networks on a single chassis, such as optical or other specialized proprietary networks connecting manufacturer-specific equipment. Because there is no central control module coordinating communication or controlling network devices, each network module has built-in processor capabilities to process input and output data while simultaneously receiving and transmitting data to the network. A built-in clock and transceiver in each CAN module helps synchronize multiplex communication between modules, so each takes an appropriate turn using the data bus to send and receive messages.

Other processing functions built into every CAN module allow it to interpret other network communication

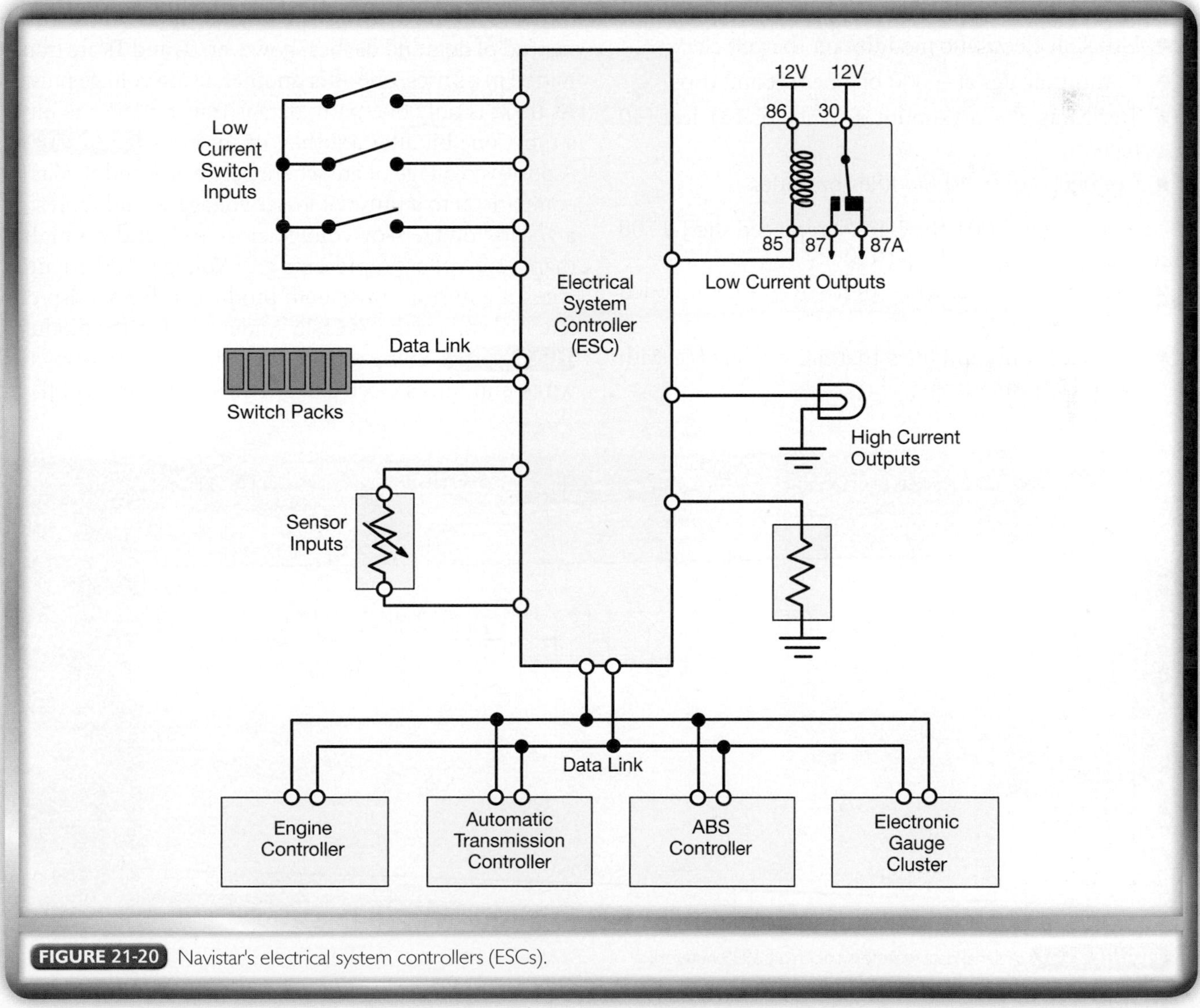

FIGURE 21-20 Navistar's electrical system controllers (ESCs).

data and control the messages it sends to the data bus. This degree of sophistication makes CAN nodes more expensive to build. Engine, transmission, and ABS modules are the largest and most common types of CAN modules. Other on-board networks are built to reduce costs and increase CAN speed.

J-1939 Versus J-1708/1587

Two different types of CANs used by on-highway trucks, buses, and highway equipment are the SAE network standards J-1939 and J-1587/1708. The J-1587/1708 CAN is identified by the six-pin DLC. It is an older network that transmits data at the relatively slow speed of 9,600 bits/second. J-1708 refers to the standards for the physical layer, or just specifications for data bus construction. J-1957 has standardized fault codes and uses an SAE set of rules to govern the communication over the J-1708 physical network. The J-1708 data bus:

- Contains two twisted wires using 18-AWG color-coded orange and green
- Links all electronic modules on the vehicle
- Communicates at 9,600 bits per second (bps)
- Transmits at a maximum distance of 131 feet (40 meters)
- Connects up to 20 modules or nodes

Beginning in 2001 the J-1939 replaced the J-1708 standard for data bus. The J-1939:

- Uses two twisted wires of 18 AWG color-coded yellow and green
- Connects only modules that are compatible with the J-1939 standard
- Requires terminating resistors
- Communicates at 256,000 bps
- Transmits at a maximum distance of 131 feet (40 meters)
- Connects up to 30 modules or nodes
- Stub connections to the twisted wire backbone are limited to 3 feet (1 meter) in length

J-1939 defines not only the construction of the data bus, but all features and characteristics of the network. Contrasted to J-1957/1708, J-1939 is like high-speed Internet access compared to dial-up in terms of the amount of data carried per second. J-1587 and J-1939 use serial data communication protocols, which have similar characteristics but differ in relation to rules about such things as message structure, transmission speed, connectivity hardware configuration, and diagnostic fault codes.

Serial Communication

Serial communication is like electronic Morse code. Instead of dots and dashes, however, 0s and 1s are transmitted in a series, one after another, using voltage pulses. As there is only one path, data is transmitted one bit at a time, one bit after another, or in series **FIGURE 21-21**. A positive voltage of anywhere between 2 and 8 volts in comparison to a pulse of lower voltage would represent a 1. No voltage—or voltage close to 0 and no higher than +1.5 volts—represents a 0. Voltage on the paired wires is a mirror opposite to produce a sharp, crisp differential voltage that is easily understood by the modules **FIGURE 21-22**. Using differential voltage and twisting the wires minimizes electromagnetic interference (EMI) in

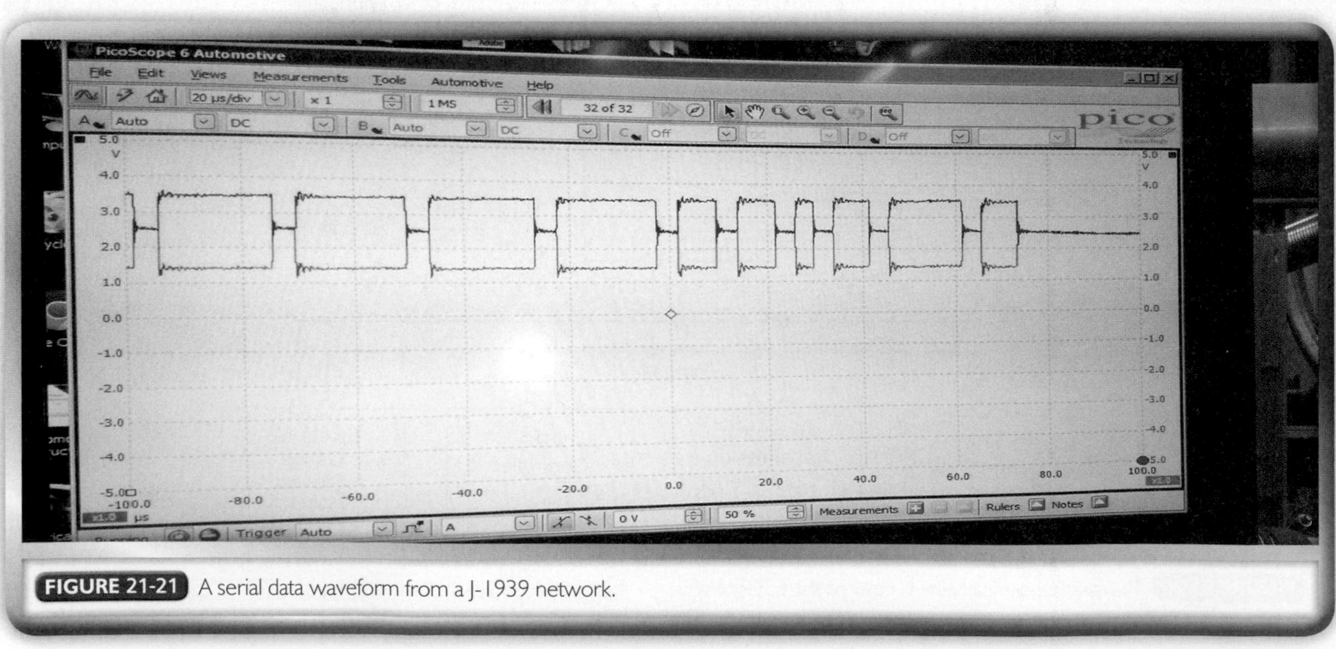

FIGURE 21-21 A serial data waveform from a J-1939 network.

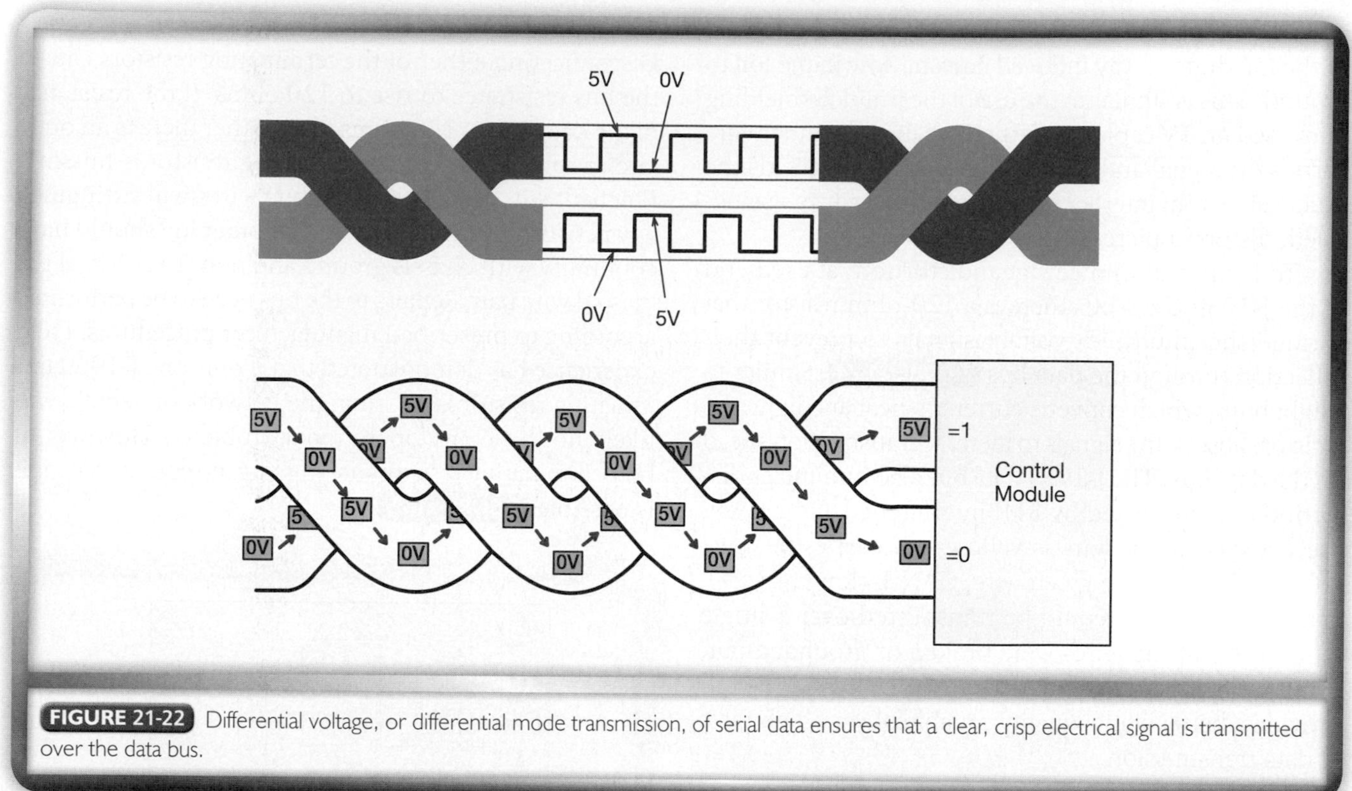

FIGURE 21-22 Differential voltage, or differential mode transmission, of serial data ensures that a clear, crisp electrical signal is transmitted over the data bus.

the wires, also called electrical noise, in wiring carrying serial data.

J-1939 communications have two wires: one wire, called CAN-hi, has a more positive voltage than the other, which is CAN-lo. Each wire will have a mirror opposite charge of the other when communication takes place.

Twisted Wire Pair Data Buses

Wires are twisted to minimize electromagnetic interference caused by magnetic fields and radio waves FIGURE 21-23. For example, magnetic fields from starters, electric motors, injectors, or radio signals from CB radios can penetrate the wires and induce voltage. Distortions to voltage signals can garble or change network messages. A cancellation effect is achieved using differential voltage signals, as the two wires carry equal and opposite voltage polarity. When the signal reaches its destination, network modules detect the voltage difference between the two wires to determine if the signal is a 1 or 0. This type of interpretation of the signal is known as **differential mode transmission**, and it provides a crisp, clear waveform. Note that J-1587/1708 networks reference the CAN voltage from ground and the differential voltage measured between the two CAN wires is slightly higher than J-1939 signals.

EMI introduced into the wires tends to affect both wires equally when wires are twisted together five turns per inch or two turns per centimeter. The low-voltage signal of the CAN data bus is even more susceptible to EMI due to the transmission speed of 256 kbps to 800 kbps. Wires are not only twisted together to resist induction of current, but on earlier vehicles, they were also covered in

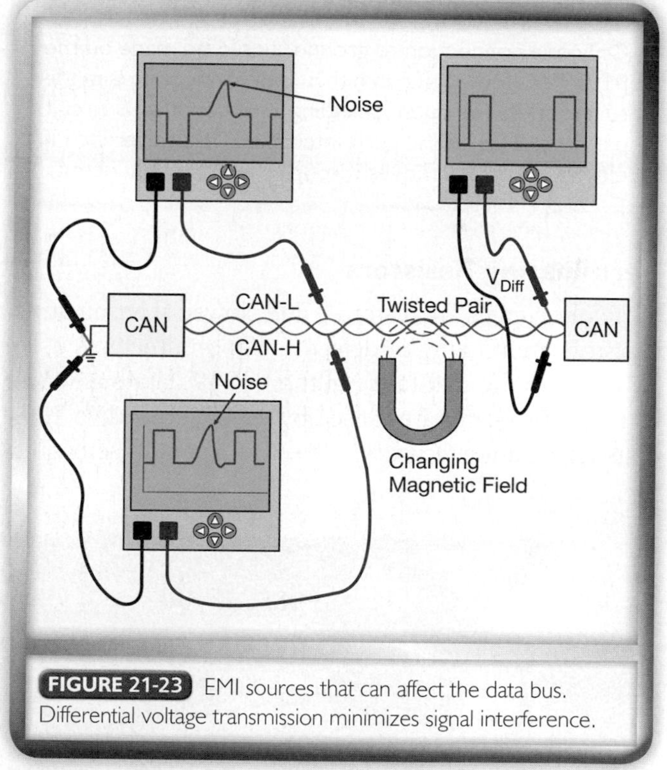

FIGURE 21-23 EMI sources that can affect the data bus. Differential voltage transmission minimizes signal interference.

a metal foil to absorb EMI signals. A third wire attached to the foil drains away induced current flow in the foil to ground. This is similar to the use of the braided shielding wire used on TV cable. With the TV cable, the inner wire carries the signal and the outer braided wire shields the inner cable from interference that would produce a static-filled, distorted picture.

To further minimize signal distortion, at each end of the J-1939 CAN-bus there is a 120-ohm resistor that extinguishes multiplex voltage signals to prevent their reflection through the data bus **FIGURE 21-24**. Similar to a light bulb, which converts current to heat and light, the resistors absorb the signals to increase transmission speed on the data bus. The J-1939 data bus also minimizes distortion of data caused by EMI interference. On a CAN, the CAN-H (high) wire is yellow and carries positive voltage (CAN+). The green wire, CAN-L (low) (CAN–), is negative. Signals could be transmitted over a single wire; if one of the wires were broken or grounded out, using the voltage-differential mode of transmission would provide a better signal quality capable of very high rates of data transmission.

> **TECHNICIAN TIP**
>
> Only one connection to ground should be made on the J-1939 drain wire. If more than one connection is made to ground, the outer shielding can become a circuit pathway. This will in turn intensify EMI interference if electrical current moves through the drain conductor.

Terminating Resistors

Network signals are distorted and slowed if terminating resistors are missing or defective. An ohmmeter is used to measure the resistance of the J-1939 data bus when network problems are caused by the data bus. Two 120-ohm terminating resistors connected in parallel across the CAN+ and CAN– wires provide 60 ohms of resistance. Disconnecting either of the terminating resistors causes the bus resistance to rise to 120 ohms. If the resistance of the data link is 120 ohms, then either there is an open circuit somewhere, or a terminating resistor is missing. Pinched, cut, or shorted data bus wires will extinguish any network communication. The outer foil should have continuity with chassis ground and none to either of the twisted wire pair. Repairs to the bus need to be performed according to prescribed manufacturer procedures. Field experience has demonstrated that if only one J-1939 terminating resistor is missing, the network or vehicle will likely not have any operational problems. However, if both terminating resistors are missing, no communication is possible **FIGURE 21-25**.

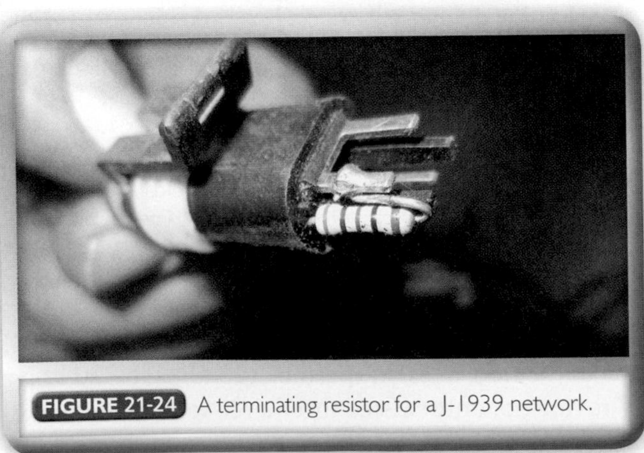

FIGURE 21-24 A terminating resistor for a J-1939 network.

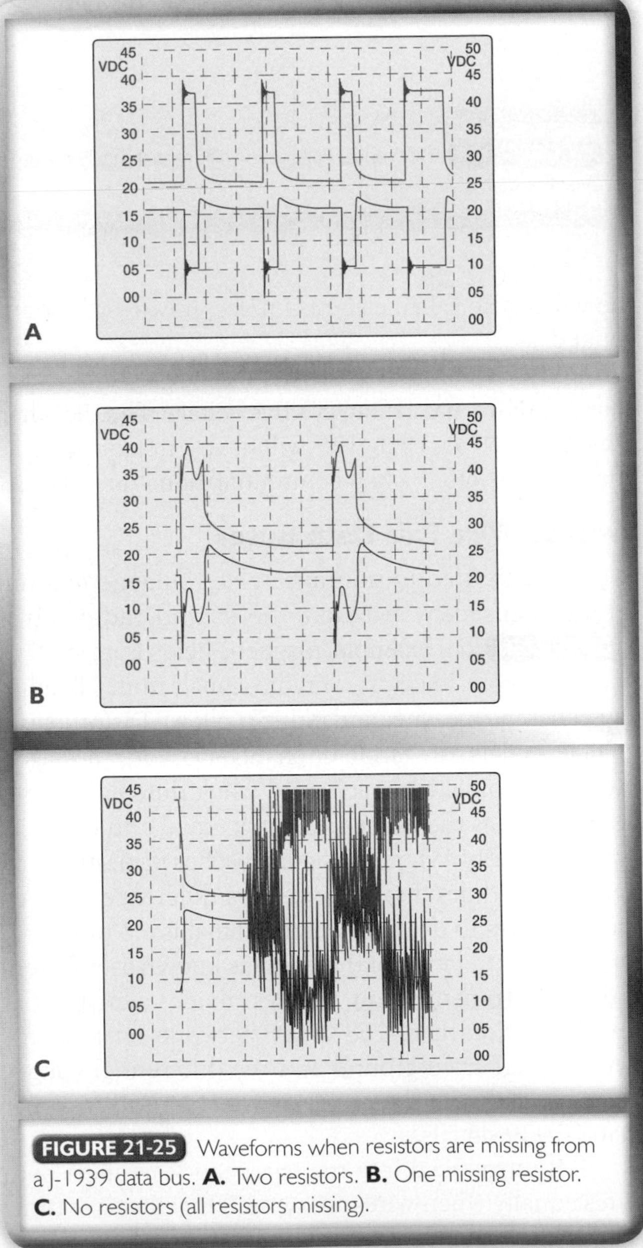

FIGURE 21-25 Waveforms when resistors are missing from a J-1939 data bus. **A.** Two resistors. **B.** One missing resistor. **C.** No resistors (all resistors missing).

To measure the resistance of terminating resistors, follow the steps in SKILL DRILL 21-1. Note that you should perform this test only after disconnecting the batteries.

Network Messages

Using CAN networks is like shouting a message in a well-ordered room crowded with people. Everyone can hear the message, but not everyone will respond or is permitted to speak at once because of message rules. Using the CAN protocols, however, is not as potentially confusing as a room full of shouting people. Instead of people, modules are communicating with one another operating under a strictly defined set of rules to control communication. To accomplish this, data carried on the CAN-bus has four distinct message formats:

- Data frame—Its message format is something like this:

  "Hello, everyone, here's some information labeled X, I hope it's useful!"

- Remote frame—Its message format is something like this:

  "Hello, everyone, can somebody please send the information labeled Y?"

- Error frame—Its message format is something like this:

  (Everyone out loud) "Can you repeat that?" This message is sent by modules that do not understand a message, if the information is garbled or is not sent according to rules.

- Overload frame—Its message format is something like this:

  "I'm a very busy transmission module sending something more important, could you please wait for a moment?"

Using these message formats that determine which module is transmitting or receiving data, problems with message transmission are eliminated while communicating huge quantities of information.

Message Format

Messages sent and received over the network are constructed in frames with a maximum message length of 130 bits. This maximum message length is, by digital data standards, short. A short message ensures the wait time for each message is as brief as possible. Each of the above messages types is further divided into sections. Examples

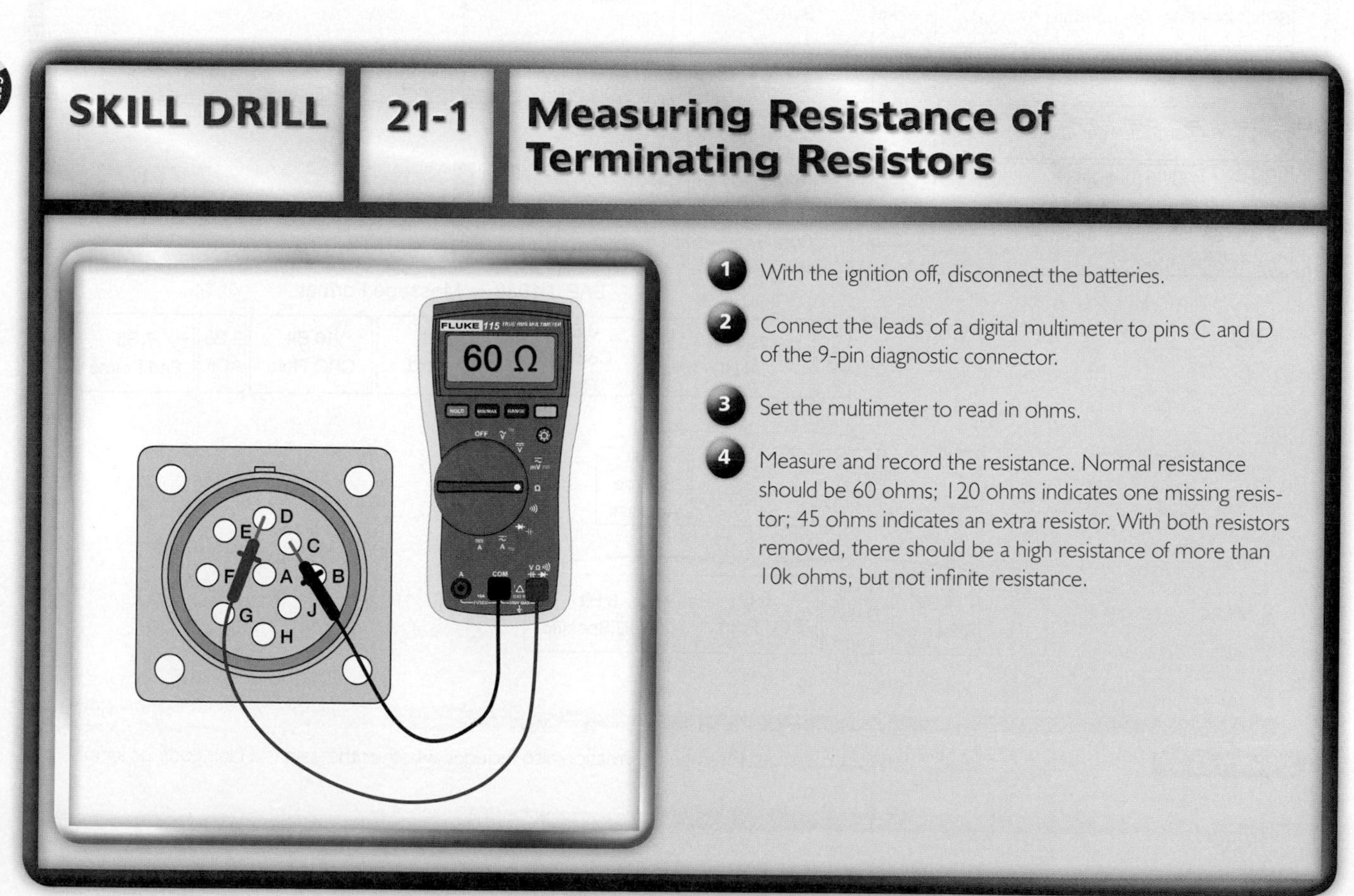
SKILL DRILL 21-1 Measuring Resistance of Terminating Resistors
FLUKE 115
60 Ω
D
E
C
F
A
B
G
J
H
COM
1 With the ignition off, disconnect the batteries.
2 Connect the leads of a digital multimeter to pins C and D of the 9-pin diagnostic connector.
3 Set the multimeter to read in ohms.
4 Measure and record the resistance. Normal resistance should be 60 ohms; 120 ohms indicates one missing resistor; 45 ohms indicates an extra resistor. With both resistors removed, there should be a high resistance of more than 10k ohms, but not infinite resistance.

of frame sets included in the above message include a start frame, which indicates the start of the message. Another frame identifies the type of message, such as whether it is from the engine or transmission, and how important or what priority it has. For example, slow-changing data, such as coolant temperature, would have less priority or urgency than, say, a wheel lock-up event reported by the ABS. Another frame within the message provides the actual data that is of interest to the modules, such as vehicle speed or whether the air conditioning is on or off. Finally, a couple of other frames are used to indicate the end of a message FIGURE 21-26.

All modules acknowledge the receipt of information from a specific module if the transmitting module by indicating there were no corrupted messages. This is like ending a telephone call with the message, "Did you hear what I said? Everyone says OK and good-bye."

No centralized special software controls the network communication. Operating instructions are imbedded in the memory chips used by the Can MODULE connected to the network. Manufacturers supplying devices connected to the network must ensure the devices are constructed to design specifications that make them network compatible. This enables the use of the plug-and-play feature of the network.

Data Bus Arbitration

Deciding which messages have priority to transmit over the network to prevent data collision between positive and negative signals is called **arbitration**. As soon as the

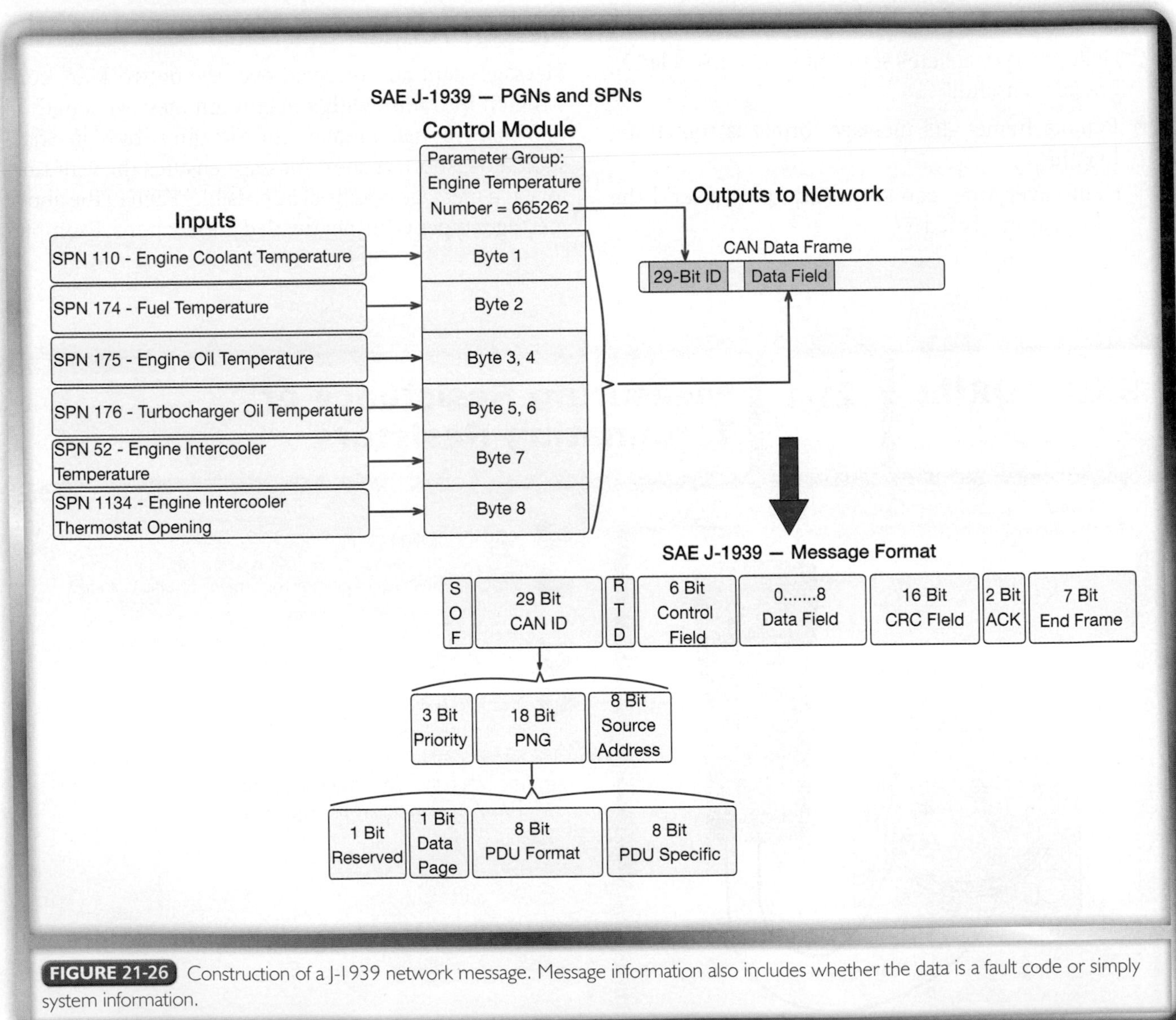

FIGURE 21-26 Construction of a J-1939 network message. Message information also includes whether the data is a fault code or simply system information.

data bus is free (i.e., the telephone line is not busy), each node or module can begin transmitting information. If two or more modules start transmitting at once, the message format decides which message has access to the data bus. For example, a wheel lock-up event or a traction control module message indicating excessive wheel slip will have priority on the data bus to supply information to the engine ECM and reduce power output. Modules with lower priority messages automatically switch from transmitting to receiving, and repeat their transmission as soon as the bus is free again.

Gateways—Joining Multiple Networks Together

Today, multiple networks exist on most vehicles. Rarely does contemporary equipment utilize only a single CAN for power train- and emission-related functions. The reason for multiple networks is primarily cost. Modules used on CANs have far more sophisticated microprocessors, software, and related electronics to operate on these networks with the complexity of communication protocols characteristic of CAN. Manufacturers can produce cheaper modules, nodes, or devices for centrally controlled networks than distributed CANs. Furthermore, manufacturers will often use their own in-house or proprietary networks for controlling unique OEM electrical devices on the network.

Many manufacturers often use **ladder logic**, a software-based control system that replicates relay-based electrical system operation. Where wiring diagrams once depicted battery current flow through electrical connections and devices and showed relays switched open or closed, ladder logic shows rules for software logic to control devices. For example, to operate a starting motor, the electrical system control software would need to confirm that a specific set of conditions is met by verifying a set of true/false statements such as these: The ignition switch is in the start position= true/false; The transmission is in neutral = true/false; Battery voltage is above 10.6-volts=true/false; The clutch is depressed=true/false. Using ladder logic, customized operational features such as International Truck's power take off (PTO) can be programmed with up to 42 rules of engagement, disengagement, and re-engagement, along with operator warnings and alarms. Controlled differential locks release above road speeds of 25 mph (40 kph) to prevent power divider damage. Features can be added or deleted, switches can be relocated, and programmable parameters can be changed. The vehicle's new file will be stored in centralized vehicle configuration data storage.

Wireless Network Communication

Cell phone and Bluetooth technology are two additional methods of network communication using wireless network interface. A Bluetooth-equipped phone, when recognized by the network, will turn down the volume of a radio, and even will transmit the call to the entertainment system for hands-free communication. Bluetooth systems are discussed in the Bluetooth Technology section. Similarly, many aftermarket consumer devices such as navigation systems, entertainment devices, security alarms, media players, and pagers can be connected to the vehicle network with a touch of a button, or even with voice commands. Bluetooth communication technology is used to connect these devices to the networks and supply information for them to operate properly or to enhance functionality. Cell phone technology is also used in system interface. **FIGURE 21-27** shows a telematics technology that continuously transmits network information from a variety of modules to a central dispatch where the data is monitored.

The vehicle network modules provide features such as:

- Remote vehicle diagnostics
- Remote door unlocking
- Locating lost or stolen vehicles
- Remote ignition lock-out if the vehicle is stolen
- Remote monitoring of trip reports, including distances, activity, logbook details, speed, fuel consumption, and start and end positions/times.

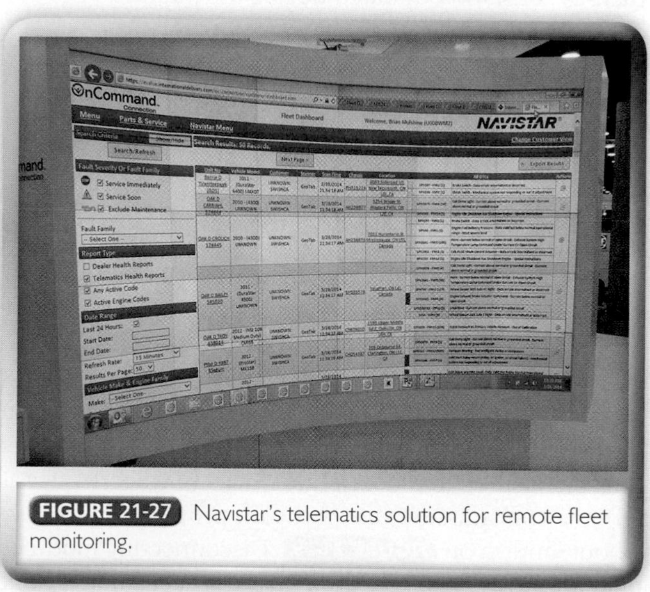

FIGURE 21-27 Navistar's telematics solution for remote fleet monitoring.

- Navigation around traffic jams
- Real-time positions, speed, status, and activities of a vehicle
- CAN-bus data acquisition, wired trailer recognition, wireless trailer temperature monitoring, and so on

Bluetooth Technology

Bluetooth is a short-range wireless technology that can automatically connect a device to a network. Cell phones are a common application for Bluetooth technology, used to connect a phone with the audio system using the on-board network. Many vehicles today are equipped or retrofitted with a wireless communication module connected to the data bus of the on-board vehicle network to communicate with Bluetooth and other radio devices, such as key fobs and cell networks. Instead of using wires to communicate with the network, Bluetooth devices, such as cell phones, use radio frequencies. Communication from the cell phone to network is also multiplexed over a wide number of shifting radio frequencies. Frequency shifting happens much like changing the radio station several times every second, with both the network and the cell phone simultaneously exchanging data on different frequencies. To start a connection, the Bluetooth device will send a signal on a predefined radio frequency, telling the wireless module or node it wants to communicate. The module, in turn, will send back a mathematical formula to the Bluetooth device telling it which frequencies to use and when. Communication can then begin between the wireless **network node** and the Bluetooth device. The communication formula determining which radio frequencies to use and when to use them is constantly updated during the interaction.

Network Problems

Problems on networks commonly originate from the following causes:

- Shorted or defective CAN modules
- Shorts to ground, power or CAN+ HI and CAN– LO wires
- Missing terminating resistors
- Additional terminating resistors

When network problems are present, the symptoms can vary widely from vehicle to vehicle, depending on the fault and manufacturer FIGURE 21-28. The vehicle may not start at all or may accelerate slowly (if it accelerates at all), the transmission may not shift properly, lights may be out, and so on FIGURE 21-29. Disconnecting modules one by one can help identify a module that is shorting out

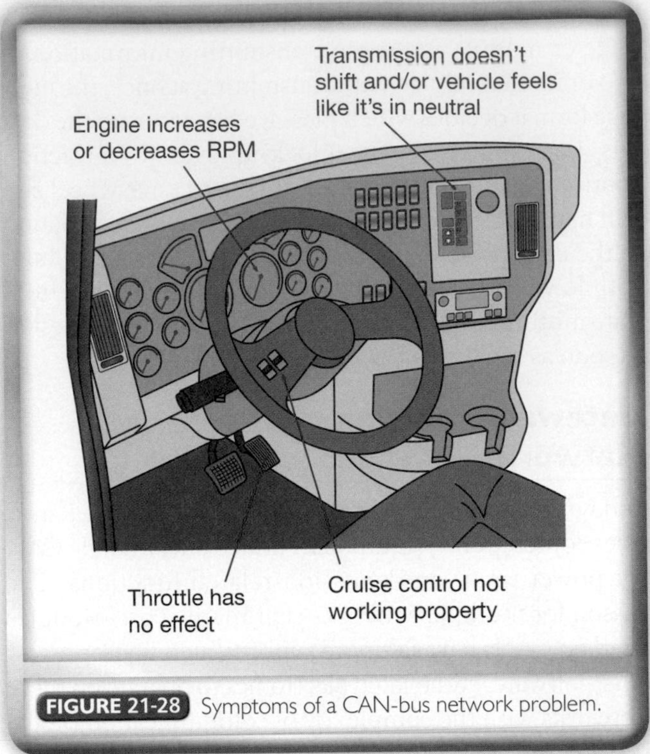
Transmission doesn't shift and/or vehicle feels like it's in neutral
Engine increases or decreases RPM
Throttle has no effect
Cruise control not working property

FIGURE 21-28 Symptoms of a CAN-bus network problem.

the CAN-bus. But the best diagnostic routine to identify a network problem is to perform resistance and voltage checks of the CAN-bus at the DLC. The HD-OBD system monitors the CAN-bus voltage and will report network faults if the voltage measurements are not correct or if there is a problem with the data. The failure of a service tool to communicate with the DLC requires a check of the voltage on the CAN pins, which should be a minimum of 1 volt. After disconnecting the batteries to remove all vehicle power, resistance checks of the terminating resistors can be performed. Too many or too few resistors will give an incorrect resistance reading. The proper resistance should be close to 60 ohms.

Power Line Carrier (PLC) Communication

PLC Multiplexing SAE J2497

PLC4TRUCKS is another commonly used multiplex systems used to provide a J-1939 connection between the tractor and trailer, primarily to power the in-dash ABS trailer lamp mandated in 2001. PLC is an acronym for **power line carrier technology**, which enables multiplex communication over constantly powered wires on the J-560 trailer plug. Many more functions can potentially be incorporated into this PLC communication bridge between

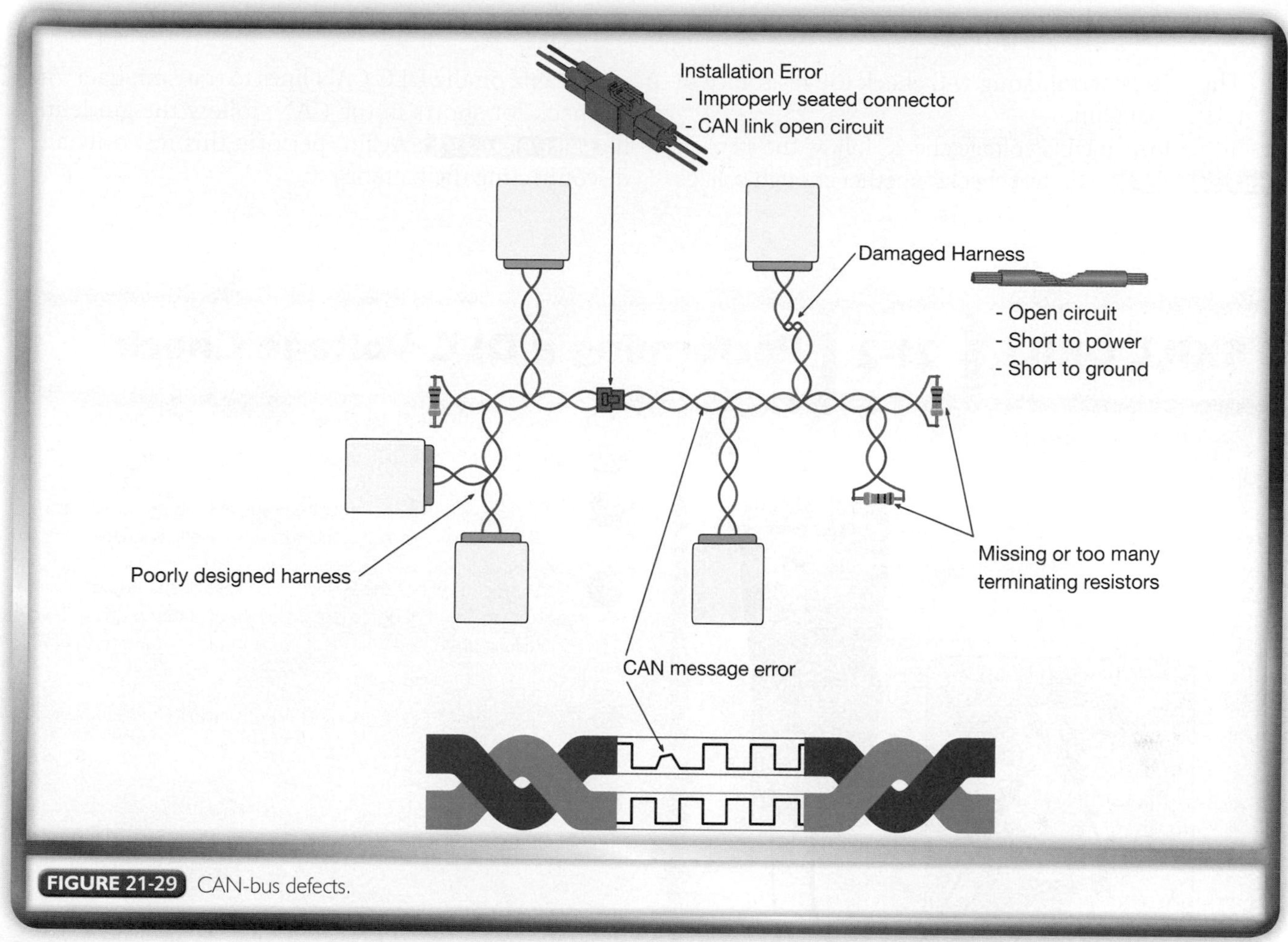

FIGURE 21-29 CAN-bus defects.

the tractor and trailer, but few are currently implemented. Network communication, when enabled, takes place over the brown and green (tail and right turn) wires of the J-560 trailer plug. Two modules, called bridges, which are located in the tractor and trailer, are used to enable communication. The system can operate in conventional mode when either a pre-2001 tractor or trailer is connected to one another. When both units are equipped with network bridges, communication can take place between the units in "smart mode." Establishing smart mode is performed automatically—no operator action is required.

PLC Smart Mode Operation

When the ignition key is turned on, the tractor bridge computer starts with J-560 outputs in conventional mode. This means the circuits to the trailer are powered as they would be during traditional operation. The blue, or auxiliary, circuit powers the trailer bridge computer. Subsequently, the trailer bridge computer also starts in conventional mode, too, but cycles a 5-ohm resistor in and out of the blue circuit at a rate of 20 Hz, producing a 20-Hz, 2.5-amp current pulse on the constant power blue circuit. The 20-Hz pulse causes the tractor bridge to listen for J-1939 communication on the green and brown circuit's tail lamp/right signal circuit, and respond to the trailer bridge module.

If the trailer bridge computer receives these messages, it sends an acknowledgment. Both bridges then switch to smart mode. If either bridge fails to receive these messages within a set period of time, the trailer bridge ceases pulsing, and the blue circuit and both bridges return to conventional mode. In smart mode, six of the seven J-560 circuit functions change. Four are used fulltime to power all the lighting circuits, and two are used for J-1939 communication. Both tractor and trailer bridges are responsible for operating the right turn and tail lamp circuits with power from the remaining four circuits, while those green and brown tail and right turn circuits are used for J-1939 communication between the trailer ABS and tractor network. The existing ground circuit remains unchanged.

The J-1939 terminating will check the resistance of the J-1939 data link.

To perform a DLC voltage check, follow the steps in SKILL DRILL 21-2. This test checks whether enough voltage is available on the DLC CAN lines to transmit data. And to check for shorts in the CAN, follow the guidelines in SKILL DRILL 21-3. Again, perform this test only after disconnecting the batteries.

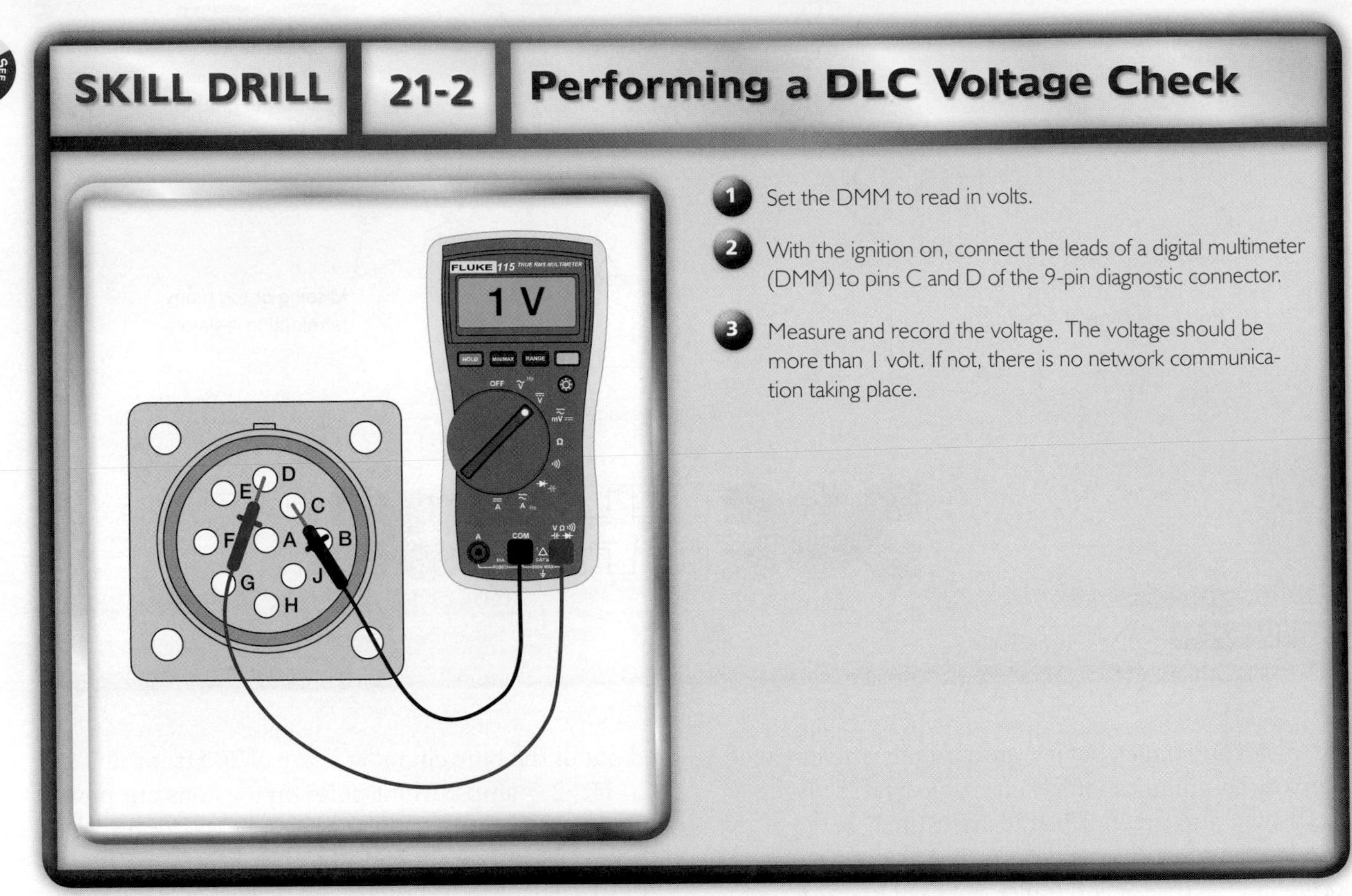

SKILL DRILL 21-2 Performing a DLC Voltage Check

1. Set the DMM to read in volts.
2. With the ignition on, connect the leads of a digital multimeter (DMM) to pins C and D of the 9-pin diagnostic connector.
3. Measure and record the voltage. The voltage should be more than 1 volt. If not, there is no network communication taking place.

SKILL DRILL 21-3 Checking for Shorts in the CAN

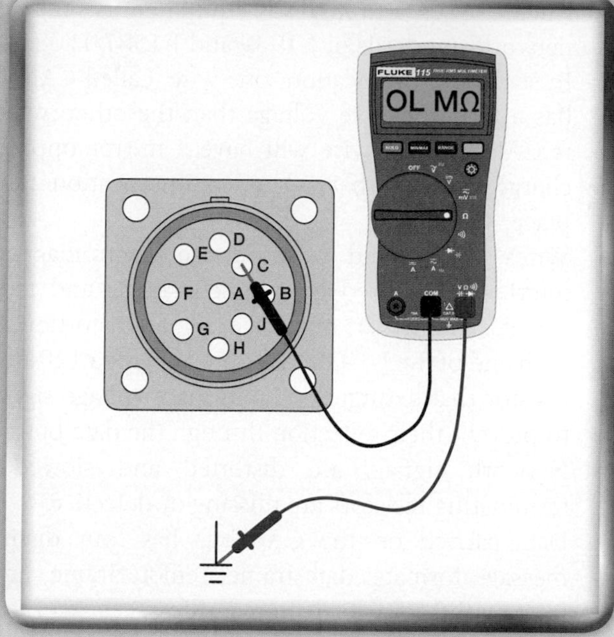

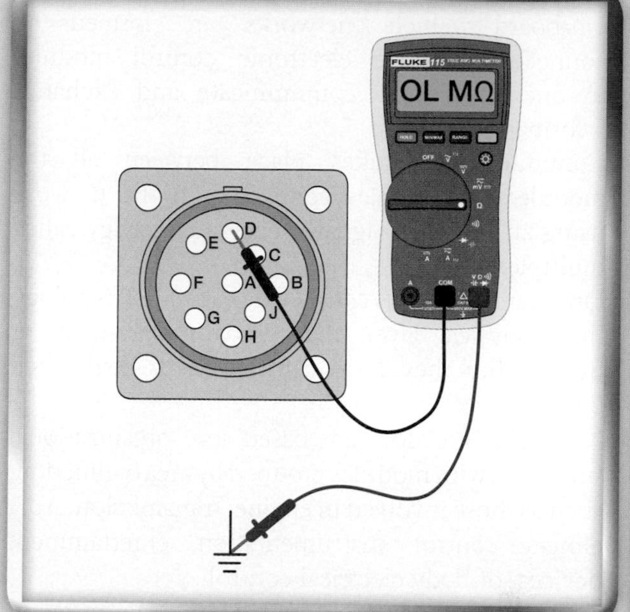

1. With the ignition off, disconnect the batteries.
2. Connect one lead of a digital multimeter to pin C of the 9-pin diagnostic connector.
3. Connect the multimeter lead to chassis ground.
4. Set the multimeter to read in ohms.
5. Measure and record the resistance.
6. Connect one lead of a digital multimeter to pin D of the 9-pin diagnostic connector.
7. Connect the other multimeter lead to chassis ground.
8. Measure and record the resistance. The resistance between chassis ground and either pins C or D should be infinite or out of limit.

Wrap-up

Ready for Review

- On-board vehicle networks are formed by connecting vehicle electronic control modules to one another to communicate and exchange information.
- Communication takes place between all the modules and devices connected to the network using an electrical signal-processing strategy called multiplexing.
- On-board networks can be categorized by typology, their physical layer, their network protocol, or by whether they have centralized or distributed control.
- Networks are formed based on organizational priorities, with modules grouped by area or function, such as those involved in engine, transmission, ABS, climate control, instrumentation, entertainment devices, or body electrical control.
- The type of multiplexing used in on-board networks works by dividing the time available to each network module or device to transmit and listen to information. Only one module is allowed to talk and all other modules must listen until it is their turn to talk.
- Advantages of multiplexing include software control of the electrical system, enabling on-board diagnostics, ease of connecting electronically controlled accessories and features, and reduction in number of sensors.
- Controlled area networks are the most widely used type of network for integrating power train operation of all the latest vehicles.
- Two different types of CANs used by on-highway trucks, buses, and highway equipment are the SAE network standards of J-1939 and J-1587/1708.
- In serial communication, one wire, called CAN-hi, has a more positive voltage than the other, which is CAN-lo Each wire will have a mirror opposite charge of the other when communication takes place.
- Wires are twisted to minimize electromagnetic interference caused by magnetic fields and radio waves. To further minimize signal distortion, at each end of the J-1939 CAN-bus there is a 120-ohm resistor that extinguishes multiplex voltage signals to prevent their reflection through the data bus.
- Network signals are distorted and slowed if terminating resistors are missing or defective.
- Data carried on the CAN-bus has four distinct message formats: data frame, remote frame, error frame, and overload frame. Messages sent and received over the network are constructed in frames with a maximum message length of 130 bits.
- Messages are prioritized to prevent data collision between positive and negative signals canceling one another.
- Cell phone and Bluetooth technology are two levels of network communication using wireless network interface.
- Disconnecting modules one by one can help identify a module that is shorting out the CAN-bus, but the best diagnostic routine to identify a network problem is to perform resistance and voltage checks of the CAN-bus at the DLC.

Vocabulary Builder

arbitration The process of deciding which messages have priority to transmit over the network to prevent data collision between positive and negative signals canceling one another.

bidirectional communication Two-way multiplex communication.

Bluetooth A short-range wireless technology that can automatically connect a device into a network.

controlled area networks (CAN) A distributed network control system in which no single central control module is used.

data bus The typology forming the communication pathway of modules in a network.

differential mode transmission A situation in which network modules detect the voltage difference between two wires to determine if a signal is a 1 or a 0.

field effect transistor (FET) A unipolar transistor that uses an electric field to control the conductivity of a semiconductor material.

gateway module A module that translates communication between different networks operating using different protocols or speeds.

ladder logic The designed-in logic of a circuit that determines what activates a specific circuit.

multiplexing Transmission of more than one electrical signal or message takes place over a single wire or pair of wires.

network node A point on a network.

on-board diagnostics (OBD) Self-diagnostic capabilities of electronic control modules that allow them to evaluate voltage and current levels of circuits to which they are connected and determine if data is in the correct operational range.

power line carrier (PLC) technology Technology that enables multiplex communication over constantly powered wires.

serial communication Communication using zeroes and ones to transmit data in a series, one bit after another in sequence.

serial data Pieces of data sent by the master module.

time division multiplexing A type of multiplexing used in on-board networks and that works by dividing the time available to each network module or device.

typology The manner in which modules are connected to one another.

Review Questions

1. What terminals of the 9-pin diagnostic connec tor are connected to a digital multimeter (DMM) to check the resistance of the terminating resistors used for the CAN-bus?
   a. A and B
   b. 14 and 16
   c. C and D
   d. 3 and 4
2. Communication between all the modules and devices in a truck connected to a network using an electrical signal-processing strategy called which of these?
   a. Networking
   b. Multiplexing
   c. Communication
   d. Linking
3. The rules or standards used to communicate over the networks are called:
   a. network protocol.
   b. typology.
   c. physical protocol.
   d. CAN (Controller Area Network).
4. Electronic control modules can easily evaluate the voltage and current levels of circuits to which they are connected and determine whether the data makes sense and is in the correct operational range. These self-diagnostic capabilities are referred to as which of these?
   a. CAN (Controller Area Network)
   b. OBD (On-board diagnostics)
   c. Network protocol
   d. Typology
5. All networks have in common the concepts of interconnected modules. The use of __________ enables digital communication between each module and time division multiplexing as a communication strategy.
   a. scan tool
   b. multiplexing
   c. serial data
   d. parallel data
6. When paired together and connected in parallel to all modules in the network, the typology forming the communication pathway is called a:
   a. bus.
   b. network.
   c. system.
   d. circuit.
7. What requires the modules and other devices to take turns, sharing the data bus communication pathway?
   a. Data sharing
   b. Time division multiplexing
   c. Network
   d. Circuit
8. When using networks, electrical system complexity is absorbed by the __________ instead of a huge array of hardwired components and circuit boards.
   a. computer
   b. controller
   c. network
   d. software
9. All electronically controlled engines and power train components have built-in self-diagnostic capabilities. To communicate this data to an electronic service tool from even a single module requires the use of:
   a. bidirectional communications
   b. factory scan tool
   c. direct communication
   d. personal computer
10. Self-diagnostic capabilities are referred to as which of these?
    a. Diagnostic circuit check
    b. Off-board diagnostics
    c. On-board diagnostics (OBD)
    d. Diagnostic control

ASE-Type Questions

1. Two technicians are discussing checking the voltage at the 9-pin diagnostic connector or datalink connector (DLC). Technician A says that voltage is checked with the ignition on at terminals C and D. Technician B says that the voltage at terminals C and D should be 12.6 volts. Who is correct?
   a. Technician A
   b. Technician B
   c. Both Technician A and Technician B
   d. Neither Technician A nor Technician B
2. When checking for shorts on the CAN-bus, which of these voltage values is a technician MOST LIKELY to find?
   a. 1 volt
   b. 0.5 volts
   c. OL (out of limits)
   d. 0.2 volts
3. Which of the following connectors do technicians use in conjunction with electronic service tools—such as scan tools, scanners, PCs, and other devices—to communicate with modules connected to the vehicle networks on late-model trucks?
   a. 6-pin diagnostic connector
   b. 16-pin DLC (data link connector)
   c. 9-pin diagnostic connector
   d. 12-pin DLC (data link connector)
4. Two technicians are discussing truck serial data communication. Technician A says that trucks using the J1939 SAE standard use a connection between the tractor and trailer, primarily to power the in-dash ABS trailer lamp called a power line carrier (PLC). Technician B says that the PLC system can operate in conventional mode only when connected to a 2001 or later tractor or trailer is connected to one another. Who is correct?
   a. Technician A
   b. Technician B
   c. Both Technician A and Technician B
   d. Neither Technician A nor Technician B
5. Technician A says that network communication, when enabled, takes place over the brown and green (tail and right turn) wires of the J-560 trailer plug. Technician B says that the MOST LIKELY diagnostic routine to identify a network problem is to perform resistance and voltage checks of the CAN-bus at the DLC. Who is correct?
   a. Technician A
   b. Technician B
   c. Both Technician A and Technician B
   d. Neither Technician A nor Technician B
6. Two technicians are discussing truck serial data communication and networks. Technician A says that data carried on the CAN-bus has four distinct message formats: data frame, remote frame, error frame, and overload frame. Technician B says that cell phone and Bluetooth technology are two levels of customization realized using wireless network interface. Who is correct?
   a. Technician A
   b. Technician B
   c. Both Technician A and Technician B
   d. Neither Technician A nor Technician B
7. Technician A says that broken mechanical systems are often diagnosed visually or with mechanical tools such as pressure gauges, dial indicators. Technician B says that self-monitoring or self-diagnostic capabilities are, therefore, built into electronic control systems to help technicians perform faster. Who is correct?
   a. Technician A
   b. Technician B
   c. Both Technician A and Technician B
   d. Neither Technician A nor Technician B
8. Which of the following safety features is LEAST LIKELY to be made possible by network communication?
   a. Headlights that are automatically switched on with wiper activation
   b. Interior bus lighting that dims to minimize windshield glare
   c. Automatic door opening when stopped for more than 5 minutes
   d. Dome or work light that shuts off after 10 minutes with door open and key off
9. Two technicians are describing the use of electronic service tools. Technician A says that fault codes, communication language, and other features of the on-board network are standardized by EPA legislation. Technician B says that only the truck manufacturer's specific scan tool or software can read the legislated fault codes. Who is correct?
   a. Technician A
   b. Technician B
   c. Both Technician A and Technician B
   d. Neither Technician A nor Technician B
10. Which of the following now come equipped with digital LCD displays that can serve as a numeric fault code reader?
    a. Scan tool
    b. Speedometer
    c. Odometer
    d. Clock

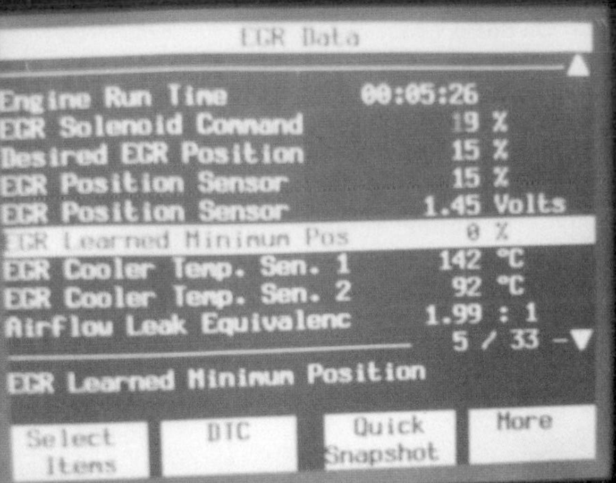

CHAPTER 22

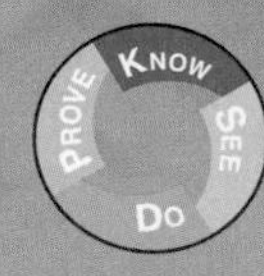

NATEF Tasks

Diesel Engines

General	Page
■ Check and record electronic diagnostic codes.	642–652

Fuel System—Electronic Fuel Management System	
■ Locate and use relevant service information (to include diagnostic procedures, flow charts, and wiring diagrams).	628, 652
■ Inspect and test switches, sensors, controls, actuator components, and circuits; adjust or replace as needed.	629–645
■ Interface with vehicle's on-board computer; perform diagnostic procedures using electronic service tool(s) (to include PC-based software and/or data scan tools); determine needed action.	642–652
■ Check and record electronic diagnostic codes and trip/operational data; monitor electronic data; clear codes; determine further diagnosis.	642–652

On-Board Diagnostics

Knowledge Objectives

After reading this chapter, you will be able to:

1. Identify and describe legislative requirements of engine manufacturer's diagnostic and heavy-duty on-board diagnostic (HD-OBD) systems. (pp 628–631)
2. Differentiate between on- and off-board diagnostics. (pp 629–643)
3. Identify and describe features of on-board diagnostic (OBD) strategies. (pp 630–631)
4. Identify and describe circuit monitoring strategies for out-of-range fault detection. (pp 630–633)
5. Identify and describe principles of fault detection and diagnosis for commercial vehicle electronic control systems. (p 632)
6. Describe and explain standards for assigning fault codes to circuit faults. (pp 642–652)

Skills Objectives

There are no skills objectives for this chapter.

Introduction

Technicians servicing today's commercial vehicles will be just as likely to use a computer as a screw driver to perform repairs. Electronic systems using microprocessors control every chassis, engine, and drive train system and provide operational capabilities far exceeding any mechanical system—and with greater precision, efficiency, and reliability.

Although electronics offer many advantages and benefits over mechanical controls, a new challenge is to identify and repair quickly any failure in systems that operate with increasing invisibility using electronic signals and software-based operating systems. To prevent a problem as simple as a broken wire from requiring huge number of labor hours to identify and repair, electronic systems have self-diagnostic capabilities. These self-diagnostic capabilities extend to the emission systems, which also must operate flawlessly for the normal service life of the vehicle to maintain almost undetectable emission levels from the latest engines.

Fundamentals of HD-OBD

The dominance of electronics makes skill development related to servicing electronic control technology one of the most important priorities for successful technicians. Understanding the operating principles of electronic control systems is foundational for choosing diagnostic strategies, using service tools effectively, and making sound repair recommendations. Nowhere are these skills more important than in comprehending and troubleshooting the operation of the HD-OBD system. This unique system is responsible for maintaining a vehicle's compliance with emission standards. The comprehensive monitoring of the vehicle performed by the HD-OBD system means electronic related faults requiring service will be identified by the OBD system.

Development of HD-OBD

The term **on-board diagnostics (OBD)** has two meanings for the technician. The simplest, most familiar definition is the diagnostic function of electronic control systems to identify or self-diagnose system faults and report fault codes. The second meaning is the legislated standards for maximum vehicle emissions levels. The legislation also establishes requirements for maintaining the lowest vehicle emissions and alerting the operator if any fault occurs that could potentially cause emissions to increase above specific thresholds or levels.

The legislation did not pop up overnight, however. It evolved over time and in stages, as we will discuss in this section.

OBD

Emission standards established for diesels beginning in the late 1970s have required a level of precision for engine control only possible through the extensive use of electronics. Electrical devices now perform the work once done by fuel system camshafts, levers, springs, flyweights, and other assorted mechanical devices. Because of the invisible nature of electronic signals and the operation of microprocessors executing thousands of lines of

You Are the Technician

You are at a customer's yard to diagnose a problem with a brand-new Class 8 highway tractor. The vehicle will start and run, but the engine will not accelerate above idle speed. After starting the engine, a red warning light immediately flashes for 30 seconds before the engine shuts down. You perform typical visual inspections of the vehicle, examine the exhaust system and wiring harnesses, and check for fuel coolant air and oil leaks. The selective catalytic reduction (SCR) tank is three-quarters full according to the dash gauge and when visually verifying the level. Nothing seems amiss, but you realize that certain emission-related and engineprotection system-related faults will produce these symptoms. Without being able to easily return to the shop with the vehicle to access diagnostic software and service information, finding the fault that is causing the severe engine power de-rate conditions and shutdown is challenging. Before calling for a tow truck to bring the tractor to the shop, consider the following:

1. What two procedures, other than using original equipment manufacturer (OEM) or other diagnostic software, can you use to retrieve fault codes?
2. Explain why the red engine warning lamp (the stop engine lamp) flashes before the engine shuts down.
3. Are SAE J-1939 fault codes retrievable from this vehicle without OEM software? Explain your answer.

software code, many hours would be spent to identify simple problems such as a broken wire or faulty sensor if these systems did not have self-diagnostic capabilities. This self-diagnostic capability, referred to as the OBD system, was originally developed by manufacturers to enable technicians to service electronic controls. Beginning in 2007, emission legislation began requiring OBD systems to monitor the operation of emission control systems and alert the vehicle operator to any potential emission increase above threshold standards. When a malfunction is detected, diagnostic information is stored for retrieval by a technician to assist in the diagnosis and repair of the malfunction FIGURE 22-1.

Engine Manufacturer's Diagnostic Systems

Before 2007, legislated standards for OBD systems were required for passenger cars, light-duty trucks, and medium-duty vehicles and engines with a gross vehicle weight of up to 14,000 lb (6,350 kg). While a form of OBD was always used by all heavy-duty diesel engine manufacturers for electronically controlled engines, in 2007, the Environmental Protection Agency (EPA) began establishing standards for detecting faults in the emissions system that were not only for electronic controls of engine, power train, and other chassis systems. A preliminary standard to the 2010 HD-OBD standard was called an engine manufacturer's diagnostic (EMD) system. The introduction of particulate filters, crankcase ventilation (CV) systems, and exhaust gas recirculation (EGR) systems in 2007 added a level of complexity to emissions systems needing monitoring to ensure they were properly functioning. The EMD standard had fewer standardized legal requirements and was less comprehensive than HD-OBD. However, EMD does continuously monitor circuit continuity and performs functional monitoring of the fuel injection system, exhaust gas recirculation (EGR), and particulate filter. A malfunction indicator lamp (MIL) was introduced for 2010 engines. The "useful life," or durability, requirement is included in the latest HD-OBD system and was incorporated in 2004 emissions legislation. Useful life standards required for diesel-powered vehicles meant manufacturers had to ensure engines complied with emissions standards over time and distance, not just on the day a representative engine from a particular engine family met emissions standards. Useful life requirements for diesel engines are:

- Light duty: 110,000 miles (177,028 km) or 10 years
- Medium duty: 185,000 miles (297,729 km) or 10 years
- Heavy duty: 435,000 miles (700,065 km) or 10 years

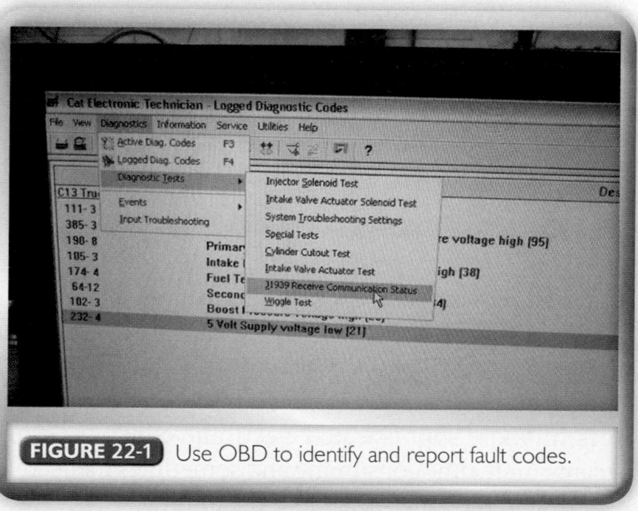

FIGURE 22-1 Use OBD to identify and report fault codes.

HD-OBD

In December 2006, the EPA revised EMD legislation by mandating more comprehensive OBD systems that functionally monitor emissions-control systems and components. Beginning with model year 2010 with a phase-in period until 2016, HD-OBD is a significant update to EMD. Unlike the sensor and limited functionality monitoring of EMD, HD-OBD is a model-based diagnostic system that uses advanced algorithms similar to artificial intelligence to identify emissions-related faults. Legislation also includes a "right-to-repair" provision for the truck/bus repair industry, directing manufacturers to make available any information necessary to perform repairs or maintenance on OBD systems and other emissions-related engine components. All OBD standards are developed by SAE International and adopted by the EPA. Engines must maintain 90–95% reduction to emissions output over the normal engine life cycle. Technical amendments to HD-OBD standards are regularly made, and legislation is updated based on SAE revisions.

Class 8 vehicle sales account for almost half of all truck sales. HD-OBD applies to approximately three-quarters of all truck and bus sales. Emissions reduction from this group, making up 5% of registered vehicles, accounts for approximately 23% of fuel consumption for all vehicles and makes a large impact on emissions levels TABLE 22-1.

Self-Diagnostic Capabilities and Approaches

Electronic systems do not have many moving parts to wear out, but the systems can be complex. When something goes wrong with a component or circuit, identifying the problem without some built-in self-diagnostic capabilities can be extremely time consuming and

TABLE 22-1: Heavy-Duty Vehicle Sales

Weight Class	2000–2001 US Average Retail Sales (Units)
3: 10,001–14,000 lb (4,536–6,350 kg)	104,686
4: 14,001–16,000 lb (6,351–7,257 kg)	49,727
5: 16,001–19,500 lb (7,258–8,845 kg)	26,763
6: 19,501–26,000 lb (8,846–11,793 kg)	46,799
7: 26,001–33,000 lb (11,794–14,968 kg)	107,089
8: 33,001+ lb (14,969 kg)	175,584
Total Class 4 and Above	**405,962**

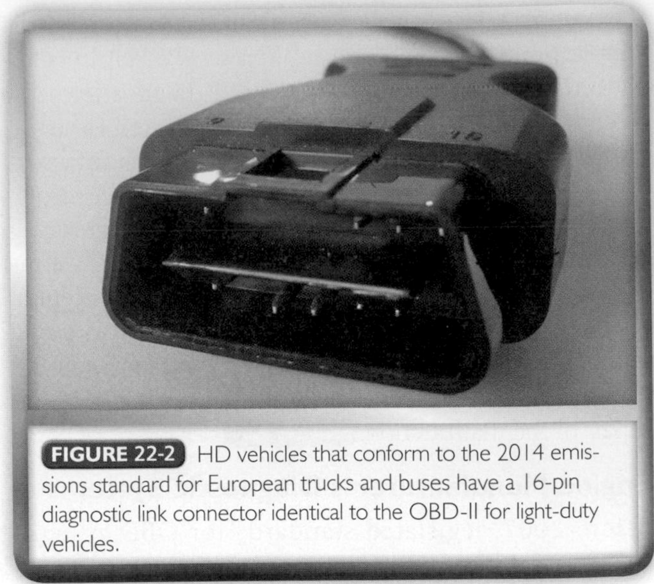

FIGURE 22-2 HD vehicles that conform to the 2014 emissions standard for European trucks and buses have a 16-pin diagnostic link connector identical to the OBD-II for light-duty vehicles.

difficult. Consider what steps would be needed to identify a problem as simple as a bent pin on a control module or a broken or worn wire on today's vehicle. Many hours, if not days, would be needed to trace every individual circuit while performing voltage and resistance checks. With built-in self-monitoring functions, electrical systems can check circuits and electrical devices, evaluate the accuracy of sensor data, and identify problems as they occur. The system records and reports when, where, and how faults occurred, enabling diagnostics on electronically controlled vehicle systems to be performed easily, often with fewer tools and in less time than on mechanical systems **FIGURE 22-2**.

The system can take one of two self-diagnostic approaches to identifying faults. The system can either use traditional self-diagnostic strategies or use a model-based approach.

Traditional self-diagnostic strategies focus on specific areas of commercial vehicle control, such as the engine, anti-lock braking, traction control, and transmissions. In vehicles where only a few control modules are used and communicate with one another, out-of-range-type fault codes and off-board fault isolation methods are adequate.

System self-diagnostic checks are generally performed by limit checking of sensors or circuit data. For example, if the signal voltage produced by a coolant temperature sensor exceeds the limits of normal operation, the system will generate an out-of-range electrical fault code **FIGURE 22-3**. The code will point to a general circuit problem requiring off-board pinpoint testing to determine whether it is the sensor, wiring, or even a disconnected or missing sensor. As system complexity evolved, the technician performed off-board diagnostics after the on-board system identified a fault. Using flow charts for a specific diagnostic code (e.g., troubleshooting diagnostic trees) in more sophisticated electronic control systems became more time consuming and sometimes ineffective, resulting in high levels of "no-fault-found."

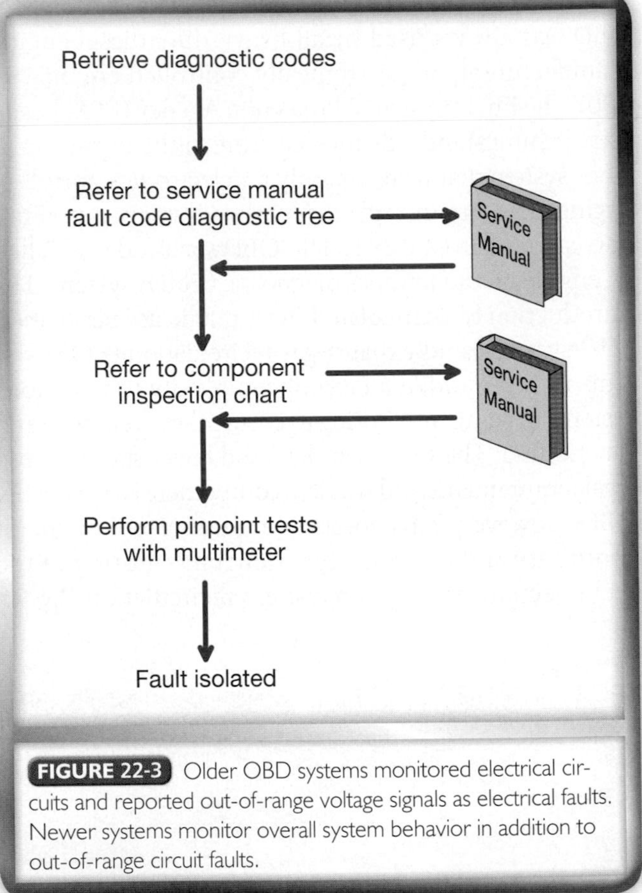

FIGURE 22-3 Older OBD systems monitored electrical circuits and reported out-of-range voltage signals as electrical faults. Newer systems monitor overall system behavior in addition to out-of-range circuit faults.

Manufacturers have also discovered incorrect component replacement and increased warranty costs are associated with high reliance on off-board diagnostic testing by technicians using service literature. Furthermore, data from a sensor as simple as the coolant temperature is even more critical to operation because monitors that evaluate emissions-control devices will run only after an engine has reached operating temperature. The cooling system operation could be within normal range, but the cooling sensor itself may not respond properly.

Model-based diagnostics compare system and component behaviors to expected patterns of operation. In addition to fault detection and isolation, the model-based approach also analyzes and categorizes the fault using advanced algorithms. System problems are generally identified without interfering with system operation by substituting suspected data from a sensor or device with a backup or default data set.

Diagnostic Definitions

A variety of terms are used to categorize abnormal system operation:

1. **Fault**: A fault is a deviation of at least one characteristic property of the system from its standard behavior. Low battery voltage, excessive oil pressure, and a missing sensor input are examples of faults. Depending on how quickly a fault occurs and whether it persists, faults are classified in four categories:
   - *Active*: This type of faults is currently taking place and is uninterrupted in action. Sudden component or circuit problems are generally active faults. An illuminated malfunction indicator light (MIL) or check engine light (CEL) indicates an **active fault**.
   - *Historical*: This type of fault, which is also called inactive, took place at one time but was corrected and is no longer active. A sensor that was temporarily disconnected is an example of a **historical fault**. Amber check engine lights can also indicate the presence of historical faults.
   - *Intermittent*: This type of fault is not ongoing and can be both active and historical. Loose connectors or poor pin contact can cause an **intermittent fault**.
   - *Incipient*: This type of fault is the result of system or component deterioration. An exhaust particulate filter filling with ash is an example of an **incipient fault**.
2. **Failure**: This refers to a fault that permanently interrupts a system's ability to perform a required function under specified operating conditions. Open or shorted circuits, cylinder misfires, or a seized variable geometry turbocharger (VGT) actuator are examples of failures. Failures produce active fault codes.
3. **Disturbance**: This is an unknown and uncontrolled input acting on the system. Electromagnetic interference, loss of mass, fluid or gas leakage from a hydraulic or pneumatic system, or excessive mechanical friction are examples of unknown or uncontrolled disturbances affecting system inputs. Low coolant level in a system without a level sensor could be an example of a disturbance.
4. **Fault detection**: This is a diagnostic strategy to determine whether faults are present in the system. An electronic control module will continuously check for voltage drops for all input and output circuits. Emissions system monitors are typical examples of a fault detection strategy used to evaluate a systems operation based on a model of expected behavior compared with actual performance of individual components or systems.
5. **Fault isolation**: This involves determining the location of the fault. Fault isolation is best accomplished using a diagnostic fault tree supplied by the manufacturer FIGURE 22-4. Examples of fault isolation include pinpoint electrical testing using a voltmeter, an ohmmeter, or commanding actuator tests.
6. **Fault accommodation**: This happens when a fault is detected. Fault accommodation, which is also known as an adaptive strategy, reconfigures the system operation or substitutes suspect data with default data to maintain normal system functionality even with the fault. One example is a newer engine that continues to run after it has lost data from a defective crank or the cam position sensor. The control modules will substitute a value derived from data from the other sensor to keep the engine running, although not as well. For example, a defective mass airflow sensor data could be replaced by intake manifold pressure and temperature data.

Types of HD-OBD Monitors

To detect conditions that can increase emissions levels beyond Federal Test Procedure (FTP) thresholds, the HD-OBD system monitors individual components and major engine emissions-control systems. Validating the operation of individual components that make up an emissions system is not enough because coordinated operation of numerous inputs and outputs form a distinct emissions-control system. What is more important is that everything is working together, and that is the job of a monitor.

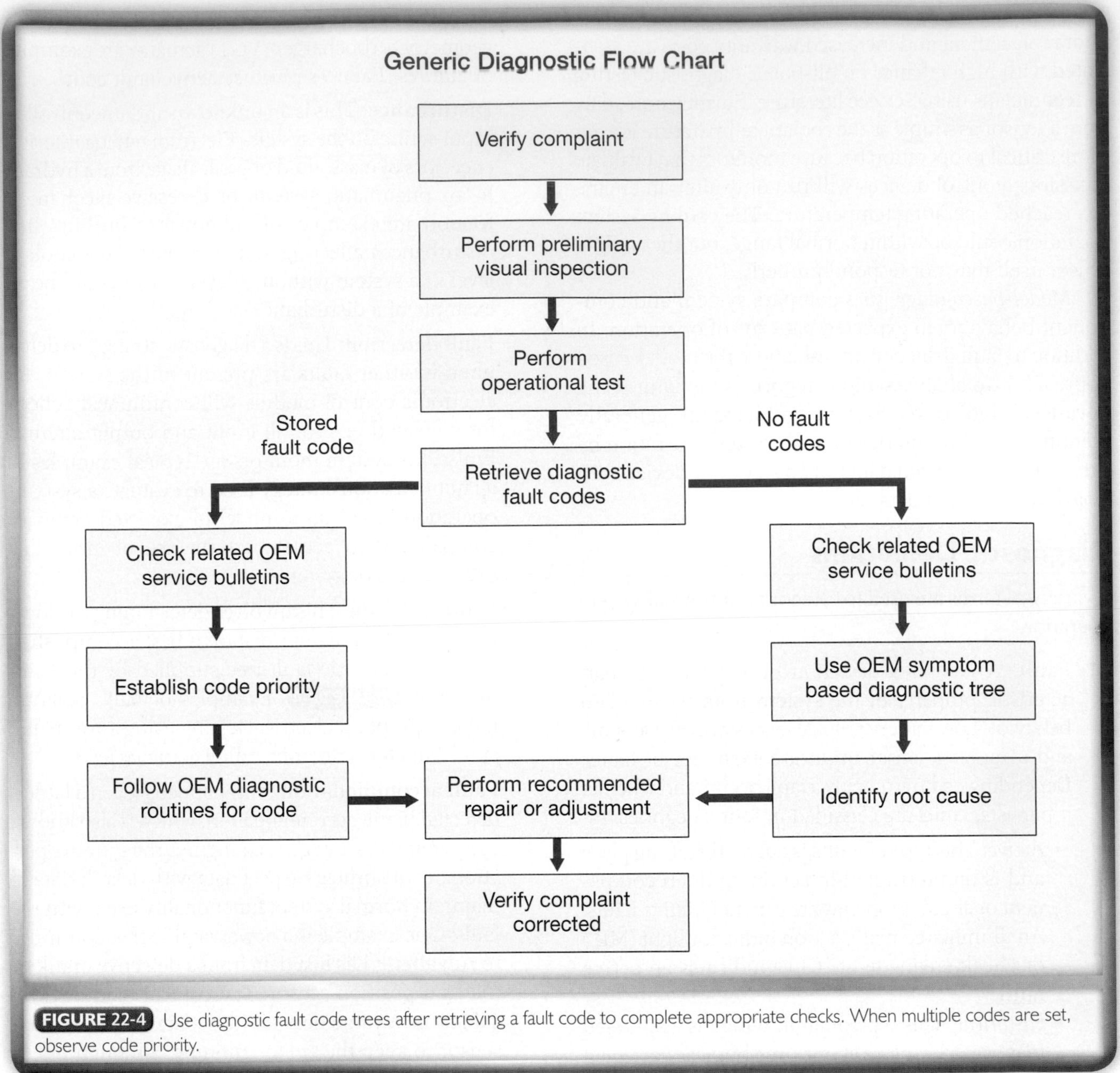

FIGURE 22-4 Use diagnostic fault code trees after retrieving a fault code to complete appropriate checks. When multiple codes are set, observe code priority.

To identify an emissions system failure, the OBD software uses a testing procedure to detect a specific system malfunction. Testing the operation of individual emissions system components using an organized procedure is known as a monitor. The OBD executive, or supervisor, function executes the diagnostic procedure used by the monitor and evaluates the system operation. This function is located in the engine control module (ECM), which consists of specialized software algorithms. The OBD executive determines when and how to run the emissions monitor.

When all the major system monitors have run, a vehicle is considered to have completed a drive cycle. An HD-OBD system executes, or runs, monitors once every eight hours of engine operation. Currently, monitors used by the diesel HD-OBD system can be divided into several general types:

1. **Threshold monitoring**: This is directly measuring the level of emissions using a sensor to identify a noxious emission. Ammonia, particulate matter (PM), or oxides of nitrogen (NO_X) sensors are examples of input devices for threshold monitors **FIGURE 22-5**.
2. **Functionality monitoring**: This is evaluating an emissions system to ensure it is operating correctly. Monitoring is generally based on a computerized

FIGURE 22-5 The NO_X sensor is an example of a component used for threshold monitoring.

model of expected or desired system behaviors developed in an OEM laboratory or through field tests. Monitoring usually includes evaluating multiple electrical signals from various sensors and performing a test during normal engine operation to evaluate system response. Moving a VGT actuator and measuring boost pressure would be an example of a simple-functional monitor that evaluates whether a system is responding correctly.

3. **Rationality, or plausibility, monitoring**: This involves evaluating the accuracy of an electrical input signal compared with other available data. For example, a coolant temperature sensor should sense a temperature similar to an oil or air temperature sensor at initial start-up if an engine has not operated for several hours. If a large difference between sensor data exists or the data does not match the engine operating conditions, such as no oil pressure when the engine is running or fuel temperature considerably colder than ambient temperature, the data is considered irrational, or implausible. Rationality faults are also called logical faults.
4. **Electrical circuit continuity monitoring**: This monitoring measures voltage drops and signal and ground return voltage from sensors or output devices to validate circuits are not open or shorted to ground and battery voltage. These types of faults produce out-of-range voltage codes. Field effect transistors (FET) sense the amount of amperage used by a circuit to detect overcurrent or undercurrent conditions caused by open or shorted circuits.
5. **Out-of-range monitoring**: This monitoring is different from out-of-range voltage codes. Out-of-range monitors validate sensor data to verify a system is operating within an expected range for a given operating condition. Out-of-range monitoring is important to enable other OBD monitors to operate. Coolant temperatures are commonly evaluated for proper response to engine warm-up. If the cooling system is slow to warm up, it is out of range.

HD-OBD legislation for diesels also includes the following features:

- An MIL
- Standardized 9-pin **diagnostic link connector (DLC)** in the driver area. The DLC is the connection point for electronic service tools used to access fault code and other information provided by chassis electronic control modules. World Wide Harmonized Diagnostic OBD (WWHD-OBD)—compliant systems use a 16-pin connector.
- Standardized emissions-related fault codes for all manufacturers
- Reading of fault codes by aftermarket electronic test equipment (i.e., scanners) for emissions system diagnosis (enabled with standardized network communication protocols)
- Display of standard emissions-related data by aftermarket electronic service tools
- Indication of the operating conditions in which a fault occurred, a feature called freeze-frame data
- Standardized names and abbreviations of components and systems
- Evaluation of the functional capability of emissions-related sensors and actuators
- Evaluation of the functions of emissions-related input and output devices for electrical-related faults (e.g., short circuit to battery positive)
- Evaluation of the rationality of emissions-related input signals and components operation, which means the accuracy of an input signal is validated while in the range of normal operation and when compared with all other available information

- Monitoring of the operation of specific emissions-related systems to validate operation. Diesel engines have unique system monitors. A readiness code is displayed once the monitor has completed a functional test of a system and found no fault FIGURE 22-6.

The EMD or the HD-OBD emissions system monitors major engine systems that influence the production of emissions TABLE 22-2. Major system monitors are essentially diagnostic strategies used to determine if an emissions system is performing properly. The **OBD manager**, software that identifies fault codes and ensures emissions systems are operating correctly, regularly evaluates malfunctions in the emissions systems unique to diesel engines.

Major System Monitors

Diagnostic monitoring of diesel engines is broken down into separate, specific hardware systems that are responsible for some specialized aspect of engine operation and

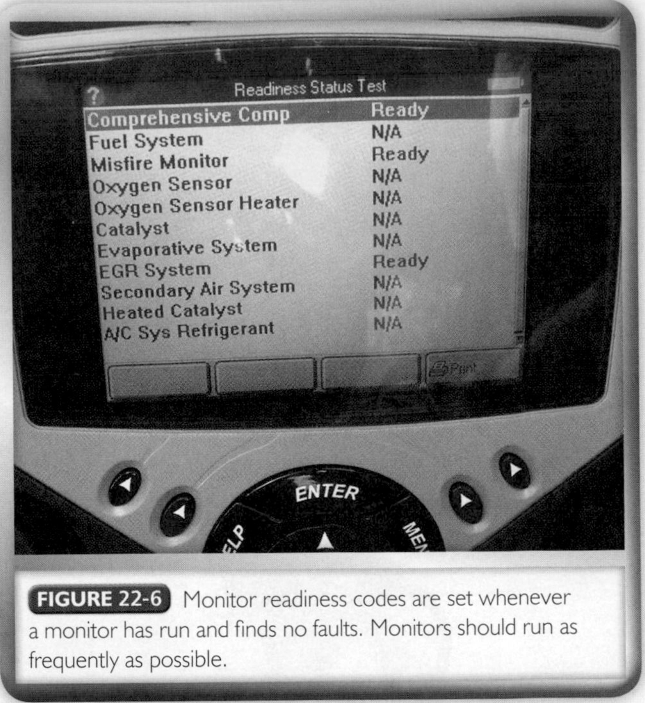

FIGURE 22-6 Monitor readiness codes are set whenever a monitor has run and finds no faults. Monitors should run as frequently as possible.

TABLE 22-2: OBD Emissions Thresholds for Diesel-Fueled/Compression-Ignition Engines Meant for Placement in Applications Greater than 14,000 Pounds (6,364 Kilograms) GVWR (G/BHP+Hr)

Component	NMHC (Non-Methane Hydrocarbons)	CO	NO_X	PM
MODEL YEARS 2010–2012				
NO_X aftertreatment system			+0.6	
Diesel particulate filter (DPF) system	2.5x			0.05/+0.04
Air-fuel ratio sensors upstream of aftertreatment devices	2.5x	2.5x	+0.3	0.03/+0.02
Air-fuel ratio sensors downstream of aftertreatment devices	2.5x		+0.3	0.05/+0.04
NO_X sensors			+0.6	0.05/+0.04
"Other monitors" with emissions thresholds	2.5x	2.5x	+0.3	0.03/+0.02
MODEL YEARS 2013 AND LATER				
NO_X aftertreatment system			+0.3	
Diesel particulate filter (DPF) system	2x			0.05/+0.04
Air-fuel ratio sensors upstream of aftertreatment devices	2x	2x	+0.3	0.03/+0.02
Air-fuel ratio sensors downstream of aftertreatment devices	2x		+0.3	0.05/+0.04
NO_X sensors			+0.3	0.05/+0.04
"Other monitors" with emissions thresholds	2x	2x	+0.3	0.03/+0.02

Source: U.S. Government Publishing Office, Electronic Code of Federal Regulations, Title 40, Chapter 1, Subchapter C, Part 86, Subpart A, Section 86.010-18, http://www.ecfr.gov

emissions-control. The high-pressure injection system and the EGR system are examples of systems that have a major monitor associated with their operation. Each of these major engine systems is assigned a monitor that tests and evaluates the system to determine whether it is functioning properly to maintain the low emissions for which the system was designed. Generally, the monitor detects conditions that would cause an emissions increase of 1.5 times the FTP for emissions testing. However, diesel engines use higher FTP thresholds for exhaust aftertreatment systems. Monitors are not required for a system where failure of a component cannot cause an increase above 1.5 times the emission limit or the failure will not cause a detectable change in emission levels. In this case, functional monitoring is required to simply ensure the system is operating within an acceptable performance range. An example of this would be a diesel particulate filter. No sensor currently measures soot from a failed diesel particulate filter (DPF). Instead, a functional monitor is used that has a diagnostic strategy to detect whether the filter is present and operational using a combination of exhaust system pressure and temperature sensors. The OBD executive evaluates the filter by comparing the measured and expected temperature and pressure values, rather than emission levels, based on a model of DPF operation TABLE 22-3.

HD-OBD legislation requires 14 mandatory major system monitors for diesel engines. If equipped with the applicable system, the following systems have monitors associated with their operation:

- Fuel
- Cold-start emissions strategy
- EGR
- Misfire
- Boost pressure
- Cooling
- Crankcase ventilation (CV)
- Comprehensive component
- Variable valve timing (VVT)

Aftertreatment monitors include:

- DPF
- Lean-NO_X Trap (LNT) or NO_X adsorber
- SCR
- Diesel oxidation catalyst (DOC)
- Exhaust gas sensors

Major emissions system monitors include:

1. Fuel system
    - Fuel pressure
    - Fuel-injection quantity
    - Multiple fuel-injection event performance
    - Fuel-injection timing
    - Closed-loop feedback controls
2. Misfire monitoring
    - Must detect misfire occurring continuously in one or more cylinders during idle
3. EGR system
    - EGR flow rate
    - EGR response rate
    - EGR cooling system
    - Feedback control
    - EGR cooler performance
    - Closed-loop feedback controls
4. Boost pressure control systems
    - Underboost and overboost malfunctions
    - Wastegate operation
    - Slow response (VGT systems only)
    - Charge air undercooling
    - Closed-loop feedback controls

TABLE 22-3: Diesel Threshold Capability by Year (Multiple of FTP Standard)

Emissions System Monitor	Hydrocarbons (HCs)	NO_X	PM
Catalyst (three-way, oxidation, NO_X SCR, or NO_X adsorber)	2007: 3–5x 2010: 2.5–3x 2013: 1.75x	2007: 3–5x 2010: 2.5–3x 2013: 1.75x	N/A
PM filter	N/A	N/A	2007: 5x 2010: 4x 2013: pending
All others (EGR, fuel system, etc.)	2007: 2.5–3.5x 2010: 2–3x 2013: 1.5x	2007: 2.5–3.5x 2010: 2–3x 2013: 1.5x	2007: 2.5–5x 2010: 2–4x 2013: 1.75–2x

5. Cold-start emissions strategies
   - Glow plugs or intake heater on-time
   - Glow plugs and intake air heaters enabled
6. Diesel exhaust aftertreatment systems: Monitor requires faults to be detected before emissions exceed standards for any of the following systems:
   - Oxidation catalyst
   - Lean NO_X catalyst
   - SCR catalyst
   - NO_X trap
   - PM trap
7. Variable Valve Timing (VVT) system: VVT system, once used by Caterpillar ACERT engines, are related to achieving the commanded valve timing and/or control within a crank angle and/or lift tolerance and to detecting slow system response prior to emissions exceeding the thresholds for other monitors. Malfunctions are monitored whenever fault conditions are met rather than monitored once per trip.
8. Engine cooling system: Cooling system malfunctions are related to slow warm-up times, which can prevent other monitors from running because coolant is not at the appropriate temperature. Proper thermostat functions and engine coolant temperature sensor readings are measured and must be reached within a specific time. Monitoring is performed monitored once per drive cycle.
9. Crankcase Ventilation (CV) system: The CV system is checked for system operation and integrity. The manufacturer may not monitor for disconnections between the crankcase and the CV valve, provided the CV system is designed to use connections that are resistant to failure and tampering.

Comprehensive Component Monitor

The comprehensive component monitor (CCM) tracks electrical circuits operating power train components that can cause a measurable emissions increase during any reasonable driving conditions or:

1. Are used for other OBD monitors
2. Are required to monitor input components for circuit and rationality faults
3. Are required to monitor output components for functional faults

The CCM is not tied to emissions thresholds. Any electrical problem will cause the MIL to illuminate.

Continuous and Non-Continuous Monitors

An emissions system may be monitored continuously or non-continuously. A non-continuous monitor requires certain conditions to be met before evaluation of an emissions system. For example, the vehicle may need to be above a particular road speed, the engine at a specific temperature, or there may even need to be an adequate level of fuel in the tank before a monitor can run. A monitor may not run if the altitude is too high, or a power take-off is operating, or some other condition is present that could jeopardize the safety of an operator or damage the vehicle. To provide an understanding of monitor operation, the following are examples of several HD-OBD monitors, along with a description of the monitor strategy and testing conditions needed to enable or activate each monitor.

Misfire Detection Monitor

Cylinder misfire occurs when a cylinder fails to produce combustion pressure similar to other engine cylinders **FIGURE 22-7**. Causes can include poor compression, improper fuel delivery, or mechanical engine failure. Because engine misfires can cause hydrocarbons and carbon monoxide (CO) emissions, the OBD system must evaluate engine operation to determine whether misfires are occurring. The threshold for diesel misfire detection is 4% per 1,000 crankshaft revolutions. This corresponds to 40 misfires per 1,000 revolutions per minute (rpm).

The misfire detection monitor is intermittent. Data from the engine sensors include oil temperature, crankshaft position (CKP), injection quantity, exhaust pressure, intake air temperature, and fuel level input. This data ensures certain conditions are met when detecting a misfire, such as distinguishing whether a vehicle is low on or out of fuel, warmed up and running, or lugging under load.

Misfire Monitor Operation

The crank position (CKP) sensor is a primary input in determining cylinder misfire. The CKP sensor produces data by sensing the movement of the teeth on a wheel located on the crankshaft. The ECM uses the speed at which the wheel passes by the sensor to calculate the time between CKP tooth edges. This data supplies rotational velocity of the crankshaft. By comparing the accelerations of each cylinder event, the ECM calculates the pressure produced from each cylinder. Cylinders producing less power will have fewer teeth pass by the CKP senor per unit of time compared with cylinders with normal or

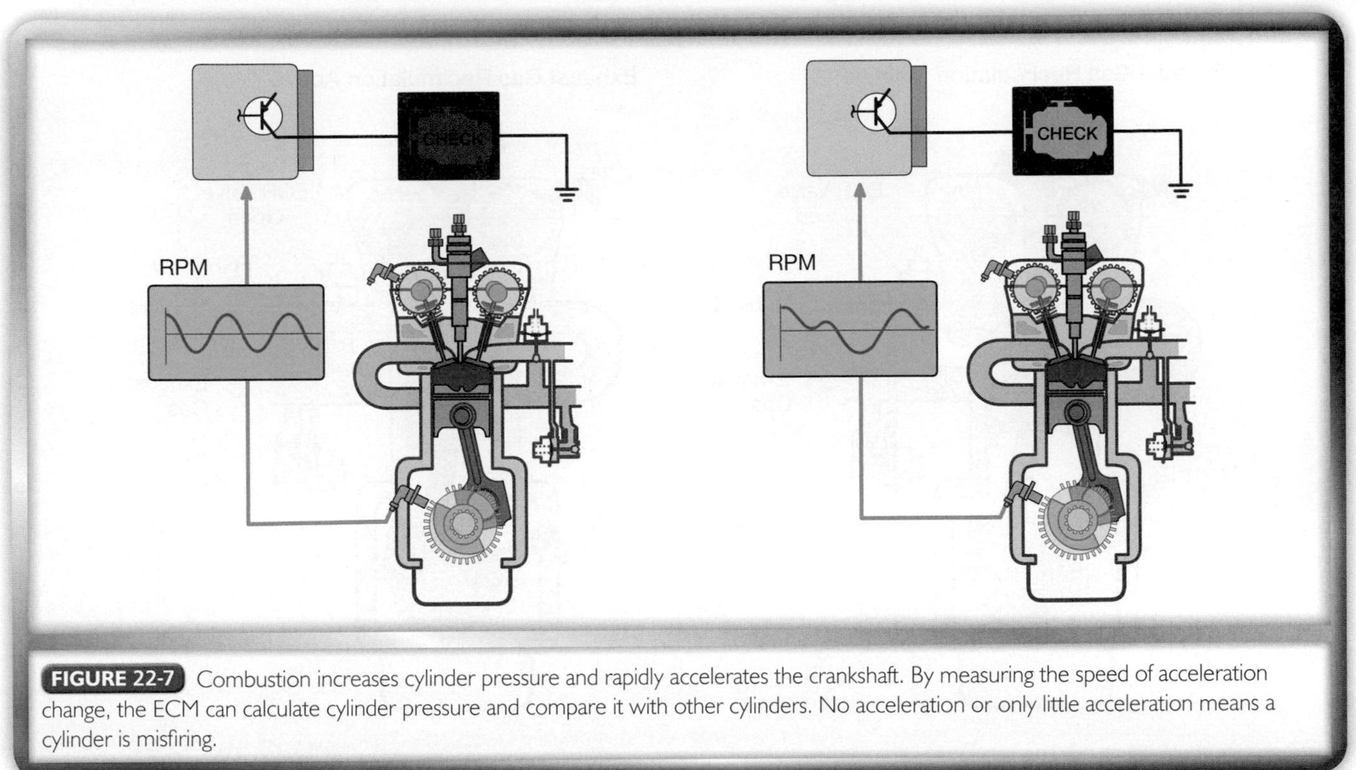

FIGURE 22-7 Combustion increases cylinder pressure and rapidly accelerates the crankshaft. By measuring the speed of acceleration change, the ECM can calculate cylinder pressure and compare it with other cylinders. No acceleration or only little acceleration means a cylinder is misfiring.

higher cylinder pressure. When the power contribution from a particular cylinder is less than an expected value and other criteria for enabling the misfire monitor are met, the cylinder is determined to have misfired. Loss of compression, worn rings, and bent connecting rods can be diagnosed by the fine resolution produced by many CKP teeth and diagnostic strategies of the latest OEM software.

EGR System Monitor

A more complex type of on-board diesel monitor is the EGR monitor. To maintain lowest production of NO_X emissions, EGR gas is recycled from the exhaust to the intake manifold, which lowers peak combustion temperatures and pressures. Failure of the EGR system to perform as it should will result in high NO_X emissions or poor performance and misfire conditions.

HD-OBD requirements for the diesel EGR monitor include detecting the following faults before emissions exceed HD-OBD thresholds:

- EGR flow rate
- EGR response rate
- EGR cooling system performance

An additional operational check includes detecting if a normally closed-loop EGR system fails to enter a closed loop or defaults to an open loop.

EGR Monitor Operation

A large variety of mechanical and electrical functions and conditions need to be evaluated by the EGR monitor, so inputs and operating strategies to check its operation are more elaborate. The electronic and mechanical functionality of the EGR valve, the EGR valve actuator, the VGT, the EGR valve position sensor, and other sensors (e.g., barometric pressure, intake boost, exhaust pressure, mass airflow, oil temperature, air inlet temperature) provide input to this monitor. Even the efficiency of the EGR cooler must be checked by the monitor to determine if the EGR system is operating correctly. Efficiency monitoring is usually accomplished by comparing exhaust gas temperature entering and leaving the cooler. Little temperature change means low cooler efficiency. The elements and components of the EGR system and associated circuits are first evaluated by the monitor before EGR flow is evaluated.

If a mass airflow sensor is used on the engine as part of the EGR monitor strategy, the following is a typical method to evaluate EGR flow. First, when normal EGR rates are being commanded and when the engine enters into either one of two specified operating ranges, a flow measurement is performed. Essentially, the intake air mass airflow (MAF) sensor will detect less fresh airflow into the engine when the EGR is enabled because EGR gas replaces fresh air intake **FIGURE 22-8** and **FIGURE 22-9**.

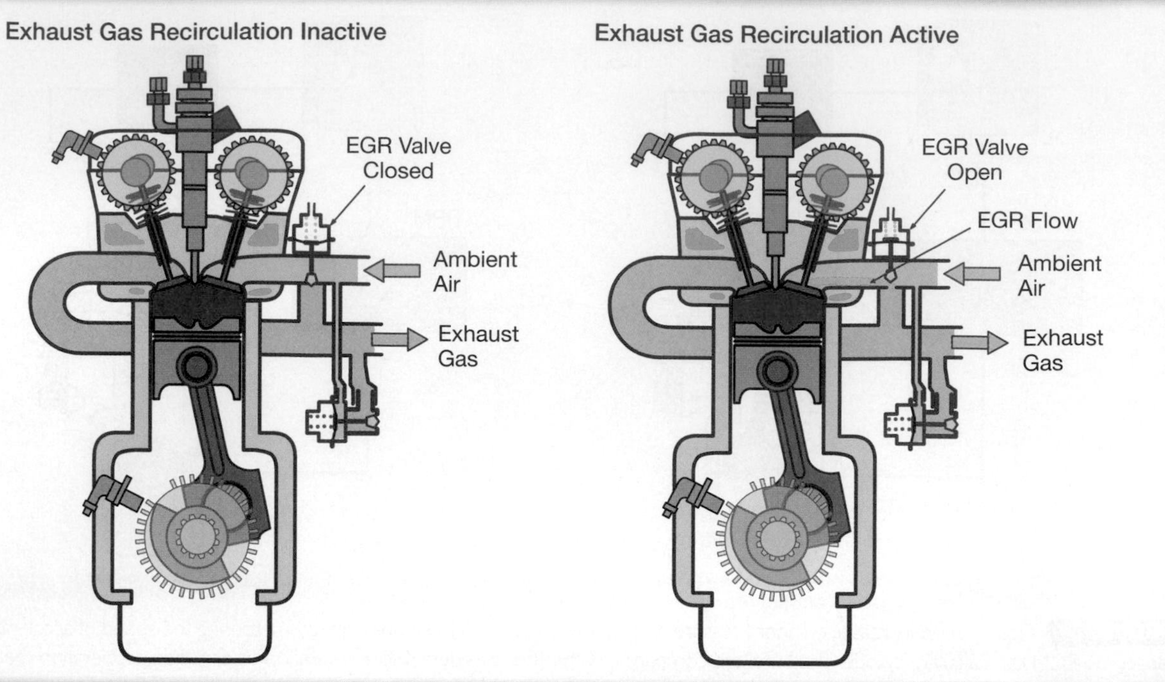

FIGURE 22-8 The difference between the measured intake airflow and the intake airflow predicted without EGR gas is calculated to find the quantity of EGR recirculated into the engine.

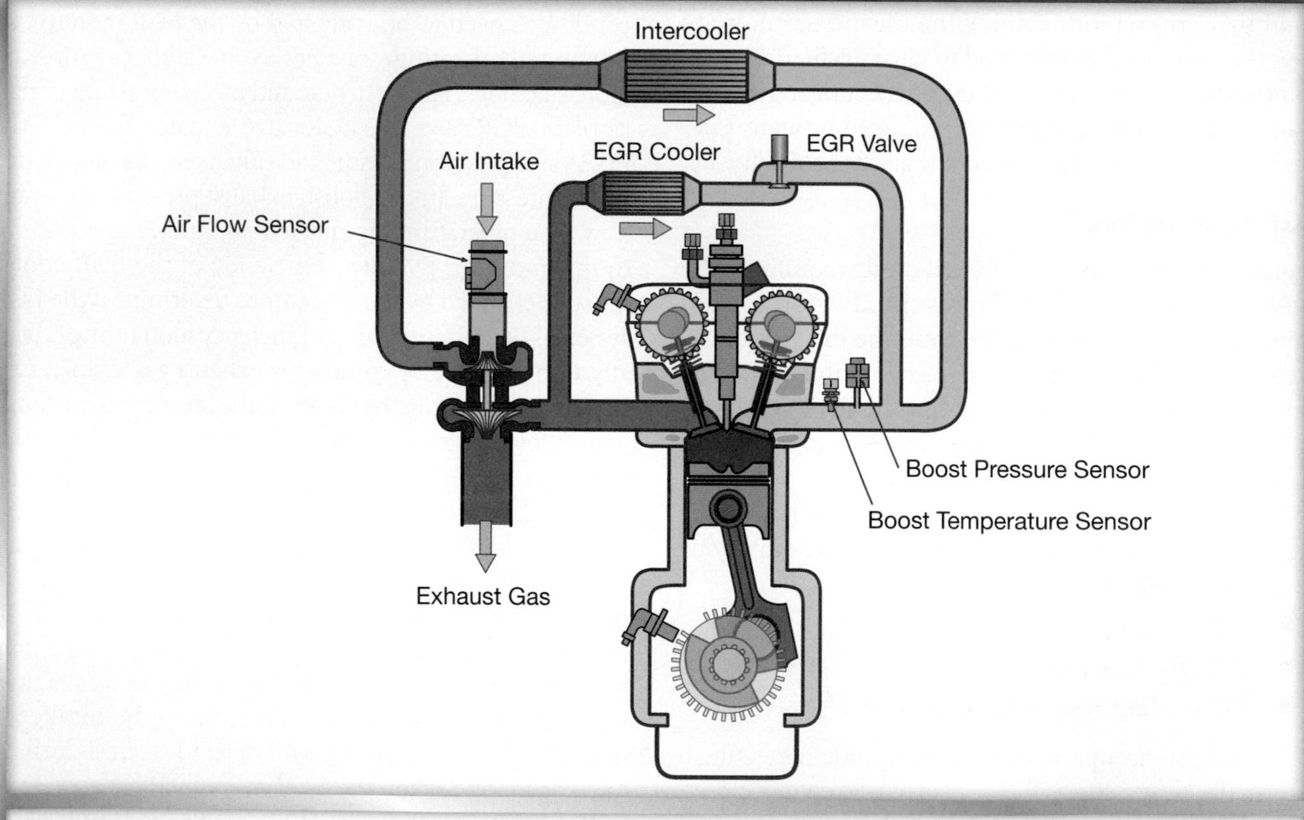

FIGURE 22-9 An EGR system configuration with an MAF sensor to provide closed-loop feedback data for EGR gas flow. Other sensors monitor cooler efficiency and EGR valve movement.

The difference in flow with and without the EGR occurs because EGR gas bypasses the MAF sensor and goes directly into the intake manifold. Two engine operating ranges are used for taking measurements to ensure an adequate amount of EGR is being supplied as requested by the engine management system and compared with an expected quantity. The variation between the quantity of EGR gas actually metered and the expected quantity by the OEM is used to determine if there is insufficient or excessive EGR gas flow.

The most basic conditions and sequence for the EGR monitor to operate occur after all the circuits, sensors, and actuators have been evaluated for correct operating range values or checked for opens and shorts and the engine is warmed up **FIGURE 22-10**. When the engine has entered the following conditions, the monitor evaluates commanded EGR flow against the actual quantity of gas inside the intake manifold as calculated by the intake temperature sensor and intake pressure sensor:

- Condition 1: The EGR flow commanded is greater than 20% and engine speed is 1,000–2,200 rpm. The injection quantity is 0.0006–0.0022 in^3 (10–35 mm^3).
- Condition 2: The EGR flow commanded is greater than 20% and engine speed is 2,200–3,000 rpm. The injection quantity is 0.003–0.007 in^3 (50–110 mm^3).

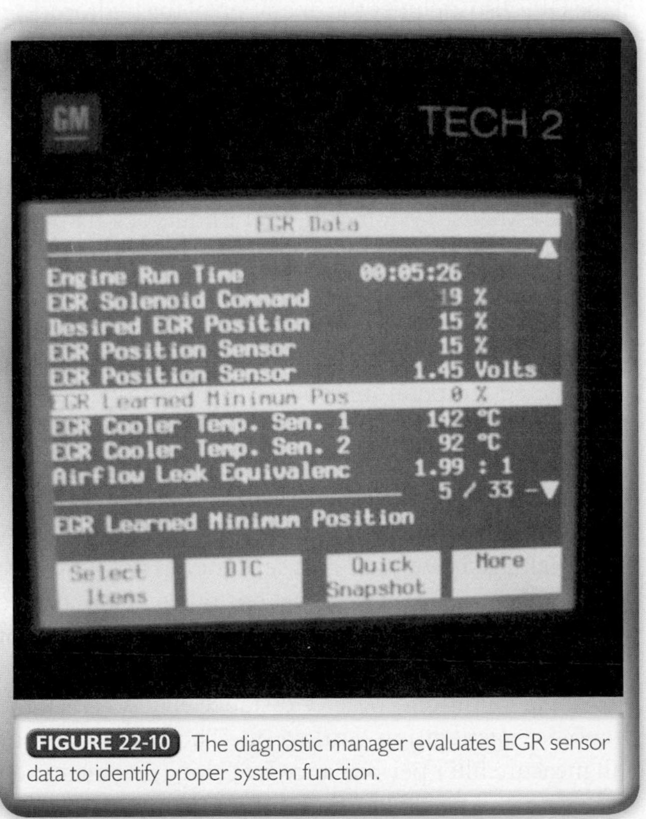

FIGURE 22-10 The diagnostic manager evaluates EGR sensor data to identify proper system function.

The limits of variations between actual and expected flow values stored in the ECM/PCM are based on engine speed and load conditions.

Another technique to monitor EGR flow is to command the EGR valve to fully open when the correct drive-cycle conditions are met. Typically, when cruising at steady speed above 50 mph (80 kph), the EGR valve is opened briefly and the turbocharger speed is measured. High EGR flow cools the exhaust gas temperature and substantially lowers turbocharger speed. If the turbocharger speed falls to an expected range, the EGR system monitor is complete, which means no faults were detected and the EGR system is functioning correctly.

Fuel System Monitors

Fuel system monitors are required to detect faults associated with the high-pressure injection system before emissions exceed OBD emissions thresholds. To do this, manufacturers will typically evaluate fuel system pressure control, fuel injection quantity, and fuel injection timing.

Fuel system monitors on common rail engines evaluate fuel pressure control by comparing expected pressure values in the fuel rail with actual pressure measured using a pressure sensor. For example, worn injectors of a common rail fuel system will set a fault indicating a loss of fuel pressure based on the shorter pulse width applied to the pressure regulator required to maintain fuel pressure in the fuel rail. Because more fuel will bypass a worn nozzle valve or other internal parts of the injectors, the fuel system will detect this as a pressure leak.

Fuel-injection quantity is monitored and calculated by measuring crankshaft speed fluctuations. Crankshaft speed is proportional to cylinder pressures, which are controlled by the amount of fuel burned inside the cylinder.

Fuel-injection timing is typically monitored by comparing a specific point when crankshaft rotational velocity suddenly increases compared with the expected angle of rotation stored in memory. Additionally, on unit injector fuel systems, signal evaluation circuits in the ECM can detect changes in the injector coil inductive signal corresponding to the beginning of injection. The needle lift sensor provides input for some electronic distributor systems.

Additional fuel monitor requirements include detecting faults of closed-loop feedback systems when they fail to enter closed loop or default to open loop.

A closed loop between the rail pressure sensor and the fuel pressure regulator is an example of a normally closed-loop system on a common rail engine. Problems with the signals or data will force the ECM to move out of closed-loop operation and use an adaptive strategy. Injector voltage is measured at the beginning and end of the injection event to check for faults in injector solenoids or electrical circuits energizing the injector.

Boost Pressure Control Monitoring

OBD diesel monitor requirements for the boost control include detecting faults before emissions exceed 1.5 times FTP emissions test standards under the following conditions:

- Underboost and overboost malfunctions
- Slow response (VGT systems only)
- Charge air undercooling

Additional requirements include detecting faults of closed-loop feedback systems if they fail to enter closed loop or default to open loop. Underboost and overboost malfunctions are typically detected by comparing expected boost pressure values stored in the engine control module (ECM) with actual boost pressure measured by the boost pressure sensor.

Slow turbocharger response times (VGT systems only) are evaluated by measuring the time the turbocharger takes to reach expected boost pressure, which is done by the boost pressure sensor and/or the turbine speed sensor. Temperature sensors located at the inlet and outlet of the intercooler or intake manifold temperature sensors evaluate charge air cooling effectiveness.

Cooling System Monitor

Other OBD monitors and emissions systems, such as the EGR, are enabled only after the engine reaches operating temperature. Engine temperature is also a variable that affects transmission shift points and injection timing. Because defective thermostats and engine temperature sensors will negatively affect engine operation, the OBD system also monitors the operation of the cooling system. The operating strategy of the cooling system monitor typically involves comparing actual operating temperature with a warm-up model based on start-up temperature, ambient conditions, and driving time. If the engine fails to reach operating temperature within a reasonable time, the monitor will set a fault. The monitor may also compare values of the coolant sensor with values of other temperature sensors, such as the oil or transmission, to check the rationality of the data.

> **TECHNICIAN TIP**
>
> Adding auxiliary heaters for passenger compartments can cause the cooling system monitor to indicate a fault. Taking heat out of the cooling system during engine warm up will delay the time to warm-up, which will illuminate the MIL.

Crankcase Ventilation (CV) System

The HD-OBD requires monitoring of the CV system of a diesel. Particulate emissions from oil vapor and blow-by gases are no longer permitted to be vented directly to the atmosphere. A plugged CV filter could also lead to engine damage from blown seals as well as oil leakage from other gaskets and engine seals. OBD crankcase ventilation system monitoring consists primarily of detecting the presence of the coalescing filter, if equipped; an open crankcase due to a missing or damaged gasket or oil fill cap; or disconnection of the ventilation system.

Aftertreatment System Monitors

Two common aftertreatment systems are diesel particulate filter (DPF) monitoring and SCR monitoring.

DPF

DPF monitoring includes the following:

- Filter performance
- Frequent regeneration
- Non-methane HC conversion
- Incomplete regeneration
- Missing substrate
- Active regeneration fuel delivery
- Closed-loop feedback control

Any disconnected sensors, missing catalysts, or invalid data will cause the MIL to illuminate. Monitoring of the DPF also includes the operation of the hydrocarbon (HC) dosing system to determine whether it is delivering fuel. Monitoring of the system operation is performed by a combination of temperature and pressure sensors FIGURE 22-11.

When the hydrocarbon dosing valve sprays raw fuel into the exhaust system, the fuel undergoes flameless combustion in the oxidation catalyst, which raises the temperature of the exhaust gas. The temperature change in and out of the exhaust system catalysts is monitored to determine whether the catalysts are operating within an expected temperature range. Missing, broken, deactivated, or tampered catalysts will not meet target temperature values, which will produce fault codes. The delta pressure (Delta P) sensor measures the pressure differential across the DPF and essentially checks for missing or damaged catalysts. This sensor does not influence when an active regeneration event takes place. Active regeneration events are based on models of expected soot loading that are derived from the amount of fuel burned, operating conditions, time or distance elapsed since the previous regeneration, and so on. The Delta P sensor will measure filter performance by comparing measured and estimated restrictions after a regeneration event. If

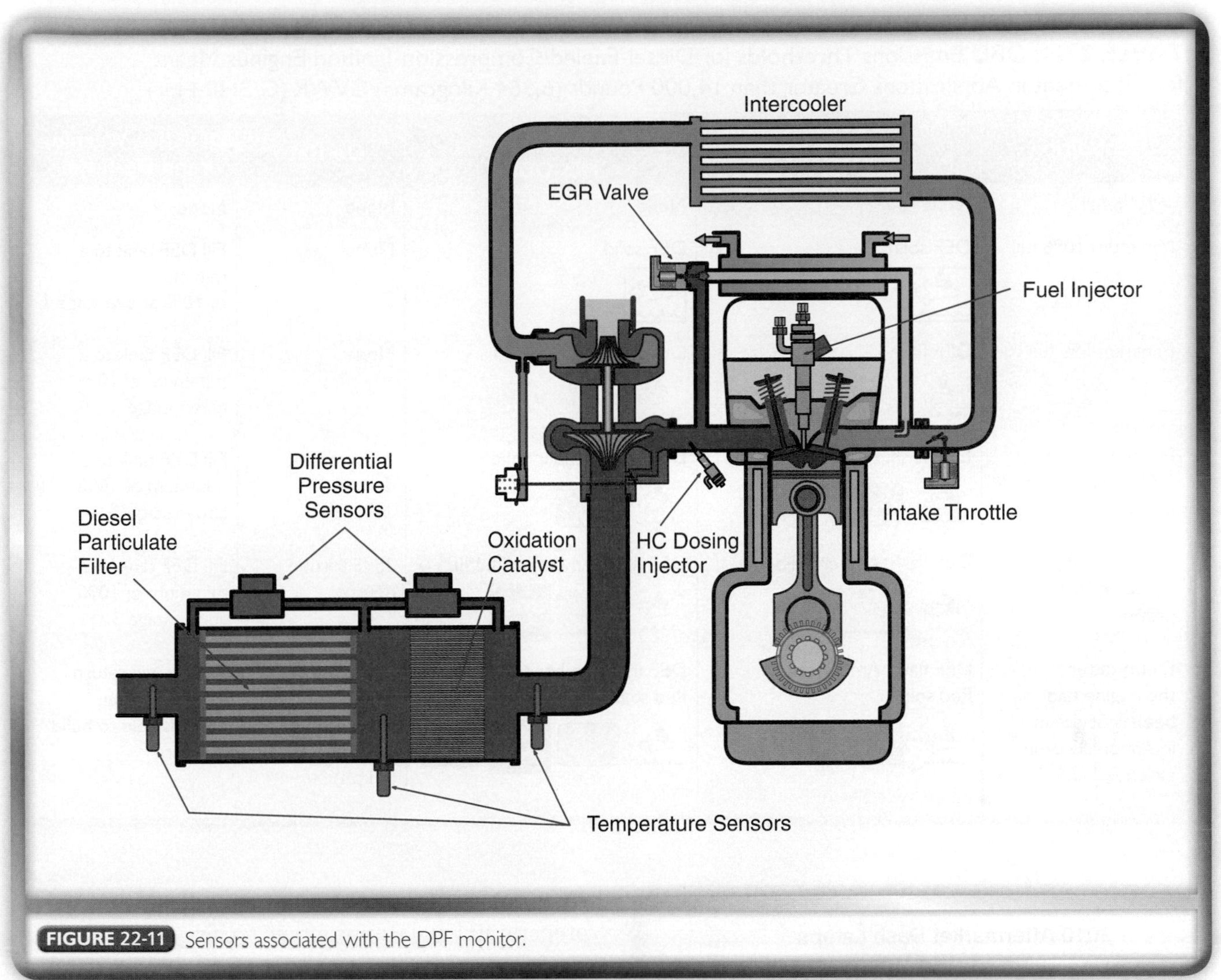

FIGURE 22-11 Sensors associated with the DPF monitor.

the values match, the system determines the filter has proper efficiency when trapping soot. A new type of soot or sensor introduced in 2015 performs as a threshold monitor for the DPF. The sensor is located downstream of the DPF filter and detects any carbon based particulate in the exhaust stream.

SCR Monitor

SCR monitoring ensures the SCR is capable of converting NO_X emissions. Two NO_X sensors measure concentrations of NO_X upstream and downstream of the SCR. When the temperature sensors in the SCR indicate the catalyst is at proper operating temperature, the monitor compares the NO_X sensor differences over time to calculate NO_X catalyst efficiency and deterioration. If the diesel exhaust fluid (DEF) dosing system is not operating correctly, the monitor will detect the absence of NO_X conversion and set fault codes, typically for identifying faults in the entire SCR system.

A DEF quality sensor can now determine the quality of DEF fluid by measuring its density. Using tuning fork technology, ultra-high frequency vibrations produced in the sensor will move at a precise rate based on fluid density.

Fault codes in the SCR system will produce de-rate conditions, depending on their severity. Running a vehicle with no DEF fluid in the reservoir will eventually cause the engine to only idle and could keep the engine from starting TABLE 22-4. FIGURE 22-12 refers to fault lamps in the instrument cluster to alert the driver to faults in the exhaust aftertreament system.

Maintaining HD-OBD

Maintaining the HD-OBD system is critical in order to identify and address emissions system deterioration and remedy failures. Technicians must understand how to use off-board diagnostics and interpret readiness and

TABLE 22-4: OBD Emissions Thresholds for Diesel-Fueled/Compression-Ignition Engines Meant for Placement in Applications Greater than 14,000 Pounds (6,364 Kilograms) GVWR (G/BHP+Hr)

Condition	Notification		De-Rate	Deactive Warning and De-Rate
	EMD+	HD-OBD		
>10% full	None	None	None	None
Minimum 10% full	DEF solid	DEF solid	None	Fill DEF tank to a minimum of 10% above stage 1
Minimun 5% full	DEF flash	DEF flash	None	Fill DEF tank to a minimum of 10% above stage 2
From minimum of 2.5% to before tank is empty	DEF flash, Amber solid	DEF flash, Amber solid	25% torque derate	Fill DEF tank to a minimum of 10% above stage 3
Lack of DEF detected by loss of prime	DEF flash, Amber solid	DEF flash, Amber solid, MIL	25% torque derate	Fill DEF tank to a minimum of 10% above stage 3
Empty, after the engine had been shut down intentionally or in extended idle	DEF flash, Amber solid, Red solid	DEF flash, Amber solid, Red solid	25% torque derate and vehicle speed limited to 5 mph (8 kph)	System will return to stage 3 after doser is able to build pressure

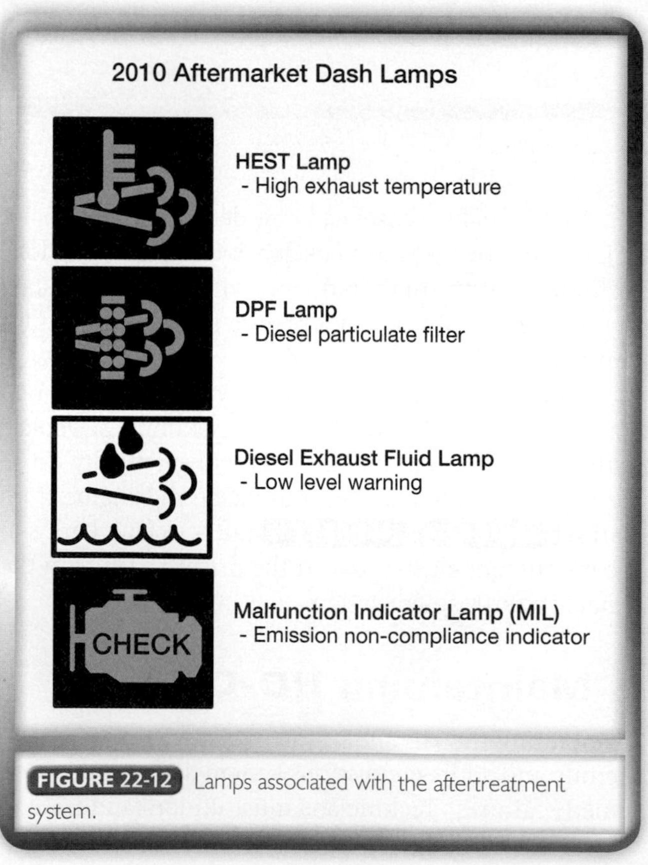

FIGURE 22-12 Lamps associated with the aftertreatment system.

diagnostic trouble codes in order to diagnose a system properly and make appropriate repairs.

Off-Board Diagnostics

When electrical faults or system problems occur in commercial vehicle control systems, electronic control modules log **diagnostic trouble codes (DTCs)** in the system memory, which are read through an instrument display cluster, a **blink code**, or retrieved by a scanner or personal computer connected to the vehicle DLC. OBD is the self-diagnostic checks by the control modules that measure circuit voltages, resistances, rationality, and other variables. More sophisticated OBD systems monitor system behavior to detect smaller faults faster. **Off-board diagnostics** and repair occur when the technician retrieves codes and vehicle data as a starting point to diagnose system problems. During off-board diagnostics, the technician may monitor system operation, perform actuator tests, pinpoint electrical tests, and inspect components. Remotely assisted diagnostics using **telematics** is also a type of off-board diagnostics. Telematics is a branch of information technology that uses specialized applications for long-distance transmission of information to and from a vehicle **FIGURE 22-13**.

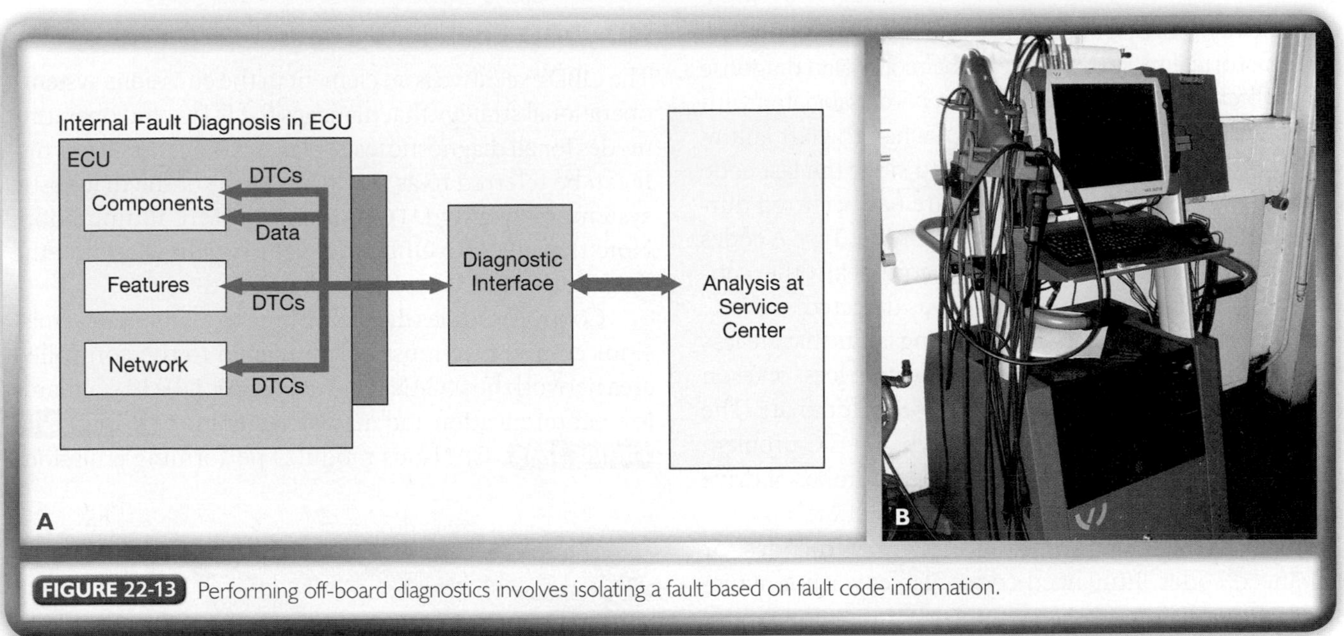

FIGURE 22-13 Performing off-board diagnostics involves isolating a fault based on fault code information.

Readiness Code

Depending on the OEM, some provision is made to validate whether a component or emissions system generating a DTC has been repaired or corrected. After a repair has been made, operating the vehicle under conditions that cause an emissions system monitor to self-check validates whether a successful repair has been completed. An HD-OBD service tool displays a readiness code indicating that a monitor has completed its functionality test and no fault was found. Each monitor requires a unique set of drive-cycle operating conditions to be met before it can properly run and evaluate the performance of an emissions system.

When an HD-OBD readiness code validates the system that has been repaired, no other fault codes associated with the system should be active. However, a message such as "system not ready" or "monitor incomplete" or "monitor not run" is displayed if the repair is not successful, or if the emission system has not met the conditions needed to enable the monitor to run.

> **TECHNICIAN TIP**
>
> After repairing a fault associated with the engine or power train, the codes should be cleared and the vehicle road tested, which involves operating the vehicle under the conditions necessary for a monitor to run (i.e., warmed up and cruising at highway speed). Recheck the vehicle for codes after the road test, before returning the vehicle to the customer. The monitor associated with the repaired fault should indicate it has "run" or is "ready."

> **TECHNICIAN TIP**
>
> Note that two-trip B-type DTCs take two drive cycles before they are logged. This means two test drives are required to ensure malfunctions have been corrected.

Emissions System Deterioration

The HD-OBD is primarily an emissions-driven diagnostic system. For diesel engines, the threshold for alerting the driver and setting a fault code generally occurs any time a condition is sensed that could cause noxious emissions to exceed the legislated FTP emissions standards 1.5 times. Higher thresholds are used for aftertreatment systems, with progressively lower threshold standards for the latest vehicle models. While malfunctions in the engine cause excessive emissions, problems with other vehicle systems also can cause the vehicle to exceed the threshold for emissions. Adaptive strategies can compensate for system deterioration. For example, wastegated turbochargers have metal springs in their actuators. Heat and time will weaken the springs so closed-loop feedback between the wastegate and the boost pressure sensor compensate for system deterioration. Common rail injectors are regularly checked using zero-fuel adaptation, which automatically updates the calibration file during vehicle deceleration.

DTCs

The HD-OBD system sets three types of codes: A, B, and C. Type A DTCs are the most critical emissions-related faults and will illuminate the MIL with only one occurrence. If a Type A code is set, the HD-OBD can store it several ways. Type A codes are generally stored in the ECM historical memory. To help the technician diagnose the problem, the code has a failure record associated with it, such as a time and date stamp of when the last failure occurred, whether the code occurred since the last code clearing event, or whether the failure has occurred during the current ignition cycle. Furthermore, Type A codes have freeze-frame data, which is a record of all other sensor data occurring when the fault was detected.

Type B codes are emissions-causing faults that are less serious than type A faults and must occur at least once on two consecutive trips before the MIL will illuminate. The MIL will also go out if a Type A or Type B DTC problem does not reoccur after a predetermined number of drive cycles (e.g., 3–5 drive cycles—varies by OEM).

Type C DTCs are non-emissions-related codes, or enhanced codes. Enhanced codes also cover non-emissions-related failures that occur outside the engine control system.

Freeze-Frame Data

The freeze-frame data the ECM stores will provide a snapshot of the engine operating conditions present at the time the malfunction was detected. This information should be stored when a pending DTC is set. If the pending DTC matures to a MIL-on DTC, the manufacturer can choose to update or retain the freeze-frame data stored in conjunction with the pending DTC. Likewise, any freeze-frame data stored in conjunction with a pending or MIL-on DTC should be erased upon erasure of the DTC.

HD-OBD Emissions Codes

The OBD executive is an element in the emissions system's operational strategy that manages the DTCs and operating modes for all diagnostic tests related to emissions systems. It can be referred to as the "traffic cop" of the diagnostic system, managing DTC storage and MIL illumination. Note that the HD-OBD MIL light is yellow, unlike the light-duty OBD-II system, which is red.

Control modules that contribute to maintaining emissions compliance must be connected to the controlled area network bus (CAN-bus) using SAE J-1939 standards for communication and network operation FIGURE 22-14 FIGURE 22-15. CAN-bus modules performing emissions

FIGURE 22-14 HD-OBD data can be accessed from the CAN-bus through the data link connector.

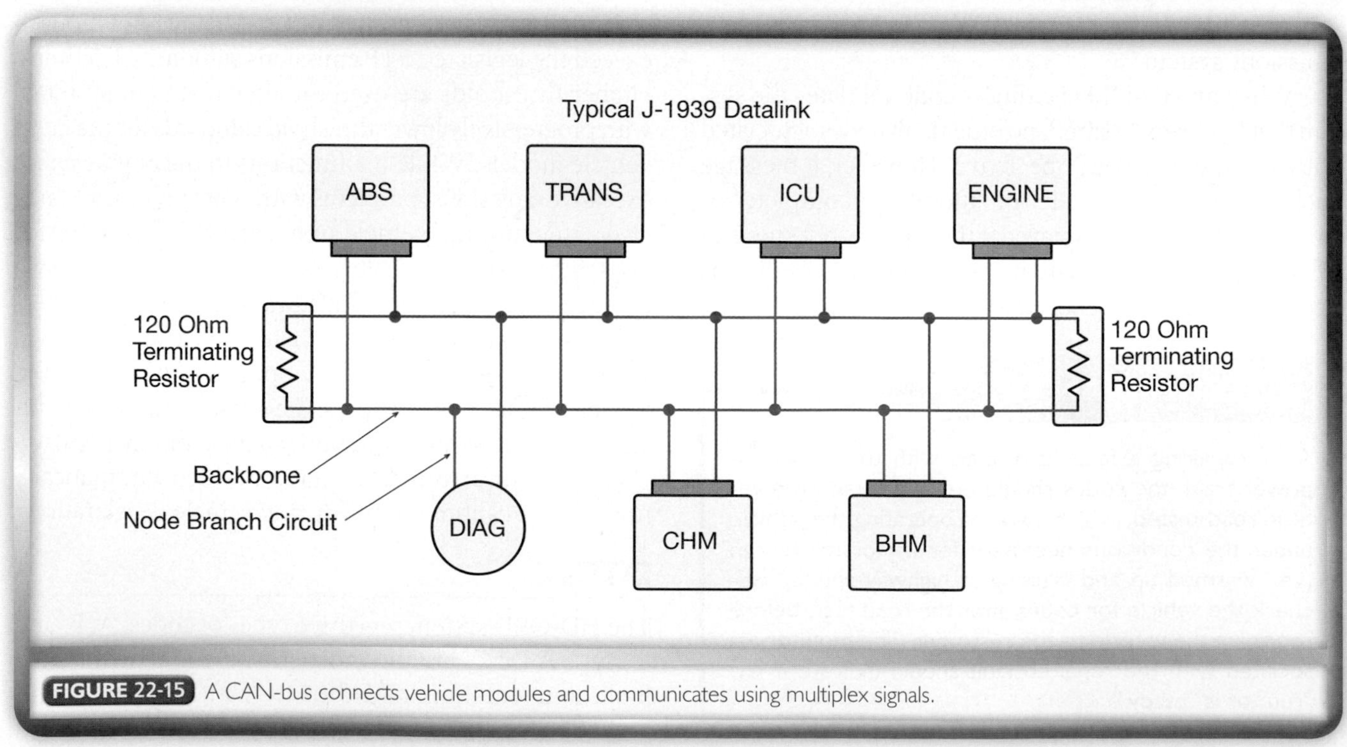

FIGURE 22-15 A CAN-bus connects vehicle modules and communicates using multiplex signals.

diagnostics will include the following types:

- Engine ECM
- Vehicle electronic control unit
- Aftertreatment control module
- Aftertreatment NO_X sensors
- Engine VGT
- EGR control module
- Anti-lock braking system (ABS)/traction control

> **TECHNICIAN TIP**
>
> To validate a repair for a fault detected by the Comprehensive Component Monitor, start the engine and let it idle for one minute. The ECM will turn off the yellow MIL when the diagnostic monitor has run. If a CCM is evaluating electrical circuits, the light will switch off after the MIL has illuminated for five seconds. For other faults, the ECM will typically turn off the MIL after three consecutive ignition cycles that the diagnostic monitor runs and passes.

Two protocols exist for identifying fault codes on heavy-duty commercial vehicles. The first is J-1587 using a J-1708 two-wire data bus. J-1587 began being used by heavy-duty and most medium-duty vehicles built after 1985. Up to 1995, individual OEMs used their own unique diagnostic connectors. J-1587, used primarily from 1996 to 2001, is easily identified by the 6-pin diagnostic connectors. Beginning in 2001, most OEMs switched to a more sophisticated J-1939 standard recognized by a 9-pin diagnostic connector. Both the J-1587/1708 and the J-1939 network connections are found in the 9-pin DLC. A specific standard exists in both protocols for identifying faults detected by the CAN-bus modules.

Proprietary Blink and Flash Codes

Manufacturers are not bound to report faults exclusively using CAN-bus codes. Specialized equipment and systems can use proprietary codes, meaning the OEM is free to define its own non-emissions-related fault codes. Blink codes are dash lights that will blink, or flash, proprietary fault codes using the red and amber engine warning lights FIGURE 22-16.

Two- and three-digit codes commonly report faults. A typical arrangement to obtain blink codes based on a proprietary code will require switching on a diagnostics switch. A warning lamp flashes to indicate a fault code. Next, the stop lamp flashes out the hundredth, tenth, and single digits of the fault code. A short pause separates the flashing of each digit, and a longer pause separates codes. Warning lamps may switch between active and inactive codes by flashing either the red for active or

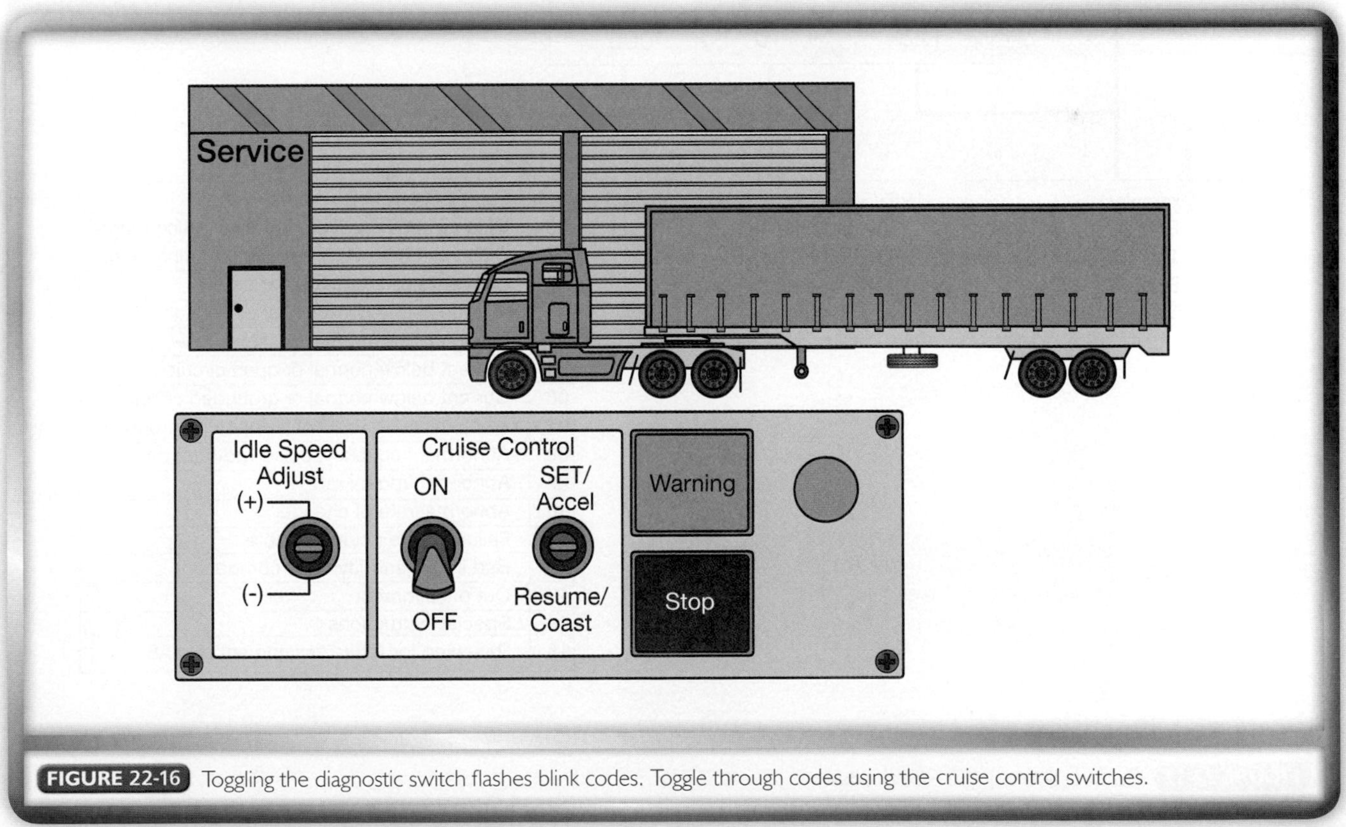

FIGURE 22-16 Toggling the diagnostic switch flashes blink codes. Toggle through codes using the cruise control switches.

yellow warning light for inactive. If no fault codes are active, the warning lamps remain lit. Late-model International trucks do not use a diagnostic switch to obtain blink codes. Instead, the ignition key is switched on while the engine is off, the park brake is applied, and the cruise control switch and resume switches are depressed simultaneously to produce diagnostic blink codes. Rather than using a diagnostic switch, other vehicles may require creating the correct conditions—such as key-on engine-off (KOEO), park brakes set, or depressing the cruise ON and RESUME switches—to prompt engine blink codes. Instrument clusters are network devices can also receive and report fault codes in the absence of a readily available service tool.

J-1587 Fault Code Construction

The SAE developed the fault code reporting standard referred to as J-1587. Six- and nine-pin diagnostic connectors carry J-1587 codes, but six-pin connectors do not include J-1939, the latest protocol. J-1587 fault codes are specifically constructed to help technicians easily isolate faults. The codes have four parts:

- Message identifier (MID) (also called module identifiers)
- Parameter identifier (PID)
- System identifier (SID)
- Fault mode identifier (FMI) **FIGURE 22-17**

Other fault code identifiers specific to an OEM may include the following:

- Proprietary parameter identification (PPID) is an OEM identification of a parameter or value used only by that manufacturer.
- Proprietary subsystem identification description (PSID) is an OEM-unique component identification.

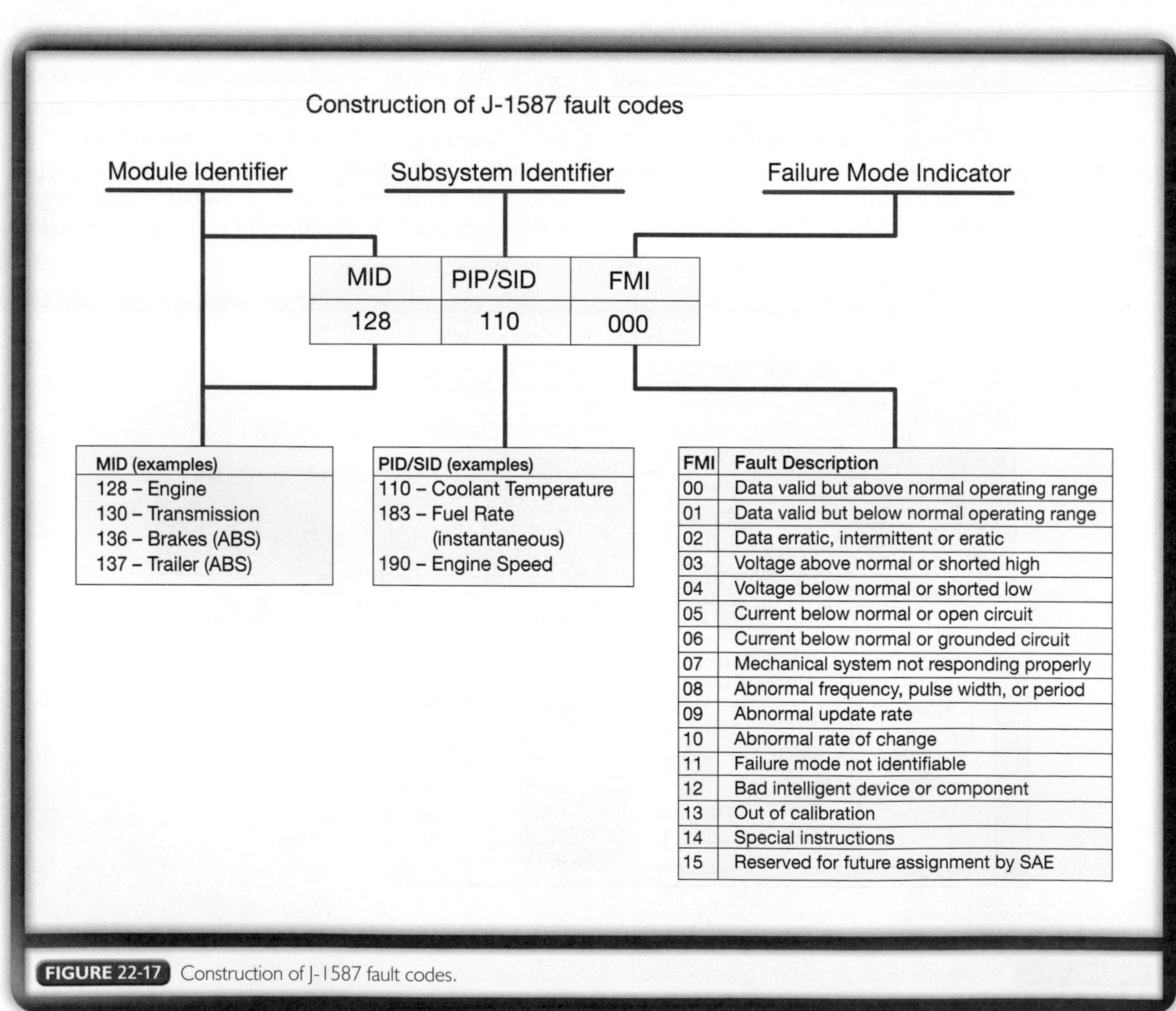

FMI	Fault Description
00	Data valid but above normal operating range
01	Data valid but below normal operating range
02	Data erratic, intermittent or eratic
03	Voltage above normal or shorted high
04	Voltage below normal or shorted low
05	Current below normal or open circuit
06	Current below normal or grounded circuit
07	Mechanical system not responding properly
08	Abnormal frequency, pulse width, or period
09	Abnormal update rate
10	Abnormal rate of change
11	Failure mode not identifiable
12	Bad intelligent device or component
13	Out of calibration
14	Special instructions
15	Reserved for future assignment by SAE

FIGURE 22-17 Construction of J-1587 fault codes.

A **message identifier (MID)** identifies which module is reporting the fault. MIDs are the first byte or character of each message that identifies which control module on the J-1587 serial communication link originated the information. A standard list of message or module identifiers exists for all vehicles regardless of manufacturer FIGURE 22-18 and TABLE 22-5.

A **system identifier (SID)** indicates a specific failed component or replaceable subsystem associated with a fault. There are several SIDs TABLE 22-6.

A **parameter identifier (PID)** is a value or identifier of an item being reported with fault data. J-1957 uses hundreds of PIDs TABLE 22-7.

The **fault mode identifier (FMI)** describes the type of failure detected in the subsystem and identified by the PID or SID TABLE 22-8. The FMI and the PID or SID, not both, combine to form a J-1957 diagnostic code. The general format of a fault message is MID-PID/SID–FMI. Now consider code 128-101-002. It breaks down as follows:

- 128: engine
- 101: intake boost pressure
- 002: data erratic, intermittent, or incorrect.

TABLE 22-5: Common MIDs Standard Across All Vehicles

MID	Description
128	ECM
130	Transmission control unit
136	ABS
140	Instrument cluster unit
180	Off-board diagnostics
181	Satellite
190	Climate control module
229	Collision avoidance
231	Cellular

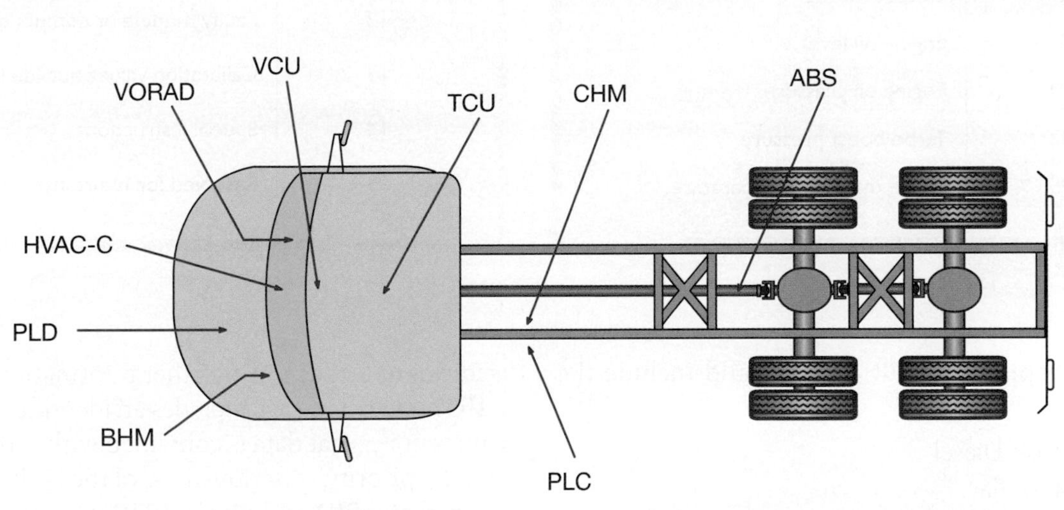

FIGURE 22-18 Location of various module identifiers or MIDs, for a chassis.

TABLE 22-6: Example SIDs

SID	Description
001	Injector cylinder 01 (on/off)
034	Reverse switch (open/closed)
100	Oil pressure or lubrication system
101	Boost pressure
103	Transmission range (high/low)

TABLE 22-7: Example PIDs

PID	Description
25	Air conditioner system status A2
33	Clutch cylinder position
40	Engine retarder
41	Cruise control switch status
91	Percent engine throttle
92	Percent engine load
93	Output torque
98	Engine oil level
100	Engine oil pressure
102	Turbo boost pressure
105	Intake manifold temperature

TABLE 22-8: Example FMIs

FMI	Description
0	Data valid but above the normal working range
1	Data valid but below the normal working range
2	Intermittent or incorrect data
3	Abnormally high voltage or short circuit to higher voltage
4	Abnormally low voltage or short circuit to lower voltage
5	Abnormally low current or open circuit
6	Abnormally high current or short circuit to ground
7	Incorrect response from a mechanical system
8	Abnormal frequency
9	Abnormal update rate
10	Abnormally strong vibrations
11	Unidentifiable fault
12	Faulty module or component
13	Calibration values outside limits
14	Special instructions
15	Reserved for future use

OEM proprietary fault codes would include the following:

- 54: Detroit Diesel
- 84: Caterpillar
- 115: Cummins

J-1939 Fault Code Construction

J-1939 codes have construction similar to J-1957 but are far more comprehensive. J-1939 uses the CAN-bus protocol, which permits any electronic control module to transmit a message over the network when the bus is idle or not transmitting other information. Similar to J-1957, every message includes an identifier that defines who sent it, what data is contained within the message, and the priority, or seriousness, of the fault or problem. Instead of a PID and SID, J-1939 uses only a **suspect parameter number (SPN)** FIGURE 22-19. The SPN is the smallest identifiable fault. Next, a failure mode indicator (FMI) notes the type of failure that has been detected.

The **source address (SA)** field designates the control module that is sending the message TABLE 22-9 and TABLE 22-10.

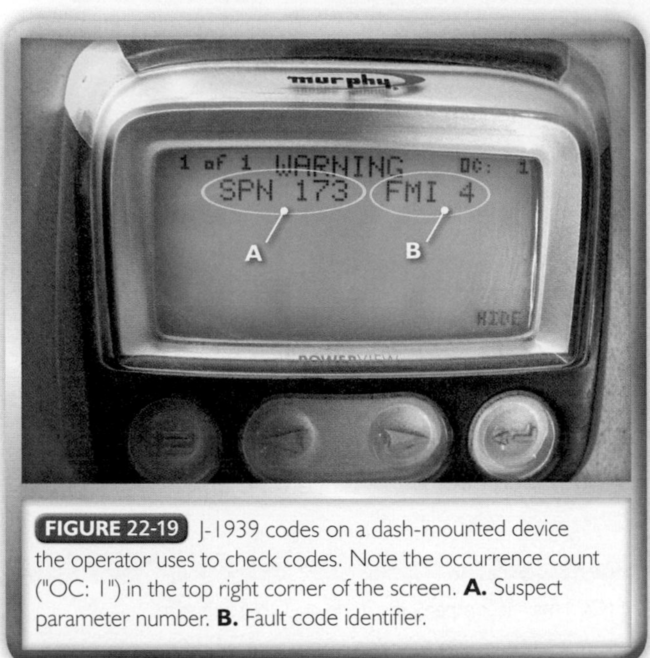

FIGURE 22-19 J-1939 codes on a dash-mounted device the operator uses to check codes. Note the occurrence count ("OC: 1") in the top right corner of the screen. **A.** Suspect parameter number. **B.** Fault code identifier.

TABLE 22-9: Example J-1939 SAs

SID	Description
1	Engine
3	Transmission
11	Brakes or ABS controller
47	Headway controller for collision avoidance system

TABLE 22-10: Comparing J-1939 and J-1587 Fault Codes

J-1939	J-1957
Source address (SA)	Message identifier (MID)
Suspect parameter number (SPN) (thousands of combinations)	Parameter identifier (PID) (hundreds of combinations)
N/A	System identifier (SID)
Fault mode indicator (0–31)	Fault mode indicator (0–15)

Suspect Parameter Number

The suspect parameter number (SPN) combines elements of J-1957 PIDs and SIDs. The SPN is used for multiple diagnostic purposes:

- Identifying the least repairable subsystem that has failed
- Identifying subsystems and/or assemblies that may not have completely failed but may be exhibiting abnormal operating performance
- Identifying a particular event or condition that requires reporting
- Reporting a component and nonstandard failure mode FIGURE 22-20 and TABLE 22-11

J-1939 FMI

The FMI defines the type of failure detected in the subsystem identified by an SPN. The failure may not be an electrical failure but may instead be a subsystem failure or condition needing to be reported to the service technician and, perhaps, the operator. Conditions can include system events or statuses TABLE 22-12 and TABLE 22-13.

Occurrence Count

The occurence count (OC) represents the number of times a fault combination of SPN/FMI has taken place.

Parameter Group Number

SPN, source addresses, and FMI information are part of a larger J-1939 message called the **parameter group number (PGN)**. PGN information includes commands, data, requests, acknowledgments, and negative acknowledgments, as well as fault codes. The package of serial data is transmitted over the CAN-bus. SPNs are assigned to each individual parameter within the PGN. This means each PGN will contain a different set of SPNs. For example, PGN 61444 is the electronic engine controller 1. Hundreds of possible messages can originate from this component because of the number of sensors and complexity of the system and its operation FIGURE 22-21 and TABLE 22-14.

PGN 61444 includes the following SPNs:

- Engine torque mode
- Driver's demand engine—percent torque
- Actual engine—percent torque
- Engine speed
- Engine starter mode
- Engine demand—percent torque

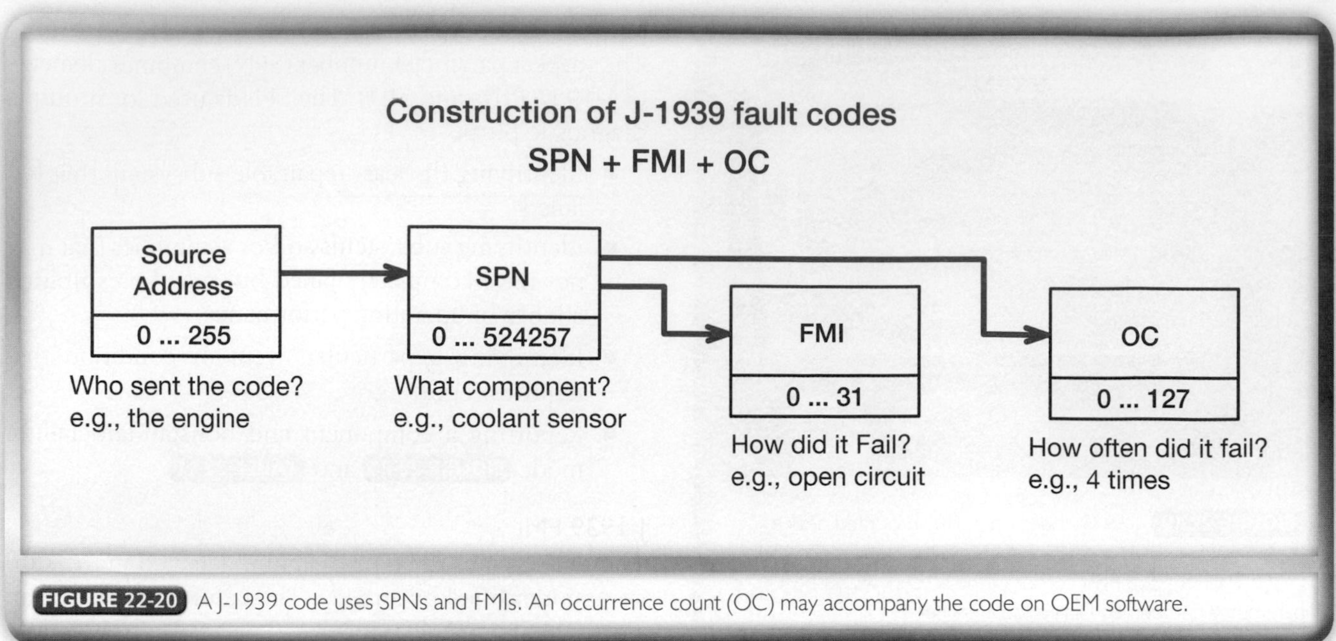

FIGURE 22-20 A J-1939 code uses SPNs and FMIs. An occurrence count (OC) may accompany the code on OEM software.

TABLE 22-11: Example SPNs

SPN	Description
031	Transmission range position
156	Injector timing rail 1 pressure
190	Engine speed
512	Driver's demand engine—percent torque
513	Actual engine—percent torque
639	J-1939 network
899	Engine torque mode
1483	Source address of controlling device for engine control
1675	Engine starter mode
2432	Engine demand—percent torque

TABLE 22-12: SAE J-1939 FMIs

FMI	SAE Text
0	Data valid but above normal operational range—most severe level
1	Data valid but below normal operational range—most severe level
2	Data erratic, intermittent, or incorrect
3	Voltage above normal or shorted to high source
4	Voltage below normal or shorted to low source
5	Current below normal or open circuit
6	Current above normal or grounded circuit
7	Mechanical system not responding or out of adjustment
8	Abnormal frequency or pulse width or period
9	Abnormal update rate
10	Abnormal rate of change
11	Root cause not known
12	Bad intelligent device or component
13	Out of calibration

Continued on next page

TABLE 22-12: SAE J-1939 FMIs, continued

FMI	SAE Text
14	Special instructions
15	Data valid but above normal operating range—least severe level
16	Data valid but above normal operating range—moderately severe level
17	Data valid but below normal operating range—least severe level
18	Data valid but below normal operating range—moderately severe level
19	Received network data in error
20–30	Reserved for SAE assignment
31	Condition exists

Message Priority

To prevent message signals from canceling out one another, signal collisions are avoided through an arbitration process that takes place while the PGN identifier is transmitted. The lower the first number is in the message, the greater importance attached to the information, requiring all other modules to listen while the information is transmitted:

- Highest priority: This is used for situations that require immediate action by the receiving device in order to provide safe vehicle operation (e.g., braking systems). This level of priority is only used in safety critical conditions.
- High priority: This is used for control situations that require prompt action in order to provide safe vehicle operation (e.g., a transmission performing an upshift, which requires a change in engine speed to control gear synchronization of damage to clutch packs) TABLE 22-15.

TABLE 22-13: Comparison of J-1939 SPN and J-1708/J-1587 Fault Codes

Description	J-1939		J-1708/J-1587	
	PGN	SPN	MID	PID
Percent load at current speed	61433	92	128	92
Engine speed (rpm)	61444	190	128	190
Distance	65248	245	128	245
Engine hours	65253	247	128	247
Coolant temperature	53262	110	128	110
Oil temperature	65262	175	128	175
Fuel delivery pressure	65263	94	128	94
Oil pressure	65263	100	128	100
Speed	65265	84	128	84
Fuel rate	65266	183	128	183
Instantaneous fuel economy	65266	184	128	184
Ambient air temperature	65269	171	128	171
Turbo boost	65270	102	128	102
Air filter differential pressure	65270	107	128	107
Exhaust gas temperature	65270	173	128	173
Net battery current	65271	114	128	114
Battery voltage	65271	168	128	168
Transmission oil temp	65272	171	128	171
Brake application pressure	65274	116	128	116
Brake primary pressure	65274	117	128	117
Brake secondary pressure	65274	118	128	118
Hydraulic retarder pressure	65275	119	128	119
Hydraulic retarder oil temperature	65275	120	128	120
Fuel level	65276	96	41	96

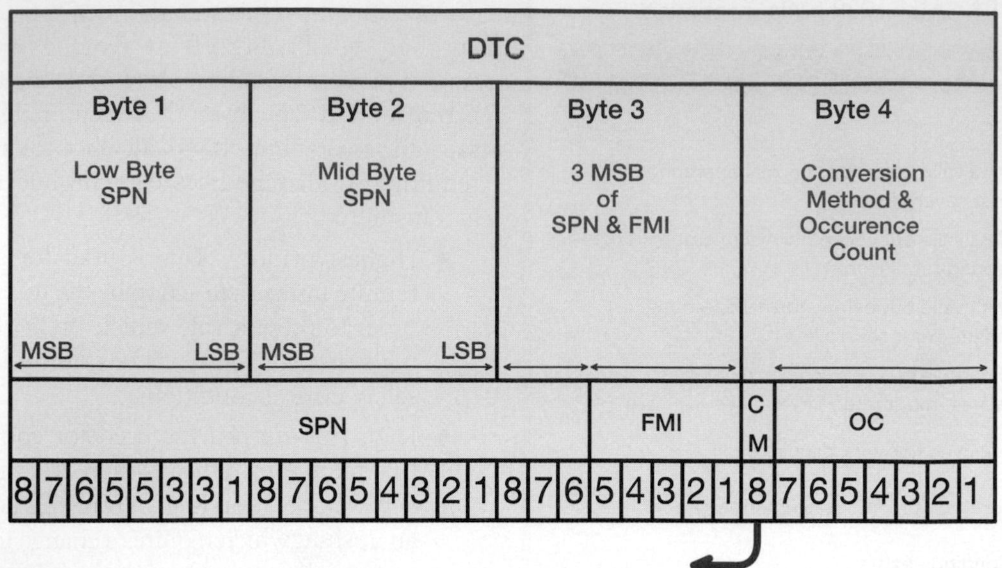

FIGURE 22-21 A J-1939 fault code is 29 bits long. The check sum (CM) field is a function of the other numbers in the code. If another module reads the code and the CM does not match, the data is rejected.

TABLE 22-14: Example PGNs

PGN	Description
61441	Electronic Brake Controller 1 (EBC1)
61442	Electronic Transmission Controller 1 (ETC1)
61444	Electronic Engine Controller 1 (EEC1)
65225	Service Information (SERV)

TABLE 22-15: Priority Fault Codes

Priority	Description
1 and 2	Reserved for messages that require immediate access to the bus
3 and 4	Reserved for messages that require prompt access to the bus in order to prevent severe mechanical damage.
5 and 6	Reserved for messages that directly affect the economical or efficient operation of the vehicle
7 and 8	All other messages not fitting into the previous priority categories

Wrap-up

Ready for Review

- Emissions standards set for diesels beginning in the late 1970s have required a level of precision for engine control possible only through the extensive use of electronics. The OBD system was originally developed by manufacturers to diagnose faults with electronic controls.
- Since 2007, emissions legislation has required OBD systems to monitor the operation of emissions-control systems and alert the vehicle operator to any emission-related faults producing excessive emissions above threshold standards.
- In the United States, the EPA revised EMD legislation by mandating more comprehensive OBD system monitors that functionally monitor emissions-control systems and components. Beginning with model year 2010, with a phase-in period until 2016, HD-OBD is a significant update to EMD.
- Electronic systems do not have many moving parts to wear out, but the systems can be complex. When something goes wrong with a component or circuit, identifying the problem without some built-in self-diagnostic capabilities can be extremely time consuming and difficult.
- With built-in electronic self-monitoring functions, electrical systems possess the capability to check the operation of circuits and electrical devices, evaluate the rationality of data, and identify problems as they occur.
- Traditional self-diagnostic strategies focus on specific areas of commercial vehicle control, such as the engine, anti-lock braking, traction control, and transmissions.
- Model-based diagnostics compare system and component behaviors to expected patterns of operation.
- A fault is a deviation of at least one characteristic property of the system from its standard behavior.
- A failure is a fault that permanently interrupts a system's ability to perform a required function under specified operating conditions.
- A disturbance is an unknown and uncontrolled input acting on the system.
- Fault detection is a diagnostic strategy to determine whether faults are present in the system.
- Fault isolation is determining the location of the fault.
- When a fault is detected, fault accommodation, which is also known as an adaptive strategy, reconfigures the system operation or substitutes suspect data with default data to maintain normal system functionality even with the fault.
- To detect conditions that can increase emissions levels beyond FTP thresholds, the OBD system monitors individual components and major engine emissions-control systems. Monitors used by the diesel HD-OBD system can be divided into several general types: threshold, functionality, rationality or plausibility, electrical circuit continuity, and out of range.
- The diagnostic manager, software that identifies fault codes and ensures emissions systems are operating correctly, regularly evaluates emission-related systems and components to detect faults in the emissions systems.
- Diagnostic monitoring of diesel engines is broken down into separate, specific hardware systems that are responsible for some specialized aspect of engine operation and emissions-control. The high-pressure injection system and the EGR system are examples of systems that have a major monitor associated with their operation.
- Emissions systems may be monitored continuously or non-continuously.
- The CCM continuously monitors electrical circuits operating powertrain components. The CCM is not tied to emissions thresholds.

- Because engine misfires can cause HC and CO emissions, the OBD system must evaluate engine operation to determine whether misfires are occurring.
- A more complex on-board diesel monitor is the EGR monitor. HD-OBD requirements for the diesel EGR monitor include detecting the following faults before emissions exceed HD-OBD thresholds: EGR flow rate, EGR response rate, and EGR cooling system performance.
- Fuel system monitors are required to detect faults associated with the high-pressure injection system before emissions exceed OBD thresholds.
- Underboost and overboost malfunctions are typically detected by comparing expected boost pressure values stored in the ECM with actual boost pressure measured by the boost pressure sensor.
- Because defective thermostats and engine temperature sensors will prevent running of other emissions system monitors, the OBD system also ensures the cooling system warms up quickly to the correct temperature.
- When electrical faults or system problems occur in commercial vehicle control systems, electronic control modules log DTCs in the system memory, which are read through an instrument display cluster or blink codes or retrieved by a scanner or personal computer connected to the vehicle DLC.
- For diesel engines, the threshold for alerting the driver and setting a fault code generally occurs any time a condition is sensed that could cause noxious emissions to exceed the legislated FTP emissions standards 1.5 times.
- HD-OBD requires monitoring of the CV system of a diesel.
- Type A DTCs are the most critical emissions-related faults and will illuminate the MIL with only one occurrence.
- Type B DTCs are emissions-causing faults that are less serious than type A faults and must occur at least once on two consecutive trips before the MIL will illuminate.
- Types C DTCs are non-emissions-related codes, or enhanced codes. Enhanced codes also cover non-emissions-related failures that occur outside the engine control system.
- The SAE developed the fault code reporting standard referred to as J-1587.
- J-1939 uses the CAN-bus protocol, which permits any electronic control module to transmit a message over the network when the data bus is idle or not transmitting other information. Every message includes an identifier that defines who sent it, what data is contained within the message, and the priority, or seriousness, of the fault or problem.

Vocabulary Builder

active fault A fault that is currently taking place and uninterrupted in action.

blink code A method of providing fault code data for a specific system that involves counting the number of flashes from a warning lamp and observing longer pauses between the light blinks.

diagnostic link connector (DLC) The connection point for electronic service tools used to access fault code and other information provided by chassis electronic control modules.

diagnostic trouble code (DTC) A code logged by the electronic control module when electrical faults or system problems occur in commercial vehicle control systems.

fault mode identifier (FMI) The type of failure detected in the SPN, PID, or SID.

historical fault A fault that took place at one time but that is now corrected and no longer active.

incipient fault A fault that is the result of system or component deterioration.

intermittent fault A fault that is not ongoing and can be both active and historical.

message identifier (MID) Also called module identifier, the electronic control module that has identified a fault. J-1587 protocols use MIDs.

off-board diagnostics Procedures to isolate a fault based on fault code information, including retrieving fault code information, monitoring system operation, performing actuator tests and pinpoint electrical tests, and inspecting components.

on-board diagnostics (OBD) Self-diagnostic capabilities of electronic control modules that allow them to evaluate voltage and current levels of circuits to which they are connected and determine if data is in the correct operational range.

OBD manager Software that identifies fault codes and ensures emissions systems are operating correctly.

out-of-range monitoring Validating sensor data to verify a system is operating within an expected range for a given operating condition.

parameter group number (PGN) A package of serial data transmitted over the CAN network that includes SPN, source addresses, and FMI, as well as commands, data, requests, acknowledgments, negative-acknowledgments, and fault codes.

parameter identifier (PID) A value or identifier of an item being reported with fault data.

source address (SA) The field that designates which control module is sending the message.

suspect parameter number (SPN) A numerical identifier that defines the data in a fault message and the priority of the fault.

system identifier (SID) A fault code used by J-1587 protocols that identifies which subsystem has failed.

telematics A branch of information technology that uses specialized applications for long-distance transmission of information to and from a vehicle.

Review Questions

1. A preliminary standard to the 2010 HD-OBD standard was called:
   a. engine manufacturer's diagnostic (EMD) systems.
   b. OBD II (On-Board Diagnostics 2nd Design).
   c. OBD (On-Board Diagnostics).
   d. CAN (Controller Area Network).
2. The HD-OBD (Heavy-Duty On Board Diagnostics) system can take one of two self-diagnostic approaches to identifying faults. The system can either use traditional self-diagnostic strategies or use (a):
   a. manufacturer-based approach.
   b. model-based approach.
   c. manufacturer-based diagnostics.
   d. case-based reasoning.
3. ________ is (are) an adaptive strategy that reconfigures the system operation or substitutes suspect data with default data to maintain normal system functionality even with the fault.
   a. Fault codes
   b. Fault accommodation
   c. Fault detection
   d. Disturbance
4. What type of HD-OBD monitor directly measures the level of emissions using a sensor to identify a noxious emission; such as: Ammonia, particulate matter (PM), or oxides of nitrogen (NO_X)?
   a. Threshold
   b. Functional
   c. Electrical circuit continuity
   d. Out of range
5. A ________ monitor tracks electrical circuits operating power train components that can cause a measurable emissions increase during any reasonable driving conditions?
   a. functional
   b. continuous and non-continuous monitors
   c. comprehensive component monitor
   d. misfire monitor
6. System self-diagnostic checks are generally performed by limit checking of ________ or circuit data.
   a. circuits
   b. sensors
   c. controllers
   d. monitors
7. Data from a sensor as simple as the coolant temperature is even more critical to operation because ________ that evaluate emissions-control devices will run only after an engine has reached operating temperature.
   a. monitors
   b. circuits
   c. sensors
   d. controllers
8. In the OBD system, a ________ is a deviation of at least one characteristic property of the system from its standard behavior.
   a. monitor
   b. fault
   c. defect
   d. failure
9. What type of OBD fault is not ongoing and can be both active and historical?
   a. Incipient
   b. Controlling
   c. Intermittent
   d. Constant
10. What is an unknown and uncontrolled input acting on the OBD system?
    a. Failure
    b. Disturbance
    c. Fault
    d. Monitor

ASE-Type Questions

1. Two technicians are discussing HD-OBD for trucks. Technician A says that the simplest, most familiar definition is the diagnostic function of electronic control systems to identify or self-diagnose system faults and report fault codes. Technician B says the automotive and light-duty truck version of OBD is called OBD II. Who is correct?
   a. Technician A
   b. Technician B
   c. Both Technician A and Technician B
   d. Neither Technician A nor Technician B
2. Technician A says that a fault is a deviation of at least one characteristic property of the system from its standard behavior. Technician B says that a historical fault took place at one time and can never be active again. Who is correct?
   a. Technician A
   b. Technician B
   c. Both Technician A and Technician B
   d. Neither Technician A nor Technician B
3. An __________ fault is not ongoing and can be both active and historical.
   a. inactive
   b. incipient
   c. intermittent
   d. historical
4. All of following are part of the HD-OBD legislation for diesels, EXCEPT:
   a. 9-pin diagnostic connector
   b. 6-pin diagnostic connector
   c. Standardized emissions-related fault codes for all manufacturers
   d. Reading of fault codes by aftermarket electronic test equipment
5. Which of these HD-OBD terms describes when the ECM stores a snapshot of the engine operating conditions present at the time the malfunction was detected?
   a. Freeze frame
   b. Diagnostic trouble code (DTC)
   c. C-type code
   d. D-type code
6. Technician A says that threshold monitoring directly measures the level of emissions using a sensor to identify a noxious emission. Technician B says Technician B says that a historical fault took place at one time and can never be active again. Who is correct?
   a. Technician A
   b. Technician B
   c. Both Technician A and Technician B
   d. Neither Technician A nor Technician B
7. What kind of monitoring measures voltage drops and signal and ground return voltage from sensors or output devices to validate circuits are not open or shorted to ground and battery voltage?
   a. Intermittent
   b. Threshold
   c. Electrical circuit continuity
   d. Out of range
8. HD-OBD legislation for diesels includes all of the following features, EXCEPT:
   a. Standardized 6-pin diagnostic link connector
   b. Standardized emissions-related fault codes for all manufacturers
   c. Reading of fault codes by aftermarket electronic test equipment
   d. Standardized names and abbreviations of components and systems
9. Which of these systems' faults is LEAST LIKLEY to be detected before emissions exceed standards?
   a. Oxidation catalyst
   b. Lean NO_X (Oxides of Nitrogen) catalyst
   c. SCR (Selective Catalyst Reduction) catalyst
   d. Glow plugs and intake air heaters X p635-636
10. Which part of the heavy duty diesel HD-OBD management system stores diagnostic information?
   a. Misfire
   b. Vehicle in vehicle out information
   c. Freeze frame
   d. Trip

CABLES BEFORE WELDING
TO PREVENT DAMAGE TO
ELECTRONIC COMPONENTS
CAUTION
HEAT TREATED
ALLOY. DO NOT
WELD TO RAIL
OR DRILL
FLANGES.
CRACKS MAY
RESULT

SECTION III

Suspension, Steering, and Brakes

CHAPTER 23 Commercial Vehicle Tires

CHAPTER 24 Wheel Rims and Hubs

CHAPTER 25 Front Axles and Vehicle Alignment Factors

CHAPTER 26 Truck Frames

CHAPTER 27 Suspension Systems

CHAPTER 28 Steering Systems and Integral Steering Gears

CHAPTER 29 Braking Fundamentals

CHAPTER 30 Air Brake Foundation Systems and Air Brake Circuits

CHAPTER 31 Servicing Air Brake Systems

CHAPTER 32 Anti-Lock Braking, Vehicle Stability, and Collision Avoidance Systems

CHAPTER 33 Fundamentals of Hydraulic and Air-Over-Hydraulic Braking Systems

CHAPTER 34 Fifth Wheels and Hitching Devices

CHAPTER 23

NATEF Tasks

Suspension and Steering

Wheels and Tires	Page
■ Identify wheel/tire vibration, shimmy, pounding, and hop (tramp) problems; determine needed action.	662–697
■ Inspect tire for proper application (size, load range, position, and tread design); determine needed action.	662–692
■ Check operation of tire pressure monitoring system (TPMS); determine needed action if applicable.	665–667
■ Identify tire wear patterns; check tread depth and pressure; determine needed action.	687
■ Remove and install steering and drive axle wheel/tire assemblies; torque mounting hardware to specifications with a torque wrench.	686–698

Knowledge Objectives

After reading this chapter, you will be able to:

1. Identify the functions, construction, composition, types, and applications of medium- and heavy-duty commercial vehicle tires. (pp 662–667)
2. Describe procedures for analyzing tire vibrations and identifying run out and imbalance conditions. (pp 662–697)
3. Identify and describe various types of tire pressure monitoring systems (TPMS). (pp 665–667)
4. Explain principles of tire inflation pressure tread design and compound for different load and speed ratings. (pp 665–669)
5. Identify and describe safety practices when servicing commercial vehicle tires. (pp 664–667)
6. Identify various types of tire failures and their causes. (pp 665–679)
7. Outline general procedures used to mount and dismount tires. (pp 686–698)
8. Describe industry standards for tire sizing and nomenclature. (pp 670–671)

Commercial Vehicle Tires

Skills Objectives

After reading this chapter, you will be able to:

1. Recommend tire replacement based on application and axle position. (pp 662–692)
2. Identify potential causes or vibration complaints. (pp 662–697)
3. Identify and analyze causes of tire failures. (pp 665–679)
4. Interpret tire codes and other tire markings. (p 670)
5. Recommend tire re-grooving, retreading or replacement. (pp 675–677)
6. Recommend tire maintenance practices and service intervals. (p 683)
7. Check and adjust the tire pressure. (p 686) SKILL DRILL 23-1
8. Check for tire wear patterns. (p 687) SKILL DRILL 23-2
9. Dismount a tire (well-based rims). (p 690) SKILL DRILL 23-3
10. Remove a tire from a wheel rim (tubeless). (p 691) SKILL DRILL 23-4
11. Fit a tire to a wheel rim (tubeless). (p 691) SKILL DRILL 23-5
12. Replace a screw-in valve stem. (p 692) SKILL DRILL 23-6
13. Balance a tire. (p 693) SKILL DRILL 23-7
14. Perform on-vehicle wheel balancing. (p 694) SKILL DRILL 23-8
15. Inspect the wheel assembly for air loss using the spray bottle method. (p 695) SKILL DRILL 23-9
16. Patch a tire. (p 696) SKILL DRILL 23-10
17. Measure tire run-out. (p 697) SKILL DRILL 23-11
18. Measure wheel run-out. (p 698) SKILL DRILL 23-12
19. Measure axle or hub flange run-out. (p 699) SKILL DRILL 23-13
20. Inspect, diagnose, and calibrate the TPMS. (p 699) SKILL DRILL 23-14

Introduction

Tires are a major component of what the trucking industry calls the wheel end. Together with hubs and rims, tires have the job of safely supporting the vehicle weight over a wide range of speed, load, and road conditions. Consequently, tires are the second highest fleet operating costs after fuel. As TABLE 23-1 shows, tires are also the most common reason for breakdowns on the road and they rank second in terms of mechanical defects related to accidents. It is easy to understand the importance of competently maintaining and servicing tires from an economic perspective.

Preventing tire failures and minimizing tire wear can save considerable expenses from downtime and roadside repair. In addition, proper maintenance of tires is critical for safety. Statistical data demonstrates that, at the worst, one in 1,000 serious accidents results in a death. If an accident involves a tire or wheel, however, that rate increases to one in 10 accidents resulting in a fatality. Liability for proper tire and wheel maintenance in many jurisdictions is the responsibility of maintenance technicians. Canadian provinces fine truck fleets up to $50,000 for each wheel separation occurrence.

Because of the wide variety tasks vehicles are expected to perform, there are enormous variations in tire technology that technicians need to properly understand in order to promote greater vehicle reliability and safety and to extend service life.

TABLE 23-1: Ranking of Reasons for Roadside Service Calls

Reason for Service Call	Percentage of All Service Calls
Tires	51.3%
Jump or pull start	7.6%
Air line or hose	4.7%
Alternator	4.1%
Wiring	3.9%
Fuel filter	3.7%
Fuel	3.5%
Brake	2.4%
All other issues	Less than 1%

Source: www.Truckinfo.net/trucking/stats.htm

Fundamentals of Commercial Vehicle Tires

Understanding tires used on heavy-duty commercial vehicles begins with understanding the differences between heavy-duty tires and those used on light-duty vehicles. It is also important that the commercial vehicle tire technician understand the functions of tires.

You Are the Technician

While working at a truck lease operation you notice there is an increase in tire-related maintenance costs. There is an above-average replacement of tires for conditions such as cupping on one side of the tire, the tread depth varying around the tires, and tire wear is often irregular. As you investigate possible causes, you examine the tire inspection preventive maintenance (PM) program. Tires are regularly checked for the correct inflation pressure at least once a month and the tires are rotated per manufacturer's recommendations. There are a variety of complaints that are even more frequently made that could be tire related. Drivers are complaining of a steering wheel shimmy from side to side, tramping noise, and general vibration at highway speeds. As you consider the mounting costs of both tire replacement and labor spent diagnosing vibration complaints, you are considering adding more inspection items to the PM inspection related to tires.

1. What inspection procedures would you consider adding to a general PM inspection for the tires? Justify your recommendation.
2. The wheels of the lease vehicles are regularly removed to inspect brake shoe wear, brake pads, calipers, hardware, and so on. How might this inspection program contribute to accelerated complaints related to tire vibration?
3. How might installation procedures of wheel rims affect the balance of wheel and tire assemblies?

Tire Differences

Two major differences exist between larger commercial vehicle tires and light-duty tires. Commercial vehicle tires contain larger air volume and produce a larger **contact patch** with the road. The larger air volume contained in heavy-vehicle tires means that a tire supports more weight with the same (or even less) tire pressure compared to other types of tires. Also, the larger road contact patch of a truck tire, of perhaps 80 square inches (203 cm^2), means less power is transmitted through each unit of contact area. Commercial truck tire construction is different than, for example, a motorcycle tire, which concentrates more weight per unit of contact patch area and transmits more torque through each unit of area in contact with the road. FIGURE 23-1 shows the power per unit of contact pressure for different applications of tires.

Those two differences explain why truck tires typically last much longer than tires on cars and motorcycles—even while carrying more weight and transmitting more power either through engine or brake torque.

Tire Functions

Tires have four basic functions, listed here and illustrated in FIGURE 23-2:

- Supporting the vehicle load
- Transmitting braking and traction forces to the road surface
- Absorbing road shocks
- Providing directional control of the vehicle.

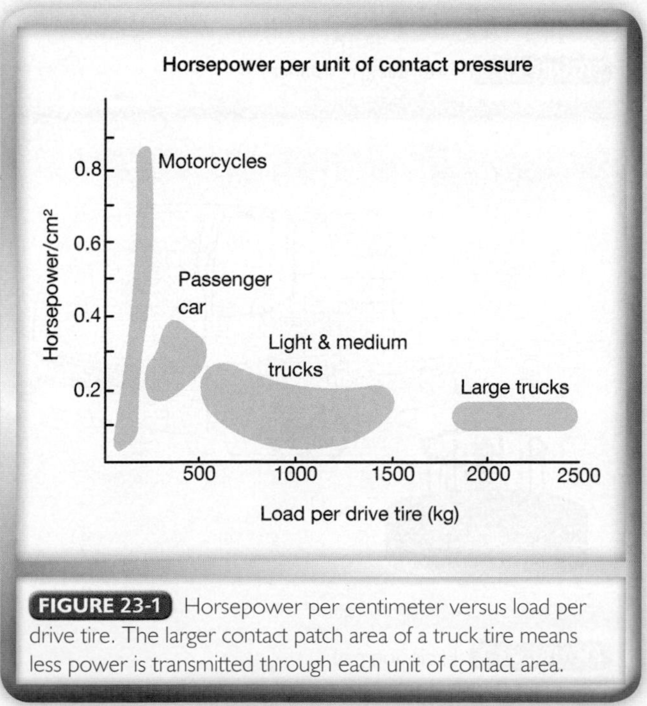

FIGURE 23-1 Horsepower per centimeter versus load per drive tire. The larger contact patch area of a truck tire means less power is transmitted through each unit of contact area.

As depicted in FIGURE 23-3, trapped air volume within the tire acts as a cushion to support the vehicle load and absorbs road shock. FIGURE 23-4 shows that the larger air volume contained in tires used by commercial vehicles supports more weight with less tire pressure compared to other types of tires.

A wide variety of tires are made to provide unique operational features for specific vehicle applications. For example, tires for on-highway trucks carrying heavy loads will be different depending on whether they are used on a steering axle, drive axle, or even trailer axles, where tires are pulled rather than steered and transmit no drive torque. The type of road surface, loading factors, fuel economy requirements, driving speed, ride characteristics, and even weight legislation are also factors influencing tire selection and design. However, the

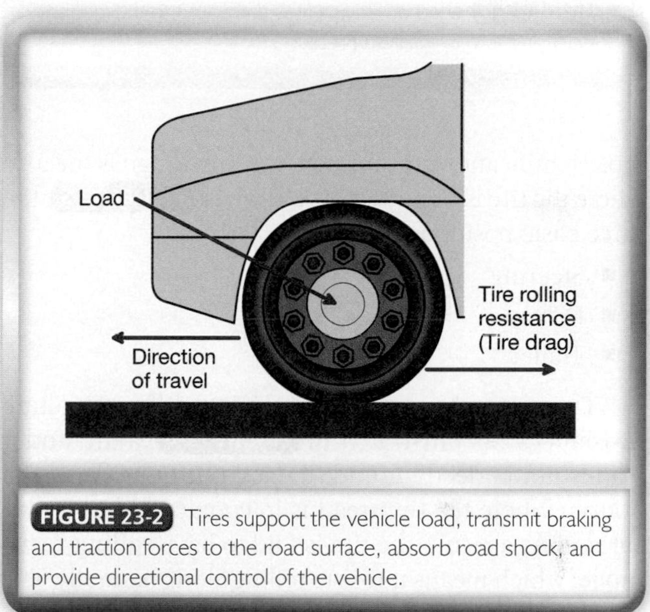

FIGURE 23-2 Tires support the vehicle load, transmit braking and traction forces to the road surface, absorb road shock, and provide directional control of the vehicle.

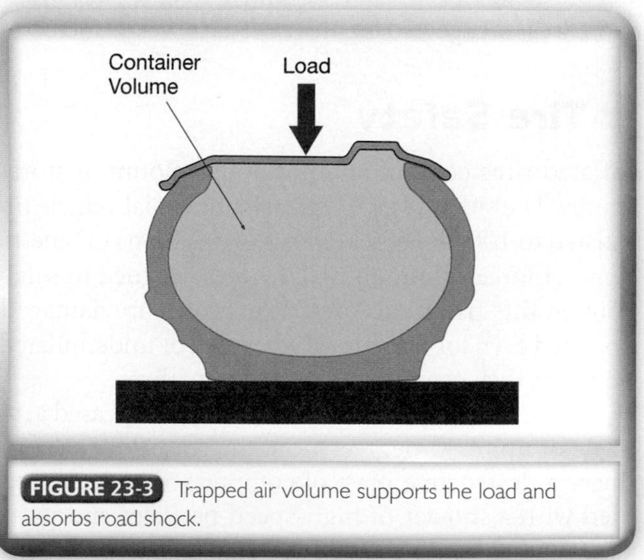

FIGURE 23-3 Trapped air volume supports the load and absorbs road shock.

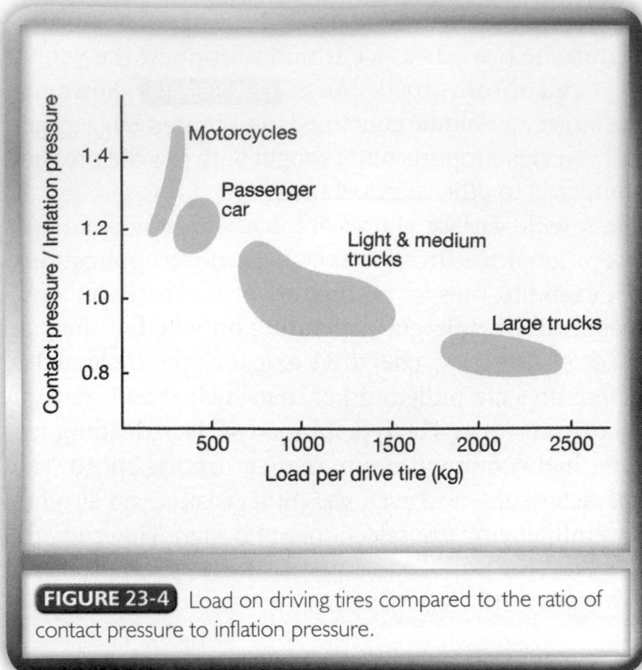

FIGURE 23-4 Load on driving tires compared to the ratio of contact pressure to inflation pressure.

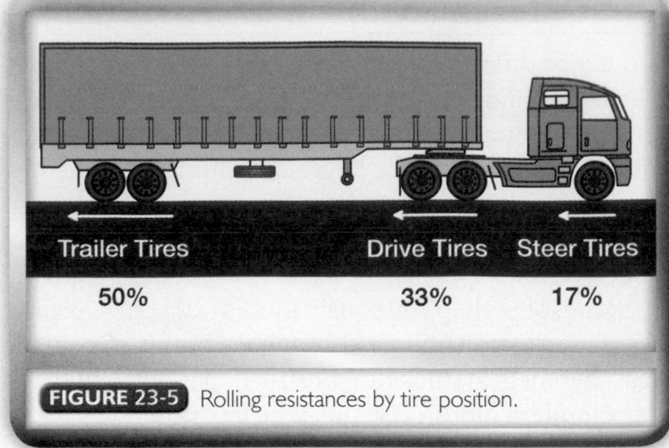

FIGURE 23-5 Rolling resistances by tire position.

most significant factor influencing tire design is the axle where the tire is mounted. As shown in FIGURE 23-5, the three basic positions are:

- Steering
- Drive
- Trailer

Tires at each position experience different rolling resistances. As illustrated in FIGURE 23-6, a tire under load is not perfectly round. In fact, it is quite flat at the bottom where the tire tread is in contact with the road surface. As a result, the tire is said to have **rolling resistance**, which means it resists rolling along naturally. The greatest rolling resistance is encountered by tires carrying the greater proportion of vehicle weight. This means more wear is expected on tires as vehicle weight increases.

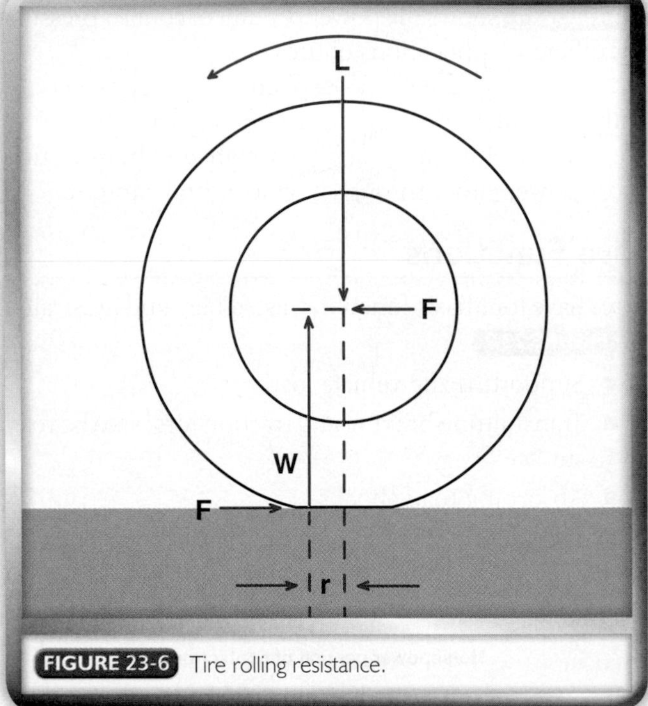

FIGURE 23-6 Tire rolling resistance.

Tire Safety

Inflated tires contain an enormous amount of stored energy. The sidewall of a typical commercial vehicle tire inflated to 100 psi (689 kPa) has over 34 tons (31 metric tons) of force acting on it! Tires are designed to safely contain this potential force. When tires are damaged, operated even for brief times when flat, or underinflated, however, they can pose a serious safety threat.

Force from exploding tires is typically released at an angle of up to 45 degrees from the rupture. That produces a destructive blast of compressed air accompanied with a shower of high-speed particles and parts. FIGURE 23-7 shows the direction of the explosion paths

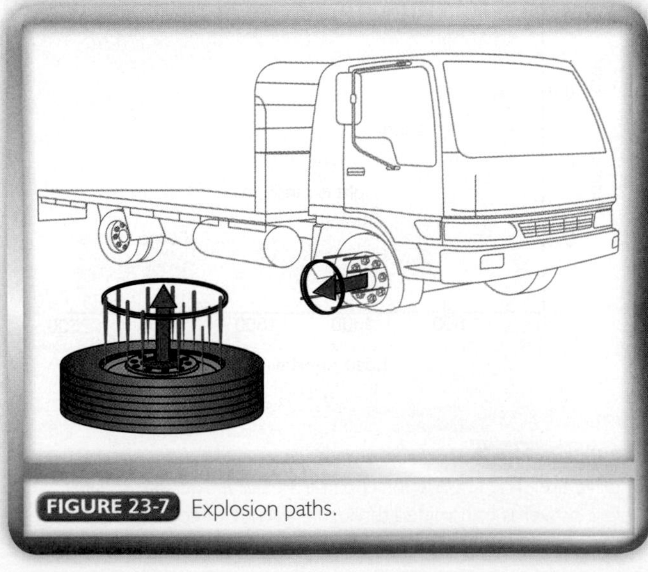

FIGURE 23-7 Explosion paths.

for a tire depending on how it is positioned. An unrestrained wheel with a tire failure can fly as much as 66 feet (20 meters) through the air, striking any bystander with lethal force. Failures of multi-piece or split rim tires have caused numerous technician fatalities.

The potential for lethal or serious injuries when working with tires cannot be overstated. Tire work should only be carried out by technicians trained in tire safety and service procedures prior to working with tires. Common hazards associated with tire work include hazards related to deflating, inflating, lifting, and moving tires.

Compressed air and debris can be released when deflating tires. Air escaping from tires while being deflated is under high pressure and releases a jet of air that can inflict serious injury by propelling dirt and debris at high speed.

While inflating tires, there is a risk of exploding tire debris and parts. Compressed air in inflated tires can explode with tremendous force. Explosion or separation of multi-piece wheel rims can occur when misassembled, damaged, or deteriorated rim and wheel assemblies fail to restrain the force of the compressed air. To help avoid accidents, when inflating tires, always use a safety cage and a remote clip-on style air hose with an accurate pressure regulator. Securing a commercial tire during inflation can be done with a horizontal restraint or a vertical safety cage while maintaining the safe operating perimeter **FIGURE 23-8**. As shown in all three illustrations, no one should enter the area of potential trajectory when tires are being inflated.

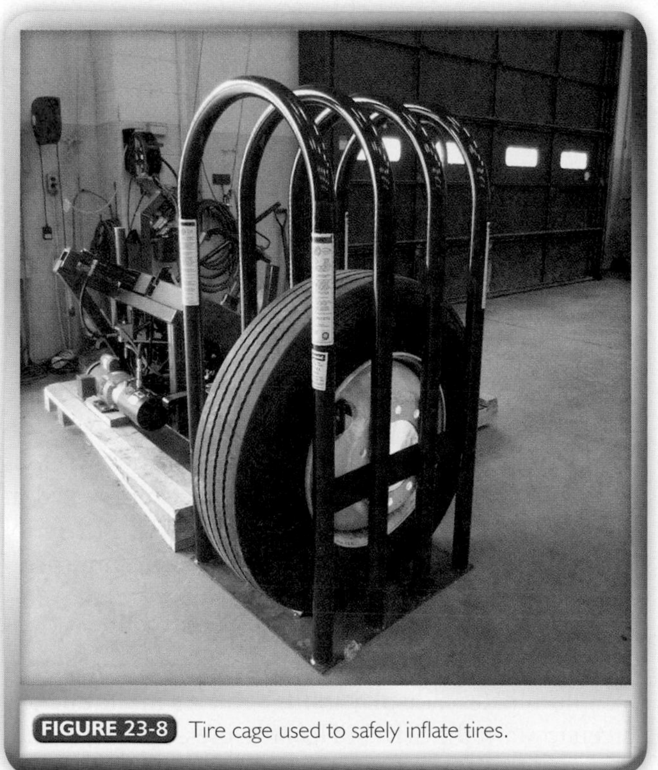

FIGURE 23-8 Tire cage used to safely inflate tires.

Unfortunately, the use of tire cages has declined in recent years due to the elimination of multi piece, split rims, and radial tires. Radial tires, however, are not indestructible, and defects can lead to tires disintegrating with explosive force. If available, safety cages should still be used even for these tires. Always inflate tires with a clip-on chuck that has an inline tire pressure gauge that enables technicians to remotely monitor tire pressure. Also, initially inflate tires to only 20 psi (138 kPa) to check for leaks and bead sealing.

Weight of the tire and rim assembly also poses a safety risk to the technician. Commercial vehicle tires and rim assemblies are very heavy and require proper lifting techniques. Finally, improper or inadequate inspection procedures and installation procedures causing wheels to separate from a vehicle are additional hazards resulting from the absence of comprehensive technician training associated with tires and wheel rims.

HDV Wheel Arrangements

Wheel and tire combinations used on heavy-duty vehicles must comply with government regulations. The reason for the regulations is that, when wheels and tires are used in an incorrect arrangement, a vehicle can become unstable in certain road conditions. Regulations state that radial tires and bias-ply tires should never be used on the same axle because of the tires' different handling characteristics.

Ideally, the tires on the same axle should be of the same make and tread pattern, as even the handling characteristics between makes vary and using different makes on the same axle can cause instability under certain road conditions. **FIGURE 23-9** shows correct and incorrect combinations.

Tire Pressure Monitoring Systems

Maintaining proper tire pressure is essential for the safety and performance of a vehicle. **Tire inflation pressure** is the level of air in the tire that provides it with load-carrying capacity and affects overall vehicle performance. It also plays a significant role in decreasing fuel consumption, reducing CO_2 emissions and extending tire life. All tires lose inflation over time and, as many modern vehicles have extended service intervals, tires can become dangerously underinflated without regular checking by the vehicle driver.

In addition to increased fuel consumption and tire wear, long periods of driving with low tire pressures can cause additional stress on the tire sidewalls. This results in increased operating temperatures that can lead to pre-

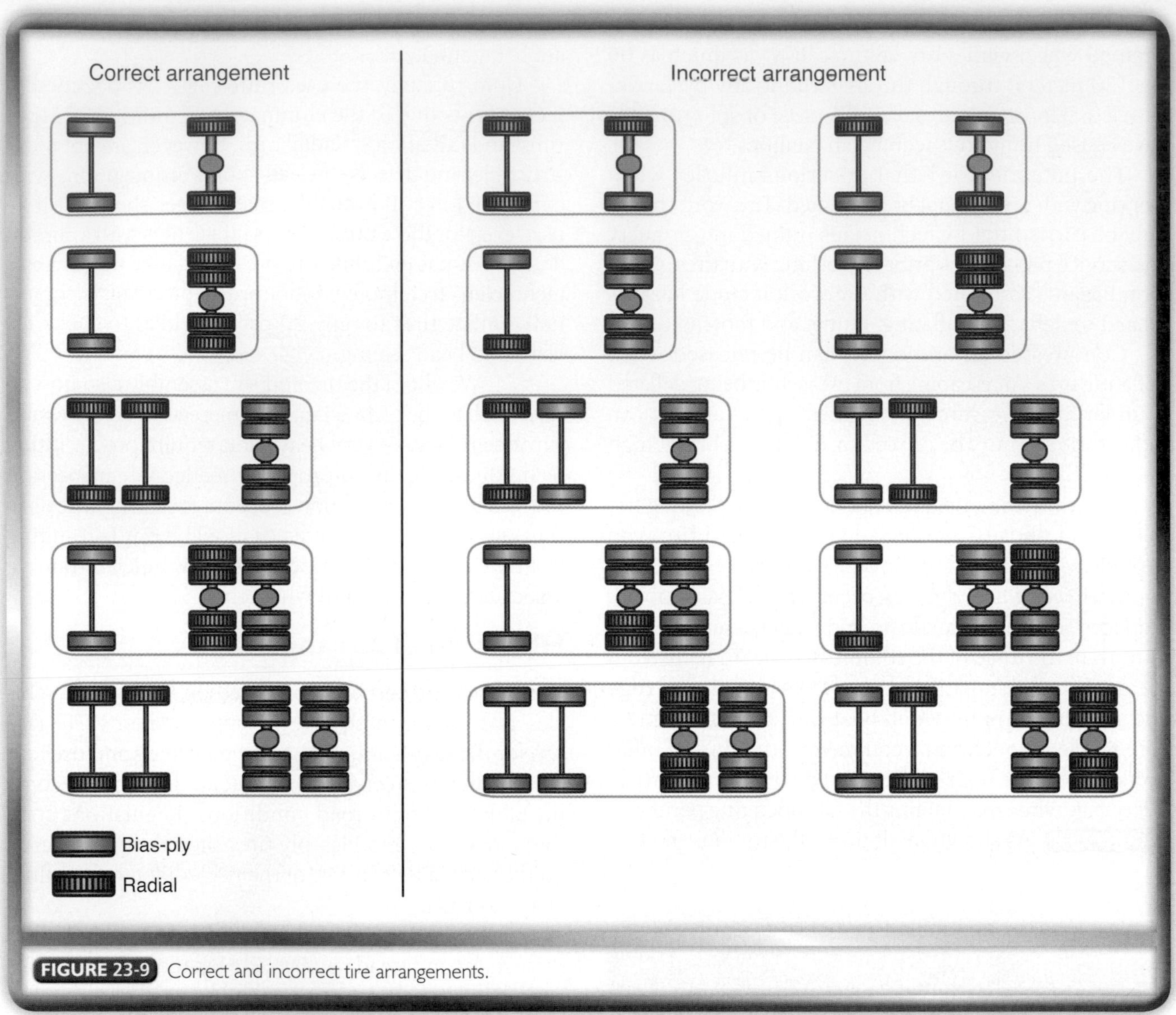

FIGURE 23-9 Correct and incorrect tire arrangements.

mature tire failure. Tires operating with low pressures can also affect the vehicle's handling and performance. In a worst-case scenario, underinflation can lead to a tire blowout or tread separation.

The automated **tire pressure monitoring system (TPMS)** provides a means of reliable and continuous monitoring of the vehicle tire pressure and is designed to increase safety, decrease fuel consumption, and improve vehicle performance. A TPMS monitors the tires for low air pressure and alerts the driver when one or more tires are lower than (or in some cases, higher than) the designated thresholds. This alert can be an illuminated warning lamp or a chime. A TPMS can be fitted to all vehicles using conventional and run-flat tires. With some TPMS systems, drivers can monitor the tire pressures and temperatures from the driver's seat to ensure that their tires are properly inflated under all operating conditions. The TPMS is designed to ignore normal pressure variations caused by changes in ambient temperature.

There are two basic configurations used to monitor the vehicle's tire pressures: direct and indirect. A **direct TPMS** directly measures the tire pressure via a sensor that is installed inside each wheel, which helps protect the TPMS from damage. Each wheel sensor is equipped with an antenna that wirelessly relays the information it senses to receivers located within the vehicle, as illustrated in FIGURE 23-10. The receivers send the signal to the control unit. The sensor is able to respond to a drop in pressure of as little as 2 psi (14 kPa). The control unit sends an appropriate signal to the driver's information circuit or, in some vehicles, the on-board computer, which in turn illuminates a display in the vehicle's multifunction screen to warn the driver of low tire pressure in a certain wheel. An audible and visual warning alerts the driver,

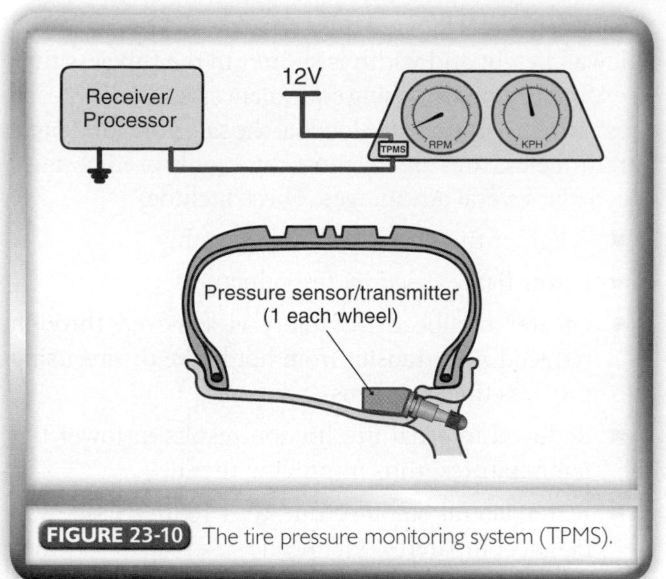

FIGURE 23-10 The tire pressure monitoring system (TPMS).

allowing time for the vehicle to stop or be driven to a service station.

The sensors are powered by an internal battery that is designed to last between five and 10 years. The use of a **centrifugal switch** in the sensor allows the sensor to go to sleep when the vehicle stops, which extends battery life. When the battery goes dead, it will need to be replaced, which usually means that the entire sensor must be replaced because the battery is typically sealed inside the sensor.

A direct TPMS can be of two types: one-way communication or two-way communication. In one-way communication, the TPMS sensor can only transmit to the receiver; it cannot receive any information. In this type of system, the sensors usually use a centrifugal switch to turn them on and off to conserve the battery energy. In a two-way communication TPMS, the sensor can receive signals as well as transmit signals. This allows the control unit to send signals to wake up or cause the sensor to sleep, thus extending the sensor's battery life. The two-way communication system is more complex and expensive than the one-way system.

An **indirect TPMS** indirectly monitors tire air pressure. The most prevalent indirect tire pressure monitoring systems in use today utilize the wheel speed anti-lock braking systems (ABS) to measure the difference in the rotational speed of the four wheels. A wheel that is rotating faster than the others indicates that the tire has lower pressure than the other tires. This is because, if a tire loses pressure, its rolling radius is reduced, which increases the speed of rotation. Since it is rolling faster than the other tires, the wheel speed sensor will send a slightly faster wheel speed signal for that wheel to the ABS control unit. The control unit monitors the changes in wheel speed, and, when a low tire pressure failure is detected, it sends a signal to the low tire pressure light and/or chime on the dashboard.

Types of Commercial Vehicle Tires

Commercial vehicle tire come in two basic types—tube or tubeless. Either type can come in a variety of sizes and profiles to meet specific vocations or needs for fuel efficiency.

Tubeless and Tube-Type Tires

Commercial vehicle tires are either tube or tubeless. What determines the type is how the air is sealed inside the tire. If the air is sealed inside using an inner tube separate from the tire casing, the tire is a **tube-type tire**. If the air is not sealed in an inner tube, the tire is a **tubeless tire**.

Tube and tubeless tires use similar construction with one exception. On a tubeless tire, a liner of rubber is applied to the inside of the tire to create an air tight seal with the casing. Different wheel rim configurations are used with each type of tire. As illustrated in FIGURE 23-11, tubeless tires use a single-piece, **drop-center wheel rim**, which is a type of wheel rim that fits over the brake drum and is concave. (Wheel rims will be covered in greater

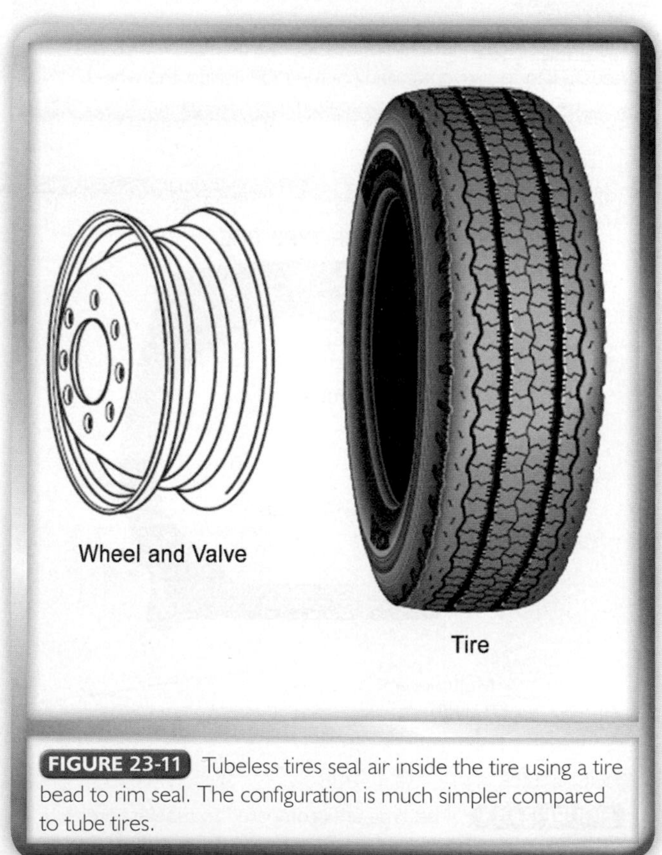

FIGURE 23-11 Tubeless tires seal air inside the tire using a tire bead to rim seal. The configuration is much simpler compared to tube tires.

detail in the chapter Wheel Rims and Hubs.) Tube-type tires use a multi-piece, flat wheel rim assembly, such as the one depicted in FIGURE 23-12. Tube-type tires also require a **tire flap**. This piece of rubber wraps around the rim to protect the inner tube from chafing, pinching, and cracking caused by friction between the valve stem slot in the rim and the edges of the tire bead. The **tire bead** is the inner circumference of the tire and is the part of the tire that connects the tire onto the rim. It could be said that it holds the entire wheel together.

FIGURE 23-13 provides a side-by-side comparison of tube-type and tubeless tires. Note the multi-piece rim and requirement for a flap in a tube-type tire. Additionally, tire sidewall height and width is shorter in the tubeless tire.

When compared using equivalent sizes, both types of tires can support the same loads at the same inflation pressure. Tubeless tires are the most commonly used because they have several advantages. These include:

- A lighter tire and wheel rim assembly.
- Fewer flats caused by tire punctures.
- Greater tire bead durability is achieved through reduced heat transfer from hot brake drums using tubeless tires and rims.
- Reduced internal tire friction results in lower tire temperatures, thus improving tire life.
- Better lateral stability due to a reduced sidewall height compared to identically sized tube-type tires.
- The use of an uncomplicated single-piece wheel rim in comparison to multi-piece rims used for tube-type tires.

This last advantage plays a key role in tire safety. Fewer parts and reduced hazards due to mismatched rim components are benefits with tubeless tires. Tube-type tires use multiple piece split rims to enable the installation of the tire over the wheel rim. Two- and three-piece styles are most common. Split rim components are not interchangeable and must be carefully matched together. Mismatching components can cause the locking split-ring to separate from the wheel with explosive lethal force. FIGURE 23-14 shows two- and three-piece rim configurations.

Locking ring, Side ring, Disc wheel, Flap, Tube and valve, Tire

FIGURE 23-12 Tube-type tires use multiple piece rims and need a flap to prevent chafing of the tube against the wheel.

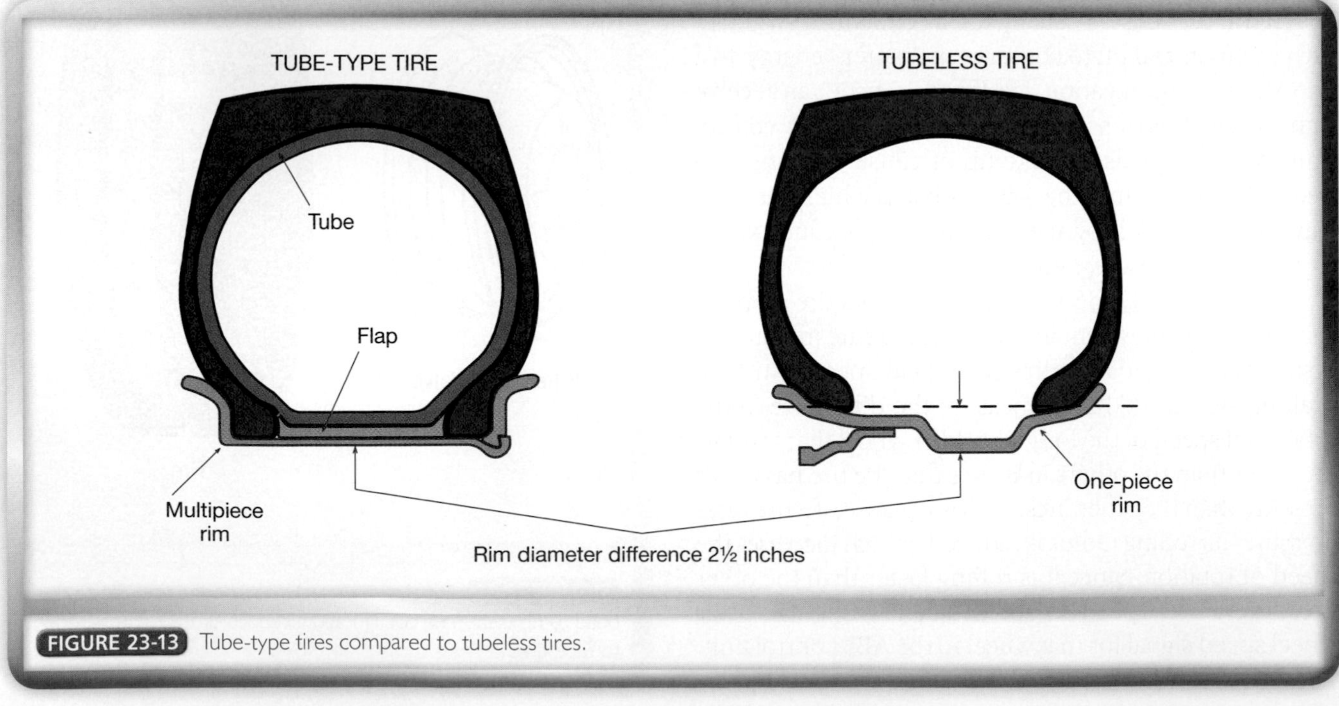

FIGURE 23-13 Tube-type tires compared to tubeless tires.

Tire Identification and Sizing

Several dimensions are important in tire sizing. The **overall diameter** is the diameter of an inflated tire at the outermost surface of the tread. The **nominal diameter** is a size code figure for reference purposes only, as indicated in the tire and rim size designation. **Section width** is the distance between the outside of the sidewalls on an inflated tire without any load on it, and **section height** is simply the height of the sidewalls. **Static radius** is the distance from the tire center to ground level. Measurements are checked on fitted tires inflated to the specified tire pressure. **Rolling circumference** is the distance covered by one revolution of the tire.

Most truck tire sizes are indicated by the section width and diameter, either in inches or millimeters, followed by R for radial, followed by the rim or wheel diameter in inches. As illustrated in FIGURE 23-15, the placement of each number and digit corresponds to specific information about the tire. For example, a designation of 11R 22.5 indicates that this tire is 11" (26.5 cm) across, from the widest point of its outer sidewall to the widest point of its inner sidewall, when mounted and measured on a specified width wheel. This is sometimes called the cross section of the tire or, as mentioned above, this measurement is referred to as the tire's section width. The R designates a radial tire while the 22.5 refers to the rim diameter on which the tire is mounted. In this case, that is 22.5" (57.2 cm).

Tire sizes and other important data are molded into the sidewalls of tires, as shown on the tire in FIGURE 23-16. FIGURE 23-17 illustrates the standard tire identification

Split Side Ring
Fixed Flange
Two Piece Rim
Rim Base
Bead Seat
Gutter
Continuous Side Ring
Split Lock Rlng
Three Piece Rim
Rim Base

FIGURE 23-14 Two- and three-piece split rim configurations for tube-type tires.

FIGURE 23-16 The tire diameter, width, and aspect ratio are molded into this tire's sidewall.

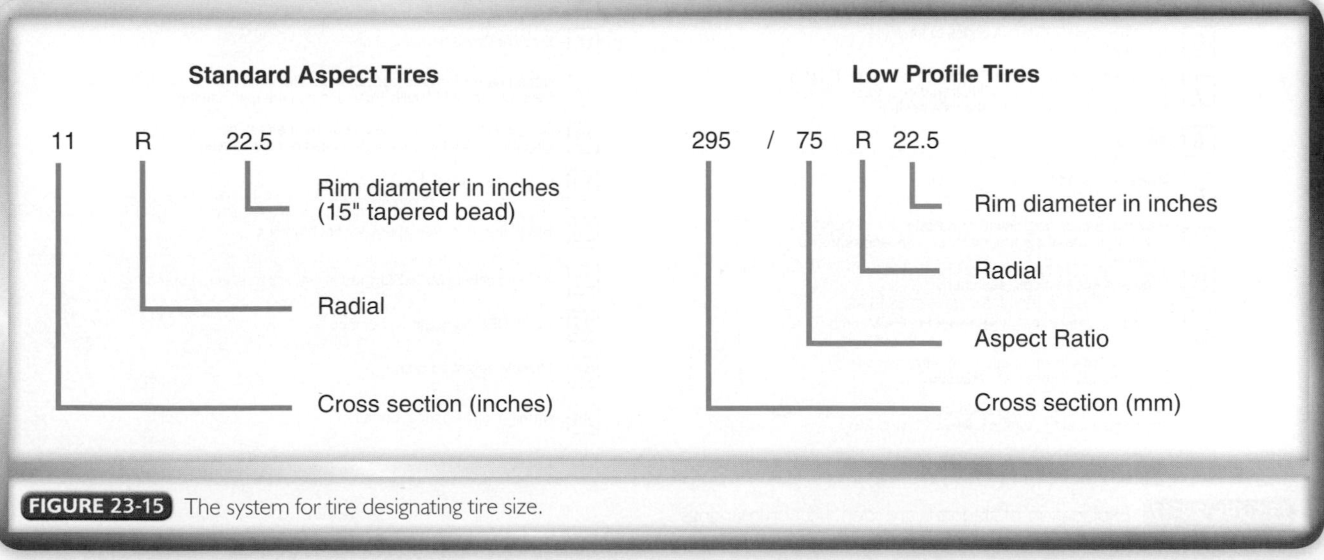

FIGURE 23-15 The system for tire designating tire size.

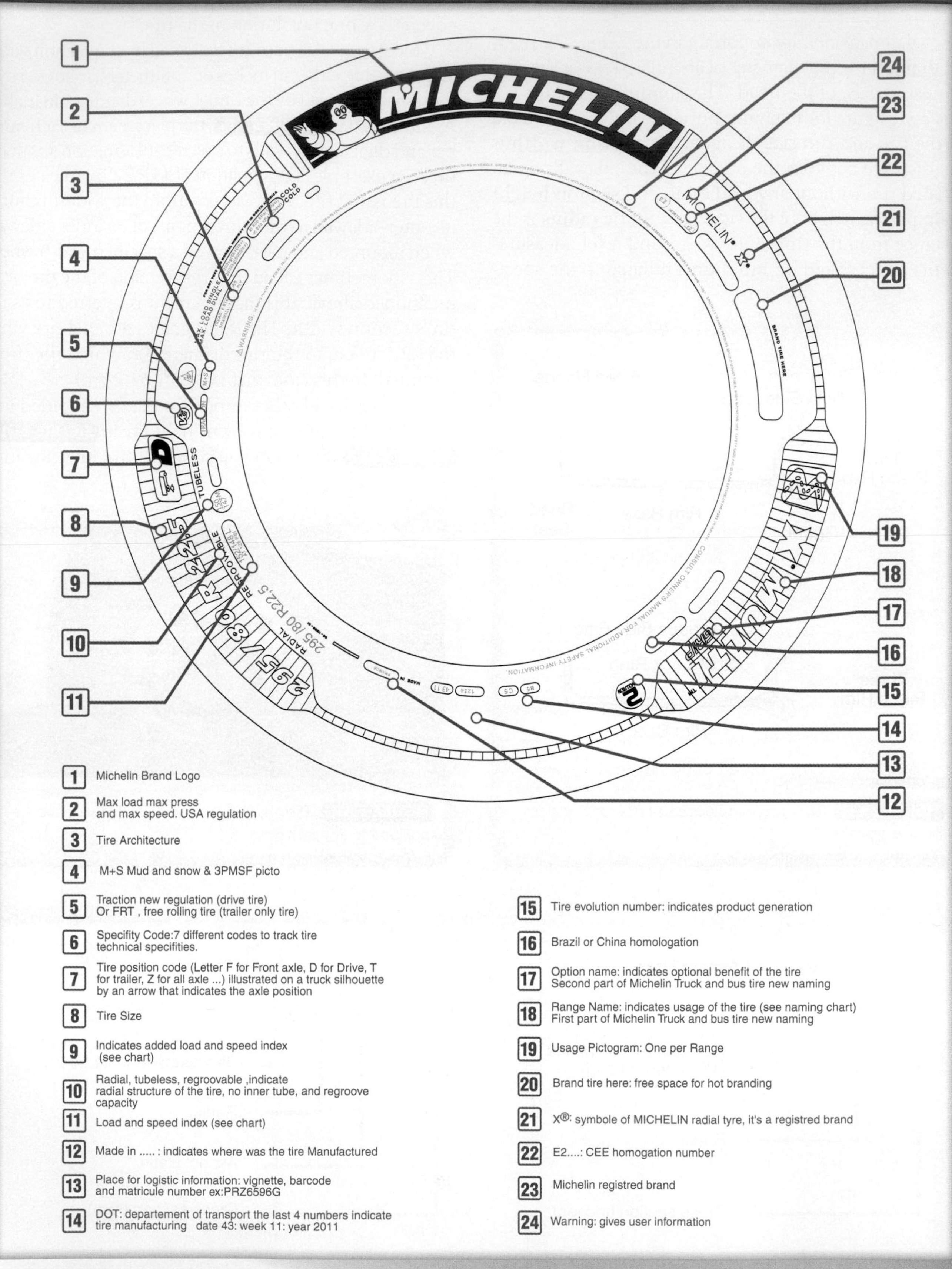
MICHELIN
TUBELESS
REGROOVABLE
RADIAL
295/80 R22.5
MADE IN
BRAND TIRE HERE
CONSULT OWNER'S MANUAL FOR ADDITIONAL SAFETY INFORMATION.
1 Michelin Brand Logo
2 Max load max press and max speed. USA regulation
3 Tire Architecture
4 M+S Mud and snow & 3PMSF picto
5 Traction new regulation (drive tire) Or FRT , free rolling tire (trailer only tire)
6 Specifity Code:7 different codes to track tire technical specifities.
7 Tire position code (Letter F for Front axle, D for Drive, T for trailer, Z for all axle ...) illustrated on a truck silhouette by an arrow that indicates the axle position
8 Tire Size
9 Indicates added load and speed index (see chart)
10 Radial, tubeless, regroovable ,indicate radial structure of the tire, no inner tube, and regroove capacity
11 Load and speed index (see chart)
12 Made in ..... : indicates where was the tire Manufactured
13 Place for logistic information: vignette, barcode and matricule number ex:PRZ6596G
14 DOT: departement of transport the last 4 numbers indicate tire manufacturing date 43: week 11: year 2011
15 Tire evolution number: indicates product generation
16 Brazil or China homologation
17 Option name: indicates optional benefit of the tire Second part of Michelin Truck and bus tire new naming
18 Range Name: indicates usage of the tire (see naming chart) First part of Michelin Truck and bus tire new naming
19 Usage Pictogram: One per Range
20 Brand tire here: free space for hot branding
21 X®: symbole of MICHELIN radial tyre, it's a registred brand
22 E2....: CEE homogation number
23 Michelin registred brand
24 Warning: gives user information

FIGURE 23-17 Explanation of standard tire identification markings.

Courtesy of Michelin

markings on a new tire and provides a legend for what each marking signifies. TABLE 23-2 shows the marking system mandated by the U.S. Department of Transportation for new tires, and TABLE 23-3 shows the same for retreaded tires.

The most important markings of those illustrated in Figure 23-17 are 295/75 R 22.5 tubeless. These letters and numbers indicate the following.

- 295 = tire width in mm
- 75 = cross-sectional ratio H:W in percent
- R = radial design
- 22.5 = nominal rim diameter of a 15 degree tapered rim (code)
- Tubeless = tubeless tire type
- Other legal and standardized markings used on the tire sidewall:
    - 156 = 8,819 lb (4,000 kg) tire load capacity S (single tire configuration)
    - 150 = 7,386 lb (3,350 kg) tire load capacity D (dual tire configuration)
    - L = acceptable speed of 75 mph (120 km/hh)
    - M = acceptable speed of 81 mph (130 km/h

Tire Profile

Determining a tire profile begins by determining the aspect ratio for the tire. The **aspect ratio** refers to a comparison between the height of the sidewall (section height) to the section width expressed as a percentage. Aspect ratio is calculated by dividing the section height by the section width. The lower a tire's aspect ratio, the wider the tire becomes in relation to the height of the sidewall.For example, a tire with a section width of 11" (265 mm) and an aspect ratio of 80% would have a sidewall height of 8.8" (212 mm). The same tire with an aspect ratio of 75% would have a sidewall height of 8.25" (209 mm).

TABLE 23-2: New Truck Tire Markings Required by the Department of Transportation

DOT	XX	XX	XXX	>0100
Meets DOT standards	Manufacturer 2-digit identification mark	Tire size 2-digit (mold/chamber) identification mark	Tire type Code (optional)	Date of manufacture (week/year) identification mark

TABLE 23-3: Retread Truck Tire Markings Required by the Department of Transportation and the States

Department of Transportation Requirements for Truck Tire Retread Markings

R	XX	XX	XXX	0100
Indicates retread	Manufacturer 2-digit identification mark	Tire size 2-digit (mold/chamber) identification mark	Tire type Code (optional)	Date of manufacture (week/year) identification mark

Additional State Requirements for Truck Tire Retread Markings

R	XX	XX	XXX	0100	RS F2
Indicates retread	Manufacturer 2-digit identification mark	Tire size 2-digit (mold/ chamber) identification mark	Tire type Code (optional)	Date of manufacture (week/year) identification mark	RS indicates retread was produced under Industry Retread Standards F2 indicates the tire is acceptable for steer axle use an d has been retreaded

Low Profile Tires

Low profile (LP) tires refer to a type of tire that has a shorter sidewall height than conventional tires. Also called low aspect ratio tires, these tires have shorter, stiffer sidewalls, resulting in less heating and tread squirm (that is, the flexibility in the tire tread between the surface of the tread and the tire carcass). Low profile tires also have a better contact patch with the road surface. Since the sidewall is smaller, low profile tires offer more responsive steering and tire stability due to greater lateral stability of tire sidewalls. That is, the sidewalls do not flex as much compared to conventional tires.

The ratio of tire section height to section width for low aspect ratio tires is generally 70% to 45% of the tire tread width. This means the tire is much wider than the height of the sidewall. Low profile construction offers the following advantages:

- Reduced tread wear and less irregular wear on steer and trail axles. Shorter sidewalls are stiffer, resulting in less tread squirm and heating plus a better contact patch with the road surface.
- Improved steering and tire stability due to greater lateral stability of tire sidewalls.
- Lighter weight.
- Smaller tire diameters, which enable trailer cube volumes to increase—potentially generating more revenue for loads.

Low profile tires cost more and have greater potential for sidewall damage through contact with curbs.

Wide-Base or Super Single Tires

Wide-base (flotation) tires are large tires with a low aspect ratio. FIGURE 23-18 shows a wide-base tire. The most common application for this profile of tire is on vehicles with high front axle loads that would exceed the loading capacity of standard tires. Dump trucks and refuse haulers that have front axle capacities ranging from 18,000 to 20,000 lb (8,165 to 9,072 kg) typically use these tires.

The most common sizes of wide-base single tire used in North America are 385/65R22.5, 425/65R22.5, 435/50R22.5, 445/50R22.5, and 445/65R22.5. In many regions, depending on load regulations, wide-base low-profile tires are used to replace two single tires on a drive axle.

Super single tires are wide-base low profile tires. Super singles are used to replace two conventional single tires on an axle to save weight and reduce wheel end parts. About 1,000 lb (454 kg) of weight are saved using these tires on a tandem axle bulk hauler application. Tire wear remains about the same as conventional dual tires, but lower rolling resistance translates into some marginal fuel savings.

When compared with standard dual tires, super single or wide-base single tires shift the bearing load centerline outwards to the axle end, as illustrated in FIGURE 23-19. This produces increased bearing and potentially more axle housing wear. Widening the tire track with these tires increases hub and axle spindle loading, resulting in increased loading of the outer wheel bearings. Bearing life can potentially be reduced and wheel ends require more frequent inspection.

FIGURE 23-18 Wide-base tire.

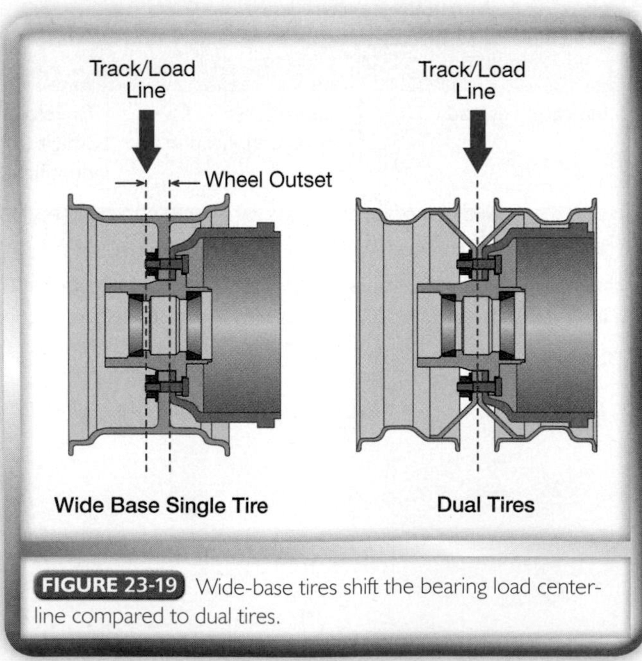

FIGURE 23-19 Wide-base tires shift the bearing load centerline compared to dual tires.

Construction of Commercial Vehicle Tires

Construction techniques and materials used by each tire manufacturer are chosen to provide operating features specific to a tire's function. For example, tire tread design influences noise, braking, torque transmission, rolling resistance, and cornering. Tire tread design even influences traction on wet surfaces and in mud or snow. So, depending on where and how the tire is used, each application needs careful analysis and selection to deliver the best performance.

Basic elements of a heavy-duty commercial vehicle tire include the tire casings, the belt, beads, sidewalls, inner liner, and tread. FIGURE 23-20 illustrates these principle elements of a tire and more.

Tire Casings

The **tire casing** forms the foundational body of the tire and consists of several layers of fabric cord, called plies, encased with a rubber compound. Common cord materials are polyester, nylon, or rayon cords, which add more strength to the tire than simply using a rubber mold to form the case. The tread, belt system (radial or bias-ply), and sidewalls are added to the tire casing.

As a foundation, the casing must withstand all of the mechanical damage from impact, twisting, and rolling forces during driving. Tubeless casings are superior in strength to a separate inner tube once commonly used to hold air. Tubeless casings easily provide the mechanical strength needed for road service, and they seal air inside the tire without the need for a tube. Lightweight casings are preferred because they reduce internal heat build-up, which leads to deterioration of rubber. The quality of tire casing construction is a factor determining how often tires can be retreaded.

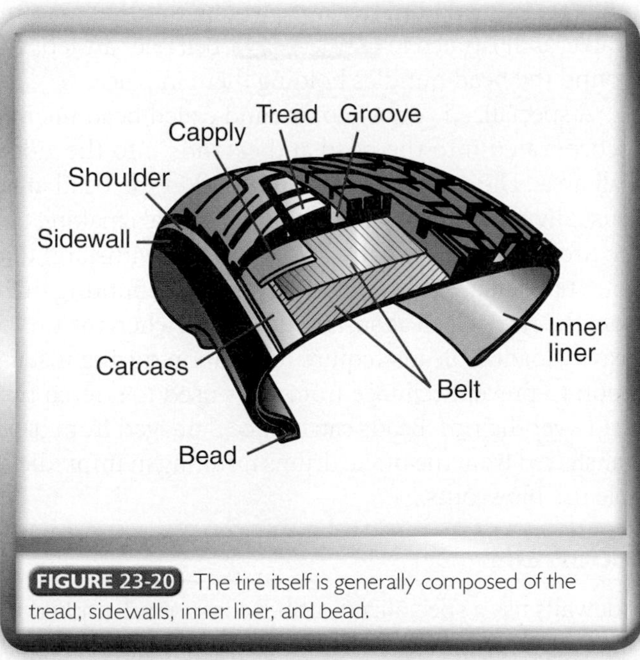

FIGURE 23-20 The tire itself is generally composed of the tread, sidewalls, inner liner, and bead.

Belt System

The belt system is attached to the tire casing. The role of the belt system is to provide stability to the tread area of the tire. Belt design, in turn, contributes to the wear, handling, and traction characteristics of the tire. Belts also work together with the tire sidewall to influence traction and cornering capabilities.

There are three basic types of tire construction: bias-ply, radial ply, and bias-belted. The construction of the different types is illustrated in FIGURE 23-21. A **bias-ply tire** is constructed in a latticed, criss-crossing structure, with alternate plies crossing over each other and laid with the cord angles in opposite directions. In bias-ply tires, the tread and tire sidewalls share the same casing and plies. **Radial-ply tires** have two or more layers of casing plies and cord loops running radially from bead to bead. As such, radial tires separate the mechanical action of the tread and sidewalls—which results in a better contact patch formed between the tire and road, as shown in FIGURE 23-22. Consequently, radial tires have better fuel economy. Additionally, rolling resistance is reduced, producing longer tread life and reduced fuel consumption. Today, most commercial on-highway vehicles use what are known as **radial placed belts**. That is, the belts are placed at 90 degrees to the tire centerline and wrapped from side to side around the tire beads. Braided steel is

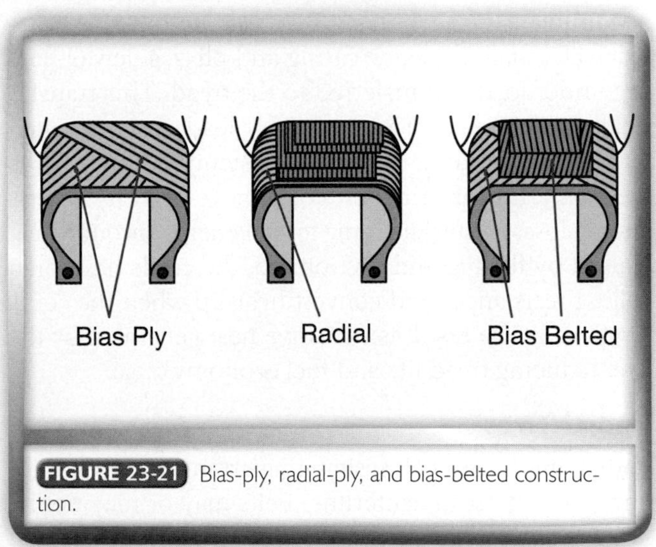

FIGURE 23-21 Bias-ply, radial-ply, and bias-belted construction.

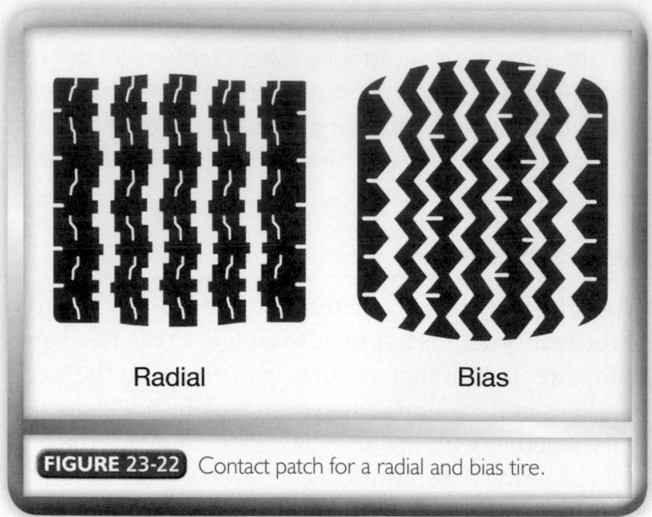

FIGURE 23-22 Contact patch for a radial and bias tire.

the most common belt material used today. Steel belts provide the best strength and stability to the tread area without adding excess weight to the tire.

Bias-Ply Tires

Bias-ply tires are an early tire construction technique that is still used today, albeit more rarely. Bias-ply belt design places tread belts at an angle or diagonally to the tire centerline. Bias-ply belt construction provides a stiffer tread and sidewall area for improved wear and puncture resistance for off-road and even military applications. Stiffer sidewalls provide better driver handling and feedback from the road surfaces and less frequent damage to sidewalls from road hazards, snags, or even rusting of steel belts used in radial construction.

Bias-ply is an inexpensively manufactured tire design used today in some applications for trucks, trailers, and farm equipment. Although inexpensive, the design has a significant disadvantage. Because the tread and tire sidewalls share the same casing and plies, sidewall flexing under load is transferred to the tread. This transfer deforms the tread formation under load. Contact patch friction, tire wear, and rolling resistance all increase as well. In addition, the belt cords have high hysteresis energy loss. Hysteresis is the loss of energy through heat caused by flexing and friction. So, the cords have high rolling resistances and convert heat-up when the cords are flexed. The result is excessive heat generated by the tire, reducing tread life and fuel economy.

Radial Tires

Radial tires have a belt system that arranges plies at right angles to the tread centerline. Belts may or may not be layered diagonally below the tread. Radial plies separate the mechanical action of the tread and sidewalls, which results in a better contact patch formed between the tire and road, which, in turn, improves fuel economy. Constructing tires this way enables the casing cords to deflect more easily under load, thereby generating less heat and producing less rolling resistance while providing better high-speed traction. Tread stiffness is added in the belt area, increasing tread life while improving handling characteristics. Radial tires are a more complex design than bias tires. Consequently, radial tires have higher material and manufacturing costs.

In summary, radial tire belt construction provides:

- Improved tread wear performance
- Improved potential for retreading, which is discussed in the section Retreading Tires
- Less rolling resistance for improved fuel economy
- A superior road contact patch for better traction characteristics

Bias-Belted Tires

In the bias-ply belted tire, as shown in Figure 23-22, the manufacturer attaches the cords in the plies and aligns them as with the bias-ply tire. The major difference comes from a rigid belt, usually of synthetic fabric, that is added. Bias-ply belted tires are reputed to have longer tread life than plain bias-ply tires. As such, bias-ply tires provides a more comfortable ride than radial-ply tires do.

Tire Beads

Tire bead bundles sit on the wheel rim and help form an airtight seal between the tire and rim. Individual tire beads are formed from steel wire wound together to form a cable, as illustrated in FIGURE 23-23. Belt plies are looped around the bead bundles holding them in place.

A specialized rubber compound called bead filler is incorporated into the bead and extends into the sidewall area. The rubber compound used in the bead area is usually harder than other rubber materials making up the tire. Bead filler is harder so that it can withstand the potential damage from mounting and dismounting tires from the rim as well as sustain deflection when the tire is heavily loaded. Beads require lubrication during installation to prevent damage from tools used to stretch the bead over the rim. Beads can also be damaged from heat transferred from the brake drums resulting in unpredictable tire blow-outs.

Sidewalls

Sidewalls use a specialized rubber compound applied to the casing. This is used to add flexibility and weathering resistance. Steel and/or nylon inserts can be added to provide quicker steering response.

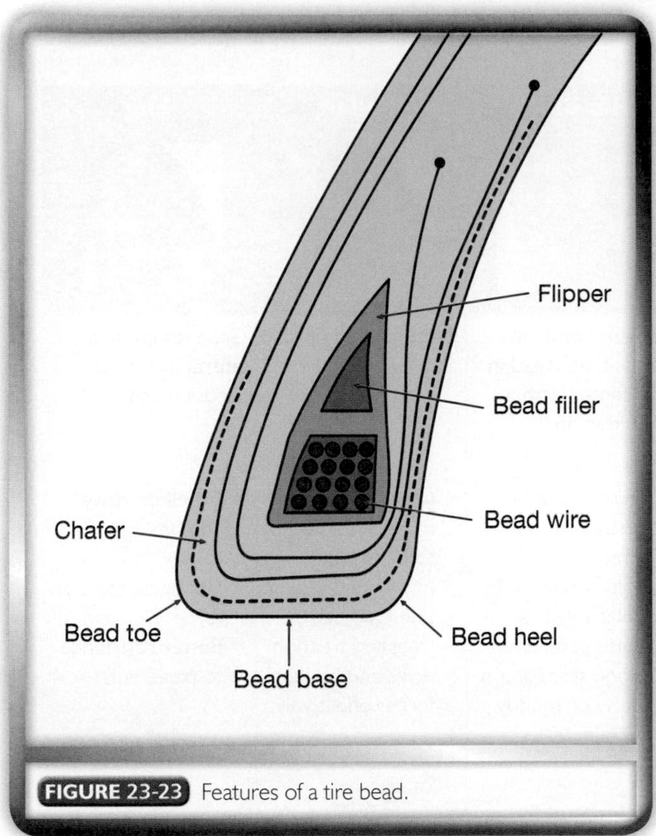

FIGURE 23-23 Features of a tire bead.

Inner Liner

The primary function of the inner liner is to seal air inside a tire and keep moisture out. A specially compounded rubber material is used. The inner liner layer has no cord reinforcement and serves a function similar to an inner tube. Abrasives and even some aftermarket tire-balancing materials rolling around inside a tire can quickly erode the liner and lead to leakage. If a damaged inner liner allows water to leak into the tire, the wheel rim can rust. The inner liner does not do a perfect job sealing the tire, however. All tires leak a small quantity of air through the inner liner. Roughly 1–3% of inflation pressure is typically lost per month. That translates to about 1 psi (6.9 kPa) in a large commercial vehicle tire. Weekly checks of inflation with a properly calibrated, direct reading pressure gauge are recommended.

Tread

Tread is a cap of molded rubber compound attached to the top of the belt system. Tread is typically made from an abrasion resistant, high grip rubber compound, formulated to combine the best traction, tire longevity, and low rolling resistance for superior fuel economy. Tread is replaceable. The tire casing can be recycled to reduce operating costs and limit the environmental impact of disposing of worn tires.

Two basic tire tread designs are the block and rib style. Block style tread is used for the drive tires to grip the road better for improved torque transmission. Ribbed tires do not transmit torque and must roll with little resistance when the direction of the tire is changed. Other tread designs are the rib-lug and lug. TABLE 23-4 compares those four basic tread designs as well as the rib-block tread design.

Most tread patterns are designed for specific applications. Traction tires are used on drive axles, and steer tires are used on front axles. Trailering tires do not requiring steering or transmitting drive torque. TABLE 23-5 compares the features and benefits of drive, steer, and trailering tire treads. Application factors that affect tread selection can include:

- Long Haul—Travel on state/interprovincial highways and normal highways at maximum speeds, with runs over 250 miles (402 km).
- Regional Service—Travel on state/interprovincial highways at normal and lower speeds, with runs under 250 miles (402 km). Vehicle may make many sharp turns and maneuvers in tight turning radiuses.
- Urban—Most travel between and around city areas. High maneuverability required.
- On-Off-Road—Travel on some highway and secondary roads with travel on gravel, muddy, snow packed, and dirt roads.

Retreading Tires

Retreading tires, illustrated in FIGURE 23-24, involves recycling the tire casing to extend its service life and is sometimes known as a "recap," or a "remold." Retreaded tires cost significantly less than the cost of a new tire (typically 40% of the cost of new) and are, therefore, widely used in commercial fleet operations. According to the Tire Retread and Repair Information Bureau, retreaded truck tires represent a savings of over $3 billion US dollars annually in North America. Retreads are also environmentally friendly. Consider that it requires approximately 22 gallons (83 liters) of oil to manufacture one new truck tire. Most of this oil is used to produce the casing which is reused in the retreading process. By contrast, a retread only takes 7 gallons (26.5 liters) of oil to produce. Retreading wide-base tires saves even more fuel. Some tires can be retreaded as often as ten times.

There are two main processes used for retreading commercial vehicle tires:

- Hot curing, also known as mold cure.
- Cold curing, also known as precure.

Both retread processes start with the inspection of the tire to determine its serviceability. Damage to sidewalls or

TABLE 23-4: Comparison of Common Tread Design

Type	Rib	Block	Rib-Block	Rib-Lug	Lug
Pattern					
Profile	Grooves cut around the circumference of a tire	Tread is chunked into individual blocks that are arranged in a pattern	Pattern combines block-type tread in the center with a shoulder rib	Combination of rib and lug patterns	Grooves cut in a lateral direction across tread
Features	• Improved driving stability • Lower rolling resistance. • Lowest tread noise • Best water drainage performance for less skidding and hydroplaning	• Good drive and braking forces. • Best traction on normal paved road	• Low rolling resistance • Smooth comfortable ride • Relatively low noise production • Good traction on snow or muddy terrain	• Rib-type pattern increases steering stability and prevents skidding • Lug-type pattern transfers traction drive and braking forces effectively	• Excellent drive and braking forces • Strongest traction force • Better resistance to tread cuts
Applications	• Best for driving on smooth cemented roads and highways • Ideal for steering or trailer tires	• Good traction performance when driving on asphalt and cement roads	• Good performance when driving on normal cemented roads • Improves fuel economy and has low tread wear	• Suitable for driving on normal cemented, asphalt roads and gravel roads at a middle/low speed	• Suitable for driving on all normal surfaces and best for muddy, off road surfaces

TABLE 23-5: Comparison of Drive, Steer, and Trailering Tire Treads

Drive Tire Tread	Steer Tire Tread	Trailering Tire Tread
• Long tread wear • Long high speed runs • Fuel economy • Wet traction • Noise reduction • Resistance to irregular wear • Dry traction • Snow traction • Wet traction	• Responsive steering • High speed runs • Long tread wear • Resistance to cutting/chipping • Resistance to road hazard penetration	• Resistance to irregular wear • Fuel economy • Long highway speed runs • Noise reduction • Resistance to rib tearing • Resistance to curbing

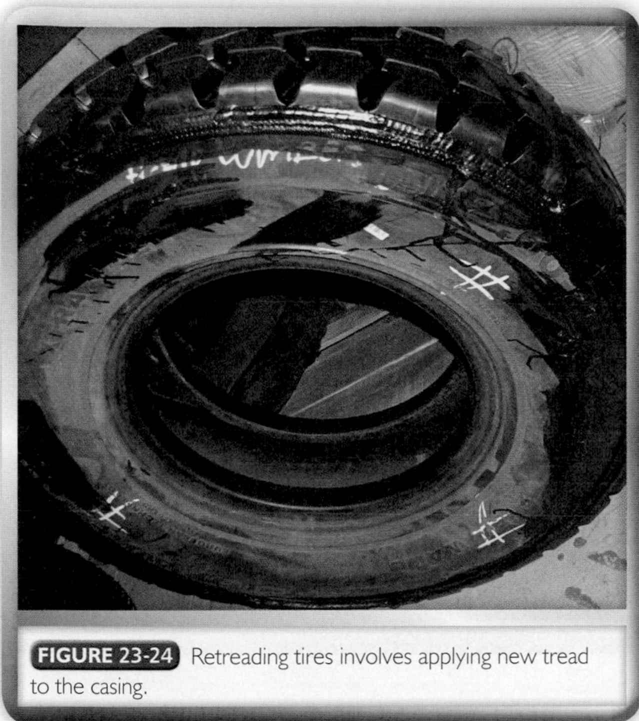

FIGURE 23-24 Retreading tires involves applying new tread to the casing.

TABLE 23-6: Comparison of Hot and Cold Curing Retread Processes

Hot Curing Retread	Cold Curing Retread
One piece tread rubber is bonded directly to the casing	Precured, preformed tread rubber is glued to the tire casing by a thin piece of cushion gum
One piece rubber is applied evenly around the tire casing No splices improves tire circumference uniformity	Precured rubber ends are glued together by a process called stitching Can be performed easier in the field
Less heat is applied to the sidewall during the curing process	High heat to the sidewall during the curing process

the belt system will disqualify the tire as a candidate for retread. Once a tire is deemed serviceable, its old tread is removed. The casing is then buffed to clean it and prepare its surface to receive the new tread.

When **hot curing**, the casing is covered with uncured rubber and then placed in a mold where it is heated. The heating process binds the tread to the casing and cures the tread. **Cold curing** uses a molded, pre-cured tread strip or tread ring which is glued to the casing. The tire is then placed in a rubber envelope with a vacuum applied to the entire tire. The enveloped tire is then placed in a heated chamber to bind the tread to the casing. **TABLE 23-6** compares the processes of hot and cold curing retread.

Tire tread separation describes the separation of the tread from the tire casing. Tire retreads or recaps are often mistakenly blamed for "road alligators," like those shown in **FIGURE 23-25**, which can litter the highway. These separated tire treads originate most often from medium- and heavy-duty commercial tires. Several studies, including a National Highway Traffic Safety Administration (NHTSA) study, have determined that tire debris on highways is not caused by retreads. Analysis of tire fragments and casings collected demonstrated that tire debris from retread tires and original equipment (OE) tires is similar to the proportion of retread and OE tires in service. Still, retreads have a bad reputation.

FIGURE 23-25 Separated tire treads known as road alligators.

Tread separations are caused by several factors, as listed in **TABLE 23-7**. Tread separations caused by heat generated by underinflation start at the edges of the steel belts where heat and stress fatigue affect the tire the most.

TABLE 23-7: Tread Failure by Cause of Separation

Cause of Tread Separation	Percentage of Failures
Road hazard	36–38%
Operational problems	32%
Manufacturing defects	16%
Excessive heat	30%

A bump forms in the tread area where the tread is separating, causing the defective tire to become unbalanced. This bump is a visual indicator that the tread is going to separate. Expansion of this bubble will increase until tire failure occurs. Another type of failure, known as a zipper rupture, is illustrated in FIGURE 23-26. Zipper ruptures are caused by impact with road debris at high speeds.

FIGURE 23-26 Zipper rupture tire failure.

> **TECHNICIAN TIP**
>
> Drive tires experience the most fatigue due to longer service life and higher heat loads from heavier tread and higher drive torque. High drive torque contributes to more casing fatigue compared with moderate fatigue on steer positioned tires and lowest fatigue for trailer tires.

> **TECHNICIAN TIP**
>
> Since tires will age more quickly if exposed to direct sunlight or heat, tires should be stored in cool, dry, dark, and moderately ventilated rooms. Tires which are not mounted on rims should be stored standing up to prevent distortion. Contact with fuel, lubricants, solvents, and chemicals can accelerate deterioration and should be avoided.

Tread Depth

Minimum tread groove depths are specified by Federal Motor Vehicle Safety Standard 119. FMVSS 119 requires manufacturers to include six evenly spaced tread depth indicators, more commonly called wear bars, around the circumference of a highway tire. Illustrated in FIGURE 23-27, wear bars are designed to have the same thickness of the tire tread when only 1/16" (1.59 mm) of tread groove depth is remaining. Vehicle operators are required to maintain at least 1/8" (3.18 mm) of tread groove depth on the front tires of any bus, truck, or truck tractor and 1/16" (1.59 mm) remaining tread depth on any other wheel positions. FIGURE 23-28 shows a tread measuring device.

Tire Regrooving

Regrooving is a process which uses a heated cutting tool to carve new tread or add stripes to a tire. Regroovable tires are manufactured to extend the tire tread life and have adequately thick tread compound between the bottom of the original tread grooves and the top of the uppermost breaker or belt depth. The depth of this area, called **undertread**, permits regrooving. It must allow a minimum of 3/32" (2.38 mm) of rubber material to cover and protect the cord after regrooving. If a tire is regroovable, a label on the sidewall (as discussed in the Tire Identification and Sizing section) designates it as such. Tire regrooving is more common in intercity coach service than in truck fleets.

Tire Inflation Factors

Maintaining the correct tire pressure for a commercial vehicle is an important factor determining the load its tires can safely carry. Maintenance of correct tire pressure

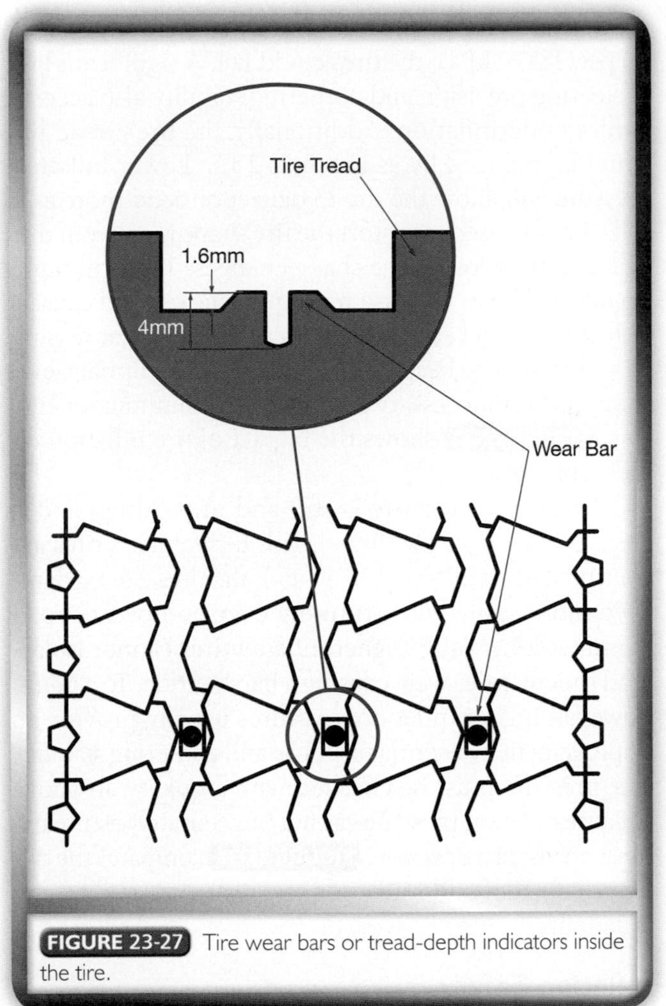

FIGURE 23-27 Tire wear bars or tread-depth indicators inside the tire.

means the tire will support vehicle weight without a problem. Fuel economy, vehicle dynamics, tire durability, and tread life are affected by inflation pressure. Too little tire pressure, the most common condition, will also eventually cause catastrophic tire failure. This happens as the individual layers of fabric and steel encased in rubber are forced to stretch beyond the elastic limits of the fabric and steel reinforcing cords. Excessive bending and flexing of tire layers during underinflation causes this condition. In addition, excessive heat produced by friction between layers within the tire, builds and causes the bonds between the various materials to weaken. The combination of mechanical stress and heat build-up eventually leads to premature deterioration and failure. FIGURE 23-29 charts the effects of tire inflation pressure on tire life.

Even if a tire does not fail immediately, once weakened, it will remain damaged even after being properly inflated. In fact, some manufactures recommend that a tire be replaced, not re-inflated, if allowed to run with less than 20% of its inflation pressure for any length of time. As mentioned in the Inner Liner section, all tires leak a small quantity of air through the inner liner—typically close to 1–3% of inflation pressure per month—and should, therefore, be checked weekly.

Determining Inflation Pressure

Vehicle weight is the primary determinant of tire inflation pressure. Heavier loads require higher inflation pressure to properly support the load. All tire manufacturers

FIGURE 23-28 Measuring tread depth. Note the location of a wear bar.

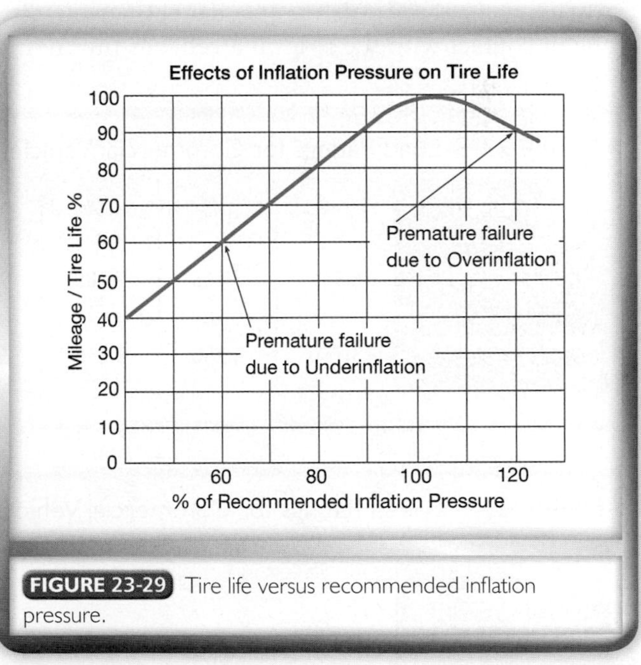

FIGURE 23-29 Tire life versus recommended inflation pressure.

supply load/inflation tables that can be used to determine the proper inflation pressure at various vehicle weights loads. Faster vehicle speeds also increase forces that can damage tires, which means less weight can be safely supported at higher vehicle speeds. TABLE 23-8 shows the load ratings for commercial vehicles and TABLE 23-9 shows the speed ratings.

Temperature and atmospheric pressure can affect tire pressure, too. For example, a tire initial inflation pressure of 100 psi (689.5 kPa) at 60°F (16°C) ambient temperature increases approximately 2 psi (13.8 kPa) for every 10°F (12°C) increase in temperature. In the summer, a tire will commonly run at 15 to 20° degrees pressure higher than its cold inflation pressure. Inflation pressures are always measured when cold, so air pressure should not be bled from a tire when warm since commercial vehicle radial tires are designed to accept this pressure change. FIGURE 23-30 shows the effect of ambient temperature on inflation pressure.

On dual wheel assemblies, maintaining identical tire inflation pressure is critical for normal tire wire. Even as little as a 5 psi (34.5 kPa) pressure difference produces a 5/16" (7.94 mm) difference in rolling diameter. Over one mile, the rolling diameter distance is equivalent to causing a tire to scuff (that is, a tire mark caused by applying enough power to a wheel to make it spin) 13' (3.96 m). And over 100,000 miles (160 km), that amounts to 246 miles (396 km) of scuffing!

Correct tire inflation levels are critical for safety, operation, and fuel economy. An underinflated tire cannot maintain its shape and becomes flatter than intended while in contact with the road. If a vehicle's tires nominally inflated to 100 psi (689.5 kPa) are underinflated by 20 psi (1,379 kPa), the tires could fail. A significant loss of steering precision and cornering stability also accompanies underinflation. Additionally, the tire's tread life could be reduced by as much as 25%. Lower inflation pressure will allow the tire to deflect or bend more as it rolls. Energy used to distort the tire shape is converted to heat and then lost as the shape changes. This will build up internal heat, increase rolling resistance, and cause a reduction in fuel economy of up to 5%. For that reason, it is imperative to keep air pressure at an appropriate level to suppress unnecessary distortion and minimize energy loss. FIGURE 23-31 shows the impact of tire inflation on fuel economy.

An overinflated tire is stiff and unyielding, and it has a contact patch with the road. If a vehicle's tires are overinflated by 20 psi (137.9 kPa), the tires can be damaged more easily when running over potholes or road debris. Additionally, higher inflated tires cannot isolate road irregularities well, causing a harsher ride. To a point, however, higher inflation pressures usually provide an improvement in steering response and cornering stability. Tire pressure must be checked with a quality air gauge because inflation pressure cannot be accurately estimated through visual inspection. FIGURE 23-32 compares the different effects of underinflation, overinflation, and proper inflation.

Inflation Safety

Tires can explode with tremendous force. A typical 11R22.5 radial tire inflated at 100 psi (689.5 kPa) contains almost 72,000 ft-lb (97,619 Nm) of potential energy.

TABLE 23-8: Load Ratings for Commercial Vehicle Tires

Load Index	148	149	150	151	152	153	154	155	156
Load capacity (lb/tire)	6,945	7,165	7,385	7,606	7,826	8,047	8,267	8,543	8,818
Load capacity (kg/tire)	3,150	3,250	3,350	3,450	3,550	3,650	3,750	3,875	4,000

TABLE 23-9: Speed Ratings for Commercial Vehicle Tires

Speed index	F	G	J	K	L	M	N
Speed in mph	50	56	62	68	75	81	87
Speed in kph	80	90	100	110	120	130	140

With this kind of force, a 180 lb (82 kg) person standing next to an exploding tire can be propelled 200 feet (61 meters). So, when inflating or re-inflating tires, always use a tire safety cage, like that shown in Figure 23-8. Always inflate tires with a clip-on chuck that has an inline tire pressure gauge which enables technicians to remotely monitor tire pressure. Also, inflate tires initially to only 20 psi (138 kPa) to check for leaks and bead sealing.

Nitrogen Fill

Well-controlled research has established that nitrogen inflated tires can reduce tire leakage about 3% compared

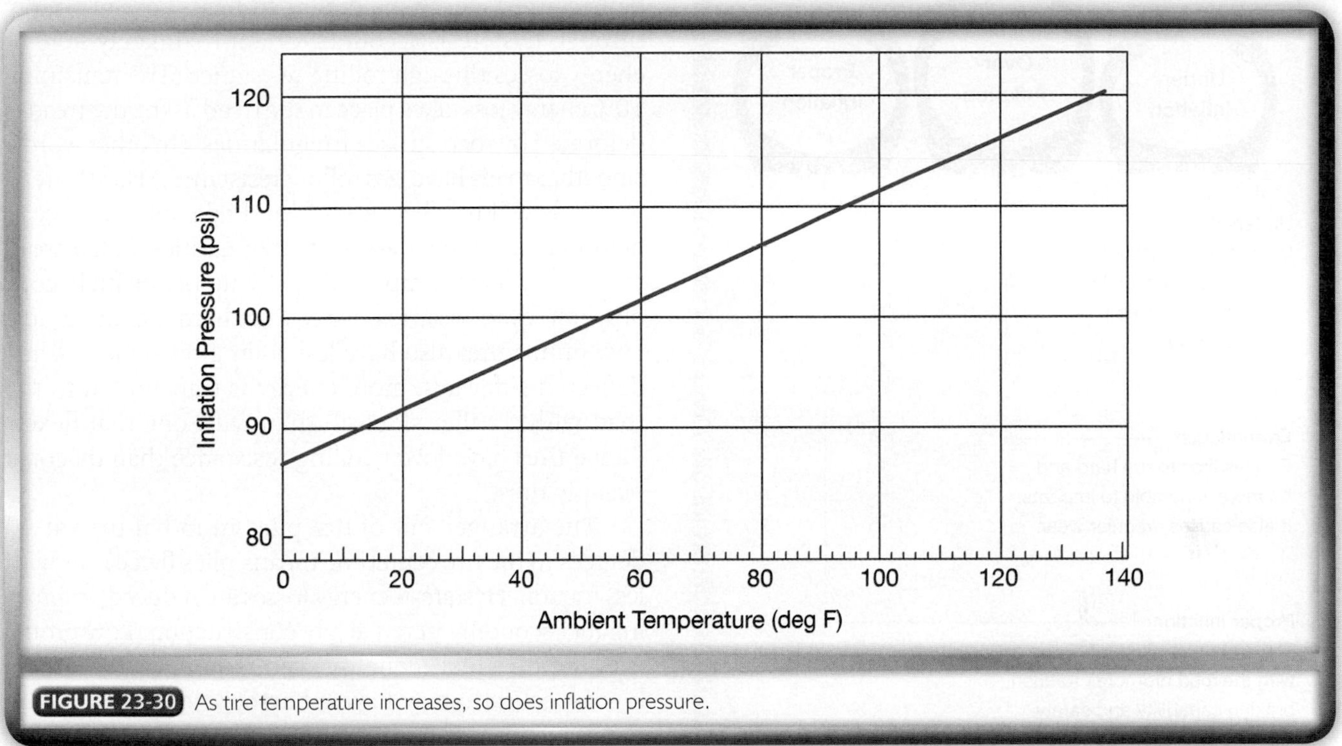

FIGURE 23-30 As tire temperature increases, so does inflation pressure.

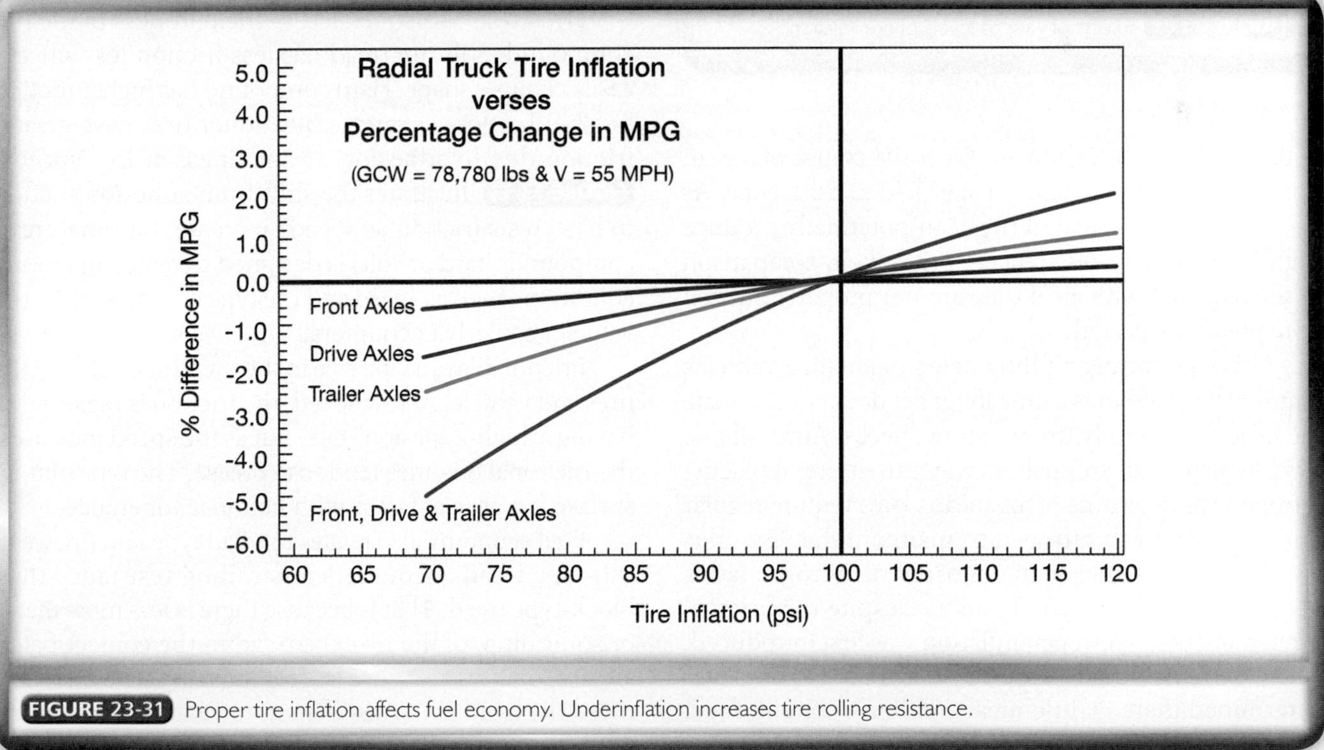

FIGURE 23-31 Proper tire inflation affects fuel economy. Underinflation increases tire rolling resistance.

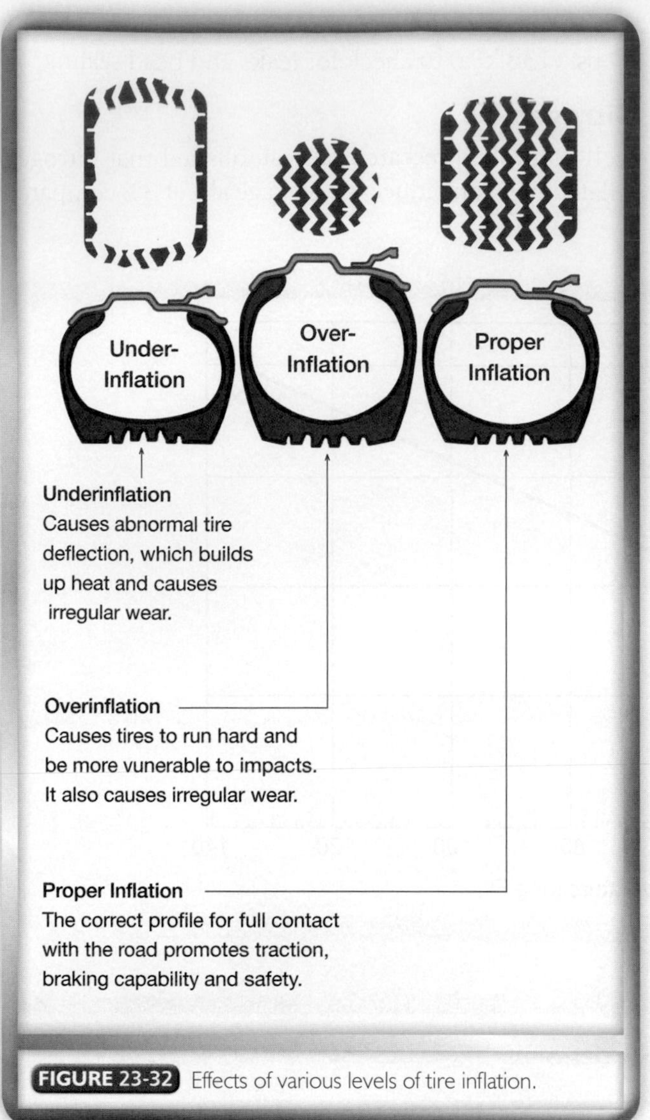

Under-
Inflation
Over-
Inflation
Proper
Inflation
Underinflation
Causes abnormal tire deflection, which builds up heat and causes irregular wear.
Overinflation
Causes tires to run hard and be more vunerable to impacts. It also causes irregular wear.
Proper Inflation
The correct profile for full contact with the road promotes traction, braking capability and safety.

FIGURE 23-32 Effects of various levels of tire inflation.

to tires inflated with shop air. Over the course of a year, this amounts to less than 3 psi (21 kPa) difference. As a result, nitrogen-inflated tires can potentially produce slightly less rolling resistance—but only in comparison to tires inflated with air if they are not properly inflated or regularly inspected.

Although nitrogen filling helps maintain a vehicle's required tire pressures a little longer, it does not eliminate the need for monthly tire pressure checks. Atmospheric oxygen also tends to push its way into a tire, replacing nitrogen gas over time. This means tires require regular purging with fresh nitrogen to maintain the 93% plus levels, or 15% higher than atmospheric nitrogen levels necessary to achieve any benefit. Despite the original excitement when nitrogen inflation was first introduced, field experience and research by tire manufacturers has determined there is little measurable reduction in fuel consumption or tread wear derived from nitrogen filling.

Nitrogen is non-corrosive and does not dissolve moisture. That can, therefore, reduce minor service limiting factors such as rim corrosion. Properly filtered-conditioned shop air, however, can achieve the same benefits.

Tire Construction and Fuel Economy

As a tire rotates, it flexes. Friction between tire plies and belts causes energy to convert to heat. Loss of energy through hysteresis accounts for approximately 90% of energy losses through rolling resistance. The remaining 10% energy loss takes place in the tread as the tire tread is deformed by road surface irregularities. (In other words, smoother roads have less rolling resistance.) Harder tread materials will not flex as easily and take more energy to deform to accommodate road irregularities. Softer tread material rubber compounds provide better fuel economy but lower wear resistance than harder compounds. Low profile tires also have less rolling resistance. When deflected sideways, more energy is transmitted to the road with a stiffer sidewall than with one that flexes. Radial tires have lower rolling resistance than diagonal bias-ply tires.

The arrangement of tire plies in radial tires at 90 degrees to the tire centerline means plies flex easier with less friction. Hysteresis energy losses are reduced, improving fuel economy in radial-ply construction. Low profile tires improve fuel economy even more. LPs that have a low aspect ratio may have a harsher ride but are more responsive because they transmit steering inputs quicker and produce less flexion of the sidewalls.

Hysteresis is also related to the hardness of the tire compound. Soft tire tread has less friction loss since it easily changes shape. Hard compound has higher friction loss but has longer service life. Softer tires have greater friction due to adhesion or stickiness at low speeds. **FIGURE 23-33** illustrates the shift from adhesion friction to hysteresis friction as speeds increase. Optimal tread compound (hard or soft) is designed to match operating conditions such as speed and the type of road surface the vehicle regularly encounters.

Friction plays a vital role in the traction motion of the tires and vehicle. At low speed, the friction is regarded as having a 'high-adhesion" rate. But as the speed increases, the frictional qualities tend to decrease. The type of road surface is a crucial factor with fictional adherence.

Fuel economy also relates to tread type and tire wear. Rib-type tread encounters less rolling resistance than block-type tread. That is because there is less movement, or squirming, of the rib-type tread in the contact patch area. Worn tires also have less rolling resistance than new tires. The tread pattern stiffens as it wears down, leading to less flexing and deformation in the tread area.

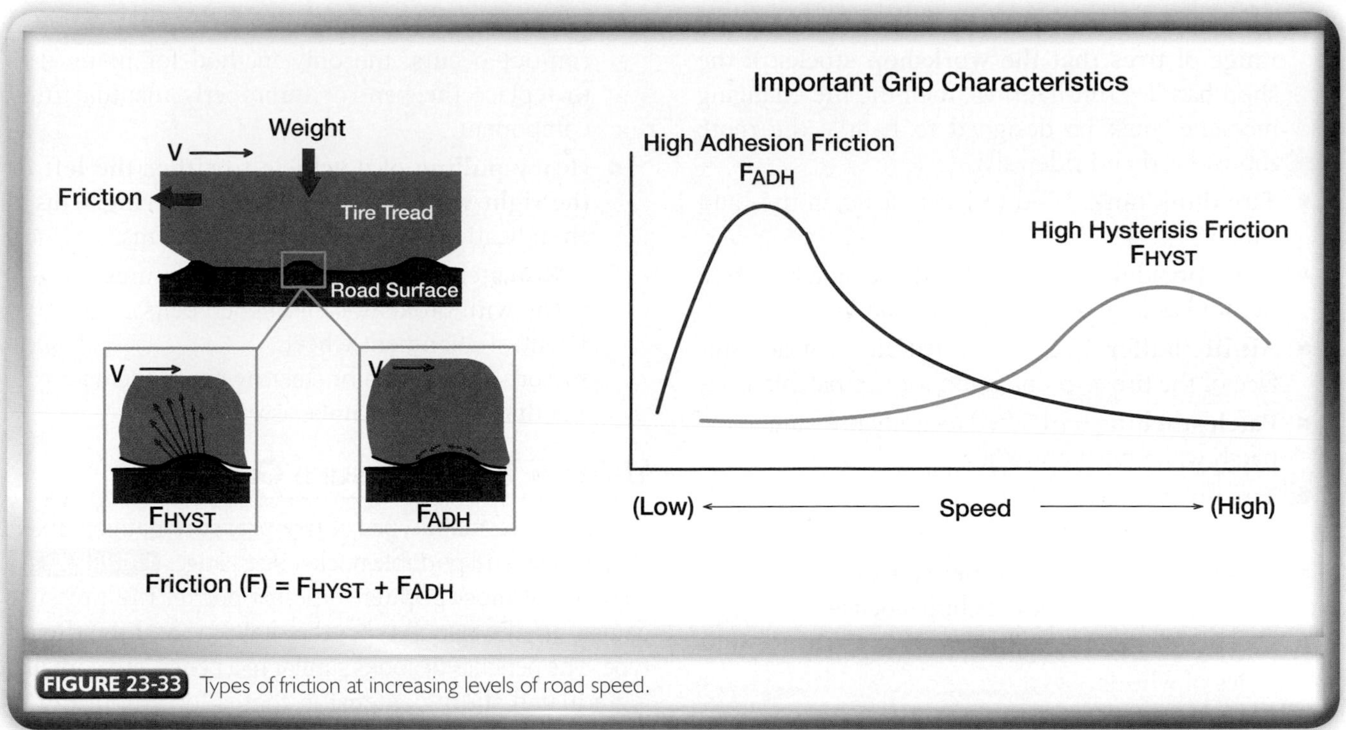

FIGURE 23-33 Types of friction at increasing levels of road speed.

The use of fuel efficient tires on all axle positions can make a significant impact on fuel consumption. A 10% reduction in rolling resistance results in approximately 3% reduced fuel consumption. This means consumption drops approximately 0.2 gallons/62 miles (0.9 liters/100 km) on a vehicle that consumes 8 gallons/62 miles (30 liters/100 km).

Changing tires can produce incorrect speedometer readings and influence fuel economy because tire revolutions per mile (rpm) may no longer be correct. Even tires with the same labeling, when supplied by different manufacturers or using different types of tread, will have different rolling circumferences. A number of electronic control modules also depend on accurate tire sizes—the ABS, traction control, engine, instrument cluster, and so on. Changing tire sizes more than 3% generally requires changing axle ratios to ensure the engine torque curves are properly matched with vehicle speed, too. After changing tires or electronic control modules, tire size or rpm may need to be reset. To properly determine tire rpm, tire suppliers should provide accurate information. Without this data, the tires rolling circumference can be divided by the number 63,360 to determine rpm. Dual inline package (DIP) switches on a speedometer are often used to change tire rpm stored in the speedometer memory. Newer vehicles only require software to modify the calculation performed by the engine or ABS module to convert pulses per mile (or kilometer) of the speed sensor to a vehicle speed displayed by the speedometer.

Maintenance and Service of Commercial Tires

Tires are one of the most maintenance-intensive parts of a vehicle. They require regular visual inspections, pressure inspections and rotations. Visual inspections of the tires and wheels should be made whenever a vehicle comes into a workshop for any work. It is common to check for any unusual wear patterns and for any embedded objects or other signs of damage. If the vehicle is not equipped with a TPMS, then the operator should be encouraged to check the pressure at least monthly. Another task is rotating the tires. Most manufacturers recommend that the tires be rotated at each oil change to even out the wear and extend the life of the tires.Research the vehicle and service information for more information.

Tools

To service wheels and tires in an efficient manner, you must have the appropriate tools and equipment. The basic equipment list should consist of:

- **Tire pressure gauge:** Used to check the air pressure in tires
- **Tread depth gauge:** Used to measure a tire's tread depth
- **Valve stem tool:** Used to remove and install tubeless valve stems in rims
- **Valve core tool:** Used to remove and install valve cores in valve stems

- **Tire-changing machine capable of handling the range of tires that the workshop stocks:** If the shop handles run-flat tires, then the tire-changing machine must be designed to handle the more robust bead and sidewalls.
- **Tire dunk tank:** Used to locate leaks in tires and rims
- **Tire spreader:** Used to spread the sidewalls of a tire for easier access during tire patching
- **Air tire buffer:** Used to lightly buff the inside surface of the tire as preparation for tire patching
- **Patch stitching tool:** Used to apply pressure to the patch when positioning it
- **Tire inflation cage:** Used to contain the tire and rim during tire inflation in the event of a tire explosion
- **Wheel balancing machine:** capable of handling the range of tires that the shop stocks
- **Variety of wheel weight styles** to cover the various styles of wheels
- **Wheel weight hammer:** Used to remove and install wheel weights onto rims
- **TPMS reset tool:** Used to reset the TPMS (not required on all TPMS-equipped vehicles)

Common Issues

Common tire and wheel issues include:

- **Air loss:** The most common issue with tires is air loss. Tires normally lose a small amount of air over time and require periodic refilling. Punctures occur that cause leaks of various sizes. Valve stems and tire beads can also allow air to leak from the tire.
- **An out-of-balance tire or wheel:** The wheel and tires should be balanced, with the weight equally distributed throughout. When a tire rotates, any points of unequal weight will cause the tire to wobble, placing stress on the shocks, bearings, and wheel assembly. Additionally, the vehicle will vibrate at speeds of about 50 to 60 kph and above, it will have a rough ride, and the steering wheel may vibrate. A wheel balancer is used to identify and correct wheel imbalances.
- **Excessive loaded radial run-out on the tire, wheel and hub assembly:** With radial run-out, the tire tread moves up and down. It is caused by incorrect manufacture or by damage to the tire, such as a broken belt. Correction involves replacing the tire.
- **Excessive lateral run-out on the tire, wheel and hub assembly:** Run-out occurs when a part of the wheel assembly becomes bent or was manufactured improperly. The result is a wobble. When lateral run-out occurs, the only method for fixing it is to replace the bent or improperly manufactured component.
- **Heavy pulling of a vehicle to either the left or the right while the customer is driving:** This is an indication of these possible problems:
  - Mismatched front tire sizes or pressures
  - Tire with broken or misaligned belts
  - Out-of-alignment wheels
  - Worn suspension or steering components
  - A dragging front brake assembly

Using a Tire Pressure Gauge

There are two main types of **tire pressure gauges**: fixed shop gauges and portable pocket-size gauges FIGURE 23-34. The three most popular types of pocket tire pressure gauges are the pencil type, the dial type and the digital type. The pencil type looks similar to a pencil and contains a graduated sliding extension that is forced out of the sleeve by air pressure when it is attached to the tire valve. The dial type has a similar chuck to the pencil type but

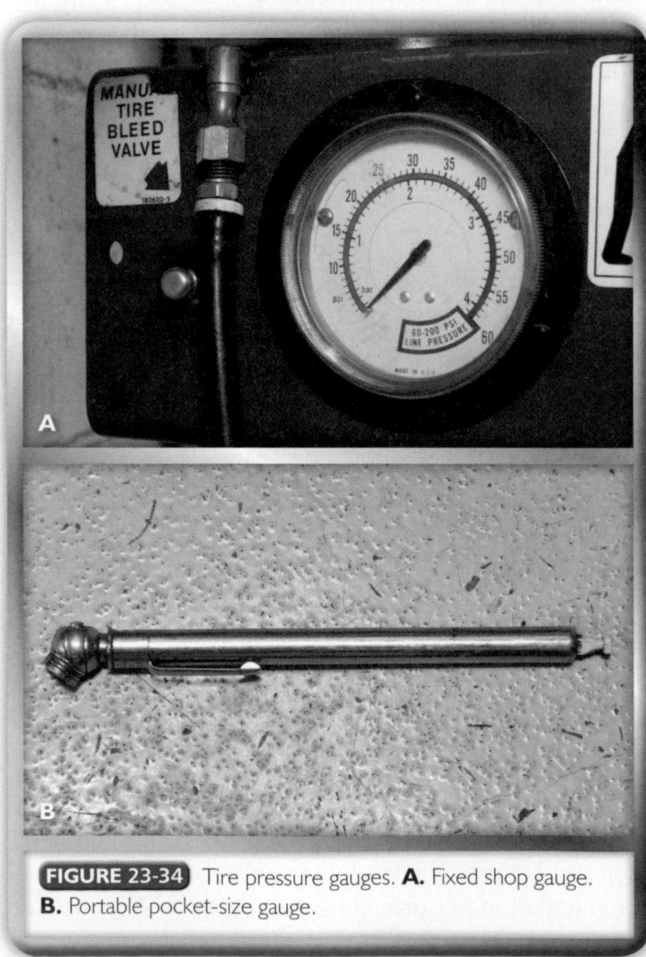

FIGURE 23-34 Tire pressure gauges. **A.** Fixed shop gauge. **B.** Portable pocket-size gauge.

includes a graduated gauge and needle. The digital type can look like any of the others, but it gives a digital reading of the pressure and is generally the most accurate. Some digital pressure gauges can also read the temperature.

Each tire pressure gauge measures pressures in kilopascals (kPa), pounds per square inch (psi) or bars. One bar is equivalent to 100 kPa or 14.5 psi. One psi is equivalent to approximately 7 kPa.

The tire pressure will vary from vehicle to vehicle, its use and driver preference. Recommended tire pressures are located on the vehicle's tire placard, usually on the driver door pillar. The maximum tire pressure is located on the tire sidewall. Never inflate the tire above the maximum pressure listed on the sidewall. The tire may explode or the wheel rim may give way and cause a blowout, which can easily be fatal.

> **TECHNICIAN TIP**
>
> A common mistake when inflating tires is to use the pressure listed on the sidewall instead of the tire placard. The pressure listed on the sidewall is the maximum pressure that the tire is designed to withstand and should never be exceeded, even when the placard lists a higher pressure! So you should always first check the placard and then verify that it is not higher than the maximum pressure listed on the sidewall. If it is, someone installed underrated tires on the vehicle.

> **TECHNICIAN TIP**
>
> If you check the tire pressures after the vehicle has been driven and the tires are warm or hot, do not release this excess pressure. If you bleed the tire pressure down to the manufacturer's recommendation, it will be underinflated when the tire is cold or at normal operating temperature. This could cause premature wear on the tires and handling issues with the vehicle. Most tire manufacturers recommend checking tire pressures before the vehicle has been driven more than 1.6 km.

> **TECHNICIAN TIP**
>
> Tire pressure should be checked when tires are cold (around 21°C). On average, the pressure in a tire will increase or decrease by about 12.5 kPa for each 2°C when the tire is above or below its normal operating temperature.

Adjusting Tire Pressure

Even brand new high-quality tires lose air over time, so tire pressure needs to be adjusted periodically. It is good practice to check tire pressure at least monthly to catch a leaking tire. Many modern vehicles are fitted with a system called TPMS, which is designed to monitor the pressures in each individual tire and alert the driver of a problem if a tire pressure is outside of the specified limits. These vehicles may have a specific tire inflation and TPMS reset procedure required by the manufacturer, so make sure you investigate that before inflating the tire.

Many tires are filled with nitrogen instead of regular air to reduce the amount of air that is lost over time as well as reduce oxidation of the rubber on the inside of the tire. It is best to fill these tires only with nitrogen to avoid introducing oxygen into the tire, but regular compressed air can be used in an emergency. Nitrogen-filled tires can usually be identified by a fluorescent green cap on the valve stem. Nitrogen-filled tires are best topped off at the manufacturer's dealership or a tire store.

To adjust the tire pressure, follow the guidelines in **SKILL DRILL 23-1**.

Checking for Tire Wear Patterns

Tires come in a wide variety of tread patterns. Patterns differ based on the manufacturer and the tire's intended purpose. For example, tires designed to wick water away from the road surface will have deep grooves angled back towards the side of the road. Racing tires will have no grooves, as the smooth tire surface grips dry road surfaces tightly, increasing friction. Regardless of the exact pattern, all four tires should be inspected regularly to ensure they are wearing evenly. Irregular wear patterns are indicative of a problem. Common irregular wear patterns encountered include feathering, one-sided wear, cupping, center wear, and edge wear.

Feathering is observed as a rib with a slightly rounded edge on one side and a sharp edge on the other. This condition can be difficult to identify visually, so the technician should run a hand across the tire in both directions, feeling for the sharp edges. Feathering is most commonly a result of the tires set with excessive toe-in or toe-out. If the tire's sharp edge is towards the outside of the treads, then the tire is toed out. If there are sharp edges towards the inside of the treads, then the tire is toed in. One-sided wear refers to ribs on one side of the tire wearing out faster than those on the other side. This type of wear indicates that the wheels are not properly aligned. Cupping is the appearance of dips around the edge of the tread, usually on just one side of the tire. It

SKILL DRILL 23-1 Checking and Adjusting the Tire Pressure

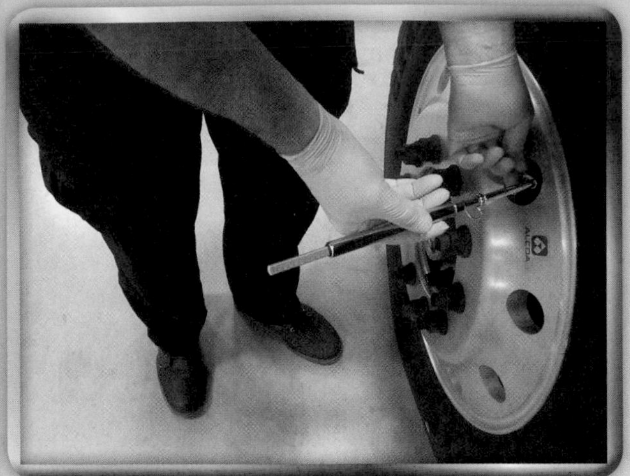

1. Park the vehicle so you can reach all tires with the air hose.
2. Check the recommended tire size and pressures on the tire placard, usually located on the driver's side door pillar or surrounding location.
3. Check the sidewall markings on the tire for the maximum operating pressure. At the same time, check the tire size and maximum load-carrying capacity of each tire, as customers sometimes install mismatched tires. If the tire markings do not meet the specifications of the vehicle, ask your supervisor for direction. Never allow a vehicle to be operated with tires that do not meet the vehicle manufacturer's specifications. Doing so can have serious safety repercussions.
4. Check the pressure when the tires are cold. Remove the cap from the valve stem on the first tire. Use a reliable tire gauge to check the air pressure in the tire. A pocket-type pencil gauge is ideal for this purpose. A gauge attached to the tire inflator is less likely to be accurate as it is more vulnerable to damage.
5. If you need to add air or nitrogen, use short bursts so you do not overinflate the tire. Recheck the tire pressure after filling it and replace the cap on the valve stem. Repeat the process for the other tires. Check the pressure in the spare tire. It may require a different amount of air pressure than the road tires.

occurs when one or more suspension parts are worn or bent. Center wear is when the ribs in the middle of the tire wear faster than those on each side. It results from driving on overinflated tires. Edge wear occurs when the ribs on the outer edges of the tire wear out faster than those in the middle of the tire (the reverse of center wear). It indicates that the vehicle has been driven with the tires consistently underinflated, or the driver regularly corners the vehicle at excessive speeds.

To check for tire wear patterns, follow the guidelines in SKILL DRILL 23-2.

Tire wear, particularly in radial-ply tires, is due to a range of reasons, which basically comes down to imbalance, incorrect inflation, or alignment issues. TABLE 23-10 shows a range of conditions and the wear signs for each condition.

Dismounting a Tire

Dismounting a truck tire is usually performed by hand with a bead breaking hammer and tire irons but can also be performed on a tire machine. These machines are very powerful, so use extreme care and closely follow the manufacturer's procedure. Tire machines are strong enough to break the bead loose from the rim as well as hold the rim while the bead is forced over the flange during removal and installation. This means the tire machine has several operations that you must become familiar with. Since different machines have different operating parameters, make sure you understand the manufacturer's specified operating procedure.

The turntable jaws on the tire changer can hold the rim by grasping it from the outside or the inside. Always

SKILL DRILL 23-2 Checking for Tire Wear Patterns

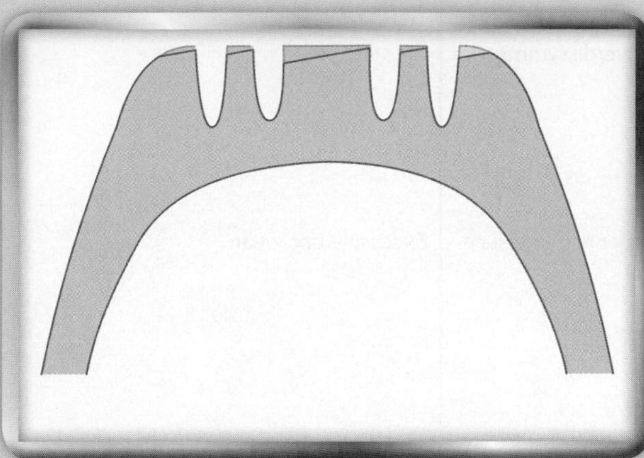

1. Inspect the tires for embedded objects in treads and remove them. If any object penetrates the tread, mark the hole with a tire crayon.
2. Look for signs of wear on all tires.
3. Check the air pressure in the tires.
4. Check the tread depth. Most tires have wear indicator bars incorporated into the tread pattern. Inspect the wear indicator bars. Front tires should have at least 4/32", (3.18 mm) while drive or trailer tires must have a minimum of 2/32", (1.59 mm). The wear indicator bars are normally set at this depth. If the tread is worn down to that level the tires are unserviceable and must be replaced.
5. Check the tread wear patterns with the vehicle's service information to indicate the types of wear that have occurred. Causes of uneven wear can include faulty shock absorbers, incorrect front alignment angles, and out-of-balance wheels. Uneven tread and bald spots can indicate over- or underinflated tires and poor alignment. Certain erratic wear patterns called river wear can show on trailer tires and are caused by unusual thrust forces that can be related to trailer axle alignment.
6. Inspect the sidewalls of the tires for signs of weather cracking and gouges from blunt objects.
7. Carefully examine the tread area for separation. This is usually identified as bubbles under the tread area.
8. Spin the wheel and see if it is running true. If it is wobbling as it rotates, report it to your supervisor.

TABLE 23-10: Ride and Wear Problems and Incorrect Tire Pressures

	Angle	Set/Condition	Result
	Toe	Excessive toe-in Excessive toe-out	Fast outside shoulder wear with feather edges pointing inside. Fast inside shoulder wear with feather edges pointing outside.
	Camber	Excessively positive Excessively negative	Fast outside shoulder wear. Fast inside shoulder wear. Pulling to the side.

Continued on next page

TABLE 23-10: Ride and Wear Problems and Incorrect Tire Pressures, continued

	Angle	Set/Condition	Result
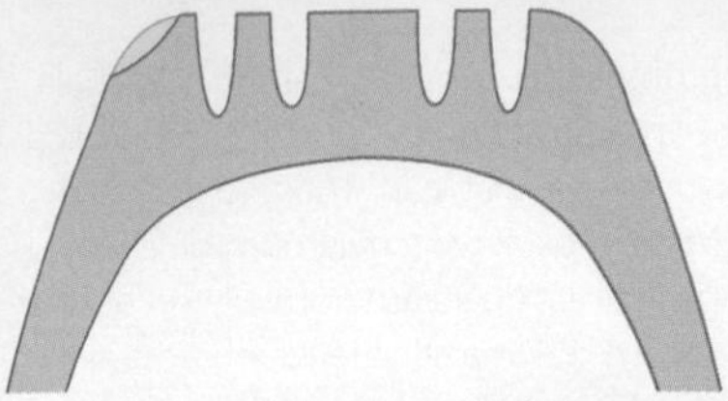	King pin offset	Positive/dissymmetric Negative/dissymmetric	Excessive tire wear.
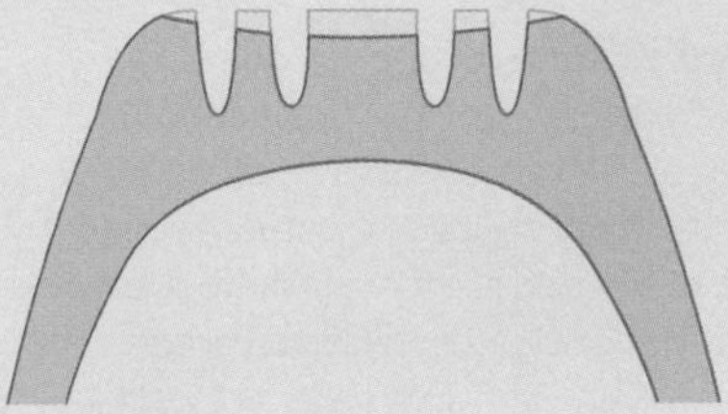	Over inflation	Incorrect tire pressure	Excessive tire wear.
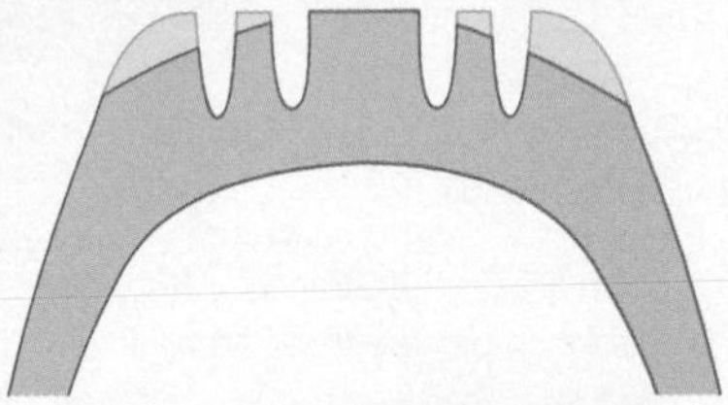	Under inflation	Incorrect tire pressure	Excessive tire wear which can lead to operational instability.
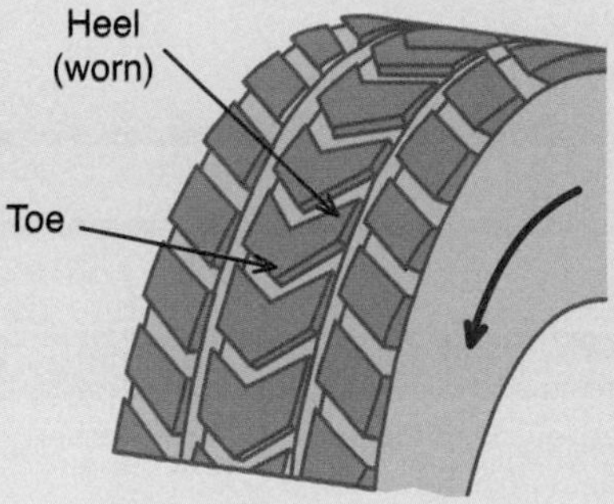 Heel (worn) Toe	Tandem rear axle parallelism	Not parallel to one another	Toe-in/toe-out type wear (different side to side).
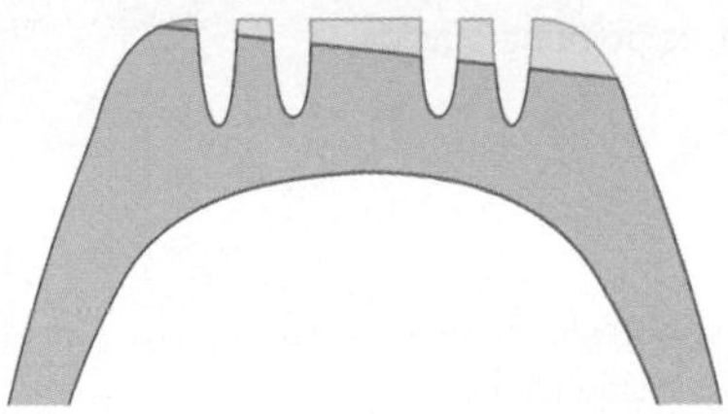	Semi trailer king pin location	Not centerd over first trailer	Tractor pulling to the side where king pin is out of center.

check the instruction manual for the tire changer you are using for the correct method of clamping a rim.

To dismount a tire (well-based rims), follow the guidelines in SKILL DRILL 23-3.

Safety

For your safety, follow these tips:

- An inflated tire is a pressure vessel that must be treated with care and respect. Always fully deflate tire before performing any repair tasks.
- Keep your hands clear of the bead breaker when it is operating. It applies great force to the tire will cause you a severe injury if your hand is trapped.
- Always use correct lifting techniques when lifting a tire on and off the tire changer and vehicle.
- The tire tread comes in contact with many unknown substances that are transferred directly to your hands. For this reason, it is recommended that you wear protective gloves when handling tires. If you do not wear gloves, wash your hands after the tire change is complete.

General Safety Precautions for Working on Heavy-Duty Wheels and Tires

It is important that you understand that every task performed on wheels presents a possible danger. As such, all the relevant safety precautions should be followed at all times:

1. Damaged tires should always be deflated before working on any other task. This can be done by removing the valve core.
2. Make sure that the tire is completely deflated before trying to remove it from the rim.
3. Always make sure that no damage occurs to any locking rings or flanges during the removal process.
4. All locking rings and flanges should be cleaned and inspected for damage.
5. Any damaged parts must be replaced before reassembly.
6. Tires should always be thoroughly inspected for damage.
7. Make sure that the correct size and type of tube, flanges and locking rings are used when assembling the wheel and tire.
8. Make sure that you use an approved tire bead lubricant.
9. Make sure that flanges and locking ring are in the correct position before inflating the wheel.
10. Always inflate the tire to the manufacturer's recommended pressure.
11. Use a safety cage when inflating a tire to the specified pressure and observe all safety precautions.
12. Always make sure that equipment used to undertake these tasks is inspected and calibrated regularly.

To remove a tire from a wheel rim (tubeless), follow the guidelines in SKILL DRILL 23-4.

To fit a tire to a wheel rim (tubeless), follow the guidelines in SKILL DRILL 23-5.

TECHNICIAN TIP

Always remove any balance weights from both sides of the rim before mounting it on the tire changer. If they are not removed, the bead remover could drag the weights around the rim, causing damage to the rim face. This is particularly important with alloy rims. The damage done by the balance weights is not repairable and usually requires the rim to be replaced, costing the shop a lot of money.

Replacing a Valve Stem

Valve stems come in a few styles, including screw-in valve stems and TPMS sensor–integrated valve stems. Screw-in valve stems normally are not replaced, but may have rubber washers or O-rings that may require replacement

SKILL DRILL 23-3 Dismounting a Tire (Well-Based Rims)

1. Before removing the tire, check to see whether the wheel is equipped with a TPMS sensor. If it is, there will be special procedures to follow during the tire replacement process. Follow the vehicle manufacturer's guidelines to avoid damaging the TPMS sensor.
2. Inspect the tread and sidewalls for barbs or pieces of steel belt that may injure you. Also inspect the tire for any obvious signs of damage. If there is any damage, the tire should be discarded.
3. Check the wheel for any balance weights, and pry them off with the wheel weight tool.
4. Locate the valve stem, unscrew the dust cap, and store it for later use.
5. Using the valve core tool, unscrew the valve core. Remember that compressed air inside the tire can cause the core to be shot like a bottle rocket if you do not hold onto it firmly, so make sure the valve stem is pointing away from your face. Also, since the air in the tire is undergoing a pressure drop as it leaves the valve stem, moisture in the airstream can form ice in the valve stem, which can become a projectile.
6. Once all the air has been removed from the tire, locate the wheel in the **bead breaker** with the outside of the rim facing towards the blade. Locate the blade close to the edge of the rim while keeping your hands at a safe distance.
7. Activate the bead breaker, which will force the tire bead away from the edge of the rim and over the safety ridge.
8. Release the blade, turn the wheel one-third to one-half of a turn, reposition the blade, and release this section of the tire as well.
9. Release the blade, roll the tire away from the machine, and reposition it with the inside of the rim facing towards the blade.
10. Set the wheel on the turntable with the shallow dish side of the wheel facing up. This will allow the drop center to be as high as possible, which will make it much easier to remove the tire. Failure to position the rim so the drop center is as high as possible will make it unlikely that you will be able to remove the tire, and will likely damage the bead of the tire permanently.
11. Position the wheel and tire assembly on the turntable and activate the jaws so the wheel is held firmly and centerd in the jaws. Activate the turntable to verify that the wheel is centerd and securely held.
12. Lubricate the top bead with tire lubricant. Make sure you get the lube on the flat bead seat, not just the side of the bead.
13. Position the bead remover against the edge of the rim; if necessary, adjust it so it has the proper clearance between the rim and the roller.
14. Use the tire lever to pry the tire bead over the bead remover knuckle, and, at the same time, push down on the sidewall on the opposite side of the tire.
15. Activate the turntable so the bead is guided off the rim.
16. Guide the lower bead into the drop center, and, using the tire lever, pry the lower bead over the knuckle and activate the turntable. The tire will come off the rim. If replacing the tire with a new one, remove the valve stem by either unscrewing it or using a valve stem tool, and discard the valve stem.

SKILL DRILL 23-4 Removing a Tire from a Wheel Rim (Tubeless)

1. Deflate the tire and loosen the bead by hammering at points close to the rim with a bead hammer.
2. Apply lubricant to the top of the bead on the open side and insert two tire irons at a distance of about 25 cm apart.
3. With one tire iron in position, pull the other one towards the center of the rim while standing on the wheel.
4. Use the first tire iron to lift the bead over the rim while holding the second tire iron in position by foot. Repeat this procedure until the top bead is completely removed.
5. Stand the tire vertically and apply tire lubricant on the second bead.
6. Insert a tire iron between the tire and rim at 45 degrees to the rim, and pry the bead right round until it is completely out.

SKILL DRILL 23-5 Fitting a Tire to a Wheel Rim (Tubeless)

1. Inspect the bead seats on the wheel rim to ensure that the bead will seat properly. Place the rim on the floor with the wider side at the bottom, ensuring that the seats are clean and free from dirt.
2. Lubricate the first bead of the tire and the upper seat of the rim and push the first bead into the wheel rim as far down as possible. The remaining section of the bead must be pushed into position using a tire iron.
3. Fit part of the second bead to the rim and use vice grips to hold it in place. Be sure not to damage the rim with the vice grips.
4. Fit the rest of the tire onto the rim and apply the recommended lubricant to the beads as required.
5. With the valve core still removed, place the wheel and tire assembly into a cage and inflate the tire to seat the beads. Then install the valve core and complete inflation according to manufacturer's recommendations.

when new tires are installed. TPMS-integrated valve stems may be made as part of the valve stem or may screw onto, or snap into, the valve stem, which is replaceable. It is important to know if the TPMS sensor is connected to the valve stem or not so you do not damage it during service and repair. Many TPMS valve stems have valve cores with coated threads and should not be replaced with non-coated threads. They should always be torqued with a valve core torque wrench.

To change the valve stem, the wheel must be removed from the vehicle. The tire is then deflated and the top bead broken. The tire is reassembled and inflated to the recommended pressure. Spray some soapy water around the valve stem and core to detect air leaks.

The nut on the valve stem is then unscrewed and the stem is removed from the inside of the rim. The old sealing washers can be replaced with new ones. Then the valve stem can be reinstalled in the rim. In some cases only the valve stem core requires replacement. In this case, the old core is screwed out and the new core is installed and the tire pressure readjusted to vehicle specifications.

To replace a screw-in valve stem, follow the guidelines in SKILL DRILL 23-6.

Mounting a Tire

Always check the instruction manual for the tire machine you are using for the correct method of clamping a rim, if that's the method to be used.

Inflating a tire for the first time is always dangerous. All tires should be inflated inside of a tire cage. Doing so contains any pieces if the tire blows up while being inflated. Always follow the manufacturer's guidelines and shop policies when inflating a newly installed tire.

TECHNICIAN TIP

Most tire changers dismount and mount the tire by turning the turntable clockwise. This is especially helpful to know so you position the tire on the turntable correctly to mount and dismount tires equipped with a TPMS.

Safety

Overinflated tires can explode. Do not inflate the tire to a pressure greater than what is listed on the sidewall. The possibility of an explosion is why tire inflators have a spring-loaded (dead man's) trigger that does not lock into position. When the tire is being inflated, use a tire cage if required, or an inflator that allows you to stand clear of the tire. Keep hands and body well away from the tire. When a tire explodes, the tire, rim or components from the tire changer may cause serious injury or death to any person nearby.

SKILL DRILL 23-6 Replacing a Screw-in Valve Stem

1. If the valve stem is a screw-in valve stem, remove the wheel from the vehicle, deflate the tire, break the top bead using the tire machine, and mount the wheel on the tire machine.
2. Unscrew the nut that holds the valve stem to the rim. Remove the valve stem from the inside of the rim.
3. Discard the old sealing washers and replace them with new ones. Place the valve stem with one new sealing washer through the hole on the inside of the rim.
4. Place a new sealing washer over the valve stem and thread the nut on by hand. Tighten the nut to the specified torque.

Dynamic Balancing a Tire

A tire that is dynamically in balance is in balance when it is spinning as opposed to when it is stationary. Dynamic imbalance occurs when a spot on either the inside or the outside of the tire's centerline is heavy. This induces a side-to-side imbalance in the tire as it rotates, which can cause a vibration as well as the steering wheel to shimmy. Dynamic imbalance is usually a result of manufacturing variations, but it can be caused by a damaged tire or wheel. Obviously, dynamic imbalance reduces ride quality and tends to increase wear on the tires and on steering and suspension system components. Dynamic balancing of the tires should be performed when new tires are installed on the vehicle as well as any time that tire imbalance is suspected.

Dynamic balancing is performed on a tire balancer that is capable of spinning the tire and then measuring the location of any dynamic imbalance. Some balancers are spun at low speed, but others are driven by the balancer at higher speeds. If the tire is spun by the balancer, embedded objects may fly off the tire, so it is important to wear safety glasses. If the wheel balancer is fitted with a safety hood, ensure that it is in place when the wheel is being rotated to further protect against flying objects.

All wheels require one of several specific designs of wheel weights. If the weights fitted to the wheel are not the correct type, they can fly off when the vehicle is driven down the road, causing possible injury or damage. It is good practice to use new wheel weights when balancing a wheel for the same reason. If the vehicle has directional tires, ensure that the wheels are reinstalled in their correct position when balancing is complete.

To balance a tire, follow the guidelines in SKILL DRILL 23-7.

SKILL DRILL 23-7 Balancing a Tire

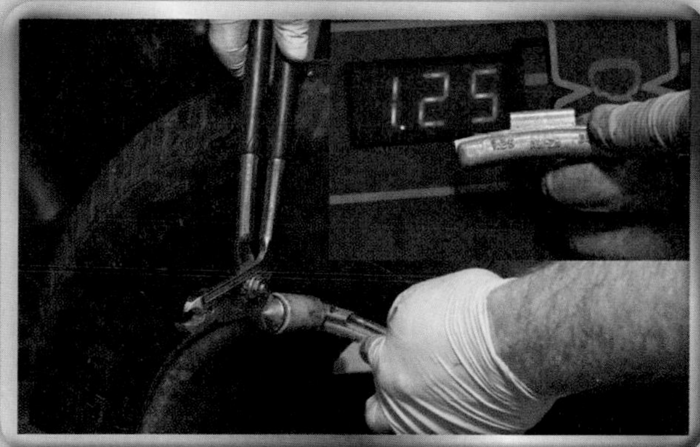

1. If using hand tools, prepare the vehicle by loosening the wheel nuts, and then raise the vehicle into a comfortable working position.
2. Check that the tires fitted to the wheels on the vehicle are the appropriate size and rating for the vehicle, as listed on the tire placard. In most cases, the vehicle should have four completely matched tires. At the very least, the front tires should match each other and the rear tires should match each other.
3. Mark the inside of the wheel or tire in relation to its location on the vehicle and then remove it. This is so that it can be reinstalled in the same position on the vehicle.
4. Check and adjust the tire pressure before balancing the tire.
5. Mount the wheel and tire on the balancer, putting the inside part of the wheel towards the balancer in most cases. Secure the wheel by screwing the hub nut assembly on the balancer shaft.
6. Calibrate the balancer to the wheel by measuring the width of the rim with a rim caliper, using the gauge on the balancer to determine the location of the flange on the wheel (offset), and the diameter of the wheel as listed on the tire.
7. Input this data into the balancer's computer, if fitted, according to the manufacturer's instruction manual. If no computer is fitted, set the balancer adjustments manually according to the instruction manual.
8. If equipped, lower the safety hood over the wheel.
9. Spin the wheel. Read the balancer's analysis, which is normally displayed visually on the machine. It tells you whether the wheel is out of balance and, if so, how much weight to use and where to put it to balance the wheel. If the wheel is out of balance, you should remove the old weights and recheck the balance of the wheel before adding new weights.
10. Install new weights recommended by the machine's display, usually by hammering them onto the edge of the rim where indicated, although some are held in place by tape on the back side of the weight.
11. Now re-spin the wheel to check for accuracy of the balancing job and to confirm that balance has been achieved. A reading of zero on both sides of the wheel means the wheel is ready to reinstall on the vehicle. Repeat the process for the rest of the wheels and tires.
12. Reinstall the wheels and tires to the vehicle, remembering to lower the vehicle just enough so the tires will be held in place while torquing the wheel nuts to the correct specification and in the correct sequence.

To perform on-vehicle wheel balancing, follow the guidelines in SKILL DRILL 23-8.

Inspecting the Wheel Assembly for Air Loss

One of the most frustrating complaints from drivers is that they constantly have to pump their tires up as the result of an air loss somewhere. To efficiently check the suspect tire, it must be removed from the vehicle and aired up to its recommended pressure. A preliminary check can be carried out with a spray bottle of soapy water. You need to spray the soapy water around the valve stem and core. In addition, spray around the bead area. Also spray the entire tread area. If there is any air leakage, soapy air bubbles will indicate where the problem is. Mark the tire where the air bubbles are coming from so that the repairs can be carried out.

To inspect the wheel assembly for air loss using the spray bottle method, follow the guidelines in SKILL DRILL 23-9.

Tire Diagnosis

Tire Repair

Driving a short distance on a tire while it is severely underinflated will cause the tire to overheat as well as weaken the sidewall belts, creating a dangerous, non-repairable condition. The damage is not visible from the outside, so every tire needing repairs must be removed from the wheel for inspection and to assess its repairability. The tire needs to be inspected externally first, then internally for any signs of serious damage, such

SKILL DRILL 23-8 Performing On-Vehicle Wheel Balancing

1. Always refer to the wheel balancing machine manufacturer's instruction manual.
2. Obtain the necessary tools and equipment as per the manufacturer's recommendations. Ensure that both equipment and associated tools are in good condition.
3. Raise the vehicle and position the balancer against the wheel so that the center of the balancer drive drum is on the tire's shoulder.
4. Position the electronic sensor as close as possible to the king pin on the inside of the axle.
5. Commence the actual wheel balancing by following the manufacturer's instructions and activating the balancer.
6. Once the wheel is rotating at the desired speed, disconnect the balancer drive drum from the wheel as per the method recommended by the balancer manufacturer.
7. Push the balancer flash button and move the machine away from the wheel. When the button is replaced, the stroboscopic flashes are stopped and balance values will be automatically shown on the balancer's display.
8. Attach the appropriate weight vertically above the center of the wheel as per the balancer instructions.
9. Repeat steps 5 through 7 to ensure that the wheel is properly balanced.
10. Disconnect and remove the balancing equipment.

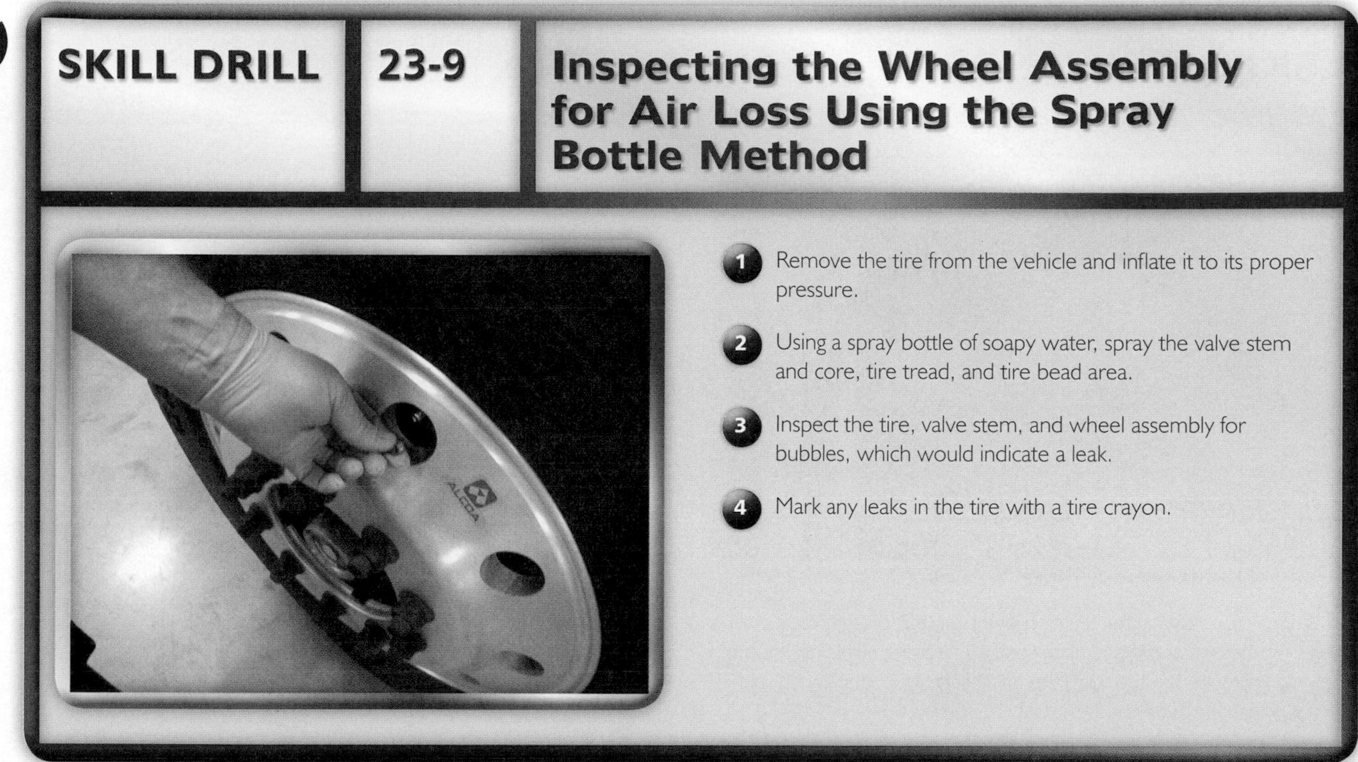

SKILL DRILL 23-9 Inspecting the Wheel Assembly for Air Loss Using the Spray Bottle Method

1. Remove the tire from the vehicle and inflate it to its proper pressure.
2. Using a spray bottle of soapy water, spray the valve stem and core, tire tread, and tire bead area.
3. Inspect the tire, valve stem, and wheel assembly for bubbles, which would indicate a leak.
4. Mark any leaks in the tire with a tire crayon.

as chaffing of the sidewalls or cords sticking through the inner liner. If the inspection shows no signs of non-repairable failure, then the tire can be repaired in accordance with the procedures recommended by the tire associations.

- Repairs from any nail or similar object should be limited to the actual tread area. Among the criteria to perform a proper repair are:
- Repairs are limited to the tread area only.
- Puncture injury cannot be greater than 6 mm in diameter.
- Repairs must be performed by removing the tire from the rim/wheel assembly to perform a complete inspection to assess all damage that may be present.
- Repairs cannot overlap. This means that if there are two or more repairs required to fix the tire, then each repair patch must not overlap.
- A rubber stem, or plug, must be applied to fill the puncture injury, and a patch must be applied to seal the inner liner. A common repair unit is a one-piece unit with a stem and patch portion. A plug by itself is an unacceptable repair.

To patch a tire, you will need a tire machine to remove the tire from the wheel, a buffer to clean the inside of the tire, glue for attaching the patch and a tire plug patch. The tire plug patch is a superior product to the old-fashioned tire plug, and, in many places, it is the only legal way to repair a hole in a tire. It is more expensive but is a much safer alternative for repairing a tire because it patches the inside of the tire in addition to filling the hole in the tire.

To patch a tire, follow the guidelines in SKILL DRILL 23-10.

Measuring Wheel, Tire, and Hub Flange Run-out

Run-out is the side-to-side or up-and-down variation in a art in the wheel assembly. In many cases, run-out issues cannot be observed when the vehicle is stationary on the ground. Instead, run-out problems can be felt as a vibration while the vehicle is being driven, usually getting more noticeable as speed is increased. If the vibration is primarily observed in the steering column or bonnet, the run-out is most likely in one or both of the front wheel assemblies.

SKILL DRILL 23-10 Patching a Tire

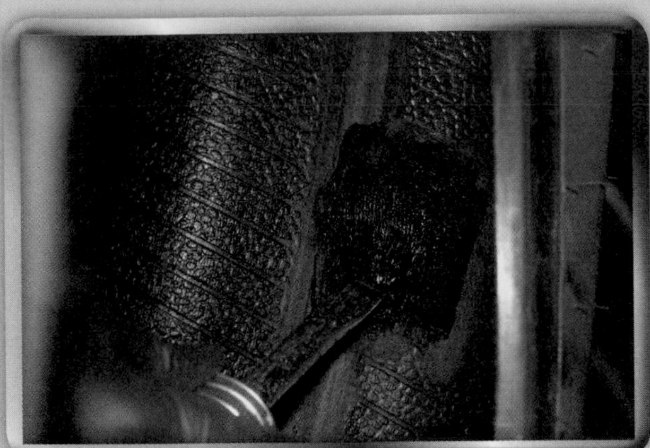

1. After marking the location of the air leak on the tread of the tire, and the position of the tire and weights on the rim, remove the tire from the rim assembly so that an internal patch can be used to rectify the problem.
2. Mount the tire in a tire spreader so that the hole can be accessed from both the inside and the outside of the tire.
3. Use an air die grinder with a pointy bit that matches the plug patch, and drill into the tire where the leak was located. This will roughen up the sides and make a cleaner hole for where the patch will be installed.
4. Use a tire buffer to smooth the area inside the tire around the hole. Smooth the area approximately 13 mm beyond the expected patch area.
5. After completing the buffing process, clean out all the accumulated debris. A vacuum works well for this.
6. Liberally apply the liquid buffing solution to a clean rag and scrub the area just buffed. Some patching systems use a liquid cleaner that is applied to the tire and scraped off with a scraper. Repeat this step once or twice, as needed.
7. Apply vulcanizing cement evenly to the inner buffed surface of the tire, and work it down into the hole. Doing so will prevent water from entering the hole and moving its way into the tire's tread. As with most contact-type cements, it needs to stand until the cement is relatively dry and is only tacky to touch.
8. After selecting the appropriate tire patch, remove the plastic protective cover that is on the sticky side of the tire patch without getting your fingerprints on the sticky side.
9. Take the pointed part of the patch and push it through the inner side of the tire's hole that was roughed previously, pushing it through to the outside of the tire.
10. Using a pair of pliers, grip the stem of the patch and pull it out so that the disc portion of the patch comes into contact with the cemented area. Pull this pointy part of the patch away from the tire's tread. The sticky side of the patch has now been tightly pressed onto the buffed surface.
11. Use a stitching tool and roll the inner side of the tire patch tight onto the inner surface of the tire. Start at the center of the patch and work outwards. This will remove any air bubbles from between the sticky side of the patch and the buffed surface. The patch is now installed properly onto the tire. It is a good practice to cover the buffed area and newly applied patch with a rubber patch sealant. Doing so will ensure a long-term, airtight repair. Trim the plug material even using a utility knife or other appropriate cutting tool.
12. After the rubber patch sealant has dried, the tire can be reassembled onto the rim in its original position and inflated to the recommended pressure. Check the wheel assembly for balance before it is reinstalled on the vehicle.

Vibration felt throughout the entire vehicle suggests that the problem is with one or both of the back wheels.

Run-out can be defined as radial or lateral. Radial run-out occurs when the component is out-of-round or off-center and is felt more as a vertical vibration. Lateral run-out occurs when the component is bent or improperly manufactured and causes the wheels to wobble side to side, creating a horizontal vibration that feels like a shimmy. Lateral run-out is felt in the steering wheel even at slower speeds.

To measure tire run-out, follow the guidelines in SKILL DRILL 23-11.

SKILL DRILL 23-11 Measuring Tire Run-Out

1. Research the procedure and specifications for measuring tire run-out in the service information. Raise the vehicle on a hoist or place a jack under the vehicle at a suitable lifting point and raise the vehicle. If using a jack, be sure to place safety stands under the frame of the vehicle and slowly lower the vehicle onto the stand.
2. Select the run-out gauge or dial indicator, attachment and bracket that fit the tire.
3. Mount the dial indicator on a firm surface to keep it still.
4. Adjust the dial indicator so the plunger is 90 degrees to the tread of the tire.
5. Press the dial indicator gently against the tire and rotate the tire one full turn. Keep pressing until the plunger settles about halfway into the indicator.
6. Verify that the plunger is still 90 degrees to the tire and lock the indicator assembly into position.
7. Carefully rotate the tire a couple of times while observing the dial readings. If the pointer hovers around a single graduation on the dial, the part has minimal run-out or surface distortion and the test is complete. If the pointer moves significantly left and right, note the variations.
8. Find the point of maximum movement to the left and move the dial so that zero is over this point.
9. Continue to rotate the tire. Find the point of maximum movement to the right and note the reading. This measure indicates the run-out value. Confirm this value by rotating the tire several more times to verify the zero point and high point. The result will be the radial run-out measurement for the tire.
10. Compare these values with the manufacturer's specifications. If the deviation is greater than the specifications, the wheel and/or hub run-out must be measured.

To measure wheel run-out, follow the guidelines in SKILL DRILL 23-12.

To measure axle or hub flange run-out, follow the guidelines in SKILL DRILL 23-13.

Inspecting, Diagnosing, and Calibrating the TPMS

Inspection, diagnosis, and calibration of the TPMS is required in several general situations. Inspection is needed whenever the tires have been dismounted from the wheels. In some cases, the TPMS sensor batteries need to be replaced and the sensor mounts need to be inspected. Diagnosis of system faults is required when the system detects a fault and turns on the warning light. This could be caused by one or more tires that are not at the proper pressure, requiring an inspection for leaks or incorrect pressures, or it could be a system fault requiring a scan tool capable of communicating with the TPMS. Calibration of the system is needed on some systems whenever a tire rotation is performed or a sensor is replaced so that the TPMS knows on which wheel each sensor is located.

To inspect, diagnose and calibrate the TPMS, follow the guidelines in SKILL DRILL 23-14.

SKILL DRILL 23-12 Measuring Wheel Run-Out

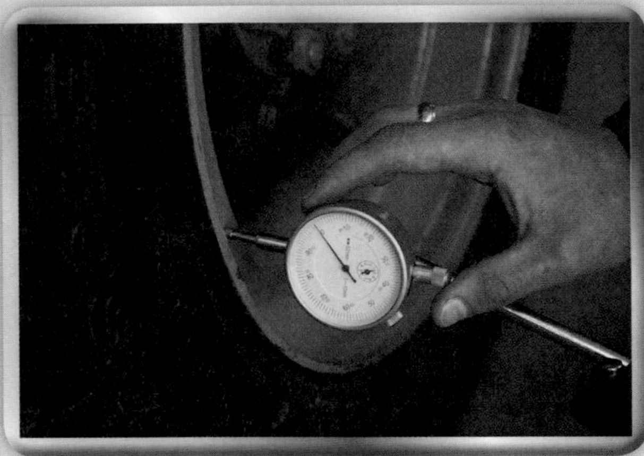

1. If equipped, remove the hubcap, mark the position of any wheel weights, and use a wheel weight tool to remove any wheel weights.
2. Select the run-out gauge or dial indicator, attachment, and bracket that fit the wheel. Mount the dial indicator on a firm surface to keep it still. Adjust the dial indicator so the plunger is 90 degrees to the flat portion of the wheel where the wheel weights are installed.
3. Press the dial indicator gently against the wheel and rotate the wheel one full turn. Keep pressing until the plunger settles about halfway into the indicator. Verify that the plunger is still 90 degrees to the wheel and lock the indicator assembly into position.
4. Carefully rotate the wheel a couple of times while observing the dial readings. If the pointer hovers around a single graduation on the dial, the wheel has minimal run-out or surface distortion and the test is complete. If the pointer moves significantly left and right, note the variations.
5. Find the point of maximum movement to the left and move the dial so that zero is over this point.
6. Continue to rotate the wheel. Find the point of maximum movement to the right and note the reading. This measure indicates the run-out value. Confirm this value by rotating the wheel several more times to verify the zero point and high point. The result will be the lateral run-out measurement for the wheel.
7. Compare these values with the manufacturer's specifications. If the deviation is greater than the specifications, the hub flange run-out must be measured to determine if the wheel or the hub is the problem.

SKILL DRILL 23-13 Measuring Hub Flange Run-Out

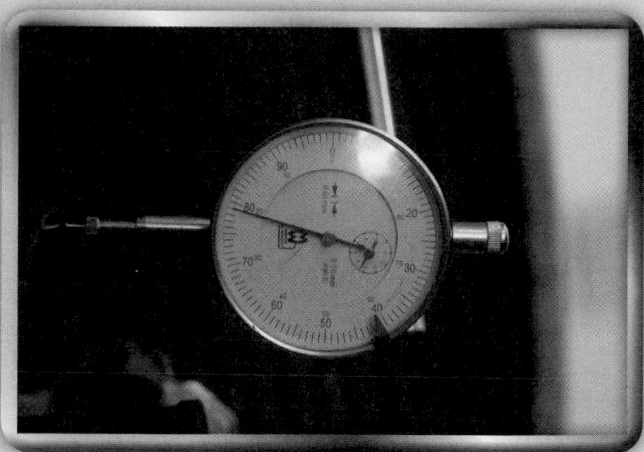

1. Research the procedure and specifications for measuring run-out in the service information.
2. Raise the vehicle on a hoist or place a jack under the vehicle at a suitable lifting point and raise the vehicle. If using a jack, be sure to place safety stands under the frame of the vehicle, and slowly lower the vehicle onto the stand.
3. Remove the wheel nuts and wheel.
4. Select the run-out gauge or dial indicator, and attachment, that will allow to index the hub flange. Mount the dial indicator on a firm surface to keep it still.
5. Adjust the plunger so it is 90 degrees to the hub flange.
6. Press the dial indicator gently against the flat surface of the hub and rotate it one full turn. Keep pressing until the plunger settles about halfway into the indicator.
7. Verify that the plunger is still 90 degrees to the hub and lock the indicator assembly into position. Carefully rotate the hub a couple of times while observing the dial readings.
8. If the pointer hovers around a single graduation on the dial, the hub has minimal run-out or surface distortion and the test is complete. If the pointer moves significantly left and right, note the variations.
9. Find the point of maximum movement to the left and move the dial so that zero is over this point.
10. Continue to rotate the hub. Find the point of maximum movement to the right and note the reading. This measure indicates the run-out value. Confirm this value by rotating the axle several more times to verify the zero point and high point. The result will be the lateral run-out measurement for the hub.
11. Compare these values with the manufacturer's specifications. If the deviation is greater than the specifications, the hub must be discarded.

SKILL DRILL 23-14 Inspecting, Diagnosing and Calibrating the TPMS

1. Turn the ignition key to the run position and observe the TPMS warning light. If the light indicates low tire pressure at any wheel, check the pressure of that wheel with an accurate tire pressure gauge. If incorrect, adjust the pressure using compressed air (or compressed nitrogen, if indicated). You may have to refer to a pressure chart if the tire is not approximately 21°C.
2. If the light indicates a system fault, connect an appropriate scan tool to the system and read any diagnostic trouble codes (DTCs). Since TPMS systems are not standardized, research DTCs in the appropriate service information, and follow the diagnostic steps listed to identify the cause of the fault.

Wrap-up

Ready for Review

- Tires are responsible for supporting the vehicle load, transmitting braking and traction forces to the road surface, absorbing road shock, and providing directional control of the vehicle.
- A wide variety of tires are made to provide unique operational features for specific vehicle applications.
- Inflated tires contain an enormous amount of stored energy, and serious safety precautions must be taken when working with them.
- Compressed air and debris can be released when deflating tires. While inflating tires, there is a risk of exploding tire debris and parts.
- When wheels and tires are used in an incorrect arrangement, a vehicle can become unstable in certain road conditions.
- Maintaining proper tire pressure is essential for the safety and performance of a vehicle, as well as decreasing fuel consumption, reducing CO_2 emissions, and extending tire life.
- The automated tire pressure monitoring system (TPMS) continuously monitors tire pressure to increase fuel economy and safety.
- Commercial vehicle tires are either tube or tubeless. What determines the type is how the air is sealed inside the tire.
- Tire sizes and other important data are molded into the sidewalls of tires. Different marking systems are used for new and retreaded tires.
- The lower a tire's aspect ratio, the wider the tire becomes in relation to the height of the sidewall.
- Low profile tires offer more responsive steering and tire stability due to greater lateral stability of tire sidewalls.
- The role of the belt system is to provide stability to the tread area of the tire.
- Three basic types of tire construction are bias-ply, radial-ply, and bias-belted.
- Bias-ply belt construction provides a stiffer tread and sidewall area.
- Radial tires produce less rolling resistance while providing better high-speed traction. They also have increased tread life and improved handling characteristics.
- The primary function of the inner liner is to seal air inside a tire and keep moisture out. Tread is typically made from an abrasion resistant, high grip rubber compound, formulated to combine the best traction, tire longevity, and low rolling resistance for superior fuel economy.
- The profile of tread used on a tire depends on the type of axle to which the tire is attached.
- Retreaded tires cost significantly less than the cost of a new tire (typically 40% of the cost of new); they are widely used in commercial fleet operations.
- Tires can be retreaded using a hot curing or cold curing method.
- Retreaded tires do not fail at higher rates than OEM tires; the failure rates are comparable.
- The depth of tire tread grooves is mandated by Federal Motor Vehicle Safety Standard 119.
- Manufacturers include wear bars around the circumference of the tire to enable technicians to determine how much tread groove depth remains.
- Regroovable tires are manufactured to extend the tire tread life and have adequately thick tread compound between the bottom of the original tread grooves and the top of the uppermost breaker or belt depth.
- Maintaining the correct tire pressure for a commercial vehicle is an important factor determining the load its tires can safely carry.
- Too much or too little tire pressure can cause catastrophic failure, and the combination of mechanical stress and heat build-up eventually lead to premature deterioration and failure.
- Nitrogen-filled tires can reduce tire leakage and rolling resistance, but properly fitted tires filled with filter-conditioned shop air can achieve the same benefits as nitrogen fill.
- Loss of energy through hysteresis accounts for approximately 90% of energy losses through rolling resistance. The remaining 10% energy loss takes place in the tread as the tire tread is deformed by road surface irregularities.

Vocabulary Builder

aspect ratio The ratio of sidewall height to section width of a tire.

bead breaker A tool used to break the tire bead seal from the rim.

bias-ply tire A tire constructed in a latticed, criss-crossing structure, with alternate plies crossing over each other and laid with the cord angles in opposite directions.

centrifugal switch A switch that is only activated when centrifugal forces are placed on a vehicle.

cold curing A retreading process that uses a molded, pre-cured tread strip or tread ring, which is glued to the casing.

contact patch The area of the tire that is in actual contact with the road.

direct tire pressure monitoring system (direct TPMS) A type of automated tire pressure monitoring system that measures tire pressure and possibly temperature via a sensor installed inside each wheel.

drop-center wheel rim A type of wheel rim that fits over the brake drum and is concave.

floatation tire Large tire with a low aspect ratio. Also called *wide-base tire*.

hot curing A retreading process in which the casing is covered with uncured rubber and then placed in a mold and heated. Also called *mold curing*.

indirect tire pressure monitoring system (indirect TPMS) A type of automated tire pressure monitoring system that uses the anti-lock braking system of a vehicle to measure the difference in the rotational speed of the four wheels to determine tire pressure.

low profile tire A type of tire that has a shorter sidewall height than conventional tires.

match mounting The process of matching up the tire's highest point with the rim's lowest point for the purpose of reducing the tire's radial run-out.

nominal diameter A size code figure, for reference purposes only, as indicated in the tire and rim size designation.

overall diameter The diameter of an inflated tire at the outermost surface of the tread.

radial placed belt A tire construction with belts placed at 90 degrees to the tire centerline and wrapped from side to side around the tire beads.

radial-ply tire A tire with two or more layers of casing plies and cord loops running radially from bead to bead.

regrooving A process that uses a heated cutting tool to carve new tread or add stripes to a tire.

retreading The process of applying new tread to an existing tire casing as a way to extend the service life of the tire.

rolling circumference The distance covered by one revolution of the tire.

rolling resistance The tendency of a tire to resist rolling along naturally when under load.

section height The height of the sidewalls.

section width The distance between the outside of the sidewalls on an inflated tire without any load on it.

static radius The distance from the tire center to ground level.

super single tire Wide-base low profile tire used to replace two conventional single tires on an axle to save weight and reduce wheel end parts.

tire bead Steel wire wound together to form a cable; when bundled together, they sit at the wheel rim to form an airtight seal between the tire and the rim.

tire casing The foundational body of the tire, consisting of several layers of fabric cord, called plies, encased with a rubber compound; a network of cords that give the tire shape and strength; also known as casing cords.

tire flap A piece of rubber that wraps around the rim to protect the inner tube from chafing, pinching, and cracking caused by friction between the valve stem slot in the rim and the edges of the tire bead.

tire inflation pressure The level of air in the tire that provides it with load-carrying capacity and which affects overall vehicle performance.

tire pressure gauge A gauge used to measure the air pressure within a tire.

tire pressure monitoring systems (TPMS) A system within wheel sensors that monitors tire inflation pressure and temperature.

tire tread separation The separation of the tread from the tire casing.

tread A cap of molded rubber compound attached to the top of a tire's belt system.

tubeless tire A tire in which the air is not sealed in an inner tube.

tube-type tire A tire in which an inner tube containing the air is separate from the casing.

undertread The depth of the area between the bottom of the original tread grooves and the top of the uppermost breaker.

weight matching The process of matching the tire's lightest point with the rim's heaviest point (generally at the valve stem) for the purpose of reducing the tire's radial imbalance.

wide-base tire Large tire with a low aspect ratio. Also called *floatation tire*.

Review Questions

1. Tire construction will change depending on whether the:
   a. tire is transmitting drive torque.
   b. tire is steering.
   c. type of road condition on which the tire is operating.
   d. All of the choices are correct.
2. Tires used by today's heavy duty commercial vehicle 8 vehicles are more commonly:
   a. tube-type.
   b. bias-ply construction.
   c. radial-ply construction.
   d. unable to be recycled by retreading.
3. When servicing tires, which of the following are the best combination of safety precautions to use?
   a. Use a safety cage during inflation and a remotely connected air chuck.
   b. Wear safety glasses, steel toed boots, and a bump cap.
   c. Use tire bead lubricant and OEM-approved pry bars.
   d. Chain tires to rims when inflating and stay out of potential tire trajectory path if it explodes.
4. What is the approximate tread width of an 11R 22.5 tire?
   a. 22" (59 cm)
   b. 11" (28 cm)
   c. 45" (114 cm)
   d. 0.78" × 11" (1.98 cm × 27.9 cm)
5. Consider a tire with a sidewall marking of 445/50R 22.5. What will be the sidewall height of the tire?
   a. 11" (28 cm)
   b. 222 mm (8.74")
   c. 445 mm (17.5")
   d. 8.8" (22.4 cm)
6. Consider a tire with a sidewall marking of 445/65R 22.5. What classification of tire is this?
   a. Low profile radial
   b. Bias-ply
   c. High hysteresis
   d. A drive axle tire only
7. Which of the following is an advantage of a diagonal bias-ply tire?
   a. It resists punctures and road damage better than other tires
   b. Lower rolling resistance
   c. Longer tread life
   d. Better road contact patch for superior traction
8. What is the most likely cause of excessive wear of one tire of a dual wheel tire pair on the same axle end?
   a. Uneven vehicle loading
   b. Unbalanced tires
   c. Uneven tire sizes
   d. Lateral tire run-out
9. What is the most likely result when the tire circumference runout is in excess of 1' (25.4mm)?
   a. Vibration felt throughout the vehicle during drive
   b. Uneven tire wear
   c. Vibration felt only when turn the vehicle during cornering
   d. None of the choices are correct
10. Tires are responsible for:
    a. supporting the vehicle load.
    b. transmitting braking and traction forces to the road surface.
    c. absorbing road shock and providing directional control of the vehicle.
    d. All of the choices are correct.

ASE-Type Questions

1. Technician A says that tires are the leading cause of all roadside breakdowns. Technician B says that tires are the second most common source of mechanical defects leading to accidents. Who is correct?
   a. Technician A
   b. Technician B
   c. Both Technician A and Technician B
   d. Neither Technician A nor Technician B
2. Technician A says "road alligators" are road debris that could be eliminated if retread tires were banned from use. Technician B says "road alligators" are not produced by the caps of a retread tire separating from the case, but are caused by under inflation of any tire. Who is correct?
   a. Technician A
   b. Technician B
   c. Both Technician A and Technician B
   d. Neither Technician A nor Technician B
3. Consider one wheel of a dual wheel combination that has been removed from a trailer to repair a flat tire. Technician A says the tire should be inflated in a safety cage with a clip-on, remote inline air chuck. Technician B says the tire should be dismounted and inspected for damage before re-inflating. Who is correct?
   a. Technician A
   b. Technician B
   c. Both Technician A and Technician B
   d. Neither Technician A nor Technician B
4. Technician A says that tires are marked with a date code indicating the date the tires must be discarded. Technician B says the date code is when the tires were manufactured. Who is correct?
   a. Technician A
   b. Technician B
   c. Both Technician A and Technician B
   d. Neither Technician A nor Technician B
5. Technician A says that a TPMS system can save the owner fuel over a period of time. Technician B says that a TPMS helps prevents blowouts. Who is correct?
   a. Technician A
   b. Technician B
   c. Both Technician A and Technician B
   d. Neither Technician A nor Technician B
6. Technician A says that using nitrogen to inflate a tire will prevent the tire from blowouts. Technician B says that when mounting and/or dismounting a tire from the rim fitted with a TPMS sensor, you must position the rim and tire properly on the tire machine or the TMPS can be damaged. Who is correct?
   a. Technician A
   b. Technician B
   c. Both Technician A and Technician B
   d. Neither Technician A nor Technician B
7. Technician A says that the tires should be replaced when the indicator bars are visible in the tread. Technician B says that faulty shock absorbers cause cupping of the tread. Who is correct?
   a. Technician A
   b. Technician B
   c. Both Technician A and Technician B
   d. Neither Technician A nor Technician B
8. Technician A says that it does not matter if you mix brands of tires on a common axle. Technician B says that the driver should check the tire pressures at least every three months. Who is correct?
   a. Technician A
   b. Technician B
   c. Both Technician A and Technician B
   d. Neither Technician A nor Technician B
9. Technician A says that all tires are the same. Technician B says that the wheel nuts must be torqued after changing a wheel assembly. Who is correct?
   a. Technician A
   b. Technician B
   c. Both Technician A and Technician B
   d. Neither Technician A nor Technician B
10. Technician A says that dynamic wheel unbalance can result in wheel shimmy. Technician B says that static wheel unbalance could cause wheel tramp to occur. Who is correct?
    a. Technician A
    b. Technician B
    c. Both Technician A and Technician B
    d. Neither Technician A nor Technician B

CHAPTER 24

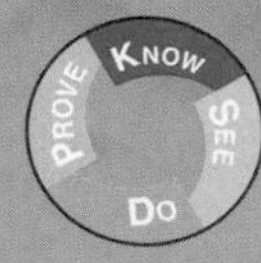

NATEF Tasks

Drive Train
Drive Axles

	Page
■ Remove and replace wheel assembly; check rear wheel seal and axle flange gasket for leaks; perform needed action.	709
■ Identify causes of drive axle wheel bearing noise and check for damage; perform needed action.	711
■ Clean, inspect, lubricate, and replace wheel bearings; replace seals and wear rings; inspect and replace retaining hardware; adjust drive axle wheel bearings. Verify end play with dial indicator method.	718
■ Inspect, repair, or replace drive axle lubrication system: pump, troughs, collectors, slingers, tubes, and filters.	722–723

Brakes
Wheel Bearings

■ Identify, inspect, or replace unitized/preset hub bearing assemblies.	718–721
■ Clean, inspect, lubricate, and replace wheel bearings and races/cups; replace seals and wear rings; inspect spindle/tube; inspect and replace retaining hardware; adjust wheel bearings. Verify endplay with dial indicator method.	718

Wheel Rims and Hubs

Knowledge Objectives

After reading this chapter, you will be able to:

1. Identify and explain the functions and applications of commercial vehicle wheels, hubs, and seals. (pp 707–716)
2. Explain the purpose, construction, and operation of wheel rims, hubs, and seals. (pp 707–716)
3. Identify and explain service procedures used to inspect and replace wheel end components. (pp 709–721)
4. Identify and analyze types of wheel end component failures. (pp 710–723)

Skills Objectives

After reading this chapter, you will be able to:

1. Prepare a wheel for installation. (p 709) SKILL DRILL 24-1
2. Manually adjust wheel bearings. (p 718) SKILL DRILL 24-2
3. Measure wheel end play. (p 719) SKILL DRILL 24-3

Introduction

Wheel rims, tires, and hubs are names given to major components making up part of the axle end or, what the trucking industry calls the **wheel end**. FIGURE 24-1A shows a wheel end for a single wheel and FIGURE 24-1B shows a wheel end for a dual wheel. Each of the wheel ends shown uses a single hub. The role of the hub is to transfer the vehicle weight from the wheels to the axle ends and enable the wheel to rotate on the axle end. FIGURE 24-2 shows a standard hub. Hub seals, bearings, and spindles also are sub-components of the wheel hub. Together these components have the job of safely supporting the vehicle weight over a wide range of load and road conditions.

Wheel ends are one of the most crucial vehicle systems to competently maintain and service from both a safety and economic perspective. Wheel-end failures and

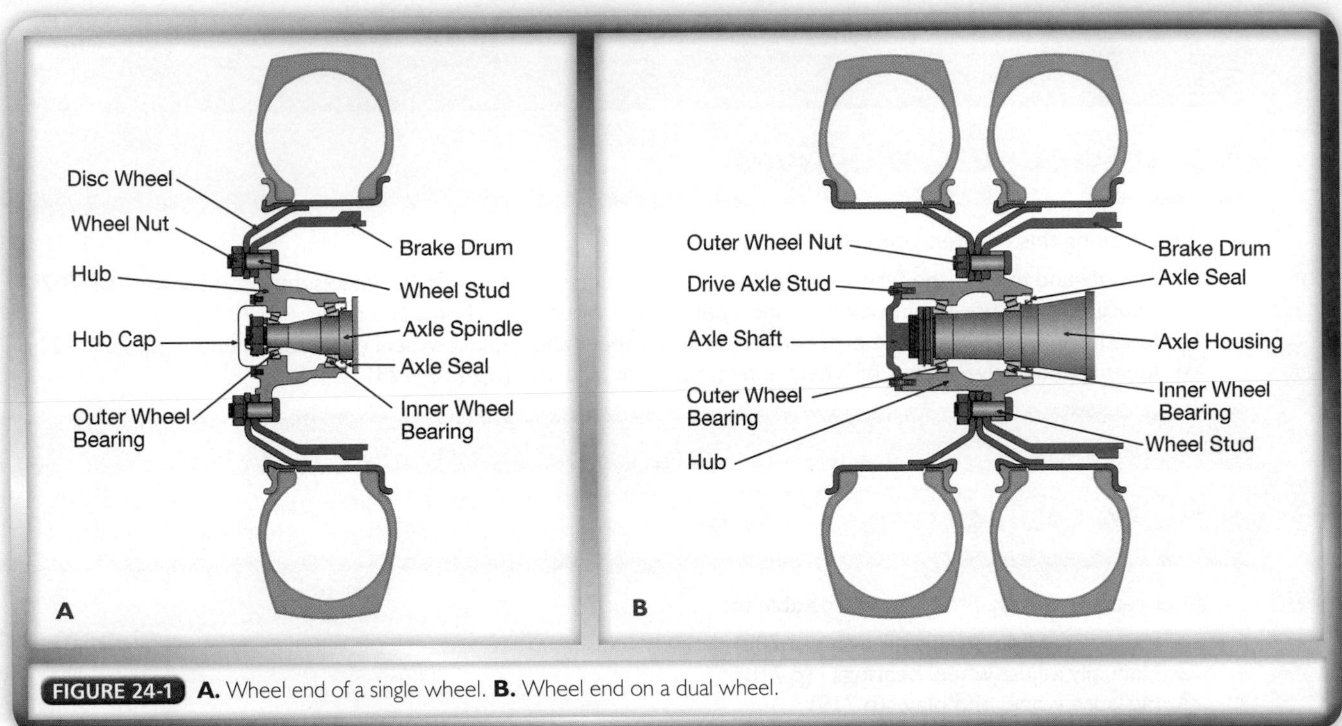

FIGURE 24-1 **A.** Wheel end of a single wheel. **B.** Wheel end on a dual wheel.

You Are the Technician

A reputable truck fleet operation recently had a wheel separation on one its trucks that caused some extensive damage to other vehicles on the road. Although a wheel separation is uncommon, it can be disastrous, if not fatal, if a separated wheel hits another vehicle, building, or person. The incident has left you concerned about the safety practices and procedure you follow in your shop whenever wheels hubs are reinstalled.

Like other technicians that service truck wheels and hubs in the shop, you have received wheel end installation service training as required by the Occupational Safety and Health Administration (OSHA) regulations. But you are considering how best to perform inspections on all wheels and hubs to make sure the assemblies are safe and in good working order. You are also contemplating revising the service standards you will use when replacing wheels and hubs. As you prepare plans for the steps to take, consider how your woudl answer the following questions.

1. What specific points inspections would you carry out for the three major types of wheels and hub assemblies serviced by your shop in the future?
2. In addition to correctly torquing the wheel fasteners, what other factors would you consider to ensure you obtain proper clamping force on wheel and rims?
3. How would you ensure that the wheel bearing end play is within the acceptable range for each vehicle?

FIGURE 24-2 Standard wheel hub.

FIGURE 24-3 Rim of the wheel.

separations can also have catastrophic consequences, not only to the vehicle, but to other users of the roadway. In many jurisdictions, wheel separations can incur fines up to $50,000 per incident, with potential for imprisonment in the case of serious negligence.

With the wide variety of tasks commercial vehicles perform, there is a corresponding variation in the technology used to construct wheel ends. And, because of the importance of wheel ends and their extensive variation, it important for technicians to properly understand wheel end construction and maintenance techniques along with the causes of wheel-end failures.

Fundamentals of Wheels and Rims

Wheels are usually made from steel or cast aluminium alloy. They are designed to be strong enough to withstand normal operational forces. Alloy wheels are popular because of their appearance and because they are lighter than steel wheels. Aluminium is a better conductor of heat, so alloy wheels can dissipate heat from the brakes and tires more effectively than steel. Alloy wheels are often called mag or magnesium wheels, but wheels made of pure magnesium are rarely used on vehicles. The terms *wheel* and *rim* are often used synonymously. Technically, the **wheel rim** is the outer circular lip of the metal on which the inside edge of the tire is mounted, as shown in FIGURE 24-3. The purpose of the rim is to hold and seal the tire to the wheel. Wheels and rims come in both imperial and metric measures. Metric rims cannot be mixed with imperial tires or vice versa.

Rim width is the distance across the rim flanges at the bead seat. The **bead seat** is the edge of the rim that creates a seal between the tire bead and the wheel. The **rim flange** is the exterior lip that holds the tire in place. The **rim diameter** is the distance across the center of the rim, from bead seat to bead seat. The width of the rim and the diameter are stated in millimeters.

Wheel Offset

The **wheel offset** is the distance from its hub mounting surface to the centerline of the wheel. Offset is important because it is typically used to bring the tire centerline into close alignment with the larger inner wheel bearing, and it reduces load on the stub axle. This requires the inside of the wheel assembly to be shaped so that there is space for the brake assembly, especially disc brakes, which are typically larger in diameter than drum brakes. The offset can be either zero, positive, or negative:

- **Zero offset**: The plane of the hub mounting surface is even with the centerline of the wheel.
- **Positive offset**: The plane of the hub mounting surface is shifted from the centerline towards the outside or front side of the wheel.
- **Negative offset**: The hub mounting surface is towards the brake side or back of the wheel's centerline.

Wheel Studs and Wheel Nuts

Wheels are fastened to the rims by wheel studs and wheel nuts. **Wheel studs** are the threaded fasteners that attach the wheel to the vehicle. **Wheel nuts** are the nuts that secure the wheel onto the wheel studs. Wheel studs and wheel nuts are highly stressed by loads from the weight of the vehicle and the forces generated by its motion. Wheel studs and nuts are made from heat-treated, high-grade alloy steel. The threads between the studs and the nuts are close fitting and accurately sized. All wheel nuts must be tightened to the correct torque and in the proper sequence; otherwise the wheel could break free from the hub.

The **bolt pattern** refers to the number and spacing of the wheel nuts or wheel studs on the wheel hub on the wheel rim, like that shown in FIGURE 24-4. As the studs are most often evenly spaced, the number of studs determines the pattern. The exact number and pattern of studs vary depending on the vehicle type and manufacturer design.

Wheel Nut Torque Versus Clamping Force

Wheel stud tension produces clamping force between a wheel and hub. Clamping force is what keeps the wheel attached to the end of the axle. As mentioned in the Wheel Studs and Wheel Nuts section, it is critical that the correct torque be used on wheel nuts. Otherwise, serious problems can occur.

Under-tightening wheel nuts allows wheels to run loose, eventually pounding and deforming wheel bolt holes. Cracks can also form in the bolt hole areas. If they are not adequately tightened, studs will fatigue and break from continuous bending. That is because tightened bolts do not bend as much as loose ones do.

Overtightening wheel fasteners also produces problems. Overtightening wheel nuts can stretch studs and cause them to fail. Applying excessive lubricant to the threads of a stud or nut can actually cause excessive tightening. That is because more torque can be applied by a torque wrench and then converted to stretching of the fastener.

As illustrated in FIGURE 24-5, the best way for a technician to produce the clamping force necessary to keep the wheels on the vehicle is through correct preparation of fasteners and the use of a torque wrench. Torque is the measure of twisting force applied to wheel fasteners and is a function of the length of a wrench and the force applied to it. Preload on the bolt—the amount of stretch—is proportional to the torque applied to the nut through the wrench. TABLE 24-1 outlines the applied torque needed to produce a certain level of clamping force for multiple types of fasteners. To prepare to install a wheel, follow the guidelines in SKILL DRILL 24-1.

TECHNICIAN TIP

When torque is applied to a nut, it stretches the stud between the nut and the head of the stud as the nut is tightened. Stretching the stud produces a spring like force called preload. Preload supplies the clamping force to retain a wheel onto a hub. Stud preload, or the amount the stud is stretched when a wheel nut is tightened, cannot be measured in the field. Technicians must control preload by torqueing wheel nuts in order to achieve an approximate amount of adequate wheel clamping force.

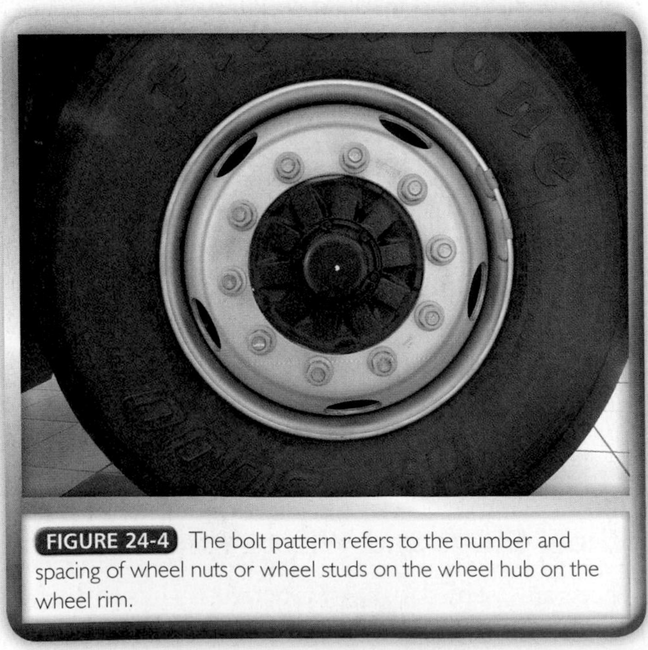

FIGURE 24-4 The bolt pattern refers to the number and spacing of wheel nuts or wheel studs on the wheel hub on the wheel rim.

FIGURE 24-5 Clamping force is produced by torqueing a fastener. The use of torque wrenches are the best way to ensure proper and consistent clamping forces on a wheel end.

TABLE 24-1: Fastener Preparations, Torque Application, and Resultant Clamping Force

Fastener Preparation Method	Torque Applied	Clamping Force
Used Stud/Used Nut (no oil)	480 ft-lb (651 Nm)	27,000 lb (12,247 Kg)
Oiled Stud/Dry Nut	470 ft-lb (637 Nm)	30,000 lb (13,608 kg)
Dry Stud/Oiled Nut	482 ft-lb (654 Nm)	40,000 lb (18,144 kg)
New Stud/New Nut	476 ft-lb (645 Nm)	47,000 lb (21,319 kg)
Oiled Stud/Oiled Nut	487 ft-lb (660 Nm)	56,000 lb (25,401 kg)
Anti-Seize Stud/ Dry Nut	488 ft-lb (662 Nm)	25,000 lb (11,340 kg)
Clean Anti-Seize then Oil	490 ft-lb (664 Nm)	40,000 lb (18,144 kg)

Wheel Types

Heavy-duty commercial vehicles commonly use two basic types of wheels—cast spoke and disc. **Cast spoke wheels** use three, five, or six cast-iron spokes integrated with a bearing hub. The wheel spoke supports one or two tire rims. A **disc wheel** is a steel or aluminum wheel rim that supports a tire and attaches to the hub using wheel studs and nuts. Two types of disc wheels are used, which are classified by the way the wheel is centered onto a hub. Let's examine these wheel types in greater detail.

Cast Spoke Wheels

Cast-iron spoke wheels are preferred in off-road or heavy-duty construction vehicle applications such as dump trucks, heavy equipment hauling, or logging. These wheels have the highest load carrying capacity. The spokes on a cast spoke wheel support the tire rim. Therefore, the more spokes there are, the greater the ability of the wheel to handle increased weight. This means

SKILL DRILL 24-1 Preparing to Install a Wheel

1. Remove debris and foreign material from all mating surfaces. When ready to install a wheel, note that the hub should be already in place. If it is not, several more steps will be required to install the hub.
2. Inspect components for damage or signs of severe wear. If installing a dual wheel, be certain that the hand hold openings are in alignment if applicable.
3. Snug the lug nuts in a star pattern to seat the wheel on the hub.
4. Torque the lug nuts to specification using a calibrated torque control tool.
5. Look for any cracks around the bolt holes or the center bore of the wheel.
6. Inspect the studs for damaged or stripped threads.
7. Inspect the lug nuts for thread or hex head damage.
8. Make sure the hub, rotor, and/or drum are properly cleaned and not damaged or cracked.
9. Snug the step wheel fasteners to seat the wheel and the drum on the hub evenly using 50 to 100 ft-lb (68 to 136 Nm) steps. Always start at the 12 o'clock position.

small diameter wheels used on equipment trailers may have only three spokes. Larger diameter wheels hauling heavier loads will use five spokes. The heaviest loads will be supported with wheels using six spokes.

The cast spoke wheel, such as the one shown in FIGURE 24-6, incorporates a hub containing wheel bearings. Brake drums are bolted to the cast spoke. Rims, such as the one shown in FIGURE 24-7, are installed over the tapered spokes to prevent the inboard side of the rim from coming off the rim. Friction between the rim and the increasingly larger diameter spoke hold everything together. The rim is held in position using wedge-shaped clamps attached to the wheel with studs and nuts. The wheel rim can be removed separately from the cast-iron spoke hub attached to the axle. As such, the rim design is also referred to as a **demountable rim** or **open-center rim**. Wheel clamps force the rim onto a taper shaped hub to secure the wheel and prevent it from rotating under torque or braking forces.

FIGURE 24-8 illustrates a single demountable rim on a cast spoke hub. Load from the tire and rim is transferred to the cast spoke hub. The rim is pushed onto the tapered

FIGURE 24-6 Cast spoke wheel using demountable rims.

FIGURE 24-7 Cast spoke demountable rim.

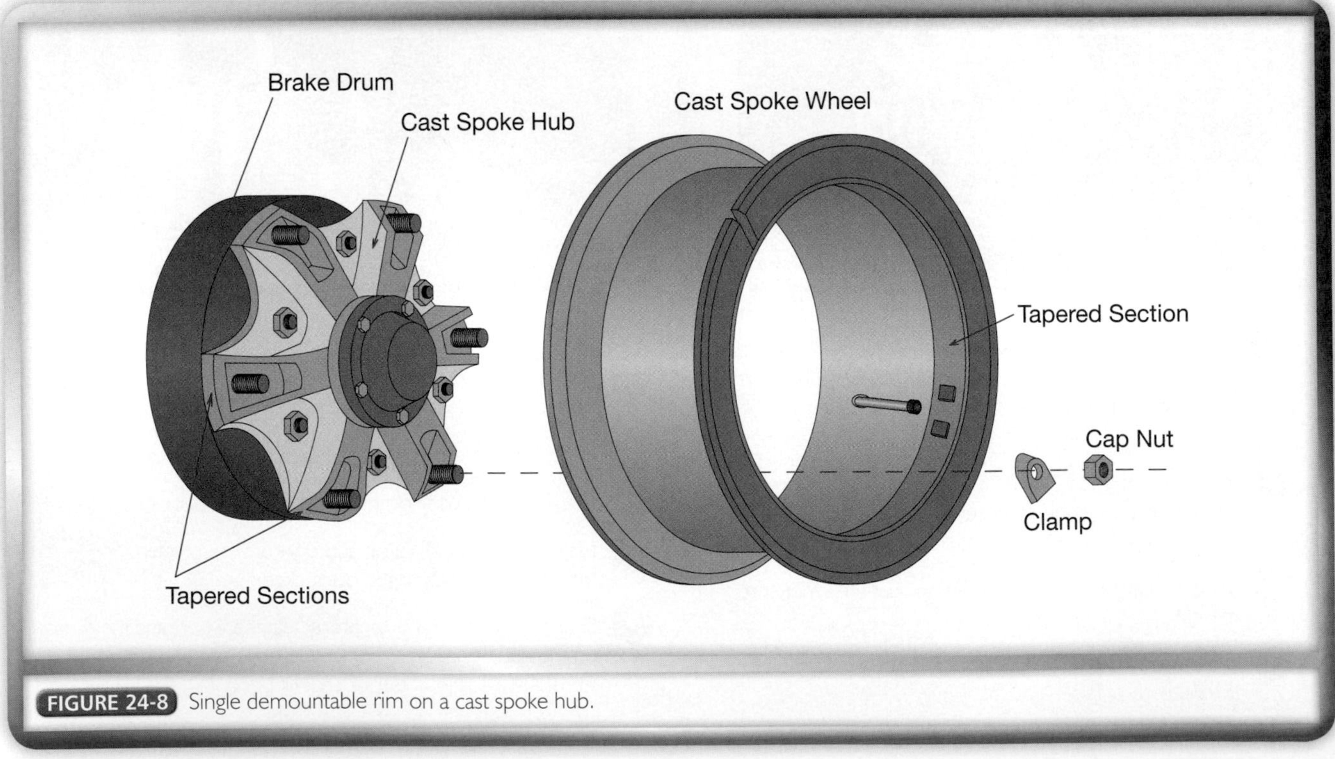

FIGURE 24-8 Single demountable rim on a cast spoke hub.

sections of the hub and will stop when the outer edge of the hub contacts the tapered inside diameter of the rim. Clamps hold the rim onto the hub. Driving the rim onto the tapered sections of the hub stretches the rim to tightly grip the hub. Clamps hold the rim onto the hub.

Cast spoke hubs are some of the oldest and most rugged types of wheel and hub configurations. The design has traditionally the fewest incidences of "wheel-off" failures due to the use of clamps to hold the rims in place.

Safety

The wheel clamps retaining demountable rims on spoke type wheels are under very high spring-like tension. When a wheel clamp is loosened, the spring forces retaining the wheel rim over the tapered spokes are rapidly released and will cause the clamp to fly off the wheel stud with considerable force. To prevent physical injury from flying wheel clamps, do not completely remove the nuts initially. Instead, first release tension on the rim by backing off the retaining nuts on all the clamps. The nuts should stay on the wheel studs with no less than two or three threads. Then, when the tension is released, hit the clamps with a hammer to loosen before removing the retaining nuts completely.

Dual Tires on Spoke Wheels

Dual demountable rims are also possible on a cast spoke hub, as illustrated in FIGURE 24-9. When dual tires are used on a cast spoke wheel, a rim spacer, such as the one shown in FIGURE 24-10, is used between the rims to transfer the clamping force of wheel clamps to the inner rim. The spacer also prevents the tires from contacting one another during vehicle operation.

Spacers are available in different widths and must be properly matched to the tire rim width and spoke width. If a spacer collapses due to excessive clamping force, the rims may move under brake or traction torque. The moving rims may contact the stops on the rim. Under this condition, a clunking noise will originate from the wheel when braking or accelerating. Collapsed or worn spacers can also lead to loose wheels and sheared tire valve stems.

Wheel Rim Run-Out

When rims are installed on spoke wheels, the lateral run out needs to be checked and adjusted. Rim clamps should be first installed and tightened in a star pattern to wedge the rim against the tapered spokes. FIGURE 24-11A shows the correct sequence for a three-spoke wheel, FIGURE 24-11B shows the sequence for a five-spoke

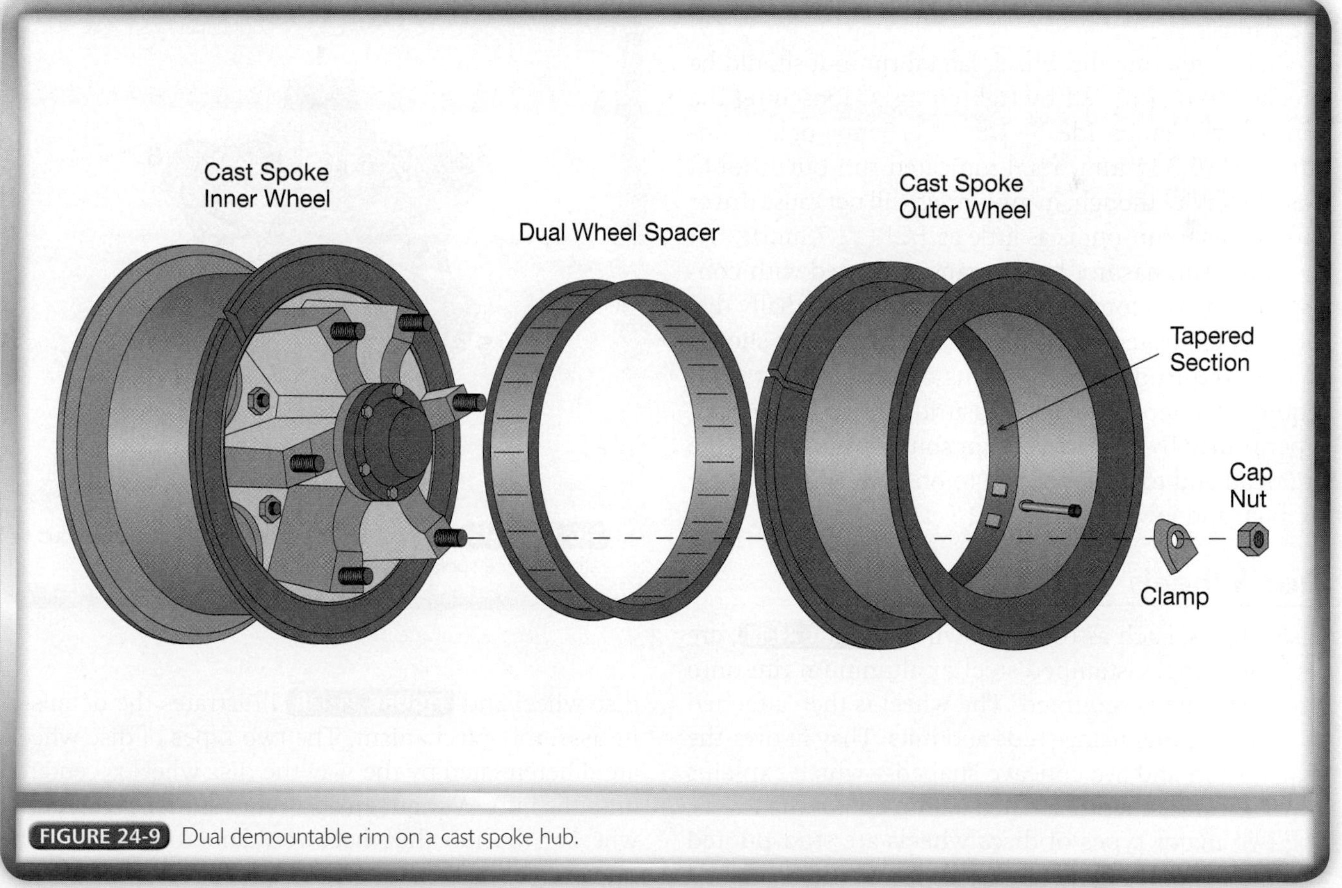

FIGURE 24-9 Dual demountable rim on a cast spoke hub.

FIGURE 24-10 Corrugated spacers used with cast spoke hubs.

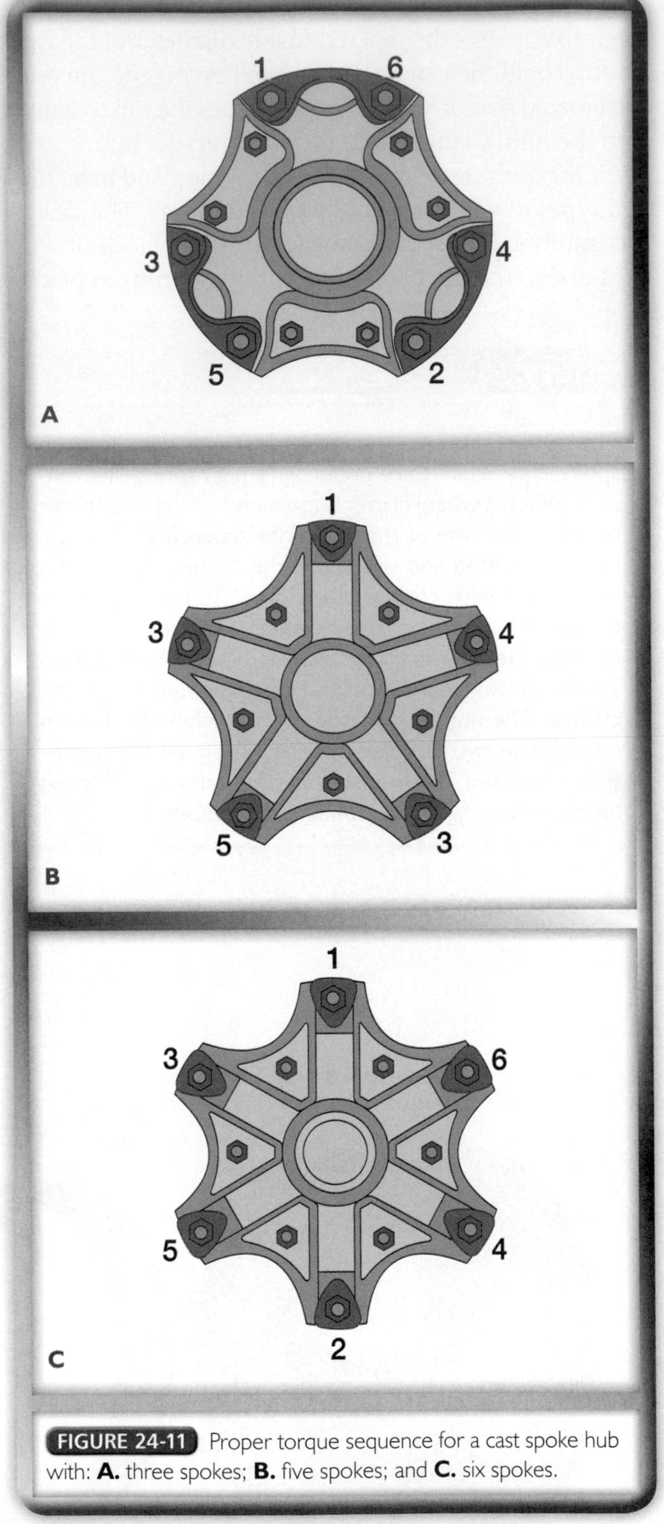

FIGURE 24-11 Proper torque sequence for a cast spoke hub with: **A.** three spokes; **B.** five spokes; and **C.** six spokes.

wheel, and FIGURE 24-11C shows the sequence for a six-spoke wheel.

Place an upright sledge hammer or a straight edge close to the outer edge of the wheel. Then rotate the wheel to check the runout. Lateral runout should then be adjusted by tightening or loosening the appropriate clamps. Ideally 1/8" (3.175 mm) or less runout should exist. Total indicated runout should not exceed 1/4" (6.355 mm). In service though, many wheels will not cause driver complaints if run-out is as much as 1/2" (12.7 mm).

While rotating the wheel, lateral run-out should be checked and adjusted by tightening or loosening the appropriate clamps. Ideally 1/8" (3.175 mm) or less run-out (1/4" (6.335 mm) total indicated run-out) should exist. In service though, many wheels will not cause driver complaints if run-out is as little as 1/2" (12.7 mm).

If the rim has not had clamps tightened with consistent and even force, the rim may become radially distorted or elongated (egg shaped). Radial run-out should be checked to determine if this condition exists and requires rim replacement. Measuring the radial run-out is performed by using a gauge or some object next to the tire tread and rotating the tire to observe whether there are high and low spots.

Disc Wheels

Disc wheels, such as those shown in FIGURE 24-12, are a simple, single, stamped steel or aluminum rim onto which the tire is mounted. The wheel is then attached to a separate hub using studs and nuts. They fit over the brake drum and are concave shaped—which explains why they are sometimes called a drop-center rim.

Two major types of discs wheels are stud-piloted and hub-piloted. FIGURE 24-13A shows a hub-piloted disc wheel and FIGURE 24-13B illustrates the details of its assembly mechanism. The two types of disc wheels are differentiated by the way the disc wheel is centered onto the hub. Without an accurate method to center the wheel on the hub, the wheel would not rotate around the same centerline as the hub.

FIGURE 24-12 Disc wheel.

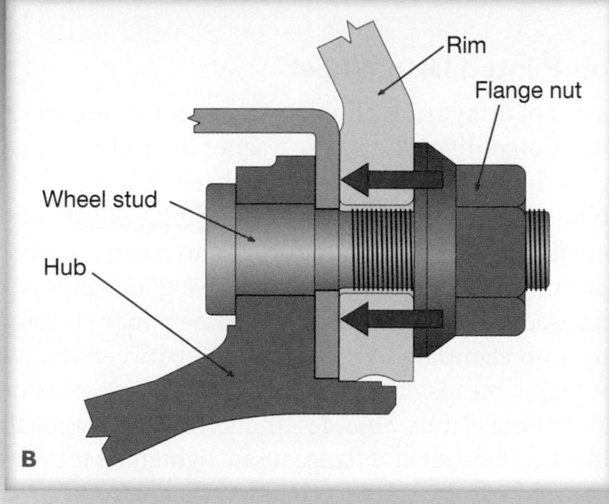

FIGURE 24-13 **A.** Hub-piloted disc wheel. **B.** Components of a hub-piloted disc wheel.

Stud-Piloted Disc Wheels

Stud-piloted disc wheels are the oldest type of wheel and no longer used on new equipment. As illustrated in FIGURE 24-14, these wheels retain the discs using studs attached to the hub and a tapered, or ball-type, wheel nut to center the disc onto the hub. The weight of the vehicle is transmitted to the wheel through the stud and nut assembly, so more studs are used to distribute the load than on a cast spoke or hub-piloted disc wheel. FIGURE 24-15 illustrates a stud-piloted mounting system. Note that the holes in the stud-piloted wheels are tapered for ball type studs and nuts. Cap nuts with square heads are used to retain the inner wheel on dual wheel axle ends.

When dual wheels are used, two nuts are needed to retain both wheels. That means twice as many nuts are required for a stud-piloted wheel compared with a hub-piloted wheel. The cap nut is installed first to hold the inner wheel against the hub. It is tightened with a higher torque than the outer ball-type nut.

Both left- and right-hand thread fasteners are used to prevent the wheel nuts from backing off. Right-hand threaded nuts are used on the right side of the vehicle and left-hand threads are used on the left side.

Because these wheels transfer weight through the studs, there is a greater likelihood of losing a wheel if the proper service procedures and hardware is not used. Different types of nuts and studs are used on steel and aluminum wheels. Aluminum wheels require longer studs due to the greater thickness of aluminum rims. And, as illustrated in FIGURE 24-16, the hardware used to retain

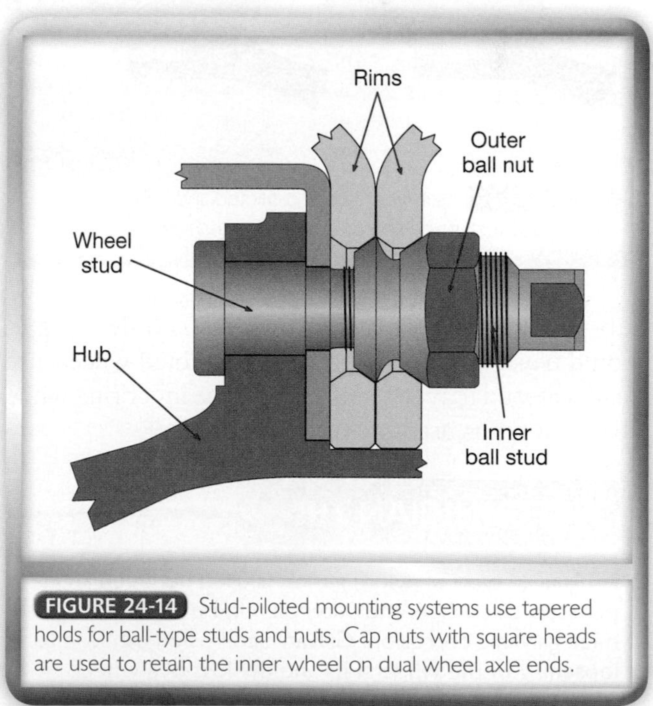

FIGURE 24-14 Stud-piloted mounting systems use tapered holds for ball-type studs and nuts. Cap nuts with square heads are used to retain the inner wheel on dual wheel axle ends.

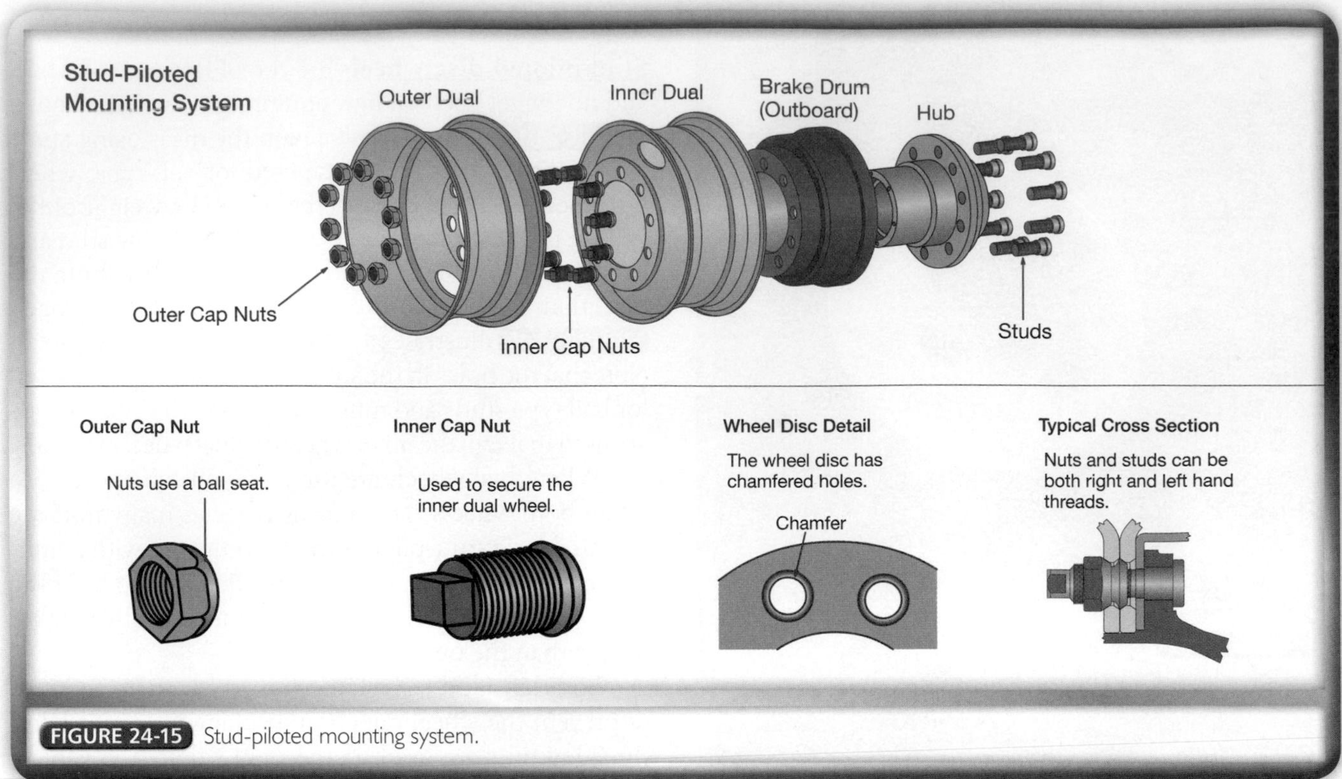

FIGURE 24-15 Stud-piloted mounting system.

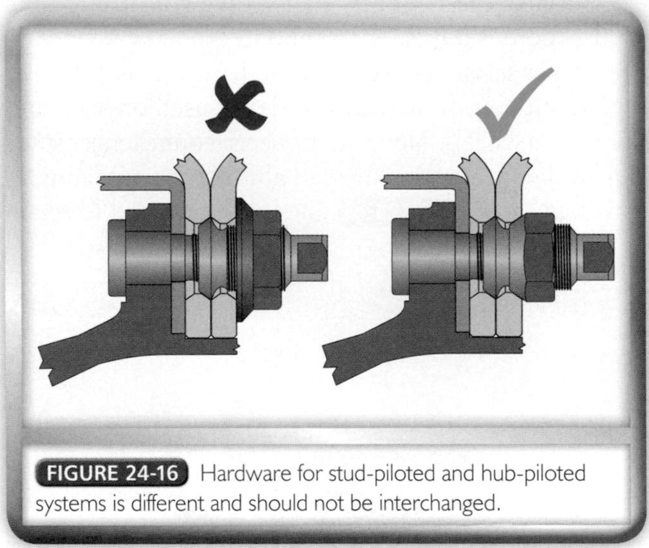

FIGURE 24-16 Hardware for stud-piloted and hub-piloted systems is different and should not be interchanged.

hub-piloted and stud-piloted wheels is different and should never be interchanged. Stud-piloted wheels use a ball seat stud to retain and support the inner rim, while a ball seat nut is used on the outer rim.

> **TECHNICIAN TIP**
>
> A Mylar (a type of nylon) gasket is used between an inner steel disc wheel and outer aluminum wheel to minimize galvanic corrosion. Galvanic corrosion can lead to loosening of the wheel nuts and the loss of a wheel.

> **Safety**
>
> Installing wheel hardware requires special attention be given to correctly tightening wheel nuts using torque wrenches. Stud- and hub-piloted wheel nuts are not interchangeable. The tapered face of the wheel nut must face the tapered seat of stud-piloted wheels. Re-torque of hub-piloted wheel nuts is essential after 30 miles (50 km) of operation since they will loosen after initial installation.

Hub-Piloted Disc Wheel

Instead of using studs and nuts to center the disc wheel, **hub-piloted disc wheels** use a series of machined pads on the hub to help center the wheel. A hub-piloted mounting system is illustrated in FIGURE 24-17. Two-piece flange-type wheel nuts are used to retain the wheel against the hub but do not carry any weight. Flange type nuts used by hub-piloted wheels convert more twisting force into clamping force. Movement between the two nut pieces means clamping forces are more consistent between wheel nuts. Since less friction exists between the lubricated hex nut and flange, more tightening torque is converted into twisting force rather than used up overcoming friction.

As illustrated in FIGURE 24-18, a small drop of oil is generally used to lubricate the two parts of the nut. Fewer

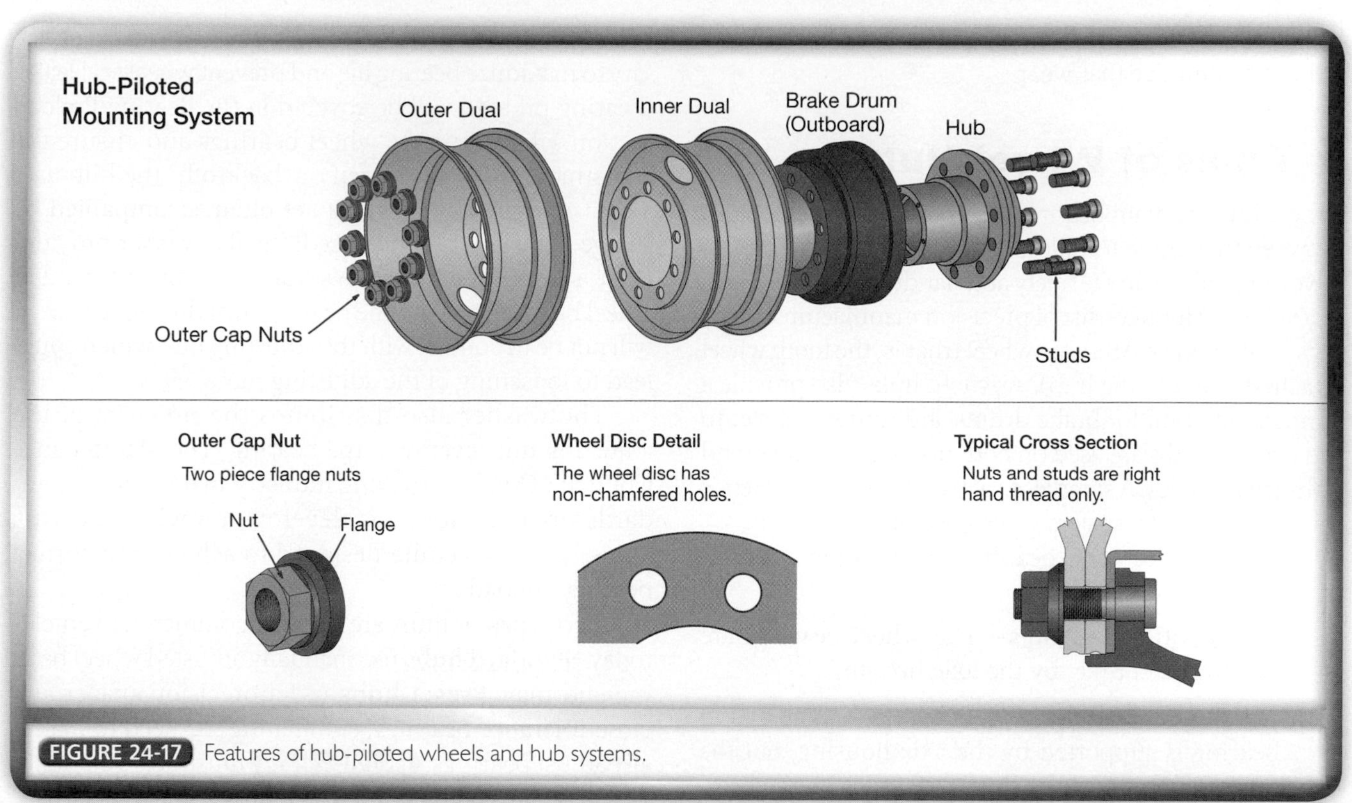

FIGURE 24-17 Features of hub-piloted wheels and hub systems.

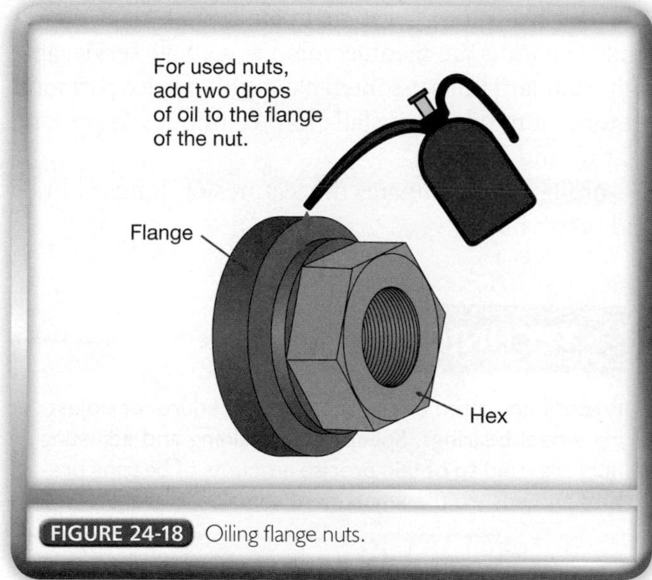

FIGURE 24-18 Oiling flange nuts.

studs and nuts are used on hub-piloted wheels. That is because hub-piloted disc wheels transfer vehicle weight through the pilot pads, as illustrated in FIGURE 24-19. **Pilot pads** are lugs attached to the bearing hub to locate the wheel assembly correctly during assembly. Unlike stud-piloted hubs, hub-piloted wheel nuts and studs only clamp the disc to the hub and do not support vehicle weight. Hub-piloted disc wheels may have wear between the pilot pads and wheel, leading to radial wheel run-out. The use of feeler blades to evenly split any clearance

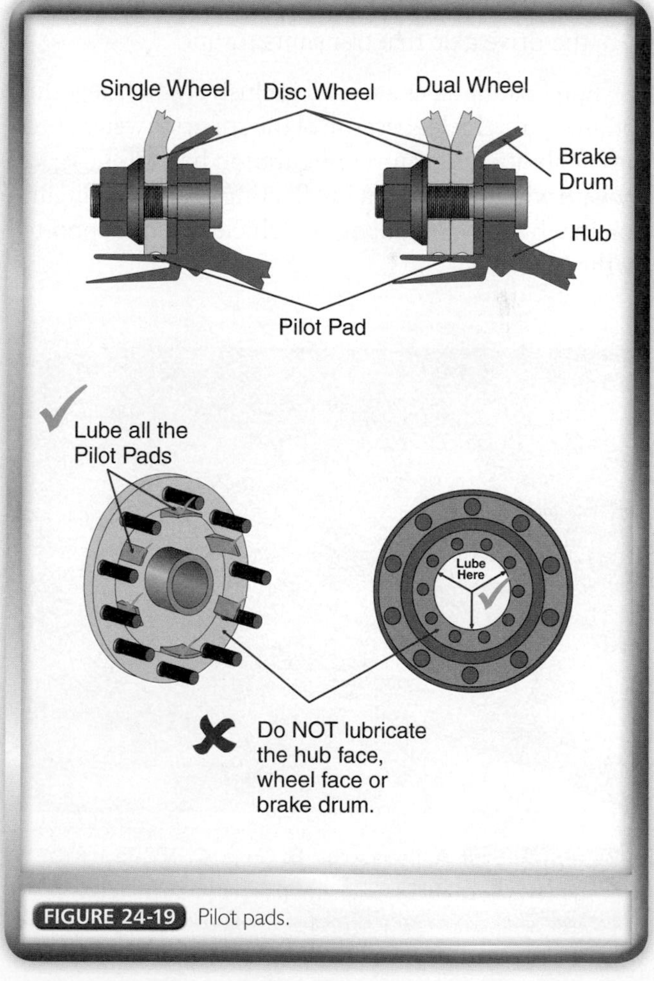

FIGURE 24-19 Pilot pads.

between the disc and pads is recommended during installation to minimize that wear.

Types of Wheel Hubs

Wheel hubs contain bearings used to reduce the friction between the stationary axle and rotating wheel. Hubs also have a crucial role in the safety and handling characteristics of a vehicle. Hubs consist of precision manufactured bearings, seals, and an ABS tone wheel (that is, the tooth wheel attached to a rotating hub). As such, hubs also provide a connection point for brake drums and torque transfer to the wheels. Hubs are used on both driving (live axles) and non-driving axles. A spindle at each end of the axle extends into the hub and transfers vehicle weight to the hub.

Three types of wheel bearing configurations are used in drive axle wheel hubs:

- **Full floating bearings**—The wheel bearings are supported entirely by the axle housing.
- **Three-quarters floating bearings**— The wheel bearing is supported by the axle housing, but the the outer flange of the drive axle rides on the bearing. This style is rarely seen today.
- **Semi-floating bearings**—Wheel bearings support the drive axle that transmits torque.

Full floating axles are used exclusively on heavy-duty commercial vehicles because of the superior weight bearing capabilities this hub configuration has. FIGURE 24-20 shows a wheel hub with a full floating bearing configuration in which the weight of the vehicle will be supported by the bearings.

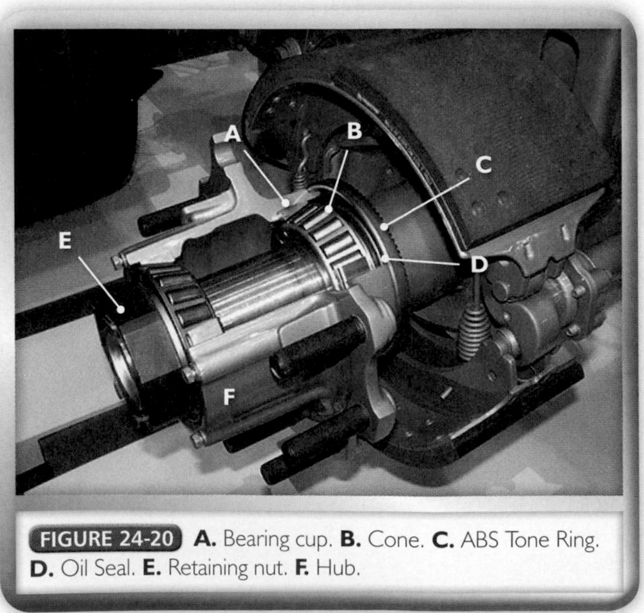

FIGURE 24-20 **A.** Bearing cup. **B.** Cone. **C.** ABS Tone Ring. **D.** Oil Seal. **E.** Retaining nut. **F.** Hub.

Precise adjustment of wheel bearing preload is necessary to maximize bearing life and prevent wheel seal leaks. (Bearing preload will be covered in the Bearing Preload section.) To adjust the wheel bearings and ensure the adjustment does not loosen or "back-off," the hub uses a pair of adjusting nuts that are often accompanied by a large flat washer. When used, the flat washer provides a flat, smooth, bearing-like surface to contact the outer wheel bearing. Should the bearing turn during service, it will not be in contact with the adjusting nut, which could lead to loosening of the adjusting nut.

The washer also distributes the pressure of the adjusting nuts evenly to the bearing. The Maintenance Council (TMC), a trucking industry maintenance standards organization, has developed a wheel bearing adjustment procedure designed to achieve the correct bearing preload.

Two types of hubs are used in commercial vehicles today. **Standard hubs** use manually adjusted wheel bearing end play. **Preset hubs** use a precision spacer and close-tolerance bearings, eliminating the need to manually adjust bearings. FIGURE 24-21A illustrates a standard hub and FIGURE 24-21B shows a preset hub.

Preset, or unitized, hubs use a precision-machined hub and bearing spacer to maintain correct bearing preload. The units are manufactured as a single serviceable unit. Standard hubs use interchangeable service parts and require more precise installation techniques to prolong bearing and seal life.

TABLE 24-2 compares the features of standard hubs and preset hubs.

> **TECHNICIAN TIP**
>
> **Preset hubs often use a different procedure for adjusting wheel bearings. Specialized retaining and adjusting nuts are used to obtain precise amounts of bearing preload and ensure the adjustment remains stable.**

Standard Hubs

Standard hubs are precision-machined aluminum or cast-iron castings used in drive, steer, and trailer configurations. Two bearing cups are press-fitted into the housing with two bearing cones. A seal is installed on the inboard side of the hub, which is used to retain oil in the hub. Bearings are installed by the technician and manually adjusted using an industry standard procedure defined by TMC RP 618, which is discussed further in the Manually Adjusting Wheel Bearings section.

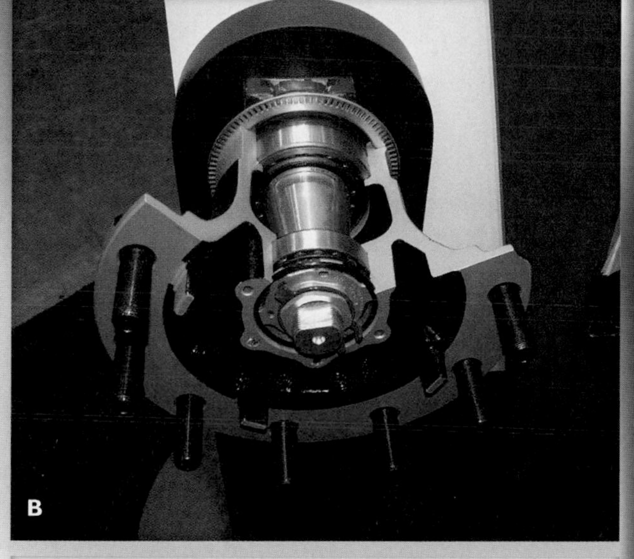

FIGURE 24-21 **A.** Standard hub. **B.** Preset hub.

TABLE 24-2: Comparison of Standard and Preset Hub Features

Standard Hubs	Preset Hubs
Individual components are assembled by a technician	Hub assembly is completely assembled from factory
Least accurate wheel bearing adjustment	Bearing end play is factory pre-set for improved accuracy
Wheel end play adjustment depends on technician skill	Adjustment made at factory and no end play errors
Labor intensive operation	Faster installation and no further maintenance required

On a standard hub, brake drums can be mounted either inboard or outboard. Outboard drums are installed over the hub and pilot on the same studs as the wheel. This means the hub does not require removal in order to replace the brake drum. Only the wheel is removed, leaving bearings and wheel seals undisturbed. Inboard drums are bolted to the inside surface of the hub, requiring hub removal during brake drum replacement.

Safety

The most common cause of wheel seal leaks is loose wheel bearings. In the 1990s, an estimated 80% of wheel-offs were caused by loss of hub lubricant. Bearing adjustment is clearly a critical service procedure. With increasing bearing end play, the wheel seal runs in an increasing elliptically shaped rotation around the axle spindle while increasing the load on the seal lip.

Bearing Preload

When adjusting wheel bearings, technicians are actually setting a bearing load factor called preload. **Bearing preload** is not a clearance; it's the load applied to a bearing before any vehicle weight or rolling loads are applied. Preload is thought of as an axial load applied to the bearing by a threaded nut.

Without enough preload, the bearings will not roll properly—some force needs to be applied to the bearing to give it traction. A negative preload occurs when hub bearings have no end play. Negative preload provides for the longest bearing life.

Negative preload cannot be measured by a technician, but bearing end play can be. Tightening the bearing retaining nut controls end play by applying an axial load to the bearing before the vehicle weight is applied. The bearing could actually be adjusted too tightly if end play is removed. For that reason, bearings are adjusted to between 0.001" and 0.005" end play, which is measurable. At that adjustment, both the bearings and the seals will have longer service life.

Manually Adjusting Wheel Bearings

TMC RP 618 is an established procedure for obtaining a wheel bearing end play of between 0.001" and 0.005" (0.025 mm and 0.127 mm). Tightening the bearing retaining nut controls end play by loading or, more accurately, preloading the bearing before the vehicle load is applied. Optimum bearing and seal life is obtained using 0.001" to 0.005" (0.025 mm and 0.127 mm) preload. To manually adjust wheel bearings, follow the steps in SKILL DRILL 24-2, in conjunction with TABLE 24-3.

SKILL DRILL 24-2 Manually Adjusting Wheel Bearings Using the TMC 618 Procedure

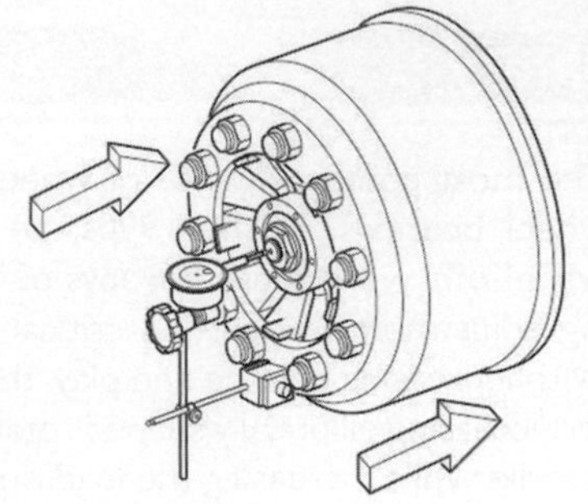

Adjust Endplay with Wheel Hub
With indicator mounted at bottom,
Push/Pull at sides of drum

1. Lubricate the bearings with clean lubricant of the same type used in the axle sump or hub assembly.
2. Install the wheel hub and bearing onto spindle and torque the inner adjusting nut to 200 ft-lb (271 Nm) while rotating the hub assembly.
3. Back-off the inner adjusting nut one full turn.
4. Re-torque the inner adjusting nut to 50 ft-lb (68 Nm) while rotating the wheel hub assembly.
5. Back-off the inner adjustment nuts as per in Table 24-3.
6. Install the locking washer.
7. Install and torque the outer jam nut as per Table 24-3.
8. Verify hub end play with a dial indicator.

TABLE 24-3: Final Back-Off for Adjustment Nuts by Axle Type and Threads per Inch

Axle Type	Threads Per Inch	Final Back-Off	Jam Nut Torque
Steer (front non-drive)	12	1/6 turn* (with cotter pin)	No jam nut used. Use cotter pin.
	18	1/4 turn* (with cotter pin)	
	14	1/2 turn (with less than 2 5/8" (6.67 cm) nut)	200–300 ft-lb (272–408 Nm)
	18	1/2 turn (with less than 2 5/8" (6.67 cm) nut)	
Drive	12	1/4 turn	With dowel-type washer 300–400 ft-lb (408–544 Nm)
	16	1/4 turn	Tang washer 200–275 ft-lb (272–374 Nm)
Trailer**	12	1/4 turn	Over 2 5/8" 300–400 ft-lb (408–544 Nm)
	16	1/4 turn	

* Install cotter pin to lock the nut.
** For positive adjustment wheel bearings (a Rockwell product), use 250 – 300 ft-lbs on adjusting nut and jam nut, as listed in the Rockwell field maintenance manual No. 14.

Bearing adjusting nuts on some axle ends may use a cotter pin with a locking tab to prevent backing off of the lock nut, as illustrated in **FIGURE 24-22**. When installing the cotter pin, never tighten the adjusting nut to align it with the cotter pin slot in the spindle. This can add excessive preload to the wheel bearings and cause a premature bearing failure. Back-off the adjusting nut instead to align the cotter pin hole.

Measuring Wheel End Play

Wheel end play is the free movement of the wheel hub assembly along the axle spindle axis. A large variety of wheel end retaining nuts are used to precisely adjust the wheel bearing end play and lock the adjustment in place. For example, the Stemco Pro-Torq nut, shown in **FIGURE 24-23**, is an example of a popular wheel retaining nut system that enables precise location and locking of the retaining nut for achieving correct end play.

Correct end play is 0.001"–0.005" (0.025–0.127 mm). Note: End play when using a ProTorq Nut is 0.001"–0.003" or (0.025–0.076 mm). To measure wheel end play, follow the guidelines in **SKILL DRILL 24-3**.

FIGURE 24-22 A conventional spindle nut on a steer axle is locked into place with a locking nut and cotter pin.

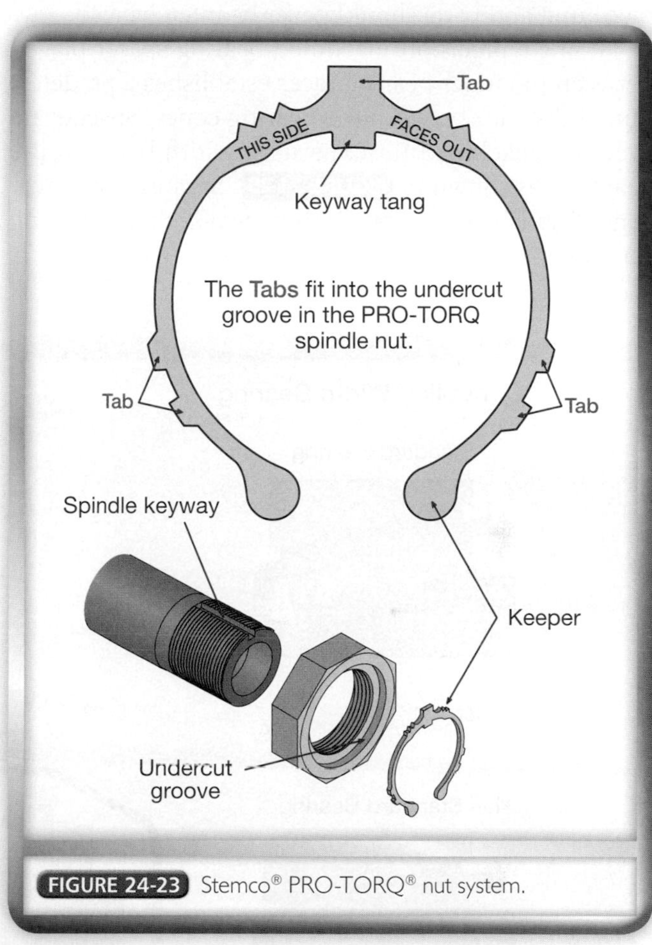

FIGURE 24-23 Stemco® PRO-TORQ® nut system.

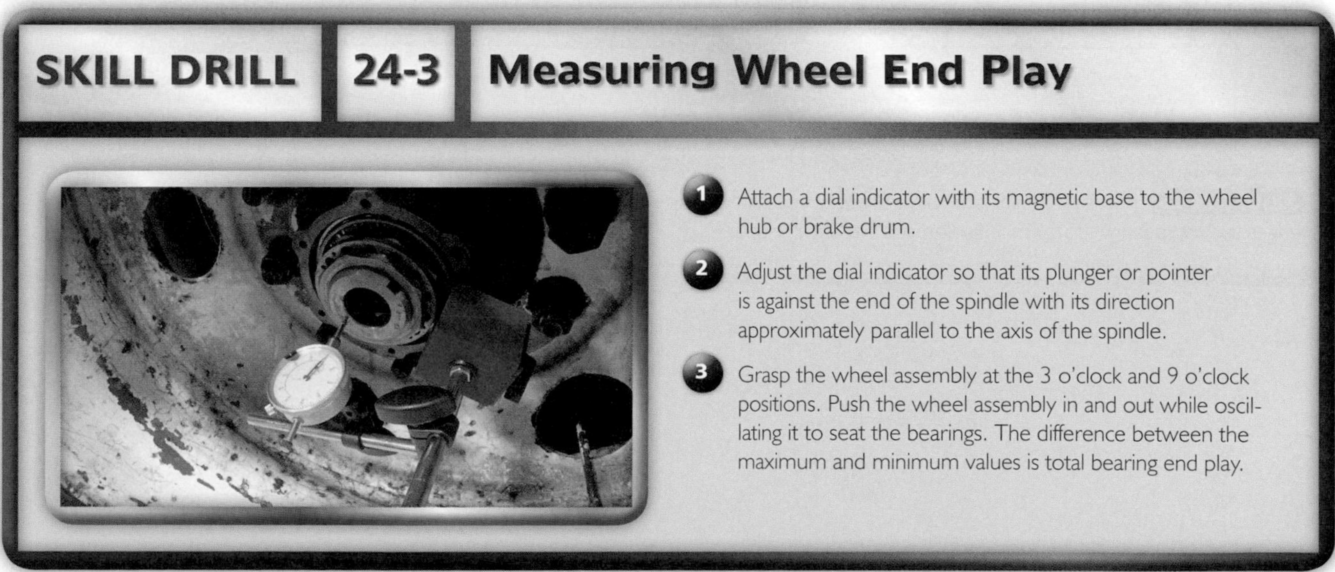

SKILL DRILL 24-3 Measuring Wheel End Play

1. Attach a dial indicator with its magnetic base to the wheel hub or brake drum.
2. Adjust the dial indicator so that its plunger or pointer is against the end of the spindle with its direction approximately parallel to the axis of the spindle.
3. Grasp the wheel assembly at the 3 o'clock and 9 o'clock positions. Push the wheel assembly in and out while oscillating it to seat the bearings. The difference between the maximum and minimum values is total bearing end play.

Preset Hubs

Standard hubs were used for decades but, beginning in 1997, a new method was devised to establish correct wheel bearing end play. In preset hubs, the bearing cup and bearing bores are machined seat-to-seat to precise tolerances in a climate-controlled factory. As illustrated in FIGURE 24-24, preset hubs are manufactured as a single piece unit and parts should never be interchanged.

Using a precision-machined bearing spacer placed between the inner bearing races establishes a predetermined distance between the bearing cones. Spacers are precisely machined for consistent width between the bearings, as shown in FIGURE 24-25. Because the spacer is not a crush sleeve, its width does not change during normal operation.

FIGURE 24-24 Preset hub unit.

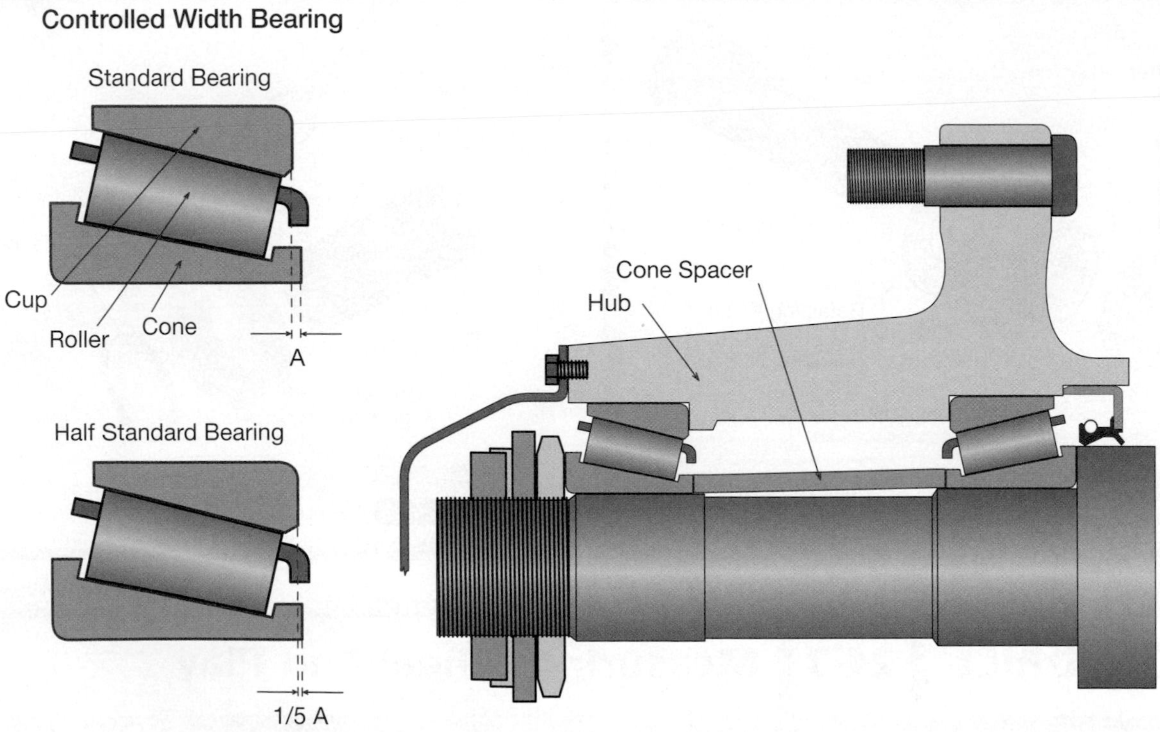

FIGURE 24-25 Precision preset hubs have precisely machined ledges for bearing cup and cone installation. The distances between the ledges and the bearing spacer maintain precise bearing preload.

When installing a new hub, a new assembly is installed on to the spindle and the bearing retaining nut is typically torqued to 250 to 300 ft-lb (339 to 407 Nm). Lubricant is added and a hubcap is installed. Wheel bearing end play is automatically set. Therefore the precision of bearing preload exceeds the accuracy obtainable for standard hubs using a manual bearing adjustment method. Preset hubs offer simplified installation procedures, improved wheel seal and bearing life, plus lower maintenance requirements. Note that preset bearings are not interchangeable with standard hub bearings.

Maintaining and Servicing Wheels and Hubs

Two principle aspects of maintaining wheels and hubs are caring for the seals and regularly lubricating the hub.

Wheel Seals

Wheel seals are an integral part of hubs used to keep oil or grease from leaking out between the wheel spindle and the rotating hub. Wheel seals also function to keep out dirt, water, and other contaminants.

Wheel seals are dynamic type seals. Dynamic seals are used in places where there is relative motion between the mating surfaces being sealed. **FIGURE 24-26** illustrates a dynamic seal.

Wheel seals are often made from metal and specialized rubber-like materials. Functionally, wheel seals must do the following:

- Withstand high temperatures produced during braking
- Be compatible with various hub lubricants that can degrade rubber materials
- Endure harsh operating conditions, such as road grit, for many miles of service

Types of Wheel Seals

A variety of seal types are available. They are classified depending on how sealing is performed, the type of installation tools used, materials the seal is made from, and whether the seal is pressed into the hub or onto the spindle shaft.

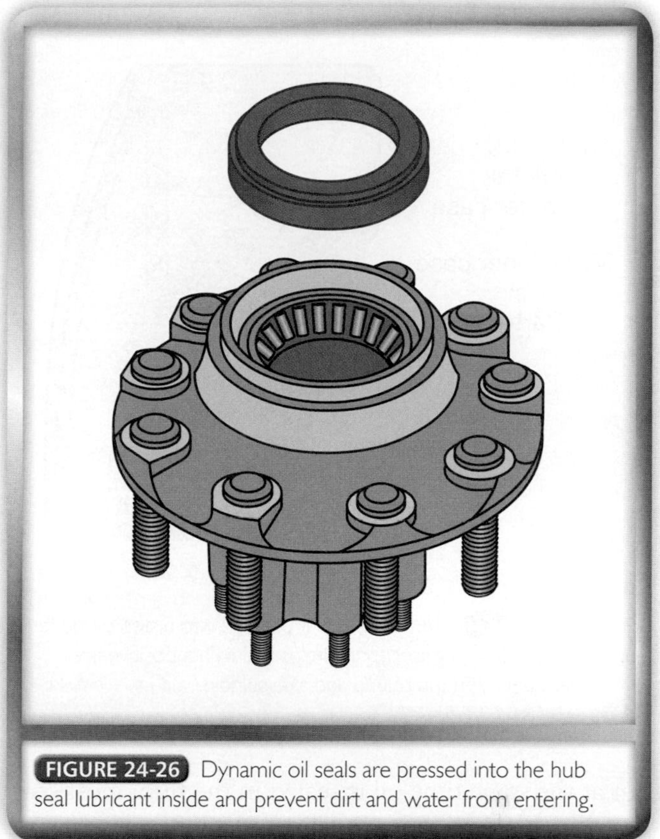

FIGURE 24-26 Dynamic oil seals are pressed into the hub seal lubricant inside and prevent dirt and water from entering.

Most seals are lip-type seals, which use a flexible piece of material to seal the rotating shaft when in contact with it. A garter spring is installed behind the seal lip to hold the seal firmly to the shaft, as shown in **FIGURE 24-27**. Any gas pressure inside the hub is used to force the seal tighter against the spindle. A small amount of hub lubricant leaks through the lip area and forms an oil film between the lip and shaft. This feature helps prevent leaks when gas pressures are high, such as when the oil or grease in the hub assembly becomes hot and expands. Various lip-type seals are illustrated in **FIGURE 24-28**.

When pressure is low and leaks are unlikely, the lower tension on the lip reduces seal and shaft wear. A slight oil film on the spindle reduces seal and shaft wear plus provides additional sealing capabilities. A good quality seal, installed properly, will not allow any oil to pass the seal lip. Because dirt and contaminants must be kept

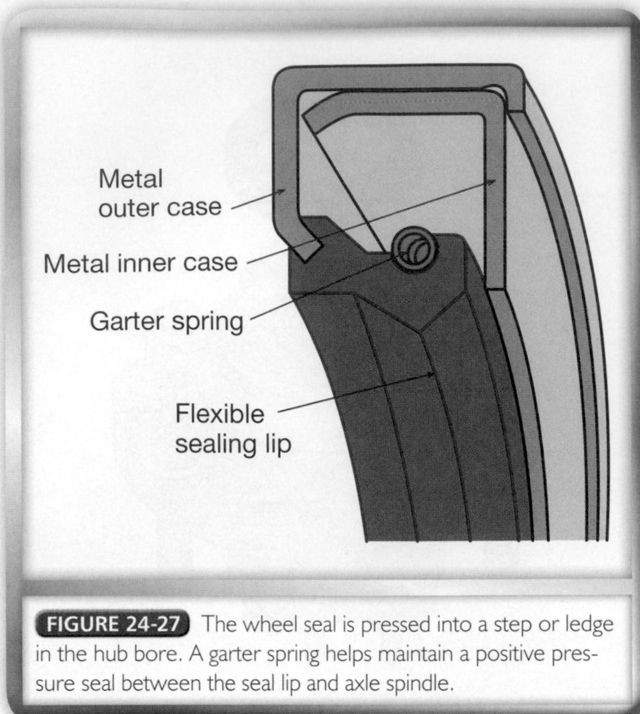

FIGURE 24-27 The wheel seal is pressed into a step or ledge in the hub bore. A garter spring helps maintain a positive pressure seal between the seal lip and axle spindle.

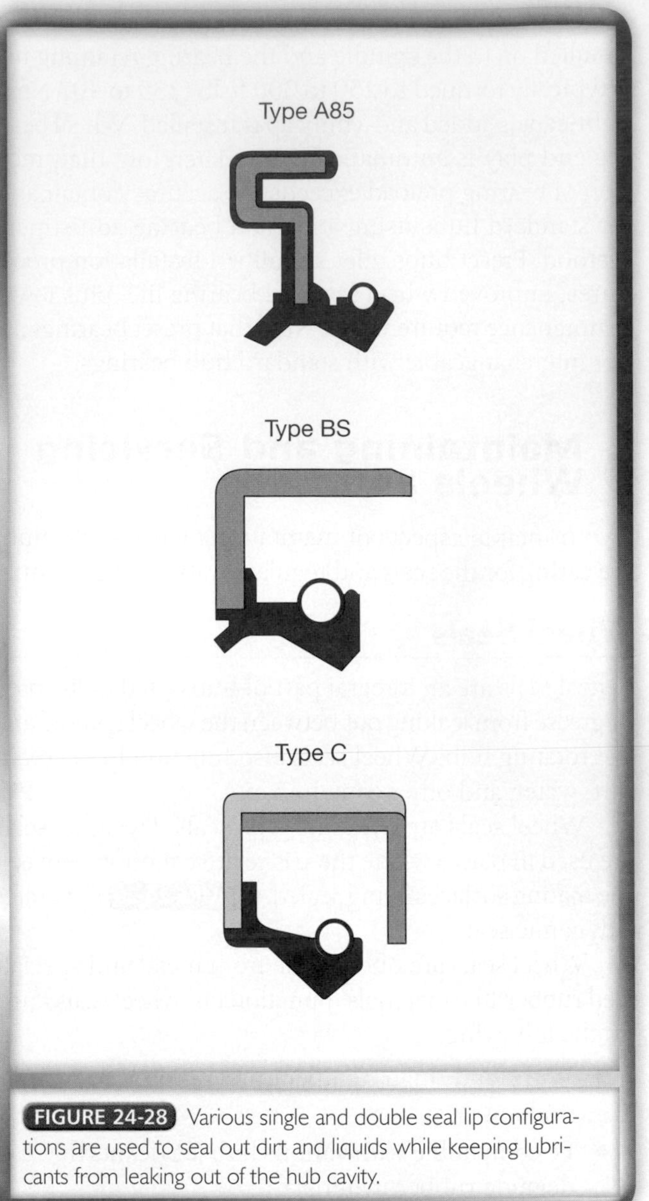

FIGURE 24-28 Various single and double seal lip configurations are used to seal out dirt and liquids while keeping lubricants from leaking out of the hub cavity.

out at the same time oil is sealed in the hub, most seals use a double lip design. One lip performs each function. Seal drivers, like the one in FIGURE 24-29, are often used to install wheel seals. Alternatively, wheel seals are hand-pressed into the hub.

Seal Failures

Wheel-end seal leaks are one of the biggest maintenance concerns among heavy-duty commercial vehicle operators. The most common failure mode for most bearings is a lack of or improper lubrication. Wheel seal leaks can quickly cause a wheel end to come off. Regularly inspecting wheel seals is critical preventive maintenance.

A leading cause of premature wheel seal failures is installation error. Damage to the seal during installation includes:

- Not lubricating the seal properly during installation
- Failing to drive the seal squarely into the hub
- Failing to correctly adjust wheel bearing end play
- Using a seal incompatible with hub lubricant
- Dirty or contaminated lubricant

Wheel Hub Lubricants

Gear oil and grease are used to lubricate wheel bearings. Good quality grease resists corrosion and water entry into the hub. Grease also helps absorb bearing shock loads and resists melting when hot.

Semi-liquid synthetic grease is commonly used in preset hubs. This grease is a semi-solid lubricant that is thick enough to stay in the bearings and provide lubrication, but thin enough to flow between parts. Lubricants used for wheel bearings generally contain the extreme pressure (EP) additive lithium or lithium soap. Lithium is a metallic element that provides additional lubrication and corrosion protection.

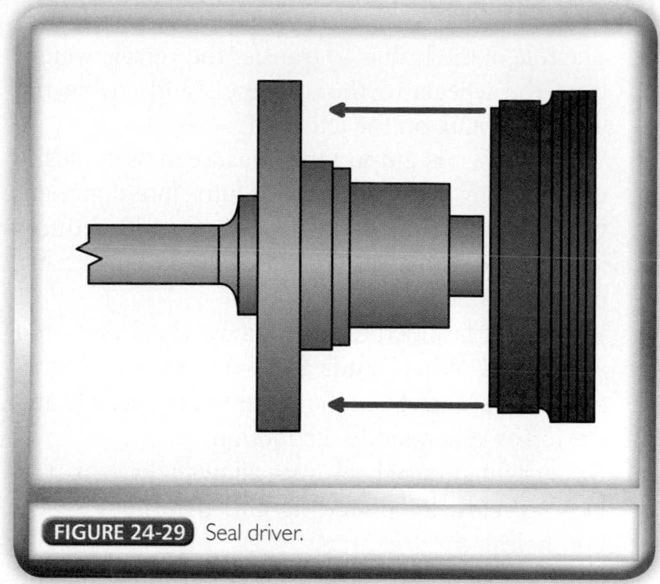

FIGURE 24-29 Seal driver.

Wrap-up

Ready for Review

- The role of the hub is to transfer the vehicle weight from the wheels to the axle ends and enable the wheel to rotate on the axle end.
- Wheel offset is important because it is typically used to bring the tire centerline into close alignment with the larger inner wheel bearing, and it reduces load on the stub axle. The offset can be either zero, positive, or negative.
- Wheels are fastened to the rims by wheel studs and wheel nuts. Wheel studs and wheel nuts are highly stressed by loads from the weight of the vehicle and the forces generated by its motion.
- Undertightening wheel nuts allows wheels to run loose, eventually pounding and deforming wheel bolt holes.
- Overtightening wheel nuts can stretch studs and cause them to fail. Applying excessive lubricant to the threads of a stud or nut can actually cause excessive tightening.
- The best way for a technician to produce the clamping force necessary to keep the wheels on the vehicle is through correct preparation of fasteners and the use of a torque wrench.
- Cast-iron spoke wheels are preferred in off-road or heavy-duty construction vehicle applications such as dump trucks, heavy equipment hauling, or logging. These wheels have the highest load carrying capacity.
- On a cast spoke wheel, friction between the rim and the increasingly larger diameter spoke hold everything together.
- When dual tires are used on a cast spoke wheel, a rim spacer is used between the rims to transfer the clamping force of wheel clamps to the inner rim.
- When rims are installed on spoke wheels, the lateral run-out needs to be checked and adjusted.
- Disc wheels are a simple, single, stamped steel or aluminum rim onto which the tire is mounted. They can be hub-piloted or stud-piloted.
- Stud-piloted disc wheels are the oldest type of wheel and no longer used on new equipment. They can use up to twice as many nuts as a hub-piloted system.
- Because stud-piloted wheels transfer weight through the studs, there is a greater likelihood of losing a wheel if the proper service procedures and hardware is not used.
- Hub-piloted disc wheels use pads instead of studs and nuts to center the wheel. Hub-piloted wheel nuts and studs only clamp the disc to the hub and do not support vehicle weight.
- Wheel hubs contain bearings used to reduce the friction between the stationary axle and rotating wheel. Bearing configurations can be full floating, three-quarters floating, or semi-floating.
- Precise adjustment of wheel bearing preload is necessary to maximize bearing life and prevent wheel seal leaks.
- Standard hubs are precision-machined aluminum or cast-iron castings used in drive, steer, and trailer configurations. Wheel bearings on standard hubs must be manually adjusted.
- Preset hubs have correct bearing end play engineered into their design and manufacture. The bearing cup and bearing bores are machined seat-to-seat to precise tolerances in a climate-controlled factory.
- Preset hubs offer simplified installation procedures, improved wheel seal and bearing life, plus lower maintenance requirements.
- Wheel seals are an integral part of hubs used to keep oil or grease from leaking out between the wheel spindle and the rotating hub. Wheel seals also function to keep out dirt, water, and other contaminants.
- Wheel seals are classified depending on how sealing is performed, the type of installation tools used, materials the seal is made from, and whether the seal is pressed into the hub or onto the spindle shaft.
- Leaking wheel seals can quickly cause a wheel end to come off. Regularly inspecting wheel seals is critical preventive maintenance.
- Gear oil and grease are used to lubricate wheel bearings. Semi-liquid synthetic grease is commonly used in preset hubs. This grease is a semi-solid lubricant that is thick enough to stay in the bearings and provide lubrication but thin enough to flow between parts.

Vocabulary Builder

bead seat The edge of the rim that creates a seal between the tire bead and the wheel.

bearing preload The load applied to a bearing before any vehicle weight or rolling loads are applied.

bolt pattern The number and spacing of the wheel nuts or wheel studs on the wheel hub on the wheel rim.

cast spoke wheel A type of heavy-duty commercial wheel that uses three, five, or six cast-iron spokes integrated with a bearing hub.

demountable rim A type of wheel rim that can be removed from the cast-iron spoke hub attached to the axle. Also called an open-center rim.

disc wheel A steel or aluminum wheel rim that supports a tire and attaches to the hub using wheel studs and nuts.

full floating bearings The wheel bearings are supported entirely by the axle housing.

hub-piloted disc wheel A type of disc wheel that uses a series of machined pads on the hub to help center the wheel.

negative offset When the hub mounting surface is towards the brake side or back of the wheel's centerline.

open-center rim A type of wheel rim that can be removed from the cast-iron spoke hub attached to the axle. Also called a *demountable rim*.

pilot pad The lugs attached to the bearing hub to locate the wheel assembly correctly during assembly.

positive offset When the plane of the hub mounting surface is shifted from the centerline towards the outside or front side of the wheel.

preload Negative endplay, or less than zero clearance.

preset hub A wheel hub that uses a precision spacer and close-tolerance bearings to eliminate the need for manual adjustment.

rim diameter The distance across the center of the rim, from bead seat to bead seat.

rim flange The exterior lip that holds the tire in place.

rim width The distance across the rim flanges at the bead seat.

semi-floating bearings Wheel bearings that support the drive axle that transmits torque.

standard hub A wheel hub that uses manually adjusted wheel bearing end play.

stud-piloted disc wheel A type of disc wheel that retains the disc using studs attached to the hub and a tapered, or ball-type, wheel nut to center the disc onto the hub.

three-quarters floating bearings The wheel bearing is supported by the axle housing but the the outer flange of the drive axle rides on the bearing, rarely seen today.

TMC RP 618 A procedure established by The Maintenance Council for obtaining acceptable wheel bearing end play of 0.001" and 0.005" (0.025 mm and 0.127 mm).

tire pressure monitoring system (TPMS) A system with in wheel sensors that monitors tire inflation pressure and temperature.

wheel end The assembly at the end of the axle.

wheel end play The free movement of the wheel hub assembly along the axle spindle axis.

wheel nuts The nuts that secure the wheel onto the wheel studs.

wheel offset The distance from the hub mounting surface to the centerline of the wheel.

wheel rim The outer circular lip of the metal on which the inside edge of the tire is mounted.

wheel studs The threaded fasteners that attach the wheel to the vehicle.

zero offset When the plane of the hub mounting surface is even with the centerline of the wheel.

Review Questions

1. Overtightening wheel nuts can:
   - **a.** stretch studs.
   - **b.** cause stress fracturing.
   - **c.** damage the stud holes.
   - **d.** distort the wheel nut.
2. Correct tightening sequence of the bearing retaining nut:
   - **a.** controls end play by preloading bearings.
   - **b.** optimizes bearing life.
   - **c.** optimizes seal life.
   - **d.** All of the choices are correct.
3. The role of the hub is to:
   - **a.** transfer the vehicle weight from the wheels to the axle ends.
   - **b.** enable the wheel to rotate on the axle end.
   - **c.** provide a mount location for the wheel assemblies.
   - **d.** All of the choices are correct.
4. Demountable rims being fitted to cast spoke hub:
   - **a.** are located by wheel studs.
   - **b.** are attached by clamps.
   - **c.** are attached by clamps and nuts onto a tapered face.
   - **d.** must be torqued to a pre-determined torque.
5. Collapsed dual wheel spacers can:
   - **a.** allow the wheels to come adrift.
   - **b.** allow the wheels to spin freely.
   - **c.** cause the wheel to move and possibly shear tire valve stems.
   - **d.** cause reduced braking forces.
6. Demountable rims installed on spoke wheel ends must be:
   - **a.** tightened to prevent movement
   - **b.** centered on wheel ends.
   - **c.** checked for lateral run-out.
   - **d.** tightened in a star pattern.
7. Wheel rims are sized according to:
   - **a.** diameter.
   - **b.** flange height.
   - **c.** width.
   - **d.** All of the choices are correct.
8. It is recommended that you should ________ the valve core when initially inflating a new tire that has just been placed on a rim.
   - **a.** adjust
   - **b.** remove
   - **c.** replace
   - **d.** assemble
9. Wheel offset is important for:
   - **a.** increasing load on the stub axle.
   - **b.** decreasing load on the stub axle.
   - **c.** maintaining equilibrium on the stub axle, regardless of load.
   - **d.** eliminating load on the stub axle.
10. ________ hubs have no end play errors.
    - **a.** Standard
    - **b.** Preset
    - **c.** Offset
    - **d.** Turned

ASE-Type Questions

1. Technician A says that you should always re-inflate a severely underinflated tire using the safety cage. Technician B says that you should use a clip-on air pressure chuck with an in-line remote mounted valve and pressure gauge. Who is correct?
   a. Technician A
   b. Technician B
   c. Both Technician A and B
   d. Neither Technician A nor Technician B
2. Technician A says when tightening lug or wheel nuts a torque wrench must be used. Technician B says that an air wrench can be used but the final tightening should be done with a torque wrench. Who is correct?
   a. Technician A
   b. Technician B
   c. Both Technician A and B
   d. Neither Technician A nor Technician B
3. Technician A says that tire markings now include load ratings on tires. Technician B says that they are only included on truck tires. Who is correct?
   a. Technician A
   b. Technician B
   c. Both Technician A and B
   d. Neither Technician A nor Technician B
4. Technician A says that tire markings now include speed ratings on tires. Technician B says that they are only included on high performance tires. Who is correct?
   a. Technician A
   b. Technician B
   c. Both Technician A and B
   d. Neither Technician A nor Technician B
5. Technician A says that tire markings now include temperature ratings on tires. Technician B says that they are only included on high performance tires. Who is correct?
   a. Technician A
   b. Technician B
   c. Both Technician A and B
   d. Neither Technician A nor Technician B
6. Technician A says mismatching tires of the same size on a heavy vehicle will generally not affect ABS operation. Technician B says that on a heavy vehicle the ABS operation will be compromised by mismatched tires. Who is correct?
   a. Technician A
   b. Technician B
   c. Both Technician A and B
   d. Neither Technician A nor Technician B
7. Technician A says that all Bias-ply tires must be rotated at regular intervals. Technician B says that directional tires can be cannot be rotated from one side of the vehicle to the other. Who is correct?
   a. Technician A
   b. Technician B
   c. Both Technician A and B
   d. Neither Technician A nor Technician B
8. Technician A says that wheel offset is the distance from the mounting surface centerline to the centerline of the wheel. Technician B says that wheel offset aligns with the inner wheel bearing. Who is correct?
   a. Technician A
   b. Technician B
   c. Both Technician A and B
   d. Neither Technician A nor Technician B
9. Technician A says that under-tightening wheel nuts can cause the wheels to loosen and become damaged. Technician B says that wheel nuts must be torqued in a set sequence. Who is correct?
   a. Technician A
   b. Technician B
   c. Both Technician A and B
   d. Neither Technician A nor Technician B
10. Technician A says that wheel bearing end play is between 0.001" and 0.005" (0.025 mm and 0.127 mm). Technician B says that wheel bearing end play is between 0.005" and 0.01" (0.127 mm and 0.25 mm). Who is correct?
    a. Technician A
    b. Technician B
    c. Both Technician A and B
    d. Neither Technician A nor Technician B

CHAPTER 25

NATEF Tasks

Suspension and Steering

Suspension Systems	Page
■ Inspect front axles and attaching hardware; determine needed action.	732–736
■ Inspect and service kingpins, steering knuckle bushings, locks, bearings, seals, and covers; determine needed action.	753

Wheel Alignment Diagnosis, Adjustment, and Repair	
■ Check camber; determine needed action.	737–739
■ Check caster; adjust as needed.	741–742
■ Identify turning/Ackermann angle (toe-out-on-turns) problems; determine needed action.	745
■ Check rear axle(s) alignment (thrustline/centerline) and tracking; adjust or repair as needed.	748–750
■ Check and adjust toe settings.	748–751
■ Identify causes of vehicle wandering, pulling, shimmy, hard steering, and off-center steering wheel problems; adjust or repair as needed.	749
■ Check front axle alignment (centerline); adjust or repair as needed.	752–755

Front Axles and Vehicle Alignment Factors

Knowledge Objectives

After reading this chapter, you will be able to:

1. Identify and describe types, styles, and construction of heavy-duty commercial vehicle axles. (pp 730–734)
2. Identify describe and explain factors affecting vehicle alignment. (pp 736–737)
3. Outline procedures used to measure wheel and axle alignment. (pp 737–746)
4. Outline methods used to inspect steering components for wear. (pp 745–746)
5. Describe the function and operation of various steer axle components. (pp 730–736)
6. Identify tools used to service front axle steering components. (pp 732–736)
7. Identify and describe problems with non-driving axles and recommend service procedures. (p 749)

Skills Objectives

After reading this chapter, you will be able to:

1. Perform a pre-alignment inspection. (p 750) SKILL DRILL 25-1
2. Measure toe-in and toe-out using a toe tester or trammel bar. (p 751) SKILL DRILL 25-2
3. Check KPI and included angle. (p 752) SKILL DRILL 25-3
4. Inspect axles for parallelism and tracking. (p 752) SKILL DRILL 25-4
5. Inspect the kingpins for wear. (p 753) SKILL DRILL 25-5
6. Lubricate the kingpins. (p 754) SKILL DRILL 25-6
7. Inspect and service tie-rods and tie-rod ends. (p 754) SKILL DRILL 25-7
8. Perform a geometric centerline alignment. (p 755) SKILL DRILL 25-8

Introduction

Several major assemblies work together in heavy-duty vehicles to power the vehicle down the road, including the clutch, transmission, transfer cases/boxes, propeller shaft, wheels, and axles. In this book, we will examine all of those systems in greater detail from the ground up, starting in this chapter with a deeper look at axles. Axles are a key component of the simple machine of wheel and axle and are used in some form in vehicles ranging from basic soapbox derby cars and go-carts, to the heaviest commercial vehicles.

Axles are straight shafts to which the wheels and tires are attached. As such, axles are part of the vehicle's steering system, as shown in **FIGURE 25-1**. Axles perform many functions. Some are load-bearing elements of the suspension system, helping support the weight of the vehicle. Others are used only to drive the wheels. A key function of axles is to maintain the position of the wheels relative to each other and the vehicle body.

In commercial vehicles, axles are used for multiple purposes, including:

- Driving
- Braking
- Steering and alignment

Types and Functions of Non-Drive Axles

There are two main categories of axles. **Live (drive) axles** are axles that are powered and can move the vehicle, like those shown in **FIGURE 25-2**. Live axles include the differential gearing and components used to transmit torque to the wheel ends. These are covered in detail in the chapter Heavy-Duty Drive Axles. Our discussion of axles in this chapter will focus on non-driving steering axles.

In contrast to live axles, **non-drive (dead) axles** do not have the capability to drive the vehicle. That is, non-drive axles do not transmit power. A typical non-drive (dead) axle is depicted in the illustration of the steering system in FIGURE 25-1.

Non-drive (dead) axles perform two main functions critical to the operation of the vehicle. First, dead axles provide a connection point for wheel ends. Second, dead axles align the vehicle wheels so that the vehicle will steer in a straight line and turn correctly. Non-drive axles also perform the important function of transmitting brake-reaction torque forces from the tire-wheel assembly to the rest of the vehicle through the suspension system. In addition, vehicle weight is distributed through the entire vehicle via its non-drive axles. Axles are used to support the weight of a fully loaded vehicle, so they must be properly designed to carry the load and resist distortion from braking "wind-up" torque as well. Finally, connection points for the suspension system are located on the axle.

There are many types of dead axles, including:

- Steering axles (front axles)
- Lift, tag, and pusher axles (rear axles)
- Trailer axles (rear axles)

Steering axles are primarily located in the front of heavy-duty vehicles. Some vehicles are also equipped

You Are the Technician

A driver with a tandem axle straight truck complains that the steering of the truck tends to pull to the curb side of the road. After performing a visual inspection, you notice most of the tires have uneven tread wear. A vehicle alignment indicates a five degree difference from recommended specification of the included angle on the right side steer axle.

1. List some likely causes of the vehicle pulling to one side of the road.
2. List the alignment angles that could cause the vehicle to pull to the right and indicate how those angles would be different.
3. What service recommendation would you make based on deviation from specifications of the included angle?

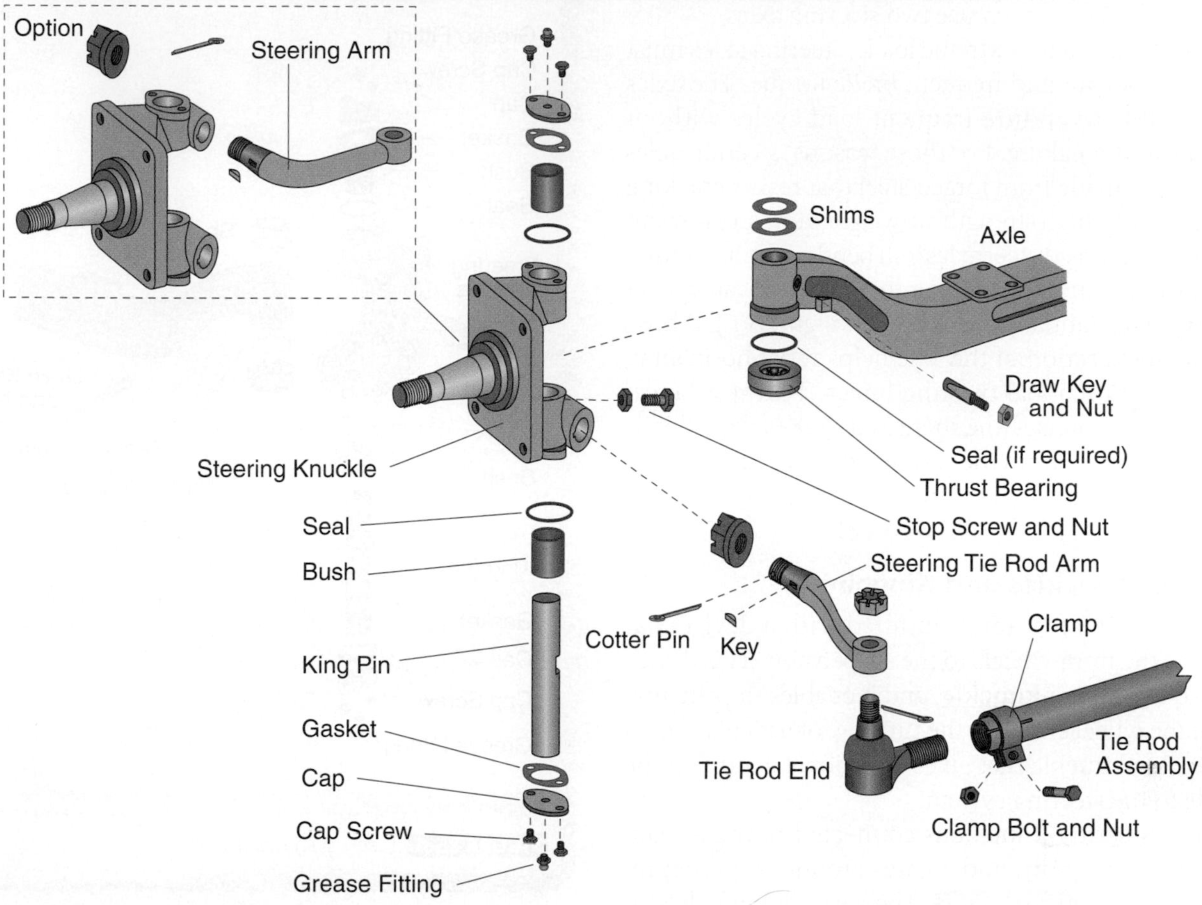

FIGURE 25-1 Typical medium- and heavy-duty steering system.

with non-drive steering axles in the rear of the vehicle. Lift, tag, and pusher axles are rear dead axles, as are trailer axles. (The section on trailer axles and axle tracking will cover trailer axles in more detail.)

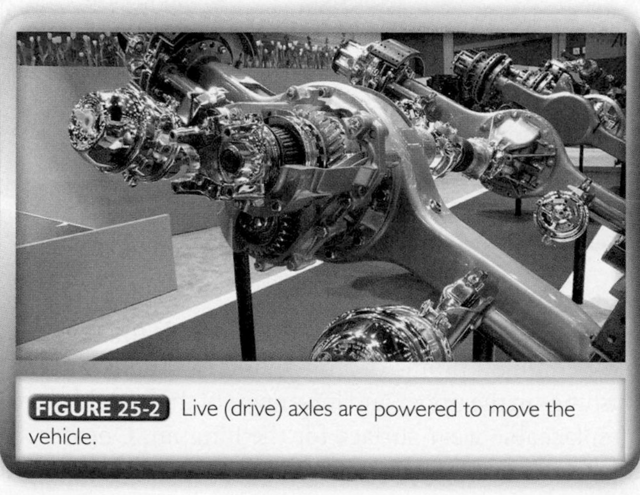

FIGURE 25-2 Live (drive) axles are powered to move the vehicle.

Steering Axles

Steering axles are used for the front axle of most medium- and heavy-duty vehicles. The most common configuration is the **solid I-beam**, a forged I-beam design named for its rigid I-shaped profile, as shown in **FIGURE 25-3**. Nominal axle weight capacities for steering axles typically range from 6,000 lb (2,722 kg) to 26,500 lb (12,020 kg).

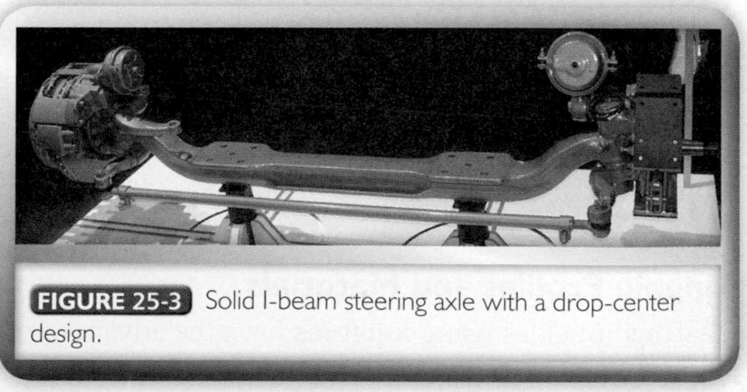

FIGURE 25-3 Solid I-beam steering axle with a drop-center design.

Very heavy commercial vehicles, such as concrete mixers and mobile cranes, often use two steering axles.

In addition to the extreme loads, steering axles must absorb significant and frequent brake torque. The axles must be able to endure frequent load cycles without fatiguing and breaking. For those reasons, steering axles are typically made from forged steel that resists cracking and produces a high strength-to-weight ratio. In the event of an impact, forged steel axles will bend and not fracture.

Newer technologies have produced fabricated steer axles that substantially reduce axle weight. A rigid box-shaped cross section of the axle helps resist horizontal, vertical, and torsional twisting forces. That resistance, in turn, helps manage the increased brake torque loads that have resulted from the shortened stopping distances mandated by changes made in 2010 to the Federal Motor Vehicle Safety Standard (FMVSS) 121.

Steering Knuckles and Kingpins

Each end of the I-beam is outfitted with a device that connects the front wheels to the suspension. This device is called a **steering knuckle**, and it enables the articulation of the wheel end. It is the turning, or articulation, of the steering knuckle that gives directional control of the vehicle to the steering system.

Each steering knuckle is connected to the I-beam through the **kingpin** and rotates around the kingpin, as illustrated in **FIGURE 25-4**. The steering knuckle also contains connection points for **steering arms** and the **tie-rod**, which is a tube that ties or connects the left and right steering arms together at each wheel end. Tying the steering arms together with a tie-rod synchronizes the movement of the steering knuckles, as shown in **FIGURE 25-5**. Two common methods are used to remove the tie rod end from the steering arm. One technique is to strike the steering arm with a heavy hammer or air-operated hammer. This will loosen the tapered joint. The other method is to use a tool called a fork or pickle fork. This tool is simply a wedge placed on both sides of the tie rod stud. Striking the fork with a hammer separates the tie-rod from the steering arm.

A single bearing located between the steering knuckle and axle transfers the weight supported by the wheel end to the axle. Without it, excessive friction between the axle and knuckle would quickly wear the two components and dramatically increase steering effort. Selective shims, located on the upper part of the axle I-beam between the knuckle and axle, as illustrated in FIGURE 25-5, take up any excessive clearance between the two parts.

Kingpin Profiles and Materials

Steering knuckles using kingpins have the advantage of being able to support much heavier weights compared to a ball-joint suspension that permits knuckle rotation. The most common profile of a kingpin is a straight kingpin. Bushings in the upper and lower part of the knuckle form a replaceable wear surface for the kingpin. One or two tapered draw keys are used to lock the straight kingpin

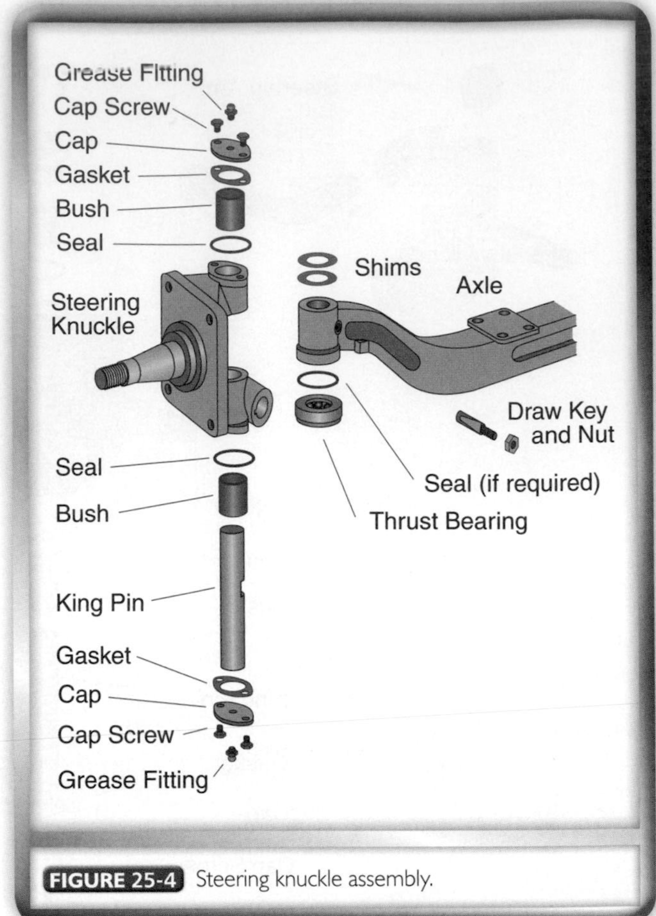

FIGURE 25-4 Steering knuckle assembly.

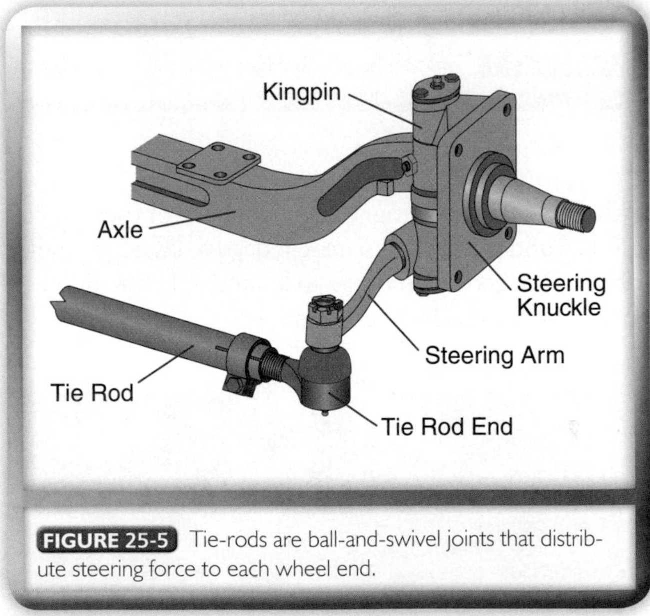

FIGURE 25-5 Tie-rods are ball-and-swivel joints that distribute steering force to each wheel end.

to the axle. FIGURE 25-6 shows various replaceable service parts for a straight kingpin with a single lock. Brass bushings are used in this service kit.

Another shape of kingpin is the tapered kingpin. Tapered kingpins have an adjusting nut that is used to adjust clearances between the pin and knuckle bushings, as illustrated in FIGURE 25-7. Unlike straight kingpins, tapered pins do not use a tapered draw key to lock the pin in place. Tapered kingpins are used on some applications such as on heavy-duty Volvo front axles. The advantage of the tapered kingpin is it has a threaded end or uses an adjusting nut that can be adjusted to compensate for kingpin and bushing wear and to minimize excessive operating clearances.

Kingpin bushings come in several materials. Most commonly, they are made from bimetal (brass and steel), nylon and steel, or similar composite materials. The steel outer shell provides strength for the bushing while the brass and nylon on the inside bushing surface provide a compatible wear surface and smooth steering rotation.

Steel-backed bronze (bimetal) bushings FIGURE 25-8A provide longer service life in severe service and can tolerate more dirt contamination. Bimetal construction makes these bushings ideal for aggregate haulers and refuse-handling vehicles. Pin-to-bushing clearances are obtained either by honing and or reaming the bushing.

Nylon bushings have the advantage of producing low steering effort and ease of installation because they do

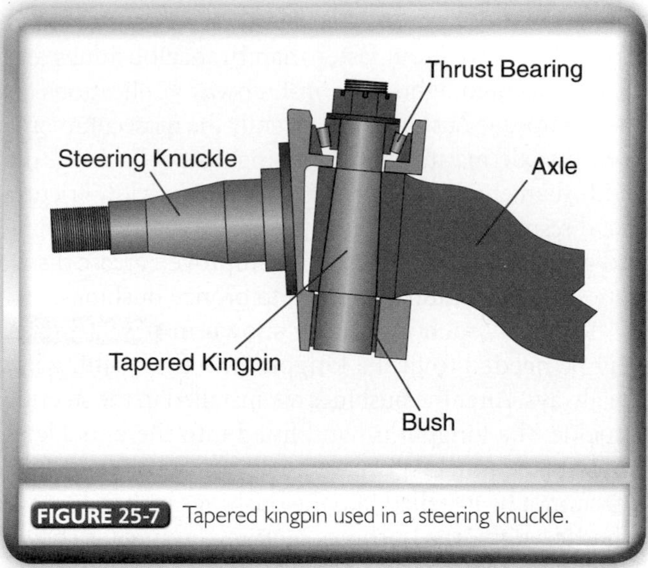

FIGURE 25-7 Tapered kingpin used in a steering knuckle.

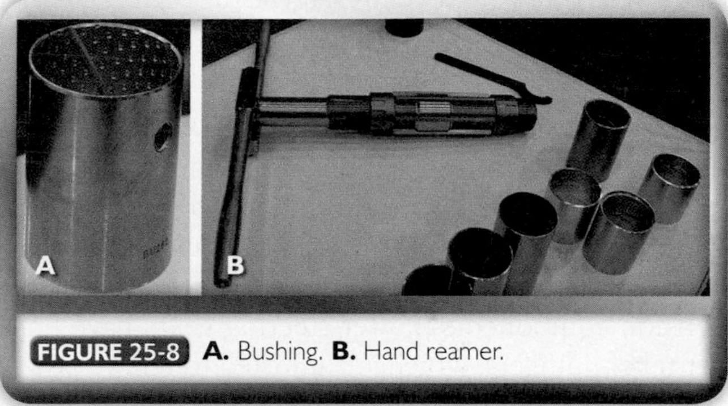

FIGURE 25-8 **A.** Bushing. **B.** Hand reamer.

FIGURE 25-6 Service kit for a straight kingpin with a single lock. **A.** Hub seals. **B.** Straight kingpin. **C.** Kingpin bushing. **D.** Tie rod end. **E.** Steering knuckle bearing. **F.** Kingpin draw keys. **G.** Steering knuckle shims. **H.** Kingpin gaskets.

not need to be reamed to fit the kingpin. These bushings typically will wear out faster than bronze bushings and are only used in light-duty, on-highway applications.

Composite bushings are currently the most commonly used by axle manufacturers. Using a steel backing, the inside diameter has a layer of plastic, such as low-friction acetyl resin polymer, applied to the steel back. Dimpling and grooving the coating enables improved grease distribution and retention compared to bronze bushings.

Reamers, such as the one shown in FIGURE 25-8B, may be needed to fit the kingpin into the bushing but not always. After the bushings are installed in the steering knuckle, the kingpin is hand fitted into the knuckle. A snug fit is required between the pin and bushings. If the pin cannot be installed into the bushings by hand, or the pin is too tight, the bushings require reaming (as shown in FIGURE 25-9), not the kingpin. When replacing kingpin bushings, a reamer is used to establish the correct internal diameter of the bushing to fit the kingpin.

Steering Stops

Steering stops are used to limit the turning angle of the steering knuckle. Adjustment of knuckle travel against the steering stops depends on the clearance of the tires and steer-axle components with the frame rails and suspension components. Power-steering gears have poppet relief plungers, which are adjusted to relieve power assist at the end of steering travel. This reduces pump wear and excessive stress on steering linkage components. Stops are adjusted to cut power assist with an additional clearance remaining of 1/8" to 3/16" (3.2 mm to 4.8 mm) between the spindle stop and the axle. Steer stops, shown in FIGURE 25-10, must be correctly adjusted first before the steering gear poppets are set to protect the power steering system. Incorrect adjustments to the stops and steering gear could cause the steering linkage to bind or allow tires

FIGURE 25-9 A cordless drill is used to drive a kingpin bushing reamer, removing material from the bushing. **A.** Steering knuckle. **B.** Holding fixture. **C.** Bushing reamer.

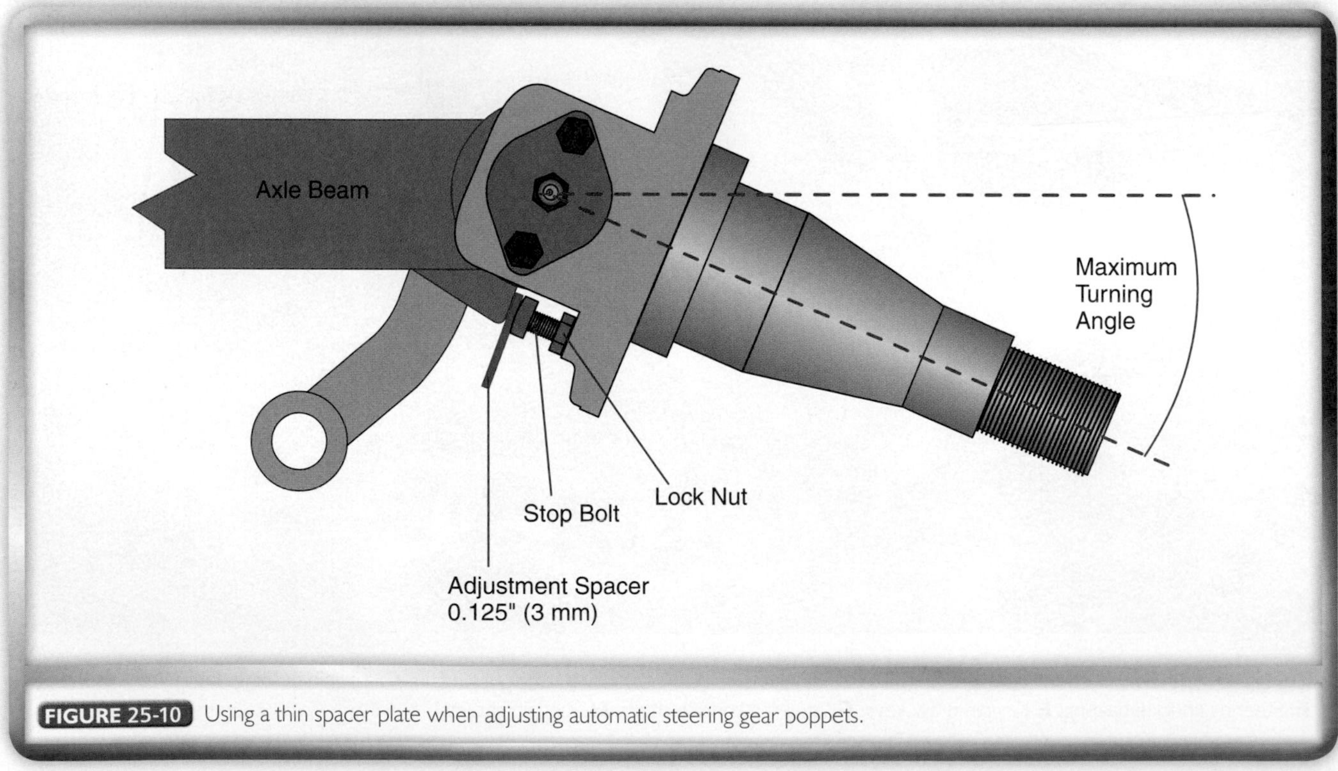

FIGURE 25-10 Using a thin spacer plate when adjusting automatic steering gear poppets.

to contact the frame or steering linkage. Incorrect adjustment could also cause the steering angle to be limited unnecessarily or, worse, cause excessive pressure to be applied to the steering linkage, potentially causing damage.

Pitman Arm

The **pitman arm**, sometimes called the **drop arm**, transfers the steering box output shaft motion to the steering linkage by converting rotational movement into linear motion. The pitman arm is typically splined to the steering gear output shaft at one end and connected through a ball stud to the drag link.

Drag Link

The **drag link**, illustrated in FIGURE 25-11, is connected to the steering arm at one end and the pitman arm at the other in order to transfer steering gear force to the steering arm. Some drag links are adjustable. That is, they incorporate an adjusting sleeve, which is used to center the steering wheel, with the straight ahead position of the wheels. In a typical drag link, the center-to-center length is critical to maintain the same number of turns from the vehicle straight-ahead position to the steering stop.

When installing an adjustable drag link, the front tires must be squared with the chassis frame. In addition, the steering wheel spokes must be correctly orientated in a straight-ahead position, and the steering box must be centered. The drag link, illustrated in FIGURE 25-12, is adjusted to the correct length to connect to the pitman arm and steering arm without moving the tires or steering gear.

Lift, Tag, and Pusher Axles

Lift, tag, and pusher axles are used to supplement the load-carrying capacity of a vehicle when required. As such, they are rear non-drive axles. What determines if an axle is a lift, tag, or pusher axle is the axle's position in

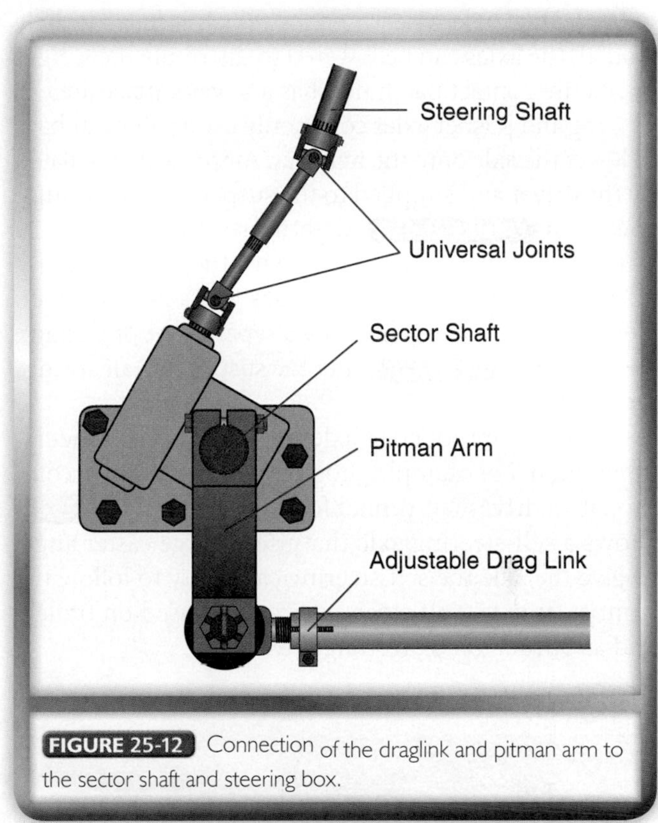

FIGURE 25-12 Connection of the draglink and pitman arm to the sector shaft and steering box.

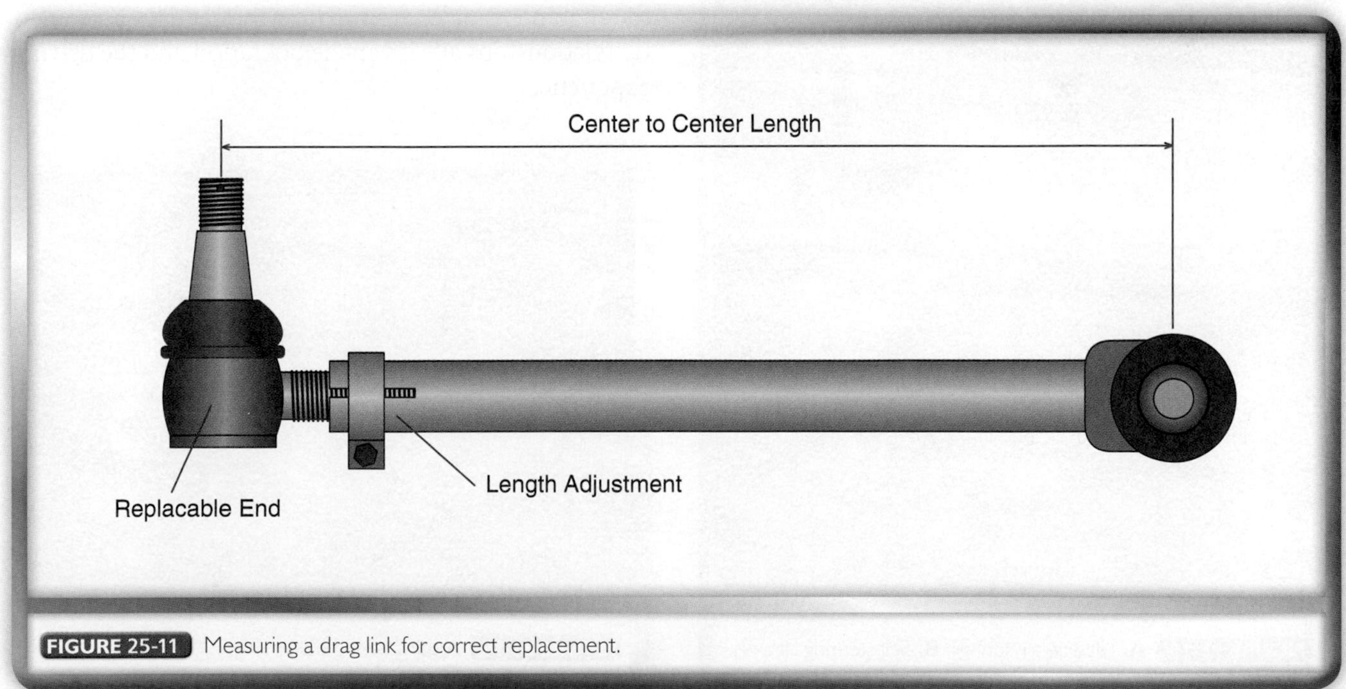

FIGURE 25-11 Measuring a drag link for correct replacement.

relation to the drive axle. **Tag axles** are mounted behind the drive axle, and **pusher axles** are mounted in front of the drive axle. Tag and pusher axles are also often **lift axles** that can be mechanically raised and lowered to meet the regulated requirements for maximum weight loads per axle. When the vehicle is empty, turning, or lightly loaded lightly loaded, the dead axles are raised to save tire wear and fuel. Likewise, when the vehicle is full or heavily loaded, the axles can be lowered to distribute the weight over a tire contact patch that has a larger surface area.

Tag and pusher axles commonly use a pair of air bags to lower the axle onto the roadway. Air pressure regulated by the driver and supplied to the suspension air springs, shown in FIGURE 25-13A, determines what percentage of the load the axle will share with the vehicle's other axles. As the air pressure increases, the axle will lower. Conversely, the axle is lifted by a separate set of air bags, shown in FIGURE 25-13B, after the suspension air springs are deflated.

Features are added to axles to better suit a particular application. For example, drop centers are used to accommodate a driveshaft tunnel for a lift axle. FIGURE 25-14 shows a self-steering axle that uses a large caster angle to give the axle the self-steering capability to follow the front steer axle. Self-steer axles can be used on trailers and as pusher axles on straight trucks.

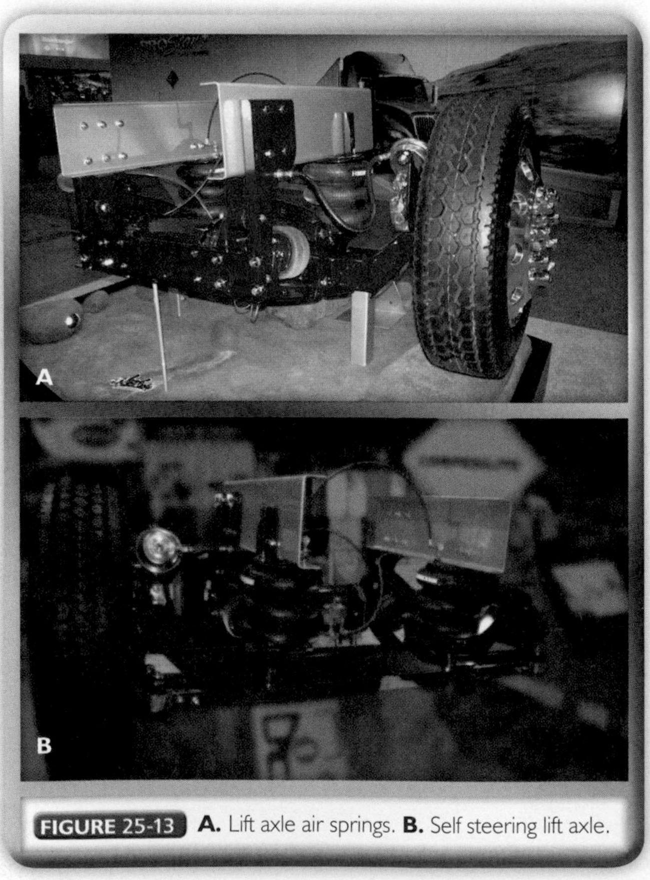

FIGURE 25-13 **A.** Lift axle air springs. **B.** Self steering lift axle.

Fundamentals of Vehicle Alignment

Wheel alignment, sometimes called **tracking**, refers to the positioning of the tires relative to the vehicle. The purpose of aligning and adjusting wheel position is to give heavy-duty commercial vehicles predictable, straight-line directional stability and the ability to correctly turn while minimizing tire wear and improving vehicle handling characteristics. Changes in vehicle loading and uneven loading alter wheel alignment, so those variables need to be taken into account by various alignment factors. Without correct wheel alignment vehicles will:

- Consume more fuel due to additional rolling resistance
- Wear tires faster since misalignment will produce uneven pressure and drag forces on tires
- Experience directional instability, as alignment strongly influences steering control
- Experience premature suspension and steering-component wear due to excessive forces applied to the components from wheel drag
- Cause increased driver fatigue due to the need to continuously correct vehicle direction, a condition known as countersteer (illustrated in FIGURE 25-15), and cause increased effort required to steering the vehicle

The positioning of the tires in relation to the vehicle results in a set of angles that, taken together, determine the vehicle's total alignment. Therefore, before you can check a vehicle's total alignment, you need to know what the alignment angles are and how they and their geometric relationships affect vehicle operation and the driving experience.

FIGURE 25-14 A self steering trailer axle.

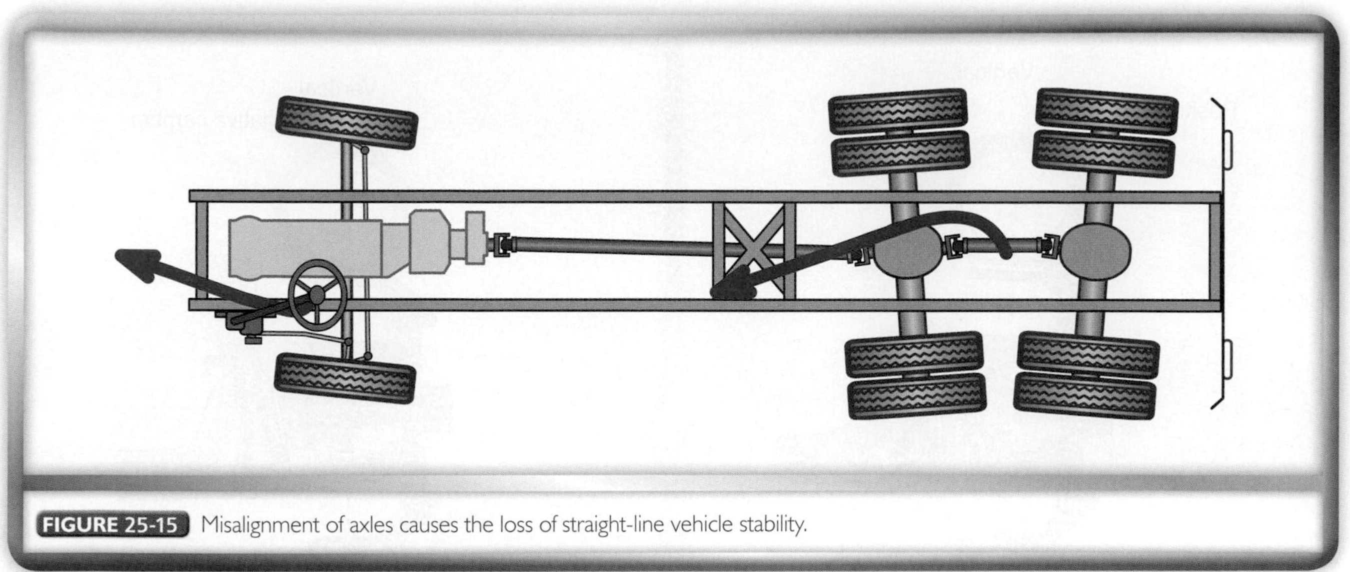

FIGURE 25-15 Misalignment of axles causes the loss of straight-line vehicle stability.

Alignment Angles

Tire alignment angles change as a result of vehicle loads. Front-axle components, therefore, contain many built-in features that enable them to optimize tire alignment for improved directional stability and vehicle handling when loaded.

Alignment angles fall into one of two categories: primary or secondary. Primary alignment angles refer to the positioning of the wheels relative to one another and to the vehicle. Many of the following primary angles are adjustable:

- Camber
- Caster
- Toe

Many vehicles allow adjustment of some of those angles, but not all are always adjustable. Secondary angles refer to the steering geometry of the vehicle produced by the design and operation of its steering and suspension components. Secondary angles include:

- Kingpin or steering axis inclination
- Included angle
- **Ackermann angle** or tire **toe-out on turns**
- Track width
- Thrust angle
- Frame angle

Camber

Camber is the side-to-side vertical tilt of the wheel. It is viewed from the front of the vehicle and is measured in degrees. Camber causes a tire to roll like a cone either inward or outward from the vehicle centerline. **Positive camber** exists when the tires are closer together at the bottom and farther apart at the top, as illustrated in FIGURE 25-16A. **Negative camber** exists when the tires are closer together at the top, as illustrated in FIGURE 25-16B.

A vehicle with camber pull will pull in the direction of the greatest positive camber. To picture why the vehicle pulls in this direction, think of a paper cone lying on its side. When the cone is rolled, it turns in the direction of the narrower end of the cone. Tires do the same thing in regard to their camber. Camber is affected by ride height on wheels with independent suspensions and can be observed by looking at the tilt of the wheel in vehicles that are lowered incorrectly.

All heavy duty commercial vehicles use positive camber because a loaded vehicle will bend the axle slightly. That bend causes the wheel to tilt inwards at the top, as shown in FIGURE 25-17A. Without some positive camber, a loaded vehicle would place more force on the inside of the tire tread, prematurely wearing out the tire. With positive camber, a loaded vehicle will allow the tire to run flatter against the road. The vehicle then places more vehicle weight on the larger inner wheel bearing. Less steering effort is required when loaded, and wear of the wheel bearing and spindle is also minimized. Axles with no camber, such as trailer axles will use identical sized inner and outer tapered roller bearings in the axle hubs.

Even though negative camber is not used on heavy vehicles, a positive or neutral camber can turn negative when the vehicle is loaded, as illustrated in FIGURE 25-17B. One benefit of negative camber is improved cornering capabilities. Camber actually causes the tires to have slightly different rolling radiuses depending on whether the inside or outside shoulder of the tire has the greatest weight loaded against it. (Recall the analogy of the paper cone.) For example, high positive camber means

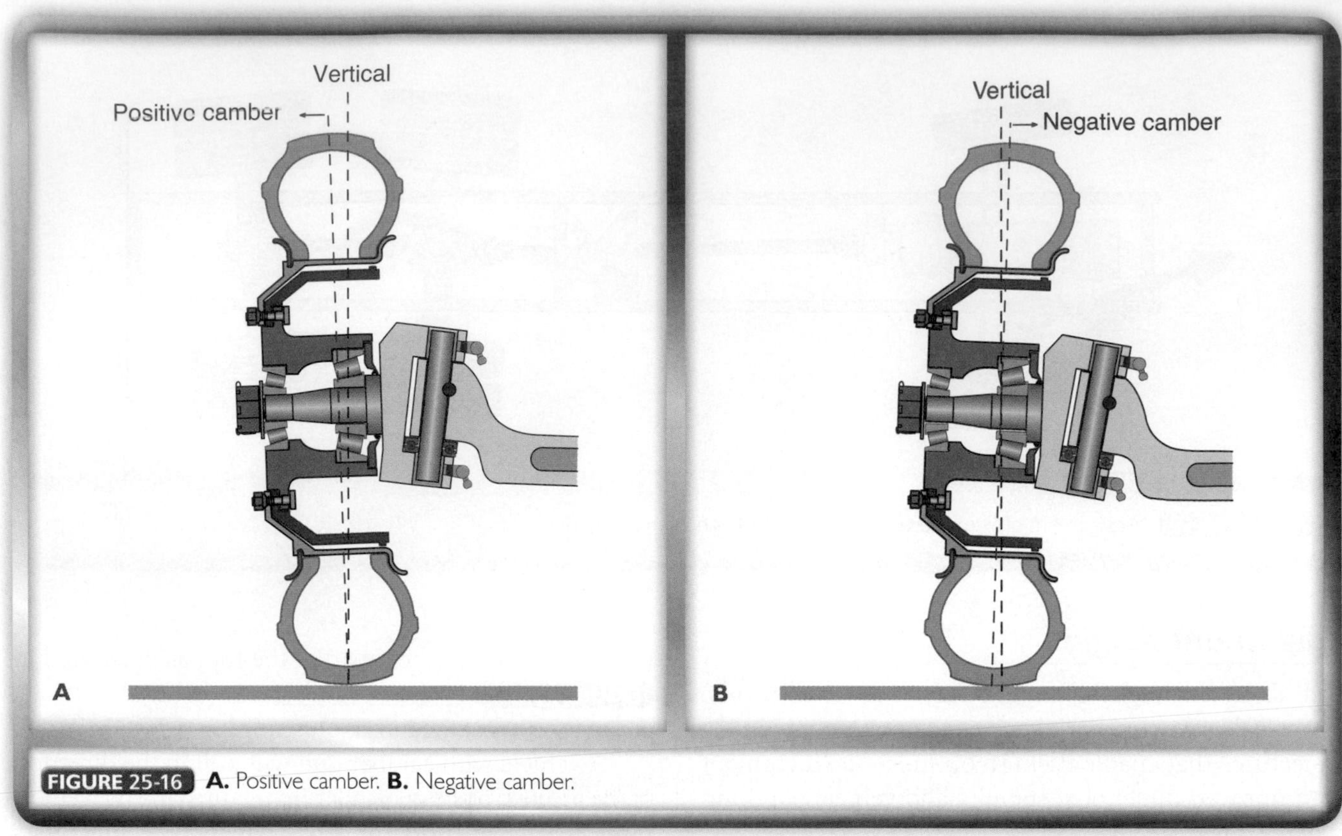

FIGURE 25-16 **A.** Positive camber. **B.** Negative camber.

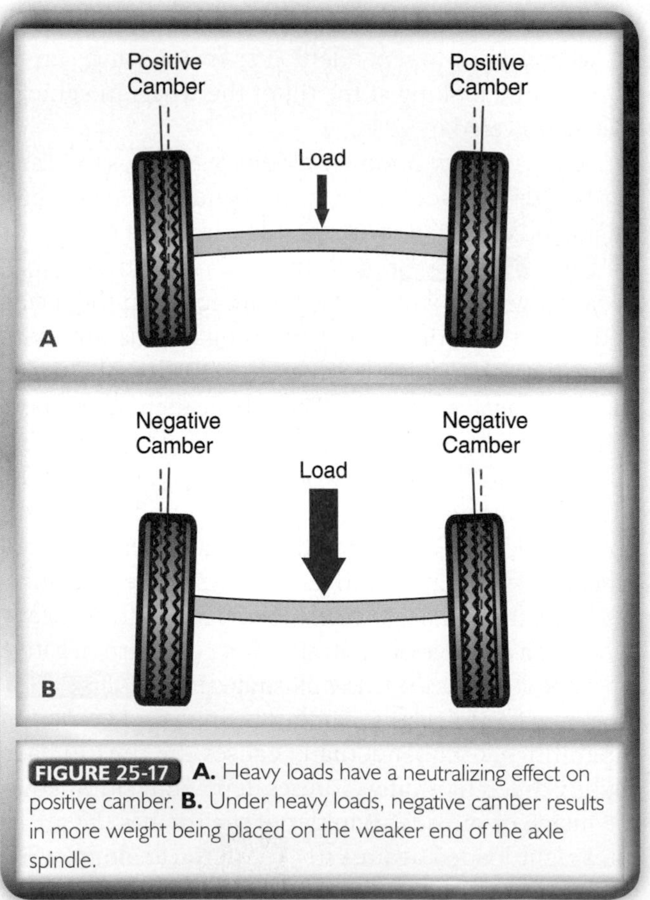

FIGURE 25-17 **A.** Heavy loads have a neutralizing effect on positive camber. **B.** Under heavy loads, negative camber results in more weight being placed on the weaker end of the axle spindle.

that more weight is applied to the outside edge of the tire, thus reducing its rolling diameter slightly compared to the inside edge. In this case, the tires tend to roll out away from the vehicle centerline. Negative camber causes tires to roll inward towards the centerline. Because camber is a tire-wearing angle, optimal camber angles are needed to produce the least wear while improving directional stability.

Roads are crowned to improve water drainage. In other words, the traffic lane is lower on the curb side than in the center. That curve allows rainwater to run off the road. Slightly reducing the degree of positive camber on the right side wheel compensates for the crown in the road, as shown in FIGURE 25-18. Without that adjustment, driving on a crowned road causes weight in a heavy vehicle to transfer to the right, which in turn causes the vehicle to pull, or drift, toward the curb.

With less positive camber on the right side, more positive camber is used on the left wheel to correct the effects of road crown. A difference of one-fourth degree more positive angle on the left wheel compared to the right wheel is typically used. The small angle will not influence direction on a flat road surface. Excessive positive or negative camber will produce uneven tire wear on either side of the tire depending on whether the camber is excessively positive or negative. TABLE 25-1 shows the

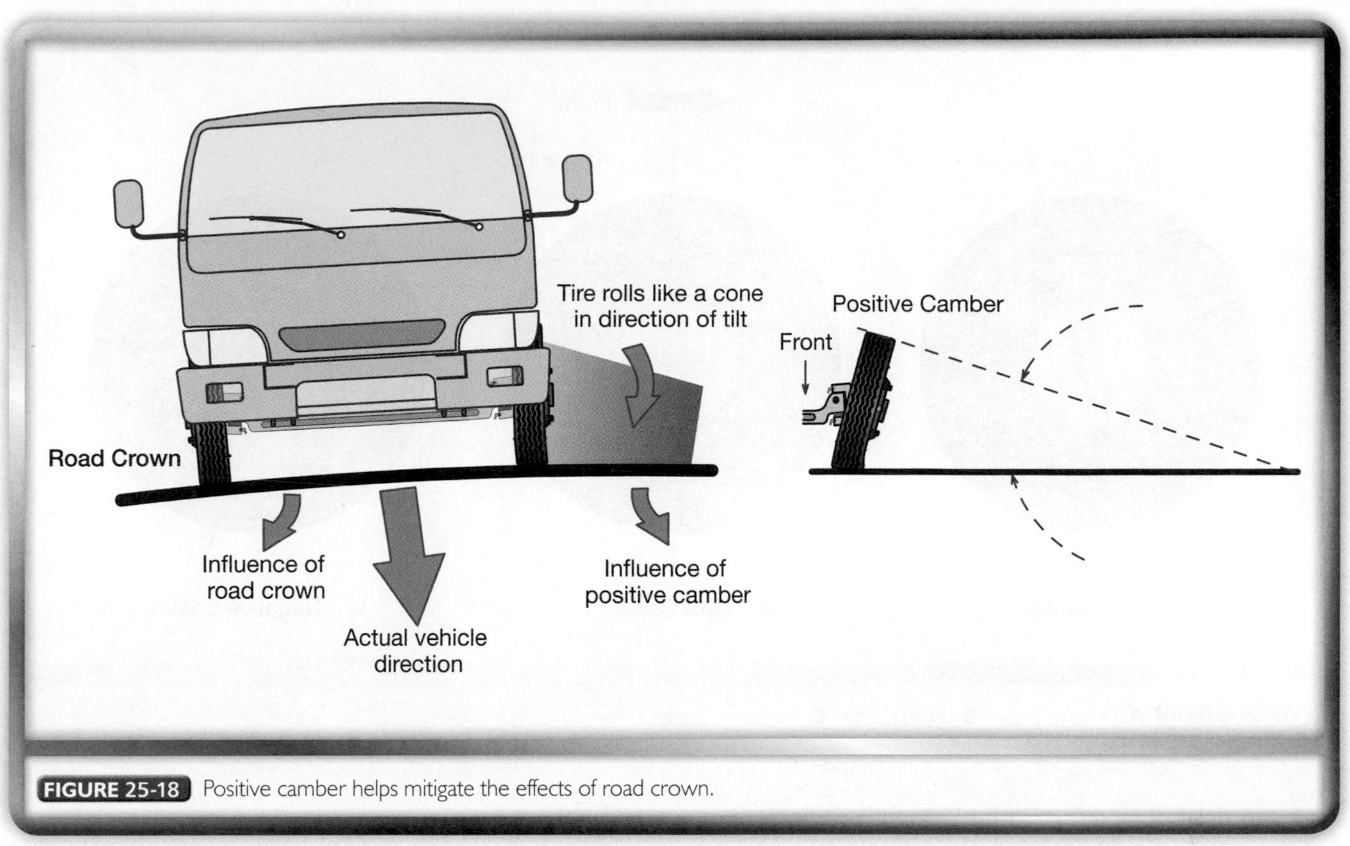

FIGURE 25-18 Positive camber helps mitigate the effects of road crown.

TABLE 25-1: Relationship of Camber Setting to Tire Life

Camber Setting (in degrees)		
Left	**Right**	**Tire Life %**
–3/4	–1	90%
–1/4	–1/2	89%
+1/4	0	100% (Optimal)
+3/4	+1/2	78%
+2	+1-3/4	73%

Source: The Maintenance Council

relationship between camber setting and tire life. Notice from the table how additional positive camber on the left wheel compensates for road crown. Improved straight-line directional stability is achieved with slightly more camber on the left than right wheel. Tire life is extended using correct camber and toe-in angles. (Toe-in angles will be discussed in the Toe section later in the chapter.)

Caster

Caster is viewed from the side of a vehicle and is the forward or rearward tilt of the steering axis from true vertical, as illustrated in FIGURE 25-19. When using kingpins, caster angle is formed between a true vertical line and an imaginary vertical line passing through the kingpin. Stated another way, caster angle is seen as a line connecting the upper and lower steering knuckle pivot points. FIGURE 25-20 illustrates the difference between caster and camber.

When the upper pivot point is more rearward compared to the lower pivot point, caster is positive. If the upper pivot point is forward of the lower pivot point, caster is negative. A maximum side to side variation of ±0.5 degrees is recommended on most vehicles. Unlike camber, caster is not a tire-wearing angle under most operating conditions.

Caster and Vehicle Stability

Today's vehicles all use positive caster for straight-line directional control stability and steering-return ability. Using a positive amount of caster at both wheels forces the wheels to return to a straight-forward point if moved to the left or right. This happens because positive caster projects the weight of the vehicle ahead of the point where tires contact the road. In other words, with positive caster,

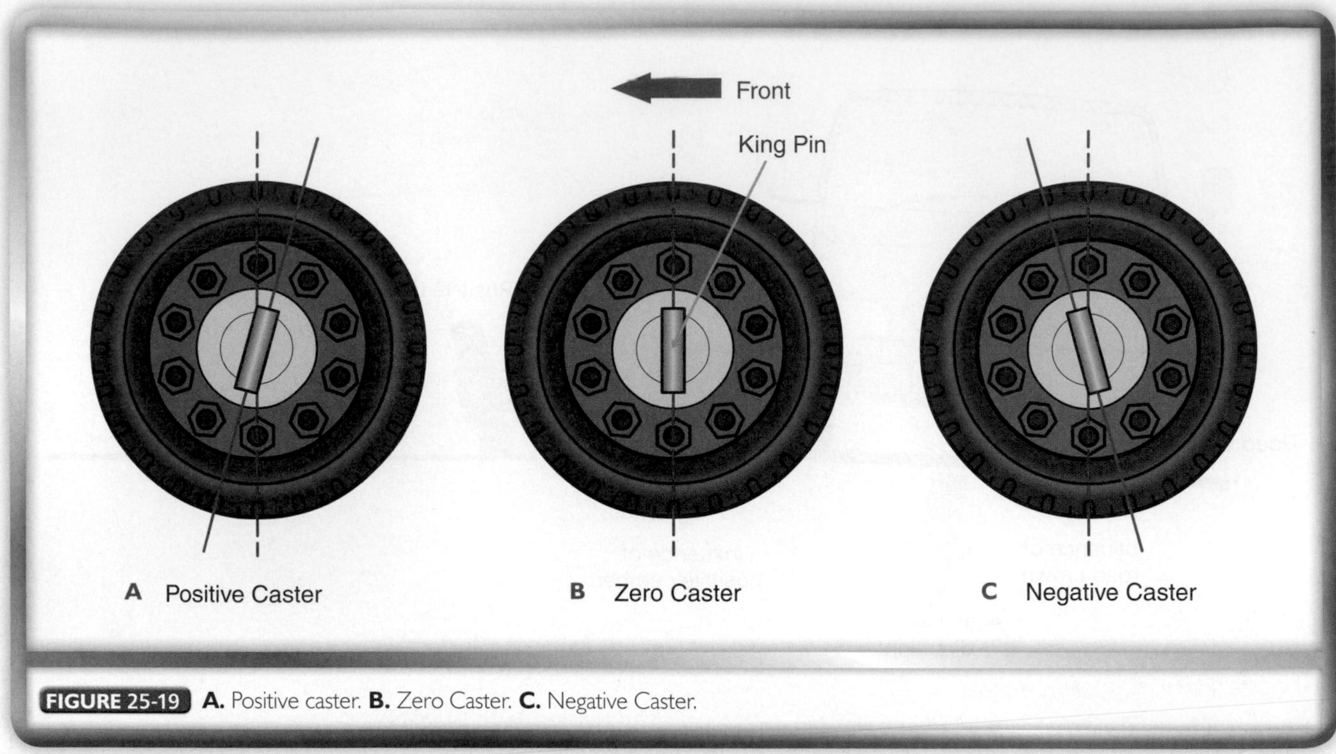

FIGURE 25-19 **A.** Positive caster. **B.** Zero Caster. **C.** Negative Caster.

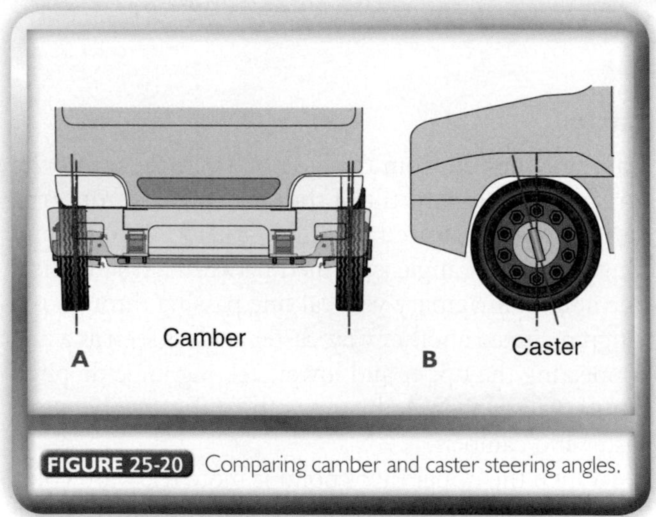

FIGURE 25-20 Comparing camber and caster steering angles.

the contact patch of the tire follows the projected weight of the vehicle, as illustrated in FIGURE 25-21.

Positive caster will produce a weight shift on the tires when moved from a straight-line direction. That shift forces the wheel to return to straight ahead position. When turning left, the left side of the vehicle will lift. That occurs because caster causes the rotation of the steering knuckle spindle to swing downwards. The left steering knuckle will lift the vehicle and tilt the tire inwards at the top. This weight shift produces force in the direction of returning the wheel to its original straight-ahead position. When turning left, the right wheel does the opposite of the left, and lowers the vehicle on the right side. The right wheel tilts out at the top. Weight transfer from both tires attempts to force the wheels to an even and level position found only in a straight-line direction. The weight transfer produced by a large degree of caster increases the amount of effort required for cornering but has the advantage of automatically returning the wheels to a straight-line direction after a turn is completed.

Like camber, a different caster angle between the right and left wheels helps compensate for road crown. The right side is adjusted with slightly more positive caster to produce a difference of no more than one-half degree between left and right.

TECHNICIAN TIP

The basic method for measuring caster angle on alignment equipment is to measure the angle of tilt when a wheel is turned. As caster angle increases, the degree the wheel will tilt in or out changes proportionally. As caster angle increases, the wheel will tilt inward—even more so when the wheel turns towards the vehicle centerline. This means when turning right, the left wheel will tilt inward at the top and the bottom turns outward. The opposite effect is seen when turning left. The caster angle is basically the difference between a wheel's tilt when the wheels are straightened and when they are turned at say 20, 30, or 45 degrees.

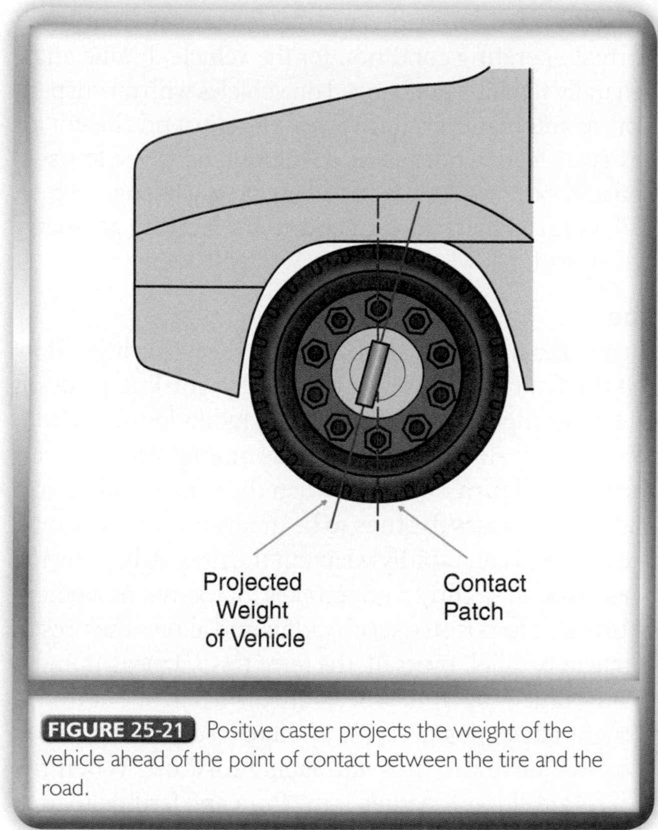

FIGURE 25-21 Positive caster projects the weight of the vehicle ahead of the point of contact between the tire and the road.

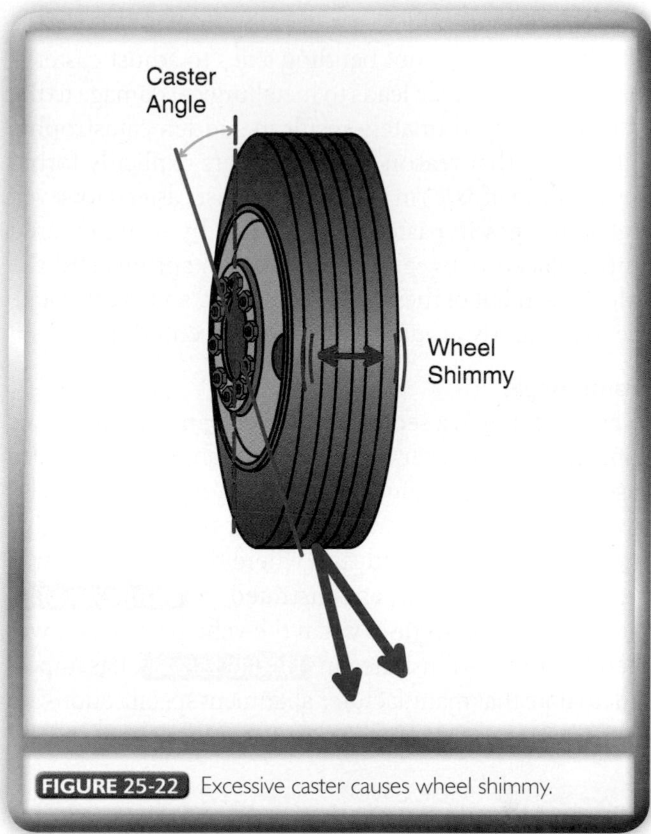

FIGURE 25-22 Excessive caster causes wheel shimmy.

Caster Shimmy

While a little caster is good, excessive caster is dangerous. Excess positive caster is responsible for a condition called **caster shimmy** that can be dangerous to vehicle control and directional stability. The effect of excess positive caster and caster shimmy is observed on furniture casters and shopping cart wheels. If you have ever tried to maneuver a cart experiencing caster shimmy, you have likely noticed the rapid—but small—side-to-side movement of the wheel, as illustrated in FIGURE 25-22. As the vehicle moves faster, the tires cannot quickly "find" the projected track they should follow and begin to swing from left to right in an attempt to find a straight ahead direction. In a heavy vehicle, this shimmy is felt in the steering wheel.

As positive camber increases, the farther the vehicle weight is projected beyond the tire contact patch, the greater the likelihood and increased intensity of caster shimmy. This also happens since caster angle affects the radius of camber roll. Increases in positive camber will produce proportional increases in the intensity and frequency of shimmy, particularly after hitting a bump. Another common cause of caster shimmy is an increase in vehicle load over the rear axle. When the rear suspension is lowered, the steering knuckle will tilt and positive caster angle increases. Shock absorbers, like those shown in FIGURE 25-23, are occasionally used on the tie-rod to minimize caster shimmy on axles with a high degree of caster.

Adjusting Caster

Caster angle is primarily built into the shape of the steering axle spindle where the kingpin passes through the steering axle or kingpin bore. Major changes to caster would require twisting the axle. Because metal tends to return to its original cold-forged position (the shape it had when originally manufactured), any changes in

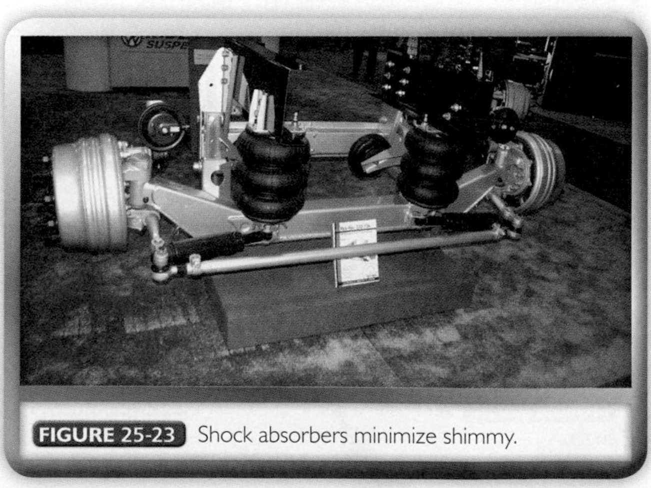

FIGURE 25-23 Shock absorbers minimize shimmy.

the field will typically revert back to original axle shape. Another reason for not bending axles to adjust caster is that bending the axle leads to metallurgical damage to the axle. That can ultimately result in sudden catastrophic failure. For that reason, manufacturers explicitly forbid any bending of axles in the field to adjust caster. However, small changes in caster can be made by using tapered shims placed between the suspension springs and the axle. Placement of these selectively sized shims can rotate the axle slightly around its horizontal centerline.

Frame Angle

Even though it is a secondary angle, **frame angle** can be considered with caster, since the frame angle can influence caster angle. Frame angle refers to the vehicle's frame relative to horizontal measurement to the ground. A **positive frame angle** is the condition where the vehicle's rear is higher than the front, as illustrated in FIGURE 25-24A. **Negative frame angle** is when the vehicle's rear is lower than the front, as illustrated in FIGURE 25-24B. It is important to note that manufacturer alignment specifications are recommended for loaded conditions because that is the normal operating condition for the vehicle. Frame angle generally remains unchanged on vehicles with air suspension, as automatic leveling valves will adjust ride height for any given load. Under some conditions, however, any suspension system's normal ride height may change, which will, in turn, affect adjustments to the steering geometry or the readings when the vehicle is unloaded.

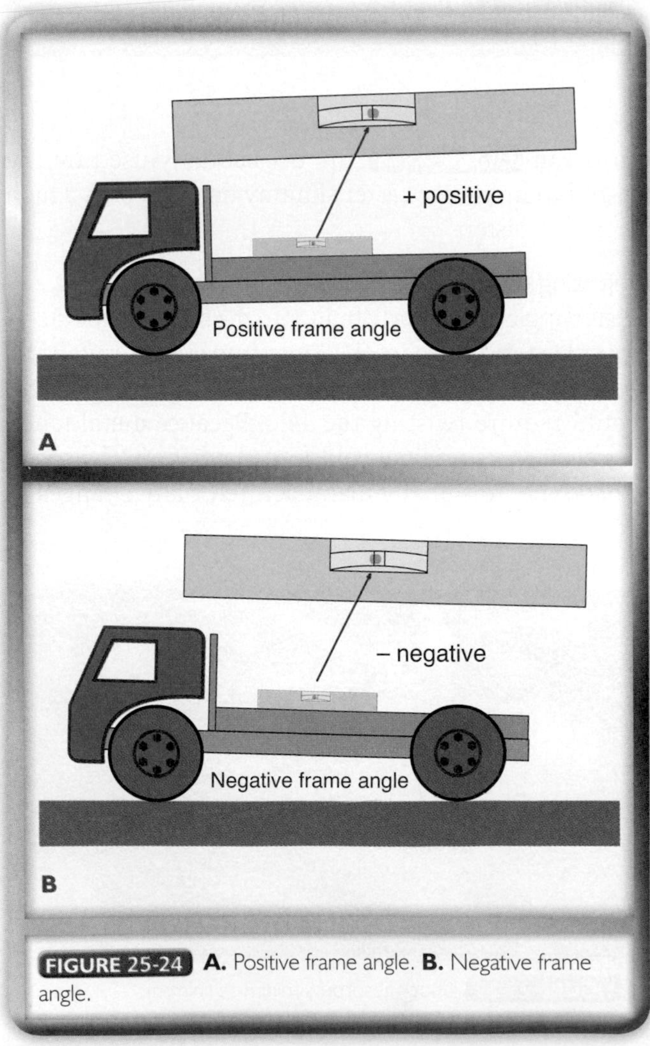

FIGURE 25-24 **A.** Positive frame angle. **B.** Negative frame angle.

Toe

Clearances in steering linkage and wheel bearings allow the tires to turn outwards from a straight-line position when moving. With a positive scrub radius found on front steer axles of almost all commercial on-highway vehicles, the tires will turn outwards when the vehicle moves forward. This causes the tires to be dragged sideways down the road and can rapidly wear out the tires. Adjusting the tires to toe-in slightly compensates for toe-out movement of tires due to positive scrub radius and allows the tires to rotate in parallel. By itself, the term **toe** is a measurement of how much the front wheels are turned in or out from a straight-ahead position. Toe is referenced from a position directly above the tires and facing forward. When the wheels are closer together at the front and farther apart at the rear, a **toe-in** condition exists FIGURE 25-25A. When the wheels are closer together in the rear than in the front, a **toe-out** condition exists FIGURE 25-25B. Rolling down the road, tires naturally toe-out to a zero toe position due to positive scrub radius.

When travelling forward, toe should be zero degrees to prevent tire wear. Excessive toe-out will wear the inside edge of both tires. Too much toe-in will wear the outside edge of tires. The difference between toe wear and camber wear is that toe wear creates a "feathering" of the tread while camber wear does not. Toe problems will affect both tires while camber wear affects one tire unless both tires have incorrect camber. TABLE 25-2 shows the life expectancy of tires based on toe dimensions.

As with some other angles, toe can be adjusted by changing the length of the tie-rod. The length is, in turn,

TABLE 25-2: Life Expectancy of Tires Based on Toe Dimensions

Toe-in	Tire Life Expectancy
0.03125" (0.794 mm)	100%
0.125" (3.175 mm)	82%
0.25" (6.35 mm)	76%

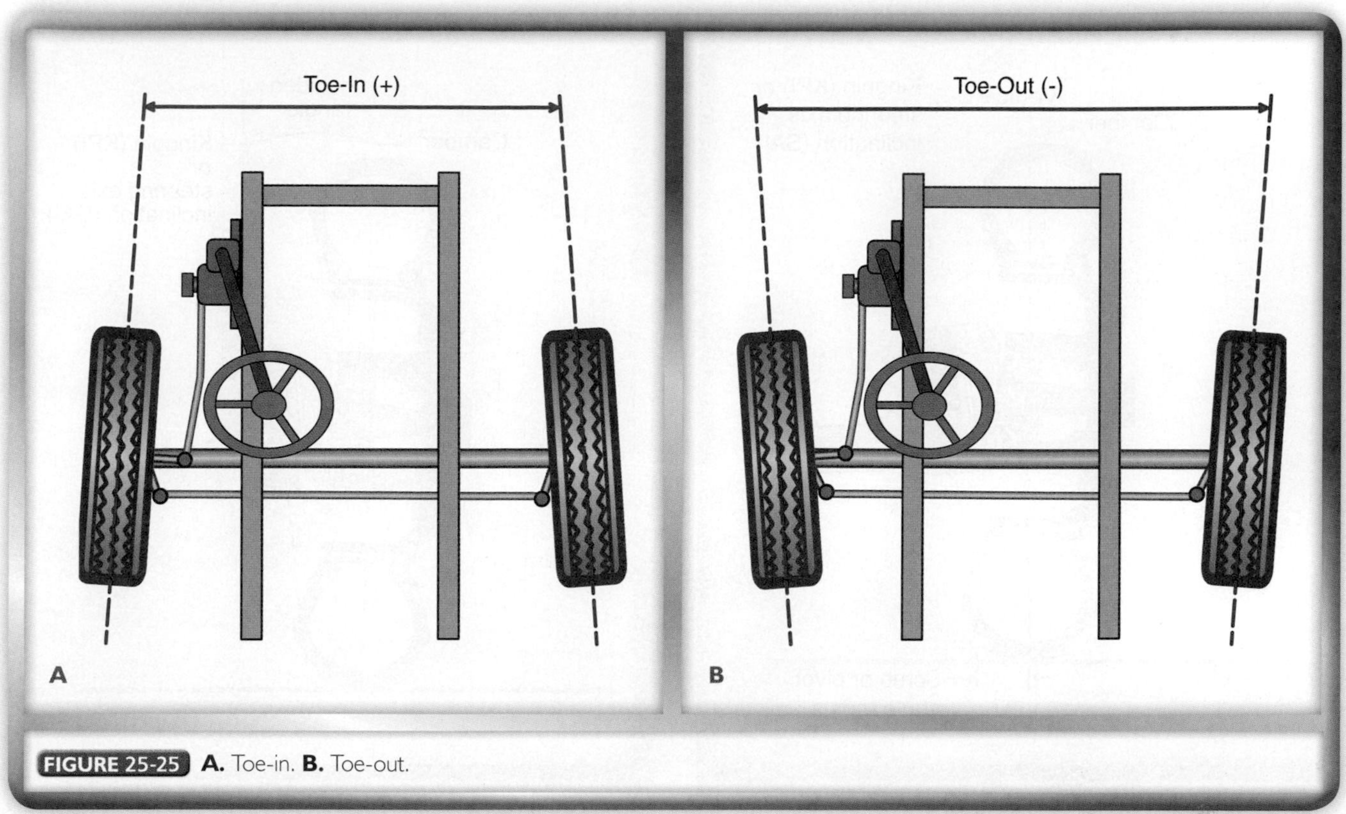

FIGURE 25-25 **A.** Toe-in. **B.** Toe-out.

changed by shortening or lengthening the tie-rod ends threaded into the tie-rod. **Tie-rod ends** are ball-and-socket joints attached to the steering knuckle steering arms. The tie-rod ends are connected together by threading into a cross tube. Each side will use a left or right hand thread to enable adjustment of tire toe by turning the cross tube that connects the tie-rod ends. As shown in FIGURE 25-26, tie-rod ends are manufactured in several designs that help prevent binding with the steering linkage.

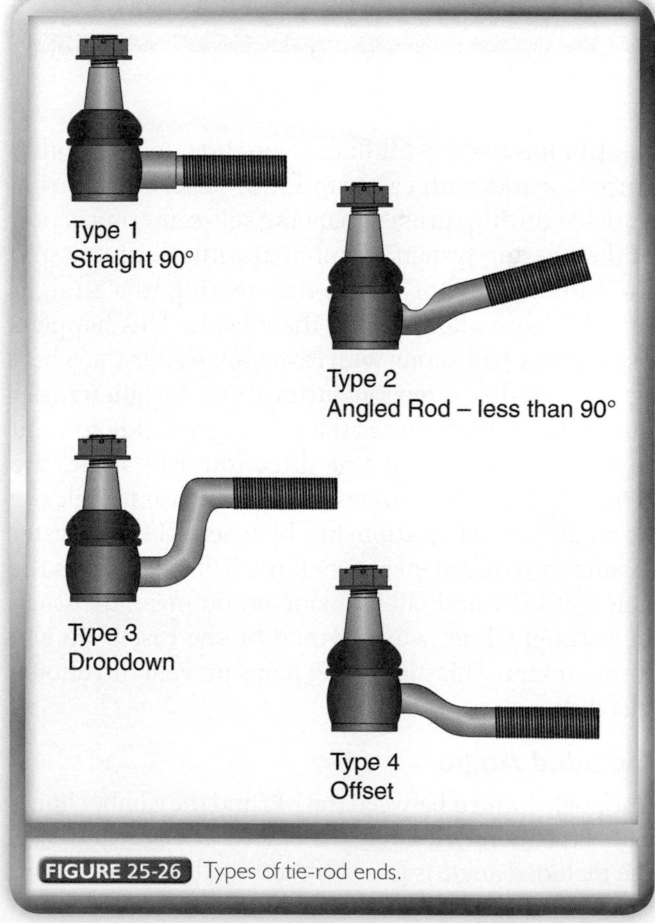

FIGURE 25-26 Types of tie-rod ends.

Kingpin and Steering Axis Inclination Angles

Steering axis inclination and kingpin inclination are industry terms used interchangeably since they refer to the same steering angle. Both terms refer to the axis around which the wheel assembly swivels as it turns to the right or left. On vehicles equipped with kingpins, this angle is naturally referred to as the **kingpin inclination angle (KPI)**. KPI is the angle formed between true vertical and the angle of the kingpin. This angle is formed into the axle during manufacture when the kingpin bores are reamed. As such, the KPI is not adjustable. As with steering axis inclination, KPI is formed by drawing a line through the center of the upper and lower pivot points of the suspension assembly as shown in FIGURE 25-27. As you would expect, then, the **steering axis inclination angle (SAI)** or KPI while described similarly to caster angle, is viewed from the front of the vehicle and not the side like caster angle.

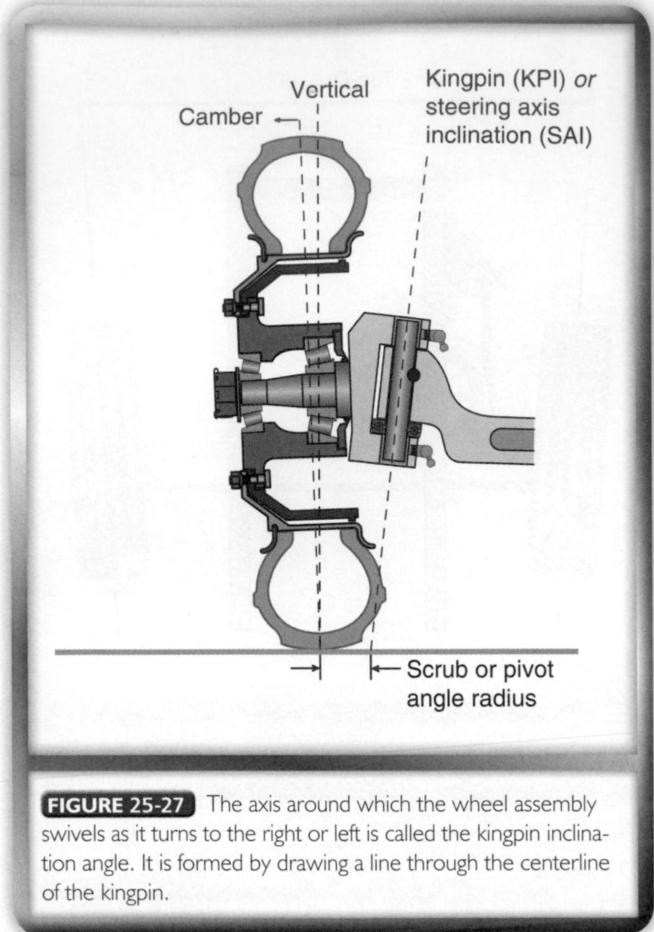

FIGURE 25-27 The axis around which the wheel assembly swivels as it turns to the right or left is called the kingpin inclination angle. It is formed by drawing a line through the centerline of the kingpin.

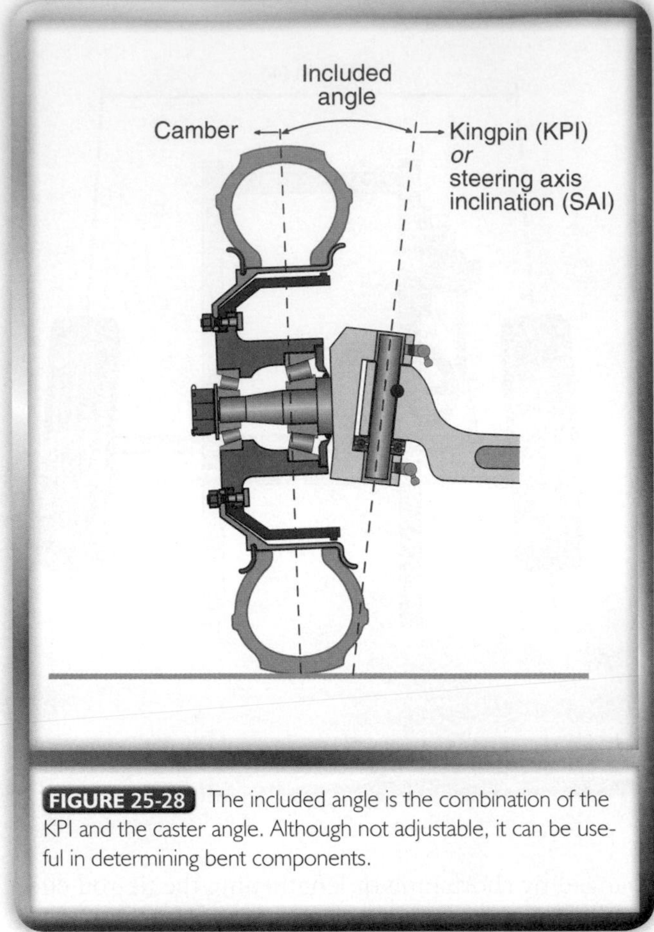

FIGURE 25-28 The included angle is the combination of the KPI and the caster angle. Although not adjustable, it can be useful in determining bent components.

KPI has the most influence on directional stability since it works with caster to lift or lower the steering knuckle during turns, enhancing self-centering action of the steering system. Combined with positive caster, the KPI angle helps return the steering to a straight line direction after turning the wheels. This happens because the KPI, along with caster angle, lifts the wheel up in an arc-like direction during turns. Weight transfer during turns then causes the steering knuckle to want to return to a straight-line direction. KPI angles are larger than camber angles and allow caster angles to be smaller. That relationship between KPI and caster results in reduced steering effort. KPI also causes the wheels to rise and fall in an arc on bumps rather than in a straight-line, which would be the case if no KPI were present. This means KPI helps prevent directional instability.

Included Angle

The angle formed between the KPI and the camber line is called the **included angle**. As depicted in **FIGURE 25-28**, the included angle is found by adding the KPI angle and the camber angle together. If the camber angle is specified as negative, then it is subtracted from the KPI angle. The included angle is not adjustable and is provided as a reference specification. When measured, the included angle can help determine if any parts are bent, such as a spindle, control arm, or steering arm.

Scrub Radius

In addition to its influence with caster, the KPI angle also determines the scrub radius of a tire. The **scrub radius** is the difference between the intersection of a point on the tire contact patch between true vertical and the KPI angle. Scrub radius forms the pivot point for the tire contact with the road. A **positive scrub radius** is formed when the KPI angle is projected inside the tire's vertical centerline, as shown in FIGURE 25-28. This means the KPI is closer to the vehicle centerline than the tire's centerline. A **negative scrub radius** is produced when the KPI projects outside the tire's vertical centerline. Whether the **scrub angle** is negative or positive affects the transmission of "road feel" back to the driver through the steering wheel. Almost all heavy-duty commercial vehicles use a positive scrub so that, when rolling forward, the positive scrub radius will cause the tire to turn outward away from the vehicle centerline. As mentioned earlier, turning tires outward causes all the clearances in the front axle, such as in wheel bearings and tie-rod ends, to be taken up, and the tires to toe-out. In addition, the increased tension on the steering linkage is transmitted to the steering wheel. Moving the steering from a straight-line position will also produce increased steering resistance, which is sensed by the driver as feedback from the road. Negative scrub radius produces what some drivers refer to as "numb" steering.

Zero scrub radius is possible without an inclined kingpin, but it requires a deeply dished wheel that places the kingpin in the vertical centerline of the wheel. It is more practical to incline the kingpin, use a less dished wheel, and maintain the self-centering effect of positive scrub radius.

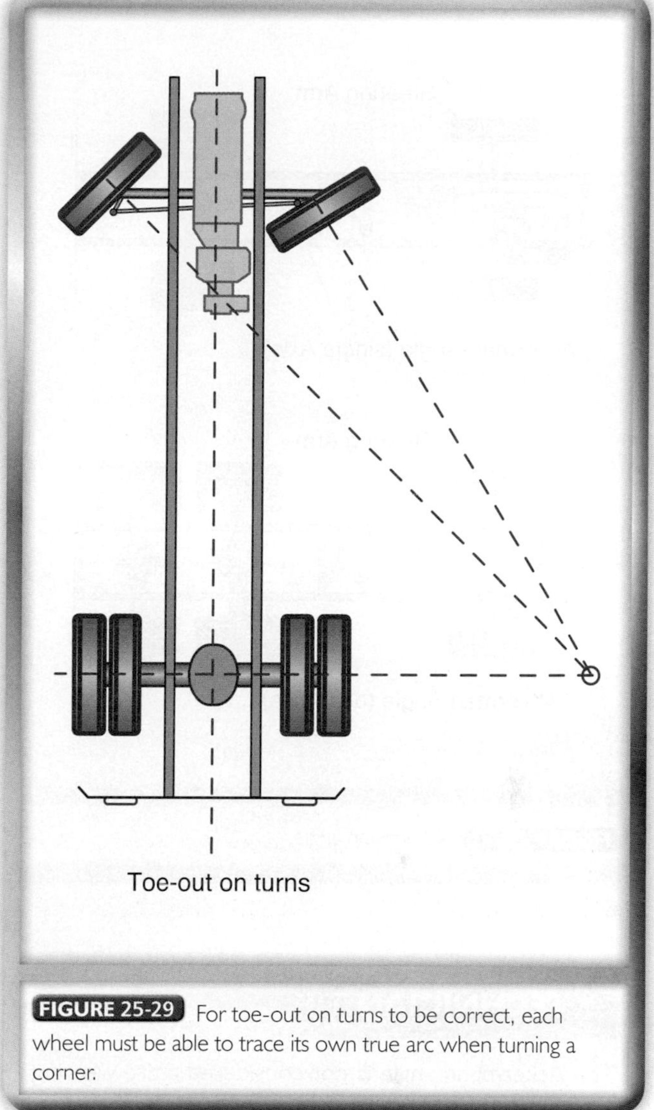

FIGURE 25-29 For toe-out on turns to be correct, each wheel must be able to trace its own true arc when turning a corner.

Basic Steering Geometry

The relationships between the steering system, the wheel positions, and the suspension system form what is called the steering geometry. **Steering geometry** is a geometric arrangement of linkages in the steering of a vehicle designed to solve the problem of keeping the wheels properly oriented through various positions of the steering and suspension systems. As the wheels move up and down relative to the body, the steering linkage swings vertically through an arc. Without steering geometry, the wheel would turn in and out as the vehicle goes over bumps. With steering geometry, the pivots for the suspension components cause the wheel to go through a similar arc as the steering components. That symmetrical motion allows the wheel to track straight ahead, or in a consistent direction if it is in a turn. Note there is a difference between steering geometry and vehicle alignment factors. Whereas steering geometry deals with the dynamics of linkage, vehicle alignment factors have more in common with the shape and position of axle components.

Ackermann Principle and the Ackermann Angle

The **turning radius** of a vehicle depends on the pivot point of the vehicle, the angle the wheels turn plus the distance between the steering wheels and pivot point. For example, since a vehicle's pivot point is at the rear axle, long wheel base vehicles have wide turning radiuses while shorter wheel base length vehicles have tighter turning circles. Efficient turning with the least tire wear and a change in vehicle direction proportional to the steering angle requires the outside wheel to turn at a smaller angle than the inner wheel. The Ackermann angle, illustrated in FIGURE 25-29, is also called tire toe-out on turns. It refers to the **Ackermann principle**, which states that the inner wheel should have a smaller turning angle than the outside wheel since it has a smaller turning radius.

This is accomplished by changing the angle and length of the Ackermann or steering arms. The ideal angle for the steering arms is produced by drawing a line between the pivot point at the center of the rear axle and the steering arm when the vehicle is steered straight ahead. In tandem axle vehicles, the pivot center is between the two axles. Theoretically, changing the wheel base would require a different steering arm. Generally, however, manufacturers will use only one steering arm regardless of vehicle wheel base. FIGURE 25-30 shows the Ackermann angle. Ackermann angle producing toe-out on turns is a non-adjustable angle. If it is not correct according to the manufacturer's specifications, then you know that steering linkage is bent, typically the steering arm. This will also cause the tires to scrub when turning corners.

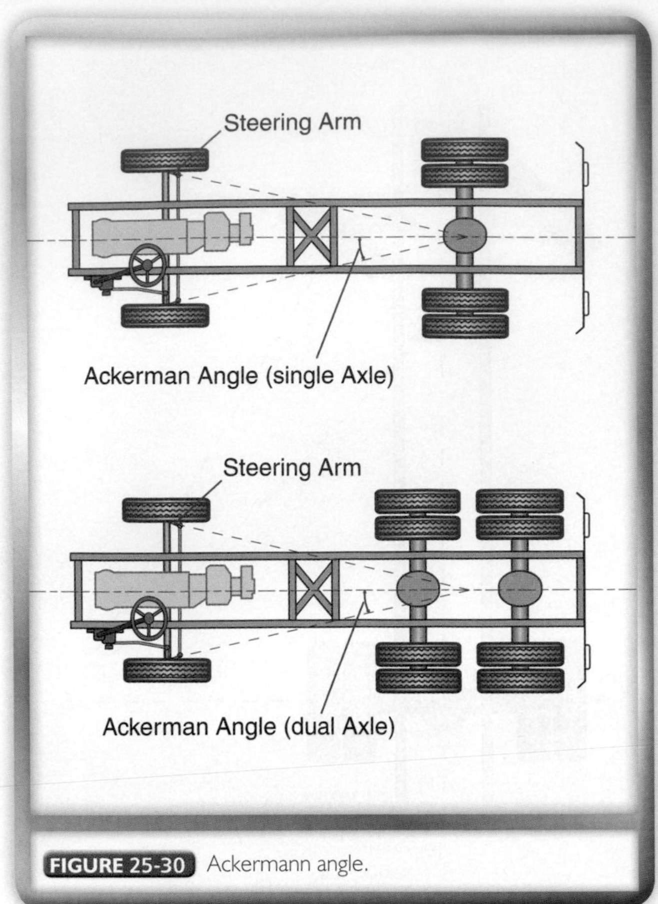

FIGURE 25-30 Ackermann angle.

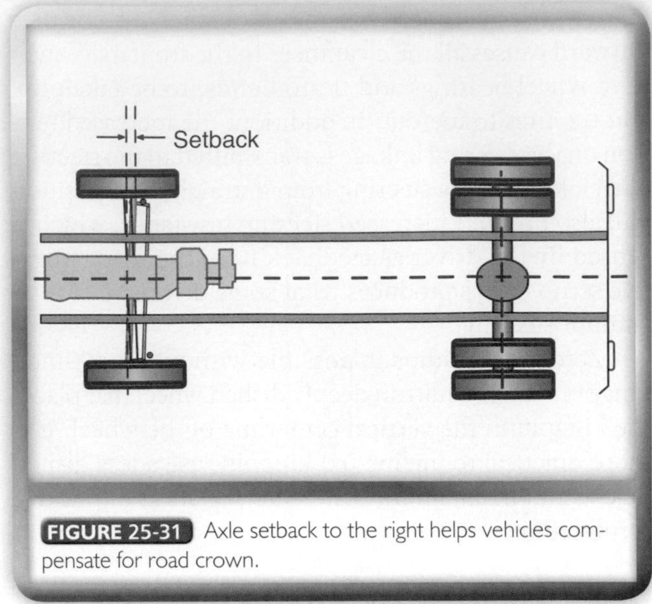

FIGURE 25-31 Axle setback to the right helps vehicles compensate for road crown.

> **TECHNICIAN TIP**
>
> The Ackermann angle is not considered a tire wearing angle under most conditions. The wrong arm, however, will accelerate tire wear for vehicles doing extensive turning, such as those operating in a city or on secondary highways with high road crowns, requiring the driver to turn the wheels slightly to correct drifting to the curb.

Axle Setback

Axle setback is **axle setback**, also referred to simple as **setback** or **skew** setback is the difference in distance between any axle end and the perpendicular centerline. For example, some trailer axles may have 0.125" (3.175 mm) set back towards the right or curb side. When the distance from the end of the right axle is measured from the trailer kingpin, the right side axle will be pulled slightly forward than the left if the measured distances are all made equal. This kind of setback will pull the right side of the axle slightly forward to compensate for high road crown, as illustrated in FIGURE 25-31. Axle setback can also be due to mismatched rims.

Trailer Axles and Axle Tracking

Trailer axles, like most steering axles, are categorized as dead axles. This means they do not transfer torque to wheel ends. Axle tracking, which refers to the ability of all vehicle and trailer tires to follow the same path, depends on axle parallelism and sharing a common centerline. Proper vehicle tracking requires all axles to be parallel with one another and to have similar amounts of offset from either the vehicle centerline or a centerline running between all axles. Tandem axles need to be parallel within 0.125" (3.175 mm) difference between the axle's centers measured on the left and the right side of the vehicle when measured at the axle end.

Axles should be perpendicular to chassis centerline within 0.125" (3.175 mm) when measured between axle end and chassis centerline. Alternatively, there should be no more than 0.25" (6.35 mm) difference between the axle end when measured from left side of frame to right axle end and vice versa. The nominal toe setting is 0" ± 1/32" (0 ± 0.794 mm). This figure is lower than a steer axle since there is no steering linkage.

> **TECHNICIAN TIP**
>
> In extreme conditions of setback or thrust angle, the tracks the rear tires make are beside those of the front. This condition is known as crabbing and can cause diagonal tire pattern wear on the rear tires as well as vehicle instability in some driving conditions. A vehicle that is crabbing will appear to be driving slightly sideways down the road.

Types of Wheel Alignment

Performing a wheel alignment will require the use of an alignment machine. In the past, simpler devices (such as using a measuring tape or a piece of string to set wheel toe) were used to align the vehicle's wheels. Today's vehicles and tires are sensitive to the position of the wheels, so simply using a tape measure to set toe is unacceptable.

Vehicle alignment equipment ranges in type from simple and inexpensive trammel bars and tire line scribing tools to sophisticated and expensive electronic systems using a variety of optical sensors, like that shown in FIGURE 25-32. Electronic alignment can identify either the vehicle centerline or vehicle frame as an alignment reference point.

Alignment is a regular part of the maintenance regimen for all heavy-duty vehicles. In addition, anytime a part that has adjustment for alignment angles is removed from the vehicle for any reason, an alignment should be performed. For example, if the front axle has adjustment slots and is being replaced, an alignment will need to be performed once the new axle is installed to ensure the correct wheel alignment angles are restored. If you are unsure if replacing a particular part will require an alignment once the new part is installed, refer to the manufacturer's service information.

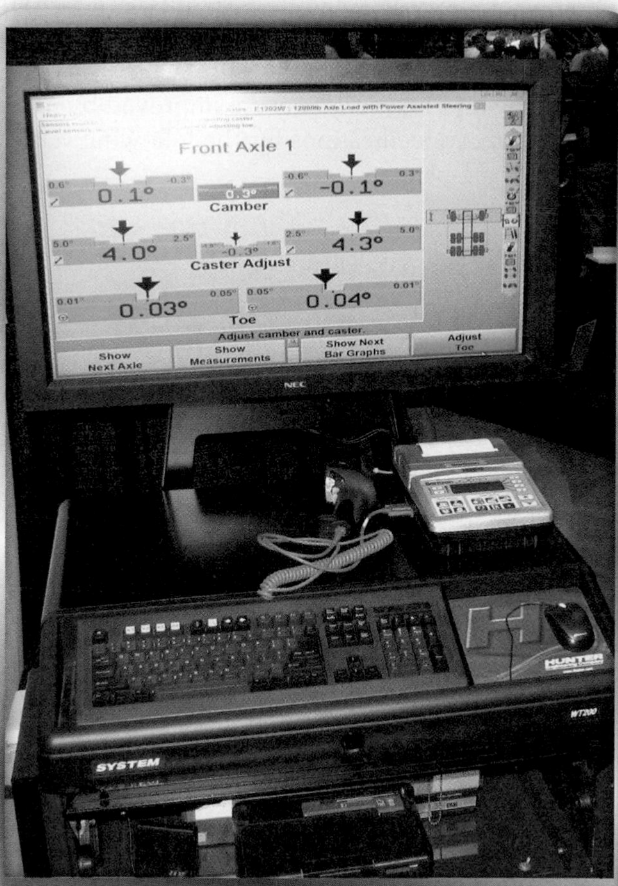

The three basic types of wheel alignment are: (1) geometric centerline (thrust angle) alignment; (2) frame centerline alignment; and (3) loaded versus unloaded alignment.

FIGURE 25-32 This Hunter alignment system uses optical sensors to measure vehicle alignment factors.

Geometric Centerline Alignment—Thrust Angle

Geometric centerline alignment is a method where a vehicle's centerline is established by placing a line from the midpoint of the front axle and the midpoint of the rear-most axle. The geometric centerline is commonly used as a reference for total wheel alignment. This method does not use frame rails or frame cross member as reference points. Instead, the alignment system will establish the geometric centerline reference point for adjustments. Ignoring the frame as a reference point eliminates error due to a bent or damaged frame.

Geometric centerline total alignment allows wheels and axles to be adjusted relative to one another to obtain the correct **thrust angle**—the angle formed between the geometric centerline and the thrust line of an axle, as illustrated in FIGURE 25-33. The term **thrust line** refers to the direction in which the rear wheels are pointing. It represents the direction the axle "points" compared to the centerline of the vehicle. Vehicles with solid, adjustable rear axles can use this method.

Frame Centerline Alignment

Unlike geometric centerline alignment, the **frame centerline alignment** method uses the vehicle frame and not its axles as the reference point for making alignment adjustments. In the field, frame centerline alignments (or checking for frame centerline alignment) can be made without using sophisticated alignment equipment. Technicians do, however, need to make very careful measurements and observations to complete the necessary calculations and interpret their results before making changes to axle alignment.

An economical electronic version uses two self-centering frame gauges hung at a right angle to the frame, one in the front and one in the rear. The gauge contains reflective targets used to identify the frame centerline. Cameras or lasers measure the angle the axles are positioned relative to the centerline of the frame. This system does not compensate for wheel run-out but allows for faster checks of alignment.

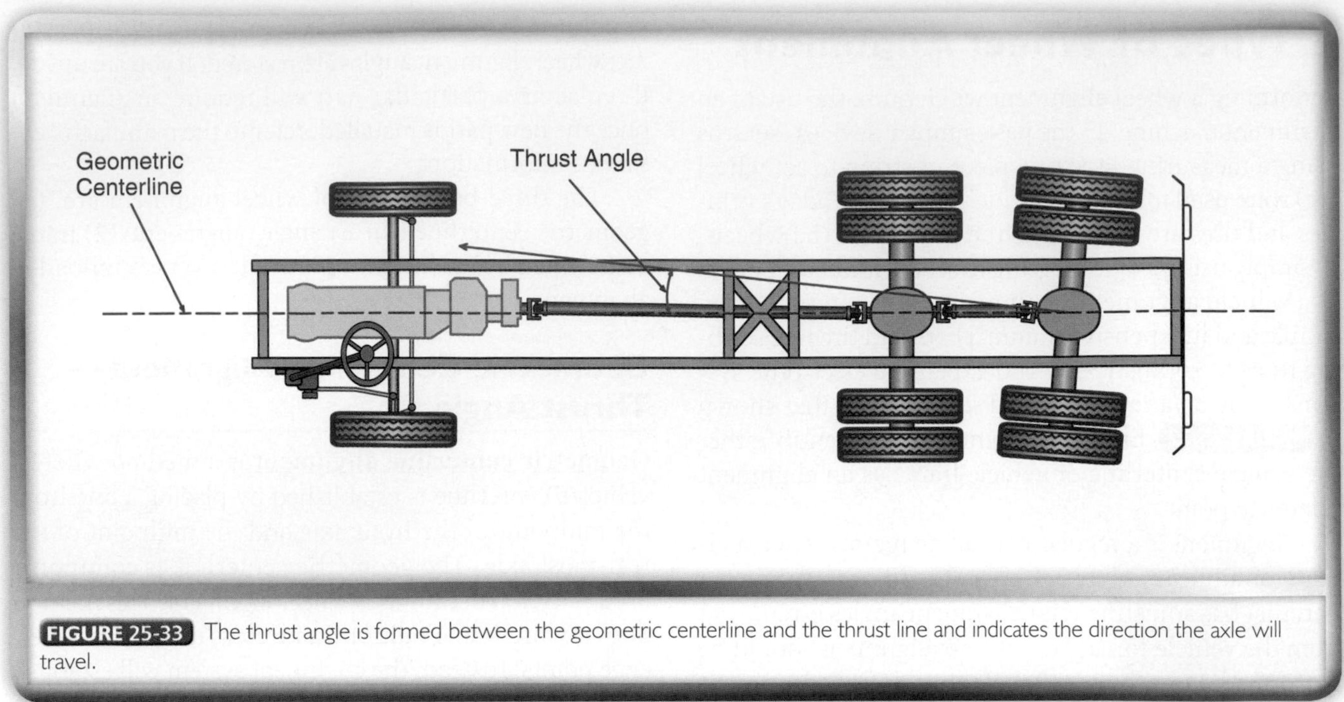

FIGURE 25-33 The thrust angle is formed between the geometric centerline and the thrust line and indicates the direction the axle will travel.

Loaded Versus Unloaded Alignment

Alignment specifications are set for unloaded vehicles. As a vehicle's load changes, however, its wheel alignment changes. That is particularly true for the Front Axles and Vehicle Alignment Factors axle. As the load increases, the axle begins to bend slightly. The bending causes the camber, kingpin inclination, and caster to change. Because axles and spring weight ratings vary by vehicle application, different alignment settings may be required to obtain the best loaded alignments.

Performing Vehicle Alignments

In-Service Wheel Alignment

Wheel alignment for modern on-highway commercial vehicles involves more than just aligning the wheels on the steer axle. Total alignment of all vehicle wheels is necessary since, without it, tire scrub increases rolling resistance, which in turn increases fuel consumption. Vehicles that do not correctly track can also increase the amount of cross-sectional area exposed to wind, which increases fuel consumption and affects vehicle handling. Premature or abnormal tire wear indicates the need for alignment but alignment should be checked whenever new steer tires are installed. Steer axles, drive axles, trailer axles, and dolly axle alignment is required for total alignment. In the total alignment procedure, every axle on the vehicle is measured and the axles are adjusted to be parallel so that all the wheels roll in the same direction and rolling resistance is minimized.

Tire life and fuel economy are improved by maintaining correct specifications for the following vehicle alignment parameters:

- Toe
- Rear tandem parallelism
- Camber
- Rear tandem **axle perpendicularity** (axles square with the frame)

TABLE 25-3 shows the The Maintenance Council's (TMC) recommended practices for drive–axle alignment.

Over its working life, every heavy vehicle will need to be inspected for alignment to ensure optimal performance, safety, and fuel efficiency. Outside of routine maintenance and inspections, drivers and technicians may notice one or more handling issues related to alignment, as outlined in TABLE 25-4.

Faced with one or more handling issues, a technician might be tempted to jump straight to performing a vehicle alignment. Before doing so, however, the technician should perform a series of inspections, measurements, and checks to determine the scope and type of alignment work that needs to be done. To perform a pre-alignment inspection, follow the steps in SKILL DRILL 25-1.

TABLE 25-3: Recommended Practices for Drive–Axle Alignment

Type of Axle	Recommendation for Drive–Axle Alignment
Steer Axles	Toe-in with a range 0–0.125" (0–3.175 mm)
Drive Axles	Tandem axles to be parallel within 0.125" (3.175 mm) measured at axle end. Axles should be perpendicular to chassis centerline within 0.125" (3.175 mm) when measured from axle end to chassis centerline, or within 0.25" (6.35 mm) when measured from left to right axle end.
Trailer Axles	Tandem axles to be parallel within 0.125" (3.175 mm) difference between the axle's centers measured on the left and the right side of the vehicle and measured at axle end. Axles should be perpendicular to chassis centerline within 0.125" (3.175 mm) when measured between axle end and chassis centerline. Alternatively, there should be no more than 0.25" (6.35 mm) difference between the axle end when measured from left side of frame to right axle end and vice versa. Nominal toe setting: 0" ± 1/32" (0 ± 0.794 mm). This figure is lower than a steer axle since there is no steering linkage.

Source: The Maintenance Council

TABLE 25-4: Handling Issues and Possible Causes

Complaint	Possible Cause
Wander or shimmy,	• Worn tie-rod ends • Worn drag link ends • Worn kingpins or kingpin bushings • Loose or shifted suspension • Weak shock absorbers • Weak or broken front springs • Incorrect front end alignment—Caster or toe-in is incorrect • Loose steering gear • Incorrectly adjusted steering gear • Incorrectly installed pitman or drop arm • Loose or worn steering column slip yoke and joints • Loose wheel bearings • Improperly lubricated fifth wheel • Low or unequal tire pressure • Unequal sized tires • Linkage binding • Steering gear binding • Front axle shifted on the springs • Looseness in steering linkage • Kingpins binding in steering knuckles • Rear axle shifted on the springs • Rear axle housing bent • Vehicle frame diamond-shaped • Loose U-bolts • Loose spring shackle ins and bushings • Uneven vehicle loading • Uneven tire wear

Complaint	Possible Cause
Thumps and knocks from front suspension	• Loose or worn kingpins • Broken steering knuckle bearing • Missing or worn steering knuckle shims • Loose front suspension attaching bolts • Loose shock absorber mountings • Worn spring bushings • Worn or seized steering column slip yoke
Irregular or excessive tire wear	• Incorrect front wheel or total vehicle alignment • Worn kingpins or kingpin bushings • Loose front suspension attaching bolts • Weak shock absorbers • Weak front springs • Bent drop arm or pitman arm • Loose or worn steering slip shaft and joints. • Worn tie-rod ends • Improper position of fifth wheel • Incorrect camber or toe adjustment • Under or over inflation • Incorrectly distributed vehicle load
Vehicle pulls to one side	• Unequal size or weight • Incorrect or unequal caster or toe-in • Defective wheel bearing • Weak or broken spring • Brakes dragging on one side • Bent steering arm or steering knuckle • Misaligned vehicle frame • Weak or broken suspension spring • Shifted rear axle

SKILL DRILL 25-1 Performing a Pre-Alignment Inspection

1. Locate and follow the procedure in the service manual. Complete the job sheet or work order.
2. Remove any heavy items from the vehicle. Do not remove any item or equipment that is supplied with the vehicle and normally kept in the vehicle.
3. Check all tires for proper tire size and adjust tire pressure to specifications.
4. Check the vehicle's ride height. It is impossible to carry out a successful wheel alignment when the vehicle's ride height is incorrect.
5. Check the play of the steering wheel. Excess play must be corrected before undertaking the wheel alignment.
6. Inspect all suspension and steering components according to service information, including the wheel bearings. Repair or replace all damaged or worn suspension components prior to aligning the vehicle.
7. Position the vehicle, making sure the front tires are positioned correctly on the turntables.
8. Attach the wheel end sensors of the alignment equipment to the wheels.
9. Perform manufacturers set-up procedures such as leveling the sensors, correcting for wheel run-out, or wheel roll compensation.
10. Compare manufacturer specifications with actual measurements.

Measuring Toe-in and Toe-out

As discussed earlier it the chapter, steering geometry must be within the manufacturer's specifications for the vehicle to operate correctly. For that reason, it is important that a vehicle's toe-in and toe-out are regularly measured. Follow the steps in SKILL DRILL 25-2 to measure toe-in and toe-out using a toe tester or trammel bar.

Checking KPI and Included Angle

As mentioned previously, the KPI is the angle formed by an imaginary line running through the upper and lower steering pivots relative to a plumb line—the vertical line created when a weight is hung from a string. It cannot be adjusted, though a technician will on occasion be asked to check the KPI to ensure it is within the manufacturer's specifications after an accident or axle repair. Generally, KPI should not vary more than half a degree, plus or minus. If KPI is incorrect, check for a bent spindle or steering knuckle. If incorrect, KPI will create an issue with the steering wheel not returning to center after cornering. To check KPI and included angle, follow the guidelines in SKILL DRILL 25-3.

Axle Tracking and Parallelism

Tracking refers to the tire path followed by the tires on a vehicle. Ideally, all tires should move in the same path. Tires that do not take the same path often have

SKILL DRILL 25-2 Measuring Toe-out Using a Toe Tester or Trammel Bar

1. Locate and follow the procedure in the service manual. Complete the job sheet or work order.
2. Perform system pre-checks, as per SKILL DRILL 25-1.
3. Park the vehicle on a level surface in a straight-ahead position over a pit if possible.
4. Mark the tire at the approximate center of the tread flange at a position that is in line with the center of the wheel.
5. Repeat step 3 on the other front tire.
6. Set up the toe tester or trammel bar per the manufacturer's specifications with the measuring pins on the marks that you have made on the front tires.
7. Tighten the slider on the trammel bar. Set the adjustable stop on the equipment to zero.
8. Remove the trammel bar and, move the vehicle forward so the wheels rotate through 180 degrees, and place the trammel bar behind the tires.
9. Measure the difference between the points on the tires in this position. An increase in the dimension is the toe-in amount. Take the measurement and compare it with the manufacturer's specifications.
10. Adjust the toe-in dimension to manufacturers specification by loosening and adjusting the tie rod.
11. Repeat the measuring process to ensure that the corrective action is within specifications.
12. List the test results and/or recommendations on the job sheet or work order.
13. Clean the work area.

different or incorrect axle offsets, or the vehicle axles are not parallel.

In the straight-ahead position, the rear wheels of a vehicle should follow the front wheels in a parallel manner. This is referred to as **axle parallelism**. If the rear axle of a vehicle is not at right angles to the chassis centerline, the front tires are affected and will have misaligned wear since the steering tires are correcting for an improper thrust angle. Failure of the wheel to track is usually due to the following causes:

- Broken or shifted main leaf spring
- Loose or broken spring center or U-bolts
- Incorrectly installed springs—back to front reversed
- Bent or twisted frame
- Locating rods, track bars, or torque rods improperly adjusted
- Worn suspension bushings for springs and torque rods

To inspect axles for correct tracking and parallelism, follow the steps in **SKILL DRILL 25-4**.

Front Axle Inspection

Kings pins, tie-rod ends, and drag links are checked for looseness or wear prior to alignment or if non-repeatable alignment measurements are observed. When properly greased, no movement between the kingpin and steering

SKILL DRILL 25-3 Checking KPI and Included Angle

1. Locate and follow the procedure in the service manual. Complete the job sheet or work order.
2. Position the vehicle on the alignment equipment turning plates.
3. Attach the wheel sensors on the vehicle to the locations specified by the alignment equipment manufacturer and compensate for tire and wheel rim run-out
4. Follow the alignment machine instructions for taking the KPI measurements and compare them with the vehicle manufacturer's specifications. Typically, the KPI reading will require turning the wheels to a specified angle while on the turning plates.
5. KPI is a non-adjustable angle; no changes can be made. The angle will help the technician to verify that steering components are not bent.
6. Calculate the included angle, if the alignment machine does not, by adding the camber reading of each wheel to the KPI of each wheel and compare with specifications.
7. List the test results and/or recommendations on the job sheet or work order.
8. Clean the work area.

SKILL DRILL 25-4 Inspecting Tandem Axles for Parallelism and Tracking

1. Park the vehicle on a flat surface. Clamp a long straight edge across the frame in front of the front axle of the tandem at exactly 90 degrees to the vehicle center line.
2. Drop a plumb bob line from the straight edge in line with the front axle hub. Using a trammel bar, measure the distance from the line to the hub, and tighten the trammel.
3. Repeat the procedure on the other side of the vehicle. Compare the measurements; they should be equal to within .125" (3.175mm). Adjust as necessary.
4. Using the trammel, check the distance between the two hubs of the tandem on the left side. Compare with the right side. Measurements should be within .125" (3.175mm). Adjust as necessary.
5. Variation of more than 0.125" (3.175 mm) must be corrected. Note that, typically, only one side of the axles is adjustable.

> **TECHNICIAN TIP**
>
> When greasing kingpins, apply grease to the fittings on both the lower and upper part of the steering knuckle. A small amount of grease should flow between the knuckle and axle to purge water and dirt from the joint. The wheel end must be raised from the ground to allow grease to evenly flow around the bushing. If this procedure is not followed, the steering knuckle sealing cap gasket will blow due to high pressure beneath the cap, which will prevent any further lubrication of the steering knuckle. If blown, the sealing cap and sealing O-ring or gasket will need replacement before additional attempts to lubricate the joint are made.

knuckle or between the tie-rod joint and steering knuckle should be observable. To perform an inspection of the kingpins, follow the steps in SKILL DRILL 25-5. To lubricate the kingpins, follow the steps in SKILL DRILL 25-6.

Inspecting and Servicing Tie-Rods and Tie-Rod Ends

Tie-rod ends and tubes should be checked for bending, cracks, looseness, and weakness at every lubrication service. To inspect and service tie-rods and tie-rod ends, follow the steps in SKILL DRILL 25-7.

To perform a geometric centerline alignment, follow the steps in SKILL DRILL 25-8.

SKILL DRILL 25-5 Inspecting the Kingpins for Wear

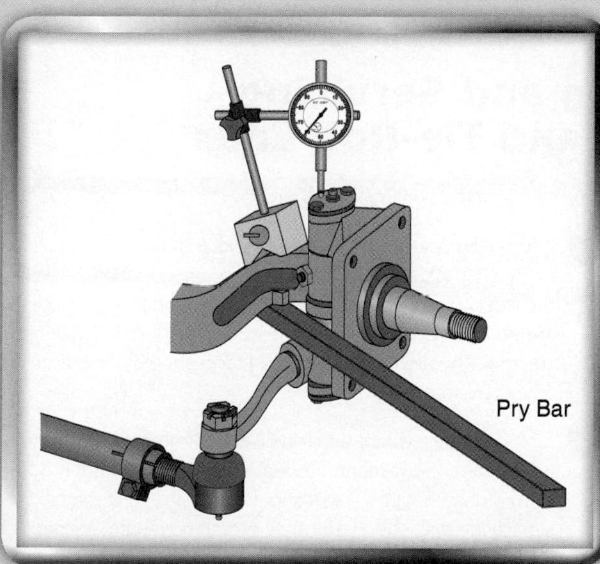

1. After supporting the front axle weight on safety stands, measure the axial (up and down) and radial (side to side) movement of the wheels to evaluate kingpin wear. Vertical movement should be undetectable. Less than 1/8" lateral movement at the steering knuckle.

2. Have a helper apply the service brakes to differentiate wheel bearing movement from kingpin bushing wear.

3. Use a dial indicator to make precise measurements. Place the dial indicator at the top and bottom of the wheel or tire to make two separate measurements.

4. Grasp the top of the tire and move the tire in and out to measure lateral movement of the kingpin. Perform the same check on the bottom of the tire to measure lateral movement of the lower end of the kingpin.

5. Measure vertical movement of the steering knuckle to check for a damaged or worn spindle bearing or worn axle-steering knuckle. Pry the tire up and down with a pry bar. No movement of the knuckle assembly should be felt and no "clunking" sound should be heard. Place a dial indicator against the lower or upper end of the steering knuckle to measure vertical movement.

6. Check OEM specifications for maximum limits of movement in the steering knuckle assembly. Note that loose wheel bearings can give a false indication of worn bushings. This is why it is necessary to have someone apply the brakes while checking kingpin movement. When the brakes are applied, only movement in the steering knuckle will be detected.

SKILL DRILL 25-6 Lubricating Kingpins

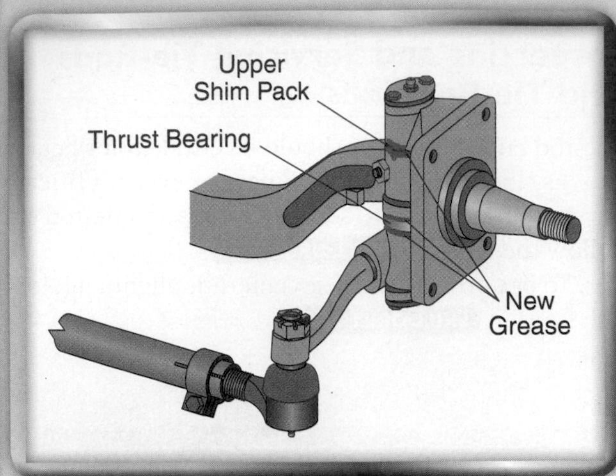

1. Relieve weight on the front axle by lifting the wheels from the ground and supporting the axle with safety stands.
2. Perform an inspection of the kingpin and steering knuckle assembly by measuring vertical and lateral movement.
3. Using a grease gun, begin lubricating the kingpins by purging water and grease from the pin with a couple of pumps of grease.
4. Stop greasing when only clean grease begins to flow from the joint connection at the lower and upper end of the steering knuckle. Do not over lubricate the assembly. Excess grease attracts abrasive dirt which can wear out the joint.

SKILL DRILL 25-7 Inspecting and Servicing Tie-Rods and Tie-Rod Ends

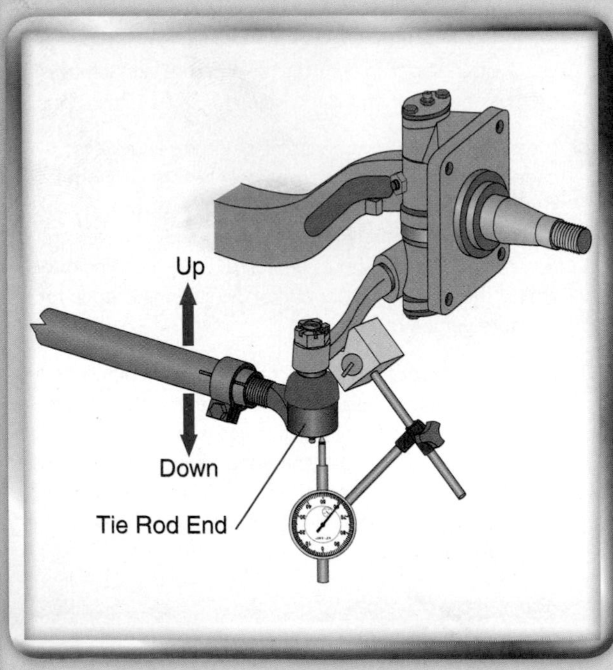

1. If removed or disabled, ball studs should have a minimum of 5 inch/lb (0.565 Nm) of resistance when turning. Shaking the steering wheel slightly back and forth while the wheels are on the ground and then measuring movement while the steering wheel is rocked back and forth should not indicate any visible free play.
2. If play is detected, use a dial indicator to measure any vertical or lateral movement. Movement exceeding 0.60" (15.24 mm) is unacceptable. Joints should be replaced at the next service interval when vertical or lateral movement exceeds 0.030" (0.762 mm).
3. Tie-rod ends, like other articulating steering system joints, are ball and socket type. A castellated nut enables the use of a cotter pin to lock the nut for added safety. Secure the thread engagement in the tube with a clamp.
4. Check that the tie-rod end is threaded adequately into tie-rod so that no gap can be observed between the end of the tie-rod and the open slot of the tube.
5. Replace any joint with a cracked boot. When lubricating the joint, grease should purge the boot of dirt.

SKILL DRILL 25-8 Performing a Geometric Centerline Alignment

1. Locate the sensors mounted on the front steer and rear axle to measure the thrust angle if present.
2. Adjust the rear axle as it is the first to point the thrust line down the vehicle centerline. The rear axle now becomes a reference point for aligning the other axles.
3. Align the front steer axle using the rear axle as a reference.
4. To adjust parallelism, loosen front U-bolts and shift the axle over the slightly oversized alignment holes in the spring seats.
5. Align the second drive axle after the steer axle is adjusted.
6. Adjust additional axles using the rear axle as a reference point.

Wrap-up

Ready for Review

- Axles are a key component of the simple machine of wheel and axle and are used in some form in vehicles ranging from basic soapbox derby cars and go-carts, to the heaviest commercial vehicles.
- There are two main categories of axles—live (drive) and dead (nondrive). Live axles are powered and can move the vehicle; non-drive axles provide a connection point for wheel ends and align the vehicle wheels properly.
- Heavy-duty vechiles commonly use I beam front axles. Each end of the I-beam is outfitted with a steering knuckle that enables articulation of the wheel end.
- Steering knuckles on medium and heavy-duty vechiles use kingpins since they can support heavy loads.
- Lift, tag, and pusher axles are used to supplement the load-carrying capacity of a vehicle when required. They are rear non-drive axles.
- Tag and pusher axles commonly use a pair of air bags to lower the axle and control axle loading.
- Wheels need to be aligned to give heavy-duty commercial vehicles predictable, straight-line directional stability and the ability to correctly turn while minimizing tire wear and improving vehicle handling characteristics.
- Tire alignment angles can change as a result of vehicle loads. Primary alignment angles are camber, caster, and toe.
- All heavy-duty commercial vehicles use positive camber because a loaded vehicle will bend the axle slightly. When normally loaded, bending the axle reduces the camber angle.
- Today's vehicles all use positive caster for straight-line directional control stability and steering-return ability. Positive caster will produce a weight shift on the tires when moved from a straight-line direction.
- Excess positive caster causes caster shimmy that can be dangerous to vehicle control and directional stability.
- Clearances in steering linkage and wheel bearings allow the tires to turn outwards from a straight-line position when moving.
- When travelling forward, toe should be zero degrees to prevent tire wear. Excessive toe-out will wear the inside edge of both tires. Too much toe-in will wear the outside edge of tires.
- Caster angle has the most influence on directional stability since it works with KPI to lift or lower the steering knuckle during turns, enhancing self-centering action of the steering system.
- Almost all heavy-duty commercial vehicles use a positive scrub which causes the tire to turn outward when rolling forward from the vehicle centerline.
- The relationships between the steering system, the wheel positions, and the suspension system form what is called the steering geometry. Whereas steering geometry deals with the dynamics of linkage, vehicle alignment factors have more in common with the shape and position of axle components.
- The turning radius of a vehicle depends on the pivot point of the vehicle, the angle the wheels turn plus the distance between the steering. According to the Ackermann principle, the inner wheel should have a smaller turning angle than the outside wheel since it has a smaller turning radius.
- Alignment is a regular part of the maintenance regimen for all heavy-duty vehicles. Performing a total wheel and vehicle alignment will require the use of an alignment machine.
- The three basic types of wheel alignment are: (1) geometric centerline (thrust angle) alignment; (2) frame centerline alignment; and (3) loaded versus unloaded alignment.

Vocabulary Builder

Ackermann angle The angle the steering arms make with the steering axis, projected toward the center of the rear axle. Also called *toe-out on turns*.

Ackermann principle The geometric alignment of linkages in a vehicle's steering such that the wheels on the inside of a turn are able to move in a different circle radius than the wheels on the outside.

axle The shaft of the suspension system to which the tires and wheels are attached; used to transmit driving torque to the wheels.

axle parallelism When the rear wheels of a vehicle follow the front wheels in a parallel manner.

axle perpendicularity When the axles are square with the vehicle frame.

axle setback The difference in distance between any axle end and the perpendicular centerline. Also called *setback* or *skew*.

camber The side-to-side vertical tilt of the wheel. It is viewed from the front of the vehicle and measured in degrees. See also negative camber and positive camber.

caster The angle formed through the wheel pivot points when viewed from the side in comparison to a vertical line through the wheel.

caster shimmy The small, rapid, side-to-side movement of the steering wheel resulting from excess positive caster.

drag link A connecting linkage that transfers movement of the pitman arm to the upper steering arm.

drop arm An arm that transfers the steering box output shaft motion to the steering linkage by converting rotational movement into liner motion. Also called the *pitman arm*.

frame angle The angle the vehicle's frame makes with regard to horizontal measurement to the ground. See also *positive frame angle* and *negative frame angle*.

frame centerline alignment An alignment method that uses the vehicle frame and not its axles as the reference point for making alignment adjustments.

geometric centerline alignment An alignment method that establishes a vehicle's centerline by placing a line from the midpoint of the front axle and the midpoint of the rear-most axle.

included angle The angle of camber added or subtracted to the steering axis inclination angle. This is the angle of the pivot points in relation to the camber angle of the wheel.

kingpin A pin that connects each steering knuckle to the solid I-beam axle.

kingpin inclination angle (KPI) The angle formed between true vertical and the angle of the kingpin. Also called *steering axis inclination angle*.

lift axle A non-drive (dead) axle that can be mechanically raised and lowered to meet requirements regulated for maximum axle weight loads.

live (drive) axle An axle that is powered and can move the vehicle. Also called a *drive axle*.

non-drive (dead) axle An axle that does not supply power to the wheels.

negative camber When the top of the tire is closer to the center of the vehicle than the bottom of the tire.

negative frame angle The condition where the vehicle's rear is lower than the front.

negative scrub radius A condition in which the point of center contact between the road surface and the tire and the point where the steering axis centerline contacts the road surface intersect above the road surface.

pitman arm A pitman arm converts the steering gear sector shaft movement to a sweeping arc resembling linear movement. Also called a *drop arm*.

positive camber When the tires are closer together at the bottom and farther apart at the top.

positive frame angle The condition where the vehicle's rear is higher than the front.

positive scrub radius A condition in which the point of center contact between the road surface and the tire and the point where the steering axis centerline contacts the road surface intersect below the road surface.

pusher axle A rear, non-drive rear mounted axle, ahead of the drive axle.

scrub angle The distance between two imaginary points on the road surface—the point of center contact between the road surface and the tire, and the intersecting point where the steering axis centerline and the tire centerline contact the road surface. The difference between the intersection of a point on the tire contact patch between true vertical and the KPI angle.

scrub radius The difference between the intersection of a point on the tire contact patch between true vertical and the KPI angle. Scrub radius forms the pivot point for the tire contact with the road. See also *positive scrub radius* and *negative scrub radius*.

setback The distance one wheel is set back from the wheel on the opposite side of the axle.

skew The difference in distance between any axle end and the perpendicular centerline. Also called *axle setback* or *setback*.

solid I-beam A type of solid steering axle named for its forged I-beam design.

steering arm An arm that extends from the steering knuckle. The tie-rods connect to these arms in order to steer the wheels.

steering axis inclination angle (SAI) The angle formed by an imaginary line running through the upper and lower steering pivots relative to vertical as viewed from the front. The angle formed between true vertical and the angle of the kingpin. Also called *kingpin inclination angle (KPI)*.

steering axle An axle that allows the vehicle to turn.

steering geometry A geometric arrangement of linkages in the steering of a vehicle designed to solve the problem of keeping the wheels properly oriented through various positions of the steering and suspension systems.

steering knuckle A device that connects the front wheel to the suspension; it pivots on the top and bottom, thus allowing the front wheels to turn.

steering stops Bolts used to limit the turning angle of the steering knuckle.

tag axle A rear non-drive axle mounted behind the drive axle.

thrust angle The relationship between the centerline of the vehicle and the angle of the rear tires.

thrust line The direction in which the rear wheels are pointing.

tie-rod A steering component that transfers linear motion from the steering box to the steering arms at the front wheels.

tie-rod end Articulating ball-and-socket joints attached to each end of the tie-rod.

toe A measurement of how much the front wheels are turned in or out from a straight-ahead position. The angle is referenced from a position directly above the tires and facing forward.

toe-in A condition that exists when, as seen from above, the wheels are closer together at the front and farther apart at the rear.

toe-out A condition that exists when, as seen from above, the wheels are closer together in the rear and farther apart at the front.

toe-out on turns A geometric steering concept that the inner wheel should have a smaller turning angle than the outside wheel. Also called *Ackermann angle*.

tracking The positioning of the tires relative to the vehicle. Also called *wheel alignment*.

trailer axle A non-drive axle used by trailers and which generally has no steering linkage unless it is a self-steering axle.

turning radius A measure of how small a circle the vehicle can turn in when the steering wheel is turned to the limit.

wheel alignment The positioning of the tires relative to the vehicle. Also called *tracking*.

Review Questions

1. What is the most common configuration of the front steering axle used on medium- and heavy-duty vehicles?
   a. Solid I-beam
   b. Solid H-beam
   c. Solid rectangular beam
   d. None of the choices is correct.
2. Which of the following types of kingpin bushings are currently the most commonly used by axle manufacturers?
   a. Nylon
   b. Composite
   c. Bronze
   d. Brass
3. The pitman arm is typically splined to the steering gear output shaft at one end and connected through a ball stud to the:
   a. center link.
   b. steering link.
   c. drag link.
   d. tie rod.
4. Which of the following is NOT a type of axle used to supplement the load-carrying capacity of a vehicle when required?
   a. Lift
   b. Auxiliary
   c. Tag
   d. Pusher
5. Which of the following is NOT a secondary alignment angle?
   a. Frame angle
   b. Cross-member angle
   c. Thrust angle
   d. Included angle
6. Most alignment specifications place a slightly more positive camber angle on the left wheel to correct for the effects of road crown on directional stability; a difference of ________ degree is typically used.
   a. 1/8
   b. 1/4
   c. 1/2
   d. 3/4
7. Concerning caster, what is the maximum side-to-side variation that is recommended for most vehicles?
   a. Plus or minus 0.1 degree
   b. Plus or minus 0.2 degree
   c. Plus or minus 0.3 degree
   d. Plus or minus 0.5 degree
8. What alignments are required for total alignment on a vehicle with multiple axles?
   a. Steer axles
   b. Drive axles
   c. Trailer axles
   d. All of the choices are correct.
9. All of the following are causes of failure of a vehicle to track properly, EXCEPT:
   a. broken or shifted main leaf spring.
   b. loose or broken spring center or U-bolts.
   c. worn suspension bushings for springs and torque rods.
   d. worn tires.
10. What front end parts should be checked for looseness or wear prior to alignment?
    a. Kingpins
    b. Tie rod ends
    c. Drag links
    d. All of the choices are correct.

ASE-Type Questions

1. Technician A says a key function of axles is to maintain the position of the wheels relative to each other and the vehicle body. Technician B says there are two main categories of axles which are drive and non-drive. Who is correct?
   a. Technician A
   b. Technician B
   c. Both Technician A and Technician B
   d. Neither Technician A nor Technician B
2. Technician A says the steering knuckle enables the articulation of the wheel end. Technician B says the steering knuckle is connected to the I-beam through the master pin. Who is correct?
   a. Technician A
   b. Technician B
   c. Both Technician A and Technician B
   d. Neither Technician A nor Technician B
3. Technician A says a snug fit is required between the pin and bushings. Technician B says if the pin cannot be installed into the bushings by hand, or the pin is too tight, the kingpin should be machined slightly smaller. Who is correct?
   a. Technician A
   b. Technician B
   c. Both Technician A and Technician B
   d. Neither Technician A nor Technician B
4. Technician A says steering stops are used to limit the turning angle of the steering knuckle. Technician B says stops are adjusted to cut power assist with zero clearance remaining between the spindle stop and the axle. Who is correct?
   a. Technician A
   b. Technician B
   c. Both Technician A and Technician B
   d. Neither Technician A nor Technician B
5. Technician A says when installing an adjustable drag link, the front tires must be squared with the chassis frame. Technician B says the steering wheel spokes must be correctly oriented in a straight-ahead position, and the steering box must be centered. Who is correct?
   a. Technician A
   b. Technician B
   c. Both Technician A and Technician B
   d. Neither Technician A nor Technician B
6. Technician A says wheel alignment refers to the positioning of the tires relative to the vehicle. Technician B says rolling resistance and correct wheel alignment is not an issue with regard to fuel consumption. Who is correct?
   a. Technician A
   b. Technician B
   c. Both Technician A and Technician B
   d. Neither Technician A nor Technician B
7. Technician A says caster can be adjusted by heating and slightly bending the axle. Technician B says caster can be adjusted by using tapered shims placed between the suspension springs and the axle. Who is correct?
   a. Technician A
   b. Technician B
   c. Both Technician A and Technician B
   d. Neither Technician A nor Technician B
8. Technician A says when travelling forward, toe should be zero degrees to prevent tire wear. Technician B says too much toe-in will wear the inside edges of tires. Who is correct?
   a. Technician A
   b. Technician B
   c. Both Technician A and Technician B
   d. Neither Technician A nor Technician B
9. Technician A says the Ackerman angle refers to a steering principle that states the inner wheel should have a smaller turning angle than the outside wheel because it has a smaller turning radius. Technician B says the Ackermann angle producing toe-out on turns is an adjustable angle. Who is correct?
   a. Technician A
   b. Technician B
   c. Both Technician A and Technician B
   d. Neither Technician A nor Technician B
10. Technician A says the geometric centerline (thrust-angle) has the advantage of eliminating error due to a bent or damaged frame. Technician B says vehicles with solid, adjustable rear axles cannot use this method. Who is correct?
    a. Technician A
    b. Technician B
    c. Both Technician A and Technician B
    d. Neither Technician A nor Technician B

CHAPTER 26

NATEF Tasks

Suspension and Steering

Suspension Systems—Frame and Coupling Devices | Page

	Page
■ Inspect, install, or repair frame hangers, brackets, and cross members in accordance with manufacturers' recommended procedures.	772–776
■ Inspect frame and frame members for cracks, breaks, corrosion, distortion, elongated holes, looseness, and damage; determine needed repairs.	777–779

Knowledge Objectives

After reading this chapter, you will be able to:

1. Describe the purpose and functions of heavy duty vehicle frames. (pp 762–769)
2. Describe resist bending moment (RBM), section modulus, and yield strength as they relate to vehicle frames. (pp 766–769)
3. Explain actual frame strength. (pp 768–769)
4. Describe and explain the materials used in frame construction. (pp 769–770)
5. Describe the different type of frame damage that can occur including impact, sag, bow, and stress risers. (pp 777–779)
6. Explain the different kinds of frame misalignment including diamond, twist, and side-sway as well as methods used to check for misalignment. (pp 777–779)
7. Explain frame alignment procedures. (p 779)
8. Describe frame repair and reinforcement procedures. (pp 782–787)
9. Describe frame welding procedures and precautions. (pp 784–785)

Truck Frames

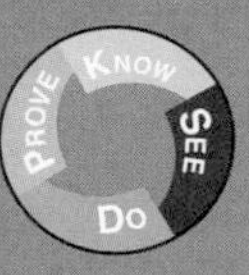

Skills Objectives

After reading this chapter, you will be able to:

1. Conduct exterior inspections of frame. (p 777) SKILL DRILL 26-1
2. Check frame alignment manually. (p 780) SKILL DRILL 26-2
3. Repair a crack between bolt holes. (p 786) SKILL DRILL 26-3
4. Repair a crack in the web or flange. (p 787) SKILL DRILL 26-4

Introduction

A vehicle frame is the backbone of the vehicle. It provides the structure to which all other vehicle components can be attached, as illustrated in FIGURE 26-1. The suspension, drive train, and vehicle body are all supported by the frame. Engineering a vehicle frame would seem very simple if all that were required of the frame was to be strong enough to carry the loads. However a vehicle frame must be capable of much more than just carrying the load of the components attached to it.

Every heavy-duty vehicle frame must be able to handle all of the forces thrown at it as the vehicle is being driven. Road shocks and bumps can more than quadruple the forces acting on the frame, so the frame must be strong enough to withstand all of those forces and more. While negotiating uneven road conditions, the frame must be flexible enough to allow some twisting as the suspension articulates over the bumps. After twisting, the frame must always return to its original shape without permanent deformation. Flexibility is critical—a frame that is too rigid risks failing due to fracture. The frame must also allow for this repeated flexing without succumbing to failure due to fatigue.

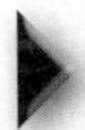

Fundamentals of Frame Design

Several frame designs can be used in the heavy-truck market. Depending on the intended vehicle use, frames can be constructed from C-channel, box rails, or I-beams, all of which are illustrated in FIGURE 26-2. **C-channel** is a C-shaped steel frame rail. **Full-box rails** are box-shaped frame rails, and **I-beams** are I-shaped frame rails. The strongest type of rail is the I-beam, but it is usually found only in very heavy off-road equipment and in some heavy hauler flatbed trailers. Some specialized heavy duty vehicles use tubular steel frame designs, which are even stronger than I-beams, but tubular rails are not normally found in on-highway trucks. The most common frame design for heavy-duty trucks is the **ladder-type frame** constructed of two parallel C-channel steel rails held together by a series of cross members. The frame construction resembles a ladder, with the cross members being the rungs, as shown in FIGURE 26-3.

All frames, regardless of their design, must be strong enough to withstand multiple forces millions of times over. In addition, the frame must be able to support not only the load that the vehicle is designed to carry, but also support all of the vehicle components connected to the frame itself. The engine, transmission, axles, suspension, cab, and the body are all attached to and, therefore, supported by the frame. At the same time the frame is supporting all of these vehicle components, it is also subjected to tremendous stresses during a normal operating day.

Forces Acting on the Frame

Road forces from uneven terrain combined with cornering, braking, and acceleration forces all cause twisting

You Are the Technician

A vehicle is brought to your repair facility for inspection prior to it being bought used by a customer. As you inspect the vehicle you notice that there has been some body repair in the front right corner of the vehicle; the body repair included a new bumper and looks like it was professionally done. You road test the vehicle and notice a slight pull to the right. As you inspect the front suspension components to find out why it is pulling, you notice that the front leaf spring shackles do not seem to be at the same angle from one side to the other.

1. What can you conclude from your observations?
2. What do you think has happened to this vehicle?
3. What next steps would you take to confirm your suspicions?
4. What is the likely repair that is required on this vehicle?
5. What abnormal wear problems could occur if the vehicle is not repaired?

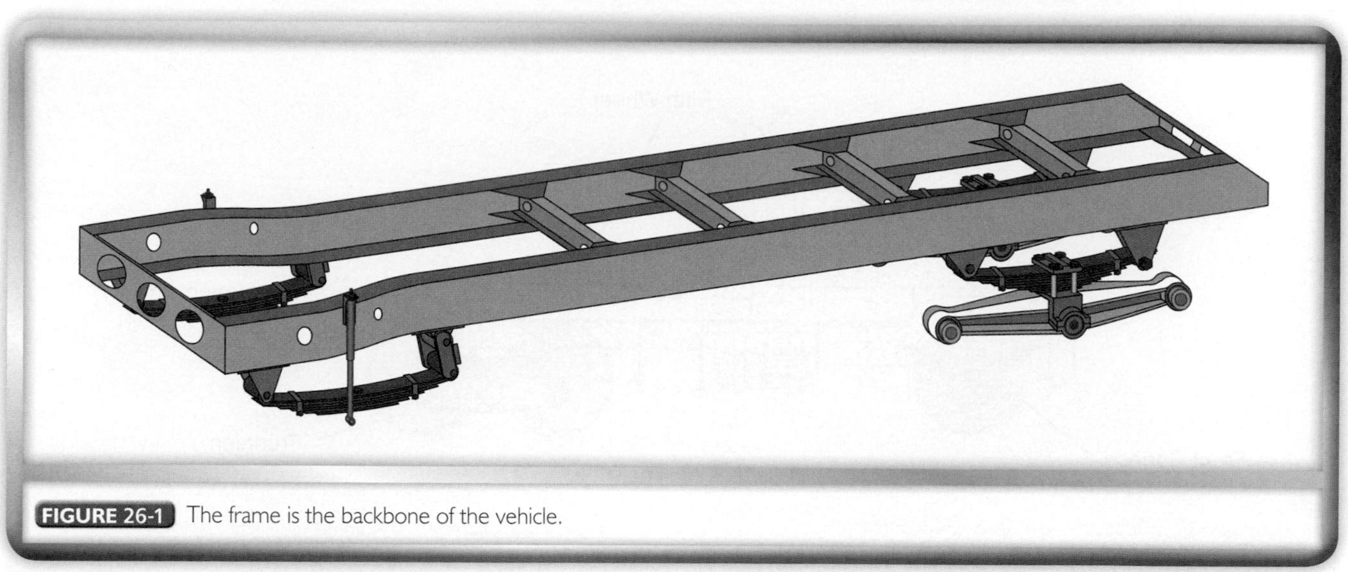

FIGURE 26-1 The frame is the backbone of the vehicle.

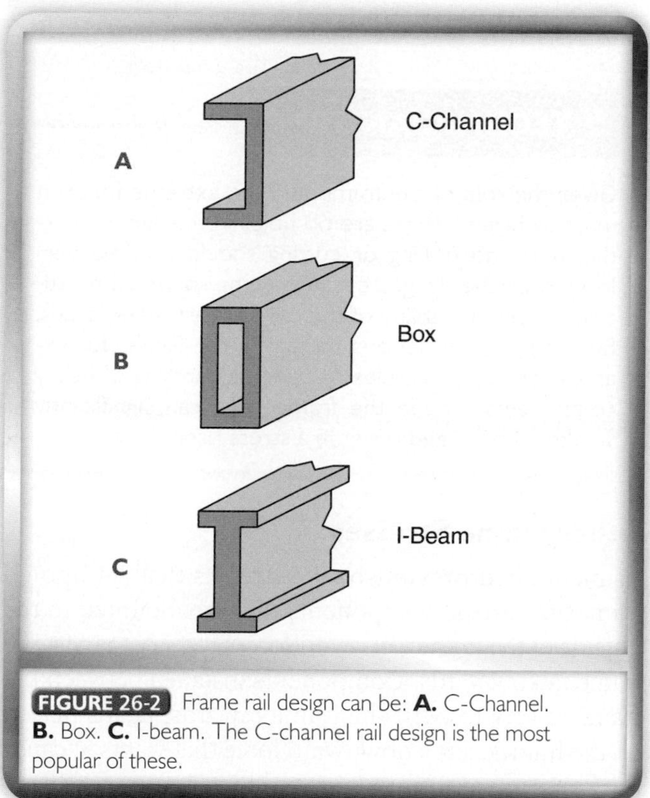

FIGURE 26-2 Frame rail design can be: **A.** C-Channel. **B.** Box. **C.** I-beam. The C-channel rail design is the most popular of these.

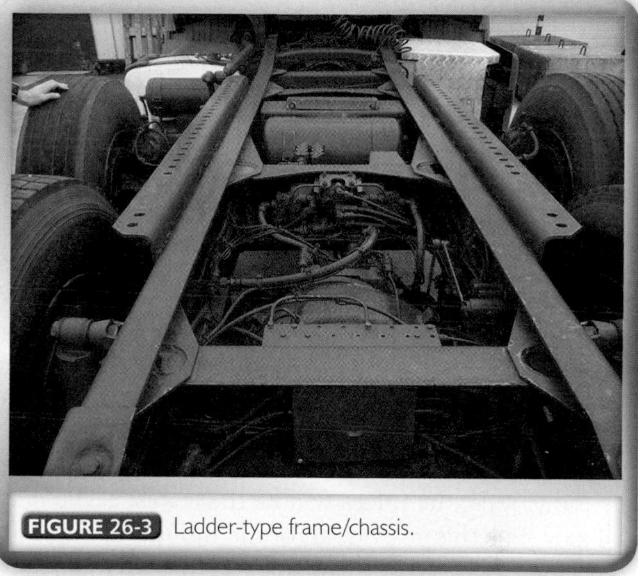

FIGURE 26-3 Ladder-type frame/chassis.

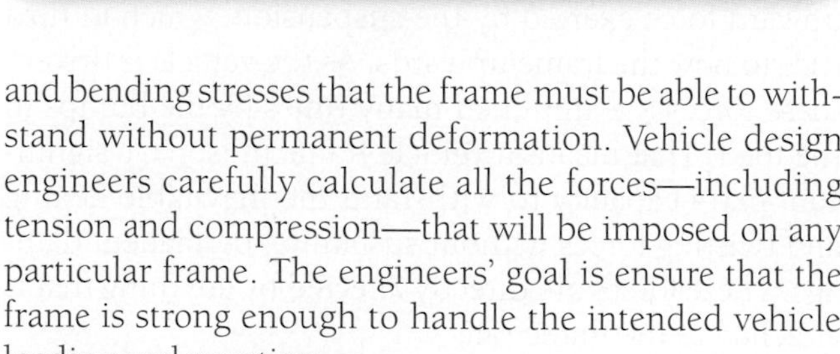

and bending stresses that the frame must be able to withstand without permanent deformation. Vehicle design engineers carefully calculate all the forces—including tension and compression—that will be imposed on any particular frame. The engineers' goal is ensure that the frame is strong enough to handle the intended vehicle loading and vocation.

Tension and Compression

Forces are exerted on multiple areas of a truck frame, but the flanges of the frame rails are particularly susceptible to high forces. **Flanges** are the flat areas at the top and bottom of the frame rail and are subjected to the greatest levels of tension and compression depending on how the frame is loaded. **Tension** is a force trying to stretch the rail apart and **compression** is a force trying to crush the rail together. As illustrated in FIGURE 26-4, the forces acting on a frame alternate from compression to tension depending on where the load is placed and where the suspension supports the frame. In most vehicles, the majority of the lower-frame flange experiences tension, while most of the upper flange experiences compression forces.

During vehicle operation, the top and bottom flanges of the frame are under either tension or compression stress depending on exactly where the load is placed and where the frame is supported by the suspension. The load pushing down on the frame creates compression on the

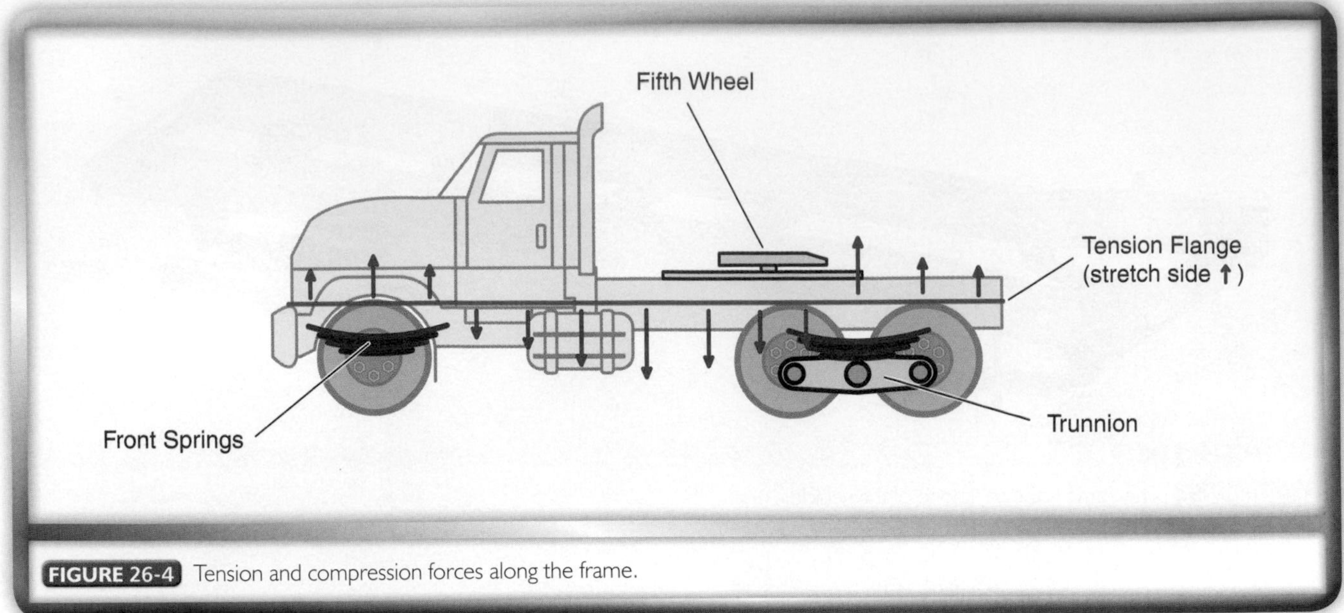

FIGURE 26-4 Tension and compression forces along the frame.

top flange of the frame rail and tension on the bottom flange. The frame supports (the suspension system) push up against the frame in the opposite direction, causing compression on the bottom flange of the rail and tension forces on the top flange.

Notice in FIGURE 26-4 that the forces at the top flange and the bottom flange are opposite each other. As a result, the forces cancel each other at the center of the **frame rail web**, which is the upright section of the frame rail. Specifically, the forces cancel out in the middle of the frame rail web in an area called the **neutral axis** or **neutral fiber**. No matter how much force is placed on the frame rails, the forces will be the lowest at the neutral axis. For this reason, all of the mounting holes for **cross members** (cross members join the two frame rails together) and the other vehicle components are located as close as possible to the center of the web of the rail where the forces acting on the rail are lowest.

A **stress riser**, also called a **stress concentration**, is anything that reduces or changes the integrity or strength of the material. Stress risers can lead to a crack in the rail, which is a serious safety risk. For this reason, any time a frame has to be raised by a jack or a hoist, the frame should be protected from damage by using wooden blocks, nylon straps, or similar cushioning devices. Extreme care should be used *anytime* work is performed around the frame that could result in a scratch or gouge.

Similarly, no extra holes should be drilled in a vehicle frame unless absolutely necessary. In the event that holes are needed in the frame, they should be drilled as close as possible to the neutral axis of the web and as far away from the highest stress areas of the frame as possible. Holes should never be drilled in the rail flanges.

> **TECHNICIAN TIP**
>
> Given the role of the frame and the extreme forces it must withstand, there are no holes in the flanges. Furthermore, no drilling or cutting should ever be performed on the flanges because doing so would drastically reduce the ability of the rail to resist these forces. Even a gouge or serious scratch in the flange, for example caused by careless jacking or handling of heavy components around the frame rails, can significantly weaken the rail and result in a stress riser.

Other Frame Stresses

As mentioned previously, the stresses that act upon a frame are varied. Components that are mounted to the outside of the frame rails exert forces that try to twist the frame rail outwards. Components installed between the frame rail try to twist the frame inwards. Loads placed on the frame exert a downward force that wants to cause the frame to sag. That downward force is opposed by an upward force exerted by the suspension, which in turn tries to bow the frame upwards. As the vehicle is driven, these forces are amplified many times by the bumps in the road. That means a vehicle frame must have significant extra capacity to withstand the inevitable flexing and twisting forces without sustaining permanent damage. These forces are directly affected by anything that is attached to the frame rail.

Calculating Frame Strength

Three basic variables used in frame design determine the strength of a given frame—resist bending moment

(RBM), section modulus, and yield strength. Although frame design is not a necessary skill for technicians, an understanding of these three terms will help when diagnosing frame damage, deciding on frame modifications, and determining repair strategies.

Resist Bending Moment (RBM)

The first of the terms used in frame design is resist bending moment or RBM. A moment is the torque or twisting/bending force applied to any component around a pivot point. The use of moment may seem strange, but it is based on an older meaning of the word. Long ago, the word moment was often used to mean "of great significance or importance," such as in "this was a discovery of great moment." (Today, this meaning comes through in the word momentous, as in "Graduation is a *momentous* occasion.")

The use of the word *moment* to describe a force, then, refers to the importance of the force in terms of where it is acting on the component. In the context of a vehicle frame, the **resist bending moment (RBM)** is the ability of the frame to support the force trying to bend it at the point where this bending force is greatest. The RBM of a frame is the actual measure of the strength of the frame. RBM is calculated by multiplying two other variables in frame design—section modulus and yield strength.

Section Modulus

Section modulus is an engineering term used to describe the strength of the shape of a certain component. As such, section modulus has absolutely no relationship to the material the component is made of. For example, the section modulus calculation is identical for a C-channel made of plastic and for a C-channel of the exact same size made from **high-carbon steel**—steel alloyed with carbon at levels of 0.9–2.5%. Therefore, section modulus is a measure of the strength of the *design*, not the material.

The section modulus calculation produces a constant for that particular shape, so the units used for the calculation do not matter. Section modulus can be stated as inches, centimeters, and so on. Two types of section modulus calculations are possible. The first is the elastic section modulus and the second is the plastic section modulus. Elastic section modulus is used for frame design, so we will use that calculation here.

For C-channel frames, the section modulus (SM) is calculated as follows:

$$SM = \frac{BH^2}{6} - \frac{bh^3}{6H}$$

Where B is the overall width of the channel at the flange; H is the overall height of the channel from flange to flange; b is the width of the inside of the flange from the inside of the web to the flange edge; and h is the height of the inside of the web between the inside of the two flanges.

If you play around with the section modulus equation for C-channel, you can quickly see that the height of the web has a much larger effect on the outcome than the width of the flanges. To demonstrate this, let's run the equation using the following figures for the C-channel:

B=2
H=6
b=1.5
h=5

The calculation using those figures is as follows:

$$SM = \frac{2\times6^2}{6} - \frac{1.5\times5^3}{6\times6}$$
$$= \frac{72}{6} - \frac{187.5}{36}$$
$$= 12 - 5.2$$
$$= 6.8$$

If we switch the figures to make the flange wider than the web is high, the outcome is much different.

B=6
H=2
b=5
h=1.5

The calculation for the wider flange is as follows:

$$SM = \frac{6\times2^2}{6} - \frac{5\times1.5^3}{6\times2}$$
$$= \frac{24}{6} - \frac{16.875}{12}$$
$$= 4 - 1.4$$
$$= 2.6$$

The difference in the results shows that the height of the component is much more important than the width, which makes sense. Imagine a typical 2" × 6" (38 × 140 mm) wooden beam used in construction. If that beam is placed on its narrow edge between two supports (such as with floor joists), it will hold a much larger load than if we place the board on its wider flat side between the two supports. The same is true in the context of a vehicle frame using C-channel rails. Making the web taller will allow the frame to carry a bigger load than making the flange wider.

Yield Strength

The second variable required to calculate RBM is the yield strength of the material used to construct the frame. **Yield**

strength is the amount of force required to permanently deform the material. Until a material reaches its yield strength, the material can deform but will return to its original shape when the load is removed. Once the yield strength is exceeded, the deformation is permanent.

Yield strength is determined by placing a piece of the material with a specific cross sectional area—typically one square inch—in a machine that will gradually exert increasing force on the material in an attempt to pull the material apart. When the material reaches its yield strength, the material shape will permanently deform and will be incapable of rebounding to its original shape. That point is also known as the elastic limit of the material.

Yield strength varies depending on the material being tested. Medium-carbon, high-tensile steel will yield and deform at approximately 50,000 psi (345 MPa). **Medium-carbon steels** are alloys with carbon at levels of 0.25–0.6%. **Tensile strength** is the amount of force required before a material deforms or breaks. Heat-treated alloy steel will yield at 110,000 psi (758 MPa) or higher. Most heavy-truck frames today use heat-treated alloy steel frames with 110,000 or 120,000 psi (758–827 MPa) yield strength. Heat-treated alloy steel allows the frame material to be thinner and lighter and the frame to retain the necessary resist bending moment (RBM) or structural strength.

Actual Frame Strength

In order to determine the actual strength of a particular frame, the resist bending moment (RBM) must be calculated and then compared to the total force acting on the frame. The RBM should be higher than the total force. In fact, RBMs must be high enough to support three times the maximum load of the frame.

To calculate the RBM, multiply the yield strength of the material by its section modulus.

$$\text{RBM} = \text{SM} \times \text{YS}$$

For example, imagine a truck has a frame with rails made of a heat-treated alloy steel rated at 110,000 psi (758 MPa) yield strength. The section modulus of that particular steel is 14.8, which is a typical section modulus of a 10 5/8 inch (270 mm) C-channel frame. The resulting RBM is:

$$\begin{aligned}\text{RBM} &= 14.8 \times 110{,}000\ (758) \\ &= 1{,}628{,}000 \text{ inch-pounds } (183{,}939\ \text{Nm})\end{aligned}$$

Before specifying this frame for a particular application, the maximum force acting on the frame has to be found and then compared to the RBM of the frame. The force the frame must be capable of supporting is determined in two steps. The first step is finding the maximum load on the frame. The second step is multiplying the maximum load by the distance in inches from the load point to the frame support point. That distance is the length of the lever arm or "moment" arm trying to twist the frame rail.

The amount of load placed on the frame is relatively easy to determine, but the point at which that force is concentrated on the frame is not as easy to identify. That point is called the **maximum bending moment** and is simply the maximum bending stress put on a vehicle frame. As illustrated in **FIGURE 26-5**, the maximum bend-

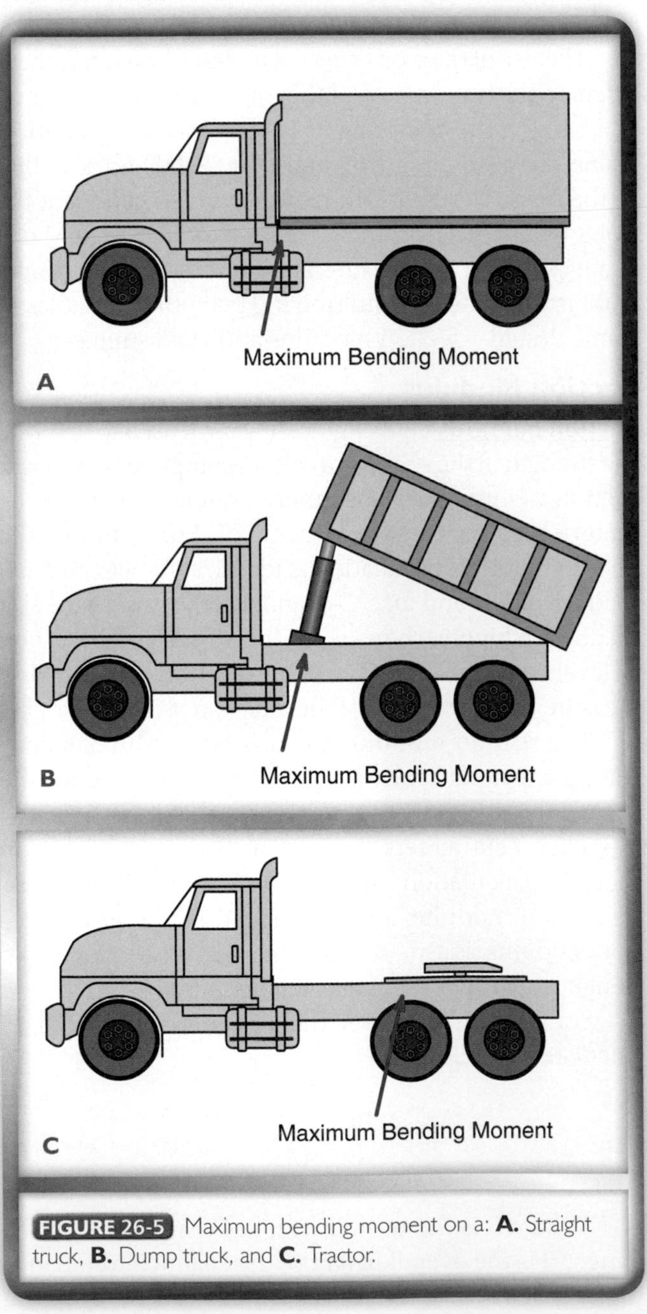

FIGURE 26-5 Maximum bending moment on a: **A.** Straight truck, **B.** Dump truck, and **C.** Tractor.

ing moment is different for every style of vehicle. The maximum bending moment for any vehicle depends on its design and where the load is placed on the vehicle, so straight trucks, dump trucks, and tractors have very different maximum bending moment locations.

The maximum bending moment of the vehicle will be the point where the load is acting on the frame at the maximum distance from the support points. The maximum bending moment is calculated by multiplying the load by the distance in inches from the support point. For example, a 34,000-pound (15,455 kg) load at a distance of 18 inches (460 mm) from the support point would equal 612,000 inch-pounds total (69,147 Nm), or 306,000 inch-pounds (34,573 Nm) of bending force per frame rail.

Frame strength is critical for heavy-duty trucks. The frame must be designed with sufficient strength to support the load placed on it and have a significant margin of safety to ensure long service life.

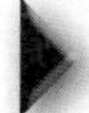

Design and Construction of Frames

The design and construction of truck frames is critical in ensuring the safe and efficient operation of the truck over its service life. The design of the components, their configuration, and the material from which they are made are all important considerations in frame construction.

Frame Material

Medium-duty truck frame rails are generally constructed using medium-carbon steels with yield strengths of up to 50,000 psi (345 MPa). To carry heavier vehicle loads, the steel plate used to manufacture these frames would have to be thicker. Using a thicker plate increases the frame's section modulus, which in turn increases the resist bending moment (RBM) of the frame.

Increasing the RBM of a frame by using a thicker plate has some disadvantages, however. A key disadvantage of using a thicker plate to increase the section modulus of the frame rail is higher weight. For example, a frame rail made of medium-carbon, high-tensile steel with 50,000 psi (345 MPa) yield strength and a section modulus of 24 has an RBM of 1,200,000 inch-pounds (135,581 Nm). That means the frame would weigh approximately 2.45 pounds per inch (0.44 kg per cm). Continuing to run the figures, the total weight of a frame 180 inches (457 cm) long would then be 882 pounds (401 kg) for both frame rails.

By contrast, a frame formed from high-performance alloy steel with 85,000 psi (586 mPa) yield strength would cut the frame weight by 30% to 40% and it would still be able to carry the same load. That is because the frame steel would be thinner and weigh less per inch.

A frame made of heat-treated chrome-molybdenum-alloy steel would cause the section modulus to drop even more, further reducing frame weight. Consider a **heat-treated alloy-steel** frame with a yield strength of 110,000 psi (758 mPa) and a section modulus of just 11. Again, this frame's height and flange width would be the same, but the steel plate would be thinner. The RBM of that type of frame rail would be 1,210,000 inch-pounds (136,712 Nm). Because the section modulus of the heat-treated, chrome-molybdenum frame is smaller, the frame will weigh only 1.125 pounds per inch (0.22 kg per cm) for a total weight of 405 pounds (184 kg). This heat treated frame would weigh less than half the weight of the medium-carbon-steel frame in the first example, yet the RBM strength is higher. The reduced frame weight also allows the vehicle to carry larger payloads.

Aluminum-alloy frames have yield strengths of 60,000 psi (414 MPa) and, with sufficient section modulus, can carry the loads required by today's heavy trucks. **Aluminum alloy** is aluminum mixed with other metals to increase its strength. The weight savings is even greater when compared to the chrome-molybdenum, alloy-steel frames. The cost of aluminum, however, can be a deterrent.

The best compromise between weight and cost for manufacturers today is the heat-treated, alloy-steel frame. Most, if not all, medium- and heavy-duty trucks currently in production are equipped with this type of frame. Lighter-duty trucks may still be equipped with medium-carbon and or heat-treated medium-carbon steel frames.

Welding on medium-carbon steel frames to alter frame length and to attach aftermarket components, such as lift gates, is a common practice in the truck industry today. Whenever modifications are made to the vehicle, care must be taken to protect the RBM of the frame. Most manufacturers prohibit welding on heat-treated frame rails and consider additional welds as voiding the vehicle's warranty. The heat from the weld can destroy the heat treatment and, thereby, reduce frame strength. Despite the risks, frame modifications are common in the industry, and many aftermarket shops perform this work on a regular basis.

Although manufacturers prohibit welding on heat-treated frame rails, they nonetheless offer instructions on frame lengthening and modifications that require welding. Clearly, there is some controversy as to the correct method of completing this kind of work—or if the work should even be performed at all. Some industry experts insist it is necessary to reinforce a welded frame at and beyond the weld in both directions to bring the frame

RBM back to specification. Other experts maintain that a reinforcement drastically increases section modulus and leads to a stress riser and frame cracking. Frame welding will be discussed in more detail in the Maintenance and Service of Truck Frames section of this chapter.

Rails, Cross Members, and Fasteners

As mentioned at the beginning of the chapter, C-channel frames, like that illustrated in FIGURE 26-6, are the most common configuration for heavy vehicles. The C-channels of the ladder frame may be formed of medium- or high-carbon steel, but today they are typically made of heat-treated alloy steel with exceptionally high yield strength. The C shape of the channel rails provides an extremely strong beam to support the vehicle components. The flat top and bottom areas of the C shape are known as the upper and lower flanges and the upright side of the C is known as the **web**.

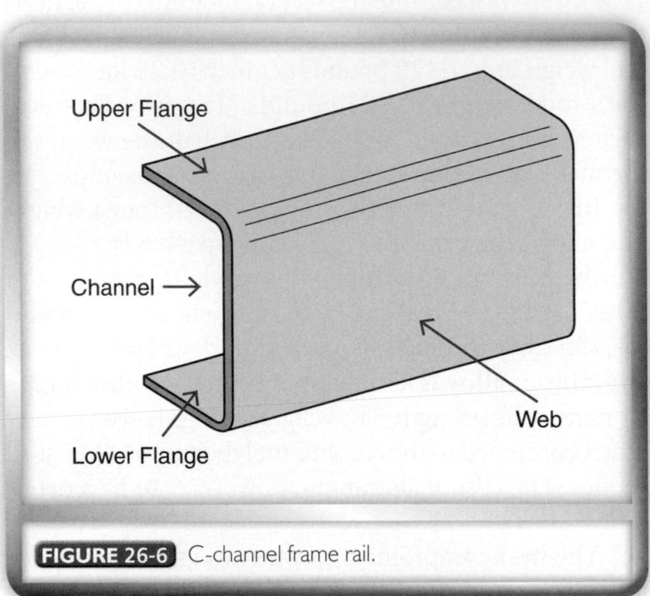

FIGURE 26-6 C-channel frame rail.

Some C-channel ladder-type frame designs are known as drop front or drop forward. As shown in FIGURE 26-7, the web height of the C-channel drops off near the front of the rails and/or the rails actually curve lower at the front. Both drop-front and drop-forward designs allow a lower mounting position for the engine and drive train, which in turn lowers the vehicle's center of gravity.

In a variation of the C-channel, ladder-type frame, the front sections of the rails will bow outward symmetrically. That means the sections will bow the same amount on each rail. This configuration was shown in Figure 26-1. In yet another variation of the C-channel, ladder-type frame, the front sections of the rails bow out asymmetrically. That is, only one rail is bowed outward. Asymmetrical configurations accommodate the engine package and front suspension.

The frame rails of the C-channel, ladder-type frame are the main load-bearing components of the frame. The connecting cross members tie the rails together both to

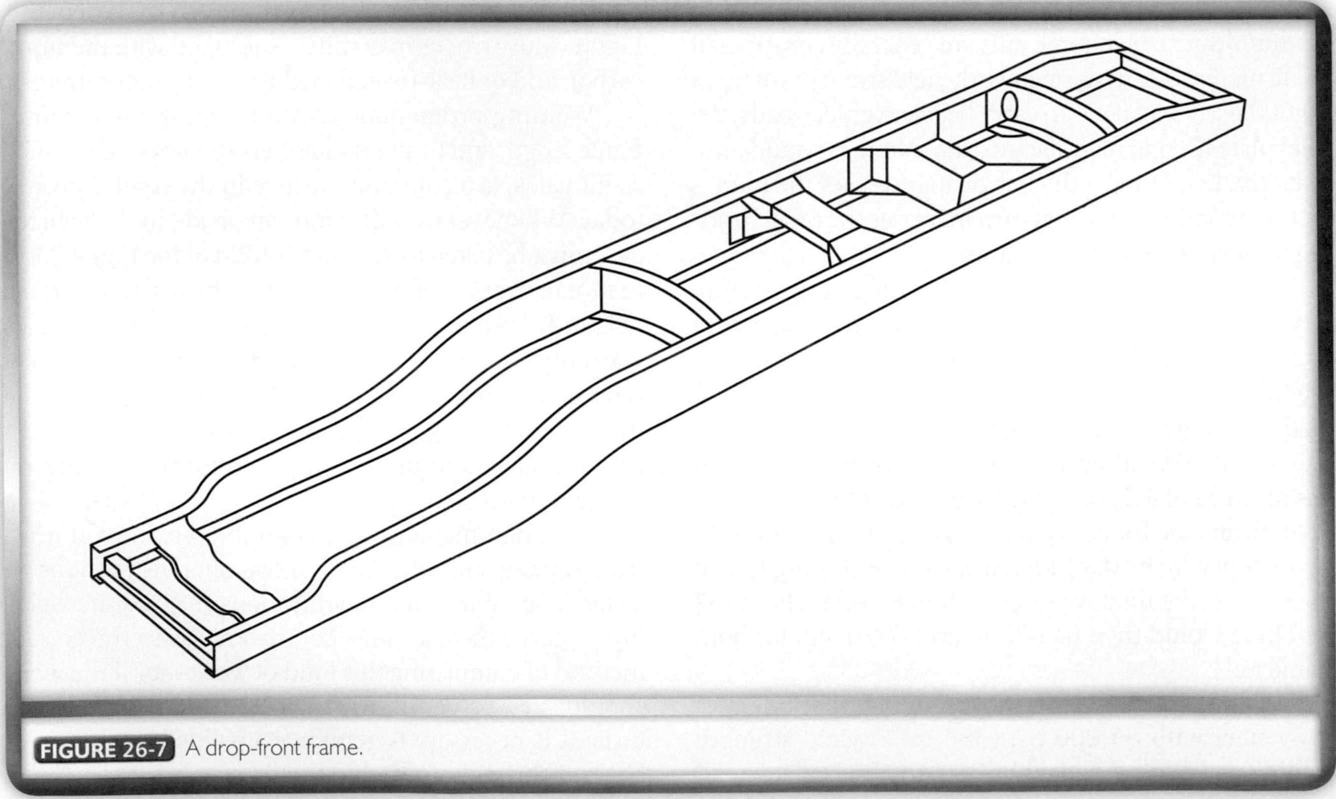

FIGURE 26-7 A drop-front frame.

maintain their alignment and to stop them from twisting under the heavy loads the rails have to carry. Frame cross members also help to control torsional stresses on the frame rails by flexing and transmitting some of the twisting stress from one rail to the other.

Frame cross members can be box, hat (as shown in FIGURE 26-8), or C-channel shaped. They may also be straight or shaped to accommodate vehicle systems such as the driveline. Often the front cross member that supports the engine is lowered. This is called a drop-center cross member, and it allows the engine and driveline mounting to be lower. As with asymmetrical ladder frames, the ability to lower the mounting of the driveline lowers the vehicle's center of gravity. The cross members also provide mounting locations and protection for vehicle wiring and other components such as air valves and piping.

Fasteners

Cross members are bolted, riveted, or attached to the rails with Huck® brand fasteners, like those shown in FIGURE 26-9. Despite appearances, **Huck® fasteners** are not nuts and bolts. Rather, the fasteners are more like a riveted connection in that the Huck® bolt has ridges instead of threads. In addition, the Huck® nut is **swaged** onto the bolt, meaning that the metal of the nut is deformed by the installation tool to precisely fit the Huck bolt. Therefore the collar cannot be tightened after the fastener is installed. As a result, these fasteners are one of the most secure attaching systems available and should last for the life of the vehicle.

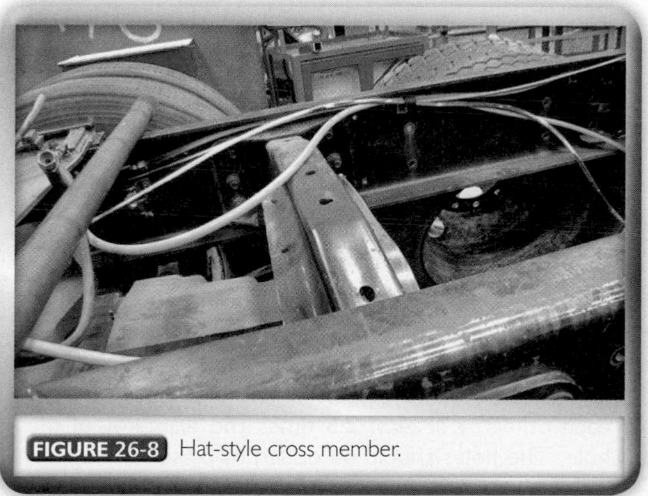

FIGURE 26-8 Hat-style cross member.

FIGURE 26-9 Huck® brand fastener.

Huck® fasteners were originally designed for use by NASA in the space program. Their versatility has caused them to be adopted for use in many industries including the truck market. Huck® bolt fasteners cannot be retorqued by traditional methods. Nonetheless, the bolts need to be inspected for looseness and for rust streaking from the frame components that are held together. Streaks can indicate movement between the components in contact. If rust streaking is found, further investigation is necessary to find out if the fasteners are loose.

Reinforced Frame Rails

In exceptionally heavy applications, manufacturers may reinforce frame rails to increase RBM by installing extra C-channel rails that fit inside the original C-channel. Two or three C-channels can be bolted together to increase the section modulus and, therefore, the RBM of the frame rails. The use of multiple channels bolted together allows the frame to be more flexible than using single extra-thick channel to increase frame RBM. Another profile of reinforcement is the **L-plate**, or inverted L-plates, which are L-shaped beams that can be bolted to the outside of the C-channel to increase the rails' RBM. FIGURE 26-10 shows several applications of different reinforcement profiles.

Reinforced frames are typically only found in off-road and heavy hauler applications because of the weight penalty they carry. Frames with three and four channels bolted together can weigh as much as 4 or 5 pounds (1.8 to 2.3 kg) per inch of rail.

Frame Reinforcement

If necessary, frame rails can also be locally reinforced when installing vehicle accessories. Local reinforcements include C-channel, L-channel plates, or fishplates. A **fishplate** is a flat, steel plate reinforcement bolted usually inside and sometimes outside the frame rail.

Great care must be taken when installing reinforcements so as not to create stress risers. The secret to successful reinforcement is tapering. That is, the edges of the reinforcing plate should be angled to spread out the stress concentration. When reinforcing a frame, the plate used should be long enough to pass the area required to be reinforced by at least half the height of the frame

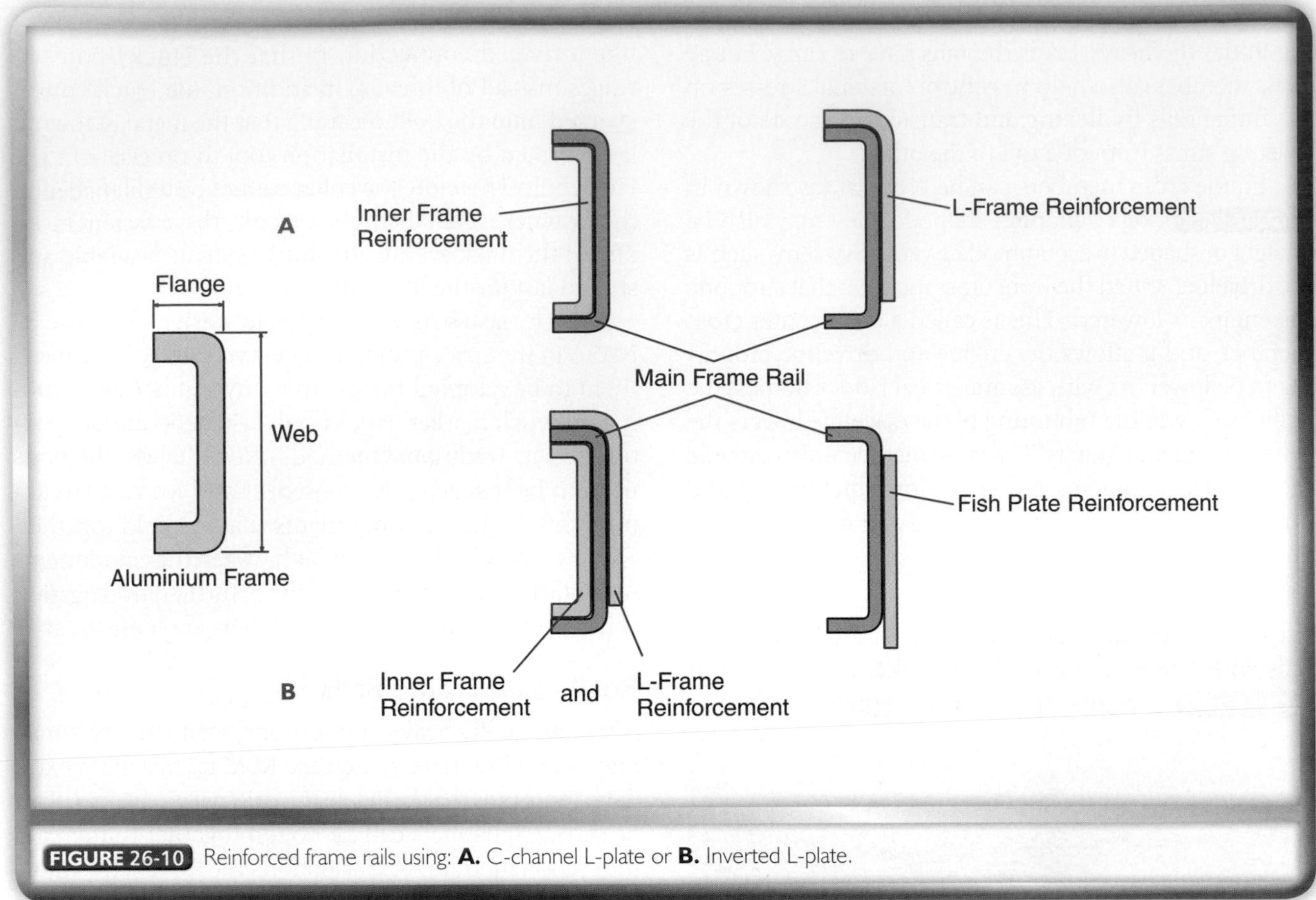

FIGURE 26-10 Reinforced frame rails using: **A.** C-channel L-plate or **B.** Inverted L-plate.

web. From there, it should taper away from those points at a rate of 25 to 60 degrees with the longest side at the tension flange of the rail. All reinforcements and bolts should be tapered and staggered. Tapering spreads out the change in section modulus and reduces the stress riser, as illustrated in **FIGURE 26-11**.

The reinforcement plate should be bolted in place using as many existing holes as possible. Only grade 8 flange-head bolts and hardened-steel washers should be used. (Soft washers will lose their torque and using no washers will damage the frame rail.) Bolt holes should be 1/32" (.03125 cm) wider than the bolts. Leaving space around the bolt allows the bolt to act as a torsion member, adding to frame flexibility; a body-bound bolt will increase localized stress.

In no case shall the holes be closer to the flanges than the factory frame holes. Never should the holes be closer than 1.5" (2.7 cm) from the flange. Remember that going from flexible to stiff in any component leads to concentrated stress. The more the reinforcement can be tapered, the better in terms of reducing the stress risers. Always stagger and taper the reinforcement plate and the attaching bolts if possible.

TECHNICIAN TIP

If holes are drilled they should be staggered so that they are not in a vertical line if possible. Never drill more holes in a vertical line than the largest number of holes drilled at the factory. Holes should be separated from each other by at least 2.5 times the diameter of the hole. The holes should be drilled as close to the neutral fiber (the center of the web) as possible. The hole should be no closer to the edge of the reinforcing plate than twice the bolt's diameter.

Frame-Supported Attachments

There are four general ways in which a vehicle body can be attached to the chassis frame: U-bolt clamps, outrigger-type mounts, fishplates, and spring-loaded resilient mounts. The choice of body mount is determined by the type of truck body being installed.

When the body is relatively flexible, such as with van bodies, it can be mounted to the frame in one of three ways: with U-bolts, outriggers, or fishplates. The least

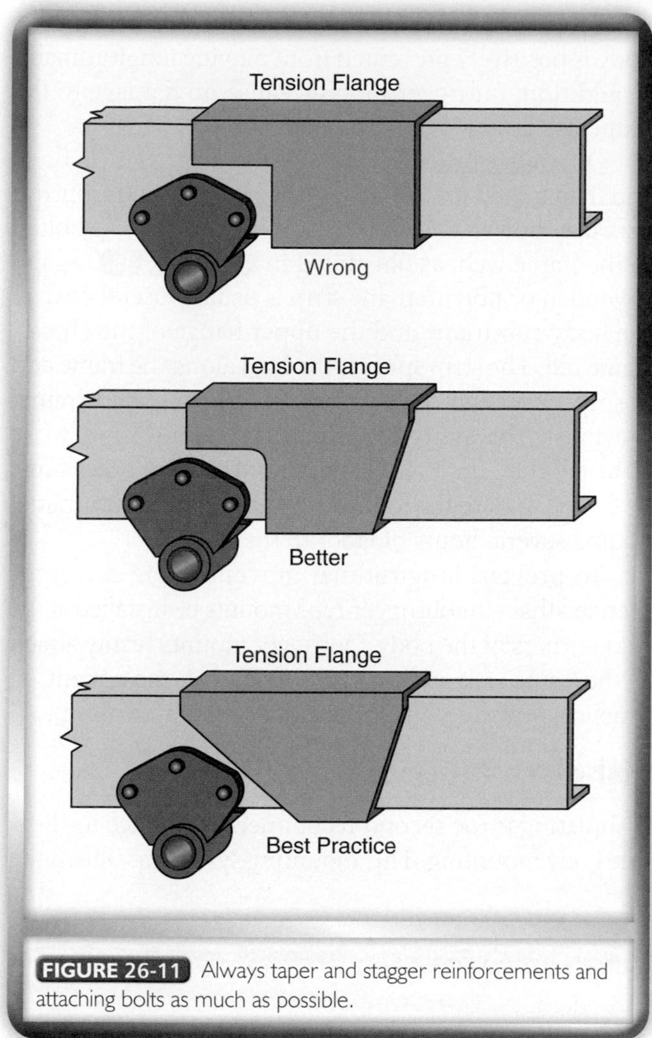

FIGURE 26-11 Always taper and stagger reinforcements and attaching bolts as much as possible.

recommended and yet most common of these is the U-bolt mounting system like that shown in FIGURE 26-12.

U-bolt Mounts

U-bolts are the least secure mounting system, but their ease of installation makes them popular with builders of truck bodies. When a body is placed on the frame, a semi-flexible material is used between the body and the frame. Polyurethane can be used, but most often the material is a strip (or strips) of hardwood such as oak. There are three primary benefits to adding semi-flexible material. First, it protects the frame flange from damage. It also adds to the flexibility of the vehicle. Finally, it helps to spread the load along the length of the frame without causing any localized stress points on the frame due to any unevenness in the body construction.

The U-bolts go over a sub-frame attached to the vehicle body and down both sides of the frame rail. They are then clamped at the bottom flange of the rail. The wood or polyurethane is clamped between the body subframe and the actual chassis frame. U-bolt mounting systems use friction between the frame, the spacer, and the sub-frame of the body to locate the body longitudinally. As a result, the body can sometimes move relative to the frame, as shown in FIGURE 26-13.

When a U-bolt mounting is used, it is also recommended that solid spacers be inserted inside the frame C-channel to stop the frame flanges from collapsing when they are clamped by the U-bolt. Steel spacers are recommended over wood because, over time, wooden blocks may contract and fall out. Again, in practice this is rarely done, and most bodies attached with U-bolts have no spacers installed at all. Quite often, the lower frame flange is bent at the U-bolt clamp point, as shown in FIGURE 26-14.

Bent flanges greatly reduce the frame strength. Flanges can bend more in vehicle service, leading to a loose U-bolt and a body that can move along the frame. U-bolt body-mounting systems are almost universal because they are easy to install and require no drilling of the frame, but these systems are the poorest of the three available choices. It is not unusual to see a U-bolt-attached body that has shifted in operation because of the short cuts taken at installation. Frame flanges that

FIGURE 26-12 U-bolt mountings.

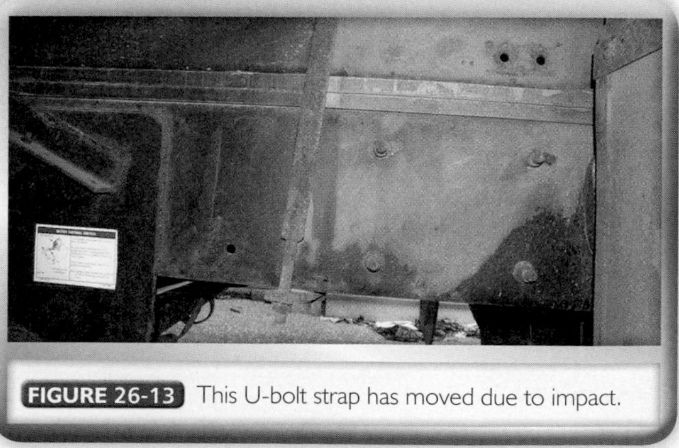

FIGURE 26-13 This U-bolt strap has moved due to impact.

FIGURE 26-14 A bent frame rail flange.

are collapsed (and therefore weakened) because a spacer was not used when installing U-bolt clamps can lead to the frame cracking at the weakened section.

U-bolt body mounting can be successful, however, if done correctly. Even though this is rarely the case, U-bolt mounting systems have been known to last for the life of vehicles with no visible problems.

Outrigger Mounts

Outrigger mounting is the recommended method of attaching flexible bodies to a ladder-type frame. Outrigger mounting is the most secure body mounting because the body is positively prevented from moving longitudinally. In addition, outrigger mounts cause no damage to the frame itself.

Outrigger brackets are welded to the vehicle body and then bolted to the frame web. Alternately, the outriggers may bolt to another bracket that, in turn, is bolted to the frame web, as illustrated in FIGURE 26-15. Again, a wooden or polyurethane strip is usually used between the body sub-frame and the upper flange of the chassis frame rail. The strip spreads the load along the frame and absorbs any high or low spots in the body sub-frame. Obviously, this system requires substantially more work to install than the U-joint system. Mounting holes must be drilled in both the frame web and the body sub-frame, adding several hours of labor to the job.

To prevent longitudinal movement, it is recommended that four outrigger-type mounts be installed at the four corners of the body. Outrigger mounts firmly attach to the frame web and prevent fore and aft movement. In practice, however, outrigger mounts are rarely used.

Fishplate Mounts

Fishplating is the second recommended choice for flexible body mounting. This mounting system, as illustrated

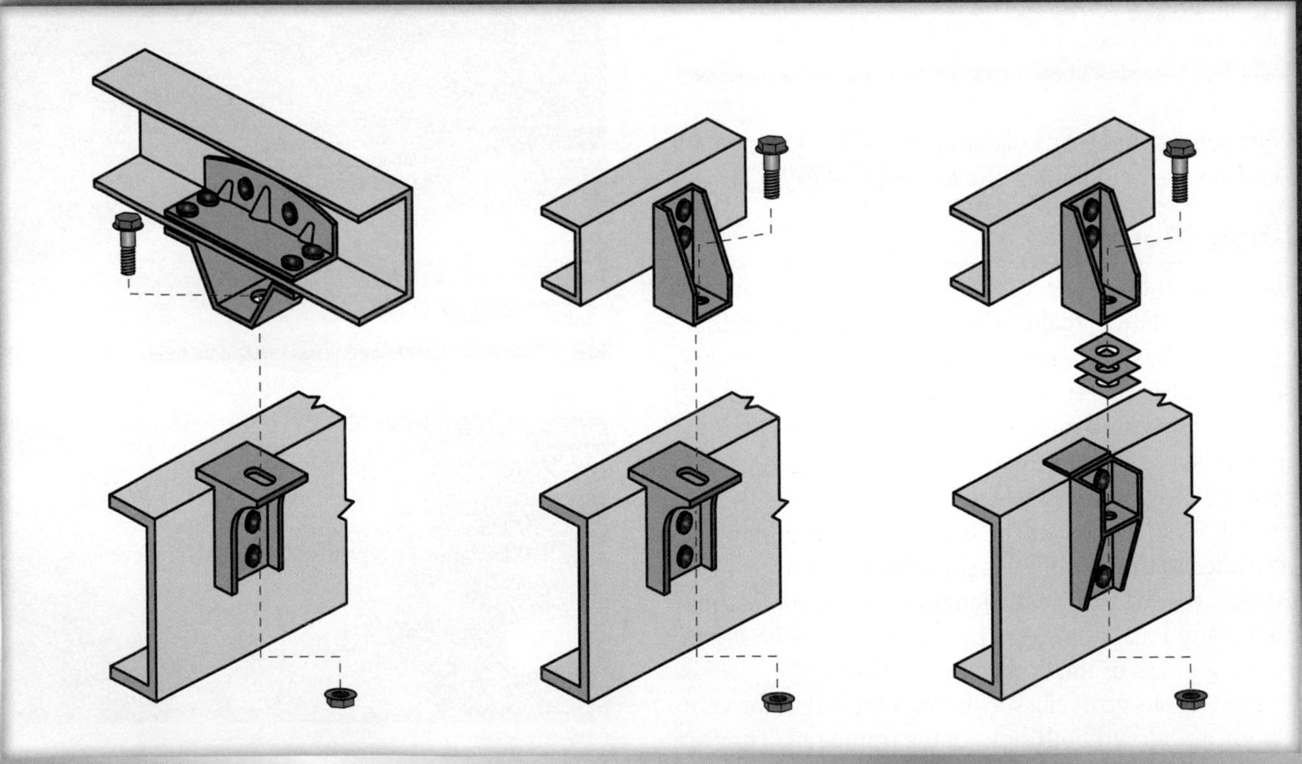

FIGURE 26-15 Outrigger mounting system.

in FIGURE 26-16, uses fishplates that are bolted to the body sub-frame and the vehicle frame web. Fishplates are flat plates used to re-enforce the frame rail. Fishplate mounts also use a wooden or polyurethane strip between the body sub-frame and the upper flange of the vehicle frame to insulate the frame and absorb any manufacturing deviations in the body sub-frame.

Fishplate systems are very secure. Like the outrigger systems, however, fishplates require holes to be drilled in the frame web and the body sub-frame. That drilling adds to the labor hours required to install the body. The extra time involved for these mounting systems is the major disadvantage that causes them to be rarely used in body installations.

Resilient Mounting Systems

When mounting a body that has reduced or very little flexibility, it is necessary to provide some movement or flexibility at the mounting points so that the body does not prevent the vehicle frame from flexing normally. Typically, installing these rigid bodies requires resilient mounting systems, these are outrigger type mounts with a flexible medium that will allow the body to move slightly up, down, or side to side.

Resilient mounts can be spring loaded or made with rubber or polyurethane elements that accommodate movement. Resilient mounts are perfect for rigid bodies, such as tankers or garbage packers. These bodies are extremely stiff and require that the mounts provide the flexibility. Tanker bodies can be mounted in a three- or four- point system that uses flexible rubber or polyurethane components. These components allow the vehicle frame to flex as necessary. Semi-rigid bodies can also use resilient outrigger mounts. FIGURE 26-17 shows a garbage packer using spring loaded resilient mounts. This allows some movement of the body as the frame flexes.

Sometimes a semi-rigid or rigid vehicle body is mounted on a frame that experiences more than normal bending and flexing because of the vehicle vocation. In those situations, another type of resilient mount called a vertical mount can be used to allow greater than normal vertical movement of the body while maintaining the

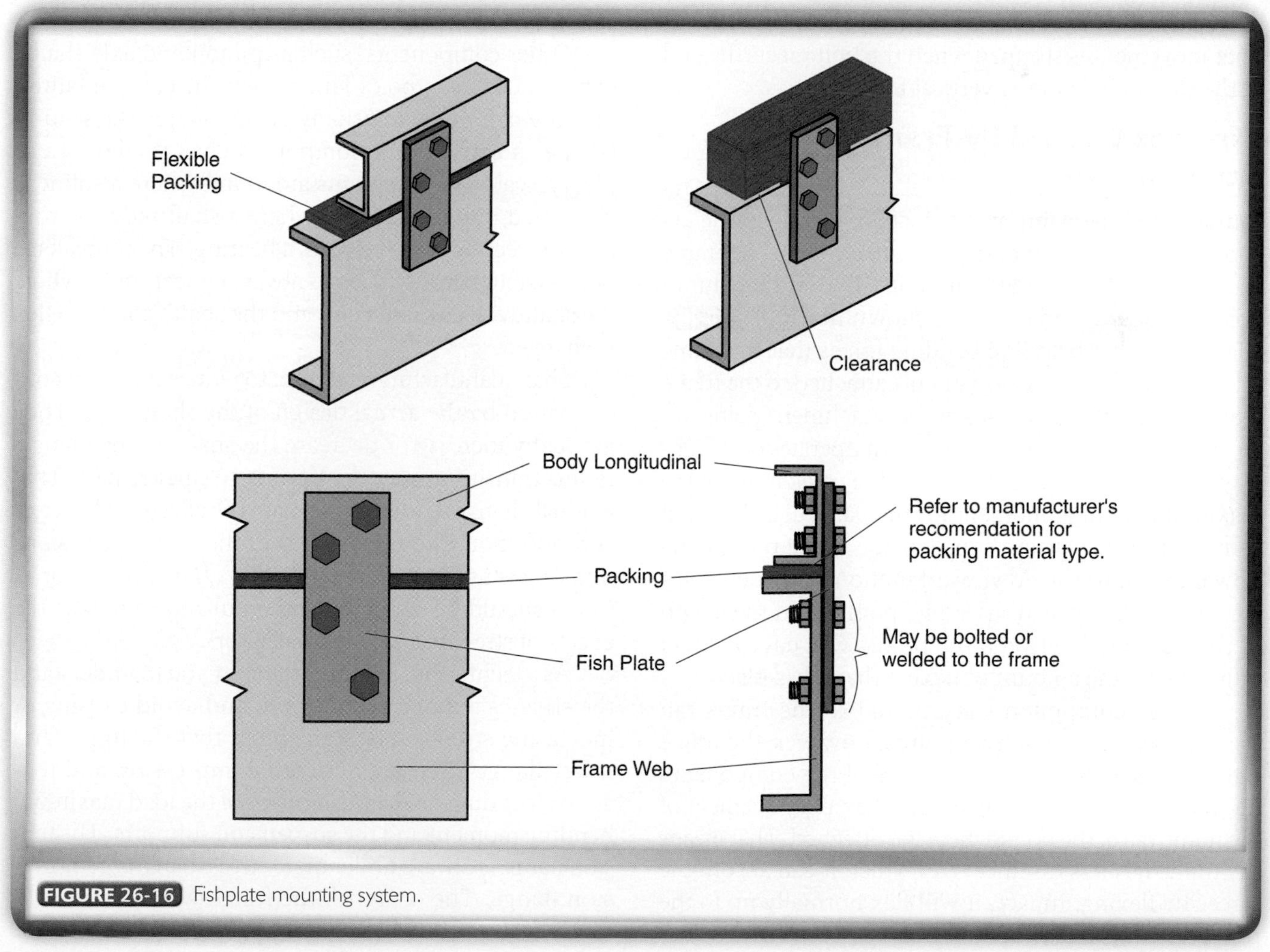

FIGURE 26-16 Fishplate mounting system.

FIGURE 26-17 A garbage packer with spring-loaded outrigger mounts.

FIGURE 26-18 Attachments such as hydraulics, dump boxes, winches, and so on add varying levels of side bending forces to the frame.

body's longitudinal position. These mounts have friction material between the vertical elements that restrict the up-and-down motion. The mounting bolts are in slotted holes that allow greater than normal vertical movement. That movement is stopped when the bolt meets the end of the slotted hole in the vertical bracket.

Stresses Caused by Frame Attachments

Almost all of the components installed on a vehicle are attached to the frame and add to the weight the frame must support. These attachments, hydraulics, dump boxes, winches, and so on, as shown in FIGURE 26-18, add varying levels of side bending forces that the frame must also withstand. Components attached to the frame tend to concentrate stresses at the attachment point.

Consider the frame of a truck as it operates on a highway. The heaviest load is resting on the truck frame at the maximum bending moment for the particular design of vehicle. The suspension supports the frame by pushing upwards against the downward motion. The frame rails flex and twist between these two points, and the length of the frame rail between the points will have a direct influence on the amount of flexing that takes place.

If large components are bolted to the frame rail halfway between these two points, however, the frame rail loses some flexibility. The mass of the component's mounting bracket restricts natural flexing movement of the frame rail at the point where it is attached. That means the frame has less distance over which it can absorb the forces by flexing. In fact, it will flex normally up to the point the attaching bracket begins, and then its flexibility decreases. Additional force such as that can cause stress risers at the beginning and end of the mounting bracket. Fatigue failures of most metal components typically occur at a stress riser.

Other components, such as pinion and axle shafts, experience this type of failure as well. Fatigue failure of those components usually occurs where the section (shape and size) of the component changes. For example, typical breakage points are found where a spline is machined into the shaft or where a shaft reduces from a raised section that supports a bearing. These breakage points occur because stress is always concentrated where the shaft widens or narrows and the shaft's ability to flex is changed.

Shaft manufacturers attempt to reduce the stress concentration by the actual design of the shaft itself. They gradually increase or decrease the shaft size by using a radius transition from the thinner to thicker part. That gradual change tends to spread out the effects of the stress concentration through the area of the radius. The same thinking is used when dealing with a frame rail. That is, forces should be spread over the rail and to reduce the effects of stress risers or concentrators.

As a technician, it is important for you to understand the stresses a frame is subject to and avoid causing or increasing stress risers. Remember that the upper and lower flange alternate between compression and tension depending on the positioning of the load maximum bending moment and the suspension supports. The tension flange is always under more stress than the compression flange. The center of the frame web (the neutral fiber) deals with the least amount of stress because the compression and tension forces cancel each other out. Therefore, any attachments should be made as close to the center of the web as possible and care must be taken to reinforce the rails, if necessary, to minimize or nullify any stress riser that may be created by large attachments.

Maintenance and Service of Truck Frames

Frame maintenance starts with a visual inspection of all the frame components as described in **SKILL DRILL 26-1**. In particular, all frame components (side rails, cross members, and brackets) should be checked for breaks, cracks, excessive corrosion, distortion, elongated holes, fastener looseness, and damage before needed repairs can be determined. If any of these defects are found, they must be repaired according to manufacturer's recommendations.

Out-of-Service Criteria for Truck Frames

Before engaging in any service activities, it is critical to understand the out-of-service criteria for truck frames. The Commercial Vehicle Safety Alliance (CVSA) is a North American organization that sets out-of-service criteria for commercial vehicles in concert with all vehicle stakeholders and enforcement agencies. The criteria apply to drivers' licensing qualifications, hours of work, and medical condition as well as the physical condition of the vehicle. The following are the CVSA out of service criteria specifically for vehicle frames.

The vehicle shall be rendered out of service if any of the following defects are present on the vehicle at the time of inspection:

- Any cracked, sagged, loose, or broken side rail that allows the vehicle body to contact moving components or otherwise suggests imminent frame collapse
- Any broken cracked or loose frame member that adversely affects the support of any suspension, steering, driveline, or body component
- Any crack 1.5" (38 mm) in length or larger in the frame web that projects towards the bottom flange of the rail
- Any crack in the frame web that extends around the radius and into the lower flange
- Any crack 1" (25 mm) or larger in the bottom flange of the side rail
- Any condition that causes the vehicle body or frame to be in contact with any part of the vehicle tires or wheel assemblies including excessive loading

The CVSA states that a vehicle shall not be put back into service until the defects are repaired.

Types of Frame Damage

Cracked frames are usually caused by fatigue failures caused by stress risers and or chronic overloading. Localized crack repair by welding is covered in the Crack Repair section at the end of this chapter. There are five other general types of frame damage that can occur when

SKILL DRILL 26-1 Conducting Exterior Inspections of Frame

1. Check the vehicle frame and the frame members for bending or other types of deformities and for any cracks and excessive rust or scale.
2. Check frame members for cracks, breaks, looseness, or sagging. In addition, inspect them for any loose or missing fasteners, including fasteners attaching functional components, such as the engine, transmission, steering gear, suspension, body parts, and fifth-wheel components.
3. Check for any condition that causes the body or frame to be in contact with a tire or any part of the wheel assemblies and for missing or unengaged locking pins in adjustable axle assemblies.

dealing with ladder-type frames, they are sag, bow, diamond, twist, and sidesway.

Sag

Frame **sag** is a downward bend of the frame rails caused by one of two factors FIGURE 26-19A. The first cause is static overload, which occurs when the load on the vehicle is more than the frame can handle. The other cause of sag is shock load to the frame caused by the vehicle dropping into a depression in the terrain; the load consequently bends the frame. Sag can also be caused by a weakening of the frame RBM, for example by drilling too many holes in the web, by holes being too close to the flanges, or by welding the frame rails and negating the properties of their heat treatment. A definitive sign of frame sag is wrinkles in the compression flange of the rail at the point of sag.

Bow

Bow is the opposite of sag. It is the upward bending of the frame rails and can be caused by uneven loading of the frame. This can occur in dump truck applications when the box is raised. The rear contact point of the box can cause the frame to bend at that point and bow upwards at the suspension. A definitive indication of frame bow is wrinkling of the lower frame flange at the point that bowing occurs.

Diamond

Diamond is a condition when one frame rail is further forward than the other FIGURE 26-19B. Diamond usually occurs as a result of impact from a collision or from a poorly reinforced plough mounting on a snow removal vehicle. Diamond can also be caused by trying to free a stuck vehicle carrying a heavy load by chaining the vehicle but to only one frame rail.

Twist

Frame **twist** occurs when one frame rail is lower than the other and also can be caused by collision damage FIGURE 26-19C. Sometimes what seems to be frame twist is not actually. For example, a broken spring will give the indication of a twisted frame, but the frame will usually return to its correct alignment when the broken spring is repaired. A truly twisted frame is one of the most difficult to repair because the rails must be simultaneously pushed and/or pulled in more than one direction to straighten them.

Sidesway

Sidesway is when the vehicle frame is bowed outward when viewed from the top FIGURE 26-19D. As with other types of frame damage, sidesway is usually caused by accident damage sustained during a side-impact collision. Shock loading while using a snowplow can also cause sidesway.

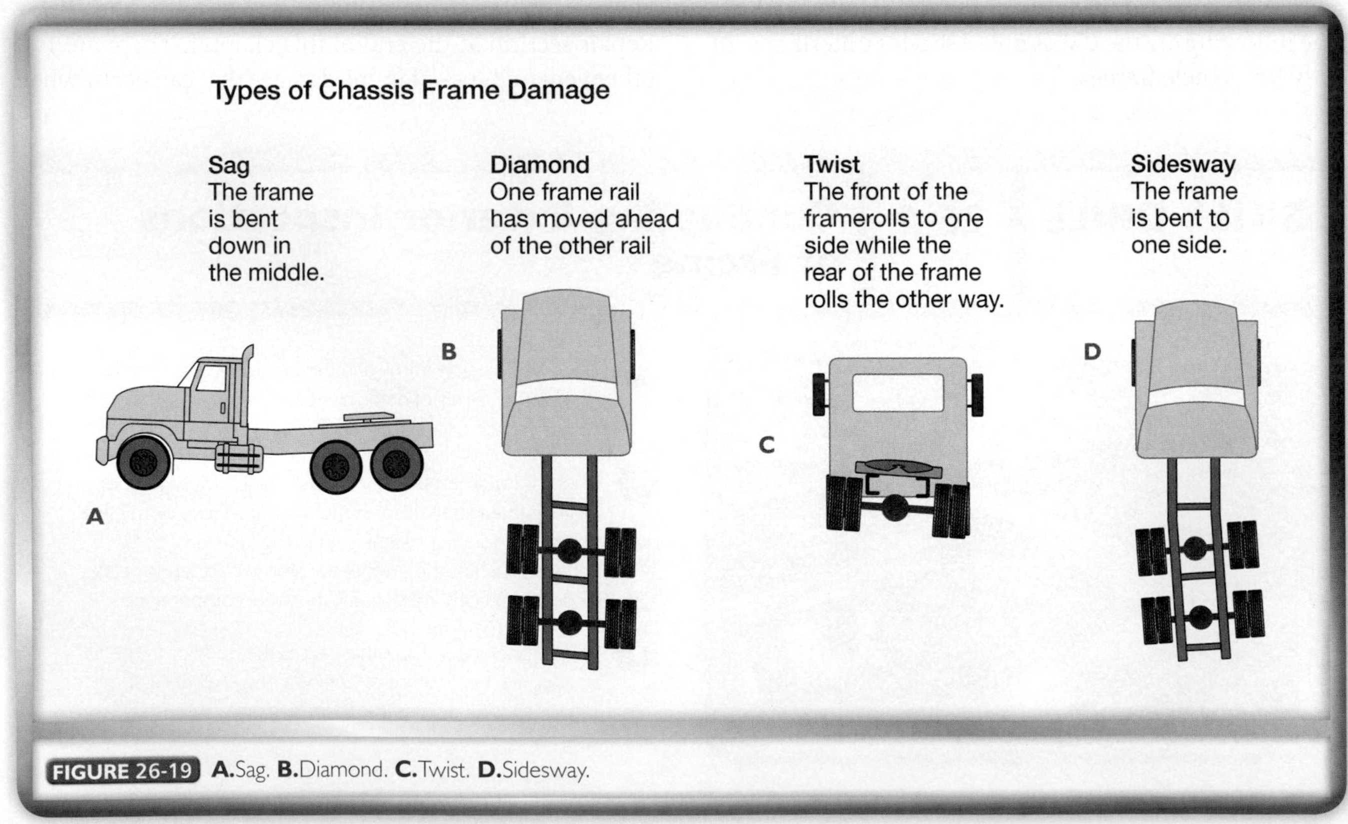
Types of Chassis Frame Damage
Sag
The frame is bent down in the middle.
Diamond
One frame rail has moved ahead of the other rail
Twist
The front of the framerolls to one side while the rear of the frame rolls the other way.
Sidesway
The frame is bent to one side.
A
B
C
D

FIGURE 26-19 **A.**Sag. **B.**Diamond. **C.**Twist. **D.**Sidesway.

Corrosion Damage

Corrosion, like that shown in FIGURE 26-20, is a constant threat to the integrity of the frame metal. Normal surface rusting of a frame does not greatly affect its strength. Always inspect the frame for rust damage while conducting vehicle service, as excessive corrosion will compromise the frame's strength.

Rust is less of a problem for today's heavy vehicles than it was in the past. Today's heat-treated high-tensile-strength frames are typically powder coated or painted using an electrophoretic process. Both of those processes lead to a much more resilient paint coating. As such, they are much less likely to sustain rust damage than older frames. Still, improper or careless work practices around the frame can damage the paint surface and cause eventual rusting. Always use due care to avoid scratching or otherwise damaging the frame coating and exposing the base metal when working on a vehicle.

A particularly troublesome type of corrosion is **galvanic corrosion**, which is the corrosion of material caused by the electrolytic effect that can occur when two dissimilar metals are in contact. This electrolytic effect can result in a heavy corrosion problem with certain chassis frames that use elements constructed from different metals.

Galvanic corrosion occurs when there are dissimilar metals in contact when an electrolyte is introduced between them. During galvanic corrosion, one metal becomes the anode and the other becomes the cathode. The metals form a galvanic cell similar to a battery. An electrical current created by the oxidation of the anode flows through the electrolyte from the anode to the cathode. The electrolyte can be anything that conducts electricity such as plain water or water mixed with road salt—either of which can be a powerful electrolyte.

The most common occurrence of a galvanic cell in a truck frame is aluminum in contact with steel. When water or salt water is present between the two, the aluminum will become the anode and the steel is the cathode. The anode (the aluminum) will oxidize resulting in a current flow but at the expense of the aluminum component.

FIGURE 26-20 Excessive corrosion.

To prevent this, anytime aluminum is used in the vehicle construction, for example as a frame cross member, there must be an insulator between the two metals to prevent a galvanic cell from occurring. Typically the metals are separated by a polymer such as Mylar. Alternatively, the two metals are coated with a corrosion-resistant insulating sealer similar to Tectyl-400C™ before they are assembled. The attaching bolts and washers are also coated with the sealer at all points where they will be in contact with the aluminum.

Any time work is performed on vehicle components with dissimilar metals, it is essential that these separators and sealers are replaced and reapplied on reassembly as required. Otherwise, corrosion will result. Galvanic cells can be created whenever any two dissimilar metals are in contact. On trucks, the most common combination is aluminum and steel, but be aware that other combinations of metal can lead also to galvanic cells. For that reason, all dissimilar metals should be insulated from each other. Needless to say, technicians working with aluminum frames must be extremely diligent to avoid creating galvanic cells and their resultant corrosion; aluminum frames are most often associated with flatbed trailers.

Frame Alignment and Repairs

In order to determine if a frame has had damage due to impact or collision, it is necessary to check frame alignment. A frame that is out of alignment will cause numerous problems. When the frame is misaligned, the axles are no longer perpendicular to the direction of vehicle travel, meaning that tire scrub will occur. This will lead to poor fuel economy, rapid tire wear, and excess wear and tear on the entire vehicle driveline. Driver fatigue will increase as the operator has to fight the steering wheel to keep the vehicle in a straight line.

Several commercial vehicle alignment systems are available to check frame alignment, but it can also be checked using a simple method requiring only a plumb-bob and a chalk-line. This method involves projecting reference points on the vehicle frame to the floor and then comparing center lines and distances. To manually checking frame alignment, follow the steps in SKILL DRILL 26-2. The procedure described is typical but may vary for a particular vehicle. Prepare to do the manual check with the following preliminary steps:

- Check the vehicle's tire pressure and adjust each tire as required.

SKILL DRILL 26-2 Checking Frame Alignment Manually

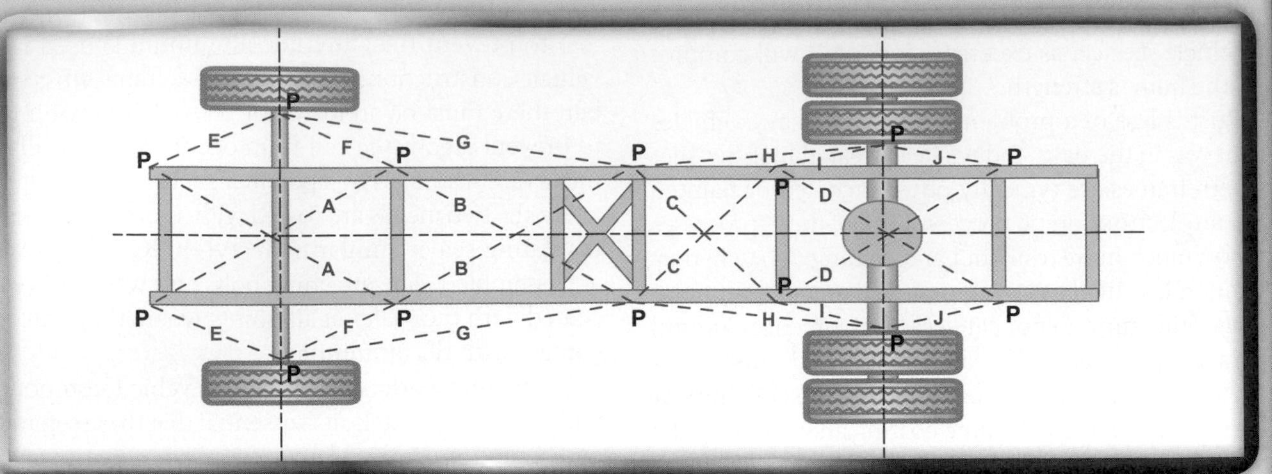

1. Select the reference points on the frame that are to be projected to the floor. (The reference points will vary from vehicle to vehicle but the points used must be the same points on each side of the frame.) Project as many reference points as possible—using more points increases accuracy.

2. If the frame being checked has rails that bow outward at the front, then use the front spring mounts as reference points to find the vehicle center line. Reference points include, but are not limited to:

   - Front suspension
   - Front and rear spring mounting bracket bolts
   - Mounting bolts on the frame cross members (use the same position bolt on each side rail)
   - Rear suspension spring mounting bracket bolts, front and rear.

   Several other reference points can be used as long as they are at the same point on each of the frame rails: using more reference points will make the alignment check more accurate. A straight edge can be clamped square to the frame rails if enough reference points cannot be found.

3. Hold a plumb-bob string in place at each of the reference points on the frame. Ensure that you are at the same side of each bolt head or rivet and that the reference point is the same on each side. If the string of the plumb bob is at the apex of the bolt hex on one side and on a flat on the other side, the points will not be the same. Hanging the plumb bob from the washer on the bolt rather than the bolt head would be more accurate. Also ensure that the reference point is the same distance from the frame rail on each side and then project its location to the floor with the plumb bob.

4. Stick a piece of tape to the floor directly beneath the plumb-bob and mark the spot on the tape or the floor. Be very precise and consistent with the marks or the test will be useless. Continue marking until all of the reference points are projected to the floor.

5. Carefully move the vehicle away from the marked spots on the floor. Measure the distance between the front plumb-bob marks from the right and left side rails. Carefully mark the exact center between these two points. That is the center line of the frame and the front.

6. Measure the distance between the rear right and left plumb-bob marks, and mark the exact center between these two points. That is the center line of the frame at the rear.

7. Using a chalk line, carefully pull the line between the two marked centers and snap the line on the ground. This is now the truck frame center line.

8. Pull the chalk line diagonally between the plumb-bob marks (i.e., between the last mark at the left rear and the second last mark at the right rear). Snap a line.

9. Pull the chalk line between the last mark at the right rear and the second last mark at the left rear. Snap a line.

10. Continue marking chalk lines until all of the plumb-bob marks are diagonally connected to form a series of Xs along the length of the frame center line as shown in the diagram. If the frame is in alignment, the exact center of the Xs should be at the frame centerline plus or minus 1/8" (2.75 mm).

11. Measure the length of the pairs of intersecting diagonals. The intersecting lines should be equal to within 1/8" (2.75 mm). If they are not, frame diamonding is present.

- Confirm that the wheel height is the same from side to side and front to back.
- Visually inspect for any obvious frame or suspension damage and repair as necessary.
- Ensure that the vehicle is on a smooth, level surface and that the front wheels are in the straight-ahead position.
- Roll the vehicle back and forth by hand to neutralize the suspension.

TECHNICIAN TIP

Out of alignment frame sections can easily be determined by the Xs that do not coincide with the frame centerline or intersecting diagonals of differing lengths.

Frame Alignment Repair

Diamond damage usually bends or displaces the cross members while the frame rails remain relatively unscathed. Examine the frame cross members very carefully to see if they have been bent or moved on their mounting bolts. Repair is then simply a matter of straightening or replacing bent cross members and, if the mounting bolts have moved, loosening the cross members, re-aligning the rails, and then re-tightening the cross members.

Frame rails damaged by sag, bow, twist, and/or sidesway can be straightened by shops with specialty equipment—provided that the damage is not severe. This type of specialized hydraulic alignment rig allows forces to be applied to the frame in many directions at once, which is required to effectively straighten a frame rail. Most of these alignment rigs are also computer assisted. The operator follows detailed setup instructions laid out by the computer, which greatly increases the success rate of the repair.

Manufacturers recommend that frame straightening be done cold, but some shops will attempt to straighten frame rails by applying heat. This practice is not sanctioned by manufacturers and will usually result in a loss of frame strength in heat-treated frame rails. In fact, most manufacturers prohibit heating or welding of any frames unless specifically authorized by their engineering department, as shown by the warning label in FIGURE 26-21.

TECHNICIAN TIP

Manufacturers have specific recommendations for frame service; most call for damaged rails to be replaced. Heating or welding of heat-treated frames is prohibited by manufacturers without express permission. Further, any liability arising from work performed on their vehicle frames without written authorization of the manufacturer is solely the responsibility of the company and person who performs the work. Careful consideration must be taken before embarking on any frame work that falls outside of manufacturer recommendations.

Trying to straighten a frame by heating the rails is a hit-and-miss operation and is rarely completely successful. Any frame rail that shows evidence of wrinkling of the metal on the rail flanges cannot be repaired and will require replacement. Wrinkling of the metal of the frame rail indicates severe impact damage to the rail and it cannot be straightened. Pay particular attention to the flange areas of the rail that are normally under compression loading to check for wrinkling. Some shops will attempt blacksmith-style repairs on wrinkled frame rails to correct the buckling of the web or the flange by using heat and sledge hammers, but this kind of repair is not recommended by any manufacturer.

Whenever a frame has been straightened, it is essential that any damaged bolts or rivets be replaced with grade 8

FIGURE 26-21 Manufacturers forbid welding on frames unless approved by their own engineers.

attaching hardware using flange bolts and hardened steel washers. All frame fasteners should be re-torqued to specification after straightening. If a frame is assembled with rivets (lighter duty frames) that have loosened, the rivets will need to be removed and replaced with bolts. Always follow the manufacturer's recommendation for bolt grade when replacing rivets with bolts. These installations may call for grade 5 bolts. Be aware that substituting grade 8 for grade 5 may reduce the frame flexibility at that point.

Safety

Read and understand these welding precautions before attempting any welding procedure on the frame or vehicle:

- Avoid welding near the fuel tank, fuel lines, or brake lines.
- Any components near the welding area that may be damaged by excessive heat must be removed or adequately protected.
- Always disconnect the battery or battery's positive and negative terminal posts.
- Check manufacturer's recommendation to protect the vehicle electronics, including disconnecting computer module grounds.
- Keep the ground connection of the arc welding machine as close to the work area as possible.
- Before welding the frame, remove the paint and or powder coating from the weld area.
- After welding, apply an anti-corrosion finishing compound to the weld and surrounding area.

Splicing Frames

Most manufacturers prefer that a vehicle be specified with the correct length frame so that lengthening and splicing is not necessary. Nonetheless, this practice has long been the norm for truck body builders and modifiers. Most, if not all, medium and heavy truck frames in production are heat-treated. Cutting and welding on heat treated frames is not generally recommended by manufacturers. Only highly competent welders such as those certified by the American Welding Society who understand the welding process and the properties of the metal being welded and with experience and proper training in pre-heating, heat treating, and tempering have the necessary skills to cut and weld heat-treated steel while maintaining the steel strength. The welded frame must be carefully preheated before welding, then heat-treated, quenched, and tempered after welding at very precise temperatures.

Welders also must understand which is the correct filler metal for the frame material and how much heat to apply. Using the wrong filler wire, like that shown in **FIGURE 26-22**, will result in a weld that is weaker than the frame metal and, as such, susceptible to breakage. Too much heat at the weld site can harden the metal at the edge of the weld to a point where it becomes brittle and will crack. Incorrect preheating and cooling will remove the heat-treating benefit of the steel and the frame steel strength will be reduced at that point. For example, a heat treated frame with 110,000 psi (760 MPa) yield strength can be reduced to 36,000 psi (250 MPa) by improper welding and finishing techniques.

In most cases, frames are welded to extend their length, and typically the design of the box or body being installed on the lengthened frame does not concentrate stress near the weld areas. That makes bringing the frame back to original strength not as critical. Manufacturers issue guidelines on frame lengthening or splicing to try and limit the risk of a frame failure because of welding. Following those guidelines helps to minimize frame weakness at weld joints by spreading out the joint and therefore ensuring that stresses are not concentrated at welds.

Frames are regularly cut and welded with straight cuts using a butt splice with few problems because the frame RBM is much greater than the load it will be subject to. If a frame is subjected to large loads near the weld area, however, it will probably break at the splice. Most experts recommend that the frame rail web section should be cut at a 45- to 60-degree angle so that bending forces are spread out over a much larger area of the welded section.

According to a major truck manufacturer, when splicing a frame, the rails should be cut on an angle following the template in **FIGURE 26-23** to avoid a concentrated stress riser in the rejoined frame. The dimensions here are for a 10.06" (25.55 cm) frame. The diagram shows the left rail. The cuts on the right rail will have opposite dimensions.

The flange section of the cut should be angled at 30 degrees from front to back. Some welders will run the

FIGURE 26-22 Flux-cored filler wire used in frame repair.

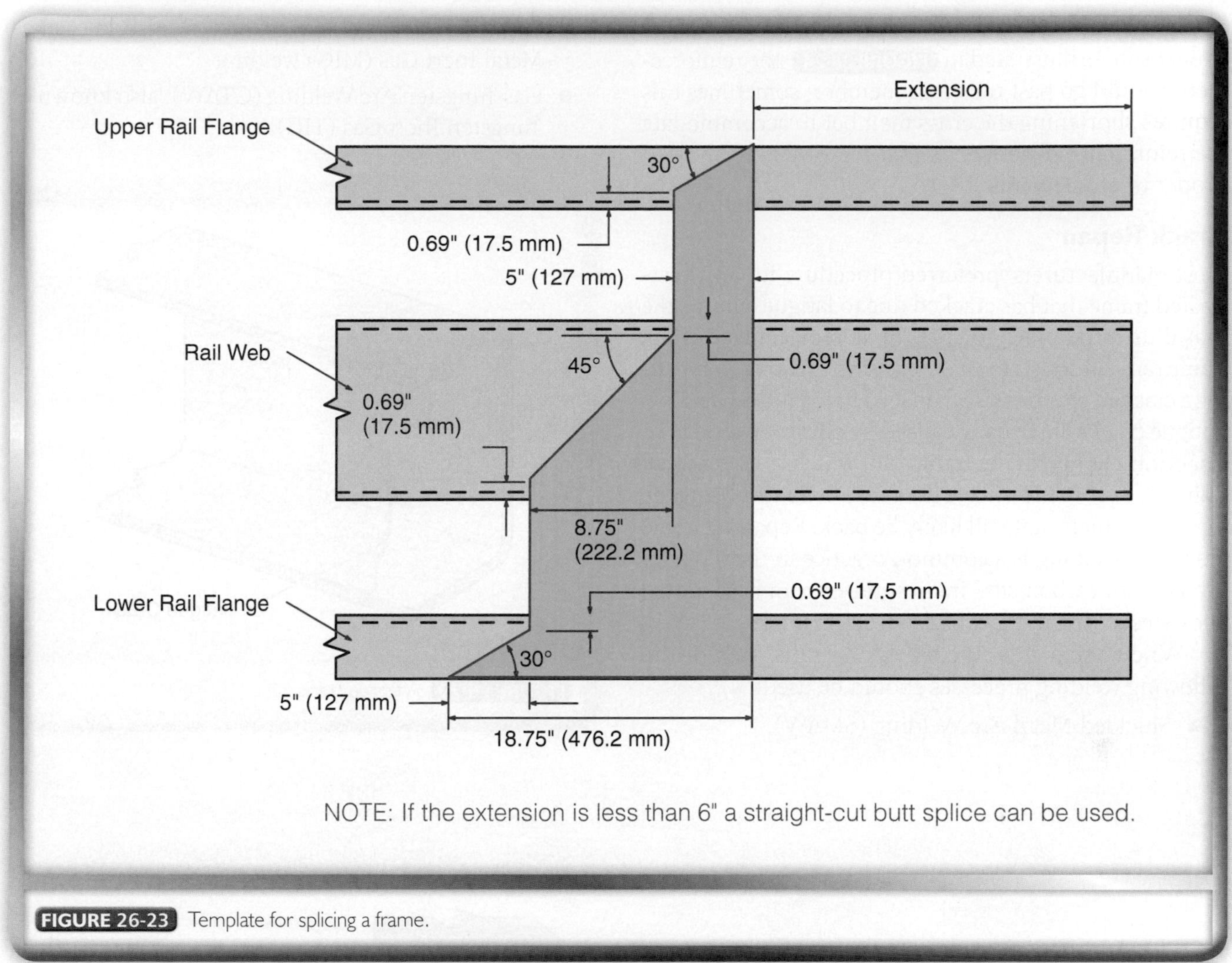

FIGURE 26-23 Template for splicing a frame.

angles on the right and left rails in opposite directions to further spread out the load across the welded frame. Opposite-side staggering is recommended by certain manufacturers. Most manufacturers also insist that if a frame is lengthened, the splice must be reinforced to attempt to bring the frame back to its original strength. In practice, however, frame splicing is quite often done without reinforcements.

The theory behind not using reinforcements is that reinforcements stiffen the frame and create a stress concentrator (riser) at the point where the reinforcement begins. Fatigue failure of the frame (cracking) is a common occurrence at a stress riser. If lengthening a frame, careful calculation is required to make sure that the vehicle's maximum bending moment is not anywhere near the welded area.

Extending a frame to carry a long body tends to spread the load over a longer surface of the frame. That is typically the reason for most frame extensions, but if heavy loads are concentrated near the weld, it is likely to fail. Most experts agree that a frame welded without reinforcements will probably fail at the tension flange side of the weld if the frame is heavily loaded at the weld point. For that reason, reinforcement of the weld is recommended.

Reinforcement should be bolted—not welded—and carried out in the manner depicted in the earlier section on reinforcement using fishplate. (Recall that using fishplate allows the frame flanges to flex more than using C-channel.) Frame reinforcements should extend past the weld point at least twice the web height and should taper away from that point at 45 degrees. Reinforcements should be made with a metal equal in thickness (never use a thicker plate as reinforcement) and yield strength to the original frame metal. Staggering the bolts and tapering the reinforcement as much as possible will do much to avoid stress concentrators and is recommended or failure is very likely. Some manufacturers even recommend reinforcements extend the length of the whole rail.

Regardless, reinforcements should never stop at or before a cross member or other section stiffener, as doing so will leave a section modulus gap causing a stress riser. As illustrated in FIGURE 26-24, the reinforcement should go past the cross member; sometimes this requires shortening the cross member to accommodate the reinforcing plate. Recall that Figure 26-10 showed proper reinforcements.

Crack Repair

Most manufacturers' preferred procedure for any heat-treated frame that has cracked due to fatigue failure, like that illustrated in FIGURE 26-25, is replacement of the frame rails, although most do offer instructions on repairing a cracked or otherwise damaged frame rail by welding. Fatigue cracks are usually caused by chronic overload or a **section change** in the frame rail, which causes a weak point. Be sure to investigate the cause before releasing the repaired vehicle or it will likely be back. Repairing frame cracks by welding is a common practice in the industry for medium-carbon-steel frames and even for heat-treated alloy steels used in most heavy-truck frames.

When repairing cracked frame rails, one of the following welding processes should be used:

- Shielded Metal Arc Welding (SMAW)
- Gas Metal Arc Welding, (GMAW), also known as Metal Inert Gas (MIG) welding
- Gas Tungsten Arc Welding (GTAW), also known as Tungsten Inert Gas (TIG)

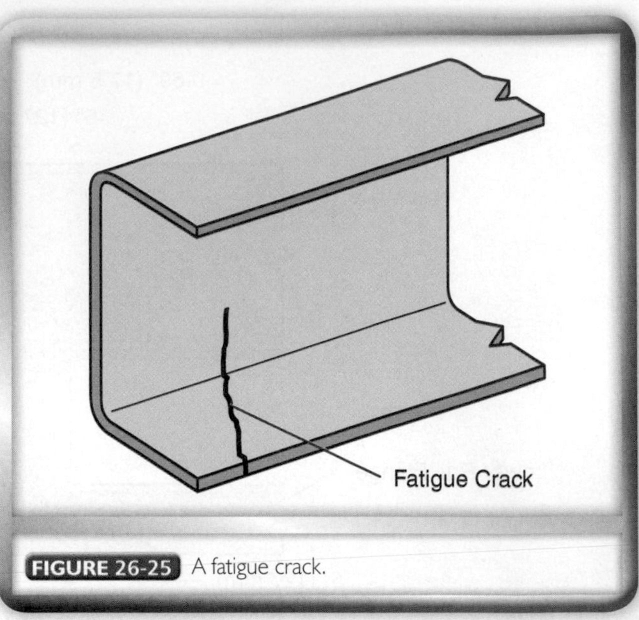

FIGURE 26-25 A fatigue crack.

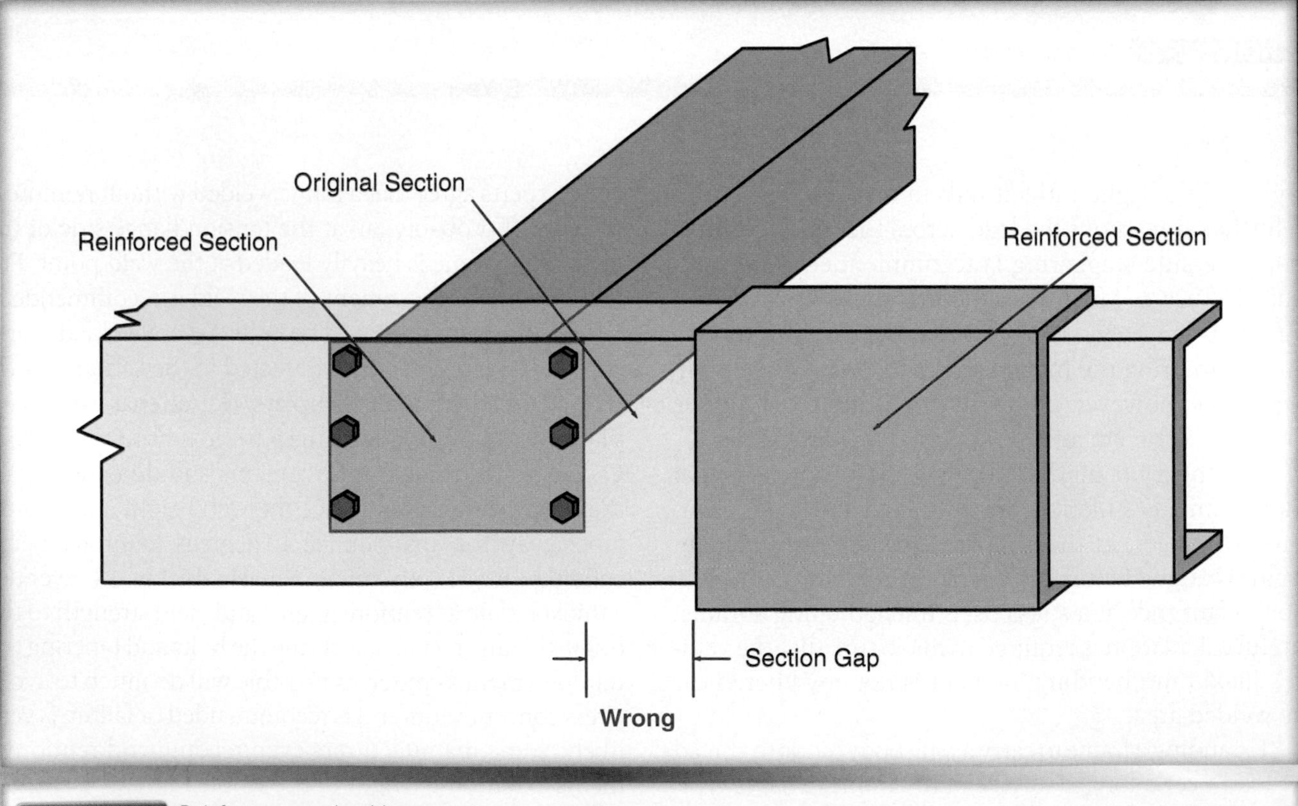

FIGURE 26-24 Reinforcements should go past the cross member.

For high-strength, low-alloy steel with tensile strengths of up to 80,000 psi (5,515 mPa), weld the crack with the appropriate low-hydrogen filler wire or electrode according to the information in TABLE 26-1. Correct amperage and voltage recommendations are shown in TABLE 26-2.

The frame metal surrounding the crack should be preheated to a temperature of 500°F to 600°F (250°C to 315°C). The Tempilstick™ shown in FIGURE 26-26 is a tool that will melt at a specific range of temperature and so help to achieve the correct temperature. Preheating helps to prevent the metal surrounding the weld from becoming brittle.

Remember to follow the welding precautions previously mentioned.

The first step in crack repair is to clean the area in and around the crack by removing all traces of rust, paint, grease, and oil. The goal is to ensure that the crack will not continue to spread after repair. Next, determine the type of crack to be repaired. Three types of frame cracks are:

- A web crack between two bolt holes or openings
- A flange crack
- A web crack that extends to or through the flange area

It is important to note here that a cracked frame indicates an overload, a stress riser, or frame damage. The vehicle should be examined carefully to determine the cause of any crack failure to avoid the problem repeating

TECHNICIAN TIP

There is controversy over frame weld reinforcement. Unless the weld is performed perfectly and with the right filler material, a loss of strength is very likely to take place on a heat-treated frame. If you undertake to reinforce a frame, be sure to stagger reinforcements and install them properly so that they do not cause a stress riser. Paying careful attention to the placement and installation of reinforcements will lessen the chance of failure of the weld in most cases.

TABLE 26-1: Recommended Electrodes and Wires

Material Strength psi	Recommended Electrode and Wire	
	SMAW	GMAW
50,000	E7018	E70S-3
60,000	–	E70S-1B
70,000	E8018	E80S-D2

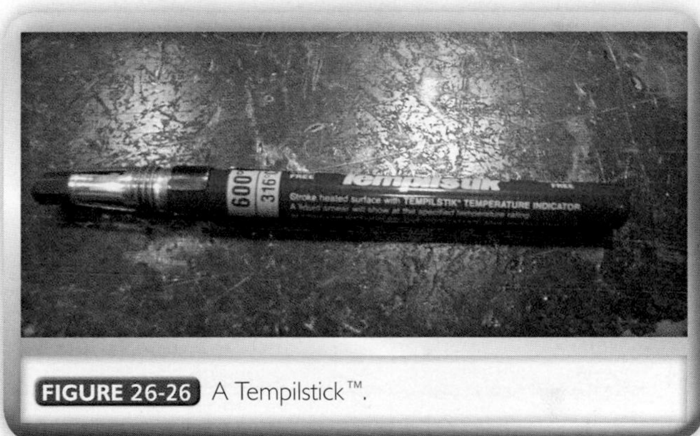

FIGURE 26-26 A Tempilstick™.

TABLE 26-2: Amperage and Voltage Recommendations for Welding

SMAW Method (HSLA Frames)				
Position	Electrode size in inches	Welding Current		Speed (In/Min)
		Amperes	Volts	
Flat	.125	–	–	–
Horizontal and Vertical	.125	110/140	20/14	24
GMAW Method (HSLA Frames)				
Position	Electrode size in inches	Welding Current		Speed (In/Min)
		Amperes	Volts	
Flat	.035	–	–	350/400
Horizontal and Vertical	.035	190/220	20/30	350/400

itself; repairing a crack in a frame that is chronically overloaded can turn into a repetitive failure if the original issue is not dealt with. After a frame failure, check to see if it cracked at the location of a newly installed accessory or if the vehicle had just undergone a change in vocation, which may have caused overload. Also, check if there has been a serious repair, such as suspension, and investigate to see if these situations might have contributed to the failure. Remember that even a deep gouge in a frame rail can cause a stress riser, leading to a crack forming at the gouge or scratch.

To repair a crack between bolt holes, follow the steps in **SKILL DRILL 26-3**. To repair a crack in the web or flange or extending from the web through the flange, follow the steps in **SKILL DRILL 26-4**. Note that the Skill Drill 26-4 includes all the steps as Skill Drill 26-3 with an added procedure for drilling a relief hole in the frame rail or web to stop the progression of the crack.

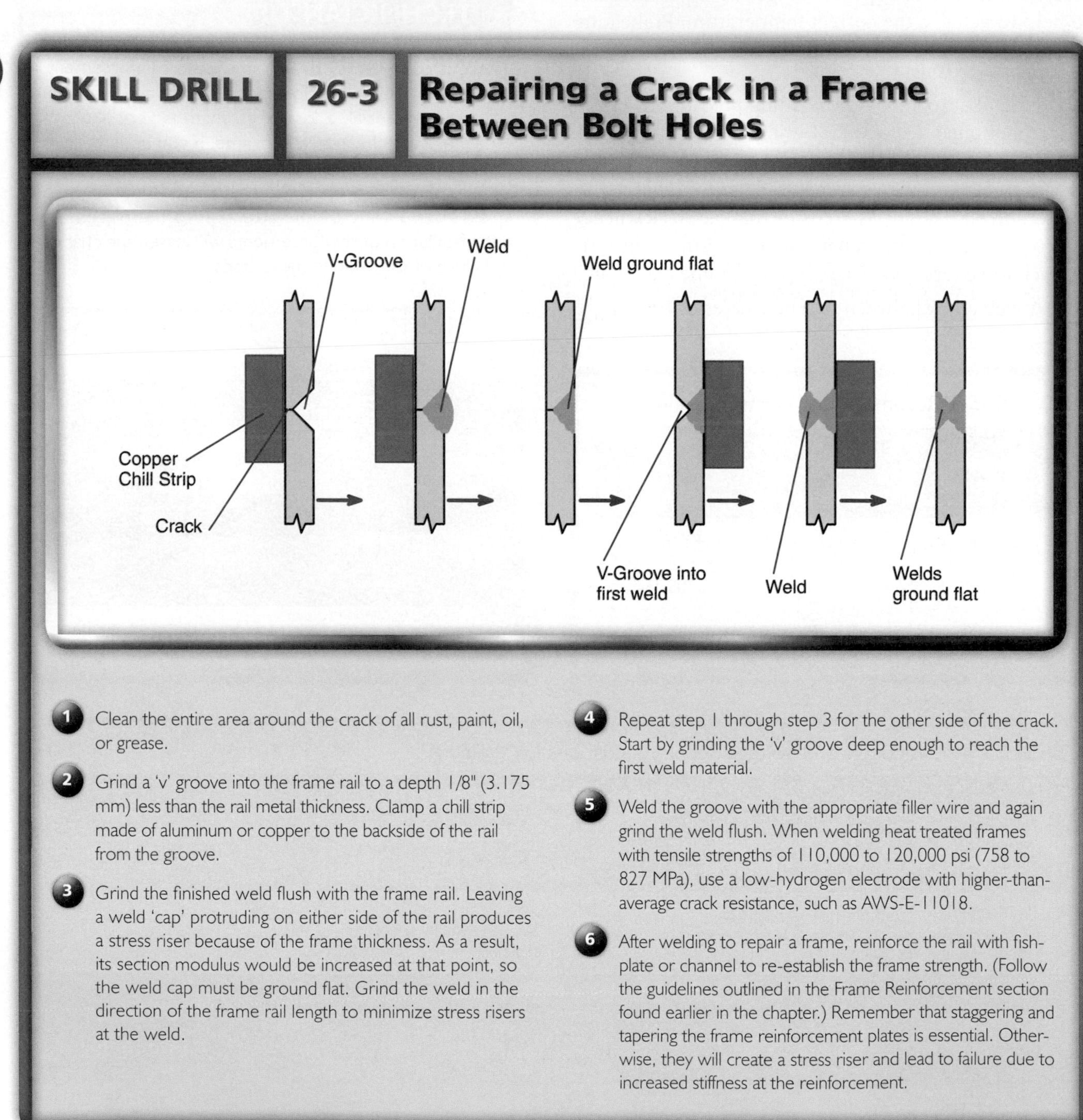

SKILL DRILL 26-3 Repairing a Crack in a Frame Between Bolt Holes

1. Clean the entire area around the crack of all rust, paint, oil, or grease.
2. Grind a 'v' groove into the frame rail to a depth 1/8" (3.175 mm) less than the rail metal thickness. Clamp a chill strip made of aluminum or copper to the backside of the rail from the groove.
3. Grind the finished weld flush with the frame rail. Leaving a weld 'cap' protruding on either side of the rail produces a stress riser because of the frame thickness. As a result, its section modulus would be increased at that point, so the weld cap must be ground flat. Grind the weld in the direction of the frame rail length to minimize stress risers at the weld.
4. Repeat step 1 through step 3 for the other side of the crack. Start by grinding the 'v' groove deep enough to reach the first weld material.
5. Weld the groove with the appropriate filler wire and again grind the weld flush. When welding heat treated frames with tensile strengths of 110,000 to 120,000 psi (758 to 827 MPa), use a low-hydrogen electrode with higher-than-average crack resistance, such as AWS-E-11018.
6. After welding to repair a frame, reinforce the rail with fishplate or channel to re-establish the frame strength. (Follow the guidelines outlined in the Frame Reinforcement section found earlier in the chapter.) Remember that staggering and tapering the frame reinforcement plates is essential. Otherwise, they will create a stress riser and lead to failure due to increased stiffness at the reinforcement.

Know See Do

SKILL DRILL 26-4 Repairing a Crack in the Web or Flange

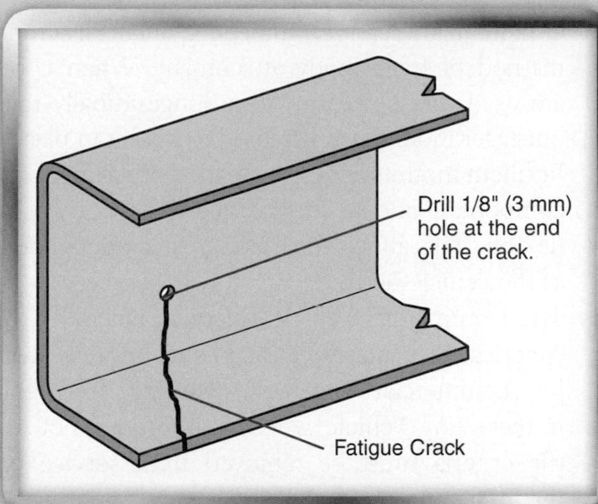
Drill 1/8" (3 mm)
hole at the end
of the crack.
Fatigue Crack

1. Follow the steps in Skill Drill 26-3 for repairing a crack in a frame between bolt holes.
2. After cleaning and grinding the first groove in the crack, determine the exact end of the crack and drill a small 1/8" (3.175 mm) hole. This will stop the crack from proceeding past the weld point. Then continue the above—outlined repair procedure.
3. Crack repairs that extend to the frame flange should be reinforced with C-channel or L-plate that reinforces the flange area as well as the web of the frame rail.

Wrap-up

Ready for Review

- Most medium- to heavy-duty vehicles use a ladder-type frame consisting of two long rails connected by a series of cross members that keep the rails in alignment.
- The frame supports all of the vehicle's components. The body, vehicle driveline, and all the suspension equipment are attached to the frame.
- Frames must be strong enough to carry these components plus the load that the vehicle is expected to carry. Frames must also be flexible enough to bend and twist in reaction to various forces without deforming as the vehicle moves along the road.
- The most common type of frame rail is C-channel, but I-beam (usually for heavier applications) and box channel can also be used.
- Frame rails can be reinforced with an L-plate, fishplate, or even another C-channel fitted inside the rail when required.
- When the frame is loaded, one flange will be subject to compression loading trying to compress the flange together, and the other flange will be subject to tension trying to pull the flange apart.
- All frame attachments should be made as close as possible to the neutral fiber.
- Frame strength is calculated using three engineering terms: section modulus, yield strength, and resist bending moment (RBM). RBM is actual strength of the frame and is calculated from the frame's section modulus and its yield strength.
- Frames can be made from mild steel that has yield strength of 50,000 psi (345 MPa) (usually light-duty vehicles); heat-treated steel that has a yield strength of 110,000+ psi (758 MPa) (heat-treated steel is used for most heavy-duty vehicles); or aluminum alloy which has a yield strength of 60,000 psi (414 MPa).
- Aluminum alloy frames are lighter than steel and are usually I-beam shaped for increased strength.
- Frame cross members hold the rails in alignment and can be box channel, C-channel, I-beam, or hat shaped. Cross members are often curved to allow passage of wiring, piping, and other vehicle components.
- Frame body attachments can be U-bolts, fishplates, or resilient mounts.
- U-bolts are the least recommended but most common method of frame body attachment. When U-bolts are used, the body can move longitudinally unless outrigger mounts are also used to hold it in place.
- Resilient mounts are spring loaded or have an elastic component and are used when the body is not flexible. This allows the frame to flex independently of the vehicle body.
- The Commercial Vehicle Safety Alliance, a North American organization, establishes service criteria for commercial vehicles including for vehicle frames. Any vehicle whose frame does not meet the criteria must be removed from service until repaired.
- Frame damage includes sag, bow, twist, diamond, and sidesway. In addition, damage can be in the form of corrosion from road salt or from galvanic cells created by dissimilar metals in contact.
- Manufacturers insist that frame straightening be done cold, but it is common practice in the field to use heat even though heat can severely reduce the yield strength of a frame rail.
- Frame re-alignment is normally performed with the use of sophisticated computer alignment machines. It can also be performed manually by taking precise measurements of the frame and projecting them onto a flat floor.
- Manufacturers forbid welding on heat-treated frames because the yield strength can be reduced from 110,000 to 36,000 psi (758 to 248 MPa) by excessive heat.
- Frame splicing is a common practice to increase frame rail length to install longer bodies or extra equipment. Frame splicing is not endorsed by manufacturers.
- Galvanic corrosion can occur when two dissimilar metals are in contact and an electrolyte is introduced between them. This creates a situation where one metal becomes the anode and the other becomes the cathode of the resulting galvanic cell. This situation can quickly lead to serious corrosion of the metals involved.

Vocabulary Builder

aluminum alloy Aluminum mixed with other metals to increase its strength.

bow A type of frame damage characterized by the upward bending of the frame rails that can be caused by uneven loading of the frame. The opposite of sag.

C-channel C-shaped steel beam that is the most common frame rail in heavy trucks.

compression A force that pushes down on the top flange of a frame rail between two support points and which tends to squeeze the flange of the frame rail together.

cross members Cross beams that join the two frame rails together to form a ladder type frame.

diamond A type of frame damage characterized by one frame rail moving forward or backward in relation to the other.

flange The flat surface at the top and bottom of a frame rail.

fishplate Flat plate used to re-enforce the frame rail or a plate bolted to the frame rail web to attach components to the frame.

frame rail web The upright section of the frame rail. Also called *web*.

full-box rail A box-shaped frame rail.

galvanic corrosion Corrosion of the material caused by the electrolytic effect that can occur when two dissimilar metals are in contact.

heat-treated alloy steel Highly engineered steel with a yield strength of at least 110,000 psi (758 MPa).

high-carbon steel Steel alloyed with carbon at levels of 0.9–2.5%.

Huck® fastener A riveted connection with ridges instead of threads and with the nut swaged onto the bolt, preventing the collar from being tightened after the fastener is installed.

I-beam I-shaped beam used for frame rails on heavier vehicles; can be aluminum or steel.

L-plate L-shaped beams that can be bolted to the outside of the C-channel to increase the rails' RBM.

ladder-type frame A frame consisting of two rails joined together by a series of cross members.

maximum bending moment The point on the frame at which the load force is concentrated.

medium-carbon steel Steel alloyed with carbon at levels of 0.25–0.6%.

neutral axis The area in the middle of a frame rail web where the tension and compression forces cancel each other out. Also called *neutral fiber*.

neutral fiber The area in the middle of a frame rail web where the tension and compression forces cancel each other out. Also called *neutral axis*.

outrigger brackets A frame-body attachment consisting of brackets welded to the vehicle and then bolted to the frame web.

resilient mounts Attachments that are spring loaded or made with rubber or polyurethane elements that accommodate movement.

resist bending moment (RBM) The frame strength calculated using the section modulus of the frame rail and its yield strength.

sag A type of frame damage characterized by the downward bending of the frame rail between two support points. The opposite of *bow*.

section change A point where a component becomes thicker or thinner or more or less rigid forming a weak point where breakage can begin.

section modulus An engineering calculation used to determine the strength of a frame rail based only on its shape, height, width, and thickness

sidesway A type of frame damage characterized by a sideways bending or deformation of the frame.

stress concentration Anything that reduces or changes the integrity or strength of the material. Also called *stress riser*.

stress riser Anything that reduces or changes the integrity or strength of the material. Also called *stress concentration*.

swaged When two metal components are fitted together by deforming the metal of one to fit the other precisely.

tension A force that tries to pull apart the bottom flange of a frame rail supported between two points.

tensile strength The amount of force required before a material deforms or breaks.

twist A type of frame damage that occurs when one rail bends up and the other rail bends down.

U-bolt A frame-body attachment that goes over a subframe attached to the vehicle body and down both sides of the frame rail before being clamped at the bottom flange of the rail.

web The upright portion of the frame rail. Also called *frame rail web*.

yield strength An engineering term used to describe the amount of force required to permanently deform a material. Yield strength occurs at the material's elastic limit—the maximum force a material can withstand and still return to its original configuration.

Review Questions

1. A frame's load carrying ability can be determined by multiplying which of the following?
   a. The section modulus by the material yield strength
   b. The section modulus by the RBM
   c. The yield strength by the RBM
   d. None of the choices are correct
2. Along with carrying the vehicle's expected load, the frame must be able to do which of the following?
   a. Support all of the vehicle accessories
   b. Flex and twist
   c. Return to its original shape after it is unloaded
   d. All of the choices are correct
3. Resist bending moment, or RBM, on truck frames refers to which of the following?
   a. The maximum load that can be put on a frame before it becomes permanently deformed
   b. The maximum load a vehicle can carry
   c. The minimum load the vehicle is designed to carry
   d. The thickness of the frame
4. Which of the following most correctly describes section modulus when discussing truck frames?
   a. An engineering formula based on the material shape and thickness
   b. An engineering formula based on the material length and thickness
   c. An engineering formula based on the material type and thickness
   d. An engineering formula based on the material type and shape
5. Most truck frames are constructed from which of the following?
   a. Box channel
   b. Tubular channel
   c. C-channel
   d. K-channel
6. Before welding a crack on a steel frame, what must be done?
   a. Drill out the ends of the crack with a 1/8-drill bit to stop its progression
   b. Seal the crack with epoxy
   c. Spread the crack with a chisel
   d. Monitor the crack through several days of vehicle operation to make sure it has finished cracking
7. In order to give a gradual increase in section modulus, frame reinforcement plates must be:
   a. cut on a 45 degree angle.
   b. cut square
   c. circular
   d. rectangular
8. When drilling holes into a frame, where is the best place to drill?
   a. As close as possible to the top flange
   b. As close as possible to the bottom flange
   c. In the flanges
   d. As close as possible to the neutral fiber
9. When drilling holes in a frame, it is best to do which of the following?
   a. Stagger the holes so no holes are in a vertical line
   b. Put only four holes in any vertical line
   c. Make sure the holes are as close together as possible
   d. Never stagger the holes as it weakens more than one section of the frame
10. What precaution must you take when bolting a steel accessory to an aluminum frame?
    a. Use Tectyl-400C™ or a similar compound to protect against electrolytic corrosion
    b. No precautions are required
    c. Use copper washers to protect against electrolytic corrosion
    d. Use high strength aluminum bolts

ASE-Type Questions

1. Tech A says that actual frame rail strength can be calculated by multiplying the section modulus by the yield strength. Tech B says that to determine actual rail strength the RBM is multiplied by the section modulus.
   Who is correct?
   a. Technician A
   b. Technician B
   c. Both Technician A and Technician B
   d. Neither Technician A nor Technician B
2. Tech A says that most frame fatigue cracks are caused by overloading of the frame. Tech B says that cracks often occur at a section change, where the frame becomes less flexible.
   Who is correct?
   a. Technician A
   b. Technician B
   c. Both Technician A and Technician B
   d. Neither Technician A nor Technician B
3. Tech A says that welding heat treated frames changes the frame strength and is not sanctioned by the manufacturer. Tech B says that damaged heat treated frame rails should be replaced not repaired.
   Who is correct?
   a. Technician A
   b. Technician B
   c. Both Technician A and Technician B
   d. Neither Technician A nor Technician B
4. Tech A says that the frame rail top flange is under compression when a load is place on it. Tech B says that the frame rails bottom flange is under tension where the suspension mounts to the frame.
   Who is correct?
   a. Technician A
   b. Technician B
   c. Both Technician A and Technician B
   d. Neither Technician A nor Technician B
5. Tech A says that the neutral fiber refers to the center of the frame web. Tech B says the neutral fiber is where most of a frame rail stress is concentrated.
   Who is correct?
   a. Technician A
   b. Technician B
   c. Both Technician A and Technician B
   d. Neither Technician A nor Technician B
6. Technician A says I-channel frames are the most common configuration for heavy vehicles. Technician B says connecting cross-members tie the rails together both to maintain their alignment and to stop them from twisting under the heavy loads the rails have to carry. Who is correct?
   a. Technician A
   b. Technician B
   c. Both Technician A and Technician B
   d. Neither Technician A nor Technician B
7. Technician A says Huck® fasteners are a type of nuts and bolts. Technician B says Huck® fasteners are one of the most secure attaching systems available and should last for the life of the vehicle. Who is correct?
   a. Technician A
   b. Technician B
   c. Both Technician A and Technician B
   d. Neither Technician A nor Technician B
8. Technician A says U-bolts are the most secure mounting system for attaching a truck body to a frame. Technician B says U-bolts and their ease of installation makes them popular with builders of truck bodies. Who is correct?
   a. Technician A
   b. Technician B
   c. Both Technician A and Technician B
   d. Neither Technician A nor Technician B
9. Technician A says outrigger mounting is the recommended method of attaching flexible bodies to ladder-type frames. Technician B says outrigger brackets are welded to the vehicle body and also welded to the frame web. Who is correct?
   a. Technician A
   b. Technician B
   c. Both Technician A and Technician B
   d. Neither Technician A nor Technician B
10. Technician A says fishplates are flat plates used to reinforce the frame rail. Technician B says fishplate does not require holes to be drilled in the frame web and the body sub-frame. Who is correct?
    a. Technician A
    b. Technician B
    c. Both Technician A and Technician B
    d. Neither Technician A nor Technician B

CHAPTER 27

NATEF Tasks

Suspension and Steering

Suspension Systems

	Page
■ Inspect front axles and attaching hardware; determine needed action.	819–822
■ Inspect shock absorbers, bushings, brackets, and mounts; replace as needed.	819–822
■ Inspect leaf springs, center bolts, clips, pins and bushings, shackles, U-bolts, insulators, brackets, and mounts; determine needed action.	819–825
■ Inspect axle aligning devices such as radius rods, track bars, stabilizer bars, torque arms, related bushings, mounts, shims, and cams; determine needed action.	819–825
■ Inspect tandem suspension equalizer components; determine needed action.	826
■ Inspect and test air suspension pressure regulator and height control valves, lines, hoses, dump valves, and fittings; adjust, repair, or replace as needed.	828
■ Inspect air springs, mounting plates, springs, suspension arms, and bushings; replace as needed.	828
■ Measure and adjust ride height; determine needed action.	828
■ Identify rough ride problems; determine needed action.	828

Suspension Systems

Knowledge Objectives

After reading this chapter, you will be able to:

1. Explain the fundamentals of heavy duty vehicle suspension and steering systems. (p 794)
2. Describe the importance of a suspension system in terms of driver comfort, load protection, vehicle control, and tire-to-road contact. (p 795)
3. Describe the function and operation of hydraulic shock absorbers. (p 799)
4. Identify the various suspension systems commonly used on heavy-duty trucks. (p 802)
5. Describe the operation and identify the components of a typical leaf spring suspension. (p 802)
6. Describe the function and identify the components of fiber composite spring suspension systems. (p 802)
7. Describe the operation and identify the components of an equalizing beam suspension system. (p 808)
8. Describe the operation and identify the components of a typical rubber spring suspension system. (p 811)
9. Describe the operation and identify the components of a typical air spring suspension system. (p 813)
10. Explain the troubleshooting procedure and out-of-service criteria for suspension systems. (pp 819–820)
11. Describe the repair and replacement procedures of various types of suspension system components. (pp 821–823)
12. Describe full suspension system alignment techniques. (p 829)
13. Perform a tandem axle suspension alignment. (p 832)

Skills Objectives

After reading this chapter, you will be able to:

1. Inspect a leaf spring system. (p 821) SKILL DRILL 27-1
2. Perform an in-service inspection of a suspension system. (p 822) SKILL DRILL 27-2
3. Remove and replace front spring components. (p 824) SKILL DRILL 27-3
4. Inspect rear spring suspension components. (p 825) SKILL DRILL 27-4
5. Inspect rear beam suspension components. (p 826) SKILL DRILL 27-5
6. Inspect and maintain air spring systems. (p 828) SKILL DRILL 27-6
7. Inspect and maintain shock absorbers. (p 829) SKILL DRILL 27-7
8. Inspect and test an air suspension system and replace the levelling valve. (p 830) SKILL DRILL 27-8
9. Adjust the ride height. (p 831) SKILL DRILL 27-9
10. Align axles. (p 832) SKILL DRILL 27-10
11. Adjust front or rear axles. (p 833) SKILL DRILL 27-11

Introduction

History has romanticized the horse-drawn chariots of ancient Rome with images of the hero speeding to victory in his chariot drawn by four thoroughbred horses, as shown in FIGURE 27-1. The reality, however, is a much different story. Roman chariots had rudimentary suspension systems, and as their speed increased, every bump from the uneven road surface was transmitted to the vehicle and its driver. In fact, the chariot races were attended not so much to see the victor but rather to view the spectacle of drivers being thrown from their speeding vehicles (sometimes to their death) as they lost control of the bumping, rattling chariot.

FIGURE 27-1 Most chariots did not have suspension systems, so they were very unstable.

Since those times, various inventors have tried to tackle the problem of a suspension system. The earliest form of suspension was a box-shape carriage supported on a wheeled cart by means of chains attached at each corner. This hanging box arrangement would swing back and forth freely as bumps were encountered, meaning that the occupants had better not be prone to motion sickness. Next was the stagecoach, which mounted the "coach" on heavy leather straps, called through braces, that helped to insulate the passengers from road shocks. The steel leaf spring appeared in the 17th century and the leather supporting straps were then fixed to springs instead of directly to the undercarriage, which further insulated the passengers and cargo from the road. Since those days, much advancement has been made in suspension systems, allowing vehicles to travel at greater speeds while still protecting the vehicle, the load, and the passengers.

Fundamentals of Suspension Systems

Suspension systems must tolerate a huge number of forces when a vehicle is being driven down the road. Think about all of a vehicle's weight being supported by the suspension system and then subjecting the parts in that system to the normal cornering, accelerating, and braking

You Are the Technician

A highway tractor is brought to your shop. The driver complains that one of the rear air bags has torn. He tells you that this is the second air bag he has had to replace since the last time the vehicle was in for a major service. You confirm the complaint—it is definitely a torn air bag. When you inspect the vehicle, everything else looks fine. The shock absorbers are new and the torque and track rods are in good shape. Explain why you might use each of the following procedures to diagnose the problem.

1. Why might you check the air bags for the proper application?
2. Why might you check that nothing is rubbing against the air spring?
3. Why might you check the shocks for proper application?
4. Why might you check all of the rear suspension components for looseness?
5. Would it make sense to talk to the air bag supplier to see if there is a problem with these particular air bags? Why or why not?

forces. On top of that, add in the abnormal forces from potholes to speed bumps. Applying a force to an object deforms it. Removing the force allows it to return to its original shape. This characteristic is called elasticity. Elasticity is the property of a material, in this instance a spring, which causes it to be restored to its original shape after distortion. A material is said to be more elastic if it restores itself more precisely to its original configuration. Vehicle suspension systems generally use the elastic properties of special metals, or air springs, to provide the springing medium that a suspension system requires.

Springs are located between the frame/chassis and the axle assemblies and are shaped to suit specific applications. For instance, some springs are designed specifically to absorb the applied force (pressure of the load) by flattening out under load.

Functions of a Suspension System

A vehicle's suspension must perform several important functions. It must ensure the vehicle stays in contact with the road and support the sprung weight of the vehicle and cargo. Another function of the suspension system is to connect the axles securely to the vehicle frame. In addition, a vehicle's suspension must control the axle torque reaction and maintain the vehicle's lateral stability. Additionally, the suspension must be able to perform all of those functions satisfactorily whether the vehicle is empty or fully loaded.

Ensuring Contact with the Road

The suspension must ensure the vehicle's tires stay in contact with the road surface. The **contact patch** between the vehicle tires and the road is relatively small—approximately 1 square foot (125 sq cm) or less for most truck tires, as shown in **FIGURE 27-2**.

These contact patches provide the traction (that is, frictional contact) through which all of the acceleration, braking, and cornering forces are transferred to the road surface. If the tires lose this frictional contact with the road, the vehicle will lose control. Therefore, maintaining contact is essential. As the wheels move upward and downward over bumps, they have a tendency to continue moving due to inertia. This rhythmic up and down motion caused by road shock is called **oscillation**. If suspension system were not able to absorb these forces, the wheels would start to hop uncontrollably. **Wheel hop** caused by excessive suspension oscillationcan lead to loss of control and extreme tire wear.

Support the Sprung Weight

The suspension system must support the sprung weight of the vehicle and cargo while stopped or moving. The

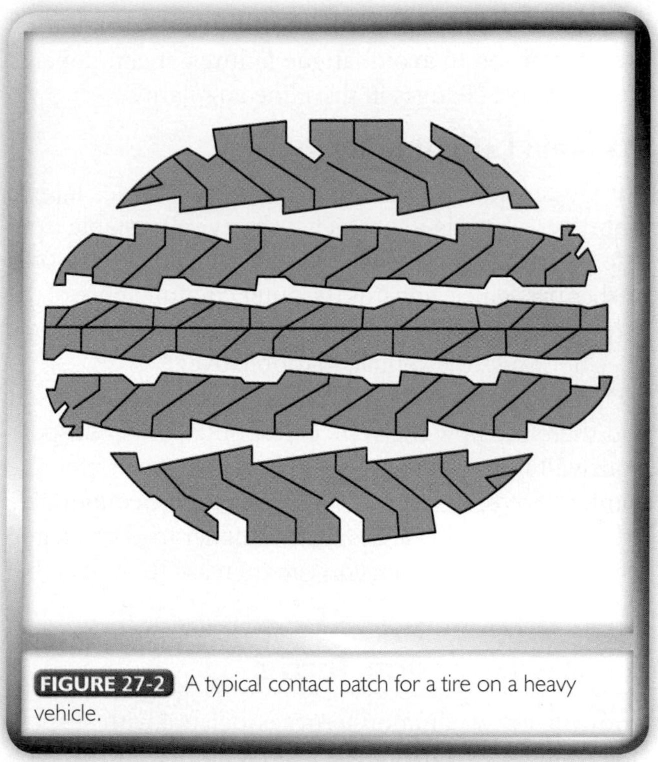

FIGURE 27-2 A typical contact patch for a tire on a heavy vehicle.

sprung weight is the weight of the vehicle components supported by the springs. The suspension must support the sprung weight regardless of the forces acting upon it, all the while insulating the vehicle body, the driver, the passengers, and the cargo from excessive road shocks. The suspension must absorb the shocks and vibrations from uneven road surfaces to ensure driver comfort and to protect the vehicle load from damage. Excessive vibration and shocks transmitted to the vehicle frame and body would lead to fatigue failures of these components.

Connect the Axles to the Frame

Another basic function of the suspension system is to securely connect the axles to the frame of the vehicle. The suspension must maintain the axle spacing and alignment as the axles articulate over uneven road surfaces and bumps. Maintaining the alignment and spacing of the axles adds to vehicle stability. Axles that do not retain their alignment while articulating would cause the vehicle to have very poor handling capabilities, excessive tire wear, and would be very hard for a driver to control.

Control Axle Torque

The suspension must control axle torque or wind-up caused by acceleration and braking forces. As the vehicle accelerates, the rear axles have a tendency to wind up with the front of the axle rising with the torque load. Under braking effort, the axles will have a tendency to wind down with the front of the axle lowering. These winding torque forces must be transferred to the vehicle frame by the suspension to avoid fatigue failures of components and excessive changes in driveline angularity.

Maintain Lateral Stability

The suspension system must maintain a vehicle's **lateral stability**, which is the vehicle's ability to be stable from side to side. As a vehicle enters a turn, centrifugal force pushes the vehicle towards the outer circumference of the turn. The springs must be strong enough that this force does not cause the vehicle to topple over.

Springs determine if the suspension is stiff or soft and therefore how the vehicle responds. Stiffer suspensions will improve lateral stability at the expense of ride comfort. Softer suspensions will offer a more comfortable ride but, in some instances such as higher road speed into cornering, a soft suspension can increase the possibility of rollover.

Basic Suspension Terms

Knowing a few common terms associated with suspension systems will provide a background for the discussion of suspension systems that follows.

Sprung Weight and Unsprung Weight

As mentioned earlier in the chapter, sprung weight is any portion of the vehicle that is supported by the suspension spring. This usually includes the chassis frame and the vehicle body. Sprung weight greatly affects the vehicle-handling characteristics, especially during hard acceleration, braking, and cornering. **Unsprung weight** is the portion of the vehicle that is not supported by the suspension system springs. Unsprung weight includes the drive and steer axles, wheels, tires, brakes, and part of the suspension system itself. FIGURE 27-3 illustrates the difference between sprung weight and unsprung weight.

The heavier the unsprung mass, the harder the vehicle is to control. Consider which would be easier to control: a beach ball versus a bowling ball. When large and heavy wheel assemblies encounter a bump or pothole, they experience a larger reaction force. In some cases, that reaction force is large enough to make the tire lose contact with the road surface. If the tires are not in contact with the road, they have lost all traction and cannot control the vehicle's direction of travel, which creates a potentially dangerous situation.

Lower unsprung weights allow the tires to follow the road contour more easily without bouncing. Heavier unsprung weights can lead to severe road shocks being sent through the suspension system. Manufacturers try to keep unsprung weight to a minimum by specifying lighter-weight aluminum wheels and lighter axle components, but the axles and the brakes must also be strong enough to support and stop the vehicle and its load. Unsprung weight is always a tradeoff between comfort and practicality.

Overslung and Underslung

Overslung suspension systems have the spring attached in position above the axles. **Underslung** will have the springs attached to the underside of the axles.

Jounce

Jounce is the upward motion of the wheel, axle, and suspension system when the vehicle encounters a bump in the road. Most suspension systems will have jounce

> **TECHNICIAN TIP**
>
> An ideal vehicle suspension would be soft enough for a comfortable ride and load protection, and firm enough for vehicle stability. Air suspension systems come close to the perfect balance of soft and firm suspension, but they are expensive and don't always respond quickly enough to the inertial shifting of the load on turns, leading to some instability. Leaf spring suspension systems are most economical, and when firm enough, they add stability to avoid rollover. In normal driving situations, however, they are stiff and give a rough ride. So, the end result is often a compromise based on cost stability and comfort.

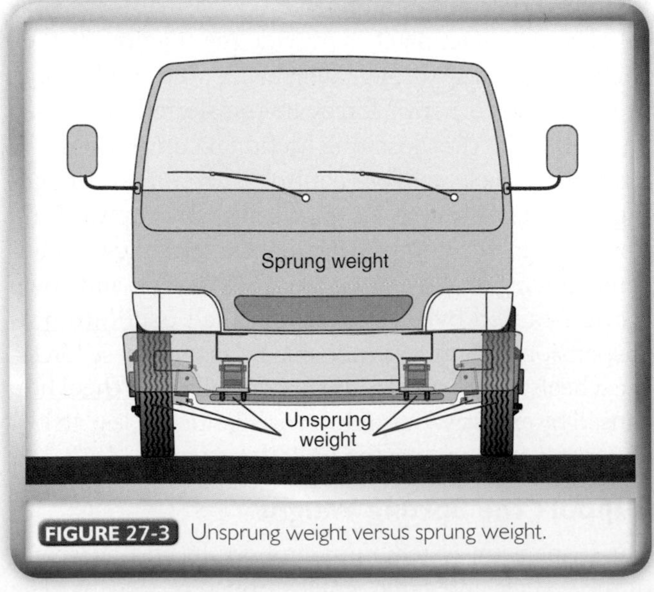

FIGURE 27-3 Unsprung weight versus sprung weight.

bumpers or blocks that prevent the suspension from being compressed so much that the axles contact the frame of the vehicle. When a jounce occurs, the spring absorbs the energy as it flexes and straightens out. That energy is then given back as the spring rebounds, or returns, to its normal shape.

Rebound

Rebound is the downward movement of the wheels and axles as the spring recovers from compression caused by road bumps or hitting a pothole or depression in the road. As such, rebound is the spring's reaction to a jounce. Together, jounce and rebound cause the suspension system to oscillate until the energy absorbed by the spring has been dissipated, as illustrated in FIGURE 27-4. It is the same as what happens when a person jumps on a trampoline. The person will continue to bounce up and down until the energy of the jump is gone.

One of the major functions of a suspension system is to minimize suspension oscillation. That is achieved either through self-dampening friction or with the use of a **shock absorber**, which, in this instance, is a hydraulic piston and cylinder arrangement designed for that exact purpose. Both of these methods absorb the springs' oscillation by converting the energy from jounce and rebound to heat. The heat conversion occurs in one of two ways. **Interleaf friction**, caused by the springs in a multileaf spring pack rubbing together, can dissipate unwanted oscillation. (Multileaf spring packs will be discussed in greater detail in the section on Springs.)

Kinetic energy generated by the shock absorber action is converted into another form of energy (typically heat) by the compression and displacement of hydraulic fluid in shock absorbers.Some suspensions use a combination of both heat conversion methods.

If a suspension fails to absorb the energy promptly, the spring oscillations may cause the wheels to hop off the ground due to the uncontrolled bouncing. This will make it very hard to control the vehicle.

Spring Rate and Load Range

Spring rate refers to the movement of the spring when it is loaded. A high spring rate corresponds to a stiffer suspension with higher lateral stability, and a low spring rate to a more comfortable ride. The amount of deflection is linear in constant-rate springs. So, if a load of 440 lb (200 kg) causes the spring to deflect 1" (2.54 cm), then a load of 880 lb (400 kg) will deflect the spring 2" (5.08 cm). FIGURE 27-5 illustrates this deflection.

A spring with a high spring rate will deflect less when loaded than a spring with a low spring rate. The load range of a spring refers to the load the spring can carry. Adding leaves to a spring pack or thickening the leaves increases the load rate and the spring rate. A spring with a low spring rate leads to a softer ride but also decreases the vehicle's load carrying capacity and lateral stability.

As mentioned in the section Maintain Lateral Stability, when a vehicle starts to turn, centrifugal forces push the load toward the outside of the turning circle. That puts more load on the outside spring. In vehicles with a low spring rate (softer ride), the vehicle will sag on the

FIGURE 27-4 A suspension system must absorb and stop spring oscillation to maintain vehicle control.

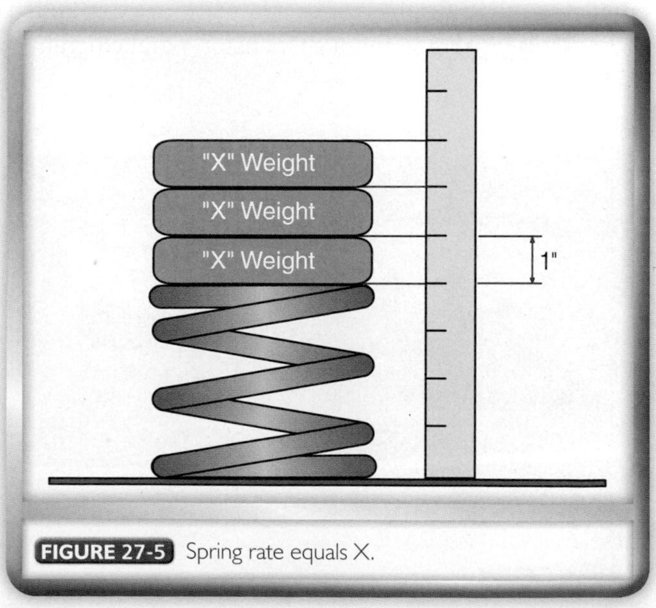

FIGURE 27-5 Spring rate equals X.

outside (lateral instability), thereby increasing the possibility of a rollover. By contrast, a high spring rate suspension adds greatly to load capacity and lateral stability in turns but makes for a stiffer, bumpier ride. Suspensions are designed as a compromise to allow the best ride possible and with the necessary load capacity and stability for the vehicle's expected vocation.

Parallelogram

Parallelogram is a term used quite often in suspension systems. A **parallelogram** is a four-sided figure in which each of the two opposite sides are parallel with each other. In suspensions, parallelograms are used to keep the wheels and axles at the proper angle or pitch during jounce and rebound.

Most light-duty and some heavy-duty vehicles will use parallelogram front suspension systems that keep the front wheels at the correct camber angle as the vehicle encounters bumps in the road. The most common type of front suspension used for this purpose is the double wishbone system. In the double wishbone system, two A-frame control arms attach to the frame at two points each, and the apex of the A-frames attach to the top and bottom of the spindle. As the wheel goes over a bump, the wheel moves up. In response, the upper and lower control arms (the A-frames) both pivot the same amount, moving closer to the frame but essentially maintaining the camber angle of the wheel. (There are slight changes to the steer angle due to tie rod position, kingpin inclination, and so forth.)

In heavy trucks, the term parallelogram is more associated with the rear suspension and uses a combination of torque rods and track rods or **trailing arms** so that, as the rear wheels encounter a bump, the suspension parallelogram keeps the rear axle housing at a fixed pitch angle. FIGURE 27-6 shows a suspension parallelogram.

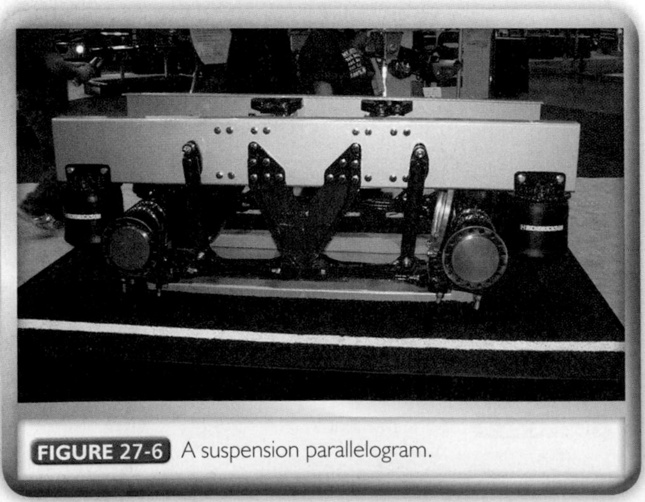

FIGURE 27-6 A suspension parallelogram.

All rear-wheel-drive vehicle suspensions have a tendency to squat during the forces of acceleration, as the pinion gear physically tries to climb up the crown or ring gear in the drive axle. The parallelogram suspension design limits the axle wind-up and the corresponding frame rise during the forces of acceleration. Limiting wind-up ensures that the drive pinion U-joint angles remain within the design specifications. This, in turn, reduces the chance of driveline vibrations caused by the suspension.

The situation changes during braking. The vehicle momentum tends to cause the rear of the vehicle to rise and the axle to wind in the opposite direction. The force on the axle builds to a point where the springs are loaded until they eventually rebound. That rebound causes the tires to lose traction with the road, leading to a condition known as wheel hop. Wheel hop is especially problematic on leaf-spring suspensions, which are explained in greater detail in the Leaf Springs Systems section of this chapter, and can reduce vehicle directional stability.

Careful design and positioning of the torque and track rods can greatly reduce wheel hop. Anti-squat and anti-wheel hop ideals are usually at odds with optimum vehicle ride characteristics. Parallelogram rear suspension systems attempt to carefully balance spring rate, anti-squat, and anti-wheel hop characteristics to optimize vehicle handling and control while providing a good ride and load protection.

Components of a Suspension System

There are several primary components of a suspension system. Components include springs, torque rods, axle stops (or jounce blocks), and shock absorbers.

Springs

The spring is the suspension's flexible component. Basic types are leaf springs, coil springs, **rubber springs**, air springs, and torsion bars. A **leaf spring** consists of a semi-elliptically curved spring steel plate clamped to an axle at its middle and which supports the body of the vehicle at both ends. When more than one steel plate or leaf is stacked together and used for a spring, it is called a **multileaf spring** or a **spring pack**. **Coil springs** are helical metal springs, and **air springs** are tough rubber bags filled with air. **Torsion bars** twist in response to the movement of the wheels and absorb their vertical movement.

Light-duty commercial vehicles usually use heavy coil springs or torsion bars at the front and leaf springs at the rear. Heavy-duty commercial vehicles predominately use leaf springs, rubber springs, or air suspension. Some

Original Equipment Manufacturers (OEM) use the torsion bar suspension in preference to the leaf spring configuration. We will discuss each type of spring in more detail later in this chapter.

Torque Rods

Torque rods are used to keep the axles in alignment with each other and with the frame. They also transfer axle acceleration and braking forces to the frame. Torque rods can be mounted longitudinally to control alignment or transversely to control centrifugal forces during turns. When mounted transversely, torque rods are called **track rods**. Some systems have torque rods mounted diagonally to control both.

Torque rods are usually adjustable. FIGURE 27-7 shows an adjustable two-piece threaded torque rod. Torque rods can also be adjusted by placing shims at the mounting locations or eccentric washers at the mounting pins.

Torque rods are mounted between the frame and the axles with rubber bushings. The rubber allows some movement while absorbing shock. The resilience of the rubber brings the axles back to alignment very quickly. This movement also allows tandem, or Tridem, axles to follow a more natural route during turns. As a tandem-axle vehicle enters a turn, the cornering forces tend to push the front axle of the tandem to the outside of the turn. At the same time, the cornering forces push the rear axle toward the inside of the turn. The rubber bushings in a suspension system can allow up to 3" (7.5 cm) of lateral movement, so each axle follows a more natural turn. Once the vehicle returns to straight-ahead driving, the rubber returns the axles to alignment.

Axle Stops or Jounce Blocks

All suspensions will limit axle movement with a rubber or a solid stop mounted between the frame and the axle, as shown in FIGURE 27-8, or between the frame and the springs. This stop is called an **axle stop**. (Axle stops are also known as **jounce blocks**.) If the suspension were allowed to articulate with no limit, the axles would bang into the frame when severe bumps are encountered. **Articulation** is the movement of the suspension due to road bumps and terrain. The axle articulation must be stopped before contact with the frame or it could lead to failure of the frame itself. Air spring suspensions sometimes have the stops inside the air springs and they are not visible from the outside.

Shock Absorbers

Some multileaf suspension systems rely on **self-dampening** caused by strong interleaf friction to dissipate the spring oscillation energy. Although these springs are quite effective at dampening oscillations, the interleaf friction leads to a very stiff and bumpy ride, particularly when a vehicle is partly or lightly loaded. In the past, heavy-duty trucks relied on this self-dampening more frequently, but today, more and more manufacturers are using leaf springs with little or no interleaf friction to provide a softer ride. Leaf springs and multileaf spring packs are discussed in greater detail in the section on Leaf Spring Systems.

Hydraulic Shock Absorbers

Leaf springs with little or no interleaf friction must use hydraulic shock absorbers such as those showing in FIGURE 27-9. Hydraulic shock absorbers absorb the

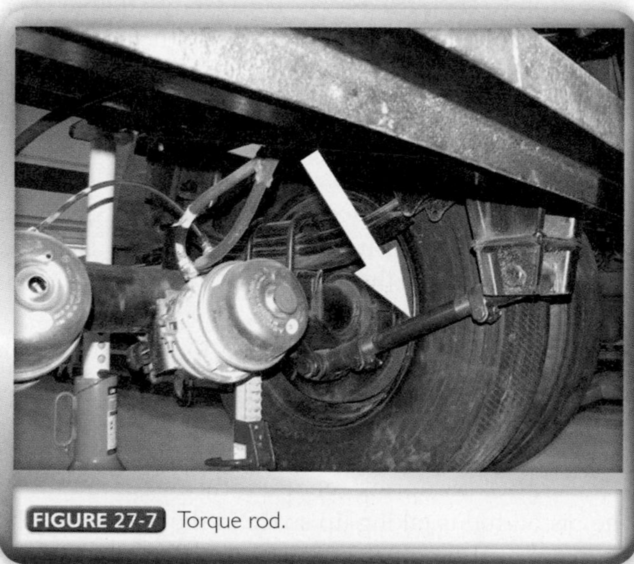

FIGURE 27-7 Torque rod.

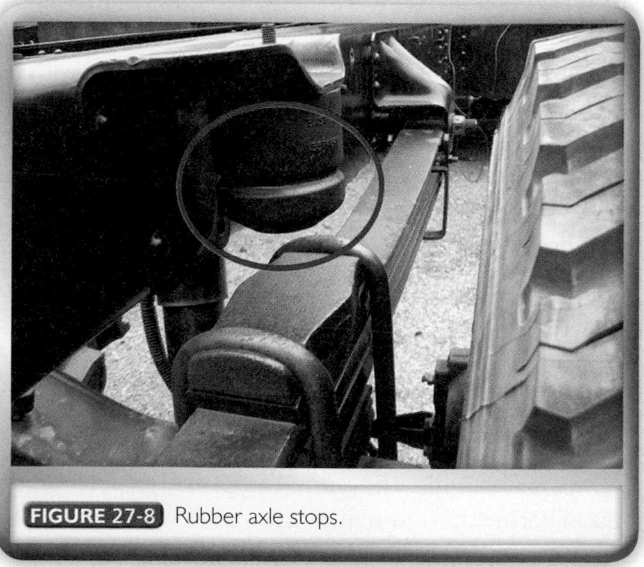

FIGURE 27-8 Rubber axle stops.

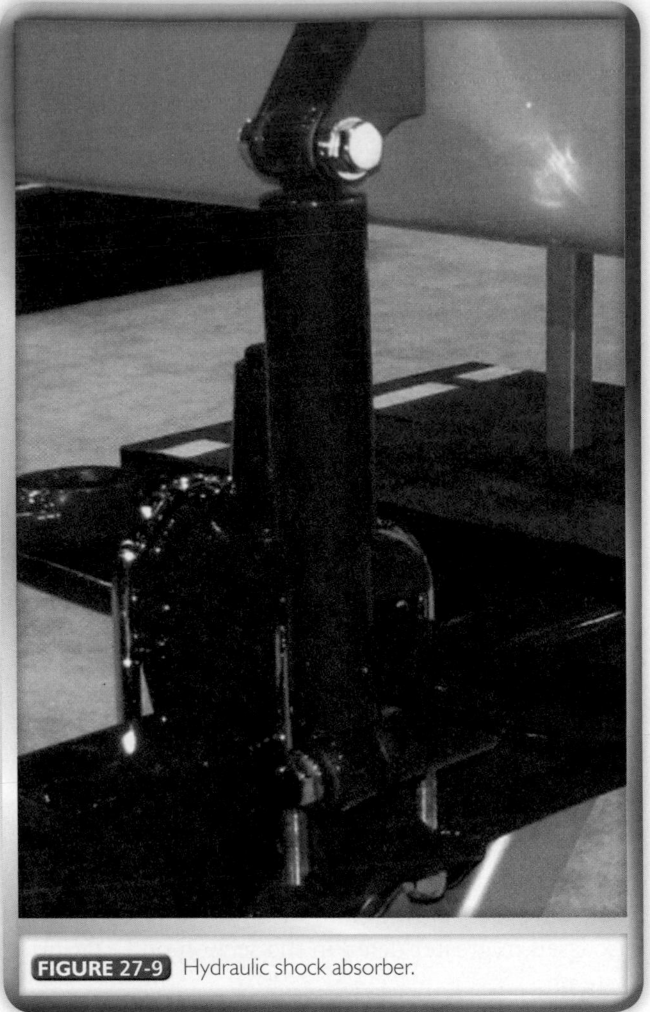

FIGURE 27-9 Hydraulic shock absorber.

spring oscillation not controlled by self-dampening to stop the wheels from bouncing off the ground. Air spring suspensions offer absolutely no self-dampening effect and must use shock absorbers or other dampers to stop spring oscillation. Otherwise, the wheels would bounce uncontrollably.

Most hydraulic shock absorbers are designed with an inner and an outer tube. The outer tube is also known as the reserve tube, and it holds a supply of hydraulic fluid. The inner tube has a piston and a base valve installed. The inner tube is full of fluid above and beneath the piston.

Shocks are dual acting. That means they absorb energy by converting it to heat on both the compression and the rebound stroke. The piston is designed with a series of orifices that will allow fluid to pass through the piston at a specific rate. All shock absorbers today are velocity sensitive. In other words, the piston orifices are controlled by flexible discs. The faster the shock compresses or extends, the more the piston restricts fluid flow. That restriction makes the shock stiffer when the compression or extension of the shock is faster.

TECHNICIAN TIP

The double-acting shock absorber dampens spring oscillation by forcing fluid through small orifices in the piston valve. The energy is transformed into heat from the resulting fluid friction, and then the heat dissipates into the atmosphere. A quick way to tell if shocks are working is to feel them to see if they are warm after the vehicle has been driven for a while over rough roads. A shock that feels colder than the other on the same axle is usually defective.

Safety

Hard-working shocks can reach 350°F (180°C) and can cause burns. To be safe, use an infrared temperature reader when measuring the temperature of shocks—not your hands.

The piston is connected to the push rod, which in turn is connected to the upper mounting eye of the shock absorber. The upper mounting eye has a rubber bushing that is bolted to the vehicle frame. The lower mounting eye of the shock is welded to the base of the outer tube. The lower mounting eye also has a rubber bushing, and it is bolted to the vehicle axle. The base valve at the bottom of the inner tube has a specifically sized orifice that allows fluid to flow into and out of the reserve tube as necessary to keep the area beneath the piston full of fluid.

When a jounce (bump) is encountered by the wheel, the axle moves upward. That motion causes the shock to compress. During this compression, the hydraulic fluid is forced through the piston orifices from the area beneath the piston to the area above. Because the diameter of the piston rod takes up space, not all of the fluid can be forced through the piston orifices. Some of the fluid flows through the base valve into the reserve tube, as illustrated in FIGURE 27-10.

The turbulent flow resulting from the fluid being forced through the orifices absorbs the energy of the jounce and transforms it into heat in the fluid. This heat is dissipated through the walls of the shock absorber out to the atmosphere.

On rebound, the opposite happens. The shock extends, and the piston is pulled upwards, forcing the fluid above the piston to flow through the orifices to the area beneath the piston. That reverse flow again absorbs the energy of the spring rebound, turning it into heat. The piston rod is taking up space in the area above the piston, so, as the piston rises, the fluid above the piston is

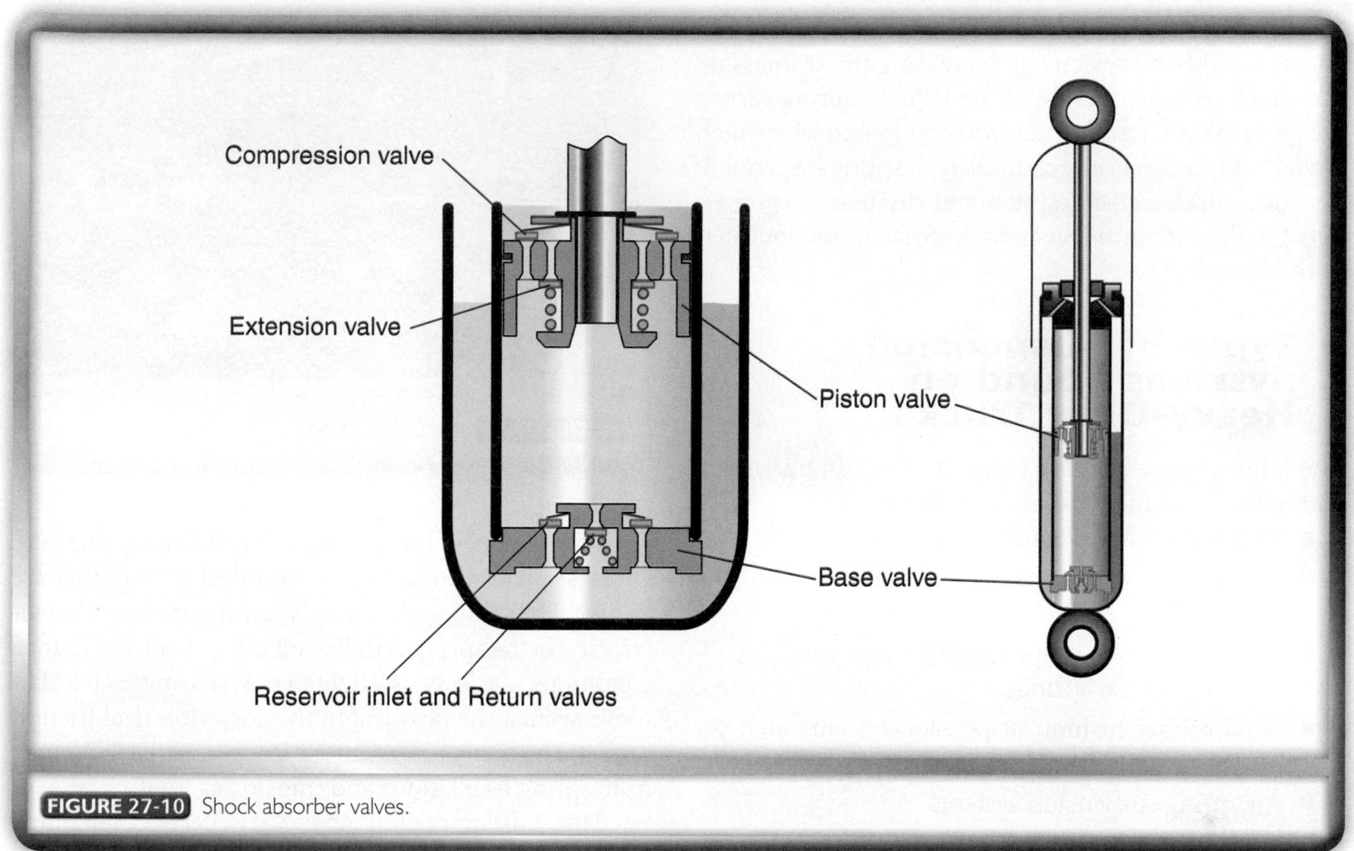

FIGURE 27-10 Shock absorber valves.

insufficient to fill the area below the piston. Fluid is then drawn through the base valve to compensate.

Due to hysteresis, the rebound force of the unsprung weight is less than the jounce force. **Hysteresis** occurs when something is deflected but does not rebound with the same force, usually due to the internal friction inherent in the material as it deflects. Many parts of the vehicle suspension system display hysteresis—the tires, rubber mounting bushings, and even the springs themselves.

Although it is dual acting, the piston valve of the shock absorber is usually biased. That means it is harder to draw the fluid back through the valve on rebound than it is to push the fluid through the valve when a jounce is encountered. Biasing the valve this way allows the shock absorber to compress more easily and not transmit a bump through the shock absorber to the frame. The suspension can then do the job of absorbing the impact of a bump in the road.

Bias is also necessary on the extension stroke. At that stroke, the shock is trying to control the movement of the vehicle sprung weight. The shock absorber then absorbs a greater amount of energy on the rebound, creating more heat as the fluid is pulled through the piston orifices. By absorbing a greater amount of energy, the shock absorbers slow the spring oscillations much more quickly, allowing for better vehicle control.

Gas Shock Absorbers

As with most fluid-filled shock absorbers, as the shock absorber works, the fluid can become aerated due to the turbulence and the suction at the base valve. Aerated fluid can severely diminish the effectiveness of a vehicle's shock absorbers. Gas shocks are designed to reduce or eliminate this aeration. Manufacturers charge the shock absorber with 100–150 psi (690–1043 kpa) of nitrogen gas. This pressure collapses the air bubbles and prevents the fluid and air from mixing, leading to more consistent shock absorber operation. Gas shock absorbers can be found on light commercial and some medium-duty vehicles.

Electronic Shock Absorbers

Electronically controlled shock absorbers have been available in the automotive market since the 1980s. Today, they are available in the heavy-truck market and can be found on some trucks with air suspension systems.

The electronic shock absorber system uses sensors that monitor vehicle acceleration, brake pressure, speed, and the pressure in the air spring bellows. The system then uses solenoids that control the orifice sizing in the shock absorber valves. As a result, electronic shock absorber systems can control shock dampening in milliseconds.

Electronic shock absorbers greatly increase vehicle stability by reducing vehicle diving and squat caused by braking and acceleration. The system also enhances lateral stability by selectively increasing the stiffness of the shocks on the outside of the vehicle during turns. Electronic shock absorber control is optimized when integrated with electronically controlled air spring suspension systems. (Air suspension systems are discussed in greater detail in the Air Spring Suspension Systems section later in this chapter.)

Types of Suspension Systems Found on Heavy-Duty Trucks

The following are popular types of suspension systems commonly used in the trucking industry:

- Steel leaf spring systems with single or multiple leafs
- Composite leaf springs (mostly found on semi-trailers)
- Equalizing beam suspension systems: solid, rubber, and leaf spring
- Solid rubber cushion suspension systems such as the Hendrickson HaulMaax suspension
- Air spring suspension systems
- Combination air and leaf spring systems
- Electronically controlled air spring systems

The following sections of this chapter will go into each suspension type in greater detail and the final section will discuss Suspension System Inspection and Maintenance.

Leaf Spring Systems

The first steel leaf spring was introduced in the seventeenth century to support the body of horse drawn coaches. Today, springs are manufactured from low-alloy, medium-to-high carbon steel that has very high yield strength, allowing the steel to return to its original shape after it has been deflected without deformation. Leaf spring leaves are shot-peened in manufacturing to reduce surface stress and lessen the possibility of a stress riser that could lead to a cracked or broken spring.

Multileaf Spring Packs

A multileaf spring pack is a stack of spring steel leaves held together with a center bolt, as shown in FIGURE 27-11. The spring pack may also have several spring alignment clips to keep the leaves parallel to each other. The top leaf, or plate, of the spring will usually have an eye formed at one or both ends for attachment purposes. Each subsequent leaf in the stack will be shorter than the one above so the spring pack will have a half diamond shape.

FIGURE 27-11 A multileaf spring.

The number of leaves in a stack will directly affect the spring's capacity or load rate. Multileaf springs that are tightly clamped together have a self-dampening characteristic. As the spring is deflected under load and jounce conditions, the leaves straighten out, causing each leaf to move against the next leaf in the pack. Interleaf friction results. The friction between the leaves absorbs the energy from spring oscillations and transforms it into heat.

This self-dampening can be very effective—so much so, in fact, that in certain applications, no other shock absorbers are needed to control spring oscillations caused by jounce and rebound. If a vehicle relies on interleaf friction for the dampening of the spring oscillations, the leaves must be kept tightly clamped together, and there should never be any lubricant placed between the individual leaves if they are to be effective.

Using interleaf friction as a sole method of shock absorption, however, causes a rougher ride. The friction tends to stop the spring's motion when a bump is encountered. Because of this, most manufacturers today use leaf spring arrangements that lessen the self-dampening effect.

The taper leaf, shown in FIGURE 27-12, and parabolic leaf springs produce less interleaf friction, leading to a softer ride. These types of springs use fewer leaves, usually two or three, to lessen interleaf friction and some springs are even assembled with nylon slipper pads between the leaves to further reduce interleaf friction. While the ride is better when the self-dampening effect is reduced, it is necessary for these springs to use carefully selected hydraulic shock absorbers to counter spring oscillation during jounce and rebound.

Composite Leaf Springs

Composite leaf springs are made from fiberglass, carbon fiber, and epoxy formed into one large semi-elliptical leaf with steel re-enforced contact points. FIGURE 27-13 shows a composite leaf spring.

Composite springs offer a large weight savings over traditional leaf springs made of steel. Composites weigh up to 75% less than a comparable steel leaf spring! They also last longer because they are not subject to fatigue damage, as steel springs are. Pricing for composite leaf springs is similar to their steel counterparts. However, even with the obvious benefits of composite springs, they have only made small inroads into the heavy-truck market and are not often seen on heavy-duty commercial vehicles. Composite springs can be used on any axle instead of steel leaf springs. They are most commonly found on tandem trailer systems that need to take advantage of the weight savings that composite springs afford.

FIGURE 27-12 A taper leaf.

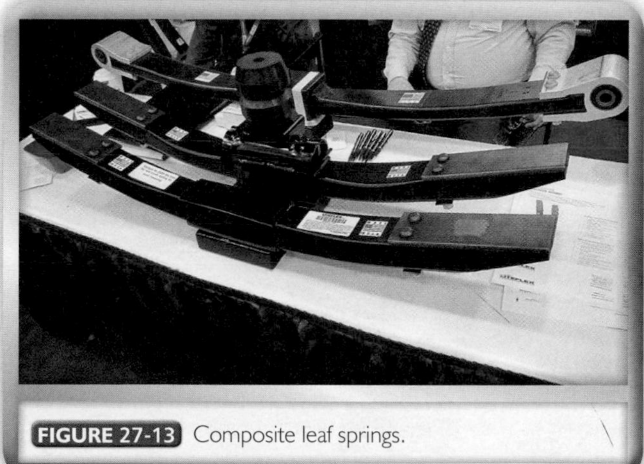

FIGURE 27-13 Composite leaf springs.

Constant-Rate Leaf Spring Assemblies

Constant-rate springs are single- or multileaf spring packs that have one or more leaves rolled into an eye at each end. As illustrated in FIGURE 27-14, the spring packs are attached to the vehicle frame through a fixed pin at one end and a shackle at the other. The fixed pin maintains axle alignment while the shackle allows the spring length to change as it is loaded. Constant-rate springs have a fixed rate of deflection. That is, as load is placed upon the spring, the spring's deflection will be consistent. If a load of 200 lb (91 kg) causes the spring to deflect 1" (2.5 cm), then a load of 400 lb (182 kg) will cause the spring to deflect 2" (5 cm).

Doubling the load on the spring doubles the spring's deflection. This is in accordance with Hooke's law of elasticity which states that the compression or extension of a spring is directly proportional to the load it is subjected to. In order for constant-rate springs to support a fully loaded vehicle, they must have a high load rate or spring capacity. Unfortunately, this means that when the vehicle is lightly loaded or empty, constant-rate springs are extremely stiff and provide little shock absorption leading to a very rough ride. For that reason, constant-rate springs are not as common as variable-rate springs today. (Variable-rate springs are discussed in more detail in the Variable-Rate or Progressive-Rate Leaf Springs section of this chapter.)

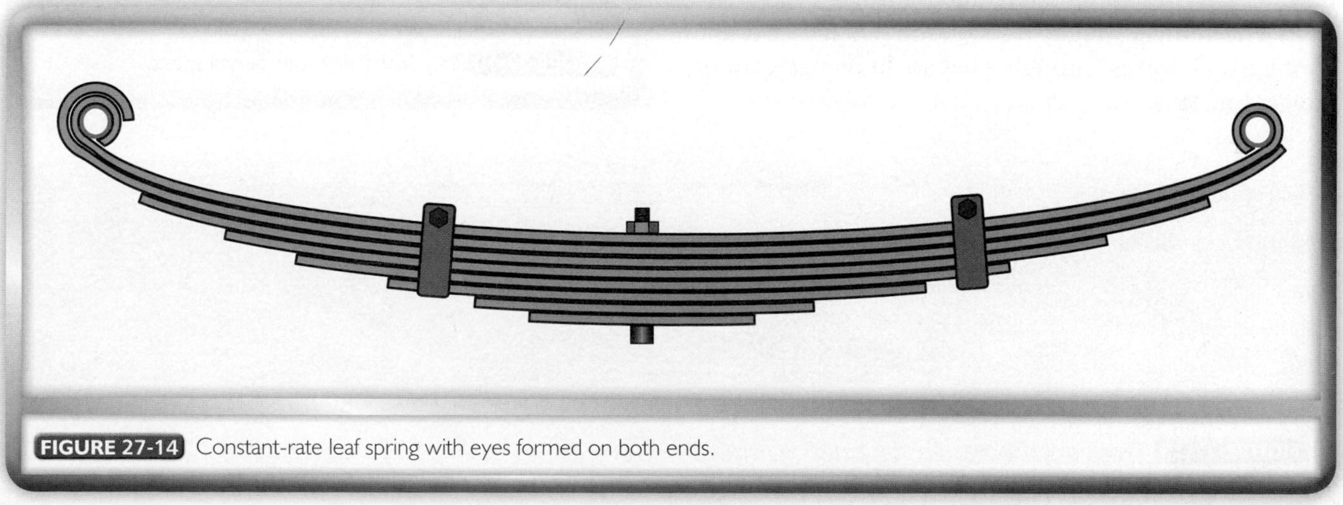

FIGURE 27-14 Constant-rate leaf spring with eyes formed on both ends.

Taper Leaf and Parabolic Leaf Springs

Taper leaf springs, like the ones in Figure 27-13, consist of a leaf spring pack in which the leaves have a varying thickness. Specifically, they are thinner at the outer ends of the leaf and get progressively thicker towards the center of the leaf.

The individual leaves are separated by low-friction spacers. That separation reduces interleaf friction and gives this spring type a softer ride. At the same time, because the leaves are full length, they can still carry the load of an equivalent semi-elliptical multileaf spring. Taper leaf springs are not variable-rate, yet the lack of interleaf friction gives the spring a softer ride throughout its operating range.

Parabolic leaf springs can be monoleaf or multileaf, such as the one in FIGURE 27-15. Parabolic leaf springs are very similar to taper leaf with one key difference—the spring taper is parabolic, meaning that the taper is engineered to precisely control the spring rate.

The width of the spring leaves can also be parabolic. That is, the width can change, leading to even more precise engineering of spring rate. Parabolic multileaf springs can be separated by low friction blocks to reduce interleaf friction and lead to much improved ride characteristics during all operating conditions. While reducing weight (as compared to multileaf spring packs), they can still carry the same loads as a much heavier multileaf spring pack when required because of the equal length spring leaves.

Variable-Rate or Progressive-Rate Leaf Springs

There are a couple of different types of variable-rate springs. The most common type uses a semi-elliptical spring pack that is not shackled to the vehicle frame. One leaf, called a torque leaf, will be pinned to the front spring bracket to maintain axle alignment. (Torque rods may be used to maintain alignment instead of a torque leaf.) The vehicle weight rests on the remainder of the spring pack's leaves through what are known as cam or hanger brackets.

The cam (hanger) brackets are semi-elliptical supports that allow the spring's contact points to easily slide along the bracket. These brackets are usually, but not always, replaceable. When the vehicle is unloaded, the ends of the spring pack rest in these hangers. As the load increases, the springs flatten out and lengthen. As that happens, the spring's contact points slide along the brackets closer to the center of the spring pack, as shown in FIGURE 27-16.

As the leaf springs flatten out, the cam (hanger) brackets cause the weight to be supported closer to the thicker part of the spring pack (the center). Spring rate increases and deflection decreases, ensuring that the spring capacity, or load rate, increases as the vehicle weight increases.

Other variable-rate springs have leaves that are separated from the main pack so that under light loads only one or two leaves support the load. Increasing the load, however, causes more leaves to compress, leading to increased spring rate and higher spring capacity. These types of springs allow a lower spring rate when lightly loaded, adding to driver comfort while still being able to support a fully loaded vehicle when required. Both of these types of springs also offer improved vehicle handling characteristics when compared to traditional leaf springs.

FIGURE 27-16 Multileaf spring with cam brackets.

FIGURE 27-15 Parabolic leaf spring.

Auxiliary Springs

Auxiliary springs are mounted on top of a carefully selected variable-rate spring. Auxiliary springs use cam brackets as contact points, making them variable-rate. As vehicle load increases, the springs can carry more weight.

The auxiliary spring is not in contact with its cam brackets when the vehicle is lightly loaded. As the load increases, however, contact results, as depicted in FIGURE 27-17. A suspension system using auxiliary springs allows a lower (softer) spring rate for driver comfort and vehicle control when unloaded, yet is still able to carry as much load as a much stiffer spring pack when required.

Leaf Spring Mounting Systems

Combination leaf spring and air systems, such as Kenworth's AG 130 and Hendrickson's AirTek system, are making inroads into the market, as are fully independent air spring front suspensions, such as Hendrickson's IFS. We will examine those systems later in chapter after first concentrating on typical leaf spring front suspension systems.

Front Steering-Axle Leaf Spring Suspensions

The front suspension systems on heavy-duty trucks are almost exclusively solid I-beam type with leaf springs.

The solid I-beam of the front axle is usually connected to the vehicle frame through two leaf springs, as shown in FIGURE 27-18. The leaf springs will normally have at least two or more leaves for safety reasons. (If one leaf breaks, the other will still support the vehicle.) The leaves may have an insulating material between each leaf to stop wear and reduce interleaf friction to obtain the smoothest ride. Some newer front suspensions are even equipped with **monoleaf springs** with only one leaf to eliminate interleaf friction all together. Multi-leaf springs are held together with a center bolt and the top two leaves at the front and the top leaf at the back are rolled to accept a bushing and a steel spring pin or a rubber mounting bushing. A typical front leaf spring suspension system is illustrated in FIGURE 27-19.

The front end of the spring is supported in the front spring bracket, which is bolted to the vehicle frame using either the spring pin or the rubber bushing and bolt.

FIGURE 27-18 Solid I-beam leaf spring suspension.

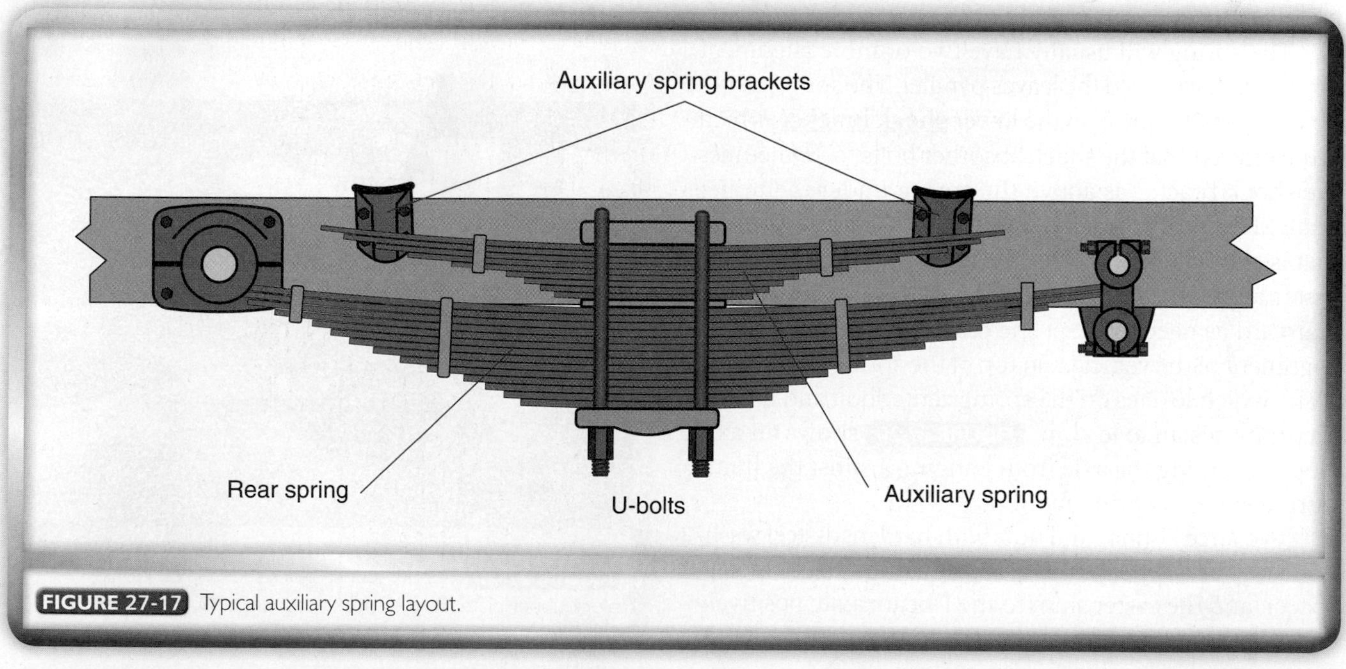

FIGURE 27-17 Typical auxiliary spring layout.

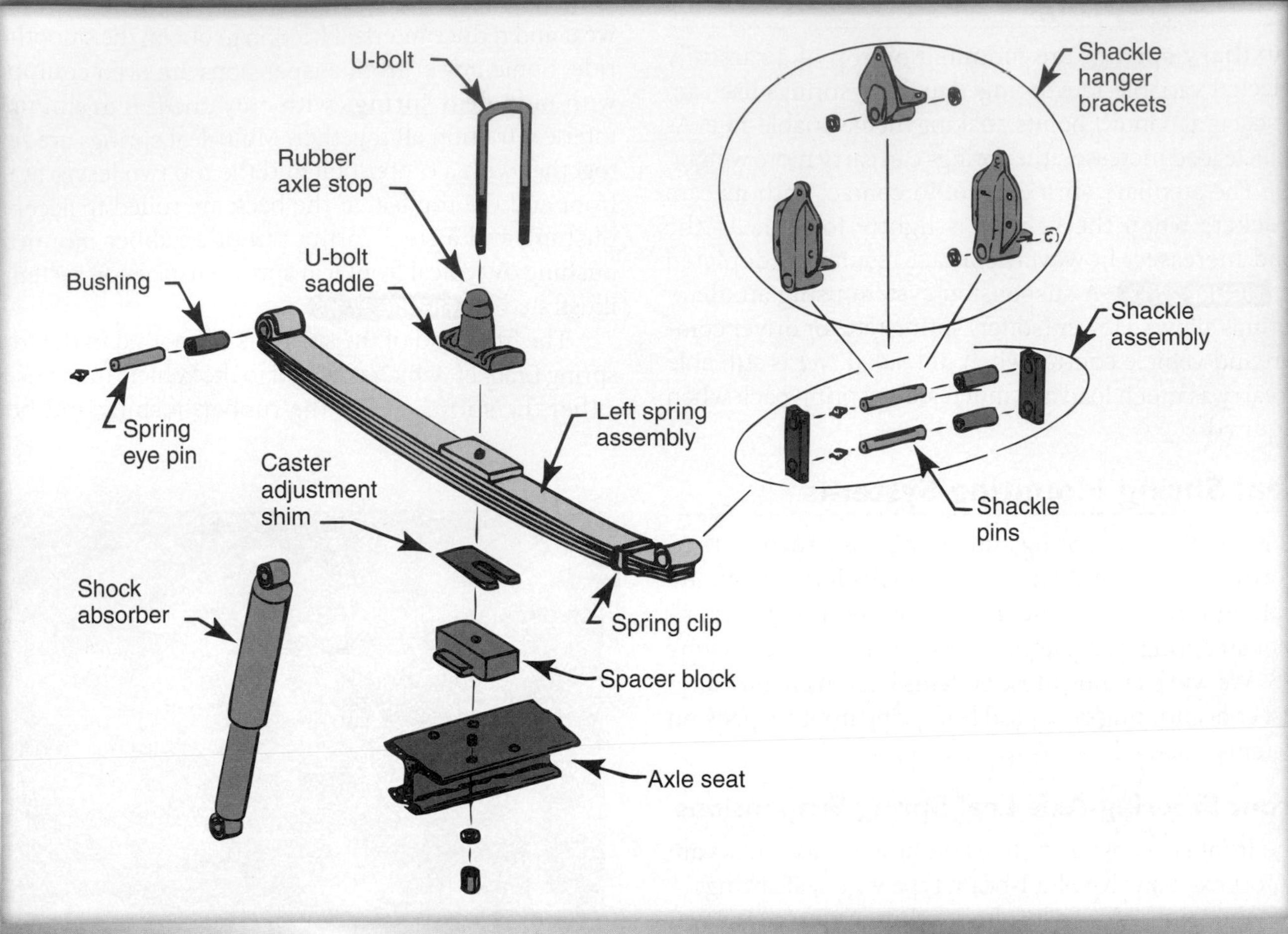

FIGURE 27-19 Front leaf spring suspension.

Systems that use the spring pin set-up need to be lubricated on a regular basis. Systems that use the rubber bushing and bolt method are maintenance free.

The spring will usually have two or more alignment clips installed to hold the leaves parallel. The spring center bolt locates the spring in the lower **shock bracket**, which is the bracket that the shock absorber bolts to. Sometimes the shock bracket is above the spring under the upper plate. The shock bracket locates on the spring spacer that is positioned above the **caster adjusting shim**. The caster adjusting shim is used to roll the axle forward or rearward as needed to set the caster angle during initial alignment of the vehicle. On top of the spring is the upper plate, which locates on the spring center bolt and usually incorporates an axle stop. **FIGURE 27-20** shows an axle stop preventing the axle from banging against the frame during extreme spring motion.

Two large U-bolts and nuts with hardened-steel washers clamp the upper plate, the spring, the shock bracket, spacer, and the caster shim to the I-beam axle, positively locating the axle to the spring. The axle will be at exactly 90 degrees to the frame. The rear of the spring is attached to the frame in one of two ways. The first way uses a spring pin that is inserted through the rolled eye. As with the

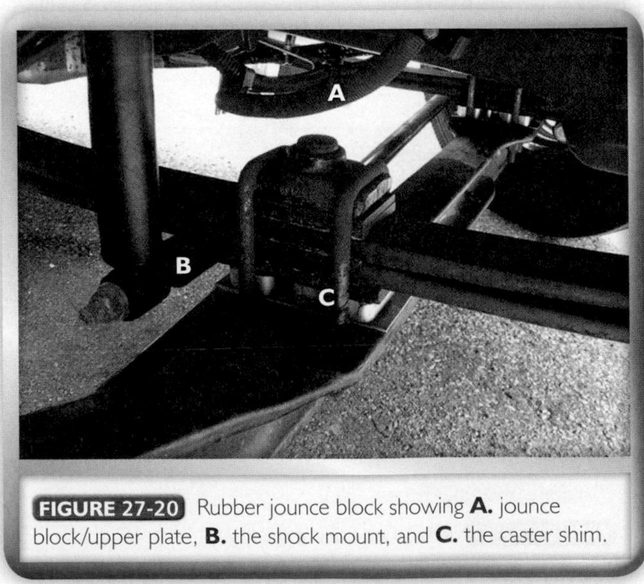

FIGURE 27-20 Rubber jounce block showing **A.** jounce block/upper plate, **B.** the shock mount, and **C.** the caster shim.

front of the spring, a rubber bushing and bolt may be used instead of a spring pin depending on the manufacturer. This pin or bushing is attached to a **swing shackle** which, in turn, is attached to the rear spring bracket that is bolted to the frame. The swing shackle allows for the lengthening and shortening of the spring as it cycles through jounce and rebound.

The second way to attach the rear of the spring is to position the top leaf of the spring straight instead of rolling it into an eye. The top two straight leaves are supported in a rubber insulator block that allows the spring length to change. This second method offers the advantage of being variable rate because the rear contact point of the spring leaves changes as the vehicle is loaded.

Drive Axle Leaf Spring Suspensions

A particular application of leaf spring suspensions is used on drive axles. Drive axle leaf spring suspensions can be used on single drive axles and tandem drive axles.

Single Drive Axle

A typical single drive axle leaf spring suspension will have a leaf spring attached to the drive axle housing in the same way as the front I-beam that is clamped on with large U-bolts. The spring mount will have a top and a bottom plate and a spring seat. The spring seat may also have an incorporated torque rod mounting bracket. There may also be an angled shim used to set the axle angle for driveline angle adjustment.

The front and rear of the spring will be supported in cam (hanger) brackets bolted to the frame. As the spring is loaded and straightens out, the cam (hanger) brackets allow the spring contact point to slide as the spring lengthens. The contact will, therefore, be closer to the center of the spring pack. This gives the spring a variable rate—a lower spring rate for a softer ride when the vehicle is lightly loaded and higher spring rate for a stiffer ride and increased lateral support when the vehicle is fully loaded.

The cam (hanger) brackets may or may not have replaceable wear pads where the springs contact the brackets. Axle alignment will be controlled by torque rods, which are bolted to the spring seat and the bottom of the front spring bracket. The torque rod on one side may be threaded so that it can be shortened or lengthened to allow axle alignment adjustment.

Other methods of axle alignment are shims used at the torque rod mounting and /or eccentric washers. The torque rods also transmit acceleration and braking forces to the frame to maintain axle rotational position and will have rubber bushings absorb the shock of these forces. If the axle is not aligned by torque rods, the spring will have a torque leaf attached to the front spring bracket for axle alignment and control of the acceleration and braking forces, as shown in FIGURE 27-21. The axle may also be equipped with transverse torque rods to control centrifugal cornering forces on the axle.

Tandem Drive Leaf Spring Suspensions

When a tandem drive axle uses a standard leaf spring suspension system, the spring is attached to the axle in exactly the same way as for a single drive axle with one exception—the rear of the front spring and the front of the rear spring are supported in what is known as an **equalizer**. As illustrated in FIGURE 27-22, the center of the equalizer itself is supported in an **equalizer bracket** on a pin so that the equalizer can pivot backward and forward.

The equalizer bracket is bolted to the vehicle frame and has internal stops that limit the equalizer's pivoting movement. The equalizer ensures that both of the tandem axles are equally loaded. As the front axle encounters a bump and moves upward toward the frame, the rear of the front spring will push the equalizer upward at the front and the equalizer's pivoting action will force the front of the rear spring downward. That action spreads the load of the vehicle equally between the front and the rear springs and axles and helps to keep all four wheels in contact with the road and is commonly referred to as a load-sharing type suspension. The pivoting action also reduces the severity of the bump at the equalizer bracket by reducing some of the upward motion. The tandem axles will be held in alignment by torque rods. As with a single axle, the torque rods can have three possible adjustment methods: they can be threaded on one side, use shims, or be mounted using eccentric washers.

FIGURE 27-21 **A.** A torque leaf and **B.** spring cam/hanger bracket.

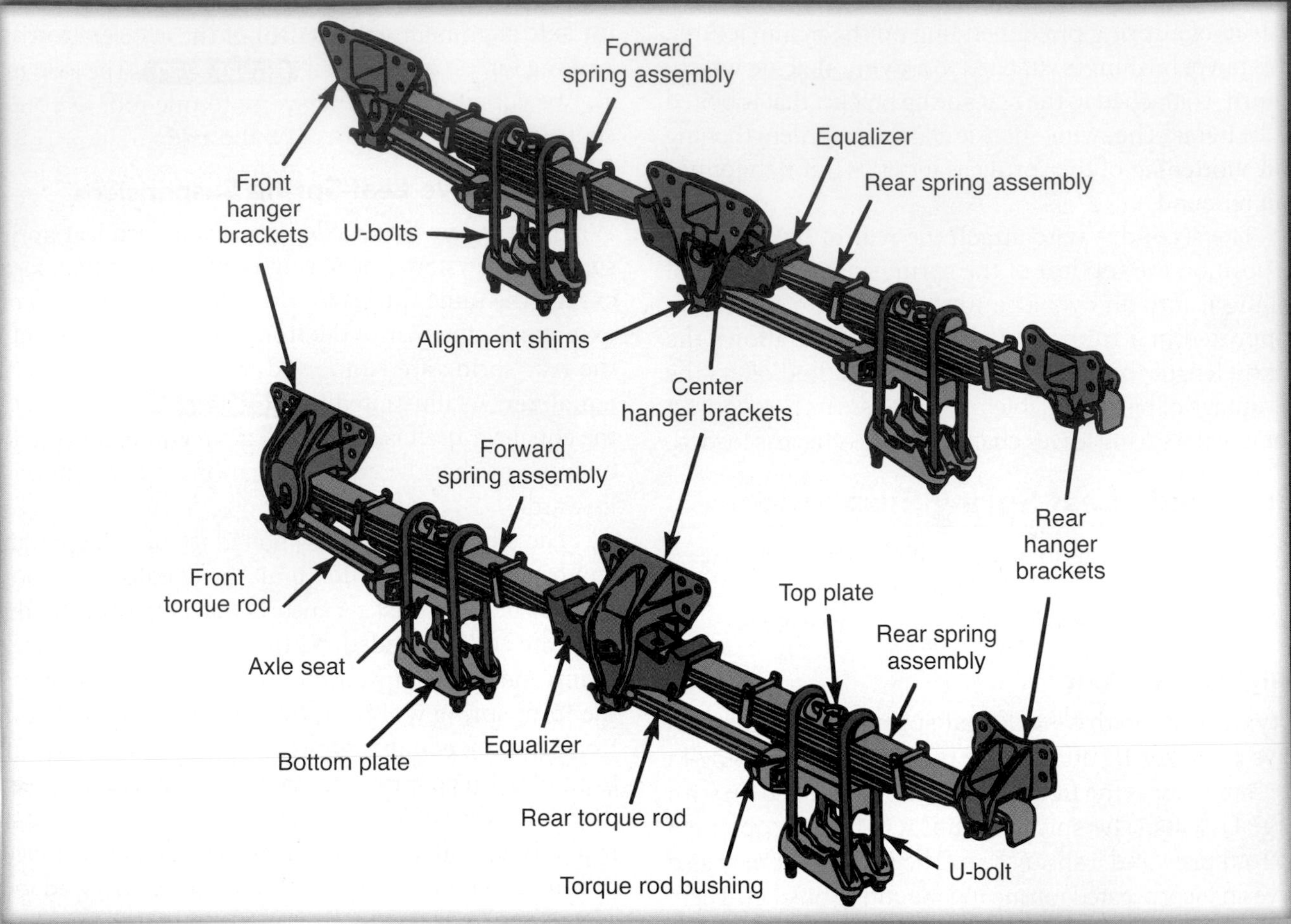

FIGURE 27-22 Typical equalizer suspension alignment of the axles is controlled by shims at the torque rod mounting bolts.

Equalizing Beam Suspensions

Equalizing beam (walking beam) suspensions are used on tandem suspension systems. Two large equalizing beams between the two axles equalize the load between the four wheels. There are four basic types of equalizing beam suspensions:

- Solid mount, with no spring at all
- Leaf spring type
- Rubber spring type, as shown in **FIGURE 27-23**
- Air spring type

Each of these types of suspensions, with the exception of the air spring type, is discussed in more details in its own subsection. Air type equalizing beam suspensions will be covered in the Air Spring Suspension Systems section. Equalizing beam suspensions are used on tandem drive axles and use the lever principle to reduce the impact of road surface irregularities.

FIGURE 27-23 Rubber spring equalizing suspension.

Typical equalizing beam suspensions have the equalizing beams mounted under the axles of the tandem. The beams—one on each side—connect the two axles together. Beam end connection points usually feature rubber bushings. The elasticity of the rubber allows for some movement but quickly returns to the original shape to maintain alignment of the axles. The low mounting position lowers the center of gravity of the vehicle, adding to lateral stability.

The centers of the beams are fitted with bronze and steel or rubber bushings and are mounted to the large spring saddles and held in place by saddle caps. The center bushing allows the beam to pivot at the saddle. The large saddle holding the beam is, in turn, attached to the vehicle frame either directly—as is the case of a solid-mount system—or through a leaf spring, rubber spring, or air spring system.

The two equalizing beams are joined at the center bushings by a cross tube. The rubber bushings used at the attachment points of suspension systems allow lateral movement as the vehicle turns a corner. As the vehicle enters a turn, the axles can move as much as 3" (7.62 cm) from side to side. This is because, as a tandem navigates a turn, the pivot point is between the two axles so the forces push the front axle to the outside of the curve and push the rear axle toward the inside. The elasticity of the rubber bushings in the torque rods and beams bring the axles back to alignment quickly when the vehicle returns to straight-ahead driving. This transition is illustrated in **FIGURE 27-24**.

The lever principle employed by equalizing beam suspension systems reduces the road shocks to the frame by 50%. When the front axle encounters a bump in the terrain, it moves up by the size of the bump. As illustrated in **FIGURE 27-25**, when a vehicle hits a bump 6" (15.24 cm) high, the axle moves up the equalizing beam. Because the equalizing beam will pivot at the rear rubber bushing, the beam acts as a lever. The center of the beam, therefore, only moves up 3" (7.62 cm). The impact to the saddle that is attached to the vehicle frame is only half of the impact to the axle. This reduces the shock to the vehicle and the cargo.

Equalizing beam suspensions typically offer a large range of suspension articulation. The wheels can move as much as much as 17" (43.18 cm) when required, so they can be used in very rough off-road conditions while still equalizing the load on each wheel and maintaining tire contact. Several manufacturers produce equalizing beam (walking) suspensions, all of similar construction.

Solid Mount Equalizing Beam Suspensions

Solid mount equalizing beam suspensions have the beam saddle bolted directly to the vehicle frame. As a result, they have very limited capabilities for absorbing shock energy other than the lever principle mentioned previously. That means they have a rough ride compared to other systems. Solid-mount systems do offer a large degree of lateral stability, high load-carrying capacity, and excellent durability from the suspension system. The suspension will have four or more torque rods to transfer the acceleration and braking forces to the frame.

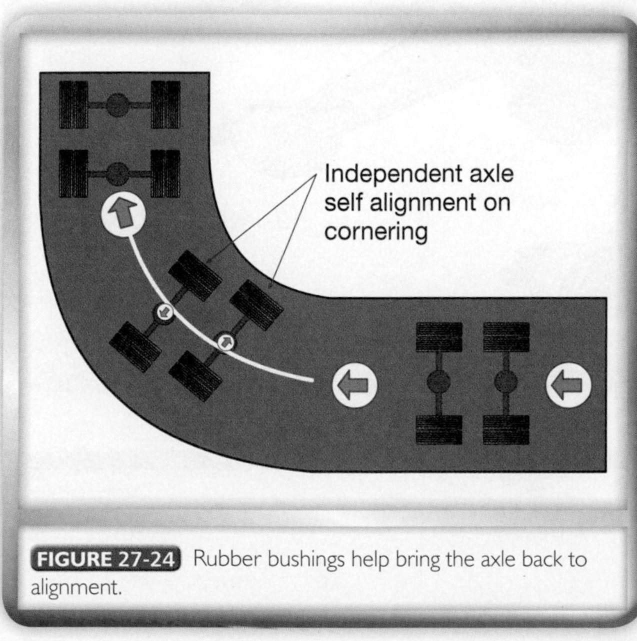

FIGURE 27-24 Rubber bushings help bring the axle back to alignment.

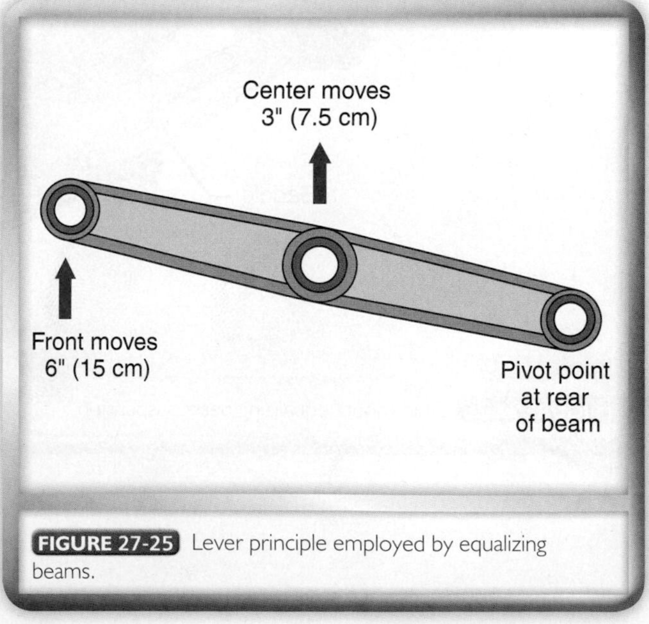

FIGURE 27-25 Lever principle employed by equalizing beams.

Solid mounted systems can be found in vehicles that have a high center of gravity. They are also common in vehicles typically operated at lower speeds in off-road environments requiring a large degree of suspension movement. Similarly, solid mounted systems are found in applications where very heavy load capacity is required, such as concrete mixers, cranes, and boom trucks.

Leaf Spring Equalizing Beam Suspensions

In equalizing, or walking, beam suspensions that utilize leaf springs, each beam's saddle will be clamped to the center of a multileaf spring pack that usually has a rolled eye at the front. The front of the spring is mounted to the front spring hanger by a pin. The pin can be rubber or solid mounted, as shown in FIGURE 27-26. The rear of the leaf spring rides on a cam (hanger) bracket in the rear spring hanger, which allows the contact point to change as the spring is loaded so the spring will have a variable rate. This suspension system can be a constant rated system, identified by the main leafs being shorter and only supported by the rear spring hanger. The vari-rate version has extended main leaves that are initially supported on the auxiliary spring hangers. Hendrickson uses these extensively and identify the variations by using RT to designate the constant rated system and RTE for the vari-rated variation.

The suspension will have two or more torque rods to transfer acceleration and braking forces to the frame. A leaf spring equalizing beam suspension will give slightly better ride characteristics than a solid mount.

Rubber Spring Equalizing Beam Suspensions

Rubber equalizing beam suspensions, like the one illustrated in FIGURE 27-27A, are similar to the leaf spring style; however, they use a variety of rubber cushion elements to absorb road shock.

The rubber components are mounted between the saddle and the frame hangers and are usually variable rate. As the load increases, more and more of the rubber element is compressed. That makes for good

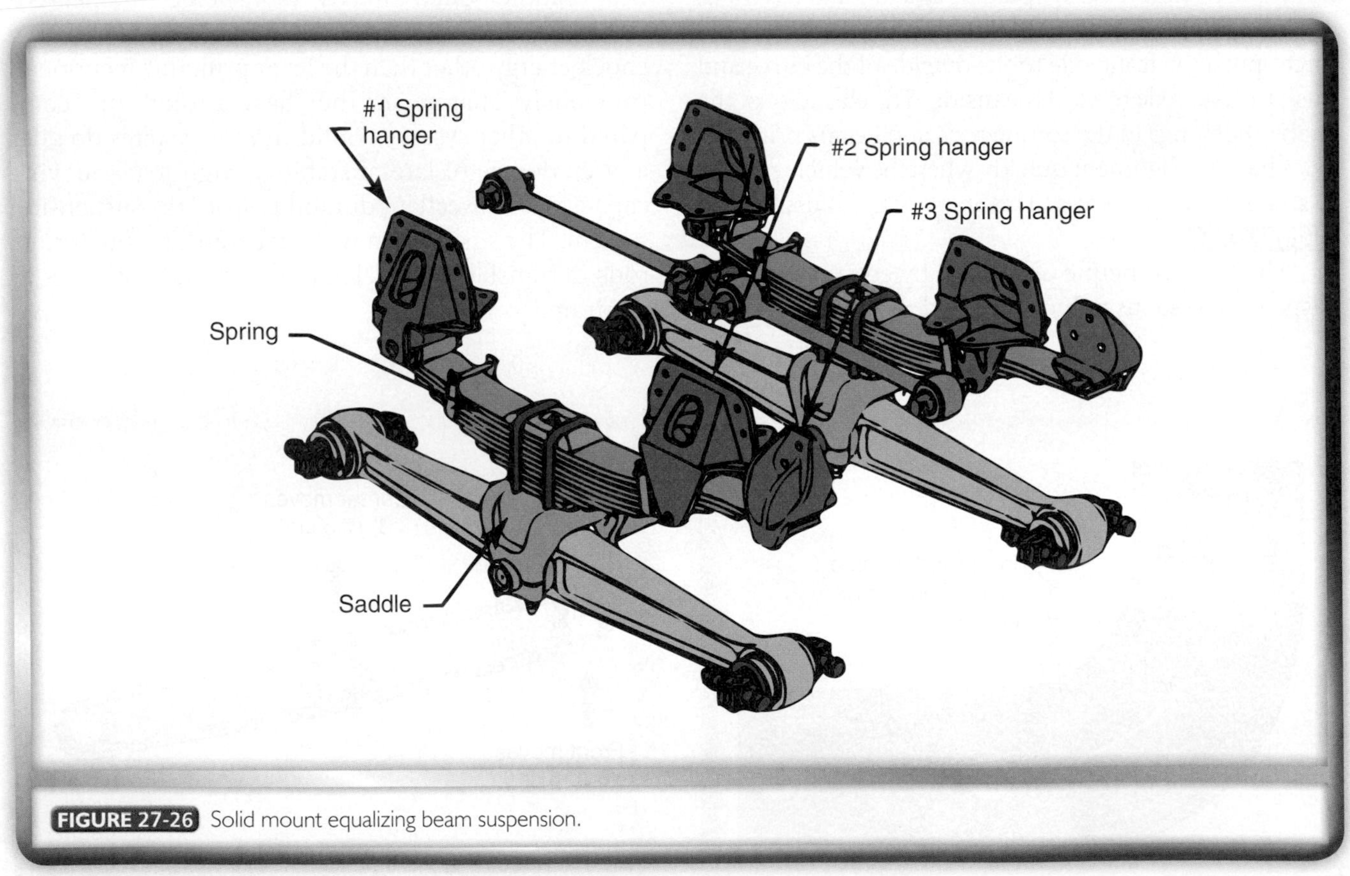

FIGURE 27-26 Solid mount equalizing beam suspension.

light-load characteristics and excellent heavy-load lateral stability.

Rubber equalizer beam suspensions will usually have four vertical **drive pins** attached to frame hangers. The drive pins pass through the rubber springs and engage drive pin bushings in the saddle. The drive pins keep the beam saddles in alignment as the rubber spring compresses and rebounds. The drive pins have rebound stop nuts and nylon bumpers. The nuts and bumpers limit the upward motion of the drive pins when the suspension encounters greater than normal rebound conditions and excessive lateral forces that would tend to pull the pins out of the saddles. The drive pins are very important for maintaining the spring and axle positioning, and they transfer driving braking and cornering (lateral) forces to the frame. The newer style of rubber spring systems use angular mounted "bolster" springs to transfer drive and braking forces through the suspension. Notice the metal plates encased in the cutaway rubber bolster spring shown in FIGURE 27-27B. This design has eliminated the vertical drive pins associated with older rubber spring systems.

FIGURE 27-27 **A.** Rubber spring equalizing beam suspension. **B.** Angular bolster springs.

Chalmers Rubber Spring Equalizing Beam Suspensions

Chalmers Suspension International manufactures an equalizing beam suspension that is unique in its design. The Chalmers system uses equalizing beams that are not solidly attached to the axles. Instead, they ride in brackets called saddles that are welded to the axles.

Chalmers suspension also uses cylindrical rubber springs that are variable rate. As the springs compress, their spring rate increases. The rubber spring elements are enveloped by spun metal restrictor "cans" such as those shown in FIGURE 27-28. The cans restrict the springs' outward motion as the springs are compressed. As such, the cans modify the spring rate as they approach maximum compression. The can attachment system is much simpler than a typical equalizer beam suspension and so is easier to service and maintain.

The rubber springs in a Chalmers suspension are free floating. They are not attached to the frame or the equalizing beams. Instead, they are compressed between a beam spring plate, which is held to the beam by two bolts, and the restrictor can, which rides free against the frame bracket. The two axles of the tandem are held in longitudinal and lateral alignment by eight torque rods mounted to cylindrical spigots.

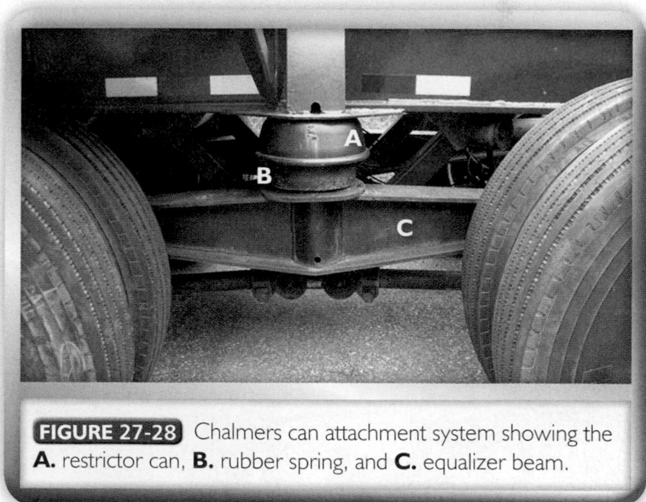

FIGURE 27-28 Chalmers can attachment system showing the **A.** restrictor can, **B.** rubber spring, and **C.** equalizer beam.

Four torque rods are mounted below the axles. Those four torque rods transfer brake and acceleration forces to the vehicle frame through the large saddle brackets, called triangular A-frames, which are, in turn, bolted to the frame. This set of four torque rods is also responsible for axle alignment to the vehicle frame. Two of the rods are adjustable to accomplish this.

The four other torque rods are mounted diagonally at the top of the axles. The ends of each pair of rods are attached to a tower welded to each axle close to its center. The other ends of this set of rods is attached to the vehicle frame near the rails forming a V shape with the rods for each axle, as shown in FIGURE 27-29. These upper torque rods control axle lateral alignment. All eight torque rods are mounted by rubber bushings and held in place by spigot caps, which compress the bushings when torqued to specification.

The rubber bushings allow exceptional articulation of the axles all while maintaining vehicle alignment. The elasticity of the bushings returns the axles to their relaxed position very quickly. As such, the Chalmers suspension system boasts one of the highest levels of wheel articulation in the market. The **variable spring rate** of the rubber springs adds excellent lateral stability. As the vehicle load shifts to one side, the spring rate on that side gets stiffer and stiffer. The more load that is applied, the more the restrictor can comes into play by intensifying the spring rate even more to stop the load shift.

As depicted in FIGURE 27-30, the Chalmers equalizing beams are not physically attached to the axles. They are actually held in place by the saddle brackets on the axles. The only fasteners used on the beams are the bolts that hold the beam spring plates that locate the rubber springs. Because the equalizing beams are not fixed to the axles, they allow for excellent articulation and less maintenance than competing systems. When the beams wear past specifications, wear pads can be welded into place to repair them.

The Chalmers suspension is extremely light when compared to standard leaf or air spring equalizer beam suspensions. The Chalmers system is also exceptionally easy to service—the entire system can be repaired and/or replaced using normal shop tools without using any expensive specialized equipment. The rubber springs are easily changed by taking the load off the springs and removing the two bolts attaching the beam spring plate to the beam. The plate, the spring, and the restrictor can are slide out and can be removed together. The sixteen rubber bushings attaching the torque rods are also easy to replace. The tension on the rubber bushing is caused by the spigot caps. Once the caps are removed, the torque rod can be easily slid off the spigots, and the bushings can be removed by simply prying them out with a screwdriver or similar tool. Furthermore, the system requires absolutely no lubrication, making it a zero-maintenance system.

Periodic inspection of the system is required, however. The restrictor cans are subject to corrosion, depending on the operating environment, and must be replaced when necessary. The rubber torque rod bushings should be checked for play while the suspension is neutralized (no torque or side loading). They should be checked for play by hand only—do not use a pry bar. If any play exists, the bushing should be replaced. Chalmers claims the rubber springs it uses are indestructible and will only require replacement if they are damaged by solvent or other chemical attack. Never use oil-based lubricants on this system. The only other components of the Chalmers system are the equalizing beams, which should be periodically checked for wear at the saddle contact area and for cracks. Excessive wear can be repaired by welding wear pads on to the beams; cracks, however, warrant replacement of the beams.

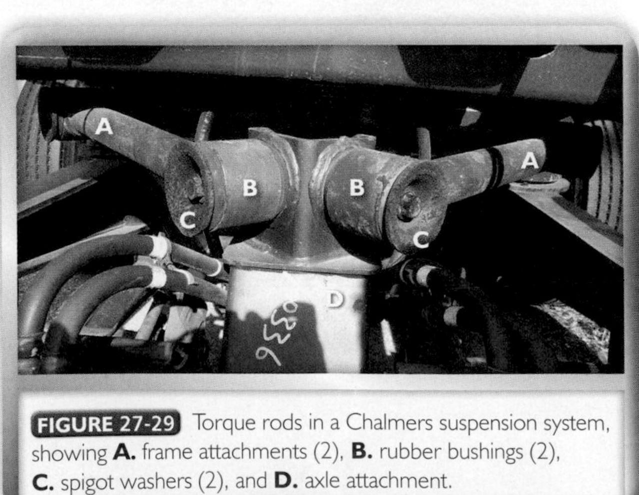

FIGURE 27-29 Torque rods in a Chalmers suspension system, showing **A.** frame attachments (2), **B.** rubber bushings (2), **C.** spigot washers (2), and **D.** axle attachment.

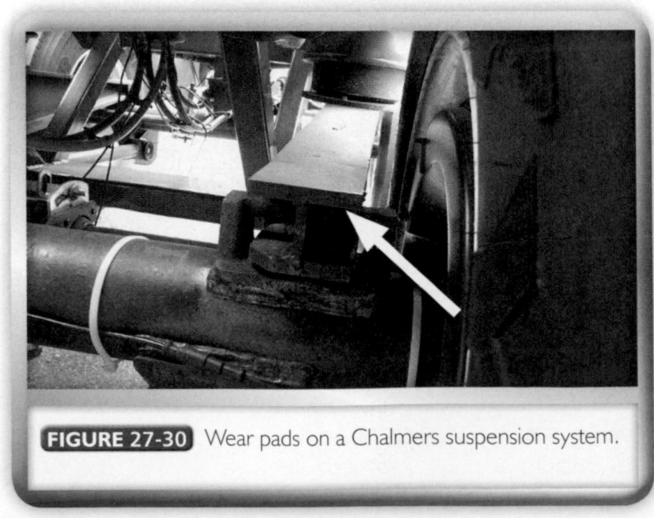

FIGURE 27-30 Wear pads on a Chalmers suspension system.

Air Spring Suspension Systems

Air spring suspensions, such as the one shown in FIGURE 27-31, are becoming the most popular suspension systems for on-highway vehicle operation. Indeed, even for vocational use, these systems are being utilized more and more.

The reason air spring suspension systems are so popular is because they provide better shock isolation than any of the other suspension systems mentioned previously. Two main advantages of air spring suspension are that the load is better protected and driver comfort is optimized. Air spring systems help prevent losses due to excessive load agitation or shock damage. The softer ride air springs go a long way to keeping drivers content. Fleet operators recognize that competent professional drivers are rare and the investment in air spring suspensions is money well spent.

Air spring systems offer excellent equalization because of all of the air **bellows**. The bellows, also known as simply the **air bag**, are the actual spring element in these suspension systems and are connected by airlines. As the pressure increases in one bag because of a jounce, the pressure also increases in the other bags. To absorb road shocks, the multiply rubber bellows are filled with air compressed by the vehicle's air system. The air spring pressure is adjustable within design limits so that the vehicle ride height remains constant whether loaded or unloaded.

When a leaf spring suspension is loaded, the operating angles of the driveline's universal joints become more severe. Severe angles can lead to vibrations and eventual failure of these and other driveline components. This does not occur with air spring suspensions unless the ride height is intentionally changed. As a result, the driveline components require service less frequently.

FIGURE 27-31 Typical drive axle air spring suspension , including **A.** upper torque rods, **B.** air spring (bellows), and **C.** trailing arm.

The adjustable air pressure also means that the spring rate for air springs is infinitely adjustable—within design limits. One of the drawbacks of air spring suspensions is that, with their lower (softer) spring rate, they offer lower lateral stability in turns. As the vehicle weight shifts to the outside during cornering, the outside spring flattens. The vehicle is then more susceptible to rollover. Note that vehicle speed when cornering plays a significant factor with this phenomena as it does with any suspension configuration. Manufacturers combat this drawback by using transverse torque rods, **stabilizer bars**, and carefully selected **reversing sleeve (rolling lobe) pistons**, which change the spring-rate profile of the air spring. Another issue with air spring systems is that they lack the self-dampening characteristics found on leaf spring systems. Air spring systems must use shock absorbers or other dampening systems to dissipate spring oscillations.

Air Spring Construction

Although the concept of an air spring was first thought of at the turn of the century, the first viable air spring was patented by Firestone in 1938. Today's air springs are manufactured of a highly durable multiply rubber similar in construction to the sidewall of an automotive tire. These walls consist of at least four layers of corded plies and a smooth air-proof inner liner.

Bellows come in two basic configurations—reversing sleeve (rolling lobe) and **convoluted air spring**. The reversible sleeve air bellows, shown in FIGURE 27-32, has only a top bead plate. At the bottom is a sleeve type piston that pushes up into the bellows as it is compressed. The convoluted type of air spring bellows, shown in FIGURE 27-33, is a double convoluted type. It has girdle hoops and a top and bottom bead plate to attach the spring. The convoluted type will have a bottom bead plate and a top bead plate. The convoluted type may have one or more girdle hoops that wrap around the bellows, effectively breaking the length of the bellows into two or more sections. Two girdle hoops are used for a double convoluted style and three for a triple convoluted style.

The convoluted style of air spring is not as commonly used as the reversing sleeve type, which is the most popular type of air spring in on-highway use. The reversing sleeve type air spring has a piston at the bottom that is forced up into the bellows as a jounce is encountered. The spring rate of the reversing sleeve type air spring can be somewhat controlled by manipulating the shape of the sleeve or piston. Outward flaring the bottom of the piston,

FIGURE 27-32 Reversing sleeve (rolling bellows) with **A.** combo stud, **B.** attachment stud, **C.** top bead plate, and **D.** reversing sleeve.

FIGURE 27-33 Convoluted bellows with **A.** air connection, **B.** top bead plate, **C.** girdle hoop, and **D.** bottom bead plate.

as illustrated in FIGURE 27-34, results in a spring rate that gets stiffer as the spring is compressed, adding to lateral stability during turns. The multiply bellows material of the air spring is held in place by bead plates at the top and bottom (in the convoluted type) or by a bead plate at the top and a clamp plate that attaches the bottom of the bellows to the piston (in the reversing lobe type).

The top bead plates will have attachment studs or threaded blind holes and an air fitting to supply compressed air to the bellows. The air fitting is sometimes fashioned into one of the attachment studs. In that case, it is called a **combo stud**. The bottom bead plate on the convoluted type will also have blind attachment holes; the reversing lobe type will have the lower attachment holes in the bottom of the piston. The reversing lobe piston can be aluminum, plastic, steel, carbon fiber, or hardened rubber. Air spring suspension systems generally use rubber jounce blocksthat restrict the maximum upward motion of the axles. These jounce blocks can be incorporated inside the air spring or may be separately mounted.

Until recently, air springs were strictly used for the rear axles of either a power unit (tractor) or for trailer suspensions. Today, air springs are typically mounted at the rear of large, box-frame-designed **trailing arms** which are held in place by rubber bushings installed in mounting brackets. Trailing arms refer to large and very strong beams. The front of the beam attaches to the vehicle frame and the beam trails behind. The axle will be attached to the beam approximately halfway along its length and the end of the beam will have a spring medium, usually air, between the beam and the frame. The trailing arms keep the axle aligned during suspension articulation. The trailing arm mounting brackets are bolted to the frame. Axle alignment is controlled by threaded torque rods that are adjustable. If the rods themselves are not adjustable, they will be mounted to the vehicle using shims or eccentric bushings to allow for adjustment to control axle alignment.

Air spring oscillations are not dampened by the springs themselves. This is one reason why they offer such a soft ride. Rather, they must use heavy-duty, dual-acting shock absorbers at each air spring to dissipate the spring's energy. Air spring suspensions typically have transverse torque rods and or stabilizer bars to control sidesway and add lateral stability during turns and excessive suspension articulation.

Combination Leaf/Air Spring

Combination leaf/air spring suspension systems are becoming commonplace in rear suspension systems. In these systems, the air spring is mounted on a specially modified leaf spring that takes the place of the trailing

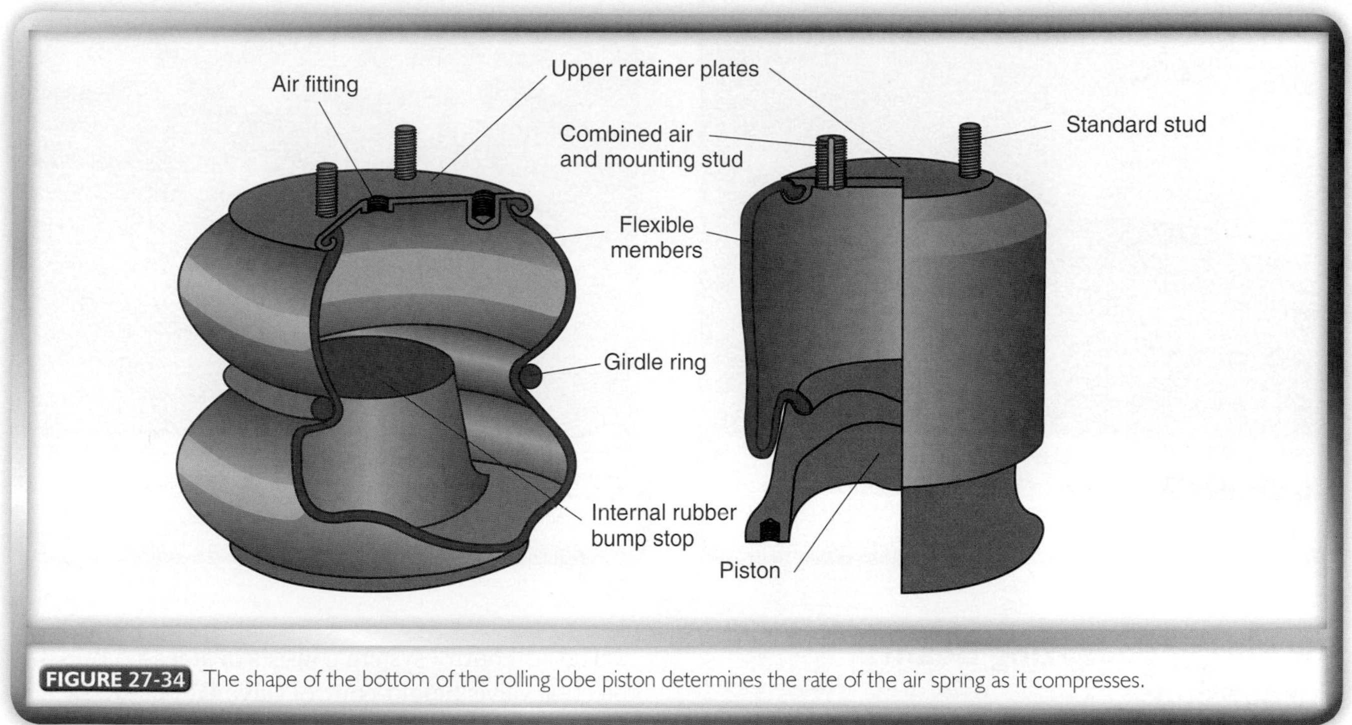

FIGURE 27-34 The shape of the bottom of the rolling lobe piston determines the rate of the air spring as it compresses.

arm. The leaf spring may be a single leaf or a two- or three-leaf pack and will be mounted at the rear, as shown in FIGURE 27-35. Combination spring suspension systems incorporate the best of both worlds. The suspension can gain the excellent lateral stability of a high-spring-rate leaf spring system while still offering the excellent shock isolation offered by air springs.

As the vehicle encounters lateral forces, the leaf spring component resists the side loading by acting as a torsional member and twisting as the load shifts to the side. This action, along with carefully selected rolling lobe pistons, enhances rollover protection and allows suspension engineers considerable latitude when designing suspensions for a particular installation.

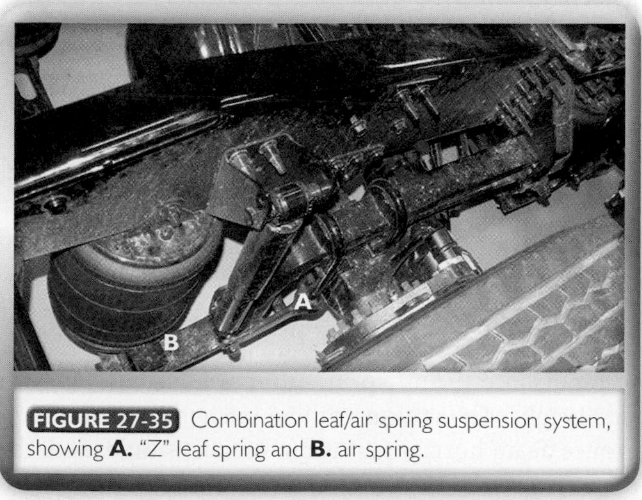

FIGURE 27-35 Combination leaf/air spring suspension system, showing **A.** "Z" leaf spring and **B.** air spring.

For a long time, air spring suspension were not considered for steer-axle applications because the uncontrolled oscillations of a typical air spring system could lead to very poor vehicle control or weak shocks. In addition, excessive loads would cause poor handling due to the front axle bouncing uncontrollably.

The introduction of combination leaf/air springs systems have now opened up the front-axle market to air spring manufacturers. Several manufacturers now offer many leaf/air spring designs that combine the softer ride characteristics of air springs with the characteristic stability of traditional leaf springs.

As with traditional front leaf suspensions, combination systems use a traditional leaf spring clamped to the front axle. The leaf spring has a rolled eye at the front, which is connected to the front spring hanger with a rubber bushing. The rear of the spring also has an eye connected to a traditional swinging shackle. The front spring connection maintains axle alignment, while the rear shackle allows for changes in the leaf length due to oscillation. The air spring bellows are mounted between the spring top plate and the frame. As the leaf spring oscillates, it also compresses the bellows, as shown in FIGURE 27-36. The air spring maintains ride height under all conditions and provides a low (soft) spring rate, while the leaf spring has a higher (stiffer) spring rate. The two spring types together give the suspension all of the desirable characteristics of both systems. The leaf springs also add lateral stability by operating as torsional devices as the vehicle experiences side forces due to turns or excessive articulation.

FIGURE 27-36 Combination leaf/air front suspension.

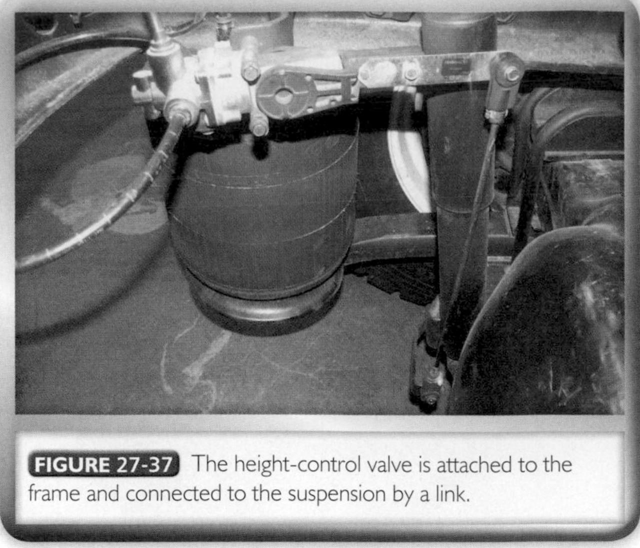

FIGURE 27-37 The height-control valve is attached to the frame and connected to the suspension by a link.

Air Spring Equalizing Beam Suspensions

Air spring equalizing beam suspensions are also relatively new. They utilize air springs as the shock absorbing element. In addition, they offer a better ride on vocational vehicles during all operating conditions over vehicles that traditionally use equalizing beam suspensions.

In this type of suspension system, the saddle that would normally attach to the leaf spring is replaced with a longer design saddle that attaches to the front frame hanger with an eccentrically mounted rubber bushing. (The bushing is eccentric to allow for axle alignment.) Two air springs are mounted between the saddle and two of the frame hangers—one directly above the axle and the second further back.

The air springs provide the same excellent ride conditions offered by other air spring suspension systems, whether the vehicle is loaded or unloaded. In addition, the suspension has longitudinal and transverse torque rods that transfer braking, acceleration, and lateral forces to the frame. Air spring oscillation is controlled by heavy-duty, dual-acting, hydraulic shock absorbers. Hendrickson currently offers a retrofit kit to change its equalizer beam suspensions with leaf spring to an air spring equalizer beam system.

Air Spring Control

Because air spring suspensions utilize compressed air inside a bellows as the spring medium, an air-control system is needed to make the system operate. The control system must keep the air springs inflated at the proper level regardless of vehicle load. Proper inflation is critical for maintaining correct vehicle ride height during all operating conditions.

The air-control system consists of at least a pressure protection valve, **height-control valve** FIGURE 27-37, and the connecting lines. The control system may have other options such as a **dump valve** (usually part of the height-control valve) and a pressure regulator valve (sometimes incorporated into the pressure protection valve). The vehicle air system supplies the compressed air to operate the system.

To allow the vehicle to build pressure on start-up, compressed air flow to the air spring system is blocked by the pressure limiting protection valve, like the one shown in FIGURE 27-38, until the air system builds to a minimum pressure of usually 65 psi (448 kPa). Once this threshold pressure is reached, the valve opens and allows compressed air to flow to the height-control valve. The pressure limiting protection valve protects the vehicle's air system from a major pressure loss in the air suspension system. The valve will not allow air to flow to the suspension until the threshold pressure is reached and will shut if pressure drops below that level.

The height-control valve, illustrated in FIGURE 27-39, is the central command for the air system. The valve is mounted solidly to the vehicle frame and controls air flow to and from the air springs. At one end of the valve a lever is attached; the other end is fixed through a link to the rear axle or the suspension components.

At the correct ride height, the height-control valve lever is usually horizontal to the ground. As the suspension is loaded, the frame lowers. That drop causes the lever to be pushed up and the height-control valve to meter air into the air springs to re-establish the correct ride height. The springs will be inflated until the lever is once again horizontal. As the vehicle is unloaded, the opposite occurs. The frame is lifted by the air spring when the load is decreased, forcing the height-control valve lever downward. That action causes the valve to exhaust air from the springs again until the lever returns to its starting, horizontal position.

The lever and the valve enjoy a certain amount of free travel (0.25–0.375" or 6–9 mm) before the valve will take corrective action by inflating or deflating the springs. There is also a delay feature inside the valve. The delay is usually controlled by the movement of a viscous fluid that slows the opening and closing of the actual valve to keep the suspension from trying to adjust pressure in reaction to every single bump in the road.

FIGURE 27-38 Pressure protection valve.

Air spring pressure may be limited to 100 psi (690 kPa) by using pressure regulating valves in combination with the pressure protection valve. When necessary under extreme loads, other systems can be inflated up to full air system operating pressures. It is important to note that when an air spring encounters a jounce, the spring collapses on itself, increasing the pressure in the spring. Because all of the springs are connected together by the air lines, the pressure increases simultaneously in all of the bellows, making for excellent load equalization between the wheels. Note that the maximum pressure an air spring is designed to contain is 200 psi (1379 kPa)—whether by inflation or by compression caused by road shocks. If the air spring inflation pressure is higher than 100 psi (690 kPa), it could indicate that the maximum pressure may be reached more easily, leading to spring failure.

Electronically Controlled Air Suspension Systems

Electronic control of air spring suspension systems, such as the one in FIGURE 27-40, have been available for over 15 years. These systems use three or more height sensors to determine (a) vehicle ride height and (b) differences between front and rear and side-to-side ride levels. When a deviation is detected, the system electronic control unit (ECU) corrects the discrepancy by activating solenoids that control air pressure to the right or left rear air springs or to the front air spring. Those adjustments allow the

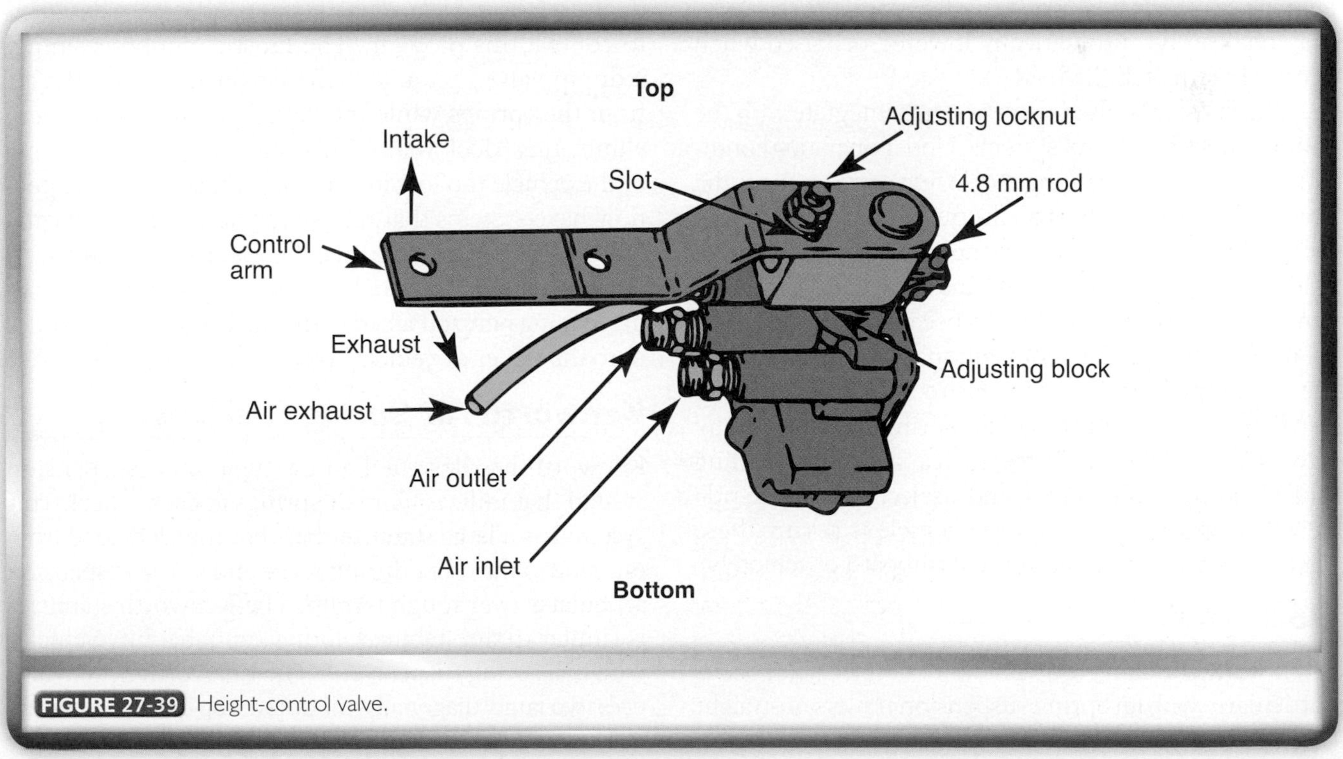

FIGURE 27-39 Height-control valve.

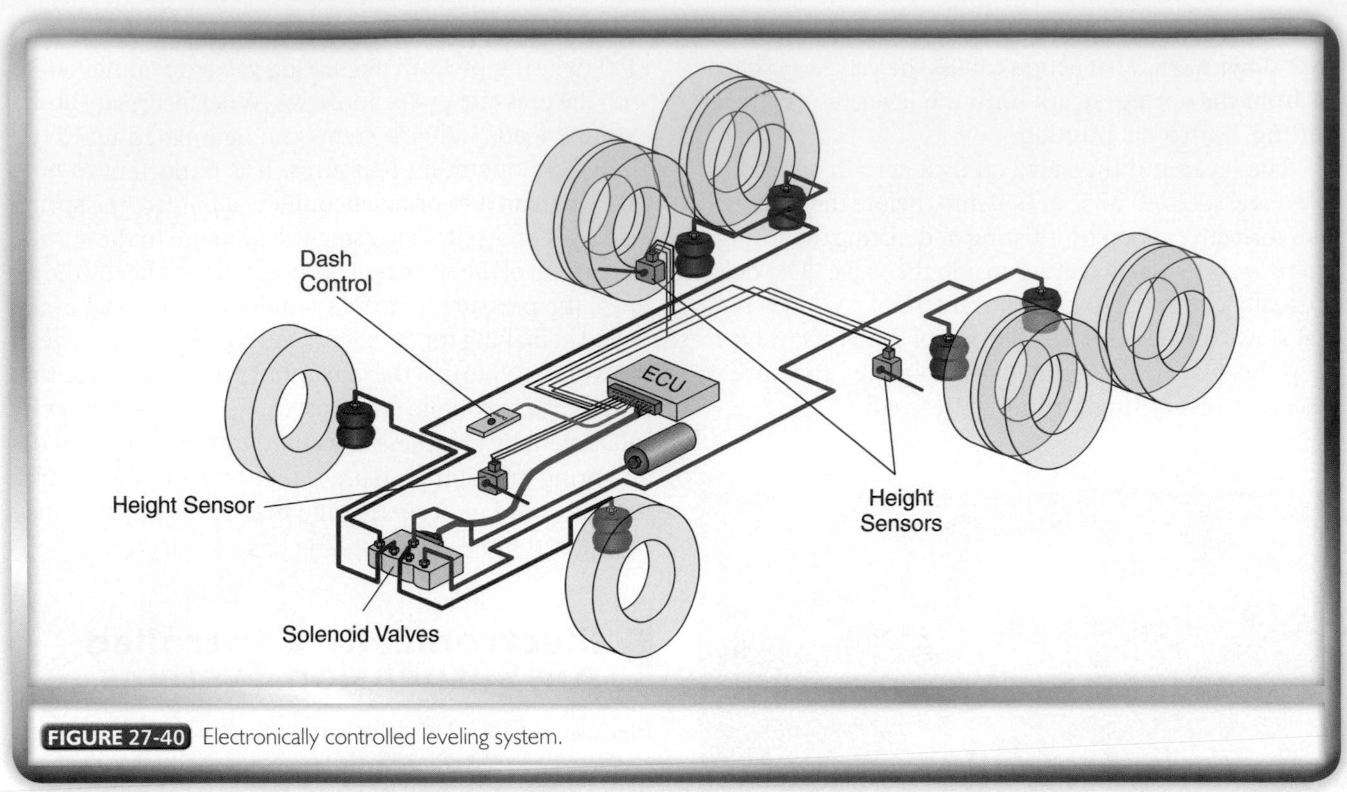

FIGURE 27-40 Electronically controlled leveling system.

system to maintain optimal ride height whether the vehicle is loaded, unloaded, or unevenly loaded from side to side.

The system ECU uses pressure sensors to monitor the vehicle load. The sensors measure the pressure in the air springs. That data is then converted to a perceived axle load. If the vehicle is equipped with a tag or a pusher axle, that axle can be automatically lowered or raised when necessary to match the load.

The latest models of these systems integrate with the ABS and traction control systems. Under operating conditions in which there is danger of losing drive traction, the pressure in the air springs on the pusher or tag axle can be reduced by the system to give more traction to the drive axles. The makers of these systems claim that the system can lead to fuel economy savings because the system uses air more sparingly than conventional systems, therefore the air compressor does not have to be as active.

Electronically controlled air spring systems usually have other selectable features, such as automatic leveling while loading or unloading, and a selectable vehicle ride height. Depending on how the vehicle is set up, these features can be selectable at the dashboard or remotely.

Dock Walk

Dock walk is a dangerous phenomenon that can occur particularly with air spring suspension trailers or straight trucks. As the vehicle is being unloaded, typically involving a forklift, the suspension will articulate from the weight of the forklift because the wheels cannot turn when the brakes are applied. This articulation tends to cause the vehicle to move away from the loading dock very slightly with each down and up motion of the suspension. This can lead to a dangerous gap between the dock and the vehicle. Many systems have been designed to combat this problem. The most common is simply a dump valve that allows the driver to release the air from the springs while the vehicle is being unloaded, eliminating "dock walk." This sometimes leaves the rear of the vehicle too low for the fork lift, so manufacturers now have systems that release the air but mechanically hold the vehicle at the correct height. In these instances, many companies use dock levers that have a compensating loading ramp attached to the dock and that protrudes onto the trailer or vehicle body.

Kenworth Air Spring Systems

Kenworth has designed a new type of air suspension system that utilizes twin air springs at each wheel. This system has a large stabilizer bar that transfers load from one side to the other during turns and as the suspension articulates over rough terrain. The Kenworth stabilizer is similar to the stabilizer found on light-duty vehicles with coil spring suspensions. The Kenworth system also uses two large, diagonally-mounted, top-mounted torque rods to maintain axle alignment. The angle of the upper torque rods prevent squatting at the rear under acceleration. The system is modular—a single axle suspension system carries spring saddles that will accept a second axle. Kenworth's system is shown in FIGURE 27-41.

Timoney Technology

An Irish company, Timoney Technology, has teamed up with Chalmers to market a fully independent, heavy-truck, front suspension system that is currently quite successful in specialized world markets. The Timoney system utilizes coil springs and double wishbone construction, making it very similar to many automobile front suspension systems. Timoney has extensive experience in building and marketing these suspension systems for municipal fire trucks, airport service, emergency vehicles, and heavy military applications. Many North American end users are looking at these suspensions for certain applications such as large fire trucks.

The ride quality and handling characteristics of Timoney suspensions is immediately apparent and noticeably better than their solid I-beam counterparts. These systems are generally quite a bit more expensive that the conventional single I-beam systems commonly used today. In a price-conscious field such as trucking, the higher price tag is slowing widespread acceptance. It remains to be seen whether Timoney will make a large impact in the marketplace with this axle.

Timoney is not the only manufacturer to produce independent front suspensions. Several manufacturers such as ZF, Meritor, and Hendrickson also manufacture independent front suspensions like that shown in FIGURE 27-42. These axles use a double-wishbone and coil-spring design. The Meritor model is also a front-wheel-drive axle. Currently Meritor markets its axle only for military equipment. Its superior ride and handling capabilities in off-road and rough terrain make it an excellent choice for those applications. Hendrickson markets its independent front suspension to the military and heavy motor-home markets.

Suspension System Inspection and Maintenance

Most of today's truck suspension systems use rubber mounting bushings, which require very little maintenance. However, all suspension systems should be thoroughly inspected for signs of damage and wear. Some systems, for example those using bronze and steel pin bushings, do require period lubrication of bushing and hangers. This section provides a brief overview of suspension inspection procedures and recommended suspension service. In no way should it be considered a complete listing of inspection and service procedures. Always check the individual manufacturer's service manual for a comprehensive list of service procedures for the vehicle being inspected.

The most common problem in suspension systems is play or looseness of the parts. Although many of the parts are designed with special connections that allow for movement (for example, to accommodate movement of the wheels), excessive play is actually a bad thing. Excessive play magnifies the feel of road imperfections and makes the steering less responsive to steering wheel input. Excessive play is potentially very damaging. It causes wear on the connecting parts and tires. Naturally, any amount of play in a fixed part is problematic and is frequently a result of part failure. Remember, unwanted looseness in the suspension system can be extremely dangerous and should be corrected as soon as possible. In some cases, the vehicle should not be driven until the vehicle has been repaired. Repair of excessive play typically means replacement of the loose part(s).

FIGURE 27-41 Kenworth's proprietary combination air leaf spring suspension for tractor drive axles.

FIGURE 27-42 ZF independent front suspension system.

Out-of-Service Criteria for Suspension Systems

The Commercial Vehicle Safety Alliance (CVSA) is a North American organization that sets out-of-service criteria for commercial vehicles in concert with all vehicle stakeholders and enforcement agencies. The criteria apply to drivers' licensing qualifications, hours of work, and medical conditions, as well as the physical condition of the vehicle.

According to the CVSA, the vehicle shall be rendered out of service if any of the following defects are present on the vehicle's suspension system at the time of inspection and the vehicle shall not be put back into service until the defects are repaired.

- Any U-bolts or other spring-to-axle clamping bolts missing, cracked, or broken
- Any axle positioning components, axle housing, axle, or spring hanger is missing, cracked loose, or broken allowing the axle position to shift
- Any leaf spring with 25% or more of the leaves cracked or broken
- Any leaf spring with a main leaf broken; a main leaf extends to the load bearing components attached to the frame (hangers or equalizers) or to the spring eye
- Any leaf spring with a separated or missing leaf or portion thereof
- Any spring with a broken torque or radius rod leaf
- Any broken coil spring
- Any missing rubber spring
- Any spring leaf displaced in such a manner that it could come in contact with the frame, rim, brake drum, or the tire
- Any deflated air spring or springs
- Any broken or cracked torsion bar on torsion bar suspensions
- Any fiber composite spring with intersecting cracks (a crack 90 degrees to the spring length)
- Any crack that extends more than ¾ of the spring length viewed from the side or the top, as illustrated in FIGURE 27-43
- Any torque or radius rod associated with axle alignment or their mounting brackets that is missing, broken, cracked, or loose and any missing bushing in torque rods, sway bars, or track rods
- Any adjustable (sliding) axle sub-frame with more than 25% of the attaching pins missing or not engaged

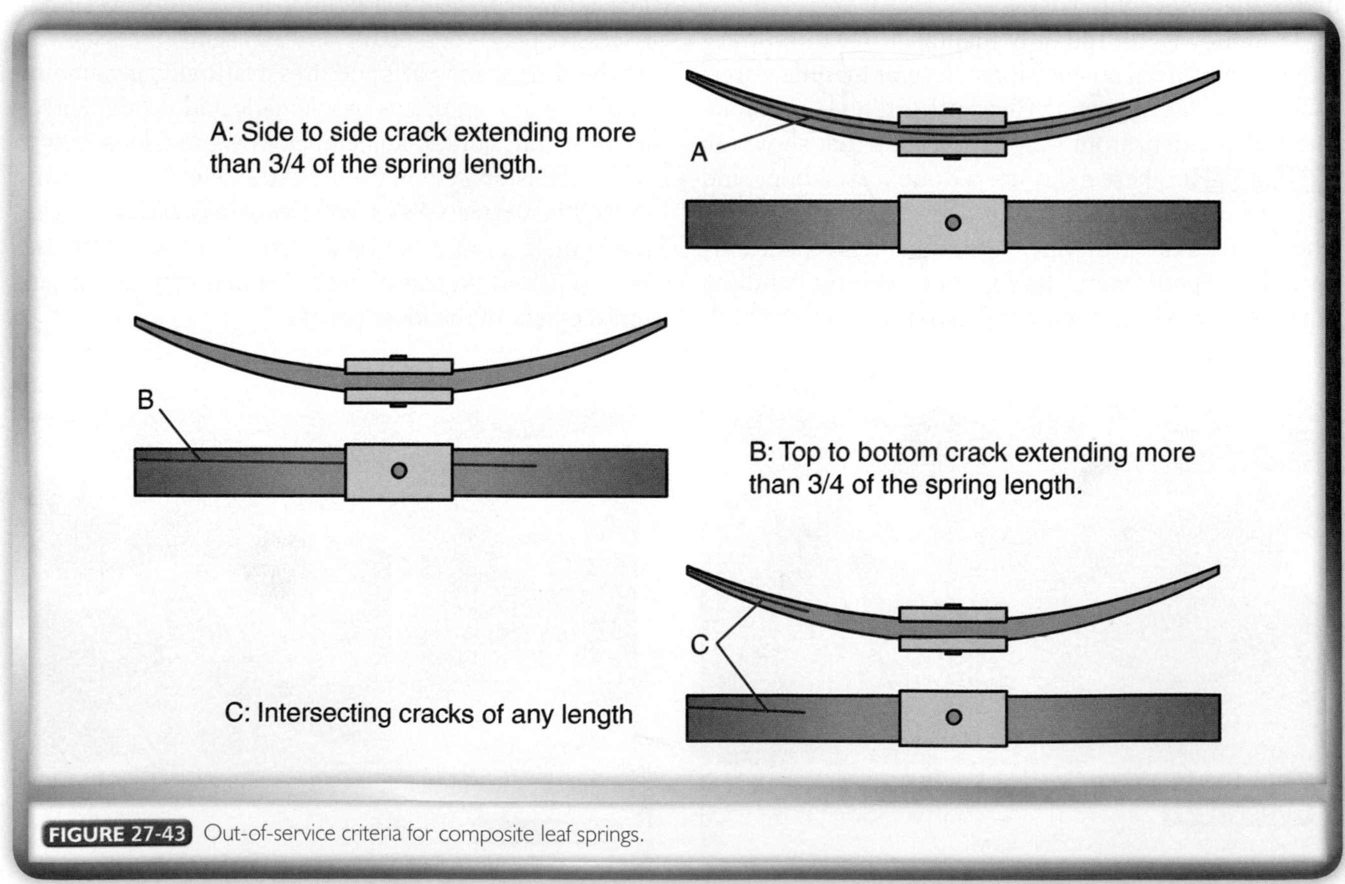
A: Side to side crack extending more than 3/4 of the spring length.
A
B
B: Top to bottom crack extending more than 3/4 of the spring length.
C
C: Intersecting cracks of any length

FIGURE 27-43 Out-of-service criteria for composite leaf springs.

There may be other out-of-service criteria enforced in certain jurisdictions.

The above list of out-of-service criteria is not meant to be a standard for vehicle maintenance targets and should in no way be construed as a measure of vehicle suitability for safe operation.

Safety

In addition to the aforementioned out-of-service criteria, it is incumbent upon authorized inspection personnel to declare any vehicle out-of-service if the loading or operation of said vehicle is, in their opinion, likely to lead to an accident or breakdown.

Inspecting the Suspension System

Before beginning any inspection, familiarize yourself with basic safety and procedural practices, such as the following:

- Manufacturers recommend that any fasteners that are removed during suspension servicing be replaced with fasteners of the same grade and sizing. Used fasteners should be discarded. **No suspension fasteners should be reused for any reason.**
- Before performing any service on suspension systems, the technician should have a good understanding of the system. Disconnecting suspension components when the system is under load can lead to severe injury or death from sudden release of spring tension or collapse of the vehicle support. **Only authorized, knowledgeable technicians should perform suspension service.**
- Never use a cutting torch or heat when removing suspension fasteners or components. Use of heat will alter the strength of the components and could lead to eventual failure, causing loss of vehicle control. Seized components can be removed by obtaining the correct tool for the job at hand.

Inspecting Leaf Spring Systems

Before a new vehicle is put into service for the first time, a leaf spring suspension system should be inspected. To inspect leaf spring suspensions, follow the steps in SKILL DRILL 27-1.

Conducting an In-Service Inspection of a Suspension System

In-service inspection should be carried out on a regular basis but, at minimum, once a year. Technicians should be on the lookout for deep scratches and/or gouges that can form stress risers and lead to spring leaf breakage. (Spring leaf breakage on a monoleaf spring will lead to loss of vehicle control.) Technicians should also look carefully for excessive abrasive wear on the individual leaves and spring packs. Follow the steps in SKILL DRILL 27-2 to conduct an in-service inspection.

SKILL DRILL 27-1 Inspecting a Leaf Spring System

1. Inspect the entire system for broken or missing components such as fasteners, bushings, spring clamps, or clips.
2. Inspect for proper spring alignment in the hangers and for suspension interference with the vehicle frame, attachments, or brake components.
3. Check and re-torque frame hangers, springs, and shock absorber mounting hardware. Most late model frames are using "Huck" brand fasteners at the frame hangers. Inspect Huck bolt fasteners for looseness. (Recall from the Heavy-Duty Truck Frames chapter that Huck bolt fasteners cannot be re-torqued by traditional methods.)
4. Check for rust streaking from the frame hanger. Streaks can indicate movement between the hanger and frame. If rust streaking is found, investigate further to find the loose fasteners.

SKILL DRILL 27-2 Performing an In-Service Inspection of a Suspension System

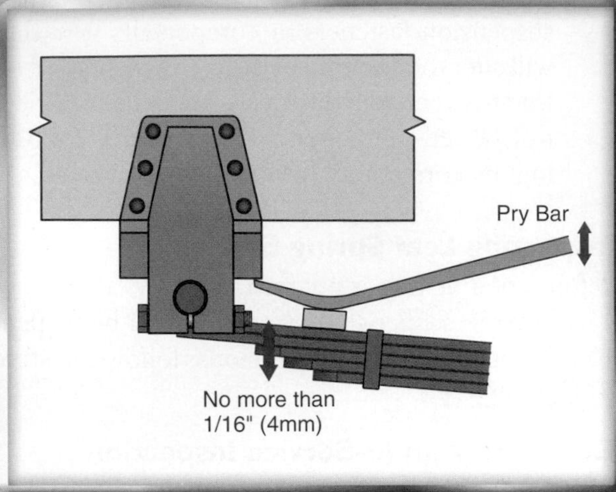

1. Check the leaf springs for missing or cracked leaves.
2. Check for deep gouges or scratches in the leaves, particularly in monoleaf springs.
3. Inspect parabolic leaf springs for missing inter-leaf spacers and/or anti-friction pads.
4. Check the spring leaves for abrasive wear. Replace any spring that shows excessive abrasive wear. Replace the individual leaves or the entire spring pack per manufacturer's recommendations.
5. Check the spring mounting fasteners, top plates, axle pads, and axle spacers for cracks and/or looseness.
6. Re-torque mounting U-bolts and hardware to specification following the pattern shown. (Most suspension manufacturers recommend that leaf spring mounting U-bolts and hardware torque be re-checked every 20,000 miles (32,000 km).) Springs should be under load while U-bolts are torqued. Failure to tighten in this order can lead to failure of the U-bolt.
7. Check spring hangers for spring alignment and signs of side rubbing in the hangers; this could indicate worn mounting bushings.
8. Use a pry bar (as shown) to check steel pin and bronze spring mounting bushings for wear and movement. Excessive movement (greater than 1/16" or 4 mm) usually requires bushing replacement, but check manufacturers specification.
9. Determine if bronze and steel pin bushings require lubrication. They should be lubricated as part of the vehicle's regular oil change and lube schedule. Check for looseness before lubricating the bushing.
10. Check rubber spring mounting bushings for any free movement. Bushings are made of rubber encased by inner and outer steel sleeves. The spring will move slightly when a pry bar is used. Any bushing that allows the spring to move freely at all should be replaced.
11. Check that the inner and outer metal sleeves of the bushing are not in contact with each other. If they are, replace the bushing.
12. Check the rubber of the bushings for end shredding, which results from excessive movement.
13. To replace shredded bushings, push the bushing out using a press. Remove the spring. Press a new bushing into place. Special tools are available to remove and insert bushings while the spring is still attached to the axle.
14. Check the rear spring shackle on front suspensions for any sideways movement or looseness of the spring or shackle at the mounting points on the frame and at the spring. There should be no perceptible movement.
15. Check unusual tire wear on the vehicle. River wear and/or cupping can indicate suspension problems (wandering and wheel hop). If the tire balance is correct, carefully examine the suspension system to determine the cause.
16. Check spring hanger slipper pads for excessive wear. Wear at the slipper pads is normal. Replace only when wear is excessive.
17. Check the insides of the spring hanger legs. Abrasive wear indicates the spring is not aligned properly or is loose in its mounting bushing. The spring should not contact the inside of the hanger legs in normal operation.
18. Visually inspect shock absorbers for oil leaks, damaged rubber bushings, and broken mounts. Drive the vehicle 50 miles (80 km) or more. The shock absorber should be warm to the touch. A cold shock absorber is not working properly.

Unloading a Suspension for Measuring Play

Play in the suspension system can be damaging to other components or can be a major safety hazard on the road. Testing for play requires the proper technique for the results to be accurate. For play to be measured, the joint must be unloaded. This means the joint cannot be under compression or tension forces. In the case of suspension ball joints, the joint cannot be supporting the weight of the vehicle or the force from the vehicle spring when measuring the play. Some suspension inspections need to conducted with an unloaded suspension system. Check the service manual if you are unsure.

Removing and Replacing Front Spring Components

To remove and replace front spring components, follow the guidelines in SKILL DRILL 27-3.

Inspecting Rear Spring Suspension Components

To inspect rear spring suspension components, follow the guidelines in SKILL DRILL 27-4.

Inspecting Equalizer Beam Suspension Systems

Equalizer beams in suspension systems are subjected to extreme compression load on the top of the beam and equally extreme tension loads on the bottom of the beam. Failure of the beam can lead to loss of vehicle control and catastrophic accidents and damage. Therefore, careful inspection of the beams themselves is a crucial part of suspension maintenance procedures.

There have been numerous failures of equalizer beams from deep gouges or scratches caused by road, or accident damage.These scratches and gouges cause stress risers which concentrate the tension forces at the scratch or gouge on the lower beam surface leading to cracking or complete breakage. Beams that exhibit heavy gouging or scratches should be replaced.

Safety

Never try to repair a cracked, gouged, or deeply scratched equalizer beam by welding the crack or building up the scratch or gouge. The heat can detrimentally affect the beam strength leading to catastrophic failure. Replace beams that are damaged.

Longitudinal and transverse torque rods should be inspected for damage from impacts. Bent or badly damaged rods should be replaced. Check the rod end mounting bushings for looseness—no excessive movement is allowed. Torque rod bushings can be either a straddle mount or tapered stud mount. Longitudinal torque rod bushings can be checked for movement by hand using a pry bar or may be checked with the suspension loaded by rocking the vehicle back and forth under power. Transverse torque rods should be checked with a pry bar. Any significant movement indicates replacement is necessary. The bushings, whether taper stud or straddle mount style, are replaced by pushing them out with a press after the torque rod is removed from the vehicle. Then a new bushing is pressed into place and the rod is re-installed. Axle alignment on equalizing beam suspensions is set by shimming the beam ends so alignment is not necessary after torque rod bushing replacement.

Inspecting Rear Beam Suspension Components

Beam suspensions may be one of two types: spring or rubber load cushions. The equalizing (walking) beams will be inspected the same way with both systems. After you identify which system you are inspecting, follow the correct procedure in the service manual. To inspect rear beam suspension components, follow the guidelines in SKILL DRILL 27-5.

Inspecting Frame Hangers

Most new rubber spring suspension systems utilize diagonally mounted rubber "bolster" springs which allow the acceleration and braking forces to be controlled by the spring and the torque rods. Older rubber spring equalizing beam suspensions use vertical drive pins in the rubber spring frame hangers that pass down through the rubber springs to the spring saddles. They are secured in the saddles by drive pin bushings. This arrangement allows the saddles to move up and down but the drive pins and bushings maintain alignment of the saddles. All acceleration, braking and cornering forces are transferred through the drive pins and bushings to the frame and therefore they require meticulous inspection.

Replacing Rubber Center Bushings

Steel and bronze equalizing beam end and center bushings are used in older applications of equalizing beam suspensions. These bushings add longevity to vehicle suspensions that are subjected to heavy loads and extremely

SKILL DRILL 27-3 Removing and Replacing Front Spring Components

1. Locate and follow the appropriate procedure in the service manual.
2. Complete the appropriate job sheet or work order with all pertinent information.
3. Chock the rear wheels, set the parking brake, and remove the ignition key.
4. Jack up the front of the vehicle and support the frame (not the axle) with axle stands. The frame should be high enough to lift the front wheels 1" to 2" (25 to 50 mm) from the floor.
5. Support the front axle with a floor jack.
6. Disconnect shock absorber from lower mount. Check the condition of the shock by stroking the shock both directions. In most cases, you will want to install new shock absorbers during a spring or spring pin replacement.
7. Remove U-bolts from spring assembly. Note: If U-bolts are extremely rusted, they will be very difficult to remove. Since they must be replaced, it may be faster, and in the long run cheaper for the customer, to cut the U-bolt with a cutting torch.
8. Remove the pinch bolts and drive the pins out of the rear shackle assembly.
9. Remove the front spring eye pins. Remember, these pins may be threaded type, requiring you to screw them out of the spring bushing. Refer to manufacturer's service manual.
10. Note the position of the caster shim and record it on the job sheet or work order. (Thick edge to front or rear?) Note: The thick edge is usually to the rear.
11. Lower the front axle and remove the spring assembly from the vehicle.
12. Record the following information on the job sheet or work order:
    - Vehicle make
    - Vehicle year and model
    - Front axle capacity (axle weight ratings may be found on the VIN label, usually located inside the driver's door frame)
    - Spring width
    - Number of leaves
    - Pad thickness
    - Length (long end and short end)

    Note: Refer to manufacturer's parts book and/or spring manufacturer's catalog to make sure you obtain the correct parts.
13. Replace spring assembly with correct part for the application.
    - Clean the axle seat and locating dowel hole.
    - Remove and install bushings with a suitable bushing driver. Note: Some spring bushings must be welded in place. Refer to the service manual for detailed instructions.
    - Install new pins and secure with pinch bolts. Now is a good time to lubricate the pins. Since there is no weight on them, grease will flow around the entire surface of the pin.
14. Position the caster shim and spacers in their original position.
15. Raise the front axle and install the top plate and U-bolts.
16. Remove the jack stands and lower the vehicle to the floor.
17. Torque the pinch bolts, U-bolts, and shock bolt to specifications. Record the recommended torques on the job sheet or work order.
    - U-bolts (diameter and torque)
    - Pinch bolts (diameter and torque)
    - Shock mounts (diameter and torque)
18. List the test results and recommendations on the job sheet or work order, clean the work area, and return tools and materials to their proper storage.

SKILL DRILL 27-4 Inspecting Rear Spring Suspension Components

1. Locate and follow the appropriate procedure in the service manual.
2. Complete the accompanying job sheet or work order with all pertinent information.
3. Chock the front wheels, release the parking brakes (must have at least 100 psi in air brake reservoirs), and remove the ignition key.
4. Inspect U-bolts for corrosion, missing nuts or washers, and the correct location in the spring saddle. Torque the nuts to the manufacturer's specifications. Important: U-bolts should be torqued with the weight of the vehicle resting on the springs.
5. Record your findings about the U-bolts on the job sheet or work order. Include the following information:
   - U-bolt condition (OK, broken, or damaged)
   - Does U-bolt fit top plate correctly?
   - U-bolt diameter and thread pitch
   - Torque specifications
6. Visually inspect the rear spring assemblies. Look for broken leaves, cracks, nicks, corrosion, and missing spring clips. Sagging (worn out) springs may cause the vehicle to lean to the right or left.
7. Record your findings about the rear spring assembly on the job sheet or work order. Include the following information:
   - Spring assemblies (OK, cracked, broken, damaged, or sagging)
   - Spring clips (OK, missing, or damaged)
8. Visually inspect shock absorbers. Look for oil leaks, damaged rubber bushings, and broken mounts. If the vehicle has just been driven (50 miles (80 km) or more), the shock absorber should be warm to the touch. A cold shock absorber is not working properly.
9. Record your findings about the shock absorbers on the job sheet or work order. Include the following information:
   - Shock absorbers (OK or leaking)
   - Rubber mounts (OK, damaged, or missing)
10. Inspect the torque arms or torque leaves and bushings. Remember, torque arms have bushings on both ends. Worn bushings can be detected by prying on the torque arm or leaf; there should be very little looseness.
11. Record your findings on the job sheet or work order. Include the following information:
    - Torque arms (OK, missing, or damaged)
    - Torque leaves (OK, broken, or center bolt sheared)
    - Bushings (OK, worn out, or missing or loose bolts)
12. Inspect the spring mounts. Jack up the rear of the vehicle and support the frame with axle stands. Visually inspect the front and rear hanger spring cam surfaces. Use a pry bar to check the equalizer bushing; it should have very little looseness. Check equalizer slipper pads for excessive wear. Check the frame hanger mounting bolts.
13. Record your findings on the job sheet or work order. Include the following information:
    - Front hanger (OK, broken, damaged, or loose or missing bolts)
    - Center hanger (OK, broken, damaged, or loose or missing bolts)
    - Equalizing arm (OK, broken, damaged, bushing worn out, or slipper pads worn)
    - Rear hanger (OK, broken, damaged, or loose or missing bolts)
14. Make replacements on required components as approved. Record findings on job sheet or work order.
    - Replace damaged U-bolts with new grade 8 U-bolts, hardened washers, and deep nuts. Use anti-seize compound to coat the threads.
    - Spring assemblies and shock absorbers should always be replaced in pairs.
15. List the test results and/or recommendations on the job sheet or work order, clean the work area, and return tools and materials to their proper storage.

SKILL DRILL 27-5 Inspecting Rear Beam Suspension Components

1. Locate and follow the appropriate procedure in the service manual.
2. Complete the accompanying job sheet or work order with all pertinent information.
3. Remove all grease and dirt from suspension area using a high pressure washer.
4. Park vehicle on a level surface, chock the front wheels, and remove the ignition key.
5. Identify whether suspension is spring type (a) or rubber cushion type (b), then follow the corresponding instructions below.
   - **a.** If the suspension is a spring type, inspect the spring hanger, forward spring hanger pin, and spring eye bushings for excessive wear or damaged parts.
   - **b.** If the suspension is a rubber cushion type, visually inspect the rubber pads or cushions for cuts or damage.

     Note: The load cushions are made of butyl and natural rubber and are not resistant to petroleum products. If the cushions become saturated with these products, they will split and disintegrate.
6. On rubber spring suspensions with frame mounted drive pins, check all the frame hangers for cracks, paying particular attention to the drive pin hangers. These will usually appear between bolt holes or from a bolt hole to the edge of the hanger bracket as shown.
7. Check carefully for signs of rust emanating from the rubber spring mounting area or from the drive pins and bushings. Rust streaks can indicate cracks or movement between components.
8. Using a jack, raise the frame slightly. If the drive pin or hanger bracket is cracked through, it will separate and it can be easily detected during this check.

   Note: Issues with any of the items checked in steps 5–8 will require hanger replacement.
9. Inspect equalizer beam for cracks, gouges, or other damage.
10. With the vehicle loaded, check the equalizing beam rubber end bushings. The bushings are under compression on the top side. The bottom of the rubber is relaxed, so the ends of the rubber will show a gap in the mounting bracket. This is normal.
11. Check the bushings for wear by placing a small jack under the beam end. Place a soft material between the beam and the jack to protect the beam from scratches. Try to raise the beam. If the inner sleeve of the bushing moves, the bushing must be replaced. Remember that the bushing is rubber mounted. Compression of the rubber is expected, but the inner sleeve should not move. Check rubber center bushings by placing a jack under the saddle cap of the beam. If the saddle raises 1/8" (3.1 mm) before the beam is raised, the bushing is worn and must be replaced.
12. Check torque on all attaching hardware according to manufacturer's recommendations.
13. List the test results and recommendations on the job sheet or work order, clean the work area, and return tools and materials to their proper storage.

tight turning situations. These conditions can wear out rubber bushings quickly. Steel and bronze bushings must be lubricated on a regular basis during the normal vehicle oil and lube schedules. These bushing are checked in the same way as rubber beam bushings, but note that there is no rubber in these bushings so all movement is wear.

Rubber center bushings allow lateral movement of up to 3" (7.5 cm) on turns. Excessive lateral movement will allow the inside of the vehicle rear tires to contact the frame. Any contact between the inside of the tire sidewalls and the frame or suspension is another indication that the rubber center bushings must be replaced. To replace rubber center bushings, follow the procedure found in the vehicle service manual.

Inspecting and Maintaining Air Spring Systems

Air spring systems usually require very little maintenance other than visual inspection, although ride height may need to be checked and adjusted from time to time. Before a new vehicle is put into service for the first time, air spring suspension systems should be inspected following the steps in SKILL DRILL 27-6.

Inspecting and Maintaining Shock Absorbers

Not all truck suspensions use shock absorbers, but shocks are becoming commonplace in most new trucks. Shock absorbers are essential for air spring suspensions which do not have any self-dampening capabilities. Unfortunately, shocks are quite often overlooked by service personnel as a maintenance item.

The Maintenance Council (TMC) has established recommended practice RP 643 which suggests that fleets include shock absorber replacement as part of a regular maintenance schedule. The reason is that, during operation, a shock absorber will lose some of its fluid due to normal misting. Oil leaks around the top seal are by design to help lubricate the shock push rod. Over time, the shock's dampening capability is reduced.

When is the right time to change a shock? On a vehicle that has travelled 150,000 miles (240,000 km), the shock absorbers have stroked approximately 30,000,000 times! Rational thought dictates that they be replaced after such extensive use.

However, there are even more compelling reasons to pay attention to shock replacement. Shock absorbers are responsible for stopping excess spring oscillation, wheel hop, and irregular tire wear. Shocks are also responsible for increasing vehicle stability. Unusual tire wear, such as river wear and tire-cupping wear, are becoming increasingly prevalent in on-highway applications. This type of wear can be caused by tires that are out of balance, but frequently this wear is attributed to worn shock absorbers on air spring suspension systems.

Newer air spring suspensions allow movement between jounce and rebound of as much as 13" (33 cm). Older leaf spring suspensions allowed movement of 3" (7.6 cm) or less. When the shocks get weak, their ability to control oscillation and stop wheel hop is diminished, which leads to the unusual tire wear. This type of wear can more than halve the life of a tire's tread. Unfortunately, this type of wear shows up rather slowly, and once it is discovered, even changing the shocks will not extend the tire's life. That is because the wear pattern is self-propagating. That is, the tire will continue to wear the same way once the wear pattern has been established. The discovery of this type of wear has led to the recommendation that shocks be changed at the same time as the tires. The relatively low cost of a set of shock absorbers is a small price to pay to protect the large investment in a set of new tires—especially if this wear cannot be traced to tires being out of balance.

Nonetheless, in-service shock absorbers should be checked following the steps in SKILL DRILL 27-7 every 25,000 miles (40,000 km) or at least once a year.

Servicing the Suspension System

Although most heavy suspension work these days is performed by specialty shops with specialized equipment and tooling, there are a couple of procedures that the technician should be familiar with—namely air spring ride height adjustment and the principles of rear axle and rear tandem axle alignment.

Adjusting the Ride Height

The height-control valve, or leveling valve, is the brains of the air spring control system; inflating and deflating the

SKILL DRILL 27-6 Inspecting and Maintaining Air Spring Systems

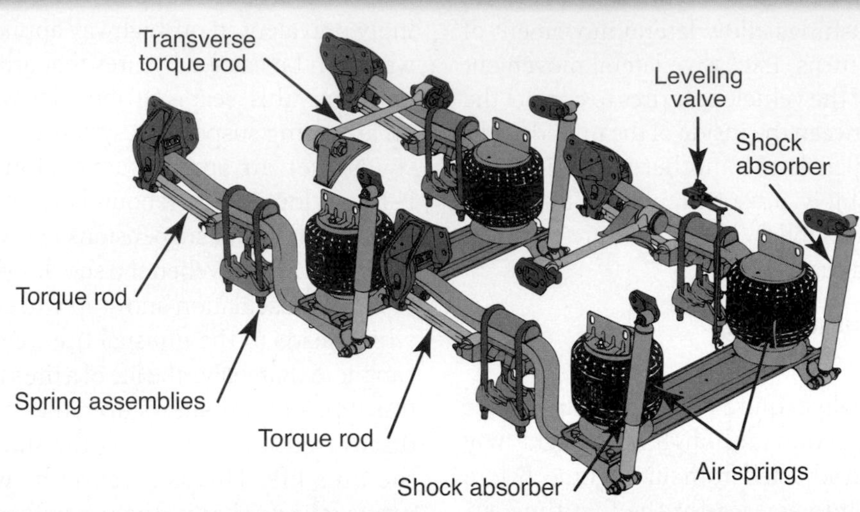

1. Inspect the entire system for broken or missing components such as fasteners and bushings.
2. Check the air system hoses and valves for proper routing, mounting, and connections.
3. Air spring system stroke from jounce to rebound can be much longer than other suspensions, so inspect very carefully for suspension interference with the vehicle frame or attachments and brake components. Pay particular attention to the air springs themselves for abrasion. Air springs will fail rapidly if they are chaffing.
4. Check and re-torque frame hangers, air spring, and shock absorber mounting hardware. Inspect Huck fasteners for looseness. Check for rust streaking from the frame hanger. Streaks can indicate movement between the hanger and frame. If rust streaking is found, further investigation is necessary to find the loose fastener.
5. Check and re-torque all suspension attaching bolts, pivot bolts, and torque rod bushing bolts.
6. Check air beam-to-axle mounting components for torque and alignment.
7. Inspect all welded connections on axles, including torque-rod brackets and frame-hanger brackets on trailer suspensions.
8. Inflate the suspension to at least 75 psi (517 kPa) and check for any air leaks in lines, connections, valves, and the air springs themselves using a bubble mixture if necessary.
9. Inspect the cross tube or channel connections for fastener torque. Check for any unusual signs of looseness, rust streaking, or metal shavings.
10. Check the height-control valve for secure air connections and proper mounting. Check the height-control linkage for damage for impact or abuse (for example, bent or broken linkage and interference with surrounding components).
11. Check the support beam (Z-spring or trailing arm) for dents, heavy scratches, or gouges and/or signs of interference with other components.
12. Check the mounting bushings and brackets for any sign of side wear or abrasion from metal-to-metal contact.
13. Check the fasteners on all torque-rod bushings for proper torque. Check the bushings for rubber shredding, metal-to-metal contact, or excessive movement. No free movement is allowed.
14. Replace the bushings if any of the preceding conditions exist.
15. Check all suspension components for impact damage, dents, bending, or heavy scratches or gouging. All damaged components should be replaced.

Safety

Before disconnecting ANY air components on an air spring suspension system (i.e., air lines, valves, air springs), it is essential that the air spring system be completely deflated or serious injury could results from explosive release of pressure and or collapse of the suspension.

SKILL DRILL 27-7 Inspecting and Maintaining Shock Absorbers

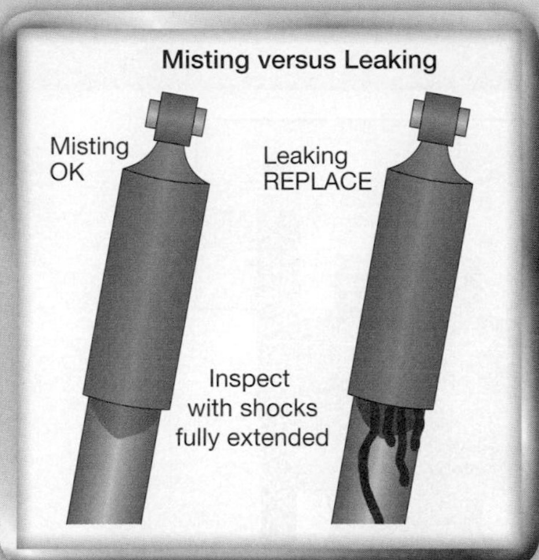

1. Check the shock mounting fasteners for correct torque. Check mounting brackets for cracked welds and metal-to-metal contact caused by worn bushings. Replace the shock if the bushing allows free movement.

2. Check the shocks for dents or bends caused by road impact. Damage to the shock casing can cause internal or external chaffing, or it may stop the shock from working altogether. Replace shocks displaying this kind of damage.

3. Check shocks for leaking fluid. Misting of oil on the inside of the dust cover and the push rod is normal and necessary for seal and rod lubrication. Any dripping fluid, however, indicates a failed shock that should be replaced. Suspect shocks can be checked using the heat method after a 15-minute road test. If the shock is working correctly, the action of the shock will cause the fluid to heat up. A weak or defective shock will stay relatively cool. If a shock on the same axle is cooler than its mate, the pair should be replaced.

Safety

Some shock absorbers are the rebound stops for air spring suspensions. Before removing the shock, ensure that the air spring is contained by the vehicle weight or that the suspension is completely deflated or serious injury and/or damage to the air spring could result.

Safety

Shocks that are heavily worked can have fluid temperatures up to 350°F (177°C). Exercise caution or use an infrared thermometer to check the temperature of the shock.

air springs as necessary to maintain vehicle ride height. The valve has an internal delay mechanism so that correction to height does not take place during normal spring oscillation.

The ride height of a vehicle can only be measured if it has matching tires, which are properly inflated, and no additional weight in the vehicle. Once these issues are taken care of, the ride height can be measured as specified by the service information. If the measured ride height is greater or less than specified, the vehicle is not in correct alignment and may be causing or contributing to the customer's concern. The use of a measuring tape from a fixed point on the frame or body of the vehicle to the component in question can help determine the cause of improper ride height. If the ride height issue is related to the air bag, then replacement of the air bag(s) may be necessary.

Follow all safety procedures outlined in the service manual. The inspection and adjustment should be performed on an unloaded vehicle. To inspect and test an air suspension system and replace the levelling valve, follow the guidelines in SKILL DRILL 27-8. If the ride height needs to be adjusted, follow the guidelines in SKILL DRILL 27-9.

Adjusting and Aligning Axles

When a vehicle requires an alignment, either front end or rear, the best course of action is to use one of the commercially available electronic alignment machines that use laser sighted electronic heads mounted at the front and rear of the vehicle. These ensure that each of the axles is perpendicular to the vehicle frame and in exact alignment. It is possible, however, to perform rear axle alignment in the shop with minimal equipment. (Front

SKILL DRILL 27-8 Inspecting and Testing an Air Suspension System and Replacing the Levelling Valve

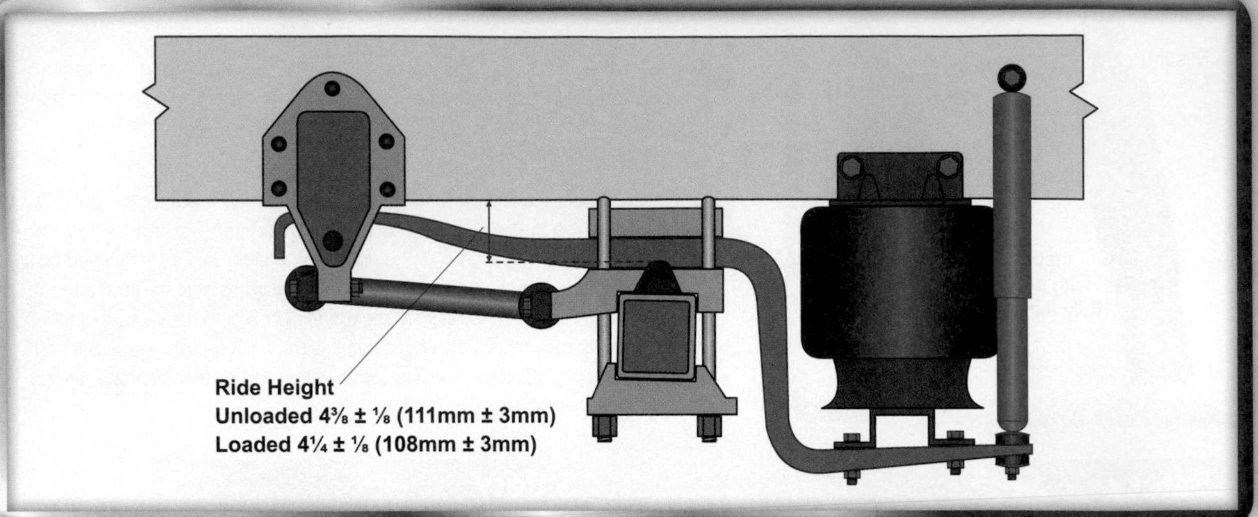

Note: The following procedure is typical, however, it is general in nature only. It is essential that you check the service manual for your particular vehicle for the correct procedure.

1. Locate and follow the appropriate procedure in the service manual.
2. Complete the accompanying job sheet or work order with all pertinent information.
3. Move vehicle to level floor area.
4. Free and center all suspension joints by slowly moving the vehicle back and forth several times without using the brakes. When coming to a complete stop, make sure the brakes are released.
5. With air system pressure at 100 psi (690 kPa), remove ignition key and chock the front wheels.
6. Inspect lines, fittings, and valves for looseness and damage.
7. Test lines, fittings, and valves for air leaks using soapy water.
8. Purge the air pressure from the suspension system system, mark the air lines for proper locations, and then remove the air lines from the leveling valve.
9. Remove the levelling valve link from the valve by removing the nut and washer. Procedures differ, so use the correct manufacturer's service manual for instructions.
10. Remove locknuts, washers, and bolts that connect the levelling valve to the frame.
11. Remove brass air fittings from the levelling valve.
12. Install brass air fitting into the new levelling valve.
13. Assemble bolts, washers, and locknuts that connect the valve to the frame.
14. Connect air lines to the levelling valve. (Making sure the air lines are in the correct locations.)
15. Assemble levelling valve threaded extension rod to levelling valve and assemble lock washer and nut.
16. Air up the system and release the parking brakes.
17. Check the ride height as recommended in the service manual to specification, as shown in the diagram. This system checks ride height between the bottom of the frame and the lower edge of the Z spring (main support member).
18. If the specification is correct, no further action is required. If it is not correct, proceed with Skill Drill 27-9.

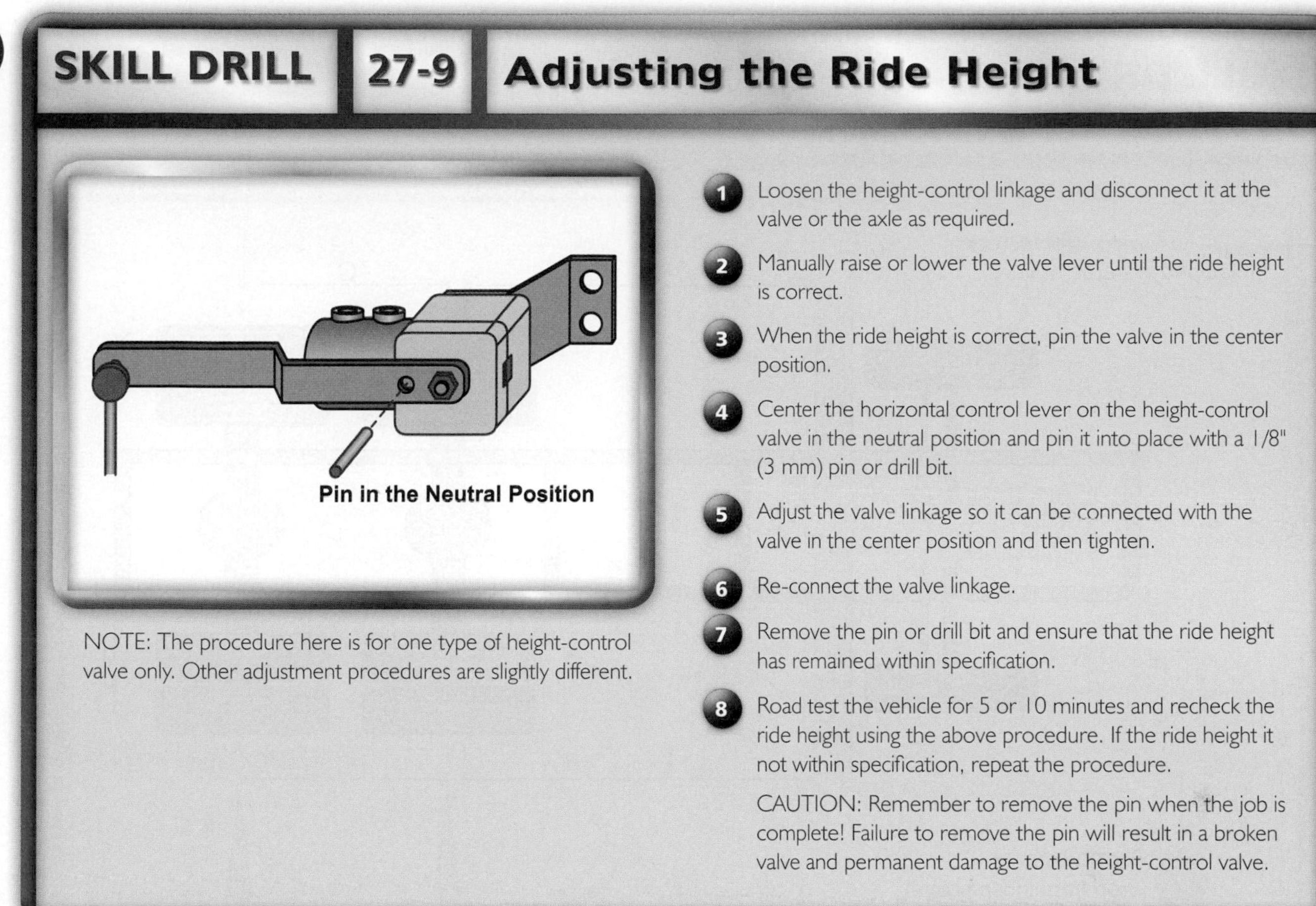

SKILL DRILL 27-9 Adjusting the Ride Height

NOTE: The procedure here is for one type of height-control valve only. Other adjustment procedures are slightly different.

1. Loosen the height-control linkage and disconnect it at the valve or the axle as required.
2. Manually raise or lower the valve lever until the ride height is correct.
3. When the ride height is correct, pin the valve in the center position.
4. Center the horizontal control lever on the height-control valve in the neutral position and pin it into place with a 1/8" (3 mm) pin or drill bit.
5. Adjust the valve linkage so it can be connected with the valve in the center position and then tighten.
6. Re-connect the valve linkage.
7. Remove the pin or drill bit and ensure that the ride height has remained within specification.
8. Road test the vehicle for 5 or 10 minutes and recheck the ride height using the above procedure. If the ride height it not within specification, repeat the procedure.

   CAUTION: Remember to remove the pin when the job is complete! Failure to remove the pin will result in a broken valve and permanent damage to the height-control valve.

axle alignment is covered in the Introduction to Front Axles and Vehicle Alignment Factors chapter and will not be discussed here.) Always consult the manufacturers' manual for the particular suspension being worked on. A general procedure for rear axle alignment is given in SKILL DRILL 27-10. A general procedure for adjusting the axles is given in SKILL DRILL 27-11. It is important to note that an axle out of alignment by ½" (12.6 mm) can decrease tire life by over 24%. In addition, that small of a difference will decrease fuel economy because of the energy required to overcome the side thrust and the increased rolling resistance.

SKILL DRILL 27-10 Aligning Axles

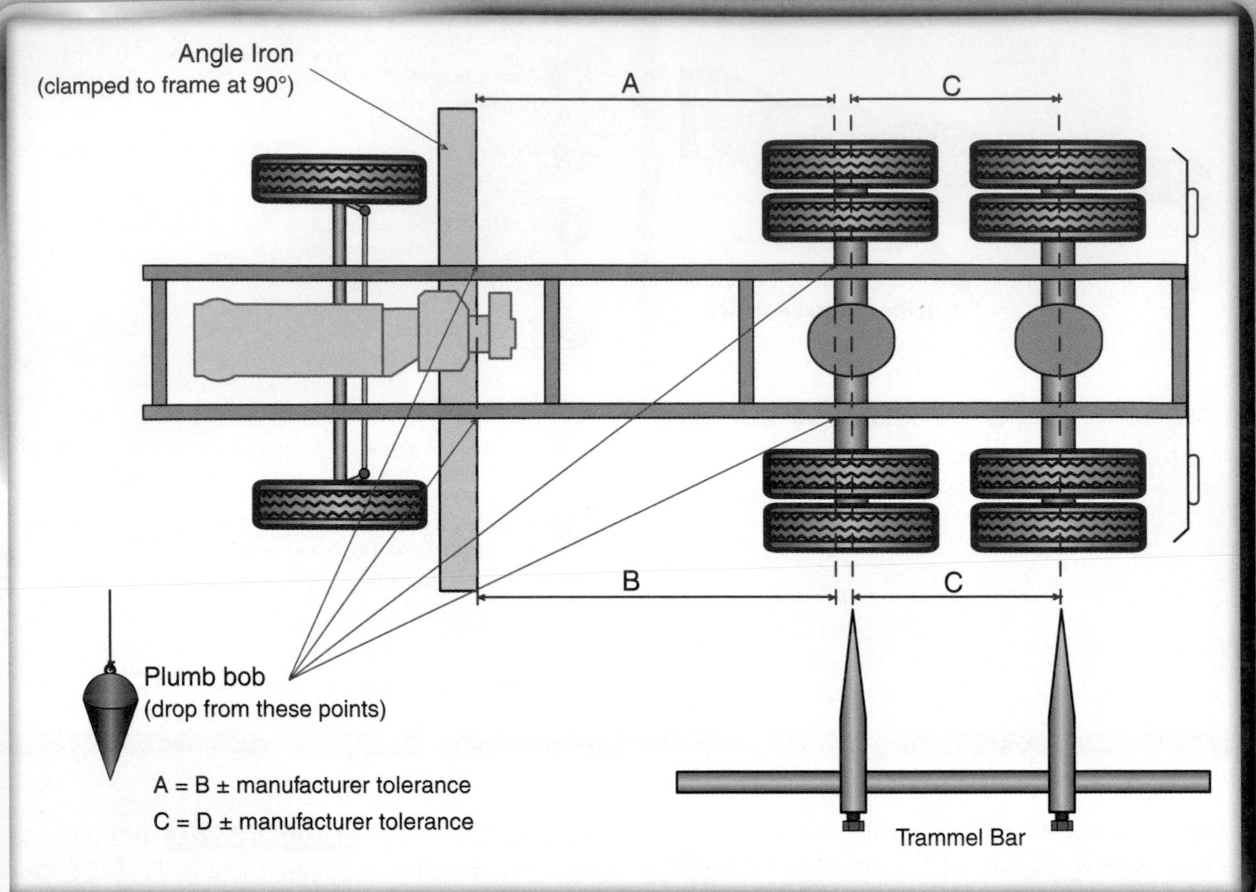

1. Park the vehicle on a level floor. Do not apply the parking brakes. Roll the vehicle backward and forward by hand to relieve stress on the suspension. Chock the front wheels to keep minimal load on the rear axle(s). Check and adjust tire pressures to the recommended level.

2. Lift the rear wheels with a jack and check for run-out and correct as necessary. Ensure the front wheels are in the straight-ahead position.

3. Using a framing square, clamp a long straight edge to the vehicle frame in front of the rear axles. Ensure that the straight edge is exactly 90 degrees to the frame rails.

4. Suspend a plumb bob from the outer edge of the frame at the straight edge on both sides of the vehicle. Measure the distance from plumb bob to the front rear axle on both sides (measurements A and B on the diagram). The distances should be equal to within 1/16" (1.5 mm). Compare the readings with the manufacturer's specification for the particular vehicle.

5. If the axle is a tandem, then measure the distance between the center of the front rear axle wheel and the rear wheel on the rear axle (measurements C and D in the diagram).

6. Use an adjustable trammel bar to take these measurements. This dimension should be equal to within 1/16" (1.5 mm). This specification is typical. Check the manufacturer's specification for the particular axle. If the front or rear axle needs to be adjusted, then proceed to Skill Drill 27-11.

SKILL DRILL 27-11 Adjusting Front or Rear Axles

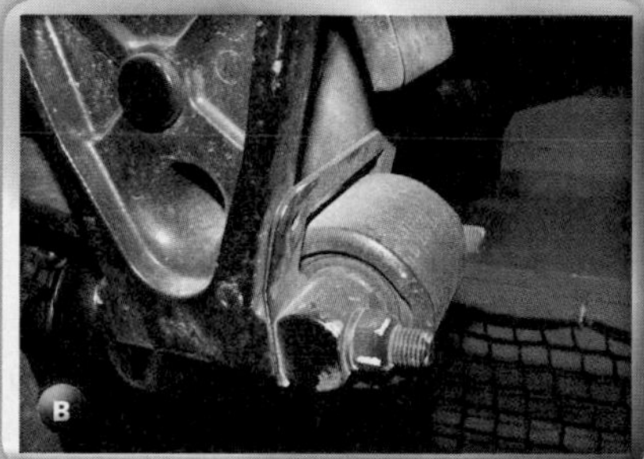

1. Determine the alignment adjustment point. This may be threaded torque rods on one side (A), shimmed torque rods on one side (B), or eccentric mounting bolts on trailing arm suspension systems (C).
2. Once the correct method is determined, adjust the front rear axle alignment to the frame.
3. Adjust the rear rear axle to the front rear axle.

Wrap-up

Ready for Review

- Suspension systems are designed to protect the passengers, the vehicle, and the load from road shocks.
- A suspension must deal with all of the forces that act upon it and minimize the impact to vehicle operation including acceleration, braking and cornering force, and road shocks.
- A suspension must ensure that the vehicle tires remain in contact with the road.
- The suspension must support the vehicle body, the drivetrain, the load, any added accessories, and the passengers. This is known as the vehicle sprung weight.
- The unsprung weight of the vehicle refers to all the components not supported by the suspension, the wheels and tires, the axles, and the brakes. Mass of the unsprung weight can greatly affect vehicle stability, so manufacturers try to keep it as low as possible while still providing adequate braking and support.
- Jounce and rebound are the terms used to describe the suspension systems reaction to road bumps. An upward motion of the tire and wheel caused by a bump in the road is a jounce, while the opposite motion, as the tire moves back down or into a depression in the road, is known as a rebound.
- Oscillation is the uncontrolled jouncing and rebounding of a suspension. It must be dissipated by using friction between the leaves of a leaf spring or by shock absorbers to maintain adequate vehicle control.
- Suspension systems use torque rods and track rods to maintain axle alignments and to transfer braking acceleration and cornering forces to the vehicle frame in heavy-duty rear suspensions. A parallelogram design strives to keep the rear drive axle at a constant angle as these forces impact the vehicle.
- In heavy-duty suspension systems, trailing arms refer to large and very strong beams. The front of the beam attaches to the vehicle frame and the beam trails behind. The axle will be attached to the beam approximately halfway along its length and the end of the beam will have a spring medium, usually air, between the beam and the frame. The trailing arms keep the axle aligned during suspension articulation.
- Axle stops are used to prevent the axles from contacting the frame during severe jounce incidents. These rubber or nylon bumpers should not normally contact the frame. If they do, the vehicle is very much overloaded or the suspension requires service.
- In the past, some heavy vehicles relied on strong interleaf friction to dampen suspension system oscillation. Today, shock absorbers are the primary method used to dampen system oscillations. Electronic shock absorbers are built with electronically changeable orifices that can react to dampen oscillations more effectively in certain conditions.
- Spring rate refer to the distance a spring is deflected when placed under load: high spring rate refers to a spring that requires a larger load to deflect and low spring rate means the spring will deflect easier. High spring rates provide more stability, especially in turns, however the ride will be noticeably rougher. Soft or lower spring rates provide more comfort but at the expense of stability. Springs that take advantage of both softer ride and vehicle stability are known as variable rate springs
- Leaf springs come in many forms: single or monoleaf, multileaf or spring packs, taper leaf, and parabolic. Leaf springs can have a variable rate or constant rate depending on design and installation.
- Auxiliary springs are used to help support the vehicle only when fully loaded. They are typically mounted above a variable rate leaf spring but do not have any effect until the vehicle is close to its load limit. They are themselves usually variable rate.

- Equalizing arms are pivoting brackets, attached to the vehicle frame, that support the rear of the front leaf spring of the tandem and the front of the rear leaf spring of the tandem. As the front spring encounters a bump, the rear of the front spring pushes up the equalizer and it pivots, pushing the front of the rear spring down and equalizing the loads they each are carrying.
- Equalizing beam, or walking beam, tandem suspensions reduce the effect of road bumps on the frame. As the front axle moves up over a bump, the front of the equalizer beam moves up with it, but the other end of the beam is attached to the rear axles and it pivots on the rear axle connection. So the beam acts as a lever and the center of the beam, where it attaches to the vehicle frame, only moves up 50% of the distance the front axle moves, reducing the impact to the frame, the vehicle body, and the load.
- Rubber springs are a very common spring medium used in very heavy-duty applications. These springs are manufactured to be variable rate.
- A Chalmers suspension system is a rubber spring suspension system that boasts the highest amount of articulation of any current suspension systems and which is extremely easy to service.
- Air springs, also known as air bellows or air bags, have instant and complete equalization in tandem applications, provide the softest ride, and yet can carry very heavy loads when required. Air springs maintain a constant vehicle ride height (loaded or unloaded) and protect the load better than any other system, while providing much greater driver comfort. One drawback of air spring systems is a slight loss of lateral stability, so many manufacturers are combining leaf springs with air springs to achieve improved stability and ride.
- Electronic suspension systems provide even better control of ride height and load distribution. These systems combine with ABS and traction control systems to optimize vehicle control. They can change ride height from side to side if necessary to account for uneven loading and can even increase pressure in the air springs on the outside of the curve during cornering to improve stability.
- Independent front suspension systems were once solely the purvey of light-duty vehicles, but more and more manufacturers are producing these systems for the heavy-duty market. The increased control and comfort of these systems make them attractive but their price and complexity are drawbacks from the standpoint of fleet operators.
- Suspension systems should be inspected on a regular basis for any component that is cracked, broken, or missing. Suspension maintenance usually involves lubrication of joints and re-torqueing of components, but technicians should always check the appropriate OEM manual for precise instructions.
- It is essential to maintain proper axle alignment; misalignment of ½" (12.6mm) can decrease tire life and severely reducing fuel economy. Alignment is normally performed using computerized alignment machines but can be accomplished relatively easily in the repair shop.
- The CVSA issues a list of out-of-service criteria for essential vehicle systems. For suspension, the list basically covers any broken, cracked, or missing component in the suspension or its attaching components. If the vehicle has any of these criteria, it is to taken out of service until repaired.

Vocabulary Builder

air bag The spring component of an air spring suspension, a tough rubber bag filled with air. Also called *air spring* and *bellows*.

air spring The spring component of an air spring suspension; a tough rubber bag filled with air. Also called *bellows* or *air bag*.

articulation Movement of axles.

auxiliary spring A second leaf spring in a leaf spring suspension that does not take any of the weight until the vehicle is close to fully loaded.

axle stop A rubber (usually) bumper that stops the axle from contacting the vehicle frame during severe suspension articulation. Also called *jounce block*.

bellows The spring component of an air spring suspension; a tough rubber bag filled with air. Also called *air spring* and *air bag*.

caster adjusting shim An angular shim used at the front leaf spring mount to roll the I-beam axle forward or back to set the caster angle.

coil spring A helical metal spring.

combo stud A mounting stud attached to an air spring that also receives the fitting to fill the spring with air.

contact patch The area of the tire that is in actual contact with the road.

convoluted air spring An air spring with a top and bottom mounting plate and one, two, or three girdle hoops. The girdle hoops add lateral stability to the spring.

drive pins Vertical pins that attach to the frame of a rubber spring equalizing beam suspension. The drive pins pass through the rubber spring elements and locate and align the spring saddles while the suspension articulates.

dump valve A driver-operated air valve to release the air from an air suspension system while at the loading dock.

equalizer The support for a tandem drive axle, using a standard leaf spring suspension system; it supports the rear of the front spring and the front of the rear spring.

equalizing beam A beam with each end attached to the axles of a tandem axle arrangement and its center attached to the frame directly or through a spring system. The beam reduces the impact of road bumps to the frame by 50% and equalizes the load carried by each of the axles. Also called a *walking beam*.

equalizing bracket A bracket connecting the rear of the front leaf spring to the front of the rear leaf spring on a tandem axle suspension; used to equalize the loading of each axle during suspension articulation.

equalizing beam suspensions Used on tandem suspension systems; two large equalizing beams between the two axles equalize the load between the four wheels.

height-control valve An air valve that maintains air spring suspension ride height.

hysteresis This occurs when something is deflected but does not rebound with the same force, usually due to the internal friction inherent in the material as it deflects.

interleaf friction Friction caused by the leaves in a multileaf spring pack rubbing together during suspension articulation; can be effective in stopping unwanted oscillation.

jounce The upward motion of the wheels and axles in reaction to road bumps or terrain.

jounce block A rubber (usually) bumper that stops the axle from contacting the vehicle frame during severe suspension articulation. Also called *axle stop*.

lateral stability The vehicle's ability to be stable from side to side.

leaf spring A spring formed by elliptical steel leaves; can be single leaf or multileaf.

monoleaf spring A leaf spring with a single leaf usually found in front spring applications only.

multileaf spring A leaf spring with more than one steel plate or leaf stacked together and used for a spring. Also called a *spring pack*.

oscillation The rhythmic up and down motion of the suspension caused by road shock. It must be stopped by dampening or vehicle stability could be lost.

overslung A suspension where the leaf spring sits on top of the axle.

parallelogram A design element in suspension systems to keep the wheels or the axles in alignment throughout suspension articulation.

rebound The downward motion of the wheel and axle after a road bump or shock has occurred.

reversing sleeve piston A type of air spring with a piston that pushes into the air spring bag or bellows as the suspension articulates. Also known as a *rolling lobe piston*.

rolling lobe piston A type of air spring with a piston that pushes into the air spring bag or bellows as the suspension articulates. Also known as a *reversing sleeve piston*.

rubber spring A suspension system utilizing rubber as the spring medium commonly found on heavier vehicles.

self-dampening The interleaf friction in a leaf spring pack that helps to stop spring oscillation.

shock absorber A (usually) hydraulic piston and cylinder arrangement designed to minimize spring oscillation.

shock bracket A bracket, usually part of the spring mounted that the shock absorber bolts to.

spring pack A leaf spring with more than one steel plate or leaf stacked together and used for a spring. Also called a *multileaf spring*.

spring rate The amount of force required to deflect the spring; a low spring rate means a softer spring and therefore ride; a higher spring rate adds more lateral stability but gives a harsher ride.

sprung weight The portion of the vehicle supported by the springs; includes the frame, the body, the load, and any accessories.

stabilizer bars Transversely mounted bars that control axle alignment and add lateral stability while the vehicle is turning by transferring some of the load from the side of the vehicle on the outside of a turn to the side on the inside of the turn.

swing shackle A spring mounting system consisting of two upright flat bars side-by-side. The top of the bars are pinned to the frame spring bracket and the bottom of the bars are pinned to the rear leaf spring eye. Shackles allow the leaf spring length to change as the suspension oscillates.

torque rod A rod that transfers acceleration, braking, and lateral forces from the axle to the frame and also maintains axle alignment. Torque rods can usually be adjusted by one method or another to realign the axles when required.

torsion bar Bars in a vehicle's suspension system that twist in response to the movement of the wheels and absorb their vertical movement.

track rod Typically, transversely mounted torque rods that counteract lateral forces acting on the vehicle.

trailing arms Refers to large strong beams attached to the vehicle frame and to the axle, they support the spring medium.

underslung A suspension system where the leaf spring is mounted under the axle.

unsprung weight The vehicle weight not supported by the suspension system; includes the axles, the tires, wheels, and the brakes.

variable spring rate A spring or suspension system where more force is required to deflect the spring as load is added; allows a soft rate when unloaded and a much stiffer suspension when loaded.

walking beam A beam with each end attached to the axles of a tandem axle arrangement and its center attached to the frame directly or through a spring system. The beam reduces the impact of road bumps to the frame by 50% and equalizes the load carried by each of the axles. Also called an *equalizing beam*.

wheel hop A situation where the wheels literally hop off the ground and lose their contact with the road, usually caused by excessive suspension wind-up due to extreme braking but can also occur on acceleration.

Review Questions

1. The purpose of a shock absorber is to:
   a. absorb road shock.
   b. support vehicle weight.
   c. control spring oscillations.
   d. increase spring capacity.
2. Which of the following is the most common type of front suspension on class 8 trucks?
   a. Twin I-beam
   b. Independent
   c. Semi-independent
   d. I-beam
3. Cam/hanger-type spring brackets are used with which type of springs?
   a. Constant-rate springs
   b. Air springs
   c. Variable-rate or progressive-rate springs
   d. Composite springs
4. Equalizing arms reduce the upward motion of road shocks to the vehicle frame by doing which of the following?
   a. Using the lever principle
   b. Absorbing the shock
   c. Using shock absorbers
   d. Transferring the motion to the drive axle
5. Why is interleaf friction important on older leaf spring installations?
   a. Interleaf friction adds to lateral stability.
   b. Interleaf friction dampens spring oscillations.
   c. Interleaf friction increases road feel.
   d. Interleaf friction is not desired and springs leaves should be lubricated to avoid it.
6. Which of the following conditions would require you to remove a vehicle from service?
   a. Deflated air bag
   b. Broken spring leaf
   c. Broken torque rod
   d. All of the choices are out-of-service criteria.
7. Hysteresis occurs when:
   a. the leaves in a multileaf spring pack rub together during suspension articulation.
   b. something is deflected but does not rebound with the same force.
   c. the upward motion of the wheels and axles reacts to road bumps or terrain.
   d. None of the choices is correct.
8. The function of the torque rod is to:
   a. maintain axle alignment and transfer lateral forces.
   b. transfer acceleration and lateral forces.
   c. transfer acceleration, braking, and lateral forces.
   d. maintain axle alignment plus transfer lateral and braking forces.
9. Which air valve is known as the central command for the air suspension system?
   a. Master control valve
   b. Weight control valve
   c. Pressure control valve
   d. Height control valve
10. An axle that is out of alignment by ______ can decrease tire life by over 24%.
    a. ¼" (6.3 mm)
    b. ½" (12.6 mm)
    c. ⅝" (15.9 mm)
    d. ¾" (18.9 mm)

ASE-Type Questions

1. Technician A says that all multileaf spring packs are variable rate. Technician B says that auxiliary springs are usually variable rate. Who is correct?
   a. Technician A
   b. Technician B
   c. Both Technician A and Technician B
   d. Neither Technician A nor Technician B

2. Technician A says that higher spring rate aids in lateral stability. Technician B says that higher spring rates lead to a much softer ride. Who is correct?
   a. Technician A
   b. Technician B
   c. Both Technician A and Technician B
   d. Neither Technician A nor Technician B

3. Technician A says that variable-rate multileaf springs change rate because the contact point between the springs and the cams changes as load is added. Technician B says that some monoleaf springs can be variable rate. Who is correct?
   a. Technician A
   b. Technician B
   c. Both Technician A and Technician B
   d. Neither Technician A nor Technician B

4. Technician A says that all torque rods are adjustable to control axle alignment. Technician B says that usually torque rods are only adjustable on one side. Who is correct?
   a. Technician A
   b. Technician B
   c. Both Technician A and Technician B
   d. Neither Technician A nor Technician B

5. Technician A says suspension systems must tolerate a huge number of forces when a vehicle is being driven down the road. Technician B says vehicle suspension systems generally use the elastic properties of special metals or air springs to provide the springing medium that a suspension system requires. Who is correct?
   a. Technician A
   b. Technician B
   c. Both Technician A and Technician B
   d. Neither Technician A nor Technician B

6. Technician A says the suspension system must ensure the vehicle's tires stay in contact with the road surface. Technician B says wheel hop caused by excessive suspension oscillation can lead to loss of control and extreme tire wear. Who is correct?
   a. Technician A
   b. Technician B
   c. Both Technician A and Technician B
   d. Neither Technician A nor Technician B

7. Technician A says a basic function of the suspension system is to securely connect the axles to the frame of the vehicle. Technician B says the suspension system must maintain the axle spacing and alignment as the axles articulate over uneven road surfaces and bumps. Who is correct?
   a. Technician A
   b. Technician B
   c. Both Technician A and Technician B
   d. Neither Technician A nor Technician B

8. Technician A says a shock absorber is effective in minimizing suspension oscillation. Technician B says interleaf friction in leaf springs is not effective in minimizing suspension oscillation. Who is correct?
   a. Technician A
   b. Technician B
   c. Both Technician A and Technician B
   d. Neither Technician A nor Technician B

9. Technician A says torque rods are used to keep the axles in alignment with each other and with the frame. Technician B says torque rods are usually not adjustable. Who is correct?
   a. Technician A
   b. Technician B
   c. Both Technician A and Technician B
   d. Neither Technician A nor Technician B

10. Technician A says most hydraulic shock absorbers are designed with an inner and an outer tube. Technician B says the outer tube is also known as the primary tube, and it does not hold a supply of hydraulic fluid. Who is correct?
    a. Technician A
    b. Technician B
    c. Both Technician A and Technician B
    d. Neither Technician A nor Technician B

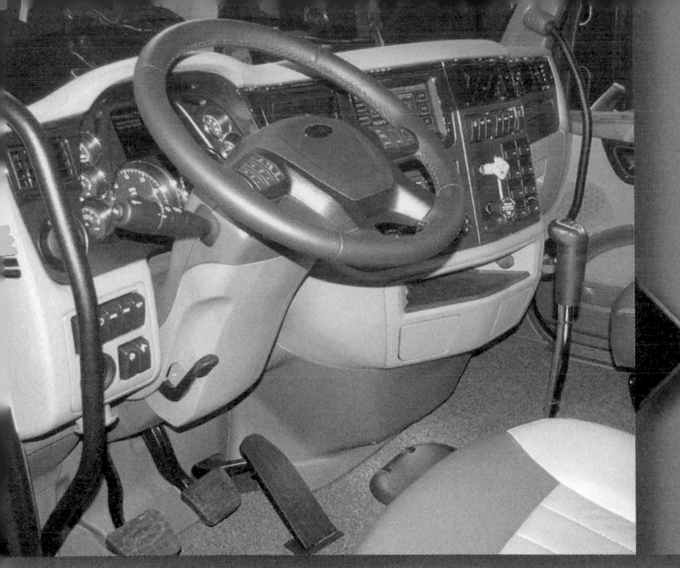

CHAPTER 28

NATEF Tasks

Required Supplemental Tasks

Shop and Personal Safety	Page
■ Demonstrate awareness of the safety aspects of supplemental restraint systems (SRS), electronic brake control systems, and hybrid vehicle high voltage circuits.	872–873

Suspension and Steering

Steering Column	
■ Inspect and service steering shaft U-joint(s), slip joints, bearings, bushings, and seals; phase shaft.	845
■ Check cab mounting and adjust ride height.	845
■ Remove the steering wheel (includes steering wheels equipped with electrical/electronic controls and components); install and center the steering wheel. Inspect, test, replace, and calibrate steering angle sensor.	845
■ Identify causes of fixed and driver adjustable steering column and shaft noise, looseness, and binding problems; determine needed action.	865
■ Disable and enable supplemental restraint system (SRS) in accordance with manufacturers' procedures.	872–873

Steering Units	
■ Determine recommended type of power steering fluid; check level and condition; determine needed action.	858
■ Inspect, service, or replace power steering reservoir including filter, seals, and gaskets.	863
■ Inspect power steering pump drive gear and coupling; replace as needed.	863
■ Inspect, adjust, or replace power steering pump, mountings, and brackets.	863
■ Inspect and replace power steering system cooler, lines, hoses, clamps/mountings, hose routings, and fittings.	863
■ Identify causes of power steering system noise, steering binding, darting/oversteer, reduced wheel cut, steering wheel kick, pulling, non-recovery, turning effort, looseness, hard steering, overheating, fluid leakage, and fluid aeration problems; determine needed action.	865
■ Inspect, adjust, repair, or replace integral type power steering gear(s) (single and/or dual) and mountings.	866
■ Perform power steering system pressure, temperature, and flow tests; determine needed action.	869–870

Steering Systems and Integral Steering Gears

NATEF Tasks, continued

Suspension and Steering Steering Units, continued	Page
■ Flush and refill power steering system; purge air from system.	871
Suspension and Steering Steering Linkage	
■ Inspect and align pitman arm; replace as needed.	854
■ Check and adjust steering (wheel) stops; verify relief pressures.	864–868
■ Inspect and lubricate steering components.	864–868

Knowledge Objectives

After reading this chapter, you will be able to:

1. Identify and describe the steering systems found on medium- and heavy-duty commercial vehicles. (pp 842–853)
2. Identify components and explain the operation of integral type steering gears. (pp 848–849)
3. Identify components and explain the operation of integral power steering assist systems. (pp 849–853)
4. Identify, explain, and recommend service and maintenance procedures associated with steering systems. (p 863)
5. Identify and explain the operation of steering wheels, columns, linkage, and related parts. (p 869–870)

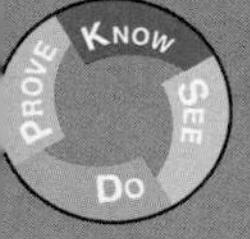

Skills Objectives

After reading this chapter, you will be able to:

1. Center the steering gear. (p 866) SKILL DRILL 28-1
2. Use a PSSA. (p 869) SKILL DRILL 28-2
3. Measure pump maximum relief pressure. (p 869) SKILL DRILL 28-3
4. Test flow volume. (p 870) SKILL DRILL 28-4
5. Test for internal leakage. (p 871) SKILL DRILL 28-5
6. Remove and replace steering wheel and center/time the SRS coil. (pp 872–873) SKILL DRILL 28-6

Introduction

While the concept of controlling vehicle direction by turning a steering wheel is familiar to every vehicle operator, steering is a "life and limb" system having significant consequences for road safety. The responsibility of technicians to choose safe work practices is needed to not only to protect the operator and vehicle, but many other road users. To properly assume these responsibilities, technicians need to be very knowledgeable about the purpose, construction, and operation of steering system components of various types of steering systems. Equipped with this knowledge, technicians can properly choose the correct service practices and tools when performing inspection, maintenance, or repairs on steering systems.

Fundamentals of Steering Systems

The **steering system** includes the steering wheel, column, steering gear, its power assist mechanism, and steering linkage connecting the steering gear to the steer axle wheels. These are the major steering components used to maintain directional control of a vehicle. Mechanically speaking, the purpose of the **steering gear** is to convert and multiply the rotational force from the steering wheel to operate the steering linkage. The gear should also function to help maintain directional stability of the vehicle, especially when it encounters bumps and irregular road surfaces while transmitting some **road feel** and minimizing road shock and vibration to the driver. Road feel is force transmitted from the tires back through the steering system to the driver.

Safety

By the sheer size and weight of a commercial vehicle, any fault in its steering system that results in a loss of steering control will have catastrophic consequences, not only for the vehicle operator but also for other road users. It is the responsibility of the technician to choose service practices that will not endanger the safety of the vehicle, its occupants, and other road users.

Heavy-duty steering systems include a combination of the following components:

- Steering wheels, columns, miter boxes, and intermediate shafts with optional tilt and telescopic options (miter boxes are used in high-angle steering columns to connect to the steering gear in specialized applications such as low-entry vehicles)
- Single or dual power steering gears; the term steering gear is also used interchangeably with steering box
- Pitman arms, drag links, tie-rods, and other steering linkage (**drag links** are a connecting linkage that transfers movement of the pitman arm to the upper steering arm)
- Power steering pumps and lines

You Are the Technician

A driver with an on-highway tractor arrives to the shop and complains the steering wheel moves forcefully to the right and left every time the vehicle hits a bump or crosses a pothole. You immediately recognize the driver's complaint as a condition called bump steer. That is, the vehicle's steering moves erratically after hitting a bump. After performing a visual inspection of the steering linkage with the wheels on the ground, you notice a new power steering hose has been installed. The driver explains the problems began after a leaking power steering hose was replaced. After listening to the driver and performing the inspection, consider the following:

1. What is likely the cause of the bump steer?
2. How will you correct the condition?
3. What other steering system inspections and service procedures would you recommend to the driver?

- **Steering angle sensors** for the vehicle stability control systems
- Steering wheel clock springs, which are used when a vehicle is equipped with a driver's side airbag (the **clock spring** supplies a movable electrical connection between the airbag and electrical system)

Even though all heavy-duty steering systems contain the same basic components, various classifications of steering systems use different combinations of those components.

Steering System Classifications

Steering systems are typically classified by the arrangement of the steering linkage and type of steering gear or power-assist mechanism. Steering linkage arrangements vary with the vehicle weight and application, and whether the steering axle is solid or, in rare instances, the vehicle has independent suspension systems at the steer tires. Some vehicles, such as concrete mixers and crane carriers, may even have two steering axles, which significantly changes the system arrangement. A **conventional steering system** with a solid I-beam front axle and a single steering gear is illustrated in FIGURE 28-1.

Today's trucks and buses exclusively use power steering gears rather than manual gears, which have no power assist. The benefit of power steering gears is that hydraulic force, produced by a power steering pump, help multiply driver input force and thereby reduce overall steering effort. The three major power steering gear systems are the integral piston system, the external power-assist system, and the rack-and-pinion system. Of these, the majority of systems use an integral piston type power steering gear—which means the power assist piston and gear assembly are incorporated into a single unit.

The integral piston classification of steering systems uses a hydraulic servo piston, also called power piston as part of the steering gear. The system, as shown in FIGURE 28-2, uses a solid, straight steering axle and a simplified steering linkage arrangement. The hydraulic servo piston multiplies the driver input force using hydraulic pressure supplied by the power steering pump.

The external power-assist steering system uses a conventional worm-gear steering box as its base. It then adds an air or hydraulic cylinder attached to the steering linkage, as illustrated in FIGURE 28-3. That cylinder provides the power assistance. Either a manual or power steering gear can be used with this type of steering system. A control valve integrated into the drag link directs fluid

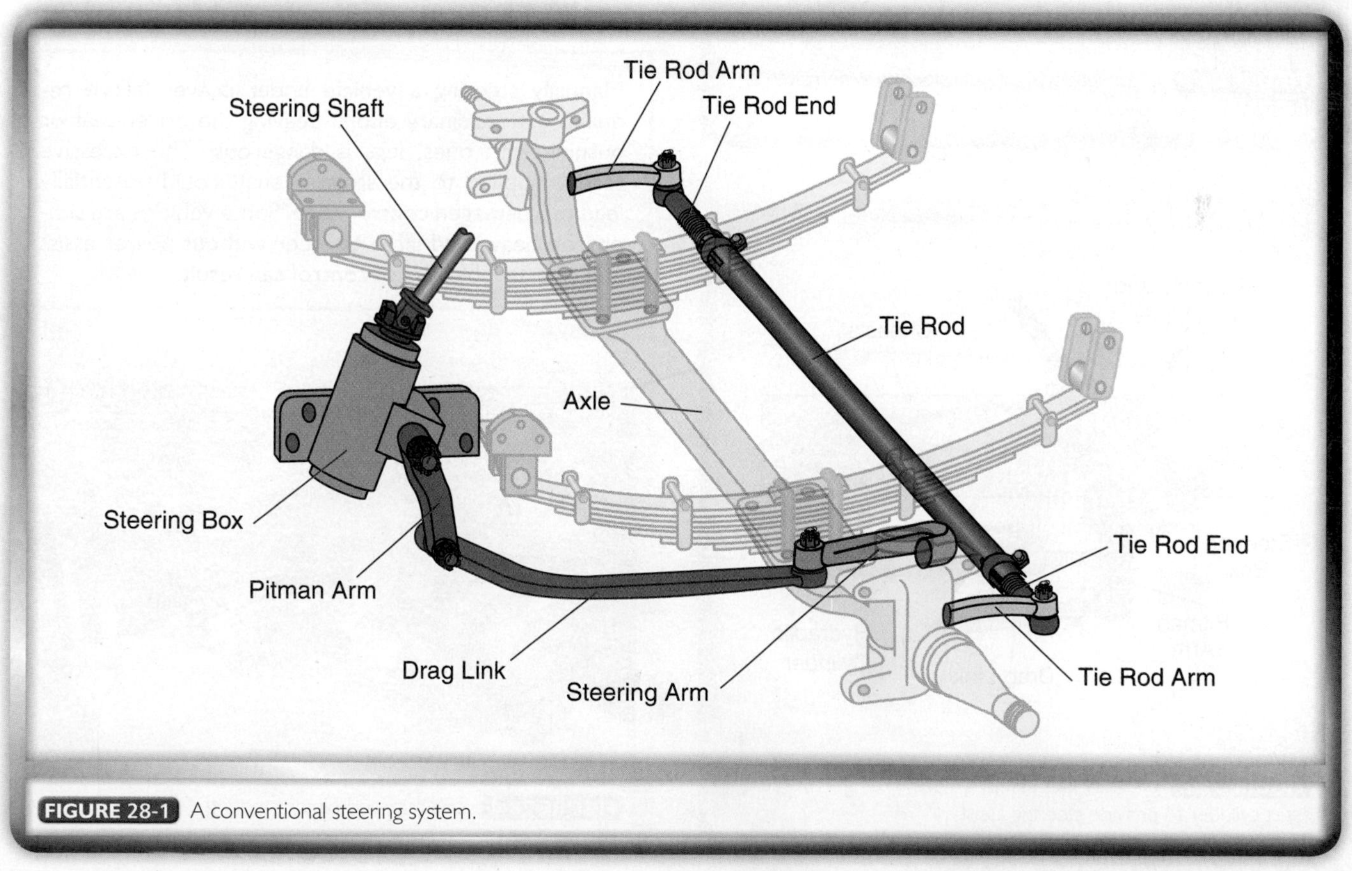

FIGURE 28-1 A conventional steering system.

or pressurized air flow into the assist cylinder. Hydraulic lines connecting the assist piston to the steering gear control valve causes the piston to operate in tandem with the steering gear to supplement the steering gear force.

Rack-and-pinion type steering integrates a power steering-assist mechanism into the steering linkage. A rack-and-pinion steering system has the advantage of providing more precise directional control. Achieving a sharper turning radius is also an advantage of rack-and-pinion steering. This system was briefly used by Freightliner but is currently discontinued. Because the rack required mounting on the front axle and excessive movement between the cab and axle limited the system's service life. ZF, a German manufacturer, is currently marketing its rack and pinion steering system in Europe and North America FIGURE 28-4.

FIGURE 28-2 A conventional integral steering system with an integrated power piston within the steering gear.

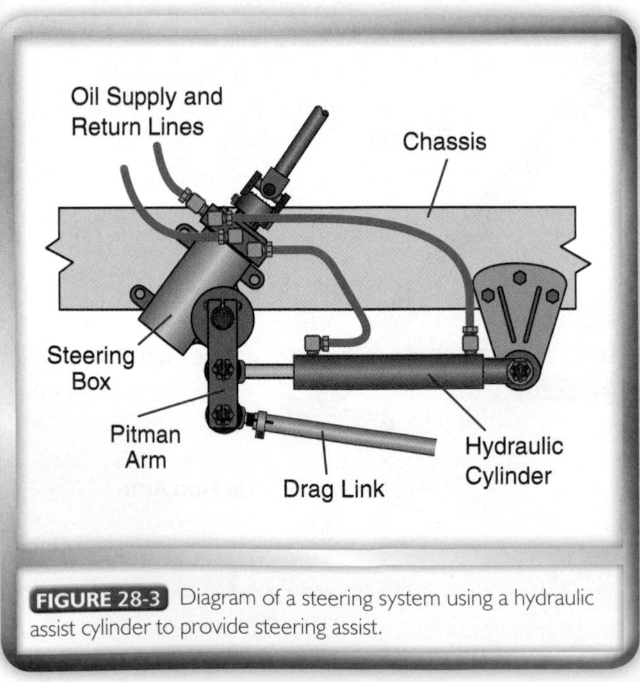

FIGURE 28-3 Diagram of a steering system using a hydraulic assist cylinder to provide steering assist.

Components of Basic Steering Systems

A basic steering system has three main assemblies: the steering wheel and steering column; the steering gear box; and steering linkage. Due to the vehicle weight and the high steering effort required to turn the steer axle tires, heavy-duty vehicles must add a power-assist system (usually hydraulic) to that basic steering system to reduce steering effort. Manual steering capabilities are built into every steering system in the event of a loss of power steering assist. If a hydraulic line breaks or the engine stalls, a vehicle can be steered, with higher effort, to the side of the road without the hydraulic assist.

Movement of the steering system starts with the driver applying effort to the steering wheel (by turning it). The steering column transmits that effort from the steering wheel through the steering column down to the steering gear. The steering gear converts the rotary motion of the steering wheel to the linear sweeping motion of the pitman arm, which is needed to pivot the wheels. The steering gear also uses principles of gear reduction

Safety

Manually steering a vehicle under power failure requires extraordinary effort. Leaving the driver seat or pushing with ones, legs is dangerous. The excessive torque applied to the steering shaft could potentially lead to a damaged control valve. Some vehicles are simply too heavy and large to steer without power assist and catastrophic loss of control can result.

FIGURE 28-4 ZF's rack-and-pinion steering system.

to give the driver mechanical advantage to overcome the high steering effort of tire resistance to turning, making it easier to steer the vehicle. The linear sweep of the pitman arm, connected to the steering gear output shaft, is then transmitted to the wheels by the drag link. Steering force is transmitted through the drag link to the **steering knuckle** by the upper steering arm. Steering arms on each of the steering knuckles are moved in unison by the tie-rod.

Steering Wheels

Trucks and buses have significantly larger steering wheels than automobiles or light-duty vehicles. Larger steering wheels provide greater mechanical advantage because more torque is required to turn steering axle wheels due to heavier vehicle weight. The larger-diameter wheel is critical in the event of a power steering-assist failure. If the power-assist fails, only manual steering is available to control the vehicle. Steering wheel diameters of 19" to 26" (48 cm to 66 cm) are common.

Size is not the only differentiating factor between the steering wheels on heavy- and light-duty vehicles. The angle of inclination is also different. In contrast to automobiles, in heavy-duty vehicles, the wheel is placed at approximately a 30 degree angle or more to the driver, as shown in FIGURE 28-5, which makes it easier to turn if power assist is ever lost. Typically the steering wheel is splined to the steel shaft of the steering column. That attachment, however, is made without a master spline. The steering wheel can therefore be removed so that technicians can relocate spokes to a straight ahead position, as illustrated in FIGURE 28-6, if adjustments to steering linkage, such as a tie-rod or adjustable drag link, are made. Always use a purpose-specific steering wheel puller to remove the steering wheel. Never use a hammer, heat the wheel, or pry the wheel off the spline.

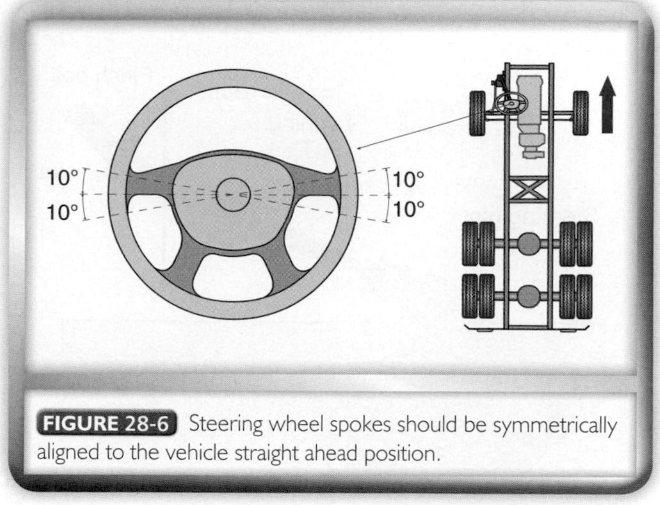

FIGURE 28-6 Steering wheel spokes should be symmetrically aligned to the vehicle straight ahead position.

FIGURE 28-5 Steering wheel with a supplemental restraint system (SRS) air bag in a heavy-duty truck.

Steering Columns and Shafts

Effort applied to the steering wheel is transferred down the **steering column**, which is made of two or more **steering shafts**, to the steering gear. Steering shafts make up the steering column, which is typically a combination of two or more steering shafts.

Steering columns in today's heavy-duty vehicles have unique and sometimes more advanced functions than previous generations of vehicles. First, heavy-duty steering columns must be capable of changing length to adapt to the flexion between the cab and frame-mounted steering gear. A sliding splined section of the column is incorporated into a pair of steering shafts, as illustrated in FIGURE 28-7. The sliding mechanism is commonly equipped with a grease fitting for lubrication.

Additionally, the movement of the steering column must be capable of changing the angle between the steering wheel and gear. Since movement between the cab and steering gear takes place continuously as the vehicle absorbs road shock and vibration, changes take place between the angles of the steering gear input shaft and the steering wheel. One or more **universal joints** (also called **U-joints**) are placed in the column to allow movement between the frame-mounted steering gear and steering column. Enabling flexion of the steering column prevents cab movement from being transmitted into the steering input shaft. When two universal joints are installed in the column, they must be phased. This means the crosses and bearing caps of the joints must exactly align with one another. If they are not aligned, the steering shafts movement can bind, which prevents the vehicle from being properly steered.

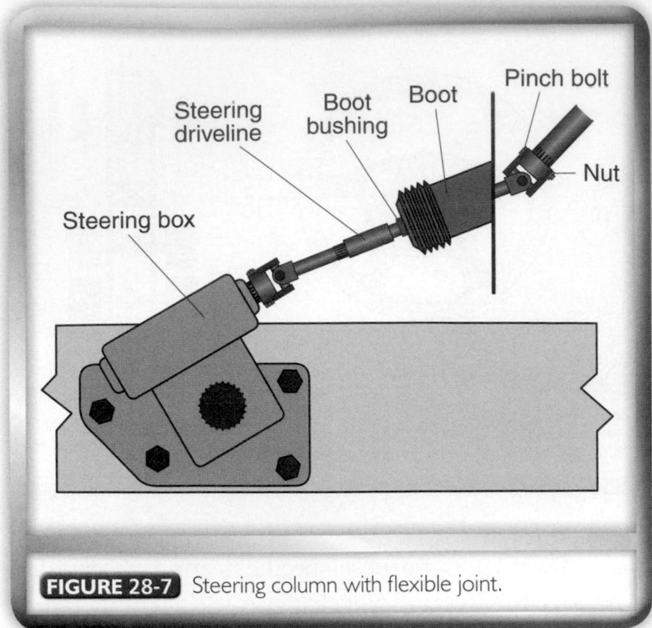

FIGURE 28-7 Steering column with flexible joint.

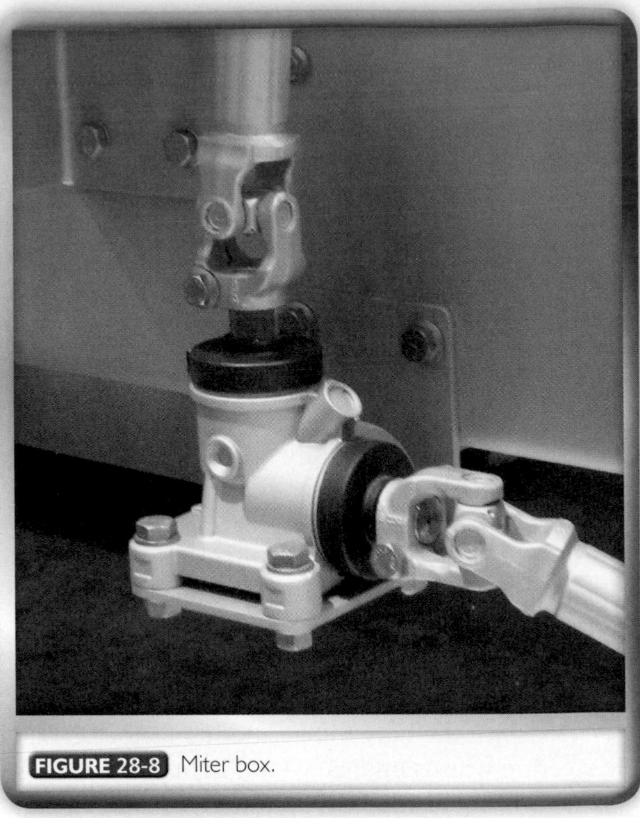

FIGURE 28-8 Miter box.

Multi-shaft steering columns using shafts connected on sliding splines, called slip yokes, enable the column to change in length. This feature is not only important to enable movement between the cab and frame-mounted gear, but it is a safety feature as well. A single, straight, steering shaft could be driven into the driver during a collision. With sliding splines however, the shafts will simply slide inside one another, shortening the shaft and preventing injury to the driver.

The location of the steering gear relative to the column sometimes requires the use of a miter box to connect the two components. **Miter boxes** are gear arrangements used to sharply change steering column angles. They are available in various angles and so enable the use of specialized cab configurations. Miter boxes are often used on cab-over-engine chassis where the steering gear is below the steering wheel, as shown in FIGURE 28-8.

> **TECHNICIAN TIP**
>
> Ensuring steering column universal joints are properly aligned is a first step during column inspection. Out of phase steering column U-joints can cause a cyclical like tightness, binding, or torque variations at the steering wheel. Proper phasing means the U-joint crosses and bearing caps must be precisely parallel to one another after the steering shafts are assembled into the column. During disassembly, separated shafts must be match-marked. During reinstallation, match marking shafts enables correct alignment of column parts to turn smoothly together.

> **TECHNICIAN TIP**
>
> When tapered studs are used to attach the steering linkage, a wedge fork will be necessary to separate the drag link from a steering arm (or pitman arm) or tie-rod ends from the steering knuckle. Common workshop practice is to shock the tie-rod end loose by striking with a large hammer. For safety reasons, castellated nuts with cotter pins are used to lock the ball stud and nut together.

Steering Gears

Steering gears fall into one of two basic categories: manual or power (assisted). Manual steering gears were occasionally used in a few applications, primarily because of their simplicity, reliability, and low maintenance. Manual steering gears provide no assistance to the driver's turning effort and rely on a high mechanical gear ratio to reduce steering effort. This means more turns of the steering wheel are required to change the direction of the steer tires. Power steering does provide assistance to the driver's effort and fewer turns of the steering wheel are required to move the steer tires. Given the weight and size of heavy-duty commercial vehicles, manual steering gears are seldom, if ever, used in heavy commercial vehicles.

Power steering gears can steer the vehicle without power assistance. Power-assisted steering systems use one of three types of gearing technology. The first is a manual recirculating-ball steering gear. Even though this gearing type is manual, the principles of its design and construction are used by all steering gears, whether manual or power. The second type of gearing technology used in power-assisted steering systems is a power recirculating-ball gear, and the third type is the rack-and-pinion steering gear.

Safety

Investigate and immediately correct any detected steering fault present. Correct any cause of steering column misalignment. Do not heat any steering component since this will cause the metal to become brittle and easily break rather than bend. Never weld or braze any broken steering component. Replace the component with original equipment only. Do not straighten any bent steering system component.

Federal Motor Vehicle Safety Standards (FMVSS) require that all vehicles are capable of being steered manually if the loss of power assistance occurs, such as during an engine or hydraulic failure. For this reason, power steering gears contain a manual steering system that is useful to examine before studying power steering systems. In this section, we'll first cover the basics of steering ratios and then move into a more detailed discussion of the three types of steering gears and gear boxes.

Steering Ratio

In manual- and power-assisted steering systems alike, steering gears play a major role in converting the rotational movement of the steering wheel into a linear motion at the pitman arm. The force to turn the wheels of a heavily loaded vehicle requires the gear to supply a significant amount of mechanical advantage to allow the driver to safely maneuver the vehicle.

On heavy-duty vehicles, the **steering ratio** refers to the mechanical advantage produced by the gear. An example of a 20:1 steering ratio means a steering wheel turned 360 degrees would turn the wheels 18 degrees (360 degrees rotation of the steering wheel /divided the ratio constant of 20 = 18 degrees of wheel turn at a 20:1 ratio) (20 × 18 = 360). Typical commercial vehicle ratios are between 16:1 and 23:1.

Although it will not transmit desirable feedback about the road conditions, a high steering ratio reduces road shock to the steering wheel and steering effort. A low ratio allows the steering to be more responsive to driver input and turn more quickly with less steering wheel movement.

In addition to being high or low, steering gears can either use a constant or a variable ratio. **Variable-ratio steering gears** use sector shafts with long and short lengths of teeth, as illustrated in FIGURE 28-9B. **Constant-ratio steering gears**, illustrated in FIGURE 28-9A,

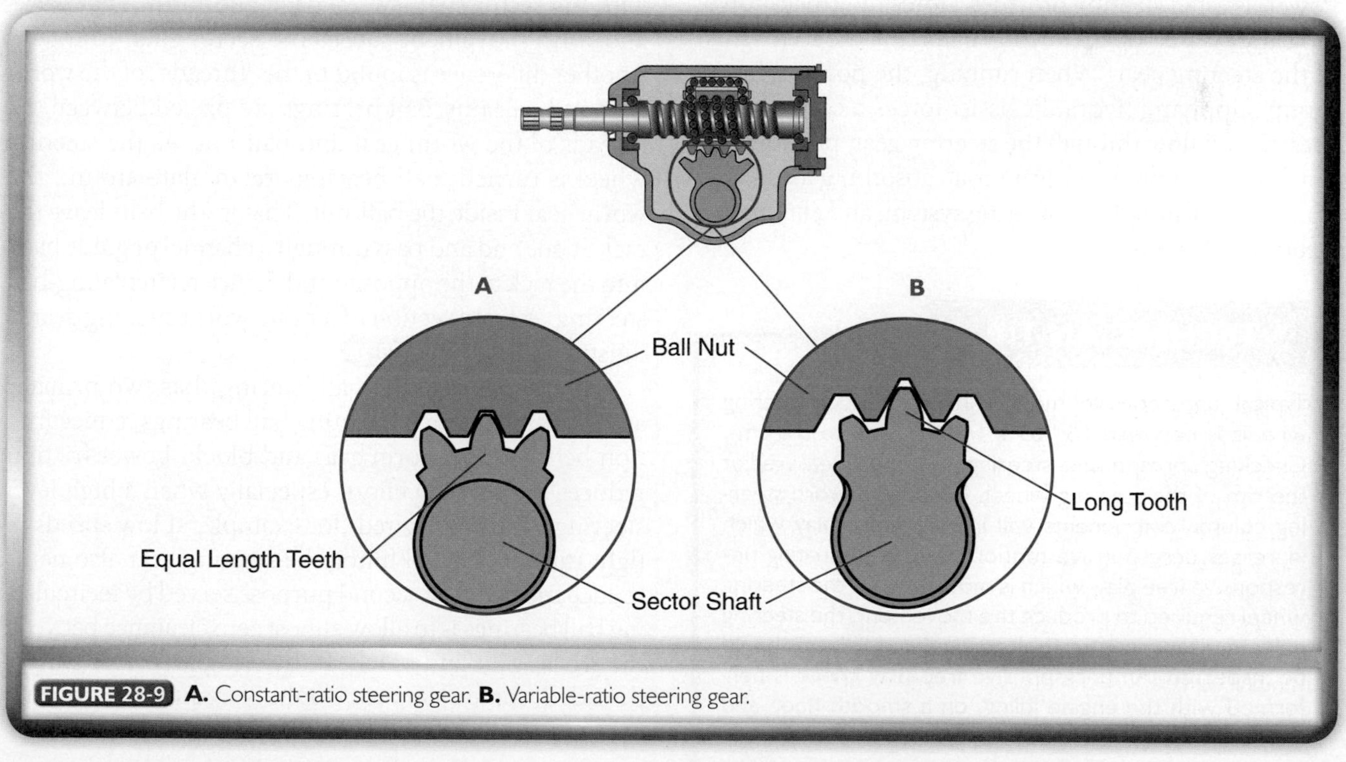

FIGURE 28-9 **A.** Constant-ratio steering gear. **B.** Variable-ratio steering gear.

use sector shafts with teeth of equal length. Variable-ratio steering produces small amounts of movement near the steering center and larger movement of the sector shaft near the ends of the worm gear or power piston travel. The longer teeth increase the ratio near the steering center while the shorter decrease the steering ratio.

Variable-ratio steering gears move relatively little when the vehicle is travelling in a near-straight direction. For this reason, drivers prefer variable-ratio steering— since little steering input is required most of the time. Because variable-ratio gears move only slightly, near steering center, they minimize a condition called oversteer—a vehicle over response to driver input when the steering wheel is first turned. Having a high steering ratio near the center of travel also reduces the tendency of a vehicle to wander when traveling straight ahead. As the vehicle wheels are turned farther from center, the steering ratio decreases.

> **TECHNICIAN TIP**
>
> Variable-ratio steering gears found on most vehicles have a wider center tooth on the sector shaft and narrower teeth toward the ends. During service, it is important that all steering components are aligned and adjusted for steering in a straight-ahead direction. Pitman arms require matching of alignment marks on the steering sector shaft as shown in Figure 28-22.

Steering force is multiplied in power-assisted systems. Power-assisted steering provides a force multiplication of typically over 2,000 lb (907 kg) of force at the sector shaft of the steering gear! When running, the power steering pump supplying hydraulic assist forces a constant low pressure oil flow through the steering gear, providing an immediate response to driver input, absorbing road shock transmitted through the steering system, and eliminating steering wheel kick.

> **TECHNICIAN TIP**
>
> Typical unresponsive motion in late model steering wheels is between 1/2" to 1 1/2" (1.3 cm to 3.8 cm). Checking unresponsive steering motion is measured at the rim of the steering wheel. Loose and worn steering column components will increase free play which increases unresponsive motion. Before evaluating unresponsive free play, which is movement of the steering wheel required to produce tire movement, the steering column, gear mounting bolt torque, and linkage should be inspected. An unresponsive free play check is performed with the engine idling, on a smooth floor, and checked on both right and left wheel cuts.

Manual Recirculating-Ball Steering Gears

The principles behind manual recirculating-ball steering gears are the same principles used by all steering gears—manual and power assisted. **Recirculating-ball steering systems** consist of a steering box with a worm gear inside a metal block called a ball-nut rack with a threaded hole in it.

The **worm gear** is a helical (spiral), grooved, shaft that is attached to the steering column and meshes with the **ball-nut rack**. The worm gear and ball-nut operate like a nut and bolt. In this case, the helix-shaped groove on the worm moves the ball-nut one tooth for each revolution of the worm. The helix-shaped groove provides smooth and quiet steering operation for the driver. It converts the rotary motion of the steering wheel to the linear motion needed to turn the wheels.

The worm gear is surrounded by a metal block, or ball-nut, containing ball bearings. The metal block has gear teeth cut into one outside edge. Those teeth mesh with another set of teeth cut into the sector shaft gear, as illustrated in FIGURE 28-10A and shown in FIGURE 28-10B. Moving the input shaft of the steering gear is like threading a bolt into a nut—only in this case the worm gear is the bolt and the metal block is the nut. Although the nut-and-bolt analogy works for envisioning the shapes and orientation of the worm gear and the metal block, it is not entirely accurate.

Unlike a nut-and-bolt arrangement, turning the steering wheel spins the worm gear in the box. As the worm gear spins, teeth on the metal block which are engaged with the sector shaft sweep back and forth. That back-and-forth movement causes the sector shaft to rotate. Another difference is found in the "threads" of the worm gear and ball-nut. Ball bearings are placed between the threads of the worm gear and ball-nut. As the steering wheel is turned, ball bearings recirculate around the worm gear inside the ball-nut. That is, the balls leave the rack at one end and pass through a channel or guide back into the rack at the opposite end, hence recirculating-ball steering. A cross section of a basic worm steering gear is illustrated in FIGURE 28-11.

Using recirculating ball bearings has two primary advantages. First, recirculating ball bearings reduce friction between the worm gear and block. Lower friction reduces the steering effort, especially when a high level steering effort is required (for example, at low speeds in tight turns). Gear oil filling the steering gear also helps reduce friction. The second purpose served by recirculating ball bearings is to allow almost zero clearance between the worm gear and block. If the two parts were simply threaded, some clearance would be required producing excessive free play in the steering system.

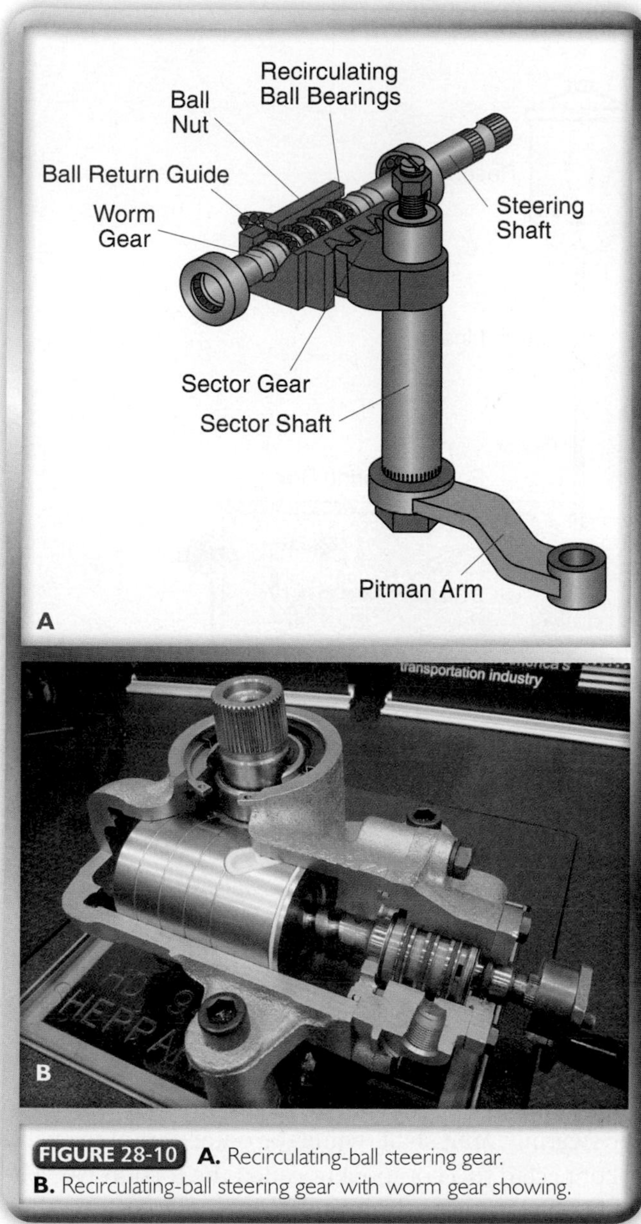

FIGURE 28-10 **A.** Recirculating-ball steering gear. **B.** Recirculating-ball steering gear with worm gear showing.

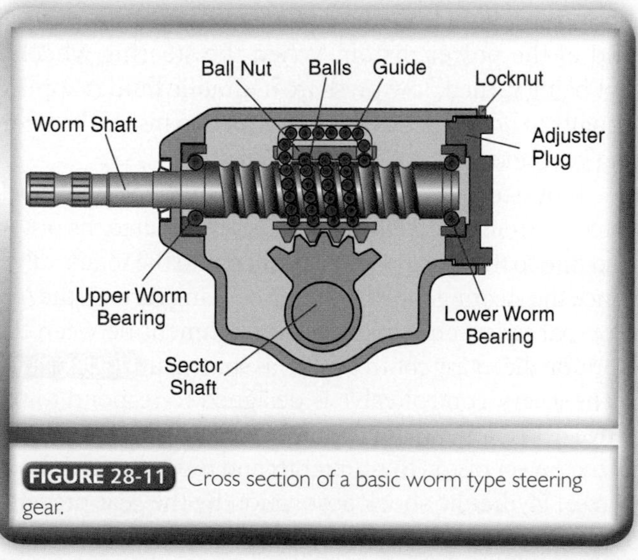

FIGURE 28-11 Cross section of a basic worm type steering gear.

Power Recirculating-Ball Steering Gears

Power steering in a recirculating-ball system operates similarly to a manual system. A key exception is the level of output force. In a power steering system, pressurized hydraulic fluid multiplies the output force of the worm gear located inside a power piston by applying pressure to a power piston moving back and forth inside the steering gear. As shown in FIGURE 28-12, the power piston has teeth machined into one side, just like the ball-nut, and those teeth engage the sector shaft teeth. The same recirculating-ball mechanism, using a worm gear and ball-nut, is located in a power steering gear; the major difference is the power piston has replaced the ball-nut.

Assist is provided by supplying higher-pressure fluid to one side of the piston. Which side of the piston receives the fluid depends on the direction the gear is expected to move. Power steering systems only engage to assist the steering effort of the driver when the driver is turning the steering wheel. This means when no turning force is being applied by the driver, such as when driving in a straight line, the hydraulic system only recirculates fluid and no assist is provided. A schematic of hydraulic assist to the steering gear is shown in FIGURE 28-13.

Two critical components of the hydraulic control mechanism of all power steering gears are the **rotary valve** (also called a **spool valve**) and the torsion bar. Together, the rotary valve and torsion bar, shown in FIGURE 28-14, are responsible for controlling the flow of hydraulic pressure inside the steering gear.

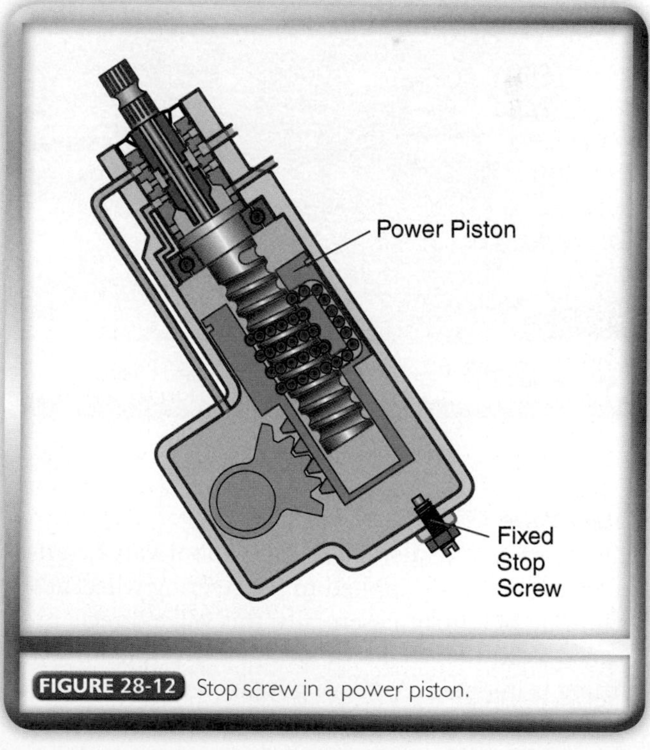

FIGURE 28-12 Stop screw in a power piston.

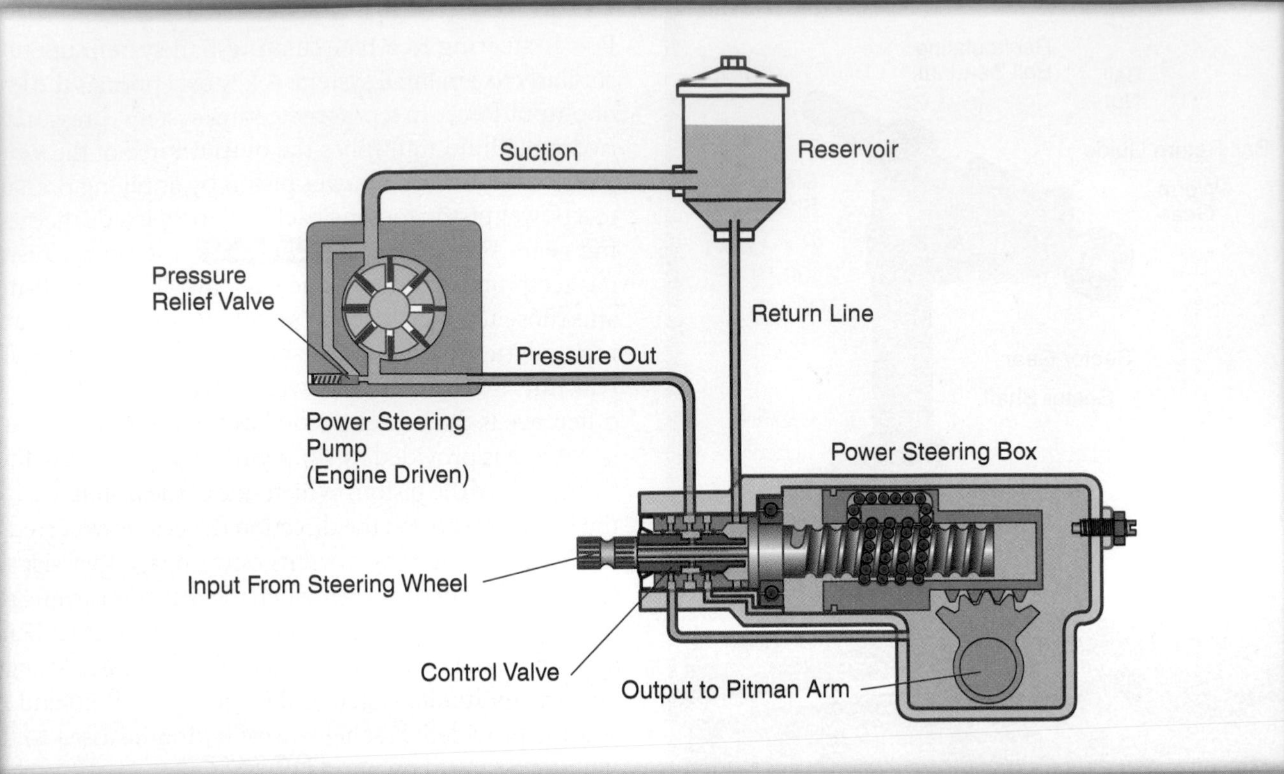

FIGURE 28-13 Hydraulic assist to the steering gear.

FIGURE 28-14 Power steering rotary valve and torsion bar.

Rotary Valve

The rotary valve, also called the spool valve, senses the change in force applied to the steering wheel at the beginning of a turn. Essentially, this valve directs pressurized fluid to either side of the power piston when turning is initiated. A steering rotary valve is illustrated in FIGURE 28-15.

The complete valve assembly, a cross section of which is illustrated in FIGURE 28-16, consists primarily of a rotary-shaped valve centered inside a valve body. The inner and outer section of the valve can move in relation to one another. The inner part of the valve is attached to the steering input shaft, while the outer part of the valve is connected to a component called the torsion bar. The torsion bar can slightly twist and transmits steering shaft input torque to the worm gear. Ports on the rotary valve body direct fluid from the power steering pump to either end of the power piston. When the steering wheel is not being turned, low pressure hydraulic fluid is applied equally to both sides of the power piston inside the steering gear housing.

If the steered wheels receive a road shock, the shock forces are transmitted through the sector shaft to the piston and into to the **worm shaft** and then into the rotary valve. Since the steering input shaft is not being turned, the torsion bar twists and changes the alignment between the ports on the rotary control valve, as shown in FIGURE 28-17 . The rotary-control valve is designed to respond to the valve deflection by sending high-pressure fluid to the end of the power piston to counteract and resist the road shock forces. Hydraulic shock absorption by the gear prevents bump steer and steering wheel kick, which was a normal

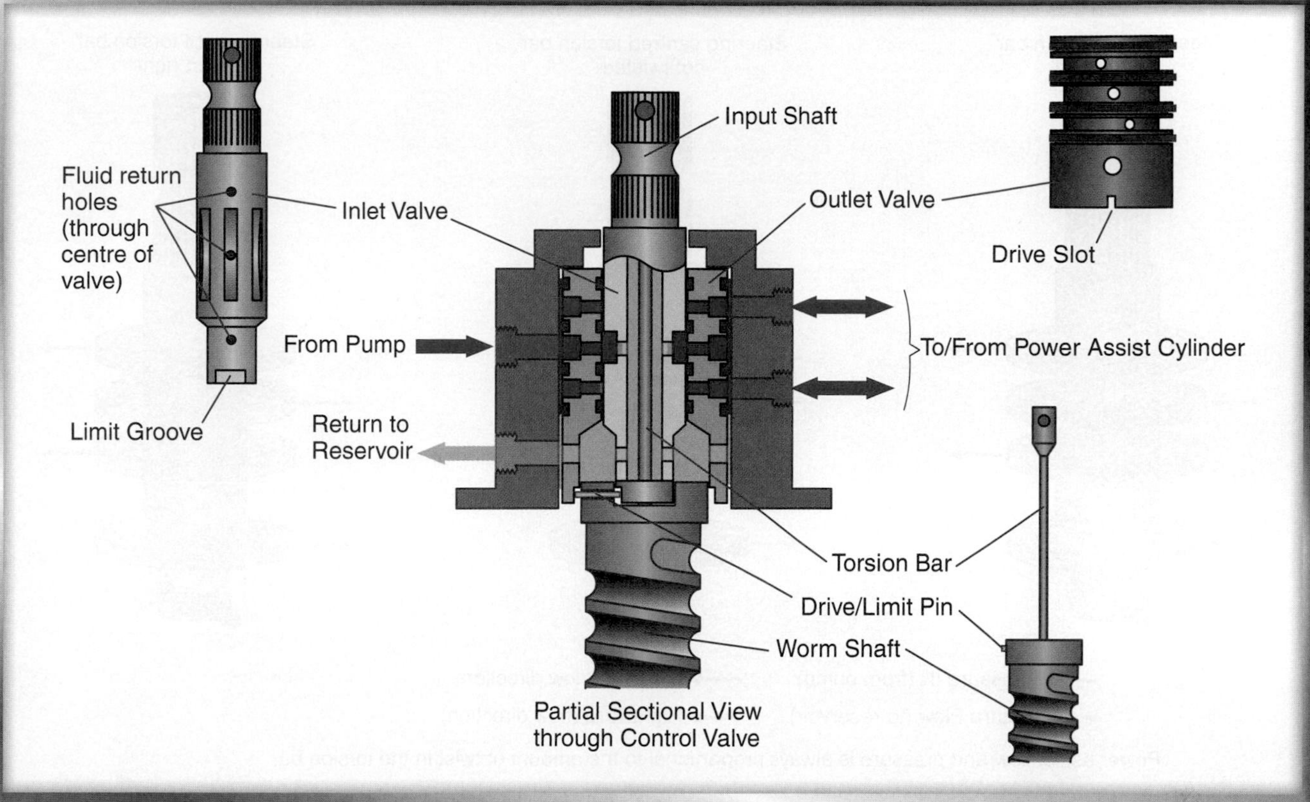

FIGURE 28-15 Steering rotary valve.

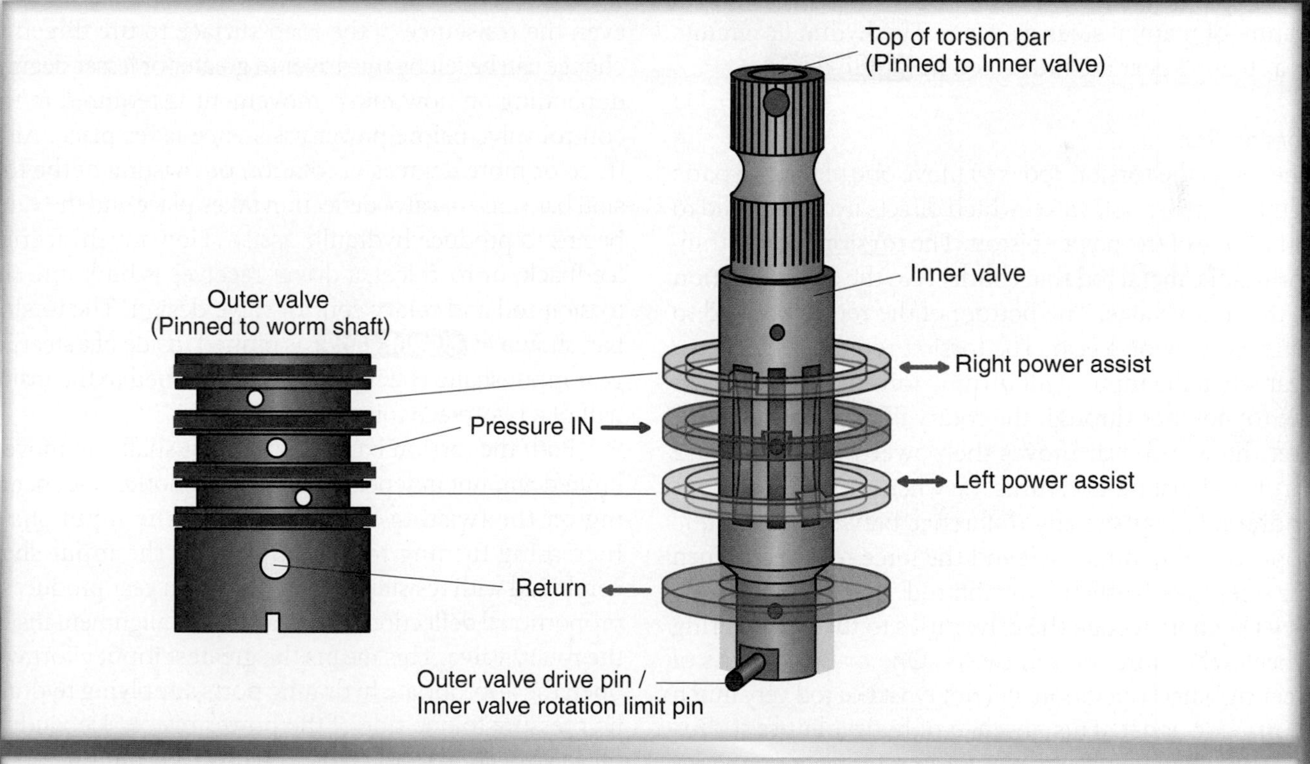

FIGURE 28-16 Cross section of rotary valve and ports.

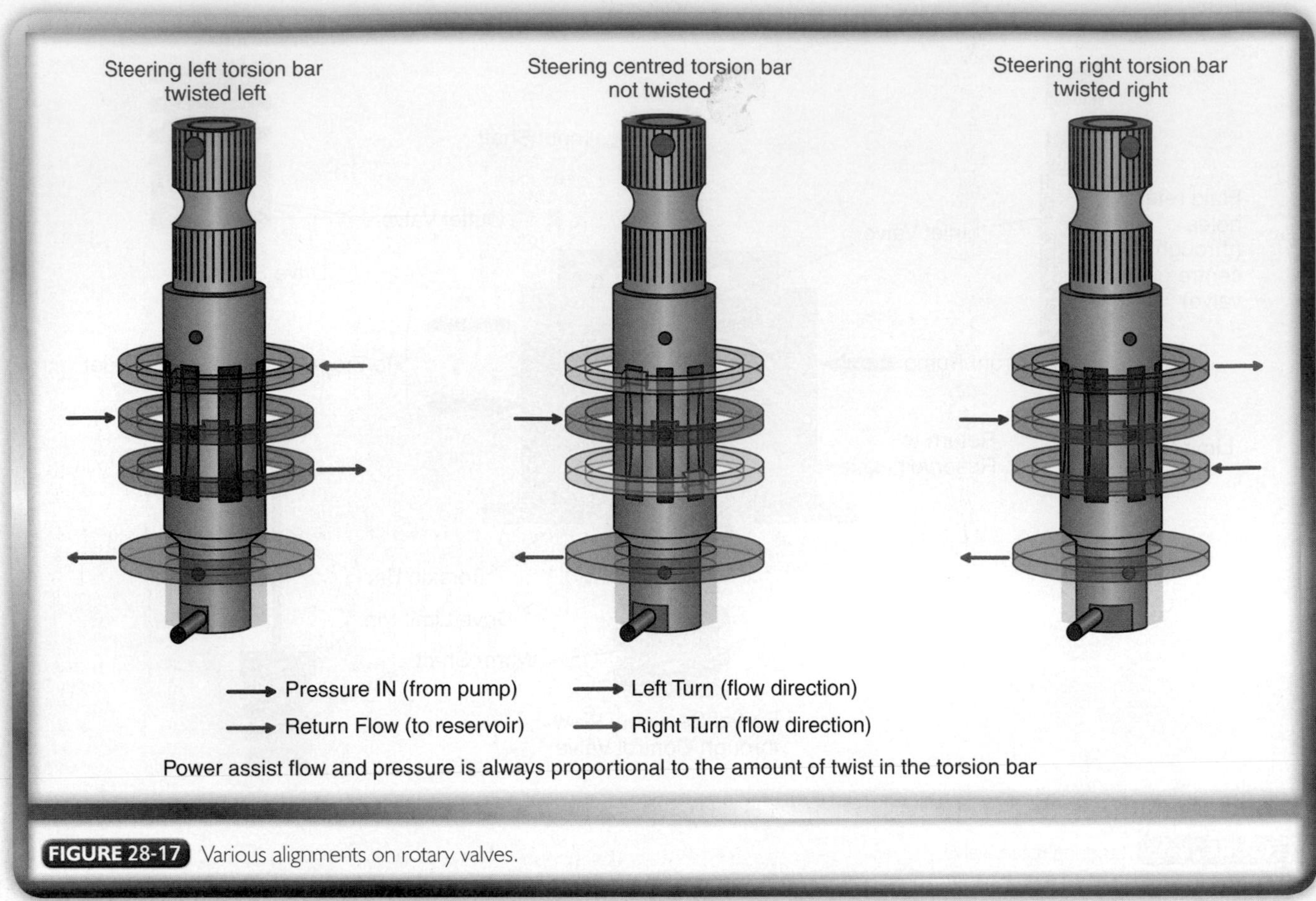

FIGURE 28-17 Various alignments on rotary valves.

feature of manual steering gears. The hydraulic circuits in a steering gear are illustrated in FIGURE 28-18.

Torsion Rod

The job of the torsion rod is to move one of the two parts of the rotary (spool) valve, which directs hydraulic fluid to either side of the power piston. The **torsion rod** is a thin, spring-like metal rod that connects to the outside section of the rotary valve. The bottom of the rod is attached to the rotating worm gear. The torsion rod turns the worm gear when the input shaft turning force is transmitted to the torsion bar through the rotary control valve. Recall that the worm gear moves the power piston back and forth, and that motion turns the wheels. With or without hydraulic pressure, any difference between the torque applied to the input shaft and the force required to turn the steer tires twists the torsion rod.

The more torque the driver uses to turn the steering wheels, the more the rod twists. One or two degrees of steering wheel operation will not twist the rod very much to provide assist. This absence of hydraulic assist during small deflection of the torsion rod is what provides some feedback about steering effort which is sensed by the driver as "road feel." Road surface irregularities and even the resistance of the road surface to tire direction change can be felt by the driver to greater or lesser degrees depending on how much movement is required in the control valve before power assistance takes place. After three or more degrees of rotation or twisting of the torsion bar, control valve deflection takes place and the valve begins to produce hydraulic assist. How much steering feedback, or road feel, a driver receives is built into the torsion rod and rotary control valve design. The torsion bar, shown in FIGURE 28-19, is pinned inside of a steering gear input shaft. The input shaft is attached to the inside half of a two-piece rotary valve.

Both the torsion bar and the input shaft can move a limited amount independently of one another—depending on the twisting force applied to the input shaft. Increasing turning torque applied to the input shaft combined with resistance from the worm gear produces a proportional deflection in the valve-port alignment inside the rotary valve. This means the greatest input effort will open the appropriate hydraulic ports supplying hydraulic pressure to one side of the power piston. Depending on the direction of the twist, pressurized fluid will pass through the valve to the top or bottom end of the steering gear power piston. If the torsion rod is broken, power

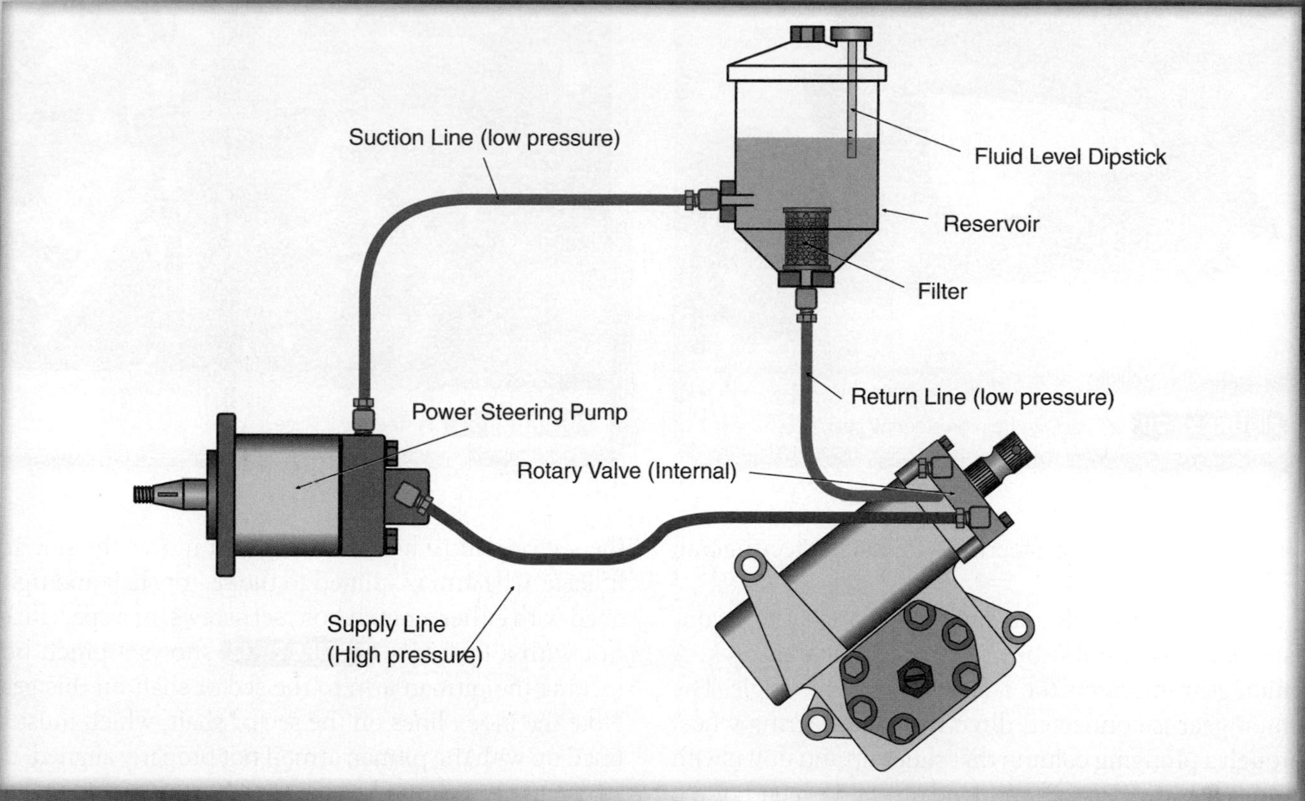

FIGURE 28-18 Hydraulic circuits for a power steering system using an integral steering gear.

FIGURE 28-19 Rotary valve and torsion bar.

assist is not possible. However, even if the torsion rod is broken, the design of the rotary-control valve allows the continuous transmission of torque from the input shaft to the worm.

Rack-and-Pinion Steering

Rack-and-pinion steering systems have been used in automobiles for decades and, in recent years, adapted for a few heavy trucks. The compact design of the system has a number of advantages. On heavy trucks, the system is 45 lb (20 kg) lighter than conventional integral steering. Rack-and-pinion steering has fewer parts and pivot points than conventional integral steering systems. Because the system has fewer parts, it also has fewer joints, which provides more precise steering response and greater reliability. The ZF rack-and-pinion steering gear, shown in FIGURE 28-20, is used by an independent suspension system in a cab-over-engine heavy-duty truck.

Rack-and-pinion steering systems do not include a pitman arm or a drag link. So, because the rack is parallel with the front axle, the problem of bump steer is minimized. **Bump steer** can occur when a wheel hits a bump and the axle lifts or drops through an arc on the side where the steering gear is located. The up or down axle movement changes the distance between the upper steering arm and the end of the pitman arm. This change in length between these two points can cause the drag link to push or pull on the steering arm, which in turn causes the vehicle to dart to one side of the road as the steering linkage is pushed or pulled. Steering pull can also sometimes occur when an axle twists due to braking torque. Without the drag link or pitman arm,

FIGURE 28-20 ZF rack-and-pinion steering gear.

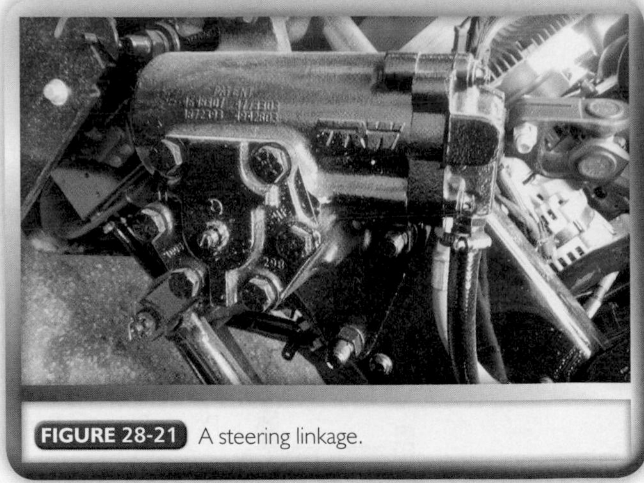
FIGURE 28-21 A steering linkage.

which rack-and-pinion steering eliminates, steering pull is minimized.

Freightliner's rack-and-pinion steering system consists of a horizontal tube containing a geared rack. A pinion gear intersects the rack at a 90 degree angle. The pinion gear is connected directly to the steering wheel through a plunging column that slides up and down with the suspension. Tie-rods protrude from each end of the tube and connect with the steering arms on the steering knuckle. A power-assist piston is integrated into the rack.

Turning the steering wheel causes the pinion gear to move the rack either to the left or right. A rotary-control valve, such as the ones found in the integral steering gears, supplies pressurized oil to two ports, one on either side of the rack piston. Without the hydraulic assist, the rack is moved left or right by only the torque transmitted from the steering wheel and into the pinion gear and rack. A torsion bar in the rack's rotary control valve varies the hydraulic pressure applied to the power piston proportionally to driver input torque.

Steering Linkage

The final basic components of any steering system are the **steering linkage**. The parts that make up the steering linkage are the pitman (drop) arm, drag link, tie-rod ends, and the upper and lower steering arms. These components were introduced in the Front Steering Axles and Vehicle Alignment Factors chapter. We will extend that introductory discussion in this section.

Pitman Arm

Recall that the **pitman (drop) arm** is attached to the output shaft, which is more correctly referred to as the sector shaft of the steering gear. The steering linkage is illustrated in FIGURE 28-21. The function of the pitman arm is to convert and transfer the rotational movement of the sector gear to linear motion that moves the steering linkage. The arm is splined to the sector shaft and tightened with either a pinch bolt, set screws, or a specialized nut with a lock tab. FIGURE 28-22 shows a pinch bolt locking the pitman arm to the sector shaft on this gear. Note the index lines on the sector shaft, which must be lined up with the pitman arm. If not properly aligned, the steering gear will not be able to rotate the steering wheel evenly between left and right turns.

It is critical that the connection of the pitman arm to the steering box sector shaft is secure. The splined shafts are often tapered to create a tighter connection. Set screws can be used to lock the arm to the sector shaft to add further security to the connection. The connection is so tight that it requires a specialized puller to remove the pitman arm from the sector shaft. An illustration for a pitman arm puller is shown in FIGURE 28-23.

An aligning mark is often used on the sector shaft and pitman arm to correctly center the wheels with the steering gear. The length of the arm affects the leverage of the steering gear on the linkage. Heavier vehicles will use longer arms. On dual box systems, the arms are different length and the right side arm, used on the slave steering gear, must always be longer than the left. If the wrong arm is installed, the slave gear will create a wheel shake on left turns. Correct pitman arm timing and drag link length is critical to prevent a similar condition.

Drag Link

Recall from the Introduction to Front Axles and Vehicle Alignment Factors chapter that the drag link is a steering linkage rod connecting the pitman arm at one end to the upper steering arm at the other. In addition to that basic bridging function, the drag link performs a leveling function. The sweeping arc the drag link moves though is enabled by the articulating ball joints at each end of the drag link. As the vehicle's suspension height adjusts as the chassis is loaded or the vehicle encounters bumps on the road, the drag link moves up and down and maintains the link between the pitman and steering arm.

While many drag links are fixed in length, others are adjustable. Adjustable drag links use a threaded center coupler or threaded rod end that enables changing the links length. On a single steering box, an adjustable link is turned to enable a technician to center the steering wheel so its position corresponds to the high point or center of the steering box travel. On dual box systems, adjustable links enable changes to equalize the turning radius of each wheel to left or right.

FIGURE 28-22 A pitman arm being locked to sector shaft by a pinch bolt.

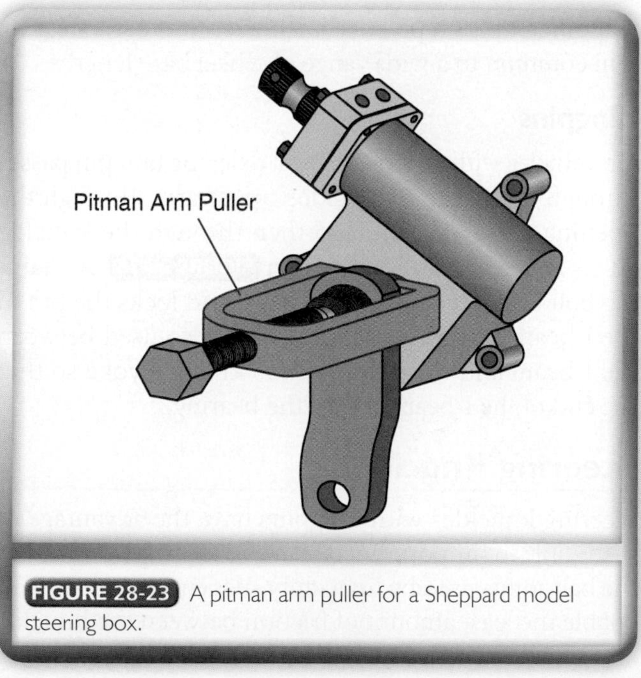

FIGURE 28-23 A pitman arm puller for a Sheppard model steering box.

Tie-Rod Ends

Tie-rod ends, such as the one shown in FIGURE 28-24, are ball and socket joints attached to both the left and right steering knuckle's lower steering arms. The ends are connected together by threading them into a cross tube called the **tie-rod**. Each side will use a left- or right-hand thread to enable adjustment of tire toe by turning the cross tube, which connects the tie-rod ends. Since the steering gear will push or pull on the upper steering arm only on one side, the movement is transferred to the opposite side through the tie-rod. Synchronizing the movement of both steering knuckles using the tie-rod means the articulating joints of the tie-rods move quite a bit. The weight of a vehicle combined with constant movement of the tie-rod ends means these parts wear the fastest of any piece of steering linkage. Frequent lubrication and maintenance inspections of these two critical joints is important to maintaining precise vehicle steering control.

A hydraulic steering dampener, illustrated in FIGURE 28-25, is sometimes connected to the tie-rod. The dampener, which operates like a shock absorber, minimizes steering wheel shimmy caused by high positive camber. Under conditions when the rear of the vehicle is heavily loaded, the frame angle may change, and the front wheels' kingpin inclination angle (KPI) tends to tilt back, which increases positive camber. Caster shimmy becomes

FIGURE 28-24 Tie-rod ends.

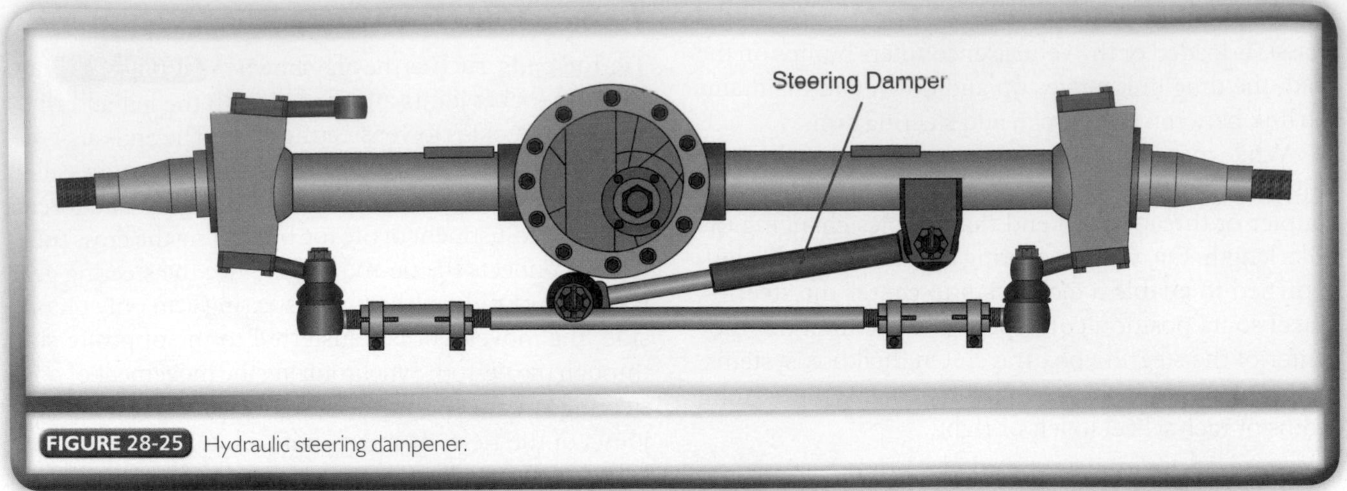

FIGURE 28-25 Hydraulic steering dampener.

even more exaggerated as vehicle speed increases. The dampener will prevent exaggerated caster shimmy and loss of steering control.

Pitman arms, tie-rods, and drag links are often designed with sharply curved shafts to prevent interference between steering or suspension components when wheels are cut sharply. Dropped tie-rod ends, illustrated in FIGURE 28-26, and tie-rod centers decrease link-to-attachment point angles. The dropped design also solves the steering geometry problem of enabling sharp turning radiuses without linkage interference by increasing the clearance between the steering arm and the tie-rod.

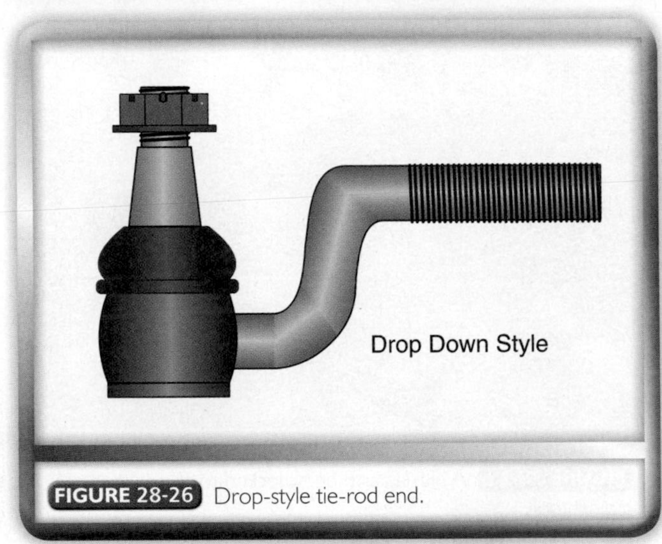

FIGURE 28-26 Drop-style tie-rod end.

Steering Arms

Steering arms are arms that extend from the steering knuckle. The tie-rods connect to the lower steering arms in synchronize steering knuckle rotation. Two steering arms are used on the left side steering knuckle: an upper arm and a lower arm. A single steering arm, also called the Ackermann arm, is used on the right when single steering boxes are used. Both lower arms are attached to the knuckle using tapered shafts and a keyway to prevent movement in the steering knuckle. A castellated nut and cotter pin are used to tighten and secure the shaft.

The lower Ackermann steering arms are forged at an angle unique to the wheel base of the chassis, as illustrated in FIGURE 28-27. By drawing an imaginary line through the shaft, the line should intersect at the vehicle's pivot point at the center of the rear axle's turning radius. Forming the shaft at this angle produces a slightly different turning radius for each wheel with the outside one toeing out on turns and the inner wheel turning more sharply than the outside wheel of the turn. Tandem axle steering arm angles should intersect with the centerline between the two axles. While the ideal steering arm angle will correspond to an angle which intersects with the center of the rear differential, in practice, manufacturers use a steering arm common to a wide range of wheel base lengths.

Kingpins

On vehicles with an I-beam front axle, the kingpin passes through the steering knuckle's upper arm, through the opening of the I-beam, and then through the knuckle yoke's lower arm, as illustrated in FIGURE 28-28. A retaining bolt keeps the kingpin in place and locks the pin in the I-beam axle. A thrust bearing is also used between the I-beam and lower arm of the knuckle yoke so that the end of the I-beam sits on the bearing.

Steering Knuckle

Steering knuckles with kingpins have the advantage of being able to support much heavier weights compared to the ball-joints used by light-duty suspension systems. To enable the least amount of friction between the knuckle and axle, a single bearing is located between the steering

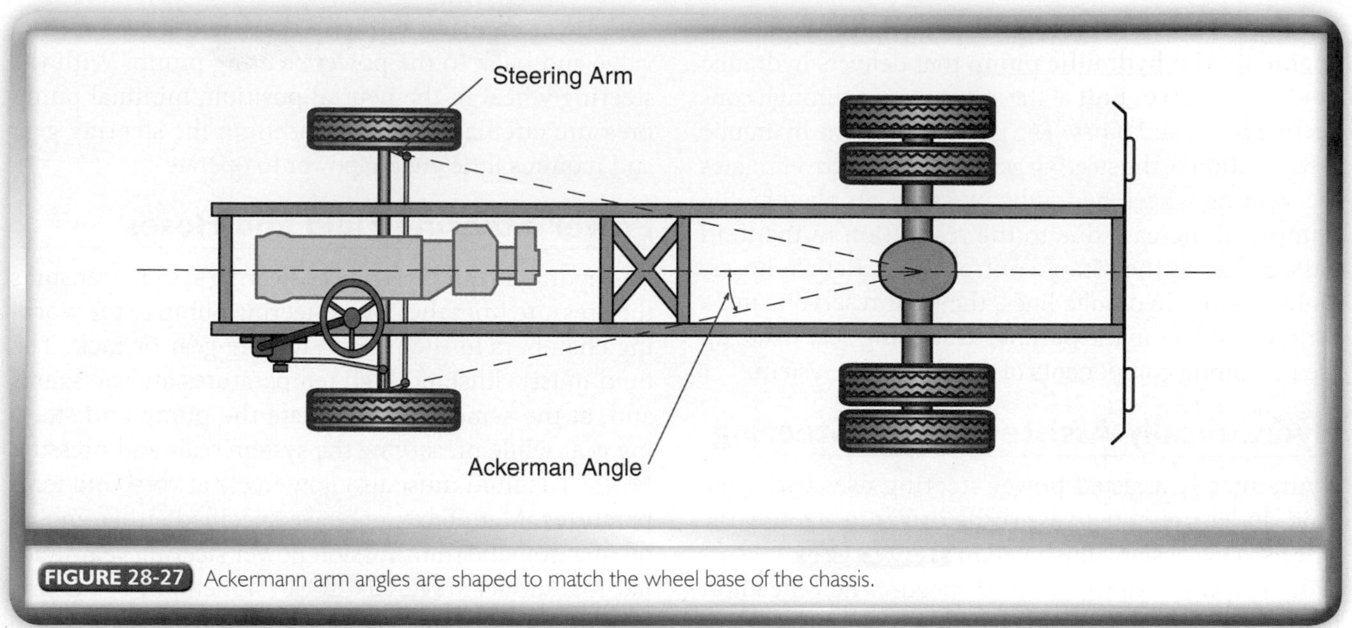

FIGURE 28-27 Ackermann arm angles are shaped to match the wheel base of the chassis.

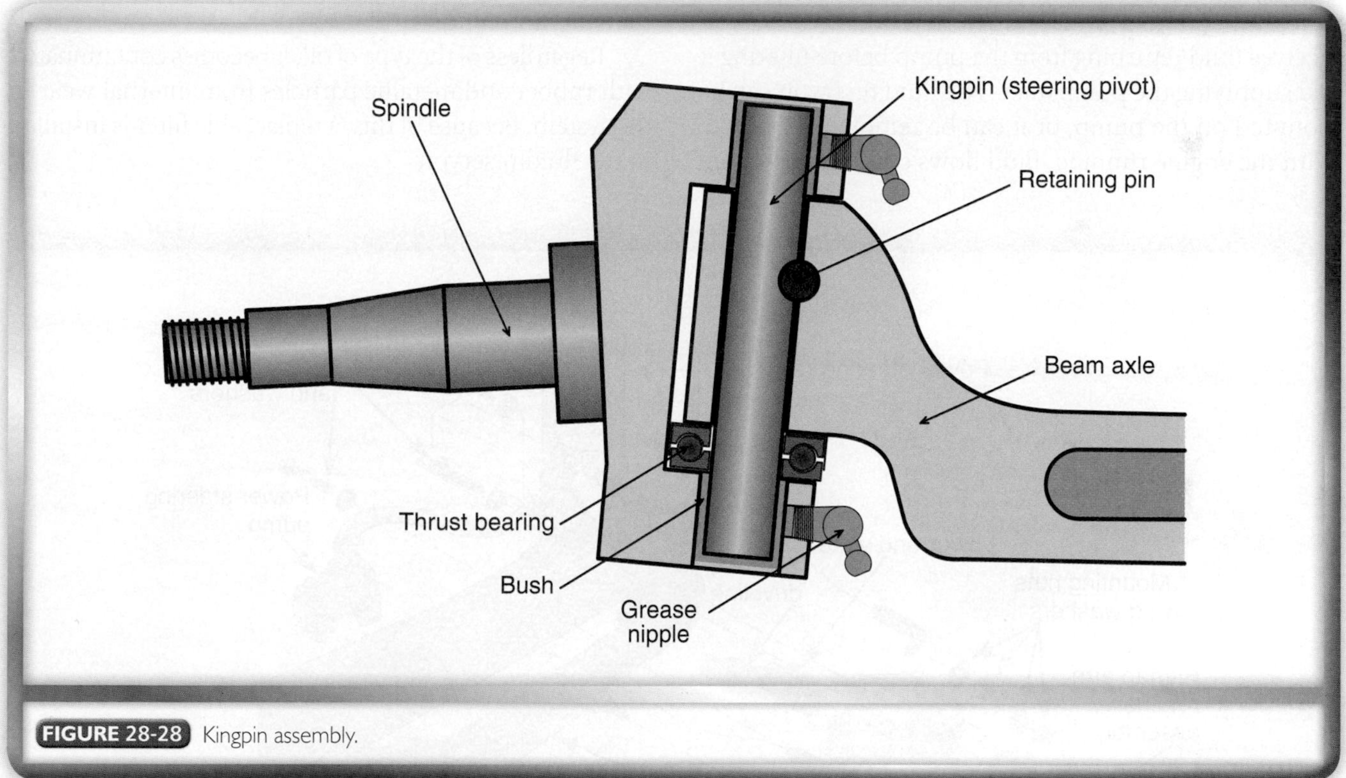

FIGURE 28-28 Kingpin assembly.

knuckle and axle, which transfers the weight supported by the wheel end to the axle. Without it, excessive friction between the axle and knuckle would quickly wear the two components and dramatically increase steering effort. The knuckle also uses adjustable steering stops, which limit the maximum rotation of the knuckle when turned. This prevents the steer tires from contacting the frame, steering linkage, or suspension components.

Hydraulic Components of Power Steering Systems

Power steering reduces the amount of physical effort required by the driver to steer the vehicle. A good power steering system not only reduces the effort required to steer the vehicle, but also provides good steering feedback (road feel) to the driver.

The most common type of power steering has an **engine-driven hydraulic pump** that delivers hydraulic fluid to the **power unit** at the steering gear through connecting hoses and pipes. The power unit is the hydraulic assist portion of the steering gear. When the driver rotates the steering wheel, hydraulic pressure supplied by the pump will increase due to the restriction in the fluid passageway in the rotary control valve. Return hoses, high-pressure hydraulic lines, the fluid reservoir, and a variety of valves in the pump and steering gear make up the remaining components of the hydraulic system.

Hydraulically Assisted Power Steering

Hydraulically assisted power steering uses hydraulic fluid under pressure to assist the driver in steering the wheels. This design, illustrated in FIGURE 28-29, is especially helpful at slower vehicle speeds when the effort required to turn the steering wheel is much higher. Two lines connect the pump to the steering gear control valve: a pressure and fluid return. A remotely mounted reservoir receives fluid returning from the pump before filtering it and supplying the pump inlet. The fluid reservoir can be mounted on the pump, or it can be remotely mounted. With the engine running, fluid flows continuously from the **power steering pump** to the steering gear control valve and back to the power steering pump. With the steering wheel in the neutral position, minimal pump pressure circulates fluid to and from the steering gear and requires little engine power to operate.

Power Steering Fluid and Hoses

The hydraulic fluid in a power steering system transmits the pressure from the power steering pump to the working chambers in the power steering gear or rack. The fluid must withstand high temperatures and pressures and, at the same time, lubricate the pump and steering gear while preserving the system seals and pressure hoses. The fluid must also flow freely at very cold temperatures. Manufacturers have specified either engine oil or automatic transmission power steering gear fluid, like that shown in FIGURE 28-30, for their power steering systems. Most engine-driven pumps use engine oil to avoid the risk of contaminating engine oil with automatic transmission fluid.

Regardless of the type of oil, it becomes contaminated with rubber and metallic particles from internal wear in the system. Because of this, a replaceable filter is installed in the fluid reservoir.

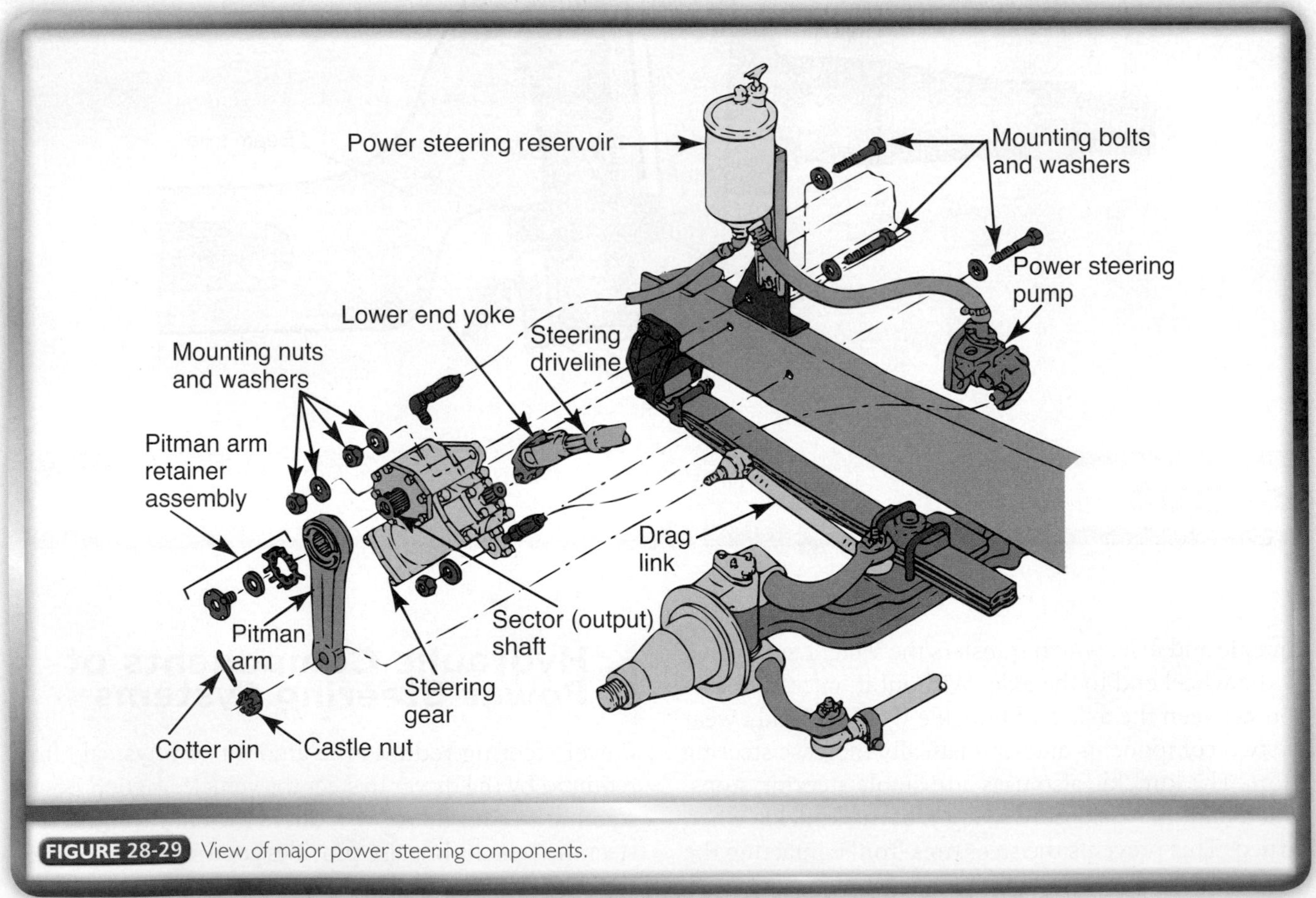

FIGURE 28-29 View of major power steering components.

Power steering hoses carry power steering fluid from the pump to the steering gear. This hose is usually made of flexible, steel-braided hose material. The return hose from the steering gear back to the pump reservoir and carries fluid under much lower pressure and is not usually reinforced.. These hoses must also allow movement between the engine and chassis, so they cannot be too stiff.

FIGURE 28-30 Power steering fluid.

Over time, power steering hoses can become weak or damaged. If they leak, they can cause a loss of vehicle control. For this reason, hoses should be inspected for seepage or wear during each service. Also, some power steering hoses use an O-ring to seal the end of each hose to the pump and steering gear. These seals can wear or leak, requiring replacement of the O-ring.

> **TECHNICIAN TIP**
>
> A power steering reservoir is often equipped with a filter needing periodic replacement. Restricted filters will lead to over-heating of power steering oil, pump cavitation, or air leaks on the suction side of the system.

As illustrated in FIGURE 28-31, when the steering gear is in the neutral or non-steering position, equal low pressure is being applied to both ends of the steering gear piston. The oil is circulating at back pressure only and provides a hydraulic cushion for the steering gear. Circulating oil is cooled in the reservoir or through a small heat exchanger which is usually a tube in the low pressure return line wrapped with cooling fins to help cool the system.

With the engine running and the steering in the neutral position, fluid flow is directed into the valve assembly

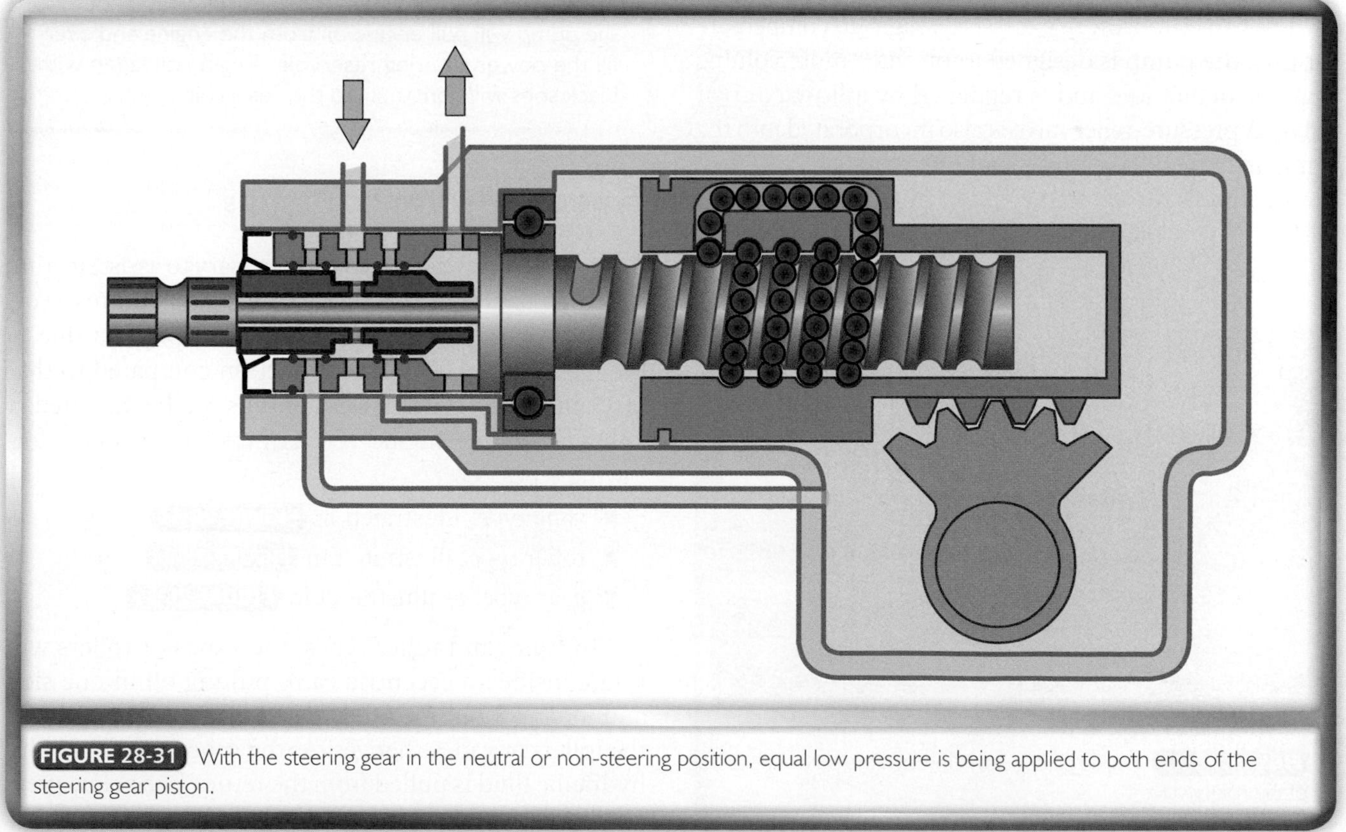

FIGURE 28-31 With the steering gear in the neutral or non-steering position, equal low pressure is being applied to both ends of the steering gear piston.

through drilled holes in the outer sleeve, like those shown in FIGURE 28-32. As soon as the steering is turned to the left or right, the slight relative movement occurs between the inner and the outer parts of the valve due to the action of the torsion rod. In the neutral position, the inner part of the valve connected to the steering input shaft lets fluid pass equally to both sides of the piston through internal passages and return to the fluid reservoir. Equal but low pressure is applied to both sides of the power piston.

When the steering wheel is turned, fluid is restricted from returning to the to the reservoir. This happens due to the action between the twisting torsion rod and the outer half of the rotary control valve. Fluid is then directed to the side that matches the turning action. At the same time, fluid on the opposite side is directed to the return circuit—back to the reservoir. Slight rotation of the valve gives a small amount of assistance, which becomes progressively greater as the torsion bar flexes when more assistance is needed.

Power Steering Pumps

To provide the hydraulic force necessary to assist steering effort, an engine-driven hydraulic pump is used. Gear-driven pumps are more popular due to the reliability of a direct connection versus a belt driven system. Gear pumps can be mounted at either end of the engine as well. These pumps can be either the vane, gear, or roller type.

Engine speed can vary, so unregulated pump output volume can be too low or excessively high. To compensate for this, the pump is designed to produce more volume than needed at idle and is regulated by a **flow-control valve**. A pressure-relief valve is also incorporated into the pump to prevent excessively high pressures such as when the steering is turned to the end of the steering stops. In addition to the pressure relief valve in the power steering pump, steering gears are equipped with relief valves that relieve pump pressure when the wheels near the steering stops at a full wheel cut. Without pressure relief, the steering system components are severely stressed and power steering oil will overheat.

Power steering reservoirs should always be located above the level of the power steering pump. Lines should always be located at a level below the reservoir. Typically, 10w-30, 15w-40, or automatic transmission fluids are used as oils. Since chemical additives in various oils may not be compatiblewith steering gear, hose, or reservoir materials, it is not a recommended practice to mix oils.

FIGURE 28-32 Drilled passageways through the outer sleeve of the rotary valve.

Power Steering Coolers

Pressurizing the power steering oil produces heat that can damage the oil. Overheated oil will oxidize and form sludge as well as harden hoses and other rubber based parts. Heated oil will lose its viscosity and leak between small clearances, causing a loss in power assist. On heavy vehicles, an oil cooler is used to prevent overheating.

> **TECHNICIAN TIP**
>
> Engine-driven power steering pumps use two seals on the drive shaft. One deflects engine oil from being pulled into the gear by pump suction, and the other prevents oil from leaving the gear. If the engine side seal is damaged or cut from by abrasive metal filings or dirt, the pump will pull engine oil from the engine and overfill the power steering reservoir. Engine oil laden with black soot will contaminate the reservoir.

Types of Hydraulic Pumps

To provide the hydraulic force necessary to assist steering effort, an engine-driven hydraulic pump and reservoir are used. Gear-driven pumps are more popular due to the reliability of a direct connection compared to that of a belt-driven system. Gear pumps can be mounted at either end of the engine, too. Pumps are one of the following types:

- vane type, illustrated in FIGURE 28-33
- roller type, illustrated in FIGURE 28-34
- gear type, as illustrated in FIGURE 28-35

In vane- and roller-types, the vanes or rollers will rotate inside an eccentric cam, pulling oil in one side and forcing it out the other side as the volume between the rollers or vanes changes. As the vanes or rollers spin, hydraulic fluid is pulled from the return line at low pressure and forced it into the outlet at high pressure.

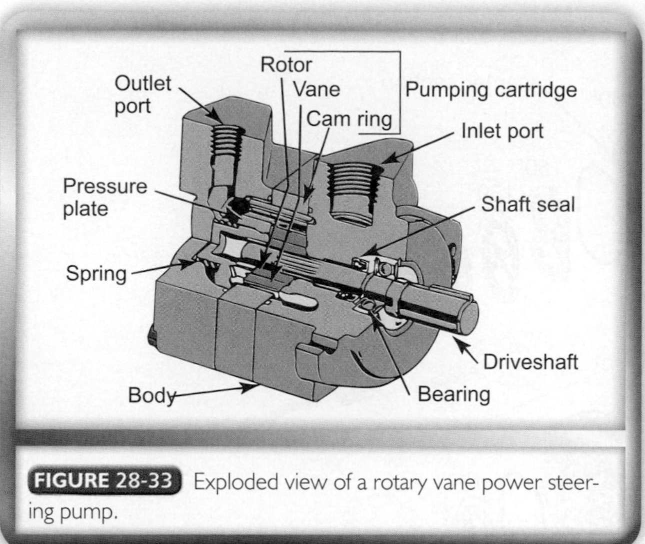

FIGURE 28-33 Exploded view of a rotary vane power steering pump.

Depending on engine speed, pump output volume can be too low or excessively high. Therefore, the pump uses a flow-control valve designed to compensate for normally low volume output at idle and decrease output volume at high pump speeds. Regulating pump volume is a flow-control needle that throttles the flow of fluid at the pump's outlet. The needle valve's position is balanced between pump outlet pressure and the position of the high pressure regulating valve. The valve position at idle is illustrated in Figure 28-35.

When both outlet volume and output pressure are low, the flow-control valve is moved to the right by the regulating valve. This allows more fluid to flow through the valve to the steering gear. **FIGURE 28-36** shows high output pressure forcing the pressure regulating valve to move left and redirect fluid back to the low pressure pump return

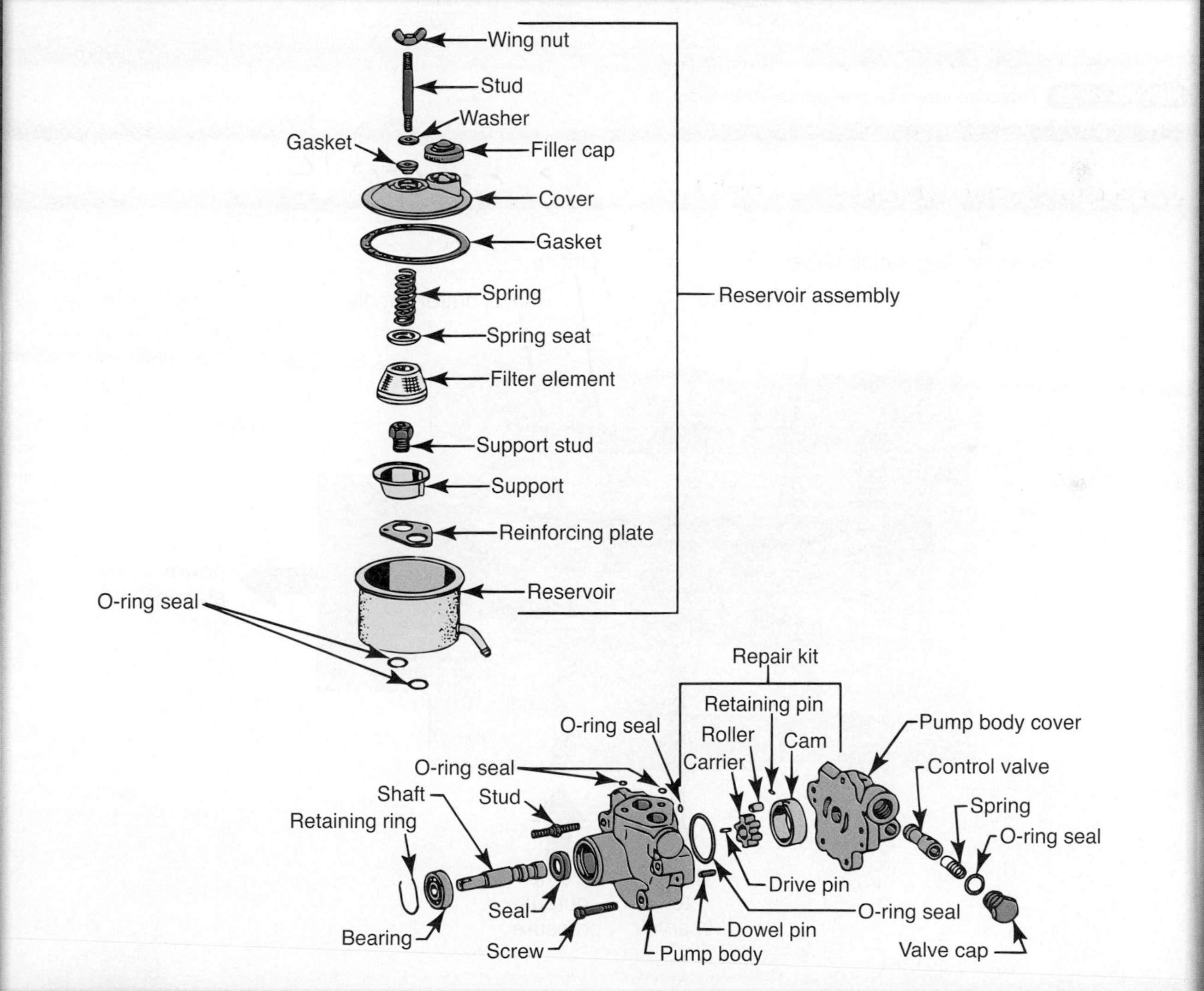

FIGURE 28-34 Exploded view of a roller power steering pump.

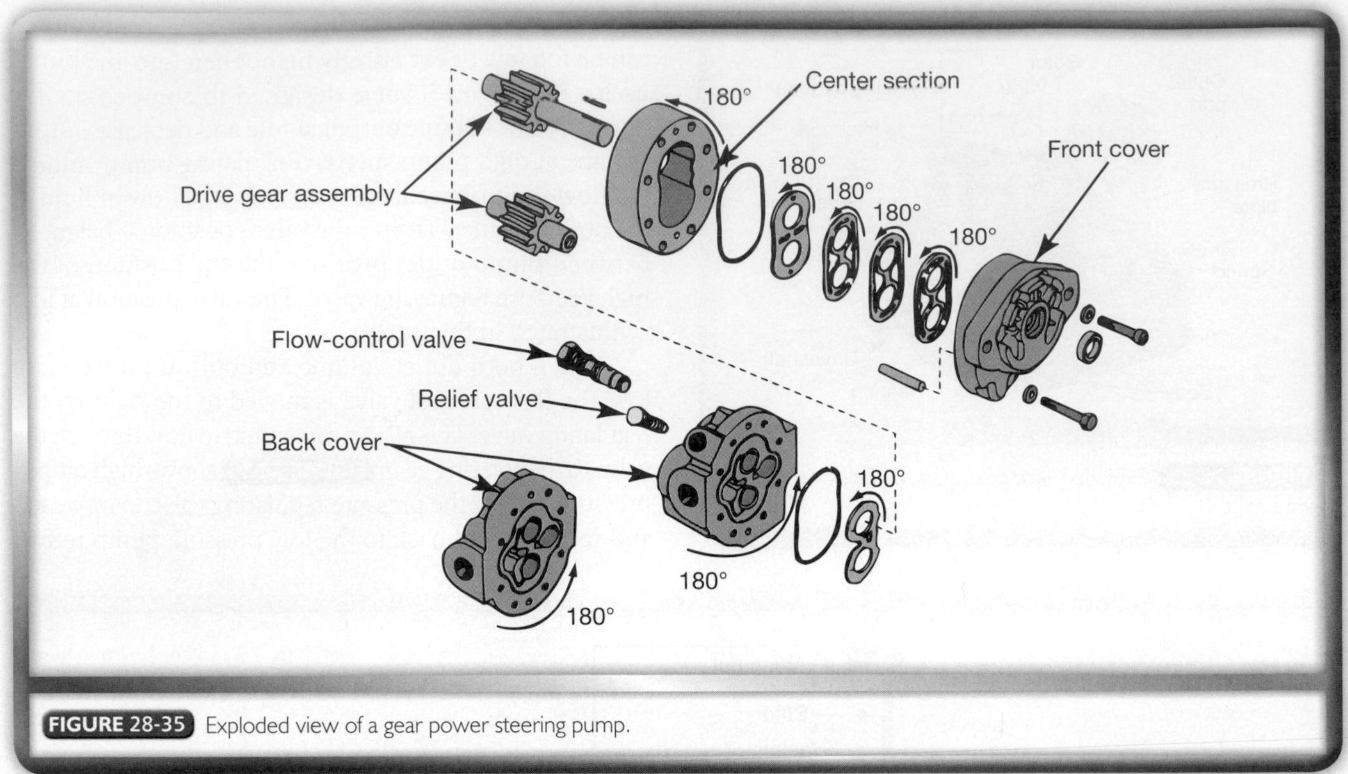

FIGURE 28-35 Exploded view of a gear power steering pump.

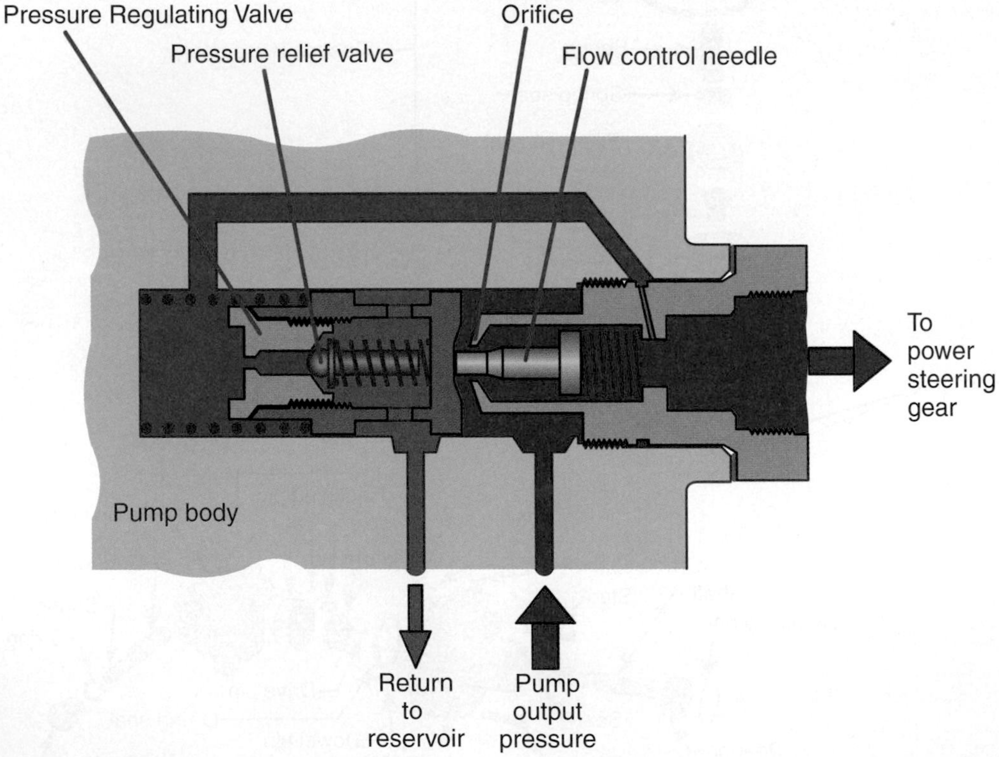

FIGURE 28-36 Position of the flow control valve at low pump speed and volume. The flow control valve's movement regulates hydraulic pressure and volume to the steering gear by moving a spring-loaded needle valve located in the outlet fitting of the pump.

circuit. At the same time the flow control valve blocks fluid flow out of the pump.

If pump outlet pressures exceed the control valve's ability to regulate pressure, an internal relief valve opens and dumps pump pressure directly back into the reservoir, as illustrated in FIGURE 28-37.

Maintenance and Service of the Steering System

The steering system is critical to a vehicle's safe operation. Always follow manufacturer procedures when working on a steering system. To maintain a vehicle in safe operating condition, it is essential to regularly inspect the steering components. This can be performed both by visually inspecting the components and joints for damage, looseness, or leakage and by operating the steering system.

To prevent dirt or other foreign matter from entering the hydraulic system, clean around dipstick filler caps before checking power steering oil level. Investigate and correct any external leak, no matter how minor, in the steering system. Comply with manufacturer's specifications and instructions for servicing the steering system. If inspection or testing of the steering system, particularly the steering gear, reveals evidence of abnormal wear or damage, or if you encounter any unusual circumstances or are unsure about choosing the correct service procedure, STOP! Then consult the vehicle manufacturer's service manual and other OEM service literature.

Steering Complaints

When a driver presents a complaint about a steering-related problem, as with any diagnosis, it is important to collect some basic information. It is important to determine what the steering is doing, when and where the problem occurs, and how the vehicle responds. A visual inspection of fluid levels, hoses, linkage and inspecting for leaks is always performed first before proceeding with more specific diagnostic procedures.

Preliminary system checks, including tire inflation pressure, tire condition, power steering level, and a visual inspection of the suspension system, should precede any major diagnostic test. For on-highway tractors, the fifth wheel should be checked to make sure it has been greased because binding between the trailer and tractor will cause

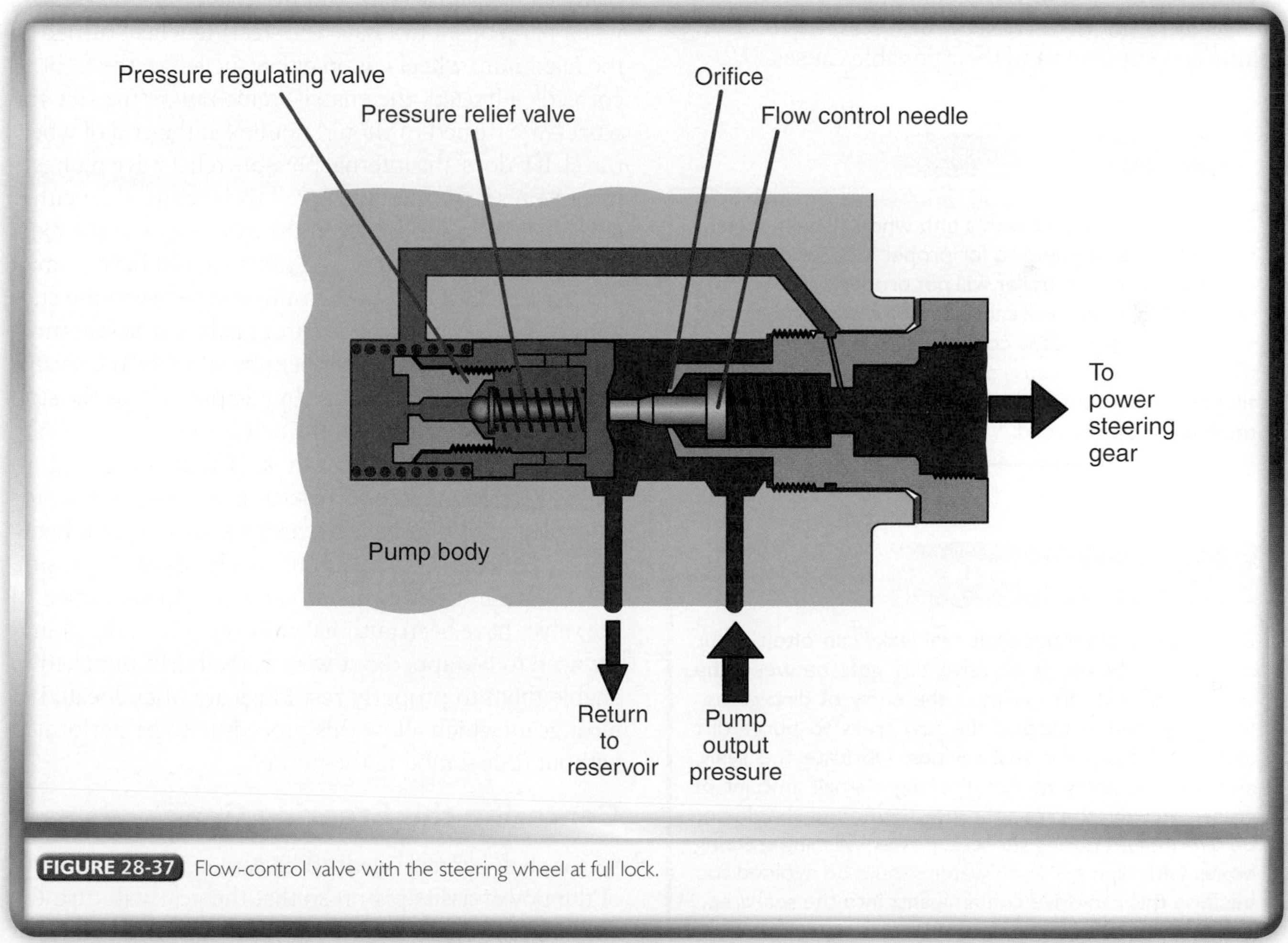

FIGURE 28-37 Flow-control valve with the steering wheel at full lock.

hard steering. Chassis parts to be checked for excessive wear or damage include:

- Kingpins
- Spring leafs, shackles, and pins
- Suspension height
- Suspension U-bolts
- Drag link(s)
- Tie-rod ends
- Steering stops
- Steering gear mounting
- Steering column slip joints and universal joints

Steering complaints fall into the following descriptive categories:

- Hard steering
- Binding
- Bump steer
- Shimmy
- Excessive turning radius
- Oversteer or understeer
- Pulling or wandering
- Noise

TABLE 28-1 provides descriptions of each of these common complaints and their possible causes.

Safety

On vehicles equipped with a fifth wheel, it is important the fifth wheel is checked for proper lubrication. Without lubrication, the trailer will not properly pivot on the wheel table, which will cause it to bind and lead to hard steering or understeer conditions. Poor lubrication of the fifth wheel can cause a loss of directional control in slippery conditions and even cause the trailer to push the tractor off the road.

TECHNICIAN TIP

Sector shaft and input shaft seal leaks can often occur on steering boxes as abrasive dirt gets between the shafts and seals. To minimize the entry of dirt, grease fittings are often used at the seal areas to purge dirt and water from the seal cavities, lubricate the seals, and prevent entry of dirt. Pushing a small amount of grease through the seals through the fittings should not be overlooked during services. Power washing steering boxes with high pressure water should be avoided too because this can drive contaminants into the seal area.

If seals are found leaking, the shaft surfaces must be inspected for wear. Abrasive dirt will wear grooves into the shafts requiring either the shaft, or the entire steering gear replacement because new seals will quickly leak. Steering input or sector shafts cannot be repaired through spray welding because the process damages the the metallurgical properties of the metal which allow the shaft to bend and not break under impact.

Steer Axle Steering Stops

All medium and heavy-duty steering systems will use steering stops to limit the range of motion of the wheels. Steering stops are adjusted to achieve a maximum wheel cut while maintaining a minimum of 1" (2.5 cm) clearance between the tires and any part of the chassis. To prevent damage to the high-pressure pump, gear, and steering linkage, the stops are used to adjust internal pressure relief valves in the steering gear. Power steering gears are equipped with internal pressure relief valves, which relieve or unload hydraulic pressure when as the steering linkage approaches the stops.

Automatic stops, which are now built into most steering gears, are set the first time the steering wheel is turned completely from stop to stop. To check this, the vehicle, when parked, should have the steering wheel turned to the maximum wheel cut on either the left or the right. If correctly adjusted, the chassis frame rail on the side the wheels are turned to should not flex at the end of wheel travel. If it does, the internal pressure relief valve plungers must be reset. If the turning radius is reduced on either side, check the gap between the axle stop and the axle. When adjusted correctly, the stops should have a small 1/8" to 3/8" (3.2 mm to 9.5 mm) gap between the stop and the contact point on the front axle just before turning effort increases. This happens because the relief valve only begins to unload the hydraulic pressure as the stop approaches the contact on the axle.

Automatic stops, such as those pictured in FIGURE 28-38, may need resetting in cases when, for example, larger tires have been installed or a gear is being installed during service. Automatically adjusted pressure relief valve in the pump can only be adjusted once. If the valves have been automatically set before, the plungers need to be tapped out with a small drift punched to enable them to properly rest Plugs are often located in most gears which allow this procedure to be performed without disassembling the pump.

Centering the Steering Gear

Sector shaft contact needs to be centered with the teeth of the power-assist piston so that the gear will turn the maximum range in each direction. Centering the gear

TABLE 28-1: Common Steering-Related Problems

Concern	Possible Cause	Remedy
Hard Steering	• The driver describes the steering with phrases such as "won't turn unless moving" • The vehicle will steer but with difficulty • Measured at the steering wheel center nut, effort requiring more than 100 inch-pounds (11.3 Nm) at the steering wheel rim is considered excessive	• Faulty supply pump • Tight or seized kingpins • High oil operating temperature • Front end load too great • Low oil level in reservoir • Air in system • Caster angle adjusted incorrectly
Binding	• Any cyclical-like tightness, locking-up, or torque variations at the steering wheel	• Steering column U-joints not phased • U-joint angles greater than 25°degrees • Seized or tight kingpins • Seized or tight steering linkage joints
Bump Steer	• The steering wheel kicks whenever the vehicle goes over a bump in the road and oscillates back and forth	• Air in steering system • Incorrect drag link, misadjusted drag link, or mismatched drag link and upper steering arm
Shimmy	• The steering wheel rhythmically shakes back and forth at low and or high speeds	• Incorrect caster angle—too much positive caster • Incorrectly loaded vehicle • Air in system • Excessive toe-in • Incorrect steering gear adjustments Wheels out of balance
Excessive Turning Radius	• The vehicle wheel cut is at a sharper angle than normal	• Steering stop relief plungers not adjusted • Steering stops not correctly adjusted
Oversteer	• The vehicle turns more than the driver wants compared to steering input • The vehicle suddenly and rapidly changes direction or darts when turned	• Oil pressure too high • Air trapped in steering gear • Looseness; worn steering linkage • Front end alignment not adjusted correctly • Overloading • Axles not parallel • Mismatched or incorrect tire and wheel rims
Understeer	• The vehicle does not respond enough to normal steering input • Steering seems sluggish	• Oil flow too low • Air trapped in steering gear • Looseness; worn steering linkage • Vehicle alignment angles not adjusted correctly • Overloading • Axles not parallel • Mismatched or incorrect tire and wheel rims • Loose or worn pitman arm splines • Loose steering gear
Pulling or Wandering	• The vehicle requires constant wheel correction to keep the vehicle traveling in a straight-line direction • The vehicle pulls consistently in a single direction (for example, to the right) • The steering can also appear to be loose, meaning there is a loss of motion in the steering system	• Vehicle angles alignment not adjusted correctly • Improper loading or tire pressure • Loose, broken, or damaged suspension (i.e., broken leaf spring center bolt) • Loose or worn steering linkage • Loose or worn pitman arm splines • Loose steering gear mounting • Loose wheel bearings • Wrong tires for application
Noise	• Clunks, buzzing, hissing, and other sounds	• Restricted oil filter • Low hydraulic fluid level • Air in system

FIGURE 28-38 Automatic steering stops (circled) adjust the first time the wheels are cut and the relief valves contact the end of the steering box.

contact is even more important on variable-ratio steering gears because the teeth have different lengths and are responsible for transferring the correct road feel. Incorrect centering can lead to steering wander, excessive looseness, and even binding of the steering gear. Even if the steering gear sector shaft and assist piston are centered, incorrect positioning of the tie-rod ends and incorrect length of the drag link can cause the steering to operate off-center. To verify on-center operation, follow the procedure in SKILL DRILL 28-1.

Worm Gear Preload Adjustment

Clearances between the worm gear and the supporting bearings are minimal. Tight clearances prevent unnecessary movement and looseness in the steering gear. Loose bearings will cause steering to wander, requiring constant wheel correction by the driver. Worm gear preload is set at the factory and may need readjustment if worm gear parts are replaced or disassembled. Bearing preload is measured with an inch-pound (newton meter) torque wrench when the sector shaft is removed from the gear. Selective shims or a jam nut is used to set the preload to manufacturer specifications.

TECHNICIAN TIP

Worm gear preload adjustment is critical to eliminate any looseness in the gear while allowing just enough pressure against the bearing without binding and still allow oil between parts.

Over Center Adjustment

Teeth on the sector shaft and power steering gear are tapered, and proper clearance between them requires

SKILL DRILL 28-1 Centering the Steering Linkage

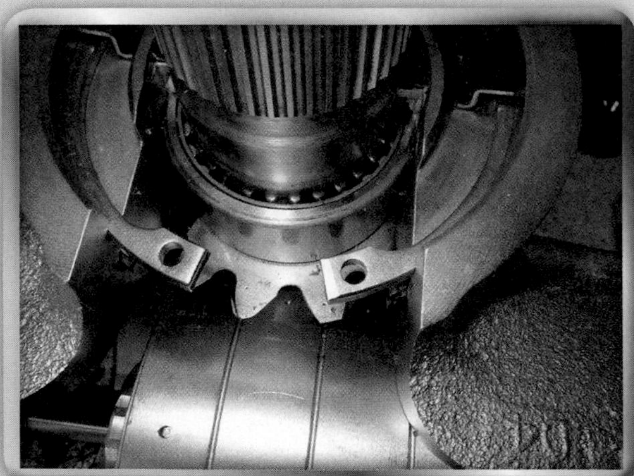

1. Square the tires with the frame so the tires are tracking in a dead straight-ahead position. This can be done by measuring the distance of the front and rear of the tire to adjust for the same distance from the frame rail.
2. Disconnect the drag link at both ends.
3. Disconnect the steering gear input shaft.
4. Check the timing mark on the pitman arm and sector shaft to verify that they line up.
5. Turn the input shaft with a 12-point socket, and count the number of turns. Precisely find and mark the halfway point between the travel limits of the input shaft.
6. Measure the distance between the hole of the pitman arm and the steering arm used by the drag link. It must be exactly the same length as the drag link. If not, the correct drag link or an adjustable drag link must be installed and adjusted.
7. Reconnect the steering input shaft, ensuring that the steering wheel spokes are aligned for a straight-ahead position.
8. If the steering wheel is not centered, remove the steering wheel and reinstall in with the spoke properly aligned to a straight ahead position.

adjustment. After worm bearing preload is completed and the sector shaft is installed and centered, the over center adjustment can be performed. As with the worm gear preload, over center adjustment is done with a torque wrench. A left-hand-thread adjusting screw on the cover at the rear of the sector shaft will move the sector shaft towards or away from the tapered teeth of the assist piston. To adjust preload to the manufacturer's specifications, rock the sector shaft through the center point using a 12-point socket to turn the input shaft. Once preload is adjusted on the sector shaft, the amount of resistance measured with an inch-pound (newton meter) torque wretch at the input shaft can be compared with manufacturer's specifications as shown in FIGURE 28-39. Total torque applied to the input shaft through the center point of the steering gear is called **total mesh adjustment**. When the torque is correct, the steering gear preload is in the proper range.

Maintenance and Service of the Hydraulic System

Oil pressure and volume requirements are established during the design of the steering system. When diagnosing steering problems, oil pressure and flow must meet certain specifications. Pressure levels determine how much force the steering system can apply to linkage, and flow, or volume, determines the speed at which the work is done. Pressure and flow specifications vary from vehicle to vehicle, but generally systems will operate at a flow rate of 2.5 to 6 gallons per minute (9.5 to 22.7 liters per minute) and approximately 1,500 psi lb per square inch (10,342 kPa).

System pressure and operating temperature must be considered during the diagnosis of the steering system. High system pressure will create heat, which thins out the oil and reduces the efficiency of the steering pump and gear. Thin oil will leak past the power piston and vanes or rollers of the power steering pump, increasing steering effort while at the same time reducing steering speed.

Power Steering System Analyzer (PSSA)

Determining whether a steering problem is present in a gear or pump, requires the use of a **Power Steering System Analyzer (PSSA)** gauge, like that illustrated in FIGURE 28-40, during diagnostics. The PSSA tool is a combination flow meter, shutoff valve, and pressure gauge. It enables a technician to measure hydraulic flow pressure in the steering system and to apply a load to the pump using the system's hydraulic lines. In other words, the PSSA analyzer will provide pressure (psi or kilopascals) and flow data (gpm or lpm) when it is installed in series with the high pressure line at the steering gear. A shutoff valve simulates a load on the system. The PSSA typically consists of a pressure gauge rated at 3,000 psi (20,684 kPa) and a flow meter with a capacity of 10 gallons per minute (gpm).

Safety

It is important to take the following precautions when performing hydraulic tests with a PSSA:

- Familiarize yourself with all moving parts that could cause personal injury.
- During test procedures, do not allow the fluid reservoir to run low on oil.
- Before beginning tests, check all components, hoses, and fittings for tightness and leaks.
- Wear appropriate safety glasses.

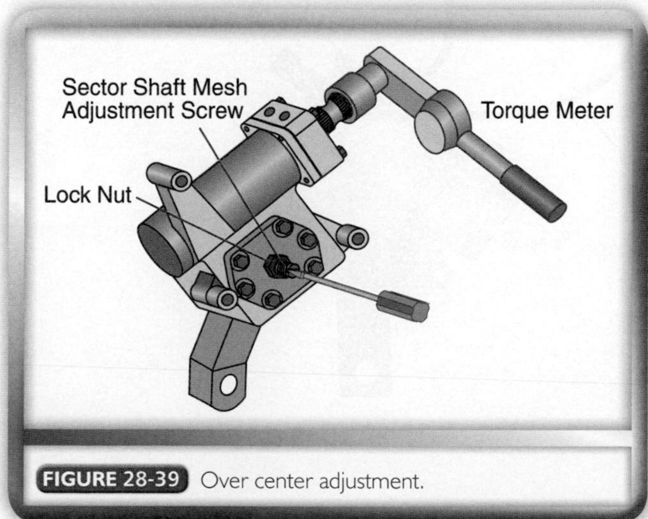

FIGURE 28-39 Over center adjustment.

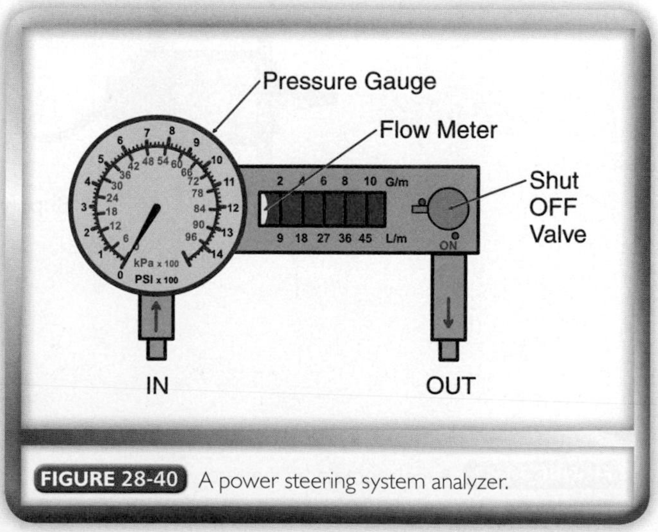

FIGURE 28-40 A power steering system analyzer.

A shutoff valve placed downstream from the pressure gauge allows the power steering pump to be isolated from the steering gear. That separation facilitates checking the pump relief pressure. A simple thermometer placed in the reservoir, as illustrated in FIGURE 28-41, will show system temperature.

Since the analyzer is connected in series, only one hose connection is opened—either at the pump output or at the pressure input—to the power steering gear housing.

To use a PSSA, follow the steps in SKILL DRILL 28-2. When thinking about hydraulic diagnostic work, it is helpful to remember the following:

- Pressure: The amount of force the steering gear can apply to linkage.
- Flow: Speed of steering, which is related to how far the piston can be displaced by oil.

To use a PSSA to measure pump maximum relief pressure, follow the steps in SKILL DRILL 28-3.

Pump output volume is measured under four conditions:

- At idle and with normal back pressure
- At idle under a 1,500 psi (10,342 kPa) load applied with the shutoff valve
- Flow at full governed RPM with back pressure only
- Flow at full governed RPM under a 1,500 psi (10,342 kPA) load applied with the shutoff valve

To use a PSSA to test flow volume, follow the steps in SKILL DRILL 28-4.

Safety

A defective pressure relief valve or missing relief valve may not relieve pump pressure when the shutoff valve is closed. This potentially can result in damage to the pump and rupture hoses. Observe the pressure gauge closely while closing the shutoff valve. If the pressure rises too rapidly or reaches 2,500 psi (17,237 kPa), immediately open the valve.

Before beginning testing or starting the engine, always verify the shutoff valve is open.

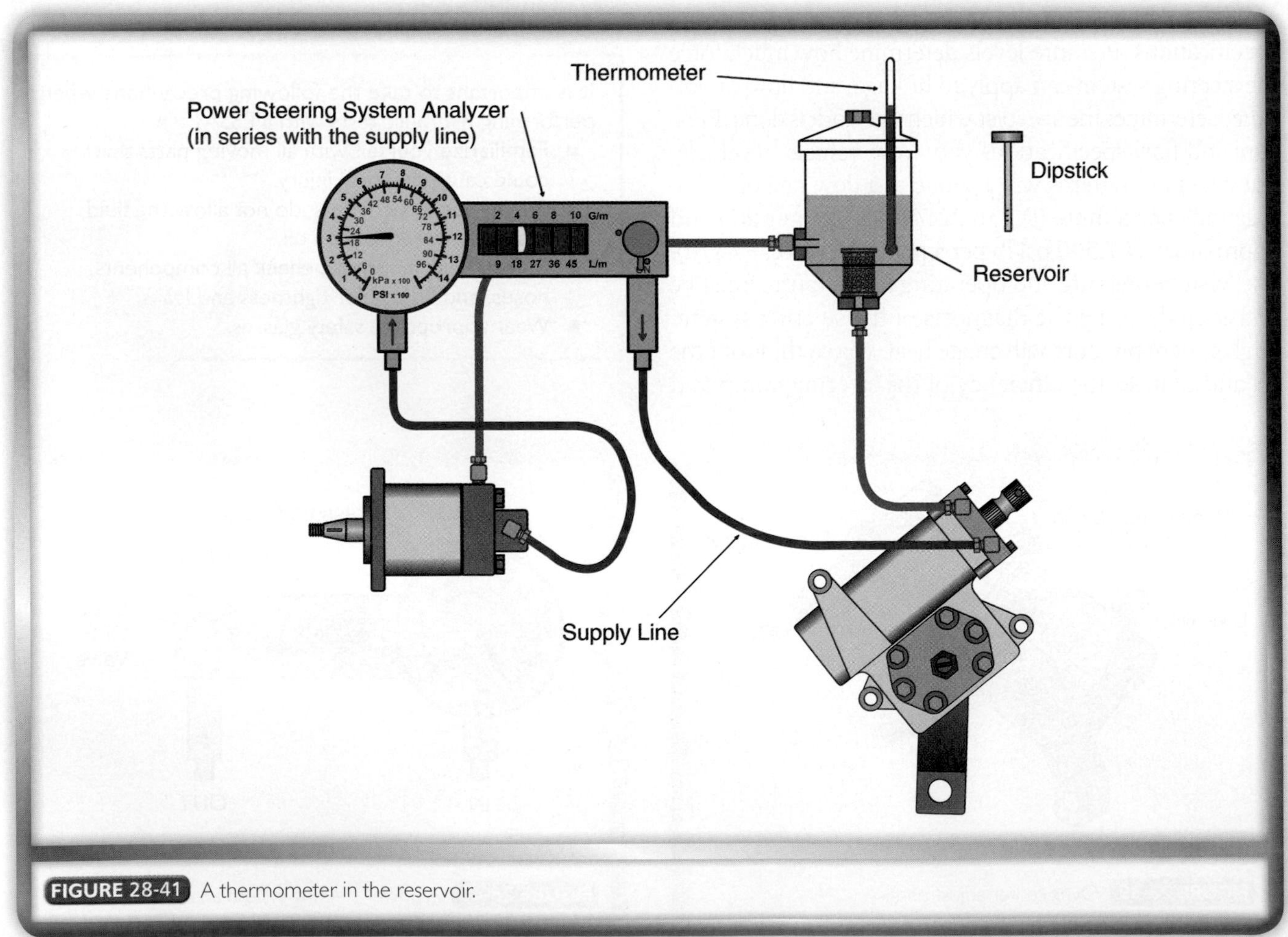

FIGURE 28-41 A thermometer in the reservoir.

SKILL DRILL 28-2 Using a Power Steering System Analyzer

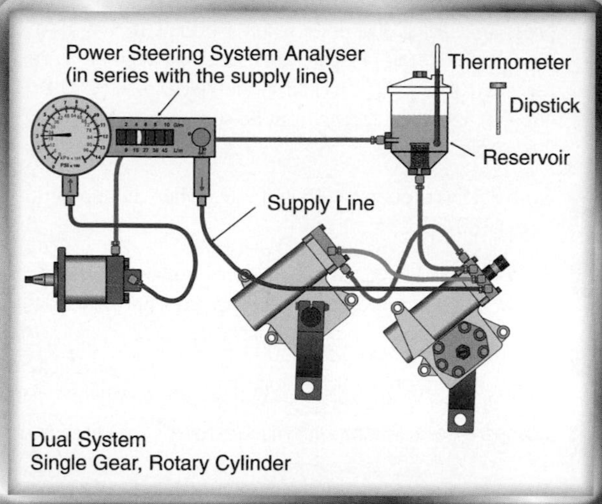

1. Connect the PSSA gauge in series with the output pressure line of the power steering pump.
2. Start and idle the engine and check the system reservoir oil level. Also, observe whether the oil is flowing in the correct direction through the gauge using the arrow on the flow meter.
3. Place a thermometer in the reservoir. A digital type thermometer with a wired probe is ideal.
4. While the engine is at idle speed, warm the system oil. This is performed by slowly closing the shutoff valve until a pressure reading of approximately 1,000 psi (690 MPa) is reached. Hold this pressure until system temperature reaches 180°F (82°C). Fluid should never reach 250°F (121°C). If it does, testing must be suspended until the fluid cools.
5. Completely re-open the shutoff valve when the temperature is 180°F (82°C).
6. Measure and record system pressure when the valve is opened, also referred to as back pressure. Normal system back pressure is between 0 and 100 psi (0 and 690 kPa) with the engine idling and no steering input. Dual-steering gear systems should have slightly higher back pressure.

SKILL DRILL 28-3 Measuring Pump Maximum Relief Pressure

1. With the engine at idle, slowly turn the PSSA shutoff valve until it is closed.
2. Measure and record the maximum pressure. This reading corresponds to the pressure at which the relief valve opens. Be sure to open the shutoff valve as quickly (within 15 seconds) as possible to avoid overheating the oil or damaging lines or the steering pump.
3. Compare observations with manufacturer's specifications.

SKILL DRILL 28-4 Testing Flow Volume

1. Connect the PSSA gauge in series with the output pressure line of the power steering pump.
2. Start and idle the engine and check system reservoir oil level. Also, observe whether the oil is flowing in the correct direction through the gauge using the arrow on the flow meter.
3. While the engine is at idle speed, warm the system oil. This is performed by slowly closing the shutoff valve until a pressure reading of approximately 1,000 psi (6,900 kPA) is reached. Hold this pressure until the system temperature reaches 180°F (121°C). Fluid should never reach 250°F (121°C). If it does, testing must be suspended until the fluid cools.
4. Completely re-open the shutoff valve when the temperature is 180°F (121°C).
5. Read the flow gauge, which measures output volume of the pump. Flow is measured in gallons or liters per minute.
6. Raise the engine speed to 1,500 rpm and record the volume observed on the flow gauge.
7. Compare observations with manufacturer's specifications.

Testing for Internal Leakage

To determine whether the steering gear has internal defects, such as worn power-assist piston seals or a worn gear cylinder, an internal leak test should be performed. This test is performed almost identically to the steering pressure relief valve test procedures. One exception is during testing; one must prevent the steering relief valves inside the steering gear from unloading as the gear is turned from stop to stop. To test a system for internal leakage, follow the steps in **SKILL DRILL 28-5**.

On dual-gear systems, the steering gears must be isolated if pump leakage occurs at a rate exceeding 2 gallons (7.6 liters) per minute. To identify which steering gear is bypassing the oil, block the lines to the slave cylinder after testing both gears together. If the slave cylinder is defective, installing plugs in the lines to the slave cylinder should reduce leakage to less than one gallon (3.8 liters) per minute.

> **TECHNICIAN TIP**
>
> **It is critical to install a spacer between the steering stops when performing the internal gear leakage test. Without the spacers, the high system pressure cannot be reached when turning the wheels and a false failure results as the steering arm unloads after contacting the steering stops.**

Checking Oil Aeration

Air mixed with the oil (aerated oil) in the steering system is inspected visually. Oil should appear clear without any signs of foaming. Entrained gas bubbles cause the fluid to compress and take on elastic qualities. Steering effort will increase and bump steer will become exaggerated as the air compresses and releases. A common cause of air leakage into the system is loose hose connections on the

SKILL DRILL 28-5 Testing for Internal Leakage

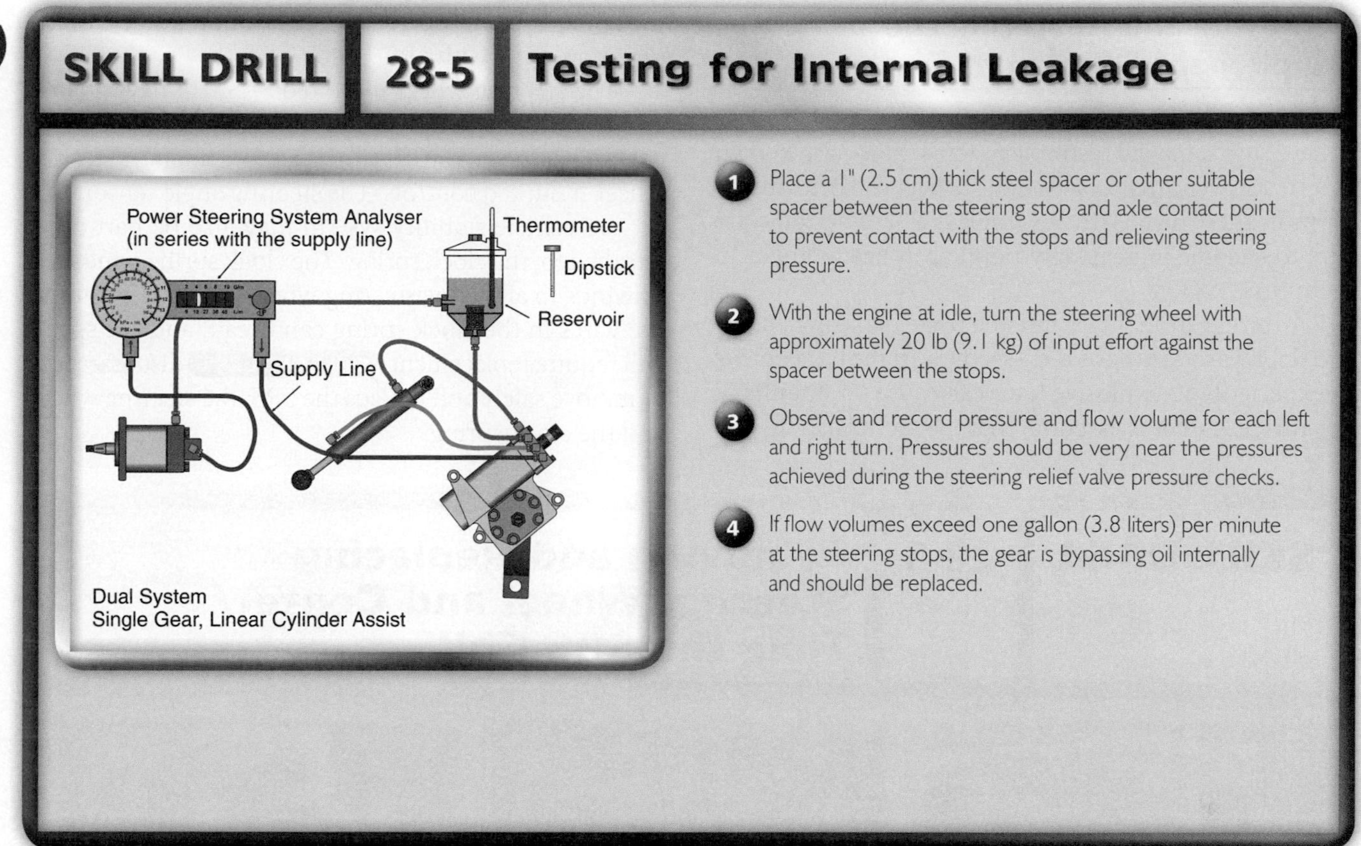

1. Place a 1" (2.5 cm) thick steel spacer or other suitable spacer between the steering stop and axle contact point to prevent contact with the stops and relieving steering pressure.
2. With the engine at idle, turn the steering wheel with approximately 20 lb (9.1 kg) of input effort against the spacer between the stops.
3. Observe and record pressure and flow volume for each left and right turn. Pressures should be very near the pressures achieved during the steering relief valve pressure checks.
4. If flow volumes exceed one gallon (3.8 liters) per minute at the steering stops, the gear is bypassing oil internally and should be replaced.

suction side. A power steering reservoir contains a filter needing periodic replacement. Restricted filters will lead to over-heating of power steering oil, pump cavitation, and air leaks on the suction side of the system.

Bleeding Air from the Steering System

Whenever a steering gear is serviced, any air in the system must be purged to restore proper operation. Turning the wheels from stop to stop while the vehicle is parked and its engine is running will not remove air. The wheels should be lifted from the floor. Only then can the wheels can be turned to help purge air. Low pressure fluid flow through the gear will gradually purge most air from the gear.

Another way to purge air from the system is by moving the wheels by hand while the engine is idling. That should only be done, however, after the steering stops are set. While the engine is idling, air-bleed screws located on top of steering gears can be loosened to also purge air.

Dual-steering boxes are more difficult to bleed. After steering stops are set, a recommended method to purge air is to disconnect the drag link at each gear and force the pitman arm from stop to stop several times while the engine is idling. Pushing fluid through the steering gear this way, when it is not pressurized by the gear during a turn, effectively removes air where circulating fluid carries air to the reservoir for purging.

> **TECHNICIAN TIP**
>
> Moving the wheels by hand from steering stop to stop while the engine is running and the wheels are raised from the shop floor is more effective at purging air than if the steering wheel is turned while the wheels are on the ground. That is because, when the wheels are on the ground, high fluid pressure required to operate the steering gear when turning will cause air to compress and break up inside the box. Smaller dispersed bubbles are much more difficult to purge.

Removing and Replacing the Supplemental Restraint System

In North America, heavy-duty trucks are not yet required to have supplemental restraint systems (SRS), also known as airbags. Some manufacturers, such as Volvo, do install them in their heavy-duty vehicles. These systems are sure to become increasingly popular in heavy trucks in the future.

An airbag in an SRS is inflated by an explosive charge and deploys in as little as 0.03 seconds. If the bag deploys unexpectedly, its explosive force can cause serious injury. For this reason, it is essential that the technician disable the airbag system before working around a steering column equipped with SRS.

The steering wheel-mounted SRS will have a clock spring mounted in the column under the steering wheel to connect the airbag, the horn button, and any steering wheel-mounted controls. The steering angle sensor used for the vehicle stability system may also be part of, or attached to, the clock spring. The clock spring winds and unwinds to allow the steering wheel to turn. Over time, the wires in the clock spring can break, and the spring will require replacement. SKILL DRILL 28-6 discusses how to remove safely and replace the SRS, the steering wheel, and the clock spring.

SKILL DRILL 28-6 Removing and Replacing Steering Wheel and Center/Time the SRS Coil

1. Find and remove the SRS fuse. Verify by turning the key on and observing that the SRS light remains lit for at least 30 seconds and does not go out. Make sure the wheels are straight ahead. Turn the key off.

2. Remove the negative battery cable and allow a minimum of 5 minutes to pass to let the SRS system's capacitors discharge. Do not use a memory minder or auxiliary power source!

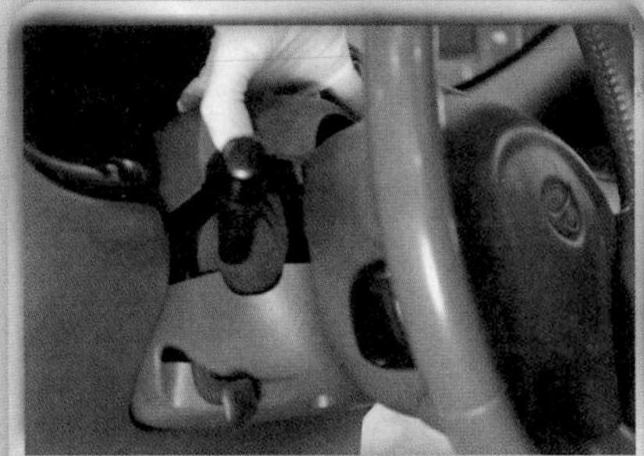

3. Locate the SRS connector at the bottom of the steering column and disconnect. Remove upper and lower trim panels.

4. Locate the bolts or spring clip on the back of the steering wheel that hold the airbag to the steering wheel, and remove or release them.

5. Lift the airbag from the steering wheel, and disconnect the airbag connector to the steering wheel harness.

6. Sit the airbag on bench face up in a safe place.

SKILL DRILL 28-6 Removing and Replacing Steering Wheel and Center/Time the SRS Coil, continued

7. Remove the fasteners that hold the steering wheel on.

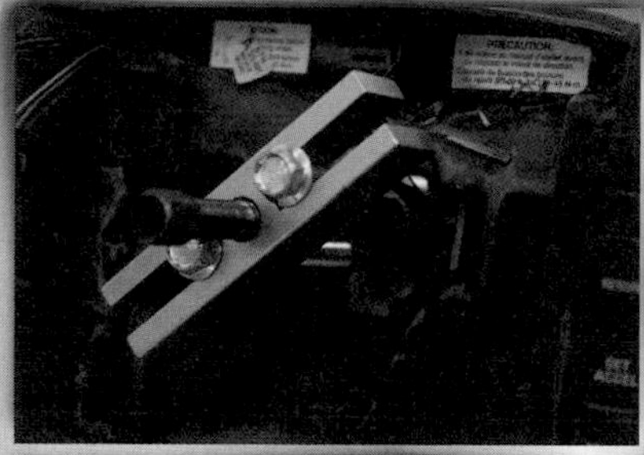

8. Remove the steering wheel with the manufacturer's recommended puller (this information can be found in the service information).

9. Remove the clock spring screws or snap ring, and lift the clock spring from the steering column shaft. Attach a thin wire to the clock spring connector (airbag connector was disconnected earlier) at the base of the steering column, and pull the clock spring and connector up through the steering column.

10. Gently pull the clock spring harness down through steering column.

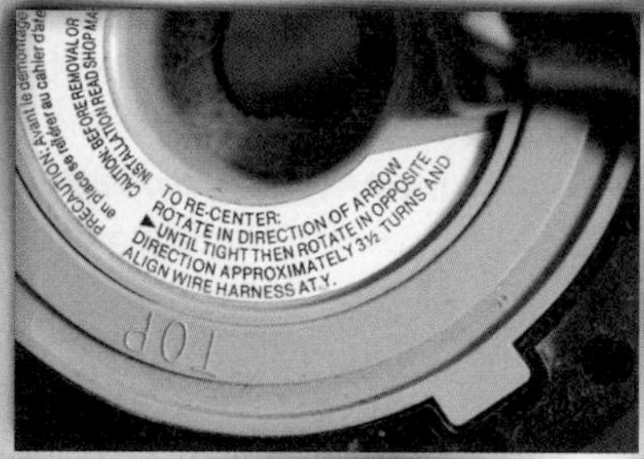

11. If the antirotation key is still installed, skip to Step 13. If the antirotation key is not installed, center the clock spring following the manufacturer's procedure. In this case, we will gently rotate the inner rotor counterclockwise until it stops.

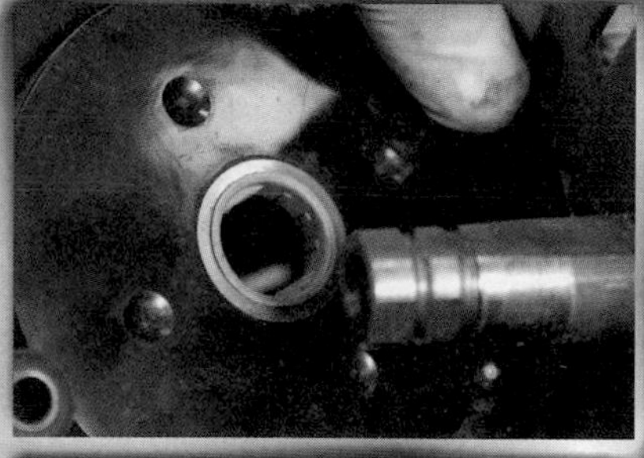

12. Rotate the inner rotor clockwise the required number of turns—in this case four full turns. Verify that all of the marks are aligned in their specified positions.

13. Reinstall the clock spring assembly in the proper orientation, and secure it with the screws or snap ring. Reinstall components in the reverse order of removal, ensuring that torque specifications are followed. Also remove the antirotation key at the appropriate step.

Wrap-up

Ready for Review

- Steering systems are life and limb systems, meaning failure of the technician to inspect and maintain the system, or to choose the correct service procedures and tools, can result in catastrophic personal injury and death.
- Steering systems multiply the rotational force applied to the steering wheel, provide directional control of the vehicle, reduce road shock to the steering wheel, and provide steering feedback to the driver called road feel.
- Miter boxes are used in high-angle steering columns to connect the steering gear to the steering column.
- Pitman arms, drag links, and tie-rods are steering linkage common to all conventional truck steering systems.
- All heavy-duty commercial vehicles use integral power steering gears, which means the power steering assist and gear mechanism are incorporated into a single steering box.
- Hydraulic steering pumps provide the main force to multiply driver input torque to the steering system.
- All integral power steering gears use a recirculating-ball steering gear.
- Recirculating-ball steering gears mechanically multiply input force and use a worm gear with a ball-nut.
- Rack-and-pinion steering is rarely used on heavy-duty commercial vehicles.
- A mechanism that enables the steering gear to steer the vehicle in the event of a loss of power assist is designed into every steering gear.
- Heavy-duty commercial vehicles use larger diameter steering wheels, which are positioned at a 30 degree or greater angle to the driver to make them easier to turn.
- Most heavy-duty commercial vehicles use multi-piece steering columns composed of two or more splined steering shafts with universal joints, which enable changes in column angle caused by movement between the cab and frame-mounted steering gear.
- Sliding splines in the steering column are called slip joints; they allow the column length to change due to movement between the cab and the frame-mounted steering gear. Sliding slip yokes also enable the steering column to shorten and thus protect the driver during collisions.
- Correct phasing or alignment of steering column universal joints is necessary to prevent steering column binding.
- A clock spring and steering angle sensor are electrical devices located beneath the steering wheel in many late-model vehicles.

- The rotary control valve directs pressurized hydraulic oil to either side of a power piston to multiply driver steering effort.
- The torsion bar connects at one end to the outer half of the rotary control valve and the lower end to the bottom of the worm gear.
- The steering input shaft is connected to the inner section of the rotary control valve.
- Twisting of the torsion bar causes deflection between the two sections of the rotary control valve and changes the direction of pressurized hydraulic oil to either side of the power piston.
- The direction of input force twisting the torsion bar changes the alignment between two sections of the control valve which, in turn, redirects pressurized oil in the steering gear.
- Road feel describes the feedback a driver receives through the steering system about the resistance the tires encounter in steering direction.
- The power steering pump uses flow control and pressure relief valves.
- The steering gear has internal pressure relief valves, which unload pump pressure when the steering linkage has contacted the steering stops.
- Steering stops are used to limit steer tire movement, which could bring the tires in contact with the suspension, frame, or steering linkage.
- Pitman arms connect to the steering gear output shaft called the sector shaft.
- Drag links connect the pitman arm to the upper steering arm and transmit steering force to the steering knuckle through the upper steering arm.
- Two lower steering arms have a unique angular shape called an Ackermann angle. The angle causes the steer tires to toe out on turns where the inner tire follows a tighter turning radius than the outer tire.
- Alignment marks on the pitman arm are used to properly center the steering linkage.
- Centering of the steering wheel can be done by changing the length of an adjustable drag link or turning the tie-rod.
- A Power Steering System Analyzer is used to diagnose hydraulic-related problems in the power steering system by measuring pump flow and pressure under different operating conditions.
- Worm gear preload adjusts bearing clearances in the steering input shaft bearing.
- The overcenter adjustment adjusts the clearances between the tapered sector shaft gear teeth and the teeth on the power piston.
- When measured with an inch-pound (newton meter) torque wrench, worm gear preload plus the over center adjustment establishes the total mesh adjustment.

Vocabulary Builder

ball-nut rack A metal block with a threaded hole that is part of the recirculating-ball steering system.

bump steer The undesired condition produced when hitting a bump where the vehicle darts to one side as the steering linkage is pushed or pulled as a result of the travel of the suspension. The steering wheel may also be violently forced from the drivers grip during severe bump steer.

clock spring A special rotary electrical connector located between the steering wheel and the steering column that maintains a constant electrical connection with the wiring system while the vehicle's steering wheel is being turned.

constant-ratio steering gears Steering gears that use sector shafts with teeth of equal lengths.

conventional steering system A steering system with a solid axle and a single steering gear.

drag link A connecting linkage that transfers movement of the pitman arm to the upper steering arm.

drop arm An arm that transfers the steering box output shaft motion to the steering linkage by converting rotational movement into liner motion.

engine-driven hydraulic pump A power steering pump driven by a belt or gear driven by the engine.

flow-control valve A valve used in power steering pumps to regulate the volume of fluid flow out of the power steering pump.

miter boxes A gear arrangement which allows sharp angle changes in the steering column.

pitman arm A pitman arm converts the steering gear sector shaft movement to a sweeping arc resembling linear movement. Also called a *drop arm*.

power steering pump A hydraulic pump that provides hydraulic pressure to the steering gear, which reduces the force required by the driver to turn the steering wheel.

Power Steering System Analyzer (PSSA) A combination flow meter, shut-off valve, and pressure gauge used to diagnose hydraulic problems in power steering systems.

power unit The hydraulic assist portion of the power steering gear.

rack-and-pinion steering system A type of steering gear arrangement that uses two gears. A smaller round pinion gear located at the end of the steering shaft connects to a linear gear called the rack. The pinion gear moves the rack from side-to-side as the pinion rotates. The side-to-side motion of the rack controls the direction of the steer tires.

recirculating-ball steering gear A steering gear that uses a worm gear inside a metal ball-nut having a threaded hole for the worm. Gear teeth are cut into one outside edge of the ball-nut, which engages the sector shaft.

road feel The force transmitted from the tires back through the steering system to the driver.

rotary valve A valve connected to the input shaft of the steering gear that controls the direction of pressurized fluid through the steering gear. Along with the torsion bar, changes in torque applied to the steering wheel and the direction of torque will alter the direction of fluid flow through the valve. Also called a *spool valve*.

spool valve A valve connected to the input shaft of the steering gear that controls the direction of pressurized fluid through the steering gear. Along with the torsion bar, changes in torque applied to the steering wheel and the direction of torque will alter the direction of fluid flow through the valve. Also called a *rotary valve*.

steering angle sensor A sensor that measures the rotational angle of the steering wheel.

steering arm An arm that extends from the steering knuckle. The tie-rods connect to these arms in order to steer the wheels.

steering column A column affixed between the steering wheel and the steering box, usually made to collapse during a crash.

steering gear A device that converts the rotary motion of the steering wheel to the linear motion needed to steer the vehicle.

steering knuckle A device that connects the front wheel to the suspension; it pivots on the top and bottom, thus allowing the front wheels to turn.

steering linkage Steel rods that connect the steering box to the steering arms on the steering knuckle.

steering ratio The mechanical advantage produced by the steering gear, which converts large turns of the steering wheel into smaller turns of the tire to ease steering for the driver.

steering shafts The shaft that connects the steering wheel to the steering gear assembly of an vehicle.

steering stops Bolts used to limit the turning angle of the steering knuckle.

steering system A term used to describe all the components and parts involved in steering a vehicle.

tie-rod A steering component that transfers linear motion from the steering box to the steering arms at the front wheels.

tie-rod end Articulating ball-and-socket joints attached to each end of the tie-rod.

torsion rod A thin, spring-like metal rod that connects to one end of the rotary valve to change its position.

total mesh adjustment A setting of the appropriate depth for the sector shaft and nut so as not to bind or have excess free play.

U-joint A cross-shaped joint with bearings on each leg where one set of parallel legs is connected to the end of one shaft and the other set of parallel legs is connected to the end of a second shaft. This arrangement allows the shafts to operate at shallow angles to each other. Also called a *universal joint*.

universal joint A cross-shaped joint with bearings on each leg where one set of parallel legs is connected to the end of one shaft and the other set of parallel legs is connected to the end of a second shaft. This arrangement allows the shafts to operate at shallow angles to each other. Also called a *U-joint*.

variable-ratio steering gears Steering gears that use sector shafts with long and short lengths of teeth.

worm gear A gear with a helical, threaded shaft that is attached to the steering column and meshes with a ball nut that transfers motion from the steering wheel to the steering linkage. Also called the *worm shaft*.

Review Questions

1. On an integral power steering gear, which of the following indicates excessive clearances between the sector shaft teeth and the power piston?
   a. Lost range of motion within steering gear
   b. Steering wheel shimmy
   c. Excessive steering effort
   d. Noise from the power steering pump when hot
2. A driver complains the steering wheel moves violently whenever the vehicle encounters a bump in the road. Which of the following is the most likely problem?
   a. An out-of-phase steering column
   b. Air in the steering gear
   c. Incorrect vehicle alignment angles
   d. A misadjusted tie-rod
3. A shock absorber-like device is attached to the tie-rod. What of the following is most likely the purpose of the device?
   a. Helps center the steering wheel
   b. Minimizes road shock and vibration to the driver
   c. Minimizes caster shimmy
   d. Prevents bump steer
4. Which of the following is the most likely problem if a steering tire contacts a drag link on sharp right turns?
   a. A misaligned steering column
   b. A steering wheel off center
   c. A drag link that is adjusted to the wrong length
   d. An incorrectly adjusted steering stop
5. What is the most likely cause for a power steering reservoir to overflow with oil?
   a. A defective power steering pump drive shaft seal
   b. Air in the steering gear
   c. Fluid that has become too hot
   d. Mixing engine oil and automatic transmission oil in the reservoir
6. Steering gear seal leakage on power steering gears due to dirt abrasion (wear caused by dirt rubbing against the seals) is minimized by
   a. using the correct viscosity of power steering fluid.
   b. greasing the steering sector shaft and input shaft seals with chassis grease during service.
   c. using a power steering fluid oil cooler.
   d. changing the power steering filter regularly.
7. Which of the following are components of the steering system?
   a. Steering column
   b. Steering gear
   c. Steering linkage
   d. All of the choices are correct.
8. The following are all power-steering gear systems, EXCEPT for the:
   a. rack-and-pinion system.
   b. integral piston system.
   c. external power-assist system.
   d. internal power-assist system.
9. Which of the following statements concerning steering columns and shafts is NOT correct?
   a. Correct any cause of steering column misalignment.
   b. Do not straighten any bent steering system component.
   c. Do not heat any steering component since this will cause the metal to become brittle and easily break rather than bend.
   d. Replace the component with original equipment only.
10. Which of the following statements concerning steering ratio is correct?
    a. The force to turn the wheels of a heavily loaded vehicle requires the gear to supply a significant amount of mechanical advantage to allow the driver to safely maneuver the vehicle.
    b. On heavy-duty vehicles, the steering ratio refers to the mechanical advantage produced by the gear.
    c. Both A and B are correct.
    d. Neither A nor B is correct.

ASE-Type Questions

1. Technician A says if the steering column input shaft is not aligned correctly it will have tight spots or bind when turned. Technician B says if the power steering fluid level is low there will be a noise when turning the steering wheel. Who is right?
   a. Technician A
   b. Technician B
   c. Both Technician A and Technician B
   d. Neither Technician A nor Technician B
2. Technician A says if the kingpins are not lubricated, the vehicle will be hard to steer. Technician B says clunking noises when turning the steering wheel are acceptable. Who is right?
   a. Technician A
   b. Technician B
   c. Both Technician A and Technician B
   d. Neither Technician A nor Technician B
3. Technician A says if the steering effort is high whenever the steering wheel is turned, one of the power steering pressure relief valves in the steering gear is defective. Technician B says if the power flow-control valve in the power steering pump is defective, the vehicle will be hard to steer. Who is right?
   a. Technician A
   b. Technician B
   c. Both Technician A and Technician B
   d. Neither Technician A nor Technician B
4. Technician A says using recirculating ball bearings reduces friction between the worm gear and block. Technician B says another advantage of recirculating ball bearings is to allow almost zero clearance between the worm gear and block. Who is correct?
   a. Technician A
   b. Technician B
   c. Both Technician A and Technician B
   d. Neither Technician A nor Technician B
5. Technician A says the rotary valve (also called the spool valve) senses the change in force applied to the steering wheel at the beginning of a turn. Technician B says that essentially, this valve directs pressurized fluid to either side of the power piston when turning is initiated. Who is correct?
   a. Technician A
   b. Technician B
   c. Both Technician A and Technician B
   d. Neither Technician A nor Technician B
6. Technician A says rack-and-pinion steering systems do not include tie rods. Technician B says rack-and-pinion steering systems do not include a pitman arm or a drag link. Who is correct?
   a. Technician A
   b. Technician B
   c. Both Technician A and Technician B
   d. Neither Technician A nor Technician B
7. Technician A says the drag link is a steering linkage rod connecting the pitman arm at one end to the upper steering arm at the other. Technician B says, in addition to that basic bridging function, the drag link performs a leveling function. Who is correct?
   a. Technician A
   b. Technician B
   c. Both Technician A and Technician B
   d. Neither Technician A nor Technician B
8. Technician A says the kingpin passes through the knuckle's upper arm, through the end of the I-beam and then through the knuckle yoke's lower arm. Technician B says a snap ring keeps the kingpin in place and locks the pin into position through the center of the I-beam axle. Who is correct?
   a. Technician A
   b. Technician B
   c. Both Technician A and Technician B
   d. Neither Technician A nor Technician B
9. Technician A says for safety reasons, castellated nuts using cotter pins to lock the ball stud and nut together are used on all steering linkage components. Technician B says it is satisfactory to use heat on rusted steering components in order to take them apart. Who is correct?
   a. Technician A
   b. Technician B
   c. Both Technician A and Technician B
   d. Neither Technician A nor Technician B
10. Technician A says pressurizing the power steering oil produces heat that can damage the oil. Technician B says on heavy vehicles an oil cooler is used to prevent overheating. Who is correct?
    a. Technician A
    b. Technician B
    c. Both Technician A and Technician B
    d. Neither Technician A nor Technician B

CHAPTER 29

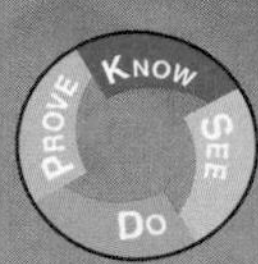

NATEF Tasks

There are no NATEF tasks in this chapter.

Knowledge Objectives

After reading this chapter, you will be able to:

1. Identify and describe factors affecting braking performance. (pp 883–904)
2. Identify and describe various types of brake systems and brake subsystems. (pp 887–890)
3. Explain friction ratings and interpret edge codes on brake shoes. (pp 898–899)
4. Explain the basic operation of foundation brake systems. (pp 890–919)
5. Identify and explain causes for brake fade. (pp 899–901)
6. Explain safe work practices related to servicing brake systems. (pp 909–910)
7. Recommend brake maintenance and service procedures for foundation brakes. (pp 913–915)

Braking Fundamentals

Skills Objectives

There are no skills objectives in this chapter.

Introduction

The enormous amount of energy contained in a heavily loaded truck or bus moving at highway speeds requires an equally powerful and reliable braking system to slow and bring the vehicle to a controlled stop. After the vehicle has stopped, the braking system of heavy trucks—not the drive train—is used to keep the vehicle parked. Even under emergency conditions such as the loss of air or brake fluid, failure of components, or even the breakaway of a trailer, commercial vehicle braking system are expected to slow and stop the vehicle safely without catastrophic consequences posed by a runaway vehicle laden with freight or passengers.

Today's braking systems are also integral to vehicle stability control, collision avoidance, rollover protection, and traction control systems. To incorporate these sophisticated features, the braking system now has a large element of electronic control operating the braking system with virtually no driver input. Brakes convert the vehicle's kinetic energy into heat energy using friction as shown in FIGURE 29-1. Heat in brake components is dissipated to the atmosphere through brake design factors as depicted in FIGURE 29-2. Unless the build-up of heat in brake parts is minimized, heat accumulations will lead to a loss of braking efficiency and damage to brake components. Legislation for truck and bus brake systems specify brake performance standards. The most recent changes in rules for brake system performance require shorter stopping distances as shown in FIGURE 29-3, with a higher level of vehicle stability while braking. Stability control, antilock braking, traction control, and improved disc brake systems are some of the technologies used to meet the latest update to brake system operation.

Innovations in technology have placed even more demands on braking systems. Improved vehicle aerodynamics, radial and low profile tires with reduced rolling resistance, plus drive trains with substantially lower

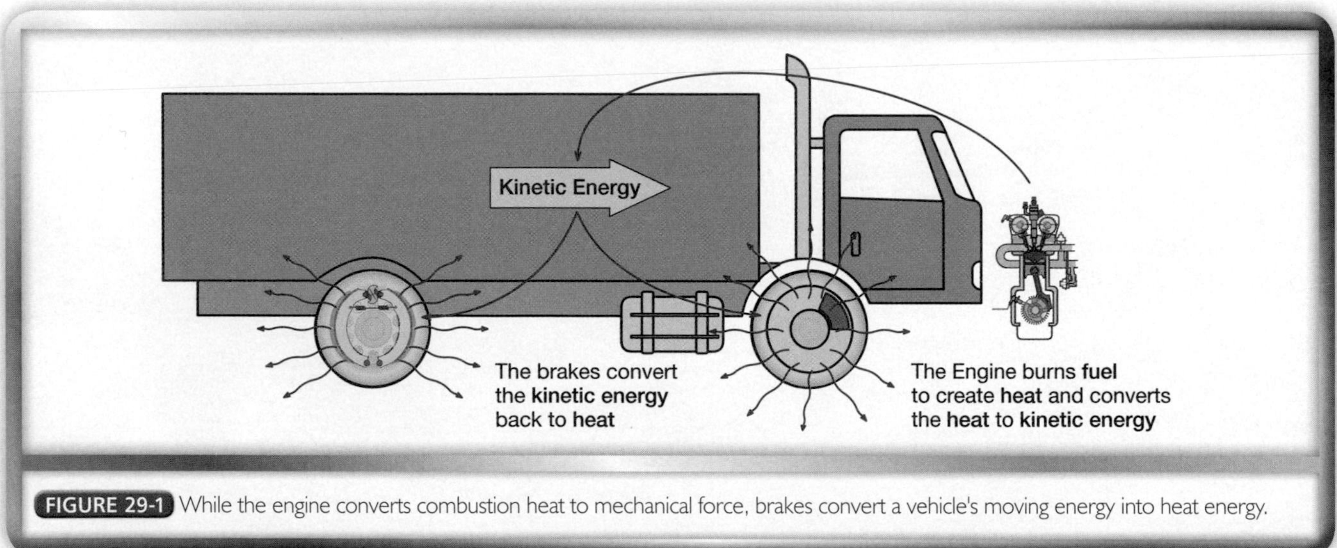
Kinetic Energy
The brakes convert the kinetic energy back to heat
The Engine burns fuel to create heat and converts the heat to kinetic energy

FIGURE 29-1 While the engine converts combustion heat to mechanical force, brakes convert a vehicle's moving energy into heat energy.

You Are the Technician

A late model tractor-trailer combination vehicle is brought to your repair facility, and the driver complains that the tractor rear brakes are grabbing when he applies the brakes. He can hear the ABS system modulators chuffing air while the vehicle is slowing down—even though he is not applying heavy pressure to the brake pedal. You accompany the driver on a road test and confirm the driver's concern—the rear tractor brakes seem as if they are about to lock up when the brakes are applied. The driver informs you that the rear tractor brakes have recently been replaced.

1. What inspections would you make of the brake system?
2. How would you confirm that all the vehicle brakes are, in fact, working?
3. How would you determine if the rear tractor brakes are working harder than the rest of the vehicle brakes?

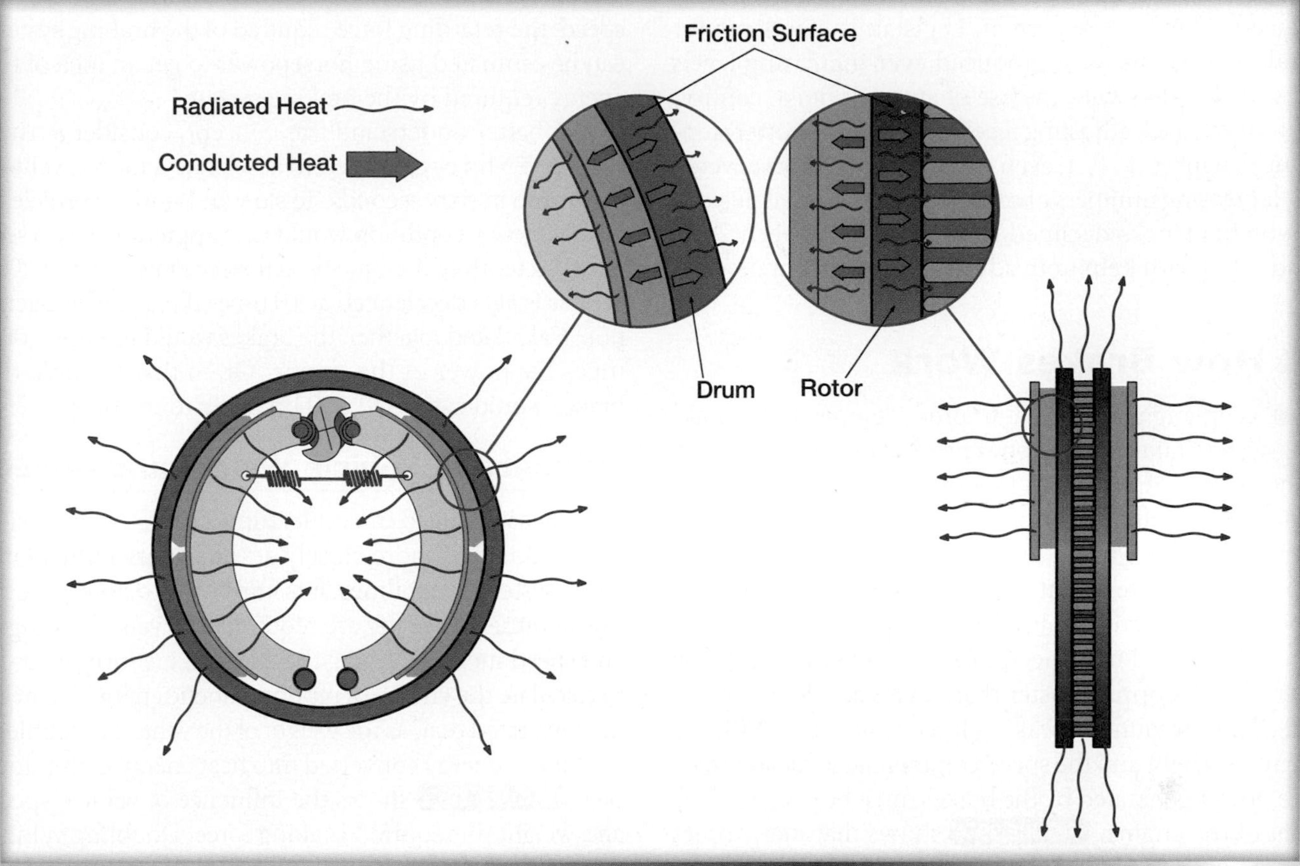

Friction Surface

Radiated Heat

Conducted Heat

Drum

Rotor

FIGURE 29-2 Unless the build-up of heat in brake parts is minimized, heat accumulations will lead to a loss of braking efficiency and damage to brake components.

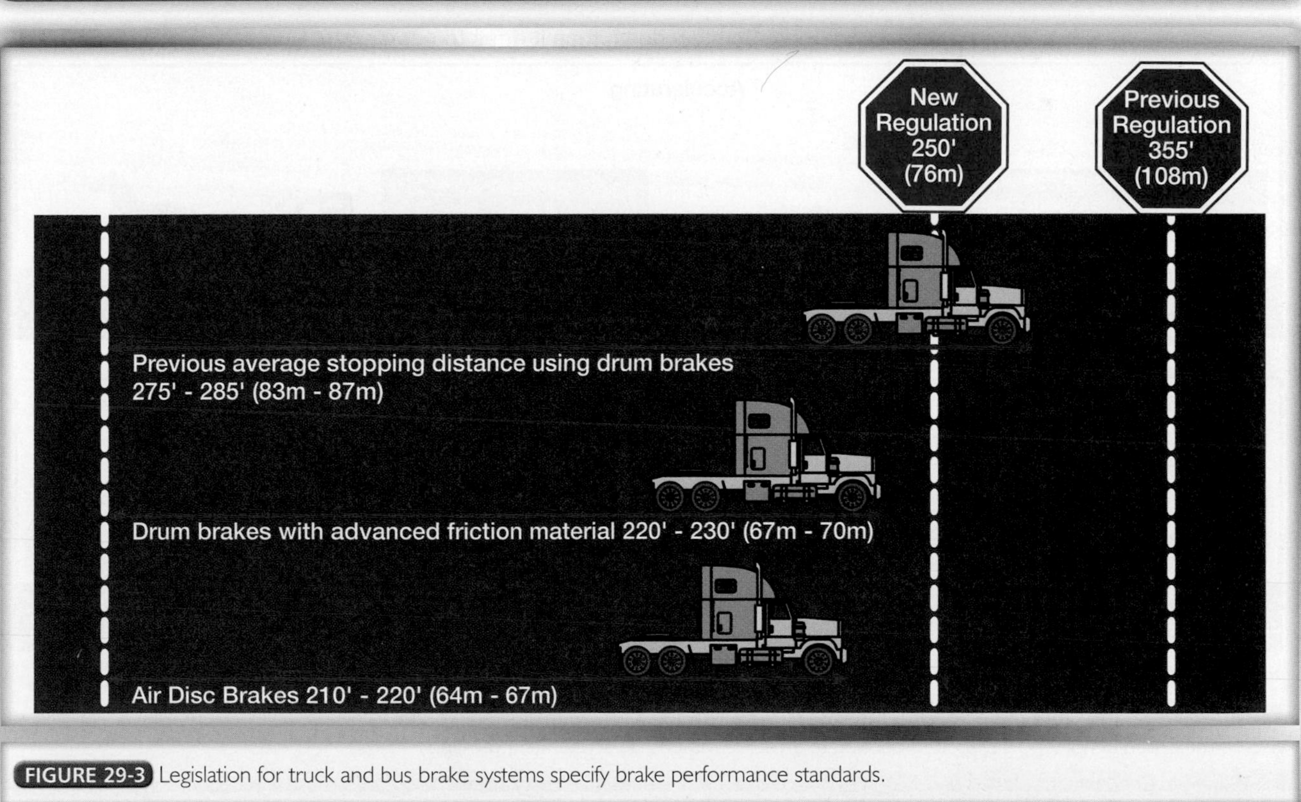

FIGURE 29-3 Legislation for truck and bus brake systems specify brake performance standards.

friction mean that higher demands to slow a vehicle are placed on the brake system. Legislative standards for braking systems have produced ever-increasing levels of vehicle safety with the use of antilock brake control, automatic slack adjusting mechanisms, and shorter stopping distances. In fact, even with more distances covered by increasing numbers of commercial vehicles, collisions involving trucks declined close to 20% between 2008 and 2009 with help from advanced brake technologies.

 How Brakes Work

Just as an engine uses heat to produce power, the braking system takes vehicle power stored as **kinetic energy** (the energy of a body in motion) and converts it back into heat through friction. Using brake drums or discs attached to the wheels, friction is produced by forcefully applying heat-resistant braking material against these rotating components. Friction's by-product—heat—is then dissipated into the air. Because a vehicle must be capable of stopping faster than it can accelerate, a tremendous amount of braking force is needed. With the heavier weight and the speed commercial vehicles travel, the power generated by the brakes must be several times that of the engine. FIGURE 29-4 shows that many times more power is required to slow and stop a vehicle than is required to accelerate a vehicle. Just as horsepower is used to measure the energy used to bring a vehicle up to speed, the retarding force required of the braking system can be estimated using horsepower to get an idea of the energy required by the braking system.

To better understand this concept, consider a truck with a 350-hp engine used to accelerate a loaded vehicle to 60 mph in sixty seconds. To slow and stop the vehicle in an emergency condition would take approximately 6 seconds—a tenth of the time used to accelerate the unit. The vehicle is also decelerated at 10 times the rate of acceleration. Calculated together, the brakes would require 1,000 times the power of the engine. Or, in this example the brakes would exert 350,000 hp of retarding force!

Influence of Vehicle Weight and Speed

The forces involved in decelerating a vehicle are considerable. Looking more closely at the factors influencing brake system capabilities, it is important to note increasing amounts of energy are required as a vehicle's weight and speed increase. Using the engineering formula used to calculate the energy of motion, kinetic energy, it can be demonstrated that, as the weight of the vehicle is doubled, the kinetic energy converted into heat energy is also doubled. FIGURE 29-5 shows the influence of vehicle speed and weight on required braking force. Doubling vehicle weight or speed needs twice the braking power for the same deceleration rate. When weight and speed are both

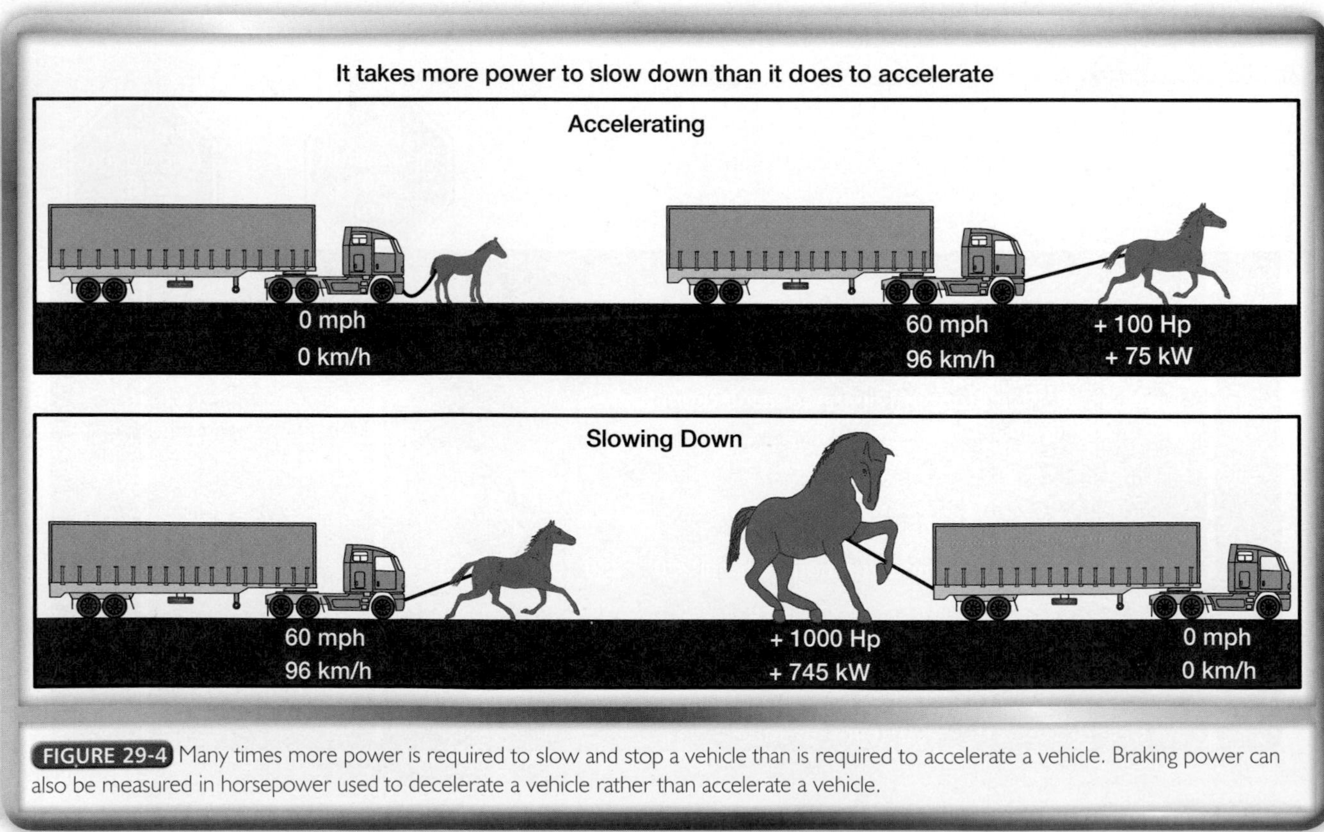

FIGURE 29-4 Many times more power is required to slow and stop a vehicle than is required to accelerate a vehicle. Braking power can also be measured in horsepower used to decelerate a vehicle rather than accelerate a vehicle.

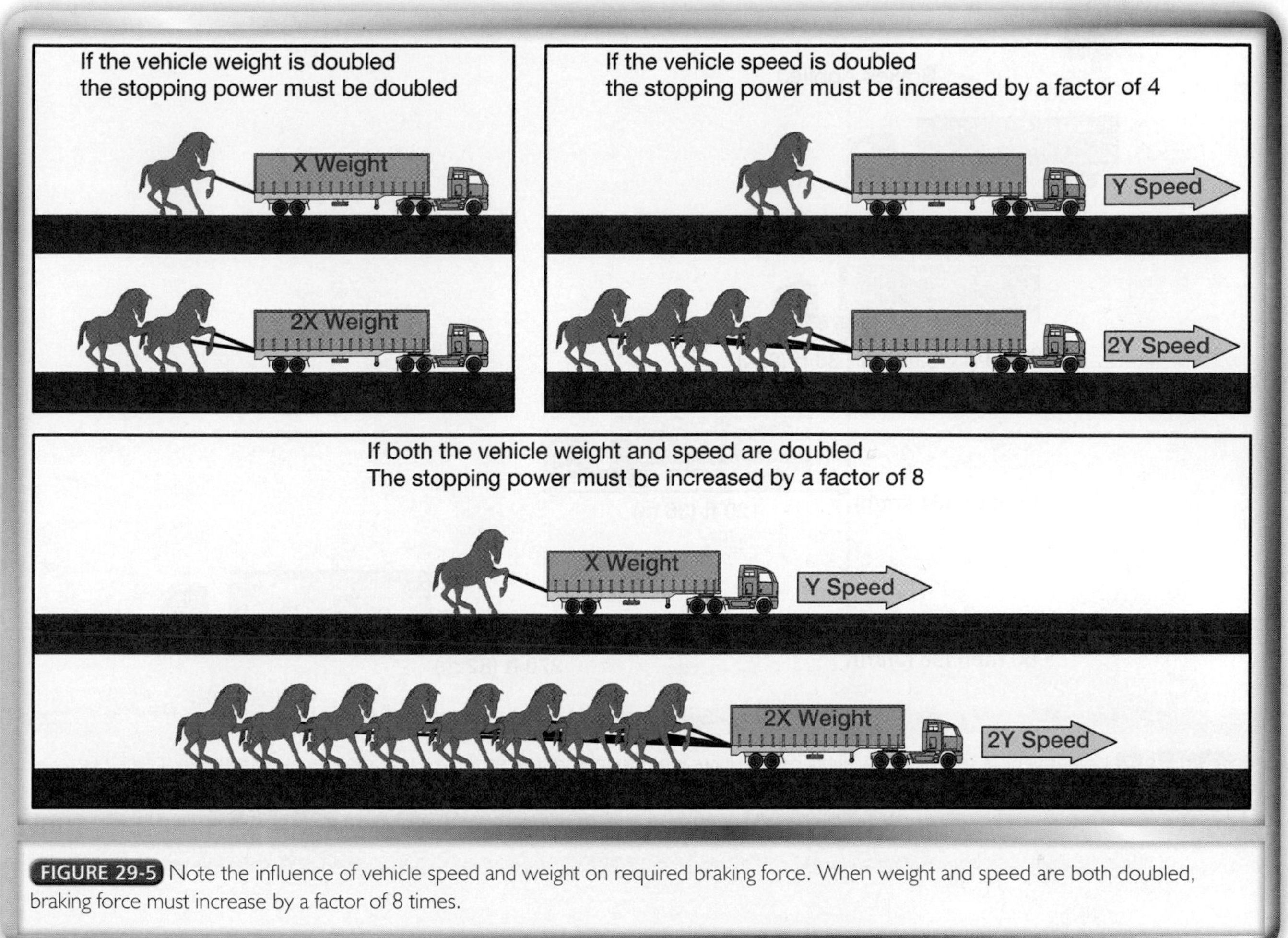

FIGURE 29-5 Note the influence of vehicle speed and weight on required braking force. When weight and speed are both doubled, braking force must increase by a factor of 8 times.

doubled, braking force must increase by a factor of eight. If the brakes cannot adequately absorb and dissipate the additional heat produced by increasing vehicle weight, braking performance and safety suffers. This explains why heavy-duty brakes are specified not by the type of vehicle but by the weight carried by an axle and its location on the vehicle.

Increasing vehicle speed has a greater effect than vehicle weight on the braking system power. Calculations of kinetic energy show braking power requirements increase by a factor of two as speed increases. This means four times as much power is required to decelerate from a speed of 40 mph compared to 20 mph. A stop from 60 mph, which is three times the speed of 20 mph, needs nine times the energy. It is understandable, then, why increased vehicle weight and speed need greater braking system pressure, larger friction surfaces, and greater capacity to absorb as well as dissipate heat. Braking power can also be measured in horsepower used to decelerate a vehicle rather than accelerate a vehicle. FIGURE 29-6 shows the influence of higher vehicle speeds on stopping distances. FIGURE 29-7 compares different brake foundation technologies and their influence on stopping capabilities.

Brake Torque & Inertia Shift

Appling brakes has two effects on a vehicle. One is the transfer of torque from the slowing wheel end to the axle through the brake mechanism. Axles will twist, and the suspension system is needed to control axle movement. Components used to attach the brake mechanism need to be capable of repeated torque transfer from the brake to the axle.

Deceleration during braking also produces a shift in vehicle weight from the rear to the front of a vehicle. The effect, called **inertia shift**, moves weight from the rear axles and transfers it forward. This effect is observed when, during hard braking, the rear suspension lifts, and the rear wheels will tend to lock up easily. The front of the vehicle dives, as weight transfers from the rear to front axles. Wheel lock-up can take place, as the rear tires will lose traction during inertia shift. Axle loads will change how much traction is available to a tire.

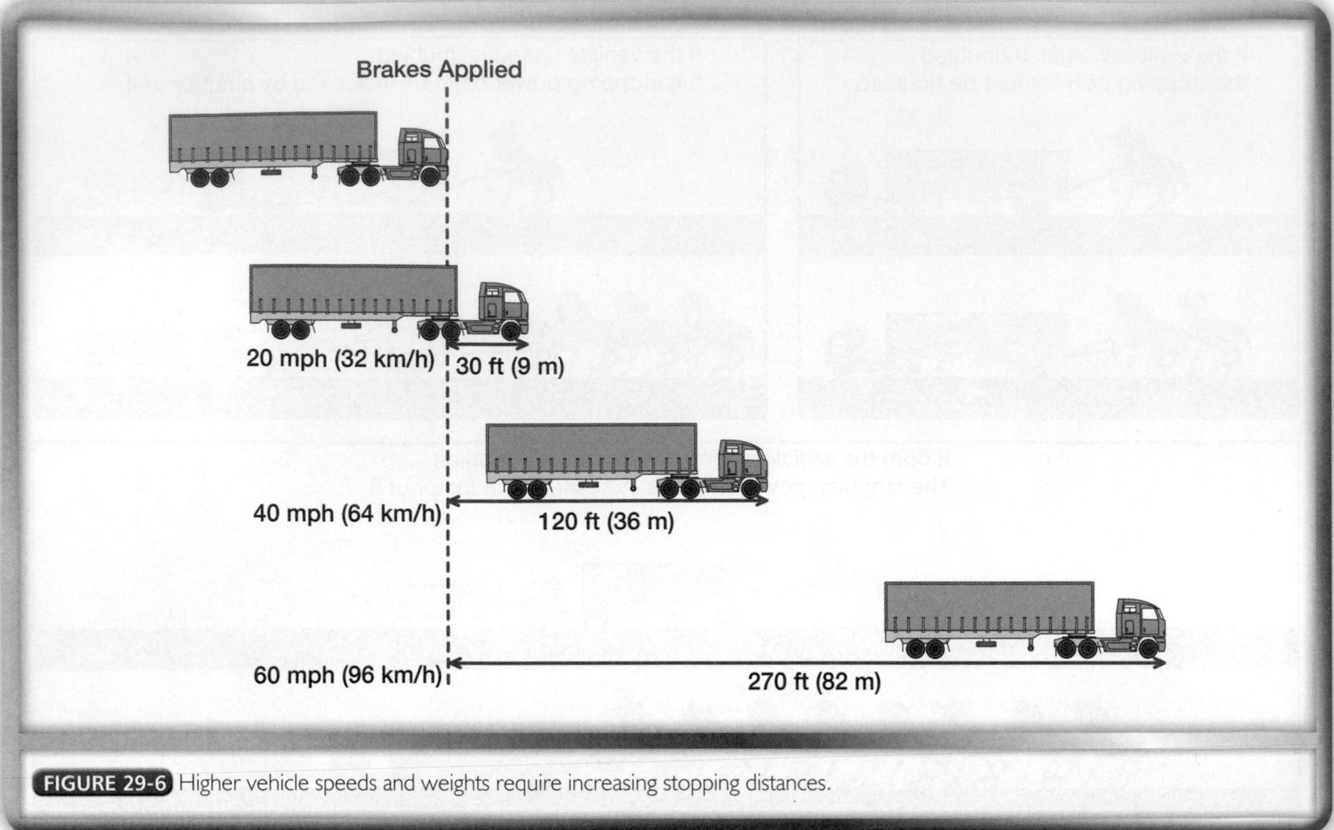

FIGURE 29-6 Higher vehicle speeds and weights require increasing stopping distances.

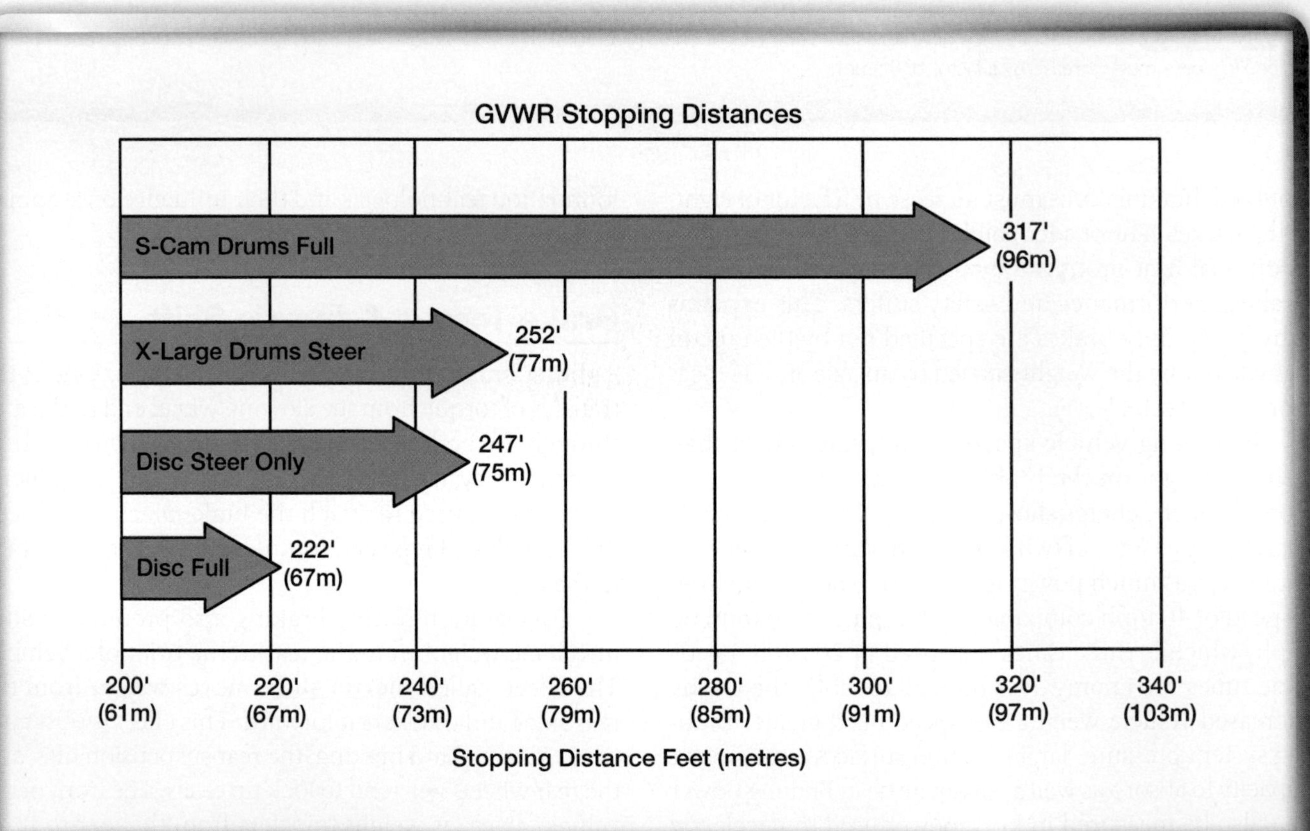

FIGURE 29-7 Comparisons between different brake foundation technologies and their influence on stopping capabilities.

The consequence of wheel lock-up is that the tires begin to skid, and the driver loses the ability to steer the vehicle. The mandatory use of antilock braking systems and other components incorporated into the braking system minimizes the likelihood of a wheel lock-up event. Other design factors—including brake size, brake type, valve opening pressures, use of specialized valves, and so on—are brake system elements that take into account the effects of inertia shift on braking and must be maintained by a technician. FIGURE 29-8 shows how vehicle weight is distributed over each axle. Too much braking performed by the front axle can cause jackknifing. Too much braking done by the rear axles can cause the trailer or rear axles to swing out. FIGURE 29-9 shows the brake torque reaction to braking force. Axles will twist in the opposite direction to the force applied to the rotating drum or rotor used to slow and stop the vehicle.

Types of Braking Systems

Because brakes require a much greater force than can be applied with a leg to slow a vehicle, brakes must multiply the input force of the operator's leg. Force multiplication is performed several ways in a braking system, but two primary methods for forcing friction material against drums and discs are using hydraulic fluid or using air pressure. Another term for brake application force is actuation pressure. A few limited production systems use both air and hydraulic pressure multiplication. Air pressure is more often used to supply force multiplication to a hydraulic actuation system.

FIGURE 29-10 depicts the force multiplication needed by the braking system to multiply the brake pedal input force enough to effectively apply the brakes. FIGURE 29-11 shows how hydraulic multiplication of driver input force can multiply brake pedal force and supply pressure to multiple wheel cylinders or brake caliper pistons. However, extra brake chambers used by multiple axles on heavy trucks and buses have higher flow requirements, making air pressure a better medium to multiply force.

Comparing Air and Hydraulic Braking Systems

Air and hydraulic braking systems each have operating characteristics that make one or the other ideal for certain applications. In heavy-duty combination vehicles, air is the best choice because of the large volume of liquid that would be needed instead of air to actuate all the brake chambers at each axle end.

Air systems also have the following advantages:

- The supply of air is limitless, which allows for minor leaks without the loss of braking.
- Connecting the tractor and trailer braking systems is easier using air lines rather than hydraulic hoses as shown in FIGURE 29-12.

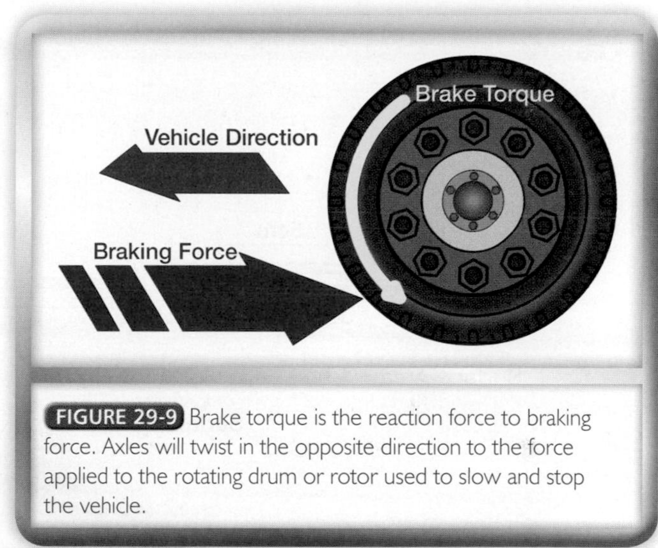

FIGURE 29-9 Brake torque is the reaction force to braking force. Axles will twist in the opposite direction to the force applied to the rotating drum or rotor used to slow and stop the vehicle.

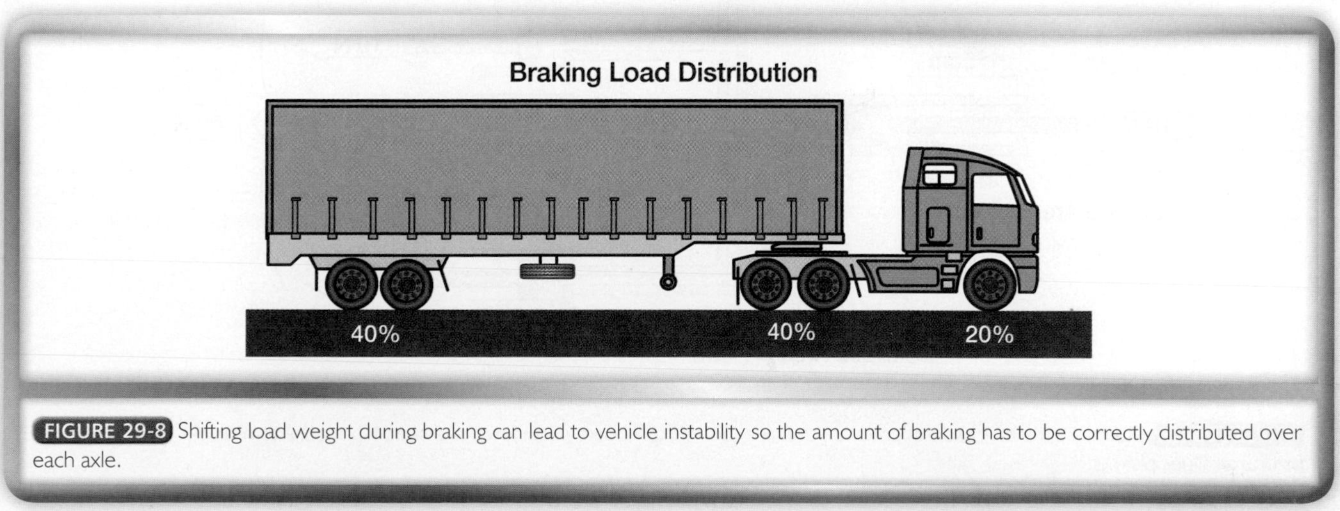

FIGURE 29-8 Shifting load weight during braking can lead to vehicle instability so the amount of braking has to be correctly distributed over each axle.

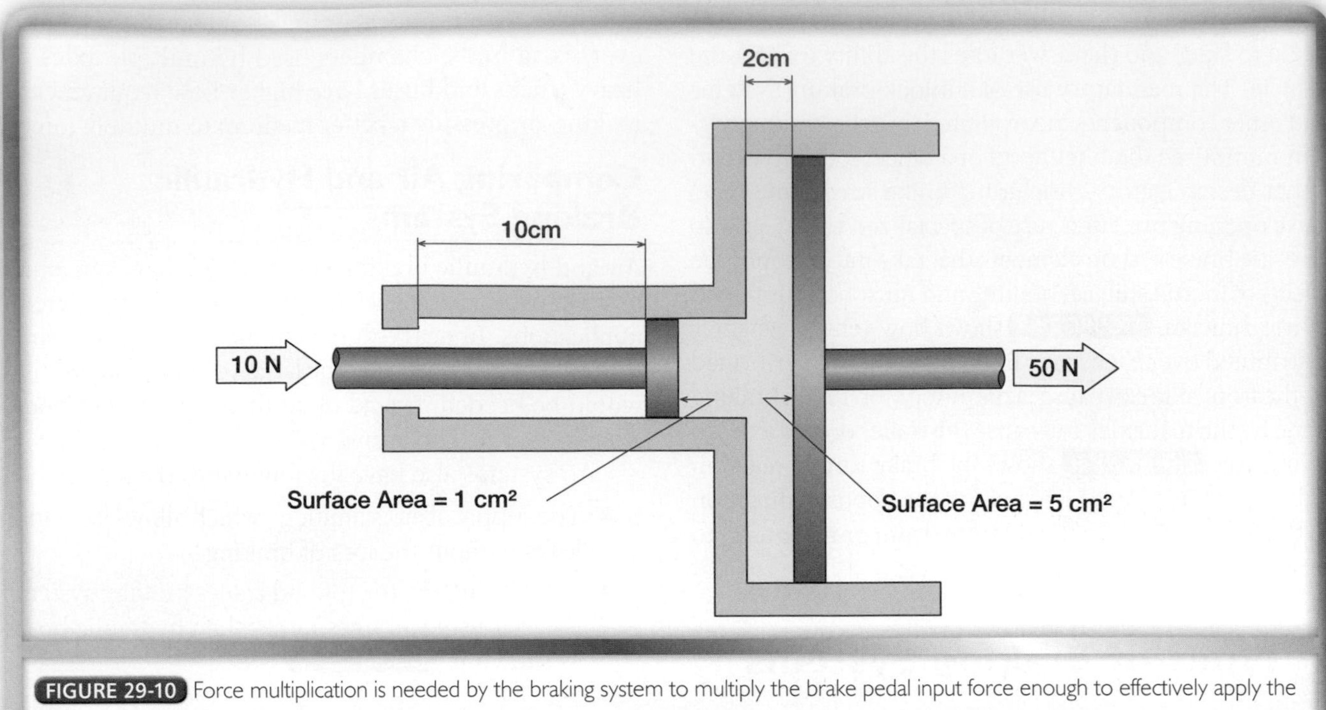

FIGURE 29-10 Force multiplication is needed by the braking system to multiply the brake pedal input force enough to effectively apply the brakes.

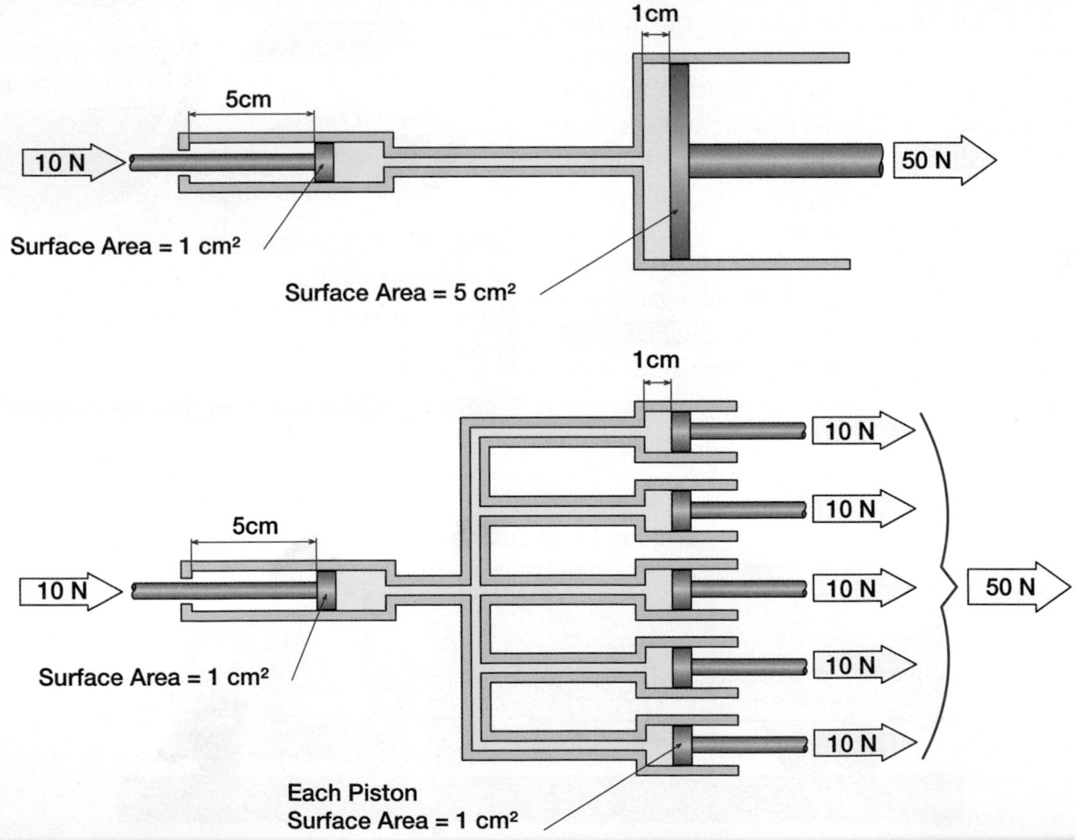

FIGURE 29-11 Hydraulic multiplication of driver input force can multiply brake pedal force and supply pressure to multiple wheel cylinders or brake caliper pistons.

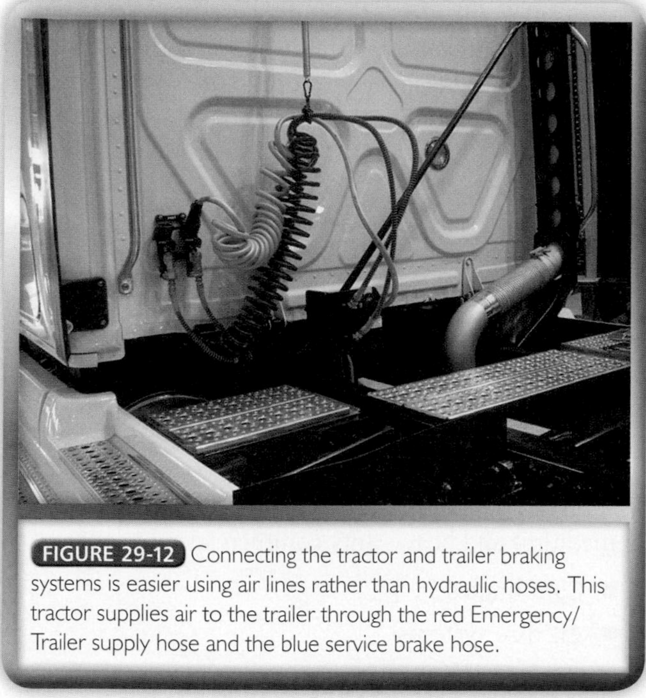

FIGURE 29-12 Connecting the tractor and trailer braking systems is easier using air lines rather than hydraulic hoses. This tractor supplies air to the trailer through the red Emergency/Trailer supply hose and the blue service brake hose.

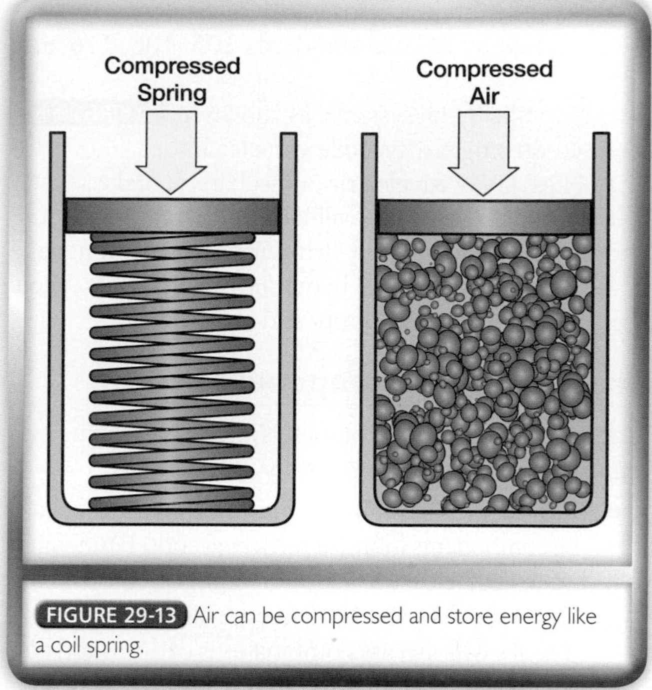

FIGURE 29-13 Air can be compressed and store energy like a coil spring.

- Air brake systems are not sensitive to altitude changes. Air can be compressed at high altitudes as well as sea level, so no loss of pressure takes place. This contrasts with hydraulic brake systems using vacuum boosters, which loose efficiency at high altitudes.
- Simpler foundation brakes—shoes, drums, and other components at the wheel ends—are simpler and fewer.
- Air can be compressed and store energy like a coil spring as shown in FIGURE 29-13.

Air systems are not without disadvantages, however, which include the following:

- The air must be pressurized, filtered, and stored in large, multiple reservoirs. This means more components are required, increasing the system complexity and cost when using air.
- The speed of air pressure transmission is much slower than a hydraulic system, which produces a longer delay between brake pedal application and brake shoe/pad actuation.
- Control of air pressure through brake circuits requires more valves and components, which adds complexity and cost to the air brake system.
- Some driver dissatisfaction with the delay occurs when an air system is empty and needs to build up pressure after the engine is started.
- Little to no feedback comes from the brake pedal about braking effort.
- Larger brake system components and diameter lines are required because air systems operate at lower pressures than hydraulic systems.
- Air brake system complexity requires that technicians have more knowledge and skill when servicing. For similar reasons, driver training and certification to operate a vehicle with air brakes is mandatory in most jurisdictions.

Air brakes system performance and safety standards are legislated by the **Federal Motor Vehicle Safety Standard 121 (FMVSS 121)**. To ensure safe braking performance under normal and emergency conditions, compliance with the standard is required by all air brake systems at the time of manufacture.

Hydraulic systems have the following advantages:

- Higher line pressures, enabling the use of smaller components.
- Faster force transmission through smaller lines. Hydraulic fluid is not compressible like air, and almost no delay takes place between brake pedal application and friction material actuation.
- Improved feedback during braking application. As the pedal is pushed further, resistance increases more than in an air system. The disadvantage is that hydraulic systems transmit annoying pressure pulsations caused by warped rotors and out-of-round brake drums back into the brake pedal.
- Lower initial cost due to fewer and smaller components.

Hydraulic brake performance and safety standards are governed by FMVSS standards 105, 106, 116, and 135.

Hydraulic brake systems, as shown in FIGURE 29-14, are used on single-drive axle vehicles under 14,000 lbs (6,364 kgs) GVW. An electric or mechanical brake booster is used on diesel-powered vehicles, as no engine vacuum is available to help multiply driver input force through the brake pedal. Note the dual hydraulic brake circuits. There is one circuit each for the front and rear axle.

Brake System Components

Regardless of the type of braking system, all braking systems will have the following subsystems.

- *Brake foundations*—**Brake foundations** are the braking components found at the wheel ends. Foundation brakes use either a drum or brake shoe combination or discs and pads. (Discs are also called rotors.) Vehicles will also use combinations of drum and disc for foundations.
- *Dual brake circuits*—Whether the actuation system is hydraulic or air operated, two separate brake circuits control the front and rear axle braking systems. Separate circuits are used to prevent a total loss of braking if a failure occurs. Only half of the brakes would be affected by a failure, and the vehicle can still be brought to a safe controlled stop. In air brake systems, the primary circuit controls the rear brakes, and the secondary circuit controls the front axle brakes. Trailers receive air pressure supplied by the secondary circuit in early model trucks. Late model vehicles supply air to the trailer from the reservoir with the highest pressure.
- *Parking brakes*—With the exception of trucks using a drive line park brake, all vehicles will use the foundation brakes for keeping a vehicle stationary when parked.

Air Brake Foundation Systems

Three basic types of brake foundation configurations found in medium- and heavy-duty commercial vehicles are:

- Cam brakes
- Air disc systems
- Wedge brakes

(This chapter examines the brake foundation system. Air brake circuits and valves are covered in a separate chapter.)

In air brake foundation systems, air pressure proportional to brake pedal travel is supplied by the primary and secondary air systems. Foundation brake components are located at the wheel ends and provide the braking action needed to slow and stop a vehicle. The wedge brakes in

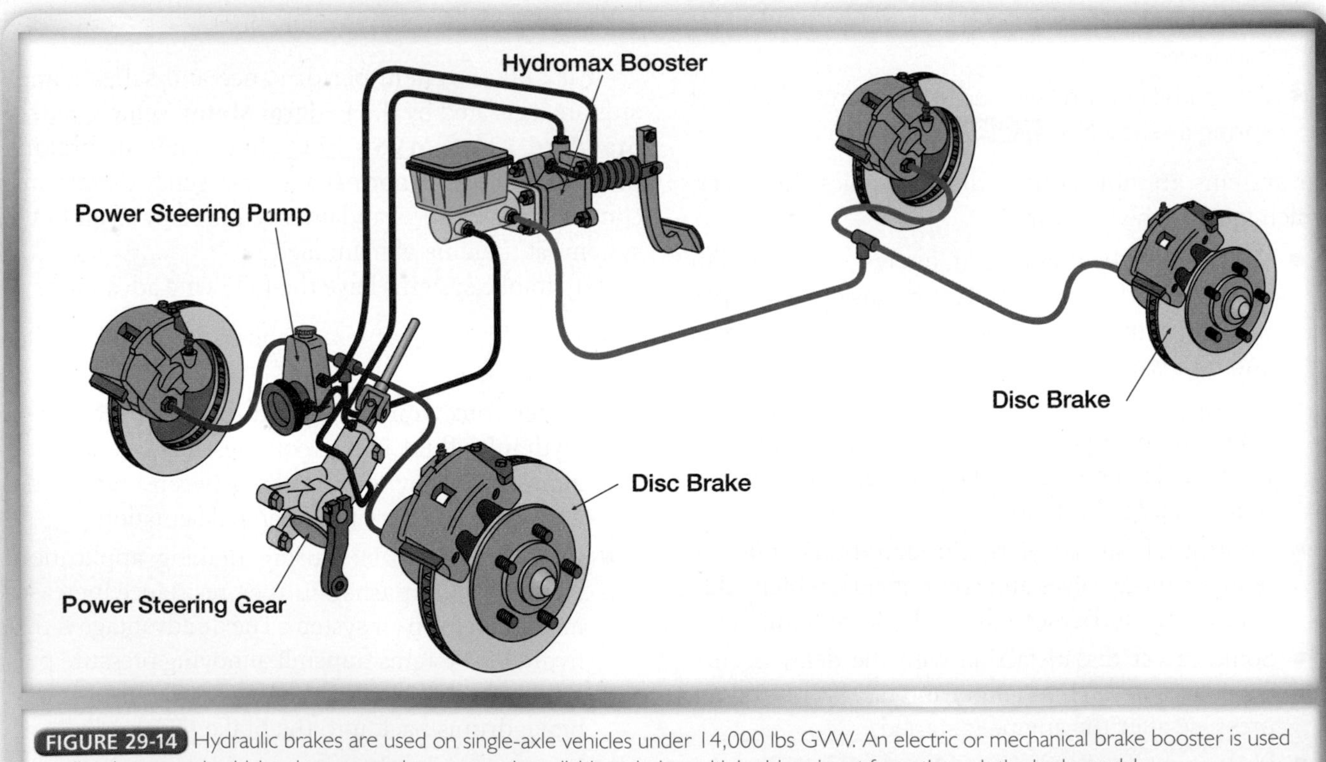

FIGURE 29-14 Hydraulic brakes are used on single-axle vehicles under 14,000 lbs GVW. An electric or mechanical brake booster is used on diesel-powered vehicles since no engine vacuum is available to help multiply driver input force through the brake pedal.

FIGURE 29-15 use shoes and rollers for the brake foundation. **Wedge brakes** use leverage to multiply braking force. A wedge pushed between two ramps, as shown in FIGURE 29-16, multiplies brake force proportional to the angle of the brake wedge. Rollers used between the ramps and wedge reduce friction force.

Disc brakes squeeze brake pads against a rotor attached to the wheel to produce braking action. Higher application force by brake pads against the rotors makes disc brake systems more efficient than other types of foundation brakes. Shorter stopping distances are easier to achieve using disc brake systems. FIGURE 29-17 shows a typical heavy-duty truck disc brake.

Cam brakes are the most common foundation brake found on heavy trucks today. These brake systems use an "S"-shaped cam that twists between two rollers to expand a

FIGURE 29-15 Foundation brake components are located at the wheel ends and provide the braking action needed to slow and stop a vehicle. The wedge brakes in this illustration use shoes and rollers for the brake foundation.

FIGURE 29-17 Disc brakes squeeze brake pads against a rotor attached to the wheel to produce braking action. Higher application force by brake pads against the rotors make disc brake systems more efficient than other types of foundation brakes. **A.** Brake rotor. **B.** Brake caliper. **C.** Actuator chamber. **D.** Brake pads.

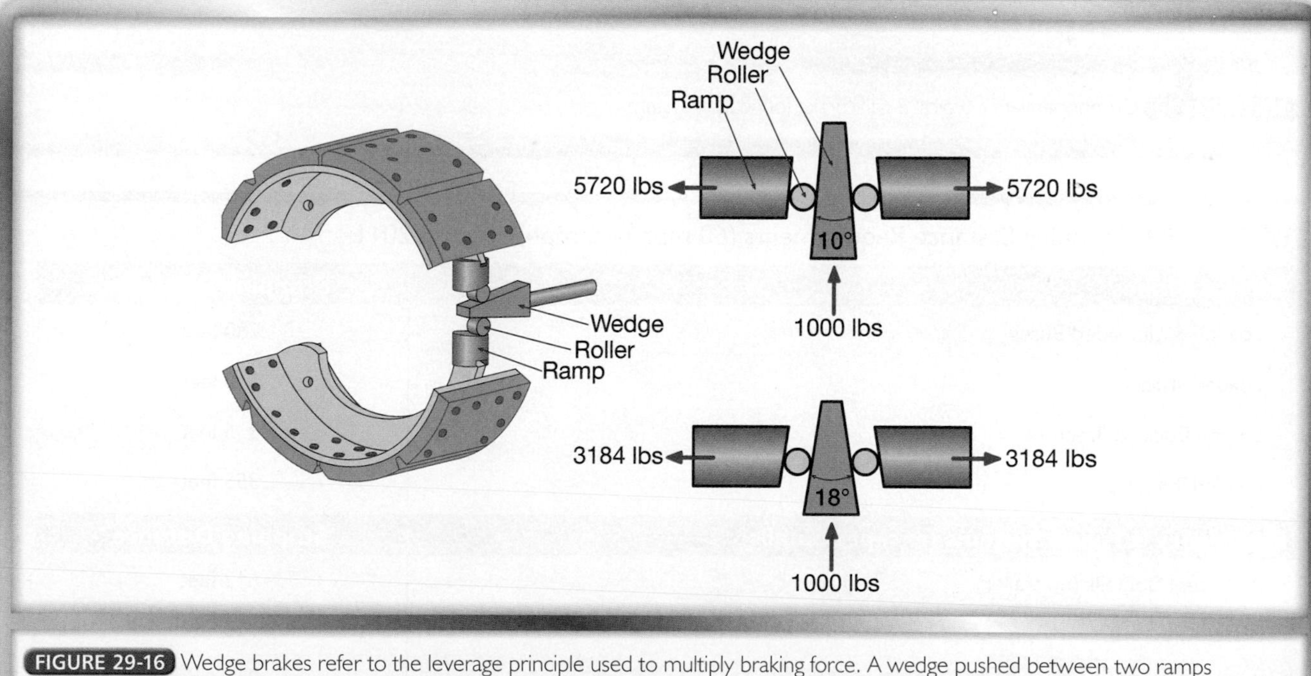

FIGURE 29-16 Wedge brakes refer to the leverage principle used to multiply braking force. A wedge pushed between two ramps multiplies brake force proportional to the angle of the brake wedge. Rollers used between the ramps and wedge reduce friction force.

set of brake shoes to apply the brakes. Because they are the most common foundation brake system, our discussion will focus primarily on the S-cam foundation brake followed by a shorter examination of disc and wedge brakes.

Cam Brake System

Operation

Cam brakes consist of an air brake chamber, automatic slack adjuster, S-camshaft, brake hardware, shoes and linings, spider, and brake drum.

The name cam brake is given because of an "S"-shaped camshaft, or **S-cam**, used to force brake shoes onto the brake drum. When torque is applied to the camshaft through the S-shaped cam ramps, rollers on the brake shoes ride up the cam, causing the shoes to contact the brake drum. Shoe-to-drum friction slows and stops the vehicle. FIGURE 29-18 shows the components of a typical S-cam brake foundation system.

Cam brakes are commonly used with 15" and 16.5" diameter drums and in varying widths from 4" to 7". TABLE 29-1 shows stopping distance requirements prior to 2011. Revisions to the year 2011 FMVSS 121 standard introduced a 30% reduction in stopping distance from the previous year. More powerful brake configurations are now necessary to meet the revised stopping distance standards. The common 16.5" × 7" rear axle brake may be replaced by an optional 16.5" × 8" or 16.5" × 8.62"

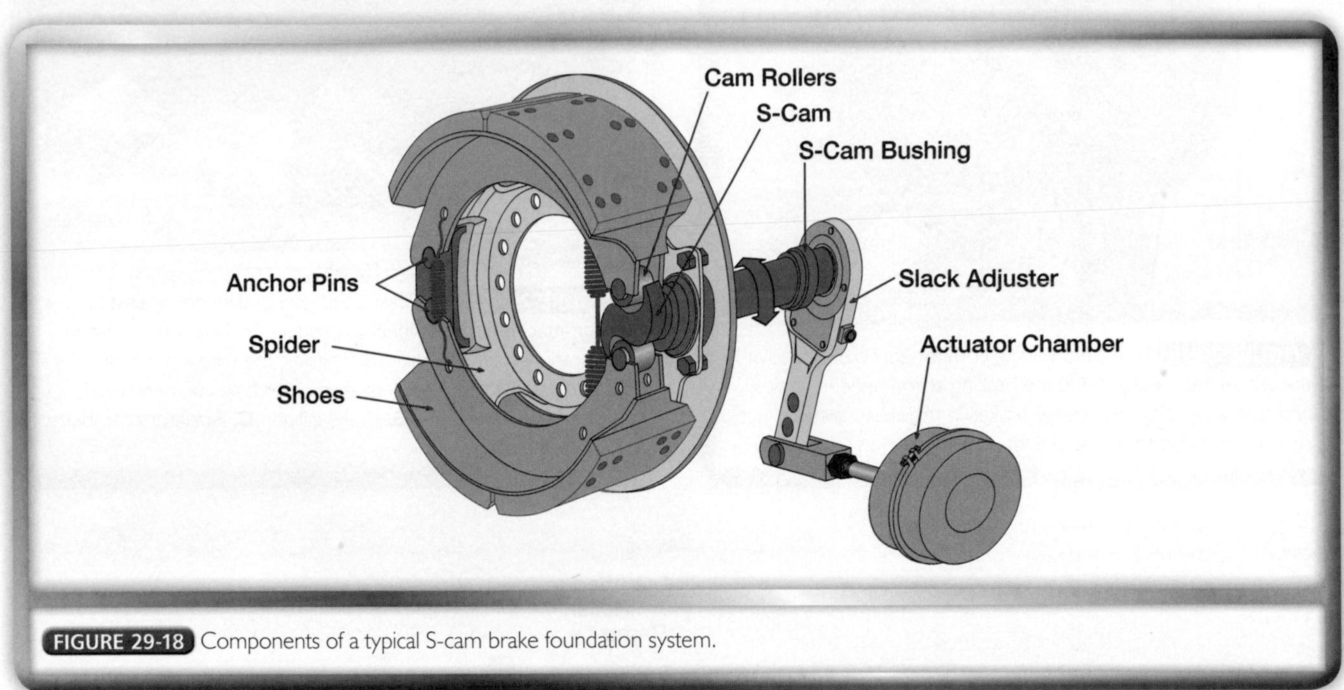

FIGURE 29-18 Components of a typical S-cam brake foundation system.

TABLE 29-1: Stopping Distance Requirements (60 mph to 0 mph) Prior to 2011

Service Brakes	Stopping Distance
Loaded & Unloaded Buses	280 feet
Loaded Trucks	310 feet
Empty Trucks & Tractors	335 feet
Loaded Tractors	355 feet
Emergency & Failed Systems (except bobtails)	**Stopping Distance**
All except Bobtails (no trailer)	613 feet
Bobtail Tractors	720 feet
Automobiles (for reference) Empty or Loaded	215 feet

brake. Traditional front axle brakes using 15" × 4" drums and brake shoes may move up to 16.5" × 5" brakes.

These stopping distance requirements must also be met with a stability requirement. During certification, the vehicle must stay within a 12' lane with no part of the vehicle leaving the lane during braking. It should be noted that the superior stopping power and fade resistance of air disc brakes (ADB) will likely replace the cam brake in most applications.

Cam brake shoes will use either a single or double anchor pin. Today's anchor pin holes are open ended to enable quick changing of brake shoes. Older shoes used closed shoe anchors, which were prone to seizing and labor intensive to remove during brake replacement. Figure 29-18 shows an S-cam brake foundation brake using double anchor pins. The S-cam shown in FIGURE 29-19 rotates in a counterclockwise direction, which makes this cam a left-hand cam. FIGURE 29-20 shows a single anchor S-cam brake. Note the actuator chamber is in front of and below the axle.

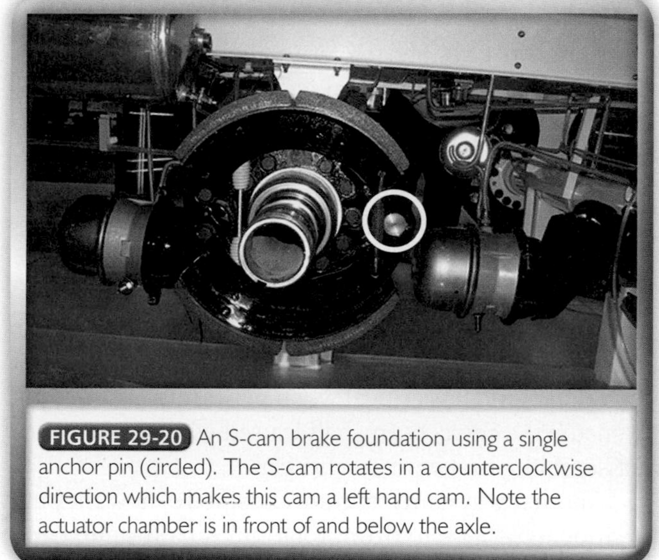

FIGURE 29-20 An S-cam brake foundation using a single anchor pin (circled). The S-cam rotates in a counterclockwise direction which makes this cam a left hand cam. Note the actuator chamber is in front of and below the axle.

Self-Energization

Cam brakes use a primary-secondary shoe design with fixed anchor points for each shoe opposite the camshaft end of the shoe. Both of these shoes are identically shaped and use two different lengths and shapes of brake lining on each shoe. What is different between the primary and secondary shoe is the direction of drum rotation acting on each shoe during brake application.

On the primary shoe, the shorter section of brake lining contacts the drum first, as it is rotated on its anchor pin against the rotating drum. Because the forward edge of the shorter lining is contacting the drum first, the direction of drum rotation causes an action called **self-energization** to take place. Self-energizing causes shoe-drum friction to rotate the brake shoe into the drum with more force. The effect is the brake will apply "harder" or "bite" into the drum with greater force thus increasing friction. Opposite the primary shoe is the secondary shoe. When it is forced against the drum, the direction of brake drum rotation forces the lining away from the drum, and less friction is produced. Self-energization can cause uneven brake shoe wear. The secondary shoe can either be on the top or the bottom position of the wheel end, left or right, depending on the location of the camshaft. FIGURE 29-21 shows the effect of self-energization.

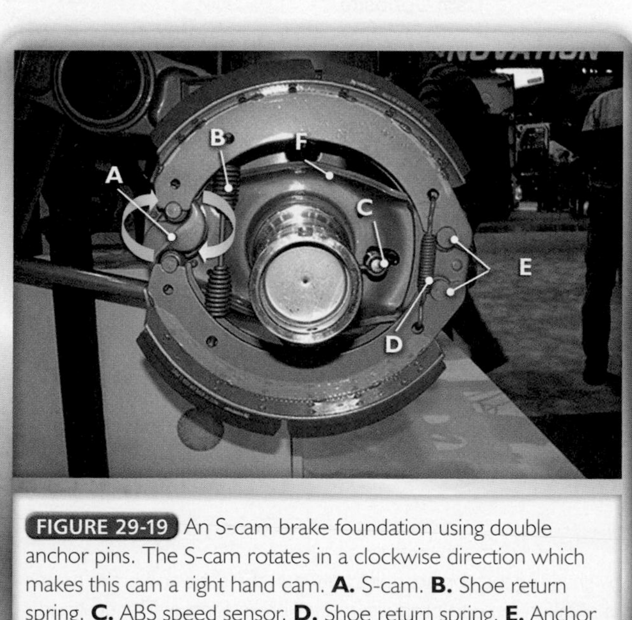

FIGURE 29-19 An S-cam brake foundation using double anchor pins. The S-cam rotates in a clockwise direction which makes this cam a right hand cam. **A.** S-cam. **B.** Shoe return spring. **C.** ABS speed sensor. **D.** Shoe return spring. **E.** Anchor pins (2). **F.** Spider.

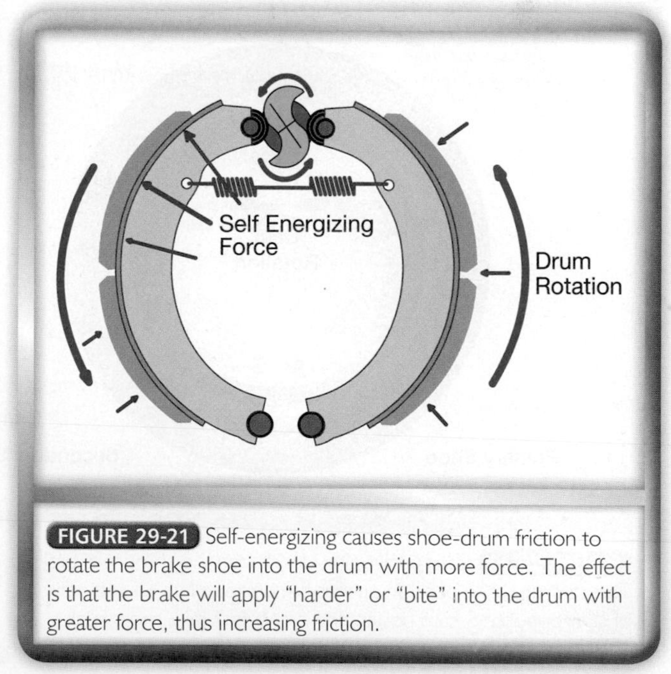

FIGURE 29-21 Self-energizing causes shoe-drum friction to rotate the brake shoe into the drum with more force. The effect is that the brake will apply "harder" or "bite" into the drum with greater force, thus increasing friction.

Left- and Right-Hand Camshafts

Camshafts are classified two ways. One is by the direction they rotate to force the brake shoes against the drum. Depending on which direction the camshaft rotates to force the primary shoe against the drum, the cam is referred to as a left- or right-hand camshaft. Left-hand cams rotate counterclockwise, while right-hand cams turn clockwise. To make it easier to remember, simply consider which way you would turn the hands of a clock, clockwise or counterclockwise. **Left-hand camshafts and right-hand camshafts** are found on either side of the vehicle, and it is critical when performing a brake job to ensure the correct camshaft is used when replacing or reassembling brakes on a wheel end.

Another way camshafts are classified is how they are positioned relative to drum rotation. A **cam-same camshaft** rotates in the same direction as the drum to energize the brakes. The primary brake shoe rollers are pushed out and down. A **cam-opposite camshaft** rotates opposite the drum's rotation to energize the brakes. The opposite rotation pushes the shoe roller up and out. Cam-opposite positioning produces more brake torque but causes the brake shoe to contact the drum at the cam end rather than closer to the center. The result is uneven brake shoe wear. FIGURE 29-22 shows the two cam positions

The major reason for different camshaft rotations is the position of the brake chambers. Some suspension systems simply do not allow enough room above or below the wheel end or in front or behind for the chamber. Positioning the chamber where the best clearances are obtained requires an appropriate type of camshaft. The location of the actuator chamber relative to the axle determines the camshaft direction of rotation. Left-hand cams turn counterclockwise FIGURE 29-23A; right-hand camshafts rotate clockwise FIGURE 29-23B.

S-cam Brackets

To support the camshaft between the brake chamber and the brake spider at the wheel end, a support bracket is used to enclose the camshaft. At least two support bushing are located at each end of the bracket. Grease seals at each end of the tube are designed to allow grease to exit at the slack adjuster end of the bracket but prevent grease from getting into the brakes.

Grease nipples are installed in the brackets to lubricate the bushings. When the bushings or camshafts wear out, movement of the S-cam in a linear rather than a rotational motion introduces more brake chamber stroke travel. Even when camshaft and bushing wear is within acceptable limits, "wheel-up" brake adjustment is a good practice to avoid adjustment error due to even slightly worn bushings. Making wheel-up adjustments involves tightening the slack adjusters with the wheels off the ground until a slight amount of brake shoe drag is obtained.

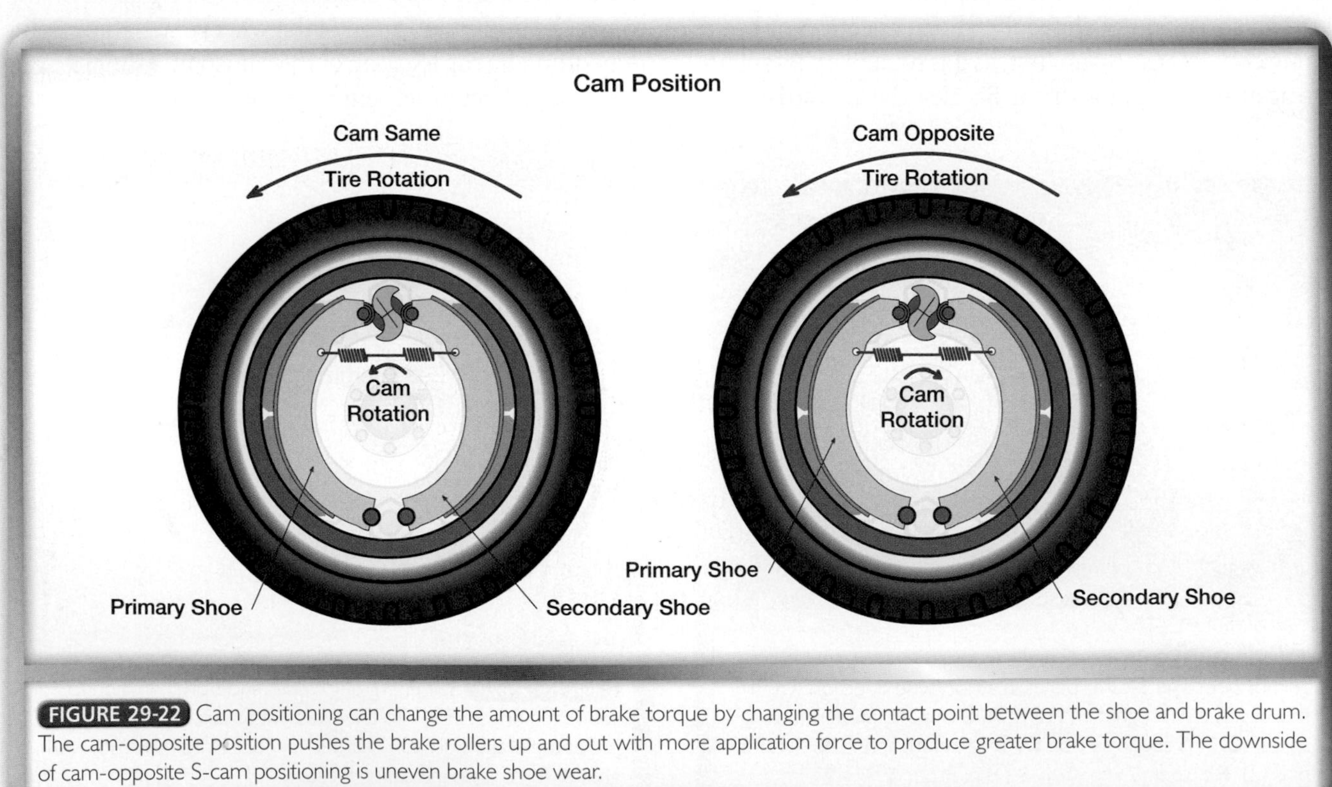

FIGURE 29-22 Cam positioning can change the amount of brake torque by changing the contact point between the shoe and brake drum. The cam-opposite position pushes the brake rollers up and out with more application force to produce greater brake torque. The downside of cam-opposite S-cam positioning is uneven brake shoe wear.

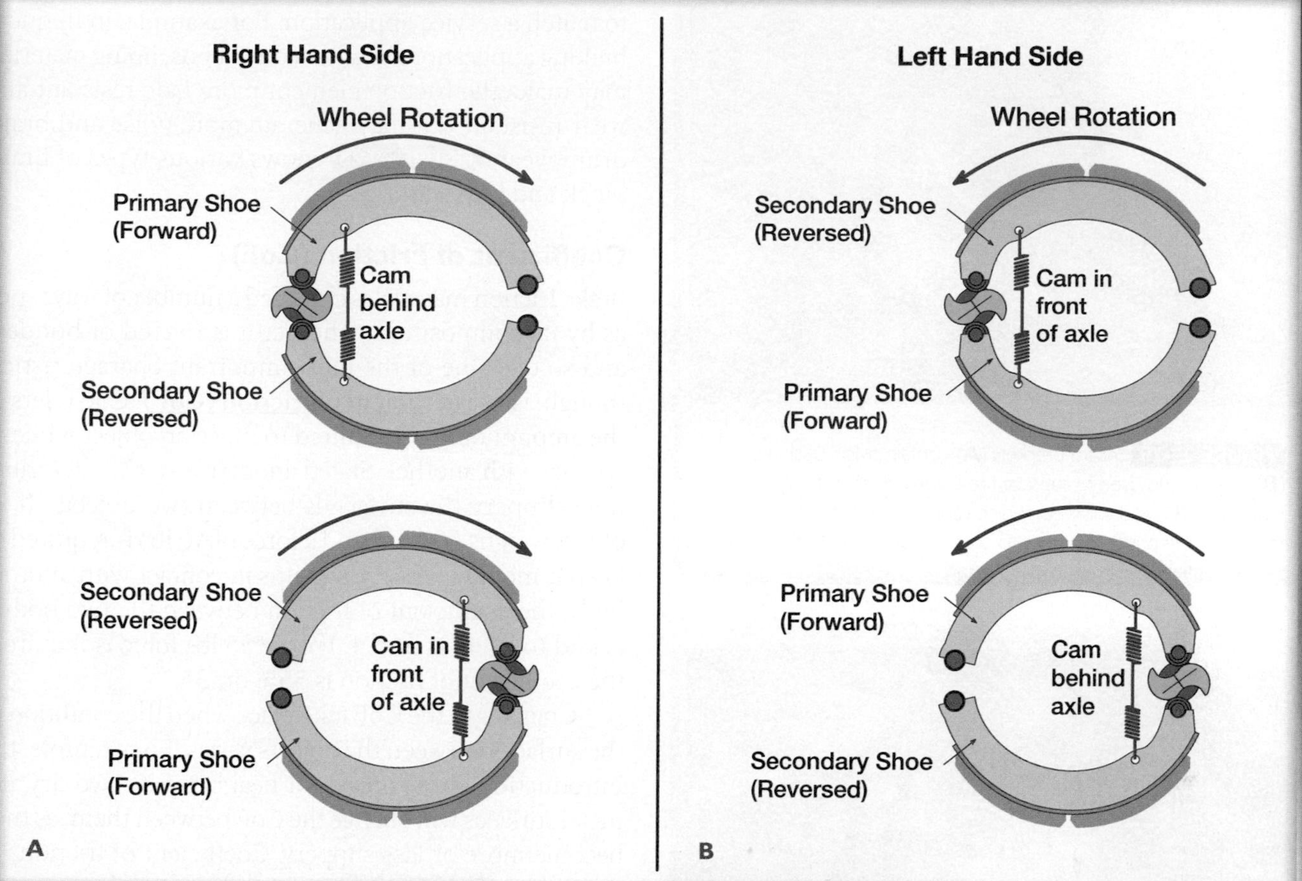

FIGURE 29-23 **A.** Right-hand and **B.** Left-hand S-camshaft classification is determined by the direction the cam rotates to apply the brakes. The location of the actuator chamber relative to the axle determines the camshaft direction of rotation. Left-hand cams turn counterclockwise. Right-hand camshafts rotate clockwise.

S-cams are shimmed with washers to prevent any excessive end play in the cam bracket. After installation, selective shims are placed between the slack adjuster and clip holding the slack adjuster onto the end of the S-cam. The S-cam bracket, shown in FIGURE 29-24, supports the S-cam and has an attachment point for the actuator chamber. Note the grease fitting in the bracket used to grease support bushing located at each end of the bracket. FIGURE 29-25 shows the S-cam nylon bushings at each end used to support the S-cam. Bushings require lubrication and will wear, which requires the actuator chamber to extend the pushrod farther to compensate for cam deflection. Selective shims installed at the end of the S-cam are used to minimize any cam end play; FIGURE 29-26 illustrates the shim positioning.

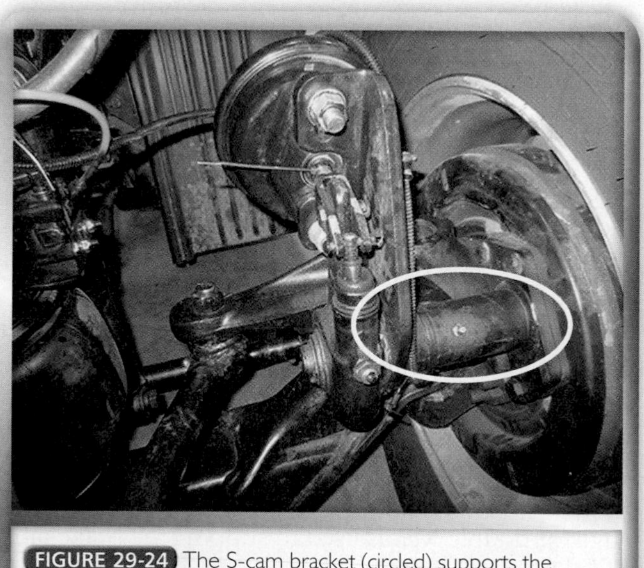

FIGURE 29-24 The S-cam bracket (circled) supports the S-cam and has an attachment point for the actuator chamber. Note the grease fitting in the bracket used to grease support bushing located at each end of the bracket.

Brake Shoes

Cam brakes use brake shoes that are made in different sizes to match an axle weight rating. The shoes have two ends—a cam and anchor pin end—and have either one

FIGURE 29-25 S-cam brackets (**A**) contain nylon bushings (**B**) at each end used to support the S-cam. Bushings require lubrication (**C**) and will wear which requires the actuator chamber to extend the pushrod farther to compensate for cam deflection.

FIGURE 29-26 Selective shims are installed at the end of the S-cam to minimize any cam end play. **A.** Shim. **B.** Snap ring. **C.** Slack adjuster.

or two pieces of lining attached. One or two pieces of friction material are attached to the brake shoe table and are called either **brake block** or **brake lining**. Brake lining and block differ in that a block is 3/4" thick and lining is 1/2" thick. Two pieces of block are required to reline a shoe and only one piece of lining.

Block and lining are riveted, bolted, or glued to the brake table. While glued friction material, called bonded lining, can withstand high temperatures, riveted lining is considered superior in heavy-duty applications because it is mechanically held to the shoe. The web is the support perpendicular to the bottom of the brake shoe table. A single or double web is used to support the brake table depending on the width of the shoe. FIGURE 29-27 shows the subcomponents of an air brake foundation. Brake block refers to ¾" thick brake shoe friction material, which is either bolted or riveted to brake shoes. Brake block, like lining, is composed of a variety of materials to match a service application. For example, in frequent braking applications such as a transit bus, lining materials may make the friction element more fade resistant and wear resistant but may generate more noise and brake drum wear. FIGURE 29-28 shows various types of brake block and brake lining.

Coefficient of Friction (CoF)

Brake friction material is classified a number of ways such as by its composition, whether it is riveted or bonded, and so on. One of the most important characteristics, though, is its **coefficient of friction (CoF)**. CoF refers to the amount of force required to move an object while in contact with another. Stated another way, CoF describes how slippery the surface is between two objects. If an object weighs 100 lbs, and a force of 40 lbs is required to keep it moving while it remains in contact with another body, the coefficient of friction between the two bodies is said to be 40% or 0.4. If only 35 lbs force is required, the coefficient of friction is 35% or .35.

Changes to the CoF take place when the condition of the surfaces between the objects varies. For example, the introduction of oil, grease, or heat between two dry, flat metal surfaces will change the CoF between them, as they become more or less slippery. Coefficient of friction, as depicted in FIGURE 29-29, is defined as a ratio between the force required to move an object compared to its weight. In the illustration, a 45-lb force applied to the 100-lb load generates a 0.45 or 45% coefficient of friction.

Brake Block Material

Brake friction material is made from a wide variety of materials to provide a varying Cof to match an application and provide other desirable performance characteristics. The perfect friction material would have the correct coefficient maintained constantly for its service life under all operating conditions of pressure, speed, temperature, and humidity. Perfect lining would not score or wear the brake drum, would operate quietly and wear slowly, and would not fade or emit noxious odor. Friction material is made from heat-resistant adhesive resin blended with materials such as glass fiber, Kevlar, mineral wool, aramid fibers, ceramic fibers, carbon fibers, slag, bronze, steel and elastomer-like compounds. Asbestos is not used in any friction material today.

Two broad categories for friction material are **non-asbestos organic (NAO) lining** and **semi-metallic linings**. Because the coefficient of friction of metallic particles in lining increases when hot, heat-resistant, semi-metallic blends are used for higher temperatures and load service ratings. The downside for semi-metallic linings

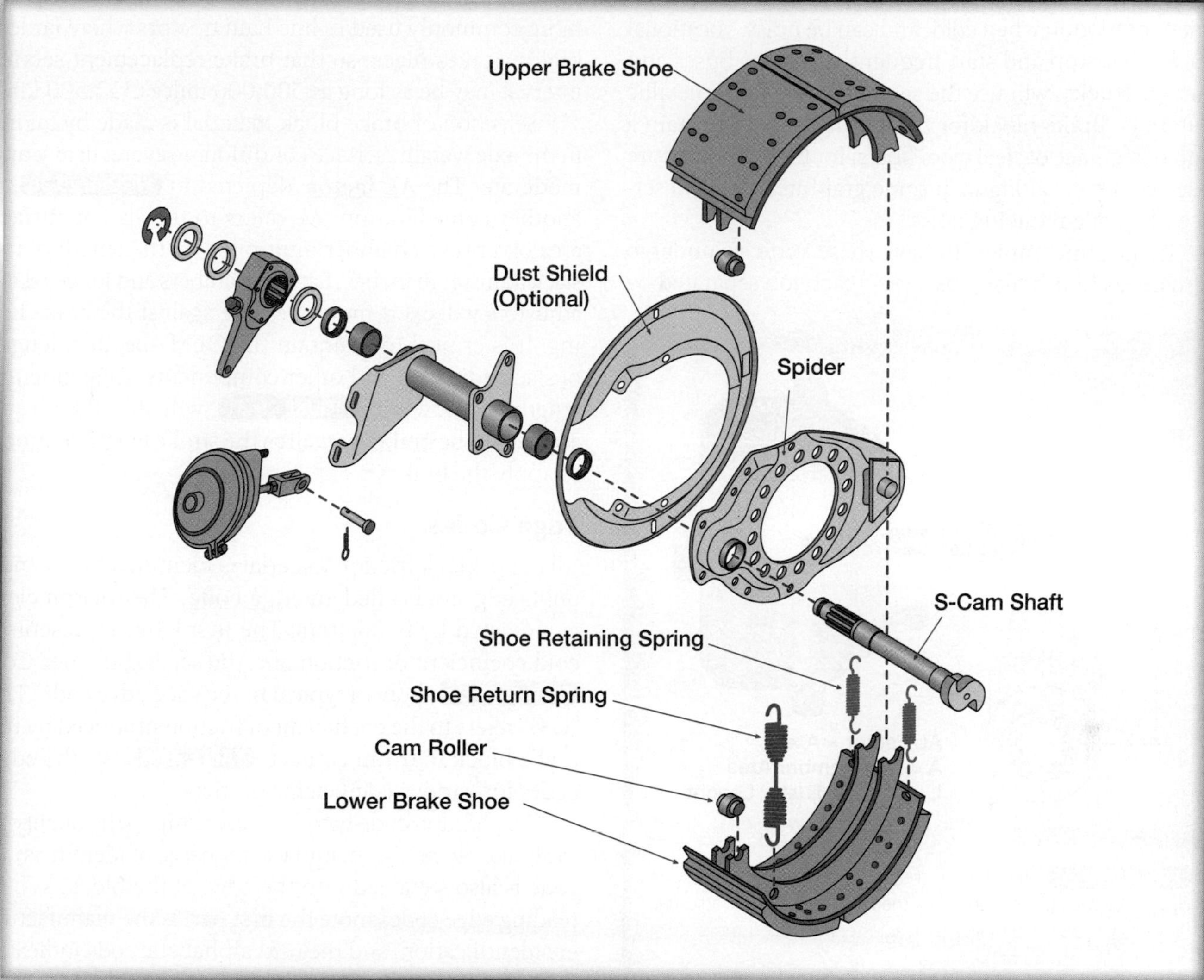

FIGURE 29-27 Subcomponents of an air brake foundation.

FIGURE 29-28 Brake block refers to 0.75" thick brake shoe friction material that is either bolted or riveted to brake shoes. Brake block, like lining, is composed of a variety of materials to match a service application.

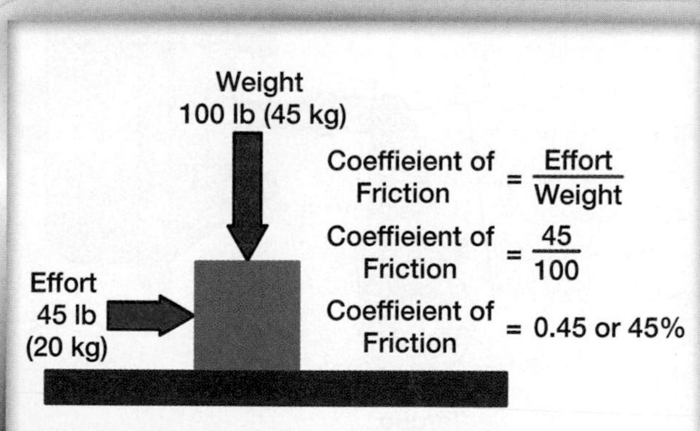

Weight
100 lb (45 kg)
Effort
45 lb
(20 kg)
Coeffieient of Friction = Effort / Weight
Coeffieient of Friction = 45 / 100
Coeffieient of Friction = 0.45 or 45%

FIGURE 29-29 Coefficient of friction is a ratio between the force required to move an object compared to its weight. In the illustration, a 45-lb force applied to the 100-lb load generates a 0.45 or 45% coefficient of friction.

is that they wear brake drums faster, have a poor coefficient of friction when cold, and can be noisy. Vocational trucks that stop and start frequently, such as buses and garbage trucks, will use the severe service semi-metallic materials. Brake block for these vehicles will contain a high percentage of steel wool fibers, for high-temperature fade-resistance, along with some graphite to extend service life while reducing noise.

It's not uncommon to have these vehicles undergo as many as four brake jobs a year, each job separated by as little as 50,000 miles (31,250 km). NOA linings are more commonly used in line haul tractors where far less braking takes place, so that brake replacement service interval may be as long as 500,000 miles (312,500 km).

Selection of brake block material is made by taking in the axle weight, service condition—severe, heavy, and moderate. The **AL factor**, depicted in FIGURE 29-30, is another consideration. AL refers to the size or surface area of a brake chamber multiplied by the length of the slack adjuster in inches. Larger chambers and longer slack adjusters will exert more pressure against the brake lining. It is critical to maintain the OEM-specified length of slack adjusters and other components. Changing the length, as shown in FIGURE 29-31, will alter the torque applied to the brakes as well as the stroke length required to apply the brakes.

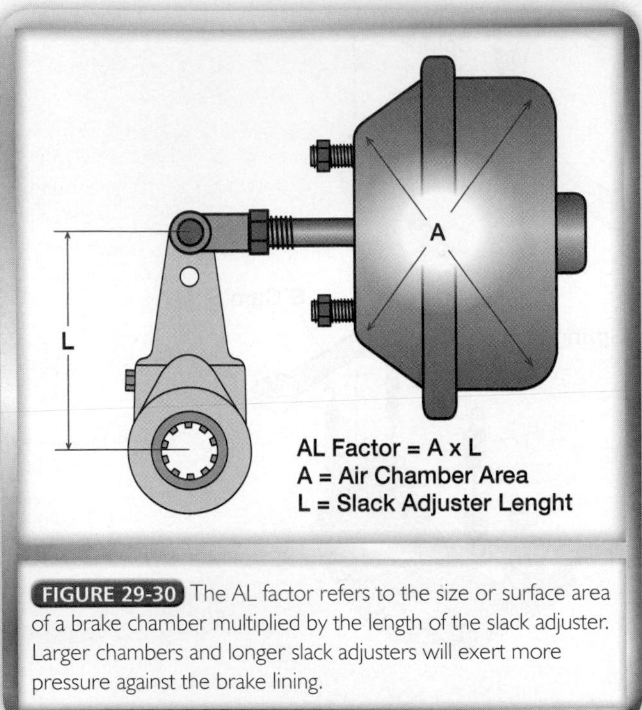

FIGURE 29-30 The AL factor refers to the size or surface area of a brake chamber multiplied by the length of the slack adjuster. Larger chambers and longer slack adjusters will exert more pressure against the brake lining.

Edge Codes

All brake block friction material is identified by a stencil on its edge and called an **edge code**. The friction class is indicated by two letters. The first letter represents a cold coefficient of friction and the second the hot CoF. FIGURE 29-32 shows a typical brake shoe edge code. The "G G" refers to the coefficient of friction produced by the brake block to drum contact. TABLE 29-2 lists the edge codes for various coefficients of friction.

The friction code has no relationship to the quality of the brake block. The manufacturer name or identification code is also stenciled into the edge of the block. When reading edge codes, note the first part is the manufacturer's identification, and the next alphabetic code indicates the composition or material the block is made from. The

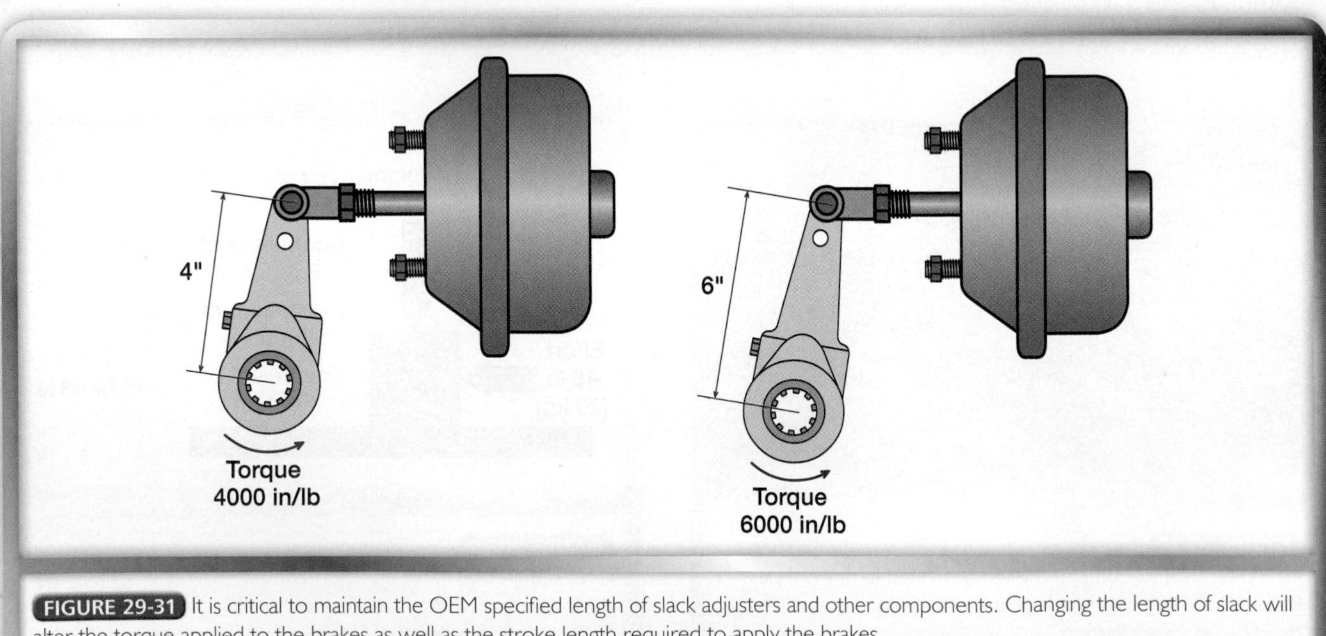

FIGURE 29-31 It is critical to maintain the OEM specified length of slack adjusters and other components. Changing the length of slack will alter the torque applied to the brakes as well as the stroke length required to apply the brakes.

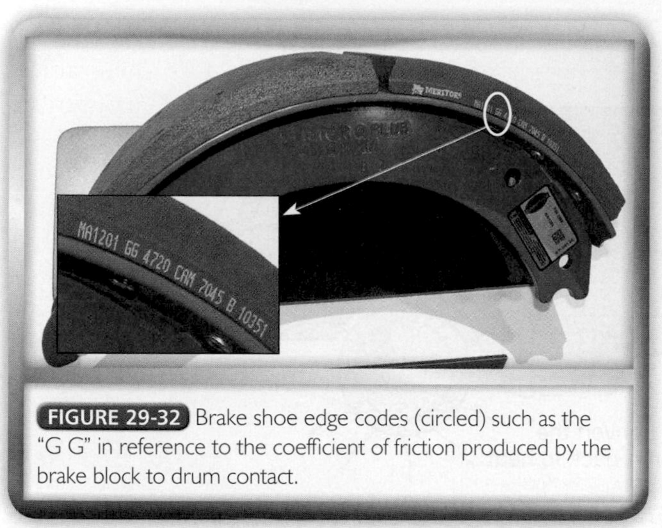

FIGURE 29-32 Brake shoe edge codes (circled) such as the "G G" in reference to the coefficient of friction produced by the brake block to drum contact.

TABLE 29-2: Coefficient of Friction Edge Codes

Coefficient of Friction	Edge Code
Over 0.25, but not over 0.35	E
Over 0.35, but not over 0.45	F
Over 0.45, but not over 0.55	G
Over 0.55	H

third two-letter code is the friction class. The first letter represents a "normal" coefficient, and the second letter represents the "hot" coefficient of friction. Each letter indicates an average coefficient of friction. Manufacturers calculate these averages from laboratory test data, where a one-square-inch sample of the lining is applied under pressure against a moving drum. As the drum heats up, normal range data to calculate cold CoF is collected between 200°F (93°C) to 400°F (204°C). The hot CoF coefficient is averaged using data from 300°F (149°C) to 650°F (343°C). Brake temperatures can climb as high as 1,000°F (538°C).

Occasionally two different pieces of block are used on one shoe to give it different characteristics. Combination lining, as it is called, will also have a direction of rotation arrow stamped on the shoe to ensure correct installation.

Brake Fade

Brake fade is a problem that can be described as the inability of the brakes to maintain their effectiveness. An operator would describe fade as the need to push the pedal harder to get the same braking effectiveness. Good quality brake linings will fade slightly upon each brake application but will immediately return to their initial state after cooling. However, the coefficient of friction of the lining may change during its service life. When the lining's CoF decreases, the vehicle develops what is known as a "hard pedal." Brake fade occurs for several reasons. During brake fade, the brakes' stopping power is reduced, as depicted in FIGURE 29-33, due to problems such as overheated brake drums and shoes, contaminated lining, or changes to the friction material, such as glazing of linings. Common types of brake fade are heat, water, mechanical, and chemical fade, as well as glazing of lining.

> **TECHNICIAN TIP**
>
> Brakes can emit noises for a large variety of reasons. Much of the noises have one common source, though—vibration. High-frequency vibration between metal brake parts or vibrating brake drums produces a loud, unpleasant noise. Loose and worn parts, hard brake lining, and the absence of lubrication between some metal parts are the source of most vibration-related noise. To minimize noise, technicians should use lubricants between moving parts of brake shoes and brake hardware. Anchor pins and cam rollers are two places where the absence of lubricant is most likely to emit noise. Lubricants dampen high-frequency vibration between the parts by absorbing vibration and resist transmitting mechanical vibration between parts. Never-Seez, a graphite-based lubricant, salt-resistant grease, or high-temperature silicone grease is recommended at points of friction and movement in the brake to prevent noise. Strong low-frequency vibration in the driving axle brakes and affecting the entire vehicle may occur at low speeds just before the vehicle stops. This type of vibration is caused by masses outside the foundation brakes being brought onto the same vibration frequency.

Heat Fade

Heat fade is the loss or reduction in the coefficient of friction as the brake temperature increases. The lining may become "slipperier," and heating of the brake drum causes its expansion and increases its internal diameter. To get an idea of the conditions producing heat related fade, consider this: a single full-stop brake application from 60 mph will raise drum temperatures to approximately 600°F (316°C)—the general limit for safe brake operation. If an axle is heavily loaded or braking is not properly distributed to all the wheels, some drums reach 800–1,000°F (427–538°C) . When heated, the internal diameter of the drum increases approximately 0.01" per 100°F rise above 50°F. This means at 600°F (316°C) the brake drums will be 0.055" larger than at 50°F (10°C). Depending on the length of the slack adjuster, brake chamber pushrod stroke will increase about 0.40", or close to half an inch.

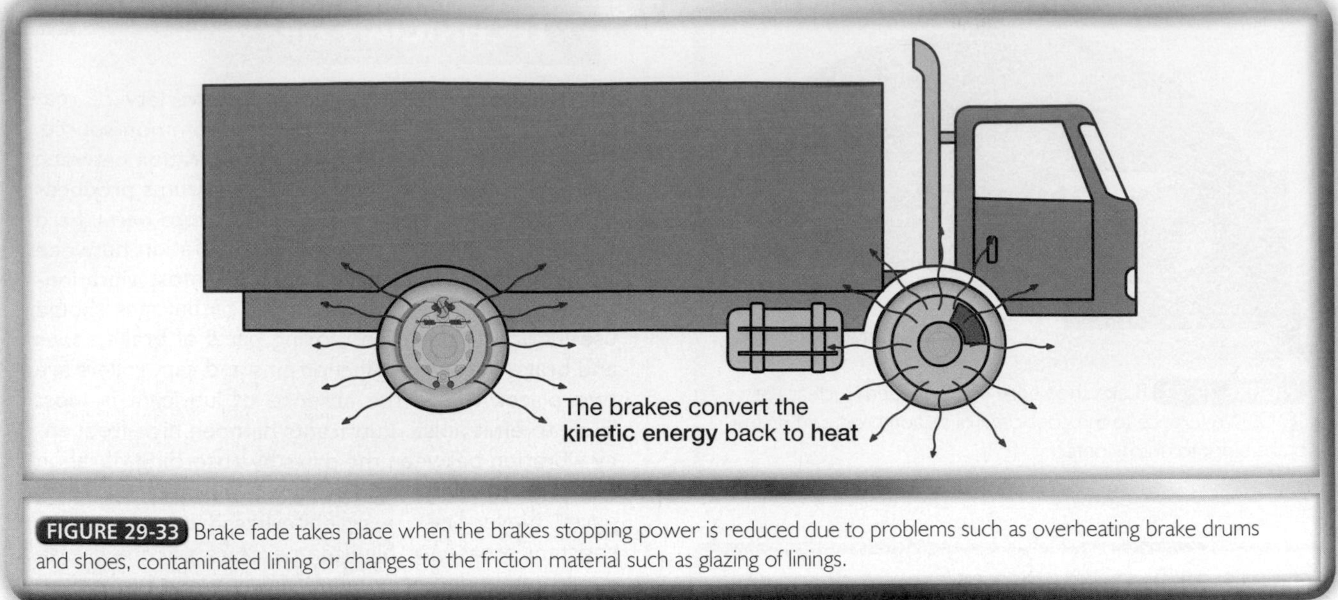
The brakes convert the
kinetic energy back to heat

FIGURE 29-33 Brake fade takes place when the brakes stopping power is reduced due to problems such as overheating brake drums and shoes, contaminated lining or changes to the friction material such as glazing of linings.

Gradual and predictable fade is engineered into lining and is a desirable characteristic. Controlled fade prevents the lining from overheating and destroying itself by maintaining its CoF. When the operator senses fade, it is a warning that the brakes have overheated and should be cooled to allow them to recover. Operating overheated brakes will result in damaged linings and drums and decreased overall performance. Disc brakes are not immune to fade, but they are less affected by heat and water than drums.

Heat fade can also take place in hydraulic brake systems due to the boiling temperature of brake fluid. Because brake fluid is hygroscopic—that is, it attracts water—moisture contained in brake fluid can turn to steam when heat transfers from the caliper piston into the fluid. Bubbles in the master cylinder can indicate the brake fluid is boiling out moisture. Alternatively, fluid that absorbs considerable heat can, in turn, boil. Specifications for brake fluids, such as DOT 3 or DOT 4 and DOT 5, differ primarily in boiling point. The highest DOT specification, DOT 5, uses silicone-based fluid and has the highest boiling point. Silicone-based fluids are hydrophobic, which means they do not attract water and will not damage paint. The latest specification, DOT 5.1, is polyethylene glycol, which is hygroscopic. **TABLE 29-3** shows boiling point specifications for different brake fluids.

Anti-fade is an opposite condition of heat fade, where the coefficient of friction increases as the brakes get hotter. If the increase in friction is too large, braking effectiveness becomes unpredictable, which can potentially cause vehicle instability problems, especially if the lining is installed on steering axles. **FIGURE 29-34** shows how disc brakes are more resistant to heat fade than drum brakes. In the illustration, stopping distances become longer with each successive brake application. Heat deteriorates drum brake performance at a greater rate than disc brakes.

TABLE 29-3: Dry and Wet Boiling Points of Brake Fluid

Dry Boiling Point	Wet Boiling Point (Contains 3.7% Moisture)	
DOT 3	401°F (205°C)	284°F (140°C)
DOT 4	446°F (230°C)	155°C (٣١١ °F)
DOT 5	500°F (260°C)	356°F (180°C)
DOT 5.1	500°F (260°C)	356°F (180°C)

Disc brakes are resistant to brake fade for a number of reasons. Better cooling through ventilation of the disc or rotor dissipates heat faster. Fins or nubs connecting one side of the disc to the other, as shown in **FIGURE 29-35**, increase surface area, which releases more heat faster.

Water Fade

Brake fade is not always due to overheating. **Water fade** occurs when water gets between the friction surfaces and the drum and acts act as a lubricant, reducing braking efficiency. Water can also be absorbed by the lining and and braking efficiency will not return to normal until the water has vaporized. Related to water fade is an erratic high friction reaction during the first two or three stops. This takes place because some linings are sensitive to humidity. Brake dust tends to attract moisture, allowing iron oxide (rust) to form on the drum after a vehicle is parked overnight.

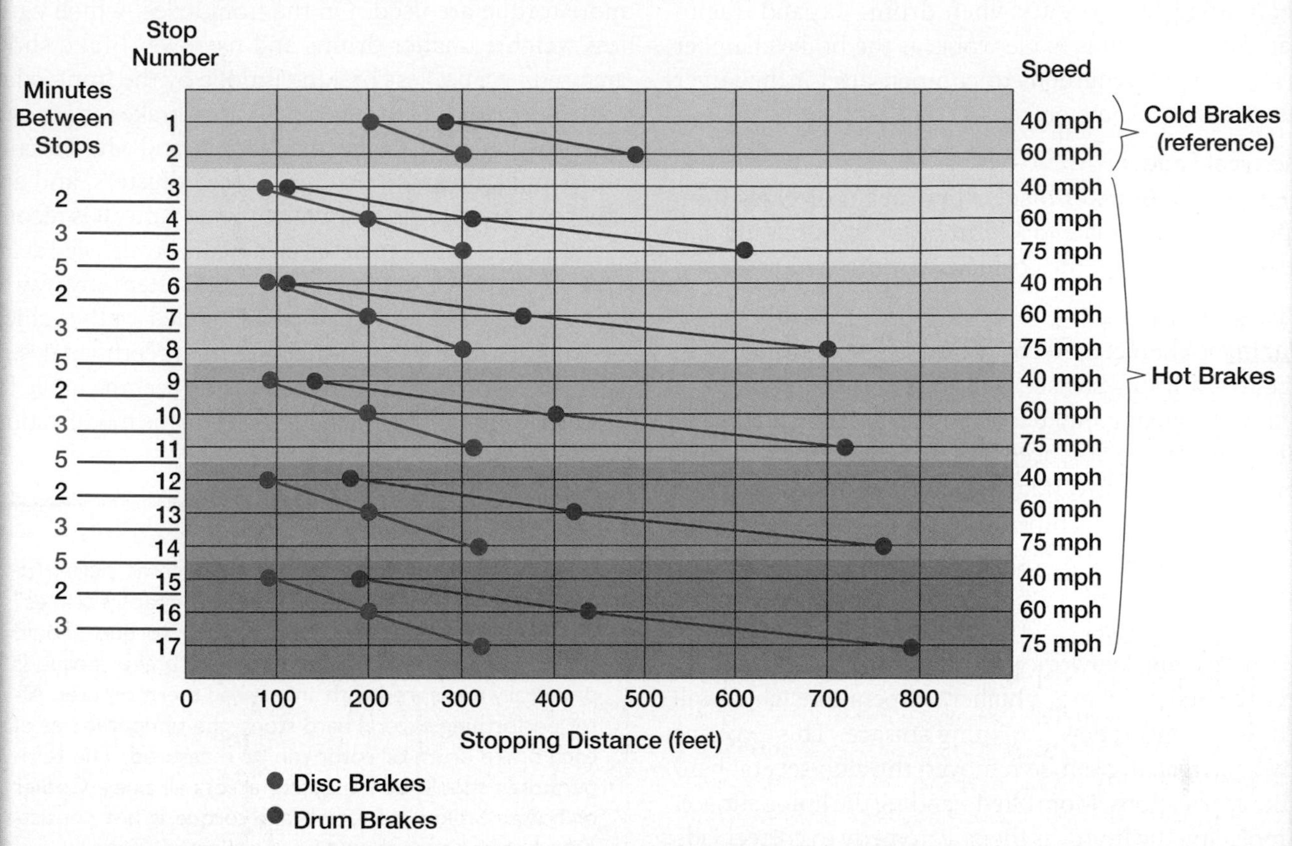

Stop Number
Minutes Between Stops
Speed

Minutes Between Stops	Stop Number	Speed	
	1	40 mph	Cold Brakes (reference)
	2	60 mph	
2	3	40 mph	Hot Brakes
3	4	60 mph	
5	5	75 mph	
2	6	40 mph	
3	7	60 mph	
5	8	75 mph	
2	9	40 mph	
3	10	60 mph	
5	11	75 mph	
2	12	40 mph	
3	13	60 mph	
5	14	75 mph	
2	15	40 mph	
3	16	60 mph	
	17	75 mph	

0 100 200 300 400 500 600 700 800

Stopping Distance (feet)

● Disc Brakes
● Drum Brakes

FIGURE 29-34 Disc brakes are more resistant to heat fade than drum brakes. In the illustration, stopping distances become longer with each successive brake application. Heat deteriorates drum brake performance at a greater rate than disc brakes.

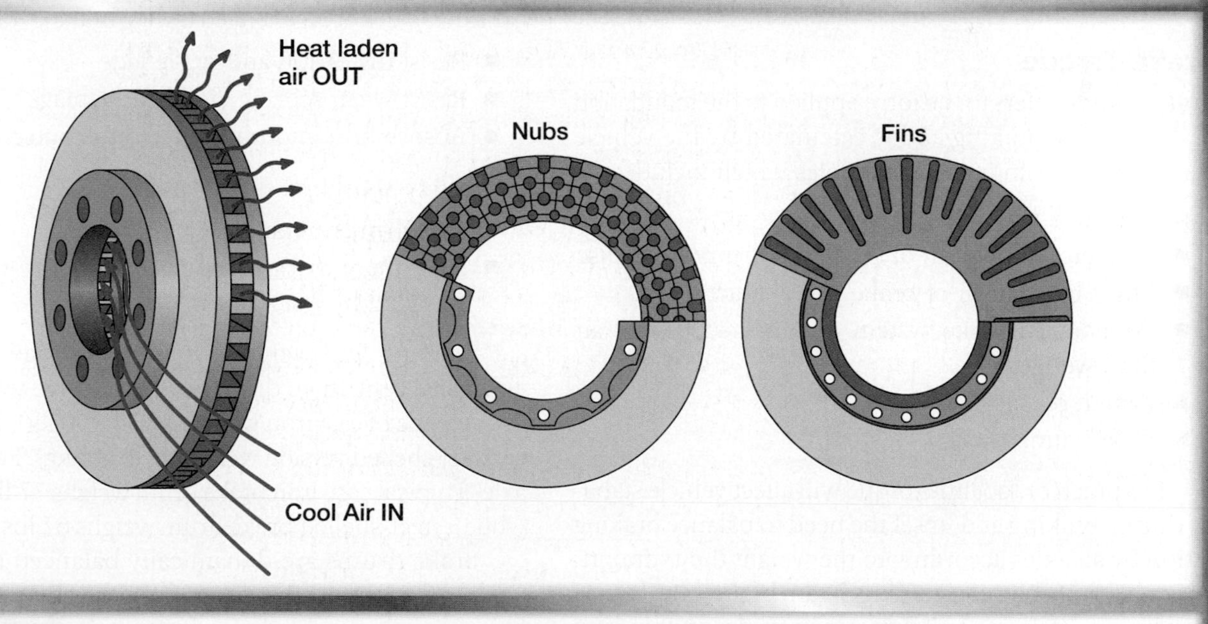

FIGURE 29-35 Disc brakes are resistant to brake fade for a number of reasons. Better cooling through ventilation of the disc or rotor dissipates heat faster. Fins or nubs connecting one side of the disc to the other increases surface area, which also speeds up heat dissipation.

Mechanical Fade

Mechanical fade occurs when drums expand due to heat. The problem is made worse as the brake chamber pushrod travel lengthens to compensate for the larger internal drum diameter.

Chemical Fade

Chemical fade takes place when steam or gases from vaporized lining materials form between hot lining and the drum, reducing the coefficient of friction.

Glazing of Brake Lining

Glazing is characterized by a hard, glassy burnt appearance to the lining surface. This hard, glassy surface is a condition causing brake fade and a "hard" brake pedal. Glazed linings are produced by slow brake applications or a brake that is lightly dragging along a drum. When this happens, the lining temperature becomes hot enough to melt resins binding the friction material, but the pressure is not adequate to wear away friction material and expose new lining surfaces.

Increasing the work per square inch of lining will force the brake to run at a higher temperature, which will wear away and renew the lining surface. This explains why some glazing can be removed through several hard brake applications. More often, sanding the lining surface, or replacing the lining, is the only remedy to correct fade or "hard pedal" conditions. The undelaying cause of high brake temperatures combined with low application force will also need correction. Defective quick release or relay valves are a common cause for glazed lining. Linings with a high CoF will glaze easier than low CoF linings because less force is required to produce the same braking effect.

Brake Torque

Brake torque refers to the force applied to the foundation brakes during braking and is calculated by the vehicle manufacturer using several variables which include:

- Designed axle weight
- Diameter and width of the brake drum/shoes/disc
- Brake lining CoF, or brake pad characteristics
- Foundation brake system design, i.e., S-cam, air disc, wedge
- Length of slack adjuster
- S-cam dimensions

Too much or too little torque will affect vehicle stability during braking and upset the need to balance braking action by all axles according to the weight they support. For example, when considering S-cam brakes, the torque is calculated relative to drum capacity, drum area, and lining area; in the case of air disc brakes, torque is relative to rotor and brake pad characteristics. More torque is needed for axles carrying heavier loads such as the rear drive axles. This means larger capacity brakes using more torque are used. On the front axles, which carry less weight, smaller drums and narrower brake shoes are used because less braking is done by the front axles.

Understanding the need to balance brake torque over all axles should help technicians understand why it is critical to replace friction material, slack adjusters, and any other part affecting torque with original parts. It is recommended that friction material on all axles be replaced at the same time. In fact, modifying the brake system any way by using incorrect parts, or parts not intended for the vehicle or application, changes the manufacturer's certified design factors. A repair facility can potentially become liable for any unfortunate consequences related to the modification.

> **TECHNICIAN TIP**
>
> When diagnosing brake complaints such as pulling to one side, hard pedal, poor braking, "grabby-brakes" and so on, even application of brake torque should be included in the checks. In the field, brake torque is practically measured with an infrared thermometer. After performing several hard stops, the temperatures of each brake drum or rotor can be measured. The temperatures should be consistent across all axles. Cooler or hotter brakes indicate brake torque is not consistent, and the cause should be investigated.

Brake Drums

Next to brake shoes, brake drums are the other critical friction-producing component in the braking system. As considerable heat is generated during braking, drums must

- Resist distortion and brake fade
- Resist wear, scoring, and heat damage
- Absorb heat and transfer it to the outer surface

Two types of brake drums are:

- **cast drums** made from cast iron
- **centrifuge drums** made with a cast iron core surrounded by a steel band

Strength and weight are the advantage of a more expensive centrifuge drum. A typical drive wheel brake drum made of cast iron weighs 110 lb (50 kg), and a typical steel-shelled version weighs 94 lb (43 kg). For the steer axle, a typical cast-iron brake drum weighs 77 lbs (35 kg), while a steel-shelled brake drum weighs 67 lbs (30.5 kg).

Brake drums are dynamically balanced at the factory. At the factory, the drum will either be machined to balance or use welded weights to balance. Both methods will provide identical performance characteristics. **FIGURE 29-36** shows the terminology used for brake drums. **FIGURE 29-37** shows the two types of brake drums—

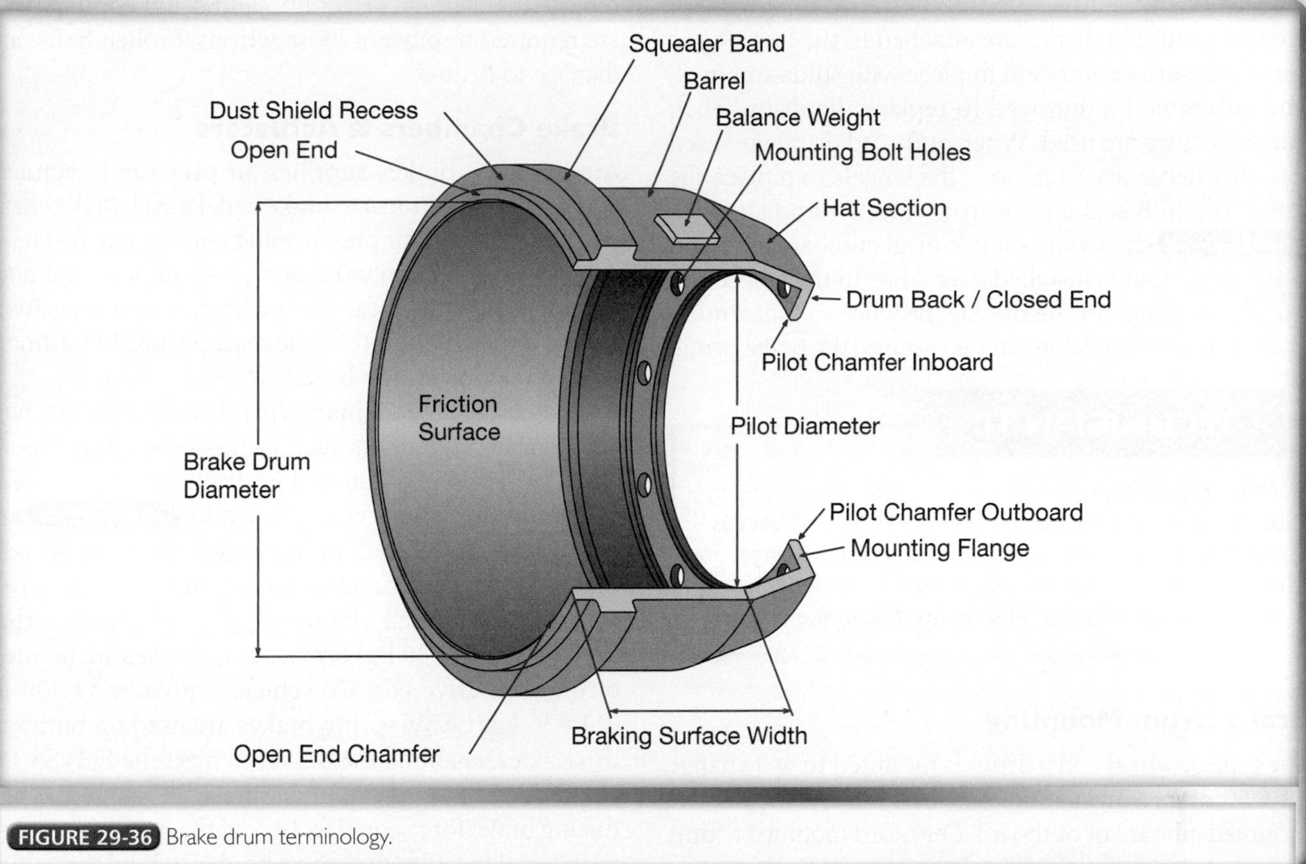

FIGURE 29-36 Brake drum terminology.

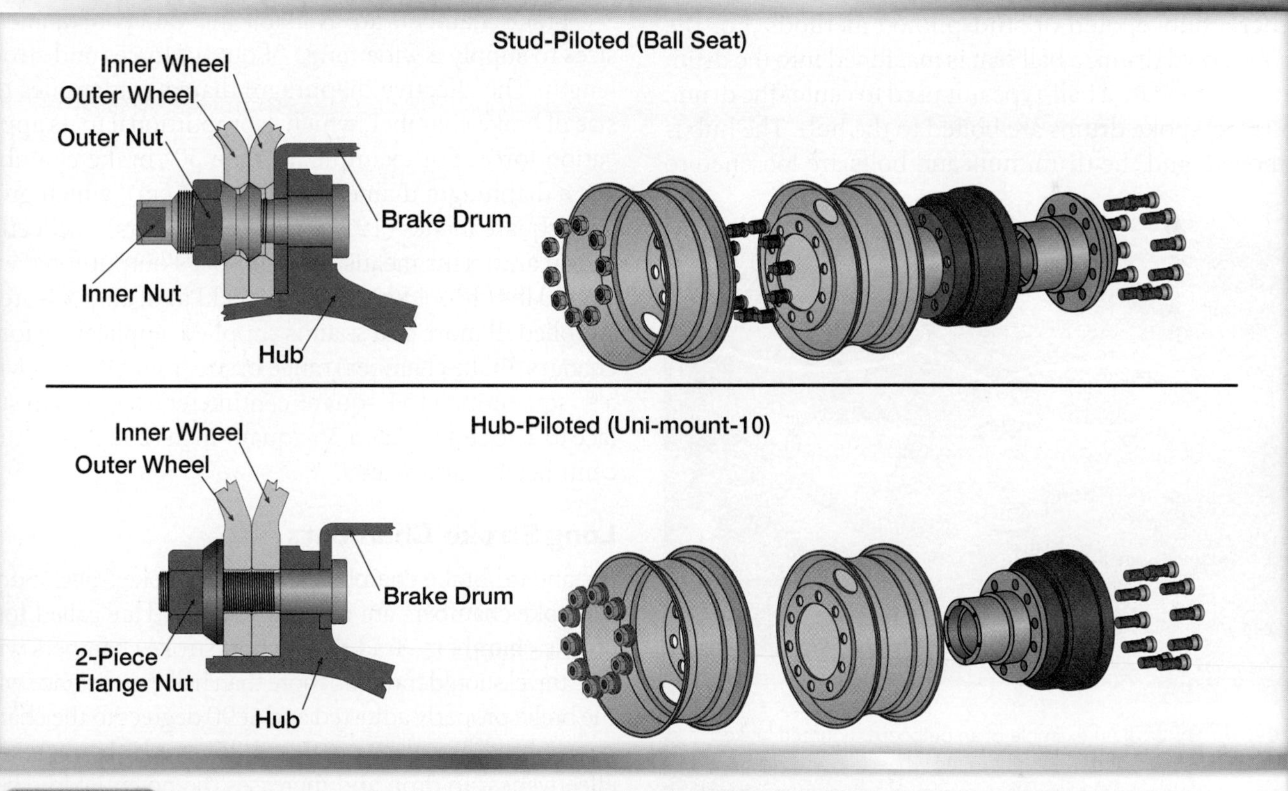

FIGURE 29-37 Brake drums can be mounted inboard or outboard on disc type wheels.. The hub must be removed to replace the drum when inboard drums are used. Outboard drums can be replaced by simply removing the wheels, the hub bearings and seal are not disturbed during brake service.

inboard or outboard—mounted on disc type wheels. Inboard mounted drums are attached to the hub on the inner hub surface and held in place with studs and nuts. The hub must be removed to replace the drum when inboard drums are used. When outboard drums are used it is only necessary to remove the wheels to replace the drum; the hub seal and bearings are left undisturbed. FIGURE 29-38 shows an example of an outboard mounted brake drum that is installed over studs in the wheel hub and clamped against the hub by the wheels. A maximum brake drum internal diameter is cast into the brake drum.

> **TECHNICIAN TIP**
>
> When brake drum types, weights, and brands are interchanged, braking can be adversely affected because the heat dissipation properties of the drum change. To maintain optimal brake performance, always change drums in pairs on axles, and do not mix brake drums.

Brake Drum Mounting

The type of wheel end a drum is mounted to will change the features of a drum. On disc wheel hubs, drums can be mounted inboard or outboard. Outboard mounted drums are simpler to remove and replace since the hub does not require removal. Drums are attached to the wheel using either a hub-piloted or stud-piloted methods. For the stud-piloted drum, a ball seat is machined into the drum to accommodate a ball-type nut used to center the drum.

Cast-spoke drums are bolted to the hub. The hub is removed, and the drum nuts and bolts are loosened to replace the drum. Correct hub and drum combinations are required to prevent loose wheels, broken bolts, and damage to drums.

FIGURE 29-38 An example of an outboard mounted brake drum that is installed over studs in the wheel hub and clamped against the hub by the wheels. A maximum brake drum internal diameter is cast into the brake drum.

Brake Chambers & Actuators

Applying the brakes supplies air pressure to actuator chambers proportional to brake pedal travel. Brake chambers then take the air pressure and convert it to mechanical force used to apply the brakes. A rubber diaphragm inside the chamber seals the pressure and acts against a push-plate, which in turn moves a pushrod that finally acts on the foundation brakes.

Actuators are like brake chambers except they have additional components such as **power springs** used to apply park brakes or internal pushrod lock mechanisms. **Spring brake** actuators, as shown in FIGURE 29-39 and FIGURE 29-40, are used on rear drive axles to apply park brakes, which are also referred to as "maxi-brakes." These actuators have dual chambers. On vehicles less than 52,000 lbs (23,636 kg) GVW, spring brakes are required on only one drive axle. On vehicles with over 52,000-lbs (23,636 kg) GVW, spring brakes are used on both rear drive axles, enabling the brakes to meet the FMVSS 121 standard. Each parking brake must be capable of producing brake force equal to 14% of the gross axle weight rating, and together they must be able to hold the vehicle stationary on a 20% grade, loaded or empty.

Brake chambers are available in a variety of diameter sizes to supply a wide range of output forces and stroke length. The effective diaphragm diameter identifies the size of brake chamber, which is proportional to its application force. For example, a "type 30" brake chamber has a diaphragm diameter of 8" (20.3 cm), which gives it 30 square inches (193 square centimeters) of effective piston area. This means the chamber's output force will be 300 lbs (136.4 kg) if 10 psi (69 kPa) of air pressure is supplied. If more or less air is supplied, application force changes. Brake chambers range in size from a 9 series with a 9 -square-inch (54-square-centimeter) diaphragm surface to a 36 series with a 36-square-inch (232.25-square-centimeter) surface area.

Long Stroke Chambers

A standard brake chamber has a 2.5" stroke travel. Some 3" stroke chambers are manufactured and are called **long stroke chambers**. Traditional short stroke chambers with 2.5" travel should travel no more than half that distance with the brake properly adjusted and at 90 degrees to the chamber pushrod. Travel greater than 1.25" causes the chamber's effectiveness to drop and increases the potential for "bottoming out," meaning that the limit of maximum pushrod travel would prevent full application of brake torque.

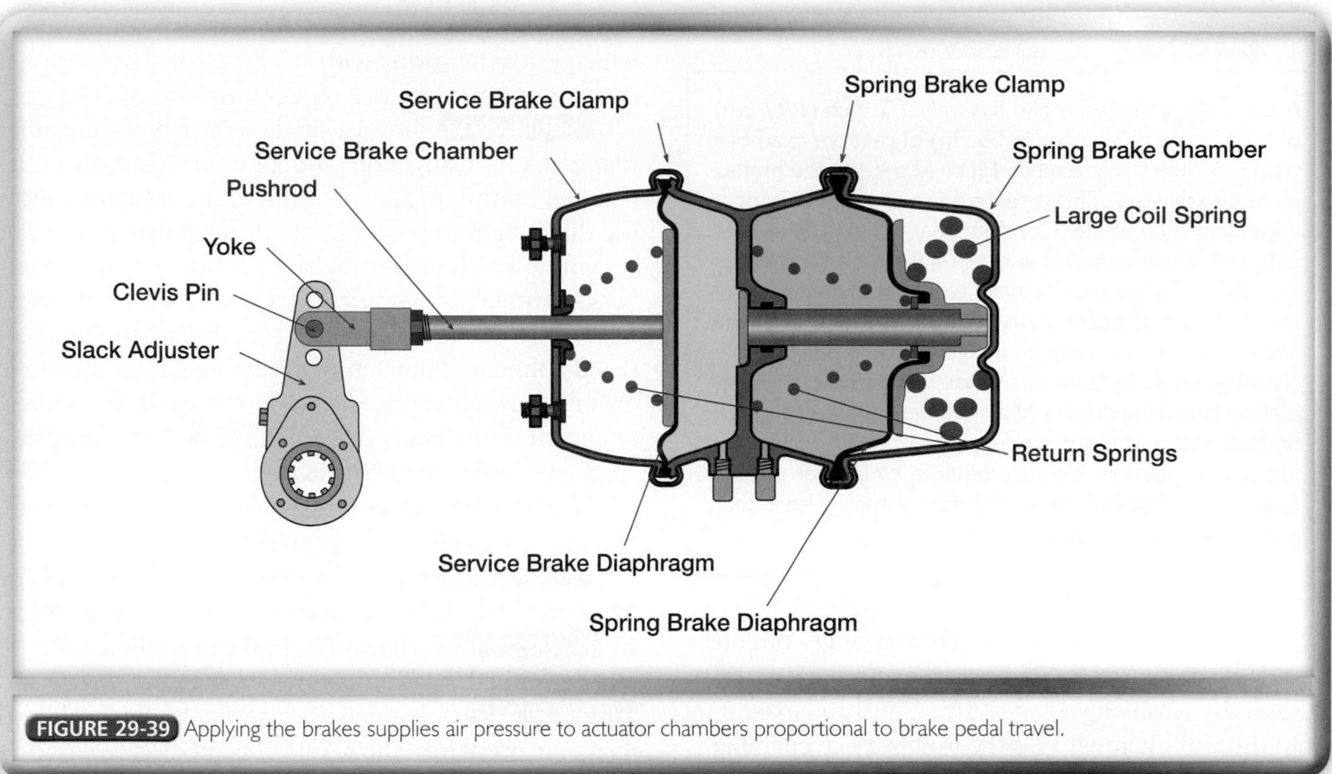

FIGURE 29-39 Applying the brakes supplies air pressure to actuator chambers proportional to brake pedal travel.

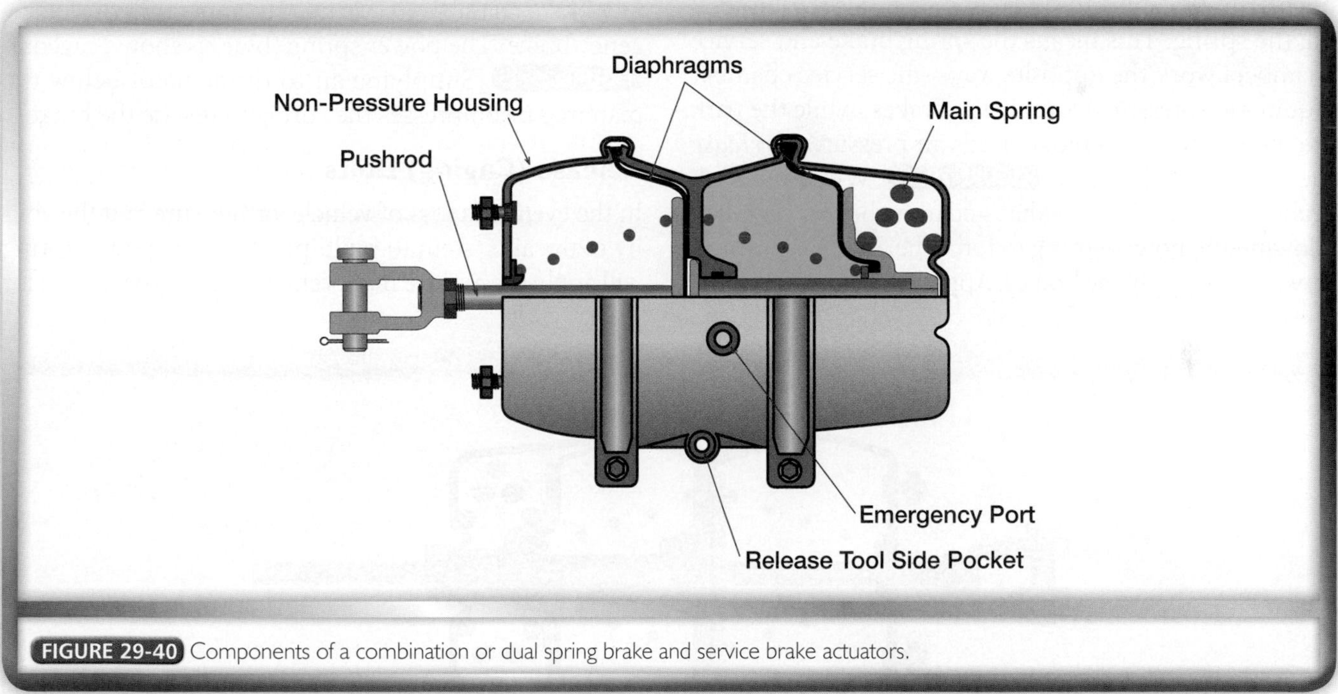

FIGURE 29-40 Components of a combination or dual spring brake and service brake actuators.

Long stroke chambers are built to help minimize the hazard of an inadequate brake stroke for a misadjusted slack adjuster or worn brakes thatwould require a longer stroke. Operational differences between these chambers do not allow for mixed use on a vehicle. Long stroke chambers have special identifying features such as square-shaped air inlet ports and yokes that are welded to the pushrod.

Dual Brake Chambers

When a brake chamber uses only a single chamber, it is called a service chamber. Dual brake chambers contain a spring brake actuator and have two separate air and mechanical actuators in a single housing. In addition to their normal parking functions, spring brakes can functions as a service brake under emergency conditions.

Safety

A correctly adjusted brake has only 1/2 inch (1.27 cm) of slack, leaving 2 inches (5.08 cm) of reserve chamber stroke. When slack reaches 1 inch (2.54 cm) the brakes must be adjusted. This is referred to as a driver's most important inch of life. Consider that during brake heat fade the drum expands and can add close to another 1/2 inch of clearance. Lining worn, the thickness of three sheets of paper adds another 1/4 inch of clearance, and it is not hard to imagine how easily a brake chamber could bottom out. Most jurisdictions have legislation requiring drivers of air-braked vehicles to check manual and automatic slack adjusters daily during the pre-trip inspection. It's also required by law for drivers to check brakes before driving down steep grades that are posted with regulatory signs.

The rear section of the dual brake chamber contains a powerful spring that is compressed using air pressure or released by removing air pressure. A pushrod extending from the rear chamber into the front service chamber is designed to push against the forward service chamber push plate and apply the brakes when no air is compressing the spring. This means the spring brake and service chambers work the opposite way—the service chamber requires air pressure to ***apply*** the brakes, while the park or emergency spring brake needs air pressure to ***release*** the brakes, as shown in **FIGURE 29-41**. When the park brakes are applied, air is exhausted from the rear chamber, allowing the power spring to force the actuator pushrod forward and apply the brakes. Approximately 75 psi (517 kPa) of air pressure is needed to release the spring brake, which loads the spring with at least 2,250 lbs (1,023 kg) of compression force in a type 30 chamber.

FIGURE 29-42 shows a single service brake chamber that contains a single diaphragm used to seal air in the actuator. Supplying air pressure to the actuator causes the diaphragm to push against the chamber piston rod assembly, which moves the slack adjuster. Brake chambers are available in a variety of diameter sizes to supply a wide range of output forces and stroke length. The effective diaphragm diameter identifies the size of the brake chamber, which is proportional to its application force, as shown in the chart in **FIGURE 29-43**. For example, a "type 30" brake chamber has a diaphragm diameter of 8" (20 cm), which gives it 30 square inches (193 square centimeters) of effective piston area.

FIGURE 29-44 shows the sequential operation of the emergency spring brake chamber and service chamber. In **FIGURE 29-44A**, the spring brake is applied since no air is supplied to the chamber. In **FIGURE 29-44B** and **FIGURE 29-44C**, the emergency spring brake is released using air pressure. The service chamber is released in B and applied in C. The power spring is located in the rear brake chamber and is used to apply the park/emergency brake. The power spring (blue) is shown caged in **FIGURE 29-45**. Supplying air to the actuator below the diaphragm compresses the spring to release the brake.

Release (Caging) Bolts

In the event of a loss of vehicle air pressure and the ability of the air system to build pressure, the power spring will apply the brakes. If the vehicle needs to be moved for

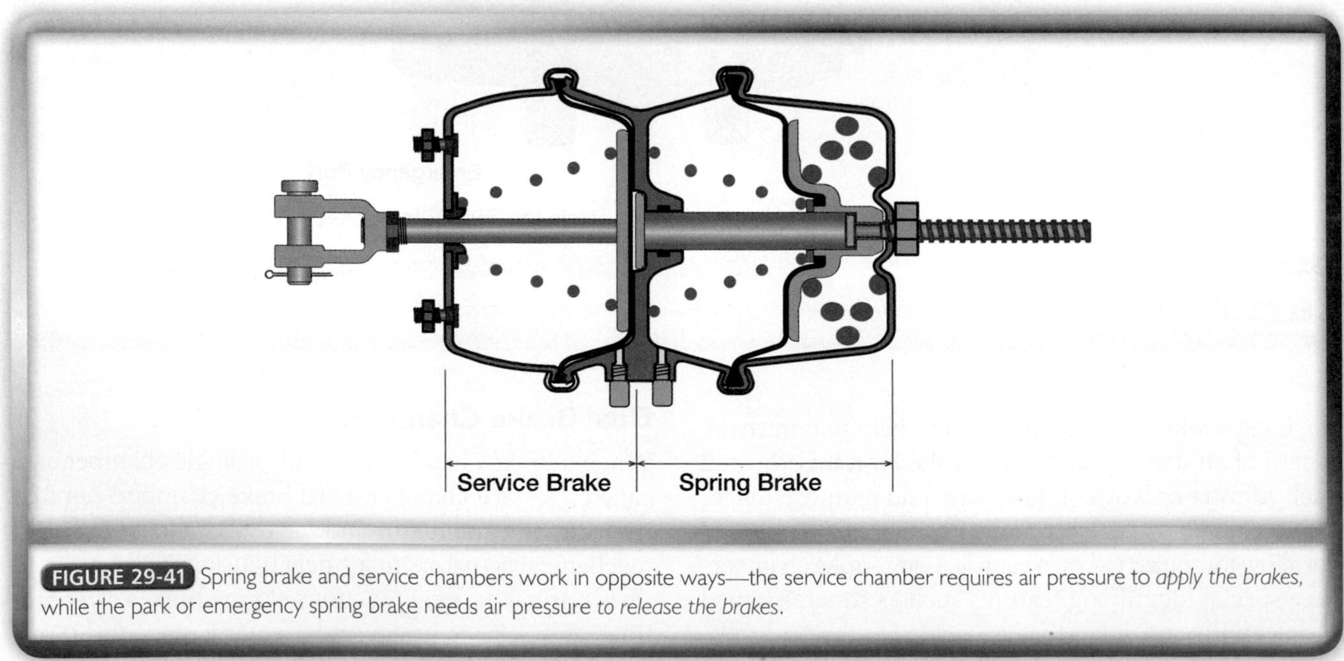

FIGURE 29-41 Spring brake and service chambers work in opposite ways—the service chamber requires air pressure to *apply the brakes*, while the park or emergency spring brake needs air pressure *to release the brakes*.

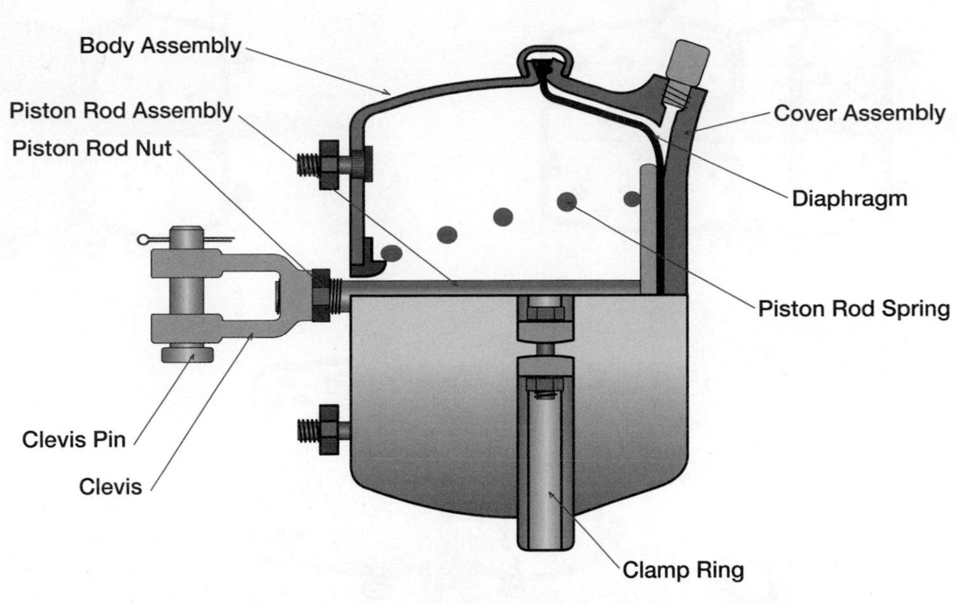

FIGURE 29-42 A single service brake chamber contains a single diaphragm used to seal air in the actuator. Supplying air pressure to the actuator causes the diaphragm to push against the chamber piston rod assembly which moves the slack adjuster.

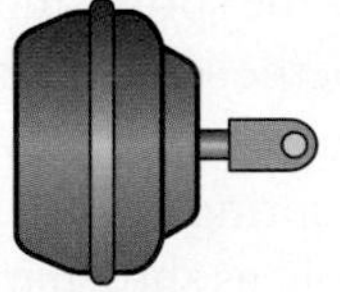

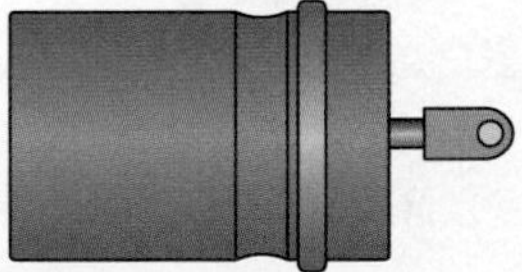

Braking Forces

Effect of Brake Chamber and Roto Chamber Sizes

Clamp Ring Type Brake Chamber		9	12	16	20	24	30	36	
Roto Chamber		9	12	16	20	24	30	36	50
Effective Area of Diaphragm (sq inches)	6	9	12	16	20	24	30	36	50
Pounds Force Developed with 60 P.S.I.	360	540	720	960	1200	1440	1800	2160	3000

FIGURE 29-43 Brake chambers are available in a variety of diameter sizes to supply a wide range of output forces and stroke length. The effective diaphragm diameter identifies the size of the brake chamber, which is proportional to its application force. For example, a "type 30" brake chamber has a diaphragm diameter of 8", which gives it 30 square inches of effective piston area.

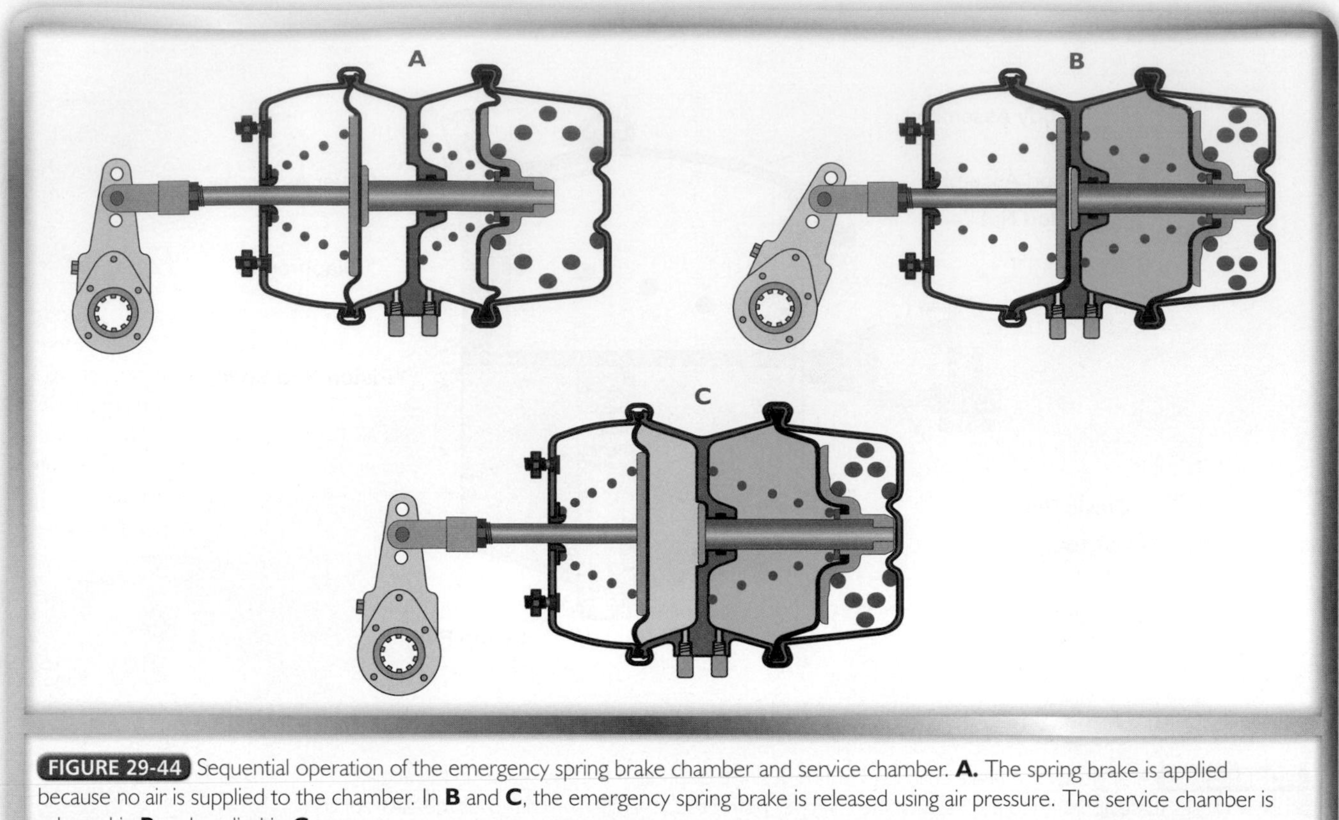

FIGURE 29-44 Sequential operation of the emergency spring brake chamber and service chamber. **A.** The spring brake is applied because no air is supplied to the chamber. In **B** and **C**, the emergency spring brake is released using air pressure. The service chamber is released in **B** and applied in **C**.

FIGURE 29-45 The power spring is located in the rear brake chamber and is used to apply the park/emergency brake. Supplying air to the actuator below the diaphragm compresses the spring to release the brake. **A.** Cage bolt. **B.** Caged power spring. **C.** Single-piece spring brake chamber clamp. **D.** Chamber separation seal. **E.** Service chamber clamp.

towing, the power spring can be released by inserting a **release bolt** into the spring and tightening the bolt. Tightening the bolt compresses the spring and releases the park brake. If the diaphragm for the service chamber is replaced, the release bolt can be used to compress the power spring to safely remove the rear spring brake chamber.

A release or caging bolt, as shown in FIGURE 29-46, is generally attached to every dual chamber brake actuator. A power spring in the rear chamber requires compressing to move a disabled vehicle without an air supply. Inserting and turning the release bolt into a keyed receptacle in the power spring and then tightening the bolt compresses the power spring. FIGURE 29-47 shows a power spring from the emergency/park brake actuator. The power spring is more commonly called a "maxi spring," forming part of the "maxi-brake."

Roto-chambers

Roto-chambers, shown in FIGURE 29-48, are actuators with a unique diaphragm construction that delivers consistent output force regardless of the pushrod position. To achieve this, the chamber has a much larger diaphragm that "unrolls" during operation. It is clamped on both the outer chamber body and the inner push plate. The rolling-type diaphragm used in roto-chambers also provides a longer service life in comparison to traditional

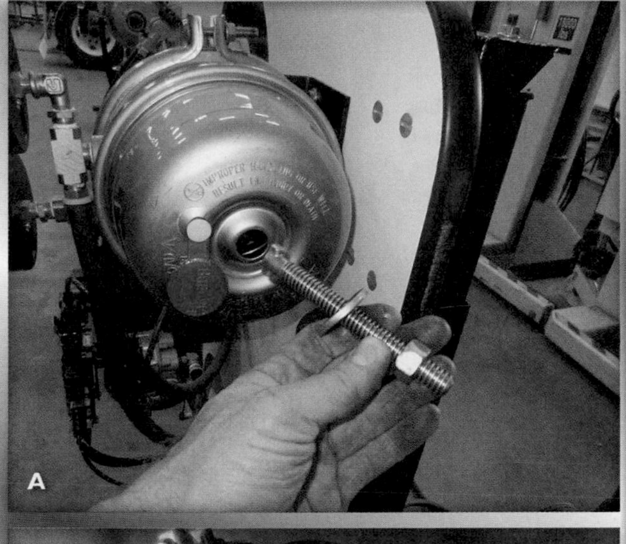

FIGURE 29-46 **A.** A release or caging bolt is generally attached to every dual chamber brake actuator. **B.** Inserting and turning the release bolt into a keyed receptacle in the power spring and then tightening the bolt compresses the power spring.

FIGURE 29-47 A power spring from the emergency/park brake actuator. The power spring is more commonly called a "maxi spring," forming part of the "maxi-brake."

Safety

Brake chambers can be disassembled by removing a clamp holding two dish-shaped halves of the chamber. Worn, leaking diaphragms are easily changed by disassembling the chamber. Because the power spring in the rear chamber is under high compression force, disassembling that chamber and suddenly releasing the spring has been proven many times to be lethal or result in serious physical injuries. To protect people and equipment from damage caused by a flying power spring, the clamp and chamber have safety features to minimize the likelihood of releasing the spring. THE CLAMP MUST NEVER BE REMOVED! It is recommended that the release or caging bolt be installed to compress the spring anytime a chamber is removed.

Safety

A spring brake or combination service/spring brake must be disarmed before disposal—and not simply disposed with other garbage. Forceful release of the compression spring may occur without warning after disposal. Specialized cages enable the power spring to be cut with a torch prior to disposal, which removes the likelihood of the potentially lethal spring causing property damage or severely injuring someone.

TECHNICIAN TIP

Broken power springs will often puncture the diaphragm in the spring brake chamber as well as prevent adequate parking brake force. Several techniques are used to inspect chamber power springs. One is to remove the end plug from the release-bolt access hole at the rear of the spring brake chamber. Using a trouble light, examine the spring to determine if it is broken. A broken spring will not allow the release-bolt hole located at the rear of the spring to line up with the access hole. Brake chamber stroke can also be checked while applying and releasing the parking brake. If the anticipated range of motion is not observed, the spring may be broken. If a rattle is heard after tapping the chamber with a hammer or shaking the chamber after it is removed, the spring is probably broken.

brake chambers. Roto-chambers are frequently found on transit buses where very high braking frequency is the norm, and safety is especially critical.

Slack Adjusters

The **slack adjuster** is a mechanical lever between the brake chamber and the foundation brake assembly. The

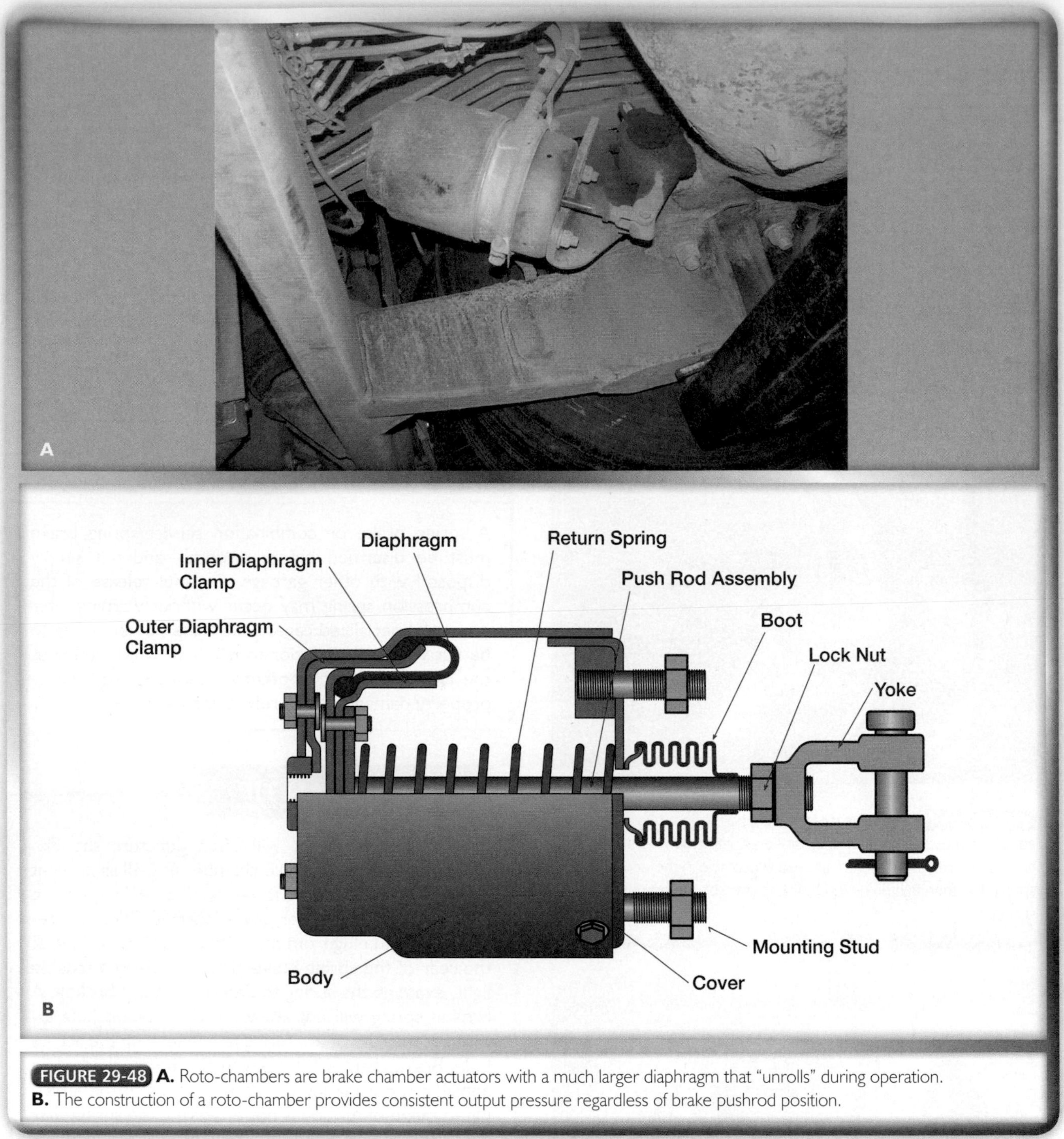

FIGURE 29-48 **A.** Roto-chambers are brake chamber actuators with a much larger diaphragm that "unrolls" during operation. **B.** The construction of a roto-chamber provides consistent output pressure regardless of brake pushrod position.

slack adjuster's primary function is to multiply the force from the brake chamber to the camshaft of the foundation brakes. A second critical function is to remove excessive chamber pushrod travel to maintain minimal clearance between the brake shoe and drum on a cam brake system. As brakes wear, the clearance between drums and shoes increases, which means the distance traveled by the brake chamber pushrod increases. Increased pushrod travel changes the angle between the pushrod and the slack adjuster, which diminishes the torque applied to the foundation brakes. Most brake chambers have a maximum stroke of 2.5" (6.35 cm), so worn brakes that have not had an adjustment could bottom out the chamber pushrod, resulting in a further loss of braking force.

In an air disc system, the slack adjuster also adjusts the clearance between the brake pads and rotor disc. Two basic types of slack adjusters are used—automatic or manual. **Manual slack adjusters**, the first type used, are now obsolete but can occasionally be found on older equipment. The second type is an automatic slack adjuster (ASA). ASAs have been mandatory on air brake vehicles since 1994. Both types remove excess free play due to brake shoe wear.

The stroke indicators attached to the chamber bracket in FIGURE 29-49 are used to visually inspect maximum pushrod travel. When the brakes are applied, the pushrod clevis pin should not travel any farther than the most distant stroke indicator. Note that the most efficient braking action is obtained when the slack adjuster arm is approximately 90 degrees to the brake chamber pushrod.

Manual Slack Adjusters

As the name suggests, slack adjusters correct excess pushrod travel from increased drum to lining clearance produced by brake wear. Most standard slacks are 5" (12.7 cm) in length, while 6" (15.25 cm) are popular on specialty applications. One, two, or three holes with bushings can be located in the arm to match specific length requirements for an application. Various arm configurations and spline types to fit camshafts are made. Bendix uses a number to designate a torque rating. For example, a type 20 represents a 20,000 inch/lbs (2,260 Nm) of torque, and a type 30 represents 30,000 inch pounds (3,390 Nm). A grease fitting is used to lubricate the adjusting mechanism and splines. Manual slacks have an adjusting screw which is locked in place by a sliding collar. To adjust, the collar is pushed inward and the screw is turned with a 9/16" wrench. A worm gear turns the slacks internal spline to reposition the camshaft.

FIGURE 29-49 Slack adjusters are used to maintain correct drum-to-shoe clearance and correct pushrod travel. The stroke indicators attached to the chamber bracket are used to visually inspect maximum pushrod travel. When the brakes are applied, the pushrod clevis pin should not travel any farther than the most distant stroke indicator.

Automatic Slack Adjusters (ASA)

When installed, **automatic slack adjusters (ASAs)** compensate for wear in brake shoe linings caused by normal braking operation. ASAs are used because shoe-to-lining clearance increases, and the brake chamber pushrod return stroke will exceed safe travel limits. To prevent this, the slack adjuster will automatically adjust brake stroke to maintain the correct shoe-to-drum clearance and reset the stroke to the correct length with each brake application. If the air brake chamber pushrod stroke is within limits during operation, no adjustment occurs. Two types of ASAs are used:

1. *Stroke sensing*—**Stroke sensing ASAs** makes adjustments to slack based on the measured rotation between a brake application and release. Stroke sensing slack adjusters were some of the earliest used but have several problems, making them nearly obsolete in new vehicles. Stroke sensing slacks adjust based on the total amount of slack travel. Many factors can change the total slack travel distance. Brake lining compression, deflection of the S-cam bracket, heat expansion of the drum, and distortion of the brake component can all increase travel distance. The increased travel distance can cause the slacks to over-adjust, leading to no running clearance for the brake shoes.
2. *Clearance sensing*—**Clearance sensing ASAs** reduce pushrod travel based on torque input to the ASA. Drum-to-shoe clearance is sensed between the mechanical position of the slack when it first moves and the point when the torque increases as the shoes contact the drums. Manufacturers use a variety of adjusting mechanisms to rotate the slack's spline gear and reduce chamber stroke travel. Correction to pushrod travel happens either during brake application and stops adjusting as resistance to S-cam rotation increases, or as the slack is released. Most manufacturers offer clearance sensing ASAs because they can more accurately maintain a nominal shoe-to-drum clearance, which is approximately one third of total chamber stroke. This happens because slack adjustment is made before braking, when the brake drums are coolest and bending of the brake system components under high torque is minimal. Overadjustment does not easily take place with this adjuster. FIGURE 29-50 shows four of the most popular ASAs.

FIGURE 29-51 shows an internal view of a Bendix clearance sensing slack. When pushrod travel becomes excessive and enough pressure is placed against the slack,

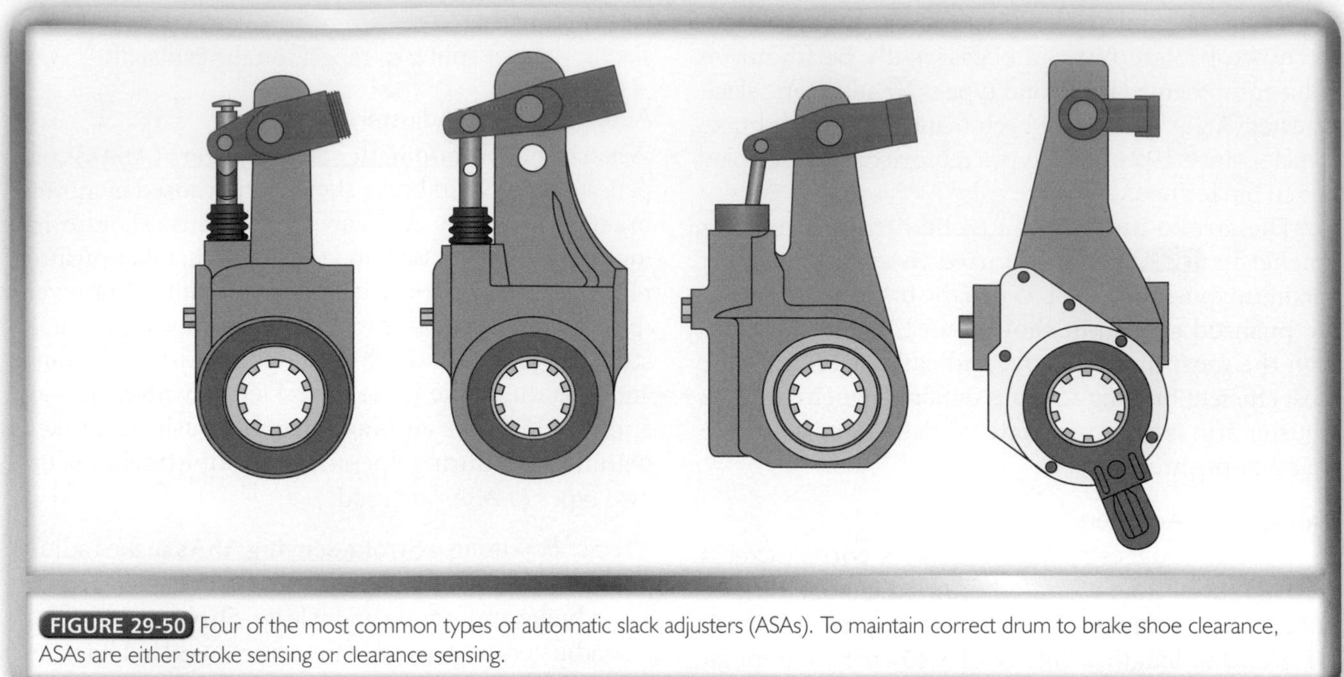

FIGURE 29-50 Four of the most common types of automatic slack adjusters (ASAs). To maintain correct drum to brake shoe clearance, ASAs are either stroke sensing or clearance sensing.

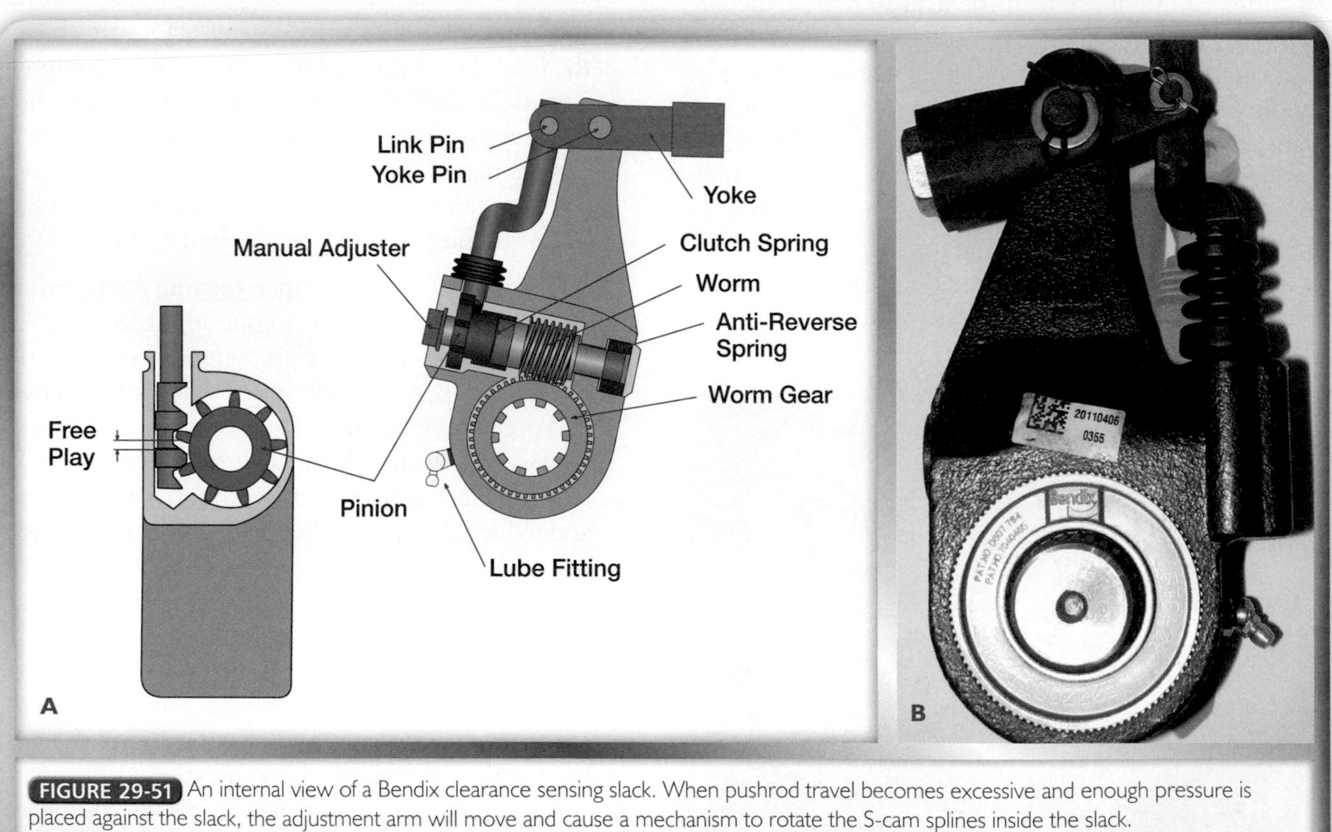

FIGURE 29-51 An internal view of a Bendix clearance sensing slack. When pushrod travel becomes excessive and enough pressure is placed against the slack, the adjustment arm will move and cause a mechanism to rotate the S-cam splines inside the slack.

the adjustment arm will move and cause a mechanism to rotate the S-cam splines inside the slack. FIGURE 29-52 shows an example of a stroke sensing ASA. When pushrod travel becomes excessive, the actuator rod will lift and rotate the slacks adjusting mechanism. While this slack can adjust for wear in brake foundation parts, it can also overadjust when brake drums expand after becoming hot. These conditions will cause the brakes to drag when the drum cools and contracts.

A correctly adjusted brake has only 1/2" (1.27 cm) of slack travel, leaving 2" (5.08 cm) of reserve chamber stroke. When slack travel reaches 1" (2.54 cm), the brakes must be adjusted. FIGURE 29-53 shows the correct way to measure stroke. FIGURE 29-54 shows a manual slack adjuster. To adjust, a locking ring is pushed down, and the adjusting screw is turned to obtain the correct stroke or brake shoe to drum clearance

ASA Maintenance

ASAs may or may not have a grease fitting, as manufacturers move to low- and no-lube sealed slack adjusters. Stroke travel should be regularly inspected by drivers and technicians. Once initially adjusted, ASA slacks should never need readjusting. If manual adjustment is required

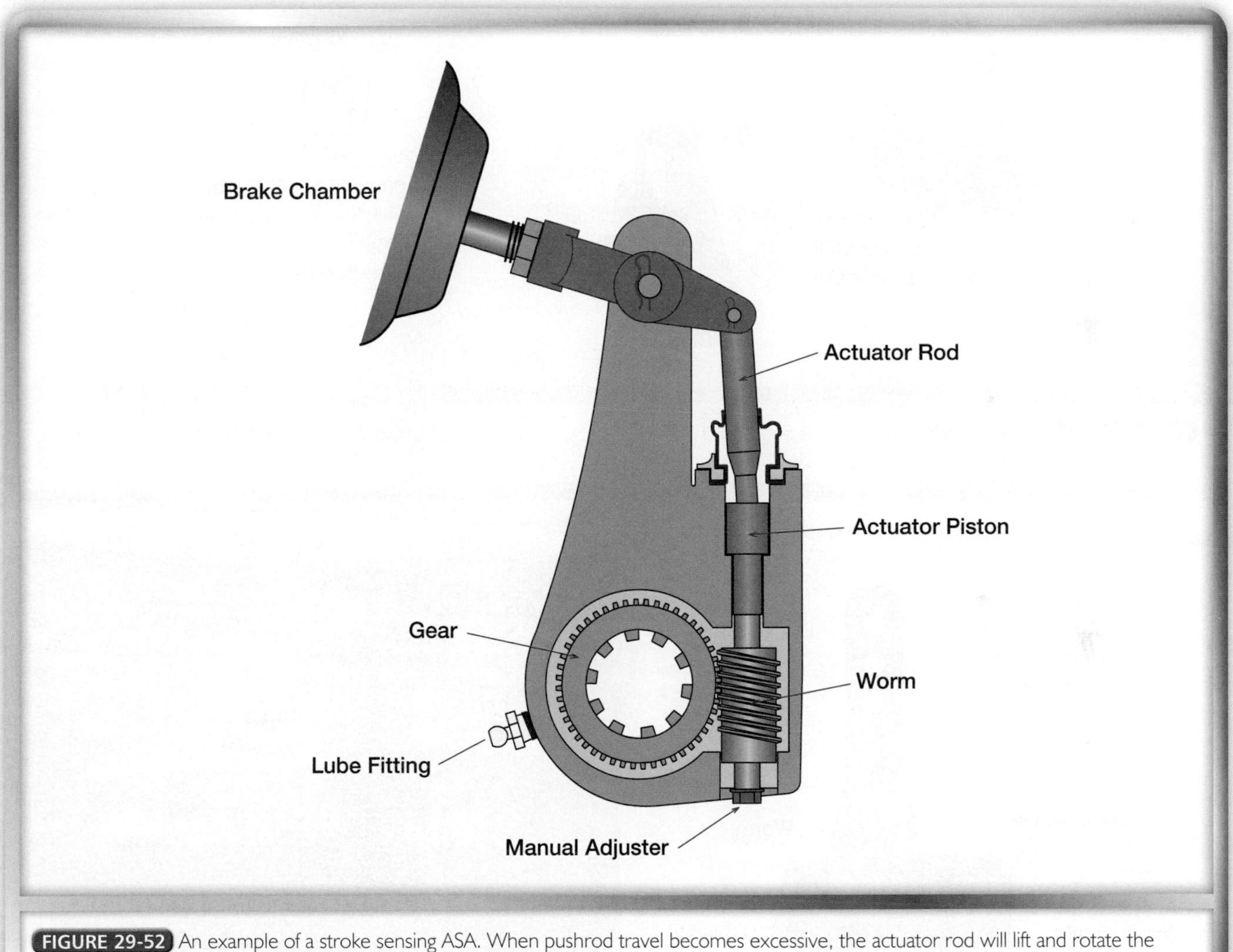

FIGURE 29-52 An example of a stroke sensing ASA. When pushrod travel becomes excessive, the actuator rod will lift and rotate the slacks adjusting mechanism. While this slack can adjust for wear in brake foundation parts, it can also overadjust when brake drums expand after becoming hot. These conditions will cause the brakes to drag when the drum cools and contracts.

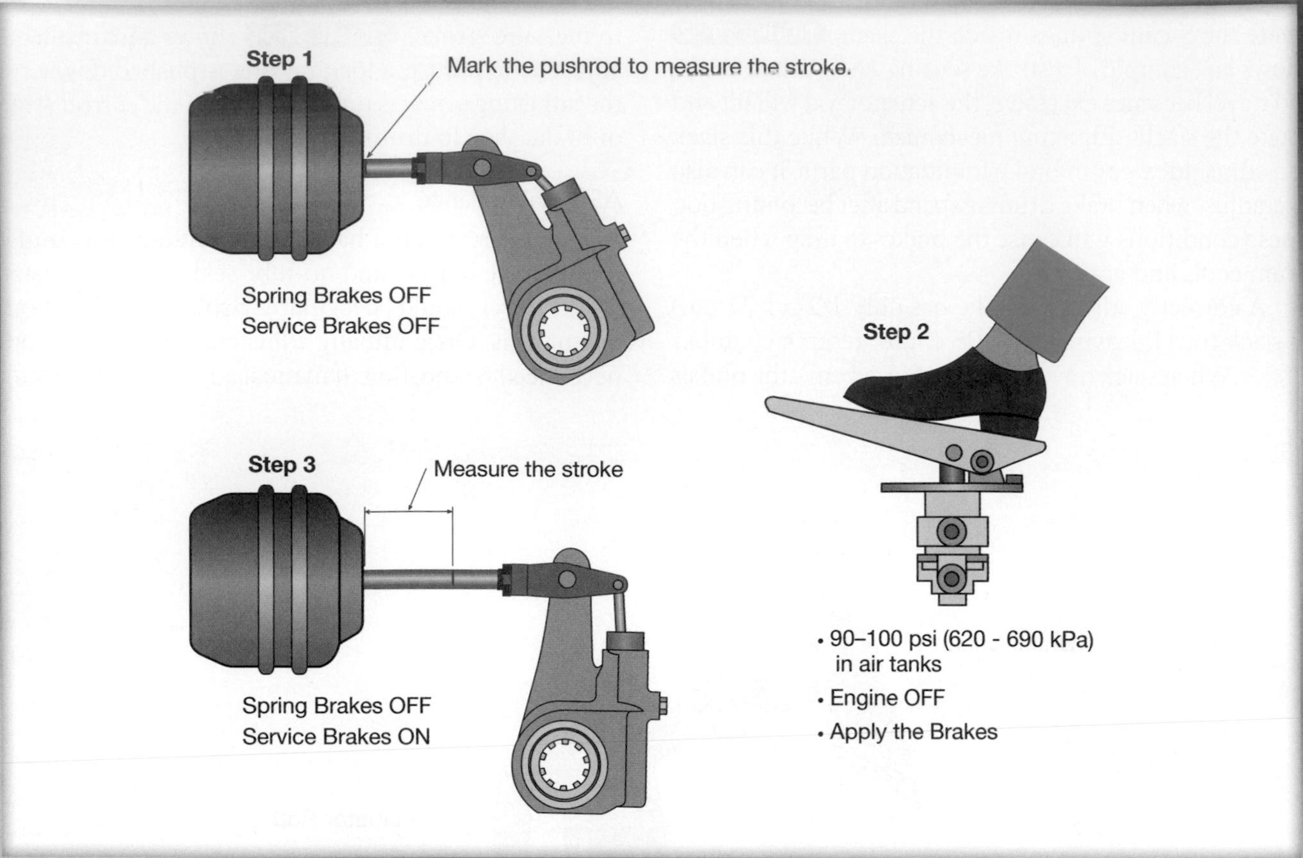

Step 1
Mark the pushrod to measure the stroke.
Spring Brakes OFF
Service Brakes OFF
Step 2
Step 3
Measure the stroke
Spring Brakes OFF
Service Brakes ON
• 90–100 psi (620 - 690 kPa) in air tanks
• Engine OFF
• Apply the Brakes

FIGURE 29-53 A correctly adjusted brake has only 1/2" (1.27 cm) of slack, leaving 2" (5.08 cm) of reserve chamber stroke. When slack reaches 1" (2.54 cm), the brakes must be adjusted.

Lock Sleeve
Worm
Adjusting Screw (Worm Shaft)
Adjusting Gear (Worm Gear)
Spline
Lube Fitting
Cover Rivet
A
A
B
B

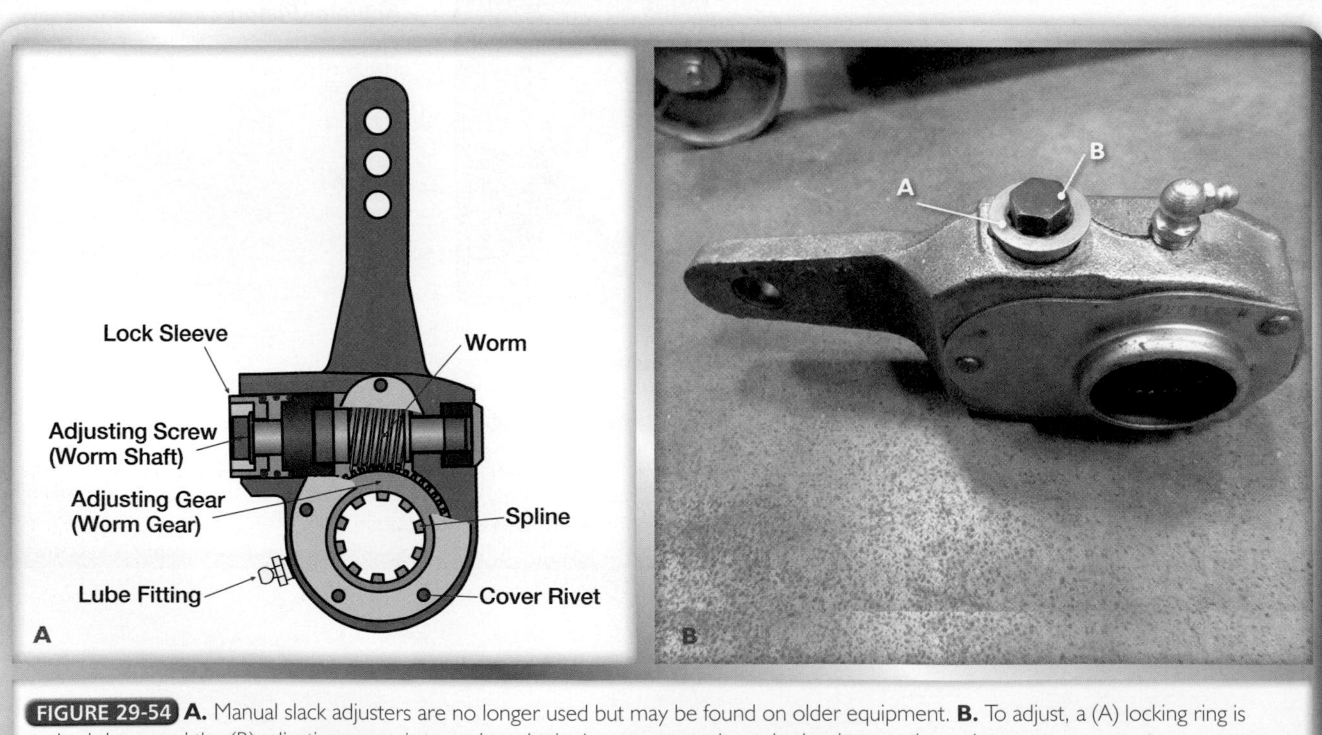

FIGURE 29-54 **A.** Manual slack adjusters are no longer used but may be found on older equipment. **B.** To adjust, a (A) locking ring is pushed down and the (B) adjusting screw is turned to obtain the correct stroke or brake shoe-to-drum clearance.

during the service life of the slack, or if stroke travel differs between two slacks on the same axle, both slacks should be replaced.

Air Disc Brakes (ADB)

Disc brakes have been commonly used on hydraulic brake systems for decades and until recently been used only on a few air-braked vehicles. However, beginning in 2011, new legislation reducing stopping distances of heavy trucks by one-third means larger, more powerful brakes are needed to meet the new safety standards. TABLE 29-4 shows the new standards.) Higher vehicle speeds are common now, with many regions having 70 mph (113 kph) speed limits, which puts even more demand on braking systems.

The need for improved braking capacity means changes to traditional S-cam systems are underway. Air disc brakes (ADB) are becoming more prevalent because of the following advantages:

- *Lower side-to-side consistency in braking torque*. Disc brakes minimize the effects of different coefficients of friction between left and right brakes.
- *Lower potential for heat- and mechanical-related brake fade*. Unlike drum brakes, as heat builds up in an air disc brake rotor, the rotor expands toward the pads and not away. Contact between the friction surfaces remains consistent even are the discs warm up. In fact, field tests prove ADB stopping capabilities far exceed drum brakes at high speed and loads due to heat and mechanical fade.
- *Better cooling with air disc brakes*. Air disc brakes use vented rotors, which dissipate heat faster than drum brakes.
- *Consistent actuation force*.Air disc brakes have fewer moving parts transferring brake force, which results in more consistent brake application and release.
- *Shorter service time*. Changing brake pads and rotors is done in much less time than changing drums and shoes.

Disc brakes, shown in FIGURE 29-55, use rotors instead of drums. Greater force can be applied to the rotor, which shortens stopping distances. Brake fade is minimal in air disc systems because rotors are squeezed rather than pushed outwards like drums. More surface area for cooling also in earlier air disc brake (ADB) systems, an actuator as well as a special slack adjuster was used to rotate a screw that squeezed the brakes. In addition to a screw-type application mechanism, a brake wedge was also used to multiply force applied to the brake pads. Early ADB systems had many problems related to maintenance and operation due to corrosion of slider pins, inconsistent operation of adjusting mechanisms, undersized rotors, and difficult access to parts. Unless regularly lubricated, parts would seize, leading to very costly repairs.

Bendix ADB series ADB22X,™ SN7,™ SN6,™ and SK7™ are an example of design change widely used for a new generation of ADB. Refer to FIGURE 29-56 for a contemporary **floating caliper** ADB design (the caliper floats on two pins), which consists of two major parts: the caliper and the carrier.

The Actuation System—Brake Applied

Bendix ADB system has an air chamber (16) used as an actuator. It is screwed into the carrier housing (2) containing a brake lever (6) and pressure piston (7). The brake multiplies force from the actuator (6) and has a fulcrum point that is supported by an eccentrically shaped roller bearing to minimize friction and variations to input brake force.

When the actuator is supplied with air pressure, braking force is transmitted through the pressure piston to the inboard brake pad by a bridge (7) and threaded spindles in the caliper piston (9).

The result is the brake pad (4) is squeezed into the rotor (3), and the opposite pad is pressed in, as the brake caliper reacts to the pressure applied to the inboard pad. Braking force is a function of air pressure, the size of the actuator piston, and the multiplication ratio of the brake lever.

Two pistons are used rather than one to eliminate taper wear of brake pads occurring when only one piston is used.

TABLE 29-4: Heavy Truck Stopping Distance Rules

Phase	Axle Configuration	GVWR	New Requirement	Compliance Date
Phase 1	Standard 6x4	Below 59,600 lbs	250'	August 2011
Phase 2	6x4 Severe Service	59,600–70,000 lbs	250'	August 2013
	6x4 Severe Service	Above 70,000 lbs	310'	August 2013
	All 4x2 Heavy Tractors	All	250'	August 2013

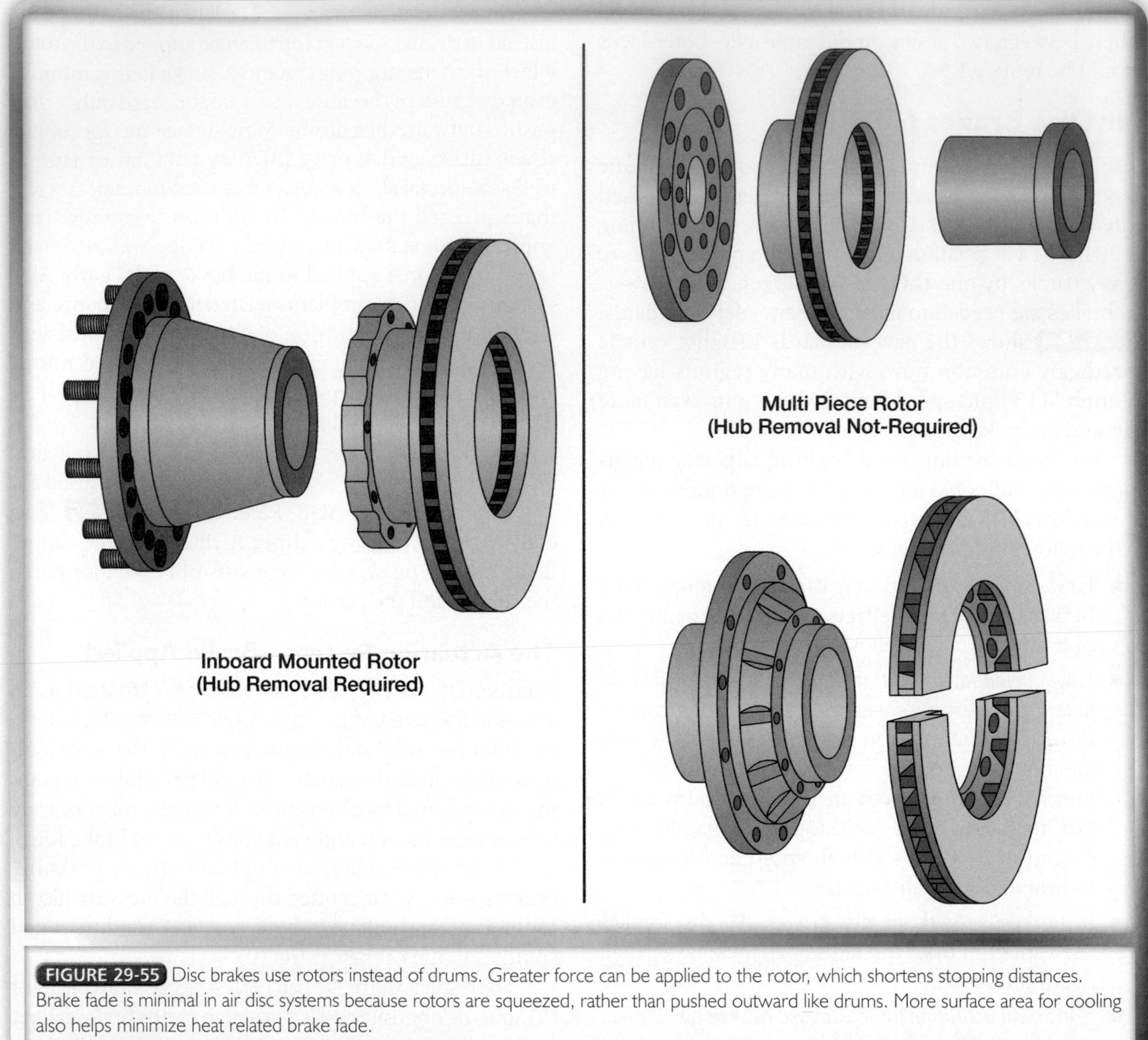

FIGURE 29-55 Disc brakes use rotors instead of drums. Greater force can be applied to the rotor, which shortens stopping distances. Brake fade is minimal in air disc systems because rotors are squeezed, rather than pushed outward like drums. More surface area for cooling also helps minimize heat related brake fade.

The Actuation System—Brake Released

When the brake actuation has finished, the brake caliper (1) will return to its initial position. A return spring located inside the power piston moves the brake lever to its non-brake position.

No pressure is exerted against the brake pad when released, and a small air gap exists between the pad and rotor. The full floating caliper design allows the caliper to slide along the caliper pins (5) and release pressure against the outboard pad.

Auto-Adjustment

To compensate for wear from the calipers' initial position, which uses a small air gap between the brake pad and rotor, an internal automatic clearance sensing adjusting mechanism is used. Clearance between the pads and rotor is maintained to ensure that the position of the brake lever is the same at the beginning of each brake application. The adjustment mechanism consists of threaded spindles, also called tappets (9), which are used to set the air gap between the pads and rotor. These spindles can be turned manually to establish the calipers' non-braked position. Spindle movement is synchronized by a chain (10) connecting the two threaded tappets. A ratcheting helix mechanism inside the tappet causes the actuating beam (8) to rotate the tappets whenever clearance increases between the pads and rotor. Rotation of the tappets is a function of piston movement. The tappets could

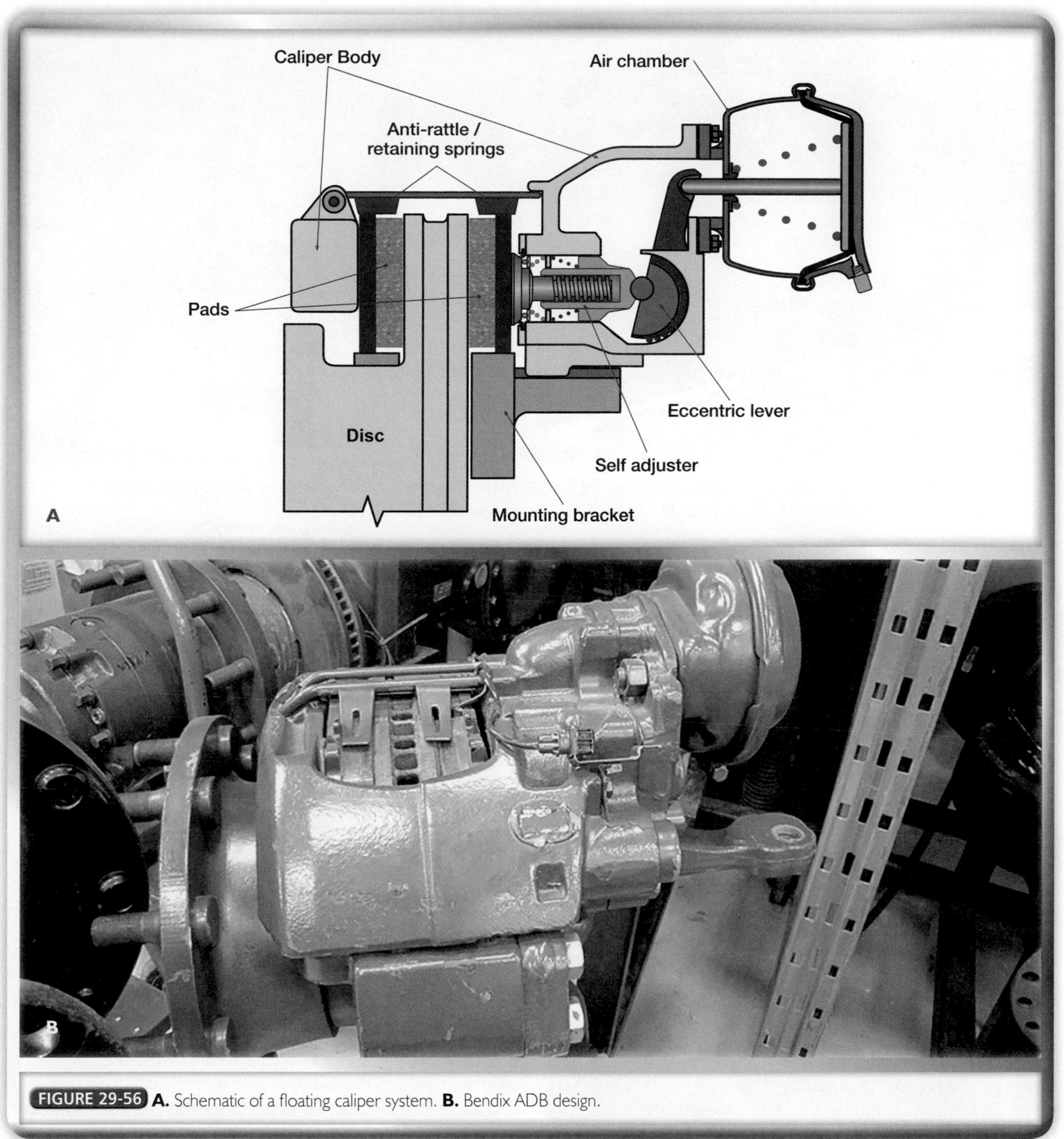

FIGURE 29-56 **A.** Schematic of a floating caliper system. **B.** Bendix ADB design.

overtighten as the caliper components are squeezed and piston travel increases. However, any preload pressure on the tappets from overadjustment will not permit rotation tappet rotation. This takes place only when zero force is applied against the tappets when the brake is released.

Meritor's air disc brake system, shown in FIGURE 29-57, is used on late-model vehicles to shorten stopping distances. FIGURE 29-58 shows a Bendix air disc brake system used on the front axle of a late model truck.

FIGURE 29-59 shows the Bendix® Air Disc Brakes Models ADB22X, ™ SN7, ™ SN6, ™ and SK7 ™. Two tappets spread braking force evenly across the surface of the inner brake pad. The sliding caliper design distributes braking forces equally between the inboard and outboard brake pad. As pads grip the rotor, the vehicle decelerates. Heavy-duty ventilated rotors minimize build-up. Wear sensors supply a continuous voltage signal that measures pad and rotor condition.

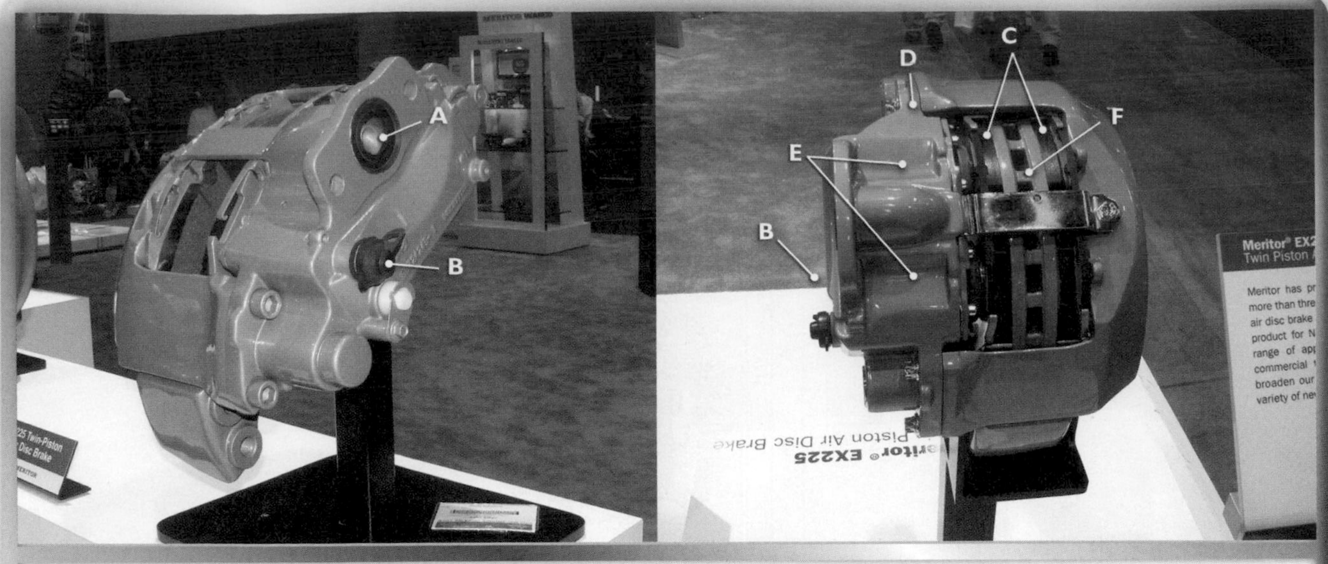

FIGURE 29-57 Meritor's air disc brake system is used on late model vehicles to shorten stopping distances. **A.** Chamber attachment point. **B.** Adjusting release screw. **C.** Brake pads. **D.** Caliper. **E.** Dual air pistons. **F.** Ventilated rotor.

FIGURE 29-58 A Bendix air disc brake system used on the front axle of a late model truck.

FIGURE 29-59 Bendix uses wear sensors in some of its ADBs, which supply a continuous voltage signal that measures pad and rotor condition. Pad and rotor wear sensor lead pins are circled.

Wedge Brakes

Before the most recent shorter stopping requirements were introduced, S-cam brakes comprised 95% of all heavy-duty North American air brake systems. A smaller niche drum brake system is the wedge brake. These systems use a ramp-and-roller design inside a wheel cylinder to multiply force supplied by an air chamber. Two wedge brake systems were built but have not been available for more than a decade. One, called the simplex system, used a single actuator, and duplex systems used dual actuators. With greater complexity, cost, and unpredictable release, wedge brakes have not had much popularity. The wedge brake's adjusting mechanism is incorporated into the housing of the brake itself. FIGURE 29-60 shows the simplex and duplex style of wedge brakes.

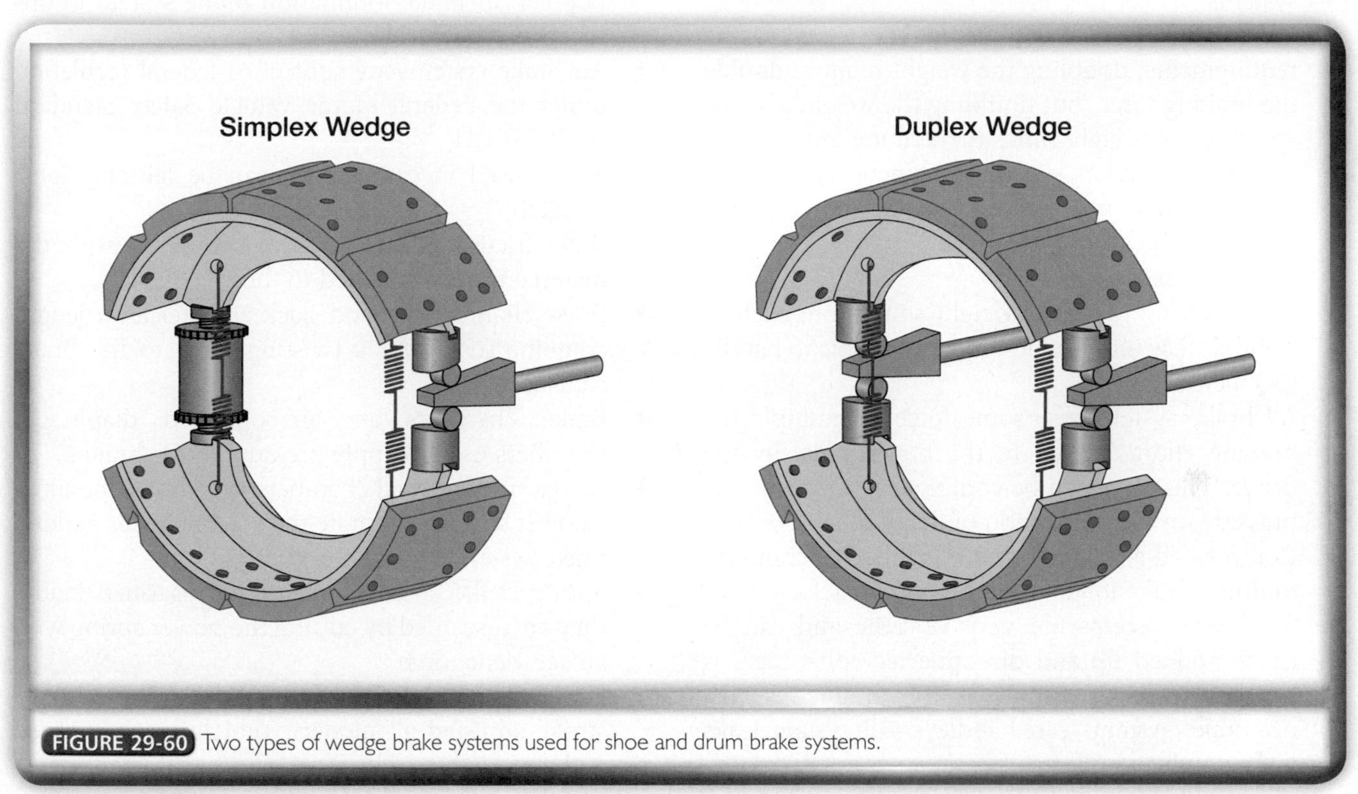

FIGURE 29-60 Two types of wedge brake systems used for shoe and drum brake systems.

Wrap-up

Ready for Review

- A moving vehicle has a tremendous amount of kinetic energy.
- To stop a vehicle, the kinetic energy must be converted into heat energy through the braking system.
- Weight and speed have different effects on braking requirements, doubling the weight requires double the braking force, but doubling the weight and the speed requires eight times the braking force.
- To operate, brakes must turn kinetic energy into heat, but they must also be capable of dissipating the heat quickly, or they will quickly lose their effectiveness.
- As a vehicle brakes, its weight shifts from back to front. Brakes must be designed to be able to handle this inertia shift.
- All brake systems use some force to multiply the braking effort applied to the brake pedal by the driver. This force can be compressed air, hydraulic pressure, or a combination of the two.
- Compressed air is the primary method of choice to multiply brake force for on highway trucks.
- Air brake systems are very versatile and can be easily hooked up and disconnected, plus there is no worry of leaks or spills, as in hydraulic systems.
- Air brake systems can handle small system leaks without adverse effects.
- All brake systems are dual brake systems, meaning that if one system fails the other can still stop the vehicle.
- Because of their simplicity, cam brakes are the most popular air brake foundation brake system in on-highway trucks.
- Air brake systems are subject to federal regulation under the Federal Motor Vehicle Safety Standard (FMVSS) 121.
- S-cam used in cam brakes can be left- or right-handed.
- Brake friction material is edge coded to ensure the material used is matched to the vehicle.
- Brake chamber size and slack adjuster lever length combine to deliver a twisting force to the brake camshafts.
- Brake chambers are air operated diaphragm chambers used to apply pressure to the brakes.
- Actuators have dual chambers with one containing a power spring to operate the emergency or parking brake system.
- Spring brake chambers must be disarmed before they are discarded by cutting the power spring with an acetylene torch.
- Slack adjusters are used to keep the brake chamber stroke adjusted all modern vehicles are equipped with automatic slack adjusters.

Vocabulary Builder

AL factor The size or surface area of a brake chamber multiplied by the length of the slack adjuster in inches.

anti-fade An opposite condition of heat fade where the coefficient of friction increases as the brakes get hotter.

automatic slack adjusters (ASAs) Automatically adjust brake stroke to maintain the correct shoe-to-drum clearance.

brake block Brake friction material that is 0.75 inch (19 mm) thick.

brake fade The inability of the brakes to maintain its effectiveness.

brake foundations The braking components found at the wheel ends.

brake lining Brake friction material that is 0.05 inch, (13 mm) thick.

brake torque The force applied to the foundation brakes during braking.

cam brakes Brakes that use an "S" shaped cam that twists between two rollers to expand a set of brake shoes.

cam-opposite. A situation when the cam rotates opposite the drum's rotation to energize the brakes.

cam-same A situation when the cam rotates the same direction the drum's rotation to energize the brakes.

cast drums Brake drums made from cast iron.

centrifuge drums Brake drums made with a cast iron core surrounded by a steel band.

chemical fade A type of brake fade that takes place when steam or gases from vaporized lining materials form between hot lining and the drum reducing the coefficient of friction.

clearance sensing ASA A type of automatic slack adjuster that reduces pushrod travel based on torque input to the ASA.

coefficient of friction (CoF) The amount of friction between two particular objects in contact; calculated by dividing the force required to move the object by the weight of the object.

edge code A code representing the CoF of a brake and its composition.

Federal Motor Vehicle Safety Standard 121 (FMVSS 121) Performance and safety standards legislation for air brakes.

floating caliper A disc brake caliper that floats on two pins.

glazing A cause of brake fade characterized by a hard glassy burnt appearance to the lining surface diminishing its CoF.

heat fade The loss or reduction in the coefficient of friction as the brake temperature increases.

inertia shift Weight that moves from the rear of the vehicle to the front during braking.

kinetic energy The energy of a body in motion.

left- and right-hand camshafts S-cams used on either side of a vehicle that rotate in opposite directions.

long stroke chambers Brake chambers manufactured with a 3 inch, (76 mm), stroke.

manual slack adjusters A manually adjusted lever between the brake chamber and the S-cam all but obsolete today.

mechanical fade Loss of brake effectiveness that occurs when drums expand due to heat.

non-asbestos organic (NAO) lining Brake friction material commonly used in line haul tractors where far less braking takes place.

power springs Springs in brake actuators used to apply park brakes or internal pushrod lock mechanisms.

release bolt A bolt that compresses the power spring of spring brakes and releases the park brake.

roto-chambers Actuators with a unique diaphragm construction which delivers consistent output force regardless of the pushrod position.

S-cam A cam shaft used to force brake shoes onto the brake drum.

self-energization A braking effect that causes the shoe-drum friction to rotate the brake shoe into the drum with more force.

semi-metallic lining Brake friction material heat resistant semi-metallic blends are for higher temperatures and load service ratings.

slack adjuster A mechanical lever between the brake chamber and the foundation brake assembly.

spring brake Brakes used on rear drive axles to apply park brakes which are also referred to as "maxi-brakes."

stroke sensing ASA A slack adjuster that makes adjustments to slack based on the measured rotation between a brake application and release.

water fade A type of brake fade that occurs when water gets between the friction surfaces and the drum and acts as a lubricant and reduces braking efficiency.

wedge brakes Brakes that use a wedge pushed between two rollers as a lever to apply the brakes.

Review Questions

1. Air wedge brakes do not use which of the following?
   a. Brake shoes
   b. Slack adjusters
   c. Air chambers
   d. Brake drums
2. The amount of force a wedge brake can develop is determined by which of the following?
   a. The air pressure applied
   b. The size of the actuator diaphragm
   c. The angle of the wedge
   d. All of the choices are correct.
3. Disc brakes are more powerful than drum brakes because of which of the following?
   a. Higher application force
   b. Larger frictional contact area
   c. More heat build up
   d. Better friction material
4. Which of the following best explains brake shoe self-energization?
   a. The secondary shoe energizes the primary shoe.
   b. The primary shoe energizes the secondary shoe.
   c. Both shoes are energized
   d. The primary shoe is pushed into the drum with more force by drum rotation
5. Which of the following statements is correct?
   a. A left hand S-cam camshaft turns clockwise.
   b. A left hand S-cam camshaft turn counterclockwise.
   c. A right hand S-cam shaft turns counterclockwise.
   d. A right hand S-cam camshaft turns counterclockwise when it is installed on the right side of the vehicle.
6. What is the recommended minimum end play for the S-cam?
   a. 0.005"
   b. 0.010"
   c. 0.015"
   d. 0.020"
7. The AL factor refers to which of the following?
   a. The effective length of the S-cam times the surface area of the brake chamber diaphragm
   b. The effective length of the slack adjuster times the surface area of the brake shoes
   c. The effective length of the slack adjuster times the surface area of the brake chamber diaphragm
   d. The effective length of the S-cam times the surface area of the brake shoes
8. A brake shoe edge code G indicates which of the following coefficients of friction?
   a. Over 0.25 but not over 0.35
   b. Over 0.35 but not over 0.45
   c. Over 0.45 but not over 0.55
   d. Over .055
9. A brake chamber having 24 square inches of surface area and actuated with 50 PSI air pressure acting on a six inch slack adjuster results in which of the following on the S-cam?
   a. 1200 pounds of force
   b. 1200 pounds foot of torque
   c. 7200 inch pounds of torque
   d. 7200 pounds of force
10. Which of the following is a reason that stroke-sensing automatic slack adjusters are almost obsolete?
   a. They are prone to over-adjustment.
   b. They may not adjust at all.
   c. They leave too much clearance between the drum and the shoes.
   d. They had too much of a failure rate.

ASE-Type Questions

1. Technician A says that vehicles require more power to stop than they do to accelerate. Technician B says that all new trucks must be equipped with antilock brakes. Who is correct?
   a. Technician A
   b. Technician B
   c. Both Technician A and Technician B
   d. Neither Technician A nor Technician B
2. Technician A says that the latest legislative requirements for truck brake systems demand shorter stopping distances. Technician B says that, to achieve shorter stopping distances, all drum brakes are legally required to be replaced by disc brakes. Who is correct?
   a. Technician A
   b. Technician B
   c. Both Technician A and Technician B
   d. Neither Technician A nor Technician B
3. Technician A says that brake systems convert potential energy to heat. Technician B Says that brakes use friction to stop a vehicle. Who is correct?
   a. Technician A
   b. Technician B
   c. Both Technician A and Technician B
   d. Neither Technician A nor Technician B
4. Technician A says that more heat helps the brakes to work better. Technician B says that a vehicle must be able to stop in less than 1/10th of the time it takes to accelerate a given speed. Who is correct?
   a. Technician A
   b. Technician B
   c. Both Technician A and Technician B
   d. Neither Technician A nor Technician B
5. Technician A says that if the vehicle weight is doubled, the stopping force must be doubled. Technician B says that if the vehicle speed is doubled the stopping force required is increased 8 times. Who is correct?
   a. Technician A
   b. Technician B
   c. Both Technician A and Technician B
   d. Neither Technician A nor Technician B
6. Technician A says that air brake systems transmit pressures much more quickly than hydraulic systems. Technician B says that compressed air stores potential energy. Who is correct?
   a. Technician A
   b. Technician B
   c. Both Technician A and Technician B
   d. Neither Technician A nor Technician B
7. Technician A says that air brake systems are better than hydraulics in tractor trailer applications because it is easier to connect and disconnect components. Technician B says that air brake system use more engine power to operate. Who is correct?
   a. Technician A
   b. Technician B
   c. Both Technician A and Technician B
   d. Neither Technician A nor Technician B
8. Technician A says that air brake systems are regulated under FMVSS 135. Technician B says that hydraulic brake systems have lower initial cost when compared to air brake systems. Who is correct?
   a. Technician A
   b. Technician B
   c. Both Technician A and Technician B
   d. Neither Technician A nor Technician B
9. Technician A says that wedge brakes are the most common foundation brake used on air brake systems. Technician B says that disc brakes are becoming more popular in air brake systems. Who is correct?
   a. Technician A
   b. Technician B
   c. Both Technician A and Technician B
   d. Neither Technician A nor Technician B
10. Technician A says that S-cams can be left or right handed. Technician B says that S-cam foundation brakes can have one or two anchors. Who is correct?
    a. Technician A
    b. Technician B
    c. Both Technician A and Technician B
    d. Neither Technician A nor Technician B

CHAPTER 30

NATEF Tasks

There are no NATEF tasks in this chapter.

Knowledge Objectives

After reading this chapter, you will be able to:

1. Outline the advantages and disadvantages of using air brakes. (pp 926–928)
2. List the four air brake circuits used in heavy-duty commercial vehicles. (pp 926–930)
3. Identify and describe the categories of commercial vehicle air brake system circuits. (pp 928–930)
4. Describe the purpose and operation of commercial vehicle air brake circuits. (pp 928–944)
5. Identify minimum performance requirements for the air system according to FMVSS 121 standards. (pp 928–933)
6. Identify and describe the air supply system's components and their functions. (pp 930–944)
7. Identify and describe the air delivery and control systems' components and their functions. (pp 930–940)
8. Identify and describe the operating factors affecting air brake system performance and efficiency. (p 935)
9. Identify and describe safety features of dual air brake system circuits and components. (pp 944–945)
10. Identify and describe the components of the park/emergency brake circuit and their functions. (pp 955–956)
11. Identify and describe the components of the trailer air circuit and their functions. (pp 957–961)

Air Brake Foundation Systems and Air Brake Circuits

Skills Objectives

There are no skills objectives in this chapter.

Introduction

Compressed air brake systems have been used since the 1870s when George Westinghouse first built air brake systems for heavy locomotives. Not long afterwards, air brakes were used in on-road vehicles. Since then, air brake systems have undergone numerous refinements to make them a highly reliable, effective braking system preferred for heavy-duty commercial vehicles because of their superior stopping power and safety.

The concept of compressed air brake systems is relatively simple. Air is pulled into an air compressor where it is pressurized, sent to a storage tank, and held at approximately 125 psi (862 kPa). When needed for braking, compressed air is piped through lines and valves to the wheel end brakes. Air-operated cylinders, or brake chambers, at the wheels convert the stored air power into mechanical force used to apply the brakes. As illustrated in FIGURE 30-1, compressed air can store energy much like a coil spring. Air brake systems multiply and transfer brake pedal force using the properties of air pressure. Because large vehicles also require an emergency brake system, compressed air is used to control heavy springs used to supply a high mechanical force that can apply brakes.

The basic principles of air brake systems are straightforward. In practice, however, safe, effective, efficient, and reliable air brake system operation relies on three major subsystems and a variety of components unique to each of those systems. This chapter specifically covers:

- Air supply system, which consists primarily of the air compressor and reservoirs
- Air delivery system, which is composed of valves and air lines arranged into specific circuits
- Emergency and park brake system, which is designed to maintain vehicle control when air is lost and to hold the vehicle when parked

The trailer air brake system is a fourth subsystem of the air brake system and works in parallel with the tractor air brake systems when a trailer is towed.

Advantages of Air Systems

In heavy-duty combination vehicles, air is used to transmit pressure and multiply the force of a driver's leg during brake application. FIGURE 30-2 illustrates how brake systems multiply force depending on the pressure and the surface area. For example, a 4:1 pressure differential will multiply 12 lb (5.4.kg) of air pressure per square inch into 48 lb (21.8 kg) of breaking force. Air is an ideal medium for transmitting and multiplying force, compared to hydraulic fluid, in large vehicles due primarily to the heavier vehicle weights and the greater number of wheel ends. Much more force needs to be applied at

You Are the Technician

You have recently begun working at a mixed fleet operation with a wide variety of medium and heavy trucks modified for specialized purposes in the mining and oil exploration industry. Some trucks were originally built as on-highway tractors and now have frame extensions to accommodate installation of 20' (6.1 m) boxes plus a fifth wheel for towing short trailers. Other chassis have had specialized installations of hydraulic booms, large air compressors, power generators, and drilling equipment. Some straight trucks have had additional axles installed, some self-steering, and others enhanced with a combination of tag and pusher axles equipped with air brakes. While most of these trucks operate in off-road conditions on rough gravel roads, a few are licensed to operate on public roads.

There have been a number of complaints from operators that the braking systems are not effective and that the vehicles become unstable and difficult to steer when braking. Some vehicles take too long to stop and require very high brake application pressures to slow the vehicles. The tire costs for the fleet are excessively high because many vehicles have tires regularly damaged with flat spots, likely due to the brakes locking up.

1. Briefly outline the steps you might take to begin to verify the operator complaints and begin to analyze potential causes of the vehicle control problems reported by the drivers.
2. List and identify problems with the braking system. What do you think could be wrong with the trucks' air brake circuits that would account for the operator complaints?
3. List the items you believe should be inspected, tested, and included in a proper preventative maintenance programs for air brakes.
4. Identify some of the diagnostic tests you might use to validate the correct operation of the air brake system components and operation in the fleet of trucks. Give reasons for using the tests.

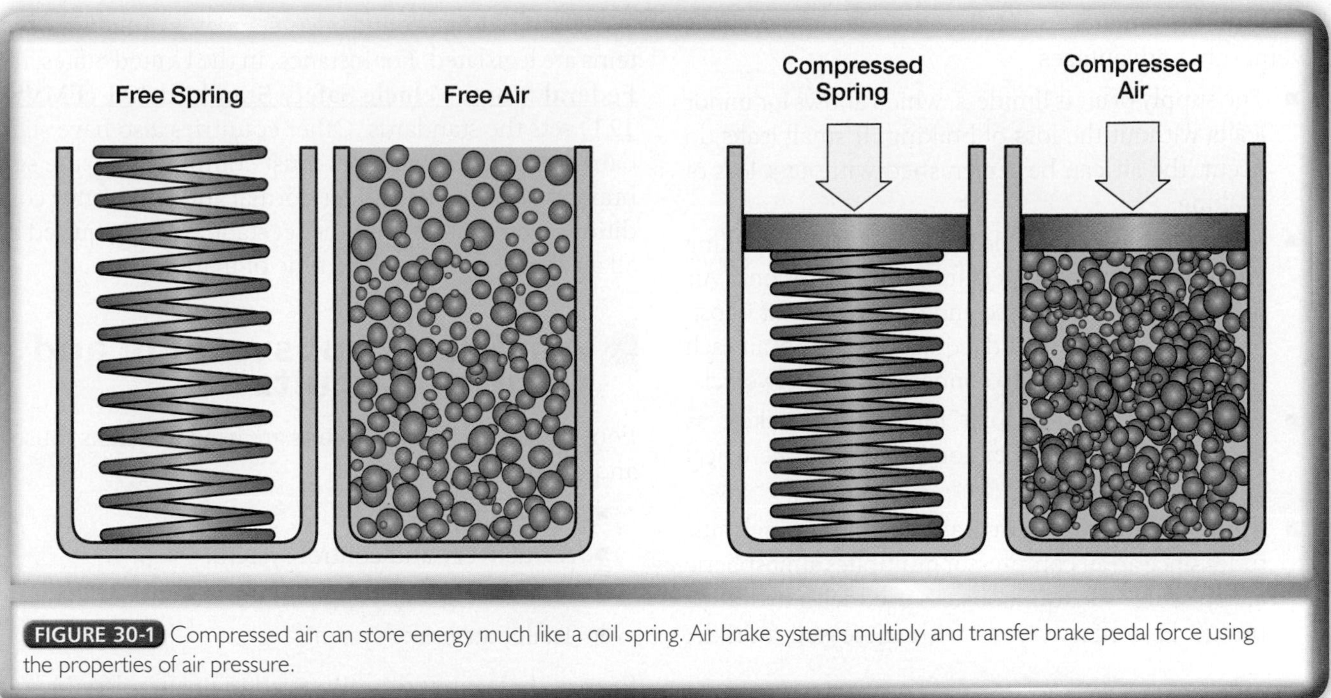

FIGURE 30-1 Compressed air can store energy much like a coil spring. Air brake systems multiply and transfer brake pedal force using the properties of air pressure.

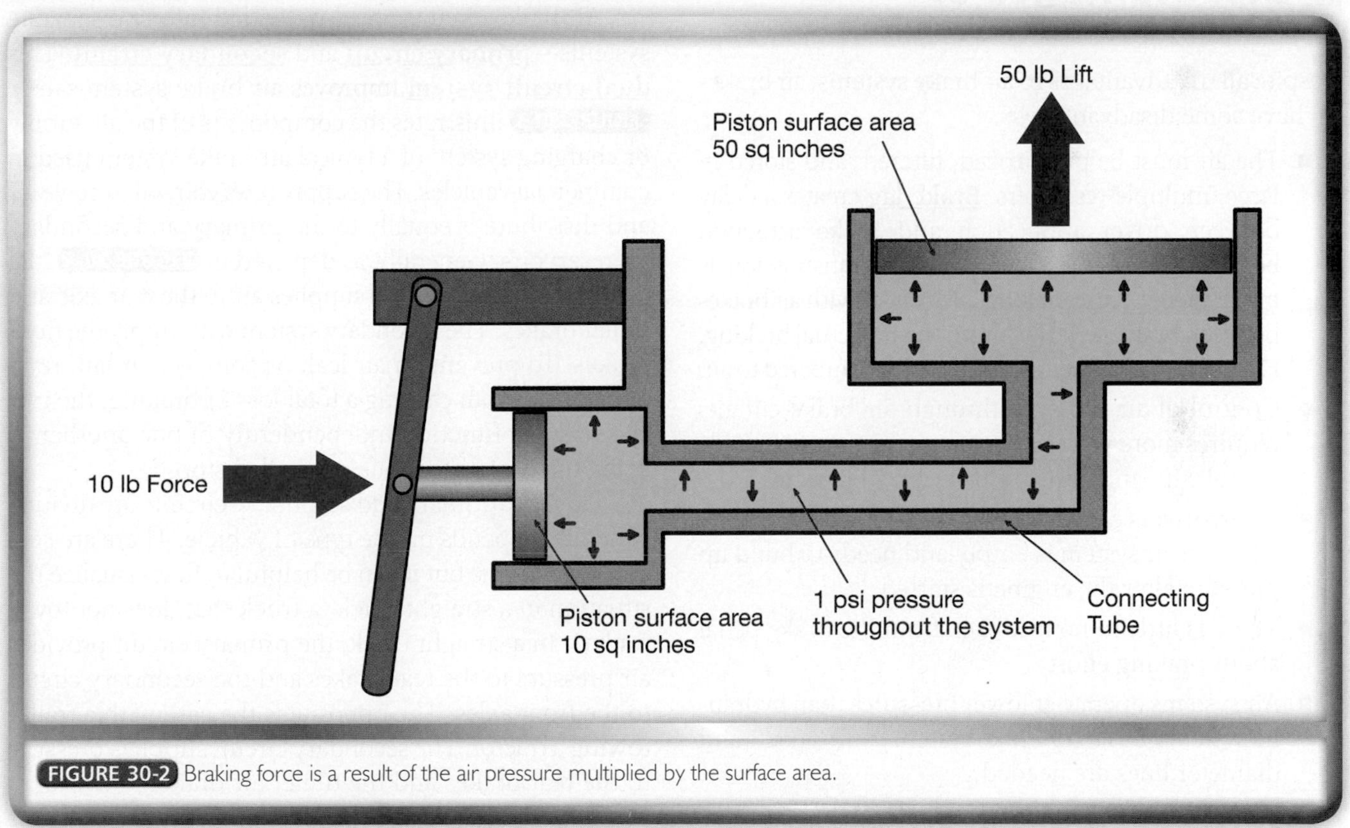

FIGURE 30-2 Braking force is a result of the air pressure multiplied by the surface area.

more wheel ends than in single-axle, light-duty vehicles equipped with hydraulic brakes.

Air pressure can be stored in an uncomplicated reservoir when a vehicle is not braking. Therefore, the greater stopping power requirements of heavy commercial vehicles are easily supplied by an engine-driven air compressor. In comparison, braking a loaded heavy-duty vehicle using hydraulic fluid would be much less efficient. It would require moving large quantities of liquids through lines and require a complex force and volume multiplication system to convert the driver's input to braking force at each wheel. When it comes to heavy-duty commercial vehicles, air brake systems have several other advantages:

- The supply of air is limitless, which allows for minor leaks without the loss of braking. If small leaks do occur, the air can be replenished without a loss of braking.
- Air brake systems enable easier and faster coupling and uncoupling of trailers from the tractor unit. Air lines can be disconnected and nothing but air is lost. Hydraulic systems would require bleeding of air each time they are opened to connect to another vehicle.
- Air systems uses simpler foundation brakes, as shoes, drums, and other components at the wheel ends are simpler and fewer.
- Air brakes can maintain brake pressure at high altitudes since an air compressor multiplies atmospheric air pressure. Vacuum boosters used with hydraulic brakes lose effectiveness with increased altitude.

Disadvantages of Air Systems

Despite all the advantages to air brake systems, air brakes do have some disadvantages:

- The air must be pressurized, filtered, and stored in large, multiple reservoirs. **Brake lag** creates a delay between driver application and brake actuation because the speed of air pressure transmission is much slower. An even longer lag exists with air brakes between brake pedal application and actual braking. Hydraulic force has little or no delay compared to air.
- Control of air pressure through air brake circuits requires more valves and components, which adds complexity and cost to the air brake system.
- Some drivers express dissatisfaction with the delay when an air system is empty and needs to build up pressure after the engine is started.
- There is little to no feedback from the brake pedal about braking effort.
- Air systems operate at lower pressures than hydraulic systems, so larger brake system components and diameter lines are needed.
- The complexity of air brake systems means more knowledge and skill are required of technicians who service the systems. For similar reasons, driver training and certification to operate a vehicle with air brakes is mandatory in most jurisdictions.
- Air can become contaminated with moisture and cause brake valves and other components to freeze up in cold weather operation.

The performance and safety standards of air brake systems are legislated. For instance, in the United States, the **Federal Motor Vehicle Safety Standard 121 (FMVSS 121)** sets the standards. Other countries also have standards to which all vehicles must comply. To ensure safe braking performance under normal and emergency conditions, compliance with the set standards is required by all air brake systems at the time of manufacture.

Air Brake Subsystems and Control Circuits

Four distinct air brake circuits are used in trucks, buses, and trailers:

- Air supply system
- Air delivery and control system
- Park-emergency/supply brake system
- Trailer air brake system

Each of these circuits is discussed in greater detail in the remaining sections of this chapter.

Air brake circuits are also divided into two separate systems—**primary circuit** and **secondary circuit**. This **dual-circuit system** improves air brake system safety. FIGURE 30-3 illustrates the components of the air supply or charging system of a typical air brake system used in commercial vehicles. The supply reservoir will receive air and distribute it equally to the primary and secondary air reservoirs. Generally, as depicted in FIGURE 30-4, the primary air brake circuit supplies air to the rear axle and trailer brakes. The secondary system will supply the front brakes. To prevent an air leak or component failure in one system from causing a total loss of braking, the two systems can function independently of one another to bring the vehicle to a safe controlled stop.

How the primary and secondary circuits are divided generally depends on the type of vehicle. There are several exceptions, but it can be helpful to first visualize the situation in a straight truck (a truck that does not tow a trailer). In a straight truck, the primary circuit provides air pressure to the rear brakes and the secondary circuit to the front axles. The opposite is the case with a trailer towing a tractor. The secondary circuit supplies pressure to the rear brakes and the trailer air brakes. Navistar is one of several OEM exceptions. It uses the primary air circuit to supply pressurized air to the rear brakes and trailer while secondary air supplies the front brakes.

Primary brake circuits are commonly color coded as green air lines. Secondary circuits generally use red. Most air supply lines are fabricated from materials such as **Synflex**, which is a brand name for tubing made from nylon and which is shown in the system in FIGURE 30-5.

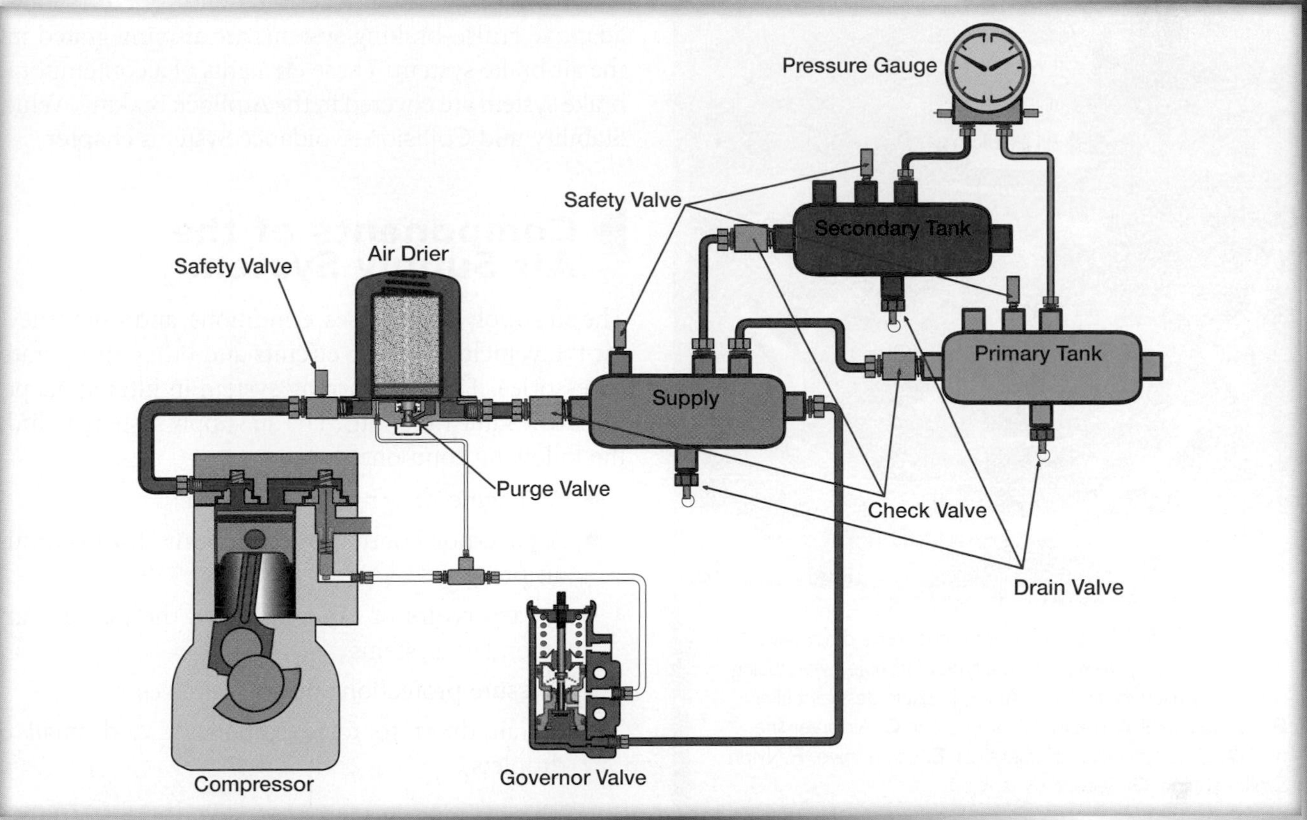

Pressure Gauge
Safety Valve
Secondary Tank
Safety Valve
Air Drier
Primary Tank
Supply
Purge Valve
Check Valve
Drain Valve
Compressor
Governor Valve

FIGURE 30-3 Components of the air supply, or charging system, of a typical air brake system used in commercial vehicles.

Brake Chamber
To Trailer Brakes
Brake Valve
Primary
Delivery to
Front Brakes
Secondary
To Rear Brakes

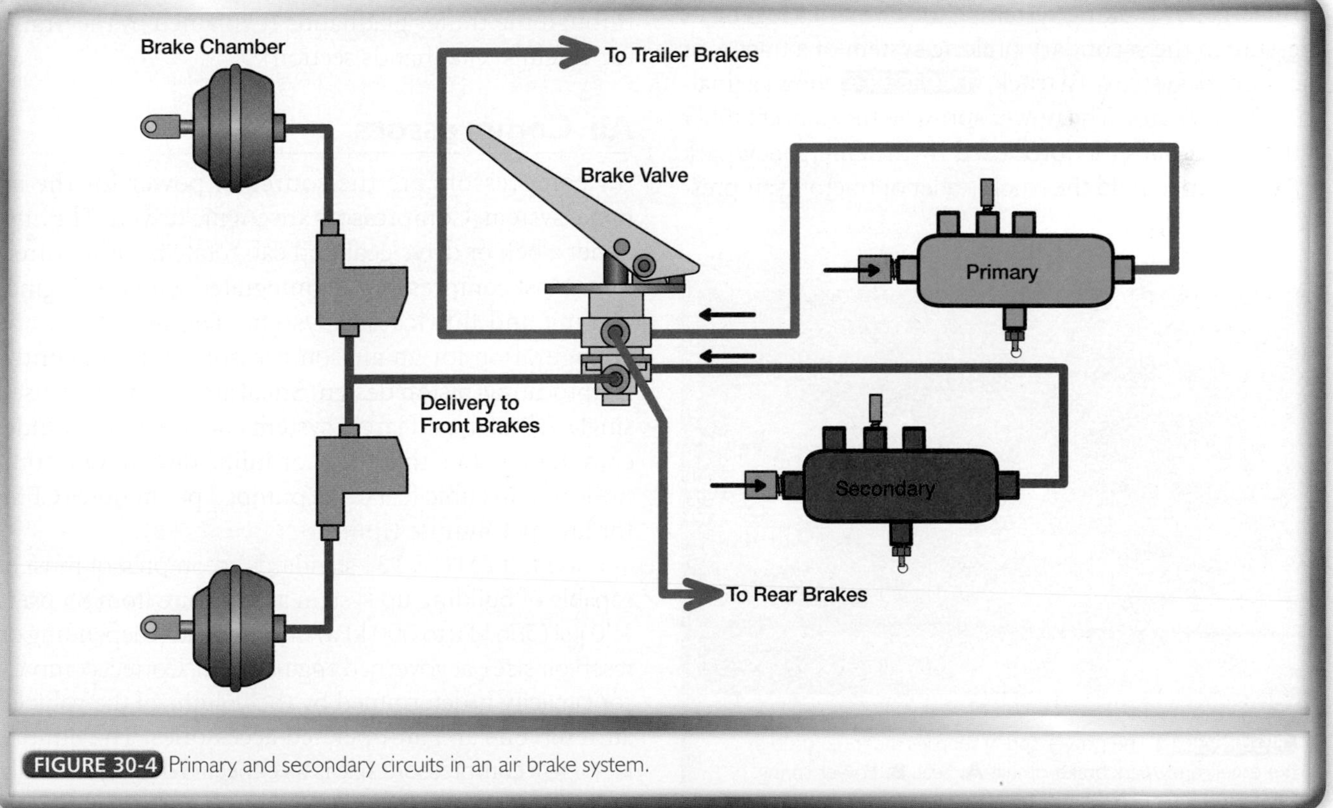

FIGURE 30-4 Primary and secondary circuits in an air brake system.

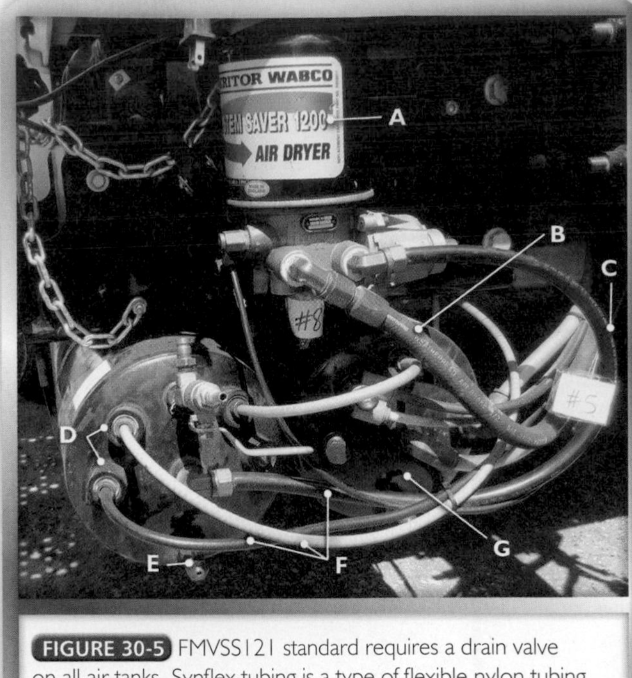

FIGURE 30-5 FMVSS121 standard requires a drain valve on all air tanks. Synflex tubing is a type of flexible nylon tubing commonly used for air lines. **A.** Replaceable dessicant filter. **B.** Braided steel air line from compressor. **C.** Air dryer line out. **D.** Quick connect air fittings (2). **E.** Drain valve. **F.** Nylon Synflex tubing. **G.** Secondary tank.

For both trucks and tractors, the **emergency brake circuit** or **park brake circuit** holds the truck/trailer or tractor stationary when parked. It also provides a backup emergency braking system in the event of a loss of air pressure in the secondary braking system of a tractor or the primary system of a truck. **FIGURE 30-6** shows a dual-chamber actuator. The power spring in the dual chamber actuator supplies the force used by the emergency/park brake circuit to hold the truck/trailer or tractor if air pressure is lost.

FIGURE 30-6 The power spring supplies the force used by the emergency/park brake circuit. **A.** Seal. **B.** Power spring.

Antilock braking, traction, stability control, and adaptive cruise-braking systems are also integrated into the air brake system. These elements of a contemporary brake system are covered in the Antilock Braking, Vehicle Stability, and Collision Avoidance Systems chapter.

Components of the Air Supply System

The air supply compresses, conditions, and stores the air for the vehicle's braking circuits and other air-operated accessories. The air charging system in filtered air performs the same functions. The air supply system includes the following components:

- An engine-driven air compressor
- A governor controlling minimum and maximum air pressure
- Air reservoirs or tanks for both the primary and secondary systems
- Pressure protection and check valves
- An air dryer to remove moisture and small oil droplets

Other vehicle systems may also use the supply of compressed air. For example, the air suspension, transmission controls, or interaxle differential lock might use compressed air. Air reservoirs for the trailer braking system receive air from the secondary air circuit supplied through the trailer gladhands (explained in the Trailer Air Circuits: Gladhands section).

Air Compressors

Air compressors are the source of power for the air brake system. Compressors are engine driven. They use either a belt or drive gear and can rotate in either direction. Most compressors are integrated with the engine's cooling and lubrication system. The most common configuration for an air compressor is a two-cylinder reciprocating-piston design. Small air systems may use a single cylinder, and larger systems can use four-cylinder compressors in either a "V" or inline design. Output is measured in cubic feet of air pumped per minute (CFM) [or liter per minute (lpm)].

To meet FMVSS 121 standards, a compressor must be capable of building up system air pressure from 85 psi to 100 psi (586 kPa to 690 kPa) in 25 seconds (depending on reservoir size), at governed engine speed. Correct compressor capacity is determined by the volume of the vehicle's air reservoirs and air-operated accessories. The limiting factor to a compressor's size is its expected duty cycle. Since compressors are designed to operate a maximum of 25%

duty cycle—that is, 25% "on time"—the compressor output must be high enough to meet and exceed air system requirements without exceeding the 25% threshold. FIGURE 30-7 shows the relationship between vehicle type and air usage. If heat produced during excessive compressor loading period is not given adequate time to dissipate, the compressor will prematurely wear out. Single-cylinder, like the one shown in FIGURE 30-8A, and multiple-cylinder compressors, such as the one shown in FIGURE 30-8B, are used to increase capacity.

The compressor typically consists of three major sections: a cylinder head, crankshaft, and the crankcase. Cast iron is used to construct the compressor. An oil line from the engine lubricates the crank bearings and cylinder walls. Piston rings help form a gas-tight seal to compress air and scrape oil from the cylinder walls and direct it back into the crankcase. Engine coolant circulates through the compressor to remove heat build-up. In most applications, a flange on the compressor crankcase provides a mounting surface to bolt the compressor onto the engine. Most compressors are coupled to the engine using a drive gear because a gear-driven coupling has the highest durability and reliability. Some single-cylinder compressors may require timing to the engine to minimize vibration caused by the inertia of the reciprocating piston. Though not as reliable or efficient, belt-driven compressors may be used in older vehicles or medium-duty vehicles with smaller air supply systems.

Compressor Operation—Loading and Unloading

The compressor is a key component for the air brake system and operates by loading and unloading as the air passes through it. Air is pulled into the compressor cylinders through the air intake valves during the piston downstroke (loading). During the upstroke, air is pushed out of the cylinders through the air discharge valves (unloading).

As illustrated in FIGURE 30-9A, on upstrokes, the air intake valves are closed by spring tension while the discharge valves are opened through air pressure. FIGURE 30-9B illustrates the downstroke. During

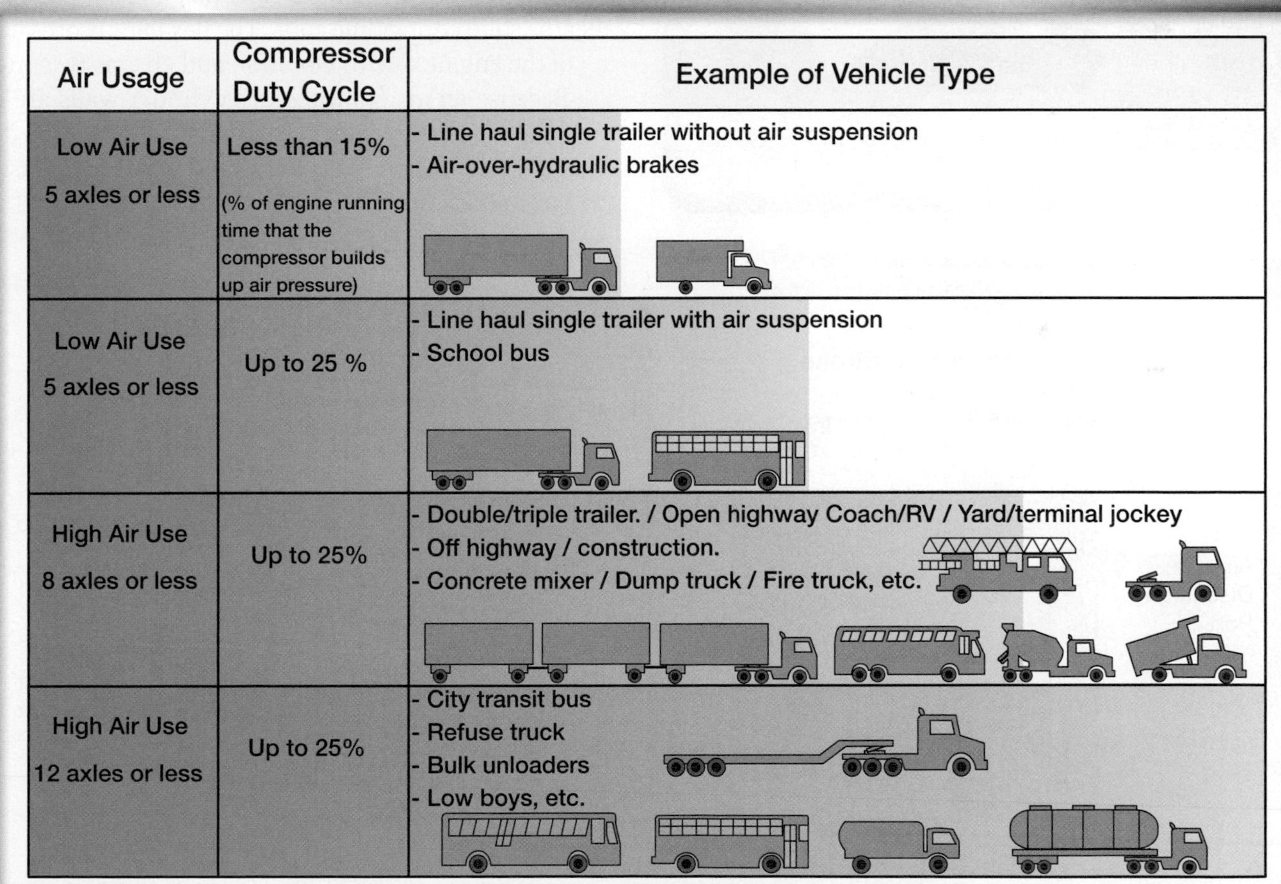

Air Usage	Compressor Duty Cycle	Example of Vehicle Type
Low Air Use 5 axles or less	Less than 15% (% of engine running time that the compressor builds up air pressure)	- Line haul single trailer without air suspension - Air-over-hydraulic brakes
Low Air Use 5 axles or less	Up to 25 %	- Line haul single trailer with air suspension - School bus
High Air Use 8 axles or less	Up to 25%	- Double/triple trailer. / Open highway Coach/RV / Yard/terminal jockey - Off highway / construction. - Concrete mixer / Dump truck / Fire truck, etc.
High Air Use 12 axles or less	Up to 25%	- City transit bus - Refuse truck - Bulk unloaders - Low boys, etc.

FIGURE 30-7 An air compressor's capacity must be selected to limit the cycle time (on/off time). Undersized compressors will build air pressure too slowly and wear out prematurely.

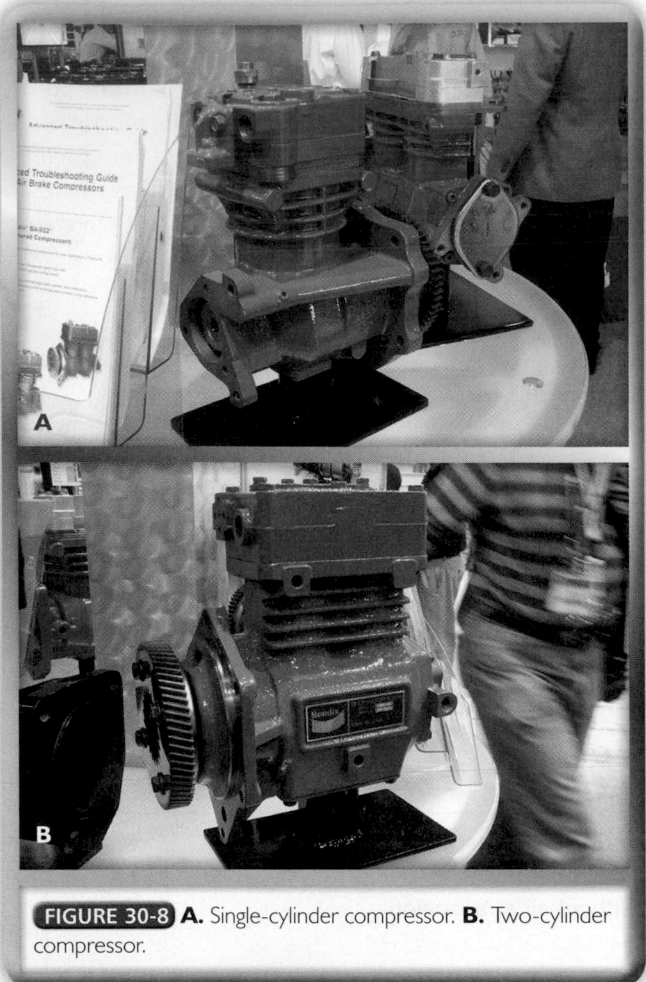

FIGURE 30-8 **A.** Single-cylinder compressor. **B.** Two-cylinder compressor.

downstroke, the intake valves are opened by a pressure differential between the cylinders and air pressure at the intake port. Atmospheric air pressure will push its way into the cylinders during the intake stroke due to the pressure differential. Pressurized air from an engine's turbocharged intake manifold air pressure will also push its way into the cylinders. Spring tension closes the discharge valves during intake stroke to prevent air from leaking back from the reservoirs and into the air compressor.

Compressor Discharge Line

High air temperatures from the compressor discharge port are lowered by using annealed copper tubing to connect the compressor with an air dryer or air reservoir. Annealed copper easily radiates heat and does not harden with time and vibration, so it will not crack. In vehicles having five or less axles equipped with air brakes, a ½" (12.7 mm) ID annealed copper discharge line of between 6" (1.8 m) and 9" (2.7 m) is used. Larger systems will use 5/8" (15.9 mm) or ¾" (19.1 mm) diameter tube up to 15' (4.6 m) long. The line should slope downward from the compressor to prevent a build-up of moisture that could freeze in the line. A stainless steel flex line is often used after the solid copper line ends. The flex line absorbs flexing of the engine due to vibration and chassis twisting.

Because an air compressor's cylinder walls are oil lubricated, some oil will always carry over into the discharge tube. Hot discharge lines can carbonize oil inside the line and lead to discharge line restriction.

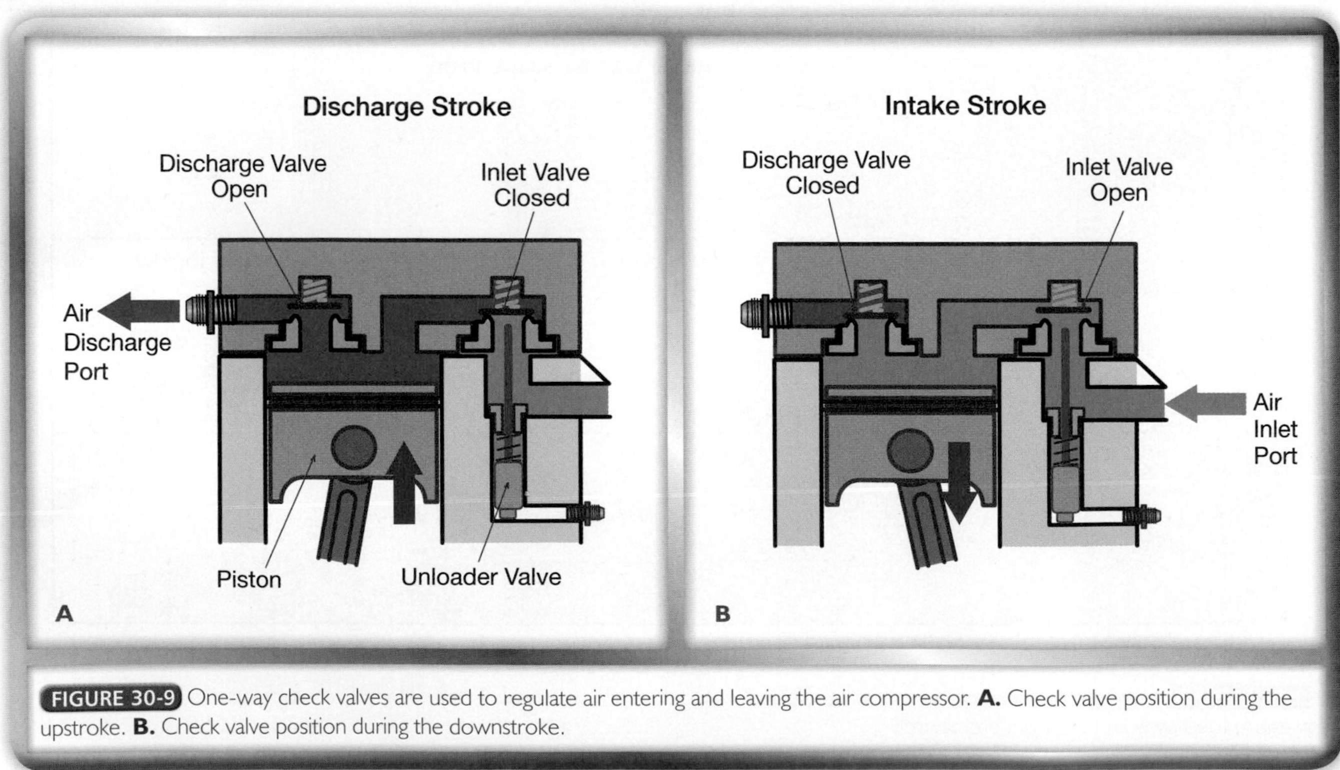

FIGURE 30-9 One-way check valves are used to regulate air entering and leaving the air compressor. **A.** Check valve position during the upstroke. **B.** Check valve position during the downstroke.

Governor

The **governor** controls air system pressure by stopping and starting compressor loading. It also controls purging of the air dryer. Current FMVSS 121 air brake standards require vehicle air pressure to fall no lower than 85 psi (586 kPa) and reach 125–130 psi (862–896 kPa) when the compressor unloads or cuts out. Cut-in pressures are generally 10 to 20 psi (69 to 138 kPa) below cut-out pressure. Governors control the cut-in and cut-out pressures of the compressor by opening or closing the unloader valves at preset pressure points. Air is supplied to the unloader valves and air dryer purge valve through the governor unloader port.

As illustrated in FIGURE 30-10, the governor has three ports:

- **Reservoir**—Measures air system pressure in the supply-service or primary air reservoir.
- **Unloader**—Air at system pressure is available at this port when cut-out pressure is reached. System pressure is exhausted and atmospheric pressure is switched to this port at cut-in pressure.
- **Exhaust**—Vents air from the unloader port when the air system reaches cut-out pressure.

As the air system pressure builds when the compressor is loaded, reservoir pressure is supplied to one side of the governor piston, which is opposed by spring pressure. As the governor piston is moved by the build-up of system air pressure supplied through the reservoir port, an exhaust valve built into the piston makes contact with an internal adjusting screw pin. The internal governor exhaust valve will then close at cut-out pressure. At that point, the unloader port is no longer open to atmosphere. At the same time, an internal air-inlet valve opens to supply the unloader port with system air pressure. Closing the exhaust passage while simultaneously opening the inlet passage enables reservoir pressure to flow around the governor inlet valve and to the unloader port. FIGURE 30-11 illustrates the governor circuit.

When the system reservoir air pressure drops to the cut-in pressure setting of the governor, the state of balance between system air pressure and governor spring pressure force will change. The piston will move to open the exhaust valve and close the inlet valve. Air in the unloader port is vented to the atmosphere and the compressor is loaded. A governor can be installed on the air compressor or remotely. An unloader line will connect the governor to the compressor's unloader port.

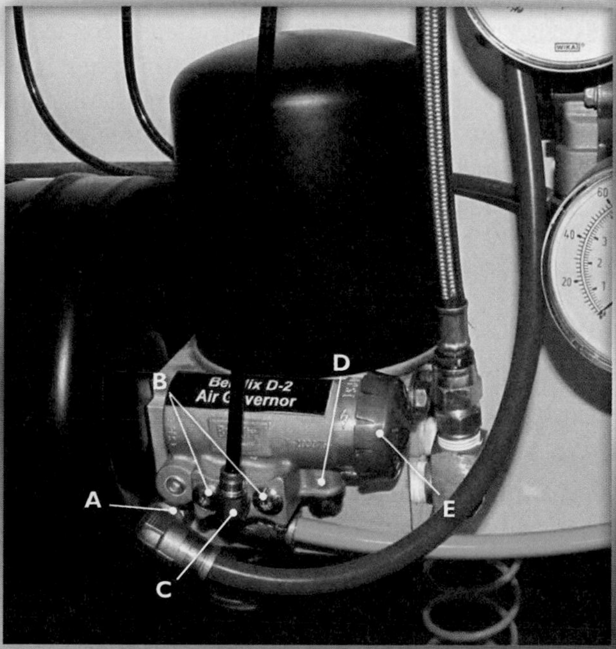

FIGURE 30-10 Governor valve with **A.** Reservoir port. **B.** Mounting bolts. **C.** Unloader port. **D.** Exhaust port. **E.** Top cover.

> **TECHNICIAN TIP**
>
> Governors are intended to be non-serviceable. Any abnormal change to system cut-in and cut-out pressures will require governor replacement and not an adjustment.

Air Reservoirs

Air reservoirs or air tanks on a vehicle store compressed air, allow it to cool, and provide a place for water and oil droplets to condense out of the air. FMVSS 121 standards require that the combined volume of all service reservoirs and supply reservoirs must be at least 12 times the combined volume of all service brake chambers at full stroke. This means the size of reservoirs is determined by the number of axles on the truck/tractor and trailer.

Reservoirs are designated as **service reservoir** (or **supply reservoir**), **primary reservoir**, and **secondary reservoir** according to the circuits they supply. Each reservoir must be equipped with a manual drain valve to remove condensed water and oil unless a third tank, the supply tank, is used. The supply tank, also called the **wet tank**, is the first reservoir receiving air from the compressor. Its function is to collect any remaining water and oil left in the compressed air.

The tank has at least two valves. One is an air pressure **safety relief valve**, which releases air if the tank

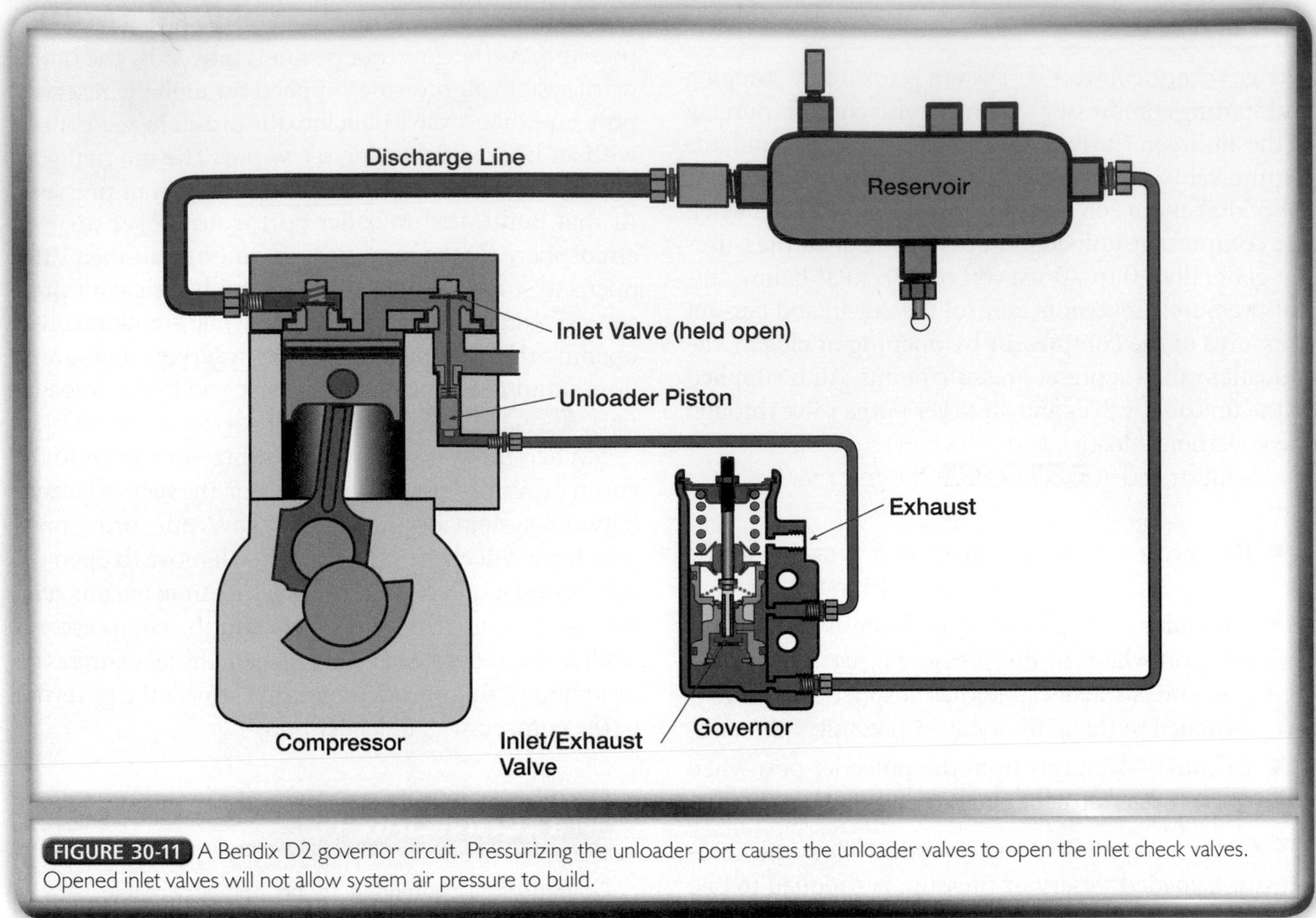

FIGURE 30-11 A Bendix D2 governor circuit. Pressurizing the unloader port causes the unloader valves to open the inlet check valves. Opened inlet valves will not allow system air pressure to build.

pressure climbs above 150 psi (1,034 kPa). The second valve is a one-way check valve between the service tank and the primary or secondary tank. Only one-way flow of air pressure, from the primary to secondary tanks, is permitted using the check valve. This valve prevents air from leaking back from either the primary or secondary tank if there is a failure causing the service tank to lose air. Air can leave the service tank but it cannot flow back into the service tank from the primary or secondary reservoir. Some reservoirs have an integral service and primary or secondary reservoir. An internal baffle separating the two tanks will contain an integral one-way check valve, which is not serviceable. FIGURE 30-12 shows a reservoir safety valve.

The service tank often has a **one-way check valve** located at its inlet to prevent a loss of air from the service tank through a failed air dryer or compressor supply circuit. Operation of the one-way check valve after the service tank can be checked by opening the drain valve on the service tank and draining the air pressure. By observing the air pressure gauges in the cab, both the primary and secondary tank pressures should remain at cut-out pressure.

Quick connect air fittings, such as the ones shown in FIGURE 30-13, are now commonly used to connect air lines to reservoirs and valves. These fitting are a "push to seal" type connecter. Simply inserting the line into the fitting and pushing will automatically seal the line. Disconnecting the fitting involves pushing the line into the fitting slightly while pushing a sliding collar around the fitting. When the collar is pushed in, the line can be pulled to release the line.

Valves

In addition to the safety relief valve and the one-way check valve, air systems use several other important valves. These include unloader valves, inlet regulating valve, a turbocharger cut-off valve, pressure protection valves, and drain valves.

Unloader Valves

Air intake and discharge valves are located in the cylinder head. Discharge or exhaust valves are one-way check valves ensuring air pushed out of the cylinder only goes to the air discharge line. The intake valves can also function as one-way check valves, except they can be mechanically

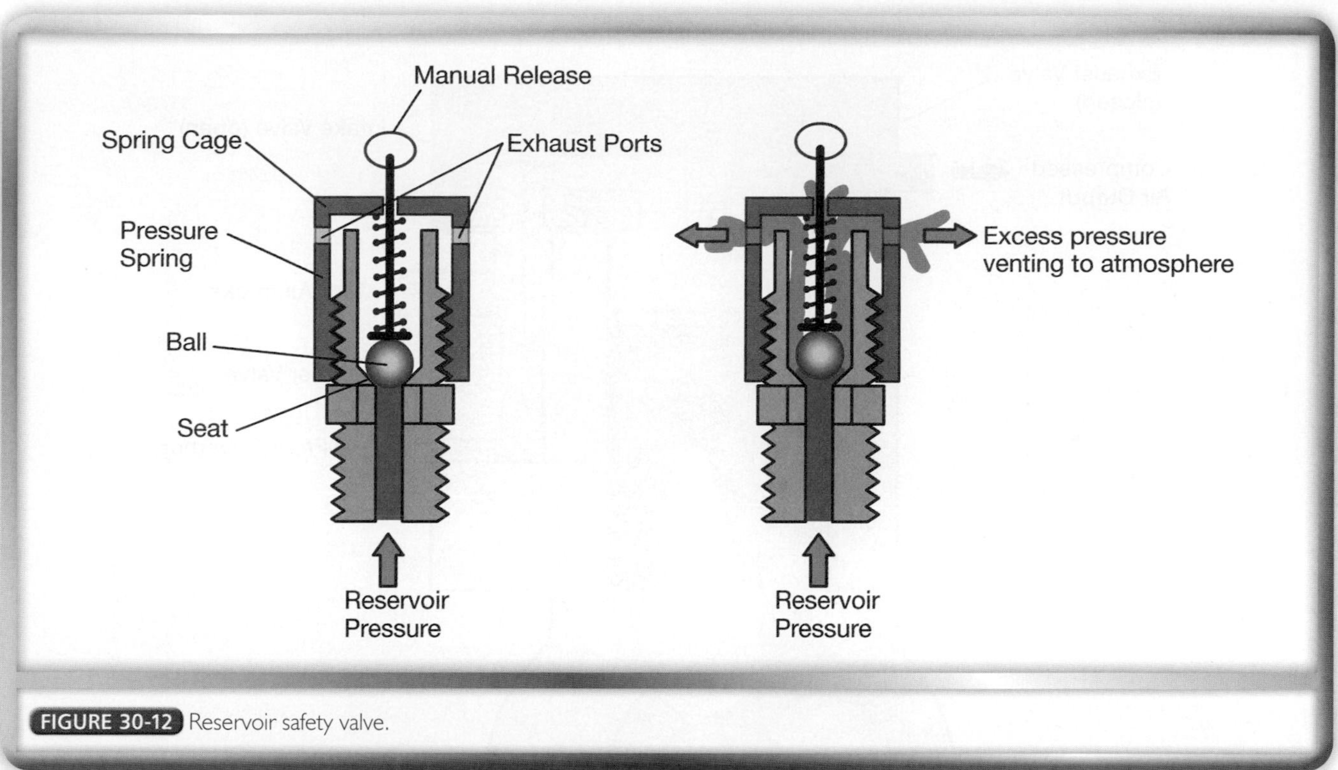

FIGURE 30-12 Reservoir safety valve.

FIGURE 30-13 Quick connect fittings (circled).

held open, allowing air to move in and out of the cylinder through the valves. Air pressure acting on small pistons will hold the intake valves open when there is no requirement to build air pressure. When system air pressure is needed, the pistons are retracted away from the intake valve stems, allowing them to function as one-way check valves. These pistons, controlling intake valve operation, are called **unloader valves**. **Unloading** refers to the state when an air compressor is not pumping air—or is unloaded. As illustrated in FIGURE 30-14, when the compressor is **loading**—that is, building up system air pressure—unloader valves have no air pressure applied to them and are retracted.

Unloader valves in some air compressors, such as Meritor's, use a sliding plate or leaf valves to load and unload the compressor. When unloaded, a sliding leaf opens an internal passageway during the upstroke, which

TECHNICIAN TIP

Slow build-up time from an air compressor may not be due to a worn compressor or a defective governor. Leaking or stuck unloader valves are often to blame. If valves have carbonized oil around their seats or if the O-ring seals around the valves are deteriorated and allow air to leak past the valve, the result is poor compressor efficiency since intake air is pushed out the intake check valves when loading. If shop air pressure is applied to the governor port on the air compressor, it *should not be heard* leaking around the unloader valves. A defective discharge valve should not leak air either. And, if air is applied to the compressor discharge port, there should be no audible air leaks. A leaking discharge valve can allow reservoir pressure to leak back through the compressor and drain the reservoir.

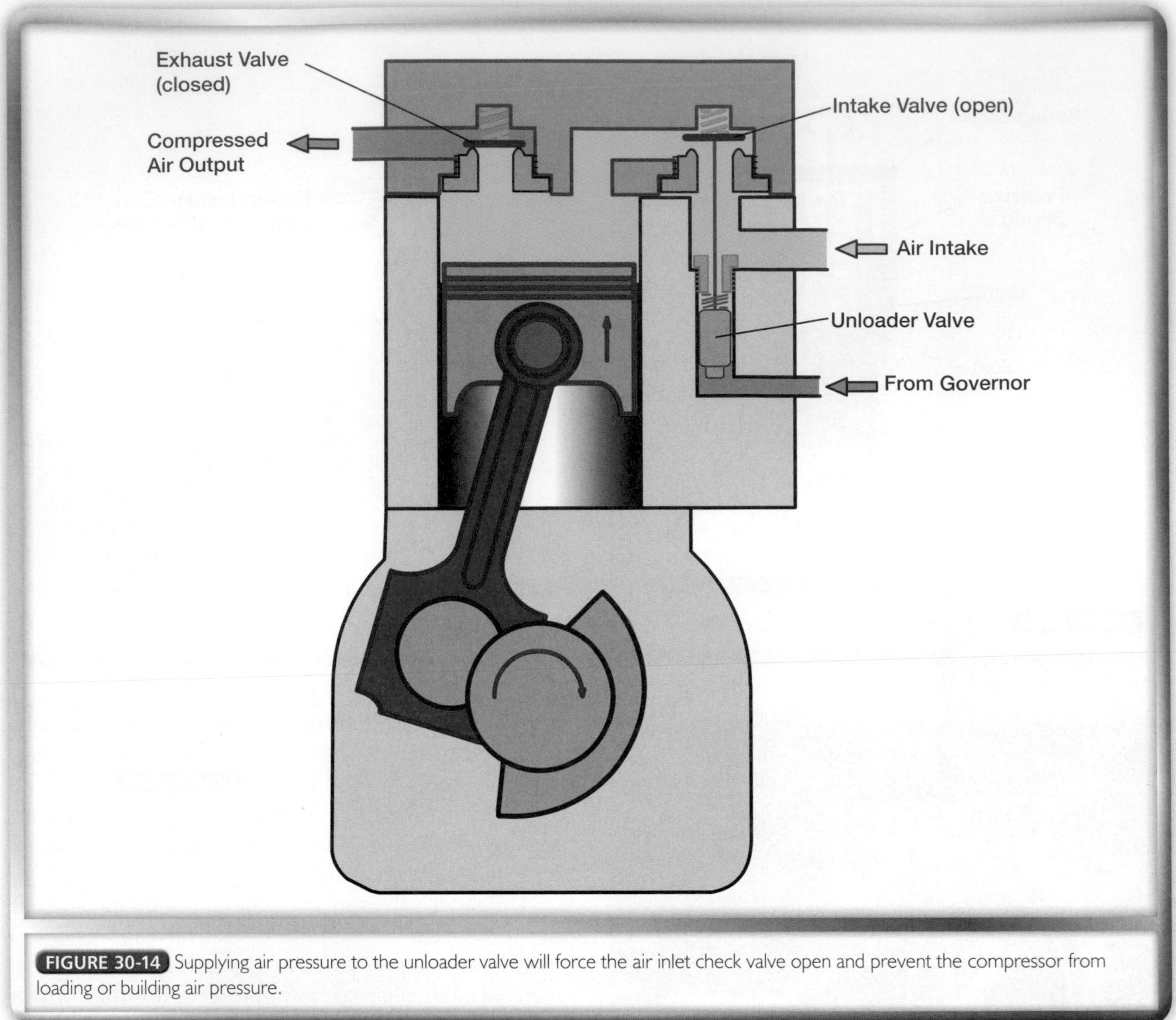

FIGURE 30-14 Supplying air pressure to the unloader valve will force the air inlet check valve open and prevent the compressor from loading or building air pressure.

allows air in the cylinder to pass back into the air inlet port and bypass the inlet check valves. Air drawn into the cylinders is simply pushed back into the air inlet of the cylinder head and pressure cannot build in the cylinders. When system cut-in pressure is reached, air is exhausted from the unloader port of the governor and the sliding leaf closes the passageway that had allowed air to bypass the inlet check valves. This means air is not dumped back into the air inlet and must pass through the compressor discharge valve or one-way check valves to leave the cylinders.

Inlet Regulating Valve

Air supplied to the compressor is filtered through the engine air filter or the air compressor's own air filter. To build up air pressure faster and prevent slow build-up of system pressure at high altitudes, the compressor can receive its air from the engine's turbocharged boosted intake manifold. An **inlet pressure regulating valve** located in the compressor intake port will limit air pressure to approximately 10 psi (69 kPa) if supplied with turbocharged air. The 10 psi (69 kPa) limit will reduce the compression temperatures of the compressed air, which can potentially damage the compressor and lead to excessively high air discharge temperatures.

Turbocharger Cut-Off Valve

On turbocharged engines, which are supplied air from the pressurized intake manifold, boost air pressure can also pass through the compressor inlet and leak out the exhaust port of the air dryer when the compressor and air dryer are unloaded. To prevent a loss of engine intake boost pressure through the compressor when it is unloaded, pressurized air from the governor unloader port will close a valve in the compressor discharge line when the compressor unloads. **Turbocharger cut-off valves** are located in either the air compressor or internal to the air dryer. On compressors that have an air inlet connected to atmospheric pressure, the cut-off valve eliminates the "puffing" noise of air passing in and out of the compressor cylinder when unloaded. FIGURE 30-15 shows a turbocharger cut-off valve.

Pressure Protection Valves

Pressure protection valves, such as the one illustrated in FIGURE 30-16, are normally closed, pressure-sensitive air control valves. When air is shared between two reservoirs or an auxiliary air circuit, the valve will flow air only above the closing setting of the valve. A typical valve setting is 70–85 psi (483–586 kPa). This means that, until reservoir pressure is above the valve setting, no air will flow to the circuit or air accessory.

FIGURE 30-15 The turbo cut-off valve is typically integrated with the air dryer inlet.

Pressure protection valves can be used in many different applications, but are typically used to protect or isolate one reservoir from another. They do this by closing automatically at a preset pressure. The valve is also commonly used to delay the filling of auxiliary reservoirs until a preset pressure is achieved in the primary or secondary air reservoirs. Reservoir pressure can then build faster to release the park brakes. Air-operated accessories that are not part of the air brake system often use a pressure protection valve to prevent a loss of air from affecting the braking system. Accessories such as the air ride suspension, air seats, horns, and so on can leak, but the pressure protection valve functions to supply air only above preset value. Once tank pressure falls below the threshold set by the pressure protection valve, air to the accessories is shut off.

Drain Valves

Each reservoir must be equipped with a drain valve, such as the one shown in FIGURE 30-17, to remove water and oil that may contaminate supply system air. The tanks should be drained regularly between 30 and 90 days. **Automatic drain valves** are also used to drain sludge-like residues as they accumulate. As illustrated in FIGURE 30-18, a typical automatic drain valve will purge sludge every time the tank pressure rises and falls. An inlet valve to the sump of

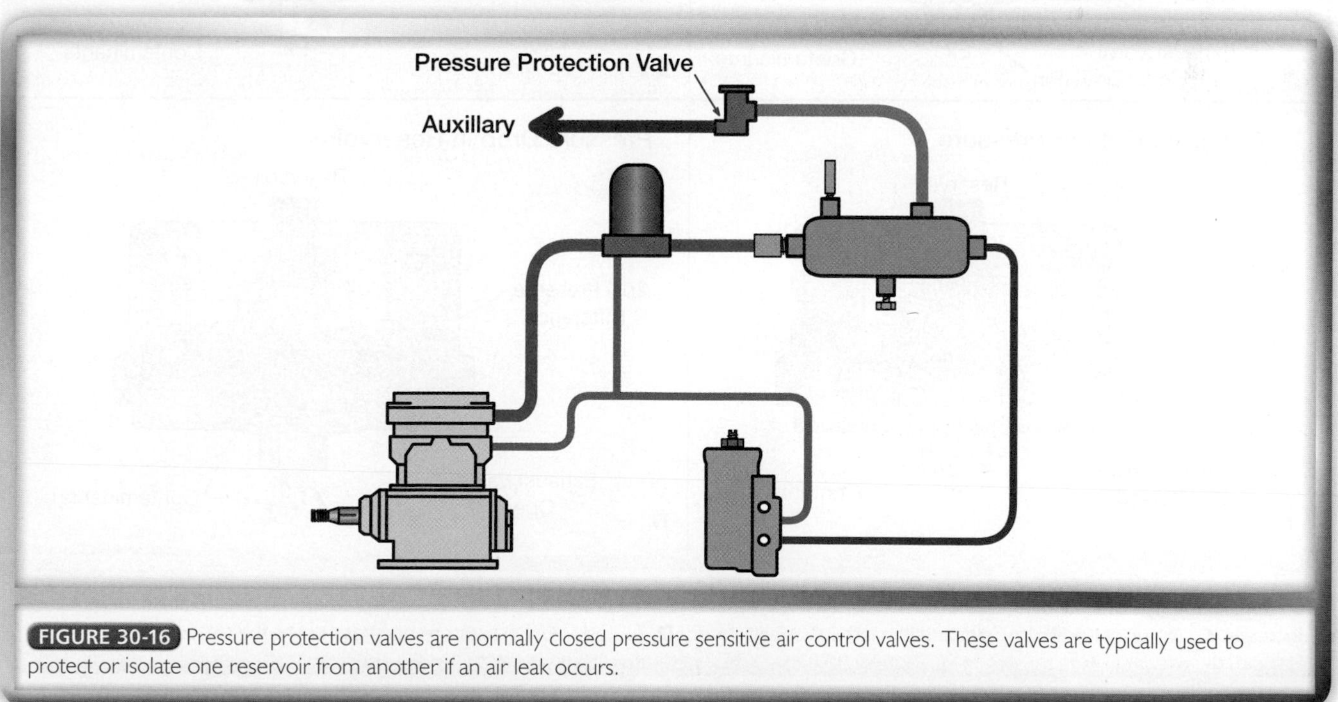

FIGURE 30-16 Pressure protection valves are normally closed pressure sensitive air control valves. These valves are typically used to protect or isolate one reservoir from another if an air leak occurs.

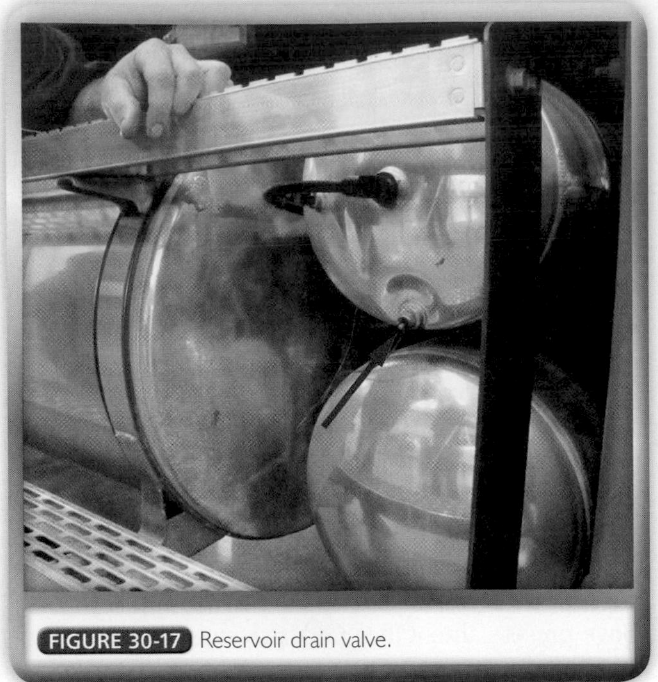

FIGURE 30-17 Reservoir drain valve.

an automatic drain valve will open when reservoir pressure is low. This allows any contaminants to drain into the valve. The same valve will close when governor cut-out pressure is reached. When reservoir pressure drops 2 psi (14 kPa), an exhaust valve in the drain valve opens due to a slight pressure differential between the upper and lower surfaces of the valve's diaphragm. The reservoir pressure drop causes the sludge accumulated in the valve sump to drain. The length of time the exhaust valve remains open and the amount of sludge purged from the reservoir depends on the air pressure in the sump just as the intake valve closes and how slowly the air pressure in the reservoir stabilizes.

Air Dryers

Air dryers are like an in-line filtration system used to remove air contaminants passed by the air compressor. Water and oil droplets discharged from the compressor can form sludge that fouls valves, blocks lines, and generally interferes with the operation of the air delivery

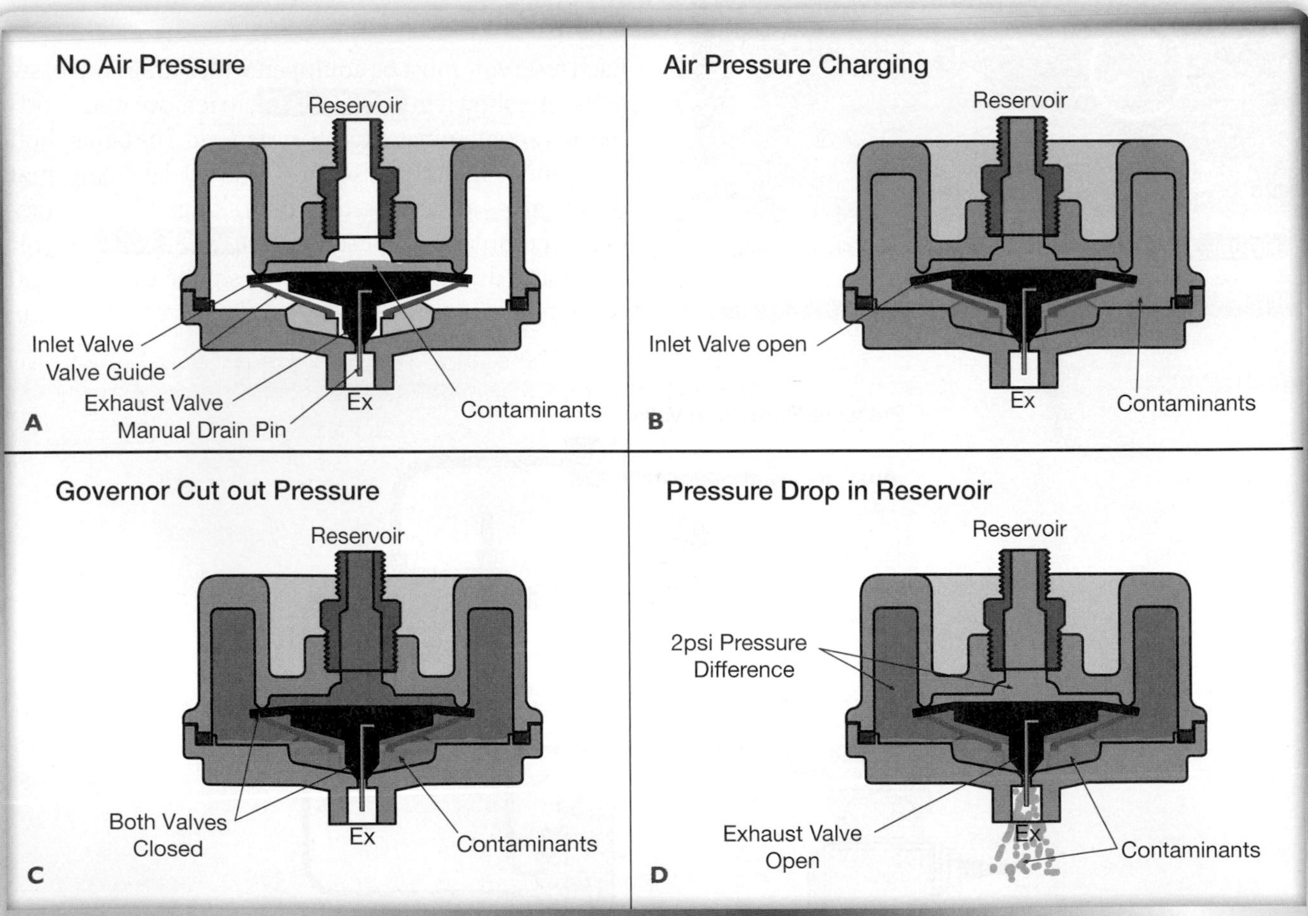

FIGURE 30-18 Automatic drain valve operation. **A.** No air pressure in reservoir. **B.** When reservoir pressure builds, contaminants increase. **C.** At cut-out pressure, inlet and exhaust valves are closed. **D.** A 2 psi (14 kPa) pressure decrease drains the valve.

system. Furthermore, in winter temperatures, moisture will freeze and block proper airflow through lines and valves.

To prolong the service life of the air brake system and reduce maintenance costs, systems generally include an air dryer. The air dryer provides clean, dry air to the components of the brake system. Daily draining of the reservoirs using manually operated drain valves can be eliminated when using air dryers.

Air dryers use a replaceable desiccant cartridge to trap oil and water discharged from the compressor by a process known as **adsorbtion**. The dryer **desiccant** is made up of tiny silica beads that are a tough granular material capable of adsorbing water and oil into their surface. Adsorbtion means that the water and oil basically sticks to the surface of the beads. FIGURE 30-19 shows the millions of beads that make up a desiccant cartridge and give the air dryer enormous adsorption capabilities.

The majority of oil droplets are first removed by the metal oil separator as the air passes into the air dryer. As shown in FIGURE 30-20, metal fibers trap oil even more effectively than desiccant. After entering the dryer, air passes through the desiccant before moving into the service reservoir. Water and any remaining oil stick to the desiccant beads as air passes through the desiccant.

FIGURE 30-19 **A.** Desiccant in an air dryer. **B.** Purge valve.

FIGURE 30-20 Air dryer with oil separator (indicated).

Charge and Purge Cycle

Air enters the dryer during the charge cycle when the compressor is loading. In its base, the dryer contains a **purge valve**. An air signal line connects the governor's unloader port to the dryer's purge valve. During this charging period, the purge valve is closed. When the compressor unloads, the dryer purge valve opens and causes the trapped air volume in the dryer to blast out the bottom of the dryer. The air carries oil and water out with it. The burst of air from the dryer lasts just a few seconds but indicates the finish of a **purge cycle**. Air may take as long as 30 seconds to completely drain from the desiccant.

The turbo cut-off valve, which is often integrated into the dryer inlet port, closes when the compressor unloads. This action prevents any further entry of air into the dryer and prevents a loss of boost pressure from the engine intake manifold into the dryer through the open compressor intake valves. A check valve at the air dryer's outlet air line prevents any reservoir air from leaking back into the dryer after it is purged. The air dryer charge cycle is illustrated in FIGURE 30-21 and the purge cycle in FIGURE 30-22.

Since moisture passes by the purge valve before exhausting out of the dryer, the purge valve can potentially freeze open in cold weather. If this happens, an open purge valve would not allow the air system pressure to build. Air would simply pass directly out of the

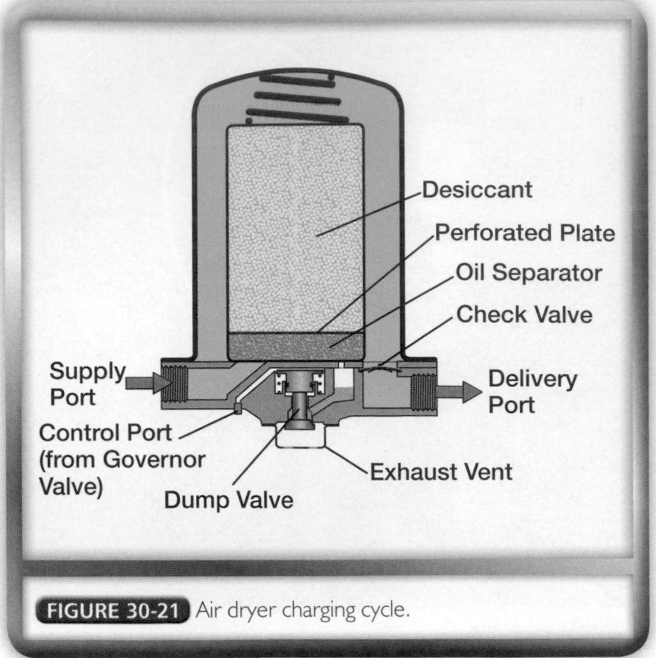

FIGURE 30-21 Air dryer charging cycle.

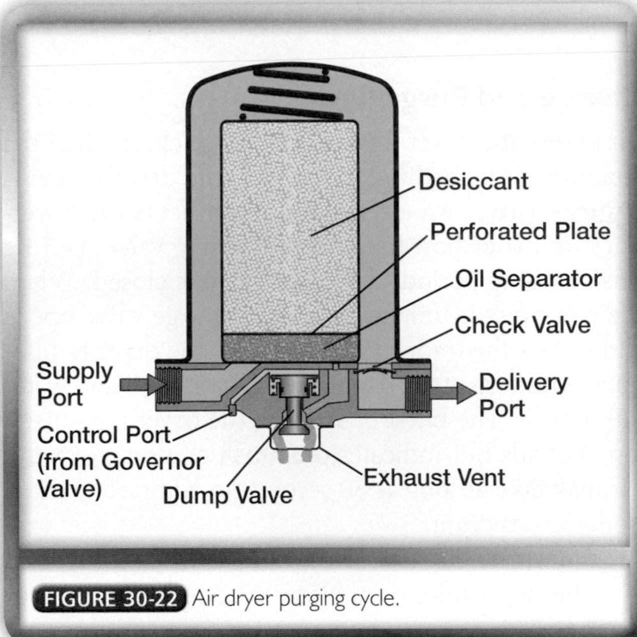

FIGURE 30-22 Air dryer purging cycle.

TECHNICIAN TIP

Most air dryers today use easy to replace, spin-on replaceable desiccant cartridges. It is important to replace cartridges at recommended service intervals and whenever an air compressor has failed. A slow air build-up may also be due to air flow restriction caused by contamination inside the dryer desiccant. For safety reasons, always completely drain air from the vehicle's air brake system since cartridges can suddenly "blow-off" the dryer housing when removed for service.

purge valve. To prevent this freezing, a thermostatically controlled electric heating element is embedded in the air dryer housing. Heating elements and other parts should be replaced during rebuild procedures. Overhaul kits containing purge valves, electric heaters, thermostats, and other components are available for overhaul.

Safety

One-way check valves between the service tank, air dryer, and even the air compressor will allow air pressure to remain in the dryer connecting lines even after draining all air reservoirs. Use caution when disconnecting these lines to minimize the hazard of whipping lines and blasts of air pressure. Lines should be slowly loosened and allowed to drain before completely disconnecting. Also make sure the purge valve is in the unloaded position before removing the cartridge.

Advanced Air Dryer Technologies

Along with every other vehicle system, air dryers have evolved technologically to improve fuel economy, reduce emissions and fuel consumption, or simplify air system design and operation.

One air dryer design by Bendix integrates the spin-on desiccant cartridge, turbocharger cut-off valve, governor, and four pressure-protection valves together into a single component. The **Air Dryer Integrated System (AD-IS)** dryer by Bendix, shown in FIGURE 30-23, works with the air supply system to isolate air brake reservoir circuits against complete pressure failures.

Since every reservoir is supplied through the dryer, pressure protection valves set to 70 psi (483 kPa) will

FIGURE 30-23 Bendix AD-IS air dryer.

automatically close to isolate a reservoir if pressure falls below that level. Even if all brake circuits fail, the dryer will maintain at least 100 psi (689 kPa) in one reservoir. That minimum level of pressure allows the vehicle to have some limited braking ability while being moved in an emergency situation. Without this reservoir protection feature, a loss of air pressure in a single tank could potentially provide only a few limited brake applications before the emergency/park brakes would apply. FIGURE 30-24 illustrates this process in the AD-IS air dryer.

The **Dryer Integrated Module (DRM)** is another version of the AD-IS dryer. As FIGURE 30-25 illustrates, the DRM features an additional small supplemental reservoir to provide additional purge volume to the dryer desiccant cartridge. Because the dessicant cartridge itself typically does not have adequate purge volume, dried air in the supplemental reservoir is used to remove more moisture and contaminants from the dryer.

The Bendix **Electronic Air Control (EAC)** shown in FIGURE 30-26 is an air supply system consisting of an electronically controlled air compressor clutch, air dryer, unloader valve, and multiple air circuit protection controls. The EAC is designed to help manufacturers meet the 2016 Greenhouse Gas Emission Standards by optimizing when the air compressor engages and disengages. The compressor clutch operates much like an on/off fan clutch except that the system collects data from a variety of vehicle sensors. The system is also connected to the vehicle's controlled area network (CAN) backbone, which provides input to software embedded into a control module.

The software contains algorithms (mathematical formulas used to solve problems) that ensure the compressor completely disengages from the engine when no air is required. This means that fuel is not wasted even due to the slight frictional losses from reciprocating pistons while unloaded.

One example of a strategy to reduce energy consumption is to have the compressor load during vehicle-engine deceleration. In the EAC, the mechanical governor is replaced with electronic control of an unloader valve, so compressor cycling is precisely controlled. Consequently, the frequency of overall compressor cycling drops. That reduction extends compressor life and generates up to 3% in fuel savings. Programmability of the system enables customized air pressure control and distributions based on customer priorities and information collected over the vehicle CAN.

Another Bendix system called the Bendix **PBS Injection Booster** and shown in FIGURE 30-27 uses an air-injection booster with the EAC dryer and compressor to reduce emissions and improve fuel economy. The

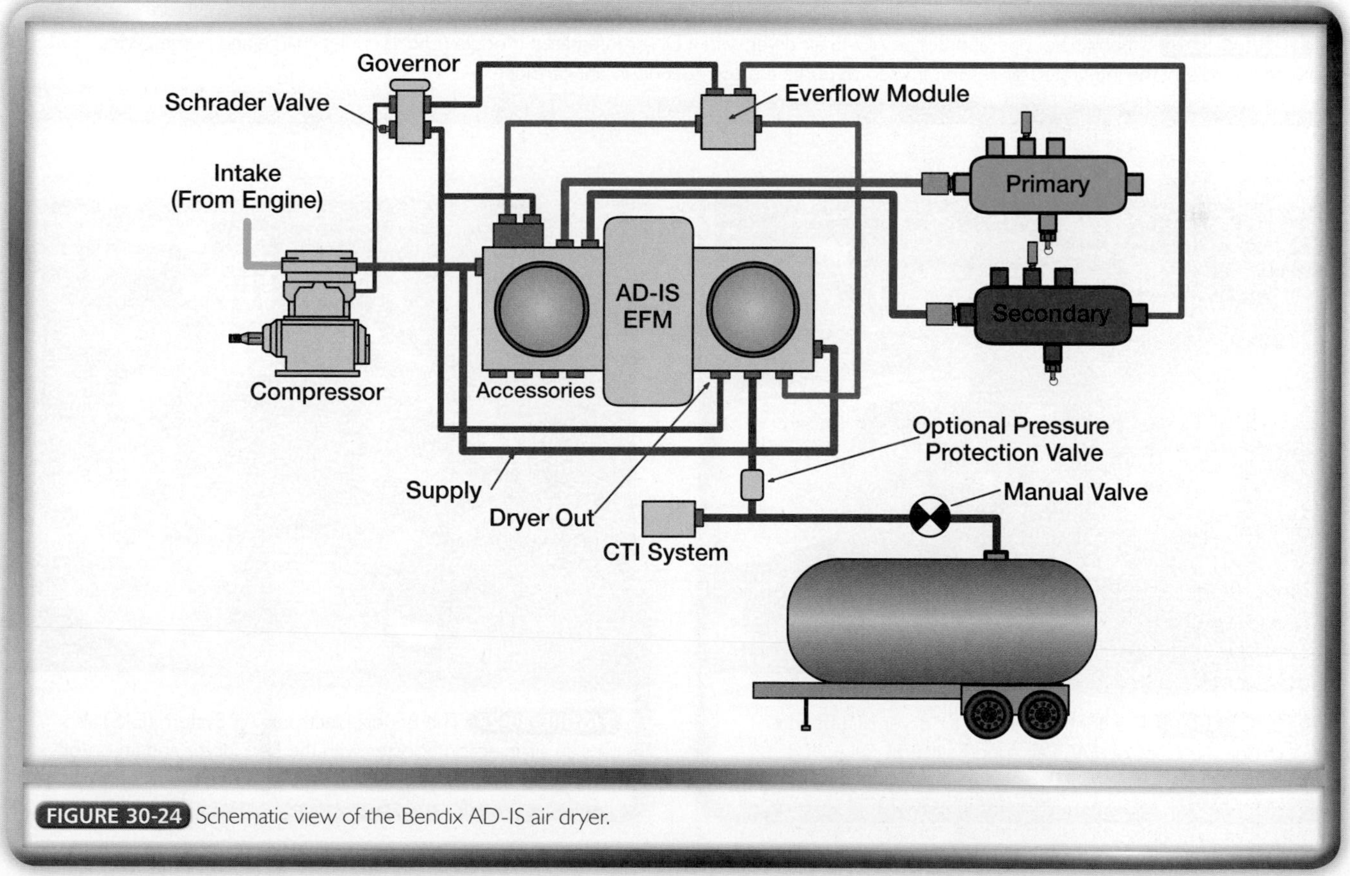

FIGURE 30-24 Schematic view of the Bendix AD-IS air dryer.

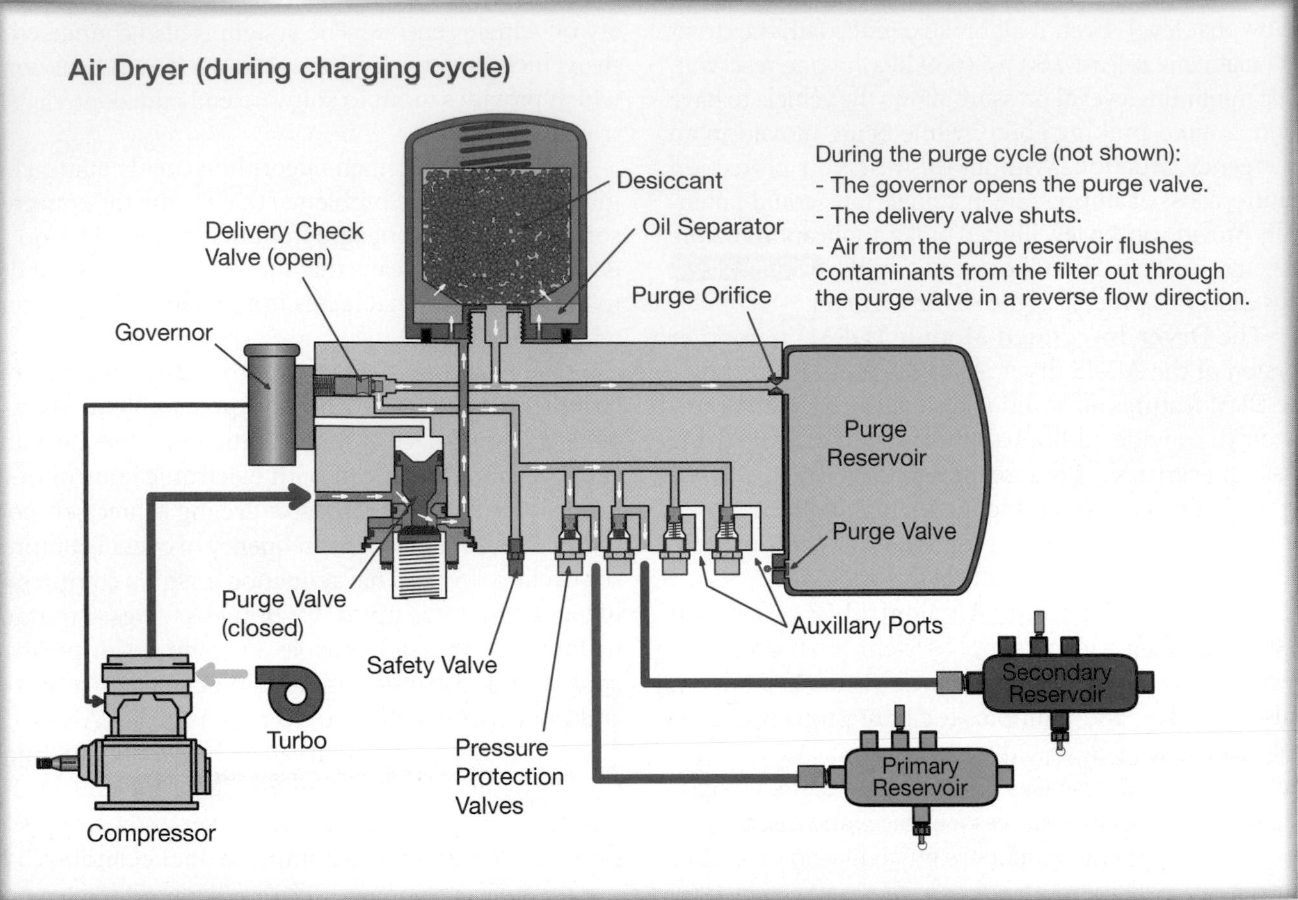

Air Dryer (during charging cycle)

During the purge cycle (not shown):
- The governor opens the purge valve.
- The delivery valve shuts.
- Air from the purge reservoir flushes contaminants from the filter out through the purge valve in a reverse flow direction.

Desiccant
Oil Separator
Delivery Check Valve (open)
Purge Orifice
Governor
Purge Reservoir
Purge Valve
Purge Valve (closed)
Auxillary Ports
Safety Valve
Secondary Reservoir
Turbo
Pressure Protection Valves
Primary Reservoir
Compressor

FIGURE 30-25 Schematic of operation of an AD-IS air dryer with a Dryer Integrated Module (DRM) during charge and purge cycles. Note the role of the integrated air reservoir used to purge the compact desiccant cartridge.

FIGURE 30-26 The control unit and air dryer of a Bendix Electronic Air Control (EAC) air supply system.

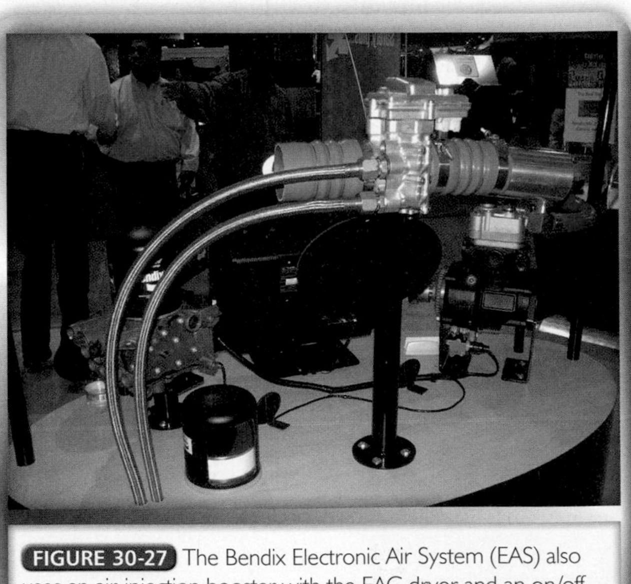

FIGURE 30-27 The Bendix Electronic Air System (EAS) also uses an air-injection booster with the EAC dryer and an on/off compressor to reduce emissions and improve fuel economy.

> **TECHNICIAN TIP**
>
> A leaking air dryer purge valve will allow air to leak from the unloader port of the governor causing frequent compressor cycling and air dryer purging. Likewise, a leaking air signal line from the air reservoir to the governor, a leaking governor gasket, or leaking unloader valves in the air compressor will cause frequent purging of the dryer. Defective O-rings sealing unloader valves can also leak air from the unloader port, resulting in unnecessary compressor cycling.

Bendix PBS works by injecting a blast of air into the intake manifold during the turbo lag period. The extra air enhances combustion efficiency, thereby reducing both emissions and fuel consumption. When the EAC dryer, air compressor with on/off clutch, and the PBS air-injection booster system are used together, Bendix claims that a vehicle will achieve up to an 8% reduction in fuel consumption.

Troubleshooting Problems in the Air Supply System

Troubleshooting problems in the air supply system begins with the dash gauges. Separate pressure gauges located in the driver's view in the instrument panel are required to indicate primary and secondary tank pressures. As FIGURE 30-28 shows, the gauges are typically color coded and labeled to distinguish pressure in the two circuits. An application air pressure gauge is sometimes located in the dash to measure air pressure applied to the service brake chambers.

Another important monitoring tool is the low-pressure switch such as the one in FIGURE 30-29. Both the primary and secondary tanks use a low-pressure switch to operate a low air pressure warning system. If either tank pressure falls below 65 psi (586 kPa), the low-pressure switch will illuminate a warning light in the driver's view and cause an audible alarm to sound.

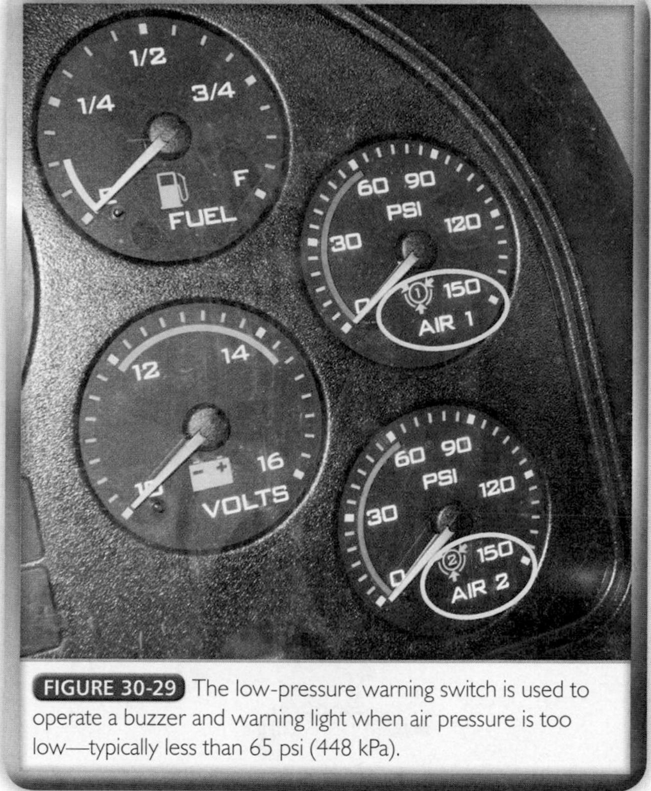

FIGURE 30-29 The low-pressure warning switch is used to operate a buzzer and warning light when air pressure is too low—typically less than 65 psi (448 kPa).

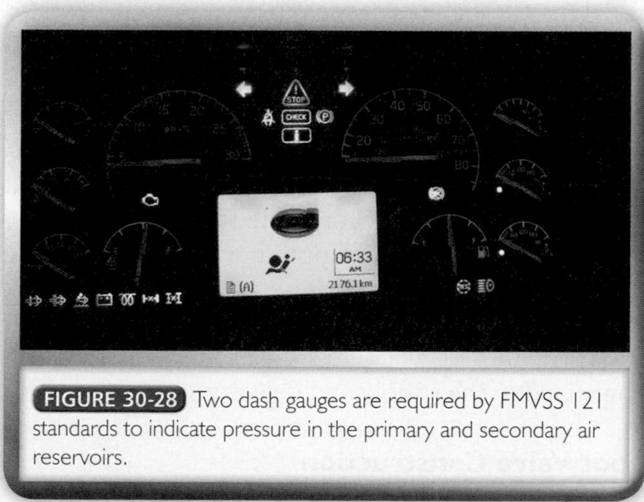

FIGURE 30-28 Two dash gauges are required by FMVSS 121 standards to indicate pressure in the primary and secondary air reservoirs.

Not all potential problems can be identified from the dashboard. For example, because oil is carried over from the air compressor and intake air has moisture, it is normal to have accumulations of oil in the reservoir tanks. To determine if the amount of oil is excessive, two oil drain tests can be performed.

The first test involves the use of a piece of paper held over the air inlet port. When the compressor is loaded, some oil droplets will spit out onto the paper. More than four or five droplets during a loading cycle of the compressor indicate an abnormal oil discharge. The likely cause is worn-out cylinders and worn or broken piston rings.

A second test involves draining the oil reservoir after service and measuring the amount of oil accumulated at the following service interval. After collecting the oil drained from the reservoir in a bottle, the amount of oil is compared against a calibrated oil level marked on the bottle. Depending on hours in service, only a limited amount of oil is considered normal. Excessive accumulations are likely caused by a defective air compressor.

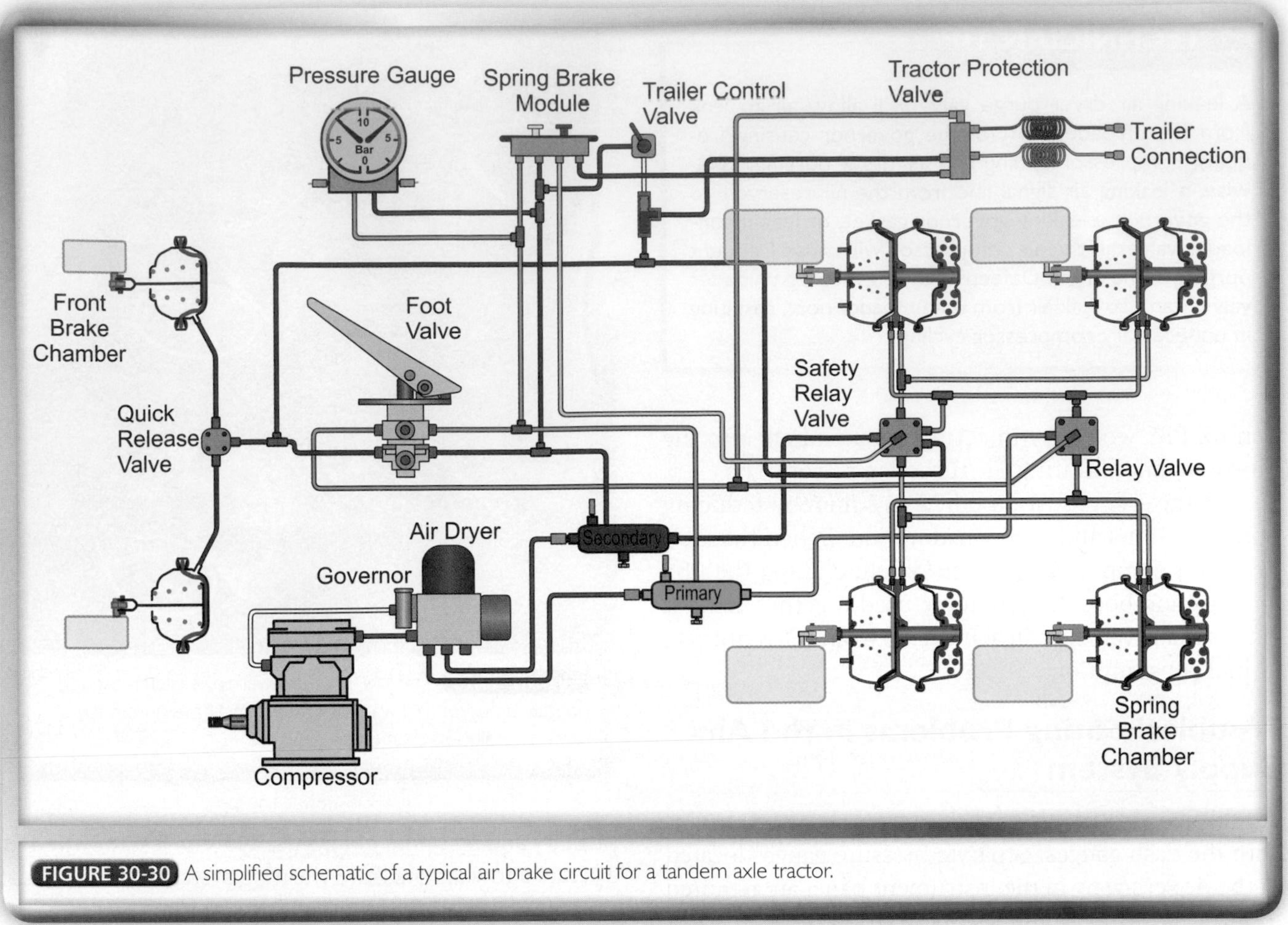

FIGURE 30-30 A simplified schematic of a typical air brake circuit for a tandem axle tractor.

Components of Air Delivery and Control Systems

In addition to having an effective air supply system, the air brakes must also have a reliable air delivery system. The delivery system transmits controlled air pressure from the reservoirs to the brake chambers. A typical system is illustrated in FIGURE 30-30 and consists of:

- A foot brake valve and often an additional hand-operated trailer service brake control valve
- Relay valves that speed up the application of air pressure to brake chambers
- Anti-compounding system design to prevent both the service brakes and the parking brakes being applied at the same time
- Proportioning valves to adjust braking force when a tractor is not pulling a trailer
- Quick-release valves to assist in releasing the brakes quickly
- Push-pull hand operated valves for parking using the spring brakes

Foot Valves

The **foot (treadle) valve**, like that illustrated in FIGURE 30-31, is the center of the delivery system. It distributes air to the brake chambers and controls the air pressure supplied for braking. By depressing the brake pedal, the foot valve delivers air pressure proportional to pedal travel. That means the further down the operator depresses the foot valve, the more air pressure is delivered to the brake chambers. Since all air brake vehicles use dual circuits, there are two foot valves contained in a single housing—one each for the primary and secondary circuits.

Two sets of ports corresponding to the primary and secondary circuits are incorporated into the foot valve. The first set includes a supply port from each of the primary and secondary air reservoirs. The second set includes two delivery ports for the primary and secondary air circuits. FIGURE 30-32 shows how a foot valve is connected to the supply and delivery systems.

Foot Valve Construction

The top part of the foot valve always contains the primary circuit control valve. The bottom part always

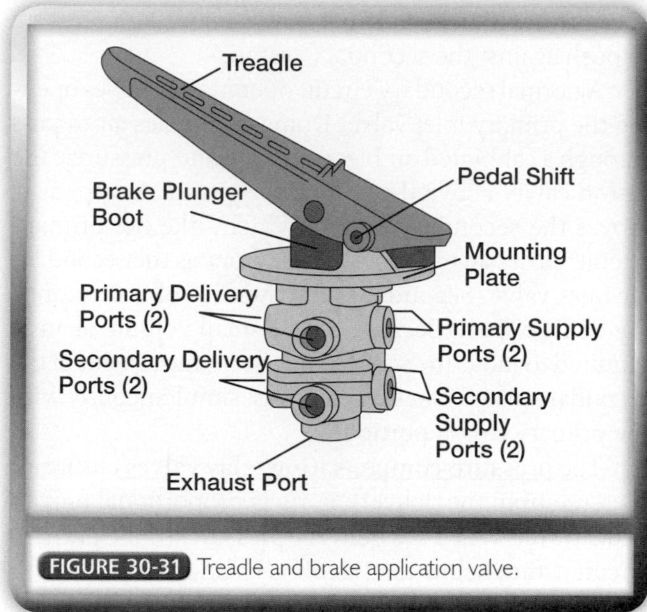

FIGURE 30-31 Treadle and brake application valve.

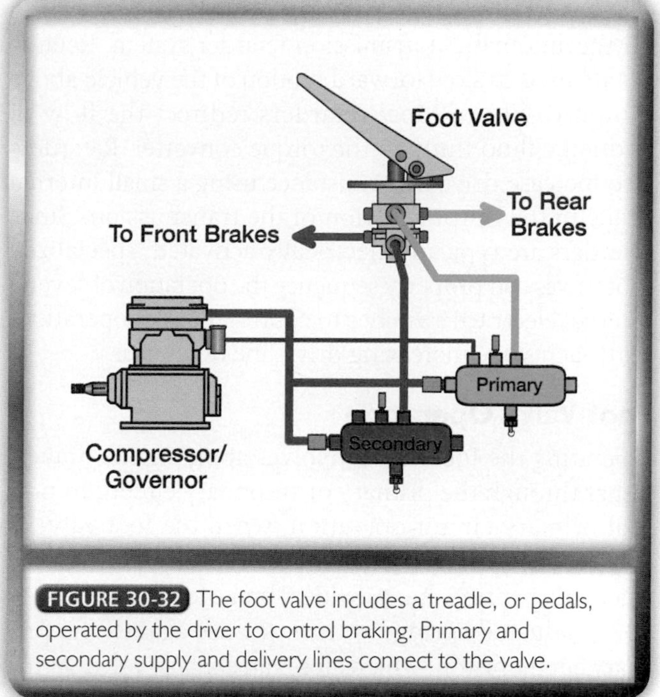

FIGURE 30-32 The foot valve includes a treadle, or pedals, operated by the driver to control braking. Primary and secondary supply and delivery lines connect to the valve.

contains the secondary control circuit. This division is done for safety reasons. The primary circuit should activate sooner than the secondary to time the brake application events from the rear of the vehicle and then forward. Also, if the primary circuit failed, pressure would be mechanically transferred to the secondary circuit's control plunger. Brake pedal "feel" is supplied by either a rubber or metal spring outside the valve, next to the primary piston. Spring tension increases the harder the pedal is pushed.

Foot valves can be either floor mounted or suspended to the firewall or bulkhead of the cab. FIGURE 30-33 shows a foot valve suspended from the firewall. The foot valve is spring loaded. Therefore, the operator feels only the spring pressure—not the pressure of the brake application as in a hydraulic brake system. Depending on the application—transit bus or on-highway truck—the valves are designed to be more or less sensitive to pedal travel. Valves for transit applications use more pedal travel to supply the same pressure than truck valves do. More pedal travel in a bus allows the operator to apply the brakes more gradually for smoother and less sensitive brake application. Smooth braking protects passengers from abrupt stops.

Foot valves are self-balancing or **pressure-balanced** devices. In other words, even if a small leak occurred in the air circuit after the valve during a brake application, the foot valve would continuously supply and regulate the application air pressure at a constant pressure to maintain consistent brake application pressure. Maximum brake application pressure can be no higher than the system reservoir pressure. When the foot valve is released, the brake application is released.

FIGURE 30-33 Foot valve designed to be mounted to the firewall.

A foot valve can also incorporate electrical switches for the automatic transmission retarder system. Retarders are used to slow forward motion of the vehicle above 5 mph (8 kpm). Most retarders redirect the flow of hydraulic fluid through the torque converter. Retarders also increase drive line resistance using a small internal brake in the output section of the transmission. Since retarders are typically electrically activated, specialized foot valves can properly sequence the operation of several internal electrical switches to control retarder operation, with each stage increasing drive line resistance.

Foot Valve Operation

Operating the foot valve involves applying the brakes, either through the primary or secondary circuit. In normal primary circuit operation, when the foot valve is depressed, a plunger in the top of the valve pushes on a graduating spring that provides "brake feel" to the driver. The graduated spring, in turn, pushes against the primary circuit piston, which closes an exhaust valve. At the same time the exhaust valve closes, the primary circuit inlet valve is opened and routes primary air supply to flow out the primary circuit delivery port. This process is illustrated in FIGURE 30-34. Pushing on the brake treadle compresses the graduating spring and transmits pedal force to the primary piston. An air bleed passageway from the delivery side of the primary valve supplies air pressure to push against the secondary piston.

A normal secondary circuit operation involves opening the primary inlet valve. Doing so enables air to pass through a calibrated air bleed passage and pressurize the piston cavity above the secondary piston. Air pressure moves the secondary piston, which, like the primary circuit, closes an exhaust valve and opens the secondary air inlet valve. Secondary air flows out of the secondary delivery port. Because only a small volume of air is required to move the secondary piston, movement of the secondary piston takes place almost simultaneously with the primary circuit portion.

The **pressure-compensating relay valves** ensure air pressure from the delivery ports is proportional only to pedal travel. When the delivery pressure for the primary circuit acting below the piston is balanced equally with the mechanical force of the brake pedal application, the air pressure will return the primary piston to a position that closes the air inlet valve. This action stops the flow of air into the primary circuit and delivery pressure stabilizes. As illustrated in FIGURE 30-35, the exhaust valve remains closed and no air is released through the exhaust port. If the foot valve is fully depressed, both the primary and secondary inlet valves remain open and full reservoir pressure is delivered to the brake chambers.

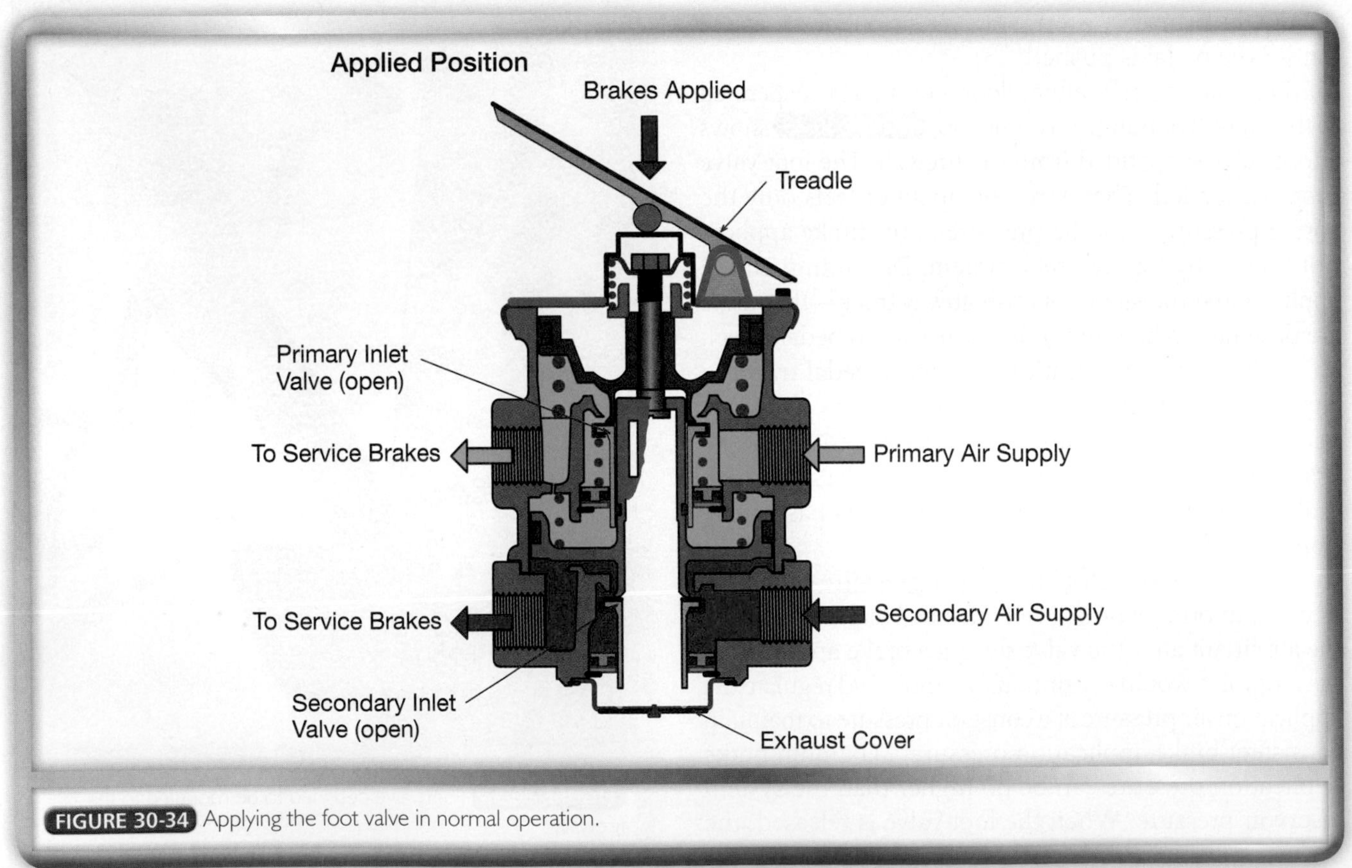

FIGURE 30-34 Applying the foot valve in normal operation.

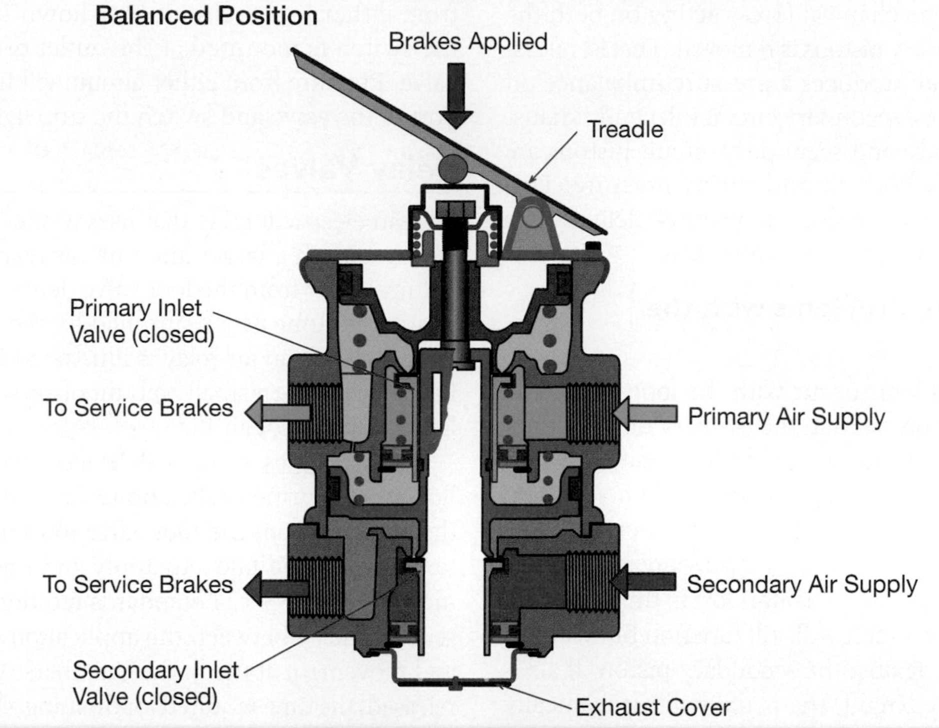

FIGURE 30-35 The foot valve in the balanced position.

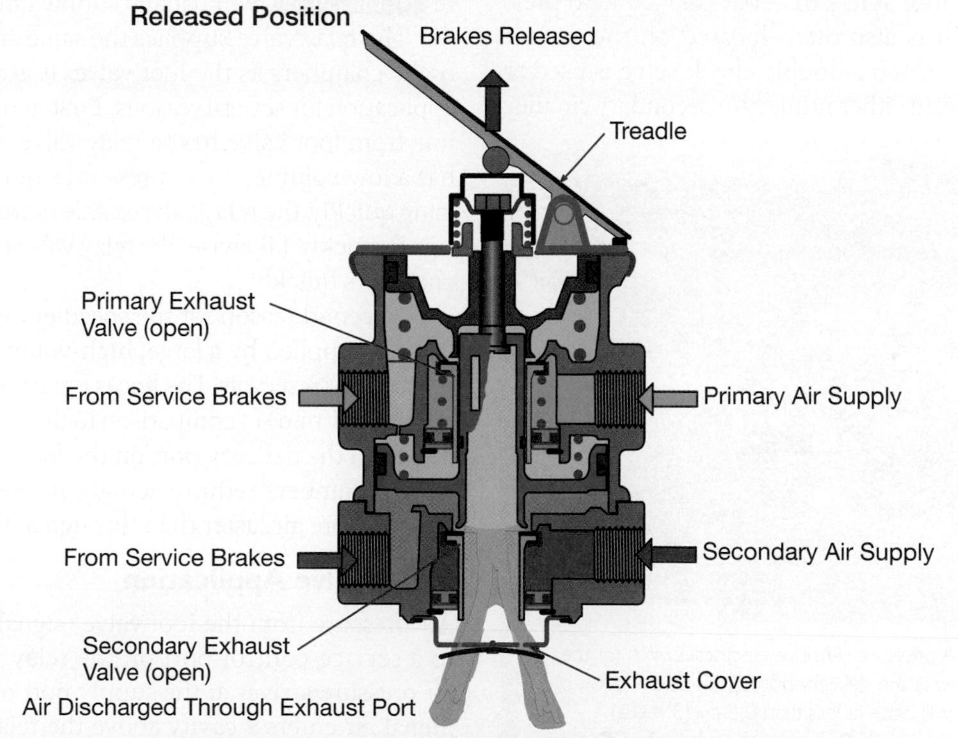

FIGURE 30-36 Releasing the brake pedal.

When the brake pedal is released, as illustrated in FIGURE 30-36, the mechanical forces acting on both the primary and secondary pistons is removed. That is, releasing the brake pedal produces a pressure imbalance on both the primary and secondary circuit inlet and exhaust valves. Both primary and secondary circuit pistons are forced upwards by both air and spring pressure. This action opens the exhaust valves, allowing all delivery line pressure to vent through the exhaust valve.

Troubleshooting Problems with the Foot Valve

Two common problems occur with the foot valve. The first is a loss of air pressure in the primary or secondary circuit. The second relates to an overly sensitive switch at the delivery port that activates the stop lights.

In the case of loss of air pressure, the foot valve can still operate. That is true whether air pressure is lost in the primary or secondary circuit. If air is lost in the secondary circuit, the primary circuit will still function but without the air-relay effect against the secondary piston. If air is lost in the primary circuit, the pedal will mechanically push the primary piston into the secondary piston to operate the secondary circuit. No air pressure will move the secondary piston downwards.

Sometimes a pressure-sensitive electrical switch located at the delivery port will activate the stop lights. The switch will close at less than 0.5 psi (3.4 kPa) pressure. This switch is also often located on the tractor protection valve. When a double check valve is used to supply pressure from either primary or secondary circuits, the stop light switch can be used to detect air pressure from either brake circuit. As shown in FIGURE 30-37, the switch is mounted at the outlet of a double check valve. Pressure from either circuit will flow to the outlet port of the valve and switch the stop lights on and off.

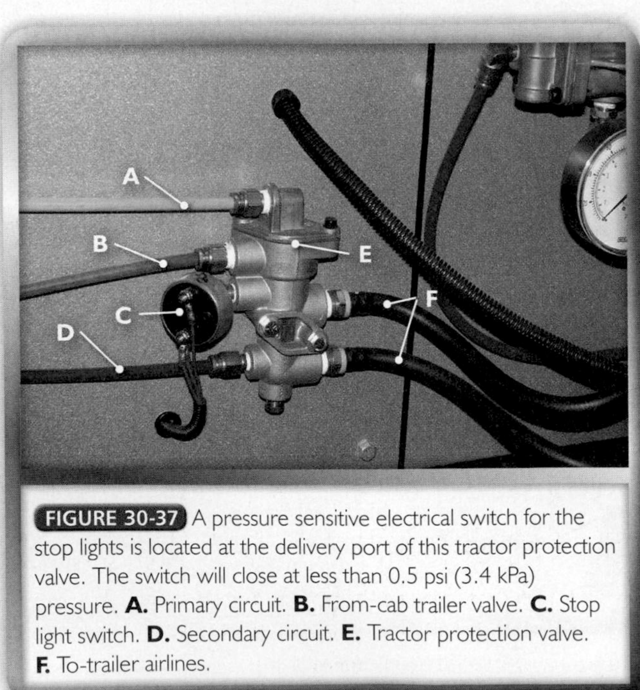

FIGURE 30-37 A pressure sensitive electrical switch for the stop lights is located at the delivery port of this tractor protection valve. The switch will close at less than 0.5 psi (3.4 kPa) pressure. **A.** Primary circuit. **B.** From-cab trailer valve. **C.** Stop light switch. **D.** Secondary circuit. **E.** Tractor protection valve. **F.** To-trailer airlines.

Relay Valves

Like an electrical relay that uses a small amount of current to switch a larger amount, air relays use the small volume of air from the foot valve delivery port to switch a larger volume of air supplied by the reservoir tanks. A circuit with an air relay is illustrated in FIGURE 30-38. Relay valves use a small amount of air volume to control larger volumes of air flow.

Relay valves are critical devices used to speed up the flow of air during brake applications and release. Since the air lines from the foot valve to brake chambers are long, the time it takes to apply and release brakes will increase. FMVSS 121 standards require less than 0.040 seconds delay between the application of the foot valve and movement at the brake chambers. When brakes are released, the time required for draining air from the chambers and lines through the exhaust port of the foot valve would take even longer than a brake application. To speed up brake application and release, relay valves are used for the rear brakes, and a quick-release valve is used for the front brakes. A single relay valve, like the one shown in FIGURE 30-39, will usually supply tandem rear axles.

The relay valve supplies the same air pressure to the brake chambers as the foot valve. It is able to speed up application for several reasons. First, it uses a small signal line from foot valve to the relay valve. Because the line has a low volume, it can pressurize quickly. By pressurizing quickly, the relay valve is able to transmit a pressure signal quickly. Likewise, the relay valve can also drain the chambers quickly.

A second reason for the speedier delivery is that the valve is supplied by a large, high-volume air supply line from the air reservoir. The line is typically 5/8" (15.9 mm) or ¾" (19.1 mm) in comparison to the ¼" (6.4 mm) signal line from the delivery port on the foot valve. When four brake chambers require actuation, the relay valve can supply more air faster than through a distant foot valve.

Relay Valve Application

Air pressure from the foot valve (signal air) is supplied to a service-control port on the relay valve. Reservoir air pressure arrives at the supply port of the relay valve. Signal air enters a cavity above the relay piston, which pushes the piston down against the spring pressure proportionally to the signal pressure. This means the relay valve piston will move a distance corresponding to the

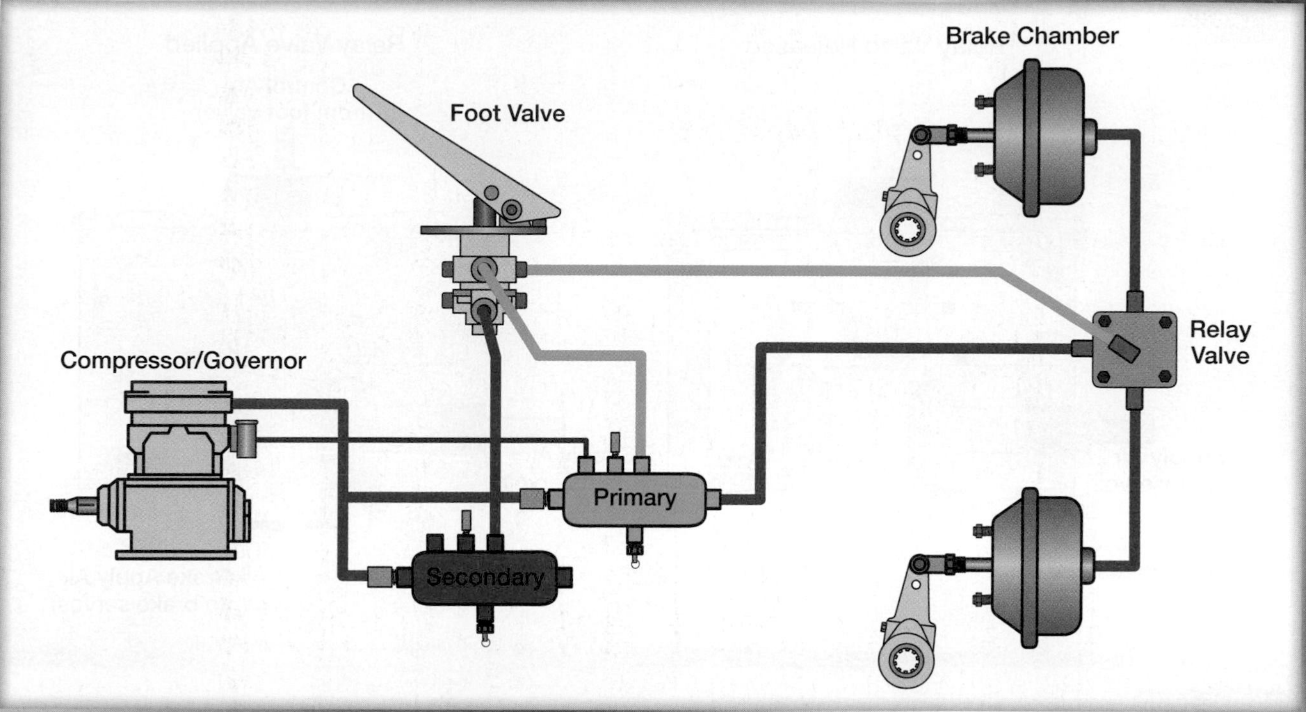

FIGURE 30-38 An air circuit with a relay valve.

force applied to the foot valve by the driver. An exhaust valve inside the relay valve seats simultaneously with the piston's downward movement, sealing off an exhaust passageway. At the same time, an air inlet port in the valve opens, so reservoir air supply flows past the open air inlet valve and into the brake chambers.

Pressure Compensating Balance

When pressure at the relay valve's outlet or delivery port equals the pressure supplied by the now open air inlet valve, air pressure beneath the relay piston equals the signal air pressure above the piston. This action causes the piston to lift slightly, which in turn closes the spring-loaded air inlet valve. That action is much like the inlet valve in the foot valve.

If no more air enters the cavity above the piston, the inlet valve remains seated and the exhaust valve remains closed, too. Air pressure to the brake chambers is held constant when inlet pressure and delivery pressure are equal. If there is a small leak at the chamber, the delivery port pressure will drop and unbalance the pressure acting on the piston. The inlet valve will open again until the state of balance returns. The **pressure-compensating balance valve** feature of air brake valves ensures a consistent delivery of air pressure is maintained in spite of leaks in the delivery system lines or air chambers.

FIGURE 30-39 Air line connections to a relay valve.

Relay Valve Release

When signal pressure from the foot valve drops due to reduced application pressure, air pressure in the cavity above the relay piston is lowered more than pressure below the piston. This condition lifts and unseats the exhaust valve, as is illustrated in FIGURE 30-40. Opening the exhaust passage vents air pressure in the brake chambers, which is expelled out the exhaust valve port, releasing the brakes.

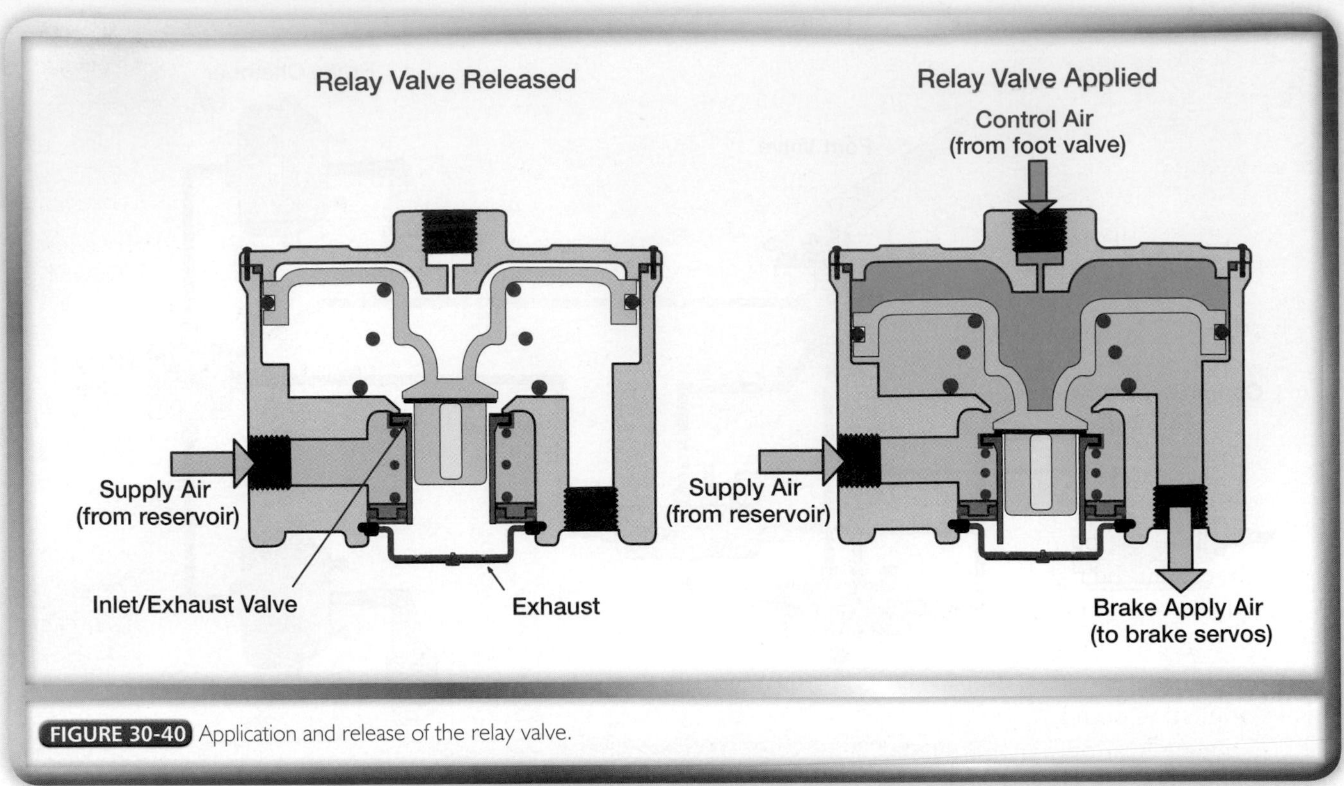

FIGURE 30-40 Application and release of the relay valve.

Pneumatic Brake Balance

Pneumatic balance is a critical aspect of brake balance. Timing brake applications in the correct sequence on each axle and having equal brake pressure at all wheel ends is necessary for safe vehicle operation. Without pneumatic balance, some brakes will work harder than others and brakes on an axle can lock up, leading to vehicle instability during braking, brake fade, and brake fires. Unequal application pressure will lead to uneven brake wear and some brakes overheating.

Without pneumatic balance, a vehicle will have a tendency to either jackknife or have the trailer swing out during hard braking events. **Jackknifing** occurs when the tractor's drive axle brakes have higher braking force than the trailer axles. If imbalance is present when road conditions are slippery or during a hard braking event, the tractor drive axles will likely lock up while the trailer axles are still rolling. Locked tractor axle brakes will cause the tractor to lose directional stability, as the tractor is sliding on the tires. A heavily loaded unbraked trailer will then push the tractor around the king pin.

During **trailer swing-out** the opposite occurs. Trailer swing-out occurs when the trailer brakes have higher levels of braking force than the tractor brakes. When trailer brakes are locked and directional stability is lost, the tractor will drag the trailer, causing it to swing out and into another lane.

Relay Valve Crack Pressures

To design an air braking system with good brake timing, where brake application occurs in the correct axle sequence, relay valves are available with different crack pressures. **Crack pressure** refers to the signal pressure required by the relay valve to begin supplying air to the brake chambers.

By changing the relay piston spring tension within the valve, which the air pressure signal is subject to and must exceed before air can be and is delivered to the brake chambers, timing of the brake application for tractor and trailer axles is varied. Ideally, the relay valve farthest away from the tractor will have the lowest crack pressure because air takes longer to travel that far. A crack pressure as low as 0.25 to 0.5 psi (1.72 to 3.45 kPa) is used on some trailer valves!

As expected, tractor relay valves will have a slightly higher crack pressure because signal air pressure reaches those valves sooner. Consider that 95% of brake applications are made at less than 25 psi (172 kPa), with 10 to 20 psi (69 to 138 kPa) being most common. At those levels, a difference of crack pressure as little as 4 psi (28 kPa) between tractor and trailer is enough to cause significant pneumatic imbalance leading to uneven brake torque.

Technicians making braking technique recommendations to vehicle operators need to understand the importance of pneumatic brake balance. Pneumatic balance is produced when air pressure is equal at all wheel ends. This means pneumatic imbalance will result if relay valve crack pressures are different. For example, a tractor may use a relay valve that has a 10 psi (69 kPa) crack pressure and a trailer being towed uses a 1 psi (7 kPa) crack pressure relay valve. Since frequent brake applications are made at less than 10 psi (69 kPa), generally only the trailer brakes would apply during controlled brake applications.

Testing done by University of Michigan Transportation Research Institute recommends that **snub braking** should be the braking technique used when downhill braking. This method requires that the truck brakes should be applied hard to slow the truck down to about 5 mph (2 kph), then hard braking should continue repeatedly until the bottom of the hill is reached. The brakes should not be lightly applied continuously. The amount of heat energy produced by the brakes is the same whether the brakes are applied hard for a short time or lightly for a long time. All of the brakes are not, however, equally applied in both situations.

If brake application pressure is between 20 and 30 psi (138 and 207 kPa) all the relay valves will open, and all the brakes—not just the trailer brakes—will work and dissipate heat. As more brakes are used by the braking system, each will operate cooler. Remember that contaminants and alcohol in the air system can also cause higher than normal crack pressures.

Pneumatic Brake Imbalance

A brake imbalance condition can be uncovered by inspecting the brake linings. If a **pneumatic imbalance** exists, the brake linings on some axles will wear faster than others. If the variation exists only between brake ends on each axle, a brake torque imbalance is likely present. Brake torque can be sensed by measuring the brake drum temperatures with an infrared thermometer after a couple of hard brake applications. Drums should be close to the same temperatures if brake torque is similar.

Crack Pressure

Nominal crack pressure (NCP) refers to the input air pressure required to produce delivery air pressure. Relay valves commonly have crack pressures varying from 2.5 psi to 10.5 psi (17.2 to 72.4 kPa), which are intended for specific applications depending on which axle the valve controls the braking pressure for. Brakes farthest away from the foot valve require the lowest pressure because signal air pressure takes the longest time to reach those valves. To produce nearly a simultaneous application of brakes, crack pressure will increase as the valve is placed closer to the foot valve. Special attention must be paid when replacing valves because different crack pressures can lead to brake imbalance.

Safety

Installing a "will fit" relay valve with an incorrect crack pressure can lead to a severe imbalance in brake application timing, which contributes to abnormal wear and even potential unsafe vehicle braking.

Anti-Compounding Relay Valves

Applying service and spring brakes at the same time combines spring and service brake force. Together, spring and service brake force applied to the slack adjuster is excessive and can lead to premature failure of the slack adjusters, or overtightening of automatic slack adjusters. To prevent foundation brake damage, an **anti-compounding valve** is used to prevent simultaneous application of the two forces. Essentially the use of this valve in the air supply to the spring brake chambers will cause the spring brakes to release when the service brakes are applied. The valve also causes the spring brakes to reapply when the service brakes are released. Anti-compounding valves are generally incorporated into the spring brake relay valve as shown in FIGURE 30-41.

An anti-compounding valve, like that illustrated in FIGURE 30-42, is a type of **double check valve**. As such, it has two supply ports and one delivery port. The double check valve only allows air to flow from either supply port to the delivery port. Air cannot change direction and flow from the delivery port to either of the supply ports. Neither can air flow from one supply port to another supply port.

One supply port of the anti-compounding valve is connected to the parking brake valve in the dash. The other supply port of the anti-compounding valve is connected to the rear axle service brake pressure signal. Pressure from either supply source will activate the spring brake relay valve and fill the spring brake chambers—thus releasing the spring brake. So if the service brakes are applied at the same time as the spring brakes, the service brake signal will apply the service brakes and release the spring brakes. Anti-compounding double check valves can be used separately, or incorporated into a relay valve, or even into quick-release valves.

For additional safety, a single axle bus or truck can also be equipped with a double check valve to apply brakes in the event of either a primary or secondary circuit failure. The input to the double check equipped relay

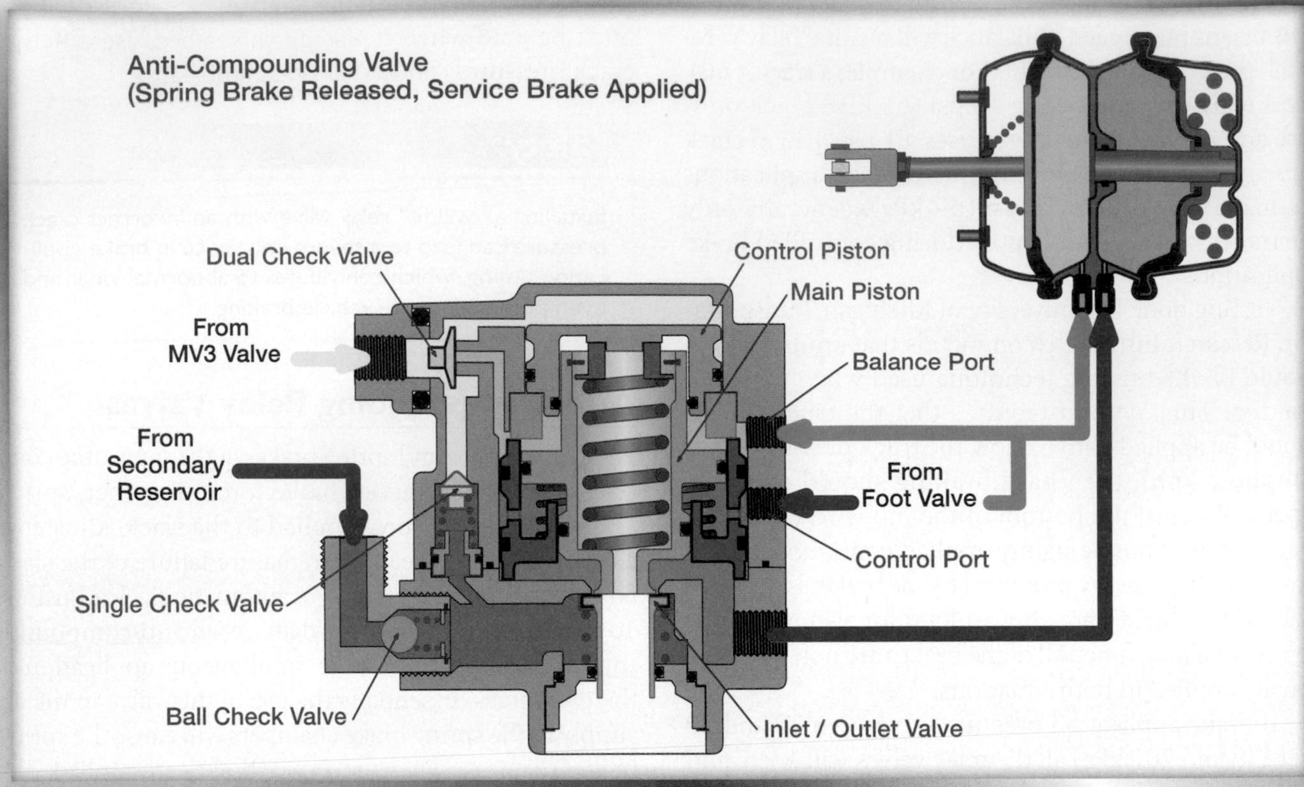

FIGURE 30-41 Anti-compounding feature prevents the service and spring brakes from applying pressure together, which would produce excessive force against the slack adjuster.

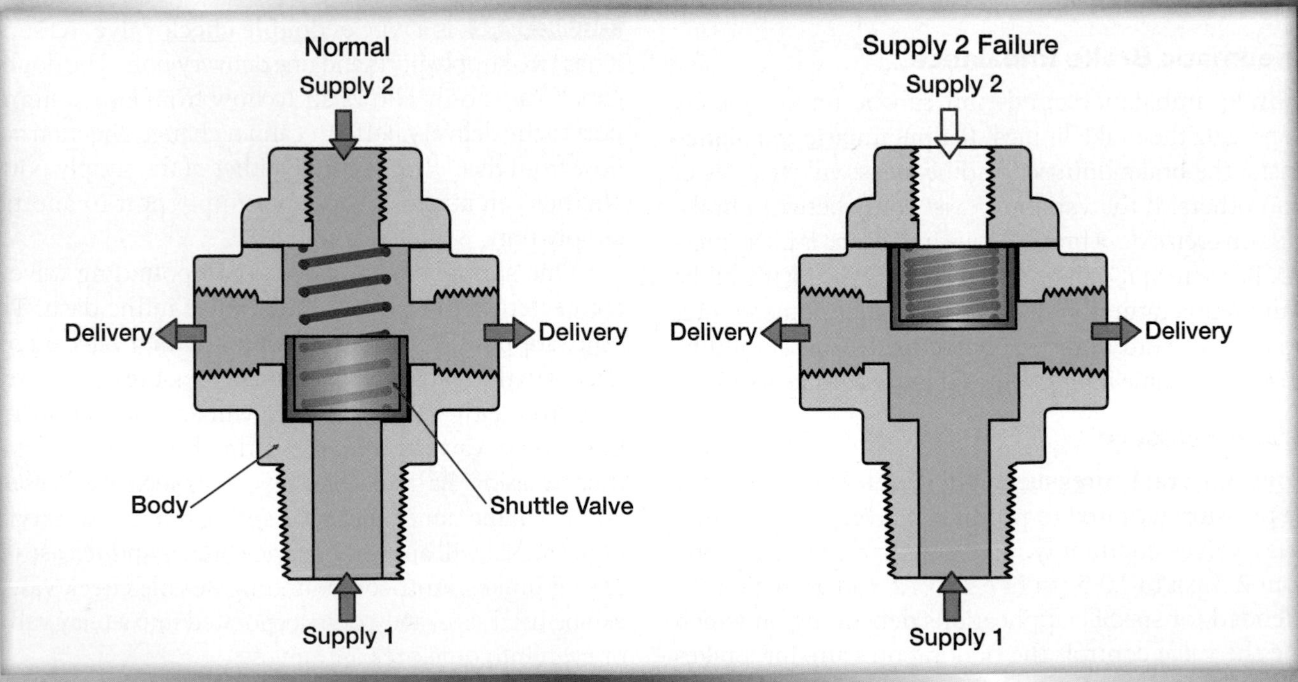

FIGURE 30-42 A relay valve with a double check valve used to prevent brake failure. The double check valve will normally block secondary pressure unless the primary circuit fails.

valve is connected to both the primary and secondary signal circuits supplied by the foot valve. In normal operation, the primary circuit will supply the double check valve with air pressure first, and prevent secondary circuit air from signaling the valve. In this normal circumstance, the valve blocks the secondary circuit signal. If the primary circuit fails and no air is supplied to the valve, the secondary circuit signal will operate the relay valve, enabling the vehicle to brake normally.

> **TECHNICIAN TIP**
>
> Just because a service brake relay valve is leaking air out of its exhaust port does not mean the valve is at fault. Sometimes a spring brake is leaking air past a seal between the rear spring brake and service chamber when the spring brake is released. If this happens, air will travel back up the service brake hose and out the exhaust port of the relay valve. Before replacing a valve that has air leaking from its exhaust, disconnect or pinch the delivery lines from that valve to determine if air is being fed back from a leaking brake chamber seal. Trailer spring brake valves can also experience this condition.

Brake Proportioning Relay Valves

When a tractor is traveling without a trailer (**bobtailing**), the absence of weight over the rear axles can easily cause the wheels to lock up even under slight brake applications. To prevent that from happening, a relay valve for tractors is designed to reduce normal service brake applications when no trailer is towed.

When the vehicle is operating in a bobtailing condition, a special **bobtailing proportioning relay (BPR) valve** is used to assist in controlling the braking performance. The valve, which is known in some locations as a "bobtailing valve," is a combination of two valves in a single housing. A typical BPR valve is shown in FIGURE 30-43. The lower half of the valve contains a conventional service brake relay valve. The upper half has an additional port connected to the cab-mounted, push-pull trailer air supply valve. It also contains a **proportioning valve**. When the trailer valve port is pressurized with air, the proportioning valve functions to change service brake application pressure. It does so by reducing rear service brake application relative to signal pressure from the foot valve when the tractor is bobtailing. The relationship between the service brake chamber pressure and the brake valve delivery pressure is charted in FIGURE 30-44.

Limiting apply pressure to the rear service brakes helps to avoid skidding and resultant loss of control when there is no trailer loading the rear service brakes. When the tractor is pulling a trailer and pressure is available at the trailer air supply port on the relay valve, the proportioning valve allows the relay valve to resume normal operation.

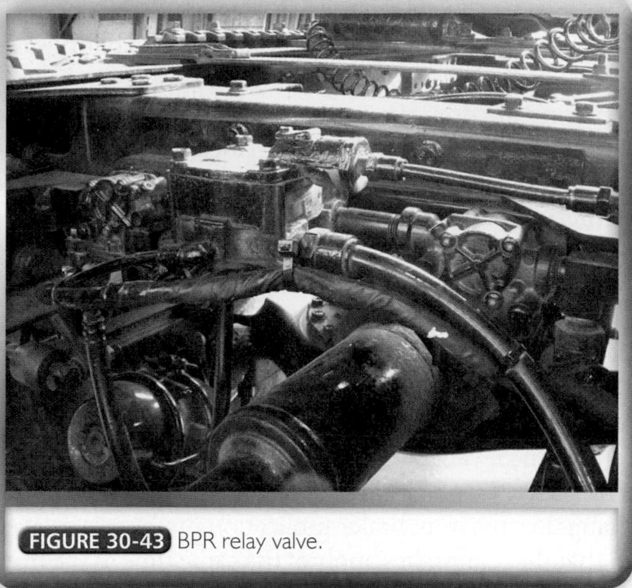

FIGURE 30-43 BPR relay valve.

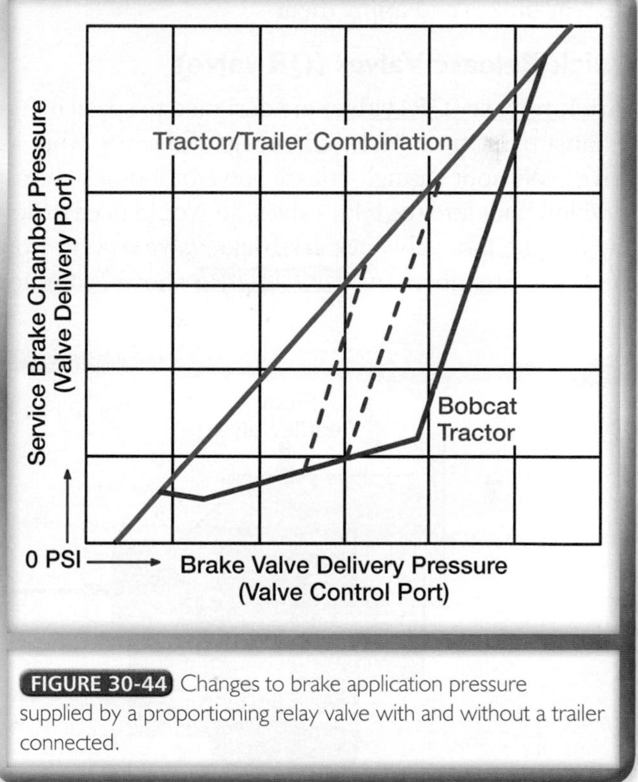

FIGURE 30-44 Changes to brake application pressure supplied by a proportioning relay valve with and without a trailer connected.

Front Axle Limiter Valves

Similar to the rear axle service brake relay valve using a proportioning valve, a **limiter (ratio) valve**, such as the one illustrated in FIGURE 30-45, is used on the steer axle of tractor air brake system. A front axle ratio control valve (limiter valve) works opposite the BPR valve. Instead of reducing air pressure to the front axle during bobtail operation, the limiter valve automatically increases brake application air pressure to improve braking lost with the reduction of rear brake torque. Full brake pressure is available to the steer axle service brakes while reduced pressure is available when towing a trailer. Limiting front brake pressure only takes place when a trailer is towed by a tractor.

Another feature built into a limiter valve improves timing of the front-axle brake application. The limiter or ratio control valve will hold off front-axle pressure until 4 or 5 psi (28 or 34 kPa) of pressure reaches the valve. By doing this, the front brake application pressure is delayed so that the rear brakes apply at the same time as the front brakes. Otherwise, the rear brake application would be delayed because of the time it takes for the air to reach the rear brakes and apply them.

Quick-Release Valves (QR valve)

Quick-release (QR) valves are designed to speed up the exhaust of air from brake chambers and some other air valves. Without a quick-release valve or a quick-release function built into the relay valves, air would need to flow back to the foot valve or park brake valve to vent from the brake chambers. As FIGURE 30-46 shows, common QR valves have three ports—a supply port at the top and two delivery ports at the side.

FIGURE 30-46 Quick-release valve. **A.** Air supply. **B.** Air delivery.

The operation of the QR valve is simple. When air pressure is supplied to the valve inlet, a spring-loaded diaphragm is pushed downward to seal the exhaust port, as illustrated in FIGURE 30-47A. Air flows out of both delivery ports to the brake chamber. When supply pressure is removed, as illustrated in FIGURE 30-47B, spring and air pressure below the diaphragm lift the QR valve diaphragm and open the exhaust passageway. Air from both the supply line and brake chambers will vent from the exhaust passage.

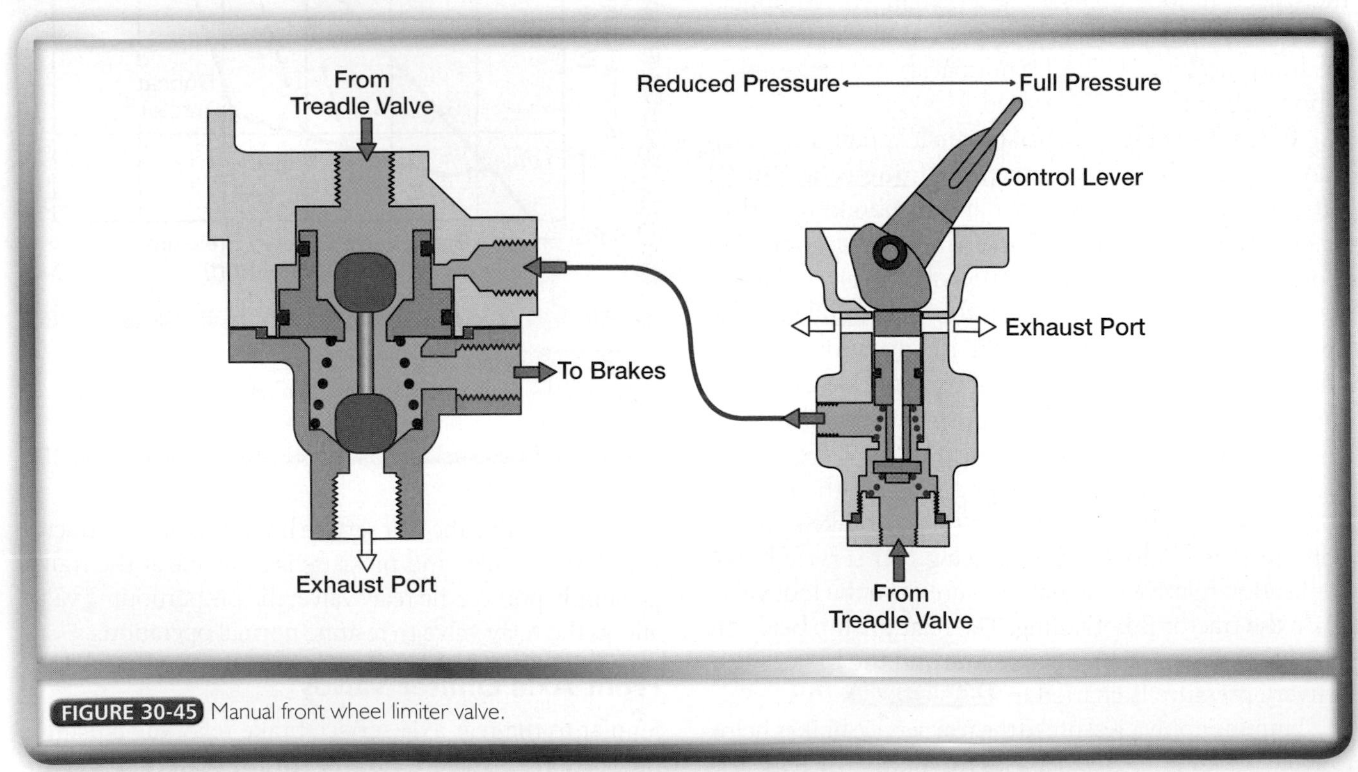

FIGURE 30-45 Manual front wheel limiter valve.

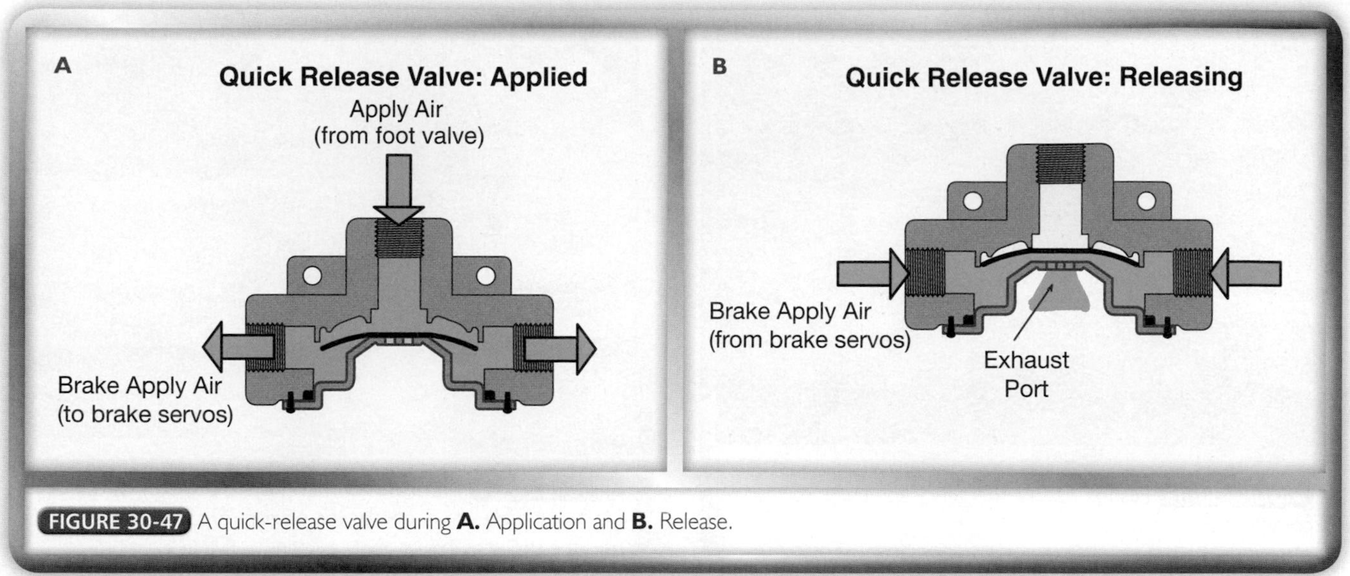

FIGURE 30-47 A quick-release valve during **A.** Application and **B.** Release.

Park/Emergency Brake Circuit

The park/emergency braking system has two major functions. The first is to control spring brake operation for parking the vehicle. Spring brakes use power springs located in the rear axle brake chambers to mechanically apply the brakes.

Air pressure of at least 30 to 45 psi (207 to 310 kPa) is needed to begin releasing the spring brakes. In straight trucks that do not tow trailers, the circuit shown in FIGURE 30-48 also has the capability to enable several "controlled brake applications" using the spring brakes instead of the normal service system air brake chambers if there is air loss to the rear brakes or primary reservoir.

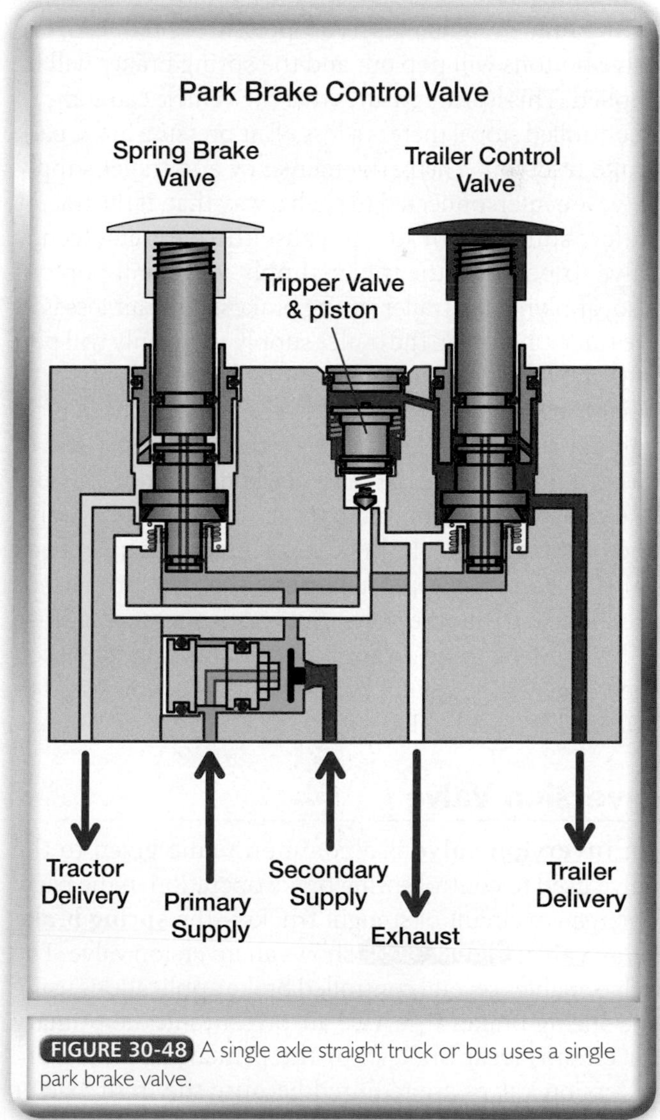

FIGURE 30-48 A single axle straight truck or bus uses a single park brake valve.

Push-Pull Control Valves

Push-pull park/emergency and trailer supply control valves are mounted in the vehicle dash, as shown in FIGURE 30-49. Supply and delivery port connections are on the valves. Both valves are normally closed to prevent air flowing through the valves unless they are depressed. When traveling over the road, the park/emergency valve button is pushed in to release the truck spring brakes, and it is pulled out for parking. Pulling the valve button out exhausts air from the air signal port connected to the spring brake relay valve. The trailer supply valve is depressed to supply air to the trailer to release its spring brakes.

The valves are pressure sensitive. That is, the valves will automatically return to the exhaust, or "button out," position when reservoir supply pressure for the spring

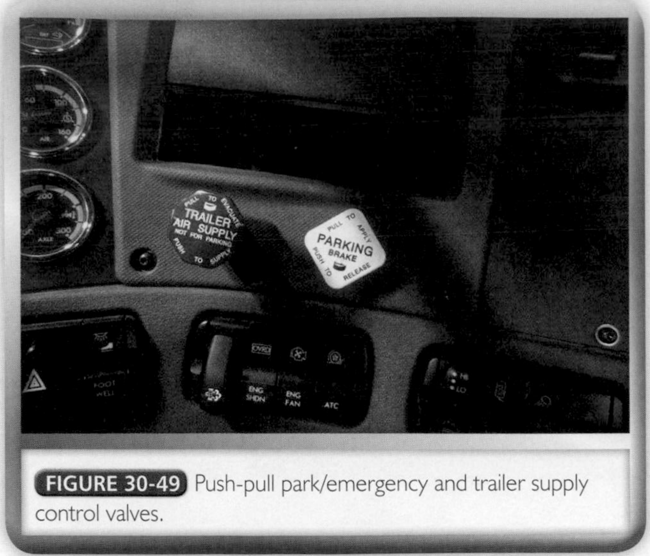

FIGURE 30-49 Push-pull park/emergency and trailer supply control valves.

FIGURE 30-50 The inversion valve, more correctly called the spring brake valve, detects the primary circuit air loss and uses the spring brakes to apply as many as five to eight brake applications. **A.** Primary applied. **B.** Secondary applied. **C.** To spring brake relay valve. **D.** From park/emergency dash valve.

brakes is below the required minimum to hold off the spring brakes. When reservoir pressure is reduced, the valve buttons will pop out and the spring brakes will be applied. This feature ensures that the vehicle can come to a controlled stop if there is a loss of air pressure in the park brake reservoir. The park/emergency and trailer supply valve are interconnected in such a way that, if the tractor suffers sufficient air loss to cause the park/emergency valve to pop out, the trailer supply valve will pop out also, applying the trailer spring brakes. If the air loss is in the trailer, however, the trailer supply valve only will pop out, applying only the trailer spring brakes. Contrary to what is commonly portrayed in the movies, the vehicle will not completely lose brakes if there is a rapid loss of air pressure. Holding the valve in when reservoir pressure is adequate will supply air to the spring brake relay valve and begin to release the brakes. An integral double check valve is used to supply air from either the primary or secondary circuit reservoirs. Automatic pressure settings will vary, depending on application. Generally, however, the valve will pop out when pressure is as low as 20 to 30 psi (138 to 207 kPa).

Inversion Valve

An **inversion valve** is a common name given to the valve used to control spring brake operation in the park/emergency circuit of straight trucks—the **spring brake relay valve**. FIGURE 30-50 shows an inversion valve. The valve enables several controlled brake applications using the spring brakes if service air pressure in the primary air circuit, (rear brakes), or the primary air reservoir. Inversion valves are required because the front axle or secondary circuit brakes alone cannot supply adequate braking force to stop the vehicle quickly enough to meet the FMVSS 121 requirements for emergency stopping. Inversion valves are not required on tractors because trailer brakes that are supplied air from both the primary and secondary reservoirs can help the tractor meet the required FMVSS 121 emergency stopping requirements and slow the tractor.

The label "inversion valve" is given to a normally open valve that requires air pressure to close. Inversion valves operate the opposite way most other air valves work—which are normally closed and require air to open. Because the spring brake valve reverses, or "inverts," the service-park brake operation when service air pressure is lost, the name "inversion valve" is commonly given to the valve, though not technically correct.

The spring brake/inversion valve detects the primary circuit air loss and uses the spring brakes to apply five to eight brake applications, depending on the secondary reservoir size. The spring brakes, not the service brakes, are used to slow the vehicle. The valve releases spring brake hold off pressure in proportion to front brake application pressure allowing the spring brakes to simulate a rear brake application. After the brake pedal is released, pressure from the secondary reservoir compresses the power spring and releases the spring brakes once again. Air from the secondary reservoir supplying the front axle is used to operate the inversion valve. Spring brake valves on straight trucks also limit maximum spring brake release pressure to 90–95 psi (621–655 kPa) rather than allowing the full system air pressure to the spring brake.

Trailer Air Circuits

The trailer park and service brakes are controlled by the tractor. Components in the brake circuit include:

- Gladhands
- Trailer air hoses
- Trailer reservoir tanks
- Pressure protection valves
- Relay valves
- Push-pull trailer air supply valve
- Trailer brake control valve (TV)

Air is supplied to the trailer circuit by the tractor's secondary air reservoir. As shown in FIGURE 30-51, two color-coded flexible hoses connect the tractor and trailer air system. Red is for the supply/emergency circuit and blue for the service brakes. The blue line supplies an air signal for the service brakes and the red line supplies air for the trailer air reservoir as well as the supply/emergency brake circuit. A service and spring brake reservoir is used on the trailer.

Supply air to the trailer is controlled through a red octagonal-shaped tractor-mounted push-pull valve. Sending air to the trailer from the cab-mounted push-pull will automatically begin to release the trailer spring brakes and begin filling the trailer reservoir, if empty. The tractor and trailer have separate valves to release and apply their respective spring brakes. Each valve can release the spring brakes independently of one another, but pulling out the square yellow tractor park/emergency valve will pop out both valves and apply both the trailer and the tractor spring brakes. Either valve can be pushed in separately to release the spring brakes, but both require pushing in to move a tractor connected to a trailer.

Trailer service brakes are activated by air pressure supplied by the blue trailer hose. An air pressure signal identical to the one supplied to the rear axle service brakes is transmitted to the trailer. Over the road, a hand-operated trailer brake control valve can also be used to apply just the trailer service brakes FIGURE 30-52.

FMVSS 121 specifies that all trailers have a means of activating the trailer brakes under trailer breakaway conditions. The loss of a trailer could potentially cause a major loss in air pressure for the tractor. To satisfy both requirements to protect the tractor and trailer, a tractor protection valve isolates the tractor during a breakaway condition while enabling the loss of trailer air pressure to activate the spring brakes for emergency stopping. Both trailer air hoses are connected to the tractor protection valve. The blue service line is closer to the tractor center, while the red emergency/supply hose is always the outside line between the two units.

Gladhands

Gladhands are the air couplers attached to the trailer hoses connecting the tractor and trailer air systems. Pictured in FIGURE 30-53, they are called "gladhands"

FIGURE 30-51 Color-coded hoses are used to differentiate brake systems. **A.** Park/emergency line. **B.** Service line.

FIGURE 30-52 The trailer brake control valve is a hand-operated pressure regulating valve that enables separate control of trailer service brakes.

FIGURE 30-53 Gladhand holders on the rear of a tractor. Red, or emergency-trailer supply, is always on the inside, the service line is on the outside. **A.** Trailer gladhands (2). **B.** Tractor protection valve.

FIGURE 30-54 Gladhands contain seals that can leak air. Seals (circled) should be regularly inspected and replaced if found defective.

because they resemble a pair of hands during a handshake when coupled. Gladhands will use a flexible rubber-like seal, shown in FIGURE 30-54, to prevent air leaks when the couplers are connected.

Trailer System Valves

Tractors that pull semi-trailers and/or straight trucks that pull full trailers require several valves to supply and control the air service brake and the spring brake systems on the trailer. Regardless of which towing vehicle is being discussed, these valves will include a valve to actuate the trailer service brakes, a valve to supply air to the trailer reservoirs, and a valve that protects the towing vehicle air system.

Trailer Brake Control (TC) Valve

Sometimes called a "broker brake," only the trailer service brakes are applied whenever this hand-operated valve is moved by the driver. **Trailer brake control valves** typically use a cam and spring mechanism to control a graduated delivery of air pressure to the trailer. Returning the handle to a rest position releases service brakes, while moving the valve handle down will increase trailer-only service brake application. Some drivers will use the valve to apply only trailer brakes to reduce tractor brake wear. However, the trailer control valve should never be used for parking.

Trailer Air Supply Valve

The red octagonal-shaped **trailer supply valve** is used to control the tractor protection system and route air from the secondary brake reservoir to the trailer brake reservoir. Like other push-pull control valves, the trailer air supply valve is a pressure sensitive, on-off control valve that will automatically pop out when reservoir supply pressure falls too low.

When the valve button is out, the trailer spring brakes are applied. FMVSS 121 requires the trailer air supply to be interlocked with the tractor park brakes. This means the tractor spring brakes cannot be applied without the trailer spring brakes also applying. This feature prevents the trailer from unexpectedly rolling away during disconnection. A two-button module is most often used. This module contains the tractor park/emergency valve with the trailer supply valve. The combination valve reduces the number of air lines and fittings required.

Tractor Protection Valves

The primary function of **tractor protection valves** is to prevent a rapid loss of air from the tractor during a trailer breakaway condition or when either the tractor or trailer develops a severe air leak. When 45 psi (310 kPa) or more of air is available at the tractor supply port, the inlet valve opens. This means the valve is now in the normal or "run" mode and is capable of allowing a trailer service brake application from the foot valve or trailer control valve. The valve is used every time the tractor and trailer are disconnected, shutting off the trailer service and supply lines when the park/emergency and trailer supply valves are pulled out. A schematic of the tractor protection valve is illustrated in FIGURE 30-55.

The valve incorporates several air control functions into a single valve. These include:

- A service line shut-off feature that prevents a trailer service brake application when tractor air pressure falls below 45 psi (310 kPa) in the tractor. Until the air pressure from the trailer air supply valve increases above 45 psi (310 kPa), the valve remains closed to service signal pressure.
- A quick-release valve for the trailer service line. This prevents air from becoming trapped in the service hose when the trailer is parked and speeds up trailer service brake release.
- Double check valves to prevent compounding of trailer service and park brakes.
- Double check valves to divert the highest service air pressure from either the tractor's front or rear brake circuits or the trailer valve.
- A stop light port for a stop light switch.

Two checks can be made of the valve operation. One is to build up tractor air pressure from 0 psi (0 kPa) while the gladhands are disconnected. While pushing the trailer supply valve in, no air should pass through

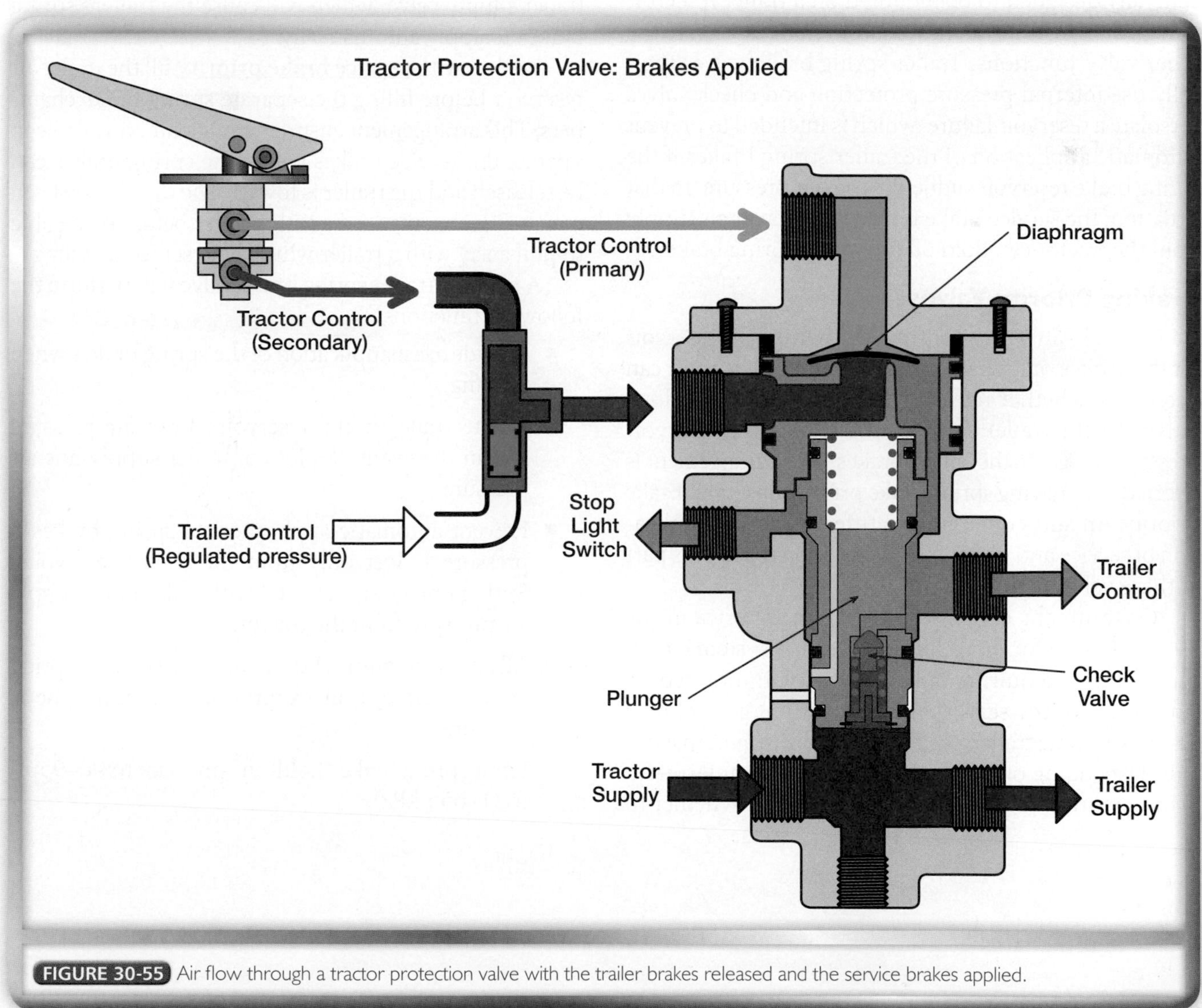

FIGURE 30-55 Air flow through a tractor protection valve with the trailer brakes released and the service brakes applied.

the red tractor hose until approximately 45 psi (310k Pa) of tractor air pressure is reached. After building up air pressure in the tractor, with the trailer supply valve pushed in, the supply/emergency gladhand should release air from the tractor until pressure falls to approximately 45 psi (310 kPa). With the tractor service brake applied, air should be released from the blue service hose and shut-off at the same time as air is cut off for the supply/emergency hose.

With just the blue service hose disconnected and the trailer charged with air, the trailer valve can be activated to check for air pressure delivery out the service hose.

Trailer Spring Brake Valves

Trailer spring brake valves are relay valves designed for use in trailer air brake systems to control the supply/emergency brake circuit. What is different about these valves, as compared to tractor spring brake valves, is that they are generally designed to be mounted on a trailer reservoir to regulate the filling of the reservoir(s) in addition to the other valve functions. Trailer spring brake valves typically use internal pressure protection and check valves to isolate a reservoir failure, which is intended to prevent automatic application of the trailer spring brakes if the spring brake reservoir suddenly loses air pressure. In that situation, the service brake reservoir or trailer air supply from the tractor can hold off the trailer spring brakes.

Braking Priority Valves

An internal valve may control whether the air reservoir for the service or spring brake is filled first. The valve can determine whether releasing the spring brakes is done only with the trailer supply air first or using reservoir pressure to release the spring brakes. This arrangement is referred to as having spring brake priority or service brake priority. An anti-compound feature preventing application of service and park brake application together is part of these valves.

Government regulations in North America in the 1990s allowed for more simplified trailer system circuit plumbing by requiring only one reservoir, not two, to supply air for the service and supply/emergency brake system on some trailers. FIGURE 30-56 illustrates that circuit. Depending on when the trailer was manufactured, manufacturers and customers could decide whether to supply air pressure to both the trailer service brakes and the spring brake reservoirs at the same time, or give priority to one or the other.

A system could, therefore, be designed and equipped for **spring brake priority**, enabling air supplied from the tractor to fill the air reservoir for the spring brakes first and even release the spring brakes before filling the air tank for the service brakes. If there is air loss to the service brakes, the spring brakes are used instead to apply the brakes. The advantage of spring brake priority systems is that they enable the trailer to be towed without waiting for the trailer air reservoirs to first fill. The disadvantage is that a trailer could be traveling without adequate air pressure to operate the service brakes. If there is a major loss of air to the trailer service brakes in a spring brake priority system, the spring brakes may remain released while no service brakes are available on the trailer. The only way to apply brakes on the trailer is to close the trailer supply valve, which will cause the trailer's spring brakes to apply automatically.

Trailers with **service brake priority** fill the trailer air reservoir before filling the separate spring brake chambers. This arrangement ensures enough air is available to operate the service brakes before the spring brakes can be released and the trailer is towed. The driver, however, may be inconvenienced a little longer before being able to pull away with a trailer while the reservoir is filling.

A popular trailer spring brake valve will perform the following functions:

- Provide a fast application of the spring brakes when parking.
- Isolate trailer brake reservoirs from air pressure loss in the event of a loss of trailer supply line air pressure.
- Prevent automatic application of spring brakes if pressure is lost only from the trailer reservoirs. Spring brakes are released with only trailer supply air pressure from the tractor.
- Allow anti-compounding of service and spring forces when the trailer supply line is at atmospheric pressure.
- Limit spring brake "hold-off" pressure to 90–95psi (621–655 kPa).

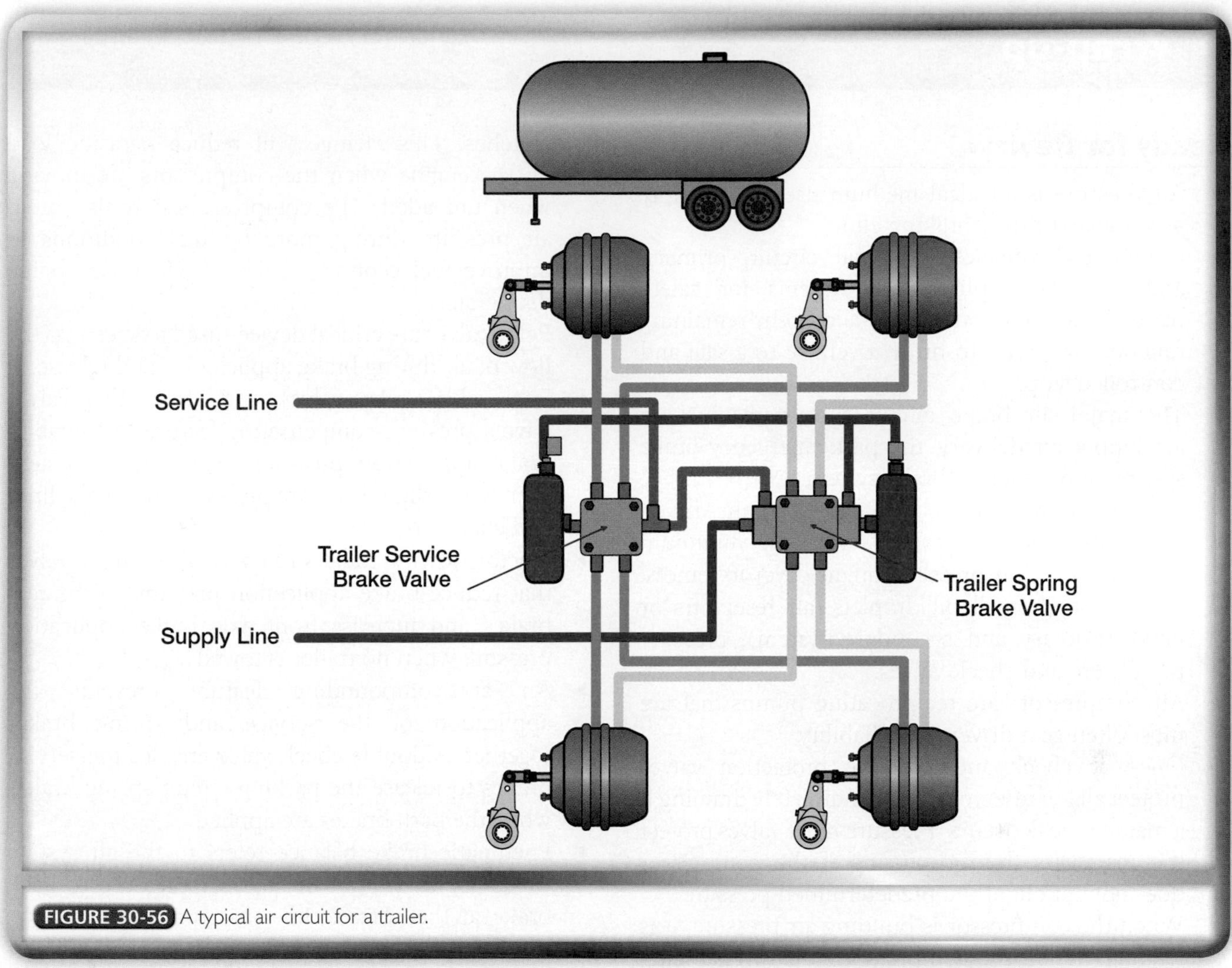

FIGURE 30-56 A typical air circuit for a trailer.

Wrap-up

Ready for Review

- Air pressure is an ideal medium used to multiply and transmit driver braking effort.
- Commercial vehicles use dual circuit, primary, and secondary split brake systems for safety reasons. Failure in one circuit allows the remaining functioning circuit to bring a vehicle to a safe and controlled stop.
- The major air brake circuit subsystems include air supply, air delivery, the park/emergency brake system, and trailer air brake system.
- The air supply system consists of an engine-driven air compressor, a governor controlling minimum and maximum air pressure, an air dryer to remove moisture and small oil droplets, air reservoirs or tanks (primary and secondary system), pressure protection, and check valves.
- Air compressors are reciprocating pumps that are most often gear driven for reliability.
- One-way check and pressure protection valves protect all the reservoirs from completely draining if a major air leak occurs. Pressure relief valves protect the reservoirs from rupturing if the compressor does not cut out at the predetermined pressure.
- When the compressor is building air pressure, it is loading. When the compressor stops pressurizing air, it is unloading. A governor controls the cut-in and cut-out systems' pressures to determine when the compressor loads and unloads.
- Unloader valves, which are small air-operated pistons, hold the compressor inlet check valves open to unload the compressor.
- Three air reservoirs are commonly used: a service-supply reservoir (often called a wet tank), a primary reservoir, and a secondary reservoir.
- The primary system circuit supplies air for the rear brakes, while the secondary system supplies air for the front brakes. Both systems can supply air to the trailer brakes and the park/emergency circuit.
- Air dryers condition system air by removing oil and water contamination. Desiccant material traps contaminants, which are purged from the dryer when the air compressor unloads.
- To meet Greenhouse Gas Emission Standards for 2016, most air compressors will be equipped with electronically controlled governors and on-off clutches. This change will reduce parasitic load on the engine when the compressors are moving when unloaded. The compressors will also build air pressure during more optimal conditions to improve fuel economy, such as when the engine decelerates.
- Relay valves are critical devices used to speed up the flow of air during brake applications and release.
- Foot valves, relay valves, and some other valves have a pressure-compensating feature that enables brake application pressure to remain consistent even when slight leaks are present in the brake lines and chambers.
- Tractors towing trailers use specialized relay valves that reduce brake application pressure to the rear brakes and increase front axle brake application pressure when no trailer is towed.
- An anti-compounding feature prevents the application of the service and spring brakes together. A double check valve enables the service brakes to release the parking circuit spring brakes when the park brakes are applied.
- Pneumatic brake balance refers to the air system capability to supply the correct pressure to each brake at the correct time. Air brake systems use pneumatic balance, which causes the rear most brakes to require the least signal pressure and to apply first. Progressively more signal pressure is applied the closer the brake is to the front of the vehicle. Correct pneumatic brake balance helps prevent tractor jackknifing and trailer swing-out.
- Dash mounted push-pull valves control the park brake operation for the truck-tractor and trailer spring brakes. The valves automatically apply the park brakes when brake pressure falls to 30–45 psi (207–310 kPa).
- A red octagonal push-pull valve in the cab supplies air to the trailer reservoir and controls the park brake operation.
- Trailer air systems can be designed for spring brake priority or service brake priority valving. Spring brake priority enables the trailer air supply to release the trailer spring brakes without first filling the reservoirs. Service priority valving ensures the service brake reservoir is filled first before the spring brakes are released.

Vocabulary Builder

adsorbtion A process in which material collects on the surface and the air dryer adsorbs moisture from the air and then discharges it in the purge cycle.

Air Dryer Integrated System (AD-IS) An air supply system component that contains an air dryer and several pressure protection valves to regulate charging of the air reservoirs.

anti-compounding valve An air control system design feature that prevents simultaneous application of the service and spring brakes.

automatic drain valve A drain valve located on the bottom of the air system reservoirs that automatically drains any accumulations of water or oil whenever the air reservoir cycles.

bobtailing A tractor traveling without a trailer.

bobtailing proportioning relay (BPR) valve A specialized relay valve used to reduce delivery pressure to the rear brakes of a tractor when no trailer is towed.

brake lag The time delay between driver brake pedal application and brake actuation due to the slower speed of air pressure transmission through air lines and valves.

crack pressure The air signal pressure required to begin delivery of air pressure from a relay valve.

desiccant Silica beads used in the air dryer to trap and hold moisture and oil until the dryer is purged.

double check valves A brake valve with two air inlets and one air outlet. Only the higher inlet pressure will leave the single valve outlet.

dryer integrated module (DRM) An AD-IS type dryer with the addition of an air reservoir used to assist purging of the spin-on dryer desiccant cartridge.

dual-circuit system A split between the air brake circuits on commercial vehicles for safety purposes. A failure in one circuit does not affect the operation of the second air brake circuit.

Electronic Air Control (EAC) A controlled area network (CAN)-operated air supply system that regulates the air compressor load and unload cycle, plus additional optional air supply system components.

emergency brake circuit The air circuit responsible for the application and release of power springs in the brake chambers. Also referred to as the spring brake circuit or *park brake circuit*.

Federal Motor Vehicle Safety Standard 121 (FMVSS 121) The legislated performance standard for air brake systems on commercial vehicles.

foot valve The center of the brake delivery system. Also called the *treadle valve*.

gladhands The air couplers attached to the trailer hoses connecting the tractor and trailer air systems.

governor An air control valve that regulates the air system cut-in and cut-out pressure. The governor also controls the purging of the air dryer.

inlet pressure regulating valve Regulates the maximum air intake pressure supplied to the air compressor from a turbocharged engine's intake manifold.

inversion valve A normally open valve that requires air pressure to close. Another name often given to a *spring brake relay valve*.

jackknifing A condition caused by incorrect pneumatic balance between a tractor and trailer. Typically, tractor brakes have applied before the trailer brakes at too high a pressure. When the tractor brakes lock, the trailer will rotate around the kingpin.

limiter valve An air pressure proportioning valve used to increase brake application pressure to the front brakes when a trailer is not towed by a tractor. Also known as a *ratio valve*.

loading The state of the air compressor when it is building system air pressure. The unloader valves are not active.

nominal crack pressure (NCP) The minimum air signal pressure required to begin delivery of air pressure from a relay valve.

one-way check valve A valve with the purpose to protect the air reservoirs and other air system storage units from completely draining if a leak occurs downstream of one reservoir.

park brake circuit The air circuit responsible for the application and release of power springs in the brake chambers. Also referred to as the spring brake circuit or *emergency brake circuit*.

park/emergency braking system The air circuit responsible for the application of the spring brakes for parking. It also has the capability to enable several controlled brake applications if a major air leak occurs in either the primary or secondary air brake circuits.

PBS Injection Booster An option for the Bendix EAC system which injects a blast of compressed air into the engine intake manifold to reduce turbocharger lag.

pneumatic balance The correct timing of brake application air pressure to each vehicle axle at the correct pressure.

pneumatic imbalance The incorrect timing of brake application air pressure to vehicle axles or brake application at the wrong pressure. Pneumatic imbalance leads to tractor jackknifing or trailer swing-out.

pressure balanced A feature of air control system valves which ensures air application pressure is consistent to the brake chambers even when small leaks drain air from delivery components such as lines and chambers.

pressure-compensating balance valve A feature of air brake valves that ensures a consistent delivery of air pressure is maintained in spite of leaks in the delivery system lines or air chambers.

pressure-compensating relay valve A relay valve having a pressure balanced inlet and exhaust valve to ensure consistent air delivery pressure to the brakes.

pressure protection valve A normally closed valve that opens after a preset pressure is reached. Pressure protection valves are used to control the charging of air system reservoirs or circuits draining out of the reservoir.

primary circuit Refers to the split brake circuit system used on commercial vehicles. The primary circuit generally operates the rear brakes while the *secondary circuit* operates the front brakes.

primary reservoir One of two air reservoirs responsible for holding pressurized air for the dual air brake system.

proportioning valve A valve that functions to change service brake application pressure. by reducing service brake application relative to signal pressure from the foot valve.

purge cycle The time between the closing and opening of the dryer purge valve, or the loading and unloading of the air compressor. Oil and moisture trapped in the dryer desiccant are purged when the air compressor unloads.

purge valve The air dryer valve, located at the dryer outlet, which controls the purge cycle. Opening the purge valve enables trapped oil and moisture to exhaust to the atmosphere through the valve.

push-pull park/emergency control valve Hand-operated dash valve used to control the operation of the spring brakes for a straight truck, tractor, and/or trailer.

quick-release (QR) valve An air valve that is used to speed up the release of air pressure from air lines. The valve exhaust closes when supplied air and then opens when air pressure drops.

ratio valve An air pressure proportioning valve used to increase brake application pressure to the front brakes when a trailer is not towed by a tractor. Also known as a *limiter valve*.

relay valve Critical devices used to speed up the flow of air during brake application and release.

safety relief valve A pressure relief valve located in the service-supply or wet tank; used to prevent tank rupture from overpressurization. The valve typically opens at pressures above 150 psi (1,034 kPa).

secondary circuit Refers to the split brake circuit system used on commercial vehicles. The *primary circuit* generally operates the rear brakes while the secondary circuit operates the front brakes.

secondary reservoir One of two air reservoirs responsible for holding pressurized air for the dual air brake system.

service brake priority A trailer spring brake relay valve which will not allow the park-spring brakes to release until the service air reservoir is filled.

service reservoir The first air reservoir to receive air from the air compressor or dryer. Water and oil condense in this tank, which supplies the primary and secondary air reservoirs. Also called the *supply reservoir*.

snub braking A braking technique that should be used when downhill braking. It requires the truck brakes to be applied hard to slow the truck down to about 5 mph (2 kph), then continued repeatedly until the bottom of the hill is reached.

spring brake priority A trailer spring brake relay valve which will allow the park-spring brakes to release with only air supplied by the trailer supply valve.

spring brake relay valve A specialized relay valve that is used to supply air to hold off the spring brakes or release air and apply the spring brakes. Also called an *inversion valve*.

supply reservoir The first air reservoir to receive air from the air compressor or dryer. Water and oil condense in this tank, which supplies the primary and secondary air reservoirs. Also called the *service reservoir*.

Synflex A reinforced nylon material used to make flexible airlines.

tractor protection valves A valve that controls the supply of air to the trailer from the tractor. The valve automatically isolates the tractor air reservoirs from being completely drained if a trailer breaks away from a tractor.

trailer brake control valve A hand-operated, cab-mounted control valve used to manually apply the trailer service brakes.

trailer supply valve A push-pull valve in the cab used to supply air pressure to the trailer air brake reservoirs.

trailer swing-out A condition caused by incorrect pneumatic balance between a tractor and trailer. Typically, trailer brakes are applied at too high a pressure, locking the trailer brakes. The trailer tires slide and cause the trailer to swing out into an adjacent lane.

treadle valve The center of the brake delivery system. Also called the *foot valve*.

turbocharger cut-off valves An air-operated valve which closes the air inlet to the air dryer to prevent engine intake boost pressure from leaking out the dryer's purge port.

unloader valves Air-operated piston-like valves used to physically hold open the air compressor's intake air check valves.

unloading The state of the air compressor when it is not building air pressure. Unloader valves hold the check valves open.

wet tank Another name for the service or supply reservoir. It is called a wet tank since moisture and vaporized oil condense in this tank.

Review Questions

1. During a normal brake application the treadle valve's secondary piston is operated by which of the following methods?
   a. Mechanically by the driver's foot
   b. By spring pressure
   c. By a relay valve
   d. By air pressure under the primary piston
2. The typical air compressor on a highway vehicle does not contain which of the following?
   a. Crankshaft
   b. Camshaft
   c. Valves
   d. Bearings
3. The purge valve on an air dryer used on a vehicle air brake system will remain open when which of the following occurs?
   a. The compressor is loaded.
   b. The compressor is unloaded.
   c. A panic stop is made.
   d. The trailer air supply button is held in.
4. When a relay valve is in the balanced or hold position which of the following is occurring?
   a. The inlet valve is closed and the exhaust valve is open.
   b. The inlet valve and the exhaust valve are closed.
   c. The inlet valve is open and the exhaust valve is closed.
   d. The inlet valve and the exhaust valve are open.
5. The ________ port is located in the top cover of a typical relay valve.
   a. supply
   b. delivery
   c. control
   d. exhaust
6. What is the function of a bobtail proportioning relay valve when in operation in bobtail mode?
   a. Increases application pressure at the front brakes
   b. Shuts off air flow to the trailer
   c. Diverts trailer air pressure to the front brakes
   d. Decreases application pressure to the rear brakes
7. Treadle valves do not contain ________ ports.
   a. supply
   b. delivery
   c. control
   d. exhaust
8. Where is a tractor protection valve is typically located on a commercial vehicle?
   a. In the cab of the vehicle
   b. Under the hood of the vehicle
   c. At the rear of the cab of the vehicle
   d. At the nose of the trailer
9. Brake pneumatic imbalance can be caused by which of the following?
   a. High governor pressure
   b. Low governor pressure
   c. Incorrect valve cracking pressures
   d. Incorrect friction material
10. If the trailer emergency/supply line breaks away from a trailer while a tractor/trailer is in motion, which of the following will occur?
    a. The trailer service brakes are fully applied.
    b. The trailer spring brakes are fully applied.
    c. Both trailer service and spring brakes are fully applied.
    d. Both the tractor and trailer spring brakes are fully applied.

ASE-Type Questions

1. Technician A says that an air brake system consists of a supply system, a delivery system, and an emergency park brake system. Technician B says that air brake systems have been used in on road vehicles for more than 100 years. Who is correct?
   a. Technician A
   b. Technician B
   c. Both Technician A and Technician B
   d. Neither Technician A nor Technician B
2. Technician A says that today's truck air brake systems will usually have two reservoirs: a primary and a secondary. Technician B says that all truck air brake systems today will use an air dryer to remove moisture. Who is correct?
   a. Technician A
   b. Technician B
   c. Both Technician A and Technician B
   d. Neither Technician A nor Technician B
3. Technician A says that the primary and secondary reservoirs are used so the system can be divided into two brake circuits: one supplying the front brakes and the other supplying the rear brake. Technician B says the primary reservoir normally delivers to the front brakes and the secondary reservoir delivers to the rear brakes. Who is correct?
   a. Technician A
   b. Technician B
   c. Both Technician A and Technician B
   d. Neither Technician A nor Technician B
4. Technician A says that the primary reservoir provides the air pressure to apply the parking brakes on an air brake system. Technician B says that a trailer can be supplied with air by either the primary or secondary reservoir. Who is correct?
   a. Technician A
   b. Technician B
   c. Both Technician A and Technician B
   d. Neither Technician A nor Technician B
5. Technician A says that air from the treadle valve is used to apply the rear brake chambers. Technician B says air from the treadle valve is used to apply the front brake chambers. Who is correct?
   a. Technician A
   b. Technician B
   c. Both Technician A and Technician B
   d. Neither Technician A nor Technician B
6. Technician A says that double check valves are used in the air brake system so that the reservoir with the higher pressure will supply a circuit. Technician B says that the tractor protection valve will close if there is a sudden full air loss in the trailer supply line. Who is correct?
   a. Technician A
   b. Technician B
   c. Both Technician A and Technician B
   d. Neither Technician A nor Technician B
7. Technician A says that air dryer desiccant absorbs water from the air. Technician B says when the air dryer purges, extremely dry air rushes over the desiccant to flush the water from its surface. Who is correct?
   a. Technician A
   b. Technician B
   c. Both Technician A and Technician B
   d. Neither Technician A nor Technician B
8. Technician A says that the air dryer purge cycle can last up to 30 seconds. Technician B says that most of the air expelled during the dryer purge exits the dryer in a couple of seconds. Who is correct?
   a. Technician A
   b. Technician B
   c. Both Technician A and Technician B
   d. Neither Technician A nor Technician B
9. Technician A says that two dash gauges are used to indicate system air pressure. Tech B says that the low air warning system usually activates at approximately 65 psi (448 kPa). Who is correct?
   a. Technician A
   b. Technician B
   c. Both Technician A and Technician B
   d. Neither Technician A nor Technician B
10. Technician A says that quick release valves are used on the front and rear brakes to speed up the exhaust of actuation air from the chambers. Technician B says that relay valves are used on the rear brake system to speed up brake application. Who is correct?
    a. Technician A
    b. Technician B
    c. Both Technician A and Technician B
    d. Neither Technician A nor Technician B

CHAPTER 31

NATEF Tasks

Brakes

Air Brakes—Air Supply and Service Systems

	Page
■ Identify poor stopping, air leaks, premature wear, pulling, grabbing, dragging, or balance problems caused by supply and service system malfunctions; determine needed action.	976–981
■ Inspect air compressor inlet; inspect oil supply and coolant lines, fittings, and mounting brackets; repair or replace as needed.	976–980
■ Inspect and test stop light circuit switches, wiring, and connectors; repair or replace as needed.	979
■ Check air system buildup time; determine needed action.	981
■ Inspect and test low pressure warning devices, wiring, and connectors; repair or replace as needed.	981
■ Inspect and test air pressure gauges, lines, and fittings; replace as needed.	981–982
■ Inspect and test air system pressure controls: governor, unloader assembly valves, filters, lines, hoses, and fittings; adjust or replace as needed.	981–982
■ Inspect air system lines, hoses, fittings, and couplings; repair or replace as needed.	982
■ Inspect and test quick release valves; replace as needed.	996
■ Inspect and test brake application (foot/treadle) valve, fittings, and mounts; check pedal operation; replace as needed.	997
■ Inspect and test brake relay valves; replace as needed.	998
■ Inspect and test emergency (spring) brake control/modulator valve(s); replace as needed.	1000–1001
■ Inspect and test hand brake (trailer) control valve, lines, fittings, and mountings; repair or replace as needed.	1002–1003
■ Inspect and test tractor protection valve; replace as needed.	1004
■ Inspect air compressor drive gear, belts, and coupling; adjust or replace as needed.	1006

Servicing Air Brake Systems

NATEF Tasks, continued

Brakes Air Brakes—Air Supply and Service Systems, continued	Page
■ Drain air reservoir/tanks; check for oil, water, and foreign material; determine needed action.	1008
■ Inspect and clean air dryer systems, filters, valves, heaters, wiring, and connectors; repair or replace as needed.	1008
■ Inspect and test air tank relief (safety) valves, one-way (single) check valves, two-way (double) check valves, manual and automatic drain valves; replace as needed.	1008–1009
Air Brakes—Mechanical/Foundation Brakes	
■ Identify poor stopping, brake noise, premature wear, pulling, grabbing, or dragging problems caused by the foundation brake, slack adjuster, and brake chamber problems; determine needed action.	976–981, 1014
■ Identify type, inspect and service slack adjusters; perform needed action.	990, 1021–1029
■ Inspect and test service brake chambers, diaphragm, clamp, spring, pushrod, clevis, and mounting brackets; repair or replace as needed.	991
■ Inspect and measure brake drums or rotors; perform needed action.	1012–1014, 1029
■ Inspect and measure brake shoes or pads; perform needed action.	1016–1018
■ Inspect camshafts, tubes, rollers, bushings, seals, spacers, retainers, brake spiders, shields, anchor pins, and springs; replace as needed.	1016–1020
■ Inspect, clean, and adjust air disc brake caliper assemblies; determine needed repairs.	1029–1031
Air Brakes—Parking Brakes	
■ Inspect and test parking (spring) brake chamber diaphragm and seals; replace parking (spring) brake chamber; dispose of removed chambers in accordance with local regulations.	986–988
■ Inspect and test parking (spring) brake application and release valve; replace as needed.	986–988

NATEF Tasks, continued

Brakes

Air Brakes—Parking Brakes, continued	Page
■ Manually release (cage) and reset (uncage) parking (spring) brakes in accordance with manufacturers' recommendations.	986–988
■ Inspect and test parking (spring) brake check valves, lines, hoses, and fittings; replace as needed.	986–999
■ Identify and test anti compounding brake function.	1008–1009
Air and Hydraulic Antilock Brake Systems (ABS) and Automatic Traction Control (ATC)	
■ Test and check operation of antilock brake system (ABS) air, hydraulic, electrical, and mechanical components; perform needed action.	990

Preventative Maintenance

Frame and Chassis—Air Brakes	
■ Check low air pressure warning devices.	981

Knowledge Objectives

After reading this chapter, you will be able to:

1. Identify and explain safety procedures to be observed when servicing air brakes. (pp 972–973)
2. Outline safe work practices related to servicing air system. (pp 972–973)
3. Identify common failures associated with brake foundations and air circuits. (pp 976–981)
4. Identify and explain causes for common braking complaints. (pp 976–981)
5. Identify and explain common failures in the air circuits system of commercial vehicles equipped with air brakes. (pp 976–981)
6. Explain and explain procedures for inspecting, servicing, and replacing foundation brake components. (pp 980–1005)
7. Recommend maintenance and service procedures for commercial vehicle air systems. (p 981)
8. Explain steps used to verify the correct operation of the air system circuits. (p 1005)
9. Identify and explain procedures for inspecting and testing brake valves hoses and connectors. (pp 1006–1010)
10. Identify and explain procedures for adjusting air brakes. (pp 1021–1029)

Skill Objectives

After reading this chapter, you will be able to:

1. Check low air pressure warning devices. (p 981)
2. Record air governor cut-in and cut-out setting (psi or kPa). (pp 981–982)
3. Check condition of air compressor. (pp 981–982)
4. Identify reasons for excessive air buildup time. (pp 981–982)
5. Test for oil consumption. (p 983)
6. Test the antilock brake system with a chuff test. (p 990)
7. Test brake balance. (pp 990–991)
8. Test air brake pressure balance. (pp 990–991)
9. Test parking brake function. (p 999)
10. Check emergency (spring) brake control/modulator valve. (pp 1000–1001)
11. Inspect coupling air lines, holders, and gladhands. (p 1002)
12. Check tractor protection valve. (p 1004)
13. Check operation of air dryer. (p 1008)
14. Drain air tanks and check for contamination. (p 1008)
15. Check condition of pressure relief (safety) valves. (p 1008)
16. Check operation of air reservoir/tank drain valves. (p 1008)
17. Identify air hose function by its color. (pp 1009–1010)
18. Inspect air lines and hoses for damage. (pp 1009–1010)
19. Measure brake drum diameter. (pp 1011–1012)
20. Test the automatic emergency brake system. (pp 988–991)
21. Identify brake timing imbalance. (pp 992–993)
22. Inspect air supply system performance. (p 981) SKILL DRILL 31-1
23. Test for air leakage. (p 982) SKILL DRILL 31-2
24. Check brake stroke length using applied stroke measurement. (p 985) SKILL DRILL 31-3
25. Inspect, test, and replace a spring brake actuator. (pp 989–990) SKILL DRILL 31-4
26. Perform a dual circuit integrity test. (p 991) SKILL DRILL 31-5
27. Inspect and test the quick release valve. (p 996) SKILL DRILL 31-6
28. Inspect, test, and replace the brake application valve, fittings and mounts. (p 997) SKILL DRILL 31-7
29. Inspect, test, and replace a relay valve. (p 998) SKILL DRILL 31-8
30. Inspect, test, and replace the parking brake hand valve. (p 999) SKILL DRILL 31-9
31. Inspect, test, and replace the inversion valve. (p 1000) SKILL DRILL 31-10
32. Inspect, test, and replace the anti-compounding circuit. (p 1001) SKILL DRILL 31-11
33. Inspect, test, and replace the trailer air supply valve. (p 1002) SKILL DRILL 31-12
34. Inspect, test, and replace the trailer brake control valve. (p 1003) SKILL DRILL 31-13
35. Inspect, test, and replace the tractor protection valve. (p 1004) SKILL DRILL 31-14
36. Inspect, test, and replace the trailer brake full function valve. (p 1005) SKILL DRILL 31-15
37. Inspect brake shoes. (p 1016) SKILL DRILL 31-16
38. Remove brake shoes. (p 1016) SKILL DRILL 31-17
39. Disassemble brakes. (p 1017) SKILL DRILL 31-18
40. Install brake shoes. (p 1018) SKILL DRILL 31-19
41. Remove the brake camshaft. (p 1020) SKILL DRILL 31-20
42. Replace automatic slack adjusters. (pp 1027–1028) SKILL DRILL 31-21

Introduction

Brake systems are a critical component of every heavy-duty vehicle. Brake system failures can have catastrophic results. As such, inspecting, maintaining, and repairing air brake systems are some of the most critical safety-related operations technicians perform.

Brake system inspection, maintenance, and service includes three major subsystems. First, service must be performed on the system's air circuits and valves. That includes the air supply compressor, supply reservoirs, and hand-operated valves such as the push-pull trailer supply and park valves. Second, technicians must routinely service the brake foundations. Components of the foundation brakes include the slack adjusters, camshafts, brake chambers, shoes, drums, retaining hardware, brake rotors (or discs), and brake pads. Finally, technicians need to ensure that the brakes on every vehicle they service are balanced. **Brake balance** is the ability of the braking system to apply the correct amount of braking torque to each wheel end at the correct time. Ideally, air should supply the all the vehicles brake chambers at the same time and pressure.

This chapter will discuss common brake system complaints and how to troubleshoot malfunctions. It will also cover multiple testing and service procedures commonly undertaken by the heavy-vehicle truck technician.

Safety During Brake System Service

Before undertaking any brake inspection, maintenance, or repair, it is essential that the technician have a complete understanding of safe shop practices for these activities. Brake repairs, inspection, and maintenance are some of the most critical life-and-limb, safety-related operations technicians perform. Not only is there a risk to public safety when a vehicle's braking system fails to operate as designed, but brake service work itself has unique safety risks to technicians. Brake dust hazards, sudden release of pressurized air, and unintended vehicle movement are just a few potential hazards facing technicians. A disciplined approach to understanding and following the best work practices and procedures during service work will ensure safe vehicle operation and minimize the likelihood of personal injuries.

When working on or around a brake system and its related components, the following precautions should be observed:

- Wear safety glasses.
- Brake chamber pushrods and slack adjusters may apply when system pressure drops. Keep hands away from chamber and related parts.
- Because a burst of air pressure may whip lines around as air escapes, never connect or disconnect a hose or line containing air pressure. Similarly do not remove a component or pipe plug unless all system air pressure has been depleted.
- Spring brakes contain power a spring that can easily maim or kill someone if released from a brake chamber. Use only the recommended, proper service tools and observe all precautions when performing any service work with these components.

You Are the Technician

You have recently begun receiving used trucks and buses at your service location and are performing a complete inspection of the equipment for resale. You note, however, that some vehicles have had specialized equipment removed. Others do not have the required "Vehicle Completed" decal located on the driver's side B pillar indicating that the vehicle conforms to all applicable Federal Motor Vehicle Safety Standards (FMVSS). The decal indicates that certification procedures, required by law, have been completed and are designed to ensure the purchaser that their completed or modified vehicle is safe, reliable, and durable.

You remember that some vehicles are allowed to leave the factory classified as "incomplete" vehicles because they undergo additional manufacturing to install bodies, specialized accessories, lighting, and other components needed to make them comply with federal standards for completed vehicles. Nonetheless, you want to make sure all vehicles at your service location conform to all FMVSS air brake safety standards.

1. Briefly outline the areas of inspection you will focus on to ensure the air brake air circuits are in FMVSS compliance.
2. Identify several specific inspections you should make of the brake foundation components to ensure the vehicles comply with FMVSS 121 standards.
3. Outline and provide a justification for any additional brake inspections items you may want to consider that would optimize the vehicle braking safety.

- Do not attempt to disassemble a component until all recommended service procedures are read and understood.
- Always validate all repairs with a thorough road test.

Vehicle Preparation

The first order of business in any brake servicing activity is to prepare the vehicle properly. Vehicles should be parked on a level surface and wheels blocked with purpose-made wheel chocks. Safety stands to support the vehicle must have the appropriate weight capacity for the vehicle. FIGURE 31-1A shows the appropriate placement of axle support stands, and FIGURE 31-1B shows correct placement of wheel chocks. The engine should be off and the key removed. Alternatively, the ignition should be locked-out to prevent starting. All the air reservoir tanks should be drained, and the park brakes should be applied.

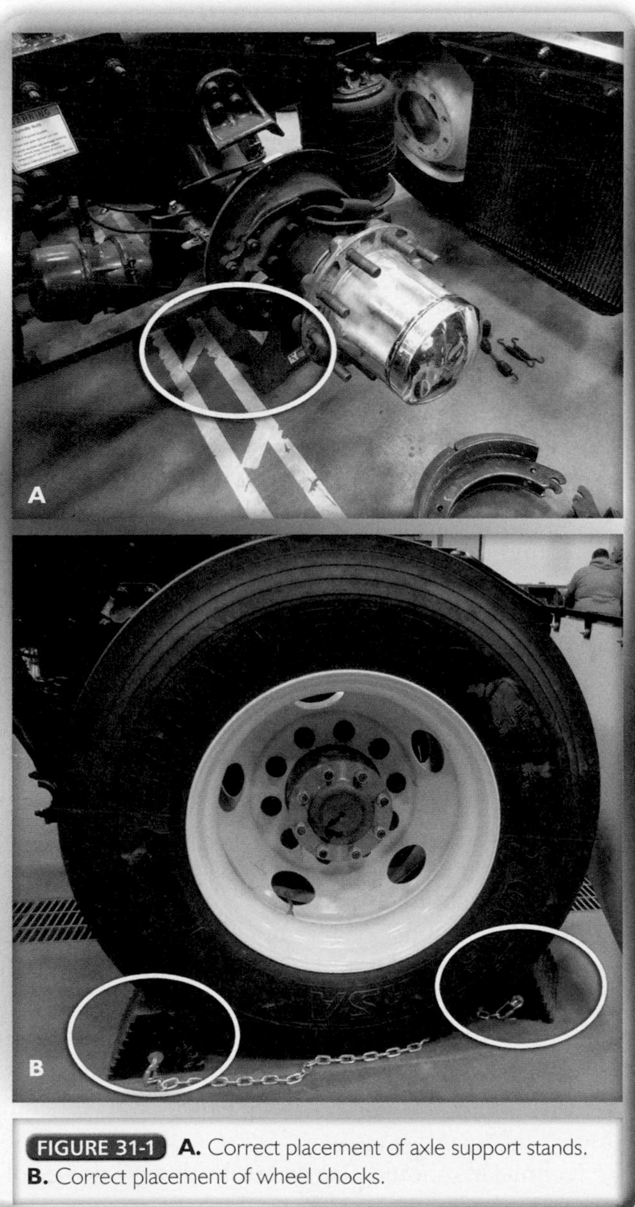

FIGURE 31-1 **A.** Correct placement of axle support stands. **B.** Correct placement of wheel chocks.

Brake Dust Hazards

The latest types of brake lining are no longer manufactured with any asbestos fibers. Instead, these linings contain a variety of ingredients, such as glass fibers, mineral wool, aramid fibers, ceramic fibers, brass, and carbon fibers. Dust produced by these materials is not specifically regulated by the Occupational Safety and Health Administration (OSHA) and are considered a nuisance dust.

Nonetheless, evidence indicates that certain diseases can develop in individuals who experience long-term exposure to some non-asbestos fibers. Manufacturers recommend that technicians use caution to avoid creating and inhaling dust. Never use compressed air or dry brushing to clean brake parts or assemblies. Doing so sends dust particles airborne. Working in the open air away from other operations is good practice. Never use compressed air or dry sweeping to clean the work area, either.

As a further precaution, the National Institute of Occupational Safety and Health (NIOSH) recommends technicians wear an N-95 disposable face mask such as the one shown in FIGURE 31-2. N-95 masks filter 95% of

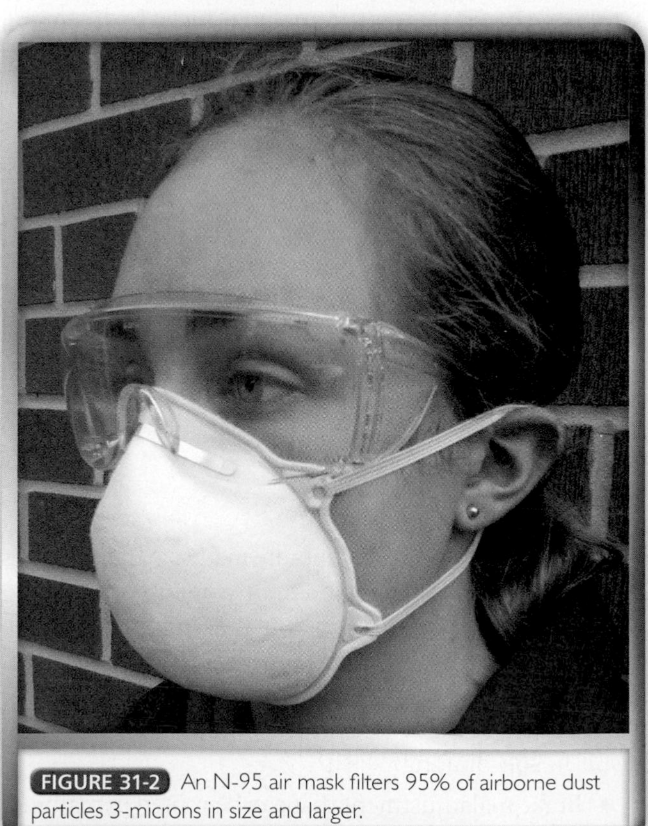

FIGURE 31-2 An N-95 air mask filters 95% of airborne dust particles 3-microns in size and larger.

all airborne particles. Technicians should wear the respirator from removal of the wheels through final reassembly.

Filtering is not reserved for PPE, however. OSHA recommends using filter cylinders to enclose the entire brake end. These cylinders have vacuums with high-efficiency particulate assistance (HEPA) filters and arm sleeves through which the technician can slide his arms while performing inspection and repairs. The arm sleeves enable the technician to work on the wheel end without coming into direct contact with parts and dust.

If individual HEPA filter cylinders are not available, then use an industrial vacuum cleaner with a HEPA filter system to clean dust from the brake drums, shoes, backing plates, and other brake parts. Then, remove any remaining dust with a rag soaked in water or by power washing the wheel end. Even hosing down the wheel ends with a garden hose can reduce breathing hazards posed by fine brake dust.

After having worked on brakes, vacuum work clothes and wash them separately from other clothing. Wash your hands before eating, drinking, or smoking. Dust residue on your hands can be ingested and lead to digestive system problems.

Diagnosing Brake System Malfunctions

Many parts of the brake system can be at fault when a complaint is made about system operation. It is important to follow a logical sequence in dealing with the complaint to identify the source of the problem. The following are complaints that a brake technician is likely to be asked to diagnose and correct on a fairly regular basis.

Common Brake System Complaints

Brake system inspection is recommended when any of complaints about soft brakes, braking noise, pulling, or general air system malfunction are made. Such complaints commonly indicate a defect is likely present in the braking system.

Soft Brakes

Slack or soft brake complaints are made when the brakes are applied and the vehicle is not slowing or stopping effectively. Typical causes of soft braking can originate in the foundation brake system, the brake linings and drums, or in the air system itself.

The following defects in the foundation brakes can result in soft braking:

- Brake maladjustment that can be rooted in malfunctioning or incorrectly adjusted brake adjustment mechanism, incorrectly brake parts, or incorrect assembly.
- Worn foundation components such as brake clevis pins and yokes, camshaft bushings, and S-cams.
- Broken park brake springs producing glazed or hardened brake linings.
- Incorrect chamber size and type
- Incorrect slack adjuster length

Soft braking can also result from certain brake lining and drum conditions, including:

- Glazed lining
- Polished drum surface
- Incorrect application of friction material
- Oil or grease contaminated linings
- Excessively worn brake lining, cracked or loose brake block

Air system malfunctions can also lead to soft braking. For example, air leaks or restrictions in the application or supply systems can decrease the force available for braking. Contaminated, malfunctioning, or worn air valves can lead to the decrease in air pressure, which results in soft braking.

Braking Noise

All air brake systems make noise—and more noise than hydraulic brakes. Air brake noise results from the buildup, release, and application of air pressure in combination with the movement of mechanical components. The forces involved in the pressure and mechanics of a heavy-duty commercial vehicle are much greater than those found in an automobile.

Brake noises from loading air compressors, purging air dryers, and air exhaust from valves are all normal sounds. However, continual air leakage and other sounds are abnormal and require corrective action. With training and field experience, a technician can differentiate normal brake noise from unusual or abnormal sounds created when the brakes are applied or while the vehicle is moving.

When diagnosing brake noises, technicians should pay careful attention to the type of noise. Is the noise a grinding, squealing, or hissing? Brake squeal is most commonly produced by some type of vibration. Correctly tightened and properly lubricated components normally do not cause brake squeal. However, some brake linings used in high temperature, frequent-stopping applications, such as a transit bus, often can be expected to generate noise.

Technicians should also carefully observe noise volume and whether it is a low or high frequency. Also, technicians should try to locate where in the system the noise is occurring as well as when the noise takes place. For example, are the brakes warm or cold when the noise occurs? Is the compressor loading or unloading? Is the noise occurring at high or low vehicle speed or at the beginning or end of the brake application. Finally, the technician needs to determine the braking condition that produces the noise. For example, is the noise heard when applying light, moderate, or heavy brake pressure? And does the noise change as the brakes are being applied? All of these observations and inquiries will help the technician start to understand the essence of the noise complaint.

The sources of squealing and grinding noises are very different. Squealing noise is typically caused by vibrating parts. Other typical causes of brake squeal during brake applications include the following:

- Glazed lining and or drums. **Glazing** is a mirror like finish produced through continuous braking pressure and pressure between lining and brake drums.
- Loose lining, brake block, or shoes
- Loose anchor pins, bushings, camshafts, and support brackets
- Missing or defective brake shoe return springs, which allow shoes to drag
- Brake drum design and weight
- Incorrect lining for the application
- Poor lining-to-drum contact
- Improper alignment of foundation parts
- Imbalanced brakes causing one axle or wheel to perform a disproportionate amount of the braking
- Dragging brakes or failure of brakes to release
- Brake shoes rubbing against a rotating drum

Typical causes of a grinding noise when the brakes are applied include:

- Foreign material embedded in friction material
- Dislocated brake parts such as a return spring, roller, or table pin.
- Metal-to-metal contact between brake shoe and brake drum
- A broken brake shoe or other foundation part failure

Pulling

Brake pull, also called **brake steer**, is an unintended left or right direction change by a vehicle during a brake application. Not all brake steer is caused by the braking system. For example, loose or worn steering linkages, wheel bearings, or kingpins can cause brake pull. Likewise, if the suspension shifts during braking, that could indicate a suspension-related issue that is causing the vehicle to pull when braking. Broken leaf springs, sheared center bolts, loose U-bolts, broken or loose torque arms, and axle alignment are a few potential causes of suspension-related pull.

Other potential causes of brake pull include the following:

- Oil or grease contaminated lining
- Improperly adjusted brakes or incorrect drum/shoe clearances
- Incorrect brake balance or brake torque
- Mismatched, defective, or worn foundation components such as brake lining, slack adjuster length, and air chambers.
- Damaged, kinked, pinch, or undersized brake hoses and or lines
- Defective or incorrect replacement air system components.

Typical causes of pulling brakes:

- Mismatched lining or drums
- Glazed ling and drums
- Spring brakes not fully releasing due to a broken spring, air leak, or insufficient release pressure.
- Slow release (worn foundation brake components, binding shoe, minimal anchor pin/shoe clearance)

Braking Odors

Complaints about smell generally indicate rapid brake wear. Smells are typically related to overheated brake lining. As the brake lining overheats, the resins binding the friction material in the brakes begins to vaporize. Similarly, leaking wheel seals can contaminate the friction material with oil or excessive grease from over lubrication of camshafts. Having grease on the friction material when the linings overheat can produce complaints related to smell.

Linings can wear faster than normal when the driver uses aggressive braking or frequent high-speed braking. Using an incorrect lining for particular application, dragging brakes, or applying improper brake torque can all contribute to accelerated lining wear as well.

TECHNICIAN TIP

Brake block and brake lining is made from materials to match operating conditions. Friction material with greater wear resistance may often be harder and more prone to noise. A trade-off for quieter brake friction materials may be shorter friction material life.

Troubleshooting Air Braking Problems

Troubleshooting problems in a vehicle's braking system must be undertaken methodically. TABLE 31-1 is a starting point for identifying common complaints in the air braking system. The information may assist in the diagnosis of air brake systems by identifying common faults and causes along with possible remedies. Always consult manufacturers' specific information for the vehicle you are working on.

TABLE 31-1: Complaints and Remedies for Components of Air Brake Systems

Component	Complaint	Remedy
Compressor	Pumps beyond "cut-out"	■ Check gauge. ■ Check governor. • Be certain it pressurizes unloader port when above "cut-out." ■ Check unloader/plungers. • Lube, kit or change head.
	Won't pump air	■ Check gauge. ■ Check compressor drive. ■ Check inlet valves and plungers. • If stuck, leak will be evident at intake when unloaded. Install unloader kit head kit or head assembly.
	Slow pressure build-up	■ Check gauge. ■ Check compressor drive. Check intake for restriction. ■ Check discharge line for restriction. ■ Check unloader function. • Lube or kit. ■ Check inlet and exhaust valves. • Leak will be evident at intake when unloaded, kit or exchange head.
	Pumps excessive oil	■ Check oil return for restriction, kink, or loop. ■ Check for gasket sealant obstructing drain. Check for undersize return line (12 mm minimum). Check for fitting restricting drain. ■ Check intake vacuum of the compressor. ■ Check for excessive engine crankcase pressure (poor engine ventilation). ■ Check compressor ring wear. • Exchange for service unit.
Wet tank	Excess oil accumulation	■ See #1 Complaint – Pumps excessive oil.
	Excess water accumulation	■ Drain daily. • Install automatic drain on wet tank.
	Damaged	■ Replace.
Low pressure indicator switch	Buzzer or light inoperable	■ Check ground and wiring on switch and buzzer/light. ■ Replace switch or buzzer/light.
	Won't operate at pressures below 60 psi (415 kPa)	■ Check dash gauge for accuracy. ■ Replace switch or buzzer/light.
Safety valve	"Pops" off excessively	■ Check system pressure. ■ Valve operating properly in venting at 140 to 150 psi (965 to 1,035 kPa). ■ Check governor/unloader.
	"Pops" off at less than 140 psi (965 kPa)	■ Replace.
	Leaks	■ Replace.
	Won't function	■ Periodic test: • Remove and test above 150 psi (1,035 kPa) with shop air. ■ Replace if non-functional.

Continued on next page

TABLE 31-1: Complaints and Remedies for Components of Air Brake Systems, continued

Component	Complaint	Remedy
Drain valves – manual	Leaks	■ Replace.
	Won't drain	■ Repair or replace.
	Won't drain in cold weather	■ Replace with heated unit.
	Leaks – malfunctions	■ Repair or replace. ■ Periodic test: • With system pressure stabilized (compressor unloaded) no leak evident at discharge port; make several foot brake applications to reduce wet tank pressure. Moisture should drain from discharge port.
Governor	Flutters	■ Check gauge. ■ Check unloader line size according to manufacturer's specifications. ■ Check air actuated accessory. • Is the air volume requirement greater than governor capacity? ■ Check for plugged governor reservoir line. ■ Repair, adjust, or replace governor.
	Won't pass air to unloader to "cut-off" compressor	■ Check governor reservoir line. ■ Repair or replace.
Single check valve	Allow bleed back to supply reservoir	■ Periodic test: • Bleed supply reservoir and observe gauges. • Check valve should maintain rear and front reservoir pressure. ■ Replace if test results are negative.
Primary and secondary reservoir	Excess oil/water	■ Drain as required. ■ Check automatic drain valve on wet tank for proper operation.
Air gauge	Incorrect reading	■ Calibrate, replace.
Dual system foot brake valve	Leaks at exhaust with hand valve applied	■ Check: • Double check valve, repair or replace.
	Leaks at exhaust with all brakes released	■ Check anti-compound double check valve for back flow. • *Caution:* Block wheels. ■ Repair or replace. ■ Check foot valve for inlet valve leak. ■ Repair or replace.
	Leaks at exhaust with foot brake applied	■ Foot valve defective. ■ Repair or replace.
Quick release valve	Leaks (when used in service brake system)	■ Replace.
	Leaks (when used in spring brake system)	■ Replace.
Service brake chamber	Leaks	■ Replace diaphragm. • Set parking brake. • Reset clamps. ■ Adjust brakes.
	Sluggish application or release	■ Check basic brake. ■ Check for air-line restriction/leak. ■ Align linkage. ■ Check chamber return spring. ■ Adjust brakes. • Angle should approach 90° on application. ■ Check for improper chamber or obstruction.

Continued on next page

TABLE 31-1: Complaints and Remedies for Components of Air Brake Systems, continued

Component	Complaint	Remedy
Slack adjuster	Sleeve will not depress	■ Clean and lubricate or replace with unit dimensionally same.
	Adjusting shaft will not turn	■ Replace with unit dimensionally same.
	Cracked housing	■ Check spring brake anti-compound system. ■ Check air chamber size. • Replace if larger than original size. ■ Check direction of travel for proper position of hex nut. ■ Hex nut must face away from chamber for unidirectional slack adjuster.
	Worn clevis pin bushing	■ Replace bushing.
Relay valve	Leaks at exhaust port with all brakes applied	■ Check seal in spring brake for back-flow of spring "hold-off" pressure through service port to open exhaust on valve. ■ Replace. ■ Check inlet valve in relay valve for leak. ■ If reservoir section of valve shows evidence of contamination, check supply lines for rusty fittings or carbon deposits. ■ Repair or replace.
	Leaks at exhaust port with service brakes applied	■ Exhaust valve not seating properly. ■ Repair or replace.
Spring parking brake (service only service chamber side of spring brake)	Parking brake drags or won't release	■ Check for: improper adjustment, restrictions or broken line. ■ Diaphragm failure. ■ System pressure too low. ■ Improper manual release. ■ Broken return spring (spring side). ■ Quick release of relay malfunction. ■ Broken power spring. ■ Replace entire unit or piggy-back emergency section.
	Sluggish park application	■ Check for: • Failed spring brake diaphragm. • Improper manual release. • Broken power spring.
	Leaks when pressurized for park and brake release	■ Check for: • Ruptured spring side diaphragm. • Push rod seal leakage.
	Service chamber malfunction	■ See service brake chamber.
Double check valve unites front brake and rear brake reservoirs to feed park control	Rear tank bleed-down also bleeds front tank or vice versa	■ Periodic test: pressure should remain in one tank after the other is drained. ■ Replace if inoperative.
Tractor-trailer park control valve (yellow diamond)	Leaks at exhaust port	■ Replace.
	Parking brake won't release	■ Check for full system pressure delivery thru valve.
	Parking brake won't apply	■ Replace if it will not release pressure.

Continued on next page

TABLE 31-1: Complaints and Remedies for Components of Air Brake Systems, continued

Component	Complaint	Remedy
Trailer charge valve (red octagonal)	Leaks at exhaust port	■ Replace.
	Driver may "over-ride" automatic trailer brakes when tractor air is below 20 psi (140 kPa)	■ Replace if T.P. system is automatic and 2-line. ■ Repair or replace T.P. system is automatic and 3-line.
	Won't apply trailer immediately when "pulled"	■ Replace if it won't exhaust. ■ Repair or replace if 2-line tractor protection valve or tractor only park valve is functional.
Tractor only park valve (blue round)	Leaks at exhaust port	■ Repair or replace.
Two-line tractor protection valve (non-automatic type) will not respond to trailer charge valve	Supply line to trailer with slow bleed down does not shut off tractor air and vent between 40 and 20 psi (275 and 140 kPa)	■ Check trailer charge valve, as it should "pop" to let T.P. valve vent trailer supply. ■ Repair or replace.
	Leaks at exhaust port or tractor service (back thru hand or foot valve) or trailer supply	■ Repair or replace.
Quick release and double check valve combination	Foot valve exhaust leak	■ Check double valve portion for feed-back to foot valve. ■ Repair or replace.
	Leaks with brakes released	■ Repair or replace.
Hand control valve-trailer service brakes	Leaks at exhaust port when released and foot valve is applied	■ Check number 23 or 24.
	Leaks at exhaust port when in applied or release position	■ Repair or replace.
Double check valve separates trailer hand valve pressure from rear foot brake pressure for delivery to trailer	Foot valve exhaust port leaks when hand valve is applied	■ Replace.
	Hand valve exhaust port leaks when foot valve is applied	■ Replace.
Double check valve separates front axle foot brake pressure from rear axle foot brake pressure and/or trailer hand valve pressure for delivery to trailer	Leaks thru foot valve	■ Replace. See number 23.
	Exhaust with hand valve applied	■ Periodic test: • Alternately loosen each inlet line and apply pressure to other. • If leak is detected, replace.
Stop light switch	Leaks	■ Replace.
	Fails to signal, sound wiring, air pressure OK, bulbs check OK	■ Replace.

Continued on next page

TABLE 31-1: Complaints and Remedies for Components of Air Brake Systems, continued

Component	Complaint	Remedy
Double dash valve with built-in w-way check. (red octagon) trailer charge (yellow diamond) tractor park	Parking brake won't release	■ Check for full system pressure delivery thru valve.
	Parking brake won't apply	■ Repair or replace if it will not release pressure.
	Leaks at exhaust port driver may "over-ride" automatic trailer brakes when tractor air is below 20 psi (140 kPa)	■ Repair or replace. ■ Replace if T.P. system is automatic and 2-line. Repair or replace if T.P. valve is automatic and 3-line.
	Won't apply trailer immediately when "pulled"	■ Replace if it won't exhaust. ■ Repair or replace number 20 if 26 is functional.
	Rear tank bleed-down also bleeds front tank or vice versa	■ Periodic test: Pressure should remain in one tank after the other is drained. ■ Replace if inoperative.
Inversion relay valve with the loss of rear service supply; application of spring brake by using the emergency section should be available along with front service brake by applying foot valve	Function test	■ Periodically test by bleeding rear service tank and observing front brake and rear spring brake application upon depressing foot pedal.
	Leaks	■ Repair or replace.
Barrier wheel oil seals	Oil leak	■ Check for proper glazing of the sealing lip. ■ Check serrations on O.D. and I.D. to see that sealing surfaces are dry. If wet, this could denote the leakage path. ■ Check area between positioning pads. If wet, suspect seal leak. ■ Check seal for damage to seal during installation. ■ Check hub bore and spindle surfaces for imperfections or irregularities. ■ Check to be sure that proper seal has been installed for the particular axle application.
Air dryer	Air leaking constantly from purge valve	■ Purge valve seal damaged. Replace purge seal. ■ Purge valve frozen. Inspect heater (see heater problems). Remove purge tube and push valve shut.
	Heater inoperative	■ Blown fuse. • Check fuse and replace with 8-10 amp fuse. ■ Broken wires or poor connections. ■ Repair or replace wiring to heater.
	Slow wet tank build-up	■ Filter and/or desiccant plugged. • Service dryer.

Conducting Preliminary Testing on Brake Systems

Before diving headlong into repairs, it is important to conduct a series of preliminary tests to collect baseline data about what is happening in the air braking system. By conducting the preliminary tests and checks in this section, a clearer picture of the various braking troubles will emerge and allow the technician to make needed adjustments and repairs more efficiently and effectively. Once preliminary tests are conducted, more advanced testing can identify problems deeper in the system.

Preliminary Testing Procedures

Conducting preliminary tests will help eliminate potential problem areas and help the technician arrive at an accurate diagnosis of the problem. Preliminary tests include testing for air brake system performance, air leakage, oil consumption, **brake stroke length**, the distance the service brake pushrod travels, parking brake function, emergency brake function, and antilock braking performance.

Testing Air Brake System Performance

A starting point for brake inspection during a preventative maintenance inspection is the FMVSS 121 Dual Air Brake System Test. This inspection should be performed on a flat level surface after blocking the vehicle's wheels to prevent it from moving. The vehicle's parking spring-brakes are applied, the transmission is in neutral, and supply reservoirs completely drained of air. To conduct a test of air brake system performance, follow the guidelines in SKILL DRILL 31-1.

Testing for Air Leakage

Technicians need to test for air leakage to determine if the amount of leakage is within acceptable levels. To conduct an air leakage test, follow the guidelines in SKILL DRILL 31-2. The results will indicate if the vehicle has an acceptable or unacceptable level of air leakage.

The acceptable level of air leakage in two minutes from either the primary or secondary supply reservoir depends on the vehicle. For a single-axle vehicle with the brakes applied, the limit is no more than 4 psi (28 kPa). For a tractor/trailer combination vehicle, a leak of no more than 6 psi is allowed, and for a tractor with two trailers, no more than 8 psi. If leaks are detected, they should be repaired and the vehicle retested to confirm the correct repair has been made. Soapy water can be used to pinpoint leaks.

Air leaks can take place at a large number of points in the vehicle air system. Air leaks from anywhere on the vehicle should be checked, including the supply reservoirs, parking brake chambers, supply lines, fittings, dash gauges, all brake valves, governor, and compressor

SKILL DRILL 31-1 Inspecting Air Supply System Performance

1. Turn the ignition key to the "on" position with the engine off. Verify the low pressure warning buzzer and light are operating.

2. Measure the air pressure build-time. Start the engine and bring the engine to high idle, which is its maximum no-load RPM. Record the following observations while building air pressure to cut-out pressure when the compressor unloads.
   - Mark the air pressure when the warning light and buzzer shut-off. Air pressure should reach approximately 60-psi.
   - Record the time it takes the air pressure to build between 85-psi and 100-psi. The time should be less than 25-seconds at governed engine RPM. If the buildup time exceeds 45 seconds, the system should be taken out of service.

3. Validate the compressor unloading cut-out pressure by recording the system pressure on both the primary and secondary reservoir dash gauges. The compressor should cut-out at between 120- and 130-psi. Compare your observations to the manufacturer's specifications.

4. Pump the service brakes to deplete the supply reservoirs. Record the pressure at which the compressor begins to build air pressure. The difference between cut-in and cut-out pressure should be 25-psi or less. Compare your observations to the manufacturer's specifications.

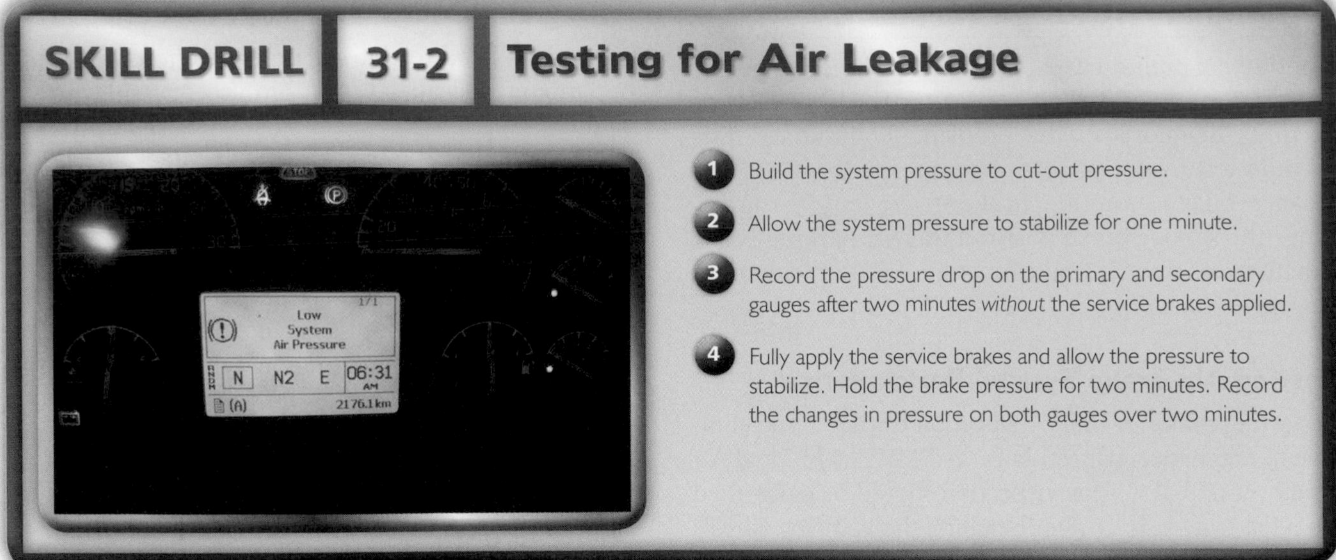

SKILL DRILL 31-2 Testing for Air Leakage

1. Build the system pressure to cut-out pressure.
2. Allow the system pressure to stabilize for one minute.
3. Record the pressure drop on the primary and secondary gauges after two minutes *without* the service brakes applied.
4. Fully apply the service brakes and allow the pressure to stabilize. Hold the brake pressure for two minutes. Record the changes in pressure on both gauges over two minutes.

discharge valves. As shown in **FIGURE 31-3A**, spring brake chambers use a seal to prevent air leakage from the power spring chamber into the service chamber. A leaking seal will cause air to continually leak from the quick release valve or the exhaust port of a relay valve associated with the service brake **FIGURE 31-3B**.

In addition, air accessories such as the air suspension, power take-off controls, and even the air seats should be investigated when inspecting for loss of air pressure. Connections to air reservoirs for vehicle accessories are one of many possible sources of air leakage. On the schematic for a coach shown in **FIGURE 31-4**, the number of air reservoirs located throughout the chassis means an extensive inspection for air leaks is required.

Air shift controls for transmissions can leak also. Worn leaking "O"-rings for range control cylinders can leak internally inside a transmission and can be hard to pinpoint. Blocking the air supply line to the transmission to determine whether the pressure will stop leaking can help identify a transmission as a source of leak.

Not all air leaks can be detected using soapy water or easily listening for telltale hissing. Leaks behind cab instrument panels and dash, body cavities, and inside transmissions and power dividers due to defective O-rings on shift mechanisms are often difficult to identify. Moving the vehicle to quiet location outside a shop can help a technician detect the sound of smaller leaks. Also helpful for locating some slow leaks causing air to leak-down over several hours are ultrasonic noise detectors. These are more commonly used to locate engine vacuum and air conditioning refrigerant leaks. A technique more often used is to isolate air circuits by disconnecting or pinching air lines. Suspected air circuits can be temporarily pinched using purpose made tools that do not damage

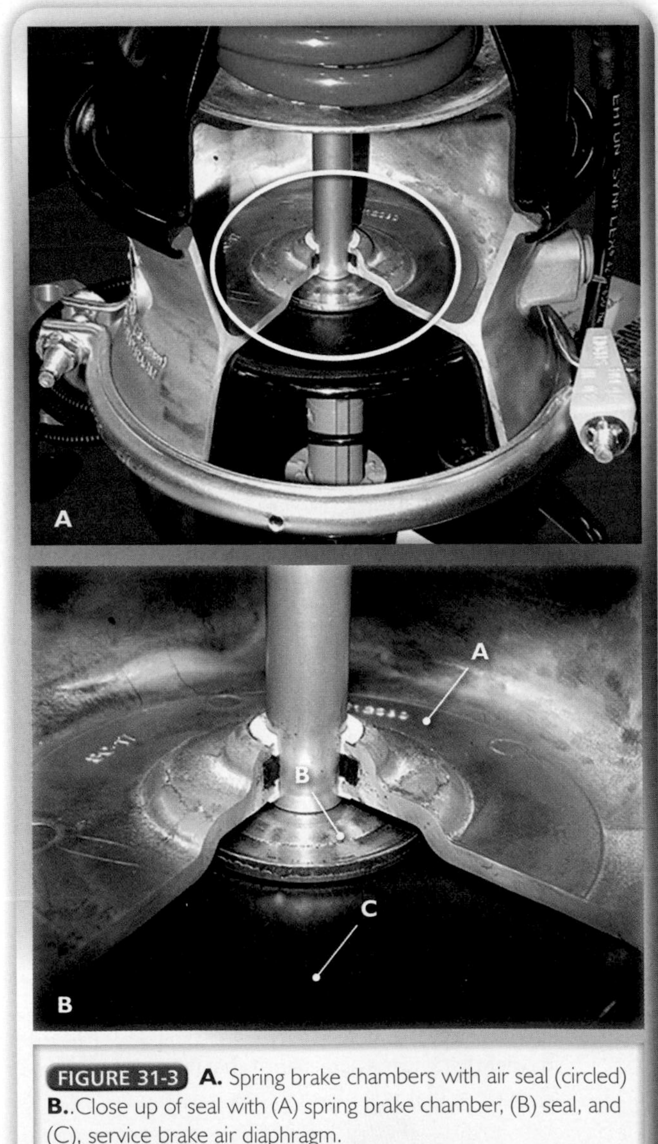

FIGURE 31-3 **A.** Spring brake chambers with air seal (circled) **B.**.Close up of seal with (A) spring brake chamber, (B) seal, and (C), service brake air diaphragm.

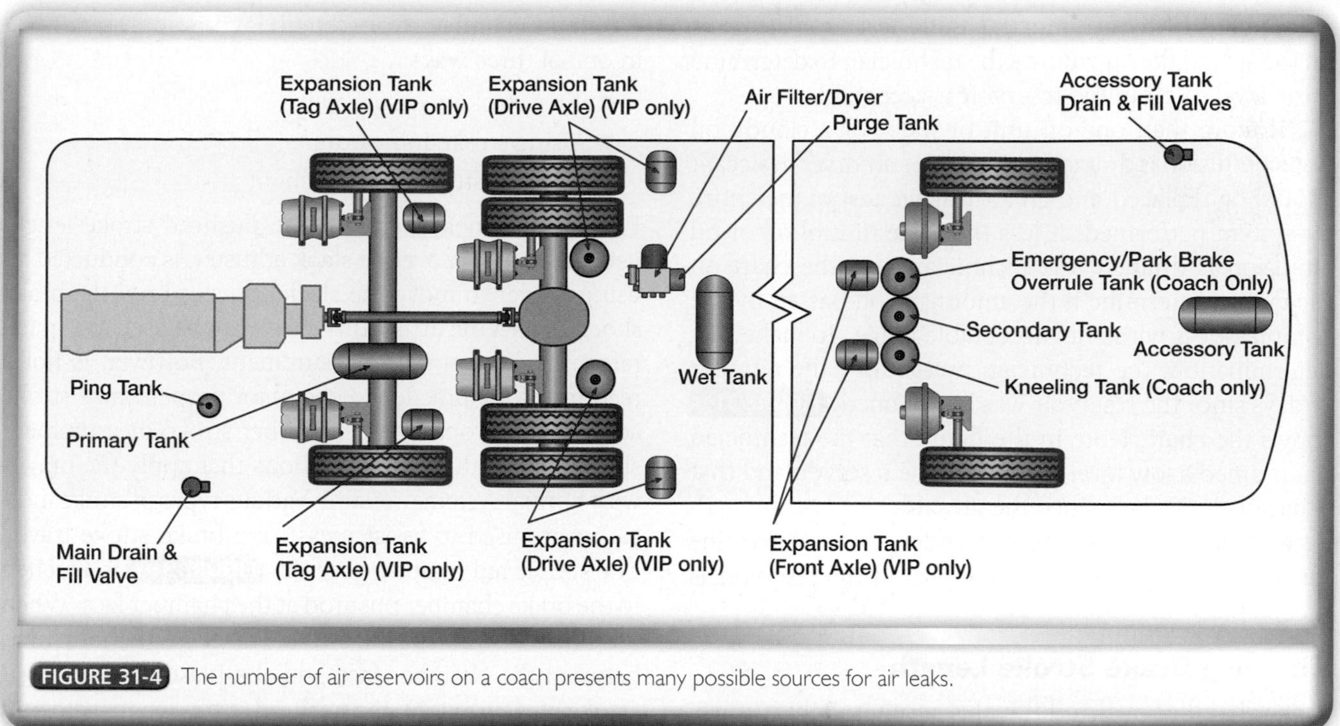

FIGURE 31-4 The number of air reservoirs on a coach presents many possible sources for air leaks.

> **TECHNICIAN TIP**
>
> Air leakage from lines and air reservoirs is the number one cause for compressors to pump excessive amounts of air. The result is that a compressor will run too hot and pass oil vapor into the system. To conduct a thorough air system leakage check, the brake pedal should be applied for two minutes while observing the air pressure gauges. An application pressure of approximately 90-psi should be used. After releasing the pedal, the gauges should be watched for two additional minutes. When the brakes are released, air leakage should not exceed 2-psi per minute with single vehicles and 4-psi for combination vehicles. With brakes applied, leakage should be no more than 4-psi for single vehicles, or 6-psi for combination vehicles.

airlines. When the pressure loss stops, the correct circuit supply line can be traced to precisely pinpoint the air leak.

Testing for Oil Consumption

Some oil is normally pumped from the air compressor. The air dryer is responsible for removing oil passed into the air supply by the compressor. Some oil can end up in the air reservoir if the oil volume is excessive, as shown in FIGURE 31-5. Oil can mix with water and gum-up air valves. At one time, a cardboard card placed over the compressor's air outlet was used to diagnose excessive oil discharge. Too much oil on the card was the justification to replace the compressor.

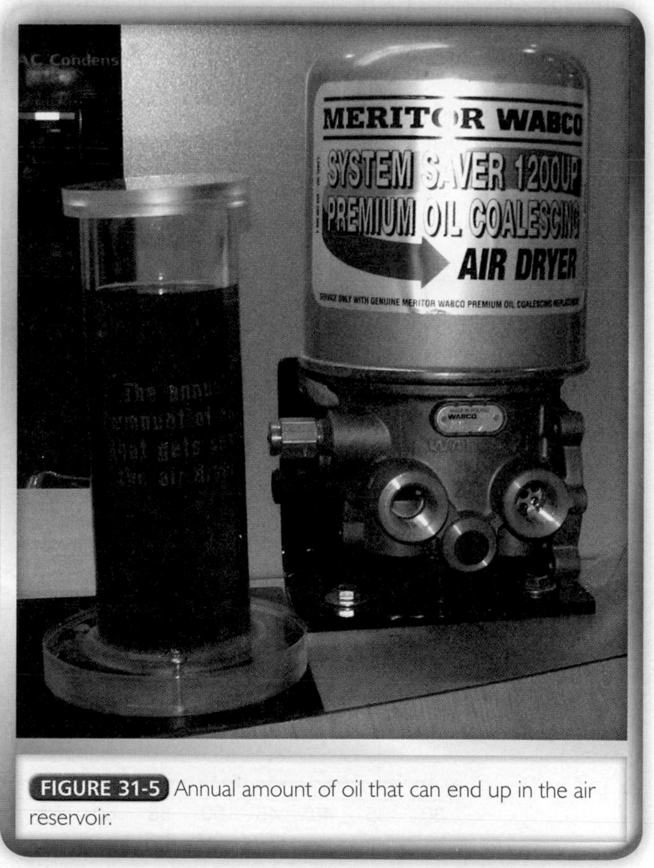

FIGURE 31-5 Annual amount of oil that can end up in the air reservoir.

Today, a more reliable and less subjective test recommended by Bendix involves the use of the Bendix Air System Inspection Cup (BASIC). After checking for external oil leaks and loose fittings, the air reservoir tanks are completely drained into the BASIC test cup. The chart on the side of the cup allows the technician to determine if the level of oil in the reservoir is acceptable.

If more than one oil unit of water or a cloudy oil water emulsion is drained, the vehicle's air dryer desiccant should be replaced and an air leakage test of the entire air system performed. If less than one unit of oil or oil emulsion is drained, the technician uses the chart on the cup to determine if the amount of oil passed by the compressor is within an acceptable range. To make that determination, the technician must know the number of days since the reservoir was last drained. FIGURE 31-6 shows the chart. Note in the figure that the technician has drained a low level of oil from the reservoir and that it has been 60 days since the air tank was last drained. Because the decision point is under the diagonal line for the acceptable level, the oil level in the reservoir is acceptable.

Checking Brake Stroke Length

Brake chamber pushrod travel is another daily requirement for a brake system inspection. Stroke travel indicates whether the brakes are properly adjusted to obtain optimal drum-shoe clearance. When brakes are properly adjusted, the angle formed between the brake chamber pushrod and the arm of the slack adjuster is approximately 90° with an 80–100 psi brake application pressure.

Brake chamber stroke length is commonly measured in one of three ways:

- Free stroke measurement
- Using stroke indicators
- Applied stroke measurement

Free stroke measurement, the pushrod stroke length using a lever to move the slack adjuster, is conducted by using a lever to move the slack adjuster until the brake shoes contact the drum; this check can be used as a quick reference. Free stroke measurement, however, is not a recommended practice to check for proper brake stroke adjustment. Proper brake chamber stroke measurement should be conducted by methods that apply the brakes with normal system pressure. Various types of stroke indicators are used to assist measuring brake stroke travel. The simple red plastic tie seen in FIGURE 31-7 is attached to the brake chamber pushrod at the chamber face. When the brake is applied, the stroke travel can be measured between the chamber face and the plastic tie. **Applied stroke measurement**, the pushrod stroke length with a 90 psi (621 kPa) service brake application, is the most acceptable procedure recommended for measuring brake adjustment. To check brake stroke length using applied stroke measurement, follow the steps in SKILL DRILL 31-3 in conjunction with the data in TABLE 31-2, which shows the maximum permissible applied brake stroke travel before requiring an adjustment. Note that these dimensions are

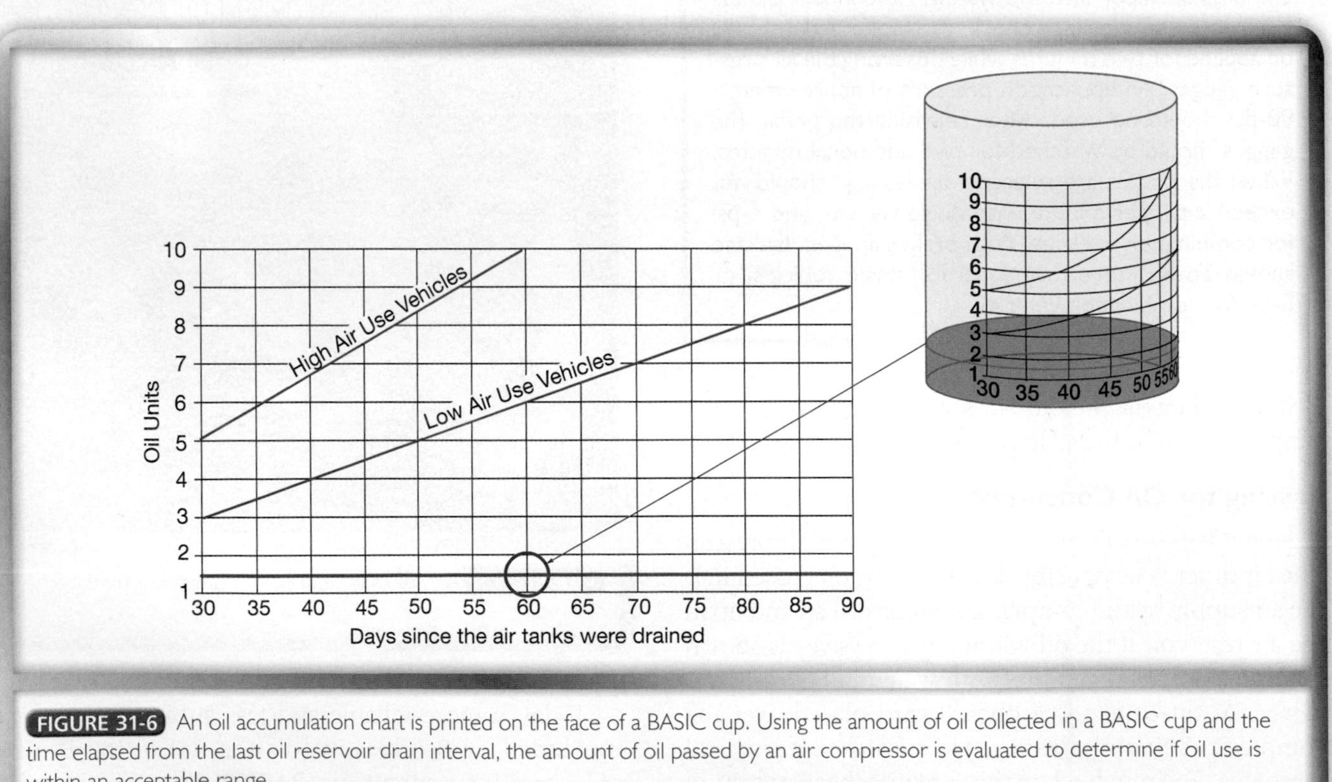

FIGURE 31-6 An oil accumulation chart is printed on the face of a BASIC cup. Using the amount of oil collected in a BASIC cup and the time elapsed from the last oil reservoir drain interval, the amount of oil passed by an air compressor is evaluated to determine if oil use is within an acceptable range.

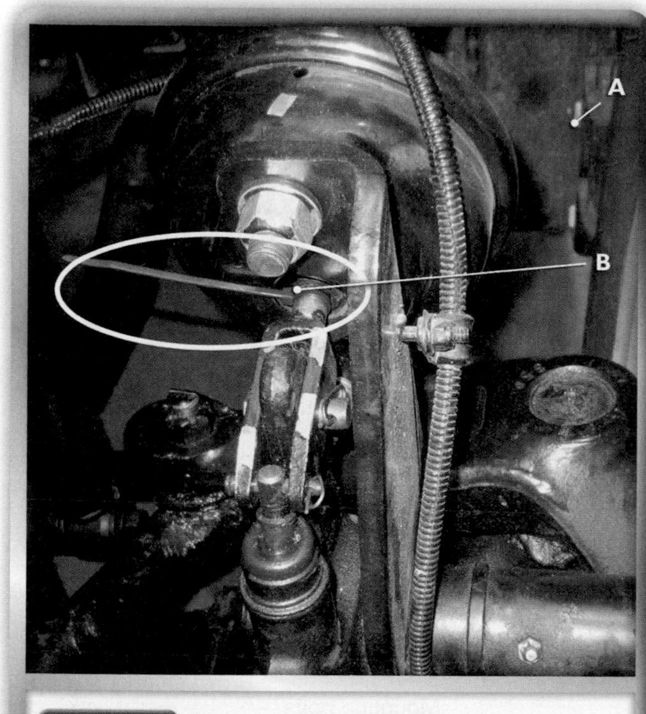

FIGURE 31-7 A red zip tie (circled) is used to assist measuring brake stroke travel. **A.** Service brake chamber. **B.** Stroke indicator.

TABLE 31-2: Actuator Stroke Table

Brake Actuator Size	Recommended Maximum Operating Stroke
Standard Stroke Actuator	
30	2" (5 cm)
24	1.75" (4.45 cm)
20	1.75" (4.45 cm)
16	1.75" (4.45 cm)
12	1.375" (3.5 cm)
Long Stroke Actuator	
30LS	2.5" (6.35 cm)
24L	2" (5 cm)
24LS	2.5" (6.35 cm)
20L	2" (5 cm)
16L	2" (5 cm)

Source: Bendix

SKILL DRILL 31-3 Measuring Brake Stroke Length with Applied Stroke Measurement

1. Using the dash gauge as a guide, adjust the air system pressure to between 80–100 psi.
2. Make a full service brake application. While holding the applied brake pressure, measure and record the distance from the brake chamber face to the center of the pushrod clevis pin.
3. Subtract the measured brake release stroke distance from the applied stroke and record. Compare your findings to the information on TABLE 31-2. Repeat at all wheel locations. On trailers, use the hand or trailer valve to apply the service brakes to measure pushrod angle.

out of service limits. A typical 30-series chamber will typically be set up to have 1" to 1.5" (25.4–38.1 mm) applied brake stroke travel using an automatic slack adjuster.

During daily inspections, when the park-spring brakes are applied, spring brake pressure will apply the brakes forcefully enough to measure the angle and stroke distance between the brake chamber pushrod and the slack adjuster arm. As showing in FIGURE 31-8, when the brakes are applied, an approximately 90-degree angle is formed between the slack adjuster and the brake chamber pushrod. The angle may vary slightly on some vehicles to prevent interference with other components.

If the angle is more than 90 degrees, the slack adjuster requires adjustment. If the slack adjuster is an automatic type, further investigation is required to determine the reason it may have lost its original 90-degree installed angle. Measure and record the distance from the brake chamber face to the center of the clevis pin with the brakes fully released. Repeat at all wheel locations.

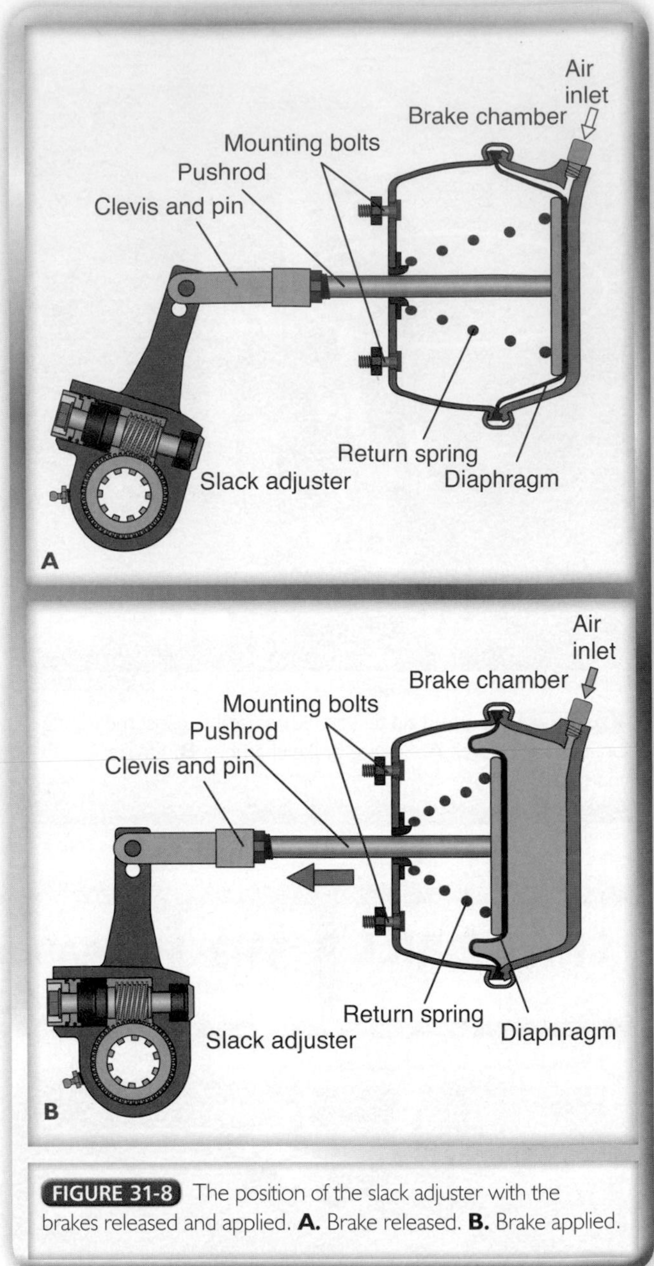

FIGURE 31-8 The position of the slack adjuster with the brakes released and applied. **A.** Brake released. **B.** Brake applied.

Testing Parking Brake Function

Ensuring the park-spring brakes are quickly applied and released validates the correct operation of park control, tractor protection, and the relay and anti-compounding valves. The operation of brake lines, hoses, spring brake chambers, and supply reservoirs are also indirectly evaluated.

On straight trucks, with air system at full pressure and the engine idling between 600 and 900 RPM, the park control valve is applied and released during this inspection. Brakes must apply and release promptly when the valve is pushed in and out. For tractor and trailer combinations, the red octagonal tractor protection control valve in the cab is used to apply and release the trailer spring brakes. Again, the brakes must respond quickly to the valve being pushed in and out.

This test requires two technicians. One needs to check brake operation if the wheels are chocked while the other operates the dash valves. Alternatively, the speed of park brake release and application can be performed by allowing the vehicle to slowly roll while in gear to no more than 3 mph. The park brake can then be applied and released to evaluate system operation.

Spring Brake Servicing

Removing the spring brake actuator will require caging the power spring. This is a simple procedure, but technicians must use extreme caution when performing this task, as the caged power spring is under extreme pressure. FIGURE 31-9 shows the correct procedure for "caging" a spring brake chamber to release the parking brake. The power spring in the rear chamber is compressed by a pressure plate when tightening the caging bolt. Note—only use hand tools. Do not use impact wrenches or air ratchets, and do not over tighten the bolt. Over-tightening the bolt will damage the pressure plate, which could potentially cause the spring to explosively release. FIGURE 31-10 shows the result of an improper stroke travel adjustment or a misaligned or damaged pressure plate in the park brake chamber, which can cause a brake to drag. A good practice is to remove the access plug from the rear of the chamber to verify the pressure plate is properly seated in the chamber.

When installing parking brake chambers, the chamber position and pushrod length are critical to achieve effective brake application. When replacing a complete spring brake actuator, the pushrod on the new chamber

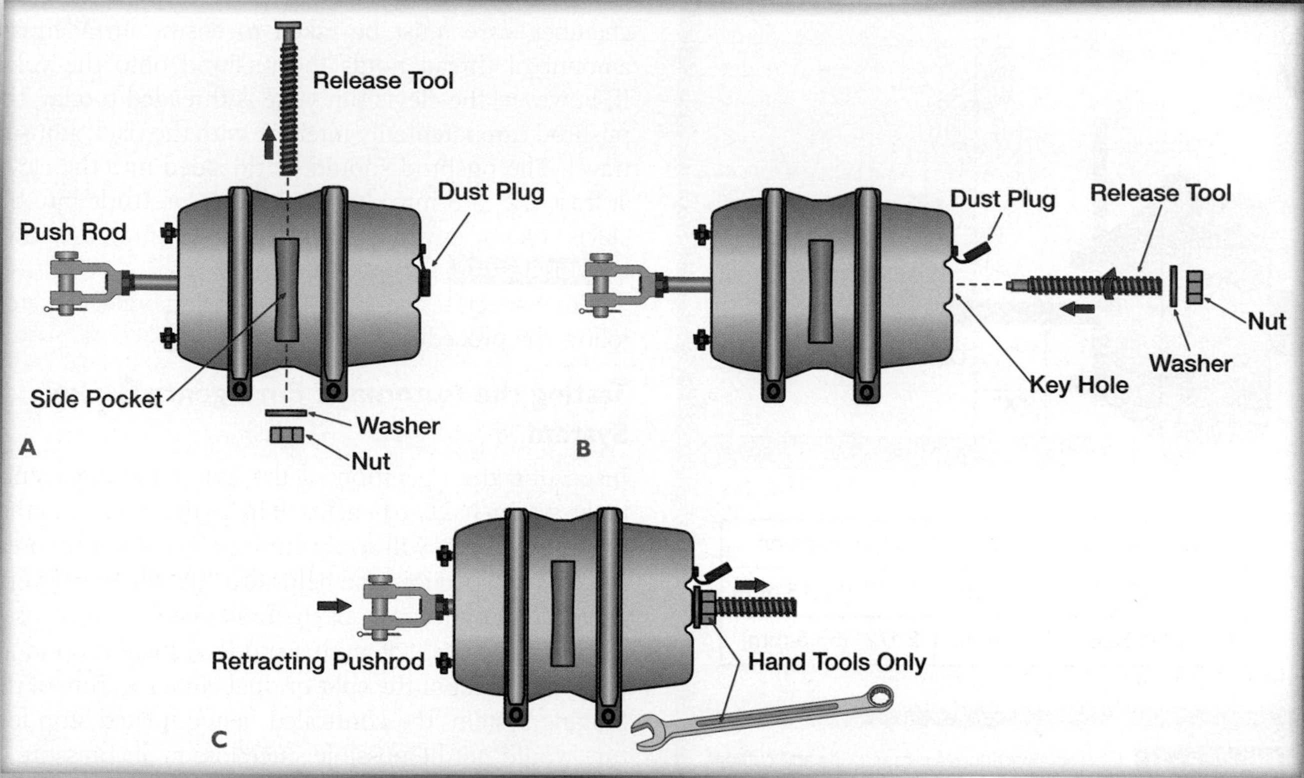

FIGURE 31-9 **A.** Insert the release tool. **B.** Release the stud by turning a quarter turn clockwise. **C.** Retract the pushrod.

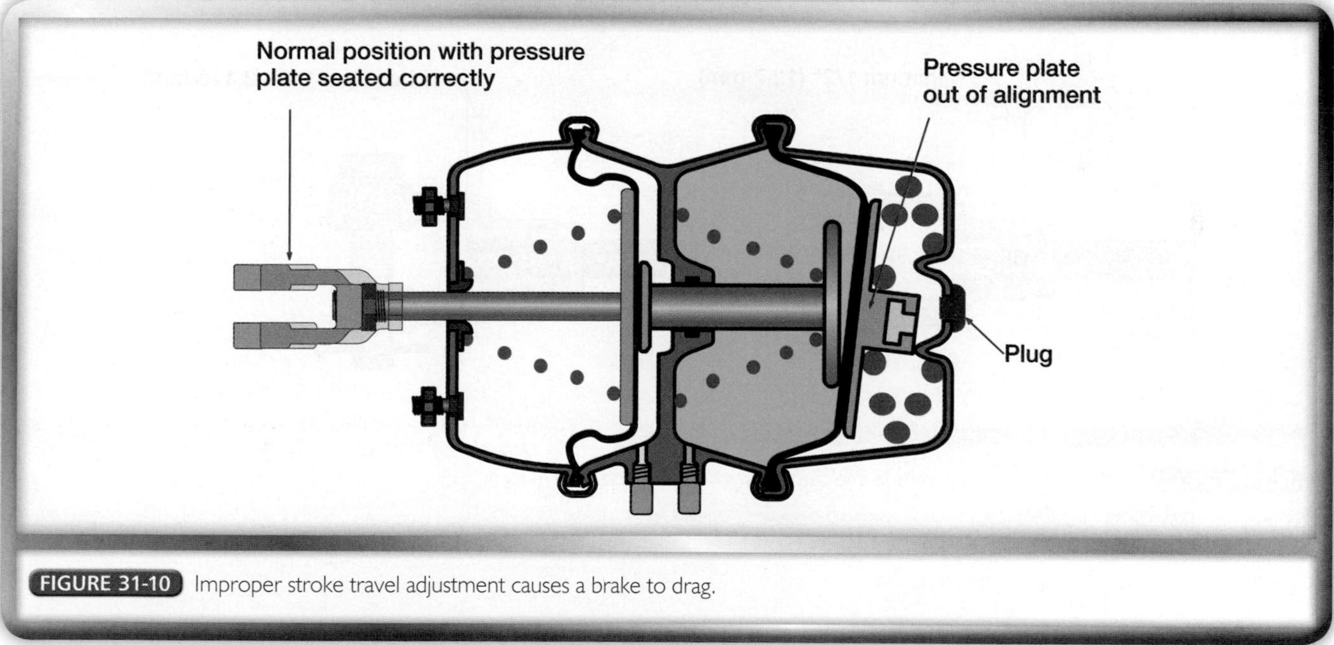

FIGURE 31-10 Improper stroke travel adjustment causes a brake to drag.

must be cut to length. To determine the correct chamber pushrod length, two measurements are required: brake stroke length and the point where the centerline of the slack adjuster intersects with the chamber pushrod when the brake is applied. A carpenter's square can be used to measure the intersection point when the slack adjuster is at 90-degrees to the pushrod. The maximum brake stroke length *x* is subtracted from the pushrod length to find the cutting point. **FIGURE 31-11** shows the correct procedure for measuring and cutting the pushrod.

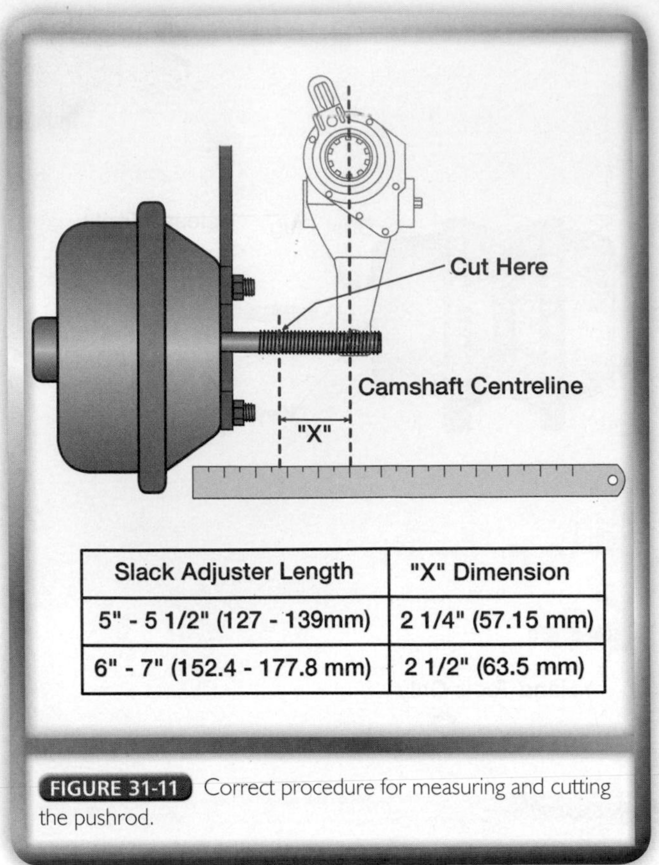

Slack Adjuster Length	"X" Dimension
5" - 5 1/2" (127 - 139mm)	2 1/4" (57.15 mm)
6" - 7" (152.4 - 177.8 mm)	2 1/2" (63.5 mm)

FIGURE 31-11 Correct procedure for measuring and cutting the pushrod.

When threading the clevis pin yoke onto the brake chamber, care must be taken to ensure an adequate amount of thread holds the pushrod onto the yoke. If, however, the clevis pin yoke is threaded too far, the pushrod can potentially interfere with the slack adjuster travel. The pushrod should be threaded into the clevis at least 1/2" (13 mm) but should not protrude into the clevis yoke by any more than 1/8" (3.18 mm), as shown in FIGURE 31-12.

To inspect, test, and replace a spring brake actuator, follow the procedure in SKILL DRILL 31-4.

Testing the Automatic Emergency Brake System

Inspecting the operation of the automatic emergency brake system has two benefits. It helps determine whether the spring brakes will apply during a loss of system pressure. The inspection also helps identify whether several controlled applications of the brake pedal can be used to help slow a vehicle with a sudden severe drop in air pressure. Without the split or dual circuit feature of the braking system, the controlled or modulated stop feature would not be possible since loss in air pressure in one reservoir could cause a loss in the entire system air pressure.

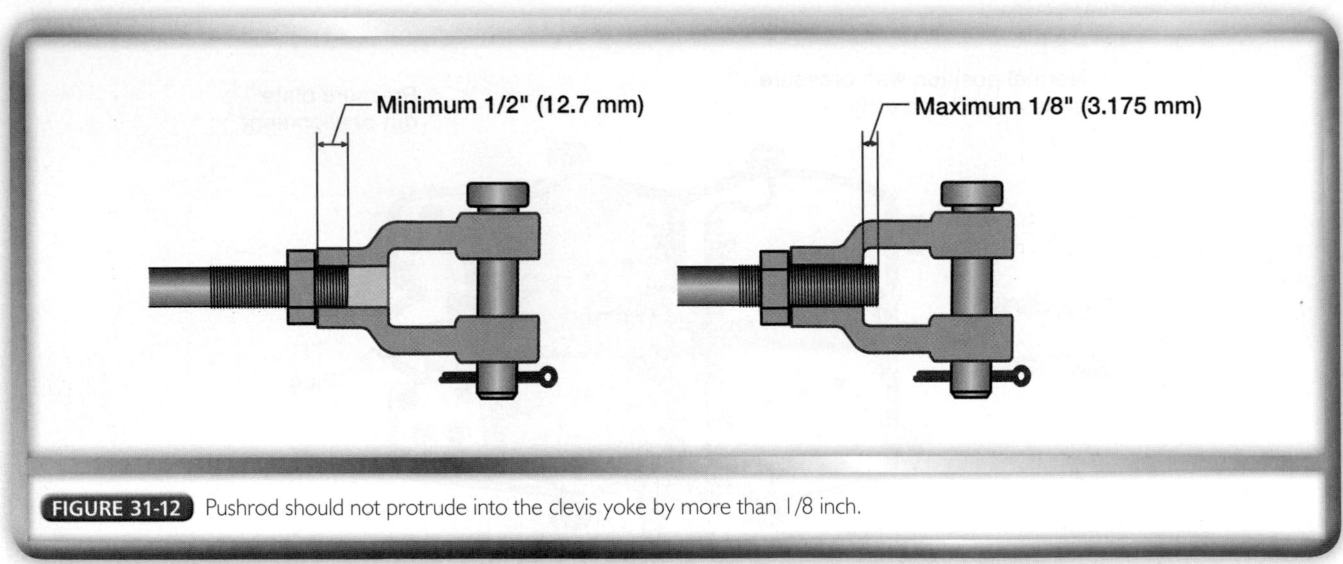

FIGURE 31-12 Pushrod should not protrude into the clevis yoke by more than 1/8 inch.

SKILL DRILL 31-4 Inspecting, Testing, and Replacing a Spring Brake Actuator

1. Locate and follow the appropriate procedure in the service manual.
2. Complete the accompanying job sheet or work order with all pertinent information.
3. Move vehicle into the shop, apply the parking brakes, and block the vehicle wheels.
4. Inspect brake chamber operation and check for air leakage.
5. Start engine and charge the air system to the compressor governor valve cut-out point.
6. Stop the engine and release the parking brakes.
7. Have an assistant apply and hold the brake pedal.
8. Apply a soap solution around the air brake chamber clamp and breather holes.
9. Verify that no bubbles appear.
10. If the bubbles appear, overhaul or replace the rear air brake chamber.
11. Remove rear brake chamber.
12. Raise the vehicle and support with safety stands.
13. Cage the power spring on the parking (spring) brake chamber.
    - Remove plug from the release tool keyhole in the center of the spring brake chamber.
    - Remove the release tool assembly from the side pocket of the adapter. *Caution:* Do not attempt to cage the power spring when the rear air brake chamber shows structural damage. Caging the power spring or disassembly of the spring brake chamber may result in the forceful release of the power spring and the chamber contents, which may cause severe personal injury. Remove the entire rear air brake chamber if it has structural damage and replace with a new unit.
14. With the parking brakes released, insert the release stud through the keyhole in the rear air brake chamber. Bottom out stud and turn the release stud 90° (¼" turn) clockwise.
15. Pull on the release stud to ensure the release stud crosspin is properly seated in the pressure plate. Assemble the release stud washer and nut on the release stud finger tight.
16. Measure the release stud length beyond the release stud nut. Check service manual for correct length. *Caution:* Do not over torque the stud nut.
17. Fully release the air brake automatic slack adjuster and remove air brake chamber clevis pins.
18. Drain air from air stands and disconnect air lines from the brake chamber.
19. Remove mounting nuts and washer from the rear air brake chamber and remove chamber.
20. Disassemble brake chamber to replace service brake diaphragm and install new spring brake chamber.
21. Mark the adapter and service hosing in relation to the clamp ring assembly.
22. Pull out the pushrod and clamp it using locking-type pliers.
23. Remove nuts and bolts on clamp ring assembly and remove clamp ring.
24. Remove diaphragm and spring brake chamber.
25. Clean and inspect parts for rust and cracks. *Caution:* Never disassemble the spring brake assembly; always replace with a new assembly.
26. Install new service brake diaphragm and new spring brake assembly.
27. Install clamp ring assembly and torque nuts and bolts.
28. Remove locking-type pliers.
29. Install brake chamber to the chamber/camshaft support bracket.
30. Install mounting washer and nuts to the rear air brake chamber and torque (108 Nm).

Continued on next page

SKILL DRILL 31-4 Inspecting, Testing, and Replacing a Spring Brake Actuator, continued

31 Install air brake chamber clevis pins and connect air lines.

32 Adjust slack adjuster to adjust the brakes.

33 Start the engine and charge the system to the air compressor governor valve cut-out point and release the parking brakes; stop engine.

34 Uncage the spring brake, and unscrew the release stud nut and washer from the release stud.

35 Turn the release stud one-quarter turn counterclockwise and remove it from the keyhole and install in the storage pocket. Install dust plug into the keyhole.

36 Remove safety stands and lower vehicle.

37 Check for proper brake operation and leaks.

38 Set parking brakes and remove wheel blocks.

39 List the test results and/or recommendations on the job sheet or work order and clean work area and return tools and materials to proper storage.

A variety of valves and circuits are evaluated during this test. Single and double check valves, tractor protection, park control, tractor control, relay, anti-lock modulators, trailer spring brake, inversion valves, and relay spring brake control valves are needed for the proper operation of this circuit. To test the functioning of the automatic emergency brake system, follow the steps in SKILL DRILL 31-5 for a performing a **dual circuit integrity test**.

Testing the Anti-Lock Brake System (ABS)

Operation of ABS modulator valves can be checked during the initial cycle of the ignition switch. After making a brake application when the ignition switch is off, the ignition is switched on. During this time, the ABS control module will briefly energize the modulator valves solenoids to test the electrical circuit operation. With the service brake applied, air pressure will exhaust from the modulator, making a short, "chuffing" sound. (This test is called the **chuff test**.) Identification of a defective modulator valve can easily be pinpointed by the absence of a sound or an unusual noise made by the valve.

Since the modulators, are energized in a particular sequence, the location of the valve can be identified. Note that the chuff test will not work unless the vehicle is stationary. FIGURE 31-13 shows a modulator. Moving the vehicle prevents performance of the test.

FIGURE 31-13 Modulator.

Conducting Advanced Brake Testing

After completing preliminary tests, the technician should undertake more involved testing procedures. Testing brake balance, brake timing imbalances, and air brake pressure balance are more involved procedures but ones that are all necessary to allow the technician to arrive at a more accurate diagnosis based on thorough examination.

Testing Brake Balance

The purpose of measuring air brake pressure between different axles is to verify correct pneumatic brake balance of the brake system. Brake imbalance happens when some wheel ends or axles work harder to brake than others. Significant brake imbalances can lead to vehicle instability during braking, brake fade, and even brake fires.

If a tractor's drive axles have a higher level of braking force than the trailer axles, the tractor drive axles can lock

SKILL DRILL 31-5 Performing a Dual Circuit Integrity Test

1. Charge both supply reservoirs to full pressure. With the engine stopped, drain the front axle reservoir (primary or secondary depending on the manufacturer) to 0 psi. Verify the following:
   - The rear axle reservoir does not lose any pressure.
   - On a tractor and trailer combination, the trailer air reservoir remains charged.
   - Tractor and trailer brakes should not apply automatically.
2. With air pressure in the front axle reservoir at 0 psi, fully depress the brake pedal to make a brake application. During this time, verify the following:
   - Rear axle brakes should apply and release.
   - Trailer brakes should also apply and release on combination vehicles.
   - The brake lights should light up.
3. Slowly drain the rear axle reservoir pressure using the reservoir drain. Verify the following events take place:
   - The park brake push pull control valve should pop out between 35–45 psi (241–310 kPa).
   - Tractor protection valve on a combination vehicle should also pop closed between 20–45 psi (138–310 kPa) and the trailer air supply hose (red) should be exhausted, usually through the tractor protection valve exhaust port.
   - Trailer park brakes should apply after tractor protection valve closes.
   - When the test is performed with a full front axle brake reservoir, the front axle reservoir should not lose pressure.
4. After closing the both reservoir drain valves, build up system air pressure. Stop the engine and drain rear axle reservoir to 0 psi. With no air pressure in the rear axle reservoir, apply and release the service brake pedal to make a brake application. Verify the following events take place:
   - Front axle brakes should apply and release.
   - On combination vehicles, the trailer park brakes should also apply and release.
   - The inverting relay spring brake control valve on straight trucks should cause the rear axle brakes to apply and release with the brake application and release.

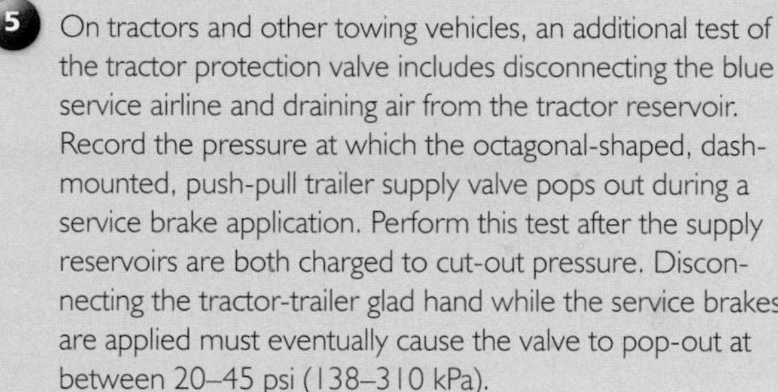

5. On tractors and other towing vehicles, an additional test of the tractor protection valve includes disconnecting the blue service airline and draining air from the tractor reservoir. Record the pressure at which the octagonal-shaped, dash-mounted, push-pull trailer supply valve pops out during a service brake application. Perform this test after the supply reservoirs are both charged to cut-out pressure. Disconnecting the tractor-trailer glad hand while the service brakes are applied must eventually cause the valve to pop-out at between 20–45 psi (138–310 kPa).

up and cause a loss of directional stability. At the same time, the rolling trailer tires enable the trailer to push the tractor and rotate around the king pin. This condition is called jackknifing and is shown in **FIGURE 31-14A**. A similar condition takes place when the trailer, rather than the tractor's, brakes lock-up. In this situation, the trailer loses directional stability as the tractor drags the trailer, causing the trailer to swing out into another lane, as shown in **FIGURE 31-14B**.

Two main categories of brake balance are torque balance and pneumatic balance. Proper brake **torque balance** is produced using properly matched and maintained system components, correctly adjusted brakes, plus properly loaded vehicles. The lack of uniform friction-material to friction-surface contact means some wheel braking torque is greater than others. In other words, if a truck, bus, or trailer unit has a torque imbalance some of the brakes will work harder and lock up easier than others.

Unlike torque balance, **pneumatic balance** is created by having equal air pressure at all wheel ends at the same time. A vehicle with a pneumatic imbalance, will allow some brakes to work harder and lock up easier than others, but the problem will affect only one axle or a set of axles, such as the tractor tandem drive axles or the trailer axles.

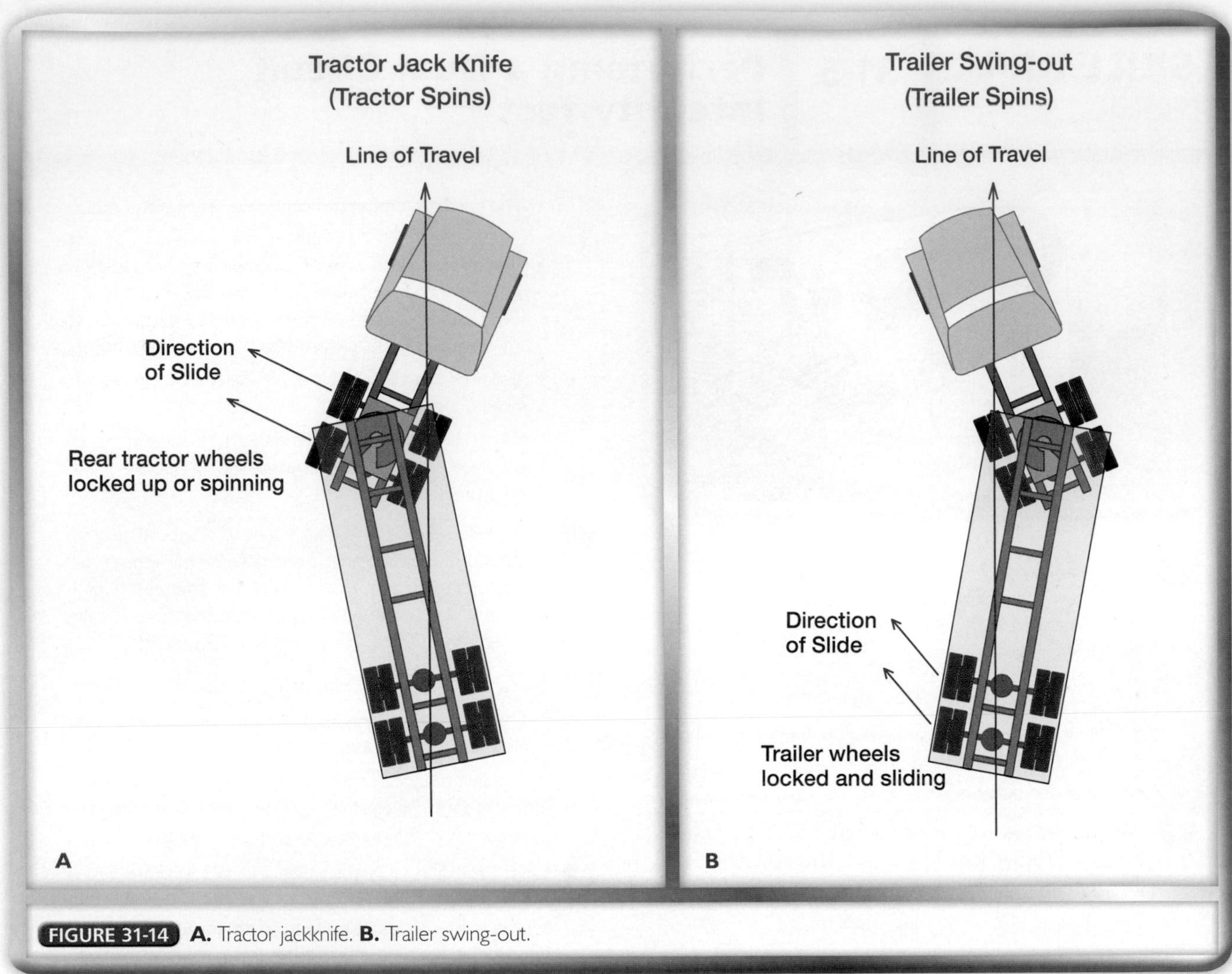

FIGURE 31-14 **A.** Tractor jackknife. **B.** Trailer swing-out.

While ABS can prevent over-braked wheels from locking-up, ABS is not a substitute for balanced braking. High application pressure braking of an ABS-equipped tractor connected to a non-ABS-equipped trailer or a trailer with a non-functioning defective ABS can lock its brakes, causing it to rapidly swing out of its lane.

Common causes of torque imbalance include:

- Oil- or grease-contaminated friction material
- Polished drums or rotors
- Glazed friction material
- Mixing friction capabilities of brake linings or pads at one or more wheels
- Oversized drums and thin rotors
- Improper brake adjustment
- Mismatched brake chambers and automatic slack adjusters.
- Improperly installed automatic slacks
- Defective or inoperative antilock brake (ABS) wheel speed sensors

A brake torque imbalance can be discovered by inspecting the brake linings. If a torque imbalance exists, the linings at some of the wheel ends will wear faster than others. Several hard braking applications will allow measurement of the brake drum temperatures. Variations of more than 50° F from side to side on the same axle, or 100° F from steer to drive and center axle, indicates a torque imbalance.

Identifying Brake Timing Imbalance

A **brake timing imbalance** occurs when some brakes receive air faster than others. FMVSS standards requires 60-psi application air pressure at each brake chamber in not more than 0.45 seconds for trucks and buses and 0.50 seconds in the case of trailers when measured from the first movement of the service brake control.

Brakes must also release quickly. With 95 psi (655 kPa) of air pressure in each brake chamber, application pressure must fall to 5 psi (34 kPa) in not more than 0.55 seconds for trucks and buses when measured from the first movement of the service brake control. On trailers, the same pressure reduction is required within 1.00 seconds. Slightly longer times are allowed in multiple trailer combinations.

To speed-up brake applications and help time brake applications, tractors and trailers use relay valves with different crack or opening pressures. These crack pressure differences are depicted in FIGURE 31-15. Crack pressure is the signal air pressure required to begin relay valve operation. It takes time to transmit air pressure over a longer distance to the trailer. Therefore, having a lower crack pressure on the trailer than on the tractor helps the brakes to apply at the same time across the vehicle. Front axle crack pressures should be the highest. Otherwise, the front axle will use a limiting valve which reduces air pressure by approximately 50% when application pressures are below 40 psi.

Testing Air Brake Pressure Balance

Pneumatic or air pressure imbalance occurs when the tractor's or trailer's air system delivers incorrect air pressures to brake chambers on a combination vehicle. The most common causes are incorrect or malfunctioning relay valves. Quick-release valves can also malfunction in ways that interfere with air pressure balance. Pinched or kinked airlines, air leaks, leaking glad hand seals, air system contamination, and a variety of other valve-related problems can contribute to pneumatic imbalance.

Pneumatic imbalance is measured with a duplex gauge such as the one shown in FIGURE 31-16. The **duplex gauge** is essentially two air gauges in a single housing. Two color-coded hoses approximately 35' long are connected to corresponding and similarly color-coded gauge indicators. This configuration allows the pressure in both lines to be observed simultaneously by a technician. Input and output air pressure at separate points in the brake system can be measured with duplex gauge.

FIGURE 31-15 Tractors and trailers use relay valves with different crack or opening pressures.

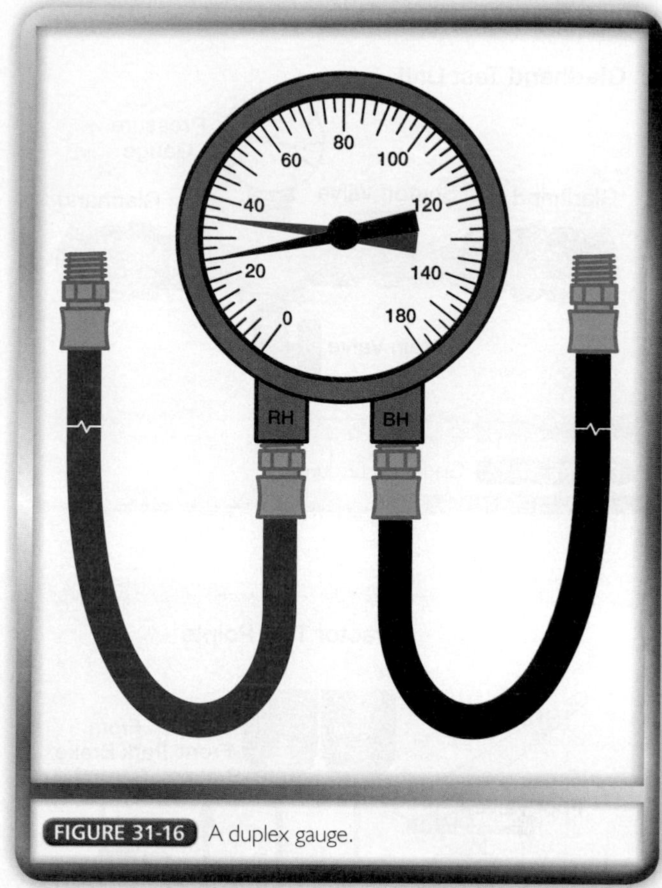

FIGURE 31-16 A duplex gauge.

Air restrictions, pressure imbalances, or inadequate air pressure are also commonly measured when diagnosing air system complaints using a duplex gauge. Comparing pressure between two points enables a relative comparison of air pressure and the time it takes for air pressure to arrive at components.

The duplex gauge can measure the pressure balance from the front steer to rear drive axle. After installing the duplex gauge to the service side of a front and rear air brake chamber, the service brakes are applied in 10-psi increments up to 80 or 90 psi. The pressure difference between the front and rear brakes should not exceed 2 psi. Since industry studies have observed 80% of all braking applications are actually 20 psi or less, the 2-psi recommendation enables consistent braking application force especially at low application pressures.

Another useful tool is the glad hand test unit. It can measure air pressure supplied to the trailer as well as the time it takes to build and release air pressure in the service line. FIGURE 31-17 shows a glad hand test unit.

Unbalanced brake pressures are typically caused by the following:

- Malfunctioning relay valves
- Malfunctioning brake application/foot valve
- Kinked or restricted lines

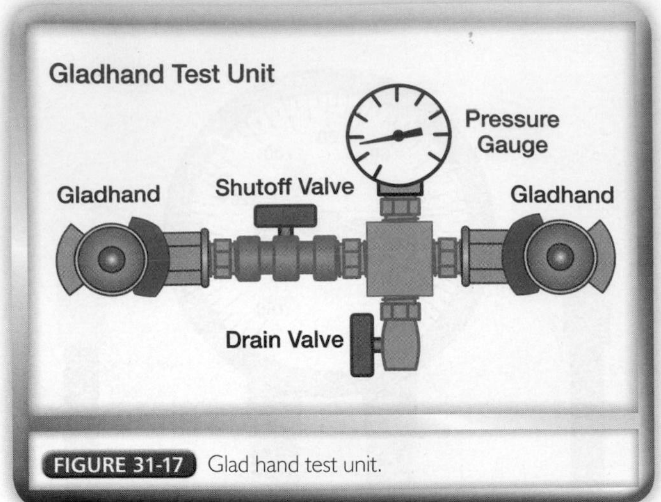

FIGURE 31-17 Glad hand test unit.

Let's consider a couple of scenarios that a technician is likely to face with regard to testing air brake pressure balance. Imagine a customer comes into the shop complaining that the trailer of his vehicle seems to be pushing the tractor. In that case, the tractor brakes are likely applying sooner and at a higher pressure than trailer brakes. To validate problem, connect the duplex gauge to points 1 and 2 as shown on FIGURE 31-18 to check application timing and pressure. If the trailer application pressure is higher, then measure points 2 and 3. If the pressures are the same, check between 3 and 4. If pressures are the same on the trailer, the problem is in the tractor system, which is sending a higher than normal signal pressure.

Still using Figure 31-18 as a guide, let's consider a different complaint. This time, the trailer brakes are slow

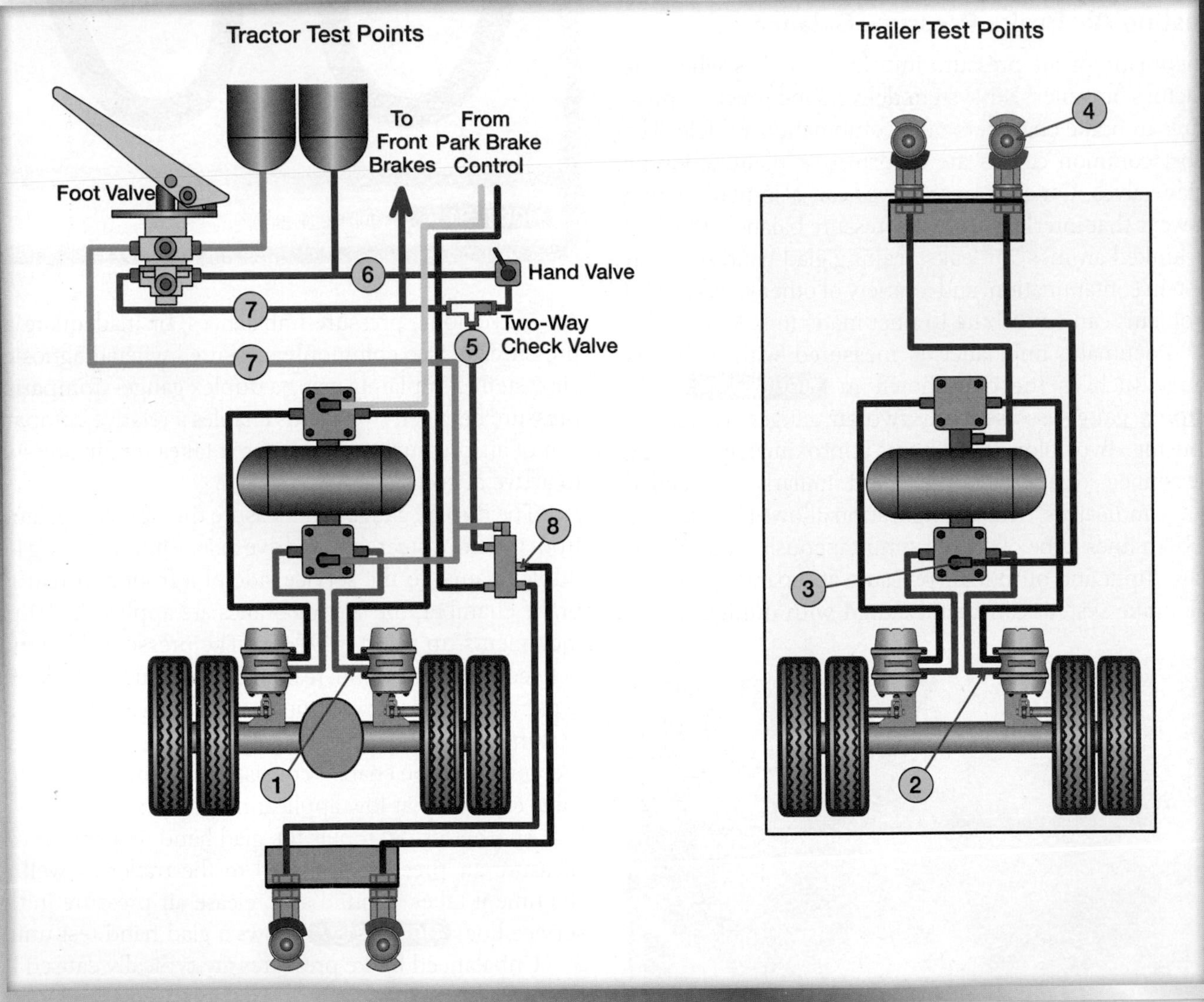

FIGURE 31-18 Pneumatic balance duplex gauge check points.

to release. Connect the duplex gauge to points 2 and 3. Make a brake application while closely observing the slack adjuster arm. If the gauges return to zero quickly together but the slack adjuster only moves after air is exhausted, there is likely a binding mechanical condition in the brake foundation. Weak brake shoe return springs, chamber defects, and dry cam bushings are several possible causes.

Inspecting and Servicing Air Brake Valves

Variations in pneumatic balance and brake timing are magnified on slippery road conditions. Not only is jack-knifing and trailer "swing out" more likely to happen but a trailer can push a tractor off the road on a curve or into the ditch if brake balance is poor. Synchronization of braking applications requires careful selection of replacement brake valves and lines – assuming a tractor and or trailer was correctly built by the manufacturer.

For instance, relay valves are especially important for pneumatic balance and timing. Relay valves not only determine brake timing but are used to speed-up both application and release of air brake pressure. By controlling the air pressure to the relay valve control port, the delivery air pressure can be graduated in order to vary brake torque to each axle. Relay valve crack pressure is the minimum air pressure required to trigger the relay valve into operation.

Not all valves are the same even though they may appear identical. There are dozens of valves to choose from with different crack pressures. Tractors use higher crack pressures than trailers to make sure the more distant brake valves of the trailer will open at the same time. This is necessary since control air takes longer to travel to the trailer valves. A trailer with a high crack pressure relay valve will have significantly slower brakes than the tractor and will tend to push the tractor when braking.

Higher crack pressures will also increase the differential between control air pressure and delivery air pressure. A tractor valve may have a crack pressure as high as 15-psi while trailers typically use valves between 1 and four psi. When replacing brake valves, both new and rebuilt valves often have a metal tag with a detailed part number. Once the valve is confirmed as defective, it is critical to replace one with exactly the same performance specifications.

The following skill drills describe how to inspect, test, and, if necessary, replace a variety of air brake system valves:

- To inspect and test the quick release valve and replace as needed, follow the guidelines in **SKILL DRILL 31-6**.
- To inspect and test the brake application (foot) valve, fittings, and mounts and adjust or replace them as needed, follow the guidelines in **SKILL DRILL 31-7**.
- To inspect and test a relay valve and replace as needed, follow the guidelines in **SKILL DRILL 31-8**.
- To inspect and test the parking brake hand (control) valve and replace as needed, follow the guidelines in **SKILL DRILL 31-9**.
- To inspect test he inversion valve and replace it as needed, follow the guidelines in **SKILL DRILL 31-10**.
- To inspect and test the anti-compounding circuit equipped with quick release (QR) and replace as needed, follow the guidelines in **SKILL DRILL 31-11**.
- To inspect and test the trailer air supply valve and replace as needed, follow the guidelines in **SKILL DRILL 31-12**.
- To inspect and test the trailer brake control valve (hand valve) and replace as needed, follow the guidelines in **SKILL DRILL 31-13**.
- To inspect and test the tractor protection valve and replace as needed, follow the guidelines in **SKILL DRILL 31-14**.
- To inspect and test the trailer brake full function valve and replace as needed, follow the guidelines in **SKILL DRILL 31-15**.

SKILL DRILL 31-6 Inspecting and Testing the Quick Release Valve; Replacing as Needed

1. Locate and follow the appropriate procedure in the service manual.
2. Complete the accompanying job sheet or work order with all pertinent information.
3. Move vehicle into shop, apply the parking brakes and block the vehicle wheels.
4. Start the vehicle and build up air pressure and release parking brakes.
5. Locate the quick release valve in the brake system.
6. Test valve for operation and air leaks.
7. Coat the exhaust port with a soap solution and check for leaks. Leakage of bubbles in three seconds is allowable.
8. Coat the valve body and cover with a soap solution. No leakage is permitted between the valve body and cover. *Caution:* Drain the air brake system by opening the reservoir drain cocks before you disconnect any air lines.
9. Mark and disconnect the air lines from the quick release valve.
10. Remove the mounting bolts and the valve.
11. Replace with new valve of the same type.
12. Install the quick release valve with the exhaust port facing down. Securely tighten the mounting bolts.
13. Connect the air lines to the quick release valve in the locations previously marked.
14. Perform the operating and leakage tests using previous steps to ensure correct operation.
15. List the test results and/or recommendations on the job sheet or work order and clean work area and return tools and materials to proper storage.

SKILL DRILL 31-7 Inspecting and Testing the Brake Application (Foot) Valve, Fittings and Mounts; Adjusting or Replacing as Needed

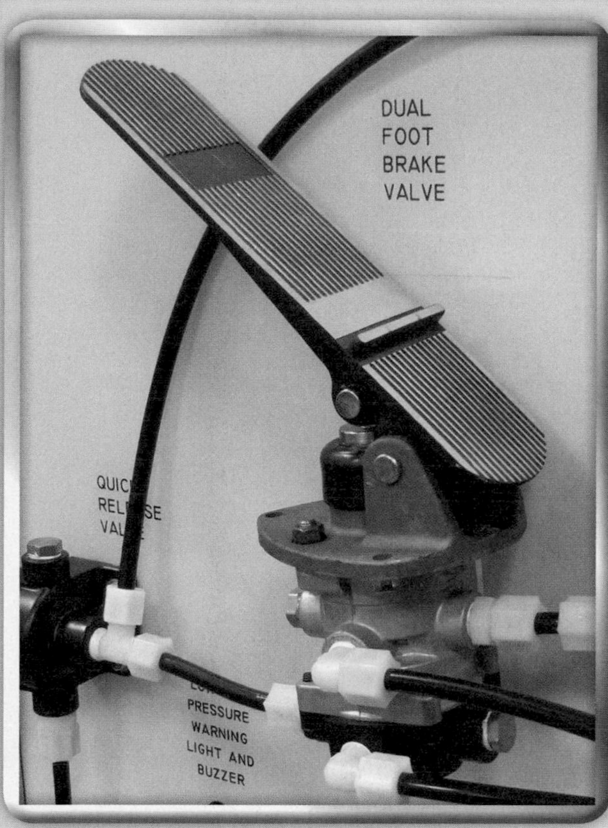

1. Locate and follow the appropriate procedure in the service manual.
2. Complete the accompanying job sheet or work order with all pertinent information.
3. Move vehicle into shop, apply the parking brakes, and block the vehicle wheels.
4. Check and inspect foot valve operation as follows.
   - Connect test gauges to the primary and secondary delivery ports on the application valve.
   - Release parking brakes and start the engine and build air pressure to 120 psi (830 kPa).
   - Depress the pedal to several different positions; check the pressure on the test gauges to ensure that it varies equally and proportionately with the movement of the brake pedal.
   - Fully depress the brake pedal, then release it. The reading on the test gauges should promptly fall to zero.
   - Make and hold a pressure application of 80 psi (550 kPa) and check the valve for leaks.
   - Coat the exhaust port and body of the valve with a soap solution, and check for leakage. The leakage permitted is a bubble every three seconds.
5. If the brake valve does not function as described above, or if leakage is excessive, replace as follows.
   - Drain all of the air reservoirs.
   - Mark the brake valve air supply and delivery lines for assembly reference.
   - Disconnect the air lines from the brake valve, and plug them to keep out contaminants.
   - Remove capscrews from the mounting bracket.
   - Remove the brake valve from mounting bracket.
   - Note the locations and positions of the double check valves and elbows, then remove them from the brake valve. Clean dirt and old sealant from the threads.
   - Make sure to replace the old valve with the same new one.
   - Apply a small quantity of pipe sealant to the male threads of each of the double check valves and the elbows.
   - Install the double check valves and elbows in the ports of the brake valves. Attach the brake valve and mounting bracket to the cab deck.
   - Clean dirt, gravel, and other foreign material from the base of the brake pedal.
   - Using a light oil, lubricate the brake pedal roller and roller pin.
   - Install brake pedal; move the pedal as needed to align the hole in the brake pedal and the mounting bracket.
   - Connect the air lines as previously marked. Tighten the nuts finger-tight. Using a wrench, further tighten the nuts.
6. Start engine, charge up the air system, inspect for air leaks and check brake operation.
7. List the test results and/or recommendations on the job sheet or work order and clean work area and return tools and materials to proper storage.

SKILL DRILL 31-8 Inspecting and Testing a Relay Valve; Replacing as Needed

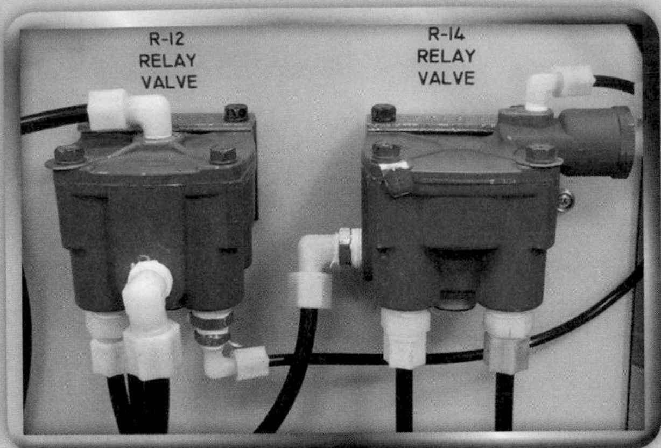

1. Locate and follow the appropriate procedure in the service manual.
2. Complete the accompanying job sheet or work order with all pertinent information.
3. Move vehicle into shop, apply the parking brakes, and block the vehicle wheels.
4. Start the vehicle and build the brake system to cut-out pressure (120 psi, 830 kPa) and release parking brakes.
5. Make several service brake applications and check for prompt application and release of the brakes, inspecting the operation of the relay valve. Check service manual for specifications.
6. With the service brakes released, apply a soap-water solution to the exhaust port of the relay valve and check for excessive leakage.
7. While holding a full service brake application, apply a soap-water solution to the exhaust port and check for air leaks. *Caution:* Open the air reservoir drain cocks to bleed air from the system before removing any lines or plugs.
8. Remove all air hoses from the relay valve, cap the hoses, and mark them for reassembly.
9. Remove the valve mounting bolts and remove the valve.
10. Replace old valve with a new valve of the same type.
11. Attach the new relay valve to the vehicle using the bolts, washers, and nuts; torque to specifications.
12. Connect the air hose fittings to the valve ports; check service manual for tightening.
13. Close the air reservoir drain cocks and start the vehicle engine to pressurize the air system.
14. Test relay valve operation using previous steps to ensure correct operation.
15. List the test results and/or recommendations on the job sheet or work order and clean work area and return tools and materials to proper storage.

SKILL DRILL 31-9 Inspecting and Testing the Parking Brake Hand (Control) Valve; Replacing as Needed

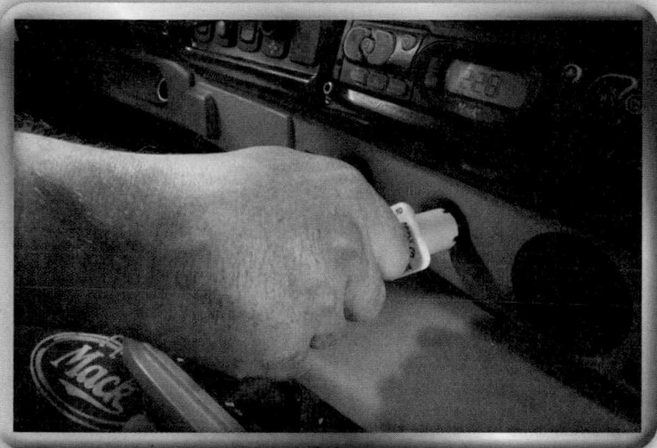

1. Locate and follow the appropriate procedure in the service manual.
2. Complete the accompanying job sheet or work order with all pertinent information.
3. Move vehicle into the shop, apply the parking brakes, and block the vehicle wheels. *Caution:* Open the air reservoir drain cocks to bleed air from the system before removing any lines or plugs.
4. To perform an operating test, connect two separate 120 psi (830 kPa) air sources to the park valve supply ports and tee an accurate test gauge into the supply lines, and provide for a means to control supply line pressure. Connect a small volume air source with a gauge to the delivery port.
5. Start the engine and build up the air pressure to the normal operating level.
6. With the valve knob pulled out, supply either supply port with 120 psi (830 kPa) of pressure. Push the valve knob in. Air pressure should rise in the delivery line and equal supply line pressure. Pull the valve knob out. Delivery pressure should exhaust to zero.
7. Build air pressure to each supply source to 120 psi (830 kPa). Decrease supply pressure at the secondary service reservoir supply port at a rate of 10 psi (70 kPa) per second. Primary supply pressure and delivery pressure should not drop below 100 psi (690 kPa). Repeat this step for decreasing primary service reservoir pressure.
8. Build air pressure to each supply source to 120 psi (830 kPa). Then, decrease both supply pressures to below 20 to 30 psi (140 to 210 kPa). The valve knob should automatically pop out when the pressure is within that range.
9. Test the valve for air leaks. With air pressure at 120 psi (830 kPa) and valve knob pulled out, coat the exhaust port and the plunger stem with the soap solution. Leakage should not exceed one bubble every five seconds.
10. Push valve knob in, then coat the exhaust port and plunger stem with the soap solution. Leakage should not exceed one bubble every five seconds.
11. If valve does not work as described or does not pass air leak test replace the valve. *Caution:* Drain air reservoirs before disconnecting air lines.
12. To replace the park control valve; remove the top-center dash panel.
13. Turn the valve knob counterclockwise and remove it from the valve stem.
14. Mark the air lines, and disconnect them from the valve assembly.
15. Remove the screws that attach the valve to the instrument panel. Remove valve.
16. Install new valve assembly in the instrument panel and install mounting screws.
17. Connect the air lines to the applicable fittings and tighten.
18. Screw the valve knob onto the valve stem.
19. Retest new valve by using the previous steps to ensure correct operation.
20. List the test results and/or recommendations on the job sheet or work order and clean work area and return tools and materials to proper storage.

SKILL DRILL 31-10 Inspecting and Testing the Inversion Valve; Replacing as Needed

1. Locate and follow the appropriate procedure in the service manual.
2. Complete the accompanying job sheet or work order with all pertinent information.
3. Move vehicle into the shop, apply the parking brakes, and block the vehicle wheels. *Caution:* Open the air reservoir drain cocks to bleed air from the system before removing any lines or plugs.
4. Tee two pressure gauges in the brake system: one in a common control and supply line and one in the delivery port.
5. Start the vehicle and build up air pressure and release parking brakes.
6. With the red dash knob pushed in and pressure coming to the control port from the trailer supply line, the valve should close. There should be 0 psi (kPa) at the delivery port.
7. With air pressure in the supply and control ports, apply soap solution around the supply port capnut. If leakage exceeds one soap bubble within three seconds, replace the O-ring. If leakage continues, replace the valve.
8. Exhaust the line coming in to the control port by pulling out the red dash knob in the cab. The pressure gauge at the delivery port should be the same pressure as is being fed the valve at the supply port.
9. Replace the valve if pressures are not at the rates specified above.
10. Remove the test gauges from the brake system.
11. To replace inversion valve, drain air system. See caution on in Step 3.
12. Identify (mark) and disconnect the three air lines from the inversion valve.
13. Remove the two bolts attaching the valve to the vehicle. Remove the valve.
14. Install new valve on the vehicle using the mounting bolts previously removed.
15. Connect the three air lines to the proper ports as marked during removal.
16. Check the inversion valve operation using the previous steps.
17. Set parking brakes and remove wheel blocks.
18. List the test results and/or recommendations on the job sheet or work order and clean work area and return tools and materials to proper storage.

SKILL DRILL 31-11 Inspecting and Testing the Anti-Compounding Circuit Equipped with Quick Release (QR); Replacing as Needed

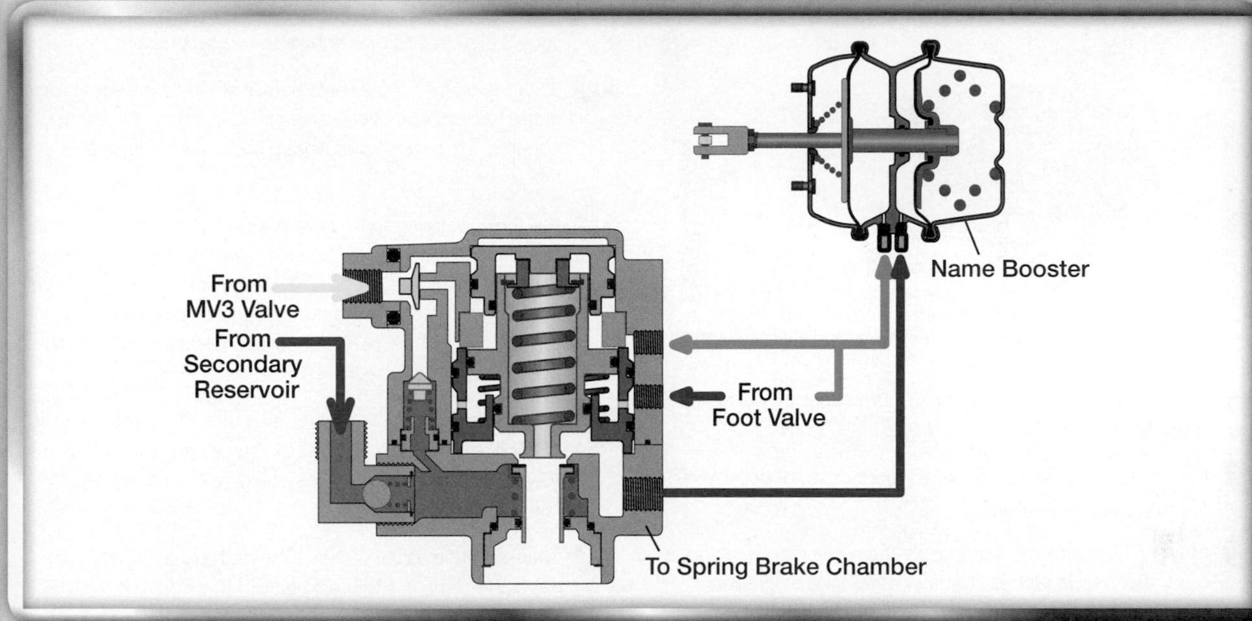

1. Locate and follow the appropriate procedure in the service manual.
2. Complete the accompanying job sheet or work order with all pertinent information.
3. Move vehicle into the shop, apply the parking brakes, and block the vehicle wheels. *Caution:* Open the air reservoir drain cocks to bleed air from the system before removing any lines or plugs.
4. Release the parking brakes.
5. Remove the air line from the valve balance port.
6. Build system air pressure to 120 psi (830 kPa). Coat the exhaust and balance ports with a soap solution; leakage of one bubble in five seconds at either port is allowable.
7. Install the air line at the balance port.
8. Apply the parking brakes. Step on the foot brake. The QR-1C valve should exhaust air at the exhaust port.
9. Drain the air system.
10. Remove the air line from the valve supply port.
11. Build system air pressure to 120 psi (830 kPa), with the foot valve depressed, coat the supply port and the seam between the body and cover with a soap solution; leakage of one bubble in five seconds at the supply port is allowable. No leakage between the body and cover is permitted.
12. Install the air line at the supply port.
13. If the valve does not function properly, or if leakage is excessive, replace the valve.
14. To replace the QR-1C valve, drain the air brake system.
15. Mark and disconnect the air lines from the quick release valve.
16. Remove the mounting bolts and the valve.
17. Install the new quick release valve with the exhaust port facing down. Securely tighten the mounting bolts.
18. Connect the air lines to the quick release valve in the locations previously marked.
19. Retest new valve using the previous steps to ensure correct operation.
20. List the test results and/or recommendations on the job sheet or work order and clean work area and return tools and materials to proper storage.

SKILL DRILL 31-12 Inspecting and Testing the Trailer Air Supply Valve; Replacing as Needed

1. Locate and follow the appropriate procedure in the service manual.
2. Complete the accompanying job sheet or work order with all pertinent information.
3. Move vehicle into the shop, apply the parking brakes, and block the vehicle wheels. *Caution:* Open the air reservoir drain cocks to bleed air from the system before removing any lines or plugs.
4. Connect the assembled hose coupling and test gauge in the tractor emergency hose coupling.
5. Start the engine and build up system pressure and check pressure reading on the test gauge as reservoir pressure builds up. There should be no pressure reading on the test gauge.
6. When system pressure reaches the 30 to 40 psi (210 to 275 kPa) range on the dash gauge, make and hold a foot or hand valve application and observe that no air escapes at the open trailer service hose coupling.
7. When system pressure reaches about 60 psi (415 kPa) the trailer air supply valve button should be pushed in. System pressure should show at once on the test gauge connected in the emergency line, and the button of trailer valve should remain in without being held.
8. Build the system pressure up to about 100 psi (690 kPa), then stop the engine. With the engine stopped, wait momentarily, then notice that the dash gauge and test gauge pressure readings equal. While still in this position, make a foot valve application, and observe that air is delivered out the open trailer service coupling.
9. With the trailer supply valve button still in, check for leakage at the valve exhaust and tripper exhaust ports. Leakage should not exceed one bubble in five seconds.
10. With the trailer supply valve button still in, check for leakage at the tractor protection valve exhaust and open service coupling. Leakage should not be more than one bubble in five seconds.
11. Pull the trailer air supply valve button out. Pressure on the test gauge connected in the emergency line should drop to zero. Make and hold a hand valve application, and observe that air delivered at the open service coupling does not exceed one bubble in five seconds. Release the hand valve application.
12. If the trailer air supply valve does not function as desired in the above test or if leakage is excessive, replace with a new valve. *Caution:* Drain the air system before removing any lines or plugs.
13. To replace the valve, remove the dash panel covering the valve and remove the bracket and valve from the dash structure. Lift the bracket and valve to a serviceable level.
14. Disconnect the supply and delivery lines from the valve and mark the lines.
15. Drive out the valve button spiral pin and remove the button.
16. Remove the valve mounting nuts, then remove the valve from the bracket.
17. Install a new trailer supply valve. Connect the line as marked and tighten.
18. Place the valve in the bracket mounting hole and install mounting nuts and tighten.
19. Install the button on the valve, and attach with the button spiral pin.
20. Install the bracket and valves in the dash. Install the dash panel.
21. List the test results and/or recommendations on the job sheet or work order and clean work area and return tools and materials to proper storage.

SKILL DRILL 31-13 Inspecting and Testing the Trailer Brake Control Valve (Hand Valve); Replacing as Needed

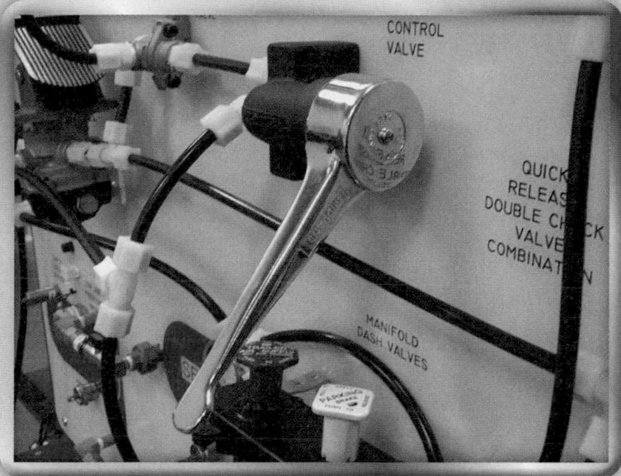

1. Locate and follow the appropriate procedure in the service manual.
2. Complete the accompanying job sheet or work order with all pertinent information.
3. Move vehicle into the shop, apply the parking brakes, block the vehicle wheels, and release the parking brakes.
4. Connect the test gauge to the delivery port of the hand valve, or connect the gauge to the service hose coupling located behind the cab. When the gauge is connected to the service hose coupling, install a dummy hose coupling on the supply (emergency) hose coupling, and place the dash valve in the trailer charging position.
5. Move the handle of the hand valve to the fully applied position. The test gauge should register full reservoir pressure.
6. Upon manual release, the gauge should immediately register zero.
7. Locate the exhaust port or exhaust line and apply a soap solution.
8. With the valve in the released position, exhaust leakage should not exceed one bubble in five seconds.
9. With the valve fully applied, leakage at the exhaust should not exceed one bubble in five seconds.
10. If the valve does not function properly or if leakage is excessive, replace the hand valve. *Caution:* Open the air reservoir drain cocks to bleed air from the system before removing any lines.
11. To replace the valve, remove dash cover if needed.
12. Mark the three air lines and disconnect the air lines from the valve.
13. Loosen the clamp that holds the hand valve mounting bracket to the steering column and remove valve from the steering column by sliding the bracket out of the clamp.
14. Remove the mounting bracket from the valve by removing the three Phillips screws.
15. Remove line fitting from old valve and install in new valve.
16. Install the mounting bracket on the new hand valve and securely tighten the three screws.
17. Slide the mounting bracket through the clamp on the steering column. Position the valve on the steering column and tighten the clamp firmly.
18. Using the reference marks made during removal, attach the air lines to the hand valve and tighten the lines firmly using two wrenches.
19. Install dash cover if removed.
20. Retest new hand valve using the previous steps.
21. Set parking brakes and remove wheel blocks.
22. List the test results and/or recommendations on the job sheet or work order and clean work area and return tools and materials to proper storage.

SKILL DRILL 31-14 Inspecting and Testing the Tractor Protection Valve; Replacing as Needed

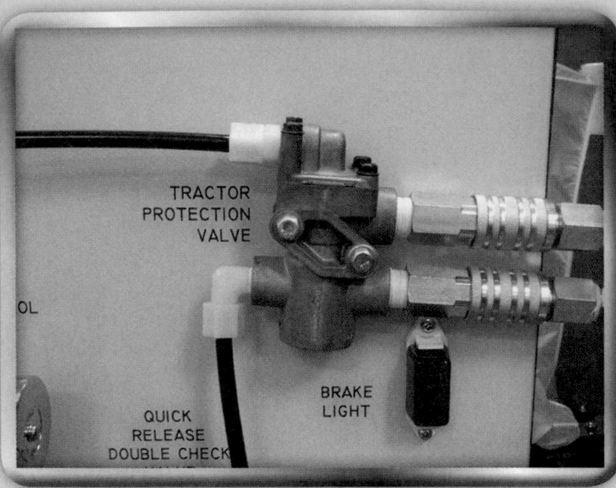

1. Locate and follow the appropriate procedure in the service manual.
2. Complete the accompanying job sheet or work order with all pertinent information.
3. Move vehicle into the shop, apply the parking brakes, and block the vehicle wheels.
4. Place the trailer air supply valve in the emergency position.
5. Disconnect the trailer air lines from the trailer supply and service couplings. Apply a soap solution to the couplings.
6. With tractor reservoirs charged to at least 100 psi (690 kPa), make and hold a full service brake application. Leakage at either tractor hose coupling should not exceed one bubble in five seconds.
7. Connect the trailer supply line hose coupling, and place the trailer supply valve in the "run" position. Leakage at the service coupling should not exceed one bubble in five seconds.
8. Connect the service brake coupling, and make and hold a full service brake application.
9. If leakage is excessive, replace the valve. *Caution:* Open the air reservoir drain cocks to bleed air from the system.
10. To replace the valve, remove the trailer hose assemblies from the TP valve.
11. Disconnect the tractor service and supply lines and mark.
12. Remove the fasteners attaching the valve to the vehicle. Remove the valve.
13. Install new valve on the vehicle, and attach it with mounting bolts and tighten.
14. Connect lines to valve as marked and tighten.
15. Close the drain cocks to the air reservoirs.
16. Start engine and build system air pressure to 120 psi (830 kPa).
17. Retest new valve by using the previous steps.
18. Set parking brakes and remove wheel blocks.
19. List the test results and/or recommendations on the job sheet or work order and clean work area and return tools and materials to proper storage.

SKILL DRILL 31-15 Inspecting and Testing the Trailer Brake Full Function Valve; Replacing as Needed

1. Locate and follow the appropriate procedure in the service manual.
2. Complete the accompanying job sheet or work order with all pertinent information.
3. Move vehicle into the shop, apply the parking brakes, and block the vehicle wheels.
4. Start the vehicle and build the brake system to cut-out pressure, 120 psi (830 kPa). Push in trailer air supply valve to charge trailer air system. Release parking brakes.
5. Make several service brake applications and check for prompt application and release of trailer brakes, inspecting the operation of the trailer full function relay valve. Check service manual for specifications.
6. With the service brakes released, apply a soap solution to the exhaust port of the trailer full function valve and check for excessive leakage.
7. While holding a full service brake application, apply a soap solution to the exhaust port and check for air leaks.
8. Record findings on work order. If valve did not pass tests, continue. *Caution:* Open the air reservoir drain cocks to bleed air from the system before removing any lines or plugs.
9. Remove all air hoses from the valve, cap the hoses and mark them for reassembly.
10. Remove the valve mounting bolts and remove the valve.
11. Replace old valve mounting bolts and remove the valve.
12. Attach the new valve to the trailer using the bolts, washers and nuts; torque to specifications.
13. Connect the air hose fittings to the valve ports. Check service manual for tightening.
14. Close air reservoir drain cocks and start the vehicle engine to pressurize the air system.
15. Test valve operation using previous steps.
16. Set parking brakes and remove wheel blocks.
17. List the test results and/or recommendations on the job sheet or work order and clean work area and return tools and materials to proper storage.

Servicing the Air Supply System

A primary function in servicing any brake system is being able to service the components of the air supply system. A technician needs to be familiar with the unique servicing issues of the air compressor, governor, air reservoirs, pressure gauges, air dryers, and the evaporator and injection systems.

Air Compressor

The air compressor often drives the engine fuel pump. Sometimes the air compressor even drives the power steering pump bolted to the rear end of the compressor. The compressor crankshaft is designed to accept a drive coupling placed between the compressor and fuel pump. A defective fuel pump or power steering pump drive seal can leak into the compressor's crankcase. Lubricating oil inside the compressor can also be pulled into the power steering pump or fuel pump. Lubricating oil for the compressor's crankshaft and pistons is supplied to the compressor by a line from the engine cylinder block oil gallery connected to the air compressor. A crankcase sump in the compressor returns oil to the oil pan through a drain hose or drains oil into the front gear-train through the compressor crankcase.

Compressors are typically driven by the front or rear engine gear train, which is a more reliable coupling than a belt driven drive. Unlike belt driven drives, no maintenance is required on a gear coupling.

Engine coolant is supplied to the compressor through two flexible hoses that are connected to engine water jackets. Intake air is supplied by either the engine air intake manifold or a separate intake supplied by filtered atmospheric air. Compressed air is forced into the metal discharge line, which sends air to the air dryer.

Common compressor problems include compressor noise and a broken compressor crankcase. Less obvious but still common compressor problems include pumping oil and slow air buildup time.

Pumping Oil

A compressor floods when its crankcase overfills with oil. This situation is often caused by a blocked or undersized oil drain. When the compressor's crankcase is flooded with oil, oil is forced past the piston rings. The compressor then produces oil discharge. Another cause for a flooded compressor is a restricted air intake. When restricted, the negative intake air pressure will cause the compressor to pull air up from the crankcase and past the piston rings.

A worn-out engine will produce excessive piston ring blow-by, causing high crankcase pressure. Blow-by contains oil droplets that will push past the compressor's piston rings only when the compressor is unloaded. When loading, air pressure in the cylinders prevents oil from moving past the rings.

An optional intake check valve is available on some models, which can hold 4 or 5 pounds of air pressure in the compressor cylinders when unloaded. The additional air pressure in the compressor cylinders surges from one cylinder to the other when unloaded. Oil is thereby prevented from passing around the piston rings and into the cylinders.

A compressor that is pumping oil will not pump it out the air intake while it is loading. That's because its air intake valves are closed during the compression stroke. Instead, oil is passed out the compressor discharge line. Note that a defective compressor piston with a hole in it, or one with broken rings, can also allow pressurized intake manifold air into the engine crankcase. Air in the engine crankcase can dramatically increase engine crankcase pressure and cause the intake manifold to lose boost pressure. Many engines have been unnecessarily rebuilt due to a defective air compressor after an assumption has been made that high engine crankcase blow-by is only caused by a worn-out engine.

All air compressors pass a small amount of oil. Discharged oil may collect in the discharge line, where it is baked by high temperature air. Baked oil gradually turns to carbon and restricts the discharge line. This explains why manufacturers recommend replacing the discharge line whenever a compressor is replaced. The compressor discharge line fitting temperature will operate normally between 200° F and 360° F (93–182° C) when charging. The copper line at the compressor end is annealed to prevent cracking due to vibration and thermal cycling. The line also enables compressed air to cool before entering the dryer. Note that the line should slope downwards to prevent the condensation of water,

> **TECHNICIAN TIP**
>
> Thoroughly clean and de-burr any air line, including the discharge line, before connecting it to the air system. Small metal particles can easily pass through the system and damage brake valves. When disturbing the discharge line, care should be taken to prevent any carbon from entering the air system by disconnecting the line at the air dryer first. After running the new compressor, the discharge line fitting temperature will operate normally between 200° F and 360° F (93–182° C) when charging.

which can potentially freeze and block the line as shown in FIGURE 31-19.

Excessive Air Buildup Time

Excessive compressor buildup time is typically caused by one of the following:

- Worn or malfunctioning air compressor
- Restriction on the air inlet side of the air compressor
- Excessive air leaks
- Loose or slipping drive belts
- Malfunctioning unloader valves

In addition, restricted air intake filters and hoses are a common factor in slow buildup time. Kinked or restricted discharge lines will slow air pressure buildup time. The discharge line must maintain a constant slope down from the compressor to the air dryer inlet fitting to avoid low points where ice may form and block the flow. If carbon buildup in the discharge line is more than 1/16" the line should be replaced.

An excessively restricted air discharge line caused by such conditions as ice or carbon plugging will cause compressor discharge pressure to increase to the point where the connecting rod will break and blow a hole in the side of the compressor.

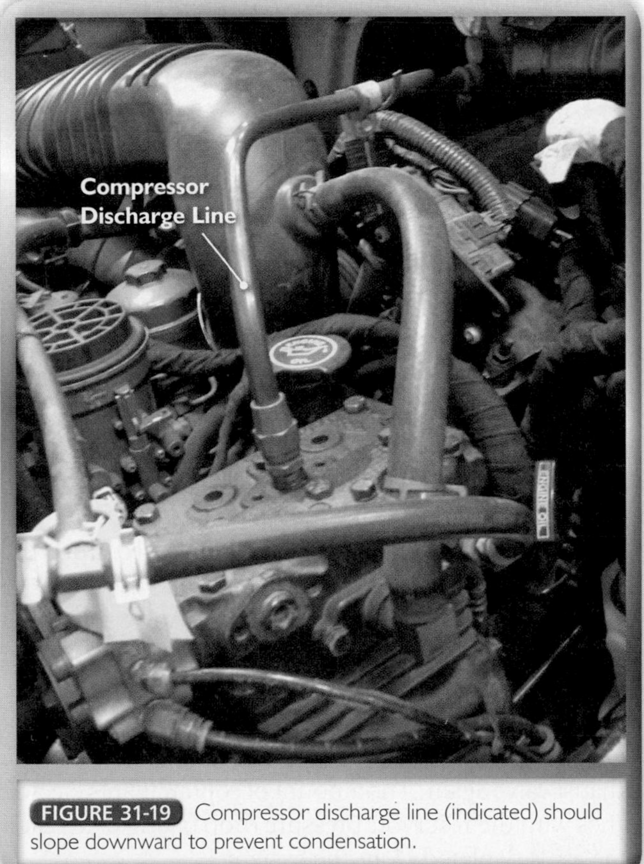

FIGURE 31-19 Compressor discharge line (indicated) should slope downward to prevent condensation.

> **TECHNICIAN TIP**
>
> Turbocharger boost pressure can be lost through a compressor connected to the engine intake system if it has damaged cylinders. Boost pressure will pass through the compressor and increase engine crankcase pressure, causing the engine to appear worn out. A leaking compressor head gasket can also pressurize the engine cooling system. Pressurization of the cooling system can cause coolant leaks and coolant loss, which may appear to be an engine head gasket or leaking cylinder liner. Unnecessary engine overhauls are frequently done due to misdiagnosed compressor problems. To isolate a cooling pressurization problem to the air compressor, the air reservoirs should be drained while the engine is running. If cooling system pressure stops increasing, the compressor is likely at fault.

Governor

The pressure at which the governor loads, is called the **governor cut-in pressure**, and the pressure at which the it unloads is called the **governor cut-out pressure**. Both should be verified against vehicle OEM specification. If the governor is malfunctioning, it should be replaced and not adjusted. (Note that the newest Greenhouse Gas (GHG) engines introduced in 2015 use fully electronic governors that do not follow conventional cut-in and cut-out pressures as part of operational strategies to reduce fuel consumption). The reservoir line to the governor should always be connected to the top of the primary air reservoir. If the air dryer and compressor are frequently loading and unloading, check the governor gasket for leakage. Unloader valves can also leak air between the governor unloader ports and the unloader valves, which causes frequent cycling of the dryer and compressor. FIGURE 31-20 shows the governor gasket and the unloader and reservoir ports.

Leaking air dryer purge valves and governor air lines can have the same effect. To check for leaking compressor unloader valves, charge the unloader port with an air hose or through a Schrader valve connected to the governor unloader port. Shut off the air supply and observe whether there is a drop in air pressure through the unloader port of the governor. A pressure gauge connected to the air hose is helpful when performing this inspection. A steady pressure reading indicates no air leakage is taking place through the unloader port. A loss of pressure indicates possible leaking unloader valves, a defective governor, leaking unloader lines, or a leaking air dryer unloader valve.

It is possible to fill the air reservoir without a running engine. The remote mounted governor in FIGURE 31-21 is equipped with a Schrader valve connected to the supply port. A shop air line can easily be clipped onto the valve and the reservoirs charged to enable the brakes to be released without a running engine or to minimize buildup time in a shop.

FIGURE 31-20 The governor gasket is located between the compressor and governor body. A leaking gasket, unloader valve, or unloader line will cause the compressor to cycle frequently. **A.** Governor gasket. **B.** Unloader port. **C.** Reservoir port.

FIGURE 31-21 Remote mounted governor with a Schrader valve (circled).

Air Reservoirs

Both primary and secondary air tanks, plus any accessory and wet air tanks, should be drained during a pre-trip inspection. Good praactice requires draining air tanks at the end of each day and leaving them open all night. In tanks equipped with automatic drain valves, reservoirs should be purged at every 12,000 miles (19,200 km) or once every year. If automatic drain valves are installed, their operation should be checked before the weather turns cold. The reservoir's pressure relief valve should be removed yearly, and its operation should be verified and compared against OEM specifications—typically 150 psi (1,034 kPa).

Oil and water contamination in the air reservoirs is detrimental to the entire air system. Valves and lines will sludge-up and fail to properly operate. Excessive water in the air reservoirs is typically caused by one of the following:

- Improper reservoir draining intervals
- Malfunctioning air dryer (i.e., the desiccant is not removing contaminants)
- Excessive air compressor duty cycle (over 25 percent)
- An air dryer purge valve frozen closed
- High inlet air temperatures to the air dryer, which prevents water condensation
- A leaking air compressor head gasket or cracked cylinder head

To minimize these causes, some vehicles use an automatic air reservoir drain valve, such as the DV-2. An automatic air reservoir drain valve ejects moisture and contaminant accumulations from air reservoirs. It operates automatically, removing contaminants every time the reservoir cycles between a pressure buildup and pressure reduction. When charging, the inlet valve opens and the exhaust valve closes due to the increasing air pressure inside the valve. Contaminants will accumulate in the sump of the valve as long as the pressure continues to increase.

When pressure stops increasing, both the inlet and exhaust valves are closed. As air is removed from the reservoir, a minimum of a 2-psi (13.8-kPa) difference in air pressure above the inlet valve and the valve sump will cause the exhaust valve to open, as pressure in the sump cavity is higher than the pressure above the inlet valve. Contaminants will be ejected from the valve sump until the pressure loss in the sump drops enough to close the exhaust valve again. The amount of contaminants ejected varies with the reservoir pressure drop taking place each time air is depleted from the system.

Dash Pressure Gauges

The dash gauge accuracy can be verified with an accurate test gauge installed in the appropriate air reservoir. A gauge will require replacement if there a difference of 4 psi (27 kPa) compared with measurements made with an accurate master gauge.

Air Dryers

The dryer's purpose is to remove moisture, dirt, oil, and other contaminants that could damage the air system components before the air enters the system reservoir. A buildup of water or ice in the reservoirs could reduce reservoir capacity, leading to frequent compressor cycling.

Desiccant cartridges contained by dryers should be regularly replaced. Typical air dryer cartridge replacement schedule is every 3 years/300K miles (480K km) for low-air-use vehicles and every year/100K miles (160K km) for high-air-use vehicles.

When inspecting the air dryer, note that it should purge when the compressor unloads. Purging is identified by the sudden exhaust of air draining from the dryer. The exhaust will contain contaminants and moisture. If the dryer does not purge, possible causes include:

- Air purge valve dryer malfunction
- Governor malfunction
- Improper governor control line connection to the reservoir

Frequent dryer purging accompanied by compressor unloading could be caused by any of the following:

- A compressor unloader mechanism malfunction (typically leaking unloader valve seals)
- An air dryer purge valve or inlet check valve malfunction
- Excessive air system leakage

FIGURE 31-22 shows an air dryer with a dessicant cartridge, purge valve, inlet port, and heating element.

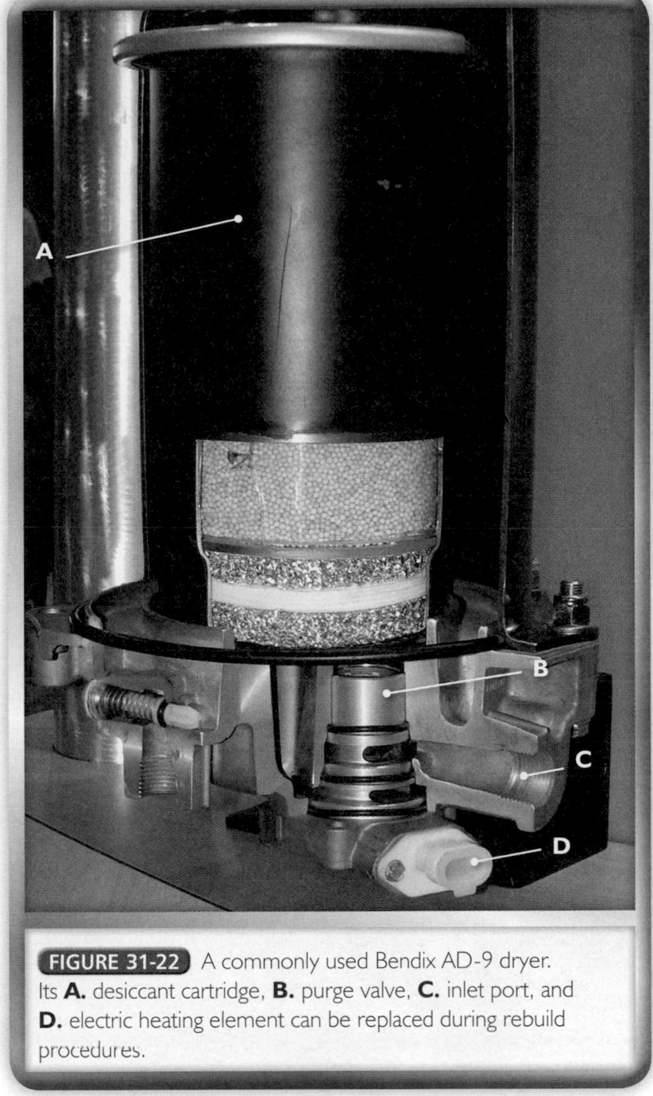

FIGURE 31-22 A commonly used Bendix AD-9 dryer. Its **A.** desiccant cartridge, **B.** purge valve, **C.** inlet port, and **D.** electric heating element can be replaced during rebuild procedures.

Alcohol Evaporator and Injector Systems

A cold weather air system accessory is the alcohol injection system. The system sends methanol into the air system to prevent moisture from freezing in the system. An evaporator is placed in series between the air dryer and primary reservoir containing the alcohol. The alcohol is atomized by the air passing from the compressor.

Alcohol evaporator systems send approximately 1 to 2 ounces (30 to 60 ml) of alcohol per hour into the air brake system whenever the compressor loaded. Air brake antifreeze is made only from methanol, not ethanol, and needs daily replenishing. If the system is using too little alcohol, it means the system is not receiving enough freeze protection. Excessive alcohol use wastes alcohol. City pick-up and delivery vehicles will cycle the air compressors more frequently due to stop-and-go driving and so will use more alcohol. On-highway vehicles will use less methanol because the brakes are not used as often, so the compressor does not operate as frequently.

Air Lines and Hoses

It is helpful to remember when diagnosing a problem with a specific brake circuit that nylon airline tubing is color coded to designate which air circuit it belongs. **TABLE 31-3** provides a guide to the color coding. Nylon line, or Synflex, is flexible, chemically resistant to deterioration, durable, and weather resistant. **FIGURE 31-23** shows nylon tubing entering a truck cab and connected to a bulkhead suspended foot valve. When replacing an air line, use nylon tubing only where it has been used previously. Nylon airlines must never be routed in areas where temperature could exceed 200° F (93° C).

Complaints such as slow brake application or slow brake release can indicate an airline is kinked, restricted, or clogged. To check for this condition, the suspected tube or hose should be disconnected at both ends and blown through to clear any blockage. Tubing and hoses can be inspected for partial restriction caused by dents or kinks. If Teflon-braided or stainless-steel hoses used in the engine compartment are replaced, they should be serviced with only the same type of hose material.

Flexible hoses like those in FIGURE 31-24 are typically used where there is constant flexing, such as for brake chamber hoses. When visually inspected, any hose that is chafed, worn, or kinked should be replaced.

All air lines should be checked for damage from cuts, swelling, kinks, and deterioration due to time and exposure to harsh operating environments. Inspect for pinched lines and the correct use of retaining clips, brackets, and ties to support hoses. Hose spring guards, such as the one in FIGURE 31-25, are used where air lines are highly flexed and should be in good condition and not distorted.

TABLE 31-3: Nylon Airline Color Designation Chart

Air Brake Circuit Color	Air Circuit
Red	Secondary
Green	Primary and delivery
Yellow	Parking brake
Blue	Suspension
Black	Accessory
Brown	Trailer brake

Servicing Foundation Brakes

In addition to servicing the air supply system, it is also important to service the foundation brakes. The life of

FIGURE 31-23 Nylon tubing entering a truck cab and connected to a bulkhead suspended foot valve.

FIGURE 31-24 Rubber flex hoses with fabric reinforced walls are used in highly flexible air connections.

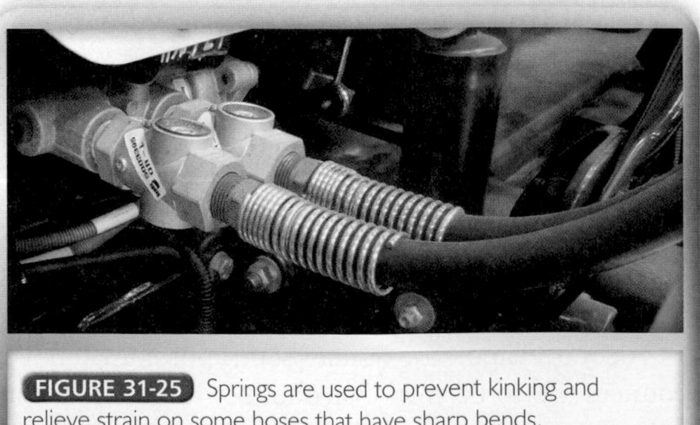

FIGURE 31-25 Springs are used to prevent kinking and relieve strain on some hoses that have sharp bends.

the foundation brakes depends on factors such as the type of brake block or lining, type and quality of drums and brake hardware, type of vehicle operation (transit, on-highway truck, vocational, etc.), and more. Aggressive driving with hard braking will also accelerate brake wear. For example, if operating conditions require frequent braking, brake lining replacement will be more frequent.

Before beginning any service procedure, it is critical that the vehicle be properly prepared and that you determine the servicing needs. To prepare the vehicle, park it on a level surface and chock the wheels with purpose-built chocks to prevent any vehicle movement. Spring brakes should be caged on all axles being serviced. The air should be drained from all air reservoirs. Axles should be raised only until the tires clear the ground. The safety stands being used should be in proper working order, and the appropriate weight must be used to support the axles. Slack adjusters should be backed off until the S-cam rollers and S-cam return to the start position of the S-cam. And, as when servicing other systems, follow the procedures in the vehicle service manual for removing wheels and drums.

Determining the service needs of the foundation brakes entails a series of tests and inspections. During regular service inspections, brake shoes should be inspected for broken welds and roller and anchor pin contact point wear. Brake blocks and lining should be examined for cracks, heat hardening, glazing, and contamination from oil or grease. No movement between the brake lining and the shoe is permissible. Camshaft wear is checked. Check for the presence of a **cam-over condition**, which can take place when the linings and or brake camshafts are worn enough to allow the cam to rotate past the rollers. This means that the S-cam rollers will crest, or pass over, the highest point of S-cam and leave the brakes applied. Cam-over conditions will keep prevent the brake shoes from returning to an off position, and the shoes are extended.

Examine foundation brakes to ensure that components are correct for the application. Chambers should have the proper length brake chambers matched and the correct size and so on. The brake drum or rotor should be cleaned and inspected for the following conditions:

- Braking surfaces should be free of scoring, excessive heat checks, and cracks.
- The drum diameter or rotor thickness should be within the maximum limits cast or stamped on the drum or on the rotor. It is recommended that at least 0.40" (10 mm) below maximum diameter or thickness should remain as a wear allowance.
- Brake drum mounting holes and pilot surface must be round and concentric.
- The mounting surface must be clean and flat.

The use of extended brake life brake parts using heavier drums and thicker linings will lengthen the service intervals between brake replacements. Standard drums for normal service weigh approximately 100 lbs (45.5 kg). Heavy-duty drums weigh approximately 120 lbs (54 kg) each, and drums for severe service can reach 135 lbs (61kg) each!

When foundation brakes need to be replaced, a service kit such as the one shown in FIGURE 31-26 is commonly used. The kit will typically include new or remanufactured shoes and hardware.

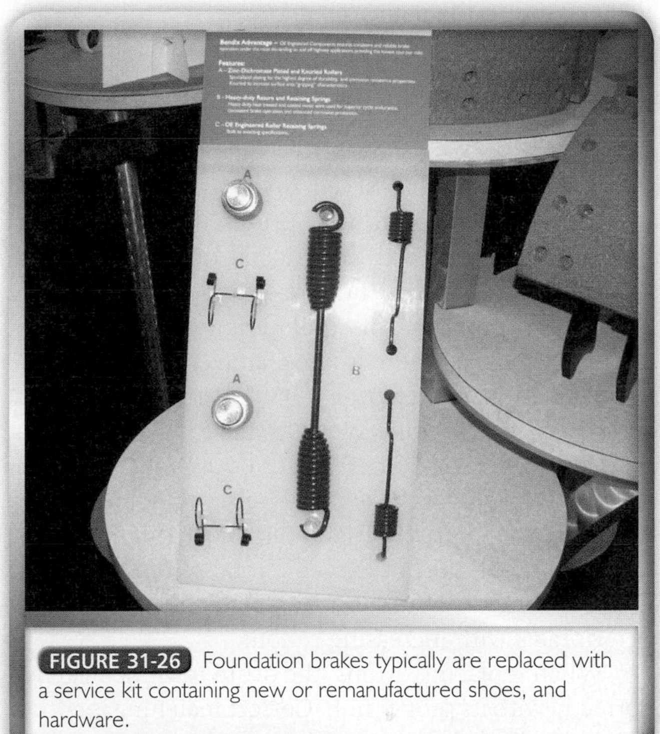

FIGURE 31-26 Foundation brakes typically are replaced with a service kit containing new or remanufactured shoes, and hardware.

TECHNICIAN TIP

Sometimes brake defects are found on only one axle end. Leaking wheel seals contaminating brake lining, a defective slack adjuster, a cracked drum, or a damaged shoe might seem more efficiently and economically repaired by replacing only the affected parts. However, braking performance will be affected because brake torque will change whenever brake parts are different at each axle end. When performing brake repairs, both ends of a common axle MUST be maintained in the same state of repair. If the brake shoes are replaced at one end, the shoes on the opposite end should also be replaced. If a brake drum is machined or replaced, the other drum should also be machined to the same dimension or both replaced to maintain consistent braking performance.

Brake Drums

Servicing brake drums FIGURE 31-27 is a critical element to the overall servicing of the air brakes. The service limit for maximum wear on brake drums is cast into most brake drums. Drum wear is measured using an inside bore gauge or drum micrometer. When placed inside a drum, the maximum diameter requiring drum replacement should be less than 16.120" for most 16.5" × 7" (42 cm × 17.8 cm) drums. Drums should not be rebored. That is, drums should not be machined to be oversize. Any boring should leave the drum 0.040" (1 mm) under the maximum diameter. That is true regardless of the reason for the boring, for example to remove scoring, heat checks, or light cracking. A minimum thickness must be maintained for additional wear.

When checking brake drum diameter for wear, the diameter should not exceed 0.120" over the original diameter. When reboring brake drums, the finished diameter should not exceed the original diameter by more than 0.080". Otherwise, brake fade and the possibility of a cam-over condition will result. For a new 16.5" drum, therefore, the maximum inside diameter will be 16.580" (42.1 cm). That is 16.5" + 0.080" = 16.580". If 0.40" (10.2 mm) remains for a wear allowance, the replacement diameter would be 16.620" (42.2 cm). Brake drum run out will not cause a brake pedal pulsation for air brakes like out of round drums will produce on hydraulic brakes; however, it should not exceed a total of 0.025" (0.635 mm), as contact between friction material and the drum deteriorates with increasing runout.

When replacing drums, the drum must be matched correctly with its proper hub. Correct matching is critical for the proper center mounting of wheel rims and for preventing "wheel-off" accidents, loose or broken mounting studs, and dragging brakes.

Hub-piloted brake drums have larger stud holes in the brake drum and a tight fit on the wheel hub pilot pads.

FIGURE 31-27 Brake drum.

It is critical to seat the brake drum properly on the drum pilot pad. FIGURE 31-28 shows an incorrectly installed brake drum. Failure to install an outboard mounted drum properly on the drum pilot pads can cause the brake drum holes to crack on the drum face as shown in FIGURE 31-29.

Ball-seat drums used with stud-piloted wheels have a tighter fit on studs. New drum designs enable the use of the same drum for ball-seat and hub-piloted wheels. However, new drum designs cannot always be used with some older stud-piloted hubs. Carefully following manufacturer directions concerning replacement parts is essential. In FIGURE 31-30, note the presence of two distinctly different hub pilot pads. One is for the wheel and the other for the brake drum.

Corrosion forming between wheel hubs and the chamfer of the brake drum pilot is a concern. This type

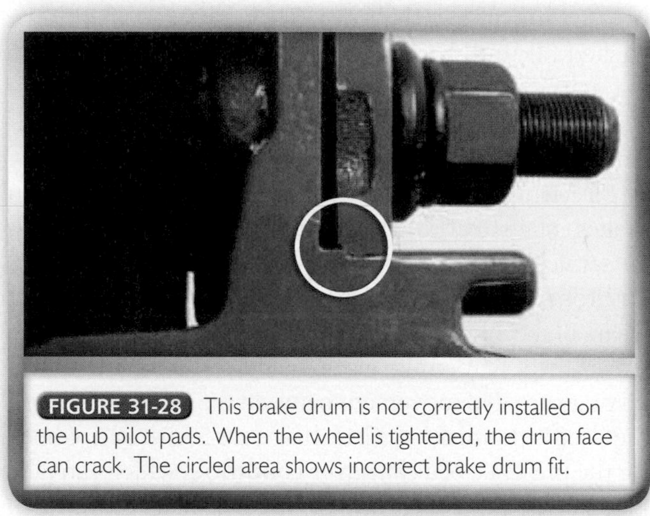

FIGURE 31-28 This brake drum is not correctly installed on the hub pilot pads. When the wheel is tightened, the drum face can crack. The circled area shows incorrect brake drum fit.

FIGURE 31-29 Cracked brake drum holes on the drum face.

FIGURE 31-30 Brake drum with two sets of pilot pads. **A.** Wheel pilot pads. **B.** Drum pilot pads.

FIGURE 31-32 A broken brake drum casting.

of corrosion generally results from improper installation, which can prevent the drum from correctly centering squarely onto the hub and against the hub flange. After the wheel nuts are tightened, the brake drum can crack as shown in FIGURE 31-31. Cracking can lead to brake drum failure as in FIGURE 31-32.

Improper drum installation will also cause irregular braking because the centerline of the drum and hub are not aligned. To prevent this, corrosion must be completely removed prior to installing the brake drum. Corrosion is best removed by chipping it and then cleaning the hub with a wire brush. Corrosion is especially a problem with aluminum hubs, which require more careful cleaning to prevent damage to the aluminum. A condition called Martensite spotting takes place when the drum braking surface is rapidly heated. Drum material changes composition to form dark, very hard crystalline structures, which are difficult to machine and prevent even drum wear. FIGURE 31-33 shows an example of Martensite spotting.

Brake drums need to be discarded if they experience any of the following conditions:

- Scoring
- Severe heat checking
- Cracking through the hat section
- Cracking through the side wall.

Brake drum service guidelines are given in TABLE 31-4, and TABLE 31-5 contains a drum replacement guide.

FIGURE 31-31 Light heat cracking is normal wear condition. The cracks do not deeply penetrate the drum braking surfaces.

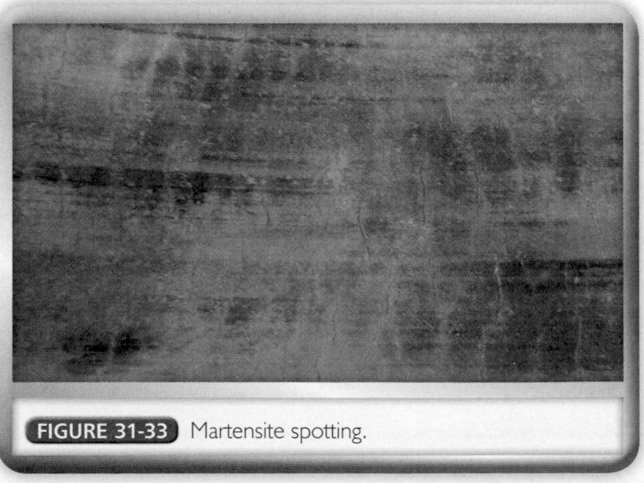

FIGURE 31-33 Martensite spotting.

TABLE 31-4: Drum Service Guidelines

Condition	Cause	Remedy
Deep, uniform drum wear	Brake drag Brake imbalance on worn wheel ends. Dirt and contaminants imbedded in the brake lining Incorrect braking and or driving technique – not snubbing brakes or downshifting on hills. Braking with hand valve on trailer brakes only.	Replace the drum Install dust shields backing plates
Eccentric drum wear (i.e., drum worn on one side only)	Brake drum dropped, bent or machined out-of-round Drum not centered on drum wheel hub pilots.	Replace the drum
Worn brake drum bolt Holes	Insufficient torque applied to wheel nuts, which also causes hub- and drum pilots to wear.	Replace the drum
Uniform heat checking (fine cracks)	Heavy braking	Replace the drum
Uniform hot spotting (black spots) on the drum's surface (Martensite spots)	Brake lining to drum contact surfaces burnished too slowly during break-in. Dragging brakes Extremely hard linings Lining swell from poor-quality linings causing brake drag	Replace the drum
Polished or glazed drums (mirror-like shine)	Low-pressure braking Incorrect brake block material for application – too soft.	Replace the drum
Scoring (Grooving) Deep grooves in the drum's surface that exceed the drum's maximum diameter. Drum can appear to be in good condition.	Dirt or contaminants in the brake system Linings worn to the rivets or not OEM-approved.	Replace the drum Scoring in the drum's braking surface that is deeper than 0.10 inch (2.54 mm) and wider than 0.030 inch (0.76 mm) requires both drum and lining replacement.
"Blue" Drum Inside of the brake drum has "blue" tint from excessive heat. Components can be deformed or damaged.	Caused by extremely high temperatures due to brake imbalance Poor driver techniques Too soft brake lining Brake drag	Replace the drum
Cracked drum	A drum can crack when the parking brake is set while the brakes are extremely hot. The cooling drum contracted on the brake shoes with enough force to crack the drum.	Replace the drum
Oil or grease contaminated lining and drums	Oil and grease spots have penetrated the drum's surface. The brake drum probably is discolored.	Replace the drum

TABLE 31-5: Drum Inspection Replacement Guide

Nominal Diameter	Discard Drum At
16.5"	16.620"
16"	16.120"
15"	15.120"

Brake Shoes

As illustrated in FIGURE 31-34, replacement or relining of brake shoes is required when lining thickness at the center of the shoe has reached 5/16" (7.94 mm) (1/4" [6.35 mm] for extended service lining). A wear line on some shoes placed at 1/4" (6.35 mm) thickness is measured at the center of the shoe and can be used as a visual guide. Alternatively, brake shoe wear can be determined by inserting a go/no-go gauge into the backing plate hole. Lastly, FIGURE 31-35 shows an optional wear indicator switch sensor is located in a brake shoe. When the brake shoe wears to less than 50%, the sensor will ground out against the brake drum, which triggers a warning indicator. Rivets or bolts attaching the brake block or lining to the shoe table should never be permitted contact the drum.

FIGURE 31-35 An optional wear indicator switch sensor (circled) on a brake shoe.

Inspecting and Removing Brake Shoes

When inspecting new or rebuilt brake shoes for wear, follow the guidelines in SKILL DRILL 31-16. To remove the brake shoes, follow the steps in SKILL DRILL 31-17.

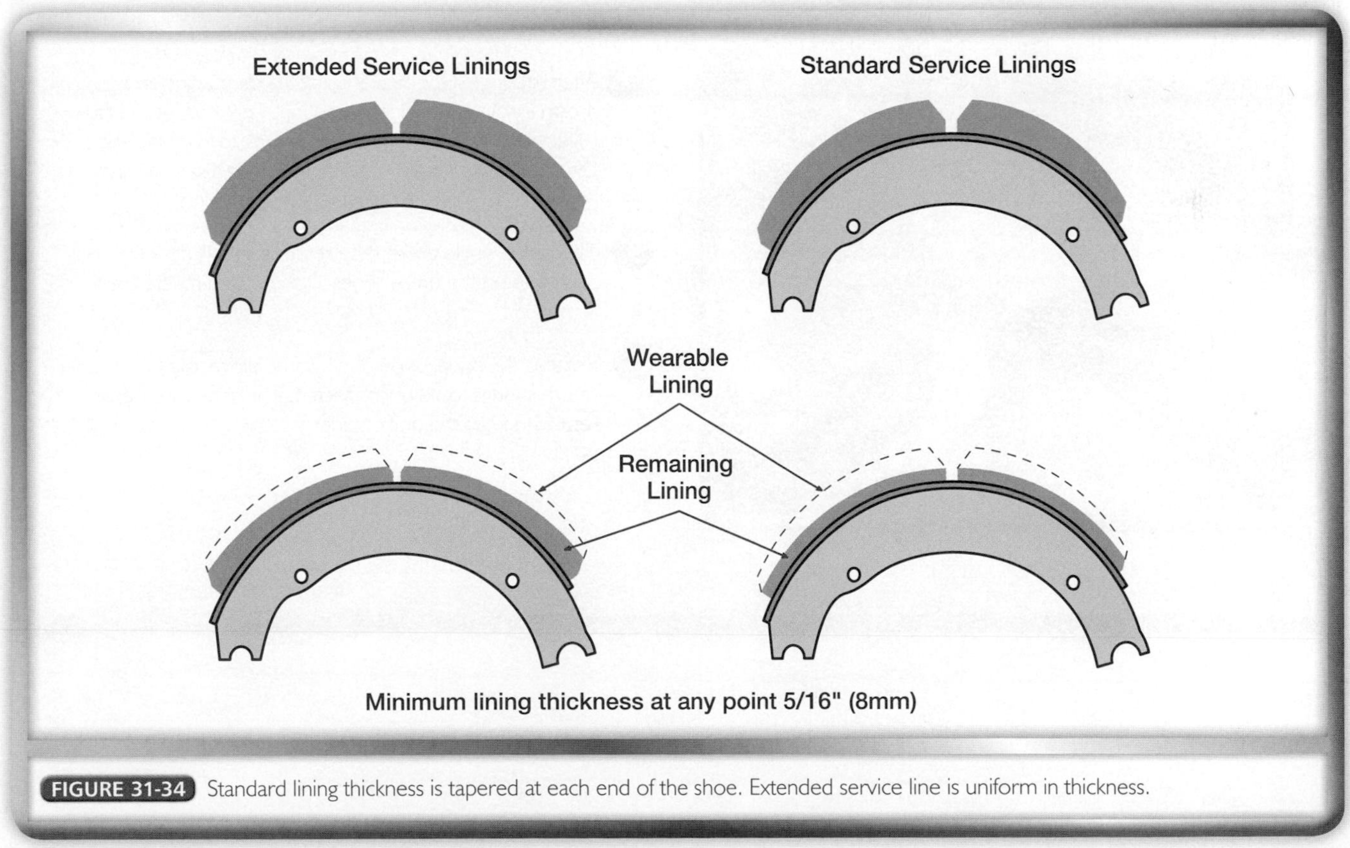

FIGURE 31-34 Standard lining thickness is tapered at each end of the shoe. Extended service line is uniform in thickness.

SKILL DRILL 31-16 Inspecting Brake Shoes

1. Determine if the shoe tables are warped are bent. Check for any small gaps between the lining and the shoe table.
2. Check for elongated rivet holes, which can cause movement between the shoe table and the lining.
3. Check for corrosion of the shoe table. Inspect for uneven fit between the lining and the shoe table. Look for visible rust at the edges.
4. Check for web-end wear, uneven, or mushroom ends. Check both the anchor pin end and the roller end for wear and elongation. Use gauges to verify the proper distance between the web ends.
5. Check for loose or broken welds. Look for cracks in the welds between the shoe table and the web.
6. Check for chips or cracks in the corrosion-resistant paint. Make sure the paint is even and that there is solid coverage.

SKILL DRILL 31-17 Removing Brake Shoes

1. After backing off the brakes using the slack adjuster, the S-cam is rotated to its start position. This enables the cam roller to be easily unclipped and removed from the shoes. Lifting the upper brake shoe slightly using a pry bar provides additional clearance to remove the cam rollers.
2. The larger, single brake shoe return spring is disconnected from pins on the brake shoes after the cam rollers are removed.
3. Rotating the lower shoe downwards allows the two smaller return springs to be disconnected. The shoes are freely removed from the brake spider.

Alternatively, brake shoes can be quickly removed by pushing out the anchor pins using a punch and hammer. These brakes use a single center return spring and have a closed hole in the shoe for anchor pin. Enclosed anchor pin holes are called "P"-type shoes. Semicircular anchor pin holes are called quick release brakes or a "QR" brake, which refers to the faster shoe replacement enabled by open anchor pin holes.

Disassembling Brakes

Two methods are used to disassemble brakes. The most common method requires only a pry bar as a lever to remove shoe rollers. To disassemble brakes using a pry bar, follow the steps in SKILL DRILL 31-18.

An alternate method for disassembling brakes involves a tool resembling a heavy-duty screwdriver with a V-shaped notch cut into the bottom of the blade. The notched screwdriver is used to disconnect both brake retain springs from the anchor pin end of brake shoes. With this method, the brake shoe springs are stretched and removed from retaining holes. The tool helps technicians avoid the pinching hazard associated with removing cam rollers while the return springs are connected. The springs can cause the shoes to snap back into position while removing the rollers and pinch fingers if a technician is not cautious. After this, the upper and lower brake shoes are pulled off the anchor pins and freed from the spider.

Installing Brake Shoes

If brake shoes are defective or need to be replaced, follow the guidelines in SKILL DRILL 31-19. New or "green" brakes require a break in procedure called burnishing. This involves driving the vehicle at moderate speeds and repeatedly snubbing the brakes hard using 20 psi or greater application pressure. The brake adjustment should be rechecked after burnishing the drums and shoes.

When installing brake shoes, anti-seize lubricant is applied to each of the brake shoe ends to minimize friction and noise production from the cam rollers and anchor pins connection points. It is important to lubricate only certain of the component parts during assembly. FIGURE 31-36 is a guide of which parts to lubricate when installing brake shoes.

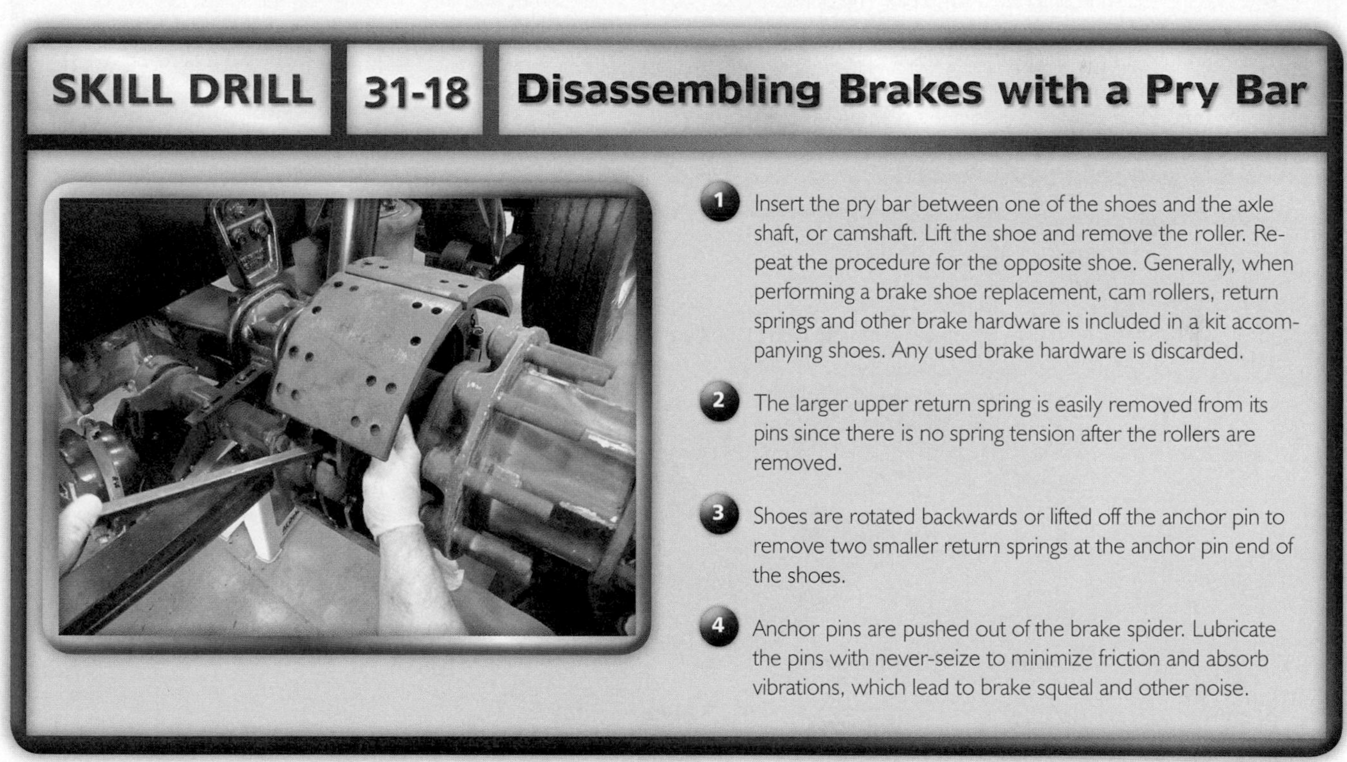

SKILL DRILL 31-18 Disassembling Brakes with a Pry Bar

1. Insert the pry bar between one of the shoes and the axle shaft, or camshaft. Lift the shoe and remove the roller. Repeat the procedure for the opposite shoe. Generally, when performing a brake shoe replacement, cam rollers, return springs and other brake hardware is included in a kit accompanying shoes. Any used brake hardware is discarded.
2. The larger upper return spring is easily removed from its pins since there is no spring tension after the rollers are removed.
3. Shoes are rotated backwards or lifted off the anchor pin to remove two smaller return springs at the anchor pin end of the shoes.
4. Anchor pins are pushed out of the brake spider. Lubricate the pins with never-seize to minimize friction and absorb vibrations, which lead to brake squeal and other noise.

SKILL DRILL 31-19 Installing Brake Shoes

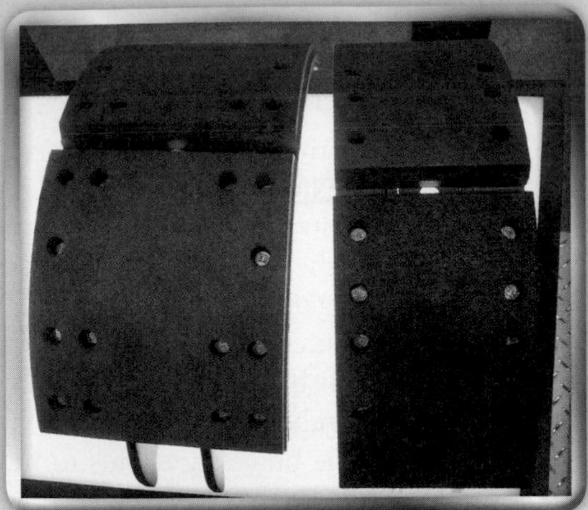

1. Install the anchor pin into the spider centering the pin in the spider. Use never-seize lubricant when installing the anchor pin.
2. Install two new brake shoe retaining springs in the anchor pin end of the shoes.
3. Place the top shoe onto the anchor pin. The opposite end of the shoe rests against the S-cam. Swing the lower shoe, with return springs attached onto the anchor pin then continue swinging the shoe towards the S-cam. Return spring tension should hold the shoes in this position.
4. Connect the hook of the larger brake shoe return spring onto the return spring pin at the cam end of the upper shoe. While holding the shoes against the S-cam, connect the other end of the hook to the return spring pin of the other shoe.
5. Using a pry bar inserted between the cam end of one of the brake shoes and the spider, pry the shoe from the cam until the brake shoe roller and pin can be installed between the S-cam and the slots in the end of the brake shoe. Duplicate the procedure on the other shoe. The roller ends connecting with the shoes require never-seize lubricant.
6. Turn the slack adjuster adjusting screw until the brake chamber pushrod yoke clevis pin aligns with the correct hole in the slacks arm. The clevis pin should be lubricated with never-seize compound and a new cotter pin installed. The cam rollers should be in lowest position on the S-cam.
7. The brake drums and wheels can now be installed and torqued to manufacturer's specifications.
8. While slowly spinning the wheel, the slack adjuster can be adjusted until a slight amount of drag is sensed as the shoe and drum clearance becomes smaller. When the service brakes are applied, both slack adjusters should move in unison, stopping at identical angles with the same pushrod stroke travel. The brakes should apply and release simultaneously.

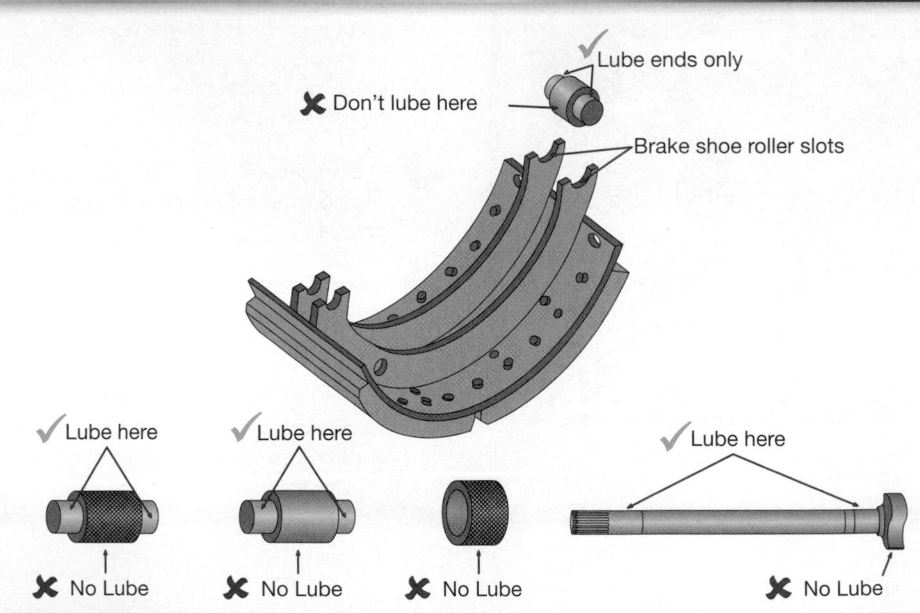

FIGURE 31-36 Not all parts in a brake shoe installation should be lubricated. In fact, some should specifically *NOT* be lubricated.

Camshafts

The camshaft, its bushings, and its bearings must be inspected regularly for signs of wear at the points indicated in FIGURE 31-37. If any of the points are observed to be worn, the cam must be discarded. Camshafts and bushings are inspected for axial (in and out along the camshaft axis) and radial play (up and down). The specifications shown are general and should be checked against specific manufacturers' recommendations. Likewise, the support bracket should be checked regularly for broken welds, cracks, and straightness as shown in FIGURE 31-38.

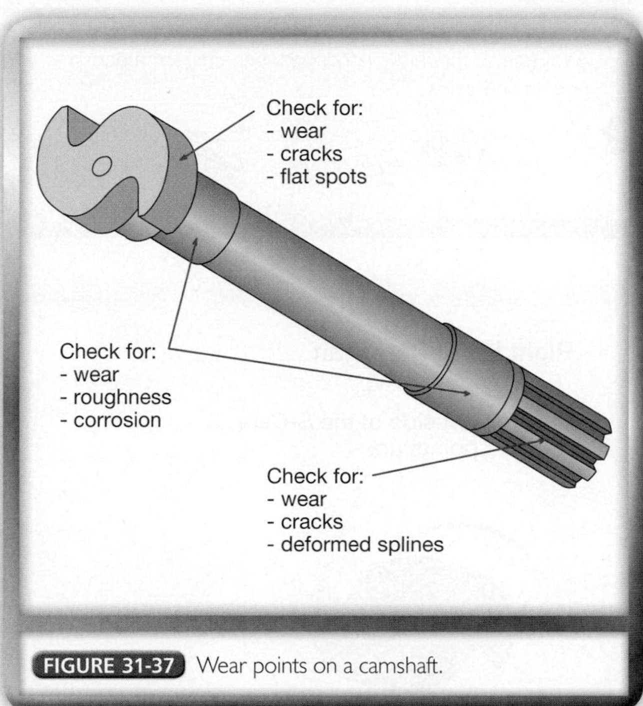

FIGURE 31-37 Wear points on a camshaft.

Radial free play, which is up and down or sideways movement of the camshaft, should typically be no more than 0.030" (0.76 mm) movement.

Allowable radial play varies between manufacturers but rarely is more than .030". Camshaft end play must be a minimum of .005" and a maximum of .030". Check camshaft play using a dial indicator with a flexible mount as shown in FIGURE 31-39. If bushings are excessively worn, both the camshaft and bushings should be replaced. Camshaft bearing surfaces should be free of wear and corrosion. Any visible wear or roughness that can be felt requires replacement. The cam head should have no cracks, and its roller surfaces free of flat spots, brinneling, or ridges.

Removing the Camshaft

To remove the camshaft, follow the steps in SKILL DRILL 31-20.

Installing a Camshaft

Camshafts are classified as left- or right-hand rotation according to the direction they rotate when the brakes are applied. Left-hand camshafts rotate counter clockwise (CCW), and right-hand camshafts rotate clockwise (CW). Camshaft rotation is illustrated in FIGURE 31-40. Failure to identify the correct direction of rotation and the appropriate installation location is a common cause of a major waste of labor time by novice technicians when performing camshaft replacement.

When replacing a camshaft and its bushings, two camshaft grease seals are replaced, one at each end of the cam tube. The direction of the seal lip placement is critical. To minimize grease entering the wheel end, the seal lip at the cam end should point inboard towards

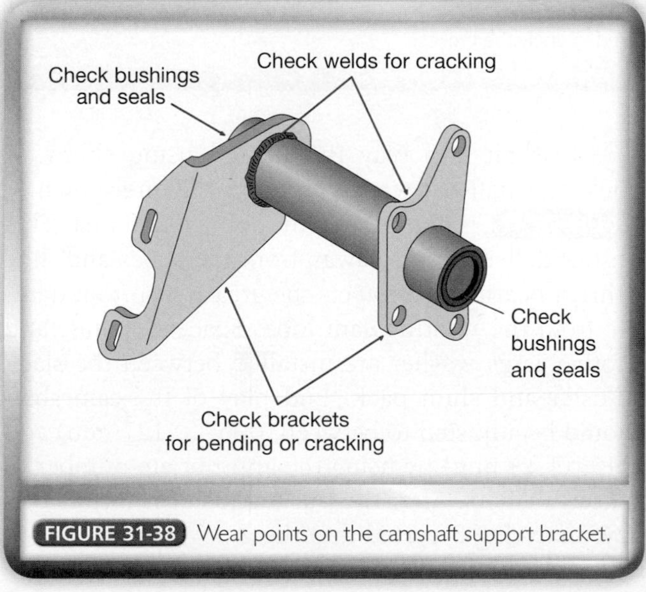

FIGURE 31-38 Wear points on the camshaft support bracket.

FIGURE 31-39 Check camshaft for radial play using a dial indicator.

SKILL DRILL 31-20 Removing the Camshaft

1. Disconnect the slack adjuster from the brake chamber yoke. Removing the clevis pin or pins frees the slack arm from the yoke.
2. Remove the snap ring and washer at splined end of the camshaft before pulling the slack adjuster from cam shaft. If the slack adjuster has worn into the camshaft splines or is seized to the camshaft by corrosion, a puller may be required. Purpose made pullers are available to remove slack adjusters.
3. Remove the spacer shims used to adjust axial end play. Also remove the thick washer between the cam support bracket and shims.
4. Slide the camshaft out of the support bracket tube from the axle end. Remove the backing plates, if equipped.

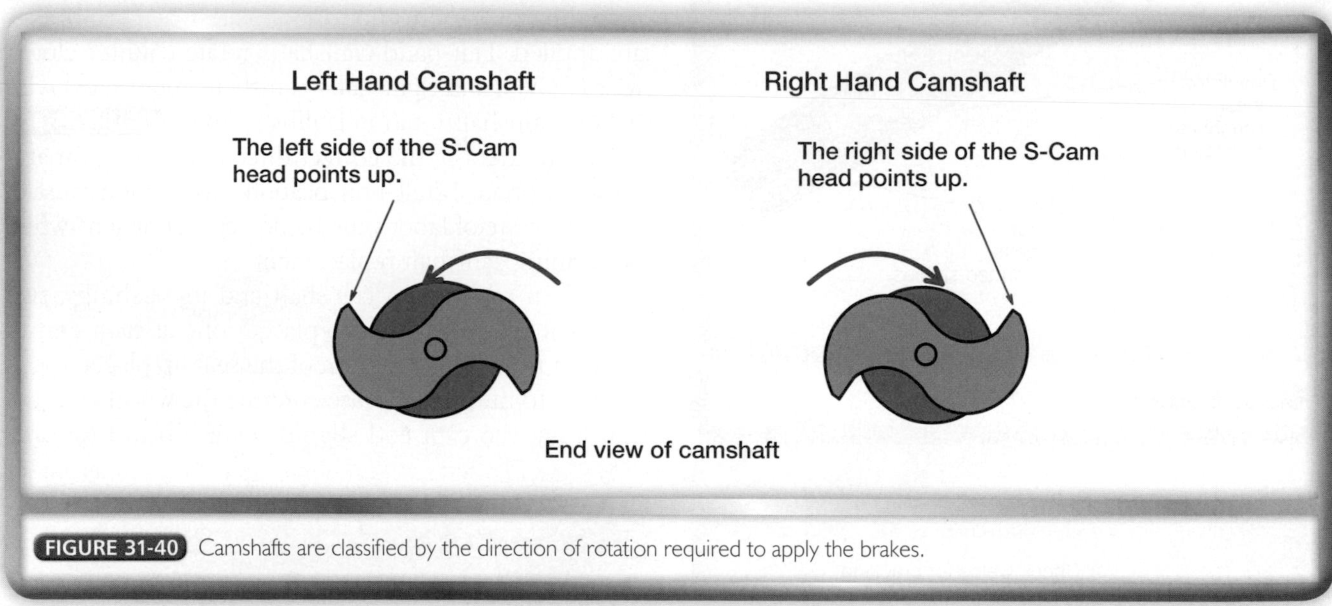

FIGURE 31-40 Camshafts are classified by the direction of rotation required to apply the brakes.

the tube center. FIGURE 31-41 shows the orientation of the lip seals.

The seal lip at the splined end should point towards the slack to enable venting and purging of old grease and contaminants in the support tube during service. It is critical to ensure that the grease holes of the bushing line-up with two grease fittings at each end of the tube. When assembling the camshaft, coat camshaft journals with a light film of chassis lube. Grease the support bracket tube until grease is forced out into the gap between the slack adjuster and support bracket tube. Grease should not appear at the cam end of the shaft where the brake shoes are. If it does, the seals have not been properly installed.

Camshaft end play is adjusted using shims. A thick camshaft flat washer, such as the one shown in FIGURE 31-42, is placed over the splined end first. This washer deflects grease away from the shoes and, like a thrust bearing, it protects the grease seal from damage from the rotating cam lobe. Spacers, shims, and another large washer are installed between the slack adjuster and shim pack. End play of the cam shaft should be adjusted to between .005" (0.127 mm) and .045" (1.14 mm) by using the appropriate number of spacer washers. After the slack adjuster is installed, a new snap ring is seated into the groove at the splined end of the camshaft.

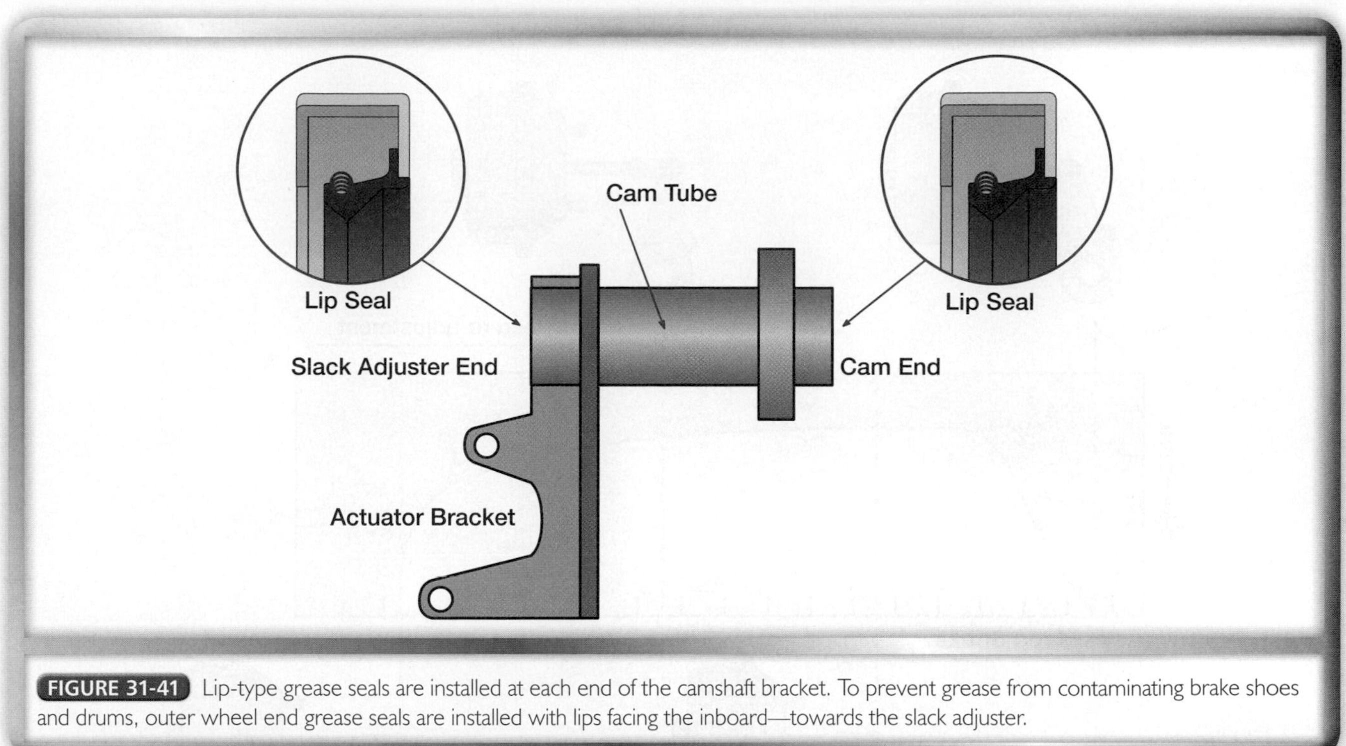

FIGURE 31-41 Lip-type grease seals are installed at each end of the camshaft bracket. To prevent grease from contaminating brake shoes and drums, outer wheel end grease seals are installed with lips facing the inboard—towards the slack adjuster.

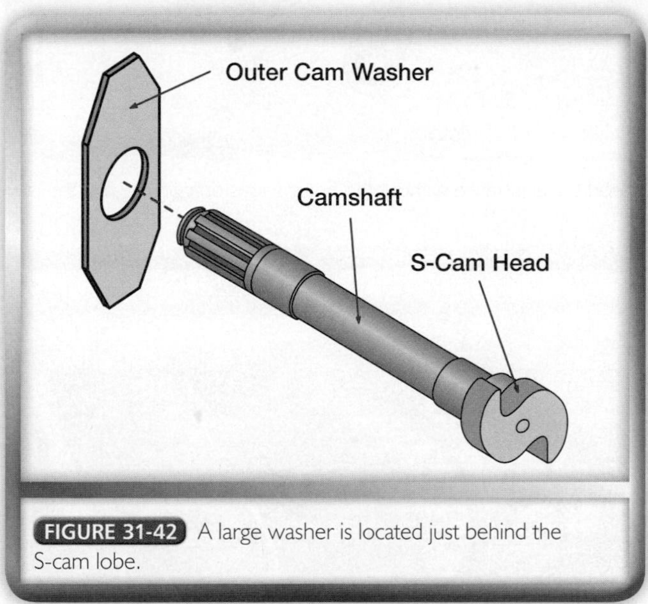

FIGURE 31-42 A large washer is located just behind the S-cam lobe.

Inspecting the Spider Plate

The brake spider plate should be inspected for cracks or broken surfaces on the spider at the cam, anchor pin, and mounting bolt holes. Lining wear tapered from side to side across shoe table indicates a bent spider. A spider can be bent if it is heated and hammered to remove seized anchor pins. A press operated with an air impact gun can be used to push out seized anchor pins. Radial clearance around the anchor pins in excess of .010" (0.25 mm) indicates excessive wear requiring brake spider replacement.

Adjusting Air Brakes

Federal and provincial laws require slack adjusters be checked daily, during the pre-trip inspection, and before driving down steep grades that are posted with regulatory signs. Since 1996, all commercial trucks and trailers with air brakes are manufactured with automatic slack adjusters. Automatic slack adjusters (ASA) maintain brake drum-to-shoe clearance more reliably than manual slack adjusters. After correct installation, automatic slack adjusters should not need manual adjustment. If an ASA is found to allow a brake stroke beyond the maximum allowable limit, the slack is defective and requires replacement. Even if the slack is temporarily adjusted, a defective slack adjuster will often lengthen rather than shorten stroke travel quickly past its maximum limit.

FIGURE 31-43 illustrates the relationship between stroke length and brake force. As the brake lining wears, pushrod travel lengthens to the point where maximum torque through a 90-degree angle disappears, and the brake stroke reaches its travel limit. Brake force rapidly diminishes when stroke travel reaches its maximum limit.

The Most Important Inch

To understand just how critical a correct brake adjustment is, consider the following. A correctly adjusted brake has only 1/2 inch (1.27 cm) of pushrod stroke travel, leaving 2 inches (5.08 cm) of reserve chamber

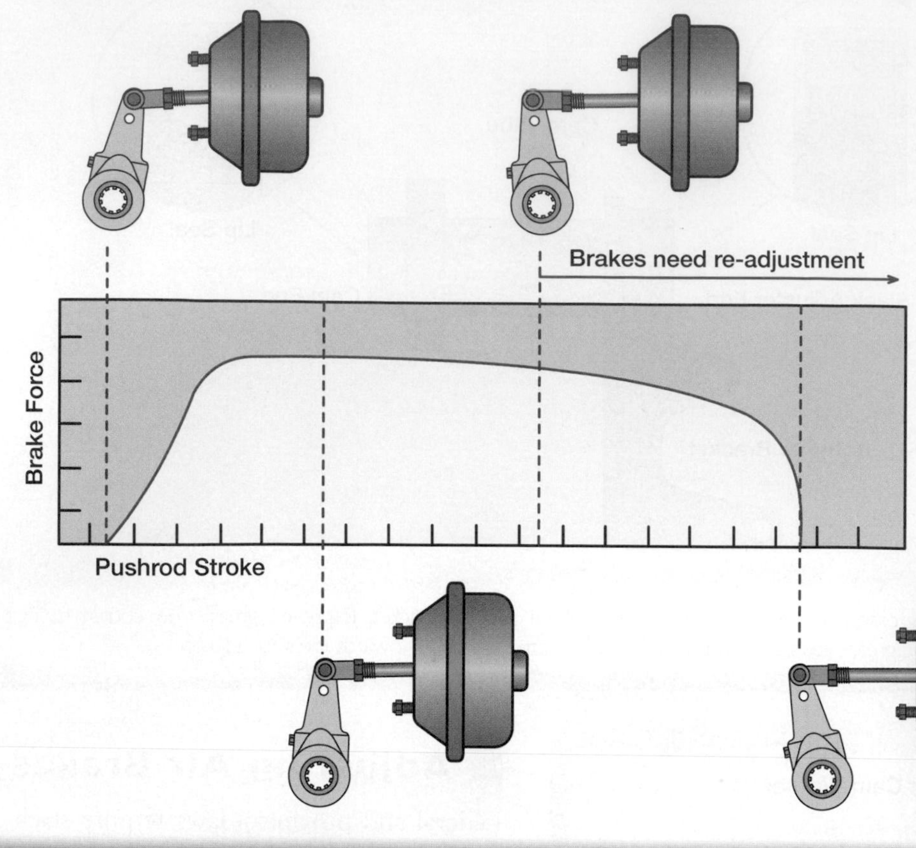

Brakes need re-adjustment

Brake Force

Pushrod Stroke

FIGURE 31-43 Air brakes are initially adjusted to obtain the shortest pushrod travel distance without the brake shoes dragging against the drum.

stroke. When the slack allows 1 inch (2.54 cm) of brake stroke, the brakes must be adjusted. This is referred to as a driver's most important inch of life.

A slack adjusted to 1" of stroke travel will move 1/4" farther at an 80 PSI application due to component stretch. A cast iron drum expands when heated, so heat fade can add close to a half inch of clearance. This leaves only 1/4" reserve stroke before the chamber pushrod potentially bottoms out. If not corrected by an automatic adjuster, lining worn the thickness of 3 sheets of paper adds another 1-4" of pushrod travel.

Brake stroke can be measured in one of two ways. One is between the brake chamber face and a marking on the pushrod. The second is by measuring the brake stroke length at the clevis pin. Both methods measure either applied or free stroke length. **FIGURE 31-44** shows a visual stroke indicator used to inspect the applied stroke length. The maximum pushrod travel measured at the clevis pin should be no more than the distance between the two yellow tabs.

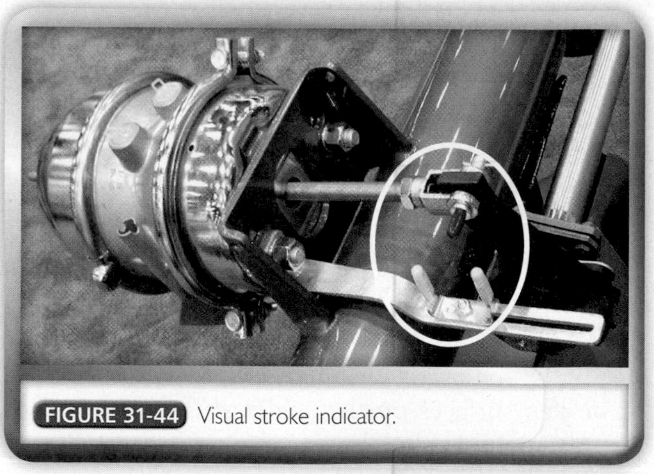

FIGURE 31-44 Visual stroke indicator.

To measure free brake stroke, start by chocking the wheels to prevent vehicle movement. Then make a chalk mark on the actuator pushrod at the chamber face with the park brakes released. By hand, pull out the actuator pushrod to its limit. Alternatively, use the open end of a 15/16" wrench as a short pry bar to pull the actuator out. To assist making a measurement of free stroke length, a purpose-made tool can be used to pull the brake chamber pushrod from a retracted position to the point where the shoes contact the brake drum. Although it is commonly used, free stroke measurement is not a recommended method to check for brake adjustment.

Finally, use a measuring tape to measure the distance the pushrod travels between the chalk mark and the face of the brake chamber. Free stroke of 1/2" (1.27 cm) to 3/4" (1.9 cm) is acceptable. If this distance is more than 3/4" (1.9 cm), the brakes should be adjusted.

The applied stroke method uses a service brake application to measure pushrod stroke travel. This requires two persons—one to apply the brakes and one to measure stroke travel. Applied stroke method is commonly used by roadside inspectors and is recommended by commercial fleet maintenance supervisors to perform brake adjustments for manual and automatic slack adjusters.

As when measuring free stroke, a reference mark is made on the pushrod at the brake chamber's face when the brakes are released. When the service brake is applied with approximately 80–90 psi (552–621 kPa) air pressure, the pushrod travel is measured. Application pressure is adjusted by pumping the brakes to deplete the air reservoir until desired pressure is reached on the dash gauge. If the slack has 1" (2.54 cm) or more travel, it must be adjusted. Slightly more travel is allowed by the applied stroke measurement compared to free stroke due to component stretch during a brake application compared to a free stroke method.

As shown in FIGURE 31-45, applied brake stroke travel is longer than the free stroke limit. With air pressure applying the brakes, greater force is used against the braking mechanism, which produces a longer stroke.

Brake Adjustment Indicators

Newer air brake chamber pushrods have a bright marking on the pushrod at the face of the brake chamber. If the pushrod travel becomes excessive, the mark will emerge to become a visual indicator that a brake adjustment must be done immediately.

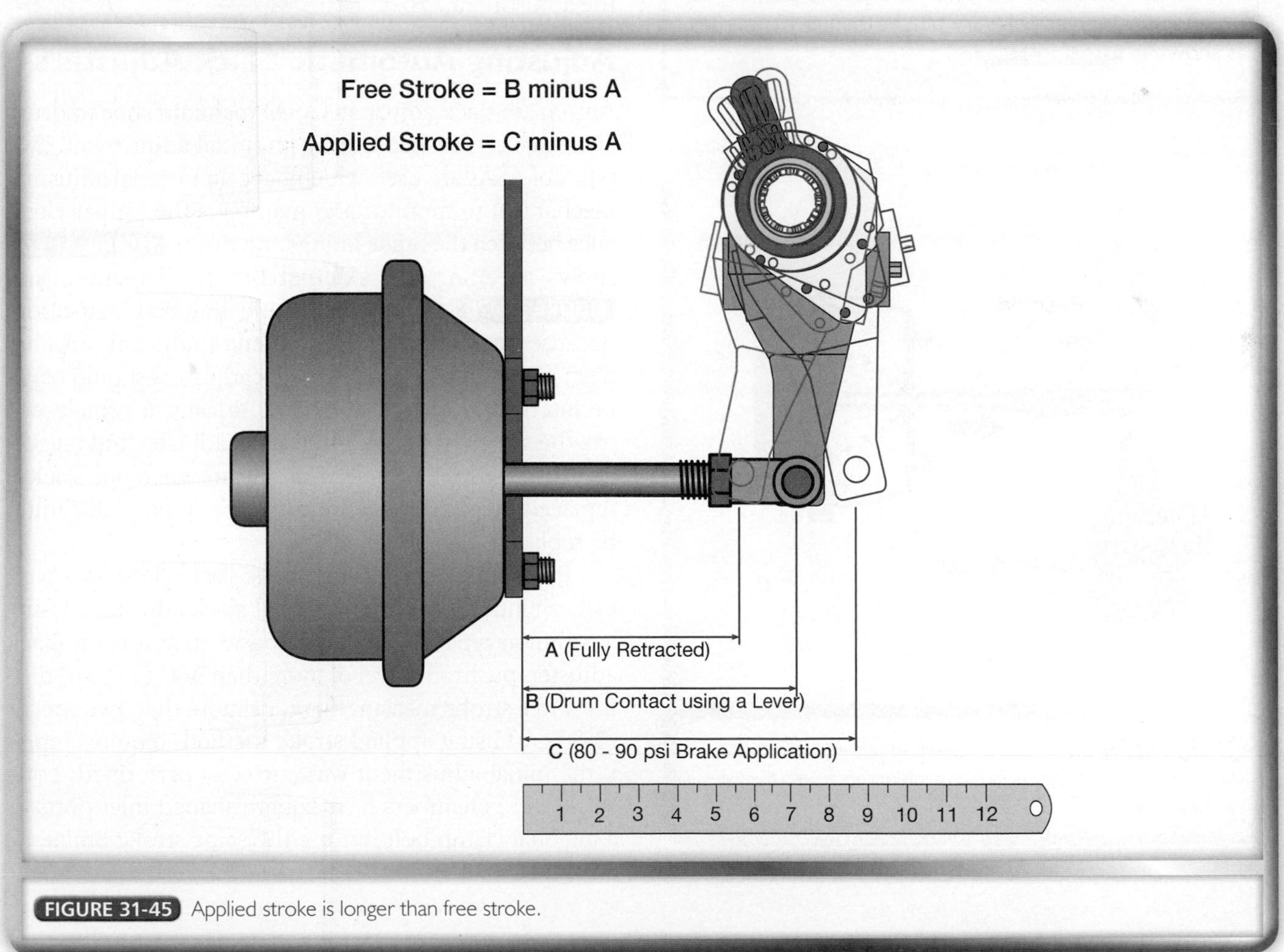

FIGURE 31-45 Applied stroke is longer than free stroke.

> **TECHNICIAN TIP**
>
> Using the parking brake control valve and the trailer supply valve to release spring brakes during an adjustment can produce an incorrect brake adjustment. Some parking brake control valves and trailer supply valves will supply air to spring brake chambers with as little as 20 psi (138 kPa) air reservoir pressure, which actually leaves the spring brakes partially applied. This explains why it is necessary to verify that air pressure is at least 90–100 psi (620–670 kPa) and that all parking brakes are released before checking or making a brake adjustment.

> **TECHNICIAN TIP**
>
> With the brakes applied, a 90-degree angle between the center of the slack adjuster arm and the brake chamber pushrod when the brakes are applied is not always a satisfactory indication that the brake adjustment is correct. The 90-degree angle depends more on the length of the chamber pushrod than the actual brake adjustment. To prevent interference between the slack adjuster and suspension or axle parts, some chamber to sack adjuster angles will vary plus or minus 10 degrees as shown in **FIGURE 31-46**.

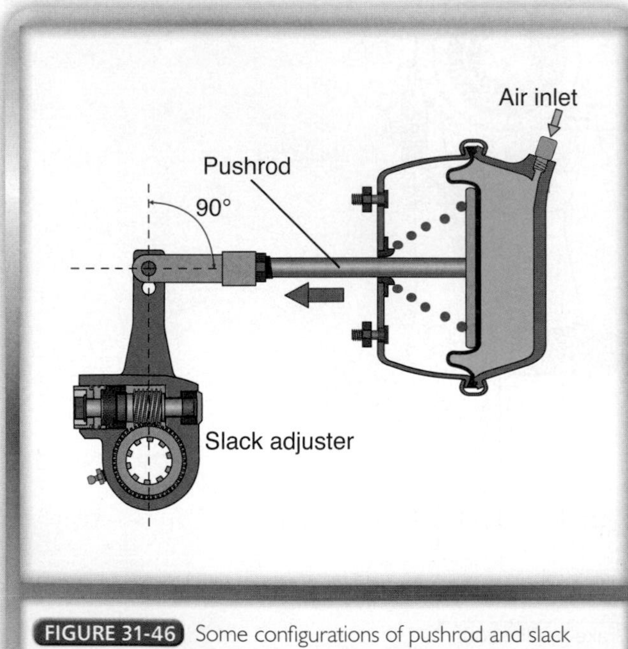

FIGURE 31-46 Some configurations of pushrod and slack adjuster use larger angles to prevent interference with the axles and attachments.

Manual Slack Adjusters

Manual slack adjusters use a spring-loaded locking sleeve, which is pressed in and held before the adjusting bolt can be turned. How the slack is orientated will determine the correct direction to turn the adjusting bolt—clockwise or counterclockwise. Using a 9/16" (14.3 mm) wrench, the locking sleeve around the adjusting bolt is pressed inwards while the adjusting bolt is turned. The slack will rotate the camshaft when turning the adjuster. Rotating the adjuster in the correct direction will rotate the cam in the same direction as a brake application.

While turning the adjuster in the correct direction, the adjustment will stop after the brake shoes have contacted the drum. By looking through an inspection hole on the back of a dust shield, a technician can visually verify that the linings have contacted the drum. Backing off the adjusting bolt about 1/3 to 1/2 of a turn should establish correct running clearance between the lining and drum. The stroke travel should then be measured to verify pushrod stroke is acceptable. Removing the wrench enables the locking sleeve to lock the adjusting bolt in place. This lock sleeve prevents backing off of the adjustment.

Adjusting Automatic Slack Adjusters

Automatic slack adjusters (ASA) maintain shoe to drum clearance established during an initial adjustment. Two types of ASAs are used which have an internal adjusting mechanism to monitor and maintains the proper clearance between the brake linings and drum. **FIGURE 31-47A** shows an ASA with external bracket actuation, and **FIGURE 31-47B** shows one with link-rod activation. Because slack adjusters use different adjusting mechanism and designs, brands of slack adjusters should never be intermixed on the same axle. Ideally, a vehicle will use the same type or brand of slack adjuster and ones of identical age on a vehicle. That means when one slack is replaced due to wear or improper operation, all should be replaced.

Pushrod stroke with automatic slack adjusters is typically slightly longer than manual slack adjusters. Using a common type 30 air chamber and an automatic slack adjuster, pushrod travel of more than 3/4" (1.9 cm) during a free stroke measurement, or more than two inches (5.08 cm) using applied stroke method, requires repair if the initial adjustment was correctly performed. Long stroke (LS) chambers have square shaped inlet ports or a tag on a clamp bolt but use the same stroke limits.

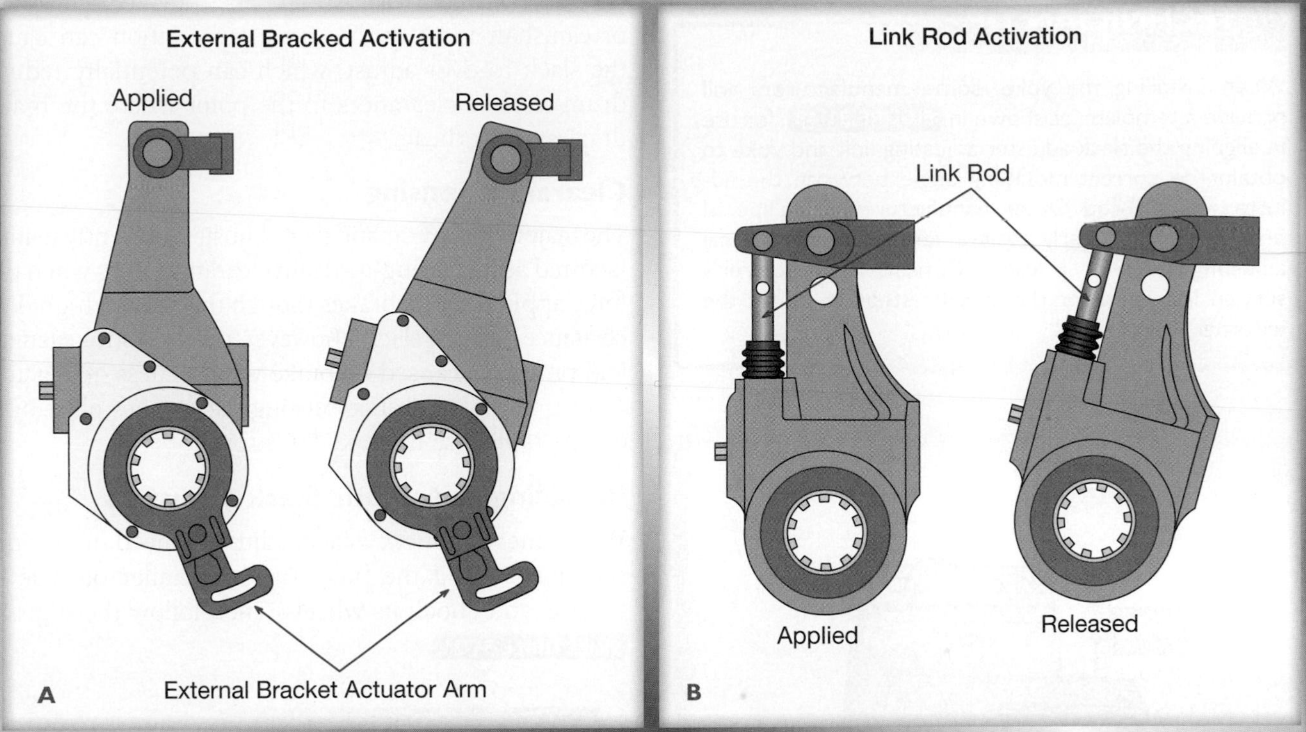

FIGURE 31-47 **A.** External bracket actuation. **B.** Link rod activation.

Automatic slack adjusters are best initially adjusted using the applied stroke method of brake adjustment. If an adjustment needs backing off, the turning force required to back off a slack is much more than a manual slack.

If the slack adjuster uses a square-shaped adjusting bolt, a spring-loaded pawl that meshes with internal teeth may need to be removed first. The pawl is disengaged by removing a 3/4" (1.9 cm) hexagonal shaped cap located on the side of the adjuster. Other adjusters using these hex caps use a round shaped "button," which can be pried out approximately 1/32" (0.8 mm) with a flat-bladed screwdriver, as illustrated in FIGURE 31-48.

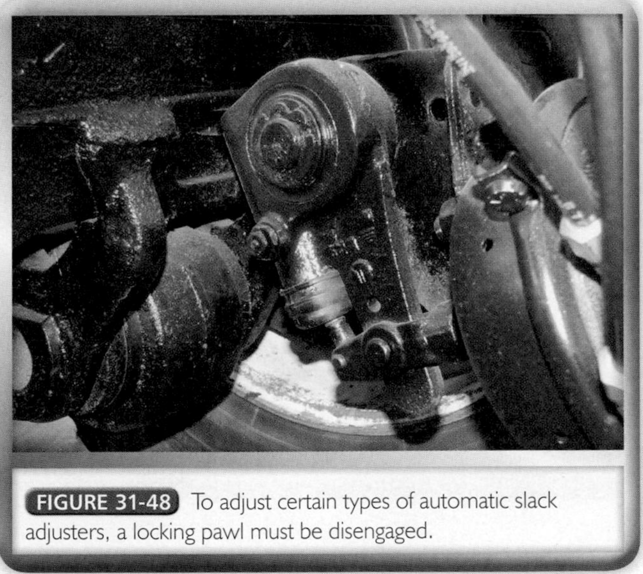

FIGURE 31-48 To adjust certain types of automatic slack adjusters, a locking pawl must be disengaged.

An automatic slack adjuster should be manually adjusted only after a brake shoe or drum is replaced or removed. Frequent manual adjustment reduces the durability of the internal adjusting mechanism. ASAs should be lubricated whenever chassis lubrication services are performed, so at 25,000 miles (40,000 km) or three months, whichever occurs first.

Stroke-Sensing Slacks

Stroke-sensing slack adjusters sense and adjust pushrod stroke. Stroke travel activates the adjusting mechanism to maintain drum-to-lining clearance. The problem with stroke-sensing slack adjusters occurs when brake parts are worn. As parts deflect, the stroke can become longer than acceptable limits even though drum-to-lining clearance is correct. Once sensed by the slack adjuster,

> **TECHNICIAN TIP**
>
> When installing the yoke, some manufacturers will provide a template, as shown in FIGURE 31-49, for use in aligning the slack adjuster adjusting link and yoke to obtain the correct mounting angle between the adjuster and pushrod. Other manufacturers use a special procedure to properly position and adjust an external adjusting lever or bracket. Consult manufacturer's service literature for the specific steps to adjust the external arm.

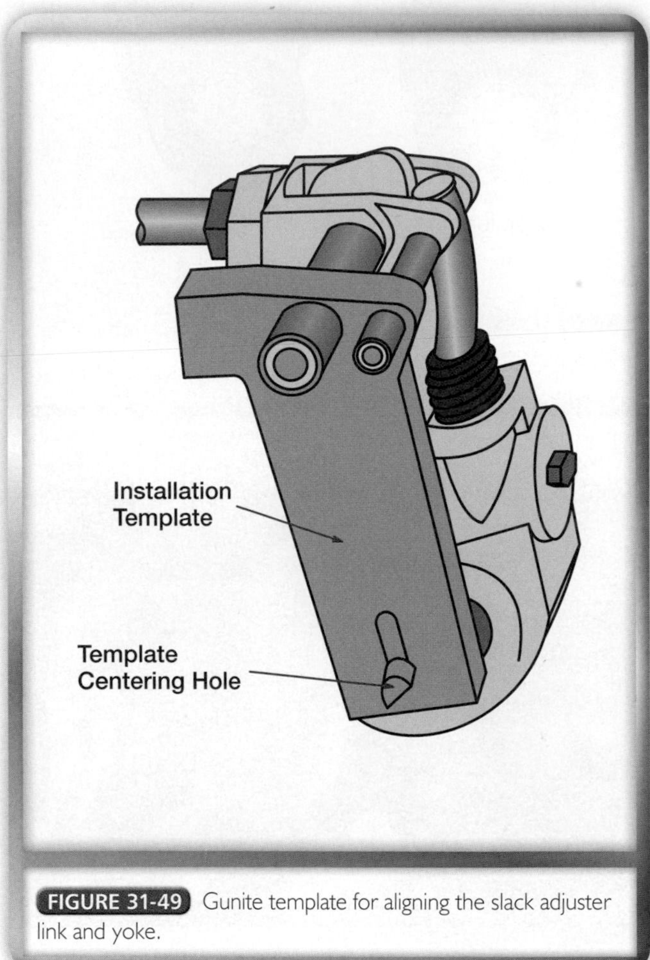

FIGURE 31-49 Gunite template for aligning the slack adjuster link and yoke.

camshaft bushing wear, air chamber bracket deflection, or camshaft twist during brake application can cause the slack to over adjust, which can potentially reduce drum-to-shoe clearances to the point where the brake drags and overheats.

Clearance Sensing

The majority of automatic slack adjusters currently manufactured adjust lining-to-drum clearances only when the force applied to the brakes though the slack is high. For clearance-sensing slacks, however, pushrod stroke length and problems caused by brake wear are less of a factor. Adjustment of clearance-sensing slacks takes place only during rapid rise in brake force torque.

Replacing Automatic Slack Adjusters

When the automatic slack adjusters need replacing, start by parking the bus, truck, or trailer on a level surface, and chock its wheels. Then follow the steps in SKILL DRILL 31-21.

> **TECHNICIAN TIP**
>
> An automatic slack adjuster that does not maintain stroke adjustment is either faulty, or there may be problems with the foundation brake. Technicians need to determine why a defective brake has excessive stroke and make the appropriate repairs. Simply re-adjusting a self-adjusting brake adjuster, or replacing it, does not ensure that the problem is corrected. The problem may exist in the foundation brake system.

> **Safety**
>
> Often the spring brakes are caged using a release tool when air pressure is not available to release the brake. It is dangerous to use an air gun to retract the power spring since damage to the internal pressure plate can cause a sudden release of the spring. Tighten the release tool stud nut no more than finger tight.

SKILL DRILL 31-21 Replacing Automatic Slack Adjusters

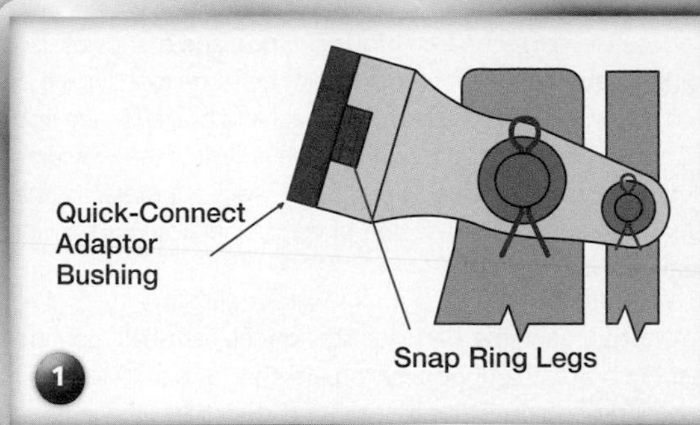

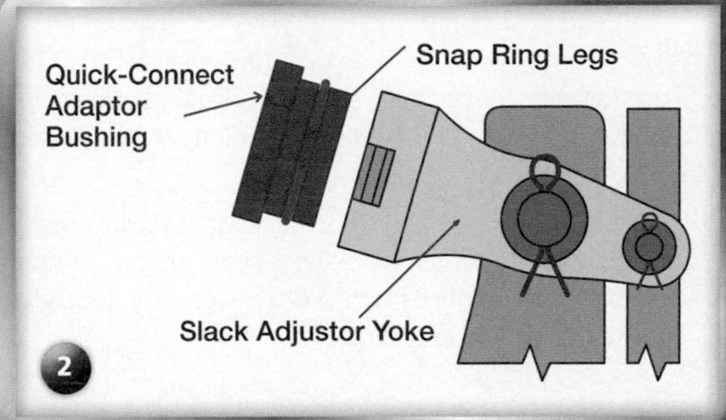

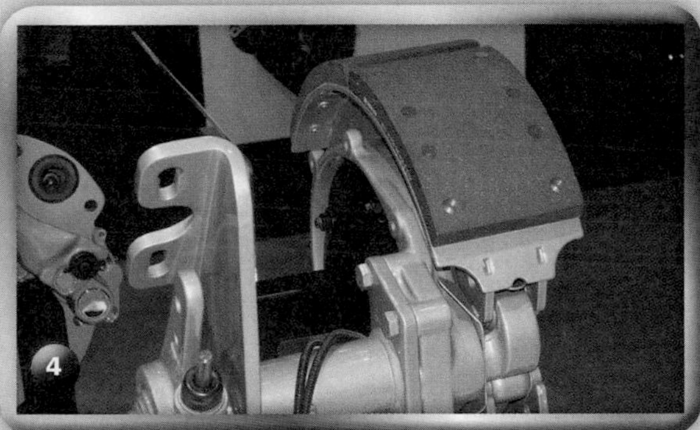

1. Release the spring brakes. If the brakes are left applied, the spring brake will need to be caged before removing the slack adjuster.

2. Disconnect the slack adjuster attaching hardware. Most slack adjusters are locked onto the S-camshaft using a removable snap-ring. Disconnect the clevis yoke clevis pins and the yoke from the chamber pushrod. If the slack used a quick-connect type clevis, it should ideally be replaced with a standard threaded type since quick-connect clevises loosen over time, contribute to longer brake stroke travel or over stroking.

3. Remove the slack adjuster from the S-cam. Slack adjusters which have been on a long time or left unlubricated may be seized and require a purpose made puller to remove. Otherwise the slack may require the use of a large hammer or cutting torch to coax the slack from the splines on the S-cam.

4. Inspect other brake foundation components. Remove the backing plate if equipped to check the condition of the brake foundation assembly. There should be adequate brake lining. The S-cam should not have excessive play due to worn bushings. The brake chamber should also be inspected for cracks, leaks, proper centering, and bent pushrods.

Continued on next page

SKILL DRILL 31-21 Replacing Automatic Slack Adjusters, continued

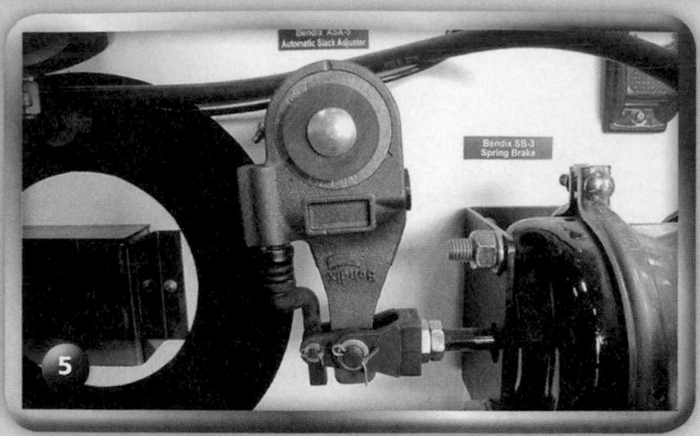

5. Choose the correct parts. Models, types, and brands of slack adjusters should never be mixed on the same axle since it can lead to variations in brake stoke travel and brake torque imbalance. Replace both slack adjusters on an axle if the matching identical slack cannot be found. Some slack adjusters are made specifically for right or left side of vehicle applications provide clearance for axle parts.

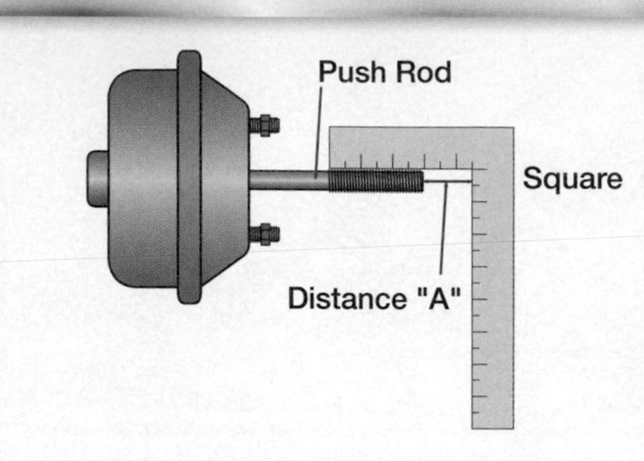

Slack Adjuster Arm Length	"A" Std Quick Connector or Easy-ON Adaptor	"A" Extended Easy-ON Adaptor
5"	1 15/16" - 3 1/32"	2 7/16" - 3 17/32"
5 1/2"	1 15/16" - 3 3/16"	2 7/16" - 3 11/16"
6"	1 3/16" - 3 1/16"	2 11/16" - 3 11/16"

6

6. Before mounting the slack adjuster on the camshaft, confirm that the brake chamber pushrod length allows a 90-degree angle between the slack adjuster and chamber or whether pushrod shortening or replacement is required. To perform this check, follow one of the following two methods:

   Method 1:

   - Place carpenter's square so that one edge is parallel to the actuator pushrod and the other edge of the square passes through the centerline of the camshaft.
   - The hole of the clevis and the vertical leg of square must pass through the centerline of the S-cam. If not, the brake chamber pushrod needs cutting or replacement depending on whether it's too long or short.

   Method 2:

   - Measure the distance from the end of the pushrod without the yoke to the edge of the square that passes though the camshaft centerline. Determine the distance needed to attach the yoke. That distance depends on the slack adjuster arm length– between 5" (12.7 cm) and 6" (15.2 cm)—and requires comparison between the slack length and the manufacturer's service information for the type of clevis yoke used.

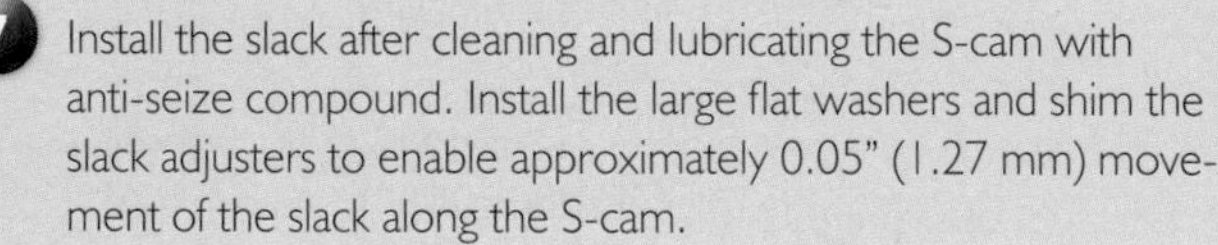

7. Install the slack after cleaning and lubricating the S-cam with anti-seize compound. Install the large flat washers and shim the slack adjusters to enable approximately 0.05" (1.27 mm) movement of the slack along the S-cam.

Continued on next page

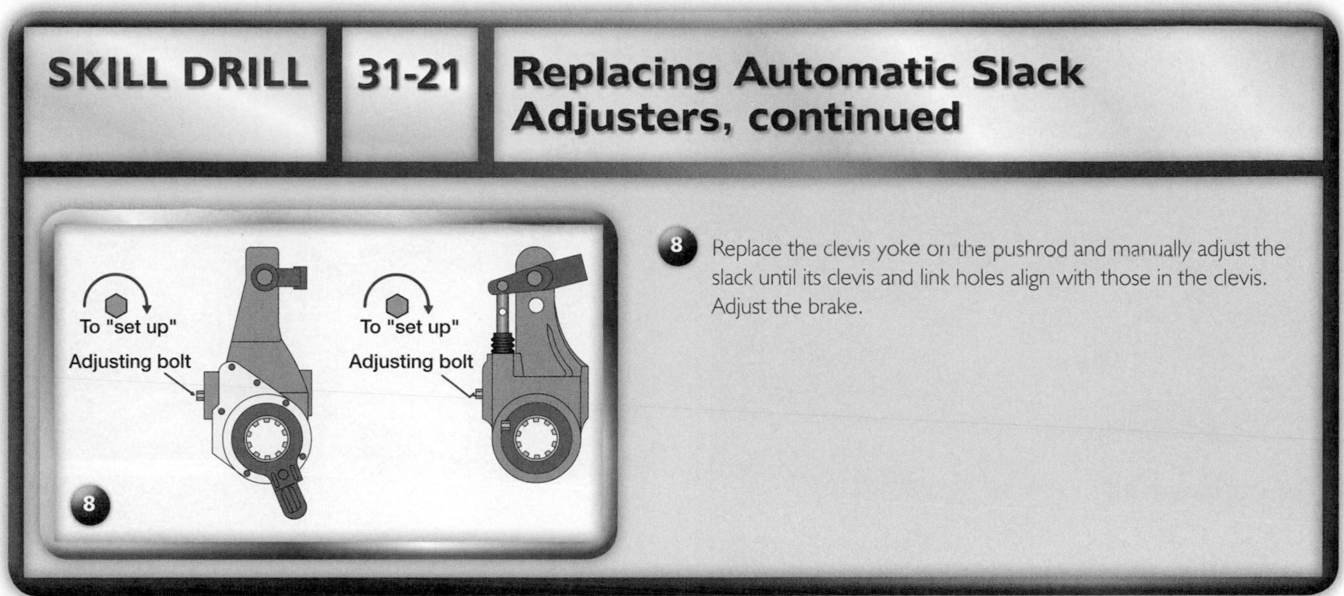

8 Replace the clevis yoke on the pushrod and manually adjust the slack until its clevis and link holes align with those in the clevis. Adjust the brake.

Maintaining Air Disc Brakes

Maintaining air disc brakes involves inspecting brake pads, rotor surfaces, and running clearance. Measuring brake pad wear is necessary for determining if the components need replacement of if brakes need adjusted.

Brake Pad Inspection

On most air disc brakes, brake pads can be visually inspected without removing the wheels. Newer model air disc brakes, such as those shown in **FIGURE 31-50**, allow the technician to check brake pad thickness visually. When the wheels are removed for a thorough inspection, the thickness of the friction material must be between 0.079" (2 mm) and 0.43" (11 mm). If it is not, the pads must be replaced. Minimum thickness depends on the type of pad being used. The manufacturer's service information must be used to determine the correct minimum specification.

FIGURE 31-50 Brake pad thickness is easily checked by visually inspecting the pads in the calipers.

Minor damage at the edges is permitted but pads must be replaced if significant damage is present on the surface of the pad. All brake pads on an axle should be replaced at the same time to prevent any side-to-side variations in brake torque.

Rotor Surface Inspection

Rotors are inspected whenever pads are replaced. Cracked and overheated rotors should be replaced. Large grooves may reduce the friction area for new pads, so turning rotors (grinding and cutting material from the surface of the rotor) can be useful but normally is not necessary. If turning is performed, a brake lathe such as shown in **FIGURE 31-51** can cut rotors while on the wheel end. Machining rotors on the vehicle is a best practice because it minimizes lateral runout due to hub and bearing irregularities caused when a rotor is transferred from an off-vehicle machine to the axle end. A minimum rotor thickness is stamped into the rotor. A caliper tool specifically for measuring rotor thickness is used.

Visually Inspecting Brake Running Clearance

Some movement of the brake caliper should be present on all disc brakes. Without some side-to-side movement, the discs will drag and overheat, causing premature wear

FIGURE 31-51 A brake lathe.

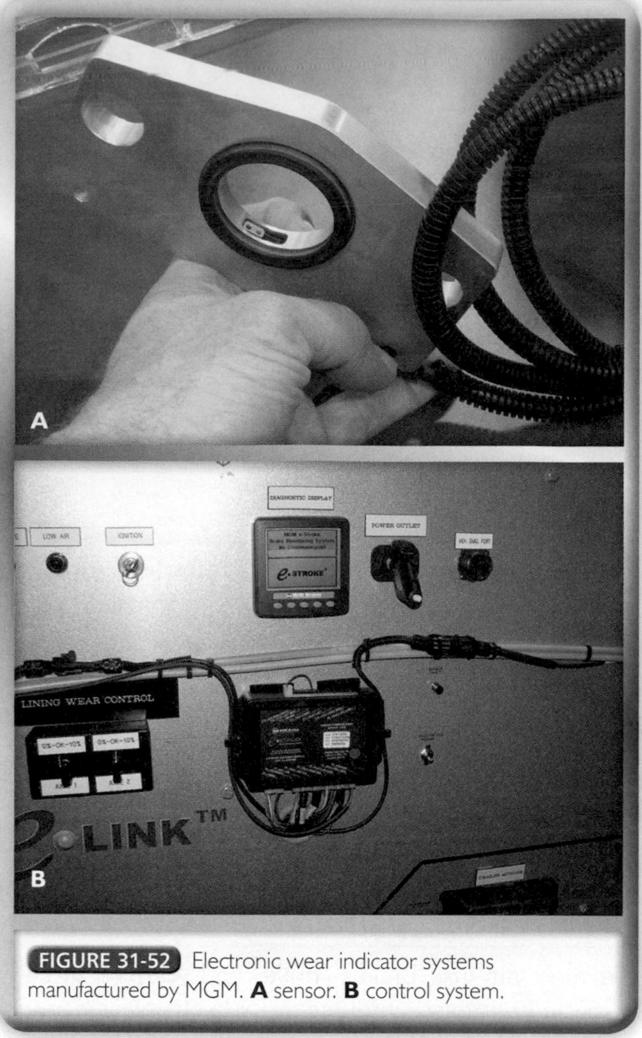

FIGURE 31-52 Electronic wear indicator systems manufactured by MGM. **A** sensor. **B** control system.

and, potentially, heat damage. If caliper movement is not present, the guide pins that attach the caliper to the steering knuckle are likely seized and need servicing. Excessive clearances can lead to brake failure.

With the wheels chocked and the parking brakes released, check movement by pushing both brake pads away from the tappets. A space between the thickness of a nickel and a dime should be measured between each pad and the tappet. Manufacturer's specifications differ between brake models. Acceptable movement means no further inspection is required.

Checking Brake Pad Wear

Disc brake pads can usually be visually inspected with little effort however certain manufacturers have indicators to assess wear. Notches cut in to the sliding caliper and the caliper bracket and or rubber boots or bushings on the caliper pins can be used to indicate when pad replacement is required. Electronic wear indicators such as the one shown in FIGURE 31-52A and FIGURE 31-52B are commonly used to measure brake pad wear. **Electronic pad wear indicators** measure brake pad wear electronically and send CAN signals to the driver when wear occurs. These indicators come in one of two types. One is simply an on-off switch that signals the driver when a certain wear point is reached. The second type uses a potentiometer to measure progressive wear; with this type, the driver will receive ongoing information on brake wear. Both systems use sensors installed in a slot in the brake pad.

For on-off indicators, when the pad wears away through use, the point is reached when the sensor contacts the rotor. Normally closed and normally open indicators are used, which either open or close the circuit for a warning light or buzzer. Sensor contact with the rotor opens or closes the circuit depending on the type of switch. Sensors are replaced when the new pads are installed.

A potentiometer-type sensor measures the progressive movement of the brake pad towards the rotor. A hand-held diagnostic tool can check individual wheel circuits or six separate circuits. A check of the potentiometer can also be performed using the tool. As shown in FIGURE 31-53, a potentiometer-type wear indicator for air disc brakes measures brake pad thickness and progressive brake pad wear. An electronic service tool can read brake wear information from a system control module or monitor the function of an individual wheel sensor.

A simple type of electronic brake wear indicator uses a switch embedded into a brake pad, as illustrated in FIGURE 31-54. The driver is alerted when pad wear is approaching minimum thickness. When the switch at the brake pad contacts the brake rotor, the circuit is grounded and will provide a warning signal for the driver.

FIGURE 31-53 A potentiometer-type wear indicator and how it connects to the vehicle for diagnostics.

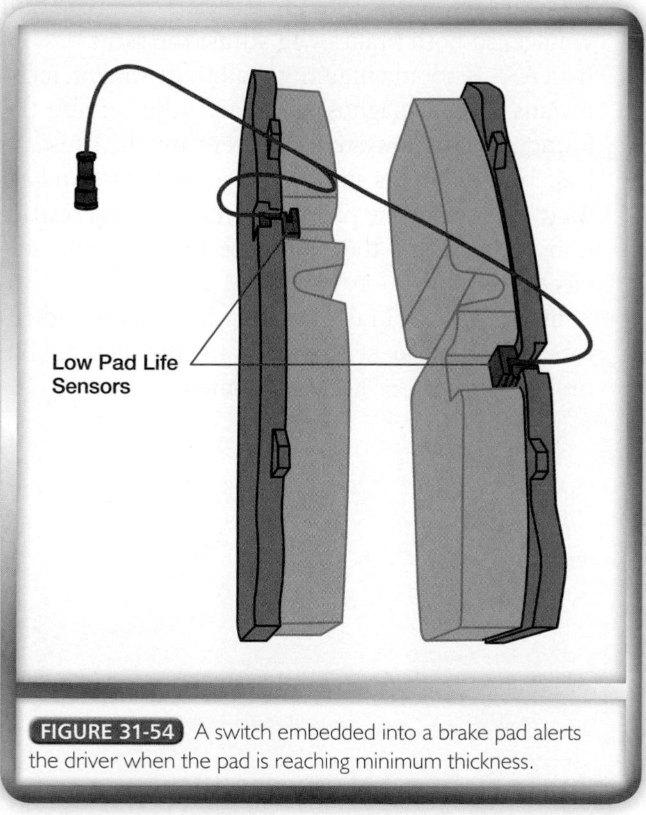

FIGURE 31-54 A switch embedded into a brake pad alerts the driver when the pad is reaching minimum thickness.

Brake Adjustment

An initial adjustment of the brakes is needed when pads are replaced. A ratcheting type adjuster beneath an adjuster cap moves the tappets in and out. With the park brakes released and the wheels chocked, the running clearances of the pads are adjusted to manufacturers' specifications as shown in FIGURE 31-55. Automatic adjustment of running clearances takes place after the initial adjustment.

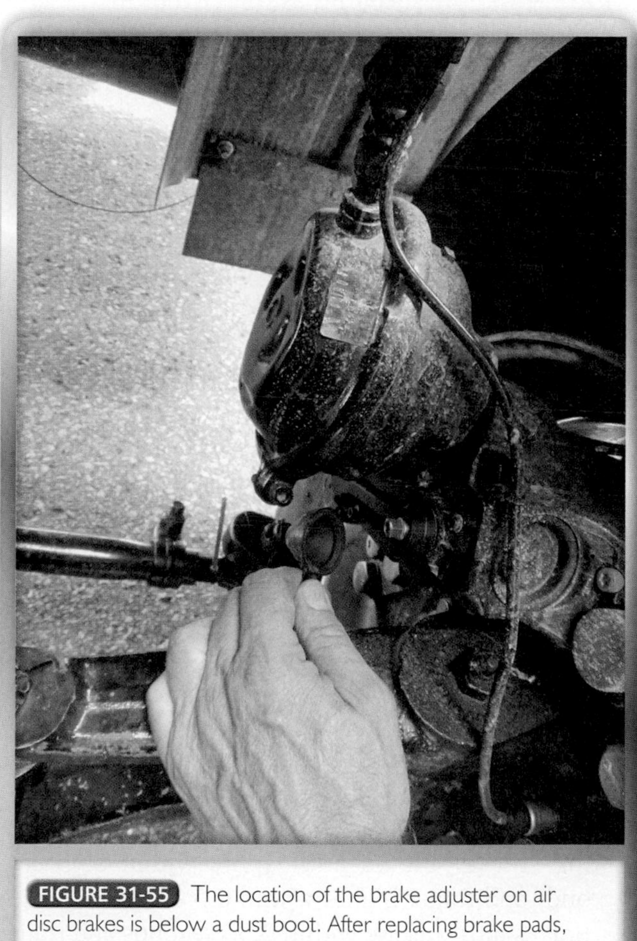

FIGURE 31-55 The location of the brake adjuster on air disc brakes is below a dust boot. After replacing brake pads, the brakes require initial adjustment, which is automatically maintained by an internal adjustment mechanism.

Wrap-up

Ready for Review

- Brake service is one of the most critical tasks that a technician has to perform because the life of the driver and all other road users is at stake if mistakes are made.
- Brakes must be balanced—both torque, or mechanical, balance and pneumatic balance are required for proper braking to occur.
- Safety is paramount when working on braking systems. Dust, whipping air lines, and the spring brake power spring all represent hazards for the technician.
- Common brake complaints include soft brake pedal, noisy brakes, pulling brakes, and odors from the brake system.
- FMVSS 121 legislation specifies standards for brake systems, including air buildup time, air leakage rate, and brake adjustment settings.
- All air compressors pump some oil into the air brake system, but excessive oil pumping must be corrected.
- Several procedures are used to test the functioning of air brake systems, such as buildup time, leakage rate, dual circuit integrity check, park brake application test, and emergency brake application test.
- When installing a new brake actuator, the technician must cut the pushrod precisely to size so that the brake functions correctly.
- Brake torque balance is maintained by the proper maintenance of the foundation brake system and brake actuators.
- Brake pneumatic balance is checked by using a duplex gauge that measures air pressure at two points at once.
- FMVSS 121 stipulates brake apply and release timing. Tractor brakes must apply within 0.45 seconds and trailer brakes within 0.5 seconds. Tractor brakes must release within 0.55 seconds and trailer brakes within 1 second.
- Relay valve crack pressure may vary from front to rear so that all of the brakes apply at once.
- When any relay valve is replaced in the system it is essential that new valve has the same crack pressure as the old one.
- Compressor discharge lines can become contaminated with carbon build up and should be replaced with the compressor.
- Air tanks should be drained daily.
- Air hoses are color coded so technicians will know what system they are connected to.
- Brake drum wear limits are .120" (3.05 mm) over nominal.
- When brake drums are installed, it is critical that they fit properly over their pilot pads on the hub.
- Brake S-cam camshafts should be checked for radial and axial play.
- Manufacturers recommend that brake stroke be measured with the brakes applied.
- All vehicles manufactured today are equipped with automatic slack adjusters. (ASAs) It is essential that all adjusters on an axle are of the same type and vintage, so both brakes will adjust the same.
- If an ASA is not maintaining brake adjustment, technicians should diagnose the slack adjuster and the foundation brake system to determine the cause.
- Disc brake calipers should move freely by hand on their pins when the pads are removed. Any restriction requires that the caliper be removed and serviced.
- Some newer air brake systems have wear indicators and/or stroke sensors to warn the driver if the brakes are worn or need adjustment.

Vocabulary Builder

applied stroke measurement The pushrod stroke length with a 90 psi (621 kPa) service brake application.

brake balance The ability of the braking system to apply the correct amount of braking torque to each wheel end at the correct time.

brake pull (brake steer) An unintended left or right direction change by a vehicle during a brake application.

brake stroke length The distance travelled by the brake chamber pushrod.

brake timing imbalance A situation in which some brakes receive air faster than others.

cam-over conditions When the linings and or brake camshafts are worn enough to allow the cam to rotate past the rollers.

chuff test A test performed on the antilock braking systems that results in air pressure being exhausted from the modulator and making a short chuffing sound.

dual circuit integrity test A test performed to verify the functioning of the automatic emergency brake system.

duplex gauge Two air gauges in a single housing.

electronic wear indicators Devices that measure brake pad wear electronically and send signals directly to the driver.

free stroke measurement The brake pushrod stroke length using a lever to move the slack adjuster.

glazing A mirror-like finish produced through continuous braking pressure and pressure between lining and brake drums.

governor cut-in pressure The pressure at which the governor loads the compressor.

governor cut-out pressure The pressure at which the governor unloads the compressor.

N-95 mask A face mask that filters out 95% of all airborne particles.

pneumatic balance The correct timing of brake application air pressure to each vehicle axle at the correct pressure.

soft (slack) brakes A situation in which the brakes are applied but the vehicle is not slowing or stopping effectively.

torque balance A situation in which braking torque is uniform for all wheels.

Review Questions

1. If a relay valve is to be replaced, which of the following is an important check?
   a. That the crack pressure is the same as the old relay valve
   b. That the new relay valve doesn't have any extra outlet ports
   c. That the relay valve doesn't have any extra inlet ports
   d. All of the above should be checked.
2. When replacing S-cam brake shoes, which of the following components should be removed first?
   a. The large return spring
   b. The small return spring
   c. The anchor pins
   d. The rollers
3. When inspecting the air brake compressor build up time, the maximum amount of time allowed for air pressure to rise from 85 psi (586 kPa) to 100 psi (690 kPa) is ________ seconds.
   a. 15
   b. 25
   c. 45
   d. 60
4. What is the maximum amount of air leakage allowed in two minutes from a tractor and one trailer combination vehicle with brakes applied?
   a. 1 psi (7 kPa)
   b. 2 psi (14 kPa)
   c. 4 psi (28 kPa)
   d. 6 psi (41 kPa)
5. When the brakes are fully applied, the angle between the slack adjuster and the brake chamber pushrod should be ________ degrees.
   a. 45
   b. 60
   c. 75
   d. 90
6. What is the lowest air pressure warning devices should normally activate?
   a. 65 psi (448 kPa)
   b. 75 psi (517 kPa)
   c. 85 psi (586 kPa)
   d. 95 psi (655 kPa)
7. What is the normal stroke limit on a standard size 30 brake actuator?
   a. 1.375" (3.5 cm)
   b. 1.5" (3.81 cm)
   c. 1.75" (4.45 cm)
   d. 2" (5 cm)
8. Which of the following is the preferred method to measure brake chamber stroke?
   a. By hand with a lever
   b. With a full service brake application
   c. With a spring brake application
   d. All of the choices are acceptable measurement methods.
9. Which of the following best describes the procedure for performing an ABS system modulator chuff test?
   a. Air system charged, apply service brake with ignition key off, then turn the ignition on.
   b. Air system charged, turn ignition on, and then apply the service brakes.
   c. Air system charged, road test the vehicle, and try to lock up the brakes.
   d. Air system charged, run vehicle on dyno, and use the dyno to lock the brakes.
10. Crack pressure on relay valves are different so brake timing can be adjusted. Which of the following would be the normal crack pressures of a tractor and a trailer relay valve?
    a. 10 psi (69 kPa) for the tractor and 4 psi (28 kPa) for the trailer
    b. 4 psi (28 kPa) for the tractor and 10 psi (69 kPa) for the trailer
    c. 4 psi (28 kPa) for the tractor and 0.5 psi (3.4 kPa) for the trailer
    d. 10 psi (69 kPa) for the tractor and 15 psi (103 kPa) for the traile

ASE-Type Questions

1. Technician A says that brake balance can be upset by replacing brakes on one wheel end only. Technician B says that brake balance can be upset by replacing an airline with one of a larger size. Who is correct?
   a. Technician A
   b. Technician B
   c. Both Technician A and Technician B
   d. Neither Technician A nor Technician B
2. Technician A says that brake dust no longer contains asbestos, so we don't have to worry about it as much as in the past. Technician B says that brake dust should be vacuumed off the wheel end with a HEPA filter equipped vacuum cleaner. Who is correct?
   a. Technician A
   b. Technician B
   c. Both Technician A and Technician B
   d. Neither Technician A nor Technician B
3. Technician A says that a cam-over condition can be caused by a failed automatic slack adjuster. Technician B says that a cam-over condition can cause a seized brake condition where the brakes won't release. Who is correct?
   a. Technician A
   b. Technician B
   c. Both Technician A and Technician B
   d. Neither Technician A nor Technician B
4. Technician A says that when testing for brake leakage, a single axle vehicle with brakes applied should leak no more than 4 psi (28 kPa) in two minutes. Technician B says that the acceptable leakage for a tractor and one trailer combination is no more than 6 psi (41 kPa) in two minutes. Who is correct?
   a. Technician A
   b. Technician B
   c. Both Technician A and Technician B
   d. Neither Technician A nor Technician B
5. Technician A says that all compressors pass some oil to the vehicle air system. Technician B says that oil passing is nothing to worry about, as it helps lubricate the air brake valves. Who is correct?
   a. Technician A
   b. Technician B
   c. Both Technician A and Technician B
   d. Neither Technician A nor Technician B
6. Technician A says that brake chamber stroke length varies widely and can be as much as 3 inches (7.6 cm) on some brake chambers. Technician B says chamber stroke length is unimportant as long as the angle between the slack adjuster and the push rod is 90 degrees or more with the brakes applied. Who is correct?
   a. Technician A
   b. Technician B
   c. Both Technician A and Technician B
   d. Neither Technician A nor Technician B
7. Technician A says that, when looking at the head of an installed s-cam camshaft, if one of the lobes points up on the left hand side, it is a left-hand camshaft. Technician B says that, when looking at the head of an installed s-cam camshaft, if one of the lobes points down on the right hand side, then it is a right-hand camshaft. Who is correct?
   a. Technician A
   b. Technician B
   c. Both Technician A and Technician B
   d. Neither Technician A nor Technician B
8. Technician A says that, when replacing a spring brake chamber system, air can be used to cage the brake, and then the caging bolt should be installed hand tight. Technician B says that, for safety, the entire system air should be drained before removing the chamber. Who is correct?
   a. Technician A
   b. Technician B
   c. Both Technician A and Technician B
   d. Neither Technician A nor Technician B
9. Technician A says that tractor and straight truck relay valves can be interchanged on a vehicle without affecting braking. Technician B says that an elbow installed on a relay valve control port can affect brake timing. Who is correct?
   a. Technician A
   b. Technician B
   c. Both Technician A and Technician B
   d. Neither Technician A nor Technician B
10. Technician A says that air system reservoirs should be drained weekly unless they are equipped with automatic drain valves. Technician B says that, if oil drains from the primary or secondary drain valve, it indicates the dryer cartridge needs to be replaced or the compressor is defective. Who is correct?
    a. Technician A
    b. Technician B
    c. Both Technician A and Technician B
    d. Neither Technician A nor Technician B

CHAPTER 32

NATEF Tasks

Air and Hydraulic Anti-Lock Brake Systems (ABS) and Automatic Traction Control (ATC)

Task	Page
■ Identify poor stopping and wheel lock-up problems caused by failure of the anti-lock brake system (ABS); determine needed action.	1038–1058
■ Observe anti-lock brake system (ABS) warning light operation (includes trailer and dash mounted trailer ABS warning light).	1041–1042
■ Test and check operation of anti-lock brake system (ABS) air, hydraulic, electrical, and mechanical components; perform needed action.	1041–1052
■ Diagnose anti-lock brake system (ABS) electronic control(s) and components using self-diagnosis and/or electronic service tool(s); determine needed action.	1042–1044, 1060
■ Diagnose automatic traction control (ATC) electronic control(s) and components using self-diagnosis and/or specified test equipment (scan tool, PC computer); determine needed action.	1042–1053
■ Verify power line carrier (PLC) operations.	1043–1044
■ Test anti-lock brake system (ABS) wheel speed sensors and circuits; adjust or replace as needed.	1044–1045
■ Observe automatic traction control (ATC) warning light operation; determine needed action.	1053

Knowledge Objectives

After reading this chapter, you will be able to:

1. Describe the features and benefits of anti-lock braking vehicle stability, and collision avoidance systems. (pp 1038–1039)
2. List the system requirements for anti-lock braking vehicle stability, and collision avoidance systems. (pp 1040–1041)
3. Describe the components of a basic anti-lock braking vehicle stability, and collision avoidance systems and their functions. (pp 1041–1052)
4. Describe the operating strategies used by ABS, vehicle stability, and collision avoidance systems. (pp 1041–1052)
5. Describe various anti-lock braking system configurations. (pp 1041–1052)

Anti-Lock Braking, Vehicle Stability, and Collision Avoidance Systems

Knowledge Objectives, continued

6. Identify the purpose of various input sensor data to operating strategies of ABS, ATC, RSC, and collision avoidance systems. (pp 1041–1052)
7. Describe the operation of the modulator valve during normal braking and anti-lock braking events. (pp 1041–1053)
8. Describe various problems with vehicle dynamics without ABS, vehicle stability, and collision avoidance systems and explain how the systems correct these problems. (pp 1042–1044)
9. Explain data transmission between the engine control unit and the anti-lock braking system. (pp 1042–1043)
10. Identify and explain common failures in anti-lock braking, vehicle stability, and collision avoidance systems. (pp 1042–1044, 1060)
11. Explain trailer to tractor fault information communication. (pp 1043–1044)
12. Explain how wheel speed sensors work. (pp 1044–1045)
13. Identify and explain terminology related to unstable vehicle dynamics. (pp 1056–1057)
14. Identify and explain adaptive strategies used by ABS systems to accommodate faults. (p 1059)
15. Recommend maintenance and service procedures for anti-lock braking, vehicle stability, and collision avoidance systems. (pp 1060–1061)

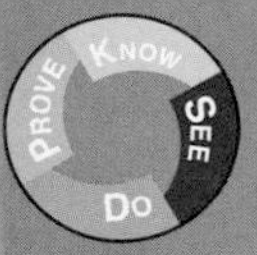

Skills Objectives

After reading this chapter, you will be able to:

1. Identify symptoms of incorrectly calibrated CAS, DSC, and RSC system sensors. (pp 1038, 1055–1060)
2. Verify the operation of an ABS system modulator valves. (pp 1041–1048, 1053)
3. Interpret ABS, ATC blink codes. (pp 1041–1044, 1053)
4. Interpret ABS fault lamp operation. (pp 1041–1044, 1053)
5. Recommend procedures and service tools for performing ABS, ATC, RSC, DSC, and collision avoidance system diagnostic tests. (pp 1042–1044, 1055–1060)
6. Outline procedure for diagnosing system faults using blink codes. (pp 1042–1044, 1060)
7. Test the functionality of a wheel speed sensor. (pp 1044–1045)
8. Adjust wheel speed sensor air gap. (pp 1044–1045)
9. Recommend a procedure for adjusting vertical and lateral adjustment of radar sensors. (pp 1059–1060)

Introduction

Before the advent of anti-lock braking systems, driving instructors (mostly parents or relatives) would tell student drivers to "pump the brakes" in a panic braking situation to avoid a skid. That lesson was good advice in theory but not so good in practice. A skidding tire has lost its frictional connection to the road surface and most of its stopping potential, so a steady brake application is better at stopping a vehicle than manually pumping the brakes. Most drivers simply panic and are unable to pump or control the application the brakes; they just push as hard as they can.

Anti-lock braking systems essentially "pump the brakes" for us, while maintaining maximum brake effort, to help retain the connection between the tire and the road and, therefore, stability. Today's brake systems are very advanced and, depending on the design, can provide traction control, vehicle stability, and even collision avoidance in addition to basic anti-lock braking. The speed of action and reaction of anti-lock braking systems are far superior to any strategy a driver could use. This chapter will introduce you to the tremendous level of sophistication of modern anti-lock brake systems.

Fundamentals of Anti-Lock Braking Systems

A vehicle's **anti-lock braking system (ABS)** is an electronic control system that works with the service brake system to monitor and automatically limit wheel lock-up events during vehicle braking. **Wheel lock-up** occurs when the drive or steer tires have stopped rotating when braking. Rolling tires can be steered better. They also transfer more braking force than locked-up, skidding tires. For those reasons, ABS dramatically enhances vehicle control and safety. In other words, a truck, bus, or trailer behaves more like a sled when wheels lock up; ABS minimizes the loss of control that takes place when tires stop rotating.

Today's ABS systems incorporate multiple features that improve the operation of the vehicle from both a functional and a safety perspective. Since their introduction in 1975, regulations and requirements have evolved to keep pace with the increased sophistication of the technology.

ABS Features and Benefits

Anti-lock braking systems provide multiple benefits to the vehicle and the driver. In addition to preventing wheel lock-up in regular driving conditions, ABS systems decrease needed stopping distances on slippery surfaces such as wet, muddy, or snow-covered roads. ABS systems also enhance steering control during hard braking, as illustrated in FIGURE 32-1. Another benefit of ABS systems is extended tire life. Using ABS prevents the formation of flat spots and uneven tread wear caused by intense, localized friction on locked, skidding tires. The likelihood of a tractor jackknife or trailer swing-out condition is

You Are the Technician

A relatively new, late-model tractor has been brought to your OEM service facility after it was involved in a rear-end collision with a school bus. The highly experienced driver of the tractor has had more than 25 years of accident-free driving. He claims he was braking the tractor when the brakes suddenly released, resulting in the unfortunate collision. The tractor brakes had already been inspected by two other repair facilities and no fault was found. Your inspection report is the final step of investigation. If, like the other technicians, you find no fault with the brakes, the driver could be fired and the company would become engaged in costly litigation.

Given the sophistication and degree of electronic control of the braking system, you balance the probability of a failure in the braking system's reliability against the integrity and skill of the driver. A few scenarios come to mind in which a new vehicle could have some previously undetected assembly errors, such as incorrectly connected air lines and wiring harnesses. You conduct a road test and apply the brakes dozens of times until they locked up. During your test, you discovered that the brakes did, in fact, release on one occasion after having been only briefly applied.

To isolate the fault, consider the following:

1. Identify how each of the vehicle's various electronic controls of the braking system operate to apply and release the brakes and under which condition.
2. Outline what steps or procedures should be taken to verify the correct operation and connections of the vehicle's braking system circuits used by the ABS, ATC, RSC, and CAS.
3. List the components or inspection points you believe would help isolate the possible causes of the brake system failure.

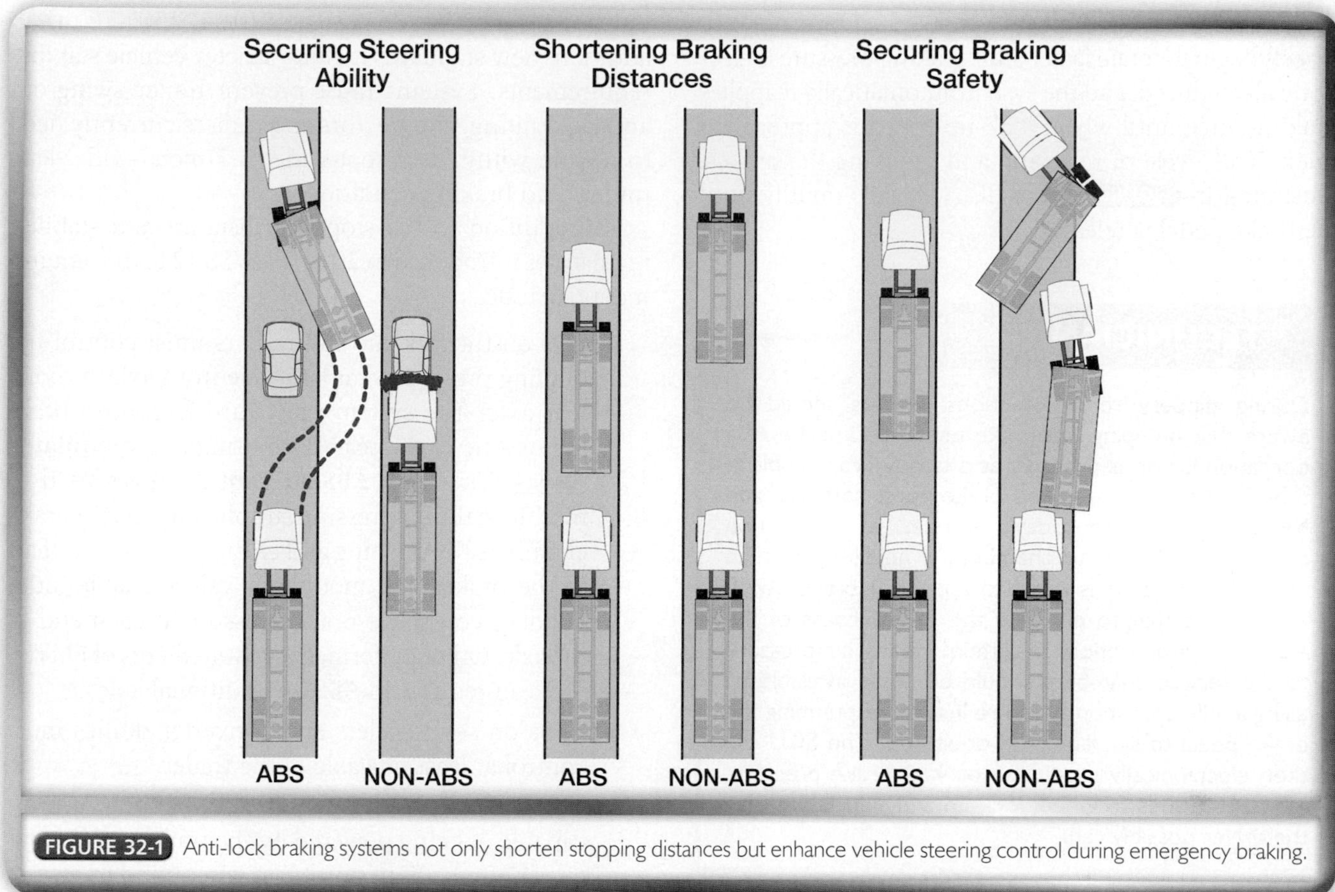

FIGURE 32-1 Anti-lock braking systems not only shorten stopping distances but enhance vehicle steering control during emergency braking.

minimized using ABS as well. TABLE 32-1 shows the key features of ABS systems and the benefits they provide.

ABS works simply by electronically measuring individual wheel speeds. Braking force applied to a wheel end is automatically reduced whenever a wheel's speed approaches lock-up (or 0 rpm under hard braking conditions). The deceleration rate of the wheels is greater during an aggressive or hard brake application, or if the vehicle is on a slippery surface. Controlled braking takes place because the software inside the electronic control unit (ECU) can distinguish between normal and abnormal deceleration using an algorithm to calculate whether

TABLE 32-1: ABS System Features and Benefits

Feature	Benefit
Electronic control of brake force to wheel ends	• Prevents wheel lock-up and skidding during braking • Improves steering control and vehicle stability during panic braking and slippery conditions • Minimizes the likelihood of tractor jackknifing and trailer swing-out • Prevents tire flat spotting
Traction control	• A feature that uses the ABS system components to minimize wheel spin during acceleration on slippery surfaces • Minimizes the likelihood of "fishtailing" to improve steering control and directional stability • Reduces the likelihood of shock load damage to driveline components after a wheel spin
Electronic control brake system operation	• Faster response than driver to wheel lock-up and spin; ABS system can "pump" the brakes on individual wheels (or pairs of wheels), independently, and with greater speed and accuracy than a driver • Default to normal braking when fault detected in electronic control system • Adaptive fault accommodation will shut off ABS only to wheel ends with ABS system faults • Self-diagnostic capabilities and capability to interface with off-board diagnostic tools

decelerating wheels are going to lock. Once slowed, wheels begin to rotate faster after braking pressure is electronically reduced, and the system automatically reapplies braking force until wheel lock-up speed is approached again. This cycle of releasing and applying the brakes, illustrated in FIGURE 32-2, will take place rapidly until the brake pedal is released.

> **TECHNICIAN TIP**
>
> During slippery road conditions, drivers should be aware that pumping the brake pedal to simulate ABS operation is not as effective as a steady brake application. Without sophisticated brake assist software and hardware found on today's vehicles, air application pressure to the brake chambers is never more than what the operator is using to apply the brake pedal. This means that to enhance the effectiveness of the ABS system operation, maximum steady air pressure to the service chambers should be made available by using a full application pressure instead of pumping the brake pedal to simulate ABS operation. The ECU can then electronically modulate, or vary brake pressure, which responds to wheel lock-up and skid faster than the driver possibly can.

ABS System Requirements

The first truck air brake ABS systems were introduced in 1975, but mandatory ABS capabilities were only legislated in phases beginning in the late 1990s and early 2000s. FMVSS 121 has introduced shorter stopping requirements for heavy trucks—stopping distances have been reduced from 355' (108 m) to as little as 250' (76 m). In addition, new standards include stricter vehicle stability requirements. Systems must prevent trailer swing-out and jackknifing, and tractors and trailers currently need to remain within a 12-foot-wide (3.7-meter-wide) lane under hard braking conditions.

In addition to the stopping distance and stability regulations introduced in 2013, FMVSS 121 ABS requirements include:

- ABS on tractors and full trailers must control the braking pressure to at least one front axle and one rear axle. The system must further control braking on one of the rear axles using two **modulator valves**. These are ABS air control valves used to modulate the air pressure supplied to service brake chambers. By opening and closing the supply of air to the brakes, the modulator valves enable independent control of brake pressure at each end of the axle. Other performance requirements of FMVSS 121 can require an ABS on additional axles.
- ABSs on semi-trailers and converter dollies must control at least one axle of the trailer.
- ABSs electronic control modules on trailers must be capable of being powered by the trailer's stop lamp circuit. Brake light power-up is required to ensure trailers equipped with ABS will still function when connected to an older, non-ABS tractor. In addition to using brake light power, tractors built after March 1, 1997 do provide a constant 12-volt current to the trailer through a #7 pin of the **J-560 trailer connector**, which is a trailer cord receptacle located at the rear of the tractor. As shown in FIGURE 32-3,

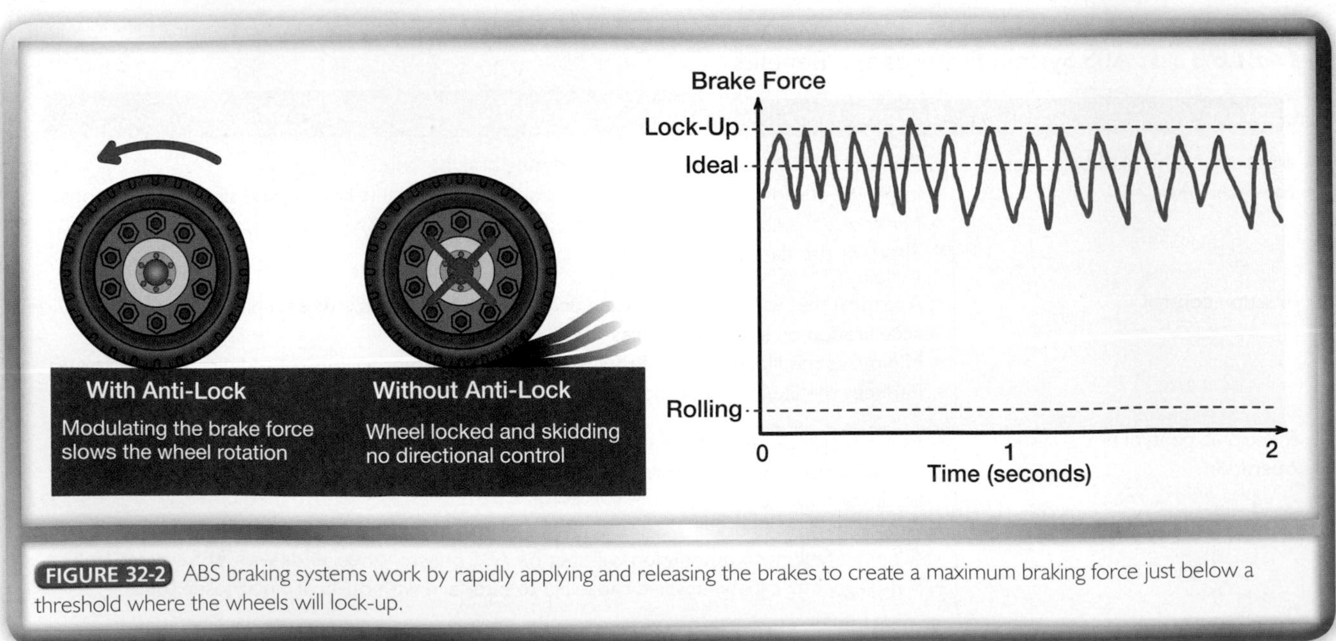

FIGURE 32-2 ABS braking systems work by rapidly applying and releasing the brakes to create a maximum braking force just below a threshold where the wheels will lock-up.

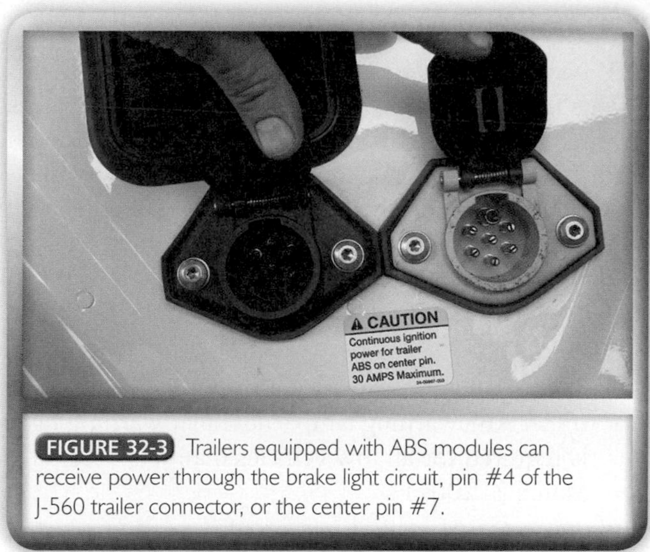

FIGURE 32-3 Trailers equipped with ABS modules can receive power through the brake light circuit, pin #4 of the J-560 trailer connector, or the center pin #7.

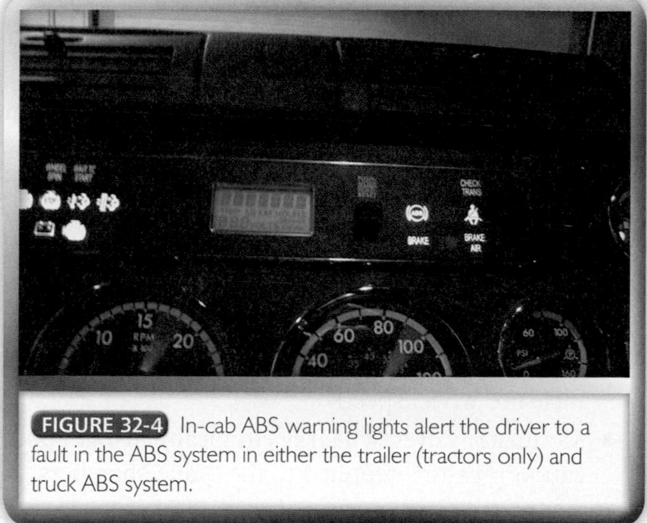

FIGURE 32-4 In-cab ABS warning lights alert the driver to a fault in the ABS system in either the trailer (tractors only) and truck ABS system.

the yellow-green trailer plug connector is used to connect trailers with ABS systems since it supplies a constant power source to the ABS module. The black connector is used on older trailers without ABS and can use the #7 pin to supply accessories such as an electrically operated lift axle. The larger ground pin accommodates higher electrical loads on trailers using ABS.

- ABS-equipped vehicles must have a dedicated yellow ABS malfunction indicator lamp. The lamp should illuminate only during an ABS system malfunction. On tractors, the ABS malfunction lamp must be in front of and in clear view of the driver, such as shown in FIGURE 32-4. On trailers, the yellow indicator is located on the left side of the trailer, near the rear side marker lamp, as shown in FIGURE 32-5. For dollies, the lamp needs to be located on the left side and visible at a distance 10' (3 m) from the lamp. On older vehicles, when the ignition key is first switched on, the bulb will illuminate for a few seconds to validate the bulb is operating properly. Depending on the system, the light can remain on until the vehicle moves fast enough to provide wheel speed data to the control module. At that point the light will go out unless a fault is detected. Since February 2009, the light should come on for a couple of seconds and then go out if everything checks out. The wheel speed sensor input is no longer required for the light to extinguish. Likewise, on models manufactured after March 2009, an external ABS light for the trailer or dolly is not required, as the tractor will have a trailer ABS light on the dash that will turn on if there is an issue with the trailer ABS.
- Air-braked tractors and trucks that tow other air-braked vehicles and that were built after March 1, 2001, must communicate with an in-cab ABS malfunction indicator lamp, which alerts the driver to any malfunction in a towed vehicle's ABS.

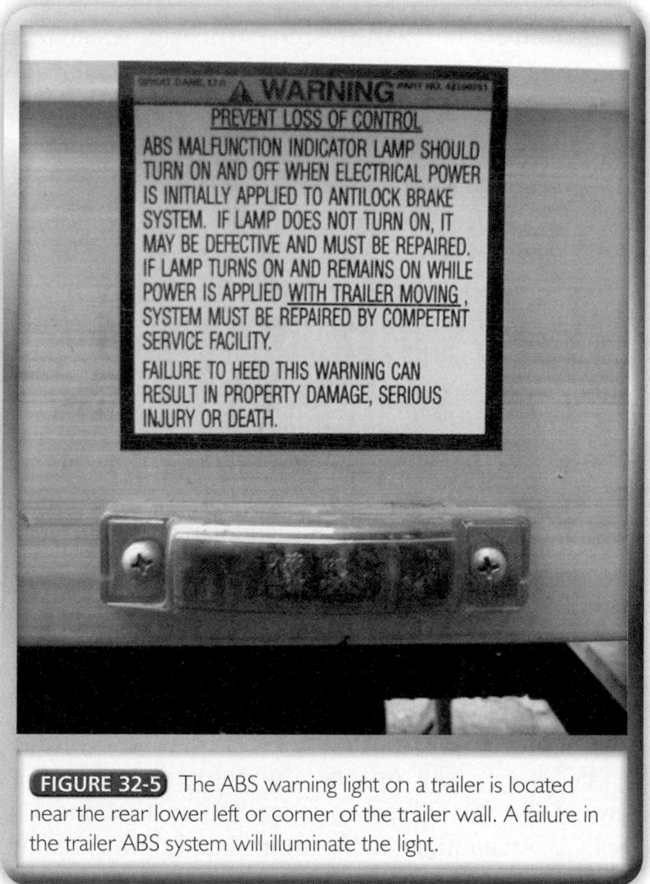

FIGURE 32-5 The ABS warning light on a trailer is located near the rear lower left or corner of the trailer wall. A failure in the trailer ABS system will illuminate the light.

ABS is used by both air and hydraulic braking systems and has been required by law on air-braked tractors since 1997, all other air-braked trucks and buses since 1998, and in hydraulic systems on vehicles over 10,000 lb (4,536 kg) GVW since 1999.

Anti-Lock Braking System Components

Electronic control of brake application force enables an ABS to adjust brake pressure faster and more accurately than a driver. Depending on the sophistication of the ABS system and vehicle configuration, a basic ABS system improves vehicle braking using the following common components:

- Electronic control unit (ECU)
- Wheel speed sensors with exciter rings—used to measure wheel speed
- Modulator valves, which electronically change application pressure supplied to the brake chambers
- ABS trailer cords
- ABS malfunction indicator lamp

We will examine a basic ABS system before examining the operation of more advanced ABS configurations in the Enhancements to Anti-lock Braking Systems section.

Electronic Control Units (ECU)

The vehicle's electronic control unit (ECU) collects information from the sensor inputs and processes the information using specialized algorithms embedded in software stored in the ECU. Algorithms are mathematical formulas used to solve a problem. In the case of ABS, the formula solves the problem of when to apply electrical signals to the modulator valves to prevent wheel lock-up.

Based on sensor inputs and instructions programmed into software, the ECU produces output signals to operate brake valves and warning lights and communicate with the vehicle network. Self-diagnostic capabilities built into the ECU can supply technicians with ABS system performance data as well as generate ABS system fault codes and other diagnostic information. ECUs are constructed to be mounted on the chassis frame or inside the environmentally protected cab.

ECUs typically operate using supply voltages of between 12 and 24 volts, depending on the model of the ECU. An ignition on/off current supply and a separate continuous battery current input are commonly connected through a 3- to 5-amp fuse and a 30-amp fuse respectively. Often the ECUs will use two ground inputs. One is for the ECU electronics, and the second is for a safety related interlock of the ABS warning light circuit and ECU. Normally, the ECU will ground out the ABS warning light whenever a fault is detected. However, with the double ground ECU input, the ABS wiring harness will automatically short the ABS warning lamp circuit to ground if the ECU connector is disconnected from the ECU.

ECU Configuration

ECU configurations vary depending on system configurations for the number of sensors and modulator valves required for a particular chassis. Additional features such as traction control, engine torque limiting capability, diagnostic outputs, and other switch inputs will add more complexity and pins to the ECU. In addition to varying by their processing speeds and memory size, ECUs can also vary according to whether they have the following features:

- An output for a cab- or dash-mounted tractor or trailer ABS warning lamp (the trailer warning light is required for all tow vehicles manufactured after March 1, 2001)
- An output for a dash-mounted automatic traction control (ATC) status/indicator lamp
- Integration with a service brake relay valve
- An optional blink code activation switch
- An optional ABS and ATC off-road switch
- Integration with a traction control valve
- J1939 serial communication to the vehicle network
- An engine brake or transmission retarder inhibit relay connection
- A stop lamp switch input (stop lamp switch status may be read from the J-1939 network data)
- Brake pressure input data from a brake pressure sensor located on the foot valve
- An odometer function that records accumulated distance
- Automatic or manual calibration of ECU software

More sophisticated ECUs will detect a system configuration immediately after the ignition is switched on. For example, the number of wheel speed sensors and modulator valves are immediately identified and the sound of electrical solenoids cycling modulator valves open and closed can be easily heard.

ABS system configuration of Meritor Wabco systems can be determined through the use of blink codes. **Blink codes**, also called **flash codes**, are a fault reporting strategy in which a fault indicator light will blink on and off to report a fault code number. Short pauses between light flashes separate numbers; long pauses separate fault codes. After the ABS diagnostic switch in the dash is pressed and released for three seconds, the module enters the clear fault mode. When pressed again for at least three seconds, then released, the system displays eight quick flashes followed by a system configuration code, if the code clearing process was successful. An ECU will not perform the configuration test when vehicle speed is detected.

ECU and On-Board Network Communication

Many vehicle features use wheel speed data, so the ABS module will average speed data and broadcast it over the J-1939 network. Speedometers, entertainment systems, collision avoidance systems, and safety interlock systems used by door locks, power dividers, and outriggers, need not duplicate vehicle speed sensors if they can simply use ABS data. Automatic traction control uses engine torque limiting, which is a strategy where the ABS ECU communicates with the engine ECU to reduce power when the wheels slip. (Torque limiting will be covered in the Torque Limiting section.) A hardwired connection to an electrical relay also enables the ABS ECU to disable the engine brake or driveline retarder, which can also cause the wheels to lock-up.

> **TECHNICIAN TIP**
>
> Engine-based braking systems, such as exhaust brakes and compression release brakes, can promote wheel lock-up conditions when activated. Driveline retarders used by automatic transmissions will lock-up wheels on slippery surfaces as well. The ABS module will have capabilities to inhibit, or shut-off, engine brakes and driveline retarders either through on-board network communication, such as over the J-1939 data bus, or directly through the use of electrical relays, which can electrically disable these devices.

Since March 1, 2001, all tractors must have an in-cab, trailer ABS malfunction indicator lamp. To transmit the status of the trailer ABS over the J-560 tractor/trailer electrical connector, ABS systems commonly use power line carrier technology. **Power line carrier (PLC) technology** is a data transmission technology enabling data exchange between the tractor and trailer ABS. PLC is needed to alert the driver, using an in-dash warning light, about any potential malfunction of the trailer ABS.

The data is not like serial digital communication over a standard controlled area network (CAN). Instead, PLC signals change (modulate) both the frequency and amplitude of a distinctly different voltage signal than is normally carried over the J-560 trailer plug #7 blue constant power wire between the trailer and tractor. When #7 pin current flow is paused, the PLC modules exchange bursts of data via high frequency voltage "chirps" in milliseconds of time. In order for PLC to function, tractors and trailers must both be equipped with PLC. The amplitude and frequency modulated voltage signal varies between 100K Hz and 400K Hz and is transmitted both ways between the trailer and tractor ABS control modules. FIGURE 32-6 shows the differences between a power line with PLC and one without PLC.

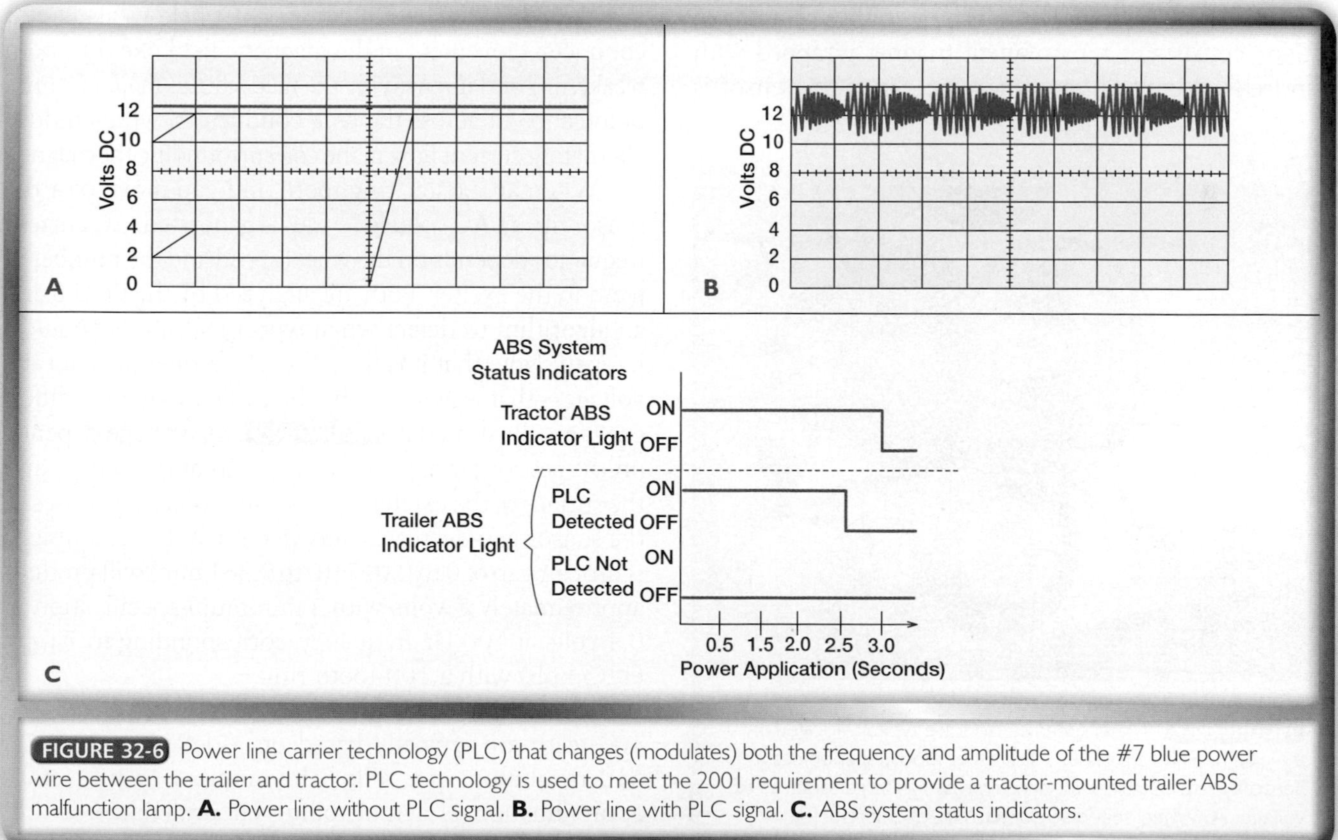

FIGURE 32-6 Power line carrier technology (PLC) that changes (modulates) both the frequency and amplitude of the #7 blue power wire between the trailer and tractor. PLC technology is used to meet the 2001 requirement to provide a tractor-mounted trailer ABS malfunction lamp. **A.** Power line without PLC signal. **B.** Power line with PLC signal. **C.** ABS system status indicators.

In addition to ABS software, specialized communication adapters can be used to check for correct PLC communication between the trailer and tractor. One example is Bendix's Trailer Remote Diagnostic Unit (TRDU). This unit not only provides blink codes to diagnose ABS problems but can clear codes and provide system configuration settings and odometer readings. If it does not establish communication due to a problem with PLC communication or a problem with the ABS ECU, the LED lights on the TRDU will illuminate in a clockwise pattern until the ABS ECU communication is established.

Wheel Speed Sensors

Wheel speed sensors are variable reluctance type sensors used to produce wheel speed data. Variable reluctance sensors use changes in a sensor's magnetic field strength to generate an alternating current signal. The frequency of the AC pulses is translated by the ECU into wheel speed. As illustrated in FIGURE 32-7, two main parts make up the wheel speed sensing system. One is a reluctor wheel, also called the tone or exciter ring. The other part is the variable reluctance sensor itself.

As illustrated in FIGURE 32-8, the **reluctor wheel** is simply a ring of raised iron teeth or a gear-like ring that moves past the sensor when the wheel rotates. The reluctor wheel (exciter ring) is pressed onto the inner wheel hub or cast into a brake drum. The **variable reluctance sensor** consists of a permanent magnet wrapped with hundreds of coils of very fine wire. Since the sensor is placed in close proximity to the exciter ring, high spots on the exciter ring will intensify the magnetic field strength in the sensor.

FIGURE 32-8 The wheel speed sensor generates wheel rotational velocity data by counting the number of teeth passing by the sensor per unit of time. One wheel rotation is typically 100 teeth. **A.** Reluctor wheel.

Magnetic fields can pass through iron much easier than through air. The magnetic lines of force increase in density when passing through the raised iron tooth. That increase in density results in intensification. Then, as the raised tooth moves past the sensor, the field weakens and contracts. Movement of the magnetic field like this, both weakening and intensifying the field, causes magnetic lines of force to cut across the wire conductors, which induce alternating current flow in the coil surrounding the magnet.

When an exciter ring tooth and gap move past the sensor tip, an AC voltage "cycle" is generated. AC current frequency depends on the wheel speed and the number of teeth in the exciter. Both are analyzed by the ECU using an algorithm to detect when wheel lock-up is about to happen. Note that it is the AC cycle frequency—not the voltage—that is analyzed by the ECU. Frequency differences are illustrated in FIGURE 32-9. AC voltage depends on the sensor air gap between the tip of the sensor and the surface of the exciter ring. Sensor voltage increases as the sensor gap decreases and vice versa. For example, a sensor air gap of 0 to 0.015" (0 to 0.381 mm) will produce approximately 5 volts with a minimum specification of 0.4 volts at 100 Hz frequency, corresponding to 7 mph (11.3 kph) with a 100-tooth ring.

Wheel speed calculations using an exciter ring with 100 teeth are typically based on a default tire size of 510 revolutions per mile. This number is an average approximation of actual rolling circumference of tires with a radius of 22.5– 4.5" (57.2–11.4 cm). A precise

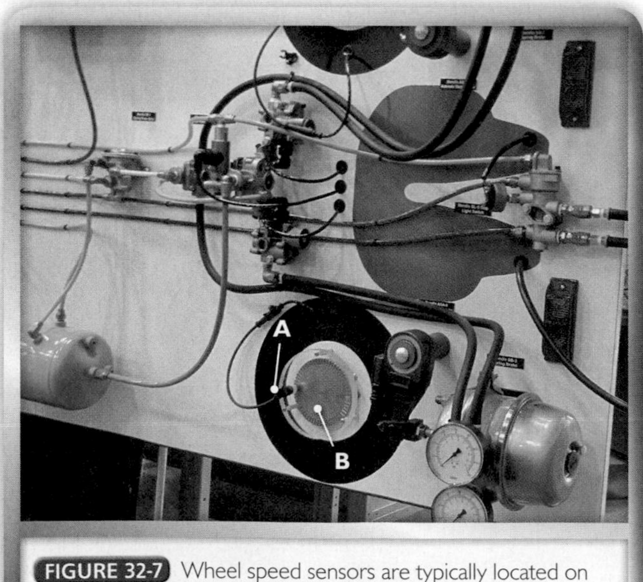

FIGURE 32-7 Wheel speed sensors are typically located on the axle hub and are either a straight or elbow-shaped design. Sensors use a variable reluctance type design to generate an AC voltage. **A.** Wheel speed sensor. **B.** Wheel end reluctor.

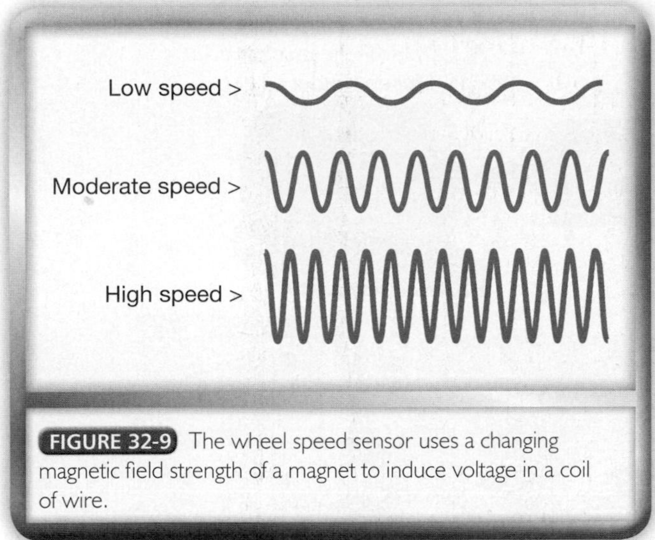

FIGURE 32-9 The wheel speed sensor uses a changing magnetic field strength of a magnet to induce voltage in a coil of wire.

number will commonly vary between 460 and 650 rpm depending on tire size, pressure tread wear, and vehicle load. The ABS sensitivity to detecting wheel lock-up is reduced when tire rolling circumference is excessive on all wheels or tire rpm is low. FIGURE 32-10 shows the relationship between tire size and revolutions.

When referencing a speed sensor or modulator valve position, the driver's seat is the vehicle's reference point. Sensors themselves are typically installed in mounting blocks welded to the axle housing. A spring-like stainless steel clip clamps the sensor with a friction fit inside the mounting block. FIGURE 32-11A illustrates the friction fit of a wheel sensor and FIGURE 32-11B shows a wheel sensor in place. An air gap is established by pushing the sensor against the exciter ring. FIGURE 32-12 illustrates the air gap. As the rotating exciter contacts the sensor, the sensor is pushed back slightly. Normal wheel bearing end play will further "bump" the sensor away from the exciter, establishing an operating sensor air gap. Loss of correct sensor air gap is a common ABS-related complaint. Sensors should be checked to see whether they are firmly in place and whether a loose wheel bearing may be interfering with the air gap.

When the ABS system configuration equips the wheels of only one tandem axle with wheel speed sensors, the sensors are usually located on the axle whose wheels are most likely to lock-up first during braking. On a tandem axle with a four-spring suspension, the sensors are generally on the lead axle. On a tandem axle with air suspension, the sensors are generally located on the trailing axle.

> **TECHNICIAN TIP**
>
> An ABS module will generate fault codes if the rpm is too low or high. To prevent tire size fault codes from being generated, the actual rolling circumference of front axle steer axle tires compared to the drive axle tires must also be within a 0.85:1.15 ratio.

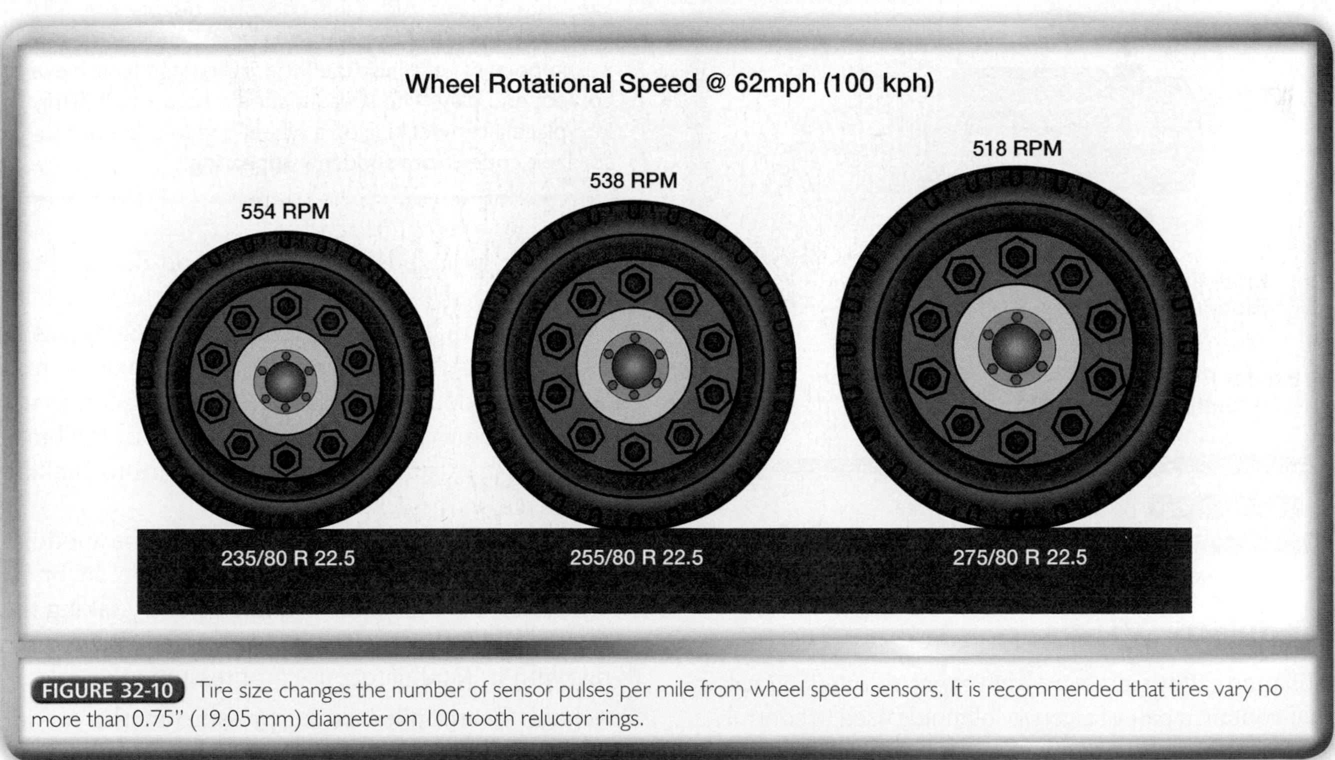

FIGURE 32-10 Tire size changes the number of sensor pulses per mile from wheel speed sensors. It is recommended that tires vary no more than 0.75" (19.05 mm) diameter on 100 tooth reluctor rings.

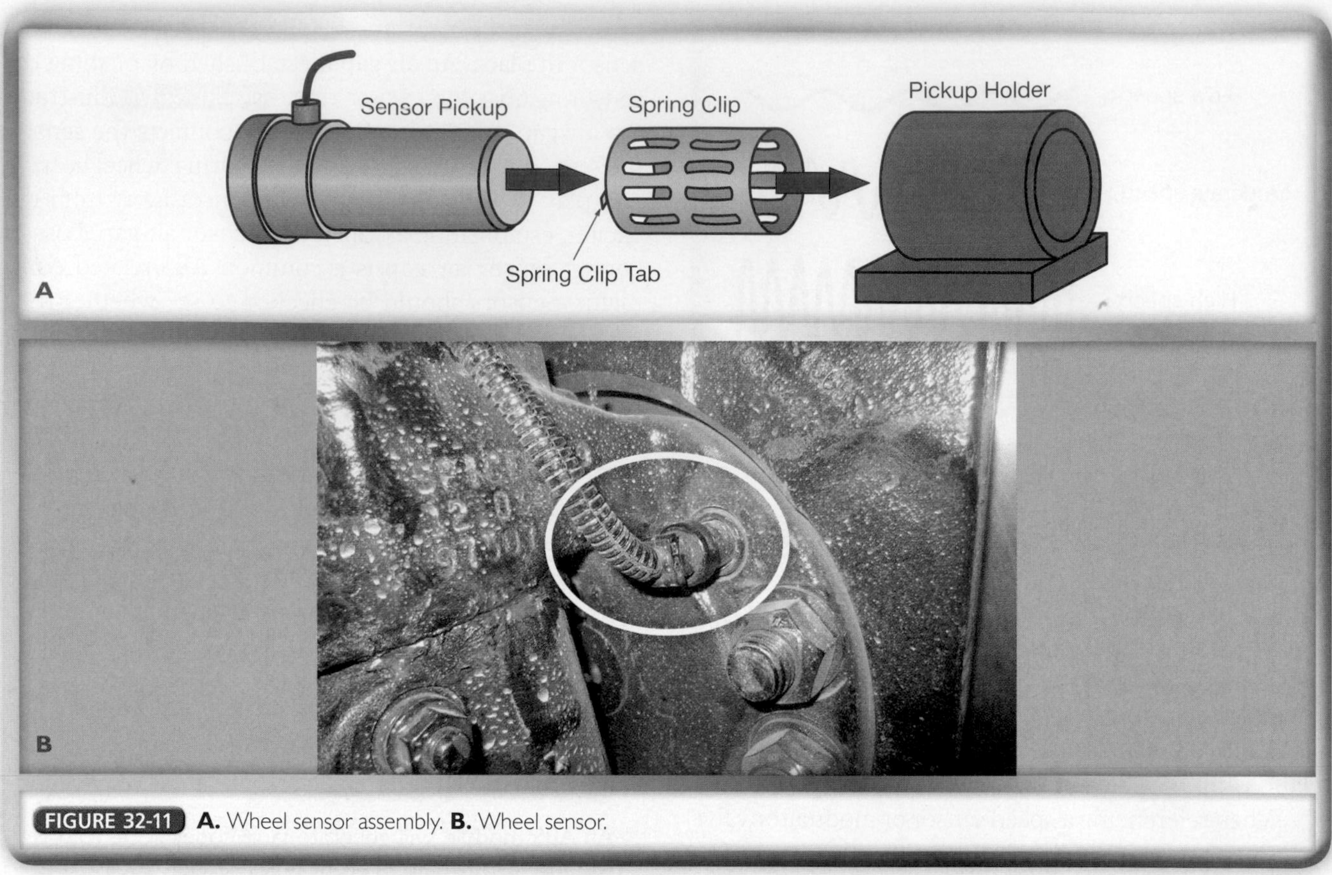

FIGURE 32-11 **A.** Wheel sensor assembly. **B.** Wheel sensor.

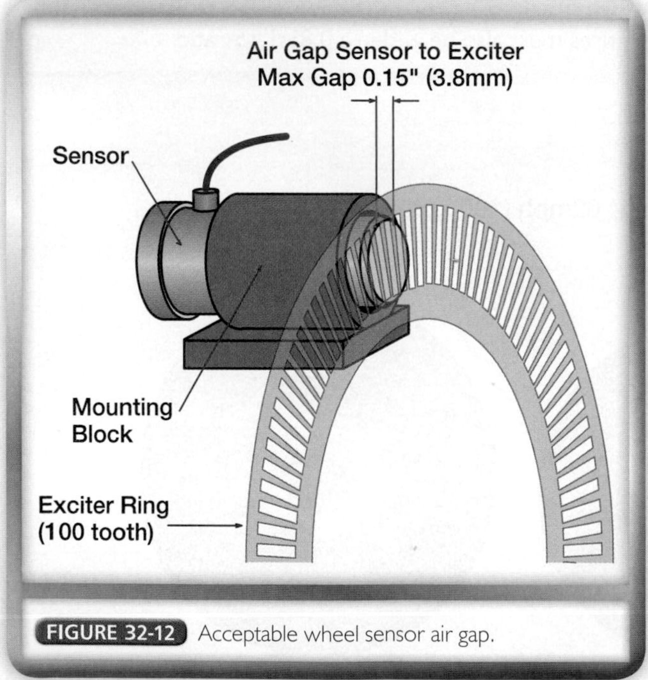

FIGURE 32-12 Acceptable wheel sensor air gap.

Modulator Valves

ABS modulator valves are high capacity, on/off air valves that contain a pair of electric solenoids used to control air brake application pressure. As these two "inlet-air" and "exhaust-air" solenoids are energized and de-energized by electrical signals from the ABS ECU, the controller can pump the brakes. That is, the controller signals to apply and release braking pressure on both axles, wheel ends on each axle, or at individual wheel ends connected to the modulator valves. FIGURE 32-13 graphs the braking action as pressure is applied to the various braking components on the vehicle.

During normal braking applications, the modulator valves are not active. When activated on air brake systems, modulators adjust braking force by taking the air pressure supplied by the foot valve and doing three things with it. Modulators use air pressure to:

- hold the supplied brake pressure in the service chambers

> **TECHNICIAN TIP**
>
> Loose wheel bearings can produce excessive sensor air gap, thus causing ABS fault codes to disable the ABS system operation. After servicing wheel ends and hubs, it is important to adjust the wheel bearings to achieve correct end play. The sensors should be pushed firmly into place after working on a wheel end to prevent sensor fault codes from suddenly appearing.

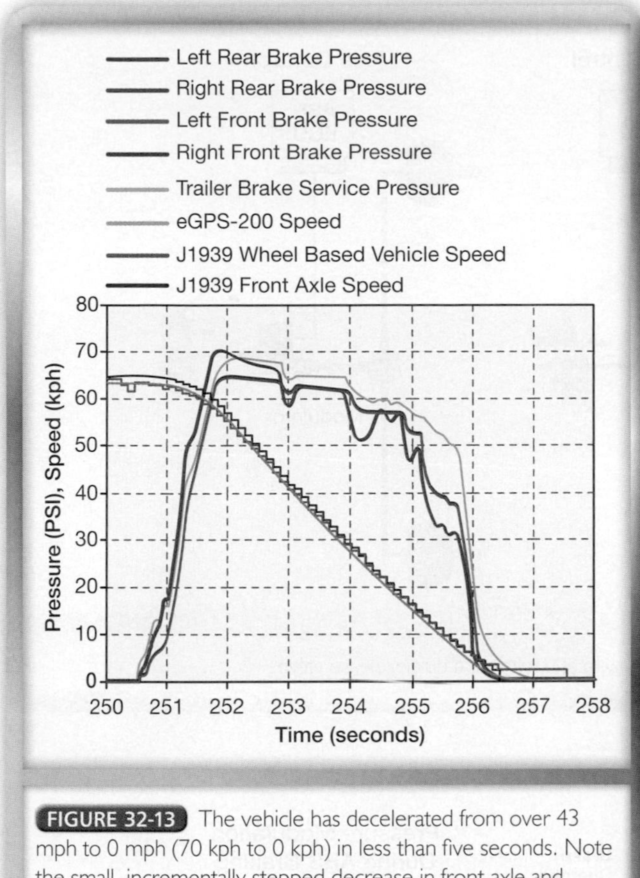

FIGURE 32-13 The vehicle has decelerated from over 43 mph to 0 mph (70 kph to 0 kph) in less than five seconds. Note the small, incrementally stepped decrease in front axle and vehicle speed made due to the changing brake modulator valve pressure in the trailer, rear, and front axle brake chambers.

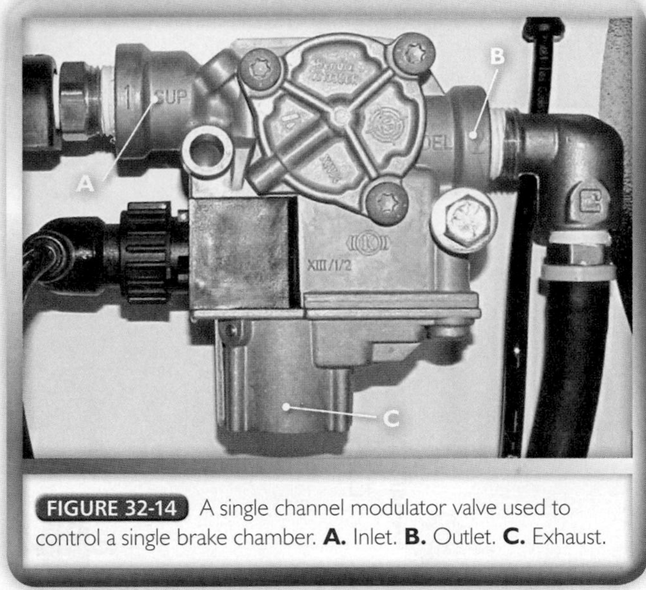

FIGURE 32-14 A single channel modulator valve used to control a single brake chamber. **A.** Inlet. **B.** Outlet. **C.** Exhaust.

- release or dump brake pressure supplied to the service chambers
- reapply brake pressure to service chambers after it has been dumped

ABS modulator valves are physically closer to the brake chambers than the driver's foot valve. Consequently, braking response is substantially faster with ABS brakes. Plus, the electronic control makes braking decisions faster and more precise because ABS systems adjust brake pressure to each wheel or set of wheels on an axle to achieve optimal braking effectiveness.

Modulators can be used to control the braking function at individual service chambers, on a pair of chambers on a single axle, or on two chambers on the same side of a tandem axle. When controlling braking at individual wheel ends, the modulator is the last control valve through which air passes before entering the brake chamber. FIGURE 32-14 shows a single channel modulator valve used to control a single brake chamber. When controlling air supply to two chambers, the modulator is often connected in series after a quick release valve. This arrangement provides a faster release of exhaust during normal service brake applications. FIGURE 32-15 shows the location and configuration of front axle modulator valves, with and without a quick release valve.

Modulator Valve Construction

Individual modulators are typically constructed from die cast aluminum body and contain two solenoids: one normally open and one normally closed solenoid. Three electrical pins connect to the solenoids and they share a common ground connection. The valves can be integrated into a conventional relay valve, too. Like other relay air valves, they have a variety of control, inlet, reservoir, and supply ports depending on how the system is configured. The modulator valve itself contains an air inlet and exhaust valve whose position is controlled by a solenoid. FIGURE 32-16 shows a trailer ABS module along with the modulator valve and sensors from a training board.

Operation Modulator Valves During Non-Anti-lock Braking

During normal service braking, both modulator valve solenoids are de-energized. The normally open inlet solenoid controlling the inlet diaphragm position enables air to pass through the valve and out the delivery port past the normally closed exhaust valve, which is opened by energizing the exhaust solenoid. In a relay-type valve, the combined modulator-relay valve will behave like a regular relay valve. The control air pressure acts on an internal piston, which simultaneously opens an inlet diaphragm and closes the internal exhaust diaphragm. Control pressure from the foot valve will regulate the flow of reservoir pressure into the valve until a state of balance between control pressure and air pressure at the relay valve's supply ports is equal.

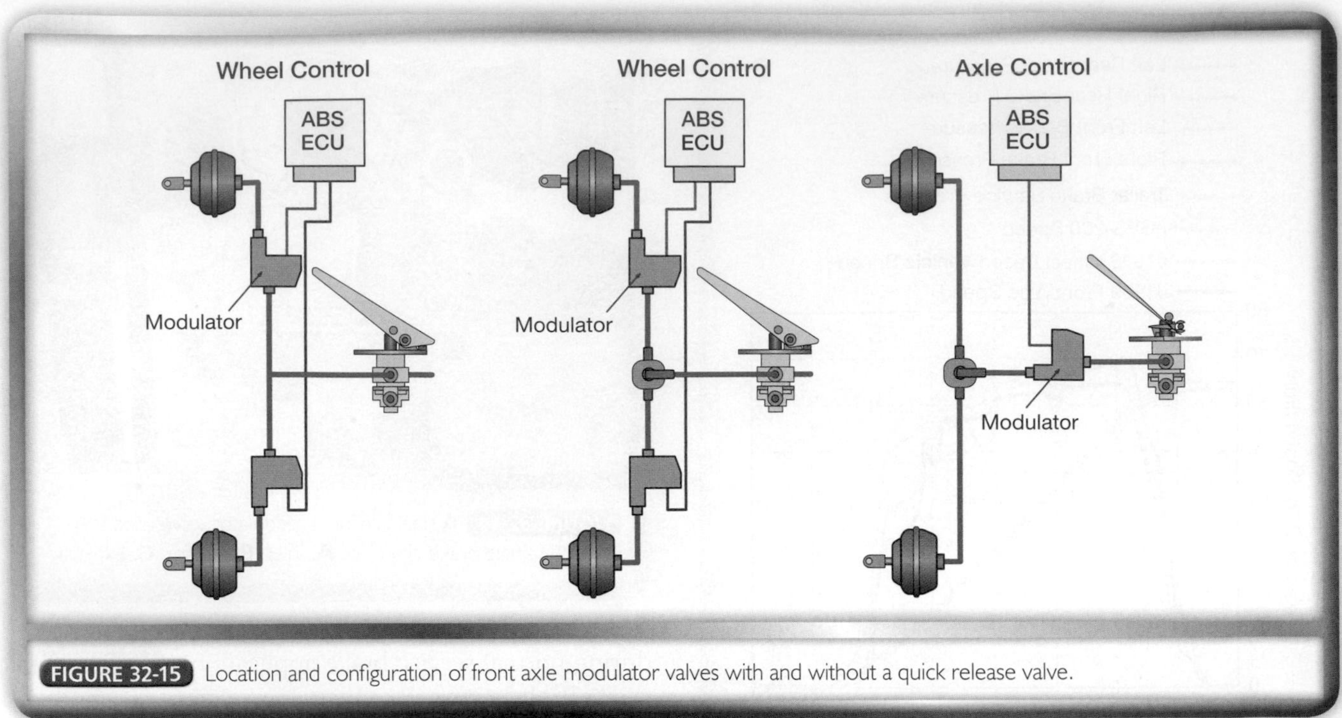

FIGURE 32-15 Location and configuration of front axle modulator valves with and without a quick release valve.

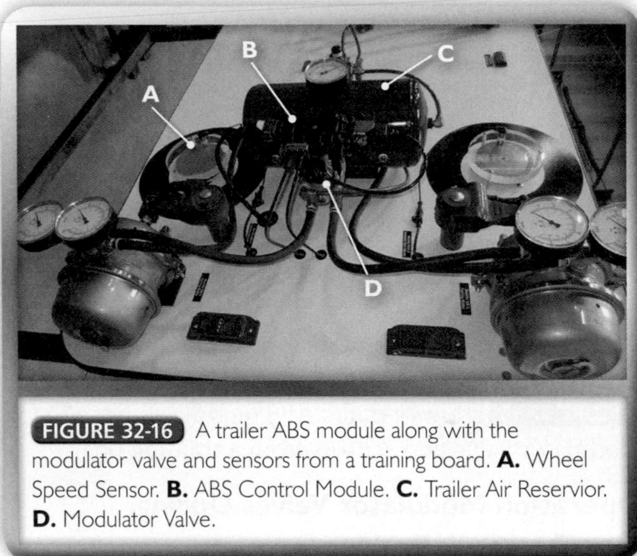

FIGURE 32-16 A trailer ABS module along with the modulator valve and sensors from a training board. **A.** Wheel Speed Sensor. **B.** ABS Control Module. **C.** Trailer Air Reservior. **D.** Modulator Valve.

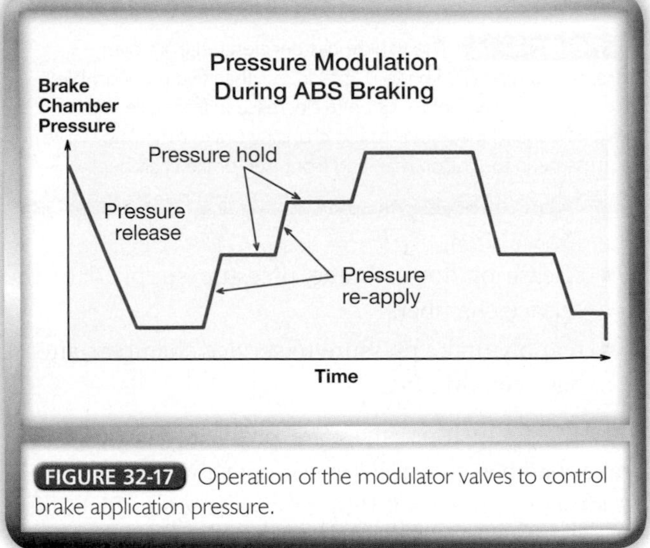

FIGURE 32-17 Operation of the modulator valves to control brake application pressure.

Operation of Modulator Valves During Anti-lock Braking

There are three distinct aspects of the anti-lock braking process:

- Exhaust
- Hold
- Reapply

Pressure changes during these phases are shown in the chart in FIGURE 32-17.

Before the first phase begins, the system is inactive, as shown in FIGURE 32-18A. The first phase is anti-lock *exhaust* and is illustrated in FIGURE 32-18B. When wheel lock-up is detected or imminent, the ECU energizes both the inlet air supply and exhaust solenoids in the modulator. Energizing the supply solenoid prevents inlet air flow into the normally open valve and opens the normally closed exhaust port to atmosphere. The modulator will remain in the anti-lock exhaust mode until the ECU senses an increase in wheel speed. At that point, the ECU can de-energize the exhaust solenoid and either open or close the air inlet solenoid. De-energizing the inlet solenoid will rebuild brake chamber air pressure, which reapplies the brakes.

The ECU can change the modulator control status by putting the solenoids into a *hold* air pressure

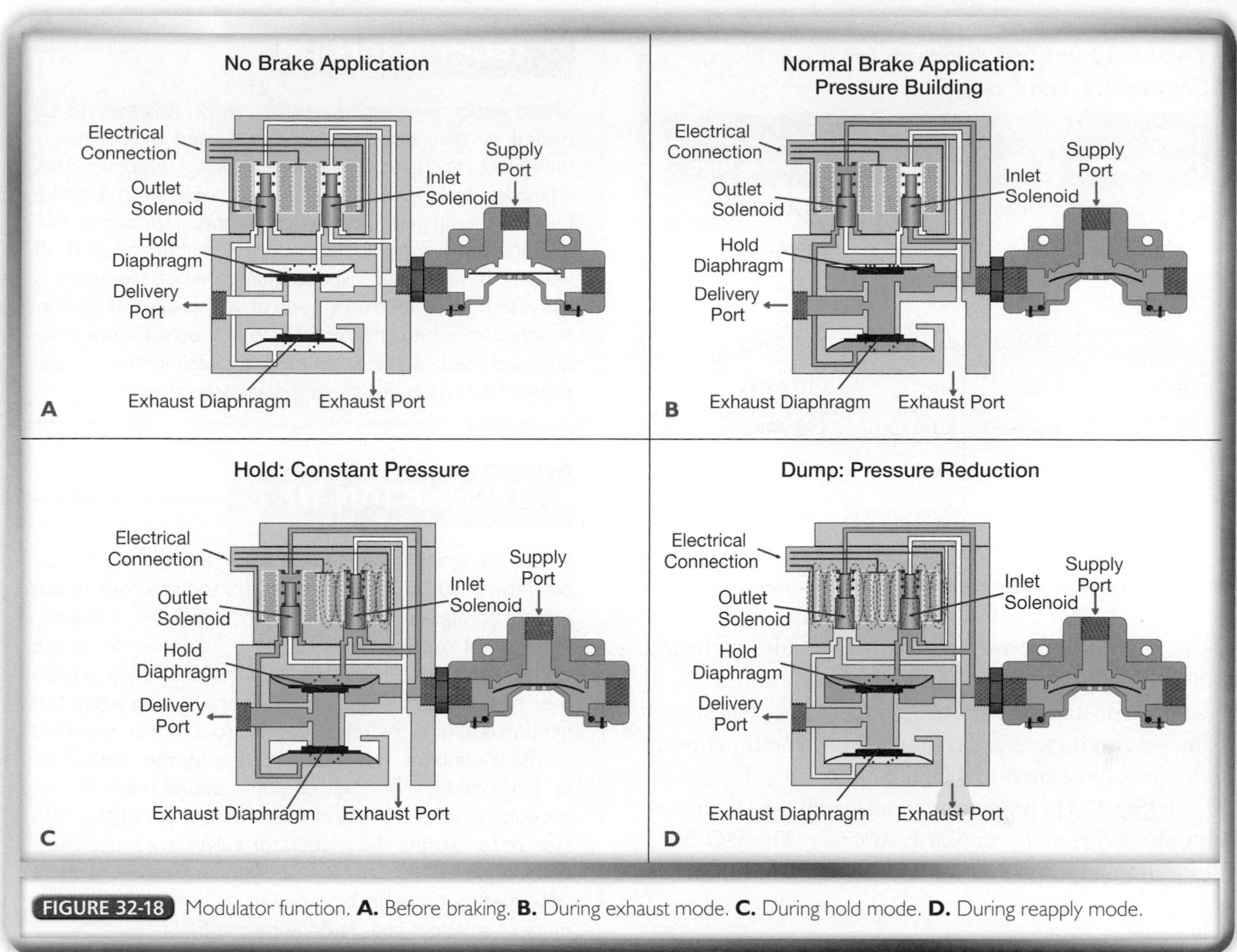

FIGURE 32-18 Modulator function. **A.** Before braking. **B.** During exhaust mode. **C.** During hold mode. **D.** During reapply mode.

position, as illustrated in FIGURE 32-18C. The ECU will do this when it senses the correct wheel speed has been achieved using the brake application pressure used at that moment. In hold mode of operation, the modulator air supply inlet solenoid remains energized, which blocks air flow into the valve. At the same time, the exhaust solenoid is de-energized. That prevents air from the brake chamber from exhausting out the service chamber(s). De-energizing the exhaust solenoid closes the exhaust outlet port. No air can be released from the chambers or supplied though the closed inlet valve. The modulator can change to an exhaust or reapply mode from the anti-lock hold mode.

In the anti-lock *reapply* mode, if the ECU senses that wheel speed has increased to the point when re-application of braking pressure is necessary, it de-energizes the supply and exhaust solenoids. With both solenoids de-energized, the modulator re-supplies air pressure to the brakes as it does in a normal braking condition. In this state, the exhaust valve is closed and the air inlet valve is open. Reapply mode is illustrated in FIGURE 32-18D.

ABS Trailer Cords

The trailer cords used in anti-lock braking systems are subject to SAE standards. Specifically, the **SAE J-560 standard** applies to the dimensional and functionality requirements for 7-pin tractor/trailer electrical connectors. It is more commonly known as the standard for the trailer electrical cord, plugs, and sockets as well as for transfers of ABS signals between the tractor and trailer. TABLE 32-2 shows J-560 standards for plugs, connectors, and cords.

Prior to the introduction of ABS, the #7 (blue) wire conductor was intended for auxiliary power purposes. Lift axles and other trailer accessories could be supplied current through this wire and switched on and off by a dash toggle switch. After the introduction of ABS, legislation required the #7 blue auxiliary power circuit be dedicated to supply continuous current to the trailer ABS system. The minimum wire gauge size increased to 12 AWG. Since many auxiliary electrical devices, in addition to the current demands of the ABS, increased the total trailer power consumption, the minimum diameter

TABLE 32-2: J-560 Standards for Trailer Plugs, Connectors, and Cords

J-560 Pin Number	Color	Purpose	Wire Gauge
1	White	Ground	8 AWG
2	Black	Clearance, marker, and I.D.	12 AWG
3	Yellow	Left turn	12 AWG
4	Red	Stop	10 AWG
5	Green	Right turn	12 AWG
6	Brown	Tail	12 AWG
7	Blue	Auxiliary and ABS	10 AWG

of the ground white wire conductor was also increased to 8 AWG. A green-colored trailer cord identifies a cord meeting SAE standards for ABS trailer cords with larger diameter conductors and ground pins. The function of each pin is illustrated in FIGURE 32-19.

An **ISO 3731 connector** is commonly used in Europe but only occasionally in North America. The ISO 3731 uses a multi-pin tractor-trailer electrical connector and can also transfer ABS signals. This connector carries power, ABS fault lamp status, and serial communications to and from trailer anti-lock braking systems.

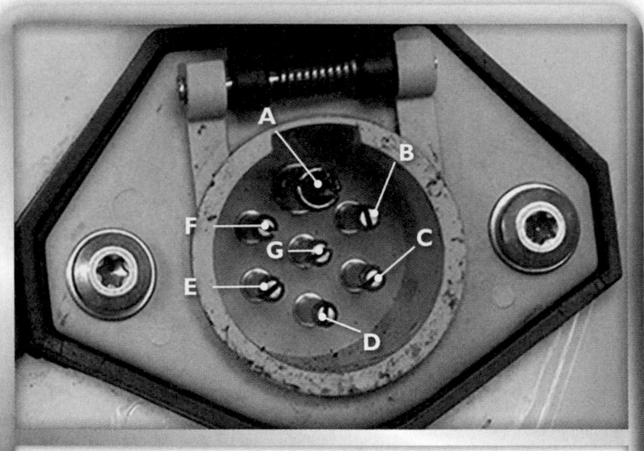

FIGURE 32-19 Power is constantly supplied through the #7 pin after the key is switched on. Each pin communicates different information.
A Pin 1: Ground Circuit
B Pin 2: Clearance, Sidemarker, ID
C Pin 3: Left-Hand Turn Signal
D Pin 4: Stop Lamp Circuit
E Pin 5: Right Turn Signal and Hazard Signal
F Pin 6: Tail Lamp, Marker Lamp, License Plate Lamp
G Pin 7*: Continuous Power or Auxiliary Circuit (Activated in "Key On" Position)

> **TECHNICIAN TIP**
>
> When performing any diagnostic work, it is easy to be misled by diagnostic fault codes caused by seemingly unrelated mechanical fault conditions. Defective slack adjusters, misadjusted brakes, or problems in a brake foundation can generate defective modulator codes. For example, an automatic slack adjuster that has backed-off will not have a wheel speed change when the valve is activated. The electronic control will assume the valve is defective when the root cause is a defective or misadjusted slack adjuster. Eliminate possible mechanical causes first when performing diagnostic checks.

> **TECHNICIAN TIP**
>
> When the ignition switch is first cycled to the on position, the ECU learns or rediscovers the anti-lock brake system configuration and performs a self-test of the solenoids. All the solenoids to the modulator valves are cycled in a particular sequence wherever they are on the chassis. By making a full brake application when the ignition is initially switched on, the sound of air supplied to the modulator valves is amplified by the exhaust of air from each valve. The "chuffing" sound made by the modulator valves is a useful functional test of the ABS system to validate the modulator valves are functioning correctly both electrically and pneumatically. Otherwise, without the brakes applied, only electrical continuity of solenoid coils is done by the ECU.

Indicator Lights and Switches

The final components in an anti-lock braking system are the indicator lights and the off-road switch. The ABS indicator lamp (amber colored) indicates the status of the anti-lock brake system. The light can illuminate to indicate normal operation or to signal a system fault. After the ignition is switched on, the ABS indicator light will typically remain lit for several seconds, and then go out if the system is functioning correctly. In addition, ABS lights are diagnostic output devices, as was discussed in the ECU Configuration section.

The ABS warning light for the trailer/dolly is not required for an in-cab light on vehicles built before March 2001. An external trailer/dolly indicator lamp is used and mandatory on vehicles built from 1998 to 2009. On vehicles built after March 2009, the external ABS light is not required.

On some vehicles, an off-road ABS switch is used to improve ABS function on poor traction surfaces such as loose gravel, sand, and dirt. The switch will allow more wheel lock-up, due to loose gravel and mud, which actually reduces stopping distances in off-road conditions.

ABS Configurations

ABS configuration is defined by the location and number of wheel sensors and modulator valves used. The most common configurations for tractors are:

- Four sensors/four modulators (4S/4M) FIGURE 32-20
- Six sensors/four modulators (6S/4M) FIGURE 32-21
- Six sensors/six modulators (6S/6M) FIGURE 32-22

Common configurations for trailers are 2S/1M, 2S/2M, 4S/2M, and 4S/3M.

Some tractors use a 4S/6M ABS system. In that system, rear drive axle wheel speed sensors are located on the front drive axle only. During hard braking, front tires are less likely to lock-up first since vehicle weight is

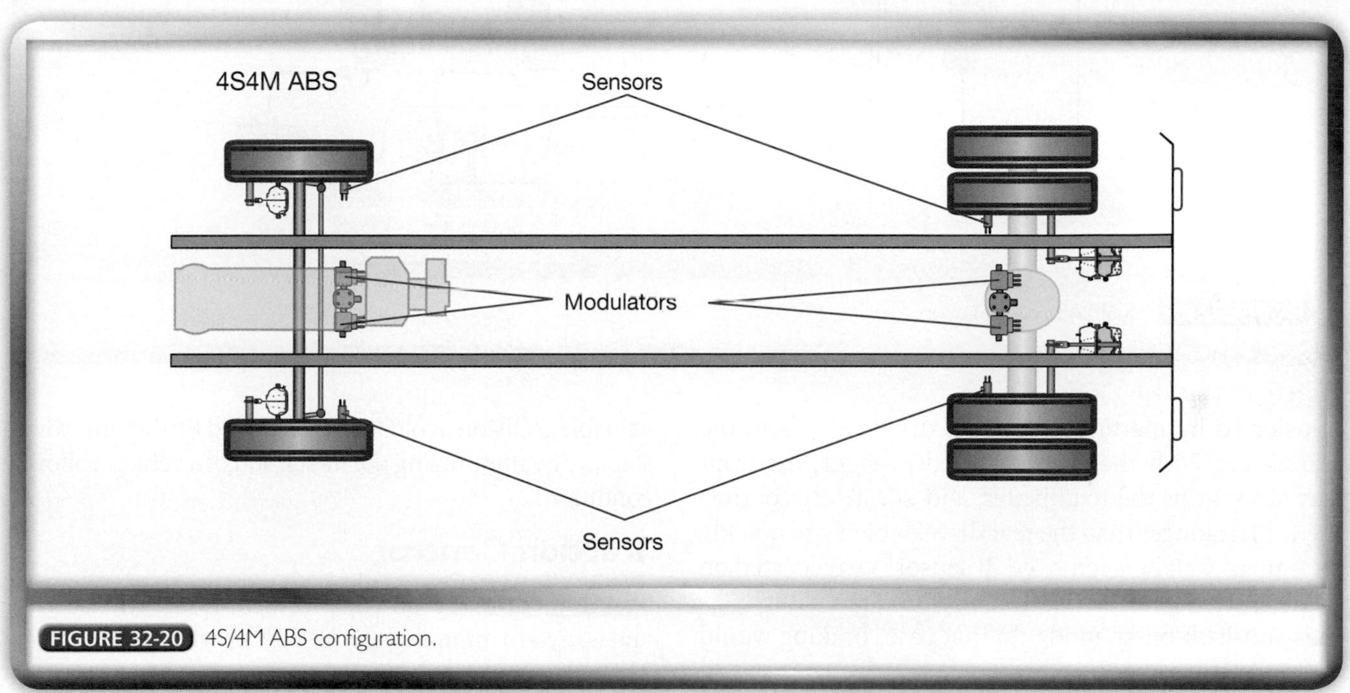

FIGURE 32-20 4S/4M ABS configuration.

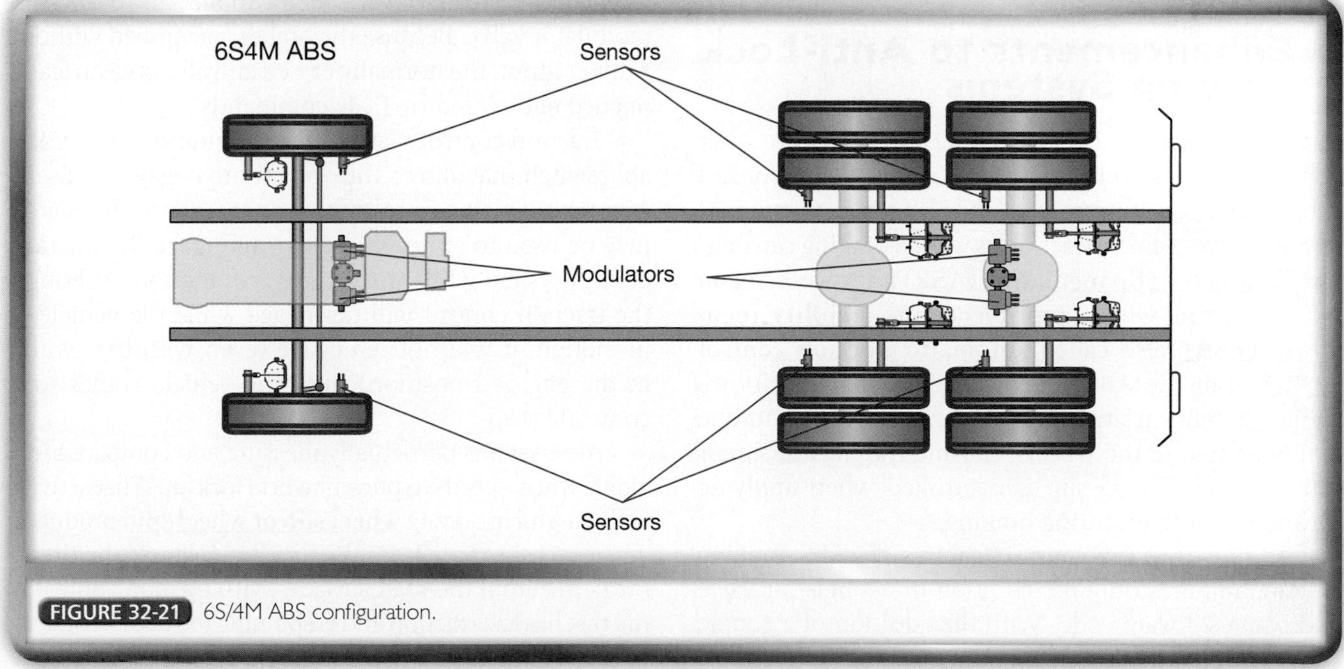

FIGURE 32-21 6S/4M ABS configuration.

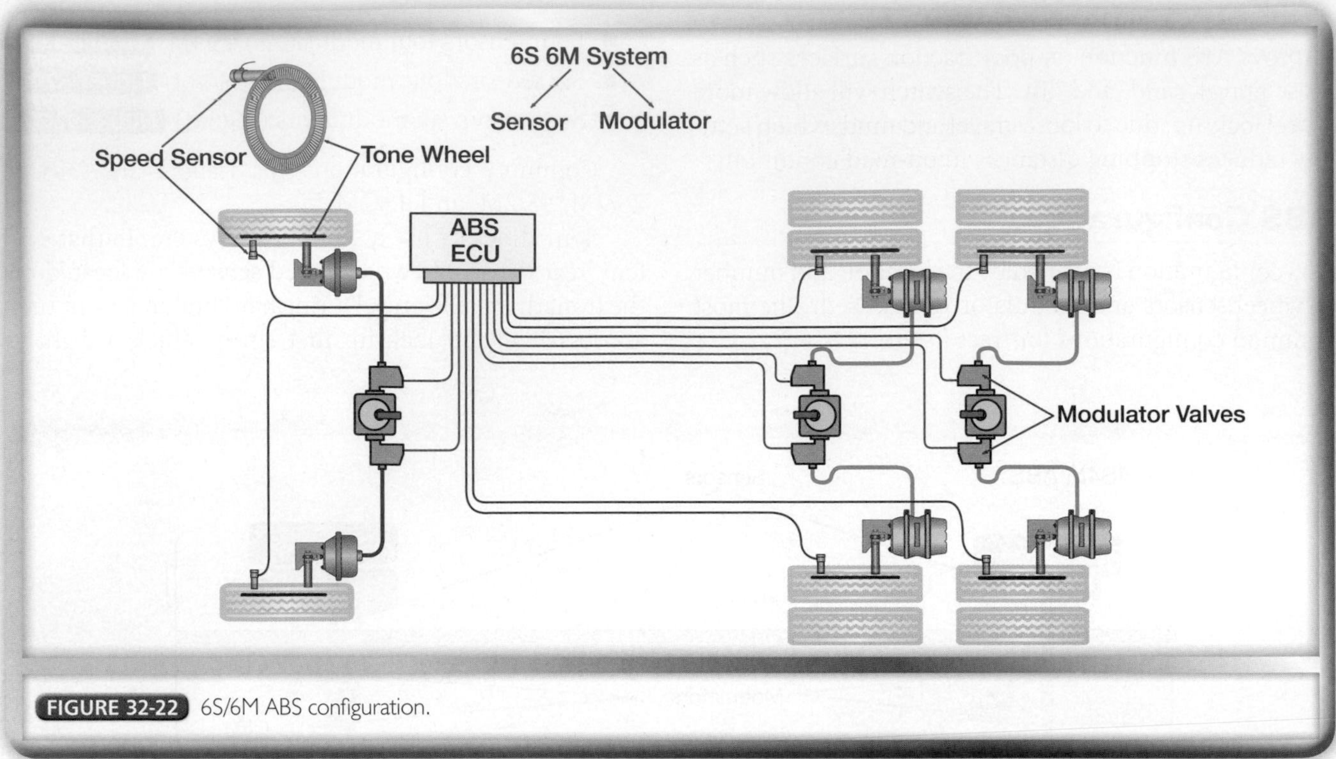

FIGURE 32-22 6S/6M ABS configuration.

transferred by inertia to the front drive axle, from the rear drive. With the additional axle weight, the front drive axle grips the road better, and effectively controls the vehicle longer than the rear drive, which will quickly lock-up as weight is removed. If sensors were located on the rear drive axle, the ABS system would prematurely go into anti-lock brake mode. In that case, braking would be less efficient because both sets of drive tires would experience brake pressure modulation.

Enhancements to Anti-Lock Braking Systems

Newer anti-lock braking systems are integrated into other vehicle control systems to provide additional safety and vehicle control features. One of the primary adaptations of ABS improves vehicle traction as well as braking capabilities. **Automatic slip regulation (ASR)** improves traction by minimizing wheel spin. **Electronic stability regulation (ESR)**, also called **automatic traction control (ATC)**, uses the ABS system components to improve vehicle stability in situations when excessive drive torque is transmitted to the wheels, causing the tires to slip or lose traction. Wheel slip is controlled when applying torque rather than during braking.

Adding traction control features to ABS braking systems requires only the addition of a single air valve and some software code. With the addition of a couple other sensors, ABS systems can be leveraged to provide a valuable collision avoidance system and further improves stability by minimizing the likelihood of a vehicle rollover condition.

Traction Control

Traction control is an enhancement to the ABS system and is used to improve vehicle stability when accelerating. The only significant change in system hardware requirements for traction control is the addition of an electrically controlled air valve, which supplies air to the ABS modulator valve. Because the brakes are applied without a driver input, the normally closed air valve is electrically opened and closed by ECU commands.

Traction control systems also include an enable/disable switch that allows the operator to engage or disengage the traction control system as necessary. The switch may be used to either engage or disengage the traction control system while the vehicle is in motion. Although the traction control will disengage while the vehicle is in motion, it will not re-engage (even with the switch in the engaged position) until the vehicle comes to a complete stop.

ABS systems perpetually measure and compare individual wheel speeds to prevent wheel lock-up. That activity is also useful in taming **wheel slip or wheel spin** produced when excess torque from the drivetrain causes the tire to break free from the road surface. With traction control, a tire that has lost traction and is spinning too fast is instantly detected through comparison with the other wheels on the vehicle, both front and rear. If wheels spin, unacceptable torque steering by the drive axles can take place.

Traction control systems commonly use two strategies to control wheel spin: torque limiting and differential braking. Both strategies are used by the ABS ECU and engine ECM independently or together. To use both options it is necessary that data sent over the J-1939 network communicate the vehicle's throttle position to the ABS ECU. Otherwise, the ATC will not function.

Torque Limiting

Torque limiting is basically a reduction in power. During a wheel slip condition, uneven wheel speeds prevent proper forward motion and can cause the vehicle to lose directional stability, as illustrated in FIGURE 32-23. The resulting understeer or oversteer risks pushing a vehicle outside its lane. By transferring torque from one side of the vehicle to the other, or reducing torque, both conditions can be prevented.

When the ABS first identifies a wheel slip condition, the ECU signals the engine to reduce the power output. With reduced engine power, the tires will again begin to grip the road surface. When both drive wheels are spinning because traction is low or absent, the ATC automatically reduces engine power through J-1939 network communication to reestablish tire-to-road traction. If the wheels continue to slip, the ATC will automatically turn on and off.

Transferring the torque to a wheel with better tire traction helps maintain vehicle stability by minimizing fishtailing also known as (**power jackknifing**). **Fishtailing** is a condition in which the drive axles of a vehicle push the rear of a vehicle and steering control is lost. Fishtailing is caused by oversteer, which occurs when the torque from the drive axle rotates the vehicle around its center point. During oversteer, the steering inputs are exaggerated; slight turns of the steering wheel when cornering during wheel spin produce a more dramatic change in vehicle direction during the turn. When the ABS transfers torque from one side of the vehicle to the other, forward momentum of the vehicle is also maintained rather than limiting engine power output. Reducing drive torque by reducing engine power, or **de-rating**, helps prevent both oversteer and understeer conditions.

Vehicles with traction control will be fitted with an indicator lamp on the dash. When the vehicle ignition is first turned to ON, the ATC lamp will come on for a few seconds as a bulb prove out. If the lamp goes out after a few seconds, the ATC system is ready; if the lamp stays on, it indicates a malfunction in the system. If wheel spin occurs at any speed above 25 mph (40 kph), the ECU will instantly blink the traction control dash lamp to advise the driver that a wheel spin is occurring. If the torque limiting feature is enabled, the ECU signals the engine control module to reduce engine torque to a level suitable for the available traction. The ECU will generally

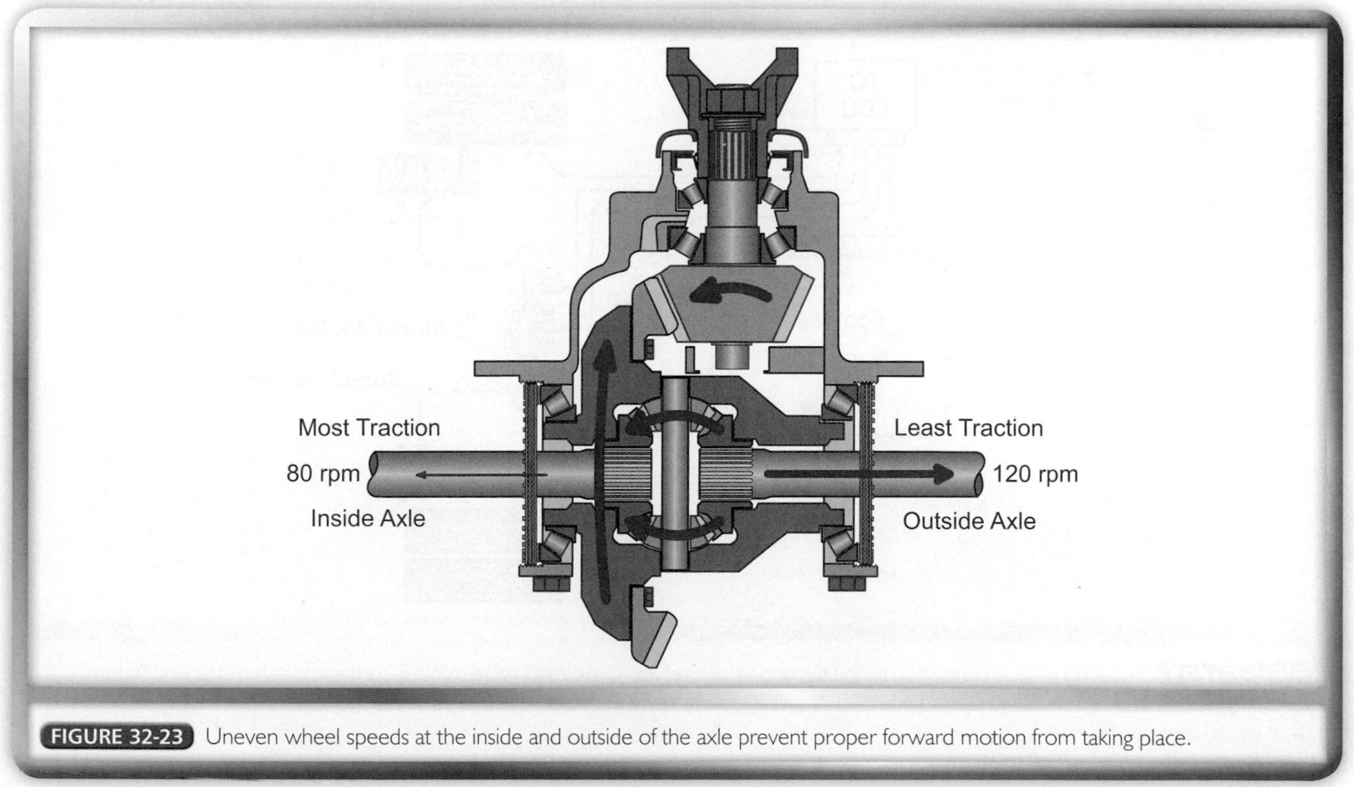

FIGURE 32-23 Uneven wheel speeds at the inside and outside of the axle prevent proper forward motion from taking place.

not signal the ATC valve to apply the brakes even slightly when wheel speed is above 25 mph (40 kph).

Differential Braking

Differential braking is a second strategy used by traction control systems. During differential braking, the brakes are applied on a slipping wheel to transfer torque to a stationary or slowly turning wheel with traction. ABS system components are repurposed independently to apply a single brake to the slipping wheel. Applying one brake on the axle with the slipping wheel will cause drive torque to transfer to a non-slipping wheel through the differential or inter-axle differential. FIGURE 32-24 shows how differential braking redistributes torque.

When a differential braking feature is configured into the system, the ABS ECU energizes a solenoid in the ATC valve that supplies air through the relay valve to each of the rear axle modulators. FIGURE 32-25 illustrates that

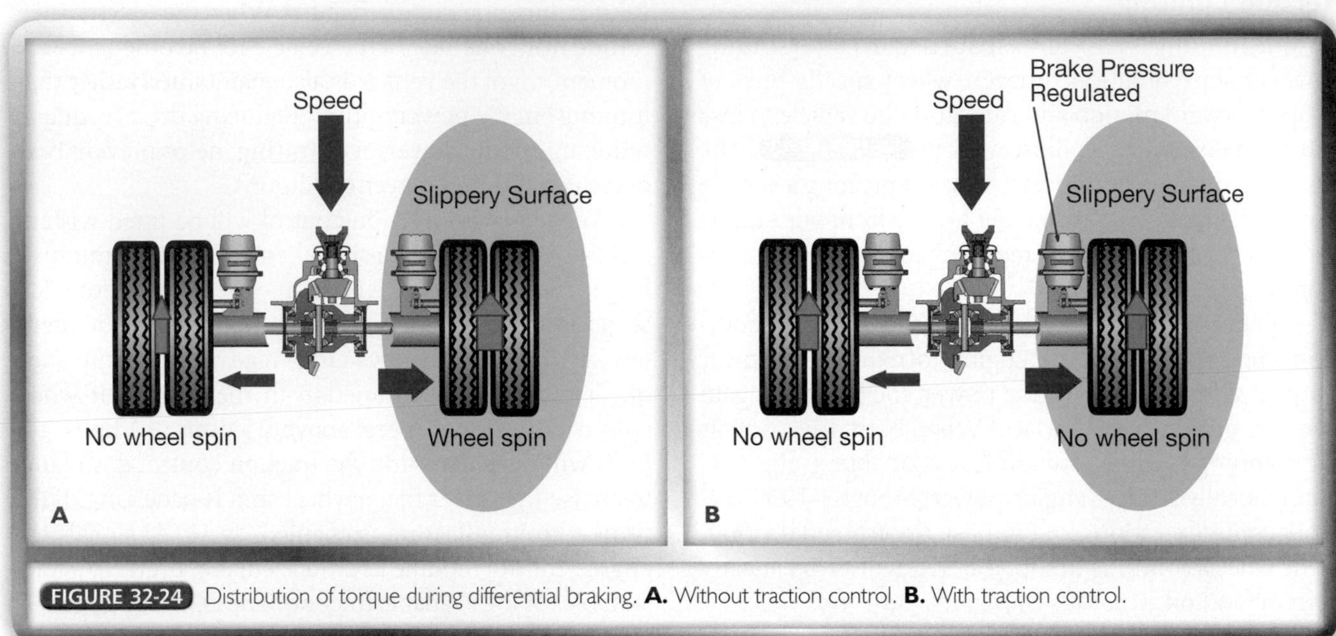

FIGURE 32-24 Distribution of torque during differential braking. **A.** Without traction control. **B.** With traction control.

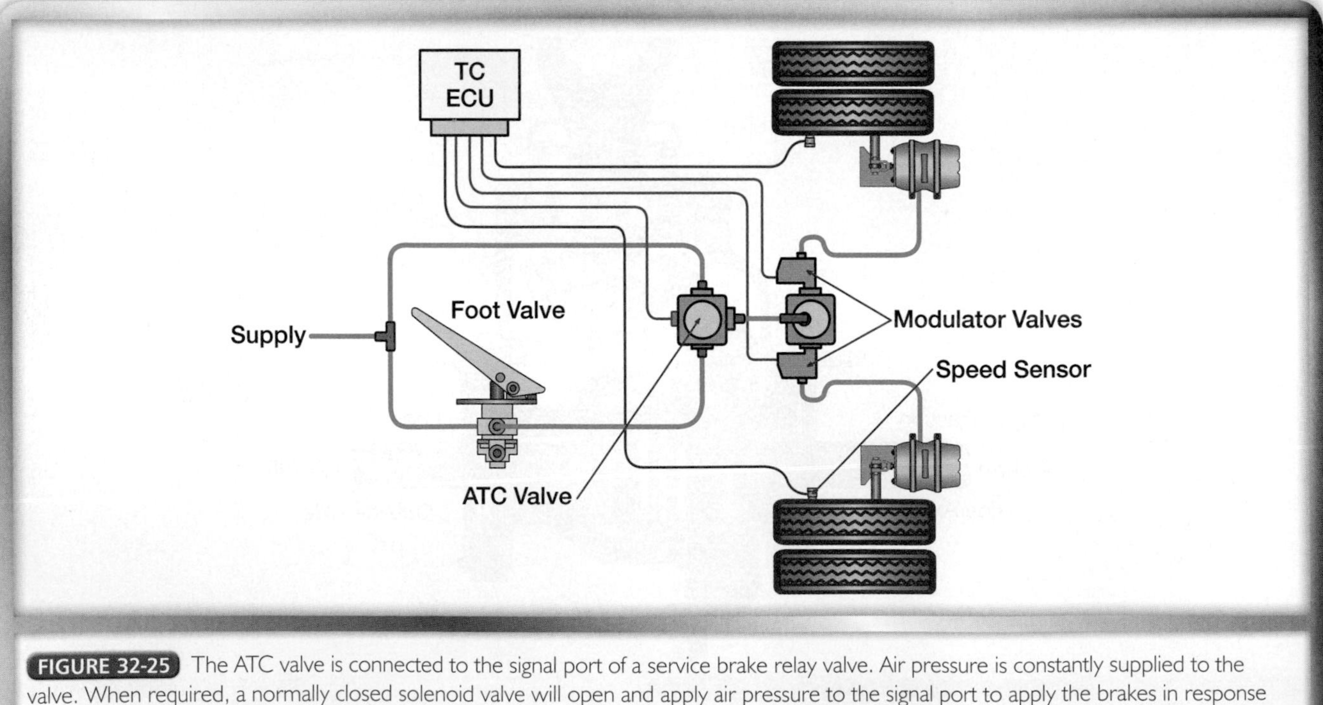

FIGURE 32-25 The ATC valve is connected to the signal port of a service brake relay valve. Air pressure is constantly supplied to the valve. When required, a normally closed solenoid valve will open and apply air pressure to the signal port to apply the brakes in response to an electrical signal.

system. Because the modulators are controlled by the common ECU, the solenoid valves in the appropriate modulator are opened and closed to gently apply and release the brake on the spinning wheel only. The gentle brake application transfers torque from the slipping wheels through the axle differential to drive the stationary or more slowly spinning wheel.

Automatic Traction Control

A designated ATC dash light will illuminate whenever the automatic traction control is activated. Once wheel spin is eliminated, the dash lamp goes out and the traction control system disengages. In some cases, traction control operation is required during extended periods without significant vehicle movement. When that occurs, the traction system will often disable traction control to prevent brake fade. The system will re-enable traction control after a short period of time. In off-road conditions, an off-road ATC strategy will allow more wheel slip in loose sand, mud, snow, and gravel. Generally, allowing more off-road wheel slip minimizes the nuisance of engine de-rating.

Advanced ATC systems will adapt the amount of wheel slip for a particular operating condition by anticipating the driver's intention. More wheel slip is permitted when the accelerator pedal is above a preset threshold than when the vehicle is lightly throttled. Faster acceleration and traction is enabled with this strategy. When driving through a curve, yaw sensors in the ECU will decrease the amount of wheel slip to maintain vehicle stability. Accelerator pedal position is transmitted to the control unit over a J-1939 compliant vehicle network.

Sometimes ATC valves are located on the service brake relay valves as shown in FIGURE 32-26. In this position, they apply air pressure to the signal port in response to a signal from the ABS/ATC control module.

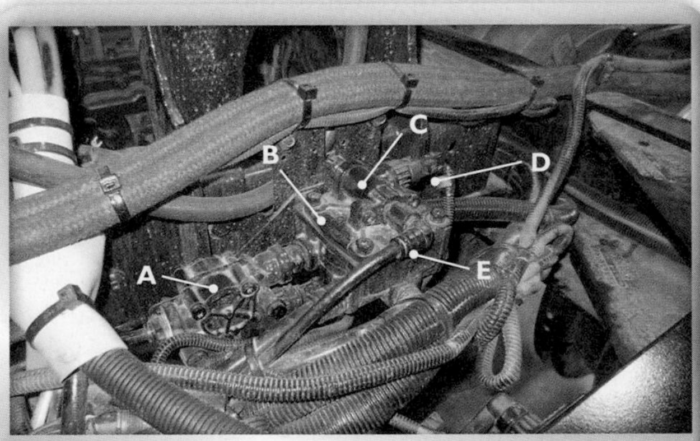

FIGURE 32-26 ATC valves located on the service brake relay valves. **A.** Modulator valve. **B.** Service brake relay valve. **C.** Traction control valve. **D.** Wiring harness. **E.** Air supply from reservoir.

FIGURE 32-27 shows an ECU, a conventional relay valve, and an ATC valve integrated into a single unit.

Stability and Safety Enhancement Systems

Stability and safety enhancement systems include a variety of electronic control systems that use the ABS to minimize the likelihood of vehicle rollovers, collisions, and a loss of directional stability. These advanced technologies vary in their operation and the type of input data used to actively respond to potential danger. Generally, they all monitor driver inputs and the vehicle's operating conditions to alert the driver of an impending collision or rollover. If action is not taken, the systems can de-rate the engine power and, in some circumstances, automatically apply the brakes.

Typical types of stability-safety enhancement systems include:

- roll stability control (RSC)
- directional stability control (DSC)
- collision avoidance systems (CAS)
- adaptive cruise control (ACC)

These systems can be standalone, but more often a variety of features are integrated together to provide varying capabilities depending on sophistication and sensor inputs.

Roll Stability Control (RSC)

Roll stability control (RSC) is a vehicle control system that measures lateral acceleration of a vehicle to minimize the likelihood of a vehicle rollover. With only a couple

FIGURE 32-27 The ECU, conventional relay valve, and ATC valve are integrated into a single unit. **A.** ABS/Traction control module. **B.** ATC valve. **C.** Service brake relay valve.

of additional sensors, ABS systems can be leveraged to minimize the likelihood of a vehicle rollover condition. Sensors measuring steering wheel angle combined with data about vehicle speed and direction are also used to predict the likelihood of a vehicle to rollover. Mathematical algorithms detect whether a vehicle is likely to rollover and a dedicated control module will send messages to de-rate engine power output, and even apply individual brakes on wheels, to slow down sideways slide or lateral vehicle acceleration.

Roll stability systems sense impending rollover conditions. The RSC automatically de-rates the engine and applies brakes to slow the vehicle even before the driver is aware of a potential rollover. The RSC uses data from the wheel speed sensors and from a lateral acceleration sensor, or "G" sensor, located inside a control module to prevent the rollover. The system corrects the vehicle dynamics through a combination of braking, use of an engine retarder, and reduction of engine torque. In addition, an accelerometer measures lateral acceleration encountered during cornering.

The RSC can only minimize the likelihood of an untripped rollover, *not* stop it. **Untripped rollovers** occur when friction is good but a truck strikes a curb and then rolls down an embankment. This type of a rollover condition is tripped and not preventable by the RSC system. If the impact energy from a vehicle collision is high enough and directed at the vehicle's center of gravity, the vehicle can also roll.

Simpler RSC systems will activate only the rear brakes of a tractor or truck through the ATC valve. To provide trailer stability control, a second electrically controlled air valve can be connected between the tractor foot valve and the tractor protection valve to operate the trailer brakes. If a rollover condition is anticipated, the valve will open and supply air from the secondary air reservoir to activate the trailer brakes and minimize the likelihood of a rollover.

More sophisticated trailer rollover protection systems use advanced algorithms, which include estimates of the trailer's mass derived from air pressure in the air suspension system. When the high lateral acceleration situation is detected, the system may briefly and gently apply the trailer brakes to test the rollover potential. If rollover is imminent, the system will simultaneously apply full braking pressure on the outer side of the trailer rolling over and lower application pressure to the brakes on the inner side of the trailer. The wheels on the inside of the curve will be lightly loaded. The centrifugal force of the turn lifts the inside wheels upward away from the ground so, by transferring the weight to the outside tires, the system attempts to prevent the rollover.

Modulation of brake application pressure by the ABS system may also help slow the trailer much faster if the tires are lightly loaded as they lift. If the trailer is stable, the system will recognize that, and no speed change will take place. Note that the driver's braking inputs have priority. If the driver applies the brakes at a greater force than the rollover protection system, the system will switch off. Some trailer rollover stability systems can operate independently of the tractor's braking system, if the tractor is operating with or without its own stability-enhancing system.

> **TECHNICIAN TIP**
>
> When disconnecting or removing the steering column of a vehicle with RSC, it is important to remember that the calibration of the steering wheel angle sensor is a critical input to the RSC algorithm. Brakes can often spontaneously apply when the steering wheel is moved if the sensor adjustment or calibration is disturbed After any service work is done to the steering system, always recalibrate and adjust the steering wheel angle sensor according to OEM procedures.

Directional Stability Control (DSC)

Roll stability systems work best when tires have good road traction, but when traction is poor on slippery surfaces, the risk to stability is yaw control. **Directional stability control systems** assist the driver in maintaining a vehicle's intended driving path by controlling yaw. **Yaw** simply refers to the rotation of a vehicle around its vertical axis. It is the difference between the vehicle's steered (intended) direction and the actual direction of travel.

Ideally, there is never a difference between intended and actual direction of travel. If, however, a vehicle is moving through a curve and its tires lose traction, the tires will slide sideways and the vehicle will have a tendency to spin. Good **yaw control** gives the driver the ability to steer a vehicle through a curve. Without good yaw control, in slippery conditions on a curve, or while turning at high speed, a truck may not respond to steering input. The vehicle may drift out of a lane, or plow out on the curve due to understeer. Or, if a trailer pushes a tractor through a curve, the tractor may rotate too much and the vehicle will jackknife due to oversteer. FIGURE 32-28 shows how DSC affects a vehicle traveling through a curve.

In terms of components, the lateral acceleration sensor in a rollover stability system is upgraded to a yaw sensor in a directional control system. As shown in FIGURE 32-29, directional stability control adds a steering wheel angle sensor, brake application pressure sensor,

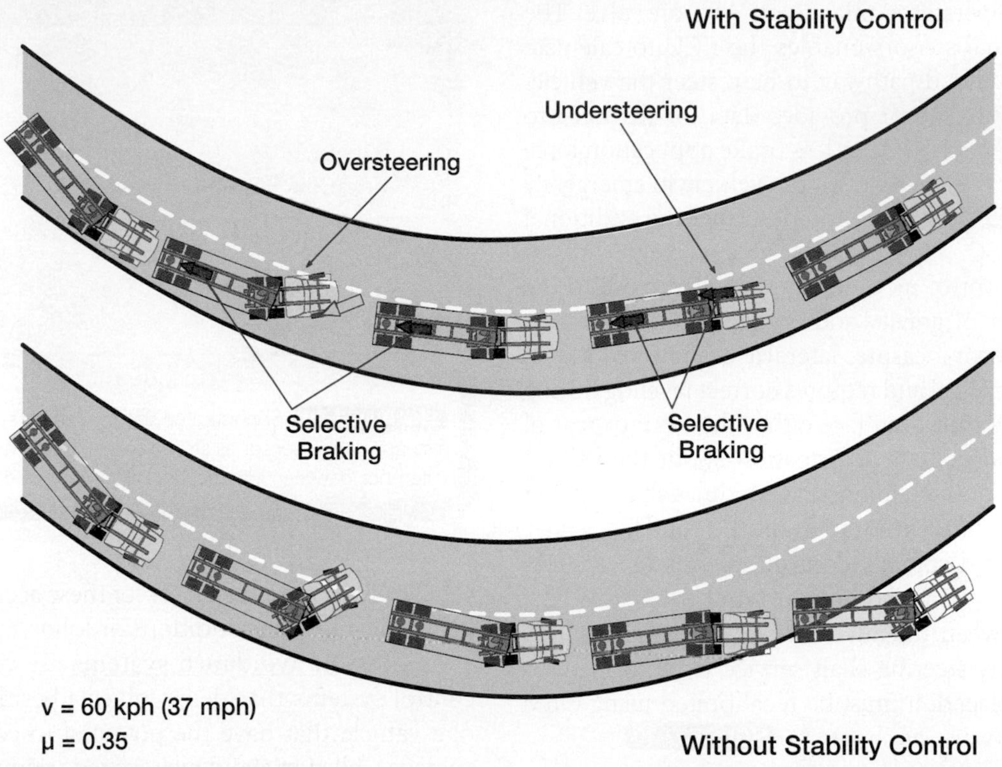

FIGURE 32-28 The ECU will selectively apply individual brakes to maintain directional stability on a curve.

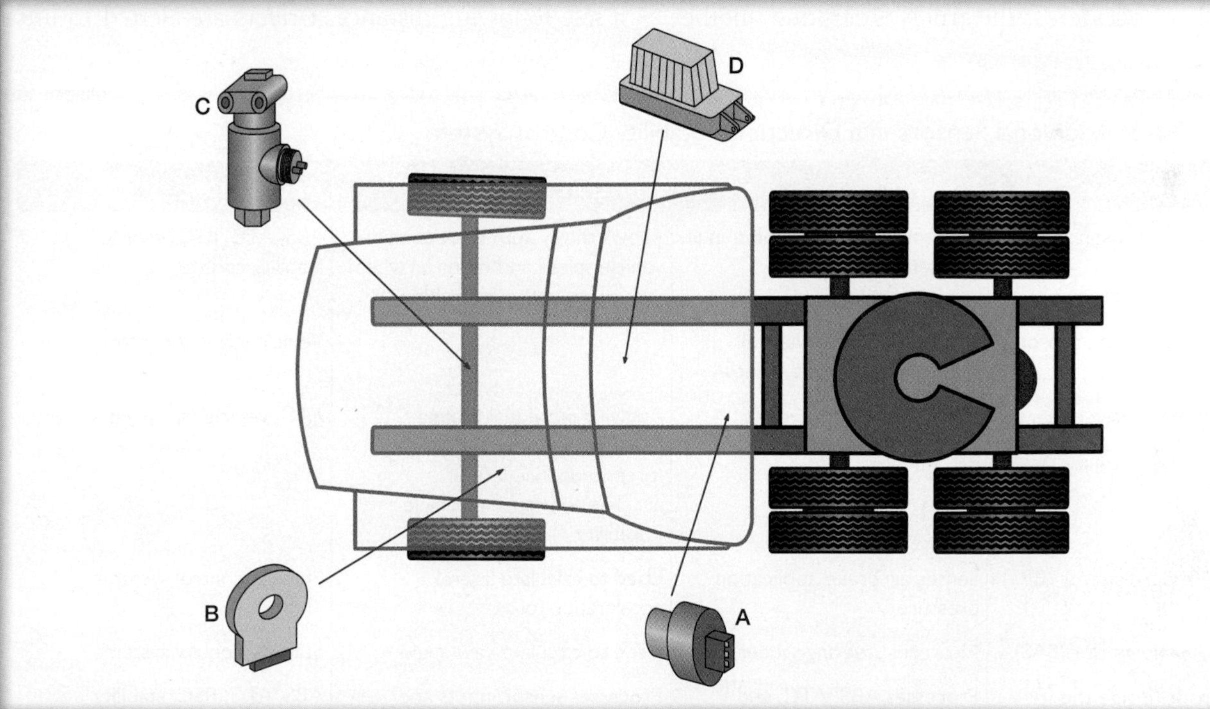

FIGURE 32-29 Components of a typical directional stability control system. **A.** Brake demand pressure sensor. **B.** Steering angle sensor. **C.** Front axle solenoid valve. **D.** ESC module.

and an air supply valve to the front axle modulator valve, which operates similar to an ATC air valve. The use of additional sensors enables the ECU to calculate the driver's intended pathway to help steer the vehicle. A brake pressure sensor provides data for the ECU to calculate how much more or less brake application force is required to precisely control the vehicle in emergency situations. TABLE 32-3 lists and describes the additional sensors in a DSC.

Stability control modules are installed close to the vehicle's center of gravity and contain an internal yaw sensor. The sensor measures lateral acceleration. Module orientation is critical and requires correct leveling during installation. Modules can face either the front or rear of the vehicle and contain information about the vehicle dimensions and other parameters. Modules should never be moved to a different location on the vehicle.

Sophisticated stability control systems use a steering angle sensor as an additional input to measure the difference between intended and actual vehicle direction. When any steering shaft service is performed, or the sensor replaced, it must be recalibrated using OEM diagnostic software, as shown in FIGURE 32-30.

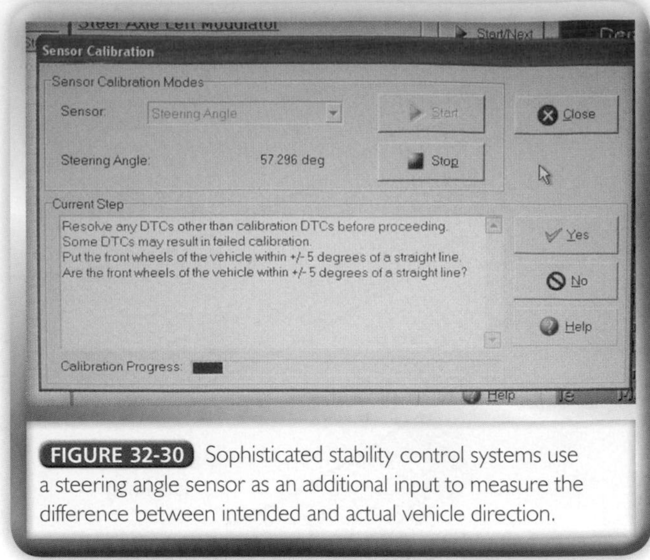

FIGURE 32-30 Sophisticated stability control systems use a steering angle sensor as an additional input to measure the difference between intended and actual vehicle direction.

Collision Avoidance Systems

According to the National Highway Transportation Safety Administration (NHTSA), rear-end collisions account for over 20% of all heavy truck crashes. In approximately 60% of these accidents, the truck is striking another vehicle. Two common causes for these accidents are driving too fast for the conditions or following too closely.

Collision avoidance systems are vehicle stability control systems that detect objects beside and in front of a vehicle that have the potential to collide with the vehicle. Collision avoidance systems minimize the likelihood of collisions two ways. The first is by alerting the driver when a pre-set following distance is shortened. A second feature in some systems is to apply the vehicle's brakes to slow the truck down safely and reestablish a safe following distance. Drivers are alerted to unsafe

TABLE 32-3: Additional Sensors in a Directional Stability Control System

Sensor	Purpose	Function	Application
Wheel speed sensor	Monitors the wheel rotation at individual wheels	Allows the system to determine vehicle speed and monitor wheel lock-up to optimize braking	ABS, ATC, RSC, vehicle stability control
Lateral acceleration sensor (yaw sensor)	Senses the side or lateral forces acting on the vehicle		Vehicle stability control
Active braking valves	Applies individual brakes	Applying individual brakes produces a counter-dynamic force to oppose lateral acceleration causing vehicle instability	ATC, vehicle stability control
Brake pressure sensor (BPS)	Senses air brake application pressure	Used to calculate lateral acceleration force	Stability control systems
Steering angle sensor (SAS)	Measures steering wheel angle	Used to calculate yaw angle	Stability control systems
Yaw sensor (inside the electronic stability control (ESC) module)	Processes ABS, ATC, and stability control data	Processes sensor inputs and produces output signals to modulator valves and warning lights	ABS, ATC, RSC, stability control systems

following distances using audible alarms and by activating the engine brake.

A key component of collision avoidance systems is radar that can detect fixed and moving objects at up to 500' (152 m) away. An electronic control unit collects radar data to determine if another object or vehicle is within the detection range. The ECU calculates the distance to the lead vehicle and the difference in speeds of the two vehicles. The radar can measure the azimuth (direction) of target vehicle and combines that information with data about the road curvature estimated from the tractor's measured yaw rate. The system uses an algorithm to calculate the time to collision and implements a collision avoidance strategy if an object is identified as being in the same lane as the truck. FIGURE 32-31 shows collision avoidance sensors. These sensors can monitor the area in front of a vehicle as well as the side in the driver's blind spot. The additional blind spot sensor can help prevent collision during lane changes.

Adaptive Cruise Control (ACC)

Adaptive cruise control (ACC) is specialized cruise mode that enables the vehicle to recognize potential collisions with vehicles or objects it is following and reduce the vehicle speed. Essentially, it is a non-emergency application of the collision avoidance system. Using the collision avoidance system, a driver can set the adaptive cruise control in one of two ways. The first option is to select the maximum vehicle speed with no objects in front of the vehicle. The second option regulates the cruise control speed according to vehicles in front of the truck or bus. If a vehicle is detected, the cruise control will adjust vehicle speed to maintain a safe travelling distance. The vehicle can de-rate the engine whenever the gap between two vehicles becomes too close, or it can activate the engine brake for a faster reduction in vehicle speed.

The driver operates the ACC system in a manner similar to conventional cruise control (CCC). Rather than selecting a constant speed for the truck to automatically maintain, with ACC, the driver is actually selecting a maximum speed, which the truck will maintain when there is no lead vehicle in the lane in front of the truck. A display screen, such as the one shown in FIGURE 32-32A, keeps the driver informed about the

FIGURE 32-31 Collision avoidance sensors.

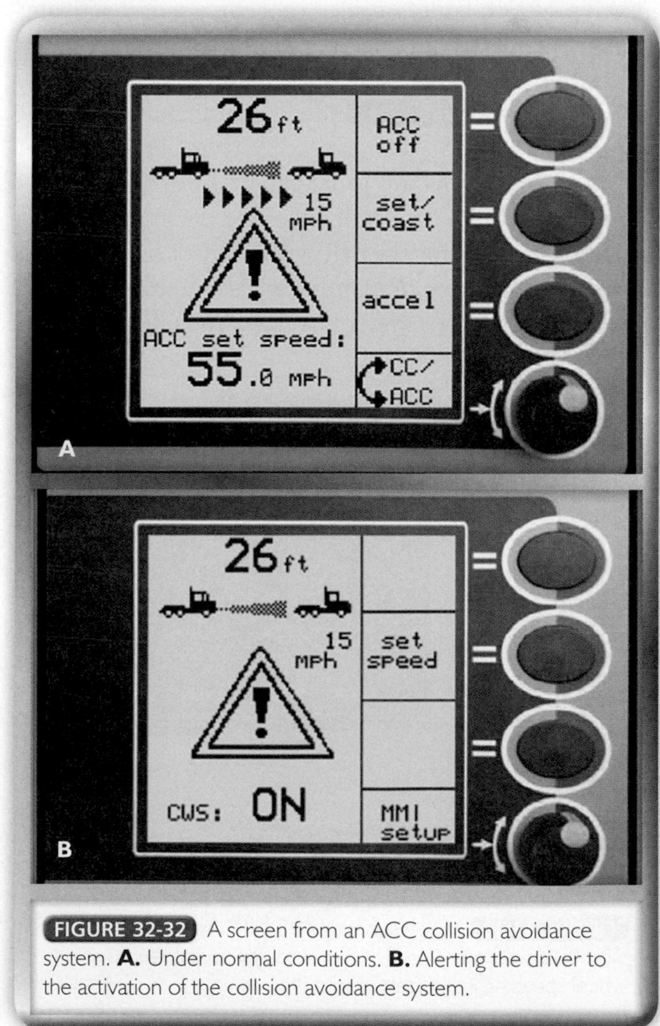

FIGURE 32-32 A screen from an ACC collision avoidance system. **A.** Under normal conditions. **B.** Alerting the driver to the activation of the collision avoidance system.

system's status. The display indicates when the system is active and its maximum set speed. If a lead vehicle is detected, the system tells the driver of the other vehicle's presence, its speed, and the gap between the two vehicles. If the truck is closing on the lead vehicle, as shown on the screen in FIGURE 32-32B, the system will reduce the vehicle speed to match that of the lead vehicle and maintain the following distance. To do so, the system will first decrease engine torque. It can also apply a transmission retarder or engine brake, downshift the transmission (if it is automatic), and apply the service brakes. If the vehicle is closing rapidly, the system can alert the driver through audible and visual signals. When there is a fault, the display also informs the driver, and the system shuts down.

Maintaining Anti-Lock Braking Systems

Basic and enhanced ABS systems and other stability control systems generally have no regular maintenance. OEM software will display system configuration data, active and inactive system faults, service procedures, and activates system outputs to validate operation. Calibration of various stability control system sensors is also performed by the software. FIGURE 32-33 shows the screen from OEM software.

When a system fault is detected, ABS and ATC functions may be fully or partially disabled depending on the fault code. Often only the axle with a sensor or modulator fault will be disabled; remaining axles will still be operating. In a four-sensor system, ABS on the affected wheel is disabled, but ABS on all other wheels remains active. In a six-sensor tractor system, one sensor fault enables the ABS system to remain active by using input from the remaining rear wheel speed sensor on the same side. The ATC will, however, be disabled. TABLE 32-4 shows the impact of faults in different sensors.

FIGURE 32-33 When servicing ABS, ATC, and ESC systems, diagnostic software is used to measure system data such as wheel speed as well as test output devices.

Sensor adjustments on anti-lock braking systems require special attention anytime the wheel ends are disturbed, such as during a brake service. When removed, sensor clips should be lubricated with dielectric type grease. This is grease that is non-electrically conductive; not chassis grease. In some instances, sensors require special attention:

- Steering Angle Sensors (SAS)—Whenever front-end alignment or steering system work is performed, Steering Angle Sensors (SAS) need recalibration.
- Yaw Rate Sensor—Whenever the electronic control module is removed or disturbed in any way, it must be reinstalled in the same precise location and in the same orientation. A recalibration process using OEM software is used.
- Stability Control Modules—These contain an internal yaw sensor and should never be moved to a different location on the vehicle.
- Front Sensor of CAS—Shown in FIGURE 32-34, this sensor is located in the front bumper and can easily be misaligned when the bumper contacts other objects. The sensor requires directional calibration to ensure it is aimed at the correct point in front of the vehicle on the roadway.
- Sensor air gap—Loss of correct sensor air gap is a common ABS-related complaint. Sensors should be checked to see whether they are firmly in place and whether loose wheel bearings may be interfering with the air gap.

Another common check to perform is on the lamps. Ensure the ABS malfunction lights are operating every time the vehicle is started. When the ignition is switched on, the ABS lamp should illuminate momentarily. The tractor ABS lamp can also be used to display tractor blink code diagnostics. The ATC and RSC/ESC functions may use the same dash indicator lamp, so understanding how the ABS and ATC/RSC/ESC lamps work is important. Generally, if the vehicle is equipped with ATC—but not RSC/ESC—the ABS and ATC lamps will illuminate for approximately three seconds when the ignition is turned to the ON position and then both go out together. When equipped with ATC and RSC/ESC, both lamps illuminate when the ignition is switched on but the ATC/RSC/ESC lamp will stay on a moment longer after the ABS lamp goes out.

TABLE 32-4: Fault Location and Impact on Anti-lock Braking System

	System Still Operating (Yes/No)					
	ABS Front		ABS Rear			
Failed Device	Left	Right	Left	Right	Traction	Standard Braking
RF Sensor	Yes	Yes	Yes	Yes	No	Yes
RM Sensor	Yes	Yes	Yes	Yes	No	Yes
LF Sensor	Yes	Yes	Yes	Yes	No	Yes
LM Sensor	Yes	Yes	Yes	Yes	No	Yes
RR Sensor	Yes	Yes	Yes	No	No	Yes
LR Sensor	Yes	Yes	No	Yes	No	Yes
RF Modulator	Yes	No	Yes	Yes	Yes	Yes
LF Modulator	No	Yes	Yes	Yes	Yes	Yes
RR Modulator	Yes	Yes	Yes	No	No	Yes
LR Modulator	Yes	Yes	No	Yes	No	Yes
Controller	No	No	No	No	No	Yes
Traction Solenoid	Yes	Yes	Yes	Yes	No	Yes
Engine Control Module[1]	Yes	Yes	Yes	Yes	No	Yes
Voltage[2]	No	No	No	No	No	Yes

[1] ABS is available in six-sensor system if mid sensor is functional.
[2] When ECM voltage or wiring "corrects" itself, system is restored.

Finally, the ABS/ATC control modules require a precise rolling circumference ratio between steer axle and drive axle tires in order for ABS and ATC to perform properly. Therefore, tire size should be regularly calibrated with the system. A default tire ratio value of 1.00 is programmed into the unit. If the automatic tire size alignment calculates a different value, the original value is overwritten in the memory to adapt the ABS and ATC function with different tire sizes on the vehicle.

TECHNICIAN TIP

During dynamometer testing of a vehicle, the ATC must be disabled. This deactivates the ATC brake torque transfer and engine de-rate strategies used by the ECM. A test mode is used to avoid torque reduction or torque increase and brake activation when the vehicle is on a dynamometer.

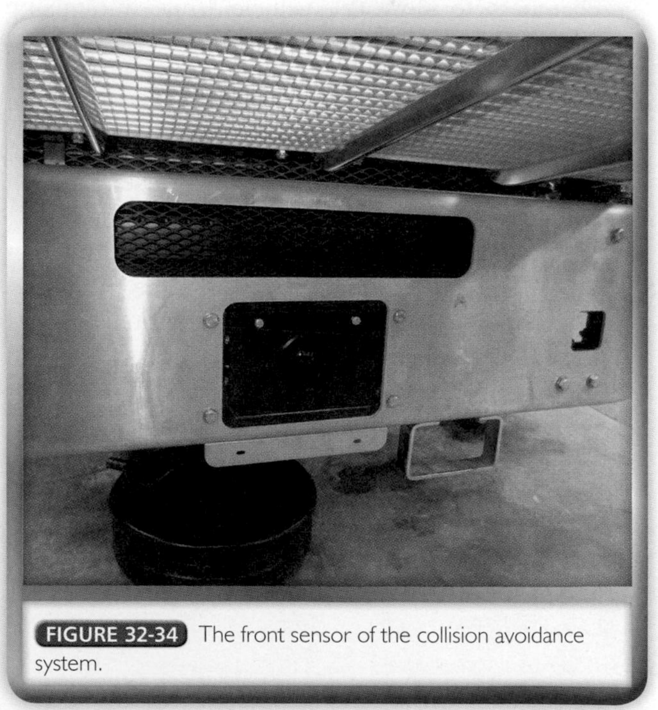

FIGURE 32-34 The front sensor of the collision avoidance system.

Wrap-up

Ready to Review

- Vehicle control, steering, and braking is better maintained when tires are rolling rather than locked. Anti-lock braking systems (ABS) monitor and automatically limit wheel lock-up events during vehicle braking.
- Tractor jackknife or trailer swing-out condition is minimized using ABS. Jackknifing can take place when the tractor brakes lock-up and the trailer pushes the tractor around the kingpin. Trailer swing-out happens when the trailer brakes lock and the trailer drifts into another lane.
- Automatic traction control, automatic slip regulation, and electronic stability control are names given to the same refinement to the ABS system, which prevents drive wheels from slipping, losing traction, or breaking free from road contact due to excessive drive torque.
- Wheel speed sensors measure tire speed and are used by the ABS electronic control unit to calculate an impending wheel lock-up event.
- Modulator valves are electrically controlled air valves that either exhaust, hold, or build-up air pressure in the brake chambers. The ABS ECU regulates the operation of the modulator valves to limit wheel speed lock-up by maintaining the optimal amount of air pressure in the service brake chambers to slow the vehicle while minimizing wheel speed lock-up.
- The ABS malfunction light will illuminate whenever a fault occurs in the ABS system. Fault codes can be extracted from the ABS ECU through the ABS malfunction light, which blinks out a sequence of short and long light flashes.
- A tractor requires a separate in-dash malfunction indicator lamp for the trailer ABS. The trailer has a yellow ABS malfunction light located on the left, lower, rear quarter of the trailer, which will illuminate whenever there is a fault in the trailer ABS.
- PLC for trucks is a communication technology that transmits data from the trailer ABS ECU to the tractor. The data is carried over the #7 blue wire.
- Power for the trailer ABS ECU is supplied by the dedicated current flow on #7 blue wire of the J-560 trailer plug. The stop lamp circuit #4 on the J-560 plug can also supply power to the trailer ABS when the brakes are applied. Trailer ABS cords are color coded green and have different sized conductors than non-ABS trailer cords.
- Wheel speed data processed by the ABS ECU is used by many other vehicle modules when it is shared over the J-1939 on-board network.
- Traction control systems use ABS system components plus the addition of an electrically signaled air valve, which supplies air to the modulator valve.
- Wheel slip caused by excessive driver torque is reduced by the traction control system in two ways. The first is to reduce engine power output. The second is to apply the brakes on the wheel end that has lost traction. Braking the slipping wheel transfers torque to other wheels through the differentials.
- Yaw refers to the difference between the vehicle's steered direction of travel and the actual direction it is moving. A yaw sensor is used by a directional stability control system to detect whether the vehicle may slide laterally from its lane.
- Stability control systems help prevent vehicle rollovers. By adding a steering wheel angle sensor and a lateral acceleration rate sensor to the traction control system, brakes can be selectively applied automatically to affected wheels and the engine de-rated to prevent a rollover.
- Directional control systems share similar hardware to stability control systems. The stability control system uses a lateral acceleration sensor, but the directional stability system uses a yaw sensor to measure the difference between the vehicle's intended steered pathway and its actual direction.
- Collision avoidance systems use radar technology to detect obstacles the vehicle could potentially collide with. The collision detection system can be integrated into the cruise control system to slow a vehicle down or even brake if a collision is impending.

Vocabulary Builder

adaptive cruise control (ACC) A specialized cruise mode that enables the vehicle to recognize potential collisions with vehicles or objects it is following and reduce the vehicle speed.

anti-lock braking system (ABS) An electronic control system that works with the service brake system to monitor and automatically limit wheel lock-up events during vehicle braking.

automatic slip regulation (ASR) A traction control system that minimizes wheel spin.

automatic traction control (ATC) A traction control system that minimizes wheel slip or spin due to excessive drive torque. Also called *electronic stability regulation (ESR)*.

blink code A method of providing fault code data for a specific system that involves counting the number of flashes from a warning lamp and observing longer pauses between the light blinks. Also called *flash code*.

collision avoidance system A vehicle stability control system that detects objects beside and in front of a vehicle that have the potential to collide with the vehicle.

de-rate Reducing drive torque by reducing engine power; used as strategy to reduce wheel slip, or loss of directional control.

differential braking Applying the brakes on an individual slipping wheel to transfer torque to a stationary or slowly turning wheel with traction.

directional stability control systems A stability control system that assists the driver in maintaining a vehicle's intended driving path by controlling yaw.

electronic stability regulation (ESR) A vehicle control system that minimizes the likelihood of a rollover, loss of vehicle direction, and wheel slip. Also called *automatic traction control (ATC)*.

fishtailing A condition when the drive axles of a vehicle push the rear of a vehicle and steering control is lost. Also called *power jackknifing*.

flash code A strategy used by ECUs to report fault codes by flashing or blinking fault lamps, using long and short pauses between the light flashes to represent numerical fault codes. Also called *blink code*.

ISO 3731 connector A type of connector commonly used in Europe that uses dedicated pins to transmit ABS information between the tractor and trailer.

J-560 trailer connector A trailer cord plug and receptacle located at the rear of the tractor.

modulator valve An electrically operated ABS air control valve used to modulate the air pressure supplied to service brake chambers.

power jackknife A condition when the drive axles of a vehicle push the rear of a vehicle and steering control is lost. Also called *fishtailing*.

power line carrier (PLC) technology A data transmission technology enabling data exchange between the tractor and trailer ABS.

reluctor wheel The toothed wheel mounted on the wheel hub, which is used by the wheel speed sensor to generate wheel speed data. Also called the *exciter ring*.

roll stability control (RSC) A vehicle control system that measures lateral acceleration of a vehicle to minimize the likelihood of a vehicle rollover.

SAE J-560 standard The SAE standards for the configuration of trailer electrical cables and plugs.

torque limiting A reduction in engine power out; used as strategy to reduce wheel slip or loss of directional control.

traction control An enhancement to the ABS system that is used to improve vehicle stability when accelerating.

untripped rollovers A vehicle rollover condition occurring when a truck strikes a curb and then rolls down an embankment.

variable reluctance sensor A sensor used to measure rotational speed, including wheel speed, vehicle speed, engine speed, and camshaft and crankshaft position.

wheel lock-up A condition where the drive or steer tires have stopped rotating when braking.

wheel slip A condition in which excess torque from the drivetrain causes the tire to break free from the road surface. Also called *wheel spin*.

wheel spin A condition in which excess torque from the drivetrain causes the tire to break free from the road surface. Also called *wheel slip*.

yaw The rotation of a vehicle around its vertical axis; the difference between the vehicle's intended direction and the actual direction of travel.

yaw control Minimizing the slip or difference between the desired or steered direction of a vehicle and actual direction a vehicle is moving.

Review Questions

1. Air anti-lock brake systems minimize wheel lock-up by:
   a. exhausting air pressure from service brake chambers.
   b. holding air pressure in service brake chambers.
   c. supplying air chambers with air during braking events.
   d. All the choices are correct.
2. Consider a tractor and semitrailer combination vehicle. If the tractor were equipped with an ABS brake system but the trailer were not, which of the following situations would most likely occur under a hard braking condition?
   a. Jackknife
   b. Oversteer
   c. Understeer
   d. Trailer swing-out
3. What type of electrical signal is supplied to the ABS ECU by wheel speed sensors?
   a. Digital
   b. Serial data J-1939
   c. Low voltage DC current
   d. Low voltage AC current
4. ABS modulator valves contain:
   a. an electrically controlled inlet and exhaust valve.
   b. only an electrically controlled air inlet valve.
   c. only an electrically controlled exhaust valve.
   d. a normally closed inlet and exhaust valve.
5. Traction control systems minimize wheel slip by:
   a. reducing engine power when the wheels spin.
   b. selectively applying brakes to slipping or spinning wheels.
   c. modulating brake pressure to wheels with traction.
   d. selectively braking wheels and reducing engine power.
6. A lateral acceleration sensor, or "G" sensor, is a system input sensor used by the:
   a. ABS system.
   b. automatic traction control (ATC) system.
   c. roll stability control (RSC) system.
   d. directional stability control (DSC) system.
7. A yaw sensor is an input used by the directional stability control system to:
   a. detect whether the vehicle's center of gravity has become too high.
   b. measure the steering wheel angle.
   c. measure the difference between "steered" and actual vehicle direction.
   d. measure the rotation of a tractor around the trailer kingpin.
8. Which of the following is the air gap setting for a typical truck wheel speed sensor?
   a. 0.005"
   b. 0.010"
   c. 0.015"
   d. There is no air gap setting.
9. Which of the following is not a stage of anti-lock operation during a potential skid situation?
   a. Hold pressure
   b. Air bleeding
   c. Exhaust pressure
   d. Reapply pressure
10. Automatic traction control brake application will normally not occur when which of the following conditions exist?
    a. Road speeds above 25 mph (40 kph)
    b. Road speeds below 5 mph (8 kph)
    c. Only when there is a system malfunction
    d. When only one wheel is spinning

ASE-Type Questions

1. Technician A says that the ABS system only exhausts air pressure from a selected brake chamber when the wheel is about to lock-up or has locked-up. Technician B says that the modulator valve can exhaust, hold, and rebuild air pressure in a service chamber when the wheels are approaching lock-up or have locked-up. Who is correct?
   a. Technician A
   b. Technician B
   c. Both Technician A and Technician B
   d. Neither Technician A nor Technician B
2. Technician A says that a modulator code fault could be caused by a defective solenoid inside the valve. Technician B says a modulator fault code can be caused by a misadjusted slack adjuster. Who is correct?
   a. Technician A
   b. Technician B
   c. Both Technician A and Technician B
   d. Neither Technician A nor Technician B
3. Technician A says that an ABS trailer electrical cord is color coded green. Technician B says that trailer electrical cords are different only as to the wire size of the conductors. Who is correct?
   a. Technician A
   b. Technician B
   c. Both Technician A and Technician B
   d. Neither Technician A nor Technician B
4. Technician A says that anti-lock braking systems improve vehicle control even though they increase stopping distance. Technician B says that, in today's vehicles, anti-lock braking systems usually incorporate some kind of traction control. Who is correct?
   a. Technician A
   b. Technician B
   c. Both Technician A and Technician B
   d. Neither Technician A nor Technician B
5. Technician A says that wheel speed sensors are usually Hall-effect sensors. Technician B says that wheel speed sensors create a digital signal. Who is correct?
   a. Technician A
   b. Technician B
   c. Both Technician A and Technician B
   d. Neither Technician A nor Technician B
6. Technician A says that ABS systems are regulated under FMVSS 121. Technician B says that every axle of a tractor trailer system must have ABS. Who is correct?
   a. Technician A
   b. Technician B
   c. Both Technician A and Technician B
   d. Neither Technician A nor Technician B
7. Technician A says that ABS systems must have a red warning lamp on the dash that lights up when an ABS system malfunction occurs. Technician B says the ABS warning lamp must come on for a few seconds when the key is switched on and then go out if the system is functioning correctly. Who is correct?
   a. Technician A
   b. Technician B
   c. Both Technician A and Technician B
   d. Neither Technician A nor Technician B
8. Technician A says that, since March 2001, vehicles that tow ABS equipped trailers must show a trailer ABS malfunction on a dash indicator light. Technician B says that trailer ABS systems communicate with the tractor by using power line carrier technology. Who is correct?
   a. Technician A
   b. Technician B
   c. Both Technician A and Technician B
   d. Neither Technician A nor Technician B
9. Technician A says that tractor ABS modulator valve solenoids are cycled when the ignition is first turned on. Technician B says that applying the brake pedal and then switching the ignition on allows the operator to check that the solenoids are exhausting air as they should. Who is correct?
   a. Technician A
   b. Technician B
   c. Both Technician A and Technician B
   d. Neither Technician A nor Technician B
10. Technician A says that blink codes must always be used to check for ABS system malfunctions. Technician B says that ABS wheel sensor air gap is set by loosening a lock nut and then adjusting the gap. Who is correct?
    a. Technician A
    b. Technician B
    c. Both Technician A and Technician B
    d. Neither Technician A nor Technician B

CHAPTER 33

NATEF Tasks

Brakes

Hydraulic Brakes—Hydraulic System	Page
■ Inspect and test brake pressure differential valve and warning light circuit switch, bulbs/LEDs, wiring, and connectors; repair or replace as needed.	1079, 1096
■ Inspect and test master cylinder for internal/external leaks and damage; replace as needed.	1091
■ Identify poor stopping, premature wear, pulling, dragging, balance, or pedal feel problems caused by the hydraulic system; determine needed action.	1091–1093
■ Inspect hydraulic system brake lines, flexible hoses, and fittings for leaks and damage; replace as needed.	1091, 1094
■ Inspect and test metering (hold-off), load sensing/proportioning, proportioning, and combination valves; replace as needed.	1096
■ Inspect/test brake fluid; bleed and/or flush system; determine proper fluid type.	1096
■ Inspect disc brake caliper assemblies; replace as needed.	1097
Hydraulic Brakes—Mechanical/Foundation	
■ Check parking brake operation; inspect parking brake application and holding devices; adjust and replace as needed.	1086–1087
■ Identify poor stopping, brake noise, premature wear, pulling, grabbing, dragging, or pedal feel problems; determine needed action.	1092, 1095
■ Inspect and measure rotors; perform needed action.	1097
■ Inspect and measure disc brake pads; inspect mounting hardware; perform needed action.	1097
Hydraulic Brakes—Power Assist Units	
■ Check emergency (back-up, reserve) brake assist system.	1081–1083

Fundamentals of Hydraulic and Air-Over-Hydraulic Braking Systems

NATEF Tasks, continued

Brakes Hydraulic Brakes—Power Assist Units, continued	Page
■ Inspect, test, repair, or replace hydraulic brake assist (booster), hoses, and control valves; determine proper fluid type.	1082–1083
■ Identify stopping problems caused by the brake assist (booster) system; determine needed action.	1080–1086
Air and Hydraulic Anti-Lock Brake Systems (ABS) and Automatic Traction Control	
■ Bleed the ABS hydraulic circuits.	1097
Preventative Maintenance and Inspection Hydraulic Brakes	
■ Inspect brake assist system (booster), hoses, and control valves; check reservoir fluid level and condition.	1081–1082
■ Check parking brake operation; inspect parking brake application and holding devices; adjust as needed.	1086–1088
■ Inspect brake lines, fittings, flexible hoses, and valves for leaks and damage.	1091
■ Check master cylinder fluid level and condition.	1093
■ Check operation of hydraulic system: pedal travel, pedal effort, pedal feel.	1093
■ Inspect calipers for leakage, binding, and damage.	1093

Knowledge Objectives

After reading this chapter, you will be able to:

1. Understand fundamental configurations for braking systems. (pp 1069–1070)
2. Identify braking system components. (pp 1071–1080)
3. Describe wheel brake actuators and associated components. (pp 1071–1072)
4. Describe hand/emergency brakes. (p 1074)
5. Describe hydraulic and air-over-hydraulic brake system components. (pp 1075–1080, 1082–1086)
6. Identify and describe hydroboost systems. (pp 1081–1082, 1093)
7. Describe the air-over-hydraulic braking system. (pp 1082–1086)
8. Remove and replace heavy-duty vehicle (HDV) brake components. (pp 1092–1097)

Skills Objectives

After reading this chapter, you will be able to:

1. Inspect hydraulic and air-over-hydraulic brake systems for fluid leaks. (p 1091) SKILL DRILL 33-1
2. Remove and replace an air-over-hydraulic master cylinder/actuator. (p 1092) SKILL DRILL 33-2
3. Remove and replace a dual-circuit master cylinder in a vacuum or hydroboost-assisted hydraulic braking system. (p 1093) SKILL DRILL 33-3
4. Remove and replace a drum brake assembly. (p 1094) SKILL DRILL 33-4
5. Test a treadle valve for leakage. (p 1094) SKILL DRILL 33-5
6. Bleed the air out of a hydraulic braking system. (p 1095) SKILL DRILL 33-6
7. Test the metering or the proportioning valve. (p 1096) SKILL DRILL 33-7
8. Test pressure differential valves. (p 1096) SKILL DRILL 33-8
9. Bleed a hydraulic ABS system. (p 1097) SKILL DRILL 33-9
10. Inspect, measure, remove, and reinstall a rotor assembly. (p 1097) SKILL DRILL 33-10

Introduction

Vehicle manufacturers must comply with government braking-performance regulations. To meet these standards, regardless of whether the brakes are air or hydraulically actuated, the manufacturer must carefully design the brake geometry, size, and power of the foundation brake components.

As heavy-duty vehicle (HDV) gross weight and available road speeds have increased over the years, regulations have required manufacturers to install more powerful systems of braking to maintain vehicle safety. A vehicle's braking system must meet the following requirements:

- To adequately and safely reduce a vehicle's speed, when required to do so
- To maintain vehicle speed on downhill gradients
- To be able to hold a vehicle stationary, even when on a gradient and the driver is away from the vehicle

An HDV hydraulic braking system's components and layout can vary, according to the vehicle's design and intended use. Generally, systems are more complex on larger vehicles than on their smaller counterparts. The principal functions of braking requirements are the same, however. Simply put, a brake is a mechanical device that inhibits motion by using friction. Although hydraulic brake systems are not common on heavy-duty vehicles in North America, they can be found on special applications such as school buses and other medium-duty vehicles. Hydraulic brake systems are also quite popular on medium-duty vehicles in other parts of the world. This chapter will focus on the basics of hydraulic brake systems and the various power-assist components used with hydraulic brakes.

Fundamental Configurations for Hydraulic Braking Systems

The heavy-duty braking system is a mechanical device that has been augmented by the addition of a power assistance component to increase braking effort.

Medium- and heavy-duty braking systems will include a foundation hydraulic braking system. Regardless of the type of power assist they use, all hydraulic brake systems include the same basic components. This basic hydraulic system will be augmented by one of two types of power assist or boost methods: a vacuum booster or a hydroboost hydraulic system.

The **vacuum booster** hydraulic braking system is predominantly found on medium-duty commercial vehicles. One of the main reasons for this system is the lower cost factor for the vehicle range. With these vehicles, the engine of choice is a diesel engine. For this reason, manufacturers must incorporate an engine-driven vacuum pump into air-over-hydraulic braking systems. The system uses this vacuum to operate the vacuum booster that provides power assistance to the braking system.

Hydroboost systems are found on many Class 4 to Class 6 commercial vehicles. The hydroboost system uses pressurized hydraulic fluid to provide brake power assist. The hydraulic pressure is supplied by the vehicle's power steering pump or by a dedicated hydraulic pump. Some lighter-duty vehicles use pressure supplied by an electric motor. As the driver presses the brake pedal, a valve is opened inside the hydraulic booster, allowing pressurized hydraulic fluid to act on a piston. This action increases the brake application effort.

You Are the Technician

You are employed in a transport company's workshop. Their fleet is a mixture of medium to heavy and heavy vehicles. They have over 50 trucks operating out of your facilities. One of the company driver's comes into the workshop and complains that the brakes on his vehicles do not feel right. You confirm the complaint—the vehicle's brakes appear not to be up to specifications. Explain why you might use each of the following procedures to diagnose the problem.

1. Why might you check the type of braking system installed on the truck?
2. Why might you study the service manual for the particular brake system?
3. Would you check for any recall bulletins that could have been issued? Why or why not?

Air-Over-Hydraulic Braking Systems

Air-over-hydraulic braking systems use an air compressor to provide power assistance over the hydraulic components to the braking system. Air-over-hydraulic systems come in two broad categories distinguished by the systems control circuit. The first type is the hydraulically controlled system. This system will have all of the same air brake supply components as full air brake systems that were covered in the chapter Air Brake Foundation Systems and Air Brake Circuits—a compressor, air dryer reservoir tanks, and lines. Air-over-hydraulic systems also use an air treadle (foot) valve to send air pressure directly or indirectly to air boosters that actuate hydraulic master cylinders to apply the brakes.

Hydraulic Braking Systems

All hydraulic braking systems on light- to medium-duty commercial vehicles include the following major components:

- A brake pedal or lever
- A pushrod (also called an actuating rod)
- A master cylinder assembly containing a piston assembly (made up of either one or two pistons, a series of seals, O-rings, and a fluid reservoir)
- Reinforced hydraulic lines
- Disc brake assemblies at each of the wheels consist of a brake caliper that actuates a pair of brake pads onto a **rotor** (which is also known as a brake disc) or **wheel cylinders** that actuate **brake shoes** onto a **brake drum** that is attached to an axle shaft. In both cases, the actuation of the brake pads or shoes is designed to bring the vehicle to a controlled halt.
- The hydraulic brake system is usually filled with a glycol-ether-based **brake fluid**. However, other fluids may also be used, depending on the particular application.

In a hydraulic brake system, when the brake pedal is pressed, a pushrod exerts force on the piston(s) in the master cylinder, causing fluid from the brake fluid reservoir to flow into a pressure chamber through a compensating port. This results in an increase in the pressure of the entire hydraulic system. This forces fluid through the hydraulic lines toward the disc brake calipers and drum brake wheel cylinders, where the fluid force acts upon the pistons. The pistons are sealed by O-rings, which prevent the escape of any fluid from around the pistons.

The brake caliper pistons then apply force to the brake pads and brake shoes to push them against the spinning rotor or drum **FIGURE 33-1**. The friction between the pads/shoes and the rotating surfaces generates a braking torque to slow the vehicle. Heat generated by this friction

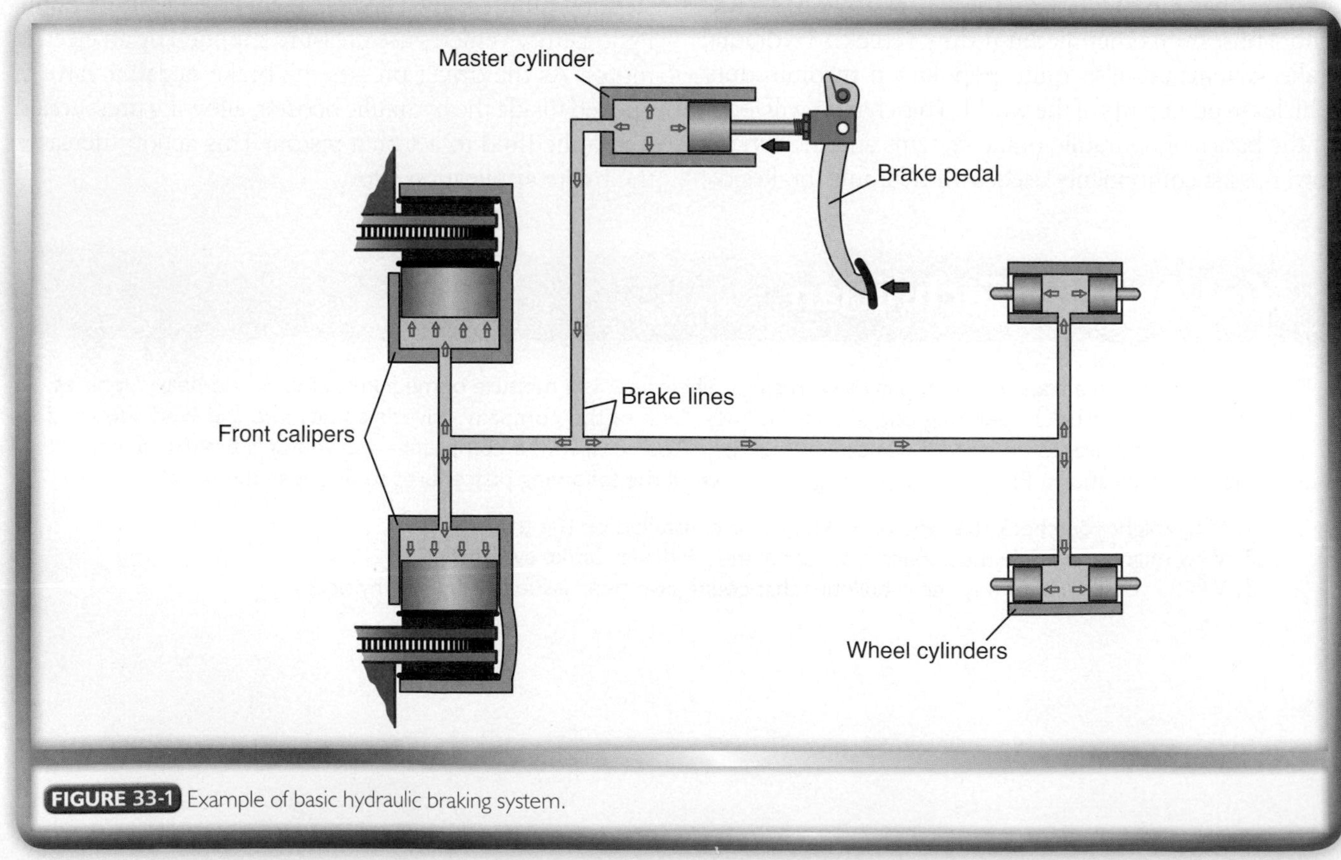

FIGURE 33-1 Example of basic hydraulic braking system.

is either dissipated through vents and channels in the rotors and drums or conducted through the pads/linings, which are made of specialized heat-tolerant materials, such as Kevlar™ or sintered glass.

Subsequent release of the brake pedal/lever allows a spring(s) to return the master piston(s) back into position. This relieves the hydraulic pressure on the **calipers** and wheel cylinders, allowing the brake pistons in the assemblies to slide back into their housings and release the brakes.

The hydraulic braking system is designed as a closed system. Unless there is a leak in the system, none of the brake fluid enters or leaves it, nor is the fluid consumed through use. In a major update in later vehicles, manufacturers introduced split braking systems. A **front/rear split system** uses one master cylinder section to pressurize the front caliper pistons and the other section to pressurize the rear caliper pistons. A split circuit braking system is now required by law in most countries for safety reasons; if one circuit fails, the other circuit can stop the vehicle.

Foundation Components of Hydraulic Braking Systems

Braking systems are complex, and their components depend in large measure on whether the system uses drum or disc brakes. Drum brakes use brake shoes in various configurations and adjusters. By contrast, disc brakes use pads. This section will explain the different components of each type of foundation braking system.

Drum Brakes

Drum brakes were once common on all wheels, but now less so. Today, drum arrangements are usually used on just the rear wheels, with disc brakes on the front in a disc/drum configuration.

The drum brake has two brake shoes with an attached lining made of friction material. These shoes expand against a brake drum's inside surface and slow the wheel down. The harder the linings are forced against the brake drum, the higher the braking force that is applied. They can be expanded mechanically or hydraulically.

The main advantage claimed for drum brakes is that the shoe mountings can be designed to assist their own operation. This is called self-energizing. Less hydraulic pressure is then needed to stop the vehicle, which is why many older drum-braked vehicles didn't need a power-assist system.

The main disadvantage of drum brakes is that the friction area is almost entirely covered by lining, so most heat must be conducted through the drum to reach the outside air to cool. With hard use, this can cause overheating and, eventually, brake "fade." Brake fade is the gradual loss of brake stopping power during prolonged or strenuous use. Very high temperatures occur at the brake drum, and that causes deterioration in the frictional value of the lining or pad material. This is common in drum brakes.

Brake Shoe Configurations and Actuation Mechanisms

The design of common brake shoe systems on medium- to heavy-duty vehicles can be in the form of one of these basic designs:

- Leading and trailing brake shoe configuration
- Two-leading-shoe configuration

Single-Leading- and Trailing-Shoe Configuration

The single-leading-shoe drum brake (SLS), which is also known as a **leading/trailing shoe drum brake arrangement**, is a basic type of drum brake design. It is typically found on the rear wheels of vehicles. While the SLS brake arrangement is not uncommon on smaller vehicles, it used to be standard on the SLS front brakes of older vehicles. An advantage of an SLS brake is that it is equally effective whether the vehicle is traveling forward or in reverse. An SLS brake is less powerful than a **twin-leading-shoe drum brake**, but that is not critical on the rear where excessive braking force can cause the rear road wheels to lock.

The term "leading/trailing" is used because there is one shoe that is "leading," that is, moving with the direction of the drum's rotation and thus exhibiting a self-applying, or self-servo, effect. In other words, the shoe is being dragged into the friction surface of the drum and in this way achieves greater braking force. The other shoe is "trailing," that is, moving against the direction of rotation, and being thrown off the drum's friction surface and not retarding the drum quite so effectively.

When the vehicle is moving in reverse, the role of the leading and trailing shoes is reversed. What would be the **leading shoe** when the vehicle is traveling forward becomes the **trailing shoe**, and vice versa. The leading shoe can be identified by observing the hydraulic wheel cylinder's mounted position and the drum brake's direction of rotation, where the hydraulic wheel cylinder forces the brake shoe outwards to contact the drum in the same direction as the drum's rotation FIGURE 33-2.

The trailing shoe is the one forced into contact with the drum via the double-acting hydraulic wheel cylinder against the direction of rotation in a forward direction. But these shoes act the opposite way when the vehicle is traveling in reverse and the brakes are applied.

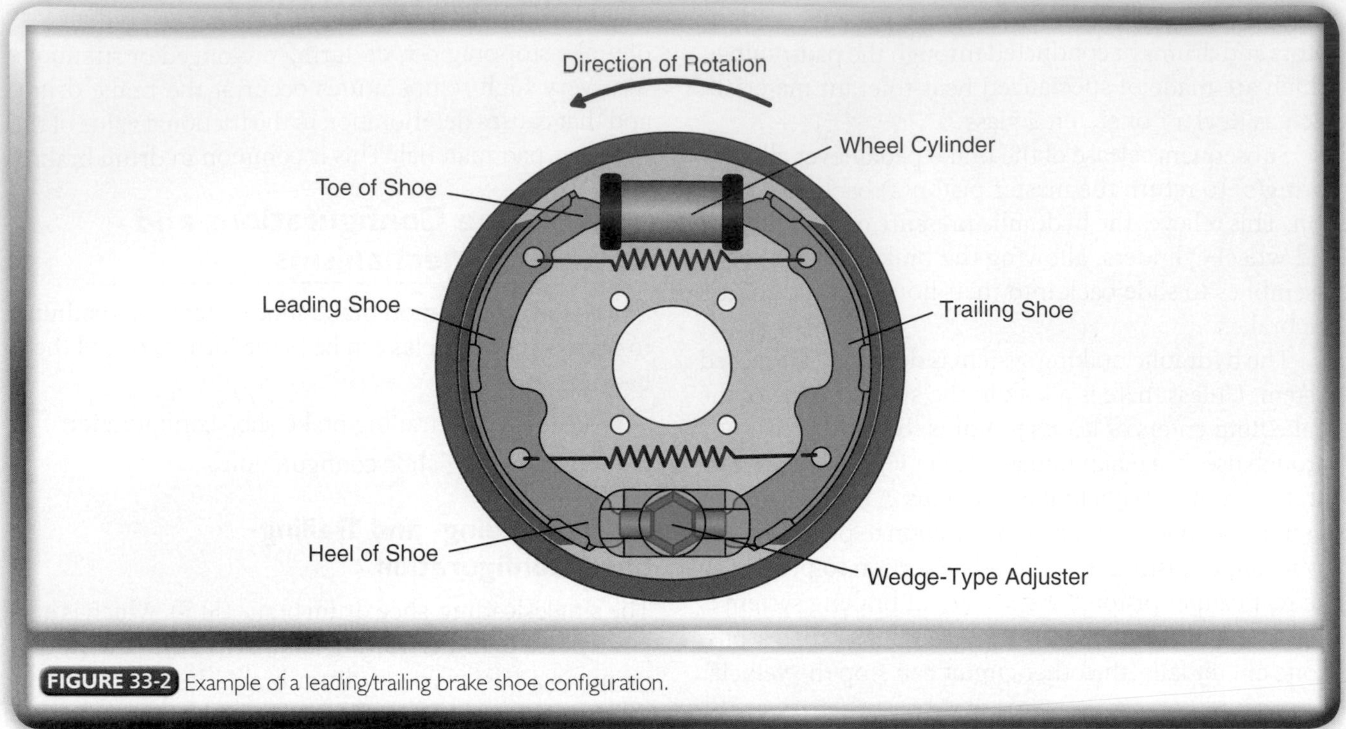

FIGURE 33-2 Example of a leading/trailing brake shoe configuration.

Two-Leading Brake Shoes

The leading brake shoe can also be referred to as the "primary" brake shoe; it is usually the brake shoe on the side towards the front of the vehicle. This is the brake shoe that carries most of the braking load. Because of this, the primary brake shoes on some vehicle applications have a thicker lining than the rear shoe. That would make the shoe on a vehicle's rear side the trailing, or "secondary," brake shoe FIGURE 33-3.

Each brake shoe in this arrangement is forced outward, with an even pressure of the linings on the drum in the direction of rotation. The **servo action** is less than that of a leading/trailing shoe arrangement but provides a more powerful and stable brake. The self-servo effect arises in the two-leading-shoe arrangement because the leading shoes are effectively dragged into the brake drum's friction surface and achieve maximum braking force. A "trailing" shoe would move against the direction of rotation by being thrown off the drum's friction surface and not retarding the drum as effectively.

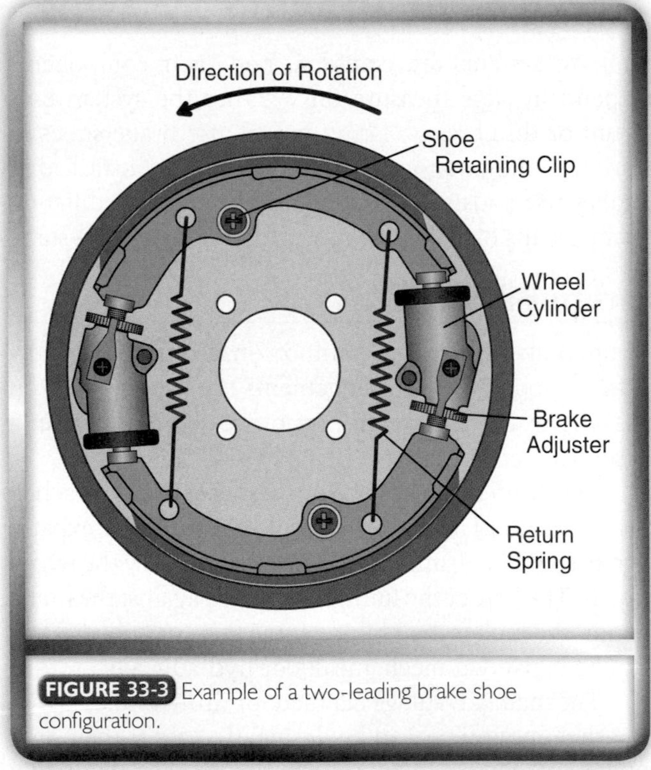

FIGURE 33-3 Example of a two-leading brake shoe configuration.

Types of Adjusters Used with Drum Brakes

Brake shoe adjusters are fitted to brake stations so that a technician can adjust the brake lining to brake drum clearance. Another function is to minimize brake pedal travel when the brakes are adjusted to manufacturer's specifications. Basically, the two types of brake lining adjusting mechanisms are:

- Star wheel-type adjuster
- Wedge-type adjuster

Both types can be found in various applications. Which type is used is often determined by the actual size of the vehicle.

Star Wheel-Type Adjuster

It is important to maintain a specified drum-to-lining clearance at all times. In some vehicles, this function is carried out automatically. But a number of manufacturers install a mechanical device that requires periodic adjustment.

An excessively large clearance between drum and linings will result in a low brake pedal and a delay in the brakes applying. But if the clearances are too tight, the brakes will drag and overheat. If the brake adjust is not equal on both sides and in front and back, then vehicle stability will be an issue under heavy braking. That is where a star adjusting screw is useful.

The star adjusting screw consists of a threaded bolt and two nuts FIGURE 33-4. They are marked either "L" (for left hand) or "R" (for right hand). Since each end of the adjusting is in contact with a brake shoe, the clearance decreases as the screws are turned. You can access the adjusting star wheels through holes in the brake **backing plate**; the holes are located on the bottom inside of the wheel on both the front and the rear.

Wedge-Type Adjuster

The wedge-type adjuster consists of a conical wedge that can be screwed in or out from the back of the backing plate between the tappets that adjust the brake lining to brake drum clearance FIGURE 33-5. It can move the linings closer or farther away from the brake drum.

This form of brake shoe adjuster has not been utilized for a number of years now, as the star wheel adjuster and self-adjusting components have become firmly established by various manufacturers.

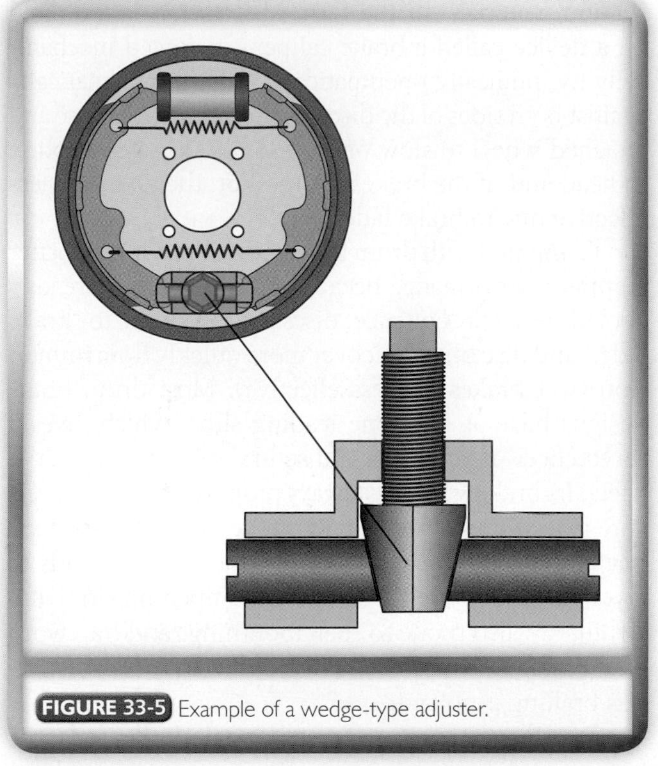

FIGURE 33-5 Example of a wedge-type adjuster.

Disc Brakes

A disc brake is a wheel brake, which slows rotation of the wheel by the friction caused by pushing brake pads against a brake disc with a set of calipers FIGURE 33-6. The brake disc is usually made of cast iron, but may in some cases be made of composites, such as reinforced carbon-carbon or ceramic matrix composites. The disc is connected to the wheel and/or the axle. To stop the wheel,

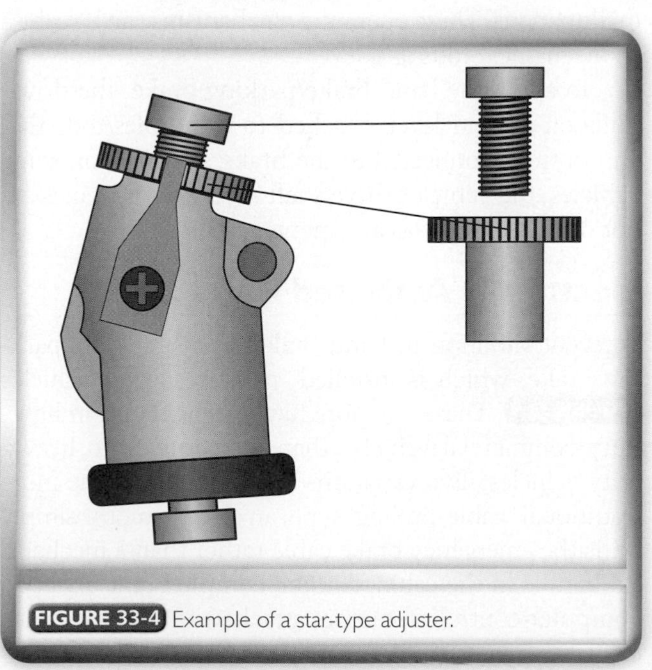

FIGURE 33-4 Example of a star-type adjuster.

FIGURE 33-6 Heavy-duty vehicle disc brake system.

friction material—in the form of brake pads mounted on a device called a brake caliper—is forced mechanically, hydraulically, pneumatically, or electromagnetically against both sides of the disc. Friction causes the disc and attached wheel to slow or stop. Brakes convert motion to heat, and, if the brakes get too hot, they become less effective due to brake fade.

Compared with drum brakes, disc brakes offer better stopping performance because the disc is more readily cooled. As a consequence, discs are less prone to "brake fade," and disc brakes recover more quickly from immersion (wet brakes are less effective). Most drum brake designs have at least one leading shoe, which gives a servo effect. By contrast, a disc brake has no self-servo effect. Its braking force is always proportional to the pressure placed on the brake pad by the braking system via any brake servo, braking pedal, or lever. This tends to give the driver better "feel" to avoid impending lock-up. Drums are also prone to "bell mouthing" and trap worn lining material within the assembly, both causes of various braking problems.

Disc brakes produce a much higher brake force per kilogram of brake weight in comparison with drum brakes. Importantly, disc brake performance improves as the components heat up, whereas drum brake performance deteriorates, producing potentially unbalanced braking when incorrectly combined on a vehicle. If used in combination with drum brakes, disc brakes tend to provide a disproportionate share of braking effort and wear out quickly, so mixing drum and disc brakes should be avoided. While the cost of disc brake parts is generally higher, their easier maintenance and lighter weight make them a very attractive technology. Disc brakes can be retrofitted.

Emergency/Hand Brakes

Heavy- and medium-duty vehicles also have emergency or hand brakes in addition to foot brakes. Hand brakes can either be mechanical or electrically activated at each of the rear brakes on the vehicle. Some other systems use a propeller (also known as a transmission or drive) shaft hand brake system as shown in FIGURE 33-7. Propeller shaft hand brakes are normally mechanically activated. The following describes the common types currently in use.

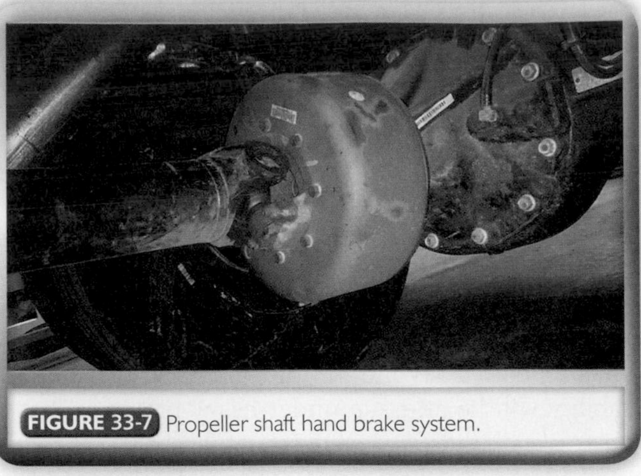
FIGURE 33-7 Propeller shaft hand brake system.

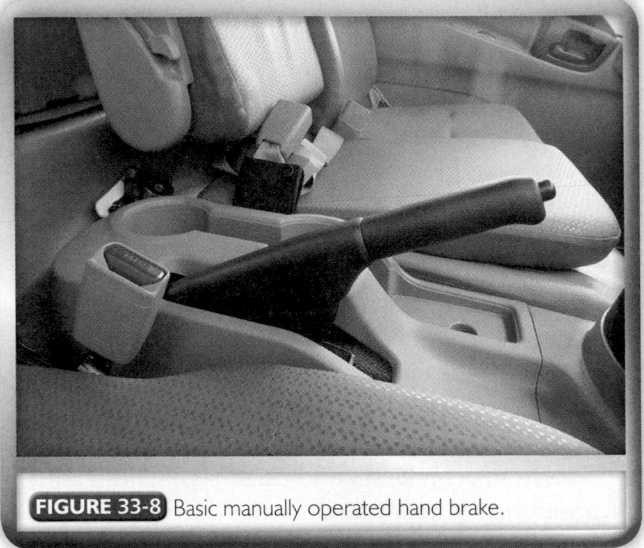
FIGURE 33-8 Basic manually operated hand brake.

Mechanical Hand Brake

Some medium-duty vehicles use a mechanically operated hand or emergency brake FIGURE 33-8. As with any parking brake, the mechanically operated hand brake's primary function is to hold the vehicle in a stationary position when parked. Its secondary function is to act as an emergency stopping brake if the primary brake malfunctions. These operating mechanisms can be cables or mechanical rods and levers.

To apply the hand brake/parking brake, the driver pulls on a hand lever attached to the cables/rods that are, in turn, connected to the brake shoes or, on some vehicles, the vehicle's drive shaft. Drive shaft brakes are not designed to act as an emergency brake.

Electrically Activated Hand Brake

A recent variation in hand brakes is the electric parking brake, which is installed in many newer vehicles FIGURE 33-9. These are more likely to be found in light-duty commercial vehicles than in medium- to heavy-duty vehicles. Two variations are available: In the more traditional "cable-pulling" type, an electric motor simply pulls the emergency brake cable rather than a mechanical handle in the cabin. A more complex unit uses two computer-controlled motors attached to the rear brake calipers to activate it.

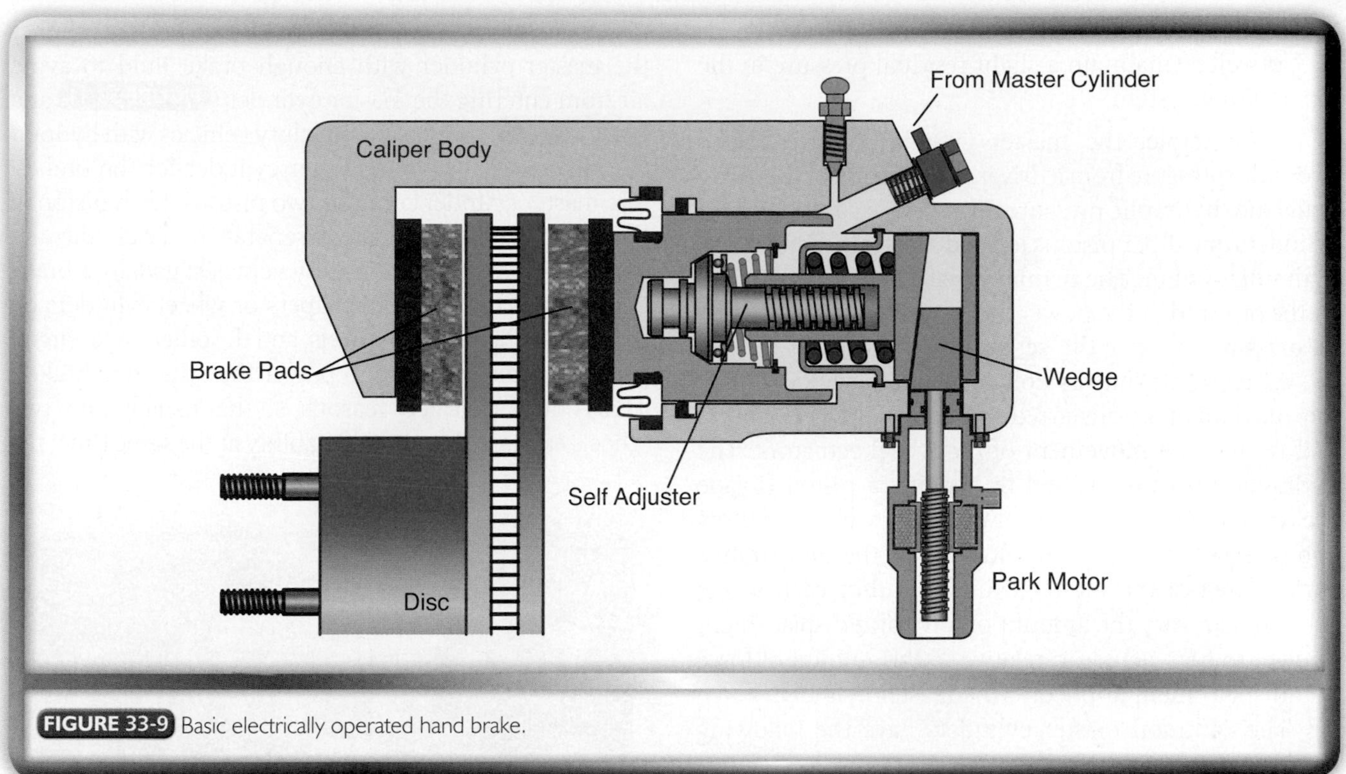

FIGURE 33-9 Basic electrically operated hand brake.

Spring Brake Park Brake

In air-over-hydraulic systems, it is common to use a spring brake arrangement that operates by using the vehicle's air system to hold the brake off when the vehicle is moving. This is done by charging the spring brake unit with air pressure from a special hand or park brake valve FIGURE 33-10.

When the actuation valve is moved to apply the brakes, air pressure is exhausted from the spring brake chamber. The power spring in the unit mechanically moves the brake components to apply the brake.

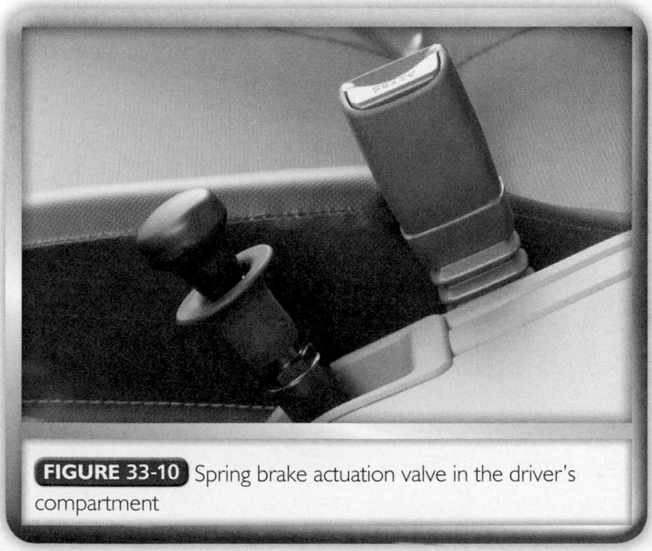

FIGURE 33-10 Spring brake actuation valve in the driver's compartment

Hydraulic Components of Hydraulic Brake Systems

All hydraulic brake systems need some kind of power assist to increase braking effort. Whether the power assist is vacuum, hydraulic, or air, all of the underlying hydraulic components will be basically the same. In this section we look at the hydraulic components common to all hydraulic brake systems.

Master Cylinder

The master cylinder's primary function is that of a pump. When activated by the foot brake pedal, it forces the hydraulic brake fluid through the brake lines under pressure to activate the wheel cylinders. **Brake lines** are tubes made of seamless, double-walled steel that are able to transmit more than 1,000 psi (6,895 kPa) of hydraulic pressure through the hydraulic brake system. The master cylinder has four main functions:

1. To develop the pressure necessary to force the wheels to expand and, thus, apply the brakes
2. To maintain equal pressure on the brake shoes/disc pads
3. To keep the braking system full of fluid to reduce the risk of possible air induction into the system as well as keep other contaminants (such as water) from entering the system

4. To compensate for wear in the brake linings/pads as well as maintain a slight residual pressure in the braking system

In principle, the master cylinder converts non-hydraulic pressure from a driver's application of the brake pedal into hydraulic pressure. This device controls wheel cylinders or caliper pistons located at the other end of the hydraulic system. The **primary piston** is moved directly by the pushrod or the power booster; it generates hydraulic pressure to move the **secondary piston**.

As a piston(s) moves along the master cylinder's bore, this movement is transferred through the hydraulic fluid and results in a movement of the wheel actuators. The hydraulic pressure created by moving a piston (inside the master cylinder's bore) towards the wheel actuators compresses the fluid evenly. But varying the comparative surface-area of the master cylinder and/or each wheel actuator can vary the amount of force and displacement applied to each actuator, relative to the amount of force and displacement applied to the master cylinder.

The common master cylinders have the following characteristics:

- Single bore
- separated into two chambers by the primary and secondary piston: and
- could contain a **residual pressure valve** for drum-type brakes (not fitted to disc brakes).

A reservoir above each master cylinder supplies the master cylinder with enough brake fluid to avoid air from entering the master cylinder (FIGURE 33-11 and FIGURE 33-12). Most medium-duty vehicles with hydraulic brakes will have one master cylinder for the brakes. The master cylinder contains two pistons. Each piston in the master cylinder operates a separate brake circuit, and for most types of medium-duty vehicles, usually a brake circuit leads to the brake calipers or wheel cylinders on only two of the vehicle's wheels, and the other brake circuit provides brake pressure to power the other two brakes. This is done for safety reasons, so that usually only two wheels can lose their braking ability at the same time; the

FIGURE 33-11 Basic tandem master cylinder.

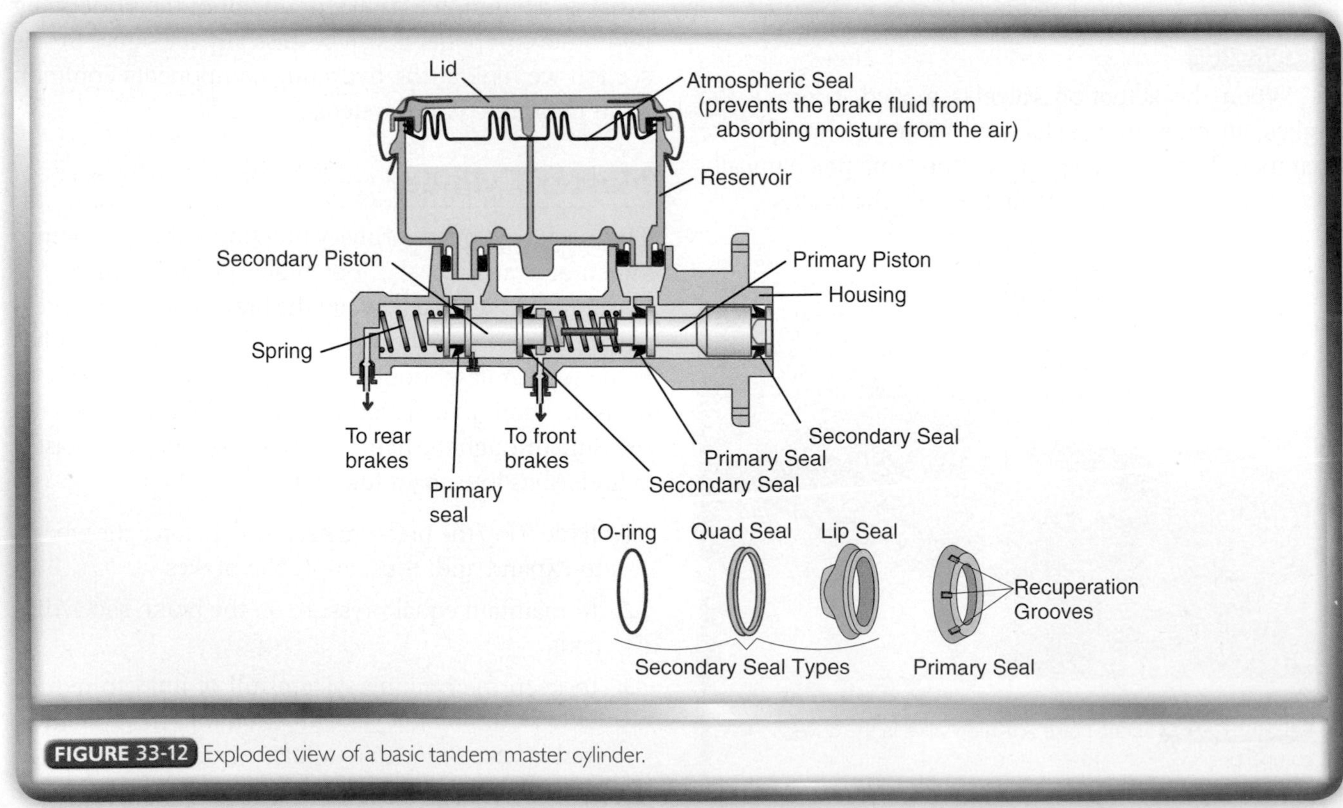

FIGURE 33-12 Exploded view of a basic tandem master cylinder.

result of such a loss would be longer stopping distances and should be fixed immediately, but at least leaves some braking ability, which is preferable to none at all.

On the front of a master cylinder's primary piston is a rubber piston cup, whose primary function is to seal the primary circuit to allow pressure buildup. A similar rubber cup is fitted to the secondary piston for the same reason, thus creating two distinct circuits within one common housing.

The actuating rod from the brake pedal is linked directly to the primary piston. This is commonly referred to as a pushrod. This pushrod has an adjustment sleeve on it that allows the rod to be shortened or lengthened to maintain a minimal end clearance and prevent excess rod movement or the rod from applying pressure to the piston.

When the brakes are in the released position, the sealing cups of both pistons are positioned between the inlet ports and the compensating ports. This allows the fluid unrestricted passage between the piston bore and the reservoirs.

When the driver applies the brake, the primary piston moves forward and covers the compensating port. This creates a pressure chamber for the trapped fluid. The trapped pressure then applies force to the secondary piston and the piston moves forward, closing the secondary circuit's compensating port. Like the primary circuit, the secondary circuit is now a complete and separate circuit. The pressure continues to build, and this pressure is applied to the wheel actuators and the brakes are applied.

If there is a failure in the secondary circuit, the primary system continues to operate normally but with increased travel. If the primary circuit fails, no pressure is generated to move the secondary piston. So, a rod attached to the front of the primary piston will push the secondary piston directly so that it still operates. A switch can warn of loss of pressure in the front or rear circuits, or one that warns of low fluid level can be fitted to the reservoir.

If residual pressure valves are fitted, they maintain fluid pressure, which aids in keeping contaminants out of the hydraulic system. These valves are normally fitted to a four-drum brake system; they are fitted into each brake line outlet fitting and allow the hydraulic fluid to flow out of the master cylinder but resist a free flow of fluid back into the master cylinder.

Split Braking Systems

Modern vehicles use tandem master cylinders on divided or dual line braking systems. A divided system is safer in the event of partial failure. Fluid loss in one half of the system still leaves the other half able to stop the vehicle, although with an increase in stopping distance. A wheel's braking ability depends on the load it's carrying during braking. So the type of vehicle is a major factor in how its system should be divided.

Typical brake line configurations consist of the following arrangements:

- Longitudinal split: The brake system has one piston in the master cylinder operating the front braking circuit and other piston to operate the rear braking circuit FIGURE 33-13.
- Diagonal split: The brake system has each master cylinder piston controlling and operating the braking

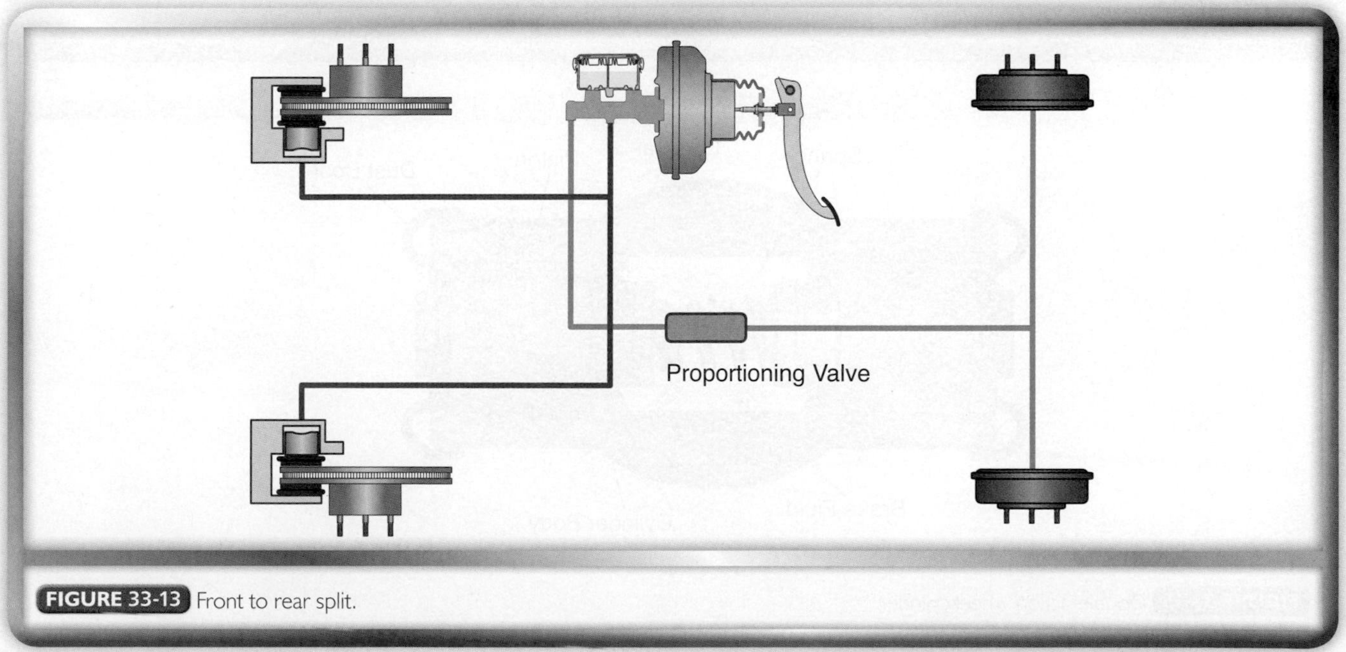

FIGURE 33-13 Front to rear split.

system diagonally. That is, one circuit will control the right front brake and the left rear brake, and the other circuit controls the left front brake and the right rear brake. This configuration helps the vehicle to brake in a relatively straight line during the failure of one of the brake circuits FIGURE 33-14. Different manufacturers advocate different layouts. Some even advocate combinations that use both types of split braking depending on load and vehicle type.

Wheel Cylinders

A wheel cylinder is a component in a drum brake system. It is located in each wheel and is usually at the top, above the shoes. Its responsibility is to exert force onto the shoes so they can contact the drum and stop the vehicle with friction. Usually, small rods shaped like a bird's beak connect these wheel cylinders to the shoes. A wheel cylinder is very similar to a master cylinder and functions in pretty much the same way, consisting of just a simple little plunger on the inside. On older vehicles, these plungers will begin to leak and hinder the brakes' performance, but they are normally inexpensive and easy to replace.

Wheel cylinders are either:

- Single piston/single action
- Dual action/double cylinder with a piston at each end FIGURE 33-15

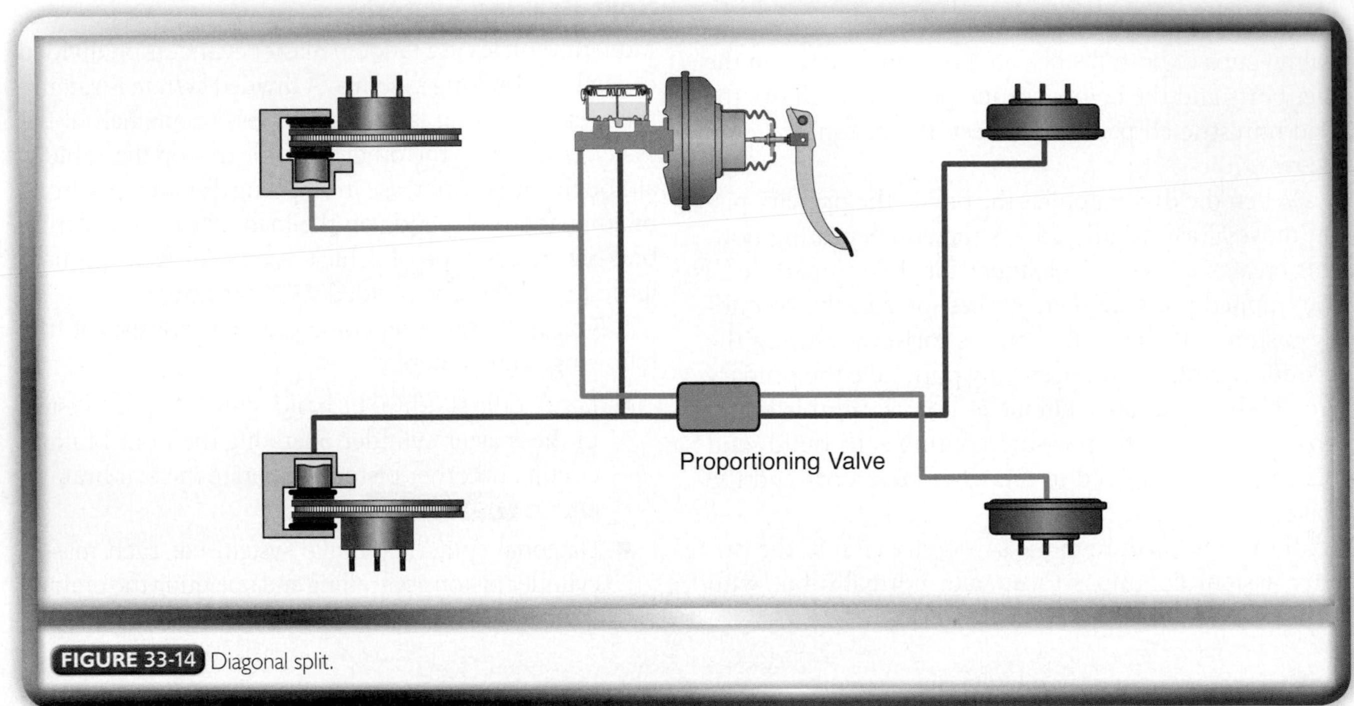

FIGURE 33-14 Diagonal split.

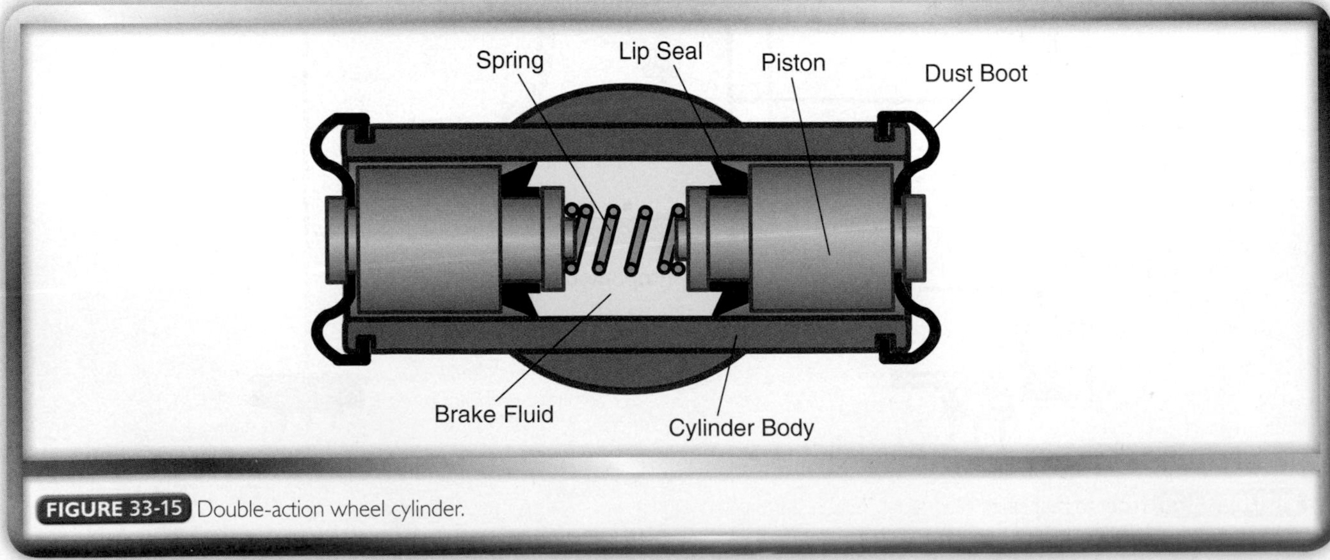

FIGURE 33-15 Double-action wheel cylinder.

They are usually made of cast iron or aluminum alloy, and they operate under difficult conditions of extreme pressures and temperatures. Some are sleeved with stainless steel so they wear longer and are more resistant to corrosion. Contamination, particularly from water, lowers the brake fluid's boiling point and may cause pitting and fluid loss. The wheel cylinder cups seal the cylinder against fluid loss.

Wheel cylinders may be fitted with a spreader and a light expansion spring to keep the lips in contact with the cylinder during retraction and while at rest. This helps keep air out of the system. Most wheel cylinders are fitted with bleed nipples to allow air to be bled from the system after assembly, and a flexible cover, or boot, allows for piston movement and also keeps out dust and moisture.

Hydraulic Brake Valves

In the past, hydraulic brake systems used several valves, such as proportioning valves, load sensing proportioning valves, metering valves, pressure differential valves, and combination valves. These valves controlled pressure to the front and rear brake circuits based on different vehicle operating circumstances and brake configurations. The advent of hydraulic anti-lock braking systems has mostly replaced these valves. Nonetheless, it is important to recognize these valves and understand their functions.

Proportioning Valves

Proportioning valves reduce brake pressure to the rear wheels when their load is reduced during moderate to severe braking. Proportioning valves can be pressure sensitive or load sensitive. The pressure-sensitive valve is in the master cylinder or in a separate unit in the rear brake circuit, while the load-sensitive type is mounted on the body or on the axle, with a mechanical connection between the axle and the frame that increases or decreases the valves operation pressures based on the ride height, and therefore, the load of the vehicle.

Metering Valves

Metering valves are used to hold off the application of the front brakes on vehicles with disc brakes on the front wheels and drum brakes on the rear wheels. Drum brakes use springs to return the brake shoes to their rest position. This means that it takes a certain amount of hydraulic pressure to overcome the tension of the return springs and move the shoes to contact the drums. Disc brakes use the much smaller force of the square-cut O-ring to return the caliper piston to its rest position, meaning that very little force is required to start the piston moving against the rotor metering valve to even the playing field, so to speak, so both the front and rear brake apply simultaneously. Depending on the brake system split, the system may have only one proportioning and one metering valve, or it may have two of each. Some hydraulic brake systems will contain combination valves that provide the functions of both the proportioning and metering valves

Pressure Differential Valve

A **pressure differential valve** FIGURE 33-16 monitors any pressure difference between the two separate hydraulic brake circuits. If there is a moderate leak anywhere in the system, it will illuminate the brake warning light on the instrument panel. The valve can be located in the master cylinder or in the combination valve.

Combination Valve

The **combination valve** shown in FIGURE 33-17 can combine the pressure differential valve, metering valve, and proportioning valve(s) in one unit. Some combination valves combine just the pressure differential valve and proportioning valve(s). On others, just the pressure differential valve and metering valve are combined. Each valve operates individually as it was designed and is collected in one unit. Combination valves are not serviceable. If they become faulty, they must be replaced.

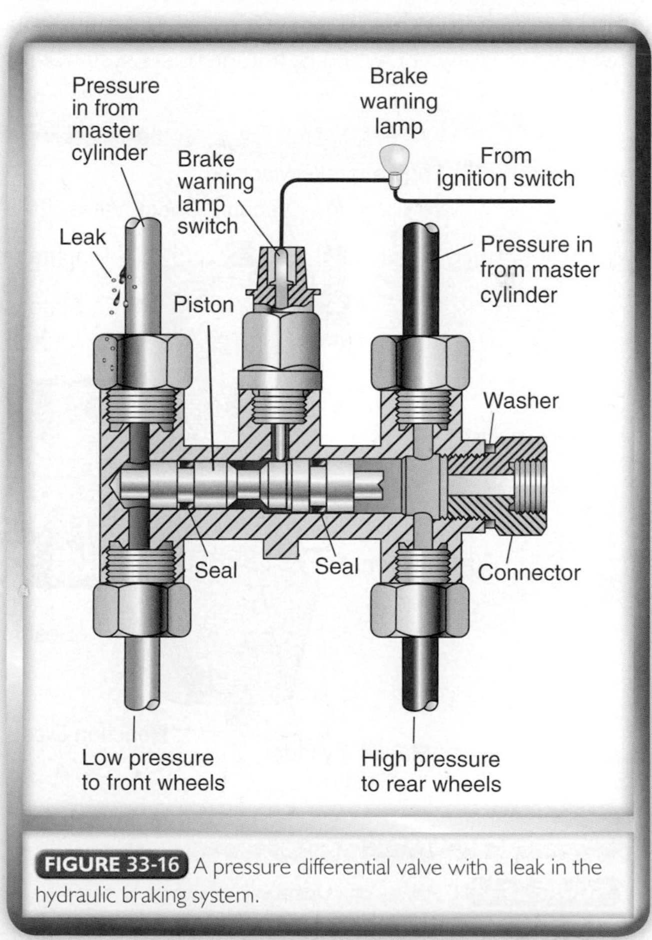

FIGURE 33-16 A pressure differential valve with a leak in the hydraulic braking system.

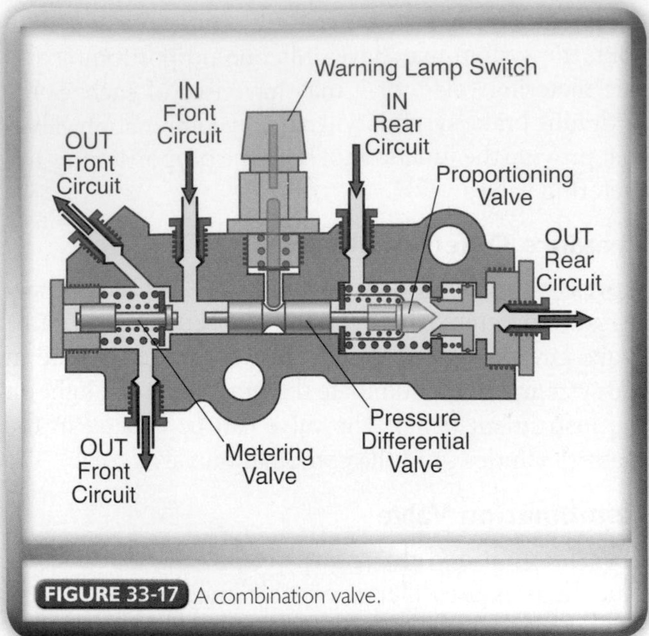

FIGURE 33-17 A combination valve.

Hydraulic Brake Power-Assist Systems

As mentioned at the beginning of the chapter, medium- to heavy-duty vehicles require a large amount of braking effort. Air brake systems can provide that effort without power assist. However, when hydraulic brake systems are used in these vehicles, the brake system requires some kind of power assist—be it vacuum, hydraulic, or air—to achieve the needed braking force. We will now look more closely at the three types of power assist systems commonly used with hydraulic brakes.

Vacuum Brake Booster or Servo (Vacuum Assist Hydraulic Systems)

A vacuum power-assist system uses a vacuum booster as shown in FIGURE 33-18 to provide assistance to the driver by increasing the braking force created by his brake pedal effort. Vacuum boosters or servos use a differential in pressure principle to increase braking force applied to the brake master cylinder.

The vacuum used to power a vacuum booster is generated in two distinct methods, depending on the type of internal combustion engine or other motive force (as in electric vehicles). In naturally aspirated spark-ignition engines, manifold vacuum can be utilized. In turbocharged and diesel engines, a separate vacuum pump is required. The engine of choice for medium- to heavy-duty vehicles is diesel, so a vacuum pump is necessary for this brake assist system. The vacuum is transferred to the booster along semi-rigid plastic lines and is stored in the booster by using a one-way check valve.

The vacuum power booster uses a large diaphragm, or sometimes two diaphragms in tandem, to supply

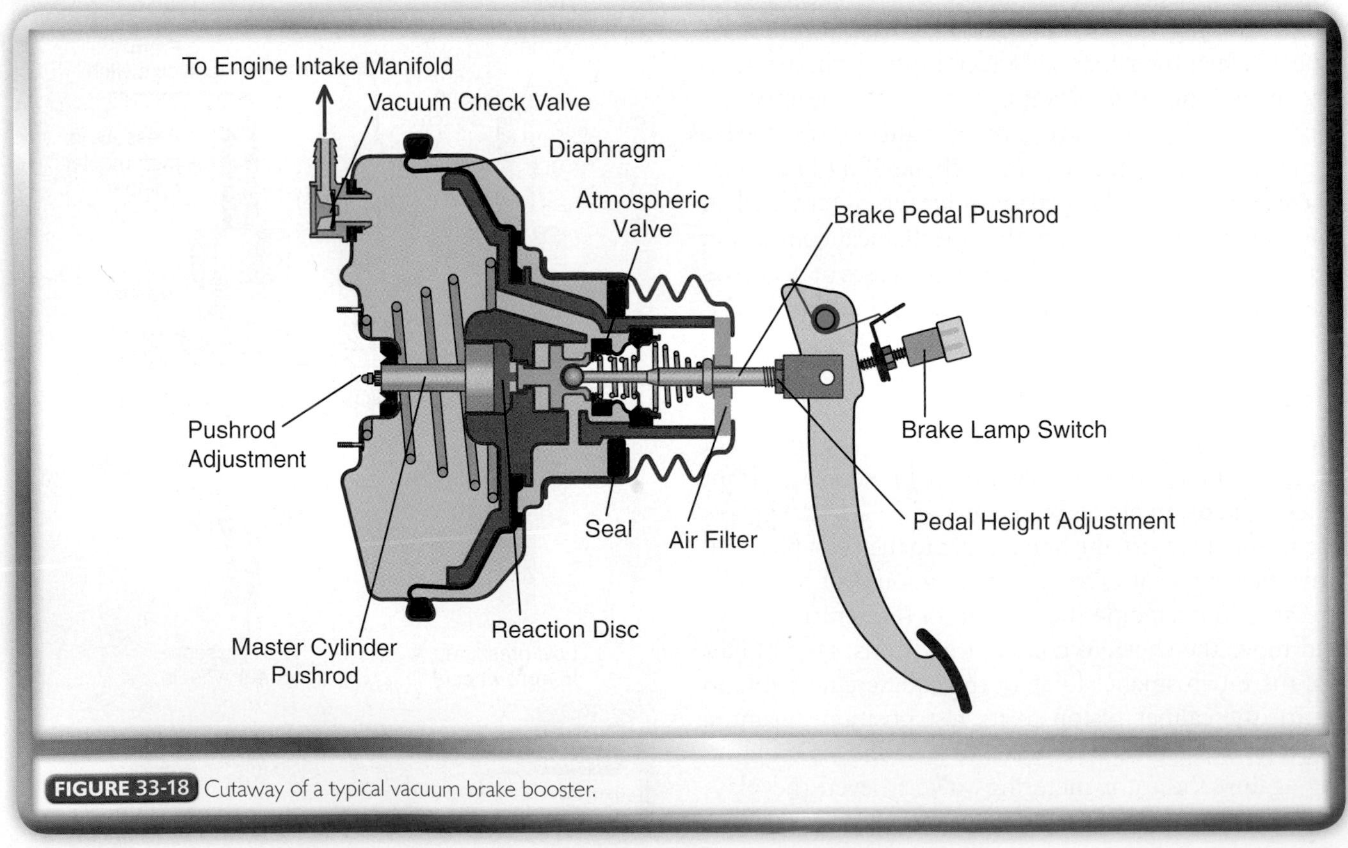

FIGURE 33-18 Cutaway of a typical vacuum brake booster.

a very large surface area for the supplied vacuum to operate on. Although these systems are called vacuum boost systems, it is actually atmospheric pressure that does the work of amplifying the braking force.

The most common booster shown in Figure 33-18 is positioned between the brake and master cylinder. When the engine is running, vacuum is supplied through an inlet check valve to both sides of the large diaphragm in the vacuum booster, creating equal low pressure on both sides. When the brake pedal is depressed, a pushrod opens the vacuum-control valve, allowing atmospheric air pressure to enter the pedal side of the diaphragm. The atmospheric air pressure pushes the diaphragm and the master cylinder pushrod towards the master cylinder, increasing the pressure on the master cylinder pistons. The level of assistance this power-boost gives depends on the pressure applied to the brake pedal. The vacuum-assist booster has three stages of operation depending on the driver's input:

1. In stage 1, the driver's foot is off the pedal, and the vacuum valve is open to both sides of the diaphragm. That equalizes the pressure so there is no power assist, and the system is released.
2. In stage 2, the driver pushes his foot on the pedal. Atmospheric pressure enters the rear side of the diaphragm and starts to push towards the master cylinder creating power assist.
3. In stage 3, the driver holds the pedal at a certain point. This allows the vacuum valve to move to a position that maintains a pressure differential between the two sides, so the assist pressure holds at a steady level.

If the engine stops running, the booster's inlet check valve holds the vacuum in the booster. Boosters are designed with enough reserve capacity to allow two to three full brake applications before the entire vacuum is lost.

To check the booster system for operating integrity, check the brake pedal movement by fully applying the brake with the engine running. Then, shut off the engine and compare the pedal movement with another full brake application. The pedal movement should remain the same in both cases. Also, immediately after the vehicle is shut off, listen carefully for any hissing sound near where the brake pedal pushrod enters the booster. A hissing sound indicates that the control valve is leaking and that the booster should be replaced.

Hydroboost Systems

Many North American Class 4 to Class 6 vehicles use a hydraulic brake system equipped with hydroboost power assist. Hydroboost systems use pressurized hydraulic fluid to provide brake power assist. The system has a hydraulic booster chamber connected in tandem with a dual circuit master cylinder a typical hydroboost system is shown in FIGURE 33-19. The booster unit is bolted to the flywheel, and the master cylinder is in turn bolted to the booster.

The hydraulic pressure used for power assist is usually supplied by the vehicle's power steering pump. Some installations, however, will use a dedicated hydraulic pump to supply pressure because the demands on the pump from the simultaneous use of the power steering and brake systems can be quite substantial. The booster unit used with hydroboost systems is equipped with an electrical back-up motor should hydraulic pressure be lost for any reason. The following four operating modes for the hydroboost system are illustrated in FIGURE 33-20:

1. In the first mode with the engine running and no brake application, hydraulic pressure is delivered to the inlet of the booster and travels through the unit unrestricted. The hydraulic pressure then returns to the pump reservoir. As the fluid exits the booster unit, the fluid opens a flow control switch that interrupts the electrical circuit to the backup electrical motor. No brake assist occurs during this mode.
2. During the second mode (braking mode), the driver pushes the brake pedal. That action moves the throttle valve, which restricts the fluid trying to exit the booster and causes pressure in the booster to rise. The rising pressure pushes on the booster's power piston, amplifying the brake pressure delivered to the master cylinder piston. Consequently, brake application pressure increases. At the same time the pressure pushes the power piston towards the master cylinder, the pressure also pushes a reaction piston towards the driver's brake pedal. This gives the driver a "feel" for the brake application.

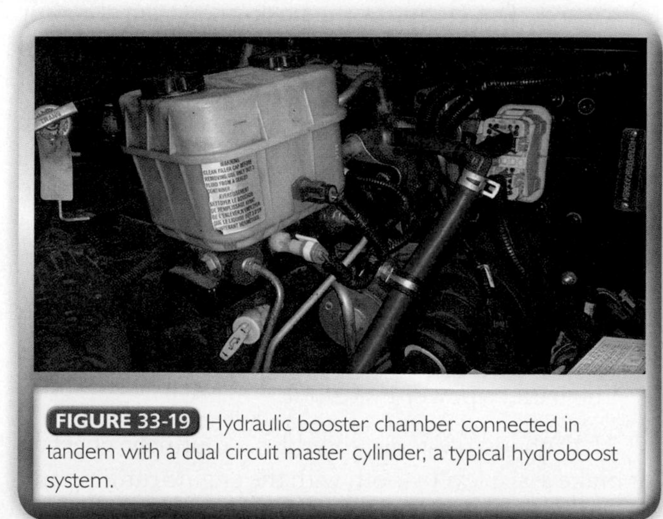

FIGURE 33-19 Hydraulic booster chamber connected in tandem with a dual circuit master cylinder, a typical hydroboost system.

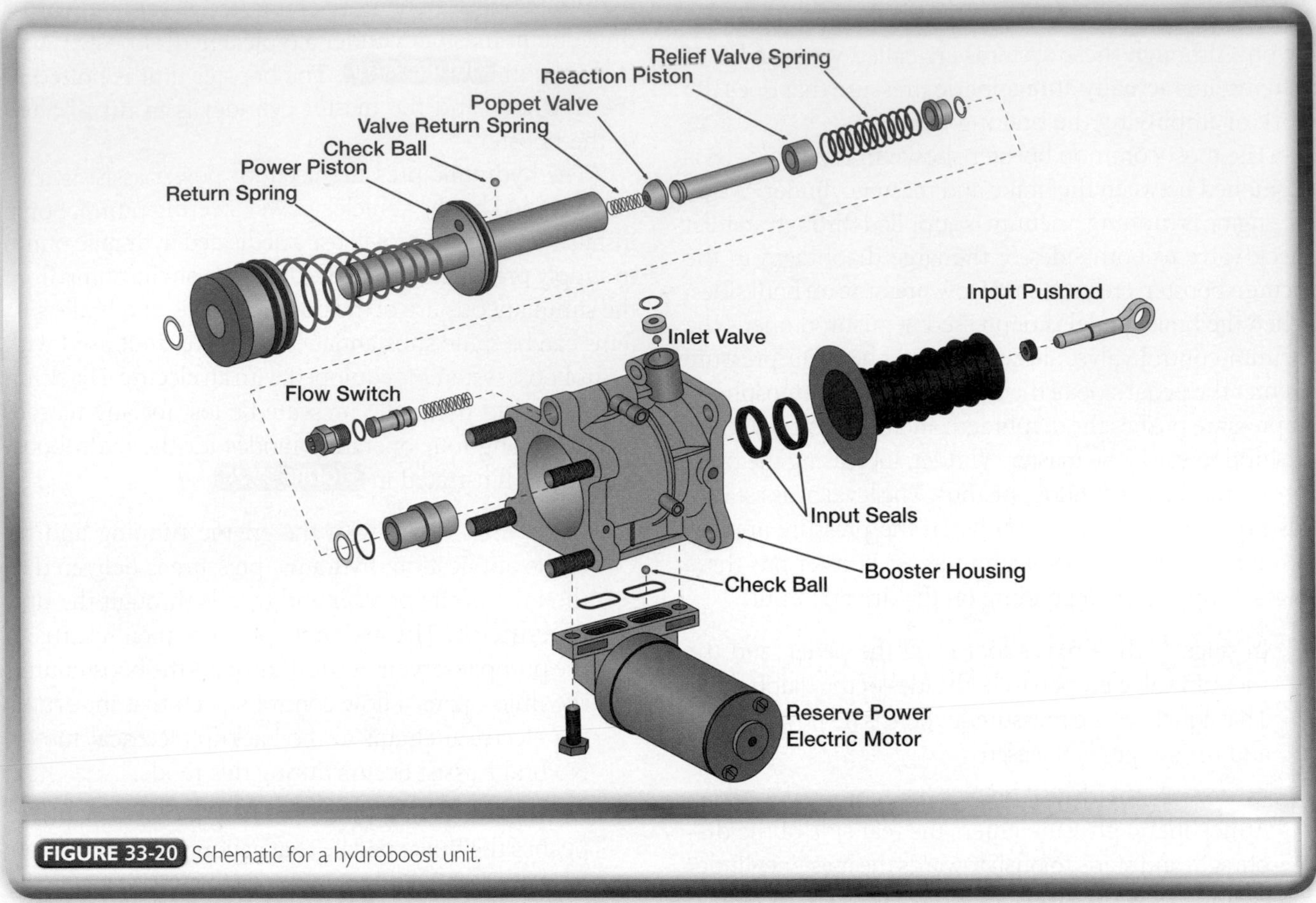

FIGURE 33-20 Schematic for a hydroboost unit.

3. The third mode of operation is when the driver holds the brake pedal depressed at any point. Doing so holds the throttle valve at an exact point and therefore the assist pressure at a steady level.
4. The fourth mode of operation is the electrical back-up motor. If there is an interruption in the hydraulic pressure exiting the hydroboost power booster from either engine failure or hydraulic system failure, the flow control switch in the booster unit remains closed. The circuit to the back-up electrical motor is therefore complete. If the driver pushes the brake pedal during this condition, the brake light switch turns on a relay that sends electrical power to the back-up motor. That powers a pump to supply pressure to the booster, and the brake assist works the same as in mode 2 and mode 3. If the driver pushes the brake pedal in this vehicle without the key on or without the engine running, the back-up motor works in the same fashion. The back-up motor provides emergency brake booster operation as long as the battery power holds out.

Hydroboost systems should be routinely checked for brake assist level—both with the engine running and shut off (to check to back-up motor)—and for leakage at the connecting hoses. Also check for leakage at the connection to the master cylinder connection and where the booster is bolted to the flywheel. Leakage at these locations means that the booster is leaking internally and should be replaced.

Air-Over-Hydraulic Braking Systems

The air-over-hydraulic system uses the same air supply system and treadle (foot) valve discussed in the chapter Air Brake Foundation Systems and Air Brake Circuits. The discussion in this section will concentrate only on the air-powered booster unit and how it increases braking effort in the hydraulic braking system.

Air Booster Units

Air boosters convert the control line air pressure from the foot brake valve into hydraulic pressure to operate the wheel cylinders or calipers and apply the brakes. There are generally two types of air boosters in common use. They are:

- An *indirect-acting type* that is generally found on heavier trucks, where the foot brake valve's control line signal acts on an integrated relay valve that in turn controls the pressure to the air booster's piston seal and provides the assistance.

- A *direct-acting type* that is generally found on lighter trucks, where the foot brake valve's control line signal acts directly on the air booster's piston seal and provides the assistance. Two air boosters are required to operate in split braking systems—one for the front brakes and one for the rear. **FIGURE 33-21** shows two direct-acting air boosters mounted on a special frame that also mounts the air tanks.

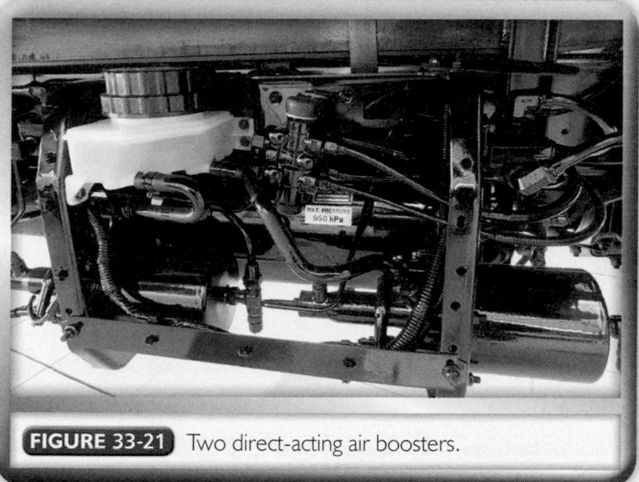

FIGURE 33-21 Two direct-acting air boosters.

Indirect Air Booster Operation

Different manufacturers have small variations in the construction of their booster units, but the principles of operation of all types are the same. **FIGURE 33-22** shows the parts of an indirect acting booster assembly. The pneumatic [air] section (on the left) and the hydraulic section [master cylinder] (on the right) are separated by seals. In this type a relay valve is also part of the assembly.

The assembly illustrated in Figure 33-22 shows the booster when the brakes are off and the booster is in the rest position. Notice the position of the components in the rest position:

1. The exhaust valve of the relay valve is open, allowing any air pressure behind the pneumatic piston to flow through the transfer tube and out the relay valve exhaust (red arrows).
2. The pneumatic piston is held in the off position by the return spring.
3. The hydraulic piston is fully retracted because the pneumatic piston and hydraulic piston are mechanically attached by the pushrod.
4. The check valve in the hydraulic piston allows brake fluid to fill the hydraulic cylinder (see arrows).

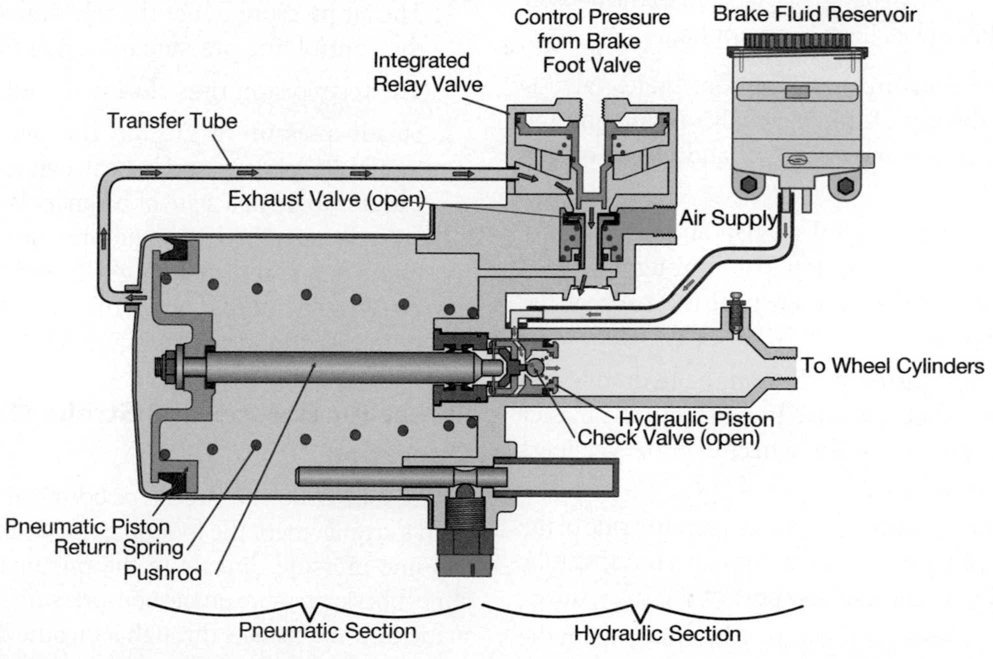

FIGURE 33-22 Indirect air booster assembly with the booster released.

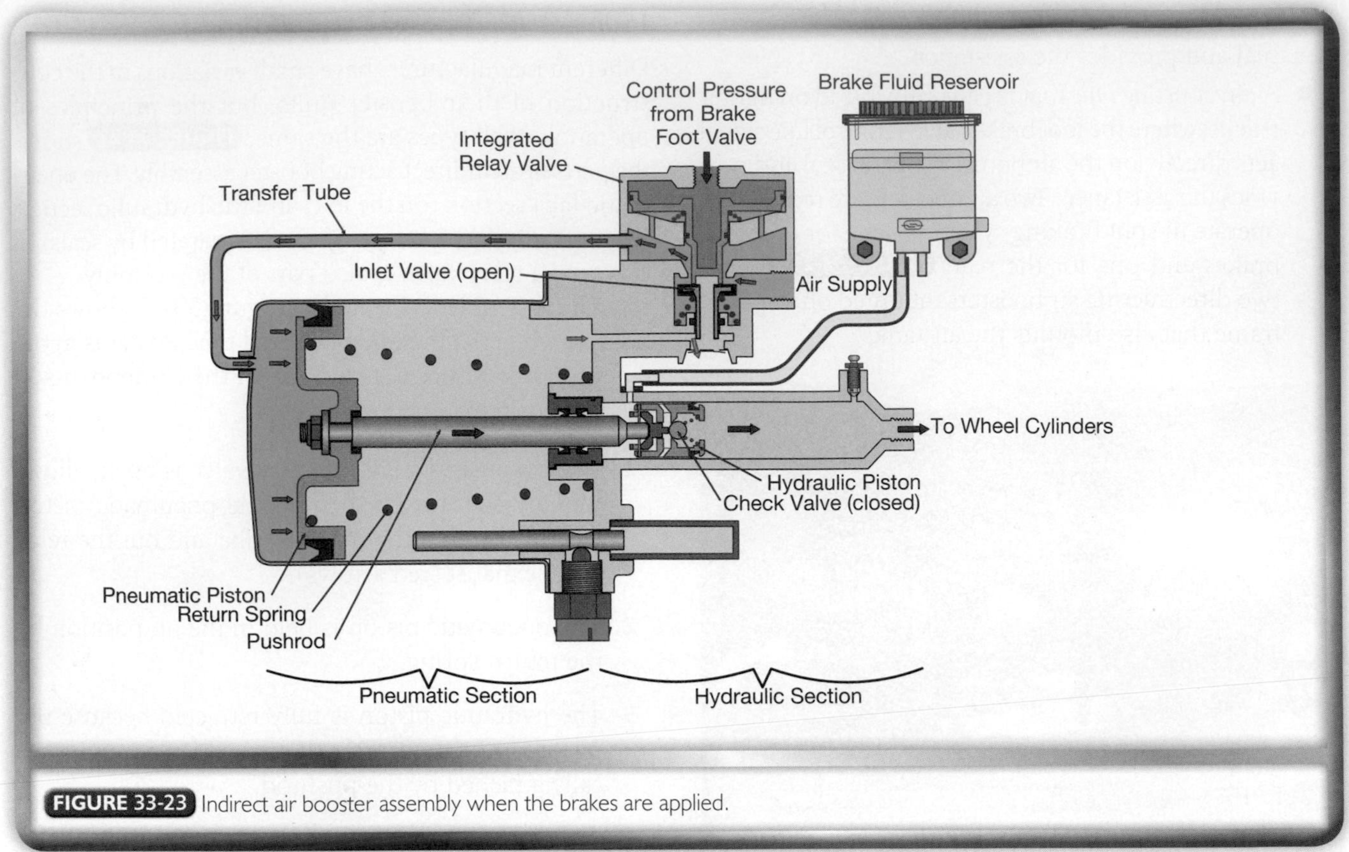

FIGURE 33-23 Indirect air booster assembly when the brakes are applied.

As you might conclude, the indirect booster operates quite differently with the brakes applied. FIGURE 33-23 illustrates the following changes that occur in the booster system when the brakes have been applied:

1. Control line pressure from the foot brake valve is applied to the top of the relay valve piston and the relay valve piston moves down and closes off the exhaust valve.
2. This action opens the inlet valve and air pressure from the air supply can now pass through the inlet valve and pressurizes the area on the back of the pneumatic piston.
3. The pneumatic piston pushes on the hydraulic piston causing the check valve to close and the master cylinder to pressurize the wheel cylinders/calipers and applies the brakes.
4. Atmospheric pressure on the non-pressure side of the pneumatic piston can exhaust through a breather tube that is linked to the exhaust port of the relay valve.
5. During this phase, air pressure is building up on the underside of the relay valve piston.

The indirect booster has a third and final position. FIGURE 33-24 shows the booster in a balanced condition. This condition exists when a steady pressure is being held on the brake pedal (foot brake valve) by the driver. In this condition, the following occurs:

1. The air pressure under the relay valve piston equals the control line pressure on top of the piston.
2. The relay piston rises closing the inlet valve.
3. Steady pressure acting on the pneumatic piston, hydraulic piston, and wheel cylinders causes the booster to be in a state of balance. When the brakes are released, the hydraulic pressure and the pneumatic piston return spring will push the pneumatic piston back. At that point, the air booster will return to released mode as in Figure 33-22.

Direct Air Booster and Stroke Detector Operation

FIGURE 33-25 shows a direct type booster in released mode. In this arrangement the foot brake valve supplies the control line pressure directly to the pneumatic piston. The atmospheric pressure on the non-pressure side of the pneumatic piston exhausts through a breather (blue arrow).

Piston Stroke Detector

If the brakes should be too far out of adjustment or a fault occurs in the hydraulic circuit, the pneumatic piston will

Brake Fluid Reservoir
Control Pressure from Brake Foot Valve
Integrated Relay Valve
Transfer Tube
Inlet Valve (closed)
Air Supply
To Wheel Cylinders
Hydraulic Piston
Check Valve (closed)
Pneumatic Piston
Return Spring
Pushrod
Pneumatic Section
Hydraulic Section

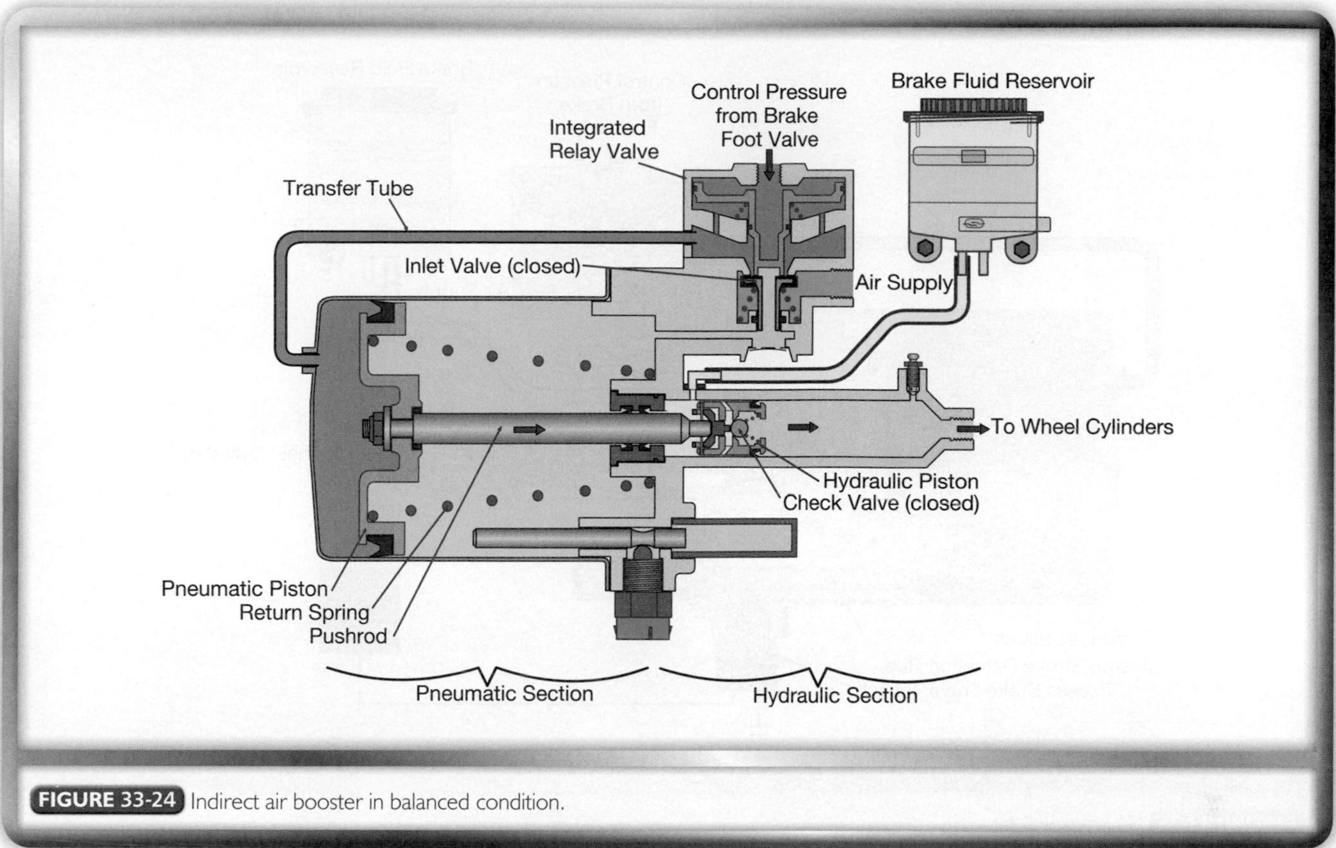

FIGURE 33-24 Indirect air booster in balanced condition.

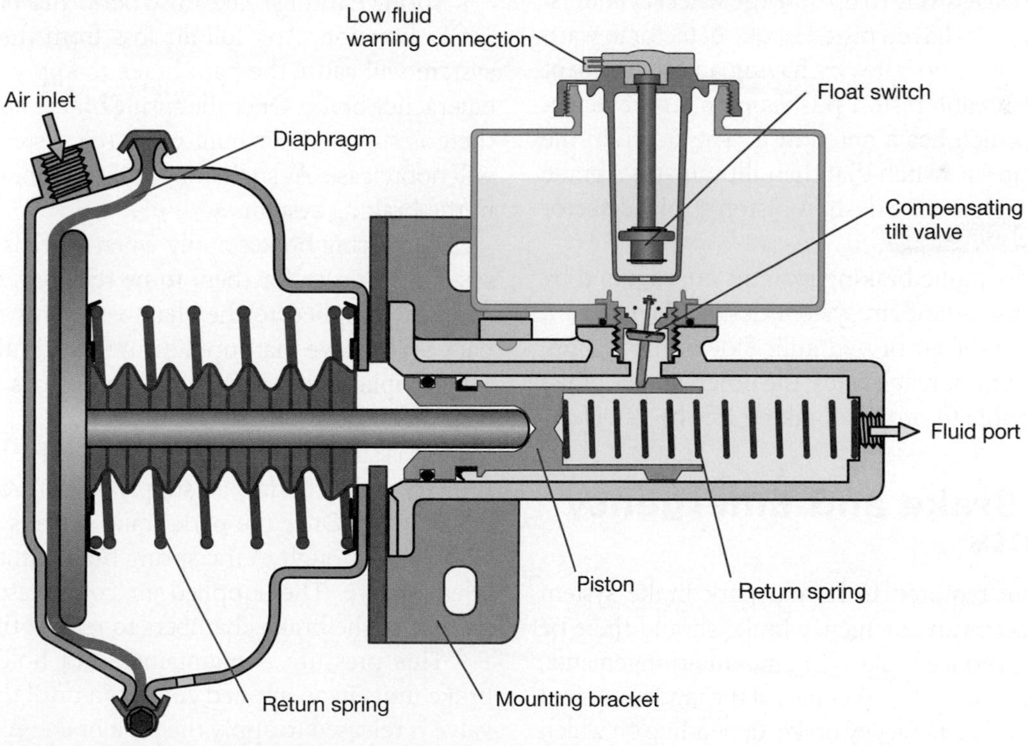

Low fluid warning connection
Air inlet
Diaphragm
Float switch
Compensating tilt valve
Fluid port
Piston
Return spring
Return spring
Mounting bracket

FIGURE 33-25 Direct-type booster in the released mode.

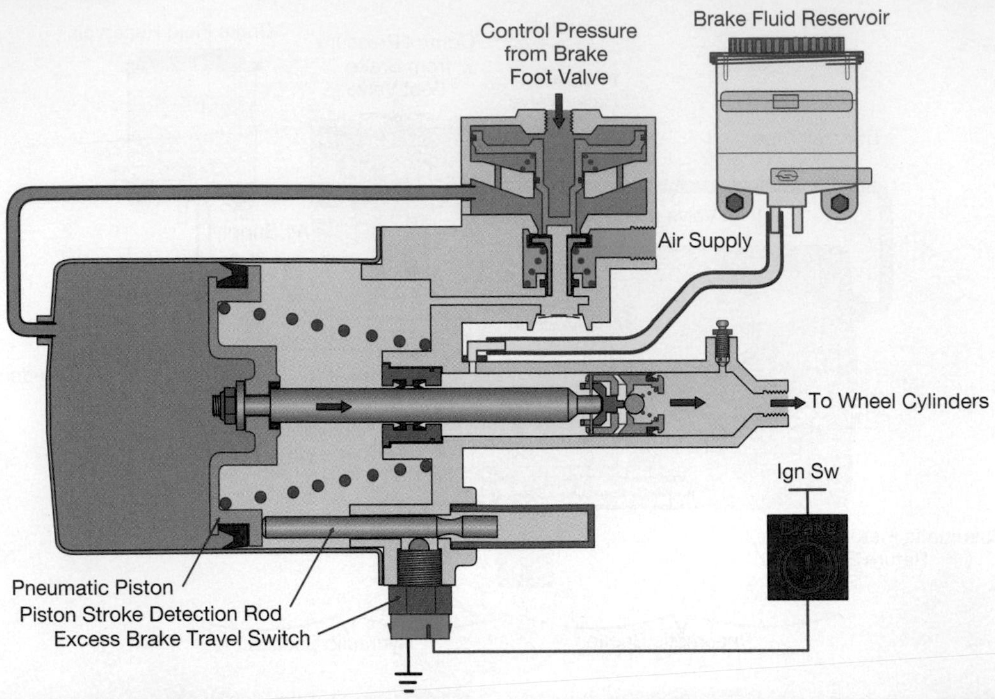

FIGURE 33-26 Piston stroke detector.

have to stroke excessively to operate the wheel cylinders. All types of boosters have a piston stroke detector to warn of this condition. It operates by having an arrangement where the pneumatic piston pushes on a stroke detector pushrod, which has a notch in it. The notch in the pushrod operates a switch that then illuminates a brake fault warning light on the dash. A piston stroke detector is shown in FIGURE 33-26.

Air-over-hydraulic braking systems are required by regulation to use a tandem system design. That way, if a fault occurs in the air or hydraulic side of the system, either on the front or rear brakes, the other vehicle brake circuit will be able to provide braking for the vehicle.

Park Brake and Emergency Circuits

All vehicles are required to have a park brake system that can also act as an emergency brake should there be a failure of the service brakes. In tandem arrangements, normally either one or the other part of the tandem system is designated as the emergency brake, depending on which service system (front of rear) fails. In most hydraulic braking systems, this park or emergency brake is the mechanically operated hand brake. In air-over-hydraulic systems, however, spring brakes are often used as parking brakes.

Spring parking brakes also perform a back-up emergency function. Any full air loss from the vehicle's air system will cause the park brake to apply and act as an emergency brake. Once the spring brakes apply, and until there is sufficient air built up in the system, the brakes will not release. As such, they act as an emergency circuit in the braking system.

The spring brakes apply when there is no air in the system. In order for them to be released, therefore, air must be supplied to the chambers. This is done via a park brake valve that supplies air to the brake chambers. The supplied air compresses the springs in the brake chambers and releases the brakes.

Air is supplied to the park brake valve from both the primary and secondary air supply tanks through a double check valve. Once the park brake valve is actuated, the air passes through to the spring brake units via a quick release valve. The supplied air compresses the power springs in the brake chambers to release the brakes.

This pressure is maintained and holds the spring brake units in an applied condition until the park brake valve is released to apply the park brake. A quick release valve is installed in the park brake circuit to vent the air quickly to the atmosphere when the park brake valve is actuated causing the power springs in the spring brake chambers to apply the brakes.

Arrangement and Operation of the Spring Brake Chamber and Wheel Cylinder

FIGURE 33-27 shows a typical spring brake chamber mounted on the rear axle of a medium-duty truck. It shows the pushrod from the chamber to the wheel cylinder with the adjusting nut in the middle.

In a typical park brake-type wheel cylinder, the design enables it to actuate the brakes when activated by the spring brake chamber, thus providing a parking brake. It also applies the wheel cylinders and thus the service brakes when pressurized brake fluid is supplied to it via the air booster.

FIGURE 33-27 Spring brake chamber mounted on a rear axle.

Initial hand brake adjustment in this arrangement is achieved by lengthening or shortening the pushrod per the manufacturer's specifications.

Park Brake Off and Applied

When park brake and service brake are at rest, as illustrated in FIGURE 33-28, the spring brake chamber is charged with air pressure from the hand brake valve. This forces the piston from its applied condition and compresses the power spring to release the park brake. The roller assembly in the wheel cylinder unit is pushed down the ramps of the wedges, enabling the pistons to retract due to the return springs that connect the brake shoes.

By contrast, the park brake illustrated in FIGURE 33-29 has been applied. In this condition, air pressure has been exhausted from the spring brake chamber. The power spring pulls on rollers in the wedge assembly. This forces the wheel cylinder pistons to move outward in the direction of their respective vertical blue arrows. Finally, the brake linings contact the insides of the brake drum with considerable force, causing the application of the park brake.

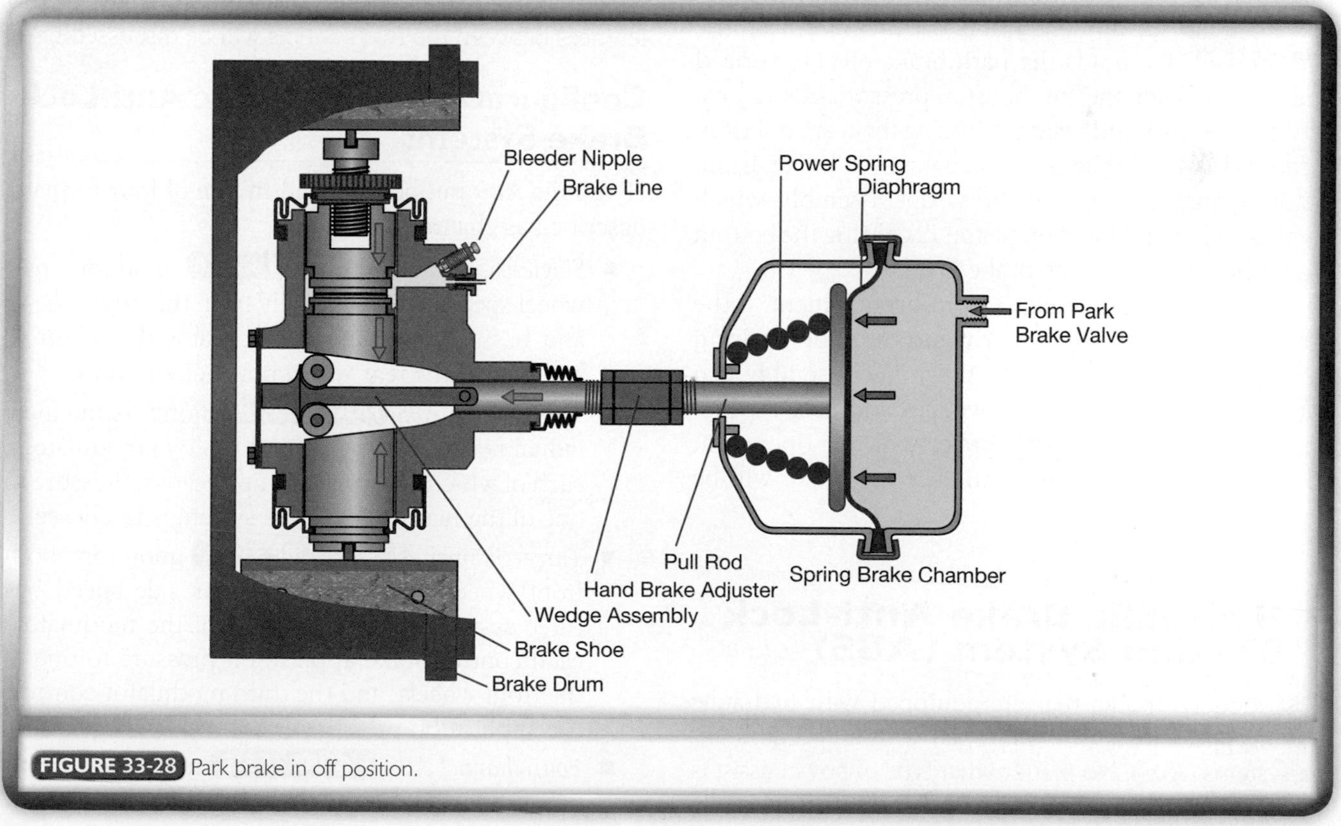

FIGURE 33-28 Park brake in off position.

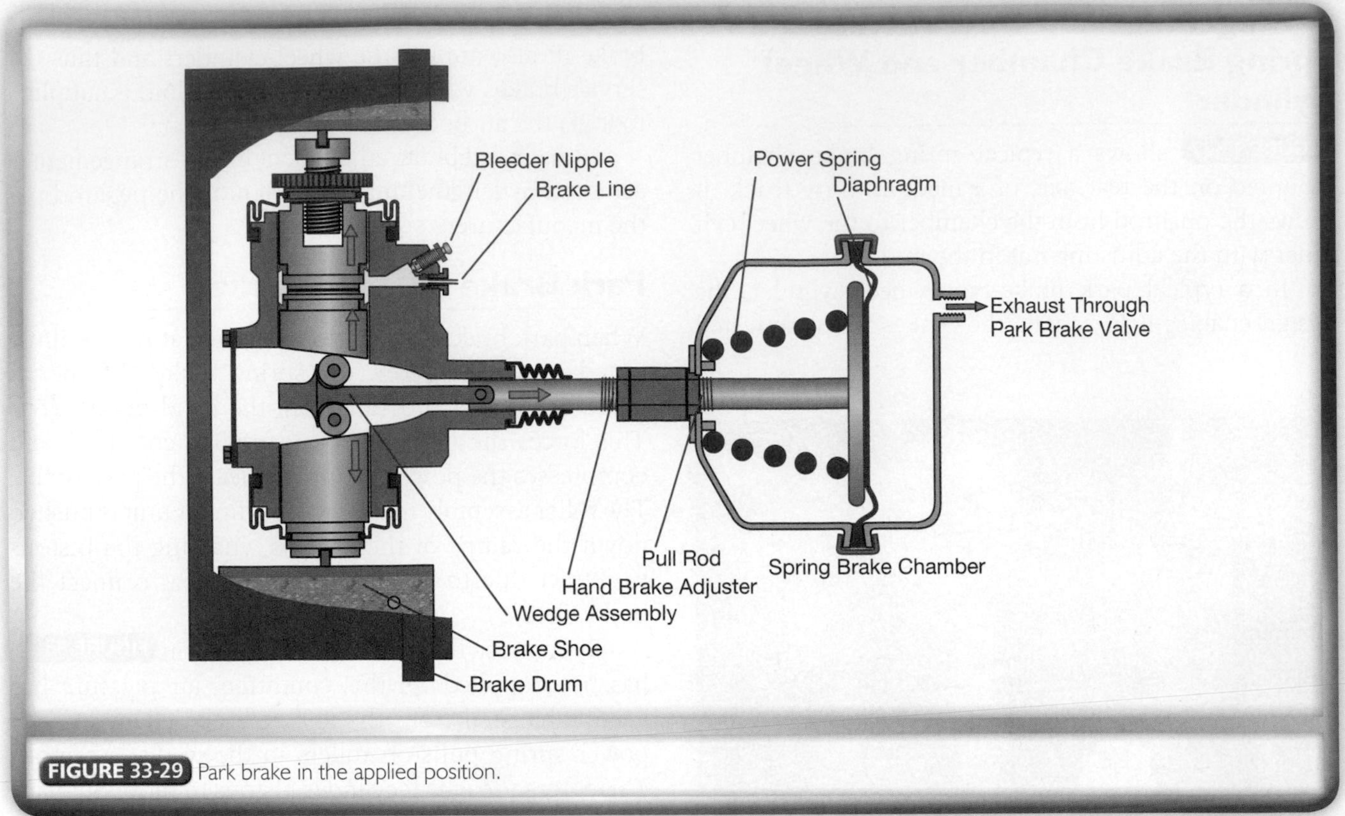

FIGURE 33-29 Park brake in the applied position.

Service Brake Applied

Sometimes, the park brake is released while the service brake is applied. That situation is illustrated in FIGURE 33-30. In this condition, air pressure from the park brake valve holds the park brake off. Pressurized brake fluid from the air booster pressurizes the area between piston X and piston Y, forcing them apart. Piston X causes the top brake shoe to contact the brake drum. Piston Y pushes down on the wedge assembly, which pivots and pushes down on piston Z, causing the bottom brake shoe to contact the brake drum

There is a disadvantage to this arrangement. If the brakes aren't adjusted regularly and the shoe-to-drum clearance gets too excessive, the roller assembly can completely pull through the wedges and past the pistons. As a result, the park brake will not operate at all, and the effectiveness of the service brake will be severely limited.

Hydraulic Brake Anti-Lock Braking System (ABS)

Most modern trucks that are equipped with hydraulic braking systems are also equipped with anti-lock braking systems (ABS). No matter what type of power assist is used, the ABS system will act in concert with the hydraulic system to prevent wheel lock-up. Air anti-lock braking was discussed in the Anti-Lock Braking, Vehicle Stability, and Collision Avoidance Systems chapter. Hydraulic anti-lock systems operate in a very similar fashion, so only the differences between the two systems will be discussed here.

Configurations of Hydraulic Anti-Lock Brake Systems

Hydraulic ABS can be designed in one of four formats, described as channels:

- *Single-channel ABS* FIGURE 33-31A monitors rear wheel speed only—typically from the drive axle—and has a single system modulator that controls pressure to the rear wheel brake circuit only.
- *Two-channel ABS* FIGURE 33-31B monitors the individual rear wheel speeds and has two modulators, each of which controls rake application pressure to one of the rear wheels. This system is rarely seen.
- *Three-channel ABS* FIGURE 33-31C monitors both front wheel speeds and the rear axle speed has three system modulators. Two of the modulators each control brake application pressure to one of the front wheels, and the third modulator controls the application pressure to the rear brake circuit.
- *Four-channel ABS* FIGURE 33-31D monitors all four wheel speeds individually, and each of the four

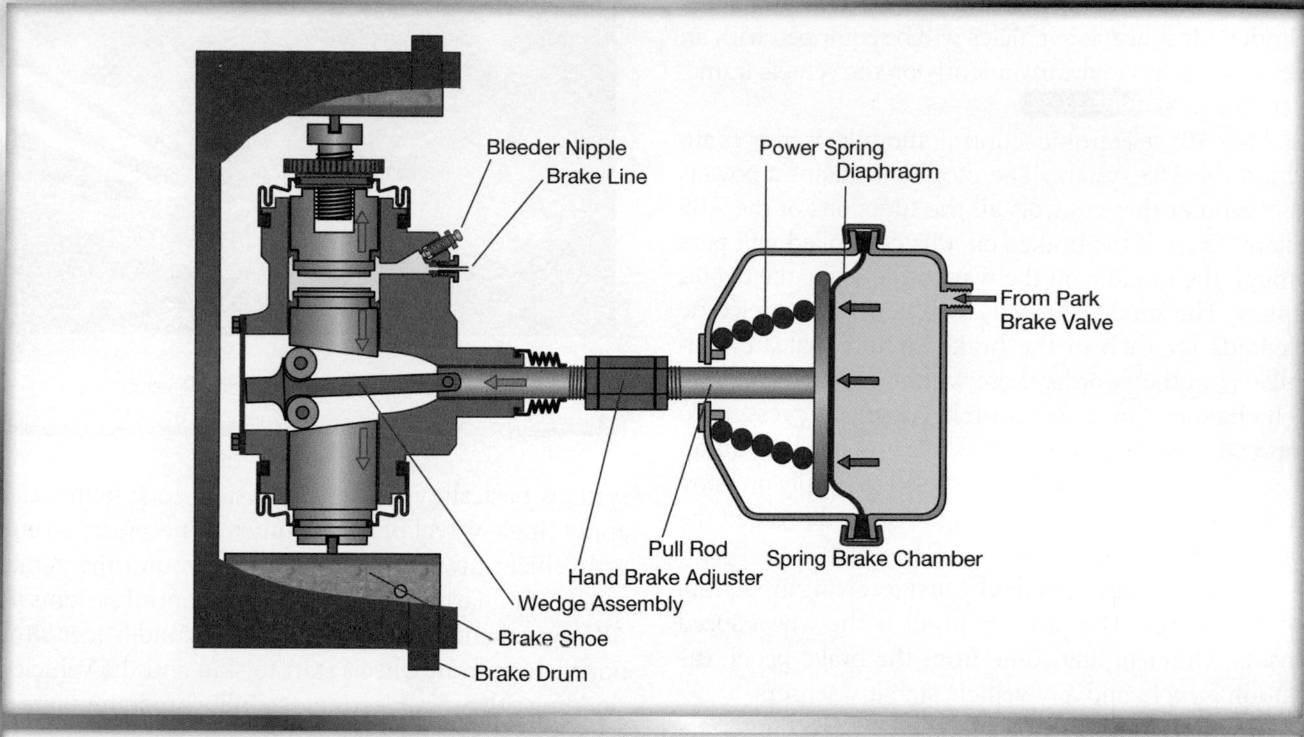

FIGURE 33-30 Service brake in the applied position when the park brake is released.

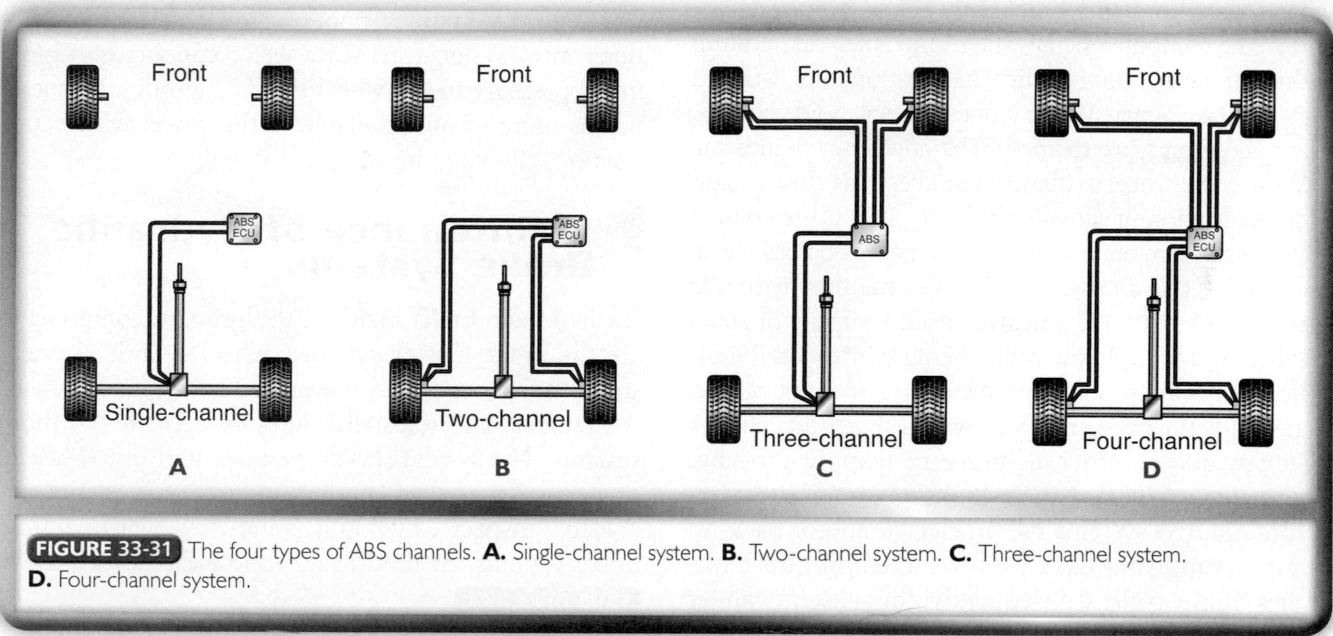

FIGURE 33-31 The four types of ABS channels. **A.** Single-channel system. **B.** Two-channel system. **C.** Three-channel system. **D.** Four-channel system.

modulators controls brake application pressure to one of the four wheels to allow the slippage of each to be individually controlled.

Of the different channels, four-channel ABS is the most commonly found today. Using four-channel ABS allows the ABS system to work in concert with a vehicle stability software program to control vehicle stability by being able to apply any of the wheel brakes when necessary to correct a skid condition.

ABS Module

Although four-channel ABS systems are the most common systems on medium-duty trucks with hydraulic brakes, lighter-duty systems may be equipped with integral ABS systems that combine the ABS module and the master cylinder. Most heavier vehicles will be equipped with an ABS module situated conveniently on the vehicle frame, as shown in FIGURE 33-32.

FIGURE 33-32 ABS module mounted to the vehicle frame.

The ABS electronic control module is the brain behind the ABS system. The module contains a powerful computer that controls all the functions of the ABS system. Each of the brake's circuits controlled will pass through the module on the way to the brake the circuit applies. The module usually will contain two electric solenoids for each of the brake circuits that are controlled. In other words, there will be two solenoids for each channel. One solenoid relieves excess pressure to stop a wheel from skidding. It is usually called the dump solenoid. The second solenoid is used to supply pressure for the brake to increase braking effort and is called the boost solenoid or the pressure solenoid.

The ABS system operates by first receiving input from several sources. The primary input is the wheel speed sensors. Other inputs come from the brake pedal, the ignition switch, and any vehicle stability sensors.

The wheel speed sensors send wheel speed information to the ABS computer, which analyzes the signal from each wheel, compares each input to all the others, and establishes an average wheel speed. Should one or more wheels drop to a threshold limit below average wheel speed, the computer signals the dump solenoid to dump excess pressure from the wheel in question until its speed matches the average. When it does, the solenoid will once again allow pressure to apply. The computer pumps the brakes on the wheel in question to keep it as close to skid as possible without actually skidding. That is the point at which maximum braking effort from the wheel is achieved.

Unlike the air brake ABS system, the hydraulic system does not have a nearly endless supply of air to exhaust and reapply the brake being controlled if multiple dumps are required. A back-up system is needed to resupply the pressure. Otherwise, the master cylinder piston would continue to move to reapply pressure, eventually leading to a no-brake-pressure situation. Hydraulic ABS systems use an electric motor back-up pump to supply the extra pressure to reapply the brake after a dump cycle. Consequently, the master cylinder pushrod does not move any further than the original brake application. The back-up electric motor pump is plainly visible in Figure 33-32.

The ABS system can be also designed to provide stability control for the vehicle. Electronic stability control systems basically use the ABS system to systematically apply single wheel brakes as much as necessary to control vehicle yaw. (Yaw is a twisting around the vehicle center.) Similarly, electronic stability control systems use ABS systematical to control oversteer/understeer situations where front wheels start to skid and the vehicle is skidding sideways. Electronic stability programs increase the safety of the operator and the vehicle.

ABS components can also be utilized to provide traction control on lighter medium-duty trucks. Traction control monitors wheel slip on acceleration. If one drive wheel starts to spin in a poor traction situation, the traction control system can use the ABS components to apply brake pressure to the wheel that is spinning. Doing so makes more torque available to the wheel with better traction, allowing the vehicle to move.

Maintenance of Hydraulic Brake Systems

In hydraulic brake systems, the primary components are the brake master cylinder, wheel cylinders, brake shoes, and drums/discs. The procedure below deals with the removal and reinstallation of components in these systems. The system should be inspected in two ways: foot-pressure applied and by conducting a system test.

To inspect hydraulic and air-over-hydraulic brake systems for fluid leaks, follow the guidelines in SKILL DRILL 33-1.

To remove and replace an air-over-hydraulic master cylinder/actuator, follow the guidelines in SKILL DRILL 33-2.

To remove and replace a dual-circuit master cylinder in a vacuum-assisted or hydroboost braking system, follow the guidelines in SKILL DRILL 33-3.

SKILL DRILL 33-1 Inspecting Hydraulic and Air-Over-Hydraulic Brake Systems for Fluid Leaks

1. Two people are required to perform these tests: one to operate the system, the other to conduct the inspection. First, inspect the system for signs of a leak at the brake component couplings and the brake lines and see if there is any evidence of a fluid leak.

2. If you find no evidence of a leak, have your co-worker put his or her foot on the brake pedal and, with foot pressure applied on the brake pedal, inspect the system and recheck for obvious leaks in and around the master cylinder.

3. With pressure still applied, check the flex lines and connections at the calipers.

4. Inspect all brake lines and line fitting connections in the hydraulic brake system for evidence of a leak or brake fluid.

5. If there is brake fluid near a connection point, perform the following activities:

   a. Clean and dry the entire area.

   b. Determine the source of the leak.

   c. Relieve system pressure (refer to the appropriate maintenance manual for complete instructions).

      1. Make the necessary repairs.
      2. Inspect any fittings for damage and, if no damage is evident, tighten the fittings by referring to the appropriate maintenance manual for torque specifications.
      3. If a fitting has been damaged, replace the fitting; again, refer to the appropriate maintenance manual for torque specifications.
      4. If any hydraulic system fittings were found loose or disconnected (brake circuit open), bleed the closed circuit after repair; refer to the brake bleed instructions given in the appropriate maintenance manual.

6. After all necessary repairs have been made and the system bled, verify that the hydraulic circuits are connected properly.

SKILL DRILL 33-2 Removing and Replacing an Air-Over-Hydraulic Master Cylinder/Actuator

1. Select the appropriate hand tools and any special tools required. In addition, locate and have available the manufacturer's workshop manual for reference. Place a collection tray under the master cylinder when removing the hydraulic pipes to collect the hydraulic fluid. Avoid getting any fluid on the vehicle's paintwork.
2. Remove as much of the brake fluid from the reservoir as possible before removing the piping, using an approved method.
3. Remove the piping and collect any fluid coming from the exposed ports. Ensure no brake fluid comes into contact with the paintwork; if it does, rinse the area thoroughly with fresh water. Do not wipe the area with a cloth, as the paint softens with brake fluid contact. Plug the pipe ends to prevent dirt from entering the master cylinder.
4. Remove all the necessary air hose connections.
5. With reference to the appropriate manufacturer's workshop manual, follow the steps listed to remove the unit.
6. When replacing the master cylinder/actuator, again follow the instructions in the workshop manual.
7. Reconnect the actuating air line and hydraulic pipes, and refill the reservoir with fresh, clean brake fluid.
8. It may be necessary to bleed the master cylinder for trapped air. Retorque all fittings to the manufacturer's specifications.
9. Carry out an integrity check on the braking system to ensure it is operating to manufacturer's specifications.

SKILL DRILL 33-3 Removing and Replacing a Dual-Circuit Master Cylinder in a Vacuum or Hydroboost Assisted Hydraulic Braking System

1. Select the appropriate hand tools and any special tools required. Locate and have available the manufacturer's workshop manual for reference. Place a collection tray under the master cylinder when removing the hydraulic pipes to collect the hydraulic fluid. Avoid getting any fluid on the vehicle's paintwork.
2. Remove as much of the brake fluid from the reservoir as possible before removing the piping, using an approved method. Ensure that brake fluid does not come into contact with the paintwork. Any spills should be rinsed thoroughly with fresh water. Only flush with water; do not wipe the area with a cloth, as the paint softens with brake fluid contact.
3. Mark the location of each of the pipes to ensure they are reconnected in the same way when reassembling. It is advisable to plug the pipe ends to prevent dirt from entering the system.
4. Using the manufacturer's workshop manual, follow the steps listed to remove the unit. However, only remove the dual-circuit master cylinder from the booster, not the complete assembly, unless the booster itself is suspected of failure.
5. When reinstalling the master cylinder to the vacuum booster or hydrobooster, ensure that the pushrod is in its correct location. Tighten securing nuts to the recommended torque as outlined in the workshop manual.
6. Reconnect the hydraulic lines.
7. Refill the reservoir with fresh, clean brake fluid. It may be necessary to bleed the master cylinder for trapped air. In some instances, it would be recommended that the entire system be bled to expel any trapped air. Retorque all fittings to the manufacturer's specifications.
8. Carry out an integrity check on the braking system to ensure it is operating to manufacturer's specifications.
9. Check that there is no fluid leakage from the bleeder screws or piping, and road-test the vehicle to determine the correct operation of the brake system.

To remove and replace a drum brake assembly, follow the guidelines in SKILL DRILL 33-4.

To test a treadle valve for leakage, follow the guidelines in SKILL DRILL 33-5.

Whenever hydraulic brake circuits are opened to replace components, air can enter the system. That air must be removed because, unlike hydraulic fluid, air is compressible. If it remains in the system, brake operation will be poor or non-existent. To bleed the air out of the system, follow the steps in SKILL DRILL 33-6.

Metering and proportioning valves are both tested in the same way. To test these valves, follow the procedure

SKILL DRILL 33-4 Removing and Replacing a Drum Brake Assembly

1. Before raising the vehicle, chock the other wheels that are not being removed. Loosen the wheel nuts/bolts from the wheel end being removed. If the wheel assembly being removed is a drive axle assembly, release the hand (parking) brake and place the transmission into neutral.
2. Raise the vehicle and place safety stands in the correct location to support the vehicle. Remove the already loosened retaining nuts/bolts, and, if necessary, as in the case of dual wheel arrangements, get help from a co-worker to remove the wheel assembly from the vehicle.
3. With reference to the appropriate manufacturer's workshop manual, remove any retaining nut and/or locking nuts (if applicable) and remove the brake drum.
4. Remove the brake shoes and return springs following the process outlined in the workshop manual. You need to be careful removing return springs to ensure the springs do not come off prematurely, as this could cause both damage and injury.
5. With the springs uncoupled from their retaining points, remove the brake shoes from their location points. Then carry out a visual inspection of all the components.
6. Reinstall the brake shoes as outlined in the workshop manual, observing all safety precautions. Make sure that the return springs are correctly seated and installed.
7. Reinstall the hub bearings as outlined in the workshop manual. Install the bearing hub and brake drum. Get a co-worker to assist you in the relocation of the hub assembly and brake drum into its operating position.
8. Replace the bearing hub adjusting nut and tighten the preload bearing to the correct torque specification. If fitted, fit and torque the locking nut and securing tab.
9. With a co-worker's help, refit the wheel assembly and screw on the nuts/bolts. Torque the wheel nuts/bolts to the specified torque setting as listed in the workshop manual.
10. Follow that correct procedure outlined in the service manual for adjusting the brakes.
11. Carry out the brake adjustment as per the manufacturer's specifications. Make sure that the wheel assembly rotates freely and does not bind on the shoes.
12. Jack up the vehicle and remove the safety stands. Make sure that there are no tools left behind, and lower the vehicle to the ground. Recheck the wheel nuts/bolts torque.

SKILL DRILL 33-5 Testing a Treadle Valve for Leakage

1. With a 100 psi (700 kPa) supply pressure in the system and the treadle valve in the released position, coat the exhaust port with soapsuds and check for leakage. There should be *no* leakage for a valve in operational condition.
2. Have a co-worker fully apply the treadle valve and hold it in the fully applied position. Coat all ports and around the top of the valve with soapsuds. There should be *no* visible signs of leakage for a valve in operational condition.
3. Should there be any signs of bubbles from the soapy water—which indicates that there is system leakage—then the components should be replaced with a new or remanufactured unit or should be repaired.

SKILL DRILL 33-6 Bleeding the Air Out of a Hydraulic Braking System

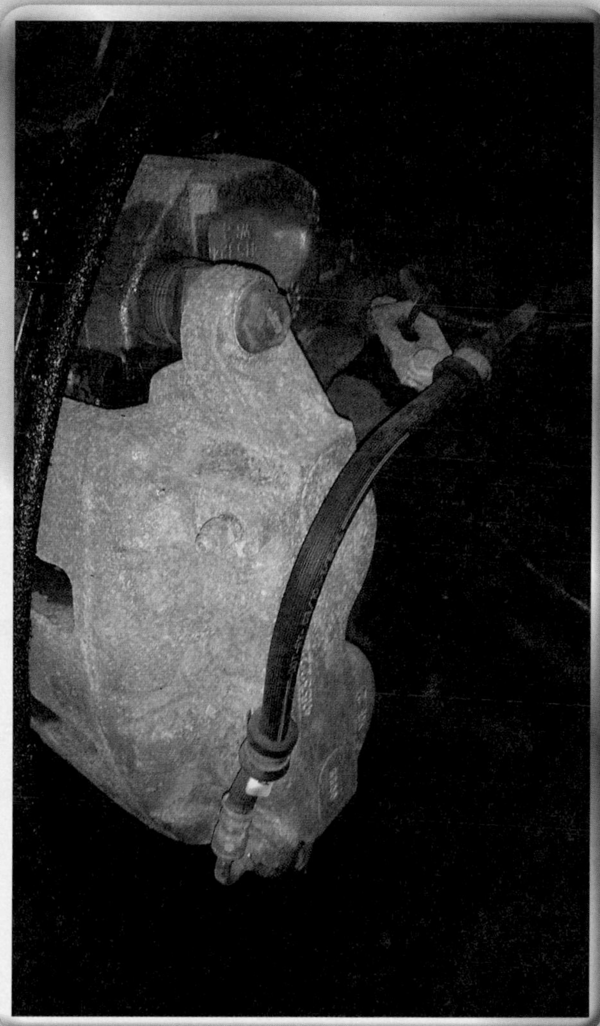

1. Clear communication between you and the assistant is required for successful bleeding.
2. Ask an assistant to slowly push the brake pedal down.
3. Starting with the bleeder screw that is the farthest from the master cylinder, attach a clear bleeder hose to the bleeder screw and insert the tube into a clear plastic container, then open the bleeder screw one-quarter to one-half turn.
4. Observe any old brake fluid and air bubbles coming out of the bleeder screw.
5. When the brake fluid stream stops, close the bleeder screw lightly and have the assistant slowly release the pedal. This allows the master cylinder to pull a fresh charge of brake fluid from the reservoir.
6. Repeat the previous three steps until there are no more air bubbles coming out of the brake unit.
7. Close off the bleeder screw and tighten it to the manufacturer's specifications. Be sure that you DO NOT bleed the system so much that the reservoir runs dry and admits air into the hydraulic braking system.
8. Check the level in the master cylinder reservoir, top it off, and reinstall the reservoir cap.
9. Repeat this procedure for each of the wheel brake units, moving closer to the master cylinder, one wheel at a time, until all of the air has been removed and the brake pedal is not spongy.
10. Start the engine and ensure the proper functioning of the brakes with the power assist operational.

in SKILL DRILL 33-7. To test the pressure differential valve, follow the guidelines in SKILL DRILL 33-8.

Bleeding hydraulic brake systems that are equipped with anti-lock braking systems can be very different than bleeding a simple hydraulic system. Each ABS system encountered will require its own specific set of instructions for successful bleeding of the hydraulic system. The steps used typically include using a scan tool to actuate the solenoids in the ABS module to ensure all air is out of the system. General guidelines for bleeding air out of an ABS system are in SKILL DRILL 33-9.

Finally, to test the hydraulic system and inspect for leaks and determine needed repairs, follow the guidelines in SKILL DRILL 33-10.

SKILL DRILL 33-7 Testing the Metering or the Proportioning Valves

1. Research the testing procedure and specifications in the appropriate service information.
2. Disconnect the inlet line and outlet line from the metering valve or proportioning valve. Use a flare nut wrench to accomplish this.
3. Connect the valve pressure tester to the inlet port and outlet port of the metering valve or the proportioning valve. Reconnect the inlet line to the valve, with the pressure gauge teed into it.
4. Operate the brake pedal and observe both pressure gauge readings; compare the findings to specifications.

SKILL DRILL 33-8 Testing Pressure Differential Valves

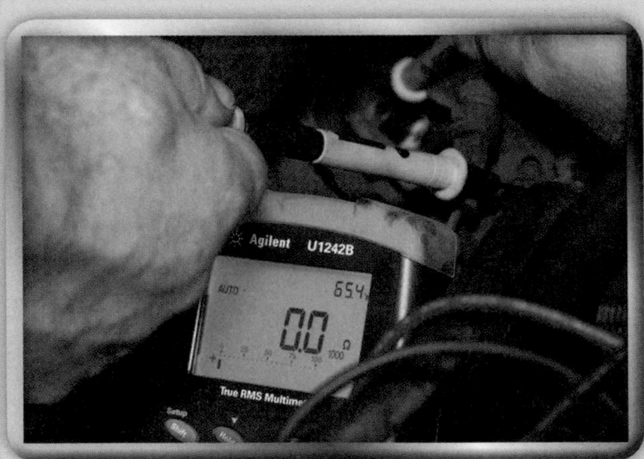

1. Research the testing procedure and specifications in the appropriate service information.
2. Disconnect the electrical connector from the pressure differential valve and connect an ohmmeter between the terminal on the valve and the body of the valve. Have an assistant lightly apply the brake pedal and hold until the bleeder screw is closed.
3. Open the front bleeder screw on the driver's side of the vehicle and watch the ohmmeter reading. It should go to zero.
4. Close the bleeder screw and move to the rear driver's side wheel. Again, with the assistant applying light pressure to the pedal, open the driver's side rear wheel bleeder screw slightly and watch the meter reading. It should go to OL and then back to zero as the valve moves to the "off" position and then to the "on" position.

SKILL DRILL 33-9 Bleeding a Hydraulic ABS System

1. Research the step-by-step bleeding process for the particular ABS system you are working on. Unless you follow the manufacturer's steps to the letter, you will be unsuccessful. The following is merely an example of the bleeding process from one manufacturer. Remember to monitor the master cylinder during the process so you do not run low on brake fluid.
2. Perform the brake bleed procedure for hydraulic system outlined in Skill Drill 33-6.
3. Install the scan tool the vehicle ECM, or if the proper electronic control equipment is available, install the scan tool directly to the modulator assembly.
4. Turn ignition switch ON or power up the electronic control equipment.
5. Push the brake pedal with maximum application force and hold.
6. Activate the ABS solenoid pulse function on the scan tool or the electronic control equipment, starting with the longest brake circuit, usually the rear.
7. Release the brake pedal for five seconds, and using the scan tool or the electronic control equipment, activate the ABS modulator valve's back-up pump for five seconds.
8. Repeat steps 5 through 7 three additional times for each of the remaining brake circuits.
9. Perform manual bleed as in Skill Drill 33-6.

SKILL DRILL 33-10 Inspecting, Measuring, Removing, and Reinstalling a Rotor Assembly

1. Locate and follow the appropriate procedure in the service manual, and refer to it for steps 2, 11, 13, and 15 if assistance is needed.
2. Remove calipers.
3. Use a C-clamp to force the caliper piston(s) back, and inspect the caliper pistons and seals for leaks.
4. Inspect and measure rotor on vehicle.
5. Check brake rotor lateral runout with dial indicator.

   Note: Tighten the wheel bearings to zero end play.
6. Record findings on job sheet or work order.
7. Check service manual to see if dimensional specifications are OK.
8. Loosen wheel bearing nut, and remove rotor hub assembly.
9. Clean rotor hub assembly and inspect.
10. Remove rotor from wheel hub. Note: Hub and rotor may be made as one unit.
11. Clean and repack wheel bearings with grease.
12. Install new rotor back on hub.
13. Install new wheel bearing seal into hub.
14. Reinstall hub and rotor assembly back on axle.
15. Adjust wheel bearing.
16. Check to make sure hub rotates freely.
17. List the test results and/or recommendations on the job sheet or work order. Clean work area, and return tools and materials to proper storage.

Wrap-up

Ready for Review

- Medium- to heavy-duty vehicle hydraulic braking systems need power assist to operate satisfactorily; the power assist can be supplied by vacuum, hydraulic pressure, or air pressure.
- Hydraulic braking with vacuum assist is typical for lighter-duty vehicles. Hydroboost systems and air-over-hydraulic systems are used on medium- and heavy-duty vehicles.
- In all hydraulic braking systems, a pushrod exerts force on the piston(s) in the master cylinder, causing an increase in fluid pressure that results in force being applied to the brake pads and shoes.
- Vacuum-assisted braking systems use atmospheric pressure to intensify braking effort.
- Hydroboost systems use hydraulic pressure supplied by the power steering pump or a dedicated pump to intensify braking effort.
- Air-over-hydraulic brake systems use a conventional hydraulic brake system. Drum brakes are the most common, but some vehicles may have disc brakes on the front axle.
- Air-over-hydraulic systems use compressed air to intensify braking effort.
- Braking systems are complex, and their components depend in large measure on whether the system uses drum or disc brakes. Drum brakes use brake shoes in various configurations and adjusters, and disc brakes use pads.
- Today, drum brakes are generally found only on a vehicle's rear wheels.
- The drum brake has two brake shoes, with a friction material called a lining attached. These shoes expand against a brake drum's inside surface and slow the wheel down.
- Even though drum brakes are self-energizing, they commonly overheat and cause brake fade.
- Disc brakes slow rotation of the wheels by the friction caused by pushing brake pads against a brake disc with a set of calipers.
- Disc brakes offer better stopping performance than drum brakes and provide a much higher braking force per lb (kg) of brake weight.
- Disc brake performance improves as the components heat up, but drum brake performance deteriorates as the components heat up.
- In addition to foot brakes, vehicles also use hand brakes that are either mechanical or electrically activated.
- Common components in hydraulic braking and air-over-hydraulic brake systems include the master cylinder, wheel cylinder, and brake booster.
- Hydraulic brake systems use a variety of valves to control system operation. These include proportioning valves, metering valves, pressure differential valves, and/or combination valves.
- Air-over-hydraulic systems also include systems for air supply, a foot brake valve, air booster units, and fail safe systems.
- Air boosters can be indirect or direct. Indirect are found on heavier trucks, and direct are generally found on lighter trucks. Boosters have three positions: released, applied, and balanced.
- As a fail safe, air-over-hydraulic braking systems are required by regulation to use a tandem system design so that one system can compensate if the other fails.
- All vehicles are required to have a park brake system that can also act as an emergency brake should there be a failure of the service brakes.
- Spring brake actuators are critical components of the park and service brake operation.
- Most hydraulic brake systems today will be equipped with four-channel ABS, meaning that each of the four wheel brakes is controlled individually.
- Vehicles with ABS system can also use the ABS system to operate an electronic stability system to enhance vehicle safety.
- ABS components can also be used to provide traction control on lighter vehicles.

Vocabulary Builder

air-over-hydraulic braking system A braking system that uses an air compressor to provide power assistance over the hydraulic components to the braking system.

backing plate A metal plate to which the brake lining is fixed.

brake drum A short, wide, hollow cylinder that is capped on one end and bolted to a vehicle's wheel; it has an inner friction surface that the brake shoe is forced against.

brake fluid Hydraulic fluid that transfers forces under pressure through the hydraulic lines to the wheel braking units.

brake lines Made of seamless, double-walled steel, and able to transmit more than 6,895 kPa of hydraulic pressure through the hydraulic brake system.

brake shoes A steel shoe and brake lining friction material that apply force to the brake drum during braking.

caliper A hydraulic device that uses pressure from the master cylinder to apply the brake pads against the rotor.

combination valve A valve that combines either all or some of the following into one housing—the proportioning valve, the metering valve, and the pressure differential valve.

front/rear split system A brake system in which the front brakes operate on one hydraulic circuit and the rear brakes from the other.

leading shoes Brake shoes that are installed so that they are applied in the same direction as the forward rotation of the drum and thus are self-energizing.

leading/trailing shoe drum brake arrangement A type of brake shoe arrangement where one shoe is positioned in a leading manner and the other shoe in a trailing manner.

metering valve A valve that delays brake application pressure to the front disk brakes until a certain level of pressure builds in the system.

pressure differential valve A valve that detects pressure loss in either of the two hydraulic systems of a split hydraulic brake system.

primary piston A brake piston in the master cylinder moved directly by the pushrod or the power booster; it generates hydraulic pressure to move the secondary piston.

proportioning valve A valve that limits brake application pressure to the rear brakes when the vehicle is not heavily loaded.

residual pressure valve (residual check valve) In drum brake systems, a valve that maintains pressure in the wheel cylinders slightly above atmospheric pressure so that air does not enter the system through the seals in the wheel cylinders.

rotor The main rotating part of a disc brake system.

secondary piston A piston that is moved by hydraulic pressure generated by the primary piston in the master cylinder.

servo action A drum brake design where one brake shoe, when activated, applies an increased activating force to the other brake shoe, in proportion to the initial activating force; further enhances the self-energizing feature of some drum brakes.

trailing shoes Brake shoes installed so that they are applied in the opposite direction to the forward rotation of the brake drum; not self-energizing and less efficient at developing braking force.

twin-leading-shoe drum brake Brake shoe arrangement in which both brake shoes are self-energizing in the forward direction.

vacuum booster A vacuum operated boost system for hydraulic brakes.

wheel cylinders A hydraulic cylinder with one or two pistons, seals, dust boots, and a bleeder screw that pushes the brake shoes into contact with the brake drum to slow or stop the vehicle.

Review Questions

1. A metering valve in a hydraulic system does which of the following?
   a. Delays application of the rear brakes
   b. Delays application of the front brakes
   c. Delays the return of brake fluid
   d. Delays the activation of the warning lamp
2. On a vehicle equipped with a hydraulic booster unit, the booster unit is most likely located:
   a. at the firewall under the hood.
   b. at the rear suspension.
   c. at the frame rail.
   d. on the engine and belt driven.
3. On a vehicle equipped with a hydraulic brake system using a vacuum booster unit, the booster unit does which of the following?
   a. Replaces the master cylinder
   b. Replaces the rear circuit on the master cylinder
   c. Increases hydraulic circuit pressure
   d. Increases hydraulic circuit fluid volume
4. During normal operation, a hydraulically boosted master cylinder is typically powered by which of the following?
   a. The vehicle's power steering pump
   b. The engine's oil pump
   c. An electric motor
   d. A hydraulic accumulator
5. Which one of the following adverse conditions will not activate the brake warning light in the instrument panel?
   a. Loss of fluid in the rear brake system
   b. A broken brake hose at a front caliper
   c. Park brake switch stuck on
   d. Vacuum booster failure
6. During normal operation of a rear drum front disc hydraulic brake system, self-energizing takes place:
   a. at the front disk brakes.
   b. at the rear drum brakes.
   c. at both the front discs and the rear drums.
   d. at neither the front discs or the rear drums.
7. Which of the following is not an advantage of disc brakes?
   a. They are resistant to brake fade from water.
   b. They are self-energizing.
   c. They are self-adjusting.
   d. They run cooler.
8. In a hydraulic brake system, where does the brake fluid transmit applied pressure?
   a. Only to the wheel cylinders or calipers
   b. In all directions equally
   c. In the direction of the applied force only
   d. Only to the system's moving parts
9. The proportioning valve on a hydraulic brake system:
   a. insures that both primary and secondary circuits are at equal pressures.
   b. reduces pressure to the front wheel hydraulic circuit during heavy braking.
   c. reduces pressure to the rear wheel hydraulic circuit during heavy braking.
   d. senses pressure loss and activates the warning light.
10. Which of the following applies to the combination valve on a hydraulic braking system?
    a. It is part of the vacuum power booster unit.
    b. It usually contains the proportioning valve and the hydraulic system failure warning light switch.
    c. It is eliminated when the vehicle is equipped with four-wheel disk brakes.
    d. It decreases the driver's pedal effort.

ASE-Type Questions

1. Technician A says that the drum-to-lining clearance must be maintained at all times. Technician B says that there would be a delay in the brakes applying if there were an excessively large drum-to-lining clearance. Who is correct?
   a. Technician A
   b. Technician B
   c. Both Technician A and Technician B
   d. Neither Technician A nor Technician B
2. Technician A says that if the drum-to-lining clearance is too tight, the result would be dragging brakes. Technician B says if the drum-to-lining clearance is too tight, the result would be overheated brakes. Who is correct?
   a. Technician A
   b. Technician B
   c. Both Technician A and Technician B
   d. Neither Technician A nor Technician B
3. Technician A says that when a driver applies the brake—and the primary piston moves forward and covers the compensating port—that this completes the primary circuit. Technician B says that when a driver applies the brake—and the primary piston moves forward and covers the compensating port—that this creates a pressure chamber for the trapped fluid. Who is correct?
   a. Technician A
   b. Technician B
   c. Both Technician A and Technician B
   d. Neither Technician A nor Technician B
4. Technician A says that the reservoir serves as a storage tank of compressed air for the air brake system. Technician B says that reservoirs may provide a location where air, heated by compression, can be cooled and the water vapor condensed. Who is correct?
   a. Technician A
   b. Technician B
   c. Both Technician A and Technician B
   d. Neither Technician A nor Technician B
5. Technician A says that brake shoes in a medium- to heavy-duty vehicle can be in a leading and trailing brake shoe configuration. Technician B says that the brake shoes can be in a screw cam operating brake configuration. Who is correct?
   a. Technician A
   b. Technician B
   c. Both Technician A and Technician B
   d. Neither Technician A nor Technician B
6. Technician A says that you would usually find a cam-operated brake on a light- or medium-duty vehicle. Technician B says that you would usually find a cam-operated brake on a large, heavy vehicle. Who is correct?
   a. Technician A
   b. Technician B
   c. Both Technician A and Technician B
   d. Neither Technician A nor Technician B
7. Technician A says that compared with drum brakes, disc brakes offer better stopping performance because the disc is more readily cooled. Technician B says that compared with disc brakes, drum brakes offer better stopping performance because the drum is more readily cooled. Who is correct?
   a. Technician A
   b. Technician B
   c. Both Technician A and Technician B
   d. Neither Technician A nor Technician B
8. Technician A says that tandem brake systems can be split from front to rear. Technician B says that tandem brake systems can be split diagonally. Who is correct?
   a. Technician A
   b. Technician B
   c. Both Technician A and Technician B
   d. Neither Technician A nor Technician B
9. Technician A says that in an air-over-hydraulic systems, the primary components are the compressor, brake master cylinder, wheel cylinders, and air actuated brake chambers. Technician B says that the system should be inspected in two ways: foot-pressure applied and by conducting a system test. Who is correct?
   a. Technician A
   b. Technician B
   c. Both Technician A and Technician B
   d. Neither Technician A nor Technician B
10. Technician A says that hydraulic brake wheel cylinders are always dual acting. Technician B says that a disc brake caliper must have at least two pistons. Who is correct?
    a. Technician A
    b. Technician B
    c. Both Technician A and Technician B
    d. Neither Technician A nor Technician B

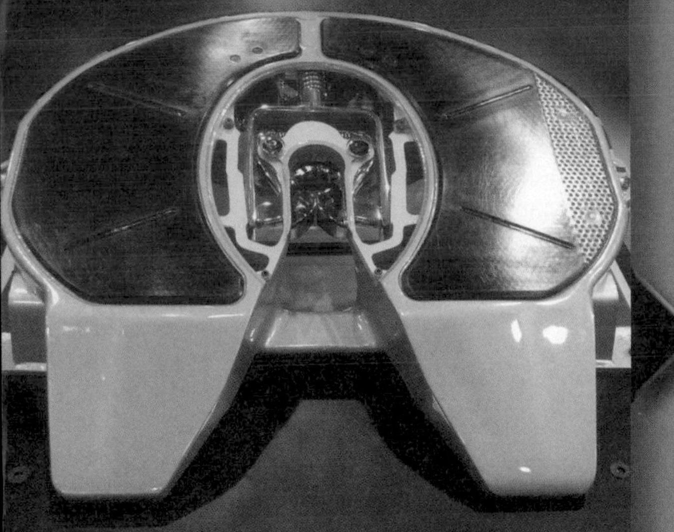

CHAPTER 34

NATEF Tasks

Suspension and Steering

Frame and Coupling Devices

	Page
■ Inspect, repair, or replace pintle hooks and draw bars , if applicable.	1109–1112
■ Inspect and service sliding fifth wheel, tracks, stops, locking systems, air cylinders, springs, lines, hoses, and controls.	1121
■ Inspect, service, and/or adjust fifth wheel, pivot pins, bushings, locking mechanisms, and mounting hardware.	1124–1128

Knowledge Objectives

After reading this chapter, you will be able to:

1. Identify and describe various configurations for combination vehicles according to connection type. (pp 1105–1107)
2. Identify various types of converter dollies. (pp 1106–1107)
3. Explain legislative requirements for combination vehicles according to vehicle weight classification, axle load weight, spread, and number. (pp 1107–1109)
4. Identify and explain the differences between fifth wheels and other coupling mechanisms. (pp 1109–1116)
5. Identify and describe types of hitching and coupling devices used on truck, tractor-trailer combinations. (pp 1109–1116)
6. Describe the procedure for correctly positioning fifth wheels. (pp 1112–1113)
7. Identify and describe types of fifth wheels used on tractors. (pp 1112–1115)
8. Identify the types and describe the function of kingpins and upper coupler assembly. (pp 1115–1116)
9. Differentiate between different fifth wheel locking jaw mechanisms. (pp 1117–1120)
10. Identify and describe inspection and testing procedures for fifth wheels and coupling devices. (pp 1122–1123)
11. Recommend and describe common fifth wheel maintenance and overhaul procedures. (pp 1122–1123)

Fifth Wheels and Hitching Devices

Skills Objectives

After reading this chapter, you will be able to:

1. Recommend the correct hitching device according to tow weight rating and application. (pp 1107–1109)
2. Locate the installation position of a fifth wheel. (pp 1112–1115)
3. Identify symptoms of incorrectly positioned fifth wheels. (pp 1112–1113)
4. Inspect and service sliding fifth wheel, tracks, stops, locking systems, air cylinders, springs, lines, hoses, and controls. (p 1121)
5. Inspect and service kingpins and upper couplers. (p 1125)
6. Inspect, service, and/or adjust fifth wheel, pivot pins, bushings, locking mechanisms, and mounting hardware. (pp 1126–1128)
7. Inspect and service landing gears. (pp 1128–1129)
8. Lubricate the fifth wheel. (p 1124) **SKILL DRILL 34-1**
9. Inspect the slider mechanism on a fifth wheel. (p 1128) **SKILL DRILL 34-2**

Introduction

To prevent damage to roadways and bridges, the vehicle weight supported by tires and axles is limited by legislation. Generally, tires should apply no more than 600 lb (272 kg) per square inch of road contact patch. Furthermore, the weight of a vehicle supported by a single axle should almost never exceed than 20,000 lb (9,072 kg).

A variety of vehicle factors and operating conditions change this general rule for maximum axle weight. The best solution to enable transportation of heavier loads is to add more axles to the vehicle configuration. Adding more axles minimizes damage to road surfaces.

Adding more axles to a rigid chassis is not without challenges, however. For vehicles loaded with tens of thousands of pounds of cargo, steering and maneuvering would become almost impossible. To solve this dilemma, trailers that allow the vehicle to articulate, or bend when turning, are used. Connecting trucks with trailers form **combination vehicles**, such as the tanker shown in FIGURE 34-1A. Fifth wheels and a variety of coupling devices are used to connect or hitch trailers to tractors while allowing articulation between tractor and towed units. A **fifth wheel** is plate type coupler with locking jaws that supports the weight of a semi-trailer and enables articulation between the tractor and trailer. In FIGURE 34-1B the front of the trailer is supported by the tractor and articulates on the fifth wheel. Fifth wheels will be discussed in greater detail in the Types of Fifth Wheels and Hitching Devices section.

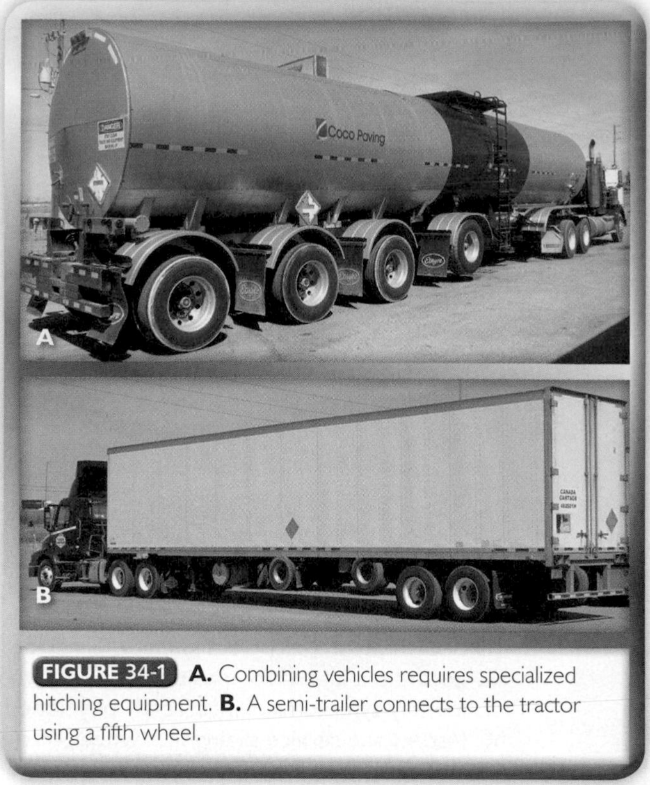

FIGURE 34-1 **A.** Combining vehicles requires specialized hitching equipment. **B.** A semi-trailer connects to the tractor using a fifth wheel.

You Are the Technician

After reading some inspection report histories of a number of tractors and trailers in a fleet operation, you discover a consistent pattern of persistent problems contributing to unusually high maintenance costs. Some of the problems include:

- Abnormal tire wear patterns on the front axle tires, leading to frequent replacement.
- Excessive tire wear on only the drive axle set of tires, resulting in frequent tire replacement.
- Steering and vehicle handling complaints, leading to unnecessary replacement of steering and suspension parts such as steering gears, which were later found to have no fault.
- Damage to the front corners of several trailers and damage to tractor's vertical exhaust stacks.
- Damage to trailer landing gear and tractor mud-flap brackets torn off several tractors.

The company has also received several fines for overloaded axles at highway inspection weigh scales.

One of the possible causes that could account for the pattern of complaints and repairs is the misplacement of a fifth wheel, leading to unequal distribution of load weight over the axles. As you begin to perform an inspection of the vehicles with the highest number of complaints, you are considering the following:

1. How would each of the above complaints relate to an incorrectly positioned fifth wheel?
2. Which complaints would be specific to a fifth wheel moved too far forward, rearward, or both?
3. Outline what items should be inspected to validate that the fifth wheel can be properly adjusted to properly distribute loads over the axles.
4. What are the maintenance practices or procedures that could be put in place to ensure the fifth wheels are correctly positioned on the tractor?

Fundamentals of Fifth Wheels and Hitching Devices

Fifth wheels and coupling devices are used to connect vehicles together into a combination vehicle. Combination vehicles allow the power unit to be used for a variety of purposes, which makes the vehicle more versatile, reduces dead time (when the vehicle is waiting between loads), and leads to increased profitability for the owner. Vehicles can be connected by using various types of hitches, couplers, and fifth wheels. This section will discuss the different types of combination vehicles and how they are connected.

Truck-Trailer Combination Vehicles

To understand when and where various coupling devices and fifth wheels are used, it is important to learn common configurations for combination vehicles. Combination vehicles can be divided into categories according to their components: tractors, trailers (semi and full) and converter dollies.

Tractors

The term tractor-engine, which was given to a motorized vehicle pulling wagons, has been replaced by the term tractor. A tractor is a commercial motor vehicle chassis designed to exclusively tow trailers. Having usually just a cab and no capability to carry cargo, tractors use high torque output engines and a fifth wheel, which is used to support the front end of a trailer.

Pulling trailers today is not fundamentally different than the wagons of a bygone era. Tractors are commonly constructed to produce substantial traction power at low speeds, hauling heavy loads through one or two drive axles. Depending on where and how the tractor is used, the cab may have a sleeper unit for the driver or driving team to use. A day cab, or conventional tractor, such as the one shown in **FIGURE 34-2**, does not have a sleeper unit and is used for short distance hauling. Aerodynamic farings reduce energy losses due to wind resistance and increase fuel economy.

FIGURE 34-2 Conventional cab forward tractors locate the engine in front of the cab.

A common tractor configuration places the engine ahead of the cab. This **cab forward (CF)** design provides the driver favorable ride characteristics and easier access to the cab. **Cab over engine (COE)** tractors have the engine located beneath the cab. This design is less commonly used in North America but is used almost exclusively in Europe because COE tractors are shorter and more maneuverable. **FIGURE 34-3** shows a cab over engine tractor.

FIGURE 34-3 Cab over engine tractors are shorter and more maneuverable but transmit more road shock to the driver.

Legislation limiting vehicle length means longer trailers can be used with cab over engine tractors. Placing the cab over the steer axles means the tractor is more easily turned in tight spaces. A disadvantage, however, is that suspension bounce and jounce are more powerfully transmitted to the cab. The wheel base length and location of the fifth wheel on a tractor are critical since the weight of the trailer must be distributed over all the axles so that no axle exceeds the maximum legal weight. Legal weight limits are covered in the Vehicle Weight Ratings and Capacity section.

A **terminal tractor**, also known as a **shunt truck** or yard tractor, is built to move semi-trailers around a warehouse yard or intermodal facility. As shown in

FIGURE 34-4, terminal tractors use unique suspensions and fifth wheels designed to get under a semi-trailer and lift a trailer without the need to raise the trailer landing gear. A hydraulic lifting mechanism integrated into the fifth wheel is designed to lift the trailer 15" (38.1 cm) with as much as 70,000 lb (31,818 kg) of force. To improve visibility, a single person cab is offset to the left of the engine.

Trailers

Trailers are the cargo-carrying portion of a combination vehicle. The most familiar combination configuration in North America is a tractor with a semi-trailer. **Semi-trailers** use one, two, or even three axles depending on their length and load carrying capacity. The position of the axles can often be moved forward and backwards along the trailer to achieve proper and even weight distribution over the axles. This is particularly useful if the load is an irregular size or weight.

The front of the semi-trailer is supported and towed by a fifth wheel, which may or may not be attached directly to a tractor. When not connected to the tractor, the trailer's landing gear supports the front of the trailer. The **landing gear** is a set of retractable legs attached to the trailer, which support a semi-trailer when it is not resting on a fifth wheel. Landing gear is illustrated in FIGURE 34-5.

FIGURE 34-5 Landing gear is a set of retractable legs attached to the trailer.

FIGURE 34-4 A shunt truck or yard tractor has a hydraulically lifted fifth wheel and is used to move trailers around a yard without needing to raise the trailer's landing gear.

Since the trailer's load is actually carried by the tractor it is referred to as a *semi-trailer*.

Different than a semi-trailer, a **full trailer** has axles at the front and rear of the trailer to support the entire weight of the trailer. FIGURE 34-6 shows a full trailer. This allows the trailer to be pulled by a vehicle with an appropriate hitching system.

Converter Dollies

Full trailers are most often semi-trailers that are converted to full trailers using a **converter dolly**, which is a fifth wheel supported by one or two axles. The converter dolly may also use self-steering axles using a high degree of positive caster to maintain straight line stability. Whenever a converter dolly is used to connect two trailers, the lead trailer is equipped with a pintle hook type hitch like the one in FIGURE 34-7. Pintle hooks will be covered in the Pintle Hooks and Couplers section.

Combination vehicles may also have multiple trailers, referred to as A-trains, B-trains, and C-trains. The trains are differentiated by the hitching mechanism connecting them to the trailers. The geometric shape of the connection is what distinguishes the different types of trailer combinations. A **draw bar** is used to connect the dolly to a lead trailer or semi-trailer.

An **A-train** is a three-unit combination of tractor plus two trailers. The second trailer is a full trailer unit connected by a draw bar to a single hitch point to the lead, or the first, trailer. The shape of the articulation point—the "A" shape of the draw bar on the converter dolly—lends the name to the tractor trailer combination. When connected to a trailer, A-type dollies form A-trains. A-trains have a significant disadvantage. Because they use only a single connection point, a greater potential exists for the

FIGURE 34-6 A full trailer.

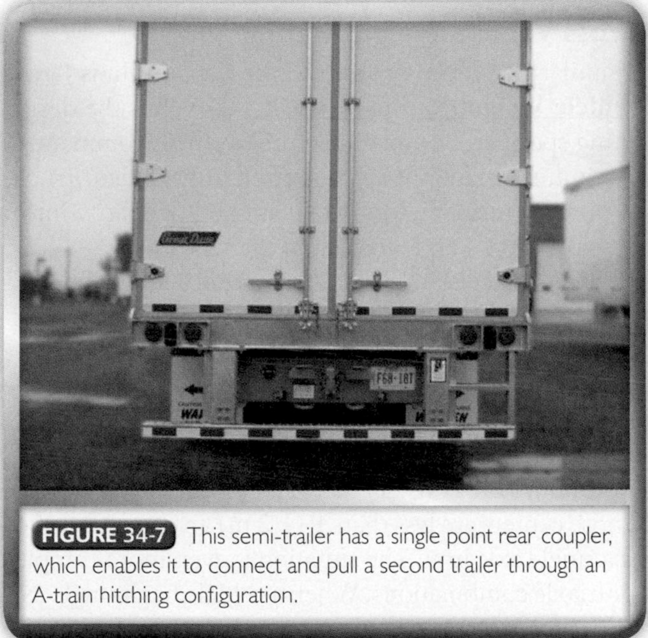
FIGURE 34-7 This semi-trailer has a single point rear coupler, which enables it to connect and pull a second trailer through an A-train hitching configuration.

FIGURE 34-8 An A-train consists of a tractor pulling a semi-trailer and a second, full trailer, behind the semi-trailer. **A.** Lead trailer. **B.** Rear trailer. **C.** Landing gear. **D.** Fifth wheel. **E.** Air hoses. **F.** Air and electrical connections.

rear trailer to become unstable and drift from the lead trailer track. For this reason, A-trains are not allowed to operate in many jurisdictions. FIGURE 34-8 shows the connection point of an A-train.

A B-train is the second trailer of a three-unit combination of a tractor and two trailers. A B combination is simply another semi-trailer connected to a fifth wheel attached to the rear section of the first trailer. The B-train does not use a converter dolly, per se. A rear frame extension of the front or lead semi-trailer will often retract beneath the lead trailer whenever it is not used. The tail area of the lead trailer with the fifth wheel is often referred to as the "bridge." B and C combinations are frequently used in North America. Since B-trains use a fifth wheel, they can support and distribute higher trailer weights than a C-train. One study found that using B-trains achieves a 78% increase in payload using only 25% more fuel. The B-train configuration is the most stable of the three combination vehicle types because a fifth-wheel connection between trailers is the best at resisting the rollover of the second trailer. FIGURE 34-9 shows the connection point of a B-train.

C-dollies have two separate draw bars used to tow each side of the dolly. The C-dolly's two horizontal parallel connection points give a C-train greater stability than an A-train. Compared to a B-train, however, the C-train is not quite as stable. The two parallel draw bars of the C-dolly ensure that the C-train will not move from a horizontal plane when towed. A C-train is similar to the A-train except that the C-train has two draw bars attached to two points on the lead trailer.

Vehicle Weight Ratings and Capacity

In the early 20th century, vehicle weight limits were legislated to protect dirt and gravel roads from damage caused

FIGURE 34-9 A B-train consists of a tractor pulling a semi-trailer and a second, full trailer, behind the semi-trailer.

by the heavy wheel weights of commercial vehicles. As truck traffic and load weights increased continually, truck weight limits began to focus primarily on gross weight limits to protect bridges from damaging truck weights. **Gross weight limits** are the maximum legal weight of a vehicle that can travel on roads and bridges.

By the mid-1970s, a law was passed to limit the weight-to-length ratio of heavy trucks to protect roads and bridges from the damage caused by the concentrated weight of shorter trucks. The law created the **Federal Bridge Gross Weight Formula** (also known as **Bridge Formula B** and the **Federal Bridge Formula**). Those formulas established the maximum weights for a commercial motor vehicle (CMV) based on the number of axles the vehicle had and the spacing between those axles.

The formula is part of US/Canadian weight and length regulations regarding interstate/interprovincial commercial traffic. Axle spacing is as important as axle weight in bridge design. Consider a vehicle with two axles carrying significant weight. If not spaced far enough apart, those two axles act like a single axle in terms of loading road surfaces. The longer the **axle spread**—a distance measured from axle center to axle center—the better weight distribution is achieved to prevent road and bridge damage.

The bridge formula, therefore, allows motor vehicles to be loaded to maximum weight only if each group of axles and their spacing also satisfy the requirements of the formula. In North America, the weight limit is typically 20,000 lb (9,072 kg) for a single-axle vehicle with a total weight on one or more axles which are not more than 40" (101.6 cm) apart. For **tandem axles** (a two-axle tractor or trailer configuration) the total weight limit is typically 34,000 lb (15,422 kg) for a vehicle with its full weight on two or more consecutive axles that are between 40 and 96 inches (101.6 and 243.8 cm) apart.

Vehicle Weight Ratings

Numerous configurations of trucks, tractor-trailers, and even buses can be classified by length, weight, number of axles, and number of wheels. In North America, one of the most common ways trucks are categorized is by **gross vehicle weight (GVW)**. GVW refers to the maximum design weight of a vehicle including a full tank of fuel, fully loaded to its capacity, and with all passengers. TABLE 34-1 shows the classifications of vehicles by GVW. The heaviest classification using this method is GVW Class 8 vehicles. Class 8 includes vehicles weighing more than 34,001 lb (14,969 kg) and which are usually considered heavy trucks.

Gross Vehicle Weight Rating

A similar classification system based on weight is **Gross Vehicle Weight Rating (GVWR)**. GVWR is the design rating specified by a manufacturer as the recommended maximum weight of a vehicle when fully loaded. Trucks or power units (tractors) are classified primarily into a class between 4 and 8 based on their GVWR.

General legislation in North America limits the gross vehicle weight of a vehicle, or a combination of vehicles, according to the number of axles and the distance between the axles. Those limits are listed in TABLE 34-2.

Many exceptions and variations are made to the general rule. As an example of how axle spacing affects maximum load, consider that vehicles with multiple axles whose centers are less than 4' (1.2 m) apart are classified as a single axle unit. The situation is even more complex for triaxle combinations. When a vehicle has a single axle with center-to-center distances closer than 10' (3.0 m) (or a steering axle closer than 9' (2.7 m)) to a triaxle unit, the single axle is considered part of that triaxle. The presence

TABLE 34-1: Classification of Chassis by Gross Vehicle Weight (GVW)

Class	Gross Vehicle Weight (GVW)
1	6,000 lb (2,721.6 kg) or less
2	6,001–10,000 lb (2,722–4,535.9 kg)
3	10,001–14,000 lb (4,536.4–6,350.3 kg)
4	14,001–16,000 lb (6,350.7–7,257.5 kg)
5	16,001–19,500 lb (7,257.9–8,845.1 kg)
6	19,501–26,000 lb (8,845.5–11,793.4 kg)
7	26,001–34,000 lb (11,793.9 kg–14,968.5 kg)
8	34,001 lb (14,969 kg) or more

TABLE 34-2: General Law Gross Weight Limits

Number of Axles	Weight Limit
2 Axles	34,000 lb (15,422.1 kg)
3 Axles	54,000 lb (24,494 kg)
4 Axles	69,000 lb (31, 297.9 kg)
5 Axles	80,000 lb (36,287.4 kg)
6 Axles	100,000 lb (45,359.2 kg)

of the additional axle does not increase the allowable legal load capacity of that triaxle unit.

Gross Combined Vehicle Weight

The **gross combined weight rating (GCWR)** is a specific maximum weight limit determined by the vehicle manufacturer. Unlike other weight ratings, the GCWR takes into account two individual (yet attached) vehicles—the tow vehicle, or tractor, and the trailer.

Types of Fifth Wheels and Coupling Devices

A variety of vehicle factors and operating conditions can change the general rules for determining maximum axle weight. The best solution for transporting heavier and larger loads is to add more axles to the vehicle configuration in order to minimize damage to road surfaces. Adding more axles is best accomplished by arranging combination vehicles and trailers to enable vehicles to articulate, or bend, when turning. Fifth wheels and a variety of coupling devices connect or hitch trailers to tractors and allow articulation between tractor and towed units. Depending on the size and type of trailer or the product transported, a number of hitching devices have been developed to tow full trailers and specialized equipment, including pintle hooks and couplers, ball hitches, and so on. Fifth wheels and upper couplers are used to connect and tow semi-trailers. We will first discuss coupling systems used with full trailers.

Pintle Hooks, Hitches, and Draw Bars

Pintle hooks are trailer hitching devices that use a fixed towing horn, which connects with a draw bar attached to the towed vehicle. Each of these components is described in greater detail in the following sections.

Pintle Hooks and Couplers

Pintle hooks are coupled by raising the draw bar eye over the pintle horn and locking it closed with a pivoting latch. **Couplers** are hitching devices that look similar to pintle hooks except the towing horn pivots and are not fixed. Since the wider opening coupler connects easier than a pintle hook, couplers are especially useful in applications with frequent trailer coupling and uncoupling. FIGURE 34-10A and FIGURE 34-10B show a pintle hook and FIGURE 34-10C shows a coupler. Pintle hooks and couplers are selected by towing and vertical weight.

To minimize shock loads when initially moving a trailer or during braking, a **snubber**, or load dampener, can be used. As shown in FIGURE 34-11A, rubber cushions or heavy springs are integrated into the device to permit some movement along the centerline and some side to side strain relief. An air-cushioned pintle hook, such as the one pictured in FIGURE 34-11B, is a rigid pintle hook equipped with an air chamber connected to

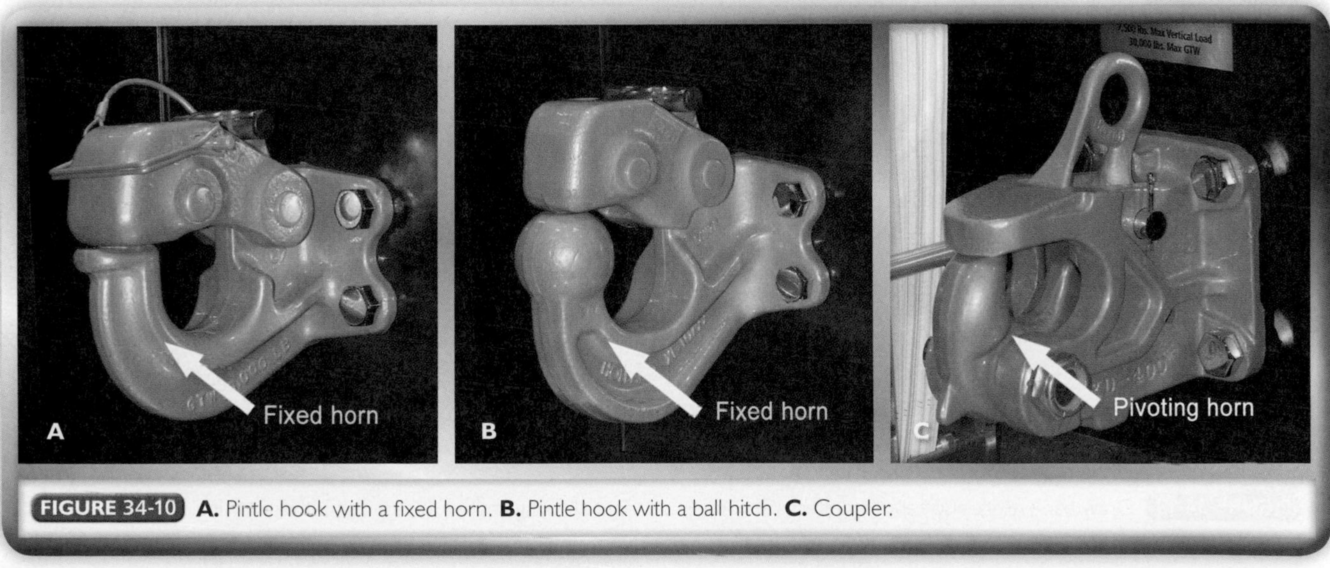

FIGURE 34-10 **A.** Pintle hook with a fixed horn. **B.** Pintle hook with a ball hitch. **C.** Coupler.

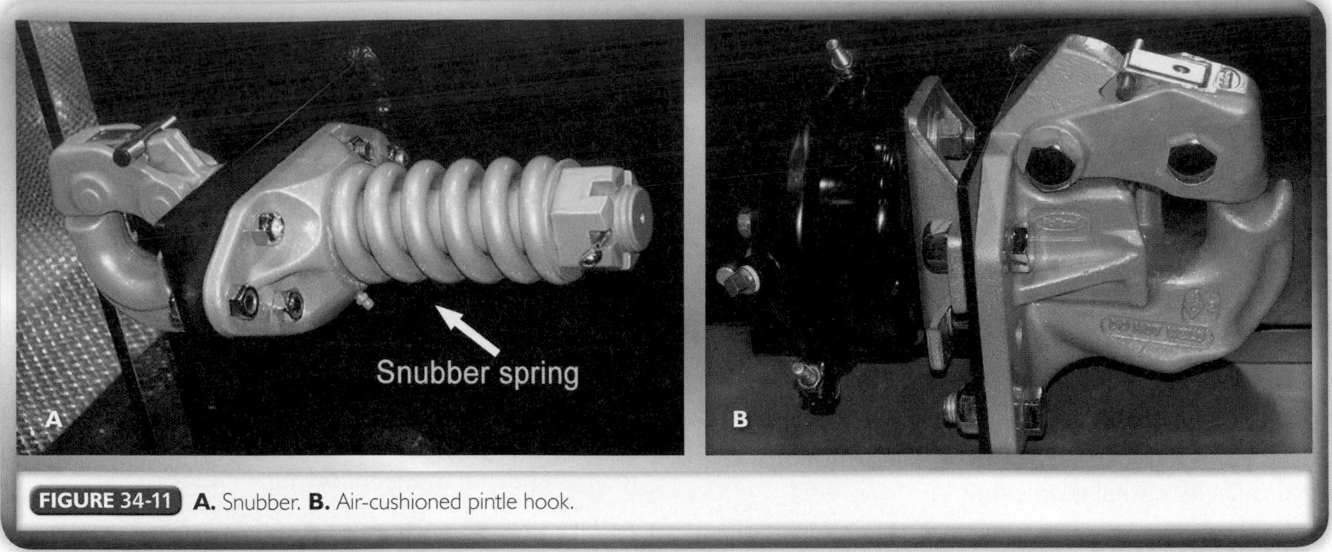

FIGURE 34-11 **A.** Snubber. **B.** Air-cushioned pintle hook.

a plunger, which removes the slack between the pintle horn and draw bar.

Draw bars are used to connect tow vehicles to a tractor or lead towing unit. Draw bars are illustrated in FIGURE 34-12. Bars are typically fabricated box-like structures or solid malleable steel material, which will bend and not crack or break under heavy strain. The bar will have an eyelet or a lunette, as shown in FIGURE 34-13, welded or bolted to the bar, which can connect to a pintle, coupler, or pin on the tow vehicle.

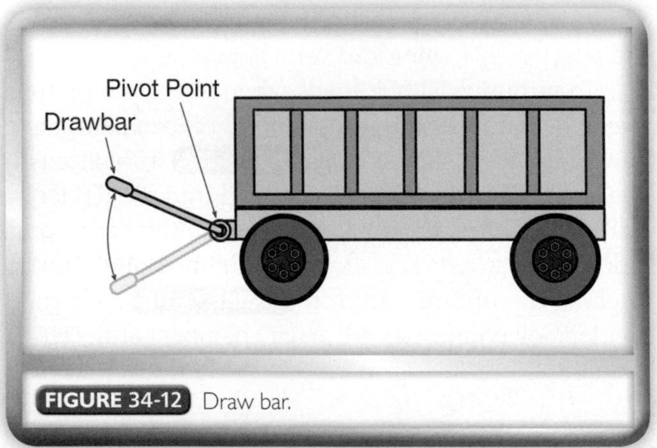

FIGURE 34-12 Draw bar.

Ball Hitches

Ball hitches are used on light- and medium-duty vehicles having a 12,000 lb (5,455 kg) towing weight capacity. The ball requires a tongue-type tow bar, which loops over a ball. Ball hitches have the advantage of providing a positive no-slack fit because the draw bar has a spring loaded tensioner at the connection point with the ball. Ball hitches, pintle hooks, and couplers will typically use rigid couplers.

Ball hitches are classified by the weight supported by the ball or **tongue weight (TW)** and the **gross trailer weight (GTW)**, which is the weight of the trailer and cargo. Different sizes of balls are used depending on the category of hitch. A 2-5/16" (5.9 cm) diameter ball coupler is the largest size for a Class 4 hitch. Class 4 hitches are

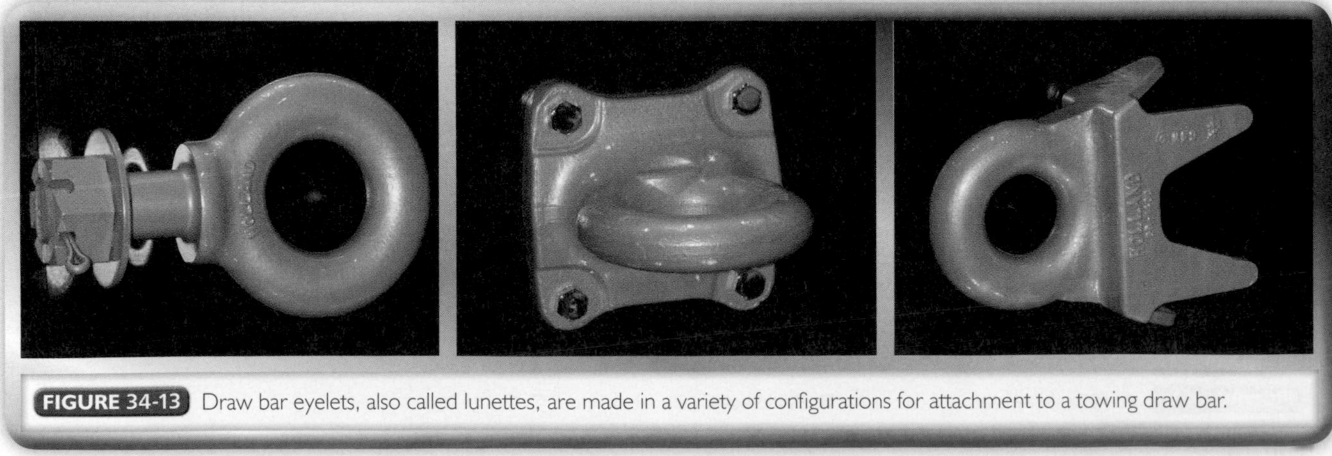

FIGURE 34-13 Draw bar eyelets, also called lunettes, are made in a variety of configurations for attachment to a towing draw bar.

classified as a hitch with weight carrying rating of up to 10,000 lb (4,545 kg) gross trailer weight and 1,000–1,200 lb (455–545 kg) tongue weight. Goose neck trailers such as those hauling large motor homes can use ball hitches mounted to the bed of a pick-up truck. The ball is fastened to a frame section of the tow vehicle, which is called a receiver. However, for vertical loads exceeding 10,000 lb (4,545 kg), fifth wheel couplers—are a more practical hitching system—even in light-duty configurations. The fifth wheel shown in FIGURE 34-14 is attached to the bed of a pick-up and pulls goose neck trailers. The various types of fifth wheels are described in the following sections.

Safety chains must supplement the ball hitch, pintle, or coupler connection in the event the trailer connection breaks away. When fabricating safety chains, the length of safety chains should be no longer than needed to provide a small amount of slack for cornering. As illustrated in FIGURE 34-15, chains are crossed beneath the tow bar to prevent it from dropping to the ground if the coupling system disconnects. Chains must be attached to the tractor and tow vehicle frame and not attached to the pintle hook or other device.

Tongue Weight

Tongue weight, or TW, is the load the draw bar places on the pintle hook, coupler, or ball hitch. As a general rule, the vertical load on the trailer tongue should be at least 10% of the gross trailer weight. When loaded properly, the weight of the load will assist stabilizing the draw bar for improved directional control when cornering, and reduce the wear out effect of surging caused by speed changes. Excessive vertical load results in accelerated wear on the tongue and tow bar. As illustrated in FIGURE 34-16, the capacity of the hitching device must match or exceed the maximum anticipated load.

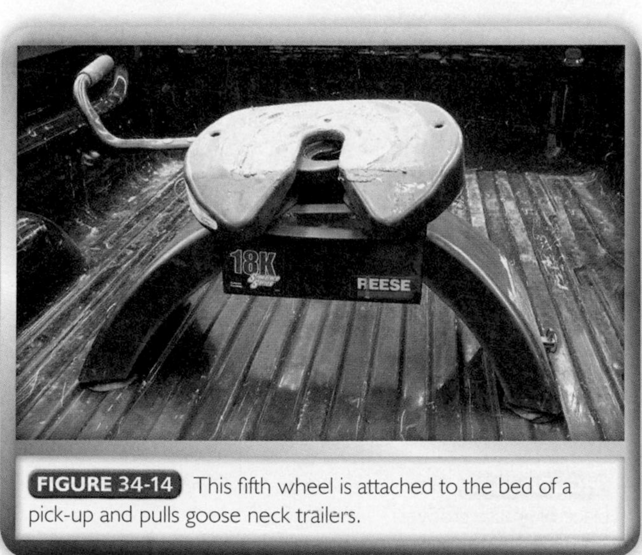

FIGURE 34-14 This fifth wheel is attached to the bed of a pick-up and pulls goose neck trailers.

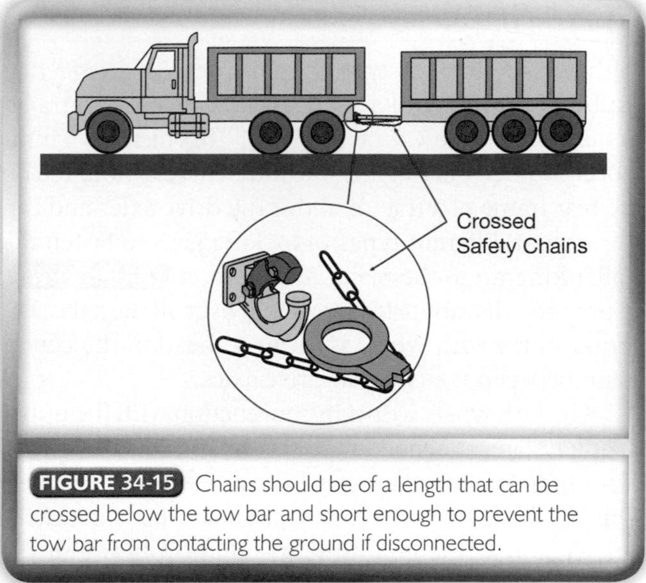

FIGURE 34-15 Chains should be of a length that can be crossed below the tow bar and short enough to prevent the tow bar from contacting the ground if disconnected.

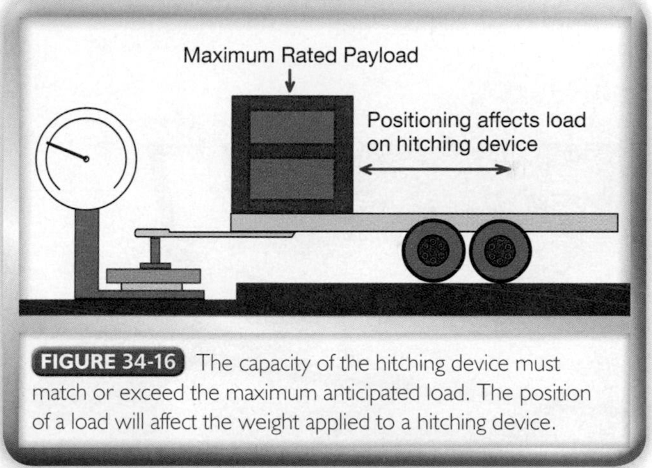

FIGURE 34-16 The capacity of the hitching device must match or exceed the maximum anticipated load. The position of a load will affect the weight applied to a hitching device.

Safety

Pintle hooks, draw bars, and couplers are made from quenched and tempered alloy steels. Heating or welding parts to repair a broken part or build up a worn surface is not permissible. Heating will change the coupler strength produced through heat treatment, potentially causing failure due to fatigue, embrittlement, or formation of a stress riser.

Safety

Hitching devices rarely fail, but when they do, the results can be spectacular. Failure to properly install, operate, adjust, or maintain a fifth wheel could result in tractor and trailer separation, causing death or serious injury to others. The most common problem for fifth wheels is failing to unlock. This often happens when they are incorrectly adjusted or some of the operating mechanisms bind or seize due to a lack of lubrication.

Fifth Wheels

Fifth wheels are plate-type coupling devices designed to support the weight of a semi-trailer and lock the trailer to the tractor or tow unit. FIGURE 34-17A pictures a fifth-wheel coupler. On tractors, the fifth wheel is mounted on the rear frame of a tractor above the drive axles and can use several different types of locking jaws to fasten the trailer kingpin to the plate. As shown in FIGURE 34-17B, to properly distribute trailer weight over all the axles, the center of the fifth wheel is located ahead of the center point between the two rear drive axles.

The fifth wheel works in conjunction with the upper coupler plate, attached to the trailer, and the upper coupler **kingpin**—together referred to as the **upper coupler**. This device distributes the trailer load onto the tractor suspension while enabling articulation between the tractor and trailer when changing direction or steering. (More information on upper couplers can be found in the Upper Couplers section.)

FIGURE 34-17 **A.** Fifth wheels are plate-type couplers. The fifth wheel is mounted securely to the rear frame of the tractor. **B.** Fifth wheel mounted ahead of the centerpoint.

To allow free and easy rotation of the trailer upper coupler and reduce wear on the fifth wheel top plate, lubrication is required. Grease grooves in the top plate typically retain and help distribute grease. Not all fifth wheels use grease, however. For example, "no lube" fifth wheels use a special Teflon-like, anti-friction plate or insert on the top plate such as the one pictured in FIGURE 34-18. Anti-friction plates are common on aluminum fifth wheels because the low-friction Teflon-like pads form a replaceable wear surface.

Safety

Without proper lubrication between the fifth wheel and upper coupler plate of the trailer, friction prevents movement between the two units. Without the ability to rotate, the trailer can literally push the tractor off the road or into another lane of traffic on a curve in the road. Steering becomes very difficult as well. Friction can also cause fifth wheel plates and coupler plates to prematurely wear.

Fifth wheels must maintain a secure connection when the trailer rolls, for example when cornering. Fifth wheels must also resist the forces of braking and acceleration. To ensure this strong connection, fifth wheels should have approximately three to six degrees of rotation around a horizontal axis, as illustrated in FIGURE 34-19. This clearance is achieved through the flexion of rubber bushings surrounding the steel pins that secure the fifth wheel to the tractor. To enable the trailer to pivot when moving up (FIGURE 34-20A) or down (FIGURE 34-20B) sharp inclines, fifth wheels pivot on the vertical plane.

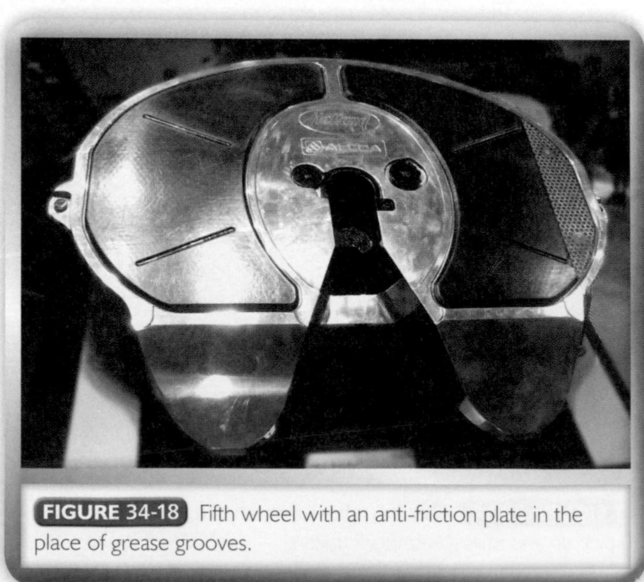

FIGURE 34-18 Fifth wheel with an anti-friction plate in the place of grease grooves.

FIGURE 34-19 The fifth wheel should be able to flex three to six degrees around a horizontal axis.

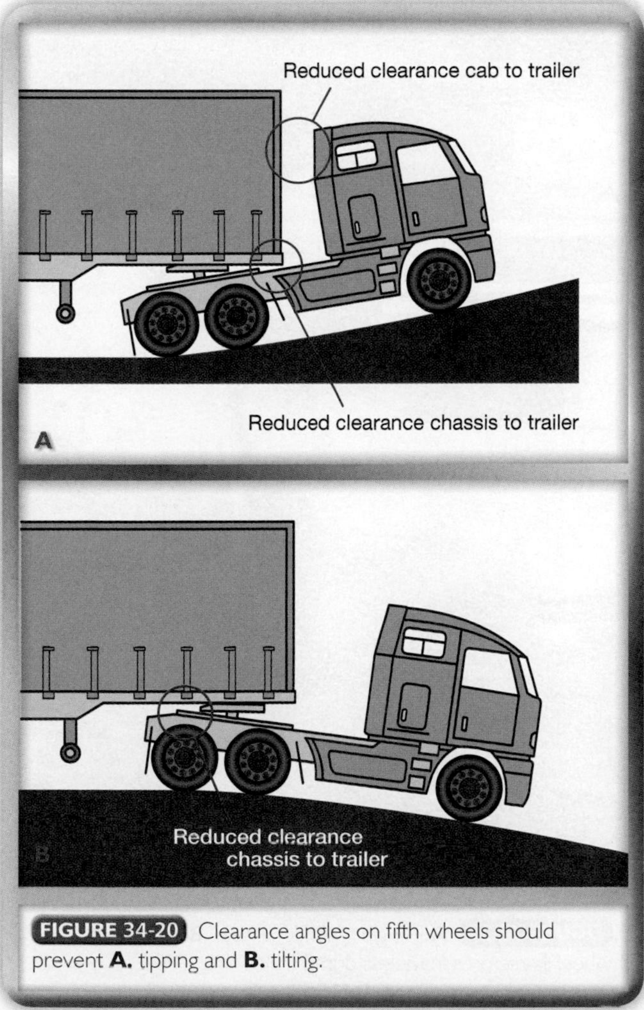

FIGURE 34-20 Clearance angles on fifth wheels should prevent **A.** tipping and **B.** tilting.

Semi-Oscillating Type

Fifth wheels that pivot slightly in both horizontal and vertical directions are called **semi-oscillating fifth wheels** and are the standard type of fifth wheel used in on-highway applications. Semi-oscillating plates can move several degrees vertically and horizontally along the vehicle's centerline. By moving vertically and horizontally, the vehicle is able to adjust to inclines and bumps in the road surface. **FIGURE 34-21** shows a semi-oscillating plate and the pivot point around which it rotates.

Fully (Double) Oscillating Fifth Wheel

Fully oscillating fifth wheels are a type of fifth wheel designed to provide front-to-rear and side-to-side movement between the tractor and semi-trailer. The significant articulation prevents the trailer body from twisting. Fully oscillating fifth wheels are ideally suited for vehicles operating in off-road conditions such as mining or logging. Liquid tankers will use fully oscillating fifth wheels to minimize cracking of the tank barrel caused by twisting of the barrel over uneven road surfaces. **FIGURE 34-22A** shows the basic design of a fully oscillating fifth wheel, and **FIGURE 34-22B** shows one in a tanker application.

Rigid Type or "No-Tilt"

A **rigid fifth wheel** does not oscillate about either axis of the vehicle. It does not articulate from side to side or front to back. Instead, it is fixed in location. **FIGURE 34-23A** shows a rigid fifth wheel.

In applications that require a rigid fifth wheel, the articulation is provided by an articulating upper coupler.

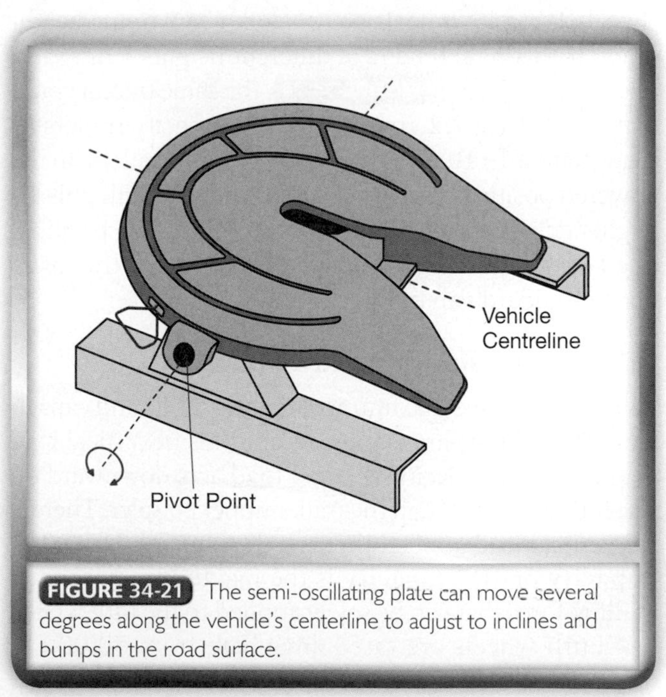

FIGURE 34-21 The semi-oscillating plate can move several degrees along the vehicle's centerline to adjust to inclines and bumps in the road surface.

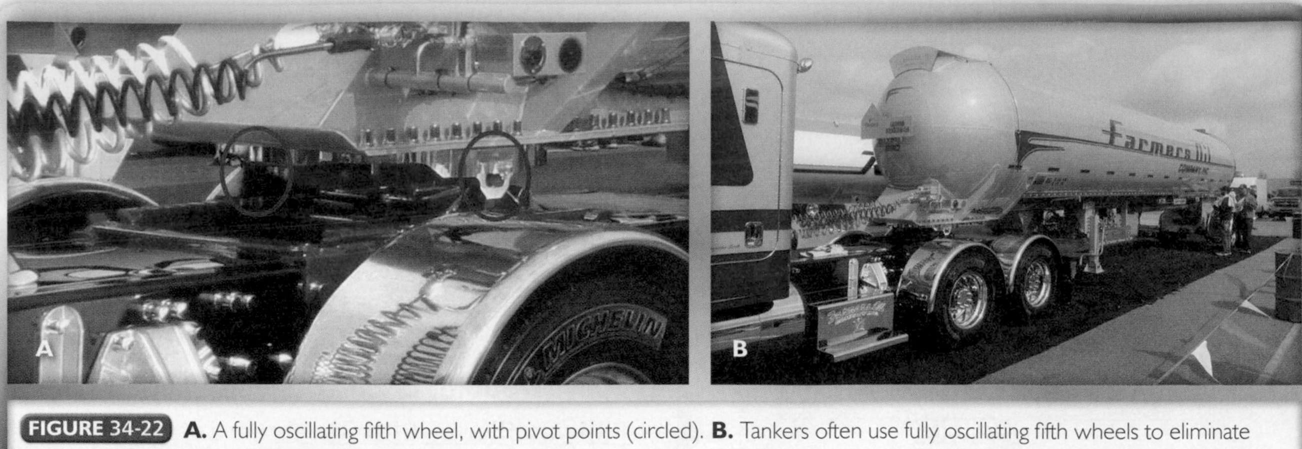

FIGURE 34-22 **A.** A fully oscillating fifth wheel, with pivot points (circled). **B.** Tankers often use fully oscillating fifth wheels to eliminate twisting between the tractor and trailer.

That design combination prevents excessive trailer rotation around a horizontal axis, which could increase the likelihood of a roll-over.

Frameless dump trailers are an example where the upper coupler articulates. A simple flip-type mechanism beneath the top plate can convert the no-tilt or rigid wheel to a standard semi-oscillating fifth wheel. FIGURE 34-23B shows a rigid fifth wheel in use on a dump trailer.

A rigid fifth wheel is different from a rigid mounted fifth wheel. The latter type is unmovable on the tractor frame and is rigidly bolted in place, preventing back and forth movement over the vehicle drive axles.

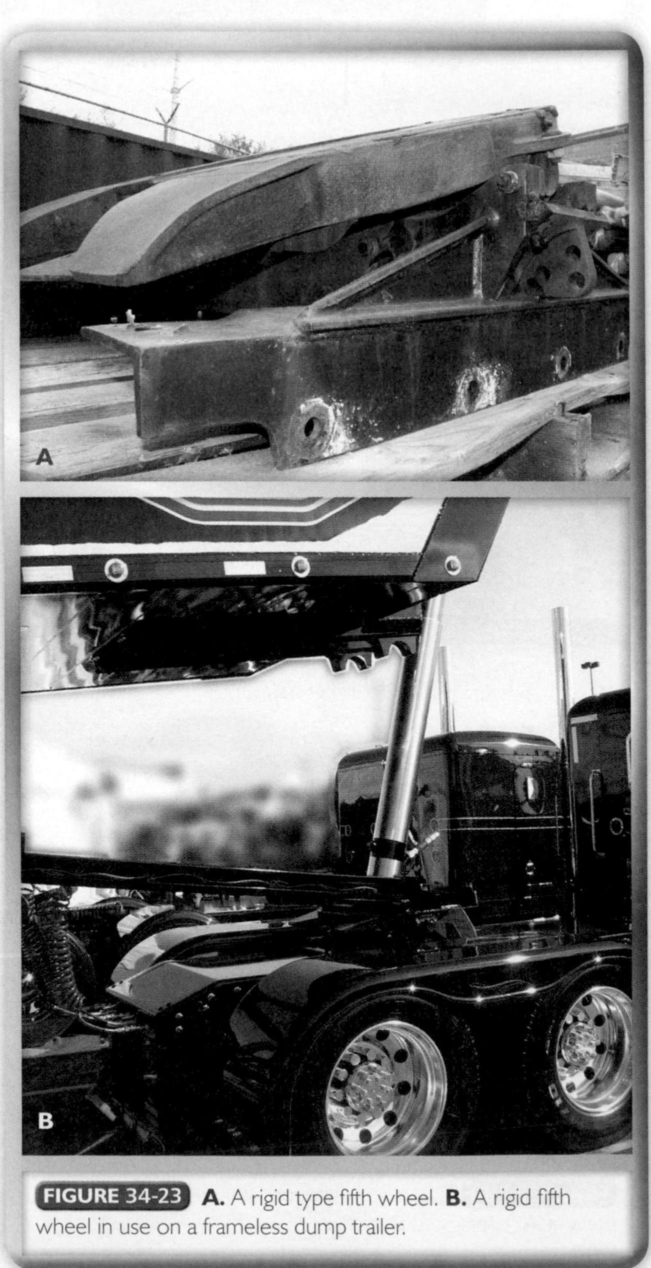

FIGURE 34-23 **A.** A rigid type fifth wheel. **B.** A rigid fifth wheel in use on a frameless dump trailer.

Two-Height Fifth Wheels

Two-height fifth wheels are a specialty stationary fifth wheel that can be either air or hydraulically operated. Two-height fifth wheels are made for low frame height tractors that haul trailers of different heights. For example, as illustrated in FIGURE 34-24, the same tractor could haul a 117" (297.2 cm) high cubic capacity trailers or pull standard 110" (279.4 cm) height van trailers. In the lowered position, the two-height fifth wheel will pull the higher cubic capacity trailer. When in the raised position, the two-height fifth wheel enables the same tractor to move standard van trailers.

Fifth Wheel Ratings and Capacity

Fifth wheels have maximum operating limits and capacities. These limits are expressed in terms of vertical load and draw bar capacity Vertical load acts downward on the fifth wheel through the trailer upper coupler. There is no vertical load applied through the kingpin. Draw bar capacity or "D" capacity is the maximum horizontal pulling force that can be safely applied to the fifth wheel.

Fifth wheels are rated anywhere from 50,000 to 70,000 lb (22,727 to 31,818 kg) vertical load capacity,

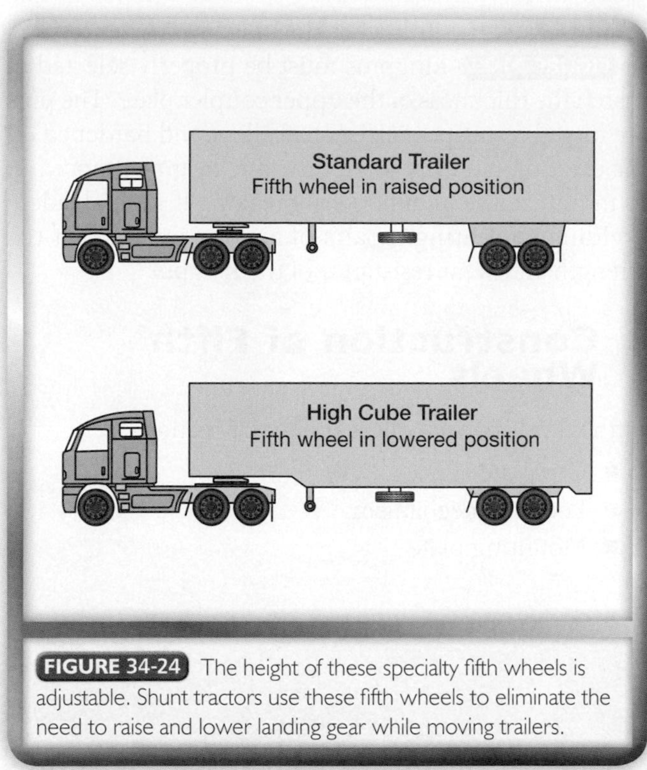

FIGURE 34-24 The height of these specialty fifth wheels is adjustable. Shunt tractors use these fifth wheels to eliminate the need to raise and lower landing gear while moving trailers.

and from 80,000 to 200,000 lb (36,367 to 90,909 kg) draw bar capacity.

Manufacturers typically rate their product in terms of operating service conditions, as illustrated in FIGURE 34-25. For example, a moderate or standard-duty coupler is suitable for most on-highway applications, while severe-duty service equipment is required for applications using multiple additional axles on trailers and abnormal stresses, such as operating off-road or where frequent hook/unhook cycles are encountered. A heavy load pulled over paved roads is less severe than a lighter load pulled in off-highway conditions where continual pounding of coupling jaws and bushings is anticipated.

Upper Couplers

The upper coupler is often referred to as the upper half of the fifth wheel. It is the steel plate, load-bearing surface on the underside of the front of a semi-trailer. The upper coupler rests on the fifth wheel of a tractor or converter dolly. The upper coupler is either bolted or welded to the trailer body. FIGURE 34-26 illustrates how the upper

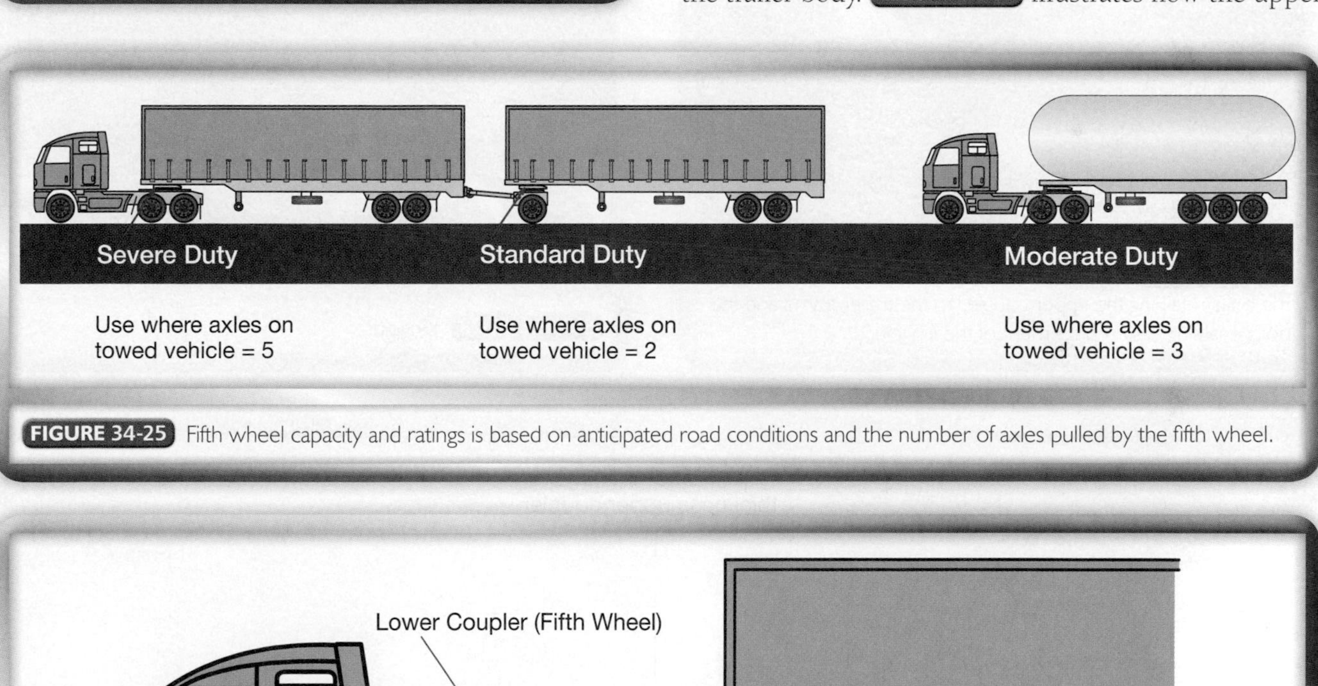

FIGURE 34-25 Fifth wheel capacity and ratings is based on anticipated road conditions and the number of axles pulled by the fifth wheel.

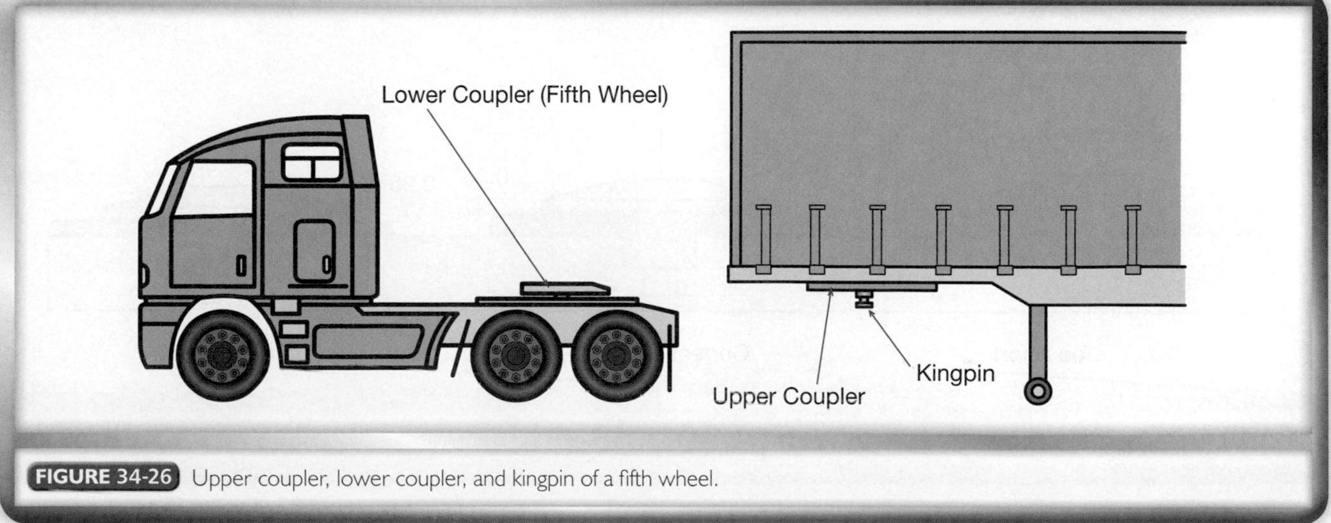

FIGURE 34-26 Upper coupler, lower coupler, and kingpin of a fifth wheel.

and lower couplers connect to hitch the tractor to the semi-trailer.

The kingpin is attached to the upper coupler, as shown in FIGURE 34-27. Kingpins come in a variety of shapes depending on the method of attaching the pin to the coupler. Three basic styles are common: mushroom, bolted, or cruciform. Mushroom-shaped kingpins are welded in place above the coupler FIGURE 34-28. Cruciform kingpins are larger, heavier, cross-shaped pins that are welded in place in a separate enclosure in the trailer subfloor.

Kingpins are either 2" or 3.5" (5.1 or 8.9 cm) in diameter. 3.5" (8.9 cm) pins are only used in specialized off road applications. Pins are either bolted into the upper coupler using a backing plate, or welded in place. A flange on the bottom of the pin prevents the pin from pulling out of the fifth wheel locking jaws. As illustrated in FIGURE 34-29, kingpins must be properly selected to match the thickness of the upper coupler plate. The pins are forged from specialized steel alloys and hardened on the exterior, not only to give the pin wear resistance but to minimize the likelihood of breaking if shock loaded. Welding or heating repairs of any type will affect the strength and wear resistance of the kingpin.

Construction of Fifth Wheels

Fifth wheels consist of several major sections:

- Top plate
- Locking mechanism
- Mounting plate

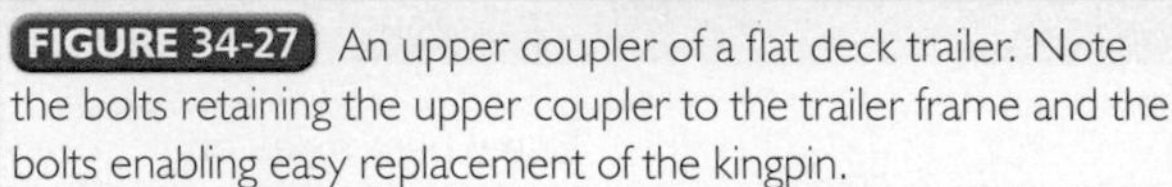

FIGURE 34-27 An upper coupler of a flat deck trailer. Note the bolts retaining the upper coupler to the trailer frame and the bolts enabling easy replacement of the kingpin.

FIGURE 34-28 Kingpin.

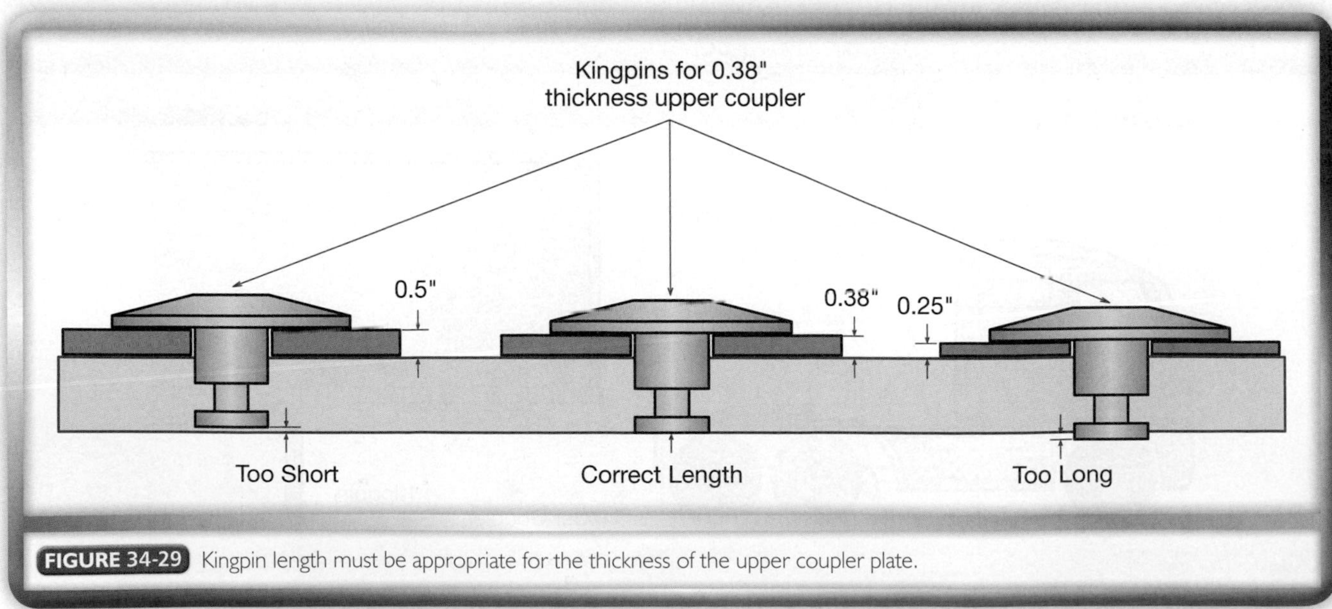

FIGURE 34-29 Kingpin length must be appropriate for the thickness of the upper coupler plate.

The major components of a fifth wheel are illustrated in FIGURE 34-30. The fifth wheel is also referred to as the lower coupler since it works together with the trailer's upper coupler containing the kingpin.

Top Plates

Fifth wheel top plates such as the one in FIGURE 34-31 are made from either stamped or cast steel. Forged aluminum wheels are also available for specialized applications. Stamped steel plates use reinforcing bars beneath the plate to increase its strength without the weight penalty of a cast iron plate.

The weight of the trailer is supported on the outer circumference surfaces of the top plate. The center section of the fifth wheel is recessed to prevent it from carrying any vertical load applied by the trailer. A weakened or "bowed" upper coupler plate can contact the center of the top plate. That contact concentrates the trailer load onto the center of the fifth wheel. As illustrated in FIGURE 34-32, center-loading can cause the fifth wheel to flex like a beam, which will lead to fatigue failure and top plate cracking. Shiny areas near the center of the plate can indicate center loading is taking place.

Locking Mechanisms

Every fifth wheel assembly uses a locking mechanism to securely hold the trailer kingpin to the fifth wheel. Locking mechanisms include coupling jaws, A- and B-type locks, and no-slack coupling.

Coupling Jaws

One method of locking the fifth wheel into place is by using coupling jaws. Backing the tractor beneath the trailer pushes the kingpin into the fifth wheel throat. That automatically locks the jaws around the pin. Jaws must prevent separation of the trailer from the fifth wheel assembly unless a positive manual release is activated.

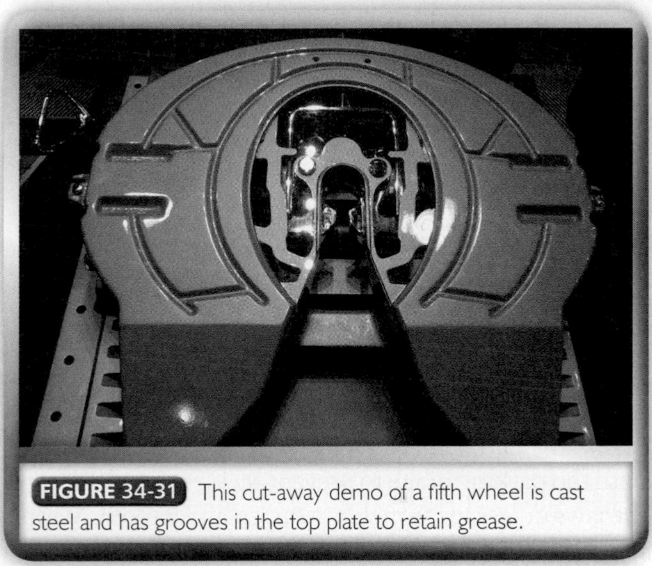

FIGURE 34-31 This cut-away demo of a fifth wheel is cast steel and has grooves in the top plate to retain grease.

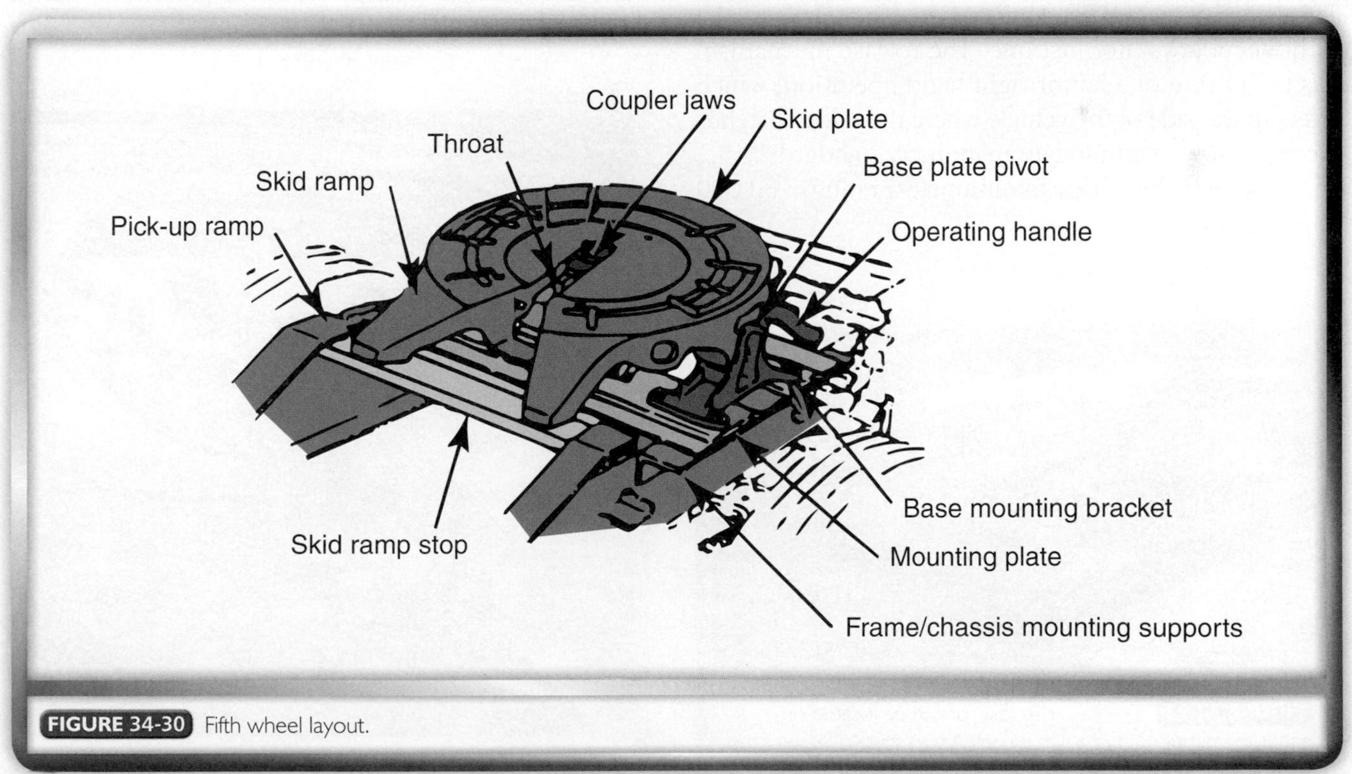

FIGURE 34-30 Fifth wheel layout.

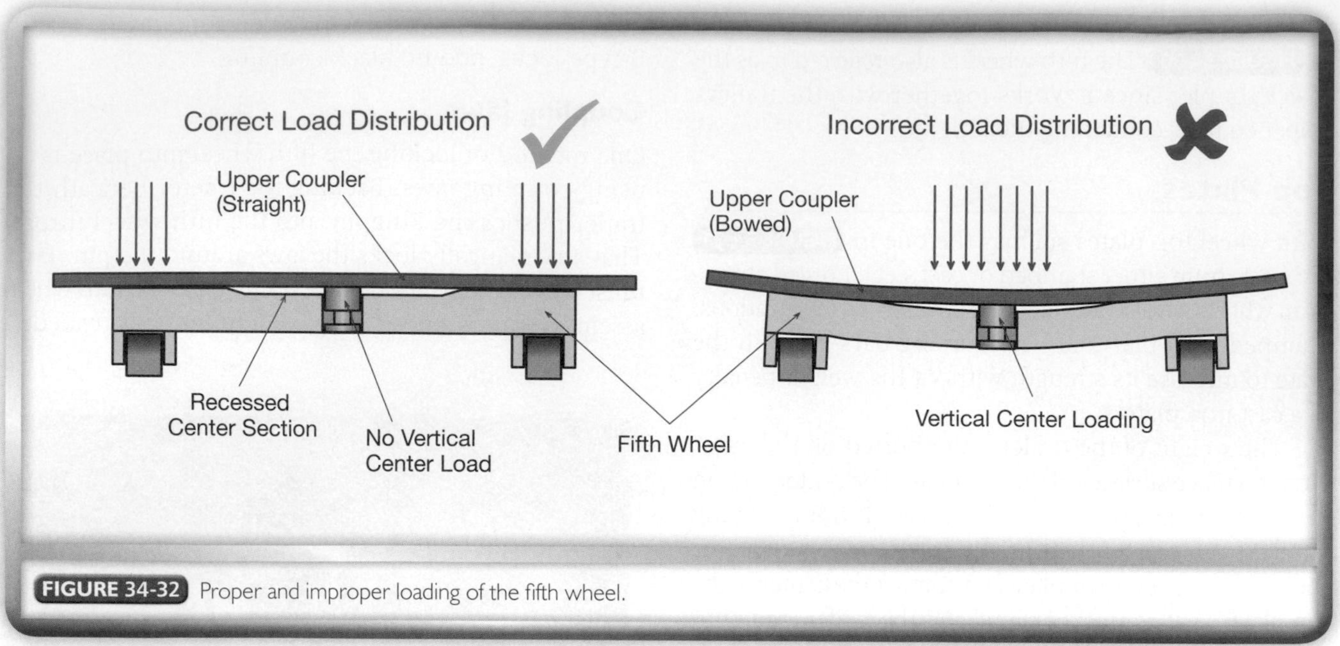

FIGURE 34-32 Proper and improper loading of the fifth wheel.

A fifth wheel release lever is located on the fifth wheel, as shown in FIGURE 34-33, and may have a remotely released air cylinder that can be activated by the driver inside the cab. Air release mechanisms are interlocked with the parking brake to prevent accidental unlocking of the jaws unless the vehicle is stopped and parked. Manual release mechanisms often use a **secondary safety latch** to minimize the likelihood of an unintended jaw release. This means a second mechanism is needed to release the fifth wheel jaws, not just one. The release mechanism has the option of a left or right hand operation, which refers to the side of the vehicle where the release latch is located. Jaws accommodate an industry standard 2" (5.1 cm) kingpin, which has a minimum tow rating of 80,000 lb (36,364 kg).

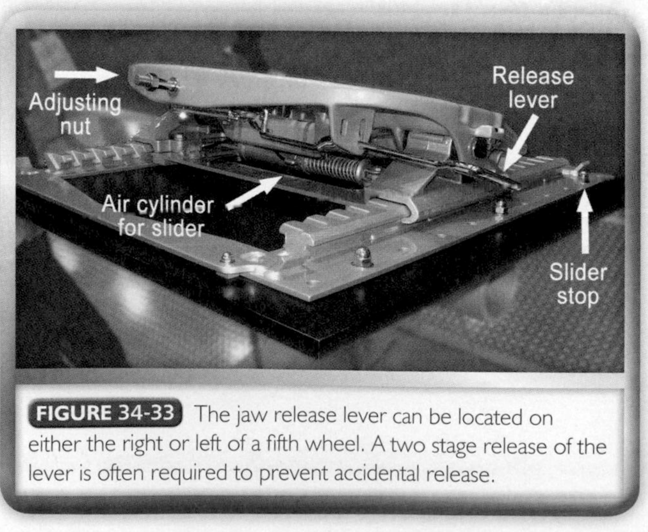

FIGURE 34-33 The jaw release lever can be located on either the right or left of a fifth wheel. A two stage release of the lever is often required to prevent accidental release.

A-type Lock

SAF Holland, manufacturer of a popular fifth wheel, uses two types of locking mechanisms. The **A-type lock** as shown in FIGURE 34-34 has a single swinging lock jaw and plunger for simple operation. When the kingpin enters the fifth wheel, pressure applied to a yoke causes the lock jaw to swing closed around the kingpin. A manually adjustable plunger wedges the swing jaw closed after it

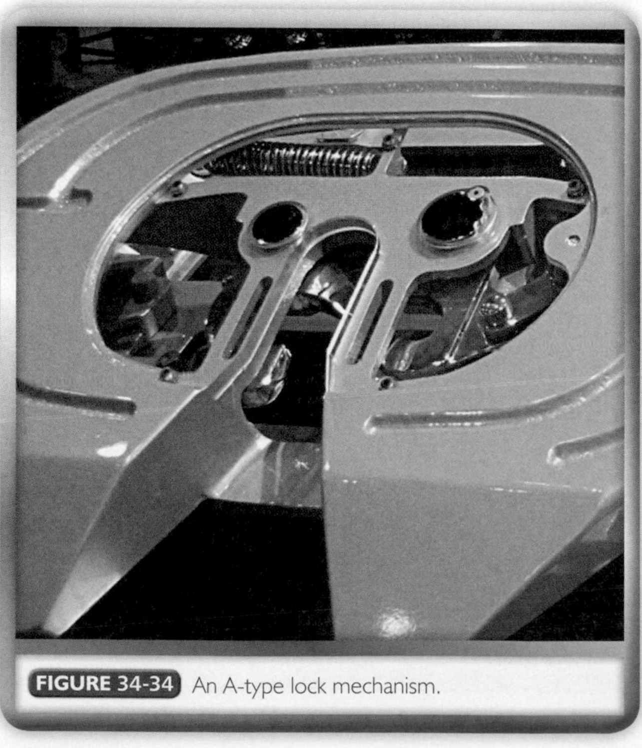

FIGURE 34-34 An A-type lock mechanism.

encompasses the kingpin. Approximately 300 lb (136 kg) of force are required to close the lock. On some plates, a replaceable wear ring is used to extend the life of a plate, which is worn by repeated hammering of the kingpin into the plate throat.

B-type Lock

A second common, but heavier, lock mechanism used by SAF Holland is the **B-type lock**. As shown in FIGURE 34-35, this mechanism uses two swinging jaws and a yoke to lock the jaws securely around the kingpin. When the pin enters the plate's throat, the open jaws pivot closed around the kingpin. A spring-loaded yoke slides between the jaws and the plate to prevent any jaw movement. Manually retracting the yoke allows the jaws to be released. The resting closed position of the yoke is adjustable as well. FIGURE 34-36 shows the underside of a Holland fifth wheel using a B-type lock.

No-Slack Coupling

ConMet, Fontaine, and Jost are all manufacturers that offer fifth wheels with a locking-bar locking mechanism called a **no-slack coupler**. As shown on the fifth wheel pictured in FIGURE 34-37, the mechanism uses a hardened steel bar, which slides behind the kingpin to lock it into place. An automatically adjusting wedge device tightens the locking bar against the kingpin almost eliminating any movement of the kingpin, which otherwise accelerates wear between the kingpin and locking bar.

A no-slack lock mechanism uses serrated edges between the locking bar and wedge. To release the locking mechanism, the wedge is simply pivoted away from the lock's serrations and retracted into an unlocked position. Without the wedge clamping the lock in position, the kingpin is easily moved rearward.

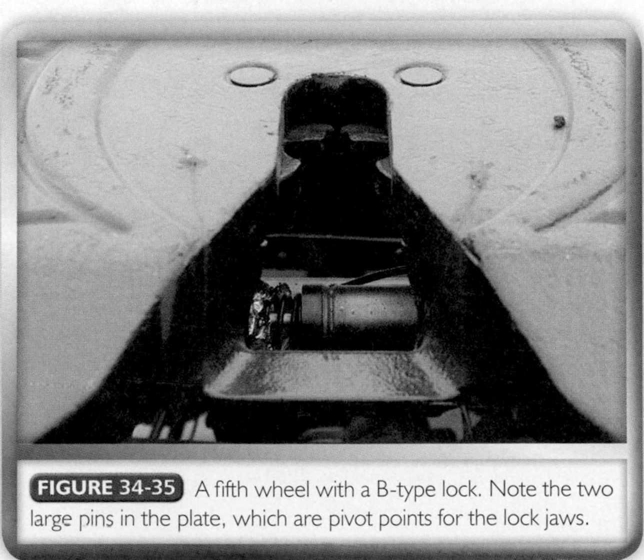

FIGURE 34-35 A fifth wheel with a B-type lock. Note the two large pins in the plate, which are pivot points for the lock jaws.

This mechanism provides the snuggest automatic fit of locking mechanisms around the kingpin since the spring loaded wedge's pressure will push the coupling into the kingpin until no clearance is available. A wedge stop rod is adjusted at the factory and should be maintained to leave a 0.25" (6.35 mm) gap between the wedge and the stop rod. If the locking bar becomes stuck and prevents the fifth wheel from unlocking, the stop rod can be hit with a hammer to push the wedge open. FIGURE 34-38A shows a wedge-type coupling in the locked position and FIGURE 34-38B shows it in the unlocked position.

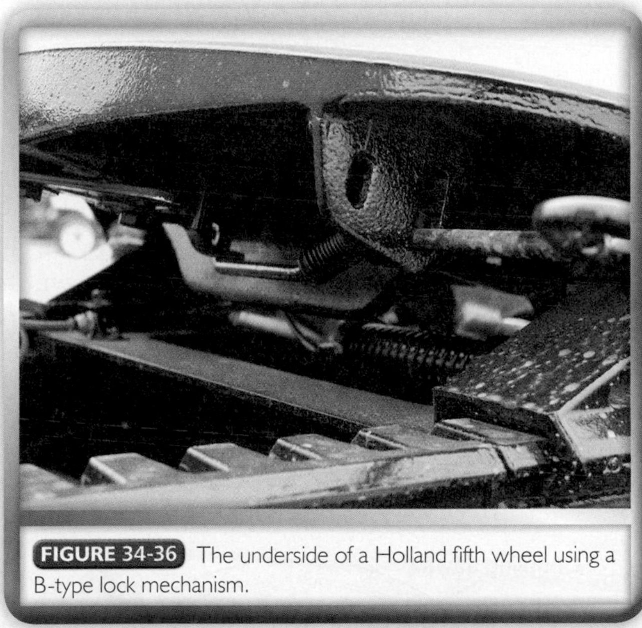

FIGURE 34-36 The underside of a Holland fifth wheel using a B-type lock mechanism.

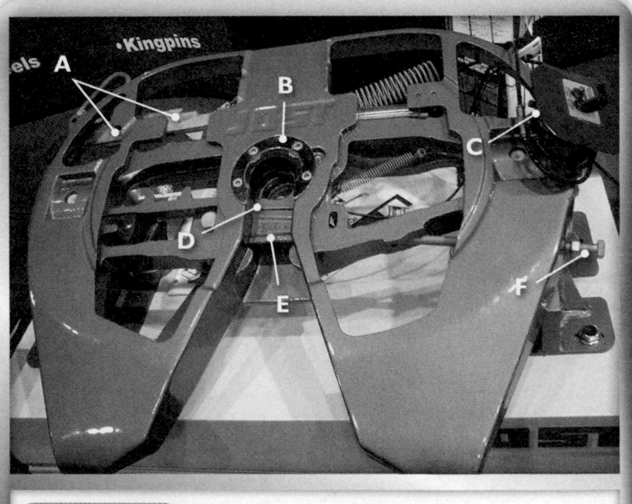

FIGURE 34-37 A no-slack wedge type lock mechanism. Serrated edges on the wedge lock the jaw in position around the kingpin. **A.** Release handle with stepped secondary lock. **B.** Replaceable wear plate. **C.** Cab located air slide release. **D.** Locking jaw. **E.** Serrated wedge. **F.** Wedge stop rod.

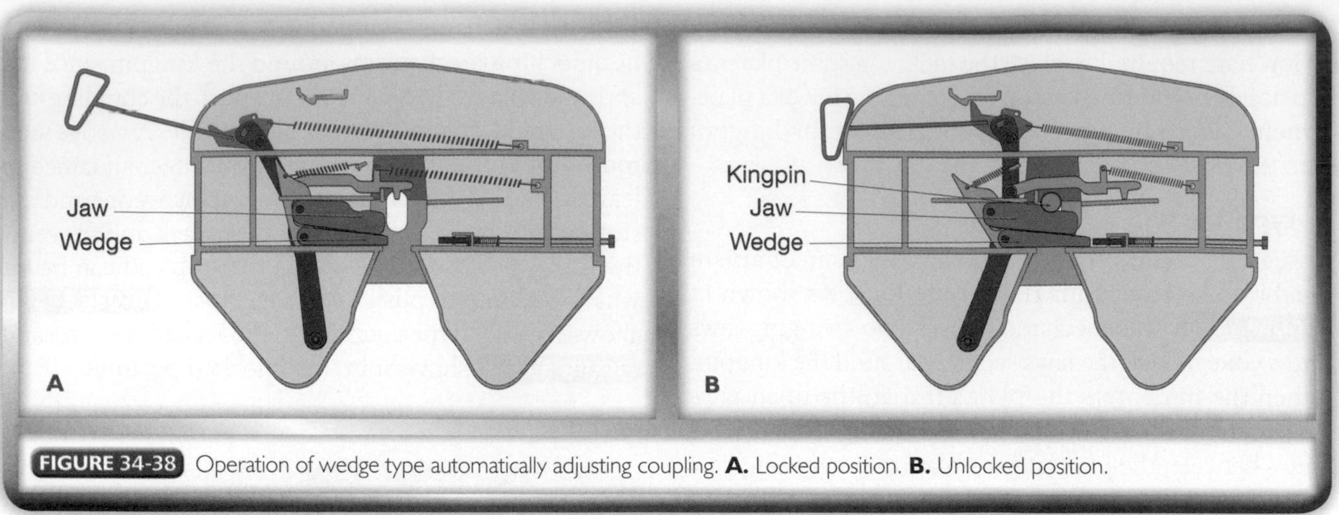

FIGURE 34-38 Operation of wedge type automatically adjusting coupling. **A.** Locked position. **B.** Unlocked position.

Mounting Fifth Wheels

Fifth wheels are attached to a baseplate typically through brackets containing a steel pin and heavy rubber bushing, as illustrated in **FIGURE 34-39**. **Flitch plates** attach the mounting plate to the vehicle frame, as shown in **FIGURE 34-40**. These are typically pieces of angle iron bolted to the tractor frame and then the base plate is welded or bolted to the angle iron. Plates must be secured to the frame of the vehicle with properly designed brackets, mounting plates, or additional pieces of angle iron and properly tightened with bolts of adequate size and grade. SAE Grade 8 bolts are the minimum tensile strength of bolt used. The installation should not cause cracking, warping, or deforming of the vehicle frame. The installation must include top plate stops or a mechanism to prevent the fifth wheel from shifting or sliding off the baseplate frame to which it is attached.

The height of the bracket is critical to obtain correct coupling height. Generally, the fifth wheel plate, when level, should be at 47" (119.4 cm) when measured from the ground with a correctly adjusted suspension system height. Ramps may be used to guide the trailer onto the fifth wheel and should allow the trailer to contact the

Coupling Jaws
Top Plate
Operating Handle
Throat
Bracket Pin
Mounting Bracket
Bracket Bushes

FIGURE 34-39 Fifth wheel mounting system.

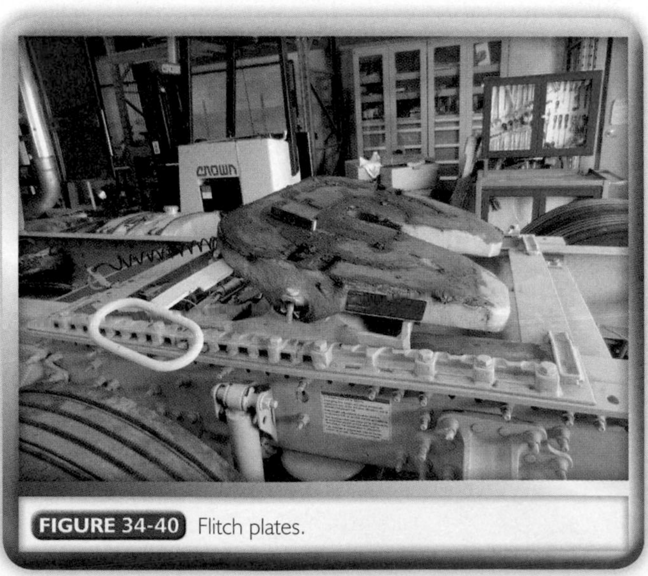

FIGURE 34-40 Flitch plates.

wheel without interference from the ramps. If the coupling height is too low when connecting to the tractor, the trailer kingpin may not lock properly or may prevent the trailer from properly articulating. Excessive coupling height will damage the trailer as it is lifted onto the tractor chassis during coupling. Coupler height is measured with the fifth wheel level and parallel with the ground. Overall trailer height should not exceed 13'6" (4.1 m), including the fifth-wheel coupler height.

Fifth Wheel Sliders

The fifth wheel can be moved forward or backward to accommodate different trailer lengths. The location of the fifth wheel can also be moved to enable even distribution of weight over the drive axles and front steer axle. To accomplish this, a **slider mechanism** enables the top plate to move forward and backward along a base frame. Sliders are a set of rails with a ratchet like mechanism that enables the fifth wheel to move back and forth between a pair of tandem axles. Sliders enable the proper distribution of trailer weight over all tractor axles. The sliding mechanism is locked in position by plungers, which lock into the racks of the base frame. A manual or air slider release mechanism is used to unlock the slider and allow the fifth wheel to move back and forth over the drive axles. FIGURE 34-41 shows a manual slide release in the locked and unlocked positions.

Proper fifth wheel positioning by the slider and during initial installation is critical. An incorrectly positioned fifth wheel will unequally load axles. If it is positioned too far ahead, the front axles will be overloaded and steering will become difficult and uneven tire wear occurs on the rear drive and steering axles. Additionally, with the trailer too far ahead, interference between the tractor and trailer landing gear can take place. The front corners of the trailer can make contact with the tractor cab and damage both units, since positioning the wheel reduces trailer **swing clearance**—the clearance remaining between a trailer and tractor when the combination vehicle is cornering. As illustrated in FIGURE 34-42, the position of the fifth wheel, whether rigidly mounted or on sliders, must allow adequate swing radius between the trailer and the tractor as well as between the tractor with the landing gear legs when turning. The swing radius is determined by the distance between the kingpin and the front of the trailer

Positioning the fifth wheel too far rearward creates another set of problems. Excessive clearance between the tractor and trailer creates power-robbing wind drag between the tractor and trailer. Drivers may prefer to move a fifth wheel farther rearward than it should be because it actually lightens the load on the front axle and reduces steering effort. If the fifth wheel slide length is too short, however, the fifth wheel may not shift far enough forward to load the front axle with the trailer weight. The rear axles may be overloaded and poor tire contact will take place on the front axle as it becomes "unloaded."

When installing a fifth wheel, the device should be positioned in the rearmost position on the slider mechanism. At this point, the fifth wheel center should be located no further back than 1" (2.5 cm) ahead of the center, between the tandem rear axles, to achieve proper weight distribution. Stops are welded to the slider mechanism to prevent the fifth wheel from moving to any position farther back along the tractor frame. The technician must take into account the swing radius of the trailers towed by the tractor.

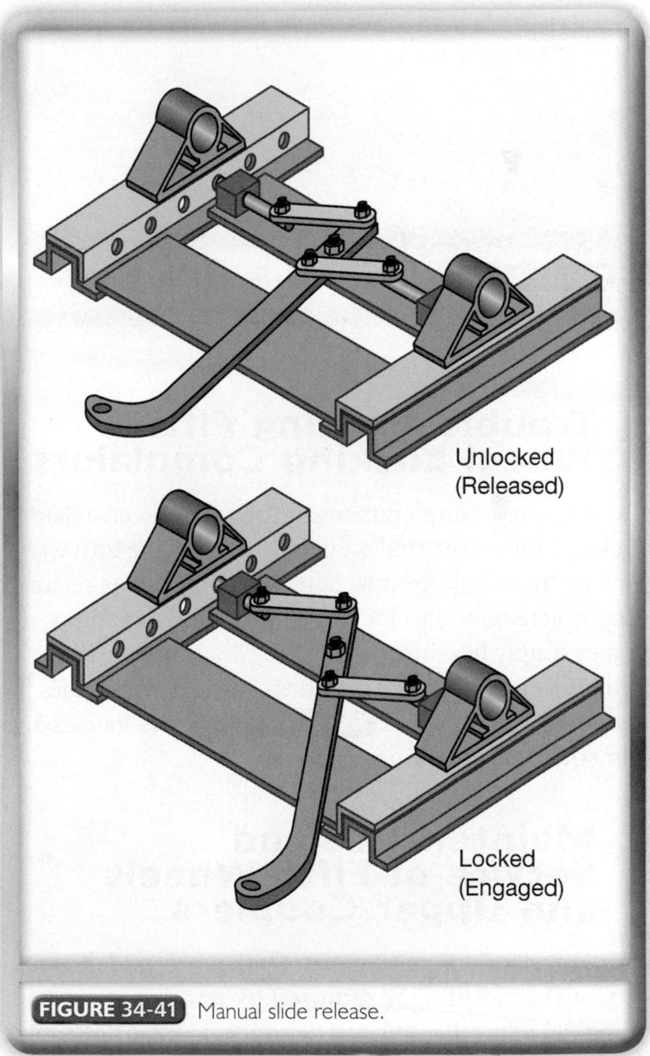

FIGURE 34-41 Manual slide release.

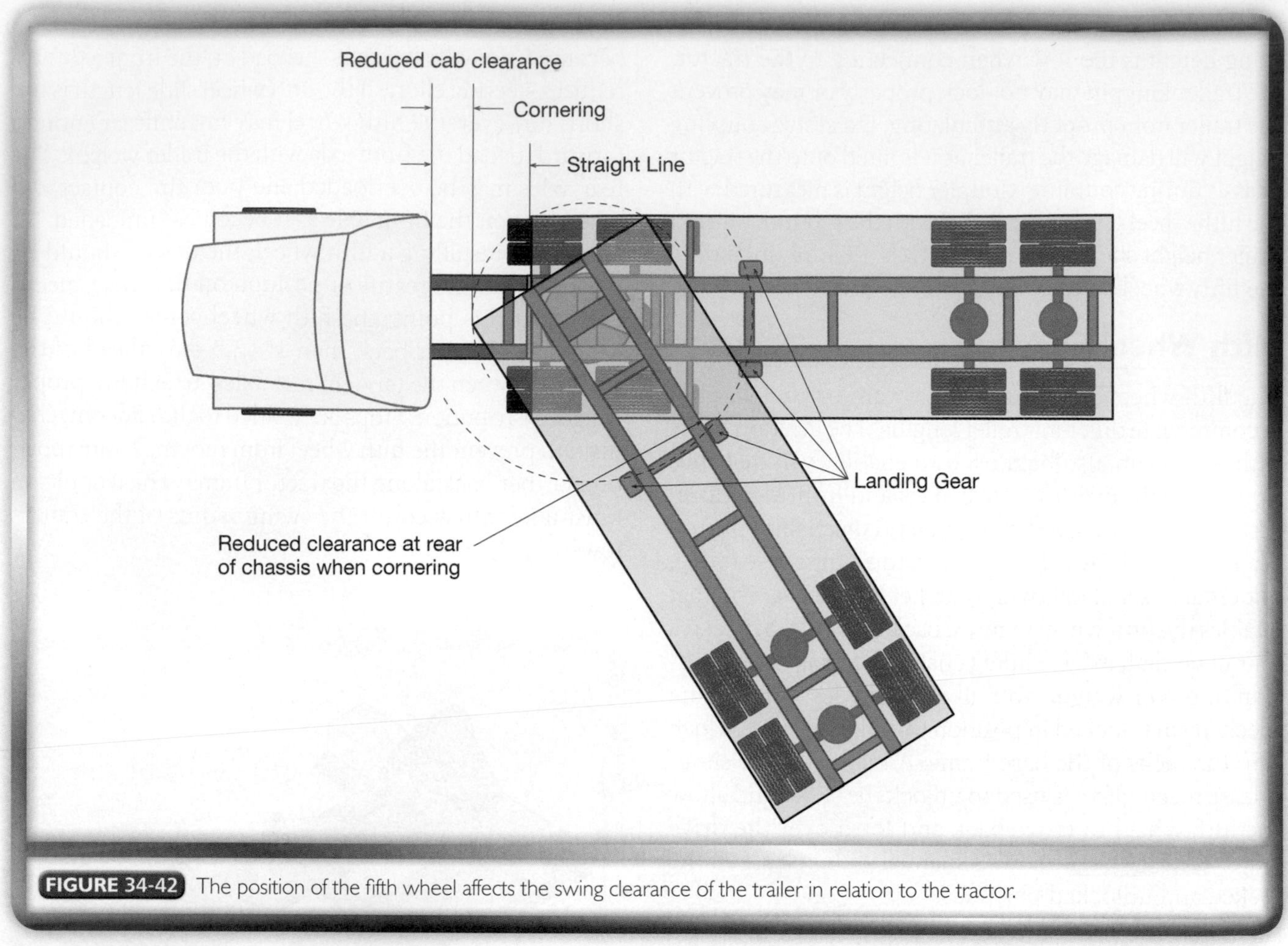

FIGURE 34-42 The position of the fifth wheel affects the swing clearance of the trailer in relation to the tractor.

Troubleshooting Fifth Wheel Locking Complaints

Two primary complaints regarding fifth wheels relate to locking. Either the trailer fails to lock into the fifth wheel or fails to unlock from it. Sometimes problems relate to a complete failure to lock or unlock and sometimes the trailer simply has difficulty locking or unlocking from the fifth wheel. TABLE 34-3 includes causes and remedies for locking problems and TABLE 34-4 includes causes and remedies for unlocking problems.

Maintenance and Service of Fifth Wheels and Upper Couplers

Periodic visual inspection of the fifth wheel and the security of the coupling is required by law. Incorrect coupling can allow the trailer to disconnect with catastrophic consequences. It is an inadequate test of the fifth wheel coupling to only perform a "tug" test—pulling the trailer with the tractor and quickly braking to check if the trailer is properly coupled. A trailer can rest on the fifth wheel without properly locking to the fifth wheel. It is critical to visually examine the lock jaws to verify they have closed around the kingpin after the trailer is connected.

When coupling, the fifth wheel must at least slightly lift the front of the trailer. When tractors with air suspension are coupled, the suspension air may be "dumped" by a manually operated dump valve. In this instance, the fifth wheel may not properly lock around the kingpin because the trailer is too high. The fifth wheel lock jaws may also be damaged by the lower flange on the kingpin. Always inflate the tractor suspension air bags.

Fifth wheel and upper coupler inspection is recommended every three months, or 30,000 miles (18,750 km). Inspection of the fifth wheel includes:

- Checking torque and replacing any missing or damaged bolts. All bolts holding fifth wheels and coupling devices must be a minimum of Grade 8 tensile strength.

TABLE 34-3: Causes and Remedies for Locking Problems Related to Fifth Wheels

Potential Cause	Remedy
Fifth wheel lock is closed	Pull both primary and secondary release handles. Open locks with a pry bar.
	Check operation of the air release cylinder. It must open and close correctly.
Lock release lever bent and binding	Inspect lever and straighten or replace as necessary.
	Check for correct handle operation according to manufacturer's service literature. [1]
Bent kingpin	Check kingpin with kingpin gauge or "go–no go gauge."
Trailer too high and not allowing the kingpin to enter lock properly	Lower trailer landing gear.[2]
Rusted, grimy, sticking lock mechanism	Clean mechanism with a solvent. Lubricate with light engine oil or diesel fuel. Open and close the lock mechanism several times to free-up operation.
Misadjusted jaw locks	Adjust lock mechanism per manufacturer instructions.
Worn-out fifth wheel lock mechanism	Remove, disassemble, and rebuild per manufacturer's instructions.
	Replace top plate and bracket bushings.
Distorted upper coupler plate	Check for warping or distortion of coupler with 48" (122 cm) straight edge.
Fifth wheel too far forward	Check position of fifth wheel.
No-lube plate too thick for kingpin	Measure kingpin length and determine whether a lube plate can be used with the trailer kingpin. Remove lube plate if kingpin length is inadequate.

[1] Normal operation for some release handles is to return "in" after unlocking the fifth wheel.

[2] The fifth wheel should lift the front of the trailer slightly when connecting to the tractor

TABLE 34-4: Causes and Remedies for Unlocking Problems Related to Fifth Wheels

Potential Cause	Remedy
Fifth wheel lock is closed	Pull both primary and secondary release handles. Open locks with a pry bar.
	Check operation of the air release cylinder. It must open and close correctly.
Bent kingpin	Check kingpin with kingpin gauge or "go–no go gauge."
Rusted, grimy, sticking lock mechanism	Clean mechanism with a solvent. Lubricate with light engine oil or diesel fuel. Open and close the lock mechanism several times to free-up operation.
Jaw locks adjusted to tightly	Adjust lock mechanism per manufacturer instructions.
Worn-out fifth wheel lock mechanism	Remove, disassemble, and rebuild per manufacturer's instructions.
	Replace top plate and bracket bushings.
Distorted upper coupler plate	Check for warping or distortion of coupler with 48" (122 cm) straight edge.
Lock release lever bent and binding	Inspect lever and straighten or replace as necessary. [1]
Lock release handle needs to be held in unlock position to disconnect	Check for correct handle operation according to manufacturer's service literature. [1]
Tractor putting pressure on locks when releasing	Back up tractor into the trailer again with the trailer brakes applied. Reattempt to disconnect from fifth wheel after moving the primary and secondary release lever to unlock.

[1] Normal operation for some release handles is to return "in" after unlocking the fifth wheel.

- Checking for broken or distorted components and repair or replace as needed.
- Inspecting the fifth wheel for bent, worn, or broken parts.
- Checking the adjustment of the fifth wheel locks and adjusting them using the recommended service tools and procedures. If the locks cannot be properly adjusted due to wear, the fifth wheel must be rebuilt or replaced.

Lubricating the Fifth Wheel

Checking the fifth wheel may also involve applying grease to the fifth wheel plate. Light oil is used to lubricate the locking mechanisms and sliders. Pin bushings have grease fittings, which use chassis grease. The actual load-bearing surface between the fifth wheel top plate and support brackets is steel on steel. Contact between the top plate and mounting brackets is steel to steel, which requires lubrication. However, most fifth wheels are held in place with rubber bushing around a urethane sleeved pivot tube. The sleeve compresses as load is applied either up or down, so about 0.5" (1.3 cm) of movement is normal on most models. Top plate bushings can be checked using a pry bar. When lifted upwards, normal travel should not exceed a 0.5" (1.3 cm) with moderate pressure applied to the bushing. To lubricate a fifth wheel, follow the guidelines in **SKILL DRILL 34-1**.

SKILL DRILL 34-1 Lubricating a Fifth Wheel

1. Grease the top plate contact surfaces using water-resistant lithium-based grease. Note that the grease fitting is on the side or under the front of the top plate. Grease the bracket supports through the fittings.
2. Fill the reservoirs with grease fittings if applicable.
3. Lubricate the cam track (indicated) and pivot with a light oil.
4. On sliding fifth wheels, spray a light oil on the rack and slide path.

Upper Coupler Checks

The upper coupler and the kingpin need to be checked for shape, size, and wear. The upper coupler needs to be checked for flatness. This can be accomplished with a 48" (122 cm) straight edge or flat bar. The flatness needs to be checked in all directions. Any bumps, valleys, or warping will cause uneven loading of the fifth wheel, which could result in damage to the top plate and poor lock life. Rippled or bent plates will also absorb grease, reducing the amount of lubrication available to the coupling. FIGURE 34-43 shows the allowable curvature for a fifth wheel upper coupler.

In addition to checking the upper coupler, the kingpin also needs to be checked for straightness, length, and wear. A critical tool for checking a kingpin is the kingpin gauge shown in FIGURE 34-44.

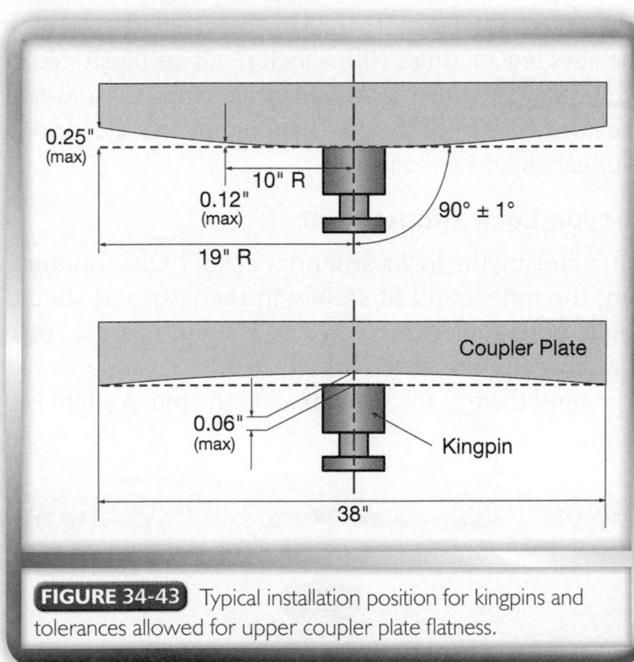

FIGURE 34-43 Typical installation position for kingpins and tolerances allowed for upper coupler plate flatness.

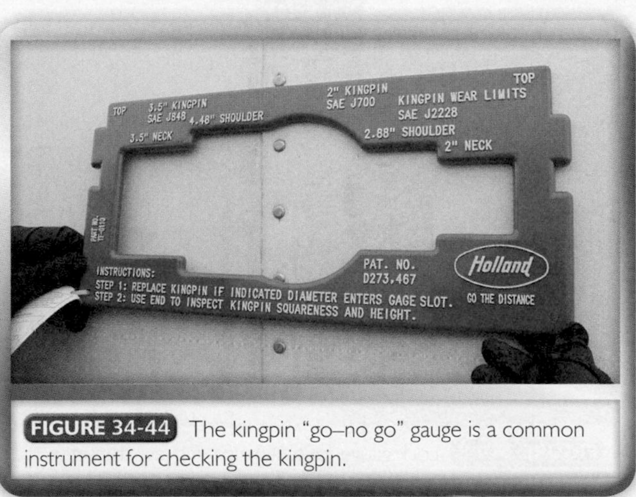

FIGURE 34-44 The kingpin "go–no go" gauge is a common instrument for checking the kingpin.

Checking Kingpin Straightness, Length, and Wear

To inspect the straightness of a kingpin, use a framing square or kingpin gauge check to see if the kingpin is bent, as shown in FIGURE 34-45A. If a trailer has rolled or nearly tipped, the pin can bend. A bent kingpin increases locking jaw wear and could also prevent the fifth wheel from properly locking. It is recommended that the kingpin should be replaced if it exceeds 1 degree from square in any direction. After kingpin replacement, the pin length should be double checked since pins must match with the coupler plate thickness. Incorrect kingpin length will prevent proper coupling if it is too short and trailer instability if it is too long. A kingpin gauge can also be used to check the kingpin's length.

Kingpins are made to an industry standard of 2" (5.1 cm) diameter. If the kingpin slides into the 2" (5.1 cm) neck diameter slot of the go–no go gauge, it is worn out and requires replacement. Excessive wear of 1/8" (3.175 mm) requires pin replacement since a loose pin will become noisy due to chucking and damage locking jaws from excessive play. If a fifth wheel is adjusted to fit a worn pin, it may not release from a trailer when a pin that is dimensionally correct is used. A micrometer or a go–no go gauge is used to check for wear, as shown in FIGURE 34-45B.

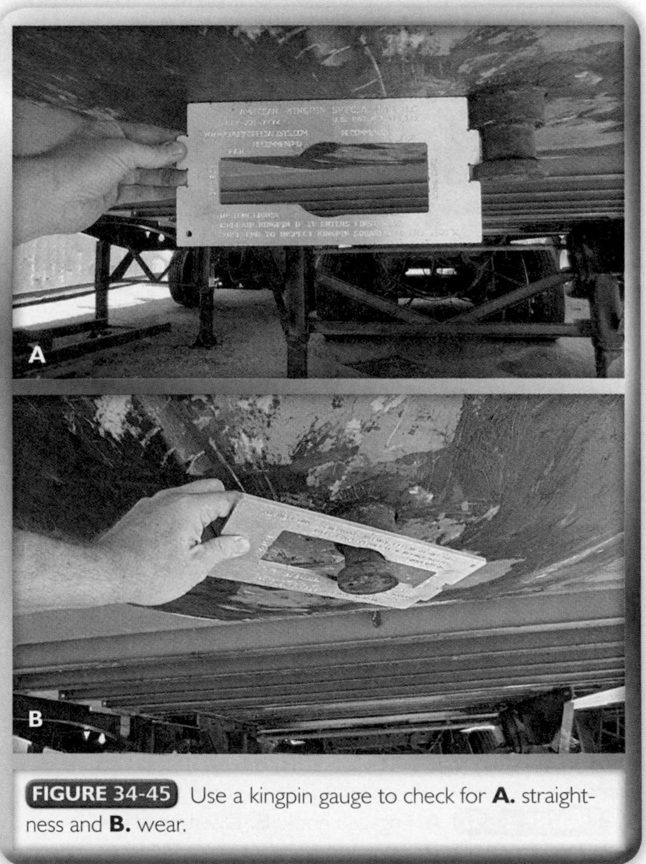

FIGURE 34-45 Use a kingpin gauge to check for **A.** straightness and **B.** wear.

In addition to checking the kingpin itself, the locking jaws around the kingpin must be checked. A kingpin service tool, such as the one shown in FIGURE 34-46, is used to measure the amount of drag in locking jaws, to check for excessive free play, and to test the unlock–lock mechanism. FIGURE 34-47 illustrates how to use the tool for this check. Engaging the hook and pushing the handle causes the locking jaws to open and close. Excessive effort required to release jaws or failure of the jaws to completely close indicates an adjustment or rebuild is required.

FIGURE 34-46 A kingpin service tool can be used to check drag in the locking jaws.

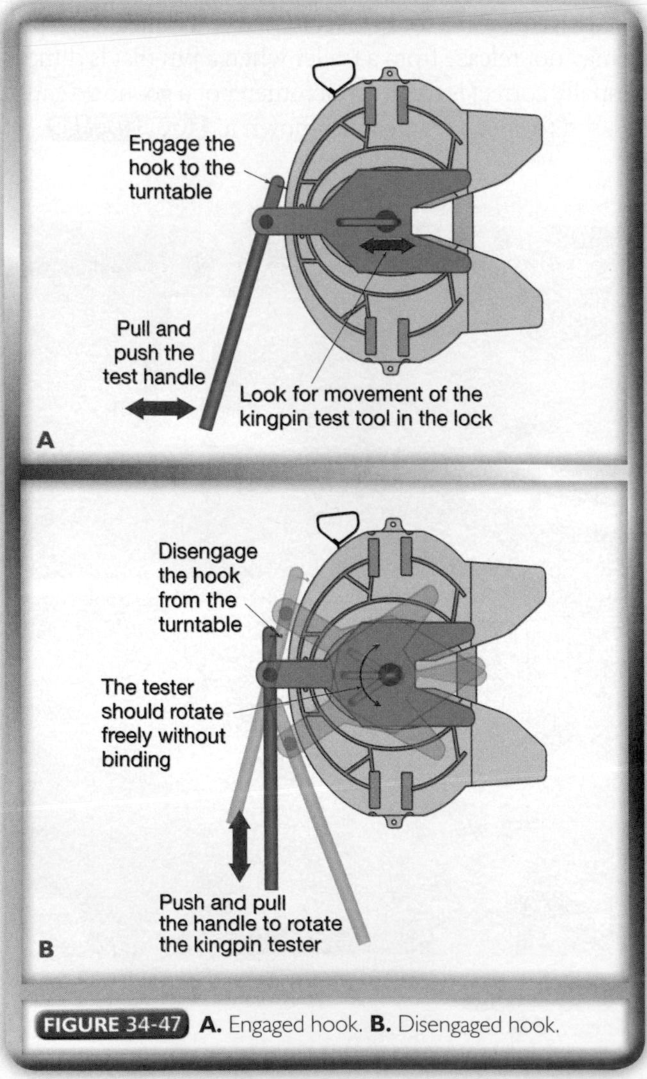

FIGURE 34-47 **A.** Engaged hook. **B.** Disengaged hook.

Fifth Wheel Service Adjustments

Fifth wheels will need to be adjusted from time to time. The adjustment procedures are different depending on the type of locking mechanism the fifth wheel uses—A, B, or no-slack locks.

A-type Lock Adjustment

The lock adjustment screw is found in the throat of the upper plate. After the lock is closed with a lock testing tool or a 2" (5.1 cm) "dummy" pin, the adjustment screw should be turned clockwise until tight. Backing out the screw 1.5 turns adjusts the fifth wheel jaws. The adjustment should be verified by locking and unlocking the jaws several times with a lock tester, as illustrated in FIGURE 34-48. When an A-type lock is correctly adjusted, the jaws must fully enclose the kingpin and the locking plunger should be visible.

B-type Lock Adjustment

After closing the locks around a 2" (5.1 cm) "dummy" pin, the pin should fit snugly in the jaws and should rotate with some hand force. If the pin is loose, turn the adjusting nut at the top of the plate counterclockwise until there is adequate drag on the pin. A slight gap

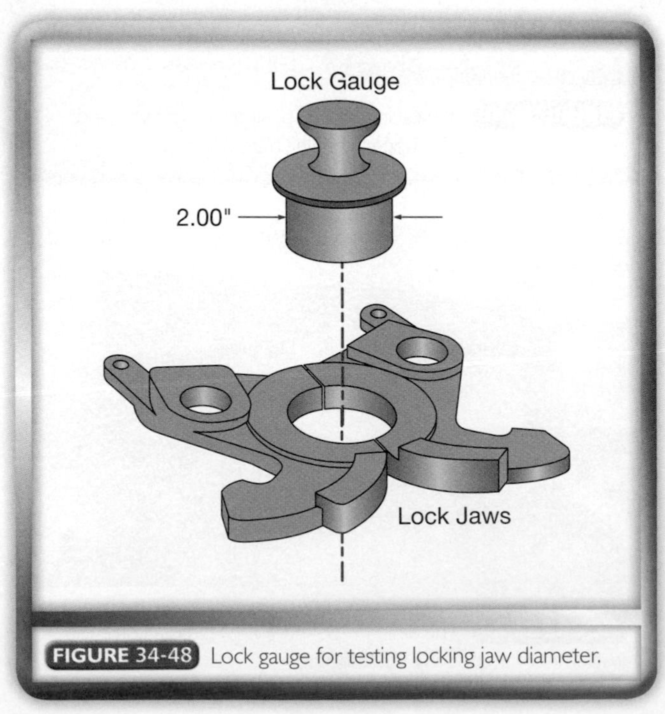

FIGURE 34-48 Lock gauge for testing locking jaw diameter.

between the flat washers and rubber bushings below the adjusting nut should be present after the adjustment is completed. The adjustment should be verified by locking and unlocking the jaws several times with a lock tester. When properly adjusted, the jaws should have no more than a 0.5" (1.3 cm) gap between each jaw after closing around the kingpin, as illustrated in FIGURE 34-49 and FIGURE 34-50.

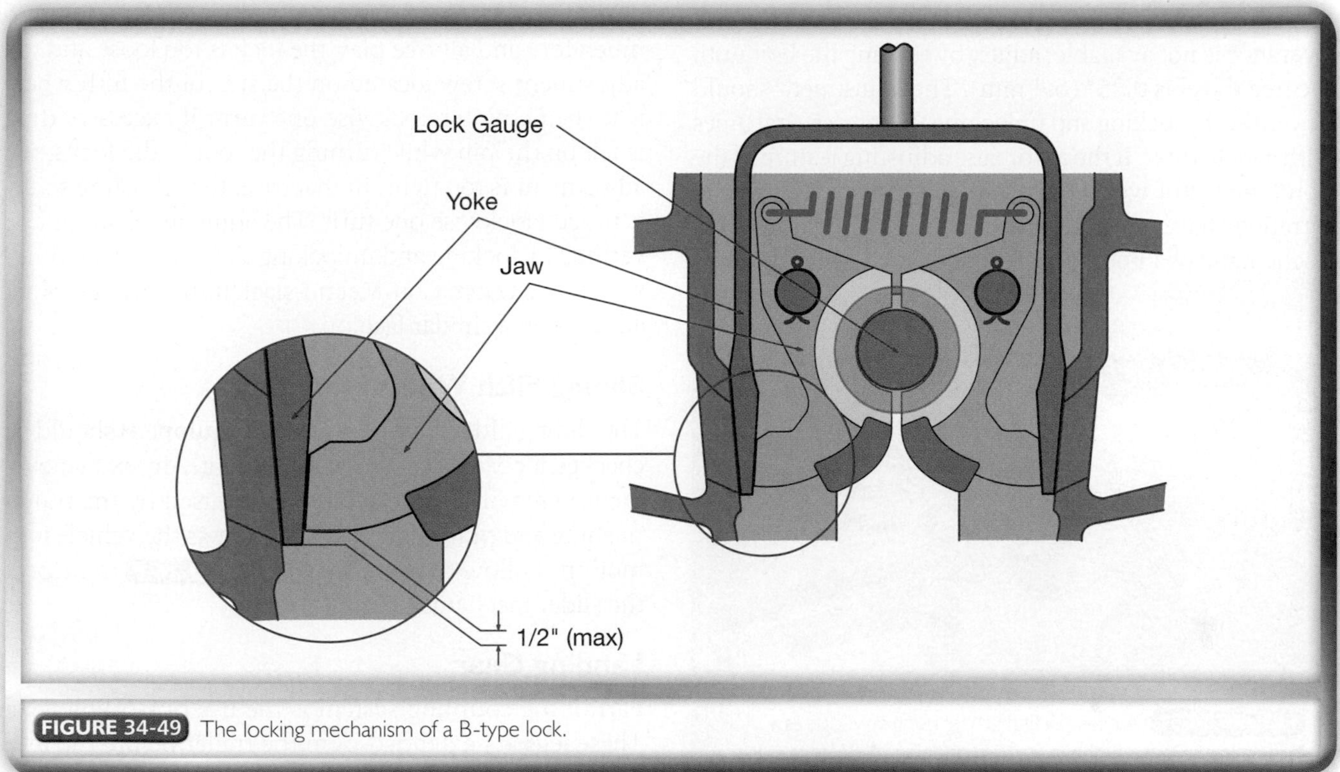

FIGURE 34-49 The locking mechanism of a B-type lock.

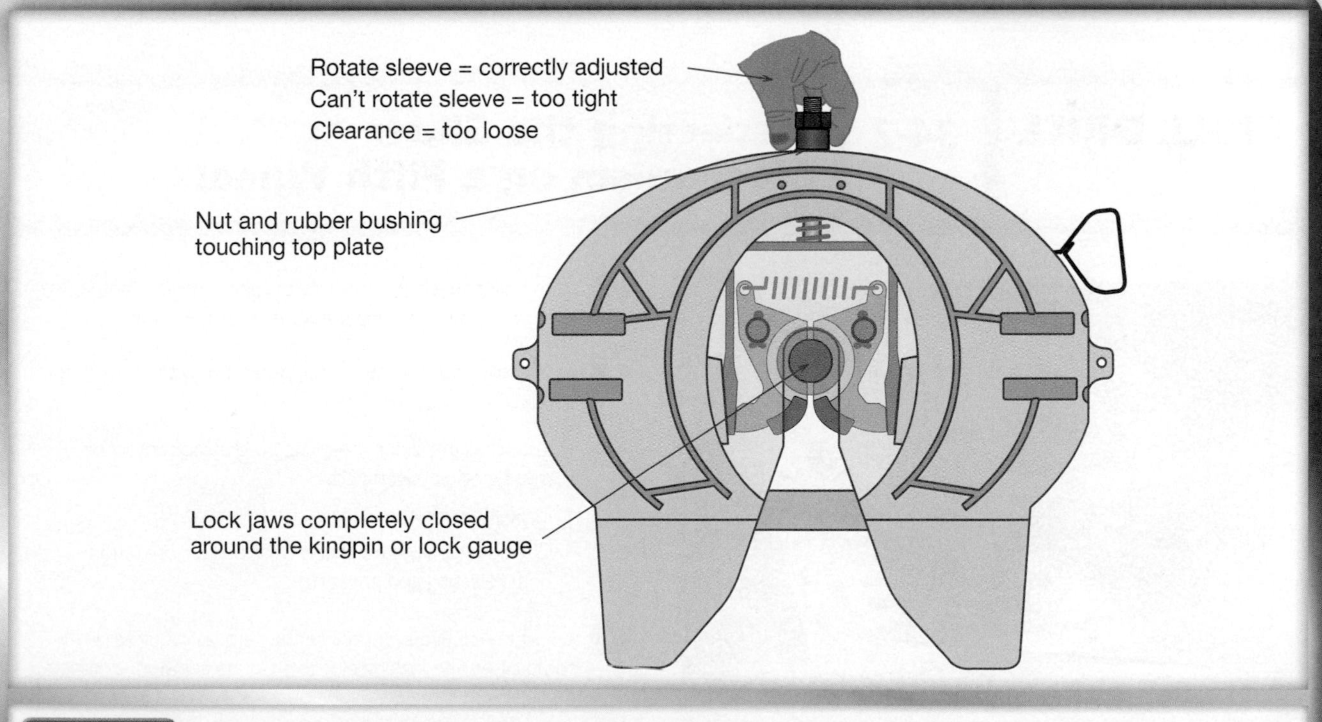

FIGURE 34-50 When properly adjusted, a B-type lock will allow the adjusting nut and a new uncompressed bushing to touch the top plate when the jaws are locked.

No-Slack Locks

To adjust a Fontaine model no-slack lock, after closing the fifth wheel with a standard 2" (5.1 cm) kingpin tool, push on the wedge stop rod until it contacts the wedge. When correctly adjusted, it should move in 0.25" (6.4 mm) with hand pressure, then spring back out. If the 0.25" (6.4 mm) clearance is not available, adjust by turning the bolt until the free travel is 0.25" (6.4 mm). The adjustment should be verified by locking and unlocking the jaws several times with a lock tester. If the automatic adjusting feature of the Fontaine is not working, it is likely the jaw and wedge serrations have worn beyond tolerances. **FIGURE 34-51** is a schematic of a Fontaine-style no-slack lock.

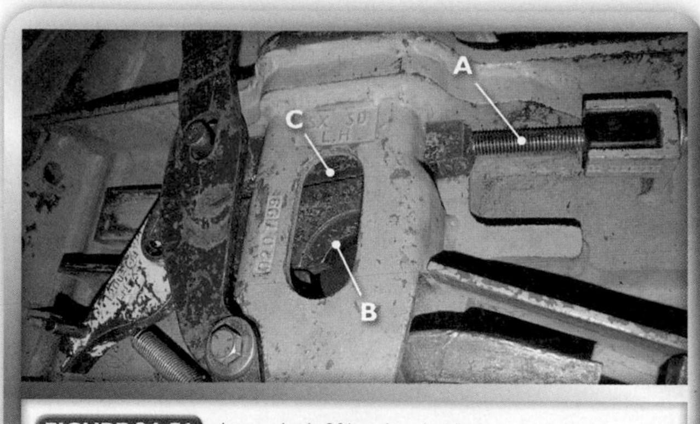

FIGURE 34-51 A no-slack fifth wheel using a wedge as a locking bar to prevent the jaws from opening. **A.** Wedge stop. **B.** Jaw. **C.** Wedge.

As with the automatic feature of a Fontaine no-slack fifth wheel, an adjustment screw is used to set the locking bar travel on a Jost no-slack locking mechanism. The adjustment is first checked by using a lock testing tool. Rocking the tool back and forth in the locks will determine whether it is correctly adjusted. If there is too much fore and aft free play, the lock is too loose and the adjustment screw located on the side of the fifth wheel is turned counterclockwise one turn. If excessive drag is felt on the pin while turning the tool in the locks, the adjustment is too tight. In that case, the adjusting screw is tuned clockwise one turn. The adjustment should be verified by locking and unlocking the jaws several times with a lock tester. Con-Met no-slack fifth wheel locks are adjusted in a similar fashion.

Sliding Fifth Wheel Mounting

The sliding fifth wheel mounting (if equipped) should be checked for excessive play or movement. Any extra movement here will lead to rapid wear caused by the trailer pushing and pulling against the slider as the vehicle is in motion. Follow the steps in **SKILL DRILL 34-2** to inspect the slider mechanism.

Landing Gear

Part of the coupling system is the use of landing gear. These legs are extended from the trailer before the fifth wheel is uncoupled from the trailer and are not raised until the trailer couples to the fifth wheel. A two-speed

SKILL DRILL 34-2 Inspecting the Slider Mechanism on a Fifth Wheel

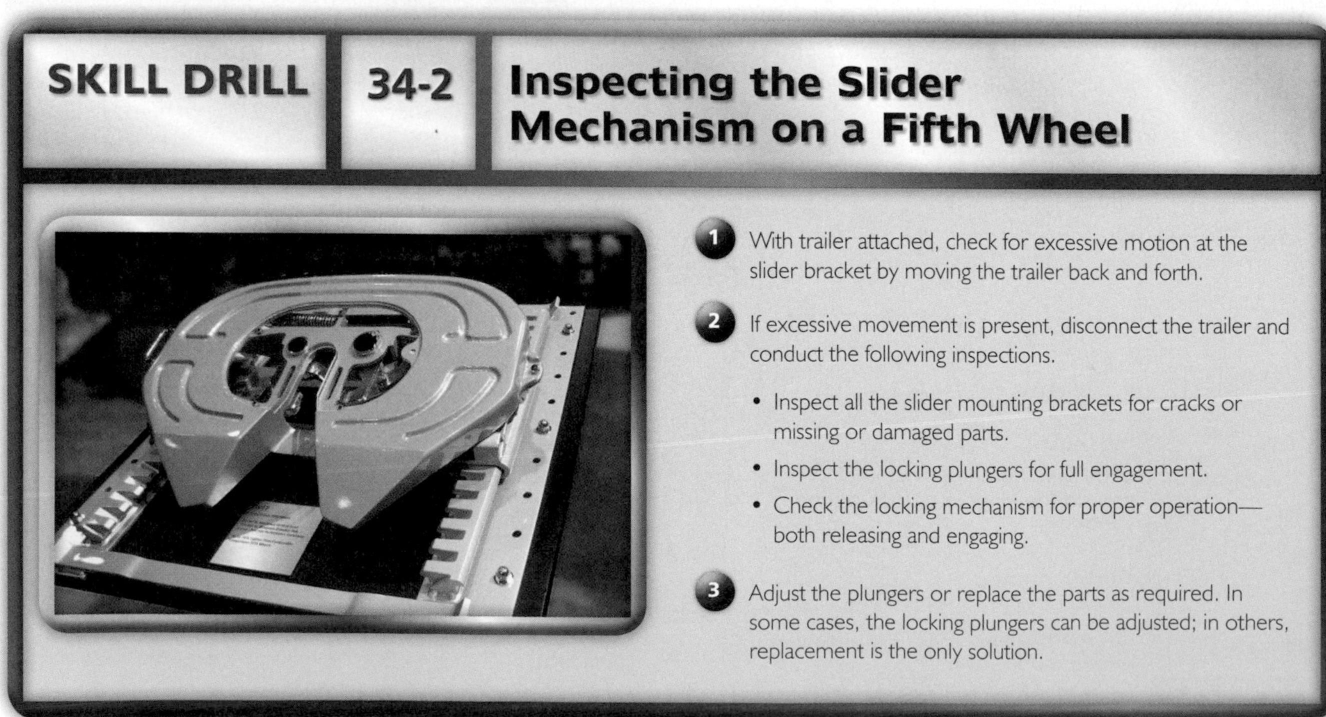

1. With trailer attached, check for excessive motion at the slider bracket by moving the trailer back and forth.
2. If excessive movement is present, disconnect the trailer and conduct the following inspections.
   - Inspect all the slider mounting brackets for cracks or missing or damaged parts.
   - Inspect the locking plungers for full engagement.
   - Check the locking mechanism for proper operation—both releasing and engaging.
3. Adjust the plungers or replace the parts as required. In some cases, the locking plungers can be adjusted; in others, replacement is the only solution.

gear mechanism is used to lower and raise the landing gear. High gear is for rapid movement of the gear when no load is resting on the legs. Low speed has a higher gear reduction ratio for partially lifting the trailer's vertical load from the fifth wheel when uncoupling. FIGURE 34-52 shows the two-speed gearing mechanism.

Several grease fittings are typically installed on the landing gear to lubricate the long internal lifting screw and the gear reduction mechanism. As shown in FIGURE 34-53, a bar connects the left and right side landing gear legs to synchronize movement of the landing gear mechanisms.

Occasionally the landing gear will bind when lifting or lowering. A common problem with landing gear is that trailers will fall on legs that have not been extended far enough when uncoupling. The shock load will typically bend the long screws in the landing gear leg and damage teeth. Disconnecting the connecting bar between the legs will help differentiate whether the problem is in one or both landing gears since one may move freely but the other not. Legs can be rebuilt or replaced when mechanisms are damaged or worn out. FIGURE 34-54 shows a landing gear with a replaceable foot.

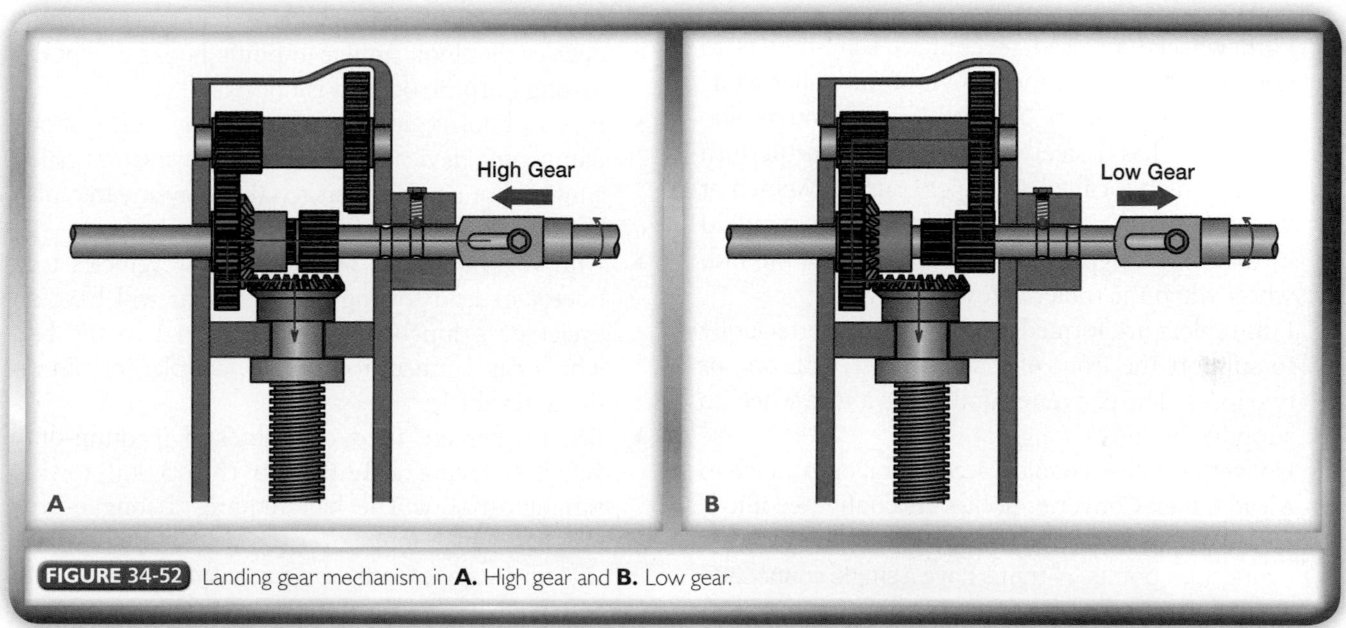

FIGURE 34-52 Landing gear mechanism in **A.** High gear and **B.** Low gear.

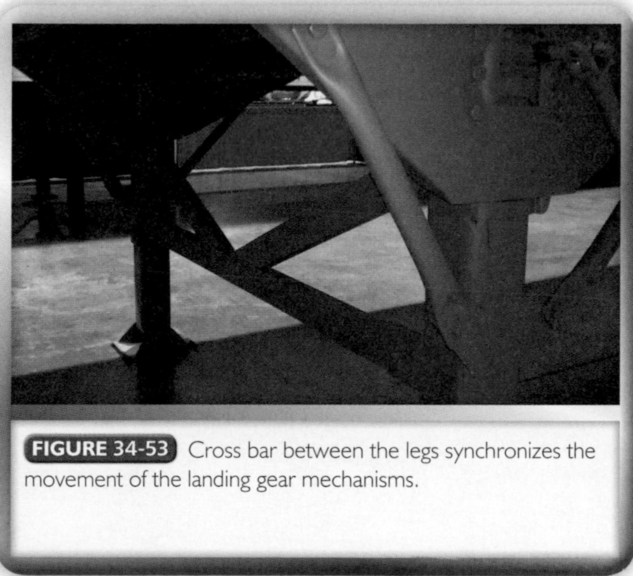

FIGURE 34-53 Cross bar between the legs synchronizes the movement of the landing gear mechanisms.

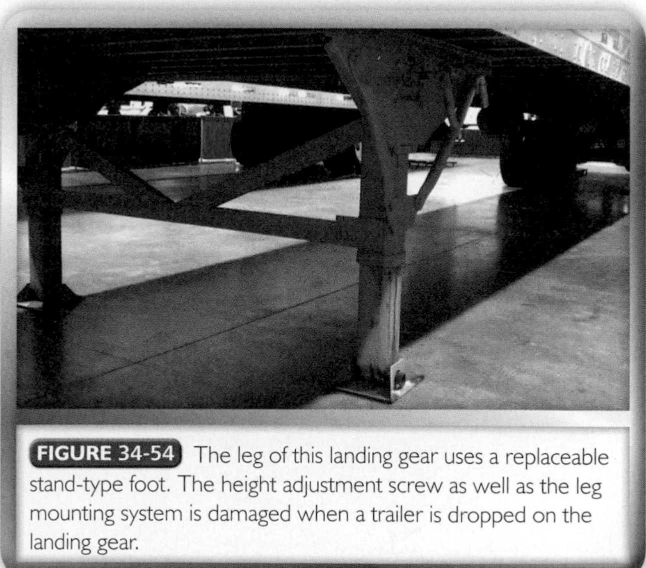

FIGURE 34-54 The leg of this landing gear uses a replaceable stand-type foot. The height adjustment screw as well as the leg mounting system is damaged when a trailer is dropped on the landing gear.

Wrap-up

Ready for Review

- Connecting trucks and tractors with trailers form what are known as combination vehicles. Combining vehicles is necessary for commercial vehicles to meet legislated requirements limiting axle weight by adding more axles to distribute vehicle weight. Fifth wheels and various other hitching devices are needed to form combination units.
- Fifth wheels are used to connect semi-trailers to tractors and support the weight of the trailer while allowing articulation between tractor and trailer. The trailer has a steel plate that rests on the fifth wheel, which is called an upper coupler. Welded or bolted to the upper coupler is an industry standard 2" (5.1 cm) kingpin, which is locked into the fifth wheel when the trailer is towed.
- Full trailers are formed by using a converter dolly to support the front of a semi-trailer with one or two axles. The converter dolly uses a fifth wheel to support the trailer weight.
- Converter dollies enable a second trailer to attach to a lead trailer. Converter dollies are configured into A and C types according to the geometric shape of the connection points. A-trains have a single connection point to the lead trailer while C-trains use two.
- B-trains are a type of combination vehicle composed of two trailers plus one tractor. A second semi-trailer attaches to the lead trailer through a fifth wheel mounted to a stub frame of the lead trailer.
- B-trains substantially increase the cargo carrying capacity of a combination vehicle with only a small increase in fuel consumption.
- Pintle hooks are trailer hitching devices that use a fixed towing horn, which connects with a draw bar attached to the towed vehicle. Couplers are hitching devices that look similar to pintle hooks except the towing horn pivots and is not fixed.
- Pintle hooks and couplers may use shock dampening devices such as rubber insulators called snubbers or air chambers to take away any free-play in the trailer connection.
- Draw bars are used to connect tow vehicles to a tractor or lead towing unit. The bar will have an eyelet or a lunette welded or bolted to the bar, which can connect to a pintle, coupler, or pin on the tow vehicle.
- Ball hitches are used on light and medium-duty vehicles having a 12,000 lb (5,443 kg) towing weight capacity. The ball requires a tongue type tow bar, which loops over a ball. Ball hitches have the advantage of providing a positive no-slack fit. Safety chains are used with ball hitches to protect

against complete loss of the trailer in the event of a break-away.

- It is important to lubricate the top plate of a fifth wheel or use a low friction, "no-lube" plate on top of the fifth wheel. Without the lubrication, articulation between the fifth wheel and trailer encounter high resistance. Steering the vehicle will be difficult and the trailer can push the tractor out of its lane when cornering. Lubrication is necessary to reduce wear on the fifth wheel top plate and trailer upper coupler.
- Fifth wheel top plates are made from cast iron, stamped steel, or aluminum. The type of jaw mechanism that locks and holds the trailer kingpin in the fifth wheel varies between manufacturers. Most locking jaw mechanisms require periodic inspection and adjustment to compensate for jaw wear. No-slack lock mechanisms are automatically adjusting.
- Fifth wheels must be properly positioned on the frame when installed to prevent interference between the trailer and tractor as well as to obtain proper distribution of trailer weight among the tractor axles. A fifth wheel should not move any farther rearward on a chassis than 1" (2.5 cm) ahead of the center between the rear tandem axles.
- The height of a fifth wheel should not allow the trailer to exceed 13' 6" (4.1 m). The height should also enable the trailer to couple properly with the tractor.
- Semi-oscillating fifth wheels are the most common type used on highway for pulling dry cube trailers. The semi-oscillating wheel will articulate several degrees side to side and back to front. Full oscillating fifth wheels articulate much more and are typically used for bulk liquid tankers to prevent tanker barrels from twisting and cracking. Rigid type fifth wheels allow the upper coupler only to move and are used on dump trailers.
- Upper couplers attach to the trailer and hold the kingpin. Kingpins are available in 2" (5.1 cm) and 3.5" (8.9 cm) for specialized applications. Upper couplers are checked for flatness during inspection.
- Kingpins are inspected for straightness, length, and wear—typically with a go–no go gauge.
- Trailer landing gear is composed of two legs, which must support the weight of the trailer when uncoupling. The landing gear has a two-speed gear reduction mechanism to quickly raise the legs (fast speed up) and reduce the load on the fifth wheel when uncoupling (slow speed–high gear reduction) to lift the trailer slightly from the fifth wheel. Legs can be replaced or rebuilt when damaged. The gear mechanism requires periodic lubrication with chassis grease.

Vocabulary Builder

A-, B-, or C-train A three-unit combination of tractor plus two trailers.

A-type lock A single swinging lock jaw and plunger for simple operation.

axle spread The distance between the centerline of two axles.

B-type lock A mechanism that uses two swinging jaws and a yoke to lock the jaws securely around the kingpin.

ball hitch A single-point connection configuration for a hitch that uses a tongue shaped draw bar, which loops over a ball connected to the tow vehicle.

Bridge Formula B See *Federal Bridge Gross Weight Formula*.

cab forward (CF) A tractor with the engine located ahead of the cab.

cab over engine (COE) A tractor with the engine located beneath the cab.

combination vehicles Two or more combined or coupled vehicle units.

converter dolly A single or set of dual axle that supports a fifth wheel. Converter dollies convert semi-trailers into full trailers.

coupler Trailer hitching device, similar to pintle hooks, but in which the towing horn pivots and is not fixed.

"D" capacity The maximum horizontal pulling force that can be safely applied to the fifth wheel. Also called *draw bar capacity*.

draw bars Bars used to connect tow vehicles to a tractor or lead towing unit.

draw bar capacity The maximum horizontal pulling force that can be safely applied to the fifth wheel. Also called *"D" capacity*.

Federal Bridge Formula See *Federal Bridge Gross Weight Formula*.

Federal Bridge Gross Weight Formula Laws that limit the weight-to-length ratio of heavy trucks with the goal of protecting roads and bridges from the damage caused by the concentrated weight of shorter trucks. Also known as *Bridge Formula B* or *Federal Bridge Formula*.

fifth wheel A plate-type coupling device designed to support the weight of a semi-trailer.

flitch plates Angle iron that is attached to the fifth wheel on one side and is bolted to the frame on another side.

full trailer A trailer that is supported at both ends with an axle and does not rest on a fifth wheel.

fully oscillating fifth wheel A type of fifth wheel designed to provide front-to-rear and side-to-side movement between the tractor and semi-trailer.

gross combined weight rating (GCWR) A specific maximum weight limit determined by the vehicle manufacturer.

gross trailer weight (GTW) The maximum carrying capacity of a trailer calculated by measuring the trailer weight and load.

gross vehicle weight (GVW) The maximum design weight of a vehicle including a full tank of fuel, fully loaded to its capacity, and with all passengers.

gross vehicle weight rating (GVWR) The design rating specified by a manufacturer as the recommended maximum weight of a vehicle when fully loaded to capacity, including all passengers and a full tank of fuel.

gross weight limit The maximum legal weight of a vehicle that can travel on roads and bridges.

kingpin The pin attached to a trailer's upper coupler which is used to lock the fifth wheel to the trailer.

landing gear Retractable legs attached to the trailer, which support a semi-trailer when it is not resting on a fifth wheel.

no-slack coupler A lock mechanism that uses serrated edges between the locking bar and wedge to ensure no play in the coupling.

pintle hook Trailer hitching device that uses a fixed towing horn, which connects with a draw bar eye, attached to the towed vehicle.

rigid fifth wheel A type of fifth wheel that does not oscillate about either axis of the vehicle. It does not articulate from side to side or front to back. It is fixed in location.

secondary safety latch An additional mechanism used as an added step to unlatch or release a fifth wheel locking jaw.

semi-oscillating fifth wheel Fifth wheels that pivot slightly in both horizontal and vertical directions; the standard type of fifth wheel used in on-highway applications.

semi-trailer A trailer that has some of its load carried by the tractor through a hitching device.

shunt truck A tractor designed to move semi-trailers around a warehouse yard or intermodal facility. Also known as a *terminal tractor*.

slider mechanism A plate the fifth wheel is attached to that has a ratchet-like set of plungers that enable the fifth wheel to be repositioned forward or backward along the tractor frame.

snubber A shock absorbing insulator used to absorb shock loads transmitted by the trailer when the tow vehicle is accelerating or decelerating.

swing clearance The clearance remaining between a trailer and tractor when the combination vehicle is cornering.

tandem axle A two-axle tractor or trailer configuration.

terminal tractor A tractor designed to move semi-trailers around a warehouse yard or intermodal facility. Also known as a *shunt truck*.

tongue weight (TW) The weight supported by the ball (tongue) in a ball hitch.

trailer The cargo carrying portion of a combination vehicle.

two-height fifth wheel A specialty stationary fifth wheel that can be either air or hydraulically raised or lowered.

upper coupler A steel plate and a kingpin fastened to the underside of the forward portion of a semi-trailer frame and designed to tow and support the weight of the trailer.

vertical load The weight supported by a hitching device, which is applied downwards by the weight of the trailer.

Review Quiz

1. Which of the following is the maximum weight load a single axle on a Class 8 combination vehicle is permitted to carry?
   a. 80,000 lb (36,287 kg)
   b. 42,000 lb (19,051 kg)
   c. 20,000 lb (9,072 kg)
   d. 10,000 lb (4,536 kg)
2. Which of the following is used to connect a single semi-trailer to a tractor?
   a. A fifth wheel
   b. A converter dolly
   c. A pintle hook
   d. A draw bar
3. What classification of hitch is used by a converter dolly connecting to a lead trailer with a single draw bar?
   a. A semi-oscillating
   b. A B-train
   c. An A-train
   d. A C-train
4. What grade of fasteners is required to fasten all fifth wheels and hitching devices to the frame?
   a. SAE Grade 14
   b. SAE Grade 8
   c. SAE Grade 5
   d. Corrosion resistant plated fasteners
5. The height of the fifth wheel from the ground should:
   a. not allow the trailer height to exceed 13'6" (4.1 m).
   b. be between 3'6" and 60" (1.1 and 1.5 m).
   c. be capable of being varied by adjusting air or hydraulic pressure.
   d. provide adequate swing clearance between the tractor and the trailer.
6. Side-to-side articulation of a semi-oscillating fifth wheel is provided by:
   a. compression in the rubber bushing beneath the top plate.
   b. a cradle mechanism supporting the top plate of the fifth wheel.
   c. pivoting of the top plate around steel pins in the plate brackets.
   d. flexing of the upper coupler plate.
7. The weight of a vehicle supported by a single axle should almost never exceed more than:
   a. 15,000 lb (6,804 kg).
   b. 20,000 lb (9,072 kg).
   c. 22,000 lb (9979 kg).
   d. None of the choices are correct.
8. Which of the following is correct concerning tractors?
   a. A tractor is a commercial motor vehicle chassis designed to exclusively tow trailers.
   b. Having usually just a cab and no capability to carry cargo, tractors use high torque output engines and a fifth wheel to support the front end of a trailer.
   c. Both A and B
   d. Neither A nor B
9. Which of the following is correct concerning trailers?
   a. Trailers are the cargo-carrying portion of a combination vehicle.
   b. The most familiar combination configuration in North America is a tractor with a semi-trailer.
   c. Semitrailers use one, two, or even three axles depending on their length and load-carrying capacity.
   d. All of the choices are correct.
10. Class 8 includes vehicles weighing more than:
    a. 30,001 lb (13,607 kg).
    b. 33,001 lb (14,969 kg).
    c. 36,001 lb (16,329 kg).
    d. None of the choices are correct.

ASE-Type Quiz

1. Technician A says that the position of the fifth wheel has to move farther forward than a conventional cab forward tractor to distribute trailer weight evenly over the axles. Technician B says that a conventional cab forward tractor needs to move the fifth wheel farther ahead than a cab over engine. Who is correct?
   a. Technician A
   b. Technician B
   c. Both Technician A and Technician B
   d. Neither Technician A nor Technician B

2. Technician A says that a fully oscillating fifth wheel is the best fifth wheel to use for a frameless dump trailer with an articulating upper coupler. Technician B says that a rigid type fifth wheel is safer. Who is correct?
   a. Technician A
   b. Technician B
   c. Both Technician A and Technician B
   d. Neither Technician A nor Technician B

3. Technician A says that a semi-oscillating fifth wheel is the most commonly used fifth wheel on tractors towing semi-trailers. Technician B says that a fully oscillating fifth wheel helps prevent liquid tanker barrels from cracking. Who is correct?
   a. Technician A
   b. Technician B
   c. Both Technician A and Technician B
   d. Neither Technician A nor Technician B

4. A fifth wheel kingpin is checked with a go–no go gauge. The 2" (5.1 cm) pin slipped into both the wider and narrower slots of the gauge. Technician A recommends replacing the kingpin. Technician B says all fifth wheel lock jaws are designed to safely accommodate variations in sizes of kingpins. Who is correct?
   a. Technician A
   b. Technician B
   c. Both Technician A and Technician B
   d. Neither Technician A nor Technician B

5. Technician A says the A-train configuration uses a fifth-wheel connection between trailers. Technician B says the B-train configuration is the least stable of the three combination vehicle types. Who is correct?
   a. Technician A
   b. Technician B
   c. Both Technician A and Technician B
   d. Neither Technician A nor Technician B

6. Technician A says that, in North America, one of the most common ways trucks are categorized is by gross vehicle weight (GVW). Technician B says that GVW refers to the maximum design weight of a vehicle including a full tank of fuel, fully loaded to its capacity, and with all passengers. Who is correct?
   a. Technician A
   b. Technician B
   c. Both Technician A and Technician B
   d. Neither Technician A nor Technician B

7. Technician A says pintle hooks are coupled by raising the draw bar eye over the pintle horn and locking it closed with a pivoting latch. Technician B says a snubber or load dampener was used in the past to minimize shock loads but are no longer being used. Who is correct?
   a. Technician A
   b. Technician B
   c. Both Technician A and Technician B
   d. Neither Technician A nor Technician B

8. Technician A says that ball hitches are used on light- and medium-duty vehicles having a 14,000 lb (6,350 kg) towing weight capacity. Technician B says that ball hitches have the advantage of providing a positive no-slack fit because the draw bar has a spring-loaded tensioner at the connection point with the ball. Who is correct?
   a. Technician A
   b. Technician B
   c. Both Technician A and Technician B
   d. Neither Technician A nor Technician B

9. Technician A says that tongue weight (TW) is the load the draw bar places on the pintle hook, coupler, or ball hitch. Technician B says that, as a general rule, the vertical load on the trailer tongue should be at least 30% of the gross trailer weight. Who is correct?
   a. Technician A
   b. Technician B
   c. Both Technician A and Technician B
   d. Neither Technician A nor Technician B

10. Technician A says that, to prevent damage to roadways and bridges, the vehicle weight supported by tires and axles is limited by legislation. Technician B says that generally, tires should apply no more than 800 lb (363 kg) per square inch of road contact patch. Who is correct?
    a. Technician A
    b. Technician B
    c. Both Technician A and Technician B
    d. Neither Technician A nor Technician B

SECTION IV

Drive Trains

CHAPTER 35 Heavy-Duty Clutches

CHAPTER 36 Servicing Heavy-Duty Clutches

CHAPTER 37 Basic Gearing Concepts

CHAPTER 38 Standard Transmissions

CHAPTER 39 Servicing Standard Transmission

CHAPTER 40 Automated Manual Transmissions

CHAPTER 41 Torque Converters

CHAPTER 42 Planetary Gear Concepts

CHAPTER 43 Hydraulically Controlled Automatic Transmissions

CHAPTER 44 Maintaining Automatic Transmissions

CHAPTER 45 Electronically Controlled Automatic Transmissions

CHAPTER 46 Driveshaft Systems

CHAPTER 47 Heavy-Duty Truck Drive Axles

CHAPTER 48 Servicing and Maintaining Drive Axles

CHAPTER 49 Hybrid Drive Systems and Series-Type Hybrid Drives

CHAPTER 50 Allison EV Drive Hybrid System

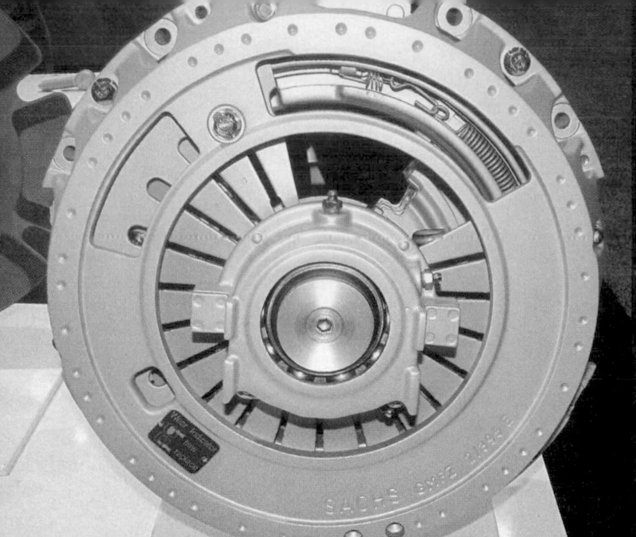

CHAPTER 35

NATEF Tasks

There are no NATEF tasks for this chapter.

Knowledge Objectives

After reading this chapter, you will be able to:

1. Describe the differences between single and multiple disc clutches. (pp 1142–1143)
2. Explain the function and operating principles of push-type clutches. (pp 1142–1146)
3. Explain the function and operating principles of pull-type clutches. (pp 1142–1146)
4. Identify clutch system components and their individual functions. (p 1147)
5. Describe the different types of flywheels used in medium to heavy trucks. (pp 1150, 1160–1162)
6. Describe and explain the purpose and function of various types of clutch brakes. (p 1153)
7. Describe the operation of the different clutch actuation systems. (p 1155)

Heavy-Duty Clutches

Skills Objectives

There are no skills objectives for this chapter.

Introduction

The clutch is an indispensable part of all power systems. It is the link between the power plant (the engine) and the rest of the vehicle driveline. All of the torque and power the engine produces must travel through the clutch. The correctly functioning clutch must provide many miles of faithful service without failure. It is the duty of every technician to fully understand the functioning, maintenance, and, when necessary, the replacement of this vital component. This chapter will help the technician to understand the purpose, function, and construction of the modern clutches commonly found in the medium- to heavy-duty truck industry.

Fundamentals of Heavy-Duty Clutches

The origin of the simple friction clutch dates back to the middle of the 19th century, circa 1835 to 1845. At that time, clutches were used for the same purposes we use them today—to connect and disconnect a power device from a mechanical system. In those days, however, clutches were typically connecting and disconnecting machinery from a steam engine. There were a multitude of designs—expanding shoe and drum types, a flat friction disc clamped against a flywheel, and the cone-type clutch.

The cone-type illustrated in FIGURE 35-1 was one of the more popular designs in its day. The cone-type clutch consisted of a female member (the cup) attached to the power source, which was usually a steam engine. A male member (the cone) attached to the gearing of the machine that needed to be driven. The cup and cone would have a running clearance in the disengaged position. When the clutch lever was actuated by an operator, the cone would be pushed into the cup, sliding along the driven shaft splines and clamped there. The friction material on

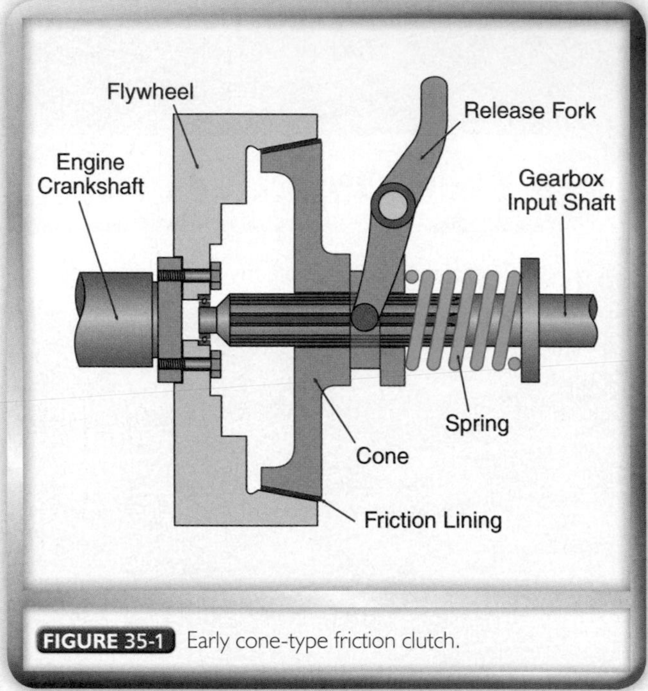

FIGURE 35-1 Early cone-type friction clutch.

You Are the Technician

A customer brings his two-year-old Freightliner truck to your shop and complains that he hears grinding from the transmission when he shifts into either first range or reverse. He says that the grinding does not happen as he is driving down the road shifting to any other gear; just first and reverse. He tells you that the problem started and has been getting worse and worse since his brother-in-law has been driving some shifts in the truck for him. You check out his complaint and find that, sure enough, there is grinding from the transmission when trying to select either first or reverse from neutral.

1. What component do you think may be to blame for this situation?
2. How would you verify your suspicion?
3. What advice could you give the driver to avoid a repeat concern?
4. What repair should be done?

the cone would grab onto, or "clutch," the driving cup and thereby transfer power to the machinery. To disengage the clutch, the actuation lever moved back, and the spring reestablished the running clearance, freeing the driven shaft again.

The cone-type clutch was an extremely important technological development. Prior to the invention of the clutch, machinery was typically directly connected to the engine. The machinery was started by closing a valve, which allowed the steam pressure to build up and provide the necessary power to drive the machine. Heavy loads would hinder the start of the machinery. The innovation of the clutch allowed the engine to be started and build up momentum in its flywheel before the load was applied. The clutch also allowed the machinery to be stopped without shutting down the engine.

Modern Clutches

The dictionary definition of clutch is to "grab or hold tightly," and this is exactly what we need a clutch to do—to grab onto a component from a running engine and transfer its motion to the driveline of the vehicle. Most people understand this to be the essential function of a clutch, but if the only purpose of a clutch were to connect two components, the vehicle could be built more simply with just a solid connection from the engine to the driveline. The clutch could be eliminated altogether.

The real purpose of the clutch is to enable the engine to be disconnected from the driveline in order to stop the vehicle or to change gears or direction. In simplest terms, the main job of the clutch is to connect and disconnect the engine from the driveline. (The clutch does have other functions. We will discuss those functions later in this chapter.)

The clutch accomplishes its job by squeezing one or more driven members or discs that are splined to the transmission input shaft between the engine flywheel and one or more driving plates that are driven by the engine.

The automotive clutch consists of two or more driving components—the flywheel and the pressure plate. The **flywheel** is a heavy, round, metal disc bolted to the end of the engine crankshaft. It provides one of the friction surfaces for a clutch disc and acts to smooth out vibrations from the crankshaft assembly. The **clutch cover** is the outside part of the clutch bolted to the flywheel and which holds all of the clutch components except the clutch disc. It is mistakenly, but commonly, called the pressure plate. The pressure plate is actually contained in the clutch cover. The **pressure plate** is the friction surface of the clutch cover and squeezes the clutch disc against the flywheel. Together, these components squeeze the friction disc(s) between them and as the disc/s are splined to the transmission input shaft this allows torque to be transmitted to the driveline, allowing torque to be transmitted to the driveline. FIGURE 35-2 shows a newer electronically actuated clutch design that has eliminated the need for a clutch pedal.

The Role of Friction

The clutch performs its duty by using **friction**, the relative resistance to motion between any two bodies in contact with one another. In simple terms, the more friction that there is between two bodies, the harder it will be to move the bodies in contact. The **coefficient of friction** is a measure of the friction that exists between two particular bodies in contact. As illustrated in FIGURE 35-3, the coefficient of friction is related to the force required to move an object across a given surface divided by the weight of the object.

FIGURE 35-2 Modern dual disc clutch assembly with an Eaton transmission.

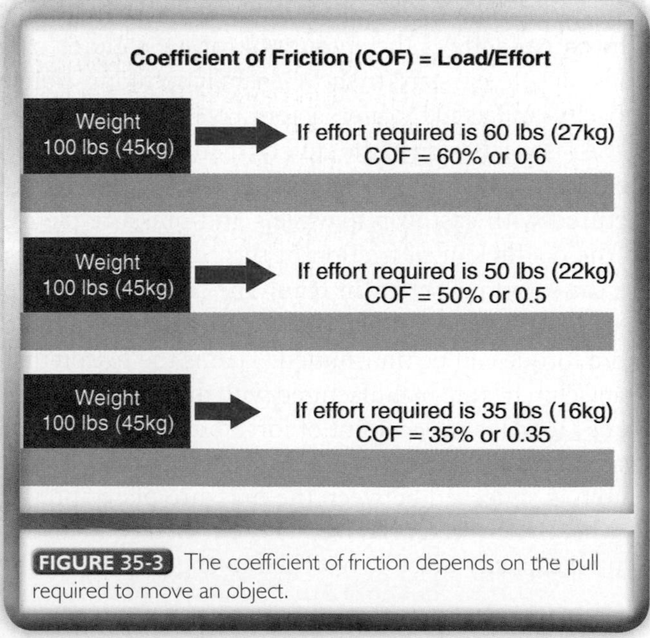

FIGURE 35-3 The coefficient of friction depends on the pull required to move an object.

Engineers carefully select material so that the coefficient of friction will give the desired result. The clutch should engage smoothly and not slip when transmitting increasing torque to the driveline. Several factors affect the coefficient of friction, such as the surface conditions of the objects. For example, rough surfaces have different coefficients of friction than smooth surfaces, as do wet and dry surfaces. Two blocks of smooth steel in contact will be easier to move than two rough surfaced bricks of the same weight. If lubricating oil is placed between the two steel blocks, they would move even more easily.

Basic Clutch Functions

As mentioned previously, clutches do more than just connect and disconnect the engine to the driveline. A clutch must allow a certain amount of slippage at engagement while the load is being taken up and the vehicle starts to move. That calculated slippage is known as **kinetic friction** and prevents driveline shock. The kinetic friction also adds to operator comfort by giving the driver a feel for the clutch. A clutch must also offer a long service life and perform hundreds of thousands of engagements and disengagements.

Perhaps the most important function of a clutch is to absorb damaging driveline torsional vibrations. **Torsional vibrations** are powerful vibrations caused by the engine firing impulses. Every time a cylinder fires, the force from the firing actually twists and accelerates the crankshaft. Torsional vibrations have increased as engine torque has increased, and the vibrations must be managed or the entire driveline will sustain fatigue damage.

Clutch Capacity

Clutch capacity is the amount of torque a clutch can transmit before it starts to slip. Generally speaking, clutch capacity is affected by three factors: coefficient of friction of the materials used in the clutch's manufacture, surface area, and clamp load. All automotive clutches are manufactured with cast iron flywheels and pressure plates, so the coefficient of friction of the cutch disc facings are the important element here. The larger the surface area of the components in contact with each other, the more torque can be transmitted. That is the reason that many clutches are manufactured with dual discs. **Clamp force (load)** is the amount of force pushing the clutch against the pressure plate and flywheel. The harder the clutch is squeezed between the pressure plate and the flywheel, the greater the torque the clutch can handle. Clutch capacity must be matched to engine torque.

Types and Design of Clutches

Two basic types of clutches are used in the medium- and heavy-duty commercial vehicle industry. They are the push-type and the pull-type. The push and pull refer to the direction the release fingers or levers have to be moved in order to disengage the clutch. In a **push-type clutch**, the release fingers or levers are pushed towards the engine flywheel to release the clutch; in the **pull-type clutch**, the levers are pulled away from the flywheel to disengage.

The single disc push-type clutch illustrated in FIGURE 35-4 is used primarily in light-duty applications, but it can be found in trucks up to class 4, 5, and 6. Push-type clutches are also available with dual friction discs for more severe-duty applications. Dual discs allow the clutch capacity to be increased without changing the clamp load.

Pull-type clutches, such as the one shown in FIGURE 35-5, are used almost exclusively in class 6, 7, and 8 trucks that use unsynchronized transmissions. Using a pull-type clutch allows the use of a clutch brake to slow and stop the transmission gearing when first or reverse gear is being selected. We will explain clutch brakes in greater detail in the Clutch Brakes section.

Pull-type clutches are also available in dual disc designs for increased clutch torque capacity. Multiple-disc clutches (clutches with more than two discs) are available for certain applications where extremely high

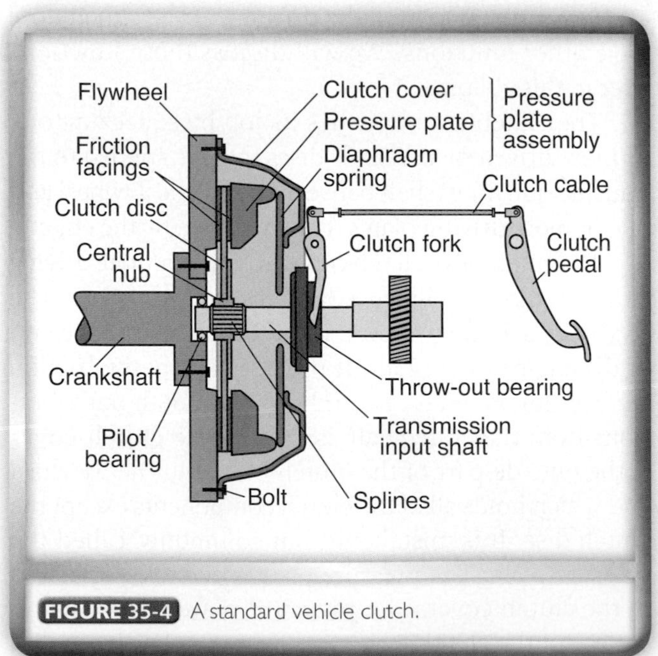

FIGURE 35-4 A standard vehicle clutch.

torque transfer capacity is needed. As yet, however, multiple-disc clutches are not prevalent in the on-highway truck market.

Clutch types are largely described by the type of cover the clutch has. The clutch cover is the component that houses the functioning parts of the clutch, the actuating levers, the springs, and the pressure plate. The clutch cover is sometimes referred to simply as the pressure plate, however, the pressure plate is just one of its components. There are three broad design categories for clutch covers:

- The coil spring style available in push- or pull-type
- The diaphragm spring style available in push- or pull-type
- The angle spring style, a pull-type clutch exclusive to the Eaton Corporation

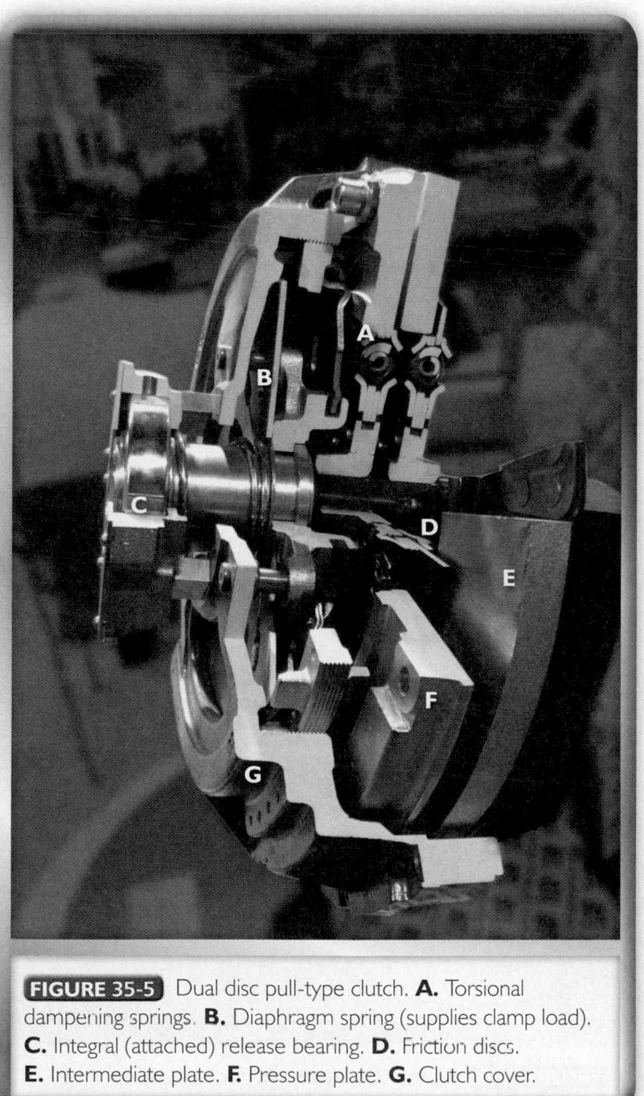

FIGURE 35-5 Dual disc pull-type clutch. **A.** Torsional dampening springs. **B.** Diaphragm spring (supplies clamp load). **C.** Integral (attached) release bearing. **D.** Friction discs. **E.** Intermediate plate. **F.** Pressure plate. **G.** Clutch cover.

These style designations refer to the method used to clamp the friction disc(s) between the flywheel and the pressure plate(s). There are self-adjusting versions of each design category as well.

Coil Spring Style Clutch

The **coil spring style clutch** uses coil springs that act directly against the back of the pressure plate to supply clamping force. In a push-type coil spring clutch, such as the one illustrated in FIGURE 35-6, a series of levers are attached to a pivot point, which is in turn attached to the clutch cover. The outer edges of the levers are attached to the pressure plate.

When disengagement is required, the release bearing is pushed against the inner surface of these levers. The **release bearing** is a hollow bearing through which the shaft passes and which allows the pushing or pulling of clutch release levers to release the clutch. The levers actually pull the pressure plate away from the flywheel, caging (or collapsing) the pressure springs. The same method is used in a pull-type coil spring clutch except, in that case, the pivot point and contact point of the levers is merely reversed. The pivot point of the levers is now at their outer edge, and the attachment point to the pressure plate is further inboard. In both push- and pull-types, as the discs wear, the pressure plate moves closer to the flywheel to compensate. This causes the coil springs to extend in order to keep contact with the pressure plate.

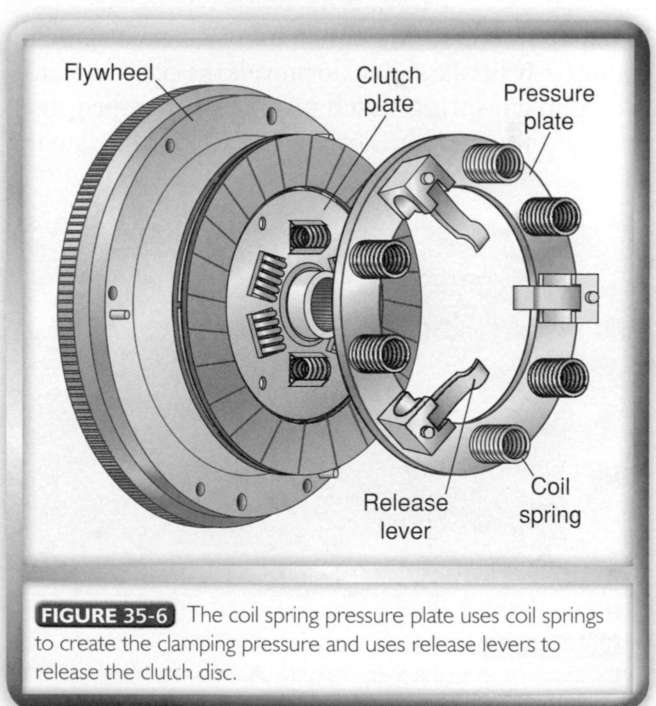

FIGURE 35-6 The coil spring pressure plate uses coil springs to create the clamping pressure and uses release levers to release the clutch disc.

Hooke's law states that the force delivered by a spring to an object is directly related to its compression or extension. That means that the more the spring is compressed, the more force it delivers to the pressure plate. As the friction disc wears, the coil springs extend. That extension of the springs reduces the force against the pressure plate. Therefore, the more that the clutch disc wears, the less the clamping force, and therefore clutch capacity, it has. To compensate for wear, coil spring clutches are built with very strong springs. The strong springs can make coil spring clutches more difficult for the driver to disengage.

In any clutch, the clutch cover is the component that is bolted to the flywheel, so the driving torque must be transferred from the cover to the pressure plate. Coil spring style clutches transfer this torque to the pressure plate in one of two ways depending on whether the cover is formed from stamped steel or is cast. The stamped steel version normally has pockets or notches formed in the stamped steel cover and drive lugs cast into the pressure plate, as shown in FIGURE 35-7. This allows positive torque transfer while allowing the pressure plate to move forward and backward as it engages and disengages. The cast cover version may use a similar arrangement to transfer torque to the pressure plate, or it may have cut outs in the cover that engage notches in the pressure plate. Coil spring clutches have mostly given way to diaphragm or angle spring clutches as the first choice of vehicle manufacturers.

Diaphragm Spring Clutch

The **diaphragm spring clutch** uses a single diaphragm spring (or Belleville spring) to provide the clamping force. A diaphragm spring clutch may have a stamped steel, cast iron, or aluminum cover. The cover is bolted to the engine flywheel and therefore turns with it. Normally in both the push-type and pull-type diaphragm style, driving torque is transmitted to the pressure plate through a series of drive straps attached to both the cover and the pressure plate.

These straps are made from laminated spring steel and have two functions. The first is to linearly transfer the driving torque to the pressure plate, as mentioned above. The second function of the straps is to act as return springs and move the pressure plate away from the clutch disc when it is disengaged. FIGURE 35-8 shows a Volvo I-Shift, electronically controlled, single-disc diaphragm, push-type clutch. Note the size of the full face organic disc compared to the quarter on the clutch disc center hub. The full face is nearly 18" (46 cm) in diameter.

In their normal, relaxed position, the drive straps are straight. As the clutch is engaged, the pressure plate moves toward the flywheel and the straps bend slightly. When the clutch is disengaged, the straps straighten out and pull the pressure plate back. As shown in FIGURE 35-9, these straps must be strong enough to withstand maximum engine torque with a safety margin. If the drive straps are overloaded, they can permanently deform, causing poor clutch release symptoms.

As illustrated in FIGURE 35-10A, a diaphragm spring clutch creates clamp load with the use of a single diaphragm spring pushing on the pressure plate. The diaphragm spring on this clutch is a single cone-shaped spring. Its outer edge rests against the pressure plate, and the inner part of the spring is cut into segments called fingers. These fingers act as the release levers. A pivot ring

FIGURE 35-7 The driving force must be transferred from the clutch cover to the pressure plate. **A.** Formed notches in the stamped steel cover engage the cast iron pressure plate to transfer driving torque. **B.** Lugs on the pressure plate.

FIGURE 35-8 Volvo I-shift clutch. **A.** Torsional dampening springs. **B.** Stamped steel clutch cover. **C.** Diaphragm spring. **D.** Clutch disc. **E.** Drive straps.

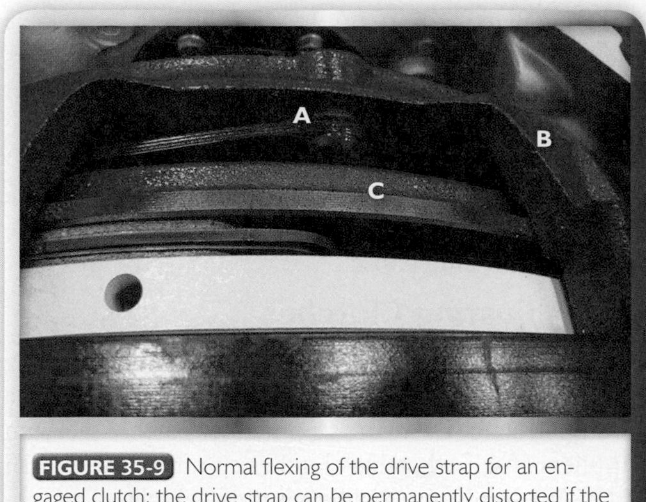

FIGURE 35-9 Normal flexing of the drive strap for an engaged clutch; the drive strap can be permanently distorted if the clutch is overloaded or shock loaded. **A.** Drive strap. **B.** Clutch cover. **C.** Pressure plate.

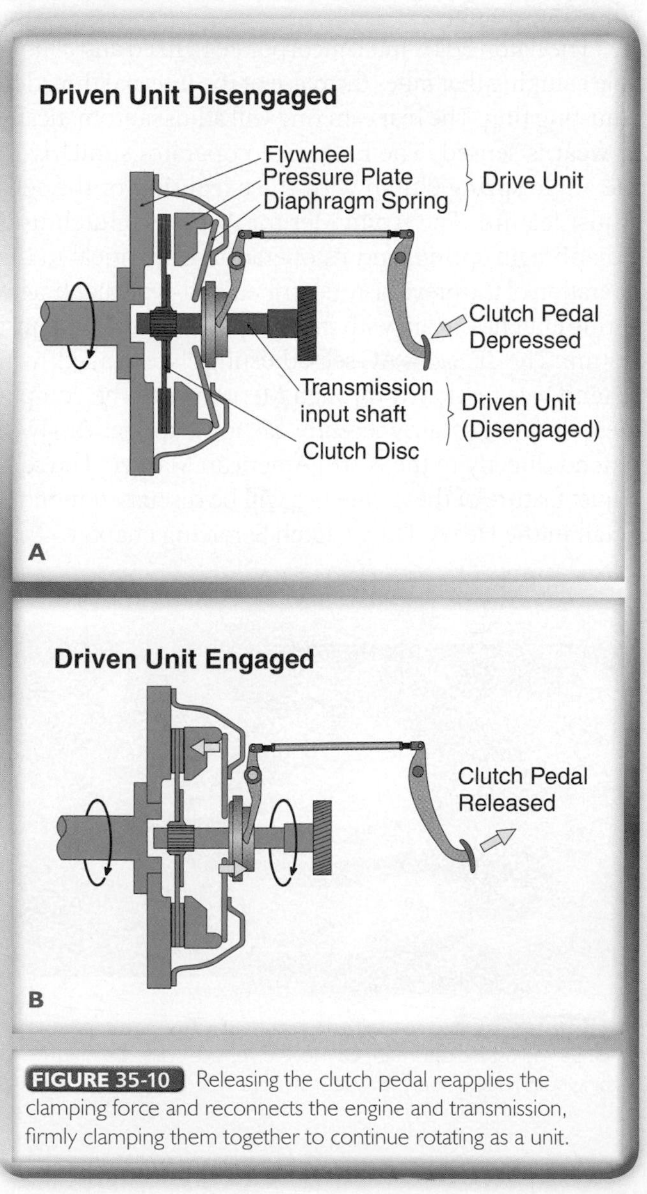

FIGURE 35-10 Releasing the clutch pedal reapplies the clamping force and reconnects the engine and transmission, firmly clamping them together to continue rotating as a unit.

is installed inside the clutch cover between the outside edge of the spring and the fingers.

To disengage the push-type diaphragm clutch, the release bearing is pushed against the release fingers. The pivot ring acts as a fulcrum, and the outer edge of the spring is pulled away from the pressure plate. The plate drive straps return to their normal straight shape, pulling the pressure plate away from the clutch disc, as illustrated in FIGURE 35-10B.

Rather than lose pressure as disc wear occurs (which happens in the coil spring type), the diaphragm spring clutch is designed to actually increase loading on the pressure plate as disc wear occurs until it is 50% worn. At that point, the pressure gradually decreases again for the second 50% of wear until the pressure returns to the original loading. This varying clamp load is accomplished through the changing contact point of the diaphragm spring with a specially designed lobe on the pressure plate and the pivot ring, which changes the effective lever length of the spring.

The pull-type version of the diaphragm spring style clutch, shown in FIGURE 35-11, arranges the diaphragm spring differently. The pivot point changes to the outer edge, and it engages the pressure plate further in towards the center. This has the effect of reversing release direction. In the pull-type diaphragm spring style clutch, the drive torque may be transferred to the pressure plate through either drive straps or pockets in the cover and lugs on the pressure plate. If the clutch does not have

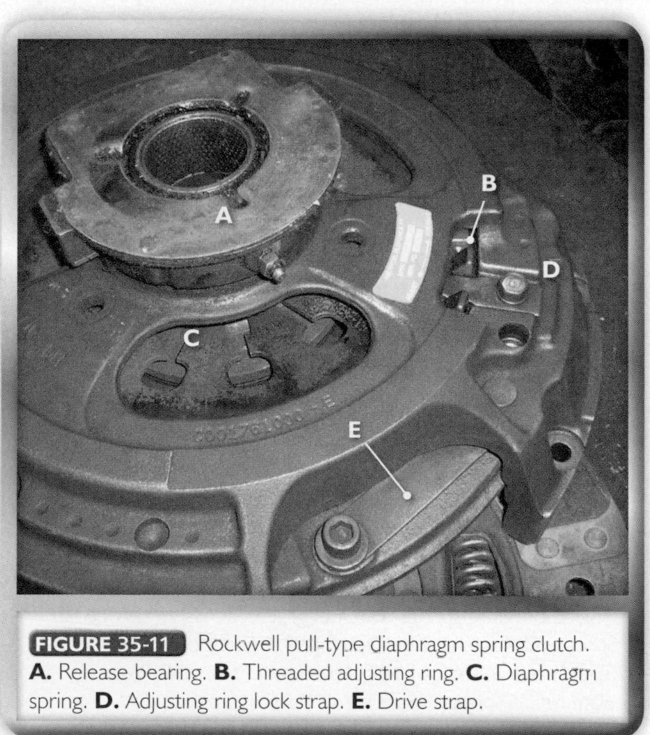

FIGURE 35-11 Rockwell pull-type diaphragm spring clutch. **A.** Release bearing. **B.** Threaded adjusting ring. **C.** Diaphragm spring. **D.** Adjusting ring lock strap. **E.** Drive strap.

drive straps, the pressure plate will be drawn away from the friction disc by several small springs when the clutch is disengaged.

Angle Spring Clutch

The **angle spring clutch** uses three pairs of angled springs pushing against the levers to supply the clamp load. The angle spring pull-style clutch manufactured by Eaton is by far the most popular in heavy-duty on-highway trucks today. Its design allows for a near constant clamp load throughout the life of the clutch discs as long as the adjustment is correct. Six angle-mounted coil springs push axially against the bearing retainer. In turn, the bearing retainer pushes against the inner edge of six equally spaced levers. These levers multiply the pressure of the springs and press against the pressure plate to create clamp load. Driving torque is transferred to the pressure plate by lugs and pockets.

The use of the levers in the clutch design allow increased clamp load with a decreased pedal effort to disengage the clutch. The Eaton angle spring clutch, shown in FIGURE 35-12, also uses three assist springs that function to reduce pedal effort on clutch release. The three assist springs are arranged so that, as the clutch releases, the springs help to hold the clutch in the release position. In fact, once the clutch is released only 30% of the pedal effort required for disengagement is needed to hold the clutch pedal down. For that reason, this type of clutch is known as the "Easy Pedal Clutch."

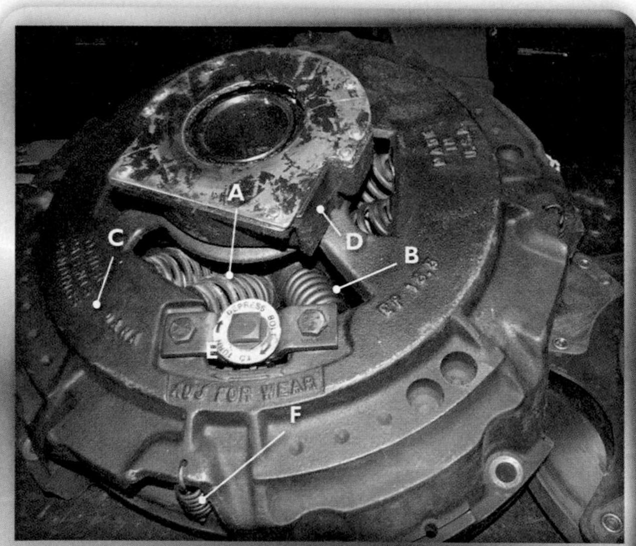

FIGURE 35-12 Eaton "Easy Pedal" angle spring clutch. **A.** Angled pressure springs. **B.** Disengagement assist (Easy Pedal) springs. **C.** Clutch cover. **D.** Integral release bearing. **E.** Quick-adjust mechanism for internal clutch adjustment. **F.** Pressure plate return springs (1 of 4).

To disengage the clutch, the integral (attached) release bearing pulls the inner edge of the release levers toward the transmission. The release levers are pivoted off the clutch cover at their outer edge and contact the pressure plate at a point closer to the center of the clutch cover. This action takes the pressure off the pressure plate and allows small return springs to pull the pressure plate away from the clutch disc.

Self-Adjusting Clutches

Self-adjusting clutches have an automatic adjusting system that relies on pressure plate movement to cause an adjustment. There are two major North American suppliers of self-adjusting clutches commonly found on today's medium-duty and heavy-duty vehicles. They are Eaton's Solo clutch, shown in FIGURE 35-13, and Meritor's AutoJust clutch, which is no longer in production. In Europe, ZF Sachs AG markets the Twin Xtend self-adjusting clutch.

The Eaton Solo clutch incorporates a fixed and a movable cam ring that takes the place of the internal threaded adjusting ring. The rear cam ring will adjust automatically as wear is sensed. The Eaton Solo operates similarly to the angle spring clutch with the exception of the self-adjust feature. The Arvin Meritor AutoJust clutch uses a diaphragm spring, and its operation is identical to the operation of the previously described pull-type diaphragm spring clutches, again with the exception of the self-adjust feature. The ZF Sachs AG self-adjusting clutch called Twin Extend was marketed through Meritor until the companies parted ways fairly recently. ZF now supplies the Twin Extend directly to the North American Market. The self-adjust feature of these clutches will be discussed in more detail in the Heavy-Duty Clutch Servicing chapter.

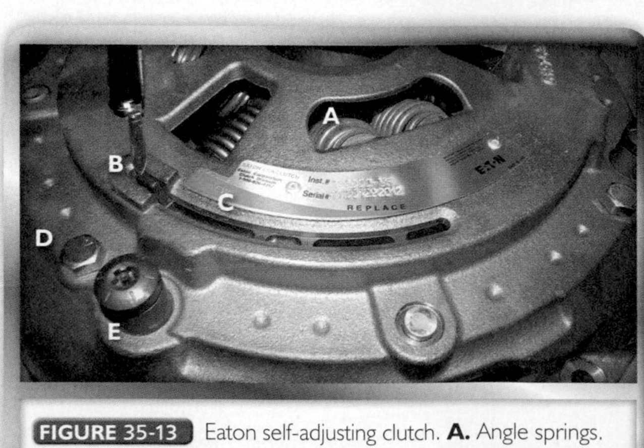

FIGURE 35-13 Eaton self-adjusting clutch. **A.** Angle springs. **B.** Self-adjust indicator tab. **C.** New to replace scale. **D.** Shipping bolts (one of four). **E.** Wear sensors.

Components of Clutches

Clutches include several other components critical to their function, including friction discs, flywheels, intermediate plates, pilot and release bearings, and clutch brakes. Additionally, regardless of type, every clutch has an actuation system that is mechanically, hydraulically, or automatically controlled.

Clutch Friction Discs

Clutch friction discs are the only driven member of the clutch assembly. The friction discs must transfer all of the engine torque to the driveline without slipping. Today's clutch discs must also absorb damaging engine torsional vibrations, cushion shock loads, and prevent gear rattle at idle. The clutch disc must do all this for many years of vehicle operation. For those reasons, the clutch discs can be thought of as the heart of the clutch. They are essential to successful clutch operation. Different types of clutch discs contribute varying benefits to the clutch system.

The friction facings on the clutch discs come in two distinct categories—organic and ceramic—both of which are available in rigid and or dampened disc styles. The dampened disc style provides vibration control.

Organic Facings

Organic facings are made of various natural materials such as cotton fibers, rubber material, aluminum, glass fibers, copper or brass fibers, and carbon material. These materials are blended together and formed into solid discs, such as the ones shown in **FIGURE 35-14**, which are then bonded or riveted to the outermost edge of the friction disc. Organic friction discs are made from a variety of carefully selected materials to give them the correct coefficient of friction.

Organic facings are usually attached to what are called cushion segments. The cushion segments are waved to create a slight space between the front and rear friction facing, as shown in **FIGURE 35-15**. On clutch engagement, these segments compress, allowing a gradual increase in friction. That gradual increase gives the vehicle a smoother start. As their name suggests, cushion segments cushion the engagement of the clutch and assist in release of the discs on clutch disengagement. Cushion segments are not normally used in heavy applications.

Organic facings are full face linings. That means that the outer area of the disc is completely covered by the facing material. Organic facings normally have grooves cut into the facing from the central hub to the outside edge to allow for heat dissipation and removal of debris by centrifugal force. Although a clutch facing (clutch lining) is very thin when new—less than 1/8" (3–4 mm)—quite a large amount of dust and debris will be present on the facing when the clutch has worn out.

Dangers of Organic Facings

Asbestos used to be the material of choice in the production of friction materials because of its high heat resistance; however since the late 1970s, asbestos has been not been used in friction materials manufactured in North America. It is important to note that friction materials manufactured overseas and installed on imported new vehicles may still contain various amounts of asbestos. Use of imported clutches or brake linings may expose a technician to asbestos. Exposure to asbestos fibers is known to cause asbestosis, which affects the lungs and is a precursor to lung cancer. Asbestos exposure is also a known cause of

FIGURE 35-14 Organic friction discs.

FIGURE 35-15 Cushion segments.

mesothelioma, a rare and almost always fatal condition affecting the outer lining of the lungs or the lining of the chest cavity. Asbestos can also affect the peritoneum, which is the lining of the stomach cavity.

Much debate surrounds the long-term effects of exposure to the newer organic friction material that contain no asbestos but may contain other fine fibers such as glass. Some critics argue that new materials are even worse than asbestos. The long-term effect of exposure to ceramic friction material dust is also not fully understood.

The safest bet for technicians is to protect themselves when servicing any vehicle by always wearing a National Institute of Occupational Safety and Health approved respirator and coveralls that protect street clothes from being contaminated by dust. Technicians should also vacuum any dust before working on clutches or brakes.

Ceramic Clutch Facings

In most medium- to-heavy applications, organic clutch discs have been replaced by discs with ceramic facings, such as the one shown in FIGURE 35-16. **Ceramic friction facings** are made mostly of man-made materials specifically designed to produce desirable characteristics. Specifically, ceramic facings have a much higher coefficient of friction and tend to have contact buttons rather than a full face lining.

Ceramic facings are made by mixing the materials together and then forming the material into the shape required and baking it. The material is then attached to a steel backing plate before being riveted to the disc. Ceramic facings have a much higher coefficient of friction and therefore do not require full face linings to give satisfactory clutch torque capability. Consequently, ceramic discs have several pads or buttons around the disc surface with spaces in between. The spaces allow for excellent cooling and better debris removal.

Ceramic facings are very rarely full face linings. Some extreme-duty applications, such as racing, may call for full face linings. Ceramic facings are not attached to cushion segments in the way that some organic facings are. The lack of attachment to a cushion segment combined with their higher coefficient of friction results in a more abrupt clutch engagement when ceramic facings are used.

FIGURE 35-16 Ceramic facing.

Rigid and Dampened Disc Styles

Both ceramic and organic discs are available in rigid and or dampened disc styles. FIGURE 35-17A shows a rigid disc and FIGURE 35-17B shows a dampened disc. Dampened discs have a set of torsional dampening springs around their center hub. The springs are designed to absorb engine torsional vibrations. By contrast, rigid discs do not absorb these vibrations. Although rigid discs are not recommended for any on highway applications in North America today they are being used in some medium duty applications in Europe combined with dual mass flywheels.

FIGURE 35-17 **A.** Rigid disc. **B.** Dampened disc.

Vibration Control

Engine torsional vibrations are caused by the acceleration of the engine crankshaft that occurs on each cylinder firing. Torsional vibrations can be responsible for severe driveline damage, including wearing of the input shaft spline, transmission input gear set, and drive axle gearing, as well as leakage of the transmission gasket and pinion seal.

A dampened disc is actually constructed of several components attached together. The central hub is splined to the transmission input shaft but it is not driven directly by the friction discs. Another disc, called the driven plate, sits around the central hub. The driven plate has a large slot that will rotate around the central hub. This driven plate has slots for the torsional springs, usually coaxial type, which is a spring inside a spring, and the friction material is attached to this plate.

Sandwiched on both sides of the drive plate are two or more spring cage plates that hold the torsional springs in place. These plates are rigidly attached to the central hub and contact the springs in the driven plate. The power flow for this arrangement then flows from the flywheel and pressure plate to the friction material attached to the driven plate. The flow continues through the coaxial torsion springs to the spring cage plates and onto the central hub and the input shaft.

This means that the drive goes through the springs before it reaches the input shaft. The springs compress to absorb the acceleration of the crankshaft due to the firing pulses effectively dampening the oscillations before they reach the driveline. Notice in **FIGURE 35-18** that the cutout in the clutch disc for the splined hub is quite a bit larger than the hub. This allows the torsional springs to be compressed as they transfer drive to the hub, thereby absorbing torsional vibrations. There are stop pins that limit how far the driven plate can move around the central hub to protect the torsional springs.

The disc in Figure 35-18 is only one design used for dampening. Many manufacturers use different designs, such as the one shown in **FIGURE 35-19**, but the effect is the same in that the friction material can only drive the input shaft through torsional springs, thereby dampening the vibrations. Regardless of the style used, **dampening discs** all allow the driven disc to rotate against springs before the drive reaches the driven hub, absorbing and dampening damaging torsional vibration.

In some applications, more dampening is required—particularly in high torque rise electronic diesel engines. These engines are capable of extremely high torque at relatively low rotations per minute (rpm). All drivelines have a **resonant frequency**, which is a point at which the driveline enters into a resonant condition where all the components start to oscillate in unison. The best example of **resonance** would be an opera singer hitting high C and shattering a crystal glass. The frequency of the singer's voice matches the resonant frequency of the crystal. The crystal molecules vibrate wildly until the glass shatters. For vehicles, resonance is the frequency at which the driveline's vibrations are the most damaging. Driveline resonance occurs when the frequency of the engine's firing pulses match the resonant frequency of that particular driveline. The matching frequencies greatly amplify the damaging twisting forces delivered by the crankshaft.

Clutch manufacturers have engineered what are commonly known as **soft-dampened clutches** to combat this situation. Soft-dampened clutches have much longer travel when dampening which allows them to combat resonance in a driveline. Soft-dampened clutches can be recognized by the larger windows in the spring cage

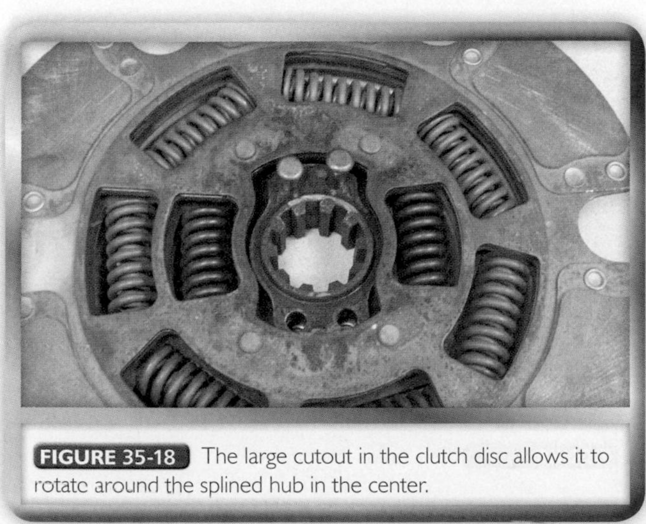

FIGURE 35-18 The large cutout in the clutch disc allows it to rotate around the splined hub in the center.

FIGURE 35-19 A dampening disc.

plates that surround their stop pins. FIGURE 35-20A shows a soft-dampened clutch with a normal travel damper and FIGURE 35-20B shows one with a long travel damper. Compare the images. Notice the difference in the available travel of the dampening discs before they contact the stop pins. These clutches have the tendency to lower the rpm of the resonance point and put it out of the normal rpm operating range of the vehicle.

Some manufacturers also use **friction dampening**. Friction dampening involves controlling torsional vibration by placing friction material between the spring cage plates of the clutch disc and the friction driven plate. In order to start dampening movement, this friction must be overcome, and that process helps to further dampen the oscillations. Some manufacturers of lighter-duty vehicles use a dual mass flywheel, such as the one shown in FIGURE 35-21, to further reduce these torsional vibrations. A **dual mass flywheel** has one section of the flywheel that is bolted to the engine crankshaft. This section drives a series of coaxial springs that in turn transmit that drive force to a second section to which the clutch assembly is bolted. Dual mass flywheels, such as the one in Figure 35-21, are not currently being used on heavy-duty applications.

Another problem associated with high-torque, electronically-controlled engines is that of transmission gear rattle at idle caused by torsional accelerations of the crankshaft. The damper springs used to absorb loaded torsional vibrations are too strong to absorb these unloaded accelerations. Consequently, the transmission gears rattle at idle. The latest clutch discs have an added set of very light dampening springs that are basically in series with the normal torsion dampening springs in the clutch disc. These light dampening springs must be compressed in order for the normal dampening springs to react. In no or very light load situations, such as idle, these springs absorb the torsional vibrations associated with gear rattle. Eaton, ZF Sachs AG, and Meritor, call this **"pre-dampening."** The lengths manufacturers go to reduce these vibrations shows that they are a very serious concern. It is important for the technician to remember, when replacing any of these components, to replace them with new parts that meet or exceed the manufacturer's specifications.

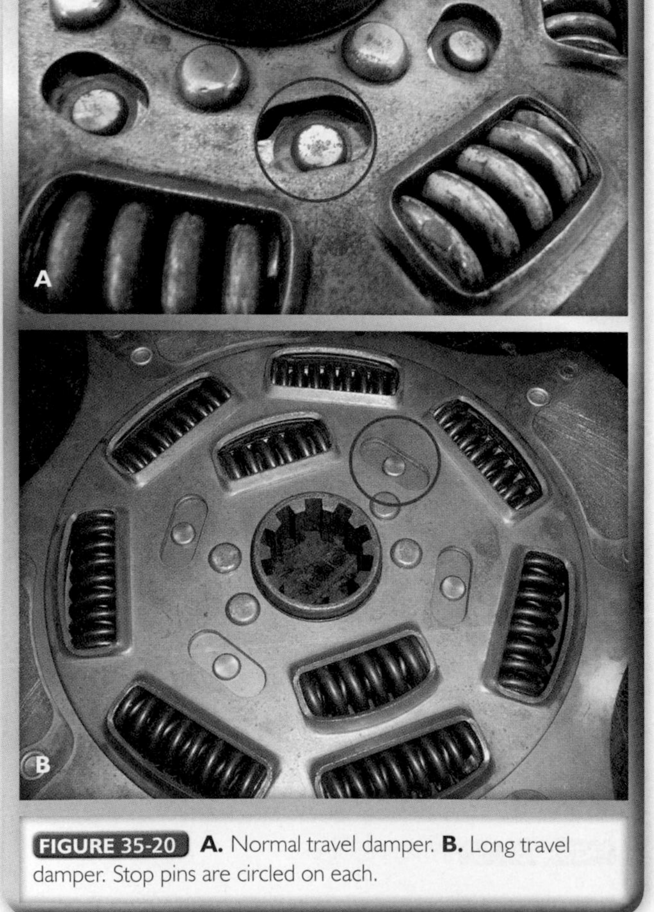

FIGURE 35-20 **A.** Normal travel damper. **B.** Long travel damper. Stop pins are circled on each.

Flywheels

As defined earlier in this chapter, a flywheel is a heavy round metal disc attached to the end of the crankshaft. The purpose of a flywheel is to smooth out vibrations from the crankshaft assembly and provide one of the friction surfaces for a clutch disc used on manual transmission/transaxle applications. Flywheels form the surface against which the friction disc is clamped. Flywheels also provide torsional dampening because of their mass. The accelerations of the crankshaft are somewhat subdued by the energy required to accelerate the heavy flywheel.

FIGURE 35-21 Dual mass flywheel.

Flywheels carry inertia as they rotate. That is, once they are rotating at a certain speed they tend to keep rotating so that the engine runs smoothly in between firing cycles. The flywheel also will usually have a ring gear attached to its outside edge to provide a means to crank the engine over.

Flywheels come in two basic designs. **Flat-type flywheels**, such as the one in FIGURE 35-22, have all of the clutch components inside the clutch cover and the cover bolts to the flywheel. This is the most common type of flywheel in use today. The second type is the 14" (35.6 cm) pot-type flywheel shown in FIGURE 35-23. In the **pot-type flywheel**, the clutch friction discs and the intermediate plate are installed into the "pot" shape of the flywheel and the clutch cover containing the pressure plate bolts to the back of the flywheel. If the flywheel has a raised bolt circle where the clutch cover mounts, it is extremely important that, when the flywheel face is resurfaced, the raised bolt circle is machined by the same amount in order to maintain the correct clamp load. If the bolt circle is not ground down by the same amount, the flywheel friction surface will be further away from the clutch pressure plate. That distance will cause the springs to extend, reducing clamp load.

FIGURE 35-22 Flat-type flywheel. **A.** Flywheel. **B.** Clutch cover. **C.** Intermediate plate. **D.** Intermediate plate drive lugs. **E.** Friction discs.

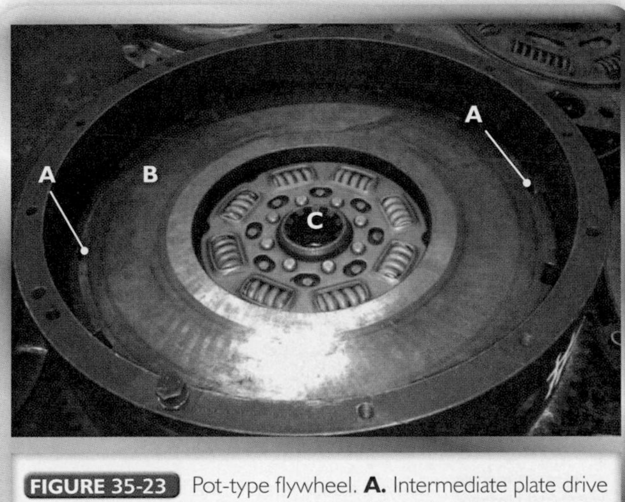

FIGURE 35-23 Pot-type flywheel. **A.** Intermediate plate drive pins. **B.** Intermediate plate. **C.** Front driven disc.

Intermediate Plates

The **intermediate plate** is the plate that contacts the back of the forward clutch friction disc and the front of the rear friction disc on dual disc clutches. This cast iron plate is necessary for all dual disc designs and creates a "friction sandwich" of flywheel, front friction disc, intermediate plate, rear friction disc, and the pressure plate. In most dual disc designs with a diaphragm and or stamped steel angle spring clutches, driving torque is transferred to the intermediate plate by means of drive straps. The intermediate plate is riveted to four or more drive straps which in turn are riveted to an aluminum spacer ring that is installed between the clutch cover and the flywheel. On other systems the, intermediate plate is driven by lugs and pockets (notches or slots in the clutch cover). In pot-type flywheel designs, the intermediate plate is driven by **drive pins** installed in the flywheel itself. Intermediate plates are indicated on the flywheels shown in Figure 35-22.

Pilot Bearings and Release Bearings

Pilot bearings are so called because they carry the pilot end of the input shaft. This often overlooked bearing is extremely important. It allows the input shaft to be supported straddle style. That is, the front of the shaft in the pilot bearing and the rear of the shaft in the transmission input bearing are mounted in the transmission case. This holds the shaft solidly when the clutch discs are disengaged and ensures the shaft remains centered.

This bearing may be as simple as a brass bushing or needle bearing mounted in a pocket formed in the rear of the crankshaft. That configuration is common on light-duty vehicles. Larger vehicles more commonly use a ball bearing mounted in the center of the flywheel, as shown in FIGURE 35-24. Regardless of the type, this bearing should always be replaced when replacing the clutch, even if it seems to be fine. The added cost to replace it during a clutch servicing is incidental compared to the costs that would be incurred to replace the bearing separately at a later date should it fail.

As its name implies, the release bearing is used to release the clutch discs. This bearing allows a stationary clutch fork to apply pressure to a rotating clutch's release levers or fingers. The pressure allows the clutch to cage the pressure plate spring(s) and interrupt power flow to the transmission. In a push-type clutch, the release bear-

FIGURE 35-24 Pilot bearing.

ing is part of a housing with a hollow center. The hollow part of this housing rides on a sleeve that is part of the transmission input bearing cover. The input shaft passes through this sleeve, and the release bearing housing is on the outside of the sleeve.

The release bearing itself is a ball bearing that is specially designed so that it can withstand both axial and radial loading. The push-type clutch release bearing shown in **FIGURE 35-25** is typical in that it is a sealed unit. That means that it cannot be lubricated periodically, but there may be a grease fitting to lubricate the release bearing housing where it slides on the input shaft sleeve. The **release fork (yoke)** is the lever that is actuated by the clutch linkage and moves the release bearing. The release fork engages a groove in the release bearing housing.

The release lever is mounted on a pivot in the clutch bell housing so that when the driver pushes the clutch pedal down the release bearing and housing move toward the clutch release levers or fingers. The release bearing in a push-type clutch does not actually rotate until in comes in contact with the release fingers or levers of the pressure plate. This is important to remember when diagnosing clutch noise complaints. Once the bearing is pushed against the fingers or levers with sufficient force, the pressure plate spring(s) is (are) caged, and the cutch is disengaged. Even though the push-type clutch release bearing is more expensive than a pilot bearing, the release bearing should always be replaced when a clutch is replaced. That is because, like the flywheel ball bearing, replacing the release bearing during a clutch replacement is less expensive than doing it separately because of failure later.

FIGURE 35-25 Push-type clutch release bearing.

Safety

The release bearing in a push-type clutch is designed only for periodic rotation when disengaging the clutch. If the driver rides the pedal or the clutch adjustment is incorrect, the bearing will be constantly rotating. That constant rotation will cause it to overheat and cause the permanent lubricating grease to liquefy and run out of the bearing, leading to premature bearing failure

In a pull-type clutch, the release bearing performs the same function as in a push-type clutch—to release the clutch—but the pull-type's design is quite different. The pull-type clutch release bearing is integral to the clutch. That means it is permanently attached to the clutch cover and in most cases is not serviced separately (see **FIGURE 35-26**). The release bearing again is a ball bearing designed to handle axial and radial thrust loads. The transmission input bearing cover used with a pull-type clutch does not have a sleeve as it does in the push-type clutch. Instead, the release bearing is encompassed in a

FIGURE 35-26 Pull-type clutch release bearing. **A.** Lubrication tube. **B.** Release bearing.

hollow housing. The outer race of the bearing is attached to the housing itself, and the inner race is attached to a sleeve. Inside the sleeve, there are two bronze bushings that allow the sleeve to ride on the transmission input shaft. This sleeve, in turn, attaches to what is commonly referred to as a retainer. It is the retainer that actually engages the release levers. Pull-type clutch release bearings usually require periodic lubrication. It is important to not overlook this service procedure.

The release fork in a pull-type clutch is "U" shaped and is attached to a cross shaft that is mounted inside the clutch bell housing. As shown in FIGURE 35-27, the "U" shape of the fork fits closely over the outside of the release bearing housing from the top, holding it stationary.

As noted earlier in this section, the inner race of the release bearing is attached to the sleeve and the retainer. The retainer is fixed to the release levers, so all three turn with the clutch. Consequently, the inner race of the release bearing is rotating any time the engine is running.

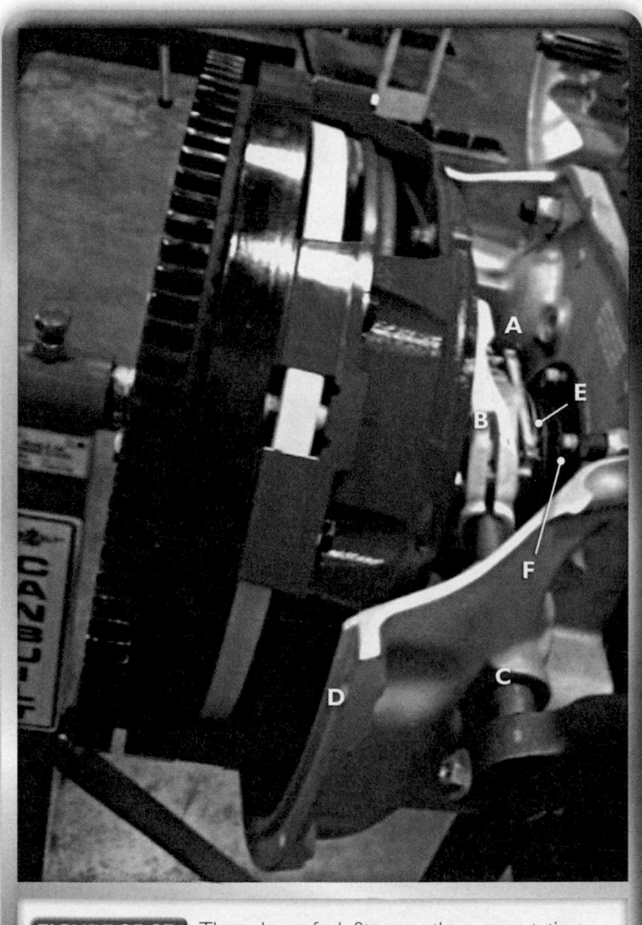

FIGURE 35-27 The release fork fits over the non-rotating release bearing housing in a pull-type clutch. **A.** Release bearing. **B.** Release fork. **C.** Cross shaft. **D.** Clutch housing. **E.** Clutch brake. **F.** Transmission front bearing cover.

To disengage the clutch, the driver actuates the clutch pedal. Actuating the pedal causes the cross shaft and the "U" shaped fork to rotate. The ends of the "U" contact wear pads located on the front of the release bearing housing and push the bearing to the rear. This action pulls the retainer and the release levers to the rear, which cages the pressure plate spring(s) disengaging the clutch. Most pull-type clutch release bearings need to be lubricated as part of regular maintenance procedures and are equipped with a grease fitting to allow this. There are, however, some permanently lubed designs as well. In some installations, a tube is attached to the release bearing and connected to a grease Zerk, or grease nipple, on the outside of the bell housing so that the bearing can be lubricated more easily. Figure 35-25 showed that release bearing with an attached tube.

Clutch Brakes

Pull-type clutches can be found in many sizes of trucks from class 5 all the way to class 8 but they are always used on class 7 and 8. These vehicles are almost exclusively equipped with twin or even triple countershaft non-synchronized transmissions. Unlike most car transmissions that have synchronizers to prevent gear clash (or grinding), these types of transmissions require the driver to match shaft and gears speeds or gear clashing will occur. The input shaft, the countershafts, and all of the main shaft gearing are rotating when these vehicles are idling in neutral with the clutch engaged. When the driver wants to select first gear or reverse, he first depresses the clutch pedal to disengage the engine. The inertia of the rotating components tends to keep them rotating, however, so if the driver were to try and engage a gear, the difference in speed between the rotating gear and the stationary main shaft would cause tremendous clashing. The rotating components have no load on them and little resistance to rotation, so they may continue to rotate for over a minute before a clash-free shift can be made.

Pull-type clutches facilitate the use of a clutch brake that can alleviate this problem. A **clutch brake** is a small frictional brake usually mounted on the transmission input shaft and designed to slow down or stop the transmission rotation when the driver wishes to engage first or reverse from a neutral position. The clutch brake is mounted on the input shaft between the release bearing and the transmission input bearing housing.

The input shaft has two splines that run its entire length, and the cutch brake has two matching teeth that fit into the splines. The rear of the release bearing housing has a smooth surface, as does the front of the transmission input bearing cover. The clutch brake has friction material on the front and back sides that will contact these smooth surfaces.

As the driver disengages the clutch, the release bearing moves backward towards the transmission. If the driver pushes the clutch pedal all the way to the floor, the clutch brake will be squeezed between the release bearing housing and the transmission input bearing cover so that the input shaft rotation will be stopped. This allows the driver to select first or reverse gear without gear clash. Stopping the input shaft with the brake saves the time needed to wait for the shafts and gears to stop spinning on their own.

A clutch brake may pose a problem for the inexperienced driver, however. The clutch brake is actuated within the last 1" (2.5 cm) of clutch pedal travel. If the driver pushes the clutch pedal to the floor when making upshifts as the vehicle is moving, the clutch brake will be destroyed very quickly. When engaged while the vehicle is moving and in gear, the clutch brake is attempting to stop the input shaft. When in gear, the input shaft is connected through the transmission gearing to the rear axle of the vehicle. The result is that, for the second before the driver actually shifts to neutral to make the shift, the clutch brake is trying to stop the entire vehicle. If the driver hits the clutch brake on upshifts and down shifts, the brake will usually fail within days.

There are three types of clutch brakes: conventional, torque-limiting, and limited torque. FIGURE 35-28 shows a variety of clutch brakes.

Conventional Clutch Brake

The conventional clutch brake is a solid piece of metal with friction material on either side. To install a conventional clutch brake, the transmission must be removed. In order to avoid the associated labor costs, aftermarket versions of this brake are made in a two-piece design that allows them to be replaced without removing the transmission. When installing a two-piece clutch brakes, the original clutch brake is carefully cut off of the input shaft using an oxyacetylene torch. The two pieces are then put into place and connected together.

Safety

Extreme caution must be taken to not damage the input shaft when using an oxyacetylene torch inside the clutch bell housing. An accumulation of grease, oil, and clutch dust can also result in a fire. Therefore, always clean the area first and be prepared with a fire extinguisher to douse any flames should fire erupt.

Torque-Limiting Clutch Brake

The torque-limiting clutch brake, like that shown in FIGURE 35-29, is the brake of choice of most manufacturers. The reason it is preferred is that it is designed to slip should the torque applied exceed its setting—typically 25ft-bl (34 Nm). The brake consists of an outer housing. Attached to the housing are the friction material and a separate inner hub that is splined to the input shaft. Two Belleville (diaphragm spring) type spring washers are placed inside the housing on either side of the inner hub to exert pressure against the hub. The brake is designed so that when approximately 25 ft-bl (34 Nm) of torque is twisting against the inner hub, the hub will slip inside the housing protecting the clutch brake. This design allows

FIGURE 35-28 Three two-piece clutch brakes and one torque-limiting clutch brake (bottom right).

FIGURE 35-29 Torque-limiting clutch brake.

a modicum of tolerance for an inexperienced driver who hits the clutch brake while upshifting. A key advantage of the torque-limiting clutch brake, therefore, is that it allows some latitude for driver error and will last longer than the conventional clutch brake if the driver actuates the brake while the vehicle is moving. If the driver uses the clutch brake repeatedly, however, even this design will fail. Driver training on the proper use of clutch brakes is essential.

Limiting Torque Clutch Brake

The limiting torque design of clutch brake is, for all intents and purposes, obsolete today; it was used for the same purposes as the brakes listed above and was also designed to assist in upshifts and so was also known as an upshift clutch brake. **FIGURE 35-30** shows the location of a typical clutch brake.

Limiting torque clutch brakes allowed a highly experienced double-clutching driver to quickly reduce engine speed in neutral during an upshift. At that point in the shift, the transmission main shaft is slowing faster than the engine and main shaft gearing because of heavy loading or steep grades. The limiting torque clutch allowed a fractional increase in shifting speed when used by a highly skilled driver.

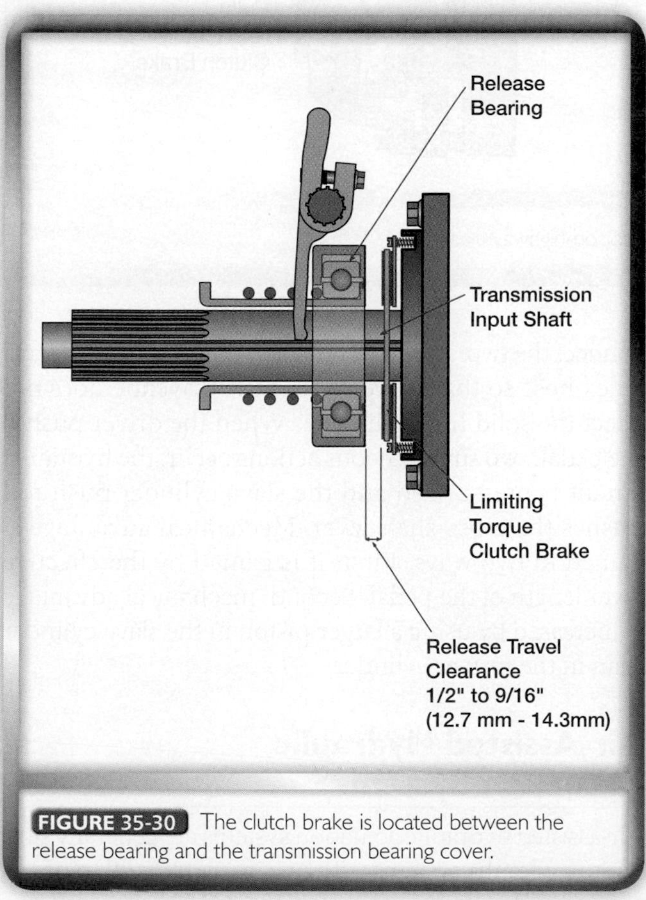

FIGURE 35-30 The clutch brake is located between the release bearing and the transmission bearing cover.

Eaton Corporation is using this faster upshifting strategy in some of its newer Ultra-Shift transmission models. Ultra-Shift transmissions use a computer controlled clutch system that also controls either an inertia brake or an actual clutch brake to manipulate engine and shaft speeds during upshifts. An **inertia brake** is a type of transmission shaft brake geared to one countershaft, which controls gearing rotational speed while shifting. Regardless of the brake type used, the result is a slight increase in shifting speed. Computer control allows perfect speed matching of gears and shafts and provides clash-free shifts—even with the most inexperienced driver.

Clutch Actuation Systems

Different clutches use different actuation systems. Most manual clutches in heavy-duty vehicles are actuated by mechanical linkage systems, but air, hydraulic, air-assisted hydraulic, automatic, centrifugal, electrical, and wet clutch actuation systems are also in use.

Mechanical Linkage

Most medium- to heavy-duty truck clutches are actuated by mechanical linkage systems. The actuation system starts with the clutch pedal. The pedal is usually a first or second class lever that helps the driver to overcome the tremendous clamp loads associated with modern clutches. Clamp loads can be more than 4,000 lb (1814 kg)! Without leverage, a driver would not be able to release the clutch. As illustrated in **FIGURE 35-31**, the clutch pedal attaches to a series of rods, bellcranks, and levers supported by the vehicle body and frame. Those components are, in turn, attached to the cross-shaft at the clutch bell housing. As expected, the release fork is actuated by the cross-shaft.

The levers in the linkage and in the clutch itself compound the force of the driver's foot on the pedal. That leverage allows a force of around 50 to 60 lb (22 to 27 kg) to cage the 3,200 lb or 4,000 lb (1451 kg or 1814 kg) clamping force. But, as we know when we use levers to compound force, we give up something in return. In this case, we sacrifice distance.

The driver may push the pedal through 10" or 11" (25–28 cm) or of travel, but the release bearing will only move 0.5" (1.3 cm) or so. The pressure plate inside the clutch cover will usually only move 0.15" to 0.20" (0.381–0.508 cm) and allow approximately 0.05" (0.127 cm) clearance on each side of each clutch disc in order for it to spin freely. With such a small amount of clearance

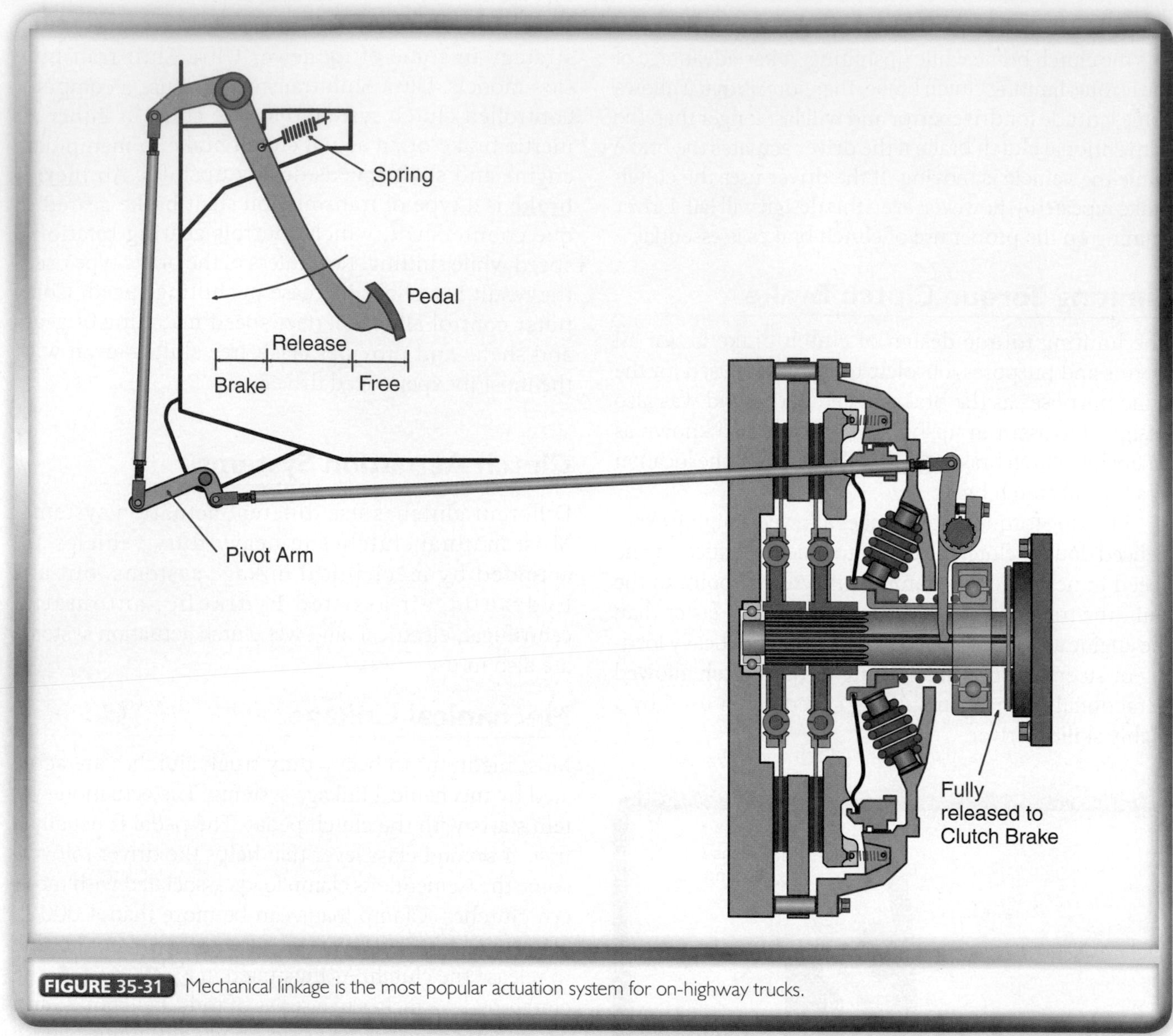

FIGURE 35-31 Mechanical linkage is the most popular actuation system for on-highway trucks.

for the discs, it is clear that any warping or damage to the discs could cause the discs to stay partially pressed against the flywheel or pressure plate when disengaged—which could cause clashing shifts. In some cases, the rods, levers, and bellcranks of a mechanical linkage system can be replaced by a cable, as illustrated in FIGURE 35-32. Cable linkage allows more flexibility in component location and the connection of components, but cable linkage systems are not as popular as mechanical linkage in heavy-duty vehicles.

Hydraulic Actuation Systems

Hydraulically actuated clutches, such as the one as illustrated in FIGURE 35-33, consist of a clutch master cylinder and push rod that will be connected to the clutch pedal. A clutch **slave cylinder** will be mounted at the transmission to actuate the cross-shaft and a hydraulic circuit will connect the two. At least a portion of this circuit will have a flex hose so that movement of the driveline does not affect the solid hydraulic line. When the driver pushes the pedal, two simultaneous actions occur: the hydraulic circuit is pressurized and the slave cylinder push rod pushes the cross-shaft lever. Mechanical advantage is gained in two ways. First, it is gained by the effective lever length of the pedal. Second, mechanical advantage is increased by using a larger piston in the slave cylinder than in the master cylinder.

Air-Assisted Hydraulic Actuation Systems

Air-assisted hydraulic actuation systems are generally similar to hydraulic systems with one important difference—instead of the master cylinder pressure acting directly on

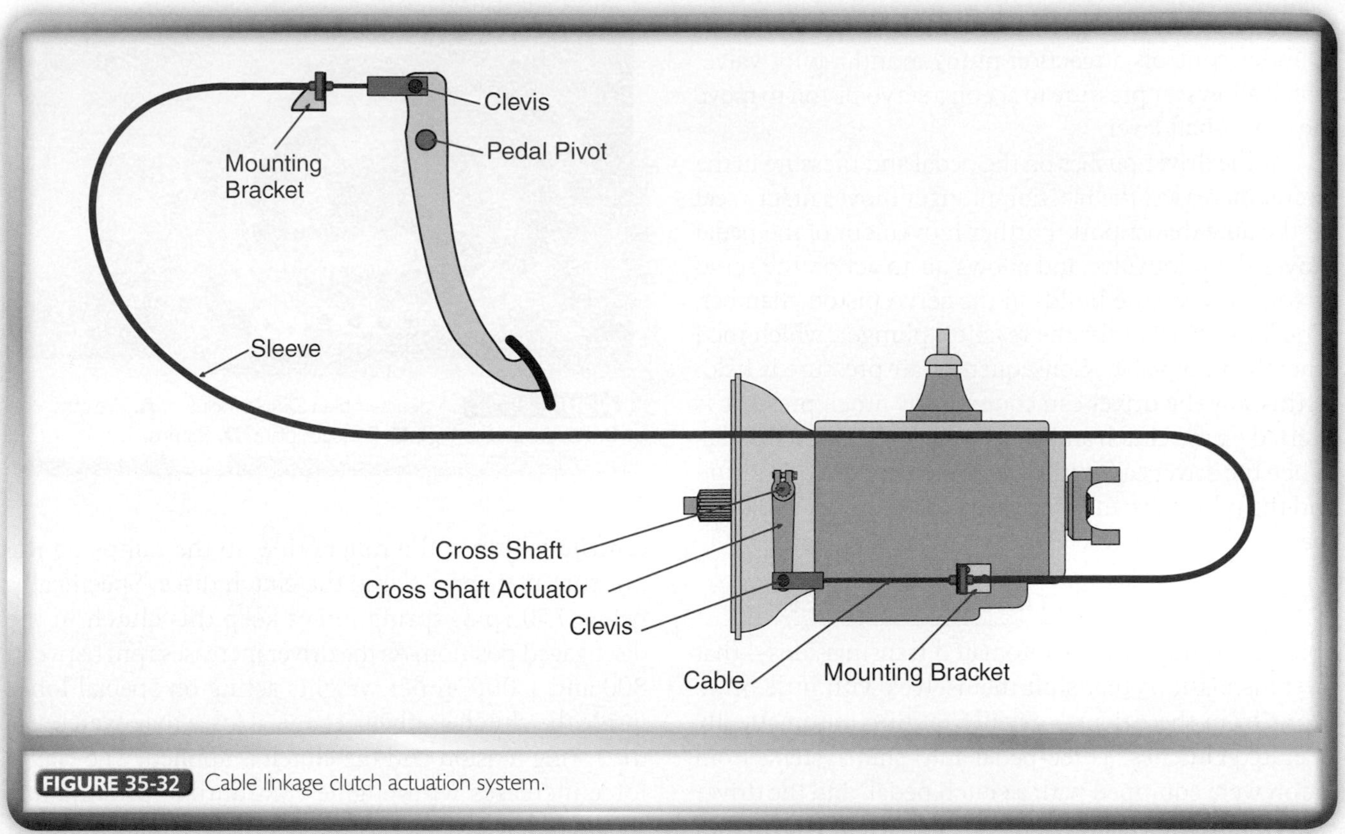

FIGURE 35-32 Cable linkage clutch actuation system.

Master Cylinder

Slave Cylinder

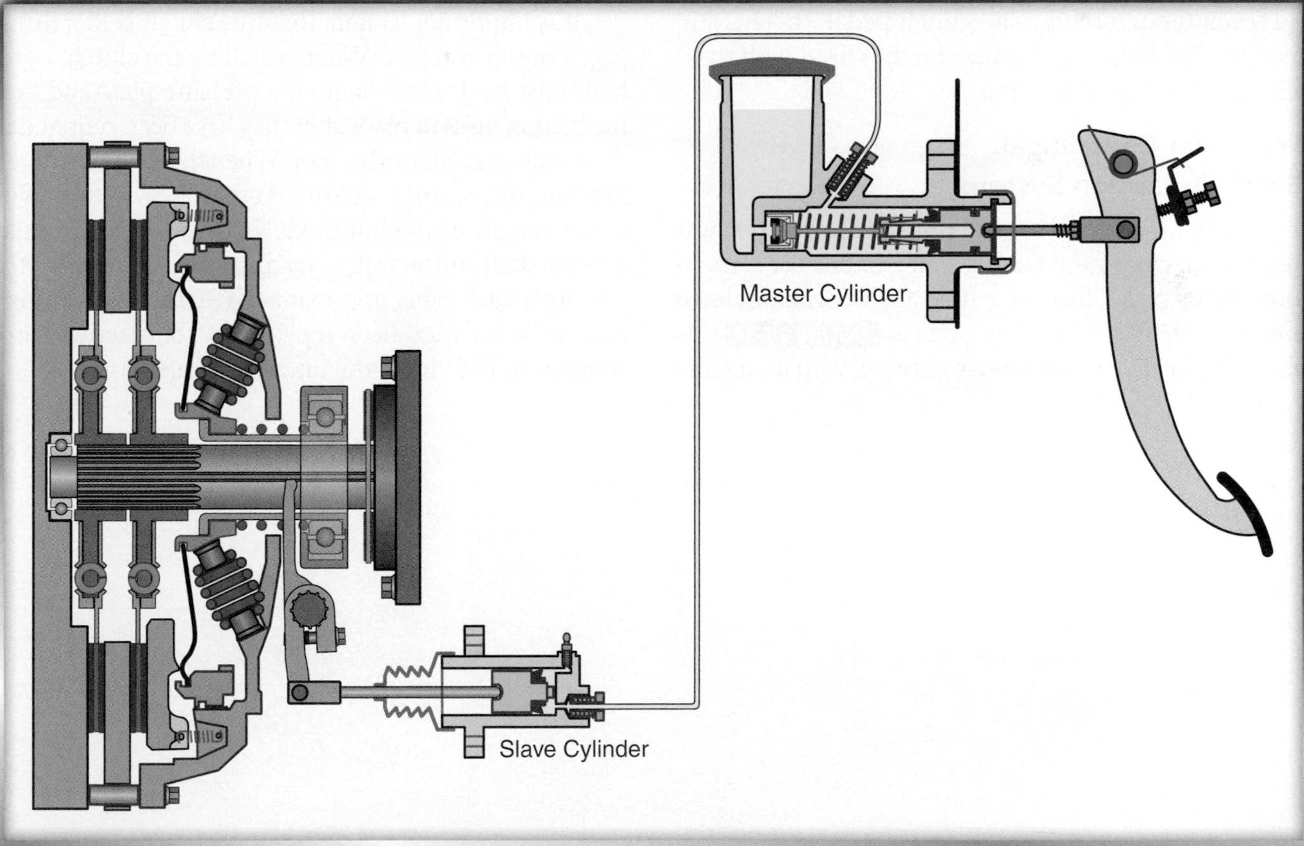

FIGURE 35-33 Hydraulic clutch actuation systems are becoming more popular today.

the slave cylinder and the cross-shaft lever, the master cylinder controls a reaction plunger and a pilot valve, which allows air pressure to act on a servo piston to move the cross-shaft lever.

As the driver pushes on the pedal and pressure in the circuit increases, the reaction plunger moves first to seal off the air exhaust port. Further movement of the pedal moves the pilot valve and allows air to act on the servo piston. As pressure builds in the servo piston chamber, it pushes back against the reaction plunger, which then seats the pilot valve. Consequently, air pressure is held. In this way the driver can control how much pressure is exerted on the clutch and gains a feel for the clutch pedal. When the driver eases up on the pedal, the reaction piston and the pilot valve move to seal off the air inlet and open the exhaust port allowing the clutch to engage.

Automatically Actuated Clutches

Vehicles equipped with automated transmissions—that is, transmissions that shift themselves with little or no input from the driver—usually require automatically operated clutches. Three-pedal auto-shift systems from Eaton were equipped with a clutch pedal, and the driver was required to use the clutch only when starting off in first or reverse. Newer systems are fully automated, and, even though there is no clutch pedal, there is still a clutch. The following are the clutches used with these fully automated transmissions.

Two-Pedal Centrifugal Clutch Actuation System

The Eaton two-pedal ultra-shift transmission system was the first system on the market that did not use a traditional clutch pedal. Instead, it used a self-engaging clutch called the DM Autoclutch (pictured in **FIGURE 35-34**). As the spring-loaded weights move outward with increasing centrifugal force, the rollers ride up the ramps on the pressure plate and clamp the clutch discs. Specifically, below 750 rpm, spring forces keep this clutch in the disengaged position. As the driver increases rpm between 800 and 1,000, roller weights acting on special lobes inside the clutch apply mechanical force that overcomes the spring tension and the clutch is applied. The clamp force increases with engine rpm until approximately 1,200 rpm, at which point the peak clamp force of around 4,000 lb (1814 kg) is achieved.

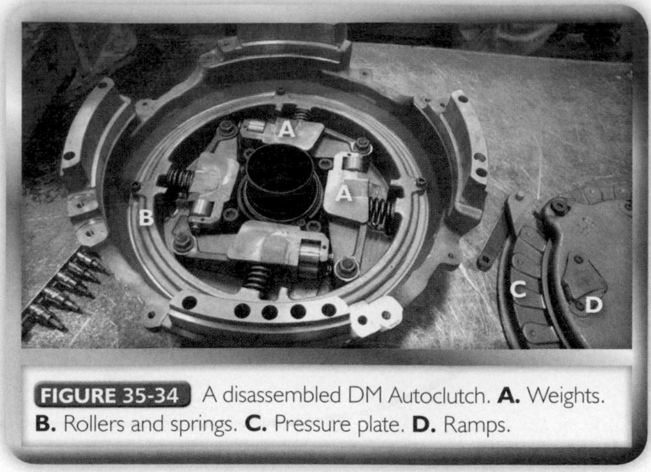

FIGURE 35-34 A disassembled DM Autoclutch. **A.** Weights. **B.** Rollers and springs. **C.** Pressure plate. **D.** Ramps.

It is important to note that this clutch is in a disengaged position at rest. When installing the clutch, a jack bolt must be used to clamp the pressure plate and hold the friction discs in place after they have been centered by the clutch disc alignment tool. When these clutches were first introduced, they were used on the heavy-duty, twin-countershaft, ultra-shift models. Medium-duty, single-countershaft, ultra-shift transmissions used an electric clutch actuator. Since approximately 2012, the centrifugal actuated clutch has been replaced by the electric clutch actuator models in all the ultra-shift transmissions.

Electrically Actuated Clutches

Eaton Corporation now uses an electric clutch actuator (ECA), as shown in FIGURE 35-35 on all medium- and heavy-duty UltraShift transmission models. The ECA uses an electric motor driving three interconnected planetary gears to release the clutch and to actuate the new heavy-duty inertia brake on the input shaft. This computer-controlled actuator is used to move the release bearing to a released position and engage the clutch. The computer-controlled actuator also applies an input shaft-mounted inertia brake (similar to a clutch brake) when needed. This allows the computer to control engine speed precisely by manipulating the inertia brake on upshifts while in neutral, leading to incrementally faster upshifts. Eaton claims that by using this procedure, its UltraShift transmission can shift through 18 speeds on a 15% grade while pulling 160,000 lb (72,574 kg)—a feat that very few professional drivers could accomplish. Many manufacturers are experimenting with automatic clutches. The latest versions of these auto-clutches feature different designs—air actuated, electrically actuated, or computer-controlled hydraulic actuation.

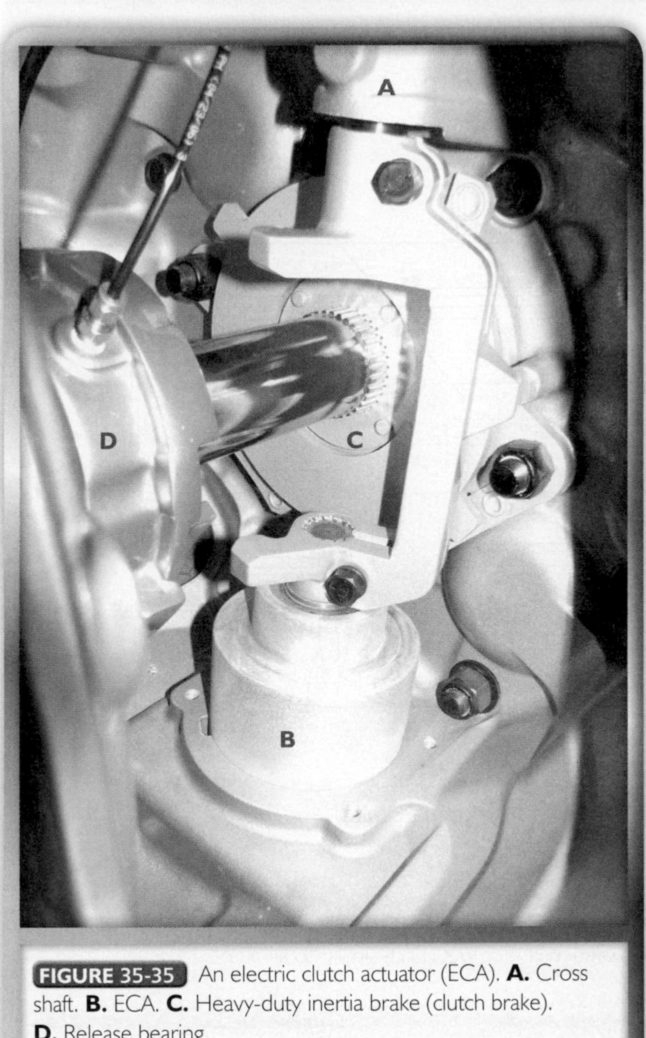

FIGURE 35-35 An electric clutch actuator (ECA). **A.** Cross shaft. **B.** ECA. **C.** Heavy-duty inertia brake (clutch brake). **D.** Release bearing.

Wet Clutches

Eaton's transmission model FO-8406-ASW uses a computer-actuated wet clutch. Wet clutches have been used in the past by Mack and many European manufacturers. Those wet clutches were typically multi-disc clutches actuated by a clutch fork in the same way as today's dry clutches. In wet clutches, however, an air-actuated reservoir would introduce cooling fluid to cool and lubricate the clutch during engagement and disengagement. As shown in FIGURE 35-36, the Eaton wet clutch is a much more sophisticated device. It consists of a hydraulically actuated wet clutch pack more similar to the type used in automatic transmissions.

The FO-8406-ASW has a hydraulic pump to supply actuating pressure and engagement and disengagement are controlled by the transmission computer. This type of wet clutch allows more control of torque transfer at vehicle take off. These types of electronically controlled auto-clutches can even be programmed with what is known as "urge to move," which makes their operation in a vehicle equipped with a manual transmission almost indistinguishable from vehicles equipped with traditional automatic transmissions.

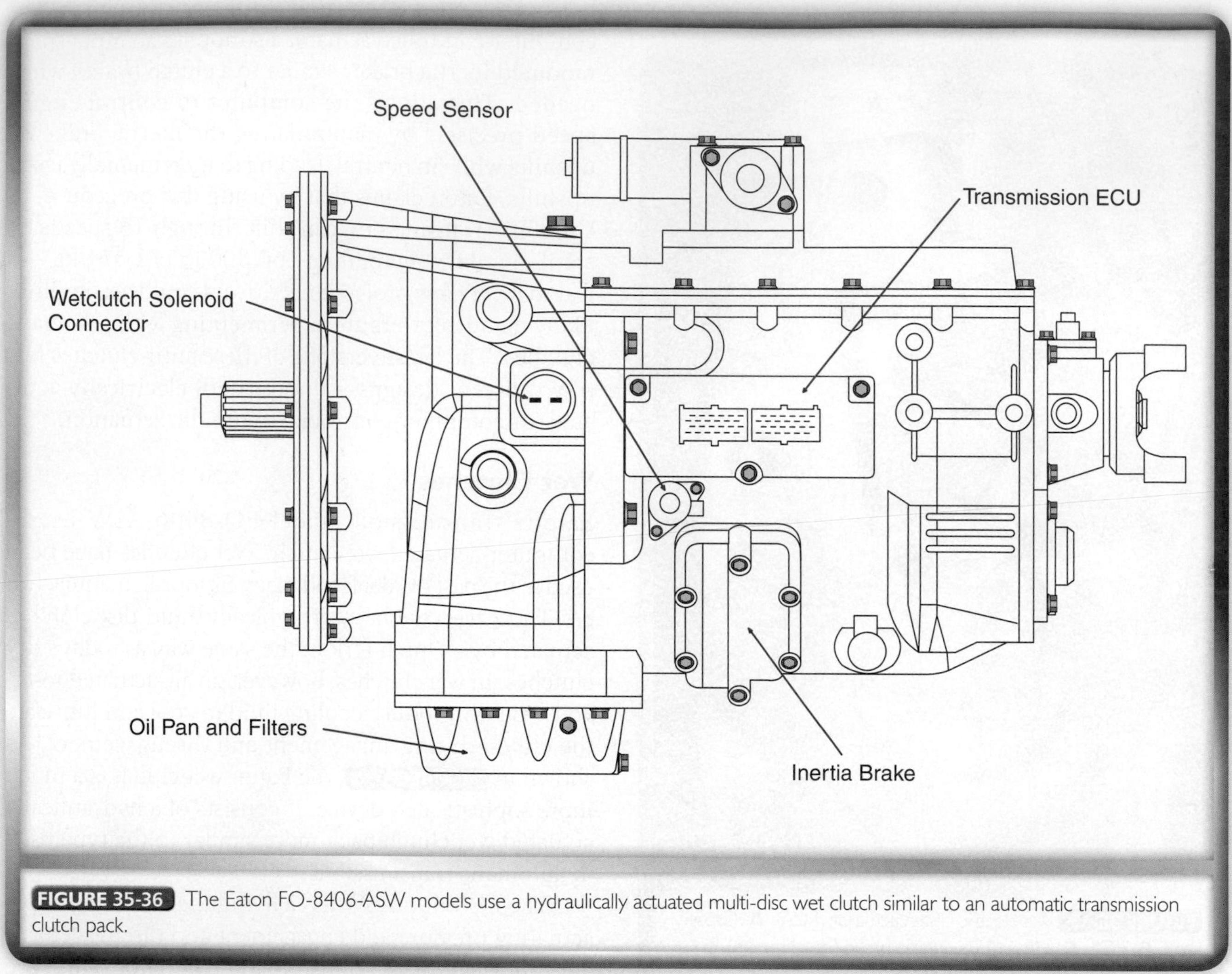

FIGURE 35-36 The Eaton FO-8406-ASW models use a hydraulically actuated multi-disc wet clutch similar to an automatic transmission clutch pack.

Wrap-up

Ready for Review

- A friction clutch has two basic functions. The first function is to transmit torque from the engine to the driveline the second is to allow the engine and the driveline to be disconnected when required.
- Clutches operate by utilizing friction, which is the resistance of motion between two bodies in contact to transmit torque.
- Clutches must handle increasingly powerful torsional vibrations that tend to twist driveline components every time an engine cylinder fires.
- Clutch capacity, or the amount of torque a clutch can handle without slipping, is affected by the coefficient of friction of the material used, the surface area in contact, and the clamp load.
- Clutches can be push-type or pull-type. This refers to the direction a clutch release bearing moves while the clutch is being disengaged.
- Coil springs can be used to supply clamping load for the clutch. As the clutch discs wear, they lose their clamping force.
- Diaphragm spring clutches are a better choice in most applications, as their clamp load is not diminished as the disc wears.
- The easy-pedal angle-spring pull-type clutch from Eaton is arguably the most popular clutch used in North American heavy-duty applications its design prevents a reduction in clamp load as long the clutch is correctly adjusted.
- Pull-type clutches allow the use of clutch brakes. Clutch brakes are splined to the input shaft of a non-synchronized transmission.
- For years, clutch friction facings were made with asbestos, which is a known carcinogen. Today, clutches manufactured in North America contain no asbestos. The long-term effects of exposure to clutch dust from modern facing materials is unknown. Technicians should always wear NIOSH-approved respirators when working in any dust-laden environment.
- Some clutches today are self-adjusting and require little or no maintenance. The Eaton Solo is one example.
- Two general types of friction materials are used today: organic and ceramic. Ceramic facings have higher coefficients of friction than organic but provide a more abrupt engagement.
- Today's manufacturers of clutches have developed clutch systems that are very good at smoothing out driveline vibrations caused by engine torsionionals, both under load and at idle.
- Engine flywheels have several important functions. They offer a friction surface for the clutch, provide inertia, and smooth out power pulsations from the engine.
- Flywheels come in two predominate designs: a flat-style flywheel and a pot-style flywheel.
- Dual disc clutches use an intermediate plate that provides a friction surface for the rear of the front friction disc and the front of the rear disc.
- Pilot bearings support the front end of the transmission input shaft and should be replaced whenever the clutch is replaced.
- The release fork (release yoke) is the lever that actually moves the release bearing to disengage the clutch.
- The release bearings in push-type clutches slide on a sleeve that surrounds the input shaft and only rotate when the clutch is being disengaged. The release bearings in a pull-type clutch are integral, and the inner bearing rotates whenever the engine is rotating.
- Most on-highway trucks contain clutches that can be actuated by mechanical linkage. Clutches can also be actuated by cable or hydraulics.
- Automated transmissions still use clutches, but in some cases they are automatically actuated by centrifugal force, air, electric, or hydraulic actuators. Automatically operated clutches will have no clutch pedal.

Vocabulary Builder

angle spring clutch A clutch manufactured by Eaton/Spicer corporation that uses three pairs of angled springs pushing against a lever to supply the clamp load.

ceramic friction facings Friction facings made mostly of man-made materials specifically designed to produce desirable characteristics.

clamp force The force squeezing the clutch disc between the pressure plate and the flywheel. Also called *load*.

clutch brake A small frictional brake usually mounted on the transmission input shaft; designed to slow down or stop the inertia of the transmission gearing so shifts into first or reverse can be made without clashing.

clutch capacity The amount of torque the clutch can safely handle without slipping.

clutch cover The outside part of the clutch that is bolted to the flywheel and which holds all of the clutch components except the clutch disc. Mistakenly but commonly called the pressure plate.

coil spring style clutch A clutch that uses coils springs mounted perpendicular to the pressure plate to provide the clamp load.

coefficient of friction (CoF) The amount of force required to move an object while in contact with another.

dampening disc A disc with a ring of torsional dampening springs around its hub designed to absorb engine torsional vibrations.

diaphragm spring clutch A clutch that uses a single diaphragm spring, also known as a Belleville spring, to provide the clamping force.

drive pin Pin used in a pot-type flywheel to drive the intermediate plate.

dual mass flywheel A flywheel with two sections separated by torsional springs; one section attaches to the engine crankshaft and the clutch cover is bolted to the other section.

flat-type flywheel A flywheel that is predominately flat, with all of its components inside the cover; the clutch cover bolts to it.

friction The relative resistance to motion between any two bodies in contact with one another.

friction dampening Controlling torsional vibration by using friction material in between the various plates in a clutch friction disc.

flywheel A heavy round metal disc attached to the end of the crankshaft to smooth out vibrations from the crankshaft assembly and provide one of the friction surfaces for a clutch disc used on manual transmission/transaxle applications.

Hooke's law A law of physics that states that force delivered by a spring to an object is directly related to its compression or extension; the greater the spring is compressed, the more force the spring delivers.

inertia brake A type of transmission shaft brake geared to one countershaft, which controls gearing rotational speed while shifting.

input shaft The component to which the clutch discs are splined.

intermediate plate A plate driven by the flywheel or the clutch cover and providing a friction surface for the back of the front friction disc and the front of the rear friction disc in a dual disc clutch assembly.

kinetic friction The friction between two surfaces that are sliding against each other

load The force squeezing the clutch disc/s between the pressure plate and the flywheel. Also called *clamping force*.

organic facings Friction facings made of various natural materials such as cotton fibers, rubber, aluminum, glass, copper or brass fibers, and carbon material.

pilot bearing A bearing that supports the front of the transmission input shaft; mounted in the flywheel or the rear of the crankshaft.

pot-type flywheel A flywheel shaped like a deep pot inside which all of the components of the clutch are housed with the exception of the clutch cover.

pre-dampening A series of small torsional dampening springs designed to prevent gear rattle at idle.

pressure plate The friction surface of the clutch cover; the plate that squeezes the clutch disc against the flywheel.

pull-type clutch A clutch with an integral release bearing, which is pulled towards the transmission to disengage the clutch.

push-type clutch A clutch in which the release bearing is pushed towards the engine to release the clutch.

release bearing A hollow bearing through which the input shaft passes, which allows for the push or pull against rotating clutch release levers to release the clutch.

release fork (yoke) The actuator that moves the release bearing.

resonance The frequency at which the driveline's vibrations are the most damaging.

resonant frequency The frequency at which the driveline enters into a resonant condition where all the components start to oscillate in unison.

self-adjusting clutches Clutches with an automatically adjusting system that relies on pressure plate movement to cause an adjustment.

slave cylinder The hydraulic cylinder used to release the clutch in hydraulically actuated clutch systems.

soft-dampened clutch A clutch with extra-long travel windows for its dampening springs; used to combat resonance in a driveline.

torsional vibrations Powerful vibrations caused by the firing force twisting and accelerating the crankshaft every time a cylinder fires.

Review Questions

1. Which of the following clutch types has an integral or attached release bearing?
   a. Push-type clutch
   b. Diaphragm type clutch
   c. Lever type clutch
   d. Pull-type clutch
2. What are the components found inside a clutch that allow us to release it with less pedal effort and also amplify clutch application pressure when it is engaged?
   a. Pressure plates
   b. Torsional springs
   c. Levers
   d. Pivot rings
3. The function of coaxial or cushion springs in a clutch disc hub is to do which of the following?
   a. Increase clutch clamp load
   b. Make the disc stronger
   c. Absorb torsional vibrations
   d. All of the above choices are correct.
4. The function of most types of clutch brakes is to do which of the following?
   a. Slow down or stop the input shaft while shifting to first gear or reverse
   b. Allow for easier up-shifting
   c. Absorb engine torque
   d. All of the above choices are correct.
5. What is the primary reason pull-type clutches are used in heavy-duty applications?
   a. Pull-type clutches will last longer.
   b. Pull-type clutches are less expensive to manufacture.
   c. Pull-type clutches require less pedal effort than push-type.
   d. Pull-type clutches allow the use of a clutch brake.
6. Which of the following affects the capacity of the clutch to handle engine power without slipping?
   a. The co-efficient of friction of the clutch disc material
   b. The surface area of the friction discs
   c. The number of friction discs
   d. All of the above affect the capacity of the clutch.
7. Why do some manufacturers use organic clutch linings even though ceramic lining offer a higher coefficient of friction?
   a. Organic linings last longer.
   b. Organic linings run cooler.
   c. Organic linings provide smoother engagement.
   d. Organic linings are better at absorbing torsional vibrations.
8. Which of the following is a correct statement about dual disc clutches?
   a. They offer smoother engagement
   b. They double clutch capacity
   c. They decrease flywheel wear
   d. None of the above is a correct statement
9. Which of the following clutch types provide constant pressure plate load regardless of clutch disc wear as long as adjustment is correct?
   a. Coil spring type clutch
   b. Angle spring clutch
   c. They decrease flywheel wear
   d. None of the above is a correct statement.
10. A new clutch disk has very small springs mounted in a circle around the clutch disk hub; these springs commonly referred to as ________ springs.
    a. torsional dampening
    b. anti-breakage
    c. engagement cushioning
    d. pre-dampening

ASE-Type Questions

1. Technician A says that a pilot bearing should always be replaced when a clutch is replaced. Technician B says that soft-dampened clutches are better at absorbing torsional vibrations. Who is correct?
   a. Technician A
   b. Technician B
   c. Both Technician A and Technician B
   d. Neither Technician A nor Technician B

2. Technician A says that since North American clutch manufacturers no longer use asbestos there is no need to be concerned by clutch dust. Technician B says that compressed air is the best way to clean the clutch housing when performing a clutch replacement. Who is correct?
   a. Technician A
   b. Technician B
   c. Both Technician A and Technician B
   d. Neither Technician A nor Technician B

3. Technician A says that coil spring clutches are the best because the heavy coil springs provide exceptional clamp load. Technician B says that diaphragm spring style clutches are a better choice because they do not lose clamp load. Who is correct?
   a. Technician A
   b. Technician B
   c. Both Technician A and Technician B
   d. Neither Technician A nor Technician B

4. Technician A says that the release bearing in pull-type clutches only rotates when disengaging the clutch. Technician B says that the release bearing in pull-type clutches is replaced whenever the clutch is replaced. Who is correct?
   a. Technician A
   b. Technician B
   c. Both Technician A and Technician B
   d. Neither Technician A nor Technician B

5. Technician A says that using dual discs in a clutch doubles the clutch capacity. Technician B says that increasing clamp load can increase clutch capacity. Who is correct?
   a. Technician A
   b. Technician B
   c. Both Technician A and Technician B
   d. Neither Technician A nor Technician B

6. Technician A says that most heavy duty truck clutches will use organic linings. Technician B says that the most common clutch type used in heavy trucks is the angle spring clutch. Who is correct?
   a. Technician A
   b. Technician B
   c. Both Technician A and Technician B
   d. Neither Technician A nor Technician B

7. Technician A says that clutch brakes help the driver up shift. Technician B says that clutch brakes can be replaced without removing the transmission. Who is correct?
   a. Technician A
   b. Technician B
   c. Both Technician A and Technician B
   d. Neither Technician A nor Technician B

8. Technician A says that a diaphragm spring clutch is a better choice than a coil spring style clutch because it doesn't lose clamp load as the disc wears. Technician B says that diaphragm spring clutches are only found in light-duty vehicles. Who is correct?
   a. Technician A
   b. Technician B
   c. Both Technician A and Technician B
   d. Neither Technician A nor Technician B

9. Technician A says that the clutch should be adjusted when the pedal free play is reduced by half. Technician B says that some clutches with hydraulic actuation systems do not require adjustment. Who is correct?
   a. Technician A
   b. Technician B
   c. Both Technician A and Technician B
   d. Neither Technician A nor Technician B

10. Technician A says that clutch wear is non-existent when the clutch is engaged. Technician B says that clutch wear will be increased on a clutch with mechanical linkage if there is no pedal free play in the cab. Who is correct?
    a. Technician A
    b. Technician B
    c. Both Technician A and Technician B
    d. Neither Technician A nor Technician B

CHAPTER 36

NATEF Tasks

Drive Train
Clutch

Task	Page
Inspect and adjust clutch linkage, cables, levers, brackets, bushings, pivots, springs, and clutch safety switch (includes push- and pull-type assemblies); check pedal height and travel; perform needed action.	1168, 1172, 1174, 1175, 1187
Inspect, adjust, lubricate, or replace release (throw-out) bearing, sleeve, bushings, springs, housing, levers, release fork, fork pads, rollers, shafts, and seals.	1170–1175
Inspect, adjust, and replace self-adjusting/continuous-adjusting clutch mechanisms.	1172, 1182
Identify causes of clutch noise, binding, slippage, pulsation, vibration, grabbing, dragging, and chatter problems; determine needed action.	1173
Inspect, adjust, repair, and replace hydraulic clutch slave and master cylinders, lines, and hoses; bleed system.	1174–1177
Inspect and/or replace clutch brake assembly; inspect input shaft and bearing retainer; perform needed action.	1178–1181
Inspect and replace pilot bearing.	1179–1183
Inspect flywheel housing(s) to transmission housing/engine mating surface(s) and measure flywheel housing face and bore runout; determine needed action.	1180–1181
Remove and reinstall flywheel and inspect mounting area on crankshaft, rear main oil seal, and measure crankshaft end play; determine needed action.	1180–1181
Inspect flywheel, starter ring gear and measure flywheel face and pilot bore runout; determine needed action.	1180–1181
Inspect, adjust, and replace single-disc clutch pressure plate and clutch disc.	1182
Inspect, adjust, and replace two-plate clutch pressure plate, clutch discs, intermediate plate, and drive pins/lugs.	1183

Servicing Heavy-Duty Clutches

Knowledge Objectives

After reading this chapter, you will be able to:

1. Describe and explain clutch system service and repair procedures. (pp 1168–1172)
2. Describe and explain the necessity of clutch maintenance operations. (p 1168)
3. Identify and explain clutch system failure causes. (p 1169)
4. Explain the procedure for removing and replacing single and multi-disc clutch assemblies. (p 1176)

Skills Objectives

After reading this chapter, you will be able to:

1. Adjust a pull-type clutch. (p 1169)
2. Replace intermediate plate drive pins on a pot-style flywheel. (p 1182)
3. Install a push-type clutch. (p 1182)
4. Install various sizes of dual disc pull-type clutch. (p 1183)
5. Install a self-adjusting clutch. (p 1186)
6. Reinstall a transmission. (p 1186)
7. Check and adjust a push-type clutch. (p 1174) SKILL DRILL 36-1
8. Check and adjust a hydraulic clutch. (p 1175) SKILL DRILL 36-2
9. Bleed and flush a hydraulic clutch system using the gravity method. (p 1176) SKILL DRILL 36-3
10. Bleed and flush a hydraulic clutch system using the manual method. (p 1177) SKILL DRILL 36-4
11. Bleed and flush a hydraulic clutch system using the pressure method. (p 1177) SKILL DRILL 36-5
12. Remove a manual transmission and clutch. (pp 1178–1179) SKILL DRILL 36-6
13. Perform required dial indicator checks during clutch replacement. (p 1180) SKILL DRILL 36-7
14. Adjust a pull-type clutch. (p 1187) SKILL DRILL 36-8

Introduction

Clutch servicing is a job that almost all heavy-duty truck technicians will have to perform during their careers. Servicing a clutch will fall into one of two basic categories. The first category is maintenance procedures, such as clutch adjustments, release bearing lubrication and inspection, and lubrication of the clutch actuation components. The clutch components include the **clutch linkage** (the connection between the drivers clutch pedal and the clutch cross shaft), the **cross-shaft** itself (the cross-shaft supports the release fork), and the release fork. The second category of service involves clutch replacement.

Safety

As mentioned in the Heavy-Duty Clutches chapter, clutch friction material contains dust and fibers that can be very harmful and even carcinogenic! Extreme care must be taken when working with clutches to protect the technician and his colleagues in the work shop Do not use compressed air to blow dust away. Always use a vacuum equipped with a HEPA filter to collect the dust. When working around clutch dust, always wear a National Institute for Occupational Safety and Health (NIOSH) approved respirator with high efficiency HEPA filters. Common sense is the key here—you do not want yourself or anyone else breathing or ingesting the dust associated with clutches.

Timely clutch adjustments and maintenance can go a long way to preventing premature clutch replacement. Technicians should be aware of signs that indicate a clutch is not being used properly due to driver error or driver abuse. Some signs to watch for include excessive dust buildup from friction material, worn clutch brakes on pull-type clutches, and any sign of overheating or burning of clutch components. If any of these indicators are present, further investigation is required to determine whether the driver or the equipment is at fault.

Preventative Maintenance of Clutches

Clutch inspection and maintenance should be performed according to the manufacturer's maintenance schedule. This schedule will vary depending on the vehicle **vocation**, (or the specific function the vehicle is designed to perform), but is usually every 8,000 to 10,000 miles (12,000 to 16,000 km).

Clutch preventative maintenance involves three basic elements.

1. **Clutch inspection.** Inspection of the clutch and its actuating system can allow a technician to prevent costly downtime by preventing potential problems. The clutch itself should be visually inspected for excess wear if possible, (on 14" (36.6 cm) pot-style flywheels the clutch discs cannot be seen), and replaced as necessary. All linkages should be inspected for wear and repaired as necessary.

You Are the Technician

A class 8 tractor is brought to your shop for a clutch adjustment. The driver says there is something wrong with the clutch, but he is not sure what it is. He says, "It just doesn't 'feel' right." He says the clutch brake does not seem to be working anymore, and he has to wait a long time before shifting into first or reverse to avoid gear clash. From your experience, the free play in the cab seems normal for this vehicle. Pedal and linkage movement seem fine. When you inspect the clutch, you see that release bearing free travel is approximately 0.75" (187 mm). Fork to release bearing clearance is correct at 0.125" (3.2 mm), and the clutch brake is still like new.

1. What can you conclude from your investigation?
2. Do you think you can solve the driver's problem?
3. What procedure would you undertake to repair the situation?
4. Do you think this vehicle requires a clutch replacement?

2. **Lubrication.** During a vehicle service, all moving components of the clutch actuation system should be lubricated, as should the release bearing, clutch release fork, and cross-shaft. Note that some systems will have **sealed release bearings**. Sealed release bearing are those that do not require periodic lubrication but still require inspection.
3. **Clutch adjustment.** Timely adjustment of the clutch is essential to its longevity. The clutch should be adjusted as necessary when the vehicle is in the shop for maintenance.

The following sections discuss the adjustment procedures for various types of medium- and heavy-duty clutches.

Clutch Adjustment Procedures

Many factors can affect the useful life of a clutch. Vehicle loading, driver skill, and highway or city operation are all important factors, but one of the most important is correct and timely clutch adjustment.

Push-Type Clutch Adjustment

A properly adjusted push-type clutch will usually have a certain amount of **free play**, or clearance, between the clutch release levers, or the diaphragm spring fingers, and the release bearing. (Some newer hydraulically actuated clutches run with no free play.)

As the clutch friction disc(s) wear, the pressure plate must move toward the flywheel to compensate. Therefore, the outer edge of the release levers or diaphragm spring fingers must move also to follow the pressure plate. This causes the inner edge of the release levers to move toward the transmission and the release bearing. Eventually, their travel will be stopped by the release bearing. Any further wear after this point will cause clutch clamp load to be lessened, leading to clutch slippage and early clutch failure.

In a push-type clutch, this adjustment is accomplished by adjusting the cable or mechanical linkage in such a way as to gain approximately 0.125" (3.175 mm) clearance between the release bearing and the release levers or fingers.

This adjustment typically leads to approximately one to two inches (2.5 to 5.1 cm) of free travel at the clutch pedal. Clutch adjustment should be performed as often as necessary when the pedal free travel is reduced by half because of disc wear, to re-establish normal clearance at the release bearing and free pedal in the cab. Push-type clutches with hydraulic actuation systems may have an adjustable slave cylinder pushrod to re-establish the 0.125" (3.175 mm) clearance. However, some hydraulic systems may operate with no clearance at all. In that case, there will be light contact between the bearing and the release levers. Always check manufacturer's specifications to be sure of the correct adjustment setting.

> **TECHNICIAN TIP**
>
> Note that the 0.125" (3.175 mm) clearance specification may vary by original equipment manufacturer (OEM). Be sure to consult the manufacturer's documentation for the clutch you are working on.

Pull-Type Clutch Adjustment

A properly adjusted pull-type clutch has a certain clearance between the tips of the release fork and the wear pads on the release bearing. In a pull-type clutch, as the disc(s) wear, the pressure plate also moves toward the flywheel to compensate. However, because the release levers or diaphragm spring pivot points are on their outer edge, the inner edge of the levers or fingers and the integral release bearing move toward the flywheel. The clutch release fork is in front of the release bearing. Eventually, therefore, it will stop the release bearing travel. Any further wear will cause decreased clamp load, which can lead to slippage and early clutch failure. Clutch adjustment reestablishes the correct free play of the release bearing and ensures the plate load is not affected by disc wear.

Pull-type clutch adjustment is significantly different than the push-type adjustment and must accomplish three things:

1. **Clutch brake actuation**, or **squeeze**, (if equipped). Clutch brake actuation is affected by total pedal travel and is adjusted by adjusting the clutch linkage. Doing this check first let the technician know if the linkage has been adjusted incorrectly. If the linkage has been adjusted to compensate for wear, the clutch brake squeeze dimension will be very low or the bearing may not touch the clutch brake at all. Using the linkage to adjust for clutch wear is a common mistake in the field.
2. **Release bearing free travel**. Sometimes called simply Release Travel. This ensures that the release bearing moves far enough to completely disengage the clutch.
3. Free play between the release fork and the release bearing. This establishes pedal-free travel in the cab and ensures that the clamp load is not affected by disc wear.

Linkage Adjustment

Linkage adjustment, or clutch brake squeeze, should be checked first because linkage adjustment will affect the other two adjustments. Linkage adjustment should rarely be required during service so long as the linkage was properly set at the factory.

The need for linkage adjustment is normally caused by wear in the linkage system. Once the worn components are replaced, adjustment is unnecessary. Linkage adjustment controls the total movement of the release fork and, therefore, when the fork will push the release bearing against the clutch brake. This should occur in the last half to one inch (12.7 to 25.4 mm) of pedal travel.

To check the clutch brake squeeze, insert a 0.010" (2.54 mm) feeler gauge between the clutch brake and the release bearing and have a colleague push the clutch pedal to the floor. While clamping the feeler gauge between the brake and the bearing, note the clutch pedal position with a tape measure. Now have the colleague raise the pedal slowly and stop when the feeler gauge can be removed. Measure the height of the clutch pedal at this point. It should be one half to one inch (12.7 to 25.4 mm) higher than the end of pedal travel noted previously. If that is not the case, the clutch linkage must be adjusted to gain proper brake squeeze. Lengthening the linkage will lower the squeeze point, and shortening the linkage will raise the squeeze point.

Safety

Clutch linkage adjustment should never be performed to compensate for clutch disc wear on a pull-type clutch. Adjusting the clutch with the linkage will lead to loss of clutch brake actuation and eventual clutch failure! Linkage adjustment should only be performed to correct the clutch brake squeeze dimension! Pull-type clutches are adjusted internally with the large adjusting ring threaded into the clutch cover or externally with a threaded release bearing sleeve—never with the clutch linkage.

Release Bearing Free Travel

Once you establish that the linkage adjustment is correct, it is time to check the release bearing free travel. Release bearing free travel is the distance the release bearing moves as the clutch pedal is depressed to the floor. As the discs wear, the release bearing moves toward the flywheel with the pressure plate and the release levers. This increases release bearing free travel at the same time it reduces free play at the release fork. Release bearing free travel is typically 0.5" to 0.5625" (1.25 to 1.4 cm) and is set by adjusting the clutch internally to move the release bearing back to where it started.

The most common form of internal adjustment involves turning a large **adjusting ring** inside the clutch cover. Clockwise movement of this adjusting ring moves the lever or diaphragm spring pivot points closer to the pressure plate. That movement causes their inner edges and the integral release bearing to move toward the transmission. That resets the release bearing free travel to 0.5" to 0.5625", (1.25 to 1.4 cm) and, if no linkage adjustment has been made, the release fork free play is re-established also.

Angle Spring Clutch Adjustment with Locking Tang

There are two adjustment systems for the angle spring clutch. As shown in FIGURE 36-1, the first system uses a **locking tang** that is bolted to the clutch cover and rests between two of the square lugs that are formed on the adjusting ring.

Safety

The clutch pedal must be depressed and the clutch disengaged in order to turn the large adjusting ring. Doing so relieves the clamp load and allows the ring to turn. Trying to turn the adjusting ring with the clutch engaged can destroy the clutch and or the adjusting mechanism.

To adjust the clutch, the engine is rotated until the locking tang is at the bottom and is accessible through the clutch inspection plate. The locking tang is then removed and an adjusting tool is bolted to the same hole as the tang bolt. Next, the clutch pedal is depressed to remove the clamp load, and the adjusting tool is used to turn the adjusting ring. The ring is turned clockwise when looking from the rear to compensate for worn clutch discs.

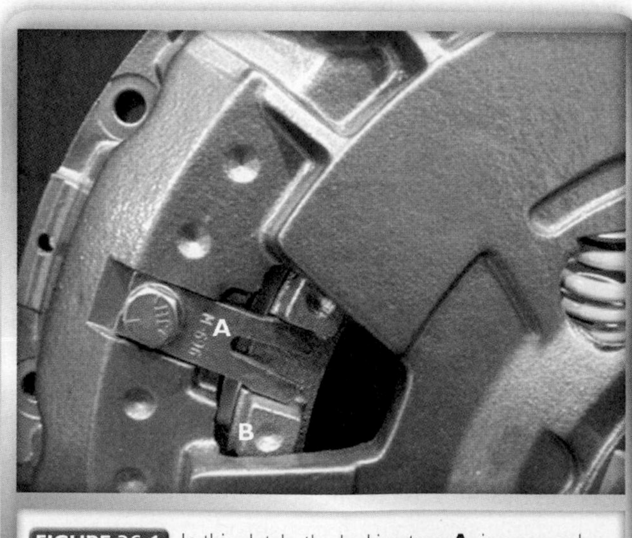

FIGURE 36-1 In this clutch, the locking tang **A.** is removed and the large adjusting ring **B.** turned clockwise to adjust for wear.

Angle Spring Clutch Adjustment with Quick-Adjust Device

The second adjusting system is exclusive to Eaton/Spicer angle spring clutches and uses a **quick-adjust** device, like that shown in FIGURE 36-2. This device consists of 5/8" (15.875 mm) bolt attached to a small pinion gear that meshes with internal teeth on the large adjusting ring. The 5/8" (15.875 mm) bolt has a spring-loaded locking system that prevents it from moving by itself. The quick-adjust device is bolted to the clutch cover. FIGURE 36-3 illustrates a properly adjusted pull-type clutch with 0.5" to 0.56" (12.4 to 14.2 mm) release bearing free travel.

To adjust the clutch with this system, the engine is again rotated until the quick-adjust is at the bottom and accessible through the clutch inspection cover. The clutch pedal is depressed to remove the clamp load and the technician uses a wrench or socket first to depress the locking bolt and then to turn the quick-adjust, which rotates the large adjusting ring in the clutch cover. The quick-adjust is rotated clockwise from the rear to adjust for worn clutch discs. One turn of the quick-adjust will equate to approximately a 0.125" to 0.2" (3.2 to 5 mm) difference in release bearing free travel.

> **TECHNICIAN TIP**
>
> Remember that, in most cases, no linkage adjustment should be required. The internal adjustment is normally all that is needed to achieve proper adjustment of the clutch.

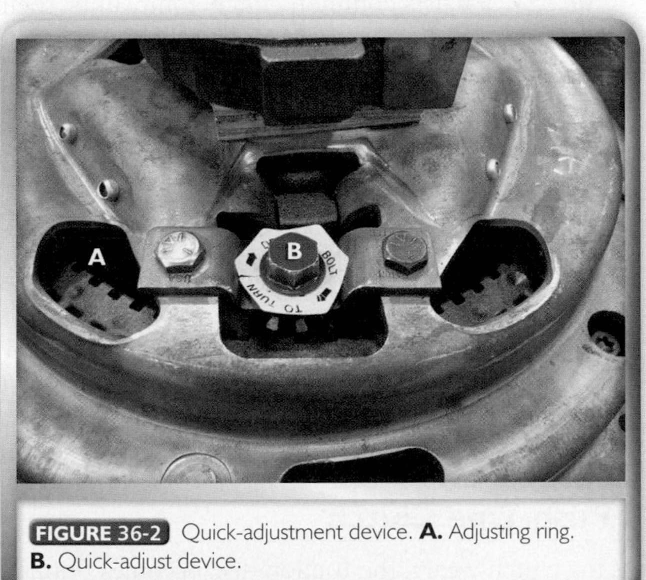

FIGURE 36-2 Quick-adjustment device. **A.** Adjusting ring. **B.** Quick-adjust device.

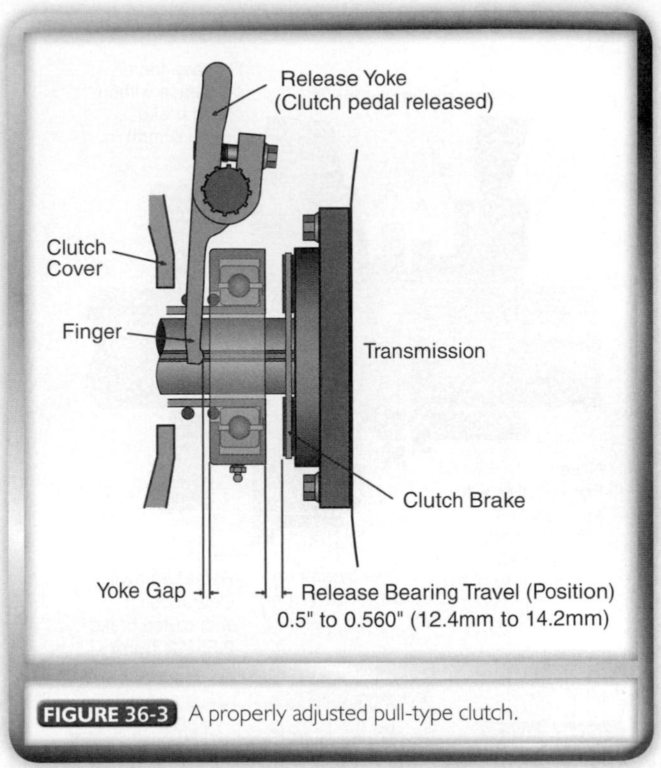

FIGURE 36-3 A properly adjusted pull-type clutch.

> **Safety**
>
> Failure to depress the clutch pedal prior to trying to rotate the adjusting ring in a pull-type clutch will cause damage to the quick-adjust mechanism. It must only be rotated with the clutch pedal fully depressed.

LIPE/Haldex Adjustment

The LIPE/Haldex brand of pull-type clutches uses a different system to adjust release bearing free travel. The release bearing spider, or retainer, which holds the inner edge of the release levers, is attached to the release bearing by a threaded sleeve with an adjusting nut and a jamb nut. To reposition the bearing, the jamb nut is simply loosened and the adjusting nut is turned. Those actions move the bearing back to its original location, thereby re-establishing release bearing free travel and release fork free play. The jamb nut is then retightened. FIGURE 36-4 illustrates a threaded release sleeve type of clutch adjusted to achieve the same 0.5" to 0.56" (1.27 to 1.43 mm) bearing free travel and 0.125" (0.32 mm) clearance at the release fork.

Release Fork Free Play

As mentioned in the Release Bearing Free Travel section, the internal adjustment to reset release bearing free travel normally results in the fork free play returning to its

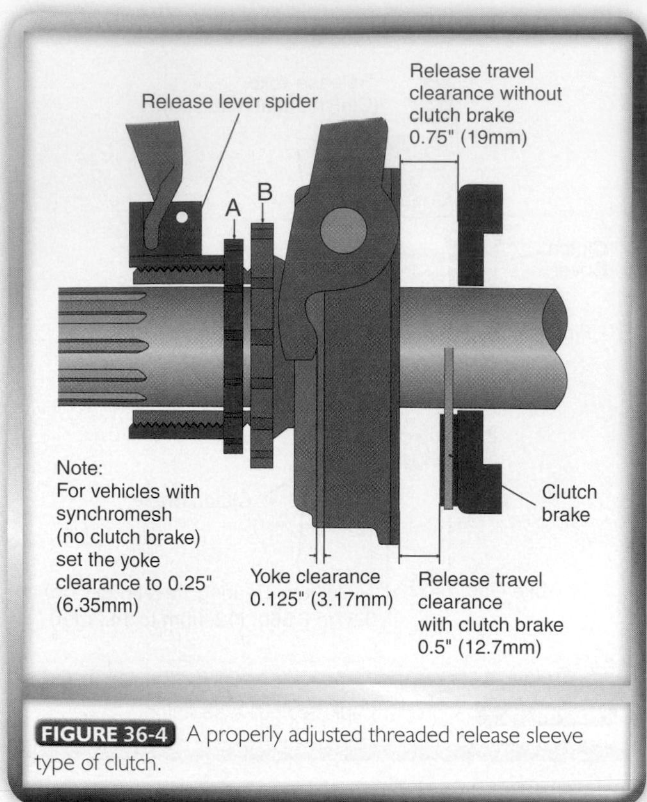

FIGURE 36-4 A properly adjusted threaded release sleeve type of clutch.

optimal setting of 0.125" (3.175 mm). This is because both are set by moving the bearing away from the fork with the adjusting ring inside the clutch. If fork clearance is not correctly reestablished after the internal adjustment, total pedal travel may need to be adjusted by raising or lowering the clutch pedal stops in the cab. The proper 0.125" (3.175 mm) free play at the fork usually equates to 2.0" to 2.5" (50.8 to 63.5 mm) of pedal free travel in the cab. Readjustment should be performed when in-cab pedal free play drops to half of the normal amount achieved after a correct adjustment.

> **TECHNICIAN TIP**
>
> Pedal free play is a result of proper adjustment and therefore may vary from vehicle to vehicle. Whatever pedal free play is established after a correct adjustment is made is the correct pedal free play for that vehicle. Drivers should be instructed to return for re-adjustment of the clutch when clutch wear causes a 50% drop in the in-cab free pedal.

Self-Adjusting Clutches

The Eaton Solo, the SACH's Twin XTend, and the Meritor AutoJust self-adjusting clutches have replaced the large internal adjusting ring with a set of **movable cam rings**. These cam rings sense plate movement as disc wear occurs and compensate by sliding one cam over the other on clutch release to reposition the pressure plate, levers, and the release bearing. These clutches are designed to require no adjustment other than initial setup procedures. These procedures are specific to each size of clutch and each manufacturer. Manufacturers publish these procedures in the installation instructions that accompany a new clutch and on their individual corporate websites.

The maintenance on these clutches is usually limited to inspection for proper functioning (making sure they are adjusting) and information on lubricating the release bearing, cross-shafts, and fork wear pads.

Troubleshooting Clutch Problems

The primary cause of clutch failure is excess heat. Excess heat causes the surface of the friction materials to liquefy, so they can no longer transfer torque. As a result, the disc starts slipping, which in turn causes more heat. At that point, complete failure occurs very rapidly.

Clutch chatter is another common complaint for clutches. **Clutch chatter** is the intermittent grabbing and slipping of the clutch while it is being engaged. Clutch chatter can be caused by issues such as a warped flywheel or pressure plate. The most common cause of chatter is an oil-soaked clutch disc caused by leaking engine oil. Shock loads can also cause severe damage to a clutch and must be avoided. Proper driver education is essential to a long and trouble-free clutch life, but the driver and the technician must work together to get the maximum life from the clutch. **TABLE 36-1** describes some common operator errors and the clutch problems they can cause.

TABLE 36-2 lists common clutch complaints, their causes, and remedies. This chart is in no way a comprehensive list of problems. Always check the manufacturer's manual when diagnosing a clutch system problem.

Maintenance and Repair of a Clutch

Every OEM will have its own detailed instructions on clutch installation procedures. OEM-specific procedures should be followed to the letter. This section is merely a general outline of clutch replacement procedures that are common to most manufacturers.

Checking and Adjusting a Push-Type Clutch

As the clutch wears, the friction disc becomes thinner. This results in the pressure plate release levers moving

TABLE 36-1: Common Operator Errors and Clutch Problems

Operator Errors	Resulting Clutch Problems
Starting in too high a gear	This causes excess slippage in the clutch because the engine has insufficient torque to pick up the load in a higher gear. The clutch must slip to make up the difference. The correct gear is the one that allows the driver to pick up the load and start moving without increasing engine speed (or with minimal increase in speed).
Proper shifting techniques	If a driver shifts to a gear that is too far away in ratio from the vehicle speed, the clutch must slip to absorb the speed difference.
Overloading the clutch	All clutches have a maximum torque capacity. Exceeding the maximum load on a clutch will cause the clutch to slip.
Riding the clutch	Pressure on the clutch pedal lowers pressure plate clamp load and can lead to a slipping clutch.
Holding the vehicle on an incline by slipping the clutch	Purposely slipping the clutch has no value other than to overheat the clutch and cause premature wear. Operators should never engage in this practice.
Coasting in gear with the clutch disengaged	Operators should always have the clutch engaged except when starting or shifting. Coasting in gear allows the speed difference between the engine and the clutch disc to vary uncontrollably. When the driver wishes to re-engage the clutch, the clutch must slip to make up the difference in speeds. Excessive disc speed can also occur by coasting down a loading ramp For example a vehicle with a 17:1 reverse gear ratio and a 4:1 final drive ratio has a total ratio of 68:1 so at 2,000 rpm engine speed the tire speed is 29.4 rpm. Heavy-duty truck tires rotate approximately 600 rpm, so, in reverse, this vehicle can achieve a top speed of approximately 3 mph (5 kph). If the driver coasts the vehicle down the ramp at 15 mph (24 kph) in reverse with the vehicle in gear and the clutch released, the speed of the clutch disc would increase to 10,000 rpm. That would far exceed the clutch's burst strength—causing the friction material to fly off the disc and leading to complete clutch failure.
Failure to request clutch adjustment or report erratic operation	The driver must be informed when the clutch is ready for a readjustment and must bring the vehicle in for service as soon as possible when it is required. The driver should also report any erratic behavior to the technician promptly so it can be seen to.

TABLE 36-2: Common Clutch Complaints, Causes, and Corrections

Symptom	Cause	Correction
Clutch slips on engagement or during operation	Insufficient release bearing clearance; no free play Riding the pedal Clutch worn out	Readjust clutch to gain correct clearance Instruct driver on proper techniques Replace worn out clutch
Pedal hard to depress	Linkage binding Release bearing wear pads grooved	Repair or replace linkage Replace release bearing or clutch assembly
Clutch does not release completely	Insufficient release bearing free travel Worn or damaged input shaft splines; discs hanging up Warped clutch disc or pressure plate Intermediate plate binding	Readjust clutch Replace input shaft Replace clutch as necessary Correct binding intermediate plate check drive pin on 14" (36.6 cm) clutch and drive slots on 15.5" (39.4 cm) clutch repair or replace as necessary
Clutch chatters on engagement	Starting in too high a gear for the load Oil-soaked discs Warped or damaged pressure plate, flywheel, or clutch disc	Instruct the driver on proper operating techniques Repair source of oil contamination and clean or replace discs Replace warped or damaged components
Clutch noisy on disengagement	Worn or damaged release bearing Worn or damaged pilot bearing; noisy only when fully disengaged Clutch adjustment incorrect on pull-type clutch	Replace release bearing Release pilot bearing If adjustment was made with linkage instead of internal adjustment, it can cause bearing retainer to contact clutch cover—readjust correctly
Gear clash on shifting	Too much free play at pedal (push-type clutch) Not enough release bearing free travel (pull-type clutch) Discs warped or damaged Pilot bearing binding	Adjust clutch linkage Adjust clutch internally Replace damaged components Replace pilot bearing

closer to the release bearing and the clutch linkage losing its operational clearance. Some clutches are self-compensating for wear, while others require checking and adjusting. You must refer to the manufacturer's workshop information to find out exactly where any adjustment should be made.

It is important to check the clutch linkage mechanism for proper operation and correct the adjustment (free play) periodically. It is common to do so during every routine maintenance service. If the clutch pedal has too little free play, the throw-out bearing could remain in contact with the pressure plate levers. As a result, the pressure plate may be unable to apply full pressure, which would result in an incomplete clamping of the disc, leading to premature wear or failure of the clutch assembly and requiring removal and replacement. Also, the pedal will have to be released a long way before the clutch starts to engage. If the adjustment has too much free play, the clutch pedal may not have enough travel to fully release the pressure plate, causing the gears to clash (grind) when shifting and resulting in heavy synchronizer wear. With this condition, the clutch will start to engage right from the floor when releasing the pedal.

To check and adjust a mechanical clutch, follow the guidelines in **SKILL DRILL 36-1**.

Checking and Adjusting a Hydraulic Clutch

It is important to check the clutch hydraulic system and components for proper operation and correct adjustment. It is common to do so during periodic routine maintenance service. If the hydraulic clutch system is improperly maintained, clutch operation could be compromised in a similar manner as the operation of a mechanical linkage clutch, resulting in pressure plate, friction disc, and

SKILL DRILL 36-1 Checking and Adjusting a Push-Type Clutch

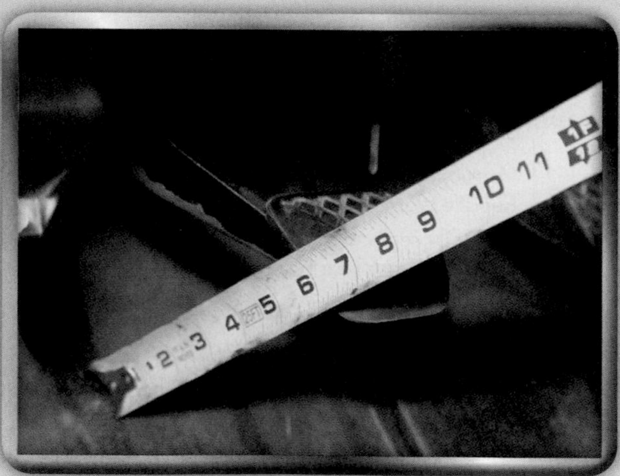

1. Research the procedure and specifications for inspecting and adjusting the clutch linkage in the appropriate service information. You are looking specifically for the proper clutch pedal height, the proper clutch pedal free play, and the procedure for making adjustments.
2. Following the specified procedure, inspect the clutch linkage parts for damage, wear, or bent or missing components. Look for signs of binding, looseness, and excessive wear.
3. Start with the clutch pedal assembly and inspect all components inside the cab. It is good practice to operate the clutch pedal while you are inspecting the components to observe any looseness or binding.
4. Check the clutch linkage components under the cab for the same signs as the components inside the cab.
5. Measure the clutch pedal height. Clutch pedal height is normally measured from the floor pan to the top of the clutch pedal pad with the clutch pedal released. Make sure there are no floor mats or other obstructions that will affect the operation of the pedal. Compare your reading with the specifications and determine any necessary actions to correct any fault.
6. Measure the clutch pedal free play. Pedal free play is normally measured from the top of the pedal at rest to where all play is taken up between the pedal and the pressure plate. This can be felt by hand or foot. Perform any adjustments as necessary, following the manufacturer's procedure.
7. Start the vehicle and depress the clutch. The clutch should engage at the proper height and have the proper free play. Make a gear selection to ensure the gears do not clash going into mesh. While in gear, slowly release the clutch and see how far the clutch pedal must travel before the clutch starts to engage in forward motion. If it is not within the manufacturer's specifications, discuss this with your supervisor.

transmission synchronizer failure. Also, improper or old fluid in the hydraulic system can cause master cylinder and slave cylinder damage.

To check and adjust a hydraulic clutch, follow the guidelines in SKILL DRILL 36-2.

> **TECHNICIAN TIP**
>
> Make sure there are no floor mats or other obstructions that will affect the operation of the clutch pedal.

Bleeding a Hydraulic Clutch System

In the case of a hydraulic clutch system failure, it may be necessary to bleed the air from the system. Bleeding is also needed whenever any hydraulic component is replaced or the hydraulic fluid becomes unfit for use due to age or contamination. Not all systems are fitted with a bleeder screw due to how the system is constructed. It may be necessary to bleed the system from the line entering the slave cylinder.

Research the procedure and specifications for bleeding the hydraulic clutch system. There are three types of bleeding: gravity bleeding, manual bleeding, and **pressure bleeding**, (a pressure bleeder forces fluid under pressure through the hydraulic system). Determine the proper method of bleeding to use by consulting the manufacturer's specifications.

After bleeding the hydraulic clutch system, fill the master cylinder to the correct level with the specified type of brake fluid.

Gravity Bleeding

Gravity bleeding uses gravity to push fluid and air from the master cylinder and lines out through the slave

SKILL DRILL 36-2 Checking and Adjusting a Hydraulic Clutch

1. Research the procedure and specifications for inspecting and adjusting the hydraulic clutch components in the appropriate service information.
2. Inspect the clutch master cylinder for correct fluid level and test the quality of the fluid.
3. Inspect all line connections to the master cylinder. If a leak at the rear of the master cylinder is suspected, it may be necessary to remove the master cylinder from the firewall to inspect behind it for leaks if no other visible external leaks are present.
4. Make sure no hydraulic lines are kinked or leaking at their connections. This will require that the system be repaired and bled of any air.
5. Check all rubber hoses for dry rot, bulges, or leaks. Make sure all hydraulic components are secure in their mountings.
6. Check the boot on the slave cylinder for seepage, which may indicate a leaking slave cylinder piston seal.
7. Check clutch pedal height. Clutch pedal height is normally measured from the floor pan to the top of the clutch pedal pad with the clutch pedal released. Compare your reading with the specifications and determine any necessary actions to correct any fault.
8. Measure clutch pedal free play using a tape measure. Pedal free play is normally measured from the top of the pedal at rest to where all play is taken up between the pedal and the pressure plate. Compare your reading with the factory specifications and determine any necessary actions to correct.
9. Note that newer hydraulically actuated clutches run with no free pedal in the cab. Always check manufacturers' specifications for the vehicle you are working on before undertaking any servicing.

cylinder bleeder screw. In most vehicles, the clutch master cylinder is quite a bit higher than the slave cylinder. The weight of the fluid can therefore be used to supply the pressure to push fluid and air out of the system.

To bleed/flush a hydraulic clutch system using the gravity method, follow the guidelines in **SKILL DRILL 36-3**.

> **TECHNICIAN TIP**
>
> Be careful of the pressure that comes out of the slave cylinder, as it may splash or spray into your eyes. Also, brake fluid will eat paint, so when handling brake fluid, quickly clean up any spilled fluid with generous amounts of water.

Manual Bleeding

The manual bleeding method uses the master cylinder to push fluid and air from the system. The procedure usually requires an assistant to hold the clutch pedal down while the other person opens the bleeder valve on the slave cylinder. Pumping of the pedal will result in a single air bubble breaking up into smaller bubbles or foam, which will require more time to bleed the system properly.

To bleed/flush a hydraulic clutch system using the manual method, follow the guidelines in **SKILL DRILL 36-4**.

Pressure or Vacuum Bleeding

The pressure or vacuum bleeding method uses pressure or vacuum to push or pull fluid and air from the system. This method works well for systems that tend to trap air in the hydraulic system that cannot be bled manually. It does require special bleeding tools or equipment.

To bleed a hydraulic clutch system using the pressure method, follow the guidelines in **SKILL DRILL 36-5**.

Removing a Clutch

A clutch will need to be replaced when it is damaged, contaminated by leaking fluid, or when adjustment can no longer correct for a slipping clutch. The transmission must be removed in order to remove the clutch, meaning that the driver's shift lever and the **shift tower** bolted to the top of the transmission must be removed. Care should also be taken to avoid fluid spills that could be caused by removing a slip yoke from the transmission output shaft. The **slip yoke** is a sliding drive shaft yoke that sometimes seals the rear of the transmission.

To safely and correctly install a new clutch requires **guide studs**, which are long threaded studs that support the clutch while the bolts are removed. In addition, you will need a **clutch alignment tool** or an old input shaft to hold the friction discs in alignment for reassembly.

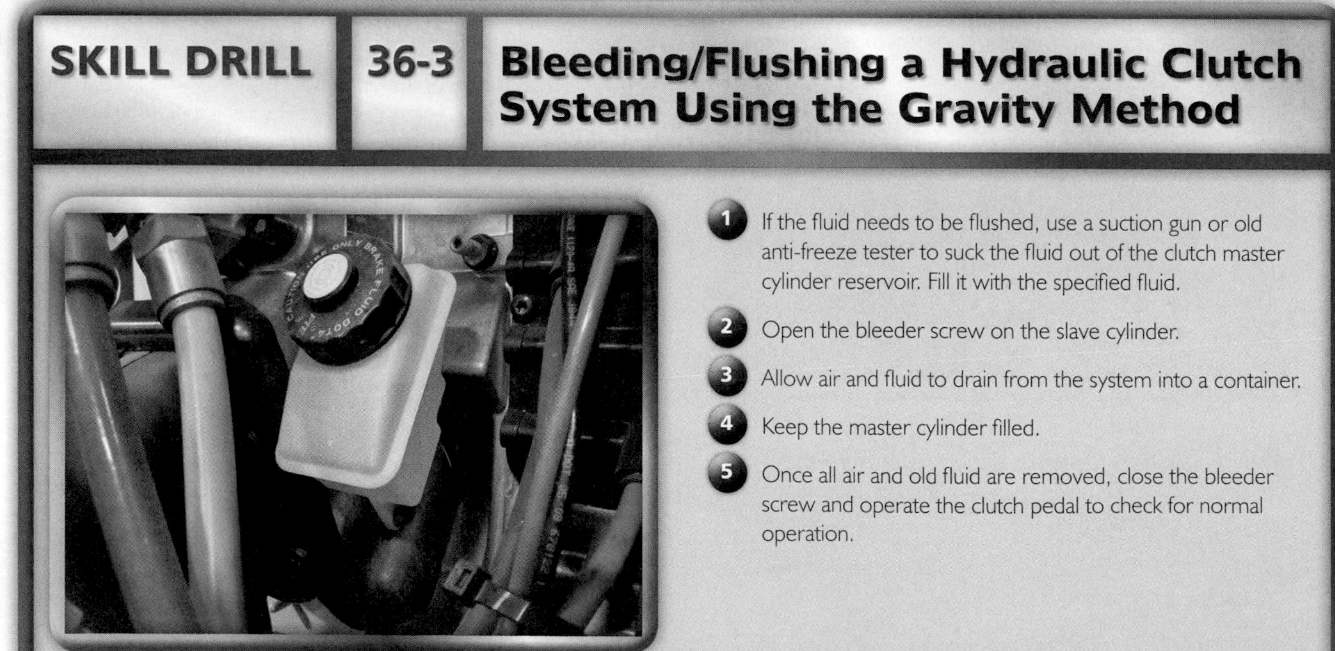

SKILL DRILL 36-3 Bleeding/Flushing a Hydraulic Clutch System Using the Gravity Method

1. If the fluid needs to be flushed, use a suction gun or old anti-freeze tester to suck the fluid out of the clutch master cylinder reservoir. Fill it with the specified fluid.
2. Open the bleeder screw on the slave cylinder.
3. Allow air and fluid to drain from the system into a container.
4. Keep the master cylinder filled.
5. Once all air and old fluid are removed, close the bleeder screw and operate the clutch pedal to check for normal operation.

SKILL DRILL 36-4 Bleeding/Flushing a Hydraulic Clutch System Using the Manual Method

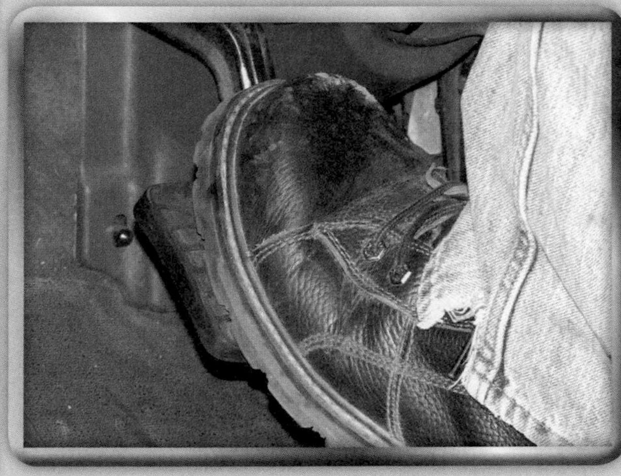

1. If the fluid needs to be flushed, use a suction gun or old anti-freeze tester to suck the fluid out of the clutch master cylinder reservoir. Fill it with the specified fluid.
2. Have an assistant depress the clutch pedal slowly. Open the bleeder valve on the slave cylinder and let fluid run out into a container.
3. When all of the fluid stops flowing, close the bleeder valve and slowly release the pedal.
4. Repeat this process until all air and old fluid are removed from the system.
5. After bleeding the clutch hydraulic system, check for correct pedal feel, and fill the master cylinder to the correct level with the specified type of brake fluid.

SKILL DRILL 36-5 Bleeding/Flushing a Hydraulic Clutch System Using the Pressure Method

1. Hook up the pressure or vacuum bleeding tool to the vehicle with the correct adapters.
2. Apply pressure or vacuum to the system.
3. Open the bleeder screw and allow the fluid and air to be purged from the system. Capture the fluid in the bleeder or use a hose to direct it into a plastic container. Repeat this process as necessary.
4. After bleeding the hydraulic clutch system, check for correct pedal feel, and fill the master cylinder to the correct level with the specified type of brake fluid.

You will also need **shipping blocks**, which are small wooden spacers that hold the release bearing of a pull-type clutch in the released position. If you are removing a SOLO or other self-adjusting clutch, four **shipping bolts** will be required to cage the clutch pressure plate for removal. Heavier clutch installations may require the use of a **clutch jack**. Make sure you have all the needed items before you begin the job.

To remove a clutch, follow the guidelines in **SKILL DRILL 36-6**.

SKILL DRILL 36-6 Removing a Manual Transmission and Clutch

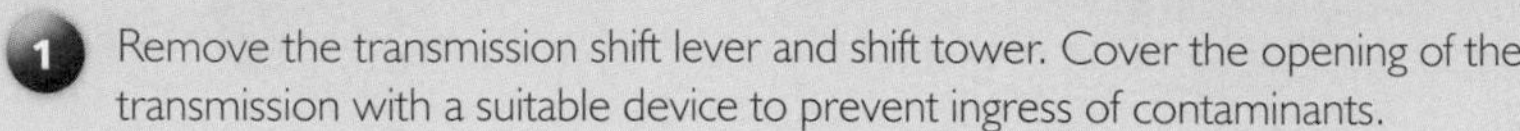

1. Remove the transmission shift lever and shift tower. Cover the opening of the transmission with a suitable device to prevent ingress of contaminants.

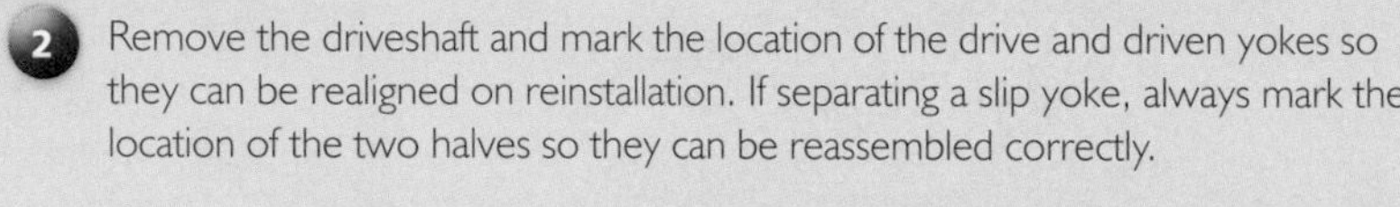

2. Remove the driveshaft and mark the location of the drive and driven yokes so they can be realigned on reinstallation. If separating a slip yoke, always mark the location of the two halves so they can be reassembled correctly.

Safety

A sudden release of air pressure can cause serious injury due to blowing particles and or air lines whipping about, so drain the air tanks as required before continuing if any air connections are to be removed. Even after the air tanks are drained, exercise caution as some air may remain in the system.

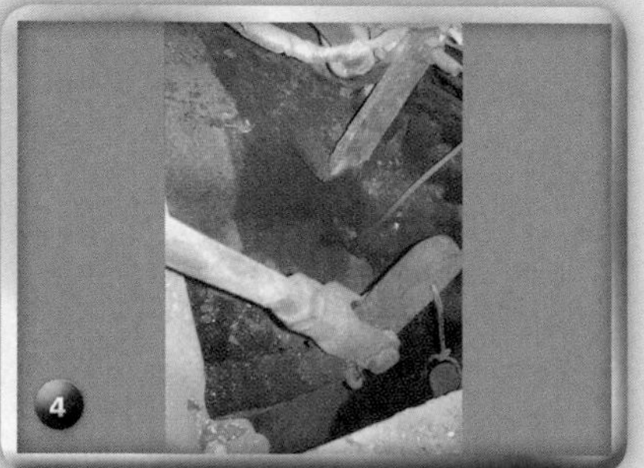

3. Disconnect the air supply and electrical connections from the transmission. If the clutch linkage has more than one possible mounting hole in the cross-shaft lever, mark the location and remove the linkage. If the clutch has a hydraulic actuating system, remove the slave valve and support it by ties or wire.

4. Support the transmission with a suitable jack. Note that the jack must have the correct attachments so that the transmission can be supported at its normal inclination. Use a safety chain to secure the transmission to the jack.

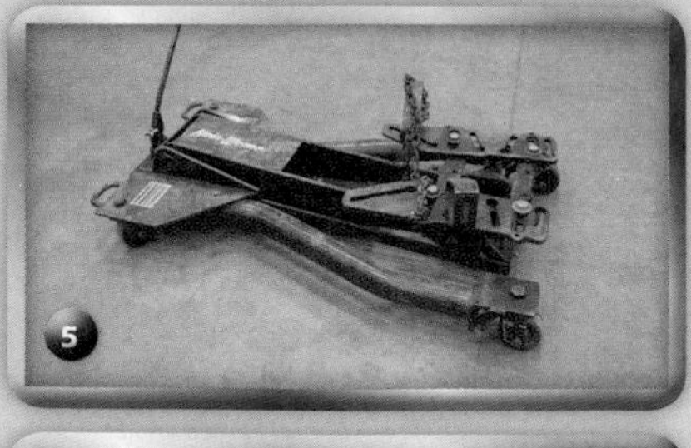

5. Remove the transmission frame supports. Remove the bolts securing the transmission to the flywheel housing. Pull the transmission straight back. Use extreme caution to ensure the transmission does not hang down from the input shaft, as damage to the transmission and/or clutch discs could result. Lower the jack and move the transmission out of the work area. Remove the clutch brake if equipped. Inspect the clutch release fork and cross-shaft for wear and smooth operation.

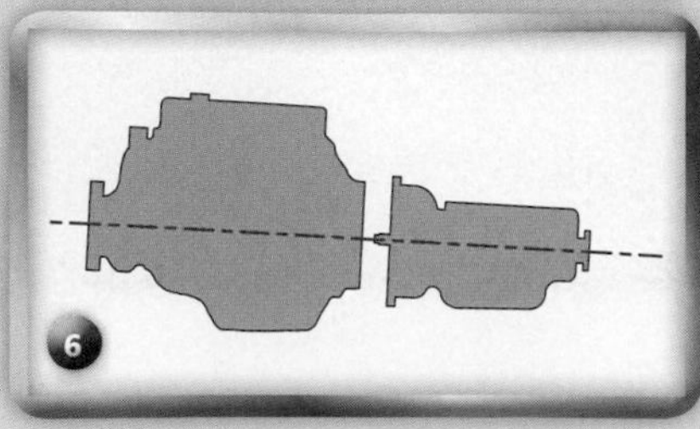

6. Before removing the clutch, inspect the clutch to determine what type it is. An Eaton Solo auto-adjust clutch, a SACH's Twin XTend, or a Meritor AutoJust clutch will need to have shipping bolts installed before removal. Failure to install the shipping bolts can lead to adjust mechanism damage and or warping of the pressure plate.

Continued on next page

SKILL DRILL 36-6 Removing a Manual Transmission and Clutch, continued

7. Install a clutch alignment tool to hold the disc/discs centered. If an alignment tool is unavailable, use an old input shaft. If using a clutch jack, use the alignment tool that comes with the jack. Dual disc 15.5" (39.4 cm) clutches can weigh in excess of 175 lb (79.4 kg), so it is advisable to use a clutch jack to take the weight of the clutch. Also beware of pinch hazards as the clutch is being removed.

8. On Eaton Solo, SACH's Twin XTend, or Meritor AutoJust clutches, install the four shipping bolts in the holes provided. Consult OEM documentation for the locations and sizes, tighten bolts until they make contact, and then turn one more turn. On all other pull-type clutches, use a clutch yoke tool to pull the release bearing back and install two ⅝" (1.6 mm) or larger wooden shipping blocks to remove the spring pressure from the pressure plate. Failure to do so may cause pressure plate warping.

9. Remove the top two clutch attaching bolts and replace them with guide studs. *Note: Guide studs can be purchased or you can cut the top off a long bolt of the correct size and thread for the particular clutch you are working on and cut a slot in the end to accept a flat-tipped screwdriver.*

10. Remove the rest of the attaching bolts following a crisscross pattern. If the clutch is not being replaced, mark the cover and the flywheel so the clutch can be reinstalled in the same location.

11. Pry the clutch back on the guide studs and remove with the clutch jack. On a 14" (36.6 cm) clutch with a pot-style flywheel, the front friction disc and the intermediate plate will likely stay in the flywheel, but be careful that they do not fall out. Use caution when you remove them from the flywheel.

12. Inspect the removed clutch carefully for signs of abuse, such as abnormal overheating, burst clutch facing, cracked friction disc hubs, and excess wear on the release bearing wear pads. All of these signs can indicate clutch abuse. If any of those signs are present, make sure that the driver is notified so as not to repeat the failure.

13. If the flywheel is to be sent for resurfacing, remove it now. Use guide studs in the top two flywheel attaching bolt positions and use caution to avoid pinching when removing.

14. Remove the pilot bearing using a driver or puller.

Safety

If removing a clutch without a clutch jack, get assistance and exercise extreme care. When removing a 15.5" (39.4 cm) clutch, the complete clutch rear disc, intermediate plate, and front disc will be removed all at once and together they can weigh in excess of 175lb (79.4 kg).

Component Inspection with Clutch Removed

Several components should be checked when the clutch is removed. Failure to do so could lead to poor clutch performance or even component failure. The transmission input shaft spline, as shown in FIGURE 36-5, should be inspected for wear. Any wear here can cause the friction discs to hang up and cause poor release. Replace the shaft if wear is excessive.

It is also important to inspect the **clutch bell housing.** The clutch bell housing is the housing that surrounds the clutch assembly and attaches to the flywheel housing. The **flywheel housing** surrounds the flywheel and bolts to the engine. It is necessary to inspect both housings for wear caused by excessive vibration. Unlike the flywheel housing wear, clutch bell housing wear cannot be measured. The technician must use his discretion when inspecting the clutch bell housing face and pilot for wear. The **clutch bell housing pilot** is the small protrusion that fits inside a mating recess in the flywheel housing known as the **flywheel housing pilot**. Most wear will usually occur between the 3 and 8 o'clock positions, as illustrated in FIGURE 36-6. Identifying wear here is subject to the technician's discretion as it cannot be effectively measured. If wear is significant, the transmission will hang down slightly and cause damage to the clutch disc, the input shaft, and the input bearing. It can also lead to gear jump out when the transmission is in direct gear. Replace the housing as necessary.

On non-synchronized transmissions, it is also important to check the input shaft bearing cover for wear. From the clutch brake, measure the distance between the forward end of the input shaft splines to the friction surface of the input bearing cover. The distance should not exceed 8.71" (22.2 cm), as shown in FIGURE 36-7. The SAE distance for dimension A is 8.657" (219.9 mm) nominal and should not exceed 8.71" (221.5 mm).

FIGURE 36-5 Inspect input shaft spline for wear.

Dial Indicator Checks

When replacing any type of clutch, the following dial indicator checks should be performed to ensure proper clutch operation and service life. While performing these tests, record the **total indicated run out (TIR),** which is the difference between the low and the high spots. Check for run out on the **flywheel friction surface** where the clutch friction disc runs. Check the pilot bearing bore in the flywheel for run out. The (**pilot bearing bore** is the bore in the flywheel that receives the pilot bearing.

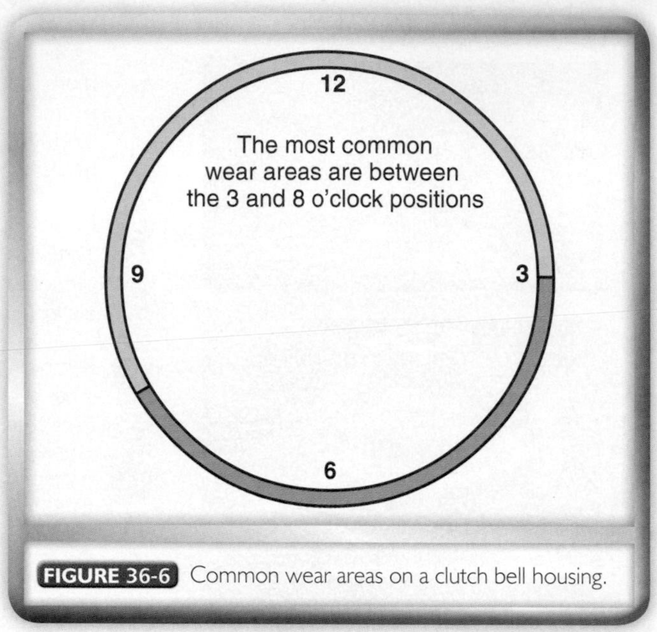

FIGURE 36-6 Common wear areas on a clutch bell housing.

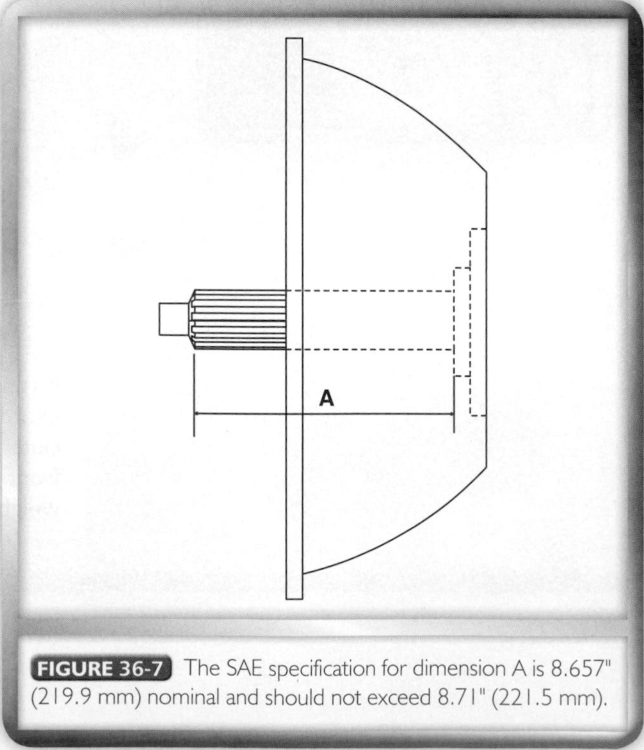

FIGURE 36-7 The SAE specification for dimension A is 8.657" (219.9 mm) nominal and should not exceed 8.71" (221.5 mm).

Check run out on the flywheel housing pilot as well. The flywheel housing pilot is the small indentation in the flywheel housing that receives the clutch bell housing pilot. Also check the **flywheel housing face** where the transmission bolts to it for run out. Failure to perform these run out checks can result in transmission misalignment, leading to gear slip out or erratic and unsatisfactory clutch operation. These checks ensure that the clutch discs will not hang up and that the center line of the transmission is directly in line with the centerline of the engine. To perform dial indicator checks, follow the guidelines in **SKILL DRILL 36-7**.

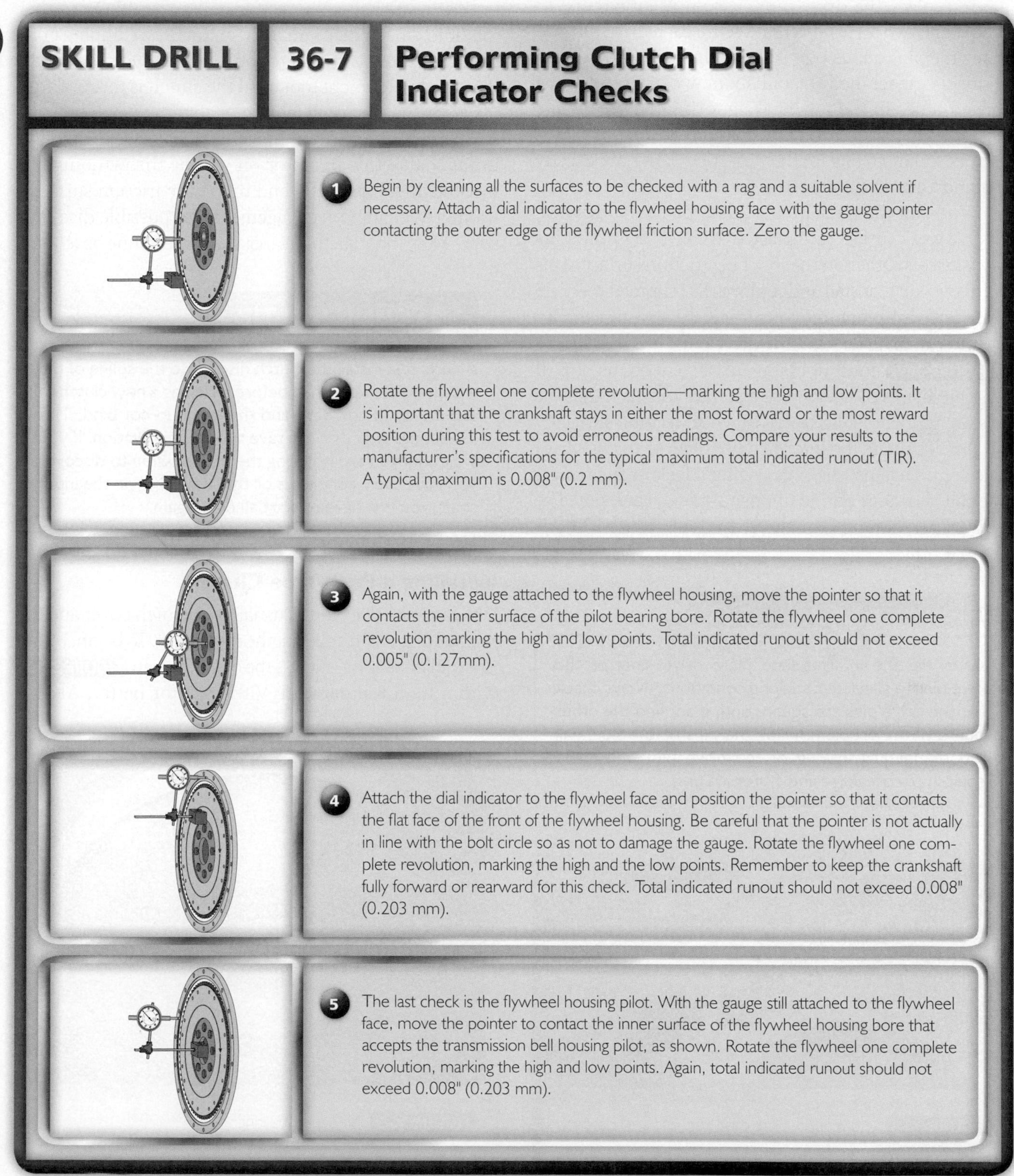

SKILL DRILL 36-7 Performing Clutch Dial Indicator Checks

1. Begin by cleaning all the surfaces to be checked with a rag and a suitable solvent if necessary. Attach a dial indicator to the flywheel housing face with the gauge pointer contacting the outer edge of the flywheel friction surface. Zero the gauge.

2. Rotate the flywheel one complete revolution—marking the high and low points. It is important that the crankshaft stays in either the most forward or the most reward position during this test to avoid erroneous readings. Compare your results to the manufacturer's specifications for the typical maximum total indicated runout (TIR). A typical maximum is 0.008" (0.2 mm).

3. Again, with the gauge attached to the flywheel housing, move the pointer so that it contacts the inner surface of the pilot bearing bore. Rotate the flywheel one complete revolution marking the high and low points. Total indicated runout should not exceed 0.005" (0.127mm).

4. Attach the dial indicator to the flywheel face and position the pointer so that it contacts the flat face of the front of the flywheel housing. Be careful that the pointer is not actually in line with the bolt circle so as not to damage the gauge. Rotate the flywheel one complete revolution, marking the high and the low points. Remember to keep the crankshaft fully forward or rearward for this check. Total indicated runout should not exceed 0.008" (0.203 mm).

5. The last check is the flywheel housing pilot. With the gauge still attached to the flywheel face, move the pointer to contact the inner surface of the flywheel housing bore that accepts the transmission bell housing pilot, as shown. Rotate the flywheel one complete revolution, marking the high and low points. Again, total indicated runout should not exceed 0.008" (0.203 mm).

Replacing Intermediate Plate Drive Pins on a 14" (36.6 cm) Pot-Style Flywheel

Fourteen inch (36.6 cm) clutch pot-style flywheels are unique in that the intermediate plate is driven by six drive pins installed in the flywheel. These drive pins should be replaced when the clutch is replaced.

To replace the drive pins, use an Allen wrench to remove the two set screws that secure each drive pin and knock the pins out using a suitable drift punch. After the flywheel is machined, install six new drive pins in the unused holes in the flywheel, ignoring the previously used holes. Use a drive pin installation tool or a small carpenter's square to ensure the pin drive flanks are exactly perpendicular to the flywheel friction surface.

When all the pins are installed, place the flywheel flat on a work surface and place two 0.5" (12.7 mm) nuts opposite each other on the flywheel friction surface. This will allow you to install and remove the intermediate plate easily without pinching your fingers. Next, test the fit. The intermediate plate on the drive pins, like that shown in FIGURE 36-8, must not hang up or stick on the pins. If the plate hangs or sticks, use a square to check that the pins are perpendicular to the flywheel friction surface.

Finally, rotate the intermediate plate so that its drive slots are up against the pins. Using a feeler gauge, measure the clearance on the opposite side of each slot. The minimum clearance for the drive pin slots is 0.006" (0.1524 mm).

Safety

Never file the intermediate plate drive slots or the drive pins to alleviate a sticking condition! Always check that the drive pins are square and, if so, find the other source of the problem. Filing the pins or the slots will lead to unequal loading of the drive pins and could result in pin breakage and system failure.

FIGURE 36-8 Intermediate plate drive pins on a 14" clutch pot-style flywheel.

Installing a New Clutch

Installing a new clutch is a relatively straightforward procedure, but remember that you will require a clutch alignment tool to line up the clutch discs before the clutch is bolted to the flywheel. Otherwise, it will be impossible to install the transmission, as the discs will not line up to the input shaft splines. If installing a SOLO or other self-adjusting clutch, you must remove the shipping bolts after the clutch is bolted to the flywheel. Do not remove the clutch alignment tool until the clutch is torqued into place, or the discs will fall out of alignment.

Do not grease or oil the splines of the transmission input shaft. Any grease or oil will be thrown outward by centrifugal force and end up on the friction surfaces, leading to chatter on engagement and possible disc slippage. Most manufacturers insist that the spline be left dry.

TECHNICIAN TIP

Always test install the clutch discs onto the spline of the transmission input shaft before installing a new clutch to see if they fit correctly and that they do not bind. This is a simple step that can save a lot of aggravation. If you wait until you are installing the transmission to discover you have the wrong discs or that they bind on the input shaft, you will have to start all over again.

Installing a Push-Type Clutch

With a push-type clutch, usually the clutch cover and the friction disc are installed at the same time. To begin, install a new pilot bearing, such as the one shown in FIGURE 36-9, with a high temperature Viton seal or better. Always

FIGURE 36-9 New pilot bearing.

replace the pilot bearing when replacing the clutch—even if the pilot bearing seems to be in good condition. The cost of replacing it is very small compared to the work required to replace it if it fails at a later date. Also, check that the clutch friction disc fits into the flywheel recess and does not contact the attaching bolts.

The next step is to install two guide studs in the top two clutch attaching holes. Test fit the clutch friction disc into the flywheel recess using the clutch alignment tool to center the disc. Make sure the correct side of the disc is facing the flywheel. As shown in FIGURE 36-10, clutch friction discs are stamped with either "flywheel side" or "pressure plate side" indications, so be sure to install the discs in the correct orientation. There should be absolutely no contact between the disc hub and the flywheel or attaching bolts.

Install a clutch alignment tool through the clutch cover and install the disc on the tool splines.

Slide the alignment tool through the clutch cover and the clutch disc and then install the disc and the clutch cover/pressure plate assembly using the previously installed guide pins. To support the cover assembly, be sure the pilot of the alignment tool enters the pilot bearing bore. Then install six attaching bolts in the open clutch attaching holes until they are finger tight (tightened by hand without using a tool). Remove the guide studs and replace them with the other two attaching bolts, again, finger tight.

Now, use an appropriate tool to tighten the bolts in a crisscross pattern starting with one of the bottom bolts. Using a crisscross pattern to tighten the bolts allows the cover to be drawn in evenly without causing warping of the pressure plate. When all bolts are tight, torque them to the manufacturer's specification, again using a crisscross pattern starting with one of the bottom bolts.

Once the plate is tightened, the alignment tool can be removed, as the clamped pressure plate will hold the friction disc(s) in place. It may be necessary to tap the end of the tool with a rubber mallet to loosen it. Run the alignment tool into and out of mesh with the splines in the disc and the pilot bearing bore to ensure it does not hang up That final check ensures that the transmission input shaft will slide easily into place.

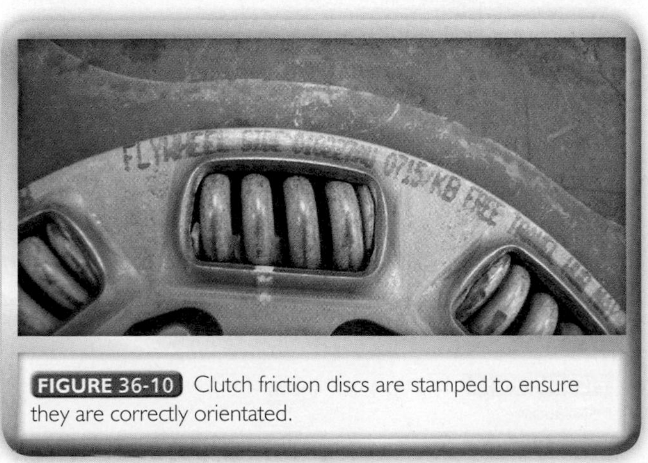

FIGURE 36-10 Clutch friction discs are stamped to ensure they are correctly orientated.

> **TECHNICIAN TIP**
>
> Some medium duty push-type coil spring clutches may have wooden shipping blocks installed between the release levers and the clutch cover, as shown in FIGURE 36-11. These blocks will be loosened as the clutch cover is tightened to the flywheel. If they do not fall out by themselves, make sure you remove these blocks after installing the clutch cover.
>
> 
>
> FIGURE 36-11 Remove wooden shipping blocks after installing the clutch.

Installing a 14" (35.6 cm) Dual Disc Pull-Type Clutch

Different types of clutches have different installation processes. For a 14" (35.6 cm) dual disc pull-type clutch, start by installing a new pilot bearing with a high temperature Viton seal or better. As with other clutch types, it is important to always replace the pilot bearing during clutch service on the 14" (35.6 cm) dual disc pull-type clutch because the cost of replacing the bearing at this point is lower than the labor cost required to replace it later.

Next, install two guide studs in the top two clutch attaching bolt holes in the flywheel. Identify and test fit in the flywheel recess, the clutch friction disc (single disc clutch), or the forward clutch friction disc (dual disc clutches). Use a clutch alignment tool to center the disc and temporarily install the disc in the recess. As shown in FIGURE 36-12, the disc will be marked "flywheel" side or "intermediate plate" side. Make sure you install the disc in the correct orientation, and then rotate the disc.

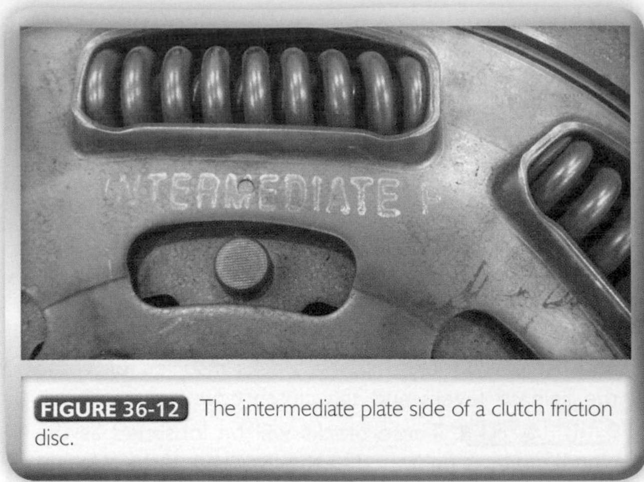

FIGURE 36-12 The intermediate plate side of a clutch friction disc.

There should be absolutely no contact between the disc and the flywheel or bolts.

With this style of flywheel, you can leave the disc where it is supported by the alignment tool. Then install the intermediate plate over the drive pins. Certain heavy-duty 14" (35.6 cm) intermediate plates require three anti-rattle springs to be installed. **Anti-rattle springs** stop the intermediate plate from rattling when the clutch is disengaged. If your clutch has these, install them now. Space them equally around the intermediate plate between the drive pins. The round edge of the anti-rattle springs' openings must point toward the flywheel, as shown in FIGURE 36-13.

Safety

The anti-rattle springs are placed between each pair of drive pins, with the semi-circular opening toward the engine flywheel. These springs are very sharp and must be pushed into place. Wear heavy gloves while installing them to avoid cuts.

FIGURE 36-13 Anti-rattle springs used on super-duty 14" (36.6 cm) clutches with pot-style flywheels.

Remove the alignment tool and install the rear friction disc with the side marked "intermediate plate" or "pressure plate" correctly orientated. Then reinstall the alignment tool through both discs. Be certain the tool pilot goes into the pilot bearing inner race. Slide the clutch cover over the alignment tool and the previously installed guide pins and install six attaching bolts in the open attaching holes and finger tighten them. Remove the guide studs, replace them with the other two attaching bolts, and, again, finger tighten them.

Tighten the bolts in a crisscross pattern starting with one of the bottom bolts to prevent warping of the pressure plate. When all the bolts are tight, as shown in FIGURE 36-14, torque them to OEM specifications in the same crisscross pattern. As the cover is drawn in, the two 5/8" (15.88 mm) shipping blocks beneath the release bearing, shown in FIGURE 36-15, should fall out. If they do not, use the yoke tool to move the release bearing until they drop out.

FIGURE 36-14 Always torque the attaching bolts to manufacturer's specification.

FIGURE 36-15 Ensure any shipping blocks are removed after installation.

The alignment tool can now be removed, as the clamped pressure plate will hold the friction discs in place. It may be necessary to tap the end of the tool with a rubber mallet to loosen it. Once again, run the alignment tool into and out of mesh with the splines in the discs and the pilot bearing race to ensure it is not hanging up.

Installing a 15.5" (39.4 cm) Dual Disc Pull-Type Clutch

Although there are many similarities in installing a 14" (35.6 cm) and a 15.5" (39.4 cm) dual disc pull-type clutch, it is important to recognize the difference in weight. A 15.5" (39.4 cm) clutch is extremely heavy and the use of a clutch jack is strongly recommended. Serious injury could result from trying to install this clutch alone without the use of a clutch jack.

Installing a 15.5" inch clutch is almost the same procedure as a 14" clutch but there are some differences. As with the 14" (36.6 cm) dual disc pull-type clutch, start by installing a new pilot bearing with a high temperature Viton seal or better. Then proceed to installing two guide studs in the top two clutch attaching holes. Once again, test fit the clutch friction disc into the flywheel recess using the clutch alignment tool to center the disc, making sure the correct side of the disc is facing the flywheel and that there is absolutely no contact between the friction disc hub and the flywheel recess or the flywheel attaching bolts.

Because the larger clutch requires a jack, first install the correct alignment spline on the jack. Then install the release bearing and clutch cover over the alignment spline. Continue by installing the rear friction disc on the alignment spline. Make sure the side stamped "pressure plate" goes toward the clutch cover. Next, install the intermediate plate and check that it moves smoothly into and out of the clutch cover drive slots, as shown in FIGURE 36-16. Always test fit the intermediate plate in the clutch cover drive slots; failure to do so could lead to a clutch that does not release properly.

FIGURE 36-16 Drive slots on the intermediate plate.

Install the front friction disc with the side marked "flywheel" toward the engine flywheel. Using the jack, raise the complete clutch into position and slide the clutch cover over the two guide studs, ensuring that the alignment tool pilot enters the pilot bearing bore in the flywheel.

Install six attaching bolts in the open attaching holes and finger tighten them. Remove the guide studs and replace them with the other two attaching bolts, again finger tightening them. Using an appropriate tool, continue tightening the bolts in a crisscross pattern, starting with one of the bottom bolts. Once all the bolts are tight, torque them to OEM specifications in the same crisscross pattern. Again, make sure that the wooden shipping blocks, like those shown in FIGURE 36-17, fall out. If they do not, use a release bearing pulling tool to move the bearing until they do.

The alignment tool and jack can now be removed because the clamped pressure plate will hold the friction discs in place. If needed, tap the end of the tool with a rubber mallet to loosen the alignment tool. Run the alignment tool into and out of mesh with the splines in the discs and the pilot bearing bore to ensure it is not hanging up.

Lightly tap the positive separator roll pins, shown in FIGURE 36-18, through the access holes in the clutch cover to ensure that the pins are flush against the flywheel. There is one pin in each intermediate plate drive lug. This ensures that there will be equal space on both sides of the intermediate plate when the clutch is disengaged.

FIGURE 36-17 Shipping blocks should be removed after installation.

FIGURE 36-18 The positive separator pins must be flush against the flywheel after installation is complete. **A.** Separator pin. **B.** Access hole. **C.** Intermediate plate. **D.** Flywheel.

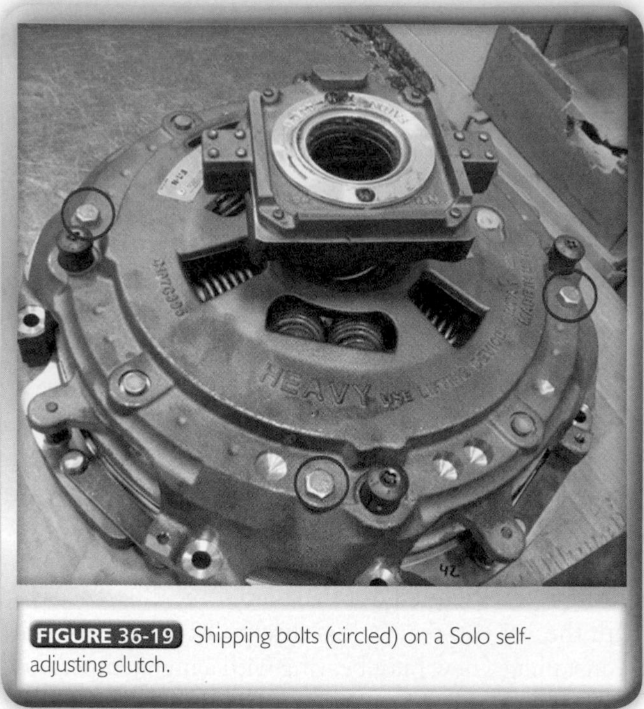

FIGURE 36-19 Shipping bolts (circled) on a Solo self-adjusting clutch.

Pull-type clutches are the most popular clutch type used in heavy-duty trucks, as these vehicles normally have non-synchronized transmissions. Using a pull-type clutch allows the use of a clutch brake that is necessary with these transmissions. To adjust a pull-type clutch, follow the steps in SKILL DRILL 36-8.

Installing Self-Adjusting Clutches

The Eaton Solo clutch, SACH's Twin XTend, and the Meritor AutoJust are types of self-adjusting clutches common in the trucking industry today. These clutches have an automatic adjusting system that relies on pressure plate movement to cause an adjustment. These clutches are packaged with shipping bolts, installed like those pictured in FIGURE 36-19. The bolts hold the pressure plate in a certain location and prevent any movement of the adjusting mechanisms.

These clutches are installed in exactly the same manner as other dual disc clutches with one exception. After the covers have been torqued to the flywheel, the shipping bolts must be removed in order for the clutch to operate. On both types, the shipping bolts are four yellow-colored or tagged bolts installed in the clutch cover. Do not remove the clutch alignment tool until these bolts are removed. While these bolts are holding the pressure plate caged or in the released position, the clutch discs can move out of alignment.

When a self-adjusting clutch is removed, the shipping bolts must be installed before the cover attaching bolts are loosened. Otherwise the clutch will over adjust and/or the pressure plate may be damaged. Keep the bolts from new installations for future use when you have to remove one of these clutches.

Reinstalling the Transmission

Reinstalling the transmission can be accomplished by following the steps listed in Skill Drill 36-5 in reverse. It is recommended that you start by installing a new torque limiting clutch brake on the input shaft, ensuring that the larger diameter side is toward the transmission bearing cover. Installing the transmission when a pull-type clutch is used requires that the release fork be rotated enough so it will pass over the release bearing as the transmission is mating up to the flywheel housing. Do not raise

SKILL DRILL 36-8 Adjusting a Pull-Type Clutch

1. Remove the clutch bell housing inspection cover. Bump the engine over until the clutch adjusting mechanism is in line with the opening.
2. Insert a .010" feeler gauge between the clutch brake and the transmission front bearing cover. Have an assistant depress the clutch pedal as far as it will go while you clamp the feeler gauge.
3. Have your assistant measure and record the distance the clutch pedal is from the floor of the cab.
4. Tell the assistant to slowly let the pedal up until you can pull the feeler gauge from between the clutch brake and the bearing cover. Then tell him/her to stop and measure the pedal distance from the floor again.
5. The difference between the two measurements is the clutch brake squeeze dimension. It should be between 0.5" and 1" (1.27–2.54 cm). If this dimension is correct, a linkage adjustment is not required. (A linkage adjustment is very rarely required on a pull-type clutch.)
6. Check the distance between the back of the release bearing and the clutch brake. This release bearing free travel dimension should be approximately 0.5" (1.27 cm). As the clutch disc wears, that dimension will increase.
7. To adjust the clutch for wear and reduce the release bearing free travel dimension, have an assistant hold the clutch pedal down to release the clutch clamp load. Use a wrench to push down on the quick adjust bolt (Photo A) if equipped, and turn the bolt clockwise 1/2 turn. Then let the pedal up and recheck the release bearing free travel dimension as in step 6. Always ensure that the quick-adjust bolt returns to the out (locked) position after adjustment is complete. (Note: If the clutch does not have a quick-adjust bolt, remove the lock strap, and turn the large adjusting ring clockwise one notch at a time while your assistant holds the clutch pedal down. Then recheck the dimension.)
8. After correcting the release bearing free travel dimension to be 0.5" (1.27 cm), check that the clearance between the release fork fingers and the contact patches on the release bearing is 1/8" (3.2 mm). (This dimension gets smaller as the clutch disc wears and will have gotten larger as the release bearing free travel dimension is corrected for wear.) If this dimension is not correct and the release bearing free travel is, then a linkage adjustment may be required. Be aware that increasing the fork-to-bearing clearance by adjusting the linkage will decrease the clutch brake squeeze dimension and vice versa.
9. Lubricate the release bearing until lubricant purges out the back of the bearing sleeve onto the input shaft. Reinstall the inspection cover.
10. Measure and record the pedal free travel in the cab. (Note: Some hydraulic actuation systems will have little or no pedal free travel.) This measurement is the normal pedal free travel. Inform the driver to have the clutch readjusted when this dimension decreases by half.

the fork to the fully horizontal position as it may contact the clutch cover, damaging the fork or the cover. Some technicians will use the release lever on the outside of the transmission as a tool to pull the transmission into the flywheel housing. This is an acceptable procedure for a normal clutch. However, if you are installing a Eaton Solo, SACH's Twin XTend, or a Meritor AutoJust clutch, you may cause the adjusting mechanism to actuate, leading to an over-adjusted clutch that will not disengage.

Once the transmission is installed, follow the clutch adjustment procedures outlined at the beginning of this chapter.

TECHNICIAN TIP

Place the transmission into gear prior to installing it. That way, you will be able to turn the input shaft to line up the splines by turning the output yoke. Never let the transmission hang unsupported in the disc splines. Even slight warping of the disc hub can cause disengagement problems and damage the input shaft bearing. Never pull the transmission in with the attaching bolts. The transmission should fit snugly to the flywheel housing with little effort. If it does not slide in smoothly, stop! Investigate the cause and correct it before proceeding.

Wrap-up

Ready for Review

- Proper and timely clutch maintenance can go a long way to extending clutch life. Clutches should be inspected and adjusted as per manufacturer's maintenance schedule.
- Adjusting push-type clutches involves adjust the clutch actuating mechanism to re-establish free pedal or release fork clearance.
- Adjusting pull-type clutches usually does not require any linkage adjustment. The clutch is adjusted internally to re-establish release bearing free travel and release fork clearance.
- Some newer hydraulic clutch actuation systems run with no clutch pedal free play. Always check the manufacturer's maintenance instructions.
- Release bearing free travel is the distance the release bearing moves while releasing the clutch on a pull-type clutch. This dimension gets larger as the clutch discs wear.
- The most common cause of premature clutch failure is excessive heat. While a clutch is engaged and not slipping, heat is basically non-existent. But if the clutch slips or the driver allows the clutch to slip too much during engagement and disengagement, the clutch will fail rapidly.
- When replacing a clutch, always follow manufacturer's procedures, which are usually available online or in written service manuals.
- When removing and installing the transmission, it is essential to keep it horizontal to the crankshaft centerline. If the transmission is allowed to hang unsupported, it can damage the input shaft splines, the clutch discs, and/or the transmission input bearing.
- Self-adjusting clutches have shipping bolts, usually yellow or tagged yellow, to cage the pressure plate. These bolts must be removed after the clutch is installed and before the disc alignment tool is removed.
- All clutch components should be inspected prior to the new clutch being installed. Pay attention to cross-shafts and bushing, input shaft splines, release forks, and pivots.
- Always replace the pilot bearing and the release bearing (push-type clutches). Their cost is far outweighed by the cost of having to again remove the transmission to replace them later.
- Dial indicator checks should be performed on the flywheel friction surface, the pilot bearing bore, the flywheel housing face, and the flywheel housing pilot. Also, check the clutch bell housing on the transmission for excessive wear.
- Always check that the new clutch discs fit freely on the transmission input shaft splines before the clutch is installed.
- Clutches are heavy. Using of guide studs can prevent you from dropping the clutch. These studs will hold the clutch in place as you remove the rest of the bolts and also as you re-install the clutch. Guide studs can be made easily by cutting the heads off bolts, or they can be purchased from tool suppliers.
- Most manufacturers recommend using a clutch jack to remove and install heavy clutches. The use of a clutch jack can make the job a lot easier, but not many shops will have them. Always ask for assistance if you require it.

Vocabulary Builder

adjusting ring A large threaded ring in the clutch cover of a pull-type clutch used to adjust the clutch internally.

anti-rattle springs Flat springs used to stop the intermediate plate from rattling on a 14" (36.6 cm) double-disc clutch with a pot-style flywheel.

clutch alignment tool A tool that holds the clutch discs in alignment as the clutch is installed and without which it is impossible to slide the transmission input shaft through the new clutch discs.

clutch bell housing The housing surrounding the clutch that bolts to the flywheel housing.

clutch bell housing pilot A small protrusion on the front of the clutch bell housing that fits into a mating recess in the flywheel housing.

clutch brake actuation The point of clutch pedal actuation on a pull-type clutch when the clutch brake is being actuated or squeezed. Also called *squeeze*.

clutch chatter The condition of the clutch alternately engaging and slipping quite rapidly when the driver engages the clutch.

clutch jack A tool with a clutch alignment tool that fits into the clutch, used to carry the weight of the clutch for installation or removal.

clutch linkage The mechanical connection between the drivers clutch pedal and the clutch cross shaft.

cross-shaft A rotating shaft that holds the clutch release fork.

flywheel friction surface The flat friction surface of the flywheel face.

flywheel housing The round housing bolted to the rear of the engine to which the clutch bell housing is bolted.

flywheel housing face The part of the flywheel housing that mates to the clutch bell housing.

flywheel housing pilot A small recess in the flywheel housing that receives the clutch bell housing pilot.

free play Clearance between two components

guide studs Long threaded studs that stop a component from falling while the attaching bolts are removed.

locking tang A small flat piece of metal that stops the large internal adjusting ring from moving when the clutch is operating.

movable cam rings Rings used in self-adjusting clutches and that take up the space of the threaded adjusting ring in the clutch cover.

pilot bearing bore The hole in the center of the flywheel that holds the pilot bearing.

pressure bleeder A device that bleeds a hydraulic system by pressurizing the fluid

quick-adjust A small mechanism used to turn the large adjusting ring in the clutch cover when adjustment is required.

release bearing free travel The distance the release bearing moves while releasing the clutch in a pull-type clutch.

sealed release bearing A release bearing with no grease nipple or zerk.

shift lever and tower The shift lever and the tower that connects it to the transmission

shipping blocks Wooden blocks that support the release bearing and cage the pressure plate on pull-type clutches.

shipping bolts Bolts used to cage the pressure plate of self-adjusting clutches, such as the Eaton Solo and the SACHs Twin Xtend.

slip yoke A splined tube that allows for driveshaft length changes.

squeeze The point of clutch pedal actuation on a pull-type clutch when the clutch brake is being actuated or squeezed. Also called *clutch brake actuation*.

total indicated runout (TIR) The difference between the high and low measurement of a flat surface, such as the flywheel friction surface.

vocation The type of service a vehicle is involved in.

Review Questions

1. Which of the following would be a driving condition most likely to cause a clutch to "burst," or throw the facings off the clutch disc?
   a. Coasting in gear with the clutch engaged
   b. Coasting in gear with the clutch disengaged
   c. Shock loading the clutch
   d. Excessive torsional vibrations

2. Normally, a properly adjusted pull-type clutch should have how much clearance at the release fork?
   a. ¼" (6.36 mm) clearance between the release fork fingers and the release bearing
   b. ½" (12.7 mm) clearance between the release fork fingers and the release bearing
   c. ¾" (19.05 mm) clearance between the release fork fingers and the release bearing
   d. ⅛" (3.18 mm) clearance between the release fork fingers and the release bearing

3. Normally speaking, pull-type clutch release bearing free travel is adjusted internally and should be which of the following dimensions?
   a. ¾" to 1" (19.05 to 25.4 mm)
   b. ¼" to ¾" (6.36 to 19.05 mm)
   c. 1" to 1 ¼" (25.4 to 31.75 mm)
   d. ½" to 9/16" (12.7 to 14.29 mm)

4. A clutch that has too much free play can cause which of the following?
   a. Wear on the clutch release fork
   b. Gear clash
   c. Clutch slippage
   d. All of the choices are correct.

5. Allowing the transmission to hang down while removing it can cause which of the following?
   a. Damage to the clutch disc hub
   b. Damage to the input shaft splines
   c. Damage to the transmission input bearing
   d. All of the choices are correct.

6. Flywheel housing face total indicated runout cannot exceed which of the following?
   a. 0.005" (0.127 mm)
   b. 0.0005" (0.0127 mm)
   c. 0.001" (0.025 mm) per inch (25.4 mm) of housing diameter
   d. 0.008" (0.203 mm)

7. The total indicated runout for the pilot bearing bore should not exceed which of the following?
   a. 0.005" (0.127 mm)
   b. 0.008" (0.203 mm)
   c. 0.0005" (0.0127 mm)
   d. 0.0005" (0.0127 mm) per inch (25.4 mm) of flywheel diameter

8. A driver reports that the free pedal in his cab is only half as much as it used to be. What could be the problem?
   a. The clutch release bearing is seized.
   b. The torsional springs are damaged.
   c. The clutch is likely overheating.
   d. This is a normal condition caused by clutch disk wear.

9. Which of the following components transfers torque from the clutch cover to the pressure plate in most diaphragm spring type clutches?
   a. Drive straps
   b. Cast lugs that protrude through the clutch cover
   c. The diaphragm spring
   d. The input shaft

10. An important purpose of the drive straps used in a clutch is to:
    a. provide higher clutch capacity.
    b. increase clutch slip on engagement.
    c. pull the pressure plate away from the clutch disk.
    d. absorb torsional vibrations.

ASE-Type Questions

1. Technician A says that, when installing clutch discs, heavy grease should be used on the input shaft splines so the discs do not "hang up." Technician B says doing so can cause grease contamination of the discs and it is not recommended. Who is correct?
   a. Technician A
   b. Technician B
   c. Both Technician A and Technician B
   d. Neither Technician A nor Technician B
2. Technician A says that angle spring pull-type clutches are adjusted by turning the large adjustment ring in the clutch cover. Technician B says that the adjustment will change the clutch brake squeeze dimension. Who is correct?
   a. Technician A
   b. Technician B
   c. Both Technician A and Technician B
   d. Neither Technician A nor Technician B
3. Technician A says that clutch brake squeeze should occur in the last inch (25.4 mm) of clutch pedal travel near the floor. Technician B says that clutch brake squeeze can be altered by a linkage adjustment. Who is correct?
   a. Technician A
   b. Technician B
   c. Both Technician A and Technician B
   d. Neither Technician A nor Technician B
4. Technician A says that a pull-type clutch with mechanical linkage should have 0.125" (3.2 mm) free play between the release fork and the release bearing. Technician B says that a pull-type clutch release bearing free travel dimension should be at least 0.5" (1.27 cm). Who is correct?
   a. Technician A
   b. Technician B
   c. Both Technician A and Technician B
   d. Neither Technician A nor Technician B
5. Technician A says that if there is no free play at the fork on a pull-type clutch with mechanical linkage, premature clutch wear out is possible. Technician B says that some hydraulically actuated clutches are designed to operate with no fork to release bearing clearance. Who is correct?
   a. Technician A
   b. Technician B
   c. Both Technician A and Technician B
   d. Neither Technician A nor Technician B
6. Technician A says that the primary cause of premature clutch failure is excessive heat. Technician B says that driver skill can greatly affect clutch life. Who is correct?
   a. Technician A
   b. Technician B
   c. Both Technician A and Technician B
   d. Neither Technician A nor Technician B
7. Technician A sees significant wear on the clutch bell housing face and recommends its replacement. Technician B states that wear in this location is normal and does not require replacement. Who is correct?
   a. Technician A
   b. Technician B
   c. Both Technician A and Technician B
   d. Neither Technician A nor Technician B
8. Technician A says that riding the clutch pedal can cause bent drive straps. Technician B says that bent or warped drive straps are caused by shock loading the driveline. Who is correct?
   a. Technician A
   b. Technician B
   c. Both Technician A and Technician B
   d. Neither Technician A nor Technician B
9. Technician A says that coasting with the clutch disengaged is a bad driving practice. Technician B says that using the clutch brake to hold a vehicle on a hill is a safe practice. Who is correct?
   a. Technician A
   b. Technician B
   c. Both Technician A and Technician B
   d. Neither Technician A nor Technician B
10. Technician A says that Eaton Solo clutches can be adjusted manually when required. Technician B says that Eaton Solo clutches are self-adjusting. Who is correct?
    a. Technician A
    b. Technician B
    c. Both Technician A and Technician B
    d. Neither Technician A nor Technician B

CHAPTER 37

NATEF Tasks

There are no specific NATEF tasks for this chapter.

Knowledge Objectives

After reading this chapter, you will be able to:

1. Describe the interaction of gears in mesh. (pp 1195–1196)
2. Explain the involute tooth profile and its significance. (pp 1196–1197)
3. Explain gear backlash and its importance. (pp 1197–1198)
4. Calculate simple and compound gear ratios. (pp 1198–1200)
5. Calculate speed and torque increases and decreases using the gear ratio. (pp 1198–1200)
6. Explain overdrive and underdrive ratios and the changes they cause in speed and torque. (p 1199)
7. Identify and describe the characteristics of spur gears. (pp 1201–1202)
8. Identify and describe the characteristics of helical gears. (pp 1202–1203)
9. Explain the advantages and disadvantages of various gearing types. (pp 1201–1205)

Basic Gearing Concepts

Skills Objectives

There are no skill objectives for this chapter.

Introduction

In order to properly diagnose and repair gear systems, technicians must have a fundamental knowledge of gearing concepts. Gears are essential to the operation of any vehicle. Gears are found in a vehicle's engine, transmission, and drive axle. The correct functioning of those gears makes the vehicle move. The basic function of a gear is to transfer torque and motion to gain mechanical advantage to either increase output power or increase output speed. **Torque** is the twisting force generated by the engine. **Mechanical advantage** is anything that allows us to move greater distances or weight with less effort.

There are many different types of gears, but all of them share common basic terms and principles. FIGURE 37-1 shows a cutaway of a typical standard transmission exposing the gearing.

FIGURE 37-1 A six-speed Fuller single countershaft transmission.

Historically, the first gears were simple wooden peg gears. As illustrated in FIGURE 37-2, one wheel of wood would have pegs installed perpendicular to its axis and these pegs would mesh with another wheel of wood on which the pegs were installed in parallel to its axis. The intermeshed pegs of the driving wheel would cause the driven wheel to turn. Motion could be transferred in this way.

As the pegs begin to mesh, however, the outer end of the driving peg contacts the driven peg first. As they continue through mesh, the driving peg will slide along the driven peg until the centers of the two wheels align. At that point, the driving peg will slide back out until it leaves mesh.

With pegs sliding in and out of mesh, the distance from the center of the driving wheels axis to the point of contact of the driven wheel's pegs is constantly changing. The constant change causes the driven wheel to turn faster at the longer contact points and slower at the shorter contact points. As a result, the speed of the driven wheel is also constantly changing.

You Are the Technician

A truck is brought to your repair shop and the driver complains that he feels a significant vibration throughout the truck in first gear that seems to get worse as he drives faster. Once he shifts into second gear, the vibration goes away. You check the transmission fluid and although the level is correct you notice the fluid has a silvery look. You recommend removing the transmission and its shift cover for a closer inspection of the components.

1. Would you recommend replacing the transmission bearings?
2. Would you inspect the gearing for wear?
3. What would you look for in the transmission to find the root of this problem?

Changing speeds would have little effect on a system such as a grain miller's grindstone being turned with a slow-moving water wheel. As speed increases, however, the constantly changing speed would become a serious vibration. Imagine what that would mean for a vehicle. It would be totally unacceptable! The whole vehicle would be trying to speed up and slow down constantly. Imagine the vibration that would result!

Modern gears are specially formed to eliminate this anomaly, so the driven gear operates at a consistent speed. This chapter will discuss basic gearing terminology and explain the construction and operation or gears in basic, universal terms. The chapter will not, however, discuss gear failure analysis. Gear failure is discussed in relevant chapters and sections on the vehicle systems that use gears.

Fundamentals of Gears

Because gears are such a foundational part of the mechanics of vehicle systems, it is important to understand how they are designed and made, how they interact, and how their ratios determine their functionality.

Gear Design

Gears can be made from a variety of metals. In medium- and heavy-duty vehicles, gears are typically made from **cast ductile iron** because it is ductile (bendable) rather than brittle. Gears can also be made of steel and undergo various methods of surface hardening. **Hardening** is a manufacturing process that makes the surface of a gear much harder than its core. Typically the surface is hardened to a depth of not more than 0.050" (1.2 mm). The idea is to produce a gear with a surface hard enough to withstand the extreme pressures that come from the sliding and then rolling contact that gear teeth are subjected to. At the same time that the exterior of the gear must be extremely hard, the gear's core must be more ductile so that it can resist fracture and absorb shock loads.

Gear Nomenclature

All gears can be described with a core set of terminology. As you read this section, consult the labeled illustration of gears shown in FIGURE 37-3.

The basic structure of the gear is its teeth, which, much as you might imagine, are the protrusions on the gear face. The apex of the tooth is called the **top land**. The **tooth face** is the area that actually comes into contact with a mating gear. The tooth face is parallel to the gear's axis of rotation. The upper portion of the tooth contact area is called the **addendum** and the lower portion of this area is called the **dedendum**.

The **root** (also called **fillet radius**) of a gear is the bottom of the valley formed between two teeth. The precise design of the fillet radius provides a gradual change in section and determines the shape of the formed tooth. The root minimizes stress risers (possible break points) to make the tooth stronger. The **root diameter** of a gear is the smallest circle of the gear measured at the fillet radius, or root, of the teeth.

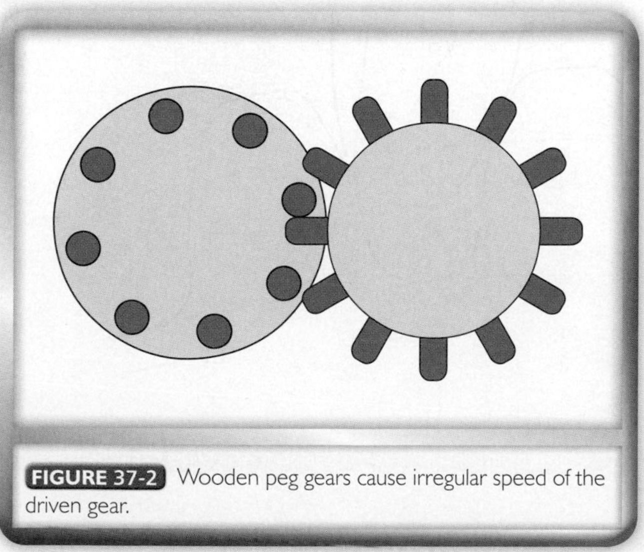

FIGURE 37-2 Wooden peg gears cause irregular speed of the driven gear.

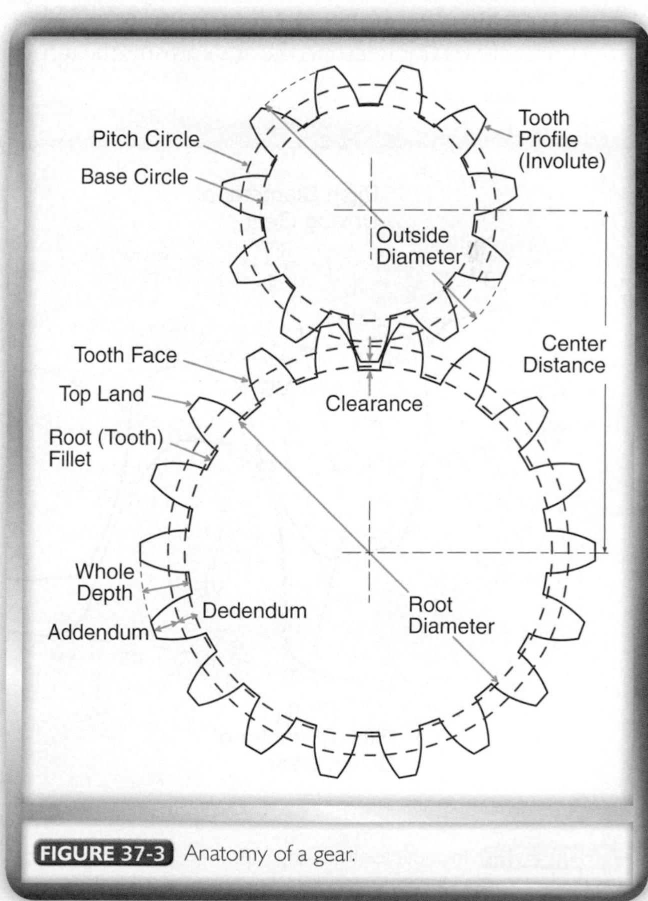

FIGURE 37-3 Anatomy of a gear.

Gear Face Contact During Mesh

As teeth on a gear engage, or mesh, with a mating gear, the contact starts at the addendum of the driven gear tooth and the dedendum of the driving gear tooth. The gears then slide into full mesh where the sliding motion stops and only rolling motion occurs between them. Then the gears slide out of mesh. At that point, contact ends between the dedendum of the driven gear tooth and the addendum of the driving tooth. The average contact point of a given tooth is its **pitch diameter** (also called the **pitch circle**). The pitch circle is the theoretical point where only rolling motion exists. The pitch diameter is usually a point approximately half way up the tooth face from the fillet radius to the top land.

A gear's **pitch** is determined by the number of teeth per unit of diameter measured at the pitch circle of the gear. For example, a gear with 60 teeth and a pitch diameter of 10" (25.4 cm) is a 6 pitch gear. This is important because only gears of the same pitch can mesh together properly. That means our example gear could only be in mesh with another 6 pitch gear.

Involute Tooth Shape

Modern gears are designed with a special tooth shape called an **involute** that compensates for the changing point of contact between gears as they rotate through mesh. On an involute tooth, the dedendum (the lower part of the tooth) is thicker than the addendum (the upper part of the tooth). This special shape is how we eliminate the speed changes noted in the introduction. Let's follow two teeth in contact through mesh and see how this is done. FIGURE 37-4 illustrates this process.

As the driving tooth comes into mesh with the driven tooth, the dedendum (thicker part) of the driving tooth comes in contact with the addendum (thinner part) of the driven tooth. As the meshing continues, the driving tooth slides down the face of the driven tooth. That slide shortens the distance from the axis of the driving gear to the point of contact of the driving tooth—just as it did in the peg wheel example described in the introduction. As the driving tooth slides into mesh, the point of contact is moving toward the thicker part of the driven tooth. The thickening causes a minute acceleration of the driven gear, canceling out the deceleration caused by the changing point of contact.

This action continues until the point of contact reaches the pitch line where there is no more sliding contact, only rolling contact. As mesh continues, the reverse happens. The point of contact slightly lengthens. As the contact point of the driving tooth slides up to its addendum (thinner part), a minute deceleration cancels out the acceleration caused by the increasing distance from the driving gear centerline.

What does all that mean? It means that, as the teeth go through mesh, the speed of the driven gear will remain consistent rather than speeding up and slowing down.

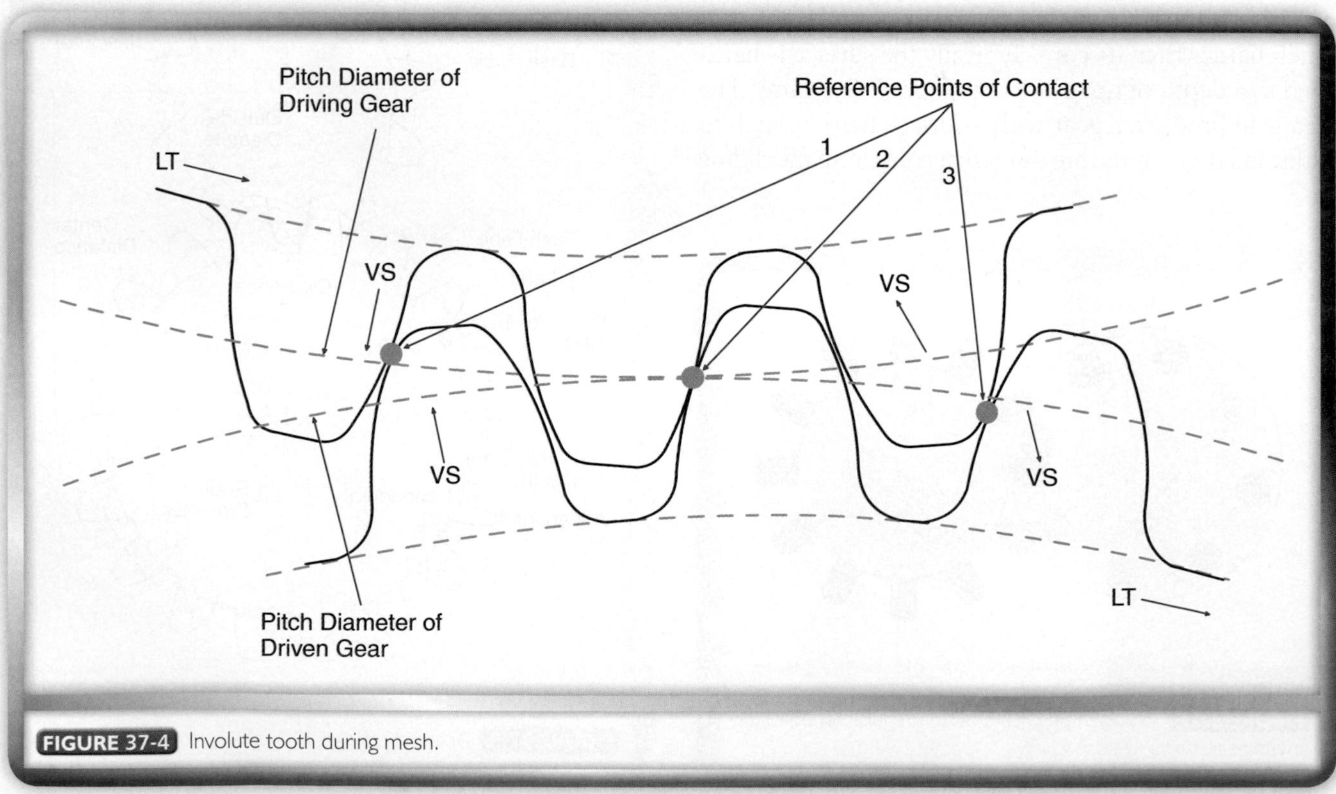

FIGURE 37-4 Involute tooth during mesh.

It is important for the technician to understand that any change in the involute shape or axial positioning of the gears caused by wear may cause this speed oscillation of the driven gear. In high-speed equipment (such as a vehicle), this speed oscillation will manifest as a vibration. Left unchecked, that vibration can cause catastrophic damage to the component—and, really to any component connected to it—because of the constant torsional stress caused by the speed changes.

Direction of Rotation

Gear rotation is described based on how the gear is moving when the flat face of the gear is viewed from the top. Rotation is normally referred to as **clockwise** when the viewed face on the gear moves to the right from the top. Rotation is **counterclockwise** when the viewed face on the gear moves to the left from the top. Clockwise rotation is usually referred to as forward rotation and counterclockwise rotation as reverse rotation.

When two external toothed gears, such as the ones shown in FIGURE 37-5, are in mesh with each other, the driven gear will turn in the opposite direction to the drive gear. Not all gears are externally toothed, however. Some gears have internally facing teeth and are called ring gears or internal gears. When a gear with external teeth is in mesh with a ring or internal gear, the driven gear will rotate in the same direction as the drive gear, as shown in FIGURE 37-6.

Gear Interaction

Gears can be mounted in many positions to accomplish the desired result. In medium- and heavy-duty vehicles, the most common mounting of gear sets is side by side on parallel axes. A notable exception to this is bevel gears, which are normally mounted at 90 degrees to each other. Gears must be mounted so that they have a certain amount of **backlash**, or the clearance between the teeth of gears in mesh. As shown in FIGURE 37-7, backlash allows for a thin layer of lubricant between the tooth contact surfaces and for expansion of the gears due to heat. Backlash must be closely controlled. Too little backlash will not allow lubricant in between teeth—leading to failure. Too much backlash can allow the gears to climb out of mesh and slip—again leading to failure. Backlash is controlled by tooth design or by moving the gears' axis closer together or further apart.

The simplest form of a gear is the lever. As shown in FIGURE 37-8, the **lever** is a simple machine that allows a large object to be moved with less force. **Simple machines** are the simplest mechanisms that allow us to gain mechanical advantage. A first-class lever has an effort arm, a load arm, and the fulcrum in the middle. Gears are essentially levers—the effort arm is the distance from the tooth face to the center of the gear's axis of rotation.

Gears have clearly evolved since the lever. As two gears in mesh rotate, the driving gear applies force or

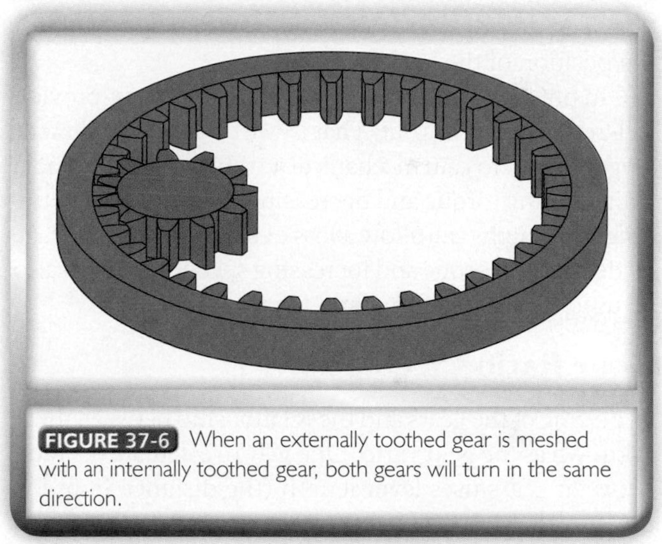

FIGURE 37-6 When an externally toothed gear is meshed with an internally toothed gear, both gears will turn in the same direction.

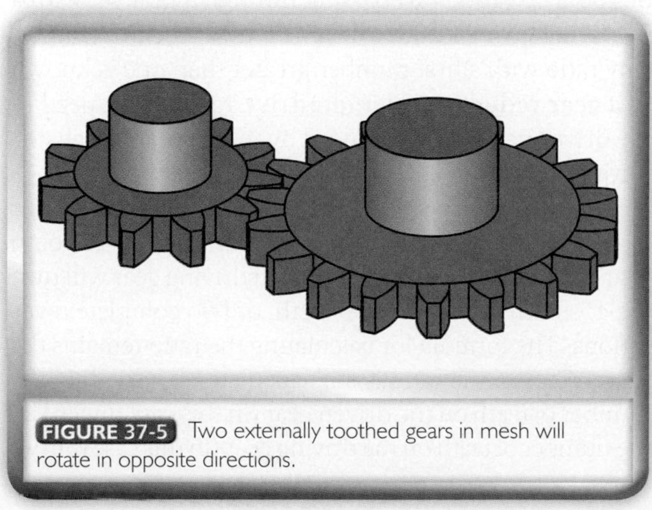

FIGURE 37-5 Two externally toothed gears in mesh will rotate in opposite directions.

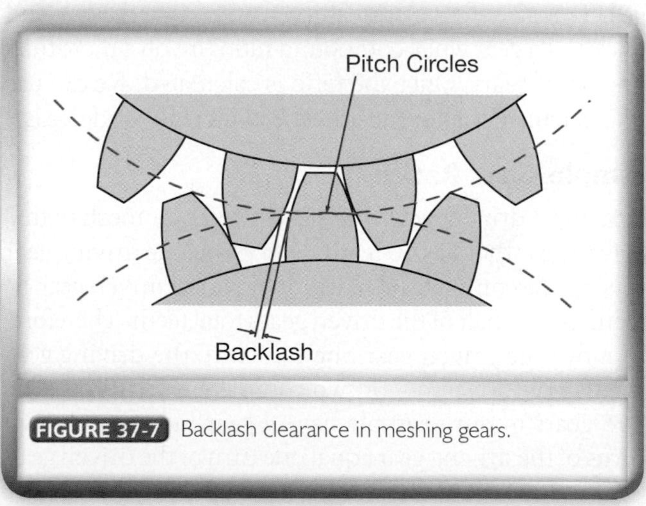

FIGURE 37-7 Backlash clearance in meshing gears.

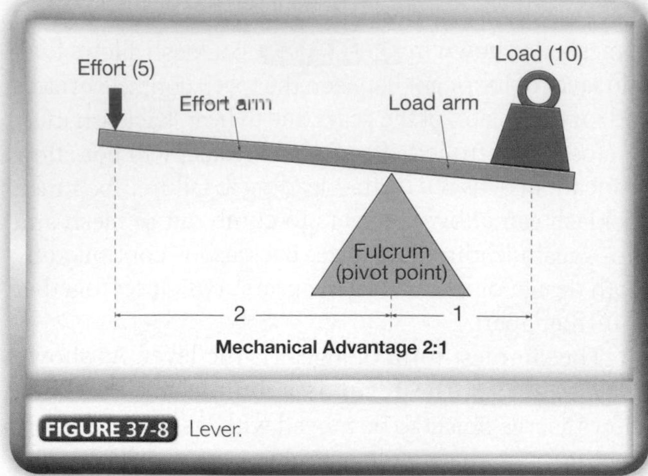

FIGURE 37-8 Lever.

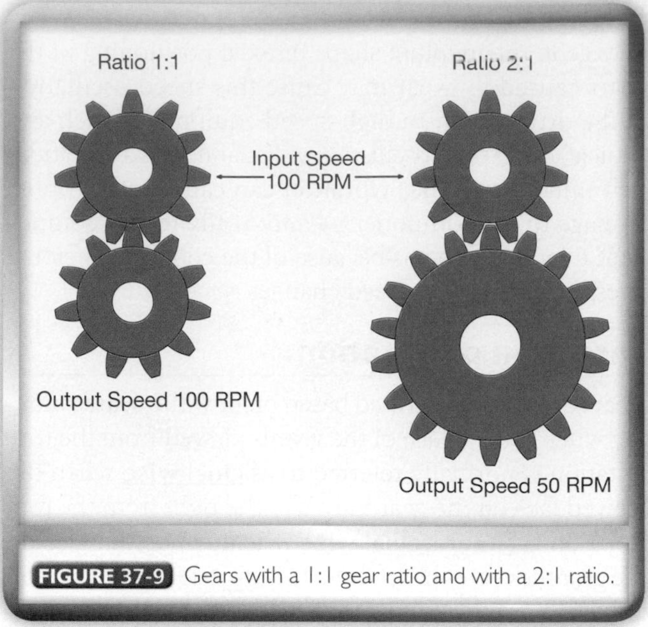

FIGURE 37-9 Gears with a 1:1 gear ratio and with a 2:1 ratio.

effort to each of the gear teeth in sequence. If we look at just one tooth through the body of the gear, we see that the distance from the tooth to the center of the gear or shaft becomes the effort arm of the lever. The center of the gear, or shaft, is the fulcrum. The load is represented by the weight on the gear or shaft that is resisting its rotation. The driving gear is, of course, a lever also but with the position of the load reversed.

In practice, different lengths of these "levers" provide different levels of output. That is, we can use the different lengths either to gain mechanical advantage—for example by increasing torque and decreasing speed. Likewise, the different lengths can allow a loss of mechanical advantage by decreasing torque and increasing speed. Gears can also be used to transfer speed and torque unchanged.

Gear Ratio Calculations

The sizing of the gears and the relationship between them is known as the **gear ratio**. One way to calculate the ratio between gears uses lever length (the distance from the center of the gears axis to the tooth contact point). A much simpler method uses the number of gear teeth. Simple gear ratios are the relationship between one driving and one driven gear while compound ratios involve more than one set of gears. Once the ratio is calculated, we can use it to calculate the torque and speed increase or decrease.

Simple Gear Ratios

Imagine a driving gear that has 15 teeth in mesh with a driven gear that has 30 teeth. Every time the driving gear rotates one complete turn, it will move the driven gear 15 teeth, or one half of the driven gears total teeth. Therefore, to move the driven gear one full turn, the driving gear must move 30 teeth—or two complete revolutions. The two gears in our example have a gear ratio of 2:1. Two turns of the driving gear equal one turn of the driven gear. This ratio is illustrated in FIGURE 37-9.

The formula to calculate this ratio is simple. Divide the number of teeth on the driven gear by the number of teeth on the drive gear:

$$30 / 15 = 2$$

The ratio is always compared to one revolution of the driven gear. Therefore, the 2 revolutions of the driving gear becomes 2 to 1 and is expressed 2:1.

What does this ratio accomplish? The ratio does two things. First, it is responsible for slowing down the speed of the driven gear. The speed of the driven gear will be the speed of the driving gear divided by the ratio. In our example, that means the driven gear will turn only half as fast as the driving gear.

Second, and more importantly, gear ratios are responsible for producing mechanical advantage. The mechanical advantage is the effort applied by the driving gear multiplied by the ratio. For example, a driving gear torque of 100 ft-lb (136 Nm) passing through a gear set with a 2:1 ratio becomes 200 ft-lb (271 Nm) at the driven gear. Any ratio with a first number greater than one is known as a **gear reduction** or **underdrive ratio**. The speed of the driven gear will be reduced by the ratio, but available torque will be increased by the same proportion.

But what happens if we reverse the two gears in our example and have the 30-tooth gear driving the 15-tooth gear? Every rotation of the 30-tooth driving gear will turn the 15-tooth driven gear 30 teeth, or two complete revolutions. The formula for calculating the ratio remains the same. That is, the ratio is still calculated by dividing the number of teeth on the driven gear (in this case fifteen) by the number of teeth on the driving gear (in this case thirty):

$$15 / 30 = 0.5$$

As with our earlier example, the ratio is always compared to one revolution of the driven gear. The 0.5 becomes 0.5 to 1 or 0.5:1. What does this ratio accomplish? Again, the ratio does two things. First, it now speeds up the driven gear. That is, the speed of the driven gear will be the speed of the driving gear divided by the ratio. That means the driven gear will turn twice as fast as the driving gear.

By gaining speed, however, we give up mechanical advantage. The torque available at the driven gear is the torque available at the driving gear multiplied by the ratio. So, 100 ft-lb (136 Nm) of driving torque becomes 100 × 0.5 or 50 ft-lb (68 Nm) of torque at the driven gear. Any ratio in which the first number is less than one is known as an **overdrive ratio**. In gears with an overdrive ratio, the speed of the driven gear will be increased by the ratio, but available torque will be decreased by a corresponding amount.

Let's walk through the basic ratio, gear speed, and torque calculations for a simple gear arrangement. As we go through the calculations, we will make the following assumptions:

- The drive gear has 20 teeth
- The driven gear has 60 teeth
- Input torque on the drive gear is 100 ft-lb (136 Nm)
- Input speed is 300 rpm

Let's begin finding the gear ratio by dividing the number of teeth on the driven gear by the number of teeth on the drive gear:

$$60 / 20 = 3$$

$$3 : 1$$

That means the gear ratio is 3:1. Because 3 > 1, 3:1 is a reduction, or underdrive, ratio.

Next, let's calculate the torque available at the driven gear by multiplying the input torque by the gear ratio:

3 × 100 = 300 ft-lb (407 Nm) of torque available to the driven gear

Notice how the calculations prove the basic premise that reduction gears increase output torque. The gear ratio of 3:1 is a reduction ratio, and the torque output is higher than the torque input.

The next calculation we perform is to find the speed of the driven gear. To accomplish that, we need to divide the input speed by the ratio:

300 rpm / 3 = 100 rpm

As we would expect, our underdrive gear ratio has caused a decrease in output speed.

Compound Ratios

In most applications there will be more than one set of gears involved in the transfer of speed and torque. When we have a ratio with more than one pair of gears involved it is called a **compound ratio**.

Let us examine briefly how compound ratios work. Consider the first gear power flow in a typical transmission. In this transmission, we will assume the input gear has 27 teeth, and it drives a countershaft driven gear with 51 teeth. The countershaft first gear has 13 teeth, and it drives the main shaft first gear which has 64 teeth. To summarize:

- Input drive gear has 27 teeth
- Driven countershaft gear has 51 teeth
- Countershaft first drive gear has 13 teeth
- Driven main shaft gear has 64 teeth

Following our formula, we divide the first driven gear by the first driving gear.

$$51 / 27 = 1.8888/1$$

$$1.89 : 1$$

Our gear ratio, therefore, is 1.89:1. This means that the input gear has to turn 1.89 times to turn the countershaft once.

Next, we calculate the ratio for the second set of gears. The second driven gear has 64 teeth and its driving gear has 13 teeth.

$$64 / 13 = 4.9230/1$$

$$4.92 : 1$$

So, the countershaft has to turn 4.92 times to turn the main shaft one complete turn.

If the input shaft has to turn 1.89 times to turn the countershaft once, and the countershaft has to turn 4.92 times to turn the main shaft once, to find the overall ratio we have to multiply how many times the input shaft must turn by how many times the countershaft must turn. Therefore,

$$1.89 \times 4.92 = 9.30$$

We see then that, in order to turn the main shaft one complete revolution the input shaft must turn 9.30 times. That means the total (compound) ratio of this scenario is 9.30:1.

Compound ratios can often involve four, six, or even more gears in the transfer of power. Calculating ratios with that many gears is more simply done by dividing the product of all of the driven gears (all of the driven gears multiplied together), D, by the product of all of the drive gears (all of the drive gears multiplied together), d. The formula for six gears would look like this:

$$\frac{D_1 \times D_2 \times D_3}{d_1 \times d_2 \times d_3}$$

Let's apply this formula to a transmission setup where the input gear has 27 teeth and it drives a countershaft driven gear with 51 teeth, the countershaft first gear has 13 teeth, and it drives the main shaft first gear which has 64 teeth.

To calculate the compound ratio for that setup, we first multiply together the number of teeth on each of the driven gears:

$$51 \times 64 = 3264$$

Next, we multiply together the number of teeth on each of the driving gears:

$$27 \times 13 = 351$$

Finally, we divide the total of the driven gears by the total of the driving gears.

$$3264 / 351 = 9.299$$

$$9.3 : 1$$

Ratios are usually rounded after two decimals, so this result would be a compound ratio of 9.30 to 1, or 9.30:1. Because 9.3 > 1, this compound ratio is a reduction or underdrive. Therefore, the input shaft must turn 9.30 times for every one turn of the transmission main shaft. Available torque at the main shaft will be input torque multiplied by the ratio. That means the available torque at the main shaft will be 9.30 times greater than the input torque. The output speed on the main shaft, however, will be the input speed divided by the ratio, or 9.30 times slower.

The same formula can be used no matter how many gear sets are involved in a ratio. It simply becomes a larger calculation with the number of teeth on each driven gear multiplied together divided by the number of teeth on each of the drive gears multiplied together. **FIGURE 37-10** illustrates how compound ratios work.

In most vehicle systems, gears sets are used in combination to produce the desired gear ratio to move the vehicle. For example, any underdrive or overdrive ratio through a transmission will have at least two ratios working together:

- The ratio of the input gear to the countershaft driven gear
- The ratio of the countershaft speed, or range gear, to its corresponding main shaft speed or range gear

Those two gears ratios combine to create a compound ratio.

Not all gears are overdrive or underdrive, however. When gears with exactly the same number of teeth are meshed, the resulting ratio is 1 to 1 (or 1:1). In this case, the gears transmit the exact speed of rotation, and torque remains unchanged.

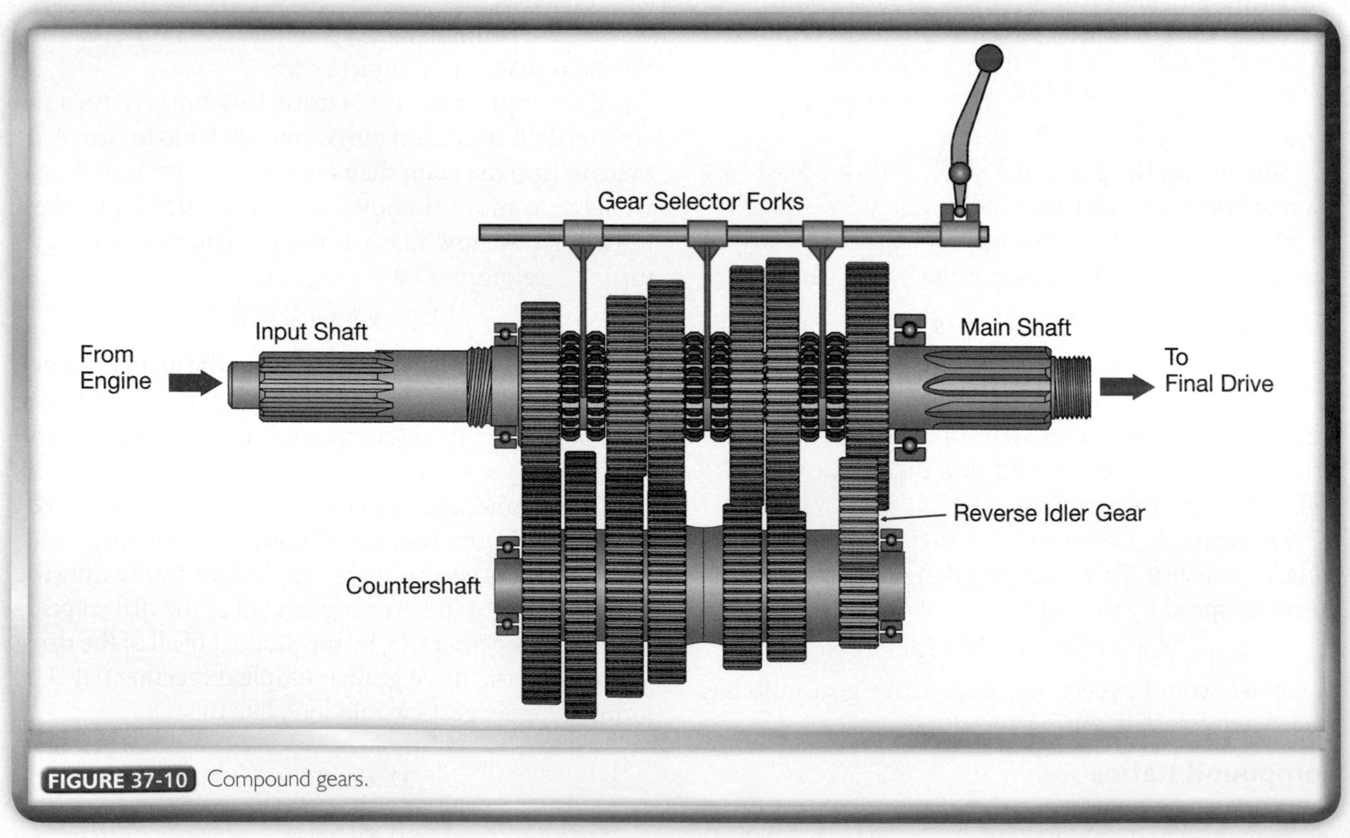

FIGURE 37-10 Compound gears.

Types of Gears

As you might expect, today's vehicles use many different types of gears in their various systems and engines. In this section, we will discuss idler, spur, helical, herringbone, bevel, worm, and rack-and-pinion gears.

Idler Gears

The gears used in most medium- and heavy-duty vehicle standard transmissions are almost exclusively externally toothed gears meshed together. When two externally toothed gears are in mesh, the driven gear will turn in the reverse direction to the drive gear. That direction suits our purpose well for all gears except reverse.

By following the power flow, we can see how this works for us. The engine turns clockwise when viewed from the front. So, too, does the transmission input shaft because it is connected to the engine through the clutch. The input shaft gear drives the countershaft driven gear counterclockwise. (That's why we call it a countershaft.) The countershaft first gear is part of the countershaft and so is also turning counterclockwise. Countershaft first gear is in mesh with the main shaft (output shaft) first gear. Therefore, the main shaft gear is driven in a clockwise direction, and the vehicle moves forward. These flow directions are repeated for the rest of the transmission gear ranges.

In reverse, however, we must turn the output shaft counterclockwise to move backward. To do this, we use an idler gear. The purpose of idler gears is to act as a bridge between two gears and reverse the direction of rotation without changing the ratio. **Idler gears** are used in transmissions to drive a vehicle backward. As shown in FIGURE 37-11, an idler gear is placed in the power flow between the countershaft reverse drive gear and the main shaft reverse gear. When the vehicle is in reverse, the input (countershaft) gear is turning counterclockwise. That causes the reverse idler gear to turn clockwise, which in turn makes the output (reverse main shaft) gear turn counterclockwise as well. The vehicle, then, moves backward.

An idler is both a driven gear and a drive gear. An idler gear is driven by the countershaft reverse gear, and the idler gear drives the main shaft reverse gear. Because the idler gear functions in both of those capacities, it has no bearing on gear ratios.

To illustrate this point, let's use the same numbers we used for first gear ratio calculation in the Gear Ratio Calculation section. This time, however, we will insert a 9-tooth idler gear into the first gear power flow and make it reverse.

FIGURE 37-11 An idler gear.

Recall our assumptions:

- Input drive gear has 27 teeth
- Driven countershaft gear has 51 teeth
- Countershaft first drive gear has 13 teeth
- Driven main shaft gear has 64 teeth
- Our newly introduced idler gear has 9 teeth
- Reverse gear main shaft has 64 teeth

First, we take the number of teeth on each of the driven gears and multiply them together:

$$51 \times 9 \times 64 = 29{,}376$$

Next, we take the number of teeth on each of the drive gears and multiply them together:

$$27 \times 9 \times 13 = 3{,}159$$

Remember that the idler gear drives the main shaft reverse gear so it is also a drive gear.

Now we divide the product of all the driven teeth by the product of all the drive teeth. That is,

$$29{,}376 / 3159 = 9.299$$

$$9.3 : 1$$

That result, 9.3: 1, is the exact same ratio that we had in the earlier calculation. Because an idler gear is both a drive and a driven gear, it cancels itself out in the calculation. Therefore, idler gears do not need to be included when calculating gear ratios.

Spur Gears

Spur gears are the simplest of modern gears used in vehicles today. As shown in FIGURE 37-12, a **spur gear** has teeth that are cut parallel to the gears axis of rotation. The advantages of spur gears are numerous. Spur gears are simpler and therefore less expensive to manufacture. Their shafts can be mounted on simple ball or roller

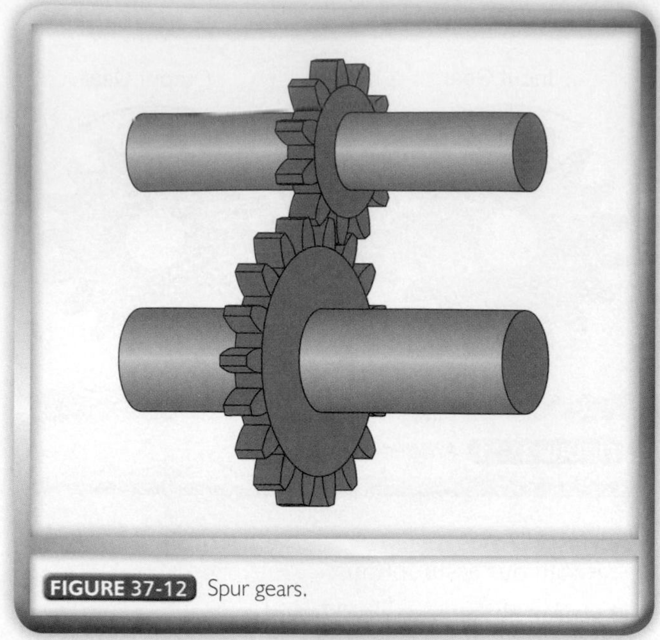

FIGURE 37-12 Spur gears.

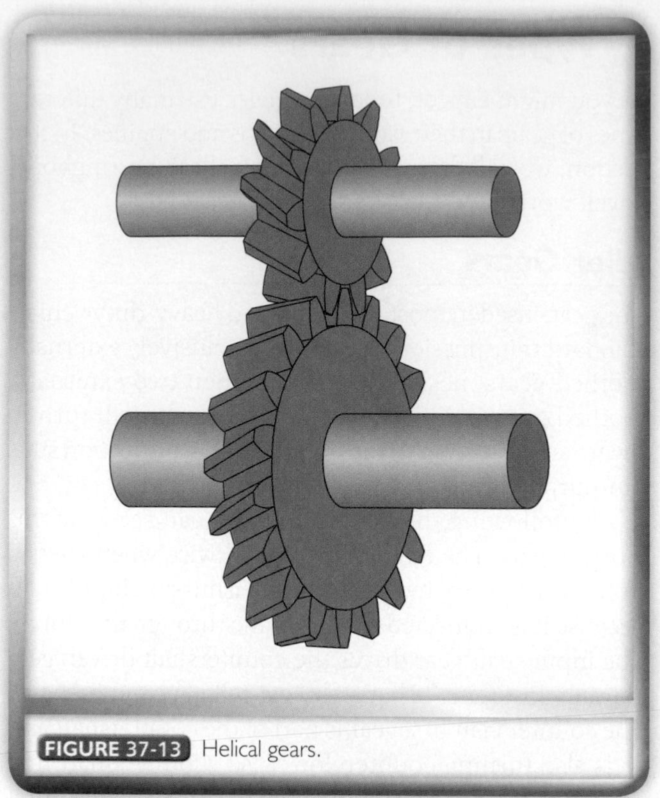

FIGURE 37-13 Helical gears.

bearings, which allows for less expensive manufacture of components. In addition, spur gears do not produce any axial thrust when they are in operation. **Axial thrust** is thrust that tries to move the gears apart along their axis. Spur gears in mesh merely produce **radial thrust**. That is, they tend to want to push away from each other radially, or perpendicular to their axis.

Spur gears do, however, have some disadvantages. First, spur gears tend to be noisy in operation. As spur gear teeth come into mesh with each other, their meshing teeth tend to impact each other, causing a clicking sound. At higher speeds, the clicking becomes a high-pitched whine. For that reason, spur gears are seldom used in light-duty vehicle manufacture. Spur gear whine may be heard when a vehicle with standard transmission is operated in reverse. Despite the whine, spur gears are commonly used for reverse gear in automobiles because the reverse gear train is usually operated for only short periods and at relatively slow speeds.

Another disadvantage of spur gears is that only one or two teeth are in mesh at any given time. That causes all of the torque transfer to be carried by those one or two teeth. Consequently, the gear must be made larger or thicker so that one tooth can carry the load alone.

Helical Gears

Helical gears have teeth that are cut spirally in reference to their axis of rotation. The design of a helical gear, such as the one shown in FIGURE 37-13, allows some advantages. First, when helical gears mesh, there is always more than one tooth in mesh at a time. As a result, helical gears do not make the characteristic whining noise that spur gears do. As the next set of teeth is coming into mesh, they do not click together. The effect is more of sliding motion as the teeth engage. Consequently, helical gears are much quieter in operation than spur gears.

Another advantage of helical gears is their strength. Because more than one or two teeth are in mesh at once, the individual teeth on a helical gear do not have to carry as much torque. Therefore, helical gears are stronger than equivalently sized spur gears. Furthermore, the design of helical gears allows gear width to be reduced with no loss of torque capacity. Transmission cases can be shorter and lighter in overall weight. Helical gears are manufactured with either left-hand helix or a right-hand helix. To determine the hand, look at a helical gear from the top. A left-hand helix appears to move down to the left, and a right-hand helix appears to move down to the right.

When used together in side-by-side applications, a left-hand gear must mesh with a right-hand gear. When mounted at right angles to each other, however, two right-hand or two left-hand helices will mesh, as shown in FIGURE 37-14. This arrangement allows the power to turn a 90-degree corner.

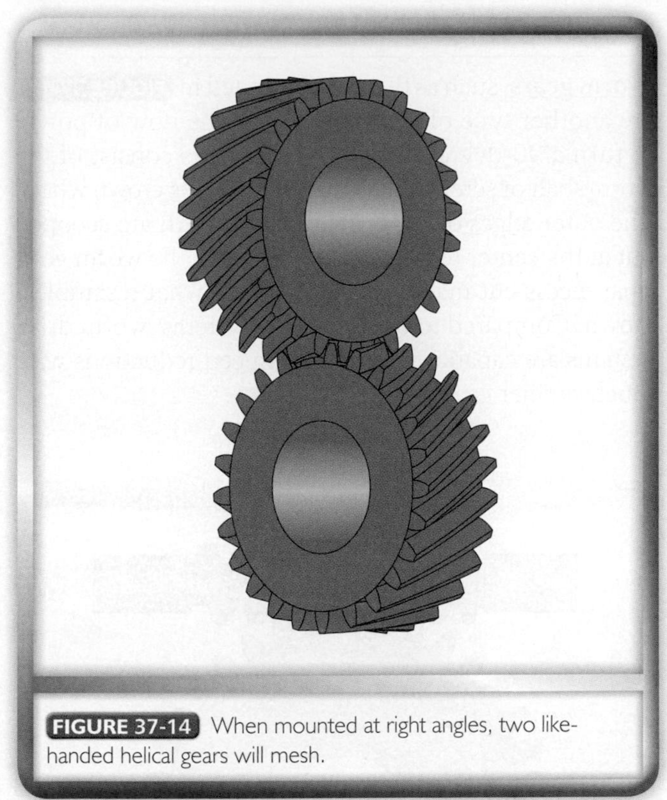

FIGURE 37-14 When mounted at right angles, two like-handed helical gears will mesh.

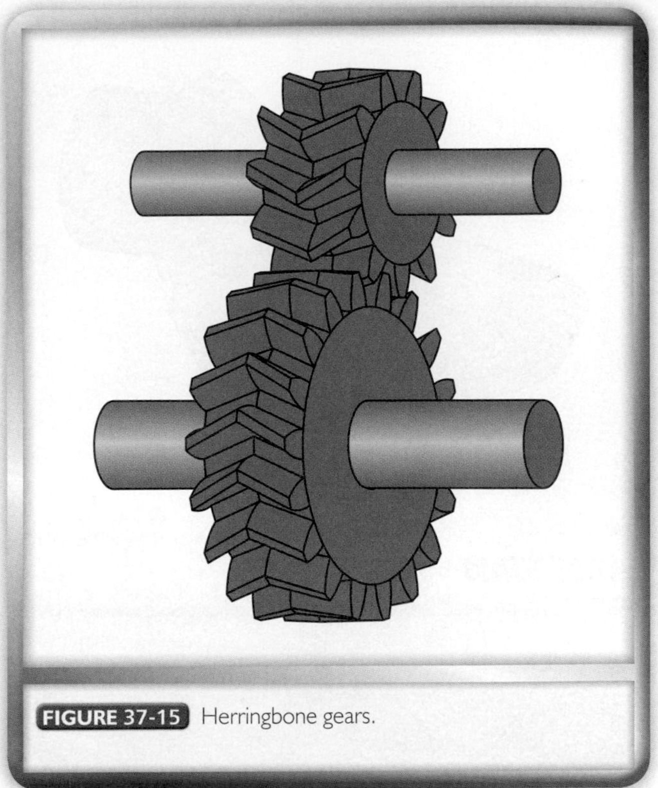

FIGURE 37-15 Herringbone gears.

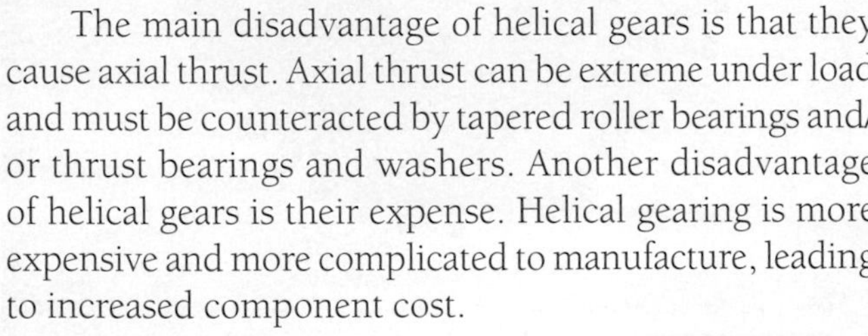

The main disadvantage of helical gears is that they cause axial thrust. Axial thrust can be extreme under load and must be counteracted by tapered roller bearings and/or thrust bearings and washers. Another disadvantage of helical gears is their expense. Helical gearing is more expensive and more complicated to manufacture, leading to increased component cost.

Herringbone Gears

Herringbone gears, such as those shown in FIGURE 37-15, have opposite helices on each side of their face. That is, one half of the tooth face is cut with a right-hand helix, and the other half of the tooth face is cut with a left-hand helix. Usually there is a groove cut at the apex of the "V" formed by the two helices to allow trapped lubricant to escape.

The advantages of herringbone gears are the same as helical gears with one key difference. The dual-cut helices on herringbone gears cause all axial thrust to be cancelled out.

These gears are obviously much more expensive to manufacture and, consequently, are not found in most vehicle applications. These gears can carry extreme loads and operate very quietly with no axial thrust. Herringbone gears are used in specialized equipment such as large turbines for generating electricity.

Bevel Gears

Bevel gears are gears cut on an angle and designed to allow the flow of power to turn a corner usually 90 degrees. Therefore, bevel gears are primarily used in drive axles to send rotating force to the drive wheels.

Bevel gears sets can be designed to allow for any degree of turning up to 90 degrees. Bevel gears consist of a cone shaped pinion gear, (a **pinion gear** is a term used to describe a small driving gear), and a ring or "crown" gear. True bevel gearing is similar to spur type gearing in that the teeth are straight cut. Bevel gears have the same inherent advantages and disadvantages of spur type gearing—bevel gears are noisy and generally weaker but cheaper to manufacture. FIGURE 37-16 shows bevel gears.

Spiral bevel gearing attempts to minimize the disadvantages of bevel gears by using helically cut teeth. The spiral bevels helical tooth configuration imparts the advantages of helical gearing to the bevel gear set, making them stronger and quieter, but they are more expensive to manufacture. FIGURE 37-17 shows spiral bevel gears.

Durapoid, hypoid, generoid, and amboid gearing are all design improvements that make spiral bevel gearing stronger and more adaptable to use in drive-axle manufacture. These designs will be discussed in more detail in the Heavy-Duty Truck Drive Axles chapter.

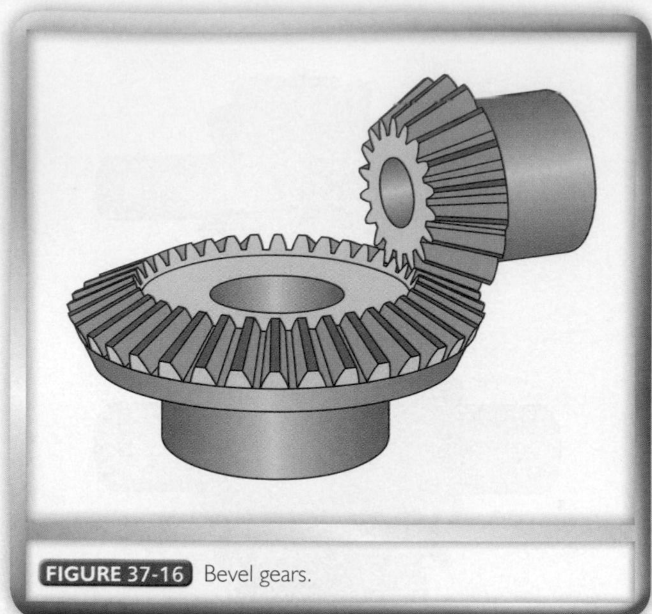
FIGURE 37-16 Bevel gears.

FIGURE 37-17 Spiral bevel gears.

Worm Gears

Worm gears, such as the one illustrated in FIGURE 37-18, are another type of gear that allows the flow of power to turn a 90-degree corner. Worm gears consist of the worm shaft or screw, which meshes with the crown wheel. The outer edges of the crown wheel's teeth are scooped out at the center to allow for the shaft of the worm gear. That recess cut makes the wheel somewhat resemble a crown. Compared to bevel gearing systems, worm drive systems are capable of very large speed reductions with much smaller gears.

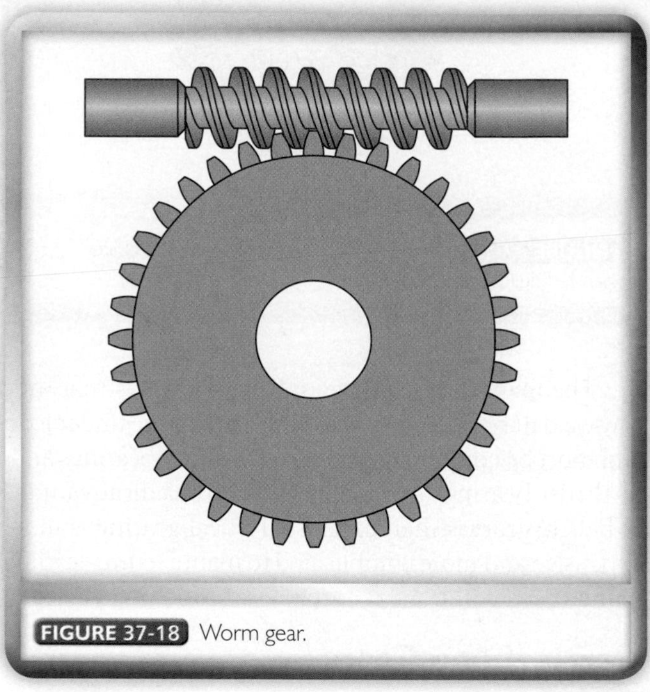
FIGURE 37-18 Worm gear.

The ratio of worm gears is set by changing the number of tooth leads or starts on the worm. With a single-start worm, the driven crown wheel will advance only one tooth with each revolution of the worm. So, a twenty tooth crown gear produces a ratio of 20:1. To achieve that reduction with bevel gears using a twelve-tooth pinion, the crown gear would have to have 240 teeth. (Just imagine the size of such a gear!)

Most worm gears will have a worm with 3 or 4 starts, which will advance the crown gear 3 or 4 teeth per revolution respectively. Worm gears are usually found in various types of machinery that require large reduction ratios.

One interesting feature of these gears is that, when a high ratio is used, the worm can drive the crown wheel easily but extremely high resistance prevents the crown wheel from driving the worm. An example of this feature is the self-locking effect of the machine heads used for adjusting guitar strings.

In the past, worm gears were used in the drive axles of vehicles. At present, worm gears are not used in North American medium- or heavy-duty vehicles.

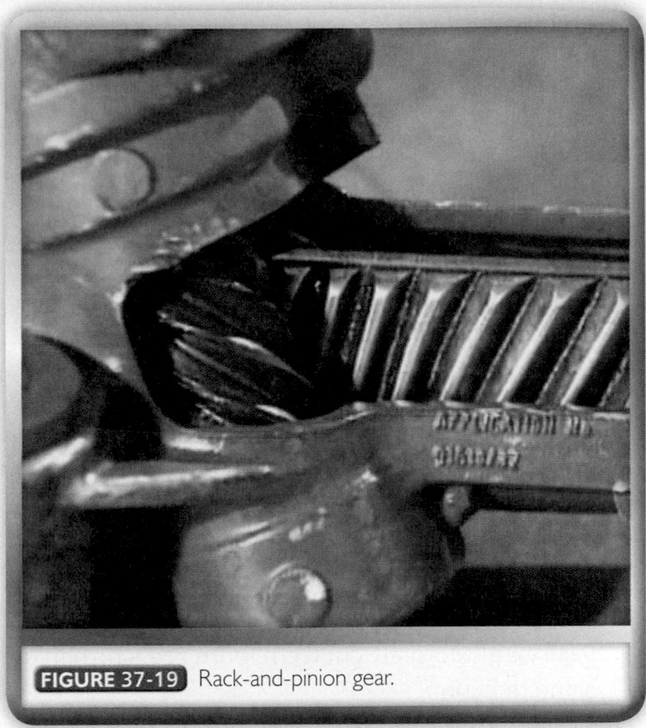

FIGURE 37-19 Rack-and-pinion gear.

Rack-and-Pinion Gears

Rack-and-pinion gears consist of a flat rack with either spur or helically cut teeth on one side and a meshing circular pinion gear. FIGURE 37-19 shows a rack-and-pinion gear. Rotation of the pinion causes the rack to move linearly or horizontally. Rack-and-pinion gears have, until recently, been predominately used in the steering mechanism of front-wheel-drive, light-duty vehicles; however, they are now becoming available in a variety of steering systems on medium- and heavy-duty vehicles as well.

Many combinations of gears are used in vehicle drivelines. As a result, a near infinite number of ratio combinations are possible to achieve the desired results. We can move a 120,000 lb (54,431 kg) load with an engine that produces only 1,500 lb (680 kg) of torque. This is achieved by sacrificing speed for torque using reduction ratios. Alternatively, we can drive a vehicle at highway speeds with an engine that is only turning at 1,400 rpm by sacrificing torque capability for increased speed using overdrive ratios.

Wrap-up

Ready for Review

- Gears are essential to the operation of any mechanized equipment—trucks and buses are no exception.
- Involute gear tooth design compensates for the natural tendency of two gears in mesh to turn at a constantly changing ratio of speed.
- Gear teeth spacing is known as gear pitch. Only gears of the same pitch can run in mesh with each other.
- Gears can have external or internal cut teeth. When externally toothed gears are in mesh, they rotate in opposite directions. A gear with internally cut teeth is known as a ring gear and, when in mesh with a gear with externally cut teeth, both gears turn in the same direction.
- Backlash is the clearance between the teeth of gears in mesh. Backlash is essential for lubrication and expansion but must be tightly controlled to prevent gears slipping over each other's teeth.
- Gear design evolved from the lever—one of the six simple machines. Simple machines allow us to gain mechanical advantage to accomplish a task.
- Gear ratio is the comparison of the input to the output result of gears in mesh. The formula to calculate ratio is the number of teeth on the driven gear divided by the number of teeth on the drive gear. If input torque is known, output torque can be calculated by multiplying input torque by the ratio. Output speed can be calculated by dividing input speed by the gear ratio.
- Compound gear ratios are those that involve more than one set of gears. All ratios where the power flows through a transmission's countershaft are compound ratios. These can be calculated by multiplying all of the driven gears together and dividing that figure by the product of all the drive gears.
- Idler gears are used to change direction of rotation. They have no influence on gear ratio, as they are both a driven gear and a drive gear.
- Spur gears are the simplest gears to manufacture. They have only radial thrust, but they are inherently noisy in operation.
- Helical gears are quieter and stronger than spur gears. Helical gears create both radial and axial thrust, and they are more complex to manufacture. Helical gears can be left handed or right handed.
- Herringbone gears have a left-hand helical cut on one side of the tooth surface and a right-hand helical cut on the other side of the tooth surface. These gears cancel out the axial thrust common to helical gears. The complexity of herringbone gears to manufacture makes them expensive and uncommon.
- Bevel gearing is used wherever a power flow must turn a corner, usually 90 degrees—at the drive axle for example. Straight bevel gearing has the same problem as spur gears in that they are noisy in operation.
- Spiral bevel gearing is quieter and stronger in operation than bevel gearing. Many different types of spiral bevel gears have been developed over the years and are all improvements to basic spiral bevel design.
- Worm gears are capable of extremely large reductions in a very small package. Reductions of 40:1 or even 50:1 can be achieved in relatively small space.
- Rack-and-pinion gears are quite popular as automotive steering systems and are starting to appear in some truck applications as well. This type of gearing gives excellent response when used in vehicle steering.

Vocabulary Builder

addendum The top, thinner part of an involute tooth contact area.

axial thrust Thrust that tries to move the gears apart along their axis.

backlash The clearance between teeth in mesh with each other.

bevel gear Gear cut on an angle allowing a power flow to turn a corner.

cast ductile iron Cast iron that is ductile (bendable) not brittle.

clockwise The clockwise direction of rotation of a gear as you look at it corresponding to the motion of the clock; also known as *forward*.

compound ratio Any gear ratio that involves more than one pair of gears.

counterclockwise The counterclockwise direction of rotation of a gear as you look at it corresponding to the motion of the clock; also known as *backward*.

dedendum The lower, thicker, part of an involute tooth contact area.

fillet radius The radius shape between the bottoms of two teeth. Also called *root*.

gear ratio The relationship between two gears in mesh as a comparison to input versus output.

gear reduction Any gear set that reduces output speed while at the same time increases output torque. Also known as *underdrive ratio*.

hardening A manufacturing process that makes the surface of a gear much harder than its core: typically, the surface is hardened to a depth of not more than 0.050" (1.2 mm).

helical gear A gear with teeth cut on an angle or spirally to its axis of rotation.

herringbone gear A gear cut with opposite helices on each side of the face.

idler gear Gear used in transmissions to drive a vehicle backward.

involute A gear design shape that compensates for the changing point of contact between gears as they rotate through mesh.

lever A simple machine that can allow a large object to be moved with less force.

mechanical advantage Anything that allows us to move greater distances or weight with less effort.

overdrive ratio A ratio that provides a speed increase and output torque decrease.

pinion gear A small driving gear.

pitch The number of teeth per unit of pitch diameter on a gear.

pitch circle The theoretical point on the tooth face halfway between the root and the top land where only rolling motion exists. Also called the *pitch diameter*.

pitch diameter The theoretical point on the tooth face halfway between the root and the top land where only rolling motion exists. Also called the *pitch circle*.

rack-and-pinion gear A gear consisting of a flat rack with either spur or helically cut teeth on one side and a meshing circular pinion gear.

radial thrust Thrust that tries to push gears in mesh apart perpendicular to their axis.

root The radius shape between the bottoms of two teeth. Also called *fillet radius*.

root diameter The smallest circle of the gear measured at the fillet radius (root) of the teeth.

simple machine The simplest mechanism that allows us to gain mechanical advantage.

spiral bevel gearing Bevel gears that are cut helically, making the gear set stronger and quieter.

spur gear A gear with teeth cut parallel to its axis of rotation.

tooth face The area that actually comes into contact with a mating gear and is parallel to the gear's axis of rotation.

top land The apex of a tooth.

torque The twisting force applied to a shaft that may or may not result in motion.

underdrive ratio Any ratio that decreases output speed while increasing output torque. Also known as a *gear reduction*.

worm gear A gear with a helical, threaded shaft that is attached to the steering column and meshes with a ball nut that transfers motion from the steering wheel to the steering linkage. Also called the worm shaft.

Review Questions

1. The input gear in a transmission has 24 teeth, the countershaft driven gear has 40 teeth. First gear countershaft has 12 teeth and main shaft first has 36 teeth. What is the first gear ratio?
   a. 1:5
   b. 0.55:1
   c. 1.8:1
   d. 5:1
2. If input torque is 1000 ft-lb (1356 Nm), how much torque will be present at the output shaft when an input gear having 24 teeth is driving a countershaft driven gear with 48 teeth, and a counter shaft second gear with 45 teeth is driving a main shaft gear with 60 teeth? Round up your answer to two decimals.
   a. 1750 ft-lb (2373 Nm)
   b. 2670 ft-lb (3620 Nm)
   c. 666 ft-lb (903 Nm)
   d. 571 ft-lb (774 Nm)
3. A gear having 48 teeth, which is rotating at a speed of 400 rpm, is driving another gear that has 78 teeth. Approximately how fast is the gear with 78 teeth rotating?
   a. 120 rpm
   b. 400 rpm
   c. 246 rpm
   d. None of the above
4. From which of the simple machines have gears basically evolved?
   a. The screw
   b. The inclined plane
   c. The wedge
   d. The lever
5. What does gear pitch refer to?
   a. The number of teeth per inch (2.54 mm) of pitch diameter
   b. The angle of the gear teeth
   c. The contact point of the gear teeth
   d. The shape of the gear teeth
6. What is the purpose of the involute shape of a gear tooth?
   a. Makes the gear contact smoother
   b. Adds strength to the gear tooth
   c. Makes the gear teeth last longer
   d. Makes the driven gear turn at a steady speed
7. Which of the following is NOT an advantage of helical gears?
   a. Quiet performance
   b. More than one tooth is in mesh at the same time
   c. Reduced axial thrust forces
   d. High strength
8. A gear with teeth machined straight and parallel to the shaft on which they are mounted are known as ________ gears.
   a. spur
   b. amboid
   c. helical
   d. spiral
9. Which of the following is a disadvantage of spur gear sets?
   a. High thrust forces.
   b. Torque losses
   c. Noise
   d. Costly to manufacture
10. Why is backlash required between meshing gears?
    a. Limits coasting whine
    b. Controls climbing
    c. Allows for heat expansion and lubrication of gears
    d. All of the choices are correct.

ASE-Type Questions

1. Tech A says that the gear attached to the input shaft on a countershaft transmission is a drive gear and the gear it meshes with on the countershaft is a driven gear. Tech B says that all the countershaft speed gears are drive gears and all the main shaft speed gears are driven gears. Who is correct?
   a. Technician A
   b. Technician B
   c. Both Technician A and Technician B
   d. Neither Technician A nor Technician B
2. Tech A says a ratio that involves more than one set of gears is known as a compound ratio. Tech B says that the formula to calculate ratio is drive overdriven. Who is correct?
   a. Technician A
   b. Technician B
   c. Both Technician A and Technician B
   d. Neither Technician A nor Technician B
3. Tech A says that all modern gearing uses an involute tooth shape. Tech B says the involute compensates for differing points of contact as a gear goes through mesh. Who is correct?
   a. Technician A
   b. Technician B
   c. Both Technician A and Technician B
   d. Neither Technician A nor Technician B
4. Tech A says that to calculate gear compound ratios you add all the driven gears together and divide by all the drive gears added together. Tech B says that idler gears are not used in gear ratio calculations. Who is correct?
   a. Technician A
   b. Technician B
   c. Both Technician A and Technician B
   d. Neither Technician A nor Technician B
5. Tech A says that externally toothed gears in mesh turn in opposite directions. Tech B says that idler gears are used to change the direction of rotation. Who is correct?
   a. Technician A
   b. Technician B
   c. Both Technician A and Technician B
   d. Neither Technician A nor Technician B
6. Technician A says that the meshing of peg gears causes an uneven speed in the driven gear. Technician B says that the distance between the contact point and the center of peg gears in mesh is constantly changing. Who is correct?
   a. Technician A
   b. Technician B
   c. Both Technician A and Technician B
   d. Neither Technician A nor Technician B
7. Technician A says that an underdrive ratio increases torque. Technician B says that an underdrive ratio creates a speed increase at the output. Who is correct?
   a. Technician A
   b. Technician B
   c. Both Technician A and Technician B
   d. Neither Technician A nor Technician B
8. Technician A says that an overdrive ratio increases torque available at the output shaft. Technician B says that an overdrive ratio is always less than 1:1. Who is correct?
   a. Technician A
   b. Technician B
   c. Both Technician A and Technician B
   d. Neither Technician A nor Technician B
9. Technician A says that bevel gears are used to make a power flow turn a corner. Technician B says that bevel gears are usually found in the drive axle. Who is correct?
   a. Technician A
   b. Technician B
   c. Both Technician A and Technician B
   d. Neither Technician A nor Technician B
10. Technician A says that rack-and-pinon gears are never found on heavy-duty trucks. Technician B says that herringbone gears are not normally used in heavy-duty trucks. Who is correct?
   a. Technician A
   b. Technician B
   c. Both Technician A and Technician B
   d. Neither Technician A nor Technician B

CHAPTER 38

NATEF Tasks

There are no NATEF tasks for this chapter.

Knowledge Objectives

After reading this chapter, you will be able to:

1. Describe standard transmission components using the proper nomenclature. (pp 1212–1214)
2. Explain the operation of various shifting mechanisms. (pp 1212–1214)
3. Explain the various types of transmissions by range selection system including sliding-gear, constant-mesh collar shift (also called sliding clutch or collar), and constant-mesh synchronized. (pp 1215–1216)
4. Describe typical power flows for single countershaft transmissions. (pp 1222–1226)
5. Describe typical power flows for multiple countershaft transmissions. (pp 1229–1230)
6. Explain the purpose and function of auxiliary transmissions. (p 1231)
7. Explain compound power flows through transmissions with auxiliary sections. (pp 1233, 1237)
8. Describe air shifting control systems for transmission auxiliary sections. (p 1243)
9. Explain the purpose and function of transfer cases. (p 1251)
10. Explain the purpose and function of power take-off devices. (p 1252)

Standard Transmissions

Skills Objectives

There are no skills objectives for this chapter.

Introduction

In order to diagnose and repair standard transmissions, a technician must have a firm grasp of basic transmission operating principles and power flows. Transmissions are not overly complex in their design, but they do have a certain mystique about them, as their operating components are hidden from view inside the transmission case.

Every day in North America, trucks are the method of choice to haul materials and products to various markets; in fact, everything that you have in your home or business at one point or another rode on a truck to get there. These truck loads can range from relatively light to extremely heavy—in some cases exceeding 120,000 lb (54,431 kg)! Meanwhile, the largest on-highway truck engines produce only around 2,100 ft-lb (2,847 Nm) of torque. Without the torque multiplication provided by the transmission, moving these loads with 2,100 ft-lb (2,847 Nm) of available torque would be impossible. The transmission, such as the one in **FIGURE 38-1**, is the component that allows us to move these heavy loads with apparent ease by using various gear ratios. This chapter will attempt to open the "box" and allow the technician to view the internal components of the standard transmission as well as learn how they function together.

Fundamentals of Transmissions

The transmission allows us to move extremely heavy loads by using torque multiplication. However, a transmission must also allow us to move loads at speeds that are appropriate for the situation. For example, an off-road vehicle like a bulldozer may only need to move at a maximum of 20 mph (32 kph) to accomplish its function, whereas an on-highway truck must be capable of highway speeds of 65 mph (105 kph) or more.

Careful selection of the transmission can allow us to have the best of both worlds—low-speed pulling power and high-speed operation for highway use. Transmissions are tailored to the vehicle they are installed in to accomplish these goals. For example, an automobile equipped with a standard transmission may have only four or five forward speeds, or gear ranges. That range gives a car

FIGURE 38-1 The right transmission selection will maximize vehicle efficiency.

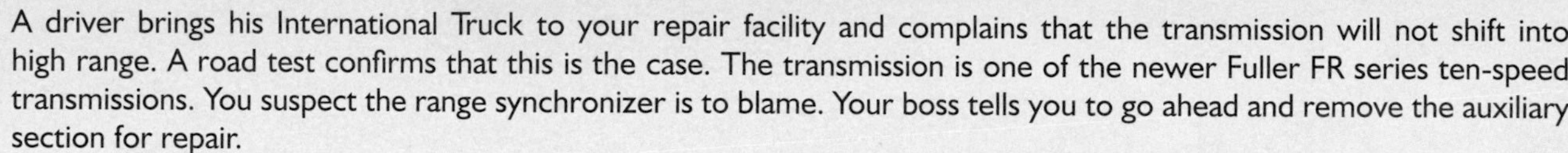

You Are the Technician

A driver brings his International Truck to your repair facility and complains that the transmission will not shift into high range. A road test confirms that this is the case. The transmission is one of the newer Fuller FR series ten-speed transmissions. You suspect the range synchronizer is to blame. Your boss tells you to go ahead and remove the auxiliary section for repair.

1. Is there anything you should do before removing the auxiliary section?
2. What things could cause the synchronizer to fail?
3. What advice should you give to the driver if it is a synchronizer failure?
4. If it is a synchronizer failure, what items would you expect will require replacement?

fairly good low- and high-speed operation. But step into a heavy-duty highway truck, and it likely has 13 or even 18 available forward speeds or gear ranges!

Why so many? The answer lies with the operating range of the engine. Most cars will have a gasoline engine that has an operating range of 3,000 to 4,000 rpm. The diesel engine in the highway truck will have an operating range of 1,000 rpm or less. To operate the truck from a stop to highway speeds, the ratio difference between each gear, or range, to the next available gear, or the **ratio steps**, must be closer together than in the car. The truck engine can only accelerate 800 or 1,000 rpm in each gear, so three or four times the number of steps are needed between low speed and high speed. FIGURE 38-2 shows the gearing in a truck transmission.

FIGURE 38-2 Trucks require transmissions with many more ranges than those required to operate automobiles.

Truck transmissions are specifically selected to match the vocation of the vehicle. Vocation is determined by many different factors. Does the vehicle spend most of its time at city speeds in stop-and-go traffic, or is it primarily an on-highway vehicle? Is the vehicle always heavily loaded or always lightly loaded? Factors like these and more are considered when specifying a vehicle's transmission.

Transmission Shafts

As illustrated in FIGURE 38-3, a basic transmission will have at least four shafts running parallel to each other and installed in a housing known as the transmission case. They are the input shaft, the countershaft, the main shaft or output shaft, and the reverse idler shaft. Engine torque is introduced to the transmission through the clutch disc or discs, which are splined to the input shaft.

The input gear is part of, or splined to, the input shaft. The **input shaft** is the input to the transmission driven by the clutch friction disc. The **countershaft** is the shaft inside the transmission, driven by the input gear. The input gear is in constant mesh with the countershaft driven gear. That is, the gears are always in mesh. The countershaft **range gears** are part of, or keyed to, the countershaft. Consequently, when the input gear turns the countershaft driven gear, all of the countershaft gears turn with it.

Main Shaft

The **main shaft** is the shaft that is driven by the countershaft and provides output for the transmission. For this reason, the main shaft is also called the **output shaft**. The

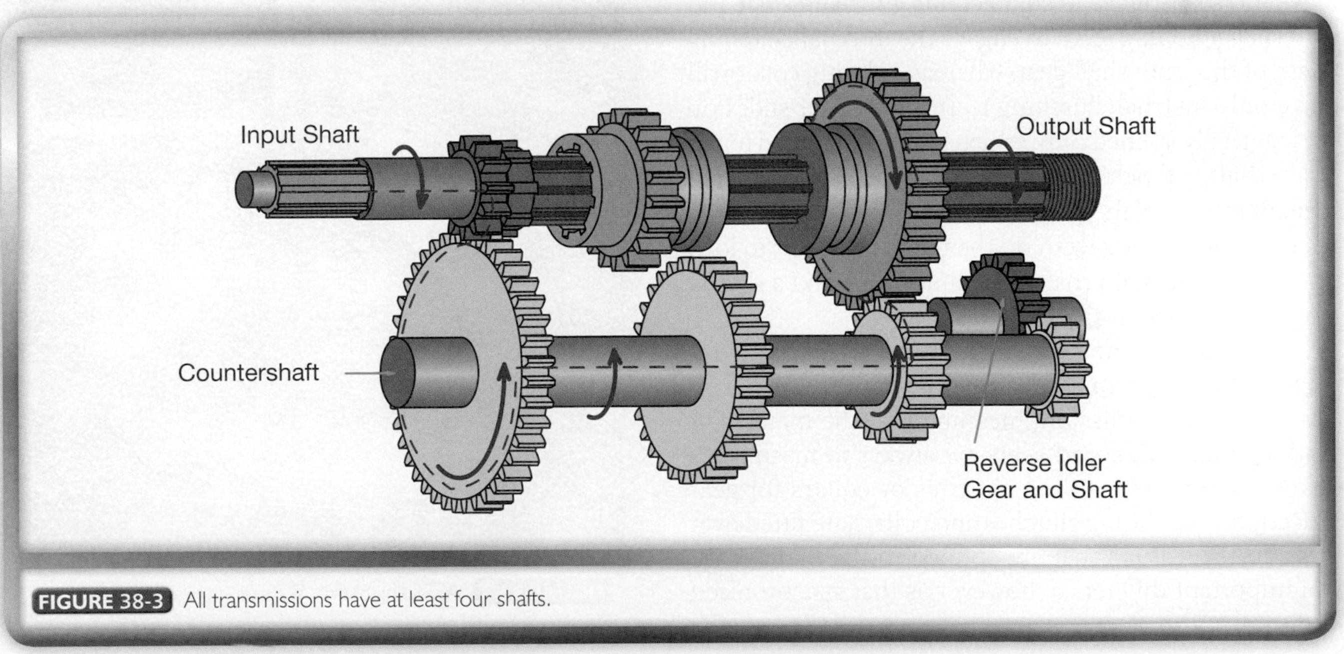

FIGURE 38-3 All transmissions have at least four shafts.

main shaft usually supports the range or speed gears on bushings or bearings. The **speed gears** on the countershaft and the main shaft create the transmission's ratios. Most modern transmissions will have all of the main shaft gears in constant mesh with their mating countershaft gears and are therefore known as **constant mesh transmissions**. The speed gears are usually not splined to the shaft and therefore are free to turn. In order for rotational power to flow through the transmission, the main shaft gears must be driven by the corresponding countershaft gears, and they then must transfer this power to the main shaft.

There are several different systems used to connect the main shaft gears to the main shaft. Transmissions are generally typed by the selection method they use. The three main types of transmission gear selection systems are the sliding-gear, sliding clutch or collar, and synchronized

The first type is the sliding-gear transmission. In **sliding-gear** transmissions, a main shaft gear that is splined to the main shaft is slid into and out of mesh with a corresponding countershaft gear to create the ratio.

The second gear selection method is the **sliding clutch**—also known as the **sliding collar** or simply a **collar shift transmission**. In this type of transmission, the main shaft speed gears are in constant mesh with the countershaft speed gears. The main shaft gears are not splined to the main shaft. The speed gears are connected to the main shaft to create a ratio by sliding collars or clutches that are splined to the main shaft. These collars or clutches slide along the main shaft to engage "dog" or clutching teeth on the gears to lock them to the shaft. The terms *sliding clutch* and *sliding collar* are used synonymously; however, to be correct a sliding clutch will have internal splines to connect it to the main shaft and external clutching teeth to engage the internal clutching teeth of the main shaft gear, whereas a sliding collar will have only internal clutching teeth. The collar slides on an externally splined hub, which is in turn splined to the main shaft and held in place by snap rings. The internal clutching teeth of the collar will engage external clutching teeth known as dog teeth on the main shaft gear to lock the gear to the main shaft. A sliding clutch and a sliding collar are shown in **FIGURE 38-4**.

The third method of gear selection is the **synchronizer**. The **synchronized transmission** is again a constant mesh transmission, meaning that the main shaft and countershaft speed gears are always in mesh. This transmission uses sliding clutches or collars for gear selection. The sliding clutches and collars are fitted over synchronizer hubs that are splined to the main shaft. An important difference, however, is that synchronized constant-mesh transmissions have a method to match shaft and gear speeds before engagement to prevent gear clash. Some transmissions will use a combination of one or more of these gear selection systems.

Reverse Idler Shaft

The final shaft essential for transmission operation is the **reverse idler shaft**, which supports the reverse idler gear. This gear is in mesh or slid into mesh (depending on the particular transmission) between the countershaft reverse gear and the main shaft reverse gear to provide a means to move the vehicle backwards. Recall from the Basic Gearing Concepts chapter that the engine and the transmission input gear both turn clockwise when viewed from the front. The input gear turns the countershaft counterclockwise, and the countershaft gears then turn the main shaft gears clockwise. The result is forward motion.

Sliding the idler gear in between the countershaft reverse gear and the main shaft reverse gear means the countershaft reverse gear turns the idler clockwise. Then, the idler turns the main shaft reverse gear counterclockwise to achieve reverse.

FIGURE 38-4 **A.** Sliding clutch. **B.** Sliding collar.

Shift Controls

Regardless of type, transmissions use many of the same basic types of controls. The transmission driver interface with a standard transmission is better known as the shift lever and is pictured in FIGURE 38-5. The **shift lever** is a shift control the driver uses to change main box gear position. The shift lever is the only part of the transmission shift mechanism that the driver sees on a daily basis.

There is much more to shifting the gears than just the lever, however. The shift lever may have the shift pattern displayed on the shift knob. If not there, the pattern is usually on a decal placed on the back of the driver's sun visor or in some other prominent position. The pattern tells the driver which way to move the lever to select a given range.

The lever can be moved forward and back and side to side to engage the various ranges. The lever itself is mounted in a **shift tower**, a raised section with a pivot into which the shift lever fits. The shift tower has a spring-loaded pivot point just above the transmission shift bar housing. The shift tower may be part of or bolted to the shift bar housing of the transmission. The spring tends to return the shift lever to the neutral position when the transmission is not in gear.

Below the pivot point the end of the shift lever forms the **shift finger**, a flat-sided piece that sits into the shift gates. It is important to note that because of the pivot point, moving the lever forward will cause the shift finger to move back. Moving the lever to the right causes the finger to move left, etc.

The **shift gates** are rectangular notches either formed into or attached to the shift rails. FIGURE 38-6 shows shift gates. The shift rails have the shift forks that actually select a particular range attached to them. **Shift forks** are forks that move the sliding clutches or collars in the transmission. Each rail, and therefore each fork, is usually responsible for two ranges: one in the rearward position and one in the forward position. In a typical five-speed transmission, the rail on the right hand side will control selection of first and reverse ranges, the center rail will control the selection of second and third ranges, and the left hand side rail will control fourth and fifth range selection. With the transmission in neutral, the shift gates all line up with each other and the finger can be moved side to side in the gates.

To select first gear in the shift gates shown in FIGURE 38-6, the driver pulls the lever towards his side of the vehicle. That action moves the finger to the right side gate. The driver then pulls the lever rearward, which moves the right shift rail to the front—engaging first range. Selecting reverse involves the same basic motion except that the driver would push the lever forward, thereby moving the rail back. FIGURE 38-7 shows shift forks attached to shift rails.

As the vehicle accelerates, the driver would depress the clutch, move the lever back to neutral, and then select the center gate and move the lever forward to select second range then rearward for third. The driver would continue through the gears until fifth range (direct drive) is reached. Direct or fifth range is the range where the sliding clutch locks the input shaft to the main shaft giving us a 1:1 ratio. (A 1:1 ratio is normally called direct.) This is the normal shift sequence for a typical five-speed transmission.

As the driver moves through the shifting sequence, the power flows through the transmission change. **Power flow** is the path that power takes from the beginning of

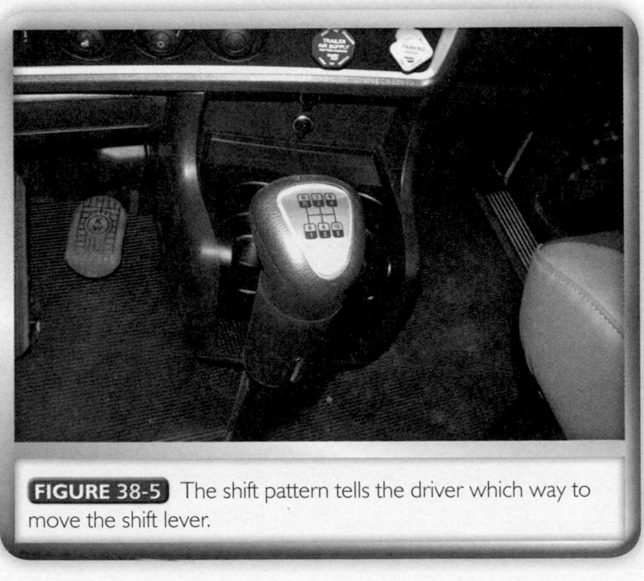

FIGURE 38-5 The shift pattern tells the driver which way to move the shift lever.

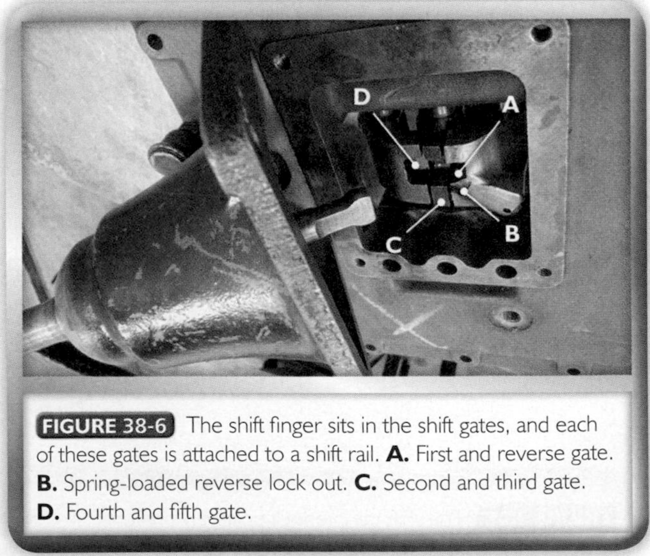

FIGURE 38-6 The shift finger sits in the shift gates, and each of these gates is attached to a shift rail. **A.** First and reverse gate. **B.** Spring-loaded reverse lock out. **C.** Second and third gate. **D.** Fourth and fifth gate.

FIGURE 38-7 Shift forks attached to shift rails move the sliding clutches to engage the main shaft gears.

an assembly to the end. In a transmission, power flow changes as different gears are selected by the driver. This is true for all transmissions.

Shift Rail Interlock

If the driver were to move more than one shift rail at once, the transmission would be in two ranges at once. In other words, the countershaft would be trying to drive the main shaft at two different speeds. That would cause the transmission to lock up and experience catastrophic failure.

To prevent this from happening, the shift rails have an **interlock system** that prevents two rails from being moved from the neutral position at once. The interlock system also prevents the other two rails from moving if one rail is not in neutral. One of the simplest forms of interlock uses two balls and a pin and is illustrated in **FIGURE 38-8**.

The shift rails are positioned parallel and close to one another. The two outside rails will have a semicircular indent on their inside surfaces. Two steel balls are placed in the shift bar housing so that they fit into each indent. The center shift rail has a semicircular indent on both sides. In the neutral position, these indents line up with the indents on the outside shift rails. The center rail also has a small cross-drilled hole that extends from one indent to the other. Inside this hole is a sliding pin.

The steels balls are particularly sized so that, for one rail to move, it must force the ball over slightly. In operation, if the center rail is moved either forward or back, the two balls are moved out of its indents and are pushed further into the indent on the outside rails. The new position blocks any movement of the outside rails. If either outside rail is moved forward or back, its ball is forced further into the indent of the center rail, preventing the center rail from moving. This action also forces the pin in the center rail to move towards the other outside rail. The corresponding ball is forced into the outside rail indent so that it cannot move either.

In addition to those basic components, there may be other components in the shift bar housing as well. For example, mistakenly selecting reverse while driving forward could be very detrimental to the transmission.

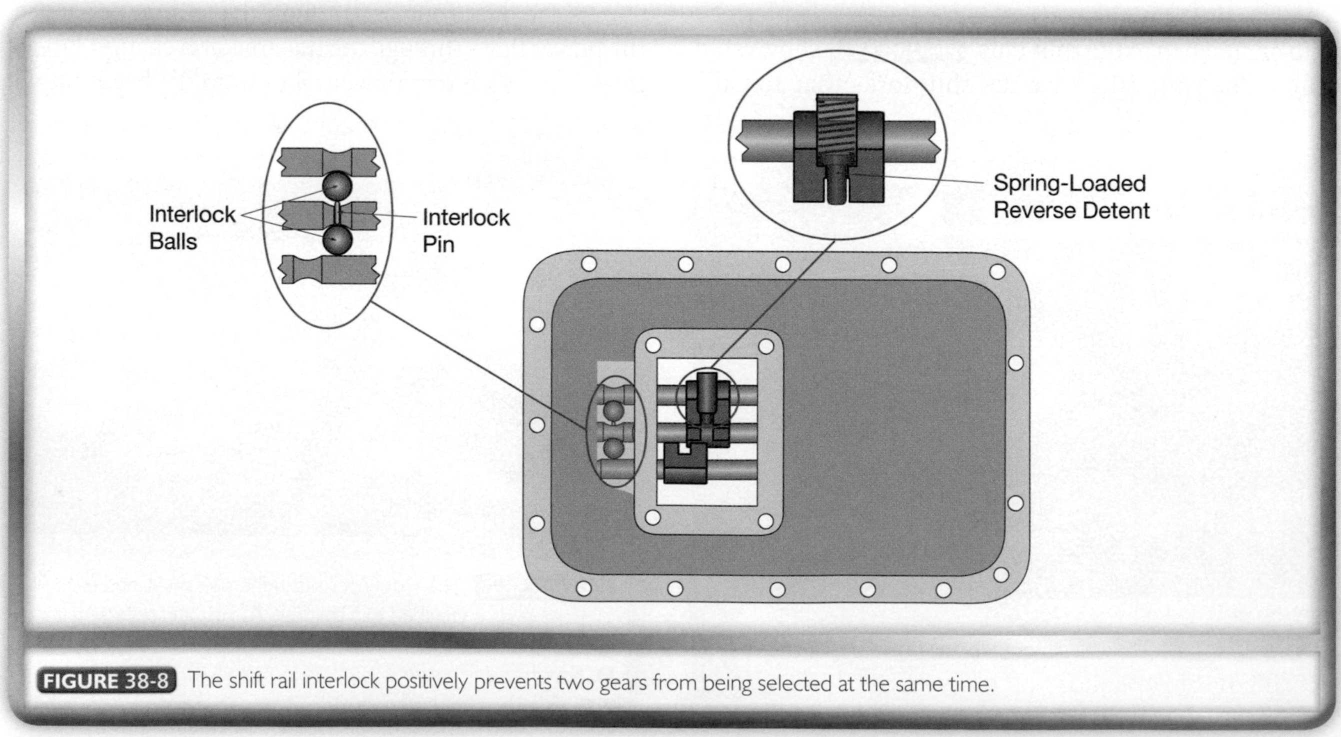

FIGURE 38-8 The shift rail interlock positively prevents two gears from being selected at the same time.

Various methods are used to discourage this. These methods may be as simple as a spring-loaded system that requires an extra effort to select reverse, as was shown in Figure 38-6, or there may be a complex reverse interlock system that positively prevents reverse from being engaged when moving forward. Most shift bar housings will also have spring-loaded **detent balls** that engage notches on the shift rails. By engaging the notches, the detent balls keep the shift rails in position when a shift is made to prevent vibration from moving the shift lever back to a neutral position.

Types of Sliding-Gear and Constant-Mesh Transmissions

As mentioned above, transmissions are classified by the method of gear selection or engagement. Sliding-gear transmissions are generally obsolete and have been replaced by constant-mesh transmissions. Technicians may still find sliding gears used for low and reverse range, (or gear) in some transmissions, however. In this section, we will explain all three types of transmissions—the sliding-gear, the constant-mesh collar shift (also known as sliding collar or sliding clutch), and the constant-mesh synchronized transmission.

Sliding-Gear Transmissions

In the sliding-gear transmission, the main shaft gears are splined to the main shaft. In the neutral position, they are not in mesh with their matching countershaft gear. The main shaft gear will have a groove cut into one side and a shift fork is installed in the groove. In order to select a range, the driver uses the shift fork to slide the gear along the main shaft until its teeth mesh with the teeth of the corresponding countershaft gear. (Refer back to FIGURE 38-3 for a diagram of a transmission shaft.) The power flows from the clutch disc to the input gear to the countershaft driven gear to the countershaft range gear to the main shaft range gear. From there power flows to the main shaft, which doubles as the transmission output shaft, and then on to the driveshaft and the wheels. This transmission type works very well from a standing start when nothing inside the transmission is moving. Selecting a range when driving down the road, however, becomes a challenge, as all the gears and shafts will be rotating at different speeds.

In order to shift ranges when this type of transmission is moving, the operator must use a **double clutch** technique to synchronize gear and shaft speed. To double clutch, the operator first disengages the clutch and moves the shift lever to the neutral position. Next, the driver re-engages the clutch and allows the engine speed to decrease to slow down the countershaft gears. That allows the speed of the countershaft gear to match the speed of the next higher range gear. He then disengages the clutch again and makes a clash-free shift. The driver then engages the clutch again.

Sliding-gear transmissions have a few disadvantages. For example, when downshifting, the countershaft gear would be turning slower than the next lower main shaft range gear. So, after re-engaging the clutch in the neutral position, the driver would accelerate the engine to speed up the countershaft gears to match the vehicle speed. Although that might sound simple, it actually involves considerable skill for the driver to get it right. Another problem with sliding-gear transmissions is that they can only use spur-cut gears and not quieter helical gears. (Helical gears cannot slide into mesh with each other.) As a result, sliding-gear transmissions tend to be noisy in operation and not as strong as they could be because of the spur gears.

Even though sliding-gear transmissions are no longer used in any North American vehicles, some constant-mesh transmissions do use a sliding-gear power flow for low range and reverse. As both these ranges are initiated from a stopped position, nothing inside the transmission case is turning.

Constant-Mesh Collar Shift Transmissions

In a constant-mesh collar shift transmission, the main shaft gears are constantly in mesh with their corresponding countershaft gears. All of the main shaft gears are turning at different speeds whenever the countershaft is turning. The differing speeds are based on the ratio between the range gears and their corresponding countershaft gears. Consequently, the main shaft gears cannot be splined to the main shaft. Otherwise, it would be trying to turn at several different speeds at once, which, of course, is impossible.

Instead, in a constant-mesh transmission, the main shaft gears are free to turn on the main shaft and are usually mounted on bearings or bushings. In order to select a range, sliding clutches or sliding collars are used. Sliding clutches have their inside surfaces splined to the main shaft and have splines cut on their outside surface as well. The outer splines are also known as clutching teeth. The sliding clutches have a circumferentially cut groove in the center that is engaged by the shift fork. Sliding clutches are splined to the main shaft in between two range gears and are used to lock one of the two gears to the shaft. As shown in FIGURE 38-9, there will be a sliding clutch between each pair of main shaft gears.

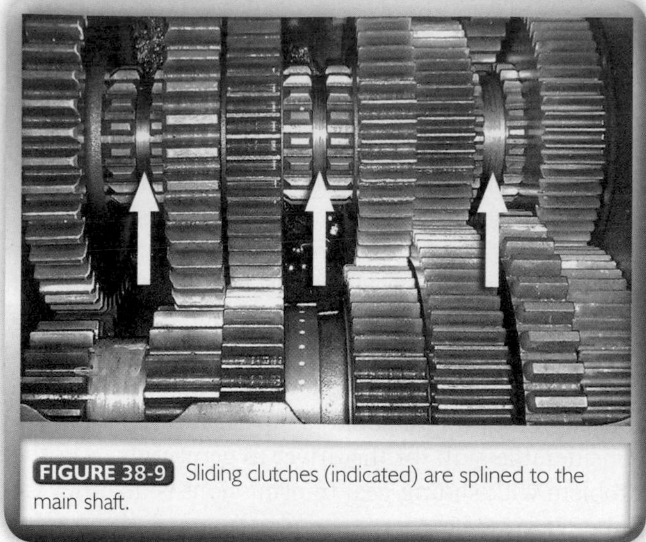

FIGURE 38-9 Sliding clutches (indicated) are splined to the main shaft.

To make a gear selection, the sliding clutch is moved forward or backward, and its outside spline is brought into mesh with matching internal splines in the main shaft gear. The main shaft gear is then locked to the main shaft, and the power flow comes from the countershaft gear to the selected main shaft gear. The power flow then travels through the sliding clutch to the main shaft and out to the driveshaft.

The terms *sliding clutch* and *sliding collar* are used interchangeably, and some manufacturers refer to the sliding clutches discussed above as sliding collars. Sliding collar, though, also refers to a ring that is splined on the inside surface of the collar. The sliding collar slides along a hub that is itself splined to the main shaft. There will be a sliding collar and hub between each pair of main shaft gears. The outside of the sliding collar has a groove to accept the shift fork. To make a shift, the collar is moved by the shift fork and its internal splines slide over external teeth that are cut on the main shaft gears. The external teeth are also called "dog teeth" because of their pointed shape. The movement of the shift fork and the internal splines of the collar locks the main shaft gear to the main shaft through the sliding collar's hub. The power flows from the countershaft gear to the main shaft gear, through the shift collar to the collar's hub, then to the main shaft, and out to the drive train. Sliding-gear constant-mesh transmissions and sliding-clutch sliding collar constant-mesh transmissions are both un-synchronized. That is, in order to perform a proper clash-free shift, both types of transmission still need to be double clutched to match gear speeds.

The constant-mesh design of these transmissions allows for helical gears to be used. Helical gearing makes the transmission stronger because of the increased tooth contact. In addition, the wiping action of helical gears makes the transmission quieter in operation. Overall, transmission length can also be shortened because the helical gears do not need to be as wide as the spur type gears to carry the same load. Transmission weight is reduced as a result.

Constant-Mesh Synchronized Transmissions

A synchronized transmission is, again, a constant-mesh transmission. Synchronization eliminates the need for double clutching techniques. The synchronizer is an assembly that matches shaft and gear speeds as a shift is being made for a clash-free engagement. The synchronizers are very similar to the sliding-collar shift system described in the Constant-Mesh Collar Shift Transmissions section. A key exception is the addition of the synchronizer components that match the speeds. There are four basic types of synchronizers: plain-type, block- or insert-type, pin-type, and disc-and-plate-type. All of the types rely on friction and some sort of shift delay system to synchronize the gear speeds.

Plain-Type Synchronizer

The plain-type synchronizer has a central hub that is splined to the main shaft and a sliding collar that is splined to the hub. A plain-type synchronizer is illustrated in FIGURE 38-10. Several springs located in the hub force detent balls into a groove cut into the center of the collar's internal splines. These detent balls tend to stop the collar from moving past the center or neutral position.

The main shaft gears have smooth, cone-shaped areas and a series of clutching teeth machined on their engagement side. Inside the plain-type synchronizer are two bronze cups that engage the cone-shaped machined area on the gear as the shift is initiated. The detent balls inside the sliding collar ensure that sufficient pressure is applied between the bronze cup and the smooth cone of the gear before the collar can slide over the clutching teeth on the main shaft gear. Ensuring the proper pressure beforehand allows the speeds to match before engagement, thereby eliminating gear clash.

Block- or Insert-Type Synchronizer

The block-type synchronizer, illustrated in FIGURE 38-11, is very similar to the plain-type, but the block-type has a more positive speed-matching system and a few more parts. The block-type synchronizer also has a central hub and a sliding collar like the plain type. Block-type synchronizers also have two bronze **blocking rings** (also known as blocker rings or baulk rings), parts that increase or decrease a gear's speed to match shaft speed so that the synchronizer sleeve can lock the gear to the shaft.

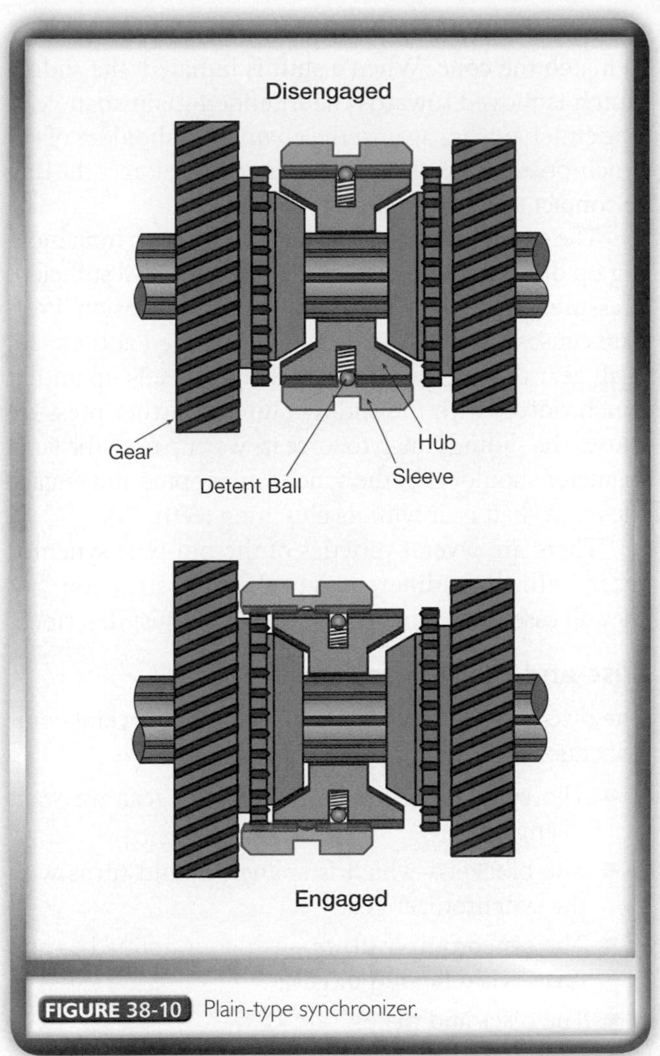

FIGURE 38-10 Plain-type synchronizer.

Blocking rings have dog teeth on their outside circumference identical to the ones on the main shaft gear. (Bronze or a similarly soft metal is usually used for blocking rings to prevent damage to the main shaft gear.) The block-type synchronizer also has three floating spring-loaded blocks (inserts) set into grooves in the central hub. The blocks, or inserts, have a raised center that engages a groove in the internal splines of the collar. This engagement tends to keep the collar in the neutral position.

The block-type synchronizer positively blocks gear engagement until the speeds match. As a shift is initiated, the shift fork moves the shift collar towards the intended gear. The groove in the moving collar drags the three blocks with it. The ends of the blocks engage three rectangular notches in the bronze blocker rings. These notches are specially sized so that the blocker ring can rotate slightly clockwise or counterclockwise in relation to the blocks or inserts. The pressure on the blocker rings forces them to contact the smooth cone-shaped surface of the main shaft gear. The inside of the blockers rings are machined with sharp ridges that help cut through the film of lubricating oil on the gear's cone.

Pressure on the blocker ring causes friction between the two components. The friction causes the blocker ring to rotate slightly left or right, depending on whether the gear is turning faster or slower than the main shaft and synchronizer. The size of the notches in the blocker rings allow this rotation to continue until the notch contacts the block. The rotation is equivalent to approximately one half of the thickness of one dog tooth. When the

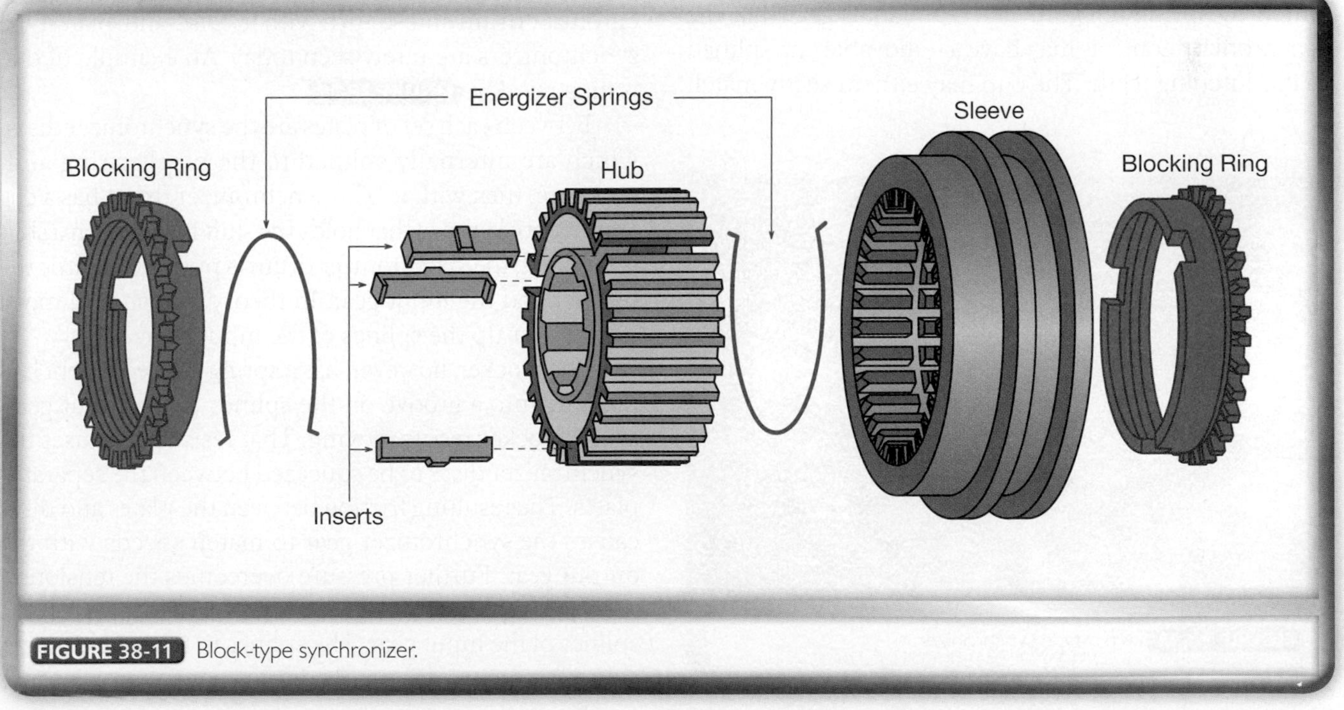

FIGURE 38-11 Block-type synchronizer.

notch contacts the block, the dog teeth on the blocker ring no longer line up with the splines on the sliding collar. Therefore, the teeth block any further movement of the collar. Blocking action continues until the gear is speeded up or slowed down sufficiently. Once the gear has sufficiently accelerated or decelerated, its momentum carries the blocker ring in the opposite direction, allowing the dog teeth to align with the splines in the collar again. The collar then slides over the blocker ring dog teeth and the dog teeth of the main shaft gear. The result is a positive clash-free shift.

Pin-Type Synchronizer

A pin-type synchronizer uses a sliding clutch or collar as its engagement device. The sliding clutch is splined to the main shaft and has a groove or a disc that is engaged by the shift fork. The pin-type synchronizer is positioned between a pair of main shaft gears and has two cone-shaped synchronizer friction rings. The surface of the friction rings can be made of bronze, aluminum, or a variety of synthetic materials. Grooves or notches are cut into the friction material to channel away lubricant and ensure contact with the gear.

The synchronizer friction rings have pins that are stepped. One section of each pin has a larger diameter and the other has a smaller diameter. A chamfer bridges the large and the small dimension. The pins fit into chamfered holes in the sliding clutch, and springs keep tension on the pins. A pin-type synchronizer is shown in FIGURE 38-12.

In the neutral position, the small dimension of each pin is held against the edge of the holes in the sliding clutch by spring tension. The main shaft gear that the synchronizer controls may have a removable cup splined to its clutching teeth. The cup may either exactly match the synchronizer cone or simply have a surface machined to match the cone. When a shift is initiated, the sliding clutch is moved towards the intended main shaft gear. The clutch pushes against the chamfered shoulder of the synchronizer ring pins and that movement forces the ring to contact the mating cup on the gear.

FIGURE 38-12 A pin-type synchronizer.

The spring tension stops the sliding clutch from moving up onto the large diameter of the pin until sufficient pressure is applied to overcome the spring tension. Pressure causes enough friction to be generated at the main shaft gear that the gear slows down or speeds up until it synchronizes with the sliding clutch. Further pressure causes the sliding clutch to force its way up onto the large diameter shoulders of the synchronizer pins and engage the main shaft gear with its clutching teeth.

There are several varieties of the pin-type synchronizer, with slight differences in their construction, but they all essentially operate in the manner just described.

Disc-and-Plate-Type Synchronizer

The disc-and-plate-type synchronizer has several components:

- The synchronizer gear—the input gear we want to engage
- The blocker—which is splined to and turns with the synchronizer gear
- The synchronizer drum—which is splined to and turns with the output gear
- The discs and plates

Several plates with external tangs, called separator plates, are placed into corresponding notches in the synchronizer drum and so turn with it. Disc-and-plate-type synchronizers are rarely seen today. An example of one is illustrated in FIGURE 38-13.

Between each set of plates are the synchronizer discs, which are internally splined to the blocker ring and, therefore, turn with it. The synchronizer drum has a circumferential groove that holds the shift fork. When a shift is initiated, the synchronizer drum is pushed towards the blocker and the input gear. In theory, this should move the blocker up the splines of the input gear.

The blocker, however, has a spring-loaded detent ball pushing into a groove on the splines of the input gear, so the blocker resists moving. That resistance causes the synchronizer discs to be squeezed between the separator plates. The resulting friction between the plates and discs causes the synchronizer gear to match speeds with the output gear. Further pressure overcomes the tension in the detent springs, and the blocker slides forward on the splines of the input gear. The splines in the synchronizer drum can now slide onto the input gear splines. Because

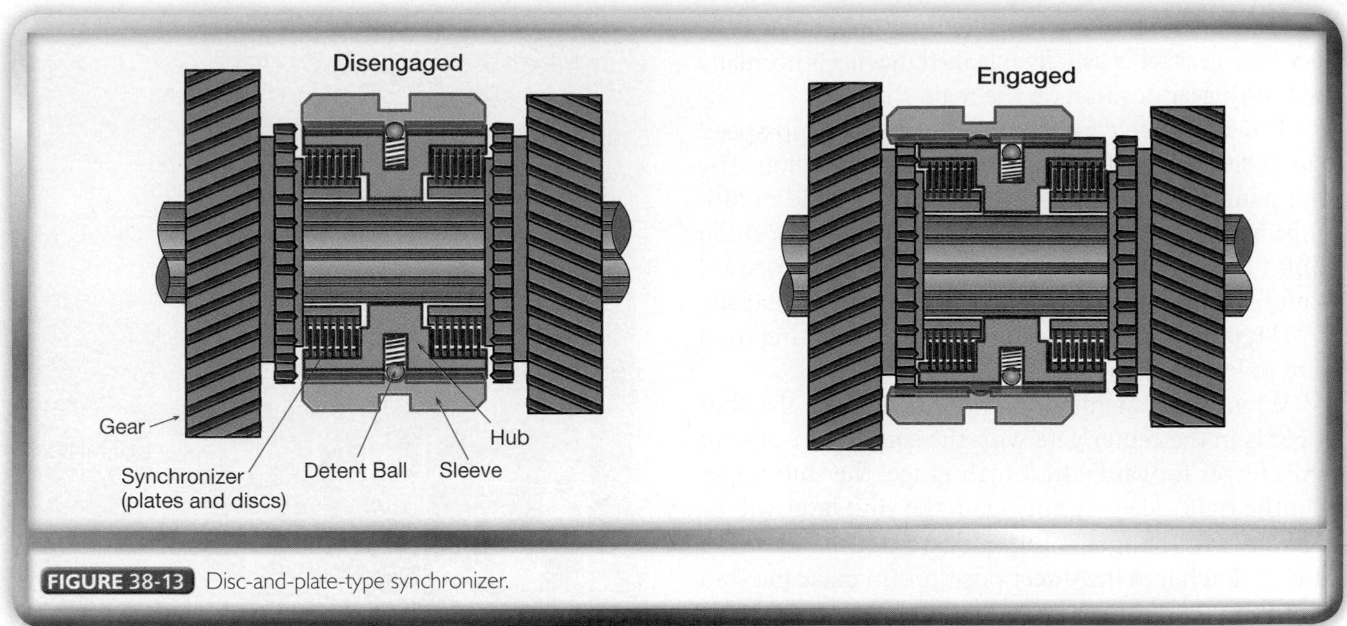

FIGURE 38-13 Disc-and-plate-type synchronizer.

the synchronizer drum splines are also still in mesh with the output gear, the gear is now engaged.

Most heavy-duty transmissions do not use synchronizers because synchronizers would not stand up to the heavy torque being transmitted by these transmissions. In vehicles with heavy-duty transmissions, the driver must double clutch and have the skill required to match gear and shaft speeds.

Single Countershaft Transmissions

At the beginning of this chapter, we noted that a transmission must match the engine and vocational requirements of the vehicle into which it is installed. A transmission must also be economically feasible for that vehicle. As their name suggests, **single countershaft transmissions** have only one countershaft and are the unit of choice for most light- and medium-duty vehicles manufactured in North America because they are relatively inexpensive to manufacture and can usually handle the requirements of the vehicle. Single countershaft transmissions are commonly available in four-, five-, and six-speed models, such as the one shown in FIGURE 38-14. Models with more forward ranges are also available.

Engines used in light- and medium-duty vehicles tend to have a wider operating rpm range than their heavier duty counterparts. As a result, more ranges or ratio steps are not usually required. If the engine's rpm range is not sufficient on its own, a two-speed drive axle can be used to double the number of ranges. (A two-speed drive axle has a low and a high operating ratio. A two-speed drive axle turns a five-speed transmission into a ten-speed—by first using the transmission gears in the low axle ratio and then shifting the axle to high and going through the transmission gears again. Two-speed drive axles will be discussed in more detail in the Heavy-Duty Truck Drive Axles chapter.)

FIGURE 38-14 Eaton FS6406 six-speed single countershaft transmission cutaway.

Overdrive Shifting

Several single countershaft transmissions are available with overdrive ratios. With overdrive ratios, the output shaft will turn faster than the input shaft. To make that happen, a set of overdrive gears is typically installed on the main shaft and the countershaft. Some manufacturers of light-duty, six-speed transmissions install the overdrive gear set after the reverse gear set. In truck applications, the overdrive gear set is usually installed in what is normally the fourth gear position on the main shaft.

The overdrive causes the high-range or top-speed gear position to no longer be in the direct position. The shift pattern becomes atypical. That is, instead of fifth range being with the shift lever in the rearward position (shift finger forward), we must move the lever forward (shift finger backward) to engage the overdrive gear set. A "U" type shift pattern is followed when shifting from third to fourth range.

When the transmission is in third range, the shift finger is in the center gate with the shift lever rearward (shift finger forward). In fourth range, the shift finger is in the right side gate and again the shift lever will be rearward (shift finger is forward), to put the four–five sliding clutch into the direct position. To make the shift from third to fourth, the operator must make an upside down "U" shape with the shift lever. Then, to shift into fifth (overdrive), the driver would move the shift lever forward, moving the shift finger rearward to engage the overdrive gear on the main shaft.

The "U" pattern can be slightly confusing to a driver who is not used to it. Most manufacturers have now eliminated it by using a bellcrank system on the fourth–fifth gear shift rail. A **bellcrank** is a shaft or lever used in a mechanical linkage with a pivot in the center that reverses the normal direction of motion. The use of the bellcrank reverses the direction the shift lever must move to select the overdrive gear making the shift pattern "normal." A simple bellcrank is used to standardize the shift pattern for fourth and fifth on a five-speed overdrive transmission, or fifth and sixth on a six-speed overdrive transmission. The bellcrank in the Fuller six-speed transmission shift bar housing is pictured in FIGURE 38-15.

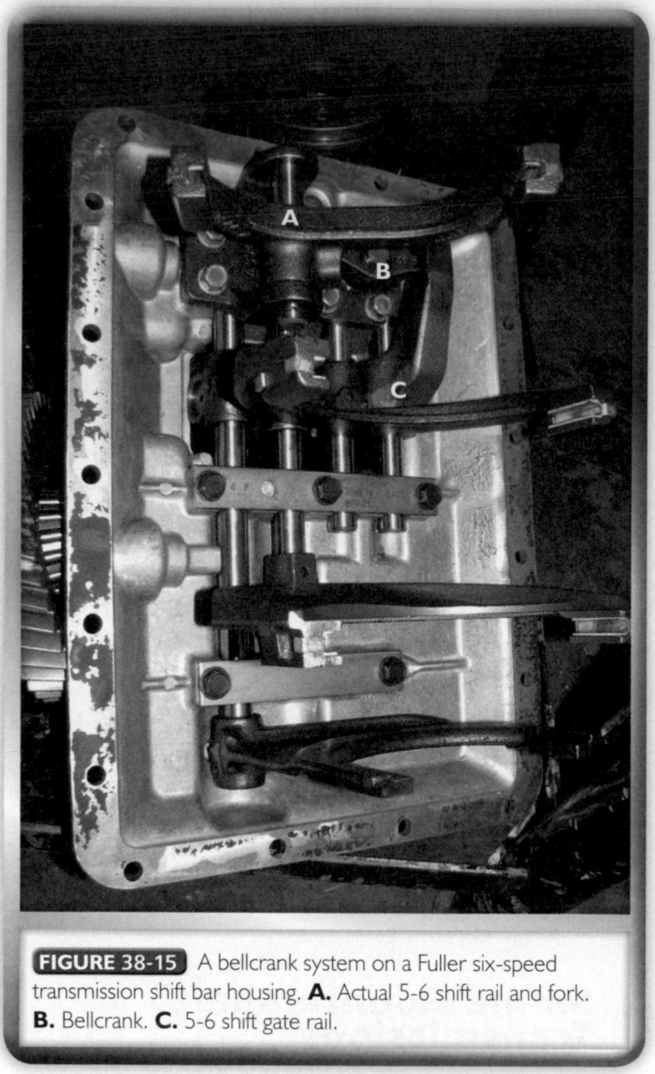

FIGURE 38-15 A bellcrank system on a Fuller six-speed transmission shift bar housing. **A.** Actual 5-6 shift rail and fork. **B.** Bellcrank. **C.** 5-6 shift gate rail.

In a shift cover with the bellcrank system, the four–five shift rail moves one end of the bellcrank, and the other end of the bellcrank actually moves the shift fork. When the shift lever is moved forward, the shift fork for the four–five sliding clutch actually moves forward instead of back. This simple system allows the shift pattern for an overdrive transmission to remain the same as for a non-overdrive model, making it easier on the operator.

Single Countershaft Transmission Power Flows

Most of today's single countershaft transmissions are constant-mesh and synchronized. (Several popular brands, however, still use a sliding gear for first range and reverse.) We will now explain the power flows for a simplified version of a single countershaft transmission.

The transmission depicted in FIGURE 38-16 is a five-speed transmission that uses sliding clutches to engage all of the main shaft gears. In non-synchronized transmissions, the driver will have to double clutch when shifting gears to match the gear and shaft speeds, as there is no system installed to do so. To engage the gears, the driver slides a sliding clutch that is splined to the main shaft into mesh with main shaft gears, which are not splined to the main shaft.

This type of transmission is quite popular in truck coach applications and is quite simple to understand. It is by no means, however, the only configuration used. Other transmission models used may be fully or partially synchronized, but the power flows will, for the most part, be similar.

- Neutral power flow. In neutral, with the engine running and the clutch engaged, engine power is transmitted through the clutch to the transmission input shaft and the input gear. The input gear transmits the rotating power to the countershaft and the countershaft gears. The countershaft gears transmit the rotating power to the main shaft gears and the reverse idler gear. Because none of the main shaft gears are engaged, the main shaft stays stationary resulting in neutral.

- Reverse power flow. As illustrated in FIGURE 38-17, the reverse power flow starts from the neutral position. The driver pulls the shift lever to the far left and forward to the reverse gear position. (Certain transmissions may have special detents or the lever may need to be pushed downward as this action is completed; this helps to stop the inadvertent

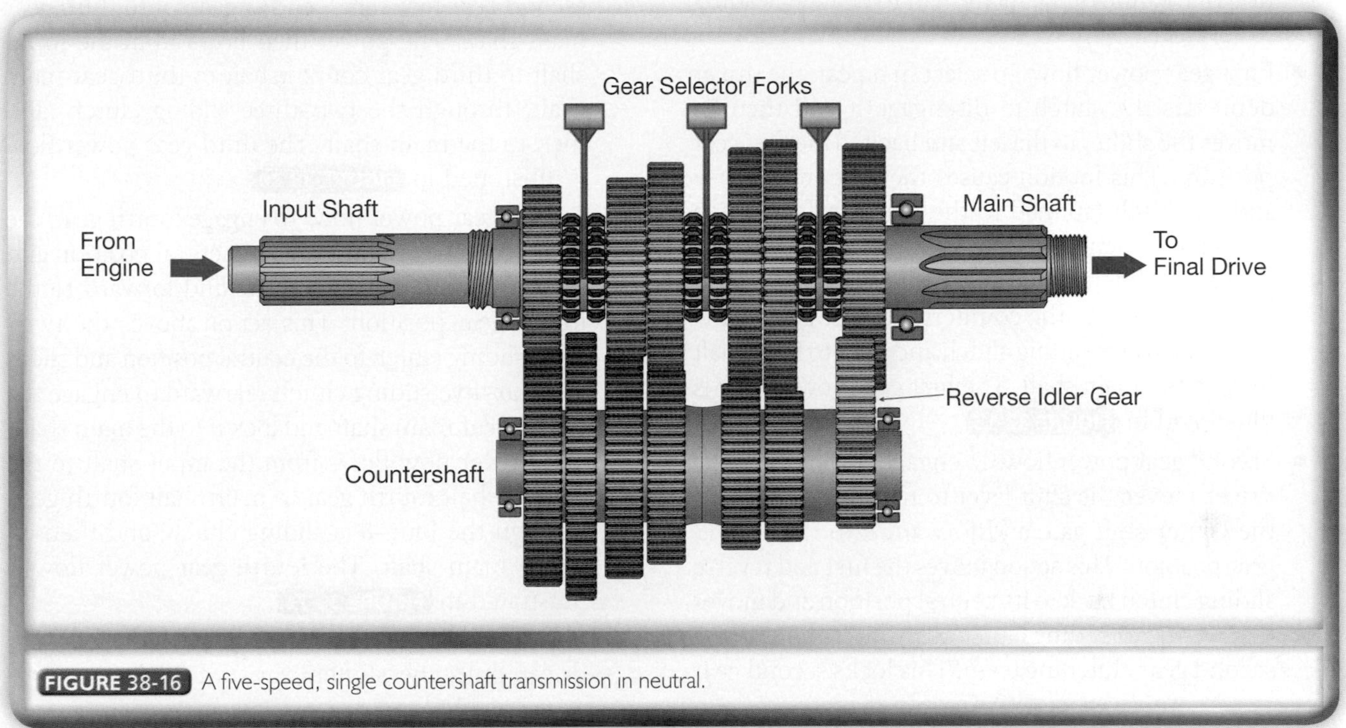

FIGURE 38-16 A five-speed, single countershaft transmission in neutral.

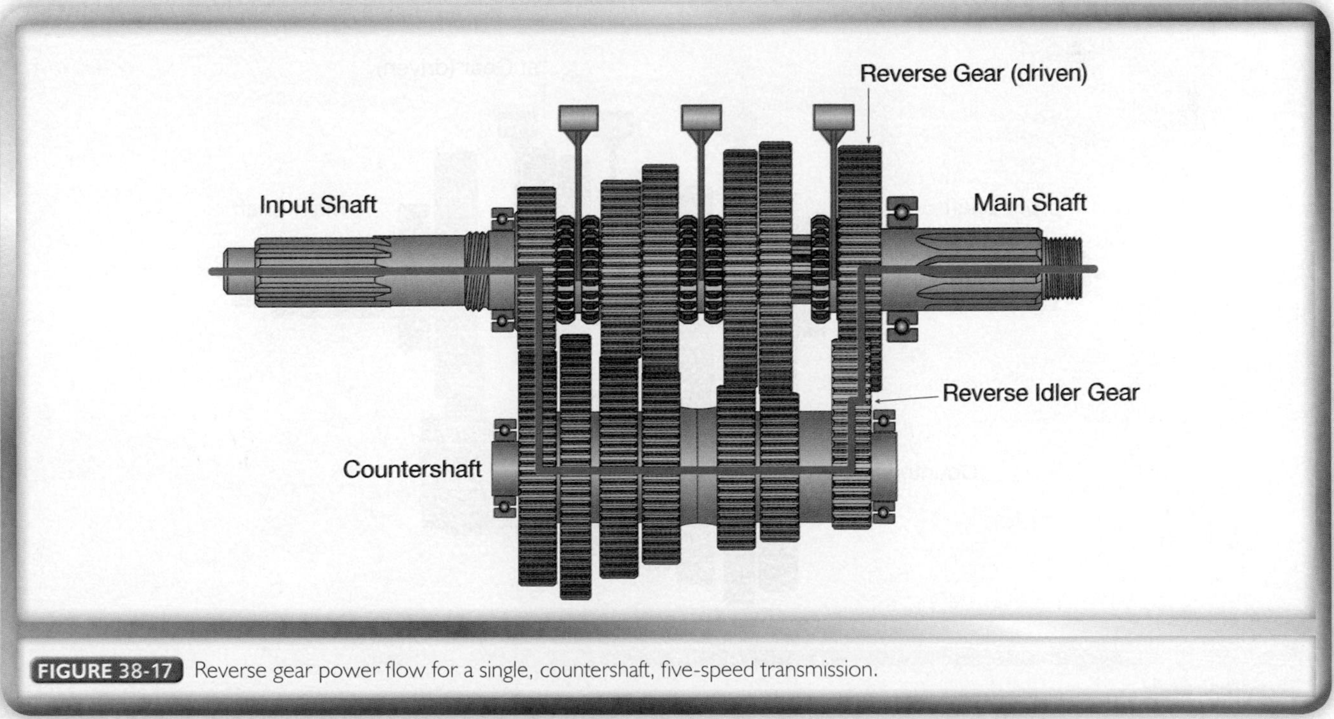

FIGURE 38-17 Reverse gear power flow for a single, countershaft, five-speed transmission.

selection of reverse when shifting out of first gear.) This action moves the first and reverse sliding clutch on the main shaft rearward and it engages the reverse main shaft gear. The power flow is as follows: from the input shaft to the countershaft reverse gear to the idler gear to the reverse gear, and then first and reverse sliding clutch, and finally to the to the main shaft. Use of the idler gear allows the direction of rotation of the main shaft to change, leading to reverse.

- First gear power flow. To select first gear, the driver depresses the clutch to disengage it and then he moves the shifter to the left and back to the first gear position. This motion causes the first and reverse sliding clutch (splined to the main shaft) to slide into engagement with first gear on the main shaft. When the clutch is reengaged, the power flows from the input shaft to the countershaft first gear to the first and reverse sliding clutch and then to mainshaft first, to the main shaft. The first gear power flow is illustrated in **FIGURE 38-18**.
- Second gear power flow. To engage second gear, the driver moves the shift lever to neutral and then to the center shift gate and forward into the second gear position. This action moves the first and reverse sliding clutch back to its neutral position and moves the two–three sliding clutch rearward to engage the second gear clutching teeth. This locks second gear to the main shaft so the power flows from the input shaft to the countershaft second gear to the main shaft gear, through the two–three sliding clutch, and then to the main shaft. The second gear power flow is illustrated in **FIGURE 38-19**.
- Third gear power flow. To engage third, the driver pulls the shift lever rearward in the center shift gate. This disengages the two–three sliding clutch from second gear main shaft and engages it to third gear main shaft. The power then flows from the input shaft to third gear countershaft to third gear main shaft, through the two–three sliding clutch, and then to the main shaft. The third gear power flow is illustrated in **FIGURE 38-20**.
- Fourth gear power flow. To engage fourth gear, the driver moves the shifter to the neutral position and then to the far right shift gate and forward to the fourth gear position. This action moves the two–three sliding clutch to the neutral position and slides the four–five sliding clutch rearward to engage the fourth gear main shaft and lock it to the main shaft. The power now flows from the input shaft to the countershaft fourth gear to main shaft fourth gear, through the four–five sliding clutch, and then on to the main shaft. The fourth gear power flow is illustrated in **FIGURE 38-21**.
- Fifth gear power flow. To engage fifth gear, the driver pulls the shifter rearward in the far right

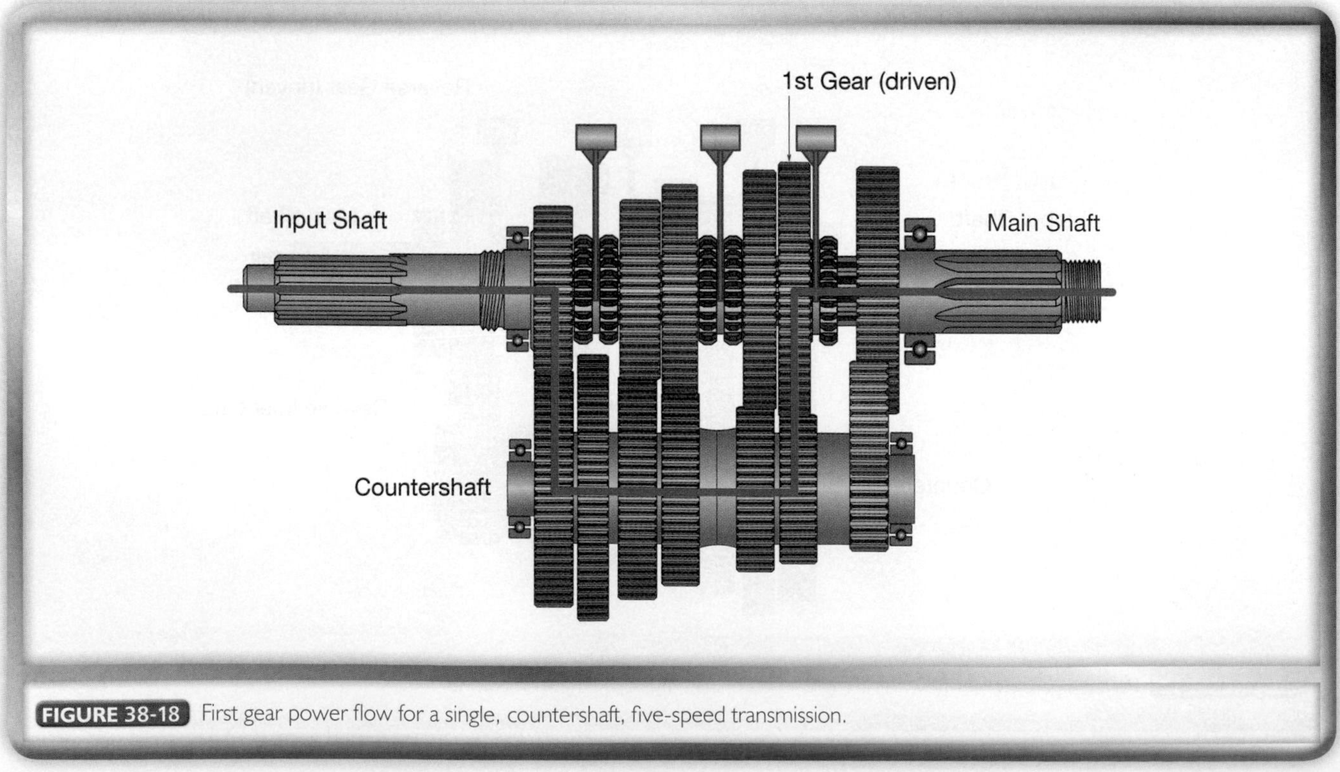

FIGURE 38-18 First gear power flow for a single, countershaft, five-speed transmission.

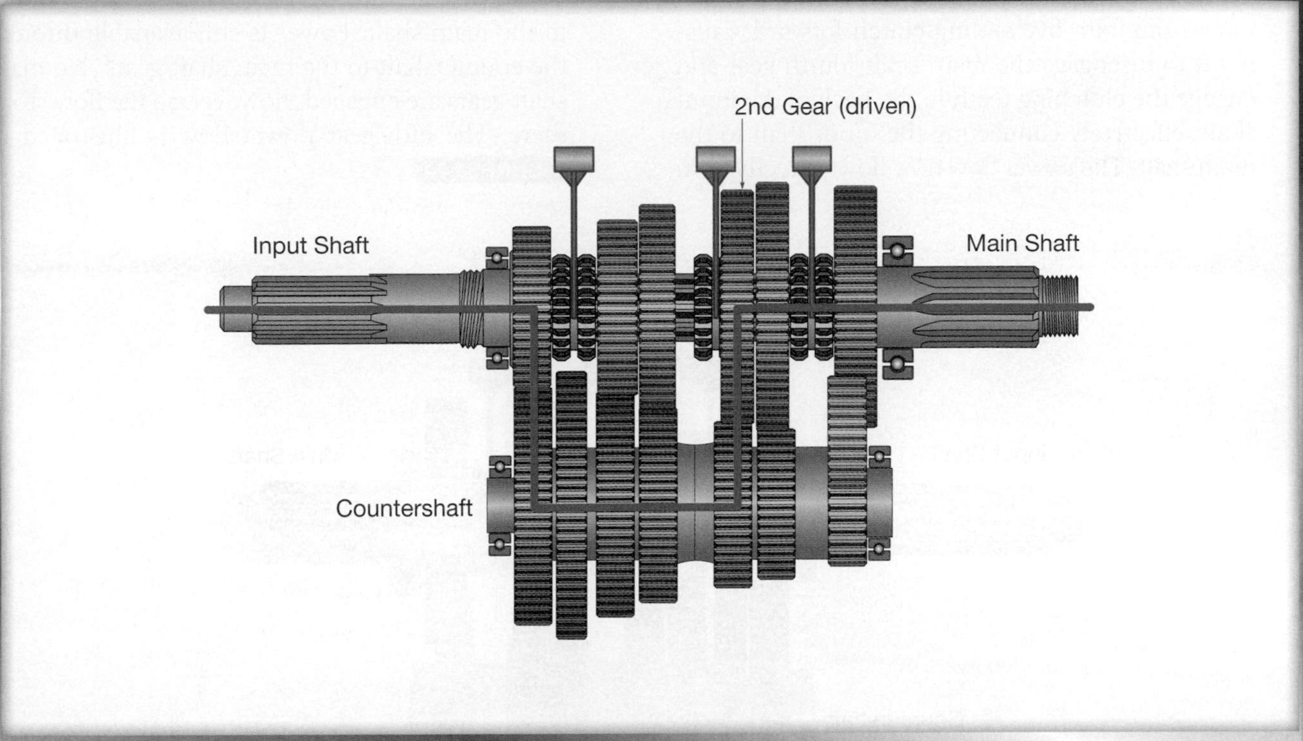

FIGURE 38-19 Second gear power flow for a single, countershaft, five-speed transmission.

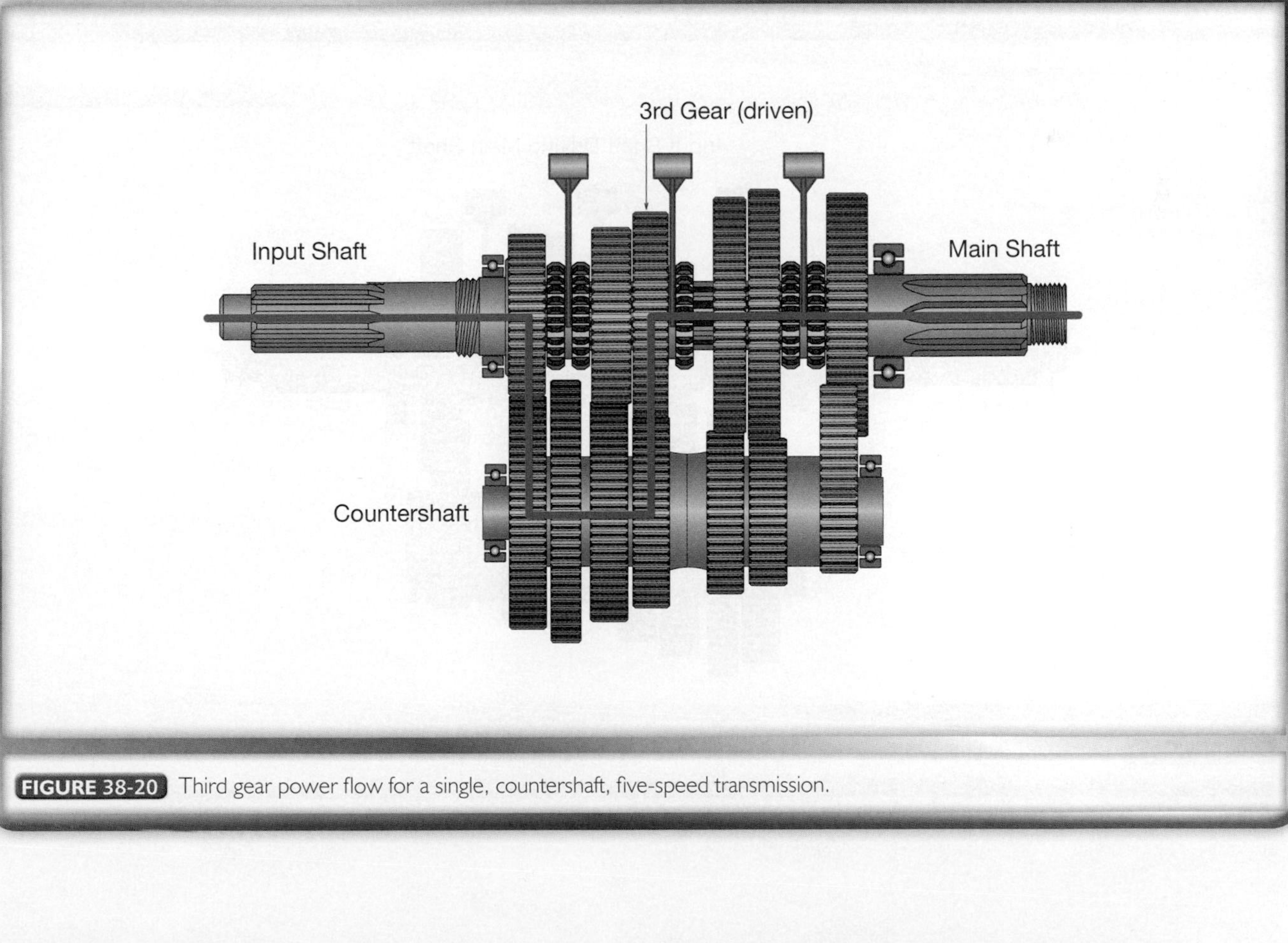

FIGURE 38-20 Third gear power flow for a single, countershaft, five-speed transmission.

shift gate into the fifth gear position. This action moves the four–five sliding clutch forward, causing it to disengage the main shaft fourth gear and engage the clutching teeth in the back of the input shaft, effectively connecting the input shaft to the main shaft. The power flow now flows directly from the input shaft through the four–five sliding clutch to the main shaft. Power is still available through the countershaft to the main shaft gears. No main shaft gears are engaged, however, so the flow stops there. The fifth gear power flow is illustrated in **FIGURE 38-22**.

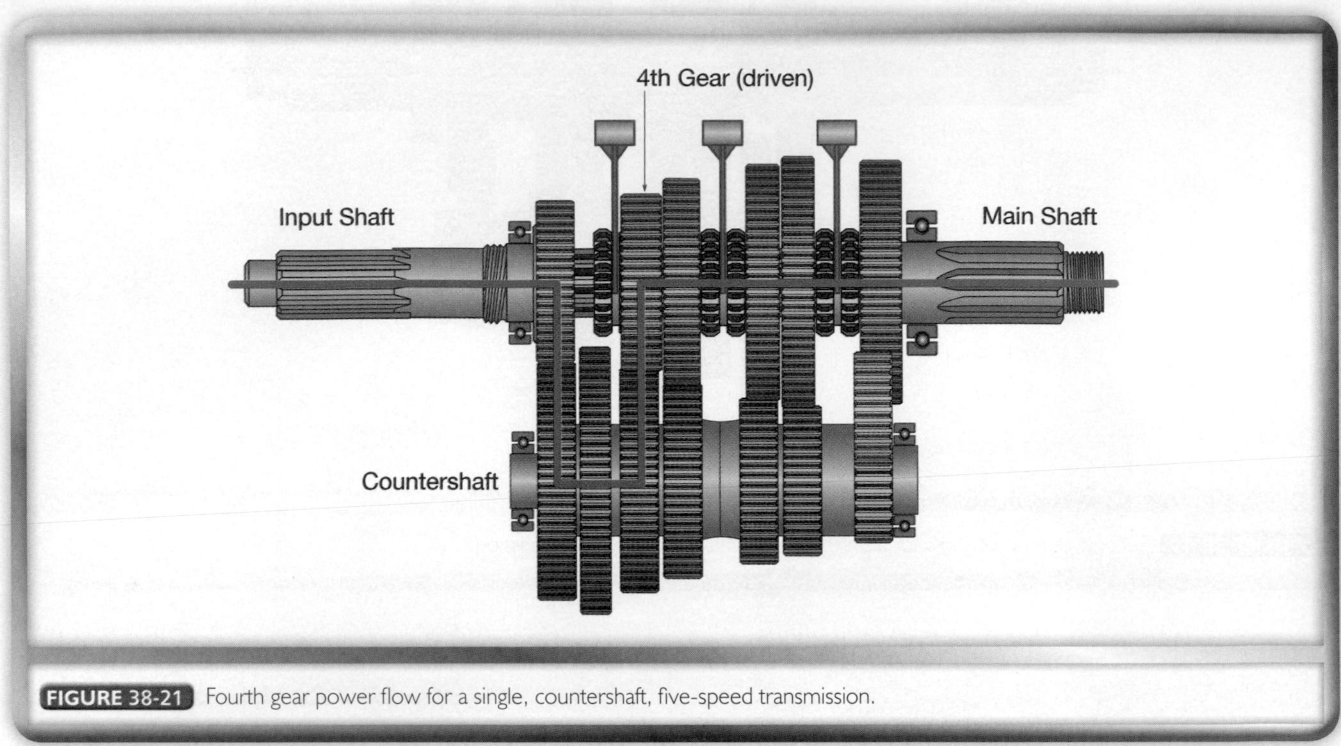

FIGURE 38-21 Fourth gear power flow for a single, countershaft, five-speed transmission.

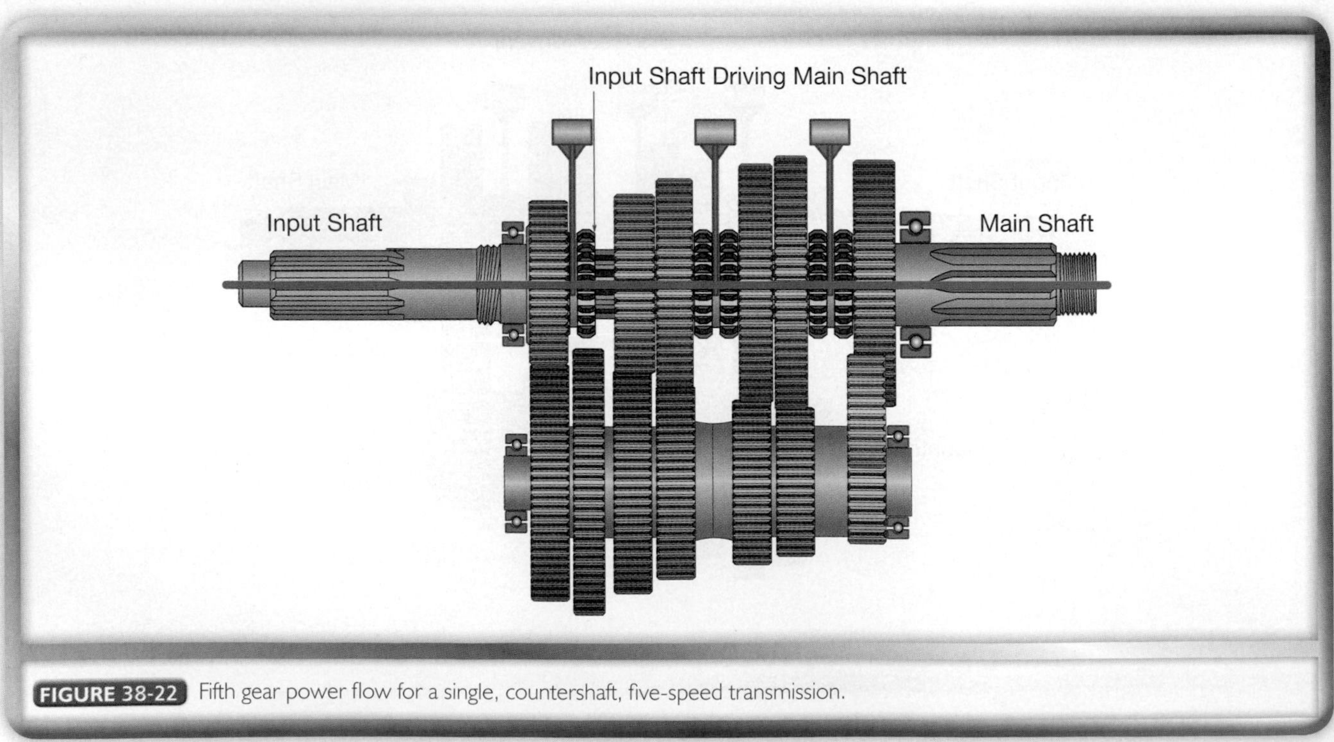

FIGURE 38-22 Fifth gear power flow for a single, countershaft, five-speed transmission.

Several manufacturers produce or have produced single countershaft transmissions for the North American medium- and heavy-duty market, including Dana/Spicer, Rockwell/Meritor, Eaton Fuller, and ZF Friedrickshafen AG. Documentation for these transmissions is readily available on the Internet. Information on each manufacturer's products can be found at the following websites:

- Information on Spicer transmissions can be accessed through www.dana.com. Spicer now concentrates on the off-highway market.
- Information on Rockwell transmissions is available at www.meritor.com. Additionally, some information on ZF transmissions used in North America can also be found at www.meritor.com.
- Information on Eaton/Fuller transmissions can be found at www.roadranger.com.
- ZF Friedrichshafen AG is a worldwide driveline manufacturing company. Until 2010, ZF marketed components for trucks in North America through Meritor. Information on those components can be accessed at www.ZF.com/us. ZF now markets directly to OEMs.

To access the correct documentation, you must have the model number of the transmission. The model number is located on the transmission's information plate. The model number indicates whether the transmission is an overdrive model or not, how many forward ranges it has, its torque capacity, and its ratio set.

To understand the information contained in a transmission's model number, let's use the information plate shown in FIGURE 38-23 as an example. The figure shows the plate for the popular Eaton Fuller medium-duty transmission; model number FS-5205-A. In this model number, each character or digit has a particular significance:

- "F" stands for Fuller.
- "S" means the transmission is synchronized. If the transmission were an overdrive model, the S would be followed by an O.
- The first "5" indicates the nominal input torque capacity. It is in hundred units. That is, 5 multiplied by 100 is the nominal input torque capacity in foot-pounds, so 500 ft-lb (678 Nm). If the digit were a "3," the transmission would have 300 ft-lb (407 Nm) of nominal input torque.
- The "2" is the design level.
- The "05" is the number of forward ranges.
- The A is the ratio set.
- The serial number is the manufacturing sequence number and is usually found beneath or beside the model number on the information tag. It may be helpful to have the serial number on hand when ordering parts for the unit.

FIGURE 38-23 Information plate from a remanufactured Eaton Fuller transmission; model FS-5205A.

Multiple Countershaft Transmissions and Auxiliary Transmissions

As transport vehicle's loads have become heavier over the years, the work the transmission has to perform has increased. With modern on-highway engines producing more than 2,250 ft-lb (3,051 Nm) of torque, the torque handling capacity of transmissions has had to increase. The only conventional way to increase the torque capacity of a single, countershaft transmission was to increase the face width of the gears and increase shaft diameters inside the transmission so they could handle the increased torque. Unfortunately, this led to longer and longer transmission cases to accommodate the larger gears. A more practical solution was a move to **multiple countershaft transmissions**, which have more than one countershaft to distribute the torque between more teeth on the main shaft and countershaft speed gears, to increase the torque capacity of the transmission.

As shown in FIGURE 38-24 and FIGURE 38-25, multiple countershaft transmissions split the input torque between two or three countershafts spaced 180 or 120 degrees apart. This allows the input gear to have two or three sets of teeth involved in transferring torque to the countershafts at all times, so the load on each set of teeth is divided. Then, when the countershaft gears bring the torque back to the main shaft, the torque once more is split between two or three sets of teeth on the main shaft gear. The load is further divided as more of the main shaft gear teeth are used to transfer the load. With more of the gear's teeth involved in torque transfer, the width of the gear's face can be smaller than on a single countershaft

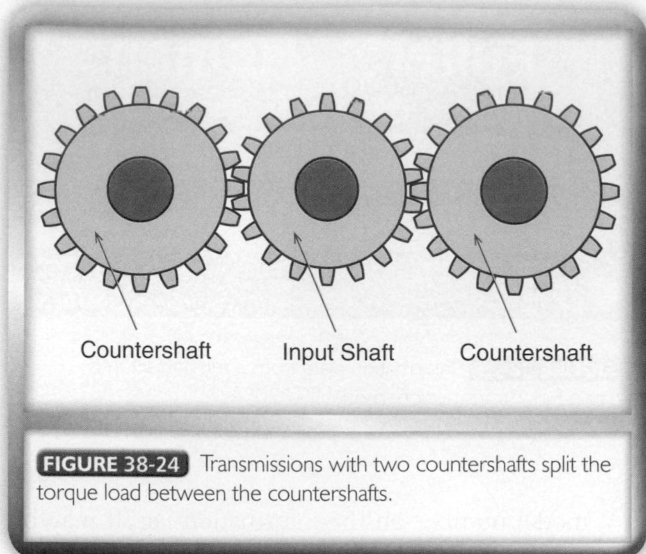

FIGURE 38-24 Transmissions with two countershafts split the torque load between the countershafts.

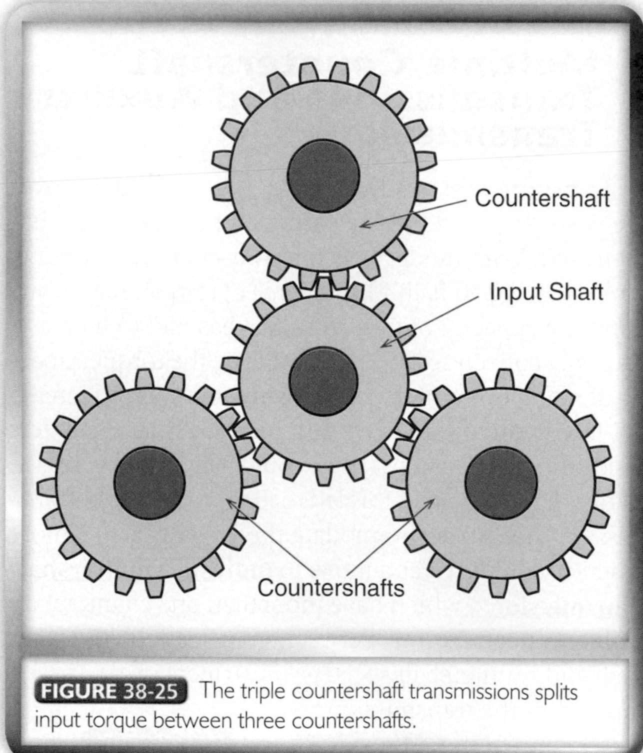

FIGURE 38-25 The triple countershaft transmissions splits input torque between three countershafts.

gear capable of carrying the same load. This leads to a shorter overall transmission length and lighter weight. A twin countershaft five-speed transmission capable of handling 1,600 ft-lb (2,169 Nm) of torque can be the same length and almost the same weight as single countershaft transmission than can handle only 900 or 1,000 ft-lb (1,220 or 1,356 Nm) of torque. The only components that need to be strengthened to carry this load are the input shaft and the output shaft, as these shafts must carry the entire load. Strengthening those shafts can be accomplished simply by increasing their diameter.

The manufacturer who dominates the North American market for twin countershaft transmissions is the Eaton Corporation. Its Fuller Roadranger transmissions have been installed in heavy-duty trucks for over 45 years. Rockwell, which later became Meritor, has also produced twin countershaft transmissions in nine- and thirteen-speed models. Spicer also manufactured twin countershaft models in the past, but does not produce on-highway models at this time. Mack, now Volvo/Mack, produces triple countershaft transmission models for its own line of trucks.

Floating Main Shaft System

The extra countershaft in a multiple countershaft transmission produces more benefits than just increased torque capacity. Because the main shaft gears are supported between two diametrically opposed countershafts, the gears virtually float between those countershafts, as shown in **FIGURE 38-26**. Because the gears are floating, they do not need to be supported by the main shaft and do not require any bushings or bearings to ride on. This makes the gears themselves and the main shaft much simpler to manufacture.

In a single countershaft transmission, when torque is being transferred between the countershaft gears and the main shaft gears, the thrust forces try to push the gears apart, putting a heavy load on the main shaft, its bearings, and the transmission case. The floating main shaft system in a twin countershaft model cancels these forces out. The main shaft has no thrust forces acting on it, so it only has to deal with the torque load.

When twin countershaft transmissions are overhauled, it is essential to time the input gear and the countershaft gears

FIGURE 38-26 Main shaft gears float between two countershafts.

to ensure that the main shaft gears do float between the countershafts. Timing is a simple matter of lining up marked teeth on the countershaft driven gears with marked teeth on the input shaft drive gear. If timing is done incorrectly, the gears will climb out of equilibrium, and the transmission will seize.

To time the gears, first find the marked tooth on each countershaft driven gear. The tooth will be marked with a "0" and is directly above the countershaft keyway. Using a highly visible marking compound, select and mark the groove between any two teeth on the input shaft drive gear. Then, mark the groove exactly 180 degrees opposite, as shown in FIGURE 38-27. Upon installation, ensure that the marked countershaft teeth mesh with the marked input shaft gear teeth, and timing will be correct.

Multiple Countershaft Transmission Power Flows

In this section on multiple countershaft transmission power flows, we will concentrate on the Eaton Fuller transmission, as it dominates the industry. Recall that most front sections, or main boxes, of twin countershaft transmissions have five forward speeds or ranges. Depending on the transmission model, the gears may be listed as one, two, three, four, and five or as low, one, two, three, and four. Regardless of the nomenclature, the power flows are the same, so we will look at the main box power flow for a typical model the RTLO-12713-A, as shown on the information plate pictured in FIGURE 38-28. This model's, nomenclature follows:

- The R stands for Eaton Fuller Roadranger transmission.
- The T is for twin countershaft.
- The L is for low-inertia auxiliary section. (The Auxiliary Sections section goes into more detail on this supplementary transmission.)
- The O indicates main box overdrive.
- The number 12 is the nominal input torque multiplied by 100 and then adding 50. This transmission can handle 1,250 ft-lb (1,695 Nm).
- The number 7 is the design level. The number 6 would be **multi-mesh gearing** in the main box. In multi-mesh gearing, the main shaft and countershaft gears have finer cut teeth—meaning more teeth are in mesh for increased strength. The number 7 shown in FIGURE 38-28 means the transmission has multi-mesh gears in the main box and helical gearing in the auxiliary section. If the number 9 were in this position, it would indicate that the transmission has an improved seal system.
- The number 13 indicates the number of forward speeds.
- The A is the ratio set, meaning the steps between shifts.

Main Box Power Flows

Recall that the Eaton Fuller transmission main boxes are all quite similar. They are twin countershaft sliding-clutch transmissions with five forward speeds. Therefore, their power flows are identical with the exception of main box overdrive transmissions and certain unique models such as the Super Ten.

As mentioned previously, the names of the forward ranges will vary depending on the transmission model. For example, in ten-speed models, the ranges are 1, 2, 3, 4, and 5. In thirteen- and eighteen-speed models, how-

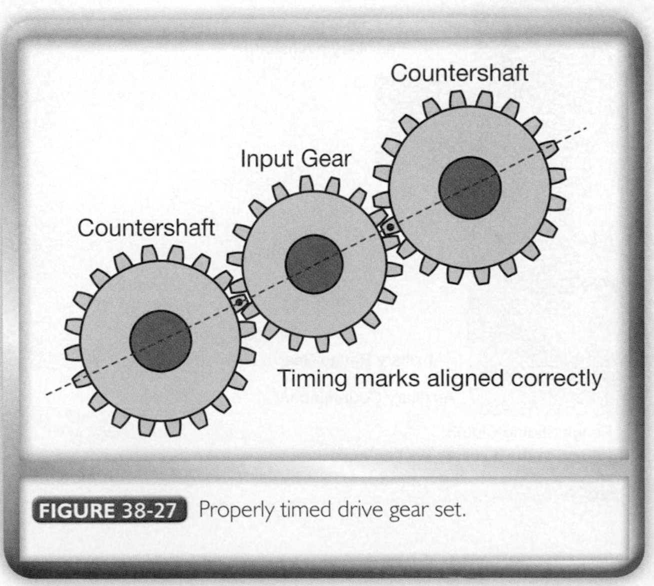

FIGURE 38-27 Properly timed drive gear set.

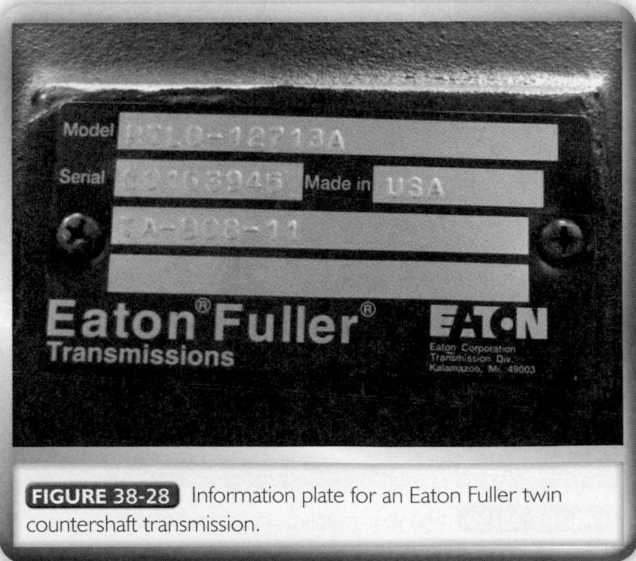

FIGURE 38-28 Information plate for an Eaton Fuller twin countershaft transmission.

ever, the ranges are listed as low, 1, 2, 3, and 4. Regardless of the names used, the flows are the same. Throughout this example, we will use 1, 2, 3, 4, and 5 for simplicity.

The transmission uses three shift rails and forks, as shown in **FIGURE 38-29**, to control the position of three sliding clutches. The right rail controls the rear sliding clutch, which can engage either the first gear or reverse gear on the main shaft. The center rail controls the next sliding clutch, which can engage either the second or third main shaft gear. The left rail controls the front sliding clutch, which can engage the fourth main shaft gear or engage the back of the input shaft to achieve direct or fifth range. Remember that the driver will pull the shifter left to select the right rail and so on.

FIGURE 38-29 The three shift rails and forks control the engagement of the three sliding clutches to lock the speed gears to the main shaft.

The power flows are quite simple. The engine delivers torque to the transmission input shaft and the input gear transfers the torque to the twin countershafts. The countershafts are in constant mesh with their mating main shaft gears. Therefore, the torque will be transmitted from the countershaft to whichever main shaft gear is locked to the main shaft by its sliding clutch. The diagram in **FIGURE 38-30** depicts first range. The power flow for all ranges is the same and merely involves a different main shaft gear.

As you can see in Figure 38-30, the main box main shaft gears from back to front are reverse, first, second, third, and fourth. Fifth, or direct, range occurs when (a) the four–five sliding clutch is engaged to the back of the input shaft and (b) the power flows from the input shaft to the four–five sliding clutch to the main shaft.

All main boxes generally share the same power flow. One exception is when a main box overdrive is installed. For a main box overdrive, the fourth main shaft gear and its corresponding countershaft gears are changed to create the overdrive ratio. The driver must then select direct

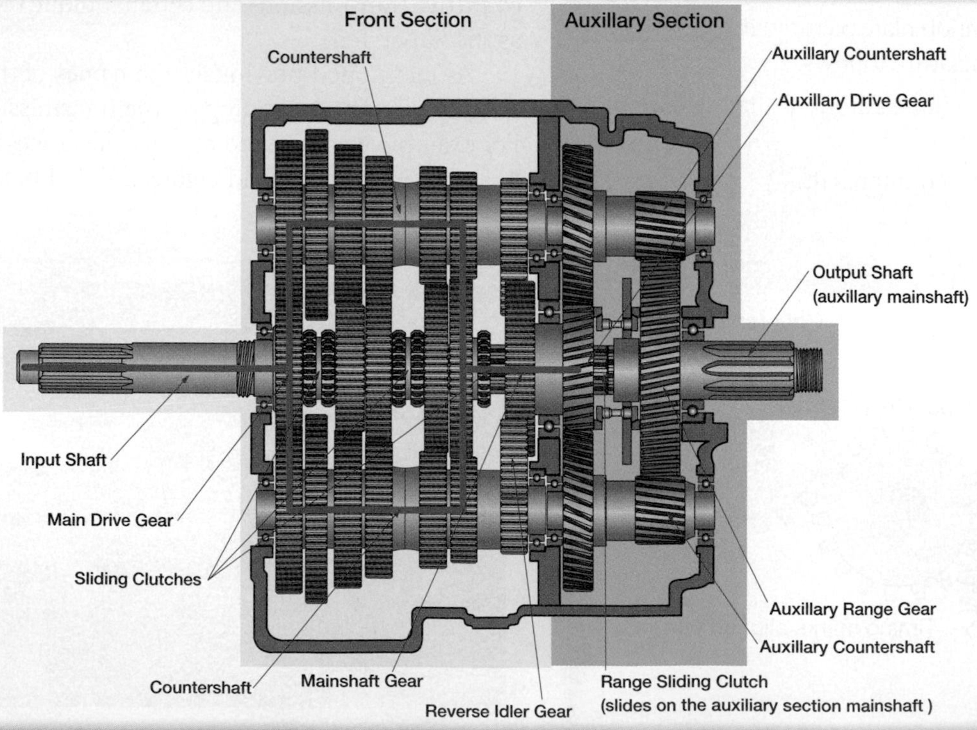

Front Section
Auxillary Section
Countershaft
Auxillary Countershaft
Auxillary Drive Gear
Output Shaft (auxillary mainshaft)
Input Shaft
Main Drive Gear
Sliding Clutches
Auxillary Range Gear
Auxillary Countershaft
Countershaft
Mainshaft Gear
Reverse Idler Gear
Range Sliding Clutch (slides on the auxiliary section mainshaft)

FIGURE 38-30 First gear mainbox, (front section), powerflow.

before selecting the fourth gear position (overdrive). In the past, the driver would simply alter the shift pattern by moving the shifter back to select direct and then forward to select the overdrive (in the normal fourth gear position). Similar to the problem in single countershaft transmissions, the awkward U-type shift pattern from third to fourth caused many unskilled drivers to continually select the wrong range first.

To eliminate driver error, all Eaton Fuller main box twin countershaft overdrive transmissions now use a bellcrank, like the one shown in FIGURE 38-31, to move the four–five shift fork in the opposite direction so that the shift pattern is normal, which makes it easier for drivers. This is the same approach used in single countershaft transmissions.

Auxiliary Sections

Today's high-torque capacity engines have very short operating ranges. Maximum torque is normally achieved at approximately 1,200 rpm, and rated speed may be as low as 1,800 rpm. The efficient operating range is limited to 600 rpm, so these transmissions require many more speed ranges than their lighter-duty counterparts. All multiple countershaft transmissions are equipped with auxiliary sections that provide additional speed ranges. **Auxiliary sections** are bolted onto the main transmission and have two, three, or four ratios to multiply the ratios available to the driver through the primary transmission.

The auxiliary section is basically another transmission attached to the main transmission. As such, the auxiliary section has its own two, three, or four available ratios—meaning the auxiliary section ratios multiply the available ratios from the main box by two, three, or four times.

In the past, auxiliary sections, then called auxiliary transmissions, were separate units attached to the main box by a short driveshaft. This arrangement required two shift levers in the cab and considerable skill from the driver in order to coordinate the shifting of both transmissions at once!

Auxiliary sections today are bolted directly to the main transmission and are controlled by air shift systems, making them much easier to operate. FIGURE 38-32 shows an auxiliary section bolted to an Eaton transmission. The main box or transmission of a twin countershaft unit is typically a five-speed sliding collar/clutch type transmission and is almost identical in design to a single countershaft five-speed with the exception of the extra countershaft. The main shaft gears are engaged by sliding clutches that lock the gears to the main shaft.

Eaton makes several different transmission models tailored to various vocations:

- The 8LL with nine forward speeds including a low-low range (for extreme pulling power).

FIGURE 38-31 The bellcrank (circled) causes the actual shift fork to move in the opposite direction to the shift rail.

FIGURE 38-32 Three-speed auxiliary section bolted to the back of the Eaton twin countershaft main box below it.

- The fifteen-speed deep-reduction has five low-low ranges (deep-reduction) for off-road and ten for on-highway (five in low range and five in high range).
- The eighteen-speed overdrive transmission is designed for high-speed, heavy line-haul operations.

Most of these transmissions will use the same design of a five-speed main box and will use different auxiliary sections to suit the application and provide the necessary range selections.

Two-Speed Auxiliary

The simplest auxiliary is the two-speed auxiliary, shown in FIGURE 38-33. The two-speed auxiliary is used in ten-speed transmission models—the five gear ranges in the front box are used twice each during acceleration, from start to highway speeds. The shifts go first through the low range of the auxiliary section and then through the high range.

The auxiliary section has its own main shaft that is not connected to the main shaft of the front section or main box. The auxiliary section also has twin countershafts. The auxiliary drive gear, which is splined to the output shaft of the main box, drives the countershafts of the auxiliary section. The low-range gears on the countershafts are in constant mesh with the large low-range gear on the auxiliary section main shaft. Range selection is controlled by an air-actuated pin-type synchronizer with a sliding clutch, which is splined to the auxiliary section main shaft.

With the synchronizer sliding clutch in the rearward position, the range gear is locked to the auxiliary section main shaft. The power flows from the auxiliary drive gear through the countershafts to the range gear. In the forward position, the synchronizer sliding clutch locks the auxiliary section main shaft to the auxiliary section drive gear. This provides high range or direct drive through the auxiliary. The countershafts and the range gears merely turn freely. FIGURE 38-34 provides a basic illustration to anchor the discussion of auxiliary power flows.

FIGURE 38-33 Two-speed auxiliary used in ten-speed transmissions.

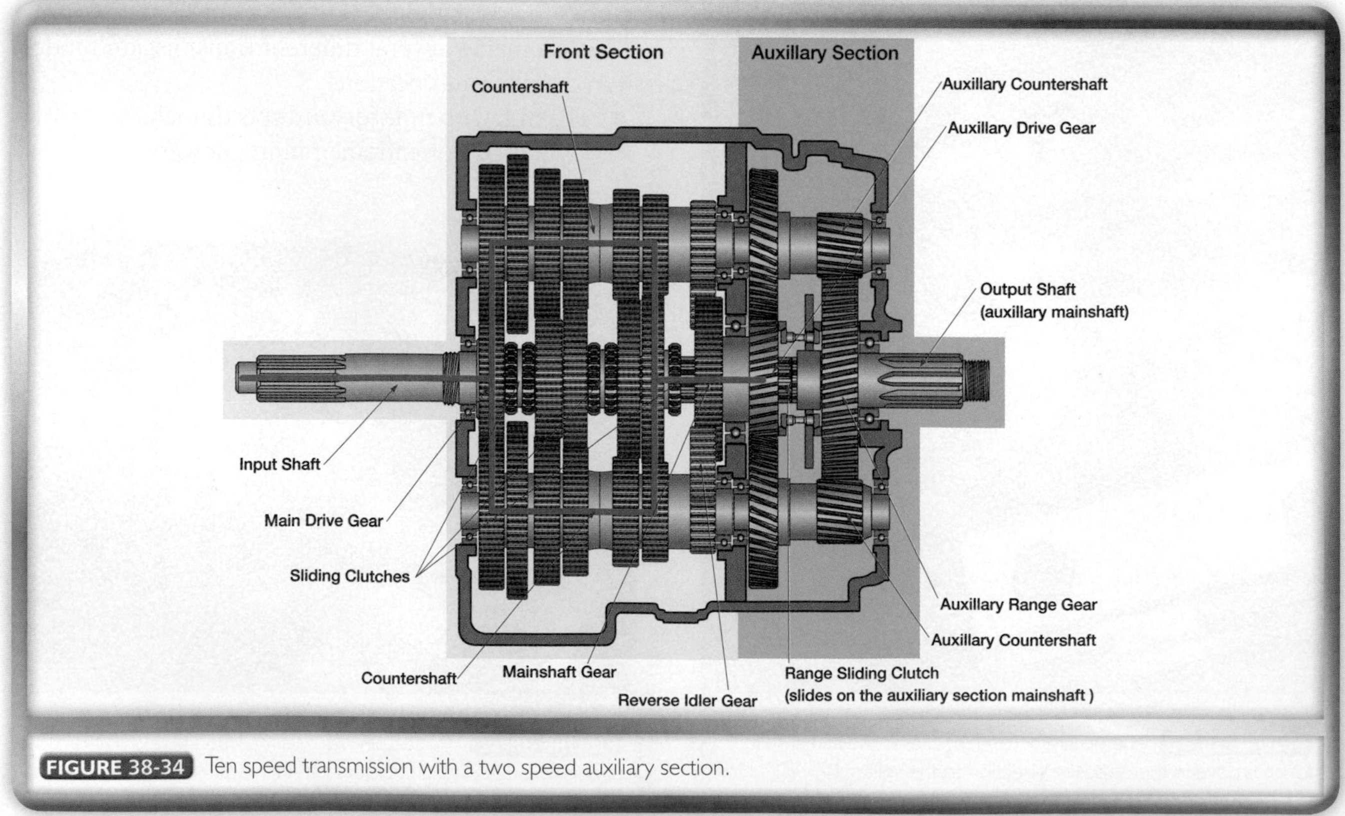

FIGURE 38-34 Ten speed transmission with a two speed auxiliary section.

Power Flow in a Two-Speed Auxiliary Section

The two-speed auxiliary has a low range and a high range. In low range, the power flows from the main shaft of the main box to the auxiliary section drive gear splined to it. The auxiliary section drive gear transfers the power to the auxiliary section countershafts and, therefore, to the auxiliary section countershaft low-range gears. The auxiliary section countershafts low-range gears are in constant mesh with the low-range gear on the auxiliary section main shaft. The range synchronizer is in the rearward position, as illustrated in FIGURE 38-35. The range synchronizers sliding clutch locks the range gear to the auxiliary section main shaft. The power flows through the range synchronizer sliding clutch and onto the auxiliary section main shaft.

In high range, the driver moves the range selector lever upward. The range synchronizer moves toward the front. This disengages the range gear from the auxiliary section main shaft and allows the gear to turn freely around the main shaft. With the synchronizer in this position, the synchronizer sliding clutch engages teeth in the back of the auxiliary drive gear. That engagement locks the gear to the auxiliary section main shaft, as illustrated in FIGURE 38-36.

So, the power flows from the main box main shaft to the auxiliary drive gear through the range synchronizer sliding clutch and onto the auxiliary section main shaft. That power flow results in a direct range (straight through) in the auxiliary. The auxiliary countershaft and the range gear are still turning as they are in constant mesh, but they are not connected to the auxiliary main shaft.

Safety

It is essential to shift the auxiliary section properly to avoid serious damage to the range synchronizer. The driver must preselect the range shift while in gear. The range interlock will allow the range to shift as the driver moves the shift lever to neutral. The sequence is as follows:

1. Starting from a stop with the auxiliary in low range, the transmission main box is shifted through the desired gear ranges until the main box top gear is reached.
2. Next with the main box still in top gear, the driver moves the range control to the high-range position.
3. Then, depressing the clutch, the driver moves the shift lever through neutral to select the first gear main box position again.

The air shift system has an interlock, shown in FIGURE 38-37, that will not allow the auxiliary section to shift range until the transmission shift lever is in the

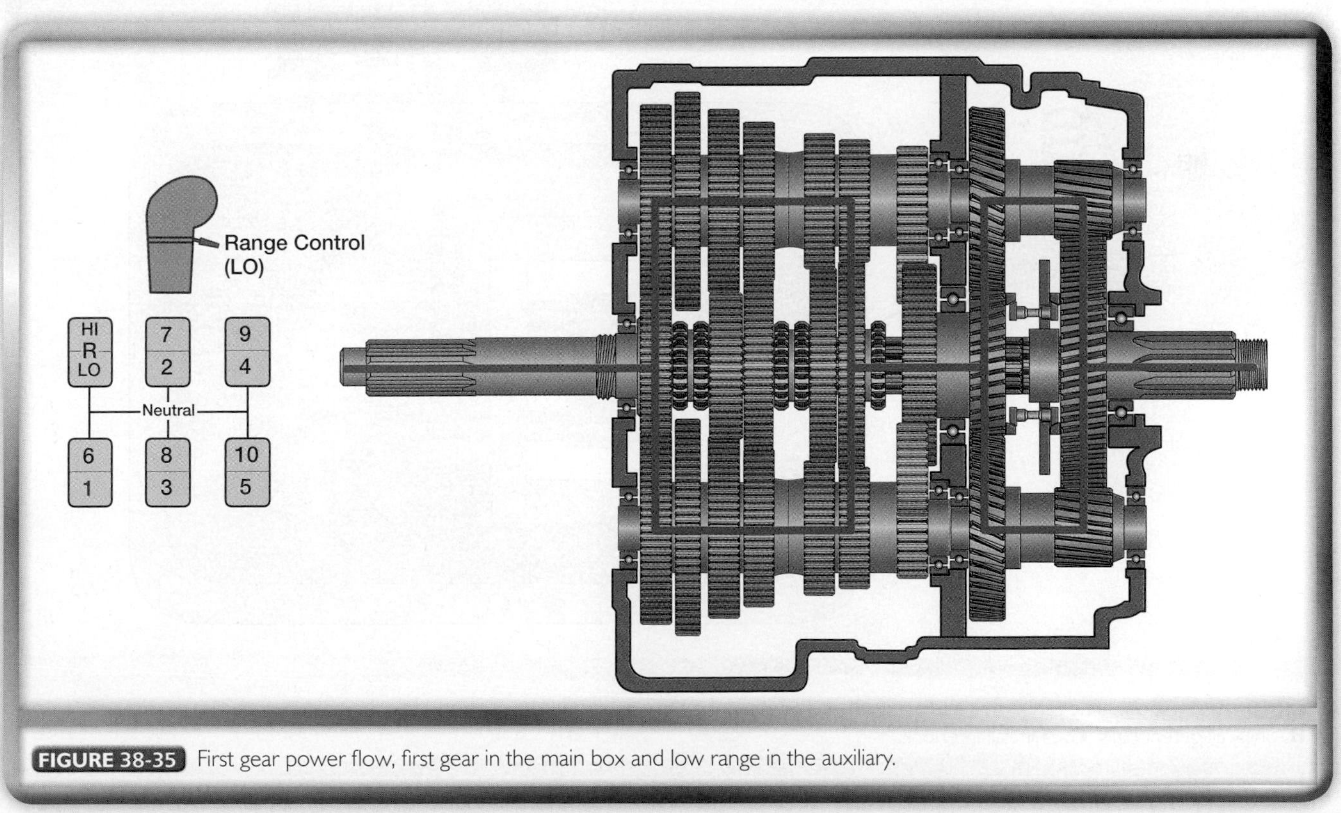

FIGURE 38-35 First gear power flow, first gear in the main box and low range in the auxiliary.

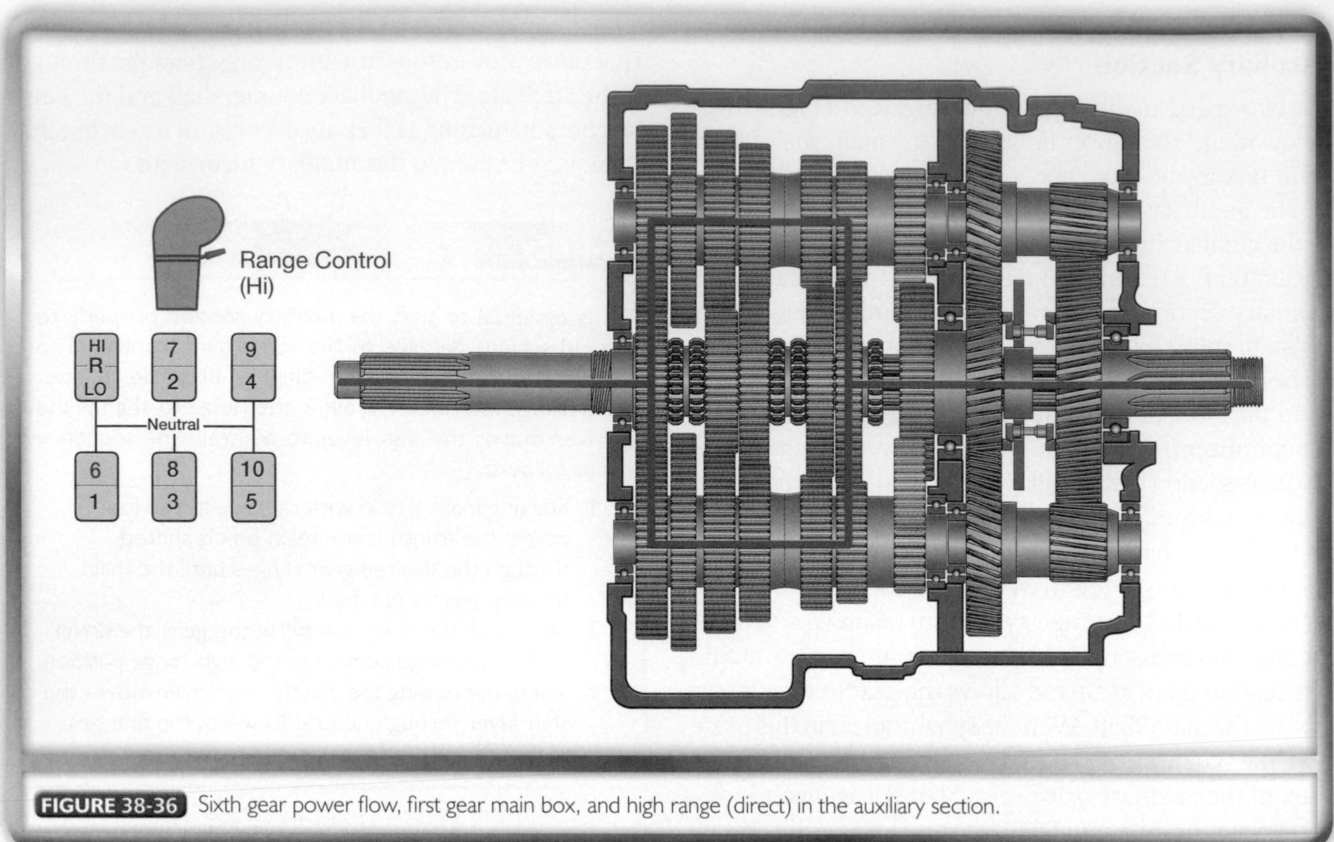

FIGURE 38-36 Sixth gear power flow, first gear main box, and high range (direct) in the auxiliary section.

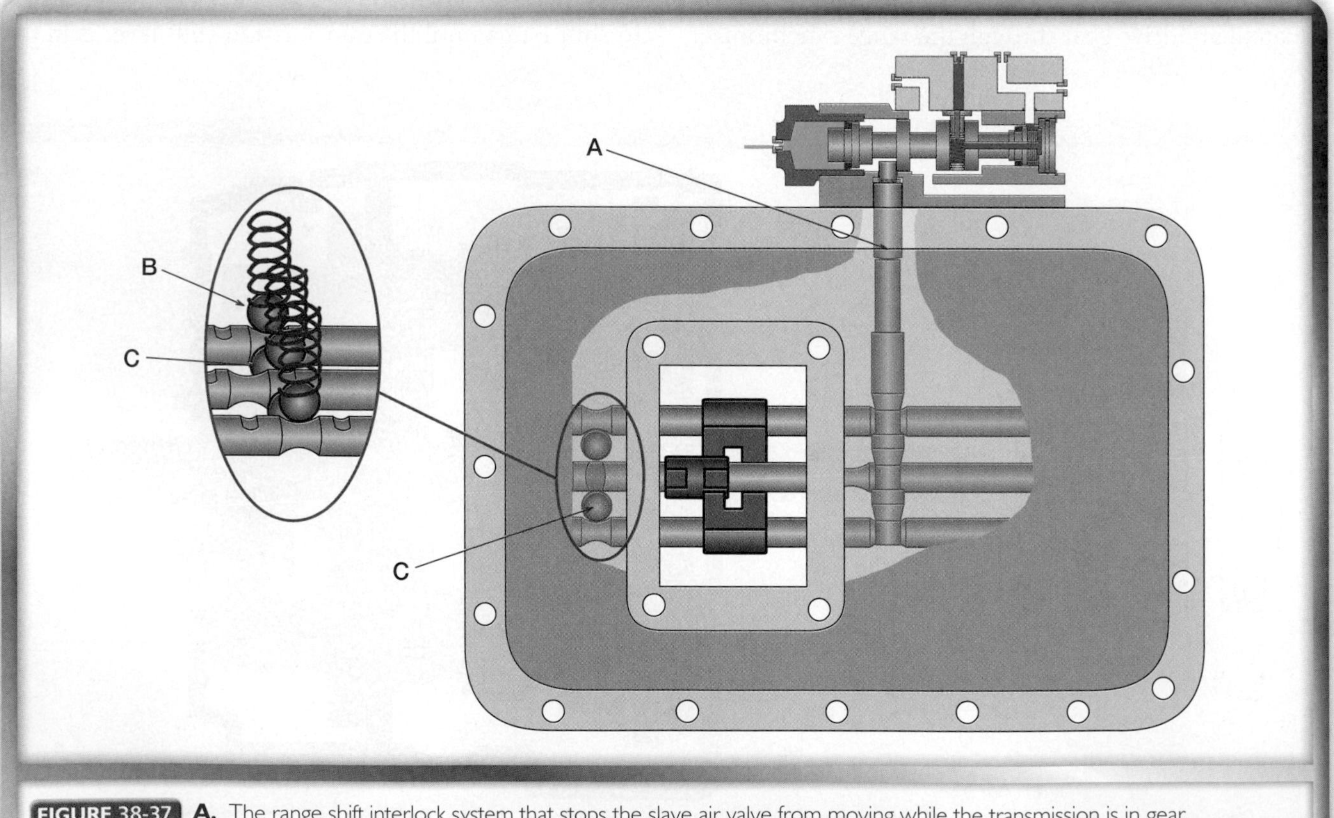

FIGURE 38-37 **A.** The range shift interlock system that stops the slave air valve from moving while the transmission is in gear. **B.** Shift rail detent balls. **C.** Shift rail interlock.

neutral position. So, as the driver moves the lever through neutral, the range shift will occur automatically and very quickly. If the driver tries to change ranges after he moves the lever to neutral, the speed difference between the auxiliary main shaft and the gears will be too great and the range synchronizer will be destroyed very quickly. On downshifting from high range, the gear shift lever is moved progressively down through the gears until the first gear main box is reached. Next, the driver preselects the low-range position and then shifts the lever through neutral towards the fifth gear main box position. As the lever moves through neutral, the range shift will again occur automatically. If the vehicle is stationary, it is permissible to perform a range shift in neutral, but never with the vehicle moving.

Three-Speed Auxiliary

There are two types of three-speed auxiliary sections: an original and a low-inertia type. We will discuss low-inertia type auxiliaries in the Low-Inertia Auxiliary Sections section later in this chapter. The original type was used with 8LL, 9L, fifteen-speed deep-reduction, and early thirteen-speed model transmissions. This auxiliary has exactly the same high- and low-range system as the two-speed auxiliary. In addition, the original three-speed auxiliary has another set of gears called the splitter gears on the auxiliary countershafts and the auxiliary section main shaft. In an 8LL, 9L or fifteen-speed deep-reduction model, the gear is known as the deep-reduction gear rather than the splitter gear, but it functions in the same way. FIGURE 38-38 and FIGURE 38-39 show a three-speed auxiliary from a deep-reduction fifteen-speed transmission.

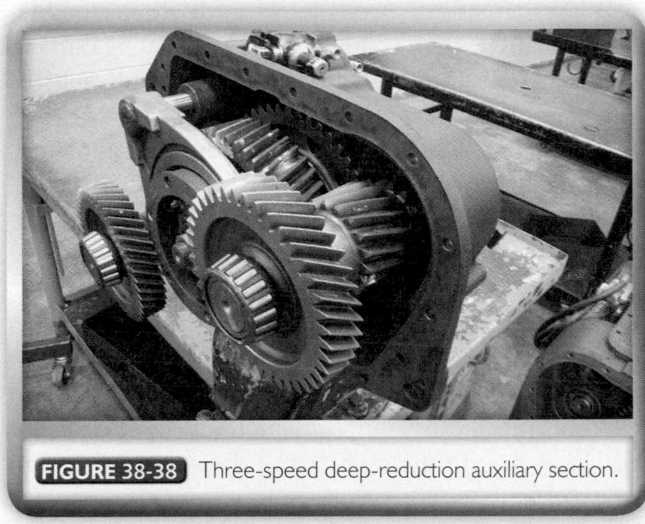

FIGURE 38-38 Three-speed deep-reduction auxiliary section.

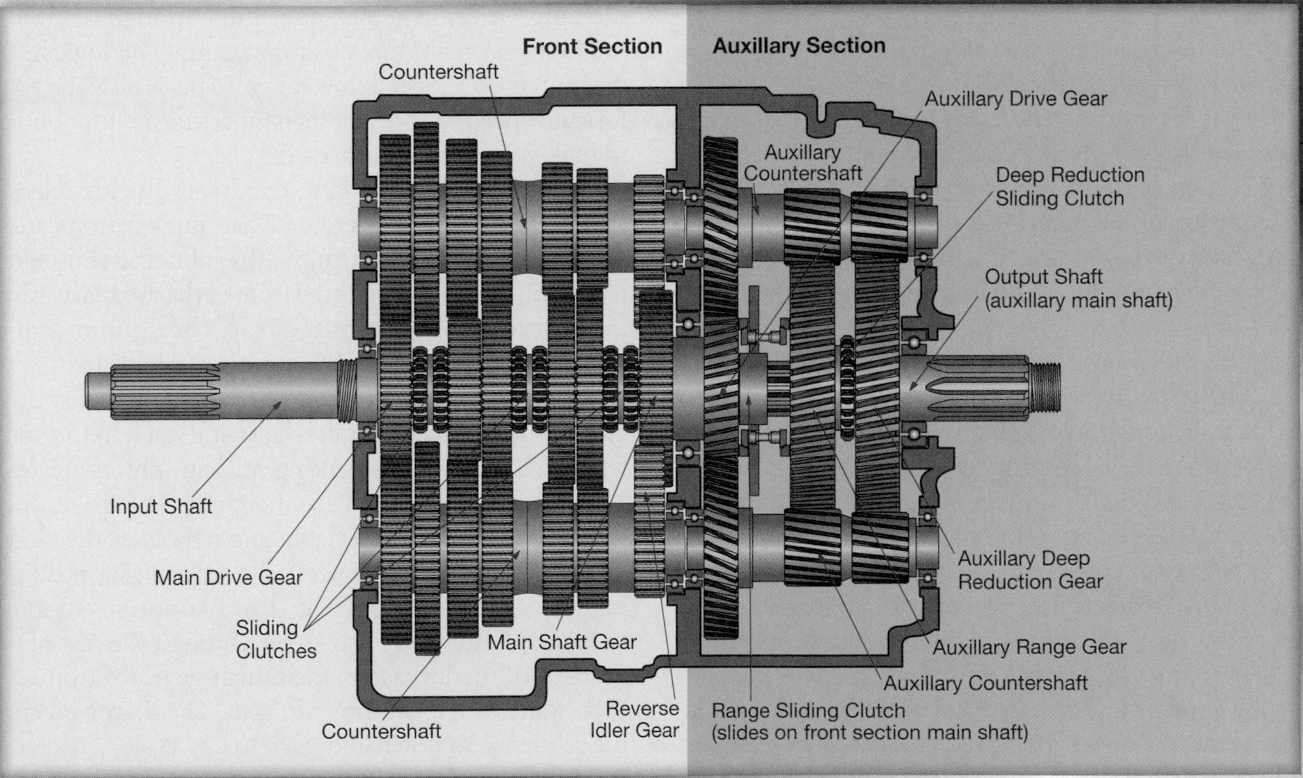

FIGURE 38-39 The extra deep-reduction gear set in the auxiliary section in this fifteen-speed deep-reduction transmission.

The auxiliary main shaft in the deep-reduction or the older thirteen-speed transmissions is split into two pieces behind the low-range gear. The splitter gear is located on the rear section of the auxiliary main shaft and the low-range gear is located on the front part of the auxiliary main shaft. The high- and low-range selection and operation are the same as in the two-speed, so we will concentrate on the splitter gears.

In older thirteen-speed transmissions, the splitter gears may provide an overdrive or underdrive ratio that allows the driver to split a ratio while accelerating through the gears. The splitter function is only available in high-range on thirteen-speed models.

In the 8LL, 9L, and fifteen-speed deep-reduction, the gears in this position produce a lower ratio than low range and provide extra low-speed pulling power. In these models, the function is only available when the auxiliary section is in low range.

The shifting mechanism for the splitter or deep-reduction gears involves a sliding clutch actuated by an air-operated shift fork. When the fork is in the rearward position, the sliding clutch locks the splitter or deep-reduction gear to the rear part of the auxiliary section main shaft. Power is forced to flow from the auxiliary drive gear to the auxiliary countershafts, to the splitter or deep-reduction gear, back to the rear section of the auxiliary main shaft, and then out to the driveline. In this rearward position, the front part of the auxiliary section main shaft is free to turn.

In the forward position, the sliding clutch engages internal teeth on a coupler collar that is also splined to the front section of the auxiliary main shaft. That locks the front section of the main shaft to the rear section of the main shaft. As this occurs, the splitter, or deep-reduction gear on the rear section of the main shaft, is disengaged and is free to turn.

In the 8LL transmission, the shift progression will be as outlined here. To begin, the main box is in low gear, the auxiliary section is in low range, and the deep-reduction gear is engaged. That starting position provides extremely low-speed and high-torque pulling power if and when necessary. If this extremely low range is not required, the driver will engage low gear main box combined with low range in the auxiliary. This will provide a normal pulling power low gear. During normal on-highway operation, the deep-reduction gear is not used, and usually the pulling power of the low gear in the mainbox is not required. In this case, the driver can start out in first gear main box and low range in the auxiliary. The driver would shift through second, third, and fourth, and then operate the air control for high range while still in fourth. The driver would then shift through neutral back to the first gear main box and go through the gears again. Eight forward speeds are available, therefore, during normal operation.

The 9L model is identical except that low gear in the main box is used both in conjunction with the deep-reduction gear and by itself during low-range operation. Nine normal forward speeds are available with one deep-reduction gear position.

The deep-reduction transmission has fifteen available speeds. The deep-reduction gear is engaged for off-road operation. With the auxiliary section in deep-reduction, the main box can be shifted through all five forward gears. Five low off-road ratios are produced. When highway operation is required, the deep-reduction gear is disengaged, and the transmission can be operated through all five forward gears, with the auxiliary in low range. The transmission can then be operated again through all five forward gears, with the auxiliary in high range. Ten on-highway speed ranges are, therefore, available.

In all of these transmissions, the shift control is interlocked to prevent shifting to deep-reduction mode unless the auxiliary section is in low range.

In thirteen-speed models, the splitter gears can only be used in high range. The driver starts out with the main box in low gear and the auxiliary section in low range. The driver then shifts through the main box gear to first, second, third, and fourth (direct). The driver then moves the range selector to high and shifts through neutral to the first gear main box position again. (The low shifter position is only used in low range.) This is now the sixth forward speed. The driver then moves the splitter button to high split while under load.

To initiate the split shift, the driver quickly releases and depresses the accelerator. That quick action causes the air-shift mechanism to move the splitter sliding clutch rearward, which detaches the front of the auxiliary transmission main shaft from the rear. The splitter gear is locked to the back half of the auxiliary main shaft.

At this point, the power flows from the auxiliary drive gear to the auxiliary countershafts and back to the splitter gear. This is now seventh gear. The splitter creates a "half" gear step between six and eight. The driver then returns the splitter to low split and depresses the clutch while moving the shift lever to the second gear position. Eighth gear is achieved. The driver continues to move to high split for nine, and so on, through the rest of the gears until the lever is in the fourth-gear position with high split, which is thirteenth gear. The driver reverses the sequence to downshift back to low gear.

Although these thirteen-speed transmissions were quite popular in the past, a technician is not likely to encounter a thirteen-speed transmission with the split auxiliary main shaft today. So, we will continue our discussion by covering the power flow only for the deep-reduction transmissions.

Power Flow Through a Deep-Reduction Three-Speed Auxiliary Section

Remember that, in a deep-reduction three-speed transmission like that shown in FIGURE 38-40, the auxiliary section main shaft is in two pieces, which can be joined or disconnected depending on whether the coupler is engaged by the splitter sliding clutch or not.

Starting in low range with the deep-reduction gear engaged, the driver selects low range by moving the range synchronizer rearward. The synchronizer's clutching teeth engage the clutching teeth of the low-range gear, locking the gear to the front part of the split auxiliary main shaft.

The deep-reduction sliding clutch is also in the rearward position. This motion does two things. First, the sliding clutch disengages from the shaft coupler, freeing the front half of the auxiliary section main shaft from the rear. Second, the sliding clutch engages the deep-reduction gear clutching teeth, locking it to the rear part of the auxiliary section main shaft, as illustrated in FIGURE 38-41.

The power flow is as follows. Power comes from the main box main shaft to the auxiliary section drive gear, which is splined to it and in constant mesh with the auxiliary section countershafts. Power flows to the auxiliary countershafts and back to the deep-reduction gear set at the rear of the auxiliary section. Power then flows down to the engaged deep-reduction gear and through the deep-reduction sliding clutch to the rear part of the auxiliary section main shaft. Power flow continues out to the driveline. Power also flows to the engaged range gear, but because the auxiliary main shaft is uncoupled, the range gear is free to turn.

In low range, the deep-reduction gear is not selected, so the deep-reduction sliding clutch will be in the forward position. This disengages the deep-reduction gear and

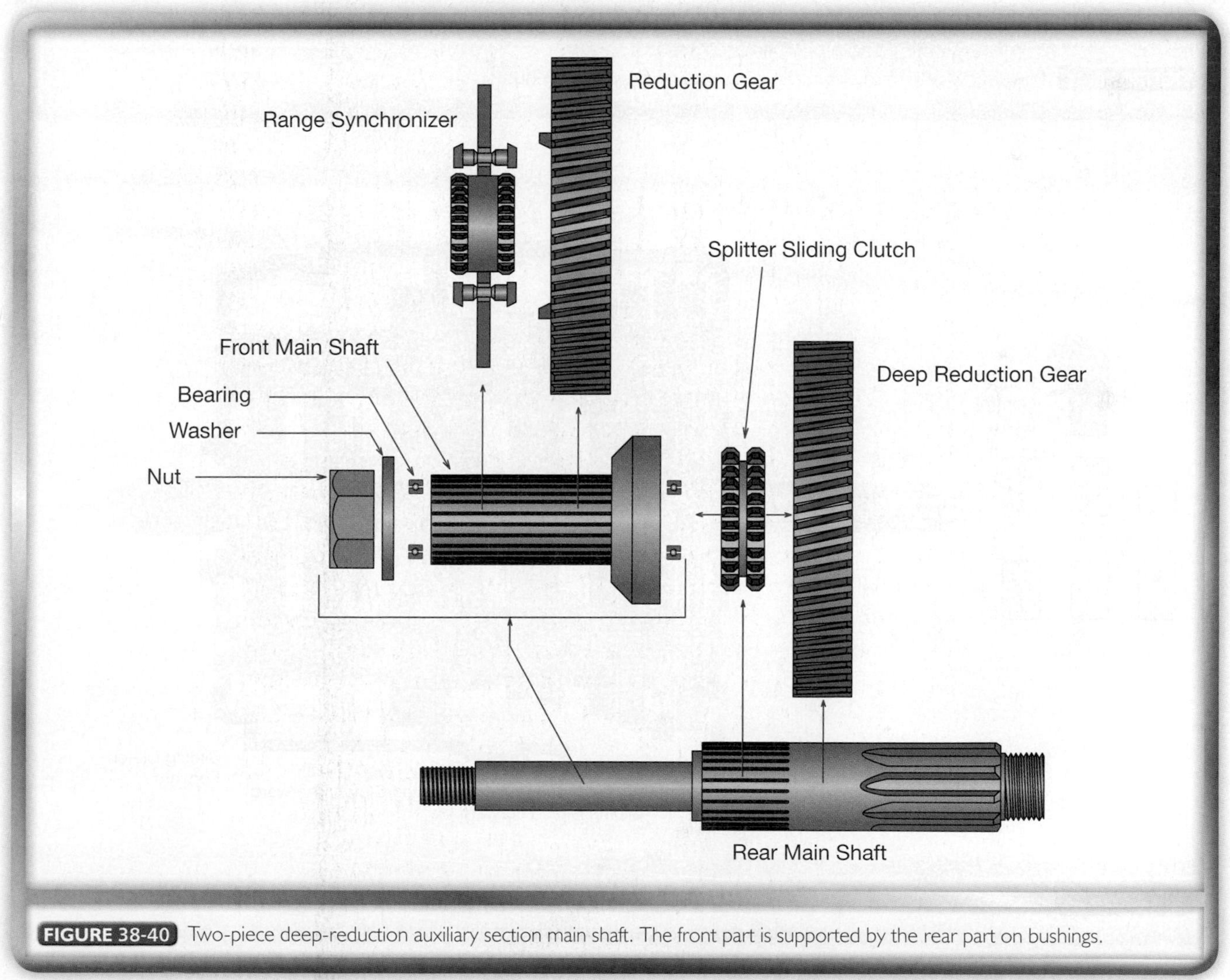

FIGURE 38-40 Two-piece deep-reduction auxiliary section main shaft. The front part is supported by the rear part on bushings.

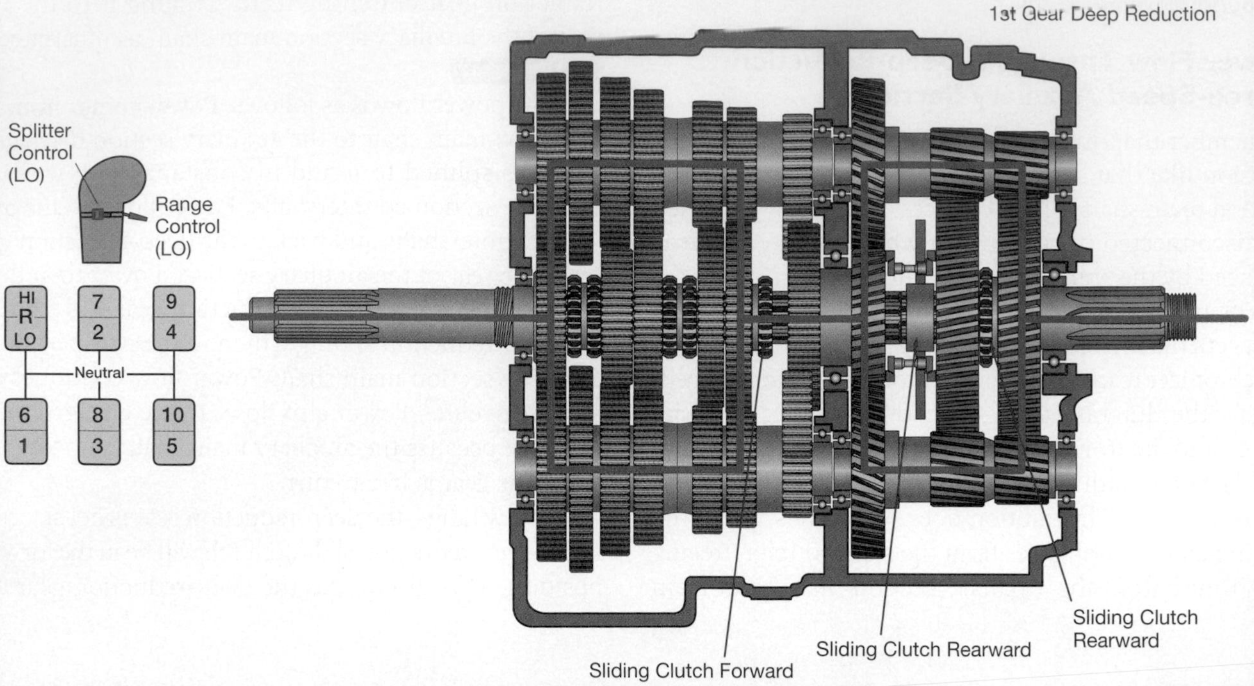

FIGURE 38-41 Power flow with main box in first gear and auxiliary in deep-reduction.

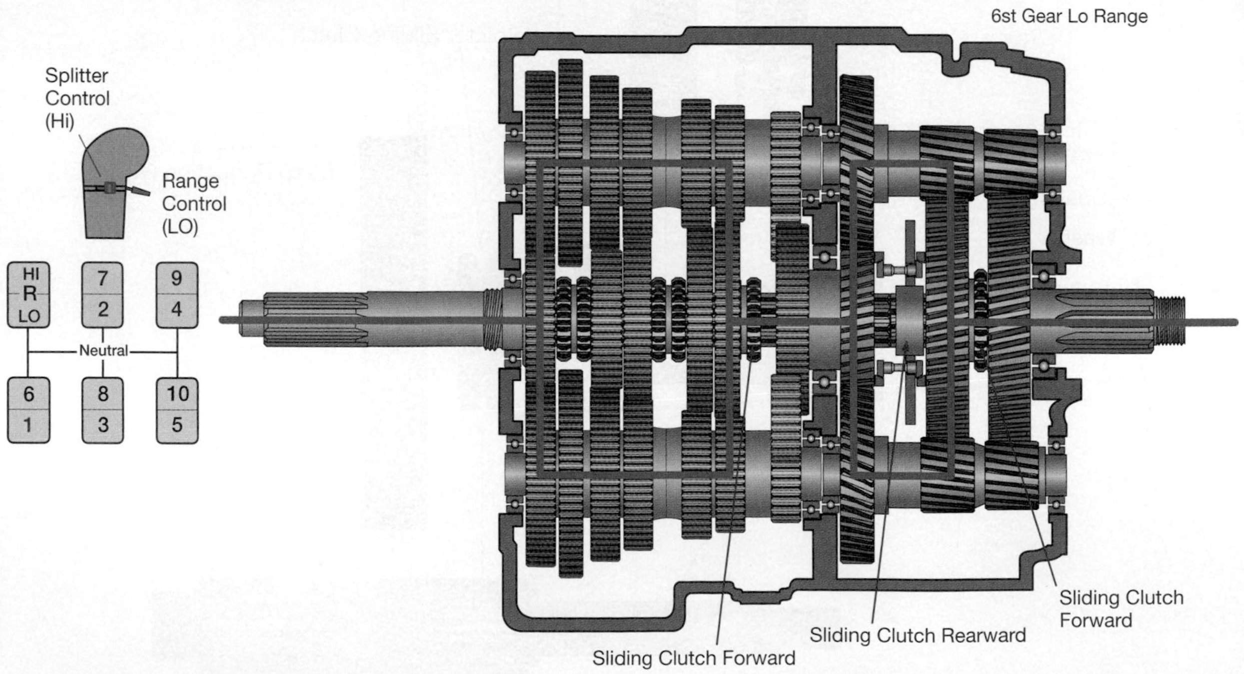

FIGURE 38-42 Power flow with main box in first gear and the auxiliary section in low range.

engages the clutching teeth of the coupler. With the clutch teeth engaged, the two pieces of the auxiliary countershaft are locked together, as illustrated in FIGURE 38-42.

The range synchronizer is still in the rearward position, locking the range gear to the front part of the auxiliary main shaft. The power flows from the auxiliary drive gear, out to the auxiliary countershafts, down through the low-range countershaft gears, to the low-range gear on the auxiliary main shaft. The power continues to flow through the range synchronizer sliding clutch, to the front part of the auxiliary main shaft, then through the coupler to the rear part of the auxiliary countershaft, and out to the drive line.

In high range, the deep-reduction sliding clutch remains in the forward position. In that position, the clutch couples the two parts of the auxiliary main shaft together, as illustrated in FIGURE 38-43. The range synchronizer moves forward. In the process, the range gear is disengaged, and the synchronizers clutching teeth engage the teeth on the rear of the auxiliary drive gear. The power flows from the main box main shaft to the auxiliary drive gear through the synchronizer sliding clutch to the front part of the auxiliary main shaft. Power then flows through the coupler to the rear section of the auxiliary main shaft and out to the drive line. The result is a direct, or one-to-one, power flow through the auxiliary section.

Low-Inertia Auxiliary Sections

The second type of three-speed auxiliary section is the low-inertia type pictured in FIGURE 38-44. **Low-inertia** designs allow the auxiliary to momentarily disengage from the main box during compound shifts, making it easier to

FIGURE 38-44 Low-inertia auxiliary section.

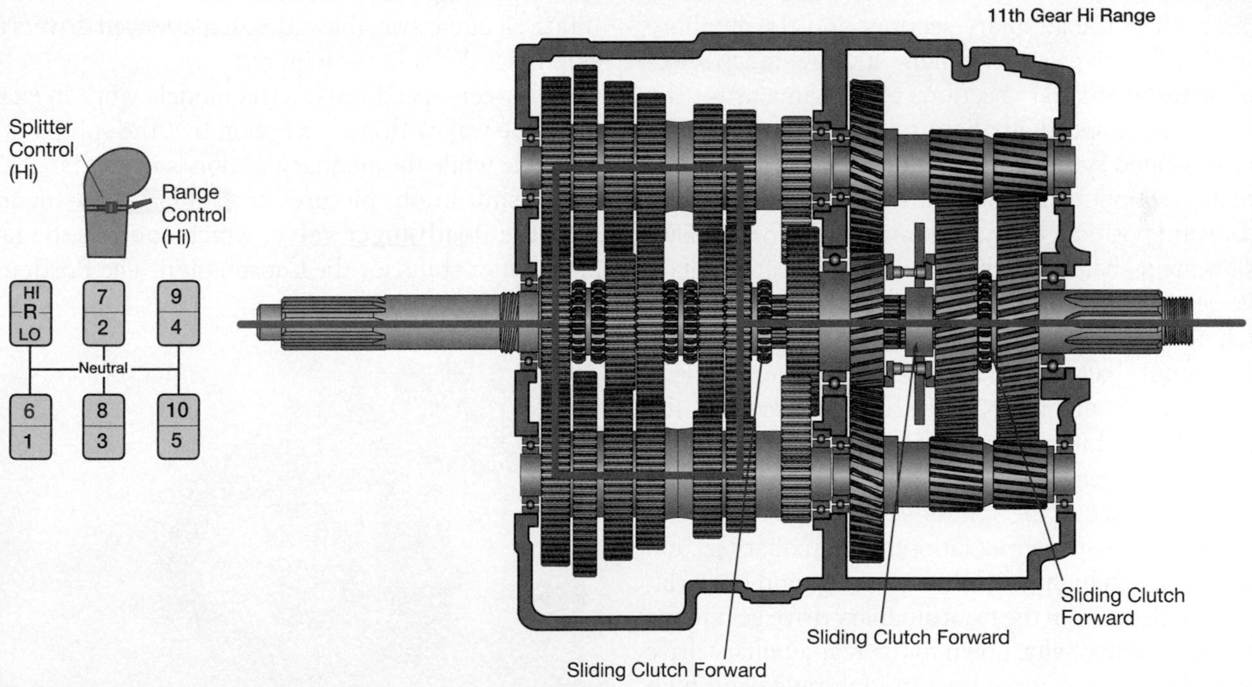

FIGURE 38-43 Sixth-gear power flow in a deep-reduction main box is in the first gear position and the auxiliary is in the high range (direct).

move the shift lever. The low-inertia type is also available as a four-speed auxiliary for eighteen-speed transmissions, but the internal components are the same—only the ratios are different. Low-inertia auxiliary sections can have three or four usable ratios, but the gearing is similar. In the three-ratio unit, the splitter sliding clutch is only used in high range.

Low inertia refers to the fact that the auxiliary section gearing is not permanently connected to the main box gearing through the auxiliary drive gear. Because there is not as much weight or inertial mass, the driver can make compound shifts more quickly and smoothly. A **compound shift** occurs when two parts of the transmission are being shifted at once; for example, where both the driver's shift lever and the auxiliary section are shifting simultaneously. In these auxiliary sections, the splitter sliding clutch is splined to the output shaft of the main box, and there are two different auxiliary drive gears: the front auxiliary drive gear and the rear auxiliary drive gear. The splitter air-shift mechanism determines which of these auxiliary drive gears will input to the auxiliary section countershafts. In thirteen-speed models, the splitter is used only in high range, but in eighteen-speed models, it is used in both high and low range.

In the old style three-speed auxiliary section, the range gear was between the input gear and the splitter gear, and the auxiliary section main shaft was in two pieces. In the low-inertia models, the range gear set is at the back of the auxiliary section, and the auxiliary main shaft is one piece. The high- and low-range selection for these auxiliary sections is the same as for the previous three-speed auxiliary section. For low range, an air-operated synchronizer locks the range gear to the auxiliary section main shaft in the rearward position. In the forward position, the synchronizer locks the auxiliary section main shaft to the back side of the rear auxiliary drive gear. In the low split position, the splitter sliding clutch moves forward to lock the front auxiliary drive gear to the output shaft of the main box and transfer torque to the auxiliary countershafts. In the high split position, the splitter sliding clutch moves rearward and locks the rear auxiliary drive gear to the output shaft of the main box.

The presence of the splitter sliding clutch provides two different possible input ratios to the auxiliary section countershafts in high range. In high range and low split, the power flows from the front auxiliary drive gear to the auxiliary countershafts, down to the rear auxiliary drive gear, and out to the drive line. In high range and high split, the rear auxiliary drive gear is locked to the output shaft of the main box and the range synchronizer sliding clutch has locked the auxiliary section main shaft to the rear side of the rear auxiliary drive gear, providing a direct power flow through the auxiliary section.

To operate an eighteen-speed transmission using all the forward gears, the driver first selects the main box low gear, with the auxiliary in low range and low split, and then accelerates. Next, the driver moves the splitter button to high split, while under load, and initiates the split shift by momentarily releasing and reapplying the accelerator.

The next shift is a lever shift. The driver first selects low split while under load and then depresses the clutch and moves the lever toward first gear position. During this process, the driver double clutches to match the shaft and gear speeds. This is called a compound shift as both the main section and the auxiliary are being shifted at the same time. The driver continues up through the main box ranges, using low and high split in each until reaching fourth gear main box, low range, and high split. At this point, the driver has gone through ten forward speeds so far.

The next shift has three elements to it. While under load, the driver will switch to high range, move the splitter to low split, and then double clutch while moving the shift lever back to the first gear main box position. As the shift lever moves through neutral, the range shift and the splitter shift will occur. The driver continues through the remaining main box gears, using each in low and then high split until he reaches the fourth gear main box, high range, and high split. That gives the vehicle eight more forward ratios for a total of eighteen speeds. On deceleration, the driver simply reverses the process.

Depending on the load, it is not always necessary to utilize all of the available ratios. Experienced drivers may skip ranges or splits as required.

Thirteen-speed low-inertia models work in exactly the same way with the exception that the splitter is not available while the auxiliary section is in low range. The driver shift knob, pictured in **FIGURE 38-45**, incorporates the **Roadranger valve**, which controls the range and splitter shifts for the transmission. The Roadranger

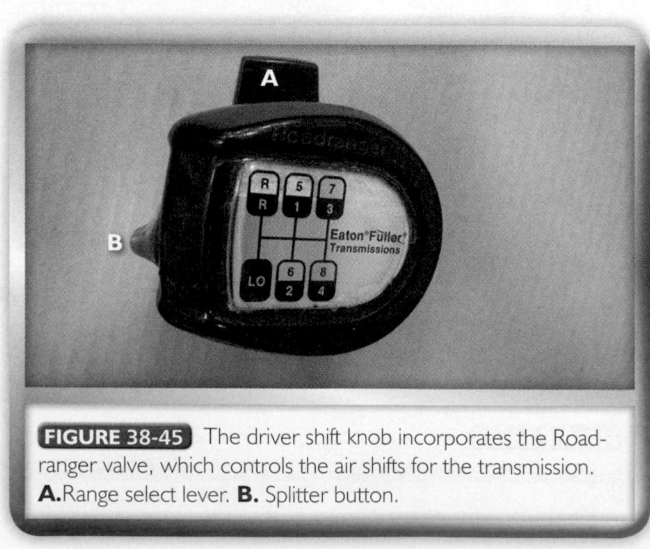

FIGURE 38-45 The driver shift knob incorporates the Roadranger valve, which controls the air shifts for the transmission. **A.** Range select lever. **B.** Splitter button.

valve will physically not allow a splitter shift while in low range. The thirteen-speed low-inertia transmission provides five speeds in low range (from low to fourth) and then four lever positions and four splits in high range for eight more ratios, bringing the total number of ranges to thirteen.

Power Flows Through an Eighteen-Speed Transmission with a Four-Speed Auxiliary

The thirteen-speed transmission's auxiliary section is identical to the eighteen-speed model except for the gear ratios used. Before discussing the power flows, let's quickly review the positioning of all the components in this type of transmission.

In the low-inertia auxiliary section, the main shaft is one piece, and the range synchronizer sliding clutch is splined to the shaft. The low-inertia box has two selectable auxiliary drive gears: the front and the rear auxiliary drive gear. The front auxiliary drive gear rotates around the main box main shaft. Even though it rotates around the main shaft, the front auxiliary drive gear is not splined to it. The rear auxiliary drive gear rotates around, but is not splined to, the auxiliary section main shaft. The splitter sliding clutch sits between the two auxiliary drive gears and is splined to the front box main shaft. All of the power exiting the main box must pass through the splitter sliding clutch to reach the auxiliary section. The position of the splitter sliding clutch determines which of the drive gears will drive the auxiliary countershafts. The range synchronizer and its sliding clutch sit just behind the rear auxiliary drive gear and just in front of the range gear.

Now, let's examine all four power flows. Recall that thirteen-speed transmissions are mechanically prevented from using the splitter in low range by the Roadranger valve (the shift selector knob).

- Low range low split. In low range low split, the splitter sliding clutch, which is splined to the main box main shaft, is forward locking the front auxiliary drive gear to the main box main shaft. The range synchronizer sliding clutch is rearward, locking the range gear to the auxiliary section main shaft. The power flow is as follows. Rotational power flows from the main box main shaft to the front auxiliary drive gear and out to the auxiliary countershafts. From the auxiliary countershafts, the power flows down to the engaged range gear, through the synchronizer sliding clutch to the auxiliary main shaft, and out to the drive line. FIGURE 38-46A shows the low-range low-split power flow.

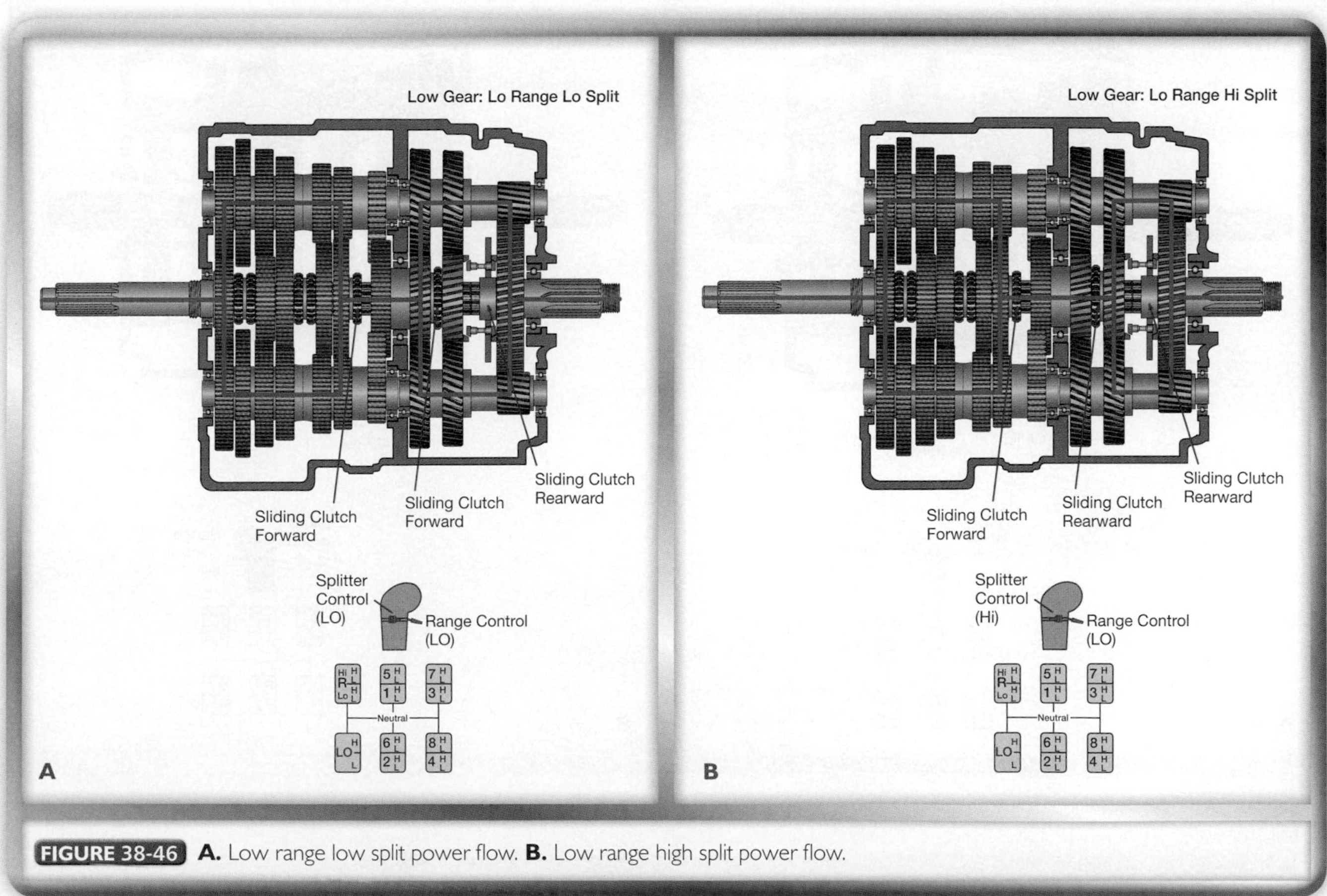

FIGURE 38-46 **A.** Low range low split power flow. **B.** Low range high split power flow.

- Low range high split. In low range high split, the synchronizer sliding clutch remains rearward, thereby locking the range gear to the auxiliary section main shaft. The splitter sliding clutch moves rearward and engages the rear auxiliary drive gear. That engagement locks the drive gear to the main box main shaft. The power flows from the main box main shaft, through the splitter sliding clutch, to the rear auxiliary drive gear, and out to the auxiliary countershafts. The power then flows down to the range gear, through the synchronizer sliding clutch, to the auxiliary main shaft, and out to the drive line. The driver splits between low and high split while moving up through the gears in low range. FIGURE 38-46B shows the low-range high-split power flow.
- Range shift. The range shift is only made once during upshifting and once during downshifting. Upon reaching top gear in low range (fourth gear main box and high split), the driver will make a compound shift by first moving the splitter button to low split. While maintaining torque, the driver will then preselect high range by pulling the Roadranger valve lever up. Next, the driver double clutches while moving the shift lever back to the first gear main box position. As the shift lever moves through the neutral position, the shifts will occur automatically as the gears reach synchronous speed.
- Power flow high range low split. To move to high range, the range sliding clutch moves forward and engages the back of the rear auxiliary drive gear. That action locks the rear auxiliary drive gear to the auxiliary main shaft. In the low split position, the splitter sliding clutch is forward. In that position, the splitter sliding clutch engages the front auxiliary drive gear and locks it to the main shaft of the main box. The power flows from the main box main shaft to the splitter sliding clutch, then to the front auxiliary drive gear, and out to the auxiliary section countershafts. Then, power continues to flow from the auxiliary section countershafts to the rear auxiliary drive gear, through the range sliding clutch to the auxiliary main shaft, and out to the driveline. FIGURE 38-47A shows a high range low split power flow.

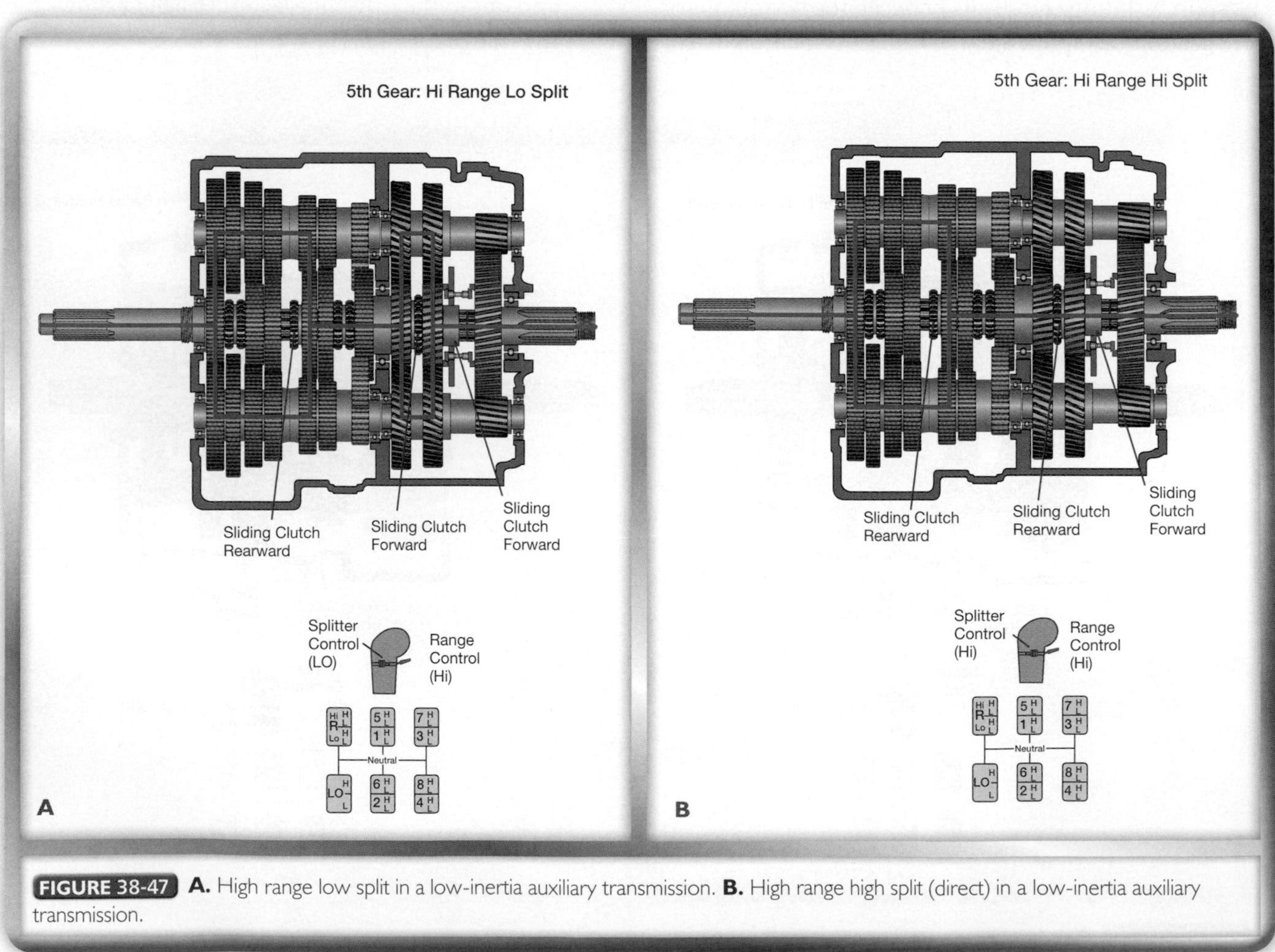

FIGURE 38-47 **A.** High range low split in a low-inertia auxiliary transmission. **B.** High range high split (direct) in a low-inertia auxiliary transmission.

- Power flow high range high split. Throughout high-range operation, the range sliding clutch stays forward, locking the back half of the rear auxiliary drive gear to the auxiliary main shaft. To achieve high split, the splitter sliding clutch moves rearward and engages the front half of the rear auxiliary drive gear. This motion makes the rear auxiliary drive act as a bridge between the main box main shaft and the auxiliary main shaft, effectively connecting the two shafts together. The power flows from the main box main shaft to the splitter sliding clutch, onward to the rear auxiliary drive gear. Power continues to flow through the range sliding clutch to the auxiliary main shaft and out to the driveline. In high range high split, the auxiliary section is in direct drive. That means the output from the main box passes through the auxiliary unchanged. **FIGURE 38-47B** shows a high range high split power flow.

Auxiliary Section Air Control

Pressurized air from the vehicle's air system is used to perform all auxiliary section shifting. The air control system starts with the master control on the shift lever. The master control is the driver's shift knob, called the Roadranger valve. The air shifting system can be broken up into two distinct parts: range shift and splitter shifting. There are hundreds of Eaton Fuller transmission models for various applications and vocations. Some will have slightly different air systems, but most of the air shift controls and shifting follow the descriptions in this section.

Range Shift Control

All Eaton Fuller twin countershaft transmissions will have a range control switch consisting of a small lever. The lever is in the down position for low range and pulled up for high range. Air from the vehicle system is supplied to a combination **air filter/pressure regulator** that is mounted to the transmission, as illustrated in **FIGURE 38-48**. The pressure regulator/filter cleans the supply air and regulates it to between 58 and 63 psi (400 to 434 kPa).

Air from the pressure regulator is piped to the **slave air valve**, a valve mounted on the side of the transmission that controls air flow to the range shift cylinder through a 1/4" (6.35 mm) air line. A spool valve piston is located inside the slave air valve. A center-drilled passage in that spool valve piston directs air to either the low- or high-range ports on the **range shift cylinder**. (The job of the range shift cylinder is to control the range

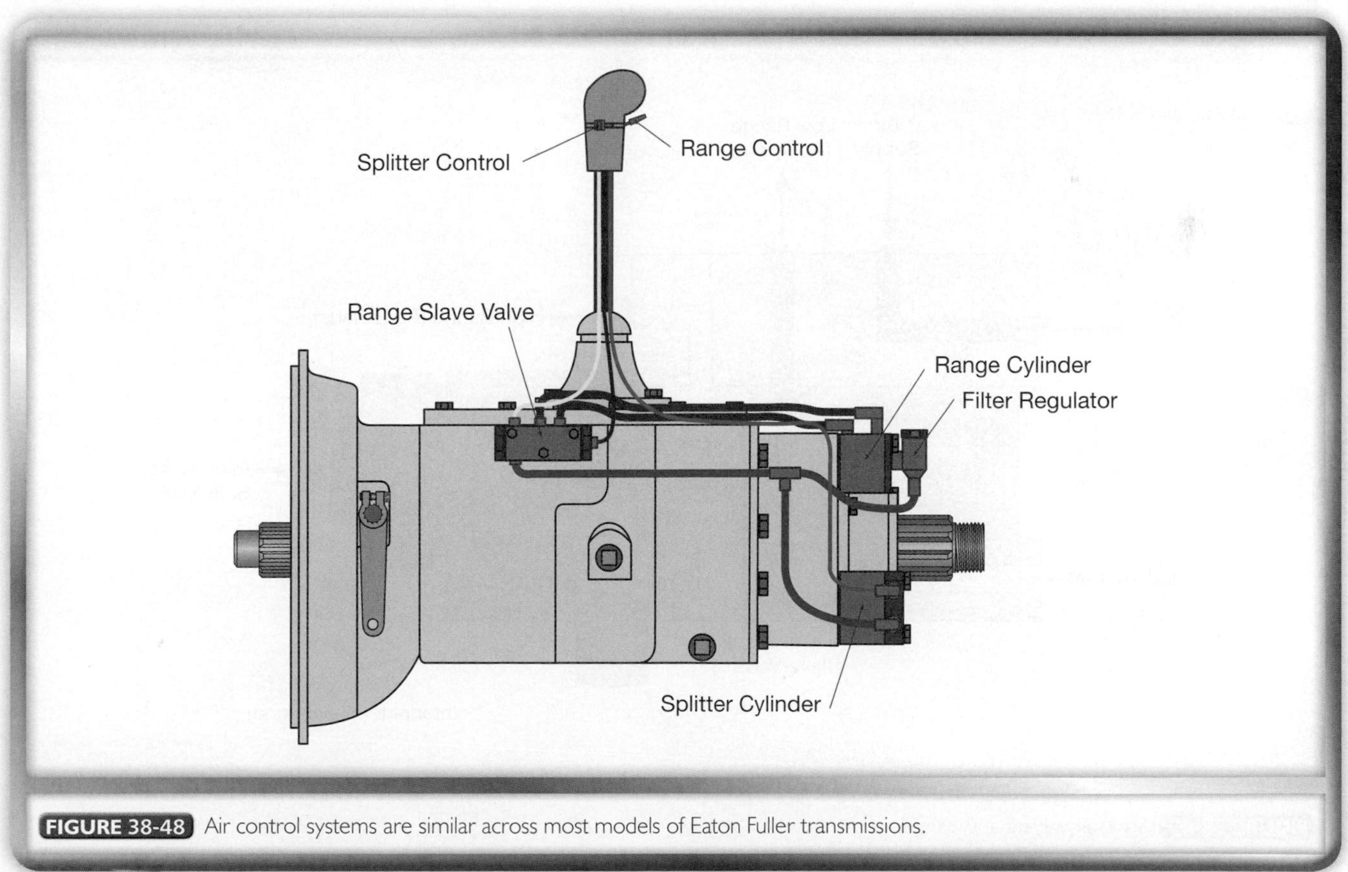

FIGURE 38-48 Air control systems are similar across most models of Eaton Fuller transmissions.

shifts in the auxiliary.) The air supply to the slave air valve is also directed to the red 1/8"or 5/32" (3.175 or 3.969 mm) air line connected to the range shift control at port "S." With the range shift lever in the down (low-range) position, the air is allowed to pass through the range shift valve and out to the black 1/8" or 5/32" (3.175 or 3.969 mm) air line connected to the range shift control valve at port "P."

The air flows down the black line and acts on the backside of the spool valve piston inside the slave air valve. The same air pressure is now pushing against the front and the rear of the spool valve inside the slave air valve. The spool valve will stay in the forward position because the surface area at the rear of the slave air valve is larger than the front, as illustrated in FIGURE 38-49. This directs the supply air through the spool of the slave air valve and through a 1/4" (6.35 mm) airline to the low-range (front) port of the range shift cylinder. The cylinder and its shift fork are moved rearward, which pushes the range synchronizer into low range by locking the range gear to the auxiliary output shaft.

When high range is selected, the range control valve seals off the supply of air to the black air line. The range control valve simultaneously exhausts the air in the black line at the master control from port "E." When this happens, the constant supply of air at the front of the slave air valve spool valve pushes the spool rearward, as illustrated in FIGURE 38-50. When the spool moves to the rearward position, it directs the flow of supply air through another 1/4" (6.35 mm) airline to the high-range (rear) port of the range shift cylinder and exhausts the air in the low-range side of the cylinder at the slave air valve. This forces the range cylinder piston forward. That forward motion moves the range synchronizer to high range by engaging the back side of the auxiliary drive gear.

All Eaton Fuller transmissions have an interlock system that prevents the slave air valve from moving unless the transmission is in neutral. The interlock system consists of a spring-loaded pin that is pushed out from the transmission and into the slave air valve spool valve. The pin physically stops the spool valve from moving. It is essential that the range shift be preselected while the transmission is in gear. Then, as the shift lever moves through neutral, the range shift will occur automatically.

Splitter Shift Control

The splitter shift is controlled by a movable button on the master shift control. For low split, this button is moved rearward; for high split, the button is moved forward. Depending on the transmission model, this button may be blue, red, or grey. The ten-speed, thirteen-speed, and eighteen-speed shift knobs are shown in FIGURE 38-51.

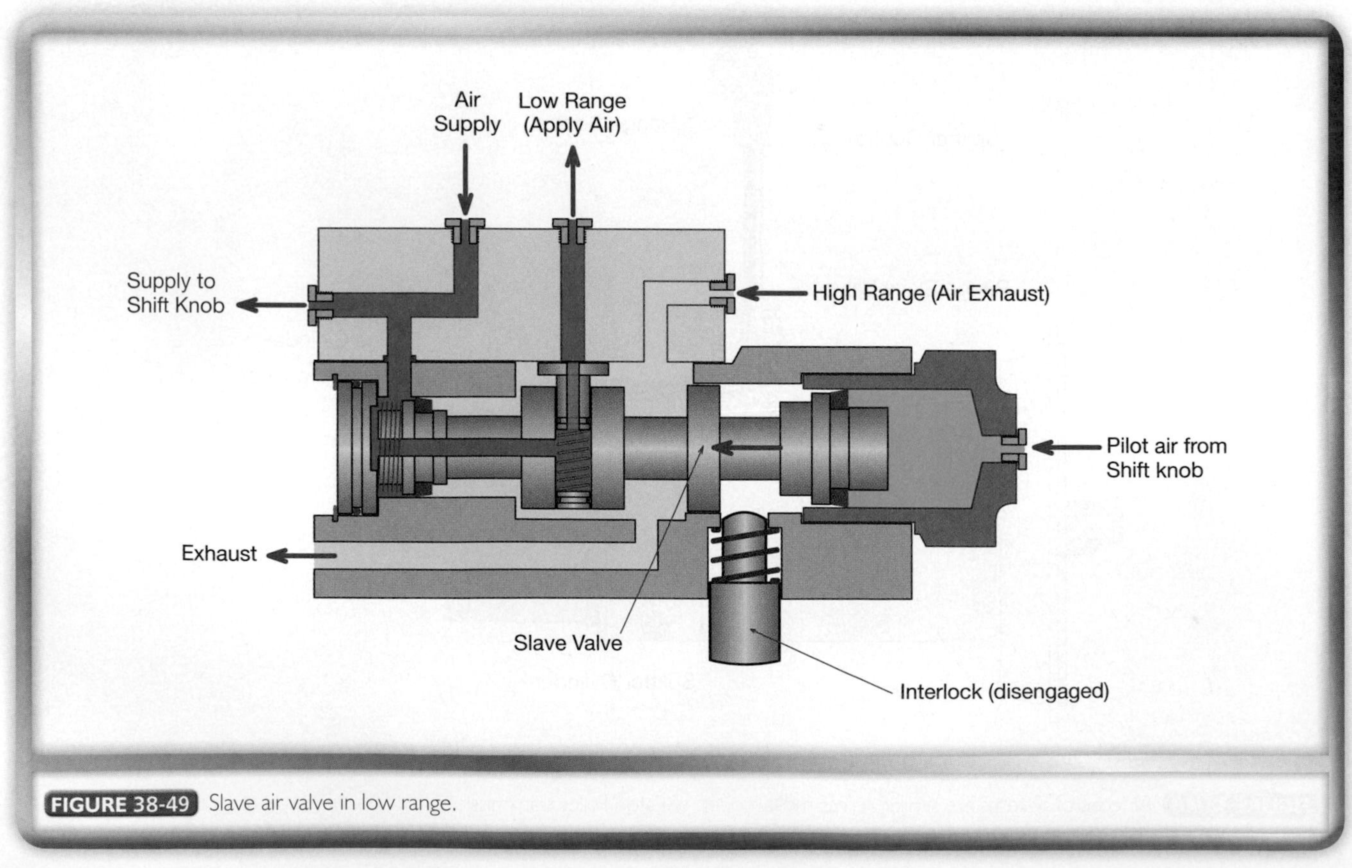

FIGURE 38-49 Slave air valve in low range.

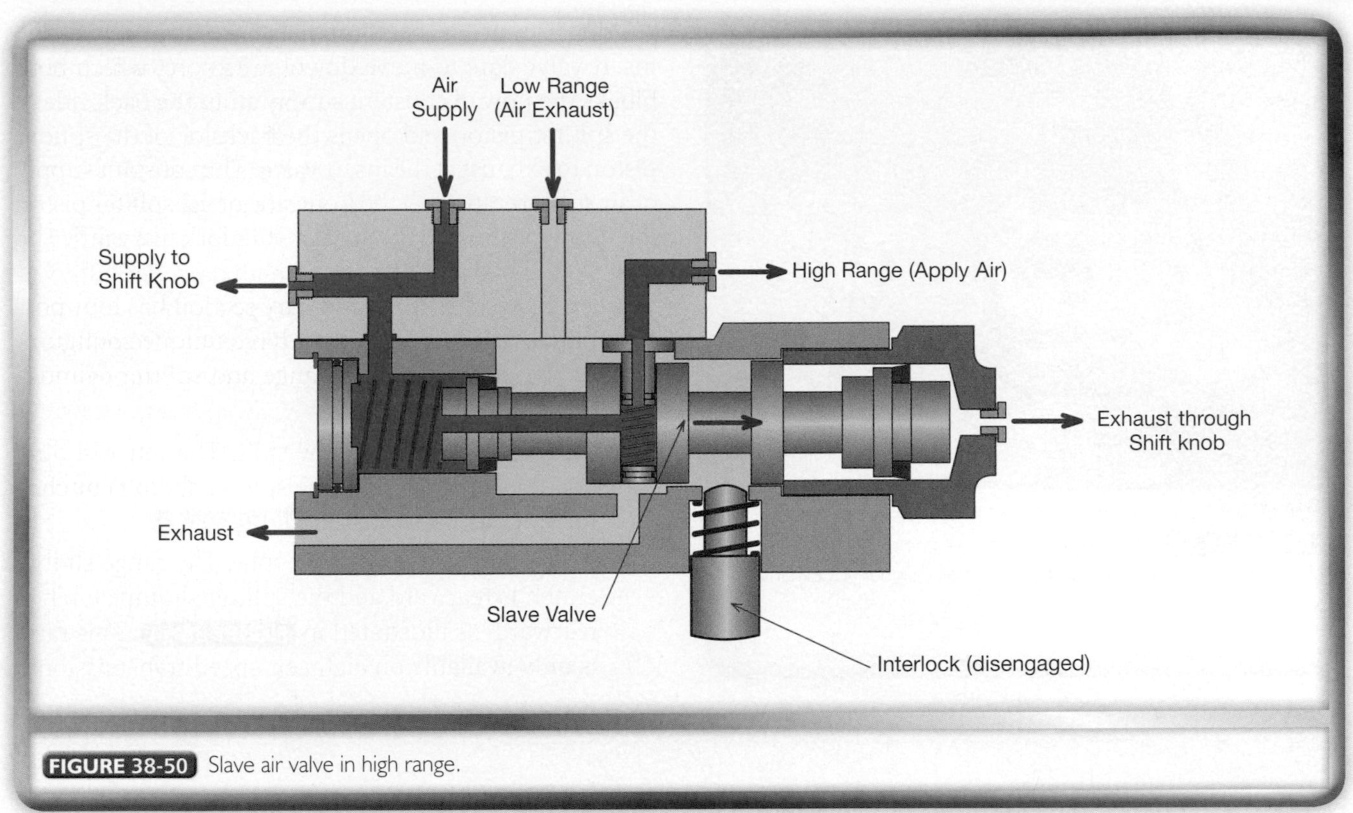

FIGURE 38-50 Slave air valve in high range.

The blue colored button is used only for deep-reduction transmissions. An interlock system in the master shift control ensures the blue button can only be used when the auxiliary section is in low range. The red button is used with a thirteen-speed transmission. Its master control interlock only allows the button to be used when the auxiliary section is in high range. The gray button is used with an eighteen-speed transmission and can be activated with the auxiliary section in both high and low range.

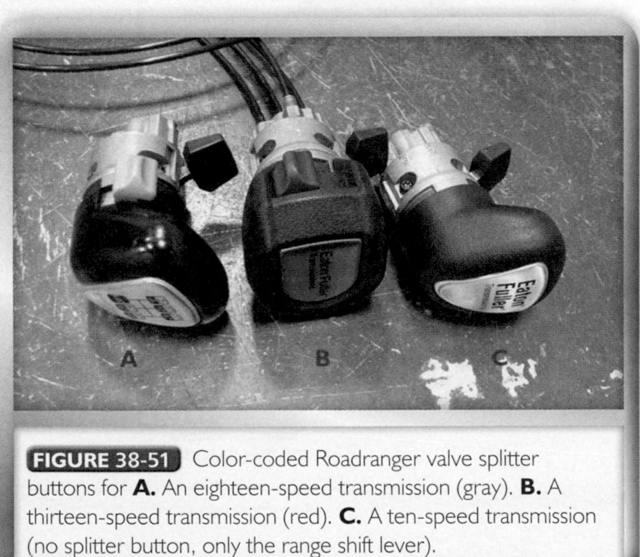

FIGURE 38-51 Color-coded Roadranger valve splitter buttons for **A.** An eighteen-speed transmission (gray). **B.** A thirteen-speed transmission (red). **C.** A ten-speed transmission (no splitter button, only the range shift lever).

A constant supply of air from the air filter/regulator is delivered to the **splitter shift cylinder** cover and, through the cover, to both the front and the rear side of the splitter shift piston. (The job of the splitter shift cylinder is to control the splitter sliding clutch.) The rear side of the piston has a larger surface area than the front so this forces the piston and the splitter shift fork forward, resulting in low split. When high split is desired, the splitter button on the shift knob is pushed forward. That forward motion connects the air from the red 1/8" or 5/32 (3.175 or 3.969mm)diameter air line at the range control lever to a third 1/8" or 5/32" (3.175 or 3.969 mm) air line connected to port "SP." The SP air line is usually blue. The other end of this air line is connected to the **insert valve** attached to the splitter shift cylinder cover that controls the air flow to the front or rear of the splitter cylinder piston. An insert valve is shown in FIGURE 38-52 . The insert valve allows air to flow to both sides of the splitter cylinder piston in low split and drains the air from the rear side of the cylinder piston in high split.

Note that, in thirteen-speed transmission models, the air to activate the splitter will be delivered from a 1/8" or 5/32" (3.175 or 3.969 mm) air line, which is usually green in color. The green air line is connected to the high-range port of the slave air valve, which brings air to the "H/L" port of the Roadranger valve. In fifteen-speed deep-reduction transmissions, the green line is connected to the low-range outlet port of the slave air valve.

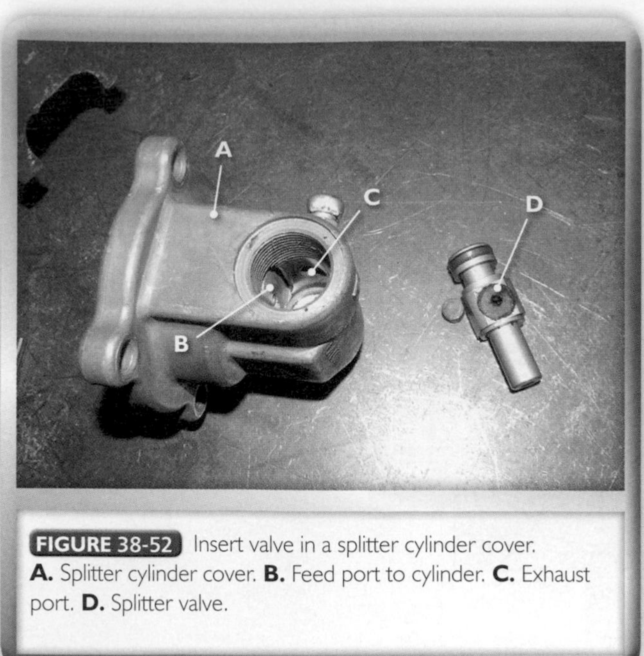

FIGURE 38-52 Insert valve in a splitter cylinder cover. **A.** Splitter cylinder cover. **B.** Feed port to cylinder. **C.** Exhaust port. **D.** Splitter valve.

This "pilot" air from the master control causes the insert valve core to move down in its bore, which both blocks the flow of constant supply air to the back side of the splitter piston and opens the backside of the splitter piston to exhaust at the insert valve. The constant supply of air still operating on the front side of the splitter piston forces the piston and the splitter shift fork rearward. The result is the high split position.

The air system in the auxiliary section has four possible ratio selections. Each ratio has a unique configuration for the positions of the range and splitter cylinder and their sliding clutches.

- Air system low range low split. The range sliding clutch is rearward and the splitter sliding clutch is forward, as illustrated in **FIGURE 38-53**.
- Air system low range high split. The range sliding clutch is rearward and the splitter sliding clutch is rearward, as illustrated in **FIGURE 38-54**. This ratio is only available on eighteen-speed transmissions.

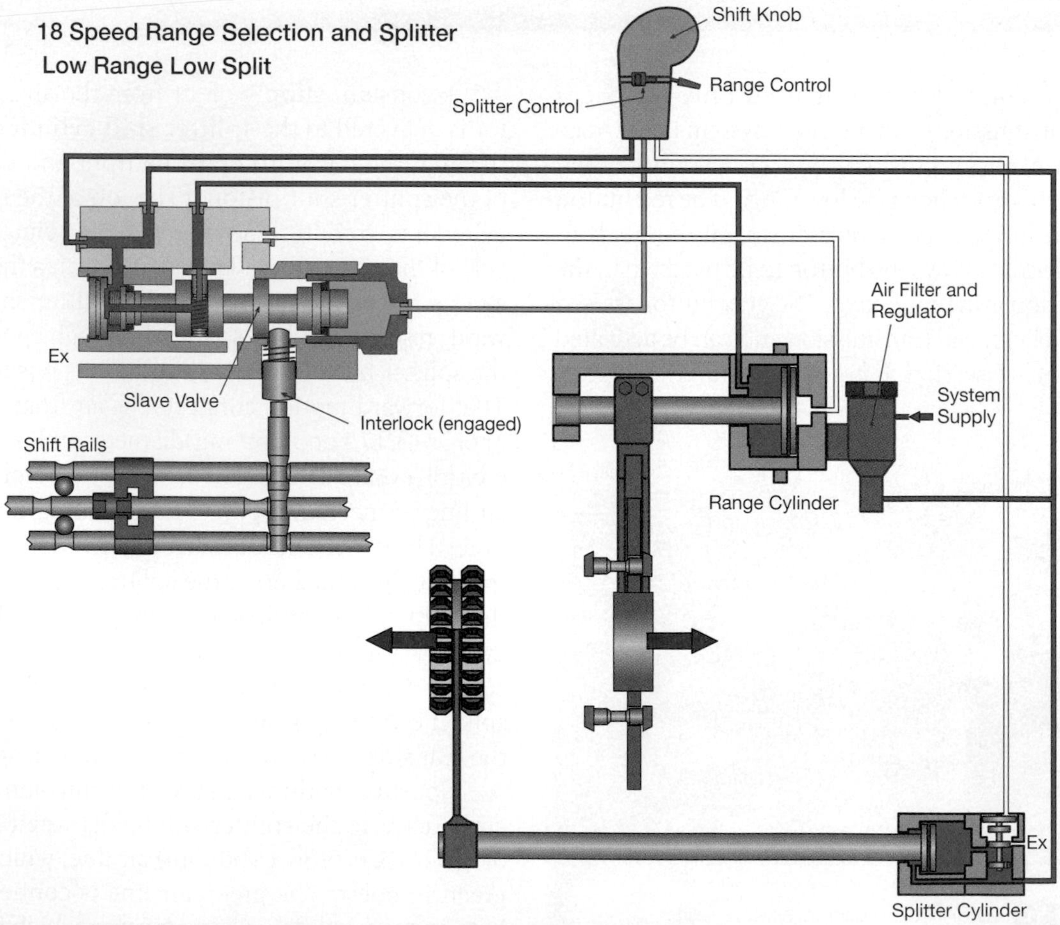

FIGURE 38-53 Air system low range low split.

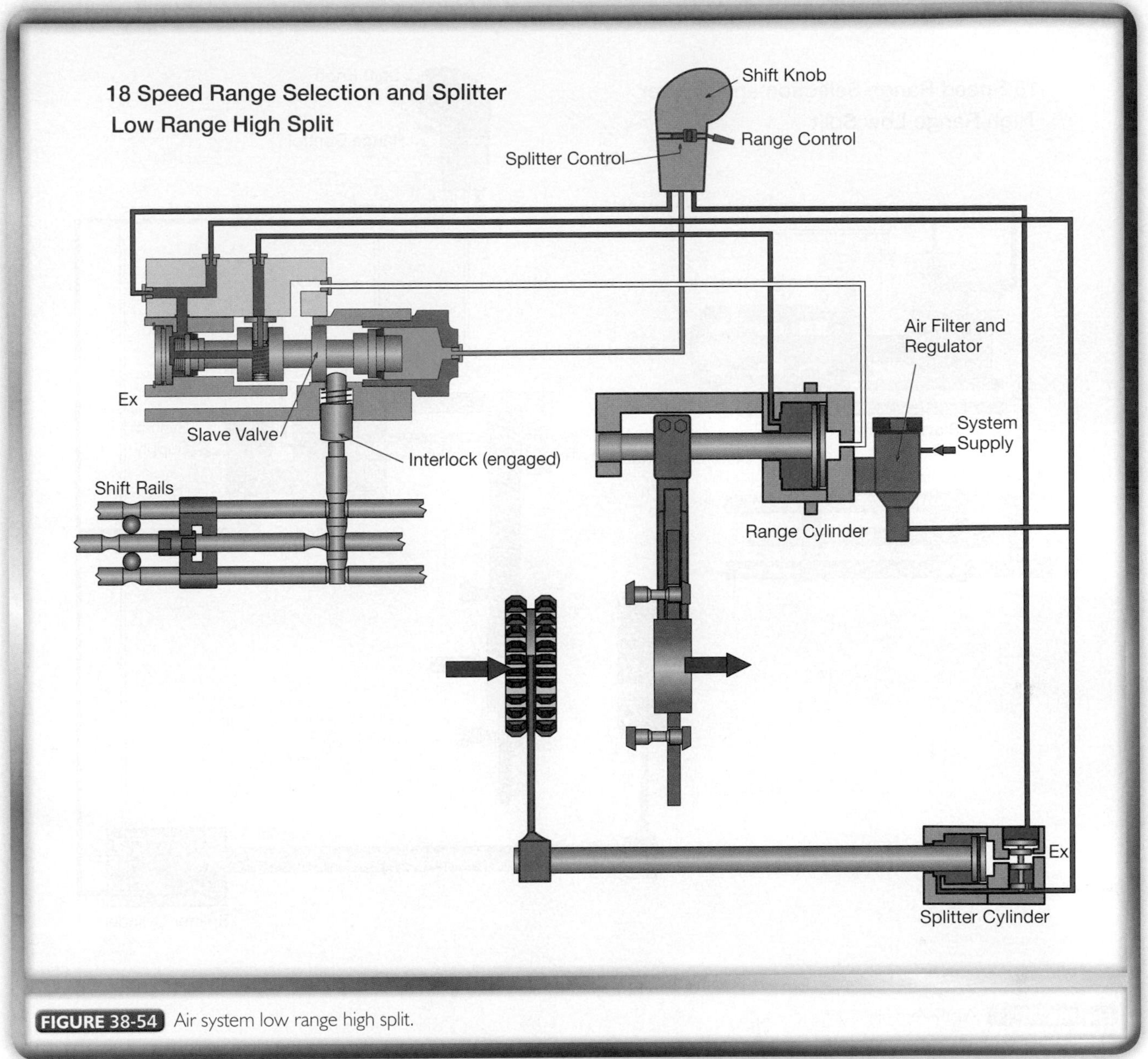

FIGURE 38-54 Air system low range high split.

- Air system high range low split. The range sliding clutch is forward and the splitter sliding clutch is forward, as illustrated in FIGURE 38-55.
- Air system high range high split (direct). The range sliding clutch is forward and the splitter sliding clutch is rearward, as illustrated in FIGURE 38-56.

FR Model Transmission Shift Controls

The newer FR model transmissions from Eaton Fuller are ten-speed transmissions that have integrated all of the air system components into a single module that is bolted to the top of the transmission shift cover. The **shift cover** is the cover on the transmission that holds the shift rails and forks. An air module from an FR model transmission is pictured in FIGURE 38-57.

A schematic of the air module is illustrated in FIGURE 38-58. This air module holds the air filter, the pressure regulator, and the slave air valve. The high-range and low-range ports consist of holes drilled into the cover and which match up to ports in the air module. These ports are sealed by O-rings, as the module is bolted to the shift cover.

The air module also has an interlock system that will not allow range shifts to occur until the shift lever is moved to the neutral position. The shift cover in the FR

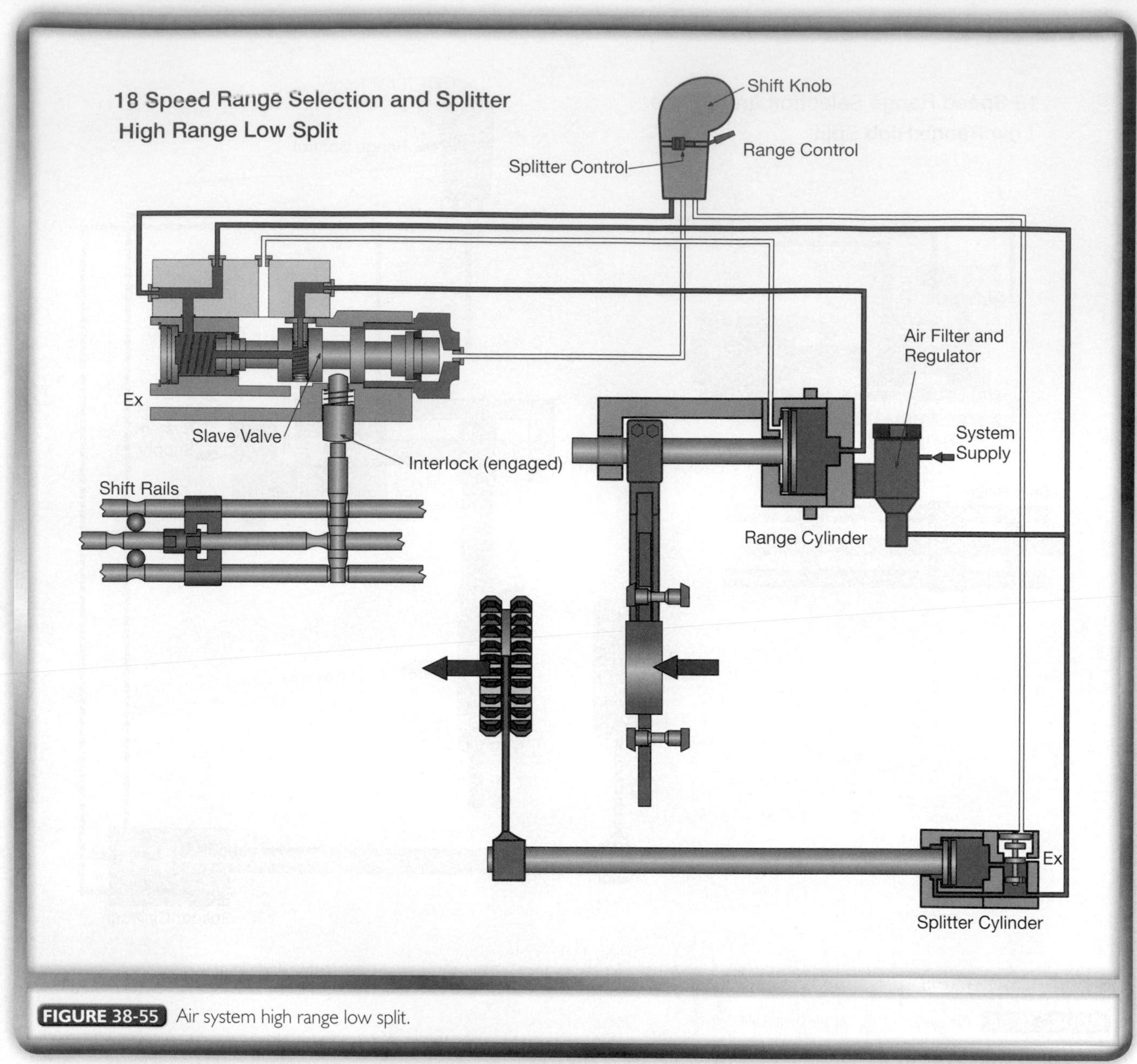

FIGURE 38-55 Air system high range low split.

series has only one shift rail, and the range cylinder is integrated with the cover, as can be seen in FIGURE 38-59, and the air module interlock finger rests against it. Whether the rail moves forward or back, the rail pushes on the interlock finger to prevent the range shift while in gear. As with the RT series of transmissions, the range shift must be preselected by the driver while the transmission is in gear. The range shift will occur automatically as the gear shift lever moves through neutral. Failure to preselect can destroy the range synchronizer!

The single module air system on the FR series transmission has some differences to the normal range control described in the beginning of the Auxiliary Section Air Control section. There are no external 1/4" (6.35 mm) lines carrying air to the range cylinder. Instead, there is only one supply line from the vehicle air system and two 1/8" (3.175 mm) lines going to and from the master shift control.

Reference Figure 38-58 as you read the following air system description. Inside the shift control module, we can see an air filter regulator system. Air is filtered and supplied to the shift control at a regulated pressure of 80 psi (552 kPa). The spool valve inside the module has an end cap whose position is controlled by the interlock shift finger. When the transmission is in any gear, the interlock finger pushes the end cap to the right, and the interlock balls clamp the spool valve in position. As with other Fuller transmissions, the driver must preselect the range shift in gear before moving the shift lever through neutral.

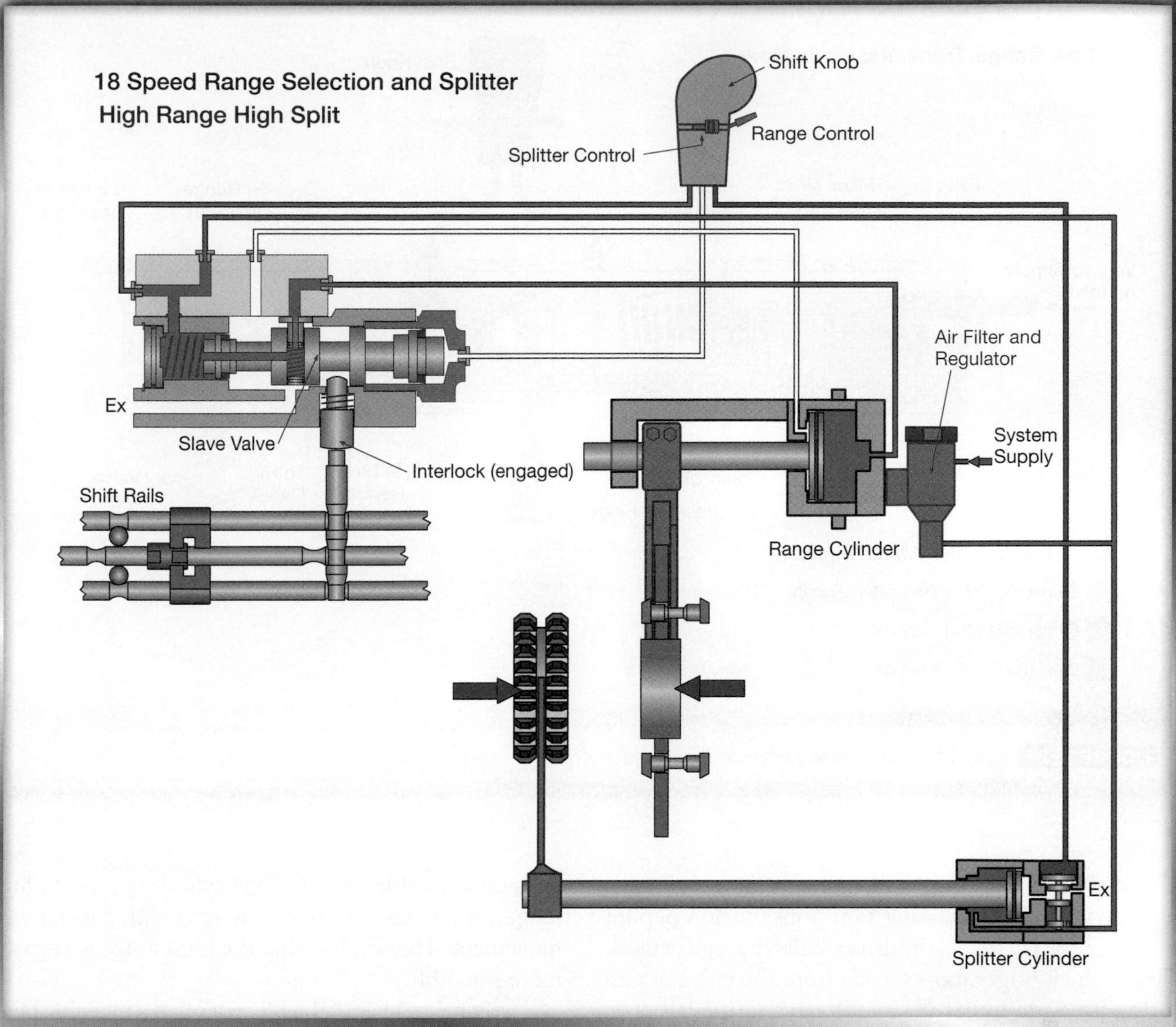

FIGURE 38-56 Air system high range high split.

As the transmission shifts to neutral, the interlock finger moves left at the top and releases the pressure on the end cap. That action frees the interlock balls, and the spool valve is allowed to move. In Figure 38-58, the transmission is in low range. Consequently, air flows from the supply to the Roadranger valve (in the shift knob). With the range shift lever in the down position, that air is directed to the pilot port and to the left side of the spool valve. The air forces the spool valve to the right against spring pressure. The spool in this position directs supply air to the low-range port and to the low side of the range cylinder piston. The range shift bar and synchronizer move rearward to engage the low range gear. Once the driver selects a gear, the interlock finger pushes the spool end cap to the right. That motion locks the spool in position.

FIGURE 38-57 The air module on the shift bar housing of the FR series Fuller transmission.

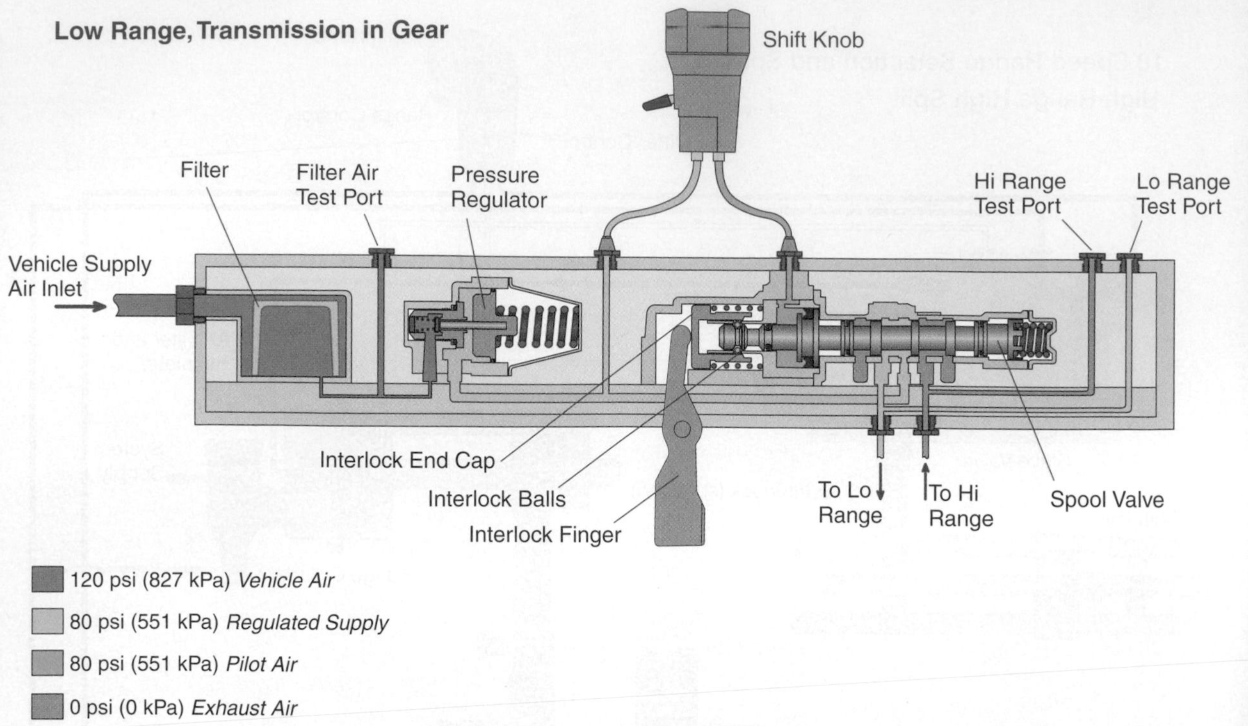

FIGURE 38-58 Schematic of air module in FR model transmission.

To shift to high range, the driver moves the range lever up while in gear. That action stops the flow of pilot air to the spool valve. As the driver shifts through neutral, the interlock finger moves away from the end cap and spring pressure forces the spool valve to the left. The low-range air is exhausted and supply air is sent to the high-range port and the back of the range cylinder piston. That air forces the range shift bar and synchronizer forward and engages the high range.

SynchroSaver

If the driver manages to select a main box gear before the air system completes the shift to high range, it can cause the range synchronizer to be damaged. The FR series transmission air module is equipped with a SynchroSaver feature designed to prevent that from occurring. If the driver achieves a main box gear shift before the high-range shift completes, the interlock finger pushes against the end cap of the spool and forces it to the right slightly. This movement aligns the spool valve outlet with both the low-range and the high-range ports. Air is then sent to both the front and the rear of the range cylinder at the same time. The rearward, or high-range, side of the piston has a larger surface area than the forward, or low-range, side. As the range cylinder moves to high range, the air pressure on the low-range side cushions the movement. The result is that the high range is engaged more smoothly.

Original models of the FR series had a movable pivot on the back of the auxiliary section that allowed removal of the auxiliary without first removing the shift cover. The

FIGURE 38-59 The range cylinder (circled) is located in the shift bar housing on the Fuller FR series transmissions.

pivot rotates the range synchronizer shaft so that it no longer engages the range shift piston shaft. Essentially, the pivot allowed the range shift bar to disengage from the range cylinder piston bar.

The pivot has two positions: locked and unlocked. Those positions are indicated by icons cast into the housing. A closed padlock symbol indicates the locked position, and an open padlock symbol indicates the unlocked position.

To remove the auxiliary, a technician must remove two bolts and rotate the pivot to the unlocked position. Then, the technician must reinstall one bolt to be sure it remains there. After the auxiliary section is reinstalled, the pivot is rotated back to the lock position. Current production FR, as shown in **FIGURE 38-60**, series transmissions do not have this pivot, so the shift bar housing must be removed to disengage the range synchronizer shaft prior to removing the auxiliary section.

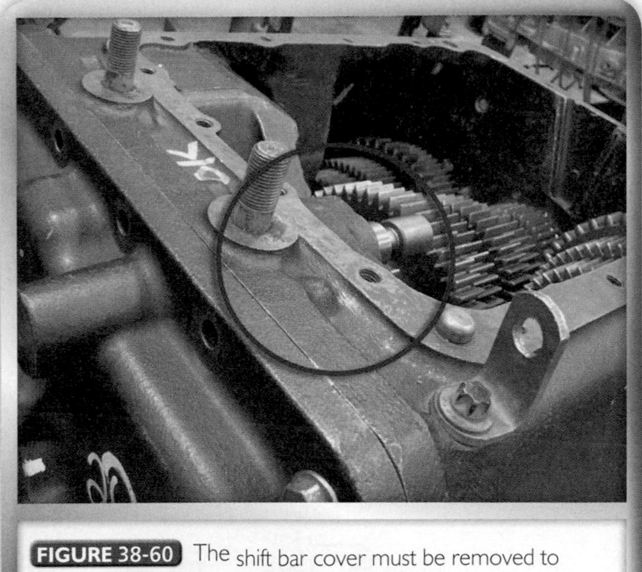

FIGURE 38-60 The shift bar cover must be removed to disengage the range shift shaft (circled) before removing the auxiliary section on newer FR series transmissions.

Safety

Technicians used to the RT and RTLO model transmissions may be accustomed to removing the auxiliary sections and replacing them with the transmission still installed. With the integrated system on the FR models, the transmission shift cover must be removed before the auxiliary section is removed. That is because the range shift piston shaft fits into a groove in the range synchronizer shaft. Damage and/or serious injury could occur from trying to force the auxiliary section out with the range shift piston still engaging the shift fork shaft.

Transfer Cases

A **transfer case** is a gear box arrangement that is either attached to the back of the main transmission or connected to it by a short drive shaft. The transfer case allows the torque from the transmission to be split between the front and rear driving axles of a vehicle. The transfer case may also provide a lower gear ratio and power take-off options. A transfer case is pictured in **FIGURE 38-61**.

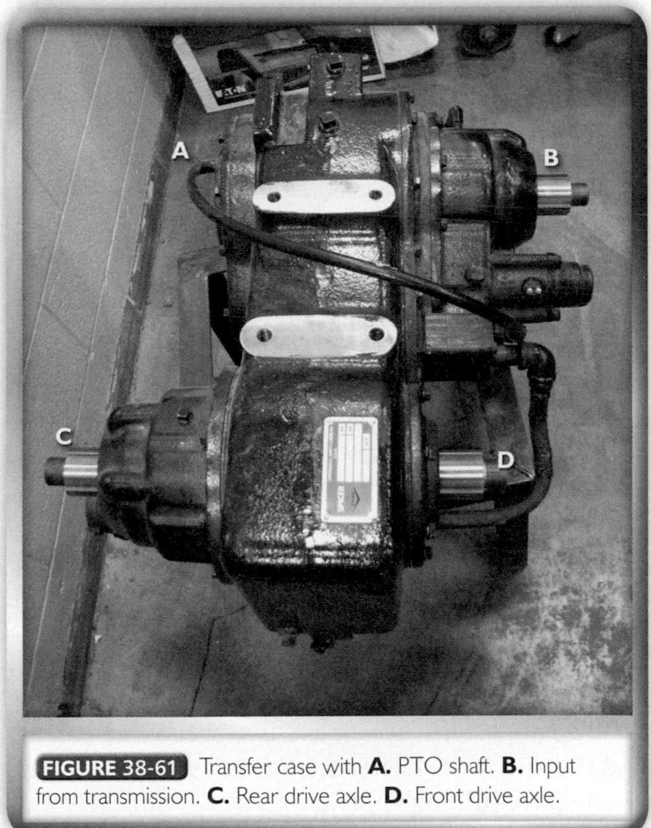

FIGURE 38-61 Transfer case with **A.** PTO shaft. **B.** Input from transmission. **C.** Rear drive axle. **D.** Front drive axle.

Transfer cases are sometimes called drop boxes, as their design allows the front drive shaft to clear the bottom of the transmission in order to go to the front axle. The transfer case will usually have at least four shafts:

- The input shaft
- The countershaft
- The front axle drive shaft
- The rear axle drive shaft

The four shafts are illustrated in **FIGURE 38-62**.

The transfer case may also contain reduction gearing to allow two speeds (low and high) through the case when desired. A two-speed transfer case will have two sets of gears that can drive the output shafts. These gear sets are selectable by the driver using a sliding clutch splined to the input shaft. The transfer case may or may not

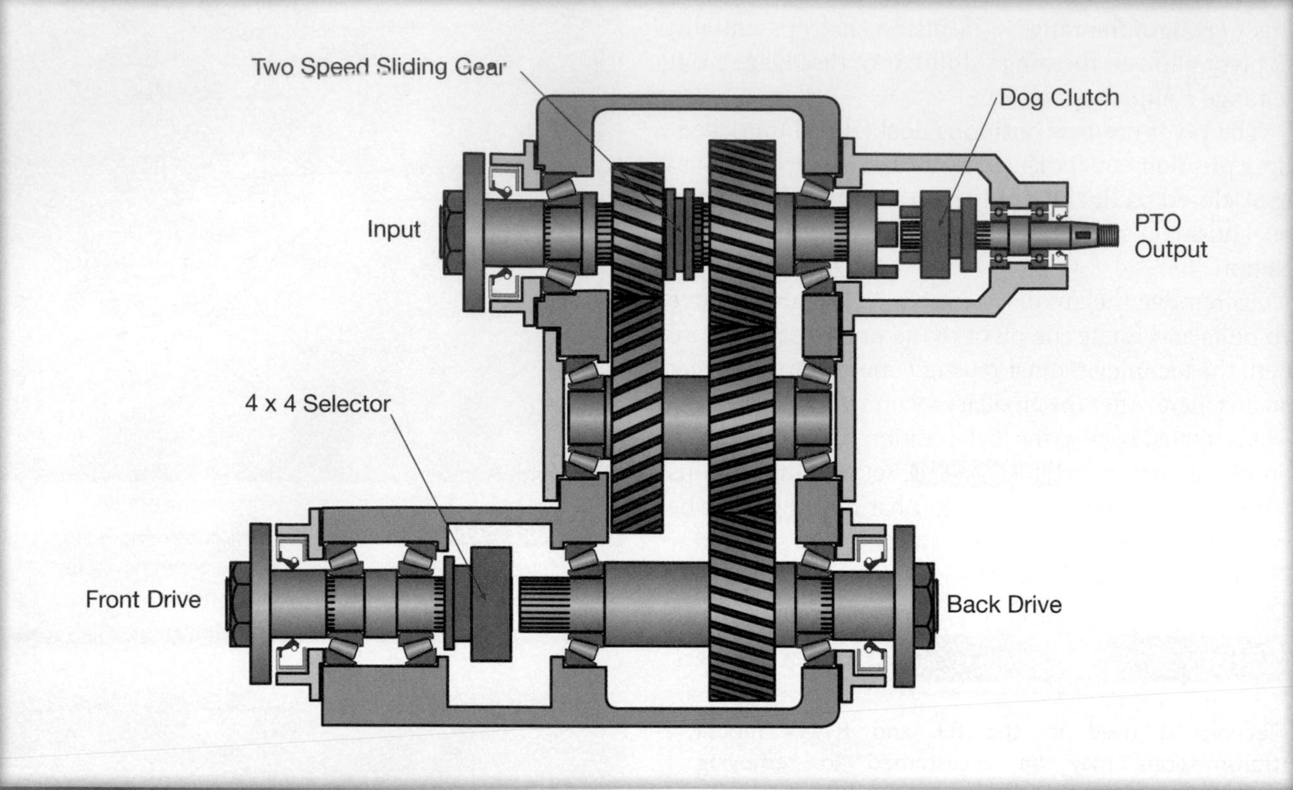

FIGURE 38-62 Schematic of a transfer case with a power take-off option.

contain an inter-axle differential gear set to allow for speed changes between the front and rear drive axles. Speed differences between the front and rear drive axles can be induced by turning and/or unequal road conditions. If a vehicle is classified as all-wheel drive, it typically means that it is in front and rear axle drive mode at all times. Therefore, the vehicle must have an inter-axle differential. If the vehicle only uses the front drive axle in off-road or poor traction conditions, the vehicle is said to have part-time front-wheel drive. In that situation, an inter-axle differential is not always required. If an inter-axle differential is present, it will normally have a lockout to prevent the differential from operating in poor traction conditions.

The front axle engagement, two-speed shift control, and the inter-axle differential lockout are all controlled by the driver through a series of air or control valves on the dash. If the vehicle does not have an air system, electric motor controls are used. It is important to note that part-time front-wheel drive systems should not be operated with the front axle engaged under normal driving conditions. Part-time front-wheel drive should only be engaged in off-road and poor traction situations.

Transfer cases come in a variety of designs. Some come equipped with one or two power take-off shaft flanges that can be used to drive accessories on the vehicle. Transfer cases use splash lubrication systems in which the lower gears rotate in a bath of lubricant and splash a steady stream of lube onto the higher gears. Some systems will use a lube pump that is filtered externally to supply pressurized oil to critical areas such as the input shaft needle bearing and gears. This lubricant will fall down through the transfer case and lubricate the other gears and shafts on the way down.

Power Take-Off Devices

Power take-off devices are quite popular in the trucking industry. These devices allow engine power to be rerouted to operate other equipment on the vehicle.

A **power take-off device (PTO)**, such as the one shown in **FIGURE 38-63**, is basically a device attached to the transmission that is gear-driven and can be used to run accessories. As such, a PTO is a gear box that is driven by the engine to power another mechanical or hydraulic component. Most PTOs are attached to the transmission through one of two provided SAE standard openings—the six-bolt or the eight-bolt opening. A PTO can be driven by the engine flywheel or even by the front gear train of the engine, but most are driven directly by the transmission's countershaft.

There are several different designs used in the manufacture of PTOs. One of the more common is the two-gear design. The two-gear design typically contains two shafts (the idler shaft and the output shaft) in the unit and three gears (the input gear, the drive gear, and the output gear). The PTO input gear is mounted on the idler shaft and is in constant mesh with the transmission countershaft gear. The output gear, also called the ratio gear, is attached to the output shaft. The drive gear is usually mounted on the input shaft but not splined to it. A sliding clutch or collar splined to the input shaft is used to engage the drive gear, which is in constant mesh with the output gear. When the sliding clutch or collar engages the drive gear, power is transmitted to the output gear to drive the PTO output shaft. The PTO output shaft can be connected directly to a hydraulic pump or to a drive shaft to power a remote hydraulic or mechanical system. The sliding clutch can be moved mechanically or by an electric or air solenoid to engage the PTO. A typical PTO is shown in **FIGURE 38-64**.

The ratio gear may be fixed to the idler shaft or free to rotate on it. If the ratio gear is freely rotating, the sliding clutch will lock it to the idler shaft to engage the PTO. (In some spur-tooth input gear PTOs, the input gear is splined to the idler shaft and slid into mesh with the countershaft gear to engage the PTO. Those types are, however, less common.) The second shaft is the PTO output shaft, which has the PTO-driven gear keyed or splined to it. Most PTOs are designed to be used when the vehicle is stationary and in neutral.

The PTO generally is engaged by moving the sliding clutch to lock the input gear to the shaft. Some models use a different configuration and have a sliding gear on the output shaft for PTO engagement. The most common application of power take-offs is to drive hydraulic pumps directly. Power take-offs can also indirectly drive air compressors/vacuum pumps, pneumatic blowers, or other mechanical components such a high pressure water pump through a driveshaft. The indirect type of PTO installation must follow all of the rules for driveshaft angles and limits mentioned in the Driveshaft Systems chapter.

There are several other types of PTOs, such as front-mount belt-driven hydraulic pumps, and PTOs provided by transfer cases. One type of PTO common in off-road equipment is sandwiched between the engine and transmission. PTOs can be retrofitted to most vehicles, and they are usually quite easy to install as long as there is sufficient clearance.

When installing a transmission-mounted PTO, care must be taken to provide the correct running clearance, or backlash, between the countershaft gear and the PTO drive gear. In most cases, this clearance runs between 0.006" and 0.018" (0.15 mm and 0.46 mm). A PTO mounted too tightly will run noisily and ultimately fail. It can also damage the transmission in the process. Conversely, a PTO mounted too loosely (with too much backlash) runs the risk of skipping teeth under load. It, too, may cause catastrophic damage from pieces of metal broken off the gears running through the transmission and the PTO.

Deciding which type and size of PTO is correct for a given application is better left to the PTO manufacturer, who can give advice on PTO speed, horsepower capability, and the suitability for a given vocation. Regardless of type, PTOs are a simple and effective way to use the powertrain of the vehicle to operate accessory devices when necessary.

FIGURE 38-63 A typical PTO driven by the transmission's countershaft.

FIGURE 38-64 A typical power take-off device. **A.** Constant-mesh gears. **B.** Sliding collar.

Wrap-up

Ready for Review

- Different vehicles are designed for different vocations or purposes. On-highway, off-highway, delivery, heavy hauling, and other vocations have specific needs when it comes to torque multiplication requirements.
- Transmissions are designed with sufficient ratio steps or increases so that they can be operated under the necessary conditions for which the vehicle is designed.
- All transmissions will have at least four shafts: an input shaft, a countershaft, a main or output shaft, and a reverse idler shaft.
- Transmissions are classified by the method they use to select gear ratios.
- A sliding-gear transmission will use only spur gears and have all of the speed gears splined to the main shaft. The spur gears must be slid into mesh with their corresponding countershaft gears to select a ratio.
- Constant-mesh transmissions have all of their main shaft speed gears and corresponding countershaft gears in mesh at all times. All of the main shaft gears turn freely on the main shaft until they are locked to it either by a sliding clutch, a sliding collar, or a synchronizer.
- Double clutching is a technique to provide clash-free shifting. The driver disengages the clutch, shifts to neutral, and then re-engages the clutch again. The driver then tries to match the engine speed to the speed of the desired main shaft gear. The driver once again disengages the clutch, selects the gear, and re-engages the clutch. Double clutching is used with sliding-gear transmissions and non-synchronized transmissions.
- Sliding clutches are internally splined to the transmission main shaft. To select a ratio, the clutch's external clutching teeth engage internal clutching teeth on the main shaft gears. This arrangement is a non-synchronized transmission.
- Sliding collars are splined to a hub that in turn is splined or keyed to the main shaft. To select a ratio, the internal splines of the sliding collar slide over external clutching (dog) teeth on the main shaft gear. This arrangement is a non-synchronized transmission.
- Synchronizers use friction to match shaft and gear speeds. Synchronizers, therefore, eliminate the need for double clutching and simplify transmission operation to the point that anyone could drive a manual transmission.
- Shift mechanisms include the shift lever, shift tower, shift cover, shift gates, shift rails, and shift forks. Two other components are also included in shift mechanisms. The shift rail interlock prevents two gears from being selected at once. The shift detents, usually spring-loaded balls, help the shift rail stay in gear.
- Overdrive transmissions sometimes present a problem for shift patterns. Most drivers are familiar with the standard H shift pattern, but the overdrive ratio must be on the main shaft, causing a U-shape shift pattern. Manufacturers use methods such as bellcranks to reverse the movement of shift rails to maintain a standard shift pattern.
- All transmission power flows will be compound flows. That is, more than one set of gears is involved in the ratio. Usually four gears are involved to create all ratios except direct, or 1:1.
- In transmissions with auxiliary sections, up to eight gears are required to finalize the ratio being selected.
- Multiple countershaft transmissions split the input torque between two or three countershafts. They utilize many more teeth on the main shaft gears to transmit torque to the main shaft and allow the transmission to handle greater overall torque. The main shaft, however, has to be made stronger, as it must carry all of the torque by itself.
- Multiple countershaft transmissions allow the main shaft to "float" or self-center, because all of the main shaft gears are directly supported by the two or three countershafts. The main shaft in these transmissions carries no load until one of the main shaft gears is locked to it by a sliding clutch. The sliding clutch will center the shaft when it engages.
- Auxiliary sections are used to multiply the number of available ratios from a transmission. Auxiliary sections typically have two, three, or four available ratios and so allow a transmission to which they are attached to have ten, thirteen, or even eighteen forward ratios respectively.

- Auxiliary section ratios are shifted by air cylinders. One air cylinder is used for range selection and one for splitter selection.
- It is essential that the driver preselects the range shift before shifting to the neutral position. Otherwise, the air-shift mechanism may not be able to complete the shift. Damage to the range synchronizer could result.
- The range shift from low to high range is used only once as the driver accelerates through the gears and once on the way back down as he decelerates.
- The splitter shift provides a half-ratio step. It is used in both low and high range on eighteen-speed Fuller transmissions but only in high range on thirteen-speed models.
- The Fuller FR series transmissions are ten-speed fleet transmissions, and they use an integrated air module to control the range shift. The range cylinder in these models is part of the transmission shift cover.
- Transfer cases are used to split the output from the transmission and send the output to both the front and rear drive axles. Transfer cases can also have a high and low gear ratio, which can multiply the overall number of ratios available to the driver.
- Power take-off devices are used to power auxiliary devices on a vehicle such as hydraulic pumps, conveyor systems, and so on. PTOs can be connected to the engine, the transmission, or the transfer case. The position of the PTO is usually dependent on when the auxiliary power is needed with the vehicle stationary, when the auxiliary power is needed with the vehicle moving, and how much power is required.

Vocabulary Builder

air filter/pressure regulator The Fuller air filter/pressure regulator cleans the pressurized air supply going to the transmission and regulates it to 58 to 63 psi (400 to 434 kPa).

auxiliary section A section bolted to the main transmission with 2, 3, or 4 ratios to multiply the ratios available to the driver.

bellcrank A shaft used in a mechanical linkage with a pivot in the center that reverses the normal direction of motion.

blocking ring A synchronizer part that increases or decreases a gear's speed to match shaft speed, so that the synchronizer sleeve can lock the gear to the shaft.

collar shift transmission A transmission that uses sliding clutches or sliding collars to select gear ratios.

compound shift A shift where two parts of the transmission are being shifted at once.

constant mesh transmission A transmission in which the main and countershaft gears are always in mesh.

countershaft The shaft inside a transmission driven by the input gear.

detent balls Spring-loaded steel balls that hold the shift rails in position.

dropbox A component that is bolted to the back of the transmission and connects the front and rear axles via the drive shaft; allows the output of a transmission to flow to both the rear and the front axles. Also called *transfer case*.

double clutch A technique drivers use to synchronize gear and shaft speed.

input shaft The component to which the clutch discs are splined.

insert valve A small valve in the splitter cylinder cover on a Fuller transmission that controls air flow to the front or rear of the splitter cylinder piston.

interlock system A system that prevents the transmission from engaging two main shaft gears at once.

low-inertia A new design auxiliary section that momentarily disengages the auxiliary from the main box during compound shifts, making it easier to move the shift lever.

main shaft The shaft that is driven by the countershaft and provides output for the transmission. Also called *output shaft*.

multi-mesh gearing Main shaft and countershaft gears that have finer cut teeth—meaning more teeth are in mesh for increased strength.

multiple countershaft transmission A transmission with more than one countershaft; used to distribute the torque between more teeth on the main shaft and countershaft speed gears to increase torque capacity of the transmission.

output shaft The shaft that is driven by the countershaft and provides output for the transmission. Also called *main shaft*.

power flow The path that power takes from the beginning of an assembly to the end. In a transmission, power flow changes as different gears are selected by the driver.

power take-off device (PTO) A device attached to the transmission that is gear-driven and can be used to run accessories.

range gear Any speed gear; in Eaton transmissions, it refers to the low-range gear in the auxiliary section.

range shift cylinder The shift cylinder to control range shifts in the auxiliary.

ratio step The difference between one ratio and the next available.

reverse idler shaft Shaft that supports the reverse idler gear.

Roadranger valve The driver's shift knob that controls range and splitter shifting.

shift cover The cover on the transmission that holds the shift rails and forks.

shift finger A flat-sided piece that sits into the shift gates.

shift forks The forks that move the sliding clutches or collars in the transmission.

shift gate Rectangular notches either formed or attached to the shift rails.

shift lever The shift control the driver uses to change the main box gear position.

shift tower A raised section with a pivot into which the shift lever fits.

single countershaft transmissions A transmission with only one countershaft.

slave air valve The valve on the side of a Fuller transmission that controls air flow to the range shift cylinder.

sliding clutch A device with splines on the inside and outside used as a gear selection method for manual transmissions.

sliding collar A device with splines on the inside only, used as a gear selection method in manual transmissions.

sliding gear transmission A transmission with a gear that is splined to a transmission main shaft and is slid into and out of mesh with a countershaft gear.

speed gears The gears on the countershaft and main shaft that create the transmission ratios, also known as *range gears*.

splitter shift cylinder The shift cylinder that controls the splitter sliding clutch.

synchronized transmission A transmission that uses sliding clutches or collars fitted over synchronizer hubs that are splined to the main shaft to select gear ratios.

synchronizer A device to match shaft and gear speeds for clash-free engagement.

transfer case A component that is bolted to the back of the transmission or connected to it by a short drive shaft; allows the output of a transmission to flow to both the rear and the front axles. Also called *dropbox*.

Review Questions

1. What is the primary reason manufacturers use multiple countershaft transmissions?
   - **a.** Multiple countershaft transmissions provide more ratios.
   - **b.** Multiple countershaft transmissions increase torque capacity.
   - **c.** Multiple countershaft transmissions are easier for the driver to operate.
   - **d.** Multiple countershaft transmissions are cheaper to produce.
2. Which of the following would NOT be an advantage of multiple countershaft transmissions?
   - **a.** Multiple countershaft transmissions shorten transmission length.
   - **b.** Multiple countershaft transmissions decrease transmission weight.
   - **c.** Multiple countershaft transmissions decrease the torque load on the transmission output shaft.
   - **d.** Multiple countershaft transmissions make the manufacturing process a little easier.
3. Which of the following BEST describes the role of the auxiliary section in a truck standard transmission?
   - **a.** Reduction of torque output
   - **b.** Multiplies the number of available gear ratios
   - **c.** Reduces transmission length
   - **d.** Enables faster road speeds in lower ranges
4. In order to rotate a countershaft transmission driven gear in the same direction of rotation as the drive gear, which of the following is a requirement?
   - **a.** The drive gear must be larger in diameter than the driven gear.
   - **b.** There must be two gears and both must have external teeth.
   - **c.** There must be an idler gear between the drive and driven gears.
   - **d.** Two gears must be in mesh with one of them driving.
5. When a Fuller Roadranger low-inertia thirteen-speed transmission is in high range, in which position is the range cylinder piston, yoke bar, and fork?
   - **a.** Fully forward
   - **b.** Fully rearward
   - **c.** Halfway forward
   - **d.** Not quite fully rearward
6. When a constant mesh transmission is in neutral, which of the following statements about the transmission's helical main shaft gears is correct?
   - **a.** They are splined to the main or output shaft
   - **b.** They are keyed to the main or output shaft
   - **c.** They are free to turn on the main or output shaft
   - **d.** They are keyed to the synchronizer hub
7. When synchronizers are used in a transmission the power flow is connected to the output shaft by the:
   - **a.** countershaft.
   - **b.** input shaft.
   - **c.** synchronizer sliding collar or clutch and hub.
   - **d.** synchronizer blocker ring.
8. What prevents transmission from being put in two gears at the same time?
   - **a.** Shift rail detent balls and pins
   - **b.** Shift rail Interlock system
   - **c.** Narrow shift gates
   - **d.** A larger shift finger
9. When a sliding gear is used in a transmission, it is connected to the main shaft by:
   - **a.** splines in the sliding gear.
   - **b.** a sliding clutch.
   - **c.** a synchronizer.
   - **d.** a shift fork.
10. What precaution must be taken when towing a vehicle with a standard transmission on the drive wheels and with the transmission in neutral?
    - **a.** Make sure the transmission is full of oil.
    - **b.** Use the emergency flashers.
    - **c.** Disconnect the driveshaft or remove the axles.
    - **d.** Lock the clutch pedal in the depressed position.

ASE-Type Questions

1. Technician A says that in order to make a range shift in a RoadRanger transmission, you move the range selector valve lever first and then shift the transmission to the correct gear. Technician B says that you shift the transmission to neutral first and then move the range selector valve lever. Who is shifting the transmission correctly?
   a. Technician A
   b. Technician B
   c. Both Technician A and Technician B
   d. Neither Technician A nor Technician B
2. Technician A says that the splitter control button on a Fuller thirteen-speed transmission can be operated in both low and high ranges. Technician B says that the splitter control button on a Fuller eighteen-speed transmission can be operated in both high and low range. Who is correct?
   a. Technician A
   b. Technician B
   c. Both Technician A and Technician B
   d. Neither Technician A nor Technician B
3. Technician A says that the splitter piston in a Fuller eighteen-speed transmission moves forward for high split. Technician B says that the splitter piston in the thirteen-speed Fuller is rearward during low range. Who is correct?
   a. Technician A
   b. Technician B
   c. Both Technician A and Technician B
   d. Neither Technician A nor Technician B
4. Technician A says that the air shift system in a Fuller thirteen-speed RTLO series transmission operates at 57–63 psi (393–434 kPa). Technician B says that the Fuller FR series transmission's air system also operates at 57–63 psi (393–434 kPa). Who is correct?
   a. Technician A
   b. Technician B
   c. Both Technician A and Technician B
   d. Neither Technician A nor Technician B
5. Technician A says that the slave air valve in a Fuller thirteen-speed RTLO series transmission is moved by air for both the low- and high-range positions. Technician B says that in the Fuller FR series transmissions the spool valve in the shift control air module moves to the high-range position by spring pressure. Who is correct?
   a. Technician A
   b. Technician B
   c. Both Technician A and Technician B
   d. Neither Technician A nor Technician B
6. Technician A says that a standard transmission noise that occurs in all gears except fifth in a five-speed non-overdrive transmission could indicate a failed output shaft pilot bearing. Technician B says that the rear output shaft support bearing could be the cause. Who is correct?
   a. Technician A
   b. Technician B
   c. Both Technician A and Technician B
   d. Neither Technician A nor Technician B
7. Technician A says that the Fuller deep reduction transmission has the deep reduction gear at the rear of the auxiliary section. Technician B says that the auxiliary section main shaft in a Fuller deep reduction transmission is in two pieces. Who is correct?
   a. Technician A
   b. Technician B
   c. Both Technician A and Technician B
   d. Neither Technician A nor Technician B
8. Technician A says that in the low split position the splitter sliding clutch is forward in the thirteen-speed fuller transmission. Technician B says that the range synchronizer is rearward when the thirteen-speed transmission is in low range. Who is correct?
   a. Technician A
   b. Technician B
   c. Both Technician A and Technician B
   d. Neither Technician A nor Technician B
9. Technician A says that, when a thirteen-speed fuller transmission auxiliary section is in low split, air is present at both sides of the splitter cylinder piston. Technician B says that, when the thirteen-speed Fuller transmission auxiliary section is in high split, air is present at the back of the splitter cylinder piston only. Who is correct?
   a. Technician A
   b. Technician B
   c. Both Technician A and Technician B
   d. Neither Technician A nor Technician B
10. Technician A says that air is present at both sides of the range cylinder piston in a Fuller thirteen-speed transmission auxiliary section when it is in low range. Technician B says that air is present at the back of the range cylinder piston only in a Fuller thirteen-speed transmission auxiliary section when it is in high range. Who is correct?
    a. Technician A
    b. Technician B
    c. Both Technician A and Technician B
    d. Neither Technician A nor Technician B

CHAPTER 39

NATEF Tasks

Drive Train

Transmission

Task	Page
■ Check transmission fluid level and condition; determine needed service; add proper type of lubricant.	1267–1268
■ Identify causes of transmission noise, shifting concerns, lockup, jumping-out-of-gear, overheating, and vibration problems; determine needed action.	1268–1273
■ Inspect for leakage and replace transmission cover plates, gaskets, seals, and cap bolts; inspect seal surfaces and vents; repair as needed.	1269
■ Inspect and replace transmission mounts, insulators, and mounting bolts.	1270
■ Inspect, adjust, and replace transmission shift lever, cover, rails, forks, levers, bushings, sleeves, detents, interlocks, springs, and lock bolts/safety wires.	1271–1273
■ Inspect, test, repair, or replace air shift controls, lines, hoses, valves, regulators, filters, and cylinder assemblies.	1274–1277, 1279
■ Inspect transmission oil filters, coolers, and related components; replace as necessary.	1278
■ Inspect and adjust power take-off (PTO) assemblies, controls, and shafts; determine needed action.	1279–1280
■ Inspect input shaft, gear, spacers, bearings, retainers, and slingers; determine needed action.	1280–1292
■ Inspect speedometer components; determine needed action.	1282–1283

Servicing Standard Transmissions

Knowledge Objectives

After reading this chapter, you will be able to:

1. Explain transmission lubrication requirements. (pp 1262–1265)
2. Diagnose transmission noise and vibration. (pp 1265, 1277)
3. Describe common standard transmission failures and their causes. (pp 1268–1273)
4. Analyze transmission component failure. (pp 1268–1273)
5. Describe standard transmission service and preventative maintenance procedures. (pp 1265–1268)
6. Diagnose shifting complaints. (pp 1270–1271)
7. Describe transmission overhaul procedures. (p 1277)
8. Describe common transmission repair tasks and procedures. (p 1277)
9. Explain how to remove and reinstall an input shaft. (pp 1280–1282)
10. Explain how to remove and reinstall an auxiliary section. (pp 1284–1285)
11. Explain how to overhaul a range synchronizer. (p 1286)
12. Explain how to overhaul and time an auxiliary section. (pp 1287–1288)

Skills Objectives

After reading this chapter, you will be able to:

1. Check the fluid level of a manual transmission. (p 1267) SKILL DRILL 39-1
2. Change the gearbox fluid. (p 1267) SKILL DRILL 39-2
3. Inspect for leakage and replace transmission cover plates, gaskets, seals, and cap bolts and inspect and seal surfaces and vents. (p 1269) SKILL DRILL 39-3
4. Inspect, adjust, service, repair, or replace remote shift linkages and control assembly brackets, bushings, pivots, and levers. (p 1271) SKILL DRILL 39-4
5. Inspect, adjust, and replace transmission shift lever assembly, top cover, and shift bar housing. (pp 1272–1273) SKILL DRILL 39-5
6. Inspect the transmission oil filter and cooler. (p 1278) SKILL DRILL 39-6
7. Inspect, test, adjust, repair, or replace air shift controls, lines, valves, regulators, filters, and cylinder assemblies. (p 1279) SKILL DRILL 39-7
8. Inspect the power take-off. (p 1280) SKILL DRILL 39-8
9. Replace the input shaft. (pp 1280–1282) SKILL DRILL 39-9
10. Replace rear seals. (p 1283) SKILL DRILL 39-10
11. Remove the auxiliary section from a Fuller Ten-Speed FR Model. (p 1284) SKILL DRILL 39-11
12. Disassemble the auxiliary section. (p 1285) SKILL DRILL 39-12
13. Overhaul the range synchronizer. (p 1286) SKILL DRILL 39-13
14. Reassemble and time the auxiliary section. (pp 1287–1288) SKILL DRILL 39-14
15. Reinstall the auxiliary section. (pp 1289–1291) SKILL DRILL 39-15

Introduction

As a technician, you will need to put your practical understandings of heavy-duty truck systems to work each day. Although you may not be servicing transmissions every day, you will come close. This chapter will cover the basic practices and procedures for maintaining and servicing standard transmissions used in heavy-duty vehicles. The focus will be on establishing certain baseline guidelines for general transmission service and maintenance.

Even though the chapter title is Servicing Standard Transmissions, it is by no means intended to be a comprehensive guide or substitute for the original equipment manufacturer's service manuals. Any information contained in this chapter is to be superseded by OEM information. It cannot be stressed enough how important it is to have access to the OEM manuals in order to properly service any transmission.

Fundamentals of Standard Transmission Servicing

Before diving into a transmission maintenance or service procedure, it is critical that you understand the fundamentals of lubrication and how lubrication varies depending on the vocation of the vehicle.

Today's medium- and heavy-duty transmissions are designed to give exceptional service and longevity. Manufacturers are warranting their products up to and including 750,000 miles (1,207,008 km) depending on vocation and load factors. These transmissions are expected to last the life of the vehicle—a life span of 2,000,000 to 3,000,000 miles (3,218,000–4,828,000 km) or more is not unheard of!

The only way these components can give this kind of service is with proper operation by the driver—and proper lubrication. Lubrication is the life blood of any mechanical component, and a transmission is no different. It is absolutely essential that the correct lubricant is used.

The most common lubricant recommended for medium/heavy duty transmissions is SAE 50 weight engine oil—either petroleum based or synthetic. Manufacturers are almost exclusively using synthetic-based lubricants for extended vehicle operation. **Synthetic-based lubricants** are manufactured rather than refined and have much longer service life. In fact, Eaton Fuller recommends its SAE-50 weight synthetic for use in all their models and even fills them with it at the factory FIGURE 39-1.

Transmissions that are filled at the factory with petroleum-based oils will usually require an initial drain and fill after 5,000 miles (8,050 km) of operation. By contrast, units filled at the factory with synthetics can go up to 500,000 miles (805,000 km) before a fluid change is required.

Gear oils with **extreme pressure additives (EP)** should never be used in vocational transmissions, as they

You Are the Technician

George's "Prostar" International tractor has 465,000 miles (748,345 km) and has come to your repair facility for a clutch replacement. The transmission is a Fuller Roadranger 13-speed model. After you remove the transmission and the clutch, you inspect all components looking for any abnormal wear or damage. You notice the input shaft splines are severely fretted where the clutch disks contact them. You recommend replacing the input shaft.

1. What could cause this kind of damage?
2. What could happen if the input shaft is not replaced?
3. Can you recommend anything to prevent reoccurrence of this problem?
4. What component would you be sure to check before re-installation of the clutch?

FIGURE 39-1 Most, if not all, Eaton transmissions are now factory filled with synthetic lubricant.

FIGURE 39-2 An integral oil cooler is an option with Eaton Fuller FR series (fleet) transmissions.

will start to oxidize at elevated operating temperatures and will cause transmission failure. Transmissions should not be consistently operated at sump temperatures of 250°F (121°C) or above as this will cause the loaded tooth contact temperature to rise to 350°F (177°C) or more. Temperatures at this level will eventually destroy the heat treatment of the gears and lead to transmission failure. The following conditions may result in operating temperatures consistently over 250°F (121°C):

- Operating at high loads/slower speed/high torque for long periods
- High ambient temperature
- Restricted transmission air flow
- Exhaust system too close to the transmission
- High horsepower operation
- Engine retarder use

If operating temperatures are at or above 250°F (121°C), the use of an external transmission oil cooler is required. Oil coolers are recommended for any vehicle with an engine of 350 hp (261 kW) and above. Eaton Fuller requires a cooler for any of the following configurations of vehicle:

- Engines of 400 hp (298 kW) and above and 90,000 lb (40,823 kg) GCW or greater
- Engines 400 hp (298 kW) and above and 1,400 lb-ft. (1,898 Nm) or greater torque
- Engines 450 hp (298 kW) and above
- Engines with 1,500 lb-ft. (2,033 Nm) torque ratings and above
- 18-speed Eaton Autoshift transmissions require an Eaton-supplied oil to water cooler or equivalent.

Eaton Fuller FR model transmissions can be fitted with an optional integral cooler as shown in FIGURE 39-2.

Most manufacturers will have their own specific lubrication requirements based on the vehicle vocation. **Line-haul** vehicles spend most of their time in on-highway operation under medium to heavy loading. **Vocational** vehicles are subjected mostly to off-road operation and typically are heavily loaded. **Severe-duty service** vehicles are operated under extreme (maximum) loading most of the time or operate on heavy grades. TABLE 39-1 lists Eaton Fuller's definitions of vehicle vocation as well as servicing recommendations.

TABLE 39-2 lists Eaton Fuller's recommendations for lube change intervals based on the above vocations. Note that Eaton states that only synthetic SAE 50 fluid must be used in all automated transmissions and with engines of 1,850 lb-ft (2,508 Nm) or greater of torque. Oil cooler filters are to be changed at oil change intervals.

Proper lubrication is essential to transmission operation. Although Table39-1 and Table39-2 are representative of a typical manufacturer's recommendation, they are by no means meant to replace OEM specifications. Always consult the OEM literature for the particular transmission being serviced to be sure the correct recommended procedures are followed.

It is important to have the transmission model and/or serial number to source the correct manual. Recall from the Standard Transmissions chapter, the model number

TECHNICIAN TIP

Transmission literature is widely available online, so there is no excuse for not having the correct and most up-to-date information for any particular transmission.

- For Eaton Fuller, visit http://roadranger.com/Roadranger/servicesalesliterature/index.htm
- For Meritor products, visit http://meritor.com/customer/northamerica/lod/default.aspx

Many more manufacturers have online applications that can be accessed for the required information.

TABLE 39-1: Vehicle Application Definitions

Line Haul (On-highway)	Vocational (Off-highway)	Severe-Duty Service
• High mileage operation (over 60,000 miles [96,500 km] per year) • On-highway or good to excellent concrete or asphalt • More than 30 miles (48 km) between starting and stopping • 4×2, 6×2, 6×4 tractor/trailer combinations and straight trucks	• Low mileage operation (under 60,000 miles [96,500 km] per year) • Off-highway or areas of unstable or loose unimproved road surfaces • Less than 30 miles (48 km) between starting and stopping • Heavy-duty, off-road, or specialized application type vehicles	• Consistent operation at or near maximum GCW or GVW ratings • Dirty or wet environments • Consistent operation on grades greater than 8%
Check fluid levels and inspect for leaks at regular preventive maintenance intervals, not to exceed 12,000 miles (19,300 km)	Check fluid levels and inspect for leaks every 50 hours	Severe-duty service will require more frequent oil changes; most manufacturers recommend that change frequency be based on oil sampling

TABLE 39-2: Eaton Fuller's Recommendations for Lube Change Intervals

HEAVY-DUTY TRANSMISSIONS					
Product	Synthetic or Mineral	Lubricant	SAE	Change Interval for Line-Haul	Change Interval for Vocational
Automated and above 1,850 ft-lb (2,508 Nm)	Synthetic	PS-164 Rev 7 or equivalent	SAE 50	500,000 miles (805,000 km) or 5 years	180,000 miles (290,000 km) or 3 years (mobile applications) or 5 years (stationary applications)
Mechanical	Synthetic	PS-164 Rev 7 or equivalent	SAE 50	500,000 miles (805,000 km) or 5 years	180,000 miles (290,000 km) or 3 years (mobile applications) or 5 years (stationary applications)
Mechanical	Mineral	Heavy-duty engine oil	SAE 50 (HD engine oil), Mil 2104 H, Cat TO-4 (SAE 40 – SAE 50)	60,000 miles (96,600 km) or 1 year	60,000 miles (96,600 km) or 1 year (mobile applications) or 500 hours or 1 year (stationary applications)
MEDIUM-DUTY TRANSMISSIONS					
Product	Synthetic or Mineral	Lubricant	SAE	Change Interval for Line-Haul	Change Interval for Vocational
Automated (includes hybrid)	Synthetic	PS-164 Rev 7 or equivalent	SAE 50	500,000 miles (805,000 km) or 10 years	180,000 miles (290,000 km) or 3 years (mobile applications) or 5 years (stationary applications)
ASW clutch module	Synthetic	Dextron III ATF	N/A	150,000 miles (241,000 km) or 3 years	150,000 miles (241,000 km) or 3 years
Mechanical	Synthetic	PS-164 Rev 7 or equivalent	SAE 50	500,000 miles (805,000 km) or 10 years	180,000 miles (290,000 km) or 3 years (mobile applications) 2,000 hours or 5 years (stationary applications)
Mechanical	Mineral	Heavy-duty engine oil	SAE 50 (HD engine oil), Mil 2104 H, Cat TO-4 (SAE 40 – SAE 50)	60,000 miles (96,600 km) or 1 year	500 hours or 1 year

will be stamped on a data plate attached to the transmission. The model number provides a great deal of information about the transmission. **FIGURE 39-3** shows the breakdown of Eaton Fuller transmission's model numbers **nomenclature**; nomenclature refers to the meaning of the text and numbers in the model number.

Other manufacturers will have similar nomenclature charts to identify their transmission models.

Preventative Maintenance of Transmissions

Key to keeping any transmission in working order is following regular maintenance procedures. Preventive maintenance is the first step. As mentioned in the section on lubrication, proper lubricant is essential to transmission operation. A regularly scheduled maintenance program should be followed to ensure the lubricant is doing its job. The air tanks should be drained and checked for contamination on a daily basis. The transmission should also be visually inspected for oil leaks every day and repaired as necessary. In addition to daily checks, the following preventative maintenance checks are recommended by Eaton at every service, or every 12,000 miles (19,000 km) whichever comes first. For off-road applications, the recommended service interval is every 50 hours of operation.

1. Air system and connections: Check the air system for leaks, worn air lines, loose connections, and bolts. Also, ensure the air system is not contaminated

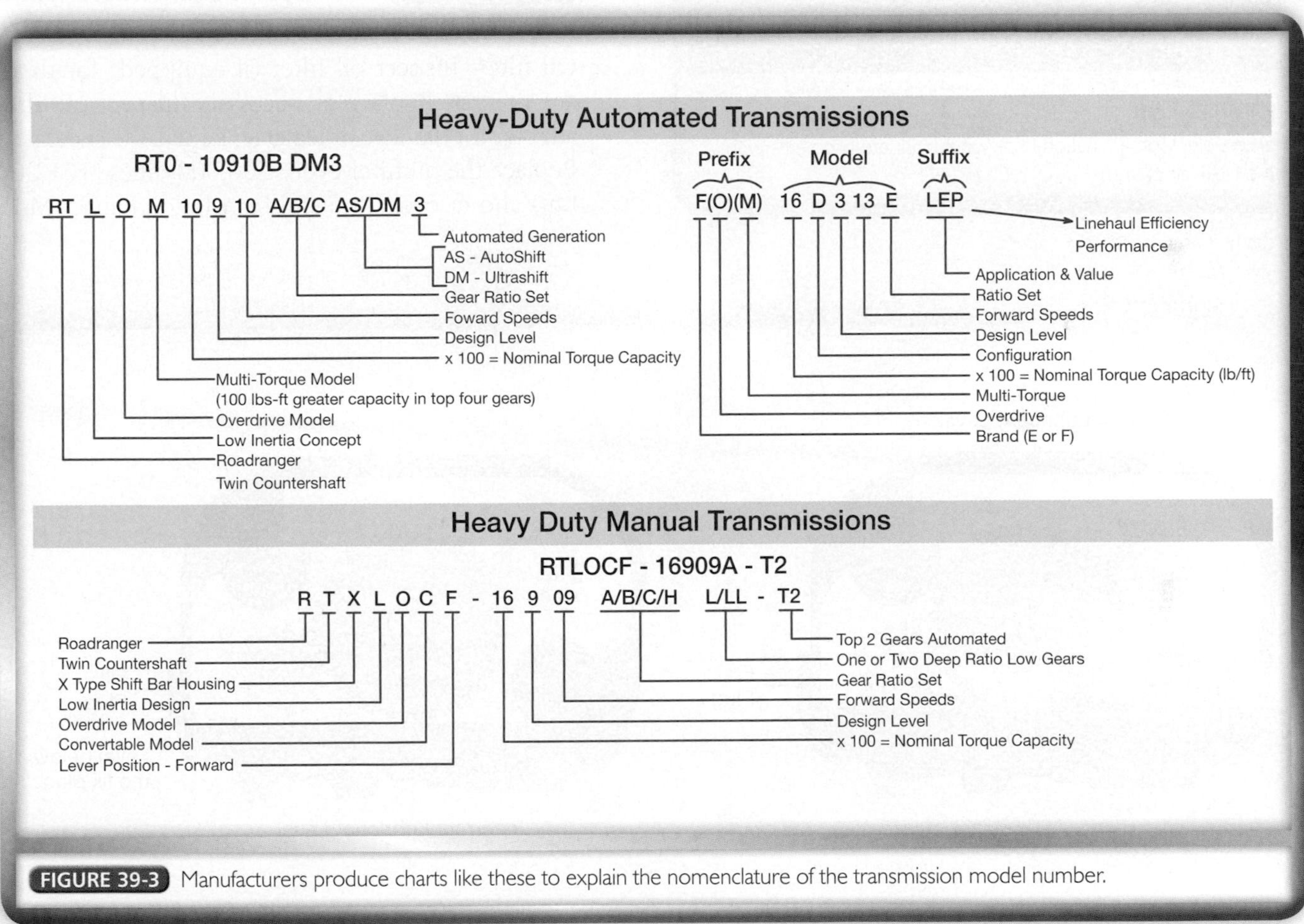

FIGURE 39-3 Manufacturers produce charts like these to explain the nomenclature of the transmission model number.

by water or oil. Check the air filter at the air filter regulator, if necessary. The sintered bronze air filter depicted in FIGURE 39-4 would show contamination very easily.

2. Clutch housing mounting: Check all mounting bolts of the clutch housing flange for looseness.

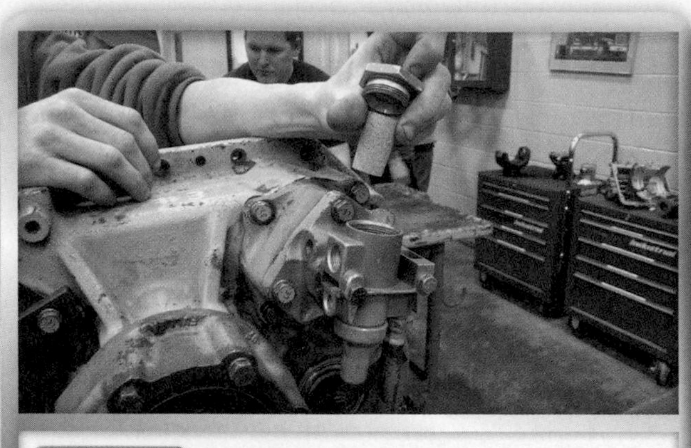

FIGURE 39-4 The sintered bronze air filter is easily accessible. Contamination here would indicate problems with the truck air system.

3. Clutch release bearing: Remove the hand-hole cover in the clutch bell housing and check radial and axial clearances in the release bearing.
4. Clutch pedal shaft and mechanism: Use a pry bar on the clutch release mechanism shafts to check for wear. If excessive movement is found, remove the clutch release mechanism and check bores and shafts on all bushings for wear. Check OEM documentation for correct clearances.
5. Lubricant: Check the lubricant level. A correct lubricant fill level is even with the edge of the check hole, as illustrated in FIGURE 39-5. Always top up fluid levels with the correct lubricant. Never mix different type or brands. To check the fluid level of a manual transmission, follow the guidelines in SKILL DRILL 39-1. To change the gearbox fluid, follow the guidelines in SKILL DRILL 39-2.
6. Oil filter: Inspect oil filter (if equipped) for damage or rust. Replace as necessary. Inspect oil filter adapter for damage or leakage. Replace as necessary. Replace the oil filter every 100,000 miles (161,000 km) and at every transmission fluid change. Most

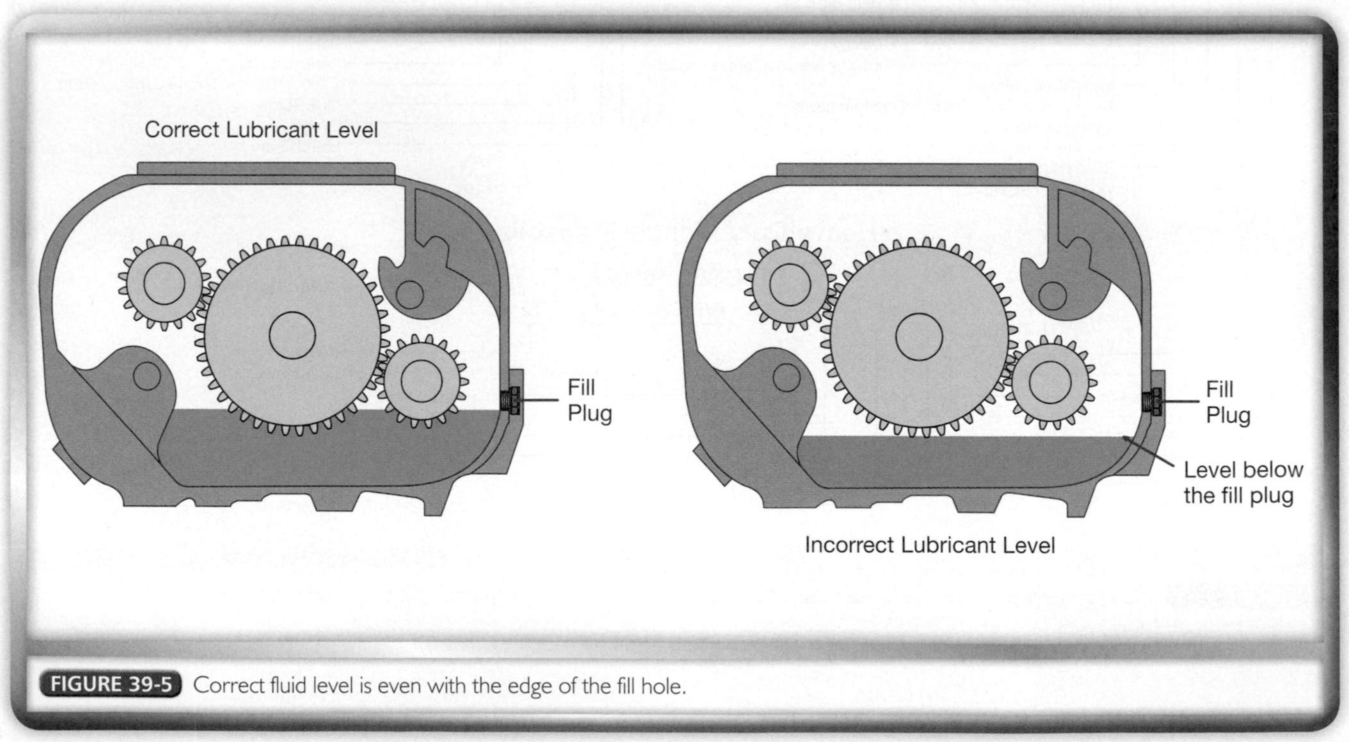

FIGURE 39-5 Correct fluid level is even with the edge of the fill hole.

SKILL DRILL 39-1 Checking the Fluid Level of a Manual Transmission

1. Safely raise the vehicle on an approved lift, making sure it is secure. Check all lift specifications and operating mechanisms, including adapters, before the vehicle is elevated.

2. Perform a visual inspection of the transmission before checking the gearbox fluid level. Obtain a clean drain pan before removing the filler plug, as fluid may spill out.

3. Remove the filler plug using the proper spanner to make sure the filler plug does not become damaged. Perform a visual inspection of the filler plug for thread damage and replace if necessary. Inspect the threads in the transmission fill hole for damage also.

4. If the gearbox fluid begins to run out as the filler plug is removed, let the gearbox fluid seek its own level before re-installing the filler plug. The gearbox fluid level should be at the bottom of the filler plug hole. If the level is left over full, aeration of the gearbox fluid could result, as well as build-up of pressure in the transmission and damage to the seals that keep the gearbox fluid at the proper level.

5. If the fluid level is low, refill with the manufacturer's specified fluid, reinstall the filler plug, and wipe the area around the filler plug hole with a clean shop towel. Tighten the filler plug to the specified torque.

SKILL DRILL 39-2 Changing the Transmission Fluid

1. Raise the vehicle using an approved lift and make sure it is secure. Check all lift specifications and operating mechanisms, including adapters, before the vehicle is elevated. Obtain a clean drain pan to put the used fluid in.

2. Inspect the transmission for any leaks.

3. Remove the drain plug from the bottom of the transmission, being careful of the hot transmission fluid. Let gearbox fluid drain until it has stopped running. If necessary, remove the drain plug for the final drive and drain the fluid.

4. Replace the drain plug(s), tighten to the manufacturer's specification, and remove the fill plug(s).

5. Refill the transmission to the proper level using manufacturer-approved gearbox fluid. Replace the fill plug and tighten to the manufacturer's specification. Use a shop towel to wipe away any spillage.

6. Road test the vehicle. If necessary, put the vehicle back on the lift and check for any leaks that may have resulted from the service. Always double check your work before returning the vehicle to the customer.

manufacturers recommend changing the filter at the same time as the transmission oil change intervals. Check the OEM manual.

7. Drain plugs: Check for leaks and tighten drain plugs securely.
8. Mounting and attaching bolts and gaskets: For applicable models, check all bolts, especially those on power take-off (PTO) covers and rear bearing covers, for looseness, which might cause oil leakage. Check PTO opening and rear bearing covers for oil leakage due to faulty gasket.
9. Gear shift lever: Check for excessive looseness and free play in housing. If lever is loose in housing, proceed with check number 10.
10. Gear shift lever housing assembly: Remove the gear shift lever housing assembly from the transmission. Check that the tension spring and washer are secure and in good shape. Check the gear shift lever spade pin (pivot) and slot for wear. Check bottom end of gear shift lever (shift finger) for wear and check slots of shift gates in shift bar housing for wear at contact points with shift lever.
11. Output shaft: Pry upward on the output shaft flange to check for radial clearance in the output shaft bearings; there should be none. Repair as necessary.
12. Rear bearing housing: Check the rear bearing housing and speedometer drive gear or speed sensor for oil leakage.

Troubleshooting Transmission System Problems

The first step in any maintenance activity is to diagnose the problem. Little good it does to start dismantling components without an idea of what could be causing the trouble! Diagnosing problems is a systematic activity that involves looking for and interpreting basic signs. As a technician, you will have to diagnose common transmission complaints such as oil leaks, noise, vibration, hard shifting, gear slip, and problems with the air system.

Oil Leaks

Oil leaks are, of course, a cause for concern with any mechanical component because they lead to a decrease in lubricant. Still, many unnecessary repairs are performed when there is only a slight weeping. An oil leak is different from an oil weep. An **oil weep** is a very minor oil seepage, usually caused by a wicking effect, and not usually a reason for repair. Oil weep can be recognized by a slight wetting of an area on the component. The area around the weep appears damp and oil has soaked in to any dirt accumulated there—but there is no dripping of fluid.

An oil weep is usually not a cause for concern. In fact, Eaton Fuller transmission rear seals are designed to experience slight weeping, so when weeping is discovered on those transmissions, no repair is needed. If an oil weep is discovered at a gasket, however, re-torque the attaching bolts and monitor the vehicle through its next few services. Depending on the state of the weep, it may not require a repair.

By contrast, a leak will always be associated with oil dripping and or an extremely wet area. Oil leaks must always be repaired. It may be difficult to see the actual path of the leak. Accumulated dirt and/or oil flow patterns may obstruct visibility. Nonetheless, it is essential that the actual leak path is determined before deciding on a repair. Remove the excess dirt and clean the affected area with an approved degreaser. Refill the transmission lube to the proper level (even with the bottom of the fill hole). Road test the vehicle until it reaches normal operating temperatures and re-inspect the suspect area. Ensure that that area is not being contaminated by oil leaking elsewhere and splashing on the area. Once the source of the leak has been identified and repaired, repeat the process to verify the repair. Poor investigation into the actual source of a leak can cause considerable wasted effort, so take the time to properly diagnose any leak. Detailed steps for diagnosing oil leakage are provided in SKILL DRILL 39-3.

Transmission Noise

A certain amount of noise is expected from a heavy-duty transmission as it does its job. Excessive or unusual noises, however, are indications of a problem. And remember that noises that appear to be coming from the transmission may actually be originating elsewhere in the driveline. The transmission may simply be acting as an amplifier. Before undertaking transmission repairs, eliminate all possible sources of the noise before condemning the transmission.

Common noises in the Eaton Fuller twin-countershaft transmission include the gears rattling at idle, knocking sounds, whining, and growling. These noises can also occur in most other transmissions as well.

Gear Rattle at Idle

A rough idling engine can cause gear rattle at idle because of the 0.006" to 0.015" (0.15 mm to 3.8 mm) clearance between the transmission main shaft gears. The small torsional vibrations set up by rough running can cause the gears to strike each other, resulting in rattle.

SKILL DRILL 39-3 Inspecting for Leakage and Replacing Transmission Cover Plates, Gaskets, Seals, and Cap Bolts; Inspecting and Sealing Surfaces and Vents

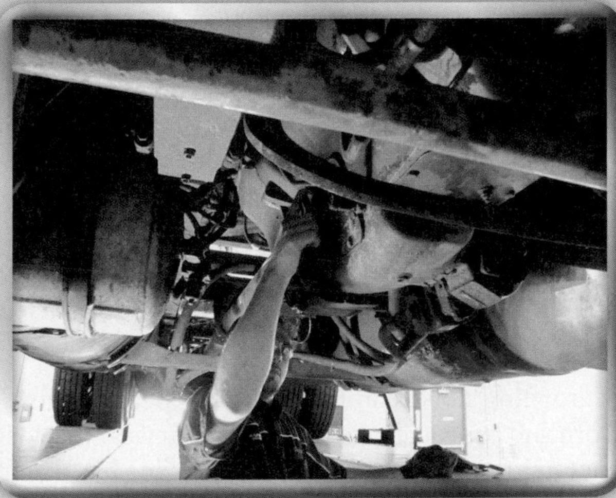

1. Locate and follow the appropriate procedure in the service manual.
2. Complete the accompanying job sheet or work order with all pertinent information.
3. Move the vehicle into the shop, apply the parking brakes, and chock the vehicle's wheels. Observe lockout/tagout procedures.
4. If the vehicle has a manual transmission, place it in "neutral"; if it has an automatic transmission, place it in "park" or "neutral." Note: Some vehicles with automatic transmission do not have "park."
5. Clean the outside of the transmission to remove oil and dirt.
6. Operate the vehicle, if necessary.
7. Inspect the following areas for leaks:
   - PTO covers on the main case
   - Auxiliary case to main case
   - Main case and the clutch housing
   - Clutch housing to flywheel housing
   - Auxiliary countershaft covers
   - Slave valve to main case
   - Shift lever and tower assembly to the top cover
   - Top cover to main case
   - Fill and drain plugs
   - Output shaft bearing retainer to auxiliary case
   - Input bearing retainer to main case
   - Speedometer bore or electronic speed pick-up in the output bearing retainer
   - Output yoke and the oil seal in the output bearing retainer on the auxiliary case

   (Note: Although the transmission must be installed to check for leaks, some of the areas where a leak might be detected cannot be "fixed" unless the transmission is removed.)
8. Remove the leaking component according to the service manual. Note: If it is determined that there is a leaking oil seal, follow the procedures outlined in the service manual for replacing the seal.
9. Use a scraper to remove all sealant/gasket material from both surfaces. Note: Do not get any dirt, sealant, or gasket material inside the transmission.
10. Clean the mounting surfaces with a chlorinated solvent.
11. Apply sealant with a sealant dispenser in a 0.125" (3.175 mm) bead. Note: Make sure you put the sealant on the right surface; it may go on the case or cover. Check the service manual.
12. Apply sealant in the applicable pattern.
13. Install the component as described in the service manual.
14. Check condition of the breather vent:

    a. Check for damage.
    b. Remove the vent by unscrewing it from the top of the transmission.
    c. Remove all dirt and oil from the screen in the breather vent.
    d. Clean or replace if necessary.
15. List the test results and/or recommendations on the job sheet or work order, clean the work area, and return tools and materials to their proper storage.

This can be lessened or eliminated by smoothing out the engine operation. Another way to minimize gear rattle is by installing a clutch with **pre-dampening** vibration control. Pre-dampening clutch systems absorb minor torsional vibrations to prevent gear rattle at idle. To accomplish this, small torsional springs are added in the damper hub to react to idling torsional vibrations. FIGURE 39-6 shows a clutch disc with pre-dampening vibration control. Finally, gear rattle can be reduced or eliminated by resetting the main shaft clearances.

Knocking

Gears are sometimes damaged before or on installation. Gears can be damaged from some other cause as well, such as something that has impacted the gear teeth, for example. Damaged gears can have bumps or swells on the teeth, as illustrated in FIGURE 39-7. These can cause a knocking or thudding sounds as the gears go through mesh. Knocking is usually pronounced when the vehicle is under load.

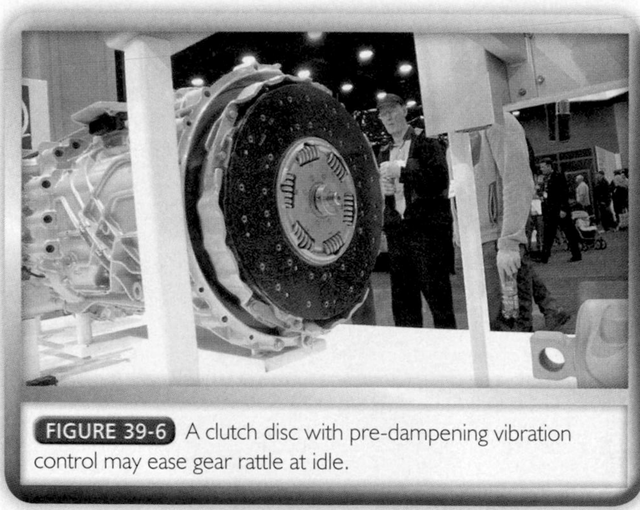

FIGURE 39-6 A clutch disc with pre-dampening vibration control may ease gear rattle at idle.

FIGURE 39-7 Bumps or swells on gear teeth due to abuse before assembly may cause a knocking sound.

Bearings that have worn spots on the bearing races or damaged rollers or balls can cause a similar noise. A gear that is cracked or broken from shock loading can have the same type of noise at low speeds. The noise changes to a howling sound as speed increases.

Whining

Spur-type gears have a natural tendency to whine. Eaton Fuller's introduction of multi-mesh gearing in design level 6 led to much quieter operation as well as increased strength. Having more than one gear tooth in contact at a time helps reduce the tendency to whine. Regardless, as gear teeth wear and pitting occurs, whining will start. As the gear teeth continue to deteriorate, the whining will become a louder howling.

Whining can also be caused by lack of backlash between gears. In addition, bearings that are improperly installed or "squeezed" (have insufficient clearance) can also cause a whining noise.

Growling

A growling noise can be caused by bearings that are worn and badly damaged. Bearings can wear due to lube contamination. Usually, bearing damage has occurred throughout the transmission, so growling can be an indication that a complete overhaul will be necessary. Growling can also be caused by timing issues. If a weld cracks or a key breaks on the countershaft, a gear may shift slightly. This results in a tooth spacing error.

Vibration

In addition to noise, another problem that technicians must commonly diagnose is vibration. Although vibrations can occur in the transmission, it is very unlikely. Usually vibrations that occur elsewhere in the driveline are amplified in the transmission. Some sources of driveline vibration are driveshaft imbalance, U-joint angularity, unbalanced wheel or brake drums, defective engine mounts, and worn suspension.

The effects of driveline vibrations can readily show up in the transmission. Signs that there is vibration in the driveline include:

- Gear rattle at idle
- Fretted gear and shaft splines (worn where they contact each other), as shown in FIGURE 39-8
- Fretted bearings or bores
- Repeated rear seal leakage
- Broken or loose range synchronizer pins
- Repeated loosening of transmission bolts and mountings
- Input shaft spline wear where the clutch disks are mounted

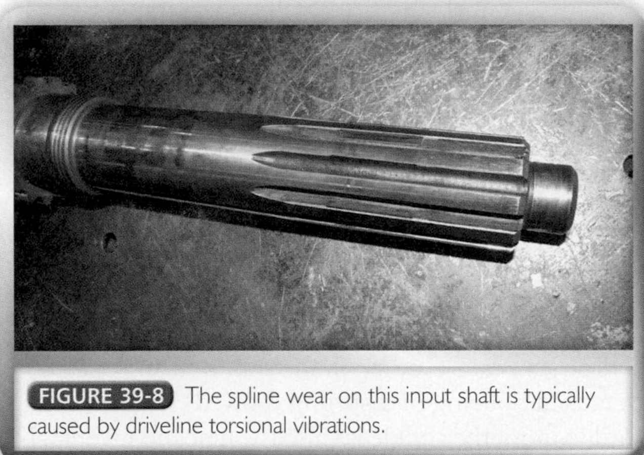

FIGURE 39-8 The spline wear on this input shaft is typically caused by driveline torsional vibrations.

Hard Shifting

Hard shifting can be caused by several factors, so it is important first to find out if the issue is inside or outside the transmission. If the transmission has **remote shift linkage**, where the shift linkage is not directly on top of the shift cover, the remote shift linkage could be the culprit. To confirm that is the case, disconnect the remote shift linkage from the shift cover and try to move the shift rails inside the transmission. (Note: Do not allow the shift detent ball and spring to be forced up and out of the cover while moving the rails.) If the rails move freely, the problem is with the remote shift linkage. Follow the guidelines in SKILL DRILL 39-4 to inspect, adjust, service,

SKILL DRILL 39-4 Inspecting, Adjusting, Servicing, Repairing, or Replacing Remote Shift Linkages and Control Assembly, Brackets, Bushings, Pivots, and Levers

1. Locate and follow the appropriate procedure in the service manual.
2. Complete the accompanying job sheet or work order with all pertinent information.
3. Disconnect linkages and remove the remote control assembly from the transmission according to manufacturer's recommended procedures.
4. Check shift linkage for straightness and rod pivot ends for wear. Replace if bent or worn.
5. Remove the set screw that fastens the outer shift lever to the shaft, and remove the shaft.
6. Remove the two straps that fasten the boot to the housing and remove the boot.
7. Remove the lock wire and set screw from the inner shift lever and pull the shaft from the housing.
8. Inspect the shaft for wear and replace if excessively worn.
9. Remove and inspect the bushings in the housing; replace if worn or damaged.
10. Fill the housing between the two bushings with grease, as specified by the manufacturer.
11. Install the shaft through the housing.
12. Put the inner shift lever in position in the housing and tighten the set screw.
13. Install the boot over the shaft and on the housing and then install new straps.
14. Put the outer shift lever on the shaft, making sure that the outer shaft lever is aligned with the inner shaft lever. Tighten the set screw.
15. Install the remote shifter onto the transmission according to manufacturer's recommended procedures.
16. Reconnect and adjust shift linkage according to the manufacturer's recommended procedures.
17. Torque fasteners to manufacturer's specifications.
18. List the test results and/or recommendations on the job sheet or work order, clean the work area, and return tools and materials to their proper storage.

repair, or replace the remote shift linkage and control assembly brackets, bushings, pivots, and levers.

Hard shifting can also be due to internal causes, such as a sliding clutch that is binding. Sliding clutches tend to bind when they have a twisted main shaft spline, as shown in **FIGURE 39-9**. The main shaft can twist in instances of heavy overloading or shock loading. A twisted main shaft will not allow the sliding clutch at the twisted area to move freely. The twist will occur when the transmission is in a gear. As a result, the transmission will remain in that gear or be very difficult to change out of that gear.

FIGURE 39-9 Hard shifting can be caused by a twisted main shaft due to severe shock load.

The movement of the sliding clutch can be affected by other deformities. The shift yoke for a particular gear can be bent and restrict the sliding clutch. The main shaft key may be distorted and cause the sliding clutch to bind. Hard shifting can also be the result of the yoke bars or shift rails binding in the shift housing because of a cracked housing or a sprung (bowed) shift rail. If it is hard to move the shift lever into the first and reverse shift gates only, the problem may be that the reverse detent plunger is over-torqued or binding due to burrs on the plunger. The reverse detent plunger purposely makes it harder to select this shift rail so that reverse is not selected inadvertently. Follow the guidelines in **SKILL DRILL 39-5** to inspect, adjust, and replace the transmission shift lever assembly, top cover, and shift bar housing.

SKILL DRILL 39-5 Inspecting, Adjusting, and Replacing Transmission Shift Lever Assembly, Top Cover, and Shift Bar Housing

1. Locate and follow the appropriate procedure in the service manual.
2. Complete the accompanying job sheet or work order with all pertinent information.
3. Remove and inspect shift tower assembly:
   a. Place the transmission in "neutral" and deplete the air from the system.
   b. Disconnect the air lines that run to the shift knob at the slave valve.
   c. Remove the cap screws and washers that fasten the housing to the top cover.
   d. Remove the shift tower housing and lever assembly and gasket from the top cover housing.
   e. Refer to the service manual for disassembling and overhauling the shift lever tower assembly. (Note: Shift towers may be made of cast iron or aluminum. Disassembly procedures differ, depending on the type of shift tower assembly.)
   f. Inspect components for cracks, tears, or other wear.
   g. Replace parts as required.

Continued on next page

SKILL DRILL 39-5 Inspecting, Adjusting, and Replacing Transmission Shift Lever Assembly, Top Cover, and Shift Bar Housing, continued

 4 Remove and inspect the top cover and shift bar housing:

a. Remove the three detent springs from the holes in the top cover. (Note: If a heavy-duty detent spring is present, it is in the bore on the slave valve side of the transmission.)

b. Remove a detent ball from each of the three holes.

c. Remove the cap screws and washers from the top cover.

d. Remove the top cover and shift bar housing from the transmission case.

e. Refer to the service manual for disassembly, overhaul, reassembly, and reinstallation of the top cover and shift bar housing.

 5 Reinstall shift tower assembly:

a. Place the transmission in "neutral."

b. Install the new gasket on the top cover housing.

c. Place the shift tower housing onto the top cover housing. (Note: Make sure the bottom of the lower shift lever is installed between the forks and the sleeves in the top cover housing.)

d. Install the mounting cap screws and torque to the manufacturer's specifications.

 6 List the test results and/or recommendations on the job sheet or work order, clean the work area, and return tools and materials to their proper storage.

Gear Slip Out

Gear slip out, or **jump out**, occurs when an engaged gear's sliding clutch moves out of engagement while the vehicle is pulling a load, causing the transmission to go into neutral. Gear slip out can occur in the main box and in the auxiliary section.

There are several reasons for gear slip in the main box. If the clutching teeth on the sliding clutch or the gear are badly worn from excessive gear clashing, slip out is very likely. FIGURE 39-10 shows a gear with badly worn clutching teeth. The presence of excessively worn clutching teeth indicates that the driver is not shifting correctly.

FIGURE 39-10 Excessively worn clutching teeth caused by gear clashing on shifts.

Gear slip out can also occur because of worn shift forks or sliding clutch grooves that will not allow the sliding clutch to fully engage with main shaft gears. Other causes of slip out include worn shift rail detents, weak or broken detent ball springs, or excessive whipping movement of long heavy shift levers, especially when operating over rough terrain.

Mechanical remote shift controls that are frame mounted can lead to slip out as the transmission moves under load. Eaton has modified the clutching teeth in later models so that the teeth have a back taper shape, as shown in FIGURE 39-11. A **back taper** is a profile of the teeth in which the outer edge is thicker than the inner edge. As the gear is loaded, the back taper actually draws the sliding clutch into a deeper mesh rather than trying to push it out of mesh.

In the auxiliary section, slip out usually occurs with the splitter gear and can be caused by worn clutching teeth. FIGURE 39-12 shows a range synchronizer sliding clutch with badly worn clutching teeth caused by failure of the driver to preselect the range shift. Damage like this on a range sliding clutch can lead to range gear slip out/jump out or failure of range engagement in the auxiliary section. Other causes of gear slip out in the auxiliary section include defective air shift systems (low pressure) and incorrect shifting by the driver (namely, failure to break torque correctly during splitter shifts).

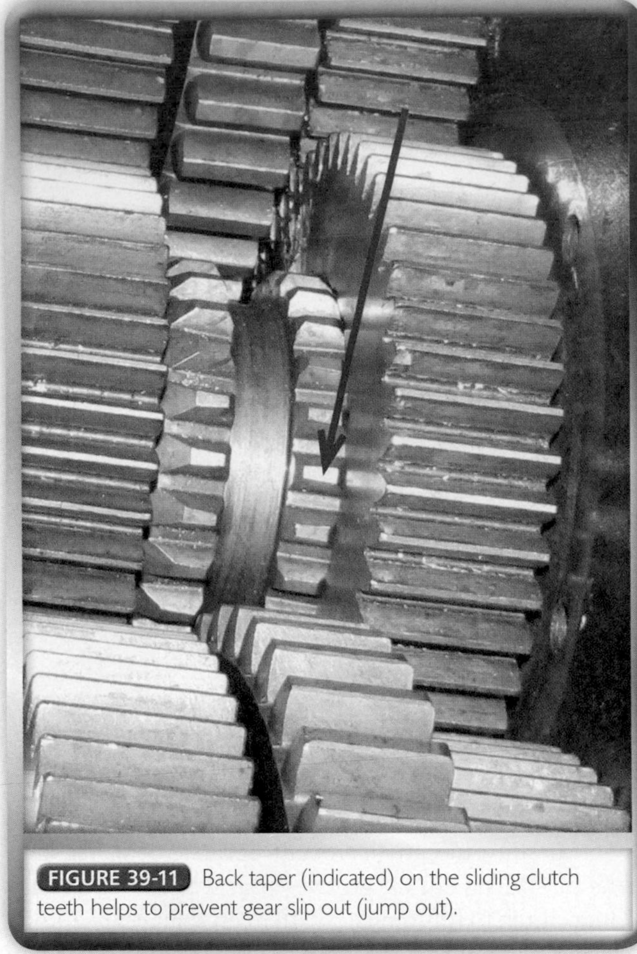

FIGURE 39-11 Back taper (indicated) on the sliding clutch teeth helps to prevent gear slip out (jump out).

FIGURE 39-12 A range synchronizer sliding clutch with badly worn clutching teeth.

Air System Problems

Different transmission models use different air shift system arrangements. FR model transmissions have a range cylinder that is integral to the shift bar housing. When the shift bar housing is installed, the range piston shaft must engage the slot in the range shift bar, as shown in FIGURE 39-13.

FIGURE 39-13 The range cylinder piston bar must engage the slot in the range synchronizer yoke bar. **A.** Range cylinder shaft. **B.** Range synchronizer shift bar.

The FR model transmissions also use an air module bolted to the top of the housing, as shown in FIGURE 39-14. This module houses the slave air valve, the air filter regulator, and the range preselect interlock system. The small metal arm shown in Figure 39-14 is forced outward by the shift mechanism when the transmission is in gear and locks the slave air valve piston in the module, preventing a range shift from occurring.

When the transmission is shifted through neutral, the arm moves, freeing the slave air valve piston. The range shift occurs. Again, the driver must preselect the range shift while in gear. The shift will happen automatically as the shift lever moves through the neutral position.

Most other transmission models use the standard type of range shift control. That is, the slave air valve is bolted to the side of the transmission and the range cylinder is mounted in the auxiliary section housing. Range shift failure can be caused by mechanical failure in the auxiliary section or by air shift problems. To locate the trouble spot, check for crossed air lines and air leaks with the engine off and the air system at operating pressure. Also check for leaks in the Roadranger valve. The Crossed Air Lines, Air Leaks, and Roadranger Valve sections that follow include general air troubleshooting procedures for ten-speed models with the slave valves mounted on the side of the transmission. Although these sections focus on the Eaton air system, other manufacturers', air system troubleshooting will be similar.

Crossed Air Lines

Crossed air line connections from the slave air valve to the Roadranger valve (driver shift knob) can be easily detected. Move the range selection lever on the Roadranger valve up with the transmission in neutral. If the air lines are crossed, a constant leak of air will be heard at the Roadranger valve while it is in high range. The leakage will stop when the valve is returned to the low position.

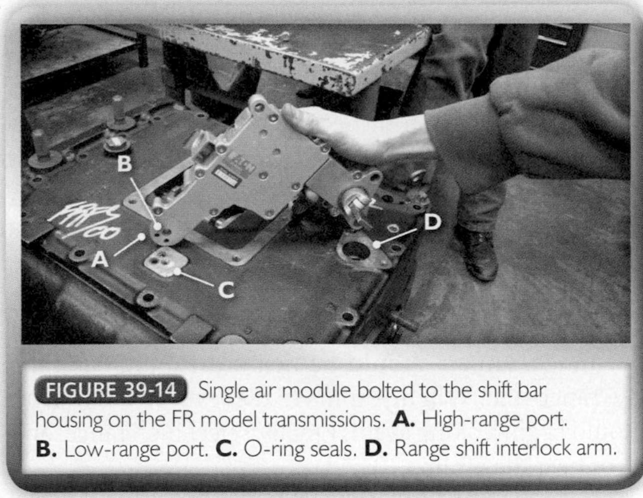

FIGURE 39-14 Single air module bolted to the shift bar housing on the FR model transmissions. **A.** High-range port. **B.** Low-range port. **C.** O-ring seals. **D.** Range shift interlock arm.

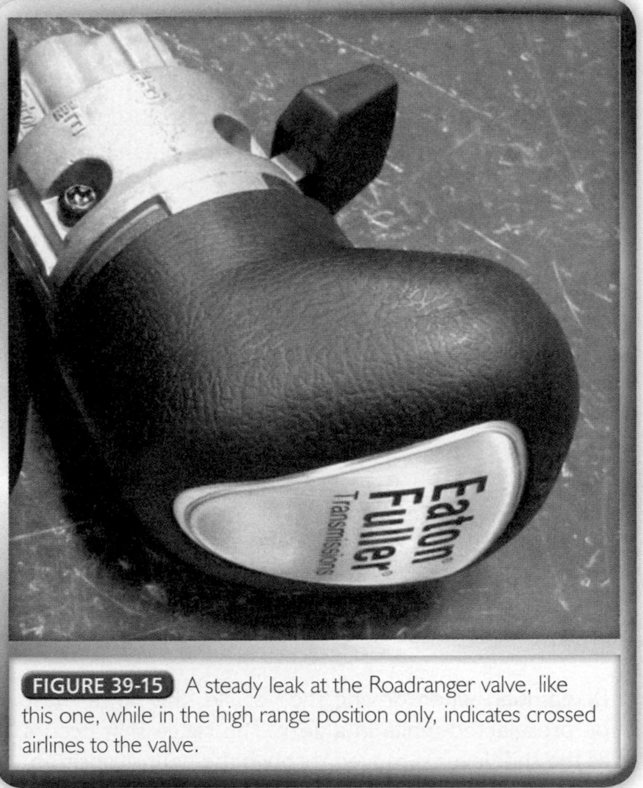

FIGURE 39-15 A steady leak at the Roadranger valve, like this one, while in the high range position only, indicates crossed airlines to the valve.

If the air lines are crossed between the slave air valve and the range cylinder, the transmission will be in high range when low range is selected and vice versa.

Air Leaks

To check for air leaks, first turn the engine off, put the transmission in neutral, and ensure the air system is at operating pressure. Next, coat all air lines and fittings with a solution of soapy water. Covering all the lines and fittings allows you to check for leaks in both the high range and low range positions. If a leak is present, the soap will start to bubble or foam. If there is a steady leak from the exhaust port of the Roadranger valve, like the one shown in FIGURE 39-15, O-rings inside the valve or worn or defective parts of the valve are to blame. The solution is to overhaul or replace the valve as necessary.

A steady leak from the breather of the slave air valve on the side of the transmission can be caused by defective piston O-rings in the valve. Again, the solution is to overhaul or replace the valve as necessary. A leak from the transmission case breather in only low range can be caused by failure of the range yoke bar O-ring, causing pressure to leak into the transmission case.

A common cause of air shift system complaints is the air filter/pressure regulator being contaminated with oil or dirt. With the air system at operating pressure, check the filter regulator for leaks. Any leakage at the breather port fails the regulator, and it should be replaced.

The filter in the air filter/regulator can be removed for cleaning by unscrewing the large end cap. Review Figure 39-3 for the location of the end cap. Drain or disconnect the air supply to the filter before servicing. The filter should be cleaned at every oil change and replaced when necessary as part of regular maintenance.

Drain the air system or cut off the pressure to the air filter/regulator. Then, install a gauge at the outlet. As you build the vehicle pressure back to normal, check that the outlet pressure is between 58 to 63 psi (400 to 434 kPa). If the pressure is not in this range, drain the air system again, and remove and clean the filter. Once again, rebuild system pressure and recheck. Never try to adjust the regulator pressure! If cleaning does not solve the problem, replace the assembly.

Roadranger Valve

A thorough check of the Roadranger valve for air leaks involves checking it generally and also checking it at high range and low range operation.

To check the overall Roadranger valve operation, start at normal operating pressure in high range with the engine off and the transmission in neutral. Disconnect the 5/32" (3.4 mm) air line at the outlet, or P port, of the Roadranger valve. Then, move the lever to low range. A steady stream of air should flow from the P port of the valve and it will shut off when moved back to high range. That indicates the Roadranger valve is functioning correctly. If the valve is not working correctly or leaks air in high range, repair or replace the valve. Reattach the air line.

To check the Roadranger valve for leakage at high range operation, turn the engine off, put the transmission in neutral with the engine off, and ensure the air system is at operating pressure. Next, disconnect the high range airline at the range cylinder. There should be no air present. Now, shift the Roadranger valve to high. You should hear a steady blast of air from the line. Shift the valve back to low, and the air should stop.

The next check tests the operation of the range preselect system. Recall from the Standard Transmissions chapter that the transmission has an interlock pin that prevents slave air valve piston movement while the transmission is in gear. The interlock pin is extended any time the transmission is in gear, and this physically prevents the valve piston from moving. This test ensures that this system is working correctly. Move the gear shift lever to any gear position and then move the Roadranger valve to the high range position. No air should be heard coming from the high range air line—indicating that the slave air valve position is locked by the interlock pin. Then move the lever to neutral. Air should be heard coming from the high range line, indicating that the slave air valve has moved.

> **TECHNICIAN TIP**
>
> Remember, when driving the vehicle, the range must be preselected while in a gear. The range shift occurs as the shift lever is moved through the neutral position. As the lever is moved to neutral, the plunger pin moves inboard, allowing the slave air piston to move and redirect the air flow to the range cylinder. Failure to preselect will quickly destroy the range synchronizer!

Checking the Roadranger valve for leakage at low range operation involves running the same test as was done in high range operation. Start again with the engine off, the transmission in neutral, and the air system at operating pressure. Select high range on the Roadranger valve, and then disconnect the low range air line at the range cylinder. Next, select low range. You should hear a steady blast of air coming from the low range line. Then, select high range, and the flow should stop. Next, place the transmission in any gear position and again select low range. No air should be heard escaping from the low range line. When you move the lever to neutral, air should begin leaking again. Finally, select high range, and reconnect the air line.

If the air shift system does not operate as described in high and low range, the slave air valve, the range shift cylinder or components, or the range synchronizer is defective.

The final place to check for air leaks in the Roadranger valve is in the range cylinder. As illustrated in **FIGURE 39-16**, the range cylinder consists of the yoke bar, the range piston, the housing, and the housing cover. The piston has an inner and an outer seal. If either of these seals is defective, range shifts to high or low will be sluggish or may not occur at all. The yoke bar has an O-ring in the range cylinder housing to seal the low range chamber of the housing from the case. If this seal fails, shifts to low

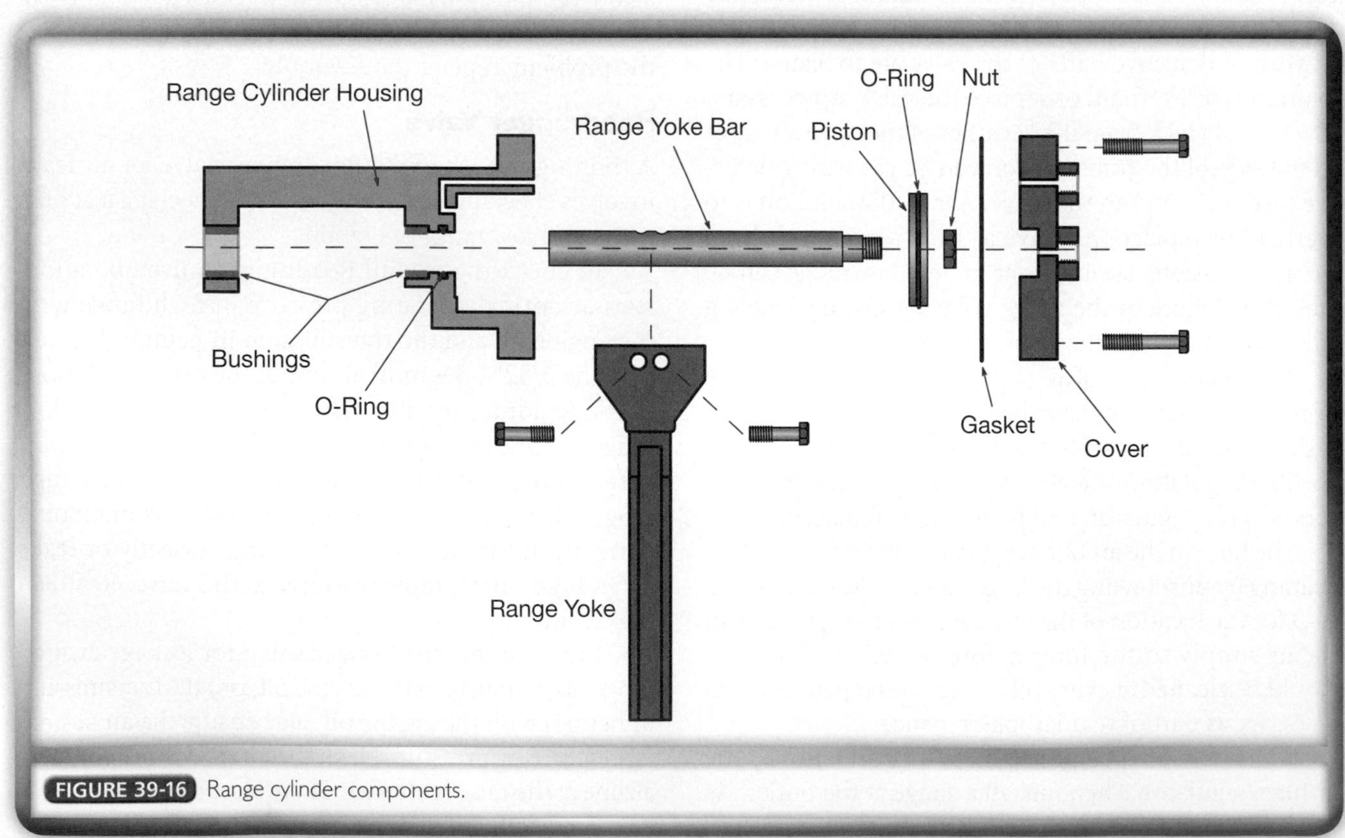

FIGURE 39-16 Range cylinder components.

range will be sluggish or not occur at all. In addition, the transmission case will be pressurized when low range is selected. The housing cover is sealed by a gasket. If this gasket leaks, range shifts to high may be sluggish or may not occur at all. Plus, air will be heard leaking from the cover when high range is selected.

Repair and Maintenance of Transmissions

Transmission overhaul is not often performed in most shops. Still, it is important to have a basic understanding of what is involved in the process. The information required to successfully rebuild a transmission is very precise and unique to the model being worked on. For that reason, we will focus our discussion on general procedures for several transmission-related tasks commonly performed in repair shops.

> **TECHNICIAN TIP**
>
> Information on overhauling or rebuilding particular transmissions is available from the manufacturers' websites. For information on the Eaton Roadranger, visit www.roadranger.com. For information on Meritor transmissions, visit www.meritor.com.

General Precautions and Procedures

As with any repair, it is critical that your work area be staged, orderly, and complete. Before beginning any maintenance or repair procedure on a transmission or auxiliary section, ensure that the following items are on hand and organized in your work area:

- The correct overhaul manual for the transmission model being serviced
- A clean dust-free area large enough to complete the repair
- All of the recommended tools found in the overhaul manual
- Replacement parts (i.e., gaskets, seals and or bearings, snap rings, and so on) for parts that will definitely or may be destroyed during disassembly

Before attempting any repair on any transmission, read and understand the following precautions and procedures:

- Bearings. Remove bearings with appropriate pullers. Carefully clean and inspect the bearings for damage and wear. Check races and balls or rollers for pitting, heat discoloration, and other damage. If there is any doubt in the bearing's condition, replace it. If the bearing is to be reused, lubricate it and wrap in protective material until ready to use. Before reinstallation, always check that the bearings fit in the bore and on its shaft. In Eaton Fuller transmissions, the bearings are a tight fit on the shaft and a light interference fit in the case bores.
- Assemblies. When disassembling various components, lay the pieces out on a clean surface in the order that they come apart and protect them from dirt and damage.
- Snap rings. Always remove snap rings with pliers designed for the job. Remember, even when they are removed correctly, snap rings are quite commonly distorted. Any distortion requires that the snap ring be replaced. Never reuse a sprung snap ring.
- Gears. Check all gear teeth for frosting or pitting. Frosting is a slight discoloration of the gear tooth face caused by tiny pits that occur naturally as the gears run together and find a common pitch line. Frosting and light pitting is usually not a cause for concern. As the gears continue to run together, frosting is usually replaced by a shiny smooth surface in a process known as healing. Moderate and heavy pitting, however, will require gear replacement—especially if it is concentrated at the pitch line of the gear teeth. Check for cracks in the gears, and carefully inspect the clutching teeth for excessive wear from clashing. If clutching teeth are worn significantly, replace the gear. Do not mistake back-tapered clutching teeth for worn teeth. Back-taper teeth are wide on the outside edge and narrower on the inside edge. Clashing wear will always progress from the outside of the tooth to the inside.
- Splines. Check all shaft splines for wear, and replace as necessary.
- Cast iron parts. Check all cast iron components for cracks and or leaks. Replace as necessary

Inspecting the Transmission Oil Cooler and Filter

Transmission oil not only lubricates a transmission's moving parts, but it may be used to cool the transmission. When oil passes over the moving parts in a transmission, it absorbs heat. In most cases, airflow over the transmission will cool the oil. When that is not sufficient, oil is routed to a transmission cooler where it is cooled before returning to the transmission. Normally, a transmission cooler is needed if the transmission's continuous operating temperature is always more than 250°F (121°C), 275°F (135°C) at intermittent operation, or the engine has a power rating of 350 horsepower (261 kW) or more.

If airflow is restricted to the transmission due to the vehicle's configuration (aerodynamics), a transmission cooler may be required. If a transmission cooler is used, it must be maintained in good working order. A fin comb may be required to assist in straightening the cooler's fins. To inspect the transmission oil filter and cooler, follow the guidelines in **SKILL DRILL 39-6**.

Inspecting the Air System

The need to troubleshoot the air shift system may become necessary if the transmission shifts too slowly or fails to shift into the desired range. Checking for leaks, proper airflow through the system, proper component operation, and the correct air system and air line connections are the primary methods for troubleshooting the system. When troubleshooting the air shift system, the engine should be turned off after building normal vehicle air pressure. Since procedures vary with the type of system (OEM differences), always consult the service manual before beginning any maintenance on the air shift system.

Air leaks can occur in any part of the air shift system. Leaks can occur at the range selector valve in the shift knob assembly, at the slave valve, range cylinder, air filter/regulator, in the air lines, or in the air line connections. The following procedure is general in nature. It is important to follow the procedure(s) outlined in the service manual for the type of transmission being serviced. Although the transmission must be installed to check for air leaks, most of the components where you might detect a leak cannot be repaired until the transmission is removed. To inspect, test, adjust, repair or replace air shift controls, lines, valves, regulators, filters, and cylinder assemblies, follow the guidelines in **SKILL DRILL 39-7**.

SKILL DRILL 39-6 Inspecting the Transmission Oil Filter and Cooler

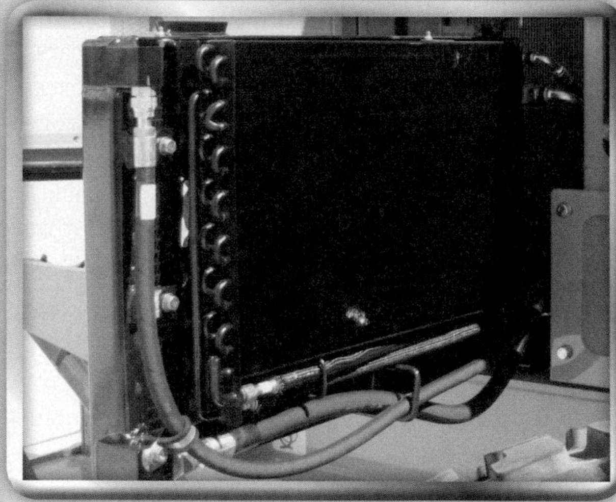

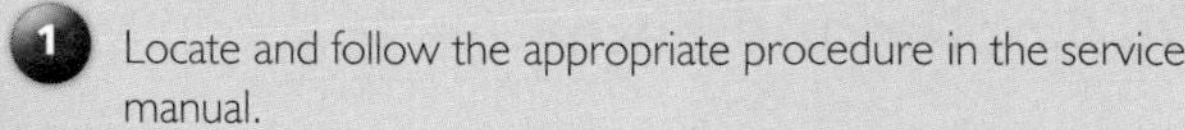

1. Locate and follow the appropriate procedure in the service manual.
2. Complete the accompanying job sheet or work order with all pertinent information.
3. Move the vehicle into the shop, apply the parking brakes, and chock the vehicle's wheels. Observe lockout/tagout procedures.
4. If the vehicle has a manual transmission, place it in "neutral"; if it has an automatic transmission, place it in "park" or "neutral." (Note: Some vehicles with automatic transmissions do not have "park.")
5. Inspect and replace the transmission oil filter:
   - **a.** Check transmission oil filter for leaks. If a leak is found, change the filter. (Note: If a filter is removed for any reason, a new one must be installed.)
   - **b.** Place a drain pan under the filter if removal is necessary.
   - **c.** Remove the oil filter using an oil filter removal tool and make sure the rubber seal from the old filter has not been left on the transmission filter housing.
   - **d.** Wipe the mating surface on the transmission clean.
   - **e.** Apply a thin coat of transmission oil to the new filter's rubber seal.
   - **f.** Screw on the new filter. (Note: It may be necessary to drain the transmission main case prior to removing the filter.)
6. Inspect and replace transmission oil cooler:
   - **a.** Check the cooler for signs of leaks. (Note: If there are leaks from the cooler, it may have to be replaced.)
   - **b.** Check all lines and hoses for any signs of leaks.
   - **c.** Check that the fins on the cooler's coils are straight. Use a fin comb to straighten the fins, if necessary.
   - **d.** Refer to the service manual for removal and replacement procedures if it is determined that a new cooler must be installed.

7. List the test results and/or recommendations on the job sheet or work order, clean the work area, and return tools and materials to their proper storage.

SKILL DRILL 39-7 Inspecting, Testing, Adjusting, Repairing, or Replacing Air Shift Controls, Lines, Valves, Regulators, Filters, and Cylinder Assemblies

1. Locate and follow the appropriate procedure in the service manual.

2. Complete the accompanying job sheet or work order with all pertinent information.

3. Move the vehicle into the shop, apply the parking brakes, and chock the vehicle's wheels. Observe lockout/tagout procedures.

4. Run the engine until normal vehicle air pressure is achieved.

5. Shut down the engine.

6. Check for air leaks in all fittings, lines, and connections:
   - a. Place gear shift in "neutral."
   - b. Coat air lines and fittings with soapy water.
   - c. Move the range selector switch up or down.
   - d. Identify air leaks at all fittings, lines, and connections.

7. Consult the service manual (air system schematics) and check that air lines are properly routed and connected.

6. Check the slave valve to ensure that there is not a constant air leak out of the exhaust port. (Note: It is normal for there to be a quick release of exhaust when a range shift is made. Generally, some slave valves cannot be repaired and must be replaced if leaks are detected.) Consult the service manual for repair or replacement of the slave valve if a constant leak is detected.

8. Check the air filter/regulator for leaks:
   - a. Place the gear shift in "neutral."
   - b. Check that no air is leaking at the breather port.
   - c. Replace the air filter/regulator if an air leak is detected. Refer to the service manual.
   - d. If not replacing the air filter/regulator, check the filter element for contamination and replace, if necessary.

9. Check the range selector valve:
   - a. Refer to the service manual for troubleshooting this valve.
   - b. Repair or replace as required.

10. Check the range cylinder:
    - a. Refer to the service manual for troubleshooting the range cylinder.
    - b. Repair or replace as required.

11. List the test results and/or recommendations on the job sheet or work order, clean the work area, and return tools and materials to their proper storage.

Inspecting the Power Take-Off

The final routine transmission inspection that is commonly undertaken in a shop is inspecting the power take-off (PTO). To inspect the PTO, follow the guidelines in SKILL DRILL 39-8.

Replacing the Input Shaft

Eaton Fuller twin countershaft transmission input shafts are replaceable without dismantling the transmission. Input shafts are commonly replaced due to excessive spline wear from the clutch disks caused by torsional vibrations. To replace the input shaft, follow the steps in SKILL DRILL 39-9.

SKILL DRILL 39-8 Inspecting the Power Take-off

1. Locate and follow the appropriate procedure in the service manual.
2. Complete the accompanying job sheet or work order with all pertinent information.
3. Move the vehicle into the shop, apply the parking brakes, and chock the vehicle's wheels. Observe lockout/tagout procedures.
4. If the vehicle has a manual transmission, place it in "neutral"; if it has an automatic transmission, place it in "park" or "neutral". (Note: Some vehicles with automatic transmission do not have "park.")
5. Check for proper engagement and disengagement of the PTO gearbox. It should shift smoothly without gear clashing.
6. Check that the PTO runs smoothly with no vibration or unusual noises.
7. Inspect linkage for looseness, broken brackets, missing clamps, security, and lubrication.
8. Inspect PTO seals and gaskets for leaks and the housing for cracks.
9. Inspect the driveline (if equipped) for loose U-joints and the correct driveline angle. (Note: Check the service manual for the procedure to check the driveline angle.)
10. Check for correct speed and output power.
11. Inspect shift system:
    - a. Inspect hydraulic shift system (if equipped) fittings, cylinders, motors, and pump. Also check that there are no leaks.
    - b. Inspect the air shift system (if equipped) for leaks and proper operation.
12. Inspect the electrical system wiring harness for cracks, security, and placement. Also check that connections are tight.
13. Inspect electrical components that control the PTO. (Note: Electrical components may include switches, gauges, overspeed protection system, and so on.)
14. List the test results and/or recommendations on the job sheet or work order, clean the work area, and return tools and materials to their proper storage.

SKILL DRILL 39-9 Replacing the Input Shaft

1. Remove the transmission according to the procedure in the Servicing Heavy-Duty Clutches chapter. Remember not to let the transmission hang on the input shaft as it is removed. With the transmission suitably supported on a transmission jack or a workbench, remove the six nuts and four bolts that secure the clutch bell housing and remove the housing. Remove the six bolts securing the front bearing cover and remove the cover and gasket. Remove and discard the rubber lip seal if present. This seal is merely for shipping purposes and is not required further.

Continued on next page

SKILL DRILL 39-9 Replacing the Input Shaft, continued

2 Using snap ring pliers, remove the front bearing snap ring from the input shaft. Use a soft iron maul to drive the input shaft to the rear as far as it will go (approximately 0.25" or 6.35 mm). A maul is a large 2" (5 cm) diameter bar approximately 8" (20 cm) long.

3 Grasp the input shaft and wiggle it. Try to move it forward as far as it will go. If it is difficult to move forward, tap the transmission housing front wall with the maul as it is pulled forward. This will expose the large snap ring on the outside of the input bearing; do not remove this snap ring.

4 Install the bearing puller #7070A kit (Owatonna tool company) or equivalent. This tool pulls on the large external snap ring on the bearing. Remove the input bearing.

5 Remove the bearing spacer from the input shaft. Remove the internal snap ring from the input drive gear using a small screwdriver. Remove the input shaft. The drive gear will remain in place in the transmission case.

6 Check and replace (as needed) the input shaft pocket bushing. This bushing supports the forward end of the main shaft. Because the main shaft "floats," the bushing rarely needs replacing. The input shaft has a spiral groove just in front of the bearing. The grooves are the oil return "threads." It is critical that they are clean and undamaged or the transmission may leak. Clean or replace as necessary.

Continued on next page

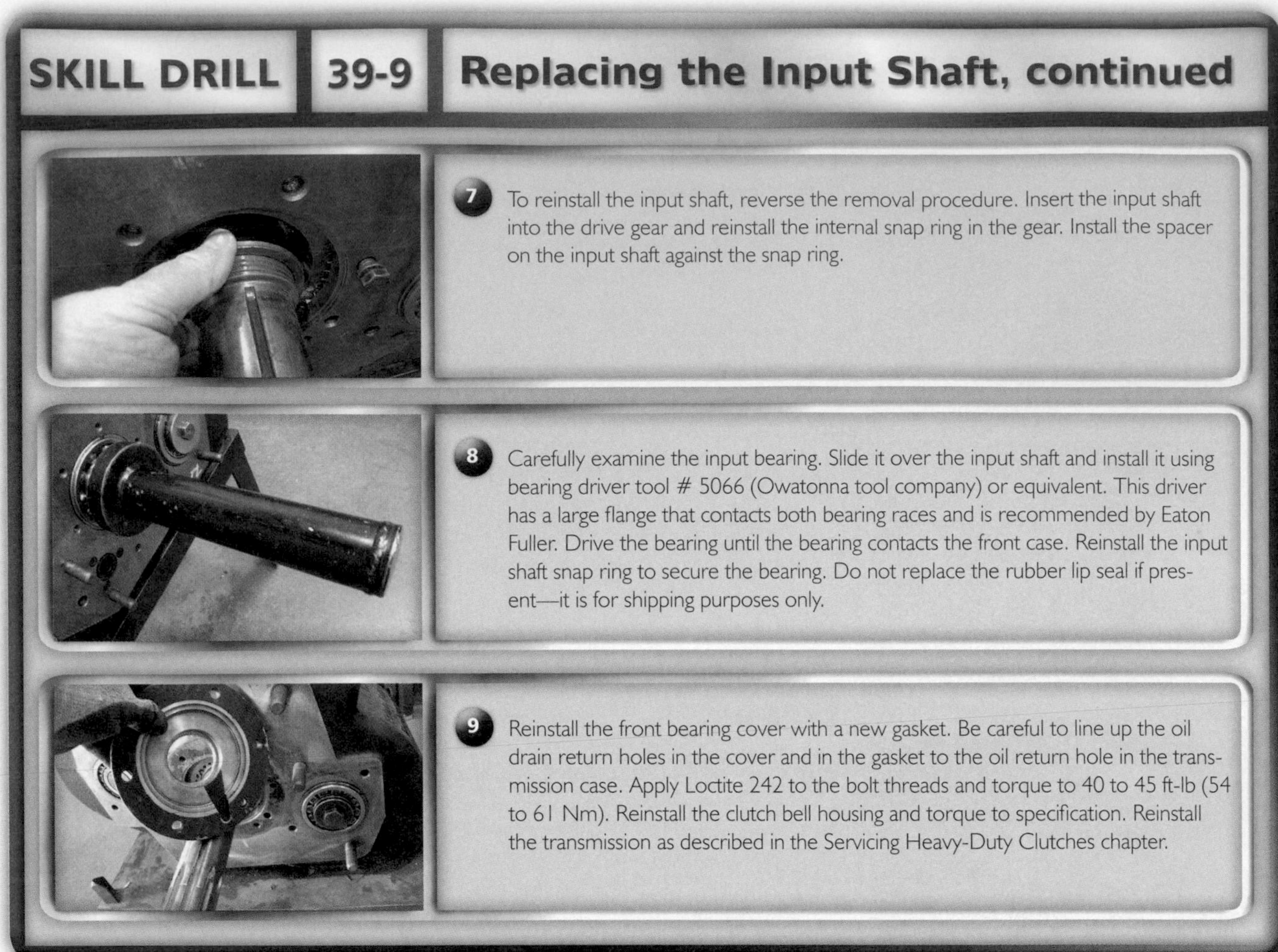

SKILL DRILL 39-9 Replacing the Input Shaft, continued
7 To reinstall the input shaft, reverse the removal procedure. Insert the input shaft into the drive gear and reinstall the internal snap ring in the gear. Install the spacer on the input shaft against the snap ring.
8 Carefully examine the input bearing. Slide it over the input shaft and install it using bearing driver tool # 5066 (Owatonna tool company) or equivalent. This driver has a large flange that contacts both bearing races and is recommended by Eaton Fuller. Drive the bearing until the bearing contacts the front case. Reinstall the input shaft snap ring to secure the bearing. Do not replace the rubber lip seal if present—it is for shipping purposes only.
9 Reinstall the front bearing cover with a new gasket. Be careful to line up the oil drain return holes in the cover and in the gasket to the oil return hole in the transmission case. Apply Loctite 242 to the bolt threads and torque to 40 to 45 ft-lb (54 to 61 Nm). Reinstall the clutch bell housing and torque to specification. Reinstall the transmission as described in the Servicing Heavy-Duty Clutches chapter.

Replacing Rear Seals

Checking and replacing seals in the transmission is a general procedure that is commonly undertaken in the shop. To replace rear seals in a transmission, follow the guidelines in SKILL DRILL 39-10. The steps listed in SKILL DRILL 39-10 cover rear seal replacement with a speed sensor. The procedure is slightly different with a mechanical speedometer. Note that on transmissions with electronic speed sensors, the speedometer reluctor doubles as the sealing surface for the rear transmission seal. A **reluctor** is a toothed wheel used with a magnetic sensor usually to measure shaft speed. If the reluctor has excessive wear from contact with the seal, it should also be replaced.

Removing and Disassembling the Auxiliary Section

Even though a complete transmission overhaul is unlikely in most shops, you may find that you need to remove an auxiliary section for maintenance and light repair. It is critical to keep the components of the auxiliary section in order as you remove them so that you can reassemble them accurately and quickly. For example, when the auxiliary countershaft bearing covers are removed, keep the caps, shims, bearing race, and countershaft from each side separate so they can be reassembled correctly. Likewise, auxiliary section countershafts are identical but they should be marked so they are reinstalled with the correct bearing and shim pack if the bearings are reused. Also note that the integral range cylinder in Fuller ten-speed FR transmissions makes it necessary to remove the shift bar housing before removing the auxiliary section. To remove the auxiliary section from a Fuller ten-speed FR model, follow the guidelines in SKILL DRILL 39-11. To disassemble the auxiliary section, follow the steps in SKILL DRILL 39-12.

TECHNICIAN TIP

If the auxiliary section is being completely replaced with a new one, step 3 in SKILL DRILL 39-10 will not be necessary to remove the old unit. The support straps will need to be installed on the new unit, however.

SKILL DRILL 39-10 Replacing Rear Seals

1. Disconnect the driveshaft at the output yoke of the transmission. Place the transmission in low gear low range. This will prevent the yoke from turning. Remove the yoke nut using a 2.75" (70 mm) socket. Remove the yoke using a yoke puller tool.

2. Remove the vehicle speed sensor (VSS). Remove the speedometer reluctor (rotor) and the O-ring from the shaft. Carefully pry the seal out with a screwdriver or pry bar inserted into the seal groove. Do not pry against the seal housing.

3. Remove the oil slinger from the speedometer reluctor (rotor) using a suitable drift punch if necessary. Check the sealing surface of the reluctor for grooving, burrs, or nicks. Do not try to repair the surface. If damaged, replace it.

4. Install the seal into the housing using a suitable seal driver. The Eaton P/N 5564501 driver is for the 7 series transmission; the 9 series transmission uses a different driver. Check the OEM manual for the correct installer. Then, install the oil slinger onto the speedometer reluctor using the proper driver. The Eaton P/N 71223 driver is for the 7 series transmission; the 9 series uses a different driver. Check the OEM manual for the proper driver.

5. Install the O-ring and the speedometer reluctor. Install the speedometer sensor. If the sensor is the thread-in type, adjust it by turning the sensor in until it contacts a tooth on the reluctor. Then back it out ½ to 1 turn.

6. Install the output yoke and torque the nut to 450–500 ft-lb (9,610–9,677 Nm). If the nylon lock on the nut is damaged or worn significantly, replace the nut. Reinstall the drive shaft and top up the transmission with the correct fluid until the level is even with the fill hole.

SKILL DRILL 39-11 Removing the Auxiliary Section from a Fuller Ten-Speed FR Model

1. Drain the oil from the transmission. Support and then disconnect the drive shaft from the transmission output yoke. Move the driveshaft away or remove it completely. Disconnect the speedometer cable or sensor. Drain the air tanks and remove the air lines going to the air module on the shift bar housing.

2. Remove the shift tower and the shift bar housing. Remove the auxiliary section countershaft bearing covers and shims. Do not mix the shims from side to side. Carefully mark the shim pack, bearing cover, bearing, and countershaft from one side so that they can be reinstalled in the correct side. Failure to do this means that the shim setting procedure must be done on reassembly.

3. Attach countershaft support brackets (indicated) to each countershaft. Buy them or make them from 0.5" flat bar stock. These will support the countershafts as the auxiliary section is removed. If supports are not installed when the bearing covers are removed, the countershafts may fall to the floor when the auxiliary section is moved away from the main box.

4. Drive the two alignment dowels forward in the transmission case by 0.5" (13 mm) to break free any rust and ease removal. Do not drive them too far or they will become loose. Remove the bolts attaching the auxiliary section to the main box. The bolts vary in length and must be replaced in their correct locations. Note the raised alignment shoulder.

5. Two or three threaded pusher holes in the auxiliary section flange area will be covered with tape. Thread the longer removed bolts into these holes, and tighten evenly until the gasket seal is broken and the auxiliary is far enough back to install the auxiliary hanger bracket. Do not move the auxiliary back any further than necessary or it may drop. If practical, install the horizontal removal hanger bracket #5061 (Owatonna tool company) or equivalent to the top of the auxiliary section flange. This tool can also be constructed following Fuller instructions.

6. Connect a hoisting device to the tool and raise it until it supports the weight of the auxiliary. If supporting the auxiliary by a transmission jack, be sure the auxiliary section is firmly secured to the jack so it does not fall. Carefully move the auxiliary section rearward to clear the main box and remove the auxiliary. Install the bottom flange of the auxiliary section to a brass-jawed vise for disassembly.

SKILL DRILL 39-12 Disassembling the Auxiliary Section

1. Remove the auxiliary section output yoke. Use a yoke puller as needed. Place a clean shop towel into the gear mesh to stop the output shaft from turning. With yoke removed, remove the speedometer reluctor and the O-ring from the output shaft.

2. Use a maul and a soft bar to drive the auxiliary output shaft forward slightly (0.5" or 13 mm) to facilitate removal of the auxiliary countershafts. Remove the countershaft support straps one at a time while holding the countershafts. Remove each countershaft and its bearing race. Mark the countershafts so they can be re-installed on the correct side.

3. Remove the range synchronizer, the yoke, and the range shift bar together from the front of the auxiliary and set aside. Drive the auxiliary output shaft forward with the maul and remove it. Do not misplace the large, steel bearing spacer. If not replacing the output shaft bearings, leave the front output shaft bearing in place as shown.

4. If replacing the output shaft bearings, place the output shaft in a press with the range gear supported by blocks. Press the output shaft through the range gear and the bearing to remove it. Note that the front and rear support bearings are different, so do not mix them up. The front rear support bearing inner diameter is slightly larger. Remove the rear bearing cover from the auxiliary section housing.

5. Remove the rear output shaft support bearing and race. Some models have a one-piece outer and inner bearing race as shown.

TECHNICIAN TIP

Certain models have one chamfered hole in the rear bearing cover, so take note of its location. This chamfered hole is sealed by a nylon collar followed by a brass washer on the retaining bolt. When reassembling, a new tapered nylon collar must be used in the chamfered hole or the cover will leak.

Overhauling the Range Synchronizer

Once the auxiliary is removed and disassembled, the range synchronizer can also be disassembled and the friction rings replaced as needed. To disassemble the synchronizer, follow the guidelines in **SKILL DRILL 39-13**. Be sure to have a clean shop towel on hand to cover the synchronizer and prevent the tension springs from flying out into the shop.

SKILL DRILL 39-13 Overhauling the Range Synchronizer

1. Place the synchronizer on a bench with the large cone shaped friction ring down. Cover the synchronizer with a shop towel. Carefully pull the smaller cup-shaped friction ring upwards until it separates. Examine both friction rings for heat discoloration, loose pins, and glazed or worn areas. Replace as necessary.

2. Examine the splines and the clutching teeth of the synchronizer clutch and replace if necessary.

3. To reassemble the synchronizer, slide the pins of the large friction ring into the three chamfered holes on the convex side of the synchronizer clutch. Place the synchronizer on the bench with the large friction ring down.

4. Install the three tension setting springs into the bores in the small friction ring. Place the small friction ring on top of the concave side of the synchronizer clutch with the springs resting against the pins of the large synchronizer ring.

5. Cover the synchronizer with a shop towel. With flat hands, twist the top friction ring counterclockwise very quickly while exerting downward force. This will compress the springs and cause the pins of the small friction ring to enter the other three holes in the synchronizer clutch. Essentially, just push down and twist. The shop towel will prevent the springs from flying out if reassembly is unsuccessful.

Reassembling and Timing the Auxiliary Section

When reassembling and timing the auxiliary section, it is important to keep track of your progress at each step in the procedure. Have a means to mark the components that you remove so you are sure to reassemble them in the proper location. This is particularly true when marking the teeth used to time the countershaft. Use a highly visible marking compound and be mindful that your marks may become obscured by the by the rear counter shaft bearing and washer on some models. To reassemble and time the auxiliary section, follow the guidelines in SKILL DRILL 39-14.

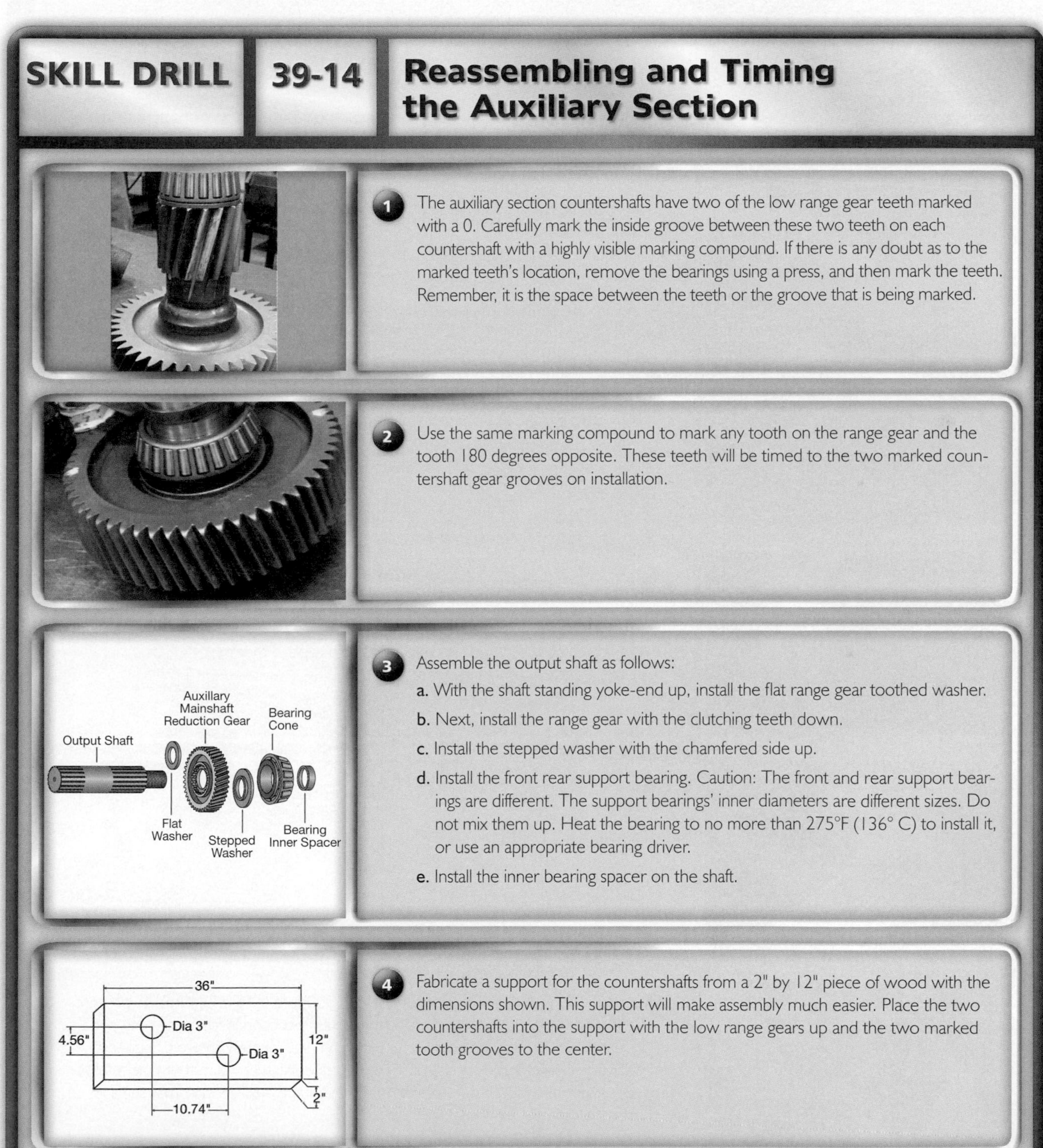

SKILL DRILL 39-14 Reassembling and Timing the Auxiliary Section

1. The auxiliary section countershafts have two of the low range gear teeth marked with a 0. Carefully mark the inside groove between these two teeth on each countershaft with a highly visible marking compound. If there is any doubt as to the marked teeth's location, remove the bearings using a press, and then mark the teeth. Remember, it is the space between the teeth or the groove that is being marked.

2. Use the same marking compound to mark any tooth on the range gear and the tooth 180 degrees opposite. These teeth will be timed to the two marked countershaft gear grooves on installation.

3. Assemble the output shaft as follows:
   a. With the shaft standing yoke-end up, install the flat range gear toothed washer.
   b. Next, install the range gear with the clutching teeth down.
   c. Install the stepped washer with the chamfered side up.
   d. Install the front rear support bearing. Caution: The front and rear support bearings are different. The support bearings' inner diameters are different sizes. Do not mix them up. Heat the bearing to no more than 275°F (136° C) to install it, or use an appropriate bearing driver.
   e. Install the inner bearing spacer on the shaft.

4. Fabricate a support for the countershafts from a 2" by 12" piece of wood with the dimensions shown. This support will make assembly much easier. Place the two countershafts into the support with the low range gears up and the two marked tooth grooves to the center.

Continued on next page

SKILL DRILL 39-14 Reassembling and Timing the Auxiliary Section, continued

5 Slide the range synchronizer onto the assembled output shaft—low range side up. Place it in between the two countershafts. Carefully time the assembly by meshing the two marked teeth on the range gear with the two marked grooves on the countershafts. The countershafts must be timed on installation to allow the floating main shaft system.

6 Place the range shift fork in the synchronizer groove. Then, place the auxiliary section housing over the assembled gearing. Install the auxiliary countershaft bearing rear races and shims in their correct locations. Install the auxiliary countershaft support straps and snug the bolts. Do not over torque them. Make sure the bearing spacer is present on the output shaft behind the front rear support bearing.

7 Install the one piece rear support bearing raceways, then install the rear-rear support bearing either by heating to 275°F (136°C) or by using an appropriate driver. (Note the two countershaft support holes drilled in the bench.)

8 Install a new seal in the rear bearing cover and install it with a new gasket, being careful to line up the oil return hole in the cover and the housing. (Note: If the rear bearing support came with a nylon collar and a brass washer on the bolt in the chamfered hole in the cover, be sure to replace them.)

9 Install the shaft O-ring and the speedometer reluctor.

10 Install the output yoke and torque to 450–500 ft-lb (610–677 Nm). To prevent the output shaft from turning, place the auxiliary section in low range and put a clean shop towel in the gear mesh. Hold the unit securely to avoid accidental damage while torque is being applied. It is essential that the output shaft is fully drawn into position before attempting to install the auxiliary or it may sag and misalignment may occur.

> **TECHNICIAN TIP**
>
> The main box and auxiliary sections on Eaton Fuller transmissions must be timed on assembly to ensure that the main or output shaft will "float" between the two countershafts. Failure to correctly time the transmission will lead to transmission seizure. In fact, the transmission will usually not even turn at all if incorrectly timed.

> **TECHNICIAN TIP**
>
> Thirteen- and eighteen-speed model auxiliary sections have an additional gear set (the splitter gear set). Nonetheless, they follow a similar procedure for overhaul. Both the range and the splitter gear will have to be timed to the countershafts on reassembly. Consult the OEM manual for the particular model being serviced.

Reinstalling the Auxiliary Section

Once the auxiliary section is reassembled and timed, it can be reinstalled. To reinstall the auxiliary section, follow the guidelines in SKILL DRILL 39-15.

Analysis of Transmission Failure

Failure analysis is a very important component of a technician's skill set. The ability to determine what specifically caused a failure to occur is essential to performing a complete repair. Correct diagnoses are also critical to preventing a repeat failure.

Drive train systems are frequently the subject of premature failures caused by overloading, driver error or abuse, or poor maintenance practices. Most manufacturers have guide books available to help determine the root cause of a failure. Remember that gears and shafts are made of ductile iron and are usually case or induction hardened, typically to a depth of no more than 0.050"

SKILL DRILL 39-15 Reinstalling the Auxiliary Section

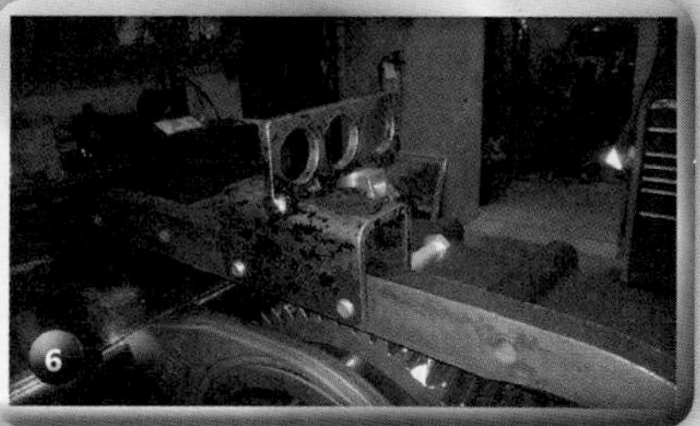

1. Install the countershaft support straps on the auxiliary section counter shafts. Snug the center bolts to center and hold the countershafts in position. Do not overtighten. The output shaft must be able to turn for installation.
2. Drive the alignment dowel pins in the main box rearward. Ensure they are positioned correctly. The dowels have shoulders that should protrude approximately 0.5" (13 mm) to the rear from the main box. These shoulders are what center the auxiliary. Make sure also that the dowel pins are clean and free of rust.
3. Clean all rust and paint from the dowel pin holes in the auxiliary section housing. Lightly grease the dowel pins and the dowel pin holes in the auxiliary section.
4. Make sure the auxiliary section is in low range so that you can turn the countershafts using the output yoke.
5. Position a new gasket on the main box flange and dowel pins.
6. Useing the hoisting tool to raise the auxiliary section level with the transmission main box or use a suitable transmission jack.

Continued on next page

SKILL DRILL 39-15 Reinstalling the Auxiliary Section, continued

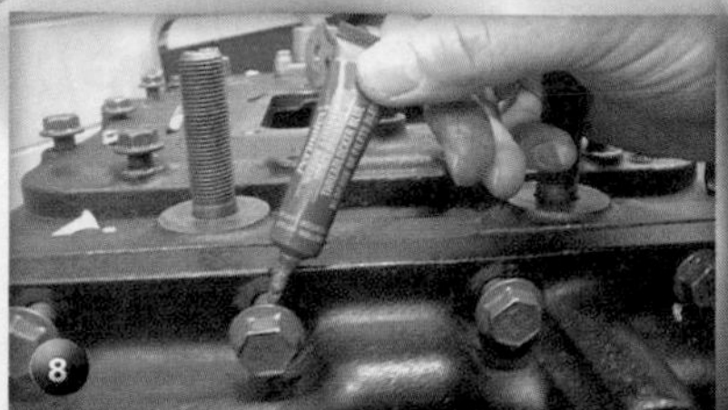

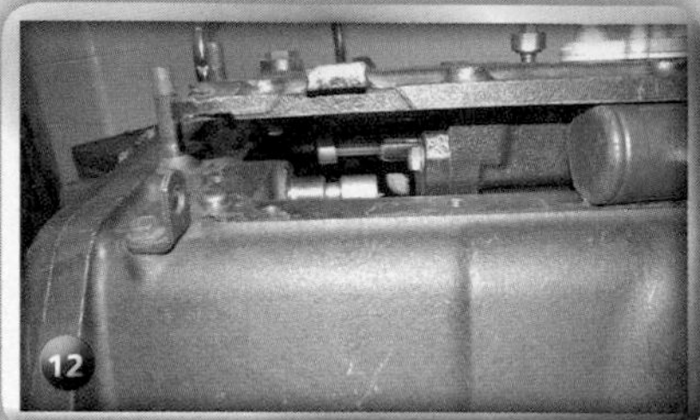

7 Position the auxiliary section level with the main case and slide the auxiliary section onto the dowel pins. Mesh the countershafts with the auxiliary drive gear as the housing is moved forward. Rotate the output yoke slightly to help the gears mesh. Slide the auxiliary forward until it is flush against the main box flange.

Safety

The auxiliary should move into place with little effort. Do not force it, and never use the attaching bolts to draw the auxiliary section in. If resistance is encountered, the most likely cause is that the timing is incorrect. Retime the auxiliary and try again.

8 Apply thread sealant or equivalent to the all the retaining bolt threads. Install the bolts to secure and torque to 40–45 ft-lb (54–61 Nm).

9 Countershaft bearing endplay must be checked and reset with shims if any of the following components were replaced:

- countershafts
- countershaft bearings
- auxiliary housing

Countershaft bearing endplay must also be checked and reset with shims if the countershafts, bearings, or shims were not properly marked on disassembly and reassembled in the same location.

10 To shim the countershaft, use the following method:

a. Clean all gasket material from the case and the countershaft bearing covers.

b. Install each countershaft bearing cover using two bolts only 180 degrees apart with a shim. Torque the bolts to 7 in-lb (0.79 Nm) only. Do not over tighten! The cover can be easily broken!

c. Alternately, use the shim setting tools available. These tools have a raised 0.100" (2.54 mm) section so the shim does not need to be installed. The tools also double as countershaft support straps.

d. Using feeler gauges, check the gap between the cover and the auxiliary housing gasket surface on both sides as close to the bolts as possible and average the two readings.

e. Compare your reading to the shim selection chart. Use **TABLE 39-3** to determine the correct shim by comparing the average feeler gauge reading to the chart.

Note: The oil pump shim is used when an auxiliary oil pump or PTO is mounted on the countershaft. The oil pump shims are smaller in outside diameter.

f. Select the proper shim and install it with a new Eaton Fuller gasket. Use thread sealant on the cover bolts and torque the bolts to specification, approximately 40–45 ft-lb (54–61Nm).

Note: This procedure sets countershaft endplay at between 0.001" and 0.005" (2.54 and 12.6 mm) and relies on the compressed thickness of the cover gasket when calculating the shim thickness. Use of an aftermarket gasket instead of genuine Fuller parts may change the endplay and result in failure.

Continued on next page

SKILL DRILL 39-15 Reinstalling the Auxiliary Section, continued

11 If shimming is not required, remove the support straps and install the correct shim, new gasket, and countershaft bearing cover. Use thread sealant on the cover bolts and torque to 40–45 ft-lb (54–61 Nm).

12 Reinstall the shift bar housing with a new gasket, being careful to line up the range cylinder piston shaft with the range yoke bar slot. Use thread sealant on the cover bolts. Torque the bolts to specification; approximately 40–45 ft-lb (54–61 Nm).

13 Install the shift tower with a new gasket. Connect all removed air lines and the speedometer connections. Reinstall the drive shaft and refill the transmission with the correct lubricant until it is level with the fill hole.

TABLE 39-3: Shim Table

Feeler Guage Average Gap (in inches)	Shim Thickness (in inches)	Standard Shim Part Number	Oil Pump Shim Part Number	Color Code
0.072–0.075	0.033–0.034	4302345	4302346	Gold
0.069–0.0715	0.036–0.037	21452	21472	Red
0.066–0.0685	0.039–0.040	21453	21473	Pink
0.063–0.0655	0.042–0.043	21454	21474	Brown
0.060–0.0625	0.045–0.046	21455	21475	Tan
0.057–0.0595	0.048–0.049	21456	21476	Orange
0.054–0.0565	0.051–0.052	21457	21477	Yellow
0.051–0.0535	0.054–0.055	21458	21478	Green

(1.27 mm). The hardening allows the component's surface to resist wear, but the ductile core allows them to flex as they are loaded so that they can absorb some shocks.

Several factors must be considered when determining the cause of failure: vehicle vocation, load, driver experience, road conditions, maintenance records, and an accurate report as to how and when the failure occurred. A more in-depth section on failure analysis is included at the end of the Servicing and Maintaining Drive Axles chapter.

Regular Wear or Maintenance Failures

Eaton Fuller twin-countershaft transmissions enjoy the largest market share in the heavy-duty commercial truck industry. These and, indeed, all twin- or triple-countershaft transmissions have certain unique wear characteristics when compared to single-countershaft transmissions. The surface of gear teeth may look smooth to the naked eye, yet all tooth surfaces are very irregular. They have numerous hills and valleys at the microscopic level. As teeth wear going through mesh with each other, these hills and valleys are worn away and the surface becomes increasingly smooth.

Spur-gear transmission wear patterns are slightly different than those with helical gears. Spur gear contact slides into mesh then rolls against its mating tooth at full mesh (when tooth loading is highest). The spur gear then slides back out of mesh. By contrast, helical gears maintain continuous sliding- and wiping-type contact. The wiping contact of helical gears tends to make the surface smoother faster than with spur-type gears. Spur gear contact leads to extreme pressure between the teeth during this rolling contact. This type of load can break off rather than wipe off the microscopic surface irregularities. As a result, the tooth surface becomes dull rather than shiny. As mentioned previously, that condition is known as frosting. Frosting is quite a common occurrence with spur-gear contact; it is not usually a cause for concern. This frosting will eventually heal. As the teeth continue to adjust to each other, the surface will heal and become shiny once again.

Spur gear contact can also lead to minor pitting caused by the lubricant being forced down through microscopic peaks and valleys on the tooth surface. Small surface fractures of the tooth result and eventually tiny pieces of metal will be broken out. This condition is known as initial pitting. As the teeth adjust to each other, the initial pitting will heal over and become shiny.

Twin- or triple-countershaft transmissions spread the torque load over several sets of teeth in contact, so the load on individual teeth is lower. The frosting and healing process can be slower than in single-countershaft transmissions—which means that wear can be observed much later in a transmission's lifespan. Also, sometimes the vocation of the transmission changes and it is subject to heavier loads. When that happens, the pitting process may restart if the increased load causes the gear teeth to readjust to each other. Deep and concentrated pitting at the pitch line indicates that these gears need to be replaced. When gear replacement is necessary, main shaft gears and their matching countershaft gears must be replaced as a set.

In addition to friction, lubrication failures due to poor maintenance, incorrect lubrication, lack of lubrication, and/or contaminated lube will always lead to eventual failure of tooth surfaces.

Abuse Failures

Transmission failure is not just the result of regular wear. It can be accelerated by abuses such as sudden load increases, dumping the clutch, backing into a loading dock at speed, spinning out, and poor gear selection.

Shock load failures occur when a component is momentarily overloaded. When a load surpasses the base strength of the material, the material will fail immediately. Driver abuse or inexperience is commonly a cause of shock load failures.

Dumping the clutch is common abuse that can be easily prevented. Dumping the clutch instead of smoothly engaging it puts enormous stress load on the entire driveline. The main failures that occur from this type of abuse are twisted main shaft in the transmission (recall the image in Figure 39-8), drive shaft torsional failures, broken universal joints, and axle shaft torsional failures.

Backing into a loading dock at speed can cause shock failures, as can backing under a trailer too roughly. Likewise, shock failure can occur if the trailer is set too low, forcing the vehicle to attempt to lift the trailer as it hooks up.

Spinout, whether in a main differential or an inter-axle differential, is another source of driver abuse that can cause catastrophic damage to the transmission. When the driver allows the wheels to spin, the drive shaft and the differential side and spider gears are rotating at enormous speeds. If the wildly spinning wheels suddenly gain traction and stop, severe shock loads are transmitted to the transmission.

Poor gear selection by the driver can also lead to severe shock loads. If, as the driver tries to re-engage the clutch, the gear selection does not match the road speed, the driveline will have to absorb the shock. In that situation, failure is possible.

See the Servicing and Maintaining Drive Axles chapter for a more comprehensive look at gear and shaft failures and their causes.

Wrap-up

Ready for Review

- Lubricant is the lifeblood of transmissions. It is essential that the quality and level be maintained for long transmission service.
- Most manufacturers now use synthetic-based lubricants, which allow a much longer service interval.
- Lubricants with extreme pressure (EP) additives are not normally recommended for heavy-duty transmission operation as they can oxidize at common transmission operating temperatures.
- Many heavy-duty transmissions are fitted with internal or external oil coolers to deal with high operating temperatures resulting from high torque loads.
- Transmission model number nomenclature can give the technician valuable information about the transmission being serviced or repaired.
- Transmission preventative maintenance today typically involves a visual inspection of the transmission for leakage, checking the mounting components for integrity, and checking the shift mechanisms and the air shifting system for leaks and correct operation.
- The use of synthetic lubricant has resulted in lubrication and filter changes becoming less common.
- Noise from the transmission can come from a variety of causes. The type of noise—knocking, growling, whining, or rattling—can help the technician isolate the cause.
- Vibration can be caused by the transmission but is more likely to be caused by other systems such as torsional vibrations from the engine, driveline vibration from the drive shaft, or wheel-end vibrations due to imbalance. However, all of these vibrations can cause transmission damage and should be corrected as soon as possible.
- Gear slip out or jump out can occur if components such as sliding clutches or shift forks are worn. Wear on these components is frequently caused by driver error or abuse.
- Newer Eaton Fuller FR model ten-speed fleet transmissions have a different air system than other transmissions. They use a one-piece air module to house all of the air control system components.
- FR models also have the range cylinder integral to the shift cover. It is essential that the shift cover is removed before the auxiliary section can be removed because the range shift bar interlocks with the range synchronizer shift rail.
- Diagnosing problems with the air shift system should always start with checking the air supply and air filter regulator for contamination and/or other problems.
- The Eaton Fuller transmission input shaft can be removed from the case without main box disassembly.
- When removing the auxiliary section, auxiliary countershaft support straps should always be used.
- The auxiliary section range gear and the main box input gear on Eaton Fuller Roadranger transmissions must be timed at installation to ensure that the gears are supported in equilibrium and allow the main shaft system to float.
- After reinstalling the auxiliary section, the auxiliary countershaft end play must be set to specification.
- Frosting is a common phenomenon with twin countershaft transmissions and is caused by microscopic imperfections on the tooth surfaces wearing off. The frosting will generally heal over as the teeth continue to work together.
- Shock loads are extremely damaging to mechanical transmissions and are usually the fault of the driver. Dumping the clutch, engaging the wrong gear, and spinning the tires and then hitting solid pavement can all cause shock loads that can cause fatigue fracture or even component breakage to occur.

Vocabulary Builder

back taper The tapered profile of the teeth on a sliding clutch such that the outer edge is thicker than the inner; the profile helps keep the clutch engaged under load.

extreme pressure (EP) additive Additives usually found in hypoid gear lube and which should not be used in Fuller Roadranger transmissions and most heavy-duty transmissions because it tends to oxidize at relatively low temperatures.

gear slip out The condition in which a transmission jumps out of gear and to neutral when under load, caused by worn components such as sliding clutches and shift forks. Also called *jump out.*

jump out The condition in which a transmission jumps out of gear and to neutral when under load, caused by worn components such as sliding clutches and shift forks. Also called *gear slip out.*

line-haul A truck that spends most of its time in on-highway operations under medium to heavy loading.

nomenclature The meaning of the letters and digits in truck transmission's model numbers.

oil weep Very minor oil seepage usually caused by a wicking effect and not usually a reason for a repair.

pre-dampening A series of small torsional dampening springs designed to prevent gear rattle at idle.

reluctor A toothed wheel used with magnetic sensors, usually to measure shaft speed.

remote shift linkage A transmission shift linkage that is not mounted directly above the shift cover and that must be properly maintained and lubricated to prevent hard shifting.

severe-duty service A vehicle that is operated under extreme (maximum) loading most of the time, or one that is operated on heavy grades.

synthetic-based lubricant A lubricant that is manufactured rather than refined and so has much longer service life; it can be a blend of natural and synthetic materials.

vocational A truck that is subject to primarily off-road operation and typically is heavily loaded.

Review Questions

1. What is the normal regulated air pressure that operates the range and splitter shifting in a Eaton Fuller Roadranger transmission?
   a. 117 to122 psi (807 to 841 kPa)
   b. 97 to 102 psi (669 to 703 kPa)
   c. 77 to 82 psi (531 to 565 kPa)
   d. 57 to 63 psi (393 to 427 kPa)
2. What must be removed before you can remove the auxiliary section on an Eaton Fuller FR model transmission?
   a. The input shaft
   b. The output yoke
   c. The shift bar cover
   d. The shift lever
3. When removing an auxiliary section in the vehicle, what is/are the recommended safe guards that you should install?
   a. Countershaft support straps
   b. Rear yoke support
   c. Guide studs
   d. Mainbox holding fixture
4. What could be the likely cause of hard lever shifting from first to second if you have eliminated the shift linkage and shift bar housing as the problem on an Eaton Fuller twin-countershaft transmission?
   a. Burned synchronizer friction rings
   b. Broken detent springs
   c. Broken synchronizer pins
   d. Twisted main shaft
5. While checking the Eaton Fuller Roadranger valve (shift knob) for correct operation of the high and low range shift, you find that air leaks constantly from the valve when in high range only. What could be the problem?
   a. Leaking Roadranger valve
   b. Crossed air lines
   c. Defective slave air valve
   d. Defective range cylinder
6. Which of the following is responsible for lubrication of most standard transmissions?
   a. A gear pump
   b. An electric pump
   c. Submersion of all components in the fluid
   d. The splash caused by the countershafts rotation
7. When assembling a Fuller twin countershaft transmission main box, you must time which of the following gears together?
   a. The main shaft gears to the countershaft gears
   b. The input gear to the countershaft driven gears
   c. The countershaft gears to the reverse idler gears
   d. The first main shaft gear to the first countershaft gears
8. When a ten-speed Fuller RoadRanger transmission (non-overdrive) main box is in fifth speed, which of the following applies?
   a. All main shaft gears are locked to the main shaft.
   b. The auxiliary section must be in direct also.
   c. All input torque is transferred to the main shaft through the countershafts and the engaged fifth speed gear.
   d. All input torque is transferred to the main shaft through the 4/5 sliding clutch
9. In the Fuller FR series transmission, where is the range cylinder located?
   a. Inside the auxiliary section
   b. Bolted to the auxiliary section
   c. Bolted to the main box
   d. Inside the shift cover
10. Which of these parts must always be removed before a damaged input shaft can be changed on a Fuller Roadranger twin countershaft transmission?
   a. The shift bar housing
   b. The auxiliary section
   c. The main shaft
   d. None of the choices is correct.

ASE-Type Questions

1. Technician A says that auxiliary countershaft end play must be checked and adjusted if the auxiliary countershaft bearing are replaced. Technician B says that the main shaft end play should be checked before reinstalling the auxiliary section. Who is correct?
   a. Technician A
   b. Technician B
   c. Both Technician A and Technician B
   d. Neither Technician A nor Technician B
2. Technician A says that the correct lubricant level in a transmission should reach the bottom of the fill plug hole. Technician B says that as long as you can feel the fluid with the first digit of your finger the level is OK. Who is correct?
   a. Technician A
   b. Technician B
   c. Both Technician A and Technician B
   d. Neither Technician A nor Technician B
3. Technician A says that transmission rattling at idle can be caused by engine torsional vibrations. Technician B says that a clutch with pre-dampening can eliminate gear rattle at idle. Who is correct?
   a. Technician A
   b. Technician B
   c. Both Technician A and Technician B
   d. Neither Technician A nor Technician B
4. Technician A says that if an Eaton Fuller Roadranger transmission is an overdrive model it will have an O in the first four letters of its model number. Technician B says that an F in the third or fourth letter position of the model number means it is a five speed model. Who is correct?
   a. Technician A
   b. Technician B
   c. Both Technician A and Technician B
   d. Neither Technician A nor Technician B
5. Technician A says that, for today's transmissions with synthetic lube, preventative maintenance is basically a visual inspection of all the transmission systems. Technician B says that transmissions equipped with straight mineral oil have oil change intervals of 500,000 miles (805,000 kilometers). Who is correct?
   a. Technician A
   b. Technician B
   c. Both Technician A and Technician B
   d. Neither Technician A nor Technician B
6. Technician A says that when overhauling a Fuller ten-speed auxiliary section, the auxiliary drive gear must be timed to the auxiliary countershafts. Technician B says that auxiliary section countershaft support straps are necessary to reinstall the auxiliary section. Who is correct?
   a. Technician A
   b. Technician B
   c. Both Technician A and Technician B
   d. Neither Technician A nor Technician B
7. Technician A says that the air filter regulator is the first place to check if a Fuller 13-speed transmission air shift system is not working correctly. Technician B says that the air supply to the air filter regulator passes through a pressure protection valve. Who is correct?
   a. Technician A
   b. Technician B
   c. Both Technician A and Technician B
   d. Neither Technician A nor Technician B
8. Technician A says that you must line up the range cylinder shift bar in the shift cover with the range cylinder shift fork while installing the shift cover on a 13-speed Fuller transmission. Technician B says that the Fuller 13-speed transmission range shift cylinder is located at the back of the auxiliary section. Who is correct?
   a. Technician A
   b. Technician B
   c. Both Technician A and Technician B
   d. Neither Technician A nor Technician B
9. Technician A says that auxiliary countershaft end play must be checked and adjusted if the auxiliary countershaft bearing are replaced. Tech B says that the main shaft end play should checked before reinstalling the auxiliary section. Who is correct?
   a. Technician A
   b. Technician B
   c. Both Technician A and Technician B
   d. Neither Technician A nor Technician B
10. Technician A says that worn clutching teeth on the range synchronizer sliding clutch are normal and the clutch does not need to be replaced. Technician B says that worn range synchronizer clutching teeth are a sign of driver abuse. Who is correct?
    a. Technician A
    b. Technician B
    c. Both Technician A and Technician B
    d. Neither Technician A nor Technician B

CHAPTER 40

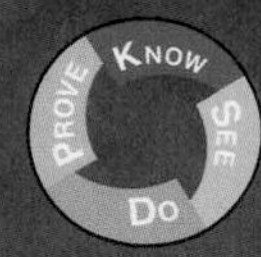

NATEF Tasks

Drive Train

Transmission	Page
■ Use appropriate electronic service tool(s) and procedures to diagnose automated mechanical transmission problems; check and record diagnostic codes, clear codes, and interpret digital multimeter (DMM) readings; determine needed action.	1330–1332
■ Inspect and test operation of automated mechanical transmission and manual electronic shift controls; shift, range and splitter solenoids; shift motors; indicators; speed and range sensors; electronic/transmission control units (ECU/TCU); neutral/in gear and reverse switches; and wiring harnesses; determine needed action.	1330–1334
■ Inspect and test operation of automated mechanical transmission electronic shift selectors, air and electrical switches, displays and indicators, wiring harnesses, and air lines; determine needed action.	1333
■ Inspect and test temperature gauge, wiring harnesses, and sensor/sending unit; determine needed action.	1334
Drive Axle	
■ Inspect and test drive axle temperature gauge, wiring harnesses, and sending unit/sensor; determine needed action.	1333–1334

Automated Manual Transmissions

Knowledge Objectives

After reading this chapter, you will be able to:

1. List the various manufacturers and types of automated manual transmissions. (pp 1302–1305)
2. Explain the difference between torque break and no torque break shifting. (p 1305)
3. Describe the operation of various types of automated manual transmissions. (pp 1306–1313)
4. Describe the electronic interface used with early J1587 systems, the controller area network used with J1939 systems, and Multiplexing as it relates to automated manual transmissions. (p 1309)
5. Describe the variety and operation of clutch systems used with automated manual transmissions. (pp 1314–1315)
6. Explain the electronically controlled shift processes used in different types of automated manual transmissions. (pp 1315–1316)
7. Explain the power flows of various automated transmissions. (pp 1316–1325)
8. Describe the on-board diagnostic capabilities of automated manual transmissions. (p 1332)
9. Explain troubleshooting procedures for automated manual transmissions. (p 1329)

Skills Objectives

After reading this chapter, you will be able to:

1. Enable the self-diagnostic mode and retrieve codes. (p 1330) **SKILL DRILL 40-1**
2. Clear inactive codes. (p 1331) **SKILL DRILL 40-2**
3. Use a diagnostic tool and procedure to diagnose automated transmission problems. (pp 1331–1332) **SKILL DRILL 40-3**
4. Inspect, adjust, repair, and replace electronic shift selectors, air and electrical switches, displays and indicators, and wiring harnesses. (p 1333) **SKILL DRILL 40-4**
5. Inspect, adjust, repair, or replace electronic shift controls, electronic control unit, wiring harnesses, sensors, control module, vehicle interface module, and related components. (p 1334) **SKILL DRILL 40-5**

Introduction

The automotive industry in general is under extreme pressure to reduce all harmful tail pipe emissions from vehicles. The trucking industry is not exempt from this pressure. Vehicles made in 2014 and later are the cleanest they have ever been. There are no more mandated reductions scheduled for traditional tailpipe emissions. The newest EPA-mandated reduction is now **carbon dioxide**.

Until recently, carbon dioxide was considered a harmless emission that simply occurred when a hydrocarbon fuel was burned completely. Today, carbon dioxide is considered a greenhouse gas thought to contribute to global warming.

The only way a vehicle can reduce its output of carbon dioxide is by supplementing the engine's power output with another energy source, such as hybrid electric technology. Bolstering the engine by another energy source provides two distinct advantages. First, less hydrocarbon fuel is used. Second, supplemental energy sources allow the engine to get more power out of the same amount of fuel by increasing **thermal efficiency**. That is, more of the fuel used is actually turned into power to drive the vehicle.

Increasing thermal efficiency is a hot topic in the trucking industry. Many new technologies and strategies are being used to achieve higher thermal efficiencies—from engine advancements to truck body shapes designed to reduce drag.

One of the more interesting strategies is the introduction of the electronically automated transmission, or what is commonly referred to as an **automated manual transmission (AMT)**. The shifting process for an electronically automated transmission is controlled by the **transmission control unit (TCU)**, also known as the **transmission electronic control module (ECM)**. The TCU works in concert with the engine control module to optimize shift points and strategies to maximize fuel efficiency. Even the most experienced driver would have trouble matching the precise shift control of a TCU. FIGURE 40-1 shows an electronically automated transmission manufactured by Eaton. This chapter will introduce the student to the various types of electronically automated transmissions and their operating systems.

Benefits of Automated Transmissions

The electronically automated transmission comes in many varieties. In the three-pedal types, a clutch is used for shifting from first to reverse only and the rest of the shifting is carried out by the transmission ECM or TCU. Two-pedal models have no clutch pedal, and the transmission's operation is entirely **shift by wire**. That is, shifting is controlled completely by the transmission electronic control. A two-pedal design is shown in FIGURE 40-2.

The primary benefit of AMT transmissions is improved fuel economy. It is estimated that AMTs improve a vehicle's fuel economy by 5% to 7% over conventional

You Are the Technician

A driver brings his truck to your service facility. The vehicle is equipped with an Eaton eighteen-speed UltraShift automated transmission. The driver is new to this vehicle and complains that when he shuts the vehicle off, it sometimes will not start when he returns to the vehicle. He says that when he turns the key on and off a few times and releases the parking brake, it will then usually start. You examine the vehicle but cannot replicate the problem. What should be your next steps?

1. Should you observe the driver as he road tests the vehicle to see if he can replicate the problem?
2. Should you check the transmission for any active or inactive diagnostic trouble codes?
3. Why should you ask the driver to explain the shut down procedure he uses for his vehicle?

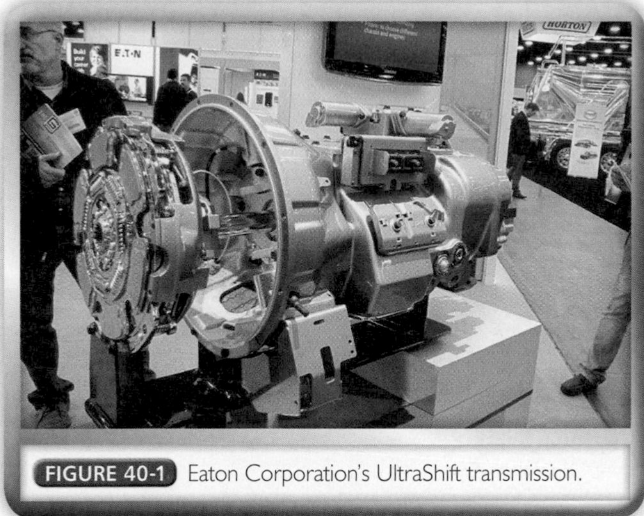

FIGURE 40-1 Eaton Corporation's UltraShift transmission.

standard transmissions because of their ability to use optimized shift strategies. Two other advantages of the AMT enhance safety: an AMT allows the driver to keep both hands on the steering wheel and AMTs are less tiring for the driver to operate because no clutching or double clutching is necessary.

AMT transmissions also reduce company expenditure on driver training. Learning to drive an eighteen-speed transmission can be a time consuming and daunting task. AMT transmissions drastically reduce the training time devoted to shifting gears. Furthermore, because the computer has control over shifting, the transmission is not subject to abuse commonly associated with unskilled drivers—and even occasionally with veteran drivers. The reduction in driver abuse means that AMTs experience longer transmission life, less down time for repairs, and higher vehicle resale value. Finally, the electronic control system also has a **self-diagnostic** capability, allowing easy troubleshooting of problems. In other words, the TCU is able to analyze its own functions.

The Role of Torque Break in Shifting

Most automated shift transmissions still use the conventional method of shifting. In other words, it is necessary to **break torque**—or unload the gear train as a shift is being made. When the gear train is under load or torque, it is nearly impossible to move the gearshift lever. Before a shift can be made, the driver must unload the drive train or "break torque".

Breaking torque means the engine must be throttled back, and the throttle must be reapplied when the shift is complete. Changing the throttle position causes a delay in overall vehicle acceleration. The deceleration and acceleration required when changing the throttle position also causes a reduction in fuel economy. Several manufacturers

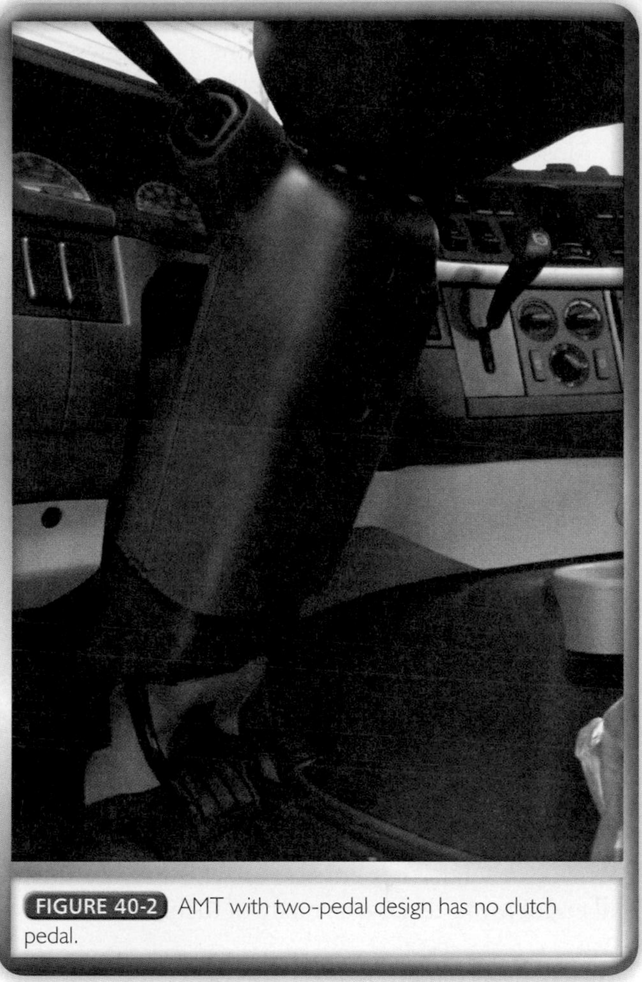
FIGURE 40-2 AMT with two-pedal design has no clutch pedal.

now have electronically automated transmissions on the market. Eaton, ZF, and Volvo all offer **dual-clutch transmissions** capable of shifting without breaking torque, thereby improving fuel economy. Dual-clutch transmissions have two separate input shafts controlled by two separate clutches.

For years, experienced drivers have been shifting truck transmissions without using the clutch pedal except for starting from a stop. Although not recommended by any transmission manufacturer, this "**gear jamming**" technique is the basis for most electronically automated manual transmissions. Essentially, what drivers were doing when making a shift was breaking torque by letting up on the accelerator in order to pull the gear stick to a neutral position. (Without breaking torque, the load on the gear shift components would make them impossible to move.) The driver would then carefully select the next gear as the engine rpm and the transmission main shaft speeds synchronized. They would complete the shift by jamming the transmission into the next gear.

To perform this technique properly required great skill and experience, and even the best drivers cause some damage to the shift collar or sliding clutch teeth. Matching the shaft speeds involved making a best guess and a less experienced driver could destroy a transmission in very little time.

Most automated transmissions use this gear jamming technique but use computer controls to break torque. Matching the shaft speeds is achieved with precision. The computer uses sensors to monitor the shaft speeds and then moves the shift forks with electric motors or air cylinders. Gear jamming is done automatically, without gear clash, and with no damage to the transmission.

Types of Electronically Automated Manual Transmissions

The internal components and power flows of Fuller electronically automated transmissions are practically identical to those used by standard transmissions. To review the internal functioning of standard transmissions, including gears and sliding clutches, consult the Standard Transmissions chapter. The North American market for AMT transmissions is dominated by the Eaton Fuller Corporation. Therefore, this chapter will focus its discussion primarily on Eaton's range of automated transmissions. There are, however, several other entries into this market and we will endeavor to discuss as many of them as possible.

Eaton Fuller's Automated Transmissions

Eaton entered the automated transmission market in 1993 with the **AutoSelect**. The transmission had limited electronics and used the older and slower **J-1587** communications to enable the engine ECM to synchronize shaft speeds during driver-initiated shifting. J-1587 is the original SAE communication protocol for commercial vehicles; quite slow in terms of data transmission at 9600 bits per second. Eaton then brought out a unique kind of transmission called the Super Ten Top Two, pictured in **FIGURE 40-3**. The shift pattern of the Super Ten is illustrated in **FIGURE 40-4**.

The Super Ten transmission had automated control over the top two split gear ranges only through a small electronic module that controlled the splitter cylinder. The control module for the top two gears is shown in **FIGURE 40-5**.

The control module provided some improvement to fuel economy and eased driver fatigue in long-haul operation. The driver would not have to be constantly shifting between ninth and tenth gears when approaching grades, for example. What made the Super Ten unique, however, was that its main box had just two forward speed gears

FIGURE 40-3 Eaton Fuller's Super Ten Top Two was introduced in 1994.

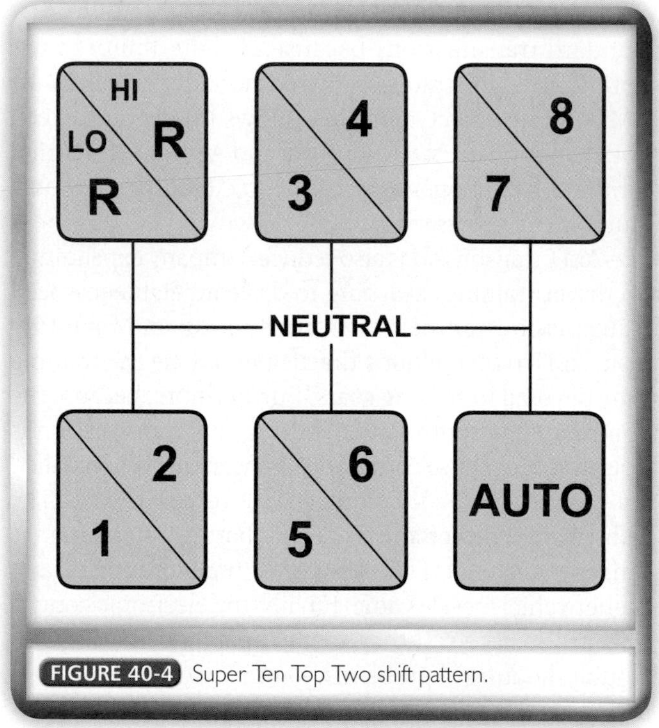

FIGURE 40-4 Super Ten Top Two shift pattern.

FIGURE 40-5 Top two transmission's control module.

on the main shaft—first and fourth speed gears only. That meant only three ratios were possible from the main box—low gear, fourth gear, and direct. The Super Ten main shaft is shown in FIGURE 40-6.

The Super Ten transmission has a special shift mechanism that only moves the first reverse rail, the fourth and fifth rail, and a three-speed auxiliary section. The shift pattern is a normal five-speed pattern, but the driver only has to move through the pattern once to get to tenth gear. The driver can split each gear stick position with the splitter button.

To operate the transmission, the driver selects first gear, which engages the first gear main shaft with the auxiliary section in low range low split. When an upshift is required, the driver moves the splitter to high split for second range. On the next upshift, the driver moves the stick to the third–fourth gear position. That engages the fourth gear in the main box and moves the splitter back to low split again. The auxiliary is still in low range. The driver then splits to high for fourth range. On the next upshift, the gear stick is moved to the fifth–sixth gear position. Direct gear is selected in the main box. The splitter is moved back to low split for fifth range and then to high split for sixth range. On the next shift to seventh and eighth stick position, the driver splits back to low for seventh. Due to the special shift rail in the main box, however, the driver is actually reselecting the fourth gear position again in the main box. The shift rails for that gearing sequence are shown in FIGURE 40-7.

The ratio change occurs because, as the driver moves through neutral to the seventh–eighth shift gate, the shift rail contacts an air switch that causes an automatic range shift to high in the auxiliary section. That puts the driver in high range low split for seventh range. The auto range shift valve is shown in FIGURE 40-8.

As the driver continues to shift, he then splits to high split for eighth range. At that point, he can move to the auto position and let the Top Two technology take over shifting for ninth and tenth. Since the debut of the Super Ten, several Fuller Roadranger models have included the TopTwo system, including thirteen- and eighteen-speed models.

The first fully automated standard transmission to hit the North American Market was the Eaton **AutoShift**. It was introduced in 1996/97 and featured the first generation of computer control. The AutoShift was a ten-speed model and had a standard dry double disc clutch that was used only when starting from a standstill. Once the vehicle was moving, its transmission was capable of automatic shifting through the entire vehicle operating range—all the way to tenth gear and back down again as necessary. FIGURE 40-9 depicts an Eaton Fuller AutoShift ten-speed transmission. Note the orientation of the shift motors. Older generations had the rail select motor orientated on the right hand side of the transmission. The present location on the left allows more room for complicated exhaust systems.

FIGURE 40-7 The shift rail of the Super Ten is arranged to reselect fourth gear main shaft on the 5/6 to 7/8 shift. **A.** Fourth and fifth shift rail. **B.** First and reverse shift rail.

FIGURE 40-6 The Super Ten main shaft has only two forward speed gears. **A.** Fourth gear. **B.** Low gear. **C.** Reverse gear.

FIGURE 40-8 The auto range shift valve is actuated by the movement of the shift rail under the top cover. **A.** Actuating pin. **B.** Auto range shift valve. **C.** Mounting hole.

Since the debut of the AutoShift, Eaton Fuller has introduced several other models of automated transmissions ranging from six to eighteen speeds and with or without clutch pedals. Eaton's latest automated transmission is the seven-speed Procision designed for the class 6 and 7 delivery truck market. This transmission is a dual wet-clutch transmission and is explained in greater detail in the Eaton Procision Automated Transmission section.

Meritor/ZF's Automated Transmissions

Meritor attempted to match Eaton's entry with a transmission model known as the **Engine Synchro Shift (ESS)** transmission. Although the driver still had to shift this transmission manually, the transmission's electronics allowed the engine speed to be manipulated during a shift. The shaft speed could be synchronized so that the clutch was only used for starting from a standstill.

FIGURE 40-9 Eaton Fuller AutoShift ten-speed transmission.

Meritor then produced the **SureShift** line of transmissions, available in nine-, ten-, and thirteen-speeds. SureShift transmissions were electronics-over-air-actuated, three-pedal, fully automated transmissions. Meritor joined forces with ZF Friedrichshafen AG of Germany and produced SureShift models of up to 16-speeds. Together the two companies marketed the **Freedomline** of two-pedal automated transmissions available in both 12- and 16-speed models. All Freedomline transmissions used an air-operated clutch and shifting controlled by the transmission computer. FIGURE 40-10 shows a ZF/Meritor Freedomline transmission.

The partnership between ZF and Meritor lasted until it dissolved in 2009. ZF now markets the Freedom transmissions directly to OEMs in North America under their European names: the **AS-Tronic** series for light-, medium-, and heavy-duty applications; these are twelve- and sixteen-speed two-pedal automated transmissions. ZF also markets the torque converter equipped **TC-Tronic** available with 12 speeds for extra heavy-duty truck applications, although Europe is the primary market for these transmissions.

ZF has just released a newer version of the AS-Tronic called the **Traxon** system that has five optional input modules, a standard self-adjusting clutch, a dual disc clutch, a torque converter module, an engine driven

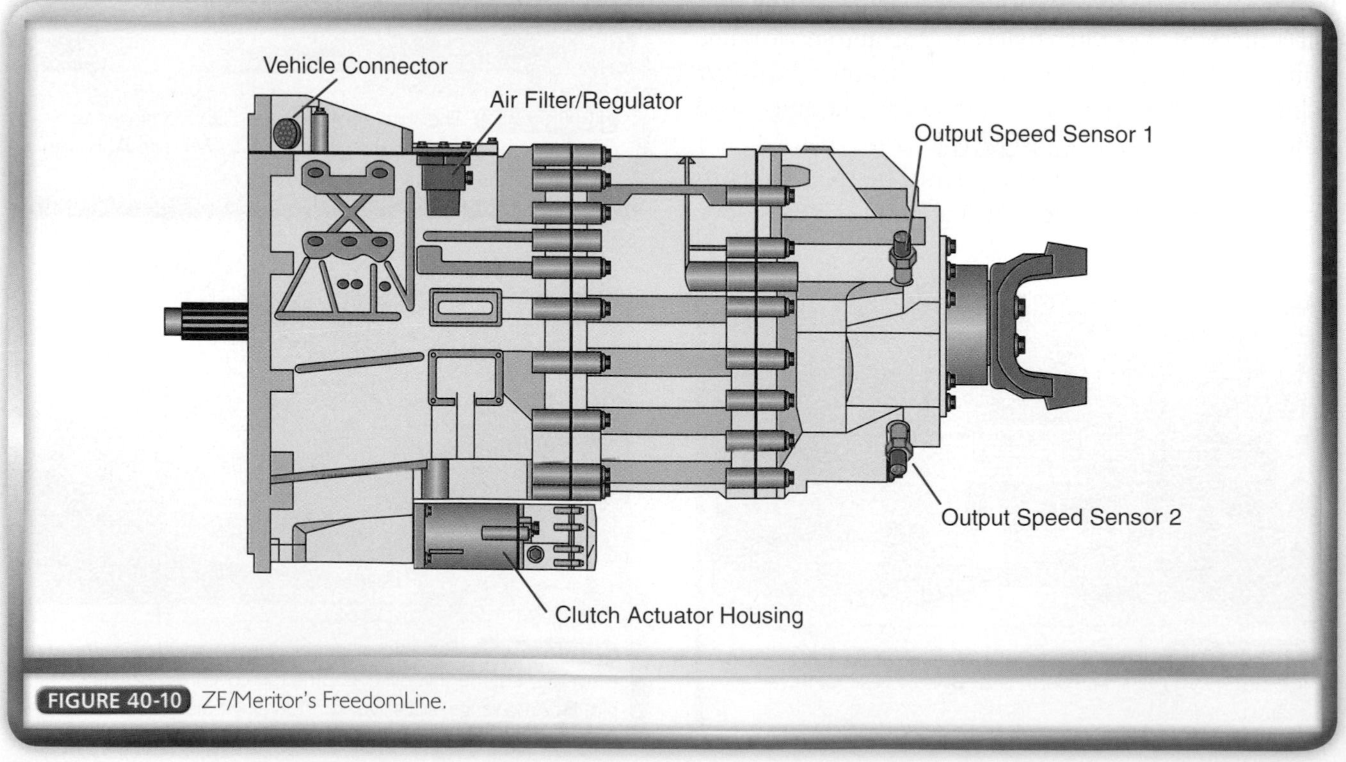

FIGURE 40-10 ZF/Meritor's FreedomLine.

power take-off (PTO) input module, and an electric traction motor that converts the system to a series hybrid. FIGURE 40-11 shows a ZF Traxon transmission.

Detroit Diesel's DT-12

Detroit Diesel has recently released a new transmission onto the North American market. The **DT-12**, pictured in FIGURE 40-12, is a twelve-speed automated transmission. It is the same transmission marketed by Mercedes in Europe in its Actros trucks. The design of the twin-countershaft transmission is very similar to that of the ZF transmission. The DT-12 system does not use a clutch pedal. Instead, the DT-12 relies on an air-actuated auto-clutch. Shifting is accomplished by an electric solenoid over air control system, which is also similar to the ZF.

Volvo Trucks' I-Shift

Mercedes was not the only manufacturer to introduce a new transmission in 2004. That same year, Volvo Trucks introduced the **I-Shift** automated transmission series in North America. As shown in FIGURE 40-13, the I-Shift is a twelve-speed, two-pedal design with electric-over-air actuation controlled by the transmission TCU. The I-Shift is available in four models, including two with overdrive, and is capable of handling up to 2,300 ft-lb (3,118 Nm) of input torque.

Volvo's latest addition to its transmission line is the new dual-clutch I-Shift. The twelve-speed overdrive transmission has been available as an option in Volvo trucks since September 2014. It is similar to the Eaton Procision transmission with one key difference—the Volvo dual clutch uses two dry friction disc clutches instead of wet clutches.

Mercedes Benz's AGS

In 2004, Mercedes Benz, known in North America as Daimler Trucks, introduced the **Automatic Gear Shift (AGS)** two-pedal, six-speed automated transmission. The AGS was designed for medium-duty trucks with up to 60,000 lb (27, 216 kg) gross vehicle weight (GVW). Shown in FIGURE 40-14, the AGS transmission uses an electronically controlled hydraulic clutch actuator for starting and stopping.

FIGURE 40-11 Traxon system with an optional hydraulic retarder called the ZF Intarder.

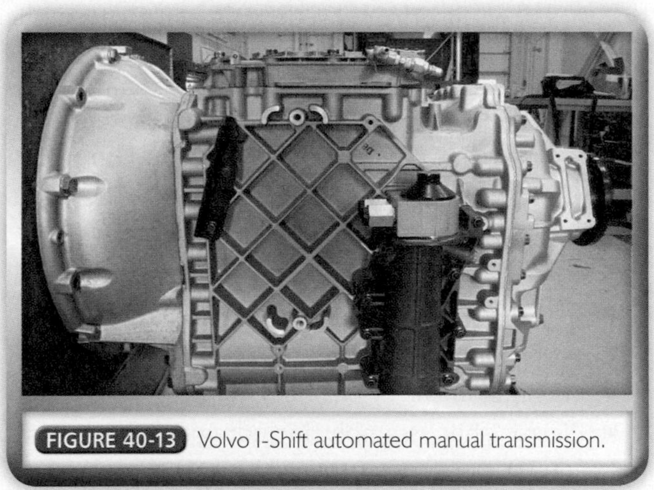

FIGURE 40-13 Volvo I-Shift automated manual transmission.

FIGURE 40-12 The Detroit Diesel DT-12 transmission.

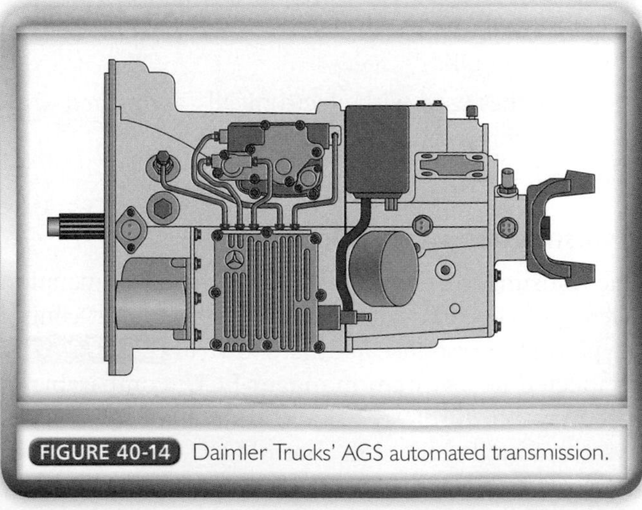

FIGURE 40-14 Daimler Trucks' AGS automated transmission.

Operation of Automated Manual Transmissions

Automated manual transmissions have unique operations and power flows compared to standard transmission. And different makes and models of AMTs operate differently from one another as well. This section will cover the operation of the Eaton Fuller AutoShift, UltraShift, and Procision; the Meritor/ZF; the Detroit Diesel DT-12; the Volvo I-Shift; and the Daimler AGS models.

Eaton Fuller AutoShift and UltraShift Operations

Eaton has two basic lines of automated transmissions available for the North American truck market. The three-pedal AutoShift line is now available in ten-, and eighteen-speed models. The two-pedal **UltraShift** line is available in five-, six-, ten-, eleven-, thirteen-, sixteen-, and eighteen-speed models with either an electronically actuated clutch or a data mechanical (DM) clutch. Data mechanical clutches are operated centrifugally. The operating systems for the two lines are of such similar design that we will discuss them together. We will point out the differences between each as we go.

The base transmission on each model is almost identical to a standard Eaton Fuller transmission. Additional components that make the transmission automated include:

- Transmission controller
- Shaft speed sensors
- Driver interface (electronic shifter)
- Start enable relay
- MEIIR Momentary engine ignition interrupt relay
- Electric shift assembly, including the shift motors and the position sensors
- Electronically controlled range valve
- Electronically controlled splitter valve
- Inertia brakes
- Clutches used with electronically automated transmissions
- Shift strategies

Transmission Controller

The transmission control used with the first generation (Gen 1) of these transmissions consisted of a shift-control keypad or lever module, like that shown in FIGURE 40-15A, connected to a **system manager** ECU, comparable to that shown in FIGURE 40-15B. The system manager ECU was connected to the shift control ECU, like that shown in FIGURE 40-15C, on the transmission.

FIGURE 40-15 First generation Eaton AMTs had three modules: **A.** The shift control; **B.** The system manager; and **C.** The transmission controller.

In second generation (Gen 2) AutoShift transmissions, the system manager and the shift lever (or push button pad) were combined. The number of electronic modules was reduced to two—one at the shift control and one at the transmission itself. Gen 1 transmissions communicated with the engine ECM over the J-1587 data link. Gen 2 models, launched in 1999, use the much faster **J-1939** data link for communication. The SAE J-1939 communication protocol features data transmission at a rate of at least 250,000 bits per second and up to 500,000 bits/second.

Shift initiation is handled by the shift control module at the driver interface. The shift control can be either push button or lever type. The controller communicates with the engine ECM to request a torque break to allow the shift. Shifts are initiated based on engine rpm and load factors. The transmission software basically monitors engine rpm and predicts an expected rpm decrease during the shift, identifying a target rpm at which to select the next gear.

If the engine rpm does not decrease quickly enough, the software can wait or initiate braking with either the engine brake or an inertia brake, if one is installed. When the rpm falls to the target rpm of the shift, the shift controller tells the transmission controller to make the shift. Upon completion of the shift, the engine ECM resumes normal rpm control.

As more and more shifts are initiated, the transmission shift control will learn the predictable rpm drop and respond accordingly. The driver can also request shifts to occur by pushing the push buttons on the shift controller or operating the transmission in the hold mode. The software will then only shift when requested by the driver.

The Gen 3 software, introduced in 2006, has only one module. As shown in FIGURE 40-16, it is mounted on the transmission. The driver interface is merely a series of switches that input to the controller, but the shift process is similar to previous generations.

The software has advanced with each generation. Gen 3 software is capable of **adaptive learning**, meaning that the software can learn and change strategy based on different factors. The software also has several preprogrammed operating modes for performance and fuel economy. The transmission control learns the terrain, the load, and the driving style of the driver and constantly adapts the shift strategies on the fly.

The TCU has self-diagnostic capabilities. It will log diagnostic fault codes and produce a data **snapshot** of each incident. A data snapshot records all the relevant TCU data before and after a diagnostic code is set to ease diagnoses. The controller is programmed to protect the transmission by prohibiting driver-initiated shifts that may damage the transmission, such as high-speed direction changes, high rpm shifts from neutral to range, or shifts that would place the engine outside of its normal rpm operating range. The controller also has a fallback strategy that actuates when a problem is detected. Fallback strategies include shift inhibits, hold in gear, down shift to last held gear, and many others. Each fallback strategy permits failsafe but limited operation if necessary.

Shaft Speed Sensors

For clash-free shifts to occur, the transmission control software must know the precise speed of the input shaft, the countershaft, the main shaft gears, and the main shaft itself.

The transmission has three speed sensors, like those shown in FIGURE 40-17, to accomplish this. The input speed sensor is at the front right corner of the transmission shift cover and targets the upper countershaft PTO gear. When the speed of the countershaft and the transmission ratios are known, the software can calculate the input shaft speed and the main shaft gear speeds.

The main shaft speed sensor is located at the left rear side of the transmission shift cover and targets the upper

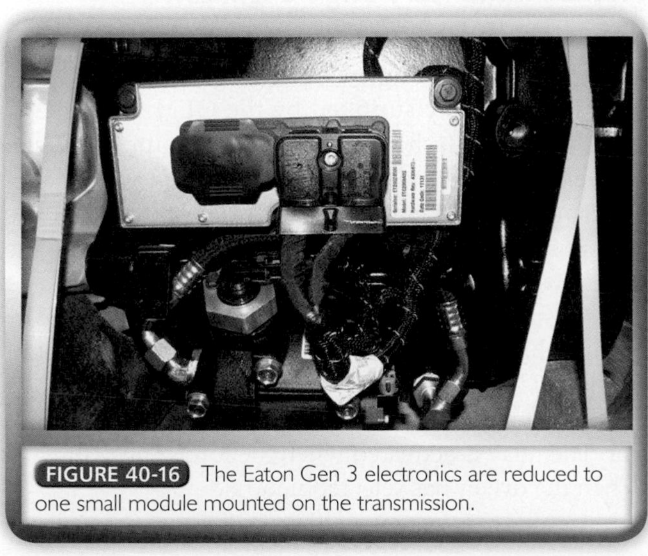

FIGURE 40-16 The Eaton Gen 3 electronics are reduced to one small module mounted on the transmission.

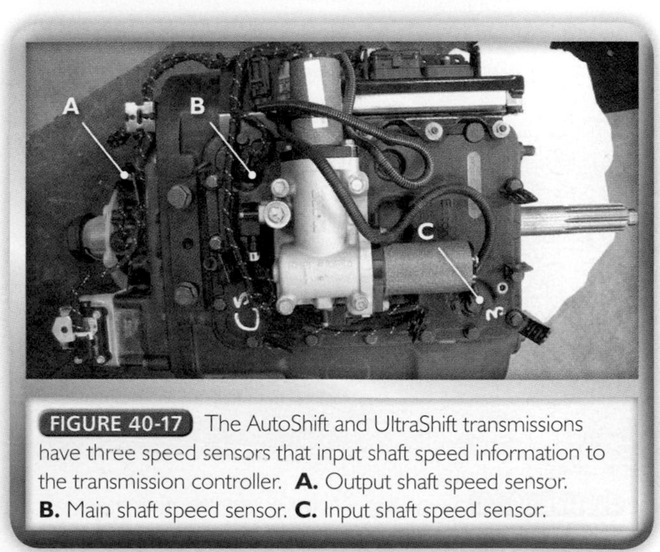

FIGURE 40-17 The AutoShift and UltraShift transmissions have three speed sensors that input shaft speed information to the transmission controller. **A.** Output shaft speed sensor. **B.** Main shaft speed sensor. **C.** Input shaft speed sensor.

auxiliary countershaft driven gear. The main shaft speed sensor monitors the speed of the auxiliary countershaft and sends that information to the transmission controller. In turn, the transmission controller can calculate the speed of the main shaft and of the sliding clutches used to engage the main shaft gears. The controller uses all of that information to tell the engine ECM to synchronize the speeds to perform a clash-proof shift.

The output speed sensor is located in the output shaft bearing support housing. The output speed sensor targets a tone wheel mounted on the shaft. The controller uses this sensor to detect output shaft speed and confirm that shifts have been made.

Driver Interface

The driver shift control in Gen 1 and 2 software versions contained an electronic module responsible for shift scheduling while the transmission controller actually handled the shifting. In Gen 3, these modules have been combined into a single module located on the transmission. The shift control can be push button or lever style. Single-module Gen 3 transmission controllers require only a series of switches for driver input. The design of the switches varies depending on the OEM. **FIGURE 40-18** shows a controller by Freightliner.

Every shifter, regardless of the OEM, has several components to it. Each control has a display that alerts the driver to gear range and shifting status and which will display diagnostic fault codes. The display can be integral to or remotely mounted from the shift control. The display indicates to the driver what gear the transmission is in.

During a shift, the display indicates the target range as a solid number. As the transmission shifts to neutral, the target range will start flashing. Once the shift completes, the range number will go back to being solid. The control has up and down buttons for driver-initiated shifts and usually has five positions or push-button choices—R for reverse, N for neutral, D for drive, M for manual, and L for low range. Drive is the position used for fully automatic operation. Selecting M will cause the transmission to remain in the current gear range. In manual, the driver can initiate shifts by using the up and down buttons. Selecting low when decelerating will allow maximum engine breaking.

FIGURE 40-18 Gen 3 shift controller from Freightliner.

The driver can also use the up or down arrows in drive to select a different start-up gear than the one selected by the software. The control usually has a service light to alert the driver to transmission malfunctions. Some UltraShift transmission installations will use an OEM-supplied shift control that may differ from the Eaton type. OEM shift controls are either resistive ladder type controllers or J-1939 controllers. J-1939 controllers have communication capabilities and can interface directly with the transmission ECM. The transmission controller also uses multiplexing to communicate with all other vehicle modules through the CAN bus line.

Start Enable Relay

The **start enable relay** is an OEM supplied relay usually mounted in the dash that is controlled by the transmission TCU. The start enable relay interrupts the circuit to the starter solenoid when it is not activated, preventing the vehicle from starting. When the driver turns on the key, the transmission controller goes through an initiation and self-check process. Next the controller will check for neutral; when it has verified the transmission is in a neutral position it will turn on the start enable relay, allowing the vehicle engine to be started. The controller will only turn on the start enable relay after the system initiation completes and it has verified that the transmission is not in any gear and that the transmission is in fact in neutral.

MEIIR Momentary Engine Ignition Interrupt Relay

The **momentary engine ignition interrupt relay (MEIIR)** is a relay supplied by the OEM and usually installed in the dash. This relay is only supplied when the vehicle has an ultrashift transmission with a data mechanical or DM clutch. The relay is controlled by the transmission controller and it will interrupt the engine ignition (or fuel supply on diesel engines) in the event of a catastrophic failure of the DM clutch. That typically occurs when the DM clutch fails to disengage. The interruption of fueling or ignition is designed to break torque to allow the transmission shift controller to pull to neutral. The relay is activated when the following occurs: When the driver has selected neutral

- When neutral is not been achieved

- After 2.5 seconds have passed since the driver selected neutral
- When engine RPM is greater than 850 or when engine torque is more than 200 ft lb (271 Nm)
- When the vehicle has an active J1939 fault

When these conditions are met, the TCU will activate the relay, momentarily shutting off engine ignition/fuelling to break torque to allow the shift control to pull to neutral. If neutral is not achieved, the system will activate the relay again and again until the conditions no longer exist.

Electric Shift Assembly

The **electric shift assembly** consists of two shift motors: the shift finger and the shift finger position sensors. The shift motors perform the actual gear selection inside the AutoShift or UltraShift main box. There are two of these motors mounted on the top of the transmission shift cover. When shifting a normal standard transmission, the driver moves the shift lever in one of four different directions—left, right, backward, or forward. The twin shift control motors are responsible for moving the shift finger side to side to select the correct shift rail and forward and back to select the desired gear. This mechanism is show in FIGURE 40-19.

At the bottom of the shift lever is a shift finger that engages one of the three shift rails when the lever is moved left to right. Each shift rail controls the position of one shift fork inside the transmission. Shift rail gates are shown in FIGURE 40-20. The shift fork engages with a sliding clutch that will lock one gear to the transmission main shaft, depending on whether the driver moves the rail lever forward or back. The right rail moves the first and reverse shift fork. The center rail moves the second and third shift fork. The left rail moves the fourth and fifth gear shift fork.

In the Eaton automated transmission, the two shift motors accomplish the same thing. A shift finger is mounted on a shift shaft. One motor moves the shift finger left to right to select the correct rail. It is called the rail select motor. The other motor moves the shift finger forward and back to select the correct gear. It is called the gear select motor.

The motors are reversible DC motors and both drive a worm shaft that controls the position of a re-circulating ball nut. This type of nut is used because it provides very smooth and precise movement and longevity. A re-circulating ball nut has a series of ball bearings running in the groove of the worm shaft. When in use, the bearings complete several circuits around the shaft. Their circuit is determined by the width of the ball nut. The bearings are returned to the beginning of the ball nut by a tube attached to the nut. The re-circulating ball nuts move the shift finger from side to side and front to back to complete a shift. FIGURE 40-21 depicts recirculating ball nuts with a shift rail nut.

FIGURE 40-20 Three shift rail gates. **A.** Left. **B.** Center. **C.** Right.

FIGURE 40-19 Shift finger and shift rail in electric shift assembly.

FIGURE 40-21 **A.** Shift rail nut. **B.** Re-circulating balls.

The electric shift assembly on earlier model AutoShift transmissions was oriented with the rail motor mounted laterally. The body of the motor protruded to the right side of the transmission case and the gear select motor protruded towards the front of the transmission. In contrast, Gen 3 AutoShift transmissions are oriented with the rail motor protruding towards the left side of the transmission case to allow more room for the installation of exhaust components on the right side.

Position Sensors

The precise positioning of the shift finger is essential to proper operation of an automated transmission. Therefore, two position sensors are used—the rail select position sensor and the gear select position sensor. Both sensors are shown in **FIGURE 40-22**. The rail select motor moves the shift finger left to right. The gear select motor will move the shift finger forward and back. In both cases, the travel distance is just over an inch (2.54 cm) in total, so exacting control is necessary.

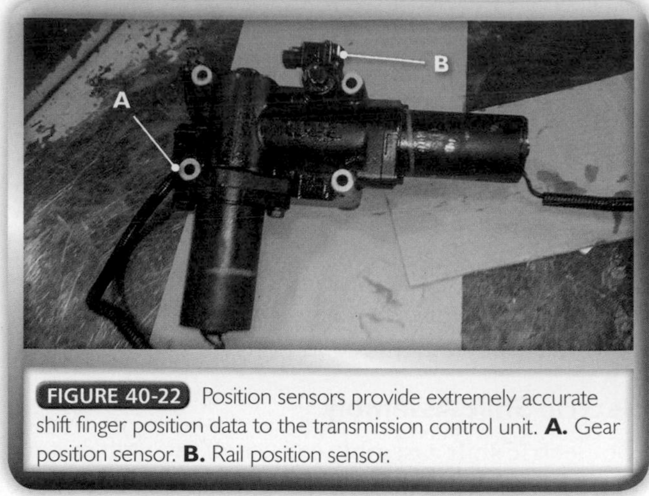

FIGURE 40-22 Position sensors provide extremely accurate shift finger position data to the transmission control unit. **A.** Gear position sensor. **B.** Rail position sensor.

The two position sensors are Hall Effect sensors that produce a digital signal and send it to the transmission control module. Every time the transmission is powered down, the shift motors and the position sensors work in concert to map the shift gate area. First, the sensors move across the gate to measure total distance from the left shift rail to the right shift rail. Next, the sensors push against the shift rail interlocks by trying to move the center and the right rail together, forward and back, and then by trying to move the center and the left side shift rail together, forward and back. This recalibration procedure gives the transmission ECU a precise map of exactly where the gates and the rails are. Once the procedure is complete, the transmission is ready for the next power up and drive cycle. **FIGURE 40-23** illustrates the sequence of the recalibration process.

Electronically Controlled Range Valve

AutoShift and UltraShift models with 10 or more forward ranges will have an auxiliary section and can be operated in high or low range depending on the operating conditions. Shifting between high and low range is done pneumatically and was explained in the Standard Transmissions chapter. In the AutoShift and UltraShift models the shifting is controlled by the transmission ECU.

The range cylinder cover is modified to accept an electrically operated air-control solenoid valve, as shown in **FIGURE 40-24**. The **air-control solenoid valve** has two electric solenoid valves that control the flow of air from the air filter/pressure regulator to the range cylinder piston. That is, the two electric solenoids direct air to the low- and high-range side of the cylinder piston as required by the control unit. The regulator holds the pressure between approximately 58 and 63 psi (400 and 434 kPa).

The operation of these valves is rather simple. To achieve low range, the transmission ECU energizes the low solenoid. Doing so allows air to flow to the front side of the range cylinder piston. The piston and its attached yoke move rearward to engage the low-range gear. The air behind the piston exhausts through the high-range solenoid.

When a shift to high range is required, the ECU de-energizes the low-range solenoid and energizes the high-range solenoid. Doing so exhausts air from the low side of the range cylinder piston through the low-range solenoid. Pressurized air is directed to the back of the piston, forcing it and the yoke forward. High range is then engaged.

Electronically Controlled Splitter Valve

On AutoShift and UltraShift models with more than ten forward speeds, there will be a splitter cylinder that controls the position of the splitter sliding clutch. Recall that the splitter shift was discussed in the Standard Transmissions chapter. Review that chapter as needed to fully understand the operation of the splitter shift.

In AMTs, the splitter cylinder cover has been modified to hold the splitter shift solenoids. The splitter shift solenoids are electric solenoids over air control valves, are controlled by the transmission, and are identical to the valves used for the range control. The ECU controls the solenoids to direct air supplied from the air filter/pressure regulator to cause one of two splits. Either the front of the splitter cylinder piston engages the high split position or, to achieve low split, air is directed to the rear of the splitter cylinder piston.

Inertia Brake

Medium-duty AutoShift and UltraShift transmissions and heavy-duty UltraShift transmissions use an **inertia brake**

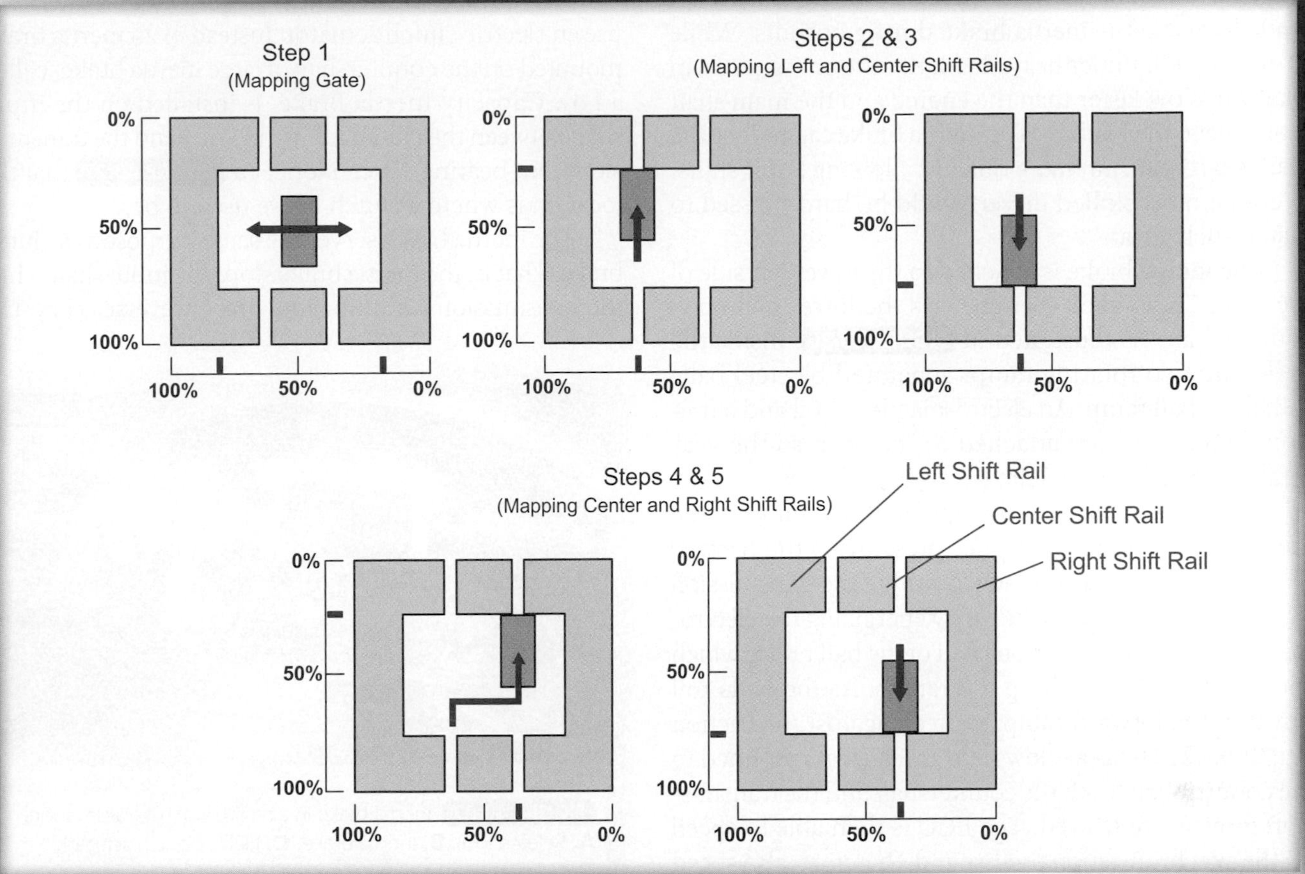

FIGURE 40-23 The recalibration procedure is performed on every system power down so the controller is ready to shift on the next drive cycle.

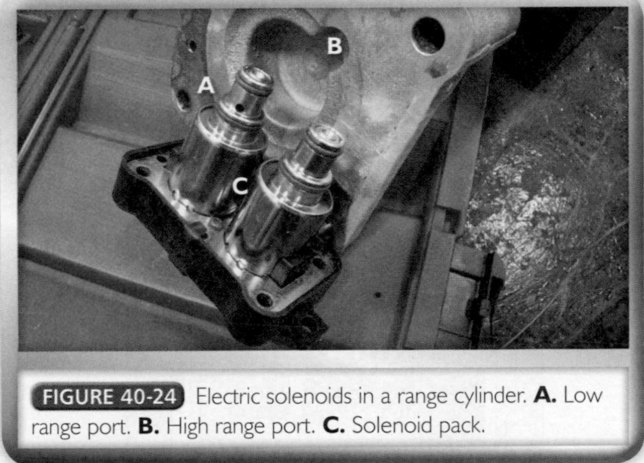

FIGURE 40-24 Electric solenoids in a range cylinder. **A.** Low range port. **B.** High range port. **C.** Solenoid pack.

FIGURE 40-25 The inertia brake mounts on the lower PTO opening of the transmission.

to slow input and countershaft speed on engagement from neutral to reverse or a forward range. Slowing the input and speed helps prevent gear clash. As shown in FIGURE 40-25, inertia brakes are typically mounted on the lower power take-off opening of the transmission.

The inertia brake can also be used to assist in gaining synchronicity of the transmission shafts and gears during upshift events. Synchronizing shafts and gears allows for slightly faster shift times. Fuller claims that an eighteen-speed UltraShift transmission can shift through all its gear ranges while pulling 160,000 lb (72,575 kg) on a 15% grade by using the inertia brake during upshifts. While climbing a hill under heavy load, the transmission main shaft can slow faster than the engine and the main shaft gears due to the loading. The inertia brake can reduce the main shaft gear rpm more quickly, allowing faster shifts. Even the most skilled driver would be hard pressed to match such a feat.

The inertia brake is attached to the lower left side of the case. The brake's gear engages the lower main box countershaft. As illustrated in **FIGURE 40-26**, inside the brake are two rotating ramps separated by steel balls called the ball ramp. An electro-magnetic coil and a friction clutch pack are attached to the gear, so the gear rotates with the countershaft.

The electro-magnetically operated ball ramp in the inertia brake assembly applies pressure to the friction plates to slow the transmission gearing. The transmission ECU actuates the inertia brake by energizing the electro-magnetic coil. This slows one half of the ball ramp, which causes the balls to roll up the ramps. As the balls roll upward, the forward ramp is forced against the friction clutch pack. The gear slows and, because it is splined to the countershaft, both the countershaft and the transmission gearing are slowed. The ECU is then able to speed up the synchronization process and, therefore, also speed up the upshift.

Newer model UltraShift heavy-duty transmissions use an electric clutch actuator. Instead of an inertia brake mounted on the countershaft, a large inertia brake, called a Low Capacity Inertia Brake, is installed on the input shaft between the clutch release bearing and the transmission front bearing cover. Notice in **FIGURE 40-27** that the location is where a clutch brake used to be.

The inertia brake serves the same purpose as a clutch brake. That is, the inertia brake stops the input shaft while the transmission is shifting into first or reverse gears. The

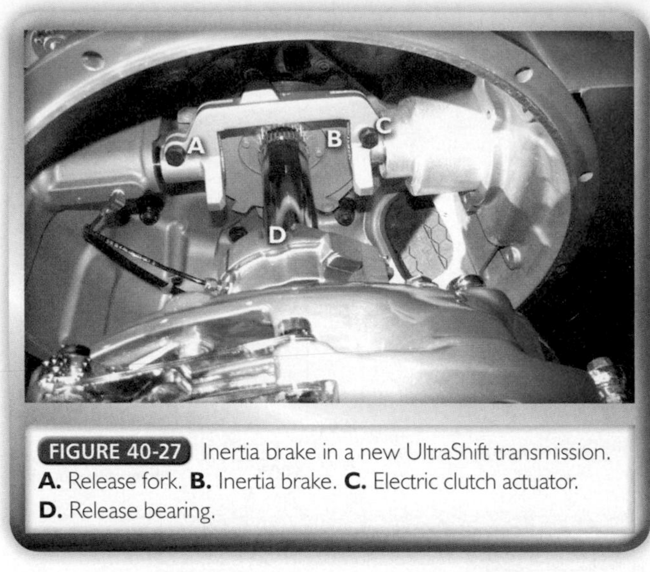

FIGURE 40-27 Inertia brake in a new UltraShift transmission. **A.** Release fork. **B.** Inertia brake. **C.** Electric clutch actuator. **D.** Release bearing.

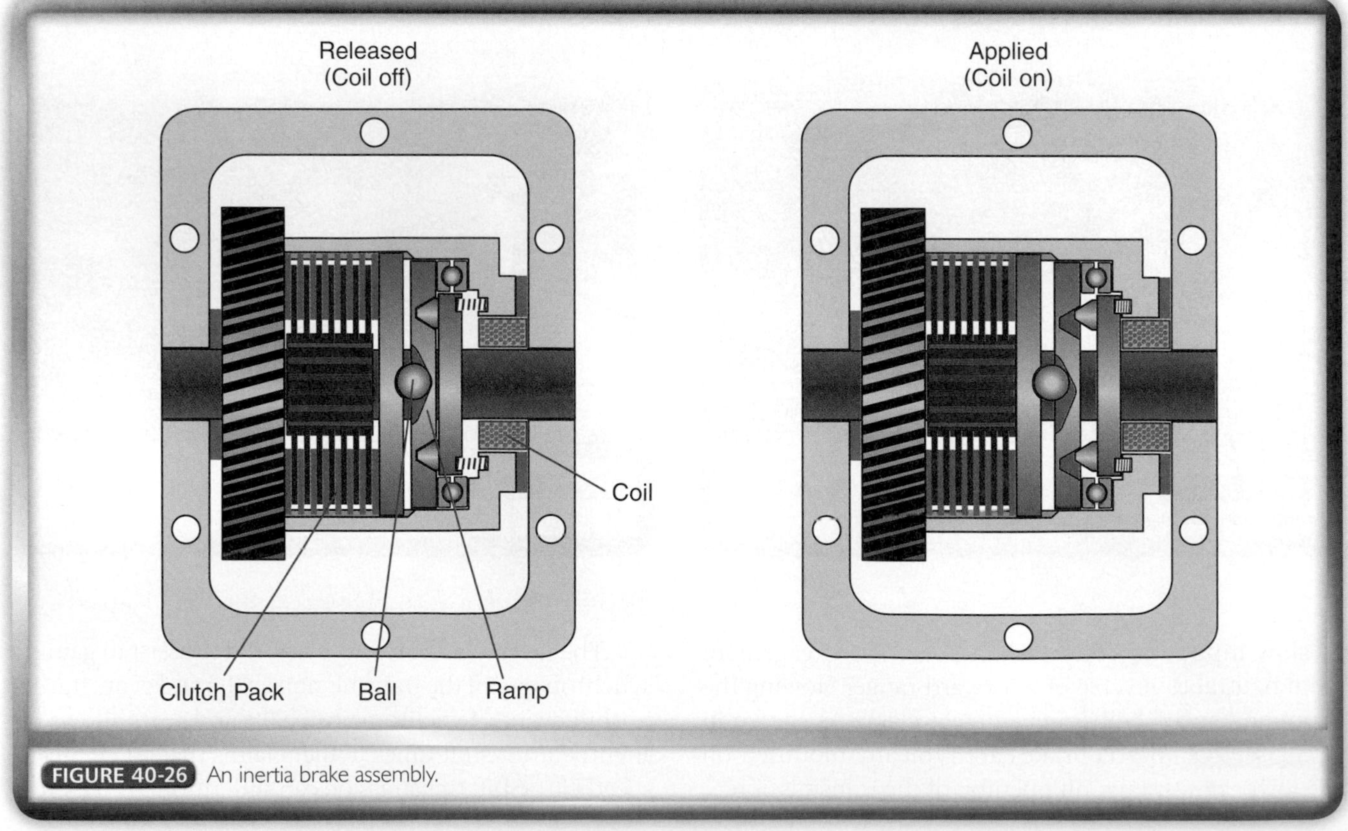

FIGURE 40-26 An inertia brake assembly.

inertia brake can also be used during upshifts when warranted by the operation of the vehicle. The electric clutch actuator is not normally used while shifting, but in certain operating conditions it is utilized to reduce engine rpm during upshifts under heavy loads.

Clutches Used with Electronically Automated Transmissions

Four different clutches are used by Eaton Fuller in its line of electronically automated transmissions: SOLO, data mechanical, electronically actuated SOLO, and wet clutch.

The SOLO self-adjusting clutch is the only manually actuated clutch supplied with the AutoShift line of transmissions. SOLO clutches used with the AutoShift are three-pedal systems. They have a clutch pedal and the driver must use the clutch when starting off shifting from neutral to reverse or forward only. The rest of the shifting is handled automatically by the transmission. **FIGURE 40-28** shows an Eaton SOLO self-adjusting clutch.

The data mechanical (DM) clutch is centrifugally applied by increasing engine rpm. The DM clutch is used with both medium- and heavy-duty models of the UltraShift line of transmissions. DM clutches use a two-pedal system with no clutch pedal. Four centrifugal weights apply the DM clutch as engine rpm increases. As the weights move out, they push against ramps built into the back of the pressure plate. That is what creates the clamp load. **FIGURE 40-29** shows the four weights in a DM clutch.

The DM clutch starts engagement at approximately 800 to 850 rpm. From there, it ramps up to full clamp load at approximately 1350 rpm. On disengagement, full clamp load remains until rpm has dropped to approximately 900 rpm. At that point, the clutch starts to release. By the time approximately 800 rpm is reached, the clutch is fully released.

FIGURE 40-28 Eaton SOLO self-adjusting clutch.

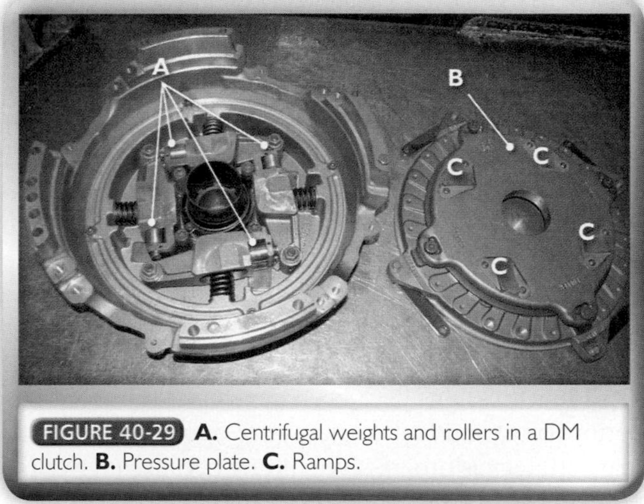

FIGURE 40-29 **A.** Centrifugal weights and rollers in a DM clutch. **B.** Pressure plate. **C.** Ramps.

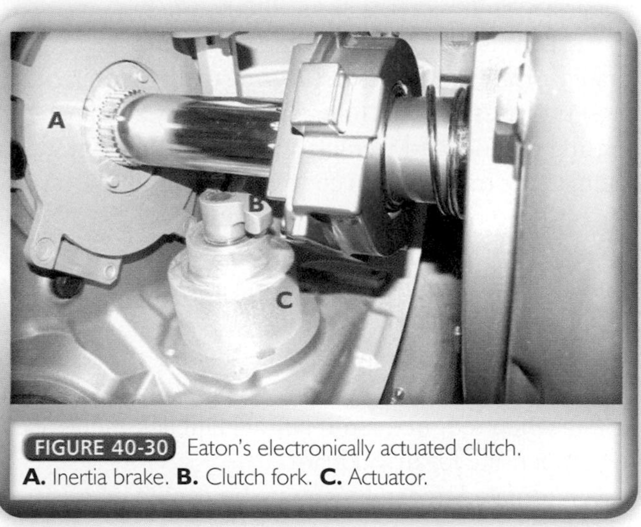

FIGURE 40-30 Eaton's electronically actuated clutch. **A.** Inertia brake. **B.** Clutch fork. **C.** Actuator.

> **TECHNICIAN TIP**
>
> The DM clutch can be subject to abuse by an unskilled driver. If the driver tries to hold the vehicle on an incline by feathering the throttle to around 800 to 850 rpm, the clutch will be constantly slipping and will burn out in very little time. As always, proper driving training is essential with any new system!

The third type of clutch used on two-pedal models of Eaton Fuller automated manual transmission models is called an electronic clutch actuation device. An example is shown in **FIGURE 40-30**. An electronically actuated clutch contains an electronic module with an integrated electric motor to operate a standard SOLO clutch. Because these transmissions are two-pedal models, there is no clutch pedal. Typically, the system will only operate the clutch when starting from a standstill or when stopping. However, the transmission may occasionally activate the clutch during shifting to aid in synchronization. This is similar to the double clutching technique discussed in the Heavy-Duty Clutches chapter.

Finally, Eaton also uses a wet clutch on some varieties of electronically automated transmissions, namely its FO-8406-ASW model. Even though these models use a two-pedal design, the clutch is similar to the multidisc hydraulic clutch found in automatic transmissions. A wet clutch of this type requires a source of hydraulic pressure to apply. The hydraulic pressure is supplied by a pump inside the transmission. Clutch application is controlled by the ECU using electronically controlled hydraulic solenoids.

Shifting Strategies

As with any new development in the automotive world, the switch to automated transmissions has been driven primarily by the need to meet increasingly stringent emission standards. Automated transmissions help to achieve new standards by being more fuel efficient than their standard transmission predecessors.

Of course, to the fleet owner, fuel is the most expensive part of the daily operation. Improvements of 3% to 7% better fuel economy are very welcome. In fact, the significant savings help to offset the higher initial expense of an automated transmission.

Shifting strategies for every conceivable vocation for these transmissions have been developed to ensure that performance and fuel economy are optimized. The primary strategy is progressive shifting because it gives the best economy. For different vocations, however, more aggressive shift patterns are desired.

The transmission ECU can be programmed to allow a range of shift strategies depending on the requirement. Most transmission controllers in use today are capable of sensing engine load, vehicle weight, and road grade or incline. The transmission controllers monitor the fueling demand and other parameters over the J-1939 CAN bus line and adjust shifting strategies based on this information. The ability to change shifting as needed optimizes performance and fuel economy.

All automated transmissions have a manual shift mode that allows the driver complete control over shift points when required. Still, failsafe fallback modes exist to compensate for driver error.

Automated transmissions are becoming increasingly popular. As their software becomes more sophisticated, it will become nearly impossible to find a driver capable of shifting with the skill and accuracy of an automated transmission while still reaching fuel economy targets.

Eaton Fuller Transmission Nomenclature

As a technician, it is important that you be able to decipher the nomenclature for the transmissions you will be working on. **TABLE 40-1**, **TABLE 40-2**, and **TABLE 40-3** will help you decipher the nomenclature on Eaton Fuller six-speed, ten-speed, and thirteen-speed transmissions.

As the company's line of transmissions has become more varied, new nomenclature is now used to reflect the variety of models available. **TABLE 40-4** contains an example of Eaton Fuller's new nomenclature. The specific changes to Eaton Fuller's new nomenclature include the following:

- "E" or "F" has been added to the prefix to identify the brand as "Eaton" or "Fuller."
- "M" has been added to the prefix to identify this transmission is approved for use with multitorque engines.
- Configuration denotes the type of clutch the transmission uses. Configurations include:
  - D—Dry mechanical
  - E—Electronic clutch actuator
  - S—Wet shifting clutch
- The design level is now a combination of the gear box design and automation platform.
- The final suffix contains the application and value code. The application and value codes include:
  - L—Line-haul
  - H—Highway (and High in 2nd position)
  - P—Performance (and PTO in 2nd position)
  - S—Severe duty
  - ST—Standard
  - V—Vocational (and Value in 2nd position)
  - M—Multipurpose (and Mixer in 2nd position)
  - C—Construction
  - X—Extreme duty
  - R—Recreational (motor home)
  - G—Generator
  - P—PTO
  - U—Utility
  - E—Efficient

Eaton Procision Automated Transmission

In September 2014, Eaton Fuller announced the addition of a brand new transmission model to its line-up. This transmission is the new seven-speed **Procision**,

TABLE 40-1: Nomenclature for six-speed FO-6406B-DM3

F	X-	X	4	06	X-	DM	3
Fuller	Overdrive if present	Input torque × 100	Design level	Forward speeds	Gear ratio	Automated with DM clutch	Gen 3 electronics

TABLE 40-2: Nomenclature for ten-speed RTO-16910A-DM3

R	T	O	IX	9	10	X	DM	3
Roadranger	Twin countershaft	Overdrive	Input torque × 100	Design level	Forward speeds	Gear ratio	Automated with DM clutch	Gen 3 electronics

TABLE 40-3: Nomenclature for thirteen-speed RTLOM-16913A-DM3

RT	L	O	M	IX	9	13	X	DM	3
Roadranger twin	Low inertia	Overdrive	Multitorque 1,750 ft-lb (2,373 Nm) in top two gears only	Input torque × 100	Design level	Forward speeds	Ratio	Automated with DM clutch	Gen 3 electronics

TABLE 40-4: Nomenclature for FOM-15D310B-LST

F	O	M	15	D	3	10	B	LST
Brand Eaton or Fuller	Overdrive	Multitorque	Input torque × 100	Clutch configuration	Design level	Forward speeds	Ratio	Application and value

fully automated, dual-clutch transmission for the class 6 and 7 truck market. The transmission has been available in North America since early 2015. Global release is expected to follow.

Dual-clutch transmissions are not a new development. They have been used with great success in the automotive market since the early 1980s. There are two basic types of dual-clutch transmissions available. The first is a twin friction disc clutch design utilizing two separate friction clutches. The second type uses two hydraulically applied multi-plate wet clutches in a single rotating housing.

In both types, one of the clutches inputs a solid primary input shaft and the second clutch inputs a hollow secondary input shaft. The gearing is usually arranged so that odd-numbered gears will be driven by the solid input shaft. Even-numbered gears are driven by the hollow secondary input shaft. This arrangement allows the transmission controller to engage the next gear before the shift occurs. To actually change to the next gear, the controller simply has to disengage one clutch and apply the other. The result is much smoother and faster shifting with no torque break losses. When torque is broken for the shift and then reapplied, fuel economy decreases. Eliminating torque break, therefore, leads to better fuel economy.

Volkswagen uses this type of transmission and calls it a Direct Shift Gearbox (DSG). The advantage of these transmissions becomes apparent when you realize that a driver shifting a standard transmission breaks torque by disengaging the clutch. That action uses approximately half a second, or 500 milliseconds, to complete the shift. An automated transmission improves that break in torque by 80% by shifting in approximately 100 milliseconds. The DSG dual-clutch transmission can shift in as little as 8 milliseconds!

The Eaton Procision transmission, shown in FIGURE 40-31, is capable of similar shifting speeds. The shifts occur under power (without torque break), and the transmission does not use a torque converter. For those reasons, Eaton claims on its website that the Procision transmission can achieve an 8 to 10% improvement in fuel economy over an automatic transmission when installed in a vehicle used for around-town deliveries.

Eaton Procision Operation

The Eaton Procision uses the second arrangement for a dual-clutch transmission. That is, the Procision has a rotating clutch module that contains the primary and secondary clutches. The rotating clutch housing is driven directly by a torsional damper bolted to the engine flywheel. The two clutches—one in front of the other in the rotating housing—again drive two input shafts. The front clutch drives the hollow (secondary) input shaft, and the rear clutch drives the solid (primary) input shaft. Inside the transmission, there are five shafts: the primary input shaft, the secondary input shaft, the main or output shaft, the countershaft, and the reverse idler shaft.

The Procision transmission has three synchronizers and one collar shift mechanism. The secondary input shaft inputs to the forward input gear, which is in constant mesh with the front countershaft driven gear. Because the front countershaft driven gear is fixed to the countershaft, they always turn together. The primary input shaft's input gear is again in constant mesh with a countershaft driven gear. That countershaft gear, however, is not fixed to the countershaft. To lock this gear to the countershaft, the second and seventh synchronizer, which is splined to the countershaft, must be moved rearward to engage the clutching teeth on the gear.

The next synchronizer shift mechanism is on the output shaft. That mechanism controls shifting for third and fifth gear. Fifth gear in this transmission is direct. The next shift mechanism is a sliding collar shift that is again on the output shaft and controls shifting for first and reverse gears. The fourth and final synchronizer shift mechanism is on the countershaft and controls shifting for fourth and sixth gears.

Movement of the shift mechanisms is controlled hydraulically. Fluid pressure is supplied by a hydraulic

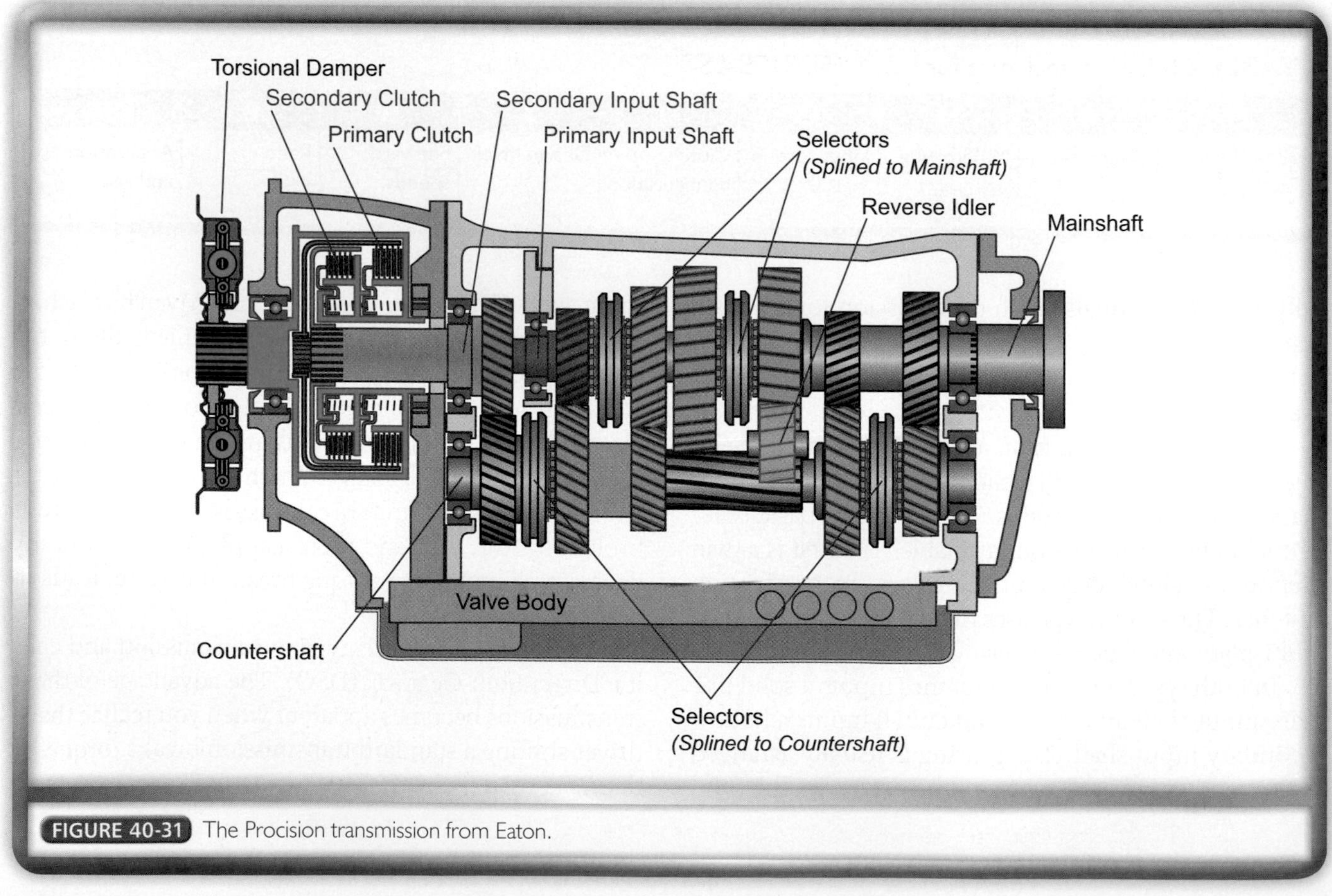

FIGURE 40-31 The Procision transmission from Eaton.

pump driven by the transmission gearing. Hydraulic pressure is also used to apply the two wet clutches.

The transmission gearing is a departure from what technicians are used to seeing. Whereas, on most countershaft transmissions all the gears are fixed to the countershaft, the Procision countershaft contains only two fixed gears. In the Procision, only the front countershaft driven gear and the first and reverse countershaft gears always turn with the countershaft. The rear countershaft driven gear is actually two gears together—the rear countershaft driven gear and countershaft third gear. This two gear block is locked to the countershaft only when the front countershaft synchronizer is in the rearward position. Fourth gear and sixth gear countershafts are also not fixed to the countershaft unless they are locked to it by the fourth–sixth synchronizer.

The main shaft in this transmission is also an anomaly. Whereas, in most transmissions all the main shaft gears are free to rotate around the main shaft unless they are locked to it by a synchronizer or sliding clutch/collar, in the Procision transmission the fourth and sixth gear main shafts are fixed to the main shaft and always turn with it. Reverse, first, and third gear main shafts are free to rotate around the shaft unless they are locked to it by the third–fifth synchronizer or the first–reverse sliding collar. While a departure from the norm in countershaft transmissions, this type of gearing arrangement is quite common in dual-clutch transmissions.

Procision Transmission Power Flows

Because the Procision transmission is unconventional, it is worth reviewing its power flows.

Neutral: In neutral, both of the wet clutches are released and the transmission receives no input, as illustrated in FIGURE 40-32.

Reverse: When reverse is selected, the first synchronizer on the countershaft moves rearward to lock the second countershaft driven gear to the countershaft. The sliding collar shift mechanism on the main shaft also moves rearward to lock reverse gear to the main shaft, as illustrated in FIGURE 40-33.

When the driver releases the brake pedal, the rear (primary) wet clutch starts to engage. The vehicle has an "urge to move" feel and also hill-hold capability for a short period. As the driver steps on the throttle, the primary clutch fully applies and reverse is fully engaged. The power flow is as follows. The primary clutch inputs the second input gear of the transmission. Then the power flows through to the second countershaft driven gear, which is locked to the countershaft by the first–seventh

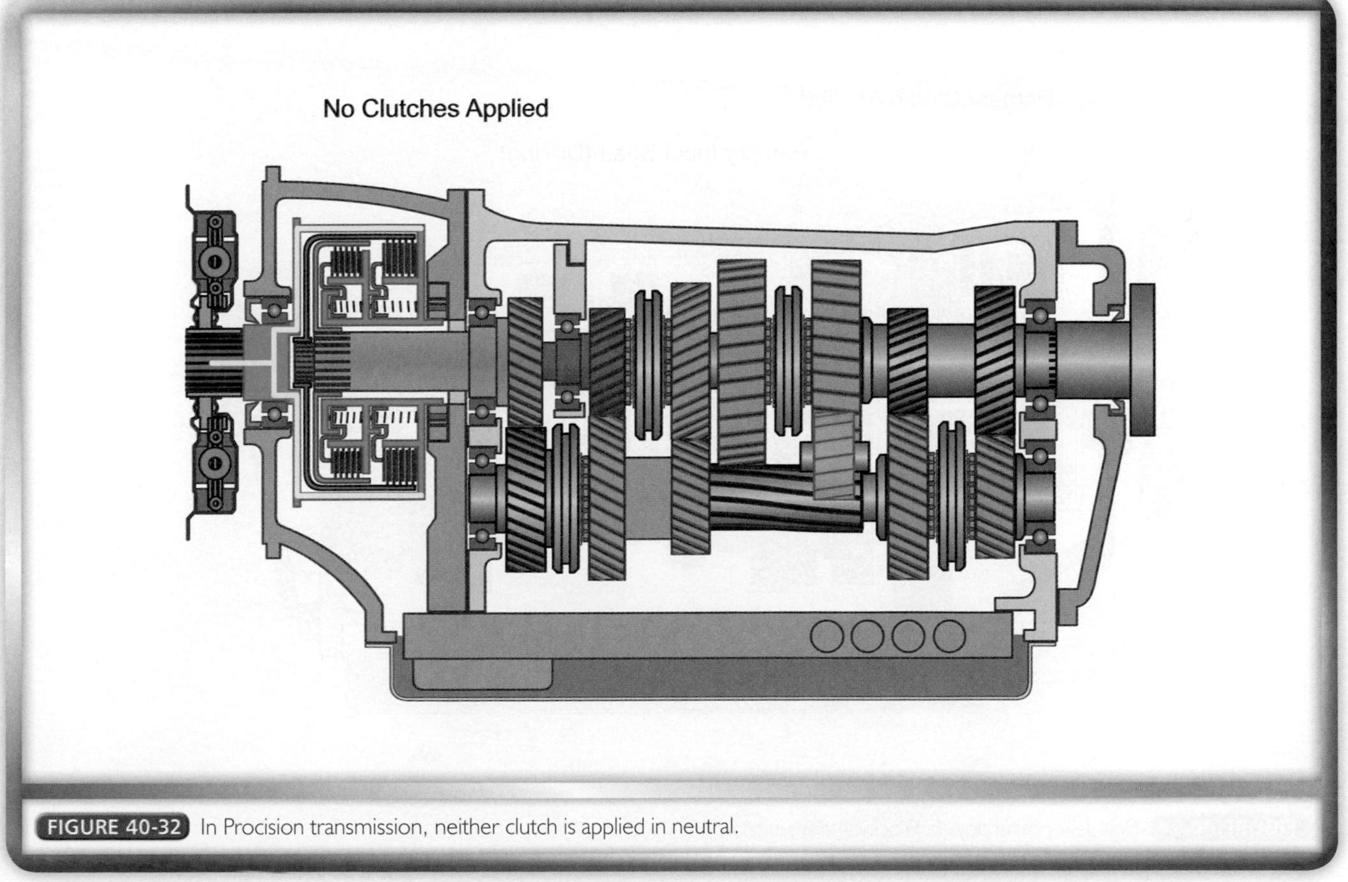

FIGURE 40-32 In Procision transmission, neither clutch is applied in neutral.

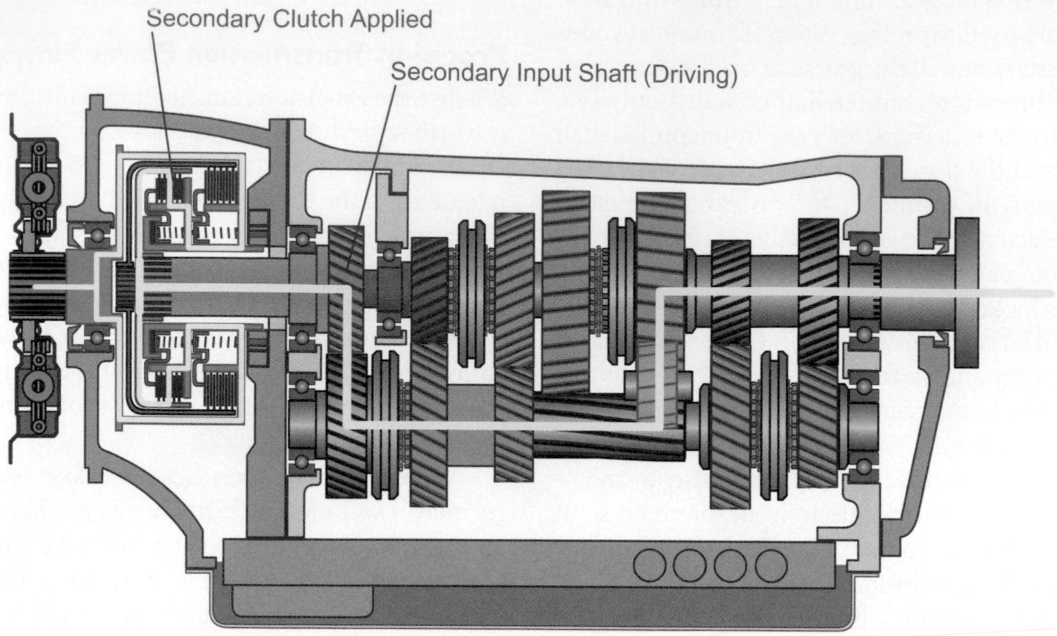

FIGURE 40-33 Reverse power flow in Procision transmission.

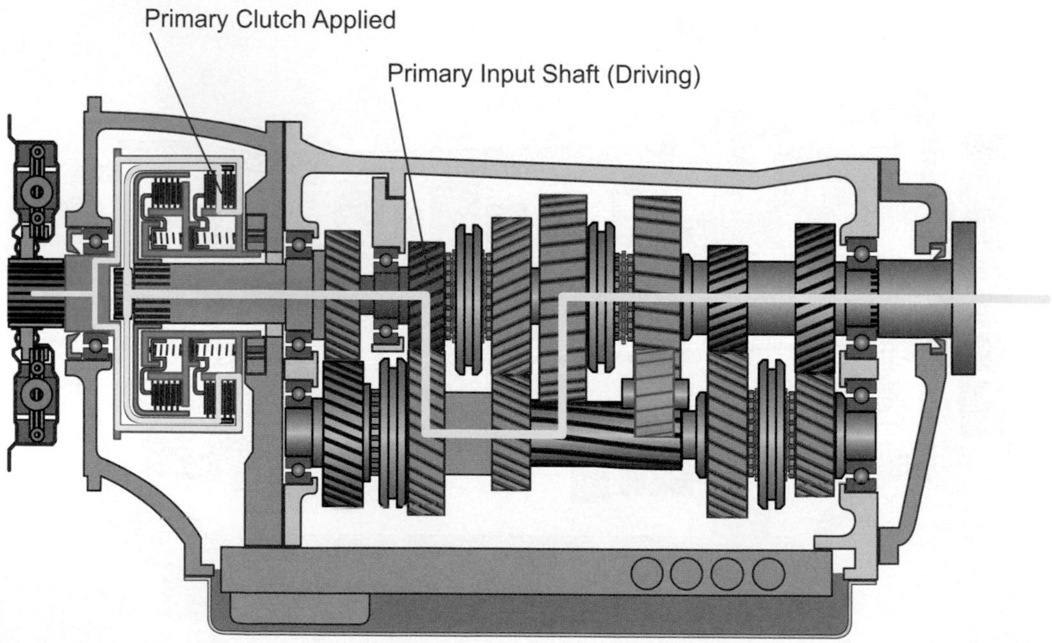

FIGURE 40-34 First gear power flow in Procision transmission.

synchronizer. Next, the power is delivered to the reverse idler gear from the countershaft. Finally, power flows to the reverse main shaft gear, which is locked to the main shaft by the first–reverse sliding collar.

First gear: When the driver selects first range, the first synchronizer on the countershaft moves rearward and locks the second countershaft driven gear to the countershaft. The first and reverse sliding collar on the main shaft moves forward, locking first gear to the main shaft, as illustrated in FIGURE 40-34. When the driver releases the brake, the primary clutch partially engages to provide urge to move and hill-hold capability for a short period. As the driver steps on the throttle, the primary clutch engages fully and the power flows from the primary clutch to the primary input gear and from there to the countershaft through the second countershaft driven gear, which is locked to the countershaft by the first–seventh synchronizer. Then power flows from the countershaft to the first speed gear, which is locked to the main shaft by the sliding collar.

Second gear: To achieve second gear, the transmission does not have to shift any gears or synchronizers; it merely switches the applied wet clutches. The primary wet clutch is disengaged, and the secondary wet clutch is engaged. The synchronizer and the sliding collar engagement as noted in first gear remain the same. The primary clutch is released and the secondary clutch is applied with no torque interruption. This then sends the power from the secondary wet clutch, to the secondary input gear, and on to the front countershaft driven gear. Power then flows from the countershaft to the still engaged first gear on the main shaft. The difference in ratio between first and second is caused solely by the different input gear driving the countershaft. See FIGURE 40-35.

Third gear: As the vehicle continues to accelerate, the transmission will preselect third gear by moving the first–seventh synchronizer to neutral and moving the third–fifth synchronizer to the rear to engage the third gear on the main shaft. When the shift to third is made, the transmission again switches input clutches from the secondary to the primary, as illustrated in FIGURE 40-36. The power flows from the primary input gear to the second countershaft driven gear. Because that gear and countershaft third are one unit, power is sent up onto main shaft third gear. The main shaft third gear is locked to the main shaft by the third–fifth synchronizer. The countershaft is not involved in this power flow. The one-piece second countershaft driven gear and the countershaft third gear merely revolve around the countershaft.

Fourth gear: As the vehicle continues to accelerate, the transmission preselects fourth gear by moving the first–reverse sliding collar to the neutral position and

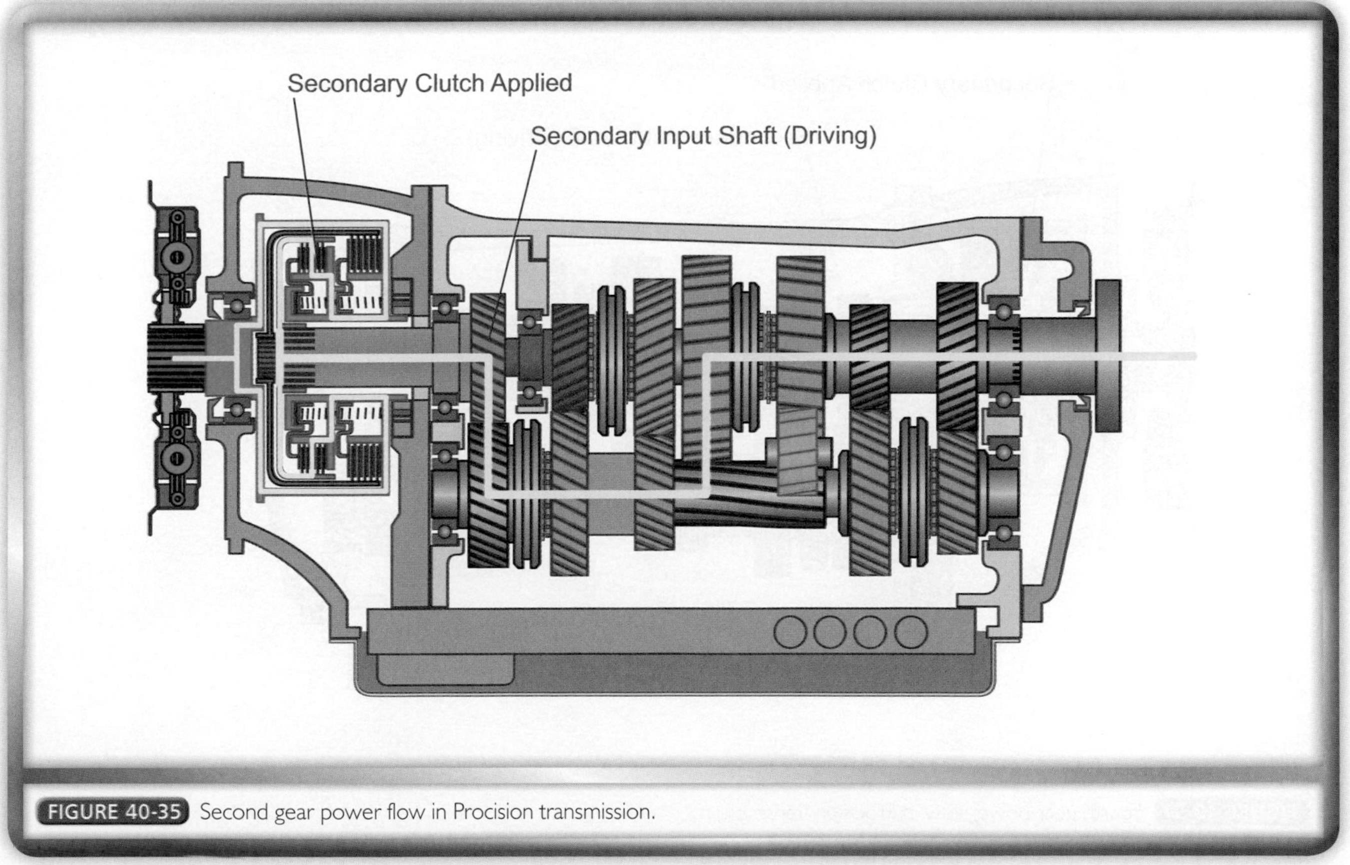

FIGURE 40-35 Second gear power flow in Procision transmission.

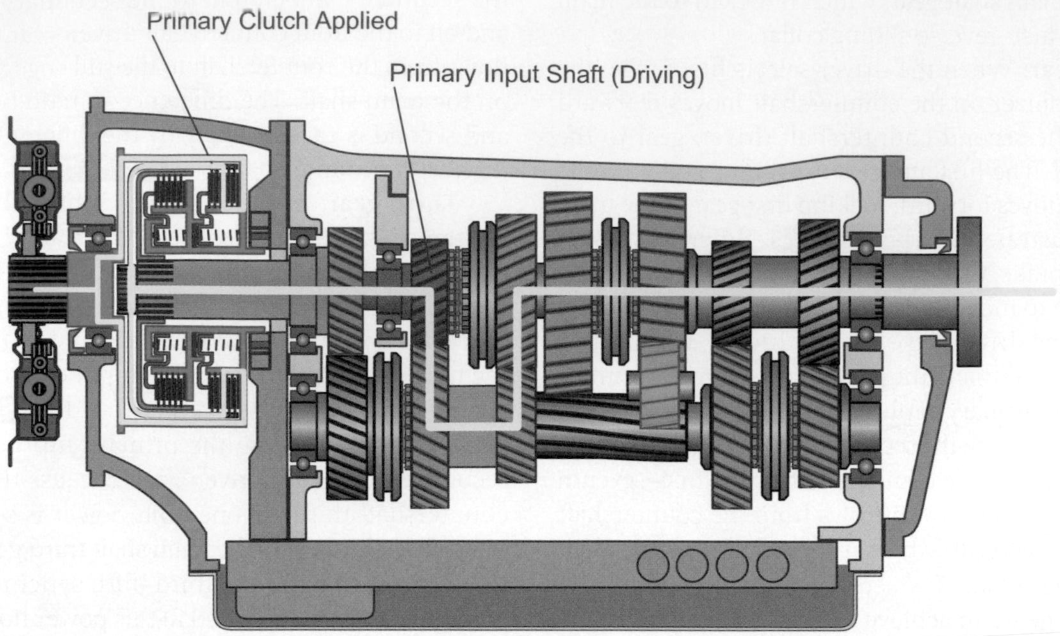

FIGURE 40-36 Third gear power flow in Procision transmission.

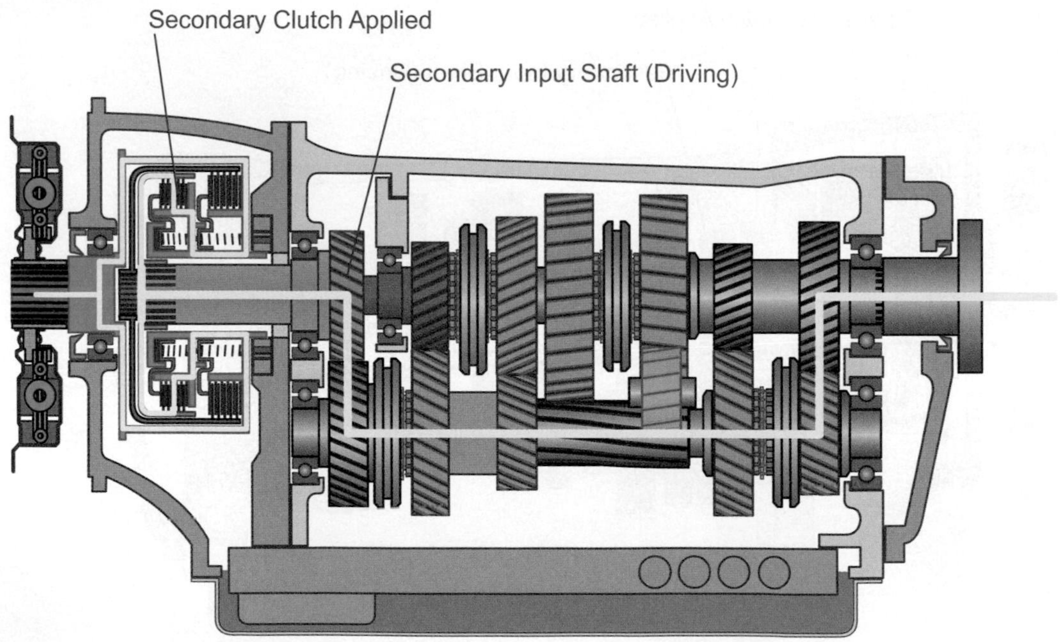

FIGURE 40-37 Fourth gear power flow in Procision transmission.

moving the fourth–sixth synchronizer to the rear to lock fourth gear countershaft to the countershaft. To actually make the shift, the transmission switches the input clutch from the primary to the secondary, as illustrated in FIGURE 40-37. The power flows from the secondary input gear to the countershaft through the front countershaft driven gear. Power then flows to the fourth countershaft gear, which is locked to the countershaft by the fourth–sixth synchronizer. Finally, power flows up to the main shaft fourth gear, which is permanently fixed to the main shaft.

Fifth gear: As the vehicle continues to accelerate, the transmission preselects fifth gear by moving the third–fifth synchronizer forward to lock the output shaft to the primary input gear. To make the shift, the transmission switches input clutches again—this time from the secondary to the primary clutch, as illustrated in FIGURE 40-38. The power is delivered to the primary input gear, which is locked to the output shaft by the third–fifth synchronizer. This power flow is direct. That is, it is a 1:1 ratio.

Sixth gear: As the vehicle continues to accelerate, the transmission preselects sixth gear by moving the fourth–sixth synchronizer forward and locking the sixth gear countershaft to the countershaft. To make the shift, again the transmission switches the input clutch; this time, however, the transmission shifts from the primary to the secondary, as illustrated in FIGURE 40-39. The power flows to the secondary input gear and to the countershaft through the front countershaft driven gear. Power continues to the countershaft sixth gear, which is locked to the countershaft by the fourth–sixth synchronizer. Finally, power travels up to the main shaft sixth gear, which is permanently fixed to the main shaft.

Seventh gear: There is no preselect for the shift to seventh gear. This is the only shift in the Procision transmission that is not a full power shift. In order for this shift to occur, the control system must break torque momentarily. The secondary clutch remains applied, and the transmission moves the fourth–sixth synchronizer to the neutral position while moving the first–seventh synchronizer rearward to lock the second countershaft driven gear to the countershaft. This process is illustrated in FIGURE 40-40. The power flows from the secondary input gear to the front countershaft driven gear. Power continues to the second countershaft driven gear, which is locked to the countershaft by the first–seventh synchronizer. Finally, power travels back up to the primary input gear, which is still locked to the output shaft by the third–fifth synchronizer.

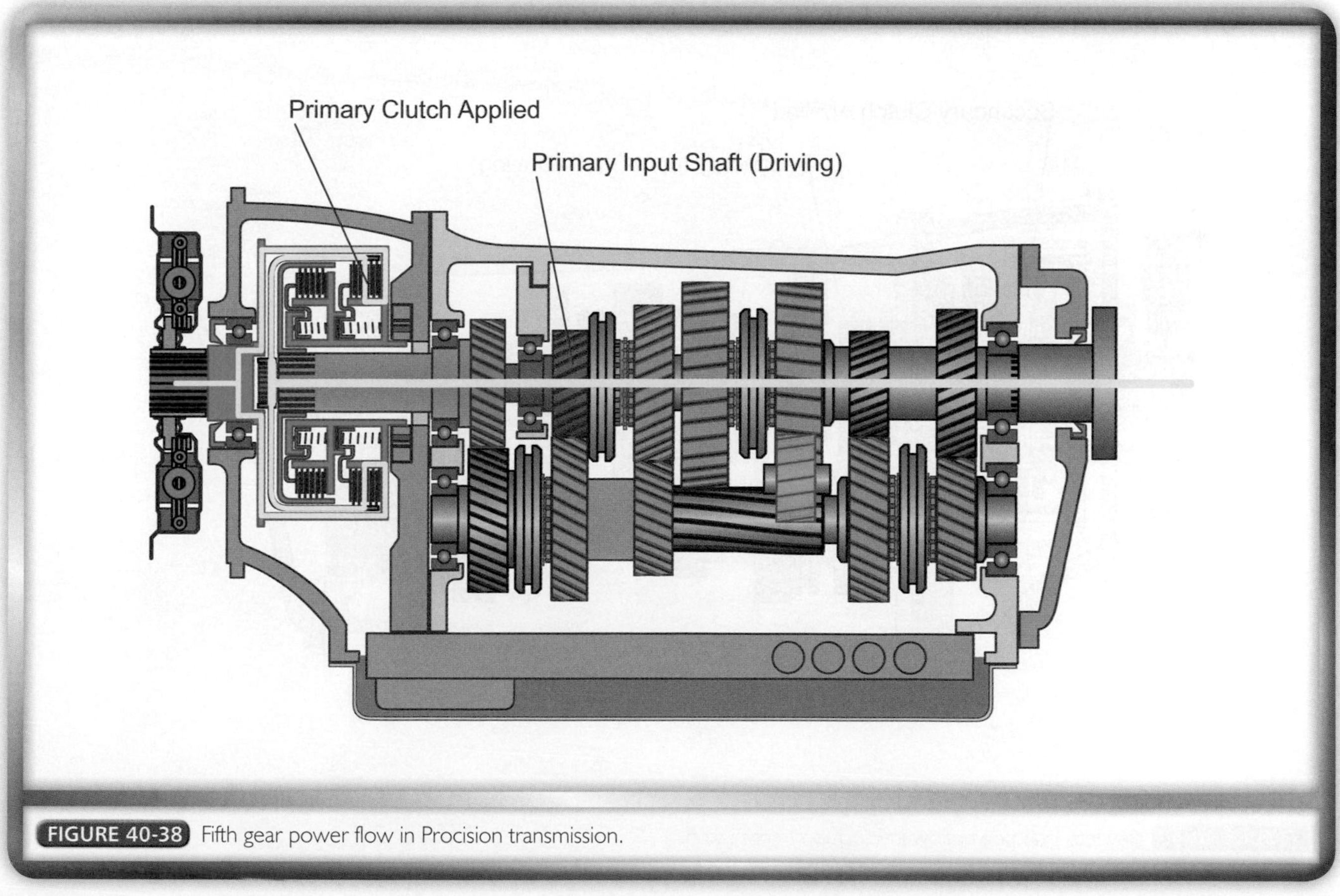

FIGURE 40-38 Fifth gear power flow in Procision transmission.

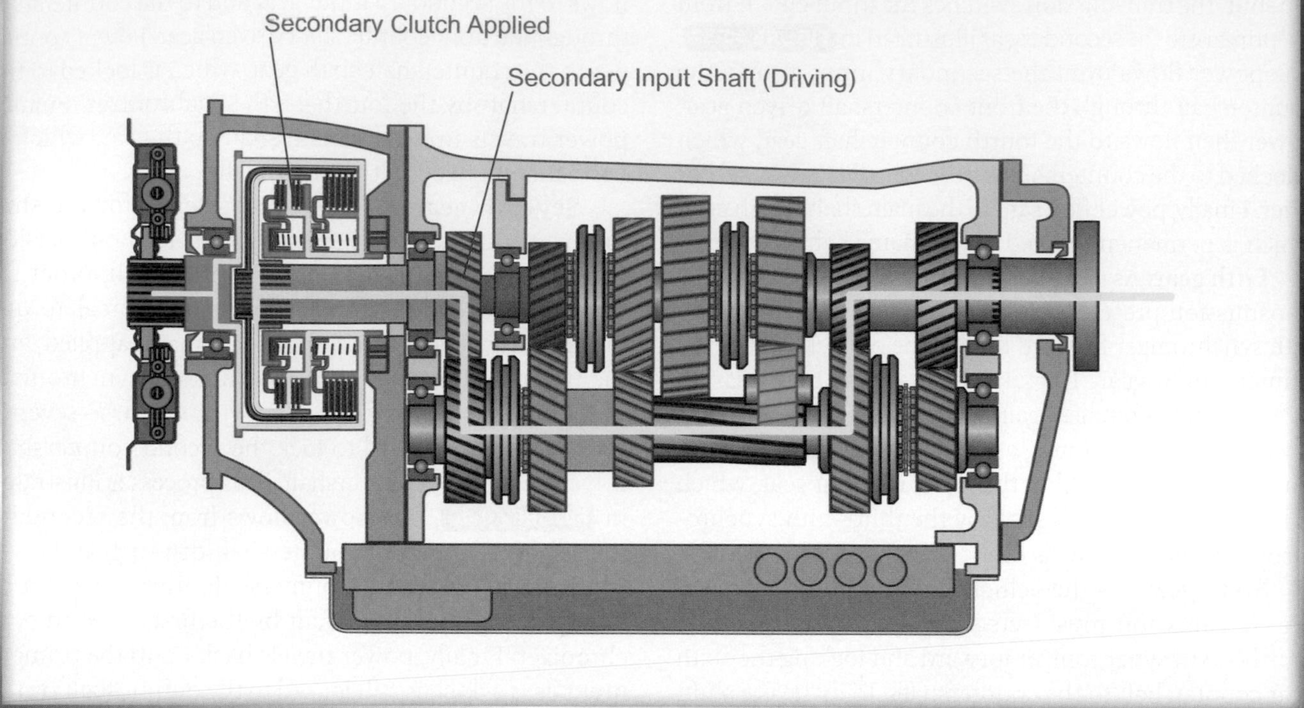

FIGURE 40-39 Sixth gear power flow in Procision transmission.

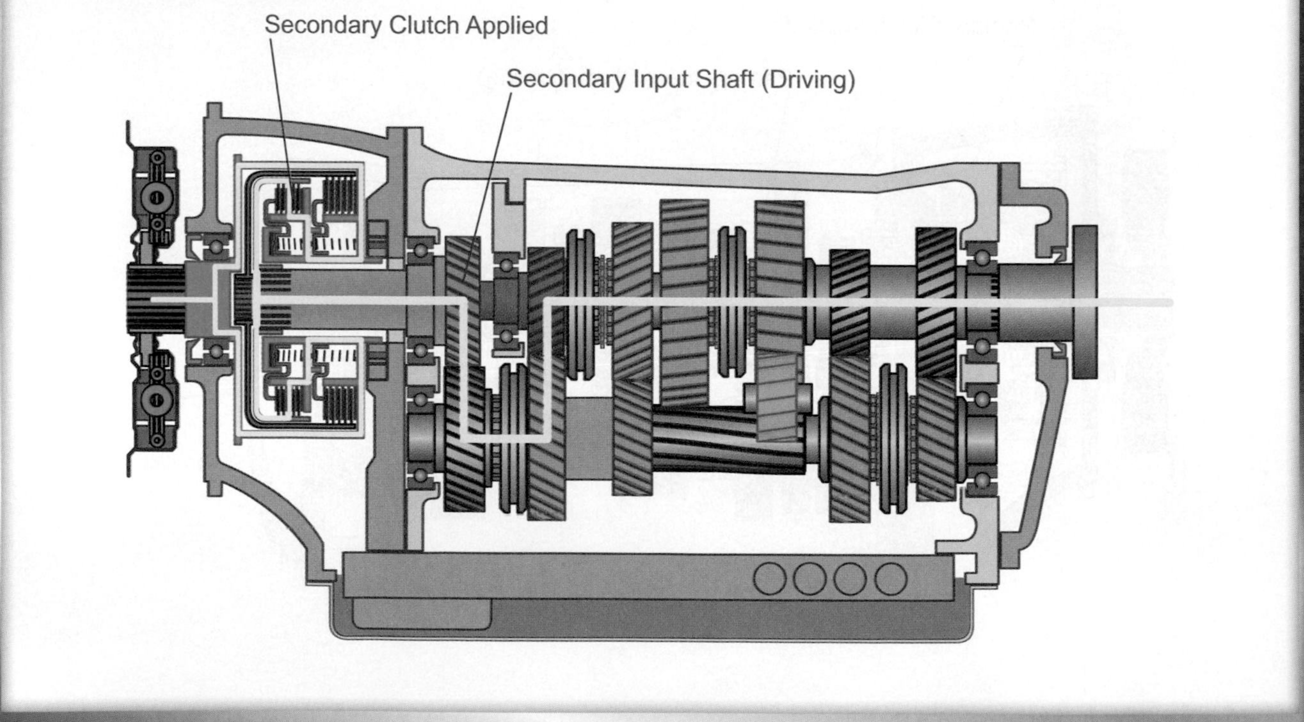

FIGURE 40-40 Seventh gear power flow in Procision transmission.

Meritor/ZF

Eaton is not the only manufacturer of electronically automated transmissions. Several other manufacturers have products on the North American market. Meritor marketed a number of automated transmissions in North America, and these were mentioned in the Introduction section of this chapter. Here we will concentrate on the transmissions Meritor marketed in partnership with ZF Friedrichshafen AG—the Freedomline and the AS-Tronic. ZF is a worldwide supplier of highly engineered and cutting edge driveline and chassis components across all transportation sectors. The ZF company name is derived from its founding business Zahnradfabrik, which means "gear manufacture" in German, and the company's home town. Its headquarters are in the town of Friedrichshafen, Germany.

ZF introduced its Freedomline of transmissions through Meritor, and Meritor was the exclusive North American supplier of the Freedomline series. In 2009, however, the partnership dissolved. ZF's truck transmission line is now known in the United States and in other parts of the world by two names depending on vocation. ZF's AS-Tronic line is for light-, medium-, and heavy-duty applications. The TC-Tronic version with torque converter is used for heavy truck applications and is primarily marketed in Europe.

The AS-Tronic is available in three basic formats: a twelve-speed, a twelve-speed with overdrive, and a 16-speed overdrive version. These are twin countershaft, heavy-duty transmissions capable of accepting up to 1,650 ft-lb (2,237 Nm) of input torque. They come equipped with a 17" (43.2 cm) organic-faced, single disc, self-adjusting clutch that is operated by the transmission electronic controller otherwise known as the ZF Meritor Transmission Electronic Controller (ZMTEC). After the split with Meritor, the controller is now called ZTEC. The transmission controller (ZTEC) controls the flow of air to an air cylinder that actuates the clutch. The state of clutch adjustment is monitored every time the clutch is disengaged and engaged. An indicator on the dash tells the driver when clutch replacement is required. The clutch is equipped with a permanently lubricated release bearing, so no maintenance is required until clutch replacement.

As illustrated in FIGURE 40-41, the ZF transmission is modular in design with an input splitter section, a three-speed main shaft section, and a planetary range section. Initial input to the countershaft from the input shaft is channeled through a splitter gear set at the front of the transmission. The front splitter gear is low split.

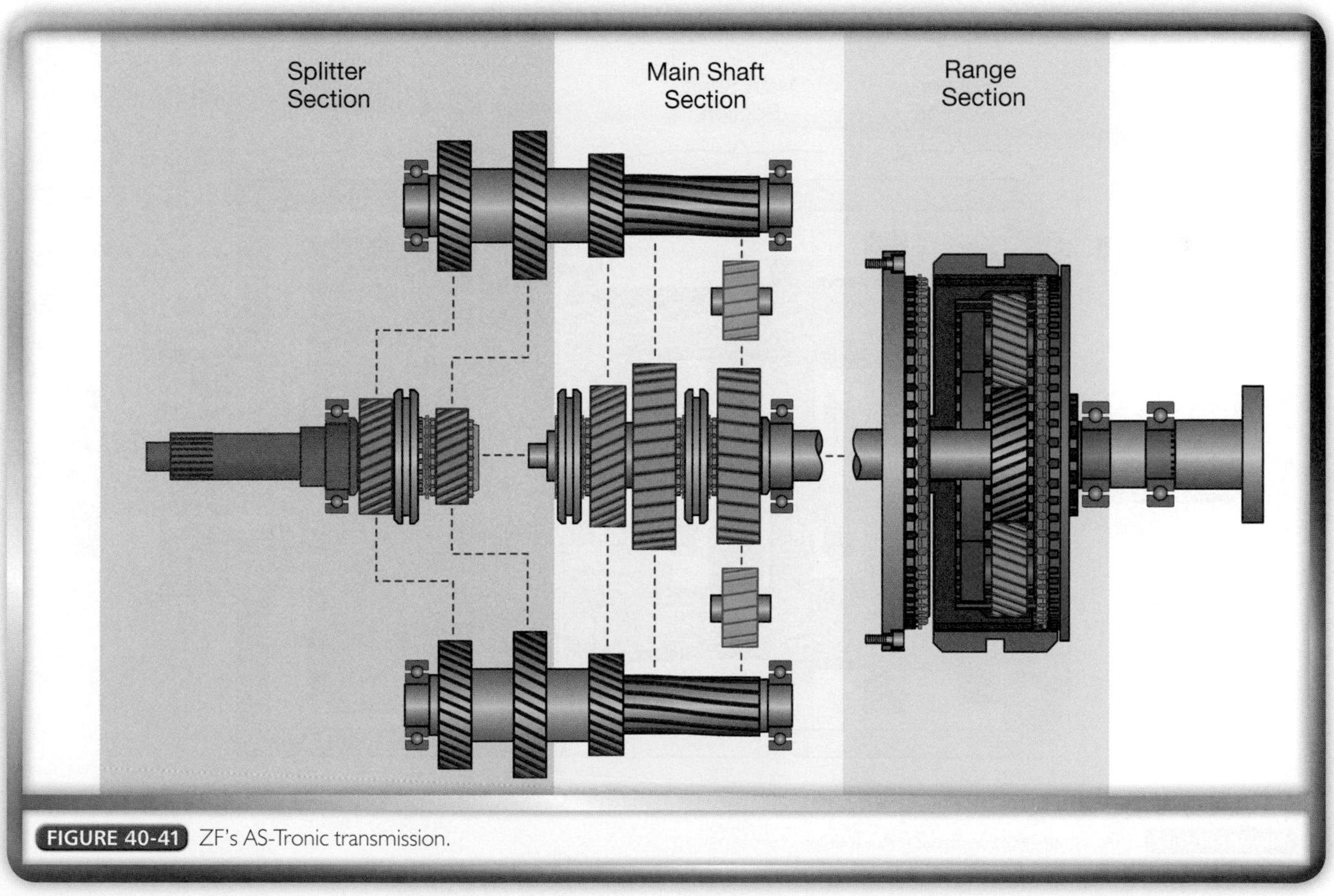

FIGURE 40-41 ZF's AS-Tronic transmission.

In non-overdrive models, the rear splitter gear is high split. In overdrive models, the front splitter is the high (overdrive) gear and the rear splitter gear is the low split. After the splitter gear set, the power is delivered to both countershafts.

In twelve-speed models, the main shaft has only two forward drive gears plus reverse. In 16-speed models, the main shaft has only three forward speed gears, plus reverse. From the main shaft, the power is delivered to a planetary range gear set in the rear of the transmission. The rear planetary gear set provides low range by inputting the sun gear, holding the ring gear and the carrier of the planetary gear set becomes output. In high range, the power passes through the planetary gear set unchanged. As illustrated in **FIGURE 40-42**, the ZF design uses each main shaft gear four times—twice in low range and twice in high range.

The ZTEC controls shifting by using solenoids to control three air cylinders and a gate or fork selector that are integral with the transmission top cover. The air cylinders control gear selection and range and splitter shifts. The four solenoid controlled air actuators, illustrated in **FIGURE 40-43**, position the shift rails when a ZF transmission shifts.

Power flows in the AS-Tronic are relatively simple. Each main shaft gear is used four times. Take the twelve-speed non overdrive model as an example:

- In first range, power is delivered to the countershafts through the low split gear set and delivered to the first gear main shaft. Power than passes through the planetary gear set in low range.
- To move to second range, the splitter gear set is shifted to the high split gear set.
- The third range returns input to the low split gear set. The second gear main shaft is selected and power passes once again through the planetary gear set in low range.
- For fourth range, the splitter gear is shifted to high split again.
- For fifth range, again the splitter gear set is shifted to low split. This time, however, the main shaft is connected to the back of the rear splitter gear set and the countershaft speed gears are not used. Once more, the power flows through low range in the planetary range set.
- For sixth range, the splitter gear is shifted to high split. This puts the front section of the transmission

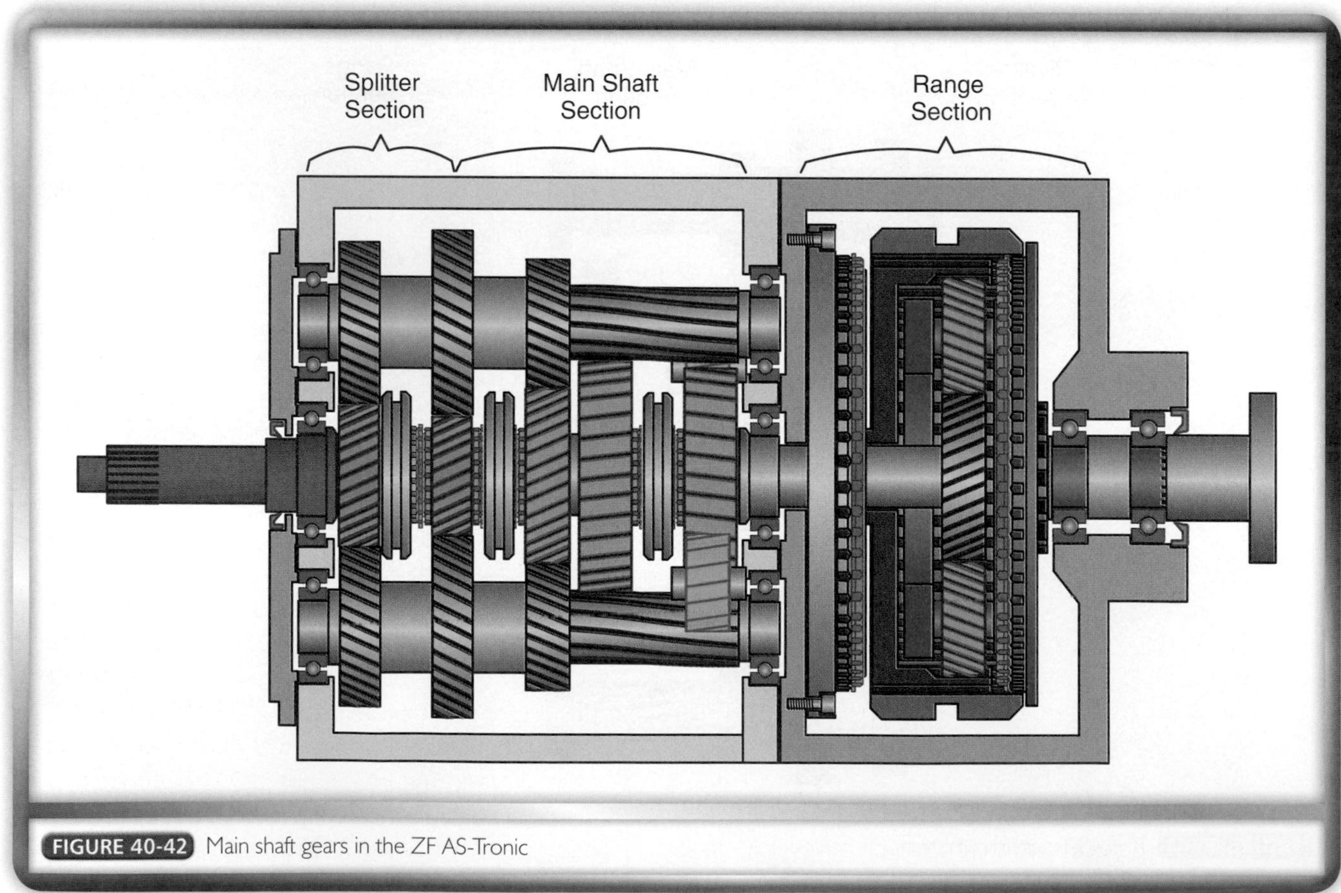

FIGURE 40-42 Main shaft gears in the ZF AS-Tronic

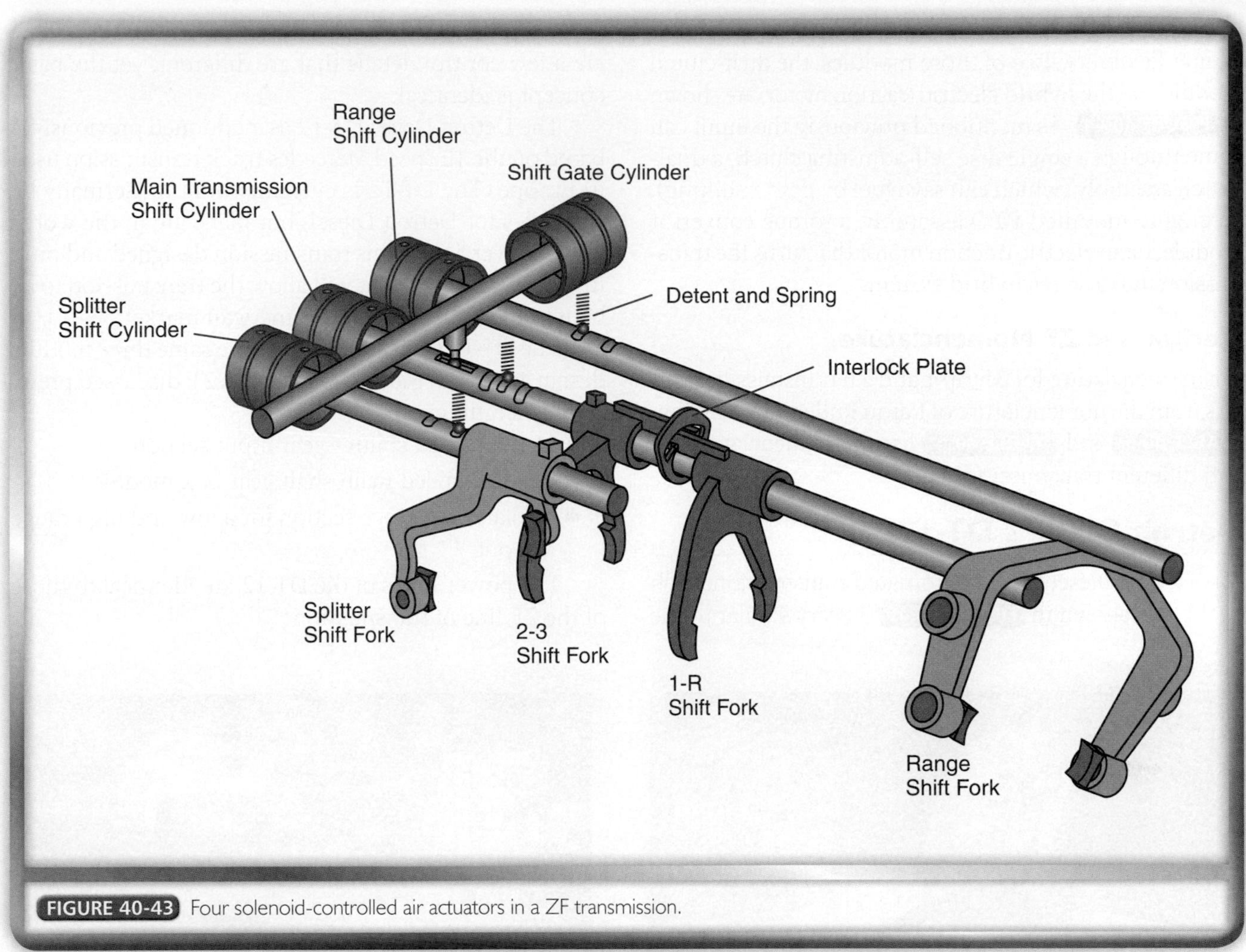

FIGURE 40-43 Four solenoid-controlled air actuators in a ZF transmission.

into direct range. In other words, the input is connected to the front side of the rear splitter gear, and the main shaft is connected to the rear of the gear. The power, however, is still flowing from the main shaft through the low range of the planetary section.

- For seventh range, the planetary range section is put into high range, or direct. At that point, power passes through the range section unchanged. The front section of the transmission repeats the exact same sequence as above from first to sixth range, ending up with twelve forward ranges in total.

The only difference between the 12- and 16-speed models is that the 16-speed model merely utilizes one more forward speed gear on the main shaft and a matching gear on each of the countershafts. Each speed is still used four times—low and high split in low range and low and high split in high range. To achieve overdrive, the splitter gear ratios are changed so that the low split set is the rear splitter gear and the front splitter gear is an overdrive gear set.

The only difference in the power flow just described is that the rear splitter gear set is used first and the front split gear set is used second. These ZF transmissions use a two-pedal design, so there is no clutch pedal. Therefore, the transmission can operate totally automatically or can be switched to manual by the driver if desired. As with all automated transmissions, though, the transmission has mechanisms to prevent abusive operation by the driver. The AS-Tronic transmission works to optimize shifting strategies for all road, load, and driver conditions.

ZF also produces a heavy-duty twelve-speed overdrive transmission with a torque converter called the TC-Tronic. Its operating principles are the same as those of the AS-Tronic with the exception of the torque converter. The inclusion of a torque converter allows for extremely smooth take-offs as well as torque multiplication and is primarily intended for use with very heavy equipment. The converter is equipped with a lock-up clutch to eliminate any losses due to converter slip.

The latest offering from ZF is the Traxon with optional input modules. This system allows the customer to select from five different input modules, which allows much greater flexibility. Two of those modules, the dual-clutch module and the hybrid electric traction motor, are shown in FIGURE 40-44. As mentioned previously, the input can come through a single disc self-adjusting clutch, a dual-clutch assembly (which can save fuel by power shifting), an engine-mounted PTO assembly, a torque convertor module, or an electric traction motor that turns the transmission into a series hybrid system.

Meritor and ZF Nomenclature

The nomenclature for Meritor and ZF transmissions differs from the nomenclature of Eaton Fuller transmission. TABLE 40-5 and TABLE 40-6 list the nomenclature for two different transmissions.

Detroit Diesel's DT-12

The Detroit Diesel DT-12 automated transmission, such as the one shown in FIGURE 40-45, is very similar to the ZF AS-Tronic described in the Meritor/ZF section. There are a few control details that are different, yet the basic concept is identical.

The Detroit Deisel DT-12 as mentioned previously is based on the 12 speed Mercedes truck transmission used in Europe. The DT-12 is currently built in Germany by Mercedes for Detroit Diesel, but plans are in the works to have a version of this transmission designed and built in North America. That will allow the transmission to be better tailored to the North American market.

The DT-12 transmission uses the same three module design as used in the AC-Tronic from ZF discussed previously, including:

- A two-speed splitter gear input section
- A three-speed main shaft gear box module
- A planetary range section for a low and high range output

The power flows of the DT-12 are identical to those of the ZF line of transmissions.

FIGURE 40-44 The dual-clutch module (left) and hybrid electric traction motor (right) for ZF Traxon transmissions.

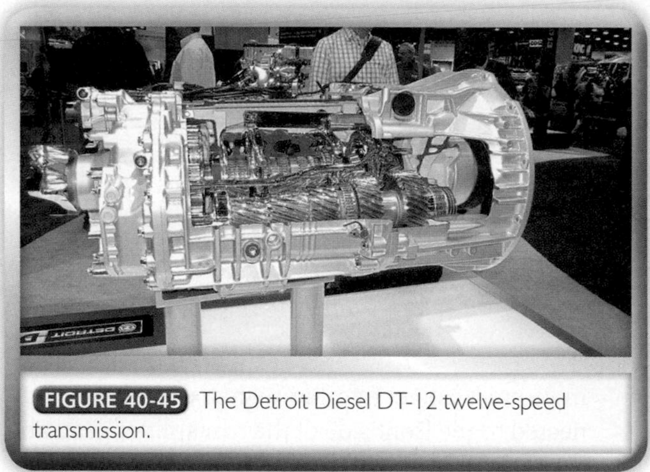

FIGURE 40-45 The Detroit Diesel DT-12 twelve-speed transmission.

TABLE 40-5: Nomenclature for Meritor RMX10-165-C2S002

R	M	X	10	165	C	2	S	002
Rockwell	M=manual S=ESS	X=overdrive no letter=Direct	# of forward speeds	Torque rating × 10	Ratio	Design level	Shift tower position	OEM specification

TABLE 40-6: Nomenclature for ZF O-16G10C-E18002

M	O	16	G	10	C	E	18	002
ZF Meritor	O=Overdrive no letter=direct	Torque rating X 100 + 50	Design platform	Forward speeds	Ratio	A=fully automated D=ESS/DDC E=ESS/ZF M=Manual S=SureShift	Highest torque in transmission × 100 + 50	OEM specification

Volvo Trucks' I-Shift

The Volvo I-Shift, shown in FIGURE 40-46, automated transmission is a two-pedal dry clutch design. The massive 17" (43.2 cm) single-disc clutch, shown in FIGURE 40-47, is actuated by an air cylinder controlled by the transmission control unit (TCU). The transmission design is very similar to the ZF transmission. One key difference, however, is that the Volvo I-Shift uses only one countershaft. Like the ZF, the Volvo transmission has a two-speed input splitter section, a three-speed main shaft section, and a planetary range section. Therefore, the main shaft gears are utilized four times each in total: twice in low range through the planetary range section; and twice in high range—for a total of 12 forward speeds.

Although the I-Shift uses a single countershaft design, it has a dual-path input system to split input torque to the countershaft for increased capacity. Shifting is accomplished by electric solenoids controlling air shifters that are integral to the transmission shift cover. This design is, again, quite similar to that of the ZF. The I-Shift transmission is available in four different models, two of which have overdrive and two of which do not:

- AT2512C—Direct Drive for Volvo D11 and D13 Engines
- ATO2512C—Overdrive for Volvo D11 and D13 Engines
- AT2812C—Direct Drive for Volvo D16 Engines
- ATO3112C—Overdrive for Volvo D16 Engines.

The transmission has adaptive shift control. Several selectable shift strategies allow the driver to optimize either performance or fuel economy—or combinations of the two. For example, strategies include:

- B = Basic
- EB = Enhanced Basic
- FE = Fuel Economy
- P = Performance
- CO = Comprehensive.

As with all automated transmissions, Volvo's transmissions can also be operated in manual mode if desired. The I-Shift controller is shown in FIGURE 40-48. Notice the "M" position for manual control.

Volvo has recently released the new twelve-speed overdrive dual-clutch I-Shift. Introduced in September 2014, the new transmission has two dry-friction input clutches. The transmission design is similar to the regular I-shift. Instead of the input going to a splitter at the front of the transmission, however, each of the clutches drive a separate input shaft, a solid inner shaft, and a hollow outer shaft. FIGURE 40-49 is a simplified diagram of the front section of the I-shift dual-clutch transmission. (The planetary range system is not shown in the diagram.)

Gear selector synchronizers are used alternately on the output shaft and on the countershaft. The two main shaft gears are driven by the countershaft either through the primary or the secondary input shafts. That allows for

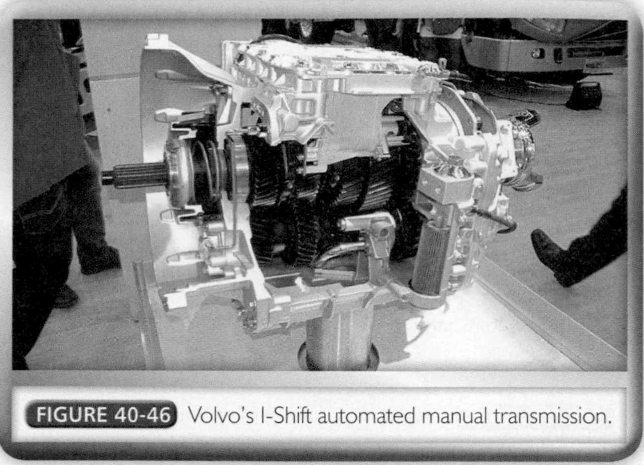

FIGURE 40-46 Volvo's I-Shift automated manual transmission.

FIGURE 40-47 The I-Shift uses a large, 17" (43.2 cm), organic-faced, single-disc clutch.

FIGURE 40-48 Volvo's I-Shift shift controller.

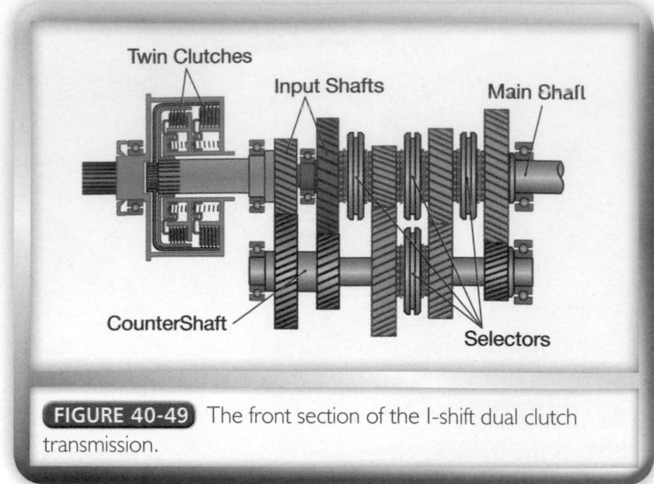

FIGURE 40-49 The front section of the I-shift dual clutch transmission.

FIGURE 40-50 Volvo I-Shift nameplate.

four different ratios. A fifth ratio can be achieved when the main shaft is driven directly by the primary input shaft when the output shaft is connected to it. With the primary input shaft connected to the output shaft, the transmission can reach a sixth ratio by switching to the secondary input clutch and driving the primary input shaft through the secondary input shaft and the countershaft.

All of those ratios pass through a planetary range gear system. That makes for six forward ratios in the low range of the planetary range system. The same six ratios are repeated in high range when the planetary range system allows the power flow to pass through unchanged. That brings the total to twelve forward ratios.

All of the transmission shifts are power shifts with no torque break except for the range shift between sixth and seventh. Compared to its traditional I-Shift, Volvo claims the new I-Shift has increased cycle time from faster shifts and improved fuel economy. Volvo's twin clutch model number is the SPO2812. It is capable of handling up to 2,065 ft-lb (2,800 Nm) of torque.

Volvo Transmission Nomenclature

As expected, Volvo has unique nomenclature for its transmissions. FIGURE 40-50 shows a Volvo nameplate, and TABLE 40-7 shows how to decipher the naming convention.

Mercedes Benz/Daimler Trucks Automatic Gear Shift

Mercedes Benz, known in North America as Daimler Trucks, has introduced two transmissions into the electronically automated transmission market since 2004. Both transmissions are Automatic Gear Shift (AGS) models—the MBT520-6DA and the MBT660-6OA. Both transmissions are six-speed models with a maximum input torque of 520 and 660 ft-lb (705 and 895 Nm) respectively. The MBT520-6DA is a direct drive model and has a maximum GVW of 40,000 lb (18,144 kg). The MBT660-6OA is an overdrive model capable of a maximum GVW of 60,000 lb (27,216 kg) and a final ratio of 73:1. Their overall gear ratio is 9.2:1 and 9.18:1 respectively. An AGS transmission is shown in FIGURE 40-51.

Regardless of model, the AGS transmission is a two-pedal design. The self-adjusting hydraulically actuated clutch is controlled electronically, and the release bearing is of the permanently lubricated type to reduce maintenance.

AGS transmissions are a completely self-contained package. They come equipped with an on-board TCU attached to the central unit that incorporates the following components:

- An attached fluid reservoir to hold the hydraulic actuating fluid for the transmission

TABLE 40-7: Nomenclature for Volvo ATO2512C

AT	O	XX	12	C
Automated mechanical transmission	Overdrive No letter = Direct	Max input torque Nm (ft-lbt) 25= 2,500 (1,850) 28=2,800 (2,050) 31=3,100(2,300)	twelve-speed	Design level

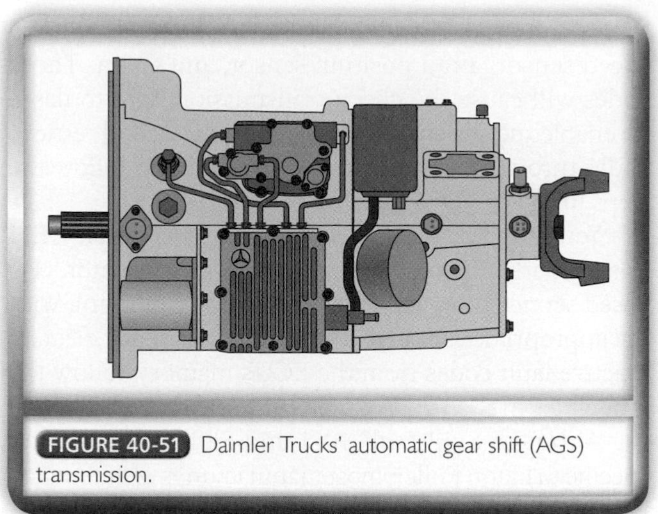

FIGURE 40-51 Daimler Trucks' automatic gear shift (AGS) transmission.

- A high pressure electric fluid pump that pressurizes fluid to 1,247 psi (8,598 kPa)
- A control valve body that holds the 12-volt electric solenoid valves that direct the flow of hydraulic fluid to operate the transmission
- A fluid accumulator that stores fluid under pressure even when the vehicle is shut down
- A hydraulically controlled X/Y shifter module that selects shift rail and gear position
- The control solenoid for the hydraulic clutch actuator (the clutch actuator is a release bearing with an integral hydraulic cylinder mounted on the transmission input shaft)

AGS transmissions also have the following sensors:

- Clutch position sensor
- Rail position sensor
- Shift rod position sensor
- Hydraulic fluid level sensor
- Input shaft speed sensor
- Two output shaft speed sensors

The TCU communicates with the engine ECU over the J-1939 data link to request torque break when a shift is required or to accelerate the engine during down shifting. The TCU communicates J-1587 fault codes when there is a system malfunction. These codes will always have several identifiers, including:

- Message identifier (MID); MID 130 identifies the transmission
- Subsystem identifier (SID)
- Parameter identifier (PID)
- Failure mode identifier (FMI) for the detected fault

The AGS series of transmissions are capable of adaptive learning and shift strategy adjustment based on vehicle load, road grade, and driver style. The transmission is able to provide changing shift schedules to optimize fuel economy and vehicle performance.

In North America, the AGS is available on Detroit Diesel, Freightliner, and Sterling trucks. Nomenclature for the MBT660-6OA is given in TABLE 40-8.

Safety

The Mercedes Benz AGS series of transmissions operates at extremely high hydraulic pressure—up to 1,247 psi (8,598 kPa). The accumulator holds this pressure even when the vehicle is not operating. Technicians unfamiliar with this transmission must consult the OEM service manual before attempting any system repairs. Inadvertent release of pressure at this level could cause fluid injection injuries, leading to serious medical problems and or death. The OEM manual has procedures to reduce the pressure before working on the transmission. Those procedures should be followed to the letter!

Troubleshooting Automated Manual Transmissions

Troubleshooting an automated transmission fault should be done in a logical sequence. First, find as much information as you can about the complaint from the driver. Then, verify the complaint. Overlooking this step has

TABLE 40-8: Nomenclature for Daimler Trucks' AGS model MBT660-6OA

MBT	660	6	O	A
Mercedes Benz Transmission	Input torque	Forward speeds	O= Overdrive D = Direct	Automatic

sent many a technician on a wild goose chase to find non-existent complaints!

Once you have established the complaint does exist, rule out any mechanical causes for the complaint, such as air system problems or transmission mechanical problems. Most AMTs will have a way to manually display fault codes.

To retrieve fault codes in an Eaton Fuller automated manual transmission, start by enabling the system's self-diagnostic mode. Alternatively, use an OEM or aftermarket electronic service tool such as Eaton's PC-based service tool, ServiceRanger, or MPSI Prolink. Be sure the appropriate cartridge is installed. Note that on Eaton Fuller's Gen 1 and Gen 2 transmissions, electronics do not flash the service transmission light for system codes, only for component codes.

Examples of system codes are the front box control system, the splitter control system, or the engine control system. System codes may or may not be associated with a recognizable symptom when they are set, but the check transmission light will not flash. Component codes are set for component problems such as the range valve, a speed sensor, a rail position sensor, and so on. Those codes will cause the check transmission light to flash. To enable the system's self-diagnostic mode and retrieve codes through the check transmission light, follow the steps in SKILL DRILL 40-1.

You can clear inactive fault codes by using an OEM or aftermarket Electronic Service tool such as Eaton's PC based service tool, ServiceRanger, or MPSI Prolink with the appropriate cartridge installed. To manually clear all inactive fault codes from the ECU's memory, follow the guidelines in SKILL DRILL 40-2.

Although Skill Drill 40-1 and Skill Drill 40-2 are specific to Eaton Fuller, most manufacturers of automated transmissions have similar procedures for reading and clearing fault code information. If the transmission is displaying a fault code, consult the manufacturer's fault code listing in the troubleshooting manual. Follow the fault code trouble tree.

The fault code trouble tree is a step-by-step method of diagnosing and repairing the fault. The Eaton Fuller

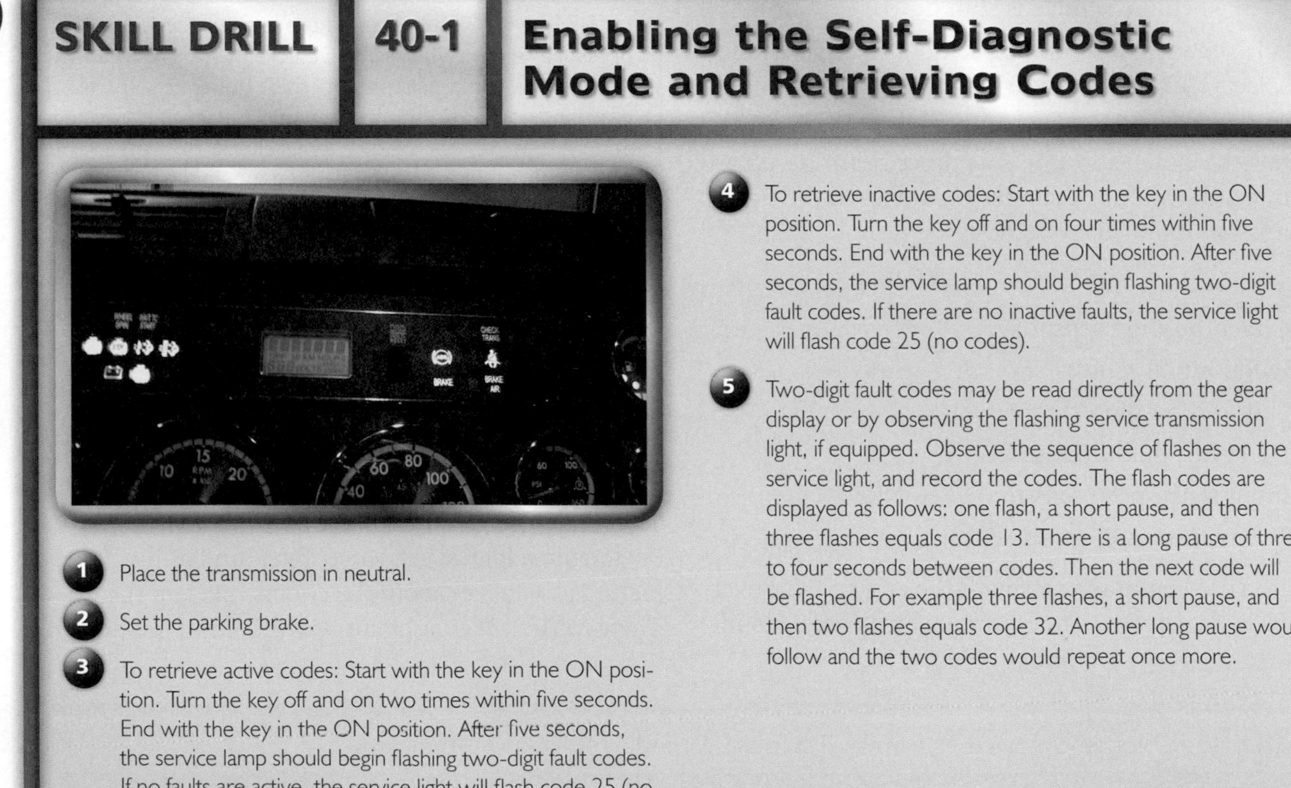

SKILL DRILL 40-1 Enabling the Self-Diagnostic Mode and Retrieving Codes

1. Place the transmission in neutral.
2. Set the parking brake.
3. To retrieve active codes: Start with the key in the ON position. Turn the key off and on two times within five seconds. End with the key in the ON position. After five seconds, the service lamp should begin flashing two-digit fault codes. If no faults are active, the service light will flash code 25 (no codes). Note: A code 88 may show up in the dash at key ON. That is a normal power-up test of the display.
4. To retrieve inactive codes: Start with the key in the ON position. Turn the key off and on four times within five seconds. End with the key in the ON position. After five seconds, the service lamp should begin flashing two-digit fault codes. If there are no inactive faults, the service light will flash code 25 (no codes).
5. Two-digit fault codes may be read directly from the gear display or by observing the flashing service transmission light, if equipped. Observe the sequence of flashes on the service light, and record the codes. The flash codes are displayed as follows: one flash, a short pause, and then three flashes equals code 13. There is a long pause of three to four seconds between codes. Then the next code will be flashed. For example three flashes, a short pause, and then two flashes equals code 32. Another long pause would follow and the two codes would repeat once more.

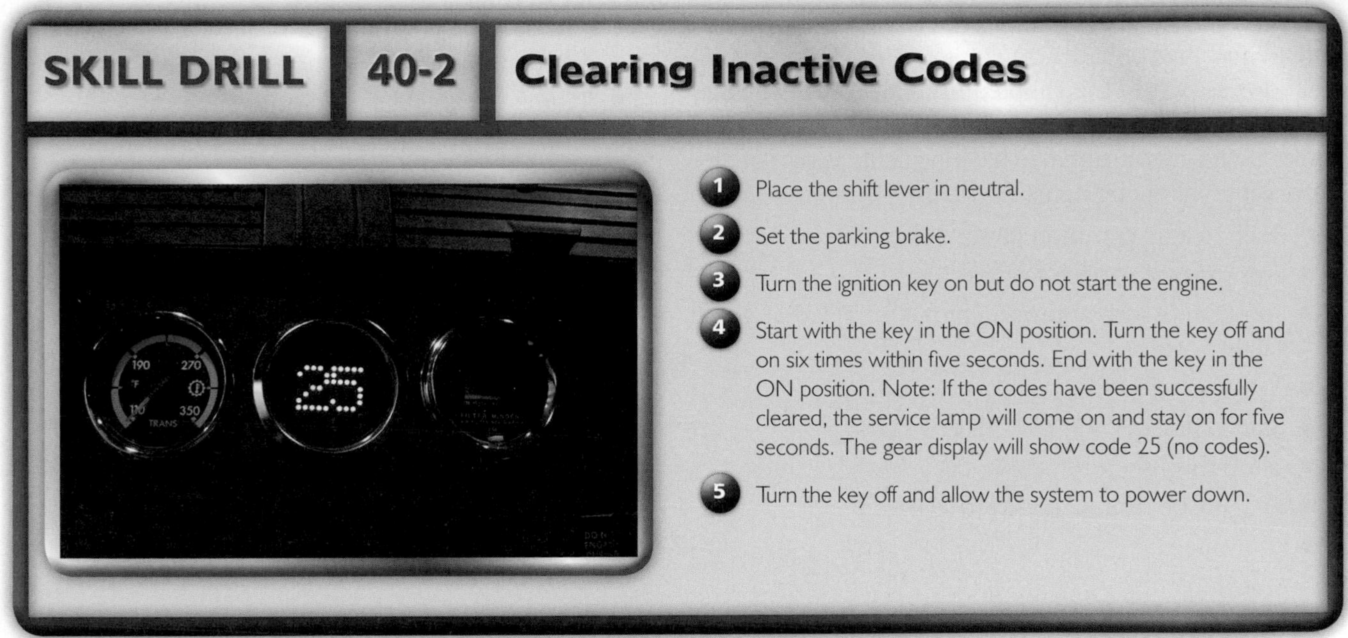

SKILL DRILL 40-2 Clearing Inactive Codes

1. Place the shift lever in neutral.
2. Set the parking brake.
3. Turn the ignition key on but do not start the engine.
4. Start with the key in the ON position. Turn the key off and on six times within five seconds. End with the key in the ON position. Note: If the codes have been successfully cleared, the service lamp will come on and stay on for five seconds. The gear display will show code 25 (no codes).
5. Turn the key off and allow the system to power down.

fault code chart lists 54 separate codes, so trying to go through them here would simply take up too much space. Manufacturers have spent millions of dollars setting up trouble trees and fault- and symptom-based diagnosis systems for their products. The best method of troubleshooting complaints is to follow manufacturer recommendations.

> **TECHNICIAN TIP**
>
> Failure to follow the trouble tree to the letter, or skipping steps, is simply a waste of your time and the vehicle owner's time. Do not be tempted to jump ahead when using a trouble tree. If you do, it is more than likely that you will end up having to start all over again.

> **TECHNICIAN TIP**
>
> You can find the OEM manuals, troubleshooting manuals, and fault code guides for Eaton Fuller transmissions on the company website at www.roadranger.com. Meritor information can be found at www.meritor.com For other automated transmissions, contact the manufacturer. There is no substitute for the OEM manual. If you cannot access one, then you would be advised not to take on the repair job.

Using a Diagnostic (Scan) Tool to Diagnose Transmissions

Using electronic diagnostic equipment to troubleshoot components has become a necessity in today's industry. Because you will work with many different diagnostic tools, it is important to locate the correct service manual procedure before attempting to retrieve trouble codes. A laptop computer, a hand-held diagnostic tool, or an on-board diagnostic component are the most common diagnostic trouble code retrieval systems. The two types of trouble codes are active and inactive. These two types of codes tell the technician what has taken place in the system. A digital multimeter is normally used to test the area where the fault code indicates that the malfunction has occurred. As you can see, it is important that a diesel technician in today's high-tech world be proficient at using electronic diagnostic tools to retrieve trouble codes and troubleshooting electronic systems.

Every technician's toolkit should contain the basic hand tools for the tasks to be undertaken, such as appropriately sized wrenches and socket sets, screwdrivers, hammers, and pliers. These items let technicians undertake the normal day-to-day activities associated with their position. In addition, special tools are always required to perform particular tasks on specific manufacturer equipment.

These are normally provided by the company the technician works for and may be, in some cases, hired in from tool suppliers because of their specialist nature. Other equipment, such as safety items, is normally provided for as part of the shop equipment. Whatever the case, before attempting a specific task on a vehicle or its components, it is essential to have available as part of the process the following items:

- Technician's common hand tools
- Appropriate service manual
- Job ticket—use appropriate one provided at your facility
- Wheel chocks
- Safety glasses
- Shop towels
- Diagnostic trouble code retrieval tool
- Multimeter
- Diagnostic equipment
- Tachometer
- Temperature gauge
- Other equipment and supplies as required by procedure

> **TECHNICIAN TIP**
>
> **Procedures vary with different types of vehicles. Always check the procedure in the service manual before beginning any service or repair.**

To use a diagnostic tool and procedure to diagnose automated transmission problems, follow the guidelines in SKILL DRILL 40-3.

SKILL DRILL 40-3 Using a Scan Tool to Diagnose Transmissions

1. Locate and follow the appropriate procedure in the service manual.
2. Complete the accompanying job sheet or work order with all pertinent information.
3. Move the vehicle into the shop and park it on level ground.
4. Apply parking brakes, chock the vehicle wheels, and observe lockout/tagout procedures.
5. If the vehicle has a manual transmission, place it in neutral; if it has an automatic or automated transmission, place it in park or neutral. Note: Some vehicles with automatic transmissions do not have park.
6. Check for active and inactive trouble codes using the appropriate service manual procedure and diagnostic tool.
7. Record any displayed trouble codes on the job sheet or work order.
8. Use a multimeter to verify the problem(s) associated with the trouble code(s).
9. Record all diagnostic readings.
10. Repair or replace the affected systems or components.
11. Clear all inactive and active trouble codes.
12. List the test results and/or recommendations on the job sheet or work order, clean the work area, and return tools and materials to their proper storage.

Servicing Electronic Shift Selectors, Air and Electrical Switches, Displays and Indicators, and Wiring Harnesses

To inspect, adjust, repair or replace electronic shift selectors, air and electrical switches, displays and indicators, and wiring harnesses, follow the guidelines in **SKILL DRILL 40-4**.

Servicing Automated Transmission ECUs, Sensors, Vehicle Interface, and Related Components

Automated transmissions come in many different types and models, so you must locate the appropriate service manual before beginning any tests or repairs. This procedure will not address any specific transmission, but will keep instructions generic.

To inspect, adjust, repair or replace electronic shift controls, electronic control unit, wiring harnesses, sensors, control module, vehicle interface module and related components, follow the guidelines in **SKILL DRILL 40-5**.

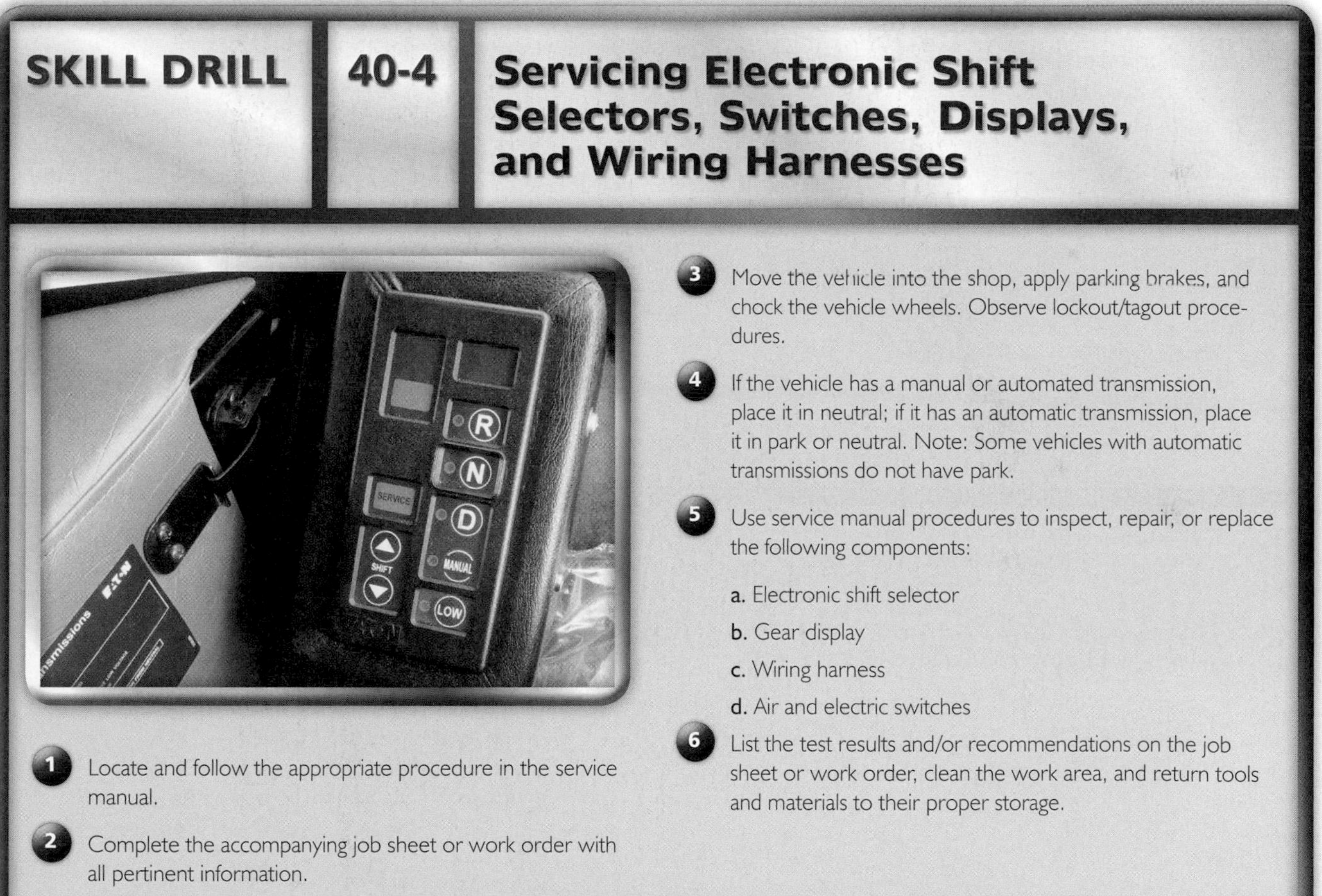

SKILL DRILL 40-4 Servicing Electronic Shift Selectors, Switches, Displays, and Wiring Harnesses

1. Locate and follow the appropriate procedure in the service manual.
2. Complete the accompanying job sheet or work order with all pertinent information.
3. Move the vehicle into the shop, apply parking brakes, and chock the vehicle wheels. Observe lockout/tagout procedures.
4. If the vehicle has a manual or automated transmission, place it in neutral; if it has an automatic transmission, place it in park or neutral. Note: Some vehicles with automatic transmissions do not have park.
5. Use service manual procedures to inspect, repair, or replace the following components:
   a. Electronic shift selector
   b. Gear display
   c. Wiring harness
   d. Air and electric switches
6. List the test results and/or recommendations on the job sheet or work order, clean the work area, and return tools and materials to their proper storage.

SKILL DRILL 40-5 Servicing Automated Transmission ECUs, Sensors, Vehicle Interface, and Related Components

1. Locate and follow the appropriate procedure in the service manual.
2. Complete the accompanying job sheet or work order with all pertinent information.
3. Move vehicle into shop, apply parking brakes and chock the vehicle wheels. Observe lockout/tagout procedures.
4. If the vehicle has a manual or automated transmission, place it in neutral; if it has an automatic transmission, place it in park or neutral. Note: Some vehicles with automatic transmissions do not have park.
5. Test the operation and retrieve diagnostic codes as outlined in the service manual.
6. Use service manual procedures to inspect, repair, or replace external/internal wiring harnesses.
7. Use service manual procedures to test, repair, or replace the following components:

   a. Electronic control unit (ECU)
   b. Vehicle interface module (VIM)
   c. Vehicle interface wiring (VIW)
   d. Engine speed sensor
   e. Transmission temperature sensor
   f. Output speed sensor
   g. Throttle position sensor
   h. Control module

8. Use service manual procedures to test, repair, or replace the electronic shift selector(s).
9. List the test results and/or recommendations on the job sheet or work order, clean the work area, and return tools and materials to their proper storage.

Wrap-up

Ready for Review

- Automated manual transmissions (AMTs) are standard mechanical transmissions adapted to computer control.
- AMTs were developed to reduce carbon dioxide emissions and to reduce fuel consumption and their development was driven by EPA-mandated reductions in exhaust emission.
- AMTs optimize shift points, leading to increases in fuel economy.
- AMTs are also a draw for new drivers because of their ease of operation and reduction in driver fatigue.
- AMTs may be three-pedal design, where the clutch is used by the driver for starting and stopping, or two-pedal design with no clutch pedal at all.
- Some newer AMTs have dual-clutch inputs that even further improve fuel economy.
- AMTs reduce driver training requirements, vehicle downtime, and vehicle driveline abuse by the driver.
- Most AMTs still require torque to be broken to complete a shift, but the newer dual-clutch models do not. Breaking torque costs fuel.
- Dual-clutch AMTs allow very quick, full-power shifting, leading to even greater fuel economy than traditional AMTs.
- Eaton Fuller's line-up of AMTs includes the AutoShift, the UltraShift, and the dual-clutch Procision. These are the most popular models of AMT found in North America.
- The brains of the AMT is the computer controller that commands the shift process. Depending on the manufacturer, this computer is called the TCU (transmission control unit) or the transmission electronic control unit (ECU).
- Meritor teamed up with ZF to market ZF's line of AMTs in North America.
- ZF now markets its AS-Tronic, TC-Tronic, and Traxon transmissions directly to North American OEMs.
- In 2014, Detroit Diesel launched its own version of the Mercedes twelve-speed AMT popular in Europe and called it the DT-12.
- The AS-Tronic and the DT-12 both have twin countershaft main boxes with a planetary range section and share very similar power flows.
- The Volvo I-shift AMT also shares a similar power flow to the AS-Tronic and the DT-12 but utilizes only one countershaft in the main box.
- AMT shifting is usually accomplished by electric motors and or electric-over-air solenoids.
- AMTs software has become increasingly sophisticated and now is capable of adaptive electronic control based on driver, load, terrain, and other operating conditions, thereby optimizing shifting strategies and fuel economy.
- To shift without gear clash, AMTs use software to read shaft and gear speeds inside the transmission.
- AMT controllers are capable of self-diagnosis and will set diagnostic fault codes, alerting the driver to problems.
- AMT software is capable of initiating failsafe strategies to protect the transmission while still allowing limited operation.
- Eaton AMTs use air solenoids to shift the range and the splitter sliding clutches in their transmissions equipped with auxiliary sections.
- Inertia brakes are used by the AMTs to control transmission shaft speeds for shifting to first or reverse from neutral and to increase shift speed synchronization when required.
- AMTs still require clutches although there may be no clutch pedal. The clutches can be standard mechanical versions (Eaton AutoShift), a centrifugally operated clutch (some Eaton UltraShifts), an electrically operated clutch (some UltraShift models), air operated clutch (used on the DT-12 and the AS-Tronic), wet clutch (used by Eaton ASW and the Mercedes AGS), or dual clutches either dry or wet (the new Volvo I-shift uses a dual dry clutch while the Eaton Procision uses a dual wet clutch for input).
- AMT TCUs record active and inactive diagnostic fault codes that can assist the technician in diagnosing complaints. These codes can usually be retrieved manually and/or by using an electronic service tool to access them.
- All manufacturers have detailed troubleshooting strategies and trouble tree sequences listed in their service manuals to assist the technician in his or her diagnosis.

Vocabulary Builder

adaptive learning Software than can learn and change strategy based on different factors.

air-control solenoid valve An electric-over-air solenoid used to control shifting by controlling the flow of air from the air filter to the range cylinder piston.

automated manual transmission (AMT) A standard manual transmission operated by electronic control.

AS-Tronic ZF's AMT for medium - and -heavy duty trucks and buses.

Automatic Gear Shift (AGS) One of Mercedes' AMTs for lighter-duty trucks.

AutoSelect Eaton's first AMT; very limited electronic control.

AutoShift Eaton's first shift by wire transmission.

break torque The unloading of the driveline to allow a shift to occur.

carbon dioxide One of the resulting gases produced when burning a hydrocarbon fuel; thought to contribute to global warming.

DT-12 A twelve-speed AMT manufactured by Detroit Diesel.

dual-clutch transmission Transmission with two separate input shafts controlled by two separate clutches.

electric shift assembly The shift actuation system for an Eaton AutoShift or UltraShift transmission that contains two shift motors, the shift finger, and the shift finger position sensors.

Engine Synchro Shift (ESS) Meritor's first AMT; limited to synchronizing engine speeds to assist the shifting process.

Freedomline 12- and 1six-speed ZF AMTs released in partnership with Meritor

gear jamming An attempt by the driver to shift without using the clutch; usually causes at least some damage to the transmission sliding clutches. Also called *float shifting*.

I-Shift The Volvo AMT; Mack trucks use the same transmission.

inertia break A component used to control the speed of the transmission countershaft and main shaft gears.

J-1587 Older SAE communication protocol; quite slow in terms of data transmission at 9600 bits per second.

J-1939 Newer SAE communication protocol; data transmission at a rate of at least 250,000 bits per second and up to 500,000 bits/second.

momentary engine ignition interrupt relay (MEIIR) A relay controlled by the TCU that cuts the engine ignition or fuelling in the event that a DM clutch will not disengage.

Procision Eaton's dual-clutch seven-speed AMT; introduced in 2014.

self-diagnostic The TCU capability to analyze its own functions.

shift by wire Shifting controlled completely by the transmission electronic control.

snapshot A snapshot records all the relevant TCU data before and after a diagnostic code is set to ease diagnoses.

start enable relay The start enable relay is controlled by the TCU and interrupts the circuit to the starter solenoid unless the TCU passes a self-check and verifies the transmission is in neutral

SureShift Meritor's first line of fully automated transmissions.

system manager A transmission control module used with older Gen 1 and Gen 2 Eaton AutoShift transmissions.

TC-Tronic A ZF AMT that uses a torque converter for input; for heavy applications.

thermal efficiency A measurement of how much of the fuel used is actually turned into power to drive the vehicle.

transmission control unit (TCU) The unit that controls the shifting in an electronically automated transmission. Also called *transmission electronic control module (ECM)*.

transmission electronic control module (ECM) The unit that controls the shifting in an electronically automated transmission. Also called *transmission control unit (TCU)*.

Traxon ZF's latest AMT with five different input modules available.

UltraShift Eaton's two-pedal AMT; completely shift by wire with no clutch pedal.

Review Questions

1. Which of the following is NOT one of the reasons that automated manual transmissions are becoming more popular?
   a. They have better fuel economy.
   b. They are less expensive than standard transmissions.
   c. They lead to reduced carbon dioxide emissions.
   d. They reduce driver training requirements.
2. The transmission shift tower is replaced by which of the following on an Eaton automated manual transmission?
   a. A shift motor
   b. A rail select motor
   c. An electric shift fork
   d. An electric shifter assembly
3. Before a vehicle with a Fuller automated manual transmission can be started, which of the following must happen?
   a. The transmission controller must conduct and pass an initiation and self-check.
   b. The transmission controller must verify a neutral position.
   c. The transmission controller must turn on the start enable relay.
   d. All of the above must occur before the vehicle can be started.
4. Each time the vehicle is shut down, which of the following occurs in the Eaton Fuller automated manual transmissions?
   a. The transmission controller conducts a self-check diagnostic.
   b. The range and splitter air shift cylinders are moved to neutral.
   c. The transmission controller maps and records the shift rail gates.
   d. All of the above happen on shut down.
5. The Eaton Gen 3 AutoShift transmission has which of the following electronic modules?
   a. A shifter module, a system manager ECU, and a shift control ECU
   b. A shifter module with built in system manager and a shift control ECU
   c. A single transmission control unit on the transmission
   d. A shifter module with a built-in, single-transmission control ECU
6. How is the auxiliary section high and low range shift accomplished on a ten-speed Fuller Ultrashift transmission?
   a. By air using two control solenoids
   b. By air using one control solenoid
   c. Electrically using one electric motor
   d. Electrically using two electric motors
7. In a Fuller Ultrashift transmission, what must the transmission controller do in order to make a shift?
   a. It must request the engine ECM to break torque.
   b. It must assume control of the engine.
   c. It must ask the driver to depress the clutch.
   d. All of the choices are correct.
8. The rail select sensor on a Fuller ultrashift transmission is a(n):
   a. induction pulse generator.
   b. potentiometer.
   c. rheostat.
   d. Hall effect sensor.
9. The output speed sensor on a Fuller ultrashift transmission is a(n):
   a. induction pulse generator.
   b. potentiometer.
   c. rheostat.
   d. Hall effect sensor.
10. What must the driver do to select high range while driving forward in an Ultrashift transmission?
    a. Preselect the range by moving the range lever to high while the transmission is in gear
    b. Preselect the range shift by pushing the up arrows
    c. Select range after the transmission shifts to neutral
    d. The driver cannot select high or low range—only gear numbers.

ASE-Type Questions

1. Technician A says that two pedal AMTs still require a clutch. Technician B says that in three pedal AMTs the driver uses the clutch only for starting off and stopping the vehicle. Who is correct?
   a. Technician A
   b. Technician B
   c. Both Technician A and Technician B
   d. Neither Technician A nor Technician B
2. Technician A says that all AMTs use a standard dry disc clutch. Technician B says that The Volvo I-Shift uses a large organic dry disc clutch. Who is correct?
   a. Technician A
   b. Technician B
   c. Both Technician A and Technician B
   d. Neither Technician A nor Technician B
3. Technician A says that the new Eaton Procision uses two multi-plate wet clutches as inputs. Technician B says that the Procision transmission has two input shafts. Who is correct?
   a. Technician A
   b. Technician B
   c. Both Technician A and Technician B
   d. Neither Technician A nor Technician B
4. Technician A says that the AS-Tronic transmission from ZF uses a splitter gear at the input to double the ratios in the front box section. Technician B says that the rearward split in the splitter section of the ZF AS-Tronic is always the High split position. Who is correct?
   a. Technician A
   b. Technician B
   c. Both Technician A and Technician B
   d. Neither Technician A nor Technician B
5. Technician A says that the twelve-speed Volvo I-Shift transmission has the same basic power flows as the twelve-speed AS-Tronic from ZF. Technician B says the twelve-speed Volvo I-Shift has only one countershaft. Who is correct?
   a. Technician A
   b. Technician B
   c. Both Technician A and Technician B
   d. Neither Technician A nor Technician B
6. Technician A says that the sliding clutches in a Fuller ultrashift transmission have wider tooth spacing than non-automated transmission models. Technician B says that the main shaft gears in a Fuller ultrashift transmission have wider tooth spacing than non-automated transmission models. Who is correct?
   a. Technician A
   b. Technician B
   c. Both Technician A and Technician B
   d. Neither Technician A nor Technician B
7. Technician A says that a Fuller eighteen-speed ultrashift transmission uses two air solenoids to control the splitter shift in the auxiliary section. Technician B says that a Fuller eighteen-speed ultrashift transmission uses two air solenoids to control the range shift in the auxiliary section. Who is correct?
   a. Technician A
   b. Technician B
   c. Both Technician A and Technician B
   d. Neither Technician A nor Technician B
8. Tech A says the MEIIR relay is controlled by the engine ECM. Technician B says that the MEIIR relay is only actuated when there is catastrophic clutch failure. Who is correct?
   a. Technician A
   b. Technician B
   c. Both Technician A and Technician B
   d. Neither Technician A nor Technician B
9. Technician A says that the Eaton Procision seven-speed transmission does not need to break torque while shifting through gears 1 to 7. Technician B says that the Eaton Procision transmission preselects seventh gear while still in sixth to make the shift quicker. Who is correct?
   a. Technician A
   b. Technician B
   c. Both Technician A and Technician B
   d. Neither Technician A nor Technician B
10. Technician A says that the ZF AS-Tronic transmission has an overdrive gear in the range section. Technician B says that the AS-Tronic can have either two or three main shaft gears. Who is correct?
    a. Technician A
    b. Technician B
    c. Both Technician A and Technician B
    d. Neither Technician A nor Technician B

CHAPTER 41

NATEF Tasks

There are no NATEF tasks for this chapter.

Knowledge Objectives

After reading this chapter, you will be able to:

1. Explain the purpose of the torque converter. (pp 1342–1344)
2. Describe torque converter components. (pp 1344–1346)
3. Explain torque converter operation. (pp 1346–1347)
4. Explain radial and vortex flow. (pp 1347–1349)
5. Describe torque converter operational phases. (p 1349)
6. Explain torque multiplication phase. (p 1349)
7. Explain coupling phase. (pp 1349–1350)
8. Describe the purpose of flex plates. (pp 1351–1342)
9. Explain the lockup clutch and operation. (pp 1352–1353)
10. Describe the torque converter hydraulic circuits. (pp 1353–1355)
11. Explain torque converter complaint diagnoses and failure analysis. (pp 1355–1356)
12. Describe stall testing procedures. (pp 1356–1359)
13. Describe torque converter service. (pp 1359–1365)

Torque Converters

Skills Objectives

After reading this chapter, you will be able to:

1. Diagnose torque converter complaints. (p 1355)
2. Perform a stall test. (p 1357) SKILL DRILL 41-1
3. Perform a stall test on engines with smoke controls. (p 1358) SKILL DRILL 41-2
4. Interpret stall test results. (p 1358)
5. Test lock-up clutch operation. (p 1360) SKILL DRILL 41-3
6. Pressure test an automatic transmission. (p 1361) SKILL DRILL 41-4
7. Inspect a torque converter for leaks and replace seals, gaskets, and bushings. (p 1361) SKILL DRILL 41-5
8. Reassemble a torque converter. (p 1362)
9. Perform a turbine end play check. (p 1363)
10. Disassemble a torque converter. (p 1363) SKILL DRILL 41-6
11. Inspect torque converter components and recommend replacement where needed. (p 1364) SKILL DRILL 41-7

Introduction

If you have read the chapters on standard transmissions, you know that most of today's truck transmissions have between 10 and 18 gear ratios in order to move the heavy loads expected of them. These ratios range from a low of 15:1, 16:1, or even 17:1 up to overdrive ratios of 0.73:1 and 0.66:1. By contrast, automatic transmissions usually have only four to six gear ratios ranging from a low of usually not more than 6 or 7:1 and ending up with the same overdrive ratios of 0.73 and 0.66:1. Still, automatic transmissions are expected to haul loads that are equal to their eighteen-speed standard transmission cousins. So, how does an automatic transmission with a low gear ratio of only 4.7:1 haul an 80,000 pound (36,287 kg) load? That is where the **torque converter** comes into play. Torque converters multiply the input torque by as much as three or four to one. In most truck applications, the multiplication is held to around two to one. Let's take the above transmission example with a 4.7:1 first-gear ratio and see what happens when we add a torque converter with a multiplication factor of 2.47:1.

Just as a gear ratio multiplies the output torque in a transmission, the torque converter multiplies the input torque. In our example, that means the overall output available to drive the vehicle amounts to the gear ratio times the torque converter multiplication factor—or 4.7 times 2.47. What results is an equivalent ratio of 11.6:1, which is ample to move the load. A torque converter multiplication factor automatically lessens as the vehicle picks up speed. When the transmission is in first gear, the overall ratio can change from the maximum of 11.6:1 all the way to the actual first-gear ratio of 4.7:1. Rather than having only four or six ratios, the torque converter allows an automatic transmission to have a constantly variable ratio within the limits of the actual gear ratios and the torque converter's multiplication factor. In this chapter, we will look at how the torque converter accomplishes this feat.

Fundamentals of Torque Converters

All vehicles, whether with standard or automatic transmissions, must have a means of interrupting the engine power from the drive line when the vehicle is stopped. Otherwise, the engine would stall. Standard transmissions have a manual or automatic clutch that performs this function. The clutch physically disconnects the transmission input shaft from the engine when the clutch is disengaged. The automatic transmission uses a torque converter to perform this function. The torque converter is a sophisticated type of **fluid coupling** that allows the vehicle to slow down and stop without any disconnection of components. The torque converter is able to accomplish this because the engine power is transmitted to the driveline through a fluid rather than a physical connection. The easiest way to visualize this power transmission

You Are the Technician

An international 4200 series truck is brought to your repair shop and the driver complains that his fuel economy has decreased steadily over the last few weeks. The vehicle has an Allison 1000 series automatic transmission. After a preliminary inspection you road test the vehicle, and the engine seems to operate as it should and has plenty of power. The transmission seems to shift gears correctly; however, the check transmission light is illuminated.

1. What could cause this lack of fuel economy?
2. What would you do next to find the problem?
3. Could the transmission cause a low fuel economy complaint?

is to imagine two electric fans facing each other. Turn one fan on, and observe the other fan. The air being pushed out by the powered fan strikes the blades of the unpowered fan. As illustrated in FIGURE 41-1, the blades of the unpowered fan start to turn even though there is no physical connection between them. The air acts as a fluid transmitting the power from the first fan into the second fan. This is the basic principle of the fluid coupler—power can be transmitted through a fluid to drive another component.

For a functioning fluid coupler to work, however, you need more than just the two fans mentioned above. Because air is easily compressed, the fans could not transmit very much torque. Plus, the fans are open at the sides, so at the first sign of resistance, the fluid (air) would merely deflect to the side. To make a proper fluid coupling, you need first to use a liquid. The reason is that most liquids are essentially uncompressible. In a transmission, hydraulic oil, usually known as transmission fluid, is used to transmit the power. Second, you must stop the fluid from being deflected to the side when the torque increases. To accomplish this, the fans in a transmission are encased in a circular housing. Third, as shown in FIGURE 41-2, the fans are placed very close to one another and the blades of the fans are slightly angled to optimize power transfer. Then, the driving fan is attached to the power source and the driven fan to the output to create a functioning fluid coupler.

Using a fluid coupler has many advantages. A fluid coupling allows equipment to start up virtually load free. When an electric motor starts up, it tends to accelerate very rapidly. A fluid coupling allows the drive to slip as the motor speed ramps up. That slippage reduces the start-up shock load, the current draw, and the potential for overheating.

A fluid coupler can also cushion the shock from overloads, machinery that jams up, or sudden speed changes by allowing the driven fan to slip. Fluid couplers are used in many applications where low speed start-up torque is not a significant issue, including conveying systems, processing equipment, and assembly-line systems, such as filling and packaging operations. Power can be supplied by electric motors, industrial engines, or power take-off units on mobile equipment, such as tractors in agricultural applications. The fluid coupler is simply designed and it can achieve nearly 100% efficiency at high speeds as long as the load applied is not too great.

The main disadvantage of the fluid coupler is that it is quite inefficient at starting speeds. When the input is much faster than the output, the coupler is also incapable of multiplying torque. During start-up operation, the driven element of the coupler is much slower than the speed of the driving element. A lot of the power is wasted and dissipated as heat, caused by the shearing force and turbulence, and is imparted on the fluid by that difference in speed. Because of this, a fluid coupler is not suitable for motive power use where heavy loads must be moved from a standing start. The torque converter, on the other hand, uses the advantages of the fluid coupler to allow the vehicle to be stopped while the engine is still running.The torque converter also allows power transfer close to 100% when conditions are correct. The torque converter also has a huge advantage over the fluid coupler because the converter can multiply torque. When starting out from a stop, the torque created by the typical internal combustion engine is quite low because the engine speed is quite low also. The torque converter multiplies this torque to allow quicker acceleration and throttle response. Depending on the torque converter design, this multiplication can be two to four times the torque the engine is producing.

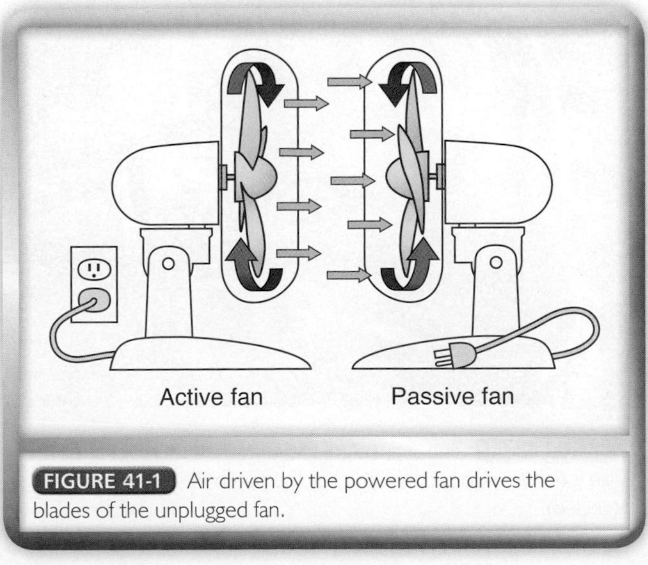

FIGURE 41-1 Air driven by the powered fan drives the blades of the unplugged fan.

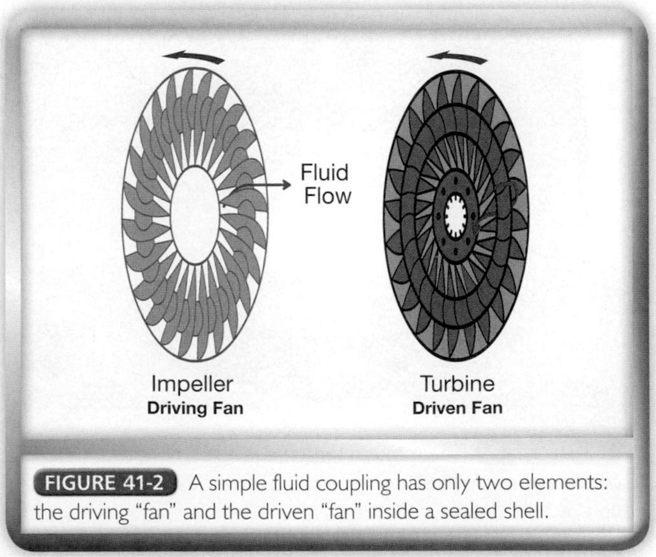

FIGURE 41-2 A simple fluid coupling has only two elements: the driving "fan" and the driven "fan" inside a sealed shell.

Most on-highway torque converters, however, multiply torque around 2:1. The torque converter, however, will never operate at 100% efficiency. The driven element (the **turbine**) can only be accelerated to approximately 95% of the speed of the driving element (the **impeller**). This is due to the turbulence caused by the other element in the converter, the stator, and by the design of the turbine itself.

Today torque converters address this inadequacy by utilizing a **lock-up clutch**. When conditions are correct, the lock-up clutch locks the turbine to the converter shell, and the engine power is transmitted one to one to the driveline, eliminating any loss in efficiency. We will look at how the converter accomplishes this as we continue this chapter.

Components of Torque Converters

In the section on the fundamentals of torque converters, we referred to the driving and driven fans in a fluid coupler because they were the simplest way to explain the basic concept. Of course, the components of a fluid couple are not actually called fans. Their correct names are the impeller (pump), which is the driving "fan", and the turbine, which is the driven "fan."

The modern torque converter, shown in FIGURE 41-3, includes several components. The shell, or housing, contains all of the component parts. The impeller (pump) is the driving member and is part of or attached to the shell. The turbine is the driven member, the stator is the reaction member, and the two halves of the split guide ring are the final components of the torque converter.

The converter also houses the components that make up the lock-up clutch. Components of the lock-up clutch include a gear or spline attached to the turbine, a friction disc that fits the spline or gear, the clutch actuation piston, and the backing plate attached to the converter housing that the piston squeezes the friction disc against. We will discuss these components individually at first and then explain how they interact with each other.

Converter Shell or Housing

The converter shell is comprised of two halves. The rear half has the shape of a hollowed-out donut, as shown in FIGURE 41-4. The donut shape is called a **torus**.

The rear half of the shell also has a hollow stub attached to its center. This is called the pump drive hub. When installed in the transmission, the pump drive hub drives the transmission oil pump gears. The front is usually flat on the outside to accommodate the placing of the lock-up clutch components. In some cases, it may have a rounded shape—especially if the converter does not have a lock-up clutch. The front half of the shell normally has a protruding pilot that will engage the rear of the crankshaft or the engine flywheel to help support the converter weight, as shown in FIGURE 41-5.

In light-duty applications, the two halves of the shell are welded together and the converter is not designed to be overhauled. Rather, it is designed to be replaced. In heavy-duty models, however, the shells are bolted together, and the converter can be disassembled for inspection and repair.

Impeller or Pump

Both impeller and pump are used to name the driving member in the torque converter. We will use the term impeller to avoid confusion with the transmission hydraulic pump. The impeller is a series of vanes. The

FIGURE 41-3 The modern torque converter housing contains all of the elements involved in power transfer and lock-up clutch operation.

FIGURE 41-4 The rear half of the converter shell is shaped like a hollowed-out donut and has the pump drive hub attached (circled).

vanes can be cast as part of the rear half of the converter shell or they may be welded to it, as seen in FIGURE 41-6. One half of the **split guide ring** is attached to the middle of the impeller's blades to provide strength and create a circular passage for fluid flow.

The torque converter shell or housing is physically attached, though not directly, to the engine crankshaft. As a result, the shell and the impeller turn with the engine. During operation, the torque converter is filled with transmission fluid. The impeller blades generate centrifugal force that flings the fluid outwards. The curved torus shape of the rear half of the shell then forces the fluid forward towards the engine.

Turbine

The turbine sits just in front of the impeller inside the converter housing. The turbine is also shaped like a donut (torus), as shown in FIGURE 41-7. When the turbine is installed in front of the impeller, the torus shape of the rear converter housing and the turbine combine to form a complete donut shape. The turbine has a series of curved blades that are designed to catch the oil being thrown forward by the rotating impeller. The second half of the split guide ring is attached to the middle of the turbine blades; again, to strengthen the blades and to help form a circular fluid flow between the impeller and the turbine and back again.

The turbine sits very close to the front of the impeller. The turbine does not, however, touch the impeller. Clearances may be as tight as 0.060" to 0.080" (1.5 to 2.0 mm), but the two components will not touch. The turbine is supported by thrust bearings or washers that locate it axially and is not connected to anything in the torque converter. The turbine is splined to the input shaft of the transmission, which enters the torque converter from the rear. The forward end of the input shaft or the front of the turbine is usually supported by a bushing inside the torque converter housing that serves to locate the turbine radially.

FIGURE 41-5 The front half of the shell tends to be flat and has a pilot (circled) that supports the converter in the crankshaft or the flywheel.

Stator or Reaction Member

The outside edges of the turbine and the impeller are very close together inside the torque convertor. In contrast, the inner edges are a fair distance apart. The **stator**, a bladed wheel most responsible for torque multiplication, sits between the turbine and impeller to take up that space. The stator is shaped like a wheel with curved blades for spokes. The outer edge of the "wheel" is positioned very close to the inner edge of the two halves of the split guide ring, as shown in FIGURE 41-8.

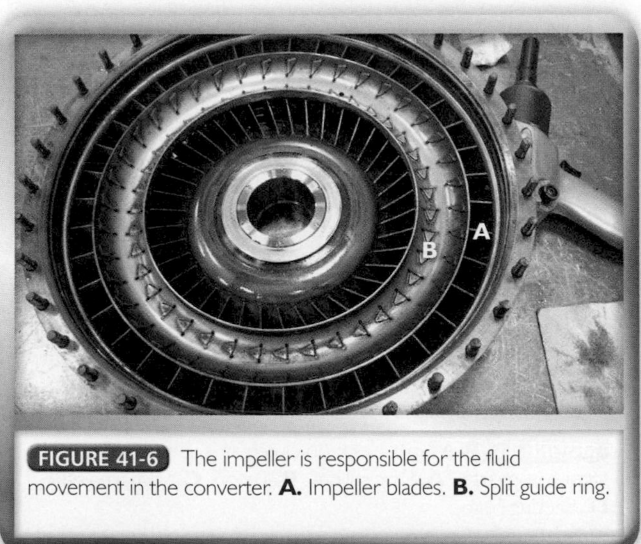

FIGURE 41-6 The impeller is responsible for the fluid movement in the converter. **A.** Impeller blades. **B.** Split guide ring.

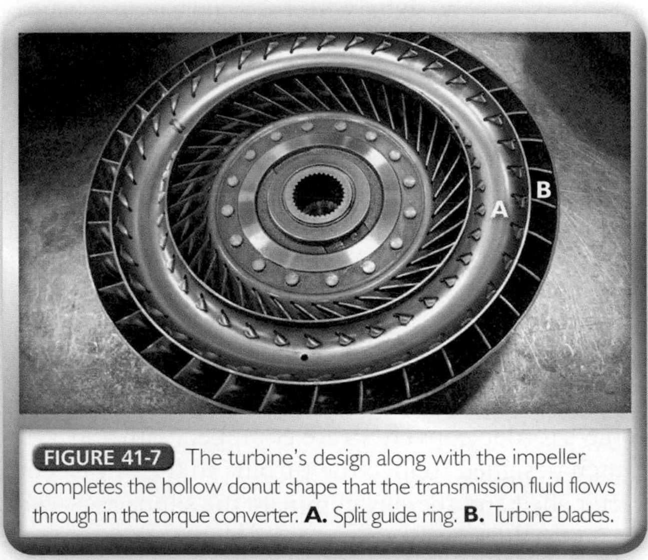

FIGURE 41-7 The turbine's design along with the impeller completes the hollow donut shape that the transmission fluid flows through in the torque converter. **A.** Split guide ring. **B.** Turbine blades.

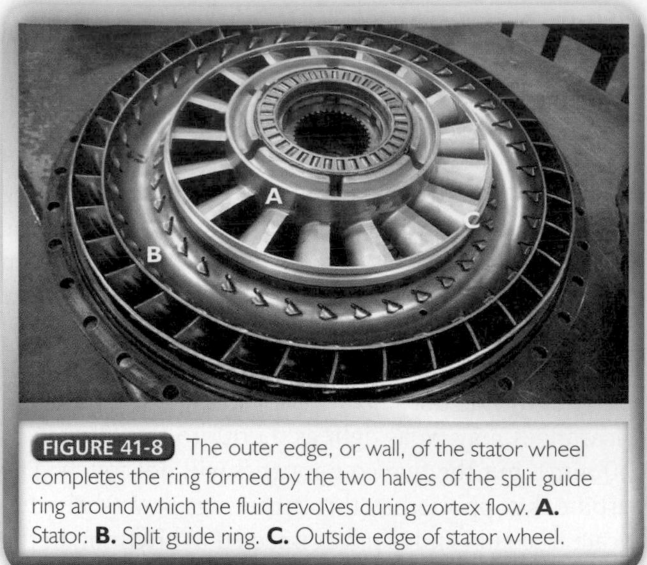

FIGURE 41-8 The outer edge, or wall, of the stator wheel completes the ring formed by the two halves of the split guide ring around which the fluid revolves during vortex flow. **A.** Stator. **B.** Split guide ring. **C.** Outside edge of stator wheel.

When the converter is assembled, the two halves of the split guide ring and the outer edge of the stator wheel create an almost complete circular ring. The fluid can flow from the impeller around the ring, through the turbine, and back to the impeller. This ring helps to reduce fluid turbulence inside the converter. The stator itself usually has three components: the inner hub, the **over-running clutch** (or **one-way clutch**), and the actual stator wheel. The inner hub of the stator is splined to the **stator support** (**ground shaft**), which surrounds and supports the transmission input shaft. Like the input shaft, the stator support enters the torque converter from the rear. The stator support (ground shaft) is attached to the transmission hydraulic pump and bolted to the transmission housing. Therefore, the stator support and the inner hub of the stator can never turn. The over-running (one-way) clutch sits on the stator inner hub and supports the stator wheel. That clutch will only allow the stator wheel to turn in one direction. The stator wheel's axial position is usually controlled by thrust bearings or washers.

Lock-Up Clutch Assembly

No matter how sophisticated the design, all torque converters allow some inherent slippage between the impeller and the turbine. That is, the impeller can never drive the turbine at engine speed. Speed loss varies but is usually in the neighborhood of 5%. In the past, that level of speed loss was acceptable. The primary focus was on performance rather than fuel economy and emission control. Today, that level of speed loss cannot be tolerated. All of today's torque converters are equipped with a lock-up clutch designed to lock the turbine to the torque converter shell and thereby eliminate the slippage. Several designs of lock-up clutches have been used in the past, but the most popular in the truck market is the piston type lock-up clutch.

Lock-up clutches usually have the following components:

- A backing plate that is either part of the front of the torque converter shell or bolted to the shell
- A hydraulic piston that is usually located in the front half of the converter shell
- A friction disc that sits in between the backing plate and the piston, as shown in **FIGURE 41-9**

The friction disc will be splined to the turbine. When the piston is actuated hydraulically, it squeezes the friction disc between the piston and the backing plate. That action locks the turbine to the shell, eliminating all slippage.

Operation of Torque Converters

The first thing we must understand about torque converter operation is that the converter must be completely filled with fluid to work properly. Any air inside the converter will cause aeration, excess heat, and very poor torque transmission. The automatic transmission oil pressure circuits prioritize fluid delivery to the torque converter to ensure it is always full. We will look at the oil pressure circuits involving the torque converter in the Torque Converter Hydraulic Circuits section.

Rotary Flow and Vortex Flow

The torque converter shell is indirectly bolted to the engine crankshaft. Any time the engine is turning, so is the torque converter shell. Remember that the impeller blades are directly connected to the rear half of the shell, so they also turn with the shell. The blades of the impeller are relatively straight (that is, they are not curved very much). The reason for that shape is that the impeller's

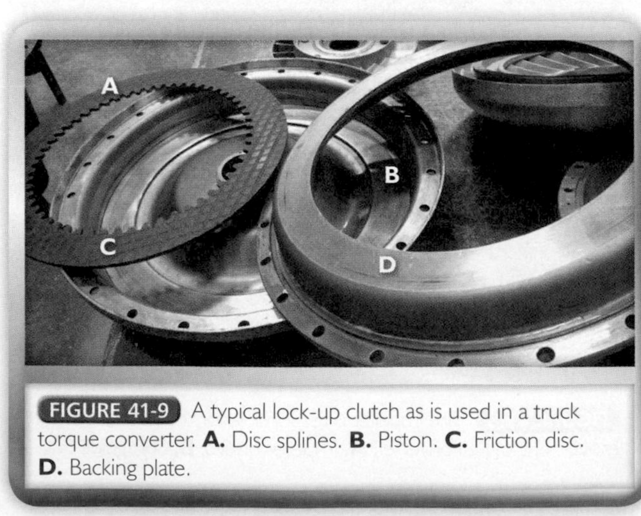

FIGURE 41-9 A typical lock-up clutch as is used in a truck torque converter. **A.** Disc splines. **B.** Piston. **C.** Friction disc. **D.** Backing plate.

job is to act on the mass of transmission fluid inside the torque converter and force the fluid towards the outside of the shell. The rotation of the shell causes **centrifugal force**, the apparent force by which a rotating mass tries to move outward away from its axis of rotation, which acts on the fluid and the blades of the impeller. **FIGURE 41-10** illustrates this centrifugal effect. The rear half of the split guide ring that is attached to the impeller blades helps to direct and smooth the flow of fluid towards the outside of the housing or shell.

The torus shape of the rear half of the torque converter shell redirects the fluid thrown outward by centrifugal force by sending the fluid forward towards the blades of the turbine. The blades in the torus-shaped turbine are curved significantly to catch the fluid. The force created by the impeller's rotation is directed against these curved blades, as shown in **FIGURE 41-11**. The curve of the turbine blades, and the front half of the split guide ring attached to them, help to direct the fluid back towards the center of the impeller.

The turbine is not attached to anything inside the torque converter, but the turbine is splined to the transmission input shaft. When an automatic transmission is started in neutral or park, the input shaft is not physically connected to the driveline. On initial start-up, then, there is no load on the input shaft or the turbine. Consequently, the force of the fluid striking the turbine blades quickly spins the turbine up to almost the speed of the impeller. Both of these elements will turn at close to the same speed because there is nothing to resist the turbine's motion.

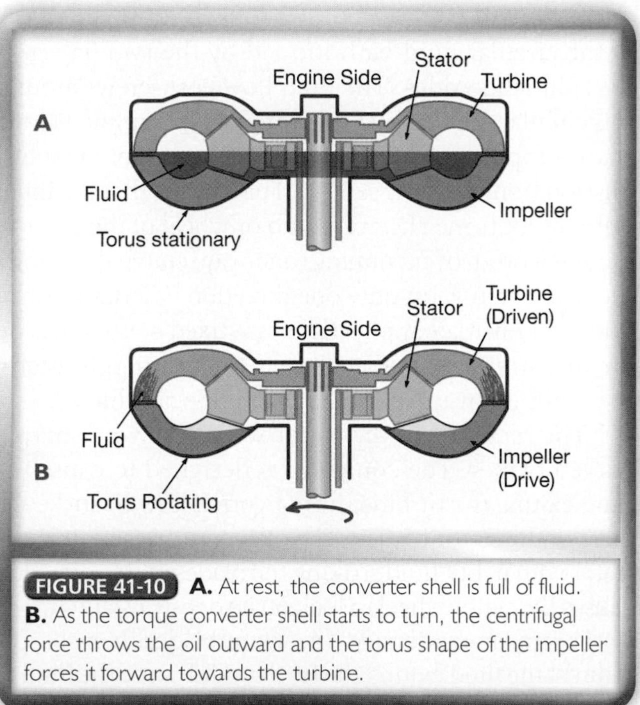

FIGURE 41-10 **A.** At rest, the converter shell is full of fluid. **B.** As the torque converter shell starts to turn, the centrifugal force throws the oil outward and the torus shape of the impeller forces it forward towards the turbine.

The mass of fluid in the torque converter in this scenario would be rotating as a solid circle of fluid traveling in the same direction. The impeller and turbine would be rotating with the converter. This type of fluid dynamic in the torque converter is known as **rotary flow** and is illustrated in **FIGURE 41-12A**. As soon as a load is placed on the turbine, however, the situation changes. For example, putting the transmission in drive connects the input shaft, and therefore the turbine, to the vehicle driveline. Assuming the vehicle is at a standstill and the engine is at idle speed, the turbine will immediately come to a stop because it now has significant load attached to it. That greatly changes the fluid dynamic inside the torque converter. What was a smooth rotary flow instantly changes to a much more turbulent flow, known as **vortex flow**, illustrated in **FIGURE 41-12B**.

In vortex flow, the fluid being thrown outward by the centrifugal force is again thrown forward by the torus shape of the rear half of the shell. With the turbine stopped, the fluid must flow through the curves of the turbine blades and return to the impeller. The front half of the split guide ring attached to the turbine blades helps to smooth the semicircular flow through the turbine.

The actual flow is as follows. First, the fluid enters the impeller near its center and flows behind the split guide ring to the outside edge due to the impellers rotation and centrifugal force. The fluid is then forced forward by the torus shape of the rear housing of the torque converter and enters the turbine at its outside edge. Fluid continues to flow around the curved blades and behind the front half of the split guide ring. The torus forces the fluid rearward, causing the fluid to exit the turbine near the center of the converter and flow back toward the impeller. Because of the sharp curvature of the turbine blades, the fluid exiting the turbine is now flowing in a direction that

FIGURE 41-11 Unlike the blades of a fluid coupler or the blades in the impeller, the turbine blades are very sharply angled in order to take advantage of as much of the force from the fluid striking them as possible. **A.** Inlet. **B.** Stator. **C.** Input shaft spline. **D.** Inside edge of outlet.

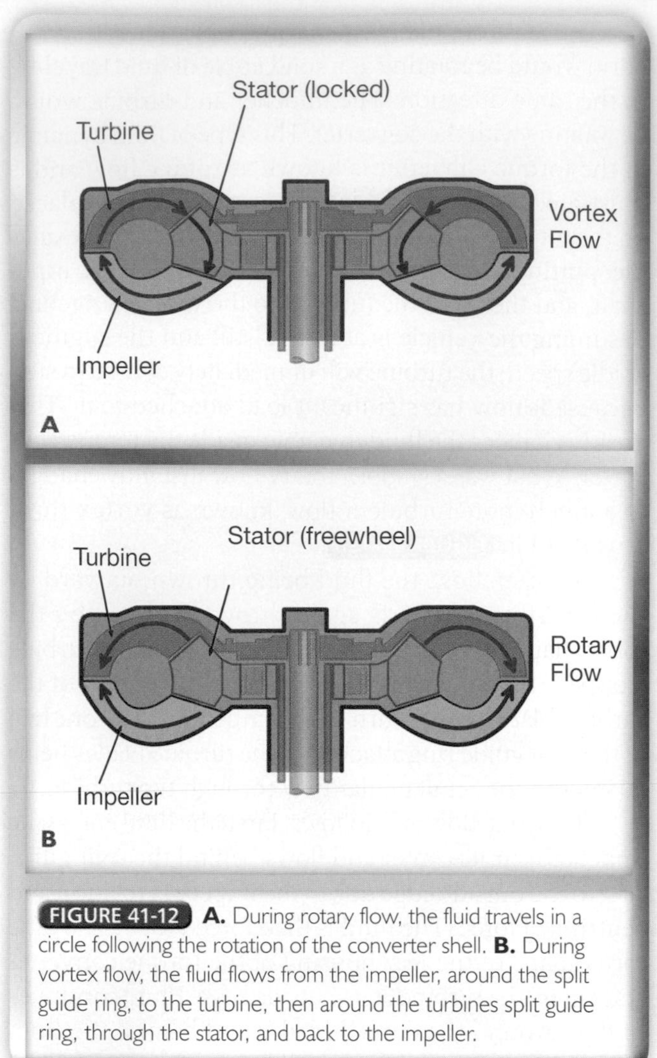

FIGURE 41-12 **A.** During rotary flow, the fluid travels in a circle following the rotation of the converter shell. **B.** During vortex flow, the fluid flows from the impeller, around the split guide ring, to the turbine, then around the turbines split guide ring, through the stator, and back to the impeller.

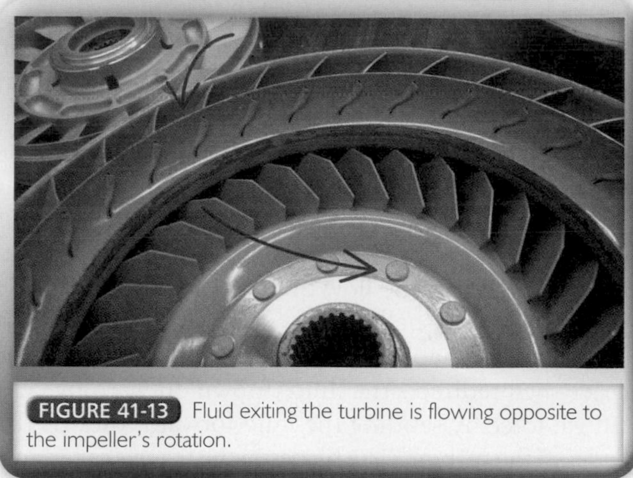

FIGURE 41-13 Fluid exiting the turbine is flowing opposite to the impeller's rotation.

FIGURE 41-14 The stator redirects fluid flow so it re-enters the impeller in the same direction as impeller rotation. This redirection adds to the effort applied to the turbine.

opposes the impeller's rotation, as shown in **FIGURE 41-13**. In effect, the fluid exiting the turbine is trying to stop the impeller from rotating.

With the vehicle in gear and at idle speed, the centrifugal force generated by the rotating impeller is very low. Therefore, the force of the fluid exiting the turbine is also very low and has little effect on the impeller's rotation. Still, as the engine accelerates, both the centrifugal force and the turbine exit force increase greatly. Increasing forces cause extreme turbulence, excess heat, and very inefficient power transfer. Why? Because the engine is trying to drive the impeller at the same time the turbine is trying to stop the impeller. To prevent this, the fluid exiting the turbine needs to be redirected so that it helps the power transfer instead of hindering it, as shown in **FIGURE 41-14**. To accomplish this, the center of the torque converter contains a stator placed in between the exit area of the turbine and the inlet area of the impeller.

The stator is a wheel with blades instead of spokes. The outer edge of the wheel completes the inner edge of the circular fluid path formed by the two halves of the split guide rings. The fluid flow corkscrews around this circular tube. The **stator inner hub** is splined to the stator support (ground) shaft, which is part of the transmission front pump assembly. That means that the inner hub cannot turn. The outer hub or wheel of the stator is mounted on an over-running (one-way) clutch that allows the wheel to turn in only one direction. (Certain heavy-duty and off-road applications use fixed stators that do not turn in either direction, but in highway applications, the stator is always mounted on a one-way clutch.)

The "spokes" of the stator wheel are very sharply curved blades. The converter is designed to cause the fluid exiting the turbine during vortex flow to strike the faces of the stator blades. The converter tries to turn the stator with it, but fluid striking the blades in this direction causes the stator wheel to lock on its one-way clutch. The stator remains stationary. The stator blades then sharply redirect the fluid exiting the turbine and cause the fluid to enter the impeller in the same direction that the impeller is turning. The force of the fluid adds to the impeller's rotation and increases the amount of torque that the engine is sending to the transmission and driveline.

It is important to realize that the torque converter does not produce torque out of thin air. The torque increase is based on three things: the angles of the turbine blades and stator blades and the speed differential between the impeller and the turbine. The angle of the blades in the turbine will determine the exit angle of the fluid and its speed. The angle of the stator blades will determine how much force the fluid will impart on the impeller when it is redirected. The speed difference between the impeller and the turbine will affect the torque multiplication. Of these three, the speed difference between the impeller and the turbine is the most significant factor in torque multiplication. In a standard transmission, when we gear down, we sacrifice speed for increased torque. In an automatic transmission, the torque converter does the same.

Torque Converter Operational Phases

Torque converters have two significant operational phases. As its name suggests, the torque multiplication phase involves increasing torque output. The coupling phase involves a slowing in the vortex flow. Let's examine these phases in more detail.

Torque Multiplication Phase

The **torque multiplication phase** occurs any time the torque converter is increasing the engine's torque output to the transmission's input shaft. Maximum torque multiplication occurs when the engine is accelerated to the maximum speed at which it can turn the impeller while the turbine remains stationary. That maximum speed is also known as the torque converter's **stall speed**. The engine cannot turn any faster because of the resistance provided by the stationary turbine. Reaching the stall speed rarely occurs in normal driving because the vehicle will usually start to move before maximum torque multiplication is reached.

The torque converter will normally only stall during a stall test procedure where the vehicle brakes are applied to prevent it from moving or if the vehicle is severely overloaded. Most on-highway torque converters are set up to have a torque multiplication factor of around 1.75:1 to 2.5:1. Recall that torque multiplication is primarily based on speed difference between the turbine and the impeller. Therefore, torque converters with higher torque multiplication typically have higher stall speeds. Within certain limitations, stall speeds and the torque multiplication factor can be manipulated in the design stage by changing the size of the torque converter elements, the angle of the turbine blades, the angle of the stator blades, and the clearance between the elements. A high-stall or high-torque-multiplication torque converter can be excellent for take-off and picking up heavy loads. A lower-stall torque converter is usually more suitable for highway operation.

Over the years, manufacturers have used many torque converter designs to optimize vehicle operation. For example, converters with **variable pitch stators** allow the angle of the stator blades to be changed hydraulically to benefit both starting off and high-speed operation. Converters with twin stators achieve much the same effect and converters with two or even three turbines fine tune vehicle performance. These modifications are not normally seen in on-highway applications today.

In normal operation starting from a stop with the vehicle in gear (usually "D" or drive range), the impeller is turning at engine speed. At this idle speed, the force of the fluid striking the turbine blades is insufficient to start turning the turbine very much. The force is usually sufficient only to hold an unloaded vehicle stationary on a slight incline. The force may be enough to start turbine creep, causing the vehicle to move forward slightly and the operator to apply the brakes to hold the vehicle stationary. As the operator steps on the throttle, the speed of the impeller increases, as does the fluid force pushing against the turbine blades. This force is redirected by the stator to assist the impeller's rotation, increasing the force again. This force will continue to increase with engine speed. The torque converter will multiply the torque from the engine within its design limitations until the vehicle starts to move. The amount of torque actually necessary to move the vehicle will depend on road grade, vehicle load, and other factors. It is important to note that, as soon as the turbine starts to turn and the vehicle begins moving, the torque multiplication factor starts to drop. It will continue to drop as the turbine speed increases and the speed difference between the impeller and turbine becomes smaller.

Vortex oil flow—the flow of fluid from the impeller through the turbine, through the stator and back to the impeller—occurs at all times during torque converter operation but is greatest at peak torque multiplication. That is, vortex flow is greatest at the converter stall speed, as illustrated in FIGURE 41-15. As the turbine speed increases, vortex flow—and therefore torque multiplication—decreases. In effect, while in operation, the torque converter has an almost unlimited number of torque multiplication ratios—from its design maximum to zero torque multiplication.

Coupling Phase

During the torque multiplication phase of torque converter operation, vortex fluid flow kept the stator held stationary

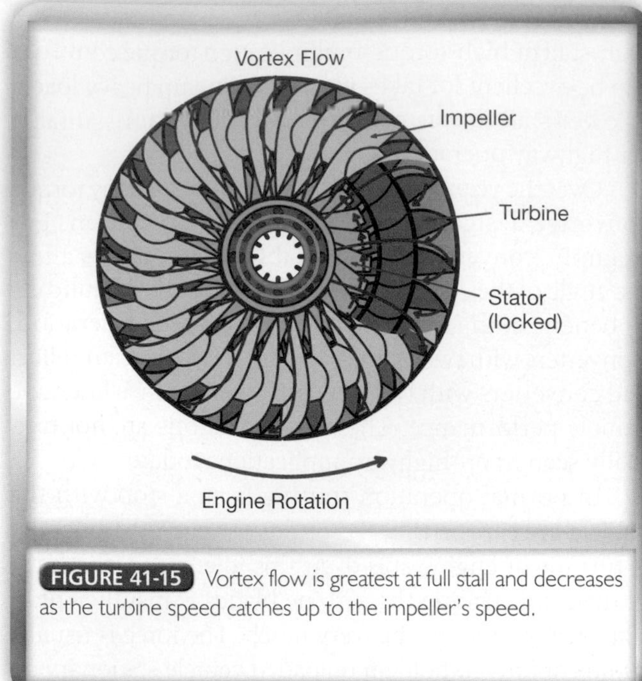

FIGURE 41-15 Vortex flow is greatest at full stall and decreases as the turbine speed catches up to the impeller's speed.

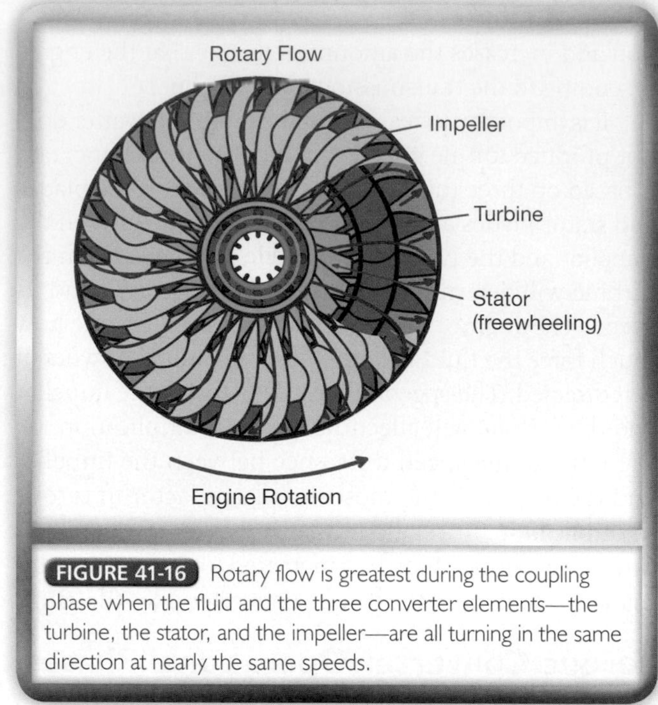

FIGURE 41-16 Rotary flow is greatest during the coupling phase when the fluid and the three converter elements—the turbine, the stator, and the impeller—are all turning in the same direction at nearly the same speeds.

on its one-way clutch to help multiply torque. As the speed of the turbine approaches the speed of the impeller, the fluid flow changes. Most of the fluid no longer exits the turbine near its center. In fact, the turbine starts to impart centrifugal force on the fluid present in its torus and starts to throw the fluid back the way it came toward the impeller. At this stage, the vortex fluid flow slows down and nearly stops in the converter. Very little fluid is flowing through the turbine blades. Most of the fluid follows the rotation of the torque converter shell. Torque converter operation has now entered the **coupling phase**, illustrated in **FIGURE 41-16**. The fluid inside the converter is basically a solid donut-shaped mass of fluid rotating in the same direction and at nearly same speed as the converter itself (that is, rotary fluid flow). In the coupling phase, however, the stationary stator we used in the torque multiplication phase would now be in the way and would restrict this rotary flow and cause extreme turbulence.

This is the reason that the stator is mounted on an over-running (one-way) clutch. When rotary flow starts to take over inside the converter, the flow of fluid starts to hit the stator blades from the back, and this unlocks the stator one-way clutch and allows the stator to turn freely in the direction of the fluid. The stator is mounted on either a sprag-type one-way clutch, as shown in **FIGURE 41-17A**, or a roller-type one-way clutch, as shown in **FIGURE 41-17B**, so that it locks in one direction and can freewheel in the other. A sprag-type one-way clutch uses a series of peanut-shaped sprags that are specially designed so that they allow rotation in only one direction. A roller-type one-way clutch uses rollers and ramps that cause the rollers to jam and lock up if they try to turn in a reverse direction.

The stator wheel is only unlocked during the coupling phase. During the coupling phase, the impeller, the turbine, the stator, and the fluid are all turning together at essentially the same speed. Also in this phase, vortex flow in the converter has almost ceased, and rotary flow is at maximum. There is always some fluid flowing around with the converter shell, so some rotary flow is always present, but it is maximum at the coupling phase and minimum at converter stall.

The coupling phase is related to torque demand and not to road speed. That means the coupling phase can happen at any vehicle speed. For example, consider a normal drive in a vehicle with an automatic transmission. You start from a standstill, and because you are in a hurry, you stomp on the accelerator. What happens? The torque converter impeller speeds up instantly with the engine, and you enter the torque multiplication phase. Vortex flow is high because there is a significant difference between the impeller and the turbine speed. Even though vortex flow and torque multiplication are very high, you are not at maximum torque multiplication because the turbine starts to turn right away to drive the vehicle. Remember that you can only achieve maximum torque multiplication at the torque converter stall speed. The stator is locked and redirecting fluid to contribute to the torque multiplication. You are continuing to accelerate when a car pulls out in front of you. Almost instantly, you

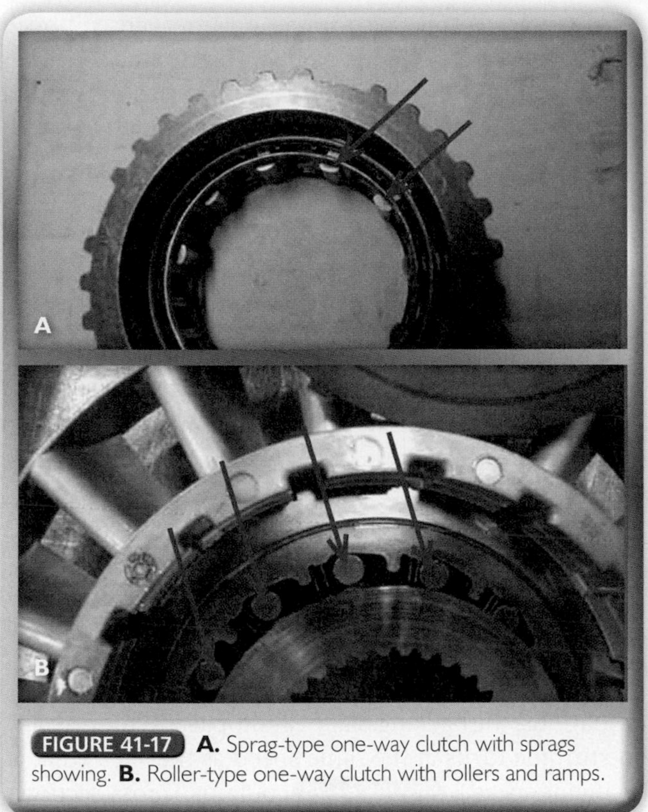

FIGURE 41-17 **A.** Sprag-type one-way clutch with sprags showing. **B.** Roller-type one-way clutch with rollers and ramps.

take your foot off the gas. The engine speed and the impeller speed will decrease until both are close to the turbine speed. The torque converter will enter the coupling phase of operation in which the impeller and turbine will be turning close to the same speed. Torque multiplication and vortex flow will have all but ceased and rotary flow is now predominant in the converter. The stator will be freewheeling with the fluid.

Now, imagine the car ahead quickly moves into the other lane. As you step hard on the gas pedal once again, the impeller speed instantly increases, locking the stator and returning the converter to high vortex flow and torque multiplication.

As you can imagine, this scenario changes constantly based on the demand for torque or acceleration. In most drive cycles, the transmission will be constantly switching from the torque multiplication phase to the coupling phase and back again. The automatic transmission has a clear advantage over standard transmissions in those situations because the automatic transmission has an automatic device that changes the torque multiplication factor within its design limit based on driver demand.

Note that converters in some off-road, slow-moving vehicles will use a fixed stator that does not freewheel and is always stationary. In these vehicles, high-speed operation is not a concern, so the stator is solidly mounted to the stator support shaft and cannot turn either direction. The torque converter elements in such vehicles are designed for high torque multiplication and low speed operation only.

Flex Plates

An engine requires a rotating mass to build inertia to keep it running between power pulses. Inertia is also critical for smoothing out the torsional vibrations created by the impact of these pulses. In standard transmission applications, those functions are accomplished by the engine flywheel.

In light- to medium-duty vehicles with automatic transmissions, the mass of the flywheel is replaced by the mass of the torque converter. The mass of the torque converter absorbs these pulsations and provides the inertia to keep the engine running between power strokes. Vehicles with automatic transmissions use a **flex plate** to connect the crankshaft to the torque converter. Heavy-duty vehicle engines usually require substantially more mass for this purpose, so heavy-duty vehicles with automatic transmissions often have a flywheel as well as a torque converter. The flex plate may have the starter ring gear attached to it.

Regardless, the torque converter cannot be coupled directly to the engine crankshaft or to the flywheel. When the torque converter is under heavy loads (while multiplying torque), its shell actually swells and contracts slightly. The fluid exerts a force over the large surface area of the converter shell to create these expansion and contraction cycles. The swelling is very slight, but over time the constant fatigue or bending forces caused by this swelling would cause the converter shell or the mounting bolts to fracture and break if it were mounted solidly to the flywheel or crankshaft. To avoid that type of failure, the converter is always bolted to an individual flex plate, like the one shown in FIGURE 41-18 (for a light-duty vehicle), or to a series of flex plates, as shown in FIGURE 41-19 (for a heavy-duty vehicle), which in turn are bolted to the crankshaft or flywheel.

In light-duty vehicles, the flex plate is usually a single plate of flexible steel bolted directly to the crankshaft. The single flex plate may also have the ring gear for starting the engine welded to it. (If the ring gear is not on the flex plate, it will be attached to the converter itself.) The converter will be bolted to the outside of the flex plate.

In heavier applications, the engine flywheel is still used and the ring gear is attached to it, usually by the heat shrink method. That is, the gear is heated to a specific temperature and placed over the flywheel. As the gear cools, it becomes fixed to the flywheel. Heat shrinking is used so that the gear can be replaced when needed. The torque converter is typically bolted to a stack of sev-

FIGURE 41-18 Flex plate for a light-duty vehicle.

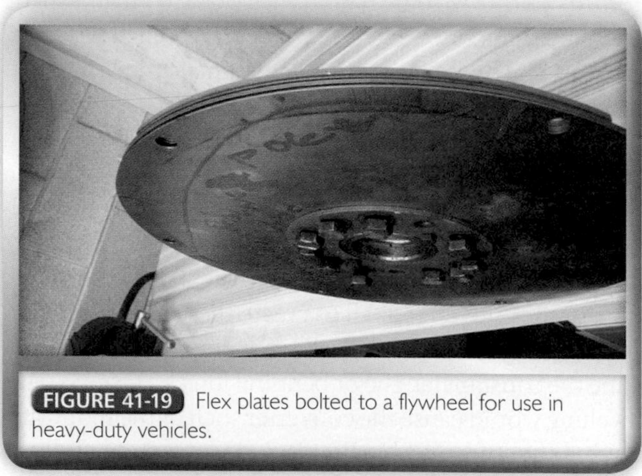

FIGURE 41-19 Flex plates bolted to a flywheel for use in heavy-duty vehicles.

eral flexible steel plates, which in turn are bolted to the flywheel. Both methods allow the converter to flex as necessary during its operation.

Lock-Up Clutch Operation

A torque converter impeller is incapable of driving the turbine at 100% of impeller (engine) speed. There will always be some amount of slippage involved. The amount of slippage is determined by many factors. The design of the turbine and impeller blades, the clearance between the torque converter elements, the viscosity of the fluid, and more can affect the amount of slippage. That slippage can cause speed differences from 5% to 10%, and put the automatic transmission at a disadvantage in terms of fuel economy and carbon dioxide emissions when compared to a standard transmission where the mechanical clutch does not allow any slippage. To compensate for that disadvantage, all modern torque converters are equipped with a lock-up clutch to lock the turbine to the converter shell. Such locking eliminates the inherent slippage and provides a 1:1 drive between the engine and the transmission.

The lock-up clutch usually consists of the three basic components, as shown in FIGURE 41-20:

- A hydraulic clutch piston, which is secured to the torque converter shell so it cannot rotate.
- A friction disc that is splined to the converter turbine. (Note that in the Allison transmission 1000, 2000, and 2400 series, the lock-up clutch friction disc and piston are combined as one unit.)
- A backing plate that is also secured, usually by bolts, to the converter shell. (In some models, the backing plate is a machined surface on the inside of the front half of the converter shell.)

When lock-up is desired, hydraulic pressure is directed to the back of the piston to squeeze the friction disc against the backing plate. All slippage is stopped, and the turbine turns at the same speed as the shell (that is, at engine speed). FIGURE 41-21 contains a cross-sectional view of a lock-up clutch system.

There are two basic control strategies for lock-up. The first is **programmed (systematic) lock-up**. The second is **modulated lock-up**. In the first type of lock-up strategy, the transmission controller engages lock-up every time the transmission reaches a certain gear range. That occurs whether the transmission controller is hydraulic or electronic. The gear range achieved may be as low as second range. Lock-up will then be engaged in every range except first. For that reason, the programmed lock-up strategy is usually the best in terms of fuel economy and, therefore, carbon dioxide emissions. The tradeoff is slower acceleration and limited overall performance after first range.

The second strategy, modulated lock-up, is performance based. With this strategy, the transmission will enter lock up at any time—even in first range—as long as certain criteria are met. For example, the transmission must usually be in second range or higher. The driver should not be trying to accelerate rapidly, and the torque converter should be nearing coupling phase. (In other words, the turbine speed is close to the impeller speed.)

When these criteria are met, the controller may engage the lock-up clutch. If any of these criteria change, for example if the driver steps on the throttle to accelerate, to pass a vehicle, or climb a hill, the lock-up clutch will usually disengage. Torque multiplication will be allowed to occur again to build speed rapidly.

FIGURE 41-20 The three components of a lock-up clutch assembly. **A.** Backing plate. **B.** Piston. **C.** Clutch disc.

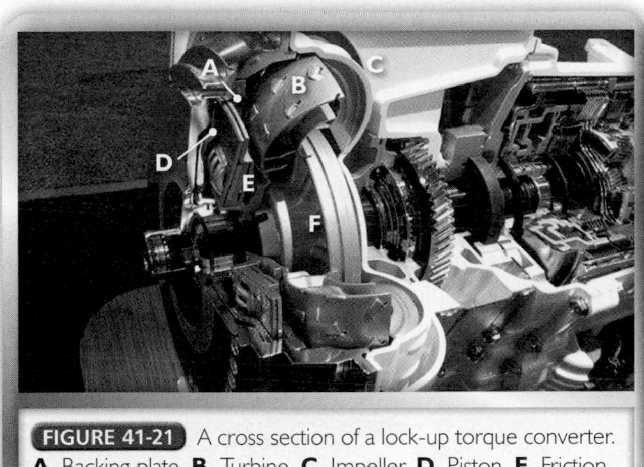

FIGURE 41-21 A cross section of a lock-up torque converter. **A.** Backing plate. **B.** Turbine. **C.** Impeller. **D.** Piston. **E.** Friction disc. **F.** Stator.

With modulated lock-up, there is no specific time when the lock-up clutch will always be engaged. In fact, the lock-up clutch may apply and release multiple times during a drive cycle even though safeguards are installed to make sure that the lock-up is not constantly engaging and disengaging. Older lock-up clutch designs would disengage as soon as the driver applied the brakes to stop. On vehicles equipped with engine brakes, the clutch will normally remain engaged to take advantage of engine braking usually until the transmission down-shifts to first range. Some newer light-duty vehicles without engine brakes utilize this strategy for enhanced engine braking in certain ranges.

One of the functions of lock-up clutches is to reduce waste in the driveline. That reduction is increasingly important as the Environmental Protection Agency has mandated reducing limits for noxious emissions from all vehicles. Limits for oxides of nitrogen and particulates are near zero, and limits for carbon monoxide are also extremely low. The next challenge for engine and vehicle manufacturers is to reduce the emission of carbon dioxide. The only way to reduce the production of carbon dioxide while burning hydrocarbon fuels is to reduce the amount of fuel consumed. So, manufacturers are pulling out all the stops in terms of maximizing engine thermal efficiencies and minimizing any parasitic load on the engine. Lock-up clutches are essential in today's automatic transmissions as one way to minimize wasted energy in the driveline.

Torque Converter Hydraulic Circuits

The torque converter must be completely full of fluid in order to operate properly. The transmission hydraulic system prioritizes fluid delivery to the converter. The hydraulic pump at the front of the transmission is driven by the pump drive hub that is welded to the back of the torque converter. As soon as the engine turns, the pump starts pressurizing fluid. As pressure builds, one of the first places the fluid is directed to is the torque converter. That is great for when the vehicle is in motion, but what happens when it is not? We still must deliver fluid from the stationary transmission to the rotating torque converter.

Directing fluid in a stationary transmission is accomplished by using a passage that is formed between the pump drive hub attached to the converter shell and the stator support or ground shaft, which enters the converter from the rear. This passage is shown in FIGURE 41-22. Fluid is sent through this passage and enters at the center of the torque converter behind the stator. There it fills the impeller blades and flows forward toward the turbine to fill its blades as well. The exit passage for the fluid is formed between the inside of the stator support shaft and the outside of the input or turbine shaft. The space between these two shafts provides the exit passage for the fluid.

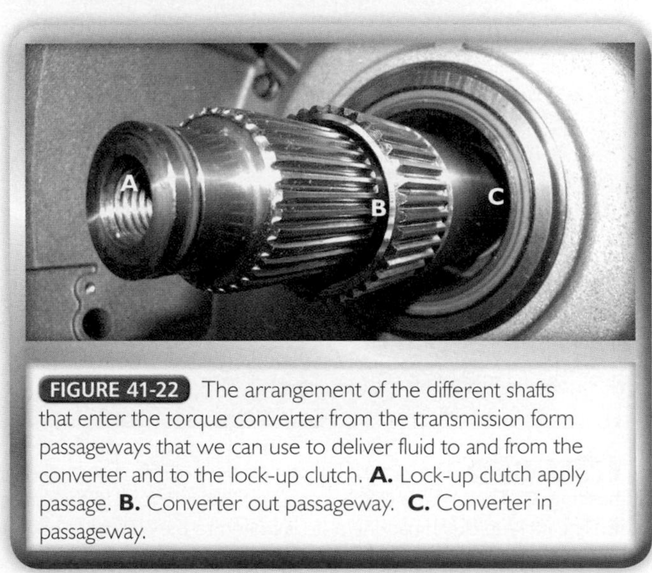

FIGURE 41-22 The arrangement of the different shafts that enter the torque converter from the transmission form passageways that we can use to deliver fluid to and from the converter and to the lock-up clutch. **A.** Lock-up clutch apply passage. **B.** Converter out passageway. **C.** Converter in passageway.

As the fluid pressure from the transmission pump builds in the torque converter, the fluid is delivered to the point where the input shaft exits the stator support shaft. That point is just behind the splines that fit into the turbine. The fluid exits through the inside of the stator support shaft.

The fluid pathway in the transmission that leads to the torque converter has a pressure relief valve to restrict converter maximum working pressure. The fluid pathway also features **anti-drain-back check valves** that ensure the fluid does not drain back out of the torque converter when the vehicle is shut off. The exit passage from the converter also includes check valves to keep the converter full of fluid even when the vehicle is not running. Without those valves, no drive would be possible on start up until the pump had refilled the torque converter. Refill can take considerable time, from 30 seconds to a minute, or even longer in cold weather when the fluid is cold and viscous. The torque converter places enormous load and shear forces on the transmission fluid that create tremendous amounts of heat. That heat must be dissipated, so the first place the fluid goes on exiting the torque converter is usually the **transmission oil cooler**. In the transmission oil cooler, the fluid flows through oil passages or tubes that are surrounded by recirculating engine coolant. As the fluid flows through the cooler, the heat is absorbed by the coolant. The fluid then exits the cooler and is returned to the transmission sump for recirculation. The converter in and out hydraulic circuits normally supply the transmission lubrication circuits. Typically, the front components of the transmission are lubricated from a passage intersecting the converter fluid-in circuit. The rear half is lubricated by the converter fluid-out circuit when it returns to the transmission from the oil cooler.

Usually, a third passage is needed into the converter to supply the hydraulic pressure or the lock-up clutch piston application. Most manufacturers use a drilled hole in the center of the input shaft to create this passage. The input shaft is usually cross drilled at a point where it passes through the rear of the hydraulic pump. That point will be sealed between two nylon or steel sealing rings. The lock-up clutch apply pressure is delivered to this point and then travels up the input shaft center drilling to the hydraulic passageway for clutch application, as indicated in FIGURE 41-23. This apply pressure flows to the front of the **lock-up clutch piston**, pushing it rearward so that it squeezes the **lock-up clutch disc** between the piston and the backing plate. That action locks the disc to the converter shell and thereby eliminates turbine slip.

FIGURE 41-23 The lock-up clutch components, **A.** The hydraulic passageway for clutch application. **B.** The turbine front support bushing. **C.** The lock-up clutch disc spline that connects to the turbine. **D.** The lock-up clutch piston is splined to the converter shell. **E.** The lock-up clutch backing plate is bolted to the converter housing.

The process just described is the most common method for hydraulic circuits to apply lock-up clutches in heavy-duty applications. The Allison 1000, 2000, and 2400 series transmissions and most light-duty automotive automatic transmissions, however, use a slightly different method of supplying fluid to and from the torque converter. This method also controls lock-up clutch operation. In these transmissions, the lock-up clutch piston and the friction disc are combined, as shown in FIGURE 41-24. This saves manufacturing costs associated with forming a cylinder inside the torque converter in which the lock-up clutch apply piston can operate. The fluid circuits used for this type of lock-up system are as follows. The converter in-circuit is through a cross and center drilling in the input shaft. The fluid from the input shaft enters the torque converter in front of the piston/clutch assembly and it exits the converter between the pump drive hub and the outside of the stator support shaft. Specifically, in the Alison 2400 series, the transmission fluid flows from the input shaft and around the outside of the lock-up clutch/piston assembly to the rear of the torque converter. This flow of fluid is sufficient to push and hold the **lock-up clutch/piston assembly** rearward and away from the front of the converter housing, keeping the lock-up clutch disengaged. To engage the lock-up clutch, the transmission control system reverses the converter fluid flow direction. With the fluid flowing from the back of the torque converter to the front, the fluid catches the formed edge of the lock-up clutch/piston assembly and pushes it forward. The fluid pressure squeezes the lock-up clutch/piston assembly against the inside of the converter shell. That motion locks the turbine to the shell. While the torque converter is in lock-up mode, the fluid does not circulate through the converter—it only applies pressure to the lock-up clutch. Turning off converter fluid flow when it is not required reduces parasitic loss due to pumping the fluid through the torque converter. Remember that, in lock-up mode, the converter is not generating any heat. To disengage the clutch, the control again reverses the flow and the piston/clutch assembly releases.

Most of the lock-up clutches in use today incorporate a spring-loaded torsional damper hub to absorb the damaging torsional vibrations created by power pulsations from the engine. These can be very simple spring dampers or more elaborate models that use coaxial springs, as shown in FIGURE 41-25. Some dampers even use internal friction dampening similar to those used on mechanical clutches. Without dampers, the power pulsations from the engine would be transmitted directly both to the transmission and the rest of the driveline when the torque converter lock-up clutch is applied. Those torsional vibrations can cause catastrophic damage to driveline components.

Troubleshooting Torque Converter Failure

Torque converters are ruggedly constructed and should last the expected service life of the transmission to which they are connected. Torque converters will not, however, stand up to serial abuse such as high-speed direction changes and vehicle overloading.

The single most common cause of failure of automatic transmissions overall is loss of fluid, and this type of failure

FIGURE 41-24 The Alison 2400 series converter. **A.** Lock-up clutch/piston assembly. **B.** Front housing. **C.** Friction material.

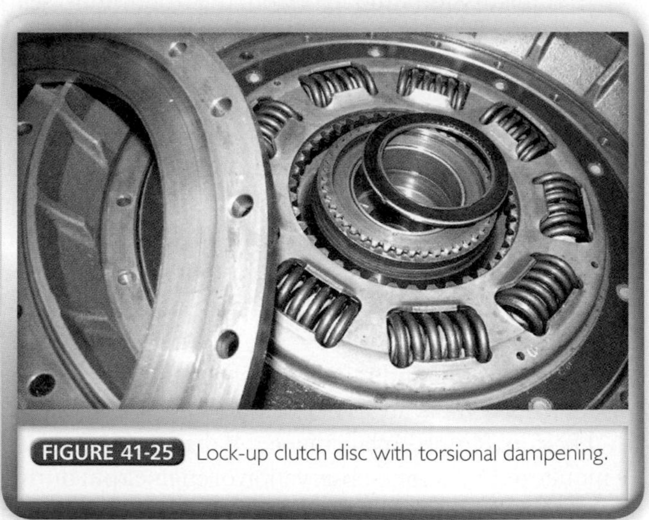

FIGURE 41-25 Lock-up clutch disc with torsional dampening.

normally requires the overhaul or replacement of the torque converter. Both the transmission and the torque converter are hydraulic devices and without fluid they will not function. Before trying to diagnose any problem with the converter or the transmission, ensure that fluid level is correct.

There are a number of failures that can occur in the torque converter alone, and they usually fall into three categories: noise, lock-up clutch issues, and performance. Noise complaints are usually caused by bearing or thrust washer failures. Lock-up clutch complaints are usually precipitated by either failure to engage or failure to disengage or shudder on engagement. Performance complaints, such as no power on take-off or the vehicle being sluggish at highway speeds, usually indicate stator problems. Regardless of the complaint, confirm that the engine performance is not to blame before condemning a torque converter.

Converter noise complaints are relatively easy to diagnose because they tend to show up only when the vehicle is placed in gear. When the transmission is in neutral or park, the converter elements are typically rotating at near the same speed because there is no load on the turbine. As soon as the vehicle is placed in gear, the turbine will come to a stop. At that point, its supporting bearings will start to turn. If the noise begins, the bearings are likely the source of the complaint. During a road test, converter noise will normally cease when the lock-up clutch engages. Whining noises that seem to emanate from the converter, but do not change, usually indicate one or more of the following:

- Transmission front pump problems
- Wear in the converter pump drive hub bushing (excessive wear here is normally accompanied with a transmission fluid leak from the front pump seal)
- Wear in the front pump gearing
- Aeration problems that can cause cavitation and rapid destruction of the pump

Aeration of the transmission fluid can be caused by one of two extremes. On the one hand, when the fluid level is too low, air is drawn in to the pump. On the other, when the fluid level is too high, the rotating components of the transmission come in contact with the fluid. What happens is like a kitchen mixer—the rotating components churn up the fluid and mix in significant amounts of air. Proper fluid level is always essential.

Lock-up clutch engagement and disengagement can be monitored by careful observation of engine rpm during a road test. As the lock-up clutch engages, engine rpm drops significantly and it will rise as the lock-up disengages. A shudder felt on lock-up clutch engagement typically indicates a failure of the clutch disc itself, a failure of the lock-up clutch piston seals, or clutch apply hydraulic circuit failure. Failure of the clutch disc will normally cause the transmission fluid to discolor from excessive heat and burnt clutch material. Shudder on engagement of the lock-up clutch can also be caused by not using the recommended transmission fluid. Many manufacturers include friction modifiers in their transmission fluid and using the wrong fluid can cause converter clutch issues and can also cause the transmission's hydraulic clutches to not engage properly. Always use the fluid recommended by the OEM or its equivalent. If lock-up clutch disengagement is the problem, it will manifest itself as a stall condition or a shudder as the vehicle is brought to stop. In that case, careful examination of the lock-up control circuit must be conducted to determine if the problem is on the control side or is an internal torque converter problem. To diagnose torque converter complaints that may involve stator operation, both a stall test and a road test are required.

TECHNICIAN TIP

Aeration of the fluid or cavitation of the front pump cause an extremely loud whining that can be mistaken as front pump or bushing failure. The sound is similar to a power steering system that is low on fluid. If you hear whining, always check the fluid level and condition before condemning any components.

Stall Testing

The stall test procedure can be used to determine engine, torque converter, and transmission performance. It is very commonly the first test a technician will perform when diagnosing transmission or converter complaints. The stall test procedure is very straight forward, but there are some preparatory steps that must be undertaken. Although the following method for stall testing an automatic transmission is very general, it does follow the usual steps necessary to determine the problem. Before testing, ensure that the engine can be accelerated to its maximum no-load speed. Also prior to conducting a stall test, check the particular manufacturer's specifications for the specific transmission model so that the test is carried out properly. You may find that certain transmission models must not be stall tested in certain gear ranges such as low or reverse. To conduct a stall test, follow the guidelines in SKILL DRILL 41-1.

SKILL DRILL 41-1 Performing a Stall Test

1. Bring the transmission up to its normal operating temperature, usually 160°–220°F (70°–104°C). With the vehicle parked on level ground, shift through all range selections and back to neutral. This ensures that the fluid level check will be accurate. Leave the engine running at idle and check the transmission oil level.

2. Check that engine coolant and oil levels are correct.

3. Transmission fluid temperature can increase very rapidly (as fast as one degree per second) during the extreme conditions created by a stall test, so install a temperature gauge at the transmission line fitting that goes to the transmission cooler. This will be the fluid output from the converter. Converter out temperature should not exceed 300°F (149°C) and sump temperatures should not exceed 250°F (121°C). Most new transmissions will be equipped with electronic temperature gauges that can be accessed with a ProLink or similar scanner. If using a scanner tool, the temperature reading is sump temperature.

4. Install a pressure gauge at the transmission line or main pressure tap. This will ensure that the transmission and the torque converter are receiving sufficient fluid pressure. Install an accurate tachometer so that the correct engine rpm can be read. (Note that steps 2–4 can usually be eliminated with electronically controlled transmissions by using an Electronic Service Tool (EST) such as a Prolink or the OEM diagnostic software, which will track all three of these items.)

5. Caution: Conducting a stall test purposely puts the torque converter into maximum vortex flow and therefore maximum torque multiplication. The vehicle must be positively prevented from moving or serious damage to the vehicle or injury to personnel may occur. Use wheel chocks, full brake effort, and chains if necessary to prevent movement. Ensure that no one stands in front or behind the vehicle during the stall test.

6. The transmission oil temperature can increase as fast as 1°F (17°C) per second during a stall test and the driveline is under great stress. Do not, under any circumstances, maintain a full stall condition for more than 10 seconds and closely monitor fluid temperature. Maximum transmission fluid temperature to the transmission cooler should not exceed 300°F (149°C) during a stall test and, if monitoring temperature with a scan tool, sump temperature should not exceed 250°F (121°C).

Safety

If engine rpm does not stabilize and continues to rise or the temperature rises above the maximum levels, stop the stall test immediately or serious damage to the transmission can occur!

7. With the vehicle's brakes applied, place the transmission in the correct range—usually first but not always. Check with the manufacturer to be sure. Accelerate to the maximum rpm the engine can achieve with the turbine stalled. After a few seconds, the engine speed should reach its maximum and stabilize. When that occurs, record the rpm on the tachometer. This is the stall speed. Gently decelerate and place the transmission in neutral.

8. To reduce fluid temperature after stall testing, shift into neutral and run the engine at 1,200–1,500 rpm for a few minutes. Doing so allows the torque converter to enter the coupling phase, so the shear forces stop and the fluid merely circulates through the converter and the cooler and back to the transmission. If, during this operation, the fluid fails to cool down, it could indicate a seized stator.

Performing a Stall Test When an Engine Has Smoke Controls

If the engine is equipped with **smoke controls**, a slightly different stall test procedure is required. Smoke controls are used on older engines with mechanical fuel injection systems, and they are designed to reduce black smoke emissions. Smoke control systems restrict the engine fueling until turbo boost is high enough. With these engines, it is not possible to obtain maximum fuel and, therefore, maximum engine rpm during a stationary stall test. Any stall test, then, produces incorrect readings. With smoke-controlled engines, a driving stall test is required. To perform a stall test on a vehicle with smoke controls, follow the guidelines in SKILL DRILL 41-2.

Interpreting the Stall Test Results

Usually the stall speed figure will allow a plus or minus of 50 to 100 rpm. If your reading is plus or minus up to 100 rpm, the engine transmission and the torque converter are functioning correctly. If the engine speed is too high or too low, then there is a problem. A high stall speed is almost always caused by a slipping clutch. Clutches will slip due to low oil level or pressure, seized or "lazy" clutch apply pistons, broken piston or transmission hydraulic circuit seals, and other problems in the clutch apply circuit. Further road testing of the vehicle or stall testing in other ranges is then required to isolate the slipping clutch.

High stall speed can also be caused by a converter that is not full of fluid. If the transmission hydraulic pressure is correct , however, this should not be an issue.

A low stall speed usually indicates an engine not performing to its capabilities. An especially low stall test speed could indicate that the stator may be freewheeling (meaning the stator one-way clutch is not holding when it should). In order for the torque converter to obtain maximum torque multiplication, the stator must be held stationary to redirect the fluid leaving the turbine. If the stator one-way clutch does not hold the fluid leaving the turbine, it interferes with the impeller rotation and causes extreme turbulence. That prevents the impeller from turning as fast as it should and stall speed will be much lower than normal. A driver complaint in this situation could be that the vehicle is very sluggish on take-off but seems normal at highway speeds or after the torque converter lock-up applies.

The opposite of this problem is a stuck stator or one that will not freewheel as it should when the coupling phase is reached. This problem will usually show up during a vehicle road test. The symptom would be that the vehicle performs normally on acceleration but cannot achieve highway speeds and it feels sluggish during cruising speeds until the converter lock-up applies. The lock-up clutch may never actually apply in this situation because of the speed difference between the turbine and the impeller. This problem is hard to detect during

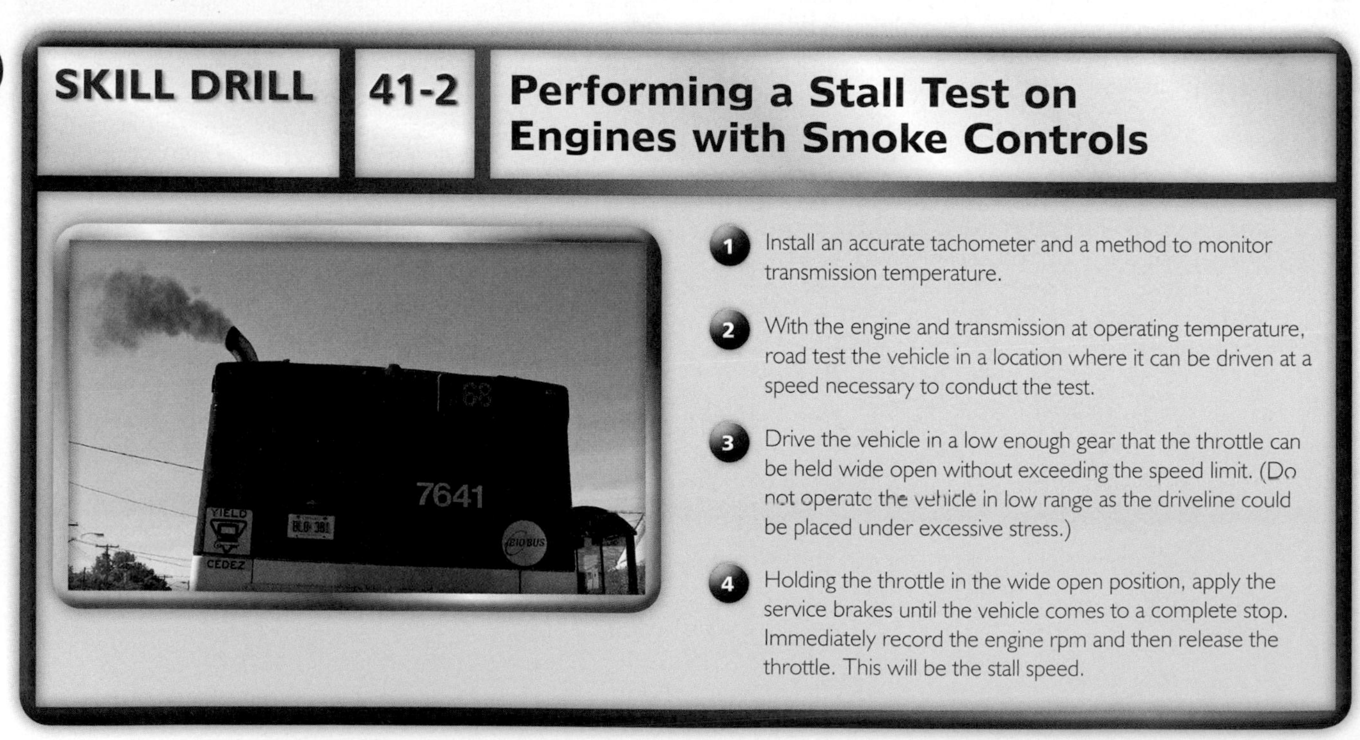

SKILL DRILL 41-2 Performing a Stall Test on Engines with Smoke Controls

1. Install an accurate tachometer and a method to monitor transmission temperature.
2. With the engine and transmission at operating temperature, road test the vehicle in a location where it can be driven at a speed necessary to conduct the test.
3. Drive the vehicle in a low enough gear that the throttle can be held wide open without exceeding the speed limit. (Do not operate the vehicle in low range as the driveline could be placed under excessive stress.)
4. Holding the throttle in the wide open position, apply the service brakes until the vehicle comes to a complete stop. Immediately record the engine rpm and then release the throttle. This will be the stall speed.

a stall test but can be verified when performing the cool down phase. After normally stall testing the converter, the fluid temperature tends to increase. When you switch to neutral and accelerate to 1,200–1,500 rpm to circulate and cool the fluid down if the stator is stuck, it will cause enough turbulence that the fluid will remain at a high temperature. The fluid temperature may even increase instead of cooling down! Internal converter problems involving the stator require removal of the transmission in order to repair them. Recall that in light-duty transmissions, the converter is not serviceable and must be replaced, but in heavy-duty vehicles, the converter can be overhauled replacing only the failed components.

Testing Lock-Up Clutch Operation

The lock-up torque converter has been used by manufacturers since the late 1970s to help improve fuel economy when the vehicle is cruising at motorway speeds. The lock-up torque converter contains a torque converter lock-up clutch, also known as simply a torque converter clutch (or TCC), which forces the turbine and impeller to match speeds. This system has several possible components that can fail, resulting in a loss of the lock-up ability or a converter that will not unlock. The system has a friction clutch disc that is actuated by a hydraulic piston and control circuit. The hydraulic control system uses an electrical solenoid valve to direct fluid away from, or to, the TCC assembly.

On electronically controlled transmissions, the operation of the TCC solenoid is monitored by the electronic control module (ECM), which controls the transmission. Different manufacturers will use different terms for this module, such as powertrain control module (PCM), transmission control module (TCM), or simply transmission ECM. We will use transmission ECM for clarity. The transmission ECM can, but will not always, set diagnostic trouble codes (DTCs) if a fault is present in the TCC circuit. For testing of a TCC on an electronically controlled transmission, a factory scan tool is invaluable. If the transmission TCM has set any codes related to the TCC circuit, look up the proper diagnostic procedure in the appropriate service information. Follow the procedure step by step.

Usually, on hydraulically controlled transmissions, the ECM will not set a DTC except in the case of an open circuit or a shorted solenoid for the TCC circuit. On a hydraulically controlled transmission, test-drive the vehicle to see whether you can feel the engagement of the lock-up torque converter. The scan tool might give data as to when the solenoid has been energized to apply the TCC solenoid, but many hydraulically controlled transmissions were built before auto manufacturers gave the technician much diagnostic data through the scan tool. If the TCC is not engaging, always check with the service information for a diagnostic procedure. Before beginning any diagnostics, check to make sure the system has power. Next, inspect and test the solenoid's ground circuit. If the power and ground circuits check out, test the solenoid with an ohmmeter. If the solenoid's resistance is within specifications, remove the solenoid from the transmission. Apply power and ground to the solenoid while attempting to blow air through the solenoid. If the solenoid operates properly, the problem is probably in the torque converter itself. If the solenoid does not allow air to flow, place it in a clean container of automatic transmission fluid and electrically cycle the solenoid to see if you can remove any blockage from the solenoid. If this does not work, it will be necessary to replace the solenoid.

To perform a lock-up converter test, follow the guidelines in SKILL DRILL 41-3.

Pressure Testing an Automatic Transmission

Automatic transmissions, whether they are hydraulically controlled or electronically controlled, use hydraulic devices inside the transmission to apply, drive, or hold mechanical devices. This means that, to perform a proper diagnosis, a technician will often have to perform a pressure test of the hydraulic system. Most manufacturers supply a test port for testing line pressure on a transmission case. Some manufacturers provide test ports for each of the different gears in a transmission and possibly for modulator pressure, governor pressure, and/or throttle valve pressure. Use the appropriate service information to determine which test ports the manufacturer has supplied and the specified pressures. It is sometimes useful to install multiple pressure gauges into the different test ports so that you can monitor the pressure in the different circuits of the transmission.

Manufacturer pressure specifications vary greatly depending on the transmission and its application. Most manufacturers specify a range for the pressure readings in particular gear ranges. Generally, line pressure should be highest in the reverse gear range. Always select a gauge that can read higher than the expected pressure you will be reading. That said, if you are expecting a reading of 120 psi (827 kPa) and you select a gauge that reads up to 400 psi (2,758 kPa), you may not get an accurate reading. A gauge that reads up to 150 psi (1,034 kPa) would be more accurate.

SKILL DRILL 41-3 Performing a Lock-Up Converter Test

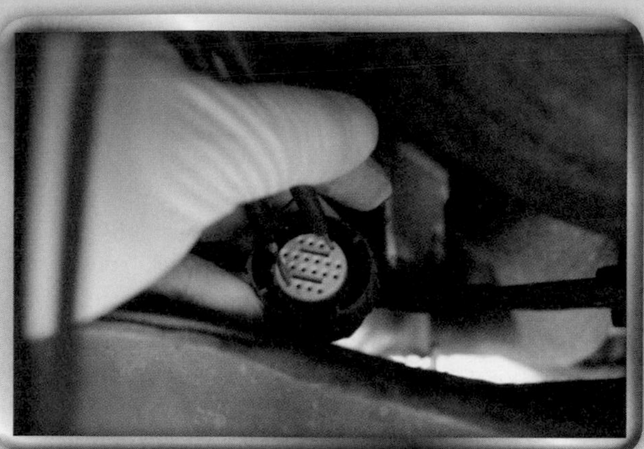

1. Scan the vehicle to identify any DTCs the transmission ECM has identified related to the TCC circuit; record your findings.
2. Look up the diagnostic procedure for the DTC in the service information and follow the step-by-step diagnostic procedure.
3. Test-drive the vehicle and observe the operation of the TCC circuit. When the TCC is applied, the TCC slippage should be less than the maximum slippage specified. (Some manufacturers specify maximum TCC slippage of 70 rpm.) If TCC slippage is greater than specifications, the TCC is not functioning correctly. First suspect an intermittent failure and check for loose wiring or connections.
4. Check the TCC circuit for power at the transmission. The system's fuse may be blown. If it is blown, determine why it blew.
5. If full power and ground are not available at the TCC connector, locate the open or high resistance using a voltmeter to measure voltage drop.
6. If power and ground are available at the TCC connector on the transmission, measure the resistance of the solenoid through the TCC connector. If out of specifications, the transmission will need to be drained and the pan removed to test the wires and solenoid. If the solenoid is not within specifications, replace the solenoid.
7. If power and ground are available to the TCC connector, and the TCC resistance is within specifications, the TCC solenoid will need to be removed and checked to see if the valve is actually opening and closing. Apply power and ground to the solenoid while attempting to blow air through the solenoid. If the solenoid operates properly, the problem is likely in the TCC itself. If the solenoid does not allow air to flow, place the solenoid in a clean container of automatic transmission fluid and electrically cycle the solenoid to see if you can remove any blockage from the solenoid. If this does not work, it will be necessary to replace the solenoid.

On electronically controlled transmissions, the procedure might involve using a factory scan tool to actuate the electronic pressure control (EPC) solenoid in order to check the PCM's ability to vary the line pressure to meet the demands of the transmission. Low line pressure can be a sign of a weak or worn front pump, a bad pressure regulation system, or internal leaks in the transmission. Follow the diagnostic procedure found in the service information. High line pressure can be a sign of a stuck pressure regulator valve or failed EPC solenoid.

To perform pressure tests, follow the guidelines in SKILL DRILL 41-4.

Checking for Leaks

Transmissions have many external seals and gaskets that can be replaced without removing the transmission from the vehicle. Examples include the extension housing seal, the vehicle speed sensor seal, the pan gasket, and the extension housing gasket. A transmission fluid leak can result in failure of the transmission due to a low fluid level. As a technician, it is important that you fix any external leaks on the transmission to prevent this failure.

Some seals, such as the extension housing seal, may require the replacement of the extension housing bushing to properly repair the leak. With a worn bushing, the driveshaft may move up and down excessively, flexing the seal and allowing transmission fluid to flow out of the transmission. Replacement of an extension housing bushing will require the removal of the driveshaft and the extension housing. The bushing can then be driven out using a driver set.

Most seals on the outside of a transmission require specialized tools to be removed and replaced without removing the transmission from the vehicle. Some of these specialty tools are universal types; others are specific for a particular model of transmission.

To inspect for leakage and replace seals, gaskets, and bushings, follow the guidelines in SKILL DRILL 41-5.

SKILL DRILL 41-4 Performing Pressure Tests

1. Refer to the appropriate service information to find the procedure to test the transmission's hydraulic pressures. Verify the correct transmission fluid level in the transmission.
2. Place a drain pan under the transmission and remove the correct pressure test port plug(s). Place the test port plug(s) off to the side where they will not be lost.
3. Install a transmission pressure tester(s) capable of measuring the maximum pressure into the test port(s) on the transmission.
4. Start the vehicle and place the vehicle in the correct operating conditions to monitor the pressure according to the manufacturer (for example, transmission at operating temperature, in drive, engine idling). Record the pressure(s).
5. Shut off the engine, remove the transmission pressure tester(s), seal the threads, and reinstall the test port plug(s).
6. Clean off any transmission fluid that dripped onto the transmission, restart the vehicle to check for leaks, and top off the fluid if necessary.

SKILL DRILL 41-5 Inspecting for Leakage and Replacing Seals, Gaskets, and Bushings

1. Place the vehicle in a safe condition for the inspection. Carefully inspect the front pump, output shaft, and selector shaft seals for leakage.
2. Inspect the transmission pan gasket, side pan gasket (if equipped), and extension housing gasket.
3. Inspect the extension housing bushing by moving the driveshaft up and down. If there is excessive movement in the driveshaft, the extension housing bushing must be replaced. Place a drain pan under the extension housing and remove the driveshaft from the vehicle.
4. Remove the extension housing from the vehicle. On some older vehicles, the seal and bushing can be replaced while it is still in the vehicle using a specially designed puller. Remove the extension housing seal using the correct tool.
5. Use the correct-sized bushing driver to remove the extension housing bushing.
6. Use the correct-sized bushing driver to carefully drive the bushing into place. Take note of any lubrication holes that need to be lined up before installation.
7. Use the correct seal installation tool to install the new seal in the housing.
8. Lubricate the edge of the seal with clean transmission fluid.
9. Reinstall the extension housing and the driveshaft.

Servicing Torque Converters

Light-duty torque converters are not designed to be serviceable, as the two halves of the converter shell are welded together. Some aftermarket shops will service these converters by cutting them open and then re-welding them after replacing worn components. This is not recommended by the manufacturer, however.

Servicing these torque converters amounts to checking turbine end play and clearances to specification and leak testing. If these converters meet these specifications, they can be reused. Unfortunately, most automatic transmission failures tend to be catastrophic. The converter may be full of debris from the failure. Virtually no amount of flushing will completely remove this debris, so converter replacement is recommended at overhaul of most light-duty vehicles.

In contrast, heavy-duty torque converters are designed to be rebuilt and are bolted together to facilitate this process. The overhaul procedures described in this section are general in nature and refer to most—but not all—heavy-duty torque converters. Always consult the manufacturer's manual for the correct procedure. The end play and leakage tests performed on heavy-duty torque converters are the same as those performed on light-duty torque converters.

> **TECHNICIAN TIP**
>
> Removing the torque converter is usually a simple matter of pulling it forward out of the front of the removed transmission. The Allison series of torque converters used in their 3000, 4000, and B series transmissions, however, have a bolt located under a plug in the torque converter front cover pilot, as shown in FIGURE 41-26. This bolt must be removed in order to remove their torque converters.

FIGURE 41-26 The bolt securing the torque converter turbine to the input shaft in the Allison World Transmission.

The torque converters used in larger vehicles are extremely heavy. Care must be taken when removing them from the transmission. Use a crane and a sling where possible to avoid injury. To disassemble a torque converter, follow the steps in SKILL DRILL 41-6. To inspect the parts after disassembly, follow the guidelines in SKILL DRILL 41-7.

Reassembling the Torque Converter

After all of the components have been checked and verified to be in working order, clean all components and reassemble the torque converter by reversing the order of disassembly. Replacing the lock-up clutch piston seal and the converter shell O-ring seal, as shown in FIGURE 41-27. It is also a good idea to replace the roller bearings that axially locate the turbine, as it is far cheaper than having to redo the job at a later date.

Special care is needed while re-installing the lock-up piston. Most pistons have locating pins or splines that stop the piston from rotating when the clutch applies. Make sure the piston fits over the locating pins properly. Note manufacturers recommend reassembly without the use of any grease, as some greases could clog fluid

SKILL DRILL 41-6 Disassembling a Torque Converter

1. Place the torque converter on a bench with a drainage system. When the converter is disassembled there will be a significant amount of transmission fluid inside, so be prepared.

2. Before removing the bolts, mark the two halves of the shell so that it can be reassembled in the exact same location. The converter elements are usually individually balanced, but it always makes sense to reinstall the halves the way they came apart.

3. Check the turbine end play dimension before disassembly. This will allow you to correct any deficiencies when you have it apart. This is accomplished by inserting a special tool that grabs the turbine and allows you to lift it. Measure the total movement and calculate the shims required to bring it to specification.

4. Remove the converter bolts (there may be as many as 50). Remove the rear half from the rest of the converter. Although it is the lighter half, it is still quite heavy, so be careful. You may need to tap the shell with a dead blow hammer to separate the halves. When they are apart, discard the sealing O-ring. Remove the stator and the thrust washers/bearings that support it, and then remove the turbine.

5. Next, remove the clutch backing plate. It may be sandwiched between the front and the rear half of the shell, or it may be bolted into the front half of the converter housing. Remove the lock-up clutch disc, and finally remove the lock-up clutch piston. It should be marked in terms of its position in the converter shell. To remove the piston, apply a small amount of air pressure to the piston apply side.

passages or interfere with valve action in transmission control. Only a light coating of the fluid type being used for the transmission should be used.

Turbine End Play and Torque Converter Leak Checks

After reassembly, there are two checks that should be made. The first check is turbine end play. Two methods are commonly used to check this. In the first method, the torque converter is placed face down on a bench and a special tool that expands to grab the splines of the turbine is installed, as shown in **FIGURE 41-28**. A dial indicator is then used to measure turbine movement as the tool is pulled upwards.

This measurement must be checked against manufacturer's specification. If adjustment is needed, it usually requires a new thrust washer in the converter.

SKILL DRILL 41-7 Inspecting Torque Converter Components

1. Inspect both the impeller and the turbine for damaged or loose blades. Inspect the two halves of the split guide ring to ensure they are firmly attached to the impeller and the turbine blades. Any looseness in the blades fails the component. Further inspect the turbine, locating bearing surfaces for any signs of wear or damage. If necessary, replace the turbine.

2. Check the bushing in the front cover of the converter shell that supports the turbine or the end of the input shaft (depending on converter). Replace as necessary. Inspect the turbine thrust washers or bearings and replace as necessary.

3. Inspect the rear half of the converter shell. Look for any impact damage or leaks. Inspect the pump drive hub surface for wear where it is supported in the front pump of the transmission. If wear is present, it usually means replacement of the shell and the front pump bushing. Pay particular attention to the surface of the hub where the front pump seal runs. The seal can cut a groove into the hub, which may cause a leak. Wear here will usually require replacement of the shell.

4. Inspect the bearing surface between the turbine and the front of the converter shell. Damage here would require parts replacement.

5. Inspect the roller bearing or washers behind the turbine, that locate it axially and replace as necessary.

6. Check the stator for movement. It should move free in one direction and not at all in the other. If it moves even slightly in the opposite direction, it must be repaired or replaced.

7. Remove the one-way clutch cover from the stator and inspect the rollers, the springs, and the ramp surfaces. Also inspect the inner hub for scoring and the bearing thrust faces. Replace components as necessary. Carefully inspect the roller ramp area of the one-way clutch for cracks or surface damage caused by high-speed direction changes.

8. Inspect the lock-up clutch piston and backing plate for signs of overheating, blueing, heat checks, and so on. Inspect the clutch disc by measuring the remaining friction material and comparing it to manufacturer's specifications. If the disc has a dampened hub, check the dampening springs for looseness.

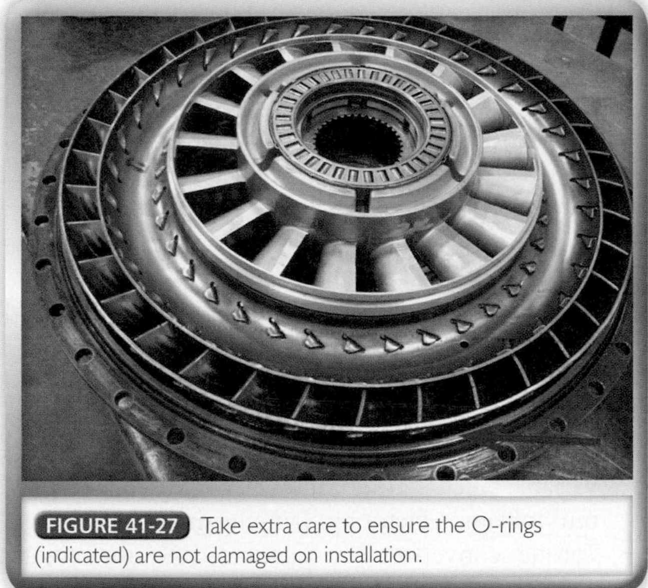

FIGURE 41-27 Take extra care to ensure the O-rings (indicated) are not damaged on installation.

The second method is used on Allison World Transmission torque converters. The Allison World 3000, 4000, and B series torque converters have a bolt under a special O-ring sealed cap in the torque converter front cover pilot. The bolt secures the torque converter to the turbine shaft and provides the hydraulic passageway for lock-up clutch operation.

To check end play in these torque converters, the converter is again placed face down on a bench and the distance from the pump drive hub to the turbine thrust face is measured (A). Next, a special tool is placed in the opening of the front cover pilot, and the converter is now placed face down on the tool. The tool forces the turbine upwards to the limit of its movement, and then the distance between the pump drive hub and the turbine is measured again (B). The difference between measurement A and measurement B is compared to a chart in the manufacturer's manual and will determine the correct shim thickness to use to provide the correct end play. Overall, turbine end play usually ranges from 0.060" to 0.080" (1.5 to 2.0 mm) in most converters, but some will have larger or smaller end play dimensions. Always check the specification. Note that converter end play is manipulated by some manufacturers to change converter stall speed. A larger end play would result in a higher stall speed. Always check OEM literature for the correct dimension.

FIGURE 41-28 This special tool locks to the turbine so it can be pulled up against a dial indicator to measure the end play.

The second check on the newly reassembled torque converter is a leak check. A special adapter is clamped into the hole formed by the pump drive hub and air pressure is applied to the inside of the converter. Leak checks are then made by either submersing the converter in water or by using a soapy water solution to check the seams of the converter housing. Pay particular attention to the weld joint of the pump drive hub.

Wrap-up

Ready for Review

- Automatic transmissions have a limited number of gear ratios available when compared to standard transmissions. To provide enough torque multiplication, automatic transmissions need a torque converter to supply the extra degree of torque multiplication.
- Fluid couplings are similar to torque converters in that they transfer power from the source to a driveline through fluid. A fluid coupling cannot multiply torque.
- Torque converters and fluid couplings both have an impeller or pump and a turbine inside a shell that is shaped like a hollowed-out donut. This shape is called a torus.
- Torque converters have an extra element inside, called a stator, which is the primary component that enables a torque converter to multiply torque.
- A torque converter's torque multiplication factor can be controlled by changing the curvature of the elements, the turbine, the stator and the impeller, the sizing of the elements, and by the clearance between the elements.
- The impeller is part of the converter housing that is bolted to the engine and so always turns with the engine.
- The turbine is splined to the transmission input shaft to deliver power to the transmission.
- The stator is mounted on a one-way clutch (usually) and can freewheel in one direction, but it will lock up if it tries to turn in the opposite direction.
- A torque converter's impeller can only drive the turbine to approximately 90 to 95% of impeller speed. This speed difference is known as slippage, so all of today's torque converters are equipped with a lock-up clutch to eliminate the 5 to 10% slippage.
- The torque converter fluid flow can be rotary or vortex. Rotary flow in the torque converter is fluid that follows the rotation of the converter housing. Vortex flow is the flow of fluid from the impeller, through the turbine, through the stationary stator, and back to the impeller.
- Rotary flow is always present in the torque converter but is greatest at the converter's coupling phase, when the turbine speed is within 10% of impeller speed.
- Vortex flow is always present in the torque converter (unless the torque converter is in lock-up) but is greatest at full stall.
- The torque converter has two distinct phases of operation—the torque multiplication phase and the coupling phase.
- The torque multiplication phase occurs anytime the converter is multiplying torque.
- The coupling phase occurs anytime the turbine and the impeller speeds are within 10% of each other.
- During torque multiplication, the stator is held stationary by the one-way clutch; during coupling phase, the stator will be freewheeling.
- Variable pitch stators can alter a torque converter's multiplication factor by changing their blade angles.
- Torque converters are connected to the engine crankshaft or flywheel through flex plates, so they can expand and contract while under load.
- Torque converter lock-up can be pre-programmed or modulated. Programmed lock-up is for fuel economy; modulated lock-up is for vehicle performance.
- Transmission fluid is normally delivered to the rotating torque converter through a passage formed between the inside of the converter's pump drive hub and the outside of the stator support shaft.
- Fluid is returned from the converter to the transmission cooler through a passage formed between the inside of the stator support shaft and the outside of the turbine shaft.
- Stall testing can help determine whether the engine, the transmission, or the torque converter is the source of a driver complaint.
- Stall test rpm higher than 100 rpm from specification usually indicates a slipping clutch or a torque converter fluid issue.
- Stall test rpm lower than 100 rpm from specification typically means an engine that is performing poorly.
- A stall test rpm that is significantly lower than specification (400 to 600 rpm lower), could indicate a freewheeling stator.
- Transmission fluid that does not cool down during the cool down phase of a stall test could indicate a stuck stator.
- Light-duty torque converters should be replaced with a new one when a transmission overhaul is required.
- Heavy-duty torque converters should be overhauled when the transmission requires an overhaul.
- The turbine position in relation to the impeller can affect the torque multiplication factor of the torque converter.

Vocabulary Builder

anti-drain-back check valves These valves try to keep the torque converter full of fluid when the vehicle is shut off.

centrifugal force Apparent force by which a rotating mass tries to move outward away from its axis of rotation.

coupling phase A torque converter operating phase when the turbine and the impeller are at close to the same speed.

flex plate A flexible plate used to connect the torque converter to the engine.

fluid coupling A power transfer device that uses fluid to transmit power to the driveline.

ground shaft A stationary shaft that holds the inner hub of the stator one-way clutch. Also called *stator support shaft*.

impeller The bladed element in a torque converter or fluid coupling that is fixed to the housing and therefore rotates with it.

lock-up clutch The clutch that locks the turbine to the converter shell when conditions are correct for 100% efficiency.

lock–up clutch disc The friction disc used in a lock-up clutch.

lock-up clutch piston The hydraulically actuated piston that applies the lock-up clutch.

lock-up clutch/piston assembly A combination lock-up clutch disc and piston assembly; used in light-duty vehicles.

modulated lock-up A lock-up clutch application strategy that is designed for maximum vehicle performance.

one-way clutch A roller or sprag type device that allows rotation in one direction but locks in the opposite direction. Also called *over-running clutch*.

over-running clutch A roller or sprag type device that allows rotation in one direction but locks in the opposite direction. Also called *one-way clutch*.

programmed lock-up A strategy that applies the lock-up clutch as soon as possible for improved fuel economy. Also called *systematic lock-up*.

rotary flow Fluid flow inside the torque converter that follows the rotation of the housing.

smoke controls A system on mechanically fuelled engines to limit smoke emissions.

split guide ring The split guide ring that is attached to the impeller and the turbine blades and creates a circular fluid passage.

stall speed The maximum speed the engine can drive the torque converter impeller with the turbine held stationary.

stator The element inside a torque converter most responsible for torque multiplication.

stator inner hub The inner race of the stator one-way clutch; it splines to the stator ground shaft.

stator support shaft A stationary shaft that holds the inner hub of the stator one-way clutch. Also called *ground shaft*.

systematic lock-up A strategy that applies the lock-up clutch as soon as possible for improved fuel economy. Also called *programmed lock-up*.

transmission oil cooler A series of oil tubes or passages that are cooled by engine coolant.

torque converter A type of fluid coupling that is also capable of multiplying torque.

torque multiplication phase Occurs whenever the impeller is turning significantly faster than the turbine.

torus The hollowed-out donut shape of the rear of the converter housing and the turbine.

turbine The torque converter element that is splined to the transmission input shaft.

variable pitch stator A stator with blades that can change the angle to alter the torque converter multiplication factor.

vortex flow The flow of fluid from the impeller, through the turbine, through the stator, and back to the impeller.

Review Questions

1. What is meant when it is said that a torque converter has a modulated lock-up strategy?
   a. The lock-up clutch will apply as early as possible during the drive cycle.
   b. The lock-up clutch will only apply when the driver requests it
   c. The lock-up clutch will apply only in high range.
   d. The lock-up clutch will apply based on a number of factors including throttle request.
2. A stall speed much higher that specified would typically indicate which of the following problems?
   a. A slipping clutch
   b. A stuck stator
   c. A freewheeling stator
   d. An engine that needs a tune-up
3. What are the two phases of torque converter operation?
   a. The torque multiplication phase and the lock-up phase
   b. The torque multiplication phase and the coupling phase
   c. The lock-up phase and the torque multiplication phase
   d. The stator phase and the lock-up phase
4. The stall test can be used to determine which of the following?
   a. The condition of the engine only
   b. The condition of the torque converter only
   c. The condition of the transmission only
   d. The condition of the engine, torque converter, and the transmission
5. Which of the following is likely the problem if a stall speed is 600 rpm or more lower than specification?
   a. A stuck stator in the torque converter
   b. A freewheeling stator in the torque converter
   c. A torque converter that is not full of fluid
   d. A transmission that has a seized clutch
6. During a converter stall test, which of the following could indicate a stuck or seized stator?
   a. Extremely low stall speed
   b. Higher than normal stall speed
   c. Low torque during the stall test
   d. No temperature decrease during the cool down phase
7. In a typical torque converter installation, what must be used between the torque converter and the engine flywheel or crankshaft?
   a. A special insulating material
   b. The torque converter front support bushing
   c. A spacer of at least 1/2 inch thickness
   d. One or more flex-plates
8. A lock up clutch in the torque converter does which of the following?
   a. Provides 100% efficiency between the impeller and turbine
   b. Increases rotary oil flow in the torque multiplication phase
   c. Allows a higher stall speed
   d. Increases vortex oil flow in the coupling phase
9. Where does the transmission fluid exiting the torque converter usually go after it leaves the converter?
   a. Straight to the transmission sump
   b. To the transmission cooler
   c. To the front lube circuit
   d. To the pump intake
10. When the engine is idling and you are in park or neutral, which of the following would be happening in the torque converter?
    a. The impeller is turning; the stator is locked; and the turbine is stopped.
    b. Both the impeller and the turbine are turning, and the stator is locked.
    c. Both the impeller and the turbine are stopped, and the stator is turning.
    d. The impeller, the stator, and the turbine are all turning at close to the same speed.

ASE-Type Questions

1. Technician A says that a fluid coupler is capable of transmitting torque to a driveline as long as the load is not too great. Technician B says that a fluid coupling can multiply torque up to four to one. Who is correct?
   a. Technician A
   b. Technician B
   c. Both Technician A and Technician B
   d. Neither Technician A nor Technician B
2. Technician A says that the primary key to torque multiplication in a torque converter is the stator. Technician B says that the angle of the blades in the turbine affects the torque multiplication. Who is correct?
   a. Technician A
   b. Technician B
   c. Both Technician A and Technician B
   d. Neither Technician A nor Technician B
3. Technician A says that the stator locks up during the torque converter coupling phase. Technician B says that the stator freewheels during the torque multiplication phase. Who is correct?
   a. Technician A
   b. Technician B
   c. Both Technician A and Technician B
   d. Neither Technician A nor Technician B
4. Technician A says that vortex flow in the torque converter is highest during full stall. Technician B says that vortex flow follows the rotation of the converter housing or shell. Who is correct?
   a. Technician A
   b. Technician B
   c. Both Technician A and Technician B
   d. Neither Technician A nor Technician B
5. Technician A says that the torque multiplication factor of a torque converter is affected by the angle of the stator blades. Technician B says that the turbine end play can affect the torque converter's multiplication factor. Who is correct?
   a. Technician A
   b. Technician B
   c. Both Technician A and Technician B
   d. Neither Technician A nor Technician B
6. Technician A says that selecting drive in an automatic transmission while the rpm is very high can damage the stator one-way clutch. Technician B says that the stator one-way clutch is usually a roller-type clutch. Who is correct?
   a. Technician A
   b. Technician B
   c. Both Technician A and Technician B
   d. Neither Technician A nor Technician B
7. Technician A says that the split guide ring in the torque converter helps to direct the flow of fluid during torque multiplication phase. Technician B says that the split guide ring in the torque converter helps to direct the flow of fluid during the coupling phase. Who is correct?
   a. Technician A
   b. Technician B
   c. Both Technician A and Technician B
   d. Neither Technician A nor Technician B
8. Technician A says that light-duty torque converters should be replaced at transmission overhaul. Technician B says that light-duty torque converters are not designed to be rebuilt. Who is correct?
   a. Technician A
   b. Technician B
   c. Both Technician A and Technician B
   d. Neither Technician A nor Technician B
9. Technician A says that turbine end play is an important check when rebuilding a heavy-duty torque converter. Technician B says that stator end play is checked after the torque converter is reassembled. Who is correct?
   a. Technician A
   b. Technician B
   c. Both Technician A and Technician B
   d. Neither Technician A nor Technician B
10. Technician A says that, during the torque multiplication phase in the torque converter, the oil exiting the stator is flowing opposite to impeller rotation. Technician B says that, during the torque multiplication phase in the torque converter, the oil exiting the turbine is flowing opposite to impeller rotation. Who is correct?
    a. Technician A
    b. Technician B
    c. Both Technician A and Technician B
    d. Neither Technician A nor Technician B

CHAPTER 42

NATEF Tasks

There are no NATEF tasks for this chapter.

Knowledge Objectives

After reading this chapter, you will be able to:

1. Explain the construction and operation of simple planetary gears. (pp 1372–1374)
2. Explain the rules for planetary gear operation. (p 1373)
3. Explain the laws of simple planetary gears. (p 1373)
4. Identify simple planetary gear power flows and ratios. (pp 1374–1378)
5. Describe brake band construction and operation. (pp 1378–1379)
6. Differentiate between sprag and roller type one-way clutches used in automatic transmissions. (pp 1379–1380)
7. Differentiate between rotating and stationary hydraulic clutch construction and operation. (pp 1380–1381)
8. Discuss Simpson, Ravigneaux, and other common planetary gear arrangements. (pp 1380–1381)
9. Describe compound planetary gear power flows. (pp 1382–1387)
10. Explain Simpson planetary gear set power flow. (pp 1382–1387)

Planetary Gear Concepts

Skills Objectives

There are no skill objectives for this chapter.

Introduction

At the heart of automatic transmission operation is the planetary gear set. Planetary gears are so called because of the way they are designed and how their components interact with each other. Planetary gear operation is quite different than conventional gearing used in standard and automated standard transmissions. All automatic transmissions rely on a combination of **planetary gears** and **power train control devices** to create their power flows. Therefore, before we start discussing automatic transmissions, a solid understanding of planetary gear concepts is required. This chapter will explain the rules and laws of simple planetary gears, how they interact with each other, and the devices used to control that interaction.

Fundamentals of Planetary Gearing

The simple planetary gear set consists of three components. First is the central externally toothed **sun gear**. Second is the externally toothed planet pinions held in a component called the **carrier**. The pinions revolve around the sun gear like planets in our solar system. The internally toothed **ring gear** surrounds the **pinion gears**, as illustrated in FIGURE 42-1. The three different gear components are in constant mesh with one another. Planetary gears are also known as **epicyclical gears**. That is, they are arranged to revolve around a common centerline.

Planetary gears are extremely versatile. They allow several ratios from one set of gears. One simple planetary gear set can be arranged to produce the following ratios:

- Two different forward reduction ratios to increase output torque while decreasing output speed
- Two different forward overdrives that increase output speed but decrease output torque
- One reverse reduction ratio
- One reverse overdrive ratio

The planetary gear set can also be used to create a direct drive, allowing torque and speed to pass through the gear set unchanged. In fact, planetary gear sets have excellent torque carrying capabilities because of the number of teeth involved to actually transfer the power. In addition, their epicyclical design allows them to cancel out most radial thrust loads.

Planetary gear sets are not without drawbacks, however. Planetary gears are normally helically cut for strength and noise reduction, but that means that they create a serious amount of axial thrust under load. Several components must be used to deal with that thrust. Planetary power train control devices are operated hydraulically, which is easily accomplished with a stationary clutch or brake band. Rotating hydraulic clutches, though, represent difficulties in supplying application pressure to the clutch as it

You Are the Technician

A truck is brought to your service facility. The vehicle has an Allison AT 541 hydraulically controlled automatic transmission. The driver complains that when his truck is heavily loaded, the engine rpms increase to a very high level when the transmission shifts to second gear. If the driver releases the throttle for a moment, the transmission seems to complete the shift, but it seems that it shifts into third gear—not second. He says the problem does not seem to be as bad when his truck is empty, but he is still not sure if the transmission actually shifts to second. You road test the vehicle and discover that, indeed, the transmission seems to skip second and go directly into third gear.

1. Should you check the transmission fluid level? Why or why not?
2. Should you pressure test the hydraulic circuit for the second gear hydraulic clutch?
3. Should you replace the transmission? Explain.

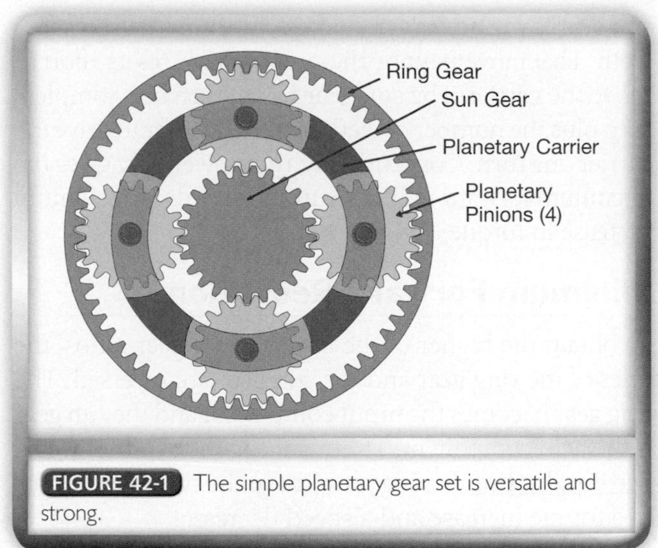

FIGURE 42-1 The simple planetary gear set is versatile and strong.

is moving. Different methods are used, but most systems use a series of sealing rings to form passages to supply the clutches. (We will look at these challenges in the Hydraulically Controlled Automatic Transmissions chapter.)

Rules of Planetary Gears

The planetary gear set can be designed with straight-cut spur-type gears or with stronger and quieter helical cut gears. Spur-cut gears will be noisier in operation, but they create no axial thrust. Helical-cut gears are stronger and quieter but create axial thrust that must be dealt with.

Planetary gears are very strong for their size. Consider a single countershaft transmission gear train. All the torque is transmitted through one or two teeth in mesh at any given time. In a planetary gear set there are at least three sets of teeth (the three pinions) transmitting the torque. In heavier applications, the number of pinions is increased, giving even more teeth in contact. Helical planetary gears also have the increased strength benefit that helical gears bring to countershaft transmissions. Because of this, planetary gears can be made very compact and yet still transmit great amounts of torque. In order for planetary gears to transmit torque, the following three criteria must be met. These criteria are known as the rules of planetary gears.

1. One of the three planetary gear components must be inputted from the power source.
2. One of the planetary gear components must be held stationary.
3. One of the planetary gear components must be connected to an output.

The only exception to the rules above occurs when we want a direct drive, or 1:1 ratio, through the gear set. To obtain a 1:1 ratio, two members of the gear set are inputted at the same speed. That causes the third component to turn with them. The third component is connected to the output so the result is direct drive. If these three rules are not met and any of the planetary gear components is free to turn, it will do so. The result will be neutral and no torque or rotational output can be transmitted.

All simple planetary gears can produce the same seven ratios regardless of size. The actual reductions and overdrives will vary, however, based on the number of teeth on the three components. The key to figuring out which ratio will be achieved is the carrier. Recall that the carrier is the component that holds the planetary pinions. The pinions merely connect the carrier to the gear set. The active component is the carrier itself. Knowing which one of the rules of planetary gears applies to the carrier—that is, whether the carrier is the input, the output, or the held member—will allow the resulting power flow to be determined.

The Role of the Carrier

The carrier is the key to planetary gear power flows; provided that the rules of planetary gears are met, the following holds true:

1. If the carrier is the **output member** of the gear set, the resulting power flow will always be a forward reduction or underdrive ratio.
2. If the carrier is the **input member** of the gear set, the result will always be a forward overdrive ratio.
3. If the carrier is the held or **reaction member** of the gear set, then the result will always be reverse.

Once it is known what the carrier is doing, figuring out what the other two planetary components are doing becomes easier.

If the carrier is output, which always gives a forward (same direction as input) gear reduction (increased output torque and decreased output speed), the sun gear and the ring gear must be either the input or the held component to satisfy the three rules of planetary gears.

If the carrier is input, the result is always a forward overdrive. That is, the direction is the same as the input and there is decreased torque and increased output speed. In that case, the sun gear and the ring gear must be either the output or the held component to satisfy the three rules of planetary gears.

If the carrier is the held component, the result will always be a reverse gear. That is, the direction will be opposite to input. The sun gear and the ring gear must be either input or output to satisfy the rules of planetary gears. If the sun gear is input, the result will be a reverse reduction, if the ring gear is input, the result will be a reverse overdrive.

Planetary Gear Power Flows

The roles and results of planetary gear sets are organized in TABLE 42-1. Note that if any two planetary gear set members are input at the same speed, the third will become the output at the same speed and direction for a 1:1 ratio or direct drive.

Throughout the sections on planetary gear power flows, planetary gear motion is described using the simplified planetary gear drawings. Each diagram uses the following legend:

- The input component direction is in **red**.
- The output component direction is in **green**.
- The held component is indicated with a black line and ground symbol.
- The reaction direction of the planet pinions is shown in brown.

Let's examine maximum and minimum forward reduction, maximum and minimum forward overdrive, reverse reduction, and reverse overdrive in greater detail.

Maximum Forward Reduction

The lower or **maximum forward reduction**, shown in FIGURE 42-2, will be obtained if the sun gear is the input because a smaller input gear always gives a lower output speed. Therefore, the ring gear would have to be the held component. In Figure 42-2, we see that the input (in red) turns the sun gear clockwise, and the ring gear is held. This turns the carrier in a clockwise direction for the output (green). Notice the reaction direction on the carrier pinion gear (brown). It has to walk around the stationary ring gear in a counterclockwise direction. This means that the carrier pinions against which the sun gear is pushing are moving away from the sun gear's teeth. That movement by the sun gear reduces its effort to move the carrier. The sun gear has to turn one complete turn plus the number of teeth on the ring gear to drive the carrier one turn. Consequently, this power flow gives the maximum forward reduction in speed and the maximum increase in torque.

Minimum Forward Reduction

To obtain the higher of the two forward gear ratios, the roles of the ring gear and the sun gear are reversed. The ring gear becomes the input component and the sun gear is the held component. This results in the **minimum forward reduction** (or higher ratio of the two) that results in a torque increase and a speed decrease.

In FIGURE 42-3 we see clockwise input on the ring gear (red). The ring gear tries to turn the carrier in a

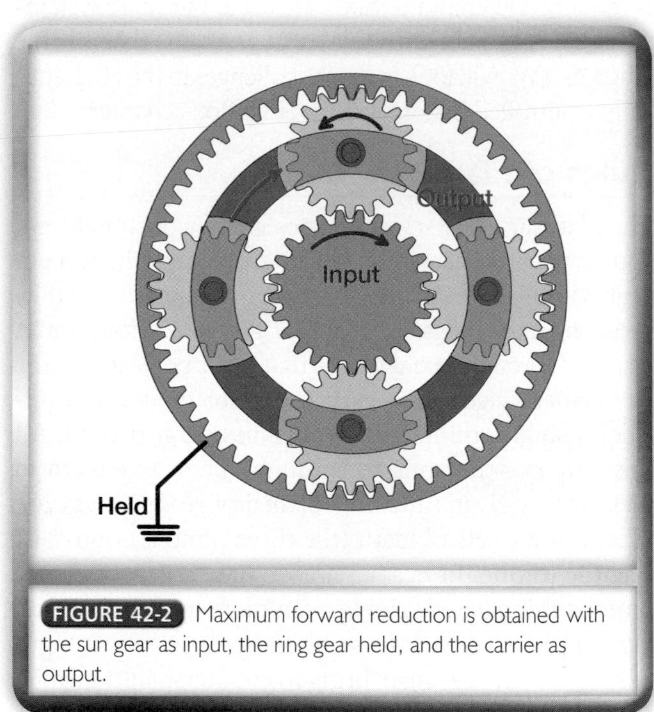

FIGURE 42-2 Maximum forward reduction is obtained with the sun gear as input, the ring gear held, and the carrier as output.

TABLE 42-1: Roles and Results of Planetary Gear Sets

Sun Gear	Carrier	Ring Gear	Speed	Torque	Direction
Input	Output	Held	Max reduction	Increase	Same as input
Held	Output	Input	Min reduction	Increase	Same as input
Output	Input	Held	Max increase	Decrease	Same as input
Held	Input	Output	Min increase	Decrease	Same as input
Input	Held	Output	Reduction	Increase	Reverse
Output	Held	Input	Increase	Decrease	Reverse

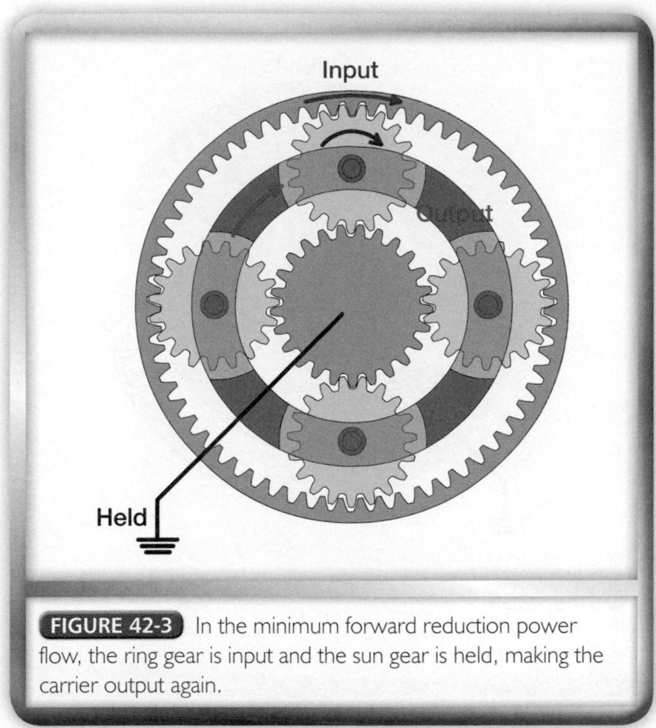

FIGURE 42-3 In the minimum forward reduction power flow, the ring gear is input and the sun gear is held, making the carrier output again.

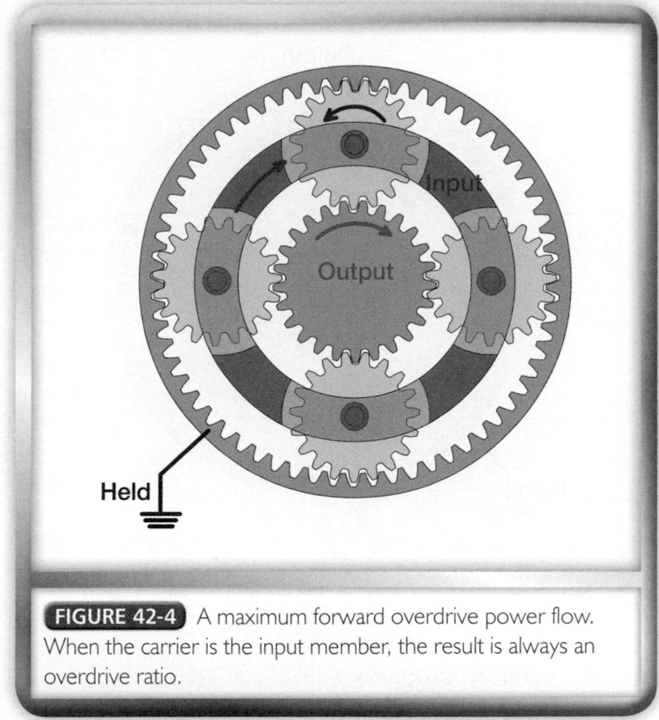

FIGURE 42-4 A maximum forward overdrive power flow. When the carrier is the input member, the result is always an overdrive ratio.

clockwise direction, as can be seen in green. However, notice the reaction direction of the carrier pinion gear in brown. It has to walk around the stationary sun gear, which causes it to rotate clockwise as well. The teeth of the carrier pinion gear are moving away from the input of the ring gear, thus reducing its effort to move the carrier. In this power flow, the ring gear will have to turn one complete revolution plus the number of teeth on the sun gear in order to drive the carrier one full turn. This results in a smaller speed reduction and a smaller torque increase than the maximum forward reduction power flow.

In a typical planetary gear set, the maximum or greater forward reduction (lower ratio) is around 3.4:1, and the minimum or lesser forward reduction (higher ratio) would be around 1.4:1.

Maximum Forward Overdrive

If the carrier is the input component, the result is always a forward overdrive—that is, there is decreased output torque and increased output speed. For forward overdrive to occur, the sun and the ring gear must either be the output component or the held component. Logically, the carrier would drive the sun gear faster than the ring gear because the sun gear is smaller and has fewer teeth. When the sun gear is the output component, we achieve the **maximum forward overdrive** (highest output speed) and, to satisfy the rules of planetary gears, the ring gear must become the held component. Following the motion in FIGURE 42-4, the carrier is input (red), and the ring gear is held stationary. The carrier rotation forces the sun gear to rotate clockwise with it, in green, but notice the reaction direction of the carrier pinion gear, in brown; it is forced to rotate counterclockwise by the ring gear teeth. The pinion gear transfers this rotation to the sun gear and therefore adds to its output speed. In this power flow, one rotation of the carrier will drive the sun gear one complete turn plus the number of teeth on the ring gear.

Minimum Forward Overdrive

To achieve the slower overdrive speed, or the **minimum forward overdrive**, the carrier is still the input component. The roles of the sun gear and the ring gear, however, are reversed. The ring gear becomes the output component, and the sun gear is the held component.

To follow this power flow, see FIGURE 42-5. The carrier is the input in red, the sun gear is held stationary, and the carrier's rotation forces the ring gear to rotate with it in a clockwise direction, in green. Again, notice the reaction direction of the carrier pinion gear, in brown, as it is forced to rotate around the stationary sun gear. The carrier pinion must turn clockwise. The pinion transfers this clockwise rotation to the ring gear, therefore adding to its speed. In this power flow, one complete rotation of the carrier will drive the ring gear one complete turn plus the number of teeth on the sun gear. The result is a slower overdrive than the previous power flow.

In a typical planetary gear set, the maximum forward overdrive ratio would be around 0.29 and the minimum forward overdrive would be around 0.76:1.

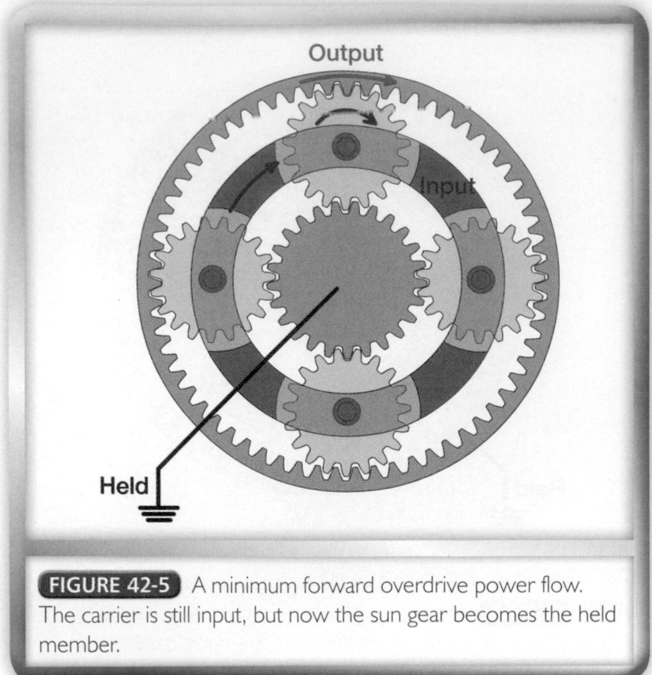

FIGURE 42-5 A minimum forward overdrive power flow. The carrier is still input, but now the sun gear becomes the held member.

FIGURE 42-6 In reverse, the carrier is the held member of the planetary gear set. If the sun gear is input, the result is a reverse underdrive.

Reverse Reduction or Underdrive

If the carrier is the held component, the result is always reverse. One combination produces a reverse overdrive and one a reverse reduction. To complete this power flow according to the rules of planetary gears, the ring gear and the sun gear must be either the input or the output component. Logically, a small gear as input will always result in a slower output speed. Therefore, when the sun gear is the input component and the ring gear is the output, the result will be a **reverse reduction**—that is, there will be a torque increase and a speed decrease. The power flow through the planetary gear set when the carrier is held is very straightforward—the carrier pinions merely act as idler gears.

In **FIGURE 42-6**, we see clockwise input on the sun gear in red. This causes the carrier pinion gears to rotate counterclockwise, as shown in brown. The pinion gears act as idler gears and transfer this motion to the ring gear, causing it to rotate counterclockwise as well, as shown in green. To turn the ring gear one complete turn, the sun gear will have to turn exactly the same number of teeth that are on the ring gear.

Reverse Overdrive

What happens, then, when the ring gear is the input component and the sun gear is the output component? Switching the sun and ring gear roles with the carrier still the held member will result in a **reverse overdrive**.

In **FIGURE 42-7**, we see the ring gear is clockwise input, in red, and the carrier is held. This rotation causes the carrier pinion gears to rotate clockwise as well, as shown in brown. Again the pinion gears act merely as idler gears and transfer this motion to the sun gear. The sun gear then turns counterclockwise, as shown in green. One rotation of the ring gear will drive the sun gear the same number of teeth that are on the ring gear, leading to a reverse overdrive.

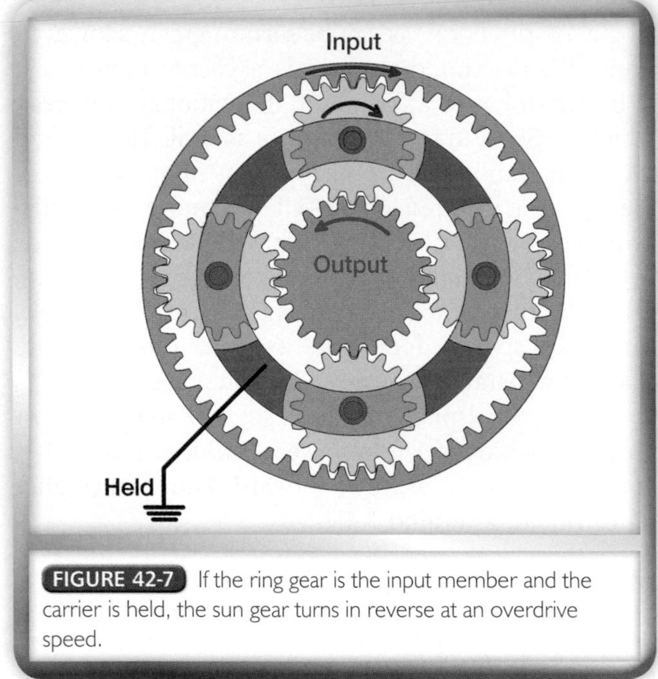

FIGURE 42-7 If the ring gear is the input member and the carrier is held, the sun gear turns in reverse at an overdrive speed.

In a typical planetary gear set, the reverse reduction ratio would be around 2.5:1, and the reverse overdrive ratio would be around 0.42:1.

To achieve the seventh possible ratio—that is, direct drive or 1:1—any two of the planetary gear components are inputted at the same speed. The sun gear and ring gear are input, as illustrated in FIGURE 42-8. Because two components are turning at the same speed, the carrier pinions cannot rotate and the third component must turn at the same speed as well. In this power flow, the planetary gear set is basically locked together and the third component will be connected to the output. What results is a 1:1 or direct ratio that allows torque and speed to travel through the gear set unchanged.

Ratio Calculations for Planetary Gears

Planetary gear ratios depend on the role of the carrier in the power flow and, therefore, there are some unique formulas used to calculate them. We still use driven-over-drive as the basic ratio formula. The carrier, however, will impact the ratio if it is the output or the input member. First, we need to know the number of teeth on the ring gear and on the sun gear. Let us assume we have a typical planetary gear set with the following number of teeth on the gears.

Sun gear (S) = 36 teeth

Ring gear (R) = 84 teeth

As they are simply connecting the ring and the sun gear, the pinion gears act as idler gears. The number of teeth on the pinions will have no bearing on the ratios.

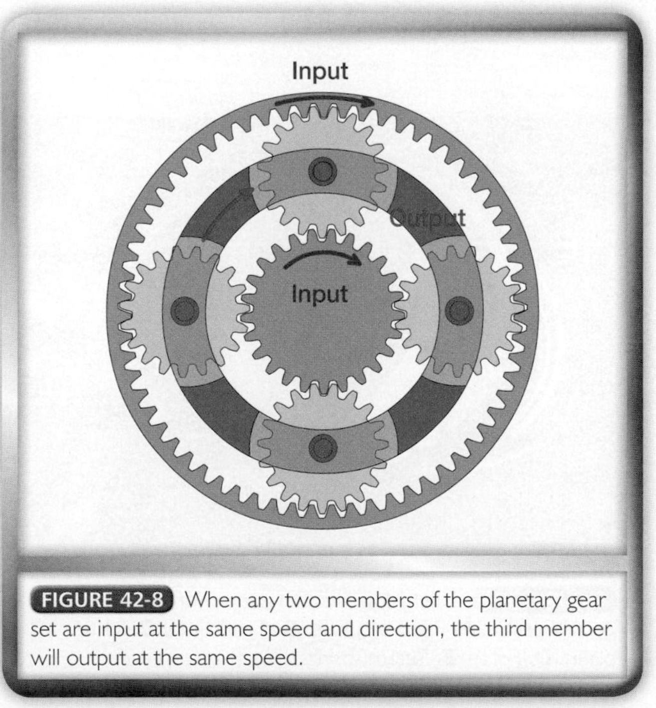

FIGURE 42-8 When any two members of the planetary gear set are input at the same speed and direction, the third member will output at the same speed.

If the carrier is the output member of the planetary gear set and the sun gear is input, the ring gear will be the held member. During this power flow, the carrier reacts against the stationary ring gear, and its teeth have a negative effect on the output. The sun gear must therefore rotate once plus rotate the number of teeth on the ring gear as well. The ratio can be found by using the following formula:

$$\text{Ratio} = \frac{R + S}{S} = \frac{84 + 36}{36} = \frac{120}{36} = 3.33:1$$

This is the maximum forward underdrive or speed reduction.

If the carrier is the output member of the planetary gear set and the ring gear is input, the sun gear will be the held member. The formula changes to accommodate the fact that the sun gear with fewer teeth is the reaction member. In that case, the formula looks like this:

$$\text{Ratio} = \frac{S + R}{R} = \frac{36 + 84}{84} = \frac{120}{84} = 1.43:1$$

This is the minimum forward underdrive or speed reduction.

If the carrier is the input member and the sun gear is the output, the ring gear must be held to satisfy the rules of planetary gears. The carrier will turn the sun gear one revolution plus the number of teeth on the stationary ring gear. That amount of rotation is due to the ring gear being the reaction member and the carrier pinions walking around the ring gear and adding their rotation to the sun gear's output. The formula in this scenario is as follows:

$$\text{Ratio} = \frac{S}{S + R} = \frac{36}{36 + 84} = \frac{36}{120} = 0.3:1$$

This is the maximum forward overdrive or speed increase.

If the carrier is the input member and the ring gear is the output, the sun gear must be held to satisfy the rules of planetary gears. The carrier will turn the ring gear one revolution plus the number of teeth on the stationary sun gear because it is the reaction member. The pinions are walking around the sun gear and adding their rotation to the ring gear's output. The formula in this scenario is as follows:

$$\text{Ratio} = \frac{R}{S + R} = \frac{84}{36 + 84} = \frac{84}{120} = 0.7{:}1$$

This is the minimum forward overdrive or speed increase.

When the carrier is the held member, the result is always reverse and the carrier pinions merely act as idler gears. The ratio in that case is simply a matter of driven-over-drive, as described below.

If the sun gear is the input and the ring gear is output:

$$\text{Ratio} = \frac{R}{S} = \frac{84}{36} = 2.33{:}1$$

This ratio is the reverse underdrive.

If the ring gear is input and the sun gear is output, the formula is as follows:

$$\text{Ratio} = \frac{S}{R} = \frac{36}{84} = 0.43{:}1$$

This ratio is the reverse overdrive.

The preceding formulas can be used to calculate simple planetary gear ratios only. Most transmissions, however, will have power flows that involve more than one planetary gear set, making them compound power flows. In some compound planetary gear sets, rather than components being held stationary, the planetary gears may be acting as the held member even though they are actually rotating slowly. In order for this to work, the acting–as held member must turn slower than the input member. Calculating ratios like these is much more difficult—and is usually unnecessary. We will discuss compound planetary gears set arrangements in greater detail in the Compound Planetary Gear Set Power Flows section.

Power Train Control Devices

To complete the power flow, planetary gears need an input component, they usually require a held component, and they must have an output component. Power train control devices are required to drive (input) or to hold the components of a planetary gear set. There are three basic types of power train control devices used in automatic transmissions—the hydraulic clutch, the brake band and servo, and the roller- or sprag-type one-way clutch.

Hydraulic Clutch

The **hydraulic clutch**, shown in **FIGURE 42-9**, can be used either to input rotational power to a planetary gear component or to hold a component stationary. When used to input the gear set, the hydraulic clutch is called a **rotating clutch** and consists of a hub or drum that is splined or attached directly (or indirectly) to the transmission input shaft. The clutch will contain a hydraulic piston, return springs to return the piston to its released position, and two sets of clutch plates known as the **friction plates** and the **reaction plates**. The friction plates are sandwiched between the reaction plates, and the set of plates is held into the hub by a pressure plate and a retaining snap ring.

The friction plates are usually internally splined to a planetary gear component. The reaction plates are normally splined to the clutch hub. When not engaged, the

FIGURE 42-9 The hydraulic clutch is the strongest planetary control device. **A.** Reaction plates. **B.** Clutch hub. **C.** Friction plates. **D.** Piston. **E.** Return springs.

hub and the reaction plates rotate around the stationary friction plates and the gear set component to which they are splined. When pressurized hydraulic fluid is introduced behind the piston, the two sets of plates are squeezed together. That squeezing action causes the rotational force to be delivered to the gear set component splined to the friction plates. When a hydraulic clutch is used to hold components stationary, there is no clutch hub or drum. The clutch reaction plates are splined directly to the inside of the transmission case and the friction plates are splined to the component we want to hold.

This type of clutch is called a **stationary clutch** and is shown in **FIGURE 42-10**. The stationary clutch will be actuated by a hydraulic piston installed in the transmission case. When pressure is introduced behind the piston, the two sets of plates are squeezed together, causing the frictions plates to hold a gear set component stationary.

The hydraulic clutch is the strongest planetary gear train control device. Its capacity can be tailored to the application by changing the clutch apply pressure and/or the number of discs used in the clutch pack. In heavy-duty applications, the hydraulic clutch is usually the only type of power train control device used.

Brake Band and Servo

The **brake band** is a metal device, either flexible or rigid, that encircles a power train component. Sometimes the device is simply called a band. The inner surface of the band is coated with a friction material and the band is split so that it has two ends. One end of the band is anchored to the transmission case and the other is attached to a hydraulic piston known as a servo piston, as illustrated in **FIGURE 42-11**.

When the hydraulic piston is actuated, the band is squeezed around the power train component, causing it to stop. Bands are only used to hold components stationary and in some cases require periodic adjustment as they wear. It is important to note that the friction material on a brake band is extremely thin and wears off very quickly in cases when the transmission slips. For that reason, adjustment can rarely be used to repair a transmission in which a band has been slipping.

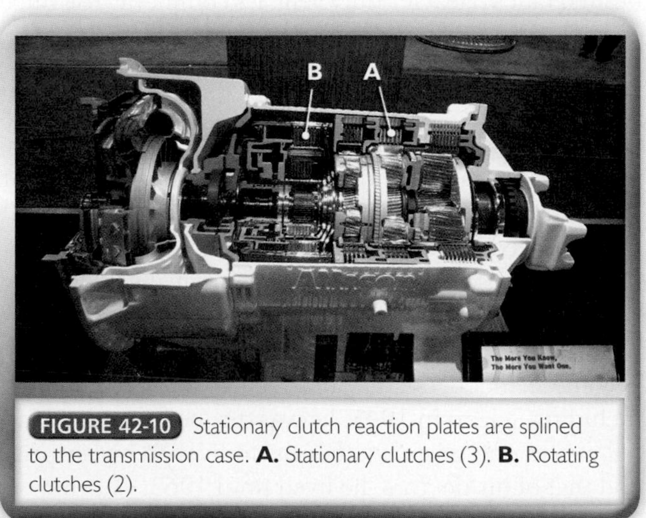

FIGURE 42-10 Stationary clutch reaction plates are splined to the transmission case. **A.** Stationary clutches (3). **B.** Rotating clutches (2).

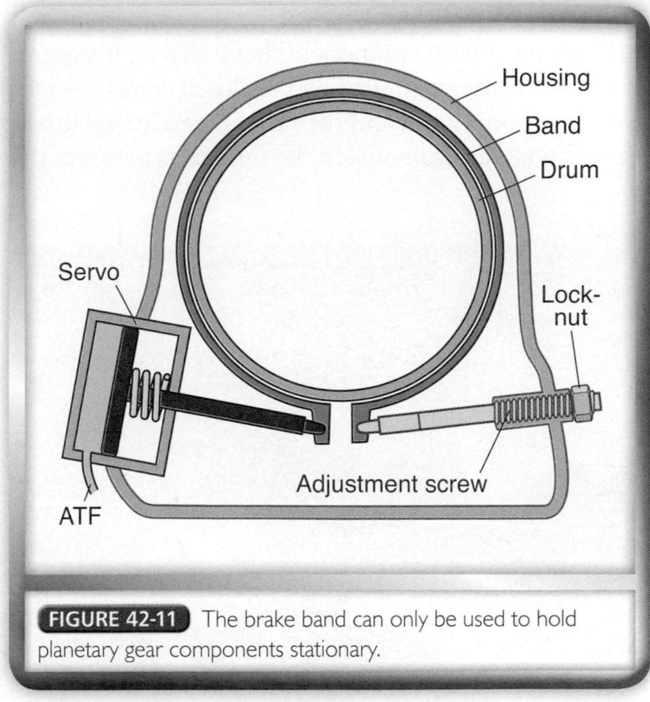

FIGURE 42-11 The brake band can only be used to hold planetary gear components stationary.

Roller- or Sprag-Type One-Way Clutches

Roller- and sprag-type one-way clutches were described in detail in the Torque Converters chapter. **FIGURE 42-12** shows a roller-type one-way clutch and **FIGURE 42-13** shows a sprag-type one-way clutch.

Inside the automatic transmission, these devices may be used to hold something stationary in one direction only and then allow it to freewheel in the other. This ability to hold and freewheel allows torque to be applied during acceleration and then have the connection broken on deceleration. This is desirable in some instances. Consider what happens when a standard transmission vehicle is accelerated in first gear and then the throttle is quickly released. The vehicle goes into severe engine braking mode. The connection from the wheels to the engine is solid, so the vehicle quickly comes to an abrupt halt.

Now, consider the same scenario occurring in a vehicle using a one-way clutch as a holding device in the automatic transmission power flow. When the throttle is released and the vehicle weight pushes the car, the one-way clutch freewheels to allow the vehicle to coast to a stop very gently. A one-way clutch can be used to the same effect by placing it between a rotating input clutch and the power train component that it drives. Instead of driving the component directly, the clutch drives one race of the one-way clutch and the other race actually drives the component. Again, when the throttle is released, the solid connection to the driveline is broken and the vehicle will gently coast to a stop.

As far as power train control devices are concerned, brake bands and sprag- or roller-type one-way clutches are not as versatile or as strong as hydraulic clutches. Consequently, brake bands and sprag- and roller-type one-way clutches are normally only found in light- to medium-duty automatic transmissions.

FIGURE 42-12 A roller-type one-way clutch. **A.** Inner race. **B.** Springs. **C.** Rollers. **D.** Ramps.

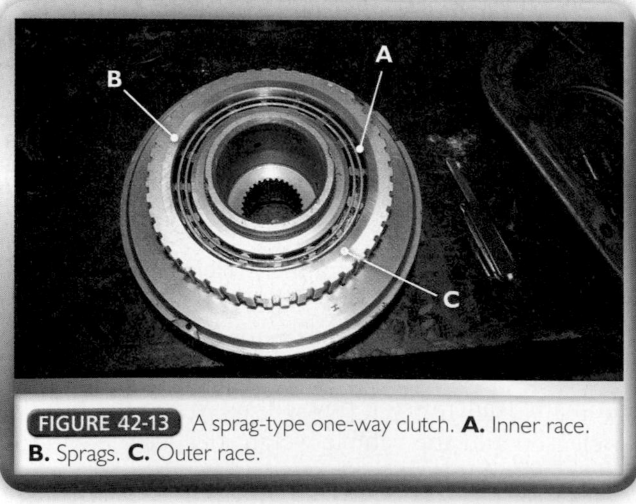

FIGURE 42-13 A sprag-type one-way clutch. **A.** Inner race. **B.** Sprags. **C.** Outer race.

Planetary Gear Set Combinations

With seven ratios available from one simple planetary gear set, it might be easy to think that only one gear set would suffice for a typical transmission. And, in theory, it could. There is a snag, however. It would be entirely impossible to have enough control devices to input and hold each of the three gear set components individually.

Therefore, most automatic transmissions use more than one set of planetary gears interconnected in such a way that we can achieve the necessary ratios for the application. Planetary gear power flows that utilize more than one gear set to produce the ratios are known as **compound planetary gear sets**.

Several different compound planetary gear designs were invented over the years, including Simpson, Ravigneaux, Wilson, Lepelletier, ZF gear sets, and others. One of the first popular arrangements was the **Simpson gear set,** which uses two planetary gear sets interconnected by a common sun gear. The Simpson arrangement is capable of producing three forward gear ratios and one reverse. The second most popular arrangement is the **Ravigneaux gear set**. Usually restricted to lighter vehicles, the Ravigneaux gear set uses two interconnected planetary gear sets sharing a common carrier capable of producing four forward ratios (including one overdrive) and one reverse. Several other arrangements are used to produce various desired ratios. Heavier-duty vehicles commonly use three or more interconnected planetary gear sets to produce six or more forward ratios.

Simpson Gear Set

One of the simplest and most popular compound gear sets is the Simpson gear set, depicted in **FIGURE 42-14**. It was invented by former Ford motor company engineer Howard Simpson. Howard Simpson originally worked for the Ford Motor Company but left in 1938 and was subsequently hired by Detroit Harvester. In 1945, he decided to become an independent consultant to various companies including Spicer. In 1947, he was diagnosed with terminal cancer and given six months to live. To his surprise and that of his doctors, he lived until 1963.

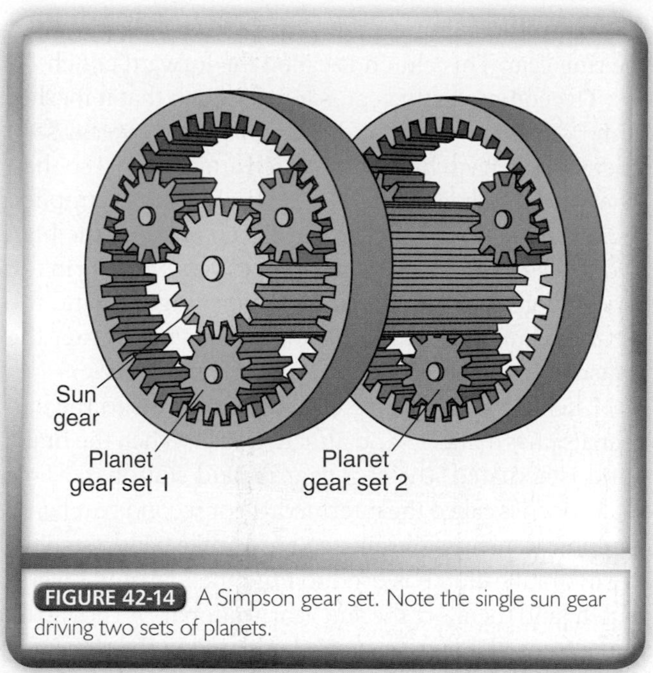

FIGURE 42-14 A Simpson gear set. Note the single sun gear driving two sets of planets.

FIGURE 42-15 The Ravigneaux gear set is very popular in light-duty automatic transmissions.

He spent much of this time after his cancer diagnosis drawing every planetary gear set arrangement he could think of—and filed patents on them all! In total, 23 patents for gear sets are attributed to him. Although Simpson fleshed out the idea for the gear set that bears his name while working for Ford, he perfected it on his own while working as a consultant. The Simpson gear set was by far the most successful and the most widely known. The Simpson gear set has been used by every North American automobile manufacturer at one time or another and is well known worldwide. A prolific inventor, Simpson was granted a total of 41 patents in his lifetime, leaving a lifetime of royalty payments to his estate.

By the early 1960s, the Simpson gear set was being used in most of North American transmissions and several foreign vehicle manufacturers' transmissions. Elements of the Simpson gear set's basic designs are still seen in many of today's planetary gear set arrangements.

Ravigneaux Gear Set

The second most common design of a compound planetary gear set is the Ravigneaux gear set patented by Frenchman Pol Ravigneaux in 1949. The Ravigneaux gear set, like that shown in FIGURE 42-15, has been used in several different North American transmissions and in foreign-made transmissions since the 1960s.

The Ravigneaux gear set consists of an interconnected planetary gear train with two separate sun gears of different sizes. One planet carrier holds three long and three short sets of pinion gears; and one ring gear meshes with the long planet pinions. The long pinions also mesh with the short pinions and with the large sun gear. The short pinions mesh with the long pinions and the small sun gear.

The Ravigneaux gear set was originally a three-speed gear set able to provide an overdrive with minor modification. Overdrive gearing became very popular in the late 1980s and 1990s to improve fuel economy. Today, this gear set is capable of producing four forward speeds, including an overdrive ratio and one reverse. (Other manufacturers achieved overdrive by modifying the Simpson gear set and adding a separate planetary gear set to provide the overdrive ratio.)

Wilson, Lepelletier, and ZF Gear Sets

The **Wilson gear set** is not as popular as the Simpson or the Ravigneaux but consists of three interconnected planetary gears that can produce five forward speeds including one overdrive.

The **Lepelletier gear set**, patented in 1990, uses a separate planetary gear set as the input to a Ravigneaux gear set and it produces six forward speeds, including two overdrives and one reverse.

ZF Friedrichshafen AG has an eight-speed automatic transmission, the 8 HP model, which has been produced for the automotive market since 2009.

Many other combinations of planetary gear arrangements are being used in light- and heavy-vehicle applications today to provide the necessary ratios for modern automatic transmission operation.

Compound Planetary Gear Set Power Flows

The Simpson planetary gear set is by far the most recognized and most widely used gear set. Its simplicity makes it a good starting place for understanding simple and compound planetary gear power flows. The only compound power flow in the Simpson planetary gear set is first gear. the other three power flows (second, third, and reverse) are simple power flows using only one of the planetary gears. For illustrative purposes, let's examine the power flow for the Simpson gear set in greater detail.

As illustrated in **FIGURE 42-16**, the Simpson gear set consists of two nearly identical planetary gears sets that share a common sun gear. The forward set's ring gear has a hydraulic clutch splined to it. When the clutch is actuated, the transmission input shaft provides rotational input to the ring gear. This clutch is called the forward clutch.

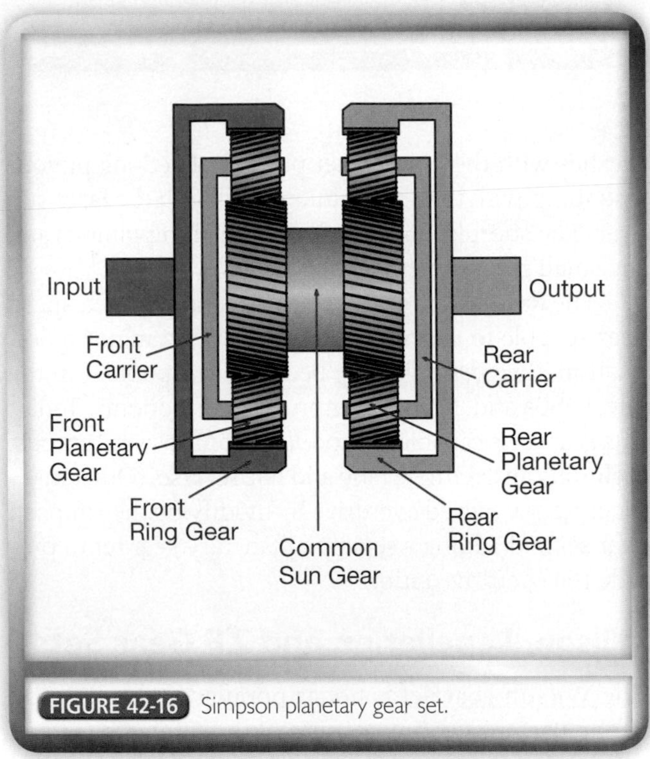

FIGURE 42-16 Simpson planetary gear set.

The common sun gear is long enough that it meshes with both the forward and the rear planetary gear sets. The sun gear has a hydraulic clutch attached to it so that, when the clutch is applied, rotational power is supplied to the sun gear. This hydraulic clutch is called the high and reverse clutch. These are the only two inputs in the Simpson gear set: the front planetary ring gear and the common sun gear. All rotational power must enter the transmission through one of these components.

The high and reverse clutch that inputs to the sun gear also has a brake band attached to it. When the brake band is actuated, the sun gear is held stationary. This brake band is called the intermediate or second gear band. (In some transmissions, instead of a brake band a stationary hydraulic clutch is used to hold the high and reverse clutch [and therefore the sun gear]stationary). The carrier of the front planetary gear set is splined to the transmission output shaft and is one of two components that can provide output power from the transmission. The rear planetary ring gear is also splined to the transmission output shaft and is the other component that can provide output power from the transmission.

The rear planetary carrier is attached to a roller-type one-way clutch that will hold it stationary if it tries to turn in a counter-clockwise direction. The rear carrier is also splined to a stationary clutch or a brake band in some transmissions so that the carrier can be held stationary in both directions. This control device is called either the low and reverse clutch or the low and reverse band.

A power train control device **application chart**, such as the one in **TABLE 42-2**, helps us to understand which control devices are in use during which power flow. Knowing which devices are operational during which range is essential to the correct diagnoses of transmission failure. For example, if a transmission with a Simpson gear set will not propel the vehicle when in drive low but will propel the vehicle when manual low is selected, the

TABLE 42-2: Application Chart for Simpson Gear Set Power Train Control Devices

Gear Range	Forward Clutch	High and Reverse Clutch	Rear Carrier One-way Clutch	Brake Band	Low and Reverse Clutch or band
Drive low	Applied		Holding		
Manual low	Applied				Applied
Second	Applied			Applied	
Third	Applied	Applied			
Reverse		Applied			Applied

problem can be narrowed down to the one-way clutch, (over-running clutch), holding the rear carrier.

Let's examine more closely how compound planetary gear power flows work by following the power flows for a Simpson gear set. Study FIGURE 42-17 to follow the Simpson gear set power flows.

> **TECHNICIAN TIP**
>
> With knowledge of the clutch application chart and a pressure tester, a skilled technician can have a good idea as to what the problem is before removing the transmission for overhaul. Without this diagnosis, the technician may overhaul the transmission only to find that the original problem still exists.

Neutral or Park in a Simpson Gear Set

In neutral and park, the transmission input shaft is connected to the torque converter turbine and the forward clutch. As a result, rotational power is available even though the forward clutch is not hydraulically applied. Power is not transferred beyond the forward clutch hub, so the clutch rotates around the stationary front planetary gear set ring gear.

First Gear (Low) in a Simpson Gear Set

First gear is the only compound power flow in the Simpson gear set. It is called a compound power flow because it uses both the front and the rear planetary gear sets to achieve the first gear or low ratio. All of the other ratios through the Simpson gear set are simple planetary power flows using only one of the two planetary gear sets.

When drive is selected by the driver, the vehicle will start in drive low, as illustrated in FIGURE 42-18. The forward clutch is applied. This brings rotational power to the front planetary ring gear. The front planetary carrier acts as a held member because it is splined to the output shaft. That means the front planetary carrier is being held by the weight of the vehicle connected to it.

It is important to remember that, with planetary gears, even though there is no control device holding a planetary gear component, the component can still act as a held member if it requires a load to cause it to turn. The front planetary sun gear becomes the output of the front gear set in reverse direction, counterclockwise, because the carrier is the held member. According to the rules for

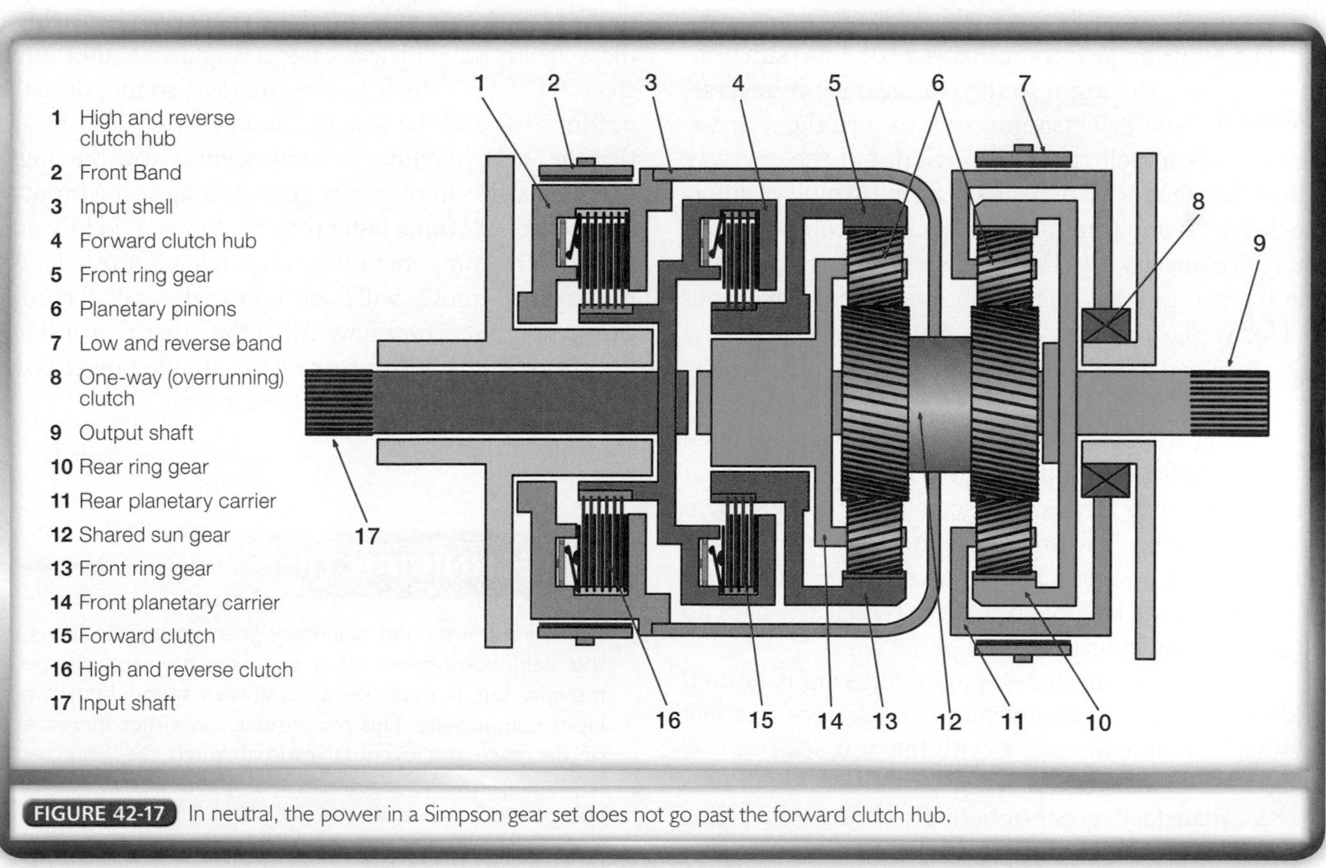

FIGURE 42-17 In neutral, the power in a Simpson gear set does not go past the forward clutch hub.

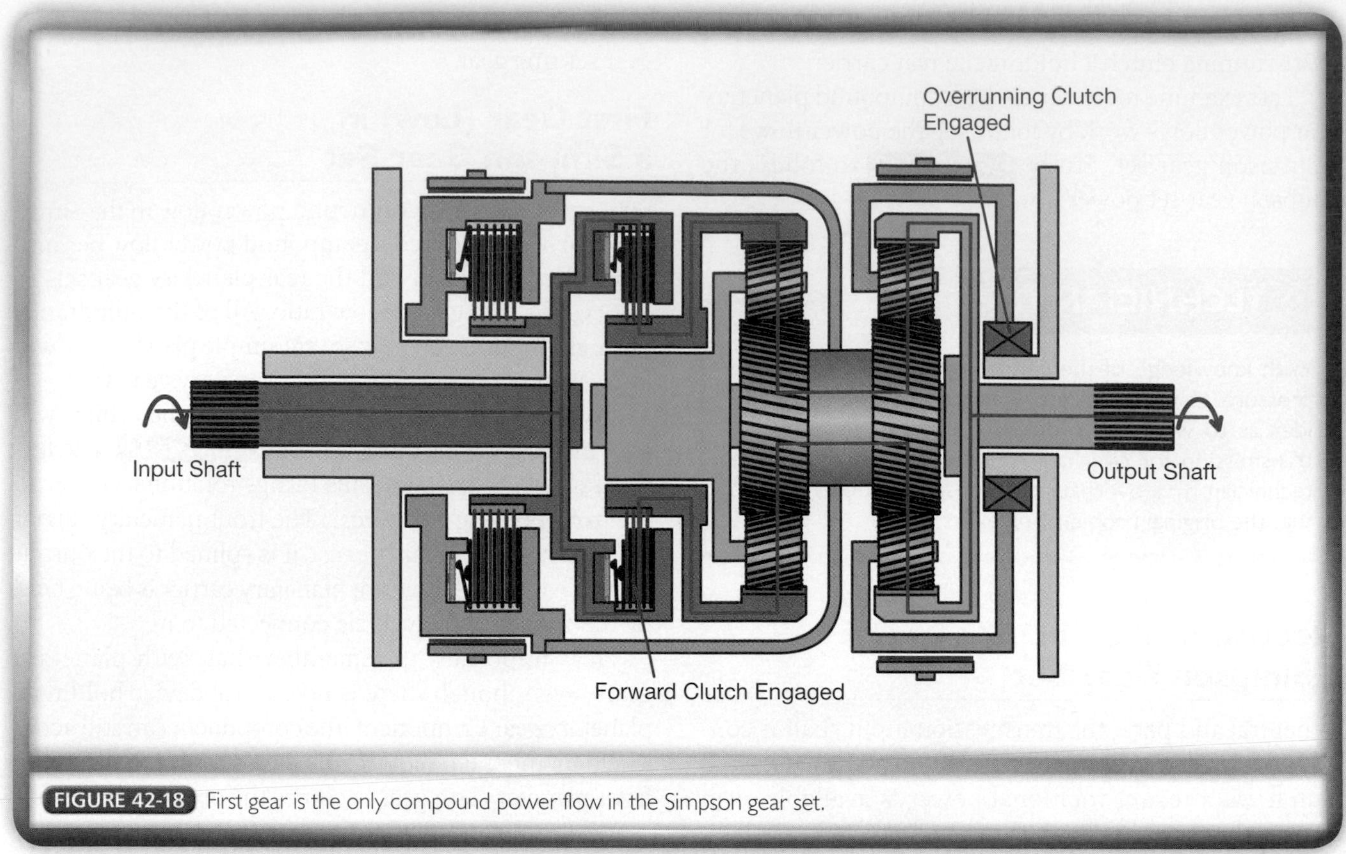

FIGURE 42-18 First gear is the only compound power flow in the Simpson gear set.

planetary gear ratios, when the carrier is the held member, the result will always be a reverse.

The Simpson gear train shares a common sun gear, so it becomes the input to the rear gear set in reverse, counterclockwise. This input tries to turn the rear carrier in a counterclockwise direction, but the one-way clutch attached to it prevents it from turning counterclockwise. Again, the carrier is the held component in the rear planetary set. This reverses the direction again, and the rear gear set ring gear becomes the final output in a forward, clockwise, direction. The rear gear set ring gear is splined to the output shaft, so power flows to the driveline and wheels.

During drive low operation, the one-way roller clutch is part of the flow. If the driver takes his foot off the accelerator, the power flow is reversed and the wheels try to drive the engine. The one-way clutch will freewheel in that direction, however. The connection from the vehicle to the engine will be broken, and the vehicle will have no engine braking in drive low.

In some circumstances, engine braking is desired and necessary. In those instances, the driver can select manual low. In manual low, with the gear selector in L or 1, the low and reverse band is applied. That holds the rear planetary carrier in both directions, and engine braking will occur.

An interesting aspect to this compound power flow involves the fact that the front planetary carrier is held by the weight of the vehicle because it is splined to the output shaft. Once the vehicle begins to move, so too, does the output shaft and the attached front carrier. That means that the "held" member or component is now moving!

This works in planetary gears as long as the input to the gear set is turning faster than the moving "held" component. The component still acts as if it is being held, yet the amount it moves will contribute to the overall ratio of the compound power flow. All of the other power flows used with the Simpson gear set are simple power flows using only one of the planetary gear sets.

TECHNICIAN TIP

In several compound planetary gear set power flows, the held component of a gear set can actually be moving, but it must be at a slower speed than the input component. This movement can either increase or decrease the eventual ratio through the gear set depending on the direction and speed of the "held" component's movement.

Second Gear in a Simpson Gear Set

As illustrated in FIGURE 42-19, second gear in a Simpson gear set is a simple planetary power flow using only the front planetary gear set. The power flow begins again with the forward clutch applied, and that brings rotational power to the forward ring gear. The band is applied, which holds the high reverse clutch drum stationary—which in turn holds the sun gear stationary through its connected input shell. The forward gear set carrier becomes output and it is splined to the output shaft.

Third Gear (High or Direct) in a Simpson Gear Set

As FIGURE 42-20 illustrates, third gear in a Simpson gear set is, again, a simple planetary power flow using only the front planetary gear set. When the transmission shifts to third gear, the brake band used for second gear is released and the high/reverse clutch is applied. This locks the high clutch to the forward clutch and provides an input to the front planetary sun gear through the input shell. The forward clutch is still applied, so there is also an input to the front planetary ring gear at the same speed. These two inputs cause the front planetary gear set to act as one unit. The carrier will turn at the same speed as well. The carrier becomes output and it is splined to the output shaft.

Reverse in Simpson a Gear Set

Reverse in a Simpson gear set is a simple planetary gear power flow using only the rear planetary gear set, as illustrated in FIGURE 42-21. Reverse is the only gear in which the forward clutch is not applied, hence its name. The forward clutch hub is, however, splined to the input shaft. When the high/reverse clutch is applied, as it is in reverse, it takes rotational power from the hub of the forward clutch and transfers it to the sun gear through the input shell. The front planetary ring gear is free to turn, so no power can be transmitted through the front planetary set.

Reverse begins with the clockwise sun gear input to the rear planetary gear set. This input tries to turn the rear planetary carrier clockwise. That makes the one-way clutch ineffective as it freewheels in this direction. In reverse, the low and reverse band is applied to hold the rear carrier stationary. The rear planetary ring gear becomes the output and is splined to the output shaft. Because the rear carrier is the held component, the output direction is reversed.

As mentioned previously, there are many different compound planetary gear set combinations, each with its own specific power flows. We only decribe the Simpson gear set power flows as an example. A good understanding of the Simspon power flows will alow you to interpret the power flows of many of the other popular gear sets.

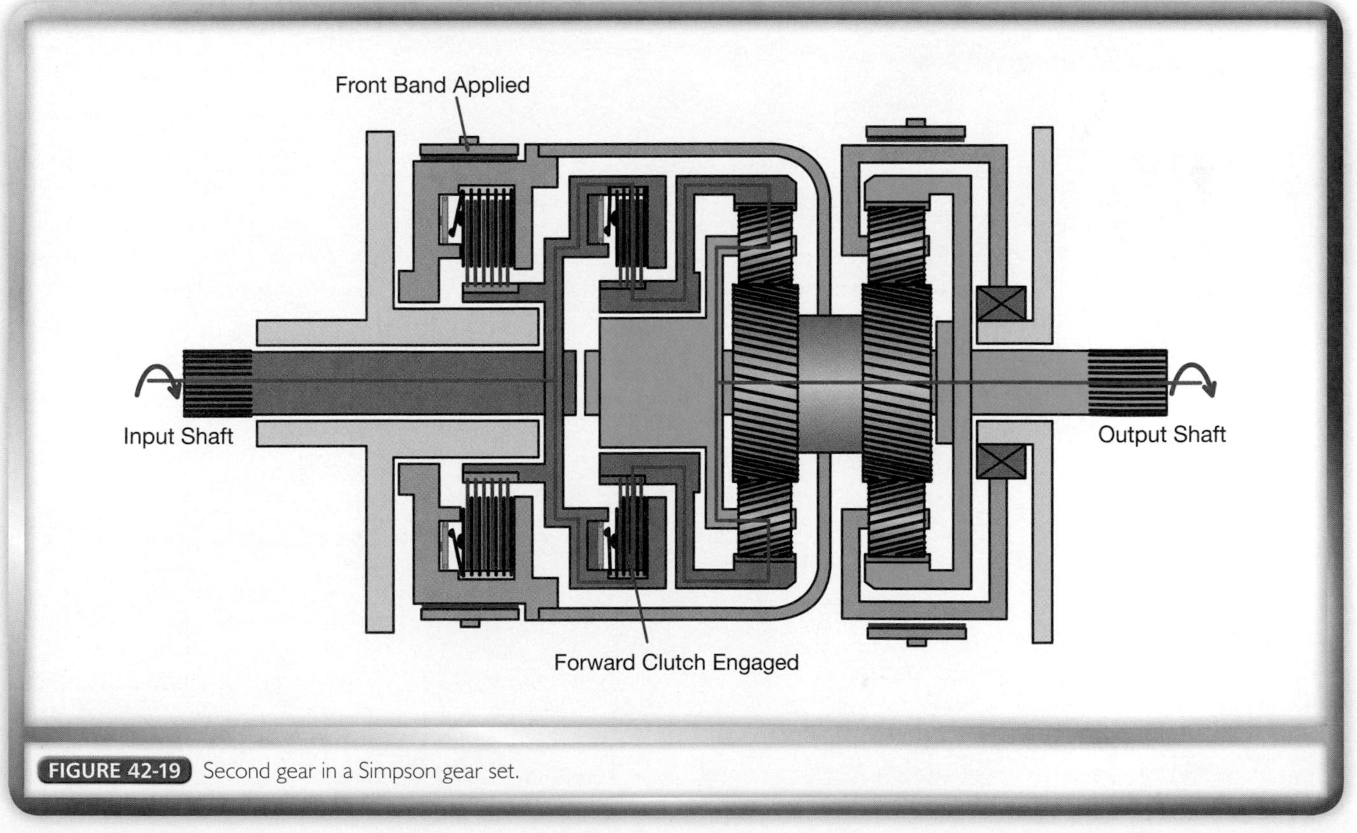

FIGURE 42-19 Second gear in a Simpson gear set.

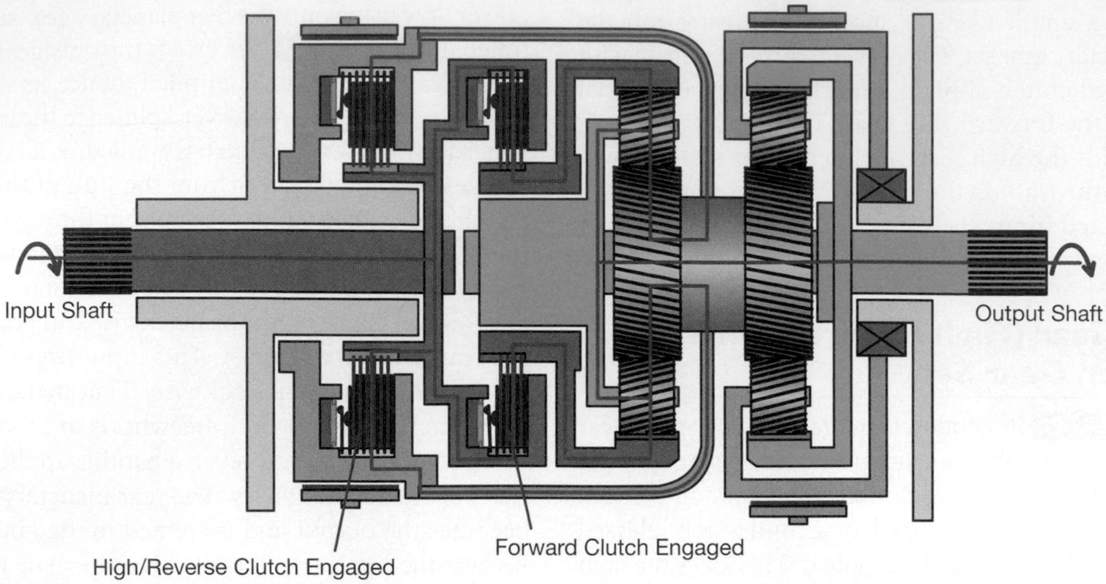

FIGURE 42-20 Third gear in a Simpson gear set is direct drive, or 1:1.

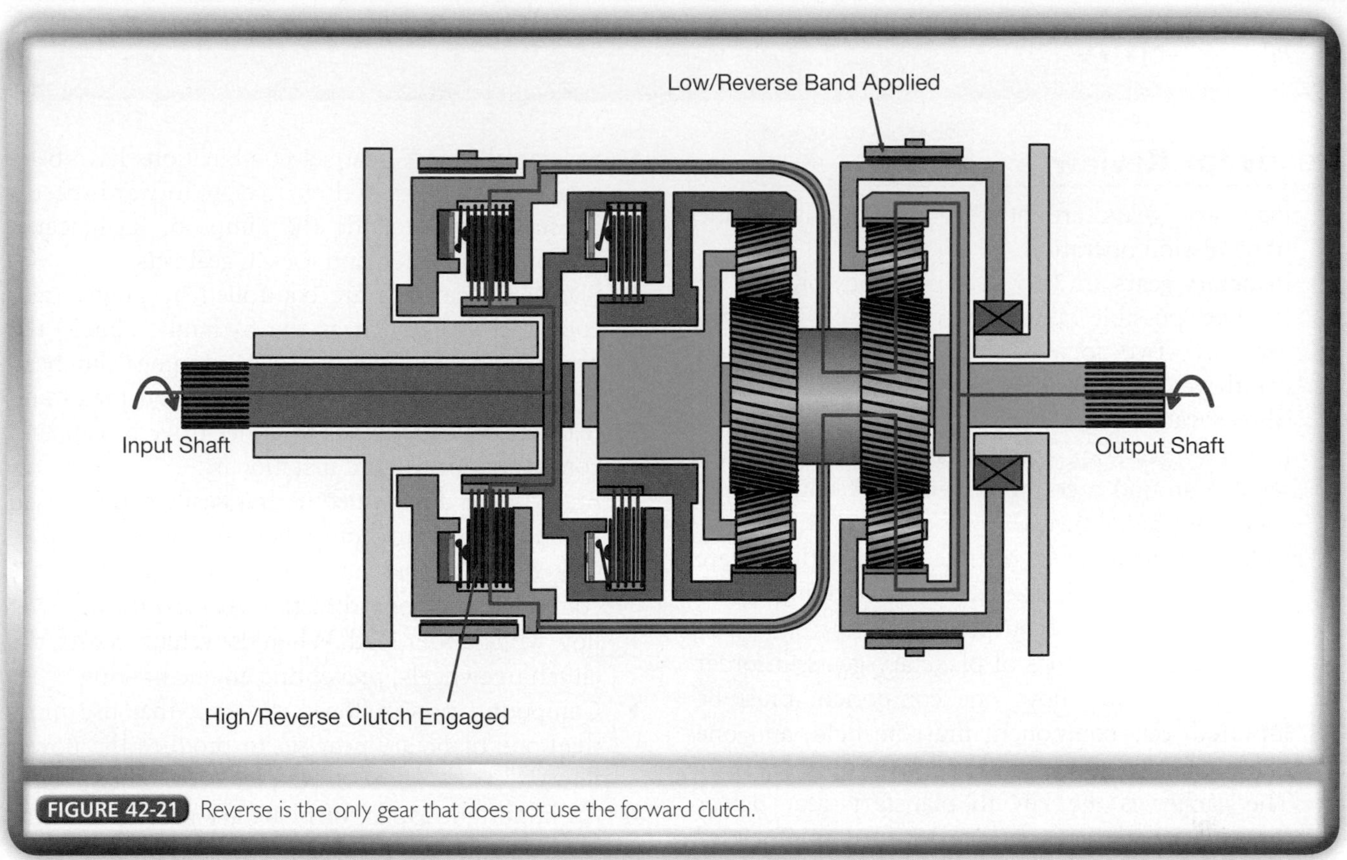

FIGURE 42-21 Reverse is the only gear that does not use the forward clutch.

Wrap-up

Ready for Review

- Planetary gears are at the heart of automatic transmission operation.
- Planetary gears are very versatile. They provide up to seven possible ratios from one simple planetary gear set—two forward reductions, two forward overdrives, two reverse ratios, and a one-to-one (direct) ratio.
- Planetary gears are epicyclical gears. That is, they revolve around a common centerline and thereby cancel out radial thrust.
- Helical planetary gears operate very quietly and are very strong for their size as they have multiple sets of teeth involved in their power flows.
- According to the rules of planetary gears, in order to have a power flow, one component must be inputted, one component must be held, and one component must be connected to an output.
- The carrier is the key to planetary gear power flows. If the carrier is output, the result is a forward reduction. If the carrier is the input, the result is a forward overdrive. If the carrier is the held component, the result will always be reverse.
- To produce a one-to-one ratio, two components of the planetary gear set are input at the same speed, and the third component is connected to the output.
- When calculating planetary gear ratios, the number of teeth on the stationary or reaction member of the planetary gear set is either added to or subtracted from the output.
- Several planetary gear set combinations have been used to provide from three to eight forward speeds. These designs include the Simpson, Ravigneaux, Wilson, Lepelletier, and the ZF gear sets.
- Planetary gear sets are controlled by power train control devices such as the hydraulic clutch, the brake band, and one-way (over-running) clutches.
- Hydraulic clutches squeeze the friction plates and reaction plates together to either drive a planetary component or to hold it stationary.
- Brake bands are applied hydraulically and are used to hold a planetary component stationary.
- One-way clutches are used to hold planetary components in one direction to produce a power flow while under load. When the vehicle coasts, the clutch freewheels, preventing engine braking.
- Compound power flows are those that use more than one planetary gear set to produce the power flow.
- An important aspect of planetary gears is that the held component in a particular power flow does not actually have to be stationary. The component can be moving as long as it is not moving faster than the input component; this is known as acting as a held component.

Vocabulary Builder

application chart A chart showing which power train control devices are used for a particular power flow.

brake band A friction faced metal band that surrounds a planetary component; when applied hydraulically, it holds the component stationary.

carrier The housing that holds the pinion gears of a planetary gear set and their shafts.

compound planetary gear set Planetary gear power flow that utilizes more than one gear set to produce the ratios.

epicyclical gear Gears that revolve around a common centerline.

friction plates Steel plates faced with friction material and used in a hydraulic clutch. They are splined to a planetary gear set component.

hydraulic clutch A hydraulically actuated power train control device that squeezes friction and reaction plates together to either drive (input) or hold a planetary gear component stationary.

input member The element of the planetary gear set that receives input from the power source.

Lepelletier gear set A compound planetary gear set consisting of three interconnected planetary gears capable of producing six forward ratios and one reverse.

maximum forward overdrive The highest (fastest) ratio possible in a planetary gear set.

maximum forward reduction The lowest (slowest) ratio possible in a planetary gear set.

minimum forward overdrive The second highest (fastest) ratio possible in a planetary gear set.

minimum forward reduction The second lowest (slowest) ratio possible in a planetary gear set.

output member The element of the planetary gear set that is connected to the transmission output shaft.

pinion gear A small driving gear.

planetary gear A gear arrangement consisting of a ring gear with internal teeth, a carrier with two or more small pinion gears in constant mesh with the ring gear, and an externally toothed sun gear in the center in constant mesh with the planetary pinions.

power train control device Device used to input or hold planetary gear components to affect a power flow. These can be hydraulic clutches, brake bands, or one-way sprag or roller clutches.

Ravigneaux gear set A popular compound planetary gear set with two planetary gear sets sharing a common carrier; capable of producing four forward speeds and one reverse.

reaction member The element of the planetary gear set that is held stationary.

reaction plates Metal plates in the hydraulic clutch; usually splined to the clutch hub or the transmission case.

reverse overdrive A reverse direction overdrive ratio through the planetary gear set.

reverse reduction A reverse direction underdrive ratio through the planetary gear set.

ring gear An internally toothed gear that surrounds the pinion gears.

rotating clutch A hydraulic clutch used to input a planetary gear component.

Simpson gear set The most common compound planetary gear set; consists of two planetary gears sharing a common sun gear; capable of producing three forward and one reverse ratio.

stationary clutch A hydraulic clutch used to hold a planetary gear component stationary and usually splined to the transmission case.

sun gear The small, externally toothed gear at the center of the planetary gear set.

Wilson gear set A compound planetary gear set consisting of three planetary gears interconnected; capable of producing five forward and one reverse ratio.

Review Questions

1. What would be the output on the ring gear of a planetary gear set when the carrier is input and the sun gear is the held component?
   - **a.** Maximum forward reduction
   - **b.** Minimum forward reduction
   - **c.** Maximum forward overdrive
   - **d.** Minimum forward overdrive
2. Which of the following will produce a direct ratio from a planetary gear set?
   - **a.** Sun gear input, carrier held, ring gear output
   - **b.** Ring gear input, carrier output, sun gear held
   - **c.** Carrier input, ring gear held, sun gear output
   - **d.** Carrier input, sun gear input, ring gear output
3. Why do manufacturers use a one-way clutch in a planetary gear set power flow?
   - **a.** To prevent engine braking.
   - **b.** They are cheaper than a hydraulic clutch.
   - **c.** They are stronger than a hydraulic clutch.
   - **d.** They are less complicated than a brake band.
4. What power flow will result from a planetary gear set if the carrier is the input member, the ring gear is held, and the sun gear is the output?
   - **a.** Maximum forward reduction
   - **b.** Minimum forward reduction
   - **c.** Maximum forward overdrive
   - **d.** Minimum forward overdrive
5. If a simple planetary gear set has 24 teeth on the sun gear and 60 teeth on the ring gear, what will be the ratio if the sun gear is input, the ring gear is held, and the carrier is output?
   - **a.** 2.5 to 1
   - **b.** 0.4 to 1
   - **c.** 1.4 to 1
   - **d.** 3.5 to 1
6. Which of the following planetary gear train control devices can be used to hold members stationary?
   - **a.** The servo and band mechanism
   - **b.** The hydraulic clutch
   - **c.** The sprag or roller type one-way clutch
   - **d.** All of the choices can be used as holding devices.
7. Which of the following planetary gear train control devices can sometimes be adjusted from the outside of the transmission?
   - **a.** The hydraulic clutch
   - **b.** The roller-type one-way clutch
   - **c.** The servo and band mechanism
   - **d.** The sprag-type one-way clutch
8. Why do we sometimes use a roller-type one-way clutch to hold a member of the planetary gear set?
   - **a.** To prevent engine braking when decelerating
   - **b.** To save money
   - **c.** To provide a much smoother engagement than a hydraulic clutch
   - **d.** All of the choices are correct.
9. Which of the following is considered the strongest planetary gear train control device?
   - **a.** Hydraulic clutch
   - **b.** Servo and band mechanism
   - **c.** Sprag-type one-way clutch
   - **d.** Roller-type one-way clutch
10. The power flow through two interconnected planetary gear sets is best described as ______ power flow.
    - **a.** double reverse
    - **b.** versatile
    - **c.** reverse
    - **d.** compound

ASE-Type Quiz

1. Technician A says that a simple planetary gear set can produce seven different ratios. Technician B says that planetary gears are epicyclical. Who is correct?
   a. Technician A
   b. Technician B
   c. Both Technician A and Technician B
   d. Neither Technician A nor Technician B
2. Technician A says that if the planetary carrier is the output member, a reverse will be the outcome if the rules of planetary gears are satisfied. Technician B says that if the carrier is input, a forward overdrive will be the result if the rules of planetary gears are satisfied. Who is correct?
   a. Technician A
   b. Technician B
   c. Both Technician A and Technician B
   d. Neither Technician A nor Technician B
3. Technician A says that helical planetary gears do not produce any thrust. Technician B says that planetary gears do not produce radial thrust. Who is correct?
   a. Technician A
   b. Technician B
   c. Both Technician A and Technician B
   d. Neither Technician A nor Technician B
4. Technician A says that holding the sun gear stationary and inputting the ring gear of a planetary gear set will produce the maximum forward reduction at the carrier. Technician B says that holding the carrier stationary and inputting the sun gear of a planetary gear set will produce a reverse reduction at the ring gear. Who is correct?
   a. Technician A
   b. Technician B
   c. Both Technician A and Technician B
   d. Neither Technician A nor Technician B
5. Technician A says that hydraulic clutches can be used to hold or input planetary gear components. Technician B says that one-way clutches are used to provide engine braking. Who is correct?
   a. Technician A
   b. Technician B
   c. Both Technician A and Technician B
   d. Neither Technician A nor Technician B
6. Technician A says that one-way clutches can be sprag or roller type. Technician B says that a one-way clutch is used in manual low in the Simpson gear train. Who is correct?
   a. Technician A
   b. Technician B
   c. Both Technician A and Technician B
   d. Neither Technician A nor Technician B
7. Technician A says that hydraulic clutches are used to drive or input a planetary gear component. Technician B says that hydraulic clutches can sometimes be adjusted from the outside of the transmission case. Who is correct?
   a. Technician A
   b. Technician B
   c. Both Technician A and Technician B
   d. Neither Technician A nor Technician B
8. Technician A says that two hydraulic clutches are used to input to the Simpson gear set. Technician B says the Simpson gear set shares a common sun gear. Who is correct?
   a. Technician A
   b. Technician B
   c. Both Technician A and Technician B
   d. Neither Technician A nor Technician B
9. Technician A says that, to achieve direct in the Simpson gear set, the front ring gear and the front sun gear are inputted and the front carrier is the output. Technician B says that reverse is a compound power flow in the Simpson gear set. Who is correct?
   a. Technician A
   b. Technician B
   c. Both Technician A and Technician B
   d. Neither Technician A nor Technician B
10. Technician A says that second gear in a Simpson gear set is a compound power flow. Technician B says that the Simpson gear set only has one compound power flow. Who is correct?
    a. Technician A
    b. Technician B
    c. Both Technician A and Technician B
    d. Neither Technician A nor Technician B

CHAPTER 43

NATEF Tasks

There are no NATEF tasks for this chapter.

Knowledge Objectives

After reading this chapter, you will be able to:

1. Name the various automatic transmission models used in the North American truck and coach market and manufactured by Allison, ZF Friedrichshafen, Voith, and Caterpillar. (pp 1394–1397)
2. Explain Allison transmission power flows. (pp 1397–1401)
3. Describe hydraulic components. (pp 1401–1412)
4. Explain the function and operation of hydraulic pumps, hydraulic control valves such as the MPRV, throttle modulator valve, governor valve, and shift valves. (pp 1401–1415)
5. Explain transmission operating pressure control, upshift and downshift control, shift point control, and shift quality control. (pp 1404–1410)
6. Describe shift cushioning devices and trimmer valves. (pp 1408–1411)
7. Describe hydraulic control circuits and schematics. (pp 1411)

Hydraulically Controlled Automatic Transmissions

Skills Objectives

There are no skill objectives for this chapter.

Introduction

Automatic transmissions have been in use in the medium- to heavy-duty truck and bus market in North America for many years. The three major manufacturers of automatic transmissions for this market are ZF Friedrichshafen, Voith, and Allison. In 2006, Caterpillar entered the truck automatic transmission market with its CX28, CX31, and CX35 models to limited success. In 2011, CAT introduced its new CT660 class eight on-highway truck, and the CX-28 is the standard equipment automatic transmission with this vehicle. The market, however, is not evenly divided among manufacturers. The lion's share of the automatic transmission market belongs to Allison.

Automatic transmissions have several benefits over their manually shifted counterparts. Automatic transmissions add to driver comfort and lessen fatigue. They allow many people to drive a vehicle without having to learn complex shift patterns and schedules. Automatic transmissions can reduce service and down time because drivers are less likely to engage in skip shifting and gear jamming. Finally, because they usually have smoother shifts, automatic transmissions enhance passenger comfort during shifting.

In this chapter, we will discover the basics of what makes automatic transmissions work and how they compare with their manual and automated manual transmission counterparts. We will focus on hydraulically controlled automatics and will concentrate on Allison automatic transmissions as they are the most common in North America. The workings of all automatic transmissions are similar, however. Electronically controlled automatic transmissions have dominated the heavy-duty truck market since the 1990s, but their operation and control is based on the purely hydraulic automatics of years past. Understanding the hydraulic controls will give the technician more insight into the logic behind the electronic control strategies, so it makes sense to start there.

The History of Transmissions in the North American Truck and Coach Market

Allison transmission is by far the largest supplier of automatic transmissions to the North American truck and coach market. As early as the 1940s, Allison was making transmission models such as the original CD-850 tank transmission. The first Allison transmission for commercial vehicles was manufactured in the 1970s. It was called the MT-25 and was followed by the AT series, including the 540, 543, and 545, which were used extensively in school bus applications and other light vehicles. The MT-640/650 was used in mid-range products; the V-730 ("V") drive series was used for inner city transit and coach applications; and the HT-740/750 was used in heavy-duty trucks and buses.

You Are the Technician

A vehicle is towed to your repair facility with a complaint that the transmission will not go into gear. You investigate and find that the vehicle is equipped with a four-speed Allison hydraulically controlled automatic transmission. You do a preliminary inspection and discover that the transmission will not go into drive or reverse. The engine runs fine and everything else seems in order.

1. What would you do next to diagnose this vehicle?
2. Could the torque converter cause this problem? Why or why not?
3. Could a failed transmission clutch cause this problem? Explain.

By the mid-1970s, Allison had sold over half a million commercial transmissions around the world and, in 1987 alone, sold a staggering 73,976 transmissions! Most of Allison's designs in these years were four-speed models—all of which used the identical gear arrangement with three interconnected planetary gears. Two designs of five-speed models incorporating a lower forward range were also available. The five-speed models used an extra planetary gear set behind the three interconnected sets and were designated deep ratio and close ratio The deep ratio transmission had a very low ratio for low gear; the close ratio had smaller ratio steps between the five gears. The Allison five-speed models are all but obsolete now and therefore will not be discussed further.

In the late 1980s, Allison moved into partial electronic control with the Allison Transmission Electronic Control (ATEC), which was eventually renamed Commercial Electronic Control (CEC). Then, in 1991, Allison introduced the World Transmission (WT), the company's first intuitive electronically controlled medium-/heavy-duty transmission. In 1999, Allison added to its line of medium/heavy WT models with the 1000/2000 and 2400 series transmissions for use in lighter-duty and mid-range vehicles. All of Allison's current transmissions are electronically controlled.

Allison is not the only manufacturer with a long history. ZF Friedrichshafen has been manufacturing automatic transmissions since the early 1960s, primarily in Europe. ZF has had several entries into the truck/coach market. ZF launched the Busmatic in 1963, the Ecomat in 1980, and the Ecolife in 2006. Most of ZF's models were available as four-, five-, or six-speed models. All of ZFs current models are completely electronically controlled.

Voith, another European manufacturer, has been making transmissions in Europe since the 1930s. Voith's business was primarily for the locomotive and industrial market, but the company started manufacturing bus transmissions in the 1950s. In 1980, Voith started to supply heavy-duty transmissions to the North American dump truck and bus markets. In 2009, Voith announced that it had more than 5,300 of its **DIWA**™ bus transmissions in service around the world! The DIWA transmissions use the torque converter as an integrated retarder to augment the vehicle brakes. Voith's current transmission models are all electronically controlled.

Fundamentals of Hydraulically Controlled Automatic Transmissions

Although all automatic transmissions used in the truck and coach market today are fully electronically controlled, the basis for that control has been developed from the hydraulically controlled transmissions used in the past. The lessons we learn in this chapter on hydraulic controls explains the thinking behind the development and utilization of electronic controls in the Electronically Controlled Automatic Transmissions chapter. This section will discuss the basic design of a hydraulically controlled automatic transmission as well as its power flows.

Transmission Design

Early four-speed models of Allison transmissions all had the same planetary gear arrangement, as illustrated in FIGURE 43-1. Because this version of the four-speed transmission is the most prevalent design in hydraulically controlled automatic transmissions, we will look at its power flow in detail. Although power flows for different manufacturers' models vary, they all share the same basic elements. The following section explains the Allison AT, MT, V, and HT series four-speed transmissions power train.

The transmission has three interconnected planetary gear sets named the front, center, and rear planetary sets, as illustrated in FIGURE 43-2. The front and the center sets are similar in design to a reversed Simpson gear set, which was discussed in the Planetary Gear Concepts chapter. The front and center sun gears are connected by the sun gear shaft and, therefore, they must turn together.

Refer again to Figure 43-1. The three planetary gear sets are interconnected except for the front planetary carrier and the rear planetary ring gear. Those two components are not connected to any other part of the gear train. Because the front and the center sun gears are splined to the **sun gear shaft** and are connected together, the front planetary ring gear, the center planetary carrier, and the rear planetary carrier are all connected together by the **connecting drum**. That means all three of the components must turn together. Finally, the center planetary ring gear and the rear planetary sun gear are part of the **main shaft**, so they must turn together.

There are five multi-disc hydraulic clutches in the transmission. From front to back, the first two clutches are the **forward clutch** (so called because it is applied in all forward ranges) and the fourth clutch. The forward and fourth clutches are rotating clutches, and they transmit rotational power to the planetary gearing. Next are the third clutch, the second clutch, and first clutch. These are stationary clutches and, when applied, they hold planetary gear components.

The forward clutch is a rotating clutch and its hub is splined to the input or turbine shaft. When it is applied, it delivers rotational power to the main shaft, so it supplies power to the center ring gear and the rear sun gear. The fourth clutch is a rotating clutch and its hub is splined

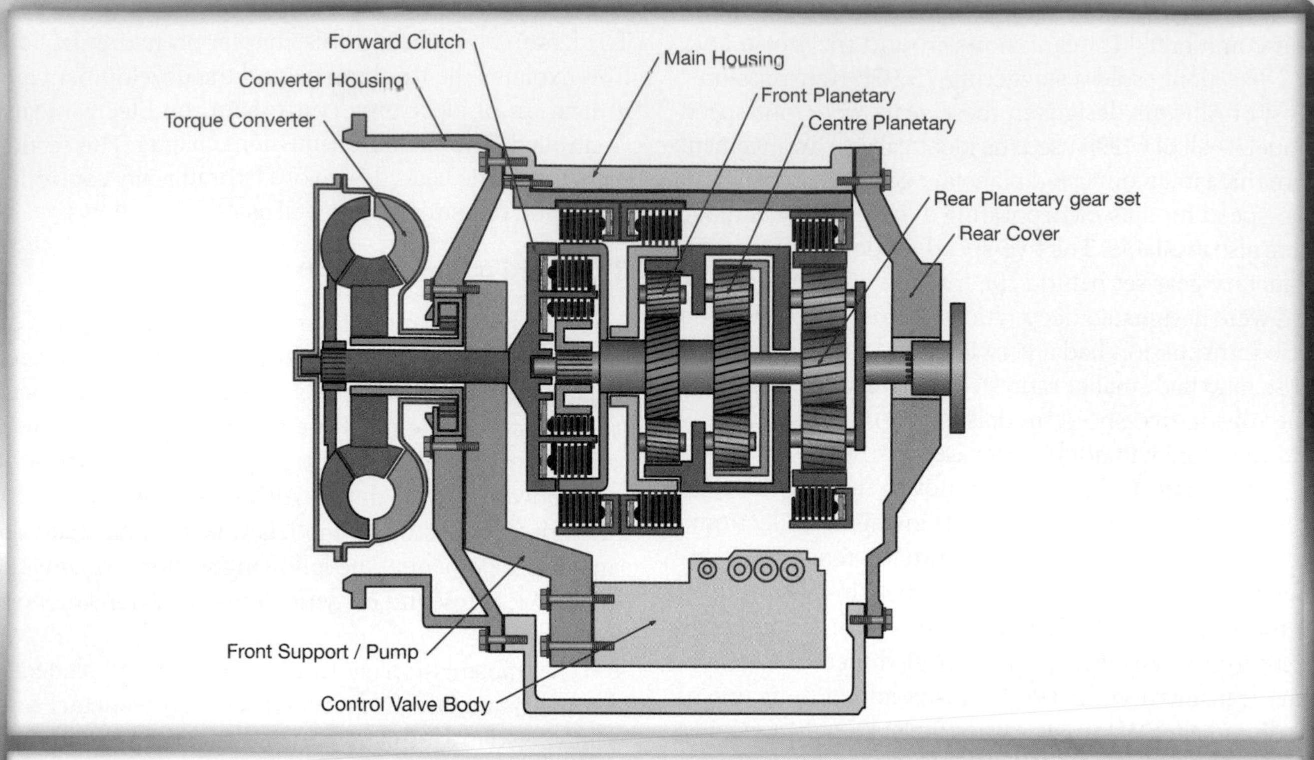

FIGURE 43-1 A cutaway view of the Allison AT 500 series transmission. The gear train, clutches, and power flows for this transmission are the same for all of the early four-speed Allison models.

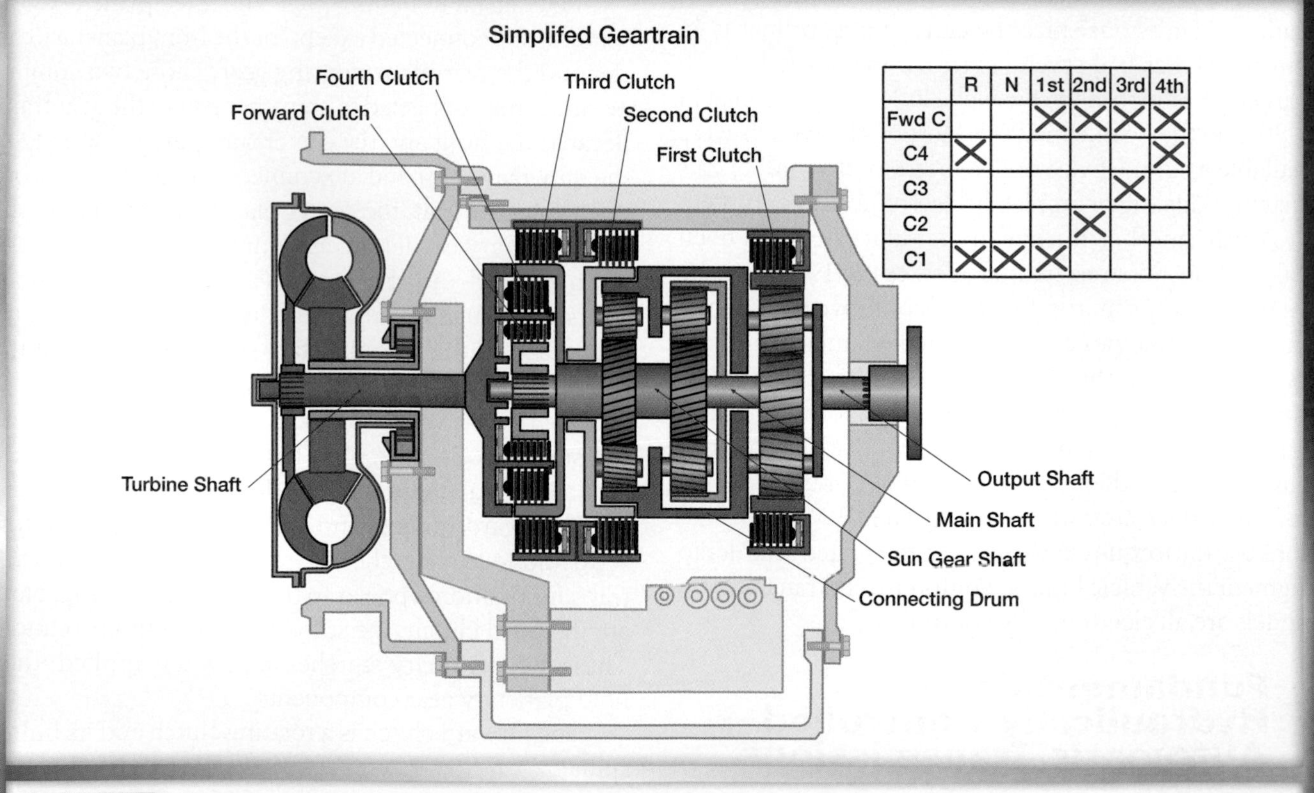

	R	N	1st	2nd	3rd	4th
Fwd C			X	X	X	X
C4	X					X
C3					X	
C2				X		
C1	X	X	X			

FIGURE 43-2 This schematic shows the three planetary gear sets and how they interconnect as well as the five hydraulic clutches. This design is common to all of the four-speed Allison models: the AT, the MT, and the HT series.

to the sun gear shaft. The friction discs in the fourth clutch are splined to an extension of the forward clutch hub. When the fourth clutch is applied, it takes rotational input from the input shaft through the forward clutch hub and delivers it to the sun gear shaft and therefore to the front and center sun gears. These are the only ways that rotational input can be delivered to the gear sets.

Third, second, and first clutch are stationary clutches—their reaction steel plates are splined to the transmission case. They hold components stationary when applied. The friction plates of the third clutch are splined to the outside of the fourth clutch hub. When the third clutch is applied, it holds the fourth clutch hub and, therefore, the front and center sun gears stationary. The friction plates of the second clutch are splined to the outside of the front planetary carrier so that, when the second clutch applies, it holds the front carrier stationary. The friction discs from the first clutch are splined to the rear planetary ring gear and, when the first clutch is applied, the ring gear is held stationary.

The only path of power out of the transmission is through the rear planetary carrier. It is the only component splined to the output shaft. Remember, though, that the front planetary ring gear, the center planetary carrier, and the rear planetary carrier are all connected together by the connecting drum. As a result, all of these components are attached to the output shaft.

Allison Transmission Power Flows

It is important for the technician to read and understand the clutch application chart when diagnosing a transmission issue. These charts tell the technician which clutches are applied and, because he knows what each clutch controls, which planetary gear components are involved in the power flow for each range (gear). Knowing which clutches are applied and what they connect to is essential to determine where the cause of the problem might originate. TABLE 43-1 is the clutch application chart for the Allison AT, MT, and HT four-speed transmissions.

Neutral

As we see from the clutch application chart and FIGURE 43-3, in neutral only the first clutch is applied. Therefore, when either first or reverse is selected, the transmission only needs to engage one of the rotating clutches—either the forward clutch or the fourth clutch—to complete the power flow. Neither of the rotating clutches is applied in neutral, so the power is delivered from the torque converter turbine to the input or turbine shaft and the forward clutch hub—but no further. The transmission is then in neutral.

First Range

When the driver selects any forward range, the transmission will always start in first range and then automatically shift sequentially to the highest selected range as road speed increases. In these transmissions, first range is a simple planetary power flow using only one of the planetary gear sets. When the driver selects a forward range, the forward clutch is applied. That action brings rotational input to the transmission main shaft and, therefore, to the center ring gear and the rear sun gear. The power flow takes place in the rear planetary set. The rear sun gear is the input and the rear ring gear is held by the first clutch. The rear carrier becomes the output and it is splined to the output shaft, as illustrated in FIGURE 43-4.

Second Range

As the transmission shifts to second range, the forward clutch remains applied, the first clutch is released, and the second clutch applies, as illustrated in FIGURE 43-5. This is a compound power flow involving the center and the front planetary gear sets.

Let's start the power flow in the center planetary set. When applied, the forward clutch connects the center ring

TABLE 43-1: Clutch Application Chart for the Allison AT, MT, and HT Series Four-Speed Transmissions

Range	Forward Clutch	Fourth Clutch	Third Clutch	Second Clutch	First Clutch
Neutral					Applied
First range	Applied				Applied
Second range	Applied			Applied	
Third range	Applied		Applied		
Fourth Range	Applied	Applied			
Reverse		Applied			Applied

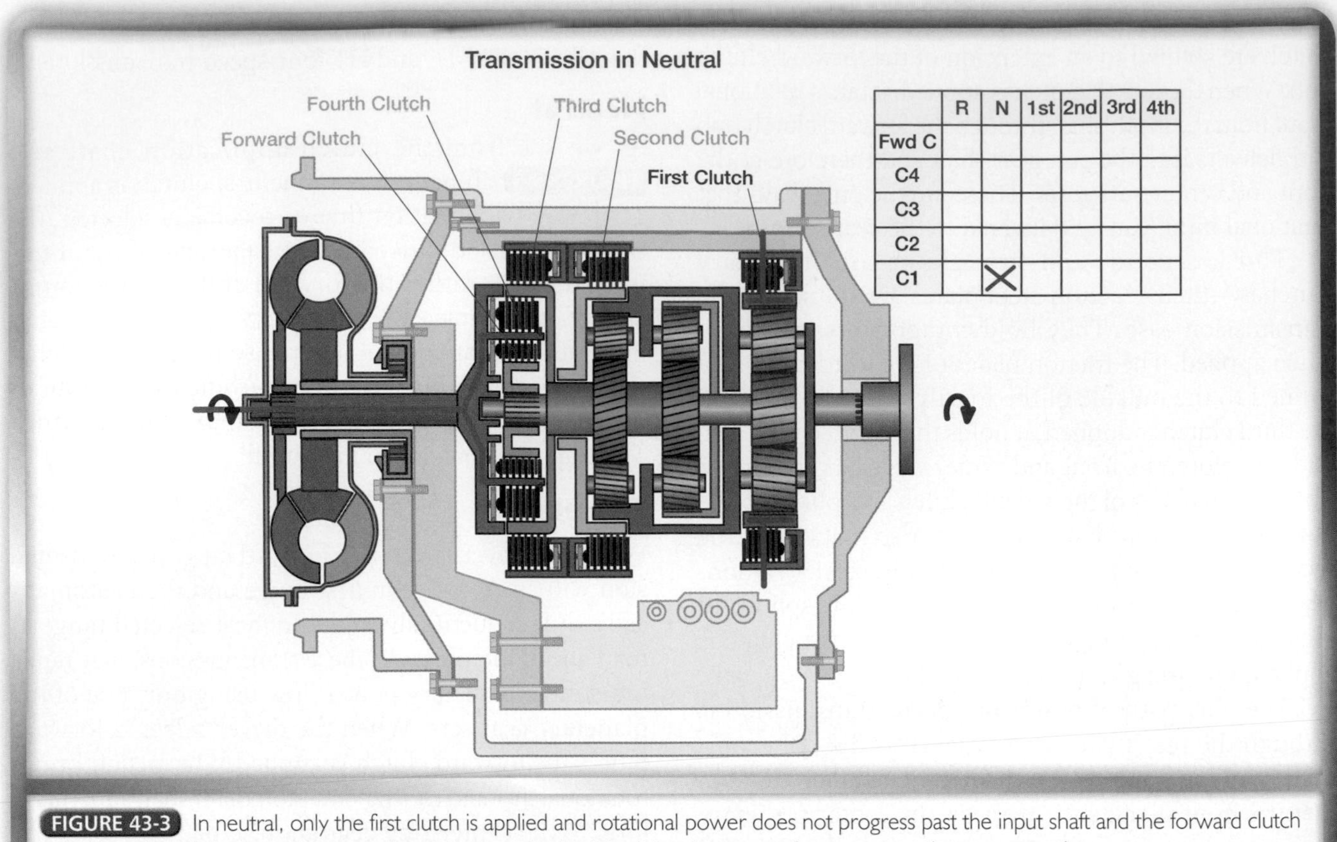

	R	N	1st	2nd	3rd	4th
Fwd C						
C4						
C3						
C2						
C1		X				

FIGURE 43-3 In neutral, only the first clutch is applied and rotational power does not progress past the input shaft and the forward clutch hub. Note that all the gears that are colored the same in all of the following power flows rotate at the same speed.

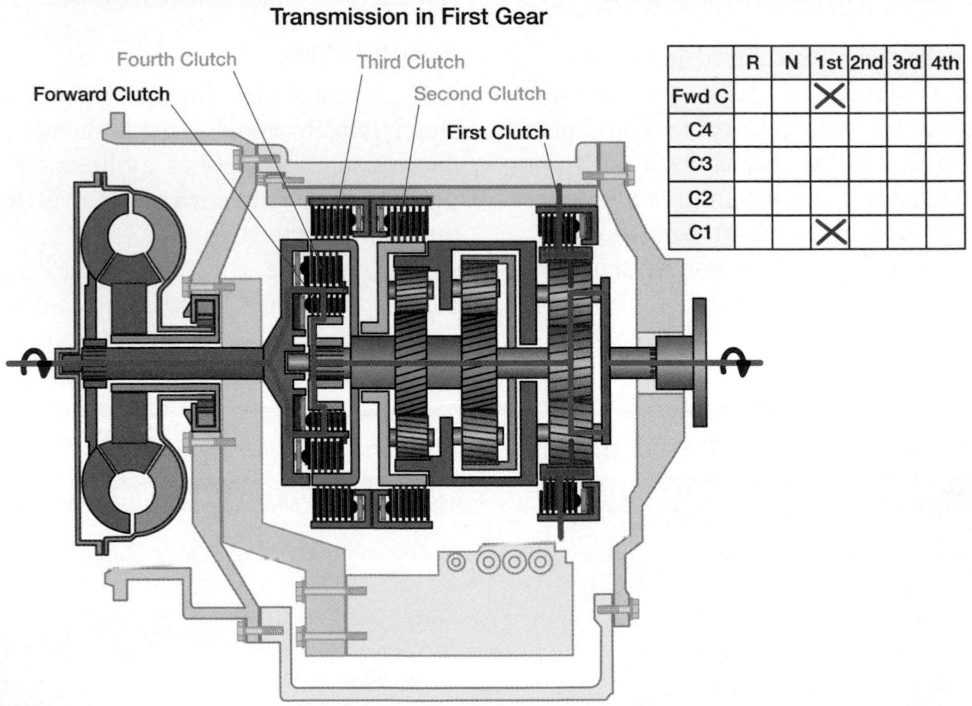

Transmission in First Gear

Fourth Clutch
Third Clutch
Forward Clutch
Second Clutch
First Clutch

	R	N	1st	2nd	3rd	4th
Fwd C			X			
C4						
C3						
C2						
C1			X			

FIGURE 43-4 First range.

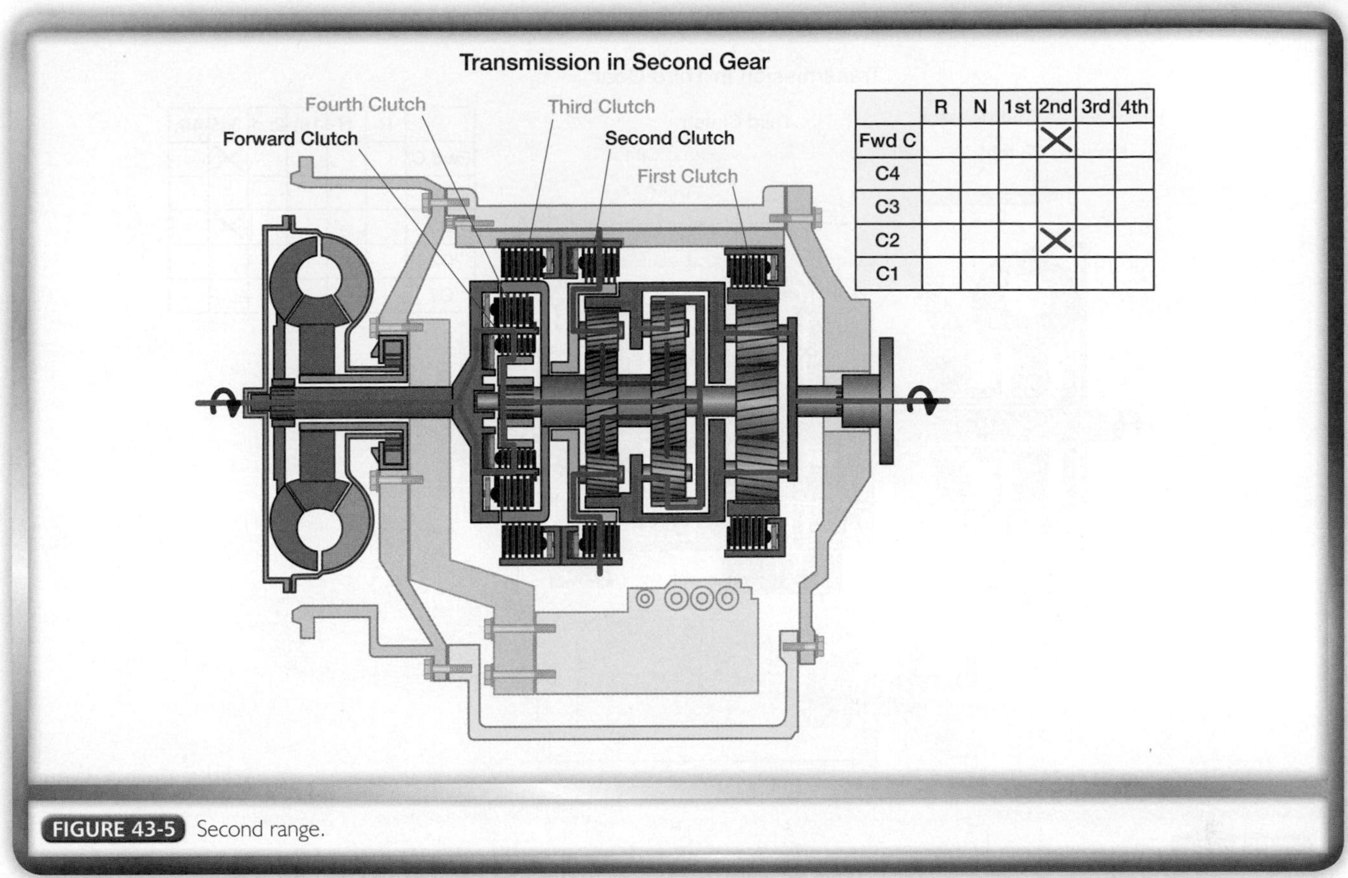

FIGURE 43-5 Second range.

gear to the input or turbine shaft so the power flow starts at that point. The center ring gear is input. The center carrier is splined through the connecting drum to the rear carrier and, therefore, to the output shaft. The weight of the vehicle is preventing the carrier from turning, so the carrier acts as a held component. This causes the center sun gear to become the output and to turn in reverse because the carrier is the "held" component. The center sun gear is splined to the sun gear shaft, as is the front planetary sun gear. The front sun gear becomes input to the front planetary set in a counterclockwise direction. The second clutch is holding the front planetary carrier stationary and the front planetary ring gear becomes clockwise output. The front planetary ring gear is splined through the connecting drum to the rear carrier and the output shaft.

This power flow is very similar to the first gear power flow through a Simpson gear set (that was explained in the Planetary Gear Concepts chapter). As the vehicle begins to move, the center planetary carrier moves with it because it is also splined to the connecting drum and the output shaft. But the center planetary carrier rotates slower than the ring gear input to the center gear set and, therefore, still acts as a "held" component to satisfy the rules of planetary gears that were discussed in the Planetary Gear Concepts chapter.

Third Range

As the transmission shifts to third range, the second clutch is released and the third clutch is applied. This power flow is illustrated in FIGURE 43-6. Third range is a simple planetary flow involving only the center planetary gear set. Forward clutch is applied, bringing rotational input to the center planetary ring gear. Third clutch is applied, and it holds the hub of the fourth clutch stationary. The sun gear shaft, which is splined to the fourth clutch hub, remains stationary as well. So the center ring gear is input, the center sun gear is held, and the center carrier becomes the output. The center carrier is splined through the connecting drum to the rear carrier and, therefore, to the output shaft.

Fourth Range

Fourth range, shown in FIGURE 43-7, again is a simple planetary power flow involving only the center planetary gear set. When the transmission shifts into fourth range, the third clutch is released and the fourth clutch applies. This bring two rotational inputs to the center planetary gear set—one through the forward clutch to the center ring gear and the other from the fourth clutch to the center sun gear. Because the center sun gear and the center ring gear are being turned at the same speed, the center

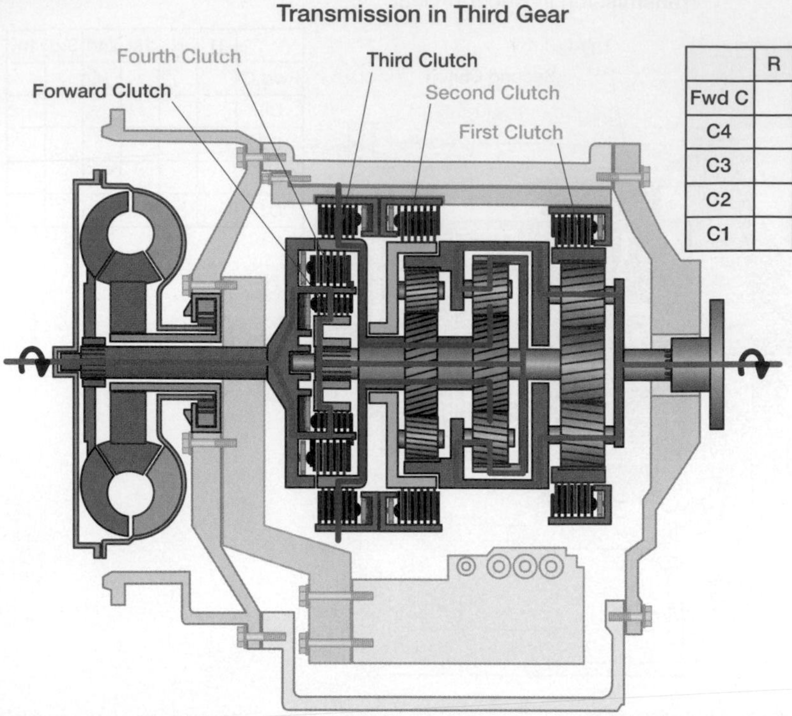

Transmission in Third Gear

Fourth Clutch
Third Clutch
Forward Clutch
Second Clutch
First Clutch

	R	N	1st	2nd	3rd	4th
Fwd C					X	
C4						
C3					X	
C2						
C1						

FIGURE 43-6 Third range.

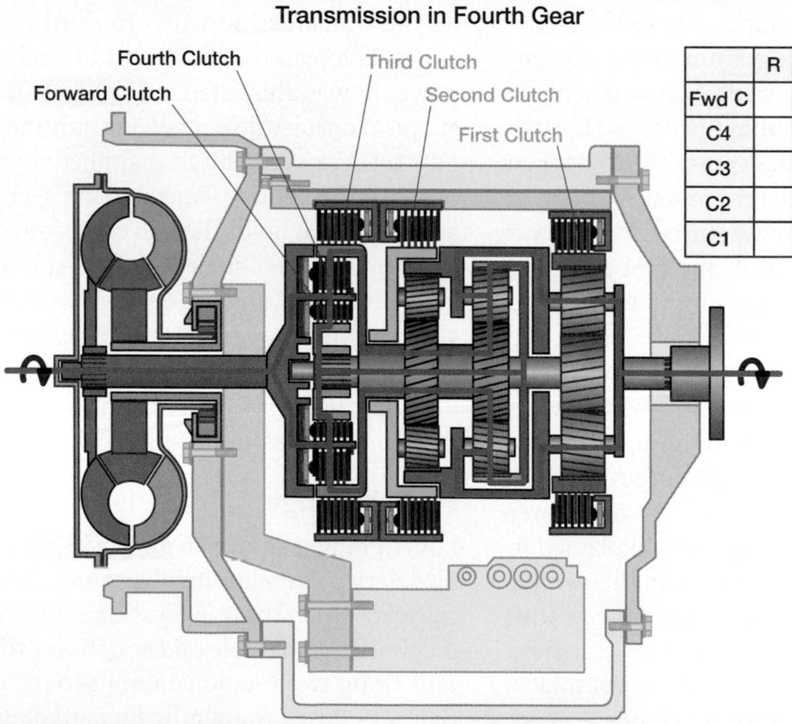

Transmission in Fourth Gear

Fourth Clutch
Third Clutch
Forward Clutch
Second Clutch
First Clutch

	R	N	1st	2nd	3rd	4th
Fwd C						X
C4						X
C3						
C2						
C1						

FIGURE 43-7 Fourth range.

carrier must also turn at the same speed and it is splined through the connecting drum to the rear carrier and the output shaft. This creates a direct-drive ratio through the center gear set even though all of the components of the three planetary gears are rotating at the same speed.

The front planetary gear set has two inputs. The first is from the sun gear. The second is from the front ring gear, which is splined to the connecting drum, so its carrier goes along for the ride. The rear planetary set has two inputs as well because the rear sun gear is part of the main shaft. Because the rear carrier is splined to the connecting drum that is turning at the same speed, the rear ring gear also goes along for the ride.

Reverse

Reverse is a compound power flow, as illustrated in FIGURE 43-8. The reverse power flow involves the center and the rear planetary gear sets. The power flow starts from the neutral position. In neutral, the first clutch is applied, holding the rear ring gear stationary. When the driver selects reverse, the fourth clutch is applied. This brings rotational power from the input or turbine shaft to the center sun gear. The center carrier is splined through the connecting drum to the rear carrier and the output shaft. Consequently, the weight of the vehicle prevents the center carrier from rotating and it becomes the "held" component in the center planetary set. The center sun gear is input. The center carrier is acting as the held component, so the center ring gear becomes the output component in a counterclockwise direction. The center ring gear is part of the main shaft, as is the rear sun gear, so the rear sun gear becomes counterclockwise input to the rear planetary set. The rear planetary ring gear is being held by the first clutch, so the rear planetary carrier becomes output in a counterclockwise direction and it is splined to the output shaft.

Transmission Hydraulic Control System Components

All automatic transmissions use hydraulic fluid to control the shifting process, to lubricate and cool the transmission, and to supply fluid to the torque converter. Most heavy-duty transmissions will use an internal **gear pump**, consisting of an internal and externally toothed gear, as shown in FIGURE 43-9, or a **gerotor pump** (the name comes from generated rotor). A gerotor pump is similar to a gear pump, but it uses a rotor operating inside a matching chamber instead of a gear. The transmission's hydraulic pump is driven by the torque converter pump drive hub to pressurize and circulate fluid throughout the

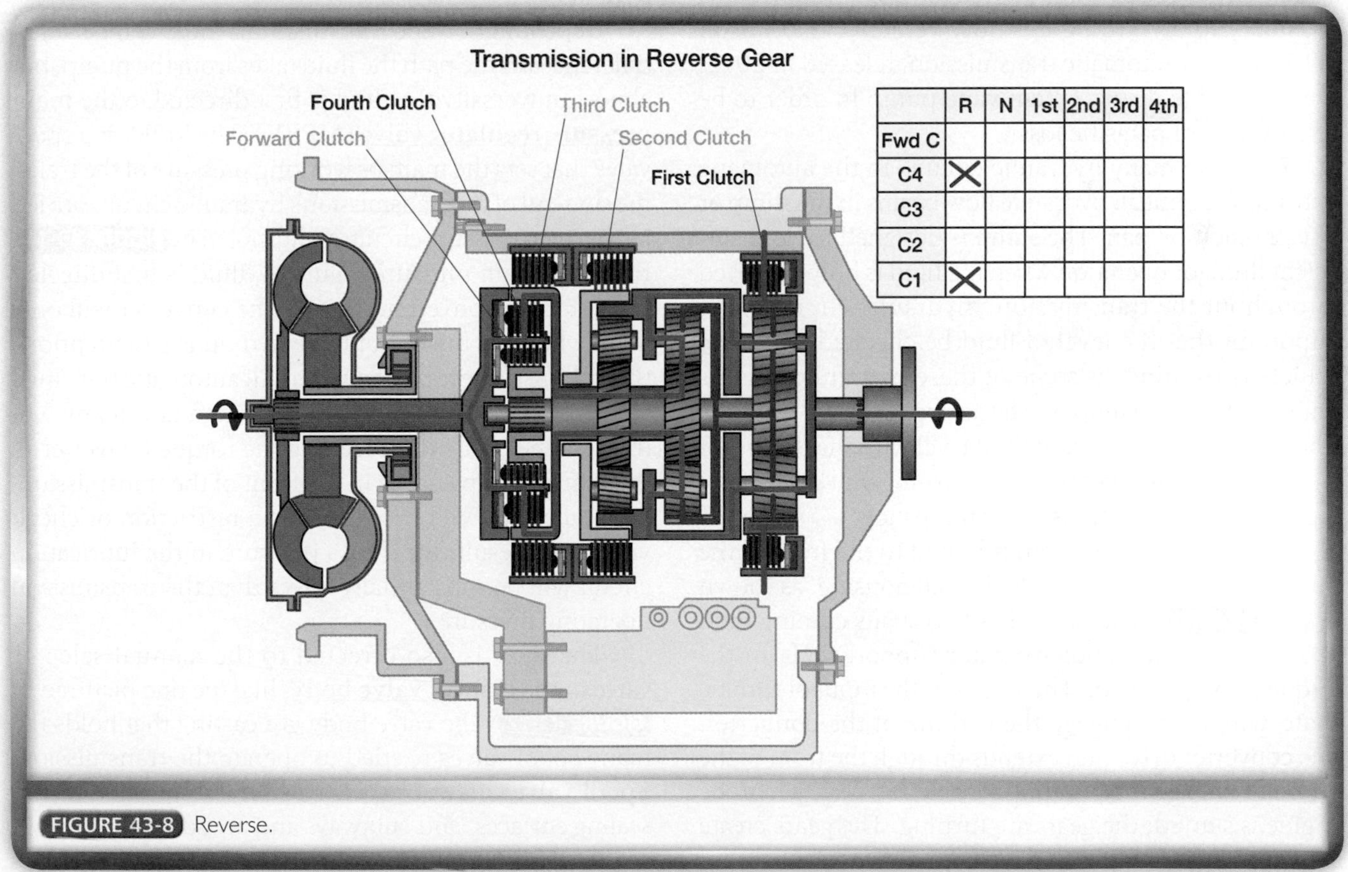

	R	N	1st	2nd	3rd	4th
Fwd C						
C4	X					
C3						
C2						
C1	X					

FIGURE 43-8 Reverse.

FIGURE 43-9 The Allison transmission uses a gear pump to supply hydraulic flow in the transmission.

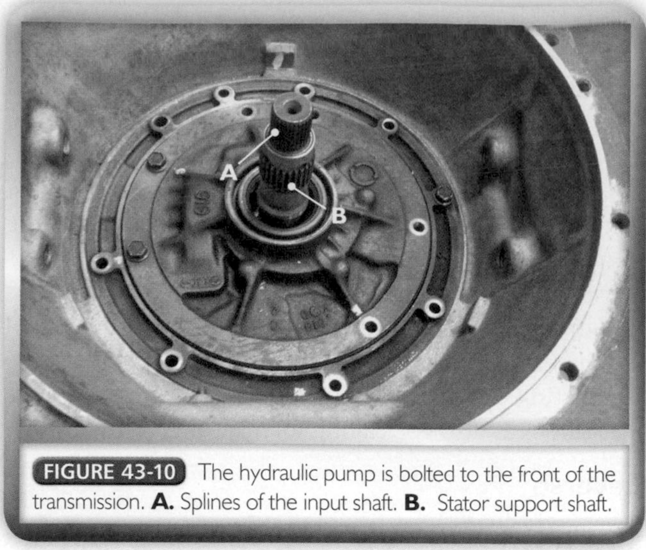

FIGURE 43-10 The hydraulic pump is bolted to the front of the transmission. **A.** Splines of the input shaft. **B.** Stator support shaft.

transmission. (If necessary, review the Torque Converters chapter to familiarize yourself with the torque converter pump drive hub.)

Some transmission models use **vane pumps**, a rotating pump with sliding vanes that hold the fluid. Vane pumps can be of fixed or variable displacement to reduce parasitic losses when high flow volume is not required. **Parasitic loss** is an unnecessary load on the engine that decreases fuel economy. Although the use of vane pumps is usually limited to lighter-duty vehicles, the Allison TC-10 class 8 automatic transmission, released in 2012, uses a variable displacement vane pump in order to be able to control parasitic loss.

There are many hydraulic circuits in the automatic transmission, but all hydraulic flow begins in the sump or transmission oil pan. The sump is designed to hold sufficient fluid for operation when the fluid is fully deployed throughout the transmission's hydraulic circuits. It is important that the level of fluid be checked while the vehicle is running, as some of these hydraulic circuits drain back to the sump when the engine is not running. Checking the transmission fluid level with the engine off and the transmission pump not turning will give a false high reading on the transmission dipstick.

The transmission pump is bolted to the front of the transmission assembly inside the bell housing, as shown in FIGURE 43-10. The pump has two shafts coming from it. The first is the stationary stator support shaft for the torque converter stator. The second is the input or turbine shaft, which will engage the turbine of the converter. The converter drive hub extends through the front of the pump to engage the pump drive gears so that, when the engine is started, the gears are turning. The gears create a low pressure area as they separate. Atmospheric pressure acting on the fluid in the sump forces it through a filter and up to the intake side of the pump. (This is why it is essential that the transmission be vented to allow the atmospheric pressure in. Otherwise, the pump's draw would create a vacuum, leading to starvation of the pump.) As the gears come back together, the fluid is pumped and exits the pressure side of the pump. From there, fluid is directed to many places in the transmission to do its job.

Depending on the transmission, there can be slight differences in the path the fluid takes from the pump, but almost universally the fluid is first directed to the **main pressure regulator valve (MPRV)**. The MPRV is a spool valve that sets the main or working pressure of the transmission. All of the transmission's hydraulic circuits are fed by the main pressure circuit, as illustrated in FIGURE 43-11. From the main pressure regulator, fluid is first directed to the torque converter. Because the converter will only work when it is full of fluid, the hydraulic system prioritizes filling the torque converter. All automatic transmissions use a pressure lubrication system and many will direct some of the fluid feeding the torque converter to the lubrication passages in the front of the transmission. This lube fluid will pass through a restriction or check valve. As a result, the fluid's pressure in the lubrication circuit will be substantially lower than the transmission operating pressure.

The fluid is also directed to the manual selector valve in the **control valve body**, like the one pictured in FIGURE 43-12. The valve body is a casting that holds the many spool valves needed to operate the transmission. **Spool valves** are valves with a series of raised lands, or sealing surfaces, and cutaways and are so called because they resemble an empty spool of thread. As spool valves

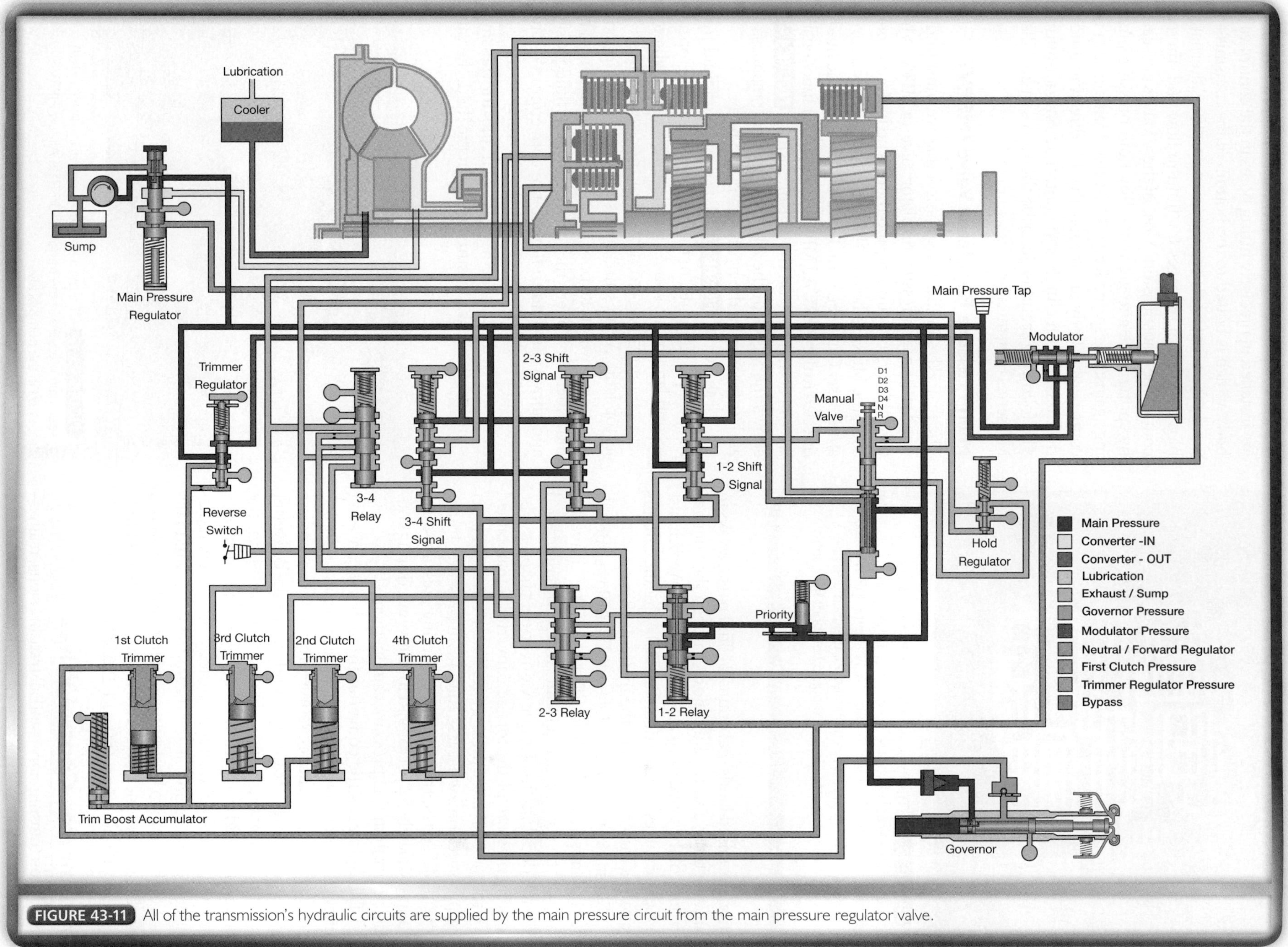

FIGURE 43-11 All of the transmission's hydraulic circuits are supplied by the main pressure circuit from the main pressure regulator valve.

FIGURE 43-12 The main valve body holds most of the spool valves necessary for the transmission's shifting and control functions. Most transmissions will have the MPRV in the valve body, but in the Allison transmission, the main pressure regulator valve is located in the oil pump body, not the control valve body.

move, the raised lands seal or unseal fluid passageways in the valve body, and the fluid flows through the cutaway portions of the valve to create a fluid circuit. We will discuss these valves in more detail in the Hydraulic Circuits section as they come up in the hydraulic flow.

Consult Figure 43-11 to follow the fluid flows through the transmission. The fluid fills the torque converter through the converter in circuit, which was described in some detail in the Torque Converters chapter. The working pressure of the torque converter is maintained by a torque converter pressure regulator valve and is set at a pressure somewhat less than main pressure. In the Allison MT series, the converter working pressure is set at approximately 52 psi (359 kPa). However, during converter operation this pressure can fluctuate.

The fluid exits the converter through the converter out circuit and is directed to the transmission oil cooler. The shear forces in the operating torque converter create tremendous heat, so directing fluid exiting the converter to the cooler makes sense. On the way back from the cooler, the fluid is typically directed into the rear lube circuit. The rear lube circuit lubricates the actual transmission gear sets and shafts. From there, the fluid falls back to the sump to be used again. Lube circuit pressures vary between models, but typical lube pressures range between 10 and 40 psi (69 and 276 kPa).

Transmission Control Valves

The Allison transmission—and all transmissions, really—use a series of spool-type valves to direct the hydraulic fluid to control the transmission's operation. Spool valves are installed in precisely fitting bores in the control valve body, which is bolted to the bottom of the transmission inside the oil pan. As the valves move, they alternately block and open passages for fluid to flow and, thereby control the transmission. Most of these valves are seated by spring force and are moved by fluid pressure pushing against the spring force. The valves contained in the control valve body are responsible for directing fluid to the transmission clutches to control automatic shifting. The following sections describe the valves in an Allison MT series transmission.

Main Pressure Regulator Valve (MPRV)

The first valve in the transmission that we must understand is the main pressure regulator valve, or MPRV. When the vehicle is not running and there is no hydraulic pressure, the MPRV is held in the seated position by a spring at its base. Once the vehicle is started, hydraulic fluid is directed to the MPRV. All MPRVs have similar function, but we will concentrate on the Allison system. **FIGURE 43-13** shows the MPRV in the Allison series of transmissions and its location in the hydraulic pump body.

As shown in **FIGURE 43-14**, transmission fluid from the pump is delivered to the MPRV between the top and second land of the spool. The fluid flows through cross and center drillings to the top of the valve to push on its top land. As pressure builds, the fluid starts to move the valve down in its bore against spring pressure. That movement first opens the torque converter fluid passage and allows the fluid to flow to the converter in circuit. The fluid is also directed through the valve to the control valve body and the necessary circuits for transmission operation. As pressure builds on the fluid, the valve

FIGURE 43-13 The main pressure regulator valve (circled) sets main pressure in the transmission. The Allison MPRV is located in the pump body.

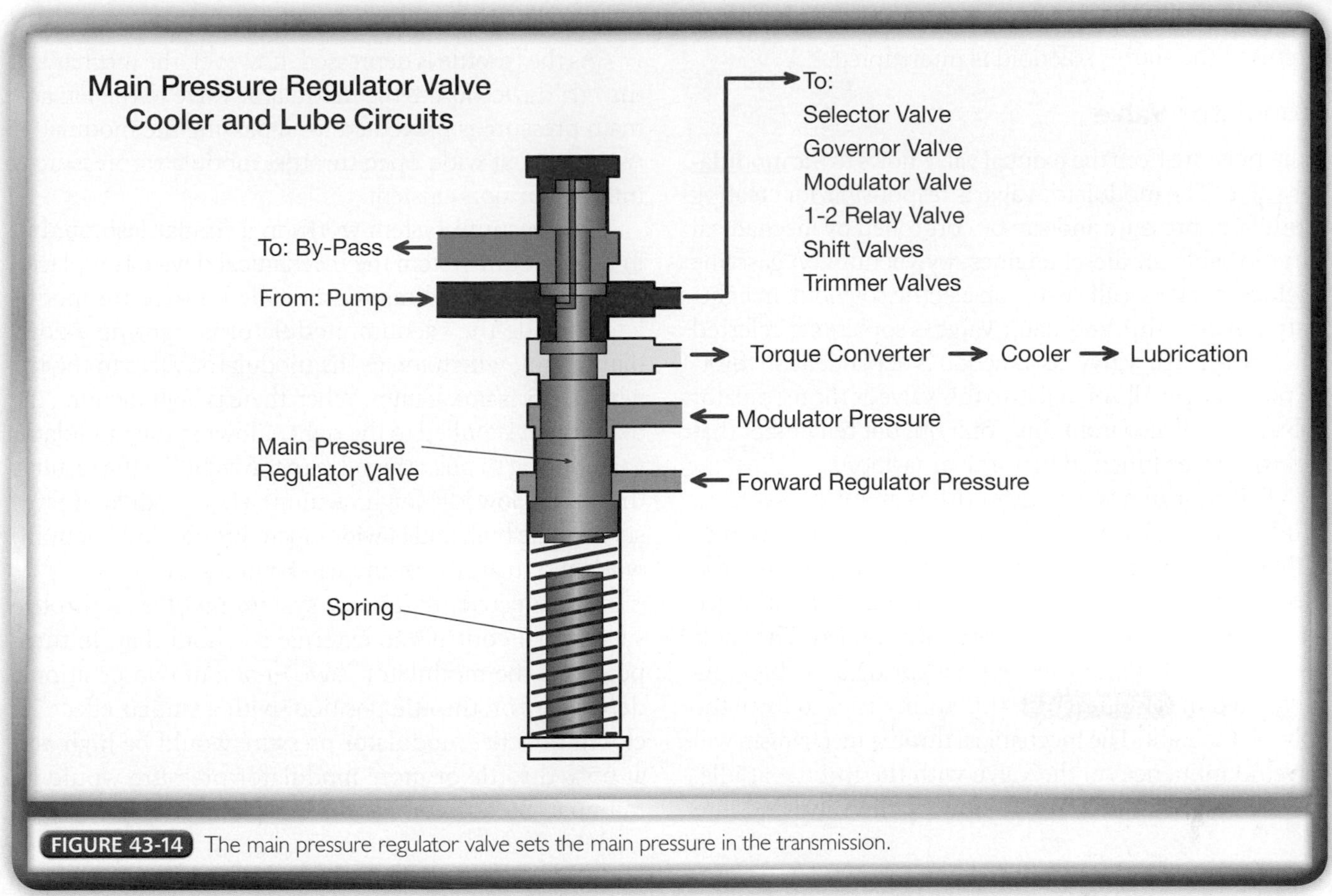

FIGURE 43-14 The main pressure regulator valve sets the main pressure in the transmission.

moves further down in its bore against spring pressure and a land uncovers a passage, allowing excess fluid flow to return to the transmission sump. At this point, the valve becomes balanced between spring and fluid pressure, and this balance sets the working pressure for the transmission.

The working (main) pressure for each transmission varies depending on the model and on other factors. Main pressure for the AT series,which can handle input torques of up to 415 ft-lb (563 Nm), ranges between 90 to 125 psi (621 to 862 kPa) at idle and 130 to 150 psi (896 to 1,034 kPa) at full stall speed. As all clutches in the transmission are hydraulically applied and the clamping force or apply pressure will directly affect clutch capacity, higher pressures are required for models that have higher torque inputs, such as the HT 740 series that is rated up to 1,300 ft-lb (1,763 Nm). The HT series main pressure can be as high as 235 to 270 psi (1,620 to 1,861 kPa) at converter stall speed under load. Main pressure is also modified by two other pressures in the transmission— neutral/forward regulator pressure and modulator pressure. Both of these pressures are derived from main pressure and are present in some models but not all. When present, these pressures act on separate lands of the main pressure regulator valve to keep the main pressure at its lower level.

Manual Selector Valve

When the vehicle is running in neutral, fluid under pressure flows from the main pressure regulator valve to all of the shift signal valves and to the manual selector valve. Pressure continues to flow also through the priority valve, the 1–2 relay valve, and on to the first clutch so that first clutch is applied in neutral. The **manual selector valve** is a spool valve in the control valve body and is mechanically positioned when the driver moves the shift selector. The manual valve is responsible for directing fluid pressure to the following circuits in these situations:

- to the forward clutch and to the neutral/forward regulator circuit in neutral or any forward range
- to the fourth clutch circuit when reverse is selected
- to the hold regulator valve, the governor valve, and to the modulator valve in all forward ranges.

To prevent automatic upshifts, the manual valve also redirects hold regulator pressure to the correct shift signal valves when manual first, second, or third is selected.

The positioning of the manual selector valve also controls the operation of the neutral safety switch, which is on the side of the transmission and connected into the starter solenoid circuit of the vehicle. This switch will only allow the vehicle to start with the selector valve in neutral. If the selector valve is in any other position, the circuit to the starter solenoid is interrupted.

Modulator Valve

Main pressure from the manual valve flows to the **modulator valve**. The modulator valve is responsible for creating modulator pressure and can be controlled by mechanical throttle cable on diesel engines, by vacuum on gasoline engines, or electrically using an electric solenoid. In light-duty vehicles, the modulator valve is sometimes referred to as the **throttle valve**, as its action is dependent on throttle position. As Allison refers to this valve as the modulator valve, we will also from this point on, but remember that throttle valves function in a similar fashion.

The modulator valve modifies main pressure to produce modulator pressure, which in turn is used to influence main pressure in some transmission models. Modulator or throttle pressure is also used to influence shift points and shift harshness or abruptness. The valve itself is a small spool valve with a spring at its base. As illustrated in FIGURE 43-15, this spring tries to force the valve to the right. The mechanical throttle mechanism will have no influence on the valve with the throttle at idle. This allows main pressure to flow by the valve and into the modulator circuit, creating high modulator pressure.

As the throttle is depressed, however, the mechanical throttle device forces the modulator valve to the left and main pressure is prevented from passing the modulator. As a result, at wide-open throttle, modulator pressure is minimal or non-existent.

The vacuum system works in a similar fashion, but in the vacuum system the mechanical device is replaced by a vacuum diaphragm unit called a vacuum modulator. Inside the vacuum modulator is a spring loaded diaphragm, which forces the modulator valve to the left when there is no vacuum. When there is high vacuum, the diaphragm is pulled to the right, allowing the modulator valve spring to push the valve to the right. So the result is the same at low idle (high vacuum) when modulator pressure will be high and at wide-open throttle (low vacuum) when modulator pressure will be minimal.

The electric modulator system involves a throttle switch that controls an external solenoid that, in turn, positions the modulator valve in one of two positions, depending on throttle position, with a similar effect. At closed throttle, modulator pressure would be high and at 65% throttle or more modulator pressure would be minimal. Because the modulator pressure is predicated

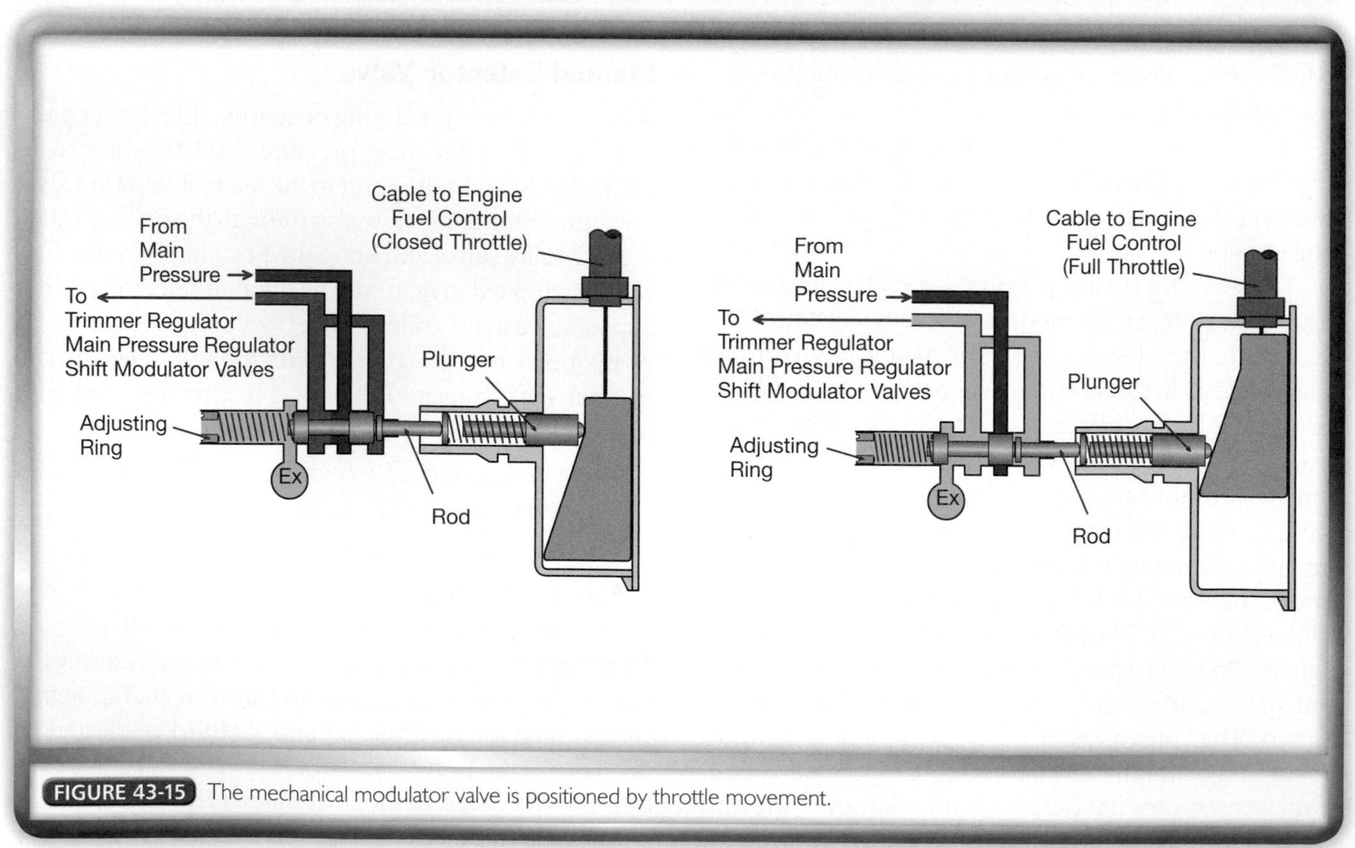

FIGURE 43-15 The mechanical modulator valve is positioned by throttle movement.

on throttle positon, the pressure becomes a "load" signal to the transmission's hydraulic control. We will discuss the modulator circuit and the necessity for this pressure in the Automatic Transmission Shifting section. Note that, in other manufacturer's transmissions, the modulator pressure is low at closed throttle and high at wide-open throttle. Regardless, modulator valve pressure influences the transmission in the same way.

Governor Valve

From the manual selector valve, fluid also flows to the **governor valve**, shown in FIGURE 43-16. This valve is mounted in a bore in the transmission case.

The governor valve itself is a spool valve mounted in a rotating tube. The tube has a gear on it that meshes with a worm on the transmission output shaft. As the output shaft turns the tube, the governor valve rotates with it. When the vehicle is at a stop, the tube is stationary also. Main pressure delivered to the valve forces the spool outwards inside the tube, which opens an exhaust passage from the governor circuit and blocks main pressure from entering the governor circuit. The tube has a pair of centrifugal weights attached to it, and as the vehicle starts to move the tube starts to turn with the output shaft.

The weights then begin to force the governor spool inward, closing the governor circuit exhaust passage and allowing main pressure to enter the governor circuit, as illustrated in FIGURE 43-17. As the output shaft speed increases, so too does governor pressure until maximum vehicle speed and maximum governor pressure is attained. As governor pressure is predicated on road speed, it becomes a "speed" signal to the transmission's hydraulic control. We will discuss what we do with this pressure in the Operation of a Hydraulically Controlled Automatic Transmission section.

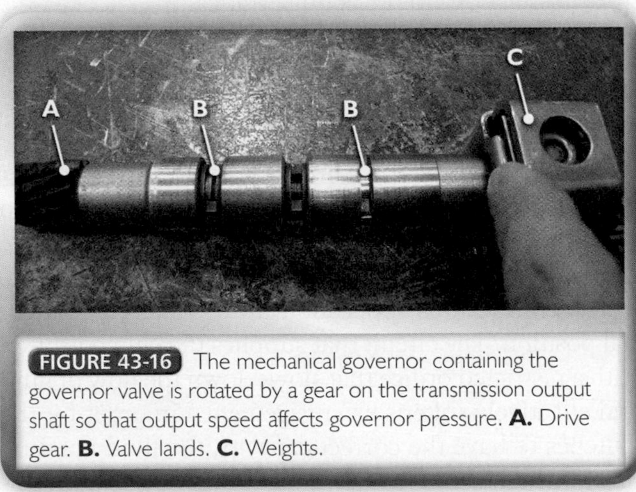

FIGURE 43-16 The mechanical governor containing the governor valve is rotated by a gear on the transmission output shaft so that output speed affects governor pressure. **A.** Drive gear. **B.** Valve lands. **C.** Weights.

Shift Signal and Shift Relay Valves

The transmission has three shift signal and three **shift relay valves**. They are essentially the same, so we will discuss all three sets at once. The shift relay valve is the simpler of the two valves, so we will look at it first. Recall the hydraulic schematic in Figure 43-11. The 1–2 shift relay valve is a spool valve and it has main pressure flowing through it and on to the first clutch. In the schematic, the valve is in the downshifted position (which appears as up on the schematic) and is held there by a spring at its base. Observing the top of the valve, there is a passage from there to the 1–2 shift signal valve above it. The valve will be moved to the upshifted position when main pressure redirected by the 1–2 shift signal valve is sent to that top land and the valve is forced down in its bore. When the relay valve moves down to the upshifted position, it connects the first clutch feed passage to the exhaust passage at the bottom of the valve. The valve also redirects the main pressure at the valve into the second clutch apply passage through the 2–3 shift relay valve. Redirecting pressure in this way applies the second clutch and the transmission attains second range.

Then, as the 2–3 relay valve moves, the fluid moves on to the 3–4 relay valve and the third clutch. And, as the 3–4 relay valve moves, the fluid will flow to the fourth clutch. This means that the same supply of main pressure is responsible for applying all of the clutches in sequence as each shift relay valve moves. This cascading fluid flow allows the clutch apply passage to be isolated by a priority valve, which we will cover in detail in the Priority Valve section.

Shift Signal Valves

The **shift signal valves** control the movement of the shift relay valves. The three shift signal valves are all set up the same and consist of two separate spool valves in one bore. The top valve is called the **shift modulator valve** and the lower valve is the actual shift signal valve.

The valves are held in the downshifted position (which is illustrated as down on the hydraulic schematic shown in Figure 43-11) and are held there by a spring at the top. The bottom land for the 2–3 shift signal valve is slightly smaller than the one for the 1–2 and the bottom land for the 3–4 shift signal valve is smaller still. Governor pressure pushes on all three of these lands to try to make the shift valves move up and so, because of the difference in the bottom land sizes, the valves move in sequence (i.e., first the 1-2 then the 2-3 and then the 3-4) as governor pressure increases with increasing road speed. Main pressure from the MPRV is directed to each

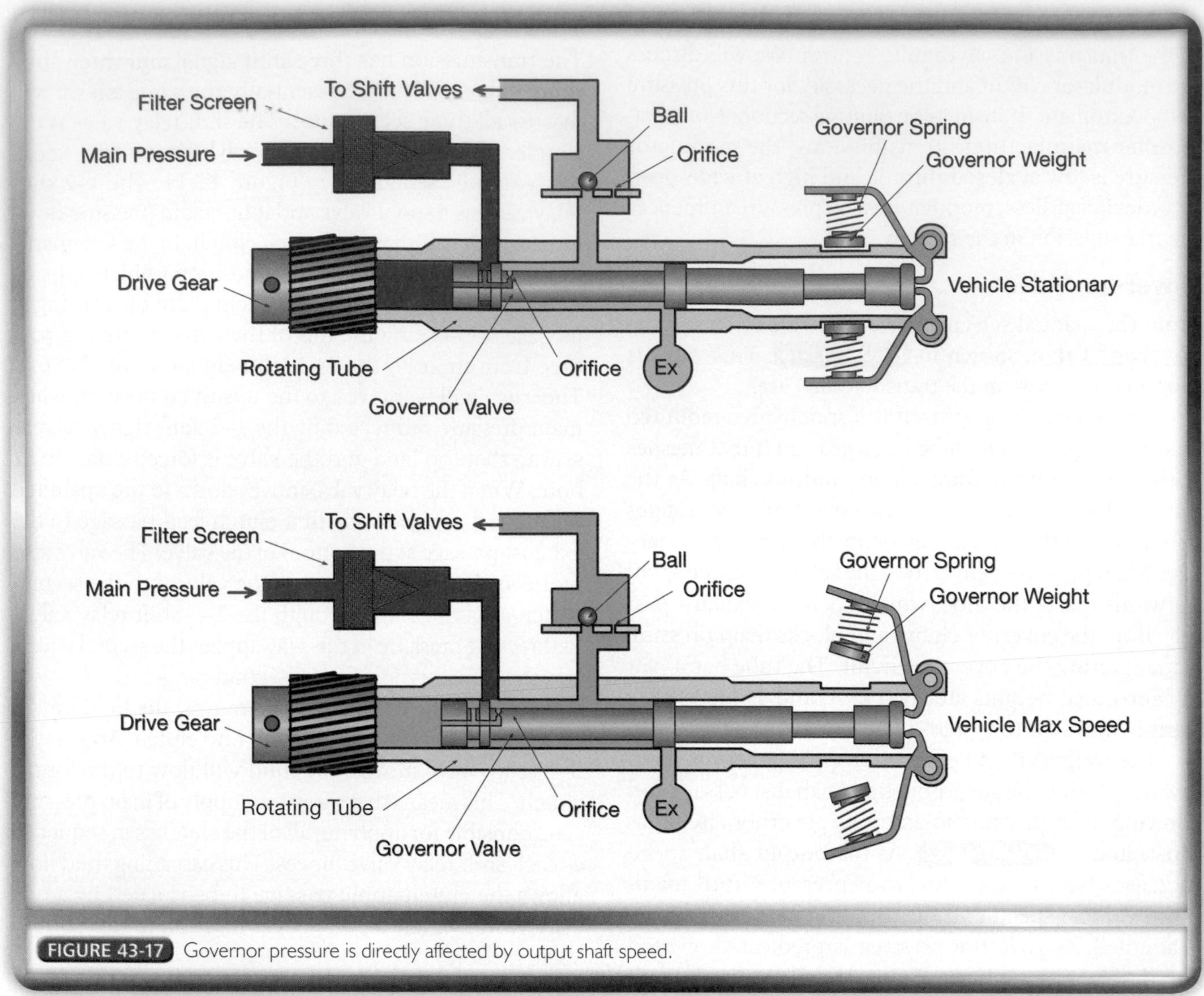

FIGURE 43-17 Governor pressure is directly affected by output shaft speed.

of the shift signal valves and deadheads at the large land, as can be seen in FIGURE 43-18.

Governor pressure is primarily responsible for moving the signal valves. Governor pressure acts on the bottom land of the valve, trying to move it up. As the valve moves, it redirects the deadheaded main pressure to the top of its corresponding shift relay valve, causing it to move. An automatic shift then occurs.

Priority Valve

All of the main pressure used to apply the clutches in the transmission flows through the **priority valve**. This valve is also a spool valve, but it acts additionally as a sort of check valve. The priority valve circuit is illustrated in FIGURE 43-19.

During certain operating modes, there is a chance that the fluid required to apply a clutch piston might momentarily exceed the transmission pump's output. The pressures that control the transmission shift valves (and other valves) may drop off. In that situation, the priority valve will close to maintain control pressure and prevent the transmission from reacting erratically.

Trimmer Valves and Trimmer Regulator Valve

Consulting again the schematic in Figure 43-11, it can be seen that there are four **trimmer valves** and a **trimmer regulator valve**. There is a trimmer valve for every clutch except the forward clutch. The job of the trimmer valve is to soften or smooth out the application of the clutches. (The forward clutch application always starts from a neutral position. The circuit that supplies the clutch is fitted with a restricted orifice that slows down the flow of fluid and effectively softens its engagement.) In order for the clutches to have the correct capacity, the fluid pressure must be high enough and the size of the application piston must be large enough to apply the correct clamping force. This might seem like common sense, but the

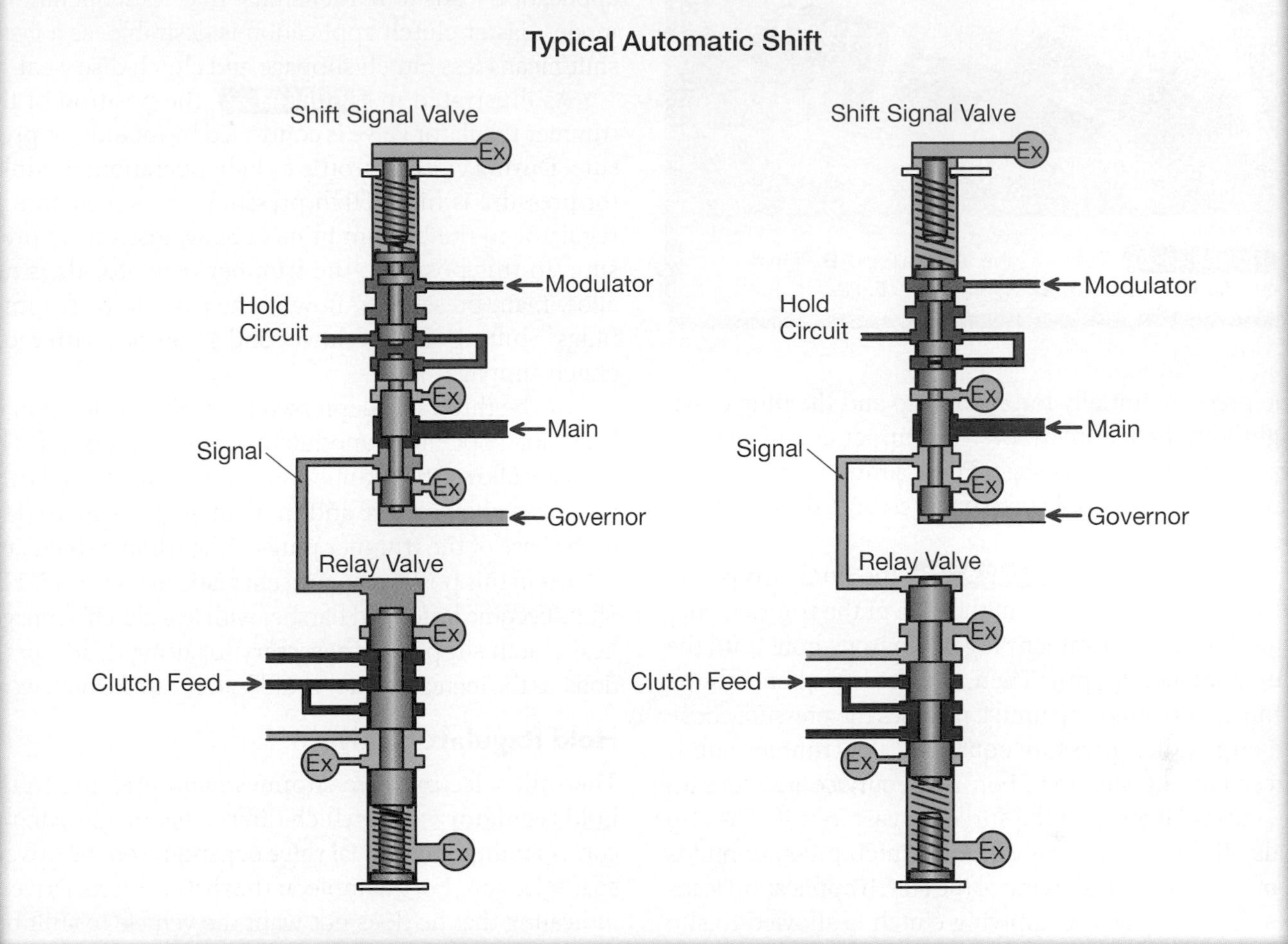

FIGURE 43-18 The shift relay and shift signal valves control the application of clutches.

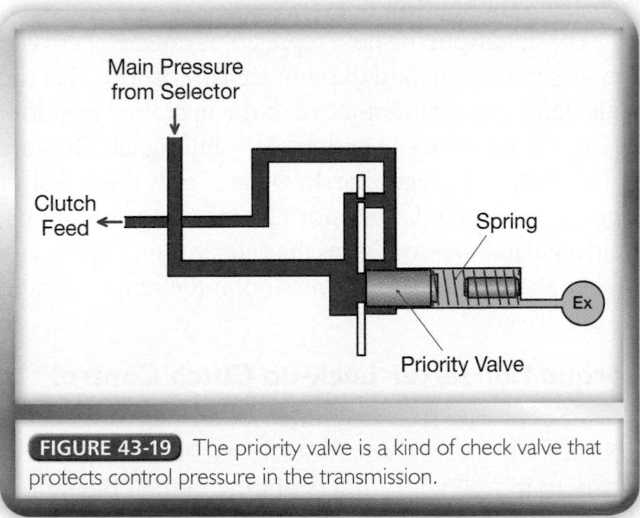

FIGURE 43-19 The priority valve is a kind of check valve that protects control pressure in the transmission.

speed at which the piston moves to apply the clutch is also influenced by these factors. Unexpected quickness in the piston movement can lead to harsh, abrupt shifting.

FIGURE 43-20 shows a trimmer valve. Notice that the trimmer cup has a smaller land at the top and a larger land at the bottom. The cup also has a small orifice that allows pressure at the top and bottom to slowly equalize.

Allison transmissions use the trimmer valves to slow down the shift slightly to make the engagement more gradual and, therefore, more comfortable for the driver and the passengers. Other transmission manufacturers accomplish this shift cushioning by using accumulators and restricted orifices in the clutch apply passage. Accumulators are spring-loaded pistons that move as the clutch applies. The clutch apply passage is similar to Allison's forward clutch passage. Allison's trimmers consist of a bore with a spring-loaded plug at its base, a pin that limits the plug's movement down in the bore, and the trimmer cup that sits on top of the plug.

Each trimmer valve is connected to the application circuit for its clutch. When the clutch is applying, the apply pressure is also delivered to the trimmer cup.

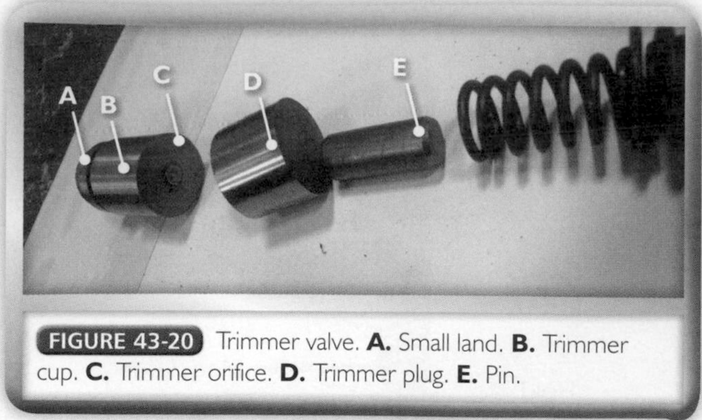

FIGURE 43-20 Trimmer valve. **A.** Small land. **B.** Trimmer cup. **C.** Trimmer orifice. **D.** Trimmer plug. **E.** Pin.

The pressure initially forces the cup and the plug down slightly in the trimmer bore. The upper end of the cup exposes an exhaust passage. Those simultaneous actions allow some of the apply pressure to escape, slowing down the clutch application.

As illustrated in FIGURE 43-21, the fluid also passes through the small orifice in the base of the trimmer cup. Fluid forces the trimmer plug down in its bore until the plug contacts the pin. Then, the pressure beneath the trimmer cup builds up until it matches the pressure above the cup. When pressure equalizes, the trimmer cup is forced back upward in its bore as the surface area beneath the cup is larger than the surface area above it. The cup seals off the exhaust passage and clutch pressure builds to maximum. This slowing of the clutch application leads to softer shifts as the applying clutch is allowed to slip more as it engages.

Trimmer Regulator Valve

The trimmer regulator valve is a spool valve that is supplied with main pressure, which is directed through the valve to the base of the trimmer valve bores. Fluid pressure here tends to accelerate the trimming action and causes the clutch application to speed up. Faster clutch application leads to harder shifts. In certain operational modes, faster clutch application is desirable, as a faster shift means less clutch slippage and clutch disc wear.

As illustrated in FIGURE 43-22, the position of the trimmer regulator valve is controlled by modulator pressure. During closed throttle or light operation, modulator pressure is high. High pressure forces the trimmer regulator to the bottom in its bore against spring pressure. In this position, the trimmer regulator does not allow main pressure to flow to the base of the trimmer plugs. Shifting will be slower and softer but with more clutch slippage.

As the throttle is depressed for rapid acceleration or heavy load operation, modulator pressure drops off. The decrease allows the trimmer regulator spring to move the valve and allows more and more main pressure to flow to the base of the trimmer plugs. (The trimmer regulator valve is in this position in the schematic in Figure 43-11.) Shifts become faster and harsher with less clutch slippage. Less clutch slippage is necessary for heavy-load operations, as the increased load could lead to rapid clutch wear.

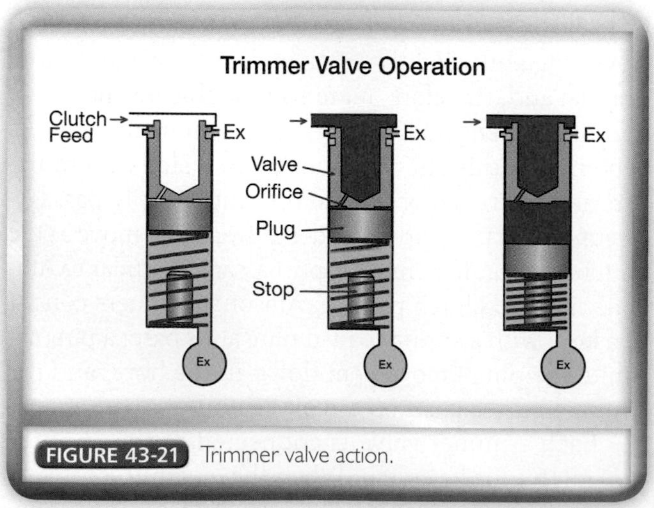

FIGURE 43-21 Trimmer valve action.

Hold Regulator Valve

The shift selector valve supplies main pressure to the **hold regulator valve**, which directs that pressure to the corresponding shift signal valve depending on the driver's gear selection. For example, if the driver selects Drive 1, indicating that he does not want the vehicle to shift out of first gear, the hold regulator valve directs fluid to three shift signal valves: the 3–4 shift signal, the 2–3 shift signal, and the 1–2 shift signal valves. Remember that the shift signal valves were actually two separate valves—the shift signal and the shift modulator valve.

The fluid from the hold regulator is directed between the shift modulator and the shift signal, ensuring that the shift signal valve cannot move to the upshifted position. In Drive 2, only the 2–3 and the 3–4 shift signal valves are fed from the hold regulator. In Drive 3, only the 3–4 shift signal valve is fed. Under normal operating conditions, hold regulator pressure stops the vehicle from shifting any higher and holds the transmission in the range selected by the driver.

Torque Converter Lock-up Cutch Control

Torque converter lock-up clutches were discussed in the Torque Converters chapter. Review that chapter if necessary to refresh your understanding of their operation. Torque converters all have an inherent slippage factor of 5–10% between the impeller and the turbine. That is, there is always a loss between the engine output and the transmission input shaft.

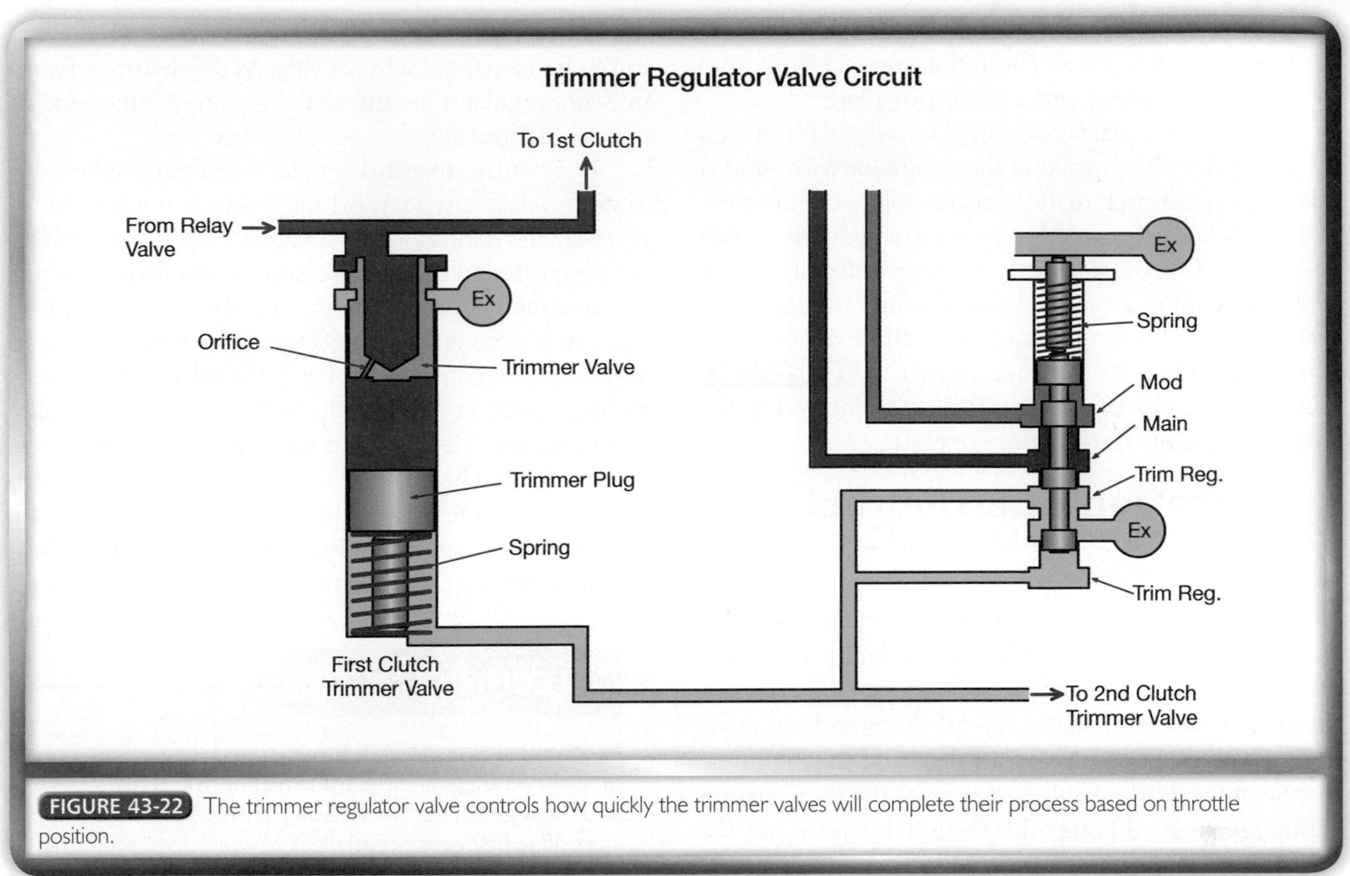

FIGURE 43-22 The trimmer regulator valve controls how quickly the trimmer valves will complete their process based on throttle position.

To eliminate this loss, all torque converters since the 1980s include lock-up clutches to lock the turbine to the converter shell and thereby eliminate the efficiency loss. The torque converter lock-up clutch is applied hydraulically by the transmission's hydraulic control system. The torque converter lock-up clutch application timing can be either scheduled or it can be modulated.

In **scheduled lock-up**, as soon as the transmission shifts into a certain range or has attained a predetermined road speed, the lock-up clutch will be applied. This application may be directly controlled by an electric solenoid-controlled valve or a spool valve that is moved by governor pressure. When these valves are moved, they direct hydraulic pressure to the lock-up clutch circuit. By contrast, **modulated lock-up** allows the lock-up timing to be affected by load and driver input conditions.

Scheduled lock-up increases fuel economy, but modulated lock-up has superior acceleration performance. Most modern commercial vehicles will have scheduled lock-up for fuel efficiency. Modulated lock-up is more commonly found in light-duty vehicles where performance—not fuel efficiency—is the key attribute.

When a vehicle has modulated torque converter lock-up, the spool valve responsible for lock-up clutch application is acted on by both governor and modulator pressure. Consequently, lock-up will occur at lower speeds under light loads and at higher speeds under heavy loads or rapid acceleration. In some hydraulically controlled transmission models, when the torque converter lock-up spool valve moves to engage the lock-up clutch, the converter will also direct fluid to a special land on the main pressure regulator valve. Fluid pressure on the land will cause main pressure to reduce, as there is less torque when the converter is in lock-up. Manufacturers commonly used this design function to reduce parasitic losses caused by the transmission's hydraulic pump.

Hydraulic Circuits

A **hydraulic circuit** is simply a pathway connecting one part of the transmission's hydraulic control with another part. There are several circuits in a transmission. Some, such as the forward clutch circuit or the fourth clutch circuit, are strictly connecting circuits. Several other circuits can be called control circuits because they control valve movement.

In the Allison AT, MT, and HT, the control circuits are the neutral forward regulator circuit (NFRC), the governor circuit, and the modulator circuit. Most circuits start at the control valve body or at the MPRV. The control valve body has a series of slots that coincide with the different lands of the spool valves. These slots are sealed off from each other by a gasket and a **separator plate**.

The separator plate has precisely sized and positioned orifices and/or openings that then coincide with various openings cast or cut into the transmission case. The openings can be directly drilled passages to a hydraulic clutch or can be "worm track" shaped passages that deliver fluid from one land of a certain valve through the separator plate and then back to a land on another valve. Worm tracks are visible in the case shown in **FIGURE 43-23**. When a valve moves, fluid pressure is redirected by the valve to make the transmission operate.

Operation of a Hydraulically Controlled Automatic Transmission

Now that we have discussed the valves in the hydraulically controlled automatic transmission and their functions, let's turn to seeing how the transmission operates. Specifically, this section will cover automatic upshifting and automatic downshifting. All of the spool valves and the hydraulic circuits must work together to control the transmission shifting process. Although this section describes only the Allison transmission, other hydraulically controlled automatic transmissions operate in a very similar fashion.

Automatic Transmission Shifting

As the discussion moves through an automatic shifting sequence, continue to refer to Figure 43-11 to follow the flow of fluid. As soon as the vehicle is started (in neutral), main pressure is established by the spring-loaded MPRV. The main pressure circuit delivers that pressure to the shift signal valves and the priority valve through the 1–2 relay valve and into the first clutch. This circuit is illustrated in **FIGURE 43-24**. Main pressure is also delivered through the manual selector valve to the neutral forward pressure regulator circuit, to the governor valve, and to the modulator valve.

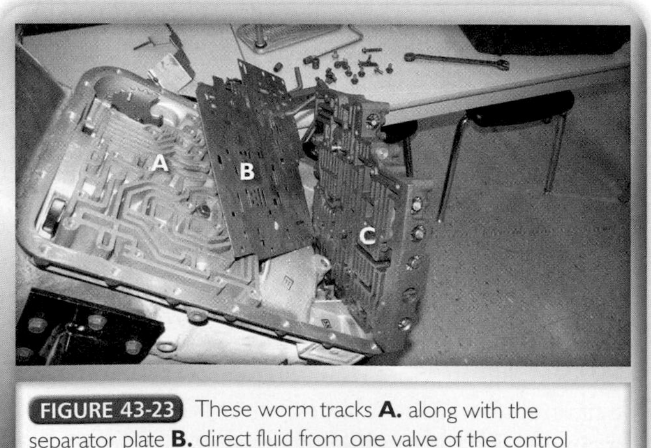

FIGURE 43-23 These worm tracks **A.** along with the separator plate **B.** direct fluid from one valve of the control valve body **C.** to another.

The neutral forward regulator pressure is present in neutral and any forward range but is not present in reverse. The neutral forward regulator pressure circuit's purpose is to lower main pressure in any forward range and neutral but allow a higher main pressure in reverse. The circuit accomplishes this by sending pressure back to a land on the main pressure regulator valve, which assists main pressure in opening the MPRV. Consequently, the main pressure is lower. This assist pressure is not present in reverse. Therefore, main pressure climbs higher to increase the clutch clamp load in reverse. This is done because reverse range has the greatest torque multiplication and, therefore, requires increased clutch clamp load.

> **TECHNICIAN TIP**
>
> In some transmissions, a driver may select either first or second range (and the transmission will actually start off in that gear), but the Allison transmission will always start off in first range regardless of which forward range is selected.

Now, let us assume the driver selects Drive 4th or simply "D." The manual valve is moved, and main pressure is directed to the forward clutch. The forward clutch is the only clutch that does not have a trimmer valve to cushion the clutch application. The forward clutch engagement is softened by placing a restricted orifice in the forward clutch apply circuit, which slows down the clutch application.

The vehicle has now attained first range. Next, the driver accelerates and the vehicle begins moving. The governor valve starts to spin and the centrifugal force on the weights begins to move the governor spool valve inboard in its bore. Main pressure starts to leak into the governor circuit and will build pressure in the circuit as speed increases. The governor pressure circuit delivers governor pressure to the base of the shift signal valves and tries to push them up in their bore.

At the same time, modulator pressure is changing, either because of throttle position (diesel engines) or vacuum drop (gasoline engines). Modulator pressure is initially quite high at idle, but as the throttle is moved, the pressure begins to drop. The modulator circuit delivers modulator pressure to the bottom land of the shift modulator valves sitting on top of the shift signal valves and tries to raise the shift modulator valves. This assists

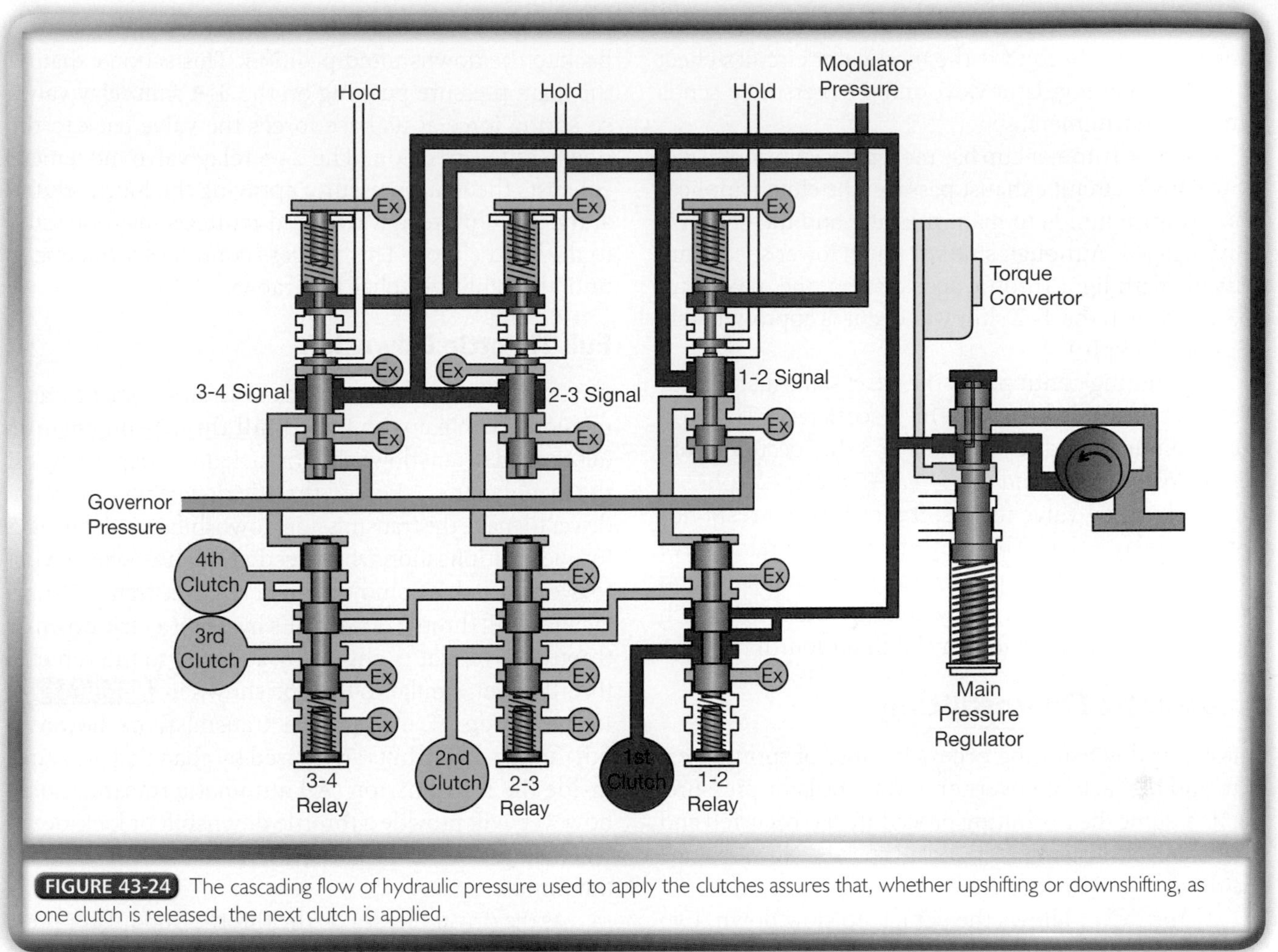

FIGURE 43-24 The cascading flow of hydraulic pressure used to apply the clutches assures that, whether upshifting or downshifting, as one clutch is released, the next clutch is applied.

governor pressure in moving the shift signal valves up. The reason for this design is so that, when throttle is light, modulator pressure is high, and the governor pressure does not have to climb as high to move the shift signal valve. An earlier shift is achieved in terms of road speed.

In some older transmission models, modulator pressure also acts on a land on the MPRV. Pressure on that land reduces main pressure so, when throttle is light and modulator pressure is high, main pressure is relatively low. The shift is softer as well because the lower pressure causes the shift to occur more slowly. This adds to passenger and driver comfort. However, when the vehicle is heavily loaded or acceleration is very rapid (wide-open throttle), modulator pressure drops to almost zero. Governor pressure alone must move the shift signal and the shift modulator valves up in their bores. To do this, road speed must increase to build governor pressure. Upshifts will then occur at a higher road speed. Plus, with modulator pressure reduced, there is no longer pressure on the land of the MPRV. Main pressure rises, causing faster, harder shifts with less slippage. So, the modulator valve is a type of load sensor that can "modulate" or adjust shift points based on load, while the governor tries to shift based on speed alone.

Recall that the 1–2, the 2–3, and the 3–4 shift signal valve bottom lands are of differing sizes, so they will shift in sequence and not simultaneously. When governor pressure based on road speed and modulator pressure based on load combine with sufficient force to move the 1– shift signal valve up in its bore, the valve moves up and redirects the main pressure. The main pressure that was deadheading at the shift signal valve is now sent to the top of the 1–2 shift relay valve, causing it to move down in its bore. The relay valve's movement causes the main pressure applying first clutch to exhaust at the relay valve. The main pressure coming from the priority valve is redirected through the 1-2 relay valve to the second clutch apply circuit.

Remember that all of the clutches except forward have a trimmer valve in their apply circuit, so the main pressure being sent to apply the clutch activates the trimmer. This slows down and softens the clutch application. The actual speed of the trimmer's operation, and therefore clutch application speed, is affected by two factors. First is the modulator circuit pressure and its effect on main pressure, if present. Second is the modulator circuit's effect on the trimmer regulator valve and the pressure it sends beneath the trimmers.

Once the trimmer cup has moved back up and sealed off the apply circuit exhaust passage, the clutch application pressure builds to main pressure and the clutch is fully engaged. Although shifts at much lower speeds are possible with light throttle acceleration, the maximum speed at which the 1–2 shift will occur is approximately 18 mph (29 kph).

The shifting continues in the exact same manner for the 2–3 and 3–4 shifts as the vehicle accelerates. The average maximum speed at which the 2–3 shift occurs would be 28 mph (45 kph) and the 3–4 at 45 mph (72 kph). As each shift signal valve moves, it moves its corresponding shift relay valve. The movement of the relay valve exhausts the applied clutch pressure and redirects fluid to the oncoming clutch apply circuit—the third clutch for third range and the fourth clutch for fourth range.

Automatic Downshifting

Automatic downshifting occurs because of spring pressure and the lack of governor and modulator pressure. Let us assume the upshifting procedure has occurred and the vehicle is cruising at highway speeds. Now, assume the driver starts to decelerate.

As the driver allows the vehicle to slow down, two things occur. First, governor pressure decreases with the decrease in vehicle speed. Second, modulator pressure increases with the decrease in throttle position. As governor pressure decreases beyond a certain point, the combination of governor and modulator pressure is no longer able to hold the 3–4 shift signal valve up against its spring. The spring force will, therefore, push the valve back to the downshifted position. This action exhausts the main pressure pushing on the 3–4 shift relay valve, so spring force at its base forces the valve back to the downshifted position. The 2–4 relay valve movement exhausts the main pressure, applying the fourth clutch at the 3–4 shift relay valve, and redirects main pressure to the third clutch. This process continues sequentially until the vehicle reaches first range.

Full Throttle Downshift

Anyone who has driven a vehicle with an automatic transmission is familiar with forced **full throttle downshifts** (also called detent downshift or kick down depending on the manufacturer). Forced throttle downshifts allow the driver to make the transmission downshift in order to gain torque multiplication when needed, such as when trying to overtake a slower moving vehicle. Some transmissions facilitate full throttle downshifts by using a kick-down or throttle valve that is physically attached to the vehicle's throttle lever, similar to the one shown in FIGURE 43-25. In the Allison AT, MT, and HT transmissions, however, full throttle downshifts are caused by changing pressures inside the transmission. All automatic transmissions, however, will provide a throttle downshift or kick-down when conditions are right and the driver steps hard on the throttle.

As the driver presses on the throttle, modulator pressure that had previously been used to assist the governor in causing an upshift, starts to drop off. Recall that modulator pressure in the Allison is high at closed throttle and almost non-existent at wide-open throttle. As modulator pressure drops, governor pressure alone may not be sufficient to hold the shift signal valves in the upshifted

> **TECHNICIAN TIP**
>
> With the exception of forward clutch, all of the clutch apply circuits have trimmer valves attached to them to cushion the shifting process. Because the vehicle will be stopped with first clutch engaged, when the vehicle starts, we need to soften the application of the forward clutch if drive is selected and the fourth clutch if reverse is selected. Forward clutch application is softened by directing the apply circuit through a small restriction, slowing down the fluid movement. Fourth clutch, on the other hand, because it is also used for fourth range, has a trimmer valve to soften its application. So why do we need a trimmer for the first clutch, as it is already applied as the vehicle is started? The first clutch trimmer is necessary to soften the 2–1 downshift.

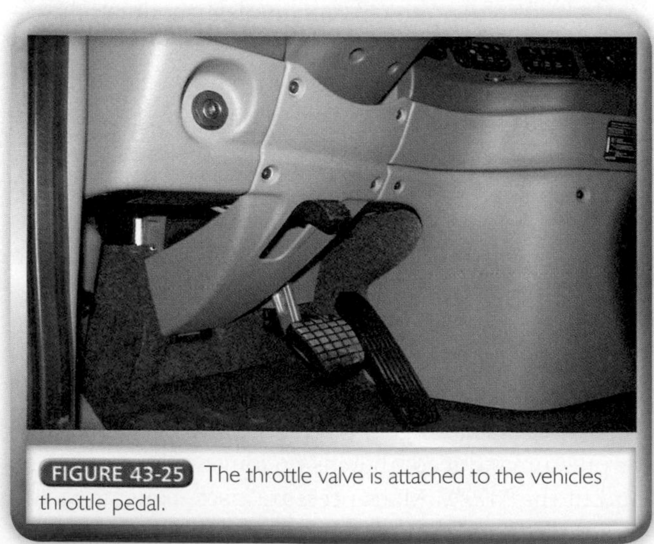

FIGURE 43-25 The throttle valve is attached to the vehicles throttle pedal.

positions. If this is the case, the shift signal valve springs will push the valves back to the downshifted position. Depending on road speed and the range the vehicle has attained, the transmission may shift from fourth all the way down to first during a forced throttle downshift. However, a full throttle downshift will usually cause a downshift of one or two ranges to give the desired torque multiplication to accelerate the vehicle.

Shift Point Control

The transmission shift points are usually adjustable and several methods are used to adjust the shift points. In lighter-duty vehicles, shift points are adjusted by controlling the spring pressure on the vacuum modulator diaphragm. In turn, that adjustment modifies the movement of the modulator valve and, therefore, adjusts the shift point. The shift point can be achieved by adjusting the throttle cable, which has the same effect.

> **TECHNICIAN TIP**
>
> Some hydraulically controlled transmissions do not have modulator valves; they have a throttle valve instead. The movement of this throttle valve will be influenced by a throttle cable attached to the vehicle throttle pedal. The overall purpose, however, remains the same—either throttle or modulator pressure will modulate the shifting and, usually, the main pressure in the transmission. Therefore, although they are created in slightly different ways, throttle pressure and modulator pressure have the same function in all hydraulically controlled transmissions and throttle or modulator pressure can, for all intents and purposes, be considered synonymous.

In the Allison transmission, precise control of shift points is accomplished in one of two ways. The first way involves adjusting the spring tension on the modulator valve itself. Adjusting the modulator spring affects all shifts throughout the transmission's operating range. The second way involves adjusting the spring tension on the individual shift signal valves, which would affect that particular shift only.

The springs are held in their bores in the control valve body by a pin and a unique ramped retainer block cam, shown in **FIGURE 43-26**. This block can be rotated by using a special tool. The tension on the spring can be increased or decreased as desired. Each notch of the retainer cam will increase or decrease the shift point by approximately 2 mph (3.2 kph).

Adjusting shift points can be accomplished in the field, but properly adjusting shift points requires a valve body test bench. The control valve body and the transmission governor are attached to the bench and road speed is simulated. The modulator pressure and individual shift points can then be set to specification for the particular vocation of the transmission. Hold regulator pressure and modulated lock-up output shaft rpm can also be adjusted on the test bench.

Reverse Hydraulic Operation

The shift to reverse begins in neutral. Remember that, in neutral, the first clutch is already applied. As the driver selects reverse, the manual valve is moved in its bore and main pressure in the neutral forward regulator circuit is exhausted through the valve. This action causes main pressure to increase as neutral forward regulator pressure is no longer pushing on the land on the MPRV to reduce it.

The main pressure is highest in reverse because reverse gear ratio can be higher than 5:1. The high ratio requires higher pressure to provide extra clamping force in the clutches. The following fluid flow begins at the bottom of the manual selector valve, as shown in Figure 43-11. Main pressure is directed from the manual valve through the base of the 1–2 shift relay valve and into the reverse circuit, which connects to the fourth clutch apply circuit through the bottom of the 3–4 shift relay valve. The fluid is directed through the base of the 1–2 relay valve to prevent it from shifting should road speed be high enough in reverse for the governor to move the 1–2 shift signal valve. If this occurs, the pressure at the top of the valve and the bottom of the valve would be equal and the valve spring would ensure the valve would not move. The reverse apply circuit also has an electrical pressure switch installed in it. The switch turns on the vehicle's reverse lights when pressure is detected in the circuit.

FIGURE 43-26 Retainer cam blocks on each shift signal valve in an Allison transmission valve body can be rotated, increasing the tension on the valve's return spring.

Wrap-up

Ready for Review

- Automatic transmissions used in today's vehicles are electronically controlled, but their function is based on their hydraulically controlled predecessors.
- Automatic transmissions increase driver and passenger comfort and reduce driver training requirements.
- Allison first started making transmissions for tanks in the 1940s and now makes a range of transmissions for trucks and busses all over the world.
- All automatic transmissions use torque converters and a set of planetary gears to create their power flows.
- Truck automatic transmission planetary gear components are controlled by either stationary or rotating multi-plate hydraulic clutches.
- Since 2000, all Allison automatics for on highway use in North America are electronically controlled.
- Truck and bus automatic transmissions use combinations of three or four planetary gear sets to create their required ratios.
- Knowledge of a transmission's clutch application chart is invaluable when trying to diagnose problems.
- Power flows in automatic transmissions may be simple (only one planetary gear set is involved) or compound (two or more planetary gear sets are involved).
- All automatic transmissions incorporate a hydraulic clutch to supply fluid pressure for transmission operation. This pump can be of fixed or variable displacement to control parasitic loads.
- In order for the transmission's pump to operate, atmospheric pressure must enter the transmission sump, so an air vent is essential.
- Automatic transmissions use a pressurized lubrication system and will have a cooler to control fluid temperature.
- Fluid exiting the hydraulic pump is directed to the main pressure regulator valve—a spool valve that balances pump output against spring pressure and other forces and creates main or control pressure. All other hydraulic circuits in the transmission are supplied by the main or control pressure.
- The manual selector valve directs main pressure to the appropriate clutches and control circuits to allow the transmission to attain a gear and shift automatically.
- The control valve body holds the spool valve responsible for shifting and shift quality control.
- The modulator valve uses main pressure to create modulator pressure. Modulator pressure is varied depending on throttle position and is, therefore, a load signal to the transmission's hydraulic control.
- Modulator pressure can be used to influence shift quality and shift timing and to increase main pressure to increase clutch capacity when required.
- The governor valve uses main pressure to create governor pressure based on output shaft speed. This pressure provides a speed signal to the control valve body.
- Upshifts are made by governor pressure and modified by modulator pressure. Without governor pressure, no upshifts are possible.
- Shift signal valves are acted upon by governor pressure and modulator pressure to control upshift points. When the shift signal valve moves, it causes the shift relay valve to move.
- Shift relay valves are moved by pressure directed from the shift signal valve. When shift relay valves move, they exhaust an applied clutch and send pressure to the on-coming clutch.
- The priority valve acts as a check valve to protect the transmission's hydraulic pressure supply.
- Trimmer valves cause a "leak" in a clutch apply circuit to soften the clutch application.
- The trimmer regulator valve allows the action of the trimmer valve to be increased or decreased based on throttle position to make shifts softer or harsher.
- All automatic transmissions use a lock-up clutch in the torque converter to eliminate the inherent 5% to 10% slippage between the impeller and the turbine and increase fuel economy.
- Torque converter lock-up in commercial vehicles is primarily scheduled, meaning that the torque converter will lock up when a specific range has been achieved to increase fuel efficiency.
- Modulated lock-up is throttle based and can increase performance.

- In the Allison transmission, the neutral forward regulator circuit (NFRC) can be used to lower main pressure in neutral and all forward ranges.
- NRFC pressure is not present in reverse, so reverse will have the highest main pressure.
- The valves in the control valve body are separated from the worm tracks in the transmission case by a separator plate and gaskets, allowing the valves to take fluid from one passage and direct it to another.
- During automatic upshifting, governor pressure acts on the shift signal valve to move it up. Modulator pressure helps the valve move up. Modulator pressure is high at closed or light throttle and low at wide-open throttle. Shifts will occur at lower speed during light-throttle operation and at higher speeds during full-throttle operation.
- Automatic downshifting is caused by the shift signal valve spring pressure overcoming dropping governor pressure.
- Full-throttle downshifts are caused by the disappearance of modulator pressure as the throttle is pushed and governor pressure alone is not able to keep the shift signal valve in the upshifted position.
- Shift points in Allison hydraulically controlled transmissions can be altered by changing spring tension on the modulator valve or the shift signal valve.

Vocabulary Builder

connecting drum A device used by Allison to connect some of the planetary gear components.

control valve body The heart of the hydraulic control; it holds the spool valve responsible for shifting.

DIWA™ A dedicated bus transmission from Voith.

full throttle downshift A downshift forced by the driver by pushing on the throttle. Also called *detent downshift* or *kick down* depending on the manufacturer.

forward clutch A clutch that is applied in all forward gears or ranges; it is not found on overdrive transmissions.

gear pump A pump consisting of an internal and external toothed gear.

gerotor pump A pump consisting of a rotor turning inside a matching chamber.

governor valve A valve that creates a pressure based on road speed.

hold regulator valve A spool valve that creates a pressure used to prevent upshifts.

hydraulic circuit A pathway connecting one part of the transmission's hydraulic control with another part.

main pressure regulator valve (MPRV) A spool valve that produces main or control pressure.

main shaft The shaft that is driven by the countershaft and provides output for the transmission. Also called output shaft.

manual selector valve The spool valve that is moved by the operator's shift linkage to select a gear.

modulated lock-up A lock-up clutch application strategy that is designed for maximum vehicle performance.

modulator valve A valve that produces a pressure based on throttle position. Also called the *throttle valve*.

parasitic loss An unnecessary load on the engine that wastes fuel.

priority valve A check valve that protects the hydraulic controls.

scheduled lock-up Torque converter lock-up that occurs at a preset point; this saves fuel.

separator plate A plate that separates the control valve body and the transmission case.

shift modulator valve A valve that is moved by modulator pressure and governor pressure for shifting.

shift relay valve The spool valve that directs clutch apply pressure to the correct clutch.

shift signal valve A spool valve that is moved by governor pressure for shifting.

spool valve A valve that has a series of lands and cutaways in a precise fitting bore.

sun gear shaft The shaft that connects the front and center sun gears in the Allison transmission.

throttle valve A valve that produces a pressure based on throttle position. Also called the *modulator valve*.

trimmer regulator valve A valve that modulates trimmer valve action.

trimmer valve A valve used to soften a clutch application.

vane pump A hydraulic pump that uses sliding vanes to move the fluid.

Review Questions

1. If the throttle or modulator valve in an automatic transmission were to stick in the closed throttle position, the probable complaint would be which of the following?
   - **a.** Soft early upshifts
   - **b.** No upshifts
   - **c.** Delayed upshifts
   - **d.** No complaint
2. Which of the following hydraulic pressures provide a load signal to the control valve body?
   - **a.** MPRV pressure
   - **b.** Governor pressure
   - **c.** Modulator pressure
   - **d.** Main pressure
3. Which of the following pressures provide a "speed" sensitive signal to the control valve body?
   - **a.** MPRV pressure
   - **b.** Governor pressure
   - **c.** Modulator pressure
   - **d.** Main pressure
4. Which of the following applies the transmission's clutches?
   - **a.** MPRV pressure
   - **b.** Governor pressure
   - **c.** Modulator pressure
   - **d.** Main pressure
5. Loss of governor pressure in an automatic transmission would cause which of the following symptoms?
   - **a.** No downshifts
   - **b.** No upshifts
   - **c.** High main pressure
   - **d.** Low main pressure
6. Which of the following statements about the lubrication circuit in an automatic transmission is correct?
   - **a.** It is a splash lubricated by the internal rotating components.
   - **b.** It is usually at line pressure.
   - **c.** It is usually supplied by the converter/cooler circuit.
   - **d.** It operates at converter pressure.
7. Which of the following is NOT one of the functions of the main pressure regulator valve?
   - **a.** It indirectly feeds the transmissions lube circuits
   - **b.** It dumps excess pressure to the pump's inlet side or to the sump when operating pressure is reached.
   - **c.** It feeds the converter-in circuit.
   - **d.** It directs oil from the converter out circuit to sump.
8. The ________ circuit can be used to raise or boost main or control pressure in automatic transmissions.
   - **a.** throttle or modulator
   - **b.** governor
   - **c.** converter-out
   - **d.** lubrication
9. In an Allison transmission, the ________ valve component has cams that can be adjusted to change shift points.
   - **a.** governor
   - **b.** shift relay
   - **c.** selector
   - **d.** shift signal
10. On Allison transmissions, the ________ valves direct clutch apply pressure to the clutch packs.
    - **a.** shift signal
    - **b.** trimmer
    - **c.** shift relay
    - **d.** modulator

ASE-Type Questions

1. Technician A says that most commercial vehicles will have scheduled torque converter lock-up. Technician B says that modulated torque converter lock-up saves fuel. Who is correct?
   a. Technician A
   b. Technician B
   c. Both Technician A and Technician B
   d. Neither Technician A nor Technician B
2. Technician A says that the trimmer regulator valve is used to modify shift harshness based on throttle position. Technician B says that trimmer valves are used to let clutches slip a bit before they are fully applied. Who is correct?
   a. Technician A
   b. Technician B
   c. Both Technician A and Technician B
   d. Neither Technician A nor Technician B
3. Technician A says that in the hydraulically controlled Allison transmissions, modulator pressure is high at wide-open throttle. Technician B says that in the hydraulically controlled Allison transmissions, high modulator pressure causes harsh shifting. Who is correct?
   a. Technician A
   b. Technician B
   c. Both Technician A and Technician B
   d. Neither Technician A nor Technician B
4. Technician A says that downshifting in hydraulically controlled Allison transmissions is caused by spring force. Technician B says that a downshift can be made at higher road speed by pushing the throttle to the floor. Who is correct?
   a. Technician A
   b. Technician B
   c. Both Technician A and Technician B
   d. Neither Technician A nor Technician B
5. Technician A says that all of the pressures found in hydraulically controlled Allison transmissions are derived from main or control pressure. Technician B says that hydraulically controlled Allison transmission lubrication circuits are at main pressure. Who is correct?
   a. Technician A
   b. Technician B
   c. Both Technician A and Technician B
   d. Neither Technician A nor Technician B
6. Technician A says that, in the Allison 500 series wwtransmission, the center planetary gear set is involved in four out of the five gear ranges. Technician B says that the center planetary gear set is not involved in first range. Who is correct?
   a. Technician A
   b. Technician B
   c. Both Technician A and Technician B
   d. Neither Technician A nor Technician B
7. Technician A says that the Allison AT 500 series transmission uses five hydraulic clutches. Technician B says the Allison AT 500 series transmission use three interconnected planetary gear sets. Who is correct?
   a. Technician A
   b. Technician B
   c. Both Technician A and Technician B
   d. Neither Technician A nor Technician B
8. Technician A says that, in the Allison AT 500 series transmission, the connecting drum is attached to the front carrier, the center carrier, and the rear carrier. Technician B says that, in the Allison AT 500 series transmission, the front sun gear is part of the main shaft. Who is correct?
   a. Technician A
   b. Technician B
   c. Both Technician A and Technician B
   d. Neither Technician A nor Technician B
9. Technician A says that the center ring gear is attached to the connecting drum in the Allison AT 500 series transmission. Technician B says that the rear carrier is attached to the output shaft in the Allison AT 500 series transmission. Who is correct?
   a. Technician A
   b. Technician B
   c. Both Technician A and Technician B
   d. Neither Technician A nor Technician B
10. Technician A says that, in fourth range in the Allison AT 500 series transmission, the two rotating clutches are turning at the same speed. Technician B says that in fourth range in the Allison AT 500 series transmission all three planetary gear sets are turning at the same speed. Who is correct?
    a. Technician A
    b. Technician B
    c. Both Technician A and Technician B
    d. Neither Technician A nor Technician B

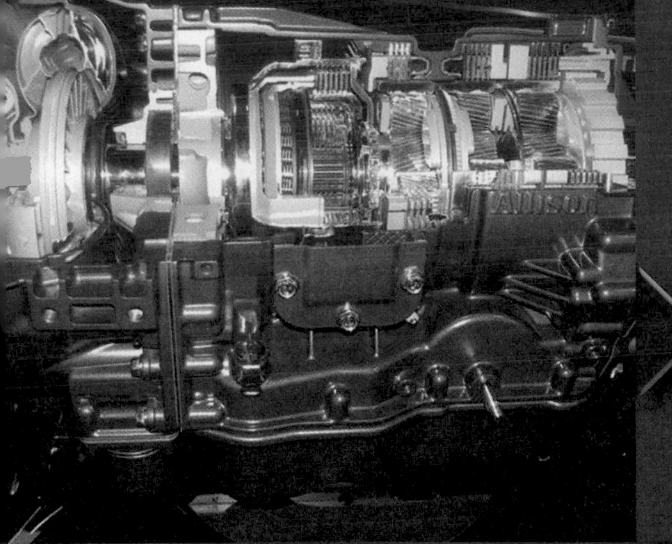

CHAPTER 44

NATEF Tasks

Drive Train

Transmission

	Page
■ Check transmission fluid level and condition; determine needed service; add proper type of lubricant.	1422–1427, 1429
■ Inspect for leakage and replace transmission cover plates, gaskets, seals, and cap bolts; inspect seal surfaces and vents; repair as needed.	1429
■ Inspect transmission oil filters, coolers, and related components; replace as needed.	1431
■ Inspect and replace transmission mounts, insulators, and mounting bolts.	1433, 1435
■ Remove and reinstall transmission.	1436
■ Inspect and test function of reverse light, neutral start, and warning device circuits; determine needed action.	1439

Maintaining Automatic Transmissions

Knowledge Objectives

After reading this chapter, you will be able to:

1. Explain the importance of fluid level and operating temperature. (pp 1423–1424)
2. Outline fluid change frequency for Allison transmissions. (pp 1424–1426)
3. Determine the correct fluid to use in a particular transmission. (pp 1426–1427)
4. Describe the different types of transmission fluid used in transmissions. (pp 1426–1427)
5. Describe basic transmission diagnostic procedures. (pp 1427–1428)
6. Explain transmission out-of-service criteria. (p 1428)
7. Adjust transmission cables and linkages. (pp 1428–1430)
8. Describe the procedure for inspecting and flushing cooler lines. (pp 1429, 1437–1439)
9. Describe the procedure for replacing a transmission support mount. (p 1430)
10. Change transmission fluid and filters. (pp 1430–1431)
11. Perform a transmission pressure test. (pp 1430, 1432)
12. Explain transmission shift point adjustment procedures. (pp 1430, 1436–1437)
13. Describe the removal and reinstallation procedures for automatic transmissions. (pp 1435–1436)
14. Describe the procedure for adjusting the transmission neutral safety switch. (pp 1437–1439)

Skills Objectives

After reading this chapter, you will be able to:

1. Identify automatic transmission fluid and filter requirements. (pp 1422–1427)
2. Perform general visual inspection of a transmission. (p 1428)
3. Inspect a transmission for fluid leakage, level, and condition. (p 1429) **SKILL DRILL 44-1**
4. Drain and replace transmission fluid and filter. (p 1431) **SKILL DRILL 44-2**
5. Perform automatic transmission pressure testing. (p 1432) **SKILL DRILL 44-3**
6. Inspect and replace powertrain support mounts. (p 1433) **SKILL DRILL 44-4**
7. Perform shift point adjustment on hydraulically controlled transmissions. (p 1434) **SKILL DRILL 44-5**
8. Remove a transmission and check the condition of its mounts, insulators, and mounting bolts. (p 1435) **SKILL DRILL 44-6**
9. Reinstall a transmission. (p 1436) **SKILL DRILL 44-7**
10. Inspect the torque converter flex plate. (p 1437) **SKILL DRILL 44-8**
11. Inspect and flush cooler lines. (p 1438) **SKILL DRILL 44-9**
12. Inspect, adjust, and replace the manual valve shift linkage and the neutral safety switch. (p 1439) **SKILL DRILL 44-10**

Introduction

Overhauling of automatic transmissions is a task rarely undertaken by most shops and requires the utmost in cleanliness and several specialized tools. For that reason, we will not attempt to discuss overhaul procedures in this chapter. Nonetheless, truck technicians must have a good understanding of what is involved in maintaining a typical automatic transmission, including the ability to diagnose basic transmission failures and recommend repair strategies. Those topics will be the focus of this chapter.

Allison is the most prolific supplier of automatic transmissions to the North American heavy truck market, so this chapter will provide a general maintenance guideline based on Allison transmission models. In no way is the information in this chapter meant to supplant Allison's or any other manufacturer's service recommendations, however. Always check the literature for your particular transmission model before proceeding. Also do not assume that the schedules and recommended fluids are interchangeable between all transmission manufacturers. Always consult the OEM manual before servicing any transmission.

Fundamentals of Transmission Fluid

Transmission fluid, like that shown in FIGURE 44-1, is the life blood of all automatic transmissions. If it is not

FIGURE 44-1 Transmission fluid requirements can vary by manufacturer, so always follow OEM recommendations.

You Are the Technician

A vehicle is brought to your shop and the driver complains that his transmission is noisy. He explains that the noise only occurs after driving for a few miles and then only when he is accelerating. He says it sounds like someone threw a bag of small ball bearings into his transmission and he is very worried about it. You do a preliminary check and discover the transmission is an Allison AT 540 series. The vehicle seems to be involved in construction, as the entire underside of the vehicle and the transmission are caked in mud. You check the fluid and find that it is at the correct level and is a normal pink color. (Note that some newer fluids are not bright pink.) Next, you road test the vehicle. Sure enough, you hear a high-frequency rattling sound as you accelerate. What are your next steps?

1. Would you inspect the transmission flex plate? If so, what would you look for?
2. What would you need to do to determine if there are ball bearings loose in the transmission?
3. Would you check the transmission vent? If so, what would you expect to find?
4. Would you recommend the transmission be replaced?

maintained at the correct level and condition, failure of the transmission is inevitable. So it is essential that the OEM's transmission maintenance schedule is adhered to.

Looking at a transmission fluid, it can be easy to assume that they are all alike. Nothing could be further from the truth. Several types of transmission fluids include **friction modifiers** that change the coefficient of friction of the transmission clutch pack. Friction modifiers also change the clutch pack's engagement and disengagement characteristics. Using fluids with friction modifiers in transmissions that are not designed for them can lead to severe oxidation issues, clutch pack slippage, and outright failure of the transmission. Transmission seal life can also be affected by using the wrong types of fluid. Leakage and clutch failure can result. Always adhere strictly to the transmission manufacturer's recommendation for the correct type of fluid and never mix fluids in a transmission.

Fluid Level

Transmission fluid performs several functions. It lubricates and cools the transmission. Fluid also transmits hydraulic power through the torque converter and acts as the hydraulic force to apply clutches. Therefore, the proper fluid level must be maintained at all times. Fluid level that is too low or too high will cause severe problems in the transmission. If the fluid is too low, the hydraulic pump will be starved of fluid during operation. Air will be drawn into the pump intake leading to **aeration** and loss of pressure. Aeration is the direct mixing of air with the fluid, which causes bubbles. Aeration can lead to burned out clutches and a loss of converter efficiency. Aerated fluid loses viscosity and so becomes less effective as lubrication.

All transmissions have a **transmission vent** that allows atmospheric pressure to enter the transmission. If that vent is not clear, the pump inlet can create very low pressures. Low pressures can cause **cavitation**, which is the formation of air bubbles in the transmission fluid as a result of the low pressure. Cavitation can damage the pump, as bubbles implode explosively and break down the actual metal. A pump experiencing cavitation will usually be extremely noisy and will eventually fail.

> **TECHNICIAN TIP**
>
> If the fluid level is correct and the fluid still becomes aerated, check the transmission vent. If the vent is blocked, it can stop atmospheric pressure from entering the transmission as the fluid is drawn in by the pump. The blockage can lead to the creation of a low pressure area which, in turn, can lead to cavitation at the pump inlet and aeration of the fluid.

The correct fluid level in an automatic transmission is normally just below the rotating components. If the fluid level is too high, aeration becomes a problem—the rotating components in the transmission run in the fluid, churning it up and aerating it. The aeration causes the same problems as occur when the fluid level is too low. Also, if the fluid is aerated because the fluid level is too high, the fluid may continue to foam and expand until it starts to leak from the vent and the dipstick tube. FIGURE 44-2 shows the dipstick tube in a heavy-duty transmission.

A missing or defective seal ring on the transmission filter(s) can also lead to aeration, allowing large amounts of air to be drawn in by the pump. For these reasons, most manufacturers insist that the fluid be checked and rechecked in a certain manner to ensure the level is correct.

Check the transmission fluid level at least twice to check the reading is consistent. If it is not, investigate the cause before proceeding. For example, a clogged transmission vent can lead to inconsistency.

Cleanliness is also very important. Before removing the dipstick, clean the area around the stick and the fill tube. If adding fluid, always use only clean fluid from a sealed container and a clean funnel. Any dirt entering the transmission can lead to stuck valves in the valve body and shifting problems. Read the manufacturer's recommendation for the fluid temperature while checking fluid level. There will usually be a large difference between the hot and cold levels of the fluid.

Most manufacturers recommend that the engine be running when checking transmission fluid levels. To check the fluid, start the vehicle with the transmission in neutral and the emergency brake applied. Place the transmission in reverse, then forward, and then back to neutral. Moving through the ranges in that manner ensures that the fluid passages are full. Then, remove

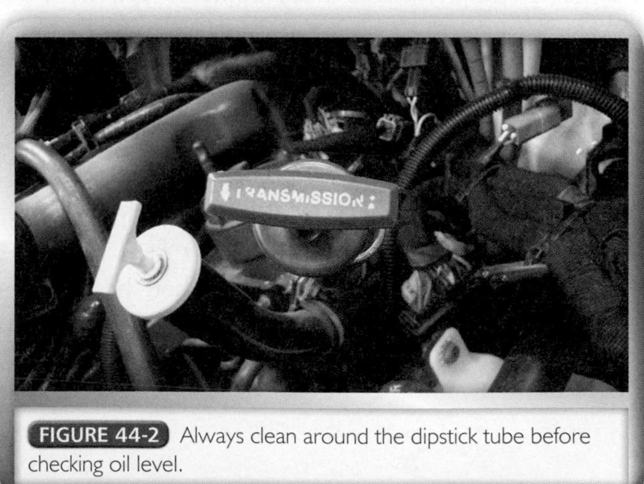

FIGURE 44-2 Always clean around the dipstick tube before checking oil level.

the dipstick and clean and replace it. Make sure it is completely installed before removing it again. Check the fluid level against the dipstick markings, as shown in FIGURE 44-3. Repeat the procedure to ensure consistency.

If necessary, transmission fluid level can be checked when the fluid is cold, say between 60°F and 120°F (16°C and 49°C), to ensure there is sufficient fluid to run the vehicle. A hot level check should be performed as soon as possible after the transmission reaches normal operating temperature of 160°F to 200° F (71°C to 93°C).

> **TECHNICIAN TIP**
>
> When checking transmission fluid, adhere strictly to the OEM-recommended procedure. Any variation could lead to a false reading. For example, if the engine speed is increased, the reading may be lower than normal due to the fluid being drawn faster by the pump. Temperature is critical as well. The difference between cold and operating temperatures can be as much as three or four liters depending on the transmission.

Minimum Operating Temperature

If a transmission is to be operated in cold ambient temperatures, the transmission fluid may need preheating before the transmission can be operated safely. Allison **TranSynd fluid** is a synthetic fluid made by Castrol to Allison specifications. If TranSynd is being used, the fluid will require preheating if ambient temperatures are below –22°F (–30°C).

If preheating is necessary because of the ambient temperature, one of these methods can be used:

- A sump heater can be installed to preheat fluid before operating the transmission.
- If no sump heater is available, allow the transmission to warm up in neutral for a minimum of 20 minutes at idle.

Allison electronically controlled transmissions have **cold operation inhibits** in their software to prevent the transmission from shifting below certain temperatures. For example, the ATEC/CEC model of Allison transmissions will not allow any shifting below –25°F (–32°C) and only limited shifting to first or reverse when the temperature is –25°F to 25°F (–32°C to –4°C).

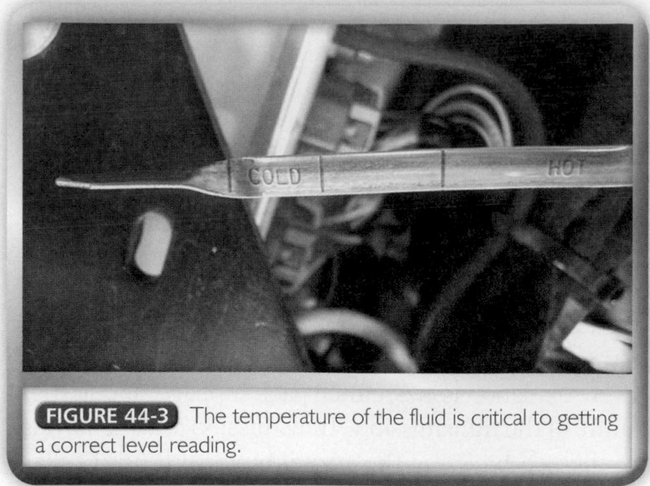

FIGURE 44-3 The temperature of the fluid is critical to getting a correct level reading.

Fluid Change Frequency

The oil change interval for Allison transmissions varies by transmission model and duty cycle or vocation. A typical oil and filter change interval for the MT series non-electronic control transmissions would be 25,000 miles (40,000 km) when using non-synthetic TES-389TM fluids. Using TES-295TM approved synthetic fluid extends the fluid change interval to 100,000 miles (160,000 km), but the filter change interval is set at 50,000 miles (80,000 km).

The fluid change frequency changes, however, for the newer computer-controlled transmissions. Since 2009, Allison computer software has been equipped with **prognostic capability**. That is, the computer's programming allows it to closely monitor the transmission's drive cycles and recommend fluid and filter changes based on actual road conditions. This option can be turned on or off by the vehicle operator through the transmission software. When Allison's **Prognostics** is turned on, the service interval is controlled entirely by the software. The software will notify the operator, through the display panel, when a fluid and or filter change is required. TABLE 44-1 is a chart depicting fluid and filter change intervals, with or without the Prognostics feature being activated, for the 4000 series transmissions.

The fluid change frequencies on other Allison series and models can differ from those depicted in Table 44-1, and early initial filter changes are required for certain transmissions. More frequent fluid changes may be required if the vehicle is operated in severe conditions

TABLE 44-1: Fluid and Filter Change Intervals on Allison 4000 Series Transmissions

4000 SERIES High Capacity Filters Fluid and Filter Change Interval Recommendations							
				Prognostics Turned Off or Not Calibrated in TCM		Prognostics Turned On	
		Transmission Model	Duty Cycle	Allison Approved TES-295TM Fluid	Allison Approved TES-389TM Fluid	Allison Approved TES-295TM Fluid	Allison Approved TES-389TM Fluid
FLUID		4000 w/ 2" and 4" Sump	General	300,000 miles (480,000 km) or 6,000 hours or 48 months	25,000 miles (40,000 km) or 1,000 hours or 12 months	When indicated by controller or 60 months, whichever occurs first	When indicated by controller or 24 months, whichever occurs first
			Severe	150,000 miles (240,000 km) or 6,000 hours or 48 months	12,000 miles (20,000 km) or 500 hours or 6 months		
FILTERS	Main Filter	4000 w/ 2" and 4" Sump	General	75,000 miles (120,000 km) or 3,000 hours or 36 months	25,000 miles (40,000 km) or 1,000 hours or 12 months	When indicated by controller or 60 months, whichever occurs first	When indicated by controller or 24 months, whichever occurs first
			Severe	75,000 miles (120,000 km) or 3,000 hours or 36 months	12,000 miles (40,000 km) or 500 hours or 6 months		
	Internal Filter	4000 w/ 2" and 4" Sump	All	Overhaul	Overhaul	Overhaul	Overhaul
	Lube/Auxiliary Filter	4000 w/ 2" and 4" Sump	General	75,000 miles (120,000 km) or 3,000 hours or 36 months	25,000 miles (40,000 km) or 1,000 hours or 12 months	When indicated by controller or 60 months, whichever occurs first	When indicated by controller or 24 months, whichever occurs first
			Severe	75,000 miles (120,000 km) or 3,000 hours or 36 months	12,000 miles (20,000 km) Or 500 hours or 3 months		

or extended duty cycles. It is essential to check the correct frequency for the specific model being serviced. The correct change frequency and fluid capacities can be found at the following Allison website:

http://www.allisontransmission.com/docs/default-source/service-documents/st1099s.pdf?sfvrsn=2

Allison also has a fluid filter change interval calculator available at the following web address:

http://www.allisontransmission.com/my-allison/customer

Fluid Analysis

When operating conditions vary from the norm, Allison recommends that **fluid analysis** be conducted to determine oil change frequencies. Fluid analysis can optimize transmission longevity and service scheduling. In order for fluid analysis to be successful, testing must be frequent and consistent so that trends can be established. TABLE 44-2 contains Allison's recommended limit for fluid conditions and contaminants.

Fluid Handling

Transmission fluid must be handled with extreme care to prevent the entry of contaminants. Never use a container that has held **ethylene glycol** or other anti-freeze solutions to transfer transmission fluid. Glycol will quickly destroy clutch plate material leading to complete failure of the transmission. Failure of or simply lack of transmission fluid is the simplest and the primary cause of automatic transmission failures and it must not be overlooked.

Types of Transmission Fluids

As with other vehicle fluids, there are many types of transmission fluids available on the market. Which fluid is used depends on the make and model of transmission being serviced. There is also a selection of additives that can be used to enhance the performance of transmission fluids. As with the fluid itself, follow the manufacturer's recommendations when determining if and which additives to use.

TABLE 44-2: Allison Transmission Fluid Limits

Condition Limit	Contaminant Limit
• Viscosity +/− 25% change from new fluid • Total Acid Number (TAN) +3.0* change from new fluid • Solids 2% by volume maximum	• Water 0.2% maximum • Glycol 0; no trace allowed. If glycol is detected the transmission will require overhaul to repair glycol damage.

* mg of KOH (potassium hydroxide), required to neutralize a gram of fluid

Recommended Transmission Fluids

Different manufacturers recommend using different transmission fluids depending on the design and construction of their transmissions. Because there is no universal transmission fluid that works for all models and manufactures of transmission, always consult the manufacturer's documentation for your transmission model before using a particular transmission fluid. This section will concentrate on Allison transmission's fluid recommendations.

TranSynd, shown in FIGURE 44-4, is a full synthetic automatic transmission fluid made specifically for Allison transmission by Castrol Ltd. TranSynd is recommended in all Allison on-highway transmissions. TranSynd meets the Allison Transmission Engineering Specification 295, or TES-295TM, fluid specification and qualifies for an extended service schedule and for severe duty operation. A list of other manufacturer's fluids that meet the TES-295TM fluids can be found at the following website:

http://www.allisontransmission.com/service/autoapp/172/viewpage.jsp?ThisPage=3.

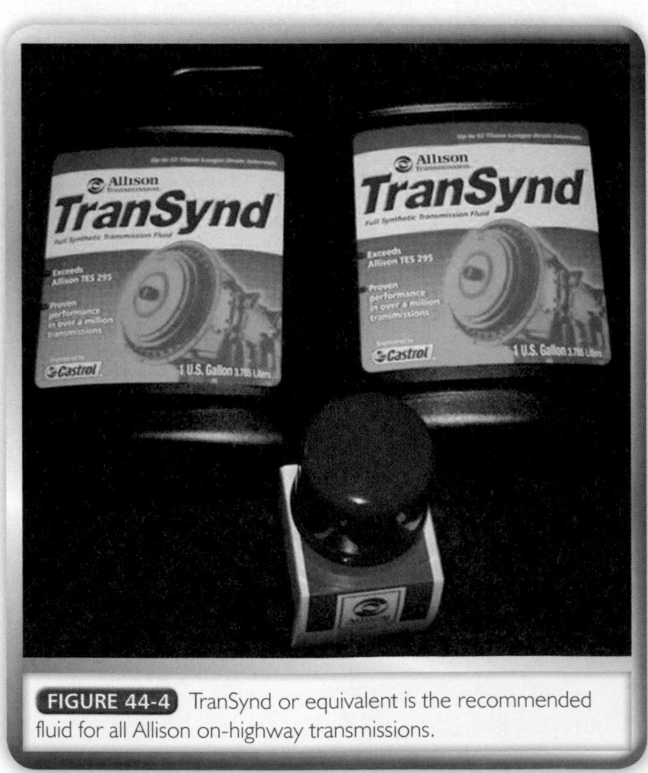

FIGURE 44-4 TranSynd or equivalent is the recommended fluid for all Allison on-highway transmissions.

In the past, Allison's TES-228TM specification for approved fluids covered non-synthetic on-highway fluids. This specification is no longer recognized. Non-synthetic fluids approved for use in Allison transmissions must now meet the Allison TES-389TM standard. A list of these fluids can be found at the following website:

https://fdlrd.swri.org/Allison/ApprovedFluidsList.aspx?Id=2.

Note: Allison highly recommends that only synthetic fluids be used in all of their transmissions.

Also in the past, off-highway model transmission fluids were classified as C-type fluids. The "C" is for construction, with the classification C-4 being the last of these. C-type fluids were automotive oil-type fluids approved for use in certain applications. Allison has done away with the "C" classification and, since November 2010, recommends that off-highway fluids all be synthetic. A current listing of these products can be found at the following website:

http://www.allisontransmission.com/parts-service/approved-fluids/on-highway-fluids.

Supplemental Additives

Most transmission manufacturers do not recommend any **supplemental additives** be used in their transmissions. Additives are products that are manufactured and marketed to increase the efficiency of transmission fluids and may alter the frictional, anti-wear, and/or oxidation properties of the fluid. Use of some supplemental additives, such as those shown in **FIGURE 44-5**, may void the transmission warranty and should not be used.

Troubleshooting Problems with Automatic Transmissions

Automatic transmissions are somewhat of a mystery to a lot of technicians, especially in the heavy truck field, as they are not as common as standard transmissions. Nonetheless, automatic transmissions are diagnosed using the same basic step-by-step process used to diagnose any failed or suspect component. As always, good understanding of the transmission's function and access to the OEM service manual are important before diagnosis is undertaken.

Automatic Transmission Diagnostics

When diagnosing problems with automatic transmissions, always stick to the basics. Check oil level and condition before starting any diagnoses. The next step is to road test the vehicle to verify any complaint. Record the pertinent information, exactly what the problem is, and when it occurs—for example during shifting or in a certain range. Does the problem occur only when the fluid is hot or cold?

When the problem is verified and recorded, the technician can then start the diagnostic procedure. Older transmissions will have symptom-based diagnostic charts for the technician to follow, and these can assist greatly in the process. Automatic transmissions with electronic controls can self-diagnose and inform the operator or the technician with detailed trouble codes. Self-diagnostic trouble codes simplify diagnostic procedures by leading the technician to the manufacturer's step-by- step troubleshooting charts to assist in the process. These charts should always be followed in sequence to eliminate any chance of misdiagnosis. There are three broad areas of failures that can occur: mechanical, hydraulic, or electronic. By following the diagnostic charts, the technician can quickly get to the root cause of the complaint.

FIGURE 44-5 Manufacturers caution against the use of any additives in their transmissions

Symptom-Based Diagnoses

A good understanding of the transmission's power flow is an invaluable asset when trying to diagnose a complaint. Knowing which clutches are involved in the power flow when a transmission problem presents itself can greatly speed up the diagnostic process. The transmission control system, whether electronic or purely hydraulic, can also frequently be the root cause of some complaints. Having a good knowledge of the control systems operation can, again, be of enormous assistance to the technician trying to pinpoint a problem.

Pressure testing can be used to determine if the problem is mechanical or hydraulic. In older transmission models, testing pressure was limited to main or line pressure testing, cooling circuit pressure tests, and flow tests. The Allison World Transmission models include pressure test points, like those shown in **FIGURE 44-6**, for each of the individual clutch apply circuits as well as the lube and main pressure.

Common transmission complaints include slipping clutches, either in drive or reverse or in a certain transmission range. Slipping clutches can usually be verified by conducting a stall test and/or road testing the vehicle after verifying the fluid level is, and will remain, correct throughout the procedure. Refer to the Torque Converters chapter for the stall test procedure.

After confirming the complaint with a stall test or road test, always refer to the transmission manufacturer's troubleshooting recommendations before proceeding further. There are myriad differences between individual manufacturer's transmissions and there is no universal procedure for their diagnoses. Always follow the OEM service manual for your transmission.

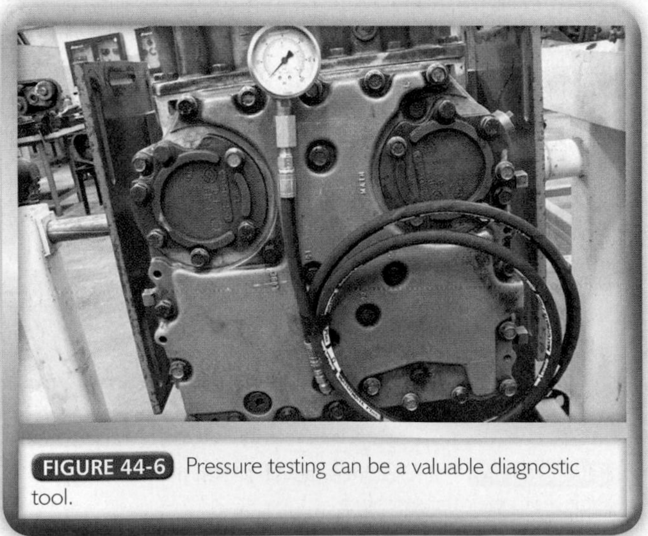

FIGURE 44-6 Pressure testing can be a valuable diagnostic tool.

Out-of-Service Criteria for Automatic Transmissions

Although the Commercial Vehicle Service Alliance (CVSA) does not specify out-of-service (OSS) criteria for automatic transmissions, the National Fire Prevention Association (NFPA) does include out-of-service criteria for vehicles covered by its standards. The following defects of the transmission shall cause a vehicle to be taken out of service according to NFPA:

- Any automatic transmission that overheats in any range
- Any automatic transmission which has a "do not shift" light illuminated
- Any transmission components that exhibit serious leakage of transmission fluid

Certain state transit organizations also list OSS criteria for automatic transmissions. The following are a selection of their criteria. A vehicle shall be taken out of service if any of the following defects are present:

- Transmission lines or hoses that have persistent leakage or a fluid leak onto any exhaust system component
- Any transmission that is loose in its mounting or has transmission mounts that are broken, damaged, or missing
- A defective neutral safety switch
- Any transmission that does not operate in any of the selected gear settings

Maintenance of Automatic Transmissions

This section will cover several maintenance procedures for automatic transmissions. It is by no means meant to replace manufacturers' recommendations for transmission service or inspection. It is merely a guideline. Always follow the relevant manufacturer's procedures for any maintenance or service task you are performing.

General Transmission Inspection

Before beginning the diagnostic procedure, it is important to inspect the transmission visually. The most important check for any automatic transmission complaint is transmission fluid level. Low or high fluid level, or deteriorated/contaminated fluid are at the root of a large percentage of automatic transmission problems.

In addition, it is important to identify visible transmission fluid leaks. If leaks are detected, take steps to ensure the fluid level remains at the full level during all diagnostic procedures. Leaks can be hard to pinpoint as air movement and vehicle vibration can spread the fluid far from the original leak point. A leak detection dye can be helpful in finding the leak. Follow the steps in SKILL DRILL 44-1 to check fluid level and determine the source of a leak.

Other important visual checks include:

- Loose fasteners (transmission and its mounting components)
- Visible transmission fluid leaks
- Transmission vent is clear (a clogged vent can lead to fluid aeration from pump cavitation)
- Correct movement and positioning of the manual shift linkage, if equipped
- Full and correct movement of mechanical throttle, **modulator cable**, or linkage and valve (if equipped)
- Leaks in air or vacuum modulator connection (if equipped); if a vacuum modulator is used, always check the inside of the vacuum line—it is a common source of an undetected transmission fluid leak
- Damaged or loose hydraulic connections and hoses
- Electrical connections and harnesses for abrasive wear and/or corrosion

> **TECHNICIAN TIP**
>
> Broken or corroded connectors and wiring are a frequent cause of problems with electronically controlled transmissions.

> **TECHNICIAN TIP**
>
> Transmissions that use vacuum modulator valves (for example, gasoline engines) can develop a pinhole in the modulator's diaphragm. This can lead to transmission fluid being drawn into the engine through the vacuum line. The transmission fluid is then consumed by the engine, leading to low fluid levels without a visible leak.

SKILL DRILL 44-1 Checking Fluid Level and Inspecting Fluid Loss

1. Look up the procedure for checking the transmission fluid level in the appropriate service information.
2. Locate the transmission dipstick (if equipped). Most but not all, transmissions are checked with the engine at operating temperature, idling, and the transmission in park. If the transmission has a dipstick, wipe it off and reinsert it into the transmission before checking the level of fluid on the dipstick. Check both sides of the dipstick; the side that is the lowest is the accurate fluid level. On some transmissions, the fluid returning to the transmission pan will splash up on one side of the dipstick, resulting in a high reading on that side.
3. If the transmission fluid level is low, add the recommended type and amount of transmission fluid. Be careful not to overfill the transmission.
4. Inspect the transmission for signs of leakage. Some places to check are the transmission pan, area around the entrance of the filler tube to the transmission, extension housing gasket, output shaft seals, selector shaft seal, area around the electrical connectors that go into the transmission case, front pump seals, fluid cooler lines, and the fittings. Also, if the vehicle has a vacuum modulator, remove the vacuum hose from the modulator and see if there is any transmission fluid in the hose. If there is, the modulator is bad. Be sure to remove the radiator cap (with vehicle cold) and check for any transmission fluid in the radiator; if present, it is an indication that the transmission cooler is leaking.
5. If the transmission has a large amount of transmission fluid or engine oil covering it, you may need to clean it with a pressure washer, some engine degreaser, or use a leak detection dye in the transmission fluid.
6. Restart the vehicle and allow it to run for a while. The leak detection dye will be easy to spot using a black light, or look for fresh transmission fluid leaking.
7. Record the location of the leak and inform the customer to obtain approval for repairs.

Performing an Oil and Filter Change

The oil and filter change procedures for automatic transmissions will depend on the model that is being serviced. What follows is merely a guideline. Always check the service manual for the transmission being serviced. Certain transmissions will require that the transmission oil pan be removed to replace the filter; with others, the filter can be accessed from the outside. Also keep in mind that a typical oil and filter change will usually not replace the quantity of fluid in the torque converter. (Some torque converters may have removable plugs to drain this fluid, but this is not conventional.) Aftermarket equipment can be installed in series with the transmission cooler circuit to flush the entire transmission torque converter and cooler with pressurized transmission fluid. These systems, however, are not recommended by manufacturers, and their efficiency is questionable at best. To change the oil and filter in a transmission, follow the steps in SKILL DRILL 44-2.

> **TECHNICIAN TIP**
>
> The Allison AT series internal filter has an O-ring on the connecting tube where it fits into the transmission housing. Failure to replace this seal can lead to fluid aeration and, if the seal is doubled up, by failing to remove the old O-ring, the filter tube can drop out of the housing after service, causing transmission failure.

> **TECHNICIAN TIP**
>
> A normal fluid and filter service will typically leave between 5 and 8 quarts, (4.5 and 7.5 liters), of the original fluid in the system that cannot be drained, so be very careful of fluid compatibility issues.

System Pressure Testing

Testing system pressure can be a valuable tool in transmission diagnoses. Hydraulic pressure is used to apply the clutches and make the transmission shift. Low pressure could indicate a failed pump, serious internal leakage, shift valve problems, and/or a failed clutch seal. High pressure could indicate a seized main pressure regulator valve. On some transmissions, it is only possible to test main pressure, where on others, such as the Allison World transmission main pressure, each clutch's application pressure and lube pressure can be tested individually. Follow the steps in SKILL DRILL 44-3 to test system pressure.

Inspecting or Replacing Power Train Mounts

Power train components are supported and aligned in the vehicle by flexible **mounts** usually made of rubber and steel. These mounts allow slight movement of the components as torque and braking forces are acting upon them. The mounts also absorb vibrations emanating from the engine and transmission and prevent those vibrations from being transferred to the vehicle frame.

These mounts are extremely resilient but can fail due to repeated flexing. Another common cause of failure is fluid contamination. If the rubber in the mount is subjected to contamination by hydrocarbon-based fluid, engine oil, fuel, transmission fluid, and so on, it will break down, and the mount will fail. Failed mounts allow excessive movement of the power train and can lead to damage and/or erratic vehicle operation. Power train mounts should be inspected regularly and replaced if defective. Follow the steps in SKILL DRILL 44-4 to inspect and replace (if necessary) power train mounts.

Allison Shift Point Adjustment

Most of today's automatic transmissions have no provision for shift point adjustment, as shifting is controlled electronically by the transmission control unit. Non-electronic Allison transmission models and certain other hydraulically controlled transmissions do allow for some adjustment of **shift points**.

Most hydraulically controlled transmissions will have either a vacuum modulator valve (gasoline engines only) or throttle cable. When a transmission is equipped with a vacuum modulator, sometimes the spring tension inside the modulator can be adjusted by turning an adjusting screw. Increasing spring tension by tightening the screw will cause shift point speeds to increase. Loosening the screw will decrease shift points. The same type of shift point adjustment can sometimes be accomplished by adjusting the throttle cable or linkage. Refer to the individual transmission manufacturer's instructions for adjusting shift points.

Hydraulically controlled Allison transmissions have an adjustable cam that holds the tension on each of the shift signal valves and on the modulator valve, as shown in FIGURE 44-7. These **valve adjusting cams** have notches that allow the cam to be rotated to increase or decrease spring tension on each individual shift signal valve.

A special tool called a J-24314 is shown in FIGURE 44-8. The J-24314 is from Kent Moore and can be used to adjust the cam's position. Each notch the cam is rotated will increase or decrease that shift point by 2 mph (3.2 kph) for the shift that valve controls. Changing the tension on

SKILL DRILL 44-2 Changing the Transmission Oil and Filter

1. Ensure that the transmission is at operating temperature.
2. Remove the drain plug, if equipped, and allow the fluid to drain completely. Pay particular attention to the consistency and color of the fluid as it drains.
   - Most transmission fluids are red and relatively clear. Note: Some newer transmission fluid may have more of a brownish tinge, so be careful not to condemn the fluid if you are not sure.
   - Fluid that has a milky or light pink color can indicate contamination with engine coolant. (Most transmissions use engine coolant to cool the fluid.) Engine coolant will destroy transmission bushings and clutch plates. If transmission fluid has been contaminated with coolant, the transmission and torque converter should be overhauled and the cooler flushed or replaced.
   - If the fluid has a shiny metallic look, it indicates an internal failure of some kind, which should be investigated. Significant metal deposits require that the transmission and torque converter be overhauled and all bearings and bushings replaced. The cooler should be also replaced. Flushing the cooler may not remove all of the metal, however, so is not recommend in this case. Some service centers will place an auxiliary filter in the return line of the cooler after flushing, but auxiliary filters can become clogged and starve the transmission of fluid. Replacement is the recommended course of action for this type of failure.
   - If the fluid is dark or smells burnt, it indicates failure of one or more of the transmissions clutch packs. Overhaul of the transmission and torque converter is required, along with flushing or replacement of the cooler.

   If the cooler is not replaced in any of the above scenarios, the cooler should be checked after reinstallation of the transmission for pressure drop across the total cooler circuit and total flow volume through the cooler circuit. If these are not in specification, replace the cooler.
3. If necessary, remove the oil pan to access the transmission filter. Newer Allison transmissions have two filters—a lube filter and a main filter accessible from the bottom of the valve body cover.
4. Remove the filter(s) and inspect for any foreign material such as clutch debris or metal. On an initial filter change, there may be a few small pieces of metal present, but any significant amounts of particles and or metal filings indicate internal failure. If the filter is accessed externally, it is not necessary to remove the oil pan, but the filter(s) should be checked in the same fashion. If the oil pan is removed, inspect it carefully for any metal or clutch debris.
5. On older hydraulically controlled models, it may be necessary to clean or replace the governor screen/filter. This may be accessible from inside the pan (AT series) or externally (MT and HT series). Check the OEM manual for exact locations.
6. After inspection, clean the filter covers and transmission pan carefully and completely before installing the new filter(s). Be careful to install the filter correctly. A missing or incorrectly installed filter seal can cause air to be drawn in by the transmission oil pump and lead to transmission failure.
7. Reinstall the transmission oil pan (if removed). Be careful not to over-torque the pan bolts. They are easily broken. Over-torqueing the bolts will also force the gasket out from between the mating surfaces and can lead to leakage. Pan bolts are rarely torqued to more than 10 to 15 ft-lb (14 to 20 Nm), but always check the service manual for exact levels.
8. Reinstall the drain plug and tighten to specifications.
9. Refill the transmission with the correct fluid to the proper level. Try not to mix fluid types, as some fluids are incompatible with each other. If unsure whether a compatibility issue exists, contact the manufacturer.
10. Start the vehicle with the emergency brake applied. Apply the service brake and select each driving range one at a time. Then place the transmission back in neutral and recheck the fluid level.
11. Road test the vehicle to bring the transmission to operating temperature of between 160°F and 200°F (71°C and 93°C). Recheck the fluid level.

SKILL DRILL 44-3 Performing Automatic Transmission Pressure Tests

1. Refer to the appropriate service information to find the procedure to test the transmission's hydraulic pressures. Verify the correct transmission fluid level in the transmission.
2. Place a drain pan under the transmission and remove the correct pressure test port plug(s). Place the test port plug(s) off to the side where they will not be lost.
3. Install a transmission pressure tester(s) capable of measuring the maximum pressure into the test port(s) on the transmission.
4. Start the vehicle and place the vehicle in the correct operating conditions to monitor the pressure according to the manufacturer (for example, transmission hot, in drive, idling). Record the pressure(s).
5. Shut off the engine, remove the transmission pressure tester(s), seal the threads, and reinstall the test port plug(s).
6. Clean off any transmission fluid that dripped onto the transmission, restart the vehicle to check for leaks, and top off the fluid if necessary.

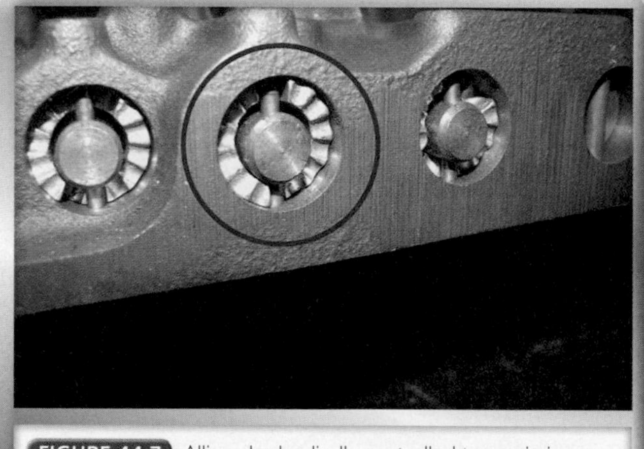

FIGURE 44-7 Allison hydraulically controlled transmissions have adjustable cams (circled) holding the shift signal valve and the modulator valve spring tension, which can be adjusted.

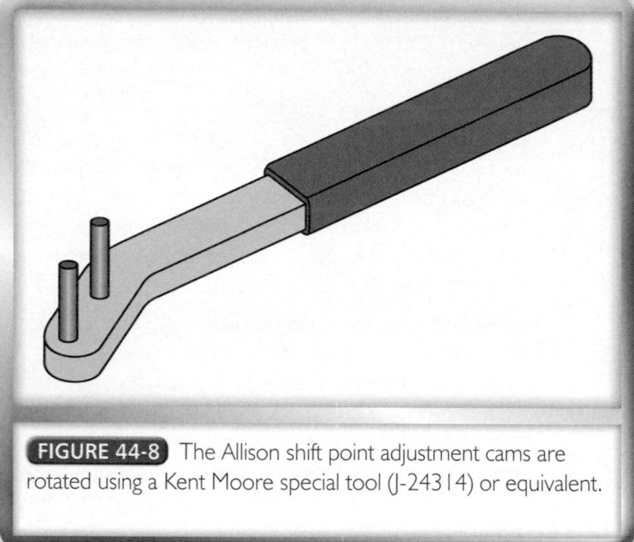

FIGURE 44-8 The Allison shift point adjustment cams are rotated using a Kent Moore special tool (J-24314) or equivalent.

the modulator valve spring will change modulator pressure and change all of the shift points at once.

These adjustable cams in the Allison transmission control valve body are accessed by removing the transmission oil pan. Allison recommends the use of a **valve body test stand**—either the Kent Moore J-25000-1 or the Aidco Model 250—in order to calibrate the shift points. To accomplish this, the valve body and modulator valve are removed and bolted to the test stand. The transmission governor is also removed and installed in the test

SKILL DRILL 44-4 Inspecting, Replacing, and Aligning Power Train Support Mounts

1. First, look up the correct procedure for checking and replacing power train mounts in the service information, especially if they are hydraulic-style mounts. Place the vehicle on a hoist to inspect the power train mounts under the vehicle.
2. Use a pry bar to carefully push up on the engine and transmission while watching the power train mounts. Look for cracks in the rubber and metal. Check that the bolts are tight. If the rubber section of the power train mount separates from the metal bracket, or if the rubber is torn, the mount needs to be replaced.
3. Lower the vehicle back down and start the engine.
4. Apply the brake and place the vehicle into gear.
5. Apply the throttle slowly and watch for excessive engine movement on the mounts.
6. Repeat step 5 with the vehicle in reverse to check the opposite mounts.
7. To remove a damaged power train mount, remove any components that are in the way.
8. Use an engine support fixture, engine hoist, or transmission jack, depending on the mount to be replaced, to raise the engine or transmission just far enough that the weight is off of the power train mount. Be VERY careful not to cause the vehicle to shift on the hoist!
9. Remove the bolts securing the mount to the transmission or engine, and then the bolts securing the mount to the frame of the vehicle.
10. Remove the old mount and compare it to the new mount.
11. Place the new mount in the correct position according to the manufacturer's service information, and lower the jack slightly. Be careful to keep your fingers away from any pinch points should the power train slip or shift.
12. Reinstall the bolts and torque them to specifications.
13. Lower the engine or transmission back down.
14. Reinstall all components that were removed to access the power train mount.

stand. (It is very important that the correct governor for the transmission model be used. Check the three-digit code stamped into the head of the governor against the OEM specification.) The test stand supplies pressurized transmission fluid and drives the governor, simulating a vehicle drive cycle. The shift points are then set to specification.

In the absence of a test stand, this procedure can be accomplished in the field by road testing the vehicle and recording the shift points at wide-open throttle. The results are then compared to the specification. If the results are not within specification, the transmission oil pan is removed and the shift signal valve tension is adjusted. Increasing the tension raises the shift point; decreasing the tension lowers it. The cams are then rotated the correct number of notches to achieve the correct shift points. If all of the shift points are low or high, the modulator linkage should be checked for proper adjustment before rechecking the shift points. After the adjustments are made, the vehicle should be road tested again to confirm shift points.

To perform shift point adjustments on hydraulically controlled transmissionmodels, follow the guidelines in SKILL DRILL 44-5.

SKILL DRILL 44-5 Performing a Shift Point Adjustment on Hydraulically Controlled Transmissions

1. Locate and follow the appropriate procedure in the service manual.
2. Complete the accompanying job sheet or work order with all the pertinent information.
3. Warm the transmission or test stand set-up to normal operating temperature. Note: Check the engine for satisfactory performance before making any adjustments.
4. Check the engine no-load governor setting and adjust if needed.
5. Check the throttle linkage that controls the modulator valve mechanical actuator and adjust if needed.
6. Check and adjust the modulator valve for satisfactory performance (see service manual).
7. Check the shift selector linkage for proper range selection.
8. To use the road test method with tachometer readings, follow the steps outlined below. Note: Before beginning the road test, compare the vehicle tachometer reading against the reading of a test tachometer to determine tachometer error.
   - a. Drive the vehicle and record the engine rpm at which each full throttle upshift occurs. Note: The 1–2 upshift should occur within 400 rpm of the governed rpm. The 2–3 upshift should be within 300 rpm of the governed rpm. And the 3–4 upshift should be within 200 rpm of the governed rpm.
   - b. Adjust as required according to the instructions in the Allison Shift Point Adjustment section.
   - c. Perform another road test to determine if the adjustments were correct.
9. To use the road test method with speedometer readings follow these steps:
   - a. Record the top speed of the vehicle in each selector hold position (first, second, and third ranges).
   - b. Select "D" (drive) and operate the vehicle at full throttle, recording the speed at which each automatic upshift occurs. Note: The 2–3 and 3–4 upshifts should occur at approximately 2 mph (3.2 kph) below the speed recorded in the previous step for the second and third ranges, respectively. The 1–2 upshift is not adjusted relative to the top speed attained in the step above, but the 2–1 downshift at closed throttle should occur at 3 to 5 mph (4.8 to 8 kph).
   - c. Adjust as required according to the instructions in the Allison Shift Point Adjustment section.
   - d. Perform another road test to determine if the adjustments were correct.
10. To use the test stand method, follow the steps outlined below. Note: Follow manufacturer's set-up procedures when using the test stand method:
    - a. Check shift point specifications as given in the service manual.
    - b. Make all determinations from output shaft speed instead of engine-governed speed.
    - c. Check individual output shaft speed ranges for each shift.
    - d. Retest to ensure that the adjustments made were correct.

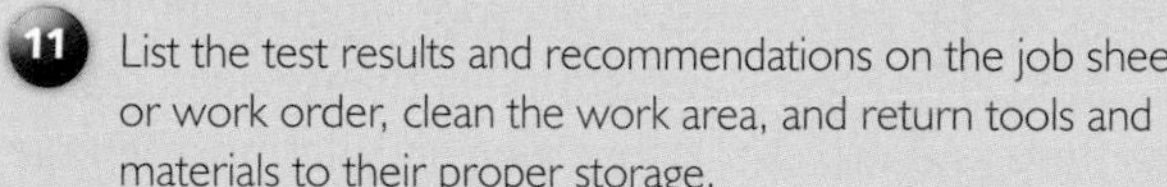

11. List the test results and recommendations on the job sheet or work order, clean the work area, and return tools and materials to their proper storage.

Removing and Reinstalling the Transmission

It is always best to try to pinpoint the problem in an automatic before the transmission is removed. Trying to diagnose an issue with the transmission on the bench or disassembled can be much more difficult without first narrowing down the complaint to a specific clutch or component. With that said, however, after careful inspection and eliminating all other possibilities, it may be necessary to remove the transmission for repair. Follow the steps in SKILL DRILL 44-6 to remove the transmission and in SKILL DRILL 44-7 to reinstall the transmission

SKILL DRILL 44-6 Removing the Transmission and Checking the Condition of Transmission Mounts, Insulators, and Mounting Bolts

1. Locate and follow the appropriate procedure in the service manual.
2. Complete the accompanying job sheet or work order with all pertinent information.
3. Move the vehicle into the shop, apply the parking brakes, and chock the vehicle wheels. Observe lockout/tagout procedures.
4. Since this is a procedure for a vehicle with an automatic transmission, place it in "park" or "neutral." Note: Some vehicles with automatic transmissions do not have "park."
5. Drain the oil from the transmission by removing the drain plug from the control module. Note: The transmission fill tube may have to be removed if it interferes with transmission removal.
6. Disconnect any hydraulic hoses from the transmission and plug all openings.
7. Drain coolant from the cooler, if present, and plug all openings.
8. Disconnect the input and output speed sensors, retarder sensors/connectors, the speedometer/ tachometer from the transmission, and the external harness from the feed-through harness.
9. Remove any linkages that may be present.
10. Mark the driveshaft yoke or flange on the transmission's output shaft. The marks will ensure that the driveshaft is properly reconnected.
11. Place a transmission jack tightly against the transmission's underside.
12. Remove the torque converter flex plate bolts that hold the transmission to the bell housing.

Safety

Do not wok underneath the transmission while disconnecting it from the vehicle. The transmission could fall, causing serious injury or death.

13. Slide the transmission away from the engine approximately 4" to 5" (100 to 125 mm) and remove the adapter ring, if used.
14. Lower the transmission to the floor.
15. Check the transmission mounts, bolts, and insulators for wear. Replace if required.
16. List the test results and recommendations on the job sheet or work order, clean the work area, and return tools and materials to their proper storage.

SKILL DRILL 44-7 Reinstalling an Automatic Transmission

1. Locate and follow the appropriate procedure in the service manual.
2. Complete the accompanying job sheet or work order with all pertinent information.
3. Check transmission housing for wear and damage.
4. Put the transmission on a transmission jack and raise it to a point where the transmission is level with the bell housing or adapter ring (if used).

Safety

Do not work underneath the transmission while connecting it to the vehicle. The transmission could fall, causing serious injury or death.

5. Move the transmission forward until the transmission mates with the bell housing.
6. Install the torque converter flex plate bolts that hold the transmission to the bell housing and torque to manufacturer's specifications.
7. Remove the transmission jack.
8. Reconnect the driveshaft to the transmission's output shaft, ensuring that the marks you made on the driveshaft yoke or flange line up.
9. Reconnect all linkages that were disconnected.
10. Reconnect the input and output speed sensors, retarder sensors/connectors, the speedometer/tachometer to the transmission, and the external harness to the feed-through harness.
11. Reconnect all hydraulic hoses.
12. Fill the integral cooler with the proper amount of coolant.
13. Reconnect the transmission fill tube, if removed.
14. Fill the transmission with the proper amount and type of automatic transmission fluid and check the level.
15. List the test results and recommendations on the job sheet or work order, clean the work area, and return tools and materials to their proper storage.

Inspecting the Flex Plate and the Torque Converter

While the transmission is operating, the flex plate that connects the torque converter to the engine crankshaft is constantly flexing and, therefore, is subject to fatigue wear and cracking. Examine the flex plate and the torque converter mounting pads, bolts, and studs carefully. Cracks in the flex plate will usually form near the torque converter mounting hardware or the bolts securing the flex plate to the crankshaft. Inspect these areas very carefully. To inspect the torque converter and the flex plate, follow the steps in SKILL DRILL 44-8.

SKILL DRILL 44-8 Inspecting the Torque Converter and Flex Plate

1. Remove the bolts securing the flex plate to the crankshaft.
2. Inspect the bolt holes used for mounting the flex plate to the crankshaft and the flex plate to the torque converter for cracks and bolt hole elongation.
3. Inspect the bolts or studs used for connecting the flex plate to the crankshaft and the flex plate to the torque converter for damaged threads.
4. Inspect the torque converter pilot for signs of damage.
5. Inspect the crankshaft pilot bore for signs of damage.
6. Inspect the torque converter mounting pads for damage.
7. Inspect the pump drive tangs for damage.
8. Install the required tool into the turbine to check for torque converter end play. Use a dial indicator to measure the amount of turbine movement.

Checking the Transmission Cooler and Lines

After transmission failure, it is common to find debris in the transmission cooler system. It is essential that this system be flushed clean or replaced when replacing the transmission. Otherwise, this debris will contaminate the new transmission.

Although replacement of the cooler is the manufacturer's recommendation, most shops will still opt for flushing. It is, however, essential that all the debris is removed. Follow the procedure in SKILL DRILL 44-9 to flush the cooler system.

TECHNICIAN TIP

When flushing cooler lines, pay particular attention to the maximum pressure recommended by the manufacturer. Exceeding this pressure could destroy the cooler and/or the lines and hoses.

TECHNICIAN TIP

Transmission coolers are usually heat-exchangers that are cooled by the engine coolant. If the transmission oil has become cloudy or milky in appearance, an internal leak of the transmission cooler is very likely. If this is the case, it is recommended the cooler be replaced.

Adjusting Shift Linkage and Neutral Safety Switch

Most transmissions today are drive by wire. That is, the shift selector has no linkage connecting it to the transmission. By contrast, older transmissions and the lighter duty 1000, 2000, and 2400 series Allison transmissions still have mechanical **shift cables** or linkage that may require adjustment. These transmissions use a **neutral safety switch** that prevents the vehicle from being started if the transmission is in any drive gear. (Some transmission OEMs refer to this switch as the PRNDL switch.) This

SKILL DRILL 44-9 Inspecting and Flushing Cooler Lines

1. First, look up the recommended transmission cooler service method in the appropriate service information, and check the instruction manual for the flush equipment you are using or for the aerosol can of transmission cooler flush. Remove the fluid cooler lines from the transmission if the transmission is still in the vehicle.
2. Using compressed air (do not exceed 30 psi [207 kPa]), blow into one cooler line while catching the residue in a container as it comes out of the other line. Switch directions and repeat.
3. Install the cooler flush machine or aerosol can lines onto the transmission cooler lines so that the flow is in the reverse direction. If using the aerosol cooler flush can, place the other cooler line into a catch can.
4. Start the flush machine or aerosol can and allow it to run for the recommended time.
5. If necessary, switch directions on the lines so they can be flushed in the other direction.
6. Remove the flush machine and blow out the lines again so no residue remains inside the lines.
7. Reinstall the lines onto the transmission or cap them if the transmission is removed from the vehicle.
8. After properly filling the transmission with fluid, start the vehicle and inspect the lines and fittings for any signs of leakage.
9. Check inside the radiator for signs of the transmission cooler leaking into the radiator.

adjustment ensures that the transmission is in the range selected according to the gear position indicator needle on the dash or the shift lever and that the neutral safety switch only allows the vehicle to be started in neutral or park. SKILL DRILL 44-10 contains steps for adjusting a general selector cable or linkage and the neutral safety switch.

SKILL DRILL 44-10 Inspecting, Adjusting, and Replacing the Manual Valve Shift Linkage and the Neutral Safety Switch

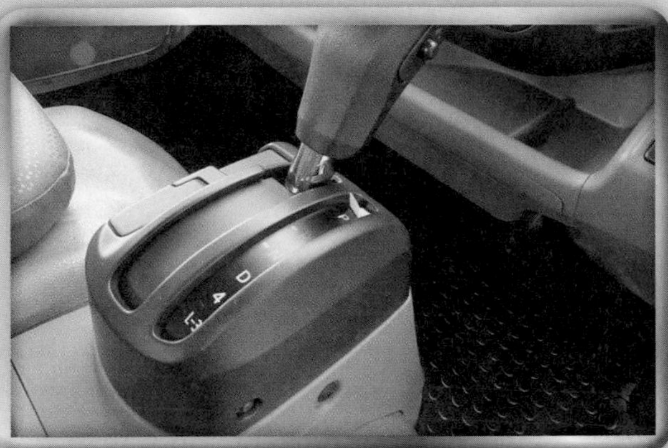

1. Look up the proper service procedure in the appropriate service information. Follow the procedure step by step to inspect and adjust the manual valve and the neutral safety switch.
2. Place the gear selector in the park position.
3. If necessary, raise the vehicle on a hoist to access the neutral safety switch and manual valve linkage.
4. Disconnect the shift linkage from the transmission.
5. Place the manual valve in the park position. The valve should snap into position.
6. The shift linkage should fit right onto the manual valve with no pulling on the linkage or the manual valve.
7. If the linkage does not line up, loosen the adjustment on the shift linkage and adjust the linkage so that it will install properly on the manual valve.
8. Tighten the adjustment on the shift linkage.
9. Double-check that the gear position indicator still indicates the vehicle is in park.
10. Use an ohmmeter to check that the neutral safety switch has continuity on the correct terminals. If not, loosen the switch and adjust its position. If continuity is never obtained, or is obtained in every gear, replace the switch. The vehicle should start only in the park and neutral positions. Make sure the brake pedal is firmly applied, then check that the vehicle starts only in the park and neutral positions.
11. Run the shifter through all of the gear ranges, checking for proper operation.

Wrap-up

Ready for Review

- Automatic transmissions are rarely overhauled in the field as most repair facilities do not have the cleanliness or special tooling required.
- Fluid is the life blood of automatic transmissions. Low, high, or contaminated fluid are by far the most frequent cause of transmission failure. So proper maintenance of fluid is essential.
- Not all automatic transmission fluids are the same. Some contain friction modifiers and/or are not compatible with transmission seals. It is essential that the manufacturer's recommended fluid is used.
- Fluid levels that are high or low can lead to aeration and rapid failure of the transmission.
- When checking fluid, always clean around the dipstick area to prevent contamination.
- Always check fluid under the correct conditions—usually with the vehicle running and the fluid at operating temperature.
- Some transmissions may have cold operation inhibits and will not function until the fluid warms up.
- Fluid change intervals vary widely based on transmission vocation, fluid type, and other factors. Always consult the manufacturer's recommendations to find the correct change interval.
- Since 2009, Allison World Transmissions have a feature called Prognostics that tracks drive cycle information and, when turned on, can tell the operator when fluid and filter changes are necessary.
- Fluid analysis may be required when fluid change intervals cannot be decided upon based on the manufacturer's information.
- TranSynd is a synthetic transmission fluid made by Castrol to Allison transmission engineering specifications and is the fluid recommended by Allison for use in all their transmissions.
- Most manufacturers do not recommend the use of any fluid additives in their transmissions.
- When diagnosing a transmission issue, always verify the complaint with preliminary checks and a road test.
- Follow symptom-based diagnoses charts when available from the manufacturer.
- On electronically controlled transmission, use the diagnostic fault code information and follow the manufacturer's trouble tree charts and/or symptom-based charts when necessary. Failure to do so will usually lead to wasted efforts.
- Stall testing can be used to check clutch function in some instances.
- Pressure testing transmissions can help to pinpoint problem areas.
- There are no CVSA out-of-service criteria for automatic transmissions; however, the National Fire Prevention Association and some state transit commissions do have out-of-service criteria.
- An oil and filter change at the proper interval is the single most important maintenance procedure on automatic transmissions.
- During an oil and filter change, it is usually impossible to remove all of the old fluid. Typically, between 5 and 8 quarts (4.5 and 7.5 liters) of fluid will remain. Always be sure of fluid compatibility.
- Power train mount hold, cushion, and alignment should be checked regularly and replaced when necessary.
- A shift point adjust could be done on older transmissions, but is rarely possible on today's electronically controlled units.
- Most failed transmissions will simply be exchanged in the field so, after diagnoses, the technician's next task is usually a transmission removal and replacement with an overhauled unit.
- The flex plate should be inspected for cracks whenever a transmission is removed.
- The transmission cooler can be a source of coolant contamination of the transmission fluid.
- When a transmission is replaced, the cooler system, lines, and hose should be flushed to remove any debris from the failed transmission.
- The shift linkage and the neutral safety switch should be adjusted when a transmission is replaced to ensure the vehicle will only start in neutral or park.

Vocabulary Builder

aeration Air in the fluid.

cavitation The formation of air bubbles in the transmission fluid as a result of low pressure at the pump inlet.

cold operation inhibit Restriction on transmission operation when the temperature is too cold for the transmission fluid to do its job.

ethylene glycol A chemical that resists freezing but is very toxic to people and animals.

fluid analysis Chemical analysis of the transmission fluid revealing contaminant levels.

friction modifier Additive in transmission fluid designed to enhance the friction characteristics of certain clutch materials.

modulator cable A mechanical cable connected to the throttle that operates the modulator valve.

mount Steel backed rubber support that holds the power train components.

neutral safety switch A switch operated by the transmission shift linkage that prevents the vehicle from being started except when in park or neutral. Also known as the PRNDL switch on some transmissions.

prognostic capability The ability by some transmission ECUs to predict fluid and filter change intervals.

prognostics Allison transmission's prognostic capability for fluid and filter change intervals; also capable of determining clutch and transmission life.

shift cable A mechanical cable connected to the driver's shift lever and the transmission manual valve.

shift point The road speed at which a shift occurs.

supplemental additive Aftermarket additive available for automatic transmissions but not recommended by manufacturers.

transmission vent A vent on the transmission that is open to atmospheric pressure.

TranSynd fluid A full synthetic fluid produced by Castrol, to Allison specification; TranSynd is the recommended fluid for all Allison transmissions.

valve adjusting cam Small cam on the end of the shift signal valves that, when turned, increase the shift point.

valve body test stand A special test stand specifically for testing and setting up Allison transmission control valve bodies and shift points.

Review Questions

1. Which of the following could cause failure of an automatic transmission?
   a. High fluid level
   b. Low fluid level
   c. Low fluid pressure
   d. All of the choices are correct.
2. Which of the following could lead to pump cavitation?
   a. Incorrect transmission fluid
   b. High fluid level
   c. Elevated fluid temperature
   d. Clogged transmission vent
3. What is meant by friction modifiers when discussing transmission fluids?
   a. Additives that change the friction characteristics of the clutches
   b. Additives that change the characteristics of the clutch seals
   c. Additives that reduce friction on bearing surfaces
   d. Additives that increase friction on bearing surfaces
4. What is meant by pump cavitation?
   a. Cavities in the pump
   b. Bubbles in the fluid caused by excess suction
   c. Bubbles in the fluid caused by component rotation
   d. Cavities in the torque converter pump
5. Approximately how much fluid is not replaced during a typical fluid and filter change on an automatic transmission?
   a. 1 to 2 quarts (0.9 to 1.9 liters)
   b. 3 to 4 quarts (2.8 to 3.8 liters)
   c. 5 to 8 quarts (4.7 to 5.7 liters)
   d. 10 to 15 quarts (9.5 to 14.2 liters)
6. An automatic transmission that has a disconnected or completely blocked modulator valve vacuum line would exhibit which of the following problems?
   a. Control or main pressure would be lower than normal.
   b. The transmission would experience early upshifts.
   c. No upshifts would occur at any speed.
   d. Upshifts would occur at much higher speeds than normal.
7. What would be the complaint or symptom in an Allison AT series transmission if a trimmer valve were stuck open?
   a. The clutch that the trimmer valve controls would have a harsh engagement.
   b. The clutch that the trimmer controls would not engage.
   c. The clutch that the trimmer controls would slip and burn out.
   d. The clutch that the trimmer controls would shift at a lower road speed.
8. Would high oil level lead to transmission slippage and why or why not?
   a. Yes, because the rotating components would aerate the oil.
   b. No, high oil level would be ok as long as it is not enough to leak.
   c. No, high oil level can sometimes keep the oil at a cooler temperature.
   d. Yes, high oil level can cause hydraulic lock, stopping the clutches from applying.
9. What is the oil drain interval for an Allison transmission is equipped with prognostics?
   a. 500,000 miles, (800,000 km), or every five years
   b. 100,000 miles, (160,000 km), or every two years
   c. 50,000 miles, (80,000 km), or once a year
   d. When indicated by the gear shift display
10. When you remove a transmission oil pan, you find black or brown fibrous dust in the oil and accumulated in the oil pan. What would you recommend as service for this vehicle?
    a. Complete overhaul of the transmission
    b. Transmission cooler flush
    c. Torque converter overhaul or replacement
    d. All of the described procedures should be recommended.

ASE-Type Questions

1. Technician A says that all automatic transmission fluids are the same. Technician B says that all synthetic automatic transmission fluids are compatible. Who is correct?
   a. Technician A
   b. Technician B
   c. Both Technician A and Technician B
   d. Neither Technician A nor Technician B
2. Technician A says using synthetic fluids greatly extends automatic transmission fluid change intervals. Technician B says that transmission vocation can influence fluid change intervals. Who is correct?
   a. Technician A
   b. Technician B
   c. Both Technician A and Technician B
   d. Neither Technician A nor Technician B
3. Technician A says that automatic transmission fluid should usually be checked with the vehicle running and the transmission at operating temperature. Technician B says that automatic transmissions using synthetic fluid can be topped up with regular fluid as long as it is not more than 2 quarts (1.9 liters) low. Who is correct?
   a. Technician A
   b. Technician B
   c. Both Technician A and Technician B
   d. Neither Technician A nor Technician B
4. Technician A says that automatic transmission fluid that looks milky or pink can mean a failed transmission cooler. Technician B says that transmission fluid that has a shiny look to it can mean internal failure of transmission components. Who is correct?
   a. Technician A
   b. Technician B
   c. Both Technician A and Technician B
   d. Neither Technician A nor Technician B
5. Technician A says that the shift points can be adjusted in most of today's automatic transmissions. Technician B says that most of today's automatic transmissions are drive by wire and the only adjustment that may have to be done is the manual shift linkage and the neutral safety switch. Who is correct?
   a. Technician A
   b. Technician B
   c. Both Technician A and Technician B
   d. Neither Technician A nor Technician B
6. Technician A says that most hydraulically controlled transmissions require regularly scheduled oil and filter changes. Technician B says that some electronically controlled transmissions can indicate when an oil change is required. Who is correct?
   a. Technician A
   b. Technician B
   c. Both Technician A and Technician B
   d. Neither Technician A nor Technician B
7. Technician A says that shift point adjustment can be performed on most hydraulically controlled transmissions. Technician B says that shift point adjustment on hydraulically controlled Allison transmissions involves removal of the transmission oil pan. Who is correct?
   a. Technician A
   b. Technician B
   c. Both Technician A and Technician B
   d. Neither Technician A nor Technician B
8. Technician A says that loss of transmission oil is the most common cause of automatic transmission failure. Technician B says that slight loss of transmission fluid over time is normal and just needs topping up from time to time. Who is correct?
   a. Technician A
   b. Technician B
   c. Both Technician A and Technician B
   d. Neither Technician A nor Technician B
9. Technician A says that "Transynd" is the fluid that Allison recommends for all its transmissions. Technician B says that, if a transmission has "Transynd" installed, it can only be topped up with "Transynd." Who is correct?
   a. Technician A
   b. Technician B
   c. Both Technician A and Technician B
   d. Neither Technician A nor Technician B
10. Technician A says that each notch of the adjustment cam on an Allison transmission shift signal valve will change the shift point by 2 mph (3.2 kph). Technician B says that the cam is turned clockwise to increase the shift point and counterclockwise to decrease the shift point. Who is correct?
    a. Technician A
    b. Technician B
    c. Both Technician A and Technician B
    d. Neither Technician A nor Technician B

CHAPTER 45

NATEF Tasks

Drive Train
Transmission

	Page
■ Inspect and test operation of automatic transmission electronic shift controls, shift solenoids, shift motors, indicators, speed and range sensors, electronic/transmission control units (ECU/TCU), neutral/in gear and reverse switches, and wiring harnesses.	1499–1500
■ Inspect and test operation of automatic transmission electronic shift selectors, switches, displays, indicators, and wiring harnesses.	1501
■ Use appropriate electronic service tool(s) and procedures to diagnose automatic transmission problems; check and record diagnostic codes, clear codes, and interpret digital multi-meter (DMM) readings; determine needed action.	1503

Knowledge Objectives

After reading this chapter, you will be able to:

1. Describe the operation of Allison Automatic Transmission Electronic Control (ATEC) and Commercial electronic control (CEC). (pp 1446–1461)
2. Describe the operation of Allison World Transmissions (WT). (pp 1462–1465)
3. Explain the power flows of the Allison World Transmission (WT). (pp 1466–1471)
4. Describe the operation of the World Transmission Electronic Control (WTEC) and later models WTEC11 and WTEC111. (pp 1471–1488)
5. Describe the operation of the electronic controls in Allison Fourth and Fifth Generation transmissions. (pp 1488–1514)
6. Describe the operation of the Allison TC-10-TS transmission. (pp 1504–1514)
7. Explain the operation of Voith transmission's DIWA Drive. (pp 1514–1521)
8. Describe ZF Friedrichshafen AG (ZF) Ecomat and Ecolife transmissions. (p 1521)
9. Describe Caterpillar CX-28, CX-31, and CX-35 transmissions. (pp 1521–1523)

Electronically Controlled Automatic Transmissions

Skills Objectives

After reading this chapter, you will be able to:

1. Scan the TCM. (p 1502) **SKILL** DRILL 45-1
2. Inspect, adjust, repair, or replace electronic shift controls, electronic control unit, wiring harnesses, sensors, control module, vehicle interface module, and related components. (p 1503) **SKILL** DRILL 45-2

Introduction

Controlling automatic transmissions electrically is not a new concept. As far back as the 1950s and 1960s, it made sense to operate the transmission electrically in certain off-road and industrial applications. Using electric controls eliminated the need for mechanical connections and meant that the controls could be located at virtually any remote location instead of having to be located precisely at the transmission. Allison invented an electrical control known as a shift pattern generator (SPG) that used pitot tube pressure to measure rotational speed. Allison used SPG primarily in its series of transmissions developed for off-highway use.

Allison was not the only early adopter of electrically controlled automatic transmissions. Voith DIWA drive transmissions were always controlled electrically, as were the ZF bus and coach transmissions (the EcoLife and the EcoMat). Over the years, however, increased competition in the business environment has caused companies to insist on ever higher fuel efficiency as a way to keep costs under control. As a result, electrical control of automatic transmissions has been replaced by increasingly sophisticated electronic control technology.

This chapter will introduce you to the electronically controlled automatic transmissions commonly used in the North American market. The dominant company in this market is Allison—throughout its history, it has produced over 5,000,000 commercial vehicle transmissions worldwide. Because Allison is the primary heavy-duty transmission manufacturer in North America, we will concentrate our discussion in this chapter on Allison products. We will also look at the Voith DIWA series transmissions and the ZF bus transmission models and will briefly discuss Caterpillar's CX series of automatic transmissions used in its CT660 on-highway trucks.

Basics of Electronic Control—ATEC and CEC

Allison's initial foray into electronic control began with its original MT-600, HT-700, and V-series (bus) transmissions. The original electronic control was called the **Allison Transmission Electronic Control (ATEC)**. This system is now called the **Commercial Electronic Control (CEC)**, but it is essentially the same system. The mechanical components of these transmissions are identical to their hydraulically controlled counterparts discussed in the chapter on Hydraulically Controlled Automatic Transmissions and so will not be discussed again in this chapter. If necessary, take time to review the mechanical transmission operation material in that chapter before continuing on in this chapter.

You Are the Technician

A vehicle with an Allison ATEC transmission is brought to your shop in northern Minnesota on a particularly icy day when overnight temperatures were well below zero. The driver complains that, when he first started the vehicle, the transmission would not go into gear for over five minutes. Then, the transmission would not shift out of first gear until he had driven for another minute, but now it seems to shift normally. The driver had not driven this vehicle previous to today and is concerned that transmission damage may have occurred. You check the fluid level, and it is correct. The fluid itself is bright red and shows no signs of contamination. You then perform a stall test and a road test and find that the vehicle is performing as it should.

1. What could be the cause of this condition?
2. Should you remove the oil pan and look for clutch damage?
3. Could this be normal operation for this vehicle?

All automatic transmissions require at least three inputs in order to be able to shift properly:

- The driver's gear selection
- A load sensitive signal
- A speed sensitive signal

Without these three inputs, automatic transmissions would not know when to shift. In hydraulically controlled transmissions, those three inputs are provided by the mechanical shift selector, the modulator or throttle valve as the load sense, and the centrifugal governor as the speed sense.

The ATEC/CEC system is completely drive by wire. That is, there is no mechanical connection to the transmission. The only connections in and out of the transmission are electrical. The driver's gear selector consists of either a push button control pad or an optional shift lever. Either way, all of the selections are made electronically. The load sensitive signal, the modulator valve, is replaced by a throttle position sensor (TPS), and the centrifugal governor input, or speed sensitive signal, is replaced by a vehicle speed sensor (VSS). These inputs and more are sent to the **transmission electronic control unit (ECU)**, also called the **transmission control unit (TCU)**. The transmission control unit, or transmission electronic control unit, is the brains of the control system. It processes the received data and decides when shifts should occur. Some manufacturers call this unit the TCM; others call it the transmission ECM FIGURE 45-1. The transmission controller then issues commands to solenoids inside the transmission to obtain the desired range.

Transmission Electronic Control Unit or ECU

The transmission control unit provides all of the shifting "thought process" for the transmission. The unit receives signals from the driver and the transmission and then decides on the best shift strategy for the operating conditions. There have been three different types of ECUs used by the Allison CEC FIGURE 45-2. The first, and now obsolete, Splash Proof model ECU was replaced by the Sealed Standard ECU. The third type, the Sealed-Plus 11, includes an additional connector which allows a remotely mounted operator interface for remote power take-off (PTO) operation and other special features.

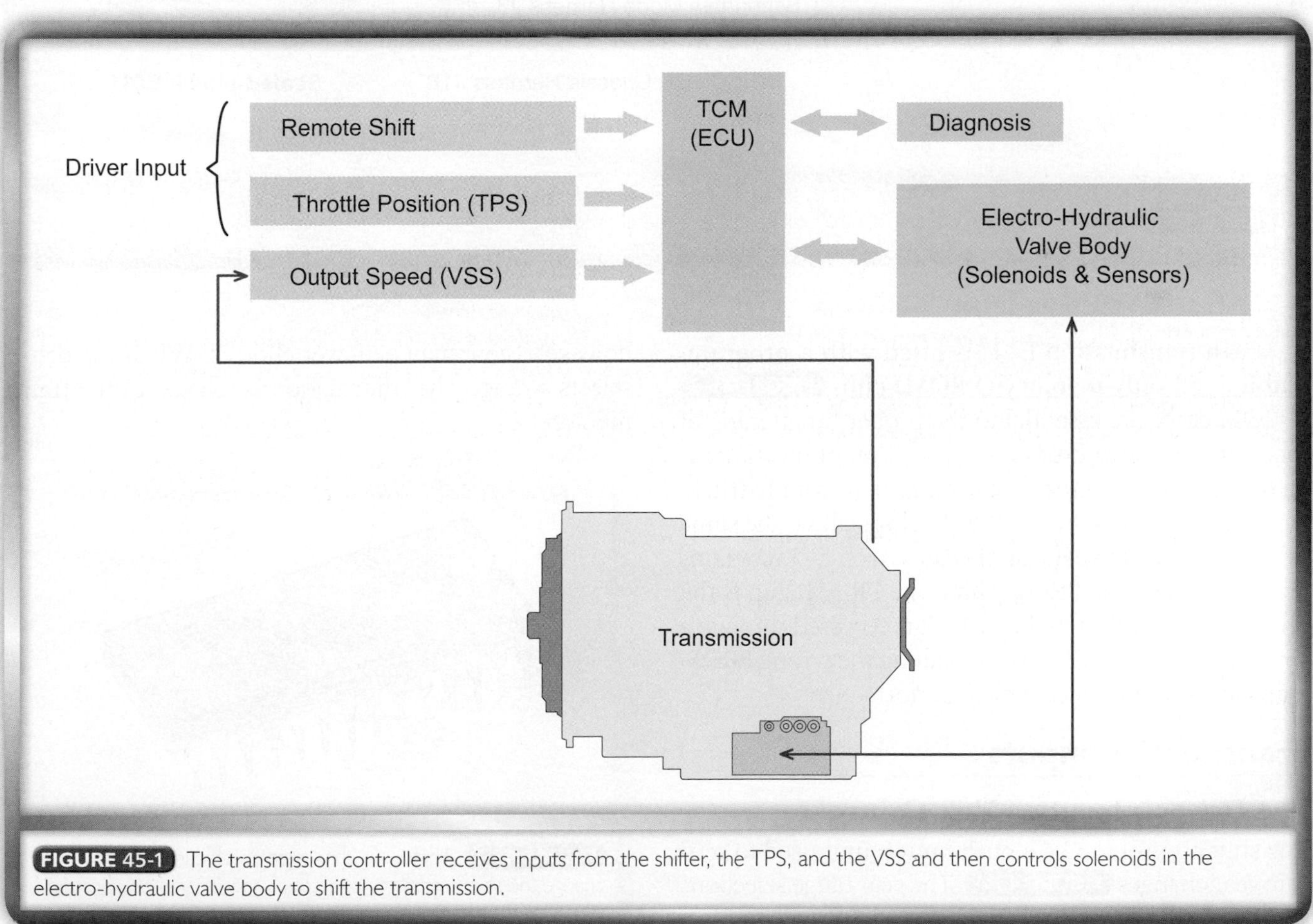

FIGURE 45-1 The transmission controller receives inputs from the shifter, the TPS, and the VSS and then controls solenoids in the electro-hydraulic valve body to shift the transmission.

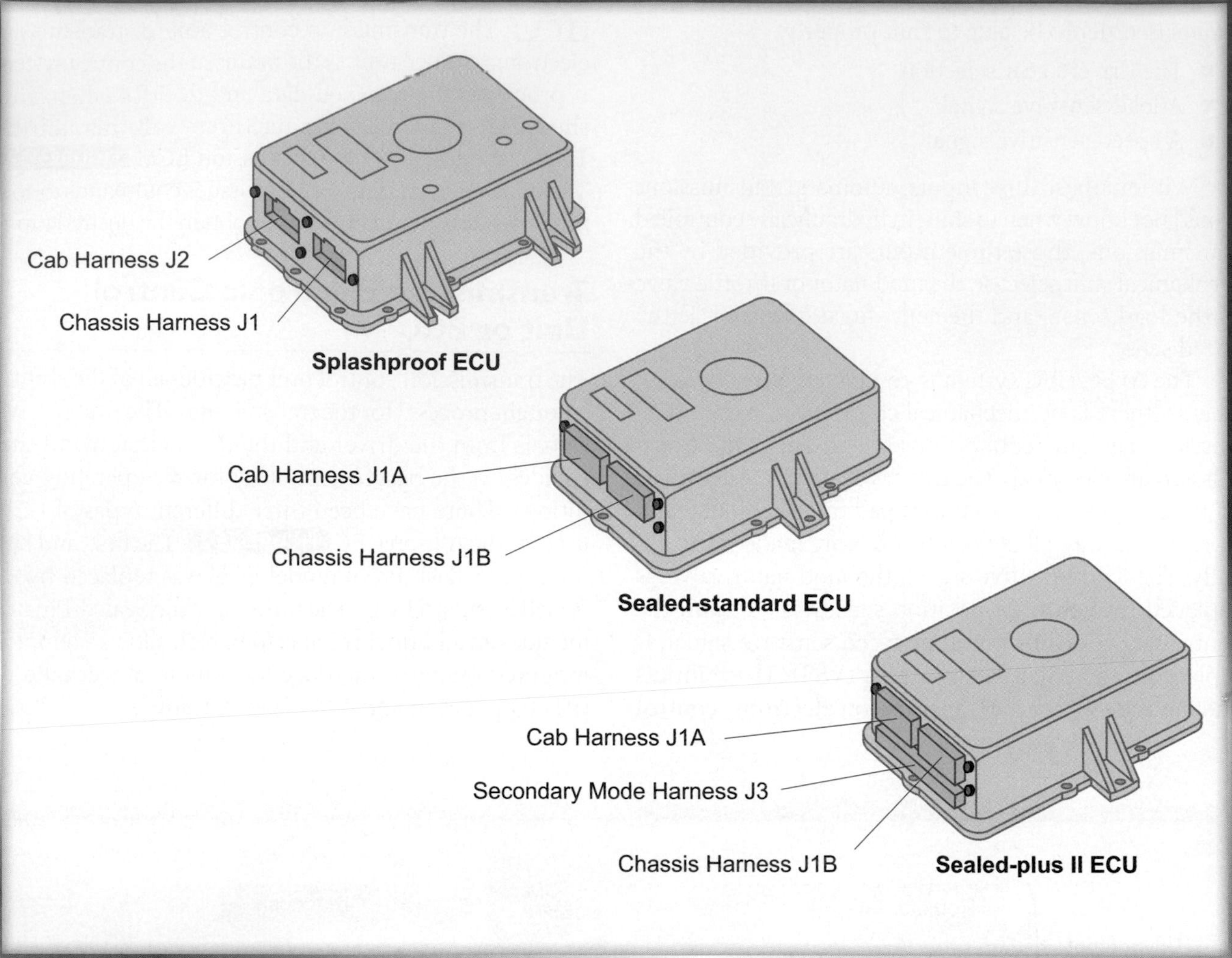

FIGURE 45-2 The ATEC/CEC electronic control unit had three generations.

Each transmission ECU is fitted with a **programmable read-only memory (PROM) chip** FIGURE 45-3 . PROM chips are essential to the proper functioning of the transmission and unique to vocation of the particular vehicle in which they are found, such as a fire truck, garbage truck, and so on. PROM chips allow the same ECU to be used in all installs because each ECU contains its own replaceable PROM chip. The PROM chip is the only serviceable part in the ECU. It is accessed through a small cover in the ECU case. Installing the wrong PROM chip can severely affect vehicle performance.

Transmission Inputs

The Driver's Input or Shift Control

The shift control can be a push button unit used to activate gear changes FIGURE 45-4. The gear range selections are usually R, N, D, 3, 2, and 1. In some applications, however, there may be fewer choices. When the driver selects a range, the information is relayed to the transmission ECU.

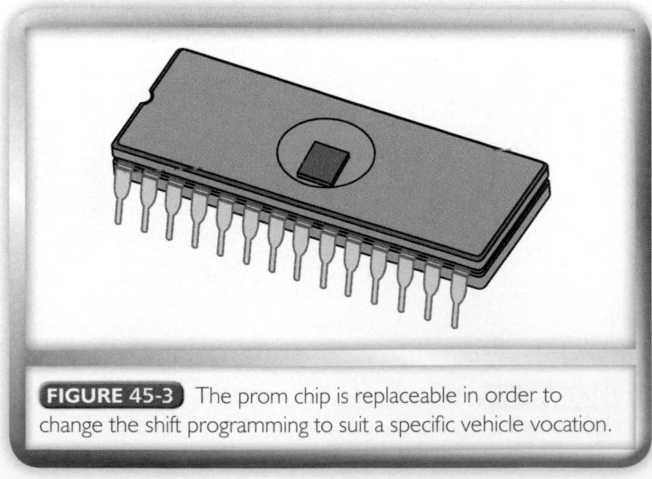

FIGURE 45-3 The prom chip is replaceable in order to change the shift programming to suit a specific vehicle vocation.

FIGURE 45-4 The driver's input can be a push button control as shown or a shift lever type.

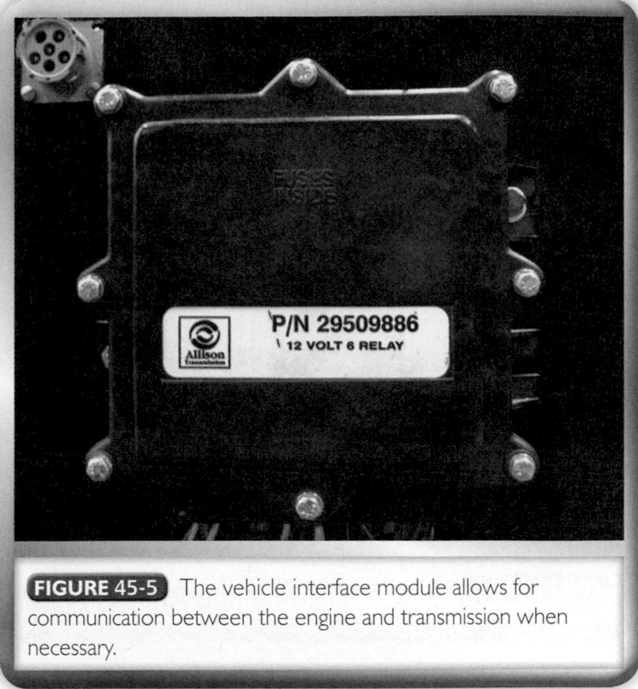

FIGURE 45-5 The vehicle interface module allows for communication between the engine and transmission when necessary.

Lever-type shift selectors usually have the same six gear positions as shift-button selectors or fewer. When the driver moves the Allison supplied shift lever, it actuates Hall effect switches. The Hall effect switches send a corresponding signal to the transmission ECU. If necessary, the vehicle can be also equipped with a remote shift control unit for special applications.

Throttle Position Sensor

On non-electronic engines, the throttle position sensor (TPS) can be OEM or Allison supplied. With an OEM-supplied TPS, the signal may have to pass through a communications adapter called a vehicle interface module before the signal can be read by the transmission ECU FIGURE 45-5.

The TPS replaces the modulator throttle valve used on hydraulically controlled transmissions and gives the transmission ECU the load sensitive signal required for shift timing and strategies. The Allison-supplied TPS is a cable-actuated linear potentiometer. As the throttle is actuated, the potentiometer sends a voltage signal to the transmission ECU, and the ECU converts this voltage into "counts." **Counts** is the term Allison uses to monitor the TPS position FIGURE 45-6.

The sensor's range is from 0 to 255 counts, which equates to the sensor's ability to travel approximately 1.5 inches. The sensor's actual movement, however, equates to only about 100 counts, or the equivalent of .75 inches. On installation, the sensor is set up so the throttle movement takes place in the middle of the sensor's range. Setting the sensor up at the midpoint allows the sensor to be self-correcting. As the throttle cable stretches over time, the sensor can reset itself so that idle and wide-open throttle still fall within the acceptable counts range. When the vehicle is shut down, the ECU records the minimum and maximum throttle positions during that drive cycle. Each time the vehicle is started, the ECU sets minimum and maximum travel at 15 counts past the last recorded reading and then adjusts the reading to reflect actual throttle movement. Those adjustments act to recalibrate the TPS on each drive cycle. Another critical adjustment that can be made by the technician is the ability to set error zones in the sensor's range. When counts from 0 to 14 and from 233 to 255 are set as error zones, the ECU can detect a broken cable or other serious problem. If the ECU reads data in the error zones, it will generate a code and turn on the check transmission/do not shift light.

Vehicle Speed Sensor (VSS)

The **vehicle speed sensor (VSS)** is an inductive pick-up sensor that reads the speed of the transmission output

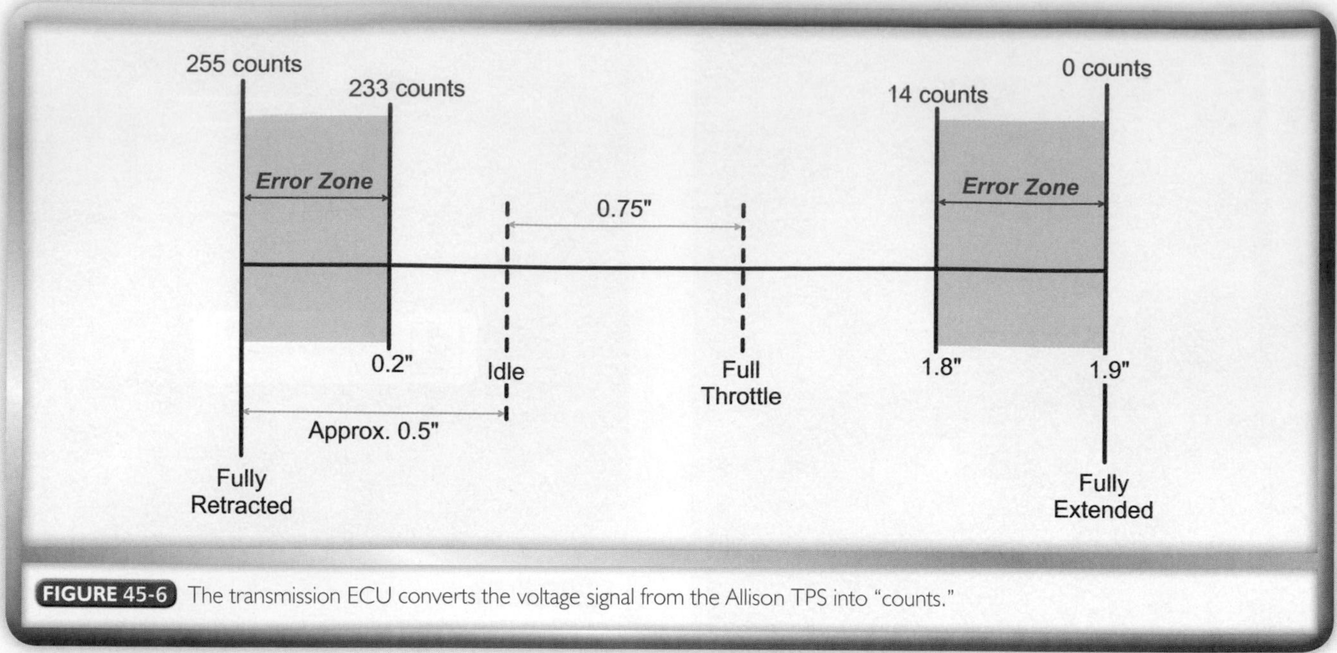

FIGURE 45-6 The transmission ECU converts the voltage signal from the Allison TPS into "counts."

shaft **FIGURE 45-7**. An inductive pick-up is simply a coil of wire wrapped around a permanent magnet core. The pick-up is placed in close proximity to a tone wheel (a toothed ring) splined to the output shaft. As the shaft rotates and the teeth on the wheel approach the magnet, the magnetic field builds and collapses.

The rising and falling levels of the magnetic field send an alternating current to the transmission ECU, which reads the voltages cross counts (i.e., the number of times the voltage changes from positive to negative) and translates the currents as output shaft speed. The VSS sensor provides a road-speed signal used with the TPS to determine shift timing. As such, the VSS replaces the centrifugal governor used on hydraulically controlled transmissions.

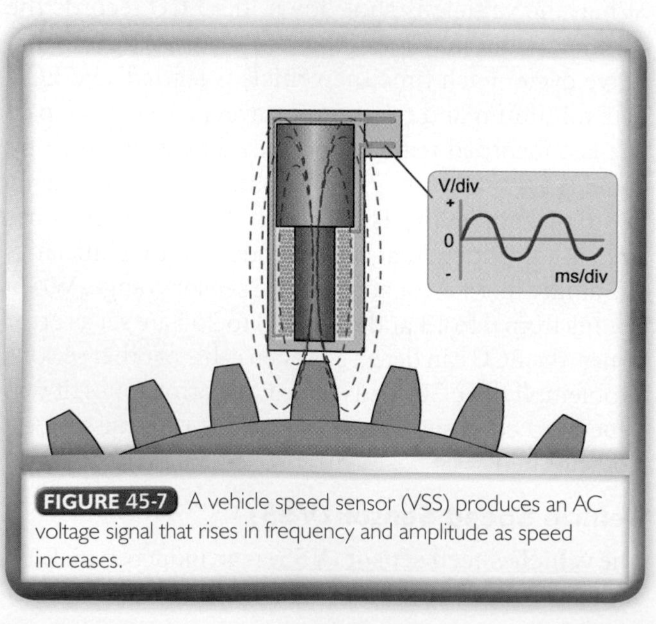

FIGURE 45-7 A vehicle speed sensor (VSS) produces an AC voltage signal that rises in frequency and amplitude as speed increases.

Fluid Sensors

Fluid sensors are a critical part of electronically controlled automatic transmissions. The most common sensors monitor pressure and temperature.

Forward and Reverse Pressure Switches

The forward and reverse pressure switches are threaded oil-pressure switches plumbed into the forward and reverse hydraulic circuits. The contacts in these switches are normally open and close, respectively, when the forward range or reverse circuit is pressurized. The transmission ECU can determine that a forward or reverse range has been achieved by monitoring these switches.

Fluid Temperature Sensor

Severe transmission damage can occur if the transmission fluid is either too hot or too cold. The transmission, therefore, has a temperature sensor that is monitored by the ECU. In on-highway models, the sensor is mounted on the valve body wiring harness inside the transmission oil pan.

The ECU will not allow shifts into any gear range if the fluid temperature is below -25°F (-32°C). As the fluid temperature rises, the controller will allow limited shifts to first or reverse only while the temperature is between -25°F and +25°F (-32°C to +4°C). If the fluid temperature increases to 270°F (132°C), the check transmission light on the shift control will be illuminated, a code will be recorded in the transmission ECU's memory, and, in on-highway models, a shift to top gear will be inhibited. Certain emergency vehicle applications will not inhibit top gear for high temperature, but the check transmission/do not shift light will illuminate and a code will be set.

Oil Pressure Switch/Sensor

The transmission ECU relies on two other inputs—the oil temperature sensor and one of three additional sensor types:

- The lube oil pressure switch
- The low oil level pressure sensor
- The fluidic oil level sensor

Inputs to those three additional sensors are used more for transmission protection rather than shift strategy, however.

It is important for the technician to know which of the above type of switch/sensor is installed because the electrical circuit for each type will react differently during testing. The installed switch can be determined by calling Allison Electronic Control Information System (ECIS), available through authorized Allison dealers, with the transmission assembly number from the plate on the side of the transmission case **FIGURE 45-8**. The PROM chip in the transmission ECU must also be programmed correctly to the type of switch, so care must be taken if either the switch/sensor or the PROM chip needs replacing.

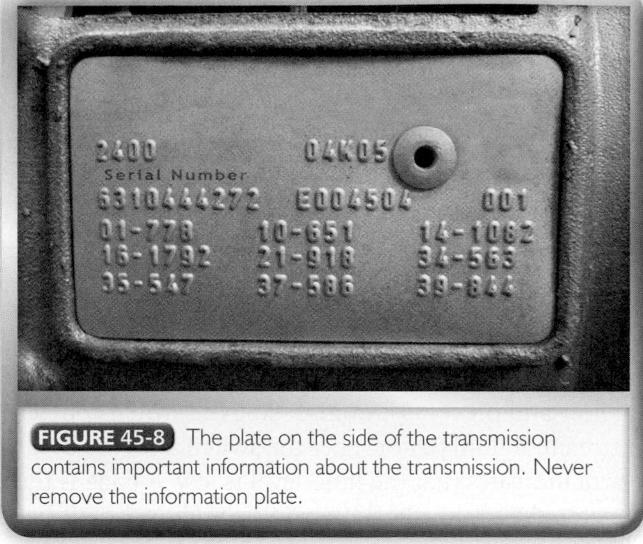

FIGURE 45-8 The plate on the side of the transmission contains important information about the transmission. Never remove the information plate.

The first type of switch/sensor is a simple oil pressure switch (called a lube pressure switch by Allison) that is plumbed into the transmission lube oil circuit. The switch contacts are normally open and close when lube oil pressure is present. If the switch contacts remain open after the vehicle is started, the check transmission/do not shift light will be illuminated and a trouble code will be set in the transmission ECU's memory.

The second type is the low oil level/pressure sensor. This sensor is bolted to the bottom of the **electro-hydraulic valve body**, also known as the **electro-hydraulic control** which is the central transmission control consisting of solenoids, spool valves, and pressure switches. The low oil level/pressure sensor bolted to the electro-hydraulic control has pressurized lube oil directed to a small orifice in the body of the sensor. The effect of the lube oil going through the orifice creates a stream of lube oil exiting one side of the sensor. A pressure switch with normally open contacts is plumbed into an opening on the other side of the sensor. The sensor is mounted in such a way that when the oil reaches operating temperature, the higher oil level caused by thermal expansion surrounds the opening on the sensor and dissipates the flow of the stream of oil exiting the sensor **FIGURE 45-9**.

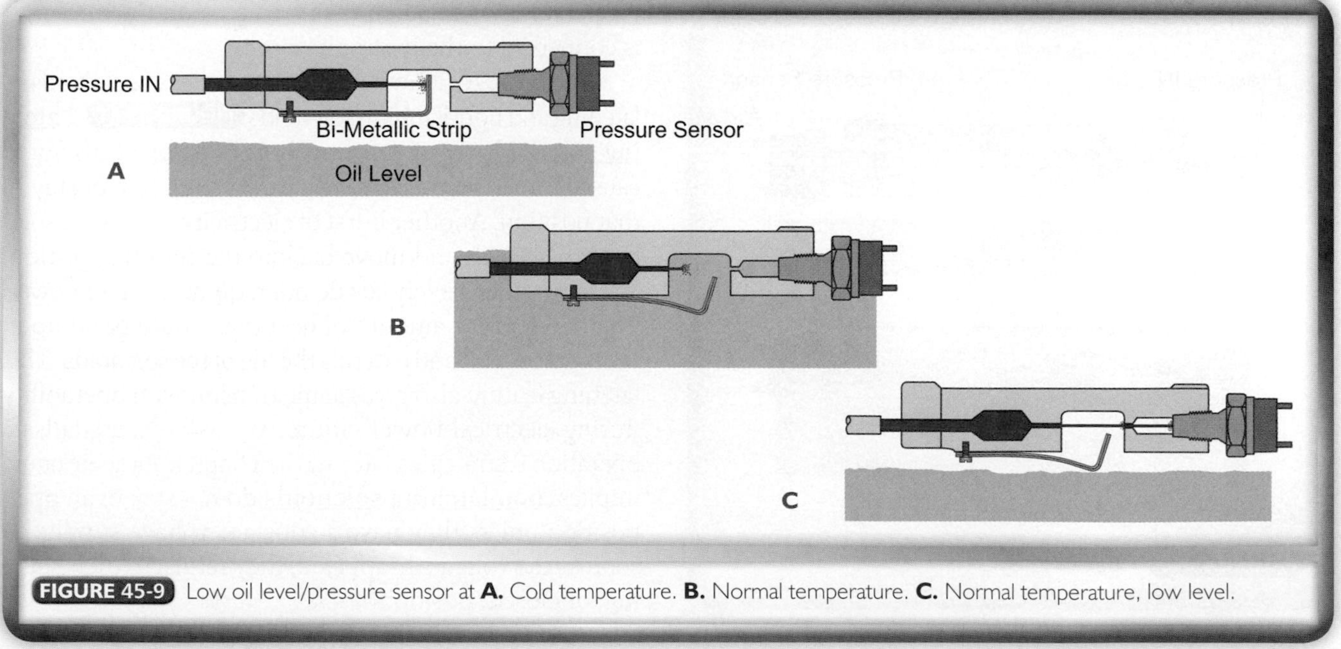

FIGURE 45-9 Low oil level/pressure sensor at **A.** Cold temperature. **B.** Normal temperature. **C.** Normal temperature, low level.

When the transmission is cold, a bi-metallic strip blocks the flow of oil, so the sensor works a bit differently. When the vehicle is started, a pressurized stream of oil flows from the orifice on one side of the switch. Because the transmission is cold at start-up, the fluid level will be below the opening in the sensor, but the bi-metallic strip will block the stream of pressurized oil from reaching the pressure switch on the other side and closing its contacts. As the transmission warms up, the bi-metal strip flexes out of the way, but, by that time, the warming transmission fluid expands and fills the opening in the sensor. The presence of the fluid in the sensor opening dissipates the oil flow and prevents it from closing the switch contacts. A stream of fluid that reaches the switch after the fluid is warm indicates that the fluid level is low. A code is then generated and the check transmission/do not shift light is illuminated.

The fluidic oil level sensor is very similar to the low oil level/pressure sensor but without a bi-metallic strip **FIGURE 45-10**. The transmission ECU is programmed to ignore signals from the sensor until the fluid temperature reaches operational levels, so the bi-metal strip is not required. The pressure switch that the fluidic sensor uses is a normally closed switch. If the fluid level is low, pressurized transmission fluid reaches the switch after the transmission warms up. The contacts open, a code is generated, and the check transmission/do not shift light is illuminated.

Wiring Harnesses

Transmissions are supported by one of two general types of wiring harness. The **chassis wiring harness** is the wiring that connects the transmission, the TPS, and the VSS to the transmission ECU. The **cab harness** connects the shift selector to the ECU and also contains the bi-directional communications connector to allow the transmission ECU to "talk" to Detroit Diesel DDEC systems and the diagnostic data link (DDL) connector, (the **diagnostic data link (DDL) connector** is the place on the vehicle where the technician can plug in diagnostic software), (Technicians using a Pro-Link or other electronic service tool can connect to the DDL and access trouble codes stored in the ECU). The cab harness also contains various interface wiring for optional transmission strategies, such as brake interlocks, low floor operating/no-shift options, and so on.

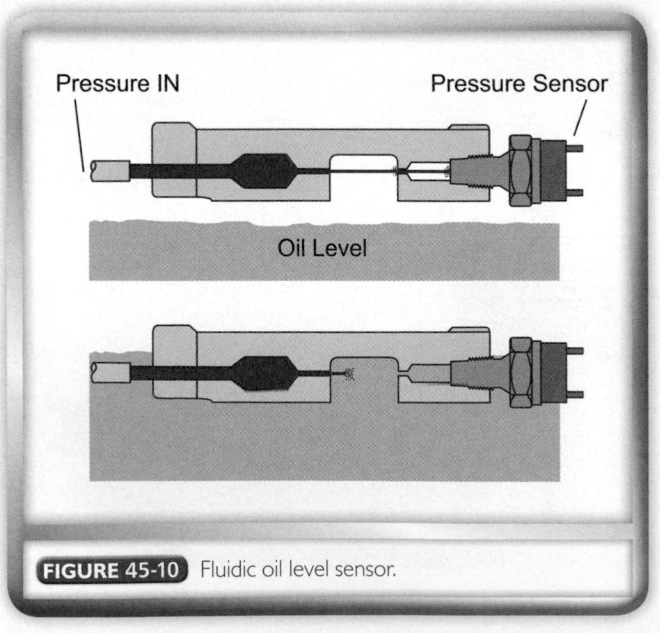

FIGURE 45-10 Fluidic oil level sensor.

Solenoids

Inside the ATEC/CEC transmission, the hydraulic circuitry is changed somewhat when compared to its hydraulically controlled predecessor. Whereas hydraulically controlled Allison transmissions use spool valves exclusively to control fluid flow, ATEC/CEC transmissions use solenoids in addition to spool valves. The solenoids direct the flow of main pressure to control the transmission shifting and other functions. The solenoids use a spring-loaded check ball to control fluid flow. Solenoids have three components:

- An inlet port controlled by the ball
- A circuit port leading to the hydraulic circuit the solenoid controls
- An exhaust port

When the solenoid is closed, the hydraulic circuit that is controlled is open to the exhaust port. When the solenoid is opened, the exhaust port is sealed, and the inlet port is connected to the hydraulic circuit.

The ATEC/CEC system uses two types of solenoids—latching and non-latching solenoids **FIGURE 45-11**. **Latching solenoids** require only a short burst of electricity to cause them to move. Once they do, they latch, or stay in that position. Another burst of electricity causes the solenoid to unlatch and move back to the starting position. Therefore, these solenoids do not require constant power. That reduces the amount of heat that would build up in the solenoid coil and extends the life of the solenoids. This latching feature also gives some transmission operability during electrical power failure. We will discuss failsafe operational strategies later in the chapter. As their name implies, **non-latching solenoids** do not stay in an open position unless they have a constant voltage supply. As soon as the voltage disappears, they return to their starting, or closed, position.

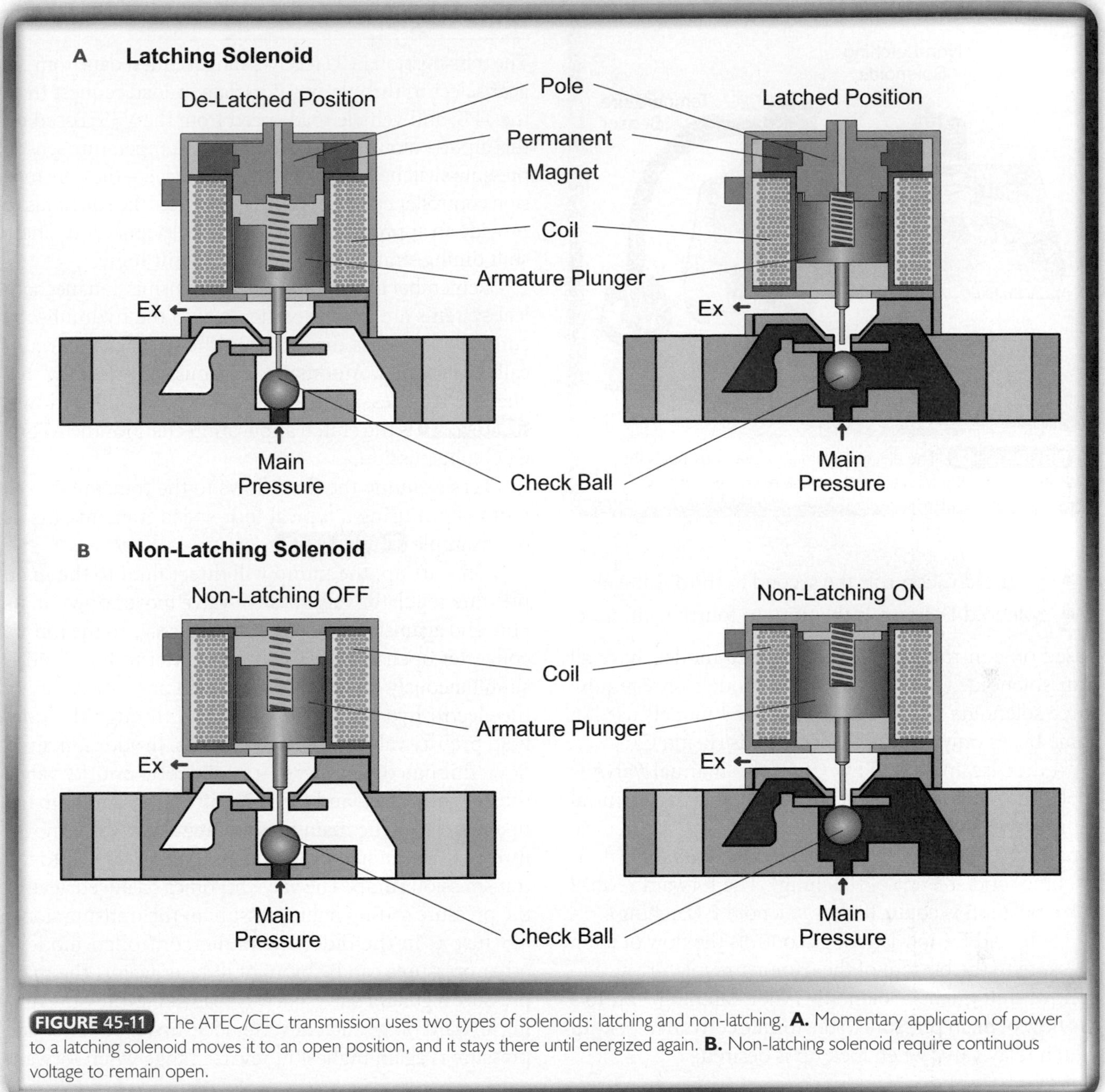

FIGURE 45-11 The ATEC/CEC transmission uses two types of solenoids: latching and non-latching. **A.** Momentary application of power to a latching solenoid moves it to an open position, and it stays there until energized again. **B.** Non-latching solenoid require continuous voltage to remain open.

Solenoid Usage

There are up to nine solenoids in the transmission: solenoids A, B, C, D, E, F, G, H, and J. (There is no "I" solenoid). The solenoids are located in an electro-hydraulic valve body and can either be clamped to or bolted to the valve body **FIGURE 45-12**.

The hydraulic circuits of the transmission are altered so that the solenoids control the flow through the main valve body. The solenoids are mounted such that they have main pressure present at their base. That pressure is blocked when the solenoid is closed, but when the solenoid is opened electrically, main pressure is redirected to the appropriate valves in the main valve body. In hydraulically controlled transmissions, the shift signal valves control the shift relay valves. In the ATEC/CEC transmissions, however, the shift signal valves are replaced with latching solenoids A, B, C, and D. The shift relay valves in the ATEC/CEC are simply called the shift valves and control the following functions:

- Solenoid A controls the low to first shift valve on five-speed models.
- Solenoid B controls the first to second shift valve.

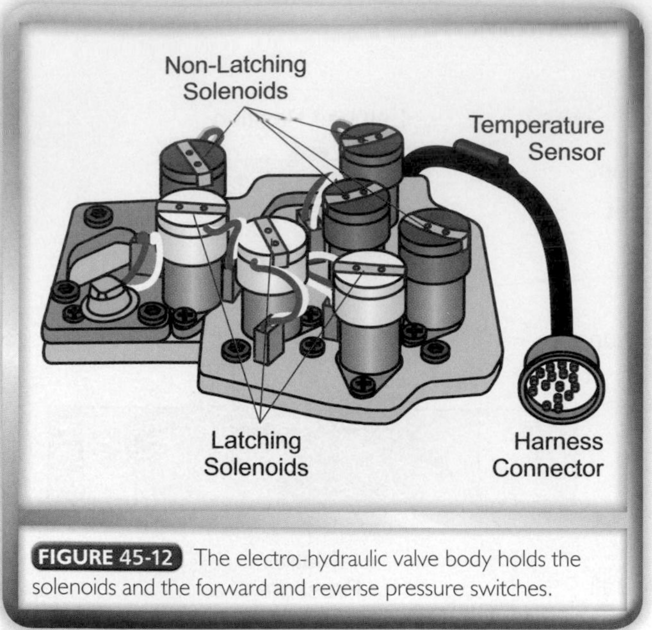

FIGURE 45-12 The electro-hydraulic valve body holds the solenoids and the forward and reverse pressure switches.

- Solenoid C controls the second to third shift valve.
- Solenoid D controls the third to fourth shift valve.

Based on control functions, five-speed models have all four solenoids (A–D). Four-speed models only require three solenoids (B–D), and three-speed models used in some buses only require two solenoids (B and C).

Likewise in the ATEC/CEC, the manual valve is replaced by two solenoid-controlled valves: the neutral range valve and the forward reverse valve. The neutral range valve position is controlled by solenoid H (non-latching) and solenoid J (latching). The forward reverse valve position is controlled by solenoid F (latching).

Solenoid E (non-latching) controls the flow of main pressure to the bottom of the trimmer regulator valve to control shift quality. Solenoid G (non-latching) controls the flow of main pressure to the torque converter lock-up clutch relay valve when lock up is desired.

Shift Logic

The transmission ECU receives range request data from the gear selector, throttle position data or load request from the TPS, and vehicle road speed from the VSS. Based on this input—along with input from the temperature sensor, pressure switches, and the vehicle interface—the transmission controller energizes and de-energizes the solenoids to provide an appropriate range for vehicle operation. These shift timing strategies are known as **shift logic**.

Remember that the ATEC/CEC transmission mechanical systems are relatively identical to the hydraulically controlled models discussed in the chapter Hydraulically Controlled Automatic Transmissions. Review that chapter if necessary to understand the power flows. TABLE 45-1 is the clutch application chart for the ATEC/CEC transmission.

Let's examine the fluid flows in the transmission in more depth using a typical four-speed transmission as our example FIGURE 45-13.

On start up, the pump will direct fluid to the main pressure regulator valve. As the valve moves down in its bore and against spring pressure, a passage to the torque converter opens, allowing the converter to fill. Fluid is simultaneously directed into the main pressure circuit of the electro-hydraulic valve body and through the solenoid priority valve to all the solenoids. In addition, fluid flows through three valves—the direction priority valve, the 2-3 shift valve, and the 1-2 shift valve—and into the first clutch. As the main pressure regulator valve moves further down in its bore, it opens a passage back to the transmission sump. The valve becomes balanced against the pressure setting main pressure in the transmission.

Just as in the older hydraulic-controlled models, other pressures can be brought to bear against the main pressure regulator valve as a way to lower its pressure during forward range and converter lock-up operation. Main pressure is again highest in reverse range when forward

TABLE 45-1: Clutch Application Chart for the ATEC/CEC Transmission

Range	Forward Clutch	Fourth Clutch	Third Clutch	Second Clutch	First Clutch
Neutral					Applied
First range	Applied				Applied
Second range	Applied			Applied	
Third range	Applied		Applied		
Fourth range	Applied	Applied			
Reverse		Applied			Applied

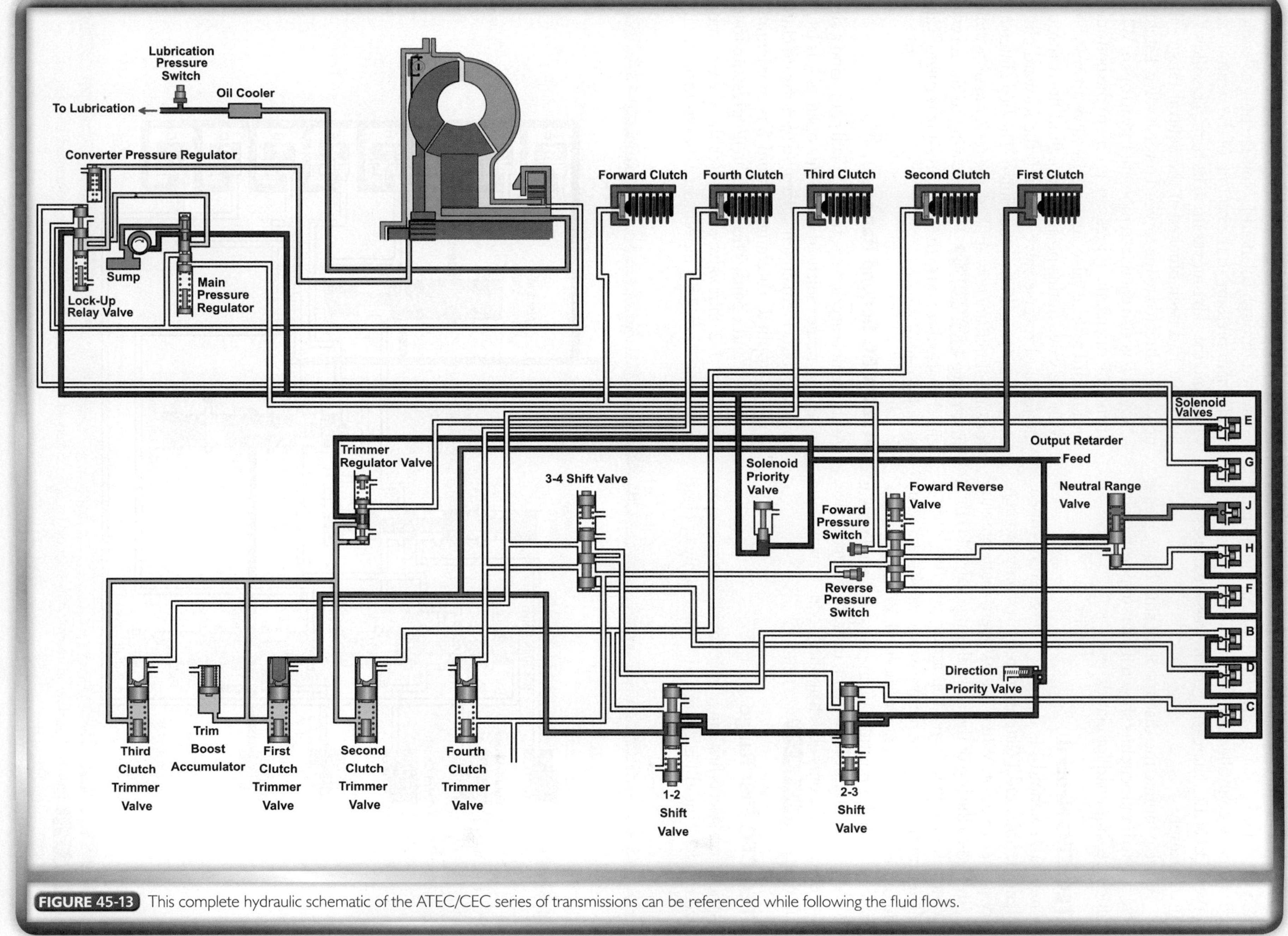

FIGURE 45-13 This complete hydraulic schematic of the ATEC/CEC series of transmissions can be referenced while following the fluid flows.

regulator and lock-up pressures are not influencing the main pressure regulator valve (MPRV). And in both the hydraulically-controlled Allison transmissions as well as in the ATEC/CEC, increasing main pressure causes first clutch to apply.

As we continue the discussion of shift logic, please note the hydraulic circuits shown in the supporting schematics are simplified for clarity.

ATEC/CEC Neutral

In neutral, solenoid J is the only energized or "open" solenoid. Solenoid J (latching) requires only momentary power to open. When J does open, main pressure is directed to the top of the neutral-range valve, keeping the valve seated in its bore. This action prevents internal leakage from causing the neutral-range valve to move up and cause an unwanted range selection. With the neutral-range valve in this position, main pressure dead heads at the valve and cannot flow to the forward reverse valve. First clutch is the only clutch applied so the transmission is in neutral FIGURE 45-14.

ATEC/CEC First Range

As the driver selects first range, solenoid H becomes energized and solenoid J is energized momentarily to close its valve. The pressure above the neutral-range valve is exhausted through solenoid J. Non-latching solenoid H sends main pressure to the bottom of the neutral-range valve, and the valve moves up in its bore. This allows the fluid that had been blocked at the neutral-range valve now to be directed to the forward reverse valve. Latching solenoid F is also energized momentarily to open. When solenoid F opens, main pressure is sent to the bottom of the forward reverse valve, moving the valve up in its bore. With the valve in this position, the fluid flows through the forward reverse valve and into the forward clutch circuit, applying the forward clutch. The first clutch and forward clutch are now applied; the transmission attains first range FIGURE 45-15. Fluid flowing to the forward clutch is also directed to the main pressure regulator valve to reduce main pressure.

ATEC/CEC Second Range

As the vehicle accelerates, the ECU will command a shift to second range. Solenoid F remains open as it is latching. Solenoid H remains energized, so the forward clutch remains applied. Latching solenoid B is momentarily energized and opens. This sends main pressure to the top of the 1-2 shift valve and causes the valve to move down in its bore. That movement exhausts first clutch at

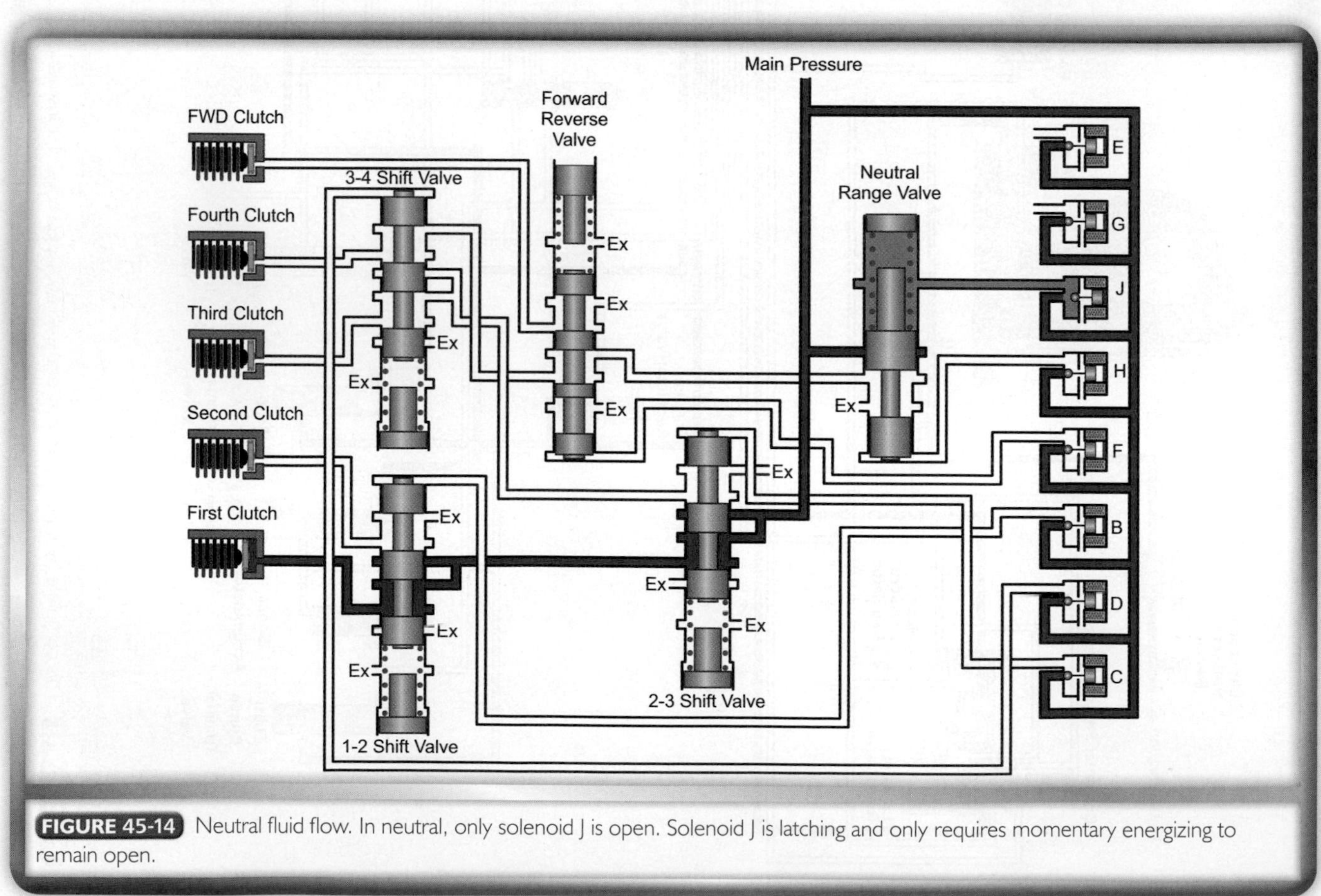

FIGURE 45-14 Neutral fluid flow. In neutral, only solenoid J is open. Solenoid J is latching and only requires momentary energizing to remain open.

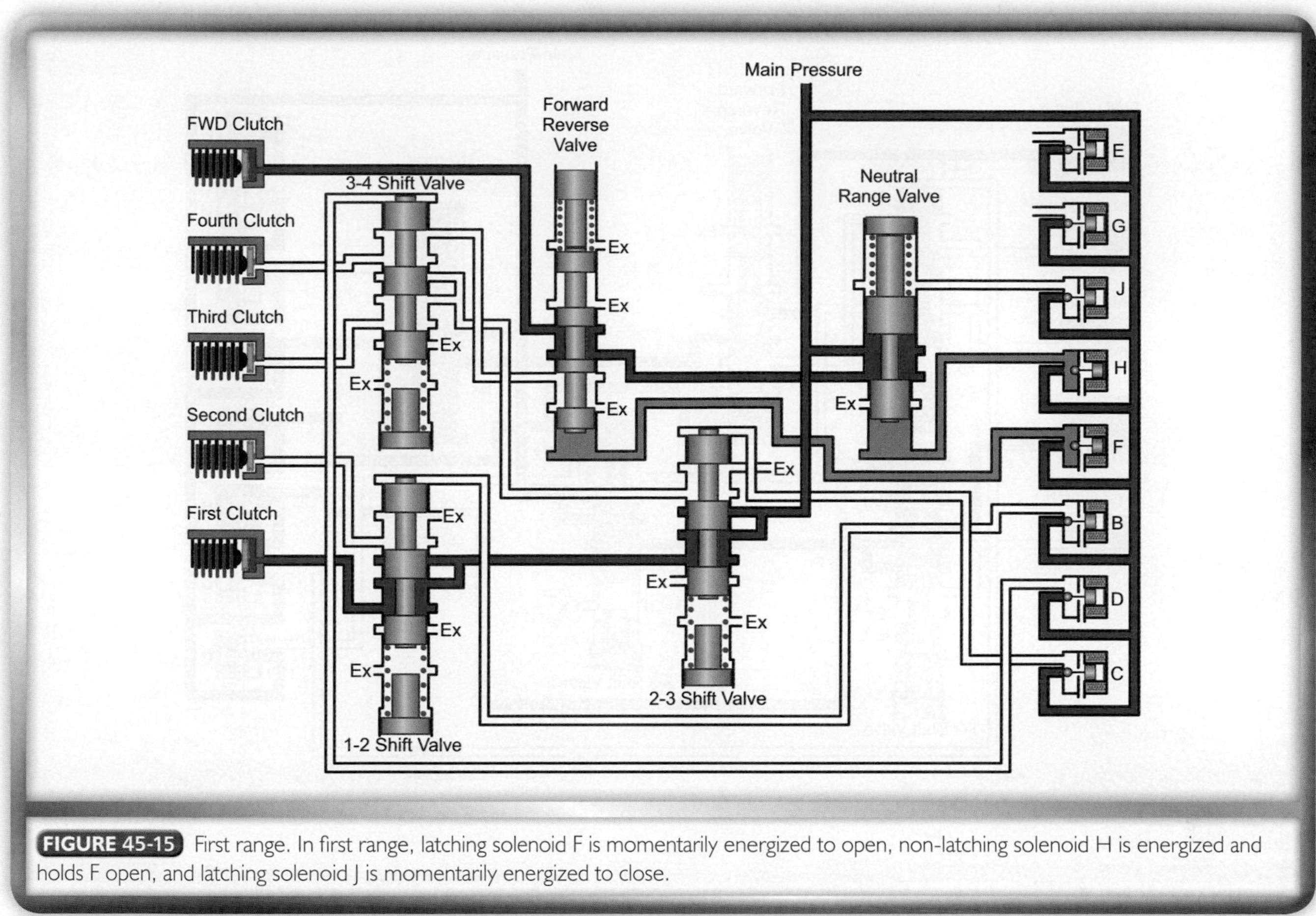

FIGURE 45-15 First range. In first range, latching solenoid F is momentarily energized to open, non-latching solenoid H is energized and holds F open, and latching solenoid J is momentarily energized to close.

the valve. At the same time, the movement sends pressure to the second clutch circuit, applying the clutch. Forward and second clutches are now applied, and the transmission attains second range **FIGURE 45-16**.

ATEC/CEC Third Range

As the vehicle continues to accelerate, the transmission ECU commands a shift to third. Solenoid F remains open as it is latching. Solenoid H remains energized, so forward clutch remains applied. Latching solenoid C is momentarily energized and opens. The opening causes the 2-3 shift valve to move in its bore and exhausts the second clutch at the valve. The motion redirects main pressure to the third clutch. Forward and third clutch are applied, and the transmission attains third range **FIGURE 45-17**.

ATEC/CEC Fourth Range

After continued acceleration, the ECU will command a shift to fourth range. Solenoid F remains open as it is latching. Solenoid H remains energized, so the forward clutch remains applied. Latching solenoid D is energized momentarily, and this causes the 3-4 shift valve to move in its bore. That movement exhausts third clutch at the valve and also redirects main pressure to the fourth clutch so forward and fourth clutches are applied, and the transmission attains fourth range **FIGURE 45-18**.

ATEC/CEC Reverse

Reverse begins with the transmission in neutral. Recall from Figure 45-13. that, in neutral, main pressure flows from the direction priority valve, down through the 2-3 shift valve and the 1-2 shift valve, and into the first clutch, applying it. Latching solenoid J is in the open position holding the neutral-range valve down in its bore, causing main pressure to be blocked at the valve. As the driver shifts the selector to reverse, solenoid J is momentarily energized to close its valve and exhaust the pressure above the neutral-range valve at the solenoid. Non-latching solenoid H becomes energized, and that sends pressure to the bottom of the neutral range valve moving it up in its bore. This redirects the fluid blocked at the neutral-range valve towards the forward reverse valve. Latching solenoid F is closed, and spring pressure holds the forward reverse valve down in its bore. The fluid is redirected through the 3-4 shift valve and on to the fourth clutch applying it. Since first and fourth clutch are applied, the transmission shifts into reverse **FIGURE 45-19**.

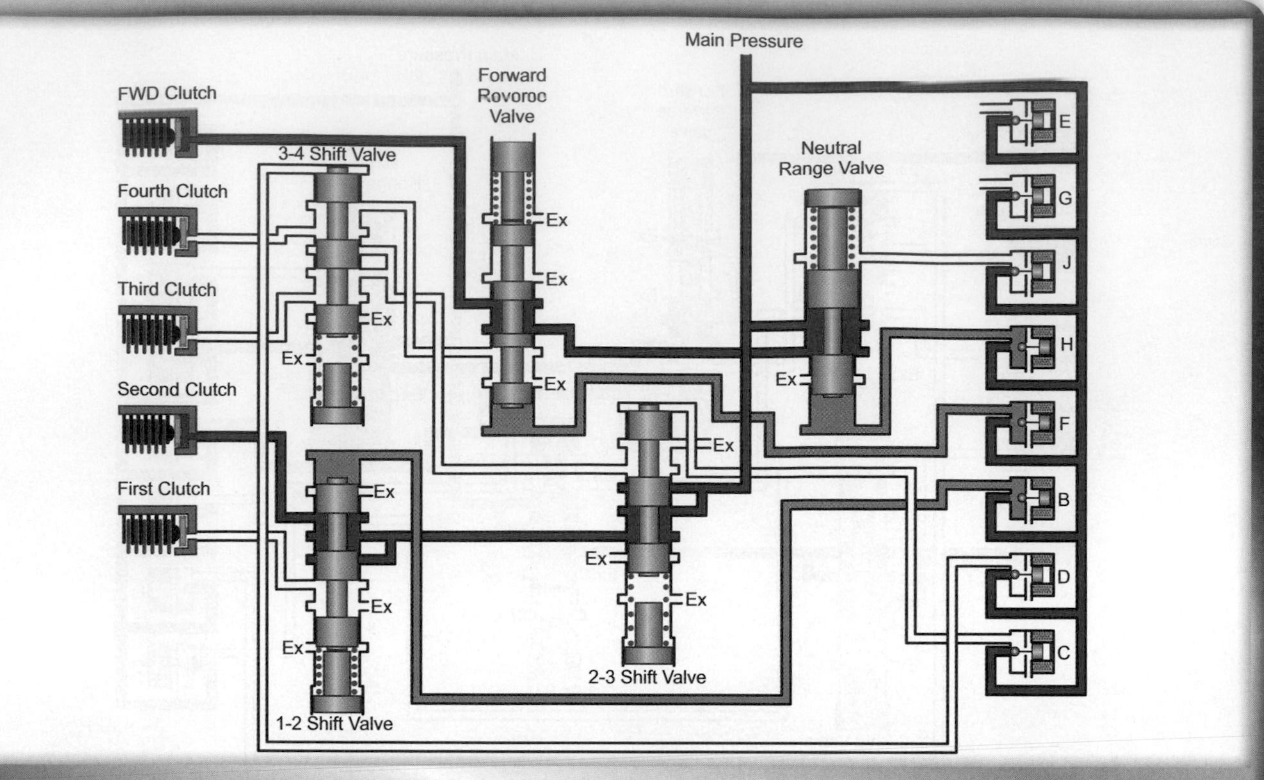

FIGURE 45-16 Second range. To achieve second range, the transmission ECU momentarily energizes latching solenoid B to open sending fluid to the 1-2 shift valve.

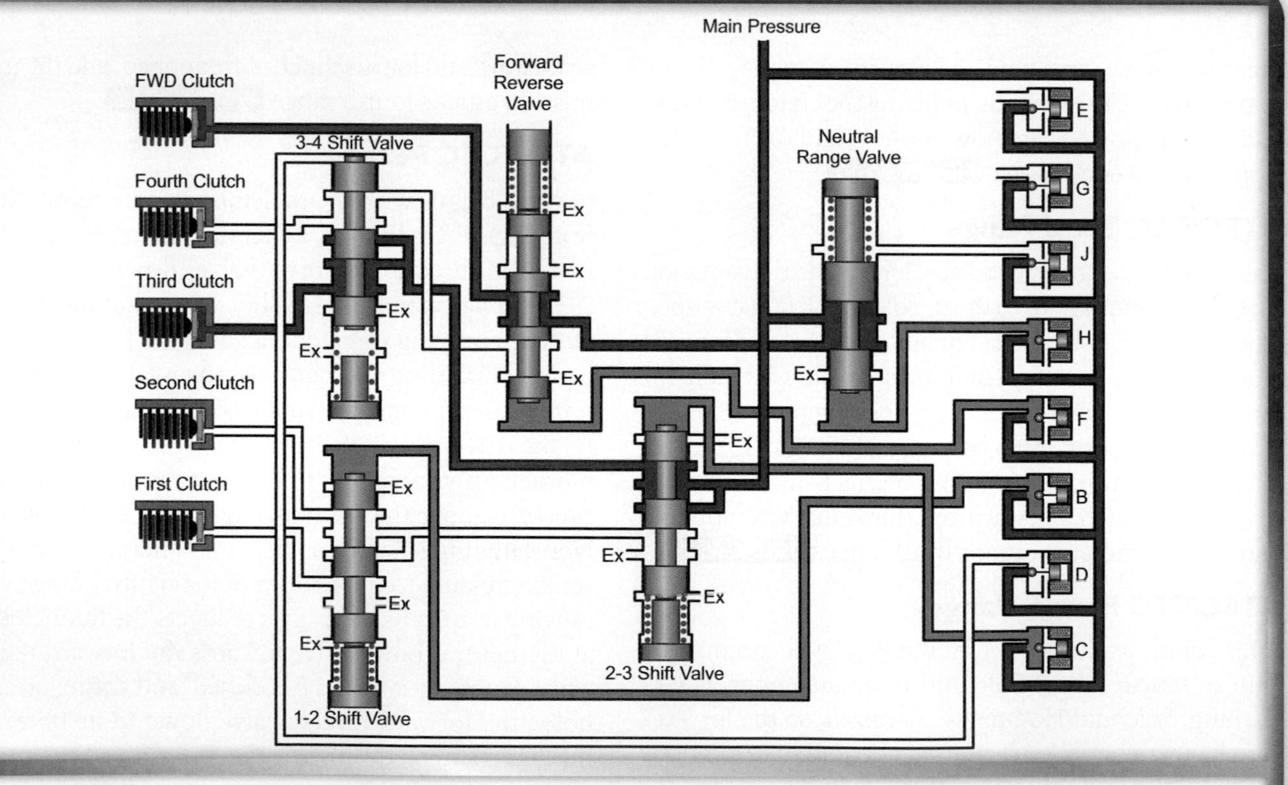

FIGURE 45-17 Third range. To shift to third, the ECU momentarily energizes latching solenoid C to open sending pressure to the 2-3 shift valve.

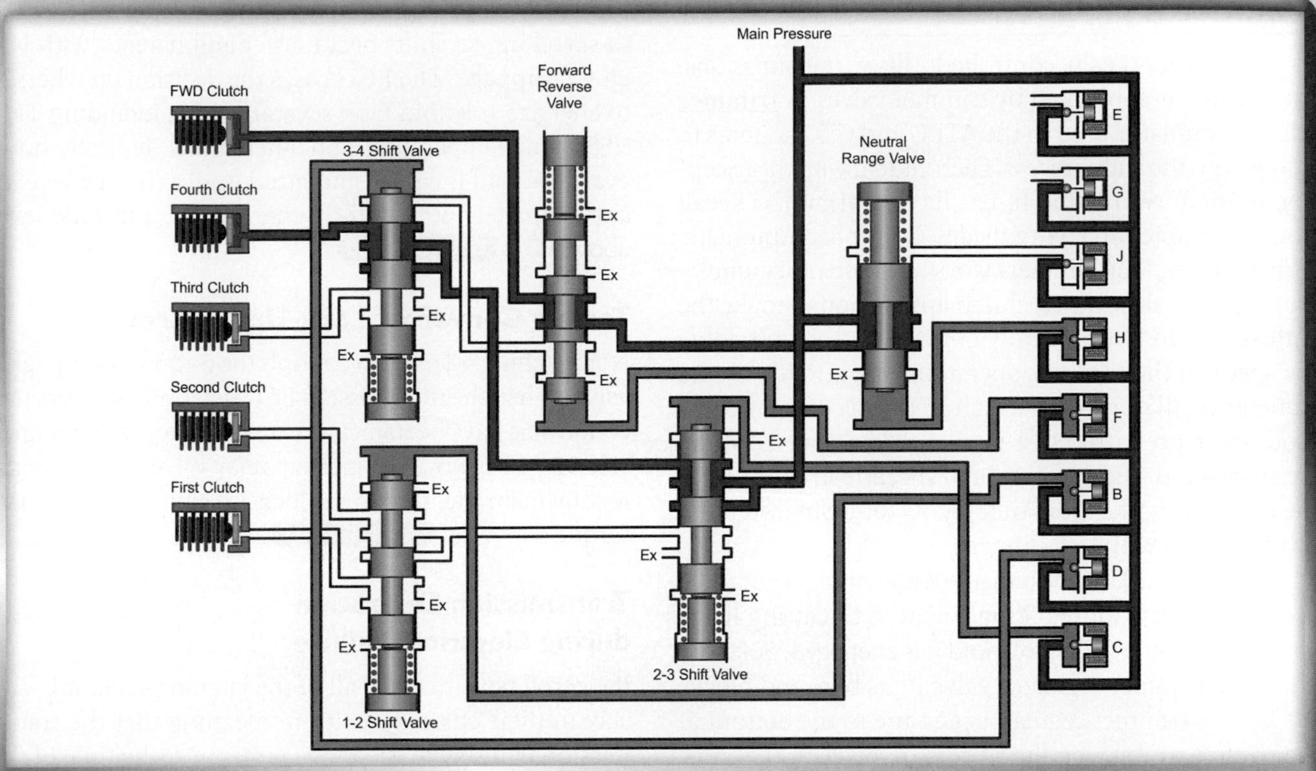

FIGURE 45-18 Fourth range. To achieve fourth range, the ECU momentarily energizes latching solenoid D to open it sending pressure to the 3-4 shift valve.

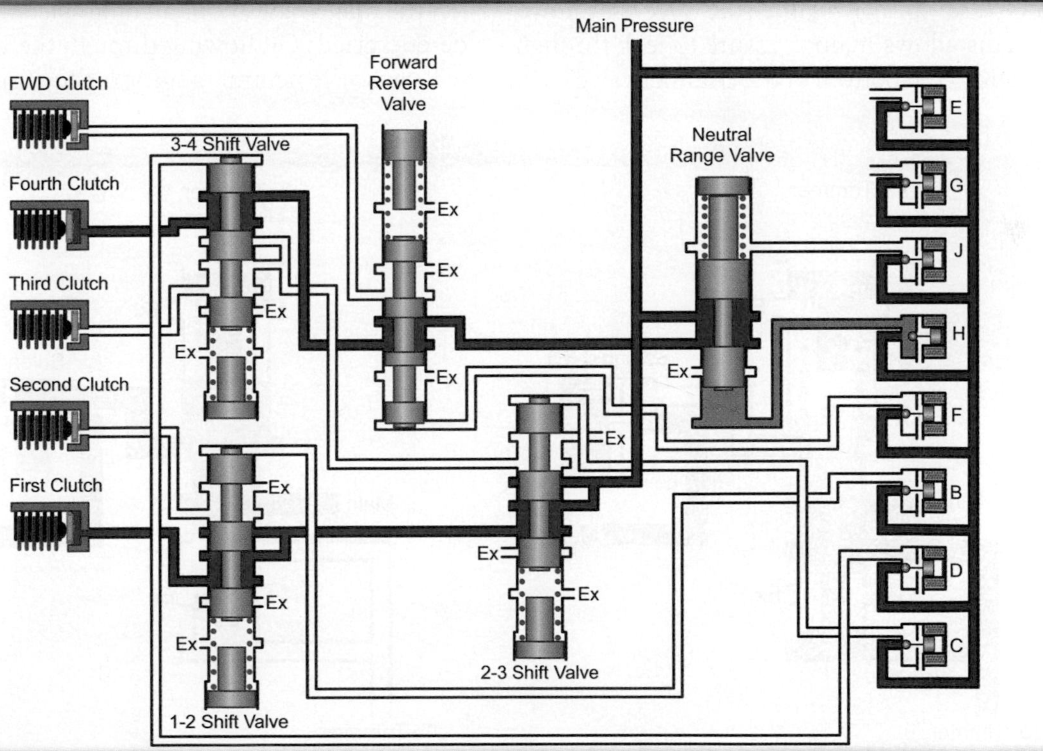

FIGURE 45-19 Reverse. The shift to reverse starts when neutral latching solenoid J is momentarily energized to close and non-latching solenoid H is energized to open.

Trimmer Operation

As in the hydraulically controlled Allison transmissions, shift quality is controlled by trimmer valves. A **trimmer** is an accumulator used in the ATEC and CEC systems to smooth out the shift process. Each clutch, with the exception of the forward clutch, has its own trimmer. Recall from the chapter on Hydraulically Controlled Automatic Transmissions that trimmers work as a kind of accumulator system to slow down clutch application to make the shift softer. In hydraulically controlled transmissions, the speed of the trimmer operation is controlled by the trimmer regulator valve, which in turn is controlled by modulator pressure. As a result, at low speeds, shifts are slower and smoother. At high speed/load conditions, the trimmer works more quickly, resulting in faster and harsher shifts with less slippage.

In the ATEC/CEC system, the trimmer regulator valve is controlled by non-latching solenoid E. During light-load, low-throttle shifts, solenoid E is energized. Solenoid E lifts the trimmer regulator valve in its bore and blocks the flow of trimmer regulator pressure to the bottom of the trimmers. With no fluid pressure beneath the trimmer valves, the trimming action takes a longer time to accomplish, so shifts are softer and slower. Under heavier loads or higher-speed shifting, the ECU will de-energize non-latching solenoid E. When this happens, the trimmer regulator valve spring will force the valve back down in its bore. This allows main pressure to leak through the valve and into the bottom of the trimmer valves. Oil pressure beneath the trimmers causes the trimming action to speed up, so shifts occur faster and harsher with less clutch slippage. The ECU bases the decision on whether to energize solenoid E on several inputs, including TPS, VSS, sump temperature, and other inputs. Typically, however, solenoid E will be energized until a throttle level of approximately 60% and de-energized at a throttle level above 60% FIGURE 45-20.

Torque Converter Lock-Up Control

Non-latching solenoid G controls the torque lock-up relay valve. When the transmission ECU determines the correct conditions have been met, the transmission will energize solenoid G to move the lock-up relay valve, thereby redirecting main pressure to the lock-up clutch piston in the torque converter FIGURE 45-21.

Transmission Operation during Electrical Failure

If electric power is lost, all of the latching solenoids will stay in their current position, meaning that the transmission will stay in the range it was in at the time of the power loss. Non-latching solenoid E will be de-energized, returning the trimmer regulator valve to its at-rest position. Non-latching solenoid G will be de-energized and release the torque converter clutch. At the bottom of the neutral range valve, non-latching solenoid H will also be de-energized. Oil flowing through the valve, however, will cause the neutral range valve to remain in the open

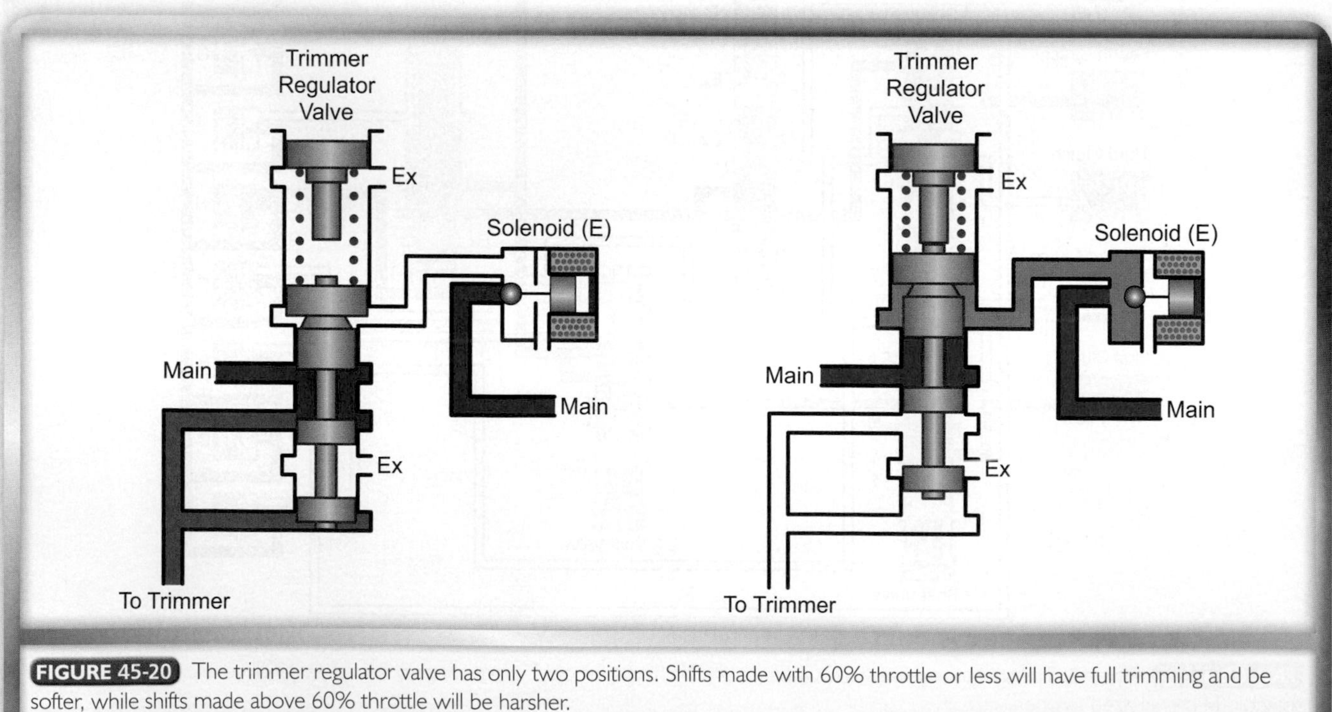

FIGURE 45-20 The trimmer regulator valve has only two positions. Shifts made with 60% throttle or less will have full trimming and be softer, while shifts made above 60% throttle will be harsher.

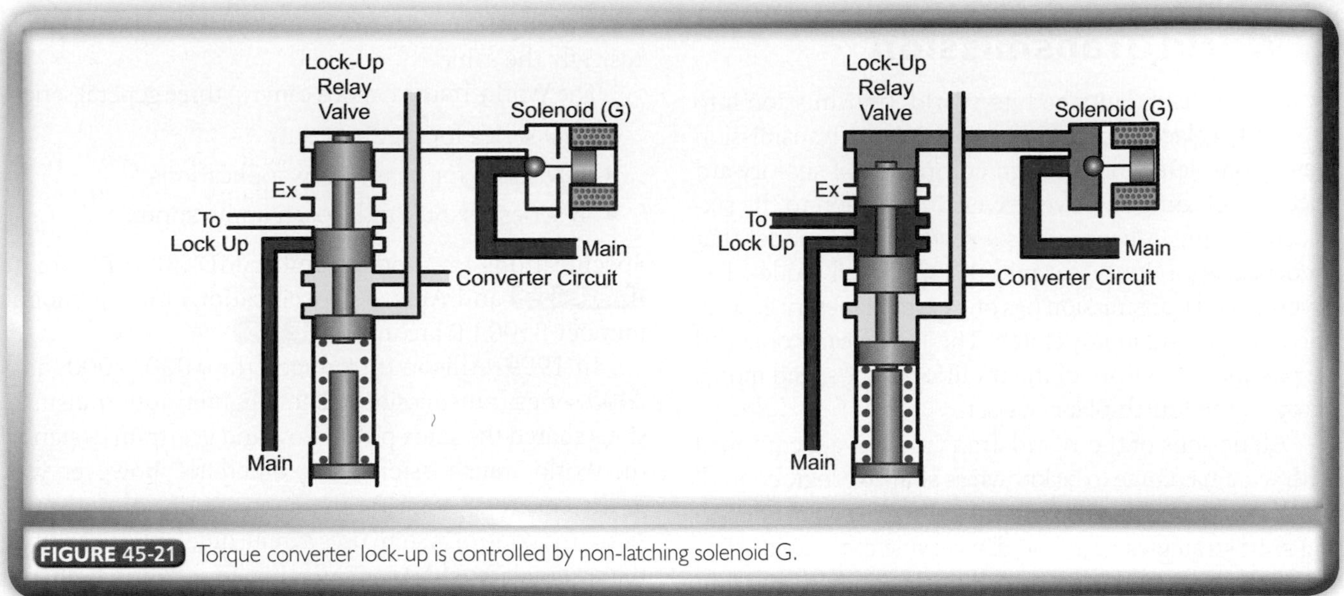

FIGURE 45-21 Torque converter lock-up is controlled by non-latching solenoid G.

position. (This occurs because of the difference in the size of the lands where the oil flows through the valve. The top land is larger in area than the bottom land, and so the valve remains open).

Once the vehicle is shut off, oil flow stops, and spring force pushes the neutral-range valve to the bottom of its bore. On restart, the latching solenoids continue to remain in position, but there is no flow through the neutral-range valve. The transmission, therefore, stays in neutral. This failsafe strategy allows the vehicle to be driven to a shop after electrical failure. Once the engine is shut off, the oil pressure holding up the neutral range valve is lost and the transmission will not go back into gear on restart FIGURE 45-22.

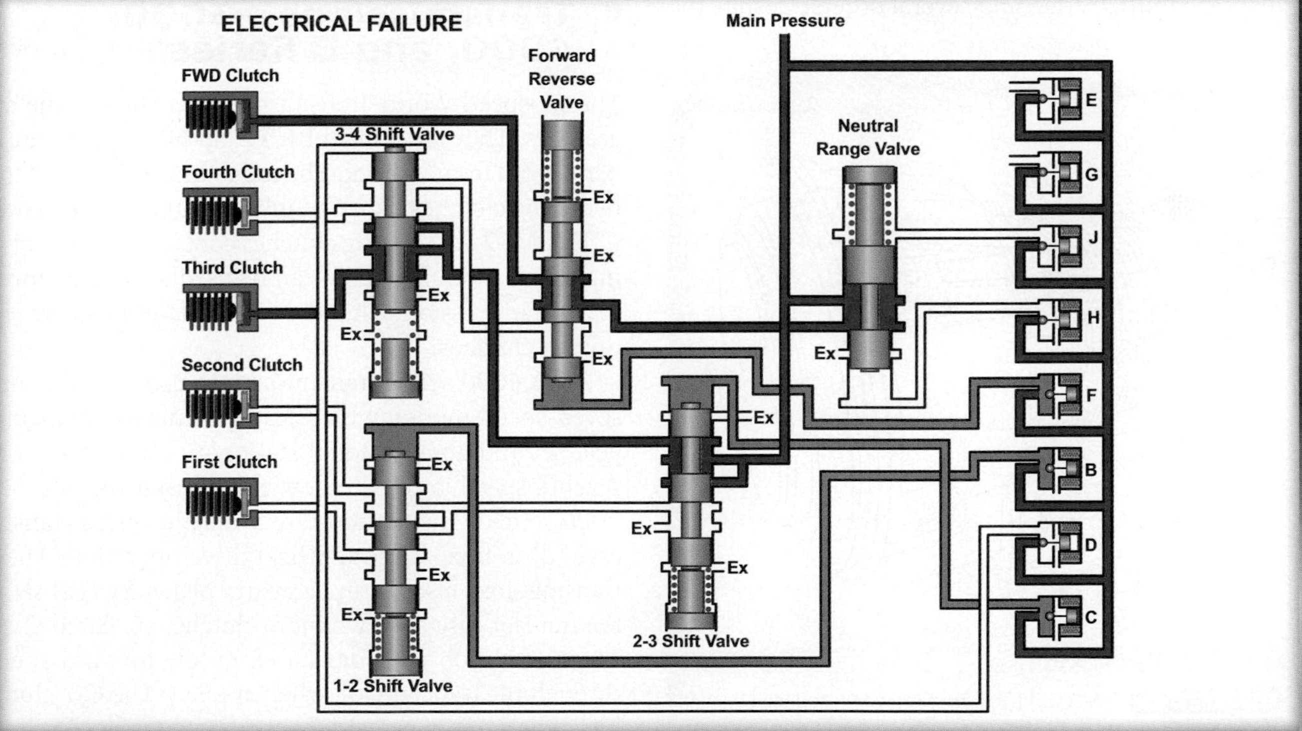

FIGURE 45-22 During electrical failure all latching solenoids remain in their positions so the transmission will stay in the range it is in until the engine is turned off.

World Transmission

In 1991, Allison launched its World Transmission into the marketplace FIGURE 45-23. The World Transmission was a completely new design comprised of six forward speeds including two overdrives. In addition to the six-speed design, Allison offers a seven-speed model that incorporates a "low" gear into the six-speed model. The seven-speed transmission has one extra planetary gear set and one extra stationary clutch. The "low" gear is obtained by passing the output of the traditional six-speed model through the fourth planetary set.

All designs of the World Transmission are equipped with what has come to be known as adaptive logic control. That means that the transmission ECU is capable of adapting shift strategies based on drive-cycle experience. The transmission ECU constantly monitors and adjusts shift points and processes to maintain optimum shift quality, fuel economy, and driver comfort. Eventually, Allison dropped the World Transmission moniker and began referring to the model line by its series numbers (e.g., the 3000, 4000, and B series). In the truck and coach market, however, the name World Transmission is still widely used. In an attempt to align model functionality with the needs of particular markets, Allison has recently created a long list of market-specific names—the Highway Series, the Rugged-Duty Series, the Motor Home Series, Transport/Shuttle Series, and several others. Despite the name changes, the transmission model numbers remain basically the same.

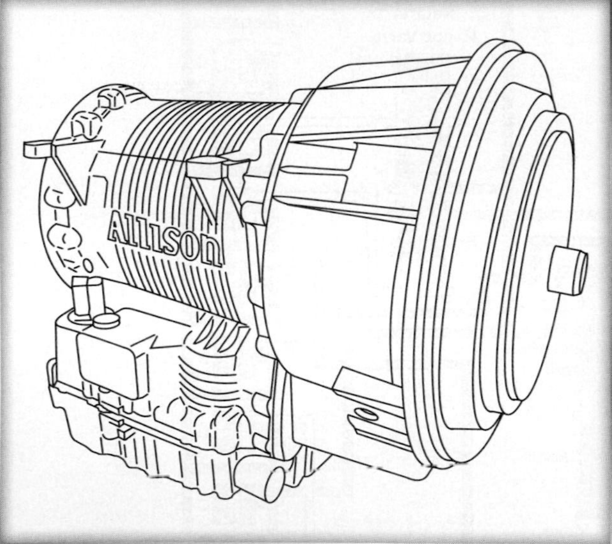

FIGURE 45-23 The World Transmission was introduced by Allison in 1991.

The World Transmissions came in three general series:

- MD series for medium duty
- HD series for heavy duty applications
- B series for Bus and Coach applications

Specifications for model number MD-3060-PR are in TABLE 45-2 and Allison's specifications for bus model number B500 PR are in TABLE 45-3.

In 1999, Allison introduced the 1000, 2000, and 2400 series transmissions. These lighter duty transmissions shared the same power flow and geartrain design as the World Transmission. A key difference, however, was in the control system. In the lighter series of transmissions, the control system uses a quite different design than the original **World Transmission Electronic Control (WTEC)** systems—WTEC, WTEC 11, and WTEC 111.

The addition of the 1000, 2000, and 2400 series transmissions enabled Allison to match transmissions to a variety of engines that produce between 165 and 565 horsepower (121–421 kW) and generate from 420 to 1,850 pound-feet of torque (568–2,508 Nm). TABLE 45-4 lists the models in Allison's Highway series and the transmission capacity rating of each.

World Transmissions—3000, 4000, and B Series

The six-speed World Transmission uses three planetary gear sets. They are named P1, P2, and P3 and are numbered from front to back. The transmission also uses five hydraulic clutches, again numbered from front to back. C-1 and C-2 are rotating clutches contained in the rotating clutch module, which can be used to provide input to the transmission. Clutches C-3, C-4, and C-5 are stationary clutches.

The 4000 series transmission is also available in a seven-speed model, which features an extra planetary gear set and an additional stationary clutch C-6. The seventh speed is an extra low gear for starting out. The 3000 series transmissions are available with a transfer case (drop box) for four-wheel drive operation. These transmissions also feature an extra planetary gear set in the transfer case and two more clutches (C-6 and C-7). The C-6 clutch provides an extra low forward speed through the transfer case when applied. The C-7 clutch locks the front and rear wheel drives together for low-traction situations.

TABLE 45-2: Specifications for Allison's MD-3060-PR Medium-Duty Transmission

MD	3	0	6	0	P	R
Medium duty or HD for Heavy Duty	#3 is medium duty #4 is heavy duty	0 is close ratio 5 is wide ratio	Number of forward speeds 6 or 7	Major revisions	Power take off provision	R is Retarder T is for drop box or transfer case

TABLE 45-3: Specifications for Allison's Bus Model Number B500 PR Transmission

B	5	0	0	P	R
Bus	Series 300, 400 or 500 higher # series can handle more input torque	0 is close ratio 5 is wide ratio	Major revisions	Power take off provision	Retarder

TABLE 45-4: Allison's Highway Series Transmissions and Their Capacity Ratings

RATINGS								
Model	**Ratio**	**Park Pawl**	**Max Input Power[1] hp (kW)**	**Max input Torque[1] lb-ft (N m)**	**Max Inport Torque w/ SEM or Torque Limiting[1,2] lb-ft (N m)**	**Max Turbine Torque[3] lb-ft (N m)**	**Max GVW bs (kg)**	**Max GCW lbs (kg)**
1000 HS	Close	Yes	340[4,7] (254)[4,7]	575 (780)	660[4,7] (895)[4,7]	950[4] (1288)[4]	19,500 (8,845)	26,001 (11,800)
2100 HS	Close	No	340[4,7] (254)[4,7]	575 (780)	660[4,7] (895)[4,7]	950[4] (1288)[4]	26,000 (11,800)	26,000 (11,800)
2200 HS	Close	Yes	340[4,7] (254)[4,7]	575 (780)	660[4,7] (895)[4,7]	950[4] (1288)[4]	26,000 (11,800)	26,001 (11,800)
2300 HS[5]	Close	No	325 (242)	n/a	450 (610)	950[4] (1288)[4]	33,000 (15,000)	33,000 (15,000)
2350 HS[7]	Close	Yes	340[4] (254)[4]	575 (780)	660[4] (895)[4]	950[4] (1288)[4]	30,000 (13,600)	30,000 (13,600)
2500 HS	Wide	No	340[4,7] (254)[4,7]	575 (780)	660[4,7] (895)[4,7]	950[4] (1288)[4]	33,000 (15,000)	33,000 (15,000)
2550 HS[7]	Wide	Yes	340 (254)	575 (780)	660[4] (895)[4]	950[4] (1288)[4]	30,000 (13,600)	30,000 (13,600)
3000 HS	Close	n/a	370 (276)	1100 (1491)	1250[6] (1695)[6]	1600[4] (2169)	80,000 (36,288)	80,000 (36,288)
4000 HS	Close	n/a	565 (421)	1770 (2400)	1850[8] (2508)[8]	2600 (3525)	–	–
4500 HS	Wide	n/a	565 (421)	1650 (2237)	1850[8] (2508)[8]	2600 (3525)	–	–

[1] Gross ratings as defined by ISO 1585 or SAE J1995. [2] SEM = engine controls with Shift Energy Management. [3] Turbine torque limit based on iSCAAN standard deductions. [4] SEM and torque limiting are required to obtain this rating. [5] Only available with VORTEC 8.1L gasoline-powered engine applications. [6] Requires Allison Transmission engine-transmission combination approval. Only available in gears three through six. [7] Check with your OEM to ensure offerings. [8] Only available in gears three through six.

Source: Information from Allison International, Inc. Permission requested.

The World Transmission design is divided into modules or major component groups FIGURE 45-24. The modules are as follows:

- Torque converter module
- Torque converter housing module
- Control module
- Front support/charging pump module
- Rotating clutch module
- Rear cover module
- Main shaft module
- P1 planetary module
- P2 planetary module
- Main housing module

Modules

Torque Converter Module

The torque converter module is a typical lock-up torque converter. The lock-up clutch incorporates a torsional damper to reduce shock on lock-up engagement and reduce the impact of engine torsional vibrations on the rest of the driveline. The torque converter hub drives the front charging pump directly on 3000, 4000, and B series without power take-off (PTO) provision. With PTO provision, the input converter drive hub drives the PTO gear which, in turn, drives the charging pump. The input torque converter has raised ribs on it. The engine speed sensor uses those ribs to sense engine RPM.

Torque Converter Housing Module

The torque converter housing module bolts the transmission to the rear of the engine flywheel housing. Likewise, the torque converter housing is also bolted to the transmission main housing. A gasket seals the connection between the torque converter housing and the main housing. The torque converter housing module also has access plates for power take-offs on the left and right side on models with PTO provision FIGURE 45-25.

Control Module

The control module is an electro-hydraulic valve body attached to the bottom of the main housing module. The module houses the electric solenoids and the various valves necessary to control the transmission operation. Also contained in the control module are the lube and main pressure filters and the pressure taps for main pressure as well as for each of the clutch-apply passages. Finally, the control module also includes the internal solenoid and switch harness and the pass-through connector that attach the module to the vehicle harness.

A gasket seals the control module to the bottom of the main housing module. Care must be taken when separating the module. First, remove all of the attaching bolts. Then, break the gasket seal only at the specified pry points.

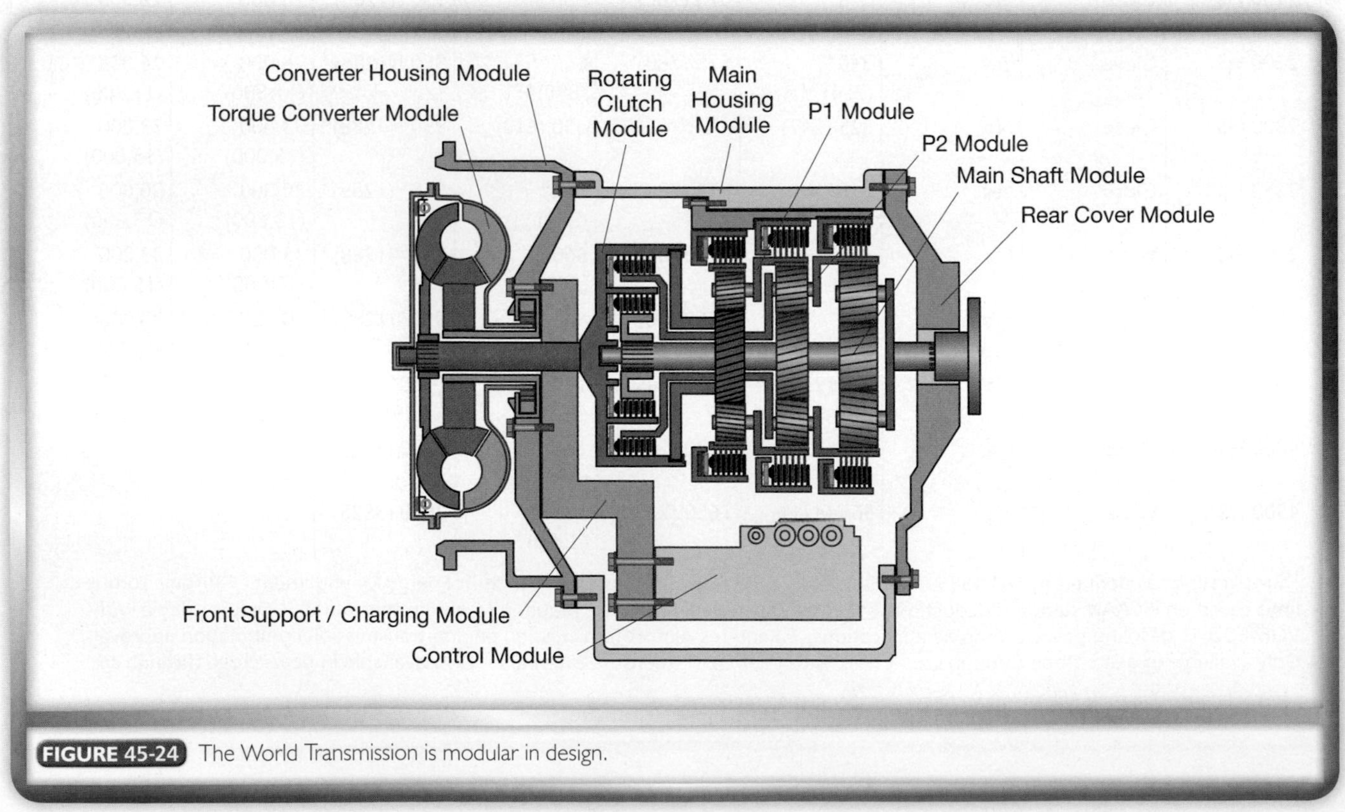

FIGURE 45-24 The World Transmission is modular in design.

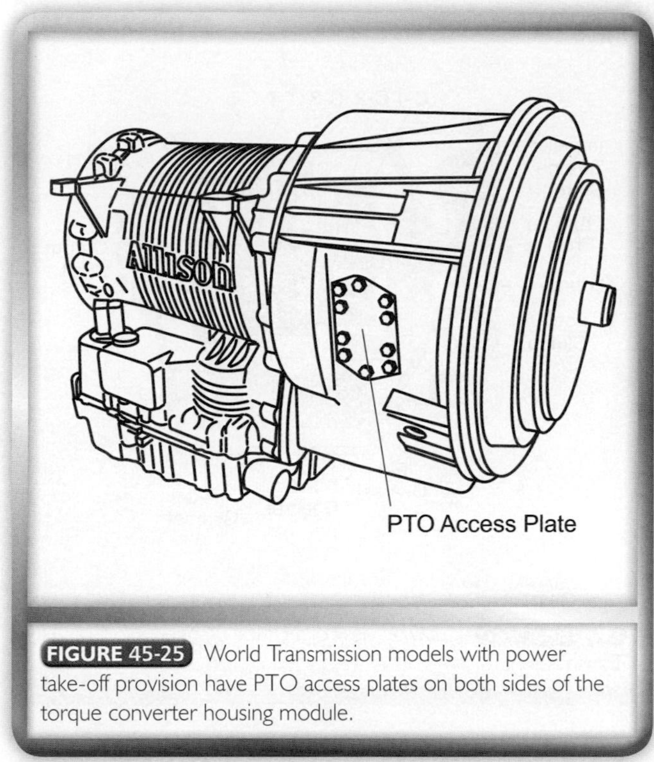

FIGURE 45-25 World Transmission models with power take-off provision have PTO access plates on both sides of the torque converter housing module.

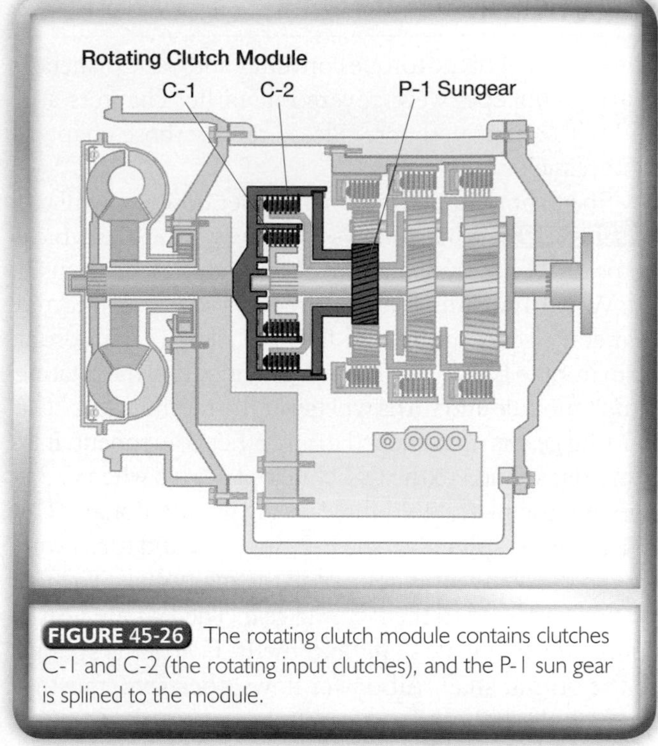

FIGURE 45-26 The rotating clutch module contains clutches C-1 and C-2 (the rotating input clutches), and the P-1 sun gear is splined to the module.

Front Support/Charging Pump Module

The front support/charging pump module includes the gerotor-style charging pump assembly, the front support bushings and bearings, and the stator support shaft. The module bolts to the main housing module and is sealed with a gasket.

Main Housing Module

The main housing module contains all of the transmission's internal components. When all other modules are removed from the housing, the C-5 clutch plates, the C-3 and C-4 clutch assemblies, and the P-1 ring gear remain in the housing.

Rotating Clutch Module

The rotating clutch module is attached to the turbine shaft and contains the two rotating clutches C-1 and C-2 FIGURE 45-26. When applied, C-1 transfers rotational power from the turbine shaft to the main shaft module. When C-2 is applied, it transfers rotational power to the P-2 carrier. There is a third piston inside the rotating clutch module called the balance piston; it is located between the C-1 piston return spring assembly and the C-1 pressure plate. The balance piston traps lubrication pressure between itself and the C1 piston. This trapped lubrication pressure is balanced against exhaust backfill pressure behind the C1 piston. The balance of pressures enhances control of exhausting and applying rotating clutches. The balance piston also provides a base for the C1 spring assembly to work against when returning the C1 piston to its seat.

Another component of the rotating clutch module is the P-1 planetary sun gear. Input torque is available at the P-1 sun gear whenever the module is rotating.

Main Shaft Module

The P-2 and P-3 sun gears are splined to the main shaft module, so rotating power is transferred to the sun gears when C-1 clutch is applied and the turbine shaft is turning.

Planetary Modules

The P-1 planetary module consists of the P-1 carrier and the P-2 ring gear. They are splined to each other and held together by a snap ring. The P-2 planetary module consists of the P-2 carrier and the P-3 ring gear. They, too, are splined to each other and held together by a snap ring.

Rear Cover Module

The rear cover module is bolted to the rear of the main housing module and sealed with a gasket. The function of the rear cover module is to contain and provide support to the output shaft. The P-3 carrier is splined to the output shaft and is part of the rear cover module. Also included as part of the rear cover module is the C-5 clutch piston. On models with an output retarder, the rear cover module is replaced with a retarder module. A **retarder** is any system used to slow a vehicle's momentum and augment the service brake.

Power Flows

The operation of the torque converter and basic planetary gearing concepts were covered in earlier chapters and will not be repeated here. Please review those chapters as necessary.

To anchor our discussion of power flows, we will use **FIGURE 45-27**, which shows a cutaway view of a typical 6-speed World Transmission. As mentioned previously, the World Transmission has three sets of interconnected planetary gears numbered P-1, P-2, and P-3 (in order from front to back). The P-1 sun gear is part of the rotating clutch module and turns whenever the module does. The P-1 ring gear is not attached to any other component. It is, however, splined to the C-3 clutch plates, so when C-3 is applied, the plates hold the P-1 ring gear stationary. The P-1 carrier is splined to the P-2 ring gear and turns with it. The P-2 sun gear is splined to the main shaft. The P-2 carrier is splined to the P-3 ring gear. The P-3 sun gear is splined to the main shaft, and the P-3 carrier is splined to the output shaft. All power flows, therefore, must go through the P-3 carrier to reach the output shaft.

As shown in **FIGURE 45-28**, there are five clutches in the transmission numbered, front to back, C-1, C-2, C-3, C-4, and C-5. Three of the clutches are stationary—C-3, C-4, and C-5—and are splined to the transmission case when applied. In addition, each stationary clutch has a specific function:

- C-3 holds the P-1 ring gear stationary.
- C-4 holds the P-2 ring gear stationary when applied. This also holds the P-1 carrier stationary as it is splined to P-2s ring gear.
- When C-5 is applied, it holds the P-3 ring gear and, therefore, the P-2 carrier stationary.

The two remaining clutches, C-1 and C-2, are rotating clutches. Both are contained in the rotating clutch module, which is splined to the turbine shaft. Both clutches enable rotational power to enter the gear train. When C-1 is applied, it brings rotational power from the turbine shaft to the main shaft and, therefore, to the P-2 and P-3 sun gears. When C-2 is applied, it brings rotational power from the turbine shaft to the P-2 carrier and, therefore, to the P-3 ring gear which is splined to it. The P-1 sun gear also enables rotational power to enter the gear train. Because the P-1 sun gear is splined to the rotating clutch module, there is always rotational power at the P-1 sun gear whenever the turbine shaft turns.

Clutch Application Chart

Even though the World Transmission (WT) has multiple clutches, not all clutches are applied in all gears. If the

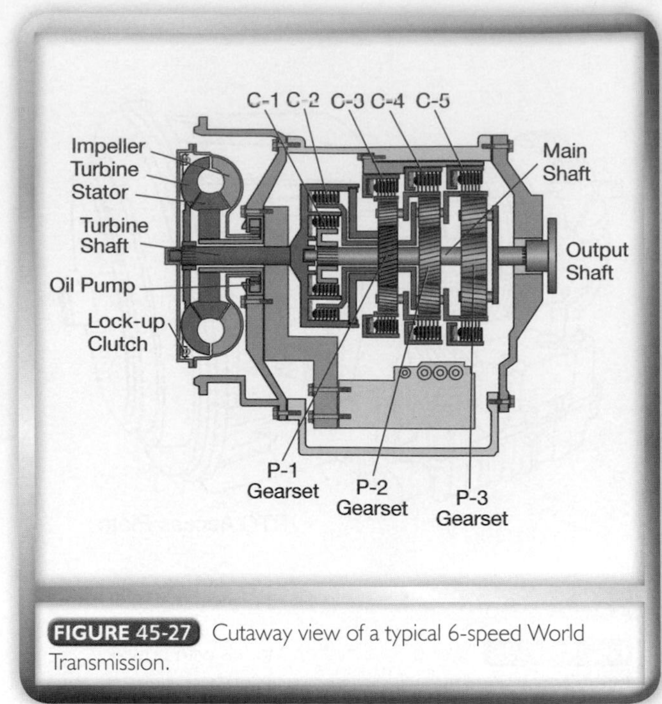

FIGURE 45-27 Cutaway view of a typical 6-speed World Transmission.

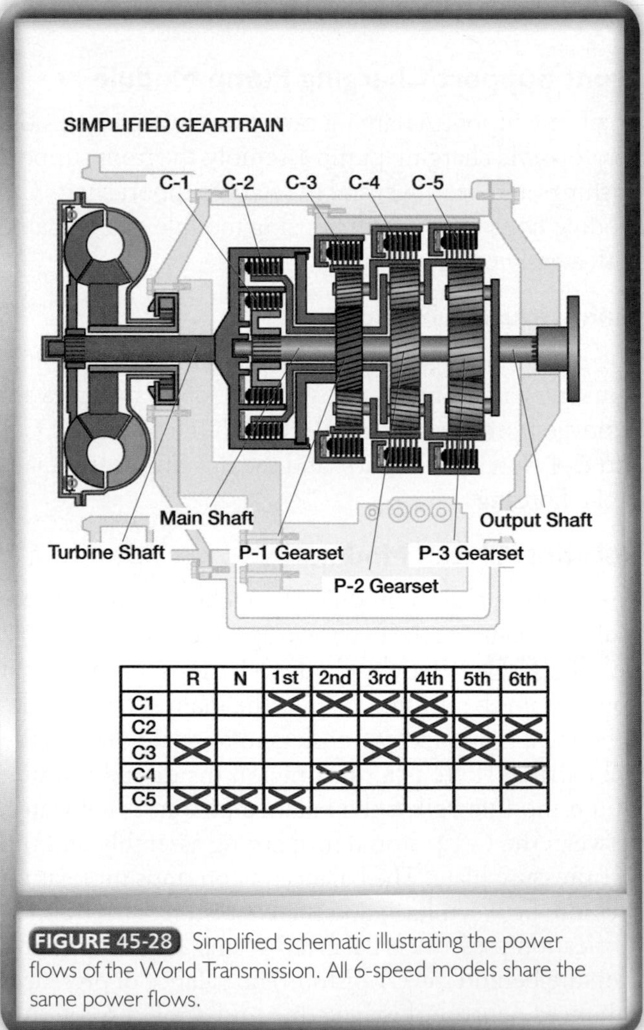

	R	N	1st	2nd	3rd	4th	5th	6th
C1			X	X	X	X		
C2						X	X	X
C3	X				X		X	
C4				X				X
C5	X	X	X					

FIGURE 45-28 Simplified schematic illustrating the power flows of the World Transmission. All 6-speed models share the same power flows.

vehicle is moving while in neutral range, the transmission will attain neutral 1, 2, 3, or 4 depending on the speed of the vehicle. This capability minimizes the rotational speed of the transmission's internal components while moving in neutral and readies the transmission for shifting into gear at that particular speed. This means that when the transmission is eventually put into a forward range, the transmission ECU only has to control one applying clutch to achieve the correct range for that speed. TABLE 45-5 illustrates how each clutch in a World Transmission is applied in each gear. As the table shows, only one clutch at a time is applied when the transmission is in neutral. Which clutch is applied depends on whether the vehicle is moving.

WT Neutral Power Flow

The transmission can obtain four different neutral power flows based on vehicle speed.

As shown in FIGURE 45-29, in neutral the C-5 clutch is applied holding the P-3 ring gear stationary. No other clutch is applied, so rotational power does not go any further than the rotating clutch module and the P-1 sun gear. Since only one clutch is applied, the transmission is in neutral. If the vehicle is moving, the applied clutch will change based on vehicle speed. As speed increases, the transmission will release and apply clutches in the following sequence:

1. Release C-5 and apply C-4.
2. Release C-4 and apply C-3.
3. Release C-3 and apply C-4 again.

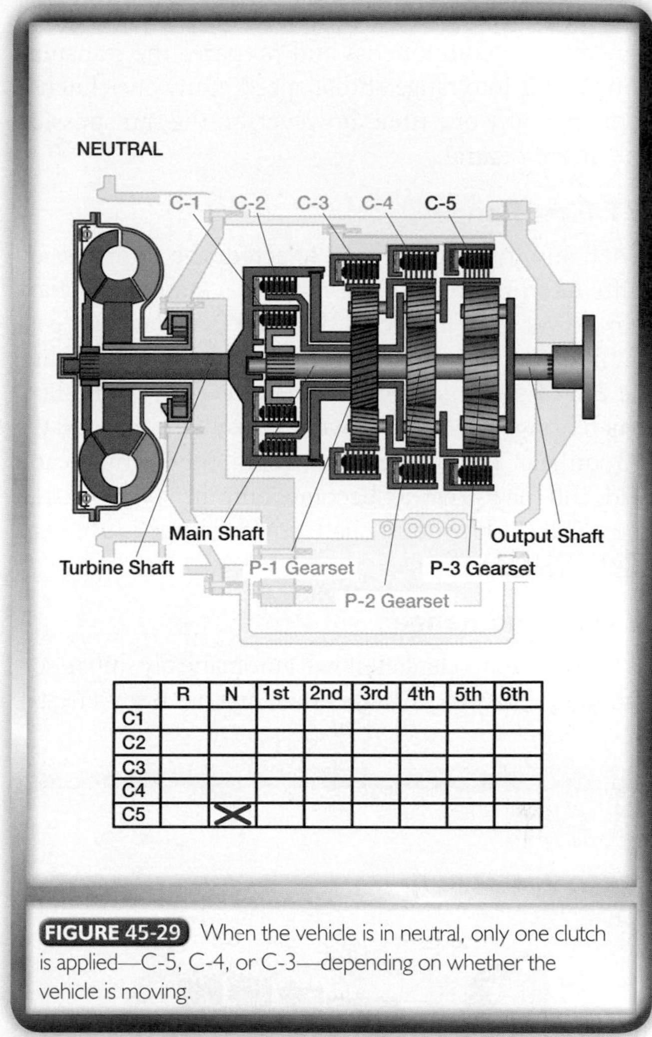

FIGURE 45-29 When the vehicle is in neutral, only one clutch is applied—C-5, C-4, or C-3—depending on whether the vehicle is moving.

TABLE 45-5: Clutch Application Chart for Allison World Transmissions

Range	C-1	C-2	C-3	C-4	C-5
Neutral 1					Applied
Neutral 2				Applied	
Neutral 3			Applied		
Neutral 4				Applied	
First	Applied				Applied
Second	Applied			Applied	
Third	Applied		Applied		
Fourth	Applied	Applied			
Fifth		Applied	Applied		
Sixth		Applied		Applied	
Reverse			Applied		Applied

*Note this chart covers all Allison World Transmissions except the seven-speed models, which have an extra clutch.

This shifting controls the rotational speed of the transmission components and prepares the transmission to shift into range at that speed. Only one clutch is applied at any one time, however, so the transmission remains in neutral.

WT First Range

When any forward range is selected, the transmission shifts into first range. First range is a simple planetary gear power flow involving only the P-3 planetary gear set. In first range, the C-5 clutch is still applied, holding the P-3 ring gear stationary. The C-1 clutch is applied, which brings rotational power to the main shaft and the P-3 sun gear. The P-3 sun gear is input, the P-3 ring gear is held, and the P-3 carrier becomes output. The P-3 carrier is splined to the output shaft, so first range is obtained **FIGURE 45-30**.

WT Second Range

As the vehicle accelerates, it will automatically shift to second range if any range higher than first has been selected. Second range is a compound planetary gear power flow involving P-3 and P-2 planetary gear sets **FIGURE 45-31**.

As the shift to second is made:

- C-5 clutch is released.
- C-4 clutch is applied.
- C-1 clutch remains applied.
- C-4 clutch holds the P-2 ring gear stationary.

Those transitions bring rotational power to the main shaft and, therefore, to the P-2 and the P-3 sun gears. The P-2 sun gear becomes input to the P-2 planetary gear set, and C-4 holds the P-2 ring gear stationary. As a result, the P-2 carrier becomes output. The P-2 carrier is splined to the P-3 ring gear, so the P-3 ring gear is turning as well. The P-3 sun gear is splined to the main shaft and so still acts as an input to the P-3 planetary gear set. This means the P-3 planetary gear set has two inputs: the P-3 sun gear and the P-3 ring gear—which are not turning at the same rate. The P-3 ring gear is turning slower than the P-3 sun gear. This makes the P-3 ring gear act as a

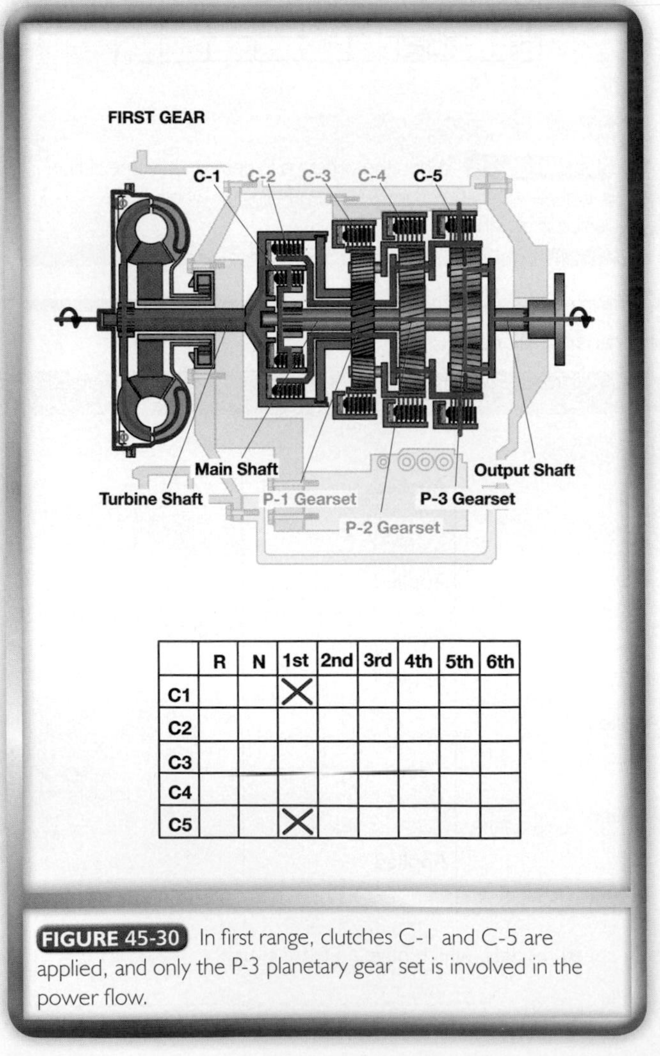

	R	N	1st	2nd	3rd	4th	5th	6th
C1			X					
C2								
C3								
C4								
C5			X					

FIGURE 45-30 In first range, clutches C-1 and C-5 are applied, and only the P-3 planetary gear set is involved in the power flow.

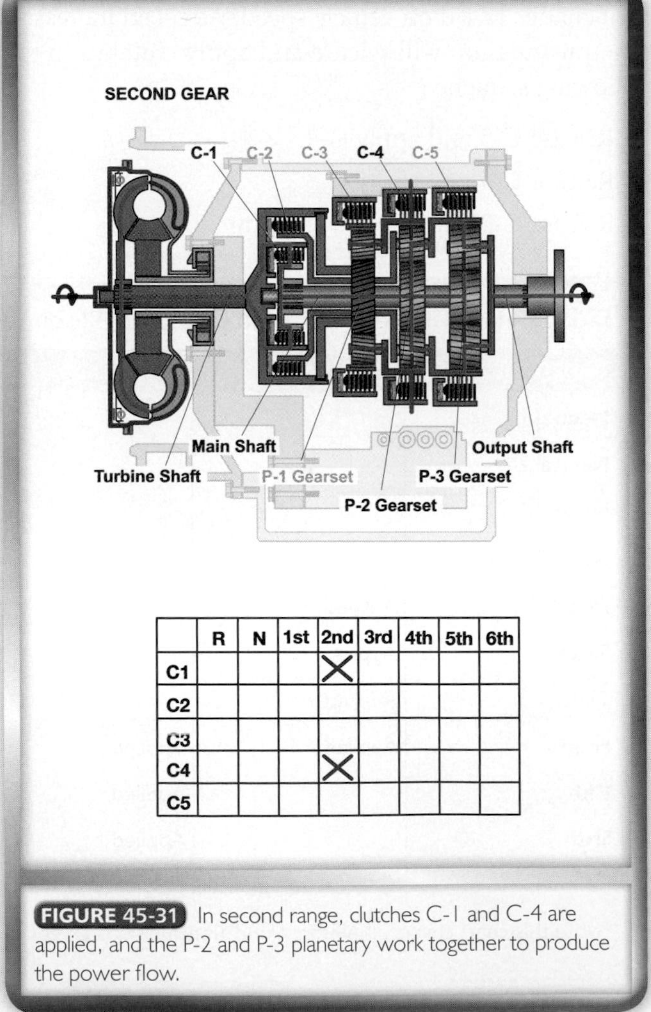

	R	N	1st	2nd	3rd	4th	5th	6th
C1				X				
C2								
C3								
C4				X				
C5								

FIGURE 45-31 In second range, clutches C-1 and C-4 are applied, and the P-2 and P-3 planetary work together to produce the power flow.

held member. In this configuration, the P-3 sun gear is input, the P-3 ring gear acts as a held member, and the P-3 carrier becomes the final output and is splined to the output shaft.

In this power flow, the only change to the output speed over first range comes from the rotation of the P-3 ring gear. Its movement adds to the rotation of the P-3 carrier.

WT Third Range

As long as the selected range is higher than second, the transmission will automatically shift to third range when conditions are correct. Third range is a compound power flow that uses all three planetary gear sets FIGURE 45-32.

When the shift to third range is made:

- C-4 clutch is released.
- C-3 clutch is applied.
- C-3 holds the P-1 planetary ring gear stationary.
- C-1 clutch remains applied.

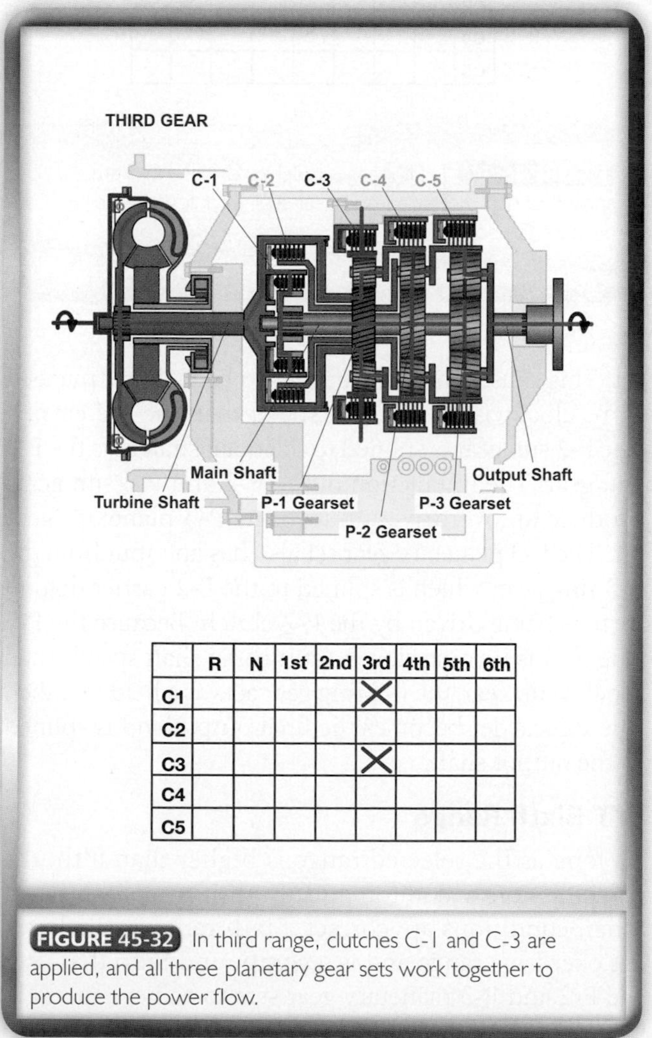

	R	N	1st	2nd	3rd	4th	5th	6th
C1					X			
C2								
C3					X			
C4								
C5								

FIGURE 45-32 In third range, clutches C-1 and C-3 are applied, and all three planetary gear sets work together to produce the power flow.

Here's how the power flow occurs in the shift to third range. The P-1 sun gear is part of the rotating clutch module and therefore rotates with it. That makes the P-1 sun gear an input to the P-1 planetary gear set. The P-1 ring gear is held by C-3, and the P-1 carrier becomes output. The P-1 carrier is splined to the P-2 ring gear, so they both rotate together. Because the C-1 clutch is still applied, the P-2 planetary gear set now has two inputs: the P-2 sun gear and the P-2 ring gear. The P-2 ring gear, however, is turning slower than the P-2 sun gear, and so the P-2 ring gear acts as a held member. The P-2 carrier, then, becomes output of the P-2 planetary gear set, and the P-2 carrier is turning faster than it did in second range because of the rotation of the P-2 ring gear. The P-2 car-rier is splined to the P-3 ring gear, so it is turning also.

As in the second range, the P-3 ring gear provides a second input into the P-3 planetary gear set, but now the P-3 ring gear is turning at increased speed. The P-3 sun gear is still being driven by the C-1 clutch and the main shaft, so the P-3 sun gear still turns faster than the P-3 ring gear. The P-3 carrier becomes the fi nal output, and it is splined to the output shaft. The ratio in third range is created by P-1 adding speed to P-2 and then P-2 add-ing speed to P-3.

WT Fourth Range

As long as the selected range is higher than third, the transmission will automatically shift to fourth range when conditions are correct. Fourth range is a simple planetary power flow that involves only the P-3 planetary gear set FIGURE 45-33.

In fourth range, C-3 clutch is released, C-2 clutch applies, and C-1 clutch remains applied. The power flow is achieved in the following sequence: C-1 clutch delivers rotational power to the main shaft and the P-3 sun gear; and C-2 cutch delivers rotational power through the P-2 carrier to the P-3 ring gear, which is splined to it. This gives the P-3 planetary gear set two inputs rotating at the same speed. The P-3 carrier must then also rotate at the same speed, as it is splined to the output shaft. This provides a direct or a one-to-one ratio.

In fourth range, even though the power flow is through the P-3 planetary gear set, the interconnections of the drive train components means that they all turn as one unit at the same speed x. Remember that the P-2 planetary has two inputs as well: the P-2 planetary carrier and the P-2 sun gear (from the main shaft). That double input makes the P-2 ring gear turn at the same speed x. The P-2 ring gear is splined to the P-1 carrier, and the P-1 sun gear is part of the rotating clutch module. That means the P-1 planetary gear set also has two inputs, and therefore its ring gear must also turn at the same speed

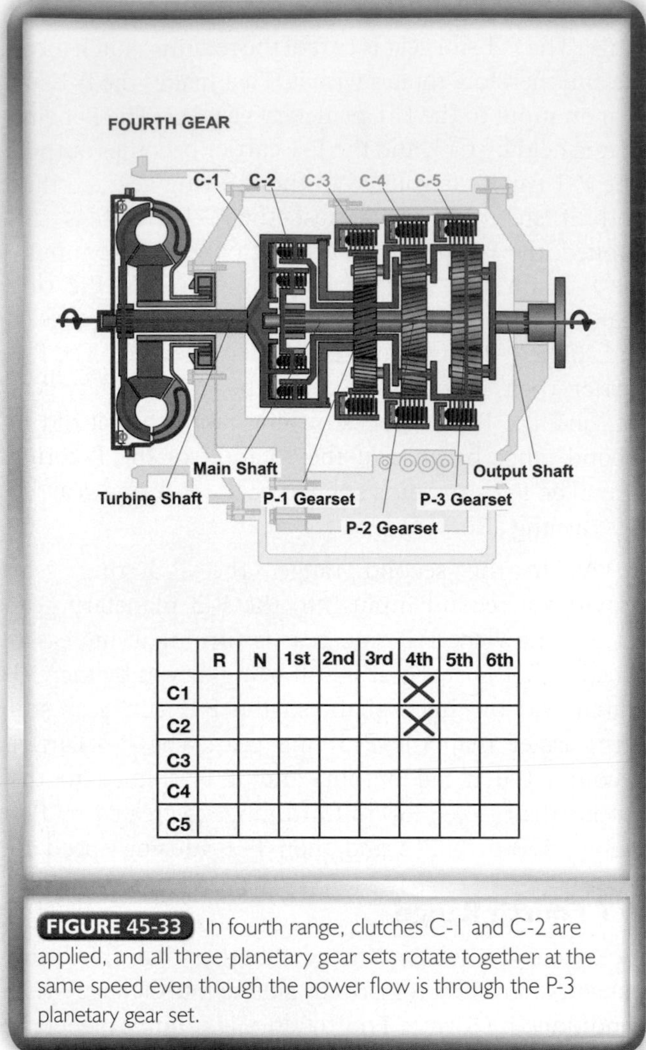

	R	N	1st	2nd	3rd	4th	5th	6th
C1						X		
C2						X		
C3								
C4								
C5								

FIGURE 45-33 In fourth range, clutches C-1 and C-2 are applied, and all three planetary gear sets rotate together at the same speed even though the power flow is through the P-3 planetary gear set.

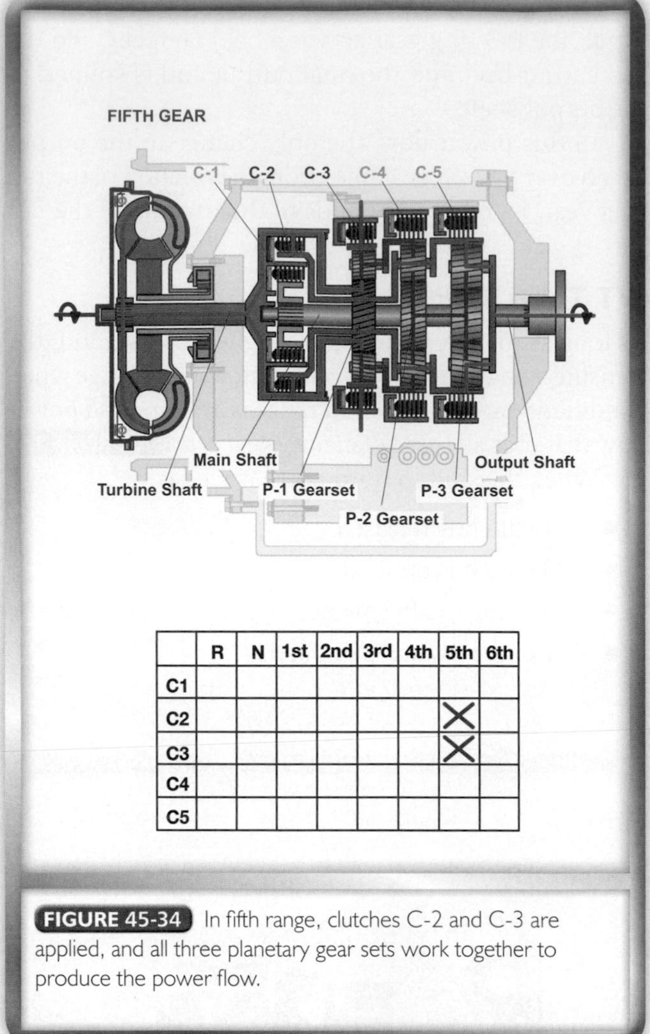

	R	N	1st	2nd	3rd	4th	5th	6th
C1								
C2							X	
C3							X	
C4								
C5								

FIGURE 45-34 In fifth range, clutches C-2 and C-3 are applied, and all three planetary gear sets work together to produce the power flow.

So, in fourth range, the rotating clutch module and all three planetary gear sets are all turning as one unit at the same speed as the turbine shaft.

WT Fifth Range

As long the selected range is higher than fourth, the transmission will automatically shift into fifth range when conditions are correct. Fifth range is the first of two overdrive ranges and is a compound planetary gear flow that uses all three planetary gear sets to achieve the final ratio **FIGURE 45-34**.

In fifth range, C-2 and C-3 are applied and produce the following power flow. The P-1 sun gear is part of the rotating clutch module and therefore always provides rotational input to P-1. C-3 is holding the P-1 ring gear stationary, and so the P-1 carrier becomes output. The P-1 carrier is splined to the P-2 ring gear, and so it becomes one of two inputs to the P-2 planetary gear set. C-2 clutch is applied and supplies rotational input to the P-2 carrier, which is the second input to the P-2 planetary gear set. This causes the P-2 sun gear to become output as it turns clockwise at a higher speed than the P-2 carrier. The P-2 sun gear is splined to the main shaft as is the P-3 sun gear. The interaction of the P-2 and P-3 sun gears produce an overdrive input to the P-3 planetary gear set. The P-3 planetary gear set also has an input from the P-3 ring gear, which is splined to the P-2 carrier that, in turn, is being driven by the P-2 clutch. Because the P-3 ring gear is turning slower (at turbine shaft speed) than the P-3 sun gear, the P-3 ring gear acts as a held member. The P-3 carrier becomes the final output and is splined to the output shaft.

WT Sixth Range

As long as the selected range is higher than fifth, the transmission will automatically shift into sixth range when conditions are correct. Sixth range is the highest overdrive range and is a compound ratio that uses the P-2 and P-3 planetary gear sets to achieve the ratio **FIGURE 45-35**.

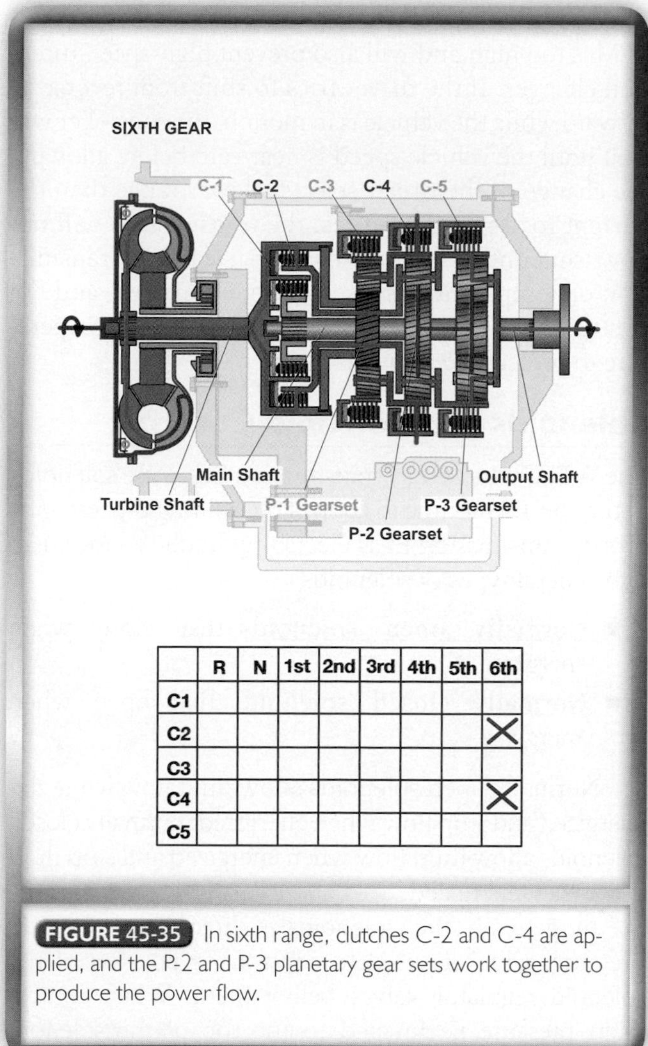

	R	N	1st	2nd	3rd	4th	5th	6th
C1								
C2								X
C3								
C4								X
C5								

FIGURE 45-35 In sixth range, clutches C-2 and C-4 are applied, and the P-2 and P-3 planetary gear sets work together to produce the power flow.

In sixth range C-2 and C-4 are applied, C-2 supplies rotational input to the P-2 carrier, and C-4 holds the P-2 ring gear stationary. That flow makes the P-2 sun gear output at an even faster overdrive than it did in fifth range. Why is it faster? Because when (a) the P-2 carrier is the input member and (b) the P-2 sun gear is the output the carrier, the pinion gears use the ring gear as a reaction member to push against in order to drive the sun gear. In fifth range, the reaction member (the P-2 ring gear) is moving away from the input member (the carrier), so the sun gear is not pushed as much. In sixth range, the ring gear is held stationary, and that allows the full reaction, or push, and allows the sun gear to have a higher speed output. The P-2 sun gear is splined to the main shaft, as is the P-3 sun gear, so the P-3 planetary gear set again has two inputs: the P-3 sun gear and the P-3 ring gear. The P-3 ring gear is splined to the P-2 carrier and, therefore, driven by the C-2 clutch. The P-3 ring gear, however, is rotating slower (at turbine speed) than the P-3 sun gear (overdrive), and so the P-3 ring gear acts as a held member. That causes the P-3 carrier to become final output, as it is splined to the output shaft.

WT Reverse

In reverse, all three planetary gear sets work together to create the power flow. Reverse range will always start from neutral gear. Recall that, in neutral, C-5 is the only clutch applied, and it holds the P-3 ring gear stationary. As the operator selects reverse, the C-3 clutch is applied and in turn holds the P-1 ring gear stationary. Neither of the rotating clutches C-1 or C-2 is applied, so the rotational input in reverse must come from the P-1 sun gear. Recall that the P-1 sun gear is attached to the rotating clutch module and turns with it at all times.

So the power flow in reverse is as follows. The P-1 sun gear is input, and the P-1 ring gear is being held by the C-3 clutch. As a result, the P-1 carrier becomes output. The P-1 carrier is splined to the P-2 ring gear, making the P-2 ring gear input to the P-2 planetary set. The P-2 carrier is splined to the P-3 ring gear, which is being held stationary by the C-5 clutch, so the P-2 carrier is the held member in the P-2 gear set. Because the carrier is held, the P-2 sun gear becomes output in reverse. The P-2 sun gear is splined to the main shaft, as is the P-3 sun gear, so the P-3 sun gear becomes reverse input for the P-3 gear set. The P-3 ring gear is being held by the C-5 clutch and the P-3 carrier becomes the final output and it is splined to the output shaft. The reverse power flow is illustrated in **FIGURE 45-36**.

Electro-Hydraulic Control—WTEC II and WTEC III

Allison's electronic control system was originally called **World Transmission Electronic Control (WTEC)**. Since the original model was launched, WTEC has gone through three revisions, including WTEC11 and WTEC111. Each revision incorporated several improvements over its predecessor. The third revision was simply known as fourth generation electronic control, and the fourth and current revision is known as fifth generation electronic control. In the fourth generation, the electro-hydraulic valve body and the control strategies were altered in major ways. For that reason, we will discuss the earlier WTEC controls separately from the fourth and the current fifth generation electronic controls. Let's start by examining the WTEC 11 and WTEC 111 versions in greater detail.

Electronic Control Unit

As with earlier Allison transmissions, in the WTEC controls system, the Allison transmission Electronic Control

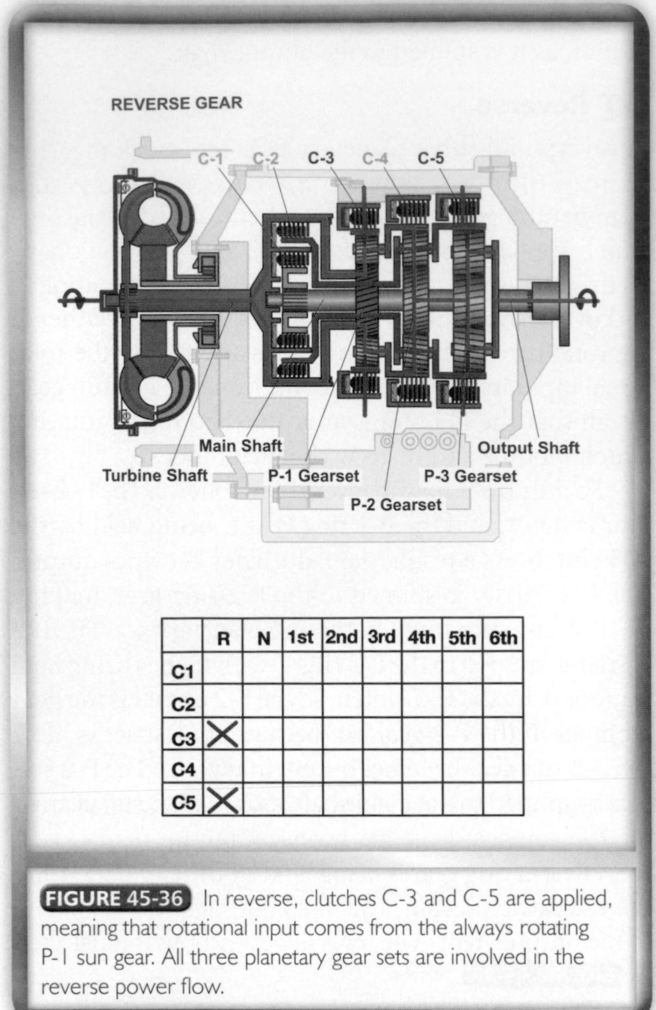

	R	N	1st	2nd	3rd	4th	5th	6th
C1								
C2								
C3	X							
C4								
C5	X							

FIGURE 45-36 In reverse, clutches C-3 and C-5 are applied, meaning that rotational input comes from the always rotating P-1 sun gear. All three planetary gear sets are involved in the reverse power flow.

Unit, or ECU, is completely drive by wire. That is, the driver has no mechanical input to the transmission.

The transmission ECU receives input information from a number of sources. Feedback information comes from the transmission itself in the form of output speed, input speed, engine speed, transmission temperature, transmission oil level, and the solenoids. The ECU also receives input from the driver's interface via the shift selector. Input from various optional input functions come through the vehicle interface wiring (VIW) or through the vehicle interface module (VIM). Finally, the ECU receives input from the electronic engine, namely from the throttle position sensor.

The transmission ECU then uses all of that information to control shifting, diagnose transmission operation, and control output and input functions that control the numerous available features of the transmission, such as shift interlocks, remote shift selectors, and power take-off operation.

The transmission control also has various self-preservation strategies to protect the transmission from abuse. The controller will inhibit neutral to range shifts if input RPM is too high and will also prevent high-speed direction changes. If the driver tries to shift from reverse to forward while the vehicle is in motion, the controller will wait until the vehicle speed is near zero before allowing the change. If the driver selects a lower range than the current road speed requires, the transmission will not downshift until a safe speed has been reached. Transmission oil temperature is also closely monitored, and the controller will modify shift capabilities based on temperature to protect the transmission.

Solenoids and Solenoid Control

The WTEC 11 and 111 transmission ECUs use solenoids in the control module to control the shifting process. The World Transmission ECU electro-hydraulic control uses two general types of solenoids:

- **Normally open solenoids** that close when energized
- **Normally closed solenoids** that open when energized

Normally open solenoids allow fluid flow while de-energized and stop flow when energized; normally closed solenoids allow fluid flow when energized and stop fluid flow when energized.

In general, the solenoids redirect control main pressure, which is used to control the position of the solenoid regulator valves below them. When control main pressure is directed to the top of the solenoid regulator valve, the valve is positioned down in its bore and directs main pressure to the appropriate clutch apply-ing it. This process is illustrated in **FIGURE 45-37** under solenoid E. Main pressure that was dead-heading at the solenoid regulator valve is thereby able to fl ow into the clutch apply passage.

Solenoids A and B are normally open (N/O) solenoids. Solenoids C, D, E, and F are normally closed (N/C) solenoids. Solenoid A controls C-1 clutch; solenoid B controls C-2 clutch; solenoid C controls C-3 clutch; solenoid D controls C-4 clutch; solenoid E controls C-5 clutch; and solenoid F controls the torque converter lock-up clutch. All models of the Allison WTEC 11 and 111 transmission contain an additional solenoid—solenoid G. Solenoid G is a normally closed solenoid that controls the position of the C-1 and C-2 latch valves. (We will cover the latch valves in greater detail later in the chapter).

The solenoids used with the WTEC controlled transmission are controlled by the transmission ECU using a pulse-width-modulated circuit. **Pulse-width modulation** means that the control command to the solenoid is pulsed on and off at a set frequency. There are two levels

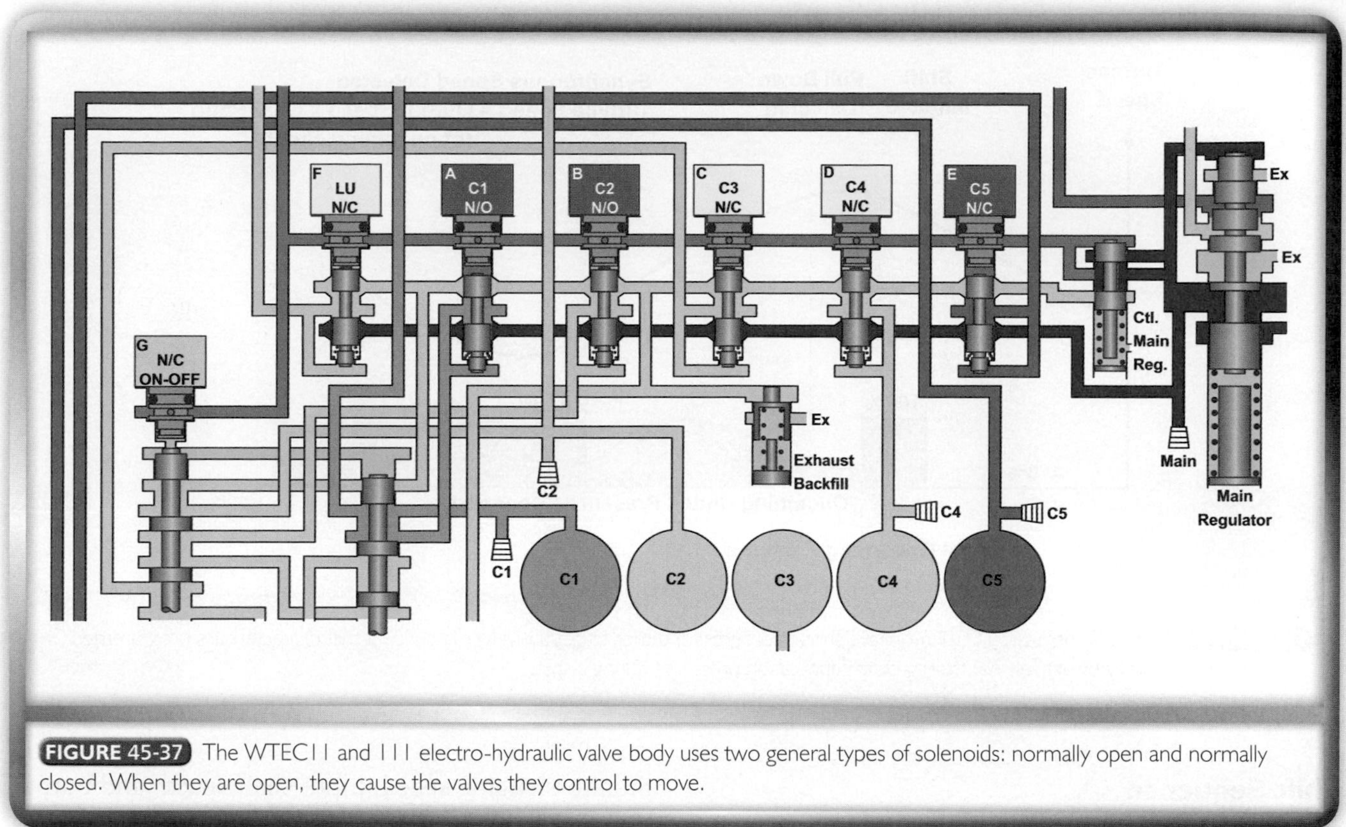

FIGURE 45-37 The WTEC I I and I I I electro-hydraulic valve body uses two general types of solenoids: normally open and normally closed. When they are open, they cause the valves they control to move.

of pulse-width modulation used—primary modulation and secondary modulation.

Primary modulation is the control used to actually open the solenoid to allow fluid flow to control the clutch application. The primary modulation control is set at 63 hertz meaning that the control current to the solenoid is turned on and off 63 times a second. The computer alters the duty cycle of the solenoid current to precisely control the speed of the clutch application. The **duty cycle** is the amount of time during each 1/63 of a second that the current is allowed to flow to the solenoid.

Secondary or (sub-modulation), means that the control current being modulated at 63 hertz and controlling the solenoids is itself being modulated at 7,812 hertz. This sub-modulation allows the transmission ECU to provide a constant average current to the solenoids. The secondary or sub-modulation is too fast to interfere with primary modulation controlling the solenoid opening but allows the ECU to increase or decrease the current to the solenoids to account for differences in operating temperature, voltage fluctuations, and solenoid degradation. The secondary modulation leads to more consistent solenoid response.

Shift Control Logic

The WTEC is programmed to adapt to provide optimum shift characteristics regardless of changes in vehicle load, terrain, and transmission component wear (e.g., solenoid degradation or clutch wear). The control has a flash memory that is programmed with the optimal shift calibrations for a given vocation. The transmission inputs—engine speed, turbine speed, output shaft speed, throttle percentage, engine and transmission temperature, and so on—allow the transmission to compare actual shifts to the pre-programmed optimal shifts FIGURE 45-38.

The controller compares each shift in progress to a set of pre-programmed values. Then the next time a shift of that kind is made, the controller adjusts the control signal of the solenoid such that the actual shift profile matches the desired shift profile.

The transmission has two adaptive modes—fast adaptive and slow adaptive. **Fast adaptive** is used when the transmission is new and makes large changes to bring the shift close to the optimal profile quickly. After the shift is close to the profile in memory (this is called convergence), the transmission switches to slow adaptive mode. In **slow adaptive** mode, the transmission makes small changes to the shifts. These small changes are designed to make up for transmission clutch wear and solenoid drift or degradation. After a transmission has been rebuilt, or if a new transmission is being installed, the controller should be reset to fast adaptive, using the Allison DOC electronic service tool or a similar device, so the shifts will reach convergence as soon as possible.

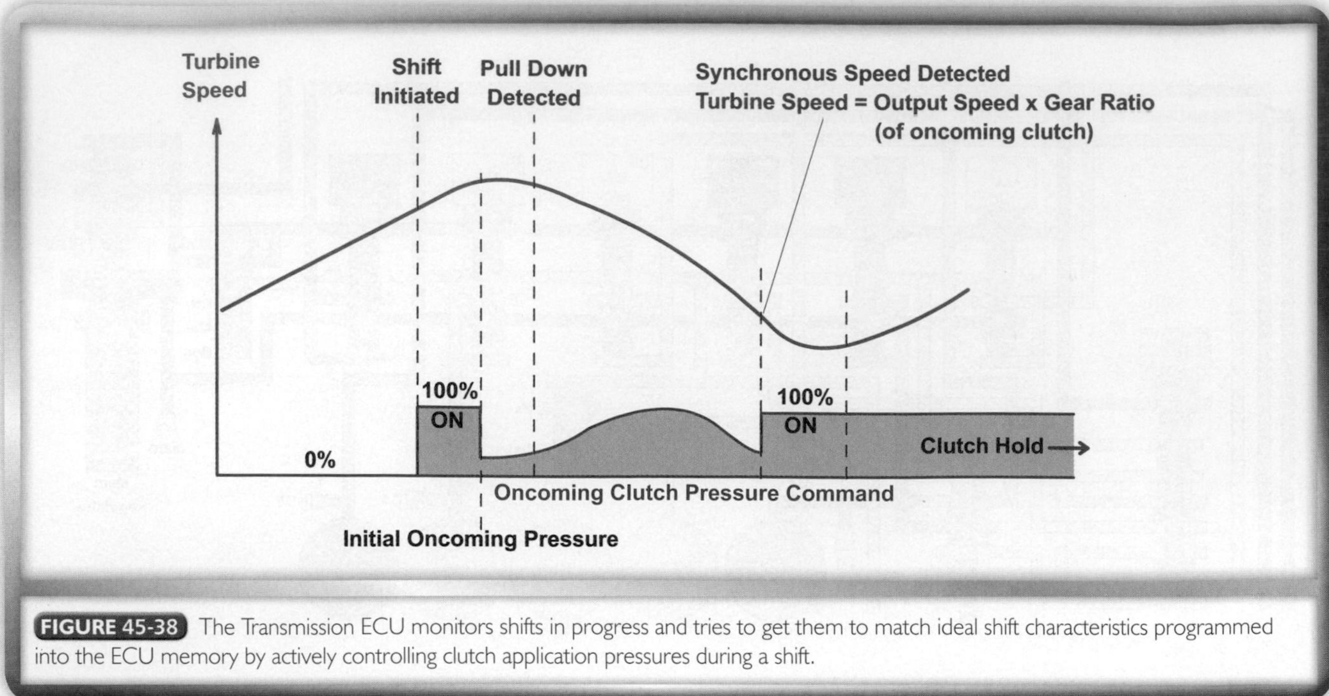

FIGURE 45-38 The Transmission ECU monitors shifts in progress and tries to get them to match ideal shift characteristics programmed into the ECU memory by actively controlling clutch application pressures during a shift.

Shift Sequence

The transmission monitors turbine speed to determine when a shift should be initiated. FIGURE 45-39 illustrates the shift sequence. As the turbine speed increases to the shift initiation point, the transmission controller commands the solenoid that controls the on-coming clutch to full pressure for a short time so that the clutch piston starts moving. This process is known as clutch fill or volume ratio. (Volume Ratio is an important diagnostic tool, for the transmission delays during this period can signal problems with specific clutches).

At the same time, the off-going clutch control solenoid is being commanded to reduce the pressure on its clutch piston. After clutch fill, the transmission applies pressure to the oncoming clutch piston at what is known as the fixed ramp rate, or **open-loop ramp rate** (meaning that the clutch pressure is being increased at a fixed rate). The off-going clutch pressure drops at a fixed **ramp-off rate** as well (meaning that the off-going clutch pressure is being reduced at a preset rate). This continues until the transmission controller detects turbine pull down. **Turbine pull down** is the reduction in turbine speed as the on-coming clutch starts to squeeze its clutch plates and the transmission is starting to attain the next range.

At this point, the off-going clutch is commanded to zero pressure, and the controller starts closed-loop control of the shift in progress. During closed loop, the controller is monitoring the decrease in turbine speed and trying to get the rate of decrease to match the ideal shift profile in its calibration. The controller constantly monitors engine speed, input shaft speed, and output shaft speed. The period of this monitoring and adjusting during a shift in progress on a World Transmission is known as **closed-loop control**.

The transmission ECU is actively adjusting oncoming clutch application pressure using pulse-width modulation to control shift quality. Closed-loop control continues until **synchronous speed** is detected. Synchronous speed occurs when the output shaft speed times the gear ratio of the oncoming range equals the input shaft speed. Synchronous speed signifies that the transmission has now attained the on-coming ratio and clutch slip is no longer occurring. At this point the controller commands the on-coming clutch solenoid to 100% duty cycle to fully clamp the piston and the clutch plates with full main pressure. This period is called **time to full apply (TFA)**. After TFA, the solenoid duty cycle is reduced to clutch hold. Full main pressure will be maintained in the clutch with less current actually flowing through the solenoid.

Range Verification and Ratio Tests

The transmission controller initiates a series of tests at each stage of a shift in progress—and even when no shifts are in progress. When no shifts are in progress, the transmission controller initiates a **range verification test** to ensure that the transmission is in a selected range FIGURE 45-40. This enables the transmission controller to compare output speed times the gear ratio to the turbine speed and determine if the clutch is slipping.

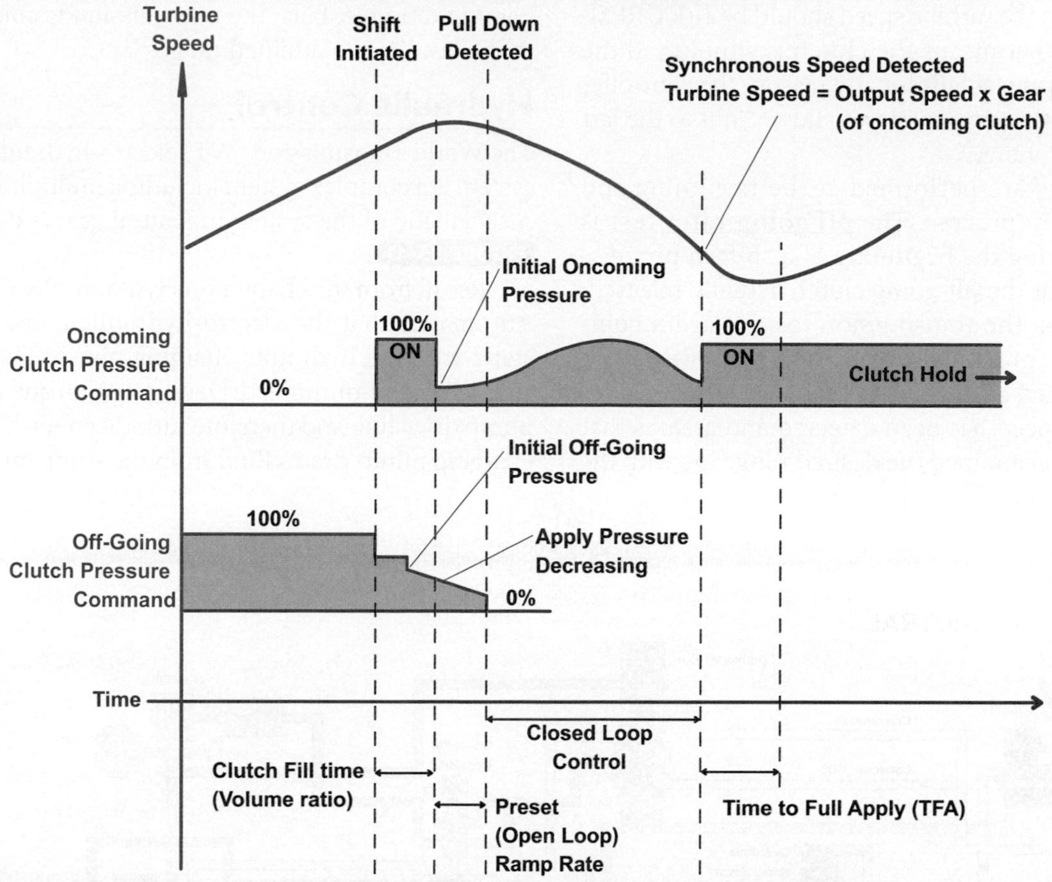

FIGURE 45-39 The transmission ECU sends signals to on-coming and off-going clutch solenoids to control the shift in progress.

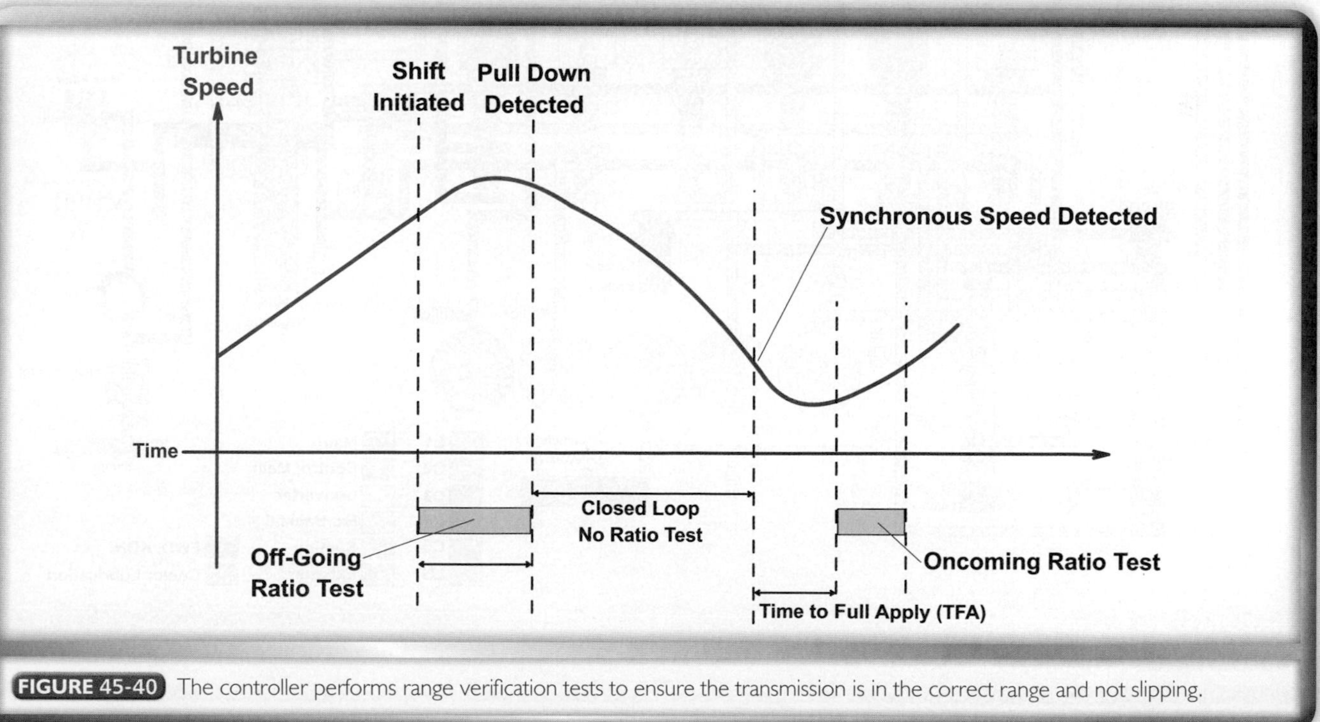

FIGURE 45-40 The controller performs range verification tests to ensure the transmission is in the correct range and not slipping.

For example, if the output speed is 250 RPM and the gear ratio is 4:1, then the turbine speed should be 1,000 RPM. If it is higher, that means the clutch is slipping. If the range verification test fails for any reason, the controller will command the transmission to down shift to the last known attained range.

Ratio tests are performed at the beginning and end of a shift in process. The **off-going ratio test** is performed during the beginning of a shift in progress and assures that the off-going clutch actually released. If this test fails, the transmission is once again commanded to the previous range. The **on-coming ratio test** is performed at the end of a shift in progress after synchronous speed has been detected and assures that the transmission attained the desired range. As with the range verification and off-going ratio tests, if the on-coming ratio test fails, the transmission is commanded to the last known attained range.

Hydraulic Control

The World Transmission (WT) electro-hydraulic control system is a complex system including multiple elements. A schematic of the system in neutral gear is depicted in **FIGURE 45-41**.

Recall from the chapter on Hydraulically Controlled Automatics that the electro-hydraulic control system starts with the hydraulic charging pump. The gerotor-style charging pump is driven by the torque converter pump drive hub and therefore turns at engine speed. The charging pump draws fluid from the sump and delivers

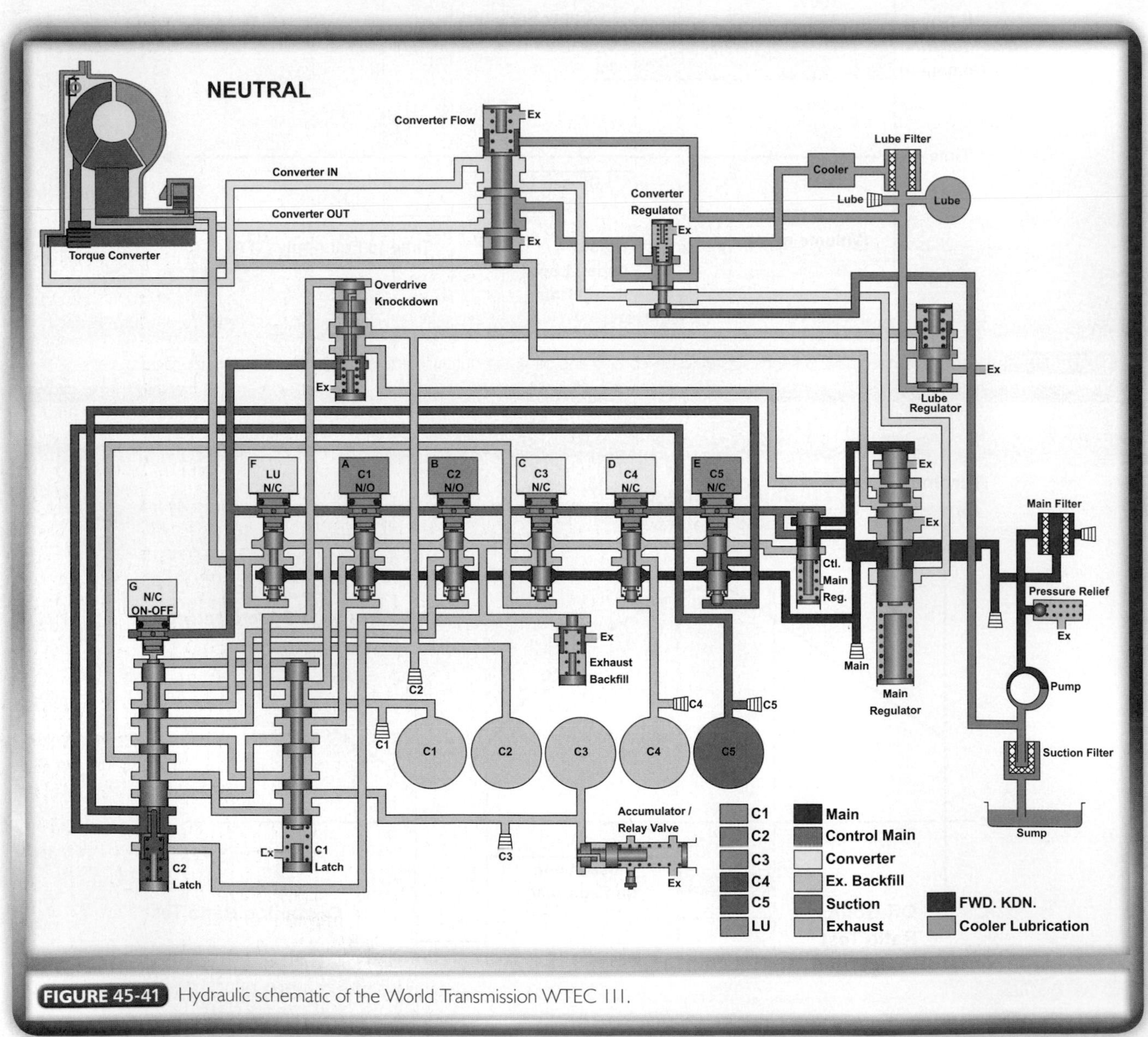

FIGURE 45-41 Hydraulic schematic of the World Transmission WTEC III.

it through the main filter and onto the main pressure regulator valve (MPRV), which is a normally closed spring-loaded valve. The fluid then flows through the MPRV and onto the solenoid regulator valves. Fluid pressure is also directed to the top of the MPRV, and as pressure increases, fluid forces the valve down in its bore. In moving down, the valve opens a passage to the torque converter. Further movement of the MPRV opens a passage to the exhaust hydraulic circuit (to the oil sump), and then the valve becomes balanced between spring force at the bottom and fluid pressure at the top.

This process sets main pressure for the transmission. In neutral and reverse, main pressure is at its highest—between 275 and 320 psi depending on transmission model. Main pressure also varies depending on the transmission range and operating mode. The circuit to the MPRV contains a pressure relief valve this valve is set to exhaust main pressure at 600 psi. TABLE 45-6 shows the ranges for main and lube pressure for each gear.

Fluid going to the MPRV is also directed to the top of the solenoid regulator valve. As pressure moves this valve down in its bore, the pressure opens a passage to the solenoids. The valve will become balanced at

> **TECHNICIAN TIP**
>
> Main pressure varies slightly from model to model up to WTEC III.
>
> The Allison Fourth Generation Electronic control has more complete control of main pressure due to the modulated main solenoid.

TABLE 45-6: Main Pressure and Lube Pressure for Each Gear

MAIN PRESSURE		
Gear	**Lock-Up**	**Pressure**
Neutral and Reverse	Lock-up not applied	275-320 psi
Forward with converter active	Lock-up not applied	239- 285 psi
2, 3, 4	Lock-up applied	165-205 psi
5, 6	Lock-up applied	155-175 psi

LUBE PRESSURE	
Gear	**Pressure**
Neutral, Reverse, 1, 2, 3	22 psi
4, 5, 6	17 psi

100 psi. This new pressure is known as control main pressure and is the pressure that transmission solenoids will redirect to control the position of the solenoid regulator valves at the bottom of each shift control solenoid (solenoids A, B, C, D, E and the converter control solenoid F).

Solenoid Fluid Flows

The solenoids control the flow of pressurized hydraulic fluid to apply the clutches necessary to attain each range. Solenoids are operated both to apply on-coming clutches and release off-going clutches as a shift occurs. Let's examine more closely the solenoid operation and fluid flows for each range.

WTEC Neutral Fluid Flow

As was illustrated in Figure 45-41, solenoids A, B, and E are energized when the transmission is in neutral. Because solenoids A and B are normally open, they stop fluid from flowing to their solenoid regulator valves and thereby prevent their respective clutches from being applied. Solenoid E is normally closed, so, when it is energized, its solenoid regulator valve is positioned down. That downward position acts to direct main pressure to the C-5 clutch. The result is that the C-5 clutch is applied, and because it is the only applied clutch, neutral is obtained. This is the process for a transmission in neutral when the vehicle is not in motion.

If, however, the transmission is in neutral while the vehicle is moving, the transmission ECU will energize solenoid E then D then C then D again, depending on the rotational speed of the transmission's components. These solenoids will correspond to clutch C-5, C-4, C-3, and C-4 again. By energizing those solenoids in that particular sequence, the ECU can control the rotational speed of the internal transmission components. Because only one of those solenoids is energized at any time, the transmission remains in neutral.

WTEC First Range

Solenoids B and E are energized in first range. As the driver selects first range, solenoid A is de-energized. Recall that solenoid A is normally open, so when it is de-energized, it directs control main pressure to the top of its solenoid regulator valve, causing the valve to move down in its bore. This action directs main pressure to the C-1 clutch applying it. Solenoid B remains energized, so C-2 clutch is not applied. Solenoid E remains energized, so C-5 also remains applied. Since C-1 and C-5 are applied, the transmission attains first range. This process is illustrated in FIGURE 45-42.

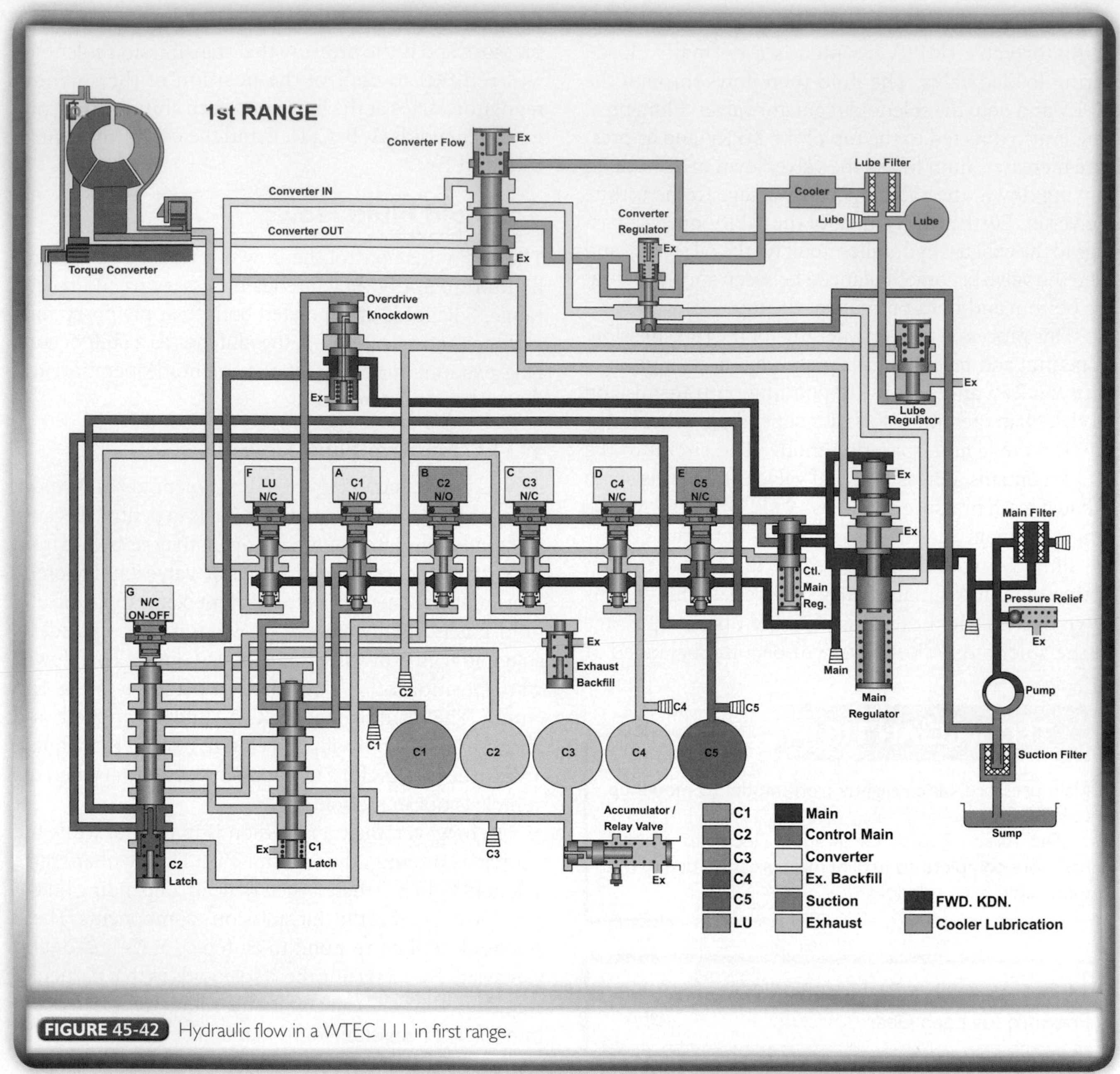

FIGURE 45-42 Hydraulic flow in a WTEC III in first range.

WTEC Second Range

In second range, the solenoids B, D, and F are energized. As the transmission shifts to second range, solenoid E is de-energized, and solenoid D is energized. That action exhausts C-5 clutch and applies C-4 clutch. Solenoid A remains de-energized, so C-1 remains applied. Solenoid B remains energized, so C-2 clutch is not applied. Because C-1 and C-4 are applied, the transmission attains second range as is shown in **FIGURE 45-43**. At this point, solenoid F is energized and applies the torque converter lock-up clutch.

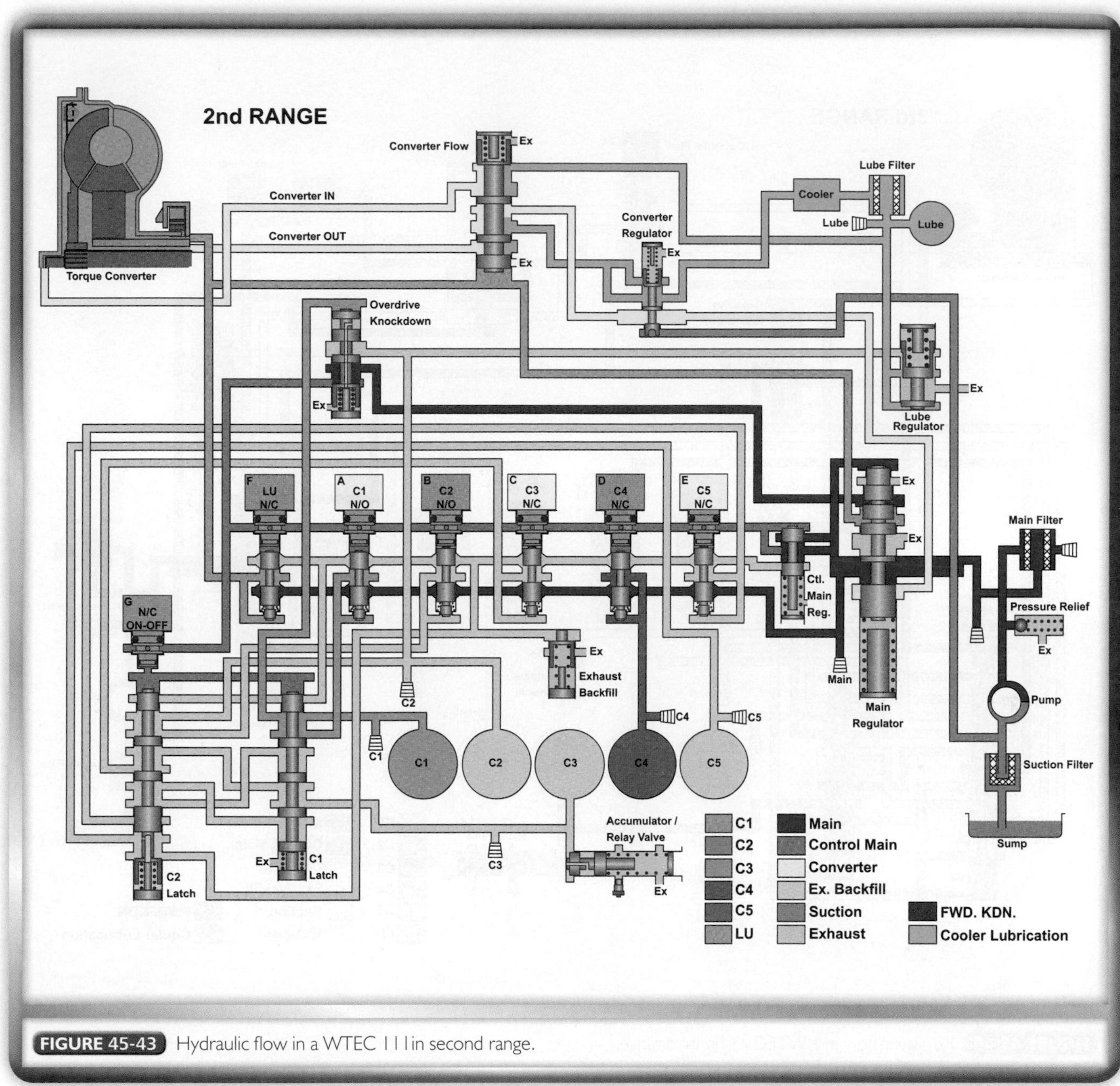

FIGURE 45-43 Hydraulic flow in a WTEC III in second range.

WTEC Third Range

In third range, solenoids B, C, and F are energized. As the transmission shifts to third range, solenoid D is de-energized, and solenoid C is energized. This process exhausts C-4 clutch and applies C-3 clutch. Solenoid A remains de-energized, so C-1 clutch remains applied. Solenoid B remains energized, so C-2 clutch is not applied. Because C-1 and C-3 are applied, the transmission attains third range, as is illustrated in FIGURE 45-44. Solenoid F remains energized applying the torque converter lock-up clutch.

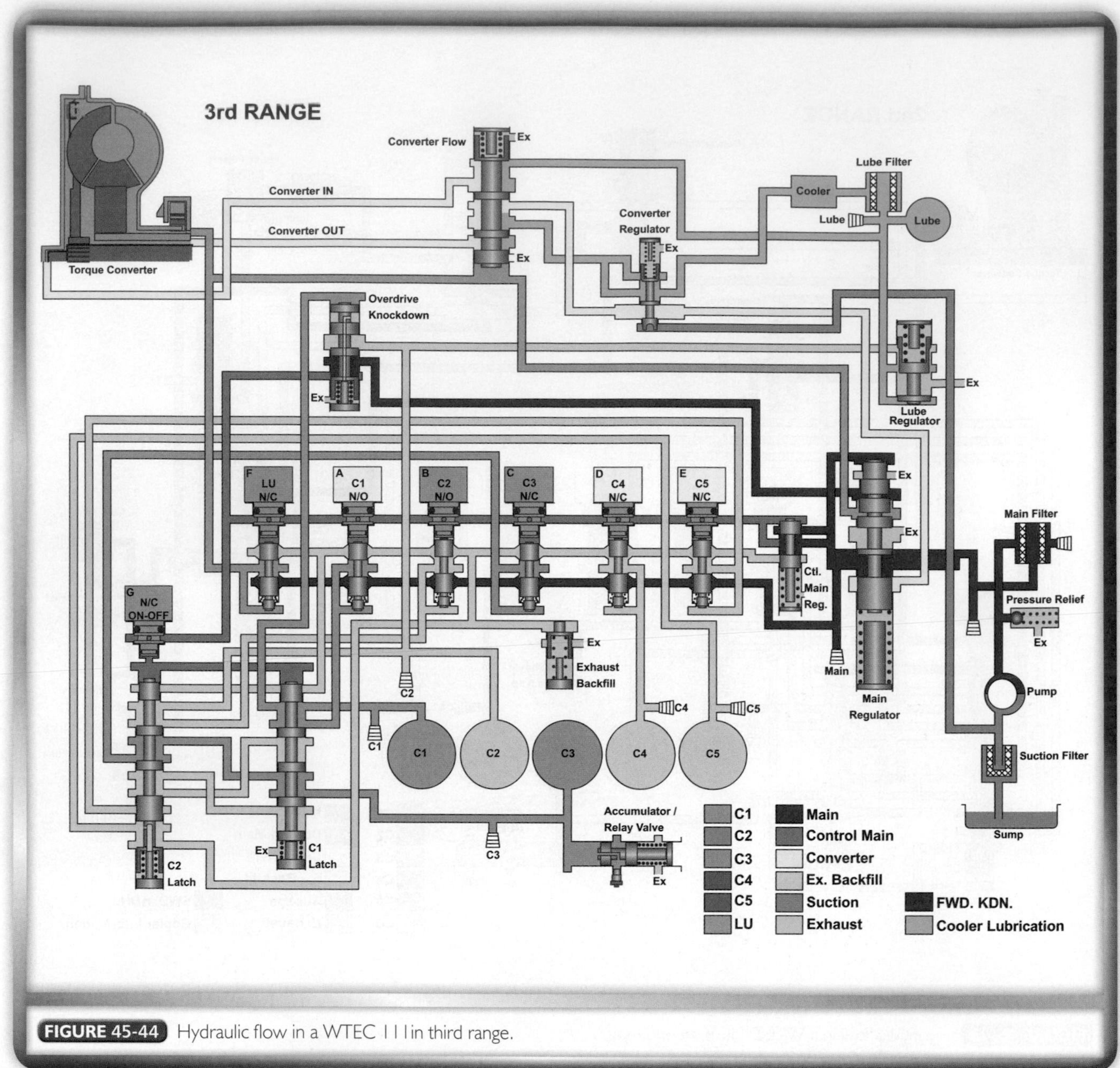

FIGURE 45-44 Hydraulic flow in a WTEC I I I in third range.

WTEC Fourth Range

When the transmission is in fourth range, solenoid F is the only energized solenoid.

As the transmission shifts to fourth range, solenoids B and C are de-energized. De-energizing solenoid C exhausts the C-3 clutch. De-energizing normally open solenoid B causes its solenoid regulator valve to move down in its bore. That process sends main pressure to the C-2 clutch and applies it. Since C-1 and C-2 are both applied, the transmission attains fourth range. FIGURE 45-45 illustrates the system in fourth range. Notice that solenoid F remains energized applying the torque converter lock-up clutch.

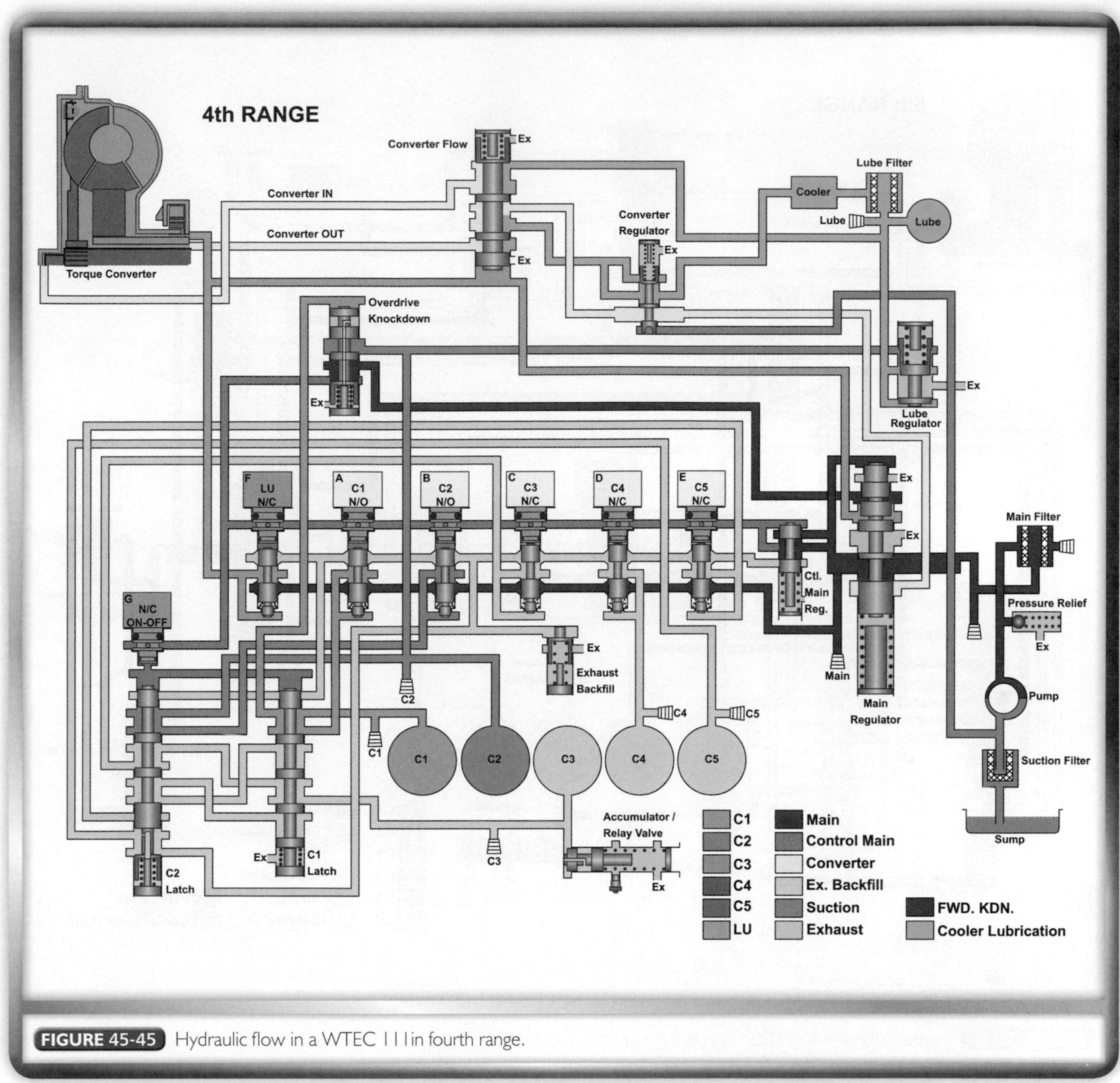

FIGURE 45-45 Hydraulic flow in a WTEC I I I in fourth range.

WTEC Fifth Range

In fifth range, solenoids A, C, and F are energized. As the transmission shifts to fifth range, solenoid A is energized, which exhausts the C-1 clutch. Solenoid B remains de-energized, keeping the C-2 clutch applied. Solenoid C is energized, and that applies the C-3 clutch. Since C-2 and C-3 are applied, the transmission attains fifth range, as is shown in FIGURE 45-46. Solenoid F again remains energized applying the torque converter lock-up clutch.

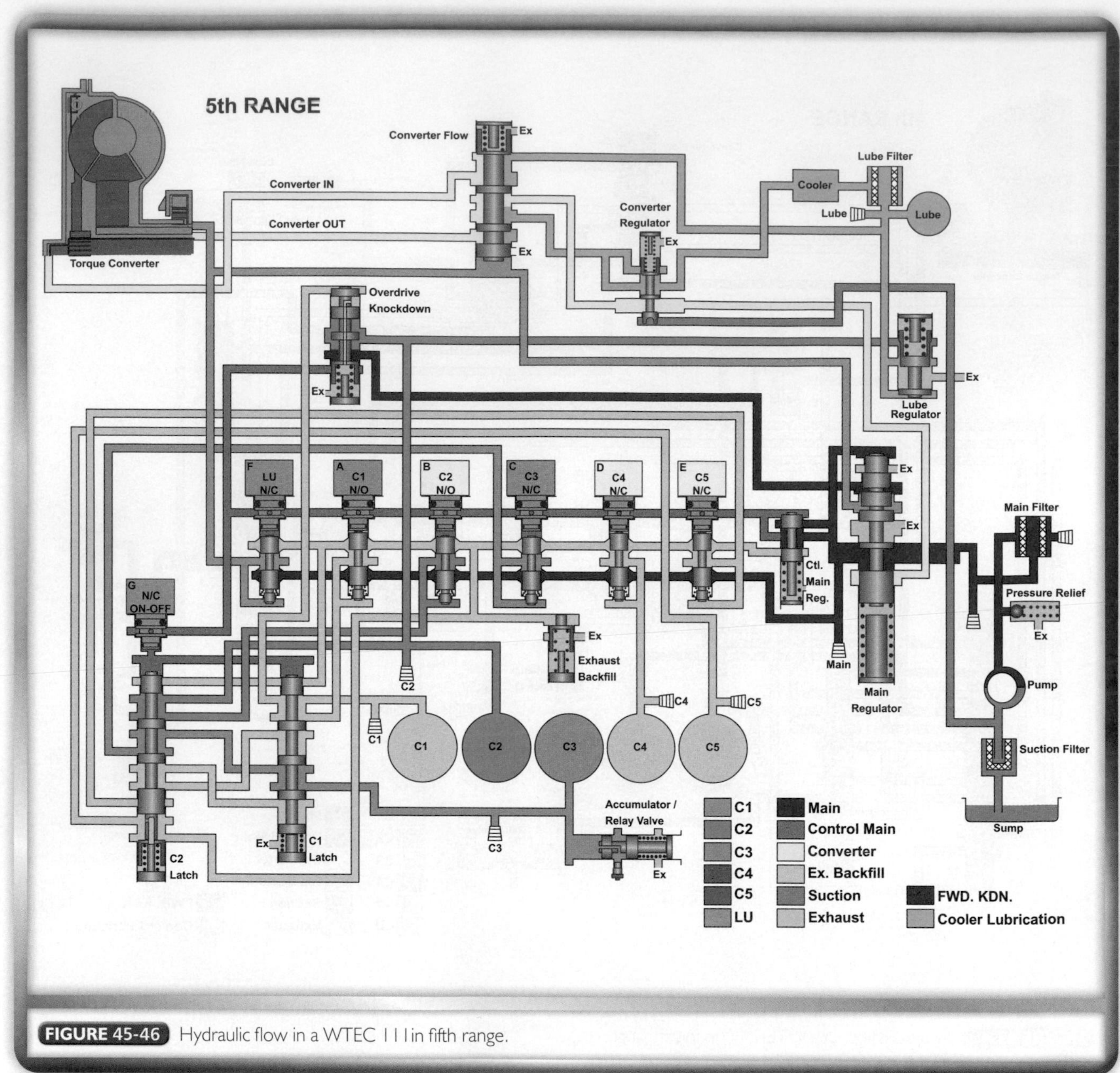

FIGURE 45-46 Hydraulic flow in a WTEC I I I in fifth range.

WTEC Sixth Range

In sixth range, solenoids A, D, and F are applied. Solenoid A remains energized keeping C-1 clutch unapplied. Solenoid B is de-energized, so C-2 remains applied. Solenoid C is de-energized, exhausting C-3 clutch. Solenoid D is energized, applying C-4 clutch. Since C-2 and C-4 are applied, the transmission attains sixth range. This is shown in **FIGURE 45-47**. Solenoid F again remains energized applying the torque converter lock-up clutch.

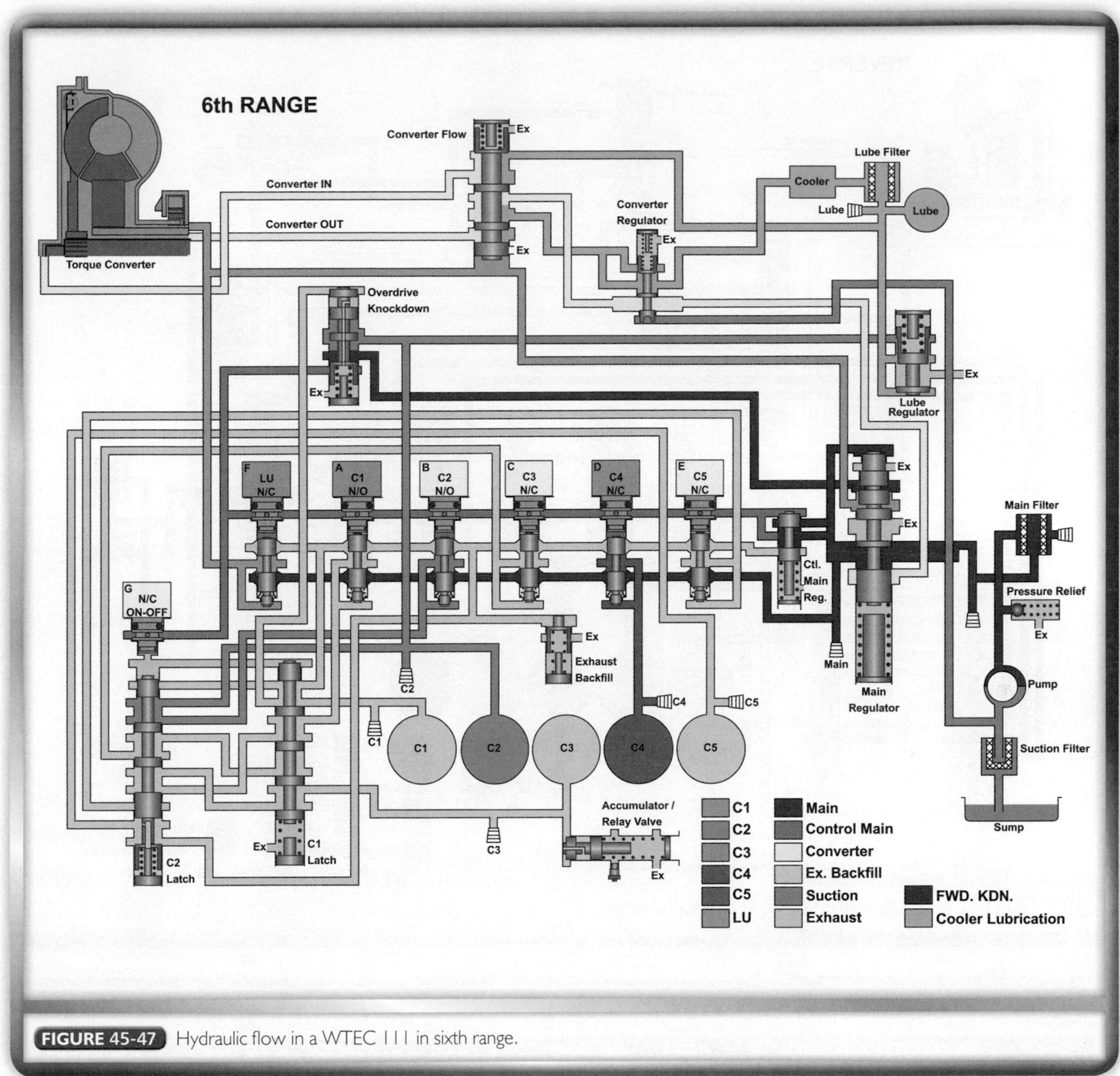

FIGURE 45-47 Hydraulic flow in a WTEC 111 in sixth range.

WTEC Reverse

In reverse, solenoids A, B, C, and E are energized. Reverse will start from a neutral position. Recall that in neutral, solenoids A, B, and E are energized. Energizing normally open solenoid A means that C-1 clutch is not applied. Energizing normally open solenoid B means that C-2 clutch is not applied. Normally closed solenoid E is energized, and that applies C-5 clutch. As the driver selects reverse, normally closed solenoid C is energized, which applies the C-3 clutch. Since C-5 and C-3 are applied, the transmission attains reverse. FIGURE 45-48 illustrates the WTEC 111 transmission in reverse.

As a review for the section on solenoid fluid flows, TABLE 45-7 shows the position of each solenoid in each range.

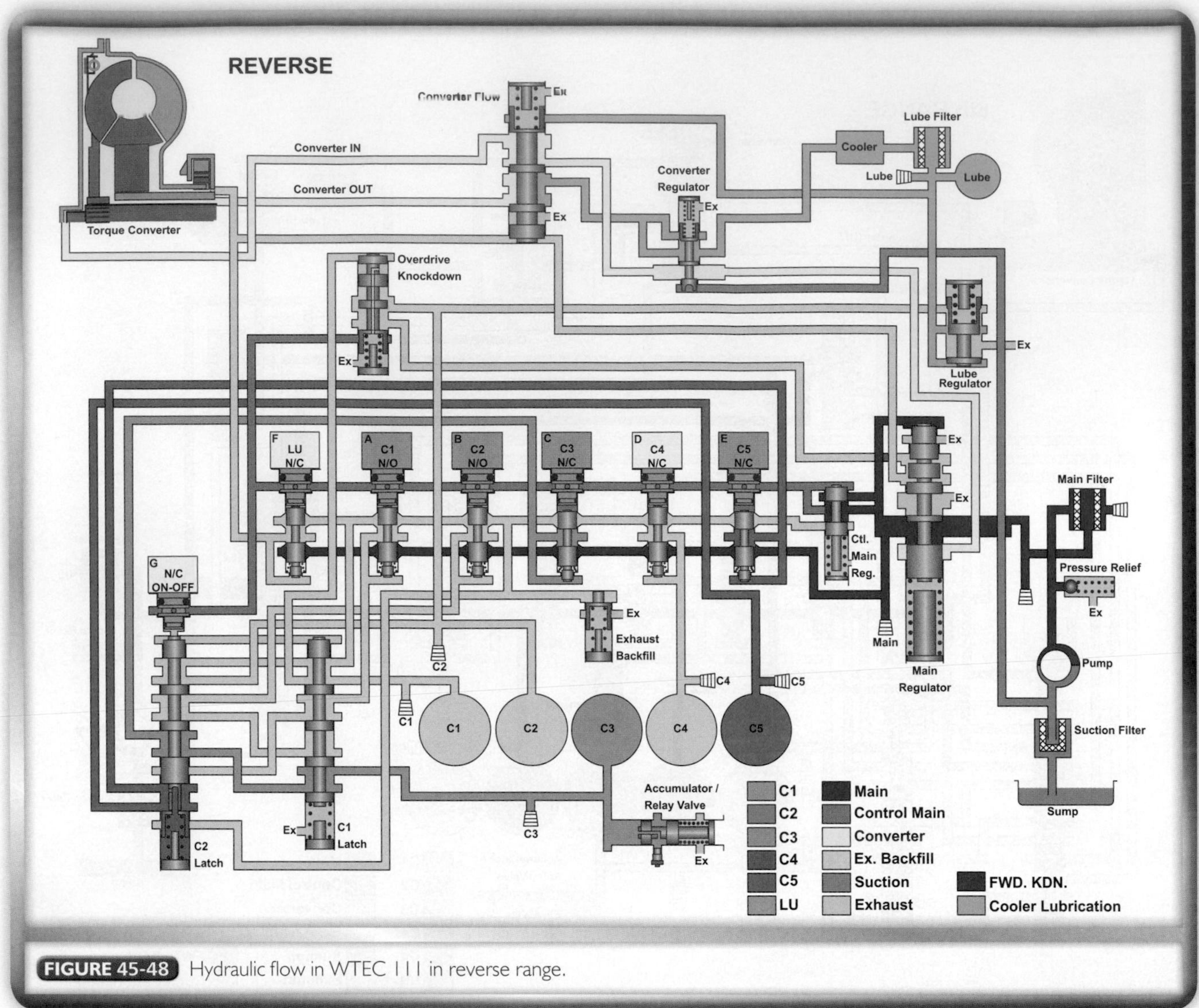

FIGURE 45-48 Hydraulic flow in WTEC 111 in reverse range.

TABLE 45-7: Solenoid Position in Each Range

Range	A (N/O)	B (N/O)	C (N/C)	D (N/C)	E (N/C)	F (N/C)	G (N/C)	Applied Clutches
Neutral 1	ON	ON			ON			C-5
Neutral 2	ON	ON		ON				C-4
Neutral 3	ON	ON	ON					C-3
Neutral 4	ON	ON		ON				C-4
Reverse	ON	ON	ON		ON			C-3 / C-5
First		ON			ON			C-1 / C-5
Second		ON		ON		ON*	ON	C-1 / C-4
Third		ON	ON			ON*	ON	C-1 / C-3
Fourth						ON*	ON	C-1 / C-2
Fifth	**ON**		**ON**			**ON***	**ON**	**C-2 / C-3**
Sixth	ON			ON		ON*		C-2 / C-4

* Solenoid F controls the lock-up and is normally energized in all ranges above first. Under certain operating conditions, however, solenoid F may be de-energized.

Latch Valves

The WTEC transmission utilizes two latch valves, C-1 latch and C-2 latch, to assure failsafe operation during electrical failure FIGURE 45-49. **Failsafe operation** occurs when the transmission control system is not operating due to electrical failure. The transmission's hydraulics are designed to allow minimal function so that the vehicle can be moved. The C-1 and C-2 latch play the main role in failsafe operation. The two latch valves are spring-loaded spool valves, and during normal operation, their position is controlled by normally closed solenoid G. The fluid is directed in such a way to apply clutches C-1, C-2, C-3, and C-5 from solenoids A, B, C, and E. That fluid must flow through one or both latch valves on the way to the clutches. Solenoids D (C-4) and F (lock-up clutch) are the only solenoids that send fluid directly to the clutches they control.

When solenoid G is energized, it directs control main pressure to the top of both latch valves. That application of pressure tries to move the valves down in their bore against spring pressure. The valves may or may not move, however, depending on the fluid flow through them. Fluid flow through the valves may keep them in a closed position—even though the G solenoid is energized.

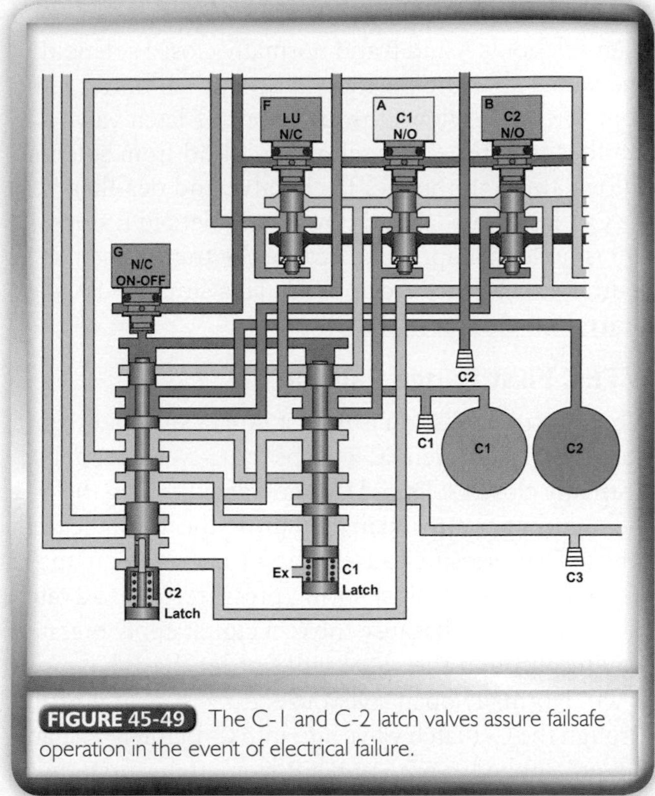

FIGURE 45-49 The C-1 and C-2 latch valves assure failsafe operation in the event of electrical failure.

Latch Valve Fluid Flows

The design of the latch valves and their fluid flows allows for the following electrical failure failsafe operational modes in each gear.

- If the transmission is in neutral or reverse when electrical failure occurs, the transmission will fail to neutral with no clutches applied (NNC).
- First range will fail to third range.
- Second, third, fourth, and fifth will fail to fourth range.
- Sixth range will fail to fifth range.

These failsafe modes allow limited (limp home) operation of the transmission during electrical failure. Refer to the hydraulic flow schematic in FIGURE 45-50 as you read the following sections on latch valve fluid flows during electrical failure.

WTEC Neutral Range Failsafe

When a WTEC transmission is in neutral, solenoids A, B, and E are energized. Fluid flow from solenoid E flows through the C-2 latch valve and into the C-5 clutch. Only C-5 is applied when the transmission is in neutral.

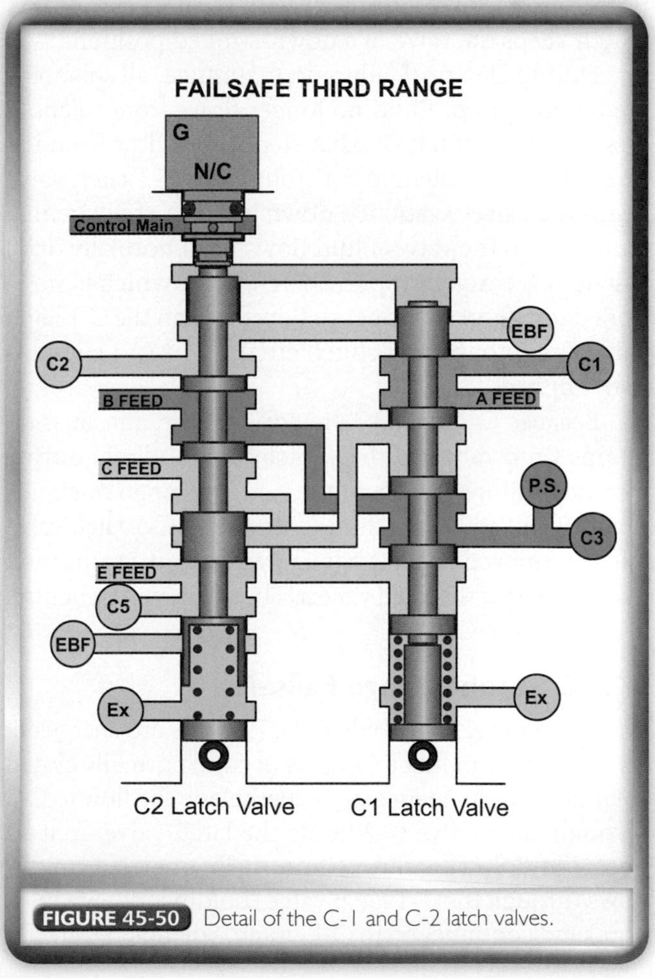

FIGURE 45-50 Detail of the C-1 and C-2 latch valves.

Electrical failure in neutral de-energizes normally open solenoids A and B and normally closed solenoid E. The latch valves are positioned up in their bores. Fluid from solenoid A flows through the C-1 latch valve and deadheads at the C-2 latch valve. Fluid from solenoid B flows through the C-2 latch valve and deadheads at the C-1 latch valve. Fluid flow from solenoid E stops, so C-5 is no longer applied. Because the transmission is in neutral, no clutches are applied. This situation is called **neutral no clutches (NCC)**.

WTEC First Range Failsafe

When the transmission is in first range, solenoids B and E are energized. Solenoid E keeps the C-5 clutch applied. Normally closed solenoid G is energized during the N-1 shift, sending control main pressure to the top of the latch valves. That pressure causes the C-1 latch valve to move down in its bore against spring pressure. The C-2 latch valve remains up because the C-5 clutch apply pressure flowing through the valve will not let the valve move down. Normally open solenoid A directs main pressure through the C-1 latch valve and into C-1 clutch. C-1 and C-5 are applied, so the transmission attains first range. After the shift, solenoid G is de-energized, but the fluid flow from solenoid A through the C-1 latch valve to C-1 clutch keeps the valve in a down-stroked position.

During electrical failure in first range, all solenoids are de-energized. Fluid no longer flows from solenoid E, so the C-5 clutch is exhausted. Fluid flow from the normally open solenoid A through the C-1 latch valve keeps the valve positioned down because of differential land sizes in the valve. Fluid flows from normally open solenoid B through the C-2 latch valve which is positioned up. Fluid continues to flow through the C-1 latch valve and into the C-3 clutch circuit. The C-3 circuit is then applied.

Because C-1 and C-3 are applied, the transmission attains third range. If the vehicle is shut down during electrical failure, on restart the normally open solenoids A and B will still allow fluid to flow. The C-1 latch valve will have moved up in its bore, however, causing the fluid to deadhead at the latch valves. The result will be neutral no clutches (NCC).

WTEC Second Range Failsafe

In second range, solenoids B, D, F, and G are energized. As the shift from first to second occurs, normally closed solenoid G is de-energized. Nonetheless, the flow to C-5 through latch valve C-2 holds the latch valve up it its bore. Fluid flowing through normally open solenoid A flows through the C-1 latch valve (holding it down in its bore) and continues on to C-1 clutch. Solenoid D directly applies the C-4 clutch—the only clutch control solenoid that does not flow through the latch valves.

As the shift is being made, normally closed solenoid E is de-energized and cuts off the flow to the C-5 clutch. After the shift has been made, solenoid G is energized, sending fluid to the top of the latch valves. As a result, latch valve C-2 will move down in its bore, and latch valve C-1 will remain down in its bore. Solenoid F is energized to apply the lock-up clutch. Because C-1 clutch and C-4 clutch are applied, the transmission attains second range.

During electrical failure in second range, all solenoids are de-energized. Normally closed solenoid D closes and stops the flow of fluid to the C-4 clutch. The fluid flow from solenoid A keeps the C-1 latch valve down in its bore and continues to supply the C-1 clutch. Fluid immediately flows from the de-energized normally open solenoid B to the C-2 latch valve, keeping it down in its bore—even though there is no pressure at the top of the valve. This fluid flows through the C-2 latch valve and on to the C-2 clutch. At that point, the C-2 clutch is applied. Normally closed solenoid F exhausts the lock-up clutch. Because C-1 and C-2 clutches are applied, the transmission attains fourth range. If the transmission is shut down, both latch valves will move back up in their bores. Upon restart, both latch valves will block the flow of fluid from normally open solenoid A and B. The result will be neutral no clutches (NCC).

WTEC Third Range Failsafe

Solenoids B, C, G, and F are energized in third range. Solenoid G keeps both latch valves down in their bores. Solenoid F applies the lock-up clutch. Normally closed solenoid C is energized. This directs fluid through the C-2 and the C-1 latch valves and into the C-3 clutch, applying it. Fluid flows from normally open solenoid A through the C-1 latch valve and into the C-1 clutch, applying it. Because C-1 and C-3 are applied, the transmission attains third range.

During electrical failure in third range, all solenoids are de-energized. Solenoid F exhausts the lock-up clutch. Solenoid C exhausts the C-3 clutch. Solenoid G exhausts the pressure from the top of the latch valves. Fluid begins to flow immediately from normally open solenoid B through the C-2 latch valve. The valve is held down in its bore. Continuation of the fluid flow applies the C-2 clutch. Fluid flow through the C-1 latch valve keeps it down in its bore and supplies C-1 clutch. Because C-1 and C-2 are applied, the transmission attains fourth range. If the vehicle is shut down, upon restart the latch valves will have moved up in their bores due to spring pressure. Flow through normally open solenoids A and

B will simply deadhead at the valves. The transmission will attain neutral no clutches (NCC).

WTEC Fourth Range Failsafe

In fourth range, solenoids G and F are energized. Solenoid G delivers pressure to the top of the latch valves, which holds them down in their bore. Fluid flows from normally open solenoid A through the C-1 latch valve and into C-1 clutch. Fluid from normally open solenoid B flows through the C-2 latch valve and into the C-2 clutch. Because the C-1 and the C-2 clutches are applied, the transmission attains fourth range. Solenoid F applies the lock-up clutch.

During electrical failure in fourth range, solenoid F exhausts the lock-up clutch. Solenoid G exhausts the pressure from the top of the latch valves, but the fluid flowing through them to C-1 and C-2 clutch keeps the valves down in their bore. Since C-1 and C-2 clutches are applied, the transmission stays in fourth range. If the vehicle is shut down, upon restart the latch valves will have moved up in their bores due to spring pressure. Flow through normally open solenoids A and B will simply deadhead at the valves, and the transmission will attain neutral no clutches (NCC).

WTEC Fifth Range Failsafe

In fifth range, solenoids A, C, G, and F are energized. Solenoid G keeps both latch valves down in their bores. Solenoid F applies the lock-up clutch. Normally closed solenoid C is energized. The energized solenoid C directs fluid through the C-2 and the C-1 latch valves and into the C-3 clutch, applying it. Fluid flows from normally open solenoid B through the C-2 latch valve and into the C-2 clutch, applying it. Because C-2 and C-3 are applied, the transmission attains fifth range.

During electrical failure in fifth range, all solenoids become de-energized. Solenoid F exhausts the lock-up clutch, and solenoid G exhausts the fluid from the top of the latch valves. Fluid flowing from normally open solenoid B through the C-2 latch valve and into the C-2 clutch keeps the valve down in its bore and the C-2 clutch applied. Fluid immediately flows from normally open solenoid A through the C-1 latch valve, keeping the valve down in its bore. Fluid flows onto the C-1 clutch, applying it. Because clutches C-1 and C-2 are applied, the transmission attains fourth range. If the vehicle is shut down, upon restart, the latch valves will have moved up in their bores due to spring pressure and flow through normally open solenoid A. Fluid flow through solenoid B will simply deadhead at the valves, and the transmission will attain neutral no clutches (NCC).

WTEC Sixth Range Failsafe

In sixth range, solenoids A, D, and F are energized. Solenoid G is de-energized. This exhausts the fluid from the top of the latch valves, and latch valve C-1 moves up in its bore. Latch valve C-2 stays down, however, because of the fluid from normally open solenoid B flowing through it and into the C-2 clutch. Solenoid F applies the lock-up clutch. Solenoid D applies the C-4 clutch. Because C-2 and C-4 are applied, the transmission attains sixth range.

During electrical failure in sixth range, all solenoids are de-energized. Solenoid F exhausts the lock-up clutch, and solenoid D exhausts the C-4 clutch. Fluid continues to flow from normally open solenoid B through the C-2 latch valve and into the C-2 clutch. Fluid immediately begins to flow from normally open solenoid A through the C-1 latch valve, which is positioned up. This fluid flows to the C-2 latch valve and through it back to another port on the C-1 latch valve. Fluid flows through this port in the C-1 latch valve and into the C-3 clutch, applying it. Because C-2 and C-3 are applied, the transmission attains fifth range. If the vehicle is shut down, upon restart the latch valves will have moved up in their bores due to spring pressure. Fluid flow through normally open solenoid A and B will simply deadhead at the valves, and the transmission will attain neutral no clutches (NCC).

WTEC Reverse Range Failsafe

When the transmission is in reverse, solenoids A, B, C, and E are energized. Solenoids A and B are normally open, so energizing them stops fluid flow. Solenoid C sends fluid pressure through the C-2 and the C-1 latch valves and into the C-3 clutch. Solenoid E sends fluid pressure through the C-2 latch valve to the C-5 clutch. Both latch valves are positioned up in their bores. Because C-3 and C-5 clutches are applied, the transmission attains reverse.

> **TECHNICIAN TIP**
>
> These failsafe strategies activate a limp-home mode to allow the vehicle to be driven to a repair depot during an electrical failure. Note that, although the vehicle can be moved during electrical failure, as soon as the engine is shut off and the transmission oil pressure drops, the transmission will then revert to neutral no clutches and the vehicle can no longer be driven.

During electrical failure in reverse, all solenoids are de-energized. Solenoid C exhausts the C-3 clutch. Solenoid E exhausts the C-5 clutch. Fluid immediately begins to flow from normally open solenoid A through the C-1 latch valve and deadheads at the C-2 latch valve. Fluid also immediately begins to flow from normally open solenoid B through the C-2 latch valve and deadheads at the C 1 latch valve. No clutches are applied, and the transmission attains neutral no clutches (NCC).

Allison Fourth Generation Electro-Hydraulic Control Valve Body

The next revision of the Allison electronic control is simply called Allison Fourth Generation Electronic Control. Fourth generation was released in the 2004–2005 model year and introduced several changes to the electro-hydraulic valve body and control strategy. For example, the solenoids used in fourth-generation systems have different functioning and locations compared to the solenoids in the WTEC 11 and WTEC 111 transmissions.

The transmission ECU is renamed **transmission control module (TCM)** FIGURE 45-51. and the clutch control solenoids have been renamed **pressure control solenoids (PCS)**. PCS1 replaces solenoid A; PCS2 replaces solenoid B; PCS3 replaces solenoids C and E; and PCS4 replaces solenoid D. Solenoid E as a standalone part has been eliminated altogether. Solenoid F has been renamed **torque converter control (TCC)**, and Solenoid G, which controls the position of the C-1 and C-2 latch valves, has been renamed **shift solenoid 1 (SS1)**. A new solenoid has been introduced called the **modulated main solenoid (Mod Main)**. The TCM uses the Mod Main to reduce main pressure when desired.

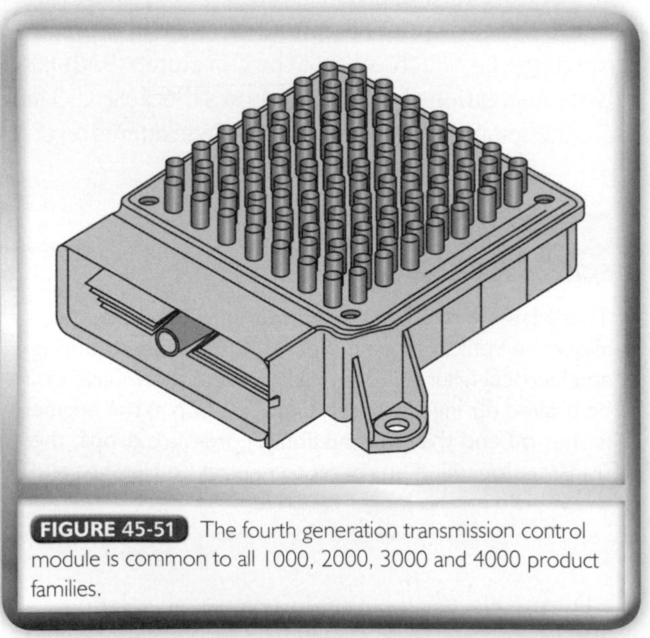

FIGURE 45-51 The fourth generation transmission control module is common to all 1000, 2000, 3000 and 4000 product families.

The pressure-control solenoids and the Mod Main solenoid are very different internally from their predecessors in the WTEC 11 and WTEC 111 controlled transmissions. The WTEC 11 and WTEC 111 solenoids had an inlet port, an outlet port, and an exhaust port. The flow of fluid was controlled by the transmission ECU using pulse-width modulation to control the opening and closing of a check ball in the solenoid. That process would direct fluid either to the outlet port or to exhaust.

In contrast, the fourth-generation control system uses variable-bleed solenoids (VBS). **Variable-bleed solenoids** control application by allowing some of the pressure going to a device to bleed off to exhaust. Variable-bleed solenoids have three ports:

- A supply port that is fed control main pressure
- A control port that sends that pressure to the solenoid regulator valve
- An exhaust port

Each pressure-control solenoid is connected to an accumulator, which absorbs pressure pulsations that can be caused by the pulse-width modulation of the solenoid. FIGURE 45-52 shows a variable-bleed solenoid in high-pressure state and in a controlling pressure state.

The TCM (formerly the transmission ECU) precisely controls the current being applied to the solenoids by changing the duty cycle of the pulse-width-modulated control circuit. Changing the duty cycle controls the size of the bleed orifice. The sizing of the bleed orifice is what allows the transmission to control precisely the speed of application of the clutch. Variable bleed solenoids are called either normally high (maximum pressure is supplied to the control circuit) or normally low (minimum pressure supplied to the control circuit).

The SS1 solenoid is not a variable-bleed solenoid. Rather, it is an on/off solenoid. PCS3 controls clutch C-5 when the C-1 and C-2 latch valves are in the up or unstroked position. PCS3 also controls clutch C-3 when the C-1 latch valve is in the down or stroked position. TABLE 45-8 is the Fourth Generation solenoid application chart for six-speed transmissions without a retarder.

The Mod Main solenoid directs pressure to a land on the main pressure regulator valve, and this reduces main pressure. In reverse the Mod Main is only used when throttle is less than 18%. Reducing main pressure when possible lowers the parasitic load the transmission hydraulic pump places on the engine.

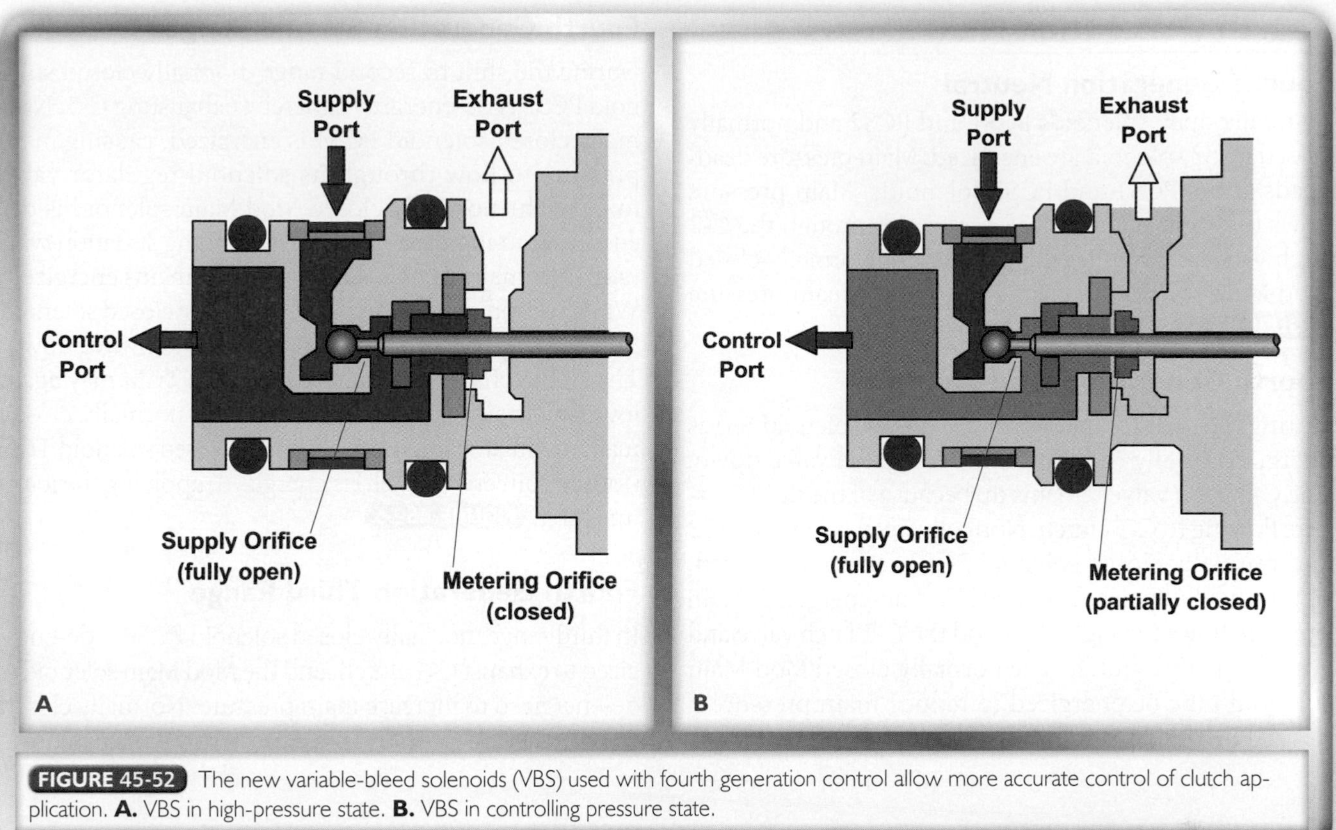

FIGURE 45-52 The new variable-bleed solenoids (VBS) used with fourth generation control allow more accurate control of clutch application. **A.** VBS in high-pressure state. **B.** VBS in controlling pressure state.

TABLE 45-8: Fourth Generation Solenoid Application Chart

Range	PSC1 N/O	PCS2 N/O	PCS3 N/C	PC4 N/C	SS1 N/C	Mod Main N/C
Neutral **	ON	ON	ON			Optional*
Reverse	ON		ON			Optional*
First		ON	ON			Optional*
Second		ON		ON	ON	Optional*
Third		ON	ON		ON	Optional*
Fourth					ON	Optional*
Fifth	ON		ON		ON	Optional*
Sixth	ON			ON		Optional*

* The modulated main solenoid may be energized by the TCM when lower main pressure is desired in any operating range.

** Four different neutral configurations can be attained if the vehicle is moving in neutral range.

As with the WTEC 11 and WTEC 111 control systems, the fourth-generation transmission can attain four different neutral configurations if the vehicle is moving while in neutral. The clutch applications depend on component rotational speed. Check the OEM manual for applications. Note that the clutch application chart and power flows for the fourth generation transmissions are identical to those for the earlier World Transmission models.

Fourth Generation Fluid Flows

Fourth Generation Neutral

Normally open solenoids PCS1 and PCS2 and normally closed PCS3 solenoid are energized. Main pressure deadheads at the PCS1 and PCS2 solenoids. Main pressure flows through the open PCS3 solenoid through the C-2 latch valve and applies the C-5 clutch. Normally closed Mod Main solenoid is energized to lower main pressure FIGURE 45-53.

Fourth Generation First Range

During the shift to first, normally closed solenoid SS1 is energized briefly to position the C-1 latch valve down. The C-2 latch valve remains up because of the fluid pressure flowing to C-5 clutch. Normally open solenoid PCS2 and normally closed solenoid PCS3 remain energized, but normally open solenoid PCS1 is de-energized. Main pressure flows through PCS1 and the C-1 latch valve and applies the C-1 clutch. The normally closed Mod Main solenoid may be energized to reduce main pressure if desired by the TCM FIGURE 45-54.

Fourth Generation Second Range

During the shift to second range, normally closed solenoid PCS3 is de-energized, thereby exhausting C-5. Normally closed solenoid PCS4 is energized, causing main pressure to flow through its solenoid regulator valve to C-4. The normally closed Mod Main solenoid is de-energized to increase main pressure if the situation warrants. Normally open solenoid PCS2 remains energized. When second range is attained, normally closed solenoid SS1 is energized, positioning the C-2 latch valve down. The C-1 latch valve remains down. The TCM may again lower main pressure by energizing the normally closed main modulator solenoid. Normally closed solenoid TCC (torque converter clutch) is energized, applying the lock-up clutch FIGURE 45-55.

Fourth Generation Third Range

In third range, normally closed solenoid PCS4 is de-energized to exhaust C-4 clutch, and the Mod Main solenoid is de-energized to increase main pressure. Normally closed solenoid PCS3 is energized, and main pressure flows

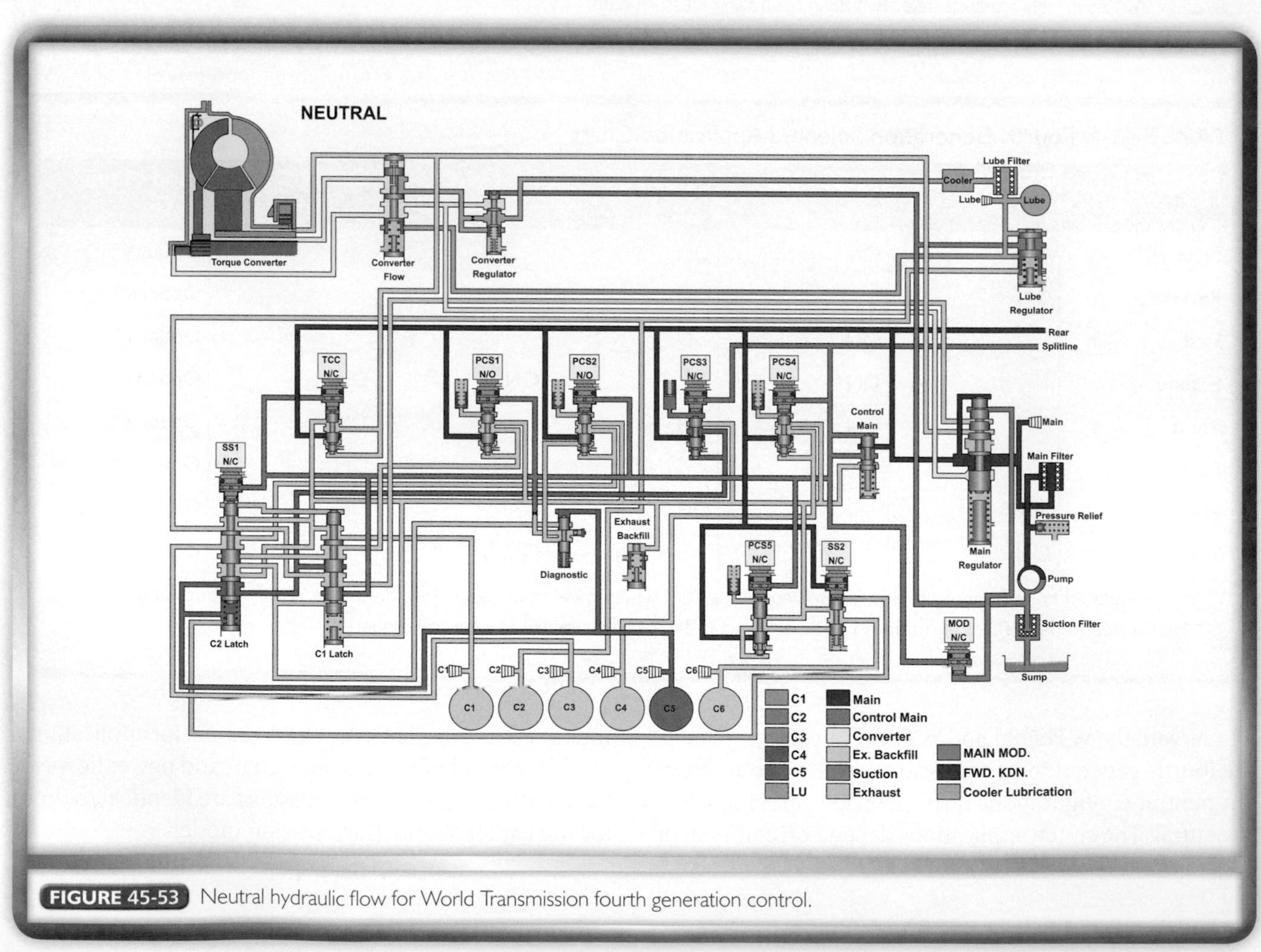

FIGURE 45-53 Neutral hydraulic flow for World Transmission fourth generation control.

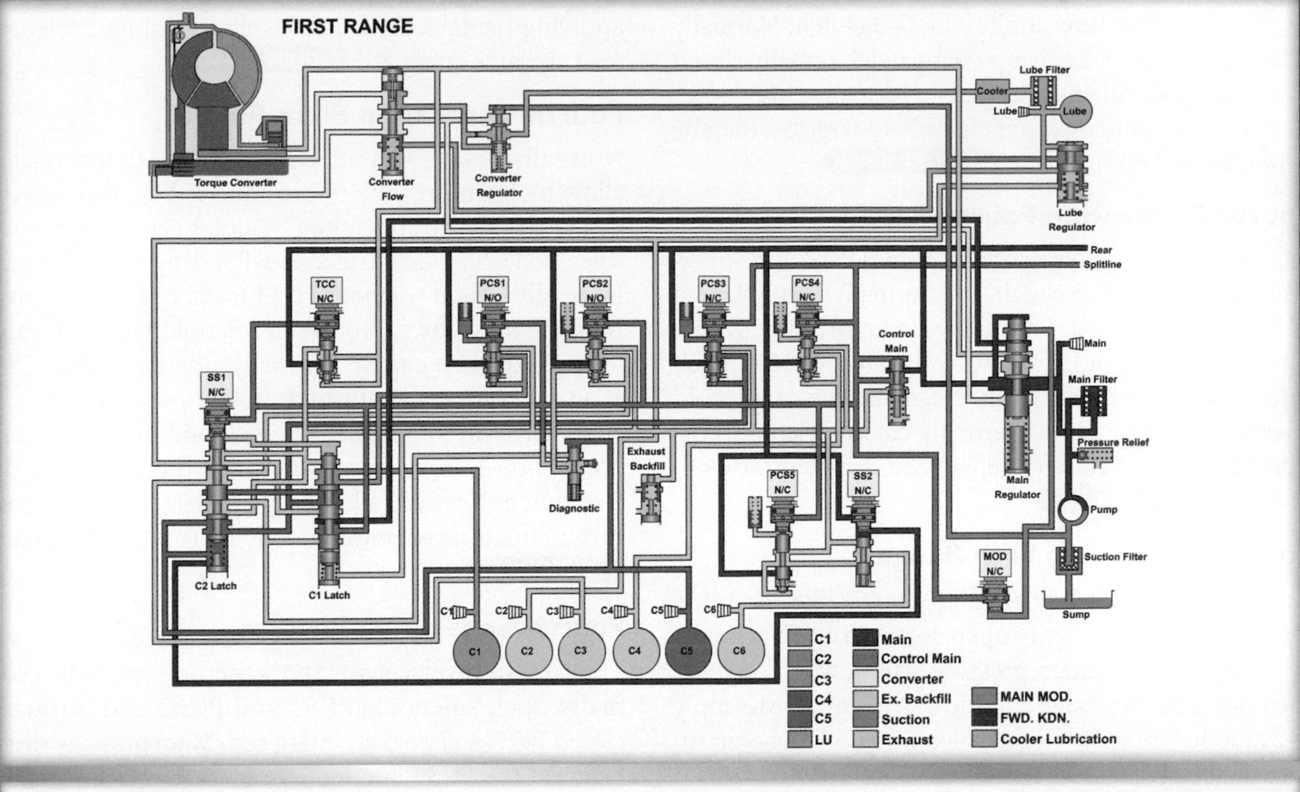

FIGURE 45-54 First Range hydraulic flow for World Transmission fourth generation control.

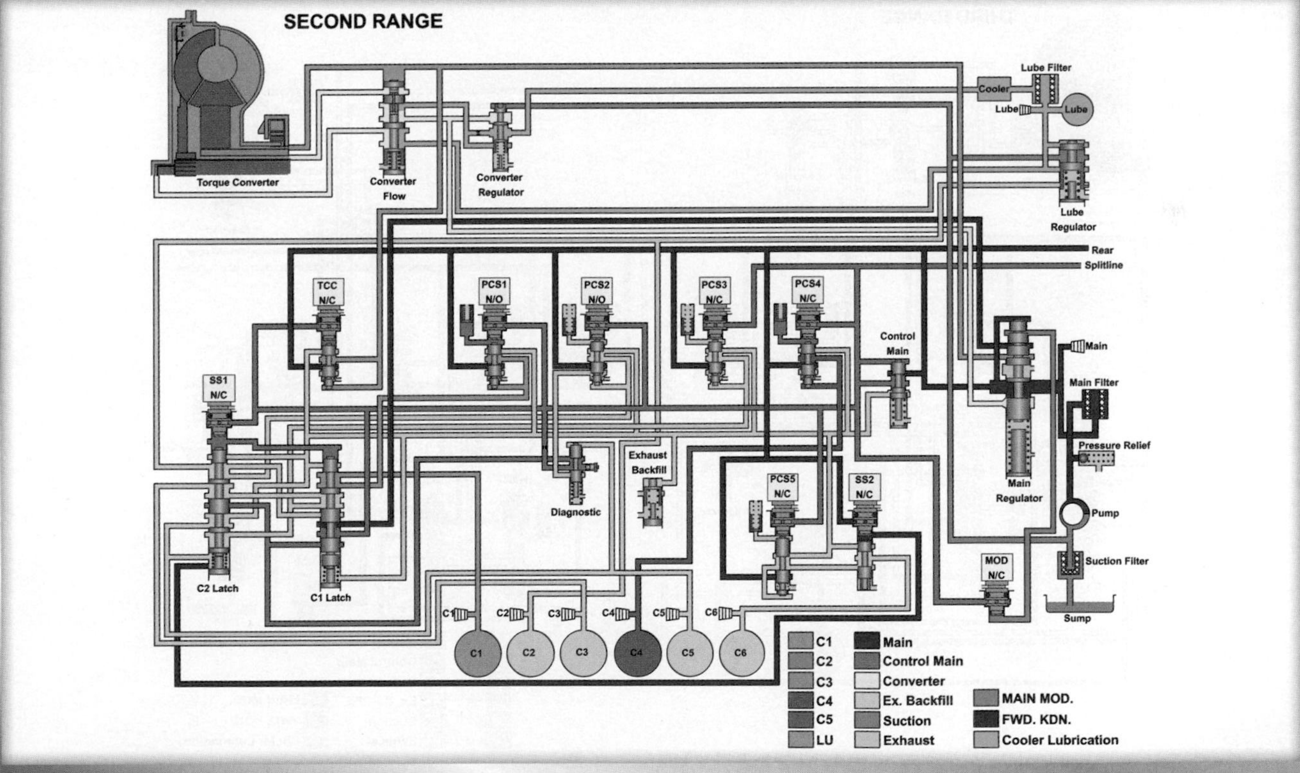

FIGURE 45-55 Second Range hydraulic flow for World Transmission fourth generation control.

through its solenoid regulator valve and the C-1 and C-2 latch valves. That flow applies the C-3 clutch. Normally open PCS2 solenoid remains energized. Normally closed solenoid SS-1 remains energized. Normally closed solenoid TCC (torque converter clutch) is energized, thereby applying the lock-up clutch FIGURE 45-56.

Fourth Generation Fourth Range

In fourth gear, normally closed solenoid PCS3 is de-energized, exhausting C-3 clutch, and normally open solenoid PCS2 is de-energized. That allows main pressure to flow through its solenoid regulator valve and the C-2 latch valve to apply the C-2 clutch. Normally closed solenoid SS-1 remains energized. Normally closed solenoid TCC (torque converter clutch) is energized, applying the lock-up clutch FIGURE 45-57.

Fourth Generation Fifth Range

Normally open PCS1 solenoid is energized, exhausting the C-1 clutch. Normally open solenoid PCS2 remains de-energized, and main pressure still flows through its solenoid regulator valve and the C-2 latch valve to apply C-2 clutch. Normally closed solenoid PCS3 is energized, allowing main pressure to flow through its solenoid regulator valve to apply the C-3 clutch. Normally closed solenoid TCC (torque converter clutch) is energized, applying the lock-up clutch. Normally closed solenoid SS-1 remains energized FIGURE 45-58.

Fourth Generation Sixth Range

Normally open solenoid PCS2 remains de-energized, allowing main pressure to continue to flow through the C-2 latch valve to apply the C-2 clutch. Normally closed solenoid PCS3 is de-energized, exhausting the C-3 clutch. Normally closed solenoid PCS4 is energized, and main pressure now flows through its solenoid regulator valve to apply the C-4 clutch. Normally closed solenoid SS-1 is de-energized, and spring pressure positions the C-1 latch valve up in its bore. The C-2 latch valve remains down, however, because of the pressure flowing to the C-2 clutch. Normally closed solenoid TCC (torque converter clutch) is energized, applying the lock-up clutch FIGURE 45-59.

Fourth Generation Reverse

The shift to reverse starts in the neutral position. Normally open solenoids PCS1 and PCS2 and normally closed PCS3 solenoid are energized. Main pressure deadheads at the PCS1 and PCS2 solenoids. Main pressure flows through the open PCS3 solenoid through the C-2

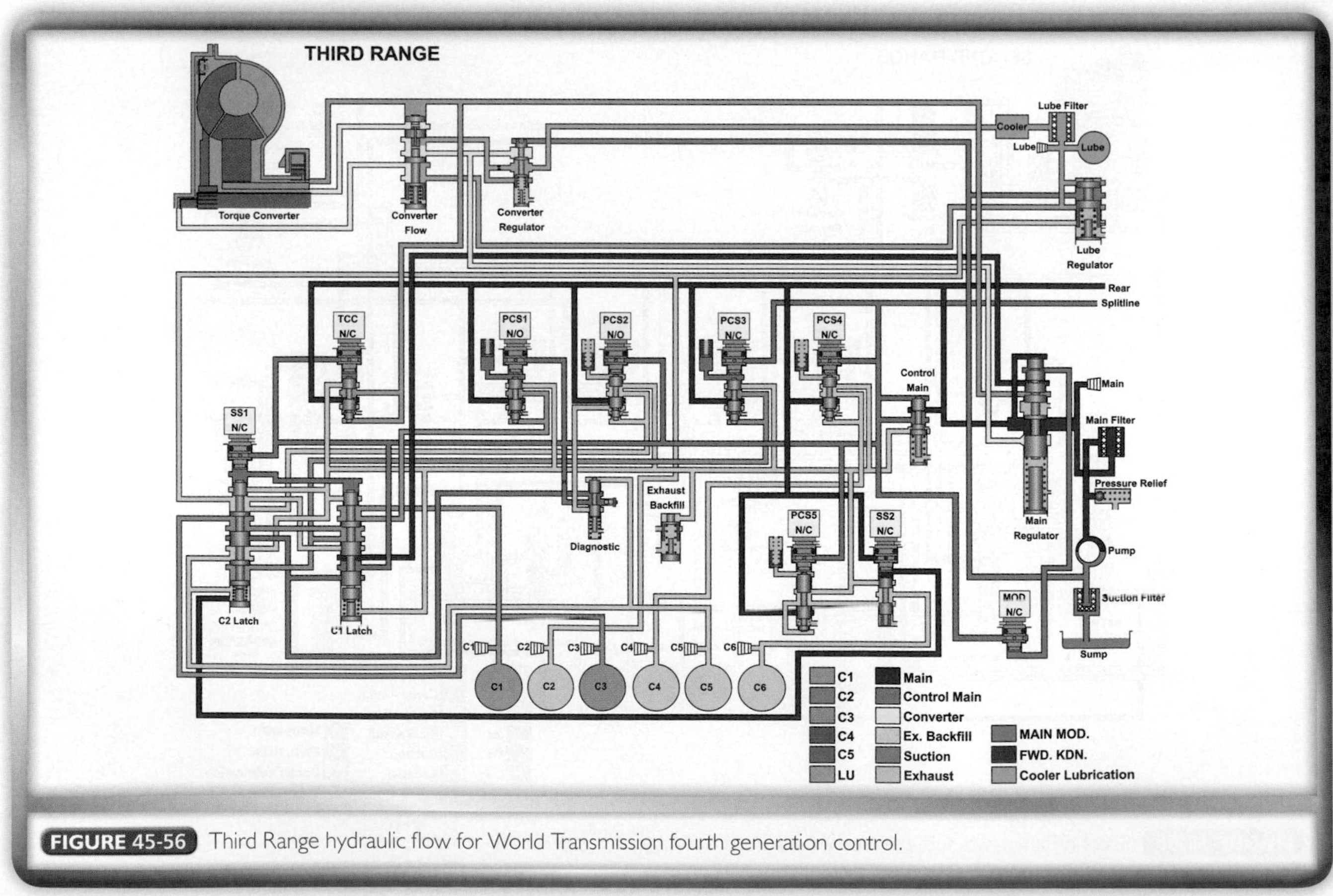

FIGURE 45-56 Third Range hydraulic flow for World Transmission fourth generation control.

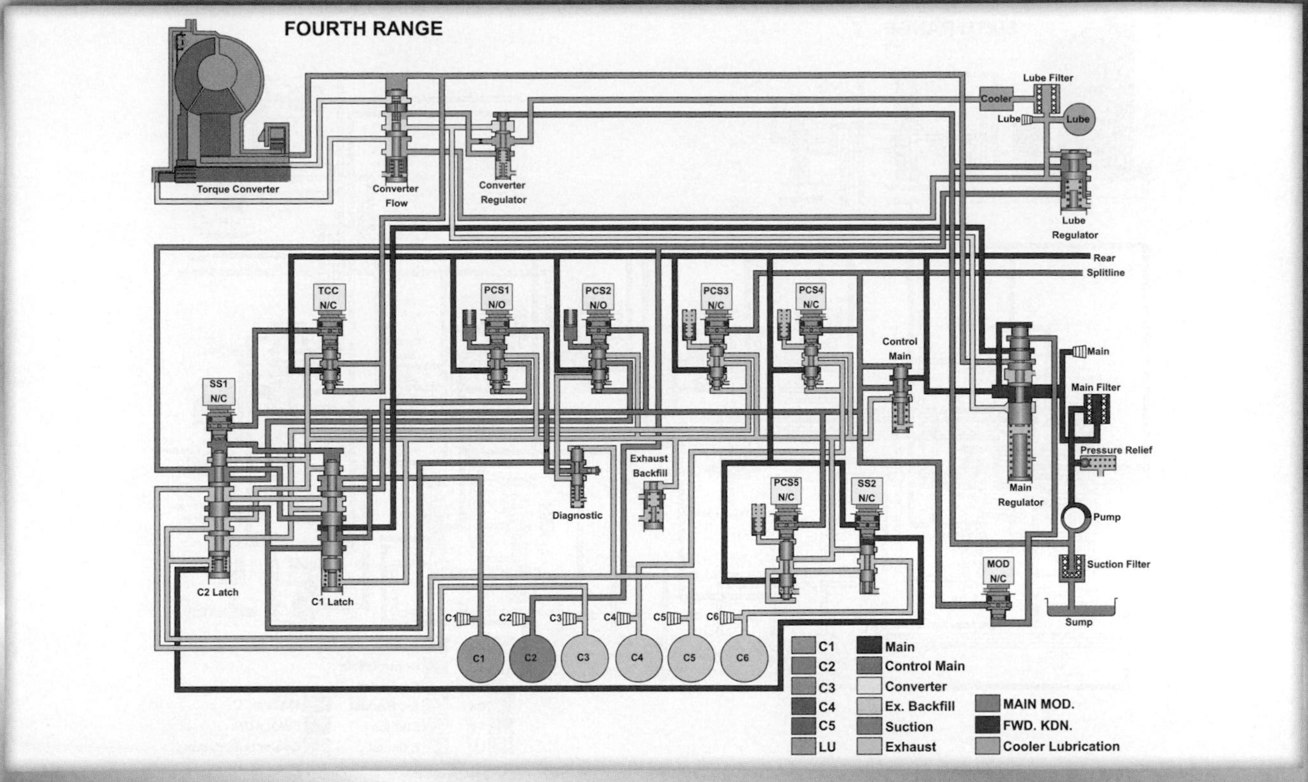

FIGURE 45-57 Fourth Range hydraulic flow for World Transmission fourth generation control.

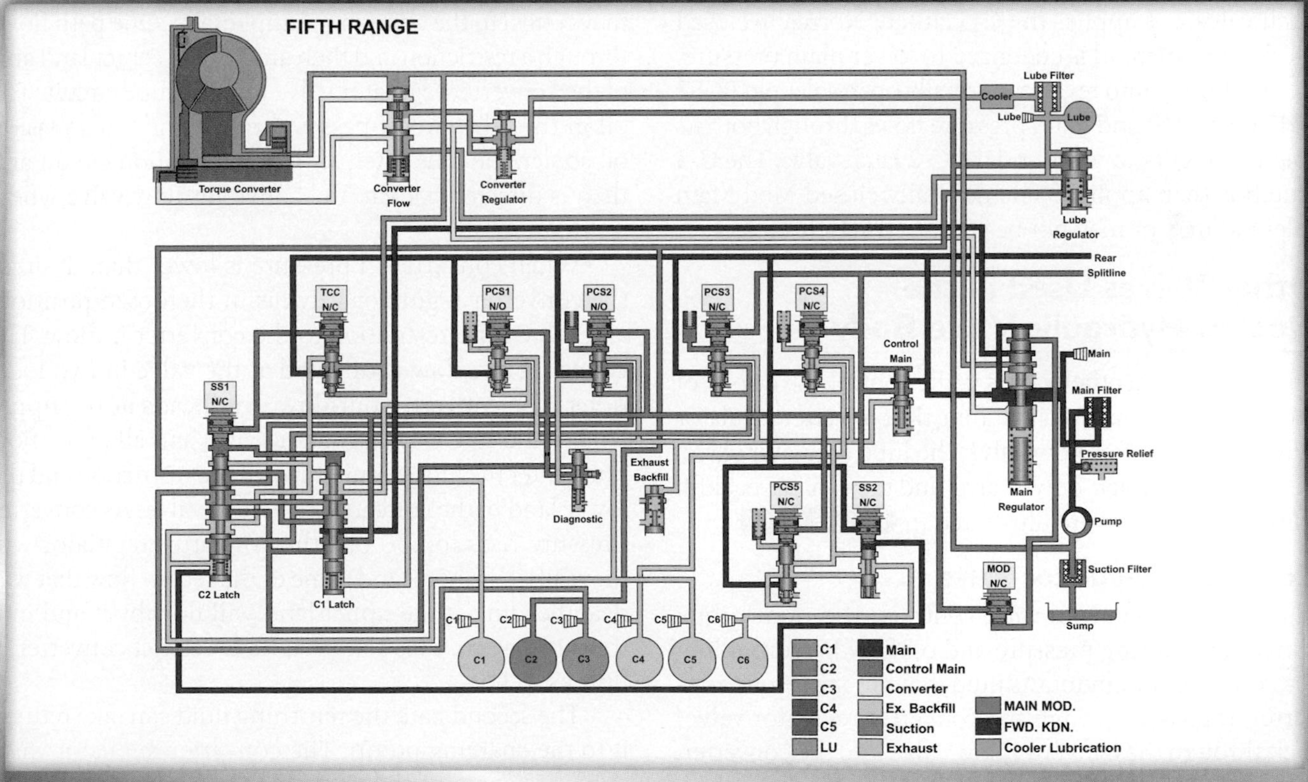

FIGURE 45-58 Fifth Range hydraulic flow for World Transmission fourth generation control.

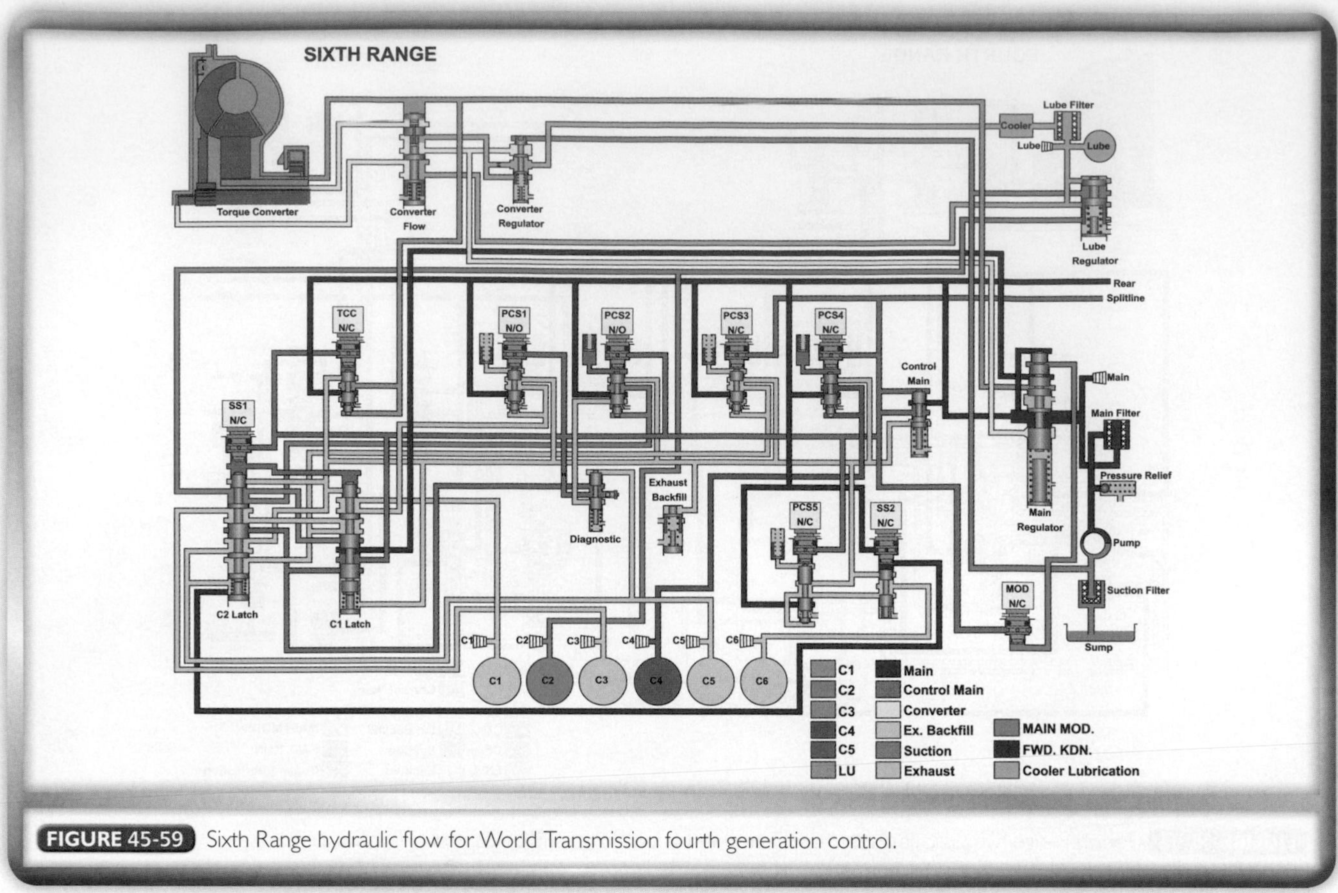

FIGURE 45-59 Sixth Range hydraulic flow for World Transmission fourth generation control.

latch valve and applies the C-5 clutch. Normally closed Mod Main solenoid is energized to lower main pressure.

In shifting into reverse, normally open solenoid PCS2 is de-energized and main pressure flows through both its solenoid regulator valve and the C-2 latch valve. The C-3 clutch is then applied. The normally closed Mod Main solenoid may or may not be energized **FIGURE 45-60**.

Other Valves Used in the Electro-Hydraulic Valve Body

There are several other valves in the control valve body of the World Transmission including the converter regulator valve, the converter flow valve, the lube regulator valve, the overdrive knock-down valve, and the exhaust backfill valve. These valves are illustrated in **FIGURE 45-61**.

Converter Regulator Valve

The converter regulator valve controls maximum torque converter working pressure and oil flow by controlling the convertor in-circuit. As fluid flows to the torque converter, it passes through the converter regulator valve, then through the converter flow valve into the converter, and back out to the converter flow valve.

From here, the returning fluid can take two separate paths. It can either flow into the lubrication circuit, or it may return to the charging pump intake. One path flows through a restriction and then around the center land area of the converter regulator valve into the lube circuit. The oil in the lube circuit passes through the transmission oil cooler, the lube filter, and the lubrication circuit and then is directed back to the converter flow valve where it deadheads.

When converter in pressure is lower than desired, the converter regulator valve is in the down position, and there is no restriction to the converter in-flow. The converter out-flow is directed at the valve in two locations. The converter out-flow deadheads at the upper land of the converter regulator valve, and all of the flow must enter the lube circuit through the restriction and the lower land of the converter regulator valve. As converter pressure rises to 130 psi, the converter regulator will move up in its bore, and some of the return flow that was dead heading at the upper land will flow by it and into the lube circuit. This action starts to restrict converter in flow as well.

The second path the returning fluid can take returns it to the charging pump. The converter regulator valve exhausts some of the converter in-flow to the pump intake. When converter pressure rises above 130 psi, the converter regulator valve moves further up in its

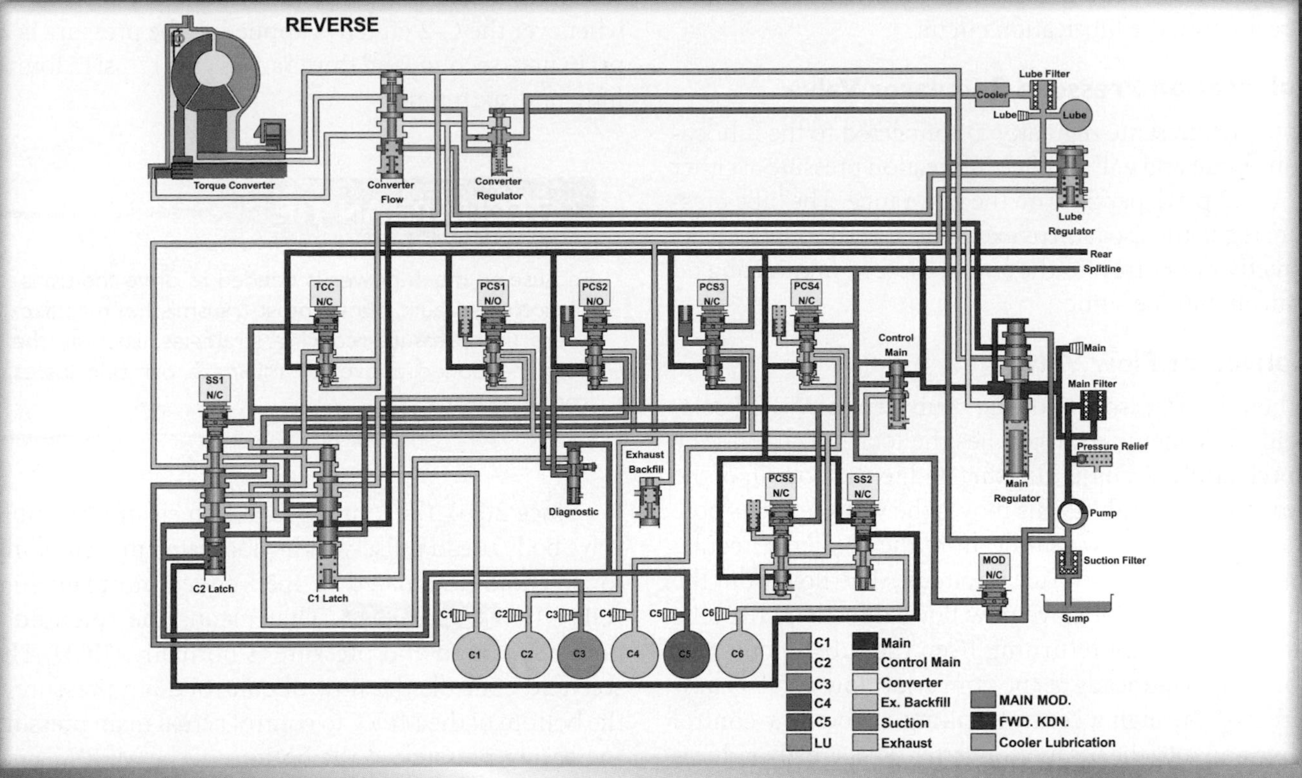

FIGURE 45-60 Reverse Range hydraulic flow for World Transmission fourth generation control.

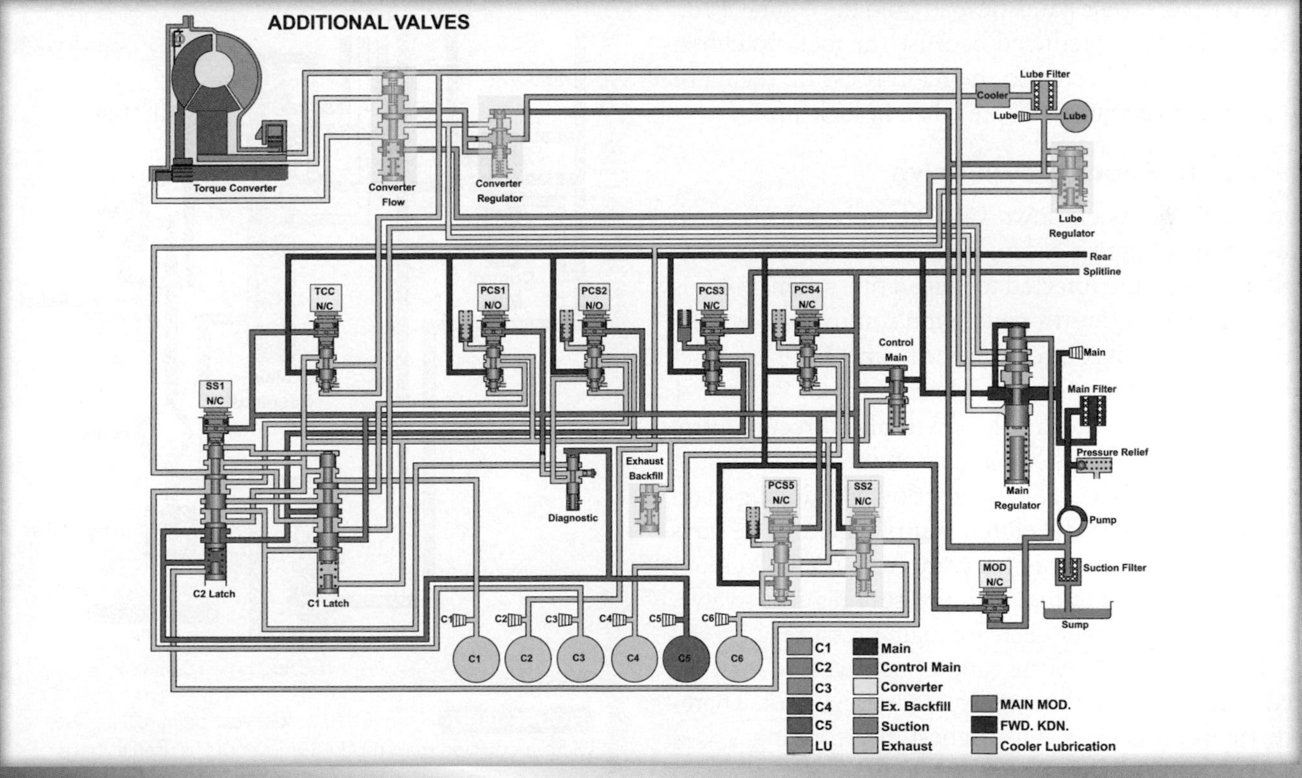

FIGURE 45-61 Additional valves in a fourth generation World Transmission.

bore and allows some of the converter in-circuit to flow directly into the lubrication circuit.

Lubrication Pressure Regulator Valve

The lube pressure regulator is connected to the lubrication circuit and will regulate lubrication pressure at either 17 or 22 psi depending on the gear range. The lube pressure regulator also returns excess fluid to the pump intake directly rather than to the sump, thereby minimizing oil churning in the sump.

Converter Flow Valve

When the TCC solenoid (the equivalent of WTEC solenoid F) is energized, it applies the lock-up clutch. The clutch apply circuit is also directed to the bottom of the converter flow valve. This moves the valve up in its bore and blocks the flow of fluid from the converter regulator valve to the converter in-circuit. The flow from the converter regulator valve now flows directly to the lube circuit. The fluid returning from the lube circuit that normally deadheads at the converter flow valve is now directed through a central drilling in the flow control valve and into the torque converter. This greatly reduces the flow through the torque converter when the torque converter is in lock up. (Recall that high fluid flow is not needed during lock-up but we must keep the converter full of fluid). Reducing the flow through the torque converter removes some parasitic load from the engine. Parasitic loss is further reduced because the lock-up clutch apply circuit is directed to the main pressure regulator valve to reduce main pressure when in lock-up.

Overdrive Knock-Down Valve

The overdrive knock-down valve actually reduces main pressure in all ranges except reverse. The valve has control main pressure directed to it at all times. This valve is not present in the fourth-generation control. Instead, the fourth-generation control uses the main modulator solenoid to lower main pressure when required. When C-1 clutch is engaged, the knock-down valve directs control main pressure (100 psi) to a land on the main pressure regulator valve. The valve moves down, reducing main pressure. When the C-2 clutch is applied, the valve stays up in its bore, and apply pressure from the C-2 clutch circuit is delivered to the main pressure regulator valve. The effect is to further decrease main pressure.

In neutral and reverse ranges, no pressure is delivered to this land on the main pressure regulator. Therefore, main pressure is at its highest in these ranges. C-2 clutch apply pressure from the overdrive knock-down valve is also directed to a land on the lube regulator valve. That application of pressure helps move the valve off its seat. The result is a reduction in lubrication pressure whenever the C-2 clutch is applied. Lube pressure is 22 psi in first, second, and third ranges and 17 psi in fourth, fifth, and sixth ranges.

> **TECHNICIAN TIP**
>
> Because so much power is needed to drive the transmission's hydraulic pump, most transmission manufacturers use pressure-reducing strategies, such as the ones mentioned above, to minimize parasitic losses from the engine.

Since 2010, the fourth generation electro-hydraulic valve body uses a pulse-width-modulated main modulator solenoid designated as open-ended, normally high (OE NH) **FIGURE 45-62**. That means the solenoid is normally closed and pressure is normally HIGH. This solenoid controls the flow of control main pressure to the bottom of the MPRV to control actual main pressure. Increasing pressure at the bottom of the MPRV causes main pressure to increase. This gives the TCM much greater control over main pressure.

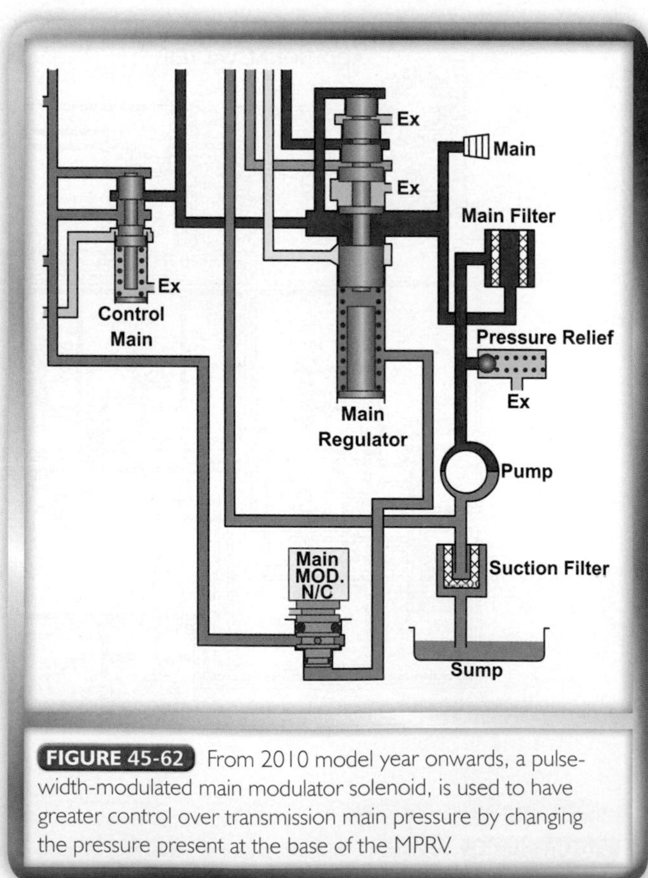

FIGURE 45-62 From 2010 model year onwards, a pulse-width-modulated main modulator solenoid, is used to have greater control over transmission main pressure by changing the pressure present at the base of the MPRV.

Exhaust Backfill Valve

The exhaust backfill valve maintains a very low pressure in the exhaust passages for the clutch packs. This minimal pressure of 2 to 3 psi is not sufficient to apply or delay release of the clutches. Minimal pressure does, however, keep the cavity behind the clutch piston full of fluid to ensure quick response during shifts.

Accumulator Relay Valve

Recall from FIGURE 45-47, in the WTEC11- and WTEC 111-controlled transmissions, the accumulator relay valve delays activation of the C-3 pressure switch until the clutch apply pressure is high. Without the accumulator, the pulse-width-modulated apply signal would cause fluctuations in the apply pressure which, in turn, would cause the switch to turn on and off rapidly. As clutch pressure builds, the accumulator is moved in its bore until the center-drilled hole in the valve communicates apply pressure to the C-3 switch. The C-3 pressure switch informs the controller whether the C-3 clutch is engaged. That is, the C-3 pressure switch signals the controller whether the transmission is in reverse, third range, fifth range, or not.

The fourth-generation valve body does not use an accumulator relay valve. Instead, fourth-generation transmissions use a valve called the diagnostic valve to control the PS1 pressure switch. As was illustrated in FIGURE 45-59, the position of the diagnostic valve is controlled by the latch valves position. The PS1 switch relays information to the transmission controller regarding the position of the PCS2 solenoid when the vehicle is second, third, fourth, and fifth range. The PS1 switch also relays information the C-5 clutch is applied in reverse.

Allison Fifth Generation Electronic Control

In 2013, Allison introduced the Fifth Generation electronic control of the World Transmission. In terms of prognostics, there are very few physical differences between the fourth and fifth generations. In the fifth-generation controls, Allison mostly added sophistication and functionality to the transmission-control software. Another difference is that filter life is actually measured by pressure differential across the filter. As pressure builds in front of the filter, the PS-2, or pressure switch valve, moves to turn off the PS-2 switch. This makes the filter life prognostics much more accurate. Pulse-width modulation of the pressure control solenoids and the open-ended solenoid (OE) is controlled at a frequency between 12,000 and 19,000 hertz.

Fifth-generation transmission controllers are common across the Allison product line but offer different software versions depending on the vocation of the vehicle. The fifth-generation controllers include an integral **inclinometer/accelerometer** to allow further refinement of transmission shifting based on topography and operating conditions such as load and road grade. Fifth-generation controllers also have other software enhancements, such as greater control over programming in/out functions and the ability to integrate and control diverse optional equipment functionality.

Retarders

Allison World Transmissions can be equipped with an optional hydraulic output retarder. As shown in FIGURE 45-63, the output retarder is mounted at the rear of the transmission in place of the rear cover.

The **hydraulic retarder** is used as a supplement to the vehicle braking system and is completely electronically controlled. The use of a retarder can increase service brake life by more than double. In addition, having a retarder on a transmission can increase braking efficiency, especially on long grades where service-brake fade can be a serious issue. Hydraulic retarders help to minimize service-brake use and keep brake temperatures down. (Lower brake temperatures result in less fade). In some instances the retarder can handle 90% of the braking effort or more.

The retarder is an assembly consisting of the following component parts:

- The rotor, which is splined to the output shaft of the transmission

FIGURE 45-63 The retarder is part of the transmission output module.

- A stationary housing
- A retarder accumulator, which is maintained full of transmission fluid
- A control valve assembly

The rotor's cast-iron components include cupped vanes formed into each side face FIGURE 45-64. The rotor sits in the middle of the stationary housing, which also has cupped vanes on its inside surfaces. The cupped surfaces of the stationary housing, however, are in the opposite direction of those on the rotor. During normal driving, the space between the rotor and the stationary cupped vanes of the housing is empty.

In order to control retarder operations, the transmission controller receives inputs from a number of sources. The controller usually receives the vehicle speed directly from the vehicle speed sensor (VSS), which is mounted on the output module of the transmission. The controller also gathers information about the arrangement of braking from the vehicle CAN BUS. (The CAN BUS is the controller area network connection on the vehicle. All of the vehicle's electronic controllers are connected together through the CAN BUS and communicate with each other). The braking information or request can be generated from multiple sources:

- A lever operated by the driver
- A separate foot pedal not connected to the vehicle brake pedal
- A variable force switch connected to the foot pedal output
- An auto-retard schedule managed by the transmission controller
- A combination of the above

FIGURE 45-64 The hydraulic retarder consists of a vaned rotor splined to the transmission output shaft and two stationary vaned elements in the housing.

In addition to speed and braking information, the dash switch sends input to the controller retarder enable switch.

When retardation is required, the controller uses pulse-width modulation to control a solenoid which in turn controls the retarder inlet valve. This valve controls transmission fluid under pressure in the accumulator that is directed to the space between the rotor and the stationary vanes. Retarder capacity is directly related to the amount and pressure of the fluid in this space. The rotor drives the fluid against the stationary cupped vanes. The friction of the fluid causes the forward momentum of the vehicle to change into heat energy. The fluid is constantly replenished by the transmissions hydraulic circuit it flows through the retarder to the outlet and on to the transmission cooler.

By increasing fluid pressure, more energy can be absorbed, but the temperature of the fluid must be closely monitored. The transmission controller monitors brake request, retarder fluid temperature, transmission sump temperature, transmission range, and output shaft speed. If any parameter is out of range, the transmission controller will disable the retardation. Specifically, the controller stops retardation when output shaft speed approaches the vehicle's calibrated minimum 165 to 450 revolutions per minute (rpm) to provide a smooth transition to the service brakes only FIGURE 45-65. Hydraulic retarders are capable of retardation equivalent to 600 horsepower (447 kW)—and more.

Most OEM hydraulic retarders function in a similar fashion, but some include extra features. For example, retarders that include a friction braking feature use a multiple-disc hydraulic clutch inside the retarder to provide even more braking effort. Hydraulic retarders generate enormous amounts of heat, so the transmission heat exchanger system (cooler) and the engine cooling system must be in good working order for them to function correctly.

Prognostics

Since 2009, Allison fourth-generation controlled transmissions have come with an optional feature called **prognostics**, which can be enabled or disabled by the operator. Fifth-generation controllers even come standard with prognostics installed in the software. The prognostics feature is software programmed into the transmission TCM that monitors and alerts the operator when the transmission fluid or filter needs changing or when the transmission clutches need servicing. The transmission controller calculates the need for service through drive cycle data and by monitoring shifts in progress.

The prognostics are accessed through the two digit display on the shift selector and the driver is alerted by a wrench symbol or the service transmission light. If the

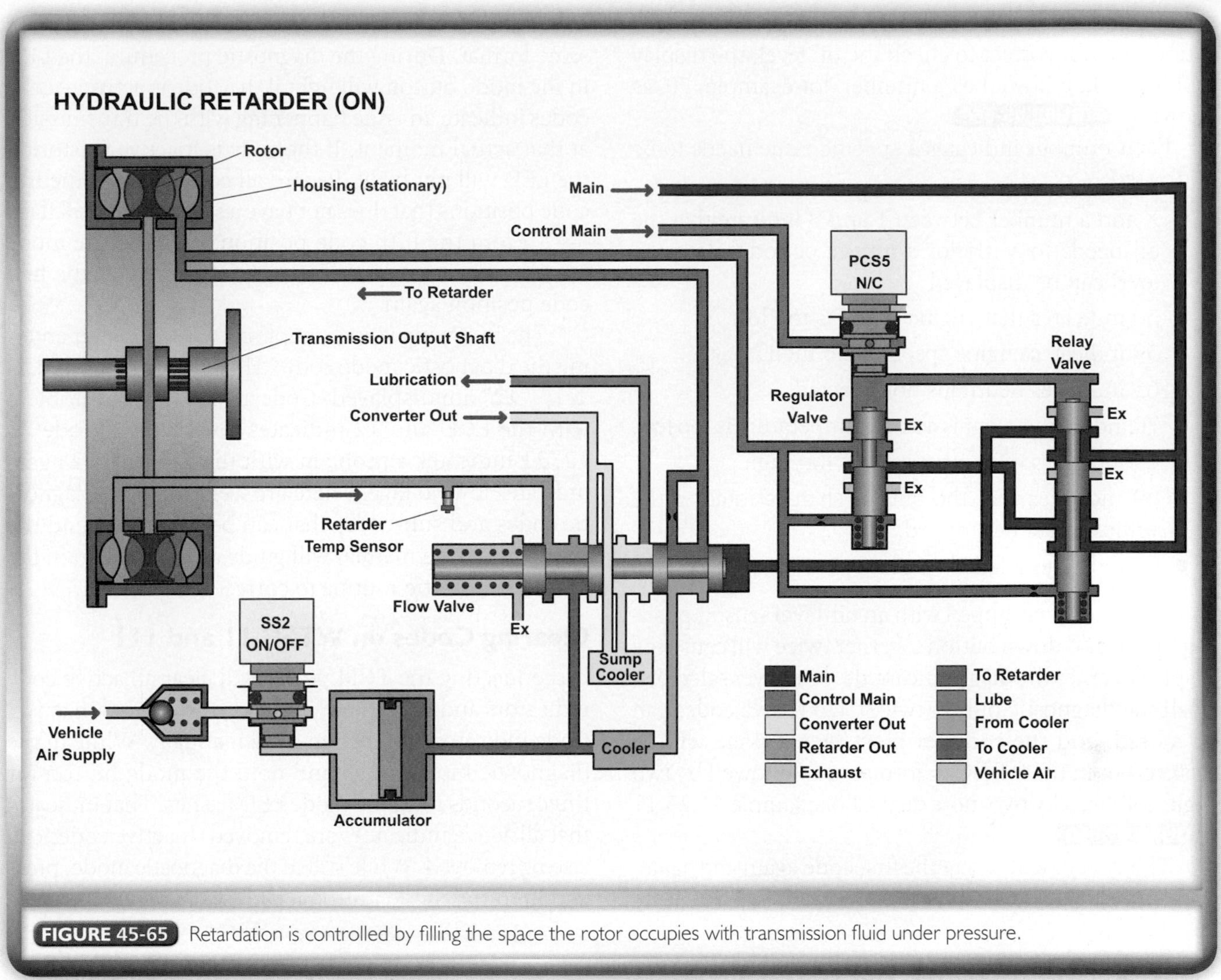

FIGURE 45-65 Retardation is controlled by filling the space the rotor occupies with transmission fluid under pressure.

wrench symbol or the service light illuminates for two minutes after drive is selected, that indicates an issue with the transmission fluid. If the wrench or the light flashes on and off for two minutes after drive is selected, it indicates an issue with the filter. Finally, if the wrench or light comes on and stays on in all ranges, it indicates that there is a problem with the transmission clutches. Understanding the warning lights allows the operator to schedule maintenance when required and before a problem gets worse.

Shift Selectors

World Transmission shift controllers perform a diagnostic function when a transmission diagnostic trouble code is set or when maintenance is required.

WTEC 11 and WTEC 111 transmissions have self-diagnostic capability only. When a problem is discovered, the transmission ECU will set a diagnostic trouble code (DTC). The codes can be accessed using the push button controller **FIGURE 45-66A**. To enter the diagnostic mode, press the up and down arrow buttons simultaneously with the key on but the engine off. The codes are set as a two-digit main code and a two-digit sub-code and are displayed in sequence on the two-digit selector display.

To display the codes for a transmission with a lever shift, press the diagnostic button (the button with the Allison logo) momentarily with key on but the engine off. If the transmission is fitted with an oil lever sensor, the oil level will be displayed first, as shown in **FIGURE 45-66B**.

After displaying the oL code to indicate "oil level," the display will show an additional code. For example, the display will read oL/ok, if the oil level is good. If oil level is low, oL/Lo will be displayed, followed by a number to indicate how low the oil is. For example, oL/Lo/2 means the oil is low by 2 quarts. If the oil level is high, the display will show oL/Hi, followed by a number indicating how much excess oil is in the system. For example, a display reading of the following 'oL' then 'Hi' then '1' indicates there is one excess quart of oil in the system. If the conditions are not correct to check the oil level, the display will flash oL, followed by a number, for example, 70, as shown in FIGURE 45-66C.

Each number indicates a specific issue needs to be addressed:

- X and a number between 1 and 8 indicate that the oil needs to settle for a longer period before the level can be displayed.
- 50 indicates that engine speed is too low.
- 59 indicates engine speed is too high.
- 65 indicates neutral is not selected.
- 70 indicates transmission oil temperature is too low.
- 79 indicates oil temperature is too high.
- 89 indicates that the output shaft is rotating the vehicle must be stopped.
- 95 indicates a failed sensor.

On vehicles equipped with an oil-level sensor, pushing the up and down button together twice will cause the display to enter the diagnostic mode. (On lever selectors, push the diagnostic button twice). Up to five codes can be stored, and the code for most recent issue will be flashed out in the following format: d1, followed by two digits followed by two more digits. For example d1,25,11 FIGURE 45-66D.

The system will repeat the first code again and again. To switch to the second code, momentarily push the mode button. The second code will be flashed out in the same format. During the diagnostic procedure, the LED in the mode button will light if the code is active. Active codes indicate an issue happening with the transmission at that actual moment. If the code is inactive (historic), the LED will not be lit. Record all codes. Any of the five code positions that does not have a stored code will flash "—". From the fifth code position, pushing the mode button momentarily will return the display to the first code position again.

The following is an example of two codes after entering the diagnostic mode code "d1," "13," "12," and "d2," "21," "12" are displayed. Code 13 indicates a problem with the ECU and 12 indicates low voltage. Code 21 12, 21 indicates a problem with the TPS and 12 again indicates low voltage. There are well over 100 diagnostic codes and sub-codes that can be displayed, and the troubleshooting manual will guide the technician in the proper diagnostic routine to correct the problem.

Clearing Codes on WTEC II and III

Disconnecting the TCM power will clear all active code indicators and keep them in the code queue as inactive. Code indicators can be removed manually. While in the diagnostic mode, push and hold the mode button for three seconds until the mode LED flashes. That indicates that all active indicators are removed. Inactive codes can also be removed. While still in the diagnostic mode, press and hold the mode button again for 10 seconds until it

FIGURE 45-66 **A.** Older WTEC II and III controller. **B.** oL indicates oil level is being shown. **C.** Code number (70 indicates that transmission oil temperature is too low to read the oil level). **D.** Display shows first of five code positions: d1, d2, d3, d4, d5.

flashes again. All inactive indicators will be cleared when the TCM is powered down.

To exit the diagnostic mode on a push-button shifter, press any range button. On lever-type selectors, push the diagnostic button once, or move the lever to any other position.

The fourth- and fifth-generation control systems use SAE J-2012 codes that are OBD 11 (on-board diagnostics) compliant. These codes contain one letter followed by four digits. Codes can be read from the Allison shift selector, with an aftermarket diagnostic reader, or using the Allison DOC software along with a computer.

The letter in a J-2012 code signifies the general component or system.

- B = Body systems
- C = Chassis systems
- P = Power train systems
- U = Network systems

The first digit after the letter code indicates DTC groupings.

- 0 = SAE/ISO controlled
- 1 = Manufacturer controlled
- 2 = SAE/ISO controlled in powertrain manufacturer controlled in any other system
- 3 = Reserved for SAE/ISO or manufacturer controlled

The second digit after a powertrain DTC refers to which system is affected. For example, 7, 8, and 9 indicate transmission issues. Some examples include P-07XX, P-08XX, and P-09XX. The XX will be the actual two-digit fault code. P-00XX, P-01XX, and P-02XX pertain to the fuel system. P-03XX is ignition systems.

The fourth-generation Allison shift selectors have a two-digit display similar to the WTEC 11 and WTEC 111, and the codes are accessed in the same way in all three models. To read the fourth-generation diagnostic codes, turn the key on, but keep the engine off. Push the up and down arrows together twice or the diagnostic button twice on lever shifters.

The order in which the codes appear is dictated by the recency of the problem (more recent troubles are indicated first). The first code to be displayed will be the position of the code (d1). The last code set will always be d1 and will be followed by a single letter (c, p, or u) and then by a sequence of two two-digit codes. For example, d1, followed by p, followed by 07, followed by 27 tells us the following information: first code position d1 is code p0727; the "p" indicates an issue with the powertrain. Code p0727 means engine speed sensor input to the transmission no signal.

To determine if a second code is present, push the mode button momentarily. You can toggle through up to five codes before the display returns to the first code. To clear the codes on a fourth generation system, press and hold the mode button for ten seconds while in diagnostic mode. This clears both active and inactive codes. Before clearing codes, always record them for future reference.

TABLE 45-9 contains a few of the fourth-generation WT control DTCs. It is by no means a comprehensive list, as there well over a hundred DTCs that can be set. Always consult the OEM manual for troubleshooting.

TABLE 45-9: Sample of Fourth Generation Trouble Codes

Diagnostic Code	Code Indicator
P063F	Auto Configuration Engine Coolant Temp Input Not Present
P0658	Actuator Supply Voltage 1 Low
P0659	Actuator Supply Voltage 1 High
P0701	Transmission Control System Performance
P0702	Transmission Control System Electrical
P0703	Brake Switch Circuit Malfunction
P0708	Transmission Range Sensor Circuit High Input
P070C	Transmission Fluid Level Sensor Circuit—Low Input
P070D	Transmission Fluid Level Sensor Circuit—High Input
P0711	Transmission Fluid Temperature Sensor Circuit Performance
P0712	Transmission Fluid Temperature Sensor Circuit Low Input
P0713	Transmission Fluid Temperature Sensor Circuit High Input
P0716	Turbine Speed Sensor Circuit Performance
P0717	Turbine Speed Sensor Circuit No Signal
P0719	Brake Switch ABS Input Low
P071D	General Purpose Input Fault
P0721	Output Speed Sensor Circuit Performance
P0722	Output Speed Sensor Circuit No Signal
P0726	Engine Speed Sensor Circuit Performance
P0727	Engine Speed Sensor Circuit No Signal

A high-quality or factory scan tool can be an invaluable asset while diagnosing an electronically controlled transmission. A generic scan tool can read codes, but a factory scan tool can also view live data from the sensors and actuators inside the transmission. To scan the TCM, follow the guidelines in SKILL DRILL 45-1.

To inspect, adjust, repair or replace electronic shift controls, electronic control unit, wiring harnesses, sensors, control module, vehicle interface module, and related components, follow the guidelines in SKILL DRILL 45-2.

Post-2009 Fourth-Generation Transmission Controls with Prognostics

The process for reading the codes is slightly different when the vehicle is equipped with fourth-generation controls and prognostic are enabled. On vehicles equipped with prognostics, a small wrench icon will momentarily be displayed between the two digits on the fourth-generation shift selector when the vehicle is started. The wrench icon should then go out. If, however, the icon remains illuminated, it indicates that maintenance is required. When the oil should be changed the wrench will illuminate for two minutes after drive range is selected and then go out. When the filter is due for a change the wrench icon will flash on and off for two minutes after drive range is selected and then go out. When clutch maintenance is required the wrench icon will come on and remain on for the entire operating time of the vehicle.

The shift controller can access the oil level, prognostic features, and the diagnostic codes by following this procedure. All of these actions are done with Key On and Engine Off with the vehicle stopped. Push the up and down arrows together once on a push type lever or the Allison diagnostic button once on a lever shifter; the display will show the oil level. Pushing the button twice displays the remaining oil life with the oM code followed by a number from 0 to 99. The number indicates the percentage oil life remaining.

Pushing the buttons three times puts the display into filter life mode. The display will then show FM followed by either "oK" if the filter is good or "Lo" if the filter should be changed.

Pushing the buttons four times puts the system into clutch life, or transmission maintenance, mode. If internal transmission maintenance is required, the display will read TM followed by either "oK" or "Lo."

While the display is in oil-life-monitor mode, pushing the mode button for ten seconds will reset that monitor. (The same is true when the display is in filter-life-monitor mode). The oil life monitor will reset to 99 and the filter monitor will reset to "oK." Note that, after model year 2010, the oil filter is monitored by pressure differential, so the filter life monitor will go back to "Lo" if the filter is clogged.

SKILL DRILL
45-1
Scanning the TCM
P0743 Torque Converter Clutch Circuit Electrical
Last Test: Failed
This Ignition: Failed MIL Requested
Since Cleared: Passed & Failed History
1 / 8
Info
1 Install a scan tool onto the vehicle's data link connector (DLC). For the location of the DLC, consult the service information.
2 Retrieve any diagnostic trouble codes (DTCs) from the vehicle. Record the codes.
3 Using the service information, research the diagnostic procedure for any codes found.
4 If there are multiple codes, evaluate the service information to see if codes are related to each other.
5 Follow the diagnostic procedure step by step until you have completed the diagnostic procedure and found the cause of the DTC.
6 Consult with the customer before completing any repair.

To access the diagnostic codes on fourth-generation systems with prognostics, press the up and down buttons

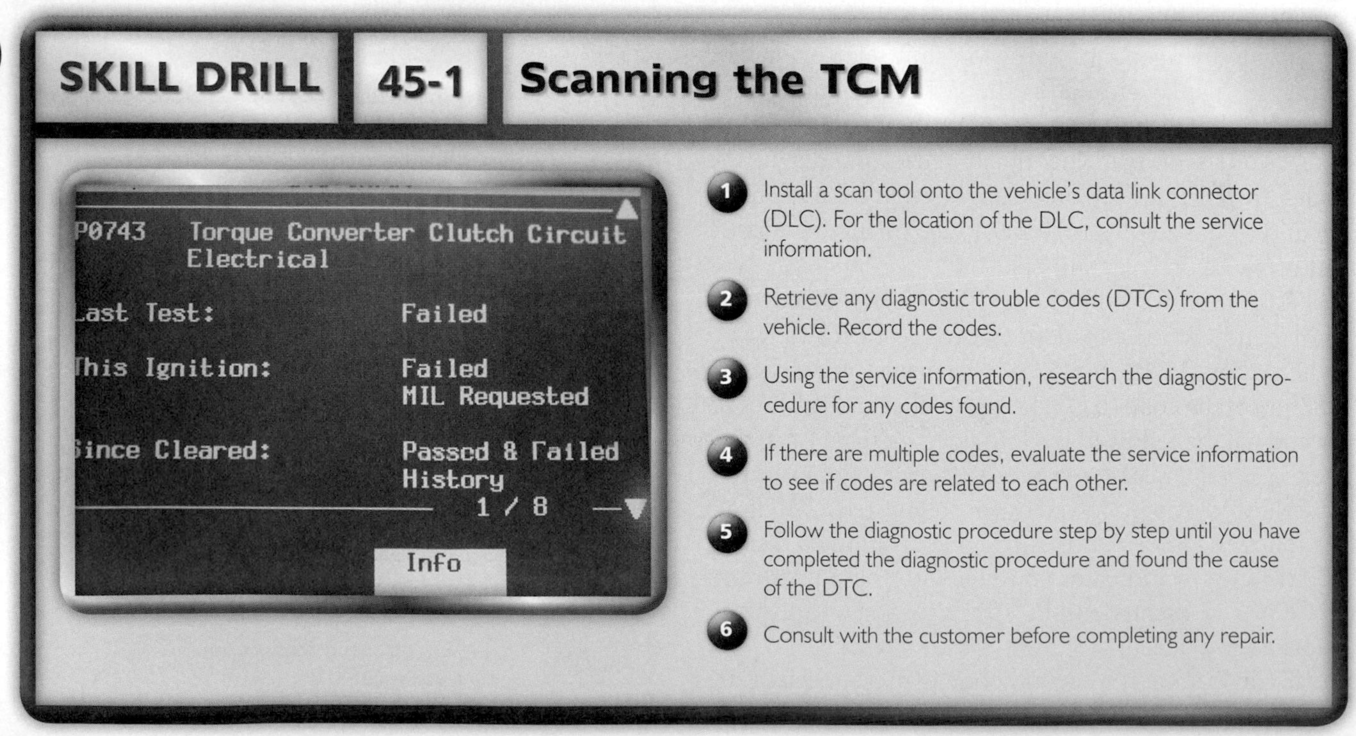

five times together on the push button selector. For level selectors, push the diagnostic button five times. The diagnostic codes will be displayed in the same format as for fourth-generation systems without prognostics described previously. To clear codes while in the diagnostic mode, push and hold the mode button for ten seconds. That clears both active and inactive codes. Be sure to record all of the codes before clearing them.

Fifth-Generation Shift Selectors

The fifth-generation Allison shift selectors are capable of displaying two digits for gear selection. These selectors also have multi-character graphic-display capabilities. That means that fifth-generation shift selectors can display prognostic information, full codes, and code descriptions, making it easier for technicians to diagnosis problems.

The process for using the shift selector to check transmission function is essentially the same as for the fourth generation with prognostics. Press the up and down arrows together on a push button selector (or push the diagnostic button once) to obtain information about transmission oil level. Push twice for the oil-life monitor, three times for the filter-life monitor, and four times for the transmission-life monitor. Although the basic process

SKILL DRILL 45-2 Inspecting, Adjusting, Repairing or Replacing Electronic Shift Controls, Electronic Control Unit, Wiring Harnesses, Sensors, Control Module, Vehicle Interface Module, and Related Components

1. Locate and follow the appropriate procedure in the service manual.
2. Complete a job sheet or work order with all pertinent information.
3. Move vehicle into workshop, apply parking brakes and chock the vehicle wheels. Observe lockout/tagout procedures.
4. If the vehicle has a manual transmission, place it in "neutral"; if it has an automatic transmission, place it in "park" or "neutral". Note: Some vehicles with automatic transmissions do not have "park."
5. Test operation and retrieve diagnostic codes as outlined in the service manual.
6. Use service manual procedures to inspect and repair or replace external/internal wiring harnesses.
7. Use service manual procedures to test, repair or replace the following components:
   a. Electronic control unit (ECU)
   b. Vehicle interface module (VIM)
   c. Vehicle interface wiring (VIW)
   d. Engine speed sensor
   e. Turbine speed sensor
   f. Output speed sensor
   g. Throttle position sensor
   h. Control module
8. Use service manual procedures to test, repair, or replace electronic shift selector(s).
9. List the test results and/or recommendations on the job sheet or work order, clean the work area, and return tools and materials to proper storage.

is the same, however, what the technician will see on the fifth-generation shift selector is more sophisticated. The fifth-generation selector will display a message rather than a simple code. For example, TRANS OIL 3 QUARTS HI, or, TRANS OIL LEVEL OK **FIGURE 45-67**.

To access diagnostic codes, push the buttons once. The display will cycle through showing the oil level function, followed by prognostics, followed by the diagnostic codes. The display will show both the code and whether it is active or not, for example, P0730 ACTIVE.

Resetting the maintenance flags and the codes is the same procedure as for the fourth generation with prognostics described previously.

Allison introduced a comprehensive dedicated diagnostic software package in 2002 called Allison DOC **FIGURE 45-68**. The software is capable of diagnosing faults and monitoring transmission operation and adaptations. Allison DOC software version 12.0 is the current package available from authorized Allison dealers. The software enables technicians to diagnose transmission operation and record operational data for all of Allison's electronically controlled transmissions—from the ATEC/CEC through all versions of the World Transmission—and is also capable of diagnosing the Allison TC-10-TS. As described in the next section, the Allison TC-10-TS is a ten-speed, twin-countershaft, fully automatic transmission designed for on-highway Class 8 tractors. Allison has offices all over the world and hundreds of qualified dealers in North America.

TC-10-TS

In late 2012, Allison released a new transmission model called the TC-10-TS, which stands for twin-countershaft (TC), ten-speed (10), tractor series (TS) **FIGURE 45-69A**. The TC-10-TS employs the blended architecture of a traditional, twin-countershaft main box, a planetary two-speed range section, and electronically controlled hydraulic clutches for shifting. With ten forward speeds and two reverse speeds, plus the comfort and ease of

FIGURE 45-67 Fifth-generation shift selectors have a graphical display capable of displaying a message rather than a simple code.

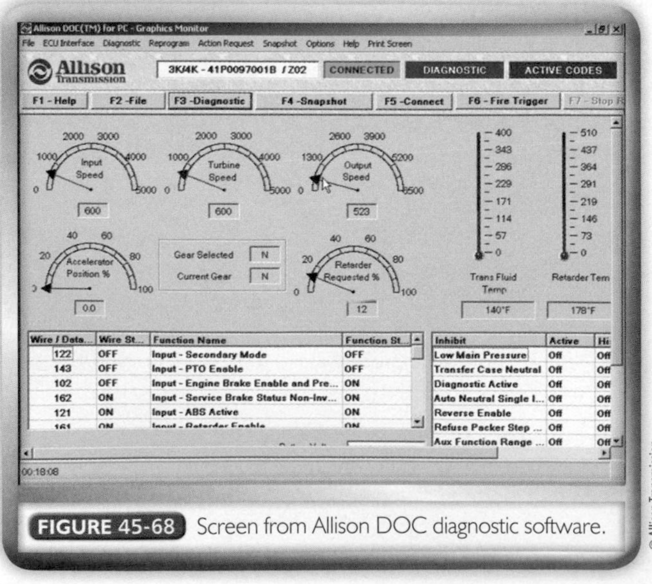

FIGURE 45-68 Screen from Allison DOC diagnostic software.

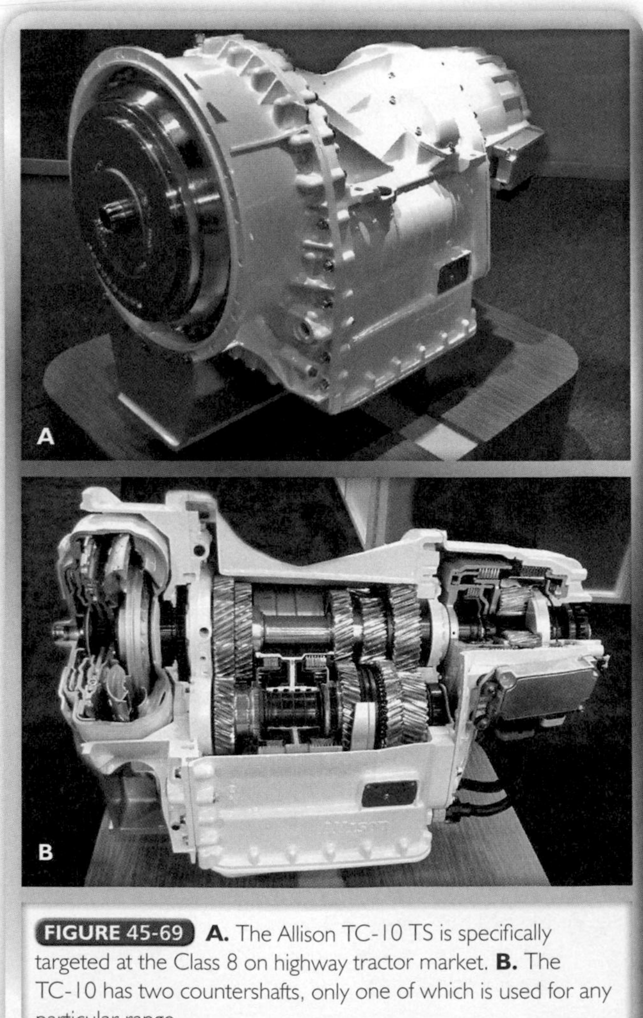

© Allison Transmission

FIGURE 45-69 **A.** The Allison TC-10 TS is specifically targeted at the Class 8 on highway tractor market. **B.** The TC-10 has two countershafts, only one of which is used for any particular range.

operation of an automatic transmission, this unit was designed to carve out a niche in the Class 8 on-highway tractor market. To date, sales of this unit have been relatively low, and it seems to appeal mainly to the markets using less-than-truck-load and around-town delivery vehicles. At the moment only Navistar (International), currently offers the TC-10-TS as an option in its trucks.

The TC-10-TS model is a completely new design that incorporates the following features:

- Torque converter input module with lock-up clutch
- Twin countershaft five-speed main gear box with five wet clutches FIGURE 45-69B
- A two-speed planetary range rear section controlled by two additional wet clutches

As shown in FIGURE 45-70, the TC-10-TS has five wet clutches in the main box. With a clutch for every gear, shifting takes place under power with no efficiency losses required when torque is broken to make a shift. The power is reduced slightly during shifts to soften the shift and, unlike in automated manual transmissions, it is unnecessary to completely break torque for a shift to occur.

Allison has historically made transmissions for use in Class 8 on-highway tractors, but the TC-10-TS is the first Allison transmission targeted specifically to the on-highway tractor market. After conducting extensive field testing of the TC-10, Allison claims the transmission can produce a 3% to 5% better fuel economy than current automated manual transmissions. Acceleration is also improved with the TC-10-TS because the transmission's clutches are basically handing off power from one to another. Under power during fleet testing, this transmission produces 20% faster acceleration. Plus, the transmission controller is adaptive. The shift can be tailored to the load and the terrain without driver input, further improving fuel economy. The TC-10-TS is available for engines with up to 600 horsepower (447 kW) and 1,700 foot-pounds (2,304 Nm) of torque. (The company states the TC-10-TS transmission is capable of handling 1,850 foot-pounds (2,508 Nm) of torque, but for now it

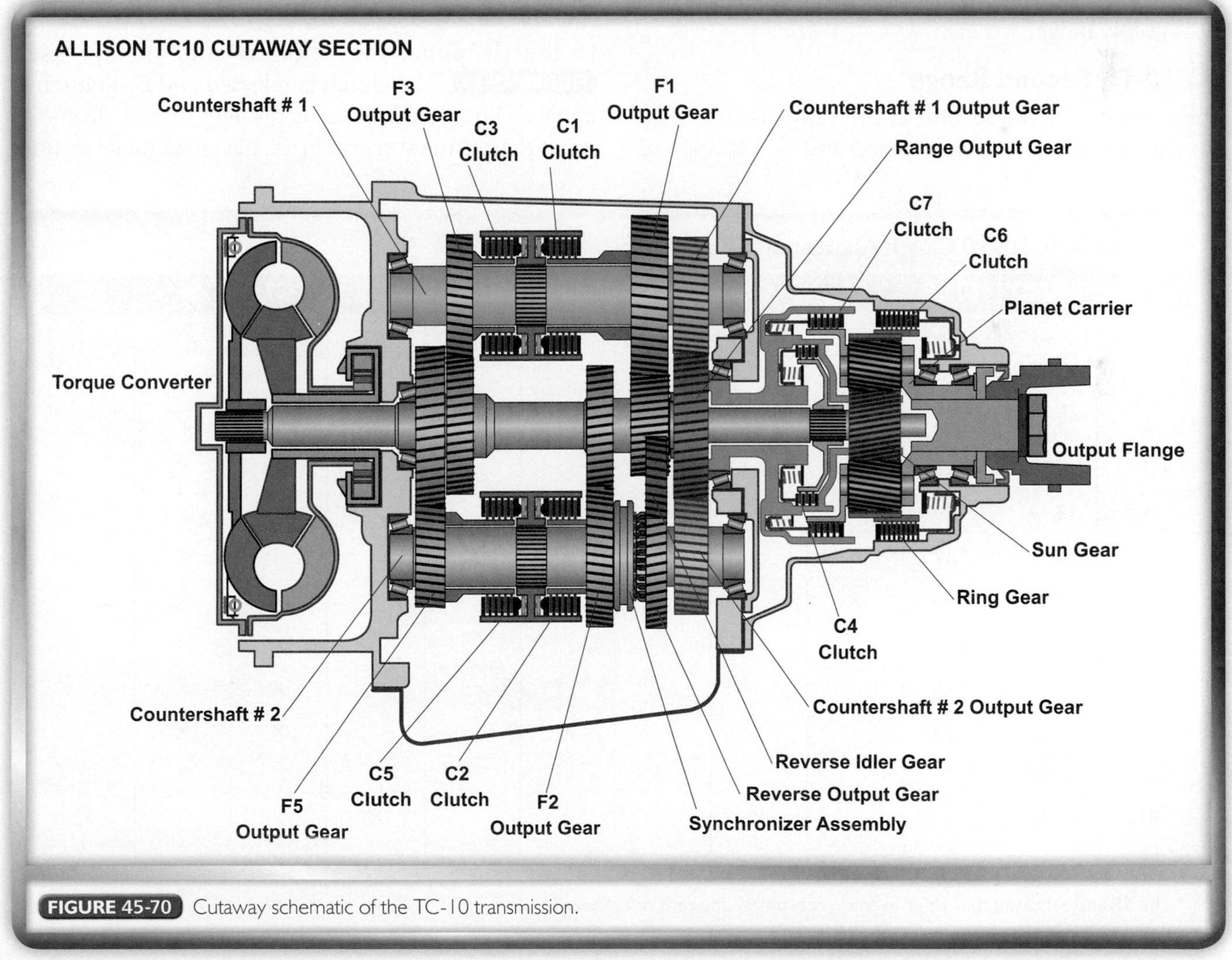

FIGURE 45-70 Cutaway schematic of the TC-10 transmission.

recommends a maximum torque of 1,700 foot-pounds (2,304 Nm). TABLE 45-10 shows the TC-10-TS clutch application.

TC-10-TS Power Flows

TC-10-TS Neutral

In neutral, the C-6 clutch is applied and holds the ring gear of the planetary gear set stationary and the synchronizer is rearward. The input shaft only will rotate with the torque converter turbine FIGURE 45-71.

TC-10-TS First Range

As shown in FIGURE 45-72, in first range, the C-1 clutch applies, and the synchronizer moves forward. C-1 clutch locks the F-1 output gear to the right-side counter shaft, and the synchro position unlocks the reverse gear. Power flows from the input shaft to the right-side countershaft through C-1. Then power flows back to the range output gear through the right-side countershaft output gear. The range output gear turns the sun gear of the planetary range section. C-6 is holding the ring gear, so the range carrier is output. That means the range planetary gear set is in low range.

TC-10-TS Second Range

The power flow for second is the same as first with the exception that C-1 is released and C-2 is applied FIGURE 45-73. C-2 locks the F2 output gear to the left-side counter shaft through the synchronizer, which is in the forward position. Note that the C-2 clutch can connect either the reverse output gear or F-2 output gear to the left-side countershaft depending on the position of the synchronizer. If the synchronizer is forward, the F-2 gear is connected by C-2. If the synchronizer is rearward, then the reverse gear is connected to the countershaft. In the second range, power is delivered to the range output gear through the left countershaft from the F-2 output gear. C-6 is still applied and holding the ring gear of the planetary range gear set. The planetary gear set, therefore, remains the same as for first gear—in low range.

TC-10-TS Third Range

In third range, the power flow switches back to the right-side countershaft FIGURE 45-74. C-2 is released, and C-3 is applied. That brings power from the input shaft to the range output gear through the F-3 output gear at the front of the right countershaft. Again, the planetary range section remains the same.

TC-10-TS Fourth Range

In fourth range, the countershafts are not used FIGURE 45-75. C-3 clutch is released and C-4 clutch is applied. Rotational power is brought directly from the input shaft to the sun gear in the planetary range section.

TABLE 45-10: TC-10 Clutch Application Chart

RANGE	RATIO	STEP	C1	C2	C3	C4	C5	C6	C7	SF*	SR*
N	–	–						X			X
1	7.40	–	X					X		X	
2	5.44	1.36		X				X		X	
3	4.25	1.28			X			X		X	
4	3.43	1.24				X		X		X	
5	2.94	1.17					X	X		X	
6	2.16	1.36	X						X	X	
7	1.59	1.36		X					X	X	
8	1.24	1.28			X				X	X	
9	1.00	1.24				X			X	X	
10	0.86	1.17					X		X	X	
R1	6.71	–		X				X			X
R2	1.96	–		X					X		X

* The SF and SR categories refer to the synchronizer forward or rearward.

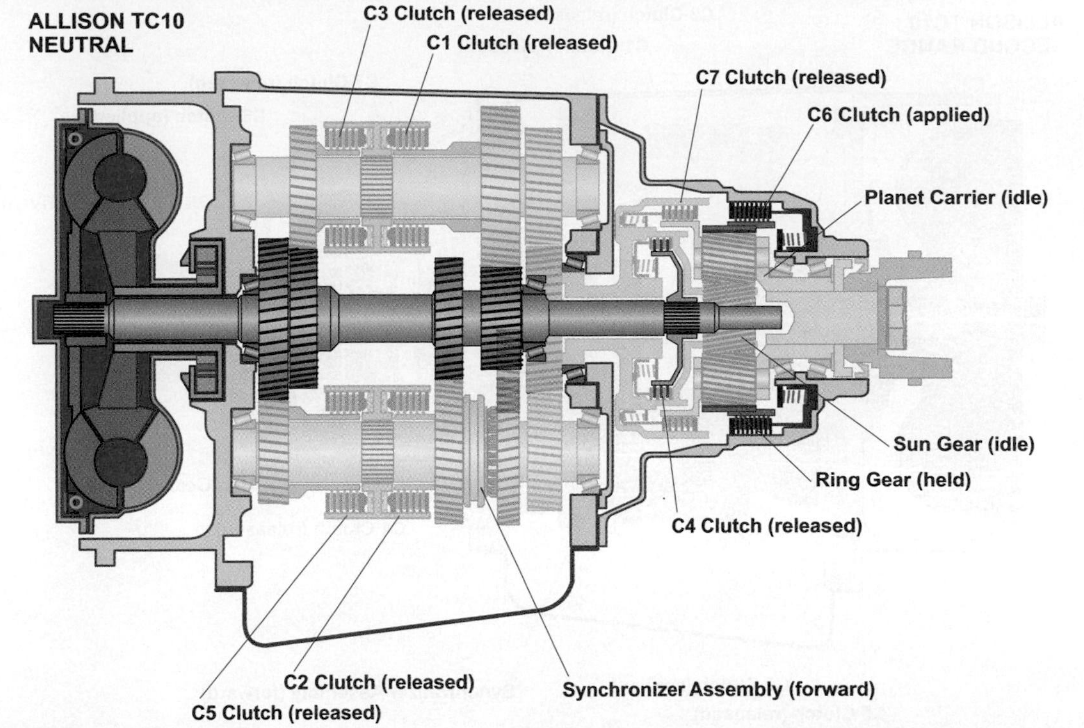

FIGURE 45-71 In neutral, no power is transmitted beyond the input shaft.

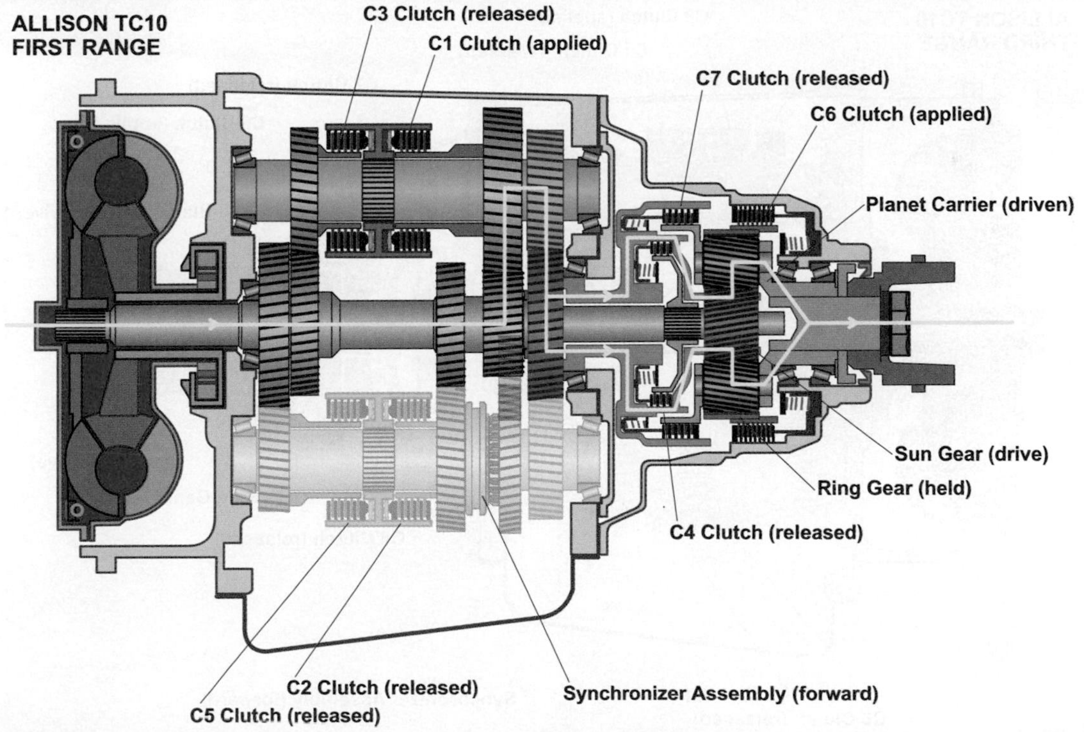

FIGURE 45-72 First range.

ALLISON TC10
SECOND RANGE
C3 Clutch (released)
C1 Clutch (released)
C7 Clutch (released)
C6 Clutch (applied)
Planet Carrier (driven)
Sun Gear (drive)
Ring Gear (held)
C4 Clutch (released)
C2 Clutch (applied)
C5 Clutch (released)
Synchronizer Assembly (forward)

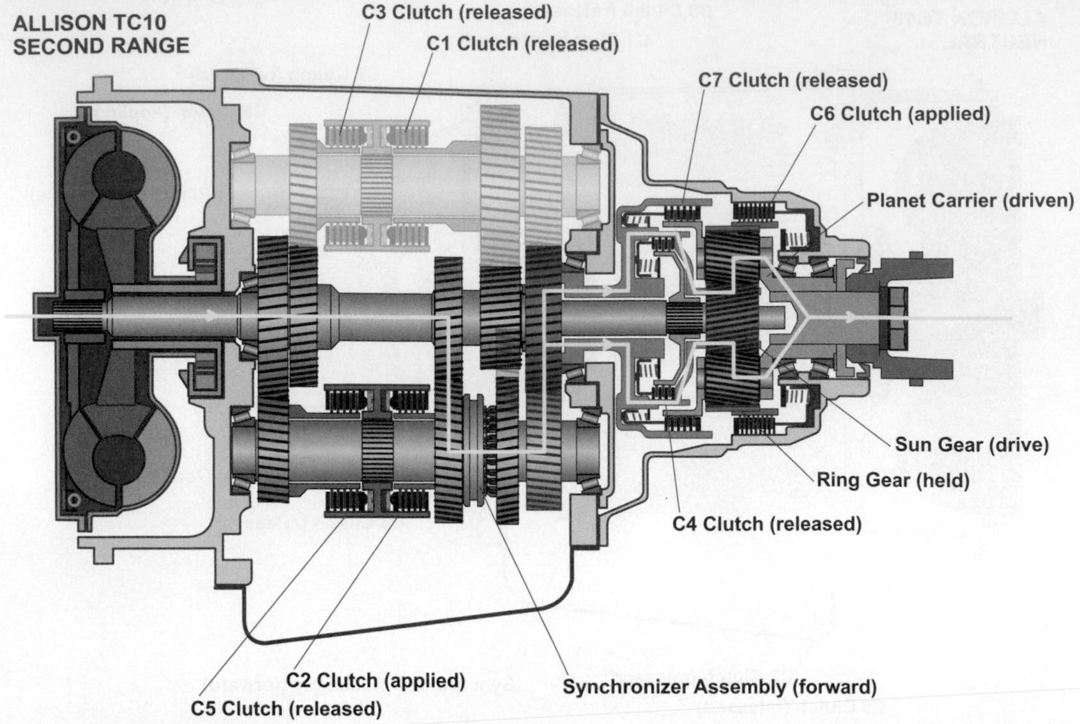

FIGURE 45-73 Second range.

ALLISON TC10
THIRD RANGE
C3 Clutch (applied)
C1 Clutch (released)
C7 Clutch (released)
C6 Clutch (applied)
Planet Carrier (driven)
Sun Gear (drive)
Ring Gear (held)
C4 Clutch (released)
C2 Clutch (released)
C5 Clutch (released)
Synchronizer Assembly (forward)

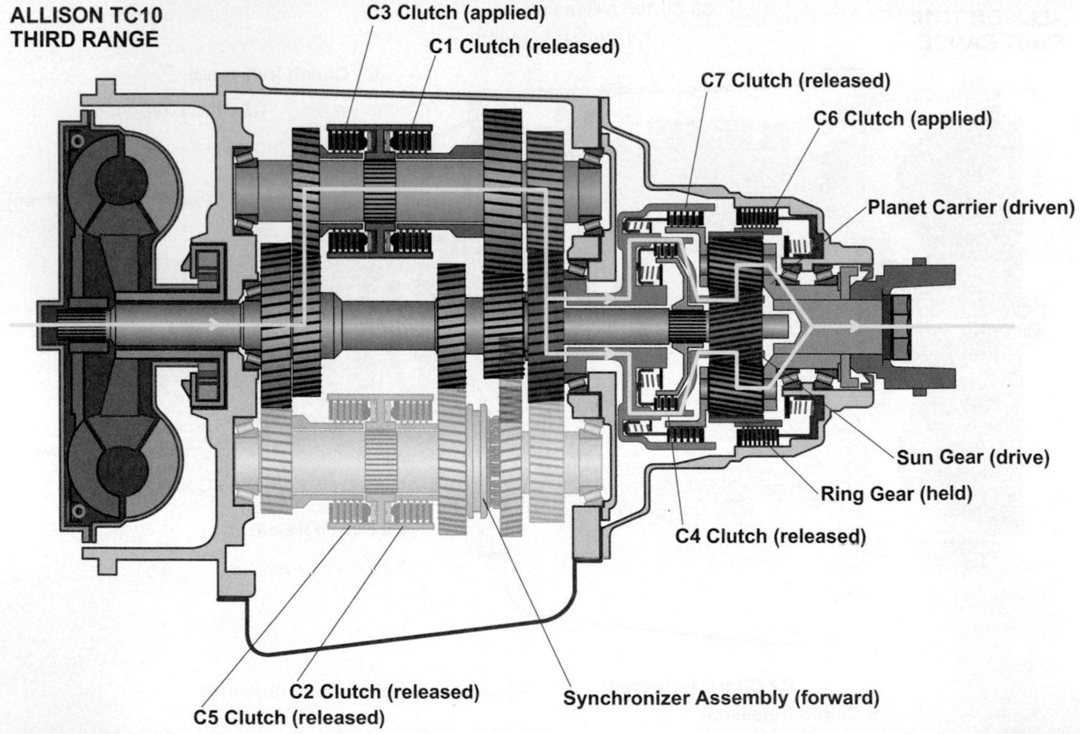

FIGURE 45-74 Third range.

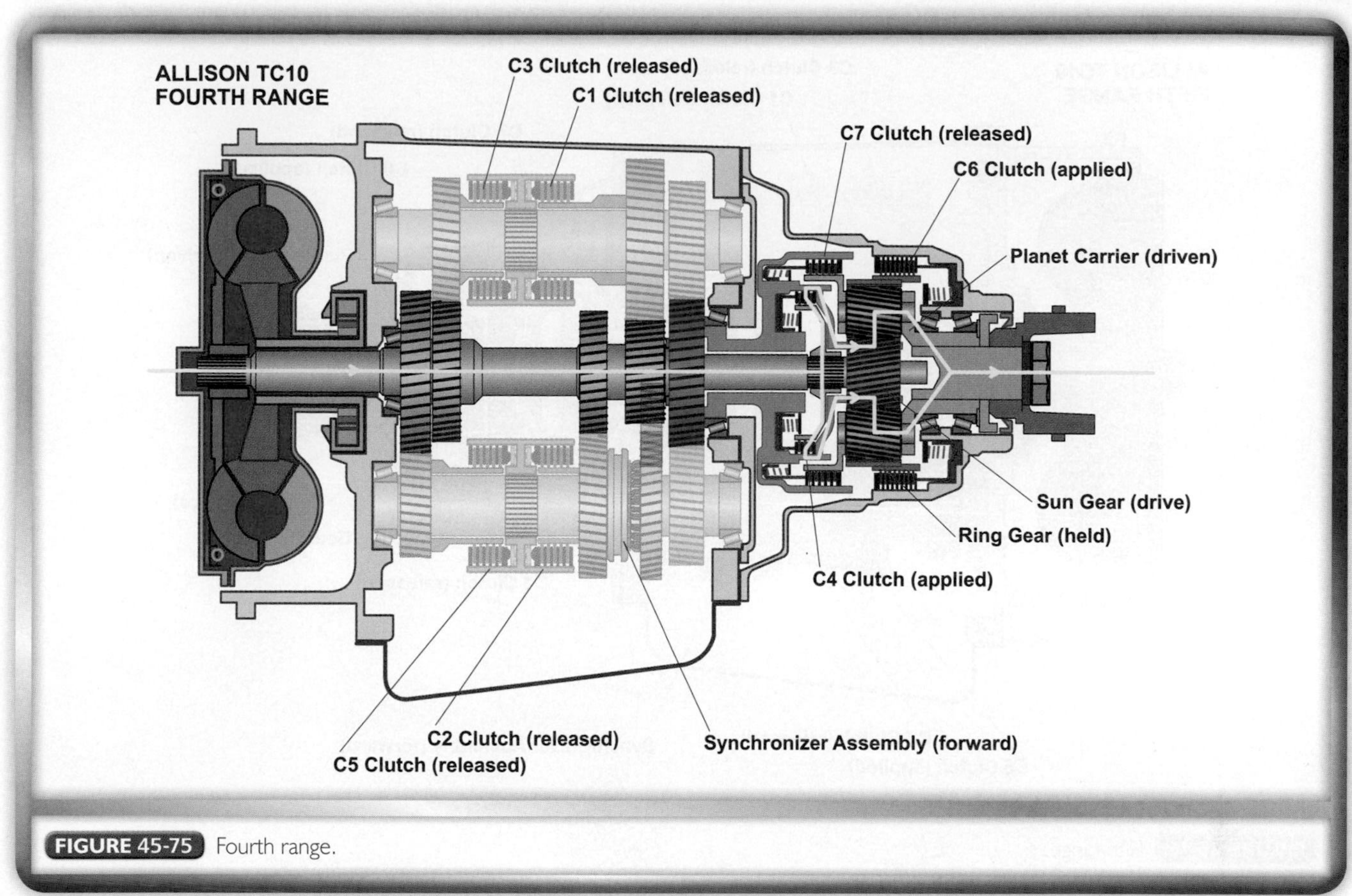

FIGURE 45-75 Fourth range.

C-6 is still holding the planetary range section ring gear, and the range planetary carrier remains the output.

TC-10-TS Fifth Range

In fifth range, C-4 is released, C-5 is applied, and C-6 remains applied. C-5 locks the F-5 output gear to the left-side countershaft. Power flows from the input shaft to the left-side countershaft through F-5 and then to the range output gear. The planetary range section remains unchanged, and the planetary carrier is still the output FIGURE 45-76.

TC-10-TS Sixth Range

In sixth range, the planetary range section changes to high range or direct (straight through operation). C-6 is released, and C-7 is applied. C-7 will remain applied for ranges six through ten. C-6 releases the planetary ring gear, and C-7 locks the planetary carrier to the range output gear and, therefore, to the planetary sun gear. This causes all three members of the range planetary to lock together and turn as one unit FIGURE 45-77.

For ranges six through ten, the first five power flows are repeated with one important exception. Instead of being reduced through the planetary range section, power flows pass straight through it unchanged. In the sixth range, then, C-1 is applied and locks the F-1 output gear to the right-side countershaft. Power flows from the input shaft through F-1 and back to the range output gear. From there, power flows directly to the output shaft through the locked together range planetary gear set.

TC-10-TS Seventh Range

In seventh range, C-7 remains applied, C-1 is released, and C-2 is applied. That sequence locks the F-2 output gear to the left-side countershaft through the synchronizer, which is in the forward position. Power flows from the input shaft to the left-side countershaft through F-2 and then to the range output gear. From there, power flows directly to the output shaft through the locked together range planetary set FIGURE 45-78.

TC-10-TS Eighth Range

In eighth range, C-7 is still applied, C-2 is released, and C-3 applies. C-3 locks the F-3 output gear to the right-side counter shaft. Power flows from the input shaft through F-3 to the range output gear and, from there, directly to the output shaft through the range planetary gear set which is locked together FIGURE 45-79.

ALLISON TC10
FIFTH RANGE
C3 Clutch (released)
C1 Clutch (released)
C7 Clutch (released)
C6 Clutch (applied)
Planet Carrier (driven)
Sun Gear (drive)
Ring Gear (held)
C4 Clutch (released)
C2 Clutch (released)
C5 Clutch (applied)
Synchronizer Assembly (forward)

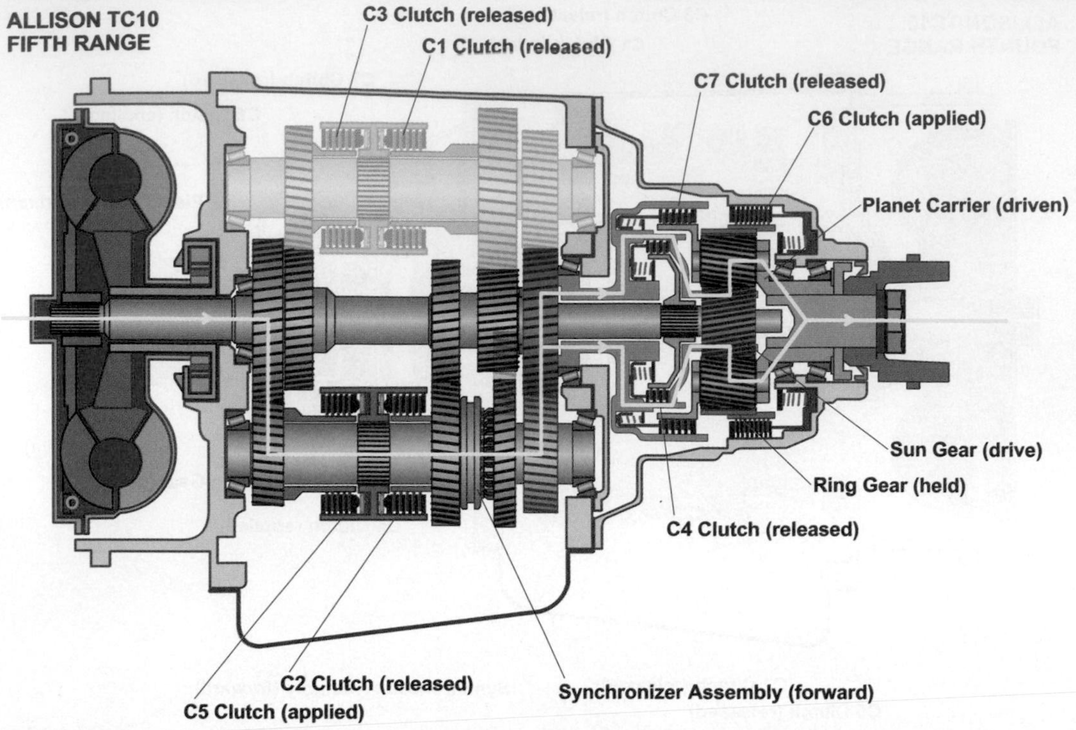

FIGURE 45-76 Fifth range.

ALLISON TC10
SIXTH RANGE
C3 Clutch (released)
C1 Clutch (applied)
C7 Clutch (applied)
C6 Clutch (released)
Planet Carrier (driven)
Sun Gear (idle)
Ring Gear (idle)
C4 Clutch (released)
C2 Clutch (released)
C5 Clutch (released)
Synchronizer Assembly (forward)

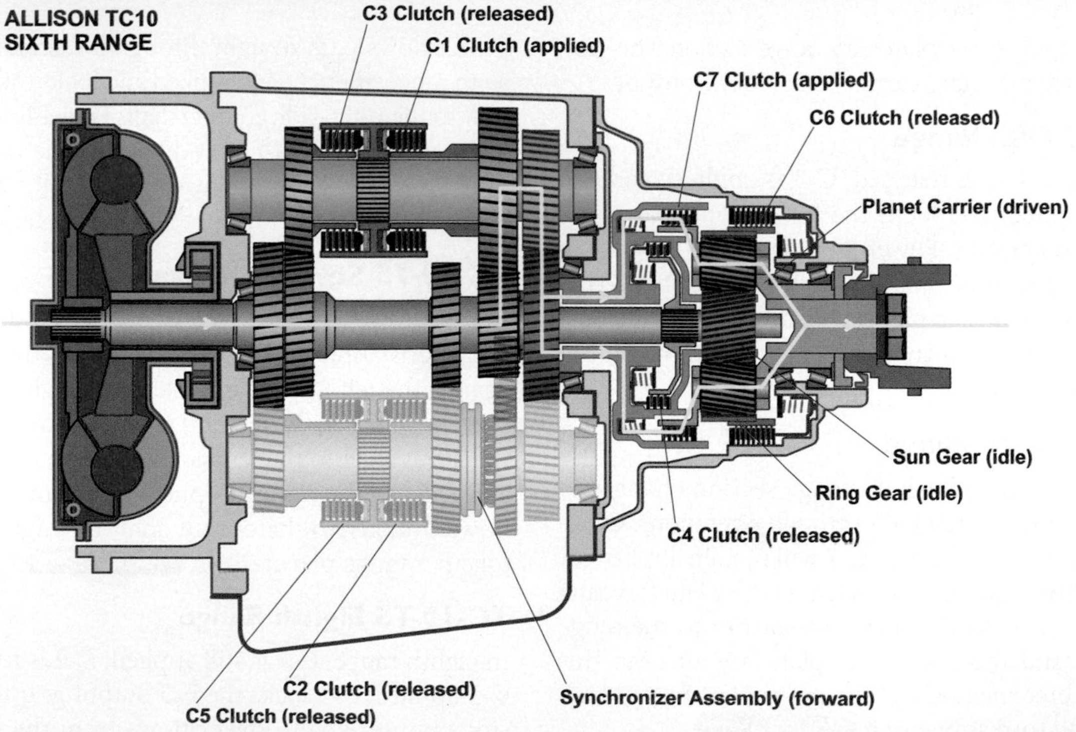

FIGURE 45-77 Sixth range.

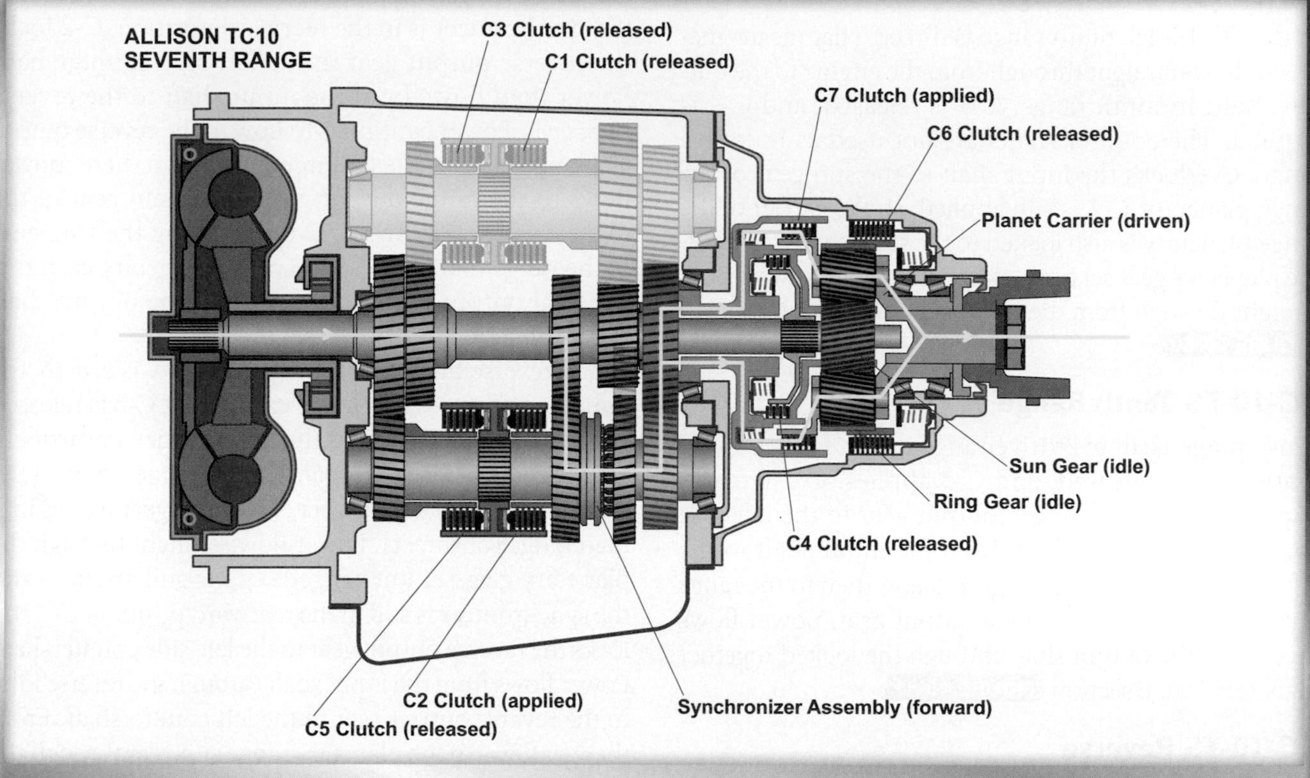

FIGURE 45-78 Seventh range.

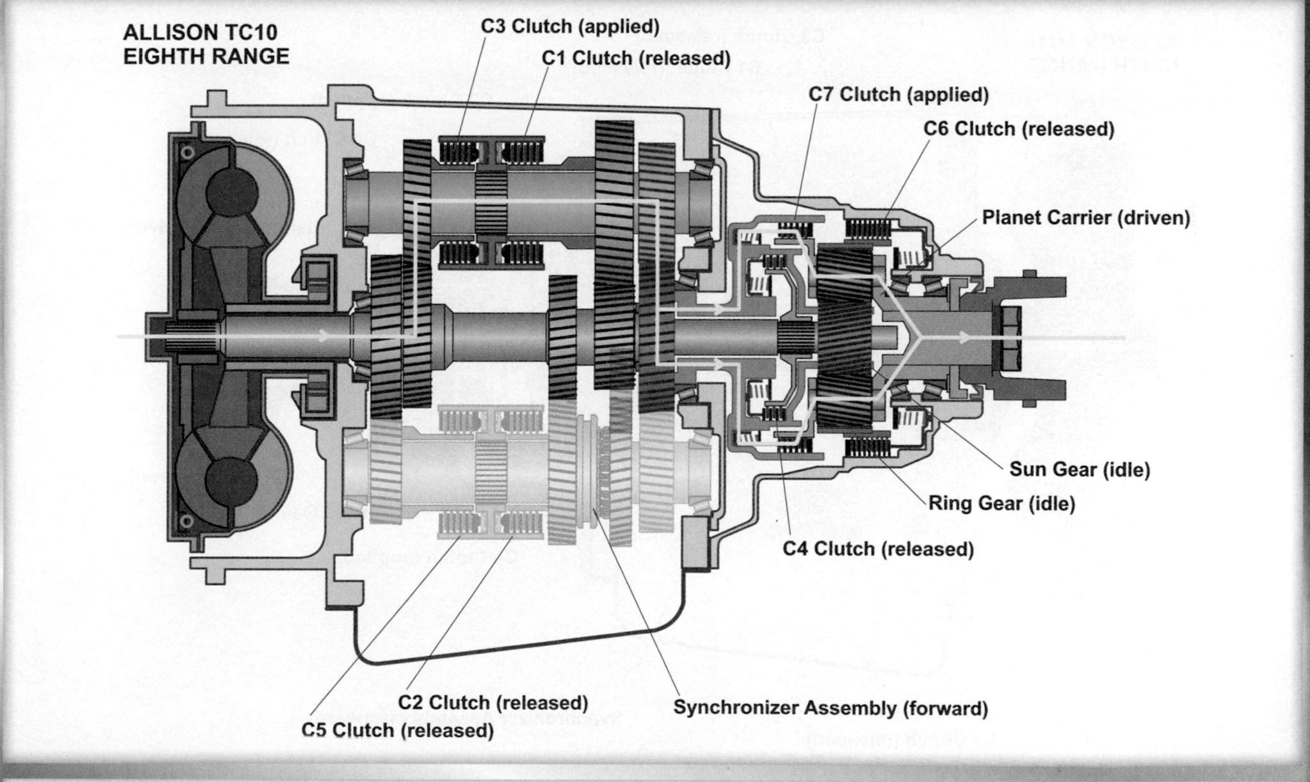

FIGURE 45-79 Eighth range.

TC-10-TS Ninth Range

In the TC-10-TS, ninth range is direct. That means that power flows straight through from the engine to the output shaft. In ninth range, C-3 is released, and C-4 is applied. The counter shafts are not used as in fourth range. C-4 locks the input shaft to the sun gear of the range planetary. C-7 is still applied, so the carrier of the range planetary is also locked to the sun gear. As a result, the planetary gear set turns as one unit, and power passes straight through from the input shaft to the output shaft FIGURE 45-80.

TC-10-TS Tenth Range

Tenth range is an overdrive range in the TC-10-TS. In tenth, C-4 is released, and C-5 applies. C-7 remains applied. C-5 locks the F-5 output gear to the left-side countershaft. Power flows from the input shaft to the left-side countershaft through F-5 and then to the range output gear. From the range output gear, power flows directly to the output shaft through the locked together planetary range section FIGURE 45-81.

TC-10-TS Reverse

The TC-10-TS has two reverse ranges: one low range and one high range. In reverse low, C-6 and C-2 are applied, and the synchronizer is rearward. C-6 holds the ring gear of the planetary range section. Because the synchronizer is in the rearward position, C-2 locks the reverse output gear to the left-side countershaft. Power then flows from the input shaft to the reverse idler gear. Power continues to flow to the reverse output gear and the left-side countershaft. From there, power flows to the range output gear to the sun gear of the planetary range gear set. C-6 is holding the ring gear of the range planetary, so the range planetary carrier is the final output and is connected to the output shaft FIGURE 45-82.

In reverse high range, the power flow is exactly the same as for reverse low range except that C-6 is released and C-7 applies. C-7 locks the range planetary carrier to the range planetary sun gear. The three members of the planetary are locked together, so reverse gear moves into high range (or direct). Power flows straight through the planetary gear set unchanged. C-2 is still applied, and the synchronizer is still in the rearward position. C-2 still locks the reverse output gear to the left-side countershaft. Power flows from the input shaft through the reverse idler to the reverse output gear to the left countershaft. From there, it flows to the planetary range sun gear through the range output gear. Because the range planetary is locked together, however, power flows from there directly to the output shaft FIGURE 45-83.

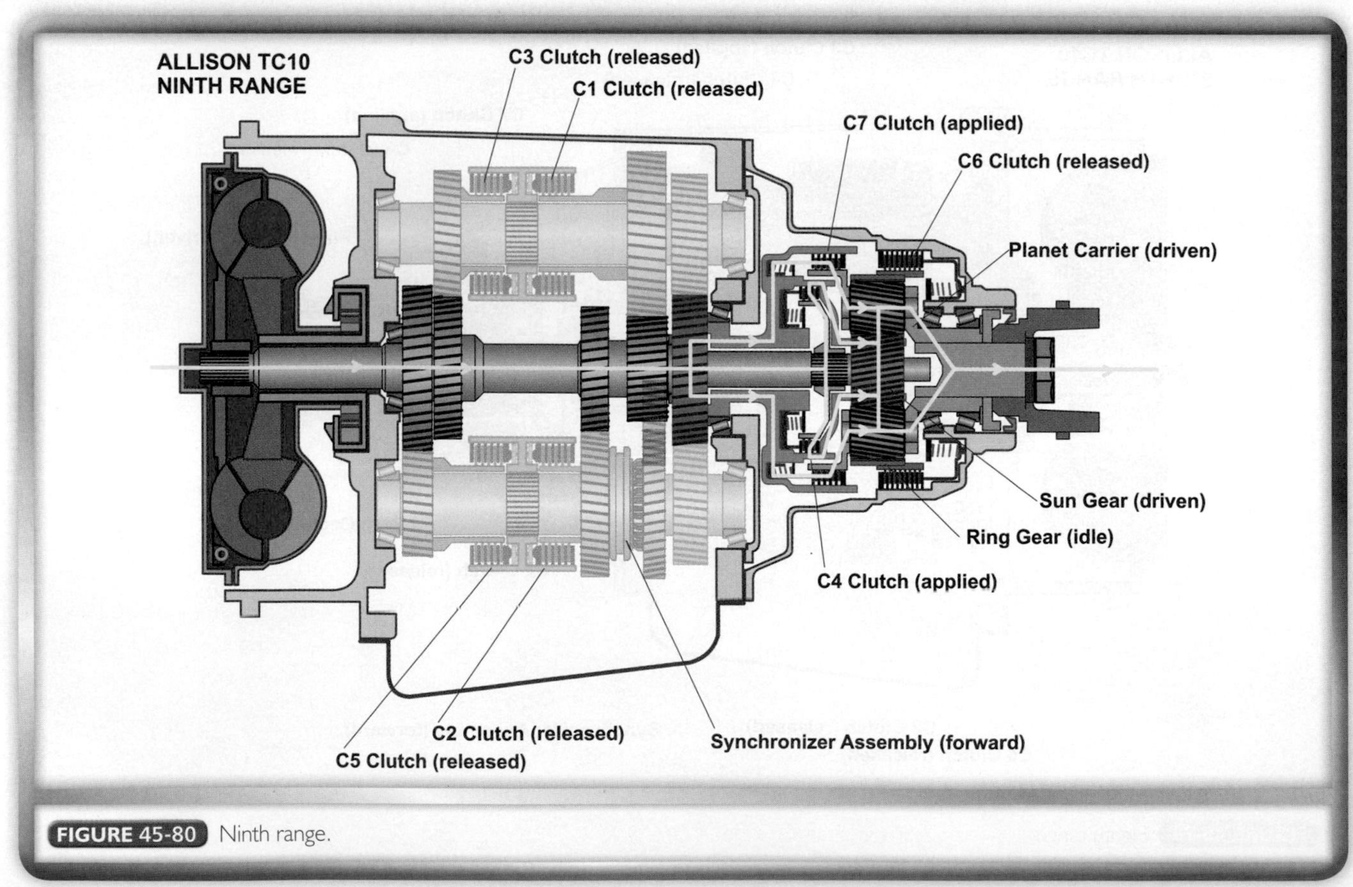

FIGURE 45-80 Ninth range.

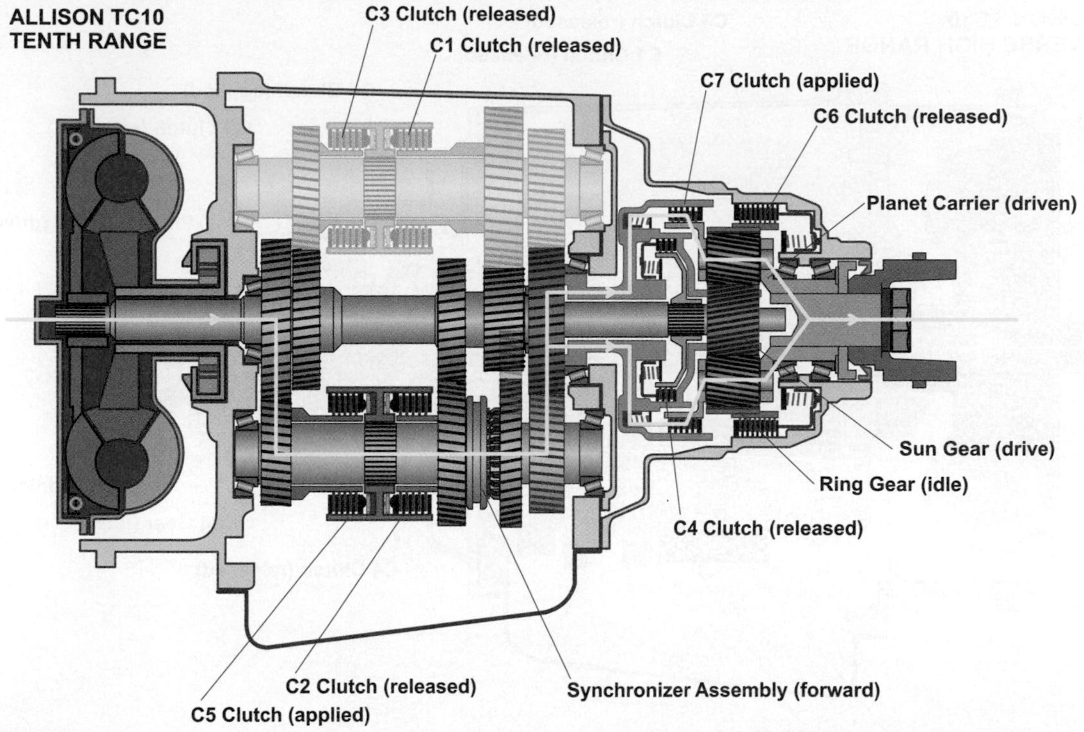

FIGURE 45-81 Tenth range.

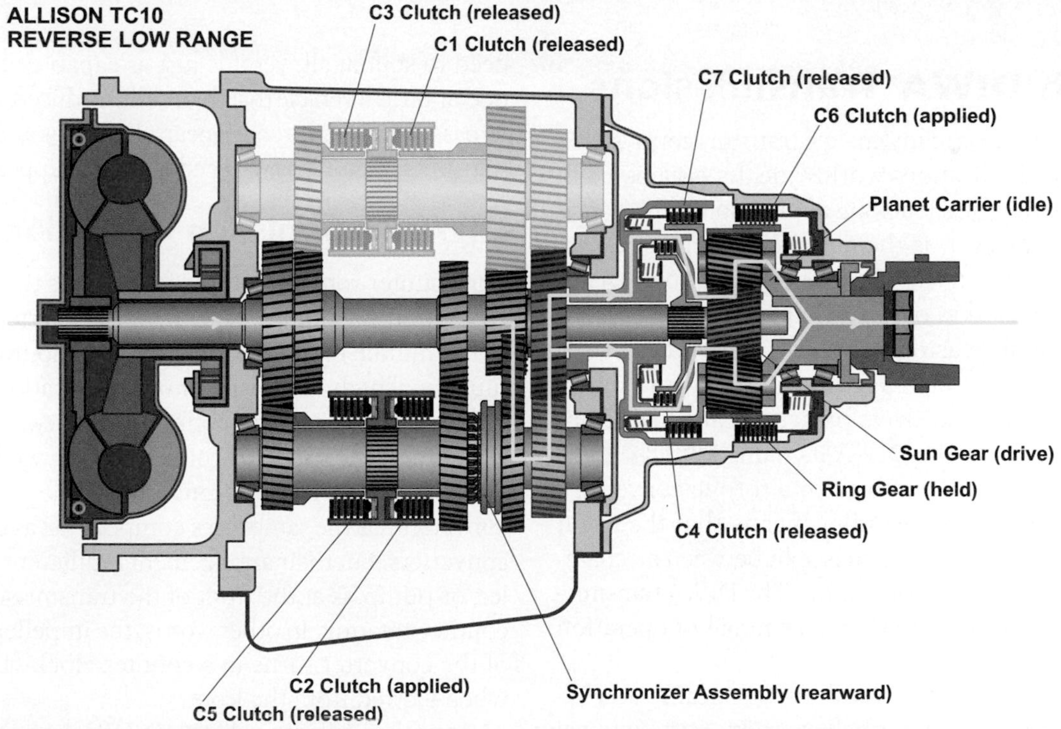

FIGURE 45-82 Reverse 1, also called reverse low range.

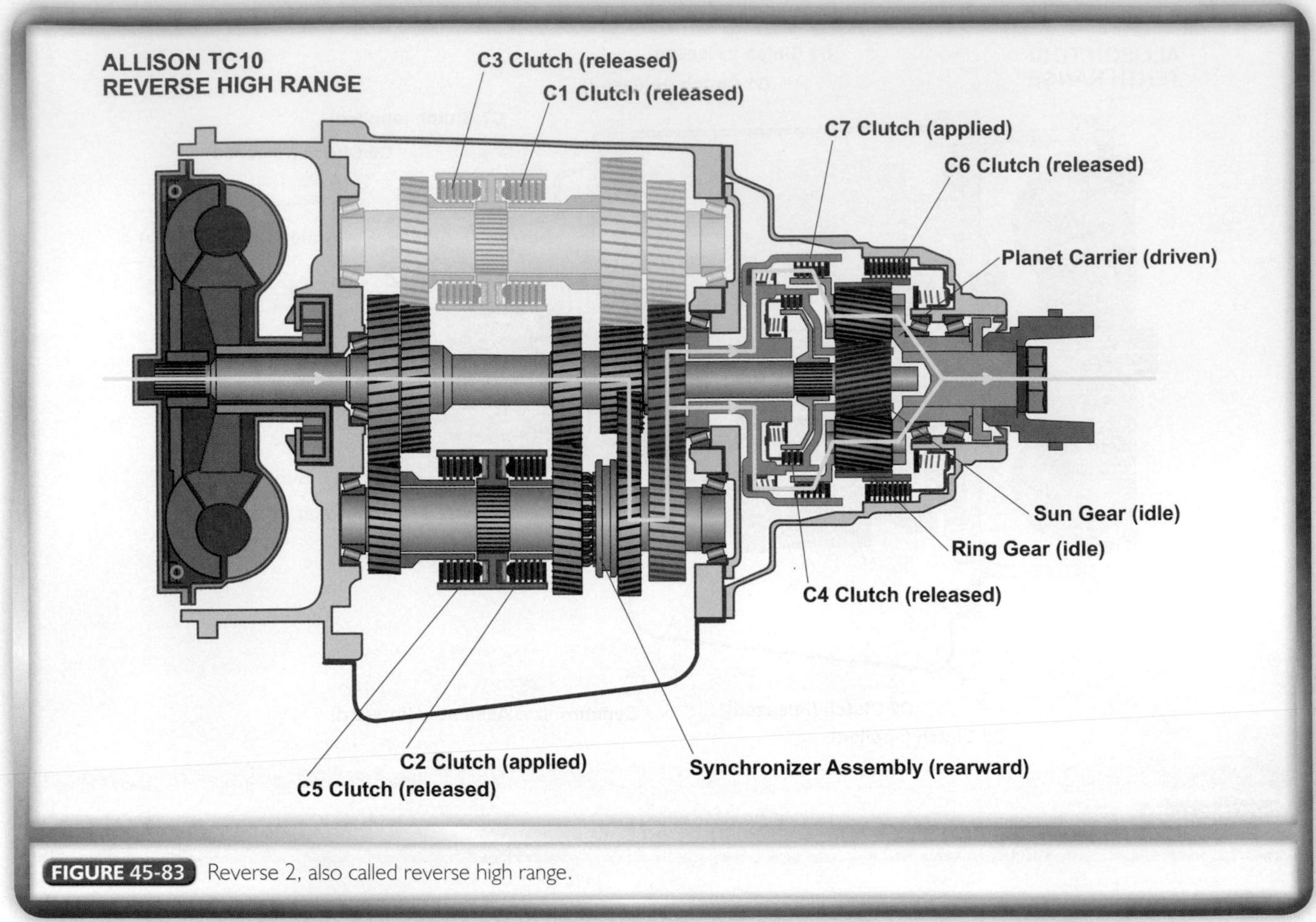

FIGURE 45-83 Reverse 2, also called reverse high range.

Voith DIWA Transmissions

The Voith Turbo Company makes transmission systems for a variety of applications worldwide. Its systems are in use in rail, marine, and trucking applications. The transit bus market, however, is the company's largest market for transmissions in terms of numbers. The Voith DIWA transmission is used in over 200,000 buses and coaches worldwide and increasingly in North America.

This transmission has a unique design with a differential torque converter drive principal called DIfferential-WAndler, giving the DIWA its name **FIGURE 45-84**. (Wandler is the German word for a torque converter). Differential drive with wandler means that the input torque during DIWA operation is split between mechanical and torque-converter operation. The DIWA transmission, therefore, has a much greater range of operation in first gear.

The DIWA transmission will use first gear to accelerate to speeds that would normally require a conventional automatic transmission to shift at least once and sometimes twice. That capability is particularly beneficial in bus applications. In stop-and-go traffic, the DIWA usually does not need to shift at all, yet it is just as capable of high-speed operation as a vehicle that does shift. Reduced shifting adds to passenger comfort and means less wear and tear on the transmission itself. Low-speed operation appears seamless.

DIWA Transmission Operation

The counter-rotating torque converter is the heart of the DIWA transmission's operation. The converter is mounted in the middle of the transmission and doubles as a fully functional hydraulic retarder on deceleration in all gears except first. The DIWA system torque converter is different from the standard converters that we looked at in the chapter on Torque Converters. The DIWA system converter has the same three components as other torque converters, but their arrangement is different. The impeller, or pump, is at the front of the transmission, but it is counter-rotating. In other words, the impeller at the front of the converter turns in a counter-clockwise direction when viewed from the front.

Another difference between DIWA and other transmissions is the position of the stator. Instead of the turbine being opposite the impeller, the stator is positioned at the rear. DIWA operation is the same regardless of

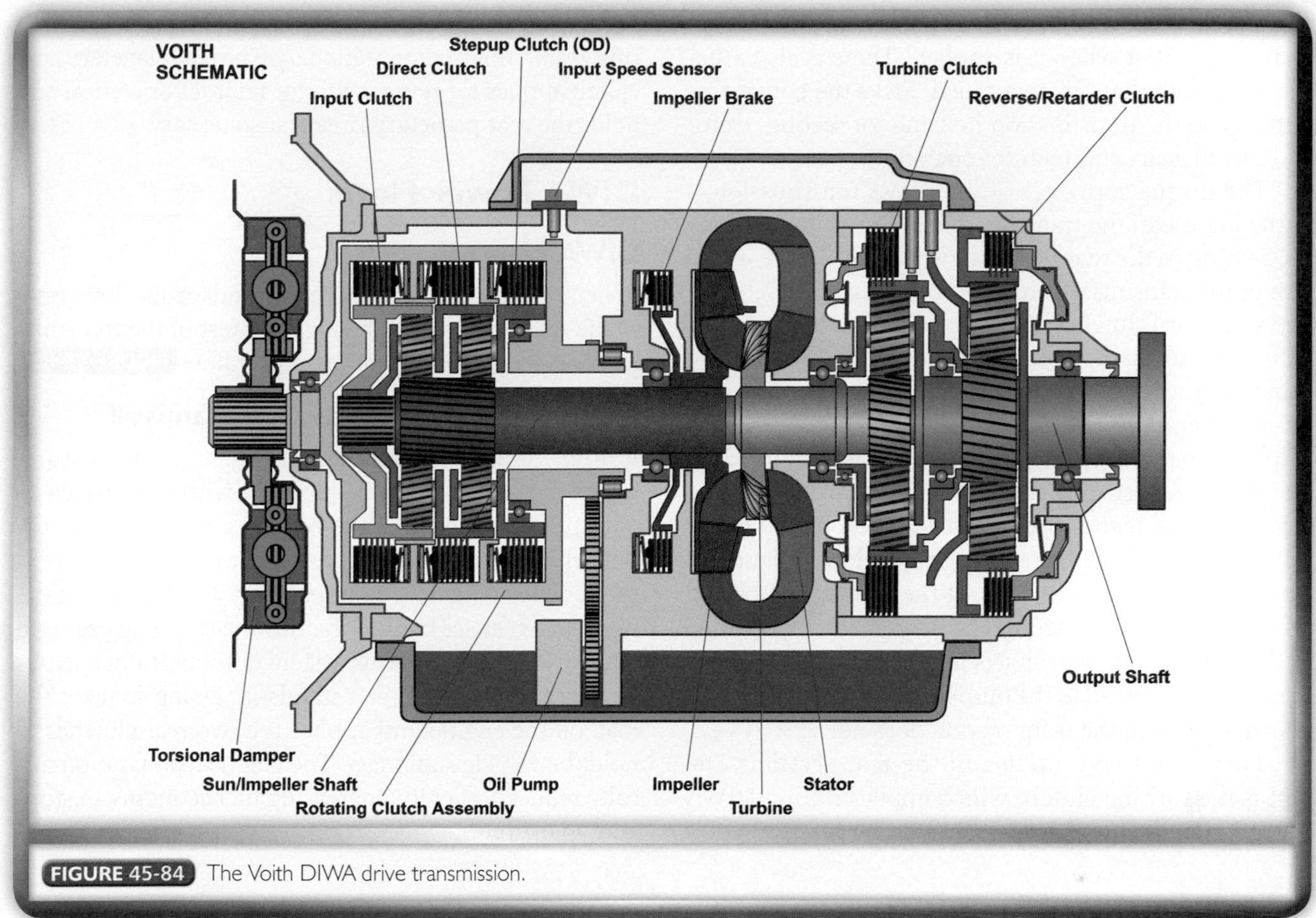

FIGURE 45-84 The Voith DIWA drive transmission.

whether the transmission is a three-speed or four-speed overdrive model.

DIWA Torque Converter Oil Flow

The DIWA torque converter is responsible for the hydrodynamic input to the transmission gearing. The mechanical portion of the differential input system will be covered later in the DIWA Power Flows section. The following is a description of the torque converter fluid flow and operation.

As the counter clockwise-rotating impeller (or pump) throws the transmission fluid outward by centrifugal force and rearward because of the housing shape, the fluid contacts the stator first—not the turbine, as is the case in most torque converters. Recall that in the DIWA system, the stator is at the rear of the torque converter. The stator re-directs the fluid flow and sends it back towards the impeller in a direction opposite to the impeller's rotation. The fluid then strikes the smaller, center-mounted turbine. The fluid striking the turbine causes the turbine to turn clockwise. The fluid then exits the turbine and enters the impeller in the same direction that it is turning, multiplying the torque. The rotating turbine provides input to the sun gear of the planetary gear set immediately behind the torque converter.

DIWA Transmission Components

All power enters the transmission through a torsional damper attached to the engine flywheel. In the front section of the overdrive transmission, a single, rotating clutch drum attached to the transmission input shaft contains three clutches:

- The input clutch
- The third gear clutch, also called the lock-up clutch as it provides 1:1 operation
- The step-up clutch (overdrive or fourth gear clutch)

Those three clutches control the operation of two planetary gears. The front planetary carrier is splined to the output shaft, and the second planetary ring gear is splined to the front carrier. The first clutch (the input clutch) in the rotating clutch module drives the front planetary ring gear when applied. The second clutch (the lock-up clutch) drives the second planetary ring gear and, by connection, the front carrier when it is applied.

The third clutch (the overdrive clutch) drives the second planetary carrier when it is applied. There is also a stationary clutch that, when applied, locks the converter's impeller to the transmission housing for second, third, and fourth gears and retarder operation.

The torque converter of the DIWA transmission is in the middle of the transmission and provides input to the gearing in the rear of the transmission. The rear section of the transmission has two planetary gear sets and two stationary clutches. The planetary gear immediately behind the torque converter receives the hydro-dynamic input from the torque converter during first gear and reverse operation. The ring gear of this planetary gear set is splined to the sun gear of the rear (reverse and braking) planetary gear set. The carrier of the first planetary ring gear set in the rear of the transmission is splined to the output shaft. The rear (reverse and braking) planetary gear set sits at the very back of the transmission, and its carrier is also splined to the output shaft. So, three of the four planetary gear sets in this transmission have their carriers splined to the output shaft. Only the second planetary gear in the front section does not.

There are two clutches in the rear section. The first is the turbine clutch, which applies during DIWA operation in first gear (when torque converter operation is necessary). The first clutch holds the first planetary ring gear in this section stationary. The rear planetary gear clutch applies for reverse and for retarder operation and holds the rear planetary ring gear stationary.

DIWA Power Flows

DIWA Neutral

In neutral, no clutches are applied, and torque flows only to the rotating clutch housing. The rest of the transmission is disconnected from the power flow FIGURE 45-85.

DIWA Automatic Neutral at Standstill

Automatic neutral at standstill is an optional feature. When the vehicle is at a standstill with the service or parking brake applied, the reverse clutch and the turbine clutch are applied at the same time. This results in the vehicle being held stationary, as two elements of the planetary gear set behind the turbine (the ring gear and the carrier) are held. This system automatically releases the front input clutch at a standstill. Doing so takes the load off the engine and applies the two rear clutches to hold the vehicle stationary. The engine load is automatically reduced, thereby increasing fuel economy in stop-and-go operation.

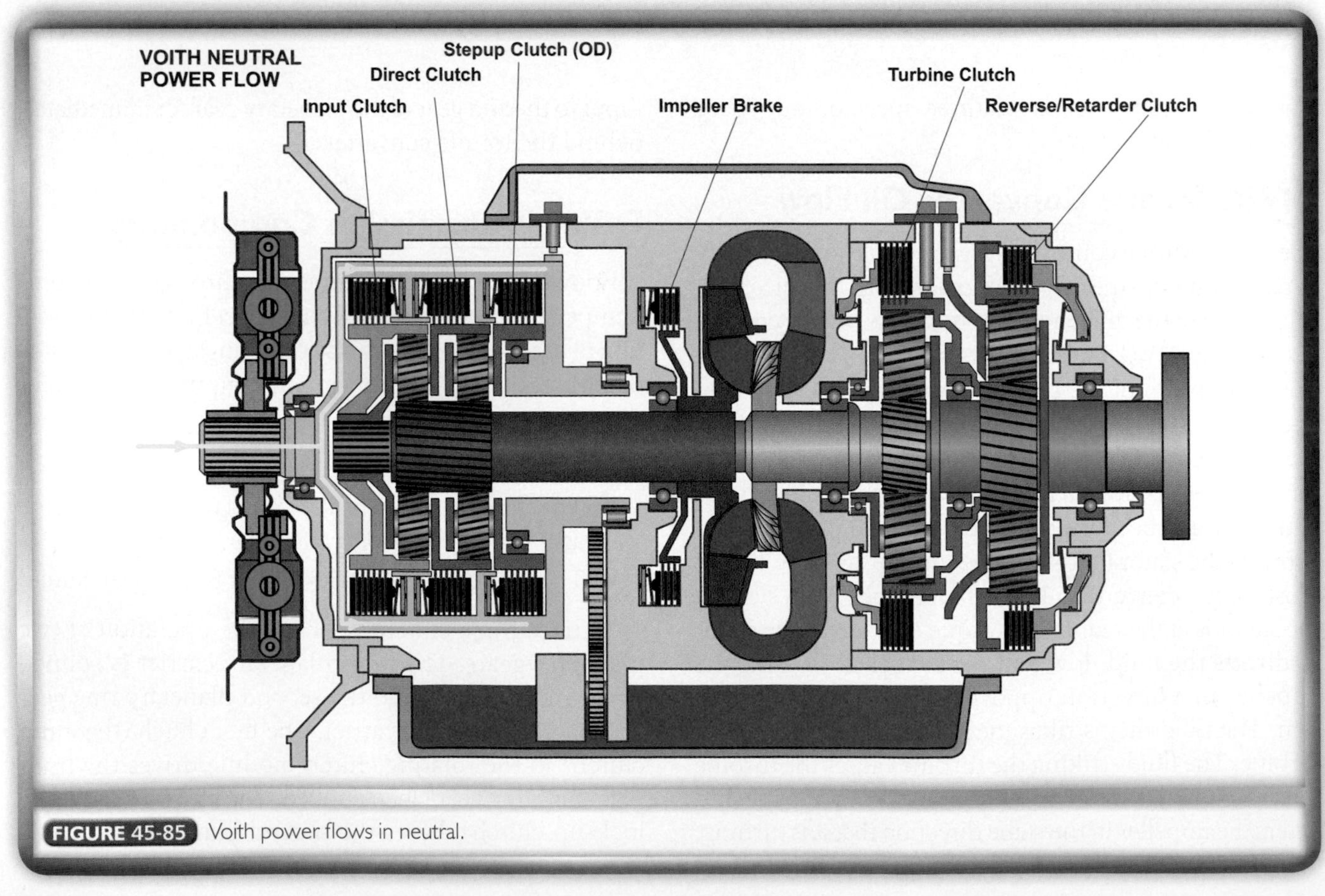

FIGURE 45-85 Voith power flows in neutral.

DIWA First Gear

In first gear, as the vehicle accelerates, the input clutch and the turbine clutch are applied, and engine torque is split between mechanical input and hydro-dynamic input FIGURE 45-86. The mechanical input comes from the front planetary gear set. The hydro-dynamic input comes from the planetary gear set directly behind the torque converter.

In the front planetary gear set, the ring gear is input by the input clutch, and the front carrier is splined to the output shaft. As such, the front carrier acts as a held member, causing the sun gear to rotate in the opposite direction. The sun gear drives the impeller of the torque converter counter-clockwise, and the torque converter turbine drives the sun gear of the planetary gear set behind the turbine in a clockwise direction. The ring gear of this planetary set is held stationary by its clutch, and its carrier becomes output. The carrier is splined to the output shaft, so this is the hydro-dynamic drive.

As the vehicle starts to move, the load becomes heavier on the sun gear driving the impeller. As a result, the sun gear starts to act as a held member in the front planetary set. The front carrier becomes output because it is splined directly to the output shaft. The load becomes stronger on the sun gear in the front planetary gear, and it acts more and more as a held member. The output from the front carrier increases as the vehicle's speed increases.

The output is a combination of the drive through the gear set behind the torque converter and the ever-increasing drive through the front planetary carrier. As the vehicle accelerates, more of the power flow is transferred from the hydro-dynamic side behind the torque converter to the mechanical side at the front planetary carrier.

DIWA Second Gear

The shift to second is controlled electronically and is essentially the same as first FIGURE 45-87. A key difference, however, is that the torque converter's operation is completely stopped. The turbine clutch is released, and the impeller clutch (brake) is applied. This holds the front planetary sun gear stationary. The front ring gear is still input, the sun gear is held, and the carrier (splined to the output shaft) is output. The result is a pure mechanical power flow.

DIWA Third Gear

In third gear, the input clutch is released, and the third, or lock-up, clutch applies FIGURE 45-88. That combination drives the second planetary ring gear, which is splined to the front carrier. In turn, the front carrier is splined directly to the output shaft, so the output shaft is driven

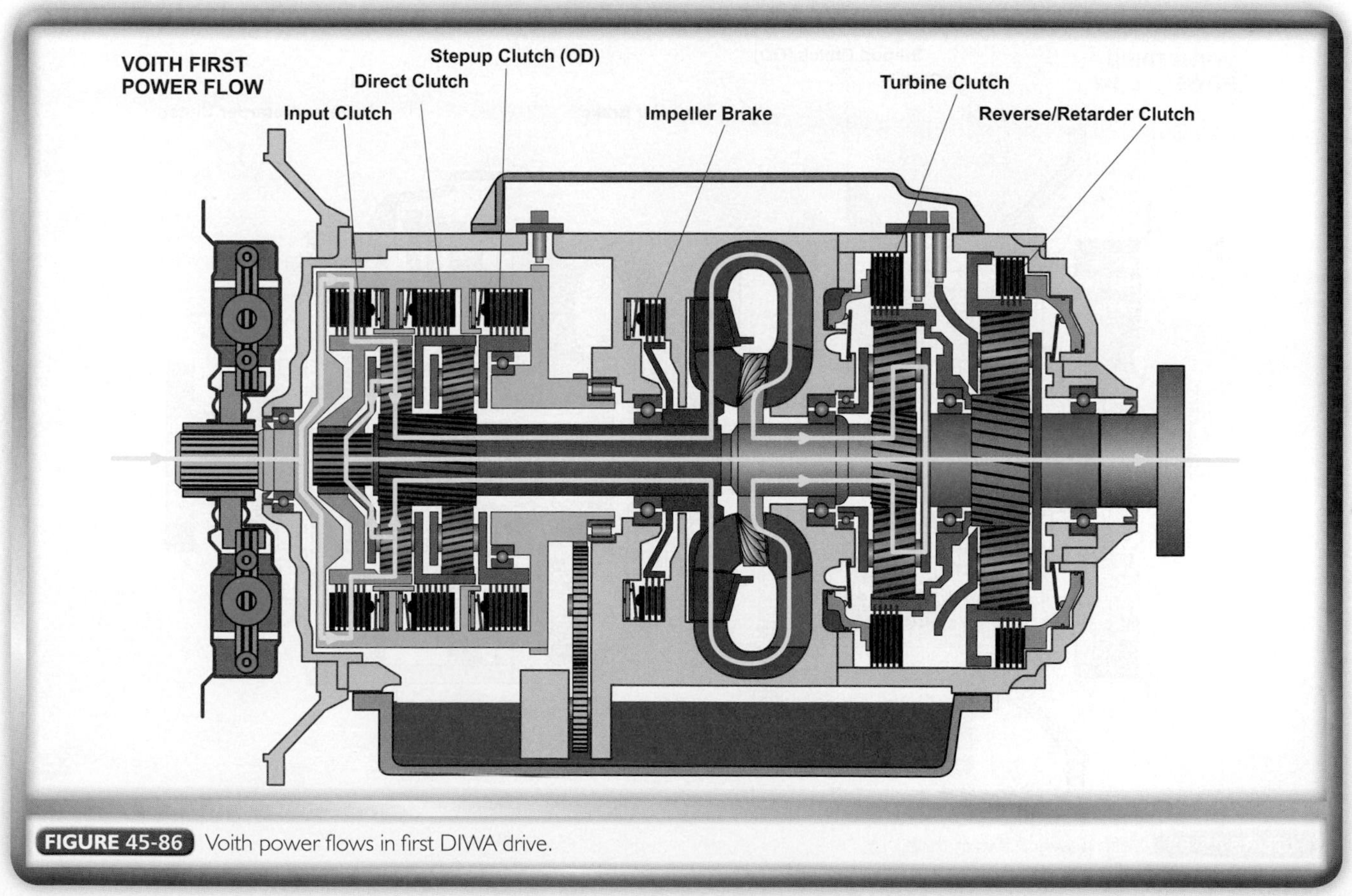

FIGURE 45-86 Voith power flows in first DIWA drive.

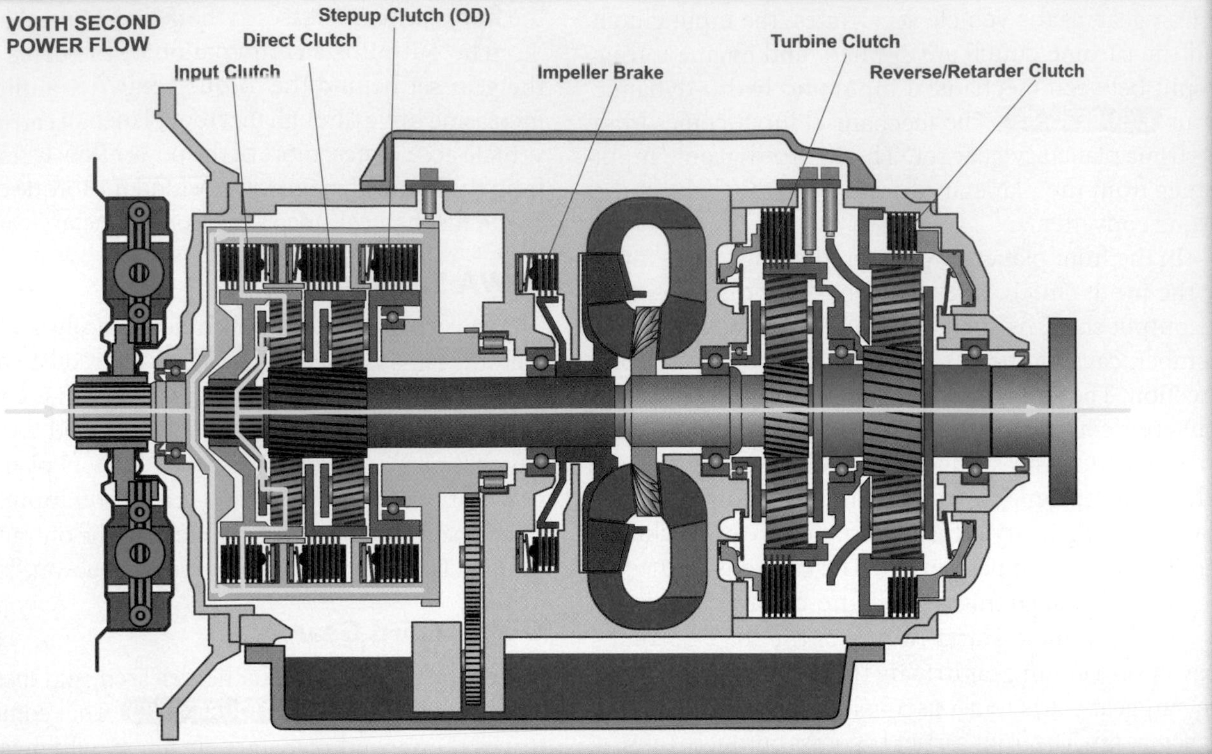

VOITH SECOND POWER FLOW
Stepup Clutch (OD)
Direct Clutch
Input Clutch
Impeller Brake
Turbine Clutch
Reverse/Retarder Clutch

FIGURE 45-87 Voith power flows in second.

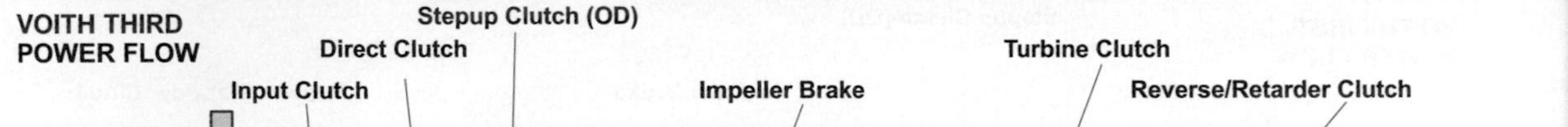

VOITH THIRD POWER FLOW
Stepup Clutch (OD)
Direct Clutch
Input Clutch
Impeller Brake
Turbine Clutch
Reverse/Retarder Clutch

FIGURE 45-88 Voith power flows in third.

directly by the rotating clutch assembly. A one-to-one ratio results.

DIWA Fourth Gear

In fourth gear, the fourth clutch applies. This inputs the carrier of the second planetary gear set. The sun gear in the second set is held by the impeller brake (clutch). With the carrier input and the sun gear held, the result is overdrive output on the second planetary ring gear. The second planetary ring gear is splined to the front carrier which is, in turn, splined to the output shaft. The result is fourth range overdrive FIGURE 45-89.

DIWA Reverse

In reverse the input is the same as for first gear FIGURE 45-90. The input clutch is applied, and that drives the forward ring gear. The turbine clutch is not applied, but the reverse/retarder clutch is applied. That combination holds the ring gear of the rear planetary gear stationary.

The power flow proceeds as follows. The front planetary ring gear is input. The front carrier has the load of the output shaft and the vehicle weight holding it stationary. That causes the sun gear to turn in reverse and inputs the impeller of the torque converter counter-clockwise. As the vehicle accelerates, the impeller begins to turn faster, driving the turbine and the sun gear of the planetary set behind the torque converter clockwise. The carrier in this set is loaded by vehicle weight, so its ring gear turns in reverse. The ring gear of this planetary set is connected to the sun gear of the rear planetary set, so its sun gear becomes reverse input to the rear planetary. The rear planetary ring gear is held by the reverse clutch, so its carrier becomes output (still in reverse), and the rear carrier is splined to the output shaft.

Retarder Operation

Retardation in first range is accomplished by lightly applying the reverse clutch with a pressure of approximately 17 to 18 pounds per square inch (1.2 bar) to slow down the output shaft FIGURE 45-91. In second, third, and fourth gears, retarder operation uses the torque converter as a hydraulic retarder. The reverse clutch, the impeller clutch (i.e., brake), and the input clutch associated with the particular range are all applied for retardation. The reverse clutch drives the turbine, which throws oil against the stationary impeller in the torque converter. The resultant retarding force slows the output shaft. The

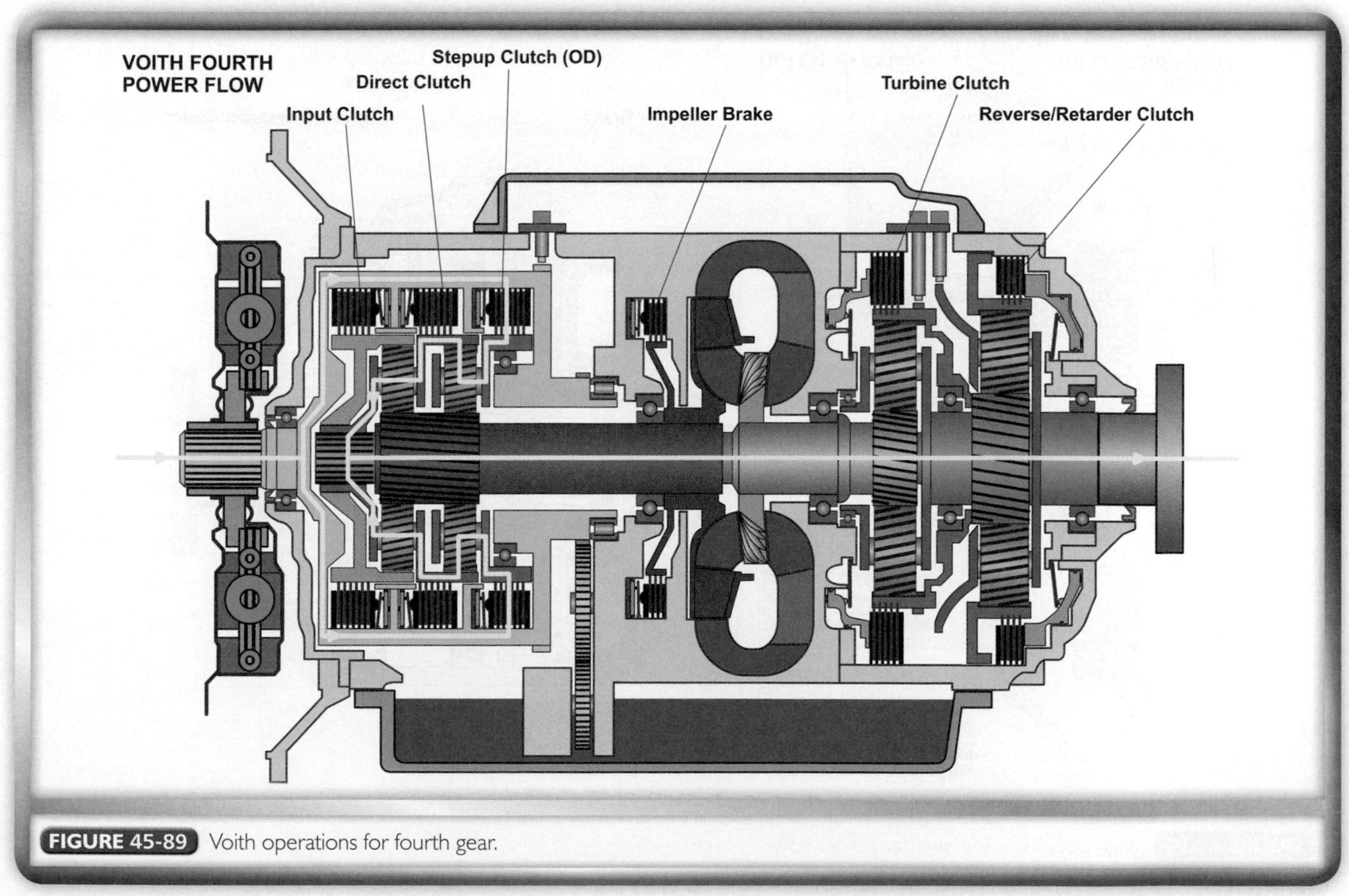

FIGURE 45-89 Voith operations for fourth gear.

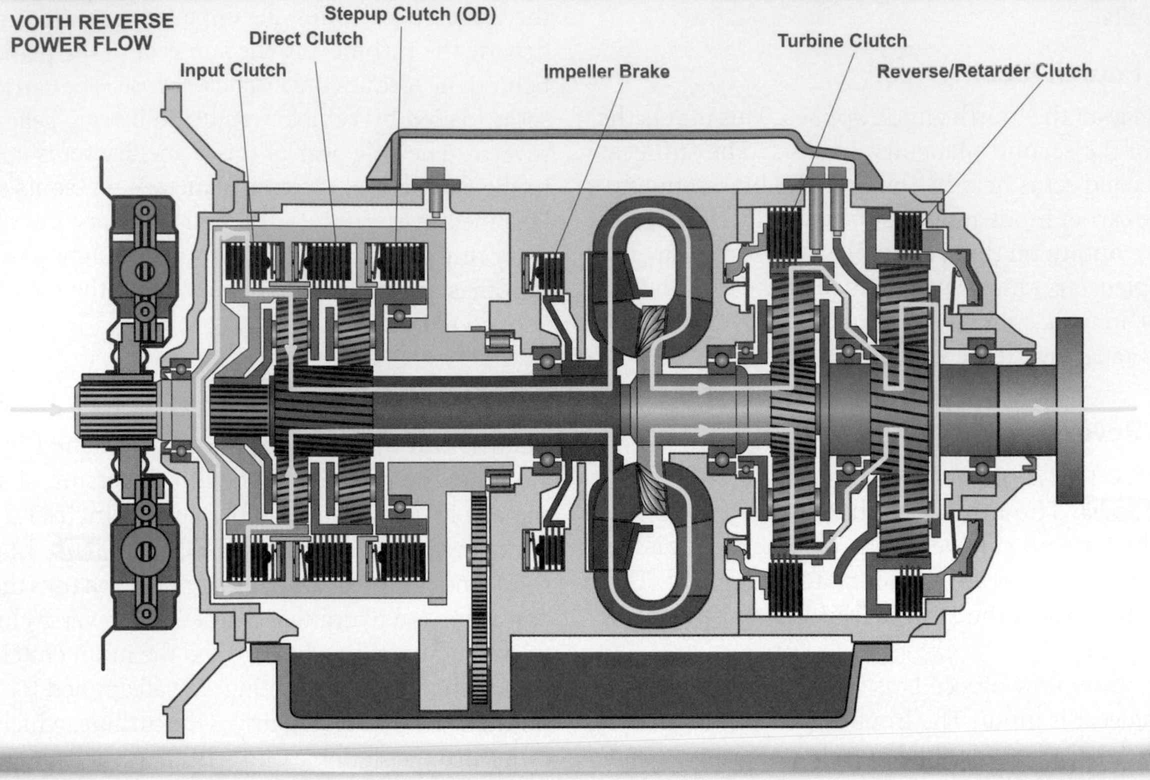

FIGURE 45-90 Voith operations for reverse.

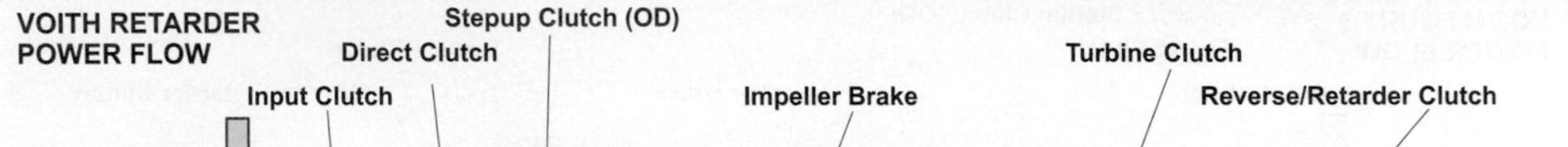

FIGURE 45-91 Voith operations for retarder power flow.

braking effort is controlled by the torque converter fluid pressure. Increased operating pressure provides greater retardation; decreased operating pressure provides less. The heat generated by the retardation is dissipated in the transmission integral heat exchanger.

Control System

The DIWA.5 Transmission with the Intelligent Control Unit E-300 comes equipped with **SensoTop**, an **adaptive control** feature that senses topography and vehicle load and adjusts shift control to obtain maximum economy and comfort. As with other transmission control systems, adaptive control allows the transmission ECU to "learn" and adapt shifts based on any number of input data. Most systems will include inclinometers or a similar component to sense road grade and gather information on load factors, fuel, rates, and more. As with most information in the system, the information collected by SensoTop travels through the controller area network (CAN) from the engine ECU.

To diagnose transmission problems and record operating events, the DIWA transmission uses a dedicated software diagnostic program called Aladin with a user friendly interface. Voith also offers a satellite monitoring system than can remotely diagnose problems with the transmission and relay them to the nearest service depot. Voith headquarters are in Hiedenheim, Germany, and the company also has offices in York, Pennsylvania and Sacramento, California.

ZF Friedrichshafen AG EcoMat and EcoLife Transmissions

ZF is a leading transmission manufacturer and has been designing and producing transmissions for various world markets for well over 50 years. ZF produces two automatic transmissions for the truck and coach market—the EcoMat and the EcoLife. The EcoMat is available in five- and six-speed models and can accept up to approximately 1,300 foot-pounds (1,762 Nm) of input torque. EcoMat is used in both trucks and buses FIGURE 45-92.

The EcoLife is ZF's latest six-speed transmission model that can handle up to 1,475 foot-pounds (2,000 Nm) of input torque. Both EcoMat and EcoLife transmissions utilize three planetary gears, six hydraulic clutches, and an integrated retarder for braking assist. ZF's proprietary TopoDyn software allows the transmission controller to learn load and road grade conditions and optimize shift profiles to suit the terrain and drive cycle. That capability leads to more efficient operation and greater driver and passenger comfort. Until 2009, ZF was in partnership with Arvin Meritor in North America, and the company still has a network of U.S. dealers marketing and servicing these transmissions.

FIGURE 45-92 ZF transmissions are sold all over the world.

Caterpillar Automatic Transmissions

Caterpillar has made electronically controlled transmissions for the off-road market for years. In 2006, the company launched its first line of automatic truck transmissions for the on-highway market. The on-highway line consists of three models:

- CX28 is a medium-duty, six-speed transmission rated for 400 horsepower (300 kW) with input torque of 1250 foot-pounds (1,770 Nm) FIGURE 45-93.
- CX31 is a six-speed model for medium-duty applications rated for up to 525 horsepower (391 kW), and 1,770 foot-pounds (2,400 Nm) of input torque.

FIGURE 45-93 Caterpillar's CX-28 Transmission.

- CX35 is a heavy-duty, eight-speed model rated for up to 625 horsepower (456 kW) and 2,150 foot-pounds (2,915 Nm) of input torque.

The CX28 and CX31 on-highway models have three planetary gear sets, five hydraulic clutches, and are capable of six forward speeds.

In all models, the clutches are numbered C-1 to C-5, and the clutch application chart and the power flows are the same as the Allison World Transmission **FIGURE 45-94**. The heavy-duty CX35 model has four planetary gear sets and six hydraulic clutches and is capable of eight forward speeds. The CX transmissions are completely drive by wire. In other words, they are solely electronically controlled. The transmission ECU has adaptive control built in so that it can optimize shifting for any operating cycle and load configuration.

The CX line of transmissions uses electronic clutch-pressure control units (ECPCs) to control clutch application. The ECPCs consist of a pulse-width-modulated solenoid that in turn controls a modulating spool valve that directs main pressure of 350 pounds per square inch (24 bars) to the clutches. When making a shift, the transmission ECU will first send a full-duty cycle signal to the ECPC solenoid. The signal tells the transmission to initiate clutch application and then will vary the duty cycle to control the quality of the shift in progress. Each clutch uses its own ECPC to control its application, and all of the ECPCs are identical **FIGURE 45-95**.

The transmissions are equipped with a lock-up converter, which locks up as the vehicle approaches maximum speed in second range. The lock-up converter is applied for all forward ranges above second. CX transmissions have two selectable operational modes:

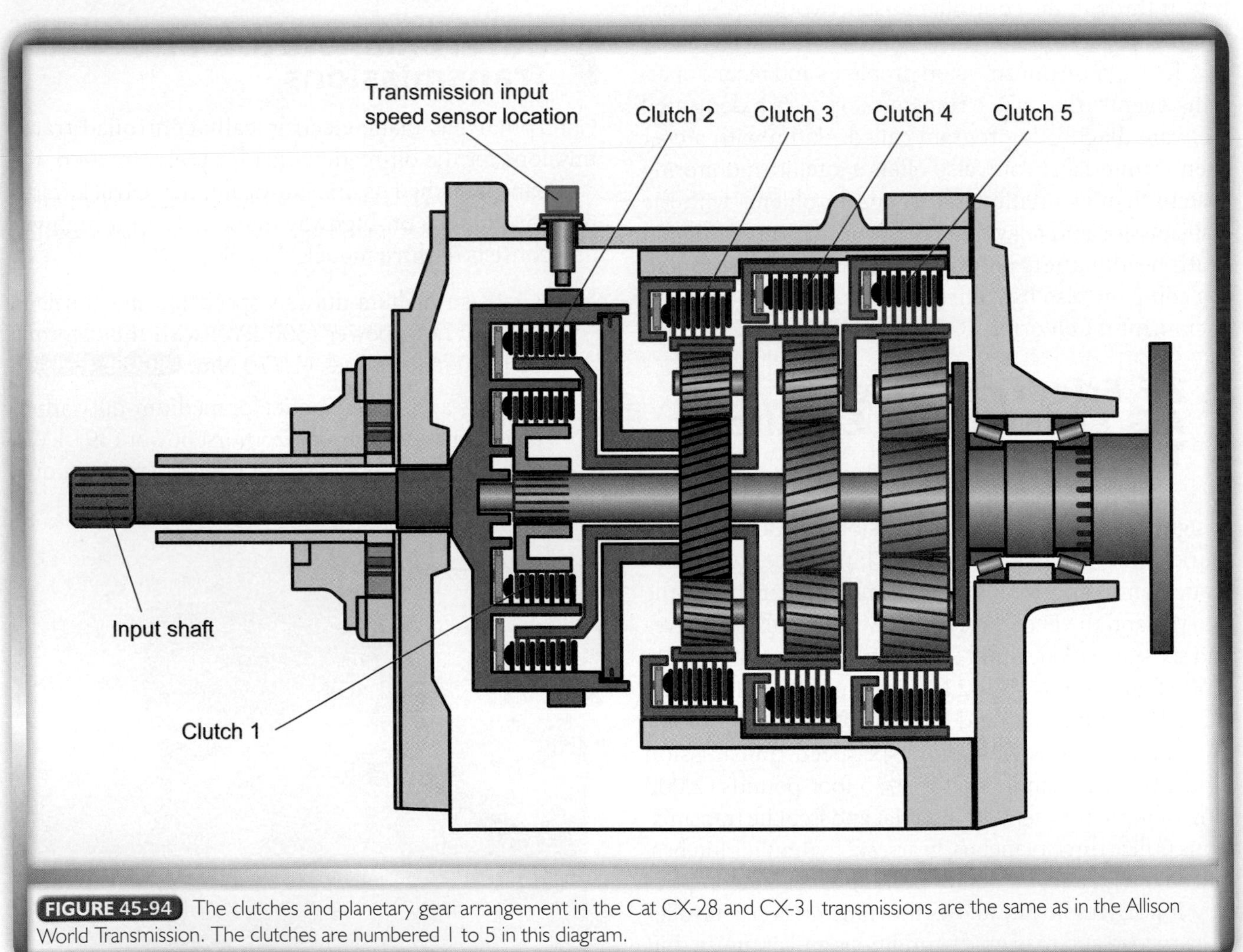

FIGURE 45-94 The clutches and planetary gear arrangement in the Cat CX-28 and CX-31 transmissions are the same as in the Allison World Transmission. The clutches are numbered 1 to 5 in this diagram.

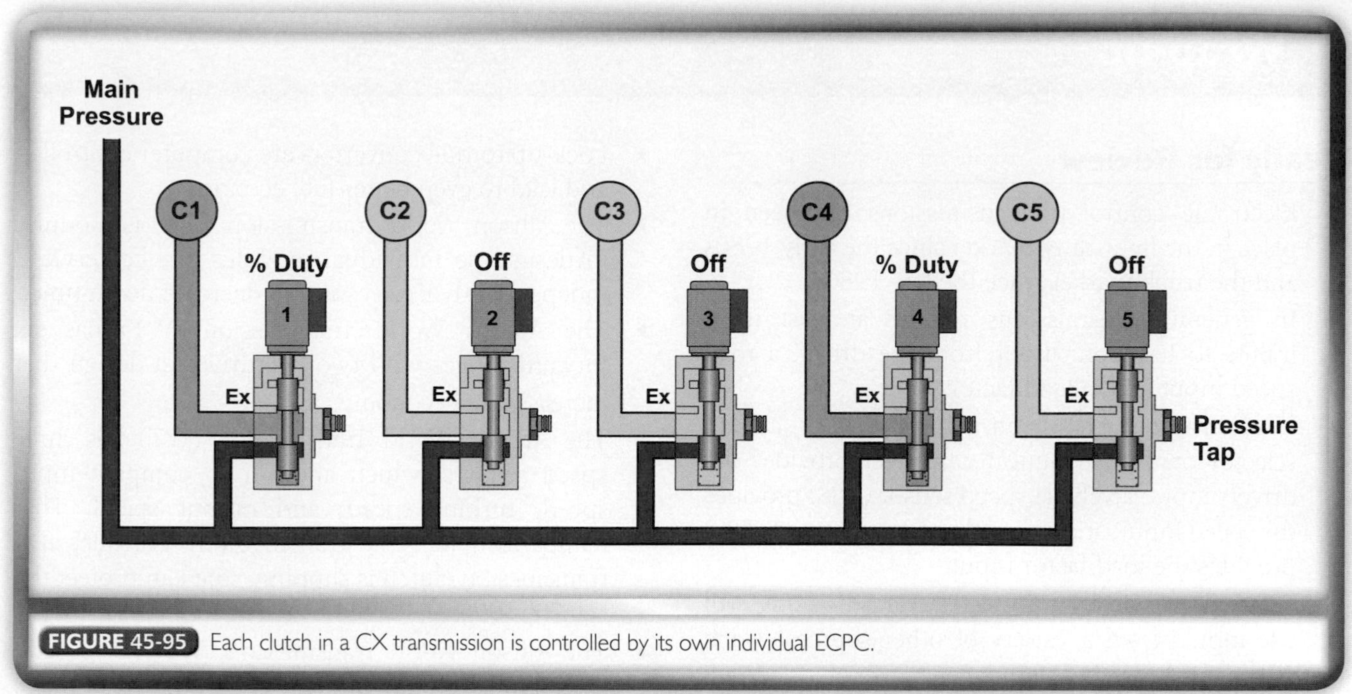

FIGURE 45-95 Each clutch in a CX transmission is controlled by its own individual ECPC.

economy mode and performance mode. In economy mode, shifting occurs at lower road speeds to save fuel. In performance modes, shifts will occur at close to the rated revolutions per minute (rpm) to allow for greater acceleration.

CX transmissions have self-diagnostic capability and will set a diagnostic trouble code (DTC) in the ECU memory and turn on an amber or red warning lamp when a problem exists. Cat Electronic Technician (ET) software is a proprietary diagnostic software program that can be utilized to access DTC information.

The ECU adaptive control on CX transmissions continuously monitors and adjusts the shifting process to make up for transmission wear and system degradation. After transmission overhaul or replacement, the adaptive control must be reset. Caterpillar calls this resetting of adaptive control "the transmission calibration procedure." It basically entails incorporating the learned adjustments to the shift process. Recalibration can only be accomplished with the Cat ET service program.

The CX series transmissions have not yet made a big impact on the North American automatic transmission market due, in part, to Caterpillar's decision to drop out of the on-highway truck engine market back in 2010. Despite reduced activity in the on-highway truck engine market, Caterpillar now produces its own line of on-highway trucks (the CT 660 and the CT 681) in which the CX31 transmission is standard equipment when an automatic is specified. These trucks currently use Navistar engines and are strictly for vocational applications—mostly dump and cement trucks. Although Cat does have a visible presence on North American highways with the CT 660 and CT 681trucks, the company has not yet garnered significant market share. As a result, the CX series of transmissions are mostly serviced only at Caterpillar dealerships.

Wrap-up

Ready for Review

- Electronic control of transmissions has been in place in the light-duty market since the early 1980s and the truck market since the late 1980s.
- In general, transmissions require at least three inputs to function: input from the driver, a road speed input, and a load factor input.
- In electronic transmission control systems, a lever selector or a push button controller provides the drivers input; a vehicle speed sensor (VSS) provides the speed input; and a throttle position sensor (TPS) provides the load factor input.
- Most electronically controlled transmissions will use inputs from a variety of other sources—such as pressure switches, temperature switches, and oil pressure sensors—to fine tune transmission shift control.
- All electronic controlled transmissions are connected to the vehicle by a multiple wiring harnesses and connectors.
- Electronically controlled transmissions use a variety of computer controlled solenoids to control shifting.
- Allison is by far the world-leading manufacturer of electronically controlled automatic transmissions.
- Allison electronic control systems have undergone several advancements through the years, starting with the Allison ATEC/CEC system, which offered minimal electronic control, through the five software versions of the Allison World Transmission series, which offers increasingly sophisticated electronic control.
- The driving force behind electronic control advancements is fuel economy.
- The careful system monitoring characteristic of electronic control results in better control of the shift timing and process leads to increased fuel economy and greatly increased transmission durability.
- Lock-up torque converters are computer controlled and lead to even better fuel economy.
- The Allison World Transmission (WT) is modular in design, so individual modules can be serviced independently if necessary to decrease down time.
- The Allison World Transmission (WT) has six forward ranges with two overdrives, a design that increases fuel economy.
- The Allison World Transmission (WT) has three speed sensors, which allow it to compare input speed, turbine speed, and output speed. That comparison tells the transmission controller if a transmission clutch is slipping, so it can protect the transmission.
- The Allison World Transmission (WT) has several protection strategies built in, such as range inhibitors when input speeds are too high, high-speed direction-change inhibitors, and temperature-based inhibitors.
- The Allison World Transmission (WT) has built-in failsafe operation that provides minimal transmission function should electrical power be lost. Failsafe operation ensures that the vehicle is not stuck on the side of the road.
- Electronically controlled transmissions have varying levels of adaptive control. That is, the transmission controller can adapt shifting to different operating conditions, load levels, and other conditions.
- The Allison TC-10-TS transmission is a fully wet-clutch-controlled electronic transmission with ten forward ranges and twin countershafts. The TC-10-TS is specifically designed for the Class 8 on-highway truck market.
- The TC-10-TS also has fully electronically controlled shifting and adaptive control.
- Allison DOC software can be used to diagnose and monitor all of Allison's electronically controlled transmissions.

- The Voith DIWA drive transmission is primarily used in transit and coach applications, as its differential inputs (mechanical and hydrodynamic) allow it to operate in first range over a wide speed range without shifting.
- The Voith DIWA is more popular in the rest of the world but is making significant inroads in North America.
- The Voith DIWA has its own dedicated software diagnostic program, known as Aladin, which can read diagnostic trouble codes and monitor transmission operation.
- ZF electronically controlled transmissions are primarily used in transit and coach operations and have yet to make a significant dent in the North American market. ZF is a huge global marketer of transmissions, and its presence in in North America is likely to grow.
- Caterpillar's CX series of electronically controlled transmissions has not yet made a significant impact on the North American market, but, with CAT poised to re-enter the on-highway engine market soon, the company may see its sales of these transmissions increase.

Vocabulary Builder

adaptive control A feature that senses topography and vehicle load and adjusts shift control to obtain maximum economy and comfort.

Allison Transmission Electronic Control (ATEC) The original version of Allison's electronic control systems which evolved into Commercial Electronic Control (CEC).

cab harness The harness that connects the shift selector to the electronic control unit.

chassis wiring harness The wiring that connects the transmission, the TPS, and the variable speed sensor to the transmission electronic control unit.

closed-loop control The time during a shift in progress on a World Transmission that the transmission ECU is actively adjusting on-coming clutch application pressure using pulse-width modulation to control shift quality.

Commercial Electronic Control (CEC) The second iteration of Allison's electronically controlled transmission.

counts The unit that Allison uses to describe throttle position based on the variable voltage signal from a TPS, Throttle Position Sensor.

diagnostic data link (DDL) connector The location on the vehicle where the technician can plug in diagnostic software.

duty cycle The percentage of time a PWM signal is ON in comparison to OFF time.

electro-hydraulic control (electro-hydraulic valve body) The valve body used to control electronically controlled transmissions and consisting of solenoids, spool valves, and, usually, pressure switches.

failsafe operation The minimal transmission function that occurs when electrical power is lost.

fast adaptive A type of adaptive control used when the transmission is new and makes large changes to bring the shift close to the optimal shift profile quickly.

hydraulic retarder Retarder systems that pump transmission fluid between a turning cupped rotor and stationary cupped housing, thereby creating fluid pressure and fluid friction that slow the vehicle.

inclinometer/accelerometer Sensors included in the transmission control system that allow it to adapt to topography and operating conditions.

latching solenoids Solenoids that need only a short burst of electricity to move to an open or closed position and they remain in that state until they are energized again.

modulated main solenoid A pulse-width-modulated solenoid that controls main pressure in fourth generation and later World Transmissions (WT).

neutral with no clutches (NCC) The status of a vehicle in neutral gear when no clutches are applied and an indication of a possible failure mode for Allison World Transmission (WT).

non-latching solenoid A solenoid that requires constant electric power to remain in the open position.

normally closed solenoid A solenoid that blocks the flow of fluid when it is not electrically energized.

normally open solenoid A solenoid that is open when not electrically energized.

off-going ratio test A test performed at the beginning of a shift in progress in the World Transmission (WT) to ensure that the off-going clutch has released.

on-coming ratio test A test performed near the end of a shift in progress in the World Transmission (WT) to ensure that the on-coming clutch has applied.

open-loop ramp rate A predictable increase in clutch apply pressure; the open-loop ramp rate is controlled by the transmission ECU.

pressure control solenoid (PCS) The term to denote clutch control solenoids in an Allison Fourth Generation Electro-Hydraulic Control transmission.

primary modulation The pulse-modulated signal sent to a solenoid to intiate fluid flow.

prognostics A self-diagnostic maintenance schedule that informs the driver when the oil, filters, or the transmission itself requires service. Prognostics are offered on the Allison World Transmissions (WTs) since 2009 and can be turned on or off by the vehicle owner if desired.

programmable read-only memory (PROM) chip A memory chip particular to the application of the vehicle in which it is found.

pulse-width modulation (PWM) An electrical signal that varies in on and off time.

ramp-off rate The specific reduction in clutch apply pressure for the clutch that is being released during a shift in the World Transmission (WT).

range verification tests Tests constantly being performed by the Allison World Transmission (WT) control system whenever there is no shift in progress the test compares turbine times the gear ratio to the output speed to ensure the transmission is not slipping.

ratio test A test performed at the beginning and end of a shift in process.

retarder Any system used to slow a vehicle's momentum and augment the service brake.

secondary modulation (sub-modulation) A very high-frequency pulse-width modulation of the current flowing through the primary modulated circuit of a World Transmission (WT) solenoid. The secondary modulation occurs at between 12000 and 19000 Htz and is used to fine tune the solenoid function.

SensoTop A system used by Voith that senses topography and adapts the shifting schedule accordingly.

shift logic The logical process created by the transmission controller using data gained from the vehicle to determine when and how shifting should occur.

shift solenoid 1 (SS1) The solenoid used in fourth-generation and later World Transmissions (WTs) to control the position of the C-1 and C-2 latch valves.

slow adaptive A type of adaptive control that involves making small changes to the shifts as a way to mitigate the effects of clutch wear and solenoid drive and degradation.

synchronous speed The point at which the on-coming clutch has applied and there is no more slippage. Turbine shaft seed times the gear ratio equals output shaft speed.

time to full apply (TFA) The point after synchronous speed has been detected at which the solenoid controlling the on-coming clutch in a World Transmission (WT) is commanded to full pressure (that is, to fully apply the clutch).

torque converter control (TCC) A control solenoid used in fourth-generation and later World Transmissions (WTs).

transmission control module (TCM) The electronic controller that issues commands to the solenoids inside the transmission to obtain the desired range. Also known as the transmission electronic control unit (ECU).

transmission electronic control unit (ECU) The electronic controller that issues commands to the solenoids inside the transmission to obtain the desired range. Also called the transmission control unit (TCU).

trimmer An accumulator used in the ATEC/CEC systems to smoothen out the shift process.

turbine pull down A decrease in turbine speed as a shift is in progress that results from the on-coming clutch starting to control its gear train component; the signal for the transmission to enter closed-loop control of the shift in progress.

variable-bleed solenoid (VBS) Hydraulic solenoids used in late-model Allison World Transmissions (WTs), which control application by allowing some of the pressure going to a device to bleed off to exhaust.

vehicle speed sensor (VSS) An inductive pick-up sensor that reads the speed of the transmission output shaft.

World Transmission Electronic Control (WTEC) Allison's original electronic transmission control system for the World Transmission.

Review Questions

1. In the Allison ATEC/CEC transmission, solenoids are used to do which of the following?
   a. Send fluid directly to clutches
   b. Act as system pressure-modulation devices
   c. Control the flow of transmission fluid to valves
   d. Replace the function of the load- and speed-sensing devices
2. What is the purpose of the transmission temperature and oil level sensors?
   a. They act as system-protection devices.
   b. They act as additional flow-control devices.
   c. They are used only as troubleshooting tools.
   d. They are installed to assist in stall testing.
3. When the fluid in an Allison ATEC/CEC transmission is extremely cold (below -25 degrees Fahrenheit), the transmission controller allows which of the following?
   a. No shifting
   b. Shifts from neutral to first or reverse only
   c. All range shifts to occur
   d. Weather does not affect the transmission shifts.
4. In Allison ATEC/CEC transmissions, what replaces the modulator valve used in hydraulically controlled transmissions?
   a. The vehicle speed sensor
   b. The transmission oil pressure control valve
   c. The throttle position sensor
   d. The transmission temperature sensor
5. What happens if you are driving a vehicle with an ATEC/CEC transmission in fourth range and electrical power to the transmission TCU is lost?
   a. The transmission immediately shifts to neutral.
   b. The transmission downshifts until it reaches first range.
   c. The transmission will shift to the next lower range (third).
   d. The transmission will remain in fourth range until the vehicle is shut off.
6. What is meant by synchronous speed as it relates to the Allison World Transmission TCU?
   a. The output shaft speed times the gear ratio equals the engine speed.
   b. The turbine speed equals the output shaft speed.
   c. The engine speed times the gear ratio equals the turbine speed.
   d. Turbine shaft speed equals output shaft speed times the gear ratio of the oncoming clutch.
7. During a shift, the World Transmission enters closed-loop control between which of the following points?
   a. Turbine pull down detected and synchronous speed
   b. Shift initiation and turbine pull down
   c. Synchronous speed and shift initiation
   d. The WT has closed loop control during the entire shift
8. During closed-loop control, the TCU is controlling shift quality by doing which of the following?
   a. Using the fixed ramp rate
   b. Applying full-line pressure to the on-coming clutch.
   c. Varying the on-coming clutch application pressure using pulse-width modulation
   d. None of the above is correct.
9. Which of the following is NOT one of three ways that the engine's rotational power can be transmitted to the gear train in a World Transmission?
   a. Through the P-2 and P-3 sun gears
   b. Through the P-1 sun gear
   c. Through the P-2 carrier
   d. Through the P-2 ring gear
10. When a World Transmission (WT) is in reverse, the input power from the engine enters the gear train through which of the following?
    a. P-1 sun gear
    b. P-1 carrier
    c. P-2 carrier
    d. P-2 and P-3 sun gears

ASE-Type Questions

1. Technician A says that the Allison transmission's TCU switches to slow adaptive mode after optimum shift quality has been attained. Technician B says that the TCU must be switched to fast adaptive mode after transmission replacement. Who is correct?
   a. Technician A
   b. Technician B
   c. Both Technician A and Technician B
   d. Neither Technician A nor Technician B
2. Technician A says that the Allison World Transmission series is a true "drive by wire" transmission. Technician B says that the World Transmission series still has a mechanical gear-shift linkage. Who is correct?
   a. Technician A
   b. Technician B
   c. Both Technician A and Technician B
   d. Neither Technician A nor Technician B
3. Technician A says the Allison World Transmision is capable of inhibiting neutral to range shifts if the engine RPM is too high. Technician B says that the TCU is capable of inhibiting downshifts if the road speed is too high. Who is correct?
   a. Technician A
   b. Technician B
   c. Both Technician A and Technician B
   d. Neither Technician A nor Technician B
4. Technician A says that the Voith DIWA drive transmission has two inputs to the transmission gear train: mechanical and hydrodynamic. Technician B says in the Voith DIWA drive transmission, torque converter doubles as a retarder. Who is correct?
   a. Technician A
   b. Technician B
   c. Both Technician A and Technician B
   d. Neither Technician A nor Technician B
5. Technician A says that the Allison TC-10 has two countershafts. Technician B says that the Allison TC-10 uses both countershafts for each power flow like the Eaton Fuller Twin countershaft transmission does. Who is correct?
   a. Technician A
   b. Technician B
   c. Both Technician A and Technician B
   d. Neither Technician A nor Technician B
6. Technician A says that prognostics in an Allison World Transmission can alert the driver when an oil or filter change is required. Technician B says that prognostics in an Allison World Transmission can alert the driver when the transmission clutches are in danger of failing. Who is correct?
   a. Technician A
   b. Technician B
   c. Both Technician A and Technician B
   d. Neither Technician A nor Technician B
7. Technician A says that the Caterpillar CX-28 transmission power flow is identical to the Allison World Transmission. Technician B says that the Caterpillar CX-28 uses two rotating clutches. Who is correct?
   a. Technician A
   b. Technician B
   c. Both Technician A and Technician B
   d. Neither Technician A nor Technician B
8. Technician A says that the four-speed Voith DIWA drive transmission has three hydraulic clutches in its rotating clutch module. Technician B says that the four-speed Voith DIWA has three planetary gear sets in the front section. Who is correct?
   a. Technician A
   b. Technician B
   c. Both Technician A and Technician B
   d. Neither Technician A nor Technician B
9. Technician A says that the four-speed Voith DIWA drive transmission has five hydraulic clutches in total. Technician B says the four-speed Voith DIWA drive transmission has four planetary gear sets in total. Who is correct?
   a. Technician A
   b. Technician B
   c. Both Technician A and Technician B
   d. Neither Technician A nor Technician B
10. Technician A says that the Voith DIWA drive transmission uses a differential input in reverse. Technician B says that the Voith DIWA drive transmission uses a differential input in all forward gears. Who is correct?
    a. Technician A
    b. Technician B
    c. Both Technician A and Technician B
    d. Neither Technician A nor Technician B

CHAPTER 46

NATEF Tasks

Drive Train

Driveshaft and Universal Joint — Page

	Page
■ Measure drive line angles; determine needed action.	1542–1560
■ Inspect, service, or replace driveshaft slip joints, yokes, drive flanges, and universal joints, driveshaft boots and seals, and retaining hardware; check phasing of all shafts.	1543–1565
■ Identify causes of driveshaft and universal joint noise and vibration problems; determine needed action.	1551–1553
■ Inspect driveshaft center support bearings and mounts; determine needed action.	1562–1565

Knowledge Objectives

After reading this chapter, you will be able to:

1. Name driveshaft components. (pp 1533–1538)
2. Explain driveshaft functions. (p 1539)
3. Explain the theory of non-uniform velocity. (p 1540)
4. Explain how to measure and calculate drive line angles. (pp 1542–1560)
5. Explain the procedure to adjust drive line angles. (pp 1542–1560)
6. Explain drive line angularity. (p 1545)
7. Explain constant velocity joints. (p 1550)
8. Describe drive line failures and their causes. (p 1552)
9. Describe drive line inspection and maintenance procedures. (p 1555)
10. Describe vehicle drive line construction. (pp 1555–1565)
11. Explain the procedure to replace drive line components. (pp 1555–1565)

Driveshaft Systems

Skills Objectives

After reading this chapter, you will be able to:

1. Check and adjust drive line angularity. (pp 1542–1560)
2. Service and maintain drive line components. (pp 1542–1560)
3. Check and adjust driveshaft phasing. (p 1543)
4. Check and repair drive line vibration and noise. (pp 1551–1553)
5. Check drive line run-out. (p 1552)
6. Inspect drive line components and recommend repairs. (pp 1555–1565)
7. Lubricate universal joints. (p 1557)
8. Disassemble and inspect a universal joint with a bolted end. (pp 1561–1562) **SKILL DRILL 46-1**
9. Install universal joints. (p 1563) **SKILL DRILL 46-2**
10. Inspect and service center support bearings. (p 1564) **SKILL DRILL 46-3**
11. Remove and reinstall the driveshaft and center support bearing and mounts. (p 1565) **SKILL DRILL 46-4**

Introduction

Before the invention of the driveshaft, rotational power from the engine of a vehicle was transmitted to the drive axle using a series of sprockets and a chain. Originally, only one of the wheels received driving power.

FIGURE 46-1 shows a chain drive from an old Cadillac. This drive system drove a differential gear set that sent power to both wheels. The system was inherently noisy, dirty, and notorious for failing.

In 1903, Clarence Spicer was issued a patent for an encased **Cardan joint** for use in vehicle driveshafts. At that time, he was the only manufacturer of these so-called **universal joints** for this purpose. Cardan joint is the original name for a universal joint. As seen in FIGURE 46-2, it consists of a cross with four machined end posts called **trunnions** over which are installed four bearing caps with needle roller bearings. These bearing caps are installed into two yokes attached to two shafts—an input or driving shaft and an output or driven shaft. The universal joint and the yokes connect the two shafts together and the joint allows the driven shaft to operate at an angle to the driving shaft.

FIGURE 46-1 Chain drives like this one were notoriously unreliable.

Mr. Spicer soon had orders from most of the automotive manufacturers of the day for his universal joint drive line system. The actual Cardan, or universal joint, that Mr. Spicer used in his patented "Casing for A Universal Joint" had been around for a long time before he considered its use in automobiles.

The invention of the universal joint is generally attributed to the Italian mathematician Gerolamo Cardano (hence the name Cardan Joint), who described the operation of the joint in detail in 1545 but did not produce it. Cardano died in 1576. The concept was studied by Robert Hooke between 1667 and 1675. In some countries, therefore, the Cardan joint is known as a **Hooke joint**. Hooke was the first to document that the joint produced **non-uniform velocity** when operated at an angle. That is, the driven shaft turns at a constantly changing speed. The Non-Uniform Velocity section discusses the concept in greater detail.

You Are the Technician

A vehicle is brought to your service facility and the driver complains of a high-pitched squeaking noise while the vehicle is moving. You ask the driver to explain the circumstances of the noise, and he says that it only makes the noise when he is going forward; not when in reverse. You do a preliminary inspection and can see nothing out of the ordinary, so you road test the vehicle and, sure enough, it does have a squeaking noise as you drive forward slowly. The frequency of the noise seems to be too fast for a wheel end. You have a closer look at the vehicle and see small streaks of rust around the front universal joint bearing caps.

1. What might the rust around the U-joint indicate, and what can be done about it?
2. If you find that there is play in the U-joint, what would this indicate?
3. Would you recommend the U-joint be replaced?

The scientific community actually traces the universal joint back to the **gimbals** used by the ancient Greeks as early as 220 B.C. and some suggest the use of gimbals began even farther back in China. Two axis gimbals have an object suspended on the center axis of a circle that, in turn, is suspended on the center axis of a second circle. That construction allows the object to stay horizontal no matter the angle of the support. For example, gimbals allow a gyroscope or compass on a ship to be kept at the exact same position even when rough seas toss the ship around. The universal joint operates on the same principle as gimbals, but the pivot points for the circles are on the inside of the joint (the cross), and the circles are actually the two shafts that the joint connects. Whatever the definitive origin of the joint, its use today in the automotive world is attributed to Clarence Spicer's patent. The universal joint is essential to the operation of most modern vehicles.

This chapter will explain the principles of operation, construction, and types of vehicle driveshafts and joints used in the medium- to heavy-duty truck and coach market. Included in the chapter will be discussions on the theory of non-uniform velocity, drive line angularity, Cardan joints, constant velocity joints, and hanger bearings. The chapter will also cover troubleshooting driveshaft vibration and typical failures as well as inspection and maintenance of driveshafts.

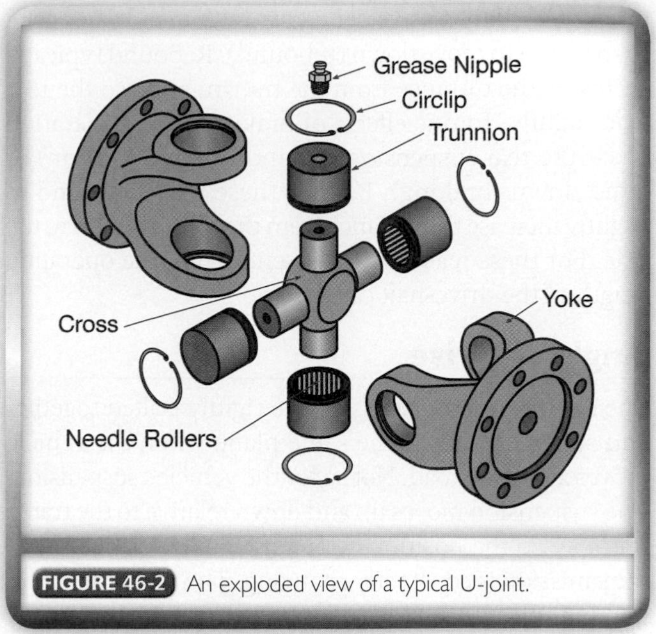

FIGURE 46-2 An exploded view of a typical U-joint.

FIGURE 46-3 A typical modern driveshaft.

Fundamentals of Driveshaft Systems

Although there are many aspects to the modern driveshaft, such as the one shown in FIGURE 46-3, any driveshaft must perform the following three basic functions:

- It must be strong enough to withstand torque from the engine.
- It must allow the shaft to change length.
- It must transmit torque through constantly changing drive angles.

Strength

The primary function of a driveshaft is to provide the strength needed to withstand the peak torque delivered from the engine while providing an ample safety margin. It might seem that increasing strength can be achieved simply by increasing the weight of the driveshaft. As the driveshaft is made heavier to carry more load, however, the shaft's maximum speed of rotation is affected. The heavier the shaft is, the lower its maximum speed can be.

As a driveshaft speeds up, centrifugal force acting on its weight will tend to move the shaft off its axis of rotation, causing a whipping action. The speed at which the centrifugal force causes the shaft to move off its axis is known as **critical speed**. If a shaft operates at or above this speed, the resultant vibration will destroy the shaft. This problem can be compensated for by making the shaft lighter, larger in diameter, or shorter in length, but careful consideration should be given to adjusting the dimensions. The overall shaft dimensions must be carefully selected to match the vehicle and vocation.

Length Changes

The second function of a driveshaft is that it must allow the shaft to change in length due to the varying distance between the engine transmission and the drive axle caused by suspension oscillations (jounce and rebound). As the vehicle encounters a bump in the road, its suspension moves upward (jounce). This movement typically decreases the distance from the transmission output to the rear axle slightly. Conversely, a dip in the road causes the suspension to move down (rebound). Rebound typically increases the distance from the transmission to the rear axle slightly. Torque effects of braking and acceleration cause the rear suspension to wind up (acceleration) or wind down (braking). Both of these reactions tend to slightly increase the distance from the transmission to the axle. For these reasons, it is essential that the operating length of the driveshaft can change.

Angle of Drive

The engine and transmission are rigidly bolted together and so are always on the same plane when the vehicle moves along the road. Not so for the vehicle's suspension. The suspension moves up and down relative to the transmission, so the position of the drive axle relative to the transmission is constantly changing. The torque forces of braking and acceleration add to this change in drive angle. A driveshaft must, therefore, be capable of transmitting torque to the rear axle while operating through constantly changing drive angles. This is the third essential function of the driveshaft.

Driveshaft Series

By far the most common driveshaft used in the heavy-duty truck market in North America is the Spicer 10 series, 1710 and 1810, driveshaft. Driveshaft capacity is the maximum torque that the shaft can handle. This capacity is denoted by the series number.

There are several other limitations on the shaft design, such as maximum shaft length, maximum rpm, maximum **torsional excitation**, and maximum inertial excitation (discussed further in the Drive Line Vibration Diagnostics section). The last two of these are extremely complicated calculations based on the diameter, length, and weight of the shaft. Excitation refers to the inherent vibration effects caused by the acceleration and deceleration of the rotating driveshaft. As such, calculating excitation levels is better left to the engineers.

TABLE 46-1 shows some of the recommended limits for the various shaft series numbers. Please note the chart is a guideline only; always consult the manufacturer for accurate and up-to-date recommendations.

Spicer recently introduced the Spicer Life series designed to supersede the 10 series. A conversion table from the ten series to the Life series is shown in TABLE 46-2.

TABLE 46-2: Ten Series Equivalents in Life Series of Spicer Driveshafts

Older Spicer 10 Series Driveshafts	Equivalent Spicer Life Series Driveshaft
1710 is replaced by ⟶	SPL-140
1760 is replaced by ⟶	SPL-170
1810 is replaced by ⟶	SPL-250

TABLE 46-1: Recommended Limits for Driveshafts by Series

Series	Tube Diameter	Maximum Shaft Length	Maximum Shaft Torque	Max Speed at 3.0° U-joint Angle
1610	4.00" × 0.134" (101.6 × 3.4 mm)	70" (177.8 cm)	5,700 ft-lb (7,728 Nm)	4,000 rpm
1710	4.00" × 0.134" (101.6 × 3.4 mm)	70" (177.8 cm)	7,700 ft-lb (10,440 Nm)	4,000 rpm
1710 HD	4.09" × 180" (103.9 × 4.6 mm)	70" (177.8 cm)	10,200 ft-lb (13,829 Nm)	4,000 rpm
1760	4.0" × .134" (101.6 × 3.4 mm)	70" (177.8 cm)	10,200 ft-lb (13,829 Nm)	4,000 rpm
1760 HD	4.09" × 0.180" (103.9 × 4.6 mm)	70" (177.8 cm)	12,200 ft-lb (16,541 Nm)	4,000 rpm
1810	4.5"" × 0.134" (114.3 × 3.4 mm)	75" (190.5 cm)	12,200 ft-lb (16,541 Nm)	3,400 rpm
1860 HD	4.59" × 0.180" (116.6 × 4.6 mm)	75" (190.5 cm)	16,500 ft-lb (22,371 Nm)	3,400 rpm

> **TECHNICIAN TIP**
>
> A vehicle uses a drive line to connect the output of the transmission to the input of the drive axle. A drive line may consist of only one driveshaft, but most heavy truck drive lines have multiple driveshafts, hanger bearings, and universal joints making up the drive line.

Components of Driveshafts/Drive Lines

Depending on the vehicle and the installation requirements, many components can be used to make up a drive line. Certain manufacturers will have a propensity for using different types of yokes, universal joints, and shaft support systems. In heavy truck installations, several driveshafts are typically used. Some straight trucks can have as many as four or even more driveshafts connected together to connect the transmission to the rear axle. The most popular components used in modern truck drive lines include the driveshaft tube, driveshaft yokes, slip joints, coupling shaft, universal joints, and fastening systems.

Driveshaft Tube

The driveshaft tube can be made from steel, aluminum, or fiberglass. Steel is the material of choice for the heavy-truck market because of its strength.

Steel tubing can be manufactured in several ways. A flat piece of steel can be bent into the shape of a tube and the seam welded. Another method of manufacture is by forging. A forged seamless tube that is extruded and has no welding is shown in **FIGURE 46-4**. A drawn-over-mandrel (DOM) tube is a welded tube drawn over a mandrel (a die the size and shape of the tube). DOM construction provides an extremely consistent wall thickness and smoothness for increased strength and stability. Forged or DOM tubes are often used in heavy-duty applications.

Regardless of construction, driveshaft tubes are hollow. Consequently, they tend to amplify any sounds like a bell. To combat this, sound deadeners made of a variety of materials—even cardboard—are placed into the tube at manufacture to stop the shaft from conducting noise.

Driveshaft Yokes

All driveshafts have yokes. Three types of yoke are prevalent in heavy-duty applications: tube, end, and flange yokes.

Tube Yokes

Tube yokes, such as the one shown in **FIGURE 46-5**, are pressed into the tube at manufacture and welded in place. Tube yokes have full round bores that accept two of the pressed-in U-joint bearing caps. There are several sizes of tube yokes to accommodate different universal joint sizes. Universal joint bearing caps are retained in the tube yoke ears by internal or external snap rings or circlips (also known as C-clip), bolt in bearing caps, or bolted spring clips.

End Yokes

End yokes are designed to be installed over the splined output shaft of the transmission, or the splined input shaft of the drive axle, as shown in **FIGURE 46-6**, or a splined shaft that is part of the driveshaft itself. End yokes are usually bolted to their respective shafts. End yokes can come in full-round or half-round designs. The full-round design allows the bearing caps to be retained by internal or external snap rings or circlips, bolt in bearing caps, or bolted

FIGURE 46-4 Driveshaft tubing may be forged or manufactured using the drawn-over-mandrel method, which produces consistent wall thickness and strength. Then the tube is welded to the yokes.

FIGURE 46-5 Tube yokes are welded to the tube and have two bores to accept the U-joint bearing caps.

FIGURE 46-6 End yokes are usually splined to a component. This transmission end yoke is of the half-round design.

spring clips. Half-round designs use attaching hardware such as U-bolts, wing-shaped bearing caps bolted to the yoke, or bolted half-round straps. Half-round yokes using straps as attaching hardware will usually have small metal tangs cast into the yoke to prevent the universal joint bearing caps from moving outward.

Flange Yoke

A **flange yoke** will hold two of the universal joint bearing caps and incorporate a flat flange with a series of mounting holes so that the flange can then be attached to a component. **FIGURE 46-7** shows a flange yoke. Universal joint bearing caps are retained in the flange yoke ears by internal or external snap rings or circlips, bolt in bearing caps, or bolted spring clips. A flange yoke is designed to be bolted to a matching flange mounted on the component called a companion flange.

FIGURE 46-7 A flange yoke connects to a drive line component with a matching companion flange.

Sometimes, a **companion flange** is matched with a flange yoke and used instead of an end yoke. The flange yoke and the companion flange bolt together when the driveshaft is installed, as seen in Figure 46-7. A companion flange is splined to the output shaft of the transmission or the input shaft of the drive axle. A companion flange does not have bores to accept the universal joint bearing caps and so must be used with a flange yoke. The flange will be held in place on the shaft by a large nut or bolt. The companion flange can be round or square in shape but must match the shape of the flange yoke that will bolt to it.

Slip Joint

A **slip joint** is a two-piece splined component consisting of a splined shaft fitted into a splined sleeve. **FIGURE 46-8** shows a slip joint. A slip joint allows the driveshaft to lengthen or shorten and is essential in a drive line to accommodate length changes caused by suspension oscillation (jounce and rebound) and the effects of braking and acceleration. Some, but not all, slip joints will have a master spline, so they cannot be re-assembled incorrectly. If they do not have a master spline, it is essential that the technician mark the mating position of the two halves of the slip joint before removal, as shown in **FIGURE 46-9**. Otherwise, a serious drive line vibration could result.

Most slip joints used on newer heavy trucks will have a coating called Glidecoat. This blue nylon coating is designed to reduce friction in the slip joint. Care must be taken not to damage the coating while removing or installing the yoke. Some slip joints will have a threaded-on seal cap, or gland nut, that must be removed before the joint can be separated. Still others will have a pressed-on seal cover that needs to be popped off to separate the joint. Spicer Life series driveshaft slip yokes are permanently lubed and feature a flexible boot that covers the slip joint.

FIGURE 46-8 A slip joint allows the driveshaft to change in length as required due to suspension oscillation.

FIGURE 46-10 A coupling shaft is a short shaft supported by a hanger bearing.

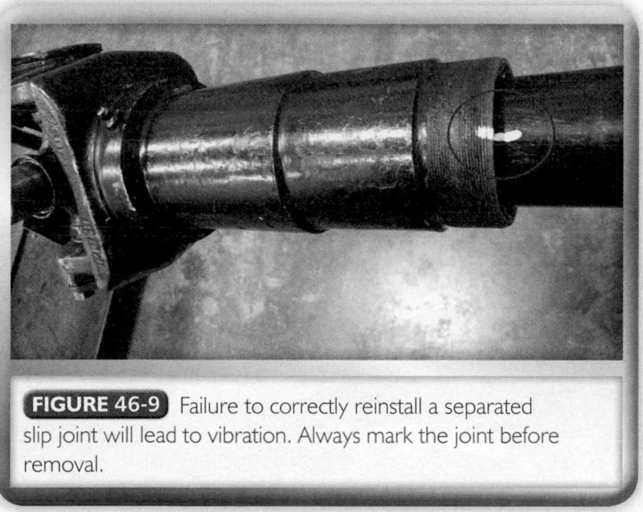

FIGURE 46-9 Failure to correctly reinstall a separated slip joint will lead to vibration. Always mark the joint before removal.

FIGURE 46-11 A hanger bearing is a rubber-encased bearing bolted to the vehicle frame that supports the driveshaft.

Coupling Shaft

A **coupling shaft** is usually a short driveshaft without a slip joint that is used in a multiple shaft drive line. A coupling shaft may also be known as a **jack shaft**. A coupling shaft is shown in FIGURE 46-10.

When a coupling shaft is used, the drive line must also have a hanger (center) bearing to support the non-drive end of the coupling shaft. A **center bearing**, also called a **hanger bearing**, is shown in FIGURE 46-11. The center bearing is used to support a multiple piece driveshaft. The center bearing consists of a bearing pressed on to a machined surface after the splined area of a driveshaft's slip yoke spline. The bearing is supported in a molded rubber cushion bracket that is, in turn, bolted to the vehicle framework. The rubber cushion used can be slotted rubber or solid depending on the severity of the expected duty cycle of the drive line. Long shaft systems may have more than one hanger bearing. Center bearings are typically permanently lubricated.

Universal Joints

The universal (Cardan) joint is essential to the operation of today's motor vehicles. It consists of a cross with four finely machined round trunnions equally spaced at 90 degrees apart. The trunnions hold the four bearing caps, which are fitted with long needle bearings to distribute the load. FIGURE 46-12 shows a universal joint with one of the bearing caps removed.

The cross is drilled with passages that connect the center of the four trunnions with a grease fitting that is installed in the cross at the center or on the outside of one or two of the bearing caps. The purpose of the passage is to supply lubricating grease to all the trunnions and bearing caps.

The bearing caps fitted over the trunnions contain thrust washers or hardened thrust surfaces to resist axial movement of the cross. A seal keeps grease in and dirt out. The seals are specially designed to allow grease to purge from the seals when the joint is lubricated, but they do not allow water or dirt to enter.

Two of the bearings are fitted into a yoke that is welded to a driveshaft component. The other two bearings are fitted to a second yoke either attached to another shaft or an end yoke fitted to a transmission or drive axle. The joint allows the two connected yokes to rotate at different angles to each other. Note that some U-joints are permanently lubricated and do not have grease fittings.

Fastening Systems

The universal joint can be attached to the driveshaft components in several ways. The caps can be a press fit into the shaft yoke and be retained with snap rings or clips. Alternatively, the caps can be held in place with straps and bolts or U-bolts and nuts. Finally, the bearing caps themselves may have a machined flange that, in turn, bolts directly to the yoke. **FIGURE 46-13** shows two popular types of attaching the joint to the driveshaft components. Bolt-on, semi-circular straps hold the joint to the half-round end yoke. Note the small cast lugs in the yoke used to prevent axial movement of the joint. In addition, the bearing caps on the tube yoke have flanges that are bolted to the yoke directly.

Manufacturers recommend that most fastening devices not be reused when servicing universal joints. Spicer states that reusing the fastening hardware may cause failure of the drive line and lead to catastrophic damage to the vehicle and even personal injury or death. Spicer Life series driveshafts use bolt-on spring-tab retainers for their bearing caps like the ones shown **FIGURE 46-14**. These caps must be replaced, along with their bolts, every time they are removed. The Life series driveshaft uses cold-formed semi-circular retaining straps, such as those shown in **FIGURE 46-15**. On quick release half-round end yokes, these straps may be reused, but not the bolts that attach them.

FIGURE 46-12 Lubrication is essential to U-joint longevity. Grease fittings, or "zerks," are provided along with a cross drilled joint to ensure that the lubricant reaches all four trunnions and bearing caps.

FIGURE 46-14 The spring-tab bearing cap retainers on this Spicer Life series driveshaft and the attaching bolts must be replaced any time they are removed.

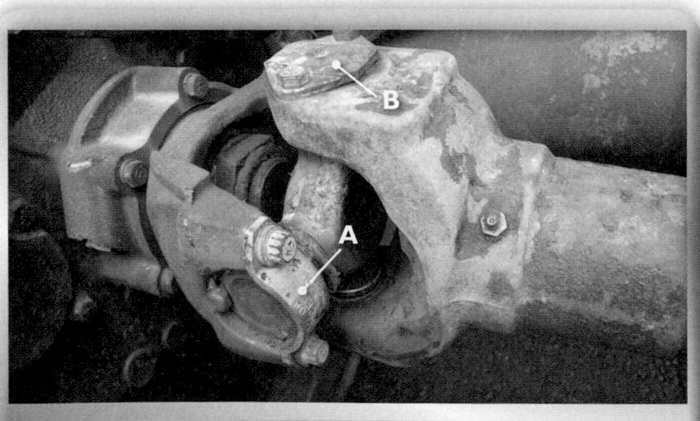

FIGURE 46-13 A U-joint fastening system using bolt-on straps (A) in the half-round end yoke and caps bolted directly to the tube yoke (B).

FIGURE 46-15 These cold-formed semi-circular straps on the Spicer Life series driveshafts may be reused, but the attaching bolts must be replaced.

Operation of Driveshafts

When a driveshaft is considered for a certain application, several things must be considered. For example, it is critical to know how much load the shaft must be capable of transmitting without failure, how fast the shaft must rotate, what angle it must operate at, and how long the shaft must be.

Shaft Mass and Critical Speed

The driveshaft and drive line must obviously be made strong enough to carry the torque load that will be transmitted through them. The crudest calculation of the peak torque that the shaft must carry is the product of the engine's peak torque multiplied by the transmission's lowest gear ratio. If the transmission is an automatic, transmission peak torque must be multiplied by the torque converter stall ratio or torque multiplication factor. Manufacturers, however, choose the strength of a driveshaft based on one of two or both of the following calculations—maximum driveshaft low gear torque or wheel slip.

Maximum driveshaft low gear torque is calculated by multiplying the following figures:

- Net engine torque (or 95% of gross engine torque)
- Transmission lowest gear ratio
- Transmission efficiency (0.8 for automatic transmission 0.85 for standard)
- Torque converter stall ratio or peak torque multiplication, if applicable.

Mathematically, that looks like this:

Net engine torque × Transmission lowest gear ratio × Transmission efficiency × Torque converter stall ratio

Manufacturers may also have to figure in the torque multiplying effect of a transfer case and its efficiency factor of about 95%.

The second calculation is based on wheel slip. The amount of torque that can be built up by the vehicle system before the drive wheels slip on regular pavement is known as wheel slip torque. It is calculated as follows:

$$\frac{0.71 \times \text{axle weight capacity rating} \times \text{tire rolling radius}}{11.4 \times \text{drive axle ratio}}$$

The lesser of the two calculations can be used in on highway applications but, in off-highway uses, the low gear torque result only should be used.

The drive line will also have a significant amount of extra strength built in as a safety margin. Recall from the Fundamentals of Driveshaft Systems section that critical speed is an issue in trying to increase the strength of a driveshaft. As the mass of the shaft increases, the centrifugal force acting on it as it rotates increases. As a result, the shaft's critical speed decreases. **FIGURE 46-16** illustrates the bow related to critical speed.

As the shaft approaches critical speed, it will start to vibrate violently. The intensity of the vibration will increase until it reaches critical speed. At critical speed, the shaft will usually fail catastrophically. To combat critical speed problems, we can reduce the mass of the driveshaft. Doing so, however, will decrease its torque carrying capability.

A second option is to decrease the shaft length. A longer shaft has more of a tendency to sag, while a shorter shaft reduces this tendency. Using a shorter shaft will decrease the overall mass of the shaft but will require the use of a multi-piece driveshaft to reach the required length. Multi-piece driveshafts can lead to vibration problems caused by non-cancelling universal joint operating angles.

A third way to combat critical speed vibrations is by increasing the diameter of the shaft tube. The larger

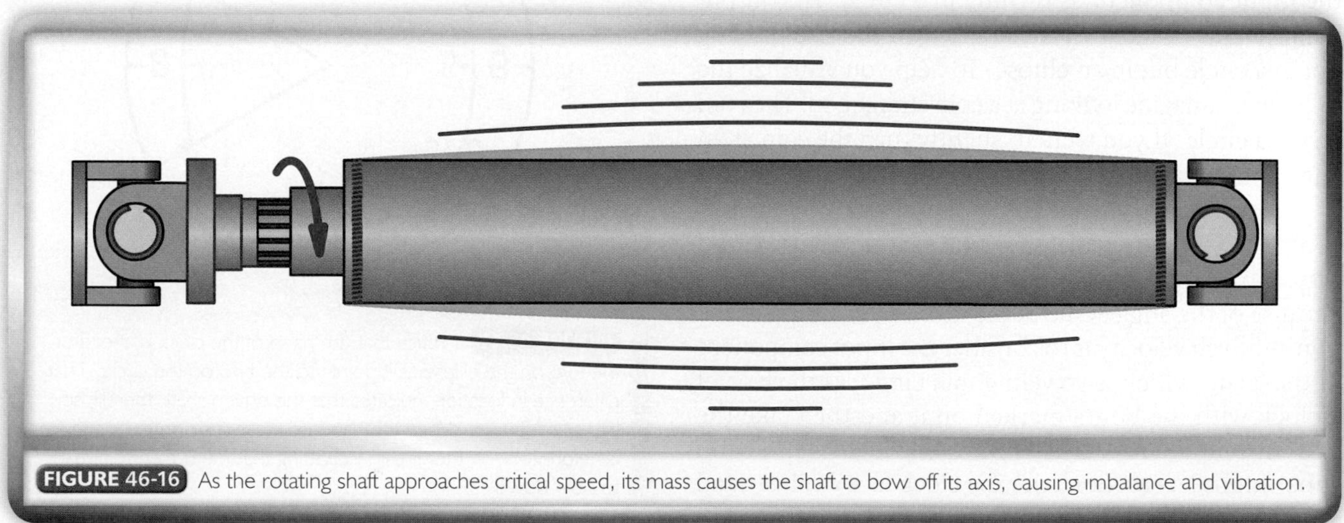

FIGURE 46-16 As the rotating shaft approaches critical speed, its mass causes the shaft to bow off its axis, causing imbalance and vibration.

diameter makes the shaft stronger and less likely to sag, but the larger diameter carries a weight penalty.

In addition to certain failure, another phenomenon called a harmonic vibration is associated with operating a driveshaft at or near their critical speed. A **harmonic vibration** is an inherent vibration that occurs at exactly half critical speed rpm and creates a noticeable vibration that will cause damage to the universal joints and, indeed, the whole drive line. Although not as severe as critical speed vibration, harmonic vibration must still be avoided for a drive line to provide worry-free service.

So, the careful selection of tubing, length, and drive line components is essential when the truck is being designed or after any modifications to drive line length, shaft speed, or torque capacity are made so that the vehicle will not be operating at or near critical speed or half critical speed during normal use. The bottom line is that a driveshaft is constructed as light as possible but as strong as necessary to do the job required of it.

Non-Uniform Velocity

All driveshafts have a natural tendency to vibrate because of a phenomenon called non-uniform velocity. Non-uniform velocity happens when any shaft with a universal joint operates at an angle different from the axis of rotation of the drive component. This concept must be understood in order to understand the dynamics of a driveshaft.

The universal joint allows a shaft to deliver torque through an angle. That is, the input or driving component of the shaft is at one angle, and the output component is at a different angle. That relationship causes the output component to turn at a velocity that is not constant. In fact, the driven shaft component will accelerate and decelerate twice during each revolution even though it is physically attached to the input.

It can be difficult to visualize this concept. Consider the input component as turning in a circle. The output component, because of the angle, will then be turning not in a circle but in an ellipse. To help you visualize the difference, imagine looking at a coin straight on. The coin forms a circle. If you were to slightly turn the coin at an angle, the coin would seem to be elliptical or oval shaped.

That is exactly what is happening with the driven component of the shaft. The yoke ears of the drive and driven parts of the joint are rotating in different planes because of the angle. One of the best ways to explain the non-uniform velocity is to consider the input component of the shaft, which is traveling in a circle, as the face of a clock with the hours marked on it and then take the driven component, which is travelling in an ellipse, and superimpose its motion over the clock face as illustrated in FIGURE 46-17.

The ellipse is inside the circle of the clock face. The two shafts are physically connected together, so they revolve around a common center point and will meet at the three, six, nine, and twelve o'clock positions. Now, draw an arrow from the center to the two o'clock position on the outer circle and look where the line intersects the inner ellipse. The line on the ellipse is at some time past two o'clock. That difference indicates that the output member (the ellipse) has accelerated in relation to the input member (the circle).

At the three o'clock position, the timing of the circle and the ellipse will coincide. But that changes at the five o'clock position. An arrow pointing to the five o'clock position on the circle (the input member) will bisect the ellipse (the output member) at some time before five o'clock. That means that the driven member has now slowed down in relation to the input member.

The process is then repeated as the input component moves towards the nine o'clock and then the twelve o'clock position. The output component must again speed up and slow down to match it. If we divide the motion into quadrants, as the input component rotates through a complete circle of 360 degrees, the driven component accelerates for the first 90 degrees of rotation or the first quadrant and then decelerates for the next 90 degrees of rotation or the second quadrant and then accelerates for the third quadrant and decelerates for the fourth quadrant. The rate of acceleration and deceleration is entirely based on the severity of the angle of drive. In other words, the higher the working angle, the greater

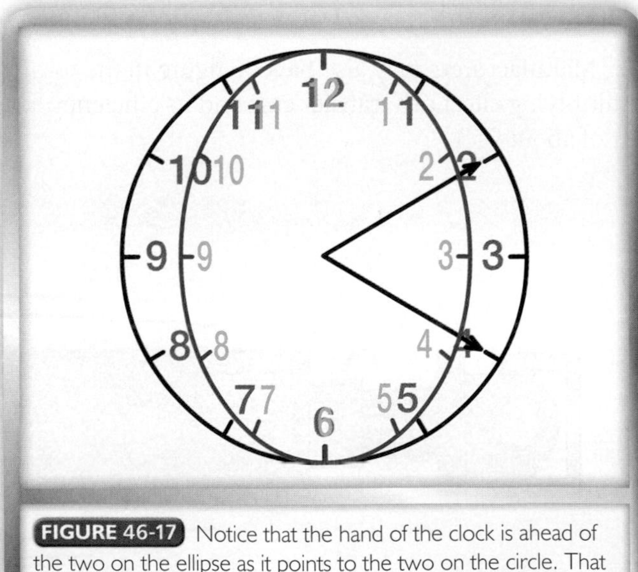

FIGURE 46-17 Notice that the hand of the clock is ahead of the two on the ellipse as it points to the two on the circle. That difference in location indicates that the driven shaft, the ellipse, had to speed up. When the hand points to four on the circle, it is before four on the ellipse, indicating that the driven shaft had to slow down.

the speed fluctuations will be. FIGURE 46-18 shows typical yoke speed vibrations.

Consider that a driveshaft has to transmit rotating power to a drive axle. If we were to connect the shaft directly to an output with this non-uniform velocity, the acceleration and deceleration would be transmitted to the drive axle and wheels. That would lead to unacceptable vibrations, as the vehicle would be trying to accelerate and decelerate constantly. In order to connect the shaft to a drive axle, we must first correct the non-uniform velocity by using another universal joint with an equal—or very close to equal—operating angle, which will cancel out the changing velocity and deliver a constant rotational speed to the drive axle, as is illustrated in the graph in FIGURE 46-19.

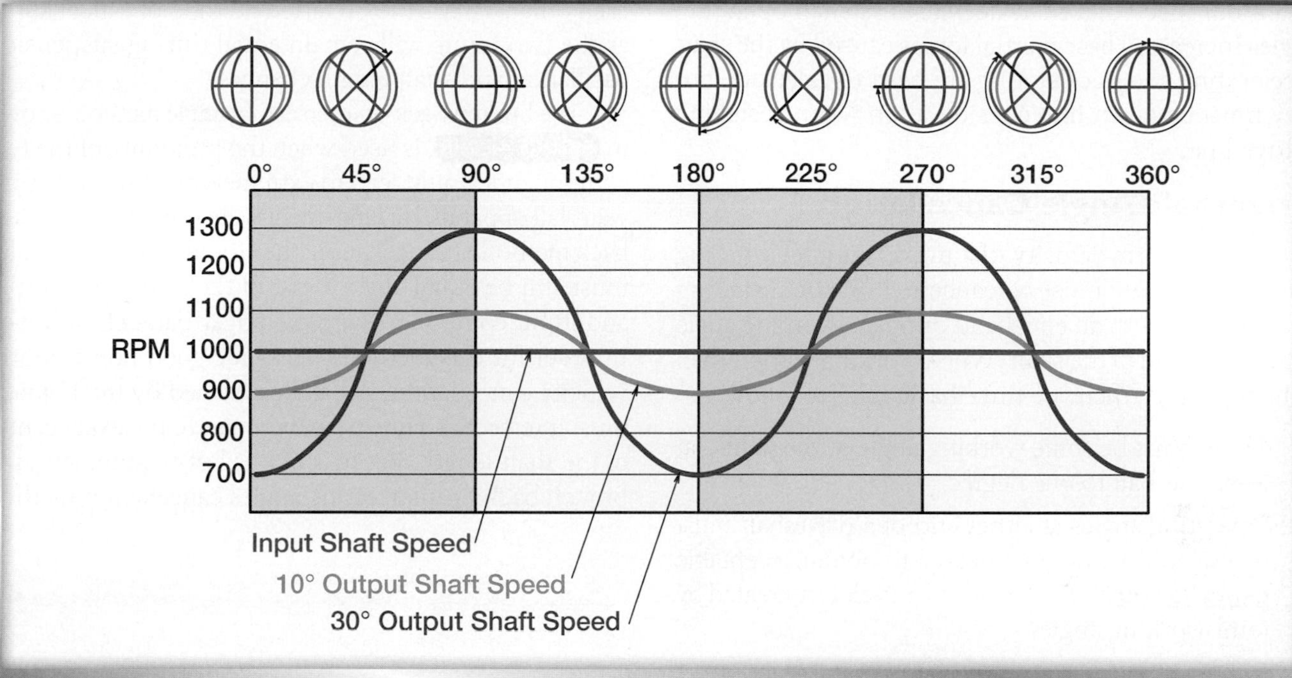

FIGURE 46-18 The frequency of the accelerations and decelerations are constant, each occurring twice per revolution. The amplitude or intensity of the speed fluctuations is based on the severity of the drive angle.

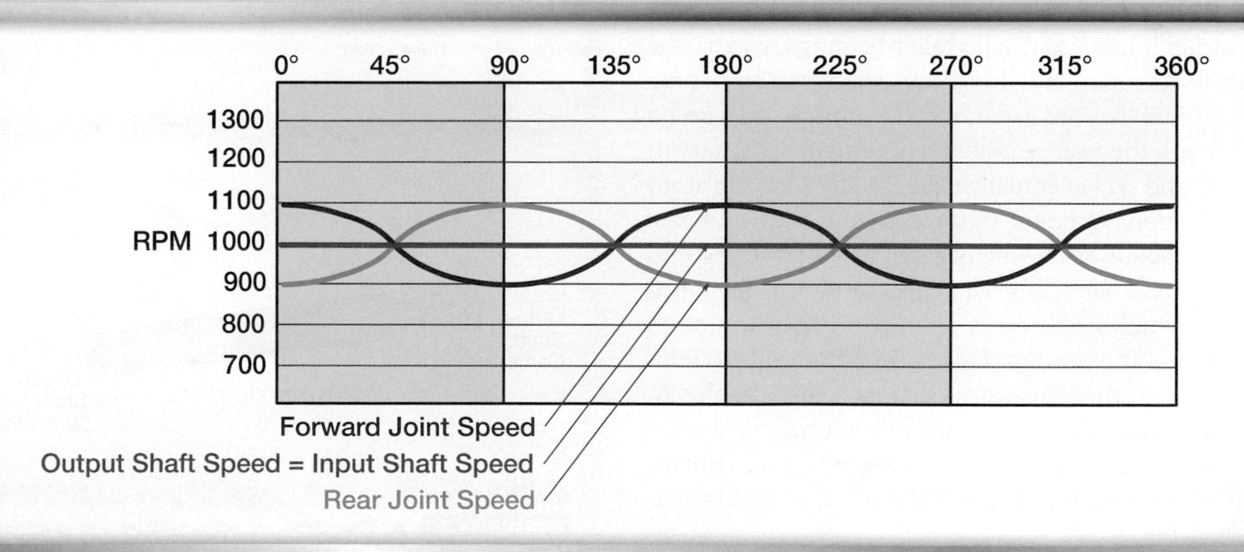

FIGURE 46-19 Installing a second universal joint with an equal and opposite angle at the other end of the driven shaft serves to cancel out the non-uniform velocity.

There is more to the story, however. This phenomenon of non-uniform velocity can lead to driveshaft vibrations even if we cancel out the speed fluctuations with a second universal joint. The inertial forces caused by the acceleration and deceleration of the driveshaft's mass can, by itself, lead to vibrations as overall shaft speed increases. The intensity of the speed fluctuations is a direct result of the severity of the operating angles and the shaft rotational speed. This means that the safe rotational speed of a shaft decreases as shaft operating angles increase. These inertial forces caused by the shaft accelerating and decelerating are hard to calculate, but they must be taken into consideration when designing a drive line.

Driveshaft Angle Cancellation

The non-uniform velocity of a universal joint working through an angle must be cancelled out by installing another joint with an equal and opposite working angle at the other end of the shaft. When working with Cardan joint angularity, there are three basic rules to follow.

1. There must be some working angle at the joint—at least one-half to one degree.
2. Operating angles at either end of a driveshaft must be equal to within one degree to obtain acceptable **cancellation** of the non-uniform velocity created by joint working angles.
3. Working angles should be kept as small as possible—three degrees or less according to most OEMs—to minimize vibrations caused by shaft inertial accelerations.

Rule Number One

All Cardan joints use needle roller bearings to carry the torque load exerted on a driveshaft. These needles require lubrication if they are to survive. If a joint works with no angle at all, the needle rollers will remain stationary in the caps and will eventually squeeze all of the lubricant out of the contact points in the caps and the trunnions. Without the lubricant, the needles will start to dig into the trunnions. This causes an effect known as **false brinelling**, which is the wearing away of the trunnion in the shape of the needles. False brinelling leads to joint failure. When the joint works at least a slight angle, for example one-half to one degree minimum, the needles will roll during operation. The rolling motion distributes the lubricant each time the needles move, so false brinelling does not occur.

Rule Number Two

The operating angles at each end of a driveshaft must be kept equal to within one degree if the non-uniform velocity caused by the joint angle is to be cancelled out. There are two ways of achieving this cancellation. The first is called the **waterfall** or **parallel joint arrangement**. The other is the **broken back** or **intersecting angle arrangement**.

In the parallel arrangement, shown in FIGURE 46-20A, the side view centerline of the transmission output and the drive axle input are parallel. The U-joint angles at either end are equal to within one degree and opposite to each other. This is the preferred method of cancellation, as the two joints will remain equal during suspension oscillation and shaft length changes.

The broken back or intersecting angle method, shown in FIGURE 46-20B, is used when the proximity of the two components would lead to extreme operating angles if a waterfall or parallel arrangement were used. In the broken back method of cancellation, the U-joint operating angles must still be equal at each end of the shaft. The output and input components are no longer parallel, however. In order for this method to provide good non-uniform velocity cancellation, the angles formed by the U-joints must intersect at a line perpendicular to the exact center of the shaft length. Because of this last requirement, the broken back or intersecting angles cancellation method

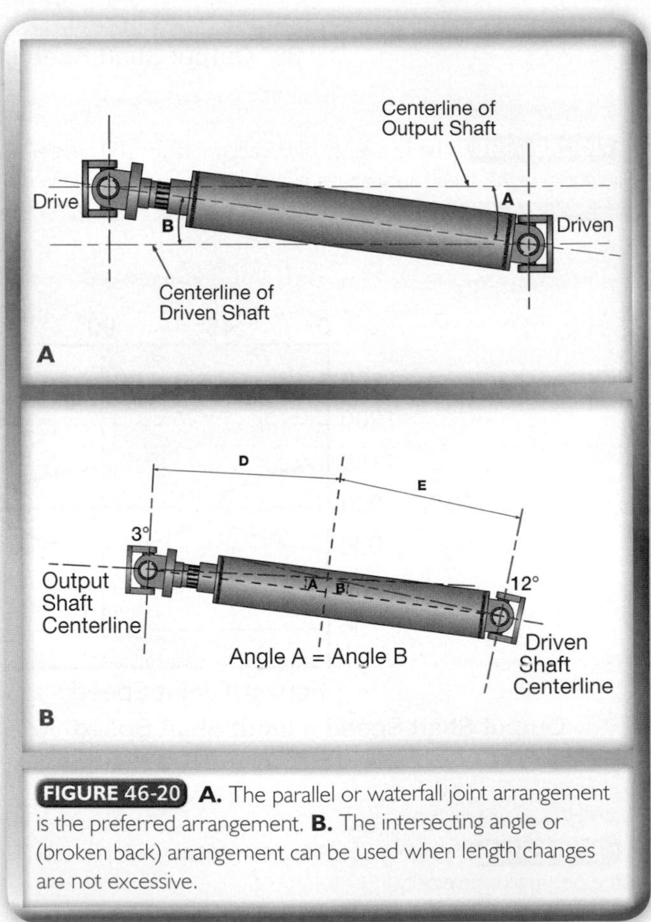

FIGURE 46-20 **A.** The parallel or waterfall joint arrangement is the preferred arrangement. **B.** The intersecting angle or (broken back) arrangement can be used when length changes are not excessive.

cannot be used where operating length changes can be excessive, as this would cause the angles to no longer intersect at the center of the shaft and lead to vibration. Broken back installations are usually only found between the two axles of a tandem drive because driveshaft length changes are minimal in this location.

Rule Number Three

The operating angles of universal joints should be kept as small as possible—preferably three degrees or less. Because of the phenomenon of non-uniform velocity of a shaft driven at an angle, all driveshafts have an inherent torsional excitation caused by the inertial forces of the shaft as it accelerates and decelerates twice per revolution. The magnitude of this torsional excitation is directly proportional to the acuteness of the angle of operation, the weight of the shaft, and the speed of the shaft. FIGURE 46-21 shows how joint operating angle will affect the expected life of the joint. Keeping angles small will allow for maximum working life.

To minimize vibration, one of three things must occur. The angle has to be lessened, the shaft must turn at a lower speed, or the shaft must become lighter. The shaft speed must be consistent with the vehicle for which it is transmitting torque. Therefore, limiting shaft speed is not one of the favored options. The weight of the shaft material can be altered, but that will have a direct impact on the shaft's torque carrying capabilities. The best solution to deal with inertial and torsional excitation is to keep the operating angle small.

Several manufacturers produce charts, such as the one shown in TABLE 46-3, specifying maximum rotational speed for a given joint operating angle. The weight of shaft must also be considered, so the maximum operating angle will change based on the "series" or load-carrying capability of the shaft in question along with its rotational speed. Universal joint longevity is also greatly affected by large joint working angles.

A universal joint operating at an angle of three degrees can be expected to last 90% or more of its normal wear life. As angles increase, this wear life reduces drastically. A joint that has a normal wear life of 100,000 miles (160,000 km) will likely last for only 60,000 miles (96,000 km) when operated at an angle of five degrees and for only 30,000 miles (48,000 km) at a 10 degree working angle. Smaller working angles reduce the chance of vibration and allow the longest wear life for universal joints.

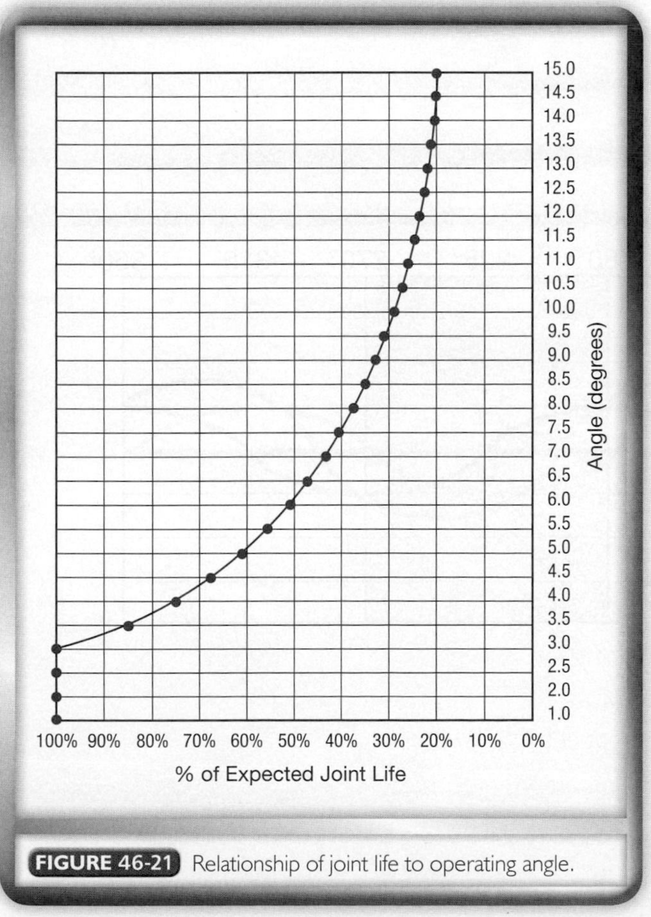

FIGURE 46-21 Relationship of joint life to operating angle.

Phasing

The working angles of a driveshaft system must be very carefully selected in order to prevent unacceptable vibration of the rotating shaft. However there is another element to the story. In order for cancellation to occur and for vibrations to be eliminated, the canceling joint angle must be in the same phase in terms of rotation.

As we discussed in the Non-Uniform Velocity section, if we divide a circle into quadrants of 90 degrees each, the driven shaft accelerates for the first 90 degrees,

TABLE 46-3: Maximum operating angles for Shaft RPM, (Max engine RPM X High gear Ratio).

Driveshaft rpm	Maximum Normal Operating Angles
5000	3° 15'
4500	3° 40'
4000	4° 15'
3500	5° 0'
3000	5° 50'
2500	7° 0'
2000	8° 40'
1500	11° 30'

decelerates for the second 90 degrees, and so on. **Phasing** of the universal joint operating angles means that the output yoke of the joint doing the cancellation of the non-uniform velocity has to be doing exactly the opposite of the driven yoke of the input universal joint—meaning that it must decelerate for the first 90 degrees of rotation and accelerate for the second 90 degrees in order to deliver a uniform velocity to the rear axle. To accomplish this, the inboard yoke ears of the driven shaft must line up. This will place their respective joints in phase with each other, as in **FIGURE 46-22**. An out-of-phase driveshaft causes the accelerations and decelerations of the joints on either end of the shafts to be out of sync with each other. The result can be seen in **FIGURE 46-23**. Failure to correctly phase the universal joints will worsen the vibration rather than cancel it.

The most common cause of out-of-phase problems is a failure by the technician to mark the slip yoke of a split driveshaft before disassembly. Always mark the slip yoke position before removal so that it can be reinstalled correctly.

Cross Phasing and Incremental Phasing Adjustments

Between 90% and 99% of all driveshaft systems are installed with the driveshafts in phase. In other words, the inboard yokes of any shaft assembly are in line with

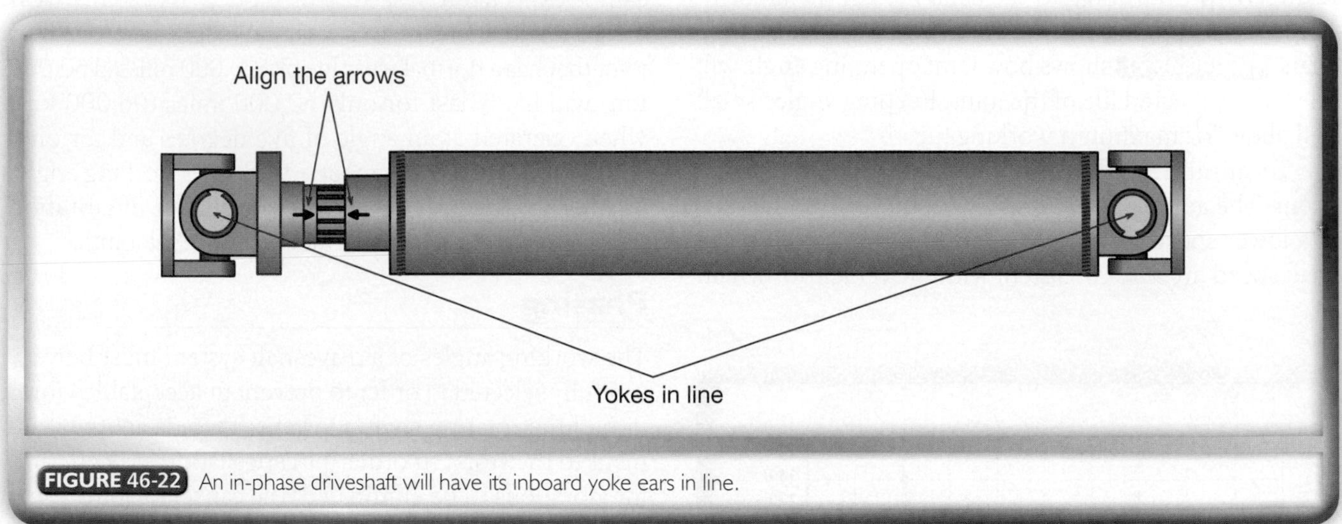

FIGURE 46-22 An in-phase driveshaft will have its inboard yoke ears in line.

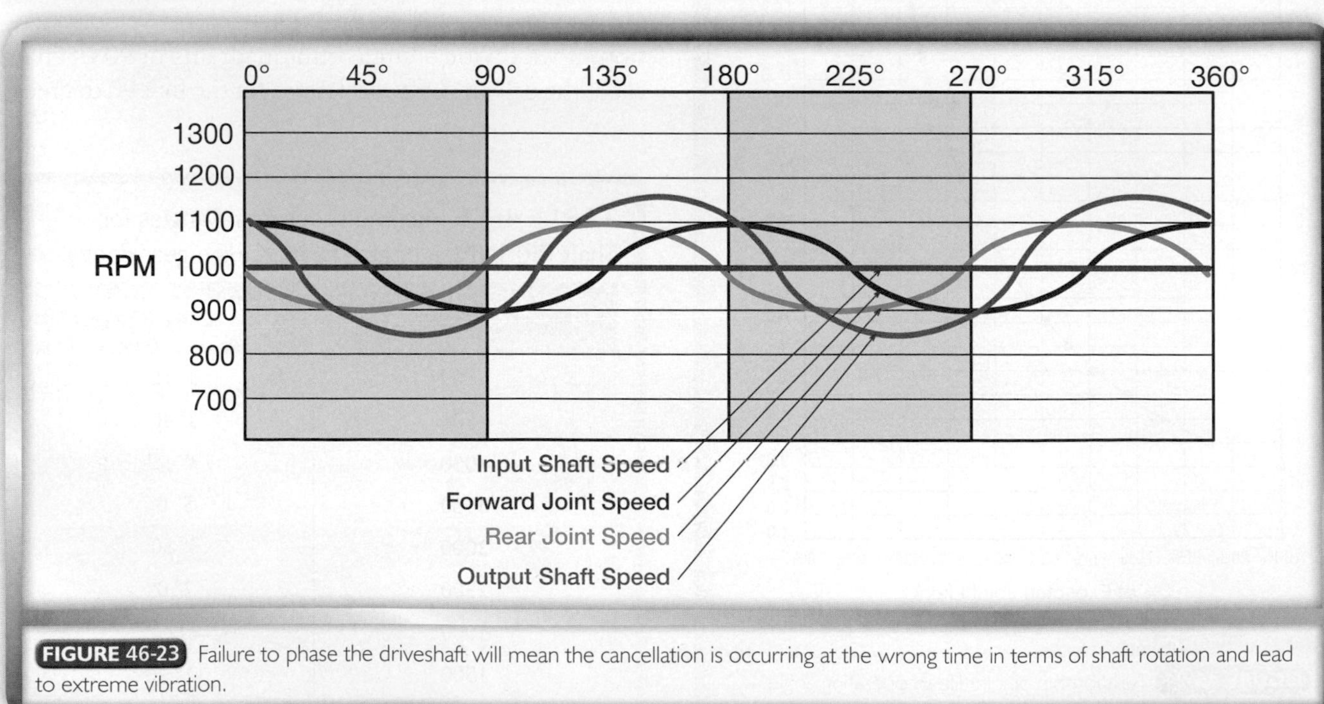

FIGURE 46-23 Failure to phase the driveshaft will mean the cancellation is occurring at the wrong time in terms of shaft rotation and lead to extreme vibration.

each other. However, certain systems are set up so that the short coupling shaft of a multi-piece driveshaft may be set at a 90 degree phase angle. This **cross-phasing** is usually done to correct an inherent vibration usually caused by the drive line system of the vehicle.

Cross-phased coupling shaft angles are kept very small to prevent drive line vibration. Sometimes the driveshaft is offset from the centerline of the transmission or drive axle—meaning that the driveshaft is angled to the left or right of the transmission or drive axle centerline. This type of installation is known as a broken back configuration. It is not to be confused with the broken back method of angle cancellation mentioned in the Driveshaft Angle Cancellation: Rule Number Two section.

A broken back installation can result in a vibration that can sometimes be dealt with by cross-phasing. These crossed-phase installations are not very common, but a technician should be aware of their existence. Certain late-model vehicles (some Volvo models for example) are purposely built with a cross-phased driveshaft that is out of phase by a number of degrees more than 90. On first observance, shaft arrangements that are not exactly in phase or cross phased at 90 degrees can seem strange to a technician. These configurations are computer designed to combat resident system vibrations in the vehicle, however, and should not be altered. For the technician, the important point is to always mark the slip yoke elements before removing the shaft so that it can be re-installed with the correct phase angle.

Drive Line Angularity

Drive Line angularity simply refers to the angles at the universal joints. For the most part, drive line angles should not need to be reset in the field. If any modification is performed on the vehicle, such as shortening or lengthening the frame or adjusting vehicle ride height, it may be necessary to check and adjust angles to avoid vibrations. This may also be necessary when diagnosing drive line vibration after all other possibilities have been eliminated.

Unless the vehicle or the drive line has been obviously tampered with, problems other than drive line angles are more likely to be the cause of drive line vibrations. One type of tampering that can lead to drive line angle problems is drivers that "soften" the ride by lowering air bag suspension pressure and ride height. Doing so can lead to excessive operating angles, which can cause vibration.

Measuring and Calculating Drive Line Angles

Most drive line manufacturers offer a computer-based program to analyze drive line angles. Software, such as the Eaton Drive Line Angle Analyzer (DAA), can determine if vibration will occur. These programs take into account drive line weight and length to determine torsional inertials and are much more accurate at predicting vibrations than simple manual calculations.

A manual calculation procedure is an acceptable preliminary check for angle issues that may cause vibration. If, after following the manual procedure, a vibration still exists, it may be due to torsional inertials that should be calculated using the computer-based programs. Drive line angles are best measured with an electronic angle gauge or inclinometer, such as the Spicer Anglemaster, to ensure that readings are accurate. Readings should be accurate to within one-quarter of a degree.

The process is relatively simple when the components of the drive line have angles only in the side view. Some vehicles, however, have angles that occur in more than the side plane. In these drive lines, the shaft may move to the right or left when viewed from above as it goes from the front to back. That is called the **plan angle**. Components that have slopes in two planes (side view and top view) create a compound angle and they must be calculated differently.

To calculate side view only angles, the angle of slope of each component in the drive line is measured and the operating angle between any two components is calculated. When a vehicle is observed from the side, any slope that goes lower as it moves towards the rear of the vehicle is a down slope and is expressed as a positive angle. If the component slope goes higher as it moves to the back of the vehicle, it is an upward slope and recorded as a negative angle.

To begin the process, on vehicles sprung with leaf springs or rubber spring systems, make sure that the vehicle is as close to its normal operating condition as possible in terms of loading. Calculating the angles to try and solve a vibration problem will not be successful if the vehicle normally operates with much heavier loads than when tested. On systems with air springs, ensure ride height is within specification before beginning the measurements also check that tire pressure is correct and the vehicle is on level ground before taking the measurements.

Most manufacturers have worksheets, similar to the one shown in FIGURE 46-24, that can be used to record the angles that will correspond to the drive line being worked on. If no worksheet is available, simply write down all of the components and record their slopes. We will use a two-piece, single-axle drive line for our example for a total of three operating angles.

The first measurement will be the frame slope. This angle, shown in FIGURE 46-25, can be eliminated when doing manual calculations but is called for when using computerized drive angle analyzer programs.

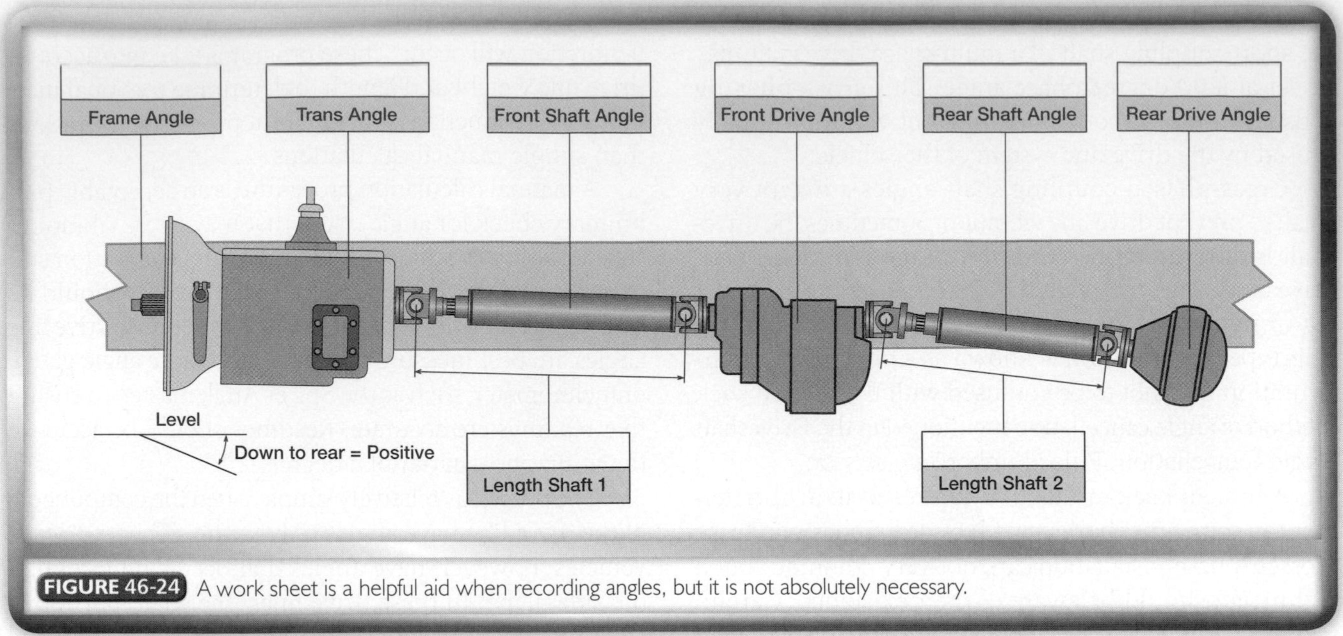

FIGURE 46-24 A work sheet is a helpful aid when recording angles, but it is not absolutely necessary.

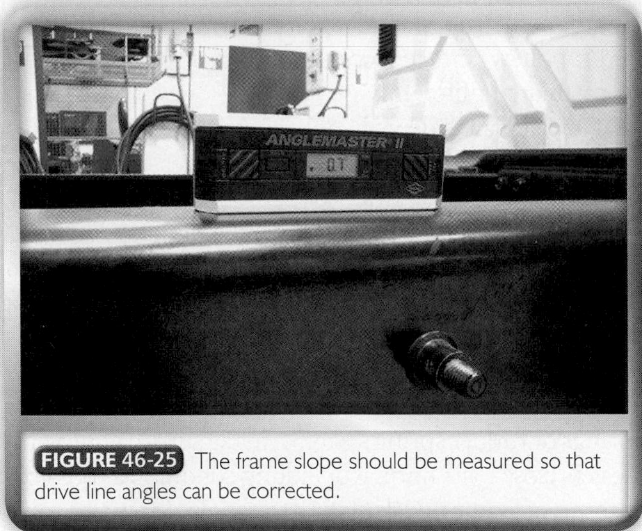

FIGURE 46-25 The frame slope should be measured so that drive line angles can be corrected.

The next measurement is the transmission slope. This measurement can usually be taken from any flat surface of the transmission that is parallel to its centerline, as illustrated in FIGURE 46-26. Alternatively, the transmission angle can be measured from its end yoke bearing caps using adapters supplied with the Spicer Anglemaster tool. Note that if you are measuring from the end yoke, the yoke ears must be positioned vertically.

Next, measure the slope of the first driveshaft, shown in FIGURE 46-27 which is usually a coupling shaft. Shaft slope measurements can be taken on any clean and smooth section of the driveshaft tube. Then, measure the slope of the next shaft and, finally, measure the slope of the drive axle.

The drive axle slope is usually measured at the flat section near the spring mounts, as shown in FIGURE 46-28, but it can be measured from the drive axle end yoke ears using the adapter. Again, the yoke ears should be vertical. If all slopes are down and all readings are positive, to calculate the working angle of each joint, simply subtract the smaller number from the larger number and that is the U-joint working angle.

Drive Line Angle Examples

Consider the following example. The transmissions slope is four degrees down, the coupling shaft is five degrees down, the second driveshaft is six degrees down, and the drive axle is seven degrees down. Given those parameters, the following are true:

- The calculation for the first U-joint angle is: 5 degrees – 4 degrees = 1 degree
- The calculation for the second U-joint is: 6 degrees – 5 degrees = 1 degree
- The third U-joint angle is: 7 degrees – 6 degrees = 1 degree

These angles satisfy the three rules for universal joint angles:

- Rule One states that there must be at least one-half to one degree of operating angle so that the needle bearings rotate.
- Rule Two states that the angles at opposite ends of a shaft must be equal to within one degree.
- Rule Three states that working angles be kept to less than three degrees.

Given the angles and their conformance to the rules, the drive line in this example should not cause a vibration because of drive line angles.

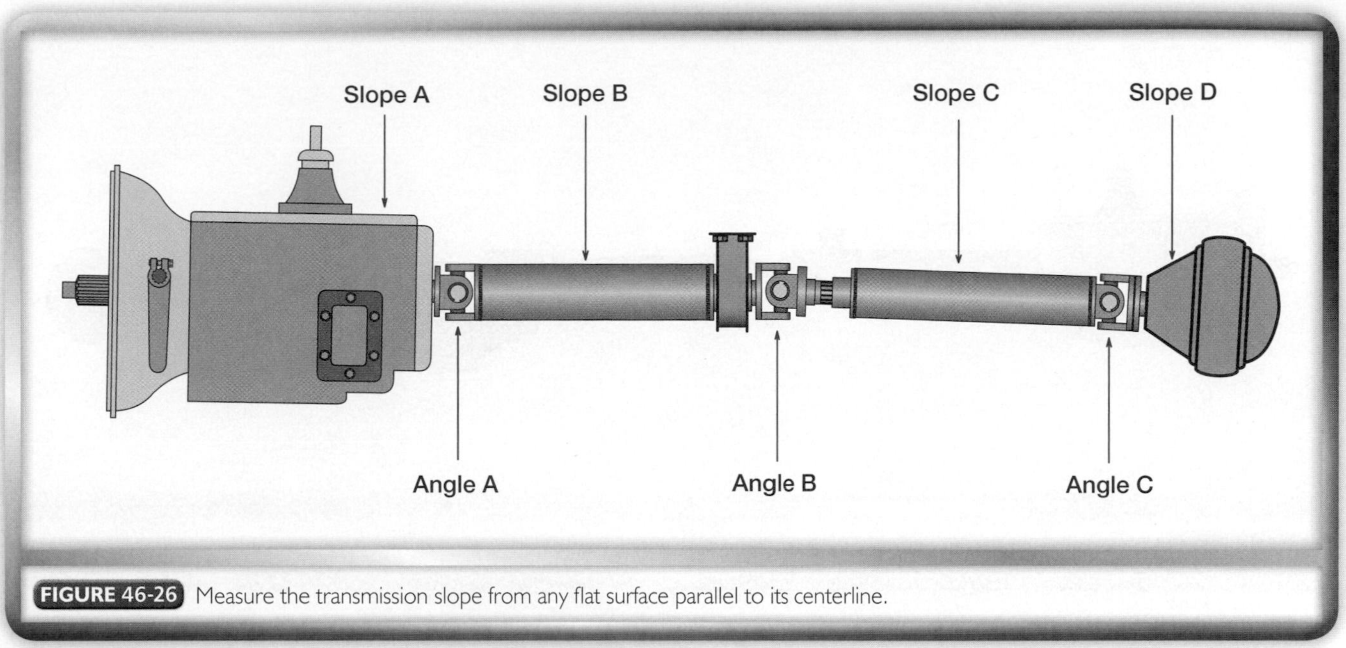

FIGURE 46-26 Measure the transmission slope from any flat surface parallel to its centerline.

FIGURE 46-27 Measure the slope of the first driveshaft.

FIGURE 46-28 The drive axle slope is measured on a flat surface close to the wheel end.

Now, let's consider another example. This time, we will use a drive line with a two-piece main driveshaft and tandem drive axles with a one-piece rear driveshaft. That makes a total of five operating angles, as illustrated in FIGURE 46-29.

Here are the parameters for this driveshaft:

- The transmission measures one degree down
- The coupling shaft measures one degree up or minus one degree
- The second driveshaft measures two degrees down
- The power-divider measures 0.5 degrees down
- The rear driveshaft measures three degrees down
- The rear-rear drive axle measures three degrees down.

Given those conditions, the operating angles are as follows:

- For the first U-joint angle, the transmission and the first shaft slopes are in different directions, so the degrees have to be added rather than subtracted—one degree down for the transmission and one degree up for the first shaft. The operating angle is two degrees.
- The calculation for the second joint angle is one degree up for the coupling shaft and two degrees down for the second shaft, so the operating angle is three degrees.
- The third operating angle is two degrees down for the second shaft and 0.5 degrees down for the power-divider, so the operating angle is 2.5 degrees.

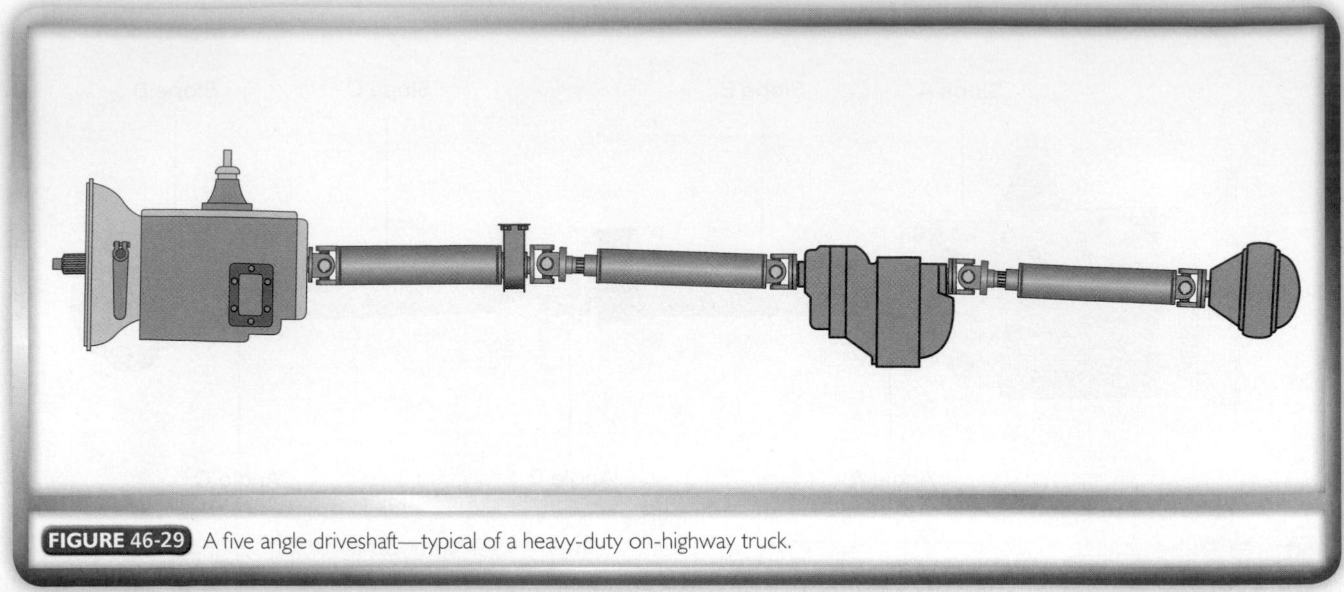

FIGURE 46-29 A five angle driveshaft—typical of a heavy-duty on-highway truck.

- The fourth operating angle is 0.5 degrees down for the power-divider and three degrees down for the rear driveshaft, so the operating angle is 2.5 degrees.
- The fifth operating angle is three degrees down for the rear driveshaft and three degrees down for the rear-rear drive axle, so the operating angle is zero degrees.

This second example meets the three rules of drive line angles for all the operating angles except for the fifth one. The fifth operating angle fails Rule Two because it is not within one degree of the fourth operating angle. Therefore it will not cancel out the non-uniform velocity in the rear driveshaft and will cause vibration. The fifth operating angle also fails Rule One in that the operating angle must be at least one-half to one degree. This angle is zero degrees, so, by itself, it will cause the bearing to wear out prematurely because the needle bearings will not rotate.

This problem can be corrected by installing shims under the rear-rear axle spring mounts to rotate the axle until it is only 0.5 degrees down. This would make the fifth operating angle 2.5 degrees and satisfy all three rules.

Compound Drive Line Angles

Compound drive line angles involve angles in two planes—the side view and the plan or top view, as illustrated in **FIGURE 46-30**. When compound angles are encountered, we must still take the same measurements as in our previous examples. However, with compound angles, we must also calculate the true operating angle by combining the measured side view angle with the plan view angle.

The only way to obtain the plan or top view angle is through careful calculation or by using a plan view angle chart, such as the one shown in **FIGURE 46-31**. This chart can be found in most manufacturers' drive line manuals. The chart's *x* axis is the driveshaft length in inches, and the *y* axis is the number of inches the shaft is offset over its length. The point of intersection is marked on the chart and then a line is drawn from the corner, where the *x* and *y* axes meet, to a circular line on the right hand side of the chart that is graduated in degrees. This is then the plan or top view angle.

Once you have determined the plan view angle, use the following formula to obtain the true U-joint operating angle.

$$C = \sqrt{S^2 + T^2}$$

where

C = true operating compound angle

S = side view angle

T = top view angle

For example, if the side view or measured angle is 2.5 degrees and the top view or calculated angle is 1.5 degrees, then the compound angle would be as follows.

$$\begin{aligned} C &= \sqrt{2.5^2 + 1.5^2} \\ &= \sqrt{8.5} \\ &= 2.92 \end{aligned}$$

When calculating the true U-joint operating angles for both ends of the shaft, the resultant angles must meet the same three rules for all drive line angles to avoid vibration and premature wear out: They must be at least one-half to one degree; they must be equal to within one degree; they should be less than three degrees.

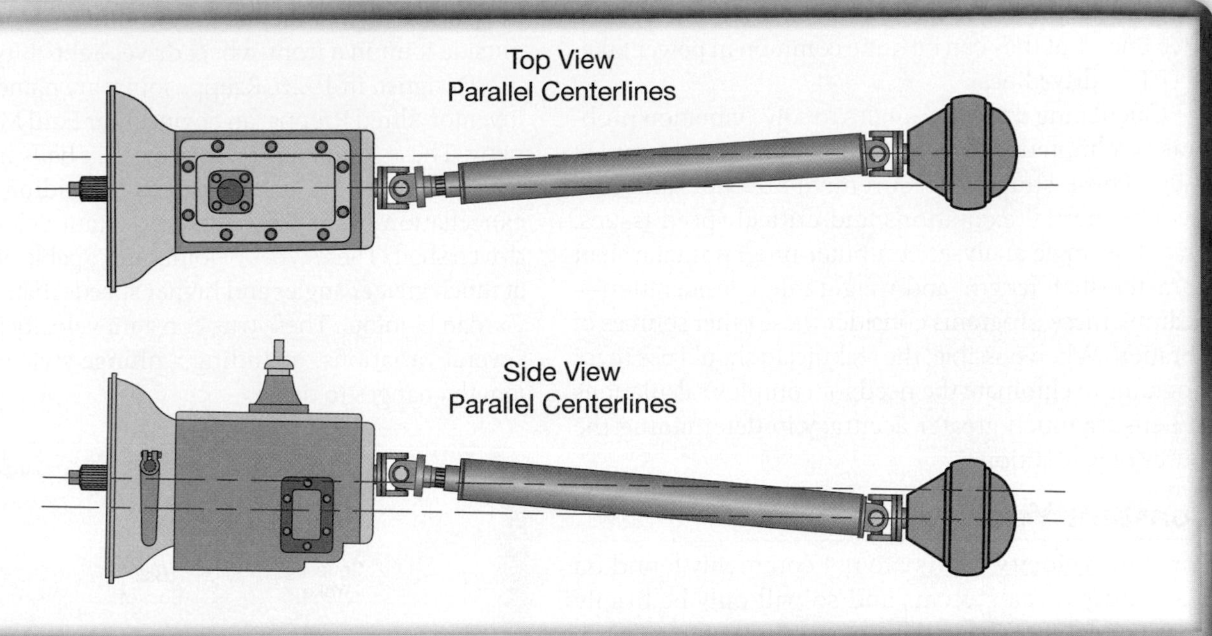

FIGURE 46-30 Compound angles are angles that exist in two planes, both from the side view and from the top view. These must be calculated differently.

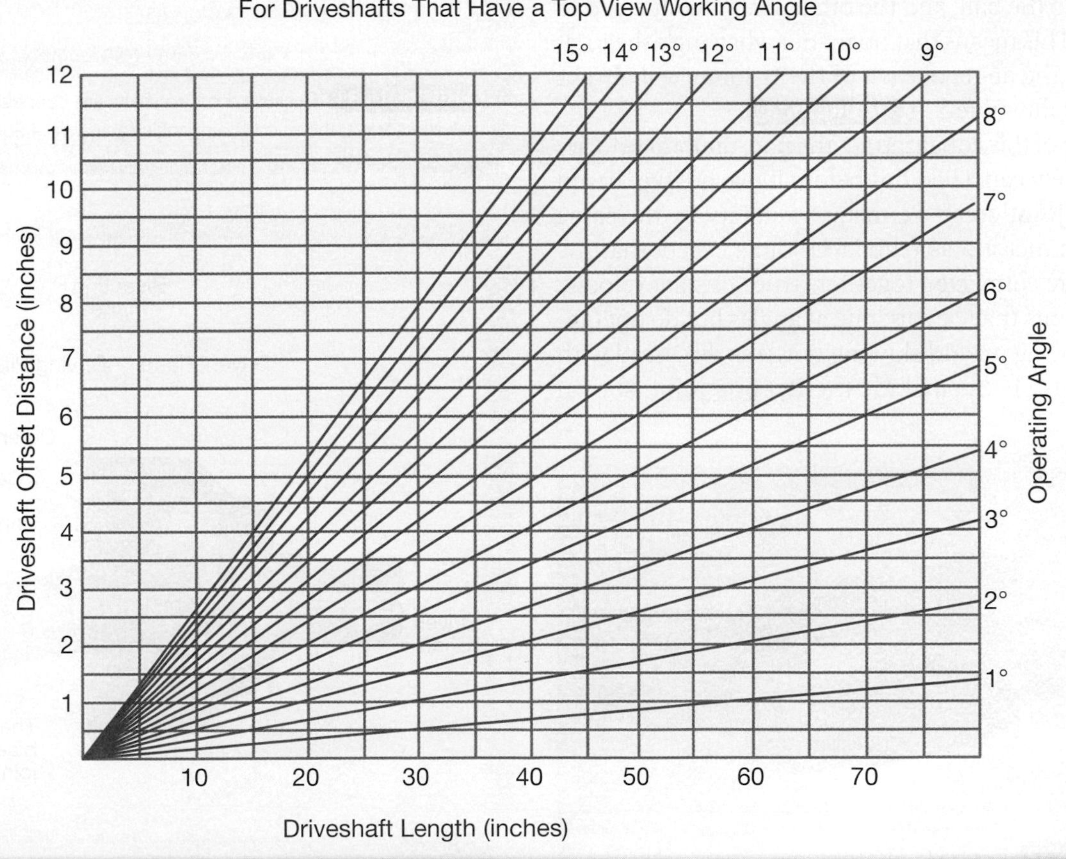

FIGURE 46-31 Plan view angle calculation chart.

Compound angles are not very common in vehicle drive lines, but they can be quite common in power take-off (PTO) drive lines.

Calculating drive line angles to solve vibration problems is a limited answer to a sometimes very complex issue. These simple measurements do not take into account inertial excitations and critical speed issues. Drive line angle analyzer computer programs take shaft diameter, shaft length, and weight into consideration—meaning these programs consider these other sources of vibration. When possible, the technician should use these programs to eliminate the need for complex calculations and ensure much greater accuracy in determining the source of a vibration.

Constant Velocity Joints

Constant velocity joints are not commonly found on heavy-duty truck systems and so will only be briefly mentioned here. The earliest style of constant velocity joint in automotive use was the double Cardan style. This arrangement had two Cardan joints in the same housing, as can be seen in FIGURE 46-32.

In between the two U-joints and inside the housing is a ball-and-socket connector. One half of the shaft is connected to the ball, and the other shaft is connected to the socket. This means that no matter what angle the joint operates at, the angle of each of the U-joints will always be equal, as illustrated in FIGURE 46-33.

Because of this equalization, the non-uniform velocity is immediately cancelled out before it reaches the driven shaft. This joint creates constant velocity by the same cancellation method as regular U-joints except that the two joints are connected together. True constant velocity joints are joints that can operate at angles but do not create the speeding up and slowing down as discussed with Cardan joints. These include the **Rzeppa joint**, shown in FIGURE 46-34, which is very commonly found as the outside joint in a front-wheel drive, light-duty vehicle.

Designed in 1926, Rzeppa joints are named for their inventor Alfred Rzeppa, an engineer for Ford Motor Company. These joints have a series of six balls inside. The drive angle always bisects the balls, leading to perfect cancellation of the angles and constant velocity of the driven shaft. These types of joints are capable of operating at much greater angles and higher speeds than traditional Cardan U-joints. These true constant velocity joints have several variations, including a plunge style that allows length changes to occur.

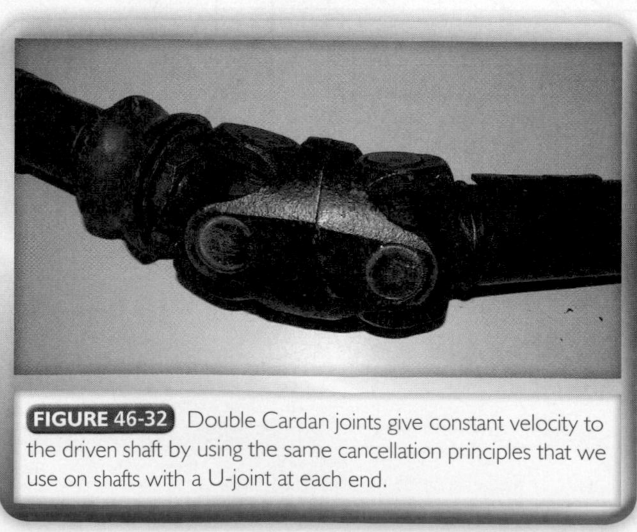

FIGURE 46-32 Double Cardan joints give constant velocity to the driven shaft by using the same cancellation principles that we use on shafts with a U-joint at each end.

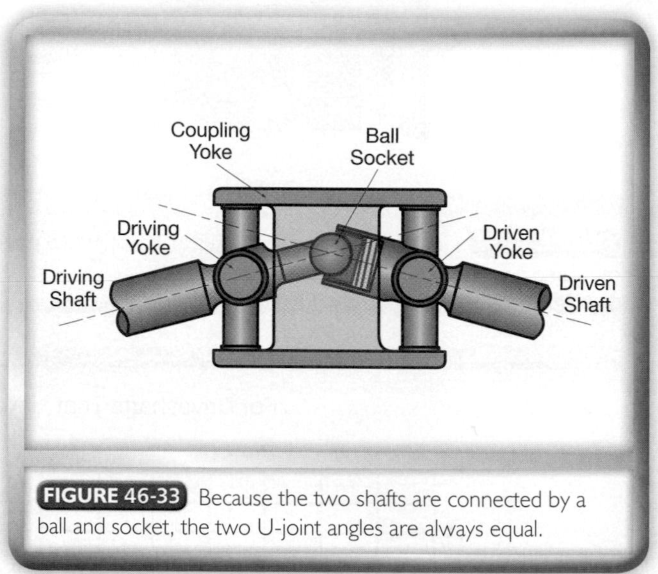

FIGURE 46-33 Because the two shafts are connected by a ball and socket, the two U-joint angles are always equal.

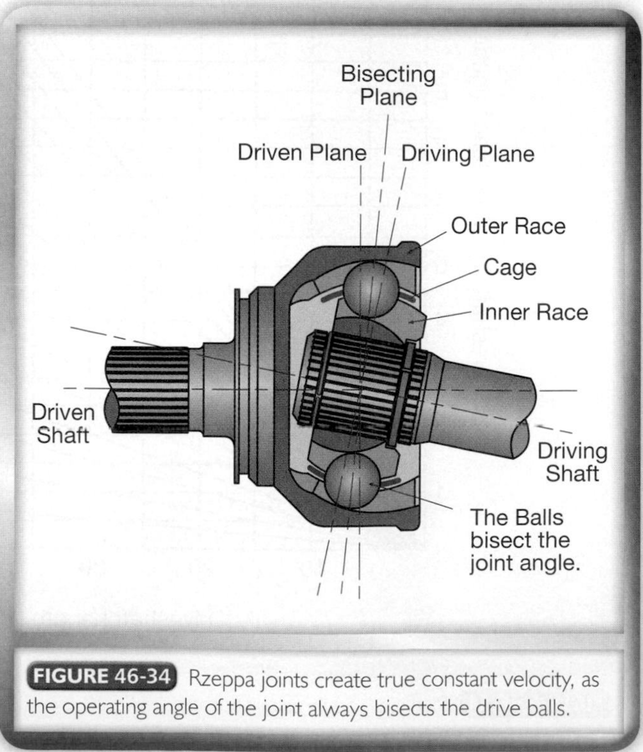

FIGURE 46-34 Rzeppa joints create true constant velocity, as the operating angle of the joint always bisects the drive balls.

Troubleshooting Vibrations and Failures

Even though drivelines can be a common source of vibration complaints, it is necessary to eliminate all other possibilities before condemning the driveshaft. Vibrations from other systems such as the engine, clutch, or wheel ends can mimic driveshaft problems. The experienced technician will usually be capable of discerning driveline vibrations from wheel end vibrations by recognizing the frequency of the vibration. Drive line vibrations occur at driveshaft speed or faster while wheel end vibrations are at least three times slower. Understanding the vibrations, measuring driveshaft runout, and analyzing driveshaft failure are all critical aspects to troubleshooting this system.

Drive Line Vibration Diagnostics

A simple road test can be used to eliminate the engine, clutch, and/or transmission as a source of vibration. Accelerate the vehicle to a speed slightly faster than the one at which the vibration is the worst. Then, depress the clutch and let the vehicle slow down through the speed where the vibration was the worst. By depressing the clutch, the engine and the clutch will slow down to idle and the transmission input is removed. No change in the vibration indicates that the engine, clutch, and transmission are not the cause, and the driveshaft could be the cause. If the drive line is, indeed, the source of the vibration, it could be one of several different kinds of vibrations. Possible drive line system vibrations include transverse vibrations, torsional vibrations, inertial excitation, and secondary couple vibrations.

Transverse vibrations are caused by an out-of-balance driveshaft or system and occur once per shaft revolution. Always check shafts for missing balance weights. These shafts are very heavy and small imbalances can cause large vibrations. Balance weights are shown in **FIGURE 46-35**.

There are two causes of **torsional vibrations** in the drive line. One source originates from the power impulses from the engine caused by the forces on the crankshaft during each power stroke. With today's engines that produce high torque at low speed, these impulses cause a twisting force to be placed on the crankshaft up to 20 times a second at rated speed. If these impulses are not properly muted by the clutch or powertrain system, they can be transmitted throughout the drive line.

The other cause of drive line torsionals is from the U-joint angles or phasing. Remember that a U-joint working at an angle causes the driven yoke to accelerate and decelerate twice per revolution. If proper cancellation is not achieved by correct angles and phasing, the driveshaft will be subjected to twisting forces. Just as a coat hanger

FIGURE 46-35 Check shaft for missing balance weights.

that is bent back and forth snaps in two, enough torsional forces in the driveshaft will lead to driveshaft failure. Vibrations from this source will occur at twice driveshaft speed.

Inertial excitation stem from the operating angles of the U-joint at the drive end of the driveshaft and are caused by the sheer weight of the driveshaft being accelerated and decelerated twice per revolution. These vibrations are hard to pinpoint. There are only two possible solutions for inertial excitation. The first is to decrease the operating angle and thereby reduce the magnitude of the acceleration and decelerations. The second is to reduce the driveshaft weight, which is seldom practical. Even though the drive line angles may be correctly canceling each other out, the larger the angle at the drive end, the more severe the inertial excitation will be.

Secondary couple vibrations are vibrations that are passed through or coupled through the hanger bearing in a heavy-duty driveshaft. These vibrations are then passed along the entire length of the drive line. Secondary couple vibrations occur at twice driveshaft speed and can affect the whole drive line. They are most often observed by failure of the hanger bearing rubber support. Secondary couple vibrations can be lessened by making sure the U-joint angle at the front of the coupling shaft is as small as possible.

Critical speed vibrations occur if the driveshaft is operated faster than its critical speed. Recall that critical speed is the speed at which the centrifugal force acting on the rotating shaft becomes stronger than the shaft material and it will start to bow off its centerline. Critical speed vibrations occur at driveshaft speed and will always cause shaft failure eventually.

Diagnosing Vibrations

Most original equipment manufacturers produce vibration diagnostic flow charts that can be used to systematically rule out all other possibilities. To begin diagnosing vibrations, gather as much information as possible from the operator about the vibration. Ask when the vibration started, if it is present at all times with the vehicle running, only when moving, or only when the vehicle or trailer is loaded, at what speed vibration occurs, and so on. This information can help to rule out other causes and pinpoint the problem.

Next, try to recreate the vibration with the driver in the vehicle if possible. Take note of the frequency, wheel speed, engine speed, or driveshaft speed. After gathering all the information necessary to narrow the problem down, follow a flow chart like the one in **FIGURE 46-36**.

If the driveshaft is isolated as the cause of the vibration, the shafts must be carefully inspected for missing balance weights or any build-up of foreign material, which could be the cause of vibration caused by imbalance. Dents in the driveshaft tubing displace shaft mass towards the center rather than the outside where it was when the shaft was initially balanced. Dents are a common cause of vibration and also weaken the tube's section modulus (strength). Dented tubing should be replaced.

Measuring Driveshaft Runout

Shaft runout is another possible cause of vibration. Driveshaft runout can be caused by a bent driveshaft, damaged yokes, or worn U-joints. A dial indicator is normally used to measure driveshaft runout.

Before measuring runout, first sand and clean around the front, center, and rear of the driveshaft to remove any uneven build-up of paint or rust. This will give the dial indicator a smooth surface for accurate measurements. Mount the dial indicator perpendicular to the shaft. The indicator base must be placed on a rigid surface floor pan, frame, or special post stand. The driveshaft must NOT be at a sharp angle during runout measurement. Make sure that the vehicle axles are in their normally weighted positions.

With the transmission in neutral, turn the driveshaft. Measure runout at the front, center, and rear of the shaft as shown in **FIGURE 46-37**. Compare your measurements to specs. Generally, driveshaft runout should not exceed 0.010" to 0.015" (0.25 to 0.38 mm), but always check the manufacturer's specification. If driveshaft runout is beyond specs, try removing and rotating the shaft 180 degrees in the rear yoke. Make sure the universal joints are in good condition and that the yokes are not damaged. If, after eliminating all other causes of vibration, runout is okay, try rotating the shaft 180 degrees in the rear yoke to possibly lessen vibration. If there is still a vibration present, the driveshaft should be sent out for balancing. Alternatively, balance weights can be added to the shaft and held in place by a gear clamp in a trial-and-error fashion, but this is a very time-consuming method and usually not worth the down time.

Drive line angles can be measured as was discussed in the Measuring and Calculating Drive Line Angles section. Measuring the angles in that way does not take inertial excitations into consideration, however. The best way to eliminate a drive line vibration is to use one of the computerized drive line angle analyzer programs offered by manufacturers, such as the Eaton DAA (Drive Line Angle Analyzer). These programs take driveshaft weight, length, and angles into consideration and are much better at eliminating driveshaft inertial excitations as well as angle vibration problems.

Analyzing Driveshaft Failure

Driveshafts can fail for a number of reasons, including brinelling, spalling, galling, fractured or broken U-joints, accelerated wear, twisted tubing, or failure of the hanger bearings.

Brinelling

Brinelling, as mentioned in the Driveshaft Angle Cancellation: Rule Number One section and shown in **FIGURE 46-38**, occurs when the rollers in the universal joint are hammered into the trunnions, leaving indentations. This can happen for several reasons. If the U-joint operates at a zero angle, the rollers do not rotate and the lubrication is squeezed out between the rollers and trunnions. This leads to brinelling-like wear on the trunnions, called false brinelling. The operating angle must be adjusted to have a least one-half to one degree or this failure will occur over and over again. Over tightening of retaining straps or distorted or damaged end yokes can cause the same problem by restricting the roller's rotation.

Excess torque can also lead to brinelling, as the trunnion metal is repeatedly overloaded. The perpetual hammering will eventually lead to brinelling. Brinelling can also occur if the slip yoke is seized. In that case, brinelling will appear on the front and rear of the trunnion rather than on the torque faces (the sides of the trunnion). As the shaft tries to lengthen or shorten, the seized slip yoke causes the front and back of the trunnions to be hammered. Brinelling can also result after a long service life as the normal wearing of the universal joint.

Spalling or Galling

Spalling and galling are the transfer of metal from one surface to the other caused by excessive friction between them. **FIGURE 46-39** shows an example of extreme spalling.

This is normally caused by either a lack of or contamination of the joint lubricant. Water and dirt are the most likely contaminants. Lack of lubricant indicates

Vibration flow chart
Step 1
Stationary inspection: check tire and rims, driveshaft tubing for dents, engine mounts, driveshaft hanger bearing
Step 2
Operate vehicle at vibration rpm. Is vibration present while stationary?
No
Yes
Road test vehicle until it passes the vibration speed and place transmission in neutral. Does the vibration go away?
Any previous engine or clutch work?
No
Yes
Yes
Problem is drive line related.
Vibration is related to the clutch or engine. Check for broken springs disks or other damage.
Engine or clutch could be causing vibration. Verify engine operating correctly and that correct clutch was installed.
Remove all axle shafts and lock in power divider, then run vehicle up to vibration speed. Is vibration still present?
No
Yes
Vibration is wheel end related. Raise vehicle on stands, keeping frame level. Remove tires and reinstall axle shafts. Operate the vehicle. Is the vibration still present?
Inspect driveshaft, u-joints, hanger bearings. Check driveshaft phasing and angularity. Check shaft runout. If all checks ok, balance the driveshaft.
No
Yes
Check tires for damage. Dynamically balance wheel and tire assemblies. Check wheels and tires for runout on reinstallation.
Check brake drums for missing balance weights, suspension system integrity, wheel bearing adjustment.

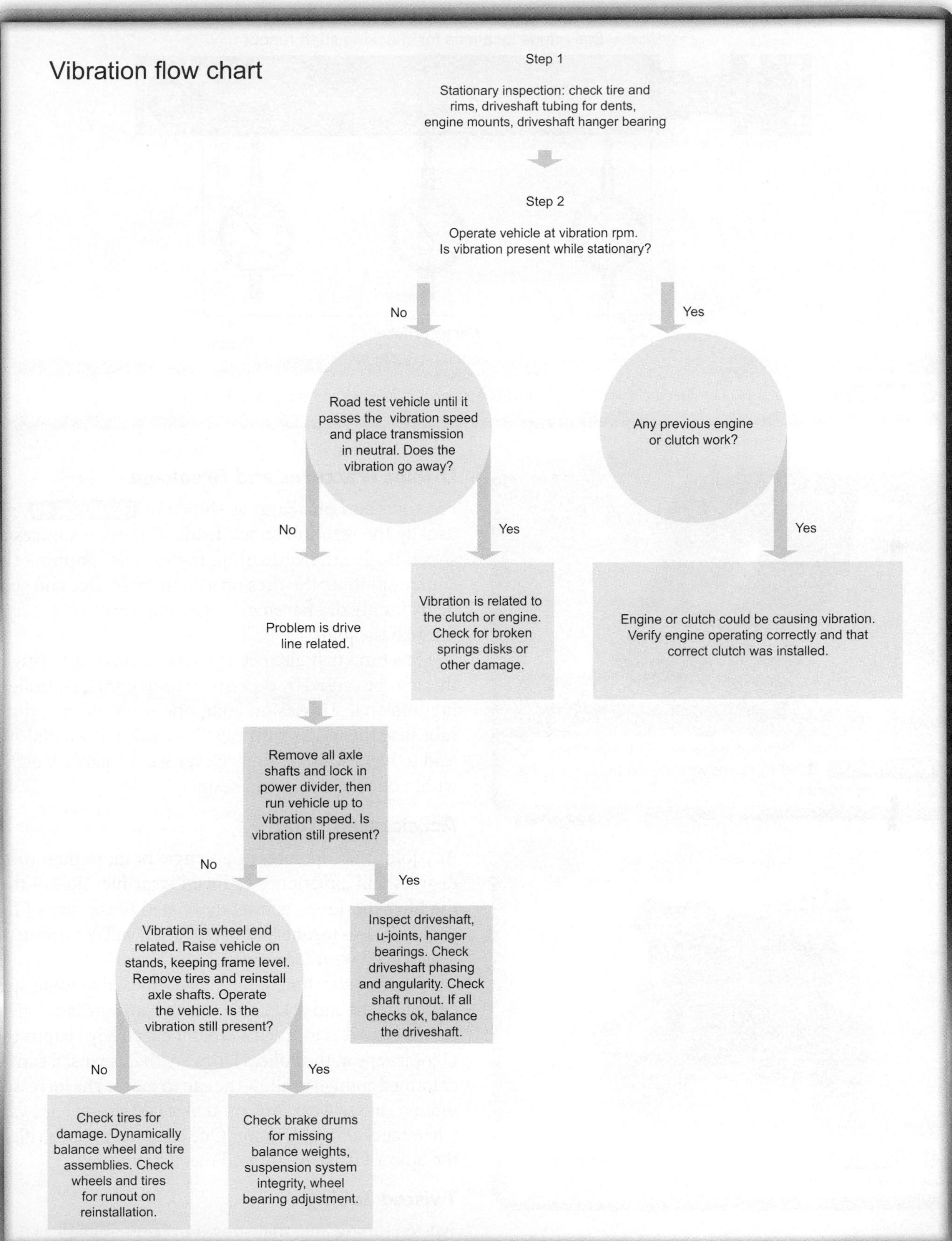

FIGURE 46-36 Vibration diagnostic flow chart.

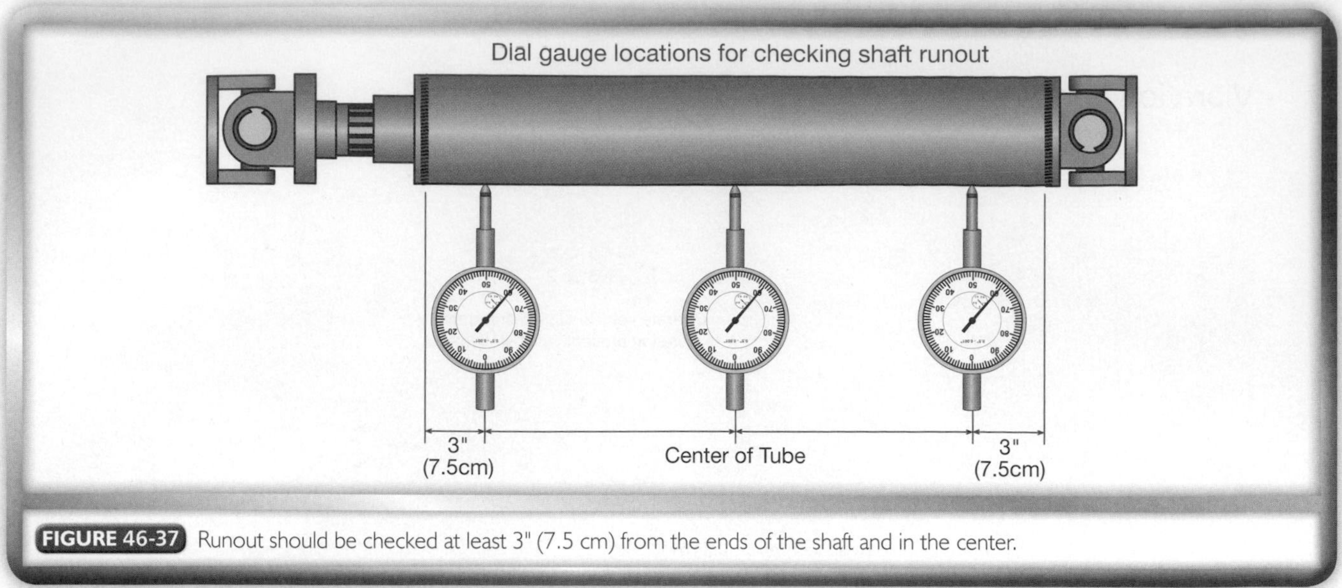

FIGURE 46-37 Runout should be checked at least 3" (7.5 cm) from the ends of the shaft and in the center.

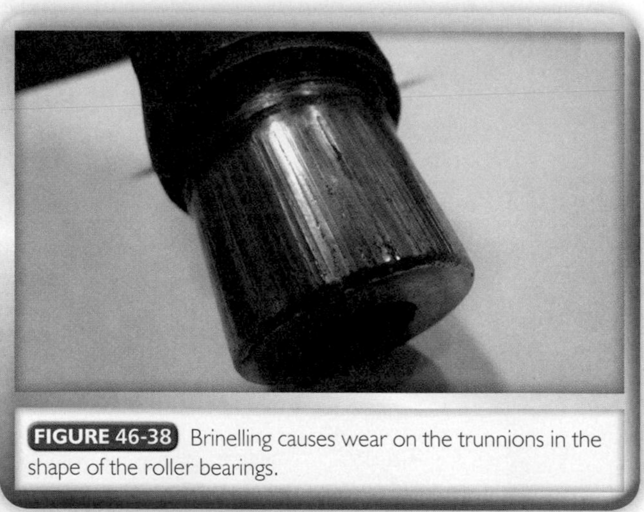

FIGURE 46-38 Brinelling causes wear on the trunnions in the shape of the roller bearings.

FIGURE 46-39 Contaminated lubricant or lack of lubricant leads to spalling. This image is an extreme case of spalling.

poor maintenance practices. Either reason can lead to burned trunnions. End galling of the trunnions is usually caused by excessive joint operating angles.

U-Joint Fractures and Breakage

Fractures and breakage, as shown in FIGURE 46-40, are usually the result of shock loads. Common sources of shock loads are overloading the vehicle, popping the clutch, spinning the tires on a slippery surface and suddenly hitting dry pavement, or sending excessive torque through the joint.

Fractures may also occur at weld seams due to fatigue that may be caused by excessive working angles introducing torsional stresses on components. Welding on the tube near the weld seams can also weaken the metal and lead to weld seam failures. Never weld balance weights within one inch of a weld seam.

Accelerated Wear

Any joint that operates at an angle of more than three degrees will experience reduced wear life. (Recall that the life expectancy is directly related to the size of the angle.) Excess torque and overloading will contribute to a shortened wear life as well.

Reusing attachment hardware can lead to wear, specifically in the end yoke. Attachment hardware is designed to stretch as it is torqued so that it effectively clamps the U-joint caps in the yoke. Hardware that is reused can be deformed enough to allow the cap to move. The increased motion causes wear. Always replace attaching hardware when reinstalling a U-joint. One exception to this rule is the Spicer Life series formed metal hardware.

Twisted Tubing

Twisted tubing, like that shown in FIGURE 46-41, is usually caused by excessive torque loading of the drive line. Excessive torque loading is typically due to driver error, such as trying to pull away with the trailer brakes applied,

FIGURE 46-40 U-joint breakage is usually caused by shock loading, as is the case in this image of a broken U-joint cross. Notice the uniform roughness of the break.

FIGURE 46-41 Extreme torque load caused this driveshaft to twist like a pretzel.

popping the clutch with excessive rpm, or slamming into a loading dock. If twisting occurs, a check should be made to determine if the drive line is capable of transferring the engine/transmission torque available.

Hanger Bearing Failures

Hanger bearing failures are actually quite rare because the bearing is sealed and permanently lubricated. The stamped steel cavity surrounding the hanger bearing does need to be packed with water-proof grease at installation. If this procedure is overlooked, the bearing will fail prematurely.

Failure of the hanger or "center" bearing is depicted in FIGURE 46-42. This type of failure usually occurs in the rubber support block and is most often caused by excessive angles at the coupling shaft drive end. This angle should be less than one and a half degrees if possible. Remember that it must also have at least one-half degree so that the rollers will turn. This problem will usually manifest as black rubber dust surrounding the hanger

FIGURE 46-42 Failed hanger bearing with collapsed slotted upper support.

bearing. On every revolution, the coupling shaft will try to straighten out its angle, and the rubber block must absorb this motion. Some heavy-duty coupling shafts can weigh in excess of 100 lb (45.5 kg). The rubber support must be strong enough for the shaft it is attached to. Hanger bearing failure is usually due to shaft imbalance or excessive torsionals leading to failure of the rubber mount. Because they are permanently lubricated, bearing failure is normally attributed to external damage to the bearing or its seals

Hanger bearing failures can also occur due to overloading the shaft or excessive drive line vibrations. A lot of hanger bearings will have a slotted rubber support. Collapsed slots are an indicator that the shaft is too heavy for the rubber support and that the slotted support should be changed for a solid rubber support.

Inspection and Maintenance of Driveshafts

Regular driveshaft maintenance is usually limited to inspecting the shaft and components for wear or damage and properly lubricating the driveshaft following the manufacturer's recommended procedures. Any inspection for wear MUST be done prior to lubricating the components. The reason is simple: the lubricant itself may mask wear in the universal joints and make it hard to detect.

Begin with a careful visual inspection of the driveshaft. Look for any broken or loose fasteners. Pay particular attention to the universal joint attaching hardware and the center bearing support bracket. Look for broken yoke tabs or missing spring clips or locks. Check the tubes for damage, dents, or missing balance weights, all of which can cause vibration problems. Also make sure that there is no foreign material stuck to the shafts, as this can also result in balance vibrations. FIGURE 46-43 illustrates how problems with the shaft can produce various vibrations.

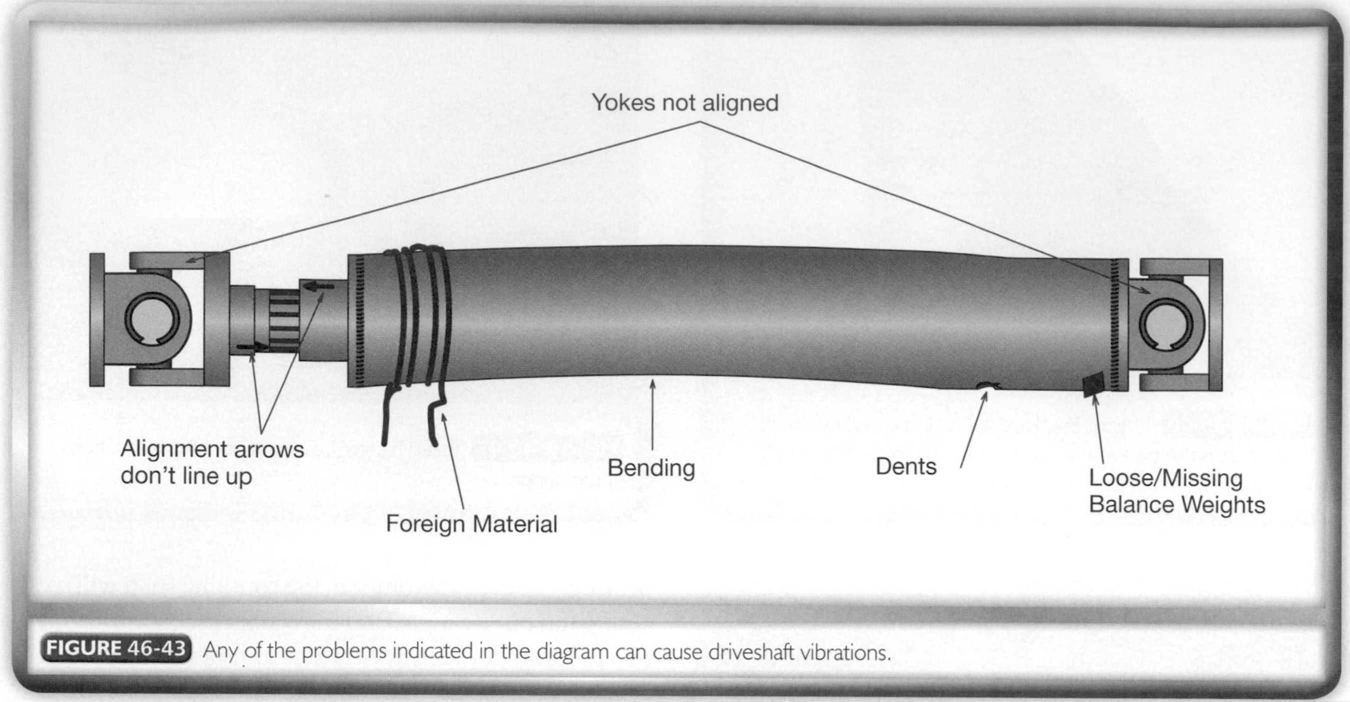

FIGURE 46-43 Any of the problems indicated in the diagram can cause driveshaft vibrations.

Look for any unusual rust streaking or rust patterns at or near the universal joints, the end yoke attaching bolts or nuts, and the center bearing hanger bolts. Rust streaking at any of these components can be a telltale sign of wear or looseness. Carefully check the center bearing rubber support. Rubber dust here is an indicator or excessive movement either from wear or vibration.

Next, check all of the universal joints for wear. Grasp both sides of each joint and try to rotate them in opposite directions to each other, checking for radial play, as depicted in FIGURE 46-44. There should be no perceptible movement between the trunnions and the caps. Even slight movement here fails the joint, and it should be replaced. Next, grasp the shaft side of the joint and move it vertically and horizontally, as shown in FIGURE 46-45, to check for end play between the joint bearing caps and the ends of the trunnions. For most manufacturers, this end play cannot exceed 0.006" (0.15 mm). Although some manufacturers recommend universal joint replacement if there is any noticeable end play, check the OEM manual to be sure.

Grasp each of the end yokes where they enter the transmission and the drive axle pinion(s) and rotate them back and forth and up and down to check for looseness. There should be no perceptible free play at these components. If play is present, consult the transmission or axle

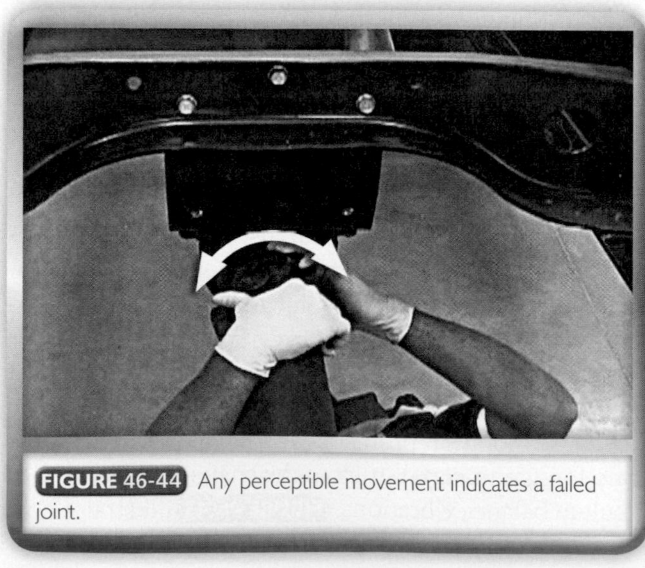

FIGURE 46-44 Any perceptible movement indicates a failed joint.

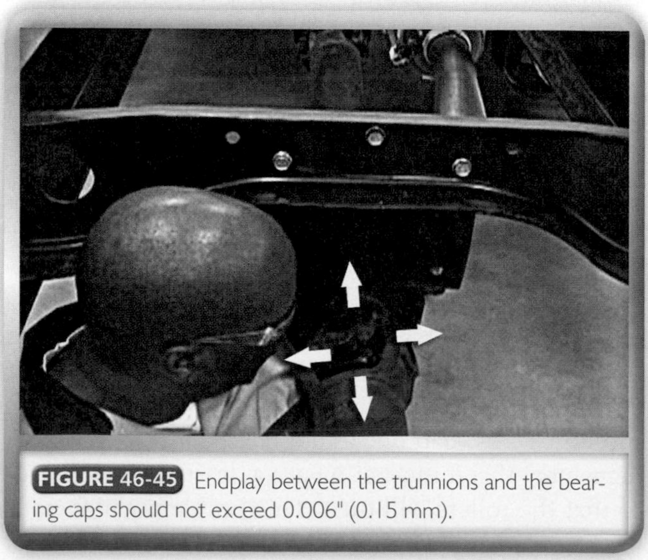

FIGURE 46-45 Endplay between the trunnions and the bearing caps should not exceed 0.006" (0.15 mm).

manufacturer's manual for instructions on how to repair the situation. There may be slight perceptible end play at the input shaft of an inter-axle differential. This is allowable, but the play should not be between the end yoke and the input shaft. Consult the manufacturer's manual for specifications if necessary.

Grasp the slip yoke and move it up, down, and radially to check splines for looseness and radial play. Maximum play should be no more than .012" (3 mm), but measurable play exceeding 0.004" to 0.006" (0.1 to 0.15 mm) should be investigated and corrected. Play in the slip joint components can cause driveshaft vibration because the play will allow the shaft to move away from its centerline while rotating.

Check the hanger bearing for wear as shown in FIGURE 46-46. The rubber supports will vary in stiffness, but there should be no play in the actual bearing itself. Also inspect the hanger bearing for any sign of rubber dust. The presence of rubber dust indicates that the hanger bearing may be failing or that the driveshaft is oscillating at the bearing for some reason. The shaft may be overloaded or sustaining excessive vibration. The reason for the rubber support wearing must be corrected or the shaft will eventually fail.

FIGURE 46-46 Slip yoke play allows the driveshaft to rotate off center, leading to vibration.

Lubrication

Lack of proper lubrication is one of the most common causes of universal joint and driveshaft failures. Regular lubrication with high quality grease that meets or exceeds the manufacturer's specifications will assist in achieving maximum joint wear life. Although each manufacturer will have its own recommendations, the lubricant used should meet the following minimum specifications:

- The grease should be good quality EP (extreme pressure) grease.
- The grease should meet National Lubricating Grease Institute (NLGI) Grade 2 specification.
- The grease should have an operating range of at least 325 °F to –10 °F (163 °C to –21 °C).
- The grease should be compatible with commonly used multi-purpose greases. When lubricating universal joints, it is essential to purge grease from all four caps until the new grease is visible exiting the cap seals. This will eliminate the old grease and lessen compatibility issues.

Knowing the correct lubricant is only one aspect of proper lubrication. In addition, the components must be lubricated at the correct intervals. Lubricating intervals vary by manufacturer and by driveshaft design. TABLE 46-4 indicates a general lubrication interval. Always check with the vehicle or driveshaft manufacturer to be certain of the correct lubrication frequency.

TABLE 46-5 provides the extended lubrication intervals for the Spicer Life series. These drive lines have booted and permanently lubed slip joints.

Dana Spicer Life series XS universal joints have an initial lubrication interval of 350,000 miles (560,000 kilometers) and 100,000 miles (160,000 kilometers) after that. The latest U-joints from the Spicer Life series are available as maintenance free. All Spicer Life series slip joints are permanently lubed at the factory. The Meritor

TABLE 46-4: Normal Lubrication Intervals

City	On-Highway	Line Haul	Off-Highway	Industrial
Every 5 to 8,000 miles, or	Every 10 to 15,000 miles, or	Every 10 to 15,000 miles, or	Every 5 to 8,000 miles, or	Every 500 hours, or
8 to 12,800 kilometers, or	16 to 24,000 kilometers, or	16 to 24,000 kilometers, or	8 to 12,800 kilometers, or	every 250 hours for continuous use, or
3 months, whichever comes first	3 months, whichever comes first	3 months, whichever comes first	3 months, whichever comes first	severe service

TABLE 46-5: Extended Lubrication Intervals for Spicer Life Series Driveshafts

City	On-Highway	Line Haul	Off-Highway	Industrial
Every 25,000 miles, or	Every 25,000 miles, or	Every 25,000 miles, or	Every 25,000 miles, or	Every 500 hours, or
40,000 kilometers, or	40,000 kilometers, or	40,000 kilometers, or	40,000 kilometers, or	every 250 hours for continuous use, or
6 months, whichever comes first	6 months, whichever comes first	6 months, whichever comes first	6 months, whichever comes first	severe service

RPL Permalube non-greasable drive line universal joints are lubricated for the life of the vehicle and so require little or no maintenance. Certain Meritor drive lines with permanently lubed universal joints may still need to have the slip yoke lubricated.

Probably the most important advice for technicians performing lubrication service on a driveshaft is to be sure that the universal joints purge grease from all four universal joint caps. If one cap fails to purge after all attempts have been made, the joint must be disassembled to find out the reason.

Using a hand or an air-powered grease gun fully lubricates each of the universal joints. As the grease is being forced into the joint, watch the bearing caps for any water or rust that purges from them. Sometimes a very small amount of clear water, one or two drops from condensation, may be present. The presence of water droplets is acceptable unless there is any sign of water contamination of the lube or rust colored material or dirt purging from the caps. In that case, the joint must be replaced. Be sure that grease is pumped into the joint caps until they are completely purged and only new grease is coming out of the caps, as shown in **FIGURE 46-47**. This ensures that there is sufficient grease in each cap and that there will not be any compatibility issues with dissimilar greases.

If one or more of the caps do not purge grease immediately, try to lessen the pressure on the cap that will not purge by using a jack with slight pressure to push the opposite cap against its trunnion while trying to get grease to purge. If this is unsuccessful and the universal joints have bolt- in caps, try loosening the bolts on the problem cap a couple of turns each and again try to purge the cap. If these methods fail, the shaft or the joint must be removed so you can investigate and remedy the situation. A universal joint bearing cap that does not purge grease while being lubricated will most certainly fail, so keep at it until it purges or replace the joint. After all caps have been purged with fresh grease, wipe up the excess grease to protect the environment and keep the vehicle underside clean.

Next, you will need to lube the slip joints. Slip joints have a Welch plug pressed into the end of the sliding tube. Where the tube turns into the yoke, the plug will have a small hole in the center for air to escape, as **FIGURE 46-48** shows.

Apply grease until it purges from the Welch plug hole and, again, watch for any signs of contamination. Even though contamination here is not as critical as with universal joint bearing caps, serious contamination should be investigated. When grease purges from the Welch plug hole, cover the hole with a finger and continue to pump the grease into the joint until it purges from the seal end. Again, purge until fresh grease is seen exiting the seal.

After completion, clean up the excess grease. If the vehicle is to be parked outside in colder climates for a significant amount of time, it is a good idea to road test the vehicle so that the slip joint will reciprocate a bit and purge any excess grease. In vehicles not road tested in cold weather, the grease can solidify while the vehicle is parked. When the vehicle is finally driven, the solid plug of grease can force the Welch plug out of the joint. After further driving, the grease will start to soften and eventually all of the grease will be thrown out of the joint by centrifugal force. This will lead to premature slip joint failure.

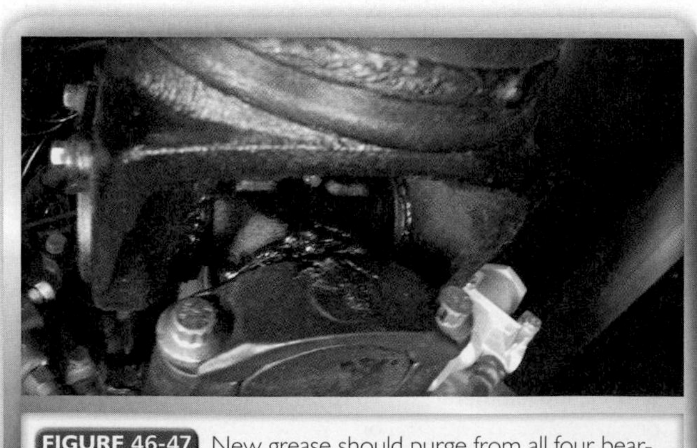

FIGURE 46-47 New grease should purge from all four bearing caps when lubricating new or in-service U-joints. If a cap fails to purge grease, it is essential to investigate the cause.

FIGURE 46-48 When lubricating a slip yoke, block the bleed hole in the Welch plug until new grease purges from the slip yoke.

Safety

If using an air-powered grease gun, use a piece of rubber gasket to seal the Welch plug hole in the end of the slip yoke. The rubber acts as a precaution to prevent grease from being injected into the skin. Although unlikely, an air grease gun may be capable of piercing the skin. Grease injection can lead to severe tissue damage.

Replacing a Universal Joint

Replacing a universal joint may or may not require that the driveshaft be removed from the vehicle. If so, the shaft must be separated from the end yokes before being taken to a work bench or press to complete the joint replacement.

The following are general steps for truck universal joint replacement procedures. Each drive line system will have individual attaching hardware styles (bolts and straps, clips, and so on), and most manufacturers insist that attaching hardware be replaced if it is removed. Therefore, before attempting to remove the shaft or any components, make sure the correct parts are on hand to complete the job. There are several different pulling and pushing tools available to replace universal joints. Regardless of the type of tool used, the same basic instructions apply when working with all driveshafts.

The most important aspects of universal joint replacement are being careful not to damage the shaft and to use as little force as possible when removing the joint. Take extreme care not to damage the shaft itself, as dents in the shaft will cause vibrations and lead to premature joint failure. Scratches and gouges can lead to localized stress risers, which weaken the shaft. The yokes can be damaged in several ways as well, so take care when working with them. The ears can be expanded by stretching them apart and be distorted or twisted by hammering and indiscriminate use of excessive force. Remember to use as little force as possible while removing universal joints. It is not recommended to use torches to heat components to ease removal because the heat can change the metallurgy of the shaft or yoke material.

Removing the Driveshaft

Driveshaft manufacturers recommend that none of the attaching hardware should be reused; any bolts, straps, or clips should be replaced, as they are torqued to yield when installed correctly and may not secure the driveshaft if they are used again. Therefore, before removing any driveshaft hardware, ensure that replacement hardware is readily available.

The first step in removal of a universal joint is to always attach slings or hangers to support the shaft before removing the attaching hardware. Be sure to use enough supports so that the shaft does not fall when one or the other end is removed. If working on a drive line with more than one shaft, each section of the shaft will require at least two slings or hangers. When removing a multi-piece shaft, start at the drive axle end and work forward.

TECHNICIAN TIP

Heavy-duty truck driveshafts can weigh well over 100 lb (45 kg) and removing the attaching bolts before supporting the shaft can lead to personal injury and or damage to the shaft. Always use a sling or other method to hold the shaft weight securely before removing any of the attaching bolts.

Before removing the sections of a multi-shaft drive line, always mark the slip joints with paint or a marking pencil so they can be reinstalled correctly. (White correction fluid from the office supplies makes a good marking compound.) If the universal joint is bolted to a half-round end yoke, after installing the correct support slings, remove the attaching hardware that holds the joint bearing caps into the end yoke. Remove the shaft to the bench to complete joint removal. As shown in FIGURE 46-49, always use a sling to support the driveshaft before removing the attaching bolts.

There are several commercially available pullers that can be used to remove the bearing caps from the shafts with a full-round end yoke. Using pullers such as the Tiger Tool U-Joint puller shown in FIGURE 46-50, is the manufacturers' recommended procedure to prevent damage to the yoke and/or shaft.

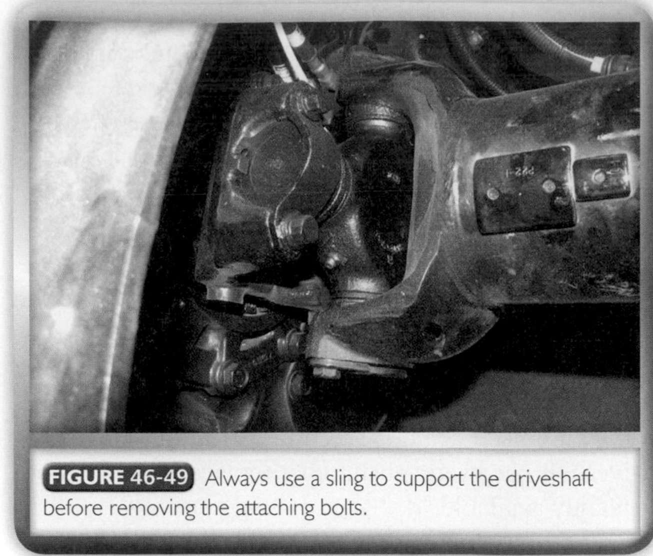

FIGURE 46-49 Always use a sling to support the driveshaft before removing the attaching bolts.

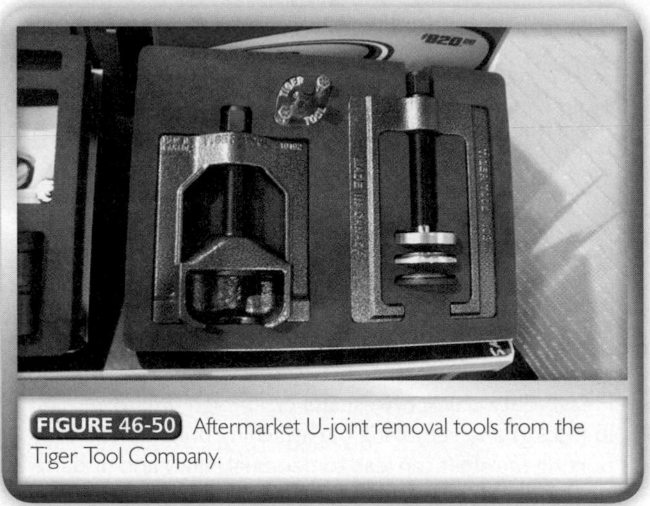

FIGURE 46-50 Aftermarket U-joint removal tools from the Tiger Tool Company.

The attaching hardware on the full-round end yoke caps should be removed and the puller installed according to the manufacturer's procedure. The puller will remove the cap using a steady pulling action that pushes against one yoke ear and pulls against another. No damage to the yoke itself will occur during this process. When the first cap is removed, the tool is re-installed to remove the other cap. The shaft is then taken to the bench to remove the other caps. If a universal joint is to be reused, ensure that the correct bearing caps are re-installed on their original trunnions. In some shops, a popular method of removing the caps is to use a floor jack and a hammer. The joint cap to be removed is placed in the vertical position and a jack is positioned close to the joint under the yoke, the jack is operated, and the weight of the vehicle is used to remove the cap. Sometimes a hammer is used to try and break the cap loose if it is seized.

No matter how common, THIS METHOD IS NOT RECOMMENDED BY ANY MANUFACTURER. We discuss the process here to try and avoid damage to equipment and or injury to technicians. It is NOT recommended.

Using the weight of the vehicle to force the cap out can cause several problems. First, the bearing cap can let go suddenly if it is seized. The jack can slip, causing the vehicle to drop, quickly resulting in crush injuries and vehicle damage. The jack itself can cause damage to the shaft by bending it or gouging at the point of contact. The yoke ears can be spread by the uneven forces being applied, and using hammers can cause damage to the shaft or yoke.

Using the proper pulling tools avoids all of these dangers and is the only procedure that should be followed. If only one universal joint is being replaced, the entire removal procedure can be accomplished with the shaft still in place on the vehicle and supported. Simply remove one cap at a time with the puller. If more than one joint is to be replaced, the shaft can be taken to the work bench and the work can be completed there, using either the puller or a suitable hydraulic press. Alternatively, if the shaft has a slip joint, the joint may be separated to remove one section of the shaft. When separating a slip joint, make sure to mark the position of the slip joint so that it can be re-installed correctly.

Some slip joints have a threaded seal cap that must be unscrewed before the slip joint can be separated, as depicted in **FIGURE 46-51**. Remember that a heavy-duty driveshaft can weigh well over 100 lb (46 kg), so get assistance when removing the shaft. There are several different pullers available for universal joints, and the method described above can be adapted to use with any one of them. The relatively low cost of these pullers

FIGURE 46-51 It may be necessary to unscrew the seal cap on a slip joint to separate it. Be sure to mark both halves so they can be reassembled correctly.

should mean that all shops will use them. Unfortunately, however, some will not and will resort to the jack method. Remember, the jack method is likely to cause injury and or shaft damage and should not be used.

After the joint has been removed, the yoke ears should be checked for wear and removal damage. Slight burrs can be removed with a small rat tail file. Remove heavy rust with an emery cloth to make the re-installation process easier.

Finally, check the yokes for distortion by using a yoke alignment bar. Slide the bar through both yoke ears. If the bar does not go through, it indicates that the yoke has been twisted due to excessive torque or disassembly damage. In that case, the yoke should be replaced.

Inspecting and Installing Universal Joints

According to most manufacturers' procedures, all driveshaft attaching hardware—bolts, nuts, straps, and lock plates—should be replaced after being removed and should never be reused. When hardware is installed properly, straps and bolts are usually torqued to yield and may be distorted. Consequently, re-using hardware may allow bearing caps to move or attachment may loosen.

Before installing a new universal joint, carefully inspect the new joint by removing all of the bearing caps and checking the rollers and the cap seals. Check for any debris or dirt in the joint and make sure that the grease zerk is in good order. Also note the location of the grease. If the grease zerk is mounted on one side (for example, towards the front or back) of the universal joint cross, that side should be installed towards the driveshaft tube. Doing so ensures that the zerk is accessible by a grease gun after installation. In some cases, it may still be possible to grease the joint if the zerk is installed towards the end yoke, but it is always better to be safe than sorry.

Remember that new universal joints are packaged with just enough lubricant to hold the rollers in place and stave off rusting. The joints MUST be fully lubricated after installation. When installing universal joint caps, it is essential that the cap and bearings be on the trunnion before forcing the cap back into the yoke ears. Otherwise, one or more of the rollers can fall between the cap and the trunnion end. Preventing that involves positioning the trunnion through the yoke, installing the cap on the trunnion, and then forcing the cap and trunnion back into the yoke ear. Universal joints should be removed and installed using steady controlled pressure only and using the proper pulling and pushing tools. A dead blow or brass hammer may be used to help seat bearing caps, but be very careful not to damage the shaft, the yokes, and/or the universal joint itself. To disassemble and inspect a U-joint with a bolted end, follow the steps in **SKILL DRILL 46-1**. To install universal joints, follow the guidelines in **SKILL DRILL 46-2**.

TECHNICIAN TIP

It cannot be stressed enough how easy it can be to "drop a roller" (when one of the roller bearings fall into the bearing cap unseen by the technician) while installing universal joints. Take extreme care to avoid this scenario. If it is suspected that a roller has dropped, be sure to re-check the joint carefully. A dropped roller will cause a new joint to fail very quickly.

SKILL DRILL 46-1 Disassembling and Inspecting a Universal Joint with a Bolted End

1. Locate and follow the appropriate procedure in the service manual.
2. Complete the accompanying job sheet or work order with all pertinent information.
3. Remove the U-joint from driveshaft:
   a. Bend tangs of lock plates away from cap screw heads.
   b. Remove cap screws and lock plates.
   c. Remove bearing caps from flange and spider. Note: If caps have to be driven out with a hammer, be careful not to damage the flange or driveshaft.
4. Inspect U-joint with bolted ends:
   a. Clean all U-joint parts.
   b. Check bearing journals for evidence of wear or heat damage; also, check ends of crosses.
   c. Make sure lubricant passages in cross are clean.
   d. Check for missing, worn, or damaged needle bearings.
   e. Apply the recommended lubricant to rollers in caps.
   f. Turn caps on journals to check for wear. Note: If any parts are worn or damaged, replace the entire U-joint.
5. List the test results and/or recommendations on the job sheet or work order, clean the work area, and return tools and materials to their proper storage.

TECHNICIAN TIP

New universal joints only have enough lube to retain the roller bearing and prevent rust. It is essential that they are completely lubricated after installation with new grease purging from all four bearing caps or failure will likely occur!

Inspecting and Replacing Center (Hanger) Bearings

The center (hanger) bearing supports the end of a split driveshaft and is a very important part of any drive line. The bearing itself is usually sealed. It cannot be lubricated, but if it has a grease zerk, it will actually require lubrication at the same interval as the rest of the drive line.

SKILL DRILL 46-2 Installing Universal Joints

1. With all of the caps removed from the cross, position it in the tube yoke with one of the trunnions protruding above the yoke ear. Install the cross in the yoke, one trunnion at a time.

2. Place the bearing cap over the trunnion, making sure that the rollers remain properly seated in the cap. Then, slide the cap into position while holding the cross so that the rollers remain engaged with the trunnion. If the cap binds in the yoke, tap it lightly with a dead blow hammer until it is flush. Always tap the center of the cap only—not the edges.

3. Install the cap retaining bolts with the lock strap if equipped, but do not fold the lock strap tangs to secure the bolt at this time. (Wait until the joint is properly lubricated.)

4. With one cap installed correctly, turn the yoke over and raise the cross sufficiently to engage the rollers of the second cap with its trunnion. Do not raise the cross so high that the other trunnion comes out of its cap. Then, push the second cap into position and secure it.

5. Rotate the joint on its bearing to be sure there is no binding. If it binds, the joint should be disassembled to find the cause.

6. If the shaft is being installed into a half-round end yoke, place the two other caps on their trunnions and tie the exposed caps together with electrical tape so they do not fall off when positioning the shaft for installation. Install the shaft and the attaching hardware.

7. If installing the shaft into a full-round yoke, repeat the installation instructions used on the bench by lifting the first trunnion through the end yoke then installing its cap so the rollers are seated. Push the cross into place. Depending on the type of joint, it may be necessary to use a pushing installation tool to install the caps. Lift the last trunnion through the end yoke just enough so that the rollers of the bearing cap are held in place by the trunnion as the cap is installed. Push it into position.

8. After the shaft is installed, follow the lubricating instructions in the Lubrication section of this chapter. It may be necessary to loosen the attaching bolts during the lubrication procedure. If your U-joint bolts have locking straps, do not fold over the lock strap tabs until you have correctly lubricated the U-joints. After lubricating the joints, correctly fold up the lock strap tangs, if equipped, to secure the attaching bolts.

The center support bearing is mounted in a rubber support to allow flexibility as the drive line moves up and down. Failure of the center bearing can cause vibration and noise in the drive line. The rubber support can become damaged by being in contact with petroleum products, which swell the rubber. Excessive vibration will weaken the rubber. The rubber can also be damaged simply by age and weathering, which will eventually cause the rubber to break down and disintegrate. Follow the procedure in **SKILL DRILL 46-3** to inspect and, if necessary, replace the center bearing. Follow the procedure in **SKILL DRILL 46-4** to remove and reinstall the driveshaft and center support bearing and mounts.

SKILL DRILL 46-3 Removing and Reinstalling the Driveshaft

1. Locate and follow the appropriate procedure in the service manual.
2. Complete the accompanying job sheet or work order with all pertinent information.
3. Move the vehicle into shop, apply parking brakes, and chock the vehicle wheels. Observe lockout/tagout procedures.
4. If the vehicle has a manual transmission, place it in "neutral." If it has an automatic transmission, place it in "park" or "neutral."
5. Jack up the rear of vehicle and place jack stands under frame.
6. Mark all joints and yokes with a center punch or paint marker to retain balance and phasing.
7. Support the drive shaft with a suitable sling and remove the driveshaft attaching bolts. Study the driveshaft to determine how it is fastened.
8. Remove the center support bearing if a two-piece driveshaft is used. Check between center support and frame for shims. If shims are used, they must be replaced when the driveshaft is reinstalled.
9. Remove the driveshaft from vehicle. Tape the U-joint bearing caps to prevent loss of needle bearings. The slip yoke should also be protected to prevent damage during removal. When removing, replacing, or servicing a driveshaft, careless handling can damage the shaft and U-joints.
10. Service the driveshaft according to the service manual.
11. Reinstall driveshaft:
    a. Place in position and check alignment marks. All mounting surfaces should be clean and free of nicks before assembly.
    b. Position all fasteners correctly and tighten evenly.
    c. Replace fasteners in center support bearing, if used.
    d. Torque all fasteners to manufacturer's specifications.
12. Jack up the rear of the vehicle and remove jack stands.
13. Lower the vehicle to floor.
14. Grease each U-joint. Continue to grease until the air is removed and grease comes from the bearing cap seals. Once grease is observed from seals, wipe seals of all grease with a shop towel.
15. List the test results and/or recommendations on the job sheet or work order, clean the work area, and return tools and materials to their proper storage.

SKILL DRILL 46-4 Inspecting and Servicing Center Support Bearings

1. Safely raise the vehicle on an approved lift. Inspect the center bearing components for any major defects, such as looseness or noises.
2. Inspect the center bearing for proper mounting.
3. Inspect the bearing mount rubber insert for dry rotting and cracking.
4. If the bearing must be replaced, follow the manufacturer's specifications and procedures for proper installation of a new bearing. Typical bearing replacement may go as follows:
   - a. Mount the driveshaft in an approved vice.
   - b. Mark the shafts so they may be properly phased when put back together.
   - c. Separate the two driveshafts.
   - d. Remove the U-shaped metal mounting bracket.
   - e. Remove the rubber mount from around the center bearing.
   - f. Remove any snap rings or circlips that may be holding the bearing in place.
   - g. Use an appropriate puller or press to remove the bearing from the driveshaft.
   - h. Check the splines for the slip yoke for any defects.
   - i. Check the slip yoke on the mating shaft for wear and defects.
   - j. Press on a new bearing.
   - k. Reinstall any necessary snap rings or circlips.
5. Install a new rubber mount around the new bearing. Reinstall the mounting bracket.
6. Put the two shafts back together, paying attention to driveshaft phasing.
7. Remove the driveshaft from the vice, and reinstall it into vehicle.

Wrap-up

Ready for Review

- Most if not all heavy vehicle drive lines consist of one or more driveshafts coupled by universal joints, also known as Cardan joints.
- Robert Hooke discovered that a shaft driven at an angle through a universal joint accelerates and decelerates twice per revolution. In some places, universal joints are known as Hooke joints because of this.
- Driveshafts must meet three criteria: They must be strong enough to transmit the maximum engine torque without failure. They must allow the shaft length to change due to suspension oscillation and torque wind up. And they must be able to operate at constantly changing operating angles.
- Most truck driveshafts are denoted by series, with the 1710 and 1810 series being the most popular in North America.
- The Spicer Life series driveshaft is fast becoming the driveshaft system of choice for most new trucks.
- Driveshaft tubing can be seamed or seamless and constructed by being welded, forged, or with a welded tube drawn over mandrel. The drawn-over-mandrel design is very consistent in tube strength and thickness.
- Driveshafts are connected to the vehicle components and to each other using various yokes. Yokes have two openings, called ears, to accept two of the universal joint bearing caps. These ears can be full-round (circles) or half-round, which require bolt-on straps.
- Tube yokes are welded to the tube ends. End yokes are splined to components such as drive axles. Both will have round or half-round ears.
- Flange yokes are splined to components and have a flat flange that, in turn, is bolted to a companion flange with two full-round yoke ears.
- Truck drive lines will usually have more than one driveshaft—requiring the use of a center (hanger) bearing for support.
- Slip yokes allow the driveshaft length to change.
- Most manufacturers recommend that driveshaft attaching bolts and most hardware be replaced and not reused.
- The critical speed of a driveshaft is the speed at which it will bow off its centerline due to centrifugal force. If operated at or beyond its critical speed, a driveshaft will fail catastrophically.
- Critical speed can be increased by reducing the shaft weight, increasing shaft diameter, or shortening the shaft's length. This is why most trucks with long drive lines have numerous short shafts connected together.
- The shaft on the driven side of a universal joint operating at an angle accelerates and decelerates twice per revolution. The rate of this non-uniform velocity increases as the operating angle of the universal joint increases.
- The intensity of the acceleration and deceleration causes inertial excitation of the shaft, leading to vibration. As the operating angles increase, maximum shaft speed must decrease or the U-joint will fail. So the speed of the shaft is restricted by its angle of operation.
- The non-uniform velocity of the universal joint must be canceled out by a second universal joint with an equal and opposite angle at the other end of the shaft.
- This cancellation can be effected in two ways: with a parallel joint arrangement (also known as a waterfall arrangement) or with an intersecting angle arrangement (also known as a broken back arrangement).
- Driveshafts with universal joints must be phased so the velocity cancellation occurs during the correct quadrant of rotation.
- Drive line angles should be at least one-half degree to ensure lubricant distribution in the joint, the angle at each end of a driveshaft should be equal to within one degree, and the angles should be kept as small as possible (three degrees or less) to minimize inertial excitation of the driveshaft.
- Constant velocity joint arrangements eliminate the need for angle cancellation and phasing because the driven shaft turns at a steady speed when constant velocity joints are used.
- Drive line vibration can be caused by a bent or dented driveshaft, foreign material build-up on the shaft, worn U-joints or slip yokes, driveshaft imbalance, drive line angles out or too steep, or a driveshaft being out of phase.
- When lubricating universal joints, it is crucial that grease purges from all four caps. Otherwise, the joint should be replaced.
- Universal joints should always be replaced using proper tooling only.

Vocabulary Builder

broken back arrangement A method of angle cancellation in which the U-joint angles will intersect at a point exactly at the middle of the shaft length. Also known as an *intersecting angle arrangement*.

cancellation The act of cancelling the non-uniform velocity in a driveshaft.

Cardan joint A joint with four trunnions and four bearing caps. Also known as a *Hooke joint* or a *universal joint*.

center bearing A bearing pressed on to a machined surface after the splined area of a driveshaft's slip yoke spline; used to support a multiple piece driveshaft. Also called a *hanger bearing*.

companion flange A splined flange attached to a vehicle component, such as a drive axle pinion shaft, that bolts to a flange yoke on a driveshaft.

constant velocity joint A joint that delivers a uniform speed to the driven shaft.

coupling shaft A short shaft usually at the front of a drive line. Also known as a *jack shaft*.

critical speed The rotational speed at which a driveshaft starts to bow off its center line due to centrifugal force, leading to vibration and shaft failure

cross-phasing When a coupling shaft is phased at 90 degrees to the second driveshaft.

drive line A series of driveshafts, yokes, and support bearings used to connect a transmission to the rear axle.

drive line angularity Refers to the angles at the universal joints.

end yoke A splined yoke attached to a component such as a transmission output shaft.

false brinelling A condition where lubricant is squeezed out from between the needles and the trunnions of a U-joint leading to wear; caused by too small or no angle at the joint so lubricant is not distributed.

flange yoke A yoke with two ears to hold a U-joint and a flat flange to bolt to a companion flange.

gimbals Two or more concentric circles used to support an item; while the circles can move, the supported object will remain stationary.

hanger bearing A bearing pressed on to a machined surface after the splined area of a driveshaft's slip yoke spline; used to support a multiple piece driveshaft. Also called a *center bearing*.

harmonic vibration An inherent vibration that occurs at precisely 50% of a shaft's critical speed.

Hooke joint A joint with four trunnions and four bearing caps. Also known as a *Cardan joint* or a *universal joint*.

inertial excitation The force caused by the speeding up and slowing down of the shaft driven through an angle. These stem from the operating angles of the U-joint at the drive end of the driveshaft and are caused by the sheer weight of the driveshaft being accelerated and decelerated twice per revolution.

intersecting angle arrangement A method of angle cancellation in which the U-joint angles will intersect at a point exactly at the middle of the shaft length. Also known as a *broken back arrangement*.

jack shaft A short shaft usually at the front of a drive line. Also known as a *coupling shaft*.

non-uniform velocity The phenomenon that a shaft driven through an angle will accelerate and decelerate twice per revolution.

parallel joint arrangement Two or more universal joint arrangements where the joint angles form parallel lines; a method of angle cancellation for use with parallel angles. Also known as the *waterfall arrangement*.

phasing Lining up the inboard yoke ears of driveshaft so that the non-uniform velocity cancellation occurs in the proper quadrant of the circle.

plan angle An angle where the driveshaft moves toward the side of a vehicle when viewed from above.

Rzeppa joint A constant velocity joint invented by Alfred Rzeppa in 1926.

secondary couple vibrations A vibration, caused by U-joint angles, that travels the length of the driveshaft.

slip joint A splined shaft and tube assembly that allows driveshaft length changes.

torsional excitation Twisting forces caused by inertial excitation.

torsional vibrations Vibrations caused by twisting forces on the driveshaft; these occur twice per revolution.

transverse vibrations Vibrations caused by shaft imbalance; these occur once per revolution.

trunnion The smooth ends of the U-joint cross that accepts the bearing caps.

tube yoke A yoke with two ears that accept a U-joint and which is welded to the driveshaft tube.

universal joint A cross-shaped joint with bearings on each leg where one set of parallel legs is connected to the end of one shaft and the other set of parallel legs is connected to the end of a second shaft. This arrangement allows the shafts to operate at shallow angles to each other. Also called a *U-joint*, a *Cardan joint*, or a *Hooke joint*.

waterfall arrangement Two or more universal joint arrangement where the joint angles form parallel lines; a method of angle cancellation for use with parallel angles. Also called *parallel joint arrangement*.

Review Quiz

1. For optimal performance, most of today's manufacturers recommend that U-joint operating angles should be no more than which of the following?
   a. 1 degree
   b. 3 degrees
   c. 5 degrees
   d. 7 degrees
2. The broken back driveshaft arrangement cannot be used in which of the following situations?
   a. When operating length changes are excessive
   b. Between the two drive axles on a tandem
   c. When operating length changes are minimal
   d. When slip joints are used
3. Double Cardan joints use two joints connected together to provide which of the following?
   a. Constant velocity to the driven shaft
   b. Higher torque capacity
   c. More driveshaft length
   d. None of these answers are correct
4. The working angle of a U-joint is restricted by which of the following?
   a. The torque it must transmit
   b. The speed at which it must operate
   c. The diameter of the driveshaft
   d. The size of the U-joint
5. U-joint working angles must be equal to within which of the following limits?
   a. 5 degrees
   b. 3 degrees
   c. 2 degrees
   d. 1 degree
6. What is the minimum U-joint operating angle that manufacturers recommend?
   a. 1/4 degree
   b. 1/2 degree
   c. 1 degree
   d. 3 degrees
7. The critical speed of a drive shaft can be increased by:
   a. shortening the shaft length.
   b. increasing the tube diameter.
   c. decreasing the shaft weight.
   d. All of the choices are correct.
8. Why does lowering the air bags sometimes cause driveline vibrations?
   a. U-joint operating angles can be increased.
   b. The drive shaft critical speed increases.
   c. Drive shaft inertial excitations are decreased.
   d. None of the choices is correct.
9. If a drive shaft has a plan angle and a side view angle, what must you do to determine the true operating angle?
   a. Add the two angles together and divide by two.
   b. Add the squares of the two angles and get the square root of the total.
   c. Add the two angles, square the result, and then get the square root of the answer.
   d. None of the choices will give the true operating angle.
10. How much radial clearance is allowed at the universal joint?
    a. zero clearance
    b. 0.006" clearance
    c. 0.012" clearance
    d. 0.010"–0.030" clearance

ASE-Type Quiz

1. Technician A says that when a driveshaft operates at an angle, the driven shaft accelerates and decelerates once per revolution. Technician B says that using a U-joint at the front and back with equal angles cancels the non-uniform velocity. Who is correct?
   a. Technician A
   b. Technician B
   c. Both Technician A and Technician B
   d. Neither Technician A nor Technician B
2. Technician A says that a drive line is made up of more than one driveshaft. Technician B says that multi-shaft drive lines must have a center or hanger bearing. Who is correct?
   a. Technician A
   b. Technician B
   c. Both Technician A and Technician B
   d. Neither Technician A nor Technician B
3. Technician A says that that drive line attaching bolts should not be reused. Technician B says that Spicer Life series spring clips can be reused as long as they are not bent. Who is correct?
   a. Technician A
   b. Technician B
   c. Both Technician A and Technician B
   d. Neither Technician A nor Technician B
4. Technician A says that some driveshafts are cross phased or phased at 90 degrees. Technician B says that, when a driveshaft slip yoke is removed, you should mark its position so that it is reassembled correctly in phase. Who is correct?
   a. Technician A
   b. Technician B
   c. Both Technician A and Technician B
   d. Neither Technician A nor Technician B
5. Technician A says that critical speed is when a driveshaft starts to bow off its center line due to centrifugal force. Technician B says that a driveshaft operating at or above critical speed will vibrate violently. Who is correct?
   a. Technician A
   b. Technician B
   c. Both Technician A and Technician B
   d. Neither Technician A nor Technician B
6. Technician A says that drive shaft angularity is the first thing to check when diagnosing drive shaft vibrations. Technician B says that a driveshaft out of phase will vibrate. Who is correct?
   a. Technician A
   b. Technician B
   c. Both Technician A and Technician B
   d. Neither Technician A nor Technician B
7. Technician A says that, as long as a drive shaft has canceling angles, it will not vibrate. Technician B says that drive shaft operating angles are limited by the speed the shaft must rotate. Who is correct?
   a. Technician A
   b. Technician B
   c. Both Technician A and Technician B
   d. Neither Technician A nor Technician B
8. Technician A says that a dent in a driveshaft may cause the shaft to vibrate. Technician B says that foreign material on the driveshaft may cause vibration. Who is correct?
   a. Technician A
   b. Technician B
   c. Both Technician A and Technician B
   d. Neither Technician A nor Technician B
9. Technician says that small amounts of rust purging from the U-joint while greasing it is expected and that you should keep greasing the joint until all the rust is gone. Technician B says that a couple of drops of water escaping the U-joint grease seals while lubricating the joint is normal. Who is correct?
   a. Technician A
   b. Technician B
   c. Both Technician A and Technician B
   d. Neither Technician A nor Technician B
10. Technician A says that, when checking U-joints, end play between the U-joint trunnions and the bearing cap should be no more than 0.006" (0.15 mm). Technician B says that slip yoke radial play should not exceed 0.030 (0.76 mm). Who is correct?
    a. Technician A
    b. Technician B
    c. Both Technician A and Technician B
    d. Neither Technician A nor Technician B

CHAPTER 47

NATEF Tasks

There are no NATEF tasks for this chapter.

Knowledge Objectives

After reading this chapter, you will be able to:

1. Explain the difference between steering, live, and dead axles used on trucks. (pp 1572–1575)
2. Describe the different types of drive axle gearing. (pp 1575–1578)
3. Explain drive axle housing types. (p 1578)
4. Explain the function and operation of differential gear sets. (pp 1578–1581)
5. Describe the function of controlled traction differentials and locking differentials. (pp 1581–1584)
6. Explain the function and purpose of double reduction helical drive axles. (p 1585)
7. Differentiate among top-mount, front-mount, and two-speed double reduction axles. (p 1586)
8. Describe the function and purpose of planetary double reduction and two-speed planetary drive axles. (pp 1586–1588)
9. Explain multi-speed axle shifting processes with air and/or electric actuators. (pp 1588–1592)
10. Explain the function and purpose of inter-axle differentials. (pp 1592–1594)
11. Explain the function of Mack wedge-type power dividers. (pp 1594–1596)
12. Explain the purpose and function of differential and inter-axle differential locks. (pp 1596–1597)
13. Define spinout and explain how to prevent it. (pp 1596–1597)
14. Describe full floating and semi-floating axles. (p 1597)

Heavy-Duty Truck Drive Axles

Skills Objectives

There are no skills objectives for this chapter.

Introduction

This chapter will explain the principles, operation, and construction of different types of axles and drive axles used in the medium- to heavy-duty truck and coach market. Included in the chapter will be sections on non-drive (dead) axles and drive (live) axles. Steering axles are discussed in the Steering Systems and Integral Steering Gears chapter, so this chapter will focus on drive axles, including single reduction and double reduction single-speed drive axles and multi-speed drive axles (including both planetary and double reduction helical two-speed types). This chapter also discusses differential gears, controlled traction differentials, locking differentials, tandem drive systems, inter-axle differentials, and differential locking systems.

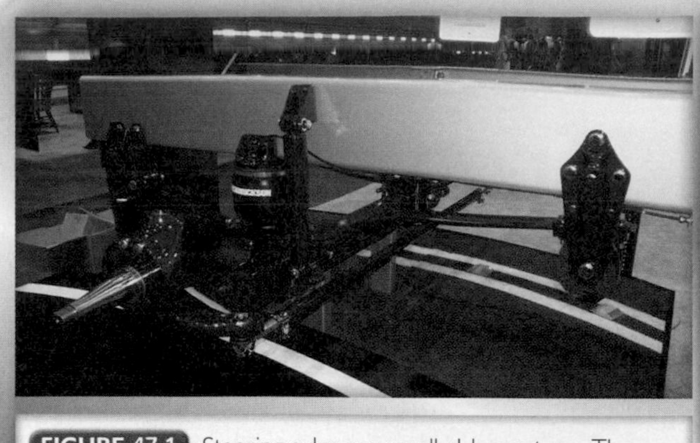

FIGURE 47-1 Steering axles are usually I-beam type. They support the vehicle weight through the front suspension and allow the vehicle to be turned.

Fundamentals of Axles

Three distinct types of axles are used in truck applications. Every vehicle will have a **steering axle**, such as the one shown in FIGURE 47-1, at the front, which allows the vehicle to turn. Not all vehicles use a single steering axle at the front. Some heavy-duty vehicles use dual steering axles. Very long vehicles, such as articulating fire trucks (tiller trucks), have steering axles in the rear. In the case of tiller trucks, the rear axle of the trailer portion of the truck can be steered to negotiate narrow streets and tight corners.

The second type of axle is called a **dead axle**. Dead axles are designed to carry the vehicle's weight and come in a variety of shapes and sizes. Dead axles can be used on trucks either in front of or behind the drive axle. When a vehicle needs to carry extra load axles, like the one shown in FIGURE 47-2, can be used as pusher axles or tag axles. These axles may be self steering or fixed. A **self-steering axle** contains wheels that will automatically follow the curve of a turn; this prevents the tire scrubbing during the turn. **Pusher axles** are located in front of the drive, or main axles, on trucks and/or trailers, and **tag axles** are located behind the drive axle. Pusher and tag axles are used to allow the

You Are the Technician

You are in the office of your Seattle service facility and one of your newer fleet drivers is recounting to his dispatcher a situation that happened to him. He is quite distraught as he tells the dispatcher what happened. Seemingly, the previous night, the driver was on the I-90 heading for Seattle carrying a load through the mountains. There were only light snow flurries, but as he climbed one stretch of mountain road, he seemed to lose traction to the rear axles of his tandem tractor. He was quite frightened by the event and eventually was able to stop the vehicle in a lay-by and engage his inter-axle and main differential locks. He said he had no more problems after locking the differentials and he made it to Seattle without further incident. The driver notices you there and asks for your input.

1. What would you tell the driver about the correct way to use differential locks in a poor traction situation?
2. What would inform the driver about the damage that could happen to the vehicle by using the differential locks in this way?
3. What service, if any, would you recommend to the driver to ensure that significant damage has not occurred in the driveline?

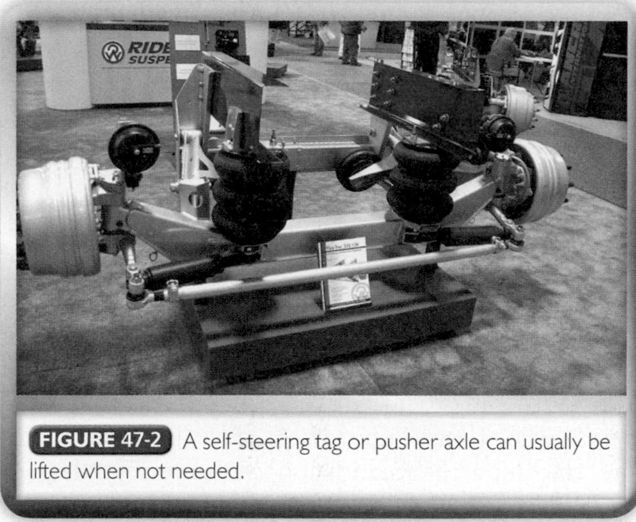

FIGURE 47-2 A self-steering tag or pusher axle can usually be lifted when not needed.

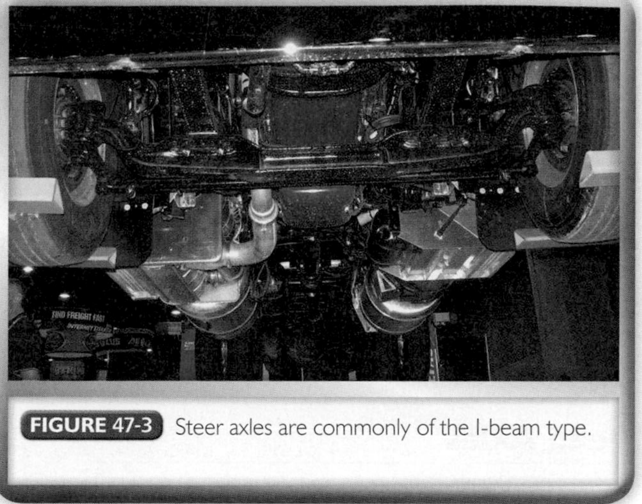

FIGURE 47-3 Steer axles are commonly of the I-beam type.

vehicle to carry more payloads and are only used when the vehicle is heavily loaded. Regardless of whether they are pusher or tag type, steerable dead axles steer in the direction of the turn, and their geometry is set so that they remain straight while going forward. These axles can typically be raised or lowered by the operator using an air control in the cab. Most steering axles are dead axles in that they only carry the vehicle weight. A steer axle may also, however, be a drive axle, as is the case with four- or six-wheel drive trucks.

The third type of axle is the **drive axle** (or **live axle**), so called because they contain the gearing necessary to drive the vehicle. Drive axles can be single- or two-speed and single or double reduction, meaning that the overall final drive ratio is the result of two separate gear reductions in the axle. They can also be arranged as a **tandem** drive where the driving force is divided between two drive axles, or **tridem** in which three drive axles split the driving force. Drive axles are usually mounted at the rear but can also be mounted at the front of the vehicle in the case of vehicles with front and rear wheel drive axles. These can be four-wheel-drive with one drive axle at the front and one at the back, or six-wheel-drive with one drive axle at the front and a tandem drive at the rear. Front wheel drive axles must also double as steering axles to turn the vehicle.

Steering Axles

All vehicles must have a way to steer. The most popular type of steer axle in trucks is the one piece I-beam style. This type of axle consists of the I-beam with flat pads to accept the spring mounts for the front suspension, as shown in FIGURE 47-3.

The wheel spindles, also known as steering knuckles, are attached to the I-beam with kingpins and bushings. The tie rod arms are attached to the bottom of the spindles and are connected together by a tie rod (also called a cross tube). The tie rod arms (also called Ackerman arms) will connect to the tie rod with tie rod ends, which are small ball joint connectors that thread into the tie rod. The left side spindle will have a steering arm at the top, which connects to the drag link. The drag link is a rod with two ball joint style ends and its length is usually adjustable so the steering can be set up properly. The drag link is moved by the pitman arm, attached to the steering box, to steer the vehicle. Note that some heavy-duty vehicles will have dual steering boxes—one on each side of the vehicle. In those cases, each steering arm will connect to one of the steering boxes. FIGURE 47-4 shows one of the two steering boxes.

FIGURE 47-4 The second power steering box is controlled hydraulically by the main power steering box.

The kingpins are retained in the steer axle by one of two methods. Either the pin is tapered and retained by a nut or the pin is straight and held in place by a wedge-shaped pin installed through an eye in the I-beam. The spindles will have bushing at the top and bottom so that they can rotate around the kingpin. A load-supporting thrust bearing allows the spindle to turn even when heavily loaded. Although the I-beam is the most common use for truck front steer axles, tubular steer axles are sometimes used.

Steering axles are covered in greater detail in the Front Axles and Vehicle Alignment Factors chapter.

Dead Axles

Truck dead axles are usually pusher or tag axles and are typically mounted on a pivoting frame. These dead axles can be raised or lowered by the driver in the cab when needed and allow the vehicle to carry more payload. A pusher axle is shown mounted on the dump truck in **FIGURE 47-5**. The amount of load the axles carry can be adjusted by the driver by controlling the air pressure in the axle's air bag suspension.

In addition to carrying the vehicle's weight, trailer dead axles serve as attachment points for the brakes and suspension. Most trailer axles are designed for specific vocations. The most common trailer axle consists of a tubular cross shaft attached to two spindles, which in turn support the wheels. Tubular axles have the strongest section modulus, so the axle can carry maximum weight. **FIGURE 47-6** shows a typical tandem trailer axle.

Drop center tubular axles are concave in the middle and are commonly found in situations when product-handling tubes and pipes are required to run under the trailer. In **crank axles**, the main beam is lower than the wheel ends. Crank axles are used with certain types of trailers with low floors, such as furniture vans. Trailer dead axle configurations can be single, tandem, tridem, or any other configuration necessary to the trailer's vocation. A tandem trailer axle arrangement can be fixed or movable, in which case the axle set can be moved forward or backward along the trailer frame.

Drive Axles

Internal combustion engines in heavy vehicles usually produce rotating power in a clockwise direction (viewed from the front) and send it through a transmission and a drive line to the rear of the vehicle. Here, the power must turn a corner in order to drive the wheels and propel the vehicle. The primary function of a drive (live) axle, therefore, is to allow the rotational power to turn 90 degrees so that we can drive the vehicle. **FIGURE 47-7** shows a typical tandem drive axle.

The drive axle will also provide a significant gear reduction—or even two gear reductions—to provide the final torque increase in a powertrain. For that reason, it is sometimes known as the final drive. The drive axle

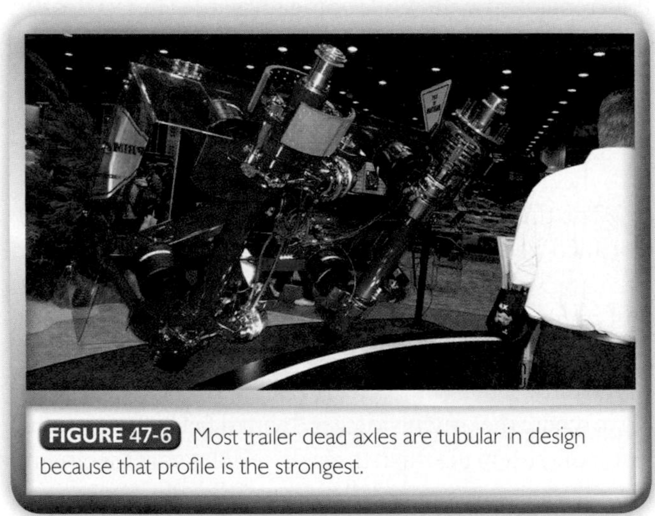

FIGURE 47-6 Most trailer dead axles are tubular in design because that profile is the strongest.

FIGURE 47-5 Dead axles, like this pusher axle, can be raised or lowered when required by the driver.

FIGURE 47-7 Drive axles allow the rotational power from the engine to turn 90 degrees so the wheel can drive the vehicle forward.

contains the **differential gears**, which allow for speed differences between the two axle shafts of the drive axle when turning. Differential gears will be discussed in the Types and Functions of Differential Gear Sets sections.

Types of Drive Axle Gearing and Housings

Drive axle gearing comes in many varieties. In addition to plain and spiral bevel gears, there are durapoid, hypoid, amboid, topoid, and generoid options. All types of gearing are protected and contained in the differential housing.

Drive Axle Gearing

In the past, **worm and crown** (or **worm wheel**) gears were used to drive the wheels at 90 degrees to the driveshaft. These older gear arrangements were capable of very high gear reduction in a compact space. Worm and crown gear sets consisted of a shaft with machined roll threads on the worm, which is in mesh with a crown gear (the worm wheel). The worm can be mounted below or above the crown wheel. A worm mounted below the crown wheel is called underslung. A worm mounted above the crown wheel is called top-mount and is shown in FIGURE 47-8.

> **TECHNICIAN TIP**
>
> In the past, worm drive axle systems with either top- or bottom-mounted worms were commonly dismissed as inefficient and prone to failure. However, a worm gear driven by a worm pinion creates less friction at the tooth contact point. For that reason, several manufacturers are currently exploring computer-designed worm drive systems. Those manufacturers are interested in how worm gears reduce the friction losses caused by bevel gears. The reason for the newfound interest is the desire to maximize fuel economy in light-duty vehicles. Some gear manufacturers estimate that worm gears can increase fuel efficiency by up to 4%.

The ratio between these gears is determined by the number of threads, or leads, on the worm—so these gears are capable of large gear reductions in a small space. Worm and crown gears were used in the early days of automobiles and trucks. Today they are, for the most part, considered obsolete. Some manufacturers are experimenting with worm gears again, however, for two main reasons: worm gears are compact and they produce less friction at the gear mesh, which may increase fuel economy.

Generally speaking, all of today's trucks use **bevel gears** that intersect at an angle to make the power turn the corner at a point 90 degrees to the driveshaft. FIGURE 47-9 shows bevel gears.

Bevel gears consist of a relatively small driving gear known as the **pinion gear** and a large gear known as the **crown gear** or **ring gear**. Bevel gears have their teeth cut at 45 degree angles from their axis, allowing them to mesh at 90 degrees to each other. The pinion gear is rotated by the drive line and drives the crown gear. The crown gear is attached to the **differential case**, which houses the differential gears. The differential gears connect to the axle shafts. Although their basic design is the same, several different types of bevel gears are used on heavy-duty trucks.

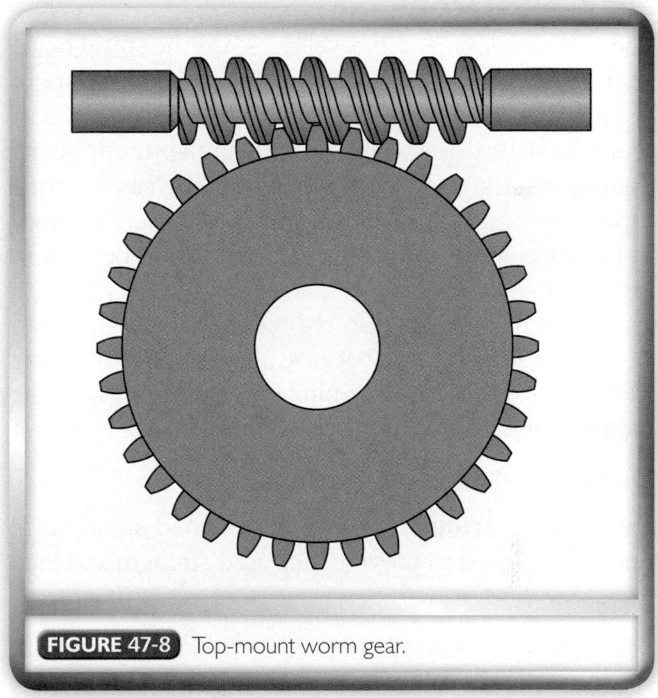

FIGURE 47-8 Top-mount worm gear.

FIGURE 47-9 Spiral bevel gears commonly used in Mack drive axles.

Plain Bevel Gears

Plain bevel gears, shown in FIGURE 47-10, have straight-cut teeth similar to the spur type gearing discussed in the Basic Gearing Concepts chapter. Consequently, plain bevel gears are inherently noisy and only have one set of teeth in mesh at any time. That is, one tooth must carry the entire torque load. Because the power flow is turning a 90 degree bend through the bevel gear set, the load and friction created at the intersection of the bevel gear teeth is extreme.

A special lubricant must be used to combat the extreme friction created by bevel gears This lubricant will have extreme pressure (EP) additives to prevent metal-to-metal contact of the bevel gear teeth. The plain bevel pinion gear is mounted at the centerline of the crown gear.

Spiral Bevel Gears

The next development in bevel gears was the **spiral bevel gear**. The teeth of a spiral bevel gear are cut in a spiral design. The spiral cuts improved upon bevel gear sets much as helical gears improved upon spur cut gears. That is, the design of spiral bevel gears increased torque capacity because more than one set of teeth were involved in torque transfer. Spiral bevel gearing can be seen in Figure 47-9.

Spiral bevel gears also reduce the noise associated with plain bevel gearing because of the wiping or sliding effect of the tooth contact. Spiral bevel gears still have the pinion gear mounted at the centerline of the crown gear.

Durapoid Gearing

Durapoid gearing is a specially designed spiral bevel gear set designed to provide increased strength and load carrying capability. The durapoid tooth design, shown in FIGURE 47-11, implements non-symmetrical tooth flanks. While the drive side of the tooth will have a relatively sheer face, the coast side of the tooth will have a sloped face. The different faces create a buttress effect for the tooth and increase the load carrying capability of the tooth.

Durapoid tooth design also incorporates a centralized tooth contact pattern. Conventional gearing has a tooth contact pattern that spreads from the inside towards the outside of the tooth under load. By contrast, the centralized pattern of durapoid gearing eliminates the end loading of the tooth. As loads increase, the contact spreads out in both directions along the tooth face. The load is then distributed more evenly. In a durapoid gear set, the pinion is mounted on the centerline of the crown wheel. Mack trucks use durapoid gearing extensively.

Hypoid Gearing

Hypoid gearing is another form of bevel gearing. Hypoid gearing was developed to increase the strength of a normal spiral bevel gear and to lower the center of gravity of the vehicle. The hypoid gear set looks very similar to a spiral bevel set with one notable exception—on hypoid gears, the pinion gear is mounted below the centerline of the crown wheel, as can be seen in FIGURE 47-12. That difference explains how the teeth of hypoid gears achieve a deeper engagement on the pinion. More teeth are in contact—greatly increasing the strength of the gear set. Having the pinion mounted lower also allows the drive train package to be lowered and that, ultimately, lowers the vehicle's center of gravity.

The hypoid gear set is the most popular design in use today on heavy trucks. The primary drawback to

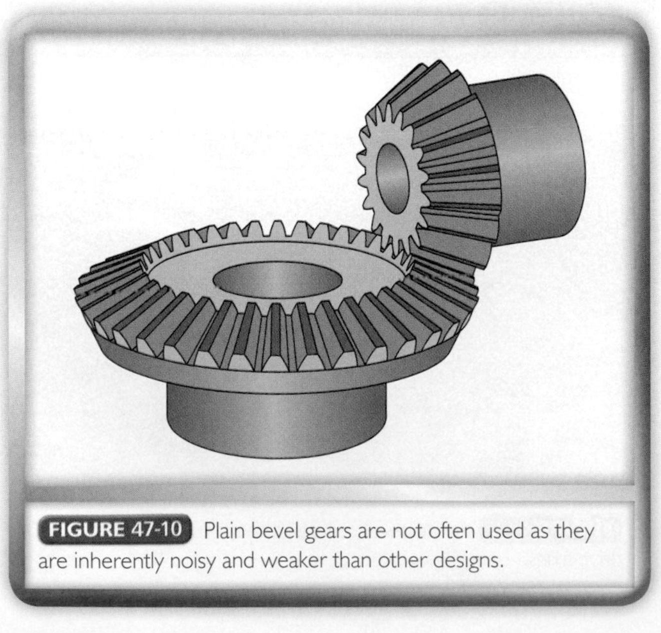

FIGURE 47-10 Plain bevel gears are not often used as they are inherently noisy and weaker than other designs.

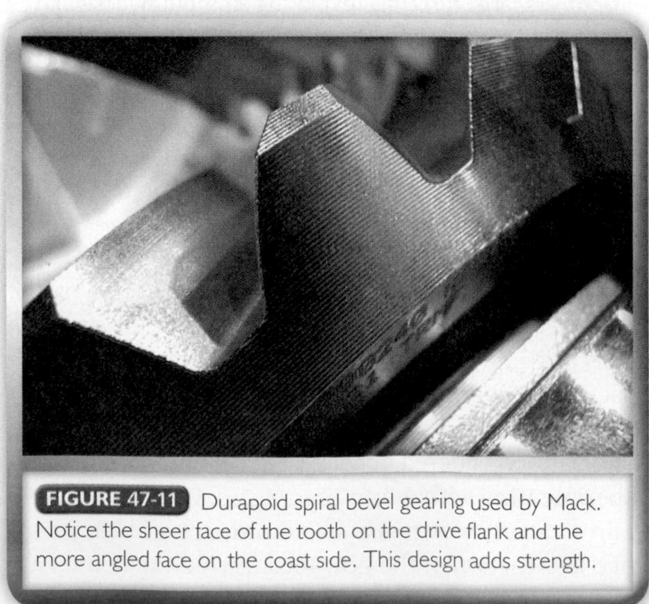

FIGURE 47-11 Durapoid spiral bevel gearing used by Mack. Notice the sheer face of the tooth on the drive flank and the more angled face on the coast side. This design adds strength.

hypoid gear sets is that the deeper mesh of the pinion gear leads to even higher friction between the gear teeth. The point at which the teeth of the crown gear and the pinion mesh is subjected to extreme pressure under load. That pressure necessitates the pinion and the crown gear to be rigidly supported. Even then, they will still try to push each other apart.

To counteract this force, sometimes a thrust screw and block are mounted in the carrier at the back of the crown wheel at the point of the gear set contact. The thrust block is adjusted so under normal conditions it has a slight clearance from the back side of the crown gear. As the load is increased and the crown gear starts to flex away from the pinion, the crown gear will contact the thrust block, stopping its flexing so that it will remain in mesh with the pinion.

Amboid

At first glance, **amboid gears** resemble hypoid but, on further inspection, it is clear that, on amboid gears, the pinion gear is mounted above the centerline of the crown gear. A second notable difference between amboid and hypoid is that the teeth on the crown gear are spiraled in the opposite directions. An amboid gear set is shown in FIGURE 47-13.

Both designs have their pinion gear teeth cut in the same direction. This means that, in the hypoid, the drive side of the crown gear teeth is the convex side. The opposite is true on amboid gears—the drive side of the crown gear teeth is the concave side. Like hypoid gearing, amboid gearing uses more than two teeth in contact to carry the torque load.

Amboid gearing was developed for use in special applications and is typically only found in the rear-rear axle of a tandem drive. Because the pinion is above the centerline of the crown gear, the input to the drive axle is higher, so the operating angles used on the connecting driveshaft universal joints can be smaller.

Topoid

Detroit Deisel has recently introduced a new style of drive axle in which the pinion position is even higher than in the amboid type. Detroit is calling this system **topoid**. A topoid gear is simply a higher mounted amboid system. FIGURE 47-14 shows a topoid system. According to Detroit, the high design of the topoid system reduces driveline angles and vibration.

Generoid

The **generoid** gear design, also known as the hypoid generoid, is similar to the durapoid in that there is a sheer drive tooth face (the convex face) and a sloped or buttressed coast tooth face (the concave face).

The generoid, shown in FIGURE 47-15, uses an asymmetrical tooth with a sheer flank on the drive side and a

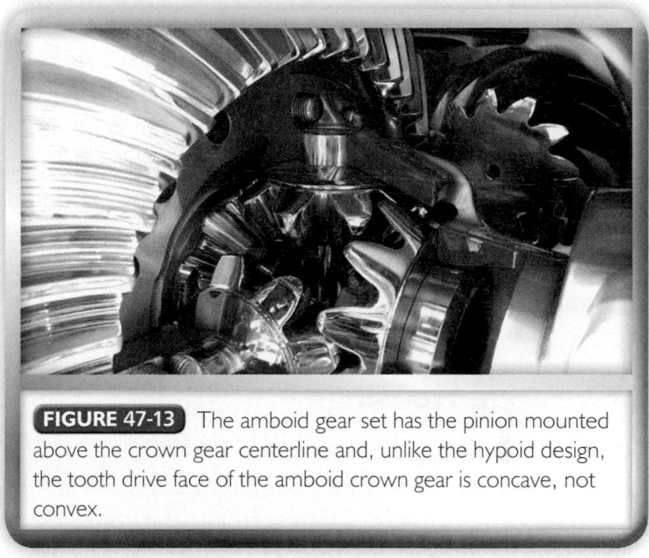

FIGURE 47-13 The amboid gear set has the pinion mounted above the crown gear centerline and, unlike the hypoid design, the tooth drive face of the amboid crown gear is concave, not convex.

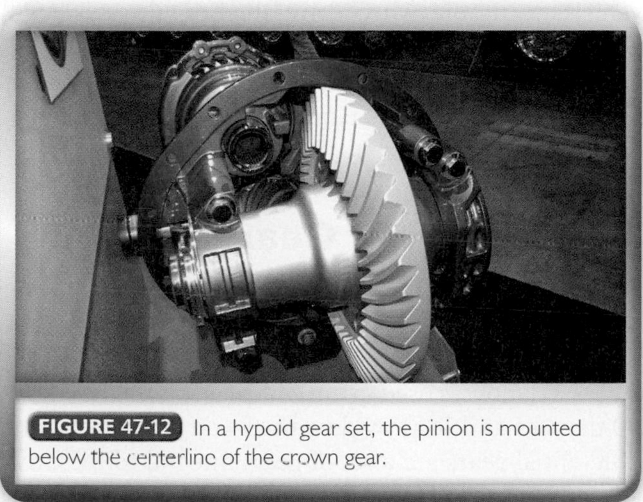

FIGURE 47-12 In a hypoid gear set, the pinion is mounted below the centerline of the crown gear.

FIGURE 47-14 Detroit Deisel's topoid system places the pinion higher on the ring gear than an amboid system.

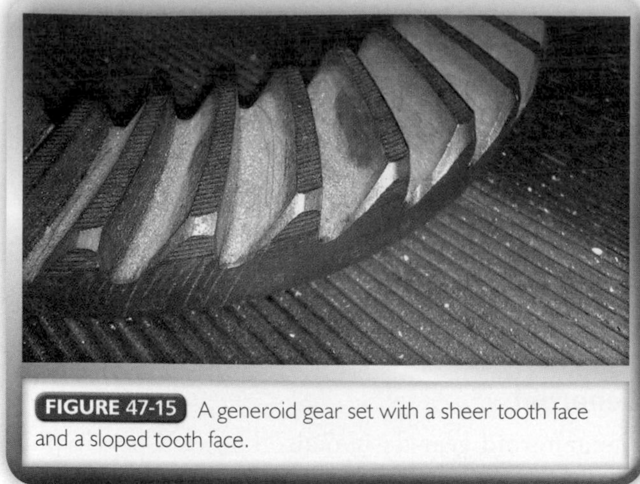

FIGURE 47-15 A generoid gear set with a sheer tooth face and a sloped tooth face.

FIGURE 47-16 The integral drive axle housing has the mounts for the drive axle bearings machined into it.

sloped buttress on the coast side. The generoid gear set also uses a centralized contact pattern, eliminating tooth end loading. That design feature gives the hypoid generoid even more strength than the traditional hypoid design.

Like the durapoid, a distinguishing feature of the generoid gear set is its tooth contact pattern, which is centered on the crown gear tooth face. Recall that the regular hypoid set has a contact pattern that starts near the toe (the inside end) of the tooth face. Drive axle gear contact patterns will be fully discussed in the Servicing and Maintaining Drive Axles chapter.

Even though some manufacturers use the generoid design, the hypoid gear set is still the more prevalent of the two.

Drive Axle Housings

Two general housing types are used for drive axles. The housings have one key point of differentiation—whether the carrier is removable. The **carrier** is the component that holds the support bearings for the drive axle gearing. In an **integral carrier housing**, shown in **FIGURE 47-16**, the carrier is not removable. The integral carrier housing is very popular in lighter duty vehicles. In the integral carrier type the, housing has all of the bearings supports machined into it. So the carrier is part of—or integral to—the housing. The drive axle gearing and bearings are accessed through a removable pan bolted to the back of the housing.

The second type of housing is the **removable carrier type**. The removable carrier housing is also known as a **banjo** housing because the shape of the housing resembles a banjo with two necks. **FIGURE 47-17** shows a removable carrier housing. In this style, the entire carrier, with all of the gears and bearings, is bolted into the front of the housing. To access the gearing or bearing for repair, the entire carrier is removed from the housing.

FIGURE 47-17 The banjo housing has the removable carrier bolted to it.

In vehicles with four- or six-wheel rear drive, all of the drive axles are interconnected by power dividers that split the torque between the available drive wheels. Power dividers will be discussed in greater detail later in the chapter in the Power Divider Components section. In vehicles with front-wheel drive, the front drive axle will be connected by a transfer case that will split the power and torque between the front and rear axles. Transfer cases are covered in the Standard Transmissions chapter.

Functions of Differential Gear Sets

The term *differential* is used mistakenly by some technicians as a synonym for a drive axle because that is where the **differential gear set** is housed. The drive axle gearing, as we know, is used to turn the power from the engine 90 degrees and to provide a final gear reduction. The differential gears are a set of gears integral to the drive axle that are for a completely different purpose than the drive axle gearing. A differential gear set is shown in FIGURE 47-18.

To illustrate the function of a differential gear set, let's consider a rear drive vehicle with four wheels—two steering and two driving. If the vehicle is traveling in a straight line, then all of the wheels will be turning at the same speed. (For the moment, we are ignoring any discrepancies in the tire sizes or irregularities in the terrain.)

When the vehicle comes to a turn, however, the situation changes. As the vehicle moves through a turn, the wheels on the inside of the turn have to turn slower than the wheels on the outside of the turn. This is because the wheels on the inside are closer to the apex of the turn than the wheels on the outside. This phenomenon can be seen in FIGURE 47-19. The inside wheels will follow a smaller curve than the outside and therefore a shorter distance.

The difference in turning radius presents no problems for the wheels on the steering axle, as they are not connected to each other and turn freely on their bearings. It is a different story for the rear wheels, however, because they are connected to the vehicle drive line. Provisions must be made for them to turn at unequal speeds. This is where the differential gears come in to play.

FIGURE 47-18 The differential gear set is held in the differential case inside the drive axle.

Differential gears allow for the wheels to turn at unequal speeds. The differential gear set is a gear arrangement that allows the available power being delivered to the crown gear to be split exactly equally between two drive wheels. The differential gear set simultaneously allows one wheel to turn faster or slower than the other when required. The need for unequal speeds is caused by vehicle turning, tire size mismatch, and uneven terrain.

The differential gears are contained inside the differential case. The case is bolted or riveted to the drive axle crown gear. When the crown gear is turned by the drive axle pinion gear, the case must turn with it. The case is made up of two halves—the flange half and the plain half—bolted together. The flange half is the side that is attached to the crown gear. In heavy-duty vehicles, the two halves of the differential case sandwich a four-legged **differential cross** (or **differential spider**) between them. The cross legs are fitted into four holes bored into the differential case, as shown in FIGURE 47-20. Therefore, the cross always rotates with the differential case and the crown wheel.

Inside the differential case are the actual differential gears. The typical differential gear set consists of four beveled **spider gears** (sometimes referred to as **differential pinion gears**) and two beveled **side gears**. The spider gears are fitted to the four legs of the differential cross, so they must rotate with it. The side gears are splined to the two axle shafts to drive the wheels. The side gears are in constant mesh with the differential spider gears. The differential spider gears and side gears normally have thrust washers between them and the differential case.

As the vehicle moves in a straight direction, the crown gear and the differential case rotate. As the case rotates,

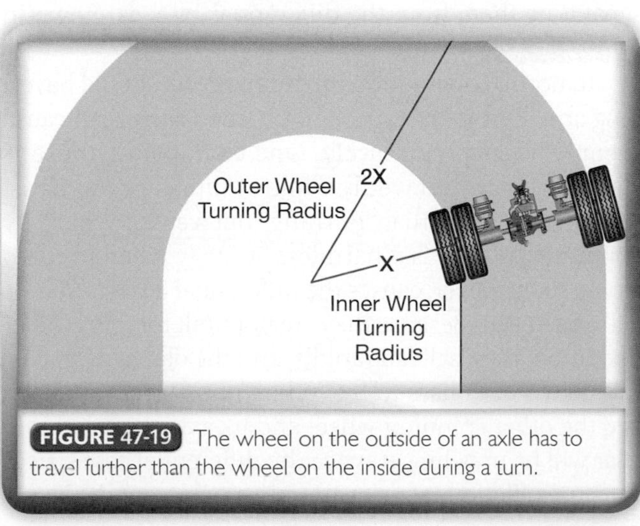

FIGURE 47-19 The wheel on the outside of an axle has to travel further than the wheel on the inside during a turn.

FIGURE 47-20 The differential cross is sandwiched between the two case halves and therefore must turn with the case.

the spider gears basically drag the side gears along as the cross tumbles end over end. In this kind of operation, the differential gears are stationary in relation to the differential case. The differential gears are not rotating inside the case. They are merely acting as a connection between the differential case and the two side gears.

The situation changes when the vehicle starts to turn. When negotiating a turn, it helps to think of the vehicle centerline as the arc the vehicle must follow through the turn. Think of the arc in terms of the speed the differential case will be turning through the turn. The wheel on the inside of the turn and its axle shaft and side gear are on a smaller arc and must turn slower than the differential case speed. At the same time, the wheel on the outside and its axle shaft and side gear must turn faster than the case. **FIGURE 47-21** illustrates these differences. As the vehicle negotiates a turn, the side gear splined to the wheel on the inside of the turn slows down and causes the spider gears to turn by that same amount. The spider gear then transfers that motion to the other side gear, causing it to speed up by the exact same amount.

The differential gear set allows this to happen because the spider gears can turn not only with the cross but they can turn on the cross as well. As the inner wheel starts to slow down during the curve, its axle shaft and side gear turn slower than the case and the spider gears. The spider gears start to walk around the slower moving inner side gear. As they do so, the spider gears' walking motion is transferred to the outer side gear, causing it to speed up by the exact same amount. This means the outer wheel speeds up by the same amount that the inner wheel slows down. The power being sent to each wheel is still exactly equal, but the wheels can turn at different speeds when needed.

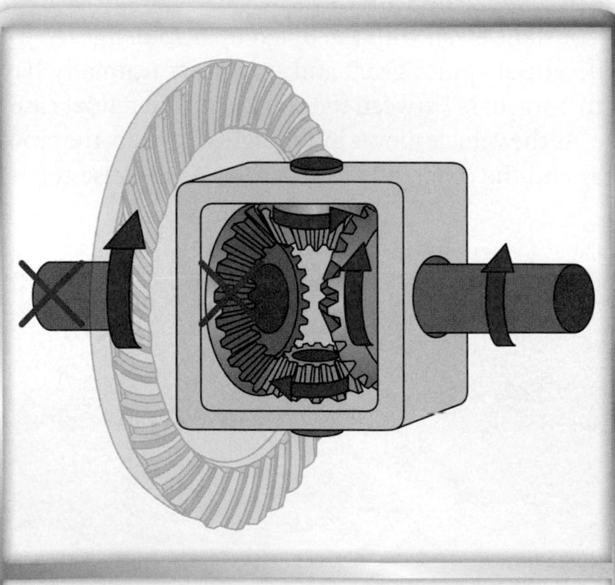

FIGURE 47-21 As the vehicle negotiates a turn, the inside side gear slows down and causes the spider gears to turn. The spider gear then transfers that motion to the other side gear, causing it to speed up.

In any driving situation, when we add the speed of the two axles together, the total will always equal 200% of case speed—no matter how much the difference in speed is. For example, on negotiating a turn, if the inner wheel, axle shaft, and side gear slow down to 96% of the differential case speed, that means that the outer wheel, axle shaft, and side gear must increase in speed to 104% of case speed to compensate. This compensation is automatic and occurs without any driver or vehicle action.

If a vehicle were built without a differential, the wheel speed differences on turns would cause the axle shafts to "wind up" in different directions during turns. The resultant twisting forces would lead to serious fatigue failures of the axle shafts. It is important to note that the difference in wheel speed encountered in normal vehicle operation is usually very slight. For example, in a drive of 1,000 miles (1,600 km), with 10% being curves, the total rotation of the differential side gears would be very small—probably 100 to 200 revolutions for the whole trip.

The rotation also occurs relatively slowly at 60 mph (96 kph). An average truck wheel will turn 500 times a minute in a straight line. On most curves at that road speed, the wheel speed difference would be in the neighborhood of 4%, meaning that the rotation of each side gear would occur at 10 rpm. Because of the relatively slow speed and small distance that they turn, side gears and spider gears do not have to be supported by bearings and run steel-on-steel. Certain models may have friction bearings (bushings) to support the spider gears, but in most cases the spider gears are simply made of hardened steel and have no bushings. The differential side and spider (pinion) gears will normally have steel thrust washers separating them from the differential case, as shown in **FIGURE 47-22**.

In normal operation, differential gears should have a long and sturdy life expectancy. Driver abuse can cause them to wear prematurely. One example of abuse is spinning one wheel wildly while in slippery conditions. Drivers may think that "burning" out a stuck vehicle by spinning the tires is a harmless strategy when needed. Doing so, however, causes the differential gears to spin at extreme speed. Because they are not built for that kind of operation, they will fail rapidly, and the damage can cost thousands of dollars to fix. When one wheel is stationary, the other spinning wheel and its axle shaft and side gear will be traveling at twice the differential case speed, causing a lifetime of wear in only a few seconds! Never allow one wheel to spin uncontrollably. The damage may not be immediately noticeable, but it will be there and the useful life of the differential gear set will be reduced. The spider gear pictured in FIGURE 47-23 has been damaged by spinning one wheel of a differential. The gear has been alternately welded to and broken away from its cross leg by the heat caused by spin out, as is evidenced by the metal transfer inside its bore.

Types of Differential Gear Sets

All differential gear sets perform the same function in the vehicle. Just because they perform the same function does not mean that all differentials are identical, however. There are, in fact, several types. Controlled traction, locking, biased torque (proportional), double reduction, and inter-axle differentials are the main types of differential gear sets. This section will describe them all in more detail.

FIGURE 47-22 Thrust washers absorb the heavy thrust loads caused by bevel gears.

FIGURE 47-23 Spider gear damaged by the heat generated from spinning out.

Controlled Traction and Locking Differentials

The major benefit of a differential is that it allows wheels to rotate at different speeds when necessary. Unfortunately, that benefit is also its major drawback. During low traction conditions, the wheel that has the least traction will spin wildly, as mentioned in the previous section. When this spinout condition is observed, it can lead a person to think that the differential is sending all of the power to one wheel only, but this is not the case. Think of it this way: If a bolt is loosely installed and the technician attempts to torque it to specification with a torque wrench, it will quickly become apparent that it is impossible to build any torque until the bolt starts to tighten in its bore. Without resistance, the bolt will merely turn freely.

The same is true for the powertrain of a vehicle. In order for the engine to build torque, there must be some resistance to motion, such as the load of the vehicle. When a wheel is on a slippery surface, the engine can only build as much torque as is required to make the wheel slip. Once the wheel loses traction, the torque required to keep it spinning is even less, as illustrated in FIGURE 47-24.

The differential gear set will still be dividing the available torque equally between the two driving wheels, but the small amount of torque needed to keep the wheel spinning is not sufficient for the wheel with good traction to move the vehicle.

In order to overcome this drawback of differential gears, engineers have developed several controlled traction and locking differentials.

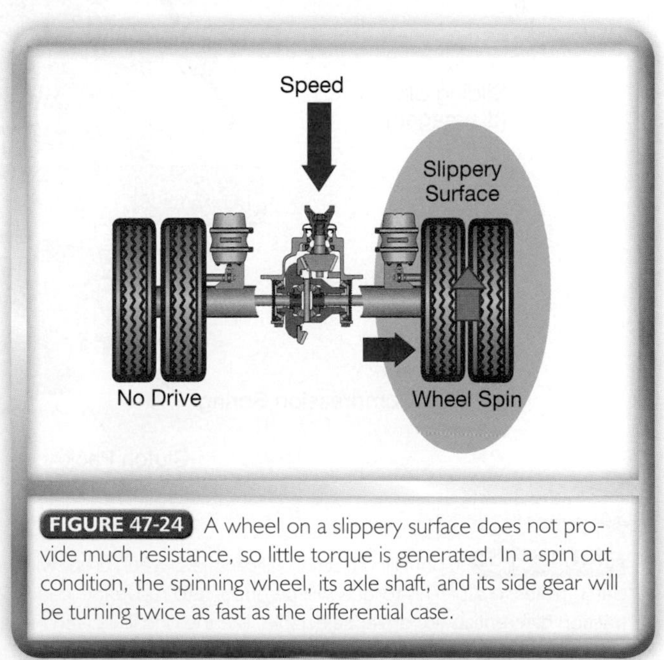

FIGURE 47-24 A wheel on a slippery surface does not provide much resistance, so little torque is generated. In a spin out condition, the spinning wheel, its axle shaft, and its side gear will be turning twice as fast as the differential case.

Controlled Traction Differentials

A **controlled traction differential** allows the engine to build more torque before the wheels can slip. There is some form of resistance that must be overcome before the side gears can move inside the differential case. Most commonly, this resistance to motion is provided by a spring-loaded clutch pack.

In a controlled traction differential, such as shown in **FIGURE 47-25**, a series of friction plates are splined to a movable spline that slides along one axle shaft. The spline has clutching teeth to engage matching teeth on one of the side gears. There is also a series of reaction plates, which are splined or lugged to the differential case. These two sets of plates are interleaved to form a clutch pack similar to the clutch packs found in automatic transmissions. Instead of being hydraulically applied, though, these clutch packs are permanently loaded by springs that pressurize the clutch pack or packs. The spline can be made to engage the side gear by using an air or electric shifter. This allows the controlled traction to be engaged or disengaged as required. Some installations will have the controlled traction permanently engaged.

The purpose of this controlled traction arrangement is to provide resistance that must be overcome before the side gear can rotate inside the case. This resistance is easily overcome by the twisting forces on the axle shafts during turns. In slippery conditions, the resistance causes more torque to build before a wheel can start slipping. The controlled traction differential will be carefully designed so that the amount of torque necessary to cause the wheels to slip is more than is required for one wheel with good traction to overcome the vehicle load and move the vehicle forward. Other designs of controlled traction differentials use a spring-loaded cone clutch design on the side gears rather than clutch plates, but they are similar in operation.

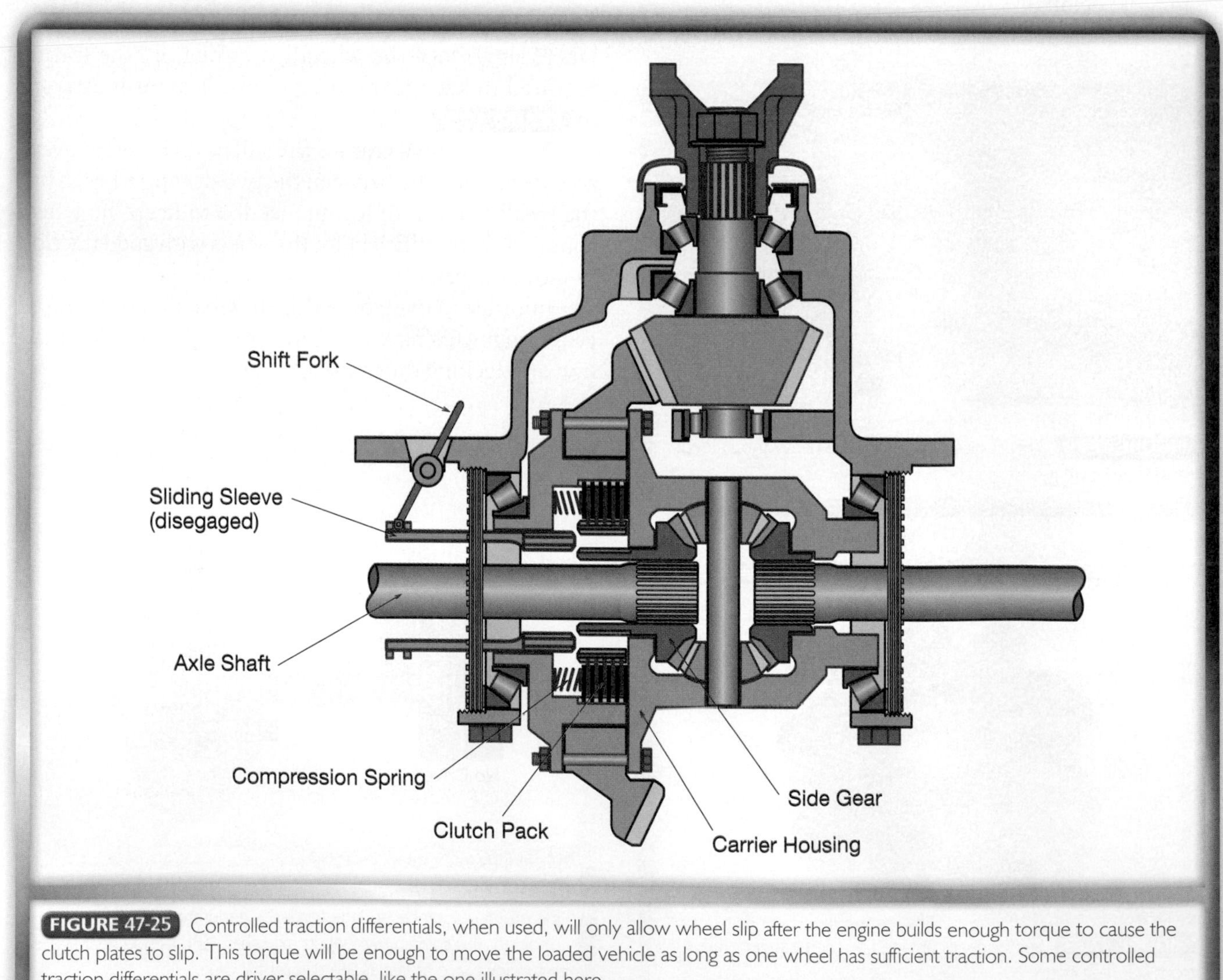

FIGURE 47-25 Controlled traction differentials, when used, will only allow wheel slip after the engine builds enough torque to cause the clutch plates to slip. This torque will be enough to move the loaded vehicle as long as one wheel has sufficient traction. Some controlled traction differentials are driver selectable, like the one illustrated here.

Locking Differentials

Locking differential systems actively prevent differential action from occurring when engaged. Heavy-duty locking differentials can be engaged or disengaged by the vehicle operator when required. These locking differentials should only be used when the vehicle encounters a low traction condition that may allow one wheel to spin. When activated, these systems prevent one side gear from turning, which stops any movement of the spider gears in the differential. This means that the second side gear cannot move either.

Most heavy-duty designs of locking differentials incorporate the following features:

- One axle shaft will have a second spline after the spline that engages the side gear.
- Mounted on this spline will be a sliding clutch or collar.
- The sliding clutch or collar will have clutching teeth on the side that faces the differential case.
- The differential case will have clutching teeth that match those on the sliding clutch or collar.

The gear is moved by a shift fork that is air or electrically operated. When the lock is disengaged, as shown in **FIGURE 47-26A**, the differential will operate normally. When the driver encounters low traction conditions, he can engage the lock. At that point, the sliding clutch or collar engages the clutching teeth on the differential case, as shown in **FIGURE 47-26B**. This effectively locks the axle shaft to the case. Because the axle shaft is also splined to the side gear, the side gear cannot rotate in the case, and that prevents any differential action from occurring. Remember that for one side gear to rotate, the other must rotate in the opposite direction. Therefore, if one side gear cannot rotate, neither can the other.

Provided there is no difference in wheel speed, the lock can be engaged at any time—whether the vehicle is moving or not. Locking the differential allows the vehicle to build enough torque to move the vehicle as long as one wheel has sufficient traction. The driver should only engage the lock during times of poor traction. As soon as possible, the driver should disengage the lock to allow the differential to resume its function of compensating for wheel speeds in turns.

Most **differential locks** are air operated and consist of a differential lock switch on the dashboard, as shown in **FIGURE 47-27**. In most cases, the shifter mechanism for the lockout is spring loaded to the unlocked position. When the lockout is engaged, air is directed to the shifter piston to engage the lock. Some tandem vehicles will have multiple locks, for example main differential locks and an inter-axle differential lock. The driver can engage the locks while stopped if he is ready to enter a low traction area or situation. Likewise, the driver can engage the locks while the vehicle is moving when conditions warrant as long as no wheels are slipping. In order to engage the locks while driving, the driver merely flips the switch to lock while he maintains speed. Next, he releases the

FIGURE 47-26 **A.** Heavy-duty locking differential with the lock disengaged. **B.** Heavy-duty locking differential with the lock engaged.

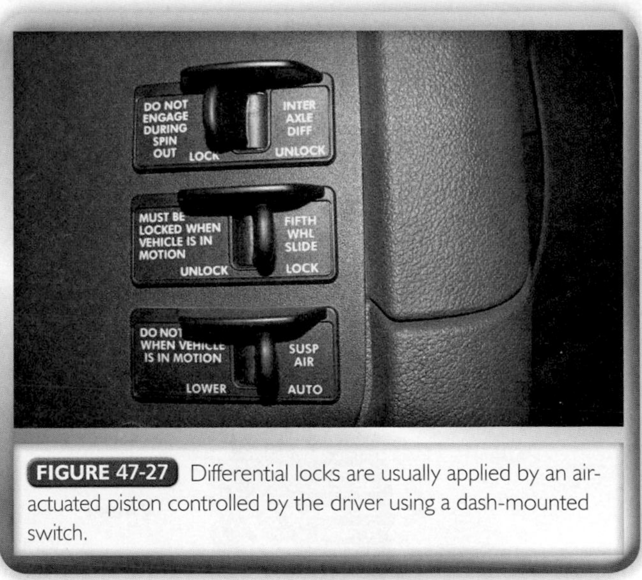

FIGURE 47-27 Differential locks are usually applied by an air-actuated piston controlled by the driver using a dash-mounted switch.

throttle momentarily and then resumes normal throttle operation. In a low traction condition when the wheels start to slip, the driver cannot engage the locks until the wheel slip stops. He would have to release the throttle first to stop the wheel slip and then engage the locks before resuming normal throttle operation.

The control switches for tandem vehicles can simultaneously control all three locks, both main differential locks and the inter-axle differential lock. Differential locks should in no circumstances be used when driving on dry pavement. Doing so will damage the drive axle.

Biased Torque (Proportional) Differentials

Several **biased torque differential** (also called **proportional differential**) systems have been developed that are capable of sending more torque to one wheel than the other when a wheel slip condition is encountered. That is, more torque is diverted to the wheel with good traction. Diverting torque in that way is commonly referred to as biasing torque. The most famous biased torque main differential is probably the **Torsen** differential by General Motors, which is illustrated in FIGURE 47-28.

The Torsen differential uses a torque biasing principle to send more torque to the wheel with good traction. These differentials have a resistance to rotation caused by gear interference. The resistance creates a bias effect and allows a multiplication of torque up to 6:1—available to the wheel with good traction. Some models offer even higher torque multiplication. If, however, one wheel is off the ground, no torque can be sent to the wheel with good traction. Logically, no torque can be created because there is no resistance (six times zero is still zero). For these vehicles to drive with a wheel off the ground, some resistance to rotation has to be introduced to the free wheel. Otherwise no torque can be created.

Originally resistance was introduced by applying the vehicle's ABS brakes selectively on the wheel with no traction. Three to six times the torque could then be sent to the wheel with traction. Similar to a controlled traction differential, the Torsen 2R has friction material inside to create some resistance. The differential then multiplies that available torque to move the vehicle using the wheel with good traction.

Eaton/Dana has recently introduced a similar design called **TruTrac**, shown in FIGURE 47-29, and Auburn gear

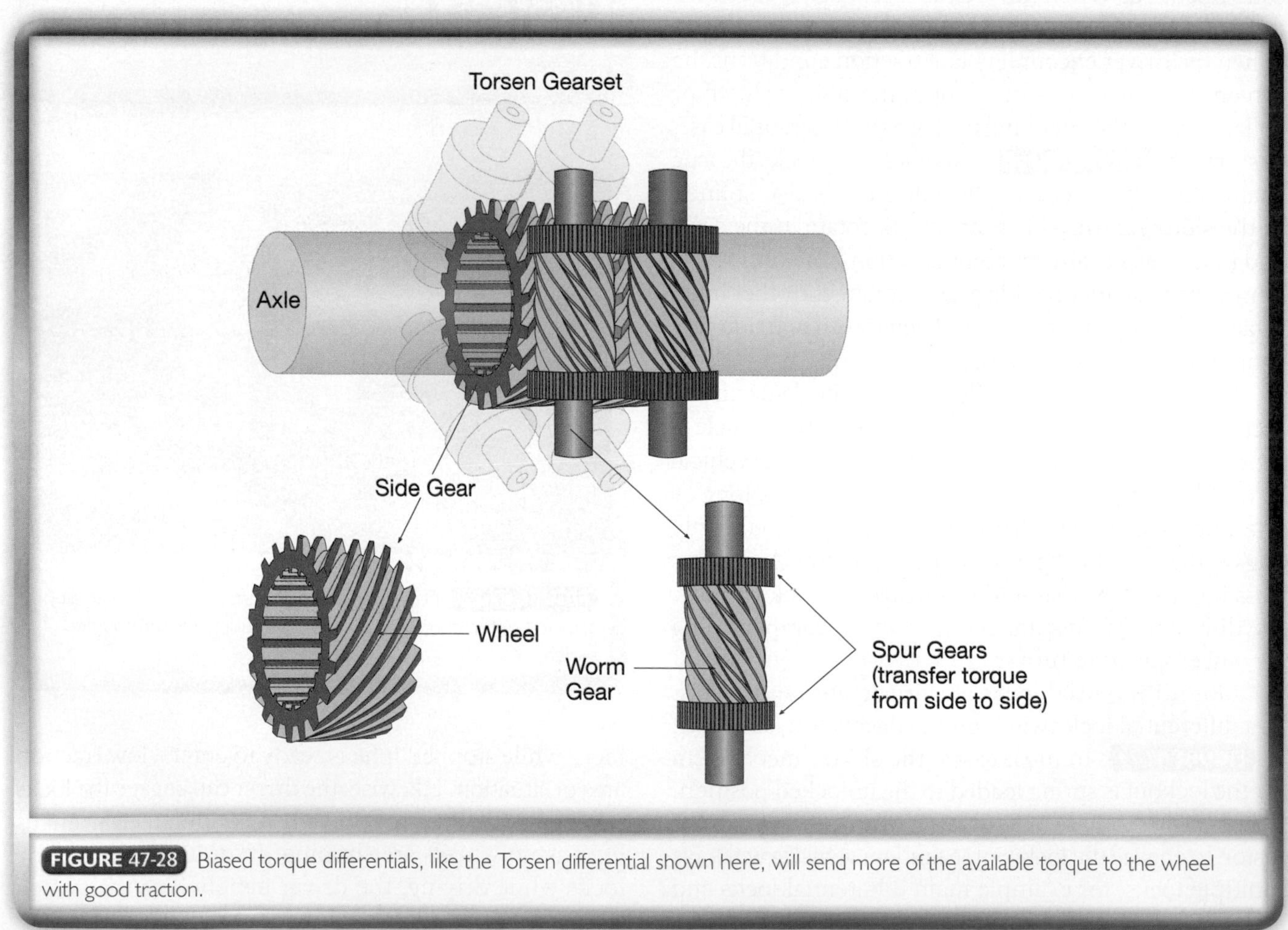

FIGURE 47-28 Biased torque differentials, like the Torsen differential shown here, will send more of the available torque to the wheel with good traction.

has developed an electronically controlled bias torque differential using clutch packs that are electrically applied.

Double Reduction and Multi-Speed Drive Axles

Double reduction drive axles use two gear reductions at all times. Double reduction drive axles come in two styles—helical double reduction and planetary double reduction.

Helical Double Reduction Drive Axles

A **helical double reduction drive axle** is a double reduction drive axle that uses a helical gear set for the second gear reduction. Although helical double reduction drive axles are not as common today as in the past, they are still used in some vehicles. Helical double reduction axles were developed for two reasons. First was to reduce the size of the crown gear and make it less likely to flex under load. The drive axle could then handle higher torque loads. The second reason was to reduce the overall size of the drive axle housing while still achieving a large overall reduction.

The first reduction in a helical double reduction drive axle consists of a small conventional crown and pinion gear set. The second reduction is accomplished by a set of helical gears. By using the two reductions together, we can achieve a large overall gear ratio with a much smaller drive axle package. Large crown gears tend to flex under heavy load as they try to move away from the pinion gear. A smaller crown gear helps to prevent this. The pinion is mounted in the drive axle as is normal, but the crown gear is not attached to the differential case. Instead, the crown wheel drives a cross shaft that has a small helical gear (called the helical pinion gear) attached to it. The helical pinion gear will mesh with a much larger helical gear that is bolted to the differential case.

In this arrangement, the power flow goes through two reductions: one with the crown and pinion gear set and the other with the helical gear set. This compounds the overall reduction through the axle. A compound gear ratio is one where two or more reductions are used to increase the overall ratio. The final drive axle ratio will be the product of the reductions (the ratios are multiplied together).

Double reduction helical drive axles are available in front mount or top mount designs depending on the needs of the application. In a top mount design, the crown and pinion gear set is mounted above the differential case. A front mount design has the differential case mounted in line with and directly behind the crown and pinion gears. Front mount designs allow for the entire drive train package to be lowered, thereby lowering the center of gravity of the vehicle.

Mack trucks quite commonly use a top mount arrangement like the one pictured in **FIGURE 47-30**, to achieve a large double reduction. In these models, the banjo housing seems to have been turned on its back with the round side (usually facing rearward) pointing down.

Helical Double Reduction Two-Speed Drive Axles

Helical double reduction drive axles are also available as two-speed models. **Helical double reduction two-speed drive axles** use two selectable sets of helical gears as the

FIGURE 47-29 Eaton/Dana now supplies a differential called TruTrac that is available for medium-duty trucks.

FIGURE 47-30 Mack uses a top mount design, double reduction drive axle quite extensively.

second gear reduction. A helical double reduction two-speed drive axle is illustrated in FIGURE 47-31. The overall reduction is selectable by the driver, effectively extending the operating ranges of the vehicle. This is accomplished by installing two different sized helical pinion gears on the cross shaft driven by the crown gear.

These helical pinion gears are in constant mesh with two large helical gears bolted to either side of the differential case. The helical pinions are not splined to the cross shaft and, therefore, are free to rotate on it. Between the two helical pinions is a sliding clutch collar that is splined to the cross shaft. When the shift fork moves the clutch collar from one side to the other, it disengages one of the helical gear sets and engages the other. The fork is moved by an electric motor or an air shifter controlled by the driver.

Adding two-speed capability to a double reduction drive axle effectively doubles the transmission ranges available to the driver for vehicle and road conditions. The driver would use the two-speed drive axle as a split shift between ratios when, and if, necessary. Although the ratios available to the driver are potentially doubled with this arrangement, to take advantage of them the driver has to perform an axle shift between each gear stick shift. The extra shift increases driver work load. Regardless of whether the double reduction two-speed is in high or low range, it always uses two reductions through the drive axle. The first reduction is through the crown and pinion gears and the second is through whichever helical gear set is engaged at the time.

Planetary Two-Speed and Planetary Double Reduction Axles

A **planetary two-speed drive axle**, as shown in FIGURE 47-32, uses a double reduction to achieve a low range ratio through the drive axle, and a single reduction in high range. The first reduction in low range is the normal crown and pinion gear. The second reduction is a planetary gear set built into the crown wheel and the differential case. For high range, only the crown and pinion gears are used to achieve the ratio. As with double reduction helical drive axles, this setup allows transmission ranges to be split and doubles the number of gear ratios available to the operator.

Some planetary two-speed drive axles, called dual range drive axles, are set up to provide a low range that is typically used only for off-road or high torque operation. The axles shift to high range for normal highway use. In a planetary drive axle, the crown gear has a set of internal teeth machined on its inner circumference. This

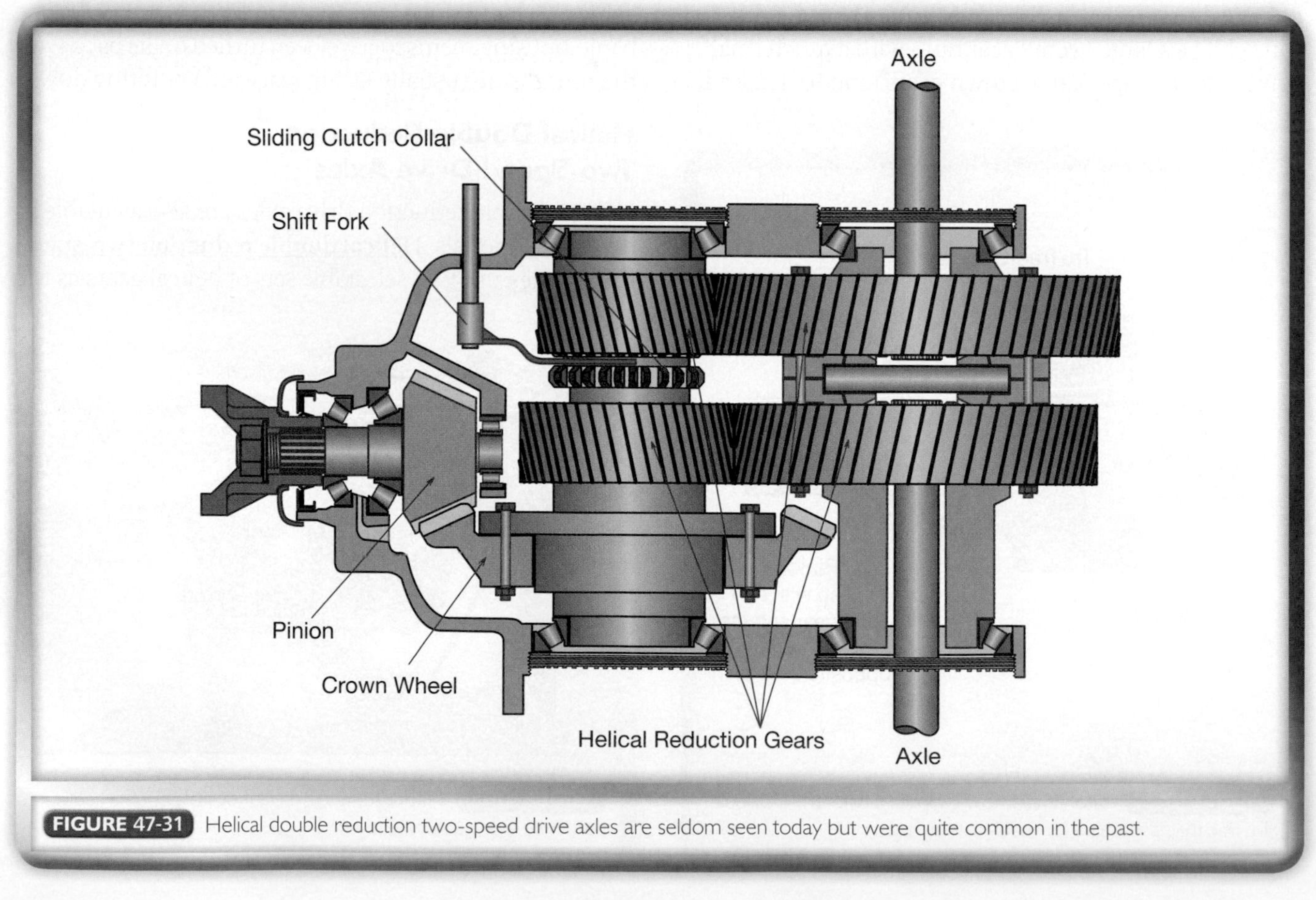

FIGURE 47-31 Helical double reduction two-speed drive axles are seldom seen today but were quite common in the past.

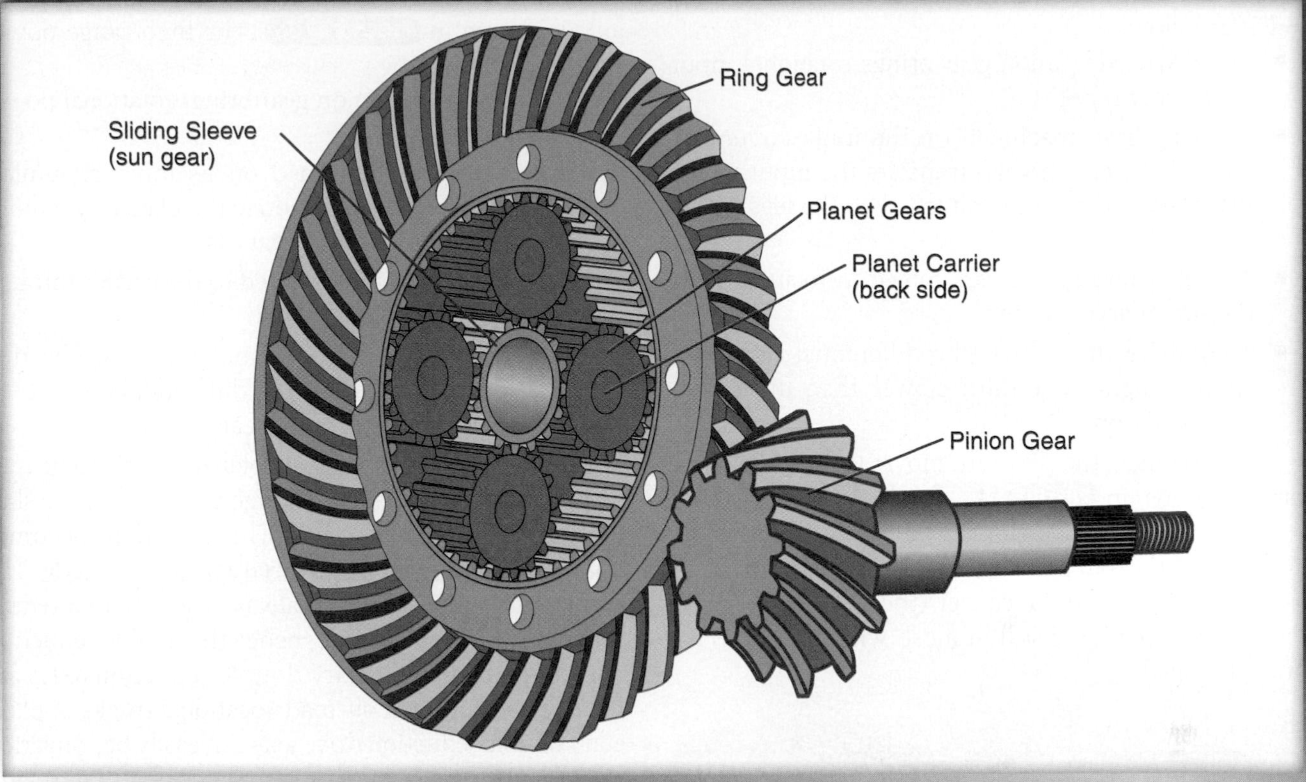

Ring Gear
Sliding Sleeve (sun gear)
Planet Gears
Planet Carrier (back side)
Pinion Gear

FIGURE 47-32 Planetary drive axles use a planetary gear to create two-speed capability.

becomes the ring gear of the planetary gear set. A housing is bolted to the crown gear instead of the differential case, so the differential case is able to rotate inside this housing.

The planetary two-speed drive axle differential case, shown in **FIGURE 47-33**, has four legs to hold the planetary pinion gears. The differential case, then, actually becomes the carrier of the planetary gear set. The sun gear is a hollow gear mounted in such a way that its teeth are constantly in mesh with the planetary pinions held on the differential case legs. Bolted to the side of the differential case on the outside of the planetary pinions is the high speed plate. It has teeth cut on its inside surface that match the teeth on the sun gear. The sun gear has another set of clutching teeth machined on its outer edge. These clutching teeth match a set of clutch teeth machined into the inside circumference of the side bearing adjuster on that side of the drive axle. The sun gear will also have a groove to accept a shift fork, which can move the sun gear in or out using an electric motor or an air shifter.

The operation of the two-speed planetary drive axle is quite simple. When low range is selected by the operator, the shifter fork moves the sun gear to an inboard position, shown in **FIGURE 47-34A**. This causes its clutching teeth to engage with the clutching teeth on the bearing

FIGURE 47-33 A planetary two-speed drive axle.

adjuster and hold the sun gear stationary. The power flow is as follows:

- The drive axle pinion gear brings rotational input to the crown gear.
- The ring gear, machined on the inner circumference of the crown gear, transfers the input to the planetary pinion gears attached to the legs of the differential case.
- The planetary pinions are forced to rotate around the stationary sun gear.
- They drive the carrier (the differential case) at a speed roughly one-third slower than the crown gear's rotation.

In high range, the shift fork moves the sun gear outward, as shown in FIGURE 47-34B, which disengages the clutching teeth from the bearing adjuster and slides the outer end of the sun gear teeth into mesh with the high speed plate bolted to the carrier (the differential case). The sun gear teeth are still in mesh with the planetary pinions as well.

FIGURE 47-34 **A.** The sun gear is moved inboard for low range, locking the sun gear's clutching teeth to the bearing retainer so it cannot turn. **B.** For high speed, the sun gear is moved outward so the sun gear engages the teeth in the high speed plate.

The power flow through a planetary two-speed drive axle is shown in FIGURE 47-35. The high range power flow is as follows:

- The drive axle pinion gear brings rotational power to the crown gear.
- The ring gear machined on its inner circumference transfers that rotation to the planetary pinions mounted to the differential case.
- The sun gear is now splined to the carrier through the high speed plate.
- The planetary pinions cannot rotate, so the ring gear drives the carrier (the differential case) at the same speed as the crown gear.

In certain vocations, a vehicle's planetary drive axle may be permanently fixed in low range by replacing the shift motor with a holding plate. This axle then becomes known as a **planetary double reduction drive axle**. The planetary double reduction always uses the two reduction through the drive axle, hence the double reduction part of its name. Planetary double reduction axles are usually only found in off-road vocational trucks. A planetary double reduction drive axle can easily be converted to a planetary two-speed by installing a shift motor and providing the necessary control circuit for the operator.

Axle Shift Control

There are two methods of control for shifting dual range or two-speed drive axles—air and electric. In both systems, the driver will have a control switch to select the different speeds. The driver may use the axle speeds as a supplement to the gear shift ratios when necessary based on load and terrain factors. In some cases, the driver may not need to use it at all.

Electric Shift Control

An electric shifter, shown in FIGURE 47-36, uses an electric motor to move the shift fork to select high and low range. The electric shift unit is attached to the drive axle housing and contains the following items:

- The motor itself
- A worm gear set
- A slider unit that moves the shift fork
- A control circuit with two switches a resistor and a diode

External to the electric shift unit are the following:

- A wiring harness
- A driver-operated control switch usually mounted on the gear shift lever
- A speedometer adapter if the vehicle has a transmission-driven speedometer

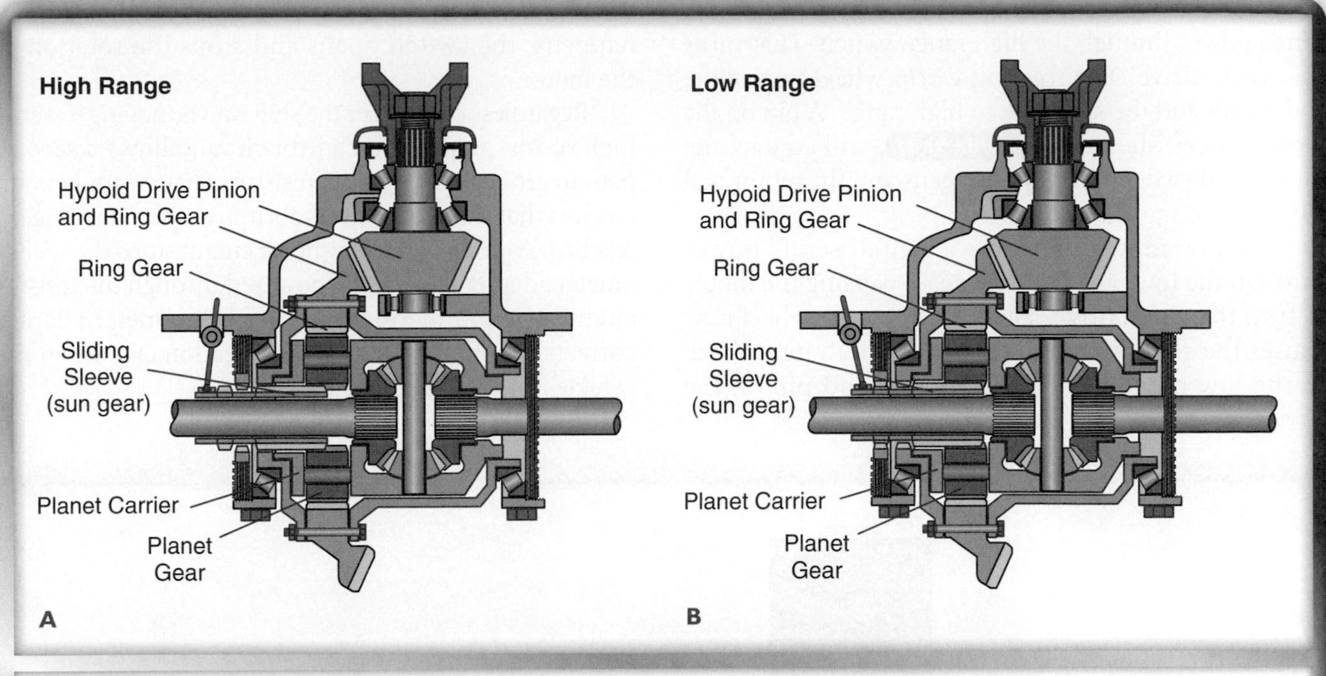

FIGURE 47-35 Power flow through a planetary drive axle. **A.** High range with the sun gear outward and locked to the high speed plate. **B.** Low range with the sun gear inward and locked stationary to the bearing retainer clutch plate.

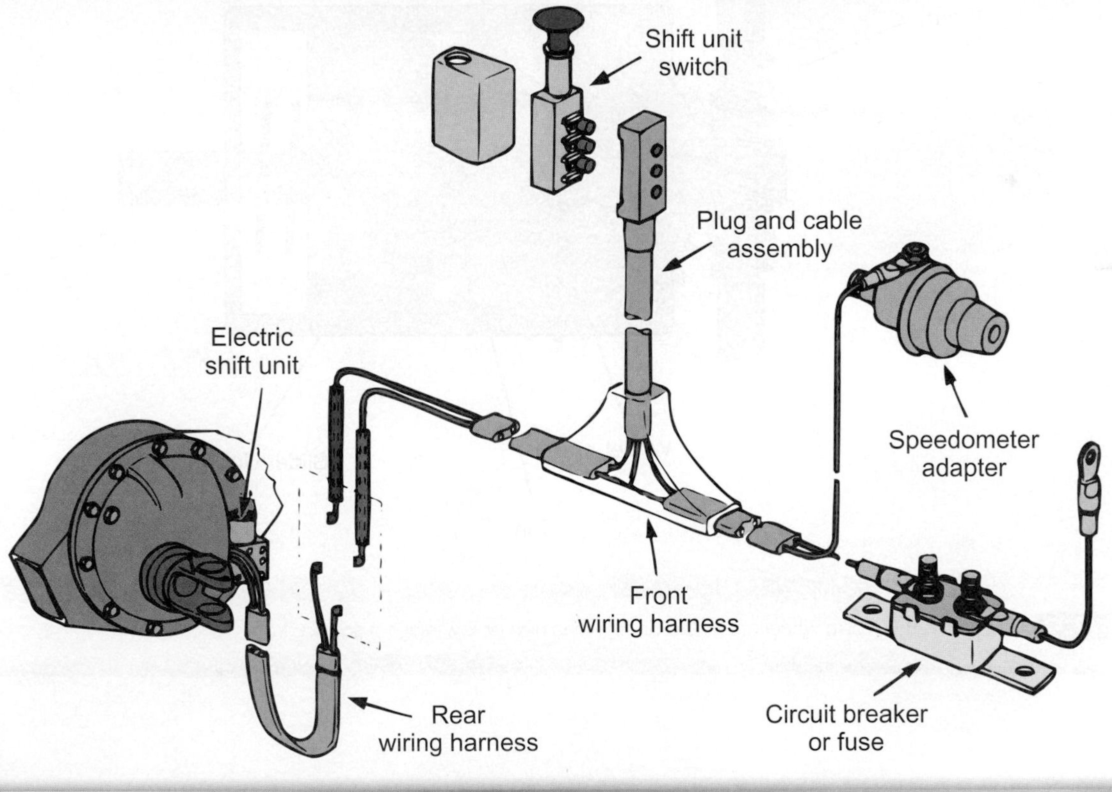

FIGURE 47-36 The driver controls the drive axle range shift by using the high–low switch on the gearstick.

When the driver requests a shift, the control switch sends power through the high range switch. That turns the worm drive. The rotating worm wheel moves the slider unit and the shift fork to high range. A pin on the worm wheel, shown in **FIGURE 47-37**, will contact the high speed switch. The switch opens and the motor will stop as high range is achieved.

For low range, the control switch sends power through the low range switch, again causing the motor to turn the worm drive. The rotating worm wheel now causes the slider unit and the shift fork to move back to the low range position until a second pin on the worm wheel contacts the low range switch. When that happens, the switch opens and stops the rotation of the motor.

Regardless of whether the shift unit is moving towards high or low range, the control circuit allows a second path to ground through the resistor. That ground circuit ensures that the motor stops abruptly when the range is reached. A diode in the low-range circuit stops the speedometer adapter from being powered through the resistor circuit when in high range. The speedometer adapter corrects the speed signal to the speedometer when the vehicle is in low range.

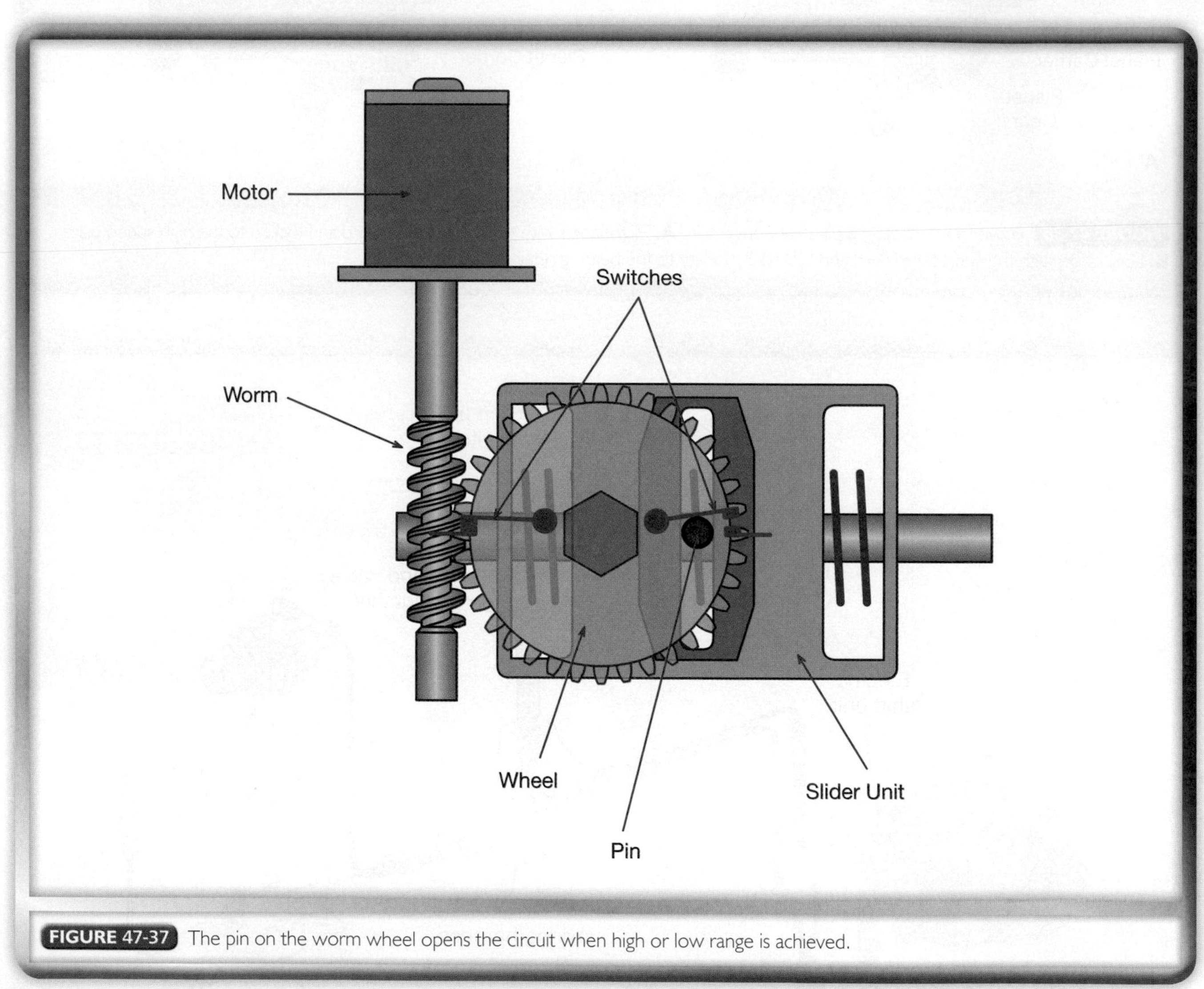

FIGURE 47-37 The pin on the worm wheel opens the circuit when high or low range is achieved.

Air Shift Control

Air shift systems, like the one shown in FIGURE 47-38, are much simpler than electric. Air shift systems consist of a shift motor unit attached to the drive axle. The shift unit contains a piston, a strong return spring, and a mechanism to engage the shift fork in the drive axle.

External to the shift unit will be the following components:

- air lines
- an air control switch (usually attached to the shift lever)
- a control solenoid
- a quick release valve
- a speedometer adapter if the vehicle has a transmission-driven speedometer; most vehicles with electronic controls will not need a speedometer adapter

The control solenoid is turned on when the ignition switch is on, allowing air to flow into the control circuit from the vehicle air tanks. Air flows to the control switch on the shift lever. When the driver places the control switch in the low range position, the air flow is stopped at the control switch. When the driver selects high range, air flows through the switch and the quick release valve to the shift unit. Air pushes against the piston and the piston then moves the mechanism attached to the shift fork. The drive axle shifts to high range.

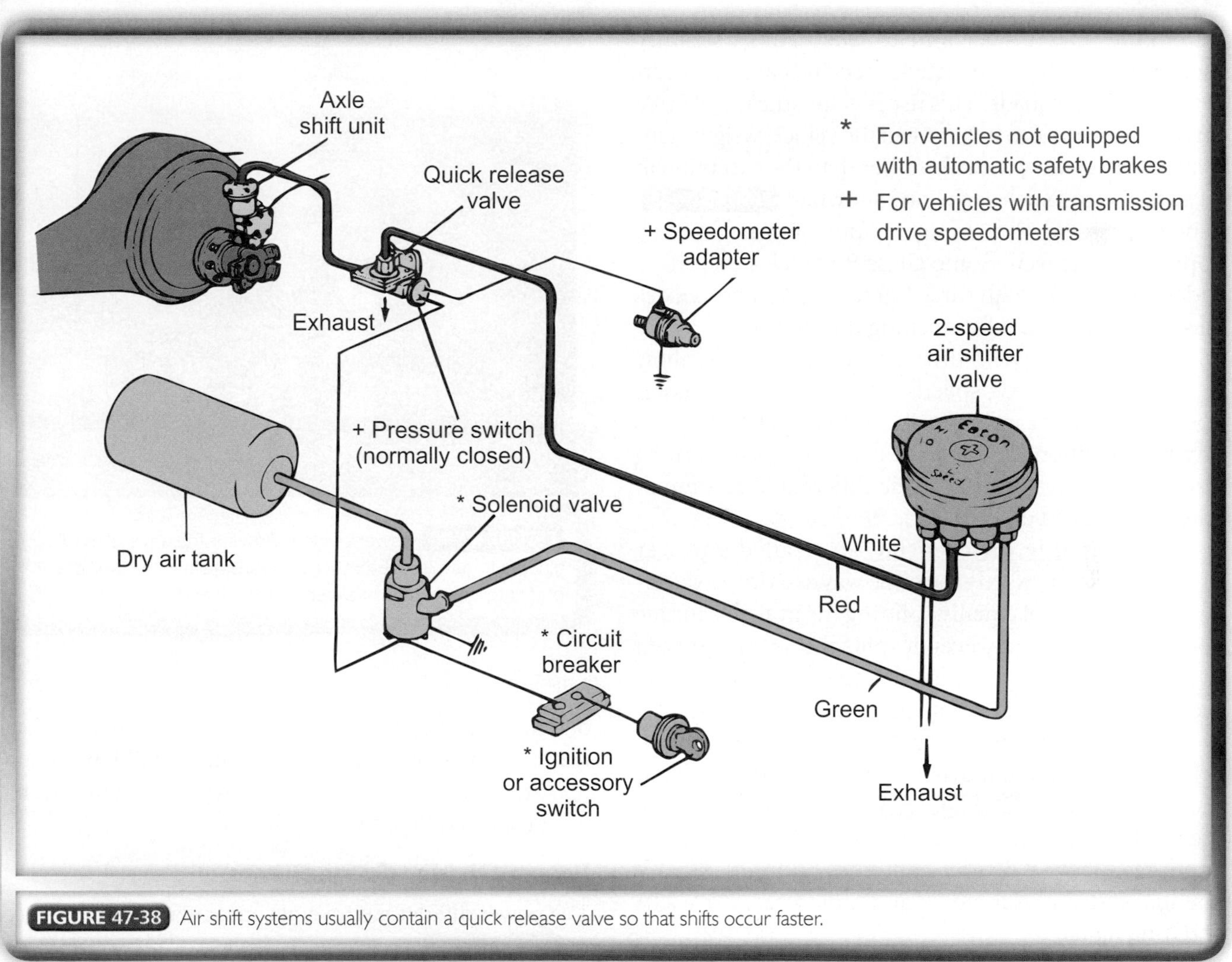

FIGURE 47-38 Air shift systems usually contain a quick release valve so that shifts occur faster.

When the driver shifts back to low range, the air flowing through the control valve is cut off. The air in the line to the quick release valve exhausts at the control switch. This causes the quick release valve to exhaust the air going to the shift control unit such that the return spring forces the piston and the shift mechanism back to the low range position. The key-on control solenoid assures that the drive axle shifts to low range when the key is turned off. If the vehicle has a speedometer adapter, it will be powered through a normally closed pressure switch that is opened when the drive axle shifts to high range. That means the adapter is used only in low range.

Inter-Axle Differentials (Power Dividers)

As engine horsepower and torque ratings steadily increased over the years, trucks became capable of carrying heavier payloads. This necessitated the use of more than one drive axle to help spread the vehicle weight. Tandem drives are now the rule rather than the exception in Class 8 tractors, such as the one shown in FIGURE 47-39. Tandem drives are increasingly popular in straight truck applications as well. Some Class 8 vehicles even have tridem drive axles with three interconnected drive axles all sharing the work of propelling the vehicle.

Tandem and tridem drive arrangements must allow for differences in axle speeds between the drive axles. Speed differences can be caused by mismatched tire sizes or wear conditions, irregular road surfaces, and turning radius differences. An inter-axle differential accommodates these speed differences.

An **inter-axle differential**, also called a **power divider**, works in exactly the same way as a drive axle differential. Instead of equally splitting the available torque to each wheel end, however, it splits the torque between two drive axles. At the same time, the differential allows the axles to turn at different speeds when required.

The inter-axle differential is contained in the front drive axle of a tandem drive. A power divider, such as the one shown in FIGURE 47-40, is commonly used in the trucking industry to accommodate wheel speed differences. A power divider combines an inter-axle differential and a regular crown and pinion gear drive axle with differential.

As its name suggests, the power divider allows the power from the vehicle drive line to be equally split between the front-rear drive axle and the rear-rear drive axle of a tandem. Even as it splits the power, the power divider allows the axles to rotate at different speeds. A tridem drive consists of three interconnected drive axles, so it requires two power dividers—one in the front and one in the center drive axle positions. The final or rear-rear drive axle of the tandem or tridem will have a normal drive axle arrangement with a regular differential for wheel speed differences.

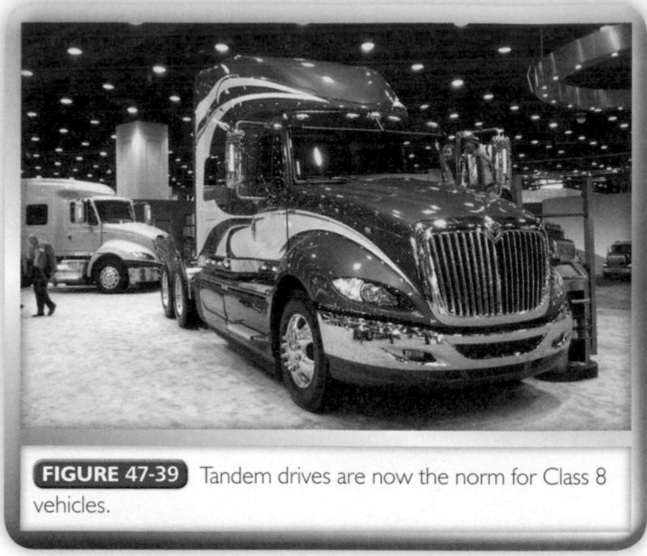

FIGURE 47-39 Tandem drives are now the norm for Class 8 vehicles.

FIGURE 47-40 Power dividers allow for the drive axles of a tandem to turn at different speeds while splitting the available driving torque equally between them.

Power Divider Components

The power divider has several components, as illustrated in FIGURE 47-41:

- the input shaft
- the helical drop gears
- the front side gear (usually part of the upper helical drop gear)
- the rear side gear (usually part of the output shaft)
- the output shaft

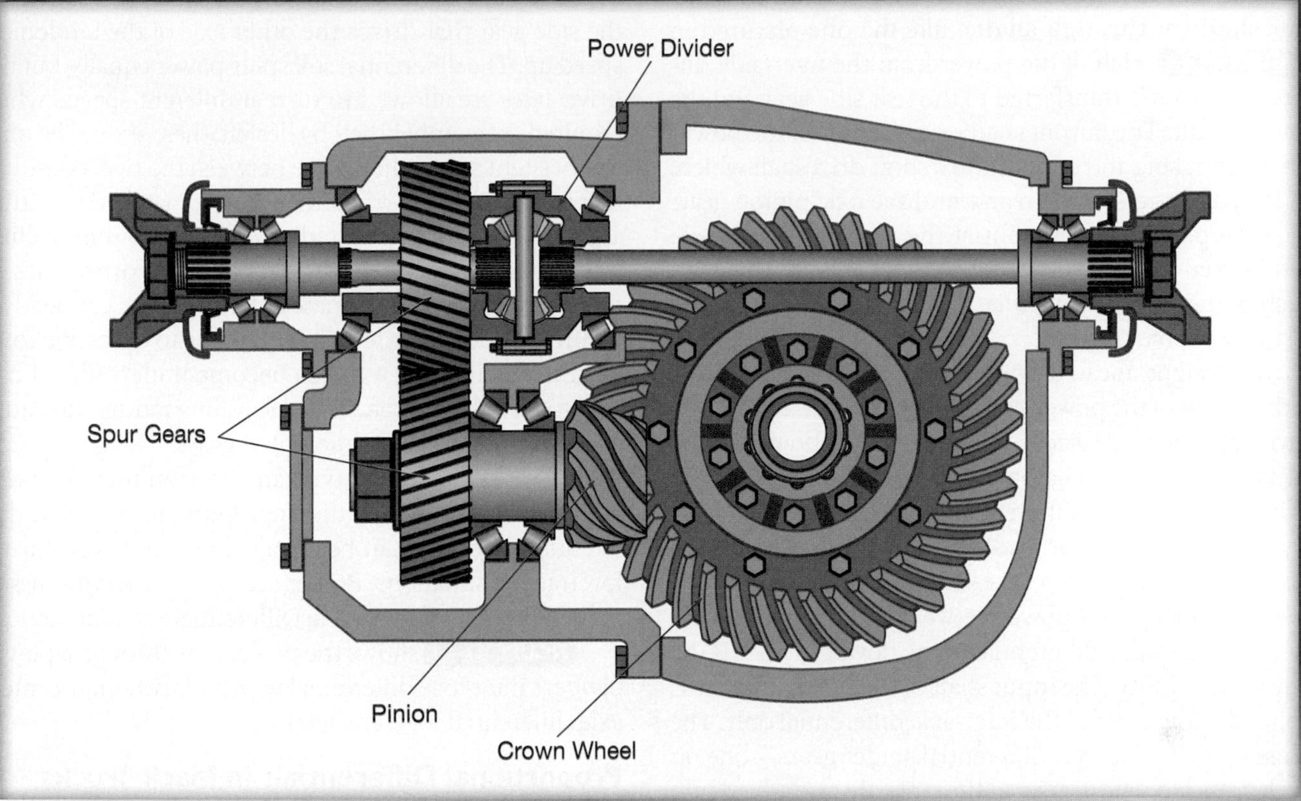

FIGURE 47-41 The major power divider components.

- the inter-axle differential with its case as well as cross and spider gears
- the crown and pinion gear set (driven by the helical drop gears)
- the wheel differential and case with its side and spider gears

In addition, the power divider will also likely be equipped with a lube pump and an inter-axle differential locking mechanism.

These components work together. The vehicle driveshaft is connected to the input shaft of the power divider and it is splined to the cross of the inter-axle differential. The cross rotates with the input shaft and delivers power in equal quantities to the front and rear side gears of the inter-axle differential. The front side gear is part of the upper helical drop gear, like the one pictured in FIGURE 47-42. The **helical drop gear** drives the pinion gear of the front drive axle of a tandem. The input shaft passes through this gear but is not attached to it. The gear rides on a bushing or bearing on the input shaft. The upper helical drop gear is in mesh with the lower helical drop gear which, in turn, is splined to the pinion gear of the front drive axle of the tandem. When the axle rotates, power is transferred to the crown gear and then to the wheel differential case. At that point, the power is split again, through the differential gears, between the two drive wheels of the axle.

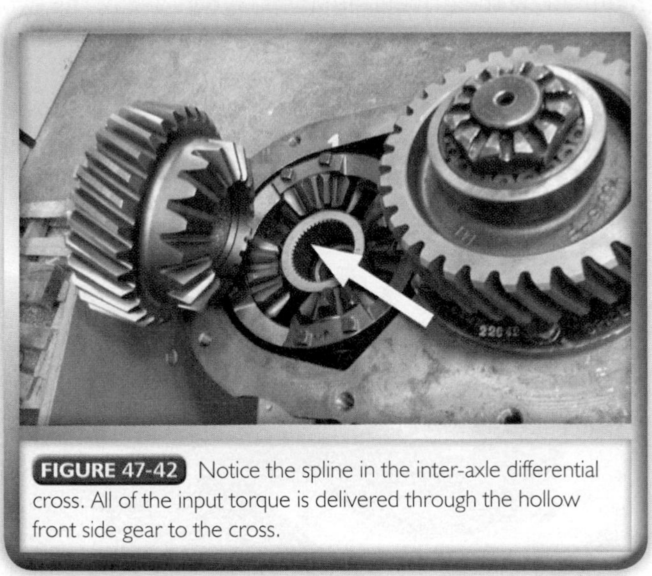

FIGURE 47-42 Notice the spline in the inter-axle differential cross. All of the input torque is delivered through the hollow front side gear to the cross.

The rear side gear is part of or splined to the **output shaft** (or **through shaft**), like the one pictured in FIGURE 47-43. Half of the power from the inter-axle differential cross is transferred to the rear side gear and the output shaft. The output shaft exits the rear of the power divider housing and connects to a short driveshaft which, in turn, connects to the rear-rear drive axle pinion gear.

The power is then split at the rear-rear drive axle differential to the rear two driving wheels. In this way, each of the four driving wheels will receive exactly 25% of the available power.

In straight-ahead driving with tires of equal size, that is the extent of the power divider operation. As the vehicle turns or when tire sizes are mismatched, however, the situation changes. The power divider must allow each drive axle to turn at different speeds. The power divider performs two functions. It allows two drive axles to rotate at different speeds when necessary while still splitting the available torque and power between them equally.

The inter-axle differential of the power divider is the key to this ability. The input shaft of the power divider is splined to the cross of the inter-axle differential only. The cross contains the four differential spider gears—one on each cross leg. The gears and the cross are assembled into a case. As the cross rotates, the spider gears essentially drag the two side gears along. The spider gears are also capable of rotating on the cross when necessary, allowing the two side gears to rotate at different speeds when required by the driving situation. When one of the two axles of the tandem is turning slower than the other due to mismatched tires, turning, or road surface variations, the side gear driving the slower moving axle slows down slightly, and the spider gears in the inter-axle differential begin to turn. The rotation of the spider gears causes the side gear that drives the other axle of the tandem to speed up. The differential still splits power equally, but the drive axles are allowed to turn at different speeds when required. Remember that, by design, there should be only a very slight speed difference between the two axles. For that reason, it is important that tires be matched to within 1/8" (3.2 mm) of rolling radius or 3/4" (9.5 mm) rolling circumference between the front and rear drive axles of the tandem. Failure to match the tire sizes can lead to failure of the inter-axle differential due to excessive rotation. Even allowing a tire to become underinflated can lead to serious differences in the rolling radius and cause excessive wear on the differential gears.

FIGURE 47-43 The rear side gear of the inter-axle differential is splined to the through shaft, so half the available torque is sent to the rear drive axle of the tandem.

Power dividers will typically have an inter-axle differential lock similar to the ones found in the main differential. The lock can be engaged by the driver during low traction situations. Proper use of this lock is discussed in the Preventing Inter-Axle Differential Spinout section.

FIGURE 47-44 shows the power flow through a power divider's inter-axle differential with and without the inter-axle differential lock engaged.

Proportional Differentials in Mack Trucks

Mack trucks have a uniquely designed proportional differential gear set, which can be used as a wheel differential or an inter-axle differential. When poor traction conditions are encountered, the Mack design, shown in FIGURE 47-45, can automatically send 75% of available torque to the drive axle wheels with the best traction

The Mack differential uses a driving cage with 24 oval-shaped wedges that drives an inner and an outer cam using the cam and wedge principal. The inner cam drives the rear drive axle of the tandem and the outer cam drives the front drive axle of the tandem. In normal operation, the driving cage and the angular position of the wedges drive the two cams at equal speeds and the entire assembly rotates as a unit. When a low traction or an unequal speed situation occurs, one of the cams will overrun (turn faster than) the driving cage. For example, if the rear drive axle loses traction, then its cam will turn faster than the driving cage. That will force the wedges up and into the outer cam and transfer more torque to the front axle, as illustrated in FIGURE 47-46. If the situation is reversed and the front drive axle loses traction, the outer cam will overrun the driving cage and force the wedges down into the inner cam. More torque will be transferred to the rear drive axle.

Mack's ingenious system allows infinitely variable speeds between the two drive axles. At the same time, the system also allows up to 75% of the available torque to be applied to the axle with better traction. The Mack

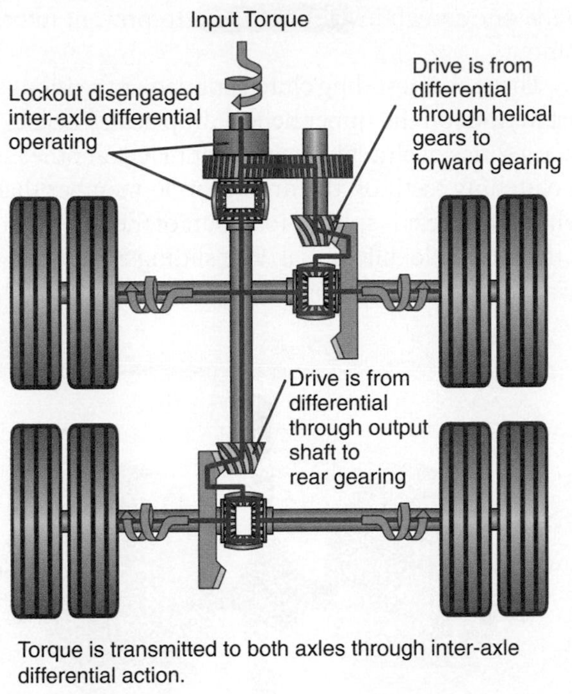

Input Torque

Lockout disengaged inter-axle differential operating

Drive is from differential through helical gears to forward gearing

Drive is from differential through output shaft to rear gearing

Torque is transmitted to both axles through inter-axle differential action.

Input Torque

Lockout engaged inter-axle differential NOT operating

Drive is from differential through helical gears to forward gearing

Drive is from differential through output shaft to rear gearing

Torque is transmitted to both axles without inter-axle differential action.

FIGURE 47-44 Power flow through the inter-axle differential. Each wheel receives 25% of the available torque.

FIGURE 47-45 Mack trucks use a proprietary inter-axle differential capable of sending 75% of the available torque to the drive axle with more traction.

inter-axle differential also comes with a driver-operated differential lock. The lock is splined to the input shaft and has a series of clutching teeth that can engage matching teeth on the inside of the differential's outer cam. When the lock is engaged, the clutching teeth mesh. As that happens, it locks the outer cam to the input shaft so that the shaft and the cam must turn at the same speed. Because the wedges cannot move, they drag the inner cam along.

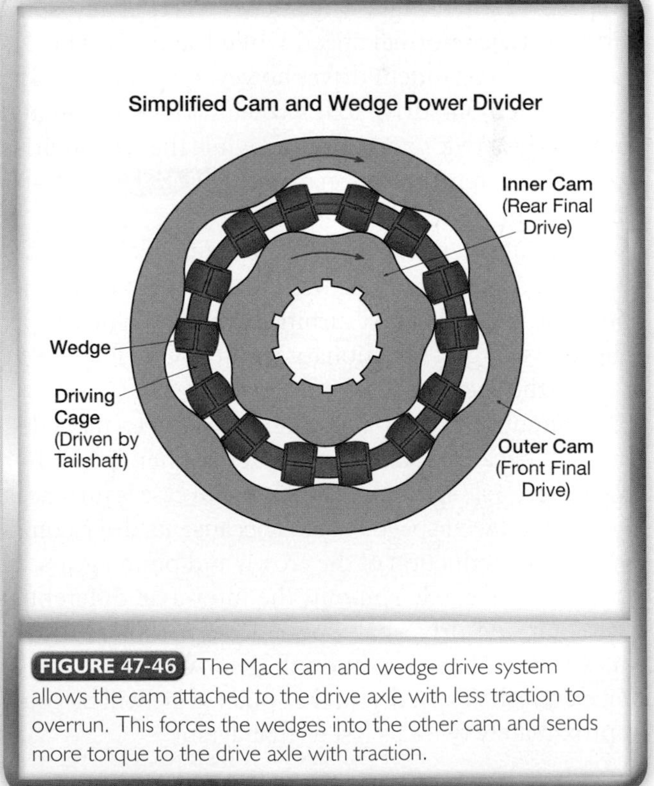

FIGURE 47-46 The Mack cam and wedge drive system allows the cam attached to the drive axle with less traction to overrun. This forces the wedges into the other cam and sends more torque to the drive axle with traction.

Both drive axles then turn at the same speed and receive the same torque.

As with all differential locks, the Mack lock can be engaged at any time provided there is no axle slip occurring. The lock should only be used in poor traction conditions.

Preventing Inter-Axle Differential Spinout

Spinout, as mentioned previously, is a situation in which one wheel of a drive axle (or one drive axle of a tandem) loses traction and spins out of control while the other remains stationary. Spinout can occur under three conditions:

- starting on a slippery surface, such as ice, snow, loose gravel, mud, or wet conditions
- driving in slippery conditions, such as climbing a hill in a snow storm; spinout in this situation can cause the driver to lose control of the vehicle
- backing under a trailer

Backing under a trailer is a condition usually unique to tandem drives. As the driver tries to back under a trailer to hook up, the rear-rear axle will become loaded first. If the conditions are not ideal, the front drive axle of the tandem can lose traction and spin out.

Careful use of the inter-axle differential locks can avoid spinout. Recall that in a single drive axle, spinout happens when a single wheel loses traction and spins wildly at twice normal speed while the other wheel is stationary. In a tandem drive, however, spinout usually occurs when one drive axle's wheels lose traction and spin wildly at twice normal speed while the second drive axle's wheels remain stationary. FIGURE 47-47 illustrates this concept.

Spinout is very damaging to the inter-axle differential gears. Consider what occurs when a single drive axle spins out. Instead of just turning several revolutions per mile, one side gear is stationary, and the other is spinning at twice the speed of the case.

Spinout in an inter-axle differential is even more detrimental because it turns at a much higher speed. In a single drive axle spinout, the differential case is turning at a greatly reduced speed. That is because its drive comes through the reduction of the crown and pinion gears. In a tandem drive axle spinout, the inter-axle differential case rotates at driveshaft speed, or up to three to five times faster. Therefore, one side gear will be turning at twice driveshaft speed, and the spider gears will be going approximately twice as fast as that again!

As a result, most if not all inter-axle differentials will be equipped with an inter-axle differential lock similar to the one shown in FIGURE 47-48, to prevent inter-axle spinout.

The lock is a sliding clutch splined to the input shaft just in front on the upper helical drop gear. The lock will have a series of clutching teeth that match another series of clutching teeth on the drop gear. Remember that the helical drop gear is splined to or part of the front side gear of the inter-axle differential. The sliding clutch is moved by an air-operated motor that the driver controls. When

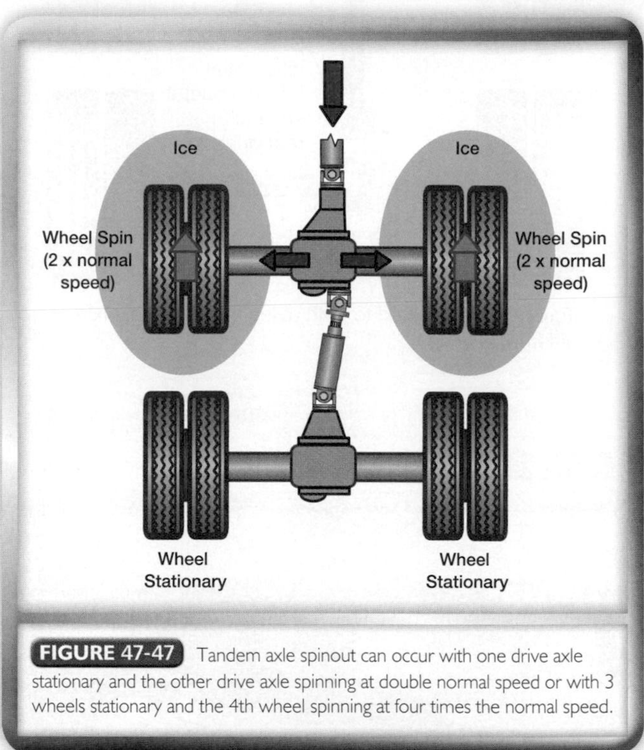

FIGURE 47-47 Tandem axle spinout can occur with one drive axle stationary and the other drive axle spinning at double normal speed or with 3 wheels stationary and the 4th wheel spinning at four times the normal speed.

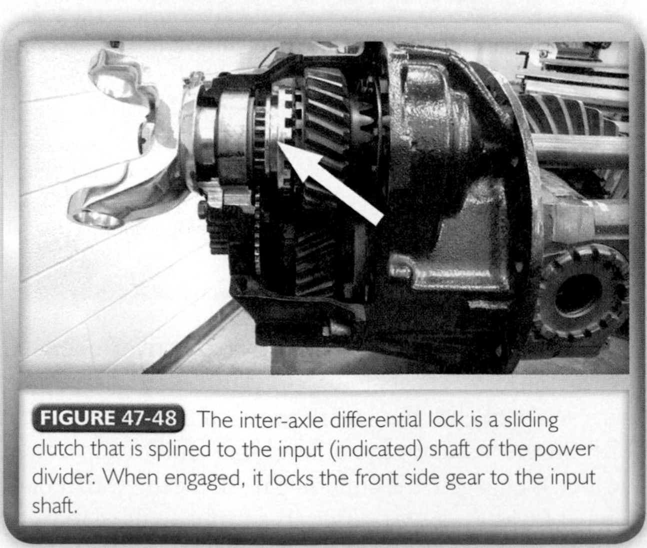

FIGURE 47-48 The inter-axle differential lock is a sliding clutch that is splined to the input (indicated) shaft of the power divider. When engaged, it locks the front side gear to the input shaft.

the driver engages the lock, the sliding clutch locks the upper helical drop gear (and, therefore, the front inter-axle differential side gear) to the input shaft. The input shaft is splined to the inter-axle differential cross as well, so the cross and the front side gear must now turn at the same speed. Because the spider gears can no longer turn, the rear side gear cannot turn either. It must go along for the ride. All inter-axle differential action stops, positively preventing spinout from occurring.

As with the single drive axle differential lock, the inter-axle differential lock can be engaged at any speed provided no wheels are spinning. To engage the inter-axle differential lock, the driver follows the same procedure as for main differential locks. The lock can be engaged while stopped or while driving. While driving, the driver maintains speed while pushing the switch to engage the lock. The driver then releases the throttle momentarily to allow the lock to engage before resuming normal throttle operation. It is essential that the wheels are not slipping while engaging the lock or damage will occur.

Types of Axle Shafts

The axle shafts that actually drive the wheel come in two basic designs: semi-floating, shown in FIGURE 47-49A, and full floating, shown in FIGURE 47-49B. With **semi-floating axle shafts**, the outer end of the axle shaft supports the entire vehicle weight at the wheel end, as the wheel is bolted directly to the axle shaft flange. The inner end of the semi-floating axle shaft "floats" in the side gear. That is, the axle carries none of the vehicle weight, hence the name semi-floating. Semi-floating axle shafts are used on light- and medium-duty vehicles only. Semi-floating axle shafts would be unable to carry the weight of a truck and its cargo.

Heavier vehicles, including most trucks, use full floating axle shafts exclusively. A **full floating axle shaft** does not carry any of the vehicle weight on either end on the shaft. The inner end of a full floating axle shaft floats in the side gear while the outer end is bolted to the wheel hub. The wheel hub is mounted on two opposing tapered roller bearings. Those bearings are supported by the spindle, which is attached to the drive axle housing. Vehicle weight is transmitted through the frame to the springs to the axle housing and then through the bearing to the wheel hub and through the tire to the ground. Vehicle torque is transmitted to the wheel hub through the axle shaft. Because the shaft carries none of the vehicle weight, it is known as full floating.

Lubricating Drive Axles

In most drive axles, lubrication is effected by the movement of the crown wheel. A fluid level plug is threaded into the drive axle housing or the rear cover (on lighter duty models) and the fluid is to be filled to the level of the

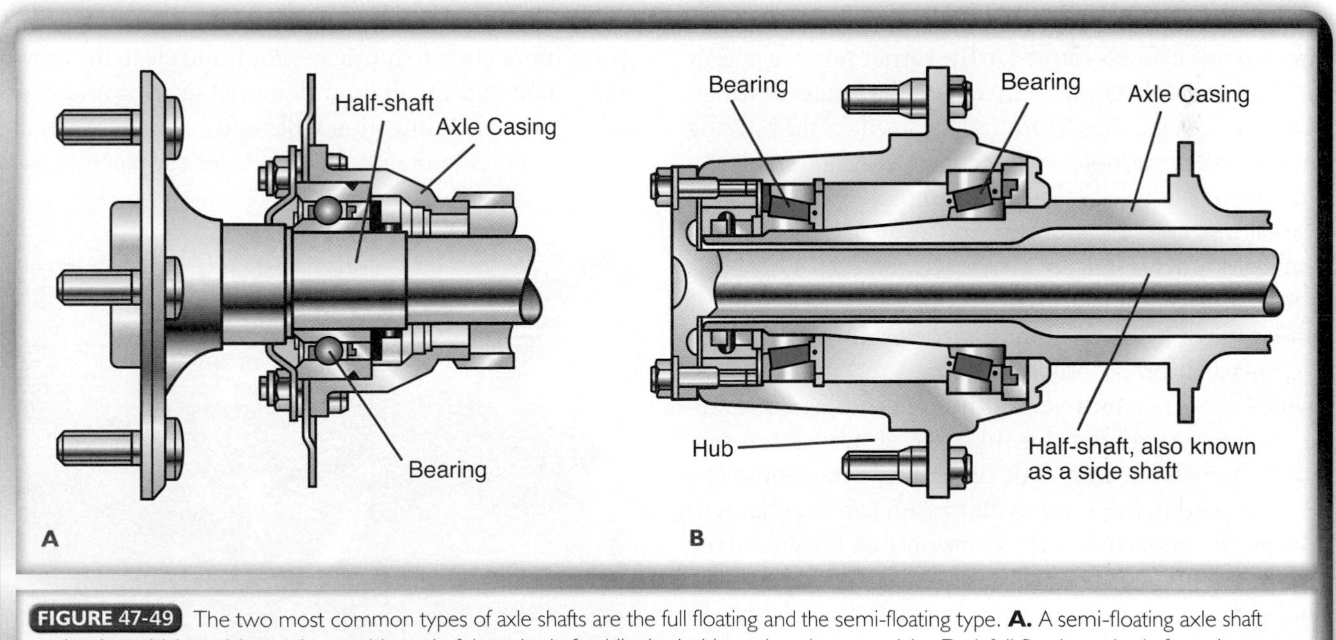

FIGURE 47-49 The two most common types of axle shafts are the full floating and the semi-floating type. **A.** A semi-floating axle shaft carries the vehicle weight on the outside end of the axle shaft while the inside end carries no weight. **B.** A full floating axle shaft carries none of the vehicle weight.

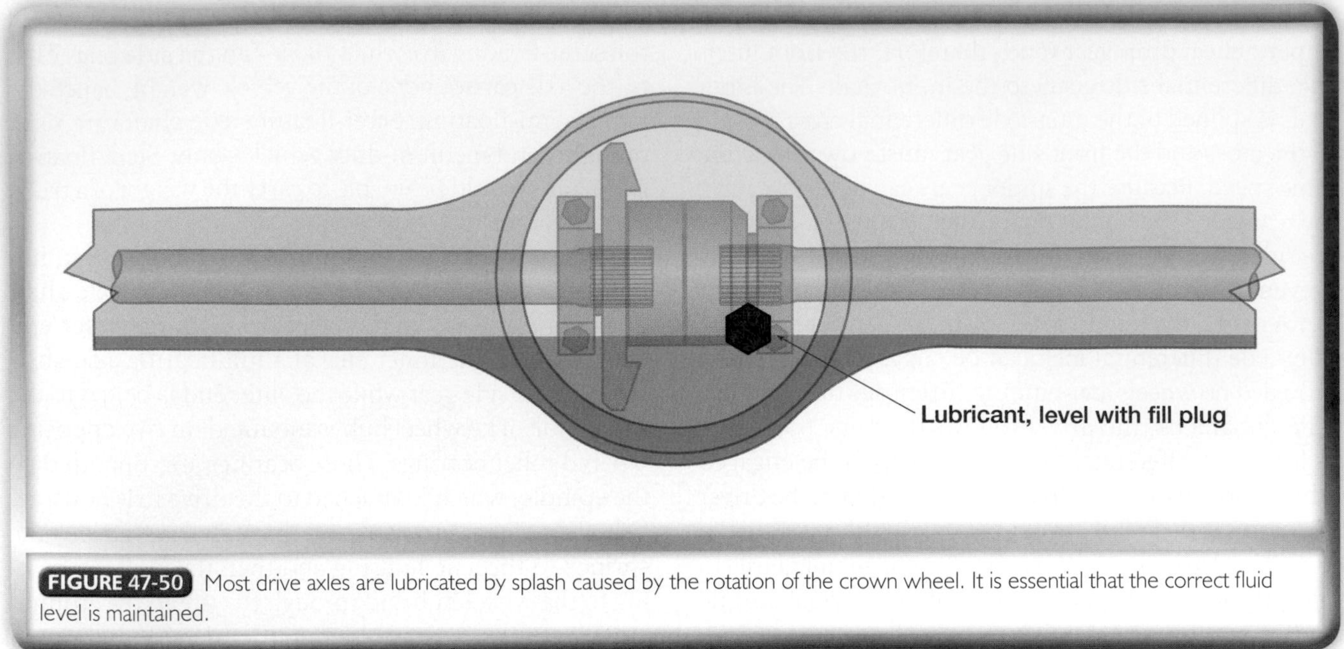

FIGURE 47-50 Most drive axles are lubricated by splash caused by the rotation of the crown wheel. It is essential that the correct fluid level is maintained.

plug, as illustrated in FIGURE 47-50. Some drive axles may have more than one level plug. In those instances, both must be filled to the level of the plugs. Always consult the manufacturer's manual to determine the proper filling sequence on these axles.

With fluid at approximately half way up the differential case, the fluid bathes the differential gears and the side bearings. As the crown wheel rotates through this fluid, its teeth throw the fluid upwards in the drive axle. The fluid then follows the curvature of the housing and is directed by channels formed in the carrier housing and/or stamped metal slingers and troughs to the pinion bearings. The fluid also splashes all around the inside of the housing onto the side bearings as well. The flowing and splashing movement allows the fluid to complete its purpose of lubricating, cooling, and carrying away foreign material from components that are in contact with each other. This type of lubrication is known as splash lubrication and is similar to what occurs in most standard transmissions.

Splash lubrication can also be used in the power divider of a tandem drive. The inter-axle differential creates a unique problem for this type of lubrication system, however. The inter-axle differential component can be lubricated in the same fashion with formed channels bringing essential lube to its components. Because of the differential's rotational speed, however, it tends to throw the lubricant away from itself by centrifugal force. To combat this problem, most power dividers are equipped with an internal or external lube pump, similar to the one pictured in FIGURE 47-51.

Although there are other designs, the most common type of gear lube pump is one that is driven by the same spline on the input shaft that the inter-axle differential lock is splined to. This gear pump then channels fluid, under pressure, through drilled passages in the input shaft. That is how lube oil is delivered to the essential components in the top part of the power divider, the input shaft front and rear support bearings, the upper drop gear bushing or bearing, and to the center of the inter-axle differential itself. The channeling of fluid ensures positive lube for those components whenever the vehicle is in motion. Nonetheless, the power divider still relies on splash lubrication to lubricate, cool, and clean the crown and pinion and the main differential gearing and bearings. Drive axle lubrication will be fully discussed in the Servicing and Maintaining Drive Axles chapter.

FIGURE 47-51 Most power dividers will be equipped with a gear driven lubrication pump (indicated) to supply vital lubrication to the inter-axle differential components.

Wrap-up

Ready for Review

- Truck axles can be divided into three categories—steer axles, dead axles, and live axles.
- Most truck steer axles will be a solid I-beam that is attached to the front suspension and has steering knuckles to allow the vehicle to be turned.
- Dead axles merely support the vehicle weight and have numerous subcategories. Tag axles are mounted behind the drive axles of the vehicle; pusher axles are mounted in front of the drive axle.
- Tag and pusher axles typically have air suspension systems and can be raised or lowered by the operator when necessary to support the vehicle load.
- Tag and pusher axles can be self-steering to prevent tire scrub on turns.
- Trailer axles come in many types depending on the trailer vocation.
- Live axles actually drive the vehicle, so they are also called drive axles.
- Drive axles allow the power from the engine to turn a 90 degree corner to send that power to the wheels.
- Drive axles usually provide the final gear reduction in a drive train and therefore are also known as final drives.
- All drive axle gears are bevel gears—meaning that they intersect at an angle (in this case, 90 degrees).
- Bevel gear sets usually consist of a large crown (or ring) gear and a smaller pinion gear.
- Bevel gears are subdivided into several types, including plain bevel, spiral bevel, durapoid, hypoid, amboid, topoid, and hypoid generoid.
- Plain bevel gears are similar to spur gears and have the same problems with noise and weakness. Plain bevel gear pinons are mounted at the crown gear's centerline.
- Spiral bevel gears are quieter and stronger than plain bevel and their pinion gears are mounted at the centerline of the crown gear.
- Durapoid gears are spiral bevel gears with an asymmetrical tooth design that adds strength.
- Hypoid gears are a type of spiral bevel gear that mounts the pinion below the centerline of the crown gear. Hypoid gearing is by far the most popular gear design used in truck drive axles.
- Amboid gears are a type of spiral bevel gearing in which the pinion gear is mounted above the centerline of the crown gear. Amboid gears are typically found only in the rear-rear axle of a tandem drive vehicle.
- Generoid or hypoid generoid gears have asymmetrical tooth flanks for extra strength.
- The drive axle is commonly misnamed the differential because the differential gear set is inside the drive axle. The drive axle and the differential are, however, different.
- The differential gear arrangement allows the power from the engine to be split equally between two axle shafts while allowing the axle shafts to turn at different speeds when required.
- The differential gear set consists of two side gears, four pinion or spider gears, and a differential spider or cross.
- The differential gears are contained in the differential case.
- As a vehicle turns a corner, the inner wheel must slow down and the outer wheel must speed up. The differential gear set allows this to happen.
- The differential always splits the available torque equally between the two wheels. Spinning wheels in a low traction condition can cause a lifetime of damage in a very short period of time.
- Controlled traction differentials allow the engine to build more torque before a wheel can spin in low traction situations.
- Bias torque differentials can send more torque to the wheel with good traction.
- Differential locks are used during low traction situations only.
- Double reduction drive axles use two gear reductions at all times.
- Planetary two-speed drive axles use a planetary gear set to produce two ratios through the drive axle.
- Tandem or tridem systems use inter-axle differentials to divide the torque between the two or three axles.
- An inter-axle differential splits the available torque between two drive axles, not the wheels.
- Spinout situations are especially damaging for inter-axle differentials because inter-axle differentials turn at driveshaft speed, not at wheel speed.
- Axle shafts on lighter duty vehicles are called semi-floating.
- Heavier vehicles use full floating axle shafts.
- Most drive axle lubrication is effected by splash from the rotation of the crown wheel.
- Power dividers typically will have a gear pump to ensure adequate lubrication of the inter-axle differential gears.

Vocabulary Builder

amboid gear A bevel gear arrangement with the pinion gear mounted above the centerline of the crown gear.

banjo A drive axle housing with a removable carrier. Also called a *removable carrier type*.

bevel gears Gears that intersect at an angle—usually 90 degrees.

biased torque differential A differential capable of sending more torque to one wheel than the other when a wheel slip condition is encountered. Also known as a *proportional differential*.

carrier The component that holds the support bearings for the drive axle gearing.

controlled traction differential A differential that will allow the engine to build more torque before the wheels can slip.

crank axle A dead axle in which the main beam is lower than the wheel spindles.

crown gear A large bevel gear that is driven by a smaller pinion gear in the bevel gear set. Also known as a *ring gear*.

dead axle An axle that supports vehicle weight only.

differential case The housing that holds the differential gears.

differential cross The mechanism that holds the differential pinion or spider gears. Also known as the *differential spider*.

differential gear A gear arrangement that splits the available torque equally between two wheels while allowing them to turn at different speeds when required.

differential gear set Consists of two side gears, four pinion gears, and a cross; allows for speed difference between the two axle shafts of the drive axle when turning.

differential lock A device that prevents differential action by locking one side gear to the differential case.

differential pinion gear A beveled gear that is a component of the differential gear set; it is fitted to the four legs of the differential cross and rotates with it. Also known as a *spider gear*.

differential spider The mechanism that holds the differential pinion or spider gears. Also known as the *differential cross*.

double reduction drive axle A drive axle that uses two gear reductions at all times.

drive axle The axle that drives the vehicle by turning the power from the driveshaft 90 degrees to deliver it to the wheels and providing the final gear reduction in the drive train. Also known as a *live axle*.

drop center tubular axle A dead axle used on trailer that drops in the middle.

durapoid gearing A specially designed spiral bevel gear set designed to provide increased strength and load carrying capability.

full floating axle shaft An axle that carries none of the vehicle weight.

generoid An asymmetrical tooth design similar to the durapoid; it gives added strength to the hypoid and amboid gear sets. Also called *hypoid generoid*.

helical double reduction drive axle A double reduction drive axle that uses a helical gear set for the second gear reduction.

helical double reduction two-speed drive axle A double reduction drive axle that uses two selectable sets of helical gears as the second gear reduction.

helical drop gear The set of gears that drive the pinion gear of the front drive axle of a tandem.

hypoid gearing A type of spiral bevel gear set that mounts the pinion gear below the centerline of the crown gear.

integral carrier housing A drive axle housing that does not have a removable carrier.

inter-axle differential A differential gear set that splits the available torque equally between two drive axles. Also called a *power divider.*

live axle The axle that drives the vehicle by turning the power from the driveshaft 90 degrees to deliver it to the wheels and providing the final gear reduction in the drive train. Also known as a *drive axle*.

locking differential A system that actively prevents differential action from occurring when engaged.

output shaft The output shaft of an inter-axle differential. The rear side gear is part of or splined to the output shaft. Also known as the *through shaft*.

pinion gear A small driving gear.

plain bevel gear A bevel gear set with straight-cut teeth.

planetary double reduction drive axle A planetary drive axle that is permanently fixed in low range.

planetary two-speed drive axle A two-speed drive axle that uses a planetary gear set for the low range.

power divider A differential gear set that splits the available torque equally between two drive axles. Also called an *inter-axle differential*.

proportional differential A differential capable of sending more torque to one wheel than the other when a wheel slip condition is encountered. Also known as a *biased torque differential*.

pusher axle A rear, non-drive rear mounted axle, ahead of the drive axle.

removable carrier type A drive axle housing with a removable carrier. Also called a *banjo*.

ring gear A large bevel gear that is driven by a smaller pinion gear in the bevel gear set. Also known as a *crown gear*.

self-steering axle An axle whose wheel will automatically follow the curve of a turn.

semi-floating axle shaft An axle shaft that carries the entire weight of the vehicle on its outer end.

side gears Part of the differential gear set; the side gears are splined to the axles.

spider gear A beveled gear that is a component of the differential gear set; it is fitted to the four legs of the differential cross and rotates with it. Also known as a *differential pinion gear*.

spinout A low traction situation where one drive wheel or one drive axle spins wildly while the other remains stationary.

spiral bevel gear A bevel gear set with spirally or helically cut gears.

steering axle An axle that allows the vehicle to turn.

tag axle A rear non-drive axle mounted behind the drive axle.

tandem Two drive axles connected by a power divider.

through shaft The output shaft of an inter-axle differential. The rear side gear is part of or splined to the through shaft. Also known as *output shaft*.

topoid A type of amboid gear set with the pinion gear mounted even higher than a normal amboid set.

Torsen A biased torque differential from General Motors.

tridem Three drive axles connected by power dividers.

TruTrac A biased torque differential produced by Eaton.

worm and crown Older drive axle gear arrangement capable of very high gear reductions in a compact space. Also known as *worm wheel*.

worm wheel Older drive axle gear arrangement capable of very high gear reductions in a compact space. Also known as *worm and crown*.

Review Questions

1. In a single-speed drive axle, the differential case always travels at which of the following speeds?
   a. 50% of crown gear speed
   b. 200% of crown gear speed
   c. 0% of crown gear speed
   d. 100% of crown gear speed
2. In a normal or non-locking differential, if one axle is turning at 96% of case speed, at what speed is the other axle turning?
   a. 96% of case speed
   b. 100% of case speed
   c. 104% of case speed
   d. 92% of case speed
3. The inter-axle differential is more susceptible to spinout damage than a main differential for which of the following reasons?
   a. It is smaller than a main differential.
   b. It turns much faster than a main differential.
   c. Its differential case is smaller.
   d. It has to carry four times the torque of a main differential.
4. Which of the following describes a double reduction drive axle?
   a. The axle has two speeds.
   b. It has a helical gear mounted on either side of the differential case.
   c. It uses two reductions (a compound reduction) through the axle at all times.
   d. It is a special axle used in low floor buses.
5. When a vehicle is moving and no differential action is taking place, which of the following is a correct statement about the spider and side gears?
   a. They are stationary inside the differential case.
   b. They are moving opposite to the case direction.
   c. They are each turning opposite directions.
   d. They are free-wheeling in the same direction.
6. A double reduction helical two speed drive axle will have which of the following?
   a. A helical pinion gear and a planetary gear set
   b. A movable sun gear
   c. A helical gear attached to each side of the differential case.
   d. A helical crown and pinon and a helical gear set
7. A(n) ________ type of housing is used with a removable carrier.
   a. integral
   b. unit
   c. banjo
   d. final drive
8. Which of the following axle types will normally result in wheel loss should the axle shaft break?
   a. Semi floating
   b. Full floating
   c. 3/4 floating
   d. Non-floating
9. Lubrication in most drive axles is achieved by:
   a. a gear-driven oil pump.
   b. pinion gear pumping action.
   c. differential action.
   d. splash from the ring gears' rotation.
10. Which of the following gears are responsible for differential action?
   a. The ring and pinion gears
   b. The ring and side gears
   c. The spider and pinion gears
   d. The spider and side gears

ASE-Type Questions

1. Technician A says that drive axles allow the power from the engine to turn 90 degrees to turn the wheels. Technician B says that a drive axle usually provides the last gear reduction in a drive train system. Who is correct?
   a. Technician A
   b. Technician B
   c. Both Technician A and Technician B
   d. Neither Technician A nor Technician B
2. Technician A says that a hypoid gear set has the pinion gear mounted above the centerline of the crown wheel. Technician B says that a generoid gear set uses a stronger tooth design. Who is correct?
   a. Technician A
   b. Technician B
   c. Both Technician A and Technician B
   d. Neither Technician A nor Technician B
3. Technician A says that a differential gear set allows for drive axle wheel speed difference in turns. Technician B says that a differential gear set can allow a single wheel on a drive axle to spin wildly while the other wheel remains stationary. Who is correct?
   a. Technician A
   b. Technician B
   c. Both Technician A and Technician B
   d. Neither Technician A nor Technician B
4. Technician A says that a controlled traction differential allows the engine to build more torque in poor traction conditions. Technician B says that controlled traction differentials prevent any differential action from occurring while engaged. Who is correct?
   a. Technician A
   b. Technician B
   c. Both Technician A and Technician B
   d. Neither Technician A nor Technician B
5. Technician A says that in a tandem drive vehicle most of the driving effort is provided by the front-rear axle. Technician B says that the rear-rear drive axle only receives 50% of the available driving torque. Who is correct?
   a. Technician A
   b. Technician B
   c. Both Technician A and Technician B
   d. Neither Technician A nor Technician B
6. Technician A says that two-speed drive axles offer more speed ranges to a vehicle operator. Technician B says that two-speed helical axles use a smaller crown gear so are less apt to flex under load. Who is correct?
   a. Technician A
   b. Technician B
   c. Both Technician A and Technician B
   d. Neither Technician A nor Technician B
7. Technician A says that an inter-axle differential divides the available power between the front and rear axles of a tandem drive. Technician B says that an inter-axle differential can split the torque between the front and rear axles of a four-by-four vehicle. Who is correct?
   a. Technician A
   b. Technician B
   c. Both Technician A and Technician B
   d. Neither Technician A nor Technician B
8. Technician A says that a durapoid bevel gear tooth is stronger than a regular bevel gear tooth. Technician B says that a durapoid bevel gear set is a spiral bevel gear set. Who is correct?
   a. Technician A
   b. Technician B
   c. Both Technician A and Technician B
   d. Neither Technician A nor Technician B
9. Technician A says that an amboid gear set has the pinion mounted below the center line of the crown gear. Technician B says that an amboid gear set's crown gear teeth are concave on the drive side. Who is correct?
   a. Technician A
   b. Technician B
   c. Both Technician A and Technician B
   d. Neither Technician A nor Technician B
10. Technician A says that most inter-axle differentials today are pressure lubricated. Technician B says that the inter-axle differential lock can be engaged while the vehicle is moving as long as there is no wheel spin occurring. Who is correct?
    a. Technician A
    b. Technician B
    c. Both Technician A and Technician B
    d. Neither Technician A nor Technician B

CHAPTER 48

NATEF Tasks

Drive Train

Drive Axle

	Page
■ Identify causes of drive axle(s) drive unit noise and overheating problems; determine needed action.	1606, 1616, 1632–1637
■ Check and repair fluid leaks; inspect and replace drive axle housing cover plates, gaskets, sealants, vents, magnetic plugs, and seals.	1607–1608
■ Check drive axle fluid level and condition; determine needed service; add proper type of lubricant.	1607–1609
■ Remove and replace differential carrier assembly.	1610–1612
■ Inspect and replace components of the locking differential case assembly.	1611–1612
■ Inspect and replace drive axle shafts.	1612–1613
■ Inspect and replace differential case assembly including spider gears, cross shaft, side gears, thrust washers, case halves, and bearings.	1612–1616
■ Inspect differential carrier housing and caps, side bearing bores, and pilot (spigot, pocket) bearing bore; determine needed action.	1616–1617
■ Inspect and replace ring and drive pinion gears, spacers, sleeves, bearing cages, and bearings.	1617–1621
■ Measure and adjust side bearing preload and ring gear backlash.	1617–1624
■ Measure and adjust drive pinion bearing preload.	1618
■ Measure and adjust drive pinion depth.	1618–1620
■ Check and interpret ring gear and pinion tooth contact pattern; determine needed action.	1622–1625
■ Measure ring gear runout; determine needed action.	1624
■ Inspect, adjust, or replace ring gear thrust block/screw.	1625–1626
■ Inspect, adjust, repair, or replace air-operated power divider (inter-axle differential) lockout assembly including diaphragms, seals, springs, yokes, pins, lines, hoses, fittings, and controls.	1627–1632
■ Inspect power divider (inter-axle differential) assembly; determine needed action.	1628–1630

Servicing and Maintaining Drive Axles

Knowledge Objectives

After reading this chapter, you will be able to:

1. Describe the drive axle overhaul process and gear set backlash. (pp 1606–1617)
2. Explain the process for setting side bearing and pinion bearing preload. (pp 1617–1624)
3. Explain the meaning and purpose of pinion depth setting. (pp 1618–1620)
4. Identify correct gear set contact patterns for conventional and drive axle gearing. (p 1625)

Skills Objectives

After reading this chapter you will be able to:

1. Inspect drive axles for fluid leaks and determine the cause. (p 1607) SKILL DRILL 48-1
2. Change the lubricant and filters on a drive axle. (p 1609) SKILL DRILL 48-2
3. Remove a differential carrier. (p 1611) SKILL DRILL 48-3
4. Disassemble a differential carrier. (pp 1612–1613) SKILL DRILL 48-4
5. Disassemble a differential case. (p 1614) SKILL DRILL 48-5
6. Remove a drive pinion. (p 1615)
7. Inspect drive axle components. (pp 1616–1617)
8. Install a pinion bearing. (p 1617)
9. Set pinion depth. (pp 1618–1620)
10. Set pinion bearing preload. (p 1618) SKILL DRILL 48-6
11. Install a pinion gear. (p 1621)
12. Reassemble the differential case. (p 1622) SKILL DRILL 48-7
13. Set gear set contact patterns. (pp 1622–1623)
14. Set side bearing preload. (p 1623) SKILL DRILL 48-8
15. Measure crown gear runout. (p 1624) SKILL DRILL 48-9
16. Install a thrust screw. (pp 1625–1626)
17. Disassemble a power divider. (pp 1628–1629) SKILL DRILL 48-10
18. Reassemble a power divider. (p 1630) SKILL DRILL 48-11
19. Check the input shaft end play. (p 1630) SKILL DRILL 48-12
20. Reinstall the differential carrier or power divider assembly. (p 1631) SKILL DRILL 48-13
21. Diagnose component failures in drive axle systems. (pp 1632–1637)

Introduction

This chapter will explain the procedures involved in the overhauling and maintenance of drive axles and inter-axle tandem drives. Although most technicians will not be required to perform this work, studying this chapter will lead to a deeper understanding of the function and maintenance of heavy duty drive axles. Included in the chapter will be the procedures for the four common adjustments required for all drive axles: **pinion depth** (the position that the pinion gear is mounted in relation to the crown gear), pinion bearing **preload** (preload is negative end play), side bearing preload, and gear set backlash.

Fundamentals of Servicing Drive Axles

Proper maintenance practices are necessary to keep drive axles in service. Always stick to the OEM's recommended maintenance schedule. They have been created to ensure that the axle will have a long service life. Failure to perform maintenance in a timely fashion can result in a costly drive axle repair. Fundamental to caring properly for drive axles is knowing how and when to lubricate them.

Drive Axle Lubrication

Use of the proper lubricant is the most basic but also one of the most important aspects of drive axle maintenance. All manufacturers require drive axle lubricants to meet the API GL-5 and or the military MIL-L-2105D standard. That is true whether the lubricant is mineral based or synthetic. Most manufacturers now recommend a synthetic formulation for their drive axle lubricant. Use of synthetics allows a much longer drain interval in most applications, and synthetics can handle severe service applications. Eaton Dana specifications for synthetic drive axle lubricant are SHAES-256 Rev C for on-highway use and SHAES-429 for off-highway vocational use. The

Safety

There is no greater consideration than personal safety and the safety of others. Always keep this as priority one when performing maintenance to the vehicle drive train. There are several precautions that must be taken to minimize the risk of injury. Failure to follow these precautions may result in personal injury, vehicle damage, or death. Observing these simple rules will create the safest environment for all.

- Always make sure the vehicle is on a level surface.
- Keep the vehicle transmission in neutral whenever possible.
- Remove the vehicle keys to prevent a person from starting the vehicle with someone underneath it. Avoid going under any running vehicle unless it is absolutely necessary.
- Chock the front and back of wheels on both sides of the vehicle to positively prevent movement.
- Always wear safety glasses, and wear a bump cap/helmet while under the vehicle.

You Are the Technician

A Class 8 tractor with tandem drive axles is brought to your shop by a tow truck. The complaint is that the engine runs but the vehicle will not move. You do a preliminary investigation with a colleague and discover that the clutch and transmission seem to be okay, as the driveshaft from the transmission to the power divider turns. You can hear a loud grinding noise coming from the general direction of the power divider and recommend its overhaul. During the overhaul you find that the inter-axle differential cross is shattered. You examine the rest of the axle components and find other issues. The front and rear side gears and the spider gears of the inter-axle differential are prematurely worn and the lubricant shows signs of severe metal contamination.

1. What do you conclude from your examination of the components?
2. What do you think might have caused the broken inter-axle differential cross?
3. What replacements and or services would you recommend for this vehicle?
4. What advice would you give to the truck owner?

lubricants are available in two weights—75W-90 and 85W-140. This lubricant (also referred to simply as *lube*) meets all the performance requirements of the majority of manufacturer's standards but, as always, check the OEM manual. TABLE 48-1 lists the various SAE Grades of drive axle lubricants and the associated ambient temperature range for each.

The level of the drive axle lubricant should be checked as often as recommended by the manufacturer. Making sure that the lubricant level is correct is a simple way of avoiding sudden catastrophic failures. It also provides an opportunity to inspect the drive axle for leaks and repair them before they can cause a serious low lube level failure. For on-highway applications, Dana Spicer recommends checking the fluid level and inspecting for leaks every 12,000 miles (16,000 km). For on-/off-highway applications, the frequency increases to checking levels and inspecting for leaks every 40 hours the vehicle is in service.

TABLE 48-1: SAE Grades by Ambient Temperature Range

Grade	Ambient Temperature Range
75W	–40° F to –15° F (–40° C to –26° C)
75W-80	–40° F to 80° F (–40° C to 21° C)
75W-90	–40° F to 100° F (–40° C to 38° C)
74W-140	–40° F and above (–40° C and above)
80W-90	–15° F to 100° F (–26° C to 38° C)
80W-140	–15° F and above (–26° C and above)
85W-140	10° F and above (–12° C and above)

To check the lube level, ensure that the vehicle is level and then remove the filler plug in the axle housing. Lubricant should be level with the bottom of the hole. If the level is below this hole, add the required amount and then re-install the plug. Do not over-torque the plug. The plug should be tightened to not more than 35 ft-lb (47 Nm). Never mix synthetic and mineral lube types as they may not be compatible. If the type of fluid is in doubt, all the fluid should be replaced.

A low level of lubricant could be a sign of leakage. In fact, drive axles can be prone to leakage. Common leak points occur at the flange gasket or in the sealant where the differential carrier is bolted to the axle housing, the pinion seal, and the unit atmospheric vent. To inspect a drive axle for fluid leakage, follow the steps in SKILL DRILL 48-1.

Lube Change Intervals and Procedures

Lube change intervals are not universal. They vary depending on the vehicle vocation. TABLE 48-2 shows typical change intervals by vocation. Note, however, that some manufacturers recommend oil sampling as the basis for setting up a change schedule.

SKILL DRILL 48-1 Inspecting Drive Axles for Leaks and Determining the Cause

1. Put the vehicle on an approved lift and make sure it is secure. Visually inspect around the housing where the axle seats for any seepage.
2. Inspect the pinion flange for any seepage.
3. If necessary, remove the rear wheels and install a dial indicator on the axle flange to check for any distortion.
4. Check and clean the breather or vent for any obstructions that may cause a pressure build-up to occur.
5. Check the differential rear cover for a leaking gasket, if so equipped. Tighten it if it is loose or replace as necessary.
6. Check the fluid level for lack of fluid or overfilling of the differential, as either one can indicate that a leak is present.

TABLE 48-2: Typical Change Intervals for Drive Axle Lubricant

HEAVY-DUTY				
Synthetic or Mineral	**Lubricant**	**SAE**	**Change Interval for Line Haul**	**Change Interval for Vocational**
Synthetic	SHAES-256 Rev C	SAE 75W-90	500,000 miles (800,000 km) or 5 years	N/A
Synthetic	SHAES-429	SAE 75W-90 SAE 80W-140	N/A	180,000 miles (288,000 km) or 3 years
Mineral Base	SAE J2360	75W, 75W-90, 75W-140, 80W-90, 85W-140	120,000 miles (193,000 km) or 1 year	60,000 miles (96,500 km) or 1 year
MEDIUM-DUTY				
Synthetic or Mineral	**Lubricant**	**SAE**	**Change Interval for Line Haul**	**Change Interval for Vocational**
Synthetic	SHAES-256 Rev C	SAE 75W-90	250,000 miles (400,000 km) or 3 years	N/A
Synthetic	SHAES-429	SAE 75W-90 SAE 80W-140	N/A	180,000 miles (288,000 km) or 3 years
Mineral Base	SAE J2360	75W, 75W-90, 80W-90, 85W-140	100,000 miles (160,000 km) or 1 year	60,000 miles (96,500 km) or 1 year

Manufacturers also list change intervals for severe duty service. The severe service recommendations should be used when the vehicle consistently operates under any or all of the following conditions:

- at or near maximum GCW or GVW ratings
- in dusty or wet environments
- on grades greater than 8%

Historically, manufacturers typically have recommended an initial fluid change at 3,000 to 5,000 miles, (4,800 to 8,000 km) for their axles when mineral-based lubricant is used. The purpose of this early fluid change (or drop) was to remove metal particles normally produced by the axle gearing during the break-in period. Today, the computerized gear-manufacturing process is much more precise. Consequently, most manufacturers no longer require this initial fluid drop, as these particles are not produced. Always check the OEM manual to be sure, however. All manufacturers have eliminated this early fluid drop when the axle is filled with synthetic lube.

Regardless of the interval, drive axle lubricant does need to be changed regularly. When changing the drive axle lube, the axle should be at normal operating temperature. If working with an axle that is equipped with a lube pump, the screen or strainer should be cleaned or the filter, if present, should be replaced at the same time as the lube. SKILL DRILL 48-2 contains guidelines for changing drive axle lubricant. An important part of this procedure is ensuring wheel hubs are filled with oil to the correct level, as illustrated in FIGURE 48-1.

TECHNICIAN TIP

Some manufacturers require that the external drive axle filter, if used, be changed every 100,000 miles (160,000 km) regardless of whether synthetic or mineral-based lubrication is used.

Drive Axle Overhaul—Removal and Inspection

Most technicians will never encounter a situation where they are called upon to overhaul a drive axle—and this text does not attempt to be a comprehensive instruction guide for doing so. When it comes to overhauling, however, all drive axles share some basic similarities, and those major points will be discussed in this chapter. It cannot be stressed strongly enough that the correct OEM overhaul manual must be used to successfully overhaul a drive axle. Attempting this process without proper documentation will lead to errors and failure.

The absolute first step in overhauling a drive axle is confirming the manufacturer and model number of the component. FIGURE 48-2 shows the breakdown of a DANA model DS404-(P) tandem drive axle. Other

SKILL DRILL 48-2 Changing the Lubricant and Filters on a Drive Axle

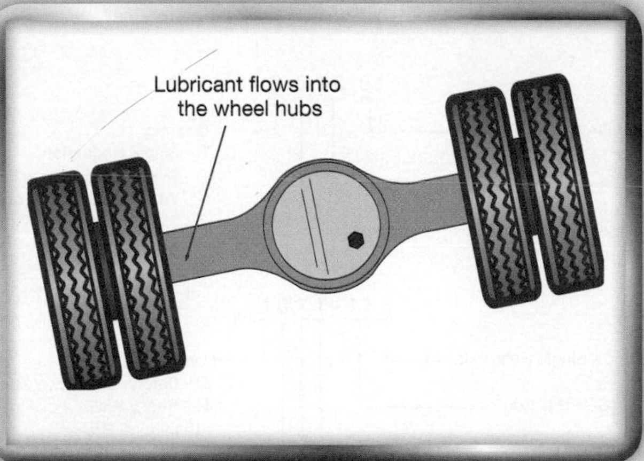

1. Remove the axle drain plug, and drain the lube into a suitable container. Allow time for the lube to drain completely. NOTE: When working with some axles, there may be more than one drain point. Consult the OEM manual for the particular model being serviced.
2. Reinstall the drain plug and torque to 35 ft-lb (47 Nm).
3. Remove the fill plug in the rear of the axle, and fill the axle with the recommended lubricant to the level of the bottom of the fill hole. NOTE: If the mounting angle of the drive axle is severe (more than 7 or 8 degrees), it may be necessary to fill from an alternate location. Check the service manual for the particular axle being serviced.
4. Raise the axle right hand side by six inches or more. Leave it sit like that for one minute before lowering the right hand side. This ensures that the wheel hubs have the correct level of lubricant.
5. Repeat Step 4 for the left hand side of the axle. Failure to perform this procedure for both sides of the axle may result in the hub bearings having a lack on lubricant and subsequent failure of the bearings!
6. Allow the axle to rest for one minute. Then check and top up the fluid as necessary until it is level with the bottom of the fill hole.
7. Reinstall the fill plug and torque to 35 ft-lb (47 Nm).

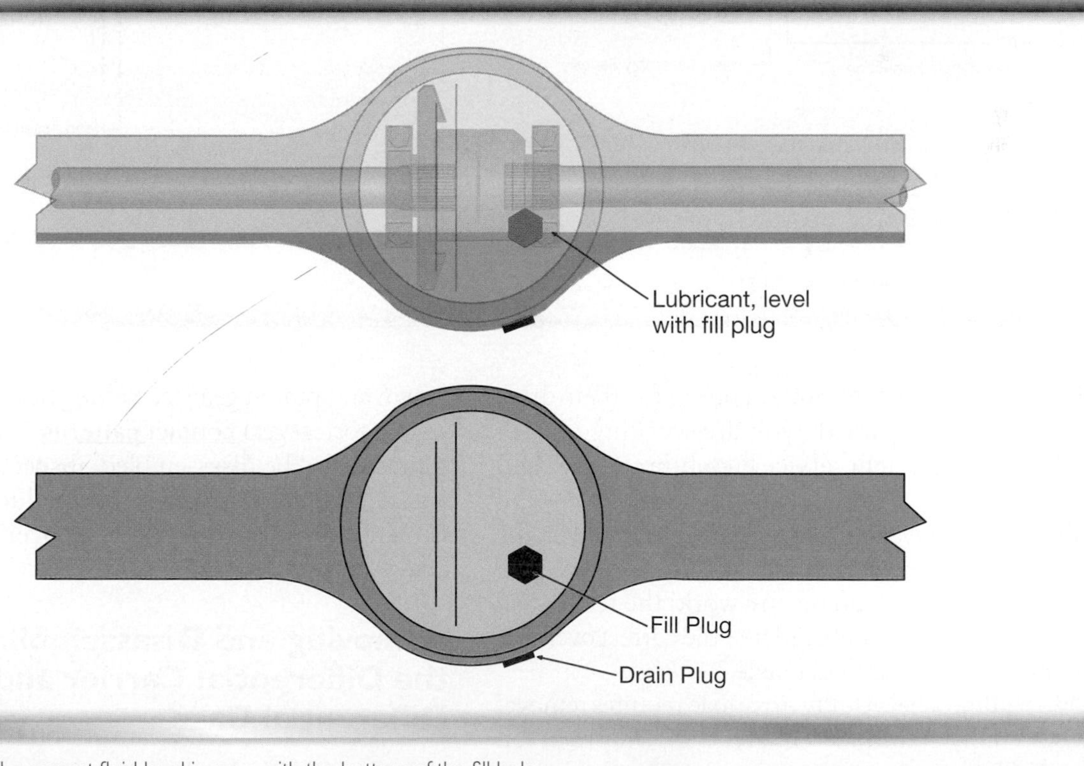

FIGURE 48-1 The correct fluid level is even with the bottom of the fill hole.

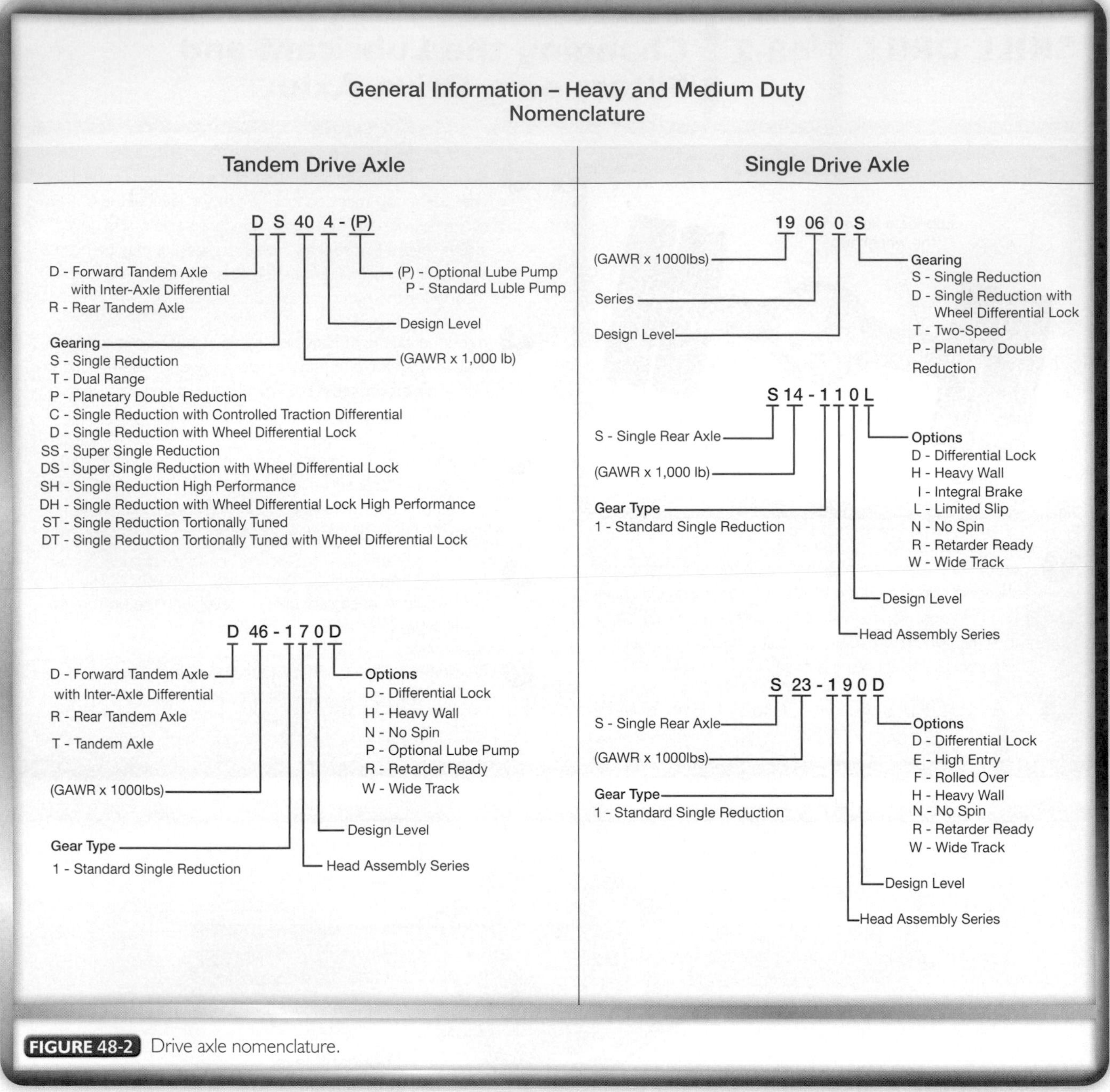

FIGURE 48-2 Drive axle nomenclature.

manufacturers will have similar coding for their drive axles. Knowing which axle you are working on will allow you to get the right service literature and the right replacement parts.

All axles will have the model number stamped on the axle or on a plate attached to the drive axle, as can be seen in **FIGURE 48-3**. Before doing any work, the technician should use the model number to find the correct overhaul information for that particular axle.

Overhauling a heavy duty drive axle requires removal and disassembly of the differential carrier. Only then can the drive axle components be inspected. The overhaul is a complex process. It requires removing, inspecting the crown and pinion gear set, setting bearing preloads, and setting correct gear **contact patterns**. The differential gear set must also be disassembled, inspected, reassembled, and reinstalled. The series of procedures in this section is merely a general overview for overhauling a typical heavy-duty drive axle.

Removing and Disassembling the Differential Carrier and Differential Case

As with most overhaul procedures, overhauling a drive axle begins with the processes of removal and disassembly.

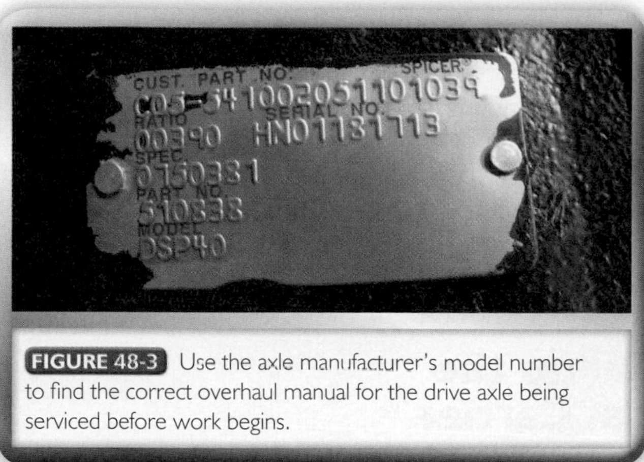

FIGURE 48-3 Use the axle manufacturer's model number to find the correct overhaul manual for the drive axle being serviced before work begins.

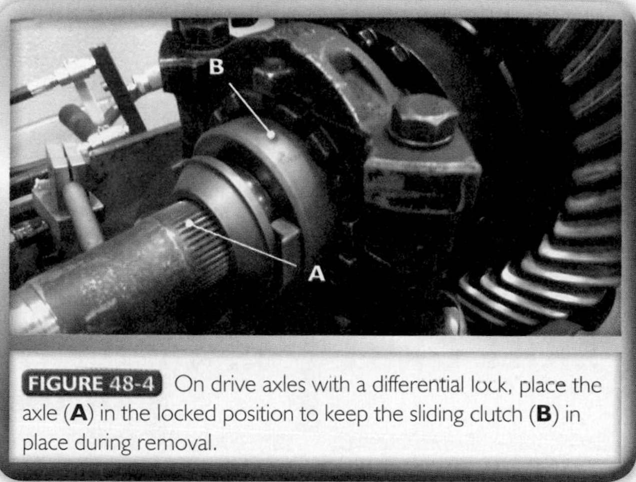

FIGURE 48-4 On drive axles with a differential lock, place the axle (**A**) in the locked position to keep the sliding clutch (**B**) in place during removal.

Specifically, the differential carrier must be removed and disassembled, and then the differential case must also be disassembled.

Safety is critical when removing the differential carrier, particularly when removing the axles only on a vehicle with a locking differential. In that case, put the axle in the locked position, as shown in **FIGURE 48-4**, and ensure it stays there. The lock sits on an outboard spline on the left axle. If the axle is removed from the vehicle when the axle is in the unlocked position, the lock will drop and it will be difficult to reinstall the axle shaft. To remove the differential carrier, follow the steps listed in **SKILL DRILL 48-3**.

SKILL DRILL 48-3 Removing the Differential Carrier

1. Support the vehicle on stands at a sufficient level that allows enough room to work beneath it and remove the differential carrier without interference from the frame and/or suspension.
2. Remove the driveshaft from the drive axle and ensure it is sufficiently out of the way to allow differential carrier removal.
3. Drain the axle fluid into a suitable container. The fluid can be an important indicator of the axle's condition. Watch for evidence of metal contamination, indicating extreme wear, or sludge, usually caused by overheating or lack of lubricant.
4. Loosen the nuts holding the axles in place at the wheel hub until they are holding by one or two threads. Leave them in place to stop the axle stud locating wedges from flying off.
5. Using a large brass drift and a hammer, strike the axle flanges to loosen the tapered locating wedges in the axles. These steel wedges center the axle shaft as it is bolted to the wheel hub.
6. Remove the nuts, wedges, and the axles and mark the axles as either right or left.
7. Support the differential carrier with a suitable floor jack and platform designed for the purpose. Restrain the front of the differential carrier to the jack. The rear side of the carrier is much heavier than the front and will try to roll off as it is removed. Before removing the differential carrier attaching bolts, ensure the carrier is securely supported.
8. Remove the differential carrier retaining cap screws or stud nuts, leaving the top two loose to hold the weight while the carrier mounting flange is loosened.
9. Loosen the differential carrier-to-housing mounting flange by using a pry bar in the pry slots on the flange or by moving the front of the housing back and forth.
10. Remove the top two retainers, pull the differential carrier forward, and lower it to the floor.
11. Mount the differential carrier in a suitable stand for overhaul.

Prior to disassembling the differential carrier, determine if the gear set is likely to be reused. If so, it is advisable to check the gear set backlash and contact pattern prior to differential carrier disassembly so that it can be reinstalled with the same settings. To disassemble the differential carrier, follow the procedure in 

.

Safety

Heavy duty driveshafts can be extremely heavy. Use a sling to support the shaft before removal!

SKILL DRILL 48-4 Disassembling the Differential Carrier

1. Mark with punch marks one of the differential side bearing bore legs (the bore in the casting that holds the side bearing races) and the bearing retaining caps (semi-circular caps that clamp the side bearing into the casting). This allows the caps to be reinstalled on the correct side.

2. If the differential carrier has a thrust screw, loosen the jamb nut and back out or remove the thrust screw. The thrust screw (circled) will be located on the ring gear side of the differential carrier housing.

3. Remove the bearing adjuster locks (cotter pins, lock plates, and so on that stop the adjusters from turning) and loosen the four (or more) bearing cap retaining cap screws. Back out the bearing adjusters (threaded rings that position the side bearings) two to three turns. Remove the bearing capscrews (A), support caps (B), and the adjusters (C). Keep each side together as a set to ensure you will be able to reinstall them in the correct location.

Continued on next page

SKILL DRILL 48-4 Disassembling the Differential Carrier, continued

4 Using a sling and a hoist, remove the differential case and crown gear as an assembly and place it on a work bench. Remove the taper roller bearings from either the differential case or the pinion gear using a wedge-type bearing puller. Place the assembly in the press with the puller vertical at first. This will allow the puller to loosen the bearing.

5 After the bearing has been loosened, retighten the wedge-type puller and install the assembly into the press horizontally to finish the removal procedure.

TECHNICIAN TIP

It may be easier to remove the side bearings after the differential case is disassembled.

6 Remove the crown gear, if replacing, by removing the retaining cap screws or drilling and punching out the rivets. The crown gear may need to be pressed off or lightly tapped off the differential case with a soft hammer. Always protect the crown gear from damage from falling.

TECHNICIAN TIP

Some differential carrier thrust screws have a thrust block swaged to the end of the screw. During the disassembly, do not remove the thrust screw completely on this type; doing so will force the block off the end of the screw.

The differential case has two halves: the **flange case half** and the **plain case half**. The crown gear is attached to the flange case half. Knowing the difference is important because disassembly of the case requires that it be placed on a bench, flange side down. To disassemble the differential case, follow the steps in SKILL DRILL 48-5.

SKILL DRILL 48-5 Disassembling the Differential Case

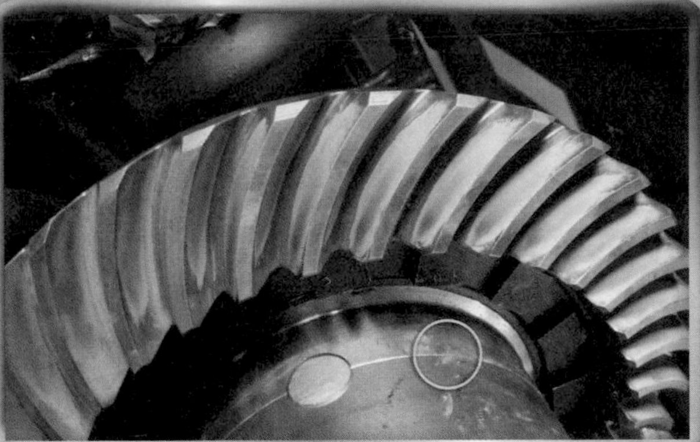

1. Place the differential case on the bench with the flange side down. Mark the differential case halves with a punch so that they can be reassembled in the correct position. Remove the differential case cap screws.

2. Remove the plain half of the differential case. The plain half of the differential case is opposite the crown gear side. It may be necessary to lightly tap the case to separate the two halves.

3. Remove the thrust washer and right hand side gear. Then remove the cross, spider gears, and their thrust washers together. Remove each spider gear and thrust washer.

4. Remove the left side gear and thrust washer and check the running surfaces of the differential case and the side gears for wear.

Safety

Not all axles have tapered locating wedges but, if they do, when the axle flange is loosened, they can fly outward from the studs and strike a person with considerable force. Always leave the stud nuts installed by a couple of threads until the axle flanges are loosened.

Removing the Drive Pinion

The drive pinion can be mounted in the differential carrier a number of different ways:

- It may be removed from the back of the differential carrier.
- It may have a pinion housing that is removed from the front of the differential carrier.
- It may simply have a pinion bearing cage bolted to the front of the differential carrier.

The last of these is by far the most popular in the heavy-duty vehicle market, and it is the type that we will discuss in this section. As always, consult the OEM manual for the particular drive axle being worked on before removing the drive pinion.

The pinion is supported by two opposing tapered roller bearings and also usually by a small **spigot bearing** (also called a **pinion pilot bearing**) that supports the pinion at the inside end. This type of mounting is called a **straddle mount pinion**. If there is no spigot bearing, the pinion mounting is known as an **overhung mount pinion**. Most heavy duty pinions are straddle mounted.

To remove the pinion yoke nut, use a yoke holding tool to stop the pinion from rotating. Pinion nuts on heavy duty axles are installed with upwards of 750 ft-lb (1,017 Nm) of torque. A torque multiplier may be necessary to remove the nut and a yoke puller, such as the one in FIGURE 48-5, may be necessary to remove the yoke.

After removing the yoke, remove the cap screws holding the pinion bearing cage to the front of the differential carrier. The **pinion bearing cage** is a plate at the front of the differential carrier that holds the two outer cups of the pinion bearings. Remove the pinion and cage as a unit. As shown in FIGURE 48-6, there will be a number of shims behind the pinion cage. It is essential that these shims are kept together as they are the pinion depth setting shims. Measure and record the thickness of the shim pack in case they are misplaced and hold the shims together with a plastic tie.

The pinion gear may be loose in the bearings. Be careful not to drop it. If necessary, use a press to push the

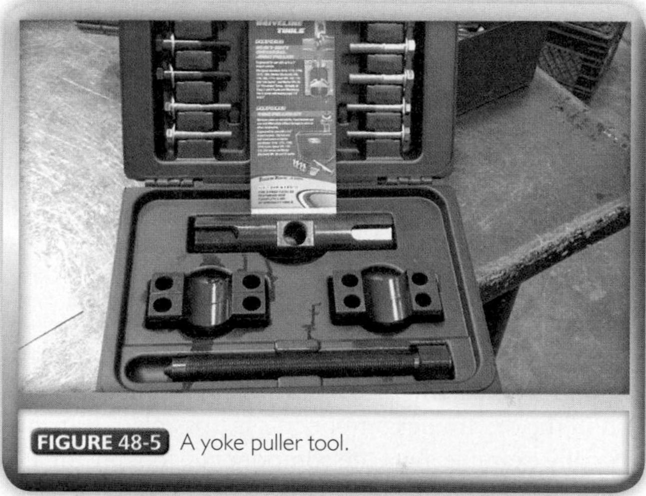

FIGURE 48-5 A yoke puller tool.

FIGURE 48-6 The correct pinion shim pack thickness is essential when reassembling the drive axle. Always measure and record the thickness and keep the shim pack together. **A.** Pinion depth setting shims. **B.** Pinion cage.

pinion out of the bearing cage. The front pinion bearing will remain in the cage and the rear bearing will come out with the pinion. Do not lose the hardened steel spacer between the two bearings—it is responsible for setting pinion bearing preload. FIGURE 48-7 shows a spacer.

Using a suitable pry bar, remove the pinion seal from the bearing cage. Doing so will free the front pinion bearing. Remove and discard the seal. Then, use a press and a suitable bearing removal puller to press the rear tapered bearing off the pinion shaft. Be sure to mount the puller vertically in the press first to start the bearing moving. Only then should you tighten the puller bolts and mount the puller horizontally to remove the bearing.

At this point, you can use the hydraulic press to remove the pinion spigot or pilot bearing from the rear of the pinion shaft, if necessary. Finally, use a puller or a soft steel drift to remove the bearing cups from the pinion cage, being careful not to damage the cage casting.

Inspecting Drive Axle Components

With the differential carrier, differential case, and drive pinion removed and/or disassembled, a careful inspection of the drive axle components is possible. Clean and carefully examine all of the components, looking for any signs of wear or damage. If a proper diagnosis was made before the axle was removed, the technician should have an idea of the kind of problem to look for.

A common problem is noise. A growling noise usually indicates one of three problems: general bearing failure; gear whine, which can be caused by worn gears; or bearing failure that allows the gear set to misalign. Clunking or banging is usually the result of gear noise. Regardless, always inspect the entire drive axle. Do not overlook the other components—even if you find the problem component right away.

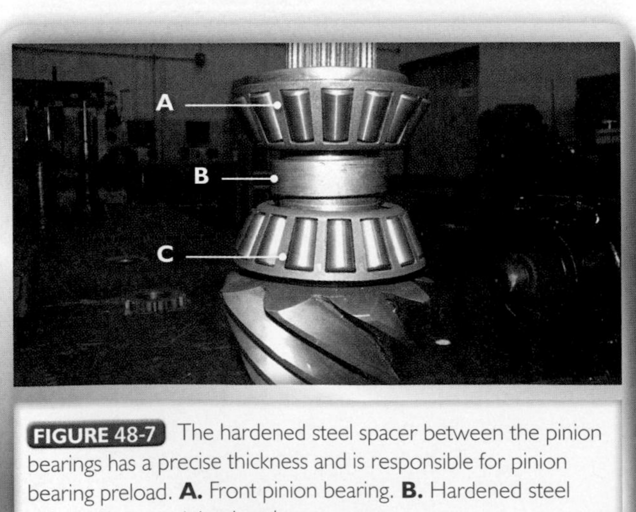

FIGURE 48-7 The hardened steel spacer between the pinion bearings has a precise thickness and is responsible for pinion bearing preload. **A.** Front pinion bearing. **B.** Hardened steel spacer. **C.** Rear pinion bearing.

If there is any doubt as to the serviceability of the problem component, replace it! The downtime necessary to redo the job makes it unfeasible to attempt reusing any questionable components. Many shops insist on replacing all bearings in a drive axle when rebuilding, regardless of their condition, as the cost of the bearings is nothing compared to having a repeat failure.

If you are reusing bearings, inspect the bearings and races very carefully. A bearing race may show signs of fatigue even while the bearing rollers still look alright. Do not be fooled! It is also difficult to see wear on the inner race of tapered roller bearings because the rollers are in the way. Make sure you check it nonetheless. Also check the bore in the differential carrier that supports the pinion spigot bearing and check the side bearings for unusual wear.

Inspect all parts for steps or grooving caused by wear. Look for any pitting or cracks on gear contact areas. Scuffing, deformation, or discoloration can be signs of excessive heat in the axle, usually caused by lubrication issues—either low lubricant level or the wrong type of lubricant. Likewise, check the teeth of the crown, pinion, and differential gears for excessive wear, pitting, and/or spalling at the contact areas.

Inspect all machined surfaces of the cast iron parts of the differential carrier and pinion cage for cracks and or scoring or obvious wear. Check for nicks or burrs on mating surfaces, and inspect all cap screws for bends, cracks, or thread damage.

After inspection, all reusable parts should be thoroughly cleaned and then lightly oiled and wrapped in rust preventative paper until reassembly.

Safety

To receive the maximum value from an axle overhaul, it is always a good idea to replace all of the lower-cost parts, thrust washers, seals, and so on. These items will prevent the axle from experiencing premature wear or loss of lubricants without adding significantly to the rebuilding cost.

The Crown and Pinion Gear Set

One component that needs special attention during inspection and throughout the overhaul process is the crown and pinion gear set. As illustrated in FIGURE 48-8, the crown and pinion gear set is a matched set and must be serviced as such. There are several numbers stamped into both the crown and the pinion gear for identification purposes. Never use a crown gear from one set with the pinion gear from another—it is a recipe for disaster.

Record the information found on the crown and pinion gears, so that the right gear set can be ordered. Heavy-duty axles are available in many different ratios and they will fit in the carrier, but the ratio could be incorrect. Installing the wrong ratio gear set can be easily done if technicians are not careful.

Drive Axle Overhaul—Reassembly

Reassembling the drive axle components begins with installing the pinion bearings. Once the pinion bearings are installed, then the bearing preload is set. After that, the pinion and the cage are reassembled into the carrier.

Regardless of the drive axle type, all drive axle overhauls will require the same four adjustments during the process. Two of the adjustments determine the gear set contact pattern and two of the adjustments ensure gear set rigidity.

The first adjustment is pinion depth. This adjustment sets the running position of the pinion gear in relation to the crown gear and affects the gear set contact pattern. Pinion depth will be discussed in the Setting Pinion Depth section.

Pinion gear bearing preload is the second adjustment. Pinion bearing preload is critical to hold the pinion gear rigid so it does not move away from the crown gear under load. Too little pinion bearing preload will allow the gear to move away from the crown gear. Too much preload, however, will cause the pinion bearing to fail rapidly. Pinion bearing preload is precisely set by steel shims. To set pinion bearing preload, follow the procedure in SKILL DRILL 48-6.

The third adjustment is side bearing preload. The side bearings support the differential case, which in turn supports the crown gear. Side bearing preload ensures that the crown gear is held rigidly and that it will not move away from the pinion gear under load. As with pinion bearing preload, too little side bearing preload will allow the crown gear to move; and too much preload will cause the side bearing to fail.

The last adjustment common to all drive axle overhauls is setting the gear set backlash. Gear set backlash allows the gears to expand while they are running. Along with the pinion depth setting, gear set backlash also controls the gear set's contact pattern.

Installing the Pinion Bearing

The basic procedure for installing pinion bearings starts by installing the tapered roller pinion bearing cups in the pinion cage. Be sure to use a suitable bearing installer that fits the cups properly. After installation, check that the cup is seated properly by checking the cup-to-seat clearance with a feeler gauge. The clearance should be less than 0.001" (0.025 mm).

Using the press, install the pinion spigot (pilot) bearing. FIGURE 48-9 shows a pinion spigot bearing. If the bearing is secured with a snap ring, install the snap ring now. If not, after installation the spigot bearing usually must be staked in position on the pinion with a staking tool.

With the spigot bearing in place, press the rear pinion tapered roller bearing on to the pinion and install it into the pinion cage. Be careful to install the correct bearing. The rear pinion may have a smaller or larger inside diameter than the front.

Finally, install the pinion bearing spacer and then the front pinion bearing. It may be necessary to press the front bearing into place on newer models with an interference fit. Lubricate the bearings liberally.

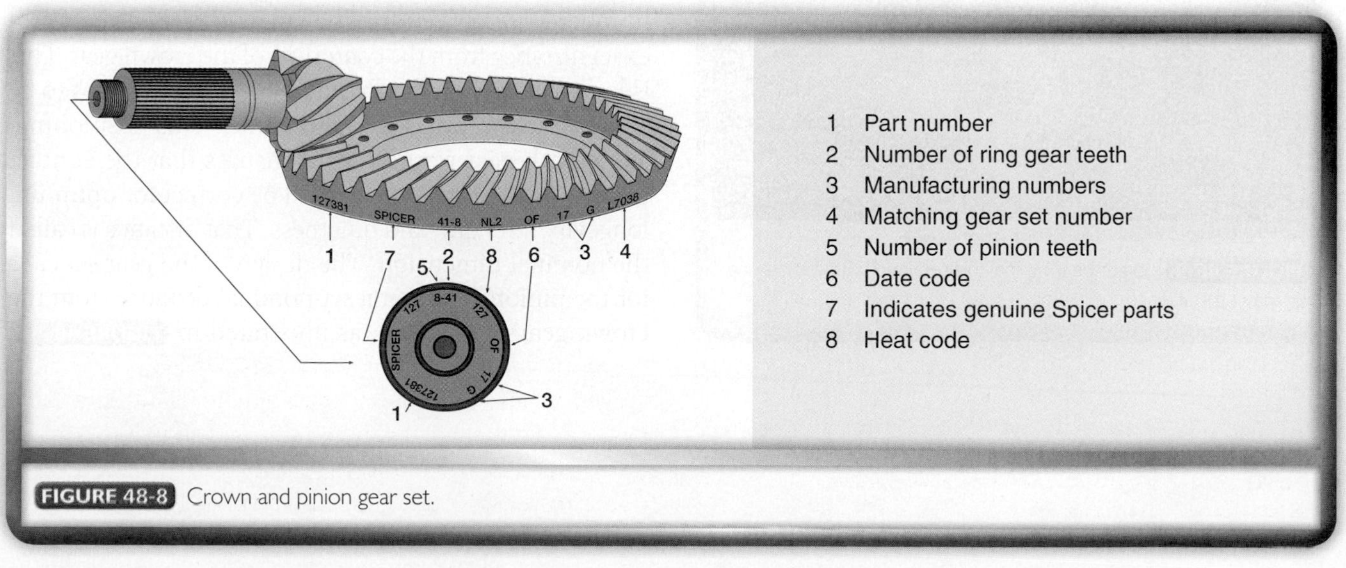

FIGURE 48-8 Crown and pinion gear set.

SKILL DRILL 48-6 Setting Pinion Bearing Preload

1. Support the pinion under a press. Then, using a correctly sized sleeve, press on the outer bearing inner race. Increase the press load to the amount recommended in the overhaul manual, typically 10 to 20 tons (9 t, 72 kg to 18 t, 144 kg). This load will accurately represent the load placed on the bearings when the pinion yoke or gear is properly torqued.
2. Tie a length of string to one of the cage mounting holes and wrap the string around the pinion cage several times. Attach a pull scale that reads in pounds or kilograms to the other end of the string. In a steady motion, start rotating the cage by hand and keep it rotating by pulling the scale.
3. Record the force required to keep the cage rotating, NOT the force required to start it rotating.
4. Multiply the pounds or kilograms pulled by the radius of the cage where the string was attached. This will indicate the rotating torque of the pinion in inch-pounds or kilograms per centimeter. Typical settings are between 15 and 30 inch-pounds or 17 and 34 kilograms/centimeter. Always check the OEM manual for the correct specification.

TECHNICIAN TIP

If replacing the pinion and crown gear, there is an additional step that must be taken to discover the correct bearing spacer to use.

5. After installing the two cage cups, oil the bearings and place them into the cage with the original spacer between them. Use the press to the correct press load, supporting the rear bearing inner race, and pressing on the outer bearing inner race. Measure the rotating torque as above, and keep adjusting the size of the bearing spacer until the torque is correct. Then select a spacer 0.001" (0.025 mm) thicker to allow for bearing growth—the bearings will enlarge slightly as they are pressed onto the pinion. This should result in the correct rotating torque on final assembly.

FIGURE 48-9 Spigot bearing may be retained with a snap ring or may be staked to the pinion.

Setting Pinion Depth

To set pinion depth, you will need the pinion variation number found on the bottom of the pinion gear. (Note that some newer pinion gears will not have a variation number.) The drive pinion of an axle is set up to sit an exact distance from the centerline of the crown gear. This is known as pinion depth. Pinion depth setting has to be accurate to within .001" (0.025mm). This positioning, along with gear set backlash, ensures that the contact pattern of the gear set teeth will be correct for optimum longevity, strength, and quietness. That distance is called the nominal dimension. The design of the gear set calls for the pinion to run at a set nominal distance from the crown gear's centerline, as illustrated in FIGURE 48-10.

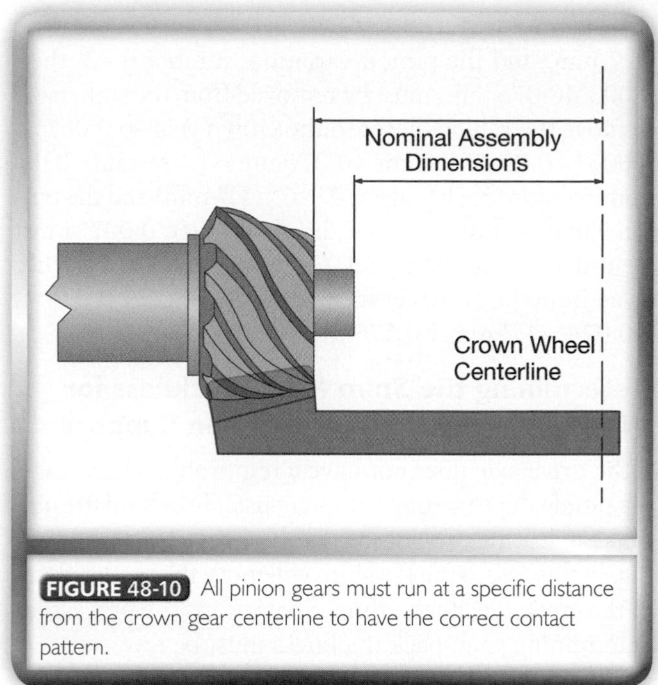

FIGURE 48-10 All pinion gears must run at a specific distance from the crown gear centerline to have the correct contact pattern.

Some pinions will have a variation number, meaning they must run at the nominal dimension plus or minus the variation amount.

Manufacturing process tolerances in the past were such that each gear set was slightly different, and each pinion would run best at a slightly different distance from the crown gear centerline. When the gear set manufacturing was completed, each set was run and lapped together on a special machine. The distance from the crown centerline was then changed until the contact pattern was perfect. So, each pinion ran best either closer to or farther away from the centerline of the crown. The pinion was then engraved with this **pinion variation number**. Positive numbers indicated a distance further away from the centerline; negative numbers indicated that the pinion was closer to the crown gear centerline. The pinion variation number shown in FIGURE 48-11 is +2. This is why crown and pinion gears were sold only as a matched set and must never be interchanged from one axle to another.

Modern drive axles, manufactured with computer-controlled machines, may not have a pinion variation number. That is because manufacturing tolerances are much finer. It is still essential, however, that the crown and pinion gear are changed as a set. In a drive axle, pinion depth is controlled in one of two ways depending on the drive axle design. When the pinion is supported by the actual axle housing, pinion depth can be controlled with shims under the rear pinion bearing cone or cup. When the pinion cage is removable, as is most common on heavy-duty axles, it can be controlled by the pinion cage shim pack, as shown in FIGURE 48-12.

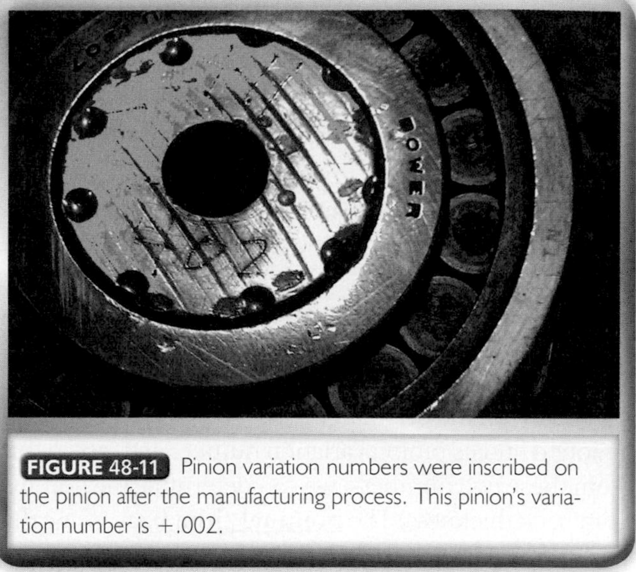

FIGURE 48-11 Pinion variation numbers were inscribed on the pinion after the manufacturing process. This pinion's variation number is +.002.

Despite being a simple process, quite often errors are made determining the shim pack thickness. If a gear set is to be reused, simply use the shims that were originally installed. After reassembly is complete, perform a contact pattern check and adjustment if necessary. If the gear set is being replaced, it will be necessary to determine the new shim pack thickness. Different procedures should

FIGURE 48-12 Pinion depth setting shims.

be followed based on whether the drive axle is fitted with a removable pinion cage or has integral pinion support.

Determining the Shim Pack Thickness for a Drive Axle with a Removable Pinion Cage

In all installations, the shim pack should consist of at least three shims. There should be a thin shim on both the outside and inside of the shim pack to promote good sealing of the pinion cage. The pinion cage, shims, and differential carrier housing all have oil return holes. These must be lined up when installing the cage.

Measure and record the thickness of the shim pack installed with the original pinion. Next, examine the old pinion to find its pinion variation number and record this. From these two numbers, we can determine the nominal shim pack thickness. The **nominal shim pack** is one that would be used if the pinion had a zero variation. If the old pinion number is negative, that means the pinion must be run closer to the crown gear centerline. Therefore, the shim pack used should have been thinner than nominal by the pinion variation number. For example, imagine you are working with a shim pack whose original shim pack thickness is 0.067" (1.7 mm) and has a pinion variation number of –5. The nominal shim pack thickness would be 0.073" (1.85 mm). That is 0.067" (1.7 mm) plus the 0.005" (0.15 mm) removed when the original pinion was installed).

If the old pinion variation number is positive, the pinion would have had to be run at the nominal distance plus the variation number. In that case, shims would have to be added to the nominal shim pack to make the pinion run correctly. To find the nominal shim pack, we would have to remove the thickness of the variation number from the original shim pack to find the nominal shim pack thickness. For example, if the original shim pack thickness is 0.067" (1.7 mm) and the old pinion variation number is +9, then the nominal shim pack would be 0.058" (1.47 mm). That is 0.067" (1.7 mm) minus the 0.009" (0.23 mm) added to make the pinion run correctly on the original installation.

Once the nominal shim pack thickness is established, check the variation number on the new pinion. If it is positive, shims will have to be added because the pinion needs to run at the nominal distance plus the variation (further away from the crown gear centerline). If the new pinion variation number is negative, shims will need to be removed because the pinion must run at nominal distance minus the variation (closer to the crown gear centerline). For example, if the nominal shim pack thickness is 0.067" (1.7 mm) and the pinion variation number is –3, then 0.003" (0.076 mm) must be removed from the shim pack to move the pinion closer to the crown gear so 0.067" – 0.003" = 0.064" (1.7mm – 0.076mm = 1.624 mm). If the nominal shim pack is again 0.067" (1.7 mm) and the pinion variation number is +7, however, then 0.007" must be added to the shim pack to move the pinion further away from the crown gear. In that case, 0.067" + 0.007" = 0.074" (1.7 mm + 0.178 mm = 1.88 mm).

Determining the Shim Pack Thickness for a Drive Axle with Integral Pinion Support

If the drive axle does not have a removable pinion cage, the pinion depth setting shims are usually behind the pinion rear bearing cone or the rear bearing cup in the housing. In this case, a thicker shim will move the pinion closer to the crown gear centerline. That means the process for determining shim pack thickness must be reversed.

If the original shim is 0.050" (1.27 mm) and the old pinion variation number is –6, it still means that the pinion must run 0.006" (0.152 mm) closer to the crown gear centerline. Because of the shim's position, however, we would have to have used a shim 0.006" (0.152 mm) thicker than normal to move the pinion closer to the crown gear. To find the nominal shim thickness, we subtract the 0.006" (0.152 mm) variation from the original shim of 0.050" (1.27 mm) to arrive at a nominal shim thickness of 0.044" (11.2 mm).

Conversely, if the original shim is 0.050" (1.27 mm) and the old pinion variation number is +3, that means that the pinion has to run 0.003" (0.076 mm) further away from the crown gear centerline. Consequently, when the axle was originally set up at the factory a shim pack 0.003" (0.076 mm) thinner than a nominal shim pack must have been used. To find the nominal shim pack in this example, we take the original shim thickness of 0.050" (1.27 mm) and add the 0.003" (0.076 mm) that would have been taken away to move the pinion further away from the crown gear centerline. Doing so gives us a nominal shim thickness of 0.053" (1.35 mm).

Once we have the nominal shim thickness, we check the new pinion variation number. If it is negative, it means that the pinion must run closer to the crown gear centerline, and a thicker shim will be needed to push the pinion toward the crown gear. For example, if the nominal shim thickness is 0.064" (1.63 mm) and the pinion variation is –5, the pinion must run 0.005" (0.127 mm) closer to the crown gear centerline. Because of the shim position, we have to add 0.005" (0.127 mm) to the shim to push the pinion gear back toward the crown gear so the shim would have to be 0.069" (1.76 mm). If the new pinion variation number is positive, we need to move the pinion away from the crown gear to make it run correctly. Therefore, a thinner shim would be required. For example if nominal shim thickness is again 0.064" (1.27 mm) and the pinion variation is +6, we must move the pinion 0.006" (0.152 mm) further away from the pinion for it to run correctly. Because of the shim position, we must use a shim 0.006" (0.152 mm) thinner, so 0.064" – 0.006" = 0.058" (1.27 mm – 0.152 mm = 1.118 mm).

This all may seem confusing, but remember this simple fact: If a pinion variation number is positive, it must run that number of thousandths of an inch *further away* from the crown gear, and if it is negative, it must run that number of thousandths of an inch *closer* to the crown gear. Finding the correct nominal shim dimension first eliminates errors caused by trying to add or subtract numbers that are positive and negative. Start with nominal shim pack (which is a zero variation shim thickness) and then move the pinion closer if negative and further away if positive by the variation number marked on the new pinion.

Setting Pinion Bearing Preload

Once the pinion bearing is installed, the next step in reassembling the drive axle is to set the bearing pinion preload. Pinion bearing preload is extremely important, as it ensures that the pinion remains rigid in the axle and will not move away from the crown gear as load is applied. Correct pinion bearing preload also ensures that the bearings are not overtightened. The preload must be set correctly or failure of the axle is likely.

Pinion bearing preload is controlled by the hardened steel spacer between the inner and outer pinion bearings. To increase preload, decrease the thickness of the spacer. A basic procedure for setting pinion bearing preload is given in Skill Drill 48-6, which is a typical pinion bearing preload setting procedure. Some drive axles use different methods. For example, lighter duty axles use a collapsible spacer between the bearing and preload is set by tightening the yoke to crush the spacer until preload is correct. (Never reuse a collapsible spacer!) Still other axles will use shims under the inner race of the front pinion bearing. Following the proper documentation for the particular axle you are working on is essential.

Installing the Pinion Gear

Once correct pinion preload has been determined, use the correct installation tool and install a new pinion oil slinger and yoke seal. An **oil slinger** is a metal ring designed to throw oil to assist lubrication. Install the pinion yoke and torque the pinion nut to the specification. The pinion nut may be reused if the nylon locking material is still in good shape. If not, replace the nut.

The pinion nut torque specification will vary widely depending upon which axle is being worked on. Pinion nut torque is seldom less than 550 ft-lb (760 Nm) and can be as high as 1,500 ft-lb (2,033 Nm). The use of a torque multiplier is strongly recommended. After the pinion is reinstalled in the pinion cage, it is time to check and set the pinion depth.

Reassembling the Differential Case and Differential Carrier

After setting the pinion depth, you can begin the process of reassembling the differential case and the differential carrier. Recall from the Removing and Disassembling the Differential Carrier and Differential Case section that removing and disassembling the carrier preceded the removal and disassembly of the case. The reassembly process occurs in reverse order. That is, the differential case must be reassembled before reassembling the differential carrier. To reassemble the differential case, follow the steps in **SKILL DRILL 48-7**.

Reassembling the differential carrier involves several key procedures, including setting the side bearing preload, checking the crown gear run out, setting gear contact patterns, and installing the thrust screw—in that order.

Setting Side Bearing Preload

Several methods are available for setting side bearing preload. Some manufacturers recommend tightening the bearing adjuster until there is no play in the bearings and then tightening two or more extra notches. Others recommend measuring the distance between the bearing caps and tightening the adjusters until the bearing caps are pushed outwards by a certain amount—indicating preload. Still others recommend using the rotating torque method used in pinion bearing preload setting. (That method only works when the pinion is not installed.) The fourth method—which is by far the easiest—is listed

SKILL DRILL 48-7 Reassembling the Differential Case

1. Press the side bearing cones on the differential case halves using a suitable driving sleeve that pushes on the inner race.
2. Assemble the differential gears and the case as follows:
   a. Put one thrust washer and side gear into the flange case half.
   b. Place the spider gears on the spider or cross and the spider gear thrust washers into place.
   c. Install the other side gear and its thrust washer.
   d. Lining up the match marks made before disassembly, install the plain case half over the assembled differential gear and torque to specification, typically in the area of 115 to 130 ft-lb (156 to 176 Nm). Check the OEM manual for the correct specifications.
3. Check the rotation of the differential gears. They may require up to 50 ft-lb (68 Nm) torque to rotate. Check the OEM manual for the specification. If the required torque is higher than specified, it indicates a problem. Disassemble and recheck the gears for damage. The gears may turn at lower torque values but there should be no perceptible play in the gears.
4. Install the crown gear onto the flange half of the differential case and tighten the nuts and bolts to specification. Note that some crown gears may need light heating to fit on to the flange. Always heat in an oven to no more than the specified temperature or damage to the gear will occur. NEVER use an oxy-acetylene torch to heat the gear as its manufacturer's heat treating will be destroyed.

step-by-step in SKILL DRILL 48-8. Note that the process can be accomplished using bearing adjusting tools that can be bought from an aftermarket supplier or they can be fabricated, like the one pictured in FIGURE 48-13.

Checking Crown Gear Runout

After the differential case and crown gear are installed, crown gear runout should be checked. Significant runout will cause problems with the gear set. Check for crown gear runout by following the procedure in SKILL DRILL 48-9.

Setting Gear Set Contact Patterns

The **gear set contact pattern** is the indication as to where the gears will contact each other during operation. The correct contact pattern is essential to ensuring that the gears are meshed correctly and will provide maximum strength and endurance. In order to check the pattern, the technician must know and understand the names of the surfaces of the crown gear teeth. The technician must also know which side of the crown gear tooth is the coast side and which is the drive side. In spiral bevel and hypoid gear sets, the drive side of the crown gear is the convex side of the tooth. In amboid gear sets, the drive side of the crown gear is the concave side of the tooth.

Gear Tooth Nomenclature

After assembly of any drive axle, it is essential that the contact pattern is checked. All conventional drive axles using hypoid gearing have the same desired hand-rolled contact pattern. Study the names of the tooth surfaces shown in FIGURE 48-14 to ensure the contact pattern check is performed correctly and the results can be properly interpreted. The contact pattern itself will consist of a **lengthwise bearing** along the **tooth face** from the **toe** to the **heel** and a **profile bearing** between the **top land** and the **root**. The correct contact pattern ensures that, as the gear set is loaded, the contact will spread toward the heel of the tooth, along its face width, so the whole tooth can carry the load. If the contact pattern runs off the tooth face at any point, the gear set will make noise. A whining noise will be heard on acceleration or deceleration depending on where the pattern runs off the tooth. This type of contact also weakens the gear set as less than the entire tooth is involved in carrying the load.

The pattern is checked on the drive side of the crown gear teeth. To check contact pattern, six or more teeth of the crown gear are lightly marked on their drive side with a tooth marking compound. The crown gear is then turned in a reverse direction while a resistance load is

SKILL DRILL 48-8 Setting Side Bearing Preload

1. Lubricate the differential side bearings and install the differential case with the bearing cups into the differential carrier.
2. Install the adjusters and the bearing caps, aligning the match marks on the cap and differential carrier bearing bore that were made at disassembly. Be very careful to ensure that the adjuster threads are not cross-threaded. Take some time and make sure they are in place correctly. Do not try to thread them in from the outside of the cap. Tighten the cap screws on the bearing cap finger tight or lightly tighten with a wrench until the caps are flush to the differential carrier.
3. Adjust the plain case half—the side opposite the crown gear—bearing adjuster outward until one thread is visible outboard of its bearing cap.
4. Install a magnetic base dial indicator so that the finger indicates the back of one of the crown gear teeth. Keep checking for backlash until the crown gear is tight against the pinion gear and all backlash is eliminated.
5. Tighten the flange side adjuster using a bearing adjusting tool, while checking for gear set backlash until there is no backlash (i.e., the crown gear is pushed up against the pinion gear).
6. Rotate the crown gear through one full rotation, again checking for gear set backlash, and tighten the adjuster at the point where the most backlash is measured until again there is no backlash. This ensures that the side bearings are properly seated.
7. Tighten the plain side bearing adjuster until measured backlash is approximately 0.002" (0.051 mm). This backlash proves that the bearing caps have moved outward from the pressure and establishes the correct amount of side bearing preload.
8. Set the gear set backlash to the specification. That is typically between 0.006" and 0.018" (0.152 and 0.457 mm) for new gearing. If using the old crown and pinion, set backlash to the amount measured before disassembly. To set backlash while maintaining the side bearing preload, back off one bearing adjuster and tighten the other one by the exact same amount. This way the crown gear can be moved toward the pinion gear (to decrease backlash) or away from the pinion gear (to increase backlash) without changing the side bearing preload already established.
9. When backlash is correct, torque the cap screws on the side bearing caps to the specification, which can be in excess of 350 ft-lb (488 Nm) on heavy-duty drive axles.

FIGURE 48-13 Bearing adjusting tool fabricated in the shop.

applied to the pinion by having an assistant hold the pinion. The load increases the chance of getting a good view of the pattern. Rotate the marked teeth through mesh in one direction a couple of times, then bring the marked teeth to the top to read the pattern.

A good, conventional hypoid pattern has the following three elements:

1. The pattern must start near but clear of the toe of the tooth.
2. The pattern should cover at least 50% of the crown gear tooth face width.
3. The pattern should be centered between the top land and the root of the tooth.

SKILL DRILL 48-9 Measuring Crown Gear Runout

1. Locate and follow the appropriate procedure in the service manual.
2. Complete the accompanying job sheet or work order with all pertinent information.
3. Place a dial indicator with magnetic base to the differential carrier's flange.
4. Position the plunger or pointer against the back of the ring gear, and set the dial indicator to zero. Make sure the indicator is stable. If not stable, you may get an inaccurate reading.
5. Rotate the ring gear and differential while reading the dial indicator.
6. Record the total indicated runout (TIR) by adding the high and low spots. For example [+ .010" (0.254 mm)] + [–0.003" (0.0762 mm)] would be 0.013" (0.330 mm) TIR.
7. Check total against manufacturer's specifications. Total runout should not normally exceed 5" (0.2 mm). If runout exceeds specifications, the differential and ring gear assembly must be removed from the carrier, and Steps 8, 9, and 10 must be completed. If runout is within specifications, the procedure is complete.
8. Check all parts of the differential and carrier for the damage that caused the runout to exceed specifications.
9. Repair or replace parts.
10. Reinstall differential and ring gear into the carrier and recheck runout.
11. List the test results and/or recommendations on the job sheet or work order, clean work area, and return tools and materials to proper storage.

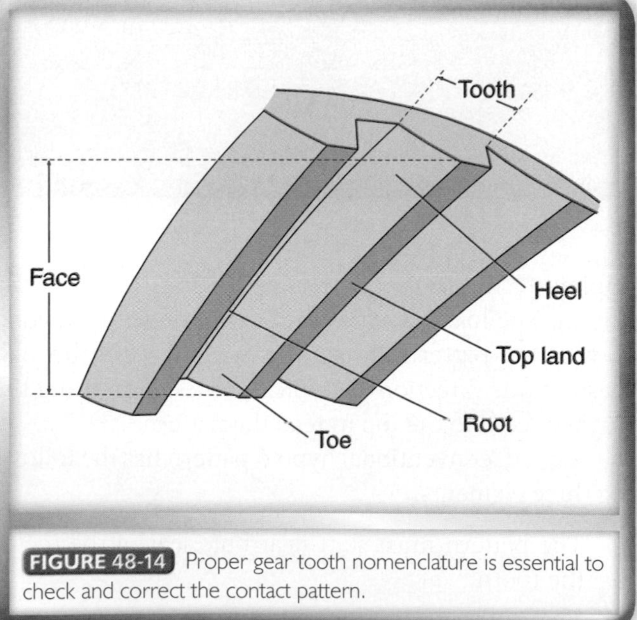

FIGURE 48-14 Proper gear tooth nomenclature is essential to check and correct the contact pattern.

The diagram in **FIGURE 48-15** illustrates the correct pattern for new hypoid gearing.

Actual contact patterns, however, are slightly different than the one illustrated. **FIGURE 48-16** shows an actual correct contact pattern for new conventional gearing. Notice that the pattern is more oval but meets the three criteria of being clear of the toe, covering half of the tooth face, and being centered between the top land and the root.

The difference in pattern shape is caused by the slight crowning of new teeth. The pattern will flatten out as the gears wear together. As a gear set wears more and more, it will create a pattern with more of a pocket (or V) shape toward the heel end of the tooth. Nonetheless, the gear set will still have the same three elements of starting near the toe, having 50% or more of the tooth covered, and being centered between the top land and the root.

The two elements of drive axle assembly that affect contact pattern are the gear set backlash and the pinion

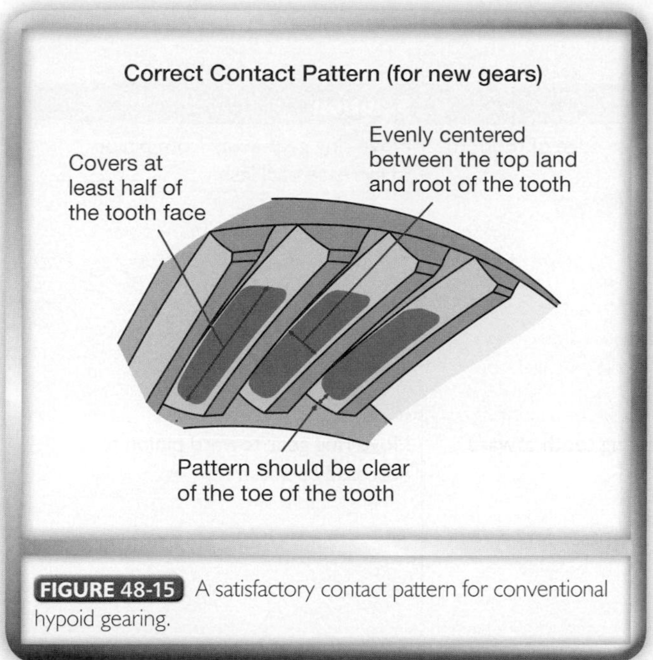
Correct Contact Pattern (for new gears)
Covers at least half of the tooth face
Evenly centered between the top land and root of the tooth
Pattern should be clear of the toe of the tooth

FIGURE 48-15 A satisfactory contact pattern for conventional hypoid gearing.

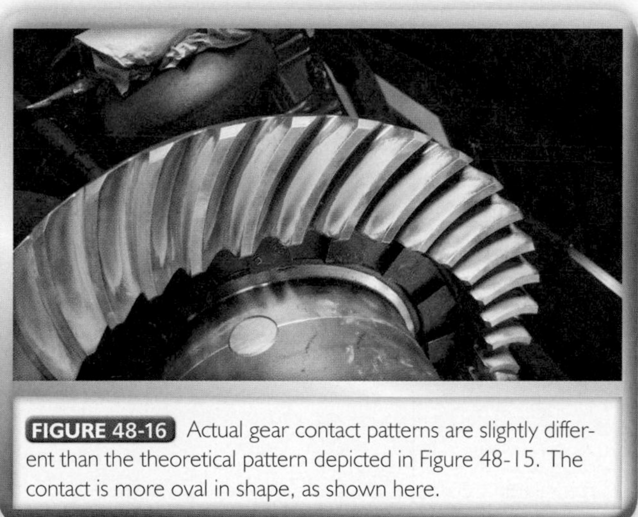

FIGURE 48-16 Actual gear contact patterns are slightly different than the theoretical pattern depicted in Figure 48-15. The contact is more oval in shape, as shown here.

depth setting. The gear set backlash affects the positioning of the pattern along the face width of the tooth. Increasing backlash will move the pattern along the tooth face toward the heel of the tooth and decreasing backlash will move the pattern along the tooth face toward the toe of the tooth. The pinion depth setting will affect the position of the contact pattern between the top land and the root of the tooth. Moving the pinion gear mounting closer to the axial center of the crown gear will move the pattern down the tooth face toward the root of the tooth while moving the pinion further away from the axial center of the crown gear will cause the pattern to move up the tooth face toward the top land of the tooth. The adjustments are somewhat interrelated in that, if the pinion gear is moved closer to the crown gear's center, it will move deeper into mesh and will decrease backlash; conversely, if the pinion is moved further from the center, backlash will increase. When a pattern adjustment is necessary, always adjust the pinion position first, if necessary, and then readjust backlash. TABLE 48-3 shows incorrect patterns and what has to be done to correct them. Take caution, though, if you have to move the pinion toward the crown gear's center. This action decreases backlash. So the crown gear should be moved away from the pinion before the pinion gear is repositioned. If this is not done, there may not be sufficient clearance for the deeper meshed pinion. This could cause damage to the gear faces.

Durapoid Spiral Bevel Gearing and Generoid Gearing Contact Patterns

Most gear sets that a technician will come across will use the conventional pattern described previously. Mack has used Durapoid Spiral bevel gearing, however, in several of their drive axles. This gearing has a different contact pattern. The same is true for hypoid or amboid generoid gearing, which looks very similar to conventional hypoid and amboid gearing, but which also has a different contact pattern. Generoid gearing has been used by Rockwell in the past and Meritor is using it in some of their drive axles. These gear sets are described in detail in the Heavy-Duty Truck Drive Axles chapter. Both durapoid spiral bevel and hypoid generoid gear sets have a centralized contact pattern, meaning that the hand-rolled pattern is centered along the face of the crown gear tooth and is also centered between the top land and the root. This is because, as these gear sets are loaded, the tooth contact spreads in both directions along the face of the crown gear tooth rather than front to back as in the conventional hypoid and amboid gears. FIGURE 48-17 is a depiction of a correct centralized pattern for both durapoid and generoid gear sets.

Without the proper OEM documentation for the axle being worked on, a technician may be fooled by this type of gearing and try to set a pattern that is unachievable. Always have the correct OEM manual for the drive axle being worked on.

Installing the Thrust Screw

If the drive axle has a thrust screw, like that shown in FIGURE 48-18, it should be adjusted after the gear set contact pattern is correctly adjusted. The typical adjustment

TABLE 48-3: Troubleshooting Tooth Patterns

Incorrect Pattern	Problem	Solution
Pattern too close to toe	Pattern too close to edge of tooth toe	Move ring gear away from pinion to increase backlash
Pattern too close to heel	Pattern too far along tooth toward tooth heel	Move ring gear toward pinion to decrease backlash
Pattern too close to tooth root	Pattern too close to tooth root	Move pinion away from ring gear, (add shims)
Pattern too close to top land	Pattern too close to tooth top land	Move pinion toward ring gear (remove shims)

of the thrust screw involves tightening the screw to a set torque or just until it contacts the back of the crown gear. Then, the screw is backed out a certain amount, usually 1/4 to 1/2 turn. Finally, the lock nut is torqued to specification while the screw is held stationary.

The thrust block normally does not contact the crown wheel during operation. Instead, it runs with approximately 0.010" to 0.020" (0.254 and 0.508 mm) running clearance. Contact with the thrust screw is made only when the crown gear flexes under heavy load.

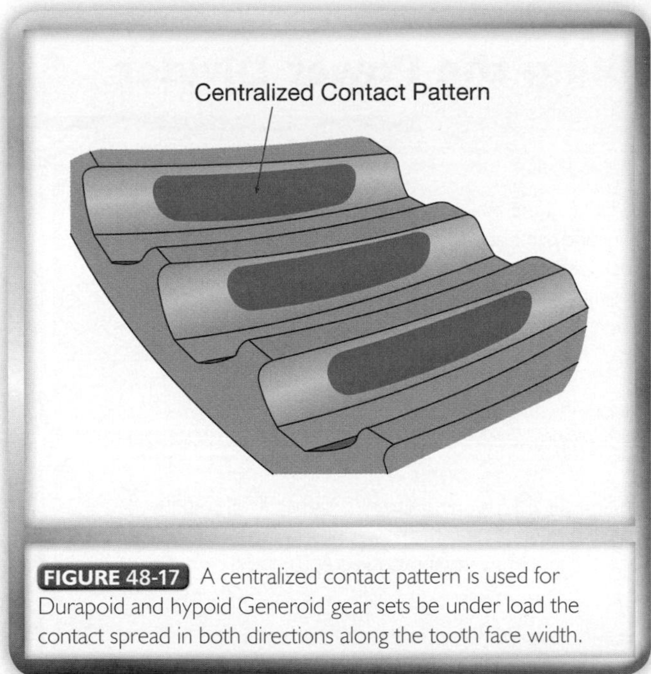

FIGURE 48-17 A centralized contact pattern is used for Durapoid and hypoid Generoid gear sets be under load the contact spread in both directions along the tooth face width.

FIGURE 48-18 Tighten the thrust screw until it contacts the back of the crown gear, then back it out ¼ to ½ turn (check OEM documentation for exact specification). This will establish the correct running clearance of between 0.010" and 0.020" (0.254 and 0.508 mm).

Overhauling the Inter-Axle Differential (Power Divider)

The power divider, shown in FIGURE 48-19, has two components: the inter-axle differential (the "power divider") and the main (or wheel) differential. The power divider removal procedures are very similar to the differential carrier removal procedure described in the Removing and Disassembling the Differential Carrier and Differential Case section. The overhaul procedures for the power divider's normal drive axle crown and pinion gear set and a main differential for wheel speed differences is very similar to the drive axle overhaul procedures discussed in the Drive Axle Overhaul—Removal and Inspection section, with the exception that it will have a drop gear attached to the axle drive pinion rather than a yoke. Therefore, this section will discuss the overhaul procedures for the power divider's inter-axle differential components only.

FIGURE 48-19 A power divider will have a normal wheel differential and an inter-axle differential.

The power divider assembly can be removed with the remainder of the main differential carrier mounted in the axle housing, by splitting the power divider housing from the main differential carrier, or with the entire assembly removed in a similar fashion to the differential carrier removal discussed in the Removing and Disassembling the Differential Carrier and Differential Case section. The only difference is that the assembled differential carrier and inter-axle differential is much heavier and more awkward to handle. Exercise extreme caution to ensure the safe removal of the unit.

Whether the differential carrier is removed with the inter-axle differential or not, the overhaul procedure is the same. We will proceed assuming the entire unit has been removed and mounted on a suitable stand.

To disassemble the power divider, follow the steps in SKILL DRILL 48-10. To reassemble it, follow the steps in SKILL DRILL 48-11. To check the input shaft endplay, follow the guidelines in SKILL DRILL 48-12 in conjunction with the

SKILL DRILL 48-10 Disassembling the Power Divider

1. Turn the support stand so that the power divider housing is facing up. Loosen the input yoke attaching nut and use a suitable puller to remove the yoke. Remove the cap screws and lock washers that secure the power divider housing to the differential carrier housing and use a sling and hoist to lift the housing clear.

2. If the power divider housing is tight to the differential carrier, lightly tap the drive yoke to loosen it or tap the housing near the dowel pins to break it free. Always support the weight of a component with appropriate equipment.

3. Remove the power divider assembly and place it on a work bench. Remove the inter-axle differential from the differential carrier housing and set aside. The inter-axle differential may be welded together and non-serviceable. If that is the case, it must be replaced.

4. Remove the front side gear/drop gear of the inter-axle differential by removing the snap ring holding the front side gear/drop gear to the input shaft. Then remove the side gear/drop gear, the thrust washer, and "D" washer (if equipped). Set everything aside. If not already removed, remove the input yoke. Hold the yoke in a holding fixture to remove the nut. The torque on this nut is usually in excess of 1,000 ft-lb (1,355 Nm). Use a puller, if necessary, to remove the yoke from the input shaft.

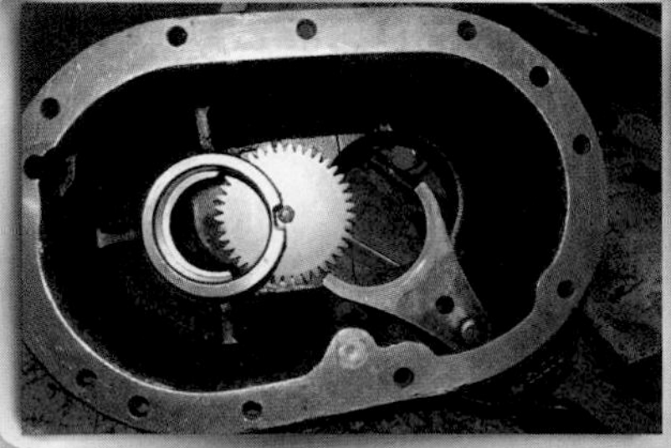

5. Remove the nut that secures the oil pump drive gear and remove the gear. Remove the differential lock cylinder from the front of the housing. Remove the shift bar nut and the shift piston and spring.

Continued on next page

SKILL DRILL 48-10 Disassembling the Power Divider, continued

6. Remove the shift bar and yoke and the inter-axle differential sliding clutch from the rear of the housing. (This may have to done as the input shaft is removed.)

7. Remove the cap screws and washers securing the input shaft bearing cage to the front of the housing. Remove the input bearing cage and its shim pack. Measure and record the shim pack thickness for use on reassembly. Be careful not to misplace the shims—these shims are responsible for setting input shaft endplay, and you will need them during reassembly.

8. Remove the input shaft from the front of the housing.

9. Remove the cap screws holding the oil pump cover to the front of the housing and remove the oil pump. Discard the seal. Remove the magnetic lube strainer screen from the power divider front cover. Remove the pipe plug in the front cover to aid in cleaning the housing lube passages. Use the inter-axle differential sliding clutch to press the input bearing from the input shaft. Place the sliding clutch on the input shaft against the back of the bearing, with clutching teeth up, and press the bearing off.

10. Remove the output shaft by pulling it up and out of the differential carrier cover. Discard the two O-rings. Remove the output shaft snap ring and remove the side gear and bearing. Replace the bearing by pressing it off the side gear with a suitable bearing puller. Replace the output shaft bearing cup in the housing. Clean all components and inspect carefully, as described previously, to determine suitability for reuse. Clean lube passages in the power divider cover.

TECHNICIAN TIP

Late model drive axles may be equipped with a spring and thrust button mounted between the input shaft and output shaft. Take care not to lose these components

TECHNICIAN TIP

At this point, if overhaul of the power divider drive axle portion is necessary, follow the procedure for drive axle overhaul discussed in the Drive Axle Overhaul—Removal and Inspection section.

SKILL DRILL 48-11 Reassembling the Power Divider

TECHNICIAN TIP

Older model inter-axle differentials could be overhauled, but late model units are permanently welded and must be replaced if there is any sign of excessive wear.

1. Press a new bearing onto the output shaft side gear. Install it on the output shaft, and install the snap ring. Install two new O-rings.
2. Replace the output shaft bearing cup in the housing and install the output shaft. If the output shaft has a spring and button, install them now.
3. Install the inter-axle differential.
4. Reassemble the input shaft by pressing on a new bearing cone and installing the side gear/drop gear and the snap ring.
5. Slide the differential lock sliding clutch over the shaft and fit the shift yoke and bar into the groove on the sliding clutch.
6. Reinstall the oil plug, the magnetic strainer, the oil pump gears, and the oil pump cover with a new O-ring seal.
7. Install the oil pump drive gear and retaining nut.
8. Slide the assembled shaft into place in the cover, feeding the shift yoke bar through the hole.
9. Install a new bearing cup and yoke seal in the input shaft bearing retainer cap and install it with the original shim pack. Leave the cap screws finger tight only.
10. Use a silicone-based gasket compound and install the assembled cover on the differential carrier. Tighten the cap screws to specification.

SKILL DRILL 48-12 Checking Input Shaft End Play

1. With the power divider cover installed, remove the input shaft bearing retainer and the shim pack. Hold the bearing retainer against the power divider cover with finger pressure and measure the clearance between the retainer and the cover with a feeler gauge.
2. Add 0.005" (0.127 mm) to the measurement above if new gearing is installed and 0.015" (0.381 mm) if the old gearing was reused. This will result in the proper endplay of 0.003" to 0.007" (0.076 to 0.178 mm) for new gearing and 0.013" to 0.017" (0.330 to 0.432 mm) for used gearing.
3. Install the correct amount of shims, then torque the bearing retainer cap screws to specification and recheck the endplay. If the endplay is in the correct range, install an input yoke washer and torque the retaining nut to specification.

torque chart in TABLE 48-4. To reinstall the differential carrier or power divider assembly, follow the procedure outlined in SKILL DRILL 48-13. Note that the procedures for reinstalling a differential carrier and a power divider are almost identical, so the general procedures in Skill Drill 48-13 apply to both.

TABLE 48-4: Torque Chart

Size	Torque in ft-lb	Torque in Nm
Input Shaft Nut		
1-5/8 – 18	780–960	1057–1301
M42 X 1.5	840–1020	1140–1383
Size	**Torque in ft-lb**	**Torque in Nm**
Bearing Cover Cap Screw		
1/2 – 13 (Grade 5)	75–85	101–115

Safety

Disassembling the power divider can be done with the differential carrier still installed in the axle housing. In that case, as the power divider housing cap screws are removed, the housing may suddenly fall free of the differential carrier. Make sure that the power divider is securely supported before proceeding. Also, take steps to ensure that the inter-axle differential does not fall from the differential carrier housing when the inter-axle housing is removed.

Diagnosing Component Failures in Drive Axle Systems

Failure analysis is a very important component of a technician's skill set. The ability to determine what, specifically, caused a failure to occur is essential to performing a complete repair and not having a repeat failure. If a power divider is disassembled and a broken inter-axle

SKILL DRILL 48-13 Reinstalling the Differential Carrier or Power Divider Assembly

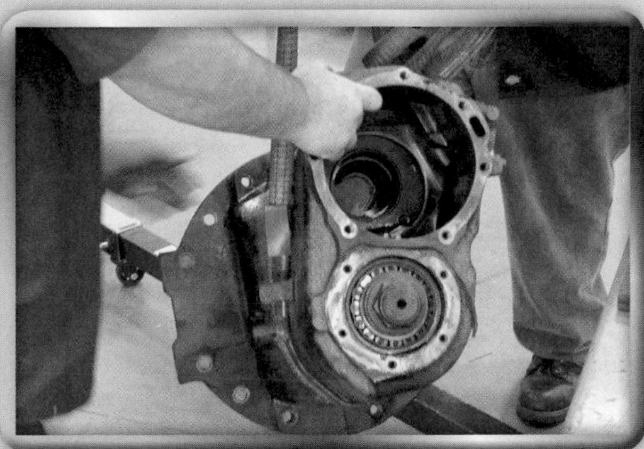

1. Clean the axle housing interior with rags and a mild solvent to remove any metal particles. Clean flange mounting surface of all old gasket material.
2. Run a new bead of silicone gasket compound or install a new gasket. Install the differential carrier by reversing the removal process.
3. Install both axle shafts with a new gasket—installing the locating wedges and nuts. Torque the nuts to the correct specification.
4. Connect all air lines. Fill the axle with the correct lubricant until it is level with the fill hole. Lift the right side of the vehicle six inches or more for one minute. Then lower the right side and lift the left side for the same amount of time. Lower the left side and let the vehicle sit for one minute. Recheck and top up lubricant as necessary. This procedure ensures that the wheel hubs have a sufficient level of lubricant and that the level in the drive axle housing is correct.

TECHNICIAN TIP

If the vehicle is equipped with a differential lock, the lock must be manually engaged with a jamb screw before the differential carrier is reinstalled. Otherwise, it will not be possible to install the axles.

differential cross is discovered, as shown in FIGURE 48-20, it cannot be simply said that the cross itself was the cause of the failure. That is where the failure happened—but what caused it?

All other parts of the axle must be examined and a determination made as to the root cause of the failure. Several things must be considered when deciding the cause of failure—vehicle vocation, load, driver experience, road conditions, maintenance records, and an accurate report as to how and when the failure occurred. If the technician simply replaces the broken components without finding the cause, the vehicle will likely be back with the same or a similar failure in the future.

The true cause of a failure can usually be determined by knowing what to look for. Most manufacturers have guide books available to help the technician decide on a failure's root cause. Drive train systems are frequently the subject of premature failures caused by overloading, driver error or abuse, or poor maintenance practices. This section will cover a methodical five-step process for diagnosing failures and then discuss the most common types of drive axle failures.

Process for Diagnosing Failures

There are five steps to diagnosing a component failure:

1. Record all the known details of the failure.
2. Investigate the vehicle history and condition.
3. Inspect the components carefully.
4. Determine the cause of the failure.
5. Ensure the cause has been corrected

FIGURE 48-20 Re-assembling a failed component without discovering the cause of failure usually means the failure will re-occur.

Step One—Record Details of the Failure

Step one of diagnosing drive axle failures is to record all the known details of the failure. Start by checking the vehicle service history. Then, talk to the driver and ask the following questions:

- What is the vehicle used for?
- Is this problem a repeat failure or the first occurrence?
- How was the truck operating when the failure occurred?
- Did the driver notice anything unusual at the time of the failure?
- Were there any noises or vibrations?
- Was the vehicle or any of its components overheating?

Step Two—Investigate the Vehicle History and Condition

The second step in the diagnosis process is to investigate the vehicle history and its condition. Start this step by looking for any leaks, cracks, or other damage that may have contributed or caused the failure. Does the vehicle look like it receives regular maintenance or is it in poorly maintained condition? Record anything noteworthy that could be a contributing factor to the failure. Something small at this point, may help once the component is disassembled!

Step Three—Inspect the Failed Components Carefully

Step three of the diagnosis process is to inspect the failed components carefully. While disassembling a unit, try to disturb as little as possible until the exact failed piece is discovered. Do not aggressively clean the parts as vital evidence may be washed away. Wait until disassembly is complete. Examine the lubricant. Is it full of metal shavings? Is the level and quality of the lubricant sufficient? Once the failed component is found, carefully examine it and all the parts it interacts with to determine what type of failure occurred. For example, was it fatigue failure, shock load failure, or was it a defect in the component?

Step Four—Determine the Cause of the Failure

Replacing a failed component without knowing why it failed is a recipe for disaster. It is up to the technician to determine what actually happened to the failed part and decide how to prevent reoccurrence.

When examining gears and shafts, remember the following: gears and shafts are typically made of ductile iron and are usually case- or induction-hardened—typically to a depth of no more than 0.050" (1.27 mm). The hardening allows the components' surface to resist wear but the ductile core allows them to flex as they are loaded so that they can absorb some shocks. This flexibility allows them to bend before they break—a characteristic that provides insight into the actual cause of a failure.

The different types of failure that can occur are covered in detail in the Types of Drive Axle Failures section.

Step Five—Ensure That the Cause Has Been Corrected

The final step is to ensure that the cause has been corrected. Merely finding out what actually happened to a component may not be sufficient in proper failure analysis. For example, while examining a failed gear tooth it can be clearly seen that a gas pocket makes up a large percentage of the break site. It would be safe to assume that the failure is a defect in material and replacing the components and rebuilding the unit will solve the problem. However if a broken tooth is found and there is evidence of a fatigue failure, for example, beach marks, a determination must be made as to the cause of the constant overloading that led to the break. Is the vehicle being used for a purpose that it is not capable of? If so, repairing the problem just means the vehicle will eventually be back with a repeat failure. When a shock load failure is discovered, it is necessary to investigate why it happened. Was it abuse? Would a driver education program help? If a lubrication failure occurred, does the vehicle maintenance program need to be revamped? It is essential that it can be honestly said that the root cause of the problem has been determined and repaired, or at least documented on the work order, before a vehicle is returned to service. This protects the reputation of the technician and the service facility and allows the vehicle owner to consider what steps he must take to prevent reoccurrence of the failure.

Types of Drive Axle Failures

Drive axles can fail in several different ways. The principal types of drive axle failure include:

- shock load failures
- fatigue failures
- abuse failures
- lubrication failures

Proper maintenance of drive axle involves recognizing the characteristics of each type of failure.

Shock Load Failures

Shock load failures occur when a component is momentarily overloaded to a level that surpasses the base strength of the material, causing it to fail immediately. A shock load failure results in a broken component. (Figure 48-20 shows an extreme shock load failure.)

If it is a shaft that breaks, the failure will usually occur at a section break. A **section break** is a point where the shaft changes in shape, thereby changing its section modulus (a measure of its load carrying capability). For example, where a spline or thread begins is a section break. So is the point where the shaft is suddenly thicker or thinner.

Shock failure breakage will leave a relatively flat and uniformly rough surface at the fracture area, as can be seen in FIGURE 48-21. Notice how the break follows the contour of the groove in the shaft. This groove constitutes a section break. Sometime a shaft will break on an angle, leaving the fractured surface uniformly rough. If the shaft has turned after the failure, the break surface may have smoothened out somewhat.

Shock load failure on a gear will usually result in a broken gear tooth. The tooth surface will, again, be uniformly rough and there will typically be a raised area on the compression side of the break. If the gear is operated after breaking, this area may be worn down. Sometimes a defect in the manufacturing process can lead to gear tooth fracture. Small imperfections known as **gas pockets** or **stringers** can occur. Gas pockets (stringers) occur during the casting process when the metal of the entire tooth is not uniformly fused together with the metal of the rest of the gear. This type of imperfection significantly weakens the gear tooth. Gas pockets can be identified by a difference in texture and shape of the fracture surface. Some of the break area will be rough, as in a normal shock load failure, but other parts of the break area will have an unusual texture. For example, it could be smooth or even hollowed out. This change in texture will be quite obvious to the technician.

FIGURE 48-21 Shock failures are recognizable by the uniform roughness (A) of the surface areas where a break has occurred. However, if a component is run after the break, there will be some areas that are smoothed out (B).

Fatigue Failures

Fatigue failures occur as the result of the component simply wearing out. They occur gradually and progress until the component fails. Fatigue can be classed into three separate types of failures—bending stresses, torsional or twisting stresses, and surface fatigue.

In bending failures, the component is stressed by load sufficient to crack the component but insufficient to break it outright. The stress occurs repeatedly until the component finally does break. Bending fatigue usually occurs with gear teeth, and the break area will be characterized by **beach marks**. Beach marks are semi-circular marks that indicate repeated cracking of the component. The crack will continue to progress until the part fails, leaving telltale beach marks in the fracture, as can be seen in FIGURE 48-22. A fatigue failure indicates repeated overloading of the component, so the technician must take steps to prevent the overloading. Otherwise, the component will fail again.

Twisting or torsional failures usually occur with shafts that are constantly exposed to twisting forces sufficient to crack the material but insufficient to break it outright. Torsional failures generally result in either a scalloped or star-type fracture. As shown in FIGURE 48-23, a scalloped-shaped fracture will show beach marks similar to a bending failure. In a star-type fracture, such as the one shown in FIGURE 48-24, some of the break area is smoothed out by the shaft spinning after the break occurred.

Surface fatigue is the final type of fatigue failure. Surface fatigue is caused by overloading to such a degree that the hard surface of gear teeth breaks down and starts flaking away. This type of failure will lead to pitting and spalling as the flaking progresses, resulting in eventual failure. There are many situations when minor pitting of a

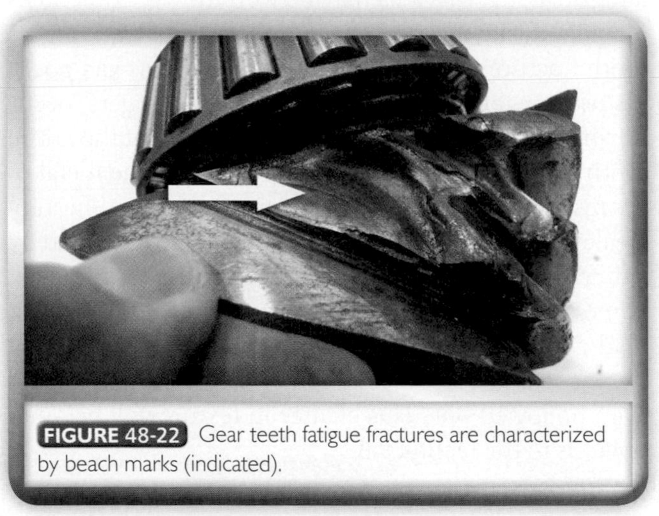

FIGURE 48-22 Gear teeth fatigue fractures are characterized by beach marks (indicated).

FIGURE 48-23 This input shaft shows classic beach marks indicative of a torsional fatigue failure.

gear tooth is not cause for concern. As pitting progresses and the tooth surface breaks down, however, the involute shape of the tooth will be lost, leading to noise and vibration. More information on spur gear wear patterns is in the Regular Wear or Maintenance Failures section of the Servicing Standard Transmissions chapter.

Abuse Failures

Several failures are the result of poor driver training and/or outright driver abuse. So-called **abuse failures** occur as a result of lack of driver training or caring. Dumping the clutch, backing into a loading dock, spinout, poor gear selection, and even downhill coasting are driver actions that can all lead to abuse failures.

Dumping the clutch is common, and yet preventable, abuse. When the driver dumps the clutch instead of smoothly engaging it, enormous stress load is placed on the entire driveline. Common failures that occur from this abuse are twisted main-shafts in the transmission, as shown in **FIGURE 48-25**, driveshaft torsional failures, broken universal joints, and axle shaft torsional failures.

Backing into a loading dock at speed is a driver abuse that can cause shock failures. Likewise, backing under a trailer too roughly or a trailer that is set too low for the tractor to pick up can also lead to failures.

Spinout—whether in a main differential or an inter-axle differential—is another common source of driver abuse that can cause catastrophic damage. When the driver allows the wheels to spin, the differential side and spider gears are rotating at enormous speeds. That creates a great deal of heat, which thins the gear lube and causes it to be thrown away from the components that need it the most. Differential spider gears can become welded to the cross legs because of the extreme heat. **FIGURE 48-26**

FIGURE 48-24 This fuller main shaft shows a star-type fracture caused by repeated fatigue stresses.

FIGURE 48-25 A twisted main shaft—typically caused by a sudden overload, like dumping the clutch.

shows an inter-axle differential cross that has sustained catastrophic damage due to spinout.

How serious is spinout? Just one instance of uncontrolled spin can cause the side and spider gears to turn more than they would for the lifetime of the vehicle if operated normally. That is a lifetime of wear is just a few seconds! Therefore, spinout should be avoided at all costs by proper driver training and the use of differential lockouts if available.

In addition to failure caused by wear, spinout can also lead to severe shock loads if the wildly spinning wheels suddenly gain traction. FIGURE 48-27 shows a side gear shattered by a sudden shock load caused by a spinning wheel suddenly gaining traction.

Poor gear selection by the driver can also lead to severe shock loads as the driver tries to re-engage the clutch. If the gear selection does not match the vehicle road speed, the driveline will have to absorb the shock,

FIGURE 48-26 Spinout can cause catastrophic failures such as in this inter-axle differential.

FIGURE 48-27 Sudden shock when a spinning wheel hits dry pavement can lead to shock failures such as this broken differential side gear.

possibly leading to failure. Related to poor gear selection is choosing to coast downhill with the clutch disengaged. Doing so is another common driver abuse that contributes to shock load failure. This commonly happens when the vehicle is going too fast. The driver panics and tries to re-engage the clutch so that he can make use of the engine brakes. The result is typically a driveline failure.

The preceding is by no means a comprehensive list of failures that can occur due to abuse. It is merely a sampling of common driver-caused failures that are totally preventable with proper training

Lubrication Failure

Lubrication failures are normally due to poor maintenance, incorrect lubrication, lack of lubrication, and/or contaminated lube. Driveline lubricants are the life blood of components, so any lubricant failure can lead directly to component failure. **FIGURE 48-28** shows an input gear from a standard transmission that basically melted during operation due to lack of lubricant. Think of the heat required to do that to a component!

Contaminated lubricant is a serious problem. Lubricant can become contaminated in several ways. One way is by mixing the wrong type of lubricants. Contamination also occurs when dirt is ingested through improperly filtered vents during normal component breathing. (All drive train components are vented to the atmosphere to allow components to breathe as the lubricant heats up and cools down.) Lubricant can also be contaminated by the introduction of foreign material during poor maintenance practices or because of component breakdown. Water can also contaminate lubricant. If the vehicle is operated in a wet area in which water rises above the component vent level, water ingestion could occur.

FIGURE 48-28 It is hard to imagine the amount of heat that can be generated when components have insufficient lube, but results like this burned input gear from a Fuller transmission are commonplace when lubrication is absent.

Wrap-up

Ready for Review

- Proper maintenance, as with all other components, is essential to the service life of a drive axle. Timely fluid checks and changes can go a long way to protecting the equipment.
- Most drive axles today are shipped with synthetic lubricant instead of a mineral oil-based lubricant.
- It was common in the past for drive axles to require an initial fluid change at 3,000 to 5,000 miles (4,828 to 8,047 km); however, with the manufacturing accuracy of today, this is usually no longer necessary.
- Always check for metal particles in the drive axle lubricant during service. This can be a good indicator of a failing drive axle.
- When filling or topping up drive axle lubricant, always use the correct fluid and be aware that some drive axles require fluid to be added in more than one location.
- Most technicians will never overhaul a drive axle but, if it is attempted, it is essential that the correct service manual for the particular drive axle be available.
- All drive axles require the same four adjustments during overhaul: pinion bearing preload, pinion depth setting, side bearing preload, and the gear set backlash adjustment.
- Always mark the components, such as the side bearing retaining caps and the differential case halves, during disassembly so they can be reassembled correctly.
- The differential case in heavy-duty drive axles has two halves, the plain half and the flange half that the crown gear is attached to.
- The differential gears, the spider gears, and the side gears run on thrust washers. These and the surfaces they contact should be carefully inspected for wear.
- Pinion gears can be overhung (only two bearing) or straddle mounted, in which case they will have a third spigot bearing supporting the end of the shaft.
- Note the position of all shims or shim packs and keep them separate while disassembling the drive axle. These are critical for setting pinion depth, pinion bearing preload, and power divider input shaft end play.
- All components in the axle should be checked for wear and damage—not just the obviously failed pieces.
- While rebuilding a drive axle, remember that the cost of replacement parts is small compared to having to redo the job. Replace all questionable parts.
- Crown and pinion gears are replaced as a set only. Most manufacturers sell replacement differential gears as a set also.
- Pinion depth may need to be adjusted to account for a pinion variation number.
- When reassembling the differential case, check the torque required to rotate the differential gears.
- Contact pattern is controlled by pinon depth and gear set backlash.
- Pinion and side bearing preload ensures rigidity in the gear set.
- After reassembling a drive axle, it is essential to check and, if necessary, correct the contact pattern.
- A conventional contact pattern should have three elements: close to but clear of the toe of the tooth, centered between the top land and the root, and extended across at least 50% of the tooth face.
- Durapoid and generoid gear sets have a centralized tooth contact pattern.
- After the contact pattern is correct, the thrust screw, if present, should be adjusted.
- Inter-axle differentials can be serviced without removing the entire power divider/differential carrier assembly.
- Power divider input shafts have end play, not preload.
- Component failures occur because of four basic issues: shock load failures, fatigue failures, lubrication failures, and abuse failures.
- When a component fails, it is essential to determine the correct cause to prevent re-occurrence.

Vocabulary Builder

abuse failure Failure directly attributed to driver or other person's actions.

beach mark Semi-circular mark in a fracture indicating repeated overload.

bearing adjuster Threaded wheel used to tighten the side bearing races.

bearing adjuster lock Lock to secure the bearing adjusters.

bearing growth The increase in bearing size as it is pressed on to a shaft.

contact pattern The contact area between two gear teeth in contact.

fatigue failure Failure of components due to repeated overload.

flange case half The half of the differential case that the crown gear attaches to.

gas pocket Imperfection in the adhesion of molten metal during the casting or forming process.

gear set contact pattern The indication as to where the gears will contact each other during operation.

heel The end of a crown gear tooth furthest from the center of its axis.

lengthwise bearing The contact pattern along the tooth face from the toe toward the heel.

lubrication failure Failure caused by incorrect lubricant, contaminated lubricant, or lack of lubricant.

nominal shim pack A shim pack that would be used if the pinion had a zero variation.

oil slinger A stamped steel ring used to throw lubricant in a certain direction.

overhung mount pinion A pinion mounted with only two opposed tapered roller bearings.

pinion bearing cage A removable casting that holds the two bearing races that support the pinion gear.

pinion depth The mounting position of the pinion in relation to the crown gear center of axis.

pinion pilot bearing A small bearing that supports the inboard end of the pinion gear when the pinion is straddle mounted. Also called *spigot bearing*.

pinion variation number A dimension to add or remove from the nominal pinion depth dimension.

plain case half The half of the differential case that does not bolt to the crown gear.

preload Negative endplay, or less than zero clearance.

profile bearing Contact pattern between the root and the top land of the tooth.

root The radius shape between the bottoms of two teeth. Also called *fillet radius*.

section break A point where the diameter of a shaft or thickness of a component changes.

shock load failure Fracture caused by one sudden shock.

side bearing bore The opening machined into the differential carrier that holds the side bearing races.

side bearing cap The cap that bolts the side bearing races to the side bearing bores.

spigot bearing A small bearing that supports the inboard end of the pinion gear when the pinion is straddle mounted. Also called *pinion pilot bearing*.

straddle mount pinion A pinion supported by two opposed tapered roller bearings and a small spigot bearing.

stringer Small inclusion in a cast or formed metal that weaken it.

thrust screw A screw that stops the crown gear from flexing under load.

toe The end of a crown gear tooth closest to the center of its axis.

tooth face TThe area that actually comes into contact with a mating gear and is parallel to the gear's axis of rotation.

top land The apex of a tooth.

Review Questions

1. Which of the following are two critical adjustments of a rear drive axle assembly not related to tooth contact pattern?
   a. Pinion depth and gear set backlash
   b. Crown gear depth and pinion depth
   c. Side bearing and pinion bearing preload
   d. Crown gear and pinion torque
2. If a drive axle's contact pattern is too close to the toe, which of the following must be done to correct it?
   a. Increase backlash
   b. Decrease backlash
   c. Move the pinion toward the crown gear
   d. Move the pinion away from the crown gear
3. If a drive axle tooth contact pattern is too low on the tooth (at the root), which of the following must be done to correct it?
   a. Increase backlash
   b. Decrease backlash
   c. Move the pinion toward the ring gear
   d. Move the pinion away from the ring gear
4. You examine a pinion gear that has broken and you see beach marks clearly present at the break point. Which of the following likely caused the break?
   a. A sudden shock the drive train
   b. A repeated overloading of the drive train over a period of time
   c. A failure of the axle lubrication system
   d. Spinout
5. You examine a failed inter-axle differential and find the inter-axle differential cross has broken in several places at once. Each of the breaks has the same uniformly rough looking surface. Which of the following could have caused this failure?
   a. A sudden shock to the drive train
   b. A repeated overloading of the drive train over a period of time
   c. A failure of the axle lubrication system
   d. Gas pockets or stringers.
6. When setting pinion bearing preload on a heavy-duty drive axle, which of the following would be a true statement?
   a. More shims between the bearings gives more preload.
   b. More shims between the bearings gives less preload.
   c. Preload should be adjusted by changing the torque on the pinion nut.
   d. Preload is adjusted by changing the bearings.
7. Which of the following is the main disadvantage of a non-locking rear drive axle differential assembly?
   a. It may not provide equal speed to both drive wheels.
   b. It will not allow for torque division.
   c. It will not redirect torque.
   d. It will allow a vehicle speed increase.
8. Pinion bearing preload and side bearing preload are critical for which of the following reasons?
   a. Pinion and side bearing preload hold the crown and pinion rigidly in position.
   b. Pinion and side bearing preload increase gear set life.
   c. Side and pinion bearing preload add to the bearings longevity.
   d. All of the choices are correct.
9. Which of the following describes a good hand-rolled, conventional tooth contact pattern in a hypoid drive axle?
   a. Close to the heel, centered between the top land and the root, and halfway along the tooth face
   b. Centered between the top land and the root and centered between the toe and the heel
   c. Close to the toe, centered between the top land and the root, and halfway along the tooth face
   d. Close to the toe, close to the heel, and full contact along the tooth face.
10. Which of the following describes a good hand-rolled generoid tooth contact pattern in a spiral bevel drive axle?
    a. Close to the heel, centered between the top land and the root, and halfway along the tooth face
    b. Centered between the top land and the root, and centered between the toe and the heel
    c. Close to the toe, centered between the top land and the root, and halfway along the tooth face
    d. Close to the toe, close to the heel, and full contact along the tooth face

ASE-Type Questions

1. Technician A says that drive axles do not usually require any regular maintenance as they are sealed units. Technician B says that some drive axles with synthetic lube will not need any maintenance for 500,000 miles. Who is correct?
   a. Technician A
   b. Technician B
   c. Both Technician A and Technician B
   d. Neither Technician A nor Technician B
2. Technician A says that a drive axle must always be filled from the plug at the rear of the housing to the correct level. Technician B says that some drive axles have more than one fill plug. Who is correct?
   a. Technician A
   b. Technician B
   c. Both Technician A and Technician B
   d. Neither Technician A nor Technician B
3. Technician A says that the pinion depth adjustment influences the drive axle's contact pattern. Technician B says that the gear set back lash influences the drive axle's contact pattern. Who is correct?
   a. Technician A
   b. Technician B
   c. Both Technician A and Technician B
   d. Neither Technician A nor Technician B
4. Technician A says that most power dividers today have lubrication pumps to lubricate the inter-axle differential. Technician B says that single axle drive axles rely on splash from the crown gears rotation to provide lubrication. Who is correct?
   a. Technician A
   b. Technician B
   c. Both Technician A and Technician B
   d. Neither Technician A nor Technician B
5. Technician A says that bearing growth refers to the increase in a bearing's size as it is pressed onto a shaft. Technician B says that bearing growth has no effect on pinion bearing preload as long as the original pinion bearing shim is used while installing a new pinion gear. Who is correct?
   a. Technician A
   b. Technician B
   c. Both Technician A and Technician B
   d. Neither Technician A nor Technician B
6. Technician A says that two-speed drive axles offer more speed ranges to a vehicle operator. Technician B says that two-speed helical axles use a smaller crown gear so are less likely to flex under load. Who is correct?
   a. Technician A
   b. Technician B
   c. Both Technician A and Technician B
   d. Neither Technician A nor Technician B
7. Technician A says that pinion bearing preload can be measured with a string and a fish scale. Technician B says that pinion bearing preload in heavy-duty axles is controlled by the torque on the pinion nut. Who is correct?
   a. Technician A
   b. Technician B
   c. Both Technician A and Technician B
   d. Neither Technician A nor Technician B
8. Technician A says that side bearing preload causes a slight flexing of the bearing mounts. Technician B says that gear set backlash is set after side bearing preload. Who is correct?
   a. Technician A
   b. Technician B
   c. Both Technician A and Technician B
   d. Neither Technician A nor Technician B
9. Technician A says that side gear support bearings should always be changed when overhauling a drive axle. Technician B says that spinout damage is usually visible as excess heat stress on the differential components. Who is correct?
   a. Technician A
   b. Technician B
   c. Both Technician A and Technician B
   d. Neither Technician A nor Technician B
10. Technician A says that, after replacing the pinion seal, installing the pinion yoke nut with a one-inch air gun is sufficient. Technician B says that some pinion nuts require as much as 1,500 foot-pounds (2,034 Nm) of torque. Who is correct?
    a. Technician A
    b. Technician B
    c. Both Technician A and Technician B
    d. Neither Technician A nor Technician B

CHAPTER 49

NATEF Tasks

There are no NATEF tasks for this chapter.

Knowledge Objectives

After reading this chapter, you will be able to:

1. Explain the operating principles and differences between hybrid drive power train systems. (pp 1645–1655)
2. Identify and explain hazards of high voltage electrical circuits. (pp 1648–1652)
3. Outline service precautions to use when servicing hybrid drive systems. (pp 1660–1663)
4. Identify the applications and advantages and benefits of heavy-duty hybrid propulsion systems. (pp 1644–1647)
5. Explain operating principles of hydraulic launch assist (HLA) hybrid drive systems. (pp 1647–1648)
6. Explain operating principles of series electric propulsion drives. (pp 1652–1663)
7. Describe the construction and operation of the BAE HybriDrive propulsion system. (pp 1652–1655)
8. Describe the operating principles of a series hybrid drive train. (pp 1652–1663)
9. Identify and explain the function of the HybriDrive propulsion system components. (pp 1655–1663)
10. Outline service precautions to use when servicing the HybriDrive propulsion system. (pp 1660–1663)
11. Outline basic service and maintenance procedures for the HybriDrive propulsion systems. (p 1663)

Hybrid Drive Systems and Series-Type Hybrid Drives

Skills Objectives

There are no skills objectives for this chapter.

Introduction

Understanding the word "hybrid" as meaning mixed or combined in nature helps explain the concept of a **hybrid electric vehicle (HEV)**—a type of vehicle that combines an internal combustion engine with an electric propulsion system into a new or hybrid powertrain configuration. Hybrids are fundamentally different from **electric vehicles**, which use only electric motors to move a vehicle. A variety of hybrid drive vehicle configurations are used in commercial vehicles. In essence, hybrid propulsion systems can use any type of engine—gasoline, natural gas, diesel, turbine, or reciprocating—assisted by an electric motor to accelerate the vehicle. In all cases, the engine will drive an electric generator used to charge batteries and help power the electric motor.

Fundamentals of Hybrid Drives

Hybrid electric vehicles are now employed in many commercial vehicle applications due to their capability to reduce simultaneously both fuel consumption and emissions produced from burning fuel. Estimates suggest that hybrids improve fuel consumption by between 20 and 60%, though real-world observed consumption in a number of applications is substantially less than those estimates suggest. Urban transit buses, intercity pick-up, delivery, and utility vehicles are the most common applications in which hybrid drive systems have the potential to excel. Even the military has seized on the hybrid advantage for situations where fuel economy is mission critical—for example, when supply lines are stretched, or when stealth is required.

Vehicles operating in urban driving conditions are best suited to hybrid use, as much of the energy derived from burning fuel is lost through idling and braking. Studies have shown that approximately 65% of energy used to accelerate a city bus is quickly dissipated into heat by frequent braking FIGURE 49-1. Garbage trucks lose 59%, while delivery vehicles picking up and moving small parcels lose half the energy produced by the engine the same way. Because hybrid drive systems are designed to produce electricity when braking, generators connected to the wheels will assist braking and store this energy in onboard batteries. In turn, the batteries will supply electric current to the traction motors for acceleration. (A **traction motor** is an electric motor that provides propulsion to a vehicle.) This feature, by which generators recover energy during braking, is called **regenerative braking**.

The inefficiencies of conventional powertrain systems are not limited to losses from idling and braking. Another inefficiency stems from idle time. Engine idle time is in the range of 50% for many vehicles operating in urban driving conditions. The stop-start feature used by some hybrid drives shuts off the engine when not

You Are the Technician

As a transit bus technician, you are skilled and qualified to work on diesel-powered bus chassis. Recently, a few of the hybrid drive buses in the fleet, which are now out of the manufacturer's warranty period, have begun to require more frequent replacement of service brakes. Brake drums are showing evidence of hard heavy braking, and brake shoes are wearing away almost as fast as the conventional bus chassis in the fleet. One hybrid bus in particular has arrived for yet another inspection of the braking system due to a driver's complaint about poor braking. Because the bus has a series-type hybrid powertrain, you realize that a significant amount of braking is supposed to be performed by the electric traction motor-generator. As you consider what elements of the hybrid system to inspect, and search OEM literature for the correct diagnostic and inspection procedures, consider the following:

1. Is there some method to adjust the amount of braking performed by the regenerative braking feature of the series hybrid?
2. List some potential problems with the hybrid powertrain that may contribute to more work being performed by the regular service brakes and not the regenerative braking system.
3. During a road test of the braking system, is there some feature that you or the driver could easily see which will verify the regenerative braking is taking place?

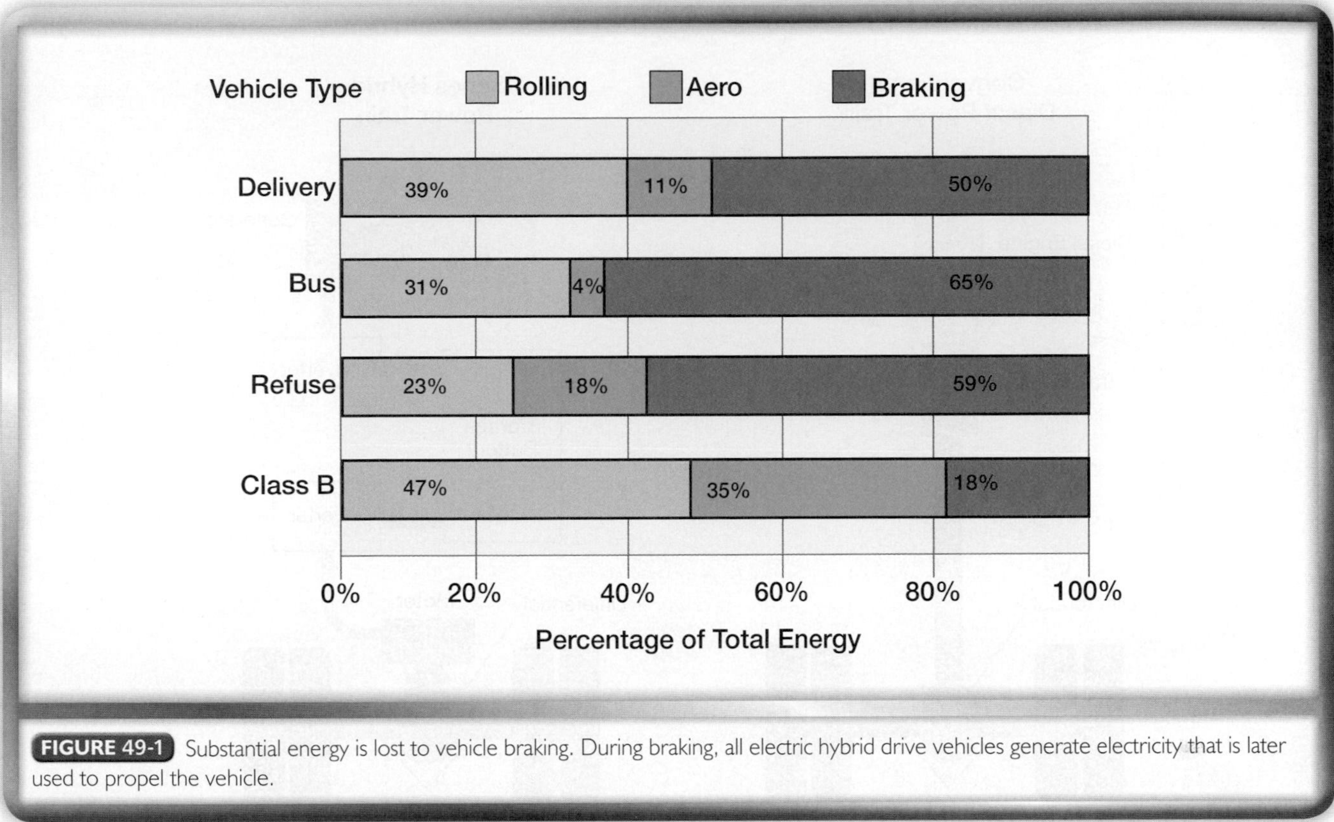

FIGURE 49-1 Substantial energy is lost to vehicle braking. During braking, all electric hybrid drive vehicles generate electricity that is later used to propel the vehicle.

in use. Also, engines required to accelerate over a wide engine rpm operating range during stop-and-go operation do not use fuel efficiently. Because hybrid drive systems can limit the rate of engine rpm change, they enable the engine to operate at its most fuel efficient, lowest emission, high torque-speed range, using less fuel while producing fewer emissions.

Other hybrid drive train advantages include:

- Increased brake life and reduced need for brake service using regenerative braking
- Extended engine life due to more favorable operating conditions
- Electric drive motors provide more torque for faster acceleration added pulling power
- Smoother acceleration
- Quieter vehicle operation
- Compatible with all fuels and engine designs so no requirement to change fueling infrastructure
- All engine emissions are reduced and less exhaust aftertreatment system service is required
- Minimum driver training required

Types of Hybrid Drives

Even though all electric hybrid systems are configured with engines, electric motors, and batteries to propel the vehicle, not all hybrid systems are alike. Different configurations offer unique advantages. The following are the most common configurations of hybrid drive systems in use:

1. Series drive—Only an electric traction motor supplies torque to propel the vehicle **FIGURE 49-2**. The engine drives a generator used to charge a bank of batteries and supply current to the electric motor (e.g., BAE Hybridrive System).
2. Parallel drive—Both the engine and electric motor work together, blending motor and engine torque to propel the vehicle **FIGURE 49-3**.
3. Series-parallel drive—A more complex system enabling an engine only, an electric motor only, and a combined engine-motor operation **FIGURE 49-4**. Also called a power-split configuration, the engine and motor operation is optimized for driving conditions (e.g., Arvin Meritor, Allison EV).
4. Plug-in hybrid electric vehicle (PHEV)—Refers to any type of hybrid electric vehicle containing a battery storage system that uses an external source to recharge the battery when the vehicle is not in operation. These vehicles also have an ability to drive or operate for an extended period in all-electric mode, lending the alternate name of extended-range electric vehicles.

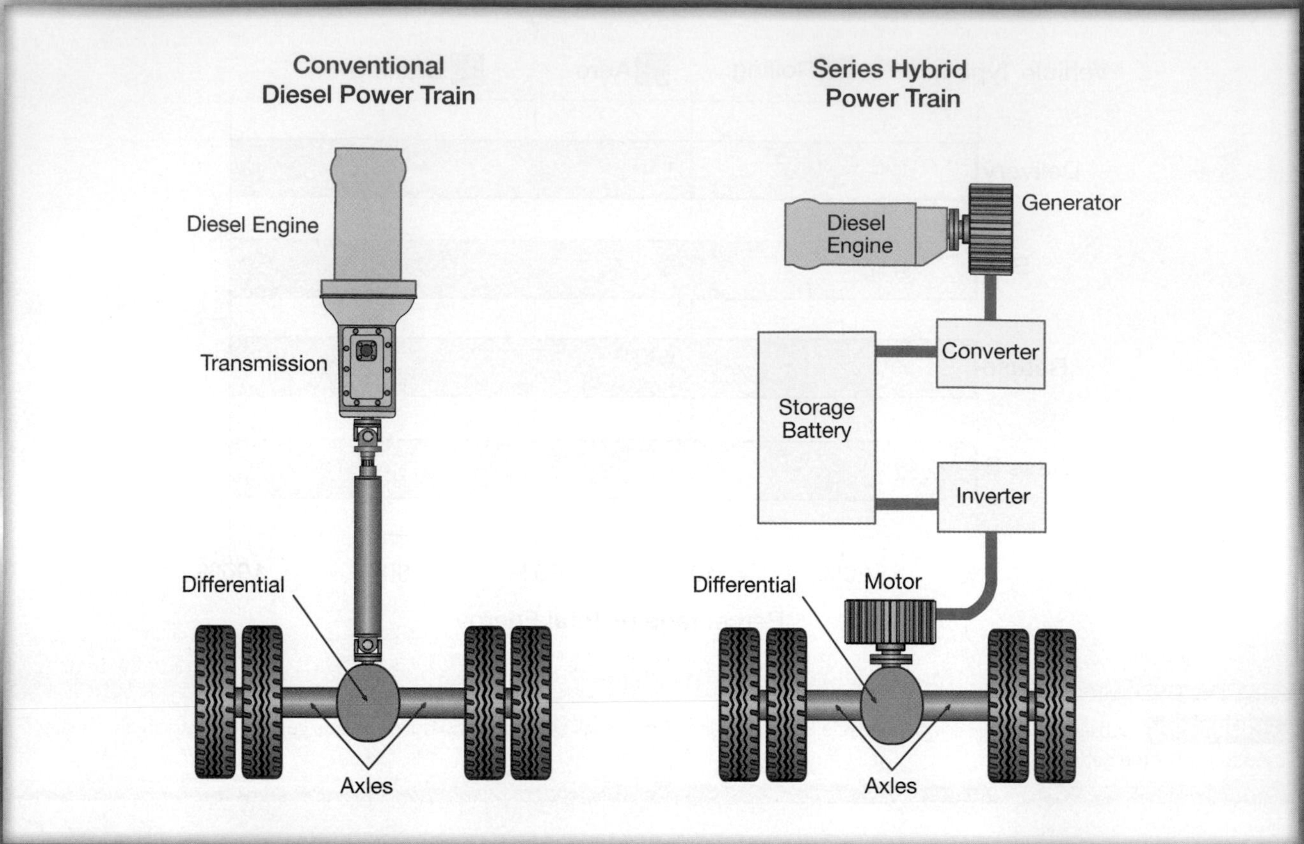

Conventional
Diesel Power Train
Diesel Engine
Transmission
Differential
Axles
Series Hybrid
Power Train
Generator
Diesel
Engine
Converter
Storage
Battery
Inverter
Differential
Motor
Axles

FIGURE 49-2 Series drive—Only an electric traction motor supplies torque to propel the vehicle. The engine drives a generator used to charge a bank of batteries and supply current to the electric motor.

Electric
Motor
Engine
Transmission
Motor
Controller
Storage
Battery

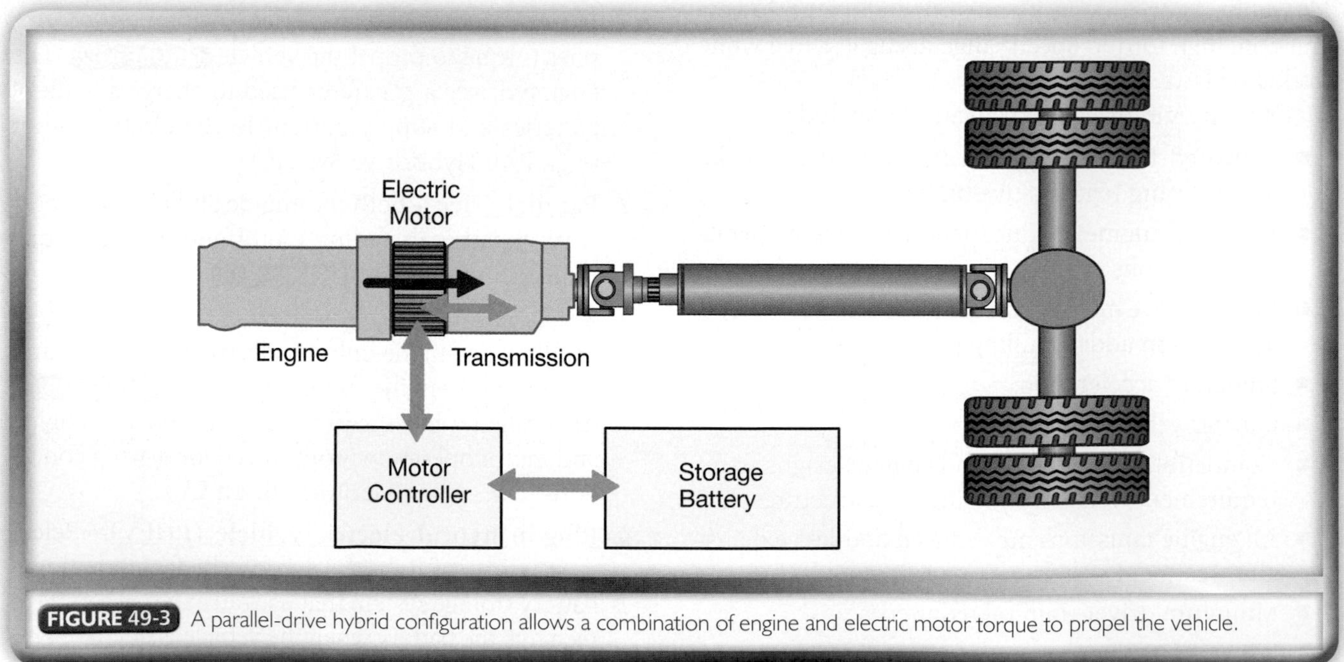

FIGURE 49-3 A parallel-drive hybrid configuration allows a combination of engine and electric motor torque to propel the vehicle.

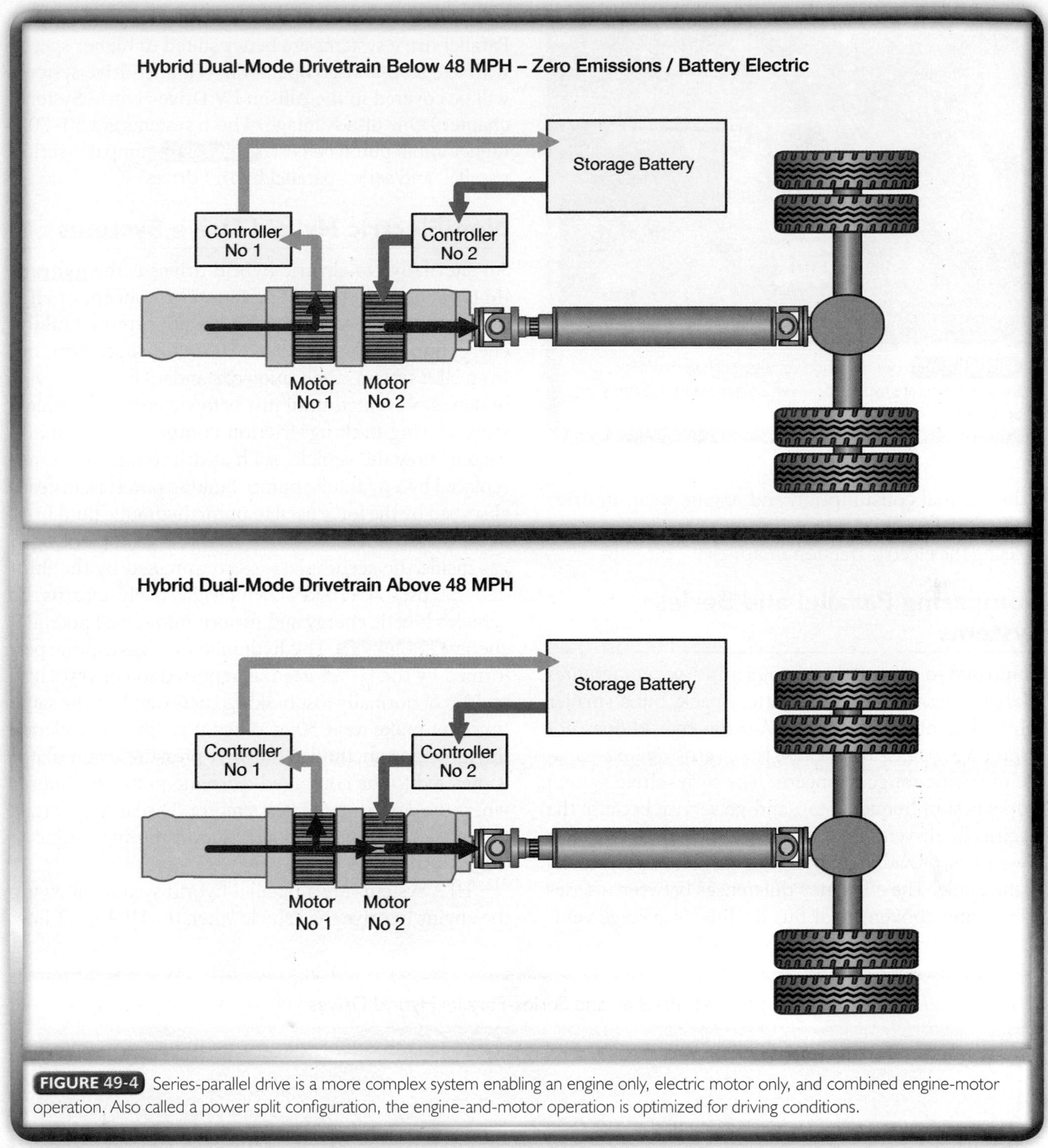

FIGURE 49-4 Series-parallel drive is a more complex system enabling an engine only, electric motor only, and combined engine-motor operation. Also called a power split configuration, the engine-and-motor operation is optimized for driving conditions.

One popular type of PHEV is the municipal utility truck. These trucks typically travel shorter distances than others but are operated in residential neighborhoods continuously for extended periods, running the lift boom, powering lights, tools, and other accessories **FIGURE 49-5**. Ordinarily, the engine is required to operate hydraulic pumps or generators. Using stored battery energy allows the vehicle to operate at a job site without engine idling, which reduces emissions from idling and exposure to diesel exhaust. Vehicle operating costs are lowered by

FIGURE 49-5 Plug-in hybrid vehicles, such as this utility truck, can operate hydraulic power equipment using battery power only.

reducing fuel consumption and engine wear. In drive mode, low-speed driving conditions are ideally suited to using the electric traction motors.

Comparing Parallel and Series Systems

Compared to a parallel system, a series system requires a larger electric motor and battery pack, but a smaller internal combustion engine. A series hybrid does not require a transmission because the electric motor is capable of a wide range of speeds. The series drive system works best in frequent stop-and-go service because the electrically-driven propulsion system has high torque at low speeds, providing smooth, fast acceleration regardless of the grade. The efficiency differences between a series hybrid and conventional bus decline as average vehicle speed increases and the number of stops decreases. Parallel-drive systems are better suited to higher speeds with less stop-and-go operation. (Parallel-drive systems will be covered in the Allison EV Drive Hybrid Systems chapter.) One disadvantage of both systems is a 50–70% higher initial purchase cost. **TABLE 49-1** compares series, parallel, and series-parallel hybrid drives.

Non-Electric Hybrid Drive Systems

An alternative to electric hybrid drives is the **hydraulic launch assist (HLA)** system. The concept of HLA uses hydraulic regenerative braking to capture braking energy and help launch the vehicle during acceleration. In an HLA system, application of standard friction service brakes is prevented until just before a complete vehicle stop. During braking, friction components normally used to slow the vehicle, such as drums and shoes, are replaced by a hydraulic pump. Braking power is, instead, absorbed by the force used to pump hydraulic fluid from a low-pressure reservoir to a gas accumulator. Nitrogen gas inside the accumulator is compressed by the fluid to 5,000 psi (34,470 kPa), which effectively absorbs the vehicle's kinetic energy and turns it into stored potential energy **FIGURE 49-6**. This hydraulic-over-gas capture performed by the HLA system is reported to convert close to 70% of normally lost braking energy and, at the same time, cut brake wear 50%. When it is time to accelerate the vehicle again, fluid in the high-pressure accumulator is metered to the combined driveline pump and motor where the device operates as a motor. The HLA hydraulic motor accelerates the vehicle by transmitting torque to the driveshaft.

HLA systems are a parallel hybrid system, allowing the engine to drive the vehicle when the HLA is off-line.

TABLE 49-1: Comparison of Series, Parallel, and Series-Parallel Hybrid Drives

	Driving Performance		Fuel Economy Improvement			
	Acceleration	Continuous high output	Idling stop	Energy recovery	High-efficiency operation control	Total efficiency
Series	●	○	●	●	◖	◖
Parallel	●	●	◖	●	●	◖
Series-parallel	○	○	○	○	●	●

● Best ◖ Good ○ Poor

FIGURE 49-6 Eaton's hydraulic launch assist (HLA) pressurizes hydraulic fluid to capture braking energy. Pressurized fluid is used to power a hydraulic motor and launch the vehicle. The primary benefits of HLA are faster acceleration and reduced emissions and fuel consumption.

Improvements to fuel economy are estimated between 15 to 30% with corresponding reductions in emissions. HLA has two modes of operation: economy and performance. In economy mode, energy stored in the accumulator during braking is used only to initially accelerate the vehicle. Once emptied, the engine will begin to propel the vehicle. In performance mode, both the engine and accumulator will provide driveline torque until the accumulator empties. Performance mode provides more torque for 2% quicker acceleration but does not provide the same reduction to fuel consumption as economy mode. TABLE 49-2 lists some common specifications of an HLA system.

TABLE 49-2: Specifications of a Typical HLA System

Weight of HLA system	1,250 lb (568 kg)
Max pressure	5,000 psi (2,272 kg)
Total system oil volume	21 gallons (80 l)
Torque	2,550 ft-lb (3,457 Nm)
Active speed range	Up to 25 mph (40 kph)
Minimum wheelbase, single	191" (4.85 m)
Minimum wheelbase, tandem	215" (5.46 m)

Hybrid Drive Electrical Safety

Hybrid drive system components use lethal high-voltage power devices operating up to 900 volts and contain energy storage systems over 700 volts DC. Although systems are designed to provide safe propulsion energy under normal conditions, during accidents or servicing personal injury, death, and expensive equipment damage can occur. Unique service procedures are outlined in mandatory training courses provided by the OEM and invigilated by local electrical authorities. Special tools must be used in addition to safety clothing (PPE) to ensure that the technician is kept as safe as possible during service procedures FIGURE 49-7.

FIGURE 49-7 Insulated service tools are required when working on high-voltage hybrid systems.

Effects of Electric Shock

Shock hazard to the human body is a function of the type of current (AC or DC), voltage, amperage, and skin resistance. Generally, ten times the amount of DC current has the same effect as AC current. Under the right conditions, 5 milliamps of AC current can be dangerous, and 500 milliamps lethal, as electricity can affect the contraction of heart muscles and muscles controlling breathing. A level of 60Hz AC is especially lethal because it closely corresponds to heart rate and can cause the heart to beat irregularly. Higher frequency AC current conducts with less resistance than low-frequency current. At high levels, electricity generates enough heat to simply destroy nerve muscle and blood tissue. The effects of electricity can be experienced as:

- Tingling sensation (AC current)
- Burning sensation
- Muscle contractions
- Ventricular fibrillation (irregular heart rhythm)
- Cardiac arrest (heart stoppage)
- Pulmonary arrest (stopped breathing)

Reactions to electricity can have serious consequences, as a person may jump or fall in response to even a light shock. High-amperage shorts can produce blinding light, fires, and explosions. TABLE 49-3 describes effects of different levels of electric current. TABLE 49-4 shows the effects of electricity on different skin conditions.

TABLE 49-3: Effects of Various Levels of AC and DC Current

Effect	AC	DC
Sensation	1 milliamp at 60 Hz	5 millamps
Muscle contraction	60 milliamps at 60 Hz	300–500 milliamps
Let-go limit	10.5 milliamps	15–88 milliamps
Minimal hazard with worst case	60 V peak AC (Not RMS)	42 V
Non-lethal under most conditions	60–150 V	60–150 V

TABLE 49-4: Electrical Resistance of Skin Under Various Conditions

Skin Condition	Resistance
Open skin (wound)	500–1,000 ohms
Wet skin	10,000–20,000 ohms
High ionic content wet skin (i.e., sweating)	5,000–10,000 ohms
Under high voltage conditions	500 ohms

High Voltage Disconnect

Disconnecting and discharging any residual current in EV components is imperative before performing any service work. Always assume the electrical system is live, even after disconnecting the battery power supply and testing for the presence of current with an approved electrical meter. Appropriate personal protective equipment safety is necessary; glasses, footwear, and gloves should always be worn, and all jewelry removed. A long-sleeved, heavy denim shirt offers protection from inadvertent upper body electrical contact. When the ignition key is switched off, most hybrid systems use a set of relays to disconnect power from the rest of the system components. A master disconnect switch is used in bus applications and should also be switched off, effectively disconnecting the vehicle batteries from the 12/24-volt electrical system. Specialized electrical connectors in the battery storage system and power cables are provided to add another level of redundancy to power disconnect procedures. Inverters and propulsion control modules should usually be disconnected, and a waiting period of several minutes is needed to allow capacitors to discharge. Additional power disconnect verification procedures are recommended by OE system manufacturers, which should be followed. For example, a lock-out device clamped on the master disconnect switch can prevent accidental energizing of high-voltage circuits when the vehicle is being serviced FIGURE 49-8.

When working on the battery storage system, two persons are required in case one person is harmed or becomes incapable of removing themselves from a live electrical circuit. Scaffolding, as shown in FIGURE 49-9, is a must when working around or servicing overhead battery systems. In addition, non-conductive body hooks and Class D fire extinguishers are required at scaffolding level.

TECHNICIAN TIP

Floating ground refers to the electrical ground separation between the chassis and the high-voltage electrical system. Dedicated circuits are used for the high-voltage system current, which does not share a ground path with the low-voltage system. An electrical system isolation monitor continuously checks to ensure that a high value of electrical resistance insulates the high from the low-voltage electrical system. Any time the potential for stray currents is detected, fault codes are logged, warning lights may be illuminated, and the vehicle may even shut-down.

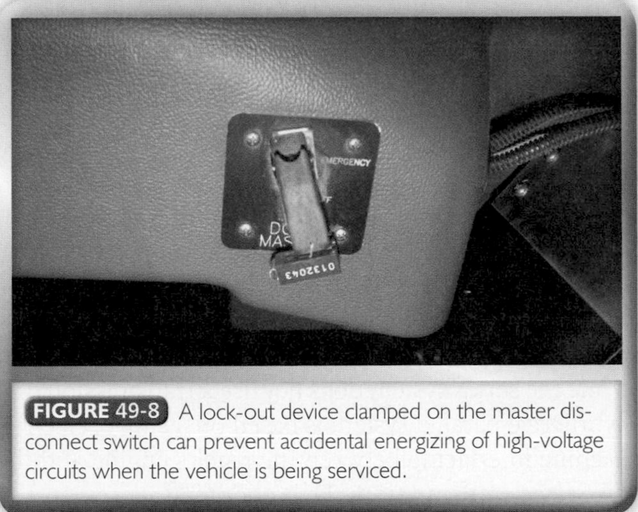

FIGURE 49-8 A lock-out device clamped on the master disconnect switch can prevent accidental energizing of high-voltage circuits when the vehicle is being serviced.

FIGURE 49-9 The use of purpose-built stairs and a buddy system is critical to safety when serving roof-mounted equipment tubs and batteries.

Insulated Gloves

One of the first lines of defense when it comes to preventing contact with energized electrical components and/or electrical power cables are insulating gloves, commonly known as lineman gloves FIGURE 49-10. OSHA requires the use of rubber insulated gloves for those persons working on or near energized circuits and/or other electrical sources that are considered either high or low-voltage applications. Lineman gloves are categorized by the amount of AC and DC voltage they have been proof-tested to in addition to the designated maximum-use voltage. The voltage protection is referenced as a Class rating, which is broken down starting with Class 00 having the lowest voltage protection up to Class 4 with highest protection. Class 0 lineman gloves recommended for use on high voltage hybrid circuits offer protection from 1,500 to 5,000 volts.

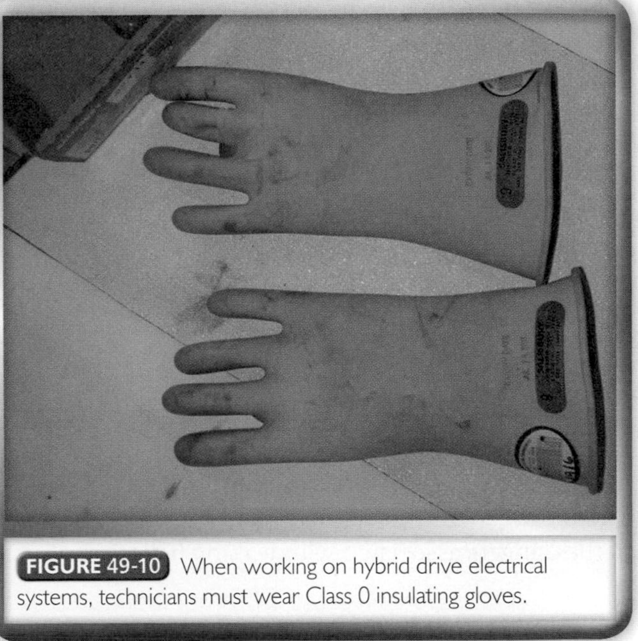

FIGURE 49-10 When working on hybrid drive electrical systems, technicians must wear Class 0 insulating gloves.

Routine Inspection

Routine periodic inspection of a hybrid drive system typically involves checking for the following:

- Loose bolts, mounting components, and grounding straps
- Loose, worn, or frayed electrical components
- Improperly routed or frayed vehicle electrical harnesses
- Damaged or loose hoses
- Fluid leaks
- Damaged, dented, or out-of-phase drive shafts
- Checking for fault codes or warning light illumination

Technicians must know the correct jacking and hoisting procedures prior to servicing the vehicle found in the OEM service manual.

Collisions

In the event of a collision:

- Turn off ignition switch, master, and battery isolator switches
- Inspect all EV propulsion system components for external damage
- Inspect all cooling lines and connections for leaks

- Place the vehicle in the service facility for a full checkout
- Emergency responders are recommended to use a Class 0 – 1,000-volt cable cutter with a 2" opening size to cut power from the battery storage to the vehicle system.
- Type D, smothering type fire extinguisher is recommended for fires

Lithium-ion and lead-acid batteries, if ruptured, will both produce flammable hydrogen gas. Corrosive battery acid will leak from lead-acid batteries. The chemical composition of the nickel-metal hydride battery electrolyte can cause severe burns to skin if it comes into contact with the body. It is essential that precautions are always followed if the hybrid vehicle has been in a collision because of the dangers associated with leaking batteries.

Series-Type Hybrid Drive Systems

BAE HybriDrive Propulsion Systems

BAE is an aerospace and defense technology company and is also one of the leading developers and manufacturers of hybrid-drive propulsion systems for the military and heavy-duty commercial vehicles. Since 1996, BAE Systems has collaborated with Daimler in hybrid electric propulsion systems for transit buses. The company's HybriDrive series-type propulsion system is currently the best-selling heavy hybrid drive and is in service in more than 4,000 transit buses in cities around the world.

HybriDrive systems are also available in parallel-type drive configurations. In 2012, BAE and Caterpillar collaborated to integrate the Caterpillar CX model transmissions into its HybriDrive parallel propulsion system. While the series system does not use a transmission, the HybriDrive parallel system is based on a single, electric, machine interfacing between the truck's engine and the CX Series transmission. This chapter focuses on the HybriDrive series system shown in **FIGURE 49-11**, as it represents one of the most common hybrid propulsion systems and also the first system, introduced back in 1998. **TABLE 49-5** compares different models of hybrid drive systems.

HybriDrive series type is available as different levels or "Generation" of hybrid systems. The differences between the systems are not obvious but, according to the manufacturer, a number of subsystems on the higher level versions have been improved including the engine,

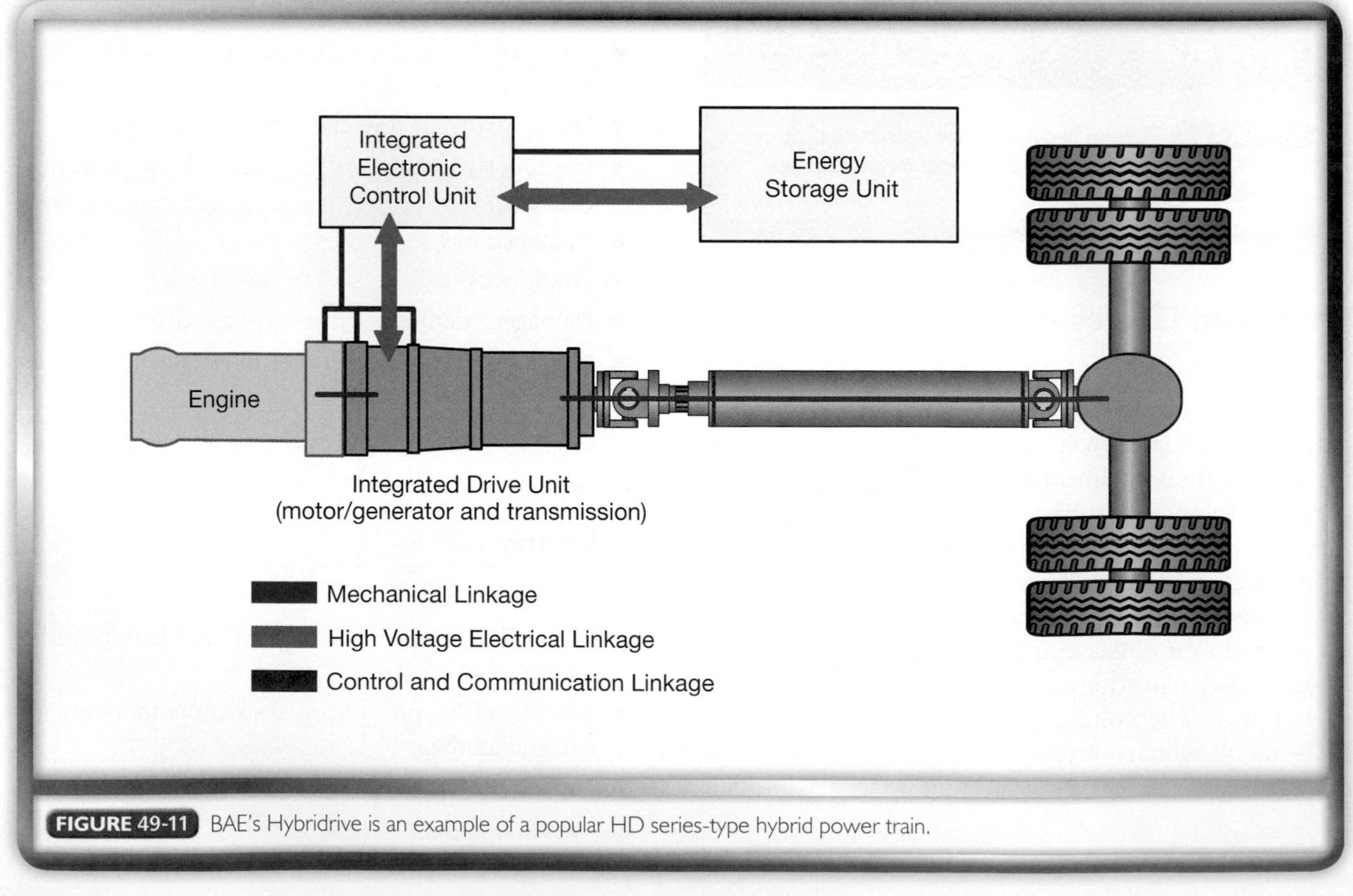

FIGURE 49-11 BAE's Hybridrive is an example of a popular HD series-type hybrid power train.

TABLE 49-5: Comparison of Different Types of Hybrid Drive Systems

	BAE Systems (HybriDrive propulsion system)	Allison EP 40	Allison EP 50
Power	• 250 hp continuous (320 hp [239 kW] peak) • Torque 2,700 lb-ft (3,660 Nm) at 0 rpm	• Continuous: 280 hp (209 kW) • Rated input torque: 910 lb ft (1,235 Nm) • Rated input speed: 2300 rpm • Acceleration power: 350 hp (261 kW)	• Continuous: 330 hp (298 kW) peak • Torque: 1050 lb-ft (1,423 Nm) • Rated input speed: 2300 rpm • Acceleration power: 400 hp (298 kW)
Engine	• Orion VI Transit Bus • Gen I Cummins B Series • Gen 2 Cummins C Series		
Electric drive motor	• Three-phase alternating current (AC) induction type	• Three-phase asynchronous induction motor/generator	• Three-phase asynchronous induction motor/generator
Motor horsepower	• 160 hp continuous using 436 VAC at 2,300 rpm • 450 ft-lbs.(610 Nm) of torque at 0 rpm • 4.69:1 gear reduction produces 2,100 ft-lbs. (2,847 Nm) of torque at 0 rpm at the output shaft yoke	• Input continuous: 280 hp (209 kW) • Rated input torque: 910 lb ft (1,235 Nm) • Rated input speed: 2,300 rpm • Acceleration power: 350 hp (261 kW)	• Input continuous: 330 hp (246 kW) • Rated input torque: 1,050 lb ft (1,420 Nm) • Rated input speed: 2300 rpm • Acceleration power: 400 hp (298 kW)
Generator type	• Permanent magnet	• Three-phase asynchronous induction motor/generator	• Three-phase asynchronous induction motor/generator
Energy storage type	• Sealed lead-acid (Gen 1) • Lithium-ion (Gen 2)	• Nickel-metal hydride (NiMH)	• Nickel-metal hydride (NiMH)
Voltage	• 520–700 VDC • 436 VAC continuous	• 600 VAC ESS Voltage Range: 432–780 VDC DPIM Voltage Range: 350 VDC	• 600 VAC ESS Voltage Range: 432–780 VDC DPIM Voltage Range: 350 VDC

VAC = Volts of AC current **VDC** = Volts of DC current

generator, propulsion control, and cooling and packaging FIGURE 49-12. The most significant difference in the systems is the energy storage components; lead-acid batteries were used in the original release of the systems, but now Lithium-ion batteries are used instead on new systems.

The BAE HybriDrive series system is designed for applications requiring low average vehicle speeds and frequent stop-and-start operation. The HybriDrive parallel system is designed for use on vehicles with operating cycles having faster operating speeds and fewer frequent stops such as medium duty trucks.

HybriDrive Series Propulsion System Overview

Many buses using the BAE HybriDrive systems are coupled to a Cummins diesel engine to obtain the highest fuel efficiency with the lowest emissions. In such installations, the engine operates at a fixed speed.

Connected directly to the engine is an electrical generator used to produce electrical power for the drive motor and to charge the batteries. A single electric drive motor coupled to the driveline has two functions. As with any series hybrid-drive system, the first function is to provide all the power necessary to propel the vehicle. The second function is to create regenerative braking, which enables the generator to convert braking force into electrical current rather than to lose energy to heat through traditional friction brakes.

On-board battery banks supply electrical current needed during acceleration and store current recovered from regenerative braking. Specialized computer software operates the propulsion control system module, which electronically controls the complete system by processing input data and sending electrical output signals to all system actuators.

The batteries compose the largest part of the electrical storage subsystem. A battery monitoring subsystem maintains the charge of each individual battery and performs battery diagnostic checks.

Hybrid vehicles produce significantly lower emissions than conventional diesel-powered buses, as the energy storage system supplies power during start-up and acceleration. At these times, the diesel engine is idling.

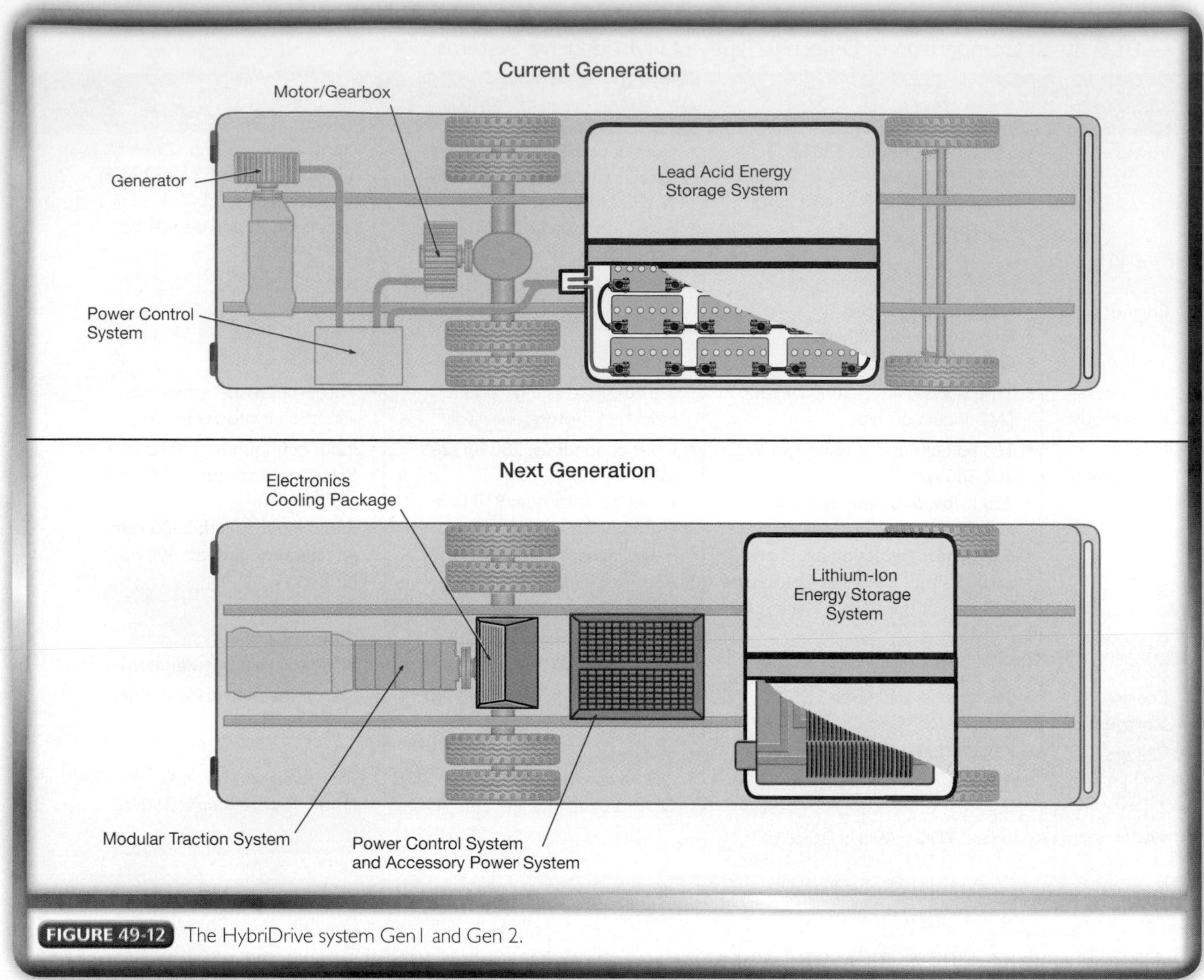

FIGURE 49-12 The HybriDrive system Gen I and Gen 2.

Major System Components of Series HybriDrive

HybriDrive includes the following major system components FIGURE 49-13

- Propulsion Control System (PCS)
- AC Traction Generator (ACTG)
- AC Traction Motor (ACTM)
- Energy Storage System (ESS) and fresh air cooling system for the ESS required for operation above 100°F (38°C)

The systems also include battery monitoring systems and current inverters, as well as diagnostic service software supplied by the manufacturer (BAE) called the Intuitive Diagnostic system (IDS). Also available is an optional data logging module that is used to record all system information available on the network data bus.

Propulsion Control System Module

The **propulsion control system (PCS) module** is the system element controlling the operation of the entire HybriDrive System FIGURE 49-14. It is a microprocessor based device that supplies electrical output signals based on input data collected from a vehicle's sensors, such as the accelerator position sensor, brake switch, gear range selector, and so on. FIGURE 49-15 shows a schematic of the HybriDrive propulsion system.

Three low-voltage connectors, each with 40-pins, form the input-output interface of the PCS with the system. Critical sensor input data is also collected from the electrical generator (ACTG), the transmission (ACTM), and the energy storage system (ESS) modules and enters the PCS through the connectors.

The ignition switch is also a critical input signal that initiates system operation by "waking-up" the PCS,

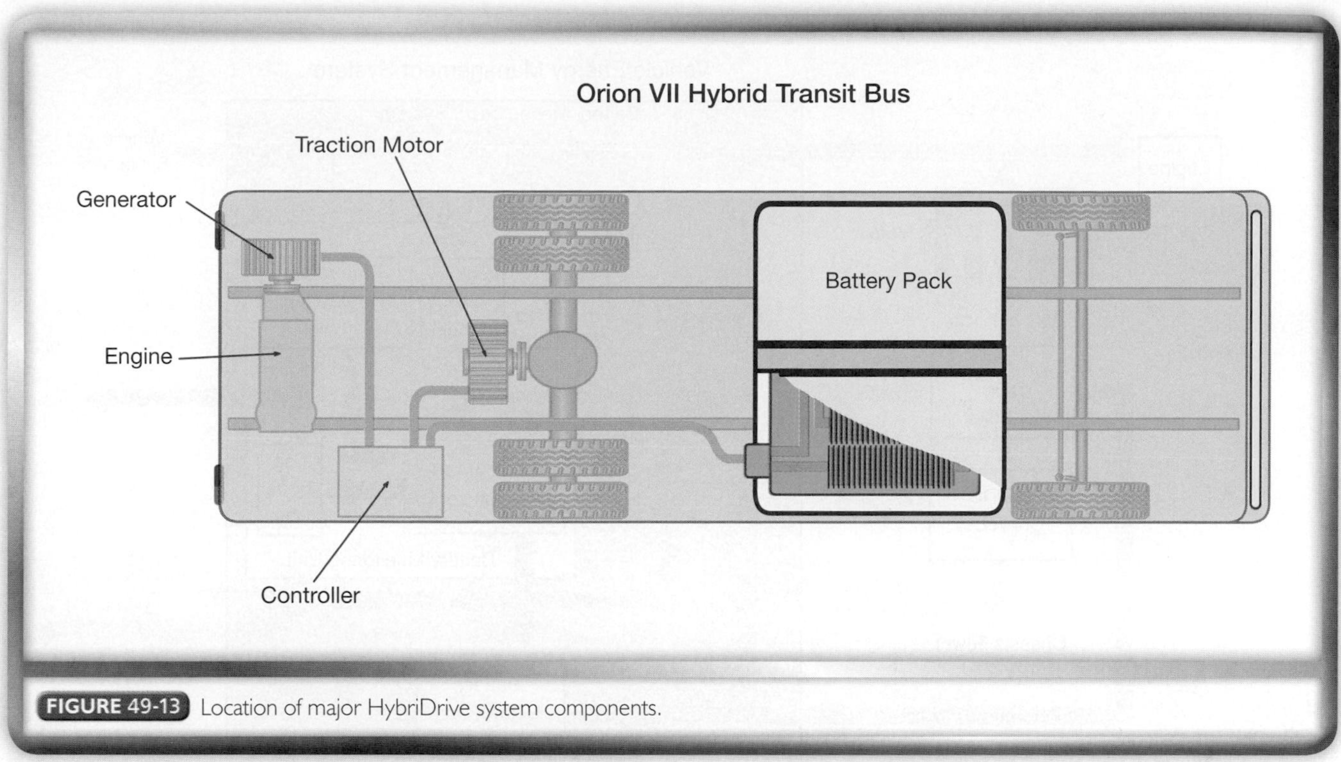

FIGURE 49-13 Location of major HybriDrive system components.

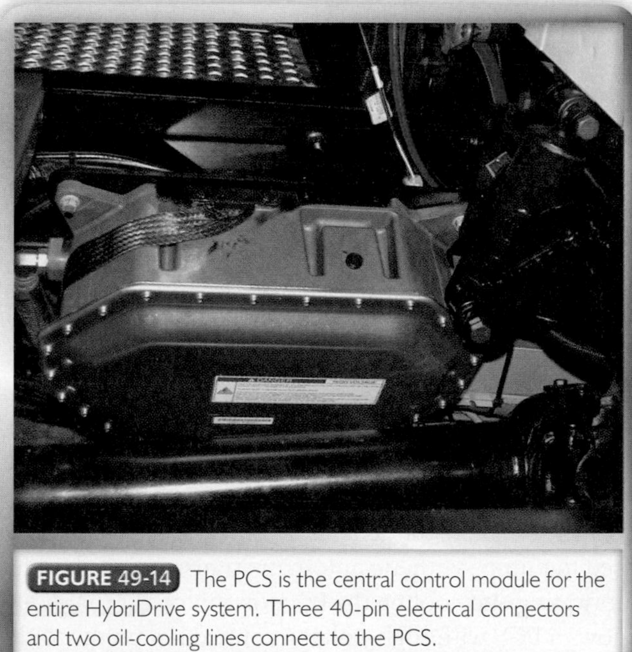

FIGURE 49-14 The PCS is the central control module for the entire HybriDrive system. Three 40-pin electrical connectors and two oil-cooling lines connect to the PCS.

which, in turn, activates other system components. Software inside the PCS containing control algorithms uses sensor data to regulate engine speed and the supply of electrical current to the inverters, which determines the output torque of the traction motor.

Even the batteries' state of charge is monitored and controlled by the PCS module. Diagnostic software continuously checks the complete system operation and sends fault information as well as system status to the diagnostic connector, where it can interface with the **Intuitive Diagnostic System (IDS)** software used by service technicians.

Fault codes are retained in the PCS non-volatile memory (NVM), which means that they can only be erased using the IDS service tool. System warning lights are also outputs of the PCS. To maintain module reliability and durability, the PCS, which weighs roughly 185 lb (84 kg), is cooled using the transmission fluid.

The system uses the following inputs and outputs to operate the system at maximum efficiency:

- PCS Inputs
  - Throttle pedal
  - Brake pedal
  - Emergency override switch
  - Gear selector switch
  - Master switch
  - Master disconnect switch
  - Engine test switch
  - Brake regeneration disable switch (optional)
  - High idle switch (optional)
- PCS Outputs
  - Stop HEV indicator
  - Check HEV indicator
  - REGEN applied indicator
  - Motor over-speed warning indicator
  - HEV maintenance required indicator

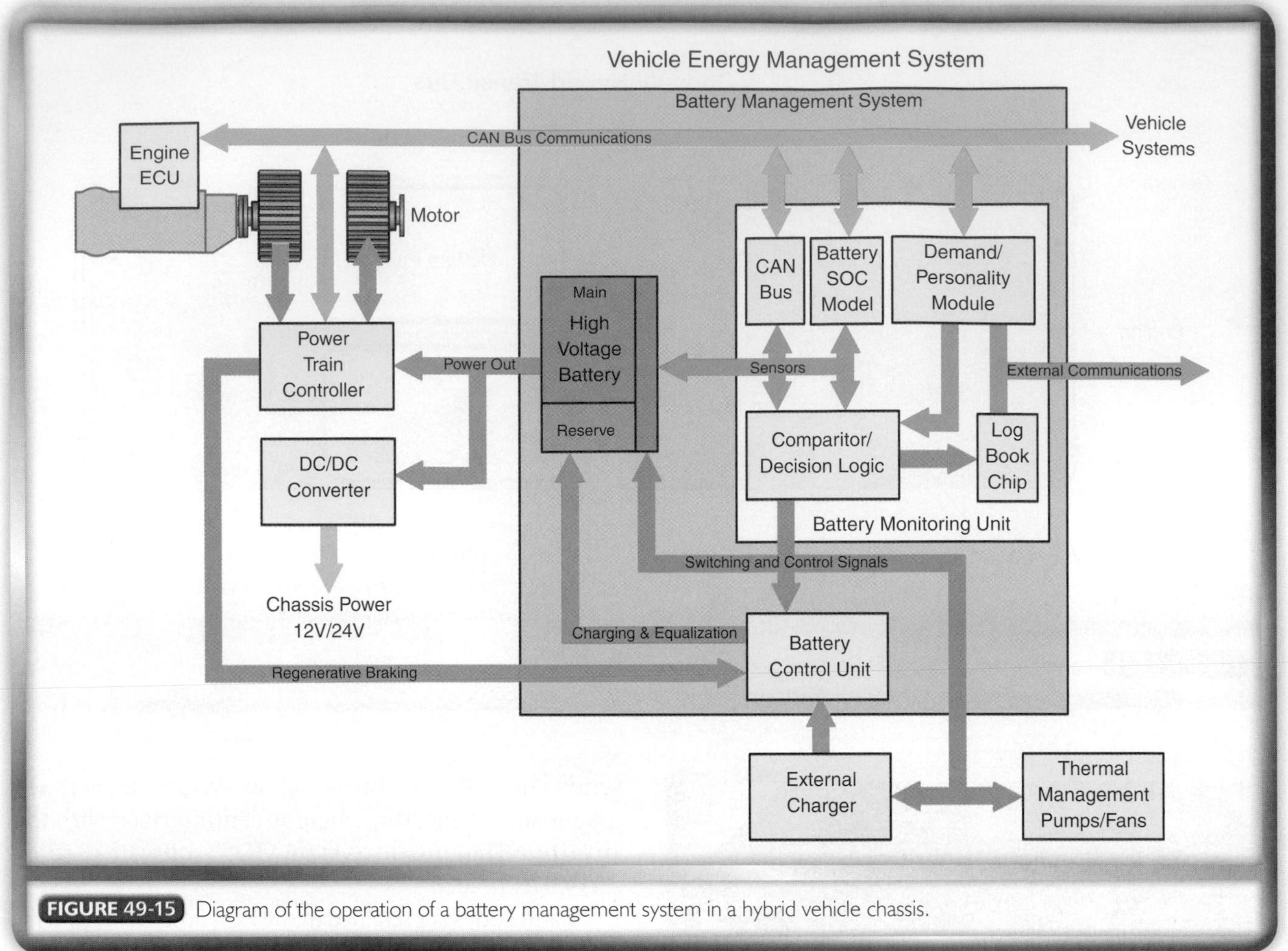

FIGURE 49-15 Diagram of the operation of a battery management system in a hybrid vehicle chassis.

- Electric current to inverters
- Battery state of charge control
- Serial data via DINEX and SAE J1939 data link

AC Traction Generator (ACTG)

Connected directly to the flywheel of the engine is the **alternating current traction generator (ACTG)**, which converts mechanical energy produced by the engine into electrical current for the propulsion system **FIGURE 49-16**. This component is a permanent magnet-brushless design generator, producing three-wave AC voltage at approximately 436 volts and 600 amps maximum with 160-horsepower (119 kW) input. Generator output is partly controlled by the speed of the engine, which is regulated by the PCS to between 800 and 2,300 rpm. Even though the generator is air cooled, heat produced during current production may require supplemental cooling using a fresh air plenum for vehicles operating in temperatures greater than 100°F (38°C). In addition to the 280 pound (127 kg) weight of the generator is an oil scavenging pump used to pump synthetic automatic transmission fluid for lubricating and cooling the traction motor. **FIGURE 49-17** shows a PCS with high-voltage connection points to the ACTM and ACTG.

FIGURE 49-16 Rear view of a typical transit bus using the HybriDrive Traction Generator (ACTG) is located directly behind the engine. No physical connection is made between the engine and drive axle. **A.** ACTG. **B.** Diesel engine.

FIGURE 49-17 High voltage connection points **A.** to the ACTM-ACTG from the PCS central control module for the entire HybriDrive system. Note the electrical connectors for sensors **B.** that also connect to the PCS.

Safety

When power washing engines, dirt washed from the engine can easily enter the ACTG. After start-up, damage occurs quickly inside the generator due to abrasive wear from the dirt. To prevent this, always use a protective apron when cleaning the engine to prevent the entry of dirt into the air-cooled generator.

Safety

The traction motor of most hybrid drive systems is not field serviceable. One of the reasons is the safety hazard created when disassembling these motors. The permanent magnets making up the motor field will draw the rotor tightly against it with tremendous force. Fingers caught between the rotor or other metal parts and field are instantly amputated and crushed. Never disassemble a permanent magnet motor of this size without the proper training and service tools.

AC Traction Motor (ACTM)

The **alternating current traction motor (ACTM)** has two functions. One is to resist driveline rotation when commanded by the PCS during braking. This effectively turns the traction motor into an electrical generator, which then sends current to charge the on-board batteries. The other function is as a high-speed, three-phase, induction-type motor FIGURE 49-18. Induction motors work well in hybrid drive systems, as they produce the greatest amount of torque at 0 rpm, when the opposing magnetic fields in the stator and rotor are strongest. In the HybriDrive system, maximum torque is 2,100 ft-lbs. (2,847 Nm) of torque at 0 rpm.

The highest torque at starting is useful to accelerate the vehicle when it is necessary to overcome vehicle inertia. Induction motors also have no brushes, which eliminates reoccurring maintenance caused by wear and extends component reliability.

Maximum speed of the motor is 15,000 rpm; however a 4.69:1 gear reduction box is used to multiply torque

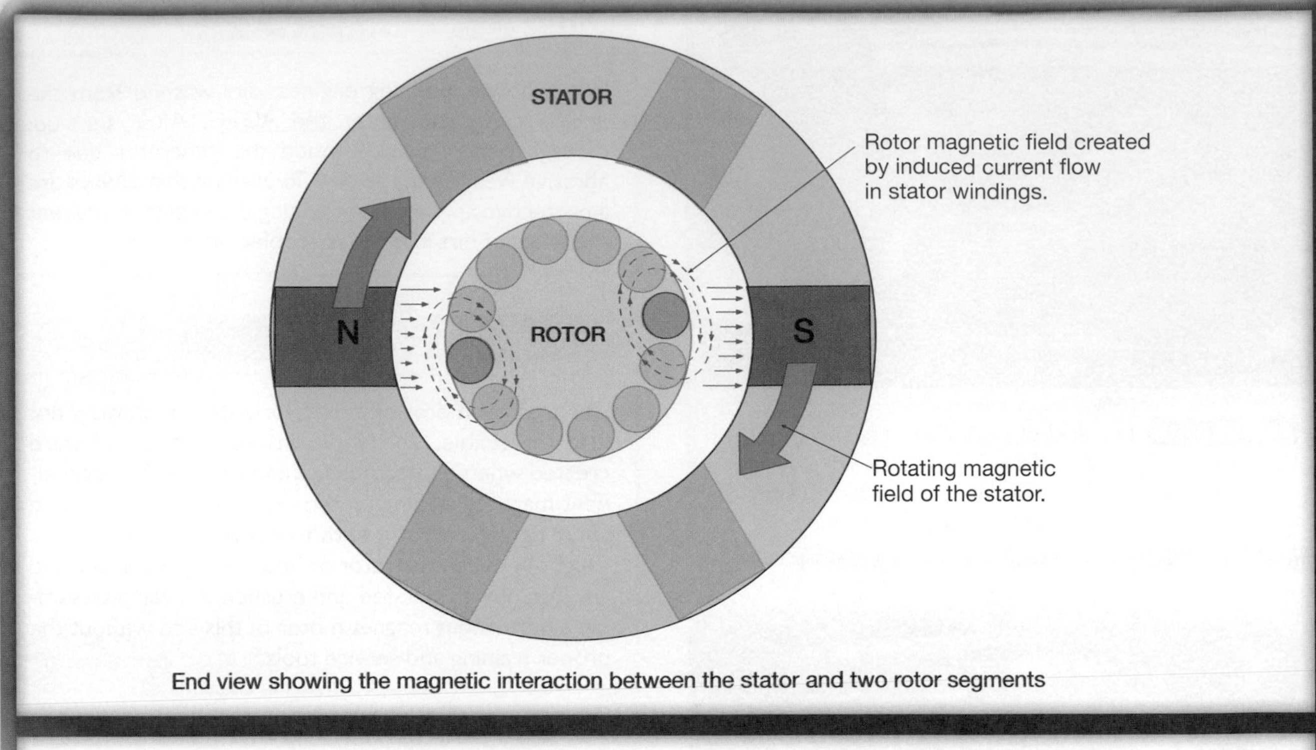

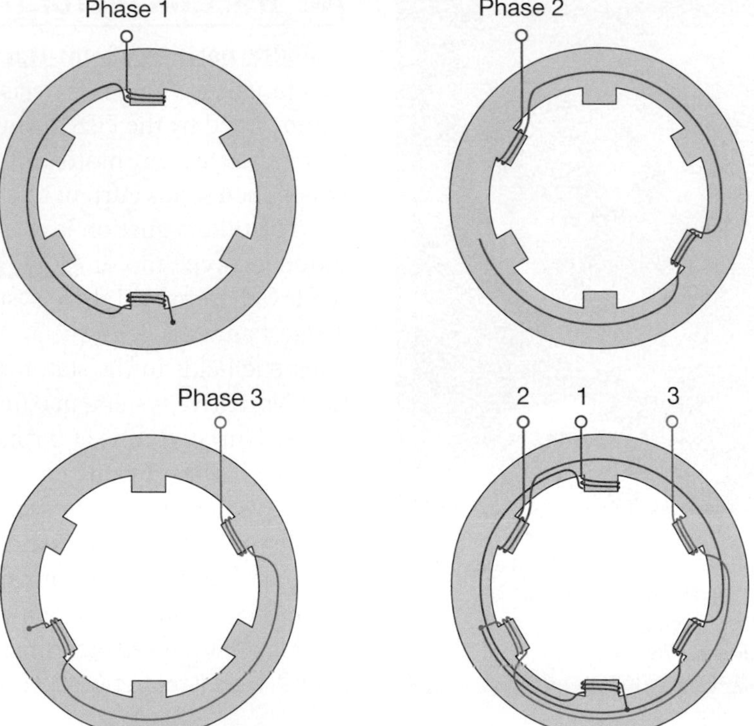

FIGURE 49-18 The ACTM is a three-phase induction motor induction which means it uses three stator winding which enables the direction of the motor to change. The polarity of each of the stator poles changes each time the AC current reverses direction. The PCS controls the phasing of stator energization, which in turn causes the motor to change direction.

output while reducing motor speed. With maximum current flow from both the batteries and the generator, the motor can momentarily produce up to 250 hp (186 kW) at approximately 600 VAC operating between 0 and 3,200 rpm. Since the motor has three phases, or windings, in the stator, the angles between the magnetic field of the stator and rotor can be electrically altered to reverse the direction of motor rotation.

A special sensor called the **resolver** measures the rotor position and speed for the PCS to properly manage the motor operation by reducing current flow and shutting down the system as needed. Because overspeed conditions will damage the motor, the resolver is a critical sensor for the PCS. The motor is connected directly to the vehicle's differential through a standard driveshaft and yoke arrangement.

During regenerative braking, reverse torque produces current to charge the batteries, which is later used to propel the vehicle. This arrangement helps the HybriDrive to reduce fuel consumption and friction brake wear. Regenerative braking energy recovered from the ACTM is automatically reduced when the batteries are fully charged. As part of the fault protection system, two temperature sensors inside the motor are used to protect the motor against overheating **FIGURE 49-19**. The motor, which weighs 450 pounds (205 kg), is also oil cooled and lubricated with synthetic transmission fluid. **FIGURE 49-20** illustrates fluid lines to the ACTM.

Safety

If a HybriDrive propulsion system needs towing, both rear axles must be removed before towing. If not removed, the lack of pressurized lubrication on rotating parts driven by the shafts will damage internal components.

Energy Storage System (ESS)

To maximize acceleration energy, the **energy storage system** supplies current to the ACTM when current demand exceeds availability from the ACTG. The ESS also stores electrical current produced during regenerative braking to maximize reductions to fuel consumption. The DC Power Link Contactor is a switch that connects the ESS to the PCS. When closed it completes the path between the Energy Storage System and PCS through the battery cables.

Elements of the ESS include battery modules, a battery management system (BMS), (the BMS manages the charging and discharging of the batteries to ensure long battery life and safe operation); an electronic cooling package (ECP), (an electronically managed cooling system for the battery modules); and system safety protection devices such as fuses and contactor switches. The original Gen 1 systems used lead-acid storage batteries, while the Gen 2 system uses lithium-phosphate ion batteries

FIGURE 49-19 The traction motor is a three-phase design, which enables precision control of speed and direction of rotation. The resolver sensor measures motor rotor angle and speed.

FIGURE 49-20 **A.** Transmission fluid line connections to the **B.** HybriDrive AC traction motor (ACTM).

stored in tubs on the vehicle roof to keep them cooler and cleaner FIGURE 49-21.

Unlike hybrid drive systems used in light-duty vehicles, in heavy-duty commercial vehicles, nickel-metal hydride (NiMH) batteries are not used because they are regarded as having reached their maximum potential. Further technological advancements and cost reductions are not expected for NiMH batteries. Lithium-ion batteries are now commonplace because they offer higher energy density than NiMH batteries and do not experience adverse memory effects due to inconsistent charging. Lithium batteries also have the lowest self-discharge rate compared to other battery technologies. That is, lithium batteries will maintain a charge for a very long time when idled.

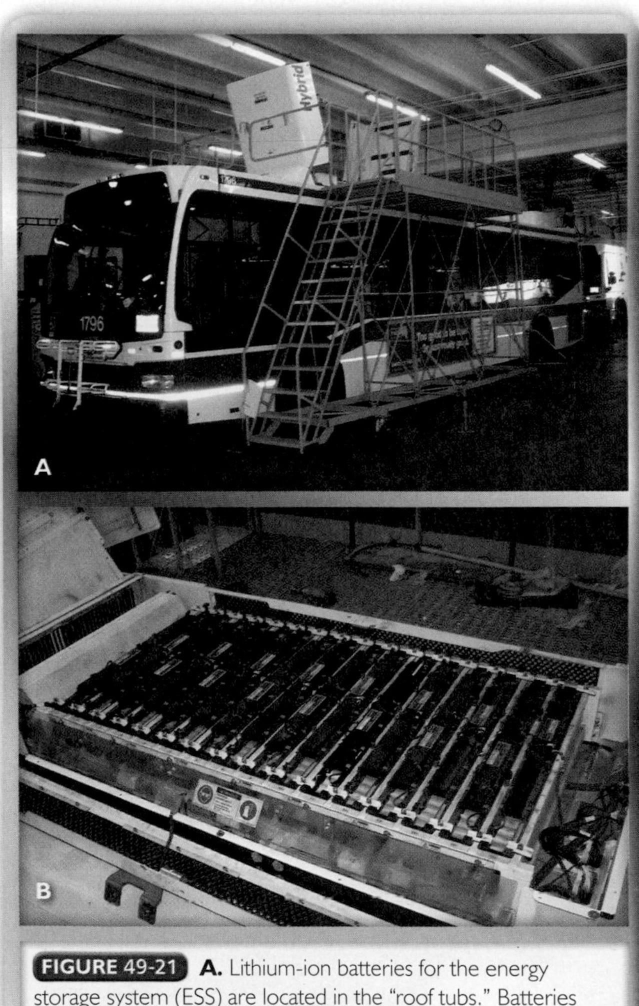

FIGURE 49-21 **A.** Lithium-ion batteries for the energy storage system (ESS) are located in the "roof tubs." Batteries are stored on the roof to keep them cooler and cleaner. Fires and battery gassing are less likely to endanger passengers. **B.** Lithium-ion battery cells are packaged in interconnected modules of 80 volts each.

Compared with lead-acid batteries, a lithium battery pack is less than one-quarter of the weight and charges faster. Upgrading to lithium batteries reduces battery pack weight from 4,100 to 1,000 pounds (1,818 to 455 kg), which means roof structures in buses do not need as much reinforcement and fuel consumption can decrease. Frequent charge and discharge cycles shorten battery life. Service life of lead-acid batteries is between two and three years compared to six years for lithium batteries.

The Lithium-ion energy storage system (ESS) contains a total of 16 Lithium-ion modules producing 39.6 V DC per module connected to total approximately 633 VDC. During **charge- depleting (CD) operating mode**, the vehicle is powered only—or almost only—by the energy stored in the battery. If an under-voltage condition is detected, current is diverted from the AC traction motor to the energy storage modules.

State of ESS Charge

In **charge-sustaining (CS) mode**, the batteries' state of charge (SOC) may rise and fall slightly. The SOC will, however, on the average, remain at its initial level and can be recharged through regenerative braking. Energy storage modules are kept at a 40% state of charge. This may seem low, but the batteries are required to have capacity to store regenerative braking energy extracted from the AC traction motor.

Without battery capacity, regenerative braking is automatically reduced when the ESS modules are fully charged, which causes the friction-type service brakes to work harder, dissipate more heat, and waste fuel.

A **master disconnect switch** located in the battery compartments enables technicians to disconnect the power circuit for maintenance or emergencies. This switch has a lock-out feature that prevents anyone other than the technician from reconnecting vehicle power.

The master disconnect switch is different FIGURE 49-22 from the master switch. This switch controls the vehicle electrical system allowing the lights, engine, and HybriDrive propulsion system to operate when it is switched to the on position.

Battery Monitoring System

The battery monitoring system operates to equalize charges evenly across all the battery modules. Because batteries will often have slightly different resistances to charging and discharging, the battery monitor controls the charge and discharge rate to each module.

Voltage to each module will change when discharging, such as under acceleration or during regenerative

FIGURE 49-22 The master disconnect and other lock-out type switches are critical safety items. **A.** Master disconnect switch. **B.** HEV fault lamp.

TABLE 49-6: Condition of Good Versus Defective Battery Modules

Condition	Good Battery Modules	Defective Battery Modules
Discharge voltage at high amperage draw	Higher voltage	Lower voltage
Charging voltage at high amperage	Lower voltage	Higher voltage
Charge time	Faster	Slower
Capacity	High discharge amperage	Low discharge amperage

braking, when batteries are charged at high amperage. Defective battery modules are identified by their inability to accept a charge. The IDS service tool does not monitor individual module amperage, so module voltage is used for comparison.

For example, operative modules in good condition TABLE 49-6 will have less internal resistance and charge at a lower voltage compared with weak or defective modules. Modules in poor condition will have the largest charging voltage differences with good modules when charge amperage is highest, such as during braking. Voltage during acceleration will drop much more compared with good modules too. Diagnostic software will flag bad battery modules under these conditions.

Current Inverters

Wave inverters are devices that change the shape of electrical current waves. A **DC-to-AC inverter** takes the straight, unchanging wave of DC current and flips, or inverts, the current's polarity to resemble an AC wave signal. Similarly, an **AC-to-DC inverter** switches the polarity of an AC current signal to resemble the straight wave polarity of DC current FIGURE 49-23.

Both types of current inverters are used in the HybriDrive system. AC current produced by the ACTG is rectified to 580 Volts DC to charge the batteries. To operate the ACTM 633-Volts DC, battery voltage is converted to three-phase 346-volts—phase-to-phase or line-to-line volts. The frequency of the voltage is varied to change the traction motor speed. At 250 hp (186 kW) maximum, 346 volts AC will have a maximum frequency of 500 Hz.

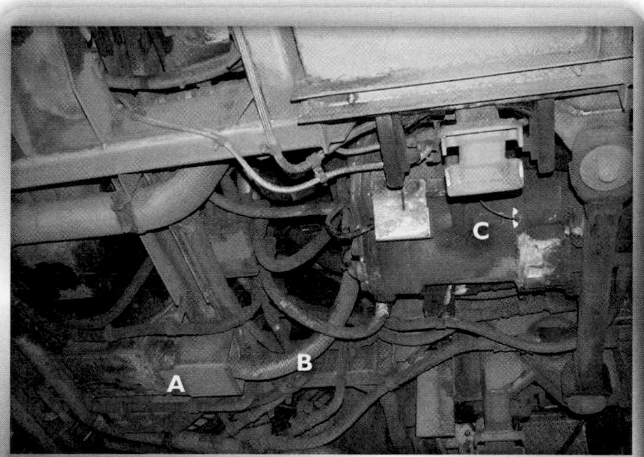

FIGURE 49-23 Three-phase voltage wave form originating from the PCS is used to operate the ACTM. Three-phase voltage operates the motor four times more efficiently a high-voltage, single-phase source. Line-to-line voltage is 346 volts AC; peak-to-peak voltage is 580 volts AC. **A.** PCS module. **B.** High-voltage cables. **C.** Traction motor.

Intuitive Diagnostic System (IDS)

The intuitive diagnostic system is BAE's service software. It is PC based and enables technicians to connect through the J-1939 connector to:

- Monitor system parameters
- View programmable parameters and make adjustments to customer programmable parameters
- View and erase fault codes
- View fault history
- Perform diagnostic tests

The IDS is able to read data and fault codes generated by the on-board diagnostic system

- Above normal component temperature
- Under and Over Voltage conditions
- Battery Under and Over Charging
- Motor Over-Speed

The PCS monitors the system for failure conditions. Under extreme conditions the system will derate or shutdown. If failures occur and the system shuts down, a PCS (Emergency) Override Switch can be pushed and held to override most shutdown conditions for up to ten seconds continuously and thirty seconds total. The PCS emergency override switch is used only to move a vehicle to a safe location if stalled on a roadway. Two dash lights indicate problems with the propulsion system.

The Stop HEV indicator is illuminated when an active severe fault is detected. In these circumstances the vehicle will not move unless the emergency override switch is pushed and a warning buzzer will sound. A Check HEV Indicator lights when a less serious but active fault is detected and the vehicle is operable in a de-rated condition. When inactive faults are logged by the on-board diagnostic system, the HEV Maintenance Required Indicator illuminates. This light is located in the engine compartment.

> **TECHNICIAN TIP**
>
> Corrosion caused by water intrusion in the wiring harness is a common cause of HEV problems and fault codes. Contributing to the problem is the position of protective split loom around vehicle cables, which can form "drip loops." These occur when water from road spray easily enters the split loom and collects. To minimize the likelihood of this problem, always orientate split in the cable loom away from the curbside engine grate and down to allow water to drain.

Unique System Inputs

To calculate the amount of torque to apply to the rear axles, a throttle pedal position sensor provides a varying voltage signal to the PCS. Based on signal values and a throttle torque map containing look-up table values, the PCS will determine the frequency and voltage supplied to the ACTM.

Brake Pressure Sensor

A brake pressure signal is needed to calculate the amount of regenerative braking performed by the ACTM **FIGURE 49-24**. Although the braking performed by ACTG is designed to simulate the action of conventional friction brakes, the brake "feel" of regenerative brakes may be too aggressive under some situations, such as on a bus with standing passengers. For safety reasons, an adjustment to the degree of regenerative braking is possible on the HybriDrive. A scale of one to ten is used for the adjustment, with ten being the most aggressive recovery of energy for greatest efficiency. In transit applications, the setting may be set as low as between three and five.

Regeneration Disable Switch

An optional switch located near the driver is available to turn regenerative braking off for one key cycle. Slippery road conditions may be one situation for which it would be desirable to turn off the regenerative braking for better control. Wheel lock-up conditions are sensed by the ABS, which will send a message along the CAN data bus to disengage the ACTM regeneration.

When the regeneration system is on, current is produced by the ACTM and ACTG to charge the batteries to a 40% state of charge. When regen is off, the ACTG charges modules ONLY when vehicle is parked in neutral. A dash light informs the driver whenever any brake regeneration is taking place.

FIGURE 49-24 The brake pressure sensor provides an input signal for the regenerative braking control. The control is adjustable between zero and ten, with zero being no regenerative braking and ten being the most aggressive braking.

Engine Test Switch

To service the engine separately from the hybrid drive system, it is preferable to disconnect all high voltage supply and operate the engine using the throttle pedal. To accomplish this, an engine test switch is used. As a two-position toggle switch, the normal position integrates engine operation into the HybriDrive system and the vehicle responds as intended. With the switch in the engine test position, only the engine responds to the throttle pedal, and all high voltage contacts are open.

Maintenance and Service

Preventative maintenance on the HybriDrive propulsion systems consists of inspections prescribed in the service manual and scheduled changes of coolant and traction motor oil. An air filter in the battery compartment is changed at two-year intervals. None of the major system components are rebuilt in the field but simply replaced after diagnostic tests have identified a replaceable unit.

Whenever the PCS is removed for replacement, it is a good practice to record all programmable parameters to adjust the replacement module efficiently. In addition to the electrical safety precautions outlined in the section, special tools like the ones shown in Figure 49-7 should be used when working on hybrid vehicles. Other electrical safety general procedures for component replacement include:

1. Switching off the master disconnect switch and locking out the switch until repairs are completed. Locking out the switch will prevent accidental reconnection of power during maintenance. The master disconnect switch disables the master switch and ignition signal, preventing the engine from starting or the PCS to energize. The master disconnect also disables the contactors in PCS and ESS.
2. Disconnect and remove all ESS high voltage connectors while wearing high voltage type 0000 lineman's gloves. Connections inside the battery storage enclosure are never to be performed without specialized OEM training.
3. Disconnect and tag external harnesses, lines and cooling connections to replacement components.
4. Validate the repair after service is completed by a proper road test or by operating the component under the appropriate condition to evaluate its performance. Faults codes should be erased before testing begins to determine whether they reoccur. Before returning the vehicle to service, any fault codes should be erased once more.

Safety

Even after the master disconnect switch is opened and locked-out, the battery system has the potential to deliver a severe shock hazard since the battery modules are not de-energized by this switch. Extreme caution must always be used when working around the Energy Storage System. Before touching any electrical conductor during HybriDrive service, always verify that an electrical circuit is de-energized by using a digital multimeter (DMM).

Wrap-up

Ready for Review

- A variety of hybrid drive vehicle configurations are used in commercial vehicles. In essence, hybrid propulsion systems can use any type of engine—gasoline, natural gas, diesel, turbine, or reciprocating—assisted by an electric motor to accelerate the vehicle.
- Hybrid electric vehicles simultaneously reduce both fuel consumption and emissions produced from burning fuel.
- Vehicles operating in urban driving conditions are best suited to hybrid use, as much of the energy derived from burning fuel is lost through idling and braking.
- The main configurations of hybrid vehicles are series, parallel, series-parellel, and plug-in hybrid vehicles.
- A series system requires a larger electric motor and battery pack, but a smaller internal combustion engine and works best in stop-and-go situations. Parallel systems are better suited to higher speeds with less stop-and-go operation.
- An alternative to electric hybrid drives is the hydraulic launch assist (HLA) system. The concept of HLA uses hydraulic regenerative braking to capture braking energy and help launch the vehicle during acceleration.
- Hybrid drive system components use lethal high-voltage power devices operating up to 900 volts and contain energy storage systems over 700 volts DC, so special tools and personal protective equipment must be used during servicing to ensure technician safety.
- BAE is an aerospace and defense technology company and is also one of the leading developers and manufacturers of hybrid-drive propulsion systems for the military and heavy-duty commercial vehicles. It manufactures series-type and parallel-type hybrids.
- HybriDrive includes the following major system components: propulsion control system (PCS); AC traction generator (ACTG); AC traction motor (ACTM); Energy Storage System (ESS)—and fresh air cooling system for the ESS required for operation above 100°F (38°C).
- The entire HybriDrive system is controlled by a microprocessor-controlled propulsion control system. Multiple inputs and outputs enable the PCS to operate the system at maximum efficiency.
- The alternating current system generator (ACTG) is a permanent magnet-brushless design generator that is air cooled.
- The alternating current traction motor (ACTM) resists driveline rotation when commanded by the PCS during braking. It also functions as a high-speed, three-phase, induction-type motor.
- Unlike hybrid drive systems used in light-duty vehicles, in heavy-duty commercial vehicles, nickel-metal hydride (NiMH) batteries are not used because they are regarded as having reached their maximum potential.
- Without battery capacity, regenerative braking is automatically reduced when the ESS modules are fully charged, which causes the friction-type service brakes to work harder, dissipate more heat, and waste fuel.
- The battery monitoring system operates to equalize charges evenly across all the battery modules. Defective battery modules are identified by their inability to accept a charge.
- HybriDrive systems use DC-to-AC and AC-to-DC inverters.
- A brake pressure signal is needed to calculate the amount of regenerative braking performed by the ACTM because the braking feel of regenerative brakes can be too aggressive in some situations, such as mass transit.
- Regenerative braking can be turned on or off by the driver.
- To service the engine separately from the hybrid drive system, it is preferable to disconnect all high voltage supply and operate the engine using the throttle pedal.

Vocabulary Builder

AC-to-DC inverter A device that switches the polarity of an AC current signal to resemble the straight wave polarity of DC current.

AC traction generator (ACTG) A device that converts mechanical energy produced by the engine into electrical current for the propulsion system.

AC traction motor (ACTM) A motor that functions as an electrical generator in a hybrid drive system.

charge-depleting operating mode (CD) A mode of operation in which the vehicle is powered only—or almost only—by the energy stored in the battery.

charge-sustaining mode (CS) A mode of operation in which the batteries' state of charge (SOC) may rise and fall slightly and energy storage modules are kept at a 40% state of charge.

DC-to-AC inverter A device that takes the straight, unchanging wave of DC current and flips, or inverts, the current's polarity to resemble an AC wave signal.

electric vehicle (EV) A vehicle in which only electric motors are used to move a vehicle.

electronic cooling package (ECP) A system of fans and electronic controls that maintains a hybrid ESS within a set temperature range.

energy storage system (ESS) A system that stores and distributes electrical current to the various components of a hybrid drive system.

hybrid electric vehicle (HEV) A type of vehicle that combines an internal combustion engine with an electric propulsion system into a new or hybrid powertrain configuration.

HybriDrive Propulsion System A series-type hybrid propulsion system developed by BAE, an aerospace and defense technology company.

hydraulic launch assist (HLA) An alternative to electric hybrid drives in which application of standard friction service brakes is prevented until just before a complete vehicle stop.

Intuitive Diagnostic System (IDS) Proprietary software system available on BAE propulsion systems to aid technicians in diagnosing service issues.

master disconnect switch A switch located in the battery compartments that enables technicians to disconnect the power circuit for maintenance or emergencies.

parallel drive A vehicle in which both the engine and electric motor work together, blending motor and engine torque, to propel the vehicle.

plug-in hybrid electric vehicle (PHEV) Any type of hybrid electric vehicle containing a battery storage system that uses an external source to recharge the battery when the vehicle is not in operation.

propulsion control system (PCS) module A microprocessor-based device that supplies electrical output signals based on input data collected from a vehicle's sensors.

regenerative braking A feature of hybrid vehicles by which generators recover energy during braking.

resolver A special sensor that measures the rotor position and speed for the PCS to properly manage the motor operation by reducing current flow and shutting down the system as needed.

series drive A vehicle in which only an electric traction motor supplies torque to propel the vehicle.

series-parallel drive A more complex system enabling an engine only, an electric motor only, and a combined engine-motor operation. Also called *power-split configuration*.

traction motor An electric motor that provides propulsion to a vehicle.

wave inverter A device that changes the shape of electrical current waves.

Review Questions

1. A series electric hybrid drive system propels the vehicle with which of the following?
   a. An electric motor only
   b. Two electric motors
   c. An electric motor and an internal combustion engine working together at all times
   d. An internal combustion engine at some times and an electric motor at others, or a combination of the two
2. What is a PHEV?
   a. A series electric hybrid drive
   b. A parallel electric hybrid drive
   c. A series-parallel electric hybrid drive
   d. An electric hybrid vehicle that plugs in to charge the batteries
3. A series-parallel electric hybrid drive system uses which of the following to propel the vehicle?
   a. An electric motor only
   b. Two electric motors
   c. An electric motor and an internal combustion engine working together at all times
   d. An internal combustion engine at some times and an electric motor at others, or a combination of the two
4. Which type of battery is used as storage in the gen 2 BAE HybriDrive series system?
   a. Lead acid
   b. Nickel-metal hydride
   c. Glass mat
   d. Lithium-ion
5. Which type of current is used to power the BAE HybriDrive series system electric motor?
   a. AC
   b. DC
   c. AC and DC together
   d. AC is used during certain operation, and DC is used during others.
6. ________ batteries are used in the storage system used with the Allison EP40 Hybrid system.
   a. Lead-acid
   b. Nickel-metal hydride
   c. Glass mat
   d. Lithium-ion
7. What is directly attached to the engine flywheel in the BAE series HybriDrive system?
   a. The electric motor/generator
   b. The transmission
   c. The AC traction generator
   d. The AC traction motor
8. How many battery modules are used in the gen 2 BAE Series HybriDrive system?
   a. 8
   b. 16
   c. 24
   d. 32
9. Much of the energy required to accelerate a city transit bus is lost to heat caused by frequent braking. What is the estimated percentage of that energy loss?
   a. 35%
   b. 45%
   c. 55%
   d. 65%
10. What cools the AC traction motor in the BAE HybriDrive system?
    a. Transmission fluid
    b. Air
    c. Engine coolant
    d. Engine oil

ASE-Type Questions

1. Technician A says that a hybrid electrical vehicle is one that has an electrical motor to drive the vehicle only and an engine to charge the vehicle batteries when necessary. Technician B says that the type of a hybrid that Technician A is describing is known as a series hybrid. Who is correct?
   a. Technician A
   b. Technician B
   c. Both Technician A and Technician B
   d. Neither Technician A nor Technician B
2. Technician A says that a parallel-drive hybrid is one in which both the engine and the electric motor combine to drive the vehicle at all times. Technician B says that series-parallel drive hybrid can use the engine, the electric motor, or both together to drive the vehicle. Who is correct?
   a. Technician A
   b. Technician B
   c. Both Technician A and Technician B
   d. Neither Technician A nor Technician B
3. Technician A says that not all hybrid drive vehicles are electric. Technician B says that hybrid drive electrical systems can be serviced in the same way as regular vehicle electrical systems. Who is correct?
   a. Technician A
   b. Technician B
   c. Both Technician A and Technician B
   d. Neither Technician A nor Technician B
4. Technician A says that electrical hybrid drive systems require an electrical storage system. Technician B says that most electrical hybrid drive systems use regenerative braking. Who is correct?
   a. Technician A
   b. Technician B
   c. Both Technician A and Technician B
   d. Neither Technician A nor Technician B
5. Technician A says that regenerative braking means that the foundation brakes can regenerate themselves after they wear. Technician B says that foundation brakes last longer when regenerative braking is used. Who is correct?
   a. Technician A
   b. Technician B
   c. Both Technician A and Technician B
   d. Neither Technician A nor Technician B
6. Technician A says that the original BAE HybriDrive system is a series hybrid. Technician B says that the original BAE HybriDrive system has two electric traction motors. Who is correct?
   a. Technician A
   b. Technician B
   c. Both Technician A and Technician B
   d. Neither Technician A nor Technician B
7. Technician A says that lead-acid batteries are used to store electricity on the latest hybrid drive systems. Technician B says that the BAE gen 2 HybriDrive system uses nickel-metal hydride batteries as a power storage system. Who is correct?
   a. Technician A
   b. Technician B
   c. Both Technician A and Technician B
   d. Neither Technician A nor Technician B
8. Technician A says that electrical hybrid drive systems use a very high voltage traction motor to propel the vehicle. Technician B says that electrical hybrid drive systems require high voltage disconnect systems to shut of the high voltage for service. Who is correct?
   a. Technician A
   b. Technician B
   c. Both Technician A and Technician B
   d. Neither Technician A nor Technician B
9. Technician A says that AC current is used to power the traction motor in BAE HybriDrive systems. Technician B says the nickel-metal hydride batteries in the BAE gen 2 HybriDrive systems are AC batteries. Who is correct?
   a. Technician A
   b. Technician B
   c. Both Technician A and Technician B
   d. Neither Technician A nor Technician B
10. Technician A says that, when a hybrid drive vehicle is brought into the shop for service, the high voltage system should be locked out. Technician B says that, when a hybrid vehicle must be towed, both axles should be removed so that the driveshaft does not rotate or damage the hybrid drive components. Who is correct?
    a. Technician A
    b. Technician B
    c. Both Technician A and Technician B
    d. Neither Technician A nor Technician B

CHAPTER 50

NATEF Tasks

There are no NATEF tasks for this chapter.

Knowledge Objectives

After reading this chapter, you will be able to:

1. Explain the operating principles of series-parallel electric propulsion drive. (pp 1670–1672)
2. Describe the construction and operation of Allison EP Hybrid drive system. (pp 1670–1679)
3. Identify and explain the function of the Allison EP drive system components. (pp 1673–1682)
4. Describe the operating principles of a dual mode hybrid drive train. (pp 1683–1684)
5. Outline basic service and maintenance procedures for Allison EP drive systems. (pp 1684–1685)

Allison EV Drive Hybrid Systems

Skills Objectives

There are no skills objectives for this chapter.

Introduction

In addition to series-type hybrids, parallel drive and series-parallel drive are two common configurations of Allison EV Drive Hybrid Systems used in heavy-duty commercial vehicles. In parallel drive hybrids, both the engine and electric motor work together, blending motor and engine torque to propel the vehicle. Series-parallel drive is a more complex system enabling an engine only, an electric motor only, and a combined engine-motor operation. Also called a power-split configuration, the engine and motor operation is optimized for driving conditions.

Arvin Meritor markets a dual-mode hybrid system specifically designed for line-haul application, but as the Allison system is the most common series-parallel hybrids, this chapter will discuss that system in greater detail.

Overview of Allison EV Drive Hybrid System

EP40 and **EP50 systems** are model names derived for Allison's Electric Propulsion system, or alternatively Allison's Electrically Variable (EV) Drive. Although the two models are almost identical in construction and operation, the EP40 is capable of continuously delivering 280 hp, (209 kW) while the EP50's output is higher at 330 hp (246 kW).

The Allison EP Drive system is primarily a parallel-type hybrid drive. Unlike series hybrid systems, such as the BAE HybriDrive, which use only an electric motor for torque, parallel systems use a transmission, which enables a combination of output torque from both the electric traction motor and engine.

A dedicated engine-mechanical pathway and an electrical motor pathway for traction torque, along with a combination of both, are possible through the power train. Allison describes the hybrid architecture as a two mode compound-split system. That is because the system's capabilities allow for only electric or only a diesel engine for traction power and an infinitely variable combination of both. FIGURE 50-1.

Torque from both sources is blended to optimally match vehicle operating conditions and the electric propulsion-drive operating state. Its automatic transmission does not used fixed gear ratios. Instead, the power continuously varies from the engine and two electric motors when the vehicle is driving in a forward direction. When decelerating, the EP system uses regenerative braking to recover braking energy. Like other hybrids, the electric **traction motors** turn into generators, producing electric current used to charge an on-board bank of NiMH batteries. Regenerative braking slows the vehicle, like a retarder would in a conventional automatic transmission, which in turn reduces brake wear and fuel consumption.

You Are the Technician

As a transit bus technician, you are skilled and qualified to work on diesel-powered bus chassis. Recently, a few of the hybrid-drive buses in the fleet, which are now out of the manufacturer's warranty period, have begun to receive more complaints about braking. Passengers are falling during braking, and there are even a few reports of injuries due to overly aggressive braking. Examining the service records, you notice the buses all have far less frequent brake service and foundation replacement than what is expected from a hybrid chassis. After inspecting all the brake foundation components on one particular chassis, you find them all to be in proper working condition. Inspection and test procedures performed on the air brake circuits and values all are within normal expected limits. While road testing the bus, you do find that even under very light brake pedal application force, the bus does brake very aggressively. As it is a series-parallel type hybrid powertrain, you realize that a significant amount of braking is supposed to be performed by the electric traction motor-generator. As you consider which elements of the hybrid system to inspect, and search OEM literature for the correct diagnostic and inspection procedures, consider the following:

1. List the safety procedures that should be followed before beginning any inspection of diagnostic work on an Allison EV hybrid powertrain.
2. Identify potential problems with the hybrid powertrain that may contribute to more work being performed by the regenerative braking system and not the service braking system.
3. What strategy do you think the Allison EV system uses to ensure there is an adequate buffer or storage capacity in the batteries for regenerative braking if the batteries become excessively charged?

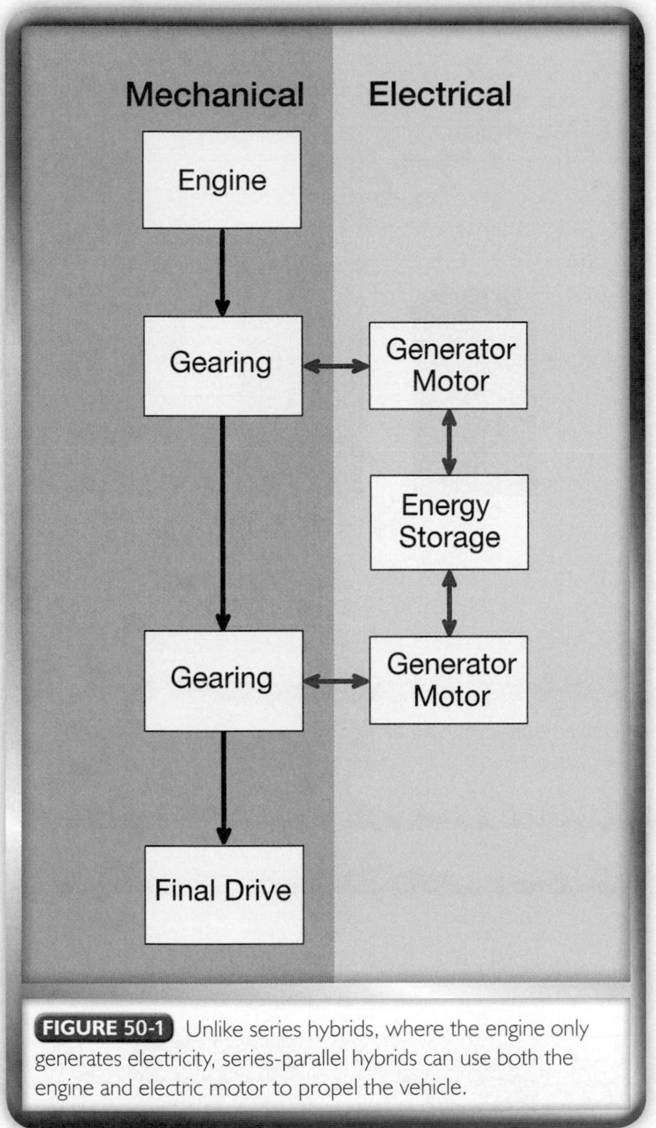

FIGURE 50-1 Unlike series hybrids, where the engine only generates electricity, series-parallel hybrids can use both the engine and electric motor to propel the vehicle.

Parallel Drive Advantages and Disadvantages

Real-world comparisons of the EP system to the series HybriDrive system show that EP offers slightly greater reduction in fuel consumption compared to the HybriDrive system operated on an identical route. The EP is capable of faster acceleration, too, if its adjustable HyGain accelerating setting feature is set-up for performance. Late-model Allison H-EP40/50s also have a unique feature referred to as **smart electrification**. This feature enables the system's motors to switch over to generating mode to produce as much as 300 amps at 24 volts at idle. Idle electrical generation at this magnitude is an ideal feature for buses replacing hydraulic-drive motors with current loads from electric accessories, such as the radiator cooling fan, charge air cooler fans, and hybrid drive cooling fans. Introduced in 2011, this feature uses a highly efficient solid state DC-to-DC converter FIGURE 50-2, eliminating the need for a traditional belt-driven alternator and associated maintenance requirements. On-board battery current is not used. Consequently, hybrid- and starting-battery life increase due to less frequent charge and discharge cycles. See FIGURE 50-3A and FIGURE 50-3B.

Despite the EP system advantages, currently less than a third of Allison EV Drive Hybrid Systems sold are Allison EP drives. The addition of the transmission and associated components adds approximately 1,500 pounds (682 kg) to vehicle weight. Additional capital purchase costs are also associated with the system. FIGURE 50-4 shows the layout of a transit bus using a series parallel-dual mode Allison EP system.

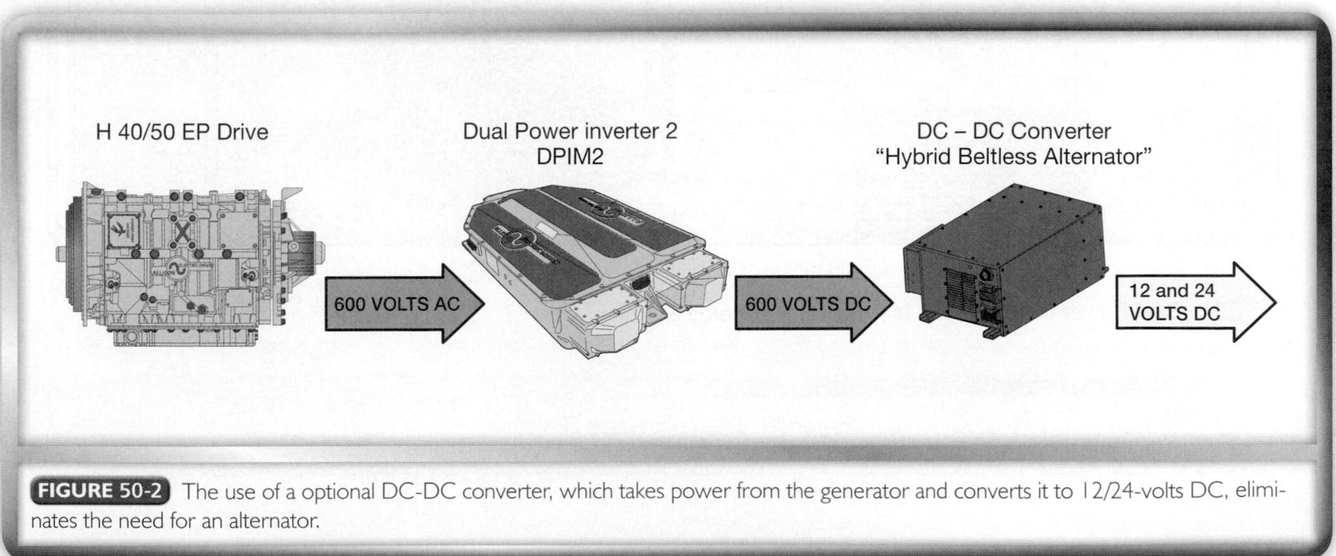

FIGURE 50-2 The use of a optional DC-DC converter, which takes power from the generator and converts it to 12/24-volts DC, eliminates the need for an alternator.

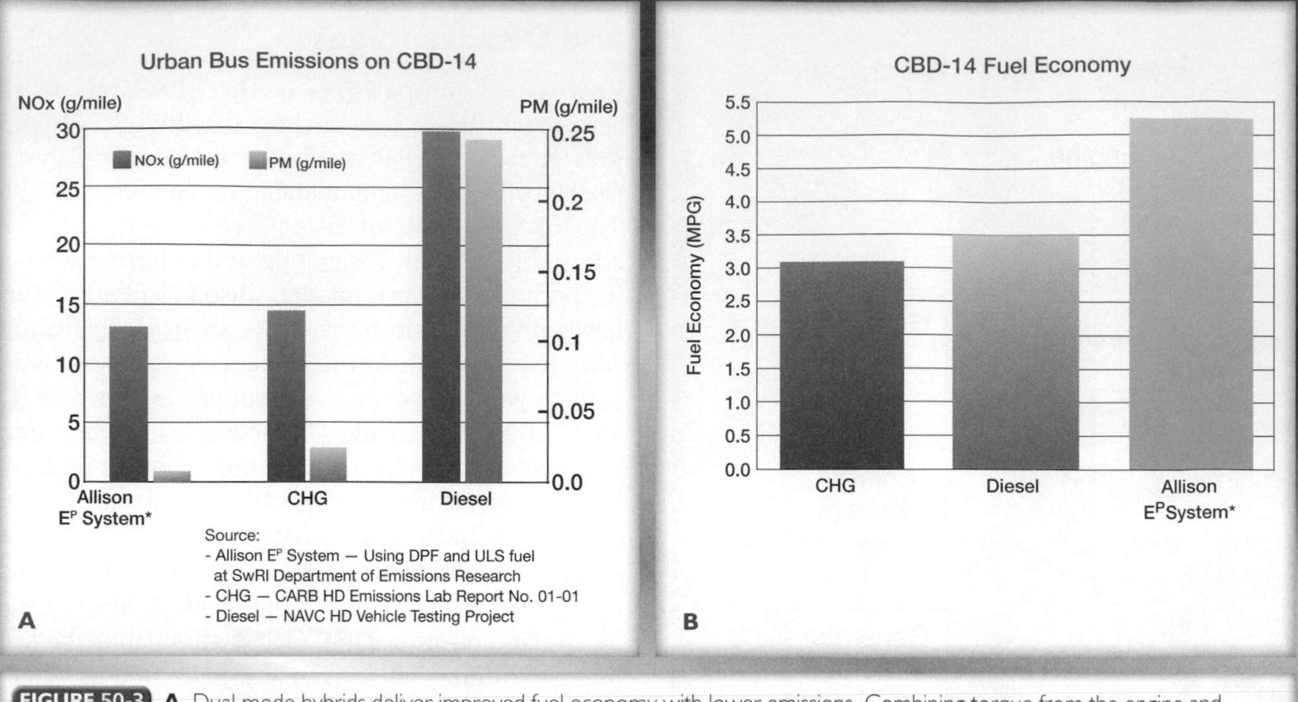

FIGURE 50-3 **A.** Dual mode hybrids deliver improved fuel economy with lower emissions. Combining torque from the engine and electric traction motor supplies superior torque. **B.** The Allison EP system has adjustable acceleration rates to balance fuel economy with performance.

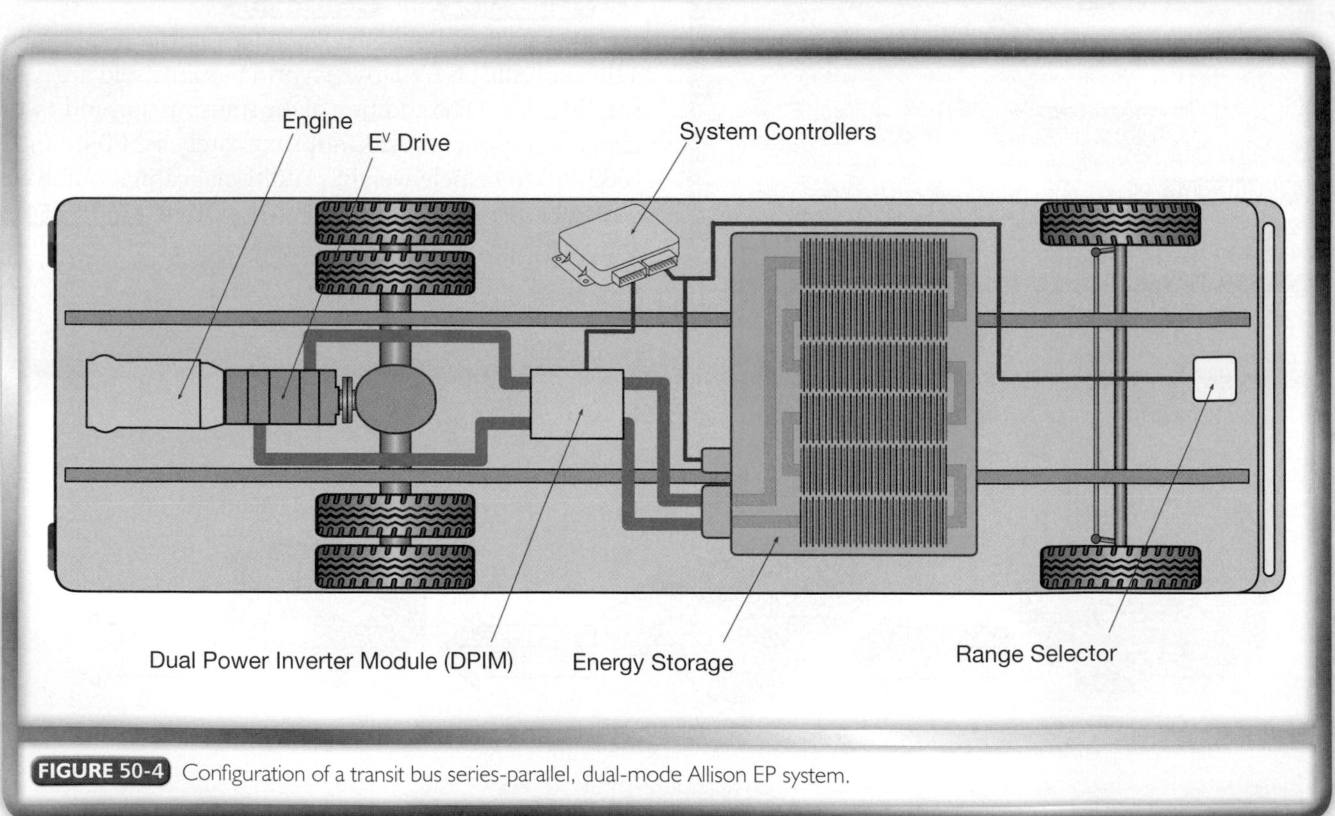

FIGURE 50-4 Configuration of a transit bus series-parallel, dual-mode Allison EP system.

System Components

The Allison EV drive system consists of the following major components:

- EV drive transmission unit
- Transmission control module (TCM)
- Vehicle control module (VCM)
- Traction motors
- Energy storage system (ESS)
- Dual power inverter module (DPIM)

EV Drive Transmission Unit

The EV Drive transmission unit provides a pathway for transmitting electric motor or engine torque (or a blend of both) using three planetary gear sets. Inside the unit, there are three planetary gear sets, two wet-type hydraulic clutches, and two motor/generators. The EV drive transmission itself consists of several standard modules illustrated in FIGURE 50-5 and FIGURE 50-6:

- Input housing module
- Main (stator) housing module
- Control valve assembly/oil pan module
- Clutch housing module
- Rear cover module

Transmission Control Module (TCM)

The **transmission control module (TCM)** is one of the most important of twelve microprocessor-based controllers the EP system uses. Most of the EP system operation is directly controlled by this processing module, which collects input signals to determine electrical outputs controlling the EV transmission operation. Torque blending, adaptive hydraulic clutch control, diagnostic system management, hydraulic oil level monitoring, and start-up and shut down routines are some of the basic important

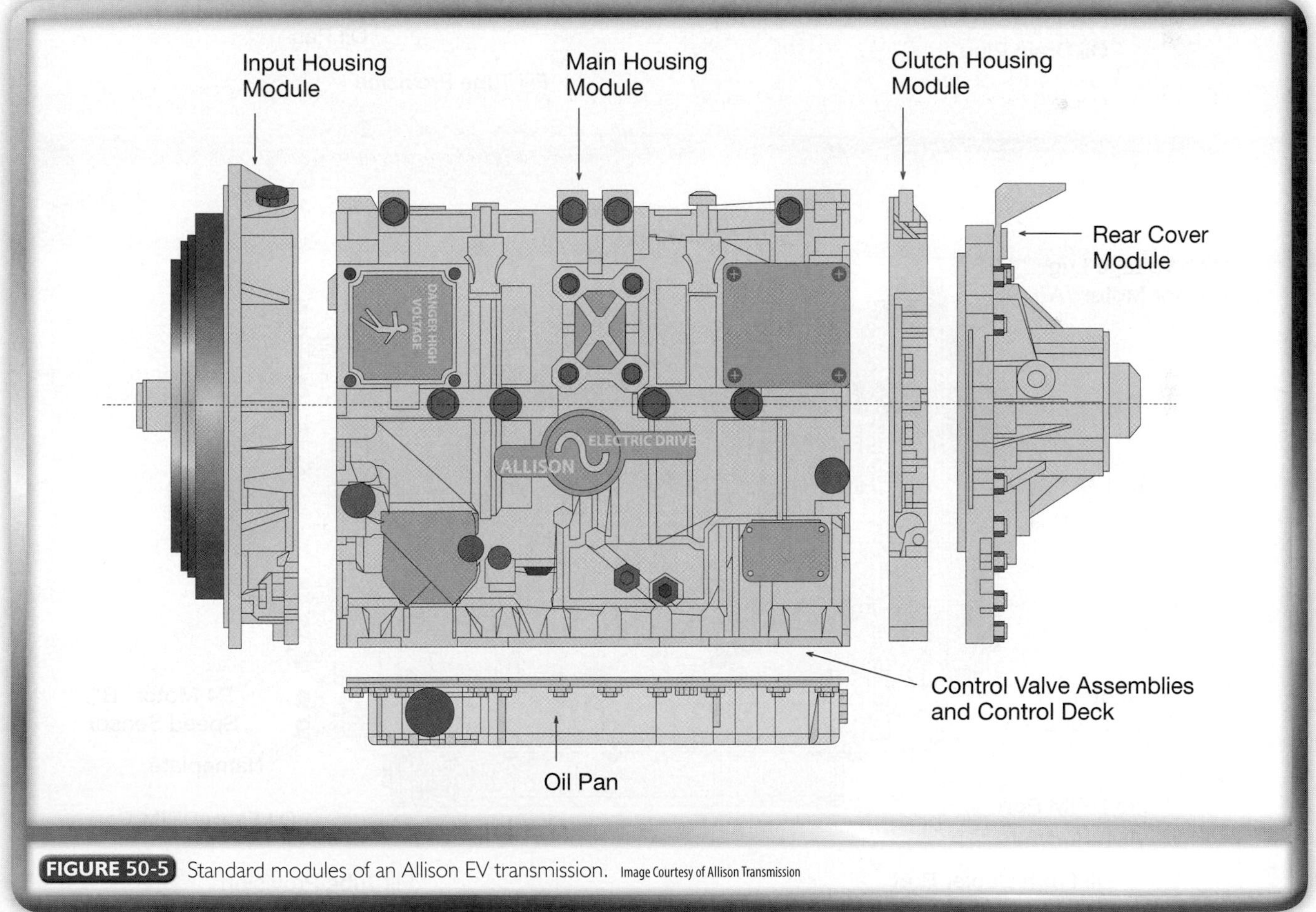

FIGURE 50-5 Standard modules of an Allison EV transmission. Image Courtesy of Allison Transmission

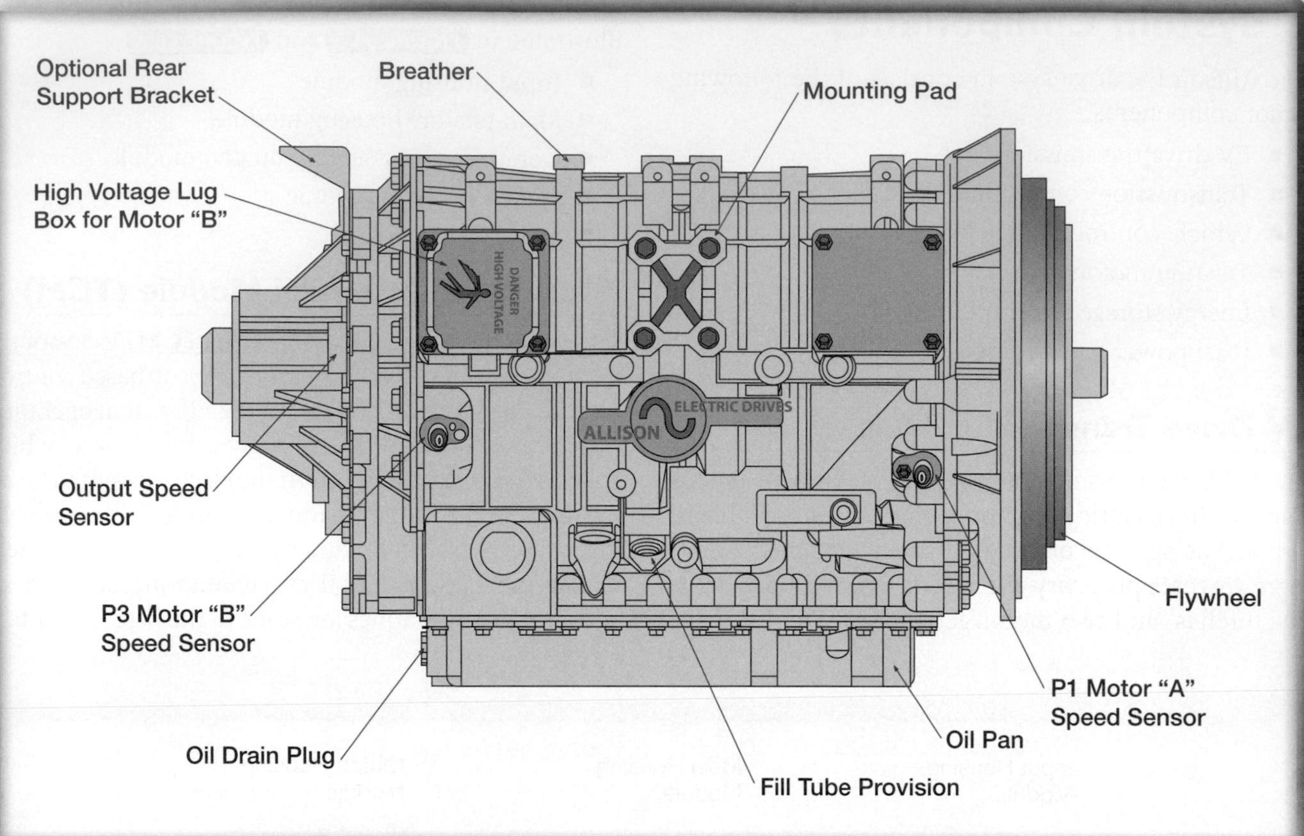

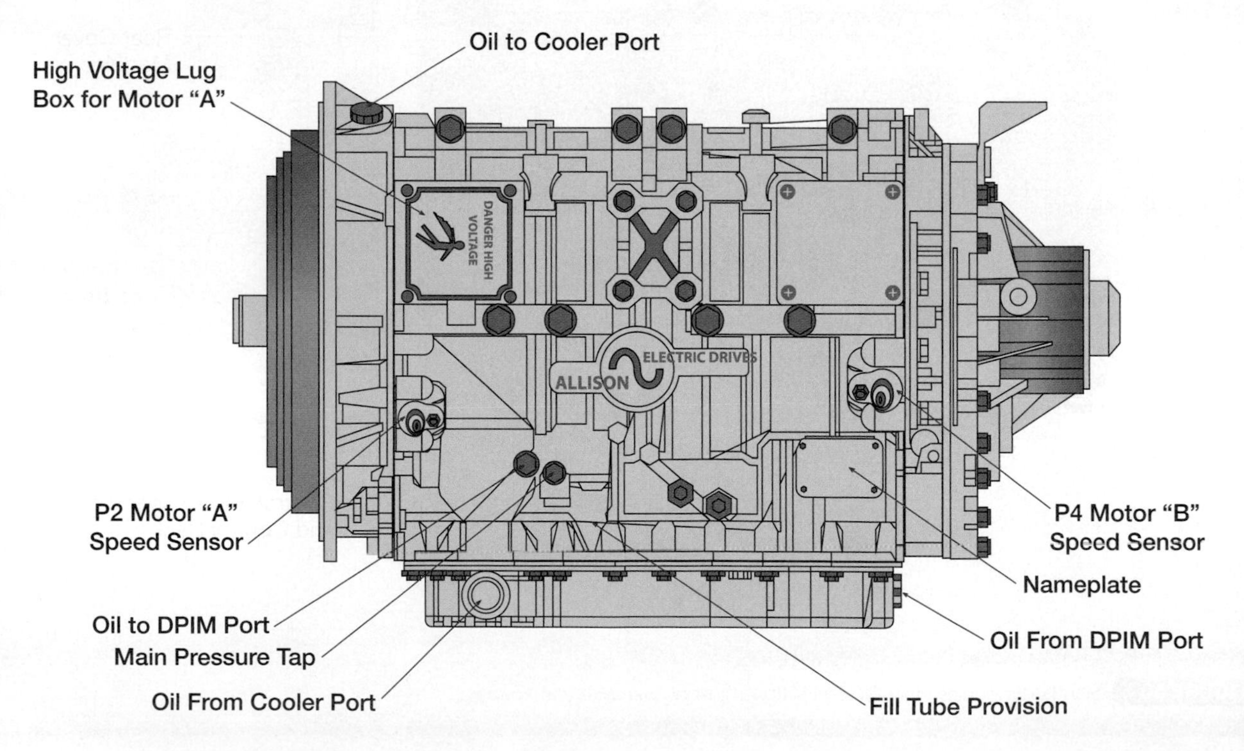

FIGURE 50-6 Side views of the Allison EV transmission. Image Courtesy of Allison Transmission

functions. In addition to J1939 CAN messages used as inputs for the TCM, a number of input circuits are connected to the TCM, such as:

- Ignition sense—Detects the ignition key switch state
- Hydraulic transmission control pressure sensors
- Transmission oil sump temperature
- Oil level sensor
- Transmission output speed
- ESS relay status
- Accelerator interlock—Disables the engine throttle, keeping it at neutral when passenger doors are open
- Fast idle switch—Increases idle speed in steps when activated
- Engine brake enable—Status of the engine brake on/off

Likewise, the TCM outputs include:

- Auxiliary function range inhibit—Prevents selection to forward or reverse range when auxiliary equipment is enabled
- Front operation—Enables vehicle start-up and operation from the driver's compartment
- Remote shutdown—Requests system shutdown
- Hydraulic clutch trim solenoids (two)
- Hydraulic clutch-blocking solenoid drivers
- DPIM wake-up signal
- ESS wake-up signal
- Engine controller wake-up signal
- Speedometer signal
- Engine brake enable
- Auxiliary brake enable indicator lamp
- PTO enable

Vehicle Control Module (VCM)

The Vehicle Control Module (VCM) is the other microprocessor-based controller FIGURE 50-7 that operates with the TCM to process data and determine electric signal outputs for the EP system and other vehicle features. Both the TCM and VCM are identical looking modules, sharing identical components. However, the VCM function concerns the vehicle-to-powertrain interface, such as limiting operation of auxiliary systems—such as rear door opening when vehicle is moving—relay control, solenoids, and warning lamp operation. The TCM and VCM both communicate over the SAE J1939 CAN network with other control modules.

VCM system inputs include:

- Vehicle switches
- Shift selector input

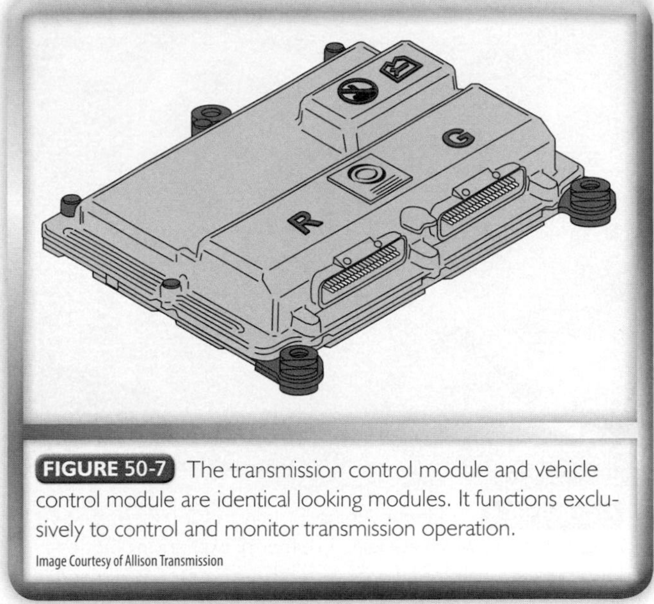

FIGURE 50-7 The transmission control module and vehicle control module are identical looking modules. It functions exclusively to control and monitor transmission operation.

Image Courtesy of Allison Transmission

- Brake pressure sensor
- System override requests

Outputs include:

- Accelerator pedal sensor supply
- Shift selector serial data link
- Dash indicator lamp control
- Main pressure boost solenoid commands
- Reverse warning
- Propulsion system inhibits
- Transmission boost solenoid

TECHNICIAN TIP

Allison's EP pushbutton shift selector features transmission fluid level reading. High fluid levels cause transmission fluid to contact rotating parts, aerating the fluid. Aerated fluid is compressible, resulting in low hydraulic clutch application force, slipping, and overheating. The power inverters (DPIMs) also use transmission fluid for cooling and can easily be damaged by aerated or contaminated fluid and or low fluid levels.

Traction Motors

EP systems use two electric asynchronous motors operating on high voltage, variable-frequency AC current. Both motors A and B are capable of continuously producing up to 100 hp (75 kw) and can rotate in either direction from 0 to 5,000 rpm. Both motors are arranged concentrically around the transmission main-shaft, with the motor nearest the engine flywheel called Motor A, and the rear motor near the output yoke called Motor B FIGURE 50-8.

FIGURE 50-8 Inside the Allison EV transmission there are two electric motors which are used in either of two driving modes-low speed or high speed operation the rear motor, low speed, is shown here.

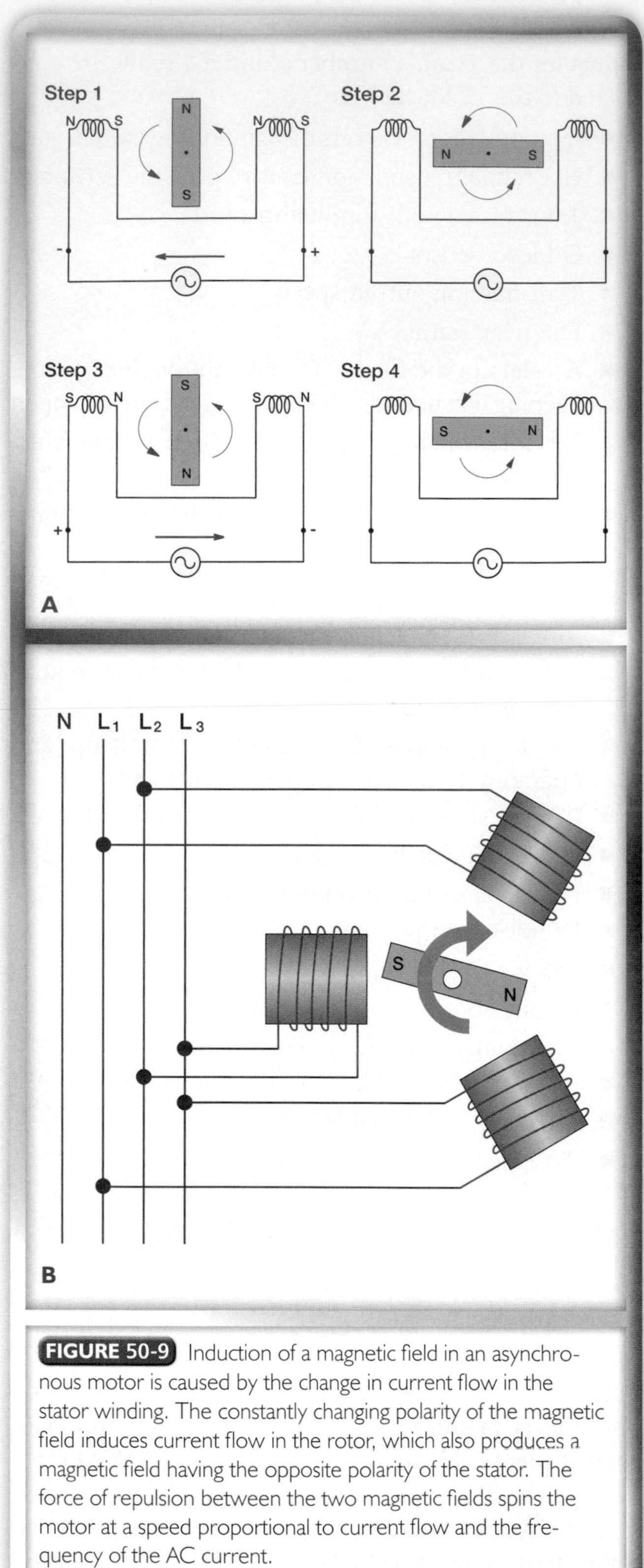

FIGURE 50-9 Induction of a magnetic field in an asynchronous motor is caused by the change in current flow in the stator winding. The constantly changing polarity of the magnetic field induces current flow in the rotor, which also produces a magnetic field having the opposite polarity of the stator. The force of repulsion between the two magnetic fields spins the motor at a speed proportional to current flow and the frequency of the AC current.

The motor stator windings are pressed into the EV stator housing and the motor has two temperature sensing thermistors embedded in the winding, which supply motor temperature data to the DPIM. For service reasons, only one sensor is connected to the DPIM. In the event one fails, the sensor wiring can be connected to the spare thermistor. A Hall effect speed sensor is located in each motors' housing. These provide motor speed and direction data to the TCM. Motor A's role is to crank the engine during start-up and to supply torque to blend with Motor B. Two of the EV's three planetary gear sets (P1 and P2) are located in Motor A's housing to enable these functions. Motor B supplies the initial traction force when accelerating from a stop. While in reverse, Motor B is the only source of torque. The third planetary gear set is located in Motor B's housing.

When the engine start button is depressed, motor speed and direction tests are performed before the engine cranks by applying a low power input to both motors.

In an **asynchronous AC motor**, the magnetic field in the rotor is induced by induction of the magnetic field in the stationary stator FIGURE 50-9. This explains why asynchronous motors are sometimes called induction motors. In asynchronous motors, no brushes are used to supply current to the rotor like a DC motor. Instead, the continuously switching direction of current flow and corresponding magnetic field polarity in the stationary stator induces current flow in the rotor windings. Flow of current induced in the rotor in turn produces magnetic fields used for repulsion forces to rotate the motor rotor. Induction in both the rotor and stator takes place as the direction of AC current flow moves from zero volts to peak volts in the stator winding. The sudden change and movement of the stators, magnetic field induces current flow in the rotor winding. Because AC current continuously switches direction, the stator current will move from peak volts in one direction to zero and then to peak volts in the opposite direction. The effect of the change in direction of current flow produces a magnetic field of the opposite polarity in the rotor. Asynchronous AC motors can use wire-wound or permanent magnets in the rotor. Rotors using permanent magnets are more efficient than wire-wound motors but are much more costly to produce FIGURE 50-10.

> **TECHNICIAN TIP**
>
> To control vehicle movement when the vehicle is stopped on an uphill grade in forward range, the EP will limit rotation of the output shaft to a near zero vehicle speed. It accomplishes this by applying reverse torque through the drive motors when the throttle is at idle stop and no service brakes are applied.

> **TECHNICIAN TIP**
>
> To simulate feedback of a conventional automatic transmission using a torque converter, creep torque is applied at closed throttle, with the service brake unapplied. Creep torque is limited to 5 mph (8 kph) and creates the impression of using a conventional powertrain system.

Energy Storage System (ESS)

ESS Function

The **energy storage system (ESS)** function is to store and supply direct current energy for the electric drive system FIGURE 50-11. Electrical energy to charge the ESS is generated by both drive motors during regenerative braking and from Motor A in mode one when not in use for propulsion. Only 40% of the electrical energy to accelerate the bus originates from regenerative braking—the remaining energy originates from the engine.

The state of charge of the ESS is carefully controlled to maintain energy levels for accelerating but, more importantly, to maintain a buffer to allow adequate battery capacity to absorb energy during regenerative braking. This means that, under most conditions, ESS batteries are never fully charged, so battery capacity is available to store energy. Without the charge buffer to absorb energy, regenerative braking cannot be used, as it would damage the batteries through overcharging. Extra friction brake wear would take place, too. One advantage of using NiMH batteries instead of other batteries is the ability of the NiMH battery to be charged and discharged repeatedly without shortening its life cycle FIGURE 50-12.

If the ESS SOC is reported to be too high, Motor A is run in the opposite direction of engine's rotation at idle to dissipate excess stored energy. Under these conditions, the TCM will request the engines ECM to command the exhaust brake to close, creating high engine exhaust back

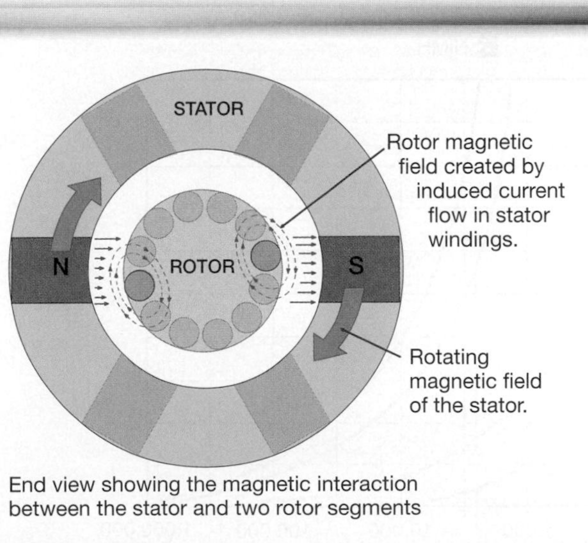

FIGURE 50-10 Three-phase motors can rotate in either direction, depending on the electrical connection to the stator. By changing which phase receives the zero-to-peak-positive or -negative current direction, the positioning of the magnetic poles will influence the direction of rotor movement.

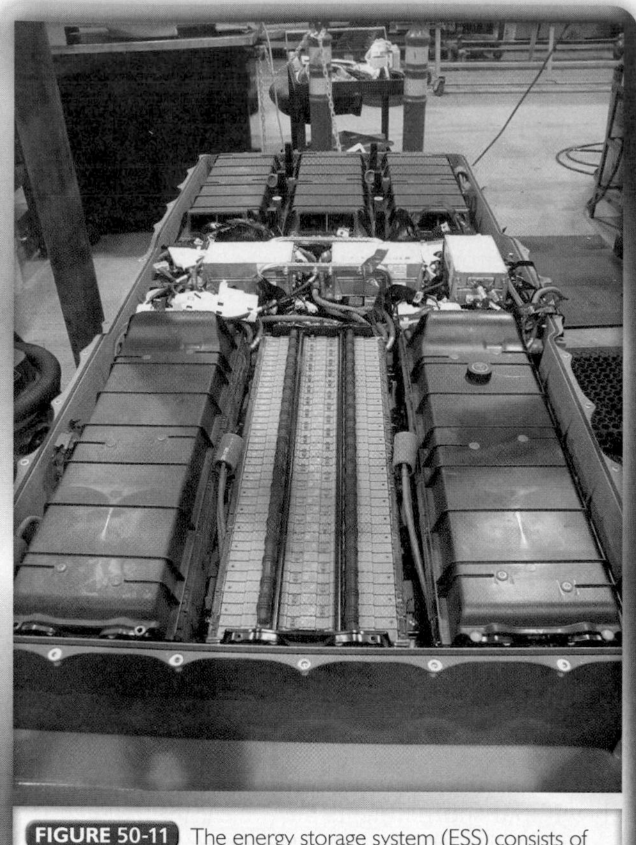

FIGURE 50-11 The energy storage system (ESS) consists of nickel-metal hydride (NiMH) batteries connected in series and parallel used to supply electric current to the motor and absorb electrical energy produced during regenerative braking.

pressure, which converts more electric motor energy into heat and rotational force.

ESS Construction

The ESS battery tub contains 240 nickel-metal hydride (NiMH) modules weighing under 1,000 lbs (455 kg) operating at a voltage range of 432–780 VDC. To achieve this voltage from a 1.2-volt NiMH cell, 40 cells are arranged to form a module. Two modules are connected to form a subpack. Two parallel connected subpacks form a substring having approximately 312 volts DC. Six battery substrings form the battery group of approximately 624 VDC enclosed in separate enclosed housing called a tub. A battery control interface module (BCIM) monitors each subpack operation and condition by measuring voltage and temperature. Data from the BCIM is reported over the CAN to the TCM module, which processes data regarding SOC, temperature, cooling fan status, and diagnostic information such as fault codes.

The TCM provides to the ESS overall system control and battery protection strategies. Since charge and discharge cycles produce heat, each subpack is fan cooled. Under excessive heat conditions, a refrigerant line to the auxiliary AC cooler can be opened to reduce inlet air temperature to the batteries. To service individual subpacks, three plastic blocks connecting cables to the batteries breaks the current path to a battery substrings. High voltage DC energy passes through the ESS tubs through

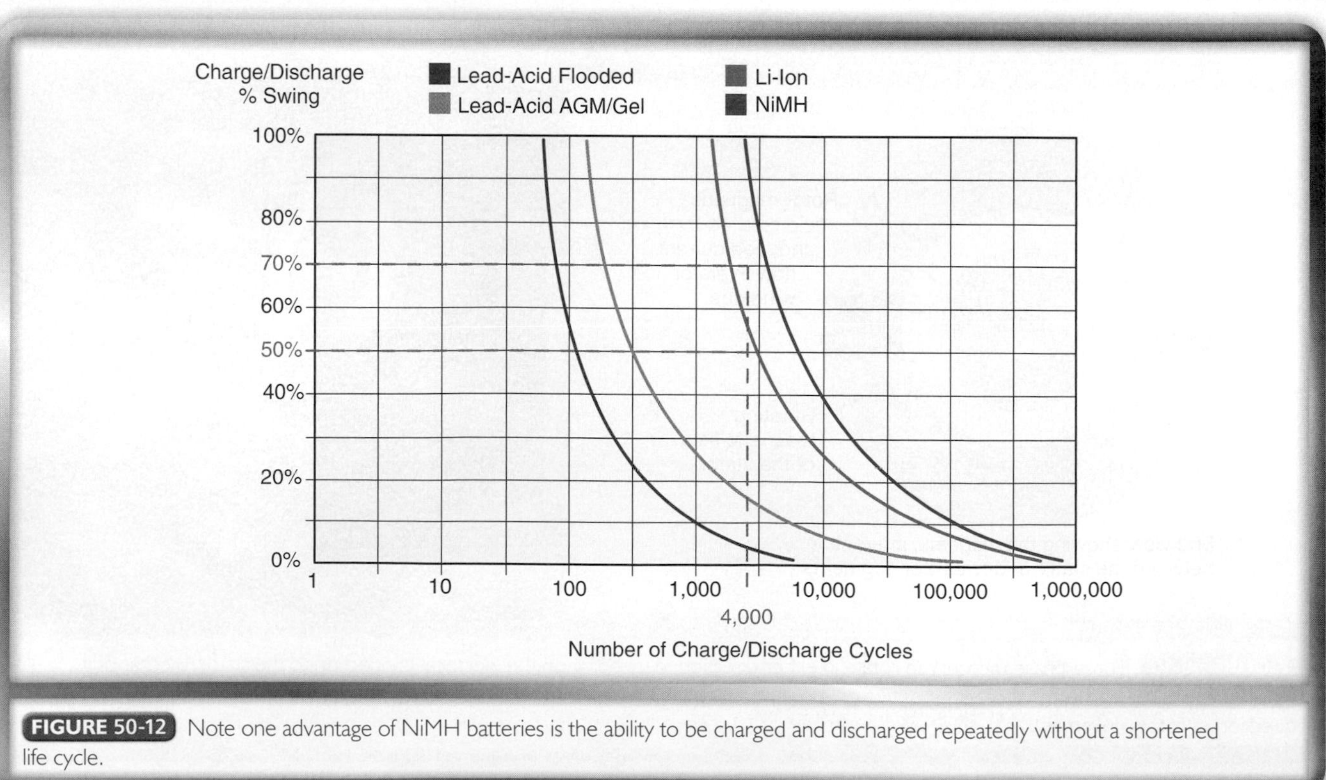

FIGURE 50-12 Note one advantage of NiMH batteries is the ability to be charged and discharged repeatedly without a shortened life cycle.

two high voltage connections, one positive polarity and one negative polarity. FIGURE 50-13 shows a schematic representation of the substrings.

Dual Power Inverter Module (DPIM)

DPIM Function and Construction

The main function of the **dual power inverter module DPIM** FIGURE 50-14 is to convert energy from the ESS into AC currents used to power the EZV drive motors. To vary motor torque and speed, the DPIM also functions to modify the frequency and voltage of the AC current. During regenerative braking, AC current produced by the motors is converted to DC current used to charge the ESS batteries. As current in and out of both motors is controlled by the DPIM, two identical wave inverters are found in the DPIM housing, each dedicated to a motor FIGURE 50-15.

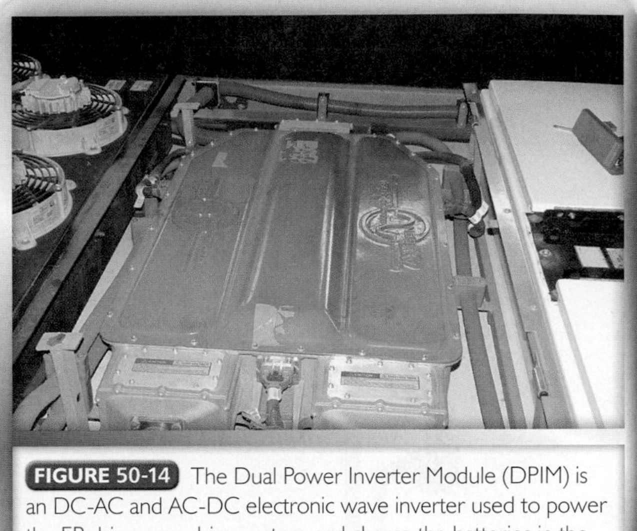

FIGURE 50-14 The Dual Power Inverter Module (DPIM) is an DC-AC and AC-DC electronic wave inverter used to power the EP drive propulsion system and charge the batteries in the Energy Storage System (ESS).

ESS Schematic

Pre-Charge Resistor
Pre-Charge Relay
High Side Relay
Pre-Charge Resistor
Pre-Charge Relay
High Side Relay
Pre-Charge Resistor
Pre-Charge Relay
High Side Relay
Subpack
Subpack
Subpack
BCIM
Fuse
Fuse
Fuse
Subpack
Subpack
Subpack
Low Side Relay
Low Side Relay
Low Side Relay
Substring 1
Substring 1
Substring 1

FIGURE 50-13 Schematic overview of the ESS and pre-charge relays used to gradually increase current into the DPIM.

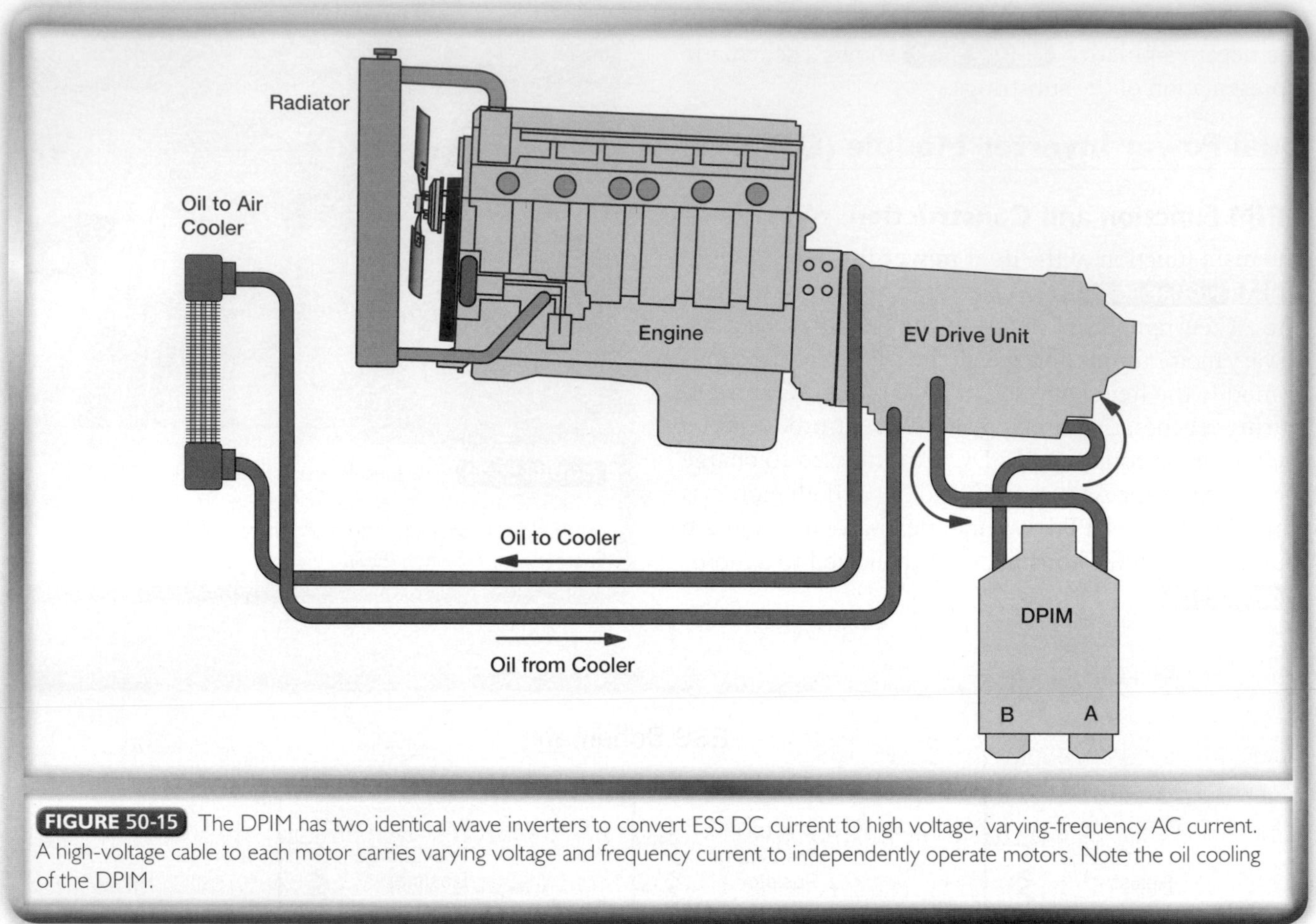

FIGURE 50-15 The DPIM has two identical wave inverters to convert ESS DC current to high voltage, varying-frequency AC current. A high-voltage cable to each motor carries varying voltage and frequency current to independently operate motors. Note the oil cooling of the DPIM.

A specialized field effect transistor (FET) called an **insulated gate bipolar transistor (IBGT)** inverts DC current to three-phase, variable-frequency, and variable-voltage AC current. IGBTs are commonly used in many home appliances and sound amplifiers, which are fast-switching, voltage-controlled power transistors capable of handling current in the order of hundreds of amperes while blocking voltages up to 6,000 volts. Heat generated by the IGBT is absorbed by heat sinks on each transistor and then removed by transmission fluid circulating around the heat sink.

The DPIM receives signals from the TCM over the CAN commanding motor torque and ESS current flow. Two microcontrollers for each inverter contain the necessary logic to control DPIM operation, run self-diagnostics, and communicate with the TCM. Three low-voltage connectors power and communicate with the DPIM, and three high voltage connections are made to the DPIM.

A high voltage DC positive and negative cable for the DPIM is connected with ESS. These high voltage circuits are isolated for use by the ESS and DPIM only and are not connected to any other positive, negative, or ground circuit. For safety reasons, DPIM self-diagnostics capabilities continuously monitor the high voltage DC circuits to ensure they remain isolated from the vehicle chassis.

DPIM Operation

A sudden in rush of DC current into the DPIM from the ESS can damage the DPIM. To enable a gradual build-up of current in the DPIM, a pair of relays located on each battery substring and a current limiting resister regulates current build-up and charging of a large voltage smoothing capacitor inside the DPIM. A fuse is also used in this to prevent catastrophic damage from over-current situations. During the one-half-second start-up period, the DPIM passes through three operating conditions:

1. Initial state—All battery relays are open, and no current flows into or out of the ESS **FIGURE 50-16**.
2. Pre-charge state—The battery pre-charge relay and the low-side relays are closed, allowing current to flow through the pre-charge resistor, which slowly increases voltage to charge the DPIM capacitor **FIGURE 50-17**.
3. Operational state—Voltage to the DPIM reaches 400V in 200 ms, achieving 85% of ESS voltage. The

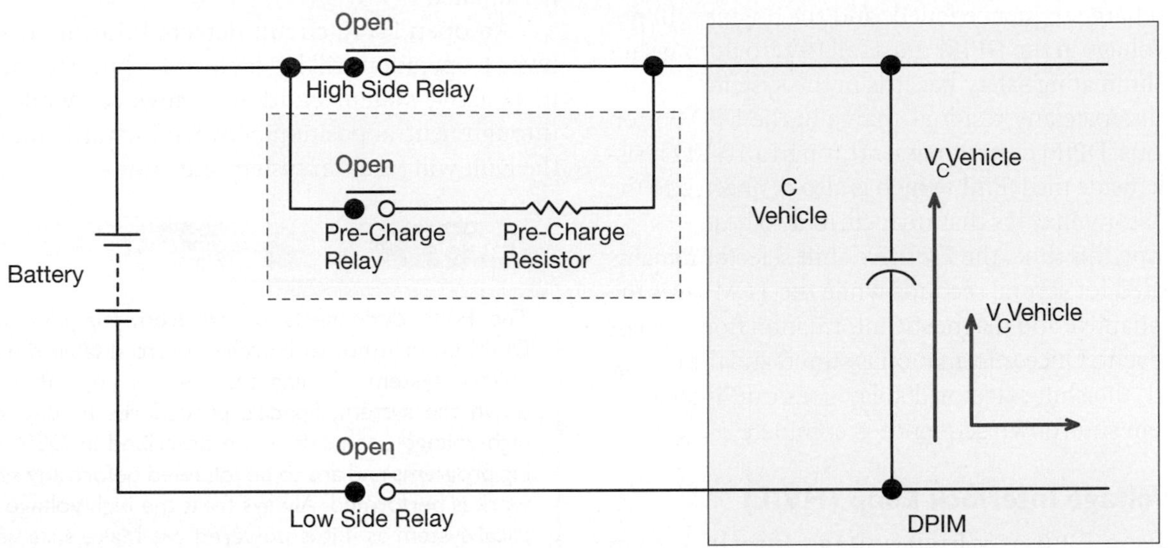

FIGURE 50-16 All relays are open during initial state, and no current flows to the DPIM to charge an internal capacitor.

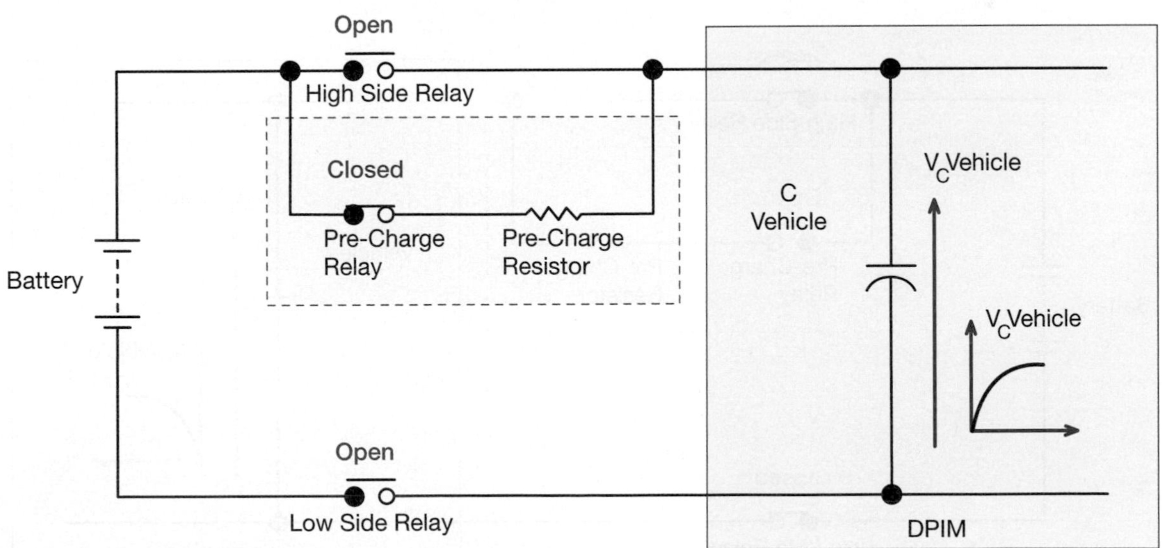

FIGURE 50-17 In the pre-charge state, the pre-charge relay and low-side relays close, allowing current to flow through resistors and slowly charge the DPIM.

high-side relays close, and pre-charge relays open to allow full voltage to the DPIM FIGURE 50-18.

If a significant voltage difference is measured between the ESS and the DPIM, fault is logged. This indicates that the pre-charge sequence failed, and the engine will not crank. Voltage in the DPIM must fall to zero during shut down, eliminating safety hazards in the system.

To dissipate any residual charge in the DPIM or on the DC bus, DPIM current passes through a 10-KΩ resistor bank inside the DPIM, which is also connected to the motor stator windings that turn current to heat.

During this time, the EV drive shift selector remains illuminated for several seconds while the TCM saves the system-adaptive and diagnostic information from the last key-on event. Once information is stored and the charge depleted, the shift selector display goes out, indicating the system shut-down sequence is complete.

High Voltage Interlock Loop (HVIL)

The Allison EP uses a **high-voltage interlock loop (HVIL)** to prevent access to potentially hazardous energized electrical circuits FIGURE 50-19. The HVIL consists of a 12V relay control circuit routed in series to switches on cover plates located on all hybrid components where potential electrical hazards exist. When any switch in an HVIL circuit is detected as open during ignition key-on, the pre-charge sequence will not take place. The engine will not crank, and the STOP SYSTEM lamp will remain illuminated.

An open HVIL circuit detected during forward or reverse operation will log fault codes but does not result in an active system shutdown. However, while passing through neutral position between forward and reverse, the fault will result in system shut-down.

Safety

The HVIL disconnects power from the ESS to the DPIM but it is not to be relied on to disable the high-voltage system. Turning the ignition key off powers down the system. Specific procedures to disconnect high-voltage connections are described in OEM training programs and are to be followed before any system work is performed. Always treat the high voltage electrical system as if it is powered on. Make sure vehicle ignition is switched off, and always follow the electrical disconnect verification procedure before performing any service work where a potentially hazardous electrical current may exist.

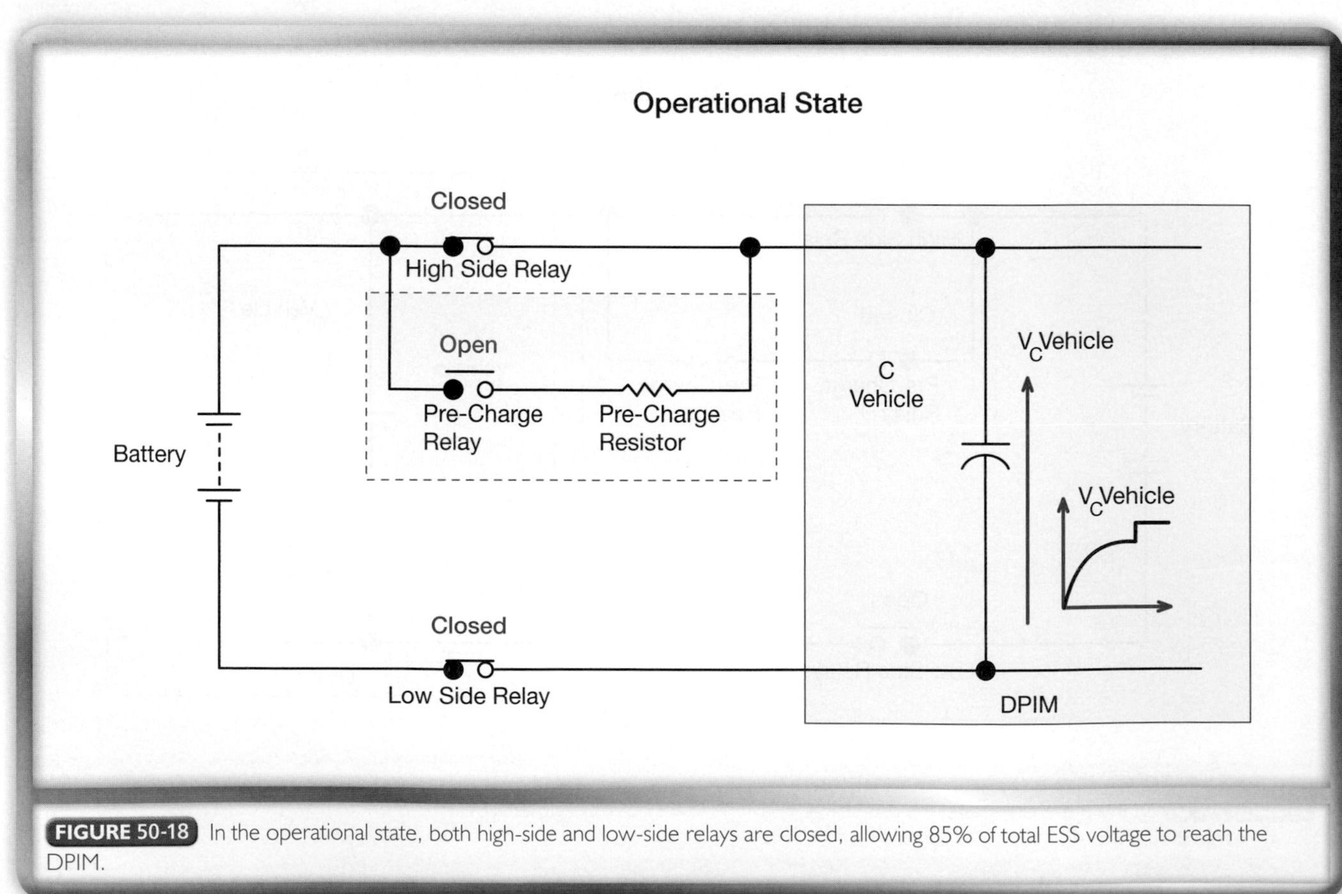

FIGURE 50-18 In the operational state, both high-side and low-side relays are closed, allowing 85% of total ESS voltage to reach the DPIM.

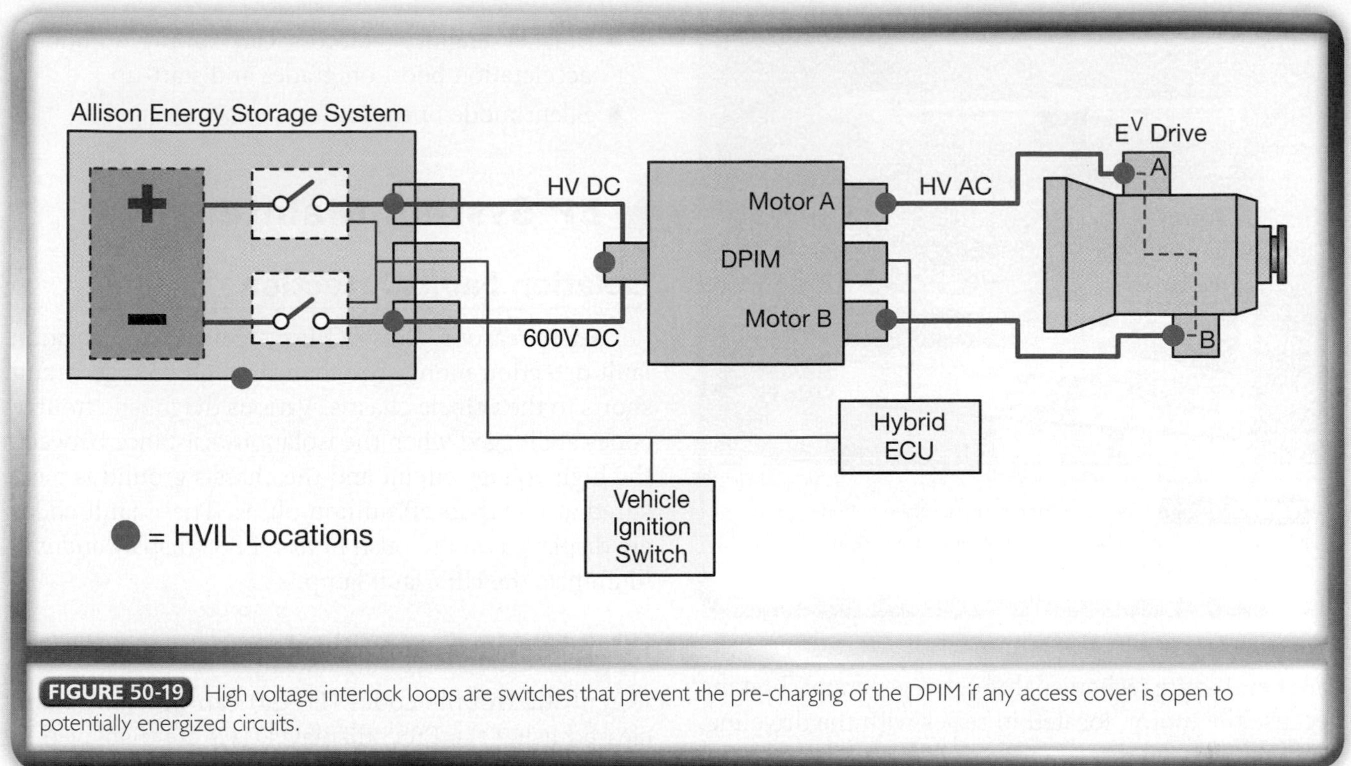

FIGURE 50-19 High voltage interlock loops are switches that prevent the pre-charging of the DPIM if any access cover is open to potentially energized circuits.

Operating Modes

Parallel hybrids can operate in various modes, for example, the capability to operate in "hush" mode. This electric-only operation minimizes noise when operating in sound sensitive areas and eliminates emissions when operating in places like long tunnels. In addition, BAE parallel hybrids can use a split-mode operation, and Arvin Meritor systems offer a dual-mode operating system.

Split-Mode Operation

The EP system has two forward modes of operation. **Mode 1** is for low-speed operation and **Mode 2** for high-speed operation. Generally, the EP control maintains Mode 2 operation until vehicle speed is under 20 or 25 mph (32 to 40 kph), at which point it will switch to Mode 1. Initially, only Motor B is used to accelerate the vehicle from rest. However, torque from the engine and Motor A are blended to supplement torque from Motor B in Mode 2. Blending torque from the motors and engine together is referred to as **compound split operation**. Exactly when the EV shifts between modes, or which torque inputs it uses, will vary based upon specific measured conditions, such as the throttle position, programmed acceleration rate, available battery current, and vehicle speed. Three planetary gear sets and two hydraulic clutches operating under electronic control of the TCM and VCM function to obtain engine-motor torque blending and forward and reverse operating modes. The split between mechanical and electric torque, EV gear ratios, and torque ratios are continuously adjusted by the TCM until maximum power output is reached. Torque blending algorithms programmed into the TCM calculate the most efficient combination to obtain best performance and lowest fuel consumption by adjusting engine speed and torque, motor speed and torque, and current consumption from power stored in the ESS batteries. FIGURE 50-20 illustrates the differences in acceleration between the Allison hybrid and a conventional diesel engine.

Dual-Mode Hybrid Drive

Although most hybrid systems today are designed for start-stop applications, Meritor produces a dual-mode hybrid drive train specifically designed for line haul trucks. The Meritor **dual-mode hybrid drive train** uses a relatively simple operating principle, combining both mechanical and electrical propulsion systems.

At speeds under 48 mph (77 kph), torque for vehicle propulsion is produced entirely by an electric motor supplied with current from lithium-ion batteries. At speeds in excess of 48 mph (77 kph), the drive train transitions to a diesel-engine power system, supplemented occasionally with the electric motor providing torque during hill climbs or passing—situations similar to a parallel hybrid system. Like other hybrid systems, the Meritor uses Li-ion

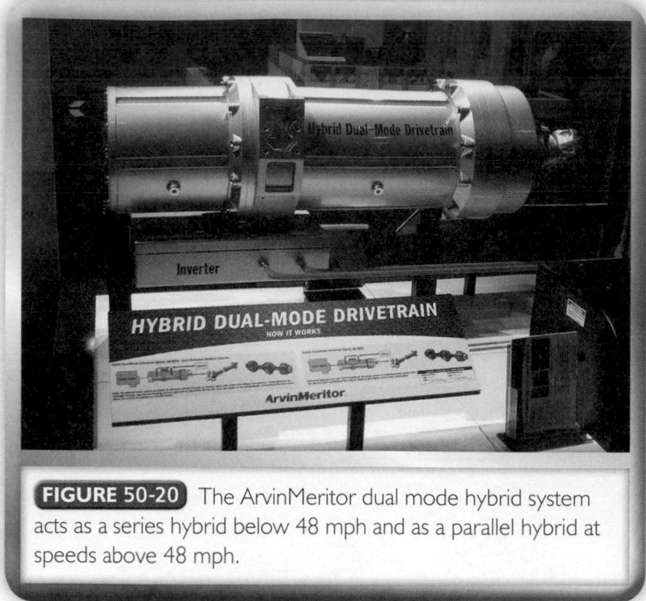

FIGURE 50-20 The ArvinMeritor dual mode hybrid system acts as a series hybrid below 48 mph and as a parallel hybrid at speeds above 48 mph.

batteries that are recharged through regenerative braking because the motor, located in series with the driveline, can switch to generation mode.

The advantages of this dual-mode system include the following:

- Fuel efficiency—Savings through regenerative braking.
- Stop-start fuel savings—Eliminates fuel consumption and emissions when vehicle is not in motion.
- Full electric, zero-emission mode in emission restricted areas.
- The electrification of accessories (e.g., air or AC compressors)—Provides further efficiency benefits, as batteries can supply continuous power during overnight rest periods, thereby eliminating the need for engine idling or other additional anti-idling systems.
- Smaller engines—Motors can supply additional acceleration boost on grades and start-up.
- Silent-mode operation

EP System Maintenance

Isolation Fault Detection

For safety reasons, Allison EP systems use an isolation fault detection monitor to identify high voltage circuit shorts to the vehicle chassis. Various diagnostic trouble codes are logged when the isolation resistance between the high voltage circuit and the chassis ground is measured at less than 50 million ohms. These fault codes are displayed on the push button PBSS display and will illuminate the HEV fault lamp.

Diagnostic Code Display

Diagnostic trouble codes (DTCs) can be viewed and cleared using the PBSS display. DTCs are displayed in the sequence in which they were logged into the TCM. All codes consist of OEM unique four-digit codes displayed as a two-digit main code followed by a two-digit sub code with more specific information about the system area where the fault has occurred. For example, the first two digits may indicate an electrical short to ground while the last two digits indicate a hydraulic pressure sensor wire.

Warning Lights

A check system warning light FIGURE 50-21 alerts the operator that an EP system fault has occurred but does not lead to a system derate or shut-down. However, a stop system warning light indicates the propulsion system will shut-down with a 30-second warning period.

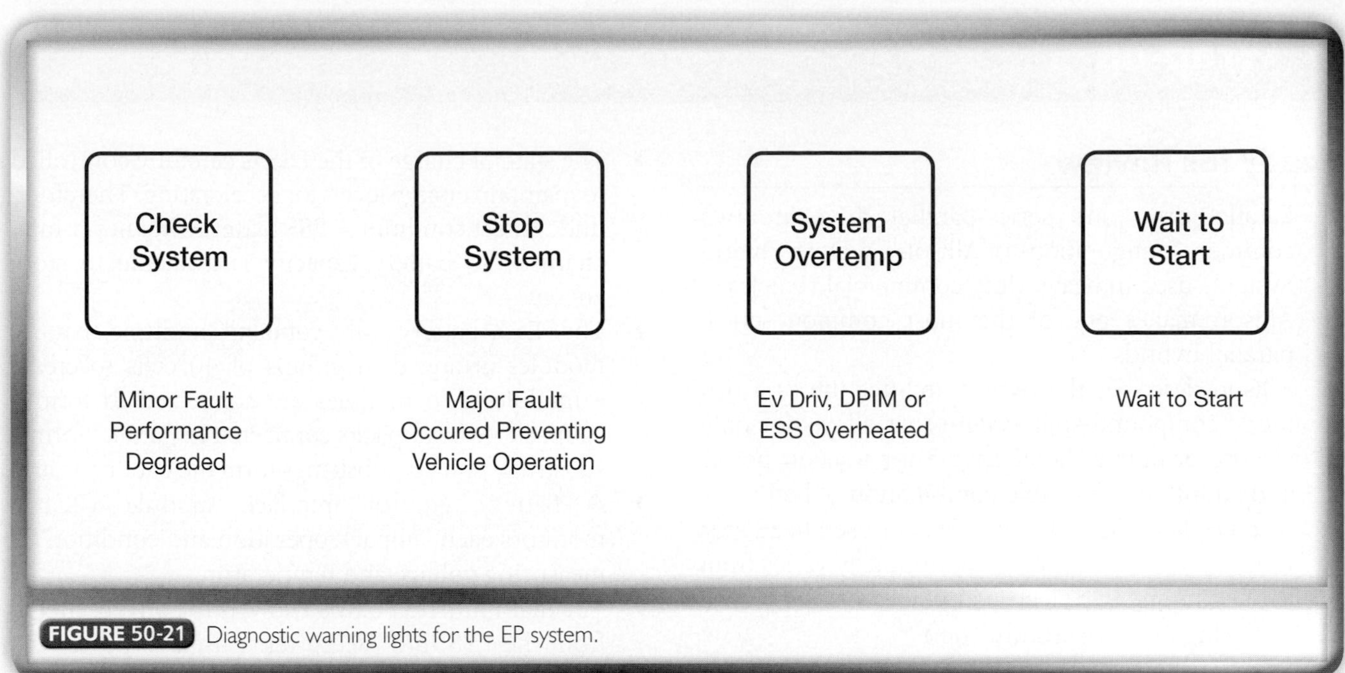

FIGURE 50-21 Diagnostic warning lights for the EP system.

A system over-temperature warning light alerts the operator when any of the EP system components are outside normal heat ranges. Over heat conditions result in reduced performance or system shut-down.

Allison DOC Service Tool

The PC-based service software for the EP system is called **Allison DOC**. (DOC is an abbreviation for diagnostic optimized connection.) Allison DOC can display logged fault codes, record snap shot data of operating conditions for later playback, and display system operating conditions in real time. The TCM contains a number of self-diagnostic routines that monitor the EP system sensors, solenoids, and speed ratios to validate that these devices are operating correctly.

Allison DOC can access and run these diagnostic routines as well. Similarly, the DPIM and ESS controllers perform diagnostic tests not conducted by the TCM, which are initiated by Allison DOC, too.

Oil Filtration

Four separate hydraulic filters are located in the EP drive transmission in the system. The filters include the:

- Suction filter screen
- Control Main filter
- Trim Solenoid filters
- Transmission fluid filter

Wrap-up

Ready for Review

- Parallel drive and series-parallel drive are two common configurations of Allison EV Drive Hybrid Systems used in heavy-duty commercial vehicles.
- Allison makes one of the most common series-parallel hybrids.
- Allison describes the hybrid architecture as a two mode compound-split system that allows for only electric or only a diesel engine for traction power and an infinitely variable combination of both.
- Its automatic transmission does not used fixed gear ratios. Instead, the power continuously varies from the engine and two electric motors when the vehicle is driving in a forward direction.
- Real-world comparisons of the EP system to the series HybriDrive system show that EP offers slightly greater reduction in fuel consumption compared to the HybriDrive system operated on an identical route.
- Allison EV drive systems consists of an EV drive transmission unit, transmission control module (TCM), vehicle control module (VCM), traction motors, energy storage system (ESS), and a dual power inverter module (DPIM).
- The EV drive transmission unit provides a pathway for transmitting electric motor or engine torque (or a blend of both) using three planetary gear sets.
- The EV drive transmission unit includes several modules: an input housing module, main (stator) housing module, control valve assembly/oil pan module, clutch housing module, and rear cover module.
- Most of the EP system operation is directly controlled by the transmission control module, which collects input signals to determine electrical outputs controlling the EV transmission operation.
- The TCM and VCM both communicate over the SAE J1939 CAN network with other control modules.
- EP systems use two electric asynchronous motors operating on high voltage, variable-frequency AC current.
- In an asynchronous AC motor (also called an induction motor), the magnetic field in the rotor is induced by induction of the magnetic field in the stationary stator.
- The state of charge of the ESS is carefully controlled to maintain energy levels for accelerating. Therefore, under most conditions, ESS batteries are never fully charged, so battery capacity is available to store energy.
- The ESS battery tub contains multiple battery modules arranged in groups of 40 cells to create a module. Two modules are connected to form a subpack; two subpacks connected in parallel form a substring; and six substrings form the battery group.
- A battery control interface module (BCIM) monitors each subpack operation and condition by measuring voltage and temperature.
- The main function of the DPIM is to convert energy from the ESS into AC currents used to power the EZV drive motors. To vary motor torque and speed, the DPIM also functions to modify the frequency and voltage of the AC current.
- During the one-half second start-up period, the DPIM passes through three operating conditions: initial state, pre-charge state, and operational state.
- The Allison EP uses a High Voltage Interlock Loop (HVIL) to prevent access to potentially hazardous energized electrical circuits.
- Parallel hybrids can operate in various modes, for example, hush mode, split mode, or dual mode.
- Hush mode minimizes noise and eliminates emissions.
- Split mode involves two forward modes of operation—one for low-speed operation and one for high-speed operation.
- The Meritor dual-mode hybrid drive train uses a relatively simple operating principle, combining both mechanical and electrical propulsion systems.
- Allison EP systems use an isolation fault detection monitor to identify high voltage circuit shorts to the vehicle chassis.
- Diagnostic trouble codes (DTCs) are displayed in the sequence in which they were logged into the TCM
- Warning lights include a check system light, a stop system light, and an over-temperature light.
- The PC-based service software for the EP system is called Allison DOC. It can display logged fault codes, record snap shot data of operating conditions for later playback, and display system operating conditions in real time.

Vocabulary Builder

Allison DOC PC-based service software for Allison's EP system.

asynchronous AC motor A motor in which the magnetic field in the rotor is induced by induction of the magnetic field in the stationary stator.

compound split operation Blending torque from the motors and engine together.

dual-mode hybrid drive train A hybrid system that combines both mechanical and electrical propulsion systems.

dual power inverter module (DPIM) The module responsible for converting energy from the ESS into AC currents used to power the EZV drive motors.

energy storage system (ESS) A system that stores and distributes electrical current to the various components of a hybrid drive system.

EP40/50 System Models of Allison's Electric Propulsion system. Also known as *Allison's Electrically Variable (EV) Drive*.

high-voltage interlock loop (HVIL) A device that prevents access to potentially hazardous energized electrical circuits.

insulated gate bipolar transistor (IGBT) A specialized field effect transistor (FET) that inverts DC current to three-phase, variable-frequency, and variable-voltage AC current.

Mode 1 In split-mode operation, the mode that is for low-speed operation.

Mode 2 In split-mode operation, the mode that is for high-speed operation.

smart electrification A feature that enables the EP 40/50 system's motors to switch over to generating mode to produce as much as 300 amps at 24 volts at idle.

traction motor An electric motor that provides propulsion to a vehicle.

transmission control module (TCM) The electronic controller that issues commands to the solenoids inside the transmission to obtain the desired range. Also known as the transmission electronic control unit (ECU).

Review Questions

1. How many ratios does the Allison EP hybrid transmission have?
   a. 3
   b. 5
   c. 6
   d. It has infinite ratios.
2. How many hydraulic clutch packs does the Allison EV drive transmission have?
   a. 2
   b. 3
   c. 4
   d. 5
3. How many planetary gear sets does the Allison EV drive transmission have?
   a. 1
   b. 2
   c. 3
   d. 4
4. The Allison EP 40 and EP 50 Hybrid systems propel the vehicle with which of the following?
   a. An electric motor only
   b. Two electric motors
   c. An electric motor and an internal combustion engine working together at all times
   d. An internal combustion engine at some times and an electric motor at others, or a combination of the two
5. What is used to cool the Allison EP HybriDrive DPIM?
   a. Air
   b. Transmission fluid
   c. Engine oil
   d. Engine coolant
6. How many traction motors are used by the Allison EP 40 and 50 HybriDrive system?
   a. 1
   b. 2
   c. 3
   d. 4
7. Which of the following describes an asynchronous AC motor?
   a. The magnet field in the rotor is induced by the stator
   b. The magnetic field in the rotor is produced by electrical current supplied through brushes.
   c. The magnetic field in the stator is induced by the rotor
   d. The magnetic field in the stator is produced by electrical current supplied through brushes.
8. How much horsepower is produced by the Allison EP 50 HybriDrive system?
   a. 180HP
   b. 230HP
   c. 280HP
   d. 330HP
9. What is meant by smart electrification when discussing the Allison EP HybriDrive systems?
   a. The traction motors can generate electricity at idle.
   b. The traction motors produce electricity during braking.
   c. The alternator is shut off when it is not needed.
   d. The starter is powered by the hybrid batteries.
10. How many battery modules are in the Allison EP drive Energy Storage System?
    a. 40
    b. 140
    c. 240
    d. 340

ASE-Type Questions

1. Technician A says that the Allison EP drive hybrid systems are series-parallel systems. Technician B says that the Allison EP drive can operate as a parallel system if required. Who is correct?
   a. Technician A
   b. Technician B
   c. Both Technician A and Technician B
   d. Neither Technician A nor Technician B
2. Technician A says that the Allison EV drive transmission has one electric traction motor. Technician B says that the Allison EV drive has three planetary gear sets. Who is correct?
   a. Technician A
   b. Technician B
   c. Both Technician A and Technician B
   d. Neither Technician A nor Technician B
3. Technician A says that the battery modules used in the Allison EP system contain 40 cells of 1.2 volts each. Technician B says that the energy storage system has 40 battery modules. Who is correct?
   a. Technician A
   b. Technician B
   c. Both Technician A and Technician B
   d. Neither Technician A nor Technician B
4. Technician A says that traction motors used in the Allison EP hybrid system use DC voltage. Technician B says that the Allison EP hybrid energy storage system operates at a voltage range of 480 to 780 VDC. Who is correct?
   a. Technician A
   b. Technician B
   c. Both Technician A and Technician B
   d. Neither Technician A nor Technician B
5. Technician A says that the DPIM converts AC to DC. Technician B says that the DPIM converts DC to AC. Who is correct?
   a. Technician A
   b. Technician B
   c. Both Technician A and Technician B
   d. Neither Technician A nor Technician B
6. Technician A says that the Allison EP hybrid system has two modes of operation—Mode 1 and Mode 2. Technician B says that, in the Allison EP system, Mode 2 is for low-speed operation. Who is correct?
   a. Technician A
   b. Technician B
   c. Both Technician A and Technician B
   d. Neither Technician A nor Technician B
7. Technician A says that the Allison EV drive transmission has six forward ratios. Technician B says that the Allison EV drive transmission has five hydraulic clutches. Who is correct?
   a. Technician A
   b. Technician B
   c. Both Technician A and Technician B
   d. Neither Technician A nor Technician B
8. Technician A says that Allison EP hybrid systems are capable of logging fault codes when a problem occurs. Technician B says that Allison EP hybrid system fault codes are two-digit main codes followed by a second two- digit sub code. Who is correct?
   a. Technician A
   b. Technician B
   c. Both Technician A and Technician B
   d. Neither Technician A nor Technician B
9. Technician A says that the Allison EP 40 and 50 save more fuel when compared to the BAE Hybri-Drive system. Technician B says that the late-model Allison transmission EV drive can generate electricity at idle. Who is correct?
   a. Technician A
   b. Technician B
   c. Both Technician A and Technician B
   d. Neither Technician A nor Technician B
10. Technician A says that the Allison EP hybrid system uses information from up to 12 microprocessors to function. Technician B system the TCM is the most important microprocessor for the EV drive operation. Who is correct?
    a. Technician A
    b. Technician B
    c. Both Technician A and Technician B
    d. Neither Technician A nor Technician B

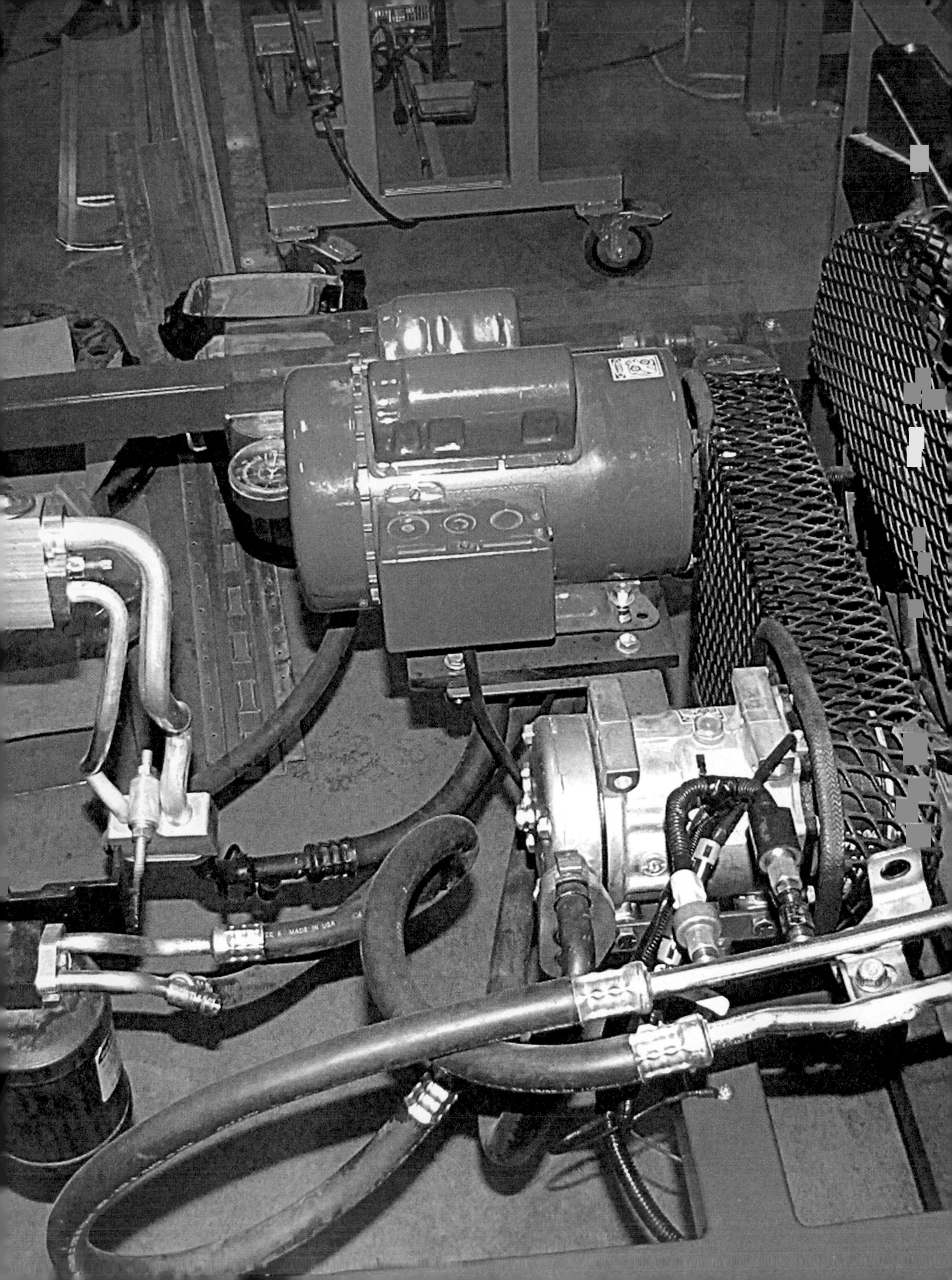
MADE IN USA

SECTION V

Heating, Ventilation, and Air Conditioning

CHAPTER 51 Principles of Heating and Air-Conditioning Systems

CHAPTER 52 Servicing Heating and Air-Conditioning Systems

CHAPTER 53 Trailer Refrigeration

CHAPTER 51

NATEF Tasks

Heating and Air Conditioning

HVAC Systems	Page
■ Identify system type and components (cycling clutch orifice tube (CCOT), expansion valve) and conduct performance test(s) on HVAC systems; determine needed action.	1708–1715
■ Retrieve diagnostic codes; determine needed action.	1725
HVAC Systems—Compressor and Clutch	
■ Inspect, test, and replace A/C system pressure, thermal, and electronic protection devices.	1721–1723
HVAC Systems—Evaporator, Condenser, and Related Components	
■ Identify the cause of system failures resulting in refrigerant loss from the A/C system high pressure relief device; determine needed action.	1715
Heating and Engine Cooling Systems	
■ Identify window fogging problems; determine needed action.	1696, 1716
■ Inspect and test thermostats, by-passes, housings, and seals; determine needed repairs.	1708-1711
■ Perform engine cooling system tests for leaks, protection level, contamination, coolant level, coolant type, temperature, and conditioner concentration; determine needed action.	1720–1721, 1724
■ Inspect engine cooling and heating system hoses, lines, and clamps; determine needed action.	1724
■ Inspect thermostatic cooling fan system (hydraulic, pneumatic, and electronic) and fan shroud; replace as needed.	1725
Operating Systems and Related Controls—Electrical	
■ Inspect and test HVAC system electrical/electronic control panel assemblies; determine needed action.	1721–1723
■ Inspect and test engine cooling/condenser fan motors, relays, modules, switches, sensors, wiring, and protection devices; determine needed action.	1723–1725
■ Inspect and test electric actuator motors, relays/modules, switches, sensors, wiring, and protection devices; determine needed action.	1723–1725

Principles of Heating and Air-Conditioning Systems

NATEF Tasks, continued

Heating and Air Conditioning Operating Systems and Related Controls—Electrical, continued	Page
■ Interface with vehicle's on-board computer; perform diagnostic procedures using recommended electronic service tool(s) (including PC-based software and/or data scan tools); determine needed action.	1723–1725
Operating Systems and Related Controls—Air/Mechanical	
■ Identify causes of HVAC air and mechanical control problems; determine needed action.	1721–1723
■ Inspect and test HVAC system air and mechanical control panel assemblies; determine needed action.	1721–1723
■ Inspect, test, and adjust HVAC system air and mechanical control cables and linkages; determine needed action.	1721–1723

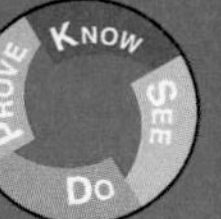

Knowledge Objectives

After reading this chapter, you will be able to:

1. Explain the principles of the heating, ventilation, and air-conditioning (HVAC) system. (pp 1697–1703)
2. Describe air-conditioning components and operating principles. (pp 1697–1717)
3. Identify and explain the three methods of heat transfer and how heat energy is measured. (pp 1698-1701)
4. Describe the purpose and operation of heating system components. (pp 1703–1717)
5. Explain the operation of rotary piston air compressors. (pp 1705–1706)
6. Explain the operating principles of a cycling clutch orifice tube (CCOT) air-conditioning system. (pp 1708–1715)
7. Explain the operating principles of a thermal expansion valve (TXV) air-conditioning system. (pp 1708–1715)
8. Identify and explain the difference between an accumulator and a receiver/filter/dryer. (pp 1716–1717)
9. Explain the purpose of refrigerant and the refrigerant classification system. (pp 1717–1721)
10. Identify the purpose and explain the function of refrigerant oil. (pp 1720–1721)

Skills Objectives

There are no skills objectives for this chapter.

Introduction

Although air-conditioning systems are now used almost universally in vehicles of all types, there was a time when mobile air conditioning installed in off-road equipment, trucks, coaches, and other heavy-duty commercial vehicles was considered by some to be strictly a luxury accessory to provide a more comfortable interior for a vehicle's operator and passengers. Furthermore, the relatively short hot-weather seasons in the extreme northern and southern hemispheres made it difficult to justify the expense and maintenance of an air-conditioning system. Nonetheless, air-conditioning systems offer important benefits that were finally realized.

This chapter will introduce you to the basics of air-conditioning systems, including how the refrigeration system works, the components of the system, the fluids used throughout the system, and system controls and diagnostics.

Brief History of Air Conditioning

The challenge of creating an air-conditioning system similar to the type used by modern vehicles was solved in the 1920s with the development of efficient refrigerant compressors and safe refrigerants. Until then, earlier crude refrigeration systems pumped toxic, flammable gases such as ammonia (NH_3), methyl chloride (CH_3C1), and sulfur dioxide (SO_2), throughout the air-conditioning system as refrigerants. Several fatal accidents occurred in the 1920s when methyl chloride leaked out of refrigerators. As a result, refrigerator owners began leaving their refrigerators in their backyards. A collaborative effort between three American corporations—Frigidaire, General Motors, and DuPont—to search for a less dangerous method of refrigeration produced today's refrigeration systems. In 1928, Thomas Midgley, Jr., aided by Charles Kettering (Detroit Diesel engine developer, founder of Delco Electric, and president of GM) invented a "miracle compound" called **Freon**. Freon was produced by reacting carbon tetrachloride, commonly used as "carb-cleaner," with fluorine gas.

Freon, a brand trademark name of DuPont Chemicals, is a colorless, odorless, nonflammable, and noncorrosive gas or liquid. Different types of Freon refrigerants were developed and were classified by DuPont as R-11, R-12, R-22, R-502, and so on based on various physical properties, such as their boiling point. Other names given to the same refrigerant made by other companies include Aircon 12, Genetron 12, Prestone 12, and Freeze 12. Because Freon was nontoxic, it eliminated the danger from refrigerator leaks. In just a few years, refrigerators using Freon would become the standard for almost all home kitchens and, later, mobile air-conditioning. In 1930, Midgley demonstrated the physical properties of Freon before the American Chemical Society by inhaling a lungful of the new gas and breathing it onto a candle

You Are the Technician

The driver of a late-model highway tractor is complaining that the truck's air-conditioning system blows warm air with increasing frequency. Some days it works well, and other days it begins to blow warm air after an hour or so of good operation. After verifying that the driver understands how to properly operate the air-conditioning system, you attempt to verify the complaint and find that the air-conditioning system is operating correctly. Air-conditioning system pressures are within normal limits, and all fan and vent controls work properly. After checking the service manual for the air-conditioning system to identify more detailed diagnostic strategies, you learn the vehicle uses an air-conditioning protection and diagnostic system (APADS) common to many heavy-duty vehicles. Using the driver's information display located in the instrument panel, you access fault codes from the climate control system module and find there is a low-voltage code for the air-conditioning compressor clutch. Before you undertake further diagnostic steps, consider the following:

1. Why would the low-voltage fault code cause intermittent operation of the air-conditioning system?
2. Why do you think APADS identifies low voltage to the air-conditioning clutch compressor?
3. How is the function of an APADS-equipped air-conditioning system restored after a fault is detected or a repair is made?

flame, which was extinguished. He had hoped that by inhaling the gas, he could demonstrate its safe, nontoxic, nonflammable properties. However, decades later, it would be discovered that the refrigerant's chlorine-based composition of a fluorine hydrocarbon compound commonly called **chlorofluorocarbons (CFCs)** damaged Earth's ozone layer. Incidentally, Midgley, who also is credited with inventing lead additives used in gasoline to increase its octane rating, died from lead poisoning just a few years after the demonstration. Although refrigerants are relatively safe, they are suffocants, meaning they can displace oxygen in the air if an evaporator suddenly ruptured inside a vehicle.

Heating, ventilation, and air-conditioning systems (HVAC) as a feature in mobile applications came as an afterthought to manufacturers years after the first vehicles were invented. Early automobiles were not comfortable. In the winter, drivers and passengers had to wear warm clothing, and in the summer, air conditioning consisted of the breeze produced from four open windows at a top speed of 25 mph. When vehicle cabs began to be closed up as a barrier to the driving elements, ventilation systems became necessary. Vents in the floors brought in more dirt and dust than cool air. In the 1940s, the first mobile air-conditioning systems were installed in automobiles. A large cooling evaporator occupied the entire trunk, and its only control was a blower motor switch. To shut off the air conditioning, one had to physically remove the belt from the compressor. Even in the mid-1980s, air-conditioning systems were installed on only about 85% of automobiles and in far fewer trucks. Today, however, almost 100% of all cars and commercial vehicles are equipped with air-conditioning systems.

Fundamentals of Air-Conditioning Systems

Air-conditioning systems absorb heat from a cab or vehicle interior through an **evaporator** and transfers that heat to the atmosphere using a heat exchanger called a **condenser**. A refrigerant gas circulated through the air-conditioning system by a pump, known as the compressor, absorbs cab heat and releases it to the atmosphere FIGURE 51-1 and FIGURE 51-2. Air-conditioning systems provide many benefits.

First, as a matter of safety, mobile air-conditioning has tremendous benefits. A comfortable vehicle environment reduces driver fatigue and distraction, as high humidity and low airflow can increase the level of driver discomfort—even when the temperature level is held constant.

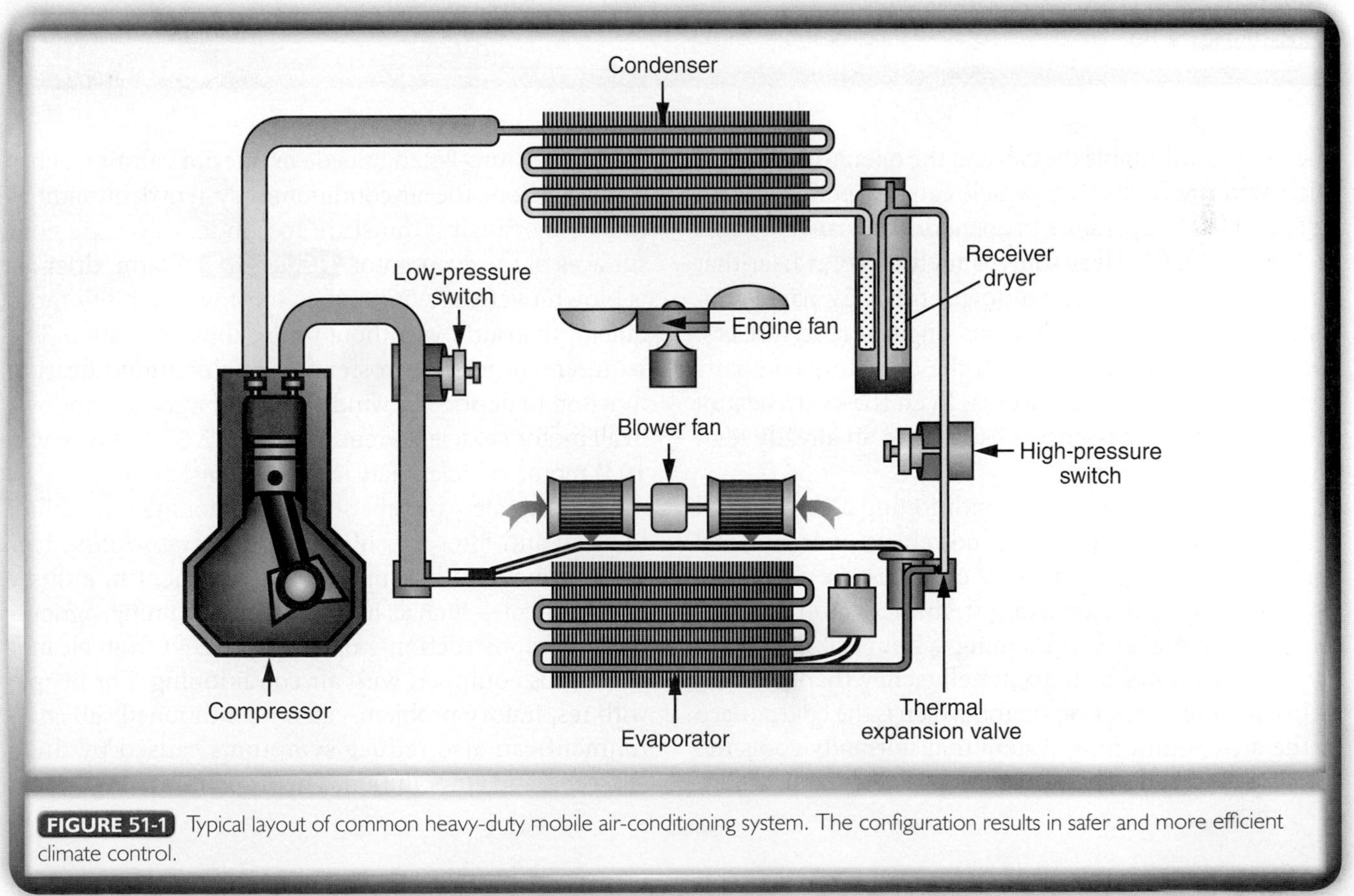

FIGURE 51-1 Typical layout of common heavy-duty mobile air-conditioning system. The configuration results in safer and more efficient climate control.

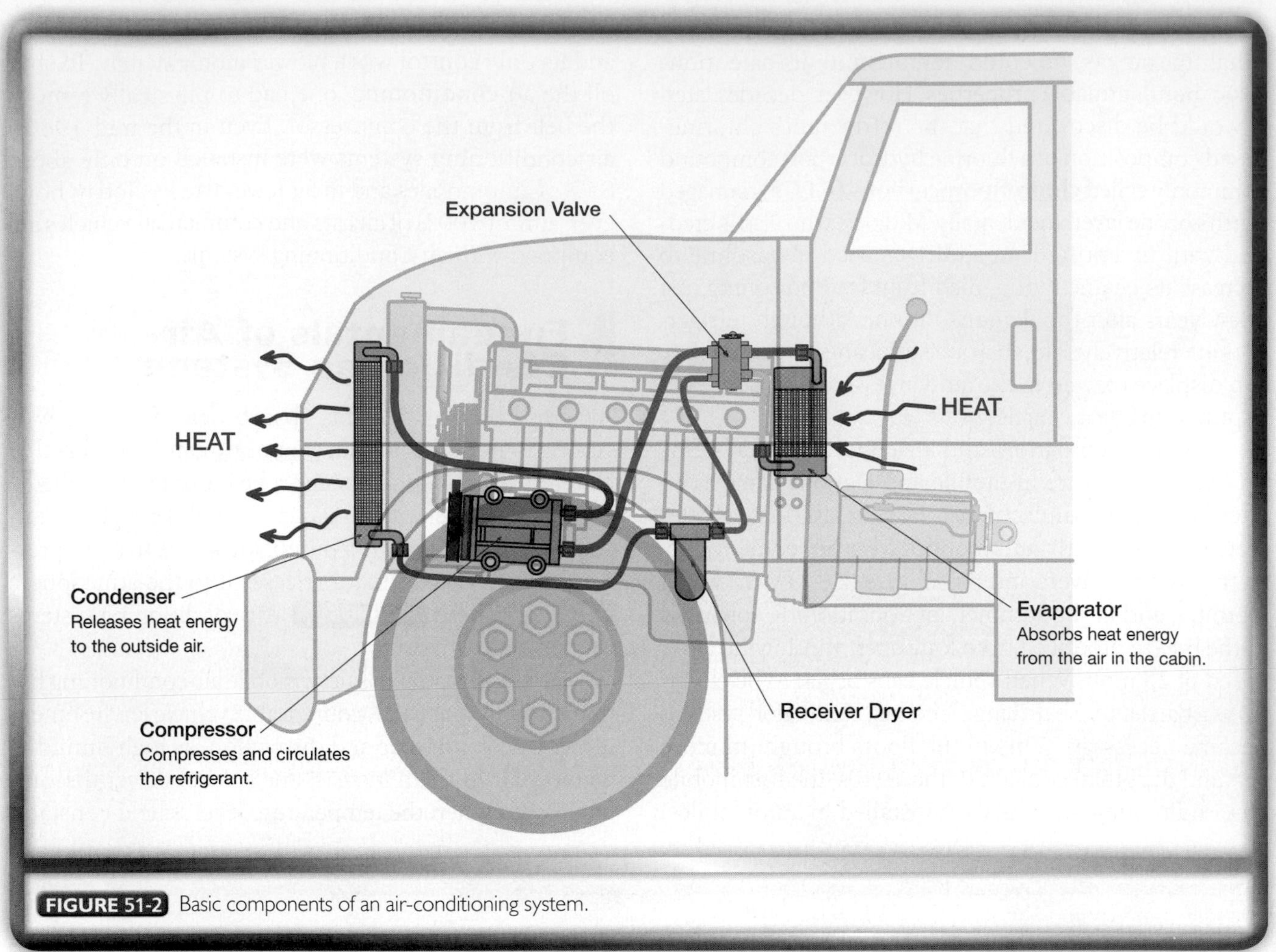

FIGURE 51-2 Basic components of an air-conditioning system.

The more comfortable the cab and the operator, the more safely and productively a vehicle can be operated. Consider that the temperature in operator's cab can be as high as 149°F (65°C). Heat sources include solar heat that enters the cab through windows and body panels but cannot leave easily. Transmissions, engines, road surfaces, and exhaust heat can also enter the operator's compartment, driving up temperatures. Even the body heat of the operator and passengers can add to an already high temperature in the cab.

A second benefit of air-conditioning a commercial vehicle is found when weather and vehicle environmental conditions converge to increase cab moisture condensation on colder interior window surfaces. In these circumstances, the air-conditioning system can operate to clear the windows with greater efficiency than a heated **defroster** alone. The evaporator, which is the cold surface of the air-conditioning system that normally cools the cab, is positioned in parallel with the heater core airflow. Before moisture-laden outside or interior cab air reaches the heater core, the air-conditioning system dehumidifies the air by causing moisture to condense on the cold surfaces of the evaporator **FIGURE 51-3**. Warm, drier air is blown over the windows to improve visibility more quickly than airflow without prior dehumidification. The requirement for a defroster and or a dehumidification function to de-fog the windshield and interior windows in all motor vehicles is required by FMVSS 103 (CMVSS 103) motor vehicle safety standard legislation.

A third safety benefit of air-conditioning is its ability to clean and filter air entering the operator/passenger compartment. When operating equipment in a dusty environment—such as in underground mining, agriculture, and construction—operators benefit from cleaner air in cabs equipped with air-conditioning. For people with respiratory problems, an air-conditioned cab environment can also reduce symptoms caused by dust, allergens, and air pollution. The air-conditioning system

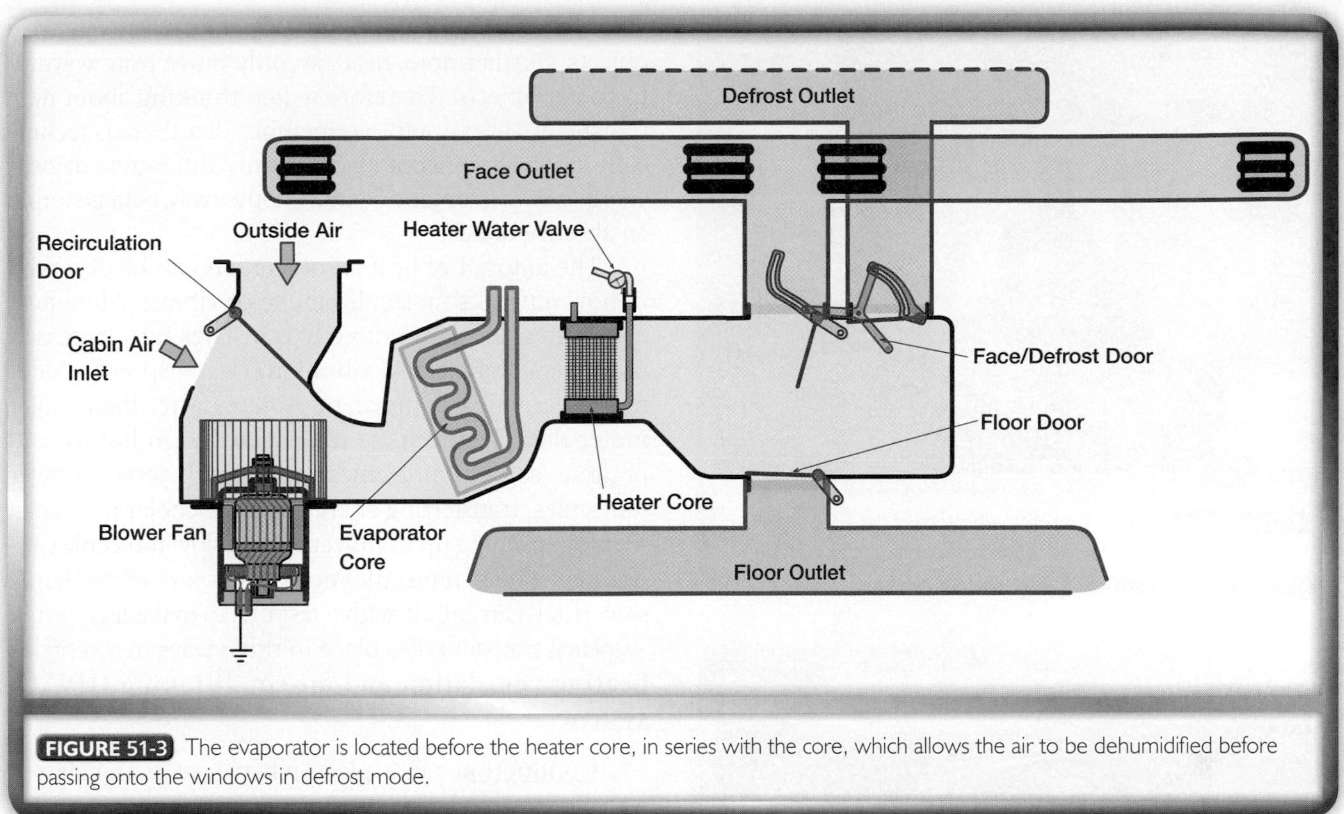

FIGURE 51-3 The evaporator is located before the heater core, in series with the core, which allows the air to be dehumidified before passing onto the windows in defrost mode.

removes dust, pollen, and particulate matter from the air by passing the incoming air over the damp evaporator. The dampness is produced by condensation of moisture in the air on the cold surfaces of the evaporator FIGURE 51-4. Dirt and condensed moisture are purged from the evaporator through a drain in the bottom of the evaporator plenum FIGURE 51-5. Today, most late-model vehicles are also equipped with an air filter located at the cab air inlet to help maintain a cleaner, dust-free cab interior FIGURE 51-6.

Air-Conditioning Operating Principles

Cabs in trucks and off-road machinery are hard to heat and cool. They have large glass areas and are not always well insulated. Hot and cold weather directly affect the temperature inside the cab. This means that any air-conditioning system must have the capacity to do a lot of heating and cooling. The ideal cab environment has a moderate humidity level and should reach a temperature of 70°F to 80°F (20–27°C) within several minutes of operation. To maintain this comfortable temperature range for the driver and any passengers, most air-conditioning

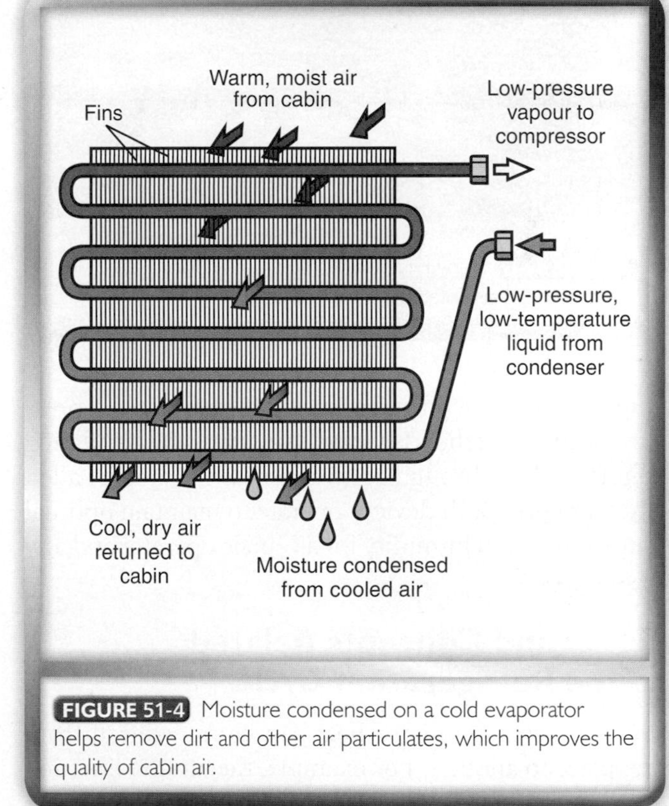

FIGURE 51-4 Moisture condensed on a cold evaporator helps remove dirt and other air particulates, which improves the quality of cabin air.

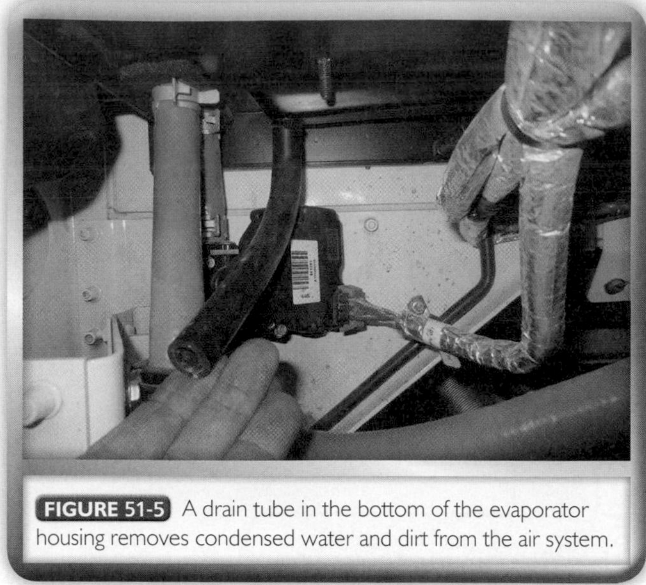

FIGURE 51-5 A drain tube in the bottom of the evaporator housing removes condensed water and dirt from the air system.

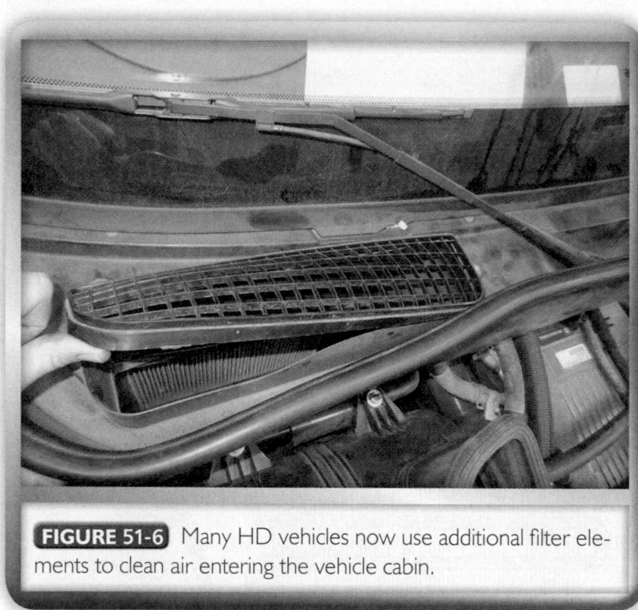

FIGURE 51-6 Many HD vehicles now use additional filter elements to clean air entering the vehicle cabin.

compressors cycle on and off using thermostatic or pressure control switches. Heating is regulated by circulating engine coolant through an in-cab heat exchanger called a **heater core**. Both devices operate to maintain optimal temperature and humidity for a vehicle operator and any passengers.

Terms and Concepts Related to the Refrigeration Cycle

Like all forms of energy, heat can be transferred from one place to another. For example, the air-conditioning system's evaporator removes heat from the cab and transfers it to the atmosphere via the condenser. The heater core uses engine coolant to transfer heat to the cab. In both of those situations, transfer cannot take place unless there is a difference in temperature between two objects. Furthermore, heat can only move from warmer to cooler objects. Therefore, when thinking about heat transfer, it's important to remember that there is technically no such concept as cold, only difference in heat energy between objects. Stated another way, cold is simply an absence of heat.

The amount of heat an object has can be observed in how much its molecules move or vibrate. More heat energy in a substance directly translates into increased movement or molecular vibration (Heat = Speed). Hotter molecules will also move, or vibrate, faster than cooler molecules. Heat transfer takes place from hot to cold because fast, hot molecules collide with cooler, slower molecules, transferring energy into the cooler molecule, thereby speeding up its movement. A slow molecule cannot make a fast molecule move faster any more than a slow truck can collide with a fast bus to make it go faster.

Heat transfer takes place in three ways in a vehicle's **heating ventilation and air-conditioning (HVAC) system**:

1. **Conduction** takes place when heat is transferred through a solid, such as a body panel, the metal fins of a condenser, or an evaporator.
2. **Convection** refers to the transfer of heat through a gas. For example, convection takes place when a denser, heavier, colder gas, such as air, displaces a lighter, less dense, warmer air, causing the air to move and circulate.
3. **Radiant heat transfer** takes place through a medium, such as a gas or vacuum, but the medium itself does not heat up. For example, sunlight will penetrate a windshield and heat surfaces inside the vehicle but not heat the air: warm surfaces do that. Heat from the sun is transferred to Earth through space by radiant heat.

Terminology of Heat Measurement

Heat is measured in a number of different ways. Probably the most familiar measurement of heat uses a thermometer. Heat measured using a thermometer is referred to as **sensible heat** because it is heat that can be sensed or felt. Ambient air temperature is an example of a measurement of sensible heat.

Another common measurement of heat is **latent heat**, which describes the quantity of heat required to produce a change of state from a solid to a liquid or a liquid to a gas. Latent heat cannot be measured with a thermometer, so it is often described as hidden heat. For example, to change water into ice (change its state), it is necessary to remove heat energy. The process of changing water to ice is called **latent heat of fusion**. There is also **latent heat of vaporization** and **condensation** FIGURE 51-7. The processes of removing and adding heat energy form the basis of refrigeration.

Finally, a third common heat measurement is the calorie, which is the basic unit for measuring the quantity of heat energy. A **calorie** is an SI or metric term for the amount of energy required to raise the temperature of 1 gram of water by 1°C. **Specific heat** is the amount of heat a substance must absorb to undergo a temperature change of 1°F. A more familiar term for heating and air-conditioning is the measuring unit of **British thermal unit (Btu)**. One Btu (252 calories) is the amount of energy required to heat or cool one pound of water 1°F FIGURE 51-8, and 144 Btu are required to change one pound of water to one pound of ice or vice versa. 12,000 Btu/hr equals one ton of refrigeration (TR), which is the amount of heat required to change one ton of ice to water in 24 hours. TABLE 51-1 compares different heating and cooling capacities.

Most truck air-conditioning units can transfer between 20,000 and 40,000 Btu/hr from the cab to the atmosphere. This is equal to 1.6–3.3 TR. For comparative purposes, an air conditioner for a medium-sized home will likely have between 1.5 and 2.5 TR capacity. Those systems may require several hours to reduce the temperature inside a home by 10–20°, whereas the truck will lower the same interior temperatures in just a few minutes. Air-conditioning units for highway coaches and transit buses have a cooling capacity in excess of 110,000 Btu/hr. Much higher capacity is needed, as each passenger emits approximately 580 Btu of heat per hour. In addition to it emanating from passengers, heat enters through open doors as passengers enter and exit a transit bus. Added to that heat load is radiant heat from the sun entering through the large areas of glass and engine heat that's conducted through the coach body.

The heating capacity of a truck's heating system is between 50,000 and 80,000 Btu/hr, with buses exceeding 125,000 Btu/hr, which is approximately the same as an average furnace of a medium-sized home FIGURE 51-9. Smaller auxiliary air-conditioning units used by on-highway tractors will supply between 6,000 and 15,000 Btu/hr FIGURE 51-10. These units will enable major

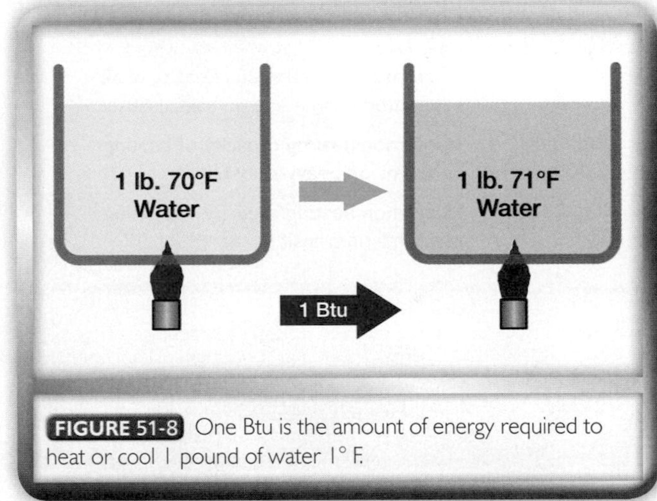

FIGURE 51-8 One Btu is the amount of energy required to heat or cool 1 pound of water 1° F.

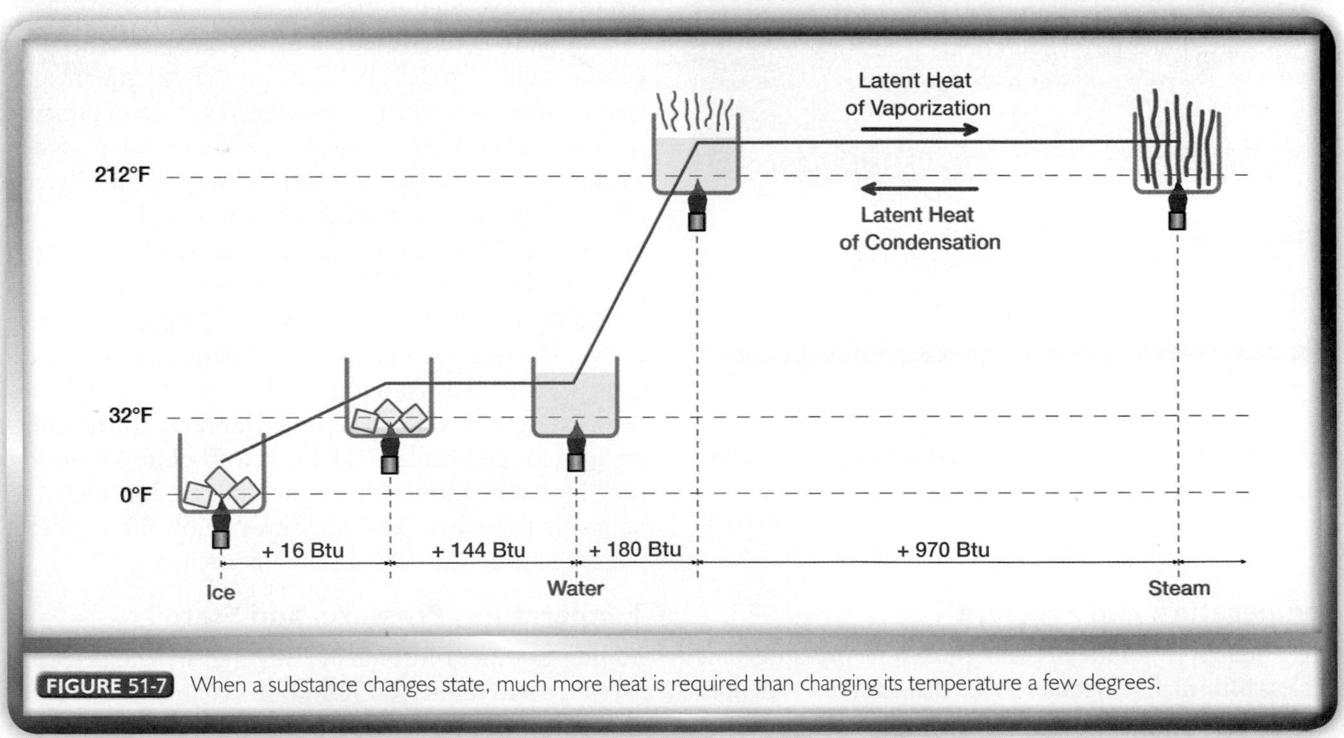

FIGURE 51-7 When a substance changes state, much more heat is required than changing its temperature a few degrees.

TABLE 51-1: Order of Magnitude for Different Amounts of Heating

Unit	Equivalent
1 Btu	252 calories Amount of energy required to heat 1 lb of water 1° F
144 Btu	Amount of energy required to change 1 lb of water into 1 lb of ice (or melt 1 lb of ice completely)
12,000 Btu/hr	1 ton of refrigeration (TR) Amount of energy needed to change 1 ton of ice to water in 24 hours
20,000–40,000 Btu/hr	1.6–3.3 TR Common refrigeration capacity of air-conditioning systems on heavy-duty trucks
110,000 Btu/hr	9.2 TR Common refrigeration capacity of air-conditioning systems on transit buses
50,000–80,000 Btu/hr	Common heating capacity of heating systems on heavy-duty trucks
125,000 Btu/hr	Common heating capacity of heating systems on transit buses

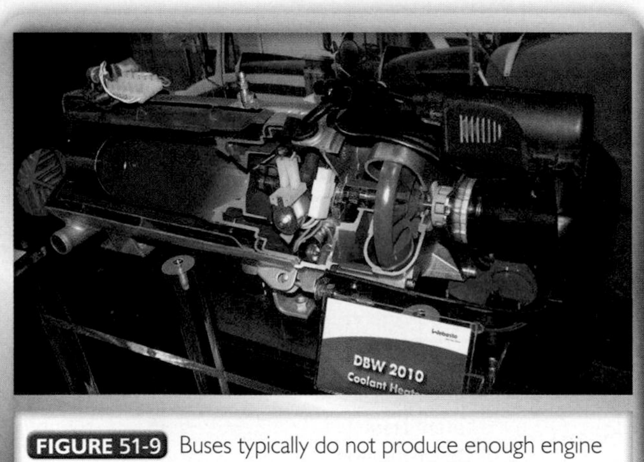

FIGURE 51-9 Buses typically do not produce enough engine heat at idle or low loads to supply enough heat for passengers. Auxiliary coolant heaters burn fuel to heat passenger compartment coolant.

reductions in engine idle time needed to keep a cab and bunk heated or cooled. The units also help drivers comply with anti-idle laws during rest breaks when cab heating and cooling are still needed.

Temperature and Pressure

The concept of temperature is related to pressure. The force with which molecules strike the sides of a container is directly proportional to the container's temperature,

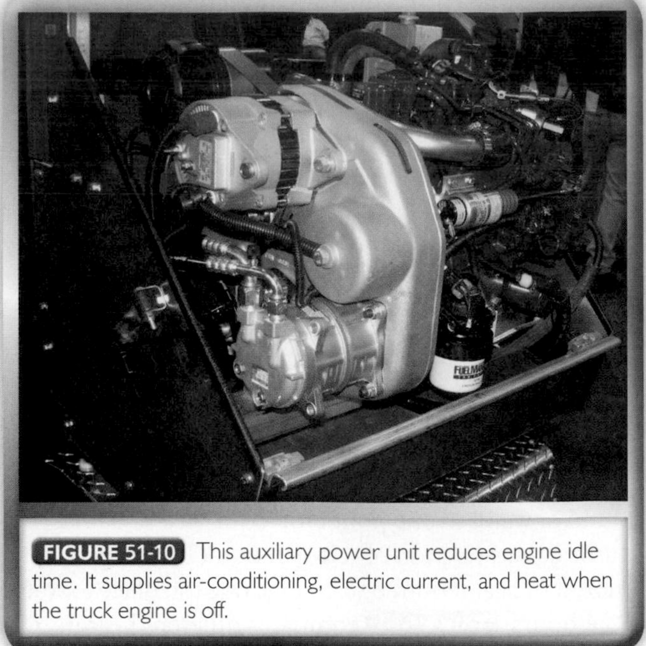

FIGURE 51-10 This auxiliary power unit reduces engine idle time. It supplies air-conditioning, electric current, and heat when the truck engine is off.

as the speed of molecular moment or vibration is related to temperature. Higher temperature produces greater molecular speed.

This concept is observed in the combustion cycle of a diesel engine where compressing air produces higher cylinder temperatures FIGURE 51-11. In a similar way, lowering the pressure of a fixed volume of gas will reduce its temperature. Technicians commonly experience this effect using air tools. Cold air will exhaust from an air tool if the compressed air driving the tool is at room temperature when it is pressurized.

Pressure is measured using a variety of units, but common units used in HVAC are pounds per square inch (psi) or kilopascals (kPa). Pressure gauges report pressure measurement using two different reference points. When a gauge is calibrated to atmospheric pressure, it will read 0 psi (0 kPa) in a room when not connected to a source of pressure. This means a gauge pressure of 0 at a room pressure of 14.7 psi (97 kPa) references atmospheric pressure, and the units for pressure will be **psig** for psi, gauge (kPaG, kPa gauge). A gauge that uses vacuum as a reference point is calibrated to read 14.7 psi (97 kPa) at sea level. This gauge reference is called absolute and the units are **psia** for psi absolute (kPaA, kPa absolute). Typically, pressures above atmospheric pressure are considered to be gauge pressures, and pressures below atmospheric pressure are considered absolute pressures.

Temperature, Pressure, and State

Boiling points of liquids are affected by the pressure exerted upon them FIGURE 51-12. (That is why cooling systems use radiator caps to increase cooling system

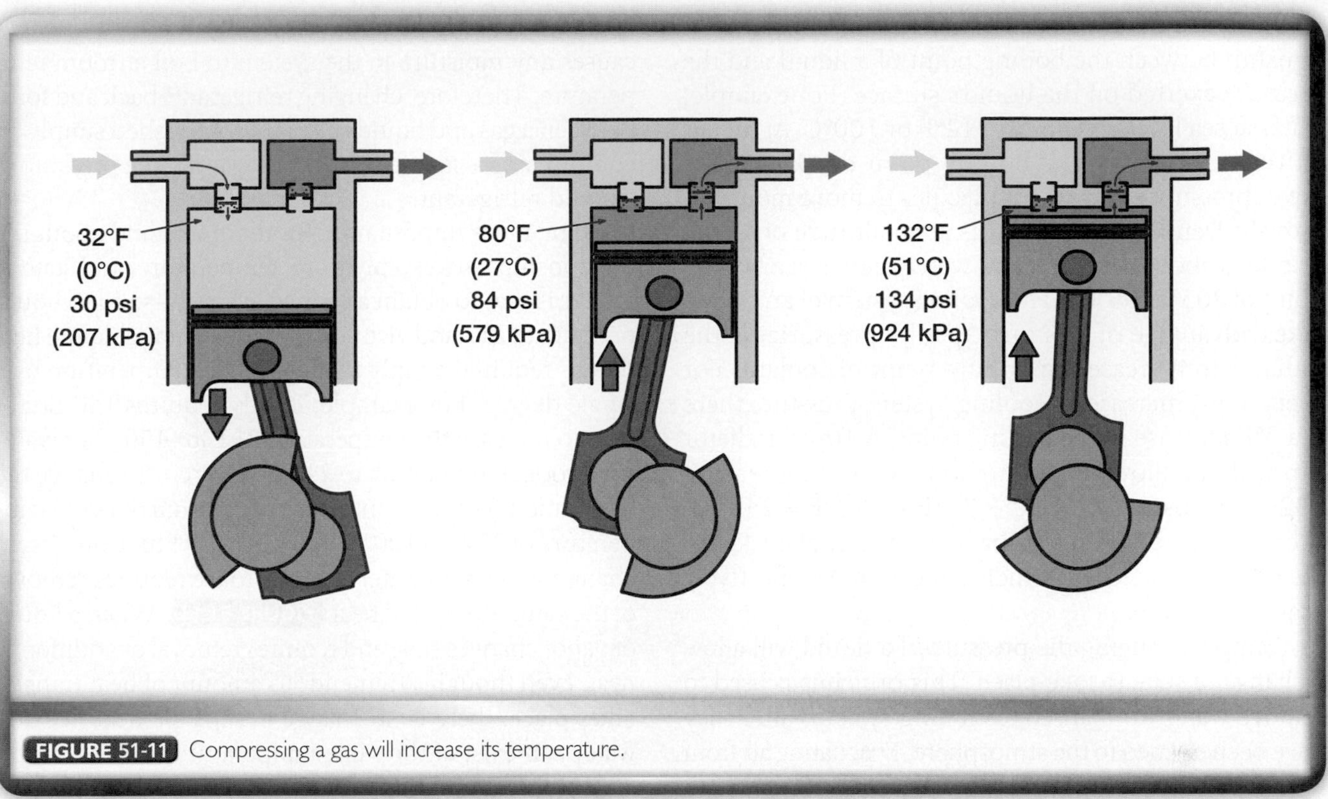

FIGURE 51-11 Compressing a gas will increase its temperature.

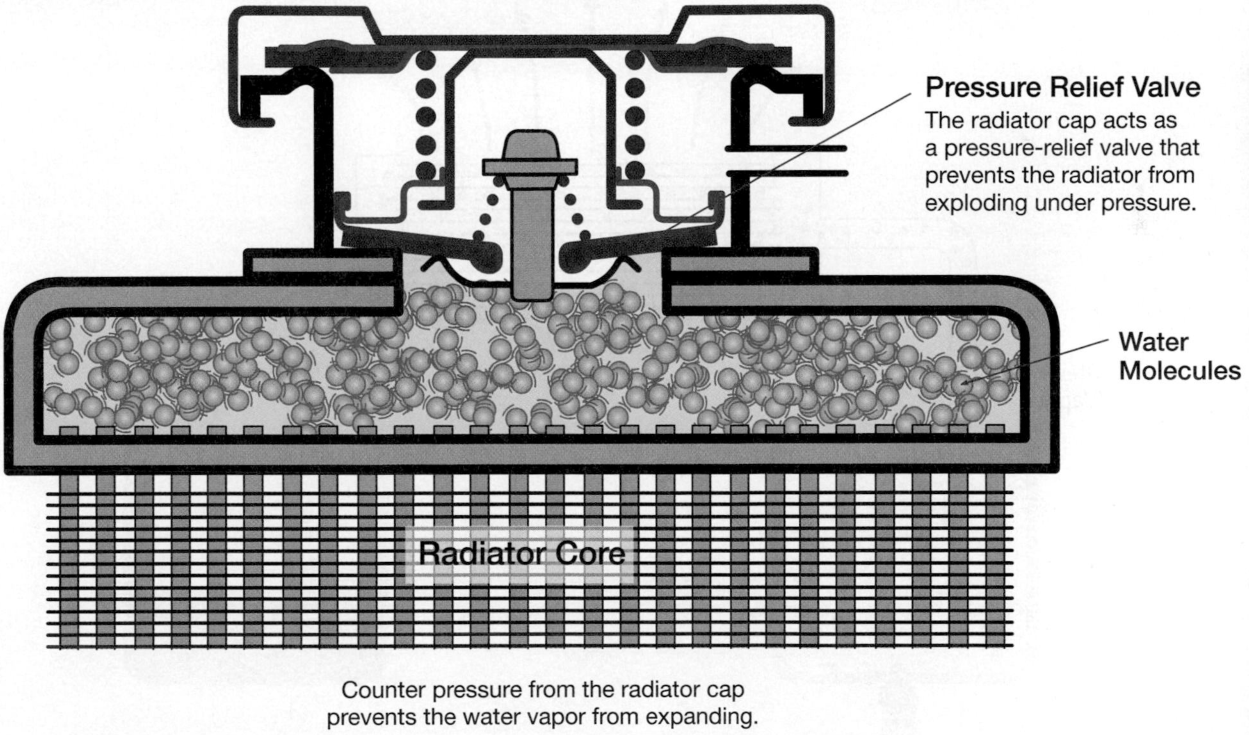

FIGURE 51-12 Increasing the pressure in the cooling system also increases the boiling point of the coolant.

pressure and boiling point.) There is also a direct relationship between the boiling point of a liquid and the pressure exerted on the liquid's surface. For example, water at sea level will boil at 212°F or 100°C. At higher altitudes, however, the boiling point drops because lower pressure allows the molecules to move more vigorously. Denver, Colorado, sits at an altitude of 1 mile (1.6 km) above sea level, and water there has a boiling point of 203°F (95°C). The cooling system of an engine takes advantage of this principle by pressurizing the radiator to increase the boiling point of coolant. For every 1-psi increase in cooling system pressure, there is a 3°F increase in the boiling point. A 10-psi radiator cap will not allow coolant to boil over until it reaches 242°F (10 psi × 3°F = 30°F 30°F + 212°F = 242°F). Increasing the boiling point of engine coolant keeps the coolant as a liquid, which can cool more effectively than water vapor.

Simply changing the pressure of a liquid will allow a change of state to take place. This principle is used to remove water from air-conditioning systems after they have been opened to the atmosphere. Evacuating air from the system, which reduces the pressure applied to water, causes any moisture in the system to boil at room temperature. Therefore, changing refrigerants back and forth between a gas and liquid state is accomplished simply by compressing a gas refrigerant or lowering the pressure of a liquid refrigerant.

One more important point to understand about the relationship between pressure, temperature, and state of matter is that to obtain a change in state—solid to liquid or liquid to gas, and vice versa—requires much more heat than is required simply to increase the temperature by a single degree. For example, it only requires 140 Btu of heat to increase the temperature of 1 lb (450 g) of water from room temperature to 212°F (100°C). To change the same amount of water into a vapor or steam having a temperature of 212°F (100°C) requires 970 Btu. Conversely, changing steam to water or water to ice requires removal of the same amount of heat **FIGURE 51-13**. When a liquid or vapor changes state and requires removal or addition of heat, even though a tremendous amount of heat transfer takes place, there is no change in sensible heat. Ice and water can exist at the same temperature, likewise water

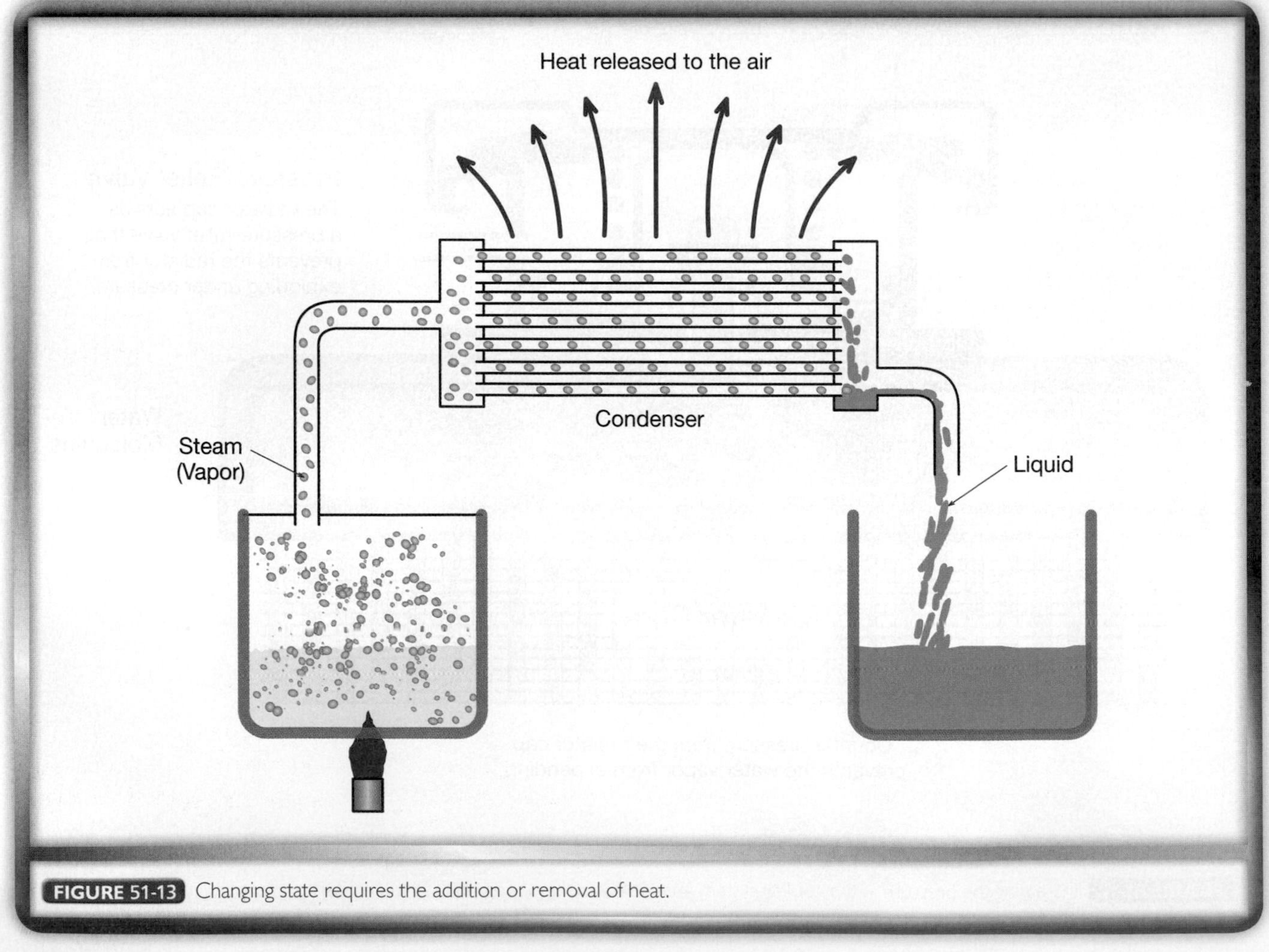

FIGURE 51-13 Changing state requires the addition or removal of heat.

and steam. Remember that heat removed or added without a change in temperature is called latent heat.

The following four rules help summarize the basic principles of refrigeration:

- **Rule 1**—To refrigerate is to remove heat. The absence of heat is cold.
- **Rule 2**—Heat can pass into anything that has less heat. Nothing can stop the movement of heat; the transfer of heat can only be slowed down.
- **Rule 3**—If a change of state is to take place, there must be a transfer of heat. For a liquid to change to a gas, the liquid must absorb heat. Heat is removed from a liquid through vapor. For a vapor to change into a liquid, the vapor must give up heat. Heat is always transferred to a cooler surface or medium.
- **Rule 4**—All refrigeration systems use two principles to move heat from one place to another. Latent heat of vaporization is used to absorb large amounts of heat inside the cab or passenger compartment. Latent heat of condensation is used to release large amounts of heat outside in the condenser. The evaporator absorbs heat; the condenser releases heat.

Simple Refrigeration Cycle

Removing heat from an object or substance is simple. Because heat always moves toward a colder object, all that is necessary for cooling is to provide an even colder substance for heat to flow into. Consider adding ice cubes to a warm drink. The warmer liquid becomes cooler as heat from the beverage flows into the colder ice. As the ice cubes absorb the liquid's heat and melt, the liquid's temperature drops. Getting sprayed with water on a warm day removes heat in a similar way. Water sprayed against the skin absorbs heat and converts to a vapor, which takes heat with it. As water gets warmer while in contact with the skin, evaporation takes place, and the skin becomes cooler. The process of removing heat through evaporation is called latent heat of evaporation.

The same principles of heat transfer apply to cooling the interior of a vehicle. A liquid refrigerant is placed in a metal-finned evaporator inside the vehicle. Reducing the pressure of the refrigerant causes the refrigerant to want to boil, or convert to a vapor. However, heat is required for the refrigerant to change into a vapor. Cabin air is the best source of heat, and so the physical properties of the refrigerant liquid will enable it to absorb heat and boil. Evaporating the refrigerant is no different than evaporating water from skin—instead of removing heat from the skin, the refrigerant removes heat from the air surrounding the evaporator. Cooler cabin air results from the heat transfer into the evaporating refrigerant. The process of evaporating refrigerant using the latent heat properties of refrigerant to absorb heat from the air removes an enormous amount of heat. Since the liquid does not simply change temperature but changes state, much more heat is absorbed by the refrigerant.

To build an efficient air-conditioning system, though, a process of continually evaporating the refrigerant is required, as is another separate process to remove heat from the refrigerant.

Once again, using a process where the refrigerant can change state will transfer much more heat than only changing the refrigerant's temperature a few degrees. Using a refrigerant compressor and a condenser, which is a type of heat exchanger, enables the process of latent heat removal from the refrigerant through condensation. The compressor will pull vaporized refrigerant from the evaporator and compress it once again to increase its temperature. Compressing the gas and sharply increasing its pressure causes the refrigerant to want to convert into a liquid **FIGURE 51-14**. If the compressed gas is circulated through a condenser, large amounts of latent heat are transferred from the gas to the atmosphere as the gas changes to a liquid.

The Refrigeration System

Air-conditioning and refrigeration systems transfer heat from the cab and passenger compartment to the air stream outside the vehicle. They also remove moisture from the air passing through the evaporator and channel it to a drain leading outside the vehicle.

The refrigeration system operates in a closed loop. This means the refrigerant is used over and over again as it circulates through the system. A typical mechanical refrigeration system consists of the six principle parts shown in **FIGURE 51-15**:

- Compressor with an electric on/off clutch
- Condenser
- Expansion device
- Evaporator
- Receiver-dryer or accumulator
- Refrigerant and oil

The Air-Conditioning Compressor and Clutch

The compressor is an engine-driven pump that increases refrigerant pressure and circulates refrigerant through the system. As the refrigerant is compressed, its temperature rises. As the boiling point of the refrigerant increases under pressure, the refrigerant returns to a liquid state. Cool, low-pressure gas from the evaporator enters the

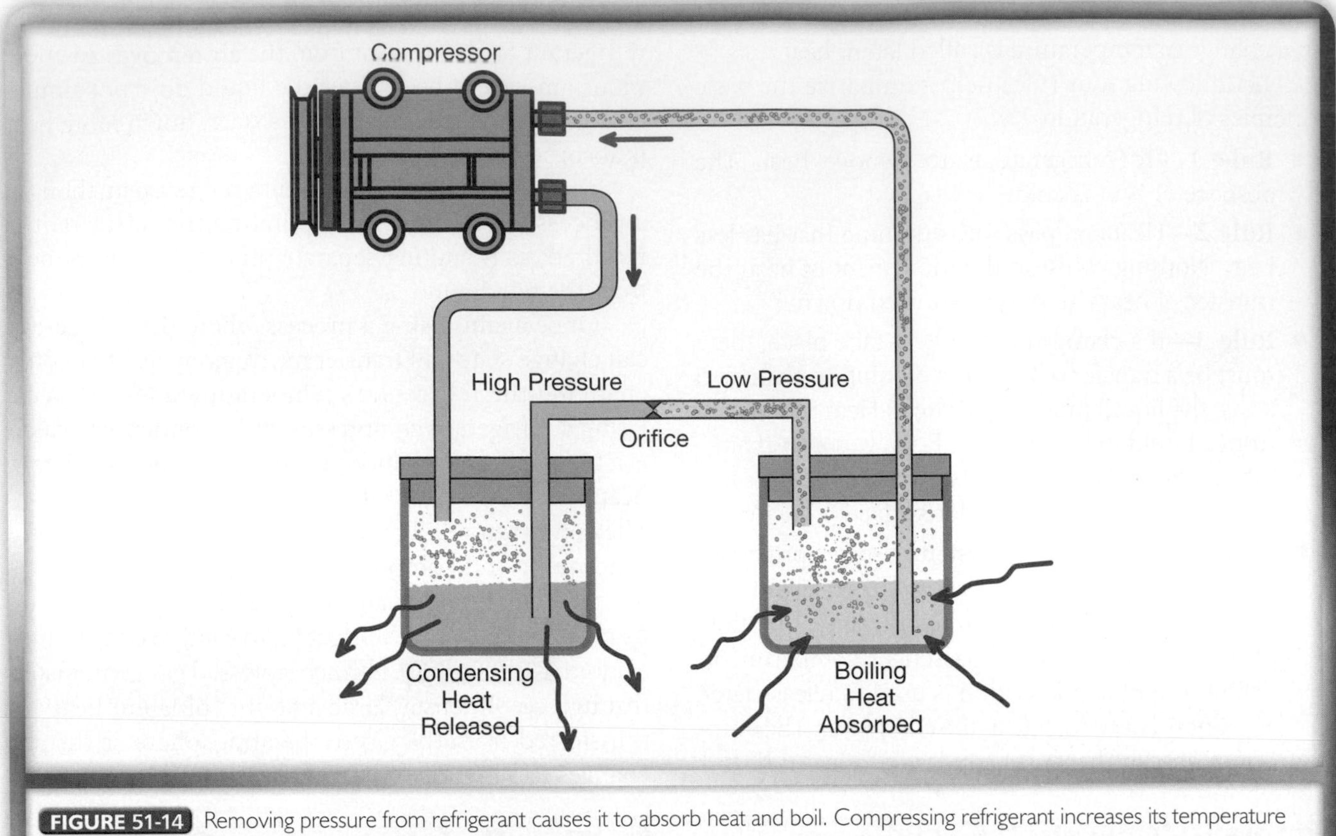

FIGURE 51-14 Removing pressure from refrigerant causes it to absorb heat and boil. Compressing refrigerant increases its temperature and causes it to want to convert into a liquid.

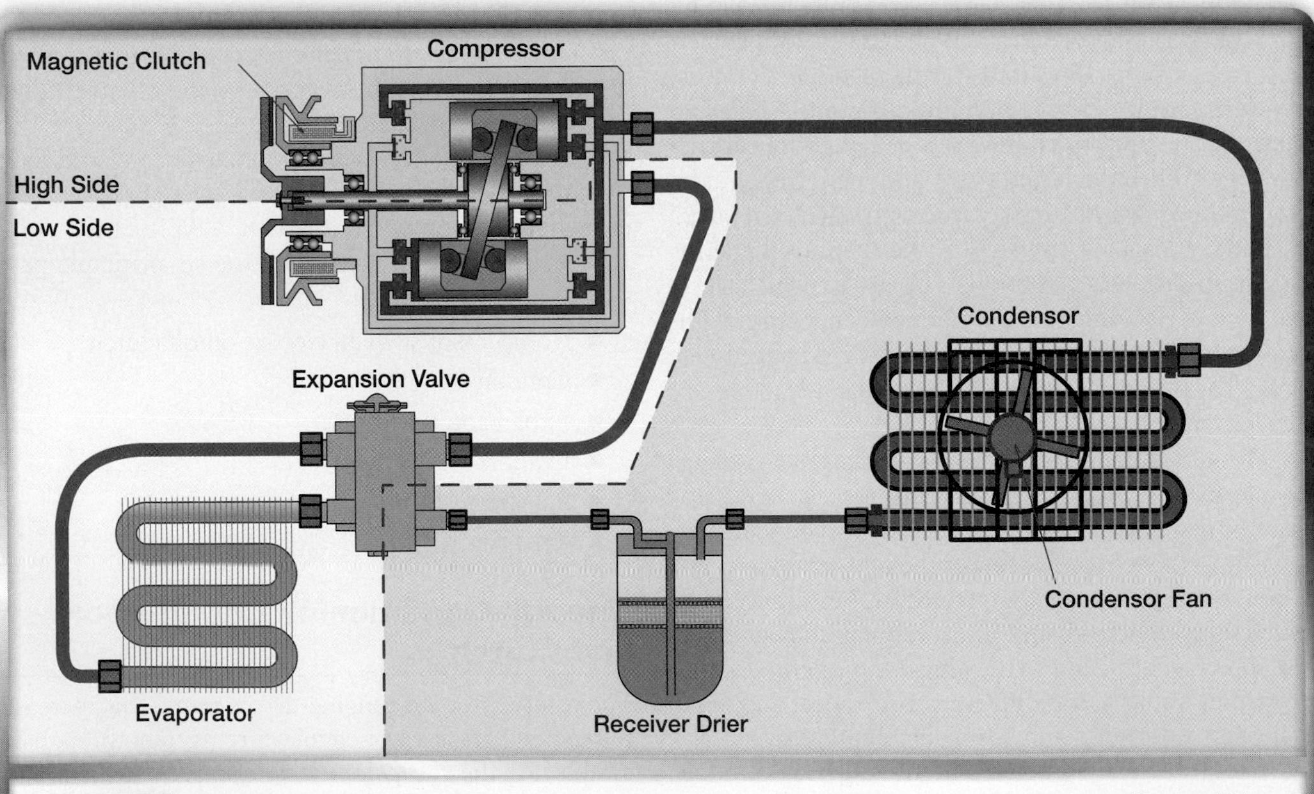

FIGURE 51-15 The components of the air-conditioning system. The compressor and expansion valve divide the system between high and low pressure sides.

compressor, where it is converted to high-pressure, high-temperature refrigerant gas leaving the compressor.

Three basic types of air-conditioning compressors can be used to build pressure exceeding 350 psi (2,413 kPa): piston, rotary vane, and scroll. Piston-type compressors are almost universally used in commercial vehicles FIGURE 51-16. Depending upon manufacturer and design, these compressors may have from 1 to 10 cylinders and may or may not have provisions to hold lubricating oil in a sump.

Compressors may have their pistons arranged in an in-line, in an axial, radial, or V design inside the compressor housing. A V type is shown in FIGURE 51-17. Generally, the compressor's capacity to move refrigerant is a primary determinant of the system's ability to remove heat. Increasing compressor displacement is proportional to the Btu capacity of the system in conjunction with other components. Highly refined mineral or synthetic oils lubricate the compressor's moving parts. These oils are specially formulated to dissolve in refrigerant and circulate through the system.

Piston compressors are designed to have an intake stroke and a compression stroke for each cylinder. On the intake stroke, the refrigerant from the low-pressure side of the system leaves the evaporator and is drawn into the compressor. The intake of refrigerant typically occurs through thin, flexible, plate-type reed valves. Another of these one-way valves controls the flow of refrigerant vapors out of the cylinder during compression stroke. During the compression stroke, the refrigerant vapor is compressed, increasing both the pressure and the temperature of the heat-carrying refrigerant.

Because compressors cannot compress liquids, they are designed to operate on refrigerant vapor only. Liquid refrigerant in the compressor will cause damage to the compressor reed valves and may also damage the compressor pistons and connecting rods through hydrostatic lock-up.

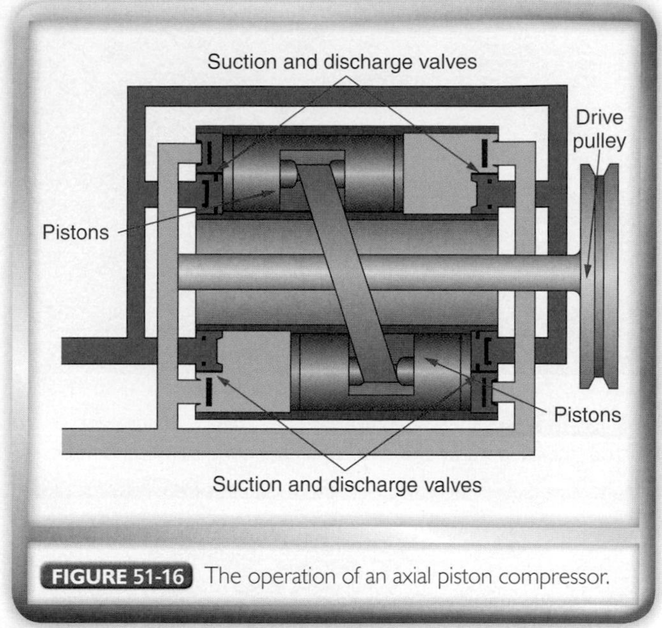

FIGURE 51-16 The operation of an axial piston compressor.

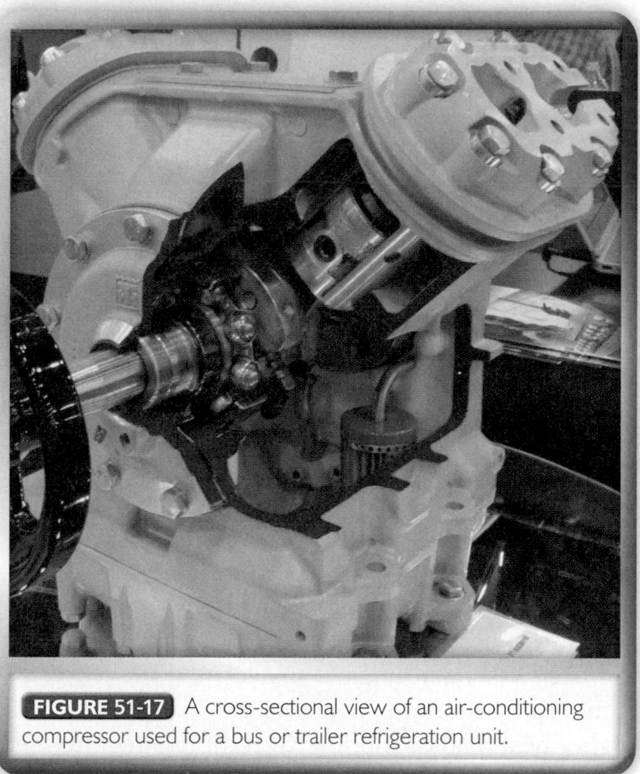

FIGURE 51-17 A cross-sectional view of an air-conditioning compressor used for a bus or trailer refrigeration unit.

Rotary Piston Compressors

Rotary piston compressors have cylindrical-shaped housings and enclose multiple pistons. In addition to being compact in design, the primary advantage of rotary piston compressors is their minimization of noise, vibration, and harshness (NVH). Consider that a 2-cylinder compressor will produce 2 large pumping pulses per rotation, whereas a 10-cylinder swash plate will create 10 smaller pulses.

Common manufacturers of rotary piston compressors found on mobile heavy-duty equipment include Sanden, Sankyo, Zexel, Calsonic, and Seltec. These compressors use a variable angle swash plate that drives pistons via a connecting rod. As the swash plate rotates through 360 degrees of motion, each piston moves through two strokes—one up, and one down. Check valves in the head of the compressor convert these pulses into suction and discharge strokes FIGURE 51-18.

Most of these compressors have variable displacement capabilities and use the pressure sensed by the low, or suction, side of the system to change the angle of the swash plate FIGURE 51-19. When little cooling loads

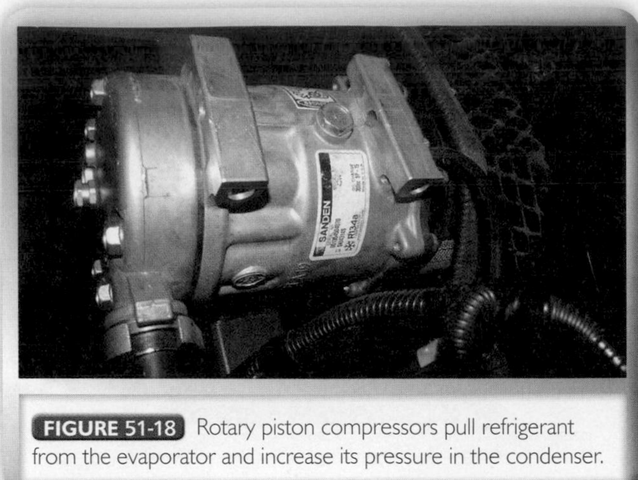

FIGURE 51-18 Rotary piston compressors pull refrigerant from the evaporator and increase its pressure in the condenser.

FIGURE 51-19 A rotary piston compressor using a variable angle swash plate changes the stroke length of its pistons.

are sensed by the compressor, such as when evaporator pressures are very low and little refrigerant is evaporating, the swash plate angle is smaller, and less refrigerant is moved by shorter piston strokes. Conversely, when a higher heat load or more refrigeration is required, the swash plate angle will increase, lengthening the piston stroke. So, at low heat loads, the compressor may have an energy efficient 2-cubic-inch displacement, while at high heat loads it may have 10 or 12 cubic inches of displacement. Considering truck compressors under maximum heat loads may draw as much as 8 hp (6 kW) and buses more than 12 hp (9 kW), reducing compressor energy consumption is important for meeting greenhouse gas emission targets. Rotary compressors in trucks will have between 5 and 10 cylinders and a displacement of 7 to 15 cubic inches.

Compressor Clutches

Mobile HD air-conditioning compressors are usually belt-driven from the engine's crankshaft. They have an electromagnetic clutch that enables the compressor to easily shut off when compressor operation is not required. Engagement and disengagement of the compressor is electrically controlled by system electronic control units, air-conditioning control panel settings, or system demands. Most systems use the clutch to cycle compressor operation on and off depending on heat loads.

When the evaporator requires refrigerant, the compressor engages and circulates refrigerant. When sufficient refrigerant pressures and quantity are available to the evaporator, the compressor disengages to conserve energy. On current air-conditioning systems, three basic parts make up the clutch: a drive plate, which is attached to the compressor shaft; a belt pulley, which is mounted on bearings attached to an extension of the compressor housing; and a magnetic coil FIGURE 51-20.

The magnetic coil engages and disengages the compressor. The coil is mounted behind the belt pulley, is attached to the compressor housing, and does not rotate with the pulley or drive shaft. Electrical connections for the clutch operation are made directly through wires, which are part of the field coil assembly FIGURE 51-21. When a magnetic field is created by applying electrical current into the coil, the drive plate is pulled against a friction surface of the pulley, causing the pulley to rotate with the compressor shaft. When not energized, the clutch allows the pulley to freewheel, minimizing parasitic energy losses as well as wear and tear on the compressor.

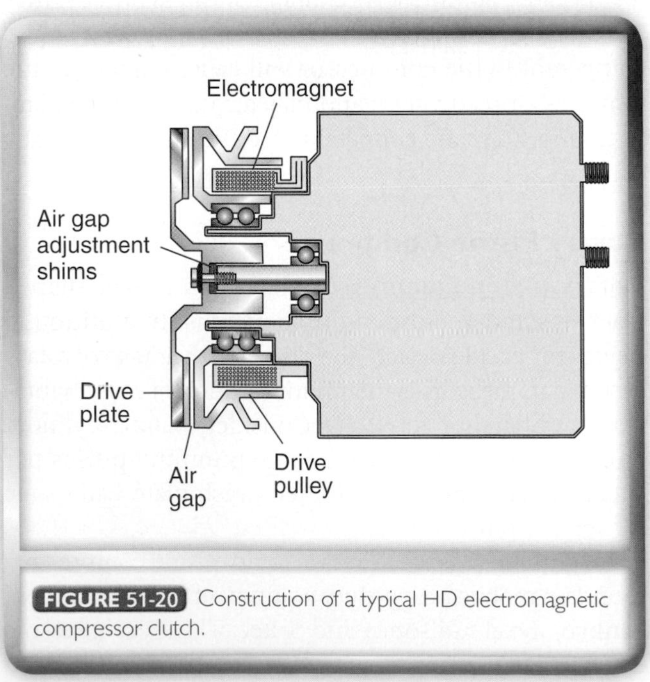

FIGURE 51-20 Construction of a typical HD electromagnetic compressor clutch.

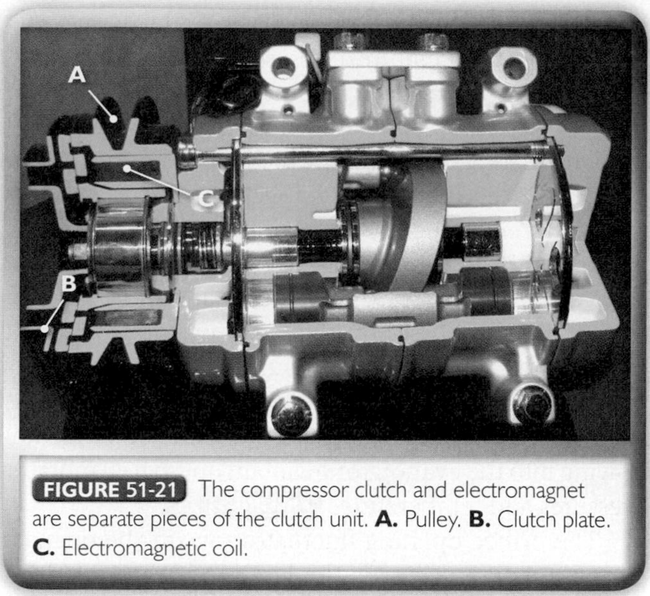

FIGURE 51-21 The compressor clutch and electromagnet are separate pieces of the clutch unit. **A.** Pulley. **B.** Clutch plate. **C.** Electromagnetic coil.

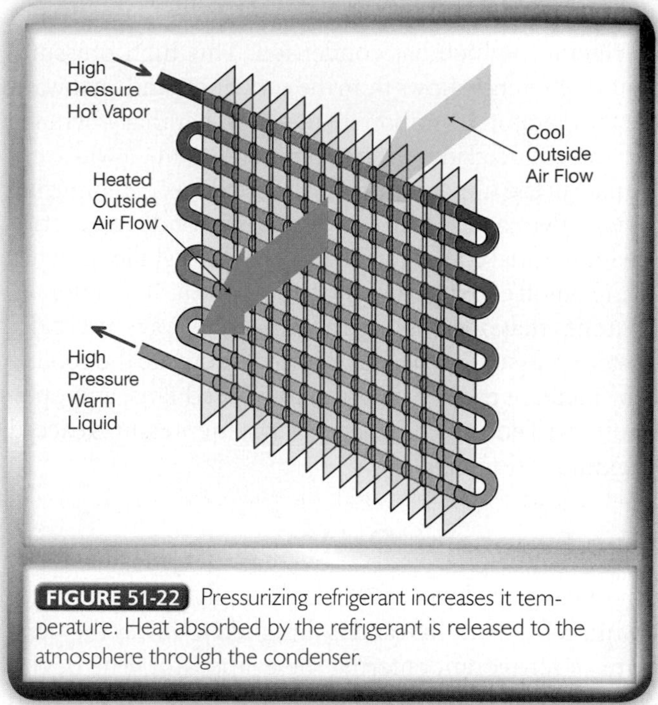

FIGURE 51-22 Pressurizing refrigerant increases it temperature. Heat absorbed by the refrigerant is released to the atmosphere through the condenser.

The Condenser

The hot, gaseous refrigerant pressurized by the compressor is sent to the condenser **FIGURE 51-22**. Outside air flows over the fins of the condenser and releases heat from the refrigerant as it converts from a gas to a liquid. Enough heat is removed from refrigerant to lower the temperature below its boiling point, and the refrigerant condenses to a liquid inside the condenser. As the gas condenses, its latent heat is removed during condensation. High-pressure, warm liquid leaves the condenser.

The condenser typically consists of coiled tubing mounted in a series of thin cooling fins. This arrangement provides maximum surface area for heat transfer using a minimum amount of engine compartment space. Some condensers consist of a tube merely bent into a serpentine shape **FIGURE 51-23A**. Refrigerant moves from top to bottom with a single pass. Newer parallel-style condensers use a manifold on each side of the condenser, creating multiple paths for refrigerant flow **FIGURE 51-23B**.

The condenser is mounted directly in front of the radiator, where it can receive full airflow created by forward vehicle motion and the engine fan. The condenser receives the heat-laden, high-pressure refrigerant vapor from the compressor's discharge hose. Refrigerant vapor enters at the top of the condenser and flows through its coils. Heat follows its natural tendency to move from hot to cold and radiates from the hot refrigerant vapors to the cooler atmosphere.

As the refrigerant vapors are cooled and flow down through the condenser, condensation eventually occurs, at which point the gas becomes liquid refrigerant. The largest amount of heat is given off by the refrigerant at the point of condensation. The refrigerant in the lower

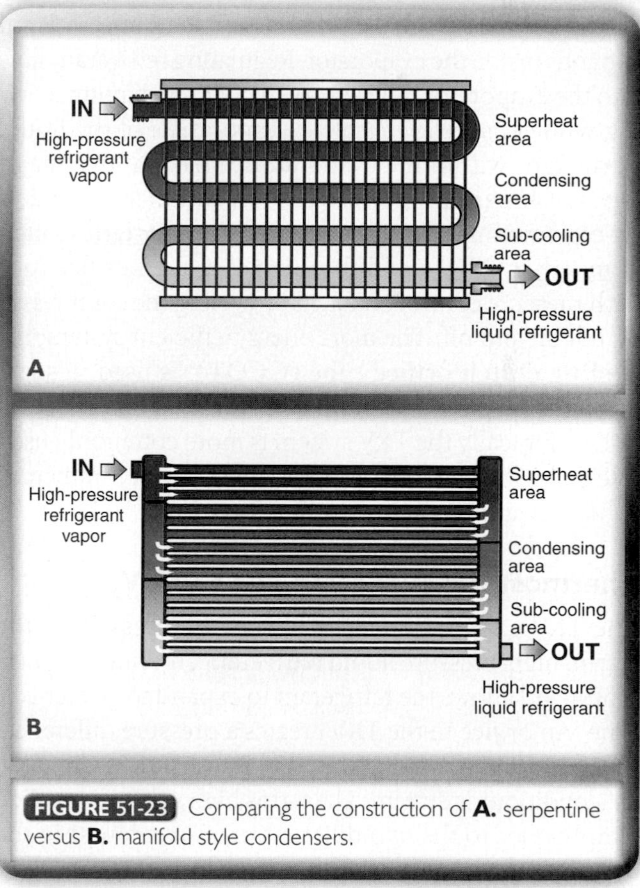

FIGURE 51-23 Comparing the construction of **A.** serpentine versus **B.** manifold style condensers.

portion of the condenser is a warm, high-pressure liquid. In an air-conditioning system operating under an average heat load, the condenser will have a combination of hot refrigerant vapor in the upper two-thirds of its coils, with the lower third of the coils containing the warm liquid refrigerant, which has condensed. This high pressure, liquid refrigerant flows from the condenser and on toward the evaporator. It's important to remember that whenever air is introduced into the refrigeration system, it will accumulate in the upper portion of the condenser, minimizing its effective capacity. Airflow across the condenser is critical for optimal cooling and component durability. Engines using on/off cooling fans will incorporate air-conditioning switches that open or close at preset high-pressure, side-system pressures. These controls will activate the cooling fan, increase the speed of variable speed fans, and open shutters (if equipped) whenever system pressures exceed maximum thresholds.

The Expansion Device

An expansion device restricts the high-pressure, warm liquid refrigerant line and is designed to lower the pressure of refrigerant entering the evaporator. The device may be a thermostatically controlled valve or a restricted orifice that meters the release of the refrigerant into the evaporator and regulates the rate at which refrigerant expands inside the evaporator. Regulating refrigerant flow into the evaporator is necessary to obtain maximum cooling while ensuring complete evaporation of the liquid refrigerant within the evaporator. There are two major types of expansion devices used in commercial vehicle air-conditioning systems. One is the **thermostatic expansion valve (TXV)**, and the other is a fixed-orifice tube with pressure control obtained by cycling the compressor clutch on and off. The more energy-efficient system, the **cycling clutch orifice tube (CCOT)**, is used in some models made by Navistar, Peterbilt, Freightliner, and Volvo. Typically the TXV system is more commonly used due to the larger capacity and physical size of commercial vehicle evaporators.

Thermostatic Expansion Valve (TXV)

The TXV expansion device lowers the pressure of the warm, high-pressure liquid refrigerant entering the evaporator and allows the refrigerant to expand to greater volume. An orifice in the TXV creates a pressure difference, forming what are called the "high" and "low" side of the air-conditioning system. The terms high side and low side simply refer to the two different pressures found in the air-conditioning system. The compressor forms the other dividing point in the air conditioning between high and low systems. Refrigerant from the receiver-dryer enters the expansion valve as a liquid under high pressure. As it passes through the metering orifice in the TXV, the refrigerant is forced through the small orifice and sprayed out into the evaporator **FIGURE 51-24**. As the refrigerant's pressure and temperature drops, so does its boiling point Atomized refrigerant can flow into the evaporator after the TXV and easily convert to a vapor.

Unlike a CCOT system, which meters refrigerant at a fixed rate, the TXV meters refrigerant into the evaporator at a variable rate. To maintain the evaporator at the correct temperature and pressure needed to produce the most efficient cooling, the TXV contains an orifice that changes diameter based on evaporator pressure and outlet temperature. Refrigerant pressure entering the TXV is lowered after passing through the internal restriction. As the orifice changes size, different quantities of refrigerant flowing into the evaporator maintain optimal evaporator pressures and temperatures **FIGURE 51-25**.

The orifice opening fluctuates toward the open or closed position to create the low pressure needed for the liquid refrigerant to effectively vaporize as it passes through the evaporator. It's important that a TXV quickly respond to changes in heat load conditions. When the evaporator pressure changes in response to varying heat loads, the valve orifice changes size to regulate refrigerant flow. For example, if high cabin temperatures evaporate more refrigerant, the evaporator pressures and temperatures increase. This requires more refrigerant to absorb and transfer more heat. In these circumstances, the TXV valve will open. The opposite will happen if evaporator temperatures and pressures drop due to less evaporation of refrigerant. Increased compressor output volume due to increased engine speed will cause the valve to move toward a closed position, restricting the amount of refrigerant entering the evaporator.

TXV Operation

The thermostatic expansion valve controls refrigerant flow by the action of a spring-loaded control valve. Evaporator temperature and pressure are two factors that change the size of the restriction opening. Temperature is sensed using a pressure differential applied to either side of a diaphragm connected to the control valve through a pin. This pressure differential is a result of pressure supplied by the temperature-sensing bulb through a capillary tube applying pressure above the diaphragm. Equalizing or balancing pressure below the diaphragm is supplied by refrigerant pressure from the low-pressure inlet side of the evaporator supplied by an internal valve passage **FIGURE 51-26**. The refrigerant pressure on the lower side of the diaphragm is proportional to temperature as well. The temperature-sensing bulb is filled with a temperature-sensitive gas, which is usually the same as the system's refrigerant. Gas pressure above the diaphragm must be higher than pressure below to open the

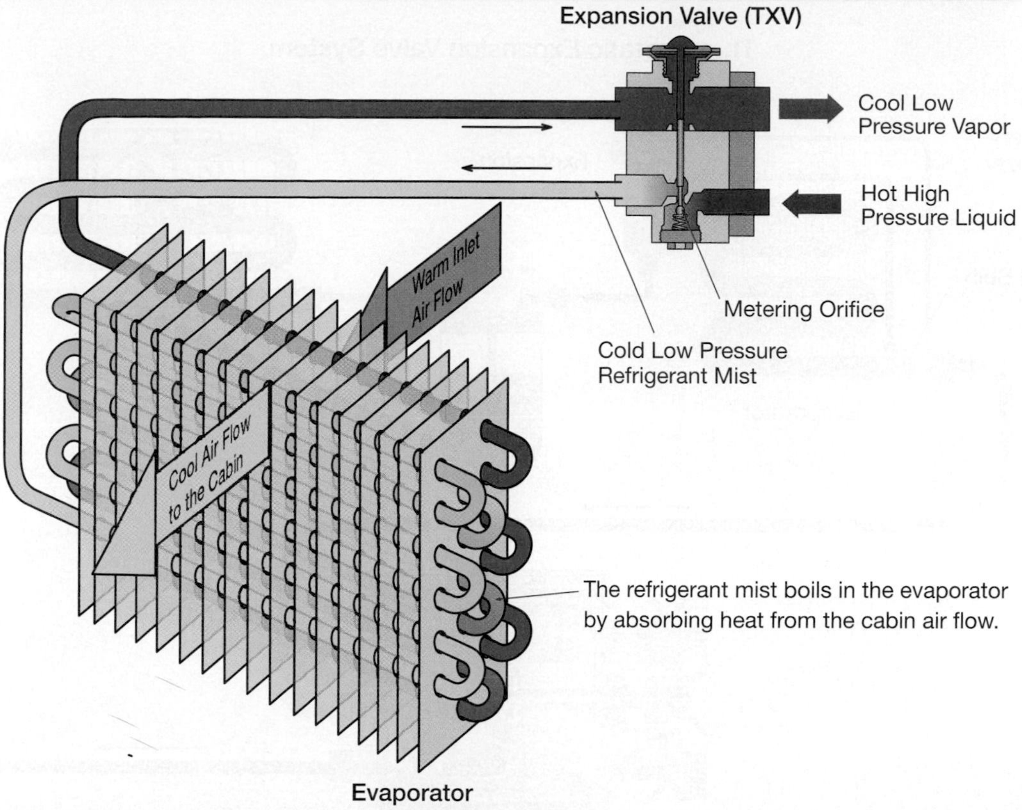

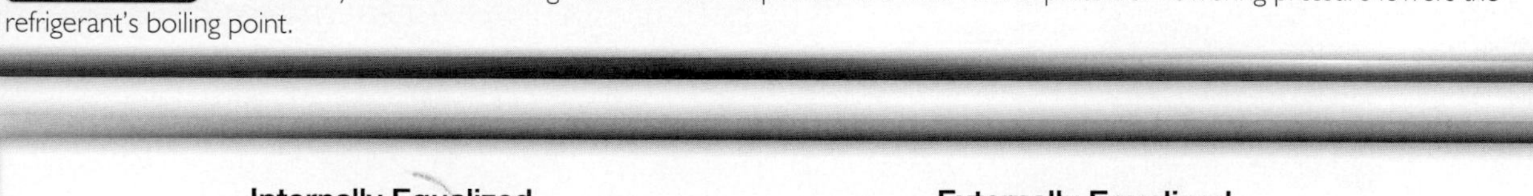

FIGURE 51-24 The TXV system meters refrigerant into the evaporator at a much lower pressure. Lowering pressure lowers the refrigerant's boiling point.

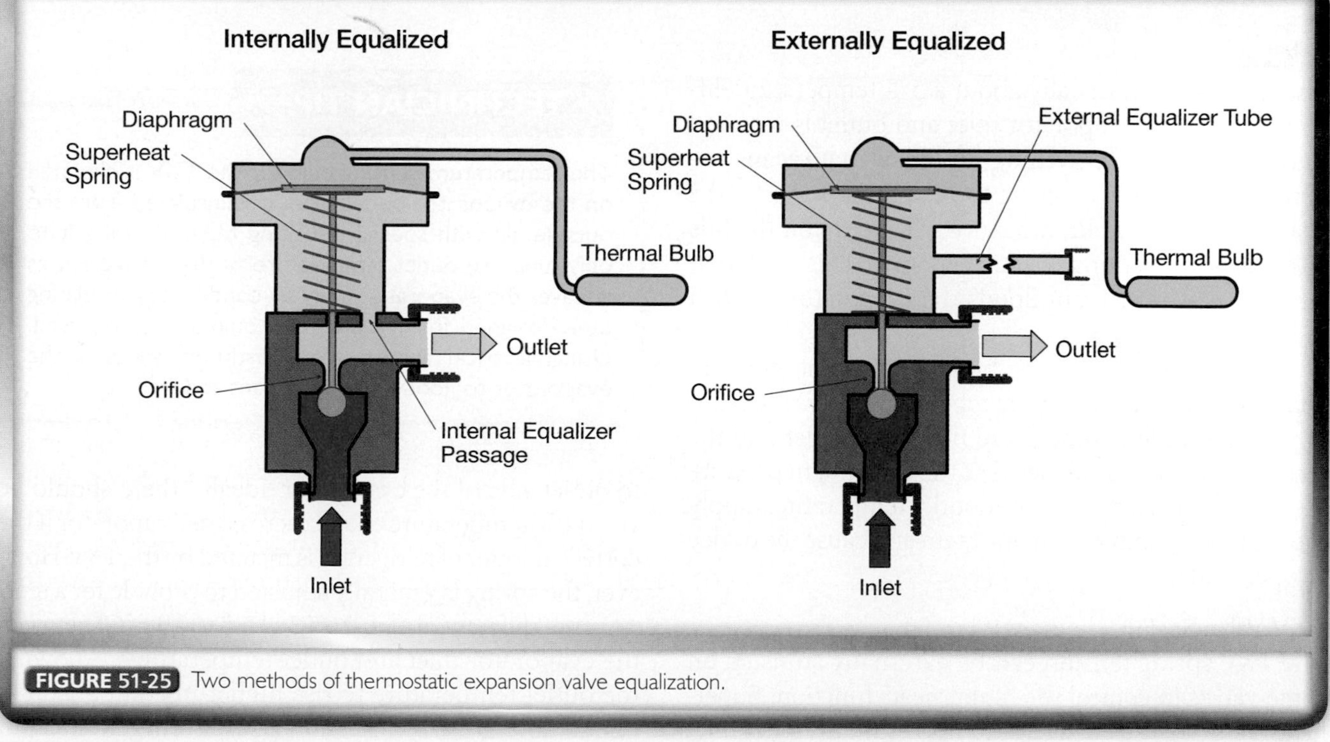

FIGURE 51-25 Two methods of thermostatic expansion valve equalization.

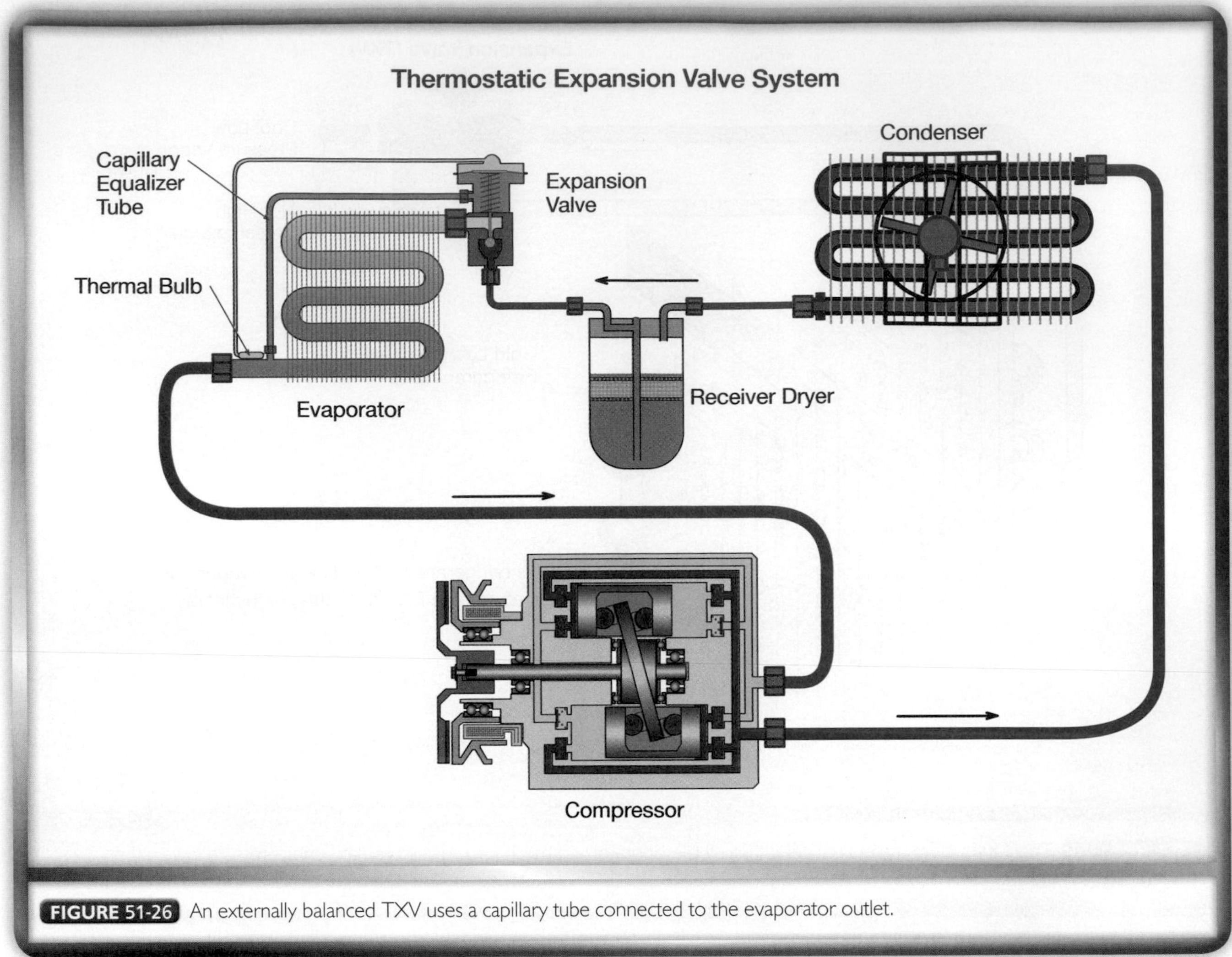

FIGURE 51-26 An externally balanced TXV uses a capillary tube connected to the evaporator outlet.

restriction orifice. Usually about a 5°F temperature difference between evaporator inlet and outlet is required to open the valve. Anything less than that means too much refrigerant is entering the evaporator. And if the evaporator is too cold, moisture will freeze on the fins and plates, preventing effective cooling. This condition where excess refrigerant floods the evaporator is called **evaporator freezing**.

Gas temperature in the bulb changes the pressure above the diaphragm. If more refrigerant enters the evaporator, the outlet temperature becomes colder and the restriction orifice is narrowed as the diaphragm pressure decreases. Warmer evaporator outlet temperatures apply more pressure above the diaphragm and cause the orifice to open wider.

TXV Valve Spring

The TXV spring tension can be externally adjusted on some valves to control the "superheat" function. Superheat is simply the change in temperature from the inlet to outlet side of the evaporator. Ideally, there should be very little temperature change across the evaporator if the correct amount of refrigerant is metered by the TXV. However, the spring is generally adjusted to provide for a temperature differential of 4–16°F (–15.5 to –8.8°C) between the evaporator inlet and outlet temperatures. Allowing the outlet temperature to rise higher in comparison to inlet temperature or pressure ensures refrigerant vapor

> **TECHNICIAN TIP**
>
> The temperature-sensing bulb for the TXV is clamped on the evaporator outlet pipe. It is insulated from the outside air with special insulating tape, allowing it to only measure outlet temperature of the refrigerant as it leaves the evaporator. Only air-conditioning insulating tape designed for insulating the bulb should be used. Using electrical tape or other substitutes will cause the evaporator to flood with refrigerant and freeze.

at the evaporator outlet will not contain any droplets of liquid refrigerant, which could cause the evaporator to freeze up due to excess refrigerant flow or potentially damage the compressor. On very large evaporators where the refrigerant travels a long way, an externally balanced TXV is used. In these valves, a capillary tube connects the outlet pressure of the evaporator to the underside of the diaphragm instead of having an internal passage supplying evaporator inlet pressure FIGURE 51-27. The lower diaphragm chamber pressure reflects the evaporator outlet temperature on externally balanced TXV to improve the superheat function of the TXV.

The "H" TXV

This TXV valve gets its name from its H-shaped design. There are two refrigerant passages through the valve, which form the legs of the H. One passage is connected to the refrigerant line from the condenser to the evaporator; it contains the ball and spring valve that meters the flow of refrigerant to the evaporator FIGURE 51-28. The other passage is in the refrigerant line from the evaporator to the compressor; it contains the valve's temperature-sensing diaphragm element. The temperature-sensing element contains a small amount of refrigerant. The expansion and contraction of the sensing element varies the amount of refrigerant flow through the system.

Early H-valves used with fixed displacement compressors had a low-pressure cut-out switch installed in the valve to sense low-side pressure at the evaporator outlet. These H-valves also used a low-pressure cycling switch to disconnect the compressor clutch and prevent evaporator freeze-up caused by excessive refrigerant flow. More recent H-valve designs used with variable displacement compressors do not use a low-pressure cycling switch.

Orifice Tube

A simple, plastic tube with a calibrated brass orifice is used on current cycling clutch orifice tube (CCOT) systems to produce refrigerant pressure drop in the evaporator FIGURE 51-29. Orifice tubes also serve the same basic function as the expansion valve but have a different construction. And, like the expansion valve, orifice tubes are

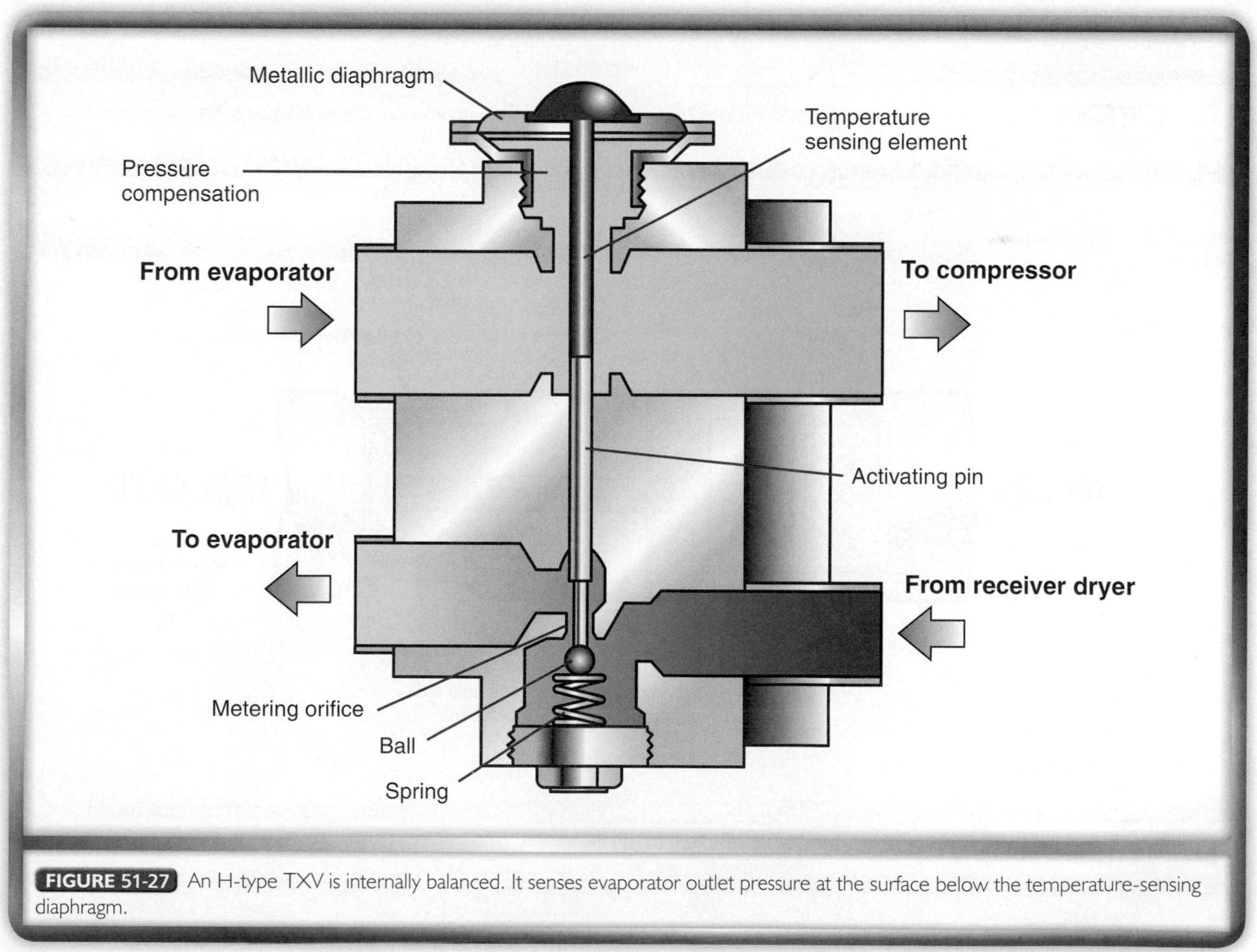

FIGURE 51-27 An H-type TXV is internally balanced. It senses evaporator outlet pressure at the surface below the temperature-sensing diaphragm.

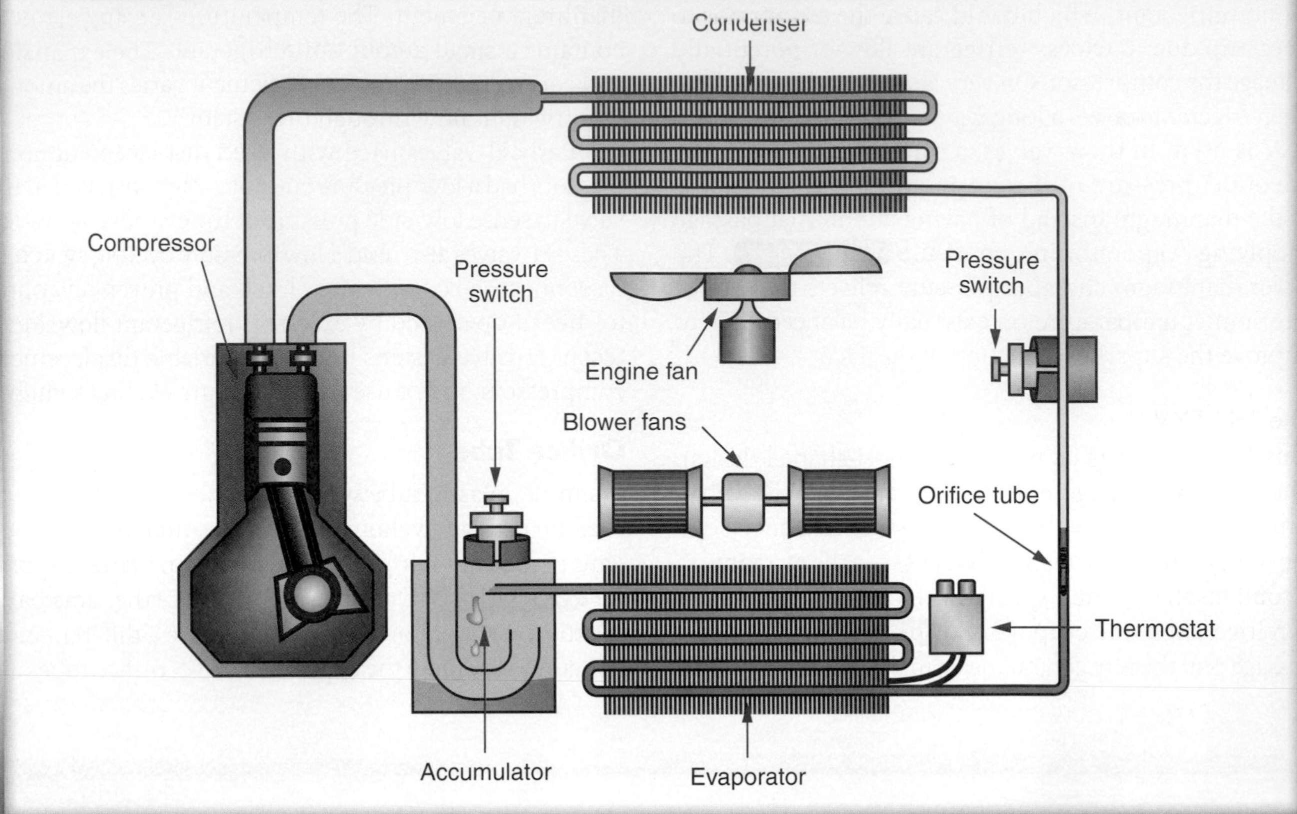

Condenser
Compressor
Pressure switch
Pressure switch
Engine fan
Blower fans
Orifice tube
Thermostat
Accumulator
Evaporator

FIGURE 51-28 CCOT systems use an accumulator located after the evaporator. The accumulator prevents liquid refrigerant from entering the compressor.

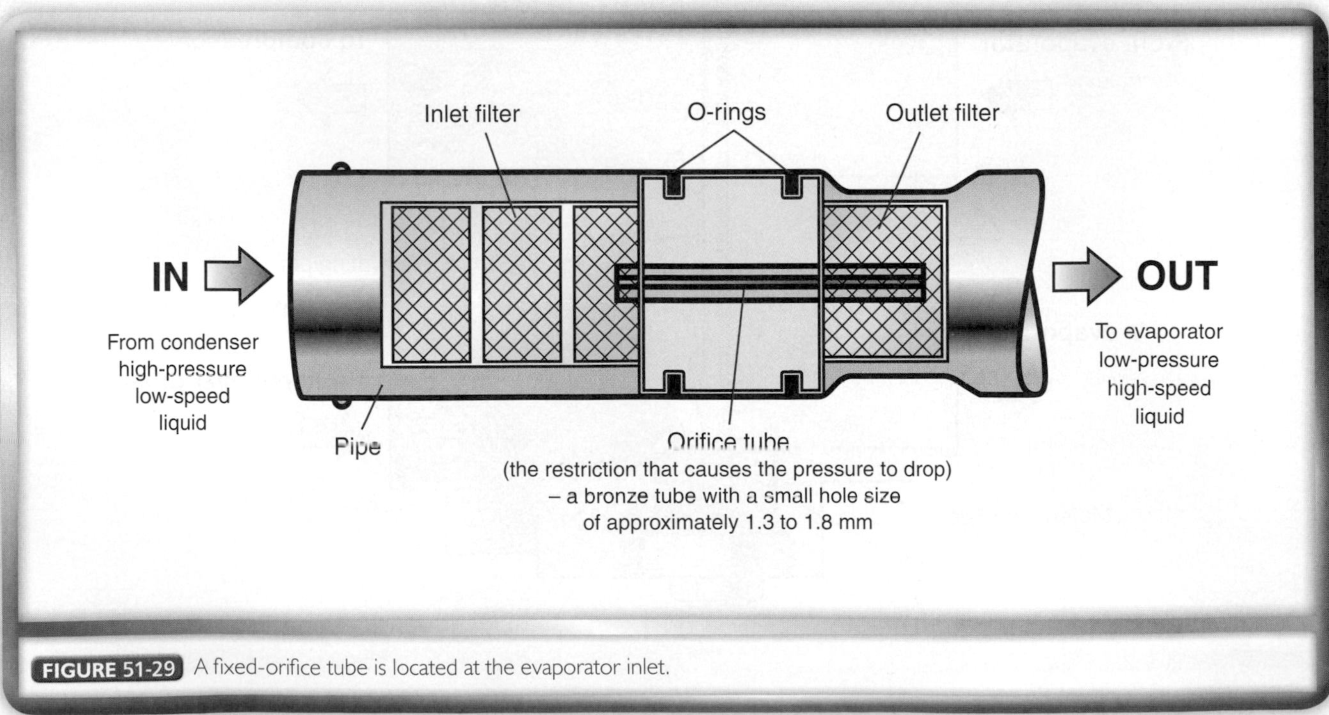

FIGURE 51-29 A fixed-orifice tube is located at the evaporator inlet.

mounted on the inlet side of the evaporator FIGURE 51-30. The tubes are enclosed with filter screens to remove contaminants that could plug a calibrated orifice tube and meter refrigerant flow FIGURE 51-31.

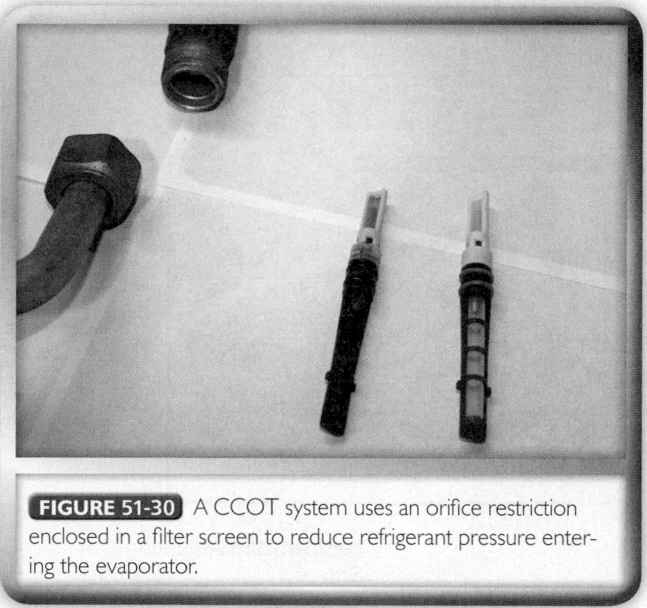

FIGURE 51-30 A CCOT system uses an orifice restriction enclosed in a filter screen to reduce refrigerant pressure entering the evaporator.

Because the orifice does not vary in size, pressure control in the evaporator is accomplished by switching the compressor clutch on and off using a pressure signal from a pressure switch located near the evaporator inlet or suction side FIGURE 51-32. The switch, called the pressure cycling switch, works along with a thermostatic switch to turn the refrigerant flow from the compressor on and off FIGURE 51-33. The switch opens when low pressure is sensed in the evaporator, which in turn regulates evaporator temperature.

When refrigerant has evaporated in the evaporator core, its pressure rises. The pressure cycling switch closes, causing the compressor to pump more refrigerant and reflood the evaporator. Cycling the compressor on and off prevents evaporator freeze-up due to excessive refrigerant flow. The switch also prevents the compressor from operating during cold weather. In subzero conditions, refrigerant gas is a liquid and incapable of dissolving and carrying oil through the air-conditioning system. If the compressor switches on with only liquid refrigerant, it will seize due to a lack of lubrication. Low levels of refrigerant detected by the pressure switch will also not allow the compressor to operate. Without adequate

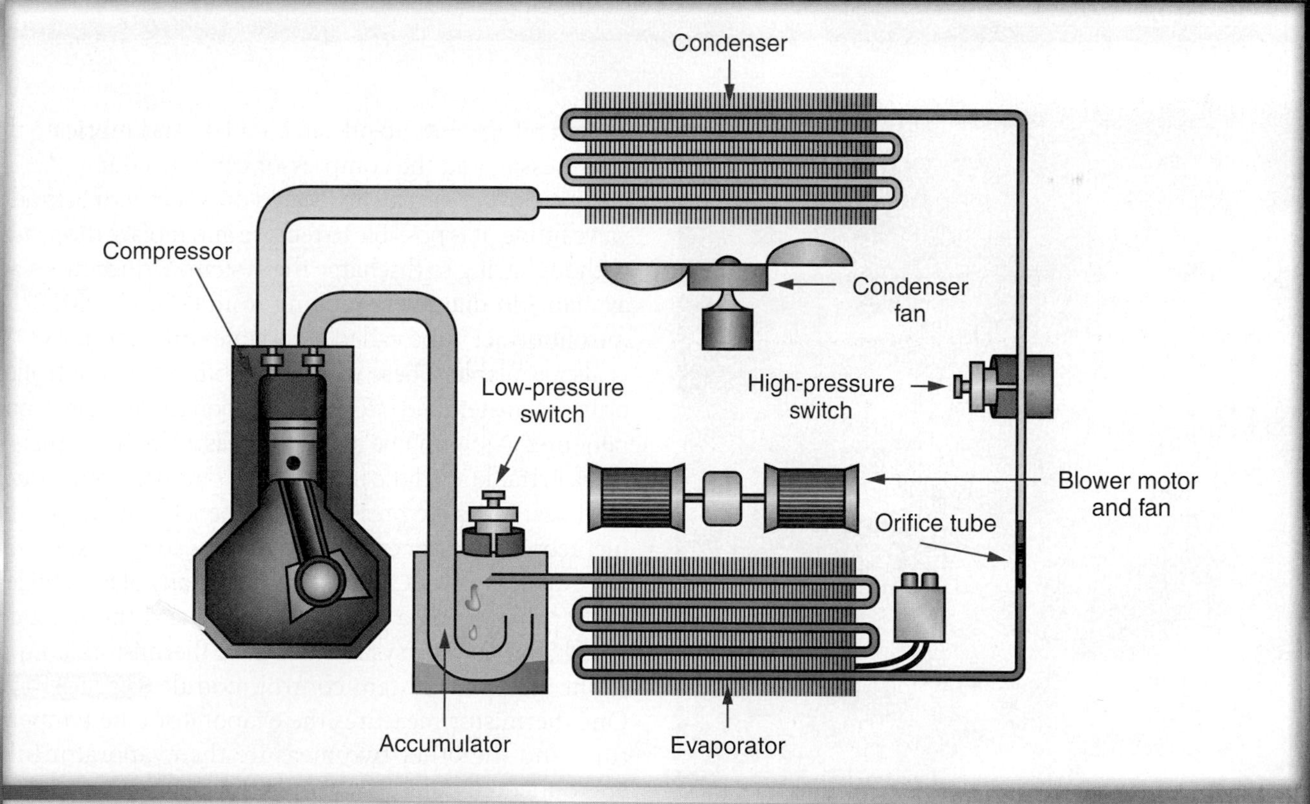

FIGURE 51-31 The pressure cycling switch is located on the accumulator of a CCOT system.

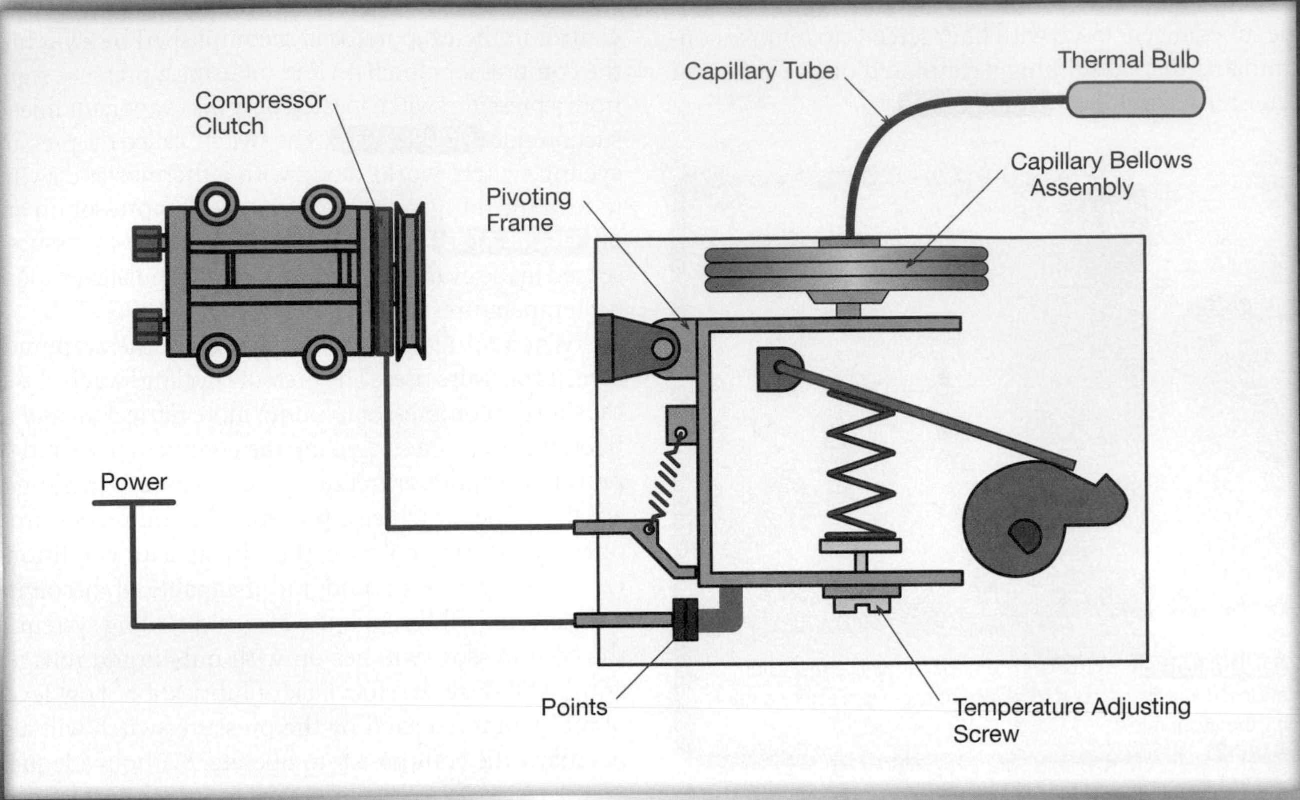

FIGURE 51-32 A mechanical thermostatic switch cycles the compressor on and off and is in series with the pressure cycling switch.

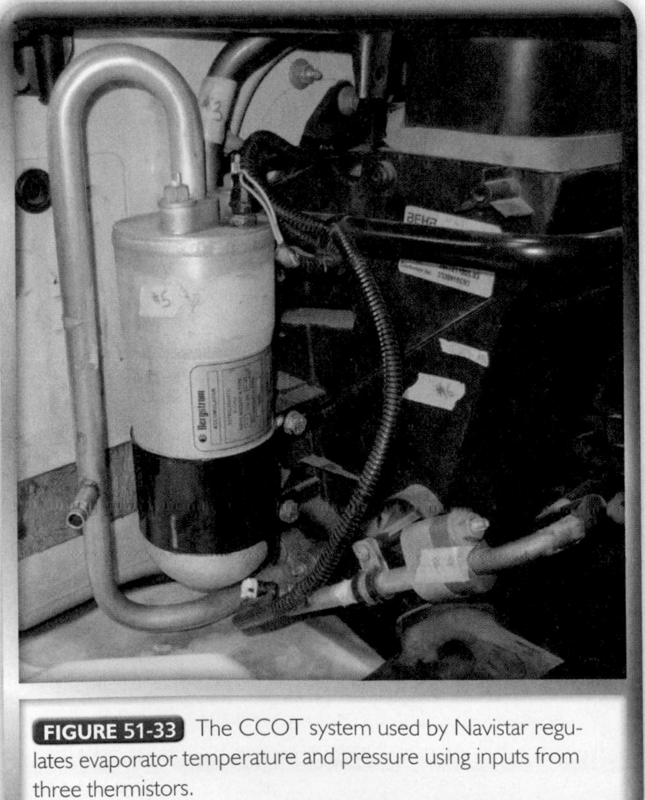

FIGURE 51-33 The CCOT system used by Navistar regulates evaporator temperature and pressure using inputs from three thermistors.

system refrigerant, no oil can circulate and lubricate the compressor, and the compressor can burn out.

This switch is usually located on a standard Schrader valve fitting. It is possible to remove and replace the switch without having to discharge the system. Orifice tubes are available in diameters ranging from 0.0047–0.078". A retrofit orifice tube called a variable orifice tube (VOV) is also available. These tubes have bimetallic-controlled orifice diameters and offer lower evaporator discharge temperatures at low engine speed, such as when the vehicle is stuck in traffic and little refrigerant is pumped even though high heat loads are present. Other benefits are improved fuel economy, lower emissions, and less compressor wear.

Navistar uses a CCOT system on many of its vehicles. Rather than using a pressure cycling and thermostatic switch, the Navistar system uses three thermistors as input to the electrical system control module **FIGURE 51-34**. One thermistor measures the evaporator core temperature, and the other two measure the evaporator inlet and outlet temperatures. By measuring the temperature difference of refrigerant entering and leaving the evaporator, the amount of refrigerant entering the evaporator or its average temperature can be accurately controlled by cycling the compressor clutch on and off. To prevent

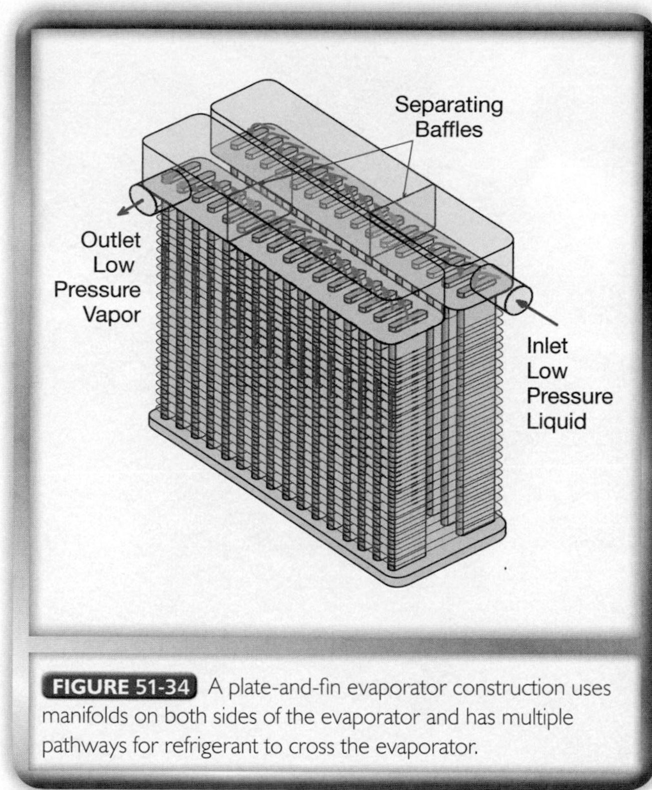

FIGURE 51-34 A plate-and-fin evaporator construction uses manifolds on both sides of the evaporator and has multiple pathways for refrigerant to cross the evaporator.

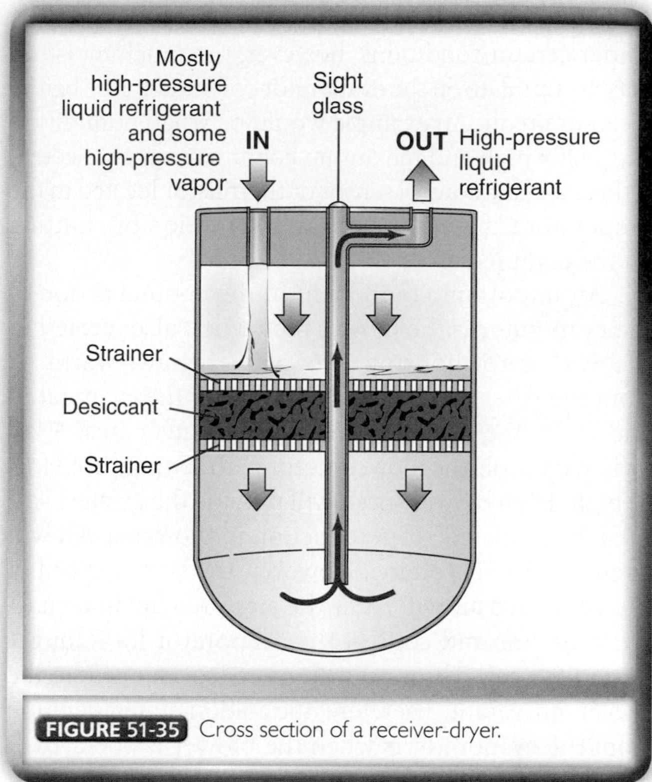

FIGURE 51-35 Cross section of a receiver-dryer.

evaporator freeze-up, sensor input from the third thermistor can provide data to the control unit to cycle the compressor clutch. Algorithms stored in the control module determine when and how long to energize the compressor clutch.

The Evaporator

The evaporator is a heat exchanger located inside the cab or passenger compartment containing the chamber where refrigerant boils and converts to a vapor. When a liquid evaporates, it must absorb a tremendous amount of heat to change state. The source of heat is warm cabin air blowing across the surface of the evaporator. The evaporator also removes moisture from the cabin air. As moist recirculated or outside air passes over the cold evaporator fins, water vapor condenses and drips to the bottom of the evaporator housing. From there it flows through a drain out of the housing.

Like the condenser, the evaporator has a couple of common constructions. The serpentine coil evaporator is constructed from a metal coil mounted in a series of thin cooling fins. The design provides a maximum amount of heat transfer in a minimum amount of space. A plate-and-fin construction uses manifolds on both sides of the evaporator and has multiple pathways for refrigerant to cross the evaporator FIGURE 51-35. Under normal operation, warm air from the passenger compartment is blown across the coils and fins.

The thermostatic expansion valve, or orifice tube, continually meters the proper amount of refrigerant required to maintain optimal heat transfer efficiency. This action also ensures that all of the liquid refrigerant will have changed to a vapor by the time it reaches the evaporator outlet. The refrigerant vapor then continues on to the inlet (suction) side of the compressor.

If too much refrigerant is allowed to enter, the evaporator floods. This results in poor cooling, as the refrigerant can neither boil away rapidly nor vaporize. It may even freeze moisture in the fins, preventing airflow and causing cooling loss. On the other hand, if too little refrigerant is metered, the evaporator starves. Poor cooling again results because the refrigerant boils away or vaporizes too quickly before passing through the evaporator.

The temperature of the refrigerant vapor at the evaporator outlet will be approximately 4–16°F higher than the temperature of the liquid refrigerant at the evaporator inlet. This temperature differential is the **superheat** mentioned earlier, which provides for optimal cooling efficiency and ensures that the vapor does not contain any droplets of liquid refrigerant that would be harmful to the compressor. The warm air blown across the evaporator usually contains some moisture (humidity). The moisture in the air normally condenses on the evaporator coils and drains off as water. Dehumidification of the air is an added feature of the air-conditioning system that adds to passenger comfort. It can also be used as a means of controlling fogging of the vehicle windows. Under certain conditions, however, too much moisture may accumulate on the evaporator coils and freeze before it can drain off. An example would be when humidity is extremely high and maximum cooling mode is selected. A thermostatic control sensor or thermistor located in the evaporator can help prevent this condition by shutting off the compressor.

An important component in the cooling action of the evaporator is the blower motor/fan, also located in the evaporator housing. The blower draws warm air from the passenger compartment, over the evaporator, and blows the cooled air into the passenger area. A fan switch controls the blower motor with settings from low to high. High blower speed will provide the greatest volume of circulated air. A reduction in blower speed will decrease the air volume. However, the slower speed of the circulated air will allow the air to remain in contact with the fins and coils of the evaporator for a longer period of time. This results in more heat transfer to the cooler refrigerant. Therefore, the coldest air temperature from the evaporator is when the blower is operated at its slowest speed.

The Receiver-Dryer

The primary function of the **receiver-dryer** is to serve as a storage reservoir for refrigerant. A second function is to absorb any moisture in the air-conditioning system. Receiver-dryers are used primarily on TXV air-conditioning systems and receive liquid refrigerant from the condenser, storing the liquid until it is needed by the evaporator **FIGURE 51-36**. Capacity of the receiver-dryer varies according to operating conditions. Typically, in truck systems the dryer will hold about half a pound (226 g) of extra refrigerant, which is used as a buffer against slight leaks and high refrigerant operating demands. Because the receiver-dryer receives liquid refrigerant from the condenser, it is mounted either adjacent to the condenser or somewhere downstream before the expansion valve. It consists of a tank, a filter, a drying agent (desiccant), a pick-up tube, and a sight glass (on some applications) **FIGURE 51-37**.

As a dryer, the receiver-dryer also acts as a moisture protection element for the system. The portion of the receiver-dryer that contains the drying agent absorbs any potential moisture from the refrigerant. If moisture does enter the air-conditioning system, it will produce ice crystals that block refrigerant flow, damaging compressors. If water overloads and contaminates the desiccant, the material will disintegrate and contaminate the system with abrasive grit that restricts system passageways.

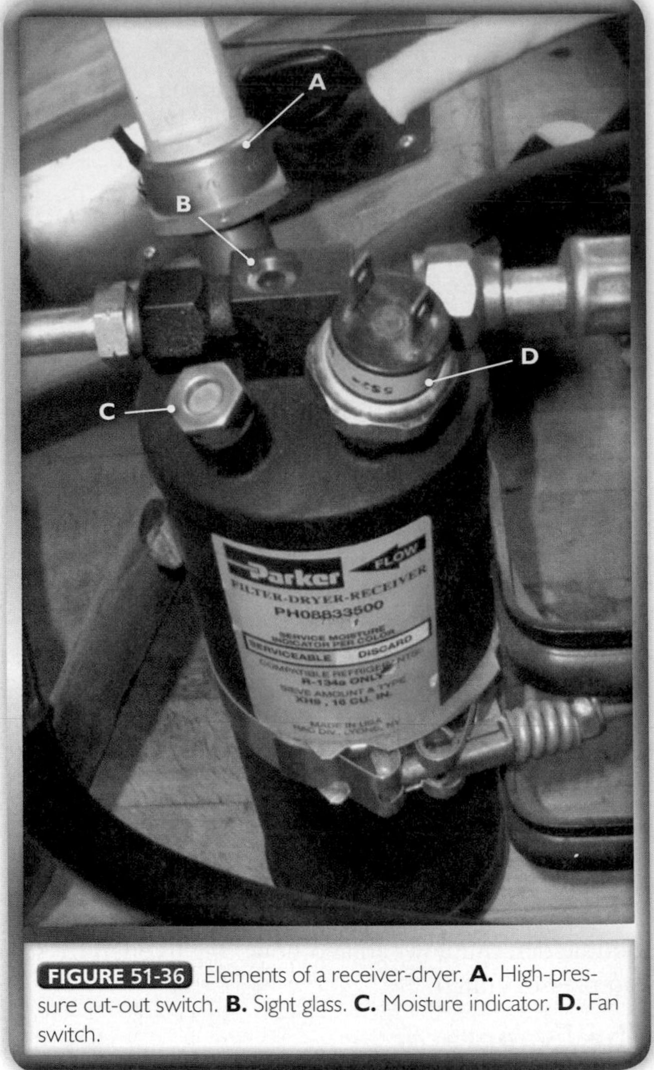

FIGURE 51-36 Elements of a receiver-dryer. **A.** High-pressure cut-out switch. **B.** Sight glass. **C.** Moisture indicator. **D.** Fan switch.

Moisture can also contribute to the breakdown of lubricating oils. In older R-12 systems, moisture would combine with chlorine to form hydrochloric acid that would internally corrode lines and other components. The removal of chlorine from new refrigerants prevents acids from forming, so line corrosion is reduced, and it is no longer necessary to check oil acidity.

Desiccant drying agents inside the receiver-dryer are compatible with refrigerant oils that can be absorbed by the desiccant. Receiver-dryers will have a moisture-indicator sight glass for determining the amount of moisture absorbed by the desiccant. This sight glass should not be confused with the sight glass for examining the condition of refrigerant. A good desiccant is light blue; a moisture-laden desiccant is pinkish or green.

Receiver-dryers often incorporate an important diagnostic aid—the refrigerant sight glass. In order to inspect the condition of the refrigerant, a glass insert at

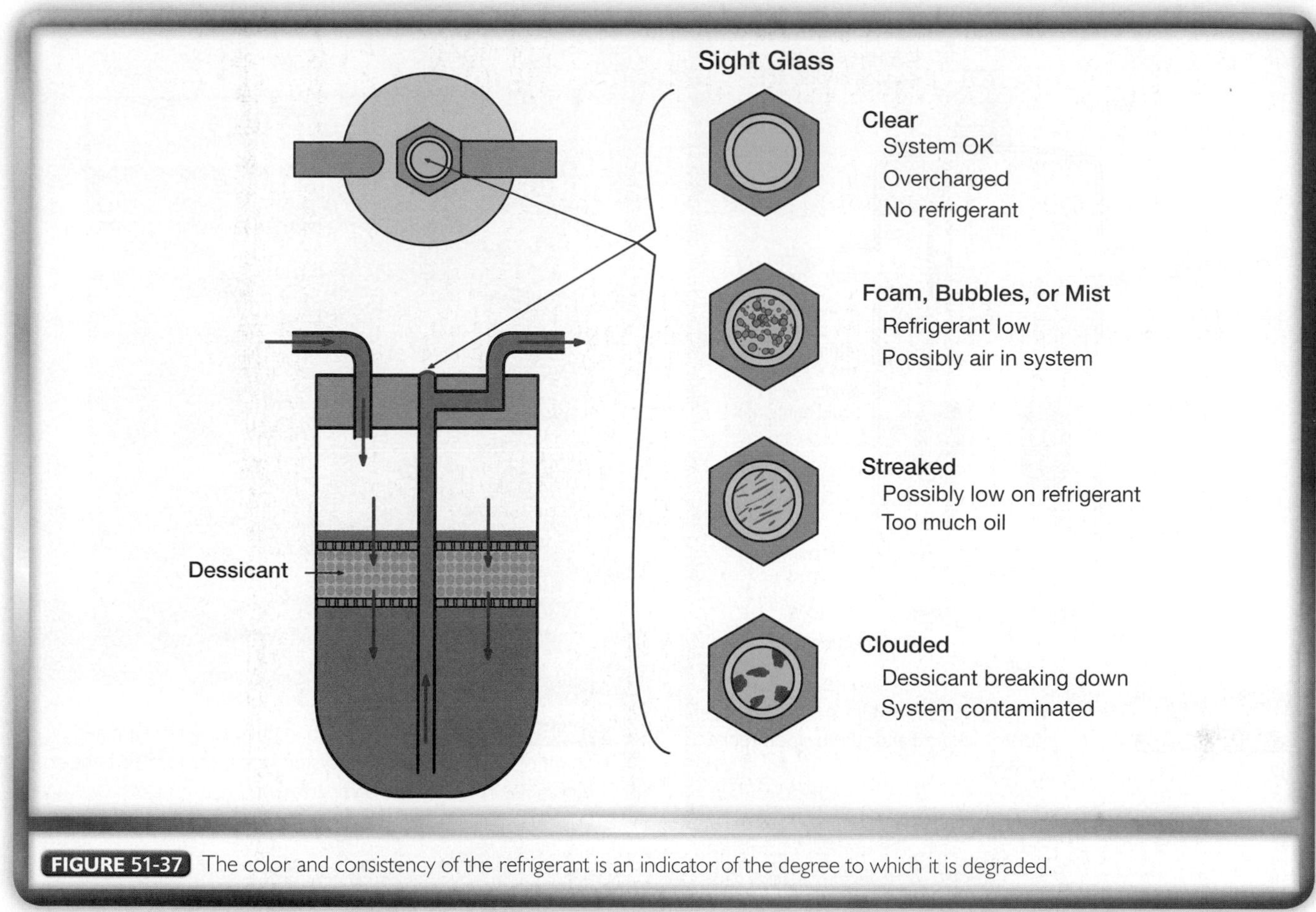

FIGURE 51-37 The color and consistency of the refrigerant is an indicator of the degree to which it is degraded.

the receiver-dryer outlet allows the technician to detect contaminated or undercharged refrigerant FIGURE 51-38. If the system is undercharged, refrigerant vapor (gas bubbles in liquid flowing into the evaporator) will be present in the glass after the system has been run and stabilized. Degraded desiccant and discolored contaminated refrigerant are also detected by examining the refrigerant flow through the sight glass.

Cycling Clutch Orifice Tube Accumulators

Accumulators are used in CCOT or fixed-orifice tube (FOT) systems. In these systems, the restriction orifice is placed in the inlet of the evaporator that has a fixed diameter. At higher engine speeds and low heat loads, the evaporator will flood with liquid. If liquid is allowed to reach the compressor, damage will result. The accumulators in these systems will collect liquid refrigerant leaving the evaporator and separate vapor from liquid before the refrigerant enters the compressor. Desiccant is placed in the accumulator to absorb moisture. A receiver-dryer may also be used in CCOT systems, but an accumulator located after the evaporator is mandatory FIGURE 51-39.

Refrigerant and Oil

Two fluids are used in automotive air-conditioning systems—refrigerant and refrigeration oil. Refrigerant itself is the central element of the entire air-conditioning process because it absorbs heat from the cab/passenger compartment air and transfers it to the atmosphere. Refrigerant also performs like a solvent of refrigerant oil in order to carry the oil through the air-conditioning system. Refrigeration oil lubricates the compressor and expansion valve. Without oil and refrigerant, the air-conditioning compressor is quickly damaged if operated. The amount of oil and refrigerant a system uses is identified on a label beneath the hood or engine compartment FIGURE 51-40.

> **TECHNICIAN TIP**
>
> Never attempt to hot-wire the operation of an air-conditioning compressor in a system low on refrigerant. Pressure switches within the air-conditioning system disable the compressor to protect it from a loss of lubricant, which is carried through the air-conditioning system by the refrigerant.

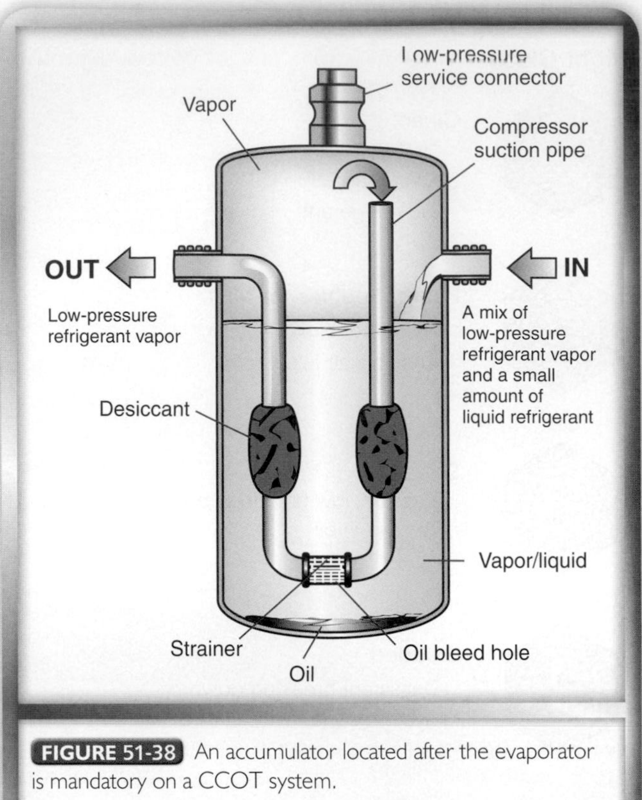

FIGURE 51-38 An accumulator located after the evaporator is mandatory on a CCOT system.

FIGURE 51-39 Labels like this one, indicating the type and amount of refrigerant and oil a system uses, are located beneath the hood or in the engine compartment.

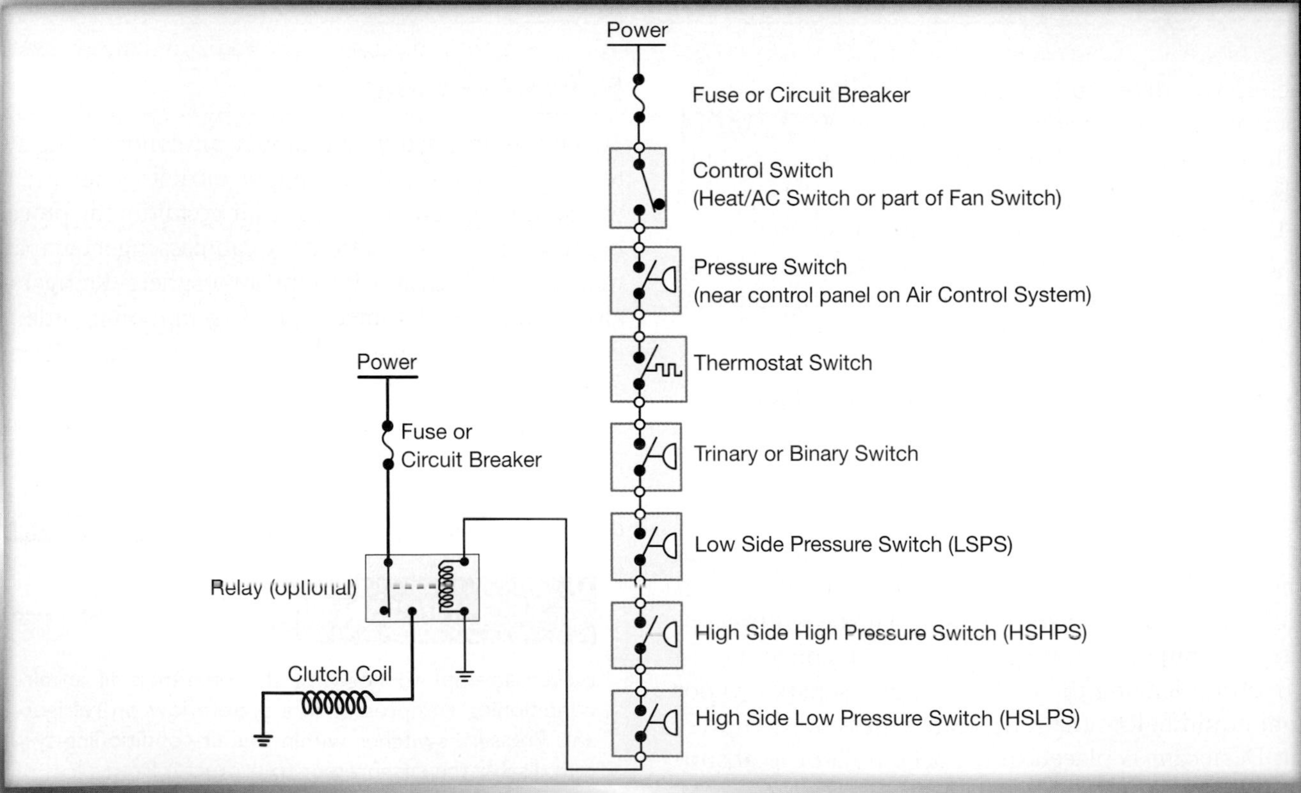

FIGURE 51-40 The switches to control the air-conditioning compressor clutch are connected in series. Opening any switch will disable the air-conditioning compressor.

Properties of Refrigerants

A variety of available refrigerants are suited to specific applications. Refrigerant used in the air-conditioning system of a truck, bus, or automobile is different from refrigerant used to freeze food products, make ice, or cool an office building. Different chemical formulations of refrigerants are used, as are blends and refrigerants having specialized additive packages to meet specific service requirements. Ideal refrigerant properties and characteristics include:

- *A low boiling point and freezing point.* Refrigerants vary according to boiling point, which ultimately determines where the refrigerant will be used. The lower the boiling point, the colder the evaporator temperature will be. R-134a refrigerant, which is commonly used in passenger compartment systems, boils at –14.9°F (–26.1°C). R-402a for trailer refrigeration boils at –56°F (–49°C).
- *A low specific heat and high latent heat.* Specific heat refers to the amount of heat that refrigerant must absorb to change its temperature by 1°F. Low specific heat means the refrigerant will easily absorb heat and change state. A refrigerant with a high specific heat loses its ability to refrigerate on a weight basis. Similarly, a refrigerant having a high latent heat capacity will absorb more heat per unit of weight. Combining a refrigerant with high latent heat and low specific heat increases the effectiveness of a refrigerant on a per-lb (per-kg) basis. If refrigerants did not have low specific heat capabilities and high latent heat properties, condensers and evaporators would need to be much larger.

Saturated Temperature

The pressure-temperature relationship of R-134a is important for the HVAC technician in diagnosing and testing air-conditioning operation. After the system has been operated, the temperature and pressure of the refrigerant follow a fixed relationship. This means that if you know the pressure of the gas, you can determine its temperature or the temperature inside a condenser or evaporator. For example, the temperature of the evaporator can be measured to determine if it is cold enough to properly cool the vehicle. For technicians using imperial measurement, the evaporator pressure will be close to the equivalent of its temperature of 20–80°F (–6.7°C to 27°C). A name given to this pressure temperature-relationship is saturated temperature. Saturated temperature refers to the temperature at which a refrigerant will change from a liquid to vapor or vapor to liquid at a given pressure. If the R-134a refrigerant in a system has a stable pressure of 30°F (–1°C), for example, its pressure will be close to 30 psi (207 kPa).

Refrigerant Types

Traditionally, refrigerants are manufactured from hydrogen, fluorine, chlorine, and carbon molecules. Two categories of refrigerant compositions are used today—hydrofluorocarbons (HFCs) and hydrochlorofluorocarbons (HCFCs). These designations refer to the chemical composition of each type of refrigerant. TABLE 51-2 lists current HFC Refrigerants. A third category of refrigerants is made from only chlorine, fluorine, and carbon (CFCs) and is no longer produced due to its destructive effect on the ozone layer.

Because the chemical names of typical refrigerants are long and complex, an industry standard method of designating refrigerants by number was developed by DuPont in 1956. Refrigerant names such as R-12, R-134a, R-402, R-404a, R-22, R503, and so on are familiar to anyone working with air-conditioning in the past decade. The method essentially counts the number of chlorine, fluorine, carbon, and other atoms in the composition.

TABLE 51-2: Current HFC Refrigerants

DuPont Number	Refrigerant Name	Application	Cylinder Color
R-23	Trifluoromethane	Low temperatures	Light gray
R-134a	Tetrafluoroethane	Automotive and residential refrigeration systems	Light sky blue
R-404a	R-125 + R-143a + R-134a	Medium and low temperature	Orange
R-407c	R-32 + R-125 + R-134a	R-22 CFC replacement	Chocolate brown
R-410a	R-32 + R-125	CFC replacement for R-12 residential air-conditioning	Rose
R-507	R-125/143a	CFC replacement for low-temperature commercial refrigeration	Light brown

R-143a used in air-conditioning and R-404a used in trailer refrigeration are both HFCs.

> **TECHNICIAN TIP**
>
> Chlorofluorocarbons (CFCs) are no longer used as refrigerants. Extensive scientific studies have proven that refrigerant made from these compounds destroys the ozone layer. The United States and Canada were among the many countries that ratified the Montreal Protocol, an agreement introduced in the 1980s to limit the production and use of chemicals known to deplete the ozone layer. As a result, environmental regulations in both countries govern the tasks of servicing the air-conditioning system. Refrigerants such as R12, commonly referred to as Freon, have been banned since 1995. Most OEMs now use R-134a. A number of refrigerants other than R-134a have been listed by EPA as acceptable under its Significant New Alternatives Policy (SNAP) program, or are under SNAP review.

Ozone Depletion

Ozone is an important component of Earth's upper atmosphere. A variation of an oxygen molecule, ozone filters out harmful ultraviolet radiation from the sun's rays and helps maintain stable Earth temperature. Stratospheric ozone is found in a layer between 10 and 30 miles above Earth's surface. Tropospheric ozone, or ground-level ozone, is harmful and a primary constituent of photochemical smog.

Research has demonstrated that CFC refrigerant molecules destroy stratospheric ozone by connecting the oxygen with chlorine. Any release or venting of CFC-based refrigerants to the air has a powerfully destructive effect on ozone, which led to the banning of CFC refrigerants. Therefore, any new refrigerants are categorized by the effect they have on the ozone.

Different from its effect on the ozone layer is a refrigerant's **global warming potential (GWP)**. GWP is a measure of a refrigerant's contribution to global warming over 100 years for a given mass compared to the same mass of carbon dioxide. Carbon dioxide's GWP is defined as 1.0. The most common refrigerant used in automotive air-conditioning systems, R-134a, has a high GWP of 1200, but as it contains no chlorine, it has no impact on the ozone layer. **TABLE 51-3** lists the properties of R-134a.

Special-Purpose Refrigerant

Some brands of refrigerants contain special additives or blends of refrigerants. For example, some refrigerants are bottled with a specific amount of refrigeration oil to allow the addition of oil to the system when replacing refrigerant. Other refrigerants use an additive with specialized lubricants to prolong the life of compressor seals and moving parts. Some aftermarket additives even contain aerobic chemical hardeners, which are intended to plug very small pinhole leaks when in contact with air.

Leak-tracing dye is the most common refrigerant additive and is often added during manufacturing. Refrigerant leaks cannot be detected directly since refrigerant instantly vaporizes. While some oil residue accompanies refrigerant leaks, smaller leaks are not visually detectable. The dyes can be seen at the location of a refrigerant leak using an ultraviolet light. Note, however, if a leak is large enough, pressure testing with nitrogen is recommended instead of leak detection with dyes. Refrigerants containing dyes should be added to a system only if it is at least 40 percent full.

Refrigeration Oil

Air-conditioning systems need lubricant for several reasons. First is to reduce friction between moving surfaces and bearings inside the compressor to ensure a long service life. Additionally, thermostatic expansion valves must be lubricated to operate freely. Lubricant also coats the inside of the air-conditioning system to prevent any corrosive substances from attacking the internal system components. Oil is helpful in keeping the system's seals soft and pliant, which reduces seepage from the system and increases compressor efficiency. In reciprocating piston compressors, the 90–120w viscosity lubricant helps the piston rings seal tightly against their cylinder walls to prevent leakage and apply maximum pressure to the refrigerant.

TABLE 51-3: R-134a Properties

Boiling Point	–14.9°F (–26.1°C)
Auto-Ignition Temperature	1,418°F (770°C)
Ozone Depletion Level	0
Solubility in Water	0.11% by weight at 77°F (25°C)
Cylinder Color Code	Light blue
Global Warming Potential (GWP)	1200

Refrigerant oil used in early systems was made from mineral oil specially formulated for air-conditioning systems. That refrigeration oil was free of sulfur, so it would not form corrosive substances. It was also non-foaming and wax-free to allow free flow through the system. Any water was removed from the oil to prevent contamination. But, as oil is hygroscopic it will absorb moisture from the air if the system is open or the storage container is not sealed. Because R-134a dissolves mineral oil and moves it through the system, new synthetic oils are needed. Two types are **polyalkylene glycol (PAG)** and **polyalphaolefin (PAO)**. PAG is used in all R-134a systems, while PAO is used in systems converted from R-12 refrigerant or special blends of refrigerant.

Air-Conditioning Controls

A variety of controls are used to regulate the operation of the air-conditioning system. These controls are necessary to:

- Adjust operator/passenger comfort levels in the cab of the vehicle
- Improve cooling efficiency of the system
- Protect major components from damage

Many of these controls are used to operate a compressor by switching the compressor clutch on and off as needed. Controls protect the compressor and other air-conditioning system components from excessive system pressures, low system pressures, and low ambient temperatures that can damage the compressor in a variety of ways.

First, if the refrigerant level is too low and the system is undercharged, oil will not be circulated through the compressor. This happens when oil is dissolved in the refrigerant and the compressor can be damaged, eventually seizing after it pushes oil out into the system. Second, during low-temperature operation, refrigerant pressure will be low, causing the same problems of oil miscibility, which is the ability of oil to dissolve into the refrigerant gas. Similarly, at low temperatures, refrigerant oil that is in the vicinity of 90–120w viscosity will also thicken to the point where it is not easily moved. Finally, compressor controls are required to protect the system from damage due to excessive system pressures. For instance, if there is little or no airflow through the condenser, heat will not be removed, and system refrigerant pressures will increase dramatically. If refrigerant pressure is high enough, hoses can burst or O-rings can begin to leak. Before that point, the high pressures can easily prompt slippage of the compressor clutch, causing damage or clutch burnout.

Compressor Controls

Common compressor controls include:

- Thermostatic switch
- Low-pressure cutout switch
- Pressure-cycling switch
- Trinary switch
- High-pressure cutout switch
- High-pressure fan switch
- Ambient temperature switch

The air-conditioning system will not use all these switches. The evaporator expansion device may not need these controls for system protection or to regulate system pressures and temperatures. The presence of an on/off engine cooling fan will also change the control configuration.

Thermostatic Switch

The thermostatic switch, also called the cold switch, is an evaporator temperature-sensing switch. It is used with either the CCOT or TXV metering systems. Using a temperature-sensitive capillary tube located where it can respond to changes in the evaporator outlet temperature, the switch will either open or close the contacts inside the switch. In turn, this action will cause the compressor clutch to be engaged or disengaged.

Two types of thermostatic switch are possible. One is built to work within a preset temperature range. It has two temperature presets—one for off, and one for on. When temperature in the evaporator coils approaches freezing, the switch contacts open, disengage the compressor clutch, and allow the refrigerant in the evaporator to absorb more heat. The temperature then rises in the evaporator due to the lack of refrigerant flow. At a preset high temperature, the switch closes, engages the clutch, and compressor operation resumes.

The second type is adjustable, so the on and off points can be varied according to system and operator requirements. Newer systems use a thermistor in the evaporator that is monitored by the body control, climate control, or electrical system control module.

Low-Pressure Cutout Switch

The low-pressure cutout switch is connected in the compressor clutch electrical circuit. When a predetermined low charge is sensed, the switch stops compressor operation. This protects the compressor from damage due to insufficient refrigerant oil. It is usually mounted somewhere in the low-pressure or suction side of the system. Low-pressure cutout switches prevent cold weather operation of the compressor because system pressure and temperatures closely match. (Trinary switches often incorporate this same switch.)

Pressure-Cycling Switch

Located on the accumulator, the pressure-cycling switch is used on CCOT (orifice-tube) systems. This switch controls the cycling of the compressor by sensing pressure in the evaporator and accumulator. Low pressure is an indicator of low evaporator temperature, just as high pressure is of higher temperature. When the evaporator pressure is low, it is an indication that the evaporator is full of liquid and no more refrigerant should be pumped into it. At around 25 psi (172 kPa), the switch opens the compressor circuit. As the refrigerant absorbs heat and the pressure rises, the cycling switch may close again at around 35 psi (241 kPa), operating the compressor and causing refrigerant to flood the evaporator once more. This switch is usually located on a standard Schrader valve fitting. It is possible to remove and replace the switch without having to discharge the system.

Trinary Switch

The **trinary switch** is mounted in the high-pressure refrigerant line. It is known as a trinary switch because of its three sets of internal contacts. Typically, the switch will serve three functions:

- Low-pressure protection
- High-pressure cutout
- Engine fan on/off

It may also have an input from the thermostatic switch to cycle the compressor on and off.

One set of switch contacts is used to signal when system pressure drops too low, about 10–15 psi (69–103 kPa). Another set of contacts is used to signal high system pressure, about 385 psi (2,654 kPa). The air-conditioning compressor clutch will be disengaged during either of these conditions.

The final set of switch contacts is used to cycle the engine fan during normal air-conditioning operation. The on/off engine fan will be engaged above pressures of 230 psi (1,586 kPa) to create airflow across the condenser and lower high-side system pressure.

A similar binary switch will have only two sets of contacts: one to shut off the clutch when system pressures are excessive, and another to cycle the engine fan on and off when system pressures are high. The binary switch is used along with a low-pressure switch to shut the compressor off if refrigerant pressures are too low.

High-Pressure Cutout Switch

If system pressures become too great, the likelihood of compressor damage and burst lines increases. Venting of refrigerant to the atmosphere is prohibited by law, so it is necessary to use a high-pressure cutout switch.

High-Pressure Fan Switch

High-pressure fan switches can also control the operation of the engine fan. When system pressures in the high side are great, more airflow across the condenser is required to lower condenser pressures. The switches are connected to an electric-over-air control valve that cycles the fan on and off. On newer electronically controlled engines, the ECM controls engine fan operation. In these cases, the ECM will use a high-side pressure switch for input to control the engine fan.

Fan Timers

Too-frequent cycling of the engine fan can cause premature wear of the fan's clutch friction discs. Many systems use a fan timer to lengthen the time a fan stays engaged after it has been signaled to cycle on. The engine fan will typically stay engaged for between 45 and 120 seconds after the request for fan engagement by the high-pressure fan switch.

Ambient Temperature Switch

The ambient temperature switch is an outside air temperature-sensing switch. It is designed to delay compressor operation when it senses a very low outside air temperature. When temperatures are low, oil can become too viscous to lubricate the compressor properly. Operating the compressor when outside air temperature is very low could damage compressor seals, gaskets, or reed valves due to cold components and lack of proper oil circulation.

At cold ambient temperatures, this sensing switch opens its electrical contacts. Current to the compressor clutch cannot pass, and compressor operation cannot occur. Compressor internal components are therefore protected. The ambient temperature switch contacts close when a preset temperature is reached, normally 32–50°F (0–10°C), depending on application. At this point, the electrical circuit to the compressor clutch is restored and compressor operation can occur. The ambient temperature switch is usually located in the engine compartment or other suitable location where it can easily sense outside air temperature.

Air-Conditioning Protection and Diagnostic System (APADS)

In order to extend the lifespan of the air-conditioning system on medium- and heavy-duty trucks, a supplier to the HD OEM industry called Index Sensors have developed systems that operate to prevent conditions that can damage the air-conditioning system and to enhance system reliability. The **APADS/air-conditioning protection unit (ACPU)** is an electronic microcontroller-based device that operates both air-conditioning controls and diagnostic systems FIGURE 51-41. Several variations of APADS are manufactured with LEDs, data bus fault code diagnostics, and various numbers of input or output connectors. Typically the unit receives input from two pressure switches and a thermostat, and may also read vehicle parameters from the vehicle SAE J1708/J-1939 data bus. The input signals are interpreted by control laws, which process outputs to the clutch coil and fan actuator circuit and generate diagnostic codes. In the APADS-equipped air-conditioning system, the controller becomes the only device through which power is switched to the clutch coil.

APADS is claimed to eliminate the problems that make the air-conditioning system one of the highest maintenance expense items for most heavy-duty commercial vehicles. A study by Index Sensors that used 55 pairs of trucks operating for 9 million miles found that those equipped with APADS spent 65% less on air-conditioning system maintenance than identical trucks without APADS. Yearly air-conditioning system maintenance costs averaged $86 per truck with APADS and $244 for non-equipped control vehicles.

Typical Air-Conditioning System Problems

The durability of the compressor and refrigerant hoses is adversely affected by operation of the air-conditioning

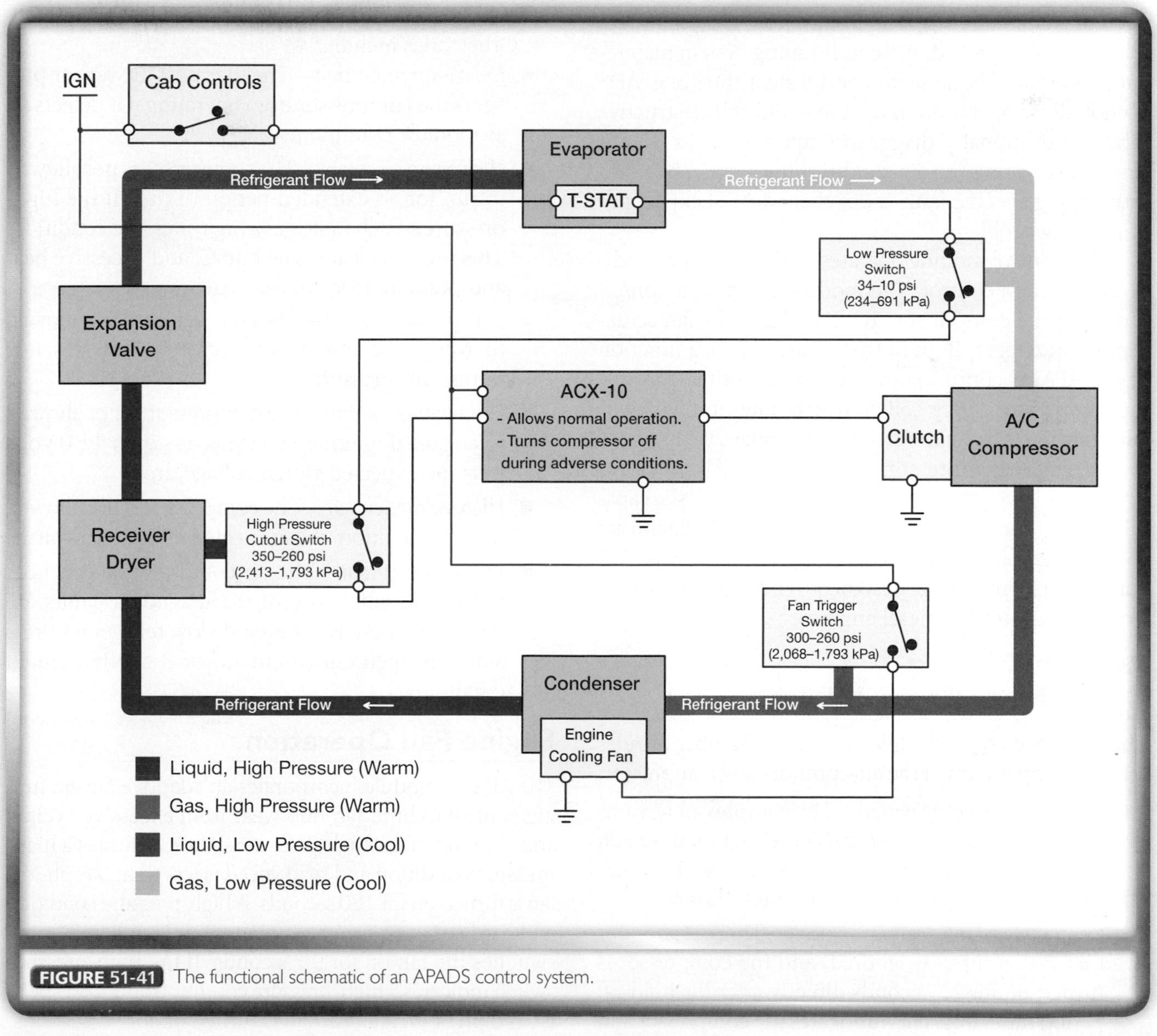

FIGURE 51-41 The functional schematic of an APADS control system.

system with reduced or excessive refrigerant charge. Operation with a partial charge of refrigerant can cause compressor lubricant starvation, compressor overheating due to rapid cycling, and seal failure, and can lead to damaged hoses and fittings due to exposure to excessive temperatures. Operation with excessive refrigerant charges can severely stress the entire air-conditioning system, causing hose and fitting leaks. Low system voltages can cause the compressor clutch to slip and overheat and loosen electrical connections, which in turn can cause erratic compressor cycling and compressor clutch failures. Traditional electrical control systems based upon a series of simple pressure switches are unable to prevent or detect these harmful modes of operation.

The APADS control system is composed of an electronic control module, two smart pressure switches, and a conventional evaporator thermostat. Because the APADS actively monitors the air-conditioning system conditions and controls the refrigerant compressor and on/off fan, reliability is improved. Air-conditioning system maintenance is reduced because the control algorithms of APADS do not allow operation in unstable and self-destructive modes. Additionally, diagnostic capabilities aid technicians in servicing the air-conditioning system by communicating specific fault codes that warn of existing or impending problems.

The control module operates as the main air-conditioning system control. The module provides an on/off output to the compressor clutch coil and the fan actuator circuit trigger. Both of these outputs are a function of the APADS control laws. Since the module controls the compressor clutch coil, it incorporates its own high-current drivers that eliminate external relays usually used to engage the compressor clutch. The APADS receives inputs from two smart switches with self-diagnostic capabilities and the evaporator thermostat. Fault diagnostic communication is established through the JJ-1708/J-1939 data bus. The module is designed to interface with electronically controlled diesel engines.

Air-Conditioning Compressor Control Rules

The APADS control module enforces a number of rules for proper operation of the air-conditioning compressor:

1. *Compressor hold-off period*—The compressor remains off for the first 15 seconds after ignition switch engagement while battery voltage is low. This prevents low-voltage compressor clutch burnout.
2. *Compressor lubrication period*—The evaporator thermostat input is ignored, and the compressor is turned on for 15 seconds directly after the hold-off period times out. This lubricates the compressor and air-conditioning system. If the high- or low-pressure switches indicate out of bound or fault conditions, the compressor is turned off.
3. *Compressor cycle limit*—All three inputs (thermostat, high-pressure switch, and low-pressure switch) that can control the compressor are governed by control logic that limits the maximum cycle rate to once every 15 seconds.
4. *Evaporator thermostat primary control*—The compressor will cycle at the frequency governed by the thermostat but is limited to a maximum of one cycle per 15 seconds (Rule 3).
5. *High-pressure reset*—When the high-pressure switch indicates an excessively high-pressure condition, the compressor is allowed to stay on for a mathematically calculated variable period, limited to 10 seconds. The compressor is allowed to turn on after the high-pressure switch resets and Rule 3 is satisfied.

Other rules include:

- *Freeze-up protection*—The thermostatic sensor prevents the compressor from operating if it detects an evaporator condition.
- *High-pressure cutout*—The compressor is not allowed to run for an extended period of time if the high-pressure switch indicates a high-pressure condition. This prevents leaks, line bursts, and excessive heat and pressure loads in the system.
- *Low-pressure cutout*—The compressor is not allowed to run if the low-pressure switch indicates low refrigerant pressure.
- *Low-voltage cutout*—The compressor is not allowed to engage if ignition voltage is less than 11.0 volts plus the expected clutch voltage drop.
- *High-voltage cutout*—The compressor is not allowed to run if ignition voltage is greater than 16 volts.
- *Diagnostic cutout*—The air-conditioning system is turned off when any of the diagnostic faults are detected. These faults include low refrigerant pressure, an open clutch circuit, or a shorted clutch circuit.

Engine Fan Operation

The APADS module incorporates an adaptive fan-on timing control to limit fan hub wear from excessive cycling and slipping. If the high-pressure switch indicates a high-pressure condition and road speed is less than 5 mph, the fan is turned on for 180 seconds. A high-pressure condition and road speed of 5 mph or greater but less than 30 mph switches the fan on for 90 seconds. If the high-pressure switch indicates a high-pressure condition and road speed is 30 mph or greater, the fan is turned on for 45 seconds.

When the parking brake is set, there is no road speed, and the high-pressure switch detects a high-pressure condition, the fan is requested until the parking brake is released or road speed is detected. During that time, if a driver shuts the air-conditioning system off, the fan remains on for two minutes to reduce system pressure.

APADS Inputs

The APADS module receives inputs from the vehicle data link, the evaporator thermostatic switch, a high-pressure system switch, and a low-pressure system switch FIGURE 51-42. Both switches have resistors connected in parallel with the electrical contacts to allow diagnosing of sensor wiring and connector faults. This switch circuit is configured to provide a low-resistance current path when it closes.

The low-pressure switch contacts are open when the pressure is sufficiently high, above 34 psi (234 kPa). Contacts close when the pressure falls below approximately 10 psi (69 kPa) and reopen after the pressure climbs back above 34 psi (234 kPa). Low-pressure switch activity is the primary indicator of a loss of charge and is also used to prevent compressor operation in extremely cold temperatures.

The high-pressure switch contacts are closed when the pressure is sufficiently low, below 260 psi (1,793 kPa). Contacts open when the pressure climbs above approximately 300 psi (2,068 kPa) and re-close after the pressure falls back below 260 psi (1,793 kPa). The high-pressure switch is the primary control for the fan and is used to prevent compressor operation when excessive discharge pressures are present.

Evaporator Thermostat

The main air-conditioning system on/off switch and the evaporator thermostatic switch are in series and are connected to the module. The series switches are configured to switch to battery voltage to command compressor operation. The thermostat contacts close when the temperature is greater than 38°F (3°C). The contacts open when the evaporator temperature drops below approximately 32°F (0°C). The thermostat is used to turn off the compressor whenever frost begins to form on the evaporator.

Diagnostic LEDs

Red and green LEDs are used on some APADS. Whenever a system fault is detected, the APADS broadcasts diagnostic information over the data bus. Diagnostic blink codes are supplied by combinations of blinking lights and colors of the LEDs FIGURE 51-43.

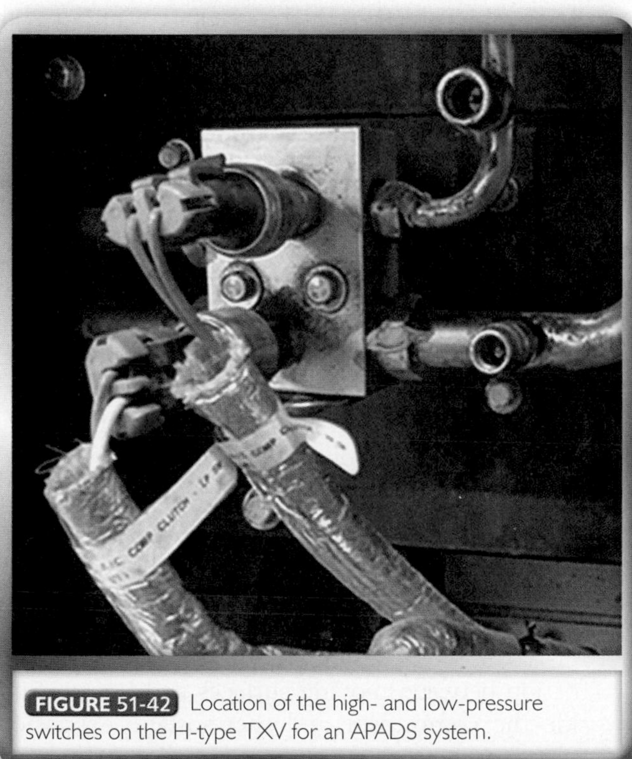

FIGURE 51-42 Location of the high- and low-pressure switches on the H-type TXV for an APADS system.

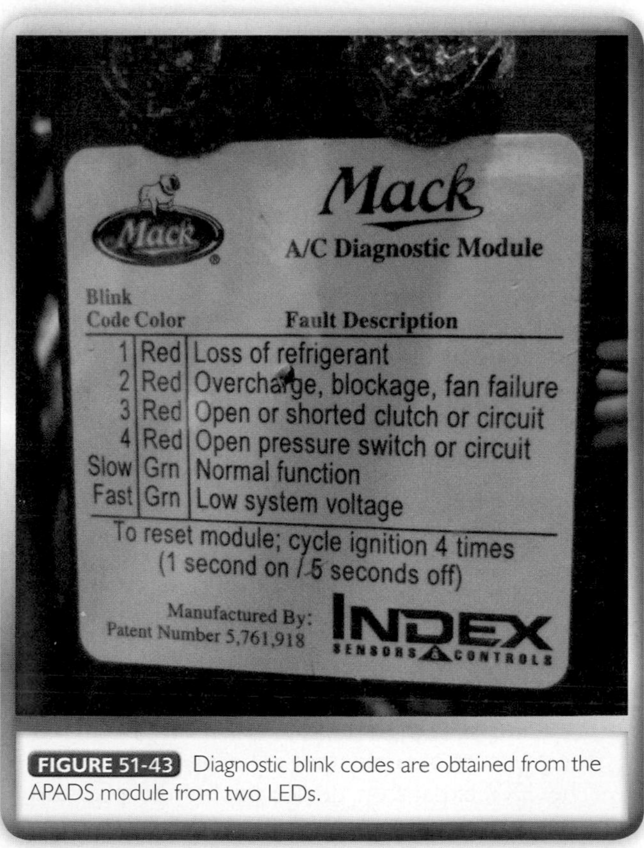

Mack
A/C Diagnostic Module

Blink Code	Color	Fault Description
1	Red	Loss of refrigerant
2	Red	Overcharge, blockage, fan failure
3	Red	Open or shorted clutch or circuit
4	Red	Open pressure switch or circuit
Slow	Grn	Normal function
Fast	Grn	Low system voltage

To reset module; cycle ignition 4 times (1 second on / 5 seconds off)

Manufactured By: INDEX SENSORS & CONTROLS
Patent Number 5,761,918

FIGURE 51-43 Diagnostic blink codes are obtained from the APADS module from two LEDs.

Wrap-up

Ready for Review

- Freon, a brand trademark name of DuPont Chemicals, is a colorless, odorless, nonflammable, and noncorrosive gas or liquid chlorofluorocarbon (CFC).
- Modern mobile air-conditioning has tremendous safety benefits. A comfortable vehicle environment reduces driver fatigue and distractions and can increase driver productivity.
- The greater the heat energy in a substance, the faster its molecules vibrate (heat = speed).
- Conduction, convection, and radiation are three types of heat transfer.
- Heat is measured in a number of different ways, most commonly with a thermometer.
- A calorie is the basic unit for measuring the quantity of heat energy.
- The concept of temperature is related to pressure.
- Boiling points of liquids are affected by the pressure exerted upon them.
- Air-conditioning and refrigeration systems operate in a closed loop in which the refrigerant is used over and over as it circulates through the system.
- The air-conditioning compressor is an engine-driven pump that increases refrigerant pressure and circulates refrigerant through the system.
- Three basic types of air-conditioning compressors can be used to build pressure exceeding 350 psi (2,413 kPa): piston, rotary vane, and scroll. Piston compressors are almost universally used in commercial vehicles.
- Rotary piston compressors have cylindrical-shaped housings and enclose multiple pistons. The primary advantage of rotary compressors is their minimization of NVH (noise, vibration, and harshness).
- Mobile HD air-conditioning compressors are usually belt-driven from the engine's crankshaft and have an electromagnetic clutch.
- The condenser typically consists of coiled tubing mounted in a series of thin cooling fins and is mounted directly in front of the radiator, where it can receive full airflow created by forward vehicle motion and the engine fan.
- An expansion device restricts the high-pressure, warm liquid refrigerant line and is designed to lower the pressure of refrigerant entering the evaporator.
- The TXV expansion device lowers the pressure of the warm, high-pressure liquid refrigerant entering the evaporator and allows the refrigerant to expand to greater volume.
- Unlike as CCOT system, which meters refrigerant at a fixed rate, the TXV meters refrigerant into the evaporator at a variable rate.
- The thermostatic expansion valve controls refrigerant flow by the action of a spring-loaded control valve. Evaporator temperature and pressure are two factors that change the size of the restriction opening.
- The orifice tube is a simple, plastic tube with a calibrated brass orifice used on current CCOT systems to produce refrigerant pressure drop in the evaporator.
- The evaporator is a heat exchanger located inside the cab or passenger compartment containing the chamber where refrigerant boils and converts to a vapor.
- The primary function of the receiver-dryer is to serve as a storage reservoir for refrigerant. A second function is to absorb any moisture in the air-conditioning system.
- Accumulators are used in CCOT or fixed-orifice tube (FOT) systems.
- Automotive air-conditioning systems use two fluids: refrigerant (to absorb heat) and refrigeration oil (to lubricate the compressor and expansion valves).
- The lower the boiling point of a refrigerant, the colder the evaporator temperature will be.
- A refrigerant with a high specific heat loses its ability to refrigerate on a weight basis. Similarly, a refrigerant with a high latent heat capacity will absorb more heat per unit of weight. Combining a refrigerant with high latent heat and low specific heat increases effectiveness of a refrigerant on a per-lb (per-kg) basis.
- Saturated temperature refers to the temperature at which a refrigerant will change from a liquid to vapor or vapor to liquid at a given pressure.
- Refrigerants are manufactured from hydrogen, fluorine, chlorine, and carbon molecules. Two categories of refrigerant compositions are used today: hydrofluorocarbons (HFCs) and hydrochlorofluorocarbons (HCFCs).
- The most common refrigerant used in automotive air-conditioning systems, R-134a, has a GWP of 1200, as it contains no chlorine and has no impact on the ozone layer.
- Air-conditioning systems need lubricant to reduce friction between moving surfaces and bearings inside the compressor and thermostatic expansion valves, and to prevent any corrosive substances from attacking the internal system components.
- Common compressor controls include the

thermostatic switch, low-pressure cutout switch, pressure-cycling switch, trinary switch, high-pressure cutout switch, high-pressure fan switch, and ambient temperature switch.

- Venting of refrigerant to the atmosphere is prohibited by law.
- Too-frequent cycling of the engine fan can cause premature wear of the fan's clutch friction discs.
- The APADS/air-conditioning protection unit (ACPU) is an electronic, microcontroller-based device that operates both air-conditioning controls and the diagnostic system.
- The APADS control system is composed of an electronic control module, two smart pressure switches, and a conventional evaporator thermostat.
- The APADS module receives inputs from the vehicle data link, the evaporator thermostatic switch, and high- and low-pressure system switches.

Vocabulary Builder

APADS/air-conditioning protection unit (ACPU) An electronic microcontroller-based device that operates both air-conditioning controls and diagnostic systems.

British thermal unit (Btu) The amount of energy required to heat or cool one pound of water 1°F.

calorie The unit of energy that reflects the amount of energy required to raise the temperature of 1 gram of water by 1°C.

chlorofluorocarbons (CFCs) A chlorine-based composition of a fluorine hydrocarbon compound.

condensation Moisture that collects on cooler surfaces as a result of hot vapors coming into contact with the cooler surface.

condenser A component of the HVAC system that transfers heat from the system to the atmosphere.

conduction The transfer of heat through a solid item, such as a body panel or evaporator.

convection The transfer of heat through a gas.

cycling clutch orifice tube (CCOT) A fixed-orifice tube with pressure control obtained by cycling the compressor clutch on and off.

defroster A heated component that operates to clear the windows.

evaporator The cold surface of the air-conditioning system that absorbs heat from a cab or vehicle interior and transfers that heat to the atmosphere through a condenser.

evaporator freezing A condition in which excess refrigerant floods the evaporator.

Freon A refrigerant produced by reacting carbon tetrachloride, commonly used as "carb-cleaner," with fluorine gas.

global warming potential (GWP) A measure of a refrigerant's contribution to global warming over 100 years for a given mass compared to the same mass of carbon dioxide.

heater core An in-cab heat exchanger that regulates heating by circulating engine coolant.

heating ventilation and air-conditioning (HVAC) system The system in the vehicle responsible for heating and cooling the air.

latent heat The quantity of heat required to produce a change of state from a solid to a liquid or a liquid to a gas.

latent heat of fusion The process of removing heat energy to matter to effect a change of state.

latent heat of vaporization The process of adding heat energy to matter to effect a change of state.

polyalkylene glycol (PAG) Synthetic oil used in all R-134a systems.

polyalphaolefin (PAO) Synthetic oil used in R-12 systems.

psia The units of pressure, in pounds per square inch, at sea level.

psig The units of pressure, in pounds per square inch, expressed relative to the environment's atmospheric pressure.

radiant heat transfer The transfer of heat through a medium, such as a gas or vacuum, which does not cause the medium itself to heat.

receiver-dryer A storage reservoir for refrigerant that also absorbs moisture from the air-conditioning system.

rotary piston compressors HVAC compressors that use cylindrical-shaped housings and enclose multiple pistons to minimize of noise, vibration, and harshness.

sensible heat Heat that can be sensed or felt

specific heat The amount of heat a substance must absorb to undergo a temperature change of 1°F.

superheat The temperature differential between the refrigerant vapor and at the evaporator and the refrigerant vapor at the evaporator inlet.

thermostatic expansion valve (TXV) An expansion device used in commercial vehicle air-conditioning systems.

trinary switch A switch with three sets of internal contacts to protect against low pressure, cutout in case of high pressure, and turn the engine fan on and off.

Review Questions

1. Which of the following is correct concerning air-conditioning operating principles?
   - **a.** The ideal cab environment has a moderate humidity level and should reach a temperature of 70°F to 80°F (20°–27°C) within several minutes of operation.
   - **b.** To maintain a comfortable temperature range for the driver and any passengers, most air-conditioning compressors cycle on and off using thermostatic or pressure control switches.
   - **c.** Heating is regulated by circulating engine coolant through an in-cab heat exchanger called a heater core.
   - **d.** All of the choices are correct.
2. ________ is NOT a common measurement of heat.
   - **a.** Sensible heat
   - **b.** Latent heat
   - **c.** Calorie
   - **d.** Standard
3. Which of the following is correct concerning temperature and pressure?
   - **a.** Pressure is measured using a variety of units, but common units used in HVAC are pounds per square inch (psi) or kilopascals (kPa).
   - **b.** Typically, pressures above atmospheric pressure are considered to be gauge pressures, and pressures below atmospheric pressure are considered absolute pressures.
   - **c.** Both A and B are correct.
   - **d.** Neither A nor B is correct.
4. ________ air-conditioning compressors are NOT commonly used in modern commercial vehicles.
   - **a.** Piston
   - **b.** Gear
   - **c.** Rotary vane
   - **d.** Scroll
5. Rotary compressors in trucks will have between ________ and ________ cylinders.
   - **a.** 2; 4
   - **b.** 4; 8
   - **c.** 5; 10
   - **d.** 6; 12
6. Which of the following is NOT one of the basic parts of the compressor clutch?
   - **a.** Drive plate
   - **b.** Clutch housing
   - **c.** Belt pulley
   - **d.** Magnetic coil
7. Which of the following is correct concerning the TXV expansion device?
   - **a.** The TXV expansion device lowers the pressure of the warm, high-pressure liquid refrigerant entering the evaporator and allows the refrigerant to expand to greater volume.
   - **b.** An orifice in the TXV creates a pressure difference, forming what are called the high side and low side of the air-conditioning system.
   - **c.** The terms high side and low side refer to the two different pressures found in the air-conditioning system.
   - **d.** All of the choices are correct.
8. Which of the following is NOT correct concerning evaporators?
   - **a.** The evaporator is a heat exchanger located inside the cab or passenger compartment containing the chamber where refrigerant boils and converts to a vapor.
   - **b.** The evaporator does not remove moisture from the cabin air.
   - **c.** Like the condenser, the evaporator has a couple of common constructions.
   - **d.** The serpentine coil evaporator is constructed from a metal coil mounted in a series of thin cooling fins.
9. In a typical truck HVAC system, the dryer will hold about ________ of extra refrigerant.
   - **a.** a quarter pound (113 g)
   - **b.** a half pound (226 g)
   - **c.** three quarters of a pound (339 g)
   - **d.** one pound (452 g)
10. What is the viscosity of the oil used in reciprocating piston compressors?
    - **a.** 10w-30
    - **b.** 15w-40
    - **c.** 85-100w
    - **d.** 90–120w

ASE-Type Questions

1. Technician A says that heat, like all forms of energy, can be transferred from one place to another. Technician B says that the air-conditioning system's condenser removes heat from the cab and transfers it to the atmosphere via the evaporator. Who is correct?
   a. Technician A
   b. Technician B
   c. Both Technician A and Technician B
   d. Neither Technician A nor Technician B
2. Technician A says that a British thermal unit, or Btu, is a common term for heating and air conditioning. Technician B says that one ton of refrigeration (TR) is the amount of heat required to change one ton of ice to water in 12 hours. Who is correct?
   a. Technician A
   b. Technician B
   c. Both Technician A and Technician B
   d. Neither Technician A nor Technician B
3. Technician A says that simply changing the pressure of a liquid will allow a change of state to take place. Technician B says that changing refrigerants back and forth between a gas and liquid state is accomplished by compressing a gas refrigerant or lowering the pressure of a liquid refrigerant. Who is correct?
   a. Technician A
   b. Technician B
   c. Both Technician A and Technician B
   d. Neither Technician A nor Technician B
4. Technician A says that air-conditioning and refrigeration systems transfer heat from the cab and passenger compartment to the air stream outside the vehicle. Technician B says that air-conditioning and refrigeration systems also remove moisture from the air passing through the evaporator and channel it to a drain leading outside the vehicle. Who is correct?
   a. Technician A
   b. Technician B
   c. Both Technician A and Technician B
   d. Neither Technician A nor Technician B
5. Technician A says that outside air flows over the fins of the condenser and absorbs heat from the refrigerant as it converts from a gas to a liquid. Technician B says that the condenser typically consists of coiled tubing mounted in a series of thin cooling fins. Who is correct?
   a. Technician A
   b. Technician B
   c. Both Technician A and Technician B
   d. Neither Technician A nor Technician B
6. Technician A says that the thermostatic expansion valve controls refrigerant flow by the action of a spring-loaded control valve. Technician B says that roughly an 8°F temperature difference between evaporator inlet and outlet is required to open the valve. Who is correct?
   a. Technician A
   b. Technician B
   c. Both Technician A and Technician B
   d. Neither Technician A nor Technician B
7. Technician A says that the refrigerant R-404a is used in vehicle air-conditioning systems. Technician B says that the refrigerant R-143a is used in trailer refrigeration. Who is correct?
   a. Technician A
   b. Technician B
   c. Both Technician A and Technician B
   d. Neither Technician A nor Technician B
8. Technician A says that the low-pressure cutout switch is connected in the compressor clutch electrical circuit. Technician B says that when a predetermined low charge is sensed, the switch stops compressor operation. Who is correct?
   a. Technician A
   b. Technician B
   c. Both Technician A and Technician B
   d. Neither Technician A nor Technician B
9. Technician A says that the pressure-cycling switch is used on CCOT (orifice-tube) systems and located on the accumulator. Technician B says that it is not possible to remove and replace the switch without having to discharge the system. Who is correct?
   a. Technician A
   b. Technician B
   c. Both Technician A and Technician B
   d. Neither Technician A nor Technician B
10. Technician A says that the APADS module receives information from the vehicle data link and the evaporator thermostatic switch. Technician B says that the APADS module receives information from the high-pressure and the low-pressure system switches. Who is correct?
    a. Technician A
    b. Technician B
    c. Both Technician A and Technician B
    d. Neither Technician A nor Technician B

CHAPTER 52

NATEF Tasks

Heading and Air Conditioning

HVAC Systems

Task	Pages
■ Verify the need for service or repair of HVAC systems based on unusual visual, smell, and touch conditions; determine needed action.	1738–1745
■ Verify the need for service or repair of HVAC systems based on unusual operating noises; determine needed action.	1739

A/C System and Components—General

Task	Pages
■ Identify causes of temperature control problems in the A/C system; determine needed action.	1738–1742
■ Identify A/C system problems indicated by pressure gauge and temperature readings; determine needed action.	1738–1739
■ Identify A/C system problems indicated by visual, audible, smell, and touch procedures; determine needed action.	1738–1745
■ Interface with vehicle's on-board computer; perform diagnostic procedures using recommended electronic service tool(s) (including PC-based software and/or data scan tools); determine needed action.	1742
■ Perform A/C system leak test; determine needed action.	1745–1749
■ Identify refrigerant and lubricant types; check for contamination; determine needed action.	1746
■ Identify contamination in the A/C system components; determine needed action.	1746
■ Recover, evacuate, and recharge A/C system using appropriate equipment.	1750–1751 1761–1763

A/C System and Components—Compressor and Clutch

Task	Pages
■ Identify A/C system problems that cause protection devices (pressure, thermal, and electronic) to interrupt system operation; determine needed action.	1741–1742
■ Inspect, test, and replace A/C system pressure, thermal, and electronic protection devices.	1741–1742
■ Inspect and replace A/C compressor drive belts, pulleys, and tensioners; adjust belt tension and check alignment.	1753

Servicing Heating and Air-Conditioning Systems

NATEF Tasks, continued

Heating and Air Conditioning A/C System and Components—Compressor and Clutch, continued	Page
■ Inspect and correct A/C compressor lubricant level (if applicable).	1751, 1763
■ Inspect, test, adjust, service, or replace A/C compressor clutch components or assembly.	1754–1755
■ Inspect, test, or replace A/C compressor.	1755
■ Inspect, repair, or replace A/C compressor mountings and hardware.	1755–1756
A/C System and Components—Evaporator, Condenser, and Related Components	
■ Identify and inspect A/C system service ports (gauge connections); determine needed action.	1742, 1746, 1750
■ Correct system lubricant level when replacing the evaporator, condenser, receiver/dryer or accumulator/dryer, and hoses.	1751, 1763
■ Inspect A/C system hoses, lines, filters, fittings, and seals; determine needed action.	1752, 1757
■ Inspect and test A/C system condenser. Check for proper airflow and mountings; determine needed action.	1756–1757
■ Inspect and replace receiver/dryer or accumulator/dryer.	1756, 1758
■ Inspect and test cab/sleeper refrigerant solenoid, expansion valve(s); check placement of thermal bulb (capillary tube); determine needed action.	1759
■ Remove and replace orifice tube.	1758, 1760
■ Inspect and test cab/sleeper evaporator core; determine needed action.	1759–1760
■ Inspect, clean, or repair evaporator housing and water drain; inspect and service/replace evaporator air filter.	1739-1740
Heating and Engine Cooling Systems	
■ Identify the cause of outlet air temperature control problems in the HVAC system; determine needed action.	1739–1746

NATEF Tasks, continued

Heating and Air Conditioning

Heating and Engine Cooling Systems, continued	Page
■ Inspect and test heating system coolant control valve(s) and manual shut-off valves; determine needed action.	1764
■ Inspect and flush heater core; determine needed action.	1764
Operating Systems and Related Controls—Electrical	
■ Identify causes of HVAC electrical control system problems; determine needed action.	1738–1739
■ Inspect and test HVAC blower motors, resistors, switches, relays, modules, wiring, and protection devices; determine needed action.	1739–1741
■ Inspect and test A/C compressor clutch relays, modules, wiring, sensors, switches, diodes, and protection devices; determine needed action.	1753
■ Inspect and test A/C related electronic engine control systems; determine needed action.	1742
■ Interface with vehicle's on-board computer; perform diagnostic procedures using recommended electronic service tool(s) (including PC-based software and/or data scan tools); determine needed action.	1742
Operating Systems and Related Controls—Air/Mechanical	
■ Identify causes of HVAC air and mechanical control problems; determine needed action.	1762–1764
■ Inspect and test HVAC system actuators and hoses; determine needed action.	1762–1764
■ Inspect, test, and adjust HVAC systems ducts, doors, and outlets; determine needed action.	1762–1764
Refrigerant Recovery, Recycling, and Handling	
■ Maintain and verify correct operation of certified equipment.	1742
■ Identify and recover A/C system refrigerant.	1746, 1750
■ Recycle or properly dispose of refrigerant.	1751
■ Handle, label, and store refrigerant.	1750
■ Test recycled refrigerant for non-condensable gases.	1746

Knowledge Objectives

After reading this chapter, you will be able to:

1. Describe the principles of the air-conditioning service process. (pp 1736–1737)
2. Discuss air conditioner capacity and why it is important to determine the proper charge. (pp 1738–1739)
3. Explain the process of performance testing the air-conditioning system. (pp 1740–1741)
4. Explain the purpose and methods of leak testing. (pp 1745–1749)

Skills Objectives

After reading this chapter, you will be able to:

1. Performance-test the air-conditioning system. (p 1740) SKILL DRILL 52-1
2. Inspect the evaporator housing water drain. (pp 1740–1741) SKILL DRILL 52-2
3. Eliminate air-conditioning system odors. (p 1741) SKILL DRILL 52-3
4. Identify refrigerant type. (p 1746) SKILL DRILL 52-4
5. Test for leaks using a sniffer device. (p 1747) SKILL DRILL 52-5
6. Perform a dye test to find a leak. (p 1748) SKILL DRILL 52-6
7. Perform nitrogen testing to find a leak. (p 1749) SKILL DRILL 52-7
8. Perform the reclaim process. (p 1750) SKILL DRILL 52-8
9. Recycle refrigerant. (p 1751) SKILL DRILL 52-9
10. Determine the need for an additional air-conditioning system filter, and perform necessary action. (p 1752) SKILL DRILL 52-10
11. Inspect, test, and replace the compressor clutch. (pp 1754–1755) SKILL DRILL 52-11
12. Remove, inspect, and reinstall the compressor. (p 1755) SKILL DRILL 52-12
13. Remove and inspect air-conditioning mufflers, hoses, lines, and fittings. (p 1757) SKILL DRILL 52-13
14. Remove, inspect, and reinstall the condenser. (p 1757) SKILL DRILL 52-14
15. Remove, inspect, and install the receiver/dryer or accumulator. (p 1758) SKILL DRILL 52-15
16. Remove, inspect, and install a thermal expansion valve. (p 1759) SKILL DRILL 52-16
17. Remove, inspect, and install an orifice tube. (p 1760) SKILL DRILL 52-17
18. Use a vacuum gauge to evacuate an air-conditioning system. (p 1761) SKILL DRILL 52-18
19. Use a micron gauge to evacuate an air-conditioning system. (p 1762) SKILL DRILL 52-19
20. Add oil to the air-conditioning system. (p 1763) SKILL DRILL 52-20
21. Change the vacuum pump oil in an air-conditioning machine. (p 1765) SKILL DRILL 52-21

Introduction

Servicing and maintaining the proper operation of an HVAC system on a commercial vehicle has greater significance than in many other modes of transportation. One reason is because cabin temperature is very important for comfort and safety reasons. Keeping windows defrosted and a driver undistracted by high heat and humidity levels not only contribute to safer operation, but it improves productivity. The cab of a commercial vehicle is, after all, a workplace for drivers. Likewise, passengers on commercial buses can spend long periods of time on board the vehicle, and a positive travel experience is beneficial for commercial success.

Heating and air-conditioning systems on commercial vehicles work even harder than those in automobiles, as commercial vehicles often have large glass areas that expose the interior to more radiant heat. Cabin climate is more difficult to maintain when it is hot or cold outside, as commercial vehicles have large exterior surface areas and are not well insulated. The system must be capable of reaching an ideal temperature of 70°F to 80°F (20°C to 26°C) after a few minutes, as well as of exchanging the air in the cabin with fresh air every few minutes to remove odors, smoke, and exhalation. Transit buses have high-demand HVAC requirements, including an air flow of between 2,500 and 3,500 cfm and the cooling capacity of 20 to 30 times that of a medium-sized home AC unit. These AC systems will operate between 1,000 and 3,000 hours a year in the climate extremes of the United States. As much as 25% of fuel cost in these applications is for producing the power required to operate AC compressors and generate electricity to drive electric blower motors for evaporators and condensers. The cost of AC system maintenance is also one of the highest vehicle servicing expenses, according to a study by Index Sensors, which identified maintenance costs averaging as much as $244 a year on heavy trucks.

Servicing AC systems has become more complex due to legislated requirements to minimize release of refrigerants into the atmosphere. The Montreal protocol, with which most countries in the world have agreed to comply, aims to reduce global warming and damage caused by refrigerants to the atmosphere's upper ozone layer. In North America, legislation in Canada and the United States demands that anyone handling refrigerants or working on air-conditioning systems must receive special training and have qualifications for working with refrigerants before undertaking any repairs. In the United States, Section 609 of the Clean Air Act outlines standards and requirements for servicing motor vehicle air conditioners (MVAC) and MVAC-like appliances. Both US law and the code outlined in technician certification for Canadian Ozone Depletion Prevention prohibit the intentional release of refrigerant.

Even though servicing and maintaining AC systems requires specialized certification and training, this chapter will focus on the fundamentals of AC service on basic mobile systems.

You Are the Technician

A roughly three-year-old refuse-hauling truck has had its air-conditioning system repaired multiple times in the past eight months. On its fourth visit to your shop, the driver complains once again that the system is blowing only warm air. After verifying the complaint, you connect a manifold gauge set to the AC system and attempt to complete an AC-system performance test. The test could not be completed, however, because after about 30 seconds of operation, the AC compressor clutch disengaged the compressor. You noticed during that time that the compressor operation was also very noisy. Examining the manifold gauge pressures during the system's brief operation, you discover that the pressures were abnormally low and likely caused by an undercharge of refrigerant. A leak somewhere in the AC system is the most likely cause for the low pressures. Before you begin any further diagnostic work or repairs consider the following questions:

1. What qualifications would be required of the technician to perform this AC repair?
2. Outline three techniques that are used to identify and locate a refrigerant leak.
3. Explain the reasons that would best account for noisy compressor operation.

The Air-Conditioning Service Process

There are many variations in the design and construction of air-conditioning and refrigeration systems used in commercial vehicles. But whether it is a medium-duty truck with a day cab, or a highway coach having the cooling capacity of a commercial office building, the following basic tasks are involved in servicing and repairing most AC systems:

1. Carrying out a *performance test* of the air-conditioning system is the first step in the diagnostic process. **Performance testing** is the term used to describe the standard air-conditioning testing process. You need to look at all of the components and compare how the air-conditioning unit is functioning versus how it is designed to function. Typically, it consists of turning on the air conditioner to its maximum setting with the windows closed and raising the engine revolutions per minute (rpm) to 1,100–1,500. The vent temperature in the cabin is checked and compared to the temperature and humidity specifications on the manufacturer's temperature chart.
2. After the performance test is complete, the next step is *diagnosing any faults* that are causing the system to operate incorrectly. This could be as simple as a slipping belt, any of the components not working properly, or a leak in the system. The next step depends on the diagnosis.
3. If the diagnosis determines that a component of the air-conditioning system is not working properly, then leak testing is not needed and you will go straight to reclaiming refrigerant. If the diagnosis is that the refrigerant is low, you will need to perform a leak test next. The electronic leak detector and dye leak tester need the air-conditioning system to be relatively full of refrigerant, while nitrogen testing requires an empty air-conditioning system. If nitrogen testing is the leak test method to be performed, proceed to the reclaim step.
4. *Leak testing* is the next step. If the system is charged, then electronic leak detectors or fluorescent dye testing are good methods. If the refrigerant has leaked out of the system, then nitrogen testing is a good method of leak testing. Use the three-step method listed in the Leak Testing section to determine whether there is a leak, and take the appropriate action. Do not forget to vent the nitrogen to the atmosphere.
5. *Reclaiming* the air-conditioning system before any repair or nitrogen testing is required by the Environmental Protection Agency (EPA), section 609 of the Clean Air Act. Reclaiming involves first checking the system to see if there has been any sealant added to it. The second step is identifying the refrigerant and removing all of it using an approved machine, then measuring and recording the amount of refrigerant and oil that was removed from the system. a significant amount of oil is removed then the air-conditioning system should be flushed and the base oil amount should be installed. Compare the amount of reclaimed refrigerant to the OEM decal in the engine compartment and determine whether the air-conditioning system may have been under- or overcharged. If undercharged, suspect a leak and leak check with nitrogen.
6. *Repair* the air-conditioning problem. Now that the air-conditioning system has been diagnosed and tested, the system fault can be repaired. Take the appropriate action and precautions that the repair requires. At this point, the air-conditioning system can be flushed and the base oil installed if needed. In small systems, if less than 1 ounce (30 mL) of base oil needs to be added to the system, this step will wait until after the evacuation is complete. Finish the repair and continue to the evacuation.
7. *Evacuation* of the air-conditioning system is the next step after all repairs are made. Evacuation is the process of creating a low pressure or vacuum in the air-conditioning system using a vacuum pump and gauges. Water boils and turns into a gas at normal ambient temperatures when placed in a vacuum, so this process can remove any moisture that entered the system. This process usually requires a strong vacuum for a minimum of 15 minutes for removal of all the moisture. Follow the proper procedure for the evacuation with a mechanical gauge or using a more accurate micron gauge. After the evacuation is complete, the oil for the air-conditioning system can be added. After the oil is added to the air-conditioning system, the vehicle is ready for the charging process.
8. *Charging* the air-conditioning system to the proper refrigerant level is an important process of the air-conditioning repair. When adding refrigerant to the system, be sure that you add the correct amount. After the refrigerant has been charged into the air-conditioning system, rotate the compressor shaft by hand to push out any liquid that may have entered the compressor during the charge process.
9. *Post-testing* of the air-conditioning system is recommended to catch any masked problems that did not appear when the original problem was diagnosed.

It is a repeat of the performance test to ensure that all moisture is removed and a recheck of the pressure gauges to be sure the high- and low-side pressures are as specified. All readings should be checked against a diagnostic chart. If you used an electronic leak detector or dye leak testing method, it is a good idea to confirm that there are no leaks. If the vehicle passes the post-test and the air-conditioning system is in good functioning order, then you are ready to contact the customer.

Determining Refrigerant Type

The only way to determine the type of refrigerant in a system is with the aid of a refrigerant identifier **FIGURE 52-1**. This easy-to-use device connects to the low-side air-conditioning fitting and takes a reading of the refrigerant. It will give a readout such as 100% R-134a, or if the system is contaminated, you may see a reading such as 60% R-134a 40% R-12. As long as the refrigerant is pure, it can be recycled using a reclaiming machine and reused. If it is contaminated by the wrong refrigerant or the wrong oil, then it is considered a hazardous waste and must be put in a separate unit and disposed of according to state law. The air-conditioning decal in the engine compartment lists the type of refrigerant and how much should be in the system.

Air Conditioner Capacity

The proper **charge** (amount of refrigerant) of the air-conditioning system is important because if the amount of refrigerant is too low or too high, the resulting change in system operating pressure will change the boiling point of the refrigerant, making it unable to effectively remove heat in the evaporator. The air-conditioning system has safety features built into it. For example, the low-pressure safety switch turns the compressor off if the pressure drops too low due to a low charge of refrigerant, and the high-pressure safety switch turns the compressor off if the pressure gets too high due to an overcharge. Since the system pressures vary greatly during operation, the switches are designed to allow operation within a wide window. Thus, they should not be used as indicators of a proper charge.

The proper charge for the air conditioner can be found listed on the OEM AC decal in the engine compartment **FIGURE 52-2**. The sticker should detail the oil capacity, charge amount, and type of refrigerant. The type of refrigerant must remain the same because cross-contamination will create a hazardous substance.

There are different ways to measure the refrigerant to be added. Some systems give you the charge amount in kilograms, pounds, pounds with ounces, and straight ounces. The machine that you use to charge the system will determine the type of measurement you will need or need to convert to. If the sticker is not under the hood of the vehicle, you will need to turn to service information or industry literature. Charging a vehicle without knowing the correct amount of refrigerant is playing a guessing game and is likely to lead to a poor-performing system and customer dissatisfaction.

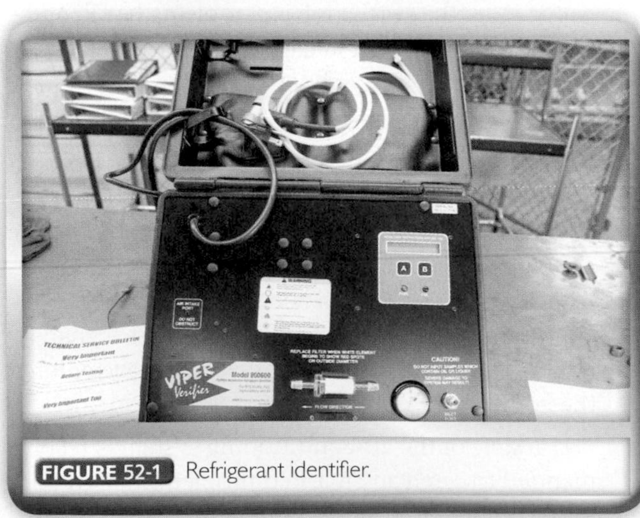

FIGURE 52-1 Refrigerant identifier.

FIGURE 52-2 An air-conditioning identification sticker.

State of Charge

State of charge in the air-conditioning system refers to the amount of refrigerant in the system compared to how much should be in the system. It is best tested by removing all the refrigerant from the air-conditioning system, comparing that amount to the manufacturer's specifications, then recharging the system with the proper amount of refrigerant, as specified by the service information. If the air conditioner cannot be discharged for any reason and the state of charge needs to be determined, then you need to start your diagnosis by performance testing the air-conditioning system on the vehicle (see the Diagnosis section). But the best way to make sure the air-conditioning system is properly charged is to remove all refrigerant from the system and reinstall the proper amount of refrigerant.

Undercharge

An undercharged air-conditioning system contains less refrigerant than the system calls for. For example, if the system is designed to hold 3.5 lbs (1.59 kg) of refrigerant but only 1.75 lbs (0.8 kg) are removed during the system evacuation, then the state of charge is half of what it should be. This air-conditioning system would be referred to as undercharged. Systems become undercharged for two primary reasons: (1) There is a leak in the system, or (2) the system was incorrectly charged.. Either way, you should plan on leak testing the system to verify that there is not a leak. The following two sections will discuss how each type of system responds to an undercharged condition.

Orifice Tube System

In a typical orifice tube system, an undercharge of refrigerant will cause a rapid cycle time (rapid turning on and off) of the air-conditioning clutch. The excessive cycling frequency is caused by inadequate flow of refrigerant into the evaporator. What little liquid refrigerant enters the evaporator quickly turns to vapor, causing evaporator pressures to increase as well. The pressure cycling switch used to regulate evaporator pressure responds to the rapid pressure changes by rapidly cycling the compressor clutch on and off. The air from the ducts will feel warm to the hand instead of cold, and the air-conditioning gauge readings will be lower than normal.

Thermal Expansion Valve System

An undercharged thermal expansion valve (TXV) system will operate with below-normal high and low system pressures. A low pressure switch located in the trinary or binary switch, or in the evaporator, will disable the AC system. The low pressure switch will typically disable the AC system if pressures fall below 10 psi (69 kPa). In an undercharged TXV system, the AC will under cool as well.

Overcharge

Overcharging the air-conditioning system will affect the orifice tube and TXV systems in the same manner. Both the low- and the high-side gauges will be running higher than normal. The air in the ducts will feel slightly cool, and the **air-conditioning compressor clutch** will run for a few seconds, then turn off for a long period of time. This behavior is caused flooding of the evaporator with excessive refrigerant or the operation of the high pressure switches disabling the AC system.

Diagnosis

The most common air-conditioning complaint that brings vehicles into the shop is simply that the air conditioner is not performing. Usually the root cause is leaks in the system. Other issues that could cause the same complaint are compressor failure, debris causing system blockages on the high or low side, or system blockages caused by moisture freezing in the system. These problems occur far less often than leaks, but do happen. Normally, a check of the gauge pressures will indicate what is going on. System normal operating pressures vary with ambient temperature, but they typically range between 25–45 psi (172–310 kPa) on the low side and 150–170 psi (1,034–1,172 kPa) on the high side at 70°F (70°C). When both gauges read low pressure, the system may be low on refrigerant. If the gauges read low pressure on the high side, high pressure on the low side, or about equal pressures, it usually means that the compressor is not working. If the low side reads as a vacuum, such as in the TXV system, the valve is blocked, and refrigerant cannot flow into the evaporator. Extremely high-pressure readings on the high side indicate that there is a blockage on the high side or an airflow restriction across the condenser.

On occasion, the problem of not blowing cold air is not the air-conditioning system at all; rather, the blend door or heater control valve is not closing adequately to keep air or hot coolant from passing through the heater core. This can be identified by checking pressures and determining that the air-conditioning system is performing correctly and moving on to the next logical cause, a heater that is not turning off.

Another driver complaint is unusual smells when running the air conditioner. The air-conditioning box has a drain tube that allows removal of water collected from the moist air as it condenses on the cold evaporator and drips into the box. If the drain is plugged, then the water will provide a breeding ground for bacteria and the smell will be distributed throughout the cabin. This problem is fixed by clearing the drain, spraying the system with a disinfectant and allowing it to sit, then running the system on high to blow everything out with all the doors open.

> **TECHNICIAN TIP**
>
> If the duct temperature is warmer than the ambient temperature, then the heater control valve is stuck open or the blend door is not positioned properly. Use hose pinch pliers to shut off the flow to the heater core and then retest the air-conditioning system.

When diagnosing air-conditioning systems, you need to look at all of the factors involved. Always refer to service information, precautions, history, and service bulletins. Some of the variable factors in air conditioning are the weather, air moisture content, temperature, overall condition of the vehicle, and type of vehicle. Obviously the temperature is important, as the hotter or colder the outside air, the harder it is to heat or cool it. Moisture in the air, through either humidity or precipitation, can stick to the fins of the evaporator and freeze. Since the evaporator is used in air conditioning and defrost to dry the air, a frozen evaporator can affect both the heating and the cooling systems. If a vehicle is running badly, the air conditioning may be turned off to try to correct the issue. Slipping belts will cause the compressor to spin slowly or not at all. Any leaks in passenger doors or windows will cause outside air to enter, which will have to be conditioned. The size and color of the vehicle make a difference. Big vehicles have more space, and the materials in the vehicle hold heat or cold; therefore, it takes longer to condition the air. A black vehicle will absorb heat and can be very difficult to cool on a hot sunny day. A cloudy day will decrease the heat load on the vehicle, increasing the air-conditioning system's efficiency and possibly giving the impression that the system is cooling fine.

> **TECHNICIAN TIP**
>
> The one rule for diagnosis of an air-conditioning system is "when in doubt, suck it out." This means if you cannot find the problem while diagnosing, remove all refrigerant and start over from a base charge. Starting with a known base charge will remove any question if the refrigerant is too low or too high or if there is any moisture causing a problem in the system.

Performance Testing

The pretest and inspection of the air-conditioning system are the first step in the diagnostic process. *Performance testing* is the term used to describe the standard air-conditioning testing process. You need to look at all of the components and compare how the air-conditioning unit is functioning versus how it is designed to function. When testing the air-conditioning system, make sure to have all of the controls at the maximum settings. The heater fan needs to be on the highest speed. The heater control knob should be on the coldest setting. The airflow should be set to the dash vents. An external fan needs to be supplying air to the condenser to simulate driving conditions.

The engine's rpm should be at 1200, which is the ideal and average rpm for the majority of air-conditioning systems on vehicles. Before testing the air-conditioning system, let the system stabilize for a few minutes to allow the refrigerant to equalize and the temperatures to reach the proper level.

To performance test an air-conditioning system, follow the steps in **SKILL DRILL 52-1**.

> **TECHNICIAN TIP**
>
> Performance testing of the air-conditioning system must be done before and after the repair. Doing so will help ensure that you identify any faults before starting the repairs, as well as verify that the faults are completely repaired.

Abnormal Noises

The compressor is the most common source of abnormal noises arising from the air conditioner. If the compressor fails internally, it may make a knocking noise. Low oil levels or low refrigerant levels will starve the compressor of oil, which produces compressor noise. While performance testing the system, abnormal noises can occur while the air-conditioning system is operating. Listen for noises that may occur when the compressor clutch is engaged. If the noise disappears when the compressor clutch disengages, then the noise is from the air-conditioning system. Be sure to listen for noises in the engine compartment as well as in the vehicle's passenger compartment. Turn off and on the compressor clutch and move the controls on the dash, listening to determine whether the noises appear and disappear.

SKILL DRILL 52-1 Performance Testing an Air-Conditioning System

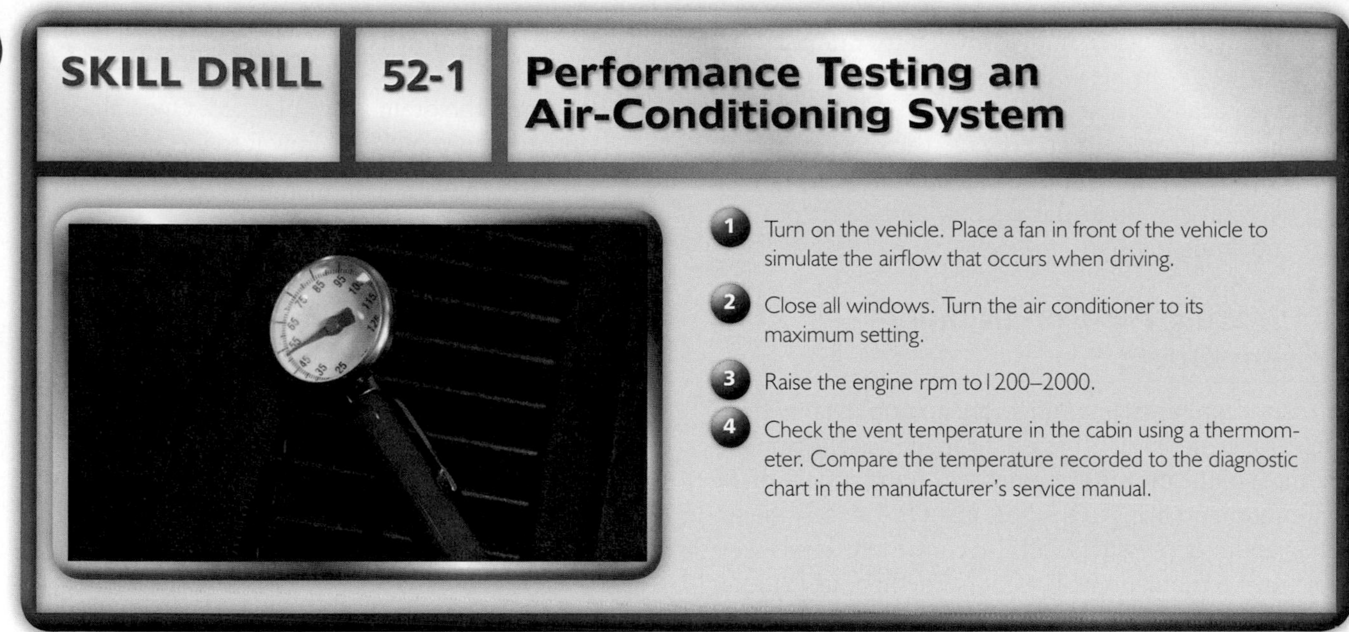

1. Turn on the vehicle. Place a fan in front of the vehicle to simulate the airflow that occurs when driving.
2. Close all windows. Turn the air conditioner to its maximum setting.
3. Raise the engine rpm to 1200–2000.
4. Check the vent temperature in the cabin using a thermometer. Compare the temperature recorded to the diagnostic chart in the manufacturer's service manual.

TECHNICIAN TIP

As a general rule, the duct temperature should be no greater than 17°F above the evaporator temperature. The optimum vent temperature is from 38°F to 48°F. The air-conditioning clutch cycle should not allow the duct temperature to have greater than a 5° swing from high to low while staying within the range of 38°F to 48°F. If the swing is out of the 5° range, the thermal switch or the pressure cycle switch may need to be replaced, if equipped.

Inspecting the Condenser for Airflow Restrictions

The condenser is normally inspected when high-side pressures are too high and the system is not cooling well. Road debris, leaves, and animal fur and feathers are common culprits, but anything that sits in front of the condenser can cause this issue. This inspection should also be performed with any air-conditioning tune-up or inspection, such as those offered by many shops before summer. Use a flashlight on the back of the condenser. Look in from the outside of the vehicle for the light coming through the condenser. Move the light across the entire condenser. If the light is not showing, the condenser needs to be cleaned.

When cleaning the condenser for debris, shop air or a water hose may be used to remove the debris, but be careful to not fold over the fins. If the shop air and a water hose do not remove the restriction, the condenser must be removed and cleaned.

TECHNICIAN TIP

There are factory adjustments on both the thermal cycle switch and the pressure cycle switch. The adjustments are for achieving optimum performance at the factory. Trying to adjust either of the switches because of an incorrect temperature swing may mask the faulty switch for a short time. If these switches are incorrectly functioning, replacement is the proper and recommended procedure for the repair.

Inspecting the Evaporator Housing Water Drain

As the air-conditioning system is running, the evaporator will sweat water throughout the day. The water collected needs to be drained from the evaporator housing. A drain hose is connected to the evaporator housing and exits through the vehicle's firewall. Checking that the drain is not plugged is a common diagnostic procedure.

To inspect the evaporator housing water drain, follow the steps in SKILL DRILL 52-2:

1. Determine that the drain tube is clogged by allowing the air-conditioning system to run while observing the drain tube for water drops. In the case of a plugged drain, no water or very few drops are found.
2. Carefully use low-pressure shop air and an air nozzle to blow air into the drain tube. Note that water will come out of the drain tube when the clog is removed and will result in a large discharge of malodorous water; stand back.

3. When the water has completely drained, the task has been performed. Advise the customer to periodically check for a water puddle under the vehicle; if one is not present, the clog may have reoccurred, and removal of the air box may be necessary to open the air box and clean out any remaining debris.

Eliminating Air-Conditioning System Odors

Air-conditioning systems are prone to unpleasant odors. Since warm, moist air is passed through the cold evaporator, most of the moisture condenses on the surface of the evaporator and drips to the bottom of the air box. Incorrect evaporator pressures will also contribute to excessive moisture accumulations. This moisture then sits in the air box and ducts where it is dark—an ideal place for mold and bacteria to grow. The mold and bacteria produce odors that are directed at the passengers when the fan is turned on. The ducts also provide an appealing space that mice and other small animals use for building their nests.

If you find that an odor is stronger in one position than in the others, the smell is likely coming from that duct. If the odor is in all positions, the problem is likely in the heater/evaporator housing. Keep testing until you can pinpoint the source of the odor. Check for odors as you try each of the following: selecting "fresh" air and turning the fan on high, selecting the dash vent, selecting each vent setting, turning the heater on high, and turning the air conditioner on.

If the drain tube becomes clogged with leaves or debris over time, the water will not be able to drain; it will stagnate and begin growing bacteria, creating an unpleasant odor. The solution to this concern is to unclog the drain tube. If odors continue to be a problem and the drain tube is open, the use of an anti-odor kit may be necessary. These kits require gaining access to the evaporator, either by complete removal of the evaporator, removal of the fan, or removal of the resistor pack, or by drilling a small hole into the air box. When access is gained to the evaporator, a spray chemical cleaner is used on the evaporator fins and allowed to dry. A follow-up chemical coating is then applied, which keeps bacteria from growing on the fins of the evaporator. If a hole was drilled into the air box according to the directions of the kit, a repair kit is usually included to repair the hole. Sometimes this will be a very strong piece of adhesive tape or a plug that will attach to the hole. Drilling a hole into the air box is not the preferred method and can result in air leaks and noise. Follow the directions of the kit to ensure a quality repair.

To eliminate air-conditioning system odors in the case of a clogged drain, follow the steps in **SKILL DRILL 52-3**:

1. Verify that the drain is not plugged. Open all of the doors on the vehicle to allow it to air out a bit.
2. Turn the blower fan on medium speed.
3. Operate the system in all zones and see if the smell is stronger in one position than the others. If so, inspect that portion of the system. If the smell is equally strong in all positions, inspect the heater/evaporator housing. If the odor is caused by mold or bacteria buildup, use an anti-odor kit to clean and kill any buildup.

Cabin Air Filter

Many vehicles now include a cabin air filter in the HVAC system to filter the air before it enters the system. The filter is housed in the air box and can be accessed from one of a variety of positions, depending on the vehicle. The access may be from under the hood near the firewall, under the windshield, or behind the glove box. It is usually fairly easy to remove and replace once you find the access cover. This filter should be inspected during every service and replaced according to the manufacturer's specified interval, typically once a year. Inspect the filter and check it for any cracks, tears, or deformities that would cause it to be ineffective.

Air-Conditioning System Conditions

Within the air-conditioning system are protective devices designed to shut down air-conditioning operations to prevent further damage. These protection devices are generally thermal units, fuses, or circuit breakers. Generally, if one of these devices is tripped, the AC system is disabled until the ignition switch is cycled.

Pressure switches, whether high or low, will have a cutoff pressure to protect the air-conditioning system. A high-pressure switch located on the high-side line may have a cutoff pressure of 400 psi (2758 kPa). At that pressure, the switch opens because the pressure is high enough to cause the **hoses** and **lines** to rupture. A low-pressure switch with a cutoff of at approximately 10 psi (69 kPa) will open because not enough refrigerant, which carries the lubricating oil, will be able to get to the compressor, and the internal moving parts may fail or overheat.

Computer-controlled air-conditioning systems have the same fail-safes as regular systems, but when the pressure switches sense a problem, they send that information to the electronic control module, which will determine if the system should be shut down until repaired. The ECM may also shut down the air-conditioning if there is a charging problem or an overheating issue and the ECM determines that the extra load on the engine created by the air conditioning needs to be shut down until the other problem is resolved.

If an electrical issue occurs, the problem must be tracked using a digital volt-ohmmeter (DVOM), which is the electrical diagnostic tool used to check voltage, current flow, and resistance of circuits. Once located, the component will need to be replaced or the wire repaired and the fuse replaced.

Low pressure normally requires refilling the air-conditioning system and finding and repairing the leak. The other issues require diagnosing and repairing the issue that caused the computer to shut off the air conditioning, then clearing the codes in the ECM so it will reset and turn the air conditioning back on. These problems are found using a scan tool to pull the codes, then diagnosing the code using a diagnostic manual.

In each of these situations, the technician must refer to the vehicle's service information and follow the steps appropriate for the vehicle type and air-conditioning model.

Maintenance and Repair

Tools

To maintain and repair air-conditioning systems, you will need the following tools:

- *Sealant detector*: Sealant detectors detect the presence of sealant in the air-conditioning system. Allowing sealant to be drawn into a refrigerant identifier or **air-conditioning machine** can ruin them FIGURE 52-3A.
- **Refrigerant identifiers**: Refrigerant identifiers hook to the low-side fitting of the air-conditioning system to determine whether the refrigerant is pure or whether it is contaminated with another refrigerant or air. Identifying refrigerant can save the costly procedure of flushing out your reclaim/recycle machine and save you from having to dispose of contaminated refrigerant FIGURE 52-3B.
- **Reclaim/recycle machine**: If the air-conditioning machine is used for any air-conditioning work on a customer's vehicle, it is required to meet the EPA requirements. This machine hooks up to the air-conditioning service ports on the vehicle and can check pressures, but also has a storage tank to hold refrigerant FIGURE 52-3C. It also has a vacuum pump to evacuate air-conditioning systems. Refrigerant must be recovered or sucked into the machine before repairs are done to the air-conditioning system. Once the repairs are done, the air-conditioning system must be evacuated or vacuumed out to create a low pressure to remove moisture. Once this is done, the machine normally can refill the vehicle's air-conditioning system either from the recycled tank, which contains refrigerant removed from vehicles, sent through a filter, then stored in the tank, or from the virgin tank, which contains new refrigerant. Most shops will draw from the recycle tank until it is too low to charge a vehicle, and then use the virgin tank.
- **Manifold gauge set**: A reliable pressure gauge set is one of the most important air-conditioning tools to obtain. Manifold gauge sets come in both mechanical

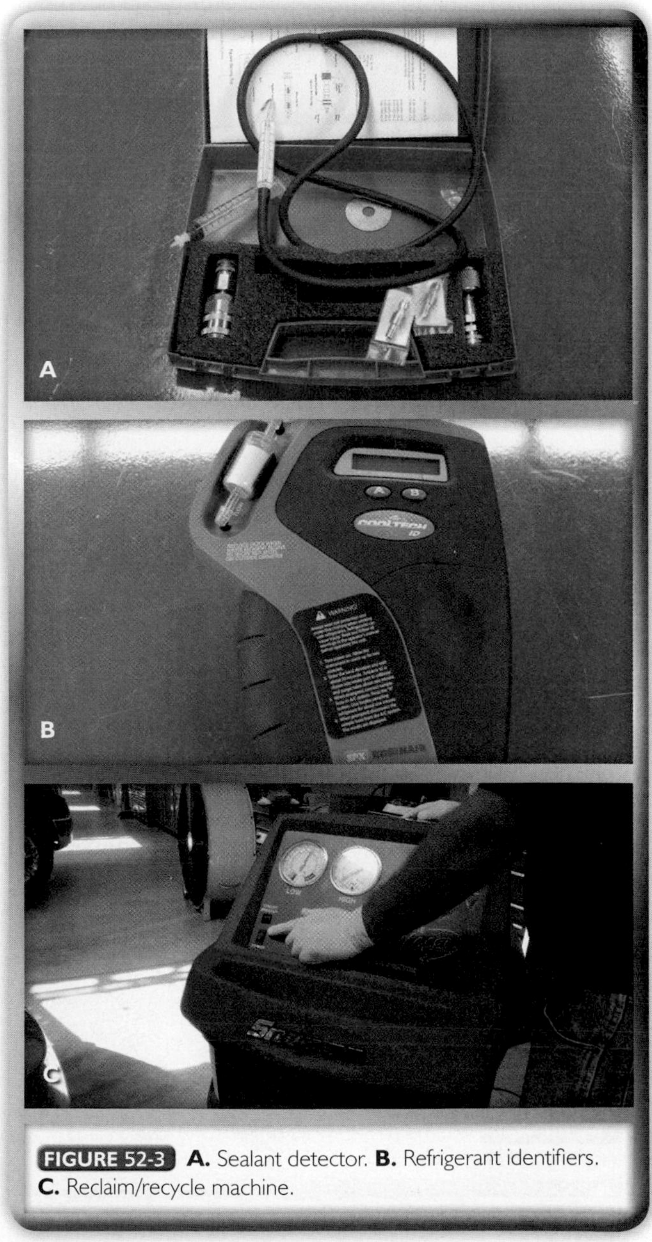

FIGURE 52-3 **A.** Sealant detector. **B.** Refrigerant identifiers. **C.** Reclaim/recycle machine.

and digital styles and are used to diagnose and service air-conditioning systems. Both types of gauge sets have a low-side and a high-side pressure gauge connected to a common manifold that can be used for manual servicing of the air-conditioning system. The hoses connect to each gauge and are connected to the manifold by valves and passageways in the manifold FIGURE 52-4 The two knobs on the front of the manifold connect the high and low hoses to the service port on the manifold. When using the gauge set, make sure both service knobs are in the closed position before connecting them to a system. The hoses on the gauge set are connected to the gauge directly; opening the service valves only connects the passageways from the hoses to the service port. On a digital gauge set, you will need to calibrate each gauge to zero so the pressures will read accurately. Follow the instructions in the operator's manual for the procedure on calibrating the gauge to zero.

Both the high-pressure and the low-pressure gauges need to be non-liquid filled if they are mechanical gauges. Oil-filled gauges do not allow the needle to move fast enough for you to see **pressure transients**, which are fluctuations observed as the gauges bounce between pressures rather than holding at one position or moving smoothly up and down the gauge. Being able to see the needle oscillations will provide valuable information when performing certain diagnostic scenarios. For example, a compressor with one bad piston will cause the high-side pressure to bounce when that piston is trying to push refrigerant. Another example is when water is in the system and freezes a line. When it starts to thaw, the affected side's gauge will bounce as the pressure changes from the temporary blockage.

FIGURE 52-4 Internal passageways of the manifold and gauge set.

Gauge sets are also built into most R/R/R machines (Recover, Recycle, evacuate, leak test, and Recharge).

> **TECHNICIAN TIP**
>
> Any air-conditioning machine can be used as a gauge set if the service valves are shut off.

- **Anemometer**: The air coming out of the vent needs to have enough flow to keep fresh air passing over the evaporator. Without air, the refrigerant will not boil. For the air-conditioning system to function properly, the velocity needs to be at a minimum of 800 feet per minute (fpm). The most accurate way to test the velocity is to use an anemometer FIGURE 52-5A. Anemometers measure the velocity of the air in fpm.
- **Retrofit kit**: This aftermarket kit has the fittings and oil to change an R-12 unit over to R-134a FIGURE 52-5B.
- **PT chart**: A PT chart, which stands for pressure-temperature chart, is used to determine what the high- and low-side pressures should be at a given outside temperature and humidity in a properly functioning system FIGURE 52-5C.
- **Vacuum pump**: Vacuum pumps are rated in the total volume of air that can be removed every minute. They are used to create low pressure or vacuum in the system. The volume is measured in cubic feet per minute (CFM). The most common pumps are the 52-CFM and 6-CFM models, although some new air-conditioning machines have a 7-CFM pump.
- *Electronic leak detector*: Sometimes called a "sniffer," this device is used to locate small refrigerant leaks by electronically reacting to refrigerant gas FIGURE 52-5D.
- *Dye leak detector*: This solution is used to detect refrigeration leaks FIGURE 52-5E.
- **Oiler**: This device is used to add oil to the air-conditioning system.
- **Vacuum gauge**: This gauge is designed to read negative pressure or vacuum FIGURE 52-5F.
- **Micron gauge**: This electronic device is designed to measure vacuum precisely FIGURE 52-5G.
- *Line wrenches*: Line wrenches are box-end wrenches or wrenches designed to go all the way around the nut or bolt with a slot cut out of the box part to allow the technician to slide the wrench over the tube or hose.

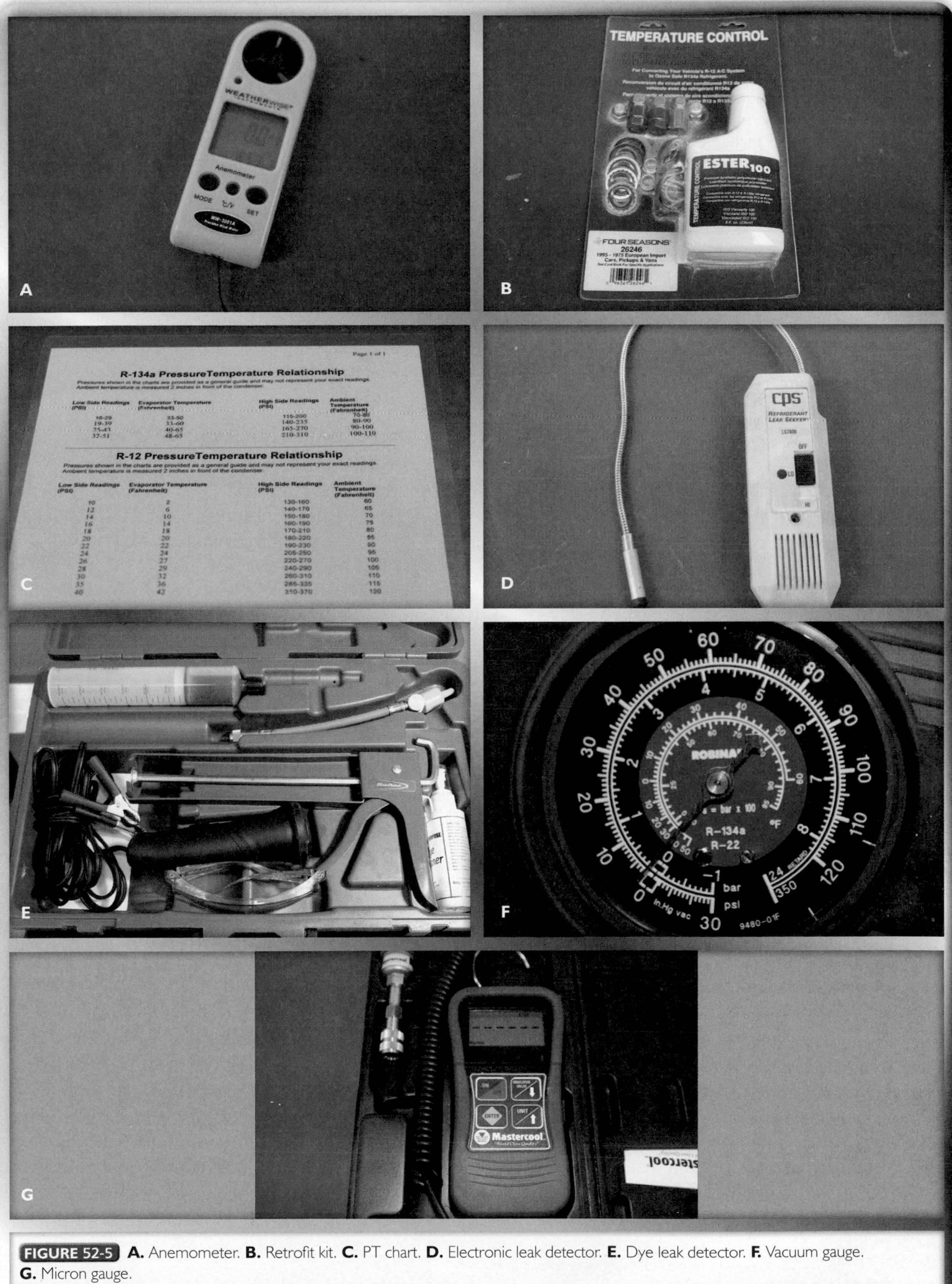

Page 1 of 1

R-134a PressureTemperature Relationship

Pressures shown in the charts are provided as a general guide and may not represent your exact readings. Ambient temperature is measured 2 inches in front of the condenser.

Low Side Readings (PSI)	Evaporator Temperature (Fahrenheit)	High Side Readings (PSI)	Ambient Temperature (Fahrenheit)
16-29	33-50	115-200	70-80
19-39	33-60	140-235	80-90
25-43	40-65	165-270	90-100
37-51	48-65	210-310	100-110

R-12 PressureTemperature Relationship

Pressures shown in the charts are provided as a general guide and may not represent your exact readings. Ambient temperature is measured 2 inches in front of the condenser.

Low Side Readings (PSI)	Evaporator Temperature (Fahrenheit)	High Side Readings (PSI)	Ambient Temperature (Fahrenheit)
10	2	130-160	60
12	6	140-170	65
14	10	150-180	70
16	14	160-190	75
18	18	170-210	80
20	20	180-220	85
22	22	190-230	90
24	24	205-250	95
26	27	220-270	100
28	29	240-290	105
30	32	260-310	110
35	36	285-335	115
40	42	310-370	120

FIGURE 52-5 **A.** Anemometer. **B.** Retrofit kit. **C.** PT chart. **D.** Electronic leak detector. **E.** Dye leak detector. **F.** Vacuum gauge. **G.** Micron gauge.

> **TECHNICIAN TIP**
>
> The low-pressure gauge is unique in that it displays both pressure and vacuum. It has a maximum pressure of about 120 psi (827 kPa) and a low pressure of 30" Hg (vacuum measured in inches of mercury, or 102 kPa). The low-pressure gauge needs to display vacuum readings for diagnostic purposes and to ensure that the proper vacuum levels are achieved when evacuating the system. The high-side pressure gauge usually has a maximum pressure of about 500 psi (3,447 kPa). Most systems will run with the high-side pressure around 120 psi (827 kPa); but if the condenser fan is not functioning, the pressure could rise as high as 400 psi (2,758 kPa). This is why you need such a large pressure range on the high-side gauge. Otherwise, if the system pressure exceeds the maximum gauge reading, the gauge could be damaged, or it could even explode.

> **TECHNICIAN TIP**
>
> Modifying the air-conditioning machine or repairing the air-conditioning machine should be performed by an authorized dealer to maintain its certification, not by the air-conditioning technician.

Identifying the Refrigerant Type

Refrigerant should be tested to determine its type any time the refrigerant will be recovered. If the refrigerant in the vehicle is contaminated and put in the recovery bottle of the air-conditioning machine, the whole bottle in the machine is contaminated and should be treated as hazardous waste. If it is not caught while in the machine, it will contaminate every vehicle that has air-conditioning refrigerant installed from that machine's recovery bottle.

Another condition that needs to be identified is whether sealer has been added to the vehicle's air-conditioning system. Many small cans of refrigerant come with sealant inside. Sealer can ruin refrigerant identifiers and air-conditioning machines. While not a lot of vehicles have sealer in them, all it takes is one vehicle to contaminate and damage your air-conditioning equipment. Most experts agree that sealant should *never* be used. If there is a leak, fix the leak! Identifying whether the system has sealer in it should be the first step in the refrigerant-identifying process.

To identify the refrigerant type, follow the steps in SKILL DRILL 52-4.

Leak Testing

The air-conditioning system is a sealed system that must not leak; however, leaks do occur and are a common reason that the air-conditioning system is not working properly. Leak testing should be performed on every air-conditioning system that is low on refrigerant or has just been repaired. Leak testing can be done by several methods: electronic leak detection, dye testing, and nitrogen testing.

The electronic leak detector and dye leak tests require that the air-conditioning system be full of refrigerant, while nitrogen testing requires an empty air-conditioning system. If a nitrogen test is the method being used, first reclaim the air-conditioning system.

Electronic Leak Detection Testing

The use of an SAE-compliant electronic leak detector is considered the safest and the most accurate method for locating a refrigerant leak. The latest SAE standard, the J-2791 electronic refrigerant leak detector, will accurately detect refrigerant leaks down to 0.1 oz (3 g) per year. Three sensitivity levels are typically available on the detector to identify large and small leaks. The detector will "beep," activate a light or both when a leak is found.

To obtain the most accurate results, leak detection must be performed with the system under pressure with no less than 50% refrigerant charge in the system. Finding smaller leaks, however, may require that the system refrigerant pressure be increased above normal before the leaks can be located.

The detector needs to be moved slowly and evenly around the components and lines. Starting with the sensitivity on a high setting and turning down the sensitivity as the alarms and lights get louder and brighter will help you pinpoint the problem. Moving with a steady hand and taking your time is critical to using this device.

When using the detector, be sure there is no wind or draft on the vehicle. A draft or air movement over the vehicle could cause the refrigerant to not enter the detector.

To test for leaks using a sniffer device, follow the steps in SKILL DRILL 52-5.

Dye Testing

Using ultraviolet (UV) light and refrigerant dye is a common way to test for leaks in an air-conditioning system. Some vehicle manufacturers add dye during the

SKILL DRILL 52-4 Identifying the Refrigerant Type

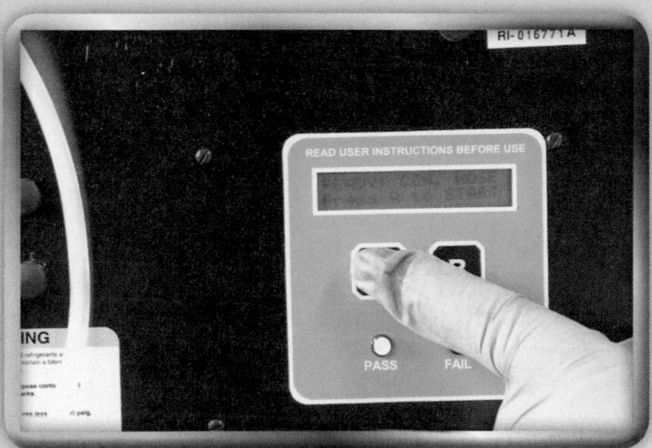

1. Use a sealant identifier to check whether there is any sealant in the system. If there is, notify your supervisor.

2. Turn on the refrigerant identifier and allow the machine to warm up.

3. Locate the high- and low-side pressure service ports. Connect the refrigerant identifier to the low side of the air-conditioning system and open the service valve. Follow the prompts on the refrigerant identifier, and record the refrigerant type and amount of air, if any.

4. Ensure that the under-the-hood sticker matches the refrigerant types on the refrigerant identifier. Turn off the service valve and disconnect the refrigerant identifier.

5. If the refrigerant does not match the under-the-hood sticker, reclaim the contaminated refrigerant into a contaminated tank and label the refrigerant for disposal. If the refrigerant is 100% pure and matches the under-the-hood sticker, continue to the next step.

6. Select the proper pressure gauge set for the refrigerant type in the vehicle. After selecting the pressure gauge set, make sure the service valves on the gauges are in the off or shut position.

7. Connect the service chuck of the pressure gauge to the air-conditioning system.

8. Open the valves and watch the high- and low-pressure gauges. Record the pressure. If the high- and low side gauges are the same pressure and you could not identify the refrigerant, then use the PT chart to determine whether there are non-condensable gases (air) in the air-conditioning system.

9. Measure the ambient temperature 15 to 20 cm in front of the condenser and the pressure on the pressure gauge set.

10. Compare the pressure to the PT chart for that type of refrigerant. If the pressure on the gauge is higher than the PT chart, the air-conditioning system has non-condensable gases. If the pressure on the gauge is lower than the PT chart, the air-conditioning system is low on refrigerant and a leak should be suspected. If the reading matches another refrigerant on the chart, then the refrigerant needs to be identified before recycling. A good reading (one in the normal ranges) on the gauge and a good temperature reading, as compared to the PT chart, indicate that there are no non-condensable gases in the system. The air-conditioning system could still be below the charge amount recommended, but it is not completely out of refrigerant.

manufacturing process. When using dye for the first time on an air-conditioning system, the dye needs to be injected as a concentrate into the system. Most machines have a special port for injecting the dye. Injecting concentrated dye into the low side of the air-conditioning system should be done with the vehicle off. When installing dye for the first time, the air-conditioning system needs to be operated so that the dye is distributed throughout all parts of the air-conditioning system.

If the vehicle already has dye installed, or after the vehicle has been test-driven after a new dye injection, locating the leak requires using a UV light. When using a UV light, make sure all safety precautions are followed, including wearing UV safety glasses. Finding leaks with a UV light is easier in the dark; installing a cover over the hood of a vehicle will help you to find the leak.

To perform a dye test to find a leak, follow the steps in SKILL DRILL 52-6.

SKILL DRILL 52-5 Testing for Leaks Using an Electronic Leak Detector

1. Make sure the air-conditioning system has refrigerant by installing a pressure gauge set and checking the readings against the PT chart.
2. Select a fairly sensitive setting for the detector. Slowly move the wand around and under all of the air-conditioning lines and components. If a leak is detected, turn the sensitivity down and pinpoint the exact location of the leak. Once the leak is located, move the wand tip from the leak to outside the vehicle. This allows the detector to "breathe" clean air, cleaning out its sensors and stopping the alarm.
3. Reclaim the refrigerant and repair the leak.
4. Always recheck for a leak after the system has been properly recharged.

SKILL DRILL 52-6 Testing for Leaks Using Dye

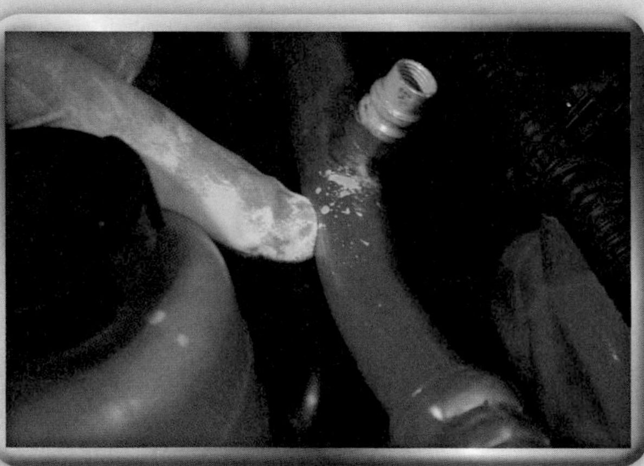

1. Check system pressure to be sure there is enough refrigerant to turn on the compressor. Turn on the compressor. If the compressor does not come on, add refrigerant in small increments until the compressor runs.
2. Add the dye through the low-pressure port using a dye injection system. Run the air-conditioning system to circulate the dye. The system may have to run for several minutes or even several days, depending on the size of the leak. If the leak cannot be located, allow the customer to drive the vehicle for a few days to a week and return the vehicle for inspection.
3. Using a black light, follow the lines, hoses, components and compressor seal, looking for the orange or green glow of the dye, which indicates a leak. If a leak is not found in the lines or hoses, it may be in the evaporator; the blower motor resistor may need to be removed to see into the air-conditioning box.
4. Recover the refrigerant in the system, repair the leak, evacuate and recharge the refrigerant and recheck for leaks.

Nitrogen Testing

Nitrogen testing has been used in the home and transport refrigeration repair industry for a long time. Nitrogen works very well for testing discharged systems or for prechecking for a leak after repairs have been made and before recharging the system. Nitrogen testing requires a nitrogen tank, pressure regulator, adapters. The nitrogen is used to simulate working conditions of the air-conditioning system and will provide enough force to make high-pressure leaks visible with soapy water.

To perform nitrogen testing to find a leak, follow the steps in SKILL DRILL 52-7.

Safety

When nitrogen testing, safety glasses, gloves, and a face shield are required. Weak components or hoses may burst under nitrogen testing conditions.

Safety

Dry nitrogen is the only gas to be used in the air-conditioning system for leak detecting and removing traces of flushing chemicals from the system. Using any other gas may cause harm and damage. Dry nitrogen is an inert gas and will not explode or ignite when in contact with other gases such as compressed air and oxygen.

Reclaiming and Recovering the Air-Conditioning System

Any time the air-conditioning system needs to be opened up, the refrigerant must be removed so that refrigerant will not be released into the atmosphere. Removing refrigerant is called **reclaiming** or **recovering**. The reclaiming process uses the air-conditioning machine to remove refrigerant from the system. It is also a good method of measuring the existing refriger-

SKILL DRILL 52-7 Performing Nitrogen Testing to Find a Leak

1. The air-conditioning system needs to be reclaimed of all refrigerant. See Skill Drill 52-8 to perform this procedure.
2. Attach the nitrogen hose of the nitrogen bottle to the low- or high-side service port on the vehicle. Once the quick coupler on the nitrogen hose has been connected and the Schrader valve depressed, start the nitrogen leak test procedure.
3. Turn the regulator on the nitrogen tank to 100 psi (689 kPa). As the pressure in the system rises, look and listen for any leaks. If a leak is located, stop the process and repair the problem.
4. Turn the regulator on the nitrogen tank to 200 psi (1,379 kPa). When 200 psi (1,379 kPa) is reached, look for bulging hoses and listen for noises.
5. Turn the regulator on the nitrogen tank to 300 psi (2,068 kPa). Once 300 psi (2,068 kPa) is reached, let the system maintain that pressure for 1 minute. Do not exceed 350 psi (2,413 kPa); doing so could cause the high-pressure relief valve to vent.
6. After 1 minute, start to spray the leak solution on all of the fittings, hoses, and air-conditioning system components. After spraying the leak solution on the air-conditioning system, it may take upwards of 20 minutes for a leak to present itself.
7. After the nitrogen test is finished, release the nitrogen to the atmosphere. Repair the leak.

ant charge in a vehicle, which will verify whether the system was undercharged, overcharged, or properly charged. The air-conditioning machine can measure the amount of refrigerant recovered from the vehicle. Comparing the amount removed to the specified capacity will allow you to determine the charge status. Another reason to recover refrigerant from a vehicle is to remove any noncondensable gases that are mixed in with the refrigerant.

To perform the reclaim process, follow the steps in **SKILL DRILL 52-8**.

> **TECHNICIAN TIP**
>
> The amount of refrigerant removed will give insight into the condition of the vehicle's air-conditioning system. Compare the weight removed to the under-the-hood sticker amount. If the amount recovered is less than the sticker indicates, there is likely a leak in the system. If there is more than the sticker indicates, then the system is overcharged. If it had the correct amount of refrigerant, then the system most likely has no leaks.

Recycling, Labeling, and Storing Refrigerant

In certain situations, the air-conditioning machine may become full of refrigerant. This will prevent you from recovering any more air-conditioning systems. Removing the refrigerant and storing the refrigerant in an approved container will allow the air-conditioning machine to continue to be used. The refrigerant tank cannot be the virgin disposable tank that the new refrigerant came in. The new virgin refrigerant tanks are a one-use-only tank and have a one-way check valve in the valve stem to prevent refilling of the tank.

To recycle refrigerant, follow the steps in **SKILL DRILL 52-9**.

> **TECHNICIAN TIP**
>
> Recycling refrigerant is one of the processes the air-conditioning machine can perform. After reclaiming the refrigerant, most air-conditioning machines automatically recycle the refrigerant. The filter system in the machine will return the refrigerant to a level of purity accepted by the EPA.

SKILL DRILL 52-8 Reclaiming and Recovering the Air-Conditioning System

1. Identify the refrigerant using the refrigerant identifier, and verify that there is no sealer in the system.
2. Start the reclaim process by hooking up the air-conditioning machine to the low- and high-side service ports.
3. Open the valves and turn on the air-conditioning machine. Select the reclaim mode and follow the prompts on the screen.
4. When the refrigerant has been removed, record the amount and compare it to the sticker on the vehicle.
5. The air-conditioning machine will drain any excess oil that might have been reclaimed. The refrigerant oil that is drained should be minimal or nonexistent. Record the amount of oil that is discharged, and install the same amount if the total oil removed is less than 30 mL. If the oil drain discharges more than 30 mL, the air-conditioning system will need to be flushed using a flush machine, removing all of the oil from the system.
6. After the old oil is flushed, reinstall the proper amount of new oil to the system.

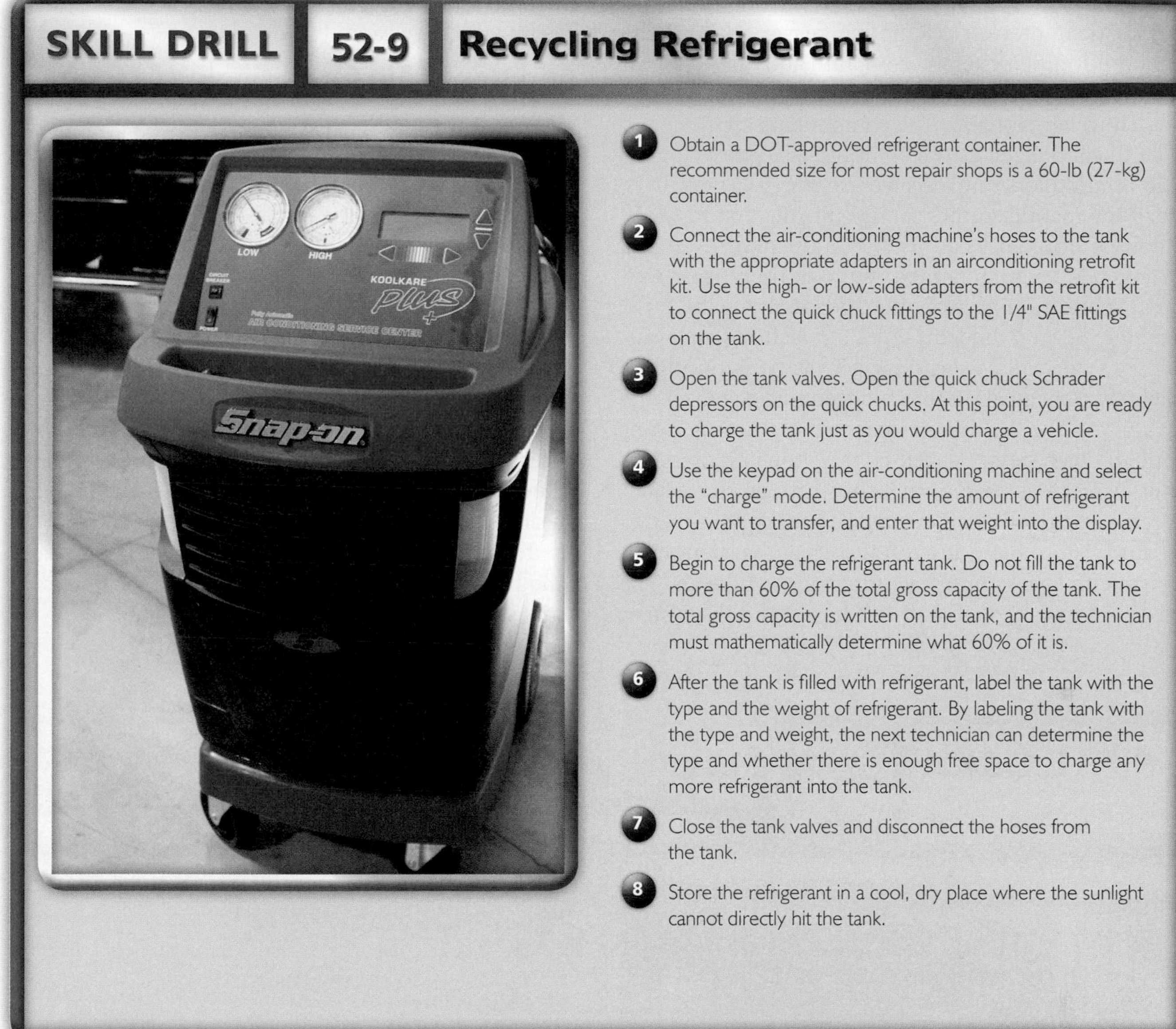

SKILL DRILL 52-9 Recycling Refrigerant

1. Obtain a DOT-approved refrigerant container. The recommended size for most repair shops is a 60-lb (27-kg) container.
2. Connect the air-conditioning machine's hoses to the tank with the appropriate adapters in an airconditioning retrofit kit. Use the high- or low-side adapters from the retrofit kit to connect the quick chuck fittings to the 1/4" SAE fittings on the tank.
3. Open the tank valves. Open the quick chuck Schrader depressors on the quick chucks. At this point, you are ready to charge the tank just as you would charge a vehicle.
4. Use the keypad on the air-conditioning machine and select the "charge" mode. Determine the amount of refrigerant you want to transfer, and enter that weight into the display.
5. Begin to charge the refrigerant tank. Do not fill the tank to more than 60% of the total gross capacity of the tank. The total gross capacity is written on the tank, and the technician must mathematically determine what 60% of it is.
6. After the tank is filled with refrigerant, label the tank with the type and the weight of refrigerant. By labeling the tank with the type and weight, the next technician can determine the type and whether there is enough free space to charge any more refrigerant into the tank.
7. Close the tank valves and disconnect the hoses from the tank.
8. Store the refrigerant in a cool, dry place where the sunlight cannot directly hit the tank.

Inspecting the Condition of Removed Refrigerant Oil

After the reclaim process, the air-conditioning machine will deposit any oil removed during the reclaim into a graduated container on the machine. By measuring the amount of oil removed, the technician will know exactly how much oil needs to be put back into the system. Only new oil should be installed.

Now that the air-conditioning system has been diagnosed and tested, the system fault can be repaired. Take the appropriate action and precautions that the repair requires. Finish the repair and continue to the evacuation.

> **TECHNICIAN TIP**
>
> **As a refrigeration technician, it is your responsibility to read the O-ring package and make sure the O-rings you are using are compatible with the type of refrigerant you are using.**

Air-Conditioning System Flush

The air-conditioning system should be flushed if the compressor comes apart or if the desiccant bag breaks open. In both of these situations, the loose parts or desiccant pellets will start to move through the system, causing blockages. Another reason to flush the air-conditioning system is contaminated oil. A special flush machine is used to flush the air-conditioning system. However, not all of the components are designed to be flushed, such as the compressor, orifice tube or TXV, accumulator, and receiver filter dryer. Be sure to check the manufacturer's service information to verify which components can safely be flushed. After the system has been reclaimed, remove the hoses from the air-conditioning machine and hook up the flush machine. Several different types of machines are available, but normally a cleaning agent is poured into the machine, then an air hose is plugged into the machine. A valve on the machine releases the cleaning agent through the system, pushed by the shop's air pressure. Another valve is used to push air through the system to remove the cleaning agent. Some shops prefer to use nitrogen to blow any residual cleaning agent from the system, as it contains no moisture, unlike air. The system is now ready to have oil added and the system recharged. Follow the instructions provided with the flushing machine carefully.

Additional Air-Conditioning Filters

While thoroughly flushing a system usually removes all debris and contaminants, it is possible that small particles can be wedged or trapped in place. Installing an additional filter provides an extra level of protection for the compressor and expansion valve or orifice tube. Additional filters are designed to catch a small amount of debris that may still be in the system, not to substitute for an adequate flush. Additional filters are generally placed in the liquid line after the condenser, but before the restriction. Any straight section of tubing between these two points can be used. The proper amount of tubing is cut out of the system so that the filter can be installed in the line. Always follow the filter manufacturer's directions when cutting the air-conditioning lines and installing the filter.

To determine the need for an additional air-conditioning system filter and to perform the necessary actions, follow the steps in **SKILL DRILL 52-10**.

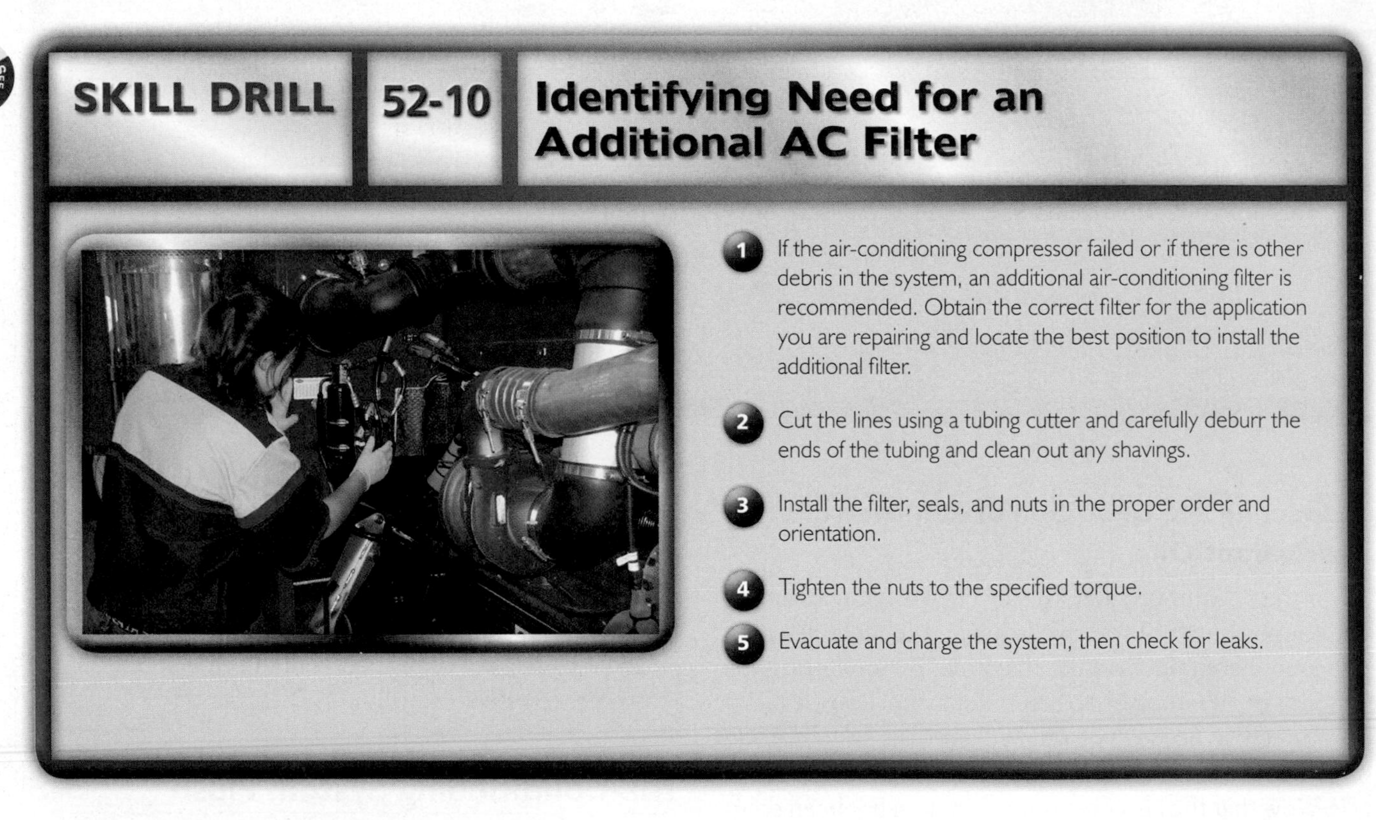

SKILL DRILL 52-10 Identifying Need for an Additional AC Filter

1. If the air-conditioning compressor failed or if there is other debris in the system, an additional air-conditioning filter is recommended. Obtain the correct filter for the application you are repairing and locate the best position to install the additional filter.
2. Cut the lines using a tubing cutter and carefully deburr the ends of the tubing and clean out any shavings.
3. Install the filter, seals, and nuts in the proper order and orientation.
4. Tighten the nuts to the specified torque.
5. Evacuate and charge the system, then check for leaks.

Inspecting and Replacing a Drive Belt

Inspecting the drive belt of the compressor is an important part of air-conditioning maintenance and repair. If the belt is worn, the engine cannot drive the compressor properly. On hot days, the refrigerant pressures are high and the compressor needs an effective drive belt to prevent slipping and causing excessive heat buildup around the clutch. The air-conditioning system requires that the compressor move the refrigerant at the correct velocity for the cooling of the passenger compartment to be at its peak efficiency. The drive belt is the first link in the system and needs to be in good condition and proper tension to ensure efficient air conditioning.

Inspecting, Testing, and Replacing the Compressor Clutch

Testing of the clutch assembly should occur when the air-conditioning pressure is high enough to turn on the clutch, but the clutch is not coming on or is not staying on. Typically, this component is checked using a DVOM. The technician needs to determine whether the clutch coil is receiving full power and ground. If it is, but still will not turn on, then the clutch coil should be checked for high resistance. If the resistance is too high according to the service information, it needs to be replaced. This number is usually 3–5 ohms. If full power and ground are not present, then wiring and switches need to be inspected and tested according to the wiring diagram.

The air gap is the space between the clutch assembly and the air-conditioning pulley. This gap needs to be checked to be sure it is correct according to specifications in the service information. If the gap is too small, the clutch will drag on the pulley, creating heat and ruining the clutch. If the gap is too large, the coil will not be able to create a strong enough magnetic pull to pull the clutch in and hold it against the pulley, or it will pull it in but will not be able to hold it in place when the engine's rpm are raised. A voltage drop in the electrical circuit that energizes the clutch coil may also prevent the compressor clutch from engaging. If it does engage, it will not be able to grip tightly enough and will begin to slip, creating heat and scoring the clutch surface.

> **TECHNICIAN TIP**
>
> A brown dust on the air-conditioning compressor clutch indicates that there is slippage that could be caused by low voltage and current to the compressor clutch circuit. Slippage could also be caused by the clutch clearance being set too large.

An air-conditioning compressor pulley or bearing may need service when noise is detected from the bearing as the engine is running. The pulley spins at all times when the engine is running and the bearing may fail and make noise. If the bearing has failed, then the pulley will have to be removed. When replacing the compressor clutch, the pulley will need to be removed as well.

> **TECHNICIAN TIP**
>
> Removing the air-conditioning compressor clutch requires special tools. Each type of compressor clutch has its own mechanism and tools necessary for removal. Before attempting to remove the air-conditioning compressor clutch on the air-conditioning compressor, make sure you follow the manufacturer's safety procedures and use the proper tools for the job.

To inspect, test, and replace the compressor clutch, follow the steps in **SKILL DRILL 52-11**.

Removing, Inspecting, and Reinstalling the Compressor

The compressor needs to be inspected any time there is a compressor failure or leaks are suspected.

To remove, inspect, and reinstall the compressor, follow the steps in **SKILL DRILL 52-12**.

Removing and Inspecting Air-Conditioning Mufflers, Hoses, Lines, and Fittings

The removal of hoses and lines is done for replacement purposes or to access another component. Some lines have male and female threaded ends that bolt together,

SKILL DRILL 52-11 Inspecting, Testing, and Replacing the Compressor Clutch

1. Inspect the air gap of the clutch. With the clutch disengaged, use feeler gauges to measure the air gap between the **drive pulley** and the clutch drive plate. If the air gap is too small, follow the manufacturer's procedure to adjust the air gap.

2. If the air gap is too large, check to see whether the pulley bearing is worn, causing the pulley to wobble and make contact with the clutch. The system should also be checked electrically using a DVOM to ensure that the clutch coil is not being energized or partially energized when it should not be. (Typically, this situation is caused by a rewiring of the system following an improper diagnosis.) Too large of an air gap is most likely caused by excessive wear of the clutch and usually requires replacement.

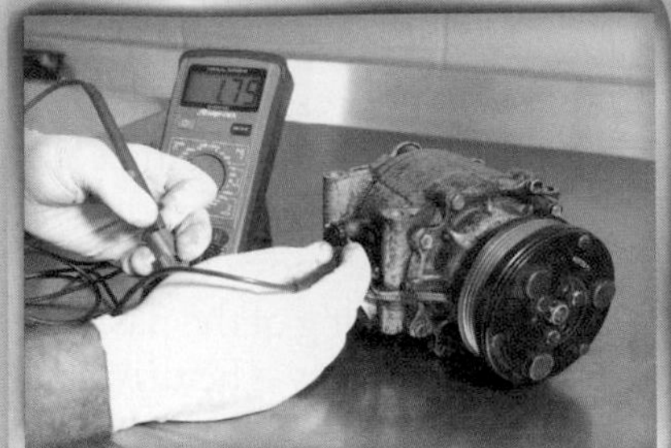

3. To check the condition of the electrical circuit, perform an amperage test to the compressor clutch. Measure the vehicle's voltage and clutch resistance (12-volt clutch resistance typically should be 3–5 ohms). Measure the amperage and compare the readings to the calculation. If the readings are in specification, adjust the clutch air gap. If the amperage is out of specification, diagnose the electrical system and replace the clutch.

4. Remove the clutch plate center bolt or nut. If the compressor uses shims, be careful to remove these for later use.

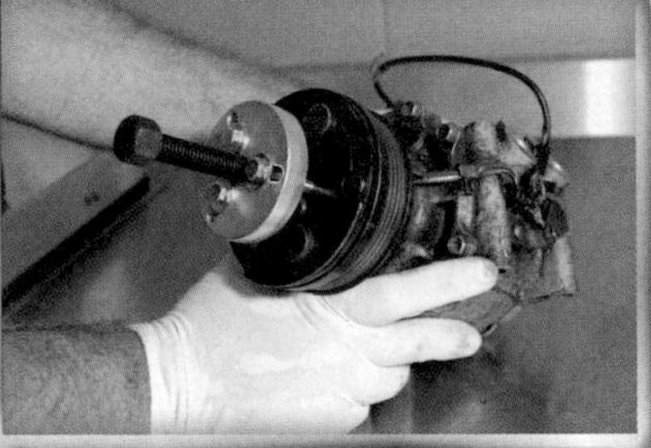

5. Using the appropriate puller, remove the clutch plate.

6. Remove the pulley snap ring, and slide the pulley and bearing off the compressor.

Continued on next page

SKILL DRILL 52-11 Inspecting, Testing, and Replacing the Compressor Clutch, continued

7 Remove the snap ring from the compressor clutch coil, and pull from compressor.

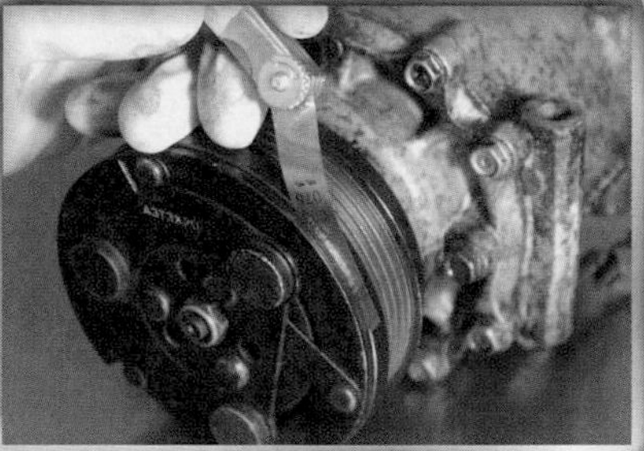

8 Reinstall the components in reverse order. When reinstalling the clutch plate, be sure to adjust the air gap (typical air gap will be 0.012" to 0.025" [0.03 to 0.06 mm]). Check specifications in your service information for the correct air gap.

9 Torque the center bolt or nut to specifications.

SKILL DRILL 52-12 Removing, Inspecting, and Reinstalling the Compressor

1 Reclaim the refrigerant, making note of the amount removed. Compare this amount to the factory specifications. Remove the belt using a serpentine belt tool or the proper wrench. Remove tension from the tensioner and slide the belt off, noting routing for reinstallation.

2 Remove the hoses from the air-conditioning system. Cap the lines.

3 Unplug the compressor clutch.

Continued on next page

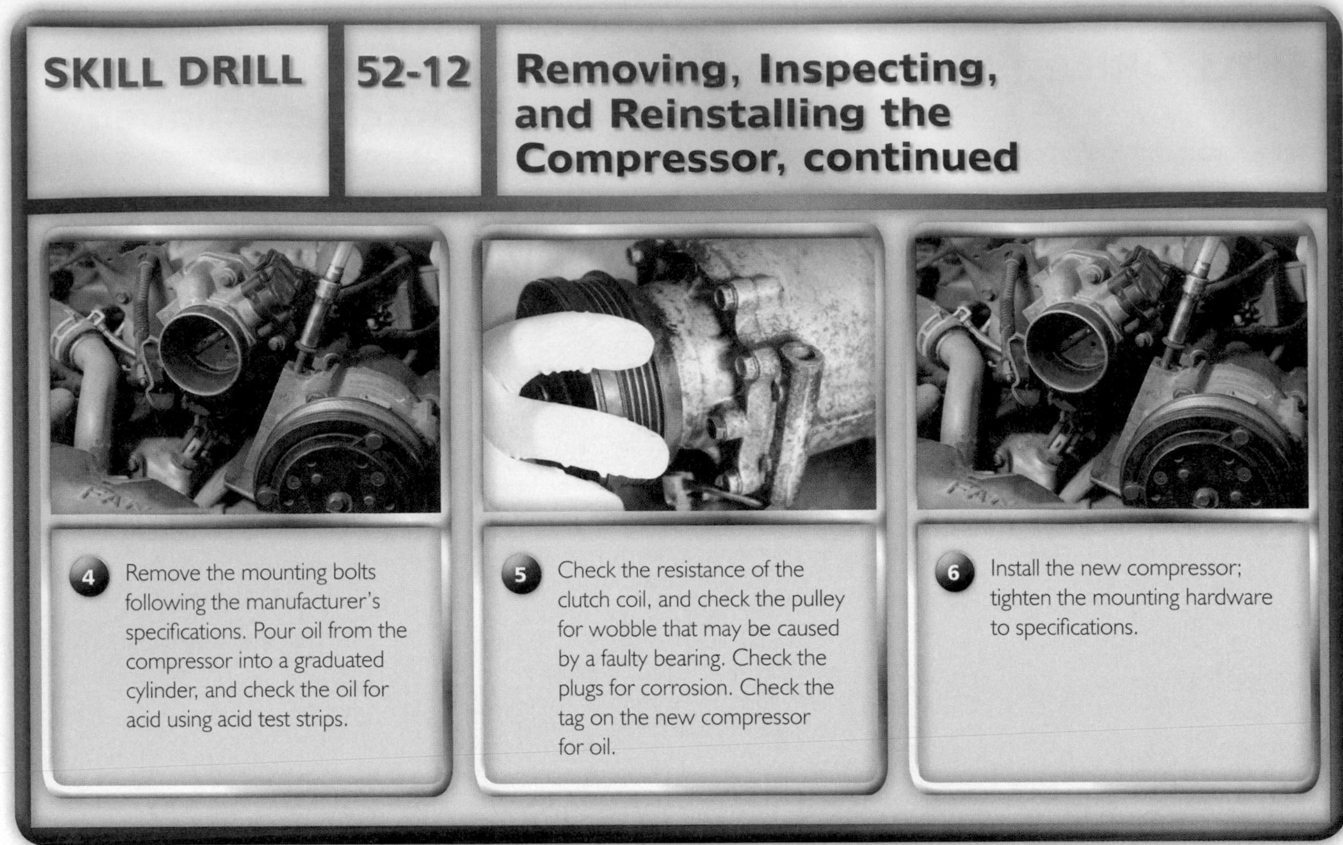

while others use retainer springs to snap them together. If the hoses are bolted together, line wrenches are used. If they use a spring lock, there is a spring lock release tool that comes in different sizes for different-sized lines. The spring lock tool goes between the fittings and spreads the spring so that the lines can be pulled apart. Any time lines are loosened, the **O-rings** in the fittings must be replaced or there is potential for leaks.

SKILL DRILL
52-12
Removing, Inspecting, and Reinstalling the Compressor, continued
4 Remove the mounting bolts following the manufacturer's specifications. Pour oil from the compressor into a graduated cylinder, and check the oil for acid using acid test strips.
5 Check the resistance of the clutch coil, and check the pulley for wobble that may be caused by a faulty bearing. Check the plugs for corrosion. Check the tag on the new compressor for oil.
6 Install the new compressor; tighten the mounting hardware to specifications.

To remove and inspect air-conditioning **mufflers**, hoses, lines, and fittings, follow the steps in SKILL DRILL 52-13.

Removing, Inspecting, and Reinstalling the Condenser

The condenser may be removed to access the radiator or if replacing the condenser because it is plugged, damaged, or leaks. Since the condenser sits in the front of the vehicle, it is damaged quite often in wrecks or by debris flying off the road. It may also have to be removed on some vans for engine removal. Some basic hand tools are necessary as well as wrenches or spring clip removal tools. The process for removing the condenser varies by vehicle type, make, and model. Refer to the service information for specific steps. Also refer to the service information to determine how much oil is needed.

To remove, inspect, and reinstall a condenser, follow the steps in SKILL DRILL 52-14.

Removing, Inspecting, and Installing the Receiver/Dryer or Accumulator

The receiver/dryer or **accumulator** needs to be removed and inspected whenever there are leaks or the desiccant is failing to dry the refrigerant. Desiccant failures arise when the system is left open for long periods of time and the desiccant absorbs too much moisture. It can also occur if the desiccant bag ruptures and desiccant

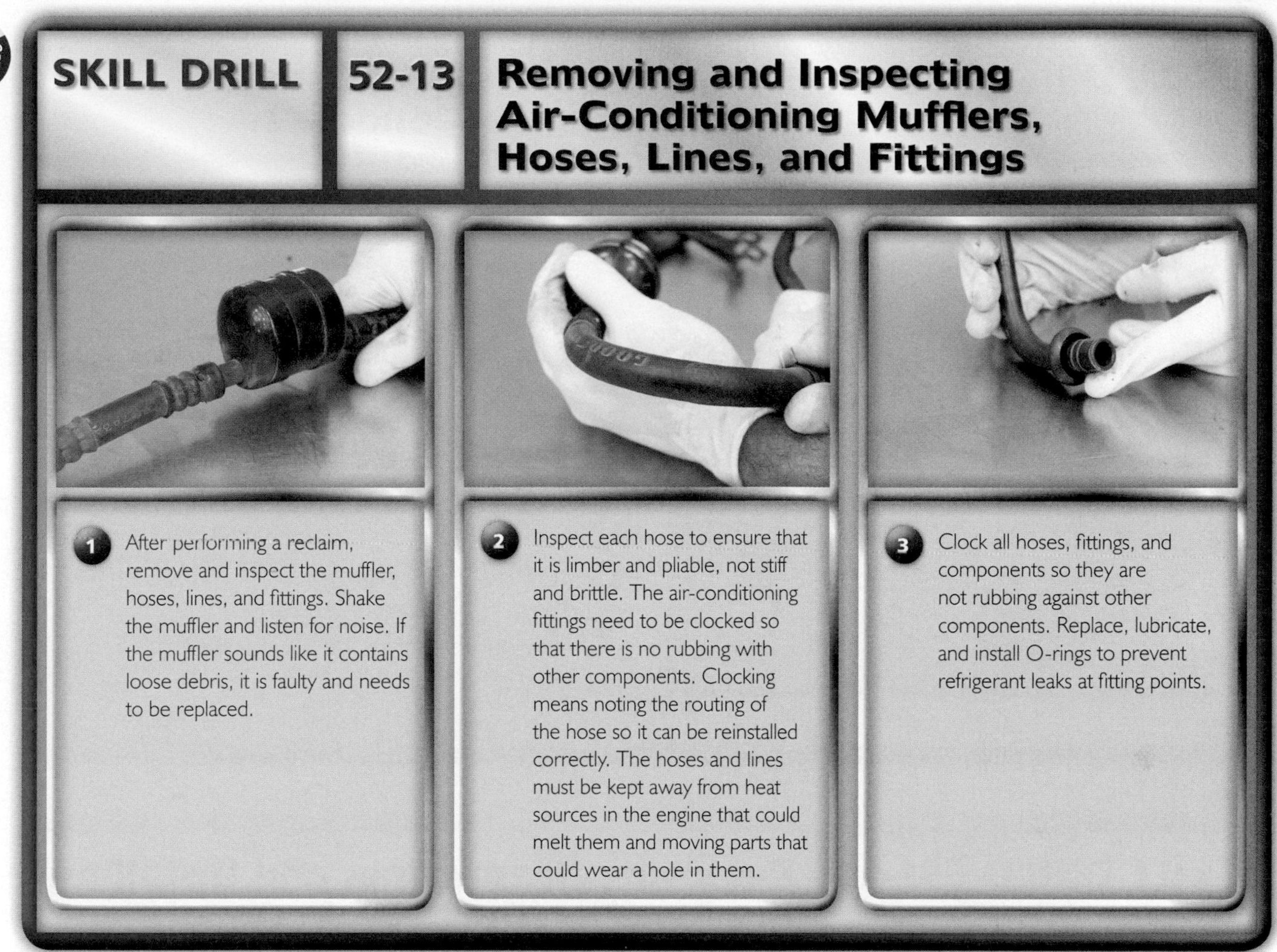

has entered the rest of the system or if the compressor has come apart internally. Refer to the service information of the vehicle for the specific procedure. Also refer to the service information to determine the amount of oil needed.

SKILL DRILL 52-13 Removing and Inspecting Air-Conditioning Mufflers, Hoses, Lines, and Fittings
1 After performing a reclaim, remove and inspect the muffler, hoses, lines, and fittings. Shake the muffler and listen for noise. If the muffler sounds like it contains loose debris, it is faulty and needs to be replaced.
2 Inspect each hose to ensure that it is limber and pliable, not stiff and brittle. The air-conditioning fittings need to be clocked so that there is no rubbing with other components. Clocking means noting the routing of the hose so it can be reinstalled correctly. The hoses and lines must be kept away from heat sources in the engine that could melt them and moving parts that could wear a hole in them.
3 Clock all hoses, fittings, and components so they are not rubbing against other components. Replace, lubricate, and install O-rings to prevent refrigerant leaks at fitting points.

To remove, inspect, and install the receiver/dryer or accumulator/dryer, follow the steps in SKILL DRILL 52-15.

Removing, Inspecting, and Installing a TXV

A TXV would be removed for inspection if the diagnostic process led to the TXV being stuck open or closed, which would be determined by gauge pressures and air-conditioning performance. If stuck open, the high-side pressures would be low and the low-side pressures would be high. If stuck closed, the high-side pressures would be high and the low-side pressures would be low and could even go into a vacuum.

When working with the expansion valve, caution must be used in all aspects of the removal and installation of the valve. Typically, the TXV is mounted on the front of the evaporator. When removing and installing the inlet and outlet lines to the evaporator, a line wrench must be used so the nuts or bolts are not damaged or rounded off. A second wrench is used to hold the other end of the line so you do not twist it and break it off. One nut will be on the line; the other nut will be on the

SKILL DRILL 52-14 Removing, Inspecting, and Reinstalling the Condenser

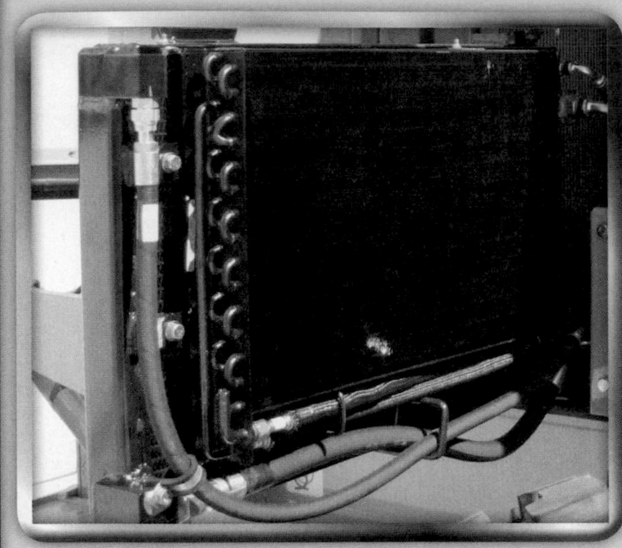

1. After reclaiming the air-conditioning system, remove all necessary components to access the condenser. This may include removing the grill, radiator, fans and coverings. Refer to the manufacturer's specific procedures on component removal.
2. Remove the inlet and outlet lines on the condenser.
3. Remove the hold-down bolts for the condenser.
4. Install the new condenser. Fasten the condenser with the mounting hardware.
5. Install new O-rings on the air-conditioning lines.
6. Install the inlet and outlet lines.
7. Replace all of the components in reverse order from removal. Evacuate the air-conditioning system if all other air-conditioning repairs are complete.

SKILL DRILL 52-15 Removing, Inspecting, and Installing the Receiver/Dryer or Accumulator

1. After reclaiming the air-conditioning system, remove the inlet and outlet lines from the receiver/dryer or the accumulator.
2. Remove the mounting clamps from the receiver/dryer or accumulator; remove the receiver/dryer or accumulator.
3. Lubricate and install new O-rings on both the inlet and the outlet lines.
4. Install the new receiver/dryer or accumulator and tighten the clamps. Install the inlet and outlet lines.
5. Proceed to the evacuation if all other repairs were made.

TXV. Twist the nut on the line and hold the nut on the TXV so as not to deform or break the TXV. A backup wrench on the expansion valve must be used also. The lines from the evaporator are aluminum, and the fittings are typically brass, so the use of an open-ended wrench will distort the brass and cause the fitting to leak. The exact procedure for removing, inspecting, and installing a TXV varies widely from vehicle to vehicle and by TXV manufacturer. Refer to the service information for the precise process.

To remove, inspect, and install a TXV, follow the steps in SKILL DRILL 52-16.

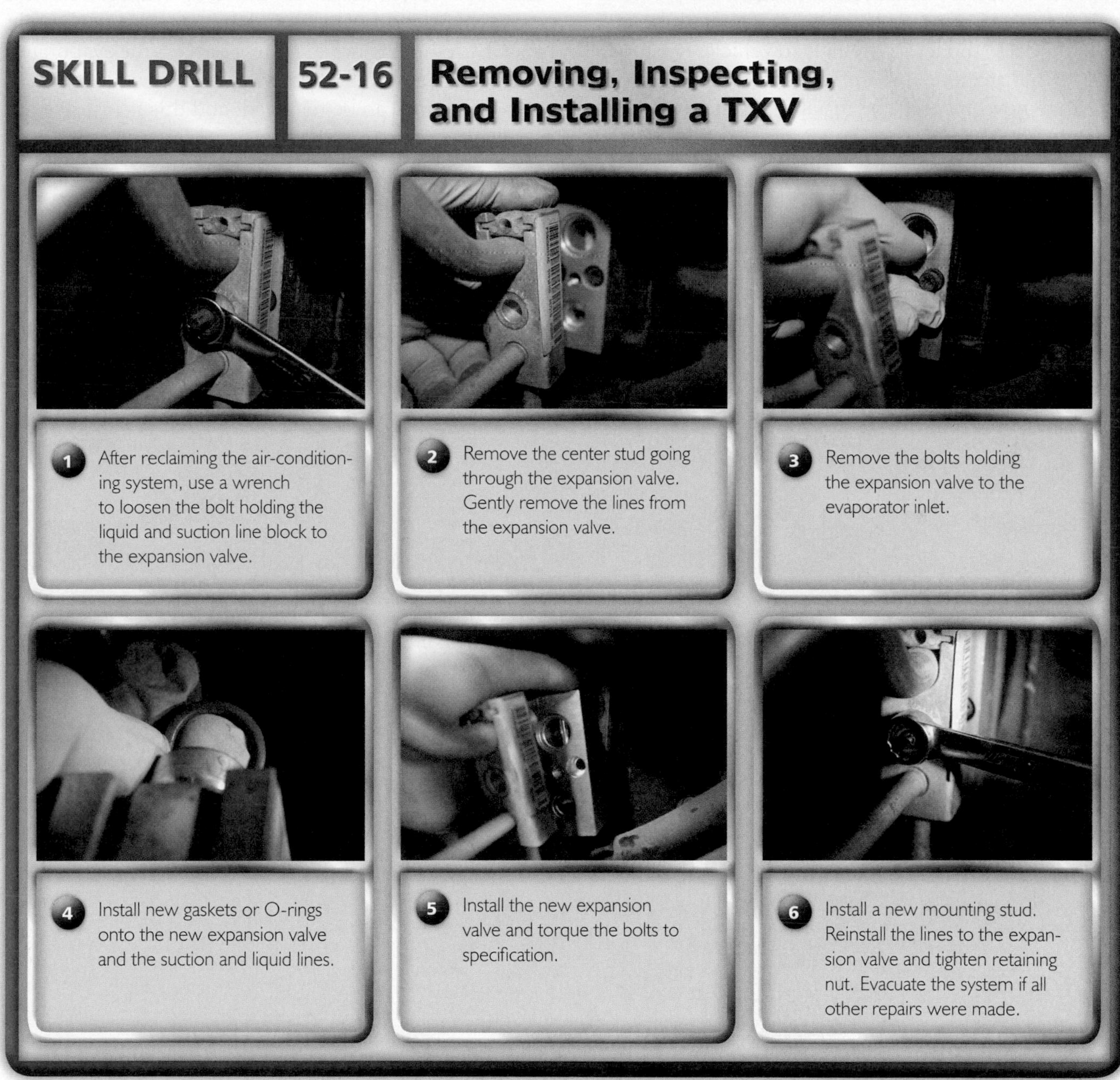

SKILL DRILL 52-16 Removing, Inspecting, and Installing a TXV
1 After reclaiming the air-conditioning system, use a wrench to loosen the bolt holding the liquid and suction line block to the expansion valve.
2 Remove the center stud going through the expansion valve. Gently remove the lines from the expansion valve.
3 Remove the bolts holding the expansion valve to the evaporator inlet.
4 Install new gaskets or O-rings onto the new expansion valve and the suction and liquid lines.
5 Install the new expansion valve and torque the bolts to specification.
6 Install a new mounting stud. Reinstall the lines to the expansion valve and tighten retaining nut. Evacuate the system if all other repairs were made.

Removing, Inspecting, and Installing an Orifice Tube

The orifice tube needs to be replaced when the same gauge readings as a blocked TXV are observed, as it can block up with debris in the system. It should also be replaced if the compressor comes apart because it can catch debris from the compressor and become clogged. The process for removing, inspecting, and installing an orifice tube varies from model to model and vehicle to vehicle. Refer to the service information for the precise procedure.

To remove, inspect, and install an orifice tube, follow the steps in **SKILL DRILL 52-17**.

Removing, Inspecting, and Reinstalling the Evaporator

Removal of the evaporator is typically done only if it is being replaced. Often, the entire dash assembly must be removed before the evaporator box can be accessed; therefore, many basic hand tools are required. Once the dash is removed, the air-conditioning evaporator box is unbolted from the vehicle, and then the case can be split open by removing more screws to access the evaporator. The lines in and out of the evaporator must be removed before the box can be removed, and this is just like the other lines. The procedure for removing the evaporator

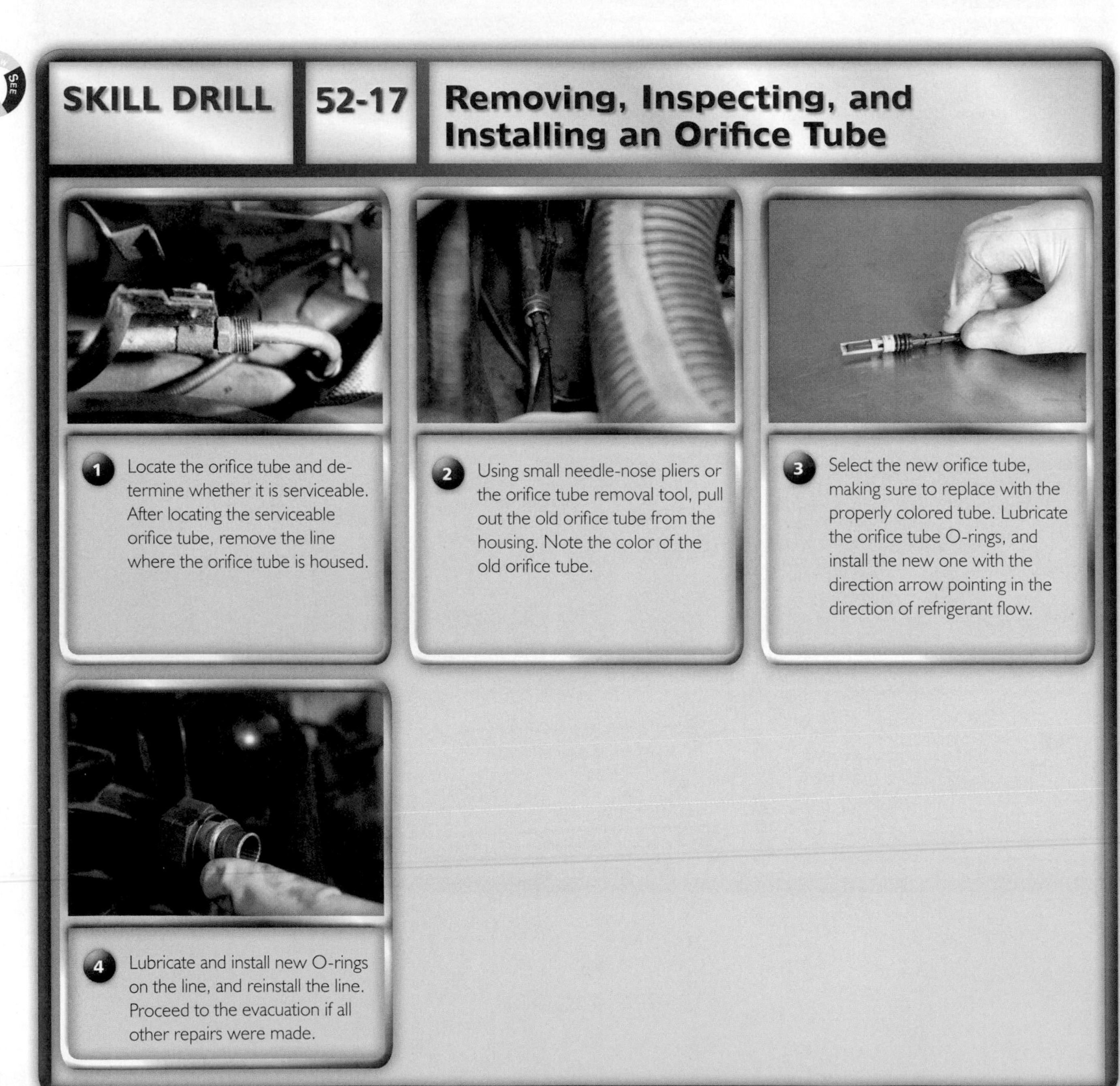
SKILL DRILL
52-17
Removing, Inspecting, and Installing an Orifice Tube
1 Locate the orifice tube and determine whether it is serviceable. After locating the serviceable orifice tube, remove the line where the orifice tube is housed.
2 Using small needle-nose pliers or the orifice tube removal tool, pull out the old orifice tube from the housing. Note the color of the old orifice tube.
3 Select the new orifice tube, making sure to replace with the properly colored tube. Lubricate the orifice tube O-rings, and install the new one with the direction arrow pointing in the direction of refrigerant flow.
4 Lubricate and install new O-rings on the line, and reinstall the line. Proceed to the evacuation if all other repairs were made.

varies greatly, as it is situated differently in each type of vehicle make and model. Refer to the service information for the particular vehicle for specific instructions. To remove, inspect, and reinstall the evaporator, you will need to follow the manufacturer's service information.

Evacuating the Air-Conditioning System

After all repairs are made, the air-conditioning system needs to be evacuated to remove all of the moisture from the air introduced into the lines from opening up the air-conditioning system. Evacuating the air-conditioning system requires either air-conditioning gauges and a vacuum pump or an air-conditioning machine. Either way, the process is the same. To remove moisture from the air-conditioning system, the pressure in the lines needs to be lowered with a vacuum pump. This pressure drop will lower the boiling point of the water in the air-conditioning system. When the system at sea level reaches a vacuum of 29.5" Hg (100 kPa), the boiling point will be lowered to 60°F (16°C). Since the boiling point is now lower than ambient air temperature, the moisture in the air-conditioning system's lines and components will boil. The vapor will be evacuated out of the air-conditioning system through the vacuum pump.

Evacuating the Air-Conditioning System Using a Vacuum Gauge

If an air-conditioning machine is unavailable, the air-conditioning system can be evacuated using air-conditioning gauges and a vacuum pump. The processes are essentially the same. When evacuating the air-conditioning system, the vacuum gauge readings need to be timed and watched. Whether a vacuum gauge or a micron gauge is being used, the time that it takes to achieve the boiling point pressure from a boiling point chart needs to be timed. The time it takes for the vacuum pump to pull down the air-conditioning system's pressure is important because there could still be small leaks that were not found during the leak test. These leaks will cause the time it takes to reach the boiling point to be longer than it should be.

When timing the vacuum gauge readings, you can use the timer on the air-conditioning machine. The time it should take to achieve the boiling point pressure at the ambient temperature with a 52-CFM pump or greater is 5 minutes. If the vacuum pump cannot pull the pressure in the air-conditioning system to the boiling point pressure in 5 minutes or less, the air-conditioning system has leaks that need to be found.

If using a mechanical vacuum gauge, once the air-conditioning system reaches the boiling point pressure, the vacuum pump needs to be left on the air-conditioning system for an additional 10 minutes to fully evacuate the air-conditioning system. You will notice that the default time for most air-conditioning machines is 15 minutes, which allows for the air-conditioning system to reach the boiling point and for the additional 10 minutes for the moisture to be removed.

To use a vacuum gauge to evacuate an air-conditioning system, follow the steps in SKILL DRILL 52-18.

Evacuating the Air-Conditioning System Using a Micron Gauge

The micron gauge is used in conjunction with the mechanical pressure gauge on your air-conditioning machine. They are able to measure vacuum very precisely. Where a vacuum gauge will have markings at 29" then 30" of vacuum, the micron gauge can measure accurately between 29" and 30" to determine exactly how well the system is being evacuated. Many vacuum pumps are measured in microns; the fewer microns it can go down to, the better. If you have two pumps and one can draw down to 500 microns and the other down to 25 microns, the second pump will do a better job of evacuating the system. Some air-conditioning machines will have a micron gauge built in. With the micron gauge, the pressure is measured in microns, or one-thousandths of 1 millimeter. To put it in perspective, in 1 inch, there are 25,400 microns. So, 0 microns equals a perfect vacuum (roughly 30" Hg), and 25,400 microns equals approximately 29" Hg. This super-fine measurement of vacuum allows you to read accurately enough to ensure that all of the moisture has been removed from the air-conditioning system.

When the micron gauge reaches 29" Hg, you still have 25,400 microns of mercury to obtain a perfect vacuum. A mechanical gauge is not accurate enough to see such small pressure movements. If using a micron gauge, watch until it hits 1,000 microns or less. A reading of 1,000 microns or less tells you that all the moisture is gone. The micron gauge should reach the boiling point of pressure within 5 minutes of turning on the pump. If it does not, then there is still a leak in the system.

To use a micron gauge to evacuate an air-conditioning system, follow the steps in SKILL DRILL 52-19.

> **TECHNICIAN TIP**
>
> If the micron does not hit 1,000 microns within the total vacuum time, then spin the clutch of the compressor and watch the pressure gauge. If the pressure rises, the clutch seal is faulty.

SKILL DRILL 52-18 Using a Vacuum Gauge to Evacuate an Air-Conditioning System

1. Hook up the high and the low side to the air-conditioning gauges.
2. Open the high- and low-side valves on the gauges.
3. Hook the pump to the center hose (normally a yellow hose), and turn on the pump.
4. After 20 minutes, turn off the pump and close the valves.
5. Note the vacuum readings. The vacuum should be around 28" Hg or 29" Hg (95 or 98 kPa). Watch the gauges for 5 minutes to be sure the vacuum holds. If the vacuum drops off, there is a leak in the air-conditioning system.

SKILL DRILL 52-19 Using a Micron Gauge to Evacuate an Air-Conditioning System

1. Refer to the boiling point chart for the boiling point pressure in microns. Connect the gauge set and vacuum pump.
2. Turn the vacuum pump on to begin the evacuation process. Evacuate for a minimum of 15 minutes. Time the pressure gauge reading.
3. The pressure gauge should reach the boiling point pressure from the boiling point chart within 5 minutes.
4. If the pressure gauge hits the pressure within 5 minutes, continue to allow the machine to evacuate the air-conditioning system until the micron gauge reaches 1,000 microns. When the micron gauge reaches 1,000 microns, the air-conditioning system is moisture free.

Determining Recommended Oil and Capacity

The refrigerant R-134a uses a polyalkylene glycol (PAG) oil. Each individual air-conditioning system will have a capacity of a specific oil. Often, if you replace just one component, the capacity chart will list how much oil should be replaced for that particular component. Unless the entire system is replaced, some oil will remain in the system. Read the manufacturer's service information for specific instructions.

> **TECHNICIAN TIP**
>
> When using a micron gauge, keep an eye on the numbers as they drop. The micron gauge may hover around 1,300. When the numbers hover at 1,300 microns, the air-conditioning system is boiling off moisture. Pay close attention at this point. If the numbers drop from 1,300 to 1,200 to 1,100 to 1,000, the air-conditioning system is okay. If the numbers fall from 1,300 directly to 1,000 and below, the moisture in the air-conditioning system just froze. The freezing of moisture is due to the lack of heat around the air-conditioning system. If the pressure gauge falls from 1,300 to 1,000 instantly, the vehicle needs to be moved to a warmer environment. The freezing of water in a vacuum cycle becomes a problem around an ambient temperature of 60°F (16°C) and below.

Adding the Proper Oil Amount

Oil should be put back into the air-conditioning system after the evacuation cycle and while pressure is lower than atmospheric pressure in the air-conditioning system. The oiler uses atmospheric pressure to push oil into the air-conditioning system. The air-conditioning system is still at a vacuum state. Since pressure in a vacuum is less than pressure outside, the oil is easily pulled in by the low pressure or vacuum. What actually happens is that the pressures try to equalize. If you have oil in the hose that is allowing outside pressure into the vacuum or lower pressure, the higher pressure pushes the oil in as it tries to equalize pressures. Most air-conditioning machines have a port that a special graduated cylinder screws into. When the port is opened with the cylinder attached, the pressure equalization forces the oil in.

To add oil to the air-conditioning system, follow the steps in **SKILL DRILL 52-20**.

Charging the Air-Conditioning System

Charging a system is performed after the air-conditioning system has been evacuated and any oil is replaced. The only tool needed is a refrigerant charging unit, with the correct type and amount of refrigerant in it. Charge the air-conditioning system to the proper factory level by reading the engine compartment decal or obtaining the amount from the manufacturer.

Refrigerant Equipment Maintenance

Regular maintenance prompts may appear as you use the air-conditioning machine. If they do, then follow the instructions on the screen. When the air-conditioning machine alerts you that it needs service, you should contact the local service department for the machine.

> **TECHNICIAN TIP**
>
> Trying to charge gas to the high side with the air-conditioning system operating will result in the compressor pushing the refrigerant back into the pressure gauge set after the compressor engages. Once the compressor engages, you will be prevented from charging the air-conditioning system due to the high pressure generated from the compressor.

Vacuum pump oil is one of the regular maintenance items that you will be prompted to change after approximately each 10 hours of vacuum use. Vacuum pump oil can be changed by the shop technician. Failure to change the oil will result in increased pump wear, as well as causing the pump to not be able to draw as deep of a vacuum. Changing the pump oil regularly will extend the life of the pump and make it reach maximum vacuum quicker. You will need a drain pan for the old oil and new vacuum pump oil for the pump.

To change the vacuum pump oil in an air-conditioning machine, follow the steps in **SKILL DRILL 52-21**.

SKILL DRILL 52-20 Adding Oil to the Air-Conditioning System

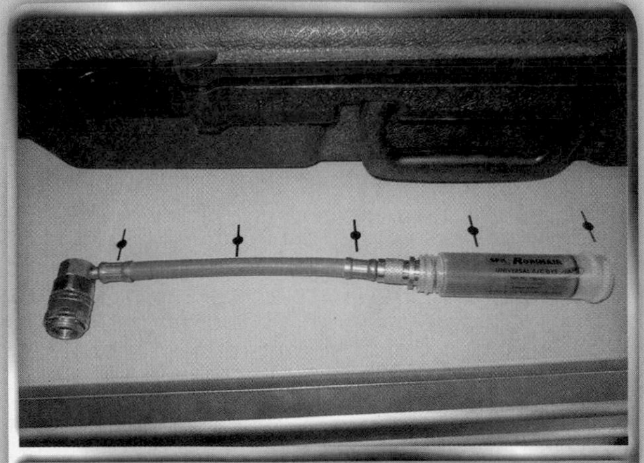

1. Evacuate the air-conditioning system and watch the vacuum gauge to ensure that it does not bleed up. If no leaks appear after 5 minutes, install the oil. Open the oiling valve as recommended by the air-conditioning machine information.

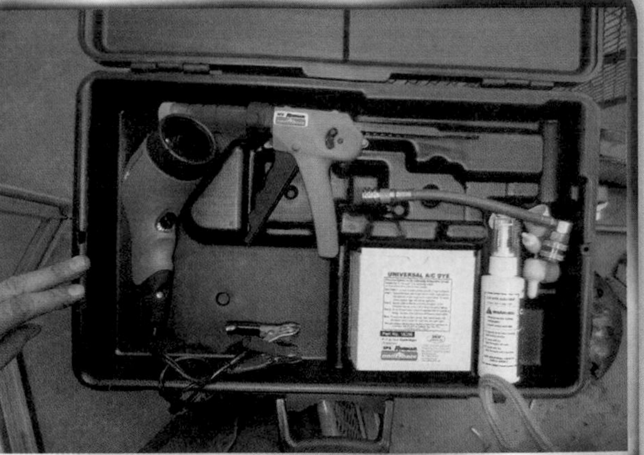

2. Shut off the valve when the proper amount of oil has been added. Recharge the air-conditioning system with the amount of refrigerant noted on the under-the-hood air-conditioning sticker or in the service information.

SKILL DRILL 52-21 Changing Vacuum Pump Oil

1. When it is time to change the vacuum pump oil, the machine will warm up the oil so it is easier to drain. In most machines, the vacuum pump is behind a cover inside of the air-conditioning machine, which must be removed before use. Remove the drain plug and drain the oil.

2. Refer to the air-conditioning machine user manual to find out what type and how much oil to install. Remove the fill plug, install the drain plug, and tighten. The fill plug will be near the top, but not normally all the way on the top. Use a funnel to add the new oil.

3. Turn on the pump and check for leaks. Check that the oil level is halfway up the sight glass. If under the halfway mark, add oil. If over, drain some oil, Recheck. Reinstall the fill plug and check for leaks.

> **TECHNICIAN TIP**
>
> Before charging the air-conditioning system, be sure to have a minimum of 5 lb (2.3 kg) plus your charge amount in the air-conditioning machine. Any less refrigerant than 5 lb will cause an insufficient refrigerant prompt on the air-conditioning machine. If this occurs, you will need to reclaim the air-conditioning system and add refrigerant to the air-conditioning machine.

Inspecting and Testing the Heater Control Valves

The heater control valves should be tested if the customer complains of no heat or poor air conditioning. The heater control valve regulates coolant flow to the heater core for heat and limits flow for air conditioning. Some are vacuum controlled and some are cable controlled. Cable-controlled models must be checked to ensure that the cable is free and working. Air-controlled models should be checked to ensure that the air is supplied to the valve at the right time and that the valve will hold vacuum. If there is a problem with cable or air operation, then the control head in the dash will probably have to be removed, inspected, and repaired. If the cable or air is working, then the operation of the valve should be checked. Have someone move the temperature lever from hot to cold while watching the valve. If the cable or vacuum servo is moving the control arm on the valve, then the valve is probably okay and the problem is elsewhere in the system, although the valve could be plugged or slipping on the shaft. Therefore, you may have to remove it from the heater hose and visually inspect that the valve opens and closes.

Removing, Inspecting, and Reinstalling the Heater Core

Heater cores are usually removed only because leaks are present. Leaks from the heater core can result in coolant misting out of the vents or coolant dripping from the same drain hole used by the AC evaporator. Because this process is different for every model of vehicle, you will need to follow the steps in the vehicle manufacturer's service information. One thing to remember is that the heater core inlet and outlet tubes are made of thin metal and soldered into thin metal tanks. Twisting the heater hoses to get them off will almost always result in ripping the heater core tubes out of the tanks. Carefully use a hose slitter or knife to slit the hose lengthwise over the heater core tubes, and then peel the hoses off of the tubes.

Wrap-up

Ready for Review

- Technicians must be EPA 609 certified to handle refrigerants.
- Performance testing of the air-conditioning system is one of the first steps in diagnosis.
- A performance test involves external cooling for the condenser, running the engine between 1,100–1,500 rpm, placing the air-conditioning on max cold, the fan on high, and measuring the duct temperature, and then comparing the duct temperature to a system performance chart from the manufacturer.
- Servicing the air-conditioning system involves performance testing the system, diagnosing any issues, leak testing, identifying the refrigerant, reclaiming the refrigerant, performing any repairs, evacuating the system, recharging, retesting for leaks, and performance testing.
- Identifying refrigerant helps avoid mixing refrigerants, which cannot be reused and must be stored separately.
- An undercharged air-conditioning system contains less refrigerant than the system calls for.
- The one rule for diagnosis of an air-conditioning system is "when in doubt, suck it out."
- The compressor is the most common source of abnormal noises arising from the air conditioner.
- If the high-side pressures are too high and the system is not cooling well, check the air flow through the condenser.
- Clearing the drain hose can clear up odors. If this does not work, an anti-odor kit may be required.
- Confirm the refrigerant in the system by using a refrigerant identifier.
- The air distribution system is designed to circulate air through the heating and cooling system, then into the passenger cabin.
- Charge refers to the amount of refrigerant in the air-conditioning system.
- Components of a heating system include: radiator, thermostat, water pump, upper and lower radiator hoses, heater core, and heater control valve.
- Steps to the diagnosis and repair of air-conditioning systems are pretest and inspection, leak test, reclaiming refrigerant, problem repair, evacuation, charging, and post-testing.
- Problems with air-conditioning system performance may be due to system leaks, compressor failure, or system blockages.
- Variable factors, such as weather, air moisture content, temperature, condition and type of vehicle, and color and size of vehicle, all affect air-conditioning system functioning.
- Air-conditioning performance testing should be done before and after a repair.
- Air-conditioning system inspection should include possible condenser airflow restrictions, evaporator housing water drain, air filter, hoses and belts, coolant pressure, radiator cap vacuum and pressure, cooling fan, fan clutch, fan shroud, air dams, and heater control valves.
- Air-conditioning systems are equipped with protective devices designed to shut down the system if refrigerant pressures are too high or low.
- Tools needed to maintain and repair air-conditioning systems include: sealant detector, reclaim/recycle machine, refrigerant identifiers, pressure gauge sets, air-conditioning machine, anemometer, retro fit kit, pressure-temperature chart, vacuum pump, electronic leak detector, dye leak detector, oiler, vacuum gauge, micron gauge, and line wrench.
- Methods of leak testing are detector testing, dye testing, and nitrogen testing.
- Any time the air-conditioning system is opened, the refrigerant must be recovered (reclaimed).
- The air-conditioning system should be flushed if the compressor comes apart, the desiccant bag breaks open, or the oil is contaminated.
- Following a repair, the air-conditioning system should be evacuated via an air-conditioning machine or air-conditioning gauges and a vacuum pump.

Vocabulary Builder

accumulator A device placed between the evaporator and the compressor to collect liquid refrigerant and prevent it from entering the compressor.

air-conditioning compressor clutch An engagement device connected to the compressor crankshaft to engage the crankshaft with a belt-driven pulley.

air-conditioning machine A machine designed to recover, recycle, evacuate, leak test, and recharge (R/R/R) the air-conditioning system.

anemometer A device that measures airflow in feet per minute (fpm).

charge The amount of refrigerant present in the system or the process of installing refrigerant in the system.

drive pulley Any belt-driven pulley used to power an accessory such as power steering or the air-conditioning compressor.

hose Flexible line used to direct liquids or gases.

lines Term used interchangeably with pipes or tubes.

manifold gauge set A set of calibrated gauges for high and low pressure that can show pressure and vacuum readings for use with air-conditioning systems.

micron gauge A device designed to measure vacuum very precisely.

muffler A device to quiet the pipes of the air-conditioning system with baffles placed inside to deaden the sound of refrigerant moving.

oiler A device used to add oil to the air-conditioning system.

O-ring Rubber-type rings available in different sizes used to seal pipe fittings.

overcharging Overfilling of the air-conditioning system; may result in poor cooling or mechanical failure of the system.

performance testing The process of recreating a driving situation to check air-conditioning performance and vent temperature.

pressure transients Minor fluctuations on the gauges that may indicate a problem.

PT chart A pressure-temperature chart that shows the relationship between air-conditioning pressures and evaporator temperature.

reclaim/recycle machine An air-conditioning machine designed to remove and recycle refrigerant for reuse.

reclaiming The process of removing refrigerant from the air-conditioning system by using an air-conditioning machine; also called *recovering*.

recovering See *reclaiming*.

refrigerant identifiers Devices used to check for impurities in the air-conditioning system.

retrofit kit An aftermarket kit that has the fittings and oil to change an R-12 unit over to an R-134a unit.

state of charge The amount of refrigerant in a system compared to how much should be in it.

vacuum gauge A gauge designed to read negative pressure or vacuum.

vacuum pump A pump used to evacuate the air-conditioning system and put it into a deep vacuum or low pressure to remove moisture.

Review Questions

1. Transit buses have high-demand HVAC requirements, including and air flow between ________ and the cooling capacity of ________ times that of a medium-sized home AC unit.
   a. 500 and 1,400 cfm; 4 to 6
   b. 1,500 and 1,900 cfm; 7 to 9
   c. 2,000 and 2,400 cfm; 10 to 18 times
   d. 2,500 and 3,500 cfm; 20 to 30 times
2. Which of the following is the first step in the diagnostic process?
   a. System pressure test
   b. Diagnosis of faults
   c. Performance testing
   d. Check for codes in computer
3. Which of the following is correct concerning determining refrigerant type?
   a. The identifier connects to the low-side air-conditioning fitting and takes a reading of the refrigerant.
   b. The only way to determine the type of refrigerant in a system is with the aid of a refrigerant identifier.
   c. The identifier will give a read-out such as 100% R-134a.
   d. All of the choices are correct.
4. Which of the following is found on the air-conditioning information sticker?
   a. Type of refrigerant
   b. Charge amount
   c. Oil capacity
   d. All of the choices are correct.
5. Which of the following is correct concerning state of charge?
   a. State of charge in the air-conditioning system refers to the amount of refrigerant in the system compared to how much should be in the system.
   b. State of charge is best determined by removing all of the refrigerant and recharging the system with the proper amount of refrigerant, as specified by the service information.
   c. Both A and B
   d. Neither A nor B
6. Which of the following is correct concerning an overcharge of the air-conditioning system?
   a. Overcharging the air-conditioning system will affect the orifice tube and TXV systems in the same manner.
   b. Both the low- and the high-side gauges will be running higher than normal.
   c. Both A and B
   d. Neither A nor B
7. Which of the following are variable factors in air conditioning?
   a. Weather
   b. Temperature
   c. Overall condition of the vehicle.
   d. All of the choices are correct.
8. Which of the following is NOT correct concerning air-conditioning system performance testing?
   a. The engine's rpm should be at 2,100, which is the ideal and average rpm for the majority of air-conditioning systems on vehicles.
   b. An external fan needs to be supplying air to the condenser to simulate driving conditions.
   c. Make sure to have all of the controls at the maximum settings.
   d. The air flow should be set to the dash vents.
9. Which of the following is correct concerning the evaporator housing water drain?
   a. As the air-conditioning system is running, the evaporator will sweat water throughout the day.
   b. A drain hose is connected to the evaporator housing and exits through the vehicle's firewall.
   c. Both A and B
   d. Neither A nor B
10. Which of the following is NOT a type of protection device used in air-conditioning systems?
    a. Thermal unit
    b. Circuit breaker
    c. Fuses
    d. Fusible link

ASE-Type Questions

1. Technician A states that the wider the gap on an air-conditioning clutch, the greater the ohm reading when checking the windings. Technician B states that the air-conditioning clutch is electromagnetically operated. Who is correct?
   a. Technician A
   b. Technician B
   c. Both Technician A and Technician B
   d. Neither Technician A nor Technician B
2. Technician A states that an air-conditioning performance test usually requires that an auxiliary condenser fan be used during the test. Technician B states that a performance test will show if the air-conditioning system is contaminated with sealer. Who is correct?
   a. Technician A
   b. Technician B
   c. Both Technician A and Technician B
   d. Neither Technician A nor Technician B
3. Technician A states that refrigerant in a vehicle should be identified before recovering the refrigerant. Technician B states that refrigerant doesn't need to be identified if you are only topping up a system with refrigerant. Who is correct?
   a. Technician A
   b. Technician B
   c. Both Technician A and Technician B
   d. Neither Technician A nor Technician B
4. Technician A states that when evacuating an air-conditioning system, the vacuum should be maintained for approximately 10 minutes after the system reaches the boiling point pressure of water. Technician B states that the primary purpose of evacuating an air-conditioning system is to remove any moisture from the system. Who is correct?
   a. Technician A
   b. Technician B
   c. Both Technician A and Technician B
   d. Neither Technician A nor Technician B
5. Technician A states that the system should be flushed if the compressor came apart. Technician B states that the system should be flushed if the oil is contaminated. Who is correct?
   a. Technician A
   b. Technician B
   c. Both Technician A and Technician B
   d. Neither Technician A nor Technician B
6. Technician A states that when using pressurized nitrogen to locate a leak, an electronic detector should be used. Technician B states that electronic detectors are used when the system has at least a minimal refrigerant charge. Who is correct?
   a. Technician A
   b. Technician B
   c. Both Technician A and Technician B
   d. Neither Technician A nor Technician B
7. Technician A states that microns are a much more accurate unit of measuring vacuum than inches of mercury (Hg). Technician B states that microns are a much more accurate measure of time than seconds. Who is correct?
   a. Technician A
   b. Technician B
   c. Both Technician A and Technician B
   d. Neither Technician A nor Technician B
8. Technician A states that to determine how much Freon is needed in a system, you must refer to identifying labels on the vehicle or the service manual. Technician B states that to determine the amount of Freon needed, you just charge the system until the pressures look correct. Who is correct?
   a. Technician A
   b. Technician B
   c. Both Technician A and Technician B
   d. Neither Technician A nor Technician B
9. Technician A states that when removing any part of an air-conditioning system, the oil should be drained from it and measured so that the same amount can be reinstalled. Technician B states that oil should only be in the compressor, and if any oil is found in any other components, it means that the receiver dryer is faulty. Who is correct?
   a. Technician A
   b. Technician B
   c. Both Technician A and Technician B
   d. Neither Technician A nor Technician B
10. Technician A states that if moisture enters the air-conditioning system, acid will be created. Technician B states that evacuating an air-conditioning system will boil moisture, which will be removed from the system as a gas. Who is correct?
    a. Technician A
    b. Technician B
    c. Both Technician A and Technician B
    d. Neither Technician A nor Technician B

CHAPTER 53

NATEF Tasks

There are no NATEF tasks for this chapter.

Knowledge Objectives

After reading this chapter, you will be able to:

1. Describe refrigerated trailer operation. (pp 1770–1773)
2. Explain the difference between vehicle-powered and self-powered refrigeration systems. (pp 1773–1774)
3. Explain how heating, cooling, and defrost cycles work. (pp 1774–1778)
4. Describe the components of trailer refrigeration. (pp 1778–1781)
5. Explain both functions of the compressor. (pp 1779–1780)
6. Explain the relationship between the condenser, expansion valve, and evaporator. (pp 1780–1781)
7. Explain the function of the refrigerant. (pp 1781–1783)

Trailer Refrigeration

Skills Objectives

There are no skills objectives for this chapter.

Introduction

Transporting temperature-sensitive goods—such as fresh produce, flowers, meat, or dairy products—requires temperature-regulated containers. In hot weather, cooling is needed to prevent products from spoiling or melting. Even though refrigeration is what immediately comes to mind when thinking about transportation of temperature-sensitive perishable goods, in the winter or in cold climates, heating is also needed to prevent damage to perishable products due to freezing. A more descriptive term than "transport refrigeration" is **transport temperature control**, which refers to heating or cooling over a wide range of outside temperatures and product storage temperatures.

This chapter will introduce you to the types of trailer refrigeration, the different heating and cooling cycles, system components and fluids, and basic maintenance of the temperature control system.

Fundamentals of Trailer Refrigeration

A number of manufacturers produce temperature-control systems, which are installed in trailers, shipping containers, and truck boxes. These systems are often called **reefers**, a common term for truck-trailer temperature-control systems. A distinction is made between these types of temperature-control units, which can both heat and cool products, and air-conditioning systems, which also use principles of refrigeration FIGURE 53-1.

Refrigeration is a process of transferring heat away from a product storage container to achieve a temperature of 65°F (18°C) or colder FIGURE 53-2. In contrast, air conditioning is designed to maintain clean, fresh, comfortable air temperatures between 65°F (18°C) and 75°F (24°C) for people. Blower fan speeds are high for the following functions: transport refrigeration, dehumidification, and refreshing the passenger compartment with clean air. Blower fan speeds are not as important in refrigeration systems as they are in air-conditioning systems. Some trailers and truck boxes have only heating systems to protect products from freeze damage, but most truck and trailer refrigeration systems are capable of both heating and cooling.

The major components and the operation of a refrigeration system are like those outlined in the Principles of Heating and Air-Conditioning Systems chapter. One major difference between the air-conditioning system and a truck-trailer refrigeration system is that heating is a critical function of a transport refrigeration system. Heating is a built-in feature of the refrigeration system necessary to defrost evaporators, which are designed to freeze product, particularly very damp products (commonly termed **wet load**.)

To reduce product temperatures to below freezing, evaporators are very cold. Moisture easily freezes on

You Are the Technician

A refrigerated trailer has arrived at your shop with the complaint that the product in the trailer is taking a very long time to cool. The driver is concerned there is a problem with the trailer reefer. The driver also reported that what he thought to be an excessive amount of water was draining from the trailer reefer and draining too frequently. So, you performed a visual inspection of the reefer and checked for any fault code displayed on the control unit, but everything appeared to be in proper working order. The trailer was cooling, and the interior temperature was approaching the temperature set point. (The temperature was only 2°F above the set point when inspected.) However, you did confirm that, based on your experience, the reefer was defrosting more frequently that it should have and drained quite a bit more water than usual. When asked about the type of product that was being transported, the driver replied that it was a fresh load of strawberries. Remembering information from a refrigeration course about the differences between the heat loads of various products, you informed the driver that the refrigeration system was functioning correctly and the observations were normal. You explained to him that the strawberries were simply a wet load. In preparing your report, you need to answer the following questions.

1. How does the type and condition of product refrigerated by a trailer affect the heat load a trailer refrigeration unit must remove?
2. How does a load with a high moisture content affect the time it takes to cool a product?
3. List at least three other factors that would affect the time it takes for the refrigeration unit of the trailer to cool the product.

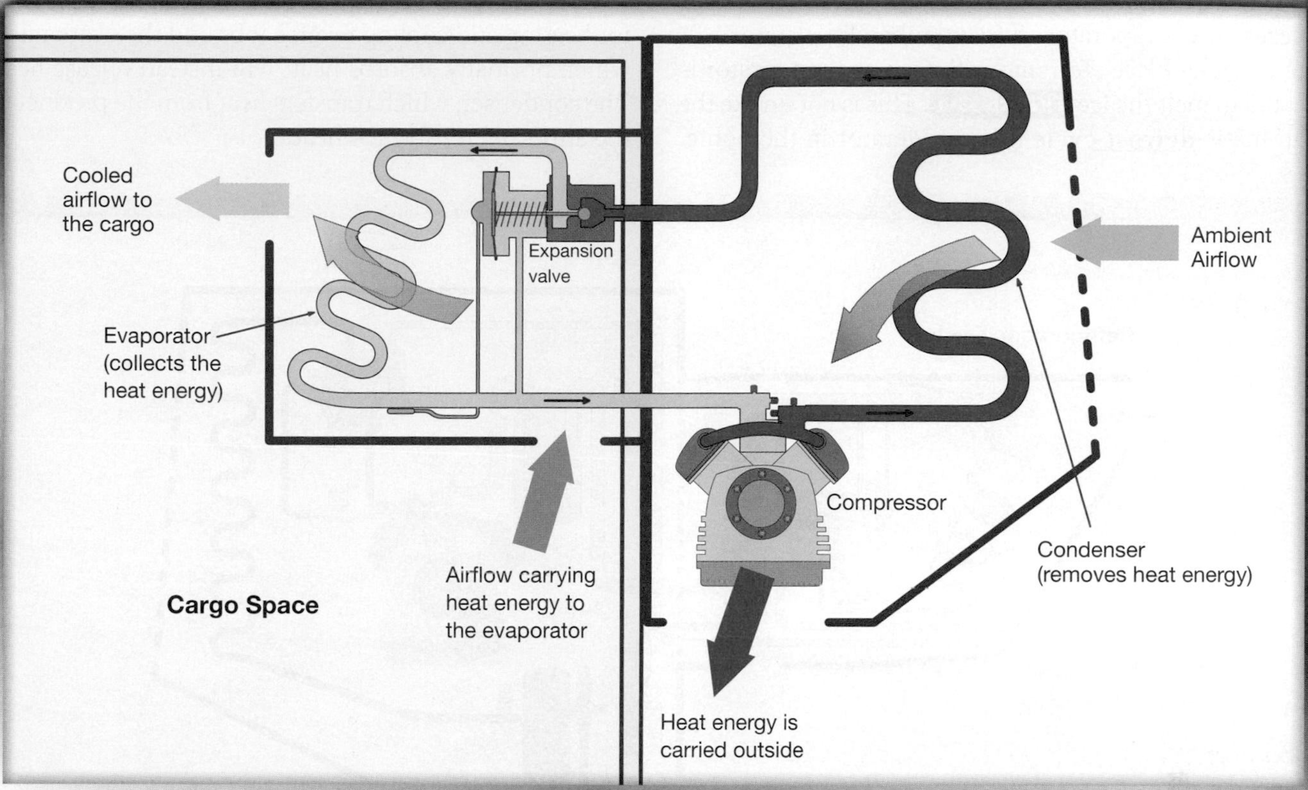

FIGURE 53-1 Refrigeration removes heat from the truck box or trailer body.

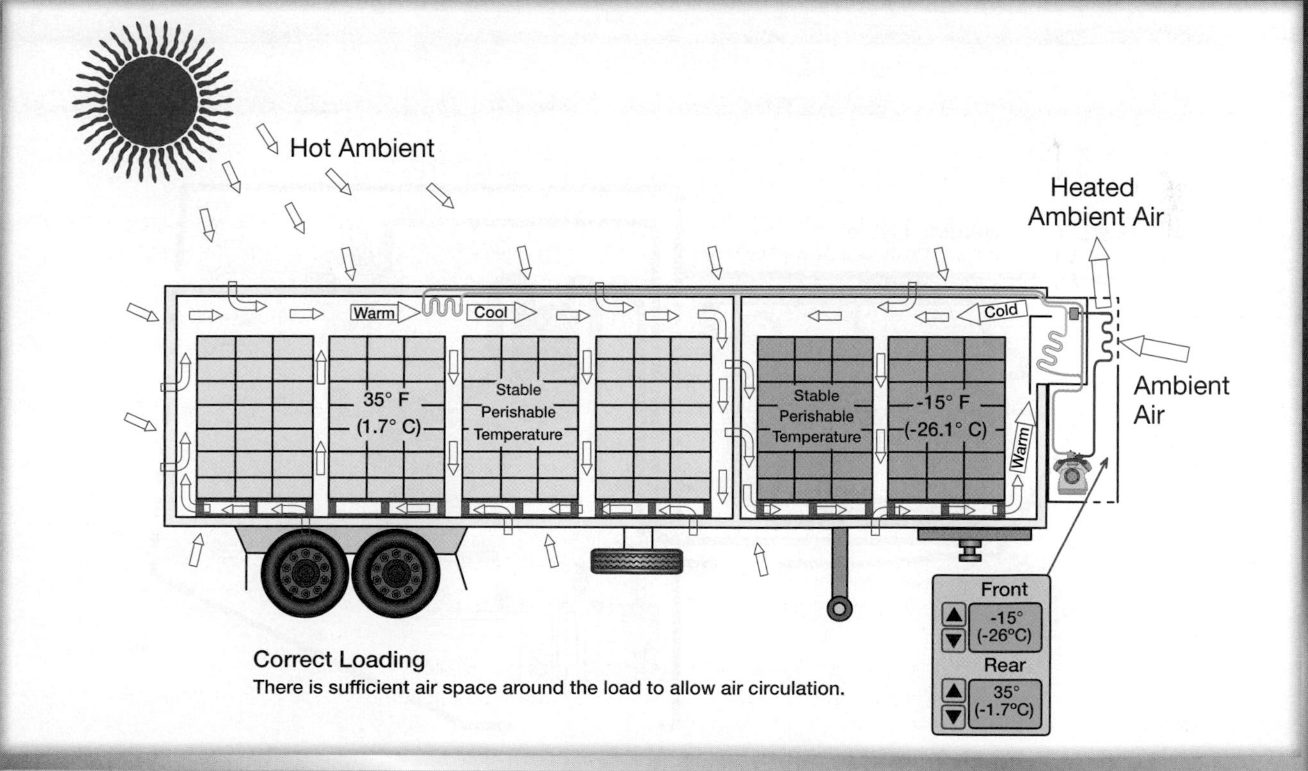

FIGURE 53-2 Refrigeration is different from air conditioning in refrigeration acheives much colder temperatures.

contact with an evaporator FIGURE 53-3. When water freezes on an evaporator's fins and tubes, little or no cooling can take place. To remove the ice, the evaporator is heated to melt the ice FIGURE 53-4. This is not unlike the automatic **defrost cycle** of a refrigerator in the home.

To defrost the reefer's evaporator, the major components for heating and cooling reverse jobs and the evaporator, which normally absorbs heat, will instead release heat. The condenser, which transfers heat from the product to the atmosphere, absorbs heat.

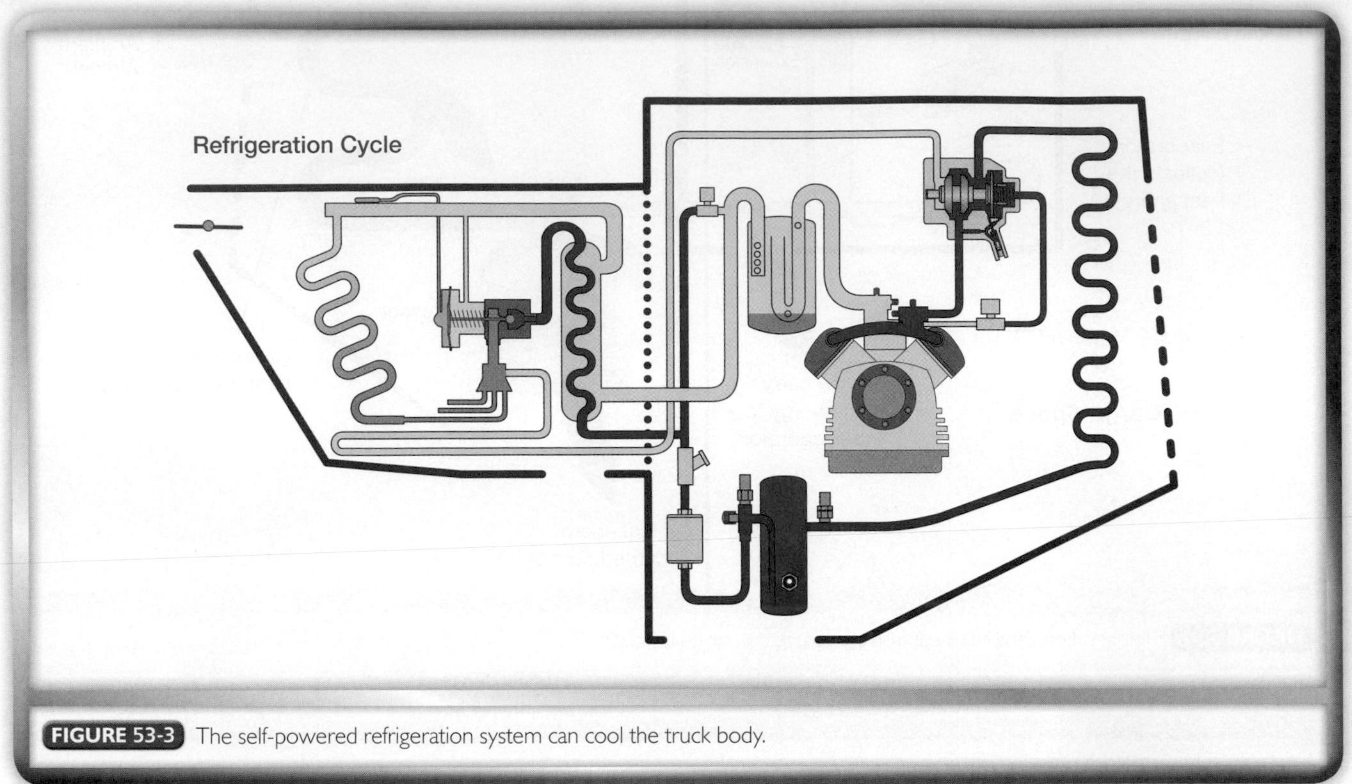

FIGURE 53-3 The self-powered refrigeration system can cool the truck body.

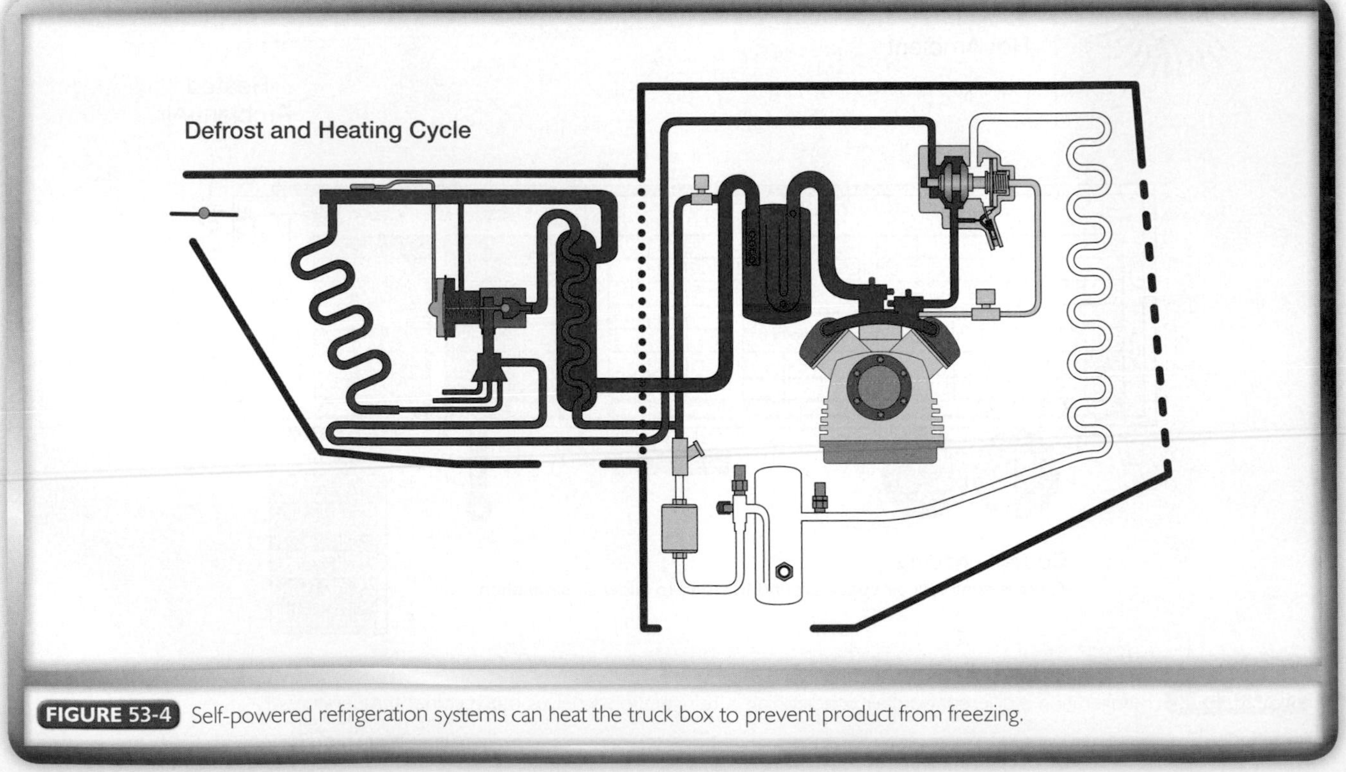

FIGURE 53-4 Self-powered refrigeration systems can heat the truck box to prevent product from freezing.

Heating Principles in Transportation Refrigeration

Like air-conditioning systems, a reefer unit removes heat from a temperature-controlled box or trailer body faster than it enters in order to cool the product. Heat enters the refrigerated area from different sources than the passenger cabin. Heat-producing sources include:

- Product that is loaded when warm
- The sun and high outside temperatures
- Doors opening during loading and unloading
- Cargo respiration

While a person may emit close to 580 Btu (146 kcal) of heat per hour, ripening product can also produce heat. For example, Thermo King, a major reefer manufacturer, notes that 2,000 pounds (909 kg) of strawberries at 32°F (0°C) produce 113–158 Btu (28–40 kcal) per hour of heat. At 40°F (4°C), the strawberries ripen faster to produce 150–283 Btu (38–71 kcal) per hour. At 60°F (16°C), the same strawberries produce up to 846 Btu (213 kcal) per hour while ripening.

To reduce heat loads from radiant heat and prevent heat absorption, trailers are often painted white or remain as reflective bright metal. Insulation in the ceilings and walls of a refrigerated truck or trailer minimizes heat transfer through conduction. Powerful evaporator fans blowing more than 3,000 cubic feet (85 cubic meters) of air per minute increase convection heat movement inside a cooled container. Door seals are carefully designed and must be maintained to keep warm, moist air out of the box.

The cooling or heating capacity of a reefer is measured in Btu per hour. A Btu is the amount of heat required to change the temperature of one pound of water one degree Fahrenheit. A reefer with 20,000 Btu/hr (5,040 kcal/hr) refrigeration capacity cooling a load containing 5,000 lb (2,273 kg) of water in it could lower the temperature 4 degrees every hour. To lower the temperature 32°F would require 2.5 hours of operation. The water content of the load has a major influence on how quickly a reefer can reach optimal temperatures. The efficiency of different refrigeration systems changes with outside temperature as well. TABLE 53-1 shows the cooling capacity of various models of transport refrigeration units at different outside temperatures.

Types of Transport Refrigeration Systems

Two major classifications of truck–trailer or transport refrigeration systems are determined by whether the refrigeration compressor is powered (i.e., driven by the vehicle) or self powered. **Vehicle-powered refrigeration units** are used in smaller delivery vans and trucks. In these systems, the compressor is located on the engine of the vehicle. Refrigerant is used both to cool and defrost the evaporator as needed. Whenever the load requires just heating, such as in the winter, the system usually does not have the capacity to supply enough heat, so engine coolant is used to transfer heat to the temperature-controlled product compartment.

Self-powered refrigeration units use a small horsepower diesel engine to power the refrigeration system. The fuel economy, durability, and low maintenance requirement, as well as the availability of high torque output at low engine speeds, make the diesel engine an ideal choice for this type of application FIGURE 53-5.

TABLE 53-1: Cooling Capacity of Various Models of Transport Refrigeration Units

Model	Btu/Hr at 35°F (2°C)	Btu/Hr at 0°F (–18°C)	Btu/Hr at –20°F (-29°C)
Trailer Unit – A	46,000 (11,592 kcal/hr)	38,500 (9,702 kcal/hr)	30,000 (7,560 kcal/hr)
Trailer Unit – B	46,000 (11,592 kcal/hr)	32,000 (8,064 kcal/hr)	21,000 (5,292 kcal/hr)
Trailer Unit – C	43,500 (10,962 kcal/hr)	27,000 (6,804 kcal/hr)	16,000 (4,031 kcal/hr)
Self-Powered Truck Unit – A	25,000 (6,300 kcal/hr)	18,000 (4,536 kcal/hr)	12,000 (3,024 kcal/hr)
Self-Powered Truck Unit – B	22,600 (5,695 kcal/hr)	12,500 (3,150 kcal/hr)	7,500 (1,890 kcal/hr)
Self-Powered Truck Unit – C	15,750 (3,969 kcal/hr)	11,000 (2,520 kcal/hr)	6,750 (1,701 kcal/hr)

FIGURE 53-5 Diesel engines efficiently power refrigeration units.

Note, however, that in most reefer systems, the engine does not always drive the compressor. In **stand-by mode**, the reefer requires a supply of electric current to operate, and that current comes from a connection to a power grid or shore power source. Furthermore, in certain instances, such as when a vehicle is parked at a yard, an electric motor is used instead of a diesel engine to drive the compressor.

These self-powered units are further classified by application depending on whether they are mounted onto smaller truck boxes, as in FIGURE 53-6, or larger trailer applications, as in FIGURE 53-7. Self-powered reefers are self-contained units integrating the compressor, evaporator, blower fans and motors, control valves, engine, and so on into a single module that can be suspended from a truck box or trailer body. In smaller units, the compressor is a two-cylinder reciprocating type, while larger units use compressors that have four cylinders arranged in a V. Smaller reefers will often use a quieter, more efficient scroll-type compressor. In addition to the compressor design, other small differences exist among the components used in various truck and trailer reefers. Nonetheless, all self-powered refrigeration systems operate in basically an identical manner.

Self-powered refrigeration systems can also be configured to control a single temperature or multiple temperatures in different areas of the trailer. On the outside, a **multi-temp unit** will look like a single temperature system FIGURE 53-8. However, multi-temp units can regulate temperature using additional evaporators mounted in the ceiling. Each compartment outfitted with its own dedicated evaporator can heat or cool product as necessary using a separate thermostatic control. The front compartment is usually reserved for frozen product and is generally cooler than the rear, which will have fresh produce and a higher temperature setting.

FIGURE 53-6 A self-powered refrigeration unit for a straight truck.

FIGURE 53-7 A self-powered refrigeration unit for a semi-trailer.

Heating, Cooling, and Defrost Cycles

Truck-trailer refrigeration systems use the same principles of refrigeration—and many of the same components—

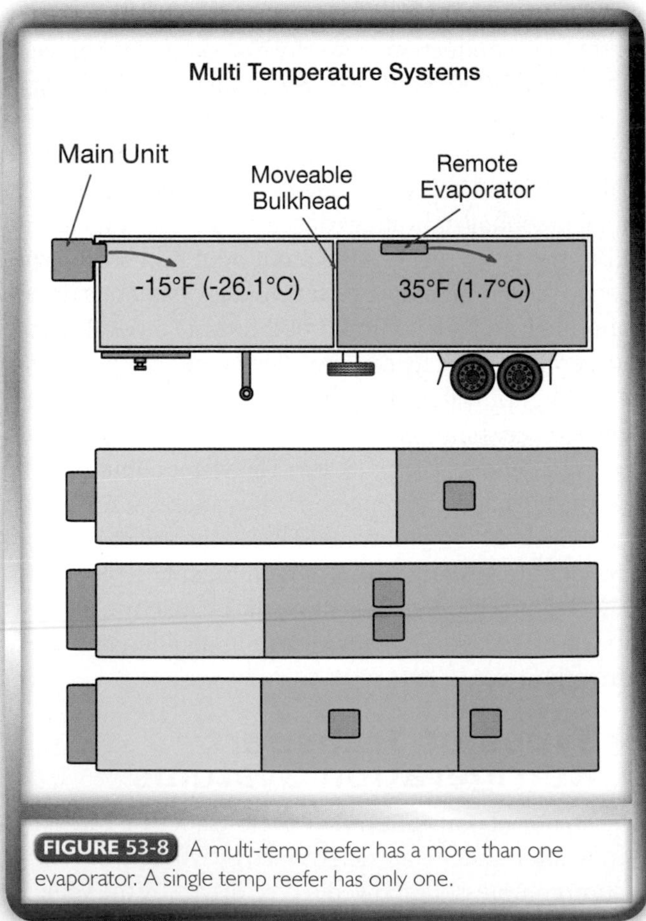

FIGURE 53-8 A multi-temp reefer has a more than one evaporator. A single temp reefer has only one.

as air-conditioning systems. Compressors, evaporators, condensers, accumulators, and expansion valves are found in both systems. (Components will be covered in the Components of Trailer Refrigeration Systems section.) What is different is that the reefer has several modes, or cycles, of operation that involve cooling, heating, and defrosting the evaporator, plus a unique valve to control the mode FIGURE 53-9.

Three-Way (3-Way) Valve

Controlling the direction of refrigerant flow determines whether the reefer is in cooling or heating mode FIGURE 53-10. Electrically controlled solenoids or a refrigerant control valve called a **three-way valve** directs hot refrigerant gas to either the condenser (when in cool mode) or directly to the evaporator (when in the heat

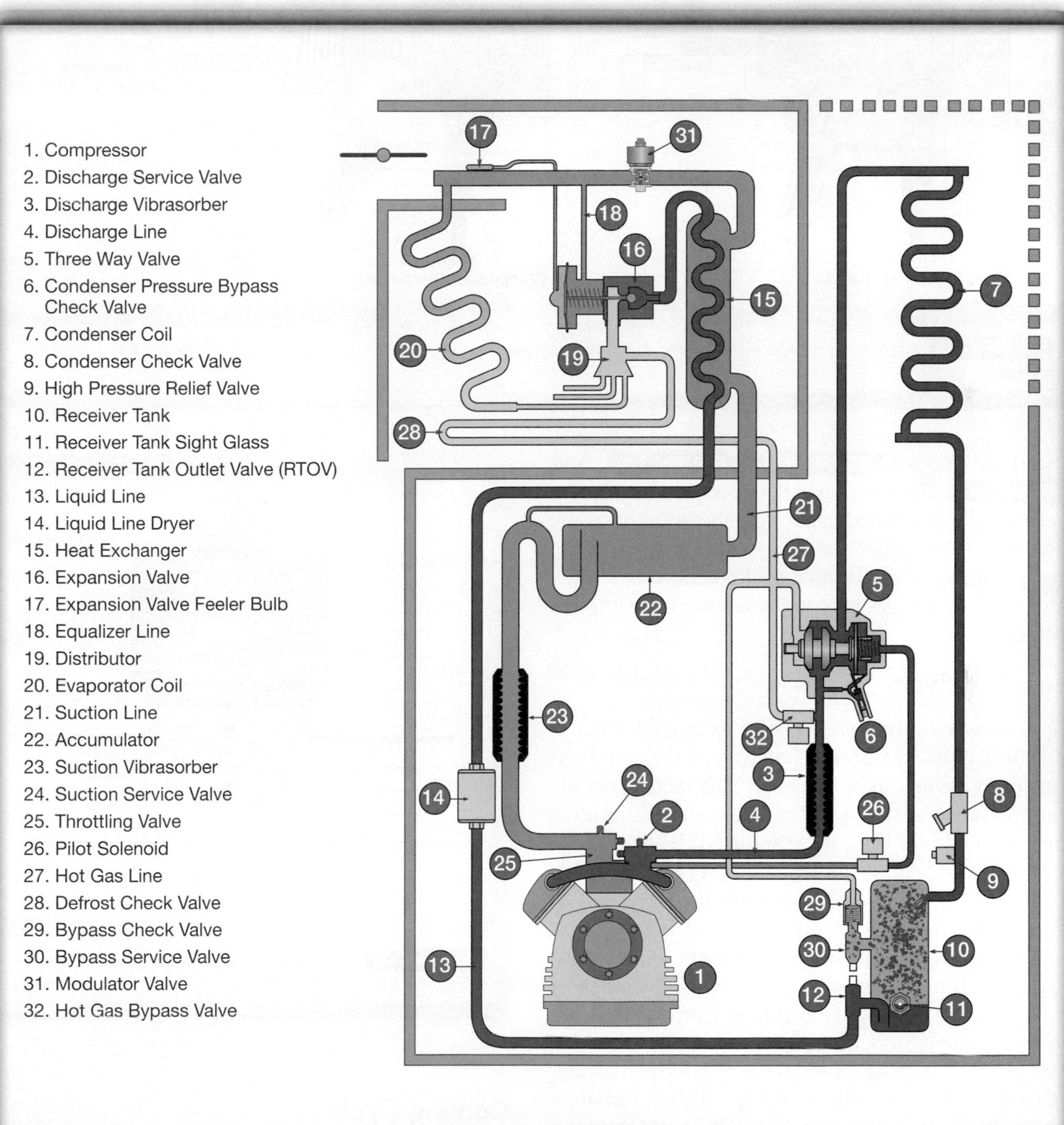

FIGURE 53-9 Refrigerant passages through a trailer refrigeration unit for heating and cooling.

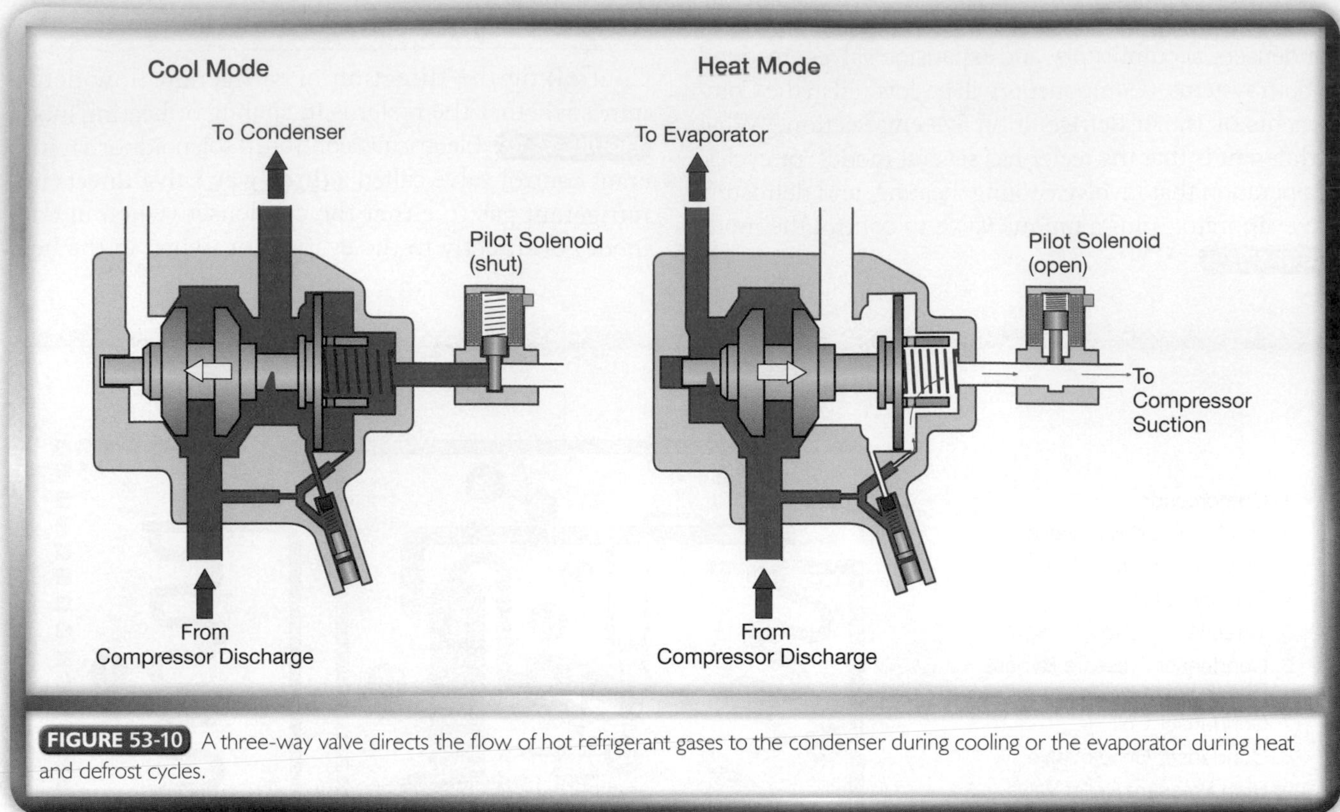

FIGURE 53-10 A three-way valve directs the flow of hot refrigerant gases to the condenser during cooling or the evaporator during heat and defrost cycles.

or defrost mode) FIGURE 53-11, FIGURE 53-12, and FIGURE 53-13. The position of the three-way valve spool is electrically controlled using a combination of spring and gas pressure. When the valve is de-energized, spring pressure moves the valve to a cool position. When the valve is energized, gas pressure forces the valve into the heat mode.

Heating Cycle

If a product requires heating, such as in cold climates and during the winter, the function of the refrigeration components can be reversed. This means that the evaporator can be used to release heat into the product compartment and the condenser used to absorb heat from the outside air. Even when it is very cold outside of the reefer, even well below zero, heat can still be extracted from the air.

During heating mode, the evaporator will be pressurized with hot refrigerant gases, and the condenser will be used to evaporate refrigerant. Even in very cold ambient temperatures, the evaporating refrigerant is able to absorb heat. Heating capabilities are not as high as cooling capacity. For example, at –0.4°F (–18°C), container temperatures may reach 40°F (5°C), and the evaporator temperature will not exceed 60°F (15.5°C). Electric heaters can supplement heating capacity of the refrigeration system in heat mode.

FIGURE 53-11 Electrically operated solenoids are used to redirect the flow of hot refrigerant.

Cooling Cycle

During cooling cycle, the refrigeration cycle is identical to one found in a conventional AC system. Refrigerant absorbs heat from the product in the trailer or box. The

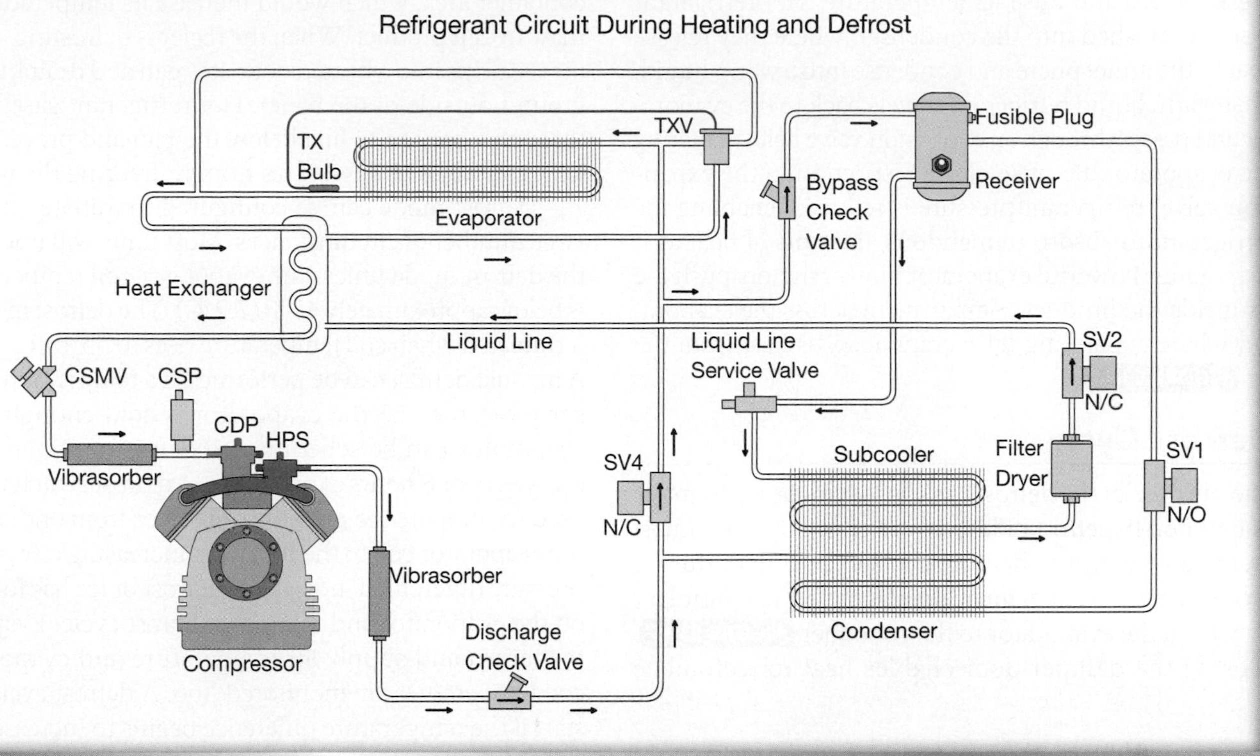

FIGURE 53-12 The operation of refrigerant solenoids in a Carrier reefer used to place the reefer in heating mode.

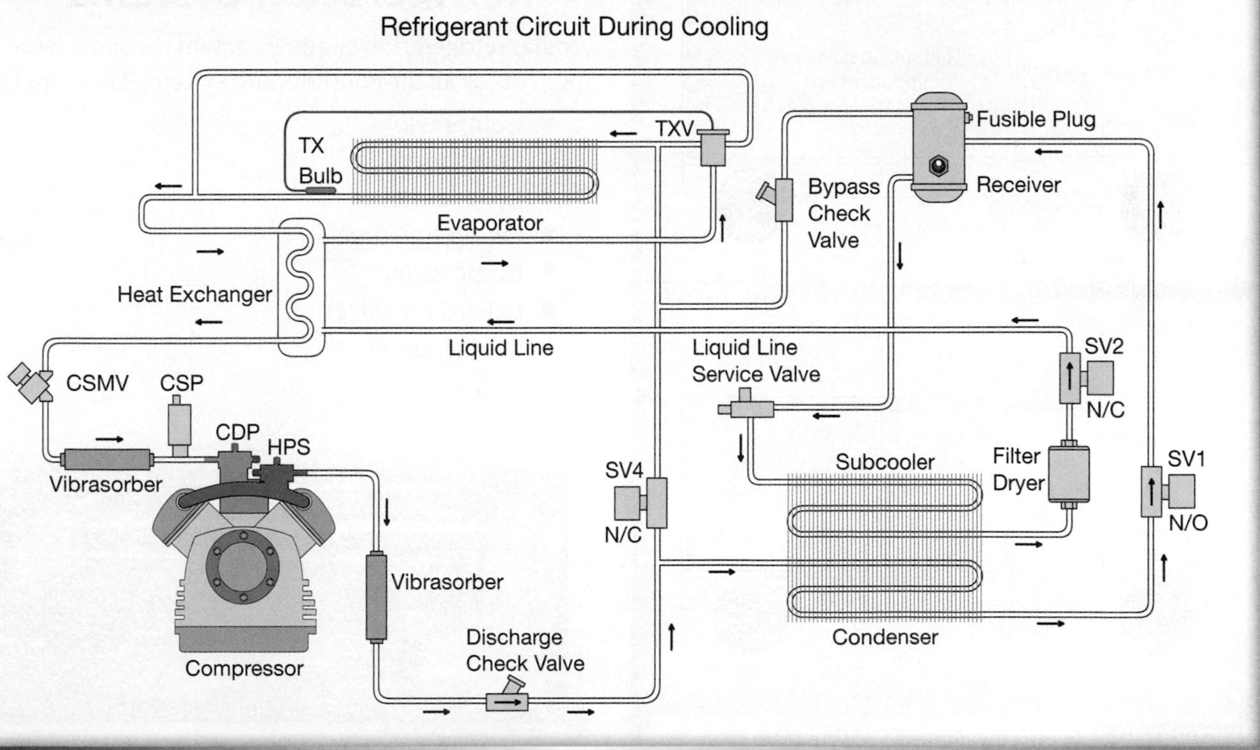

FIGURE 53-13 The operation of refrigerant solenoids in a Carrier reefer used to place the reefer in cooling mode.

compressor pulls the refrigerant into its cylinders to compress the gas and raise its temperature. Hot refrigerant gases are pushed into the condenser, where they release heat to the atmosphere and condense into a warm liquid. That warm liquid refrigerant travels back to the evaporator and passes through an expansion valve before entering the evaporator. Because of the restriction in the expansion valve, refrigerant pressure is reduced, enabling the refrigerant to absorb tremendous amounts of heat as it evaporates. Powerful evaporator blower motors push the air inside the product compartment across the evaporator, where expanding refrigerant absorbs heat from the air FIGURE 53-14.

Defrost Cycle

The purpose of the defrost cycle is to remove ice from the evaporator. In defrost mode, the reefer will operate almost identically as in the heating cycle except that, during the defrost mode, a damper door is closed to control air flow from the evaporator to the container FIGURE 53-15. Closing the damper door enables heat to recirculate around the evaporator and not flow into the refrigerated container area, which would increase its temperature or thaw frozen product. When the reefer is defrosting, melting ice drips into a heated defroster pan and drains to the ground outside of the reefer. Hot refrigerant gases pass through a section of line below the pan and prevent the cold container temperatures from re-freezing the water.

Defrost mode can be configured to initiate under a large number of circumstances. Most units will not enter the defrost mode unless the evaporator coil temperature is below approximately 45°F (7.2°C). The defrost mode is terminated when coil temperature rises to 55°F (12.8°C). A manual defrost can be performed if a temperature sensor indicates that the evaporator is cold enough. The evaporator can be scheduled to defrost automatically every 4, 6, or 8 hours of operation. A defrost switch is also used to compare the pressure difference from one side of the evaporator coil to the other. An increasing refrigerant pressure differential indicates that frost or ice has formed on the evaporator and initiates a defrost cycle. Evaporator return and supply air temperature and evaporator coil temperature are monitored, too. A defrost cycle can start if the temperature difference begins to increase and the evaporator is cold enough to indicate the possibility of frost or ice.

FIGURE 53-14 Reefers transfer heat from the cargo compartment to the atmosphere using latent heat of evaporation and condensation to move large quantities of heat.

Components of Trailer Refrigeration Systems

Trailer refrigeration systems contain the same basic components as an air-conditioning system. These include:

- Compressors
- Condensers
- Receiver tanks
- Liquid line dryers
- Evaporators
- Expansion valves
- Refrigerant

FIGURE 53-15 Damper doors allow for better control of the air flow, which makes for more efficient defrosting.

Compressors

To provide the cooling capacity for the large cargo areas of truck-trailer refrigeration systems, compressors need a much greater ability to move refrigerant. While smaller rotary-piston compressors may be found on vehicle-powered systems, reciprocating-piston compressors are the most common type used in self-powered refrigeration systems. The Thermo King compressor shown in FIGURE 53-16 has a compression ratio of 50:1 and operates up to 350 psi (2,413 kPa).

When the piston is at the bottom of its stroke, refrigerant travels from the crankcase sump and enters the cylinder through a port on the side of the cylinder. Downward movement of the piston forces vapor through ports to the chamber above the piston FIGURE 53-17. When the piston moves upwards, highly compressed refrigerant vapor passes through the one-way discharge valve plate and enters into the discharge manifold.

Compressors use a throttling valve designed to limit the amount of refrigerant entering the compressor. Excessive refrigerant flow produces too much discharge pressure and overloads the compressor. That excessive load can increase engine fuel consumption and overload the

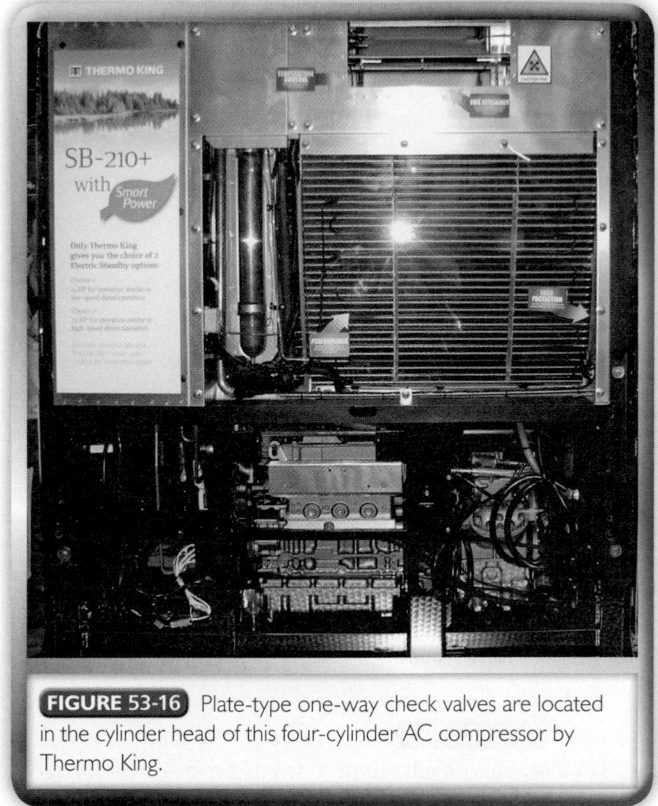

FIGURE 53-16 Plate-type one-way check valves are located in the cylinder head of this four-cylinder AC compressor by Thermo King.

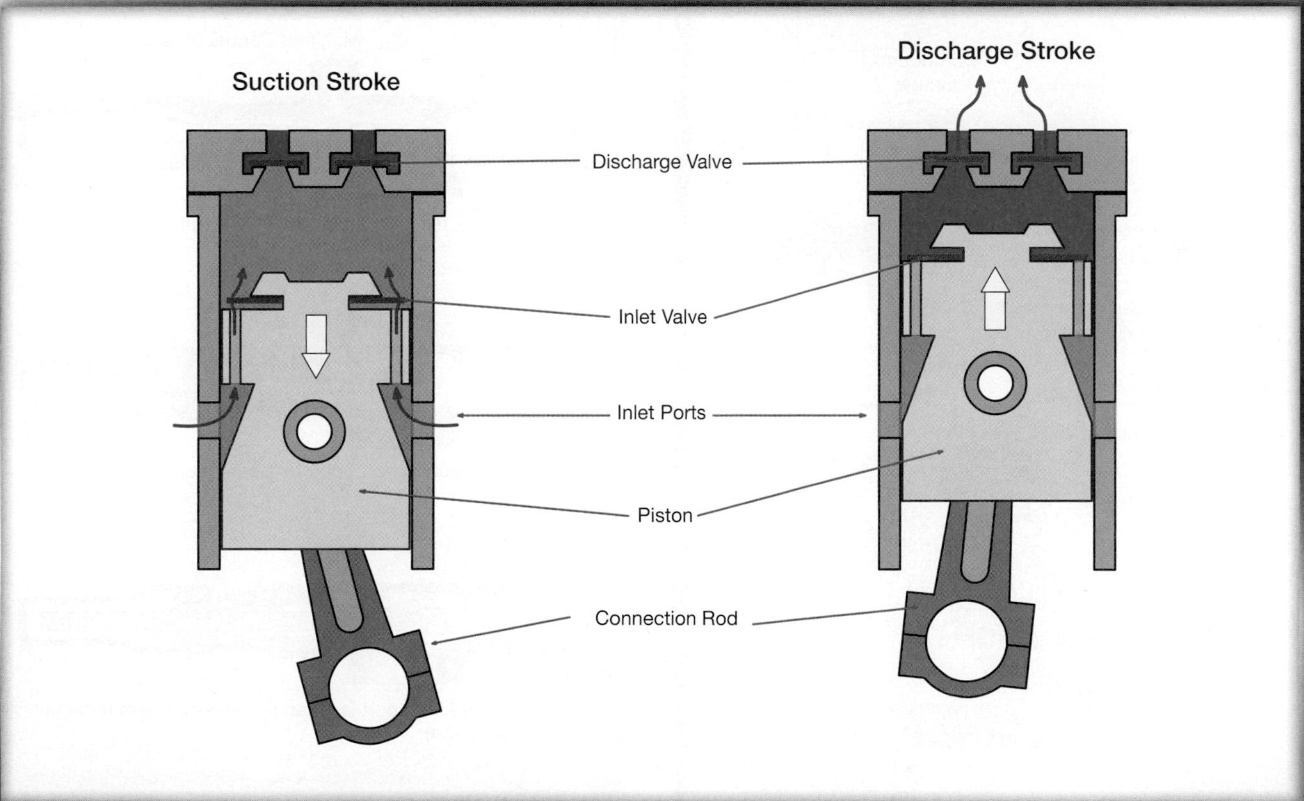

Suction Stroke

Discharge Stroke

Discharge Valve

Inlet Valve

Inlet Ports

Piston

Connection Rod

FIGURE 53-17 Operation of a reciprocating design AC compressor.

electric motors of units with optional electric stand-by systems. Four-cylinder compressors have the throttling valve mounted on top of the compressor.

The throttling valve has little impact on compressor operation when cargo temperatures are low, as refrigerant pressures are correspondingly low. However, during heating and defrosting, when system pressures are higher, flow correspondently increases. A properly adjusted and functioning throttle valve begins to limit the flow of refrigerant into the compressor as system pressures increase. Shims are used to adjust the operation of the valve. A deteriorated or improperly adjusted throttle valve can cause inadequate refrigerant flow, which starves the compressor and causes the whole system to lose effectiveness, reducing cooling and heating performance.

Discharge and Suction Service Valves

The discharge and suction service valves are located on top of the compressor. These valves are points at which system pressures are measured and the system can be isolated from the compressor if the compressor requires removal FIGURE 53-18. Because the valve stems used in the service valves can leak a small amount of refrigerant around the seals, a tightly-sealed protective cap is required when the system is operating. Back seating the service valves is required to enable flow of refrigerant. Forward seating valves isolates the compressor from the remaining AC system FIGURE 53-19.

Vibrasorbers

Flexible braided stainless steel lines connect the compressor inlet and outlet to the system. The lines are called **vibrasorbers**, and, as the name suggests, they absorb compressor movement and vibrations that would otherwise be transmitted to the more fragile copper refrigerant lines. Continuous line vibration will work-harden copper, leading to cracking and refrigerant leakage.

The Condenser

During cooling mode, the refrigerant leaves the compressor, passes through the three-way valve, and enters the condenser. Because the boiling point of refrigerant vapor increases when the liquid is pressurized, the vapor will want to condense. In doing so, tremendous amounts of heat are released into the atmosphere, as the refrigerant passes through the condenser, changing from a vapor to a liquid. When the refrigerant changes from a vapor to a liquid, latent heat energy contained in the refrigerant is

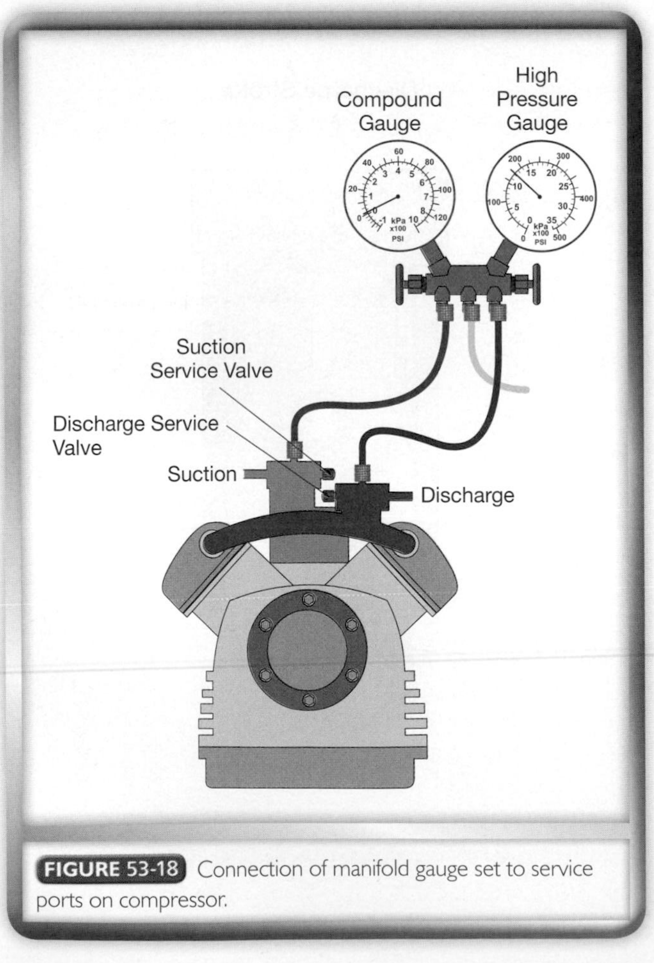

FIGURE 53-18 Connection of manifold gauge set to service ports on compressor.

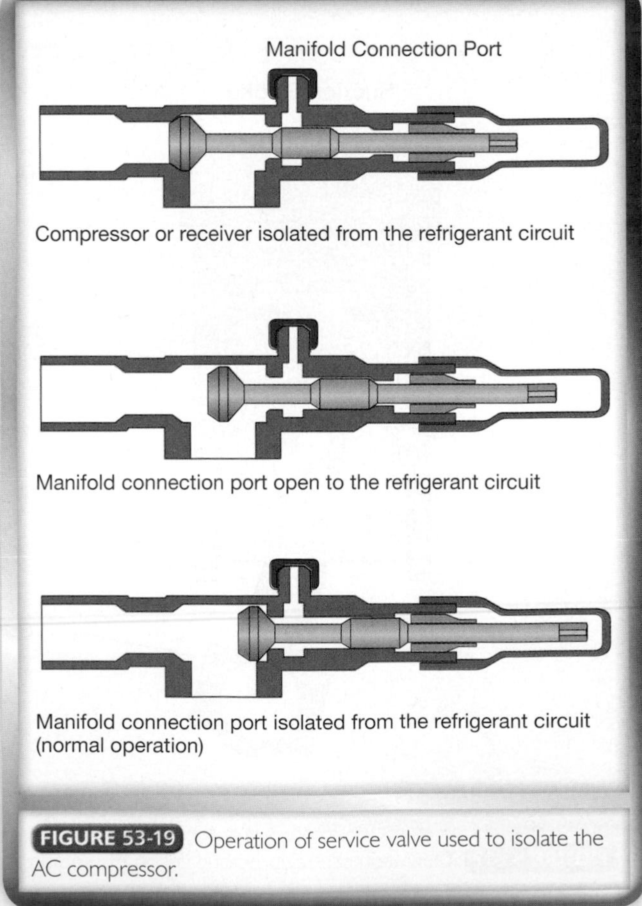

FIGURE 53-19 Operation of service valve used to isolate the AC compressor.

released into the atmosphere. Typically, the vapor passing through the condenser is about 30°F higher than ambient temperature.

Condenser Check Valves

Check valves are used in the reefer to permit refrigerant flow in only one direction. A refrigerant check valve at the condenser outlet allows refrigerant to flow during the cool mode and blocks refrigerant flow during the heat mode.

Receiver Tank

Because the amount of refrigerant needed during reefer operation depends on a variety of factors, such as ambient and container temperature, storage of extra refrigerant by the receiver tank is needed for efficient reefer operation. Often the tank has a sight glass on the top and/or bottom to provide a means of checking the system refrigerant level. Warm liquid refrigerant from the condenser pours into the receiver tank and pools at the bottom, so the lower sight glass should always be filled during operation. High-pressure liquid is pushed through the receiver tank outlet valve (RTOV) to the liquid line that connects it to the evaporator. A bypass check valve in the receiver is closed during cooling mode and opens during heating mode to connect the receiver with the evaporator FIGURE 53-20.

The Liquid Line Dryer

The liquid line dryer located after the receiver tank operates like a filter and a device to remove moisture and other contaminants from the refrigerant during unit operation. These dryers have a service interval and require regular replacement—or replacement whenever the system is opened to the atmosphere. A heat exchanger encloses the suction line between the dryer and the expansion valve. Cooler refrigerant leaving the evaporator absorbs heat energy from the warm liquid suction line. By pre-cooling the refrigerant in the liquid line before it reaches the expansion valve, evaporator temperatures can be colder, increasing cooling capacity.

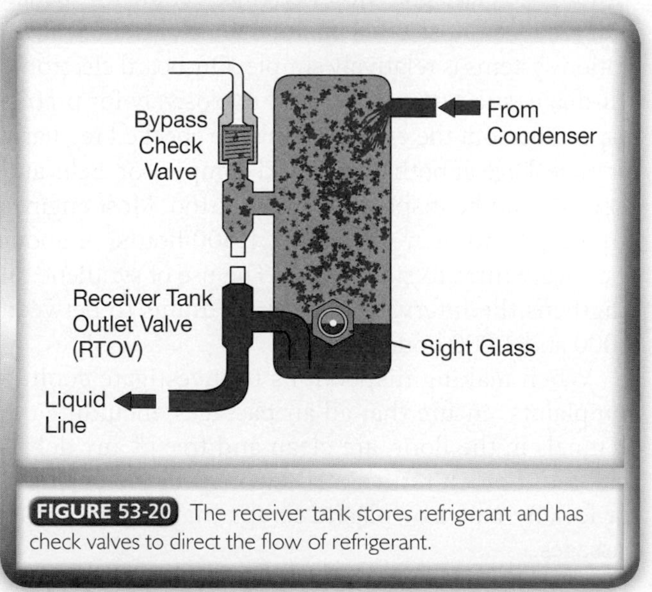

FIGURE 53-20 The receiver tank stores refrigerant and has check valves to direct the flow of refrigerant.

The Evaporator

The evaporator absorbs heat from the temperature-controlled product compartment. Reefer evaporators are very large and extend into the product compartment. High-velocity blower fans push air through the evaporator coils, keeping the air 10–15°F warmer than the evaporator. A powerful evaporator fan draws cargo air through the evaporator coil. Using R-404a refrigerant, an evaporator pressure of about 15 psi (103 kPa) provides a temperature of 0°F (–18°C) in the reefer.

The Expansion Valve

The thermostatic expansion valve (TXV) regulates the flow of liquid refrigerant into the evaporator to produce the low evaporator temperatures. Lowering refrigerant pressure reduces the refrigerant's boiling temperature. As the boiling temperature of refrigerant drops, tremendous amounts of latent heat are absorbed by the refrigerant during the change of state.

A temperature-sensing bulb filled with refrigerant is attached to the evaporator outlet line. The bulb will allow the opening diameter of the expansion valve to change and adjust the flow of refrigerant into the evaporator. A cold evaporator outlet will reduce refrigerant flow, while a warm outlet increases the diameter of the valve's variable orifice size. An equalizer line connects the TXV to the evaporator's outlet FIGURE 53-21. When the bulb accurately senses the temperature of the evaporator outlet, it adjusts refrigerant flow through the TXV to ensure that as little liquid as possible leaves the evaporator and that most of the refrigerant converts to a vapor.

Located between the expansion valve and the evaporator coils is a distributor. This part of the evaporator supplies refrigerant to several routes to improve the evaporator's efficiency.

Unique Refrigeration Fluids

Like air-conditioning systems, trailer refrigeration systems also use unique refrigeration fluids, including refrigerant and compressor oils.

Refrigerant

The boiling point of refrigerant primarily determines whether it is used for air conditioning or refrigeration. All current truck-trailer refrigeration systems use R-404a

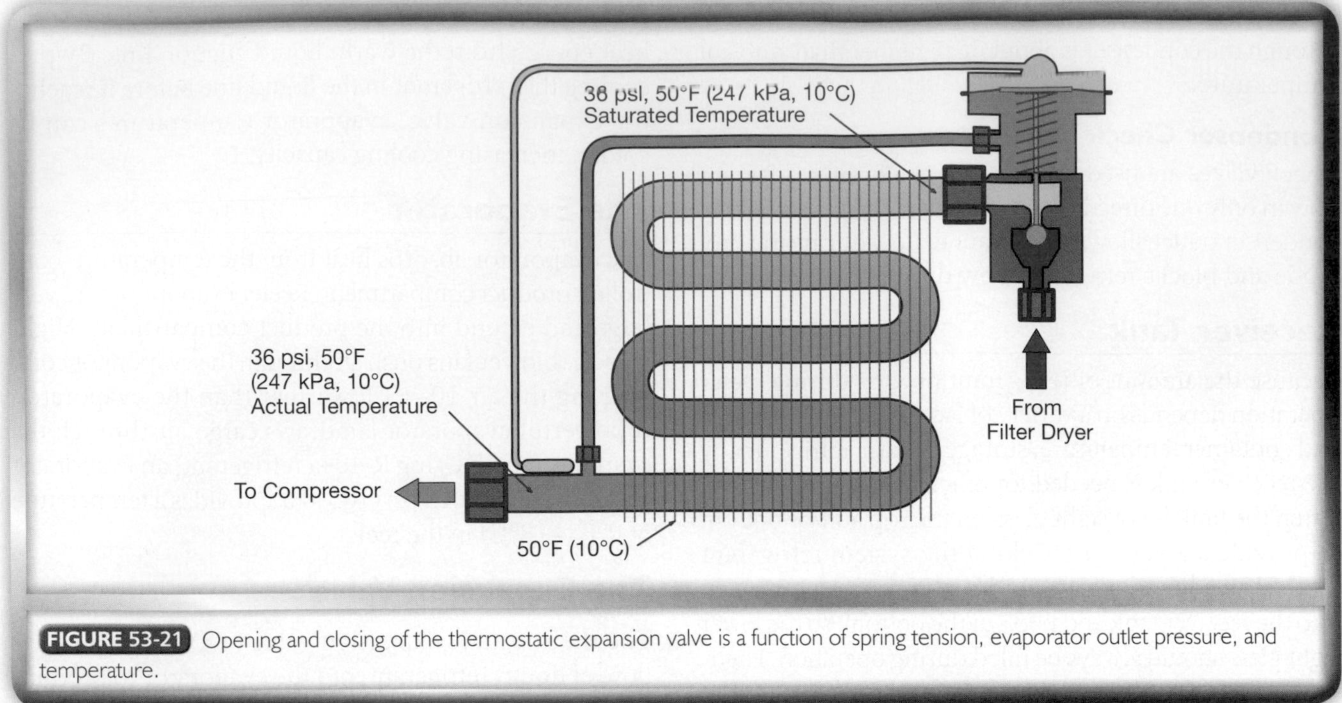

FIGURE 53-21 Opening and closing of the thermostatic expansion valve is a function of spring tension, evaporator outlet pressure, and temperature.

refrigerant. Refrigerants with very low boiling points are capable of refrigerating temperatures well below 0°F (–18°C). TABLE 53-2 compares R404a which boils at –50°F (–45.5°C), to R134a, which boils at –15°F (–26.5°C) and is commonly used in air-conditioning systems. Each refrigerant is assigned a unique color code to prevent cross contamination and allow easier identification.

After CFC refrigerants were banned in the mid-1990s, no suitable alternative refrigerant was available. In the interim period, refrigerant R502, a hydrochlorofluorocarbon (HCFC),was chosen as a transitional refrigerant until reliable chlorine-free refrigerants were available. Today, truck-trailer refrigeration units use a chlorine-free refrigerant known as R404a, which is a hydrofluorocarbon (HFC). R-404a is currently recommended for temperature control to –20°F (–29°C), and R134a is recommended for applications no lower than 0°F (–18°C).

TABLE 53-2: Boiling Points of Common Refrigerants at Sea Level

Type	Boiling Point	Container Color
R134a	–15.7°F (–26.5°C)	Light blue
R12	–21°F (–29.4°C)	White
R502	–49°F (–45°C)	Purple
R404a	–50°F (–45.5°C)	Orange

Compressor Oils

Refrigeration compressors are much like engines, with moving parts that require constant lubrication. Without oil, a compressor quickly overheats and destroys itself. Using transitional R-502 required alkylbenzene-type compressor lubricant. With the production of chlorine-free refrigerants, polyolester oil (POE), which is compatible with R134a and R404a, is now used.

Refrigeration System Maintenance

Although reefers use diesel engines requiring special maintenance, most other maintenance of trailer refrigeration systems is relatively simple. On-board electronic self-diagnostic systems are used extensively for pretrip inspections, but the engine should be checked regularly for oil leakage at both engine and compressor. Belts and hoses should be inspected regularly, too. Most engines require oil and filter changes at 1,500 hours, or about once every three to six months. The use of synthetic oil lengthens the interval between oil drains to between 3,000 and 4,000 hours.

When making inspections to investigate cooling complaints, ensure that all air passages, including the channels in the floor, are clean and free of any debris that could block return airflow. Inspect the evaporator for any paper or plastic scraps that may block air passages.

Wrap-up

Ready for Review

- Although they operate on the same principles as other air-conditioning systems, refrigerated trailers utilize a far more sophisticated air-conditioning system than a regular vehicle.
- One major difference between an air-conditioning system and a truck-trailer refrigeration system is that heating is a critical function of a transport refrigeration system.
- Modern fresh air exchange systems primarily operate through the use of a heat exchanger where older "refrigerated air" is used to cool incoming fresh air as it is vented from the reefer.
- Many reefers can be divided into different compartments or zones through the use of specially constructed movable bulkheads. This enables the simultaneous transportation of different types of perishable goods within the same reefer.
- The cooling capacity of a particular reefer is dependent on a number of factors including its construction, the size of the reefer, the products it is designed to carry, whether it will carry varied product in different cooling zones, and whether the cargo must remain frozen or merely cooled.
- Poor circulation is a major contributor to cargo deterioration during transportation.
- Most reefer cooling units are driven by a small diesel engine. Modern units are required to have modern emissions systems for auxiliary power units (APUs), common rail (CR) fuel systems, exhaust gas recirculation (EGR), and diesel particulate filters (DPFs).
- The compressor performs two functions: it creates the required pressures to facilitate the "change of state" required for operation of the system, and it moves refrigerant through the system to carry heat absorbed from the evaporator to the condenser.
- Along with the vehicle's air-conditioning system, the refrigerant is the "lifeblood" of trailer refrigeration. It is responsible for absorbing heat from the inside of the insulated compartment and releasing it to the air outside the compartment from the condenser.
- The system is effectively divided into two sides by the compressor and the expansion valve. The high-pressure side is the part of the system between the compressor outlet and the expansion valve inlet, and the low pressure side is the part of the system between the expansion valve outlet and the compressor inlet.

Vocabulary Builder

defrost cycle A situation in which the evaporator releases heat instead of absorbing it, and the condenser absorbs heat instead of transferring it.

multi-temp unit A reefer configured to control multiple temperatures in different areas of the trailer.

reefer A truck-trailer refrigeration temperature-control system.

self-powered refrigeration units A transport refrigeration system powered by a small horsepower diesel engine.

stand-by mode A reefer operating mode during which the engine is not driving the compressor.

three-way valve A valve that directs hot refrigerant gas to either the condenser (in cool mode) or directly to the evaporator (in heat or defrost modes).

transport temperature control Heating or cooling over a wide range of outside temperatures and product storage temperatures.

vehicle-powered refrigeration units A transport refrigeration system that is powered by a compressor located in the vehicle's engine.

vibrasorbers Flexible stainless steel lines that connect the compressor inlet and outlet to the trailer refrigeration system and absorb compressor movement and vibration.

wet load Very damp products.

Review Questions

1. Refrigeration is a process of transferring heat away from a product storage container to achieve a temperature of:
   a. 60°F (16°C).
   b. 62°F (17°C).
   c. 65°F (18°C).
   d. 68°F (20°C).
2. Which of the following are sources of heat that enter the refrigerated area of the trailer?
   a. Product that is loaded when warm
   b. Heat from the sun and high outside temperatures
   c. Opening doors during loading and unloading
   d. All of the choices are correct.
3. Which of the following components is unique to reefer refrigeration operation?
   a. Compressor
   b. Expansion valve
   c. Condenser
   d. Three-way valve
4. Which of the following is correct concerning the heating cycle?
   a. If a product requires heating, such as in cold climates and during the winter, the function of the refrigeration components can be reversed.
   b. The evaporator can be used to release heat into the product compartment and the condenser used to absorb heat from the outside.
   c. Both A and B are correct.
   d. Neither A nor B are correct.
5. Which of the following is correct concerning the cooling cycle?
   a. During cooling cycle, the refrigeration cycle is identical to one found in a conventional AC system.
   b. Refrigerant absorbs heat from the product in the trailer or box.
   c. Powerful evaporator blower motors push the air inside the product compartment across the evaporator, where expanding refrigerant absorbs heat from the air.
   d. All of the choices are correct.
6. Which of the following is correct concerning the defrost cycle?
   a. The purpose of the defrost cycle is to remove ice from the evaporator.
   b. When defrosting, melting ice drips into a heated defroster pan and drains to the ground outside of the reefer.
   c. Defrost mode can be configured to initiate under a large number of circumstances.
   d. All of the choices are correct.
7. What type of compressor is commonly used in self-powered refrigeration systems?
   a. Vane type
   b. Reciprocating piston
   c. Gear type
   d. None of the choices are correct.
8. The Thermo King compressor has a compression ratio of:
   a. 20:1.
   b. 30:1.
   c. 40:1.
   d. 50:1.
9. Which of the following is NOT correct concerning the liquid line dryer?
   a. The liquid line dryer located after the receiver tank operates like a filter and a device to remove moisture and other contaminants from the refrigerant during unit operation.
   b. These dryers are designed to last for the life of the vehicle and do not have a service interval.
   c. A heat exchanger encloses the suction line between the dryer and the expansion valve.
   d. Cooler refrigerant leaving the evaporator absorbs heat energy from the warm liquid suction line.
10. What type of refrigerant is used in modern truck-trailer refrigeration units?
    a. R143a
    b. R404a
    c. R22
    d. R162

ASE-Type Questions

1. Technician A says that most engines require oil and filter changes at 1,500 hours, or about once every three to six months. Technician B says that the use of synthetic oil lengthens the interval between oil drains to between 2,000 and 2,500 hours. Who is correct?
   a. Technician A
   b. Technician B
   c. Both Technician A and Technician B
   d. Neither Technician A nor Technician B
2. Technician A says that a number of manufacturers distribute refrigeration temperature-control systems which are installed in trailers, shipping containers, or truck boxes. Technician B says that these systems are more familiarly called reefers, a common term for truck-trailer refrigeration temperature-control systems. Who is correct?
   a. Technician A
   b. Technician B
   c. Both Technician A and Technician B
   d. Neither Technician A nor Technician B
3. Technician A says that the cooling or heating capacity is measured in Btu per hour. Technician B says that Btu per minute is the amount of heat required to change the temperature of one pound of water one degree Fahrenheit. Who is correct?
   a. Technician A
   b. Technician B
   c. Both Technician A and Technician B
   d. Neither Technician A nor Technician B
4. Technician A says that vehicle-powered refrigeration units are used in smaller delivery vans and trucks. Technician B says that self-powered refrigeration units use a powerful electric motor to power the refrigeration system. Who is correct?
   a. Technician A
   b. Technician B
   c. Both Technician A and Technician B
   d. Neither Technician A nor Technician B
5. Technician A says that controlling the direction of refrigerant flow essentially determines whether the reefer is in cooling or heating mode. Technician B says that the three-way valve directs hot refrigerant gas to either the evaporator (when in cool mode) or directly to the condenser (when in the heat or defrost mode). Who is correct?
   a. Technician A
   b. Technician B
   c. Both Technician A and Technician B
   d. Neither Technician A nor Technician B
6. Technician A says that heating capabilities are not as high as cooling capacity. Technician B says that electric heaters cannot supplement heating capacity of the refrigeration system in heat mode. Who is correct?
   a. Technician A
   b. Technician B
   c. Both Technician A and Technician B
   d. Neither Technician A nor Technician B
7. Technician A says that most units will not enter the defrost mode unless the evaporator coil temperature is below approximately 45°F (7.2°C). Technician B says that timed defrosts can be scheduled to defrost the evaporator automatically every 1, 3, or 5 hours of operation. Who is correct?
   a. Technician A
   b. Technician B
   c. Both Technician A and Technician B
   d. Neither Technician A nor Technician B
8. Technician A says that trailer refrigeration systems contain the same basic components as an air-conditioning system. Technician B says that some of the basic components are compressors, condensers, evaporators, expansion valves, and refrigerant. Who is correct?
   a. Technician A
   b. Technician B
   c. Both Technician A and Technician B
   d. Neither Technician A nor Technician B
9. Technician A says that, because the amount of refrigerant needed during reefer operation depends on a variety of factors, such as ambient and container temperature, storage of extra refrigerant by the receiver tank is needed for efficient reefer operation. Technician B says that often the tank has a sight glass on the top and or bottom to provide a means of checking the system refrigerant level. Who is correct?
   a. Technician A
   b. Technician B
   c. Both Technician A and Technician B
   d. Neither Technician A nor Technician B
10. Technician A says that refrigeration compressors are much like engines, with moving parts that require constant lubrication. Technician B says that without oil, a compressor quickly overheats and destroys itself. Who is correct?
    a. Technician A
    b. Technician B
    c. Both Technician A and Technician B
    d. Neither Technician A nor Technician B

WARNING
FAILURE TO FOLLOW
CAUTIONS & WARNINGS
LISTED ON SEPARATE
SHEETS ENCLOSED
WILL CAUSE SERIOUS
& POSSIBLE FATAL
INJURY AND/OR DEATH
SAE 100R17 210 BAR (3045 PSI)

SECTION VI

Hydraulics

CHAPTER 54 Hydraulics

CHAPTER 54

NATEF Tasks

Hydraulics

General System Operation	Page
■ Identify system type (closed and open) and verify proper operation.	1791–1794
■ Read and interpret system diagrams and schematics.	1815–1816
■ Perform system temperature, pressure, flow, and cycle time tests; determine needed action.	1827–1828
■ Verify placement of equipment/component safety labels and placards; determine needed action.	1826, 1832
Pumps	
■ Identify system fluid type.	1794
■ Identify causes of pump failure, unusual pump noises, temperature, flow, and leakage problems; determine needed action.	1814–1815
■ Determine pump type, rotation, and drive system.	1806–1814
■ Remove and install pump; prime and/or bleed system.	1812–1819
■ Inspect pump inlet for restrictions and leaks; determine needed action.	1827–1828
■ Inspect pump outlet for restrictions and leaks; determine needed action.	1827–1828
Filtration/ Reservoirs (Tanks)	
■ Identify type of filtration system; verify filter application and flow direction.	1797
■ Identify causes of system contamination; determine needed action.	1799–1832
■ Service filters and breathers.	1828–1830
■ Take a hydraulic oil sample for analysis.	1828
■ Check reservoir fluid level and condition; determine needed action.	1828–1830
■ Inspect and repair or replace reservoir, sight glass, vents, caps, mounts, valves, screens, and supply and return lines.	1828–1830

Hydraulics

NATEF Tasks, continued

Hydraulics Hoses, Fittings, and Connections	Page
■ Inspect hoses and connections (length, size, routing, bend radii, and protection); repair or replace as needed.	1798–1806
■ Assemble hoses, tubes, connectors, and fittings in accordance with manufacturers' specifications; use proper procedures to avoid contamination.	1798–1806
■ Inspect and replace fitting seals and sealants.	1804–1806
■ Diagnose causes of component leakage, damage, and restriction; determine needed action.	1827–1830
Control Valves	
■ Perform control valve operating pressure and flow tests; determine needed action.	1819–1823
■ Inspect, test, and adjust valve controls (electrical/electronic, mechanical, and pneumatic).	1819–1823
■ Identify control valve leakage problems (internal/external); determine needed action.	1819–1823
■ Inspect pilot control valve linkages, cables, and PTO controls; adjust, repair, or replace as needed.	1819–1823
■ Pressure test system safety relief valve; determine needed action.	1822–1823
Actuators	
■ Identify actuator type (single/double acting, multi-stage/telescopic, and motors).	1817–1819
■ Identify the cause of incorrect actuator movement and leakage (internal and external); determine needed repairs.	1817–1819
■ Inspect actuator mounting, frame components, and hardware for looseness, cracks, and damage; determine needed action.	1817–1819
■ Remove, repair, and/or replace actuators in accordance with manufacturers' recommended procedures.	1817–1819
■ Inspect actuators for dents, cracks, damage, and leakage; determine needed action.	1817–1819
■ Identify the cause of seal failure; determine needed repairs.	1827–1829
■ Purge and/or bleed system in accordance with manufacturers' recommended procedures.	1829

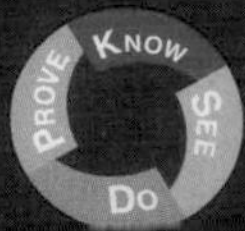

Knowledge Objectives

After reading this chapter, you will be able to:

1. Explain the fundamentals of the hydraulic system. (pp 1791–1796)
2. List the different types of hydraulic fluids. (p 1794)
3. Explain the basic operating principles common to all hydraulic systems. (pp 1791–1796)
4. Describe the relationship between flow rate and pressure. (pp 1795–1796)
5. Identify the common components of a hydraulic system. (pp 1796–1802)
6. Differentiate between the different types of lines used in hydraulic systems. (pp 1798–1804)
7. Describe the different fittings used on hydraulic lines and when it is appropriate to use each. (pp 1804–1805)
8. Identify and compare the different types of positive-displacement pumps.(pp 1807–1808)
9. Calculate pump displacement, theoretical flow rate, volumetric efficiency, and pump power. (pp 1809–1810)
10. Describe the operation of the various types of hydraulic pumps. (pp 1811–1812)
11. Describe the operation of variable-displacement pumps. (pp 1812–1813)
12. Explain the causes and effects of pump cavitation. (p 1814)
13. List the common causes of pump failure. (pp 1814–1815)
14. Differentiate between linear and rotary actuators. (pp 1815–1817)
15. Describe how hydraulic actuators are built. (pp 1818–1819)
16. Identify and describe the types of valves used in hydraulic systems. (pp 1819–1824)
17. Identify the types of hydraulic accumulators. (pp 1824–1826)
18. Describe how to operate and work with accumulators safely. (pp 1826–1827)
19. Identify the main areas of preventative maintenance for hydraulic systems. (pp 1827–1830)

Skills Objectives

After reading this chapter, you will be able to:

1. Change hydraulic fluid. (p 1829) SKILL DRILL 54-1
2. Change a hydraulic filter. (p 1830) SKILL DRILL 54-2

Introduction

This chapter introduces the fundamental concepts of hydraulic applications. It describes the advantages and disadvantages of hydraulic systems and offers everyday examples of their applications, as well as discusses the types of systems in common use. It goes on to describe the purposes of hydraulic fluids, the operating principles of hydraulic systems, and how power transfer occurs. Finally, it covers the organizations that govern industrial standards and provides illustrations of common hydraulic symbols along with the terms used to describe them.

Fundamentals of Hydraulic Systems

The fundamental operating concept of all hydraulic applications is the use of fluid as power. One of the main advantages of hydraulic systems is that they can be designed to lift very heavy objects through the use of **mechanical advantage** and by using the fluid as the transfer medium. This means that mechanical linkages are unnecessary, as flexible pipes can be used to transfer the required force from the component exerting the initial force to the component exerting the moving force.

Hydraulically powered equipment also has the advantage of having fewer mechanical parts that can wear and break down. Hydraulic systems are self-lubricating and compact, and rely on multiplication of forces, whereby a small force can control large forces.

There are also disadvantages to hydraulic systems, such as the potential for equipment failure when hoses fail and the hydraulic fluid leaks. However, the disadvantages are far outweighed by the advantages of these systems, as shown in TABLE 54-1.

Basic Types of Hydraulic Systems

There are numerous applications for hydraulic equipment. These fall into three principal categories: industrial and civil, mobile, and aerospace. Examples of applications are listed in TABLE 54-2. Regardless of application, hydraulic systems fall into two basic types: open loop and closed loop.

In an open-loop system, fluid flows from a reservoir to the pump, through the system and back to the reservoir, where it is directed to the pump again FIGURE 54-1. Most hydraulic systems are of this type. By contrast, in a closed-loop hydraulic system, no reservoir is used. Fluid circulates from the pump, through the system, and directly back to the pump FIGURE 54-2. Hydrostatic transmissions are closed systems.

The Role of Hydraulic Fluids

Hydraulic fluid is the underpinning ingredient of any hydraulic system due to the vital functions it performs:

- Transmitting energy
- Lubricating components
- Preventing rust and corrosion
- Sealing clearances

You Are the Technician

You are assigned a work order for a late-model utility truck that has extensive hydraulic accessories. On initial inspection, you discover that the vehicle has a closed-center hydraulic system and that the system is powered by an engine driven multi-piston pump. The vehicle has several hydraulic actuators including a lifting boom, outrigger stabilizers, and a hydraulic lift platform at the rear of the vehicle. The complaint is that the hydraulic accessories are working slower than normal and the system is running hotter than usual.

1. What would you check for at the hydraulic system reservoir that could contribute to this problem?
2. If the reservoir checks out, how would you establish whether system performance is at or below normal level?
3. If the system is indeed operating at a lower level than normal, what system components could be the root cause of this issue?

TABLE 54-1: Advantages and Disadvantages of Hydraulic Systems

Advantages		Disadvantages	
Simplicity	Hydraulic systems do not require complicated systems of gears, cams, cables, or linkages, and the wear and distortions associated with these components is eliminated.	High pressures	Hydraulic systems require strong components to withstand the pressures and the forces created by them.
Precise control	Position, speed, and other control parameters can be controlled very precisely and can be performed the same way repeatedly.	Relatively low efficiency	The efficiencies of components (particularly pumps and hydraulic motors), as well as pressure losses in valves and piping, lead to low overall system efficiencies compared to most other types of power transmitting systems.
Force multiplication	Hydraulic systems allow for relatively small actuators at the point of force application compared to other types of systems.	Cleanliness requirements	To ensure long life and best efficiency, hydraulic fluids must be kept clean and free of contaminants.
Flexibility	Components can be conveniently located at widely separated points.	Safety	High-pressure fluids can be a safety hazard in the case of hose ruptures or broken pipes and tubing.
Construction	Although numerous components may be required, the actual construction of the system is fairly simple.	Fire hazard	All hydraulic fluids will burn under certain circumstances. Fluids must not be exposed to open flames or high-temperature heat sources.
High control ratios	Very large forces can be controlled by very small forces.		
Ability to turn corners	Fluid conduits can be designed to transmit fluids up, down, and around corners without significant losses in efficiency.	Leaks	Fluid leaks and spills can be hazardous.
Seamless speed control	Speed variations can be accomplished without shifting gears or interrupting the power flow.	Disposal	Disposal of hydraulic fluids can be costly.

TABLE 54-2: Everyday Applications for Hydraulics

Industrial and Civil	Mobile	Aerospace
• Presses • Rolling mills • Robots • Pick-and-place mechanisms • Elevators	• Cranes • Earth movers • Mining equipment • Pavers • Fork lifts • Aerial lifts • Brakes • Power steering • Wheel motors	• Flight controls • Rocket nozzles • Aircraft brakes • Cargo handling

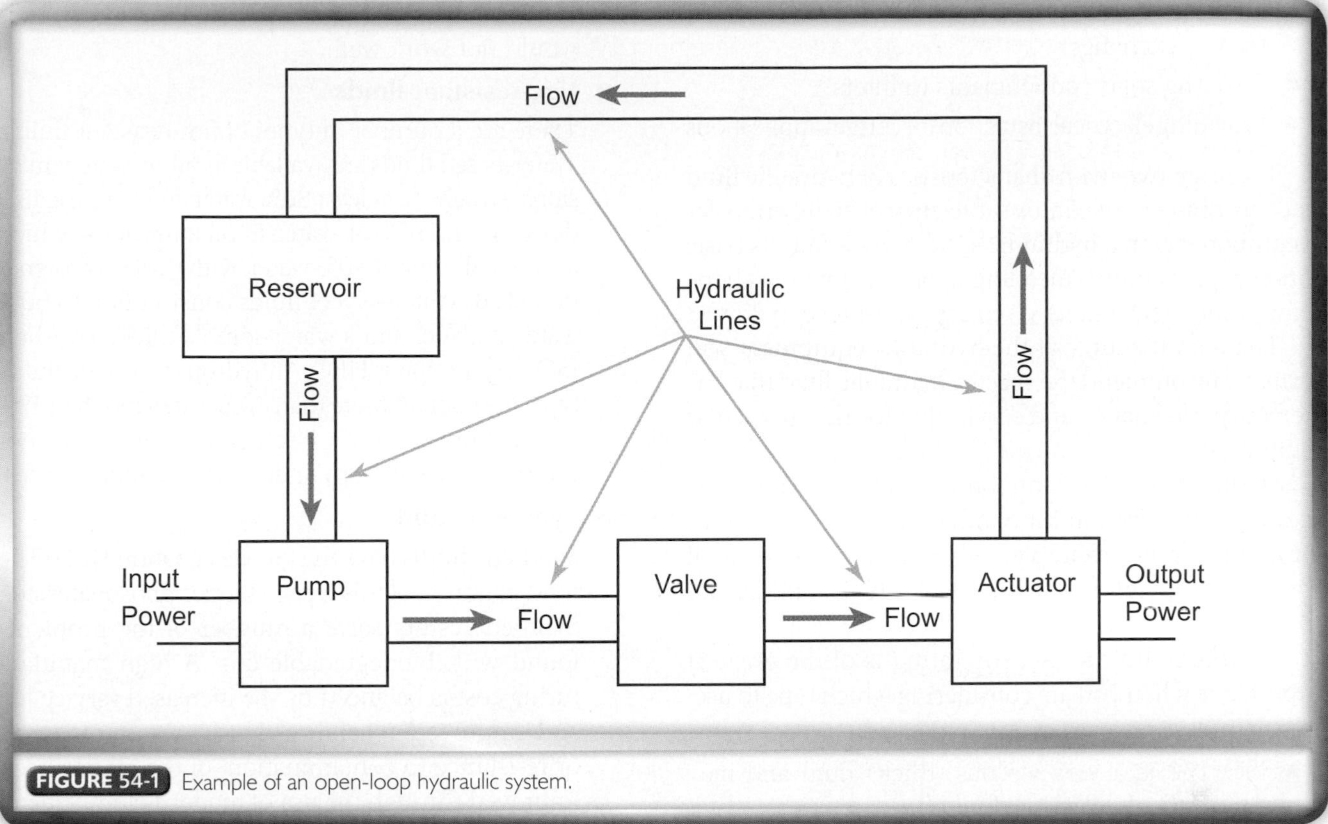

FIGURE 54-1 Example of an open-loop hydraulic system.

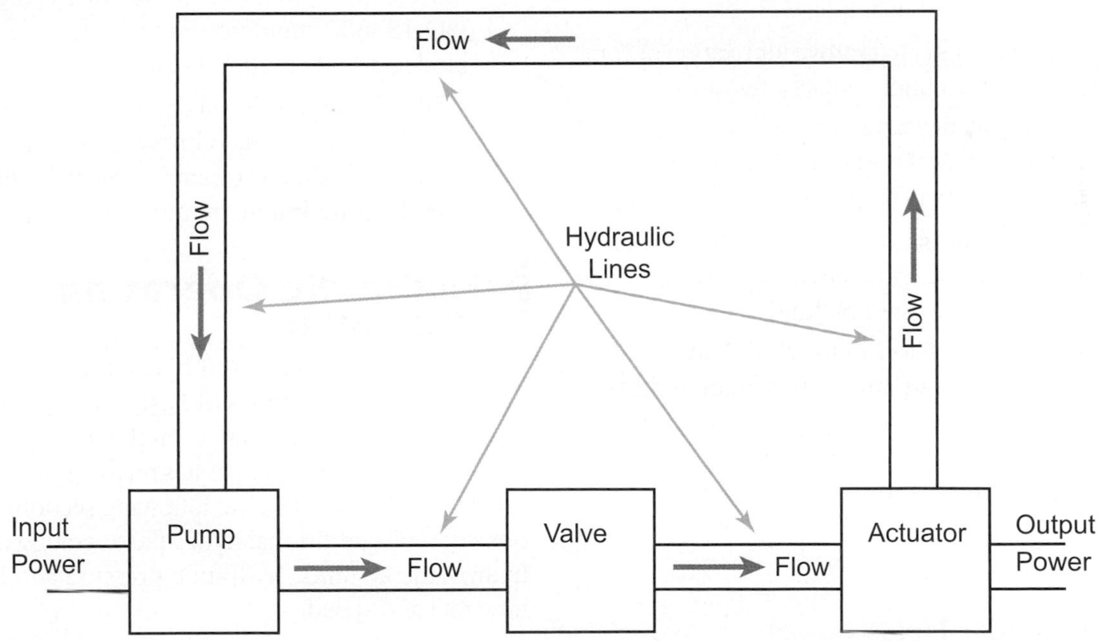

FIGURE 54-2 Example of a closed-loop hydraulic system.

- Transferring heat from components to the reservoir or heat exchanger
- Carrying solid contaminants to filters
- Providing electrical insulation for certain applications

There are two main characteristics of hydraulic fluid that contribute to maximum efficiency of energy transfer to components in a hydraulic system or circuit: its basic non-compressibility (meaning it can assume the shape of any container) and its **viscosity** (resistance to flow).

The manufacturer of the hydraulic equipment will normally recommend the specific hydraulic fluid that has the best performance and service life for that particular equipment.

Hydraulic fluid is commonly identified by an International Organization for Standardization (ISO) number and letter. For example, ISO 32 HH is a mineral oil of viscosity 32 centistokes at 104°F (40°C) and has no inhibitors.

Hydraulic fluid's viscosity rating is of the greatest importance when you are considering which type to use. For example:

- ISO 150 is a very viscous (thick) fluid and may have difficulty flowing through a system when cold.
- ISO 10 is a thin fluid, and its lubrication value will be reduced when hot.

Additives and viscosity improvers may also be added to the hydraulic fluid. For example:

- Anti-wear additives can improve lubrication of components subject to high contact pressure.
- Anti-foaming agents can improve the separation of air from the fluid and reduce foam inside the tank.
- Demulsifiers can help separate water from fluid.
- Corrosion inhibitors can reduce rust formation on exposed surfaces, such as the inside surfaces of the tank that are not covered by fluid.
- Automatic transmission fluid (ATF) can maintain its viscosity at higher temperatures than traditional hydraulic fluid; it also may contain additional anti-foaming agents, making it suitable for power steering circuits and compact hydrostatic drive systems, where space for large reservoirs and coolers is limited.

Types of Hydraulic Fluids

There are four basic types of hydraulic fluids:

- **Petroleum-based fluids**

  Petroleum-based hydraulic fluids are refined oils with additives to improve certain fluid properties. Without the additives, petroleum-based fluids would not work well.
- **Fire-resistant fluids**

  There are a number of types of fire-resistant fluids: Water-based fluids are available as oil-in-water emulsions, which are at least 80% water and have the ISO designation HFA; or water-in oil emulsions, which are typically about 40% water, with the ISO designation HFB. Water–glycol fluids consist of up to 60% water, a glycol and a water-soluble thickener; their ISO designation is HFC. Anhydrous synthetic fluids typically contain more than 80% water and their ISO designation is HFAS. Fire-resistant fluids are not fire-proof; all will burn under certain circumstances.
- **Synthetic fluids**

  Synthetic fluids have the ISO designation HFD. The most common of this type of fluid is phosphateester. Synthetic esters solve a number of the problems found with biodegradable oils. A high manufacturing cost is balanced by the increased service life and improved reliability. The water intolerance, or resistance to contamination, of the oil has been improved through the use of modern demulsifiers.
- **Biodegradable fluids**

  Biodegradable hydraulic fluid or oil is now used in most industries, especially where machinery comes into contact with the environment. According to the ISO 153830 standard, there are four categories of biodegradable hydraulic oil:
  - HETG – hydraulic oil environmental triglyceride
  - HEPG – hydraulic oil polyalkylene glycol (PAG)
  - HEES – hydraulic oil environmental syntheticester
  - HEPR – hydraulic oil mixed hydrocarbon/ester

Hydraulic Operating Principles

The operating principles of hydraulics are embedded in the scientific principles of **Pascal's law**, which dates from the 1600s. To this day, even the most sophisticated modern equipment still operates on these principles. Pascal's law is described in the following section. Later sections describe additional hydraulic operating principles: hydrostatic systems, hydraulic pressure and force, and flow rate and speed.

Pascal's Law

In the 1600s, Blaise Pascal observed the effects of pressure applied to a fluid in a closed system. Pascal's law states that "pressure applied to a fluid in one part of a closed system will be transmitted without loss to all other areas of the system." This means that pressure exerted on a confined fluid at rest is transmitted equally in all directions, is the same at any point in the liquid, and is exerted at right angles to the walls of the container.

Taking hydraulic braking systems as an example, Pascal's law can clearly be seen as the operating principle behind this everyday application: Pressure created in the master cylinder is transmitted through the hydraulic braking system as long as the system remains closed and has no leaks. In a closed system, hydraulic pressure is transmitted equally in all directions throughout the system. What happens to the pressure levels if there is a leak in the system? According to Pascal's law, a substantial leak will prevent the pressure from building up and therefore the pressure within the system will be equally low. This means that the vehicle may lose some or all of its braking ability if a leak develops.

Pascal's law also helps in diagnosing problems with hydraulic systems. For example, in the case of a brake system, if the brake pedal is squishy (soft or spongy), there is a good chance that the hydraulic braking system has air in it and needs to be bled. If the brake pedal slowly sinks to the floor, there is likely a small leak in the system that needs to be found. If the vehicle pulls to one side, it could be that a brake hose is plugged up and is not transmitting pressure to one of the brake units. An example of Pascal's law is illustrated in FIGURE 54-3.

Hydrostatic Systems

Modern hydraulic systems are almost exclusively hydrostatic systems. Hydrostatic systems take mechanical rotary output from a power source and convert it to a hydraulic power source power using a hydraulic pump FIGURE 54-4. The hydraulic power is transferred through a system of pipes, tubes, and control valves, and is then converted back into mechanical power – either as linear motion, with linear actuators, or as rotary motion, with a hydraulic motor.

Hydraulic Pressure and Force

The pressure in a hydraulic system is determined, for the most part, by the load the system must move. Varying amounts of mechanical force can be extracted from a single amount of hydraulic pressure. Because pressure is force per unit area (e.g. 50 psi, or 345 kPa), the same pressure applied over different sized surface areas will produce different levels of force. As a practical example, this principle allows engineers to design automotive brakes to have a precise amount of braking force at each wheel. For instance, the front wheels on some front-wheel drive vehicles can produce up to 80% of the vehicle's stopping power due to the weight distribution and weight transfer. For these vehicles to brake smoothly, more pressure must be applied to the front brake units than the rear brake units. This is accomplished through the front and rear brake pistons. The larger brake pistons on the front wheels give greater mechanical force and braking power to the front wheels.

FIGURE 54-5 illustrates a hydraulic system that has cylinders of different sizes. When the brake pedal is pressed, the force against the piston in the master cylinder applies pressure to the brake fluid. This same pressure is transmitted equally throughout the fluid, but

1 lb effort

10 lb effort

Piston surface area = 1in^2

Piston surface area = 10in^2

Pressure = lb/in^2

FIGURE 54-3 Force is multiplied ten to one in this hydraulic system.

FIGURE 54-4 Example of a hydrostatic drive motor.

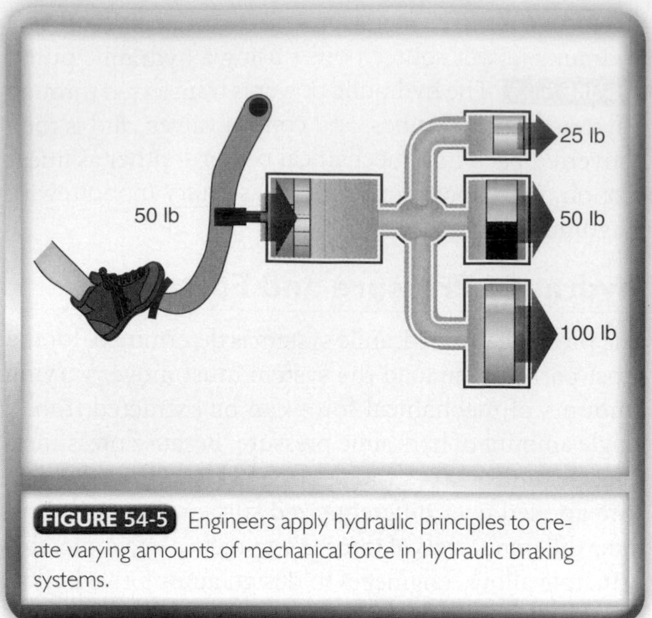

FIGURE 54-5 Engineers apply hydraulic principles to create varying amounts of mechanical force in hydraulic braking systems.

each output piston develops a certain amount of force depending on its diameter (surface area). The top cylinder is smaller than the master cylinder, so the amount of force it exerts will be less than the force applied to the master cylinder. The middle cylinder is the same size as the master cylinder, so the force will be the same. The bottom cylinder is larger than the master cylinder, and so its force will be greater.

> **TECHNICIAN TIP**
>
> Input force, output force, and working pressure are optimized during the design of the hydraulic system based on a specific equipment application. This is one reason why it is never acceptable to arbitrarily substitute hydraulic components from another piece of equipment.

There are three variables to consider when talking about pressure and force in hydraulic systems:

1. **Input force**: The force applied to the input piston is measured in pounds (lb), kilograms (kg), or newtons (N). For example, if 20 lb (44 kg) of force were applied to the input piston, this force would be labelled as 20 lb (44 kg).
2. **Working pressure**: The working pressure of the hydraulic fluid is expressed as the amount of force per specified area. To find the working pressure, take the input force and divide it by the area of the input piston. For example, Figure 54-5 shows the force within the system given the different surface areas of the cylinders.
3. **Output force**: Output force is exerted by the output piston and is expressed as kilograms, newtons, or pounds. Finding this measurement is fairly simple: Take the working pressure and multiply it by the surface area of the output piston, as shown in Figure 54-5.

Flow Rate and Speed

The speed at which a load can be moved depends on the available flow rate. Hydraulic oil must circulate within a system for it to transmit energy to the working components. Without oil flow, most systems cannot work. Hydraulic flow is normally produced by using a positive displacement pump. There are three main principles that are critical to understanding hydraulic flow.

For anything to move in a hydraulic system, the hydraulic fluid must transmit force to an actuator. An actuator is a mechanical device, like a **hydraulic cylinder**, or **ram** , or rotary motor, that moves or controls a mechanism that does the work. For instance, on an earth mover the ram controls the movement of a scraper or shovel.

The rate of flow is calculated in gallons per minute (gpm) (liters per minute, lpm, in metric), and the flow rate varies the speed of the actuator when controls are moved by the equipment operator.

The actuator speed changes when the volume of fluid changes on the actuator surfaces, depending on the demand placed on the system by the equipment operator.

Common Components of Hydraulic Systems

All hydraulic systems have a number of components that work together to complete the system and allow it to perform tasks. Depending on the purpose of the system, several other components may be required.

Pumps

All systems require a pump of some sort to create hydraulic flow through **displacement**, or the volume of fluid moved by the pump in one complete revolution. Positive displacement pumps, which include vane, gear, and piston type pumps, are crucial to maintaining oil flow in a hydraulic system. Pumps will be discussed in detail in the Hydraulic Pumps section.

Hydraulic Lines and Fittings

Lines and fittings are used to connect the hydraulic system together and as such they are extremely important. Lines and fittings are covered in further detail in the Lines and Fittings sections.

Actuators

Actuators are the devices that control the mechanical work functions inside a hydraulic system. Without an actuator the hydraulic system has no purpose. There are different types of actuators that perform an assortment of tasks, which are explained in the Hydraulic Actuator section.

Reservoirs

A reservoir is a tank used to store the system fluid. The hydraulic fluid tank, or reservoir, holds excess hydraulic fluid to accommodate volume changes caused by cylinder extension and contraction, temperature-driven expansion and contraction, and leaks. The reservoir is also designed to aid in separating the air from the fluid and to work as a heat accumulator to cover losses in the system when peak power is used. **FIGURE 54-6** shows a vented tank or reservoir.

FIGURE 54-6 Example of a hydraulic tank or reservoir.

Filters

Filters remove contaminants (usually solid) from the fluid. Hydraulic systems are very sensitive to any form of contamination, and contaminant particles can be as small as the width of a human hair. As a result, a number of key filters are used in hydraulic systems to prevent contamination from damaging internal components **FIGURE 54-7**.

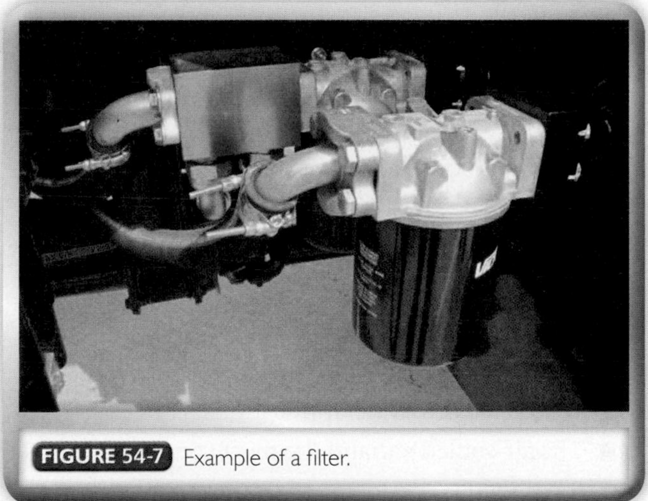

FIGURE 54-7 Example of a filter.

Contamination can be removed from a hydraulic system by filters located at six different points within the system:

- **Air breather cap filter**: Large volumes of air can move in and out of a hydraulic tank. The air has to be filtered to remove water and dust particles before they contaminate the tank. In addition, vapors released to the atmosphere from the hydraulic oil have to be removed to prevent air pollution.
- **Hydraulic tank**: The tank acts as a sediment filter whereby large particles and water can settle at the bottom of the tank and be collected during an oil change.
- **Suction filter**: Suction filters or lines range from a coarse strainer of 250 microns (60 mesh) to a fine element of 25 microns (550 mesh). Suction filters clean the oil before it enters the pump, but they can also restrict flow, causing damage to the pump.
- **Pressure filter**: A pressure filter or line can be installed between the pump and the directional valves to remove fine particles, down to 3 microns (4800 mesh) in some systems.
- **Return filter**: A return filter filters the oil returning to the tank from the valves and actuators. Keeping the hydraulic tank clean of contaminants is important.
- **Off-line filter**: The filtration system filters only part of the system's oil flow, so a dedicated pump and filtration system is often installed. Components can be smaller and the finest of filters used without affecting the performance of the main system.

Accumulators

A hydraulic **accumulator** stores hydraulic energy. It performs a number of functions, including the following:

- Acting as an emergency power source in the event of pump or engine failure
- Providing a pressure source to hold loads in place with the pump shut down
- Providing additional energy during peak load demand and recharging during low-demand periods, just like a battery and alternator in a car
- Removing pressure and flow pulsations created by actuators or pumps

- Providing fluid flow to supplement the pump in order to increase actuator speed
- Acting as a shock absorber for an actuator (an accumulator can operate faster than a relief valve)
- Operating as part of a suspension system for a vehicle or machine
- Starting up an emergency lubrication system
- Acting as part of an engine starting or cranking system for marine or mining application

A hydraulic fluid cannot be compressed or changed chemically. Therefore, for a hydraulic accumulator to work, the hydraulic energy must be changed into mechanical or pneumatic energy. There are several types of accumulators, and they are discussed in the Hydraulic Accumulators section.

Heaters and Coolers

Heaters and coolers help to regulate fluid temperature. To maintain fluid temperatures within the required operating range, an oil cooler may be required to dissipate waste heat that is generated by the hydraulic system FIGURE 54-8. The quantity of waste heat increases as the components wear; therefore, the maintenance of the cooling circuit becomes more important. Two types of oil coolers are generally available:

- The liquid-cooled type, used in torque convertor systems and marine applications
- The air-cooled variant, the most common in mobile equipment

Hydraulic oil cooler circuits operate with a design similar to an engine cooling system. When the hydraulic fluid is cold, a thermostatic or pressure-based bypass valve directs cold fluid directly to the reservoir. As fluid temperature rises and viscosity reduces, a greater volume of fluid is passed through the cooler.

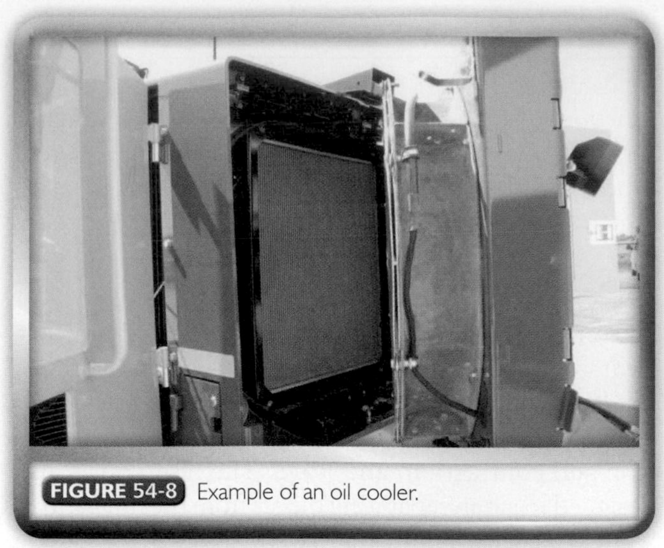

FIGURE 54-8 Example of an oil cooler.

FIGURE 54-9 Different types of hydraulic lines.

Lines

Hydraulic fluid is distributed between components through a combination of rigid steel pipe or tubing and flexible hose assemblies FIGURE 54-9. The selection of lines used in hydraulic circuits is governed by the Bernoulli principle, which describes the behavior of a fluid, gas, or liquid as it flows through a hydraulic line. Daniel Bernoulli stated that if the flow of a fluid remains constant, the measures of the fluid remain constant; changing one of the two measures (up or down) affects the other oppositely. The two measures used for fluid are velocity and **pressure**. Velocity and pressure react opposite to each other. When velocity increases, the pressure must drop if the flow is to remain constant. In other words, fluid pressure and speed will vary as the line narrows or widens. As the line narrows, the speed of the flow increases and the pressure decreases. As the line widens, the speed of the flow decreases and the pressure increases FIGURE 54-10. The Bernoulli principle applies to all three types of hydraulic lines: pipes, tubes, and hoses.

Both rigid and flexible lines have their respective advantages, and their use depends on the particular application. Flexible hose assemblies allow movement of actuators, can reduce the transmission of vibrations, and absorb pressure spikes better than comparable rigid steel tubing. Rigid steel tubes can assist in cooling the fluid, are cost effective, and take up less space than comparable flexible hoses.

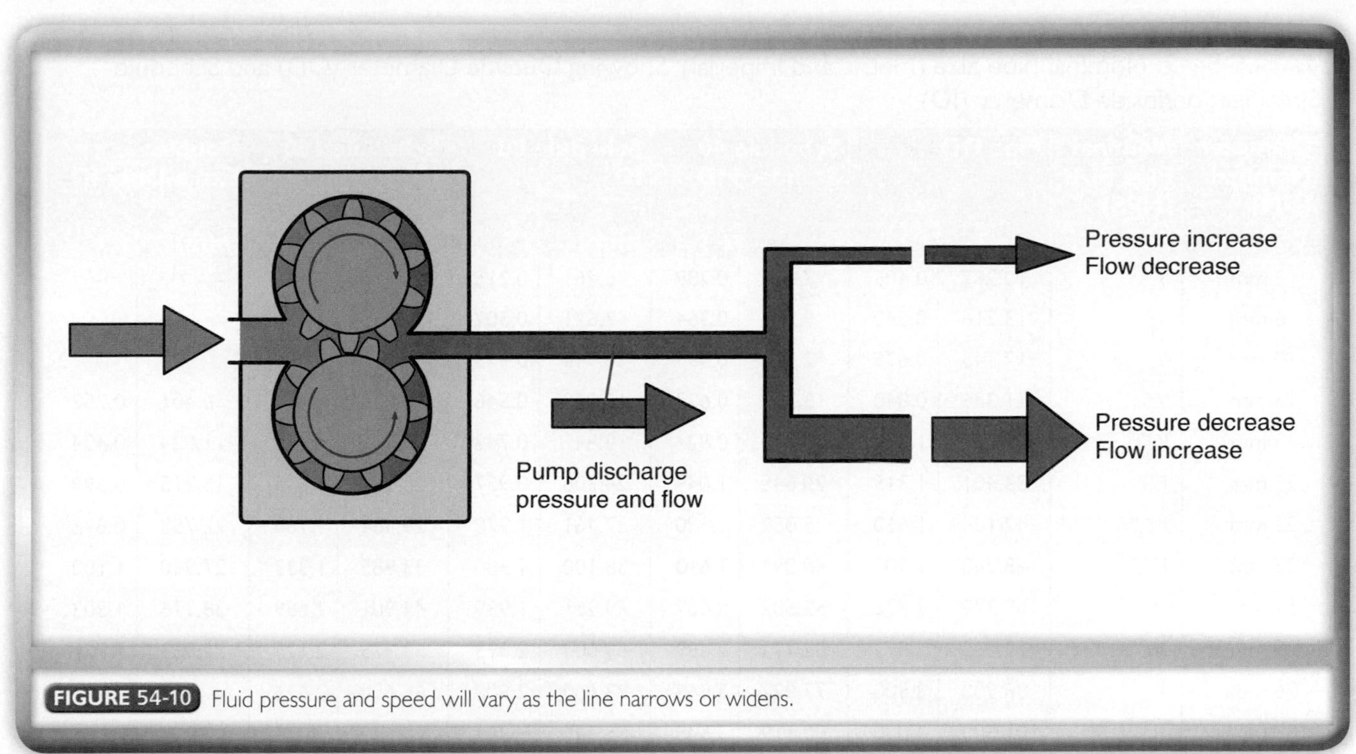

FIGURE 54-10 Fluid pressure and speed will vary as the line narrows or widens.

Rigid Lines (Pipe and Tubing)

There are two types of rigid fluid conductors, defined by two terms that are often confused: pipe and tubing. The main differences between pipe and tubing are their construction materials and applications. The next section discusses the two types of rigid lines.

Pipe is typically constructed from cold-drawn seamless or welded steel but may also be made from **stainless steel** for special applications. The use of pipe as opposed to tubing is intended for industrial applications requiring long, straight runs – pipe is not normally bent or shaped other than in smooth turns (not tight angles). It is treated by heating and is then slow cooled, or annealed, to allow bending and flaring.

Pipe dimensions are normally specified by diameter nominal (DN) in metric, or nominal pipe size (NPS) in inches – which are not the actual **outside diameter (OD)** measurements TABLE 54-3. Schedule specifications refer to a table of specifications that define the wall thickness and **inside diameter (ID)** for a specific size of pipe. FIGURE 54-11 illustrates how the wall thickness increases as the inside diameter decreases.

Metric sizes are not direct equivalents to the imperial sizes in either size or capacity, but there is little difference between the maximum working pressures of the metric size and its closest equivalent imperial size.

TECHNICIAN TIP

Never use galvanized pipe or fittings for hydraulic system applications. The coating can react with the hydraulic fluid and come off the pipe walls and fittings, causing contamination and damaging components.

TECHNICIAN TIP

Most pipe manufacturers provide specific data on their products. When you are designing or replacing pipes, you should always refer to the manufacturer's data to ensure that the correct selection is made.

Tubing is normally made from **seamless** steel, but may be made from stainless steel for special applications. Normally used for on-machine plumbing, tubing is designed to be bent and shaped to accommodate the installation on the machine. Its dimensions are specified by the actual OD and the actual wall thickness.

Metric sizes are not direct equivalents to the imperial sizes in either size or capacity, but there is little difference between the maximum working pressure of the metric size and its closest equivalent imperial size. For example, a 12-mm OD by 2-mm wall tube is expressed as a 12 × 2 tube, which has a working pressure of 3697 psi

TABLE 54-3: Nominal Pipe Size (Metric and Imperial), Showing Outside Diameter (OD) and Schedule Specification/Inside Diameter (ID)

Diameter Nominal (DN)	Nominal Pipe Size (NPS)	Pipe OD		Schedule 40 Standard ID		Schedule 80 ID		Schedule 160 ID		Double Extra-Duty ID	
		(mm)	(″)	(mm)	(″)	(mm)	(″)	(mm)	(″)	(mm)	(″)
3 mm	1/8″	10.287	0.405	7.341	0.289	5.461	0.215	—	—	—	—
6 mm	1/4″	13.716	0.540	9.246	0.364	7.671	0.302	—	—	—	—
10 mm	3/8″	17.145	0.675	12.522	0.493	10.744	0.423	—	—	—	—
13 mm	1/2″	21.336	0.840	15.799	0.622	13.868	0.546	11.836	0.466	6.401	0.252
19 mm	3/4″	26.670	1.050	20.930	0.824	18.847	0.742	15.596	0.614	11.024	0.434
25 mm	1″	33.401	1.315	26.645	1.049	24.308	0.957	20.701	0.815	15.215	0.599
32 mm	1 1/4″	42.164	1.660	35.052	1.380	32.461	1.278	29.464	1.160	22.758	0.896
38 mm	1 1/2″	48.260	1.900	40.894	1.610	38.100	1.500	33.985	1.338	27.940	1.100
51 mm	2″	60.325	2.375	52.502	2.067	49.251	1.939	42.901	1.689	38.176	1.503
64 mm	2 1/2″	73.025	2.875	62.713	2.469	59.004	2.323	53.975	2.125	44.983	1.771
76 mm	3″	88.900	3.500	77.927	3.068	73.660	2.900	66.650	2.624	—	—
89 mm	3 1/2″	101.600	4.000	90.119	3.548	85.446	3.364	—	—	—	—
102 mm	4″	114.300	4.500	102.260	4.026	97.180	3.826	87.325	3.438	—	—
127 mm	5″	141.300	5.563	128.194	5.047	122.250	4.813	109.550	4.313	103.200	4.063
152 mm	6″	168.275	6.625	154.051	6.065	146.329	5.761	131.801	5.189	—	—

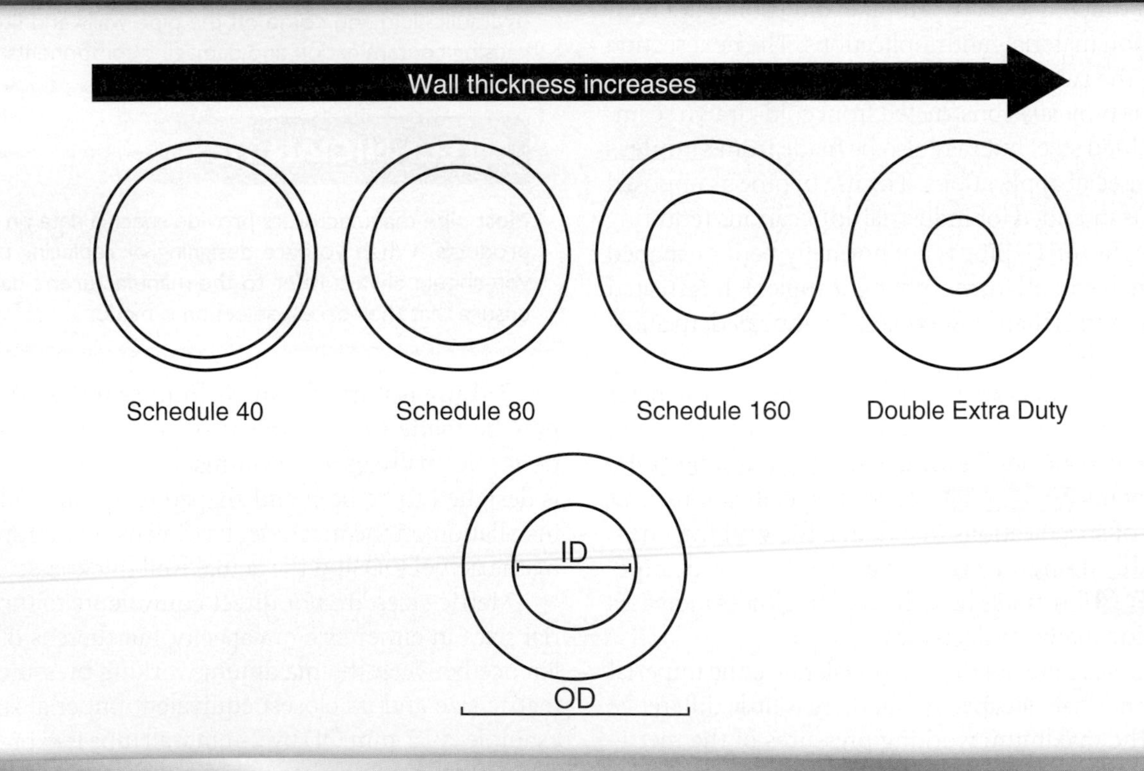

FIGURE 54-11 Schedule specifications for wall thicknesses and pipe sizes.

(25,489 kPa). Its closest inch equivalent is a 1/2-inch by 0.0854-inch tube, which has the same working pressure. Line size selection and pressure ratings will be discussed in the Line Sizing section.

TABLE 54-4 provides an outline of the range of operating pressures that can be used with tubing. You will notice that the thickness of the wall of the tube has a direct influence on the possible working pressures.

> **TECHNICIAN TIP**
>
> Most tube manufacturers provide specific data on their products. When you are designing or replacing tubes, you should always refer to the manufacturer's data to ensure that the correct selection is made.

> **TECHNICIAN TIP**
>
> Never use copper tubing for hydraulic system applications. It is too soft to withstand the pressure.

Flexible Line (Hoses)

Flexible hoses are intended for use where there is vibration or relative movement between components on a machine. Hoses for hydraulic system applications are rated by international standards to withstand specific pressures and temperatures. The appropriate rating is printed on the side of the hose. Hydraulic hoses have the following characteristics:

- They must comply with SAE J517 hydraulic hose standards.
- They are of the 100R-series and designated as 100R1, 100R2 etc., depending on materials and construction.
- They are designated by a dash number that indicates the inside diameter of the hose in sixteenths of an inch (multiples of 1.58 mm). For example, a -8 (dash 8) hose has an eight-sixteenths (one-half inch) ID, which in metric is 12.64 mm (8 x 1.58).

> **TECHNICIAN TIP**
>
> Hose manufacturers provide specific data about their products, and you should always refer to the manufacturer's data when replacing hoses to ensure that the correct selection is made for the specific application.

Hydraulic **hoses** are constructed from layers of material that are selected to meet the required operating pressure, type of fluid, and application FIGURE 54-12. Hydraulic hoses normally consist of three layers: an inner tube (usually a synthetic rubber or thermoplastic); a reinforcement layer, which is one or more wraps of a steel or textile braid; and an outer cover of synthetic rubber or thermoplastic.

They may have additional layers of various materials to anchor the three primary layers and prevent **chafing**—including an external, braided wire cover.

TABLE 54-4: Metric Tubing Sizes: Outside Diameter × Wall Thickness and Working Pressure (Metric and Imperial)

Tubing OD × Wall Thickness	Working Pressure (bar)	Working Pressure (psi)
8 mm × 1 mm	333.91	4843
8 mm × 2 mm	539.86	7830
8 mm × 2.5 mm	649.83	9425
12 mm × 1.5 mm	189.95	2755
12 mm × 2 mm	254.89	3697
12 mm × 2.5 mm	319.92	4640
15 mm × 1 mm	184.92	2682
15 mm × 1.5 mm	279.93	4060
15 mm × 2 mm	335.91	4872
15 mm × 2.5 mm	408.86	5930
22 mm × 1 mm	124.93	1812

For conversions from bar to MPa/kPa, see front of this text.

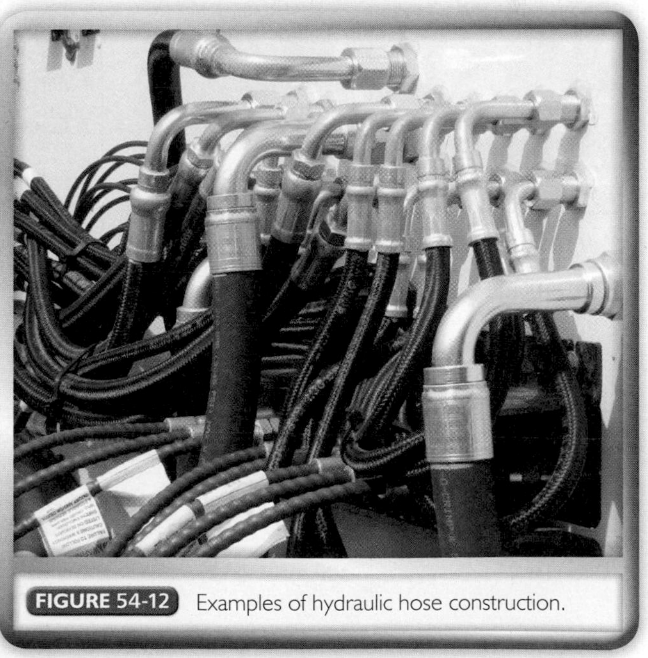

FIGURE 54-12 Examples of hydraulic hose construction.

TABLE 54-5 lists various hoses according to their rating by the Society of Automotive Engineers (SAE) and describes their construction.

Selecting the Appropriate Line

When determining the correct materials for a particular application, it is important to know the intended use of the equipment and its operational conditions. The following summarizes appropriate applications for pipe, tubing, and hoses:

- Pipe: Used in fixed, permanent (in-plant) systems, such as lifts and permanent pumping stations **FIGURE 54-13**.
- Steel tubing: Used in on-machine applications, such as hydraulic cranes, where a rigid line is desired, but the line must be bent and shaped to conform to the machine structure **FIGURE 54-14**.
- Hoses: Used in on-machine applications, such as excavators and mobile plant equipment, where vibration is expected or where there is relative motion between machine elements **FIGURE 54-15**.

Line Sizing

For ideal operating conditions, a constant flow rate should be maintained in hydraulic systems. The internal bore, or inside diameter (ID), of the line is important to the efficient flow of the hydraulic fluid. If the internal diameter is too small, then the flow is restricted, which causes higher fluid **velocity** and **turbulence**. This leads to higher pressure drops, fluid heating, and wasted energy. The correct internal diameter will create a smooth flow, described as laminar flow. Line size is therefore critically important.

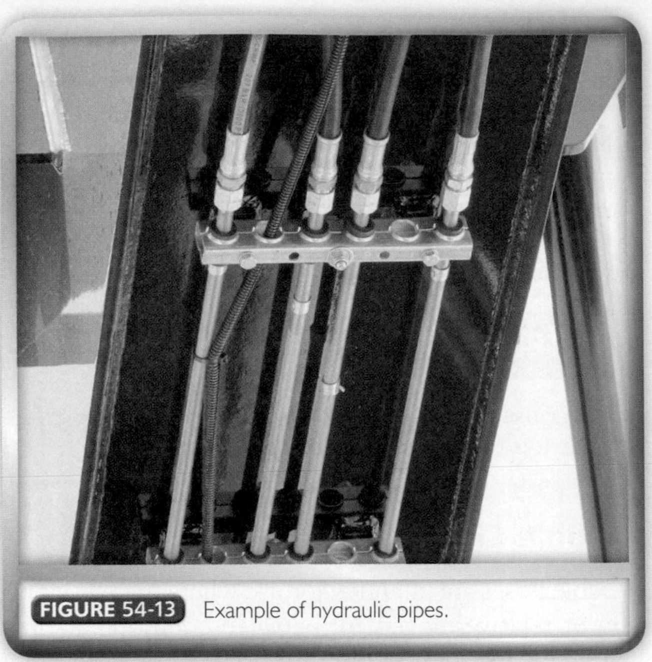

FIGURE 54-13 Example of hydraulic pipes.

TABLE 54-5: SAE-Rated Hoses

SAE Number	Inner Tube	Reinforcement	Cover
SAE 100R1	Synthetic rubber	1 High-tensile steel coating	Synthetic rubber
SAE 100R2	Synthetic rubber	2 Wire braids 2 Spiral plies 1 Wire braid	Synthetic
SAE 100R3	Synthetic rubber	2 Textile braids	Synthetic
SAE 100R4	Synthetic rubber	Braided textile fibers or spiral-body wire	Synthetic
SAE 100R5	Synthetic rubber	1 Textile braid 1 High-tensile steel wire braid	Cotton braid
SAE 100R6	Synthetic rubber	1 Textile braid	Synthetic rubber
SAE 100R7	Thermoplastic	Synthetic fiber	Thermoplastic
SAE 100R8	Thermoplastic	Synthetic fiber	Thermoplastic
SAE 100R9	Synthetic rubber	4 Spiral plies wrapped in alternating directions	Synthetic rubber
SAE 100R10	Synthetic rubber	4 Spiral plies of heavy wire wrapped in alternating directions	Synthetic rubber
SAE 100R11	Synthetic rubber	6 Spiral plies of heavy wire wrapped in alternating directions	Synthetic rubber

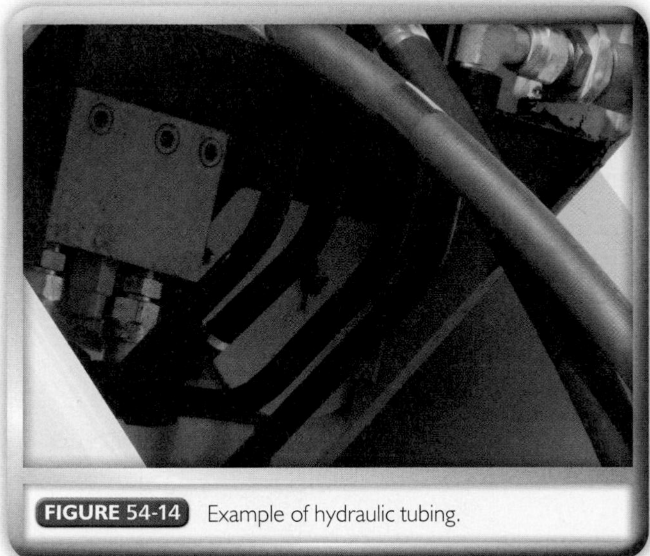

FIGURE 54-14 Example of hydraulic tubing.

FIGURE 54-15 Example of hydraulic hoses.

Although desirable, laminar flow is difficult to achieve in mobile hydraulic systems. A compromise is required between the physical space available and the function of the hose or tube. To achieve the same fluid flow rate within a circuit, three different conditions have to be considered:

1. The supply from the tank or reservoir to the pump is subject to very low pressures and requires a large internal diameter to allow free flow of fluid to the pump inlet FIGURE 54-16.
2. Lines subject to high pressure can be considerably smaller in diameter than pump supply hoses and will still maintain laminar flow.
3. Fluid returning from the directional valves to the tank or reservoir is subject to an intermediate pressure and requires an intermediate diameter.

Proper Routing of Hydraulic Lines

General guidelines to consider when routing hydraulic lines include the following:

- Support long runs of pipe or tubing at regular intervals.
- Avoid contact of lines with sharp corners where chaffing can occur. Use standoffs or padding FIGURE 54-17.
- Keep lines away from hot components such as exhaust systems and furnaces.
- Route lines to protect them from impact damage, wherever possible.

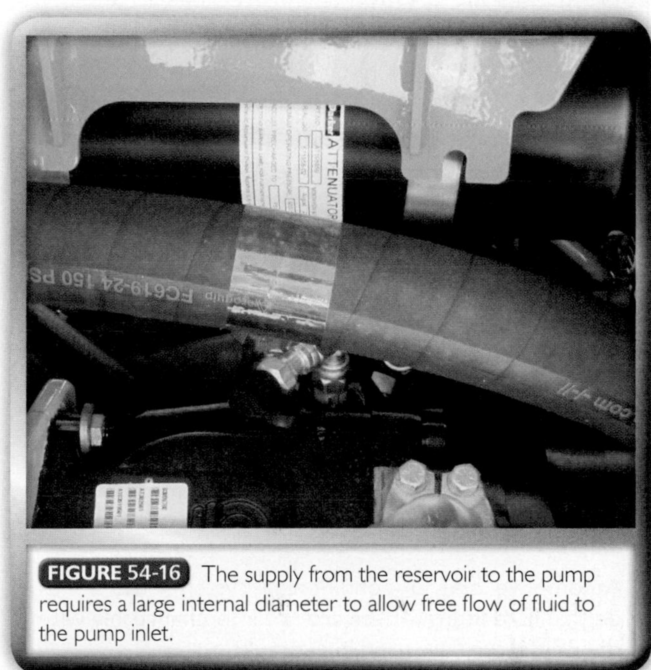

FIGURE 54-16 The supply from the reservoir to the pump requires a large internal diameter to allow free flow of fluid to the pump inlet.

FIGURE 54-17 Example of standoffs.

As you have learned, where relative movement, vibration, or flexing are anticipated, flexible hose is the appropriate choice. Specific guidelines for routing flexible hose are discussed in the next section.

Fittings

Fittings are used to connect rigid and flexible hydraulic lines to other components in the system. Although they perform a similar function, tube fittings and hose-end fittings are different and are used in specific applications.

Tube Fittings

Tube fittings are divided into three basic categories: flare fittings, compression fittings, and straight thread connectors.

Flare fittings and compression fittings are used to connect a tube to a component or device such as a valve block, pump, or actuator. They are available in several different types shown in TABLE 54-6:

- Flare fittings Note: Always use Style B 37-degree (formerly JIC) flare fittings in hydraulics applications.
- Ferrule compression fittings
- Sleeve compression fittings
- O-ring compression fittings

> **TECHNICIAN TIP**
>
> Automotive and air-conditioning systems use a 45-degree flare fitting. These are not interchangeable with the 37-degree flare used in hydraulic systems.

> **TECHNICIAN TIP**
>
> Each type of tube fitting is recommended by its manufacturer for specific applications. You should always follow the equipment manufacturer's repair manual when replacing these items.

Straight thread connectors are used for joining tubing to components. At the end of a run of tubing, a fitting has to be provided to enable it to be connected to a component or hose. Some straight-cut thread connectors are fitted with an adjustable locking nut. There are two types of straight thread connectors:

- Straight thread SAE O-ring connector
- Straight thread SAE O-ring elbow connector

Hose End Fittings

You should always use a hose end fitting made by the same manufacturer as the hose you are working on. There are three types of hose ends: permanent, reusable, and quick-disconnect.

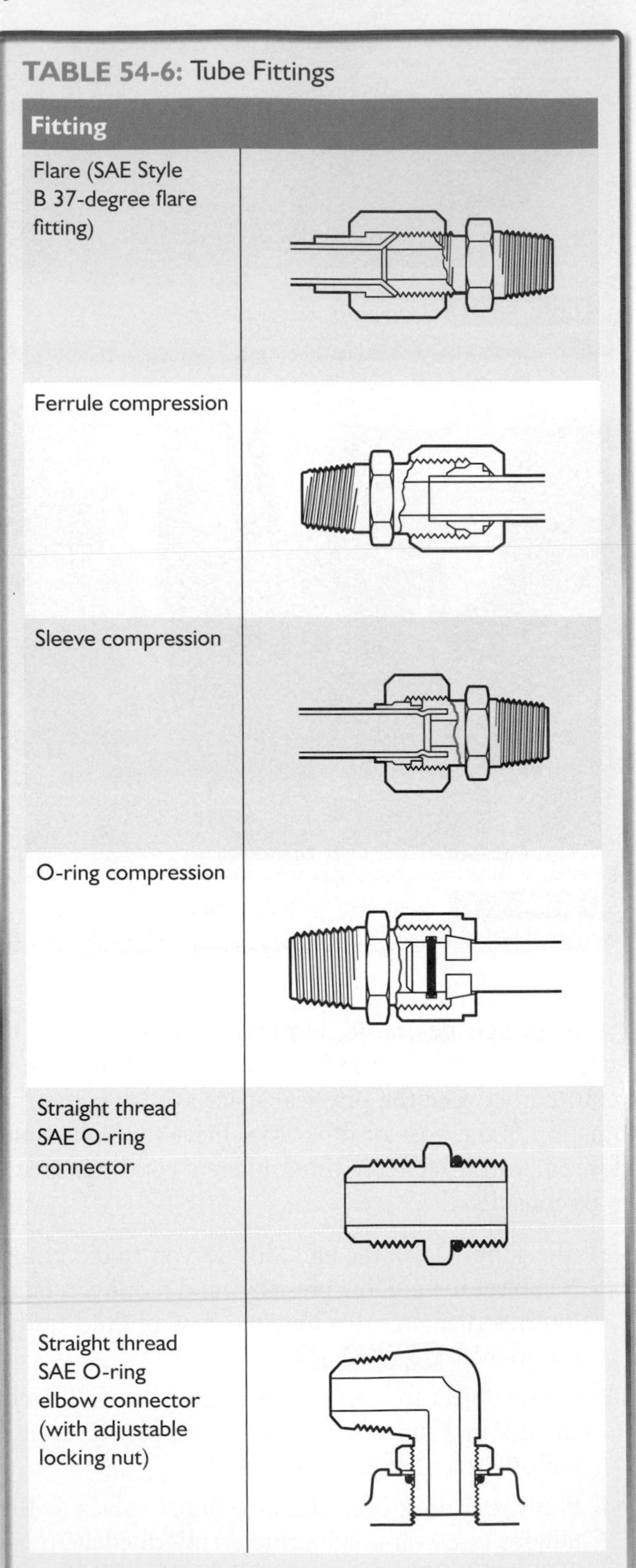

TABLE 54-6: Tube Fittings

Fitting	
Flare (SAE Style B 37-degree flare fitting)	
Ferrule compression	
Sleeve compression	
O-ring compression	
Straight thread SAE O-ring connector	
Straight thread SAE O-ring elbow connector (with adjustable locking nut)	

Permanent hose ends are either **swaged** or **crimped** onto the hose end; they cannot be removed and used on another hose assembly FIGURE 54-18A. By contrast, reusable hose ends use a nut that is tightened over a barb that has been inserted into the end of the hose. They can be salvaged to use on another hose assembly FIGURE 54-18B. The third type of hose end is the quick-disconnect hose end. These are often used wherever it is necessary to frequently make and remake hose connections FIGURE 54-18C. Hose ends may require **skiving** (or cutting thin layers off) the end to reduce its thickness before the fitting is crimped onto the end of the hose using a special machine.

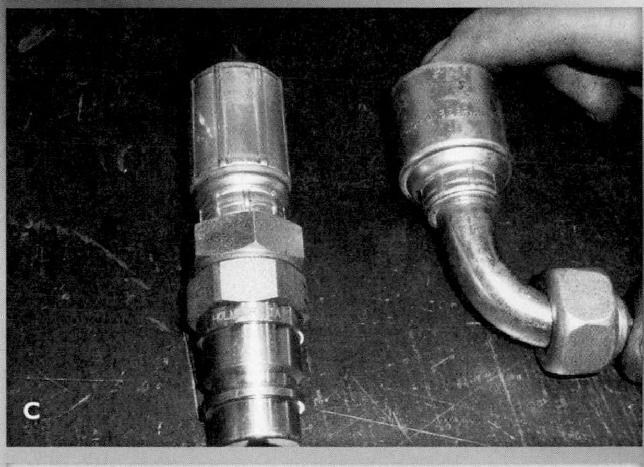

FIGURE 54-18 Hose fittings. **A.** Permanent hose ends. **B.** Reusable hose end. **C.** Quick-disconnect hose end.

> **TECHNICIAN TIP**
>
> Never use hose end fittings from one manufacturer with a hose from another manufacturer.

Flexible Hose Guidelines

Specific guidelines for routing flexible hose include the following:

- Leave extra length to accommodate length changes when hose is pressurized FIGURE 54-19.
- Make hose sufficiently long to distribute movement in flexing situations and to avoid abrasion FIGURE 54-20.

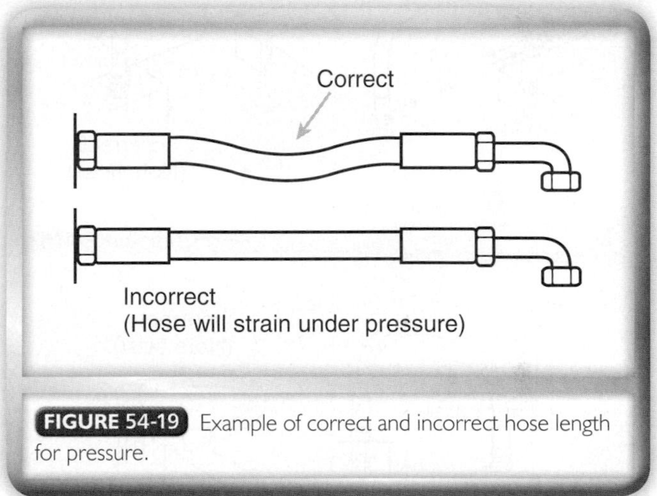

FIGURE 54-19 Example of correct and incorrect hose length for pressure.

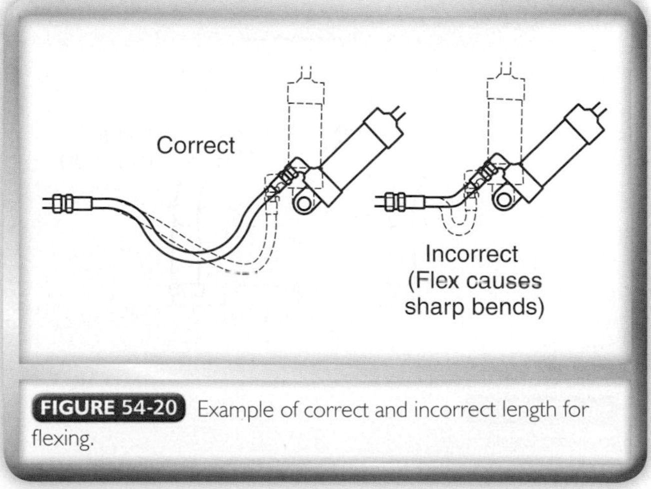

FIGURE 54-20 Example of correct and incorrect length for flexing.

- Avoid twisting of hose bent in two planes by clamping the hose at the change of plane **FIGURE 54-21**.
- Avoid tight bends through use of appropriate fittings **FIGURE 54-22**.
- Avoid abrasion with proper bracketing **FIGURE 54-23**.
- Avoid hose collapse through use of sufficient slack **FIGURE 54-24**.
- Protect hoses from hot surfaces in the system **FIGURE 54-25**.
- Simplify hose routing where possible **FIGURE 54-26**.
- Simplify connections where possible **FIGURE 54-27**.

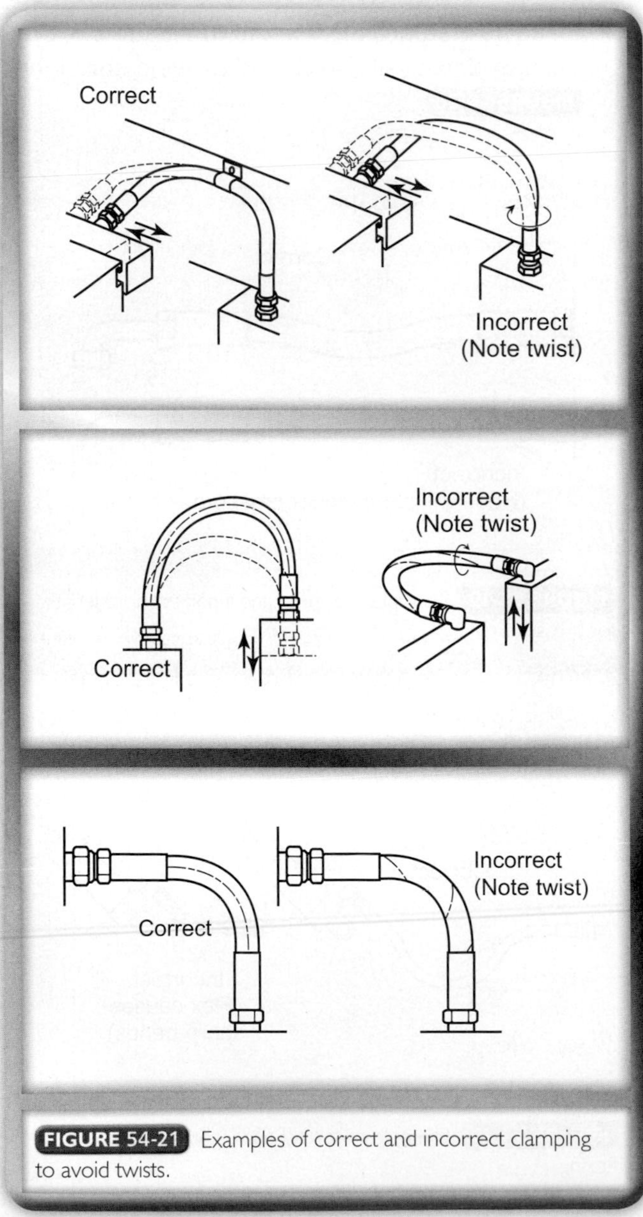

FIGURE 54-21 Examples of correct and incorrect clamping to avoid twists.

Hydraulic Pumps

Hydraulic pumps convert mechanical rotary motion from the prime mover (the electric motor or internal combustion engine) to hydraulic power to operate the system. Various types of pump are in use in hydraulic systems, and they all operate in basically the same way, even

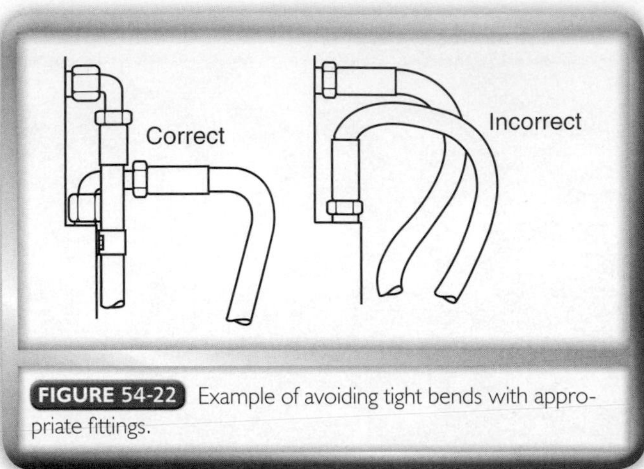

FIGURE 54-22 Example of avoiding tight bends with appropriate fittings.

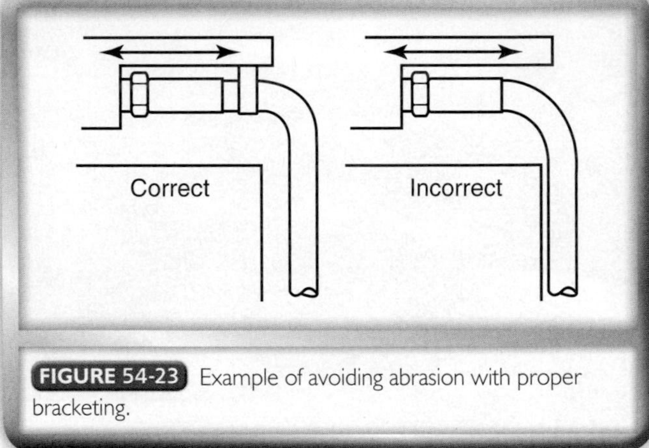

FIGURE 54-23 Example of avoiding abrasion with proper bracketing.

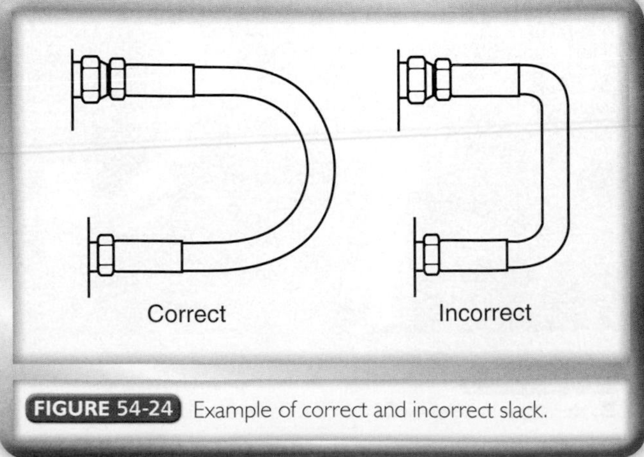

FIGURE 54-24 Example of correct and incorrect slack.

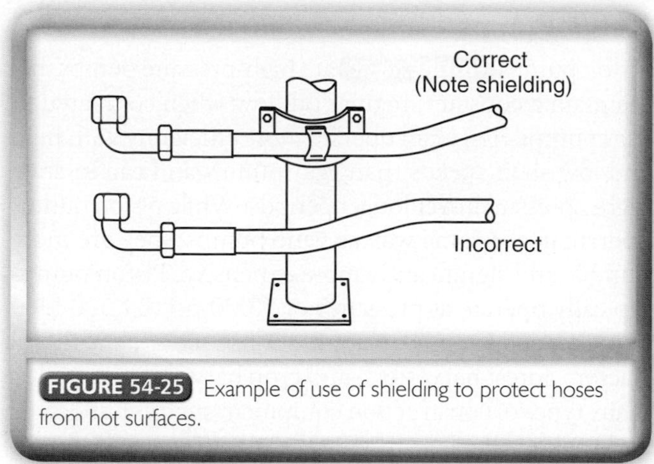

FIGURE 54-25 Example of use of shielding to protect hoses from hot surfaces.

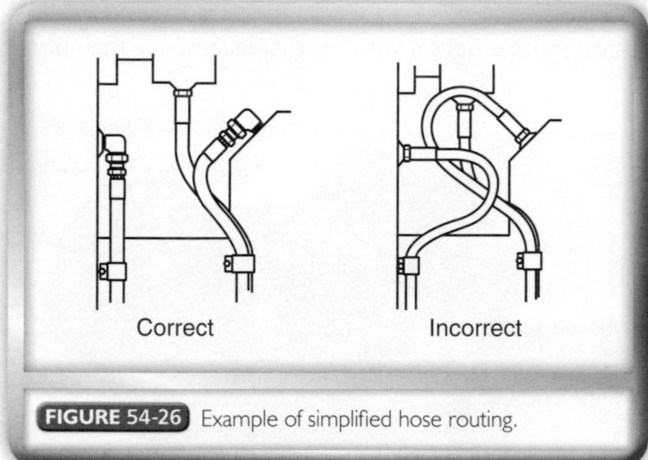

FIGURE 54-26 Example of simplified hose routing.

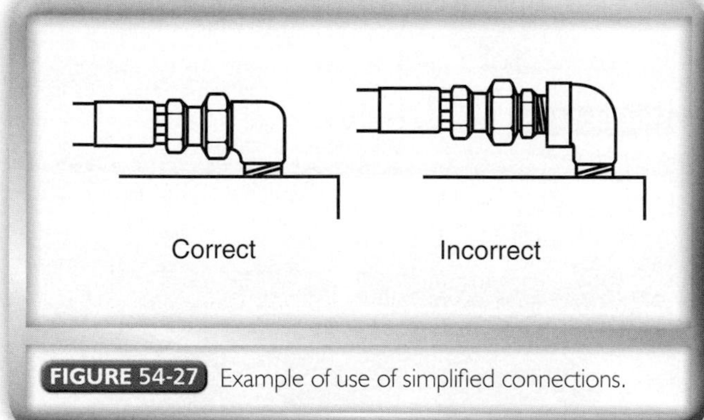

FIGURE 54-27 Example of use of simplified connections.

though they have very different mechanisms. This section describes the different types of positive displacement pumps; provides the formulae for such critical calculations as pump displacement, theoretical flow rate, volumetric efficiency (VE) and pump power; and describes in detail the operation of different types of pumps.

The purpose of a hydraulic **pump** is to provide the system with a constant supply of hydraulic fluid. It does this by producing **flow** in the system. The fluid flow is used by actuators in the system to perform work.

Pumps do not produce pressure. The pressure in a system results from the resistance to the flow produced by the pump. This resistance is primarily due to the load the system must move. Some types of valves also produce resistance.

All pumps operate in basically the same way, even though they have very different mechanisms. Through the rotation of the interior mechanism, the pump volume is increased at the pump inlet. This creates a low-pressure area at the inlet, allowing fluid to be pushed into the pump by atmospheric pressure, a **fluid head**, or both. That fluid is then carried to the outlet port where the action of the mechanism decreases the volume in the pump, forcing the fluid out through the outlet port.

There are two basic categories of hydraulic pump: non-positive displacement pumps (also known as dynamic pumps) and positive-displacement pumps.

A *non-positive displacement (dynamic) pump* is designed in such a way that a buildup of pressure at the outlet causes the fluid to recirculate or leak back inside the pump housing. As a result, the output flow rate decreases as the outlet pressure increases. These pumps are primarily used as fluid transfer pumps and charge pumps rather than fluid power pumps.

A *positive-displacement pump* is designed in such a way that a buildup of pressure at the outlet has little effect on the output flow rate of the pump. Most fluid power pumps used on hydraulics equipment are of this type.

Types of Positive-Displacement Pumps

There are three main categories of positive-displacement pumps—gear pumps, vane pumps, and piston pumps TABLE 54-7. Each type has distinct construction and applications.

TABLE 54-7: Positive-Displacement Hydraulic Pump Categories

	Fixed displacement	Variable displacement
Gear Pumps		
External	X	
Internal	X	
Vane Pumps		
Balanced	X	
Unbalanced	X	X
Piston Pumps		
Axial-inline	X	
Bent-axis	X	X
Radial	X	X

Gear Pumps

Gear pumps are typically limited to operating pressures of 2,500 psi (17,200 kPa) and are used in applications such as conveyor and baggage handlers, where a fixed displacement (or a constant amount of fluid for each revolution) is required. Some gear pumps are designed to function as either a motor or a pump. Gear pumps normally contain two equal-sized gears in constant mesh. One gear wheel has an extended drive shaft and is attached to the power source, which is usually an internal combustion engine or electric motor. The powered gear is called the driver while the second gear is called the driven gear. The gears revolve inside a close-fitting casing, and the fluid is carried around in the space between the gear teeth. The tips of the teeth must maintain a seal with the outer casing to prevent leakage FIGURE 54-28. Gear pumps can be described as having a pulsating oil flow compared to vane or piston pumps, which have a constant flow.

Vane Pumps

Vane pumps are typically limited to operating pressures of 2,000 psi (13,800 kPa) and are used in applications such as dump trucks and loading shovels FIGURE 54-29. They consist of a rotor containing sliding vanes in slots. The pumping action of vane pumps is created by the changing volume between the sliding **vanes**. Sliding vane pumps are quieter and have lower flow pulsations than comparable gear pumps. A small amount of ring and vane wear can be compensated for by the sliding vanes. Some vane pumps have a **variable displacement** capability, discussed in a later section. There are three main types of sliding vane pump: unbalanced fixed displacement, unbalanced variable displacement, and balanced fixed displacement.

Piston Pumps

Piston pumps FIGURE 54-30 are high-pressure pumps that maintain a constant, regular oil flow when compared to gear pumps. They can operate more efficiently with high and low shaft speeds than gear pumps and can tolerate higher pressures over longer periods. While piston pumps operate in the same way as vane pumps, they are more durable and significantly more expensive. Piston pumps typically operate at pressures of 5,000 psi (34,500 kPa) or higher and are used in applications such as agricultural tractors, forest harvesters, and crop harvesters, as well as many types of construction equipment such as bulldozers and backhoe loaders. They come in two general forms—axial piston pumps and radial piston pumps—described in detail in the Piston Pump Operation section. Some piston pumps have a variable displacement capability.

FIGURE 54-29 Example of a vane pump.

FIGURE 54-28 Gears from a gear pump.

FIGURE 54-30 Example of a piston pump.

Hydraulic Pump Calculations

When working with hydraulic pumps, you will need to be able to make various calculations to determine hydraulic pump displacement, theoretical flow rate, volumetric efficiency (VE), and pump power. Equations and examples are included below.

Calculating Hydraulic Pump Displacement

Pump displacement is commonly shown on the pump identification label.

If you need to calculate hydraulic pump displacement, use the following formula:

$$d = \frac{Factor \times Q}{N}$$

Where:

d = Displacement, in cubic centimeters per revolution (cm^3/rev, or cc/rev) or cubic inches per revolution (in^3/rev)

Q = Pump flow rate, in liters per minute (lpm) or gallons per minute (gpm)

N = Pump speed, in revolutions per minute (rpm)

Factor = 1000 for metric units and 231 for imperial units (US gallons)

Example

A pump that is rotating at 1000 rpm is producing a flow rate of 20 lpm. What is the displacement?

$$d = \frac{1000 \times 20}{1000} = 20 \text{ cm}^3\text{/rev}$$

Calculating Hydraulic Pump Theoretical Flow Rate

The theoretical oil flow is calculated from two figures:

1. The pump's displacement, which is commonly shown on the pump's identification label.
2. The input shaft speed of the pump.

To calculate hydraulic pump theoretical flow rate, use the following formula:

$$Q = \frac{N \times d}{Factor}$$

Where:

Q = Pump flow rate in liters per minute (lpm) or gallons per minute (gpm)

N = Pump speed in revolutions per minute (rpm)

d = Displacement in cubic centimeters per revolution (cm^3/rev, or cc/rev) or cubic inches per revolution (in^3/rev)

Factor = 1000 for metric units and 231 for imperial units (US gallons)

Example 1 (metric)

A 20 cc pump whose input shaft is operating at 1000 rpm will, in theory, deliver 20 000 cubic centimeters (cm^3) of fluid per minute. Dividing 20 000 by 1000 will convert the answer to liters per minute (lpm). Therefore, a 20 cc pump operating at 1000 rpm will theoretically deliver 20 liters of fluid per minute.

This is expressed by the equation:

$$Q = \frac{1000 \times 20}{1000} = 20 \text{ lpm}$$

Example 2 (imperial)

A 1.22 cubic inch pump operating at 1000 rpm will deliver 1220 cubic inches (in^3) of fluid per minute. There are 231 cubic inches in a US gallon. (This example uses US gallons. Note that there are 277.42 cubic inches in an imperial gallon.) This is expressed by the equation:

$$Q = \frac{1000 \times 1.22}{231} = 5.28 \text{ gpm}$$

Converting gpm to lpm

To compare these two answers, use the conversion:

$$3.79 \text{ liters} = 1 \text{ US gallon}$$

$$5.28 \text{ gpm} = 3.79 \times 20.01 \text{ lpm}$$

The difference in the answers is due to the rounding off to two decimal points of the various results. The flow rate formula and examples determine the theoretical flow rate. The actual flow rate can be determined only by using a flow meter to measure it.

Calculating Pump Volumetric Efficiency

Volumetric efficiency (VE) is the comparison of theoretical pump flow to the actual flow that can be measured. For example, a 20 cc hydraulic pump, when manufactured, is calculated to have a theoretical oil displacement of 20 cubic centimeters (cm^3) per shaft revolution (cm^3/rev, or cc/rev).

However, most hydraulic components are not internally 100% leak free. This may be by design, to provide lubrication, or it may be the result of the limitations of the materials used. Components also expand and contract with temperature changes, so it is difficult to maintain the close tolerances required to prevent leakage.

A pump manufacturer will quote the volumetric efficiency of a pump at a specified pressure and using a known viscosity of oil. Hot, thin fluid at high pressure will produce more leaks, and reduced volumetric efficiency, than a cold, viscous fluid at low pressure. Different fluids, temperature, and pressure will affect the volumetric efficiency: increased pump wear, reduced oil quality, and raised operating temperatures will reduce measured efficiency.

To calculate volumetric efficiency (VE), use the following formula:

$$VE = Actual\ flow\ rate \div Theoretical\ flow\ rate$$

Example

The pump of 20 cc displacement would, if rotated at 1000 revolutions per minute (rpm), theoretically deliver a flow of 20 000 cm^3 or 20 liters per minute (lpm). If a flow test is performed on this pump, the result may be correct at a low pressure of 50 bar, but at a higher pressure of 150 bar internal leakage will be more apparent and the measured flow will be reduced, for example to 19 lpm.

If the actual (measured) flow of 19 lpm is divided by the theoretical flow rate of 20 lpm, it can be calculated that this pump has 95% volumetric efficiency:

$$VE = \frac{19}{20} = 0.95 \text{ or } 95\%$$

Calculating Hydraulic Pump Power

A hydraulic pump converts mechanical energy into hydraulic energy. The maximum hydraulic power available from a fixed-displacement pump can be calculated by multiplying the maximum system pressure by the actual flow when measured at maximum pressure. Similar calculations can be made for variable pumps. For fixed-displacement pumps, pressure and flow rate are multiplied together (Power × Pressure × Flow rate) and divided by a constant conversion factor: For metric unit calculations, use the formula:

$$kW = \text{Pressure in bar} \times \text{Flow rate in lpm} \div 600$$

Or:

$$kW = \frac{p \times Q}{600}$$

Where:
kW = Output power in kilowatts
p = Pressure in bar
Q = Flow rate in liters per minute (lpm)
600 = Metric conversion factor

For US unit calculations, use the formula:

$$HP = Pressure\ in\ psi \times Flow\ rate\ in\ gpm \div 1714$$

Or:

$$HP = \frac{p \times Q}{1714}$$

Where:
HP =Output power in horsepower
p = Pressure in pounds per square inch (psi)
Q = Flow rate in US gallons per minute (gpm)
1714 = US conversion factor

Example

A 20 cc displacement pump is measured to deliver 19 lpm at the maximum system pressure of 150 bar.

To calculate output power:

$$kW = 150 \text{ bar} \times 19 \text{ lpm} \div 600$$

Or:

$$kW = \frac{150 \times 19}{600} = \frac{2850}{600} = 4.75 \text{ kW}$$

To calculate the mechanical power required to drive the hydraulic pump, the mechanical and volumetric efficiency have to be factored in. Energy lost due to internal fluid leakage, mechanical friction, and noise can reduce overall pump efficiency to between 80% and 90%.

For this example, a figure of 90% will be used:

$$kW = 150 \text{ bar} \times 19 \text{ lpm} \div 600 \times 0.9$$

Or:

$$kW = \frac{150 \times 19}{(600 \times 0.9)} = \frac{2850}{540} = 5.28 \text{ kW}$$

This example shows that a pump requires 5.28 kW of mechanical power to create 4.75 kW of useful hydraulic power.

Gear Pump Operation

Gear pumps consist of a housing, a drive gear (driven by the shaft), a driven gear, and other mechanisms such as pressure plates. As they rotate, the gears separate at the pump inlet, allowing fluid to be forced into the pump. The fluid is carried in the spaces between the gear teeth and the pump housing to the outlet port. The meshing of the teeth forces the fluid out through the outlet port and into the system. Gear pumps are typically limited to operating pressures of 172 bar (2500 psi).

There is a large diameter inlet port at the lower side of the gears, and a smaller diameter outlet port at the top. The right-hand gear rotates counterclockwise, and the left hand gear clockwise, to carry the fluid from the bottom to the top. The fluid is delivered in pulses as the gear teeth create dead spots in the fluid flow. A gear pump can be described as having a pulsating oil flow compared to a vane or piston type pump, which have a constant flow. Thrust plates or bushes at either end of the gears prevent fluid leakage over the gear faces. Pump pressure acts on the thrust plates to hold them tight to the gear face. The thrust blocks are normally made from aluminum and contain plain bushes for the gear shafts. International standards are applied to the size of drive shafts and mountings for hydraulic pumps, but there are also many specialist designs that are mounted on engines and transmission gearboxes.

Generally gear pumps are either external or internal. External gear pumps have two spur gears that mesh with each other. One gear is driven; the other is an idler and is turned by the driven gear **FIGURE 54-31**. Internal gear pumps use an external gear, known as the rotor, and an internal spur gear, which is the idler. These gears also have a crescent located in the housing, which separates the pump into two chambers. The fluid being pumped is forced around the crescent, and this is how the pressure is increased.

There are also derivatives of gear pumps in use. Lobe pumps are similar to external pumps; however, unlike direct gear pumps, the lobes do not make contact. Gerotor pumps are similar to internal gear pumps but without the crescent in the housing.

Vane Pump Operation

A vane pump consists of a rotor containing sliding vanes in slots. The rotor is offset from the centerline of the housing **FIGURE 54-32**. As the mechanism rotates, the volume in the pumping chambers created between the vanes increases at the inlet port, creating the low-pressure area that allows fluid to be pushed into the pump. The fluid is carried around the pump in pumping chambers between the vanes and the pump housing. As the volume decreases at the outlet port, the fluid is forced out of the pump and into the system. Some vane pumps have a variable displacement capability. Vane pumps are typically limited to operating pressures of around 2,000 psi (13,800 kPa).

Piston Pump Operation

Piston pumps are high-pressure pumps that maintain a constant, regular oil flow. They can operate more efficiently with high and low shaft speeds, can tolerate higher pressures over longer periods, and are generally less noisy than gear pumps. They operate similarly to vane pumps, but they are much more durable—and more expensive. Piston pumps come in two forms, axial or radial, with axial piston pumps available as either the inline or bent-axis type:

- Inline axial piston pumps: In inline axial piston pumps, the pistons operate parallel to the axis (drive shaft) of the pump. In an inline arrangement, the pistons are connected to a **swash plate** in order to make them move in their pumping chambers.
- Bent-axis piston pumps: In bent-axis piston pumps, the pistons operate at an angle to the axis (drive shaft) of the pump.
- Radial piston pumps: Radial piston pumps operate perpendicular to the axis of the pump. They are rather like a radial engine in that the pistons rotate.

> **TECHNICIAN TIP**
>
> Piston pumps are extremely sensitive to contamination.

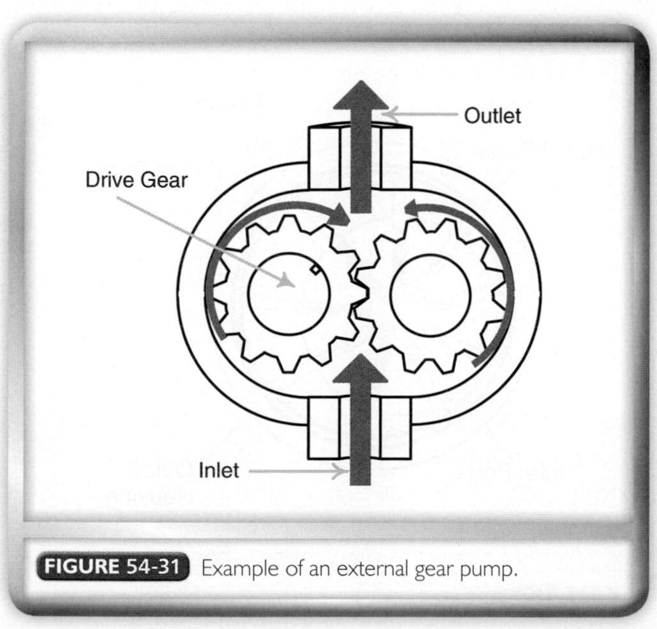

FIGURE 54-31 Example of an external gear pump.

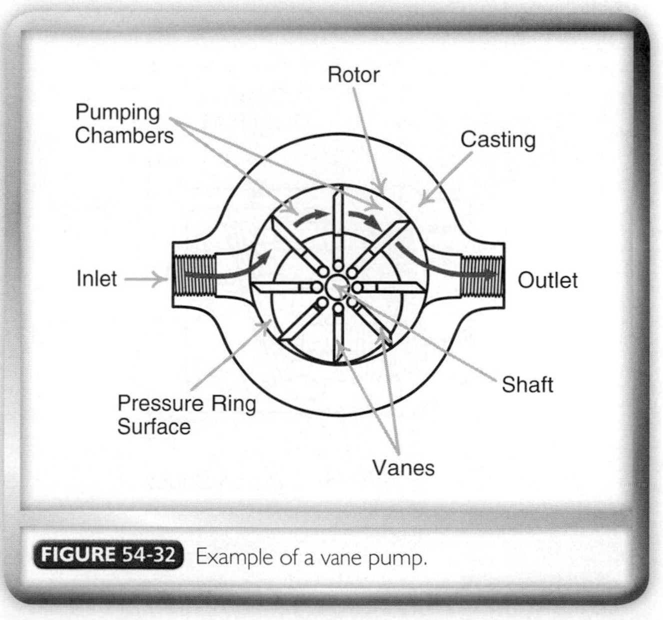

FIGURE 54-32 Example of a vane pump.

Axial Piston Pumps

Axial piston pumps have a rotating cylinder unit that contains a number of pistons. The pistons reciprocate in and out of the cylinder unit. The gear wheels maintain the correct alignment between the shaft and cylinder assembly, and the pistons force the oil out through the outlet port. Each piston has a number of metal sealing rings, similar to an automotive engine. Axial piston pumps can typically operate at pressures of 5,000 psi (34,500 kPa) or higher.

The angled swash plate of an inline axial pump controls the piston position. As the piston barrel rotates, some pistons pull away from inlet port, allowing fluid to be pushed into the pump, and some pistons are pushed in towards the outlet port, forcing fluid out of the pump and into the system FIGURE 54-33.

Bent-axis pumps operate in the same way as inline axial piston pumps, except that the piston barrel is set at a fixed angle to the swash plate rather than having the swash plate set at a fixed angle to the pistons FIGURE 54-34.

Radial Piston Pumps

Radial piston pumps work on the same principle as radial piston engines. The piston block rotates around a fixed **pintle** (crankshaft), allowing pistons to reciprocate inside their pumping chambers, alternately drawing the hydraulic fluid in and then pushing it out into the system FIGURE 54-35. Radial piston pumps can typically operate at pressures of 5,000 psi (34,500 kPa) or higher.

Variable-Displacement Pump Operation

Vane pumps and piston pumps (but not gear pumps) can have a variable-displacement capability. Variable-displacement pumps have a mechanism that allows the displacement to be changed.

Variable-Displacement Vane Pumps

Variable-displacement vane pumps have a moveable pressurizing, or stator ring, inside the pump,

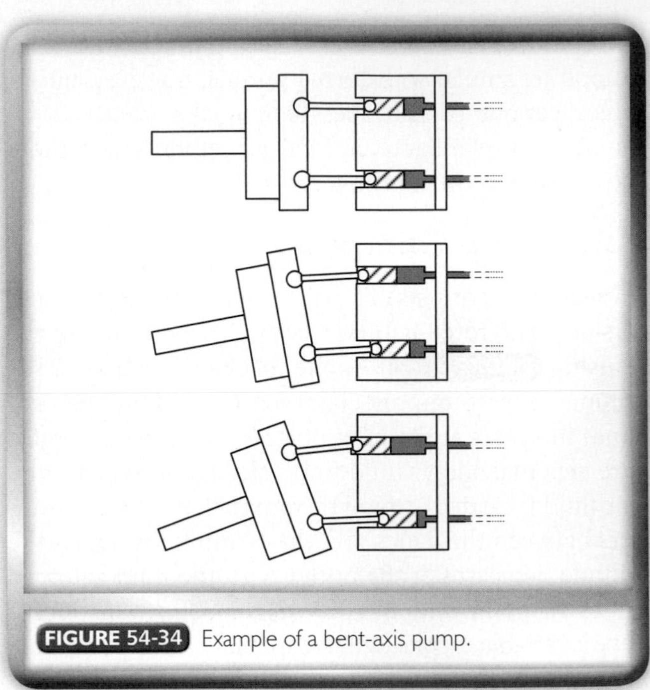

FIGURE 54-34 Example of a bent-axis pump.

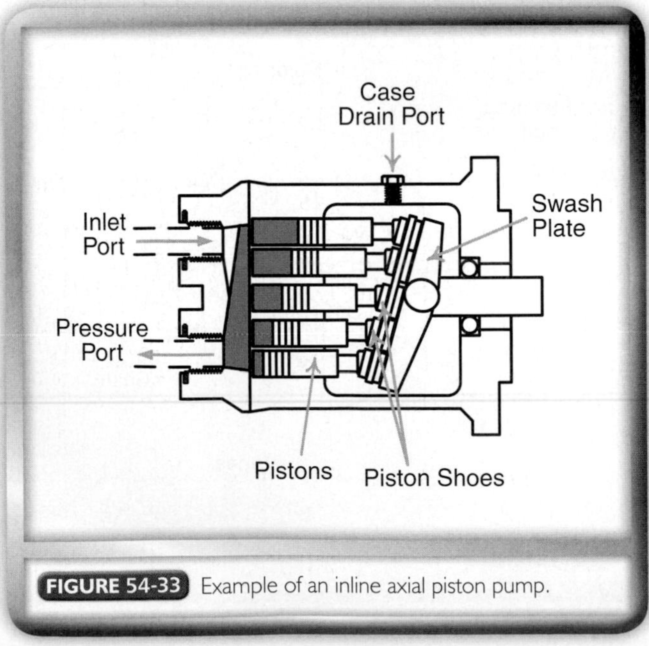

FIGURE 54-33 Example of an inline axial piston pump.

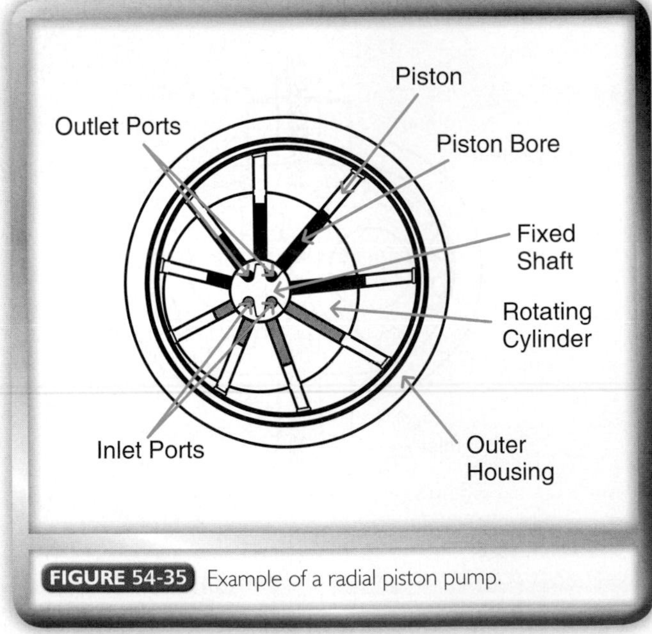

FIGURE 54-35 Example of a radial piston pump.

and a screw adjustment positions the pressure ring FIGURE 54-36. The stator ring can be positioned anywhere between the zero-flow position and the maximum-flow position. It can automatically adjust the amount of volume it displaces at each rotation by centering the rotor when the pressure in the system starts to build. This type of pump protects itself against excessive pressure by reducing power consumption as the flow rate decreases. When pressure reaches a set value, the compensator spring force equals the hydraulic piston force. As pressure continues to increase, the compensator spring is compressed until maximum set pressure is achieved. At this point, the pump is protected because it produces no more flow, resulting in no power loss and no fluid heating.

Variable-Displacement Piston Pumps

A variable-displacement piston pump is designed to deliver oil flow on demand through a series of reciprocating pistons housed in a rotating cylinder. The stroke of these pistons is controlled either mechanically or electronically by control cylinders attached to a swash plate that is part of a moveable yoke. The yoke (swash plate) angle varies the piston stroke, increasing or decreasing pump displacement. An external screw mechanism is used to adjust the swash plate angle FIGURE 54-37. When the swash plate moves, the pistons draw in oil like syringes and force it into the valve block. The pistons have brass shoes called slipper plates that run against a cam plate. The angle of the cam plate forces the pistons to reciprocate in and out. A metal disc, called the **valve plate**, interfaces between the rotating cylinder and the pump's inlet and outlet ports. A thin film of oil provides lubrication and maintains the seal between the stationary valve plate and the rotating cylinder. The valve plate or rotary cylinder face may be coated with a softer metal to provide a bearing surface.

A negative-control pump is used in an open-loop, or constant-flow system. When no function is operated within this system, unused oil flowing back to the tank generates a negative control signal, which moves the pump swash plate to reduce the piston's stroke and reduce oil flow. When the operator engages a control—in an excavator, for example—oil flow is directed away from the tank and out to the required actuator. The reduction in unused oil flow to the tank reduces the negative signal, which allows the swash plate to pivot. This action increases piston stroke and pump flow to meet the demand from the operator. If the equipment operator releases the controls, the swash plate moves to the minimum flow position. Negative-control systems are common in larger fluid-powered equipment applications where many actuators are in operation simultaneously and require good flow control and cooling.

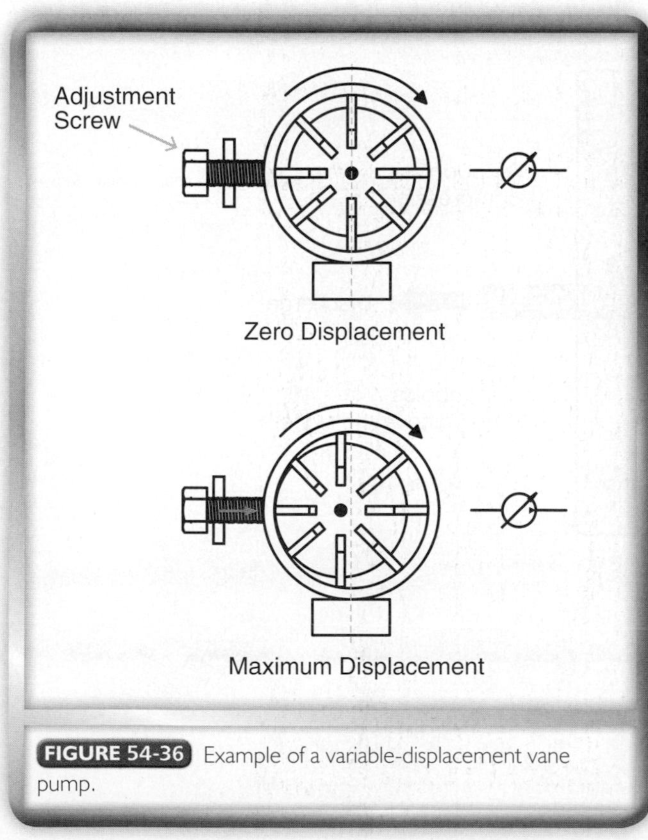

FIGURE 54-36 Example of a variable-displacement vane pump.

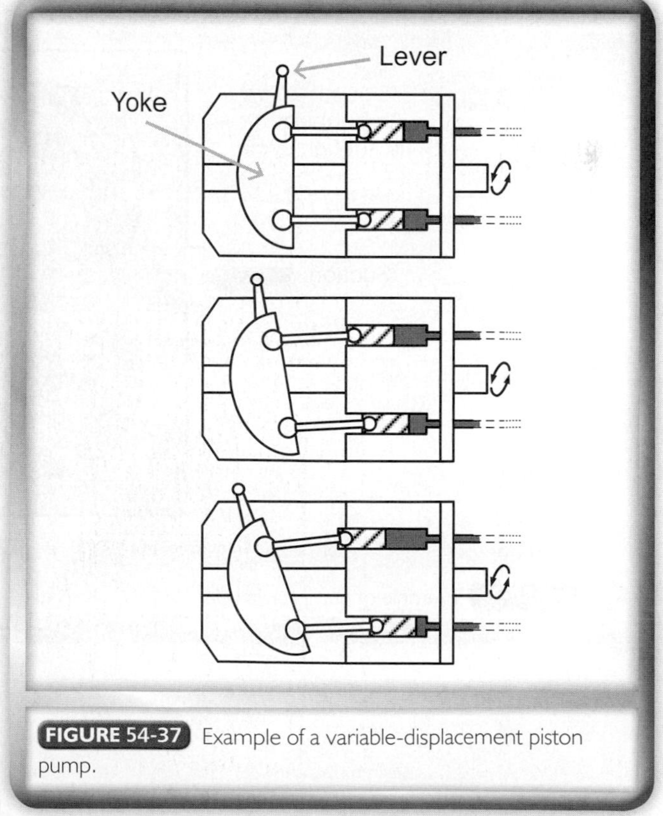

FIGURE 54-37 Example of a variable-displacement piston pump.

A similar type of pump known as a closed-center pump is used in closed-loop load-sensing systems to provide for a positive control signal when a function is operated. No signal is present when the valves are in neutral, and closed-center pumps reduce fluid flow to practically nothing when no function is operated. Most equipment that uses a load-sensing system relies on variable-displacement pumps to deliver hydraulic fluid.

Pump Cavitation

Cavitation is the formation of air or gas bubbles at the inlet of the pump because the pump does not completely fill with fluid FIGURE 54-38. The term is also used to denote the collapse of air and gas bubbles in the pump, which creates a distinctive noise.

Causes of Pump Cavitation

True cavitation results from a restriction in the pump suction line, allowing a high vacuum in that line. True cavitation allows vapor bubbles to form in the fluid, and air bubbles to evolve from the fluid. True cavitation can be caused by a clogged suction filter, items stuck in the suction line, a kinked suction line, a collapsed hose line, a suction line that is too small or too long, or a clogged reservoir breather.

Fluid **aeration** means excessive air in the fluid. It can be caused by a low fluid level; leaking fittings in the suction line; leaking seals somewhere in the system, allowing air to enter; new components being installed without being filled with fluid; or foaming in the tank.

Effects of Pump Cavitation

It is important to inspect hydraulic pumps for cavitation because the effects can be damaging to the system. Some of the effects of pump cavitation include:

- Excessive pump noise
- Excessive pump wear due to bubbles and cavities imploding and damaging the pump components
- System contamination due to debris from pump component damage

Common Causes of Pump Failure

Pump inspections and installation and maintenance procedures should be followed carefully to avoid some of the common causes of pump failure. These include:

- Contaminated fluid (the most common cause of pump failure)
- Cavitation
- Incorrect fluid
- Running dry

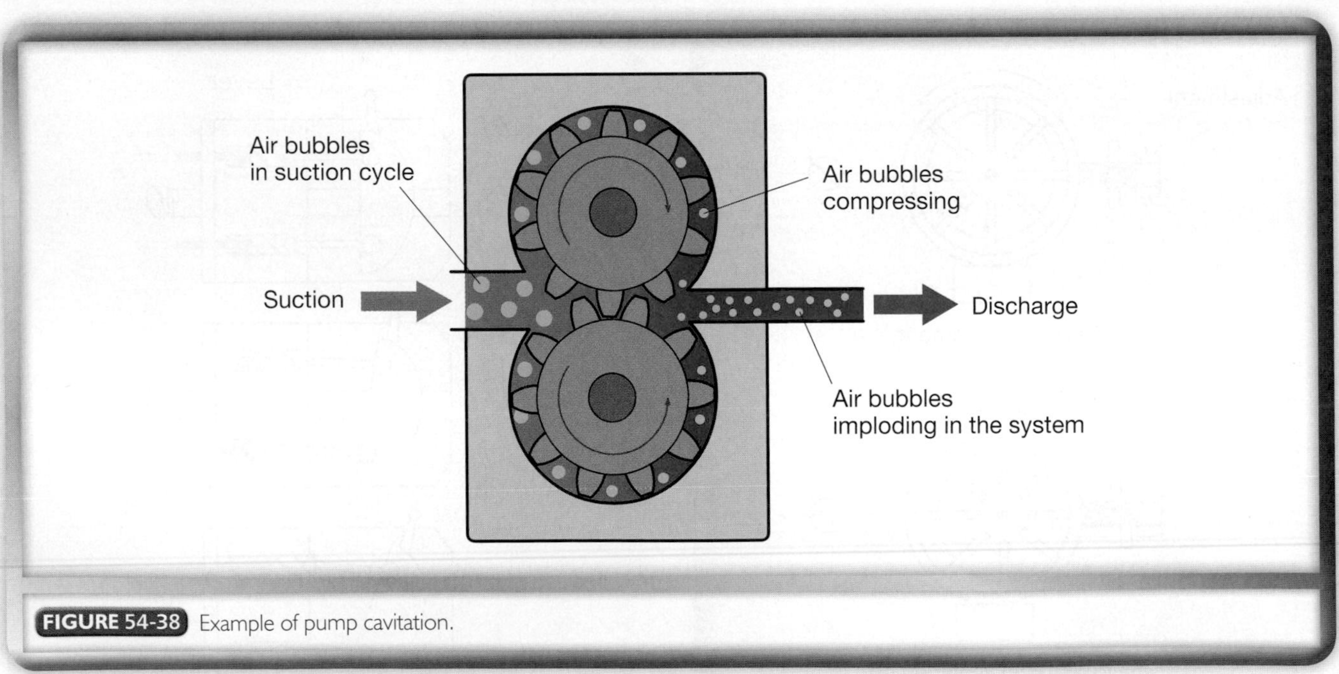

FIGURE 54-38 Example of pump cavitation.

- Shearing shafts due to excessive system pressure causing pump mechanism to stall
- Clogged or kinked case drain lines
- Abuse and incorrect operating procedures (examples: excessive pressures or speeds)

> **TECHNICIAN TIP**
>
> Contaminated fluid is the most common cause of pump failure.

These problems can all be avoided by keeping the equipment regularly serviced and maintained, and operating within the system's designed capacity.

Pump Symbols

FIGURE 54-39 shows some common pump symbols used in hydraulic circuit diagrams. Note that the symbols for pumps do not distinguish between piston, vane, and gear pumps.

Hydraulic Actuators

Hydraulic actuators convert the fluid energy back into mechanical energy to move the load. They can come in two forms: linear actuators, such as hydraulic cylinders, or rams; and rotary actuators or hydraulic motors. This section describes the two basic types, their common identifying symbols, their functions and applications, and identifies the parts of each type of actuator.

FIGURE 54-40 shows the actuator symbols used in hydraulic circuit diagrams. Note that the symbols for hydraulic motors do not distinguish between piston, vane and gear motors.

> **TECHNICIAN TIP**
>
> Many variations on these basic symbols exist. Consult any hydraulics textbook or perform a simple keyword search online for additional examples.

Linear Actuators (Hydraulic Cylinders)

Hydraulic cylinders are used to do everything from steering cars and upending trays on dump trucks, to moving giant shovels in open-pit mines. They can be used to provide either **angular** or linear motion.

Cylinders used for angular motion are **trunnion** or mounted so that the cylinder is free to move from its original alignment. This allows the load to move in an arc. An example of an application of angular motion is a cylinder that extends the bed of a garbage truck.

Cylinders used for linear motion are mounted rigidly so that they cannot move from their original alignment. All motion resulting from their extension or retraction is linear and along the centerline of the cylinder. Hydraulic **cylinders**, or rams, are **linear** actuators: They provide for a linear form of energy transfer to produce either linear or angular motion. In fluid power mechanics, the hydraulic cylinder, which houses the ram, enables the lifting of heavy materials in mobile equipment applications

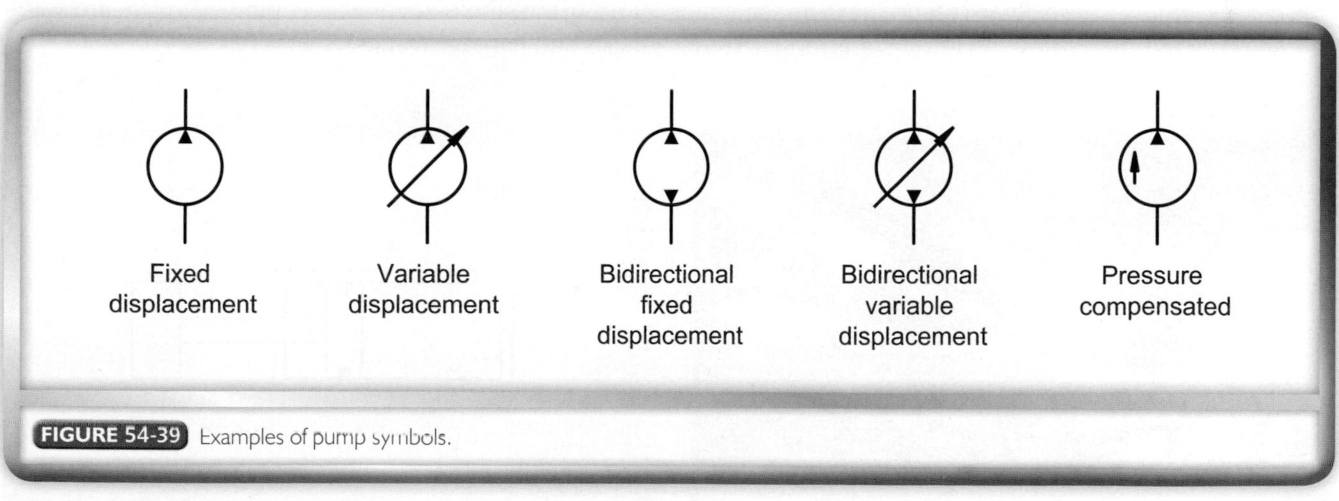

FIGURE 54-39 Examples of pump symbols.

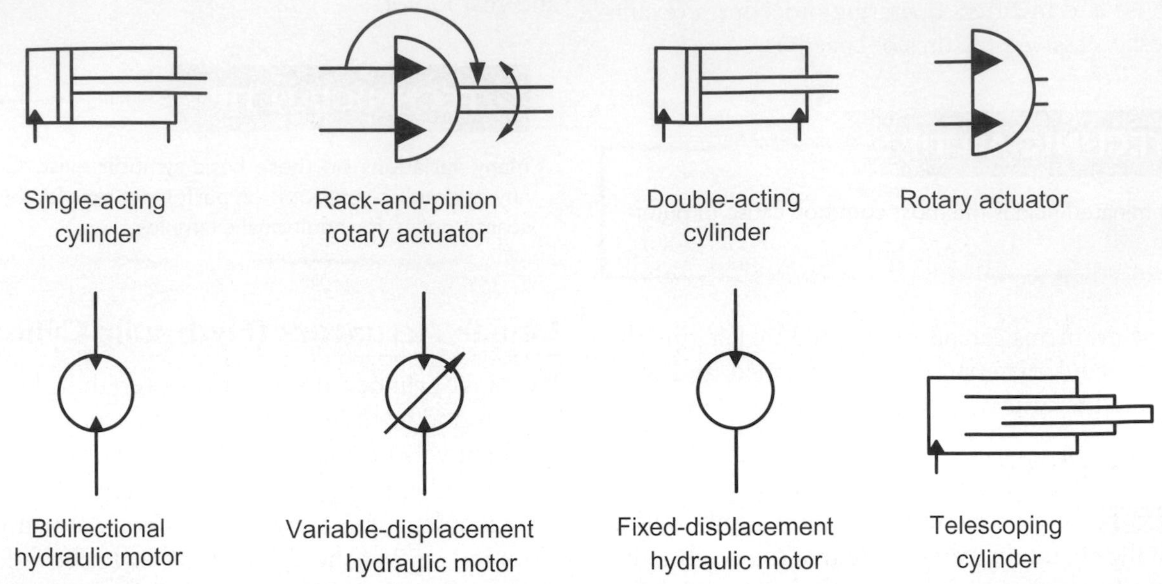

FIGURE 54-40 Symbols for common types of hydraulic actuators.

FIGURE 54-41. They come in various types: single-acting and telescoping cylinders, and double-acting cylinders.

Single-Acting and Telescoping Cylinders

In a single-acting cylinder, the oil flows into only one side of the cylinder, normally to extend the cylinder, and can be retracted by oil flow. Cylinders are returned to their original positions by either the load or a spring **FIGURE 54-42**.

Telescoping cylinders are usually single-acting cylinders that have two or more sections that are extended **sequentially** **FIGURE 54-43**. Some examples of applications using single-acting telescoping cylinders are crane masts and garbage trucks.

FIGURE 54-41 Example of a hydraulic cylinder.

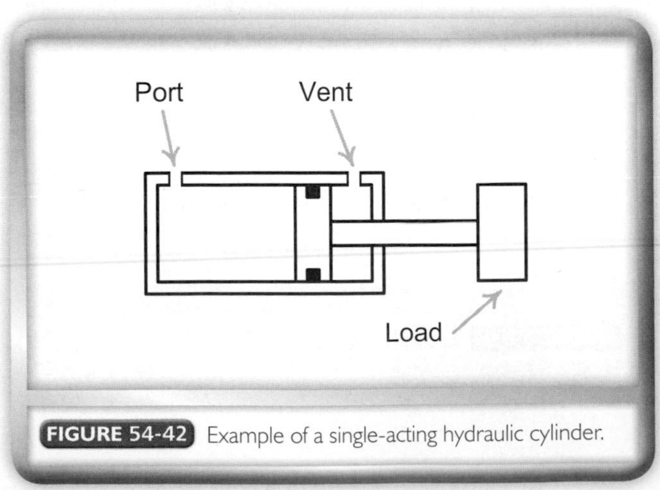

FIGURE 54-42 Example of a single-acting hydraulic cylinder.

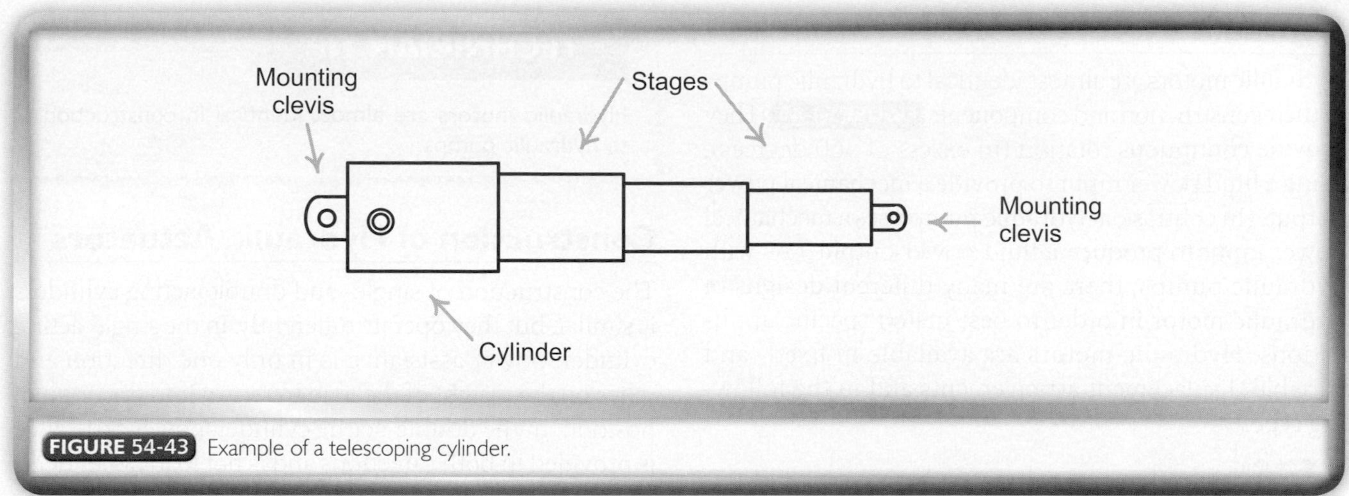

FIGURE 54-43 Example of a telescoping cylinder.

Double-Acting Cylinders

Double-acting cylinders have two oil **ports**. Oil flows into one port to extend the cylinder, and oil flows into the other port to retract the cylinder FIGURE 54-44. An example of an application of a double-acting cylinder is the packer-ejector in a garbage truck.

Rotary Actuators

Typically, hydraulic motors provide continuous rotary motion whereas rotary actuators provide a limited rotation, usually up to a maximum of 720 degrees. They provide for a rotary form of energy transfer to produce rotary motion, providing torque as the force output to the load. An example of an application of a rotary actuator is a device in a production line that picks up a part, rotates to deliver it to a machining operation, and then rotates back to pick up the next part. Hydraulic motors provide continuous rotary motion and are used in a wide range of applications:

- External gear types can be used on equipment like cutting decks for lawn tractors.
- Internal gear types are designed for low-speed, high torque applications to directly drive components like propulsion wheels, conveyors, and road brushes.
- Vane types can be used on a hydraulic crane or arm, along with a grapple, clamshell bucket, or any other attachment that requires a rotary motion to assist in positioning.
- Inline axial and bent-axis piston types are used where high speed, low torque, and high pressures are required, such as on drilling decks of oil rigs.
- Radial piston types are very low-speed but high torque motors and are ideal when a compact direct drive solution is required: for example, to drive wheels on a forklift, ship container handler, or a cement mixer drum.

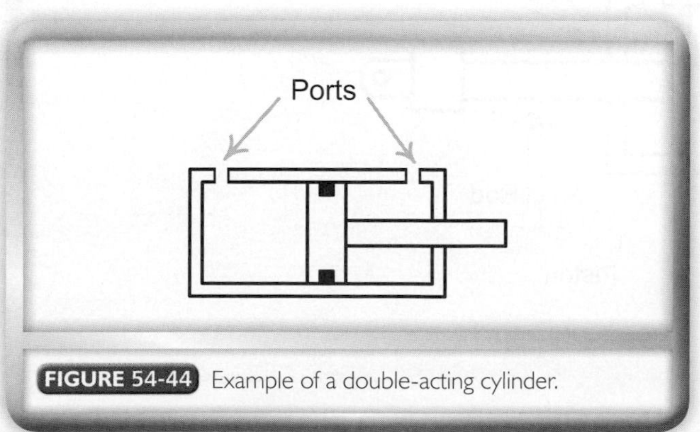

FIGURE 54-44 Example of a double-acting cylinder.

Vane-Type Actuators

Vane-type actuators are similar to hydraulic motors except that the rotation is limited to 300 degrees or less. These actuators normally have two oil ports, and oil flow rotates the actuator clockwise or counterclockwise (depending on the direction of the flow).

Rack-and-Pinion Actuators

Rack-and-pinion actuators convert linear motion to circular motion. They utilize a linear **piston** (**rack**) with gear **teeth** on its shaft. The rack is driven by oil entering one of the ports at each end of the piston. The **pinion** is a gear attached to the output shaft that is rotated by the movement of the rack. The shaft can be rotated from a few degrees to more than 360 degrees, depending on the stroke of the piston and the number of gear teeth. To increase the output torque capability, two racks may be used to rotate the pinion.

Hydraulic Motors

Hydraulic motors are almost identical to hydraulic pumps in their construction and components **FIGURE 54-45**. They provide continuous rotation (in excess of 360 degrees), using a fluid power input to provide a mechanical power output. (In contrast, a hydraulic pump uses a mechanical power input to produce a fluid power output.) As with hydraulic pumps, there are many different designs of hydraulic motor in order to best match specific applications. Hydraulic motors are available in fixed- and variable-displacement arrangements and in the following types:

- Gear
- Vane
- Piston

FIGURE 54-45 Example of a hydraulic motor.

> **TECHNICIAN TIP**
>
> Hydraulic motors are almost identical in construction to hydraulic pumps.

Construction of Hydraulic Actuators

The construction of single- and double-acting cylinders is similar, but they operate differently. In the single-acting cylinder, power assistance is in only one direction and relies on the weight of the load to return it to the original position. In the double-acting cylinder, power assistance is provided in both directions and is not load dependent.

Both types of cylinder are constructed in a similar way. That is, each has a housing that enables mounting to a secure location, fixing it at one end. The **housing** has a **bore** inside it within which a piston can move. Connected to the piston is a **rod** that moves with the piston, thereby providing linear movement to anything that is attached.

Single-acting cylinders have a **vent** at one end to allow the cylinder to remain at atmospheric pressure on that side of the cylinder, whereas the double-acting cylinder has hydraulic fluid at each side of the piston.

The parts of a single-acting cylinder are shown in **FIGURE 54-46** and the parts of a double-acting cylinder in **FIGURE 54-47**.

Vane-type rotary actuators **FIGURE 54-48** have a construction similar to vane type pumps. The vane motor is an alternative solution to the external gear actuator when used for high-speed, low-torque applications. Just like a

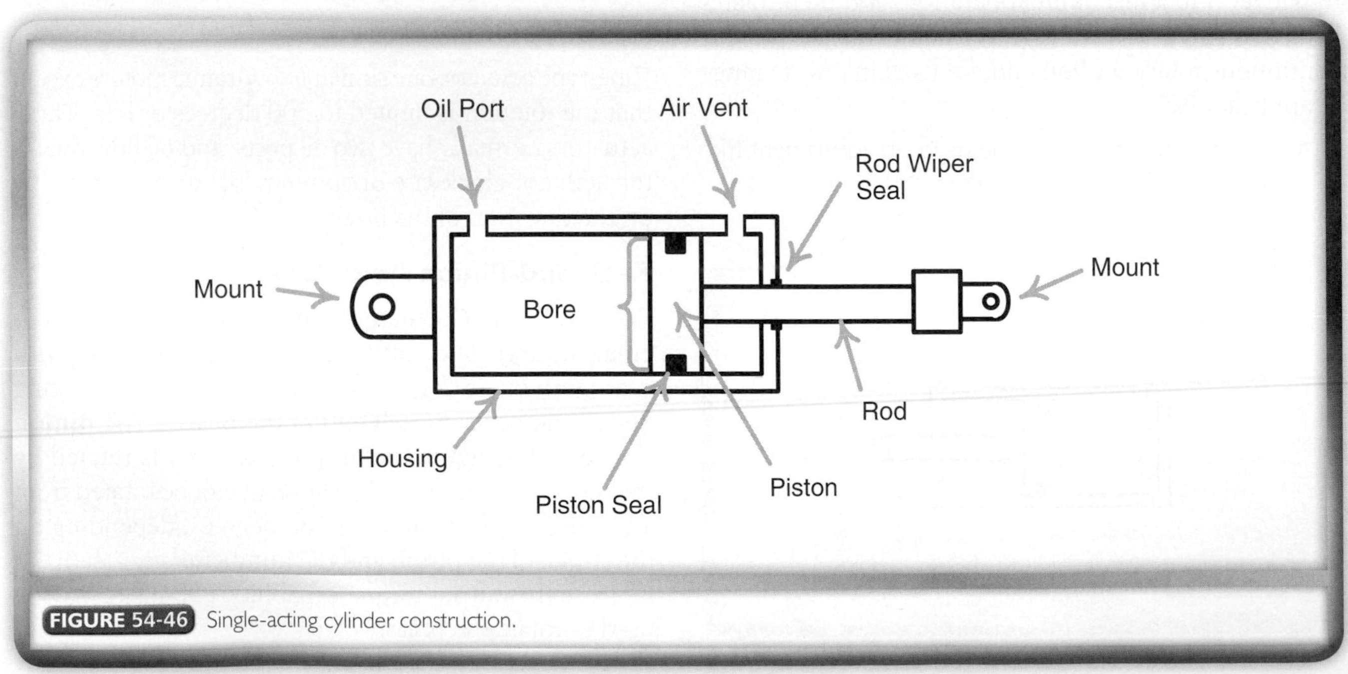

FIGURE 54-46 Single-acting cylinder construction.

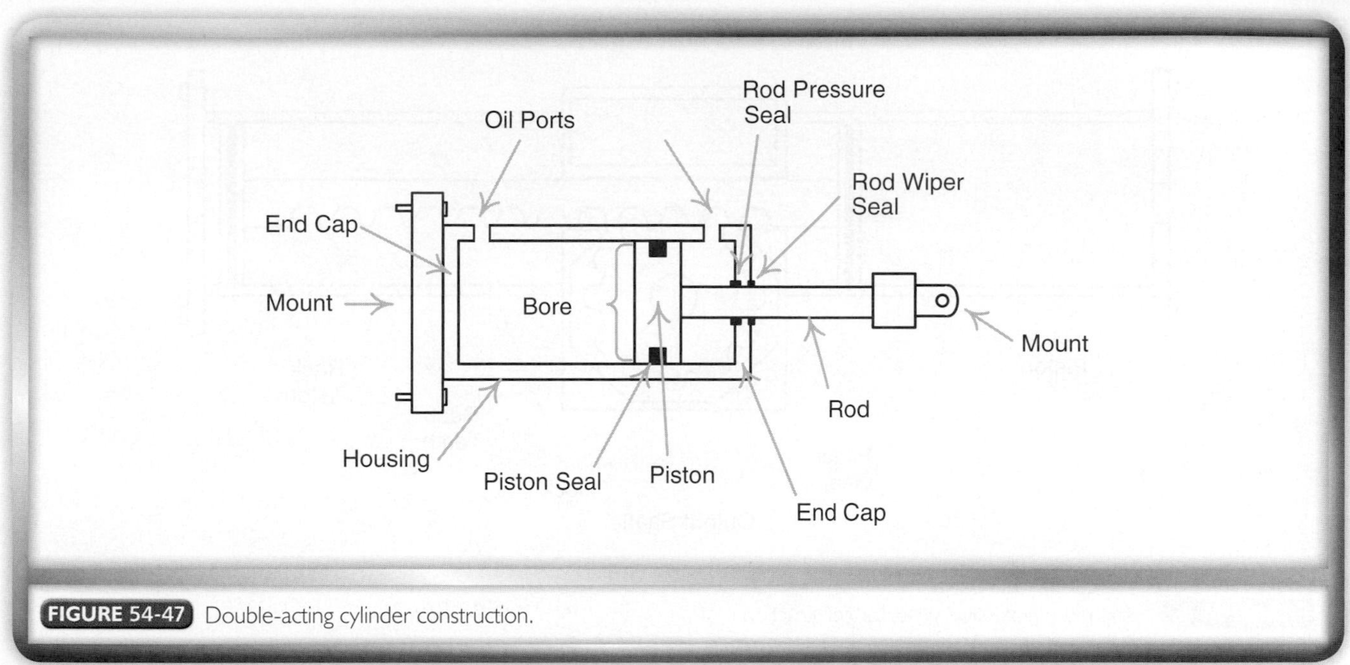

FIGURE 54-47 Double-acting cylinder construction.

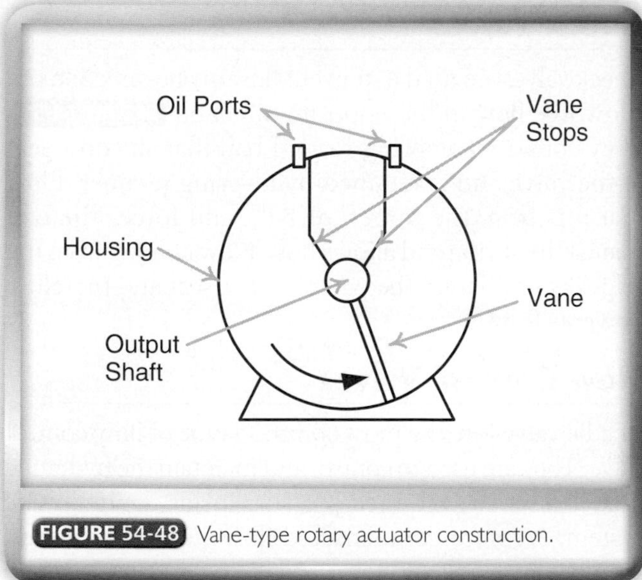

FIGURE 54-48 Vane-type rotary actuator construction.

vane pump, it is constructed of vanes that rotate inside a housing, and the center of the motor is connected to an output shaft that turns. Fluid enters the oil port on one side of the motor and leaves from the oil port on the other side.

The rack-and-pinion rotary actuator FIGURE 54-49 has two opposing single-acting linear actuators attached to a common piston rod, or rack. The rack piston has teeth machined into it, which rotate a pinion gear when the pistons move back and forth, according to which end of the piston hydraulic fluid is applied. Rotation can be less or greater than 360 degrees.

In a hydraulic motor FIGURE 54-50, the hydraulic fluid enters the inlet port and passes around the gears in the chamber, forcing the gears to turn. It then leaves through the outlet port. The driving gear drives the output shaft via a keyway to drive the item being rotated. The driven gear acts as an idler in this example.

Valves

Valves are the control components in a hydraulic system. Today, the most commonly used types of valves are pressure control valves, check valves, flow control valves, directional control valves, and pressure relief valves.

Pressure Control Valves

The main types of pressure control valves are:

- **Pressure-relief valves**: Pressure-relief valves determine or limit the maximum operating pressure in the system and provide a safety valve to prevent system over-pressurization. They are often used to set the pressure for a process.
- **Unloading valves**: Unloading valves are remotely piloted valves that unload the pump so that it operates at low pressure when certain pressure conditions are met in the system.
- **Sequencing valves**: Sequencing valves are remotely piloted valves that are used to control the sequence, or order, of operation of actuators in the system.
- **Pressure-reducing valves**: Pressure-reducing valves limit the maximum pressure that can occur in a

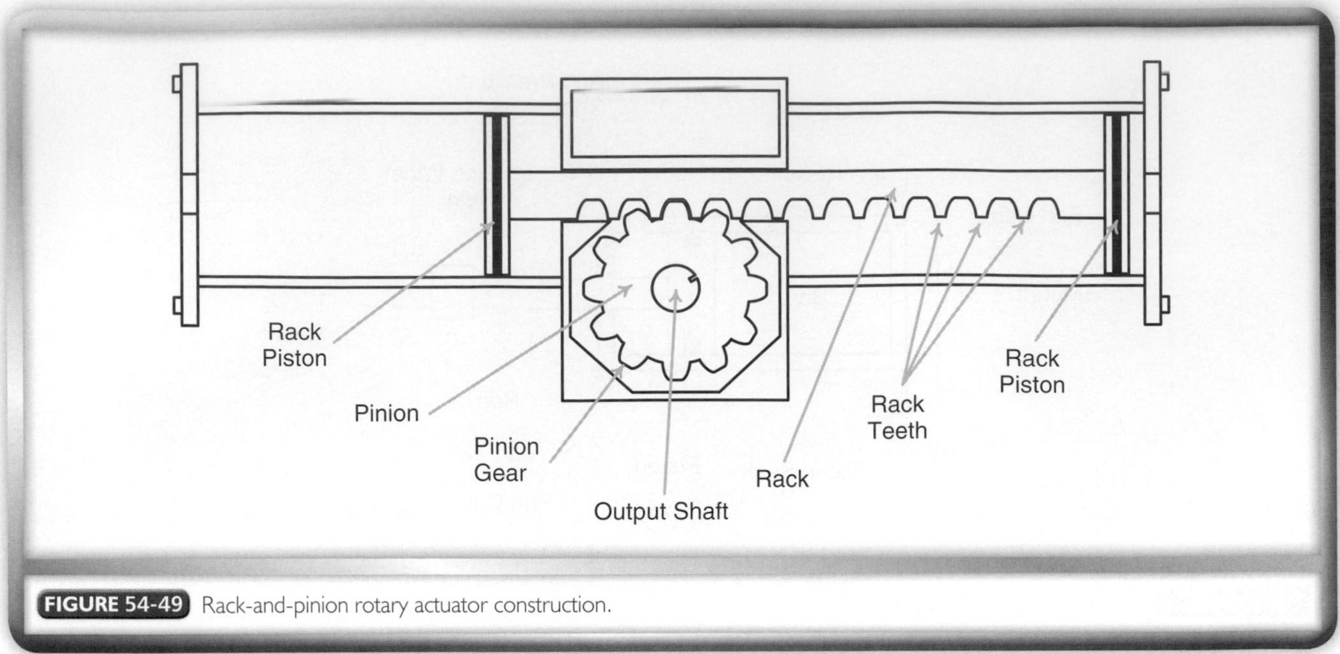

FIGURE 54-49 Rack-and-pinion rotary actuator construction.

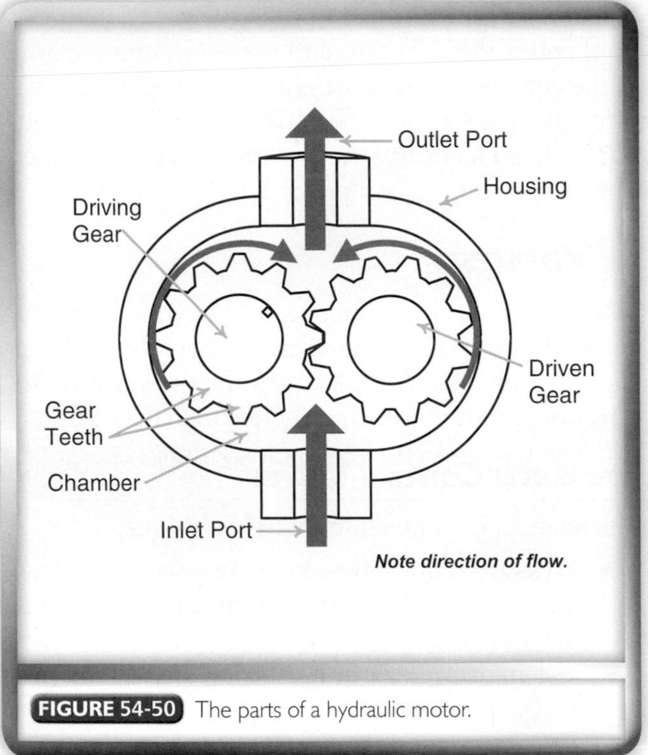

FIGURE 54-50 The parts of a hydraulic motor.

portion or branch of a system (unlike the pressure-relief valve, which controls the entire system).

- **Brake valves**: Brake valves provide back pressure to limit speed on a hydraulic motor operating an over-running load (such as a piece of earth-moving equipment going downhill).
- **Counterbalance valves**: Counterbalance valves provide a back pressure to hold a vertical load in place until certain pressure requirements are met.

Check Valves

Check valves are used to prevent flow in one direction but allow free flow in the opposite direction FIGURE 54-51. They consist of a spring-loaded ball that sits on a seat in the valve and is retained by a spring retainer. Flow that hits from the upper, or ball, end forces the ball against the spring and allows flow. Flow coming from the opposite end forces the ball onto the seat and therefore prevents flow.

Flow Control Valves

Needle valves are the most common type of flow control valve. They are used to control and maintain the hydraulic fluid at a set and required pressure inside the hydraulic system. Pressure-compensated flow control valves are used when a constant flow needs to be maintained.

Needle Valves

Needle valves use a **tapered** device, which moves within the valve throat to adjust the size of the flow opening and, consequently, the flow rate through the valve. The head of the valve is normally designed with an adjusting knob or screw.

The flow through the valve is dependent on the pressure drop across the valve (inlet pressure minus the outlet pressure) FIGURE 54-52.

> **TECHNICIAN TIP**
>
> Most flow control valves are needle valves.

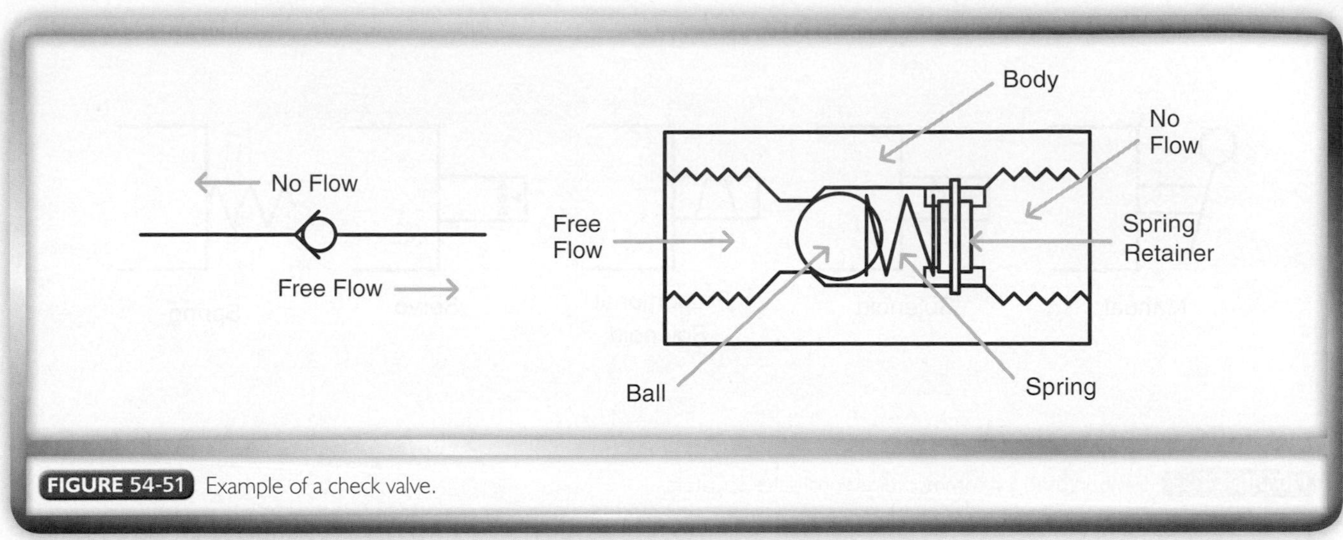

FIGURE 54-51 Example of a check valve.

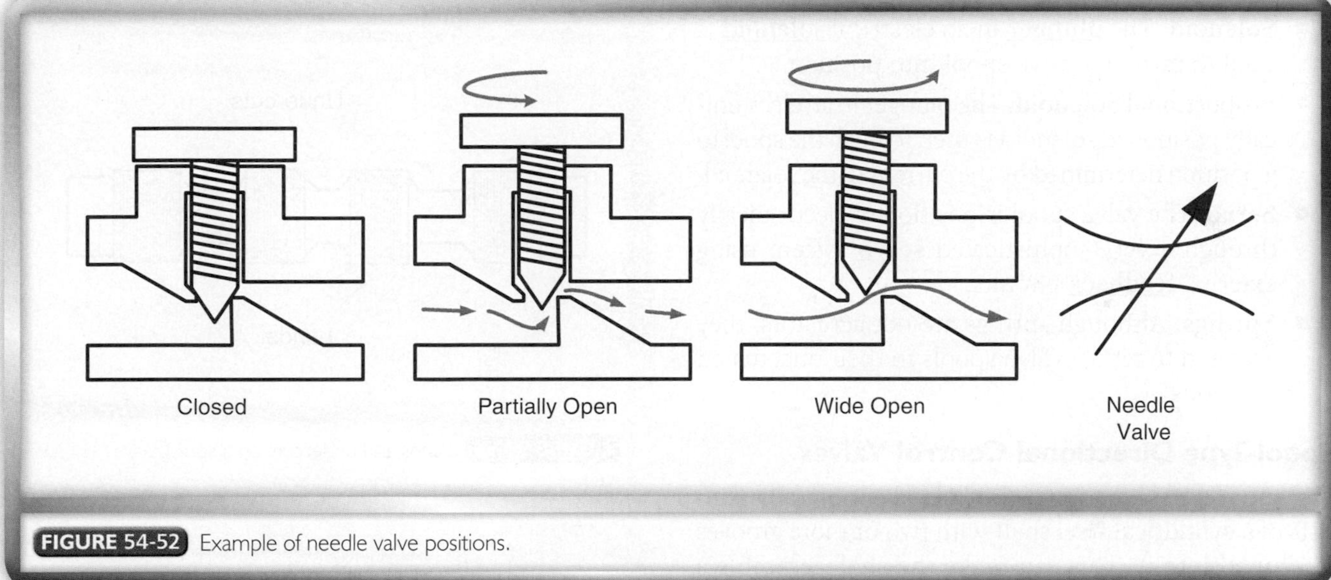

FIGURE 54-52 Example of needle valve positions.

Directional Control Valves

A directional control valve is an important component within a hydraulic system. Its function is to direct hydraulic oil flow within the circuit. For example, when a driver pulls a lever inside the cabin to extend a linear actuator (hydraulic cylinder), it is a directional valve that is connected to the driver's lever. This valve controls the oil flow to and away from the actuator. There are four directional control valve mechanism types:

- **Spool-type**: Spools are by far the most common directional control valve mechanism for hydraulic applications.
- **Sliding plate**: The sliding-plate mechanism opens and closes ports using a sliding plate that allows or prevents flow. They are normally designed to provide for multiple directional operation of hydraulic equipment. For example, in a fork lift truck operation, it may be desirable to lift, tilt and otherwise control the load all at the same time.
- **Rotating plate**: The rotating-plate mechanism allows hydraulic fluid to flow by rotating to open and close ports.
- **Cartridge**: The cartridge mechanism normally consists of a solenoid-operated valve that allows or disallows flow depending on the valve's activation or non-activation by an electric current.

Similarly, there are numerous methods for moving the spools in directional control valves. The most common actuators are FIGURE 54-53:

- **Manual**: A hand-operated lever is used to push the spool into position.

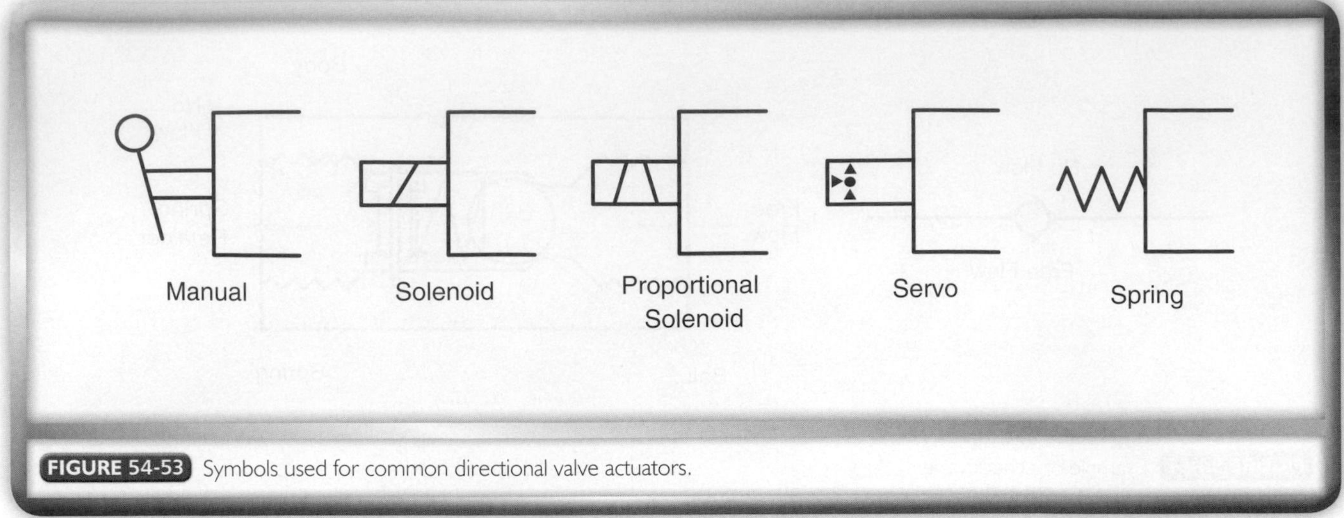

FIGURE 54-53 Symbols used for common directional valve actuators.

- **Solenoid**: The **plunger** in an electrical **solenoid** is used to push the valve spool into position.
- **Proportional Solenoid**: The plunger in an electronically positioned solenoid is used to push the spool to a position determined by the current to the solenoid.
- **Servo**: The valve spool is positioned electronically through a very sophisticated **servo** system using external **feedback** circuits.
- **Springs**: Although springs are not actuators, they are used to return valve spools to their unactuated positions.

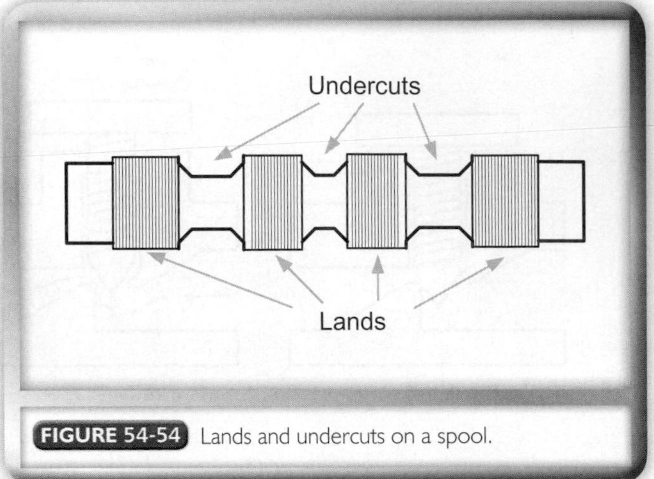

FIGURE 54-54 Lands and undercuts on a spool.

Spool-Type Directional Control Valves

The spool-type directional control valve normally consists of a cylindrical steel shaft with two or more grooves machined into it. This can make the shaft resemble a bobbin or spool used for storing yarn—hence the origin of the term "spool" for this type of valve. A spool-type directional control valve has a sliding spool that moves within a bore in the valve to cover and uncover flow paths in the valve. The raised parts of the spool (the parts with the larger diameters) are called **lands**. These play an important role in the valve's operation by blocking internal flow paths. The lowered parts of the spool (with smaller diameters) are called **undercuts**. These provide the flow paths between the valve ports FIGURE 54-54.

Depending on the spool design, a directional control valve may have two or three functional positions, which are discussed in the following sections.

Two-Position Directional Control Valves

A two-position valve has two functional positions that control the direction of operation of an actuator. The two positions are extend and retract for a cylinder; and forward and reverse for a hydraulic motor FIGURE 54-55.

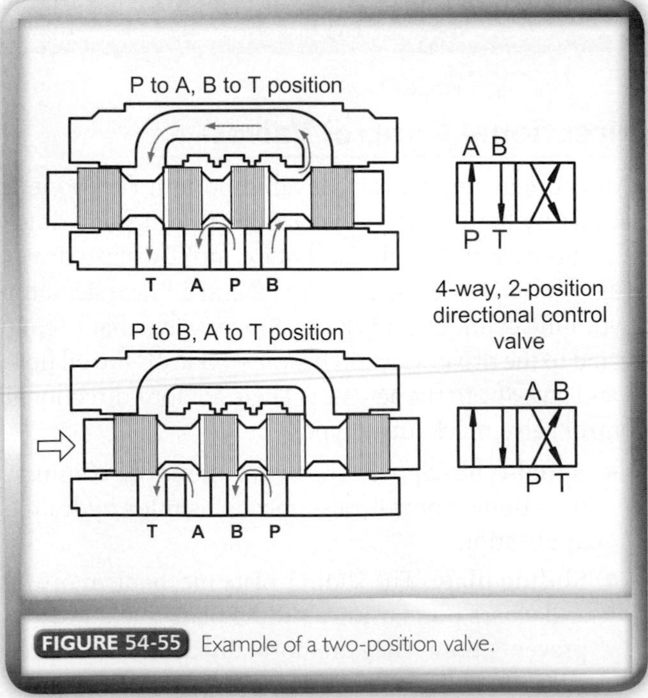

FIGURE 54-55 Example of a two-position valve.

With a two-position valve, the actuator cannot be stopped and held except at the ends of its **stroke**.

Three-Position Directional Control Valves

A three-position valve spool incorporates a third functional position that allows for additional functional operations when the spool is placed in its center position. Three-position valves will normally have a spring on each end of the spool to return it to its center position when the valve is not actuated. There are four common center positions:

- **Closed center**: In the closed-center position, all four ports are blocked FIGURE 54-56.
- **Open center**: In the open-center position, all four ports are connected FIGURE 54-57.
- **Tandem center**: In the tandem-center position, the two actuator ports are blocked and the pressure and tank ports are connected FIGURE 54-58.
- **Float (or motor) center**: In the float-center position, the pressure port is blocked and the rest of the ports are connected together FIGURE 54-59.

> **TECHNICIAN TIP**
>
> Servo valves are extremely sensitive to contaminated fluid.

Pressure-Relief Valves

Relief valves are pressure-limiting devices used to protect hydraulic systems and their components. They are available in a number of configurations to meet the hydraulic circuit's requirements. For example, a relief valve that regulates the whole system pressure will operate at a higher flow rate and more frequently than one that is intended

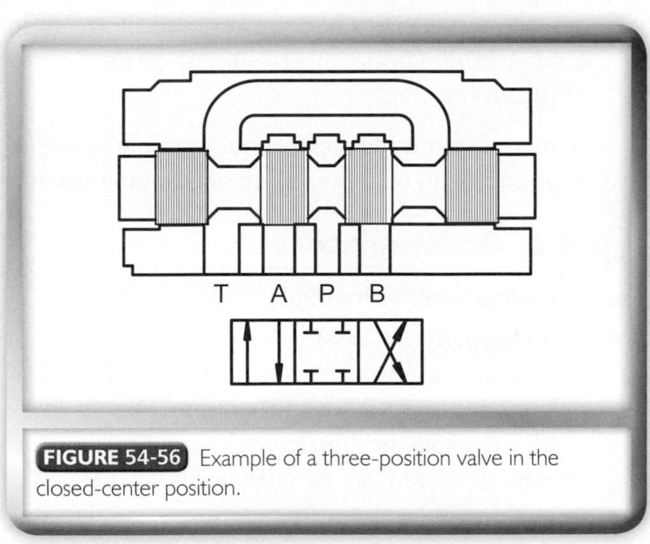

FIGURE 54-56 Example of a three-position valve in the closed-center position.

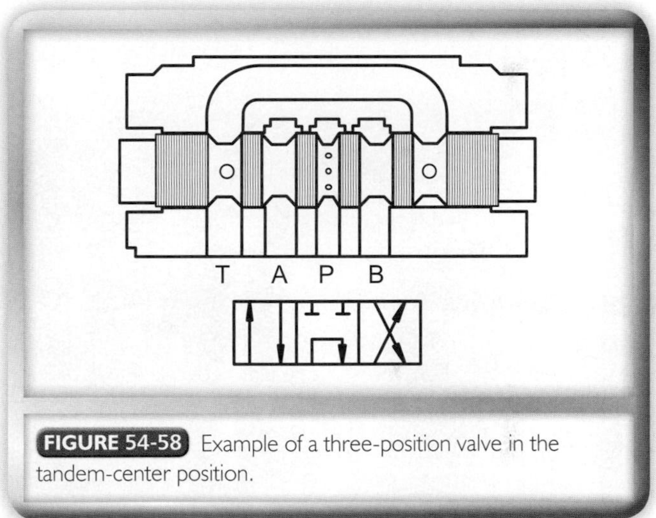

FIGURE 54-58 Example of a three-position valve in the tandem-center position.

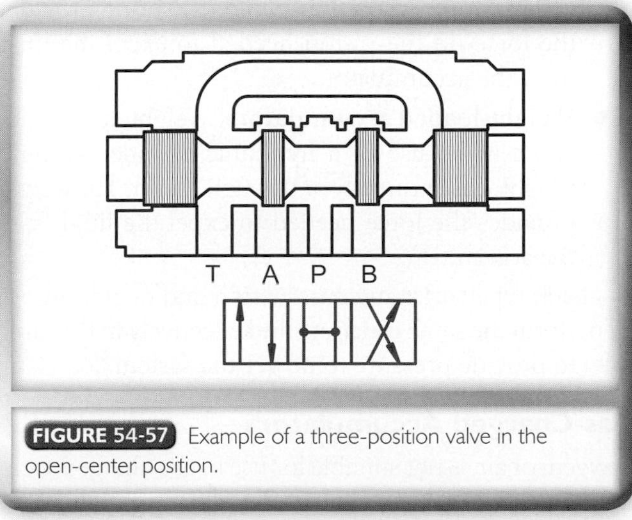

FIGURE 54-57 Example of a three-position valve in the open-center position.

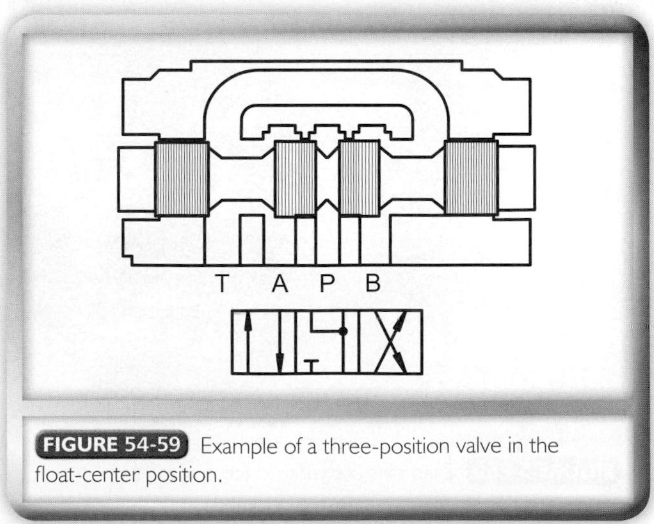

FIGURE 54-59 Example of a three-position valve in the float-center position.

to protect a hydraulic cylinder from intermittent shock loads. There are two types of pressure-relief valves: direct acting and pilot operated.

Hydraulic Accumulators

An accumulator is an energy storage device FIGURE 54-60. Since hydraulic fluid cannot be compressed or changed chemically, for a hydraulic accumulator to work, the hydraulic energy must be changed into mechanical or pneumatic energy.

In the case of a gas-charged bladder-type accumulator, hydraulic fluid is passed into the bladder at system pressure. The bladder is filled with gas; the gas gets compressed by the fluid at system pressure; and the pressure in the bladder increases.

The gas becomes even more compressed when the fluid is pressurized by the pump in the system. If the system pressure drops because of a system failure, then the pressure in the bladder becomes higher than the pressure in the system, and it is that pressure that provides the power to the system.

FIGURE 54-60 Examples of hydraulic accumulators.

Accumulators perform four main functions:

- **Storing energy**: Energy cannot be destroyed, but it can be changed and stored in a different form. Accumulators do this by changing the energy—either mechanically or pneumatically—and storing that energy for use when the system pressure is less than that of the energy stored in the accumulator. They then release the stored energy to support the system at that time.
- **Absorbing shock**: Accumulators act as a shock absorber for an actuator. (An accumulator can operate faster than a relief valve.) They also operate as part of a suspension system for a vehicle or machine.
- **Maintaining pressure**: Accumulators remove pressure and flow pulsations created by actuators or pumps.
- **Providing emergency flow**: Accumulators act as an emergency power source in case of pump or engine failure. They provide additional energy during peak load demand and recharge during low demand periods, just like a battery and alternator in a car. Accumulators can also start up an emergency lubrication system.

For marine or mining applications, accumulators can also act as part of an engine starting or cranking system.

Types of Accumulators

There are three types of hydraulic accumulators:

- **Gas-charged (or gas-loaded) accumulators**: In gas-charged accumulators, also known as hydropneumatic accumulators, the gas provides the force needed to expel the fluid from the accumulator, and the energy stored can be retrieved when needed.
- **Spring-loaded accumulators**: Spring-loaded accumulators replace the gas with a spring—usually the coiled compression type—and the spring provides the force on the piston needed to expel the fluid from the accumulator.
- **Weight-loaded accumulators**: Weighted accumulators make use of a hydraulic cylinder lifting a weight, either directly or through a lever. The weight provides the force needed to expel the fluid from the accumulator.

Each type varies in construction and operation but all perform the same function, and effectively in the same way: to provide pressure to power the system.

Gas-Charged Accumulators

Oxygen, or air, is not suitable for use in gas-charged accumulators, as they may cause an explosion if they come into contact with the hydraulic fluid. Nitrogen, which is almost inert in its natural state, is commonly used. (An inert gas is a gas that does not undergo chemical reactions or change under different sets of conditions, such as temperature change.) Gas-charged accumulators are used in many different applications.

The common types are piston-type, bladder-type, or diaphragm-type:

- **Piston-type gas-charged accumulator**: A piston type gas-charged accumulator has a cylindrical body with a piston separating the fluid and the gas FIGURE 54-61.
- **Bladder-type gas-charged accumulator**: A bladder type gas-charged accumulator uses a bladder made from a rubber-like material to separate the fluid and the gas, and to provide the force needed to expel the fluid from the accumulator FIGURE 54-62.
- **Diaphragm-type gas-charged accumulator**: A diaphragm-type gas-charged accumulator has a spherical or cylindrical body with a diaphragm separating the fluid from the gas FIGURE 54-63.

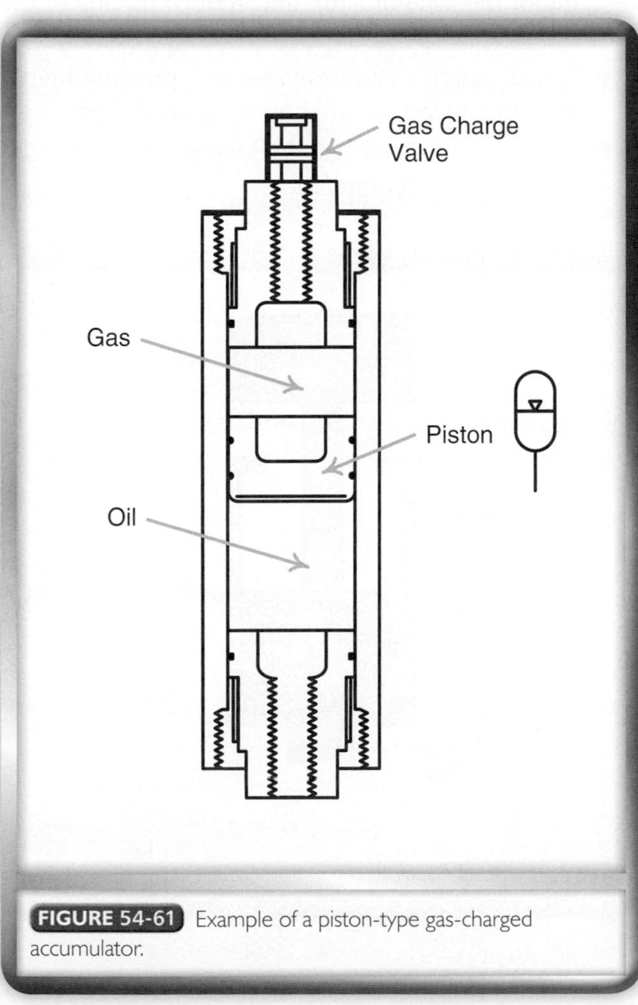

FIGURE 54-61 Example of a piston-type gas-charged accumulator.

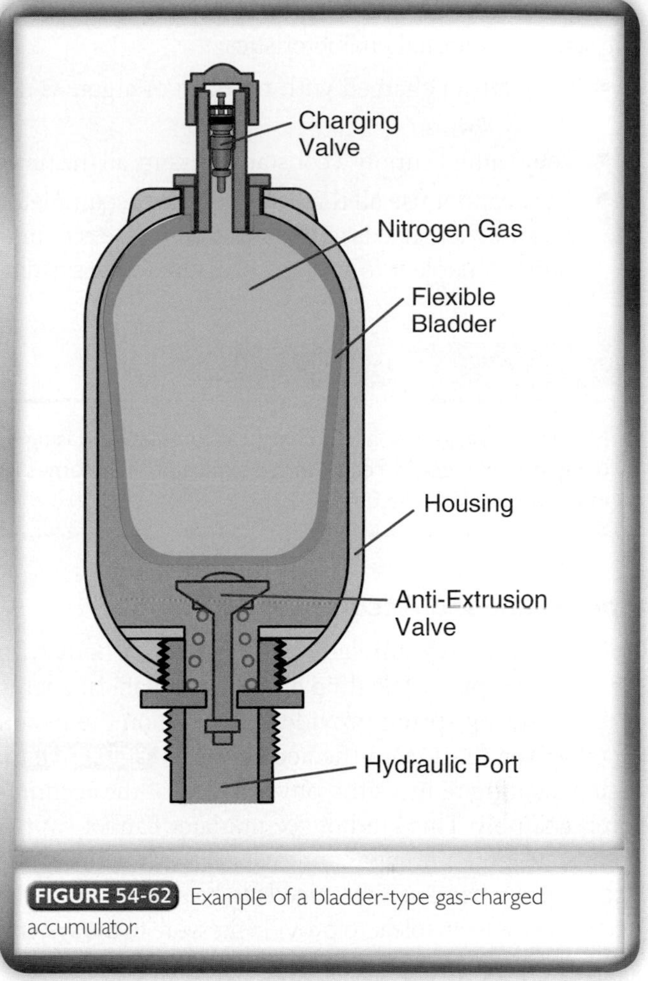

FIGURE 54-62 Example of a bladder-type gas-charged accumulator.

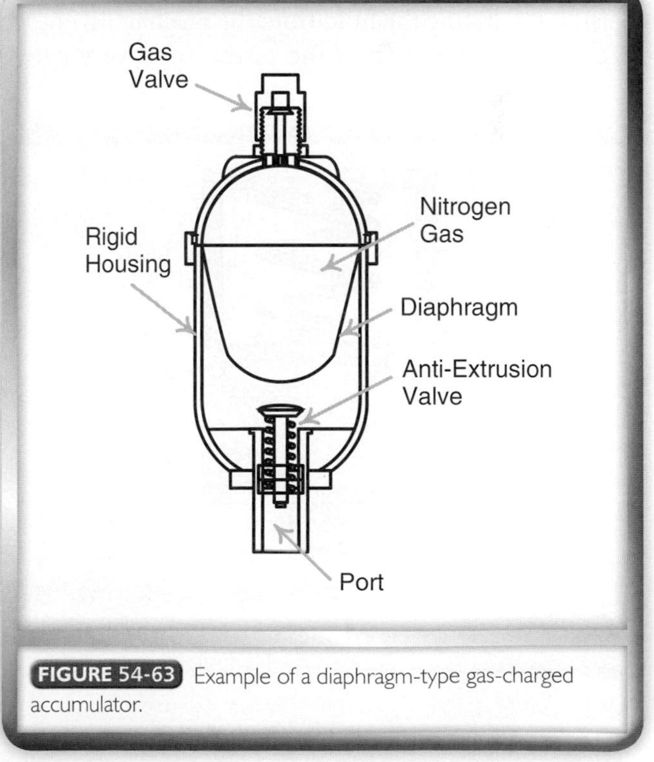

FIGURE 54-63 Example of a diaphragm-type gas-charged accumulator.

No matter the type, gas-charged accumulators all exhibit the same operational characteristics:

- They are all charged with nitrogen or argon as the charge gas.
- They cannot supply a constant pressure all the time.
- They cannot use all the fluid from the accumulator because there needs to be some fluid in the accumulator to enable it to provide pressure to the system.

Safety

Never use oxygen or air to charge accumulators! Using oxygen or air could result in an explosion if it comes into contact with the fluid.

Spring-Loaded Accumulators

A spring-loaded accumulator has a cylindrical body with a piston to separate the fluid and the mechanical energy force. A strong spring provides the force on the piston to expel the fluid from the accumulator FIGURE 54-64. Using a spring reduces the physical size of the accumulator assembly. This kind of accumulator cannot supply a constant pressure, nor can it use all the fluid from the accumulator because there needs to be some fluid in the accumulator to enable it to provide pressure to the system.

Weight-Loaded Accumulators

A weight-loaded accumulator has a cylindrical body with a piston separating the fluid from the mechanical energy force. A weight on top of the piston (or a very heavy piston) provides the force on the piston to expel the fluid from the accumulator FIGURE 54-65. This type of accumulator is often constructed in place because of its large size.

Unlike gas-charged and spring-loaded accumulators, weight-loaded accumulators provide a constant pressure, and therefore allow all the fluid from the accumulator to be used.

Safety Precautions for Hydraulic Accumulators

Accumulators are used to store energy and therefore can pose significant safety hazards. Make sure you understand the hazards and always use appropriate safety precautions:

- Always discharge stored hydraulic fluid from the accumulator before removing it from the system by operating the entire system without the pump running.
- Always pre-charge the gas side of an accumulator according to the manufacturer's instructions. Too high or too low a pre-charge can cause damage to the accumulator, interfere with the proper functioning of the accumulator, and reduce the life of the accumulator.
- Never charge an accumulator to a pressure higher than that recommended by the manufacturer.
- Always use an inert gas such as nitrogen or argon to charge an accumulator.

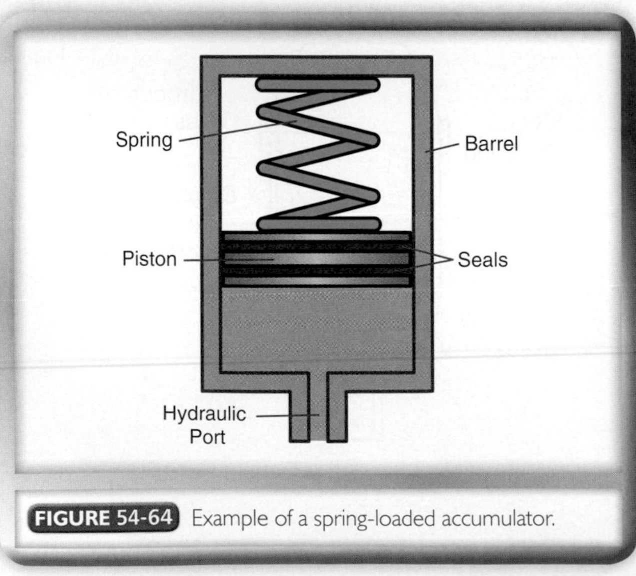

FIGURE 54-64 Example of a spring-loaded accumulator.

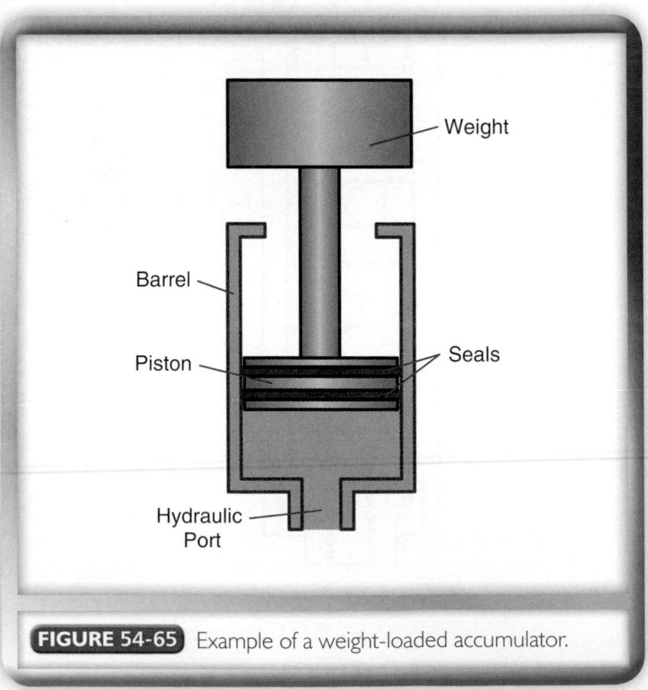

FIGURE 54-65 Example of a weight-loaded accumulator.

- Leave some fluid in the accumulator to enable it to provide pressure to the system.
- Never use oxygen. Using oxygen could result in an explosion if it comes into contact with fluid.
- Never use air to charge an accumulator since air can contain water vapor and sufficient oxygen to cause an explosion.
- Water vapor can also cause the accumulator to rust and eventually weaken to the point of structural failure.
- Before disassembling an accumulator, release both the gas and hydraulic pressures.
- Use extreme care in removing the springs from spring-loaded accumulators.

Safety

Never use oxygen or air to charge an accumulator. Using oxygen or air could result in an explosion if it comes in contact with the fluid. Air contains sufficient oxygen to cause an explosion and also can contain water vapor, leading to rust and eventual failure.

Safety

Before disassembling the accumulator, ensure that the pressure on both the fluid and the gas sides of the accumulator has been completely discharged.

Hydraulic System Preventative Maintenance

As with every heavy-duty vehicle system, preventative maintenance is critical for the hydraulics on a vehicle. There are important benefits to regular preventative maintenance of hydraulics systems, including:

- It prolongs the life of the system.
- It reduces system down-time.
- It reduces or eliminates preventable failures.
- It reduces operational costs.
- It reduces repair costs.
- It reduces lost productivity.

Although regular preventative maintenance may initially increase down-time, it will prevent longer, more expensive repairs in the future. Ideally, preventative maintenance should be performed when a machine is not scheduled to be in use.

Common Sources of Damage

There are several basic factors that can damage a hydraulic system. These include:

- Excessive speed
- Excessive heat
- Excessive pressure
- Contamination

Excessive speed, heat, and pressure can result from operator error. Often, however, they are the result of initial damage caused by contamination. Contaminated fluid is the most common source of hydraulic system damage. In most environments, it is readily preventable with regular maintenance.

Common Problems Encountered During Inspections

Typical problems that may be identified when carrying out a preventative maintenance inspection include:

- Not enough hydraulic fluid in the reservoir, which can cause the system to run erratically
- Clogged or dirty oil filters, which can reduce system life
- A loose inlet line, which can result in a loss of system pressure
- Contaminated or incorrect fluid in the system, which can result in expensive repairs
- Leaks in components, hoses, or lines, which can be caused by loose lines

To identify these and other problems, it is helpful to create and use an inspection log.

Scheduling Preventative Maintenance

Manufacturers provide inspection and maintenance schedules as part of the manufacturing process. There are several items that form the basis for scheduling preventative maintenance:

- The age of the equipment
- The frequency of use
- The intensity of use

There are also a number of predictable conditions affecting maintenance scheduling, such as going into or coming out of storage and seasonal peak use patterns.

> **TECHNICIAN TIP**
>
> The more frequently equipment is used, the more often it should be inspected.

Unusual conditions that can affect maintenance scheduling include:

- Weather fluctuations, such as an unseasonably late snowstorm
- Temperature extremes, such as 115°F (46°C) heat in a normally temperate zone
- Unusual working environments, such as desert (high heat and dust) or rain forest (prolonged heat and excessive humidity)

> **TECHNICIAN TIP**
>
> Tailor equipment maintenance patterns to accommodate the environmental conditions in which the equipment operates.

Preventative Maintenance Best Practices

Anumber of best practices should be followed when undertaking preventative maintenance procedures. Best practices will vary depending on the type of equipment. The following is not an exhaustive list but provides some general guidelines:

- Conduct daily visual and auditory inspections.
- Maintain a daily inspection log.
- Conduct routine fluid analyses.

Know and follow the manufacturer's maintenance recommendations, including:

- Fluid and filter types
- Fluid cleanliness recommendations
- Fluid and filter replacement indications (housing pressure drop indicators) or schedule
- Normal system operating conditions
- Schedule routine maintenance before it becomes urgent.
- Schedule routine maintenance when machine is normally off-line whenever possible.
- Anticipate replacement of system components based on their expected life and use patterns.

> **TECHNICIAN TIP**
>
> Replacement of aging and worn parts before they fail minimizes the possibility of consequent damage to other system components.

Performing Preventative Maintenance

At a minimum, the following steps should be accomplished during a routine preventative maintenance inspection:

- Clean the exteriors of system components, hoses, and lines before beginning a preventative maintenance inspection in order to detect leaks and to check for wear.
- Check the fluid level before starting the system.

Note: A low fluid level may indicate system leaks.

Inspect for leaks by checking the machine and the floor around it for fluid stains.

Note: Leak inspection should be done both with the system operating, and with the system shut down.

- Inspect hoses, lines, and system components for visible wear.
- Check outputs for proper system operation, including pressure and temperature gauges.

> **TECHNICIAN TIP**
>
> Replacing fluid can be a very costly and time consuming action. Fluid should be changed only if it has had its chemical structure damaged to the point that it cannot be returned to its original condition. Fluid that is simply dirty can usually be filtered to return it to a usable state. Fluid samples taken before scheduled preventative maintenance will provide the information needed to make this decision.

> **TECHNICIAN TIP**
>
> New fluid is not necessarily clean fluid.

- Check for normal actuator functionality.
- Listen for unusual sounds.
- Look and feel for unusual vibrations.
- Replace fluid and filters according to the manufacturer's recommendations.

Note: Exceed the manufacturer's recommendations if the conditions warrant.

Predict maintenance needs and schedule **planned down-time** to accommodate them.

Changing Hydraulic Fluid and Filters

To change hydraulic fluid, follow the guidelines in **SKILL DRILL 54-1**. To change a hydraulic filter, follow the guidelines in **SKILL DRILL 54-2**.

> **TECHNICIAN TIP**
>
> Filters should be changed only when they have reached the terminal pressure drop recommended by the manufacturer. Pressure drop indicators, or other devices on the filter housing, should be used to make this decision.

> **TECHNICIAN TIP**
>
> Follow shop guidelines and your instructor's directions about proper disposition of filter media and used hydraulic fluid.

SKILL DRILL 54-1 Changing Hydraulic Fluid

1. Assemble the following tools and materials:
   - Appropriate tool to fit hydraulic drain plug
   - Clean, lint-free shop towels
   - Hydraulic fluid according to manufacturer's specifications
   - Safety glasses or goggles
   - Gloves
2. Put on safety glasses or goggles, and gloves.
3. Operate the levers to release system pressure.
4. Slowly open the reservoir filler cap to relieve pressure on the reservoir.
5. Drain the hydraulic fluid by removing the drain plug in the reservoir.
6. Open the inspection plate on the reservoir.
7. Remove any dirt and foreign material that has settled to the bottom of the reservoir.
8. Replace the inspection plate and drain plug.
9. Remove, clean, and replace the inlet screen, if present.

   Note: If the filter needs changing, change it after this step (see Skill Drill 54-2).
10. Fill the reservoir to the fill line with clean hydraulic fluid.
11. Bleed the system if necessary.
12. Operate the system and check for leaks.
13. Check the fluid level to ensure it is still within specifications.
14. Clean the work area, and return tools and materials to their proper storage.

SKILL DRILL 54-2 Changing a Hydraulic Filter

1. Assemble the following tools and materials:
   - Wrench for removing filter
   - Clean, lint-free shop towels
   - Appropriate new filter
   - Safety glasses or goggles
   - Gloves
2. Put on safety glasses or goggles, and gloves.
3. With the system shut down, operate the levers to relieve system pressure.
4. Clean the area around the filter.
5. Remove the old filter.
6. Clean the filter housing (if it is a cartridge-type filter).
7. Install a new filter and tighten to the manufacturer's specifications.
8. Operate the system and check for leaks.
9. Clean the work area, and return tools and materials to their proper storage

Wrap-up

Ready for Review

- The fundamental operating concept of all hydraulic applications is the use of fluid as power. One of the main advantages of hydraulic systems is that they can be designed to lift very heavy objects through the use of mechanical advantage and by using the fluid as the transfer medium.
- There are numerous applications for hydraulic equipment, which fall into three principal categories: industrial and civil, mobile, and aerospace.
- Hydraulic systems fall into two basic types: open loop and closed loop. In an open-loop system, fluid flows from a reservoir to the pump, through the system, and back to the reservoir, where it is directed to the pump again. In a closed-loop hydraulic system, no reservoir is used. Fluid circulates from the pump, through the system, and directly back to the pump.
- Vital functions of hydraulic fluid include: transmitting energy, lubricating components, preventing rust and corrosion, sealing clearances, carrying solid contaminants to filters, and providing electrical insulation for certain applications. These capabilities make hydraulic fluid the underpinning ingredient of any hydraulic system.
- Pascal's law states that "pressure applied to a fluid in one part of a closed system will be transmitted without loss to all other areas of the system." This means that pressure applied to a fluid in one part of a closed system will be transmitted equally to all other areas of the system.
- The main differences between pipe and tubing are their construction materials and applications. Piping is intended for industrial applications requiring long, straight runs, and is not normally bent or shaped other than in smooth turns. Tubing is designed to be bent and shaped to accommodate the installation on the machine.
- Never use galvanized pipe or fittings for hydraulic system applications. The coating can react with the hydraulic fluid and come off the pipe walls and fittings, causing contamination and damaging components.
- The Bernoulli principle describes the behavior of a fluid, gas, or liquid as it flows through a pipe, tube, or hose. Bernoulli stated that if the flow of a fluid remains constant, the measures of the fluid remain constant; changing one of the two measures (up or down) affects the other oppositely.
- The two measures used for fluid are velocity and pressure. When velocity increases, the pressure must drop if the flow is to remain constant. Fluid pressure and speed will vary as the line narrows or widens.
- You should always use a hose end fitting made by the same manufacturer as the hose you are working on. There are three types of hose ends: permanent, reusable, and quick-disconnect.
- The purpose of a hydraulic pump is to provide the system with a constant supply of hydraulic fluid. It does this by producing flow in the system. The fluid flow is used by actuators in the system to perform work.
- Pump displacement is commonly shown on the pump identification label. If you need to calculate hydraulic pump displacement, use the following formula: $d = Factor \times QN$.
- To calculate hydraulic pump theoretical flow rate, use the following formula: $Q = d = N \times dFactor$
- To calculate volumetric efficiency (VE), use the following formula: $VE = Actual\ flow\ rate \div Theoretical\ flow\ rate$.
- Gear pumps consist of a housing, a drive gear (driven by the shaft), a driven gear, and other mechanisms such as pressure plates.
- A vane pump consists of a rotor containing sliding vanes in slots. The rotor is offset from the centerline of the housing.
- Piston pumps are high-pressure pumps that maintain a constant, regular oil flow. They can operate more efficiently with high and low shaft speeds, can tolerate higher pressures over longer periods, and are generally less noisy than gear pumps.
- Vane pumps and piston pumps (but not gear pumps) can have a variable displacement capability. Variable displacement pumps have a mechanism that allows the displacement to be changed.
- Cavitation is the formation of air or gas bubbles at the inlet of the pump because the pump does not completely fill with fluid. The term is also used to denote the collapse of air and gas bubbles in the pump, which creates a distinctive noise.
- Hydraulic actuators convert the fluid energy back into mechanical energy to move the load. They can come in two forms: linear actuators, such as hydraulic cylinders, or rams; and rotary actuators or hydraulic motors.

- The main types of pressure control valves are pressure-relief valves, unloading valves, sequencing valves, pressure-reducing valves, brake valves, and counterbalance valves.
- Check valves are used to prevent flow in one direction but allow free flow in the opposite direction.
- Needle valves are the most common type of flow control valve. They are used to control and maintain the hydraulic fluid at a set and required pressure inside the hydraulic system.
- A directional control valve is an important component within a hydraulic system. Its function is to direct hydraulic oil flow within the circuit.
- An accumulator is an energy storage device. Since hydraulic fluid cannot be compressed or changed chemically, for a hydraulic accumulator to work, the hydraulic energy must be changed into mechanical or pneumatic energy.
- Oxygen, or air, is not suitable for use in gas-charged accumulators, as they may cause an explosion if they come into contact with the hydraulic fluid. Nitrogen, which is almost inert in its natural state, is commonly used.
- A spring-loaded accumulator has a cylindrical body with a piston to separate the fluid and the mechanical energy force. A strong spring provides the force on the piston to expel the fluid from the accumulator.
- A weight-loaded accumulator has a cylindrical body with a piston separating the fluid from the mechanical energy force. A weight on top of the piston (or a very heavy piston) provides the force on the piston to expel the fluid from the accumulator.
- Accumulators are used to store energy and therefore can pose significant safety hazards. Make sure you understand the hazards and always use appropriate safety precautions.
- Regular preventative maintenance prolongs the life of the system, reduces system down-time, operational and repair costs, and potentially eliminates preventable failures. Ideally, preventative maintenance should be performed when a machine is not scheduled to be in use.
- Excessive speed, excessive heat, excessive pressure, and contamination can all damage a hydraulic system.

Vocabulary Builder

aeration Air in the fluid.

angular Consisting of, or forming, an angle.

bladder An inflatable bag, or sack, that contains fluids or gas.

bore The inside diameter of a tube.

cavitation The formation of air bubbles in the transmission fluid as a result of low pressure at the pump inlet.

chafing Wear or abrasion due to prolonged or constant friction.

crimp Join two pieces of material by folding and pinching together.

cylinder An actuator that converts hydraulic power into linear mechanical force. Also known as *ram*.

diaphragm A flexible partition separating two cavities.

displacement The volume of fluid that is moved by the pump in one complete revolution.

feedback A sensed output parameter that is compared to the input command.

flow How much fluid is being moved in relation to the work that is being done.

fluid head In fluid dynamics, head is the concept that relates the energy in an incompressible fluid to the height of an equivalent static column of that fluid. In the case of a hydraulic pump, because the tank is above the pump and the fluid will run to the pump inlet by gravity, the height of the tank equals the fluid head.

galvanized Coated with zinc, for rust protection.

hose Flexible line used to direct liquids or gases.

housing An enclosed case for a mechanism.

hydraulic accumulator A device that stores hydraulic energy and acts as an emergency power source in the event of system pump failure.

hydraulic cylinder or ram A device that uses hydraulic fluid pressure and convert it to Linear mechanical movement.

input force The force applied to the input piston, measured in either kilograms (kg), newtons (N), or pounds (lb).

inside diameter (ID) A precise measurement of line capacity.

land The largest diameter in a spool; used to block flow paths.

linear Extending or moving in one dimension only.

mechanical advantage Anything that allows us to move greater distances or weight with less effort.

output force Force that equals the working pressure multiplied by the surface area of the output piston, expressed as newtons or kilograms.

outside diameter (OD) A general measurement (often a nominal specification, rather than an actual measurement) used in specification of pipe.

Pascal's law The law of physics that states that pressure applied to a fluid in one part of a closed system will be transmitted equally to all other areas of the system.

pinion A gear or cog with a number of small teeth; used with a rack to convert linear to circular motion.

pintle A bolt or pin forming the pivot of a hinge.

pipe A rigid tube of metal, plastic, or other substance, used to convey fluids.

piston A solid disk that moves within a tube (or cylinder) under fluid pressure.

planned down-time The practice of scheduling major repairs and overhauls before declining performance or system failure makes them urgent (and thus expensive).

plunger A mechanical device that provides a thrusting motion, such as a piston.

ports Openings for intake or outlet of a fluid.

pressure The force per unit area applied to the surface of an object.

pump A device that generates a flow of fluid.

rack A bar with teeth; used with a pinion to convert linear to circular motion.

rod The part of a linear actuator that transfers force from the piston to the load.

seamless Formed in one piece; lacking seams, and thus smooth and regular.

sequentially Operating in a series, or in logical order.

servo A control system that compares the output feedback signal to the input command signal and makes automatic adjustments to provide the commanded output.

skive To pare, or cut thin layers off an object to reduce its thickness.

solenoid An electromagnetic switch.

stainless steel A rust-resistant steel alloy containing chromium; normally resistant to stain and tarnish.

stroke The range of motion of a cylinder.

swaging A method of joining a fitting to a fluid conductor by deforming either the fitting or the conductor to form a strong joint.

swash plate A displacement unit on which displacement pistons are arranged axially to a drive shaft.

tapered Having a gradual decrease in diameter or width.

teeth Uniform projections in a piece of machinery that engage and transfer motion to or from a complementary piece of machinery.

telescoping Extending from a series of nested sections.

trunnion Paired cylindrical projections used for support, as on a cannon.

tubing Metal pipe that is intended to be bent and shaped to fit an application.

turbulence Movement of the hydraulic fluid not related to speed.

undercuts The smallest diameter in a spool; used to create a flow path when the valve is open.

valve plate A unit that has two semicircular ports that allow inlet and outlet of hydraulic fluid.

vanes A fin or blade, attached radially to a cylinder, that moves (or is moved by) hydraulic fluid or air.

variable displacement The capability to change displacement, as in a pump with a mechanism that allows the displacement to be changed.

velocity The speed of movement of the hydraulic fluid.

vent An opening used to release or discharge a fluid or gas.

viscosity The measurement of the thickness of a liquid.

working pressure The pressure within a hydraulic system while the system is being operated.

Review Questions

1. Which of the following variables in a hydraulic system is expressed in amount of force per specified area?
   a. Input force
   b. Working pressure
   c. Output force
   d. Latent pressure
2. Which of the following components in a hydraulic system stores hydraulic energy?
   a. Actuator
   b. Reservoir
   c. Pump
   d. Accumulator
3. Which type of tubing has the largest inside diameter?
   a. Schedule 40
   b. Schedule 80
   c. Schedule 160
   d. Double
4. Which of the following types of positive-displacement pumps operates at the highest pressure?
   a. Gear pump
   b. Vane pump
   c. Piston pump
   d. All of the choices have the same operating pressure range.
5. Which type of rotary actuator is likely to be found on the drilling deck of an oil rig?
   a. External gear type
   b. Vane type
   c. Inline axial type
   d. Radial piston type
6. Which of the following is one of the main functions performed by a hydraulic accumulator?
   a. Absorbing shock
   b. Maintaining pressure
   c. Providing emergency flow
   d. All of the choices are correct.
7. When a three-position directional control valve is in the ________ center position, the pressure port is blocked, and the rest of the ports are connected together.
   a. closed
   b. open
   c. tandem
   d. float
8. A needle valve is a type of ________ valve.
   a. pressure control
   b. check
   c. flow control
   d. directional control
9. Which component in a hydraulic system controls the mechanical work functions within the system?
   a. Actuator
   b. Reservoir
   c. Pump
   d. Accumulator
10. The selection of lines used in a hydraulic circuit is dictated by:
   a. the Bernoulli principle.
   b. Pascal's law.
   c. Ohm's law.
   d. Newton's first law of fluid dynamics.

ASE-Type Questions

1. Technician A says that a single-acting cylinder relies on the weight of the load to return it to the original position. Technician B says that a double-acting cylinder is also load dependent. Who is correct?
   a. Technician A
   b. Technician B
   c. Both Technician A and Technician B
   d. Neither Technician A nor Technician B
2. Technician A says that check valves allow flow in both directions. Technician B says that check valves prevent flow in one direction and allow free flow in the opposition direction. Who is correct?
   a. Technician A
   b. Technician B
   c. Both Technician A and Technician B
   d. Neither Technician A nor Technician B
3. Technician A says that oxygen should be used to charge an accumulator. Technician B says that the accumulator should be fully charged before it is removed from the system. Who is correct?
   a. Technician A
   b. Technician B
   c. Both Technician A and Technician B
   d. Neither Technician A nor Technician B
4. Technician A says that spring-loaded accumulators can hold a constant pressure. Technician B says that only weight-loaded accumulators can hold a constant pressure. Who is correct?
   a. Technician A
   b. Technician B
   c. Both Technician A and Technician B
   d. Neither Technician A nor Technician B
5. Technician A says that angular motion is used to extend the bed of a garbage truck. Technician B says that rams can produce both angular and linear motion. Who is correct?
   a. Technician A
   b. Technician B
   c. Both Technician A and Technician B
   d. Neither Technician A nor Technician B
6. Technician A says that positive-displacement pumps are mostly used as fluid power pumps. Technician B says that dynamic pumps are primarily used as fluid power pumps. Who is correct?
   a. Technician A
   b. Technician B
   c. Both Technician A and Technician B
   d. Neither Technician A nor Technician B
7. Technician A says that long runs of hydraulic pipe should not need to be supported at regular intervals. Technician B says that it is okay to run hydraulic lines near hot exhaust components. Who is correct?
   a. Technician A
   b. Technician B
   c. Both Technician A and Technician B
   d. Neither Technician A nor Technician B
8. Technician A says that the same pressure applied over different sized surface areas produces the same level of force. Technician B says that the same pressure applied over different sized surface areas produces the different levels of force. Who is correct?
   a. Technician A
   b. Technician B
   c. Both Technician A and Technician B
   d. Neither Technician A nor Technician B
9. Technician A says that most hydraulic systems are open-loop systems. Technician B says that most hydraulic systems are closed-loop systems. Who is correct?
   a. Technician A
   b. Technician B
   c. Both Technician A and Technician B
   d. Neither Technician A nor Technician B
10. Technician A says that petroleum-based hydraulic fluids need additives to work well. Technician B says that fire-resistant hydraulic fluids will actually burn under certain circumstances even though they are made mostly of water. Who is correct?
    a. Technician A
    b. Technician B
    c. Both Technician A and Technician B
    d. Neither Technician A nor Technician B

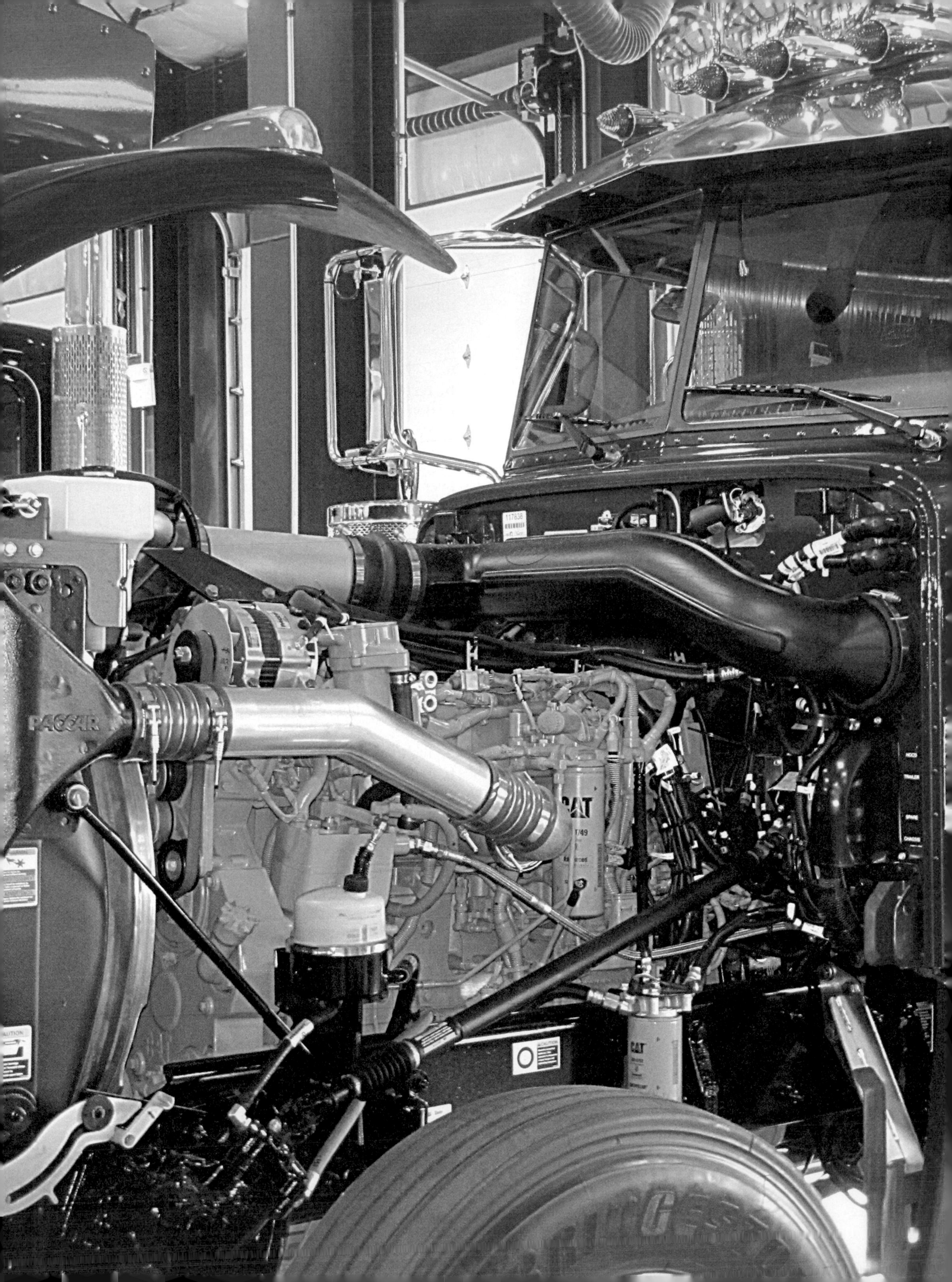
PACCAR
CAT

SECTION VII

Preventative Maintenance and Inspection

CHAPTER 55 Preventative Maintenance and Inspection

CHAPTER 55

NATEF Tasks

Preventative Maintenance and Inspection Engine System—Engine	Page
■ Check engine for oil, coolant, air, fuel, and exhaust leaks (Engine Off and Running).	1858, 1863
■ Check engine starting/operation (including unusual noises, vibrations, exhaust smoke, etc.); record idle and governed rpm.	1860
■ Inspect engine mounts for looseness and deterioration.	1873
■ Inspect vibration damper.	1875–1876
■ Inspect belts, tensioners, and pulleys; check and adjust belt tension; check belt alignment.	1875–1876
■ Check engine oil level and condition; check dipstick seal.	1875–1876
■ Check engine compartment wiring harnesses, connectors, and seals for damage and proper routing.	1875–1876
Engine System—Fuel System	
■ Check fuel tanks, mountings, lines, caps, and vents.	1863
■ Service water separator/fuel heater; replace fuel filter(s); prime and bleed fuel system.	1868
■ Drain water from fuel system.	1878
Engine System—Air Induction and Exhaust System	
■ Check exhaust system mountings for looseness and damage.	1866–1867
■ Check engine exhaust system for leaks, proper routing, and damaged or missing components to include exhaust gas recirculation (EGR) system and after treatment devices, if equipped.	1866–1867
■ Check air induction system: piping, charge air cooler, hoses, clamps, and mountings; check for air restrictions and leaks.	1878
■ Inspect turbocharger for leaks; check mountings and connections.	1878
■ Check operation of engine compression/exhaust brake.	1879–1880

Preventative Maintenance and Inspection

NATEF Tasks, continued

Preventative Maintenance and Inspection Engine System—Air Induction and Exhaust System, continued	Page
■ Service or replace air filter as needed; check and reset air filter restriction indicator.	1878
Engine System—Cooling System	
■ Pressure test cooling system and radiator cap.	1878
■ Inspect coolant hoses and clamps.	1878
■ Inspect coolant recovery system.	1878
■ Check coolant for contamination, additive package concentration, aeration, and protection level (freeze point).	1878
■ Service coolant filter.	1878
■ Inspect radiator (including air flow restriction, leaks, and damage) and mountings.	1878
■ Check operation of fan clutch.	1879–1880
■ Inspect fan assembly and shroud.	1879–1880
Engine System—Lubrication System	
■ Change engine oil and filters; visually check oil for coolant or fuel contamination; inspect and clean magnetic drain plugs.	1875–1876
■ Take an engine oil sample for analysis.	1875–1876
Cab and Hood—Instruments and Controls	
■ Inspect key condition and operation of ignition switch.	1860
■ Check warning indicators.	1860–1861
■ Check instruments; record oil pressure and system voltage.	1860–1861
■ Check operation of electronic power take off (PTO) and engine idle speed controls (if applicable)	1860

NATEF Tasks, continued

Preventative Maintenance and Inspection Cab and Hood—Instruments and Controls, continued	Page
■ Check HVAC controls.	1860
■ Check operation of all accessories.	1860
■ Using electronic service tool(s) or on-board diagnostic system; retrieve engine monitoring information; check and record diagnostic codes and trip/operational data (including engine, transmission, ABS, and other systems).	1860
Cab and Hood—Safety Equipment	
■ Check condition of spare fuses, safety triangles, fire extinguisher, and all required decals.	1859
■ Inspect seat belts and sleeper restraints.	1859
■ Inspect wiper blades and arms.	1860
■ Check operation of electric/air horns and reverse warning devices.	1860–1861
Cab and Hood—Hardware	
■ Record all observed physical damage.	1858
■ Inspect windshield glass for cracks or discoloration; check sun visor.	1859
■ Check seat condition, operation, and mounting.	1859
■ Check door glass and window operation.	1859
■ Check operation of wiper and washer.	1860
■ Inspect steps and grab handles.	1862
■ Inspect mirrors, mountings, brackets, and glass.	1862
■ Inspect and lubricate door and hood hinges, latches, strikers, lock cylinders, safety latches, linkages, and cables.	1862, 1866–1867
■ Lubricate all cab and hood grease fittings.	1866–1867
■ Inspect cab mountings, hinges, latches, linkages, and ride height; service as needed.	1866–1867
Cab and Hood—Heating, Ventilation, & Air Conditioning (HVAC)	
■ Check A/C system condition and operation; check A/C monitoring system, if applicable.	1860–1861
■ Inspect A/C condenser and lines for condition and visible leaks; check mountings.	1877
■ Inspect A/C compressor and lines for condition and visible leaks; check mountings.	1877
■ Check HVAC air inlet filters and ducts; service as needed.	1877
Electrical/Electronics—Battery and Starting Systems	
■ Inspect battery box(es), cover(s), and mountings.	1864
■ Inspect battery hold-downs, connections, cables, and cable routing; service as needed.	1864

NATEF Tasks, continued

Preventative Maintenance and Inspection Electrical/Electronics—Battery and Starting Systems, continued	Page
■ Check/record battery state-of-charge (open circuit voltage) and condition.	1864
■ Perform battery test (load and/or capacitance).	1864
■ Inspect starter, mounting, and connections.	1864, 1875–1876
■ Engage starter; check for unusual noises, starter drag, and starting difficulty.	1875–1876
Electrical/Electronics—Charging System	
■ Inspect alternator, mountings, cable, wiring, and wiring routing; determine needed action.	1875–1876
■ Perform alternator output tests.	1879–1880
Electrical/Electronics—Lighting System	
■ Check operation of interior lights; determine needed action.	1859
■ Inspect and test tractor-to-trailer multi-wire connector(s), cable(s), and holder(s); determine needed action.	1864–1865
■ Check all exterior lights, lenses, reflectors, and conspicuity tape; check headlight alignment; determine needed action.	1866–1867
Frame and Chassis—Air Brakes	
■ Check low air pressure warning devices.	1860–1861, 1869–1870
■ Inspect coupling air lines, holders, and gladhands.	1860–1861, 1869–1870
■ Check brake chambers and air lines for secure mounting and damage.	1864–1865, 1869–1870
■ Check operation of air dryer.	1864–1865, 1869–1870
■ Inspect and record brake shoe/pad condition, thickness, and contamination.	1864–1865, 1869–1870
■ Check operation of parking brake.	1869–1870
■ Record air governor cut-in and cut-out setting (psi).	1869–1870
■ Check operation of air reservoir/tank drain valves.	1869–1870
■ Check air system for leaks (brakes released).	1869–1870
■ Check air system for leaks (brakes applied).	1869–1870
■ Test one-way and double-check valves.	1869–1870
■ Check emergency (spring) brake control/modulator valve, if applicable.	1869–1870
■ Check tractor protection valve.	1869–1870
■ Test air pressure build-up time.	1869–1870
■ Inspect and record condition of brake drums/rotors.	1869–1870

NATEF Tasks, continued

Preventative Maintenance and Inspection Frame and Chassis—Air Brakes, continued	Page
■ Check anti-lock brake system wiring, connectors, seals, and harnesses for damage and proper routing.	1869–1870
■ Check operation and adjustment of brake automatic slack adjusters (ASA); check and record push rod stroke.	1869–1870
■ Lubricate all brake component grease fittings.	1869–1870
■ Check condition and operation of hand brake (trailer) control valve, if applicable.	1869–1870
■ Perform anti-lock brake system (ABS) operational system self-test.	1869–1870
■ Drain air tanks and check for contamination.	1869–1870
■ Check condition of pressure relief (safety) valves.	1869–1870
Frame and Chassis—Hydraulic Brakes	
■ Check master cylinder fluid level and condition.	1867–1868
■ Inspect brake lines, fittings, flexible hoses, and valves for leaks and damage.	1867–1868
■ Check parking brake operation; inspect parking brake application and holding devices; adjust as needed.	1867–1868
■ Check operation of hydraulic system: pedal travel, pedal effort, pedal feel.	1867–1868
■ Inspect calipers for leakage, binding, and damage.	1867–1868
■ Inspect brake assist system (booster), hoses and control valves; check reservoir fluid level and condition.	1867–1868
■ Inspect and record brake lining/pad condition, thickness, and contamination.	1867–1868
■ Inspect and record condition of brake rotors.	1867–1868
■ Check anti-lock brake system wiring, connectors, seals, and harnesses for damage and proper routing.	1867–1868
Frame and Chassis—Drive Train	
■ Check clutch adjustment; adjust as needed.	1859
■ Check transmission case, seals, filter, hoses, lines, and cooler for cracks and leaks.	1859
■ Check operation of clutch, clutch brake, and gearshift.	1859–1861
■ Check clutch linkage/cable for looseness or binding, if applicable.	1860–1861
■ Inspect transmission breather.	1874–1875
■ Inspect transmission mounts.	1874–1875
■ Check transmission oil level, type, and condition.	1874–1875
■ Inspect U-joints, yokes, driveshafts, boots/seals, center bearings, and mounting hardware for looseness, damage, and proper phasing.	1874–1875

NATEF Tasks, continued

Preventative Maintenance and Inspection Frame and Chassis—Drive Train, continued	Page
■ Inspect axle housing(s) for cracks and leaks.	1874–1875
■ Inspect axle breather(s).	1874–1875
■ Lubricate all drive train grease fittings.	1874–1875
■ Check drive axle(s) oil level, type, and condition.	1874–1875
■ Change drive axle(s) oil and filter/screen, if applicable; check and clean magnetic plugs.	1874–1875
■ Check transmission wiring, connectors, seals, and harnesses for damage and proper routing.	1874–1875
■ Change transmission oil and filter, if applicable; check and clean magnetic plugs.	1874–1875
■ Check interaxle differential lock operation.	1874–1875
■ Check transmission range shift operation.	1874–1875
■ Check hydraulic clutch slave and master cylinders, lines, fittings, and hoses, if applicable.	1875–1876
Frame and Chassis—Suspension and Steering Systems	
■ Inspect steering gear for leaks and secure mounting.	1858
■ Check steering wheel operation for free play and binding.	1859
■ Check and record suspension ride height.	1865
■ Lubricate all suspension and steering grease fittings.	1866–1867
■ Check wheel bearings for looseness and noise.	1871
■ Check oil level and condition in all non-drive hubs; check for leaks.	1871
■ Inspect shock absorbers for leaks and secure mounting.	1871
■ Inspect air suspension springs, mounts, hoses, valves, linkage, and fittings for leaks and damage.	1871
■ Inspect steering shaft U-joints, pinch bolts, splines, pitman arm-to-steering sector shaft, tie rod ends, and linkages.	1872
■ Check kingpins for wear.	1872
■ Check axle locating components (radius, torque, and/or track rods).	1872
■ Inspect springs, pins, hangers, shackles, spring U-bolts, and insulators.	1874–1875
■ Check power steering pump, mounting, and hoses for leaks, condition, and routing; check fluid level.	1877
■ Change power steering fluid and filter.	1877
Frame and Chassis—Tires and Wheels	
■ Inspect tires for wear patterns and proper mounting.	1871
■ Inspect tires for cuts, cracks, bulges, and sidewall damage.	1871

NATEF Tasks, continued

Preventative Maintenance and Inspection Frame and Chassis—Tires and Wheels, continued	Page
■ Inspect valve caps and stems; determine needed action.	1871
■ Measure and record tread depth; probe for imbedded debris.	1871
■ Check and record air pressure; adjust air pressure in accordance with manufacturers' specifications.	1871
■ Check wheel mounting hardware; determine needed action.	1871
■ Inspect wheels for cracks, damage, and proper hand hold alignment.	1871
■ Check tire matching (diameter and tread) on single and dual tire applications.	1871
Frame and Chassis—Frame and Fifth Wheel	
■ Inspect fifth wheel mounting, bolts, air lines, and locks.	1864–1865
■ Check quarter fenders, mud flaps, and brackets.	1864–1865
■ Check pintle hook assembly and mounting, if applicable.	1864–1865
■ Inspect frame and frame members for cracks and damage.	1864–1865
■ Test operation of fifth wheel locking device; adjust if necessary.	1866–1867
■ Lubricate all fifth wheel grease fittings and plate, if applicable.	1867–1868

Knowledge Objectives

After reading this chapter, you will be able to:

1. Define preventative maintenance. (p 1846)
2. Identify various types of maintenance practices. (pp 1846–1847)
3. Learn which federal agencies regulate the operations of commercial vehicles. (p 1847)
4. Identify the basis of establishing a PMI schedule. (p 1847)
5. Identify legislated requirements for vehicle inspections. (pp 1847–1850)
6. Explain why preventative maintenance is important. (p 1850)
7. Outline responsibilities regarding preventative maintenance (PM) and vehicle safety inspections. (pp 1850–1851)
8. Describe what is involved in planning a PM program and identify the inspection requirements for commercial vehicles. (pp 1851–1854)
9. Identify items for an inspection checklist. (pp 1851–1853)
10. Develop and use inspection schedules and inspection reports. (pp 1851–1854)
11. Distinguish between the various types of PMI. (pp 1848)
12. Identify the requirements of PMIs. (pp 1850–1854)
13. Identify requirements of the Commercial Vehicle Safety Alliance Inspection Program. (p 1853)
14. Identify the requirements of PMI record keeping. (pp 1853–1854)
15. Understand the qualifications of an inspector. (pp 1854–1855)
16. Distinguish between the qualifications of a vehicle inspector and a brake inspector. (pp 1854–1855)
17. Identify the lubricants used in PMI. (p 1855)
18. Identify how to find information on recalls. (pp 1855–1856)
19. Distinguish between shop and vehicle rules. (p 1856)
20. Identify specialty tools used in PMIs. (pp 1855–1856)
21. Describe the PMI process. (pp 1858–1880)

Skills Objectives

After reading this chapter, you will be able to:

1. List the general guidelines for conducting preventative maintenance inspections. (p 1857) SKILL DRILL 55-1
2. Perform a walk-around inspection. (p 1858) SKILL DRILL 55-2
3. Perform an in-cab inspection, including key-off inspection, key-on inspection, and engine-on inspection. (p 1859) SKILL DRILL 55-3
4. Perform an internal key-on inspection. (p 1860) SKILL DRILL 55-4
5. Perform an internal cab engine-on inspection. (pp 1860–1861) SKILL DRILL 55-5
6. Perform a cab door inspection. (p 1862) SKILL DRILL 55-6
7. Inspect body and component mountings. (p 1863) SKILL DRILL 55-7
8. Inspect batteries and mountings. (p 1864) SKILL DRILL 55-8
9. Inspect lines and mountings on fifth-wheel couplings. (pp 1864–1865) SKILL DRILL 55-9
10. Inspect the vehicle frame and suspension and verify suspension ride height. (p 1865) SKILL DRILL 55-10
11. . Inspect the vehicle's electrical components, its exhaust system, and its lubrication system. (pp 1866–1867) SKILL DRILL 55-11
12. Inspect hydraulic and air-over-hydraulic braking systems. (pp 1867–1868) SKILL DRILL 55-12
13. Perform a full inspection of the vehicle's air brake systems. (pp 1869–1870) SKILL DRILL 55-13
14. Inspect vehicle tires and wheels. (p 1871) SKILL DRILL 55-14
15. Inspect the vehicle for proper wheel alignment. (p 1872) SKILL DRILL 55-15
16. Inspect and check under-vehicle frame, its mountings, and electrical and exhaust components. (p 1873) SKILL DRILL 55-16
17. Inspect the vehicle's transmission and drive train. (pp 1874–1875) SKILL DRILL 55-17
18. Perform an engine-off engine compartment inspection. (pp 1875–1876) SKILL DRILL 55-18
19. Inspect the steering and air-conditioning components during an engine-off engine compartment inspection. SKILL DRILL 55-19
20. Inspect the fuel, intake, cooling, and cab-tilt systems during an engine-off engine compartment inspection. (p 1878) SKILL DRILL 55-20
21. Inspect the vehicle for leaks, fluid levels, and operating systems during an engine-on engine compartment inspection. (pp 1879–1880) SKILL DRILL 55-21
22. Inspect cargo-handling devices. (p 1880) SKILL DRILL 55-22

Introduction—What Is Preventative Maintenance?

Preventative maintenance and inspection (PMI) is really the starting point for understanding all the critical systems in medium- and heavy-duty vehicles. PMI is critical to making sure heavy-duty vehicles conform to federal, state, and local laws for roadworthiness and safe operation.

Commercial vehicles are built ruggedly to withstand continuous daily operation in extreme operating environments. In spite of their robust construction, time and a variety of other wear factors eventually produce deterioration to the point a vehicle cannot operate efficiently, safely, or reliably. Common points of wear and deterioration include the braking system, engine oil that loads with contaminants, and chassis components that lose lubricant. Preventative maintenance (PM) and its associated regular inspections (PMI) are a set of service operations that involve scheduled inspections, adjustment, cleaning, testing, parts replacement and vehicle repair to prevent unexpected breakdowns, extend service life, and minimize vehicle downtime. From a business perspective, PM has the added benefit of increasing resale value and **return on investment (ROI)**, lowering overall lifetime cost of operation plus increasing productivity since the vehicle will provide more efficient service with improved reliability FIGURE 55-1. Preventative maintenance adds resale value to a vehicle. Many operators

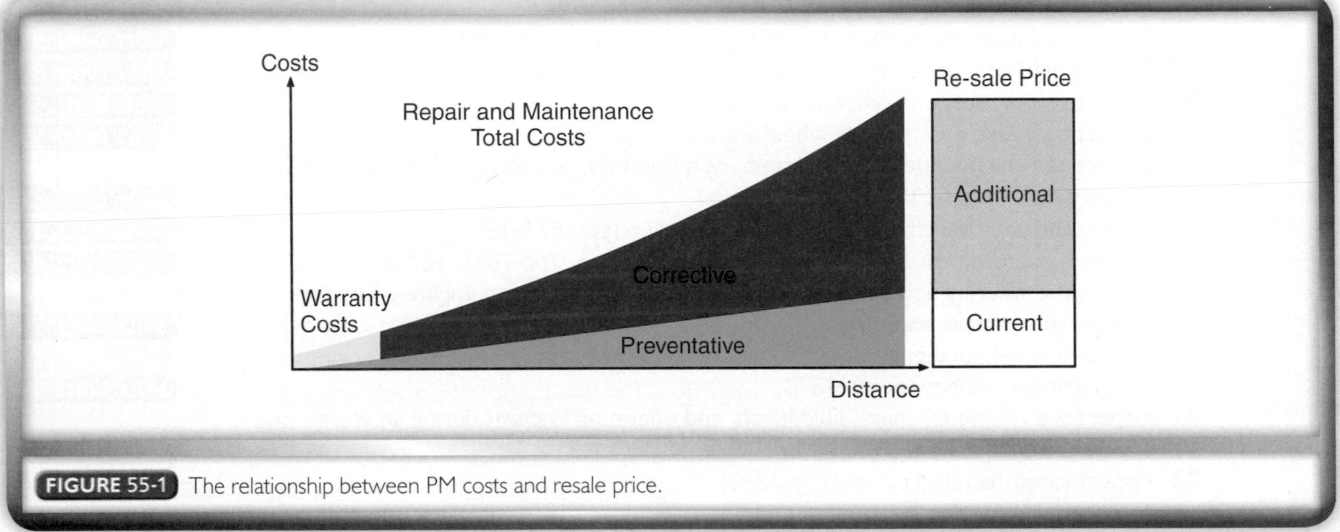

FIGURE 55-1 The relationship between PM costs and resale price.

You Are the Technician

A large number of transportation-related businesses depend on your shop to provide running repairs as well as to perform regularly scheduled maintenance and safety inspections for a variety of types of trucks and buses. One of the difficulties you have when making service recommendations to customers is providing the best advice to clients with different expectations for the level of maintenance support you can provide. Some customers want to keep repair and vehicle maintenance costs as low as possible and want only the minimum amount of work performed in order to keep the equipment operating on the road. Other customers want the security of knowing their vehicles are in the best condition to avoid unexpected break-downs and disruptions to their business operations. Some customers prefer to do most of their own repairs and need only annual safety inspections, which you can provide. As you prepare your recommendations for each of these categories of customers, consider the following:

1. List in point form the reasons for performing proactive maintenance inspections.
2. For each of the categories of customers above, which type of PM schedule (PM- A, B, or C inspection, if any at all) is likely to be used by the customer? Explain your answer.
3. List in point form the requirements for facilities and technicians to perform safety inspections and meet the standards for issuing a Commercial Vehicle Safety Alliance (CVSA) safety inspection decal.

operate vehicles for a set period based on time or mileage. Regular PM ensures that they will get the maximum return on their investment when they trade the vehicle for a replacement.

Fleet operators cannot afford to have their vehicles out of service for longer than is necessary. Any PMI must include careful attention to detail when it comes to inspecting wires, hydraulic lines, braking systems, and fluids and running the tests needed to ensure that all systems are operating properly before the vehicle is placed in service. The general visual inspection also includes checking the security, safety, and proper operation of mountings, fasteners, cabling, driveline phasing, and tire condition and wear patterns.

Safety legislation requires all commercial motor vehicles (CMVs) to undergo PM. The legislation defines a CMV as a vehicle that is used in an interstate commerce business and meets one or more of the following specifications:

- Weight of in excess of 10,001 pounds
- Designed for transportation of 16 passengers, including an unpaid driver
- Designed for transportation of 9 passengers, including a paid driver
- Involved in transporting hazardous materials within state or interstate in a quantity requiring placards

As an example, companies that operate commercial vehicles within the United States to move freight, passengers, or transport any cargo interstate, must be registered with the **Federal Motor Carrier Safety Administration (FMCSA)**. Any hazardous materials carriers who move enough materials requiring a safety permit must also register for a **United States Department of Transport (USDOT) number**. The USDOT number functions as a unique identifier used to collect and monitor a company's safety information.

Schedules and Types of Preventative Maintenance Inspection (PMI)

There are three primary bases for the establishment of a preventative maintenance inspection schedule.

- Time (number of months or hours)
  - Engine hours are used for long-haul vehicles.
  - Months are used for shorter-haul vehicles.
- Mileage
  - Recommended by manufacturer for normal use (shorter-haul and long-haul mixture use).
- Amount of fuel consumed
  - Easily monitored by the cost of fuel and mileage traveled.

PMI falls into three basic categories, and each category has a scheduled interval with its own checklist. Typical PMI programs include:

- **PM-A**—This inspection generally is a visual check of all safety-related items such as brakes, tires, horn, wipers, steering components, suspension components, and lighting. The chassis is lubricated and fluid levels are checked. Minor adjustments are also performed. The normal interval for a PM-A is approximately halfway between normal oil change intervals. So a PM-A would take place every 10,000 miles or 16,000 km.
- **PM-B**—This inspection is more comprehensive than a PM-A. It includes all checks and adjustments performed in a PM-A as well as an oil change and oil and fuel filter change. The inspection items include the engine and driveline plus greater detail checks of the braking, steering, and other chassis systems. A PM-B is performed at every oil change, while a PM-A is performed between PM-B inspections and only the chassis is greased—no oil is changed.
- **PM-C**—This is typically an annual inspection that includes all the items in PM-A and B plus a comprehensive inspection of all chassis components. Scheduled fluid changes and component adjustment, repair, or replacement are performed at this time **FIGURE 55-2**. This inspection is often referred to as an annual safety inspection or DOT inspection required to maintain operational certification.

PM is generally proactive, which means maintenance work is scheduled to prevent unexpected breakdowns from occurring. **Proactive PM** is typically based on distance traveled, engine hours, time, or fuel used. **Proactive maintenance** reflects the understanding that the cost of repairing an unexpected breakdown is usually much greater than preventative maintenance. Small problems are corrected before they turn into bigger, more expensive problems and cause unanticipated downtime or become a liability due to unsafe service conditions. Experience has demonstrated that not following a proactive maintenance strategy, and instead pursuing a cost-minimization maintenance strategy or a **reactive maintenance** strategy, meaning service is performed only after equipment is broken, may keep vehicle and fleet operating costs low only temporarily **TABLE 55-1**. But as time passes and distance traveled increases, the cost of repairs eclipses what

B & C PM PREVENTIVE MAINTENANCE CHECKSHEET FOR SERVICE TRUCKS

FHWA ANNUAL INSPECTION - INITIAL BOX IF PERFORMED

COMPANY NAME:

INSPECTION DATE: | UNIT#: | MILES: | HOURS:

EMPLOYEE NAME: | BRANCH:

DENOTES MANDATORY FHWA ITEMS, WHICH MUST BE FREE OF DEFECTS TO CERTIFY!

	AT EVERY B-PM SERVICE DO THE FOLLOWING ITEMS: 1 THROUGH 64	INITIALS
01	FHWA INSPECTION DUE: ☐ YES ☐ NO	
02	CHECK SAFETY EQUIPMENT - REFLECTOR KIT, CONES, WHEEL CHOCKS & FIRE EXTINGUISHER	
03	WARNING DEVICES: ☐ WATER ☐ AIR ☐ OIL	
04	HORNS: ☐ AIR ☐ ELECTRIC	
05	WIPERS & BLADES	
06	FLOOR MAT SHIFT BOOT	
07	SEATS SEAT BELTS	
08	GLASS & WINDOW OPERATION ☐ MIRRORS	
09	CLUTCH FREE PLAY & CLUTCH BRAKE OPERATION (IF EQUIPPED)	
10	BACKUP ALARMS	
11	FOOT BRAKE PARKING BRAKE	
12	☐ VERIFY CHECK VALVE OPERATION ☐ INTERLOCK OPERATION (IF EQUIPPED)	
13	☐ 4-WAY WHEEL LOCK OPERATION (IF EQUIPPED) ☐ AIR SHIFT OPERATION (IF EQUIPPED)	
14	☐ CHECK GEAR SHIFT ☐ CHECK FOR CURRENT & PROPER REGISTRATION AND PERMITS	
15	ALTERNATOR OUTPUT & RECORD	
16	☐ NOISE IN ENGINE ☐ EXCESSIVE SM0KE	
17	ENGINE OIL PRESSURE: @IDLE @MAX RPM	
18	ACCELERATOR PEDAL	
19	EASE OF STEERING & NOISE - EXHAUST MUFFLER & PIPING	
20	AIR DRYER OPERATION IF EQUIPPED)	
21	LIGHTS SIGNAL LAMPS STOP LAMPS	
22	☐ MUD FLAPS ☐ AIR TANK DRAINS ☐ BATTERY BOX	
23	CAB MOUNTS: FRONT REAR	
24	☐ SHEET METAL ☐ IDLER PULLEY	
25	COOLANT - RECORD ANTFIREEZE PROTECTION ______ ☐ DCA ☐ FULL	
26	RADIATOR MOUNTING DEV CES0 RADIATOR HOSES	
27	WATER PUMP (CLEAN OUT WEEP HOLE) ☐ INSPECT BELTS, AND FAN HUB	
28	ENGINE AIR COMPRESSOR & LINES OR MASTER CYLINDER AND LINES AS EQUIPPED	
29	STARTER, MOUNTING & WIRING	
30	CHANGE ENGINE OIL AND FILTER	
31	CHECK FUEL SYSTEM / FILTER CHANGED (BY MANUFACTURERS SCHEDULE) ☐ YES ☐ NO	
32	AIR FILTER CHANGED (BY RESTRICTION GUAGE OR MANUFACTURERS SCHEDULE) ☐ YES ☐ NO	
33	INSPECT AIR INTAKE PIPING, CHARGE AIR COOLER, AND HOSES	
34	POWER STEERING & STEERING SYSTEM COMPONENTS	
35	CHECK BATTERIES - HOLD DOWNS, CLEAN TERMINALS	
36	MOTOR SUPPORTS	
37	CHECK TRANSMISSION FLUID LEVEL, INSPECT FOR LEAKS, MOUNTING BOLTS AND BRACKETS	
38	CHECK DIFFERENTIAL, INSPECT FOR LEAKS, MOUNTING BOLTS AND BRACKETS	
39	DRIVE SHAFT & U-JOINTS	
40	BRAKE ADJUSTMENT & OVERALL SYSTEM OPERATION	
41	BRAKE SHOES	
42	CHECK WHEEL SEALS AND HUBS	
43	CHECK SUSPENSION AND FRAME	
44	INSPECT PTO SYSTEM HOSES AND MOUNTING BRACKETS	
45	CHECK TREAD DEPTH & AIR TIRES TO SPECIFICATIONS	

		INITIALS
46	LUBRICATE ALL FITTINGS	
47	OVERALL BODY CONDITION, CHECK FOR DAMAGE, DENTS, HOLES, DECALS & MARKINGS	
48	INSPECT LIFT GATE AND ALL DOORS,AND LATCHES	
49	INSPECT FLOOR,LOAD SECUREMENT DEVICES,	
50	VERIFY ALL WARNING DECALS IN PLACE	
	PTO DRIVEN COMPRESSOR SECTION (If gasoline powered use the Compressor PM form)	
51	CHECK FOR HYDRAULIC OIL LEAKS	
52	CHECK HYDRAULIC OIL & FILTER AND CHANGE ACCORDING TO MANUFACTURERS GUIDELINES	
53	INSPECT OIL SEPERATOR & CHANGE ELEMENT ACCORDING TO MANUFACTURERS GUIDELINES	
54	INSPECT GAUGES AND INSTRUMENTS	
55	INSPECT ALL PIPING AND CONNECTIONS (HYDRAULIC AND AIR)	
56	TEST AUTOMATIC SHUTDOWN (IF EQUIPPED)	
57	INSPECT ALL MOUNTINGS & BRACKETS (TIGHTEN AS NEEDED)	
58	INSPECT ALL ELECTRICAL CONNECTIONS	
59	CHANGE COMPRESSOR CRANKCASE OIL (CHANGE FILTER IF EQUIPPED)	
60	INSPECT COMPRESSOR AIR FILTER AND CHANGE IF NECESSARY	
61	INSPECT ALL GUARDS AND BRAKETS,REPAIR OR REPLACE AS NECESSARY	
62	INSPECT DRIVE COUPLER AND OR BELTS (AS EQUIPPED)	
63	CHECK AND CLEAN SCAVENGER ORIFICE & RELATED PARTS PER MAINTENANCE SCHEDULE	
64	INSPECT PTO MOUNTING AND BE SURE PUMP SPLINES/ COUPLING ARE PROPERLY LUBRICATED	
	AT EVERY C-PM SERVICE ADD THE FOLLOWING ITEMS: 65 & 66	
65	CHANGE TRANSMISSION FLUID AND FILTERS	
66	CHANGE FUEL FILTER	

COMMENTS:

FRONT: /32ND PSI, /32ND PSI

REAR: /32ND PSI (×8)

FHWA ANNUAL INSPECTION COMPLETE THE FOLLOWING:

VIN# ______________________

INSPECTOR'S NAME (PRINT) | SIGNATURE:

I CERTIFY THIS VEHICLE TO BE FREE OF ANY DEFECTS AS DESCRIBED IN 49 C.F.R. PART 396.17

THIS INSPECTOR MEETS THE QUALIFICATION REQUIREMENTS IN SECTION 396.19. ☐ YES

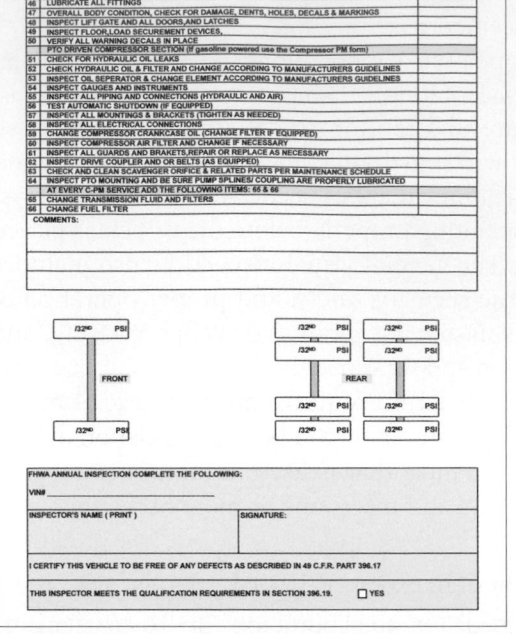

FIGURE 55-2 A PM inspection sheet used for both PM-B and PM-C inspections. During a PM-B inspection, the items under the PM-C section are simply not performed.

TABLE 55-1: Reactive Maintenance Versus Proactive Maintenance

Reactive Maintenance	Proactive Maintenance
Late detection of problem by operator	Early detection by skilled technician or advanced monitoring techniques
Immediately out of service with indefinite downtime	Planned service with scheduled return to service
Expediting parts at high cost and waiting for parts	Parts on hand and best value obtained by preordering parts
Dispatching a technician for possible road call; disrupting employee work schedules	Scheduling labor and planned allocating of resources
Idle driver and/or passengers; disruption to freight delivery schedule	No disruption to driver passengers or freight delivery
High costs and safety risks	Low costs and safety risks
Consequential damage from failure	Corrective action limiting consequential damage

proactive PM would have cost, and vehicle uptime falls **FIGURE 55-3**. Unexpected failures, faster component wear out, consequential damage from failures, and downtime due to unexpected repairs, drive up the maintenance costs on a vehicle that does not have preventative maintenance performed.

Predictive PM is based on a statistical analysis of when equipment and component failures are likely to occur and replacing parts or equipment before that point. For example, large truck leasing and rental companies will sell used vehicles at an optimal point in vehicle lifecycle before repair costs sharply increase and before resale value falls. Some equipment or parts may be prone to high-frequency failures because of operating conditions. Engine overhauls or vehicle rebuild procedures are also performed based on anticipated service life rather than at the point of failure. The results of a study by a major engine manufacturer compared the operational costs of engine run to failure and one overhauled using predictive maintenance. Running to failure increased repair costs as much as 60% **FIGURE 55-4**.

To maximize equipment's service availability, regular PM service is performed on a scheduled basis. However,

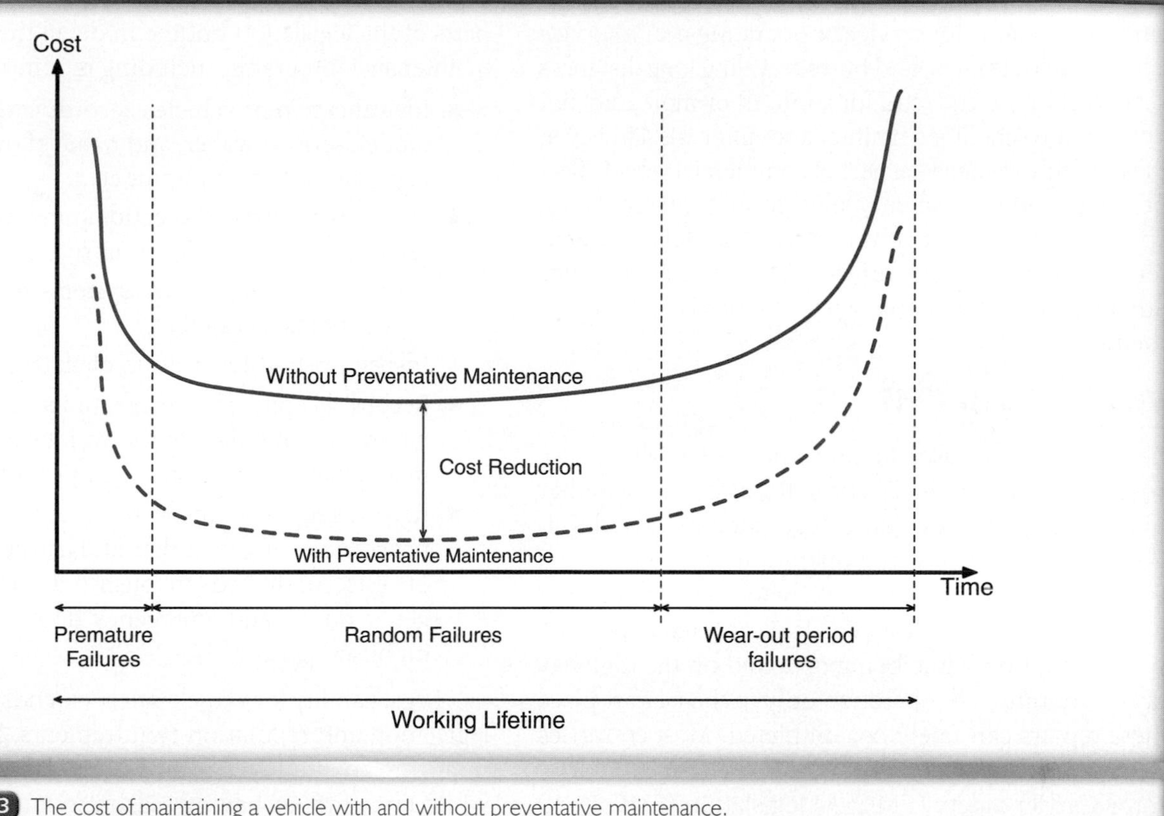

FIGURE 55-3 The cost of maintaining a vehicle with and without preventative maintenance.

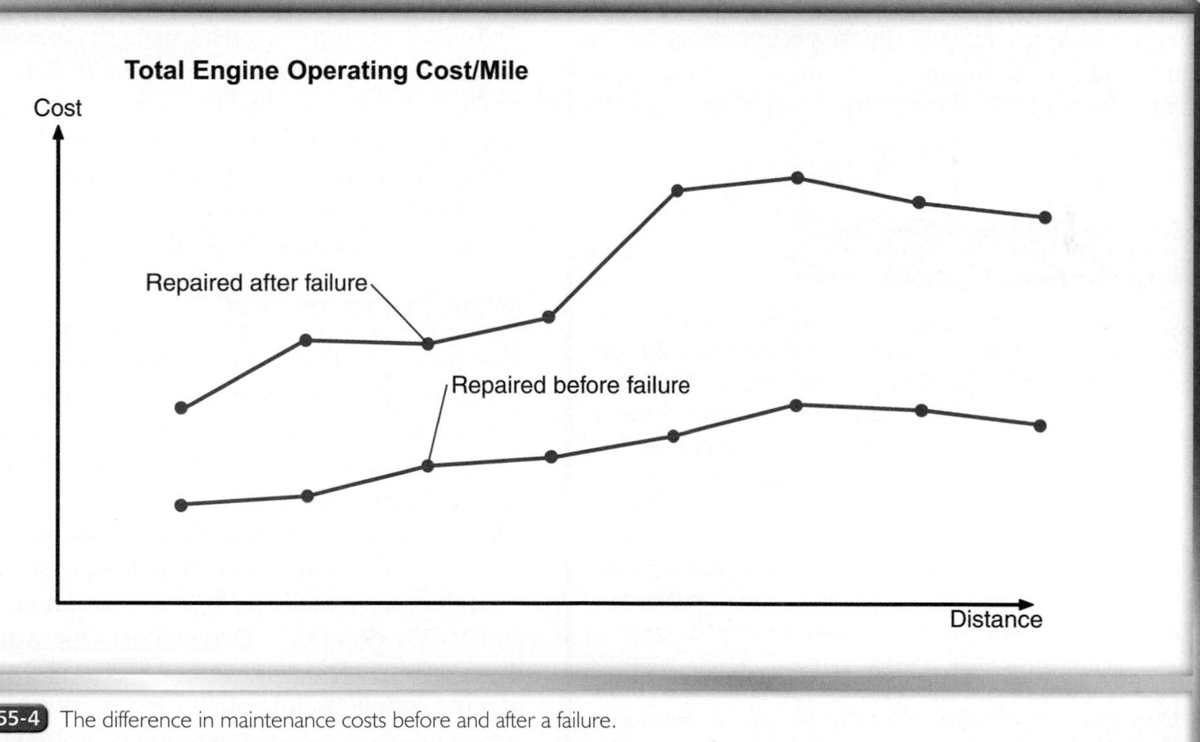

FIGURE 55-4 The difference in maintenance costs before and after a failure.

when PM is performed is also dependent on whether a vehicle is available for service or operating near a service facility. Trucks, trailers, and buses traveling long distances every week or on the road for a month or more may not fit neatly into scheduled maintenance intervals. However, PM is a highly managed aspect of commercial vehicle fleet operation, and to efficiently allocate shop time, manage expenses, maintain warranty requirements, follow recommendations by manufacturers, and ensure compliance with a variety of legislative safety standards, most PM is scheduled.

Why Perform PM?

The most obvious reason for implementing a maintenance program is that it reduces costs. Regardless of whether it makes good business sense, legislation in most developed countries forbids the operation of a commercial motor vehicle in a condition likely to cause an accident or breakdown. Any motor vehicle discovered to be in an unsafe condition while being operated on the highway may be continued in operation only to the nearest place where repairs can safely be completed. Most countries mandate regular inspections. In the United States, Federal Motor Carrier Safety (FMCSA) legislation (FMCSA 49 CFR Section 396.3: Inspection, Repair, and Maintenance) demands that every motor carrier and equipment provider must systematically inspect, repair, and maintain, or cause to be systematically inspected, repaired, and maintained, all motor vehicles and intermodal equipment subject to its control. The object of the legislation is public safety for operators and other road users. Other parts of the legislation outline in detail the scope of the maintenance programs, including requirements for:

- Identification of vehicles according to year, make, model, serial number, and name of owner or company owning the equipment.
- Systematic safety inspections and procedures to remove unsafe vehicles from service.
- Vehicle components and systems to be inspected for safety inspections.
- Inspection and lubrication of chassis.
- Record keeping for inspections identifying the nature and due date of the various inspection and maintenance operations to be performed.
- Record keeping of inspection, repairs, and maintenance indicating their date and nature; and a record of tests conducted on push-out windows, emergency doors, and emergency door marking lights on buses.

Legal liability for vehicle safety extends beyond most legislation and regulation requirements. For instance, requiring an employee to operate a dangerous vehicle while knowing, or having reason to know, that use of the vehicle creates unreasonable risk or harm makes the organization's manager liable for negligent entrustment. Having a proper PM program with good record keeping will enable a company and its managers to avoid prosecution in the event of a collision or fatality. If the steering or brakes failed and resulted in a serious accident or fatality and the vehicle were impounded for investigation, vehicle maintenance records would be examined to determine whether the vehicle was properly inspected and maintained in a safe operating condition.

> **TECHNICIAN TIP**
>
> CSA 2010 basic scores are calculated ratings on compliance, safety, and accountability initiated by the Federal Motor Carrier Safety Administration (FMCSA). The system uses the Safety Measurement System (SMS), which is used to identify carrier companies for safety audits. Scores are calculated based on Behavior Analysis and Safety Improvement Categories (BASICs), which includes measures involving driver fitness, collisions, traffic violations, and so on. It is good practice to perform regular PM inspections to avoid an increase in BASIC scores since any safety defects related to maintenance will trigger audits. The Canadian equivalent to BASIC scores is the Commercial Vehicle Operator Registration (CVOR) record. It measures the safety performance of carriers also to improve its commercial vehicle safety performance.

Who Performs PM?

Drivers are the first persons responsible for identifying potential safety issues and the possibility of imminent breakdowns. When the driver communicates vehicle problems, proactive maintenance can take place. In the United States, FMCSA legislation requires drivers to prepare a report in writing at the completion of each day's work for each commercial vehicle the driver has operated that day. Specifics of the legislation are contained in FMCVS 49.396.11: **Driver Post-Operation Vehicle Inspection Report (DVIR)** FIGURE 55-5. Inspection reports supply useful data for PM work and alert management to any unsafe operating condition. Inspection reports supply useful data for PM work and alert management to any unsafe operating condition.

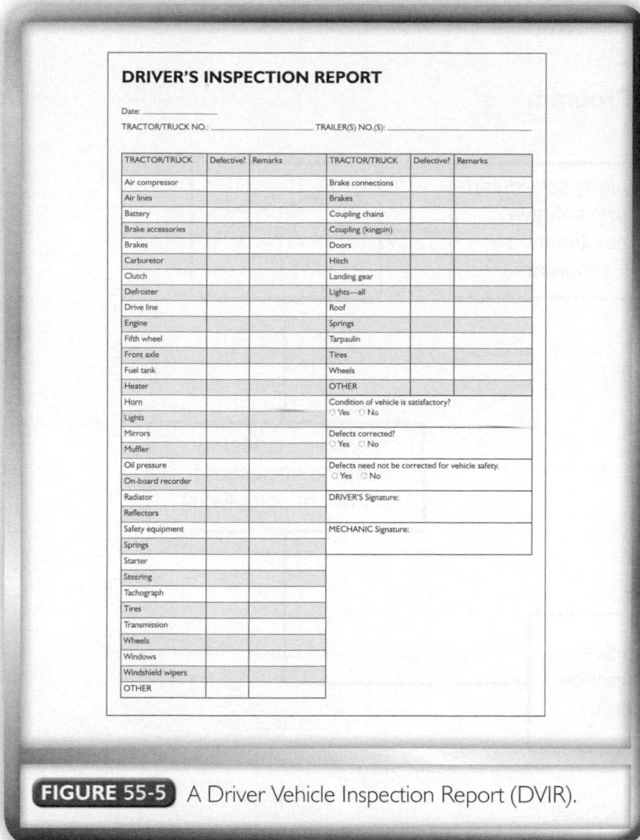

DRIVER'S INSPECTION REPORT

Date: ______

TRACTOR/TRUCK NO.: ______ TRAILER(S) NO.(S): ______

TRACTOR/TRUCK	Defective?	Remarks	TRACTOR/TRUCK	Defective?	Remarks
Air compressor			Brake connections		
Air lines			Brakes		
Battery			Coupling chains		
Brake accessories			Coupling (kingpin)		
Brakes			Doors		
Carburetor			Hitch		
Clutch			Landing gear		
Defroster			Lights—all		
Drive line			Roof		
Engine			Springs		
Fifth wheel			Tarpaulin		
Front axle			Tires		
Fuel tank			Wheels		
Heater			OTHER		
Horn			Condition of vehicle is satisfactory? ○ Yes ○ No		
Lights					
Mirrors			Defects corrected? ○ Yes ○ No		
Muffler					
Oil pressure			Defects need not be corrected for vehicle safety. ○ Yes ○ No		
On-board recorder					
Radiator			DRIVER'S Signature:		
Reflectors					
Safety equipment			MECHANIC Signature:		
Springs					
Starter					
Steering					
Tachograph					
Tires					
Transmission					
Wheels					
Windows					
Windshield wipers					
OTHER					

FIGURE 55-5 A Driver Vehicle Inspection Report (DVIR).

The driver is required to monitor and report on the following vehicle parts and systems:

- Vehicle safety items such as the tires, rims, wipers, horn, brakes, steering, trailer brake connections, coupler condition, and parking brake.
- Vehicle glass, body condition, lighting, mirrors, and emergency equipment (i.e., flares and a first-aid kit).

It's helpful to a fleet operation for drivers to also report **drivability items** such as misfires, rough idle, and check engine and other warning lights.

PM is performed by normally certified technicians attached to a fleet operation or by service repair centers with the capability to properly complete PMIs and repairs. PM work is detail orientated and requires technicians to develop good powers of observation gained through training and experience.

Effective PM Program Development

PM Service Intervals

Legislation governing commercial vehicle maintenance and safety only requires a carrier to "systematically inspect, repair, and maintain, or cause to be systematically inspected, repaired, and maintained, all motor vehicles and intermodal equipment subject to its control." Parts and accessories required in the regulations "shall be in safe and proper operating condition at all times." It is therefore the responsibility of a carrier to develop a PM program to meet those performance standards and have records documenting that vehicles are being maintained and repaired as needed **FIGURE 55-6**.

Several factors are used to determine the frequency of a PM schedule. One is the operating condition of the vehicle. Dusty conditions, extreme cold or heat, stop-and-go driving, off- or on-road operation, and traveling at continuous on-highway speeds are just a few operating conditions that influence **PM service intervals**. Most commercial vehicles operate under severe conditions rather than normal conditions. **Severe service operating conditions** include:

- Towing or hauling heavy loads
- Extensive idling and/or stop-and-go, low-speed driving encountered in inner-city traffic
- Delivery
- Off-road dusty conditions
- Multiple drivers

Manufacturer recommendations for PM schedules found in service literature and owner's manuals differentiate between **normal service operating conditions** and severe service operating conditions, and the recommendations should be followed. Experience with a particular piece of equipment may require a modified PM schedule. For example, hydraulic brake calipers may require lubrication of sliders twice a year rather than once a year to minimize lining wear caused by sticking caliper sliding surfaces.

Developing a PM Service Checklist

At a minimum, a **PM service checklist** should include an itemized task list of procedures that includes mechanical safety items related to braking, steering, suspension, lighting, mirrors, wipers, horns, tires, wheels, and so on. The task list should also include items related to maintenance on engines, drivelines, electrical system, body/cab, fluids, filters, and other items regularly requiring periodic adjustment, lubrication, or replacement. Inspection of fire protection, emergency exit, and evacuation equipment is critical for buses and motor coaches. The type of checklist as well as the inspection schedule will vary with vehicle type and operating service. A procedure should be in place ensuring that safety-related vehicle defects discovered during inspections are reported, repaired, and validated before the

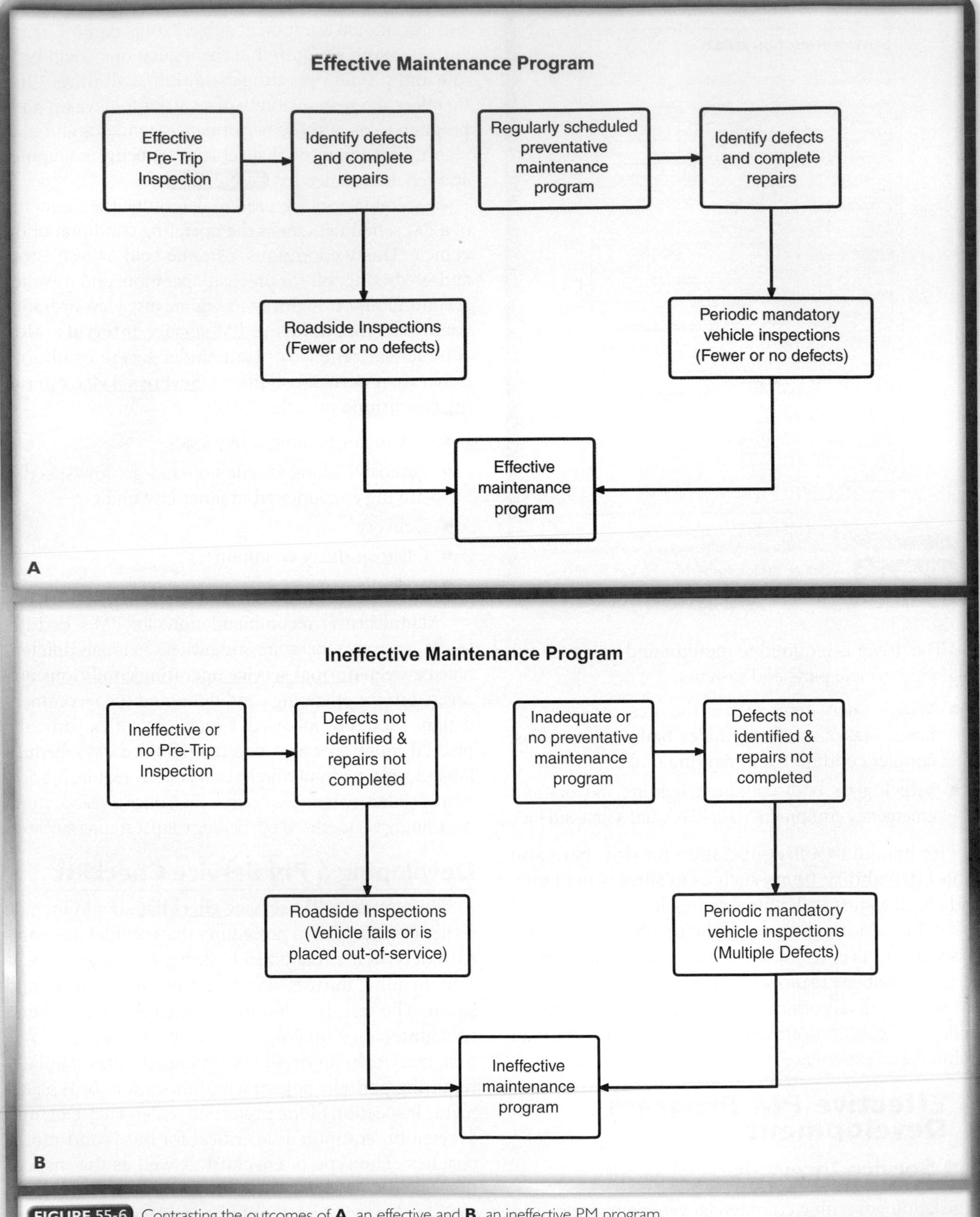

FIGURE 55-6 Contrasting the outcomes of **A.** an effective and **B.** an ineffective PM program.

vehicle is released for operation. Driver Vehicle Inspection Records (DVIRS) and other driver communications should have a procedure to ensure equipment managers are promptly notified about vehicle defects.

Commercial Vehicle Safety Alliance Inspections

The **Commercial Vehicle Safety Alliance (CVSA)** is a nonprofit organization dedicated to improve the safe operation of commercial vehicles in North America by establishing a uniform, reciprocal enforcement of commercial vehicle safety standards. The driving force behind the organization was the recognition that commercial vehicle highway safety was nearly the same in most U.S., Canadian, and Mexican jurisdictions. Even though a common criteria for regulation and inspection was used in most states and provinces, there was no mechanism to recognize enforcement standards in each region. A significant duplication of work and record keeping by government agencies and the motor carrier industry was taking place until a North American standard for commercial vehicle safety was in place.

The CVSA establishes transportation safety standards for motor carriers, drivers, vehicles, and inspectors through compliance, education, training, and enforcement programs. The organization has also developed policies and procedures requiring drivers to immediately notify management of any roadside vehicle out-of-service order (OOSO) and has recommended various minimum inspection standards and criteria that its members agree to follow. Not only are the standards uniform, but each enforcement jurisdiction recognizes each other's work in inspecting commercial vehicles, their drivers, and their cargo.

CVSA's core functions are to support the North American Standard Inspection Program and all of its components, which include:

1. North American Standard Inspection Procedures
2. Training curriculum
3. Inspector certification
4. North American Standard Out-of-Service Criteria
5. CVSA decal program

Of particular interest to technicians are the **North American Standard Out-of-Service Criteria (OOSC)**. This standard is used by all law enforcement agencies throughout North America. Two of its four parts outline out-of-service safety standards. Part two of the standard describes the critical vehicle inspection items and provides direction to each commercial vehicle inspector in North America to identify at what point a commercial motor vehicle can no longer be safety operated for fear of causing an accident or breakdown. Part four of the standard establishes criteria for placing a motor carrier out of service. The standards are minimum requirements, and the CVSA encourages the use of higher safety standards. Other parts deal with drivers out of service and transportation of hazardous waste. The only difference between the U.S. and Canadian editions of the North American Standard Out-of-Service Criteria is that the U.S. edition references the **Federal Motor Carrier Safety Regulation (FMCSR)** violation codes.

A commercial vehicle may qualify for a CVSA decal if it passes a Level I or V inspection and no defects are found in critical inspection items listed in the CVSA OOSC. This means the vehicle is free of any mechanical-, cargo-, and driver-related safety violations. The decal is valid for three months FIGURE 55-7. Defects that are noted during inspection that are not critical inspection items do not affect decal qualification.

Record Keeping

The use of software-based record keeping is almost universal in fleet operations. Software can customize maintenance schedules, create and track work orders, track fuel consumption, record maintenance histories, track tire service, record accidents, monitor labor, and

FIGURE 55-7 A CVSA decal.

produce invoices. Managers can accurately monitor the cost of PM and associated vehicle costs to make decisions and have insight into business operations. Navistar's "On Command" system is an example of the latest sophisticated service reporting software. The software not only tracks all service work and electronically stores inspection reports plus work orders, it also has a GPS feature **FIGURE 55-8**. Service software like Navistar's GPS will track a vehicle and in the event of a problem, it can perform a customized search and direct the operator to the nearest repair facility

Additionally, engine software from many manufacturers typically has a programmable engine parameter that can alert the driver when a PM is due **FIGURE 55-9**.

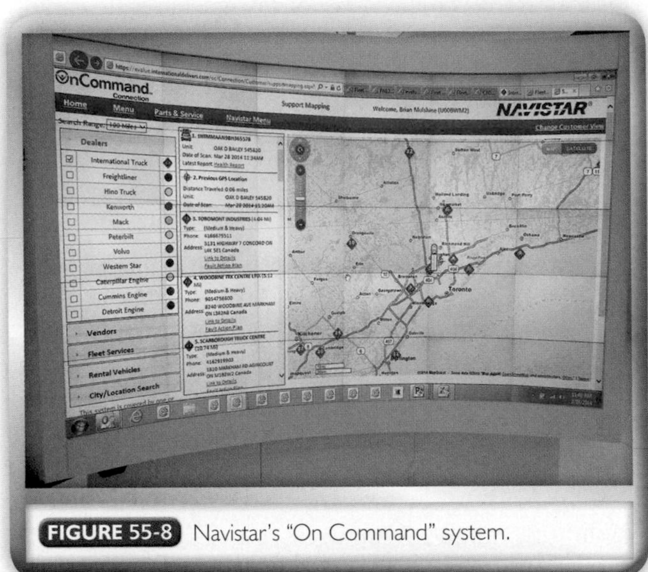

FIGURE 55-8 Navistar's "On Command" system.

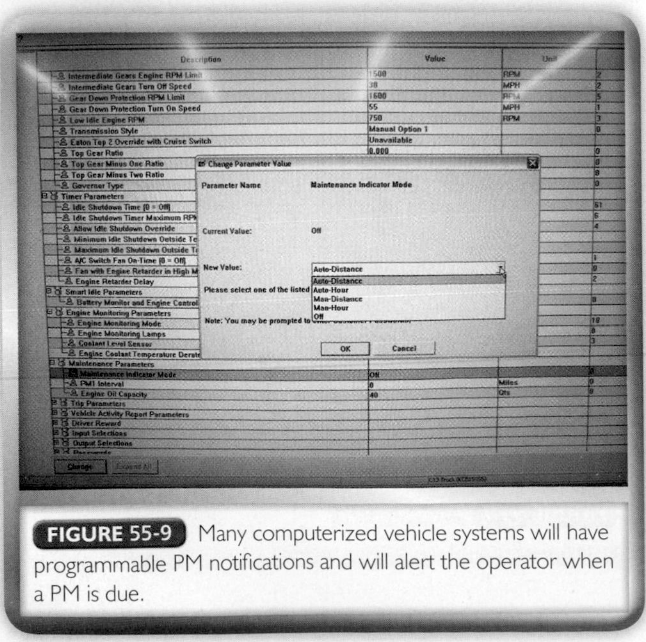

FIGURE 55-9 Many computerized vehicle systems will have programmable PM notifications and will alert the operator when a PM is due.

Normally a maintenance light in the dash will light up to alert the driver when the programmable preset value for time or distance is reached. For example, as vehicles are required to become more environmentally compliant, they are fitted with features like exhaust aftertreatment systems, which add new maintenance considerations. Diesel particulate filters typically require service between 250,000 and 450,000 miles. Ash accumulations in the filters need purging. Selective catalyst reduction (SCR) systems also use a filter for the diesel exhaust fluid (DEF), which needs replacement. This is a classic example of where good record keeping is particularly pertinent.

PMI Record-Keeping Requirements

Record keeping is an essential component of the PMI process. Inspections have to be carried out by duly authorized inspectors who can demonstrate both training and experience. Normally, evidence of the inspector's qualifications is required to be held on the operator's premises. In the United States, record-keeping requirements fall under the regulation 49 CFR, part 396.21. The qualified inspector performing the inspection must prepare a report that identifies:

- The individual performing the inspection and the date the vehicle was inspected
- The motor carrier operating the vehicle
- The vehicle components inspected and the results of the inspection, including those components not meeting the minimum standards

The original or a copy of the inspection report must be retained by the entity responsible for the inspection for a period of 14 months. The inspection report must be available for review on demand of an authorized federal, state, or local official. A decal or sticker may be placed on the vehicle instead of carrying the report. If a decal is used, it must contain the name and address of the motor carrier or other entity where the inspection report is maintained and certain other information as outlined in 49 CFR, part 396.17.

Inspector Qualifications

In most countries, an inspector carrying out this work is required to be registered and appropriately qualified. In the United States, the requirements are as follows:

Criteria: He or she must understand the inspection criteria set forth in 49 CFR, part 393 and appendix G, and must be capable of identifying defective components.

Master: He or she must have mastered the methods, procedures, tools, and equipment used when performing an inspection.

Capability: He or she must be capable of performing an inspection by reason of experience, training, or both, through the successful completion of a state- or federally sponsored training program and have a combination of training and/or experience totaling at least one year. The training and/or experience may consist of the following:

- Participation in a manufacturer-sponsored training program or similar commercial training program designed to train students in truck operation and maintenance.
- Experience as a mechanic or inspector of another commercial vehicle.
- Experience as a commercial vehicle inspector for a state, provincial, or federal government.

Evidence of an individual's qualifications must be retained by the motor carrier while the individual is performing annual inspection and for one year thereafter.

Brake inspectors are expected to meet similar, but separate, qualifications to inspect brakes.

Lubricants Used in PMI

The lubricants used in PMI include oils, transmission and axle lubricants, chassis lubricants, and even trailer lubricants.

Oil

It was once normal practice for engines to need one grade of oil for summer and another for winter. Oils are graded or classified by the American Society of Automotive Engineers (SAE) through the viscosity index. Engine oil with an SAE number of 50 has a higher viscosity, or thickness, than SAE 20 oil. Oils with low viscosity ratings (such as SAE 5W, 10W, and 20W) were tested at a low temperature, around 0°F (–18°C), and were used for cold conditions. Oils with high viscosity ratings (such as SAE 20, 30, 40, and 50) were tested at a high temperature, around 210°F (99°C), and were used for hotter conditions. Modern oils are blends of oils that combine these properties. Today's oils are blended with additives, called viscosity index improvers, to form multi-grade, or multi-viscosity, oils. They provide better lubrication over a wider range of climatic conditions than do monograde oils.

Oil is also classified by the American Petroleum Institute (API) service classification. Oils for spark-ignition engines use the prefix S, and diesel or compression-ignition engines use C. Some oils have additives that make them suitable for both. Manufacturers recommend the ideal viscosity and API classification for a particular engine. Always refer to the service manual for guidance in making the proper selection.

Transmission and Axle Lubricants

Most manufacturers recommend the use of single-viscosity lubricants based on the highest ambient operating temperature.

Chassis Lubricants

Chassis lubricants are greases classified in terms of their penetrating ability. There are two popular types of on-board chassis lubrication systems:

- *Automatic chassis lubrication system (ACLS):* Used in air- or electric-driven systems and uses progressive feeders, piston distributors, or metering valves at the ends of the dispensing lines.
- *Manual-manifold or distribution block:* Contains 12 to 24 grease lines connected to critical lubrication points.

Trailer Lubrication

Lubricate as outlined in the trailer service manual.

Finding Information on Recalls

Given that there are thousands of vehicles built every day, it is to be expected that something will go wrong in the construction process. In the medium- and heavy-duty truck industry, errors occur due to a particular component failure that is often discovered at the time of a system failure or at a scheduled service time.

Manufacturers are required to provide information about component failures to their clients (normally through the dealer network) and to the government department that deals with such matters. Normally, the clients are informed and asked to have the vehicle made available for repairs to be made at the manufacturer's cost.

When carrying out an inspection, it is good practice to identify whether the vehicle you are inspecting has been subject to a recall and whether the repair has been completed. Depending on the issue, information can be sought through the appropriate manufacturer or regulatory body. There are several ways of finding out this information; some of the methods include the following:

1. Check the particular vehicle service history.
2. Check the manufacturer service bulletins.
3. In the United States, the National Highway Traffic Safety Administration (NHTSA) of the U.S. Department of Transportation provides recall information, including vehicle and equipment campaigns from 1966 to present. The campaigns include motor vehicle products that experienced a safety-related defect or did not comply with federal motor vehicle safety standards.

4. The Environmental Protection Agency's Office of Transportation and Air Quality is responsible for ensuring that motor vehicles comply with the federal emission standards throughout the useful life of those vehicles. The EPA can require manufacturers to recall vehicles when a substantial number of a class or category of vehicles fails to meet emission standards. Vehicle manufacturers can voluntarily issue recalls for emission-related problems.

Shop and Vehicle Rules for PM and PMI

It is very important to use the right tool or piece of equipment and to not substitute the wrong tool for the right one. Failure to use the correct tool or piece of equipment could result in personal injury and damage to equipment.

If customers observe that service personnel take care of vehicles by driving carefully and installing fender and seat covers, and if the shop is well maintained, the service department's image will be greatly enhanced in the customer's eyes.

Always obey the shop and vehicle rules and principles, consider how the shop is laid out, and educate yourself on specialty tools that make the job easier and prevent damage.

Shop Rules

- Keep the shop floor and workbenches clean.
- Store flammable liquids and oily rags in an EPA-approved container.
- Properly tag malfunctioning equipment and report it to your instructor.
- Maintain shop equipment in good working order.
- Never use a tool unless you have been trained on its operation.
- Use the right tool for the right job.

Vehicle Rules

- Where appropriate, install fender covers before beginning any shop work, and install seat covers before entering the cab for any reason.
- Check that the garage door is open enough to allow vehicle entry and exit.
- Check brake operation before operating any vehicle.
- Check around the vehicle for objects or personnel before attempting to start a vehicle.
- Treat the customer's vehicle as you would treat your own.

Shop Setup

It is very important that the shop be set up for functionality FIGURE 55-10. Proper PM and PMI functionality dictates that there are lights, air hoses, tools, equipment, refuse and oil containers, jack stands, and other equipment present and in proper position to complete the inspection. Since there are many types of vehicles built by a variety of manufacturers and equipped with different components, it is impossible to compile a single list of specific procedures for every PMI. However, the generic guidelines in SKILL DRILL 55-1 are suitable when completing a PMI. Note that all manufacturers specify maximum wear limitations before a vehicle OOSC is reached. It is crucial that these specifications are adhered to at all times.

Specialty Tools

When conducting inspections, there are a number of tools that not only make the job easier, but will also prevent potential damage to the vehicle itself. The tools listed in TABLE 55-2 are the fundamental tools that should be available to technicians. The list is not exhaustive, and some manufacturers specify particular tools for their vehicles.

PMI Process

The PMI process can be carried out in a range of ways, but a methodical approach is best to ensure task efficiency and to avoid missing items due for inspection. The process should begin with a walk-around inspection.

FIGURE 55-10 A shop is set up to perform preventative maintenance inspections.

SKILL DRILL 55-1 Conducting PMIs : General Guidelines

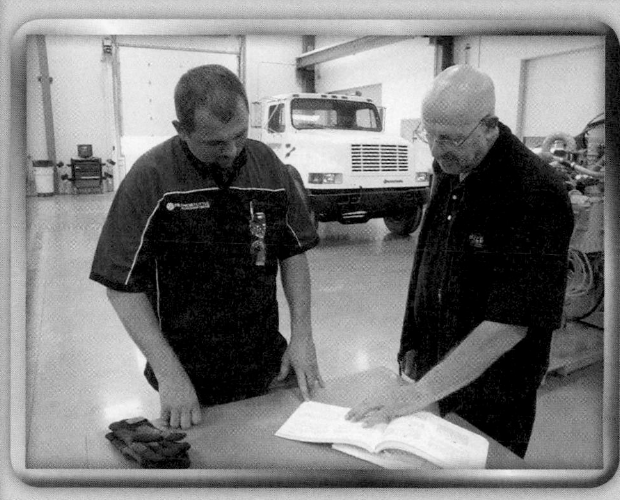

1. Locate and use the appropriate service manual for the vehicle and/or component you are servicing.
2. Document every discrepancy for follow-up by a qualified technician.
3. Do only those repairs you are qualified to perform.
4. Use the right lubricant for the component being serviced. Lube procedures may differ by vehicle and component. Always refer to the service manual. Use a lubrication chart when available as a guide.
5. Always dispose of hazardous materials in the proper manner.
6. When determining whether a discrepancy is cause for the vehicle to fail an inspection, refer to the vehicle service manual.

TABLE 55-2: Specialty Tools and Their Uses

Tool	Usage
Brake lining measurement tool	Used to measure the thickness of a brake lining to see whether it is within specifications
Belt tension gauge	Used to measure tension on a belt
Headlight adjustment tool	Used to adjust headlights to specifications
Portable light tester	Used to test trailer lights and antilock brakes when there is no trailer supplying power
Tire mating square	Used to ensure that the tires on an axle are square to each other
Battery load tester	Used to check battery load and capacity
Coolant tester (refractometer)	Used to test the ethylene glycol (antifreeze) mixture in the cooling system. A standard hydrometer can also be used, but the Technology Maintenance Council (TMC) recommends the use of a refractometer for testing antifreeze strength.
Coolant system pressure tester	Used to test for cooling system leaks when there is coolant loss or overheating problems
Scan tools	Used to retrieve diagnostic codes from the vehicle's computer

Tool	Usage
Dial indicator gauge	Used to measure runout, roundness, and wear on various components such as bushings, tie rods, and ball joints
Tire tread depth gauge	Used to check tire wear to determine tire replacement need
Light bulb socket scrubber	Used to clean corrosion from light bulb sockets
Bazooka tubes	Used to align a trailer from the fifth wheel pin to the rear tandem axles
Digital volt-ohmmeter (DVOM)	Used to test current, voltage, resistance, and frequency of electrical and electronic components
Test strips and coolant	Used to measure nitrate concentration and pH of vehicle coolant
Thermometer	Used to measure the temperature of various liquids and components
Fifth wheel test pin	Used to test the fifth wheel latch
One-foot ruler	Used for making various measurements
Torque wrench	Used to ensure that items like lug nuts are secured correctly
Wheel alignment equipment	Used to check and adjust the wheel alignment

Performing a Walk-Around Inspection

A walk-around inspection should be undertaken prior to beginning a PMI to assess the general condition of the vehicle. You should perform the walk-around inspection with the driver/operator present to identify existing problems and discuss the procedures for checking items. Document on an inspection form all items checked and anything found requiring later attention or rectification. The steps of a walk-around inspection are given in **SKILL DRILL 55-2**.

Performing Internal Cab Inspections

A follow-up inspection ensures that every item is thoroughly inspected after an initial walk-around inspection. After the initial walk-around inspection, the inspector should continue in a sequential manner commencing with an internal cab inspection. There are three components to an internal cab inspection:

- Key-off inspection **SKILL DRILL 55-3**
- Key-on inspection **SKILL DRILL 55-4**
- Engine-on inspection **SKILL DRILL 55-5**

SKILL DRILL 55-2 Performing a Walk-Around Inspection

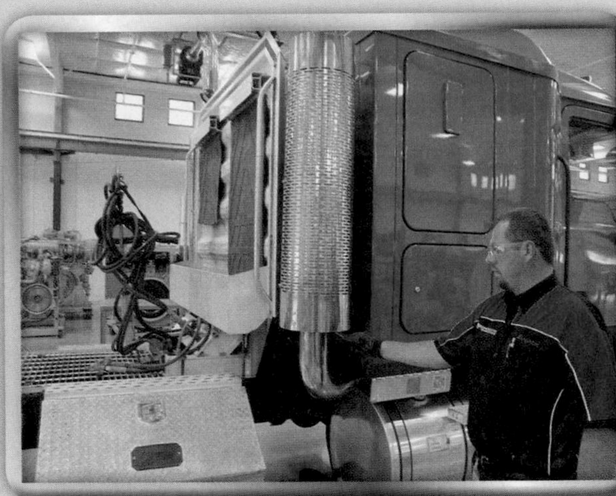

1. Identify leaks. Look around for leaks from the various vehicle systems, including:
   - Fuel
   - Grease
   - Engine oil
   - Transmission fluid
   - Power steering fluid
   - Brake fluid
   - Hydraulic fluid
2. Both the inspector and operator should look for, and document, obvious problems such as flat tires.
3. Both the inspector and operator should look for, and document, obvious problems such as broken springs.
4. Both the inspector and operator should look for, and document, obvious problems such as objects or parts out of place.
5. Both the inspector and operator should look for, and document, obvious problems such as cracked or bent frames or rims.
6. Both the inspector and operator should look for, and document, obvious problems such as dents in the body or trailer.
7. Both the inspector and operator should look for, and document, obvious problems such as missing or damaged parts.
8. Both the inspector and operator should look for, and document, obvious problems such as improper driveline connections.
9. Both the inspector and operator should look for, and document, obvious problems such as broken glass.

SKILL DRILL 55-3 Performing an Internal Cab Key-Off Inspection

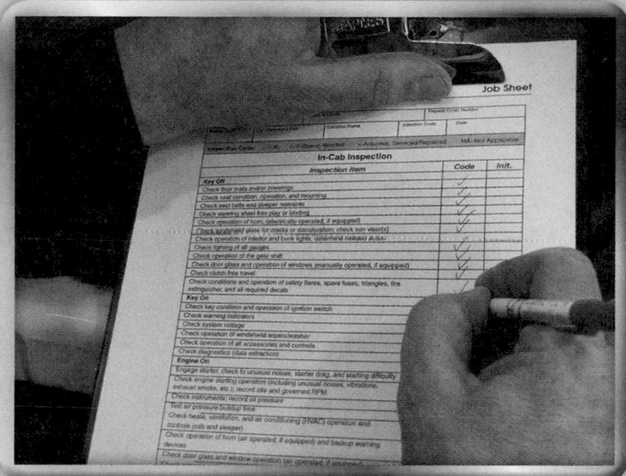

1. Begin the inspection process with the key off.
   - Check the floor mats and coverings to ensure that they are in good condition.
   - Check that the gear shift boot has no holes or splits in it.
2. Next, check both the driver and passenger seats.
   - Check the front and back of both seats for signs of wear and tear.
   - Check the seats for smooth operation and secure mounting.
   - Check any seat adjustment controls to ensure that they are functioning correctly and that any locking mechanisms work correctly.
   - Get into the seat and check the security and operation of seatbelts and sleeper restraints, if fitted.
3. While seated in the driver's seat, inspect gauges and controls near the steering wheel.
   - Check the steering wheel for free play or binding and ensure that the results are within recommended specifications.
   - Check the operation of the horn.
   - Check the windshield glass for chips, cracks, or discoloration and the sun visors for condition and operation.
   - Operate the lighting controls and check that all the gauges illuminate.
   - Check the operation of any cab interior and bunk lights.
4. With the clutch depressed, check the operation of the gear shift by shifting it through the gears.
   - Note if there are any obstructions, binding, looseness, or any other condition that may seem abnormal and may prevent operation.
5. Check the clutch-free travel by applying light pressure to the pedal with your hand.
   - Measure how far the clutch pedal must be depressed before engaging the clutch, and ensure that the free travel is within recommended specifications.
6. Now, look at the condition of the door glass and operation of any movable windows, their channel guides, and their locking devices.
7. Check the condition and documentation of safety flares, spare fuses, triangles, fire extinguisher, and all required decals.
   - Depending on location and operation of the vehicle, regulations determine the type of equipment to be carried. For instance, in the United States it is normal to carry three bidirectional reflective triangles, an approved fire extinguisher (properly charged and mounted), spare fuses for all sizes used on the vehicle, and three liquid-burning emergency flares.

SKILL DRILL 55-4 Performing an Internal Cab Key-On Inspection

1. First, check the ignition key condition and operation of the ignition switch, making sure it operates in all positions.
2. Leave the key in the ignition in the on position.
3. Now check all the warning indicators:
   - The low oil pressure light, for example, should be illuminated and a buzzer should sound if it is part of the dash design.
   - Check the illumination of any electronic engine or braking system warning lights. It is important to remember that these lights will normally cycle through various stages, so make sure you observe their operation and compare the results to the original equipment manufacturer's (OEM) guidelines.
   - Check the system voltage. Note the reading on the voltage gauge and record it on the checklist. Then crank the engine, which should show a gauge reading decrease. When the engine starts, check the system voltage again. When increasing the revolutions per minute (rpm), the gauge reading should increase.
4. Shut down the engine and then return the key back to the on position.
   - Check the operation of windshield wipers and washers by moving the switch through its positions; check also that the wipers park correctly when turned off. Ensure that the washer spray nozzles function and are adjusted properly.
   - Check the operation of all other accessories and controls such as remote mirrors, heated mirrors, cruise control (the on and off function only), powered windows, and any other installed accessories.
5. Extract the engine monitoring information. The correct method of retrieving such vehicle fault codes varies with each manufacturer.
   - Some vehicles are equipped with a diagnostic request switch, while others may require the use of a scan tool, a laptop computer, a voltmeter, or some other device. Make sure you extract any monitoring information from the vehicle computer using the method prescribed in the service manual.

SKILL DRILL 55-5 Performing an Internal Cab Engine-On Inspection

1. With the engine running, check all of the vehicle instruments:
   - Tachometer
   - Fuel gauge
   - Coolant temperature gauge
   - Oil pressure gauge
   - Voltmeter gauge
   - All other engine system gauges

   Record the oil pressure and voltage on the checklist.

2. Test the air pressure build-up time by depressing the brake pedal and any other air system operating controls to reduce all air pressures to less than 80 pounds per square inch (psi) (553 kPa).

Continued on next page

SKILL DRILL 55-5 Performing an Internal Cab Engine-On Inspection, continued

- Run the engine at a minimum of 1,200 rpm and measure the time it takes to go from 85 psi (586 kPa) to 100 psi (689 kPa). The time should not exceed 25 seconds. If it does, further investigation is needed to discover why the pressure is not building.

3. Check the heater, ventilation, and air-conditioning controls in the cab and the sleeper (if fitted).
   - To make sure the operating cables are moving smoothly, place the control levers in each of the positions. If the controls are vacuum operated, listen for the vacuum motors to work.
   - Check that all air vents are opening and closing properly and that the fan motor operates at every available speed selection position.
   - Check that the air conditioner is operating by listening for the noise of the air conditioner compressor clutch engaging when the air conditioner is turned on.
   - When this occurs, check that the air coming from the ducts is getting colder.
4. Check air-operated horns (if equipped), and any backup warning devices by operating them so they sound.
   - Check that any fitted backup warning devices (lights and beepers) work properly when the transmission is placed in reverse.
5. Check door glass and window operation for binding, cracked or broken glass, or missing channels.
6. Check the operation of the parking brake holding power by trying to move the vehicle after you set the brake.
   - If the vehicle moves, it may simply mean that the parking brake is out of adjustment, and further investigation will be required.
   - Check that the parking brake releases properly by moving the vehicle after releasing the brake.
7. Check the operation of the clutch and clutch brake (if fitted) by putting the vehicle in gear and slowly releasing the clutch until the vehicle moves. Make sure the clutch brake engages when the clutch pedal is 1/2" from the floor.
8. Check for the following shut-down operations:
   - Mechanical
   - Electronic
   - Emergency

   At a minimum, turning the key to the off position should shut down the engine.

After completing the key-off inspection tasks, you should continue the inspection in the key-on state. To complete the steps in this part of the inspection, the key must remain on after the first step or task.

After the key-on inspection, you can complete the engine-on inspection. With the engine on, and when checking the system voltage, the starter operation should be checked again to identify any unusual noises, starter drag, or starter difficulty. Once started, listen for noises like hesitation, stumbling, or engine miss, and look for excessive exhaust smoke when the throttle is depressed. Then increase the rpm and check the voltage gauge reading. It should increase. This test is a good indicator of whether the charging system is operating properly and whether the gauge is working correctly.

Performing Exterior Inspections

This inspection covers the cab doors, body and component mountings, batteries and mountings, lines, fifth wheel coupling mountings, frame and suspension, suspension ride height, electrical components, exhaust, and lubrication. To inspect the cab door, follow the steps in **SKILL DRILL 55-6**.

After the inspection of the cab door and the catwalk, move on to inspecting the mirrors, cab, and fuel systems. To inspect the body and component mountings, follow the guidelines in **SKILL DRILL 55-7**.

The next exterior inspection involves battery inspection and load testing. You should check battery boxes, their covers, and their mountings to ensure that they are securely attached and have no missing hardware. Check for any damage, holes, and tears to the cover and box, which should be securely attached to the vehicle. Look for any cracked or missing mounting components. Ensure that there is no corrosion on the inside bottom of the box. To inspect the batteries and their mountings, follow the procedure in **SKILL DRILL 55-8**.

SKILL DRILL 55-9 has guidelines for inspections that involve air lines and the fifth-wheel coupling mountings. The next step in exterior inspections is to check the frame and suspension of the vehicle, as described in **SKILL DRILL 55-10**.

SKILL DRILL 55-6 Performing a Cab Door Inspection

1. Begin by checking the cab door operation. Ensure that the locks, latches, and hinges do not bind when the door is opened or closed. Ensure that they are securely attached.

2. Check that the doors lock and unlock from the outside when using the key and from the inside. Check the locks for ease of operation.

3. Check all components on the cab door.
   - Pull the straps and test the handles to make sure they are in good condition.
   - Check for any missing or flat rollers.
   - Check the tracks to ensure that they are not loose or bent.
   - Ensure that no cables are frayed.

4. Look at the panels and hinges for damage and determine whether the seals are in good condition. Also check any stops in the end of the tracks to ensure they are in place and are tight.

5. Check the condition of any grab handles, steps, and catwalks. Note any missing grab handles, and make sure the handles on the vehicle are securely attached.

6. Ensure that catwalk assemblies are inspected for nicks or gouges that could result in personal injury. Look at the steps and check that they are securely attached to the vehicle and that the tread hardware is in place. There should be no loose or missing rivets, bolts, or screws.

7. Look at any catwalks that are fitted to the vehicle for damage from contact with the trailer. The catwalks need to be securely attached to the vehicle.
   - Look for any loose or missing hardware.
   - Make sure there is no grease or oil present.

SKILL DRILL 55-7 Performing a Body and Component Mountings Inspection

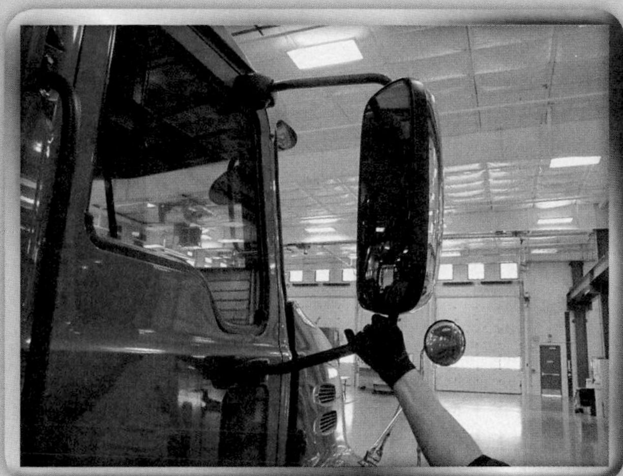

1. Check the vehicle mirrors for secure mountings and brackets.
   - Mirror glass should be free of cracks or chips and should be securely fastened in its frame.
   - If mirrors are heated, make sure the heating controls are working properly.
2. Look for and record all physical body damage in the cab and sleeper area.
   - Note any dents, breaks, or cracks in fiberglass or broken/missing rivets or bolts.
   - Check for rust in any of the fixtures, mountings, or fittings. While some surface corrosion is acceptable, there must not be any holes in the sleeper or cab.
   - If the vehicle has a body, then check for any missing fasteners and for any damage to the exterior skin.
   - Check welds for cracks.
3. Check the fuel tanks, lines, caps, and vents for any seepage or leakage in the fuel system.
   - Ensure that the lines are not within 6" (150 mm) of any exhaust component unless they are shielded.
   - Check that the lines are tight at the fittings and that the tank fill caps do not have any missing gaskets or seals.
4. Inspect the fuel tank mountings to ensure they are not loose, broken, or missing any mounting bolts or brackets. Remember that some fuel tanks use springs or rubber bushings to permit movement.
   - Make sure that tank straps and strap insulators are in the proper position. Look for any cracks in the mounts themselves and check that vents are not blocked.
   - The vent tubes should not have kinks in them. Check for dirt accumulation around the vent to prevent potential blockages from occurring in the future.

SKILL DRILL 55-8 Inspecting Batteries and Mountings

 Check the battery hold-downs, connections, cables, and cable routing for their security and make sure they are attached to the battery box frame.

- Make sure that the hold-downs fit properly and that they do not crush or distort the battery box or contact any of the terminals.
- Check any fasteners for rust or other corrosion, and inspect connections, cables, and cable routing for corrosion. Ensure that there are no holes or tears in the cable insulation and that the battery connections are tight.
- Check the condition of the ground connection, and check that any other cables do not rub on any other components.

 Record the battery's state of charge and capacity by checking the open circuit voltage of each battery. The results should be 12.4 volts or higher on a 12-volt battery.

- Conduct a battery load test and compare the voltage and temperature readings to the service manual figures.

SKILL DRILL 55-9 Inspecting Lines and Fifth-Wheel Coupling Mountings

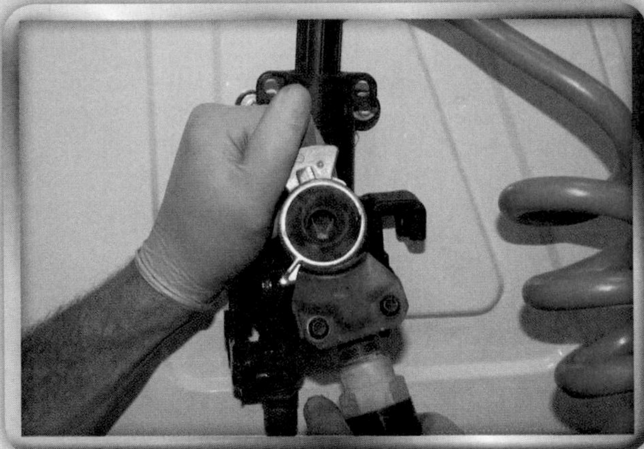

 Inspect coupling air lines, their holders, gladhands, and the multi-wire connectors.

- Check the air lines for chafing or rubbing on the catwalk, kinks, knots, or twisting in the lines. Make sure they are securely mounted.
- Check for any broken or missing fasteners, and check that the holders keep the lines and cords from dragging on the catwalk or other components.
- Check that the rubbers on the gladhands are not torn, and inspect for cracks or looseness of the flange. Ensure that the fittings are not loose.

 Inspect the multi-wire connection by checking each circuit for power using a test light or by turning on the appropriate light switch and determining whether the system is working. Check any trailer cords for chafing, and ensure that the cord ends are not worn or broken.

Continued on next page

SKILL DRILL 55-9 Inspecting Lines and Fifth-Wheel Coupling Mountings, continued

3. Check the air drier drain valve, mounting, fittings, and connections for leaking air. Check that any associated electrical connections are secure.

4. Inspect the components for loose, broken, or missing mounting bolts, and check the brackets for cracks.

5. Check the fifth-wheel coupling for cracked mounting plates or feet, loose bolts, broken or damaged side rails, or worn bushings.

6. Inspect for missing or damaged slide locking pins. If fitted, the system should also be inspected for a damaged air hose or cylinder, which could impede the proper operation of slide latches. Check for a damaged or inoperative safety latch and locking mechanism.

7. Using a fifth-wheel test pin, check that the locking jaws fully lock into the closed position. Check for any excessive play between the test device and jaws. There should be some play between the test device and jaws; refer to the service manual for acceptable limits.

8. If the vehicle has a pintle hook towing arrangement, the assembly and mounting should be inspected for loose or missing fasteners. A fastener is not considered missing if there is an empty hole in the device but no corresponding hole in the frame, or vice versa.

9. Check for cracks in the frame or mounts, cracks in the hook assembly, or any welded repair. In accordance with DOT regulations, there cannot be any welded repairs to the pintle hook itself. Ensure that the latch locks the pintle hook in the closed position, and check for the presence of a safety pin. Check for excessive play in the pintle hook latch.

SEE

SKILL DRILL 55-10 Inspecting Frame and Suspension and Suspension Ride Height

1. Check the vehicle frame and the frame members for bending or other types of deformities and for any cracks and excessive rust or scale.
   - Check frame members for cracks, breaks, looseness, or sagging. In addition, they should be inspected for any loose or missing fasteners, including fasteners attaching functional components such as the engine, transmission, steering gear, suspension, body parts, and fifth-wheel coupling.

2. Check for any condition that causes the body or frame to be in contact with a tire or any part of the wheel assemblies and for missing or unengaged locking pins in adjustable axle assemblies.

3. Check and record the vehicle's suspension ride height. Checking the vehicle's suspension ride height is an important aspect of exterior inspections. Every manufacturer has its own procedure for this. Some of the most common methods are:
   - Measuring from level ground to the bottom of both frame rails.
   - Measuring from level ground to the bottom of the rear-most air bag.
   - Measuring from level ground to the tip of the fifth-wheel plate.
   - Measuring from the bottom of the air bag to the bottom of the frame rail.
   - Measuring from the top of the axle housing to the bottom of the frame rail.

Inspections of the electrical components, exhaust, and lubrication come next. Prior to beginning these inspections, it is important to:

- Turn on all the vehicle lights and turn signals. It may be helpful to have someone in the cab for these checks.
- Check all exterior lights, lenses, covers, and reflectors for secure mounting and correct location. There are laws that determine the lighting and reflector requirements for all vehicles, including tractors and trailers.
- Check for cracked lenses and internal moisture and for proper operation.
- Check any visible wiring for general condition.

To inspect electrical components, exhaust, and lubrication, follow the steps in SKILL DRILL 55-11.

Inspecting the Braking System

Brakes are a special area of extreme importance in terms of operational efficiency and safety. As such, brakes are one of the highest priorities in PMI, and if they are found defective the vehicle must be designated out of service until rectification of the defects are attended to. To inspect hydraulic or air-over-hydraulic brakes, follow the steps in SKILL DRILL 55-12.

SKILL DRILL 55-11 Inspecting Electrical Components, Exhaust, and Lubrication (Including Fifth Wheel)

1. Check license plates and brackets to ensure that the license has not expired and that the brackets are securely mounted. Ensure that license plate lights are working.
2. Check the exhaust system for leaks, proper routing, and damaged or missing components by inspecting the pipes and mufflers.
   - It is especially important that the exhaust system not be leaking at a point forward of, or directly below, the driver/sleeper compartment. Ensure that the exhaust outlet is behind or above any part of the vehicle designed to be occupied.
   - Check that the exhaust system does not rub or contact any other objects and that no part of the exhaust system is positioned in a location that could result in burning, charring, or damaging the electrical wiring, fuel supply, or any combustible part of the vehicle.
3. Check mountings for looseness and damage, and check that mufflers are securely mounted to the vehicle and to their associated pipes or exhaust stacks.
   - Check for any missing fasteners on the exhaust pipes and mufflers, and inspect any supports for excessive rust or cracks.
   - Check the muffler for holes, dents, or other damage or missing components.
4. Check front and rear cab mounts for wear and secure attachment to the frame and cab structure, and ensure that all fasteners are present and tight.
   - Check the cab rear air ride height and adjust if fitted. In such cases, the cab should sit approximately in the center of its limits of travel.
   - Check the cab latches and cables for secure attachment, wear, or damage and for binding and secure attachment.
5. Check wiper blades for deterioration, cracks/tears, hardening, missing pivot parts, and secure attachment to the arm assembly. Operate wipers/washers to make sure the wipers cover the whole window with no streaks.
   - Wiper arms should be inspected for damage, looseness, or wear in linkage and for bends and spring tension.

Continued on next page

SKILL DRILL 55-11 Inspecting Electrical Components, Exhaust, and Lubrication (Including Fifth Wheel), continued

- Windshield washer nozzles should be examined for build-up of foreign material and their hoses for attachment, wear, and proper routing.

6. Check the headlight alignment using a marked screen wall, mechanical headlight aimer, or photoelectric aimer.

7. Lubricate all cab and hood grease fittings and wipe grease fittings. Replace any fittings that are damaged.
   - All grease fittings should take grease; if they do not, they should be replaced.
   - Lubricate door and hood hinges, latches, strikers, lock cylinders, safety latches, linkages and cables.

8. Lubricate all fifth-wheel grease fittings and plate. Wipe grease fittings and replace any fittings that are damaged.
   - All grease fittings should accept grease; if they do not, they should be replaced. This process should be undertaken while rocking the fifth wheel front to back to disperse the lubricant evenly on the pivots.
   - Lubricate the fifth wheel plate (unless it is Teflon coated) by applying a liberal amount of lubricant to the throat and back half of the plate. Smooth the lubricant over the back half of the plate, from about the front edge of the throat to the back of the plate.

SKILL DRILL 55-12 Inspecting Hydraulic and Air-Over-Hydraulic Brakes

In hydraulic brake systems, it is critical to detect leaks and ensure proper fluid levels.

1. Check the master cylinder fluid level and condition.
   - Remove the top of the master cylinder, check the fluid level, and make sure the fluid is not discolored or burnt. Discoloration or burning indicates the presence of water or another contaminant.
   - Add fluid as necessary, ensuring that you use the correct type.
   - Check for external leaks around the cylinder and inspect all connecting lines and hoses for leaks or kinks.
   - Check that the cylinder is securely mounted.

2. Make sure the power brake boosters are securely mounted before looking for any external leaks. Check the control valve and all lines and hoses for leaks or kinks.

3. Check wheel cylinders/calipers, brake lines, fittings, flexible hoses, and valves for leaks and damage.
   - Check the vehicle's brake lines, valves, and fittings visible under the hood for leaks, damage, and proper routing.
   - Check that they are supported appropriately.
   - Then continue under the vehicle, looking for visible signs of leaks from the backing plates. Any wheel cylinder leaks will be evident here.

4. If the drums are removed, give the wheel cylinders a thorough check by pulling back the dust boots on the cylinders and looking for leaks or rust.

5. Check calipers (on disc brake systems) for leaks, and check that the fastening bolts are tight and that any flexible hoses are not cut, snagged, kinked, collapsed, or leaking.

6. If there are signs of collapsed spots on the flexible hoses, replace the hoses.

Continued on next page

SKILL DRILL 55-12 Inspecting Hydraulic and Air-Over-Hydraulic Brakes, continued

7. Check the record brake lining/pad condition and thickness.
   - Most brake lining measurements can be made without removing the wheels by looking through the sight holes in the backing plates and measuring the brake linings at their thinnest point. Record the measurement on the checklist.

8. With the parking brake set, check and record the condition of the front and rear brake drums/rotors.
   - If removed, check all brake drums for excessive scoring, cracks, gouges, discoloration, and unusual wear patterns. Record any discrepancies on the inspection checklist.
   - Inspect the brake rotors for excessive scoring, cracks, gouges, discoloration, and unusual wear patterns. Record any discrepancies on the inspection checklist.

9. Check parking brake operation, and inspect parking brake application and holding devices. Set the parking brake, start the engine, and build up air pressure or create a vacuum (where there needs to be sufficient reserve for one full-brake application after the engine has stopped).
   - Vacuum hose/line restricted; worn through the outer cover to cord ply; crimped, cracked or broken; or collapses when vacuum is applied.
   - Now, place the vehicle in gear and slowly release the clutch until the engine's rpm drops. Do not allow the vehicle to move. If the vehicle does move, it may mean the parking brake is out of adjustment.
   - Next, release the parking brake to make sure the vehicle will move freely.

10. On vehicles with hydraulic park control, turn the ignition to the run position and open the driver's door with the parking brake released.
    - Check that the "apply brake" warning light illuminates.
    - Now place the vehicle in neutral, shut off the engine, and apply the parking brake.
    - Move to the underside of the vehicle and check the application of the parking brake and holding devices.

11. Check the operation of the hydraulic system, pedal travel, pedal effort, and pedal feel.
    - First, apply the brakes several times with the engine off.
    - Then, apply and hold the brakes and start the engine.
    - As the engine starts, you should feel the brake pedal go down, but by no more than half its travel distance. If the pedal goes past halfway, the brakes may need to be adjusted.
    - Now release the brake, reapply the pedal, and check for a firm feel.

Defective Brakes Criteria

A vehicle or combination vehicle is designated OOSC if 20% or more of its service brakes have one of the following defects:

- Any steering-axle brake defect listed in next section.
- Won't actuate effectively or friction material won't contact drum/rotor.
- Audible air leak.
- Missing brake on any axle required to have brakes.

Inspecting Full Air Brake Systems

With air brakes, the truck's air pressure system has to be operating properly. There is a series of tests you will need to perform on the air brake system. These tests may require two people. To perform a full inspection of the air brake system, follow the procedure in SKILL DRILL 55-13.

Inspecting Tires and Wheels

Inspecting wheels and tires is critical to the safe operation of any road transport vehicle. Underinflated tires, tires with poor tread, mismatched tires, and poorly mounted tires can contribute to poor handling in bad road conditions at the very least, and can lead to blowouts and accidents in worst-case scenarios.

The following Skill Drills may seem routine, but finding potential trouble spots requires a sharp eye. Checking the condition of the wheel bearings is normally also part of this inspection process. To inspect tires and wheels, follow the steps in SKILL DRILL 55-14.

Inspecting Wheel Alignment

Performing a wheel alignment inspection is good practice for the safe operation of any road transport vehicle. Incorrect wheel alignment can contribute to the unnecessary

SKILL DRILL 55-13 Inspecting Full Air Brake Systems

1. Check parking brake operation, and check for air leaks with the brakes applied and released. To do this:
   - Set the parking brake, start the engine, and build up system air pressure.
   - Next, place the vehicle in gear and slowly release the clutch until the engine's rpm drops. Do not allow the vehicle to move. If the vehicle moves, it may mean the parking brake is out of adjustment.
   - Place the gear selector to "neutral," shut off the engine, check the air gauges, and note any air loss on the gauge. There should not be any loss of air pressure on a healthy system.
   - Exit the cab, move to the underside of the vehicle, and listen for air leaks. Now, move to the rear parking brake chambers to look, listen, and feel for air leaks.
   - Return to the cab and release the parking brake. Depress the brake pedal and note any air loss on the gauge. There should be no more than a 3-psi (21-kPa) air loss in one minute. Air loss more than this amount indicates an air leak.
2. Make sure the brake chambers are mounted securely with no missing bolts, and check for rust and any cracks on the surface of the chambers.
   - Make sure that the air lines are securely mounted.
3. Check air governor cut-in pressure, record air governor cut-out setting, and check air drier drain valve operation.
   - Set the parking brake, start the engine, build air pressure, and observe the air gauge readings.
   - Record the maximum pressure on the gauge on the checklist after the compressor cuts out. Normally the air pressure should stabilize at 120–130 psi (827–896 kPa).
   - Now, drain the air in the system by activating the foot valve repeatedly, and check that the compressor kicks in at approximately 85–90 psi (586–621 kPa) to fill the system back to 120–130 psi (827–896 kPa).
   - When this occurs, the system governor should cut out, and you should hear the air drier purge out its exhaust port.
4. Check the one-way and double-check valves.
   - To check the one-way check valve, build up the system to full air pressure, and then release the brakes.
   - Shut off the engine and drain the wet tank completely. Check the dash air pressure gauges and note any loss in pressure. If there is a loss of air pressure on either gauge, there is a problem with the one-way check valve.
   - To check the double-check valve, build up the system to full air pressure, and then release the brakes on the tractor and trailer (if attached). Now shut off the engine and drain the primary air reservoir using the petcock, but leave the petcock open.
   - Check that the secondary air gauge holds pressure even though the primary air gauge is losing pressure. Any loss of air pressure indicated by a drop in pressure on the secondary air gauge indicates an air leak on that side of the double-check valve.
   - Finally, complete the task by closing the petcock on the primary air reservoir.
   - To check the tractor protection valve, build up the system to full air pressure, and then release the brakes on the tractor and trailer (if attached).
   - Shut off the engine and remove the red emergency hose from the trailer or the holder on the cab.
   - After the hose is disconnected, air pressure will drop, and the trailer valve should pop out.
   - Listen for the trailer valve to pop out as air escapes the system. The valve should pop out before the gauge drops to 45 psi (310 kPa).
5. Check the pressure-warning devices and build-up time. When checking low air pressure warning devices, build up the system to full air pressure and then release the brakes.
   - Shut off the engine, drain the primary air reservoir using the petcock, and leave the petcock open.
   - Turn the key on and check that the low air warning light or buzzer comes on between 55 and 60 psi (379–414 kPa).

Continued on next page

SKILL DRILL 55-13 Inspecting Full Air Brake Systems, continued

- Now, close the air reservoir drain petcock, start the engine to build pressure, and observe when the low air warning light goes out or the buzzer stops.
- Raise the rpm to 1,200 when the air pressure reaches 85 psi (586 kPa) and measure the amount of time it takes to raise the air pressure from 85 psi (586 kPa) to 100 psi (689 kPa). This should take no longer than 25 seconds.

6 Inspect and record the condition of brake lining/pads and brake drums/rotors, and check the condition of the camshaft and bushing.

- This task can normally be done without removing the road wheels. However, in some cases, it may be necessary to remove the tires or the brake drums on the vehicle. It may also be necessary to remove the dust shield on the front brakes.
- Set the parking brake. Use a brake lining gauge to measure the brake pad thickness of all brakes, and record the results on the checklist. The minimum lining thickness should not be less than 1/4" (6.5 mm). Many brake linings have indicators that allow this to be clearly seen.
- If the drums have been removed, check for scoring, cracks, or unevenness, and record their condition on the checklist.
- Also check the S cam, which actuates the brake shoes, for bushing wear or any other excessive wear.

7 Check manual and automatic slack adjusters.

- Set the parking brake, start the engine, and build the system air pressure to 120 psi (827 kPa).
- Safely raise the wheel(s) off the ground and, with the vehicle correctly supported, release the brakes.
- Rotate the wheel manually. If the adjustment is correct, the pad should just touch the drum and cause the wheel to stop turning freely.
- Make any adjustments as necessary according to the service manual.
- Now check actuator rod travel by marking the rod flush with the brake chamber and applying full brake pedal pressure.
- Measure from the brake chamber to the mark you made and compare the distance traveled with the specifications.
- To check an automatic or manual slack adjuster push rod travel, set the parking brake, start the engine, and build the air pressure to 80–90 psi (552–621 kPa).
- Now, release the brakes, mark the rod flush with the brake chamber, and apply the brake and hold on.
- Measure the rod again and compare the readings with service manual specifications.

8 Check the condition and operation of the hand brake (trailer control valve). The process to check the trailer control valve may require two people.

- Start by setting the parking brake, starting the engine, and building the system to full air pressure.
- Release the brakes, apply the trailer hand brake, and observe full reservoir pressure on the gauges.
- Move to the rear of the trailer and confirm that the brakes are engaged by observing the positions of the brake chamber rods and determining whether the brake lights are illuminated on the trailer.
- Release the trailer hand brake and check that the pressure is depleted and the brake lights are now off.

9 Perform an antilock brakes system (ABS) test. The steps below are a general test, and you should refer to the appropriate service manual for a more specific test. This test may require two people.

- First, build the system to full air pressure and then set the brakes.
- Shut off the engine and turn the key to the on position, but do NOT start the engine.
- Listen for the ABS to apply the brakes, starting with the front brakes and working around the vehicle to the rear.
- Check that the ABS light on the dash cycles through in the time specified by the service manual.

10 Check the spring brake inversion system. Checking the spring brake inversion system will require two people.

- First, chock the front wheels, build the system to full air pressure, and then shut off the engine.
- Next, release the parking brakes and drain the primary air tank completely.
- Depress the foot valve and observe that the push rods of the spring brake chambers extend.
- Release the foot valve and check that the push rods retract to the released position.

SKILL DRILL 55-14 Inspecting Tires and Wheels

1. First, check tires for irregular wear patterns.
   - Run your hand over the tread and feel for areas of uneven wear and confirm with a visual inspection.
   - Take note of any bald spots on the tread.
   - Irregular tire wear patterns may indicate other problems such as loose front-end linkages, worn wheel bearings, over- or underinflated tires, bad shock absorbers, out-of-balance wheels, or poor alignment.
2. Next, look for the proper mounting of directional tires. This involves noting any missing balance weights and making sure the tires are a matched set. Note any discrepancies.
   - You will need to make sure the tire diameter and tread are the same on all tires on each axle. This is particularly important on dual tire installations.
   - Ideally, all tires across the same axle should be matched in tread design and by manufacturer. You can still operate the vehicle safely if two tires on one side of the axle are different from the matching set on the other side of the axle.
   - NOTE: Bias and radial tires should NOT be mixed on any vehicle, regardless of tread design.
3. Check the overall condition of the tire, tread, and sidewalls. Note any of the following:
   - Cuts
   - Tears
   - Cracks
   - Bulges
   - Feathered edges
   - Spotty or excessive wear on the outside ribs
   - Excessive heel and toe wear on lug-type tire
   - Broken wheel studs
4. Check the valve caps and stems.
   - Note any loose or leaking caps, oxidized or rotted grommets, or missing caps.
   - Make sure valve stems are properly aligned (180 degrees apart on dual wheels).
5. Check and record tread depth, and probe for embedded debris.
   - Check the tread depth by measuring in three places with a tread depth gauge at equal intervals around the center of the tire.
   - Record the tread depth on a checklist sheet. The minimum depth allowed by the FMCSA is 4/32" (3.175 mm) on the steering axle and 2/32" (1.5875 mm) on drive trailer axles.
   - In all cases, your local government regulations will have all the updated technical specifications.
   - Next, check the tire treads for embedded debris, and remove the debris where appropriate.
6. You will also need to check and record air pressure. Find the recommended tire pressure sticker or placard (usually mounted on a door post) and note the maximum and minimum tire pressures.
   - Use an appropriate tire pressure gauge to measure the pressure on each tire, recording the pressure on the PMI checklist.
   - A vehicle should not be driven if the tire pressure is less than 80% of the maximum recommended pressure.
7. Next, inspect lugs, spacers, wheels, and mounting hardware.
   - Look and feel for cracks, corrosion, missing lugs, broken studs, and rust streaks between mating surfaces and the wheels around the studs.
   - Note any oil or grease leaks from the hubs, slipped wheels, loose lugs, and any other obvious damage.
   - It is important that the lugs are torqued to the manufacturer's specifications, so use a torque wrench to verify the correct tightness on the lugs.
8. On vehicles with tandem wheels, check dual mating with a square. Measure the difference in tread between the two tires on each dual set using the mating square.
   - The difference in tread should not be more than a 1/4" (6.35 mm), and the smaller tire must be on the inside.
   - Mismatched dual tires overload the larger diameter tire, causing it to overdeflect and overheat. The smaller diameter tire, lacking proper road contact, wears faster and unevenly. Tread or ply separation, tire body breaks, and blowouts may result from mismatched tires.

rapid detrition of tires and also affect handling of the vehicle itself.

The guidelines for performing a wheel alignment inspection in SKILL DRILL 55-15 may seem routine, but by following the procedures outlined, you can significantly reduce wear and tear on the vehicle.

Performing Under-Vehicle Inspections

The under-vehicle inspection should focus mainly on the transmission and drive train of the vehicle. Drivelines in most medium- and heavy-duty vehicles are long, so you will often need to get under it on a creeper unless it can be raised on a hoist or accessed from a pit.

In general, you will be looking for:

- Any signs of leaks
- Correct phasing of the driveline
- Any missing bolts or fasteners
- The steering linkages to be intact and not corroded

You will be able to carry out the bulk of the inspection more easily if you can drive the vehicle over an inspection pit or raise it on a hoist. You must always use the correct size wrench to remove drain plugs to check drive axle fluid levels. During this inspection, you should also be checking for fluid leaks that might indicate ruptured seals. You will also be visually checking the vehicle exhaust system components for signs of damage or wear. Your under-vehicle inspection should start with the vehicle frame.

Frame, Mountings, Electrical, and Exhaust

The vehicle frame takes a great deal of weight stress and is prone to cracks, so it is a good place to start this inspection. Check all the frame areas, especially frame members, for bending or other types of deformities. Note any cracks or excessive rust or scale, which will indicate a potential weak point. SKILL DRILL 55-16 contains guidelines for performing inspections on the under-vehicle frame, mountings, electrical, and exhaust.

SKILL DRILL 55-15 Inspecting Wheel Alignment

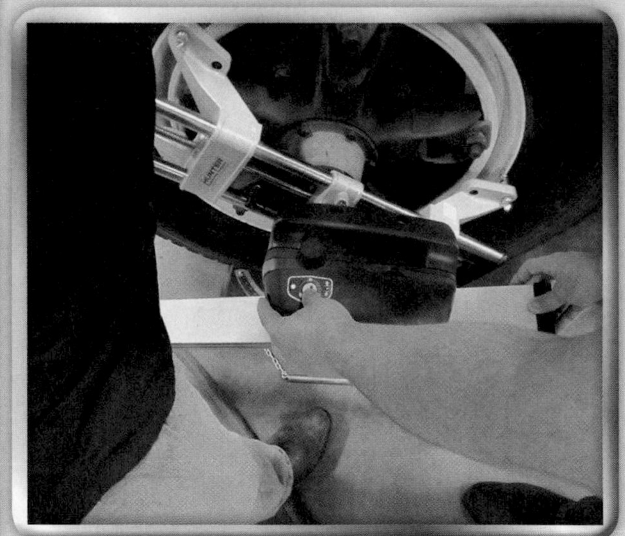

1. Check the front axle kingpin wear by checking for excessive play between the kingpin and the spindle.
   - With the vehicle raised just off the ground, insert a pry bar under the tire and move the bar in an up-and-down motion.
   - Check the thrust bearing for excessive play using the same method.
2. Check tandem axle alignment and spacing by visually verifying that the axles are perpendicular to the vehicle centerline. Axles out of alignment can cause the steering wheel to rest in an off-center position and the front tires to scrub and wear quickly. Misalignment can also cause the vehicle to oversteer when turning in one direction and understeer when turning in the other direction.
3. Check toe-in using the appropriate alignment equipment. This may involve mounting alignment sensors on wheels and checking each tire.
   - When the front end of the tire points inward toward the vehicle, the tire has toe-in. When the front end of the tire points outward from the vehicle, the tire has toe-out. Toe-in is designed into the vehicle by the manufacturer to counteract the natural tendency of the tires to toe-out when the vehicle is driven.

SKILL DRILL 55-16 Inspecting Under-Vehicle Frame, Mountings, Electrical, and Exhaust

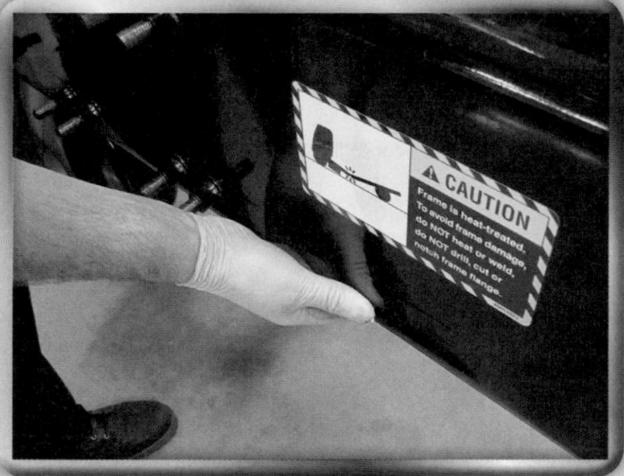

1. Check for any loose or missing fasteners, especially those attaching functional components such as the:
   - Engine
   - Transmission
   - Steering gear
   - Suspension
   - Body parts
   - Fifth wheel
2. Check for any condition that causes the body or frame to be in contact with a tire or any part of the wheel assemblies. This is a potentially dangerous condition that could result in a blowout.
3. Check for missing or unengaged locking pins in the adjustable axle assemblies.
4. Inspect engine mounts for looseness and deterioration.
   - Look for missing or loose fasteners.
   - Check the rubber mounts for cracks, deterioration, and splitting.
   - Check that any mounting pads have not shifted.
5. Check the vehicle wiring, routing, and hold-down clamps and ensure the wire insulators are not cracked, chafed, or charred.
   - Be sure that the wiring is clear of moving parts and heat-producing sources such as exhaust.
   - Ensure that the wiring is not pinched.
   - Check for missing hold-downs, and make sure all hold-downs are securely attached and do not pinch the wiring.
6. Check the under-vehicle exhaust system.
   - Check the exhaust system for leaks, proper routing, and damaged or missing components.
   - Check the mountings for looseness and damage.
   - Ensure that the muffler is securely mounted to the vehicle, and check the pipes or exhaust stacks. Inspect the muffler for holes, dents, or other damage that may indicate a leak.
   - It is not permissible for the exhaust system to be leaking at a point forward of, or directly below, the driver's sleeper compartment.
   - Check engine parts for signs of exhaust leakage, and make sure the exhaust system does not rub or contact any other objects. This is particularly important where there is a potential of damage to electrical wiring, fuel system, or any combustible part of the vehicle.
7. Inspect the clutch linkage/cable.
   - Check for looseness in the joints, binding, kinks, and fraying.
   - Make sure the linkage/cable does not rub against other components.

Transmission and Drive Train

The next area to inspect is the transmission and drive area. To perform this inspection, you will need to check that the bolts attaching the transmission to the flywheel housing are present and tight. Check the mounting area for any cracks and the rubber isolators for wear, oil contamination, and damage. Also look for gaps between the transmission case and flywheel housing. To perform an under-vehicle transmission and drive train inspection, follow the steps in SKILL DRILL 55-17.

Inspecting the Engine Compartment

The engine compartment inspection focuses on pumps, pulleys, belts, the air-conditioning unit, steering linkages, and vital fluids. This inspection involves steps with the engine off and with the engine on. To perform an

SKILL DRILL 55-17 Inspecting the Under-Vehicle Transmission and Drive Train

1. Inspect the transmission case, seals, lines, cooler, and fittings for leaks and cracks.
   - Check the fittings for tightness.
   - Check the case plugs and fittings for seepage.
   - Check the cooler lines for chafing, leaks, or seepage.
   - If the vehicle is equipped with airlines, check the lines for signs of leakage and wear, and make sure the lines are not routed near moving parts.
   - With transmission breathers, make sure the vent is open and is not clogged with any debris to restrict flow, and make sure the cap is present.
2. If your vehicle has a standard transmission, check the transmission oil.
   - Check the oil level, type, and condition.
   - Make sure the oil level is flush with the bottom of the fill hole.
   - Check the oil for the presence of water or metallic particles, and observe if it is a milky color or has a silver sheen.
   - Make sure the oil does not smell burned.
   - If you need to add oil, be sure it is the type recommended by the manufacturer. For transmission and axle lubricants, most manufacturers recommend the use of single-viscosity lubricants based on the highest ambient operating temperatures.
   - To add oil to an automatic transmission, the method recommended by the manufacturer should be followed. In such cases, normally the transmission oil level is checked with the transmission in neutral or park and with the engine running.
3. Check U-joints, yokes, drivelines, and center support bearings. For this next inspection, you will need a creeper unless the vehicle is parked over a pit.
   - Check for looseness, damage, and proper phasing.
   - They are considered in phase when the driveline yokes are in the same position along the drive shaft.
   - Check each U-joint for wear in the trunnion or cross.
   - Check for loose trunnion retaining bolts and for excessive play.
   - Make sure the seals are intact.
4. Check the drive shaft for damage and missing counterweights and inspect the welds on the drive shaft for cracks and the input and output yokes for looseness.
   - Check each slip yoke by twisting it in opposite directions and pushing up and down while looking for excessive play.
   - Check for loose bearings or insulating rubber in the supports.
   - Check that all fasteners are present and tight and that the supports are aligned vertically and horizontally.
   - Check the center support bearing and mounting for looseness and deterioration by attempting to move the driveshaft up and down and from side to side.
5. Inspect the axle housings for cracks and leaks, and check the axle breather.
   - Look for leads at the mounting gaskets, bolts, pinion seal, rear cover, and axle housing.
   - If you find caked grease around the axle housing, rear cover, or spring hangers, carefully check the differential housing for cracks.
   - Make sure all fasteners are present and secure.
   - Turn the protective cap to check that the breaker vent is open, not caked with dirt, and has a protective cap.
6. Check the drive axle(s) oil level, type, and condition.
   - You will need to remove the drain plug first, being careful not to spill the fluid.
   - Using a finger or a piece of bent wire, check that the oil level is flush with the bottom of the fill hole.
   - Check the oil for the presence of water (milky color) or metallic particles (silver sheen).
   - Use the recommended type of oil when adding oil to the axle.
   - When you reinsert the fill plug, check for leaks around the mating surface.

Continued on next page

SKILL DRILL 55-17 Inspecting the Under-Vehicle Transmission and Drive Train, continued

7. Check the oil level and condition in all non-drive hubs.
   - Check that the oil level is flush with the bottom of the fill hole.
   - Check for the presence of water or metallic particles.
   - Top off any fluid with the manufacturer-recommended oil.
   - Check for leaks around the fill plug and mating surface.

8. Check the two-speed axle unit operation and oil level.
   - To check the proper axle operation, rotate the drive shaft by hand with the transmission in neutral and the two-speed selector on low. The axles should not rotate.
   - Check again by attempting to rotate the drive shaft by hand with the two-speed selector on high. It should rotate some, and then catch in gear.

engine-off engine compartment inspection, follow the steps in SKILL DRILL 55-18. The following Skill Drills cover the various aspects of each.

Steering and Air-Conditioning Components

This engine compartment inspection focuses on the power steering pump and AC components. All inspections revolve around the principles of secure mounting, condition, and leak detection. To perform an engine-off engine compartment inspection specifically on the steering and air-conditioning components, follow the steps in SKILL DRILL 55-19. To perform an engine-off engine compartment inspection specifically on the fuel, intake, cooling, and cab tilt systems, follow the procedures in SKILL DRILL 55-20.

During the engine-on inspection, when you are checking for leaks, you must first start the vehicle and let it idle for a few minutes. One person should stay in

SKILL DRILL 55-18 Inspecting Engine-Off Engine Compartments

1. Check the belts, pulleys, and tensioners.
   - Check the belts for cracks, blazing, jagged or streaked sidewalls, tensile breaks in the cord body, and uneven ribs on serpentine belts.
   - Check that the belts ride slightly above the pulley, not down into the pulley.
   - Worn out pulleys will wear out belts quickly.
   - Stretched belts indicate a worn out pulley.
   - Check that the tensioners are holding tension on the belt. If the vehicle has an auto-tensioner and the belt is loose, the belts and the tensioner will need to be replaced as the belts cannot be adjusted.
   - Check that the pulleys do not have excessive play or wobble and that they are aligned.
   - Ensure that the pulleys do not have embedded foreign objects.

Continued on next page

SKILL DRILL 55-18 Inspecting Engine-Off Engine Compartment, continued

2. Check the engine oil.
   - Always clean around the dipstick with a clean rag before removing the dipstick to check the oil.
   - Check that the oil is at the proper level and check the dipstick for signs of coolant and fuel contamination (e.g., dirt, milky color, burnt).
   - Check the entire engine compartment for any visible signs of leaks, focusing on seals, gaskets, hoses, filters, and drain plugs. NOTE: It can be hard to determine where leaking fluids are coming from.

3. If the servicing mileage/km specifications have been reached, take an oil sample. To take an oil sample:
   1. Start and warm the vehicle to operating temperature.
   2. Drain the oil and check the magnetic drain plug for contamination.
   3. Take an oil sample following recommended Test Monitoring Center [TMC] procedures using the oil sample syringe

NOTE: Samples should be taken from oil midway through the draining. Evidence of metal shavings or other contamination on the magnetic drain plug could indicate problems within the engine.

4. If the servicing mileage/km specifications have been reached, change the engine oil in accordance with the manufacturer's specifications.
   - Inspect and clean the magnetic drain plugs.
   - Replace the oil filter and refill with oil to the correct specification.

5. Check electrical wiring, routing, and hold-down clamps, including the engine control module (ECM) and powertrain control module (PCM). Check that the wiring is clear of moving parts and heat-producing sources such as the engine, and that it is not pinched.
   - Wire insulators should be free of cracks and should not show chafing or charring.
   - Wires should also not rub together.
   - Hold-down clamps should be secure and should not pinch the wiring.
   - For ECMs and PCMs, check that all sensor wires are no closer than 6" (15.24 cm) to any hot surfaces. NOTE: If any wires are closer than 6" (15.24 cm) and cannot be rerouted, make sure they are protected by heat shields.
   - Also check all wiring and connectors on computer units.

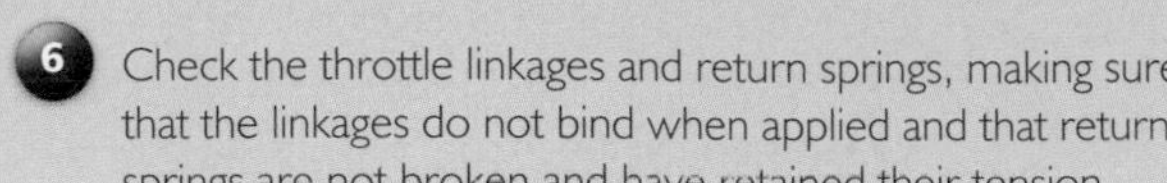

6. Check the throttle linkages and return springs, making sure that the linkages do not bind when applied and that return springs are not broken and have retained their tension.
   - Check the starter mounting and connections to be sure they are securely mounted.
   - All electrical connections should be tight, and wiring should not be rubbing or chafing.
   - Check the alternator mounting, wiring, and wire routing to make sure all the electrical connections are tight and not corroded and that there is no rubbing or chafing.
   - Check that the windshield washer fluid container is filled to the proper level.

7. Check the hydraulic clutch slave and master cylinders' fluid levels and look for any indication of leaks (if fitted). Also look for any leaks on lines, hoses, and fittings, and make sure the lines are properly routed.

8. Check power brake booster(s), hoses, and check/control valves for secure mounting. Inspect all lines and hoses for leaks or kinks.

SKILL DRILL 55-19 Conducting an Engine-Off Engine Compartment Inspection: Steering and Air-Conditioning Components

1. Check the power steering fluid and filter.
   - Locate the power steering reservoir and clean around the dipstick before removing it to check the fluid level.
   - Add the recommended fluid if necessary. Never mix fluid types.
   - Check for leaks if the fluid is low.
   - Inspect the filter located in the reservoir and clean or replace it if necessary.
2. Check the power steering pump.
   - Check the power steering pump, mounting, and hoses for leaks, condition, and routing.
   - Pay close attention to the seals and fitting around the pump and make sure the pump is securely mounted.
3. Check the steering gear for leaks and secure mounting.
   - Check all fittings and seams for seepage or leakage.
   - Check input and output shafts for any leakage.
   - Check that mounting hardware is present and secure.
   - Check for cracks or other damage to the gear mounting areas.
4. Check the Pitman arm-to-steering sector shaft.
   - Check the mounting of the Pitman arm-to-steering gear output shaft for looseness.
   - Check that the splines on the Pitman arm-and steering output shaft align and are tight.
   - Check for excessive play in the steering gear output shaft.
5. Check the steering shaft U-joints.
   - Check all steering shaft U-joints for excessive side and rotational play and for secure attachment to steering shafts.
   - Check the pinch bolts at the steering shaft.
6. Check the tie rod ends and drag links.
   - Check tie rod ends for excessive axial play (in/out of joint).
   - Check drag link joints for excessive axial play (in/out of joint).
   - Check that the threaded portion of the tie-rod end assembly is inserted into the cross-tube for adequate clamping.
7. Check the linkage-assist power steering cylinders.
   - Check for secure attachment.
   - Check for leaks at fittings, hoses, and piston seals.
8. Locate the air-conditioning condenser/compressor and check the front side of the condenser for debris that might cause an airflow restriction.
   - Make sure the condenser is mounted tightly and the condenser lines are not showing signs of leakage.

   Check the compressor for:

   - Broken brackets
   - Loose or missing bolts
   - Alignment of belt and pulleys
   - The condition of the refrigerant hoses

   NOTE: All service ports must have dust caps.

SKILL DRILL 55-20 Conducting an Engine-Off Engine Compartment Inspection: Fuel, Intake, Cooling, and Cab Tilt Systems

1. Check the fuel pump and fuel line mountings. Road and engine vibrations may damage the pump if it is not secure.
   - Check the water separator/fuel heater.
   - Check the water separator, drain off excess water, and check that the fuel heater functions properly.
   - Replace the fuel filter(s) according to the service manual.
   - Prime and bleed the fuel system according to the service manual.

2. Check the intake system.
   - Check the air filter and replace it if required.
   - Check the reading on the filter monitoring device, and reset the air filter restriction indicator to zero.
   - Visually inspect the turbocharger for leaks; check mountings and connections.
   - Check the charge air hoses and pipes.

3. Check the radiator for leaks, damage, and air flow restrictions caused by debris.
   - Make sure the radiator is securely mounted.
   - Check the coolant filter according to the service manual.
   - Check the coolant recovery system for holes and proper mounting.
   - Make sure the coolant recovery system cap is secure.
   - Check the radiator hoses for leaks and cracks, and check the clamps for tightness.

4. Check the coolant for contamination, additive concentration, and protection levels.
   - Contaminants may be oil, rust, or debris.
   - Check the coolant for proper inhibition either by the test strip or titration method, and record your reading on the checklist.
   - Check the protection or freeze point level using a refractometer, and record your reading on the checklist.
   - The protection level should be between –25 and –35°F (–32 to –37°C).
   - If the system has the correct protection level but additional coolant is needed, fill with the manufacturer's recommended coolant.

5. Pressure test the cooling system and radiator cap (according to the manufacturer's recommendations) to ensure correct pressure in the coolant system.
   - Check the fan assembly and shroud mounting.
   - Check that the blade assembly is free of cracks.
   - Grasp the fan blades and check for excessive play in the shaft.
   - Check for adequate clearance between all moving parts.
   - Check the air supply system with the brakes applied, and then check the system for leaks with the brakes released.

6. If fitted, check the tilt cab system's hydraulic pump.
   - Make sure there is adequate clearance in front of the cab before activating the tilt system.
   - Make sure there is nothing loose in the passenger compartment that could go through the windshield when the cab is jacked up.
   - Check the tilt cab system hydraulic lines and cylinders for leaks and damage.
   - Check the oil level and service as required.

   NOTE: If the vehicle does not have a hydraulic tilt cab system, make sure the safety locking devices are working properly.

the cab, and a second person can do the inspection. To perform an engine-on engine compartment inspection to check for leaks, levels, and operation of systems, follow the steps in SKILL DRILL 55-21.

Inspecting Cargo-Handling Devices

When inspecting cargo handling equipment, there are two types of operating lift gate systems that use hydraulic power: the single-acting hydraulic cylinder and the double-acting hydraulic cylinder. When checking the hydraulic fluid, you first need to know which type of system you are inspecting.

The single-acting hydraulic cylinder uses hydraulic power in one direction of the lift only. It should always be checked with the cylinder(s) in its non-working position (collapsed or extended).

The double-acting cylinder uses hydraulic power in both directions. It should always be checked with the cylinder in the collapsed position (cylinder all the way in). Check the condition of the hydraulic fluid to ensure efficient operation of the equipment, and change any dirty fluid.

To inspect cargo-handling devices, follow the guidelines in SKILL DRILL 55-22.

SKILL DRILL 55-21 Conducting an Engine-On Engine Compartment Inspection: Leaks, Levels, and Operation of Systems

1. After the engine has been running, check all oil, coolant, air, and fuel lines for leaks.
   - Check the air induction system by inspecting the charge air cooler and piping for leaks.
   - All hoses should be free from cracks and any blockages, and they should be mounted securely.
2. If the vehicle is equipped with an automatic transmission, the oil level should be checked to make sure it is at the full mark on the dipstick.

   NOTE: On some trucks equipped with automatic transmissions, you may need to check fluid level with the engine running. Always consult the appropriate service manual.
   - The oil should be checked for the presence of water or metallic particles, which may indicate undue wear in the transmission.
   - Make sure the oil does not smell burned. If you need to change or add transmission oil, make sure it is the recommended manufacturer type.
3. Check the alternator current and voltage outputs and record your results.
   - Check the air conditioning to ensure that the entire system is functioning properly.
4. While in the cab, you will need to verify the operation of the engine/exhaust brake.
   - To test the engine brake, consult the appropriate service manual.
   - For the exhaust brake, build the air pressure to at least 85 psi (586 kPa).
   - With the engine idling, activate the exhaust brake with the switch on the dash. The brake should exhaust, releasing the brake's air supply system. Accelerating the engine should release the brake.
5. Check operation of the fan clutch following the manufacturer's procedures.
   - The clutch should engage at the correct engine temperature.
   - All fan clutches will engage when the engine reaches a predetermined temperature above the thermostat opening temperature.
   - The clutch may also engage when the air-conditioning system is turned on. Next, ensure that the heating, ventilating, and air-conditioning (HVAC) inlet filters are clean and that the inlet ducts are clear of debris.

Continued on next page

SKILL DRILL 55-21 Conducting an Engine-On Engine Compartment Inspection: Leaks, Levels, and Operation of Systems, continued

6. Check the exhaust system for leaks, proper routing, and damaged or missing components; and check the mountings for looseness and damage.
   - Check the muffler(s) for secure mounting to the vehicle, pipes, or exhaust stacks.
   - Check for missing fasteners on exhaust pipes and mufflers.
   - Check the supports for excessive rust or cracks.
   - Check the muffler for holes, dents, or other damage.
   - Check for missing components (such as mufflers).
   - Check pipes and mufflers for any sign of leaks.

   NOTE: It is not permissible for the exhaust system to be leaking at a point forward of, or directly below, the driver/sleeper compartment.
   - Check that the exhaust outlet is aft (above) any part of the vehicle designed to be occupied.
   - Check that the exhaust system does not rub or contact any other objects.

   NOTE: No part of the exhaust system should be positioned in a location that could result in burning, charring, or damaging the electrical wiring, fuel supply, or any combustible part of the vehicle.

SKILL DRILL 55-22 Inspecting Cargo-Handling Devices

1. Check all hydraulic components for leaks, taking care to also check hoses for any cracking, chafing, or incorrect routing.
2. Inspect all electrical components.
   - Identify any frayed wiring.
   - Check the condition and operation of switches.
   - Check the condition of connections.
   - Check the security of the electric motor that drives the hydraulic pump.
   - Check for the presence of a protective cover over the components.
3. Check lift gate components and operation by ensuring that the lift gate operates both up and down and does not drift down or lower too fast.
   - It should operate smoothly (not jerkily) and not rise too slowly.
   - Make sure there are not any unusual noises during operation.
4. Check for broken welds, and ensure that there is no binding at pivot points and no frayed lift cables. Also check the presence of warning/operation decals, and check that any safety catches operate correctly.
5. Check that all stops, safeties, and chains work properly.
   - Tracks should be clear of debris, and the lift gate should not bind during operation.
6. Finally, lubricate the ramp according to the procedures in the service manual.

Wrap-up

Ready for Review

- Preventative maintenance and inspection (PMI) is critical to making sure heavy-duty vehicles are roadworthy and conform to federal, state, and local laws for safe operation.
- Preventative maintenance (PM) has the added benefit of increasing resale value and return on investment (ROI), lowering overall lifetime cost of operation, and increasing a vehicle's reliability.
- In the United States, commercial vehicles moving freight or passengers, or transporting any cargo interstate must be registered with the Federal Motor Carriers Safety Administration (FMCSA) and have a United States Department of Transport (USDOT) number.
- Time, mileage, and amount of fuel consumed are the three bases for the establishing a PMI schedule.
- PM-A is a visual check of all safety related items such as brakes, tires, horn, wipers, steering components, suspension components, and lighting.
- PM-B is a comprehensive inspection that includes all the items found in a PM-A, and adds an oil and fuel filter change.
- PM-C is typically an annual inspection that includes all the items in PM-A and PM-B, with additional inspection of all chassis components. Scheduled fluid changes, component adjustment, and repair or replacement are performed at this time.
- PM is generally proactive, which means maintenance work is scheduled to prevent unexpected breakdowns from occurring.
- Proactive maintenance reflects the understanding that the cost of repairing an unexpected breakdown is usually much greater than preventative maintenance.
- Drivers are the first persons responsible for identifying potential safety issues and the possibility of imminent breakdowns.
- In the United States, FMCSA legislation requires drivers to prepare a report in writing at the completion of each day's work for every commercial vehicle that driver has operated that day.
- It is the responsibility of a carrier to develop a PM program to meet performance standards and have records documenting that vehicles are maintained and repaired as needed.
- At a minimum, a PM service checklist should include an itemized task list of procedures that include mechanical safety items related to braking, steering, suspension, lighting, mirrors, wipers, horns, tires, and wheels.
- The use of software-based record keeping is almost universal for fleet operations. Software can customize maintenance schedules, create and track work orders, track fuel consumption, record maintenance histories, track tire service and accidents, monitor labor, and produce invoices.
- The nonprofit organization Commercial Vehicle Safety Alliance (CVSA) enforces uniform standards for commercial vehicle safety across the United States, Canada, and Mexico.
- A commercial vehicle may qualify for a CVSA decal if it passes inspection, meaning that no defects are found during a Level I or V inspection.
- Record keeping is an essential component of the PMI process. Inspections have to be carried out by duly authorized inspectors who can demonstrate both training and experience.
- Oils are graded or classified by the American Society of Automotive Engineers (SAE) through the viscosity index.
- Given that there are thousands of vehicles built every day, it is it is to be expected that something can go wrong in the construction process. When carrying out an inspection, it is good practice to try to identify whether the vehicle you are inspecting has been subject to a recall and whether the repair has been completed.
- In the United States, the National Highway Traffic Safety Administration (NHTSA) of the U.S. Department of Transportation provides recall information, including vehicle and equipment campaigns from 1966 to present.

- It is very important to use the right tool or piece of equipment. Do not substitute the wrong tool for the right one.
- It is essential that a shop be set up for functionality. This means that there are lights, air hoses, tools, equipment, refuse and oil containers, jack stands, and other equipment present and in proper position to perform preventative maintenance inspections.
- Brakes are of extreme importance in terms of operational efficiently and safety. Of all the PMI areas, brakes are one of the highest in priority, and if they are found defective, the vehicle must be designated out of service.
- With air brakes, the truck's air pressure system has to be operating properly. There is a series of tests you will need to perform on the air brake system. These tests may require two people.
- Inspecting wheels and tires is absolutely critical to the safe operation of any road transport vehicle. Underinflated tires, tires with poor tread, mismatched tires, and poorly mounted tires can contribute to poor handling in bad road conditions at the very least, and can lead to blowouts and accidents in worst-case scenarios.
- Performing a wheel alignment inspection is good practice for the safe operation of any road transport vehicle. Incorrect wheel alignment can contribute to the unnecessary rapid detrition of tires and affect handling of the vehicle itself.
- The under-vehicle inspection should focus mainly on the transmission and drive train of the vehicle. Drivelines in most medium- and heavy-duty vehicles are long, so you will often need to use a creeper, unless it can be raised on a hoist or accessed from a pit.
- To perform an inspection of the drive area, you will need to check that the bolts attaching the transmission to the flywheel are present and tight.
- When inspecting cargo-handling equipment, there are two types of operating lift gate systems that use hydraulic power: single-acting hydraulic cylinder and double-acting hydraulic cylinder.

Vocabulary Builder

Commercial Vehicle Safety Alliance (CVSA) A nonprofit organization dedicated to improve the safe operation of commercial vehicles in North America by establishing a uniform, reciprocal enforcement of commercial vehicle safety standards.

CSA 2010 basic score Calculated ratings on compliance, safety, and accountability initiated by the Federal Motor Carrier Safety Administration (FMCSA).

drivability items Warning lights such as misfires, rough idle, and check engine.

Driver Post-Operation Vehicle Inspection Report (DVIR) In the United States, FMCSA legislation requires drivers to prepare a report in writing at the completion of each day's work for each commercial vehicle the driver has operated that day. Specifics of the legislation are contained in FMCVS 49.396.11.

Federal Motor Carrier Safety Regulation (FMCSR) Regulations issued by the Federal Motor Carrier Safety Administration (FMCSA), published in the U.S. Federal Register, and compiled in the U.S. Code of Federal Regulations (CFR).

Federal Motor Carrier Safety Administration (FMCSA) All companies that operate commercial vehicles within the United States to move freight, passengers, or transport any cargo interstate, must be registered with the FMCSA.

North American Standard Out-of-Service Criteria (OOSC) Defects that require a vehicle to be taken out of service until repaired.

PM-A PM-A inspections are visual assessments of all safety-related items such as brakes, tires, horn, wipers, steering components, suspension components, and lighting.

PM-B PM-B inspections include all of the checks and adjustments performed in PM-A, as well as an oil change, and oil filter and fuel filter changes. The inspection items include the engine and driveline, as well as greater detail checks of the braking, steering, and other chassis systems.

PM-C PM-C inspections are annual and include all the items in PM-A and B, as well as comprehensive checks of all chassis components. Scheduled fluid changes and component adjustment, repair, or replacement are performed at this time.

PM service checklist An itemized task list of mechanical safety procedures.

PM service intervals The frequency of a PM schedule.

predictive PM A statistical analysis of when equipment and component failures are likely to occur, including replacing parts or equipment before malfunctions happen.

proactive maintenance Reflects the understanding that the cost of repairing an unexpected breakdown is usually much greater than preventative maintenance.

proactive PM Preventative maintenance that is typically based on distance traveled, engine hours, time, or fuel used.

reactive maintenance Service is only performed after equipment is broken, temporarily keeping vehicle and fleet operating costs low.

return on investment (ROI) The ratio of dollars spent on a vehicle for its purchase and maintenance compared to how much the vehicle earns.

severe service operating conditions Conditions consist of towing or hauling heavy loads, extensive idling and/or stop-and-go, low-speed driving encountered in inner-city traffic, delivery, off-road dusty conditions, and multiple drivers.

United States Department of Transport (USDOT) number Any hazardous materials carriers who move enough materials requiring a safety permit must also register for a USDOT number.

Review Questions

1. An oil and fuel filter change takes place at:
   a. PM A.
   b. PM B.
   c. PM C.
   d. PM D.
2. Federal regulations require that every motor carrier must systematically ________ all motor vehicles subject to its control.
   a. inspect
   b. repair
   c. maintain
   d. All of the choices are correct.
3. A procedure should be in place ensuring that safety-related vehicle defects discovered during inspections are ________ before the vehicle is released for operation.
   a. reported
   b. repaired
   c. validated
   d. All of the choices are correct.
4. The Commercial Vehicle Safety Alliance (CVSA) membership includes:
   a. the United States.
   b. Canada.
   c. Mexico.
   d. All of the choices are correct.
5. Fleet operation software can accomplish tasks such as:
   a. customize maintenance schedules.
   b. create and track work orders.
   c. track tire service.
   d. All of the choices are correct.
6. The following must be included on the PM inspection report EXCEPT:
   a. the individual performing the inspection and the date the vehicle was inspected.
   b. a description of the uses of the vehicle such as over the road, local delivery or other uses.
   c. the motor carrier operating the vehicle.
   d. the vehicle components inspected and the results of the inspection, including those components not meeting the minimum standards.
7. Which of the following are correct concerning vehicle rules for PM and PMI?
   a. Check that the garage door is open enough to allow vehicle entry and exit.
   b. Check brake operation before operating any vehicle.
   c. Check around the vehicle for objects or personnel before attempting to start a vehicle.
   d. All of the choices are correct.
8. Which of the following items should a shop have on hand for PM and PMI service?
   a. Lights
   b. Air hoses
   c. Tools
   d. All of the choices are correct.
9. Which of the following are components of the internal cab inspection?
   a. Key-off inspection
   b. Key-on inspection
   c. Engine-on inspection
   d. All of these are components of an internal cab inspection.
10. Severe operating conditions include:
    a. towing or hauling heavy loads.
    b. off-road, dusty conditions.
    c. vehicles used by multiple drivers.
    d. All of the choices are correct.

ASE-Type Questions

1. Technician A says that the type of checklist as well as the inspection schedule will vary with vehicle type and operating service. Technician B says that inspection of fire protection, emergency exit, and evacuation equipment is critical for buses and motor coaches. Who is correct?
   a. Technician A
   b. Technician B
   c. Both Technician A and Technician B
   d. Neither Technician A nor Technician B
2. Technician A says that a DVIR is a driver vehicle inspection report. Technician B says that a DVIR covers vehicle safety items such as the tires, rims wipers, horn, brakes, steering, trailer brake connections, coupler condition, and parking brake. Who is correct?
   a. Technician A
   b. Technician B
   c. Both Technician A and Technician B
   d. Neither Technician A nor Technician B
3. Technician A says that the CVSA is the commercial vehicle safety alliance. Technician B says that the CVSA does not include a training curriculum. Who is correct?
   a. Technician A
   b. Technician B
   c. Both Technician A and Technician B
   d. Neither Technician A nor Technician B
4. Technician A says that the use of software-based record keeping is almost universal for fleet operation. Technician B says that managers can accurately monitor the cost of PM and associated vehicle costs to make decisions. Who is correct?
   a. Technician A
   b. Technician B
   c. Both Technician A and Technician B
   d. Neither Technician A nor Technician B
5. Technician A says that record keeping is an essential component of the PMI process. Technician B says that inspections have to be carried out by duly authorized inspectors who can demonstrate both training and experience. Who is correct?
   a. Technician A
   b. Technician B
   c. Both Technician A and Technician B
   d. Neither Technician A nor Technician B
6. Technician A says that, in most countries, an inspector carrying out this work is required to be registered and appropriately qualified. Technician B says that, in the United States, the requirements include, in part, at least five years of experience as a commercial vehicle mechanic. Who is correct?
   a. Technician A
   b. Technician B
   c. Both Technician A and Technician B
   d. Neither Technician A nor Technician B
7. Technician A says that flammable liquids and oily rags should be stored in an EPA-approved container. Technician B says to use the right tool for the right job. Who is correct?
   a. Technician A
   b. Technician B
   c. Both Technician A and Technician B
   d. Neither Technician A nor Technician B
8. Technician A says that it is very important that the shop be set up for functionality. Technician B says that some manufacturers specify maximum wear limitations before a vehicle out-of-service criteria (OOSC) is reached. Who is correct?
   a. Technician A
   b. Technician B
   c. Both Technician A and Technician B
   d. Neither Technician A nor Technician B
9. Technician A says that the PMI process should begin with a walk-around inspection. Technician B says that you should perform the walk-around inspection alone so that you can concentrate on your inspection. Who is correct?
   a. Technician A
   b. Technician B
   c. Both Technician A and Technician B
   d. Neither Technician A nor Technician B
10. Technician A says that you should check all exterior lights, lenses, covers, and reflectors for secure mounting and correct location. Technician B says that you should check any visible wiring for general condition. Who is correct?
    a. Technician A
    b. Technician B
    c. Both Technician A and Technician B
    d. Neither Technician A nor Technician B

APPENDIX A

2014 NATEF Medium/Heavy-Duty Truck Accreditation Task List Correlation Guide

NATEF Task List	NATEF Priority Number	Chapter
Required Supplemental Tasks		
Shop and Personal Safety		
1. Identify general shop safety rules and procedures.	N/A	3
2. Utilize safe procedures for handling of tools and equipment.	N/A	4
3. Identify and use proper placement of floor jacks and jack stands.	N/A	5
4. Identify and use proper procedures for safe lift operation.	N/A	5
5. Utilize proper ventilation procedures for working within the lab/shop area.	N/A	3
6. Identify marked safety areas.	N/A	3
7. Identify the location and the types of fire extinguishers and other fire safety equipment; demonstrate knowledge of the procedures for using fire extinguishers and other fire safety equipment.	N/A	3
8. Identify the location and use of eye wash stations.	N/A	3
9. Identify the location of the posted evacuation routes.	N/A	3
10. Comply with the required use of safety glasses, ear protection, gloves, and shoes during lab/shop activities.	N/A	3
11. Identify and wear appropriate clothing for lab/shop activities.	N/A	3
12. Secure hair and jewelry for lab/shop activities.	N/A	3
13. Demonstrate awareness of the safety aspects of supplemental restraint systems (SRS), electronic brake control systems, and hybrid vehicle high voltage circuits.	N/A	28
14. Demonstrate awareness of the safety aspects of high voltage circuits (such as high intensity discharge (HID) lamps, ignition systems, injection systems, etc.).	N/A	17
15. Locate and demonstrate knowledge of material safety data sheets (MSDS).	N/A	3
Tools and Equipment		
1. Identify tools and their usage in automotive applications.	N/A	4
2. Identify standard and metric designation.	N/A	4
3. Demonstrate safe handling and use of appropriate tools.	N/A	4
4. Demonstrate proper cleaning, storage, and maintenance of tools and equipment.	N/A	4
5. Demonstrate proper use of precision measuring tools (i.e. micrometer, dial-indicator, dial-caliper).	N/A	4
Preparing Vehicle for Service		
1. Identify information needed and the service requested on a repair order.	N/A	2
2. Identify purpose and demonstrate proper use of fender covers, mats.	N/A	2
3. Demonstrate use of the three C's (concern, cause, and correction).	N/A	2
4. Review vehicle service history.	N/A	2
5. Complete work order to include customer information, vehicle identifying information, customer concern, related service history, cause, and correction.	N/A	2
Preparing Vehicle for Customer		
1. Ensure vehicle is prepared to return to customer per school/company policy (floor mats, steering wheel cover, etc.).	N/A	2

Continued on next page

NATEF Task List	NATEF Priority Number	Chapter
Workplace Employability Skills		
Personal Standards		
1. Reports to work daily on time; able to take directions and motivated to accomplish the task at hand.	N/A	2
2. Dresses appropriately and uses language and manners suitable for the workplace.	N/A	2
3. Maintains appropriate personal hygiene.	N/A	2
4. Meets and maintains employment eligibility criteria, such as drug/alcohol-free status, clean driving record, etc.	N/A	2
5. Demonstrates honesty, integrity, and reliability.	N/A	2
Work Habits/Ethic		
1. Complies with workplace policies/laws.	N/A	2
2. Contributes to the success of the team, assists others, and requests help when needed.	N/A	2
3. Works well with all customers and coworkers.	N/A	2
4. Negotiates solutions to interpersonal and workplace conflicts.	N/A	2
5. Contributes ideas and initiative.	N/A	2
6. Follows directions.	N/A	2
7. Communicates (written and verbal) effectively with customers and coworkers.	N/A	2
8. Reads and interprets workplace documents; writes clearly and concisely.	N/A	2
9. Analyzes and resolves problems that arise in completing assigned tasks.	N/A	2
10. Organizes and implements a productive plan of work.	N/A	2
11. Uses scientific, technical, engineering, and mathematics principles and reasoning to accomplish assigned tasks.	N/A	2
12. Identifies and addresses the needs of all customers, providing helpful, courteous, and knowledgeable service and advice as needed.	N/A	2
I. DIESEL ENGINES		
All NATEF tasks for this standard can be found in *Fundamentals of Medium/Heavy Duty Diesel Engines* (ISBN 978-1-2840-6705-7).		
II. DRIVE TRAIN		
A. Clutch		
1. Identify causes of clutch noise, binding, slippage, pulsation, vibration, grabbing, dragging, and chatter problems; determine needed action.	P-1	36
2. Inspect and adjust clutch linkage, cables, levers, brackets, bushings, pivots, springs, and clutch safety switch (includes push- and pull-type assemblies); check pedal height and travel; perform needed action.	P-1	36
3. Inspect, adjust, repair, and replace hydraulic clutch slave and master cylinders, lines, and hoses; bleed system.	P-2	36
4. Inspect, adjust, lubricate, or replace release (throw-out) bearing, sleeve, bushings, springs, housing, levers, release fork, fork pads, rollers, shafts, and seals.	P-1	36
5. Inspect, adjust, and replace single-disc clutch pressure plate and clutch disc.	P-1	36
6. Inspect, adjust, and replace two-plate clutch pressure plate, clutch discs, intermediate plate, and drive pins/lugs.	P-1	36
7. Inspect and/or replace clutch brake assembly; inspect input shaft and bearing retainer; perform needed action.	P-1	36
8. Inspect, adjust, and replace self-adjusting/continuous-adjusting clutch mechanisms.	P-1	36
9. Inspect and replace pilot bearing.	P-1	36
10. Remove and reinstall flywheel, inspect mounting area on crankshaft, rear main oil seal, and measure crankshaft end play; determine needed action.	P-1	36
11. Inspect flywheel, starter ring gear, and measure flywheel face and pilot bore runout; determine needed action.	P-1	36
12. Inspect flywheel housing(s) to transmission housing/engine mating surface(s) and measure flywheel housing face and bore runout; determine needed action.	P-2	36

Continued on next page

NATEF Task List	NATEF Priority Number	Chapter
B. Transmission		
1. Identify causes of transmission noise, shifting concerns, lockup, jumping-out-of-gear, overheating, and vibration problems; determine needed action.	P-1	39
2. Inspect, test, repair, or replace air shift controls, lines, hoses, valves, regulators, filters, and cylinder assemblies.	P-2	39
3. Inspect and replace transmission mounts, insulators, and mounting bolts.	P-1	44
4. Inspect for leakage and replace transmission cover plates, gaskets, seals, and cap bolts; inspect seal surfaces and vents; repair as needed.	P-1	44
5. Check transmission fluid level and condition; determine needed service; add proper type of lubricant.	P-1	44
6. Inspect, adjust, and replace transmission shift lever, cover, rails, forks, levers, bushings, sleeves, detents, interlocks, springs, and lock bolts/safety wires.	P-2	39
7. Remove and reinstall transmission.	P-1	44
8. Inspect input shaft, gear, spacers, bearings, retainers, and slingers; determine needed action.	P-3	39
9. Inspect transmission oil filters, coolers, and related components; replace as needed.	P-2	44
10. Inspect speedometer components; determine needed action.	P-2	39
11. Inspect and adjust power take-off (PTO) assemblies, controls, and shafts; determine needed action.	P-3	39
12. Inspect and test function of reverse light, neutral start, and warning device circuits; determine needed action.	P-1	44
13. Inspect and test transmission temperature gauge, wiring harnesses, and sensor/sending unit; determine needed action.	P-2	40
14. Inspect and test operation of automated mechanical transmission and manual electronic shift controls, shift, range and splitter solenoids, shift motors, indicators, speed and range sensors, electronic/transmission control units (ECU/TCU), neutral/in gear and reverse switches, and wiring harnesses; determine needed action.	P-2	40
15. Inspect and test operation of automated mechanical transmission electronic shift selectors, air and electrical switches, displays and indicators, wiring harnesses, and air lines; determine needed action.	P-2	40
16. Use appropriate electronic service tool(s) and procedures to diagnose automated mechanical transmission problems; check and record diagnostic codes, clear codes, and interpret digital multimeter (DMM) readings; determine needed action.	P-1	40
17. Inspect and test operation of automatic transmission electronic shift controls, shift solenoids, shift motors, indicators, speed and range sensors, electronic/transmission control units (ECU/TCU), neutral/in gear and reverse switches, and wiring harnesses.	P-2	45
18. Inspect and test operation of automatic transmission electronic shift selectors, switches, displays, indicators, and wiring harnesses.	P-2	45
19. Use appropriate electronic service tool(s) and procedures to diagnose automatic transmission problems; check and record diagnostic codes, clear codes, and interpret digital multimeter (DMM) readings; determine needed action.	P-3	45
C. Driveshaft and Universal Joint		
1. Identify causes of driveshaft and universal joint noise and vibration problems; determine needed action.	P-1	46
2. Inspect, service, or replace driveshaft, slip joints, yokes, drive flanges, and universal joints, driveshaft boots and seals, and retaining hardware; check phasing of all shafts.	P-1	46
3. Inspect driveshaft center support bearings and mounts; determine needed action.	P-1	46
4. Measure drive line angles; determine needed action.	P-1	46
D. Drive Axle		
1. Identify causes of drive axle(s) drive unit noise and overheating problems; determine needed action.	P-2	48
2. Check and repair fluid leaks; inspect and replace drive axle housing cover plates, gaskets, sealants, vents, magnetic plugs, and seals.	P-1	48
3. Check drive axle fluid level and condition; determine needed service; add proper type of lubricant.	P-1	48
4. Remove and replace differential carrier assembly.	P-2	48

Continued on next page

NATEF Task List	NATEF Priority Number	Chapter
5. Inspect and replace differential case assembly including spider gears, cross shaft, side gears, thrust washers, case halves, and bearings.	P-3	48
6. Inspect and replace components of locking differential case assembly.	P-3	48
7. Inspect differential carrier housing and caps, side bearing bores, and pilot (spigot, pocket) bearing bore; determine needed action.	P-3	48
8. Measure ring gear runout; determine needed action.	P-2	48
9. Inspect and replace ring and drive pinion gears, spacers, sleeves, bearing cages, and bearings.	P-3	48
10. Measure and adjust drive pinion bearing preload.	P-3	48
11. Measure and adjust drive pinion depth.	P-3	48
12. Measure and adjust side bearing preload and ring gear backlash.	P-2	48
13. Check and interpret ring gear and pinion tooth contact pattern; determine needed action.	P-2	48
14. Inspect, adjust, or replace ring gear thrust block/screw.	P-3	48
15. Inspect power divider (inter-axle differential) assembly; determine needed action.	P-3	48
16. Inspect, adjust, repair, or replace air-operated power divider (inter-axle differential) lockout assembly including diaphragms, seals, springs, yokes, pins, lines, hoses, fittings, and controls.	P-2	48
17. Inspect, repair, or replace drive axle lubrication system: pump, troughs, collectors, slingers, tubes, and filters.	P-3	24
18. Inspect and replace drive axle shafts.	P-1	48
19. Remove and replace wheel assembly; check rear wheel seal and axle flange gasket for leaks; perform needed action.	P-1	24
20. Identify causes of drive axle wheel bearing noise and check for damage; perform needed action.	P-1	24
21. Inspect and test drive axle temperature gauge, wiring harnesses, and sending unit/sensor; determine needed action.	P-2	40
22. Clean, inspect, lubricate, and replace wheel bearings; replace seals and wear rings; inspect and replace retaining hardware; adjust drive axle wheel bearings. Verify end play with dial indicator method.	P-1	24
III. BRAKES		
A. Air Brakes		
1. Air Supply and Service Systems		
1. Identify poor stopping, air leaks, premature wear, pulling, grabbing, dragging, or balance problems caused by supply and service system malfunctions; determine needed action.	P-1	31
2. Check air system build-up time; determine needed action.	P-1	31
3. Drain air reservoir/tanks; check for oil, water, and foreign material; determine needed action.	P-1	31
4. Inspect air compressor drive gear, belts, and coupling; adjust or replace as needed.	P-3	31
5. Inspect air compressor inlet; inspect oil supply and coolant lines, fittings, and mounting brackets; repair or replace as needed.	P-1	31
6. Inspect and test air system pressure controls: governor, unloader assembly valves, filters, lines, hoses, and fittings; adjust or replace as needed.	P-1	31
7. Inspect air system lines, hoses, fittings, and couplings; repair or replace as needed.	P-1	31
8. Inspect and test air tank relief (safety) valves, one-way (single) check valves, two-way (double) check valves, manual and automatic drain valves; replace as needed.	P-1	31
9. Inspect and clean air dryer systems, filters, valves, heaters, wiring, and connectors; repair or replace as needed.	P-1	31
10. Inspect and test brake application (foot/treadle) valve, fittings, and mounts; check pedal operation; replace as needed.	P-1	31
11. Inspect and test stop light circuit switches, wiring, and connectors; repair or replace as needed.	P-1	31
12. Inspect and test hand brake (trailer) control valve, lines, fittings, and mountings; repair or replace as needed.	P-1	31
13. Inspect and test brake relay valves; replace as needed.	P-1	31
14. Inspect and test quick release valves; replace as needed.	P-1	31

Continued on next page

NATEF Task List	NATEF Priority Number	Chapter
15. Inspect and test tractor protection valve; replace as needed.	P-1	31
16. Inspect and test emergency (spring) brake control/modulator valve(s); replace as needed.	P-1	31
17. Inspect and test low pressure warning devices, wiring, and connectors; repair or replace as needed.	P-1	31
18. Inspect and test air pressure gauges, lines, and fittings; replace as needed.	P-2	31
2. Mechanical/Foundation Brakes		
1. Identify poor stopping, brake noise, premature wear, pulling, grabbing, or dragging problems caused by the foundation brake, slack adjuster, and brake chamber problems; determine needed action.	P-1	31
2. Inspect and test service brake chambers, diaphragm, clamp, spring, pushrod, clevis, and mounting brackets; repair or replace as needed.	P-1	31
3. Identify type, inspect, and service slack adjusters; perform needed action.	P-1	31
4. Inspect camshafts, tubes, rollers, bushings, seals, spacers, retainers, brake spiders, shields, anchor pins, and springs; replace as needed.	P-1	31
5. Inspect, clean, and adjust air disc brake caliper assemblies; determine needed repairs.	P-2	31
6. Inspect and measure brake shoes or pads; perform needed action.	P-1	31
7. Inspect and measure brake drums or rotors; perform needed action.	P-1	31
3. Parking Brakes		
1. Inspect and test parking (spring) brake chamber diaphragm and seals; replace parking (spring) brake chamber; dispose of removed chambers in accordance with local regulations.	P-1	31
2. Inspect and test parking (spring) brake check valves, lines, hoses, and fittings; replace as needed.	P-1	31
3. Inspect and test parking (spring) brake application and release valve; replace as needed.	P-1	31
4. Manually release (cage) and reset (uncage) parking (spring) brakes in accordance with manufacturers' recommendations.	P-1	31
5. Identify and test anti compounding brake function.	P-1	31
B. Hydraulic Brakes		
1. Hydraulic System		
1. Identify poor stopping, premature wear, pulling, dragging, balance, or pedal feel problems caused by the hydraulic system; determine needed action.	P-2	33
2. Inspect and test master cylinder for internal/external leaks and damage; replace as needed.	P-1	33
3. Inspect hydraulic system brake lines, flexible hoses, and fittings for leaks and damage; replace as needed.	P-1	33
4. Inspect and test metering (hold-off), load sensing/proportioning, proportioning, and combination valves; replace as needed.	P-3	33
5. Inspect and test brake pressure differential valve and warning light circuit switch, bulbs/LEDS, wiring, and connectors; repair or replace as needed.	P-2	33
6. Inspect disc brake caliper assemblies; replace as needed.	P-1	33
7. Inspect/test brake fluid; bleed and/or flush system; determine proper fluid type.	P-1	33
2. Mechanical/Foundation Brakes		
1. Identify poor stopping, brake noise, premature wear, pulling, grabbing, dragging, or pedal feel problems caused by mechanical components; determine needed action.	P-2	33
2. Inspect and measure rotors; perform needed action.	P-1	33
3. Inspect and measure disc brake pads; inspect mounting hardware; perform needed action.	P-1	33
4. Check parking brake operation; inspect parking brake application and holding devices; adjust and replace as needed.	P-2	33
3. Power Assist Units		
1. Identify stopping problems caused by the brake assist (booster) system; determine needed action.	P-3	33
2. Inspect, test, repair, or replace hydraulic brake assist (booster), hoses, and control valves; determine proper fluid type.	P-3	33
3. Check emergency (back-up, reserve) brake assist system.	P-3	33

Continued on next page

NATEF Task List	NATEF Priority Number	Chapter
C. Air and Hydraulic Anti-Lock Brake Systems (ABS) and Automatic Traction Control (ATC)		
1. Observe anti-lock brake system (ABS) warning light operation (includes trailer and dash mounted trailer ABS warning light); determine needed action.	P-1	32
2. Diagnose anti-lock brake system (ABS) electronic control(s) and components using self-diagnosis and/or electronic service tool(s); determine needed action.	P-1	32
3. Identify poor stopping and wheel lock-up problems caused by failure of the anti-lock brake system (ABS); determine needed action.	P-1	32
4. Test and check operation of anti-lock brake system (ABS) air, hydraulic, electrical, and mechanical components; perform needed action.	P-1	32
5. Test anti-lock brake system (ABS) wheel speed sensors and circuits; adjust or replace as needed.	P-1	32
6. Bleed the ABS hydraulic circuits.	P-2	33
7. Observe automatic traction control (ATC) warning light operation; determine needed action.	P-3	32
8. Diagnose automatic traction control (ATC) electronic control(s) and components using self-diagnosis and/or specified test equipment (scan tool, PC computer); determine needed action.	P-3	32
9. Verify power line carrier (PLC) operations.	P-2	32
D. Wheel Bearings		
1. Clean, inspect, lubricate, and replace wheel bearings and races/cups; replace seals and wear rings; inspect spindle/tube; inspect and replace retaining hardware; adjust wheel bearings. Verify end play with dial indicator method.	P-1	24
2. Identify, inspect, or replace unitized/preset hub bearing assemblies.	P-2	24
IV. SUSPENSION AND STEERING		
A. Steering Systems		
1. Steering Column		
1. Identify causes of fixed and driver adjustable steering column and shaft noise, looseness, and binding problems; determine needed action.	P-1	28
2. Inspect and service steering shaft U-joint(s), slip joints, bearings, bushings, and seals; phase shaft.	P-1	28
3. Check cab mounting and adjust ride height.	P-2	28
4. Remove the steering wheel (includes steering wheels equipped with electrical/electronic controls and components); install and center the steering wheel. Inspect, test, replace, and calibrate steering angle sensor.	P-1	28
5. Disable and enable supplemental restraint system (SRS) in accordance with manufacturers' procedures.	P-1	28
2. Steering Units		
1. Identify causes of power steering system noise, steering binding, darting/oversteer, reduced wheel cut, steering wheel kick, pulling, non-recovery, turning effort, looseness, hard steering, overheating, fluid leakage, and fluid aeration problems; determine needed action.	P-1	28
2. Determine recommended type of power steering fluid; check level and condition; determine needed action.	P-1	28
3. Flush and refill power steering system; purge air from system.	P-2	28
4. Perform power steering system pressure, temperature, and flow tests; determine needed action.	P-3	28
5. Inspect, service, or replace power steering reservoir including filter, seals, and gaskets.	P-2	28
6. Inspect power steering pump drive gear and coupling; replace as needed.	P-3	28
7. Inspect, adjust, or replace power steering pump, mountings, and brackets.	P-3	28
8. Inspect and replace power steering system cooler, lines, hoses, clamps/mountings, hose routings, and fittings.	P-2	28
9. Inspect, adjust, repair, or replace integral type power steering gear(s) (single and/or dual) and mountings.	P-2	28
3. Steering Linkage		
1. Inspect and align pitman arm; replace as needed.	P-1	28
2. Check and adjust steering (wheel) stops; verify relief pressures.	P-1	28
3. Inspect and lubricate steering components.	P-1	28

Continued on next page

NATEF Task List	NATEF Priority Number	Chapter
B. Suspension Systems		
1. Inspect front axles and attaching hardware; determine needed action.	P-1	25
2. Inspect and service kingpins, steering knuckle bushings, locks, bearings, seals, and covers; determine needed action.	P-1	25
3. Inspect shock absorbers, bushings, brackets, and mounts; replace as needed.	P-1	27
4. Inspect leaf springs, center bolts, clips, pins and bushings, shackles, U-bolts, insulators, brackets, and mounts; determine needed action.	P-1	27
5. Inspect axle aligning devices such as radius rods, track bars, stabilizer bars, torque arms, related bushings, mounts, shims, and cams; determine needed action.	P-1	27
6. Inspect tandem suspension equalizer components; determine needed action.	P-3	27
7. Inspect and test air suspension pressure regulator and height control valves, lines, hoses, dump valves, and fittings; adjust, repair, or replace as needed.	P-1	27
8. Inspect air springs, mounting plates, springs, suspension arms, and bushings; replace as needed.	P-1	27
9. Measure and adjust ride height; determine needed action.	P-1	27
10. Identify rough ride problems; determine needed action.	P-3	27
C. Wheel Alignment Diagnosis, Adjustment, and Repair		
1. Identify causes of vehicle wandering, pulling, shimmy, hard steering, and off-center steering wheel problems; adjust or repair as needed.	P-1	25
2. Check camber; determine needed action.	P-2	25
3. Check caster; adjust as needed.	P-2	25
4. Check and adjust toe settings.	P-1	25
5. Check rear axle(s) alignment (thrustline/centerline) and tracking; adjust or repair as needed.	P-2	25
6. Identify turning/Ackermann angle (toe-out-on-turns) problems; determine needed action.	P-3	25
7. Check front axle alignment (centerline); adjust or repair as needed.	P-2	25
D. Wheels and Tires		
1. Identify tire wear patterns, check tread depth and pressure; determine needed action.	P-1	23
2. Identify wheel/tire vibration, shimmy, pounding, hop (tramp) problems; determine needed action.	P-2	23
3. Remove and install steering and drive axle wheel/tire assemblies; torque mounting hardware to specifications with a torque wrench.	P-1	23
4. Inspect tire for proper application (size, load range, position, and tread design); determine needed action.	P-2	23
5. Inspect wheel/rims for proper application, hand hold alignment, load range, size, and design; determine needed action.	P-2	24
6. Check operation of tire pressure monitoring system (TPMS); determine needed action if applicable.	P-3	23
E. Frame and Coupling Devices		
1. Inspect, service, and/or adjust fifth wheel, pivot pins, bushings, locking mechanisms, and mounting hardware.	P-1	34
2. Inspect and service sliding fifth wheel, tracks, stops, locking systems, air cylinders, springs, lines, hoses, and controls.	P-2	34
3. Inspect frame and frame members for cracks, breaks, corrosion, distortion, elongated holes, looseness, and damage; determine needed repairs.	P-1	26
4. Inspect, install, or repair frame hangers, brackets, and cross members in accordance with manufacturers' recommended procedures.	P-3	26
5. Inspect, repair, or replace pintle hooks and draw bars, if applicable.	P-2	34
V. ELECTRICAL/ELECTRONIC SYSTEMS		
A. General Electrical Systems		
1. Read and interpret electrical/electronic circuits using wiring diagrams.	P-1	16
2. Check continuity in electrical/electronic circuits using appropriate test equipment.	P-1	10
3. Check applied voltages, circuit voltages, and voltage drops in electrical/electronic circuits using appropriate test equipment.	P-1	10

Continued on next page

NATEF Task List	NATEF Priority Number	Chapter
4. Check current flow in electrical/electronic circuits and components using appropriate test equipment.	P-1	10
5. Check resistance in electrical/electronic circuits and components using appropriate test equipment.	P-1	10
6. Locate shorts, grounds, and opens in electrical/electronic circuits.	P-1	8
7. Identify parasitic (key-off) battery drain problems; perform tests; determine needed action.	P-1	13
8. Inspect and test fusible links, circuit breakers, relays, solenoids, and fuses; replace as needed.	P-1	8
9. Inspect and test spike suppression devices; replace as needed.	P-3	9
10. Check frequency and pulse width signal in electrical/electronic circuits using appropriate test equipment.	P-3	19
B. Battery		
1. Identify battery type; perform appropriate battery load test; determine needed action.	P-1	13
2. Determine battery state of charge using an open circuit voltage test.	P-1	13
3. Inspect, clean, and service battery; replace as needed.	P-1	13
4. Inspect and clean battery boxes, mounts, and hold downs; repair or replace as needed.	P-1	13
5. Charge battery using appropriate method for battery type.	P-1	13
6. Inspect, test, and clean battery cables and connectors; repair or replace as needed.	P-1	13
7. Jump start a vehicle using jumper cables and a booster battery or appropriate auxiliary power supply using proper safety procedures.	P-1	13
8. Perform battery capacitance test; determine needed action.	P-2	13
9. Identify and test low voltage disconnect (LVD) systems; determine needed repair.	P-2	13
C. Starting System		
1. Perform starter circuit cranking voltage and voltage drop tests; determine needed action.	P-1	14
2. Inspect and test components (key switch, push button, and/or magnetic switch) and wires and harnesses in the starter control circuit; replace as needed.	P-2	14
3. Inspect and test starter relays and solenoids/switches; replace as needed.	P-1	14
4. Remove and replace starter; inspect flywheel ring gear or flex plate.	P-1	14
D. Charging System Diagnosis and Repair		
1. Test instrument panel–mounted volt meters and/or indicator lamps; determine needed action.	P-1	15
2. Identify causes of no charge, low charge, or overcharge problems; determine needed action.	P-1	15
3. Inspect and replace alternator drive belts, pulleys, fans, tensioners, and mounting brackets; adjust drive belts and check alignment.	P-1	15
4. Perform charging system voltage and amperage output tests; perform AC ripple test; determine needed action.	P-1	15
5. Perform charging circuit voltage drop tests; determine needed action.	P-1	15
6. Remove and replace alternator.	P-1	15
7. Inspect, repair, or replace cables, wires, and connectors in the charging circuit.	P-1	15
E. Lighting Systems		
1. Interface with vehicle's on-board computer; perform diagnostic procedures using recommended electronic service tool(s) (including PC-based software and/or data scan tools); determine needed action.	P-1	17
2. Identify causes of brighter than normal, intermittent, dim, or no headlight and daytime running light (DRL) operation.	P-1	17
3. Test, aim, and replace headlights.	P-1	17
4. Test headlight and dimmer circuit switches, relays, wires, terminals, connectors, sockets, and control components/modules; repair or replace as needed.	P-1	17
5. Inspect and test switches, bulbs/LEDs, sockets, connectors, terminals, relays, wires, and control components/modules of parking, clearance, and taillight circuits; repair or replace as needed.	P-1	17
6. Inspect and test instrument panel light circuit switches, relays, bulbs/LEDs, sockets, connectors, terminals, wires, and printed circuits/control modules; repair or replace as needed.	P-2	17
7. Inspect and test interior cab light circuit switches, bulbs/LEDs, sockets, low voltage disconnect (LVD), connectors, terminals, wires, and control components/modules; repair or replace as needed.	P-2	17

Continued on next page

NATEF Task List	NATEF Priority Number	Chapter
8. Inspect and test tractor-to-trailer multi-wire connector(s); repair or replace as needed.	P-1	17
9. Inspect, test, and adjust stoplight circuit switches, bulbs/LEDs, sockets, connectors, terminals, wires, and control components/modules; repair or replace as needed.	P-1	17
10. Inspect and test turn signal and hazard circuit flasher(s), switches, relays, bulbs/LEDs, sockets, connectors, terminals, wires, and control components/modules; repair or replace as needed.	P-1	17
11. Inspect and test reverse lights and warning device circuit switches, bulbs/LEDs, sockets, horns, buzzers, connectors, terminals, wires, and control components/modules; repair or replace as needed.	P-1	17
F. Gauges and Warning Devices		
1. Interface with vehicle's on-board computer; perform diagnostic procedure, verify instrument cluster operations using recommended electronic service tool(s) (including PC-based software and/or data scan tools); determine needed action.	P-1	18
2. Identify causes of intermittent, high, low, or no gauge readings; determine needed action.	P-2	18
3. Identify causes of data bus-driven gauge malfunctions; determine needed action.	P-3	18
4. Inspect and test gauge circuit sensor/sending units, gauges, connectors, terminals, and wires; repair or replace as needed.	P-2	18
5. Inspect and test warning devices (lights and audible) circuit sensor/sending units, bulbs/LEDs, sockets, connectors, wires, and control components/modules; repair or replace as needed.	P-1	18
6. Inspect, test, replace, and calibrate (if applicable) electronic speedometer, odometer, and tachometer systems.	P-2	18
G. Related Electrical Systems		
1. Interface with vehicle's on-board computer; perform diagnostic procedures using recommended electronic service tool(s) (including PC-based software and/or data scan tools); determine needed action.	P-1	18
2. Identify causes of constant, intermittent, or no horn operation; determine needed action.	P-2	8–18†
3. Inspect and test horn circuit relays, horns, switches, connectors, wires, clock springs, and control components/modules; repair or replace as needed.	P-2	8–18†
4. Identify causes of constant, intermittent, or no wiper operation; diagnose the cause of wiper speed control and/or park problems; determine needed action.	P-2	8–18†
5. Inspect and test wiper motor, resistors, park switch, relays, switches, connectors, wires, and control components/modules; repair or replace as needed.	P-2	8–18†
6. Inspect wiper motor transmission linkage, arms, and blades; adjust or replace as needed.	P-2	8–18†
7. Inspect and test windshield washer motor or pump/relay assembly, switches, connectors, terminals, wires, and control components/modules; repair or replace as needed.	P-3	8–18†
8. Inspect and test side view mirror motors, heater circuit grids, relays, switches, connectors, terminals, wires, and control components/modules; repair or replace as needed.	P-3	8–18†
9. Inspect and test heater and A/C electrical components including: A/C clutches, motors, resistors, relays, switches, connectors, terminals, wires, and control components/modules; repair or replace as needed.	P-3	8–18†
10. Inspect and test auxiliary power outlet, integral fuse, connectors, terminals, wires, and control components/modules; repair or replace as needed.	P-3	8–18†
11. Identify the cause of slow, intermittent, or no power window operation; determine needed action.	P-3	8–18†
12. Inspect and test motors, switches, relays, connectors, terminals, wires, and control components/modules of power window circuits; repair or replace as needed.	P-3	8–18†
13. Inspect and test block heaters; determine needed repairs.	P-2	8–18†
14. Inspect and test cruise control electrical components; repair or replace as needed.	P-3	8–18†
15. Inspect and test switches, relays, controllers, actuator/solenoids, connectors, terminals, and wires of electric door lock circuits.	P-3	8–18†
16. Check operation of keyless and remote lock/unlock devices; determine needed action.	P-3	8–18†
17. Inspect and test engine cooling fan electrical control components/modules, wiring; repair or replace as needed.	P-2	8–18†
18. Identify causes of data bus communication problems; determine needed action.	P-2	8–18†

†All the necessary techniques and information to test and repair these components are covered between chapters 8 through 18.

Continued on next page

NATEF Task List	NATEF Priority Number	Chapter
VI. HEATING, VENTILATION, & AIR CONDITIONING		
A. HVAC Systems		
1. Verify the need for service or repair of HVAC systems based on unusual operating noises; determine needed action.	P-1	52
2. Verify the need for service or repair of HVAC systems based on unusual visual, smell, and touch conditions; determine needed action.	P-1	52
3. Identify system type and components (cycling clutch orifice tube—CCOT, expansion valve) and conduct performance test(s) on HVAC systems; determine needed action.	P-1	51
4. Retrieve diagnostic codes; determine needed action.	P-3	51
B. A/C System and Components		
1. A/C System—General		
1. Identify causes of temperature control problems in the A/C system; determine needed action.	P-1	52
2. Identify refrigerant and lubricant types; check for contamination; determine needed action.	P-1	52
3. Identify A/C system problems indicated by pressure gauge and temperature readings; determine needed action.	P-1	52
4. Identify A/C system problems indicated by visual, audible, smell, and touch procedures; determine needed action.	P-1	52
5. Perform A/C system leak test; determine needed action.	P-1	52
6. Recover, evacuate, and recharge A/C system using appropriate equipment.	P-1	52
7. Identify contamination in the A/C system components; determine needed action.	P-3	52
8. Interface with vehicle's on-board computer; perform diagnostic procedures using recommended electronic service tool(s) (including PC-based software and/or data scan tools); determine needed action.	P-2	52
2. Compressor and Clutch		
1. Identify A/C system problems that cause protection devices (pressure, thermal, and electronic) to interrupt system operation; determine needed action.	P-1	52
2. Inspect, test, and replace A/C system pressure, thermal, and electronic protection devices.	P-2	51
3. Inspect and replace A/C compressor drive belts, pulleys, and tensioners; adjust belt tension and check alignment.	P-1	52
4. Inspect, test, adjust, service, or replace A/C compressor clutch components or assembly.	P-2	52
5. Inspect and correct A/C compressor lubricant level (if applicable).	P-2	52
6. Inspect, test, or replace A/C compressor.	P-1	52
7. Inspect, repair, or replace A/C compressor mountings and hardware.	P-2	52
3. Evaporator, Condenser, and Related Components		
1. Correct system lubricant level when replacing the evaporator, condenser, receiver/dryer or accumulator/dryer, and hoses.	P-1	52
2. Inspect A/C system hoses, lines, filters, fittings, and seals; determine needed action.	P-1	52
3. Inspect and test A/C system condenser. Check for proper airflow and mountings; determine needed action.	P-1	52
4. Inspect and replace receiver/dryer or accumulator/dryer.	P-1	52
5. Inspect and test cab/sleeper refrigerant solenoid, expansion valve(s); check placement of thermal bulb (capillary tube); determine needed action.	P-3	52
6. Remove and replace orifice tube.	P-1	52
7. Inspect and test cab/sleeper evaporator core; determine needed action.	P-3	52
8. Inspect, clean, or repair evaporator housing and water drain; inspect and service/replace evaporator air filter.	P-1	52
9. Identify and inspect A/C system service ports (gauge connections); determine needed action.	P-1	52
10. Identify the cause of system failures resulting in refrigerant loss from the A/C system high pressure relief device; determine needed action.	P-2	52

Continued on next page

NATEF Task List	NATEF Priority Number	Chapter
C. Heating and Engine Cooling Systems		
1. Identify causes of outlet air temperature control problems in the HVAC system; determine needed action.	P-1	52
2. Identify window fogging problems; determine needed action.	P-2	51
3. Perform engine cooling system tests for leaks, protection level, contamination, coolant level, coolant type, temperature, and conditioner concentration; determine needed action.	P-1	51
4. Inspect engine cooling and heating system hoses, lines, and clamps; determine needed action.	P-1	51
5. Inspect and test radiator, pressure cap, and coolant recovery system (surge tank); determine needed action.	P-1	*
6. Inspect water pump; determine needed action.	P-1	*
7. Inspect and test thermostats, by-passes, housings, and seals; determine needed repairs.	P-2	*
8. Recover, flush, and refill with recommended coolant/additive package; bleed cooling system.	P-1	*
9. Inspect thermostatic cooling fan system (hydraulic, pneumatic, and electronic) and fan shroud; replace as needed.	P-2	51
10. Inspect and test heating system coolant control valve(s) and manual shut-off valves; determine needed action.	P-2	52
11. Inspect and flush heater core; determine needed action.	P-3	52
D. Operating Systems and Related Controls		
1. Electrical		
1. Identify causes of HVAC electrical control system problems; determine needed action.	P-1	52
2. Inspect and test HVAC blower motors, resistors, switches, relays, modules, wiring, and protection devices; determine needed action.	P-2	52
3. Inspect and test A/C compressor clutch relays, modules, wiring, sensors, switches, diodes, and protection devices; determine needed action.	P-2	52
4. Inspect and test A/C related electronic engine control systems; determine needed action.	P-2	52
5. Inspect and test engine cooling/condenser fan motors, relays, modules, switches, sensors, wiring, and protection devices; determine needed action.	P-2	51
6. Inspect and test electric actuator motors, relays/modules, switches, sensors, wiring, and protection devices; determine needed action.	P-2	51
7. Inspect and test HVAC system electrical/electronic control panel assemblies; determine needed action.	P-2	51
8. Interface with vehicle's on-board computer; perform diagnostic procedures using recommended electronic service tool(s) (including PC-based software and/or data scan tools); determine needed action.	P-2	52
2. Air/Mechanical		
1. Identify causes of HVAC air and mechanical control problems; determine needed action.	P-3	52
2. Inspect and test HVAC system air and mechanical control panel assemblies; determine needed action.	P-3	51
3. Inspect, test, and adjust HVAC system air and mechanical control cables and linkages; determine needed action.	P-3	51
4. Inspect and test HVAC system actuators and hoses; determine needed action.	P-3	52
5. Inspect, test, and adjust HVAC system ducts, doors, and outlets; determine needed action.	P-3	52
E. Refrigerant Recovery, Recycling, and Handling‡		
1. Maintain and verify correct operation of certified equipment.	P-1	52
2. Identify and recover A/C system refrigerant.	P-1	52
3. Recycle or properly dispose of refrigerant.	P-1	52
4. Handle, label, and store refrigerant.	P-1	52
5. Test recycled refrigerant for non-condensable gases.	P-1	52

*All NATEF tasks for this standard can be found in *Fundamentals of Medium/Heavy Duty Diesel Engines* (ISBN 978-1-2840-6705-7).
‡Tasks 1 through 5 should be accomplished in accordance with appropriate EPA regulations and SAE "J" standards.

Continued on next page

NATEF Task List	NATEF Priority Number	Chapter
VII. PREVENTIVE MAINTENANCE AND INSPECTION		
A. Engine System		
1. Engine		
1. Check engine starting/operation (including unusual noises, vibrations, exhaust smoke, etc.); record idle and governed rpm.	P-1	55
2. Inspect vibration damper.	P-1	55
3. Inspect belts, tensioners, and pulleys; check and adjust belt tension; check belt alignment.	P-1	55
4. Check engine oil level and condition; check dipstick seal.	P-1	55
5. Inspect engine mounts for looseness and deterioration.	P-1	55
6. Check engine for oil, coolant, air, fuel, and exhaust leaks (Engine Off and Running).	P-1	55
7. Check engine compartment wiring harnesses, connectors, and seals for damage and proper routing.	P-1	55
2. Fuel System		
1. Check fuel tanks, mountings, lines, caps, and vents.	P-1	55
2. Drain water from fuel system.	P-1	55
3. Service water separator/fuel heater; replace fuel filter(s); prime and bleed fuel system.	P-1	55
3. Air Induction and Exhaust System		
1. Check exhaust system mountings for looseness and damage.	P-1	55
2. Check engine exhaust system for leaks, proper routing, and damaged or missing components to include exhaust gas recirculation (EGR) system and after treatment devices, if equipped.	P-1	55
3. Check air induction system: piping, charge air cooler, hoses, clamps, and mountings; check for air restrictions and leaks.	P-1	55
4. Inspect turbocharger for leaks; check mountings and connections.	P-1	55
5. Check operation of engine compression/exhaust brake.	P-2	55
6. Service or replace air filter as needed; check and reset air filter restriction indicator.	P-1	55
7. Inspect and service crank case ventilation system.	P-1	*
8. Inspect diesel exhaust fluid (DEF) system, to include tanks, lines, gauge pump, and filter.	P-1	*
9. Inspect selective catalyst reduction (SCR) system; including diesel exhaust fluid (DEF) for proper levels, leaks, mounting, and connections.	P-2	*
4. Cooling System		
1. Check operation of fan clutch.	P-1	55
2. Inspect radiator (including air flow restriction, leaks, and damage) and mountings.	P-1	55
3. Inspect fan assembly and shroud.	P-1	55
4. Pressure test cooling system and radiator cap.	P-1	55
5. Inspect coolant hoses and clamps.	P-1	55
6. Inspect coolant recovery system.	P-1	55
7. Check coolant for contamination, additive package concentration, aeration, and protection level (freeze point).	P-1	55
8. Service coolant filter.	P-1	55
9. Inspect water pump.	P-1	*
5. Lubrication System		
1. Change engine oil and filters; visually check oil for coolant or fuel contamination; inspect and clean magnetic drain plugs.	P-1	55
2. Take an engine oil sample.	P-1	55
B. Cab and Hood		
1. Instruments and Controls		
1. Inspect key condition and operation of ignition switch.	P-1	55
2. Check warning indicators.	P-1	55
3. Check instruments; record oil pressure and system voltage.	P-1	55

*All NATEF tasks for this standard can be found in *Fundamentals of Medium/Heavy Duty Diesel Engines* (ISBN 978-1-2840-6705-7).

Continued on next page

NATEF Task List	NATEF Priority Number	Chapter
4. Check operation of electronic power take off (PTO) and engine idle speed controls (if applicable).	P-2	55
5. Check HVAC controls.	P-1	55
6. Check operation of all accessories.	P-1	55
7. Using electronic service tool(s) or on-board diagnostic system, retrieve engine monitoring information; check and record diagnostic codes and trip/operational data (including engine, transmission, ABS, and other systems).	P-1	55
2. Safety Equipment		
1. Check operation of electric/air horns and reverse warning devices.	P-1	55
2. Check condition of spare fuses, safety triangles, fire extinguisher, and all required decals.	P-1	55
3. Inspect seat belts and sleeper restraints.	P-1	55
4. Inspect wiper blades and arms.	P-1	55
3. Hardware		
1. Check operation of wiper and washer.	P-1	55
2. Inspect windshield glass for cracks or discoloration; check sun visor.	P-1	55
3. Check seat condition, operation, and mounting.	P-1	55
4. Check door glass and window operation.	P-1	55
5. Inspect steps and grab handles.	P-1	55
6. Inspect mirrors, mountings, brackets, and glass.	P-1	55
7. Record all observed physical damage.	P-2	55
8. Lubricate all cab and hood grease fittings.	P-2	55
9. Inspect and lubricate door and hood hinges, latches, strikers, lock cylinders, safety latches, linkages, and cables.	P-1	55
10. Inspect cab mountings, hinges, latches, linkages, and ride height; service as needed.	P-1	55
4. Heating, Ventilation, & Air Conditioning (HVAC)		
1. Inspect A/C condenser and lines for condition and visible leaks; check mountings.	P-2	55
2. Inspect A/C compressor and lines for condition and visible leaks; check mountings.	P-2	55
3. Check A/C system condition and operation; check A/C monitoring system, if applicable.	P-1	55
4. Check HVAC air inlet filters and ducts; service as needed.	P-1	55
C. Electrical/Electronics		
1. Battery and Starting Systems		
1. Inspect battery box(es), cover(s), and mountings.	P-1	55
2. Inspect battery hold-downs, connections, cables, and cable routing; service as needed.	P-1	55
3. Check/record battery state-of-charge (open circuit voltage) and condition.	P-1	55
4. Perform battery test (load and/or capacitance).	P-1	55
5. Inspect starter, mounting, and connections.	P-1	55
6. Engage starter; check for unusual noises, starter drag, and starting difficulty.	P-1	55
2. Charging System		
1. Inspect alternator, mountings, cable, wiring, and wiring routing; determine needed action.	P-1	55
2. Perform alternator output tests.	P-1	55
3. Lighting System		
1. Check operation of interior lights; determine needed action.	P-1	55
2. Check all exterior lights, lenses, reflectors, and conspicuity tape; check headlight alignment; determine needed action.	P-1	55
3. Inspect and test tractor-to-trailer multi-wire connector(s), cable(s), and holder(s); determine needed action.	P-1	55

Continued on next page

NATEF Task List	NATEF Priority Number	Chapter
D. Frame and Chassis		
1. Air Brakes		
1. Check operation of parking brake.	P-1	55
2. Record air governor cut-in and cut-out setting (psi).	P-1	55
3. Check operation of air reservoir/tank drain valves.	P-1	55
4. Check air system for leaks (brakes released).	P-1	55
5. Check air system for leaks (brakes applied).	P-1	55
6. Test one-way and double-check valves.	P-1	55
7. Check low air pressure warning devices.	P-1	55
8. Check emergency (spring) brake control/modulator valve, if applicable.	P-1	55
9. Check tractor protection valve.	P-1	55
10. Test air pressure build-up time.	P-1	55
11. Inspect coupling air lines, holders, and gladhands.	P-1	55
12. Check brake chambers and air lines for secure mounting and damage.	P-1	55
13. Check operation of air dryer.	P-1	55
14. Inspect and record brake shoe/pad condition, thickness, and contamination.	P-1	55
15. Inspect and record condition of brake drums/rotors.	P-1	55
16. Check anti-lock brake system wiring, connectors, seals, and harnesses for damage and proper routing.	P-1	55
17. Check operation and adjustment of brake automatic slack adjusters (ASA); check and record push rod stroke.	P-1	55
18. Lubricate all brake component grease fittings.	P-1	55
19. Check condition and operation of hand brake (trailer) control valve, if applicable.	P-2	55
20. Perform anti-lock brake system (ABS) operational system self-test.	P-1	55
21. Drain air tanks and check for contamination.	P-1	55
22. Check condition of pressure relief (safety) valves.	P-1	55
2. Hydraulic Brakes		
1. Check master cylinder fluid level and condition.	P-1	55
2. Inspect brake lines, fittings, flexible hoses, and valves for leaks and damage.	P-1	55
3. Check parking brake operation; inspect parking brake application and holding devices; adjust as needed.	P-1	55
4. Check operation of hydraulic system: pedal travel, pedal effort, pedal feel.	P-1	55
5. Inspect calipers for leakage, binding, and damage.	P-1	55
6. Inspect brake assist system (booster), hoses, and control valves; check reservoir fluid level and condition.	P-1	55
7. Inspect and record brake lining/pad condition, thickness, and contamination.	P-1	55
8. Inspect and record condition of brake rotors.	P-1	55
9. Check anti-lock brake system wiring, connectors, seals, and harnesses for damage and proper routing.	P-1	55
3. Drive Train		
1. Check operation of clutch, clutch brake, and gearshift.	P-1	55
2. Check clutch linkage/cable for looseness or binding, if applicable.	P-1	55
3. Check hydraulic clutch slave and master cylinders, lines, fittings, and hoses, if applicable.	P-1	55
4. Check clutch adjustment; adjust as needed.	P-1	55
5. Check transmission case, seals, filter, hoses, lines, and cooler for cracks and leaks.	P-1	55
6. Inspect transmission breather.	P-1	55
7. Inspect transmission mounts.	P-1	55
8. Check transmission oil level, type, and condition.	P-1	55

Continued on next page

NATEF Task List	NATEF Priority Number	Chapter
9. Inspect U-joints, yokes, driveshafts, boots/seals, center bearings, and mounting hardware for looseness, damage, and proper phasing.	P-1	55
10. Inspect axle housing(s) for cracks and leaks.	P-1	55
11. Inspect axle breather(s).	P-1	55
12. Lubricate all drive train grease fittings.	P-1	55
13. Check drive axle(s) oil level, type, and condition.	P-1	55
14. Change drive axle(s) oil and filter/screen, if applicable; check and clean magnetic plugs.	P-2	55
15. Check transmission wiring, connectors, seals, and harnesses for damage and proper routing.	P-1	55
16. Change transmission oil and filter, if applicable; check and clean magnetic plugs.	P-2	55
17. Check interaxle differential lock operation.	P-1	55
18. Check transmission range shift operation.	P-1	55
4. Suspension and Steering Systems		
1. Check steering wheel operation for free play or binding.	P-1	55
2. Check power steering pump, mounting, and hoses for leaks, condition, and routing; check fluid level.	P-1	55
3. Change power steering fluid and filter.	P-1	55
4. Inspect steering gear for leaks and secure mounting.	P-1	55
5. Inspect steering shaft U-joints, pinch bolts, splines, pitman arm-to-steering sector shaft, tie rod ends, and linkages.	P-1	55
6. Check kingpins for wear.	P-1	55
7. Check wheel bearings for looseness and noise.	P-1	55
8. Check oil level and condition in all non-drive hubs; check for leaks.	P-1	55
9. Inspect springs, pins, hangers, shackles, spring U-bolts, and insulators.	P-1	55
10. Inspect shock absorbers for leaks and secure mounting.	P-1	55
11. Inspect air suspension springs, mounts, hoses, valves, linkage, and fittings for leaks and damage.	P-1	55
12. Check and record suspension ride height.	P-1	55
13. Lubricate all suspension and steering grease fittings.	P-1	55
14. Check axle locating components (radius, torque, and/or track rods).	P-1	55
5. Tires and Wheels		
1. Inspect tires for wear patterns and proper mounting.	P-1	55
2. Inspect tires for cuts, cracks, bulges, and sidewall damage.	P-1	55
3. Inspect valve caps and stems; determine needed action.	P-1	55
4. Measure and record tread depth; probe for imbedded debris.	P-1	55
5. Check and record air pressure; adjust air pressure in accordance with manufacturers' specifications.	P-1	55
6. Check wheel mounting hardware condition; determine needed action.	P-1	55
7. Inspect wheels for cracks, damage, and proper hand hold alignment.	P-1	55
8. Check tire matching (diameter and tread) on single and dual tire applications.	P-1	55
6. Frame and Fifth Wheel		
1. Inspect fifth wheel mounting, bolts, air lines, and locks.	P-1	55
2. Test operation of fifth wheel locking device; adjust if necessary.	P-1	55
3. Check quarter fenders, mud flaps, and brackets.	P-1	55
4. Check pintle hook assembly and mounting, if applicable.	P-2	55
5. Lubricate all fifth wheel grease fittings and plate, if applicable.	P-1	55
6. Inspect frame and frame members for cracks and damage.	P-1	55

Continued on next page

NATEF Task List	NATEF Priority Number	Chapter
VIII. HYDRAULICS		
A. General System Operation		
1. Identify system type (closed and open) and verify proper operation.	P-1	54
2. Read and interpret system diagrams and schematics.	P-1	54
3. Perform system temperature, pressure, flow, and cycle time tests; determine needed action.	P-1	54
4. Verify placement of equipment /component safety labels and placards; determine needed action.	P-1	54
B. Pumps		
1. Identify system fluid type.	P-1	54
2. Identify causes of pump failure, unusual pump noises, temperature, flow, and leakage problems; determine needed action.	P-1	54
3. Determine pump type, rotation, and drive system.	P-1	54
4. Remove and install pump; prime and/or bleed system.	P-2	54
5. Inspect pump inlet for restrictions and leaks; determine needed action.	P-2	54
6. Inspect pump outlet for restrictions and leaks; determine needed action.	P-2	54
C. Filtration/Reservoirs (Tanks)		
1. Identify type of filtration system; verify filter application and flow direction.	P-1	54
2. Service filters and breathers.	P-1	54
3. Identify causes of system contamination; determine needed action.	P-2	54
4. Take a hydraulic oil sample for analysis.	P-1	54
5. Check reservoir fluid level and condition; determine needed action.	P-1	54
6. Inspect and repair or replace reservoir, sight glass, vents, caps, mounts, valves, screens, and supply and return lines.	P-1	54
D. Hoses, Fittings, and Connections		
1. Diagnose causes of component leakage, damage, and restriction; determine needed action.	P-2	54
2. Inspect hoses and connections (length, size, routing, bend radii, and protection); repair or replace as needed.	P-1	54
3. Assemble hoses, tubes, connectors, and fittings in accordance with manufacturers' specifications; use proper procedures to avoid contamination.	P-1	54
4. Inspect and replace fitting seals and sealants.	P-1	54
E. Control Valves		
1. Pressure test system safety relief valve; determine needed action.	P-1	54
2. Perform control valve operating pressure and flow tests; determine needed action.	P-1	54
3. Inspect, test, and adjust valve controls (electrical/electronic, mechanical, and pneumatic).	P-1	54
4. Identify causes of control valve leakage problems (internal/external); determine needed action.	P-1	54
5. Inspect pilot control valve linkages, cables, and PTO controls; adjust, repair, or replace as needed.	P-1	54
F. Actuators		
1. Identify actuator type (single/double acting, multi-stage/telescopic, and motors).	P-1	54
2. Identify the cause of seal failure; determine needed repairs.	P-1	54
3. Identify the cause of incorrect actuator movement and leakage (internal and external); determine needed repairs.	P-1	54
4. Inspect actuator mounting, frame components, and hardware for looseness, cracks, and damage; determine needed action.	P-1	54
5. Remove, repair, and/or replace actuators in accordance with manufacturers' recommended procedures.	P-1	54
6. Inspect actuators for dents, cracks, damage, and leakage; determine needed action.	P-1	54
7. Purge and/or bleed system in accordance with manufacturers' recommended procedures.	P-1	54

GLOSSARY

A-, B-, or C-train A three-unit combination of tractor plus two trailers.

absorbed glass mat (AGM) battery A type of lead acid battery that uses a thin fiberglass plate to absorb the electrolyte; prevents the solution from sloshing or separating into layers of heavier acid and water.

abuse failure Failure directly attributed to driver or other person's actions.

AC ripple A pattern produced by voltage fluctuations from the alternator that create differences between the peak voltage of an AC sine wave and the minimum voltage found in the trough between sine waves.

AC traction generator (ACTG) A device that converts mechanical energy produced by the engine into electrical current for the propulsion system.

AC traction motor (ACTM) A motor that functions as an electrical generator in a hybrid drive system.

accumulator A device placed between the evaporator and the compressor to collect liquid refrigerant and prevent it from entering the compressor.

Ackermann angle The angle the steering arms make with the steering axis, projected toward the center of the rear axle. Also called *toe-out on turns*.

Ackermann principle The geometric alignment of linkages in a vehicle's steering such that the wheels on the inside of a turn are able to move in a different circle radius than the wheels on the outside.

active fault A fault that is currently taking place and uninterrupted in action.

active sensor A sensor that uses a current supplied by the ECM to operate.

AC-to-DC inverter A device that switches the polarity of an AC current signal to resemble the straight wave polarity of DC current.

adaptive control A feature that senses topography and vehicle load and adjusts shift control to obtain maximum economy and comfort.

adaptive cruise control (ACC) A specialized cruise mode that enables the vehicle to recognize potential collisions with vehicles or objects it is following and reduce the vehicle speed.

adaptive learning Software than can learn and change strategy based on different factors.

addendum The top, thinner part of an involute tooth contact area.

adjusting ring A large threaded ring in the clutch cover of a pull-type clutch used to adjust the clutch internally.

adsorbtion A process in which material collects on the surface and the air dryer adsorbs moisture from the air and then discharges it in the purge cycle.

aeration Air in the fluid.

air bag The spring component of an air spring suspension; a tough rubber bag filled with air. Also called *air spring* and *bellows*.

air drill A compressed air-powered drill.

Air Dryer Integrated System (AD-IS) An air supply system component that contains an air dryer and several pressure protection valves to regulate charging of the air reservoirs.

air filter/pressure regulator The Fuller air filter/pressure regulator cleans the pressurized air supply going to the transmission and regulates it to 58 to 63 psi (400 to 434 kPa).

air hammer A tool powered by compressed air with various hammer, cutting, punching, or chisel attachments. Also called an *air chisel*.

air nozzle A compressed-air device that emits a fine stream of compressed air for drying or cleaning parts.

air ratchet A ratchet tool for use with sockets powered by compressed air.

air spring The spring component of an air spring suspension; a tough rubber bag filled with air. Also called *bellows* or *air bag*.

air-conditioning compressor clutch An engagement device connected to the compressor crankshaft to engage the crankshaft with a belt-driven pulley.

air-conditioning machine A machine designed to recover, recycle, evacuate, leak test, and recharge (R/R/R) the air-conditioning system.

air-control solenoid valve An electric-over-air solenoid used to control shifting by controlling the flow of air from the air filter to the range cylinder piston.

air-impact wrench An impact tool powered by compressed air designed to undo tight fasteners.

air-over-hydraulic braking system A braking system that uses an air compressor to provide power assistance over the hydraulic components to the braking system.

AL factor The size or surface area of a brake chamber multiplied by the length of the slack adjuster in inches.

alkalis Chemical compounds that have a pH value greater than 7. They are commonly used in toy batteries and bleaches.

Allen head screw Sometimes called a cap screw, it has a hexagonal recess in the head which fits an Allen key. This type of screw usually anchors components in a predrilled hole.

Allen wrench A type of hexagonal drive mechanism for fasteners.

Allison DOC PC-based service software for Allison's EP system.

Allison Transmission Electronic Control (ATEC) The original version of Allison's electronic control systems which evolved into Commercial Electronic Control (CEC).

alternating current (AC) A type of current flow that continuously changes direction and polarity.

alternator ripple The top of the waveform.

aluminum alloy Aluminum mixed with other metals to increase its strength.

amboid gear A bevel gear arrangement with the pinion gear mounted above the centerline of the crown gear.

ammonia sensor A sensor used in selective catalyst reduction (SCR) that provides data to the ECM that is used to determine if ammonia values are out of anticipated range.

amperage The measurement of the quantity of electrons in electric current movement.

ampere (amp) The unit for measuring the quantity of electron flow past one point in a circuit per unit of time.

amp-hour A measure of how much amperage a battery can continually supply over a 20-hour period without the battery voltage falling below 10.5 volts.

analog meter A meter that uses a sweeping needle that continuously measures electrical values.

analog signal An electric current that is proportional to a continuously changing variable.

analog to digital conversion The process when an analog waveform is sampled and measured many times a second to generate a digital representation of the waveform.

anemometer A device that measures airflow in feet per minute (fpm).

angle grinder A portable grinder for grinding or cutting metal.

angle spring clutch A clutch manufactured by Eaton/ Spicer corporation that uses three pairs of angled springs pushing against a lever to supply the clamp load.

angular Consisting of, or forming, an angle.

anisotropic An object that has unequal physical properties along its various axes. Used in head gaskets to pull heat laterally from the edge surrounding the combustion chamber to the water jacket.

anti-compounding valve An air control system design feature that prevents simultaneous application of the service and spring brakes.

anti-drain-back check valves These valves try to keep the torque converter full of fluid when the vehicle is shut off.

anti-fade An opposite condition of heat fade where the coefficient of friction increases as the brakes get hotter.

anti-lock braking system (ABS) An electronic control system that works with the service brake system to monitor and automatically limit wheel lock-up events during vehicle braking.

anti-rattle springs Flat springs used to stop the intermediate plate from rattling on a 14" (36.6 cm) double-disc clutch with a pot-style flywheel.

anti-seize compound Neutralizes a chemical reaction that can prevent threads and fasteners from sticking together and freeze spark plugs in place in aluminium cylinder blocks.

APADS/air-conditioning protection unit (ACPU) An electronic microcontroller-based device that operates both air-conditioning controls and diagnostic systems.

application chart A chart showing which power train control devices are used for a particular power flow.

applied stroke measurement The pushrod stroke length with a 90 psi (621 kPa) service brake application.

arbitration The process of deciding which messages have priority to transmit over the network to prevent data collision between positive and negative signals canceling one another.

armature The only rotating component of the starter; has three main components: the shaft, windings, and the commutator.

articulation The movement of the suspension system in reaction to road bumps or terrain.

aspect ratio The ratio of sidewall height to section width of a tire.

AS-Tronic ZF's AMT for medium - and -heavy duty trucks and buses.

asynchronous motor A motor in which the magnetic field in the rotor is induced by induction of the magnetic field in the stationary stator.

A-train A combination vehicle in which the second trailer is a full trailer unit connected by a draw bar to a single hitch point on the lead (first) trailer.

A-type lock A single swinging lock jaw and plunger for simple operation.

automated manual transmission (AMT) A standard manual transmission operated by electronic control.

automatic disengagement lockout (ADLO) A device that prevents the starter motor from operating if the engine is running.

automatic drain valve A drain valve located on the bottom of the air system reservoirs that automatically drains any accumulations of water or oil whenever the air reservoir cycles.

Automatic Gear Shift (AGS) One of Mercedes' AMTs for lighter-duty trucks.

automatic slack adjusters (ASAs) Automatically adjust brake stroke to maintain the correct shoe-to-drum clearance.

automatic slip regulation (ASR) A traction control system that minimizes wheel spin.

automatic traction control (ATC) A traction control system that minimizes wheel slip or spin due to excessive drive torque. Also called *electronic stability regulation (ESR)*.

auto-ranging multimeter A multimeter that has fewer positions on its range selection knob and will automatically select the correct range when meter test leads are connected to a circuit.

AutoSelect Eaton's first AMT; very limited electronic control.

AutoShift Eaton's first shift by wire transmission.

auxiliary section A section bolted to the main transmission with 2, 3, or 4 ratios to multiply the ratios available to the driver.

auxiliary spring A second leaf spring in a leaf spring suspension that does not take any of the weight until the vehicle is close to fully loaded.

aviation snips A scissor-like tool for cutting sheet metal.

axial thrust Thrust that tries to move the gears apart along their axis.

axle The shaft of the suspension system to which the tires and wheels are attached; used to transmit driving torque to the wheels.

axle parallelism When the rear wheels of a vehicle follow the front wheels in a parallel manner.

axle perpendicularity When the axles are square with the vehicle frame.

axle setback The difference in distance between any axle end and the perpendicular centerline. Also called *setback* or *skew*.

axle spread The distance between the centerline of two axles.

axle stop A rubber (usually) bumper that stops the axle from contacting the vehicle frame during severe suspension articulation. Also called *jounce block*.

back taper The tapered profile of the teeth on a sliding clutch such that the outer edge is thicker than the inner; the profile helps keep the clutch engaged under load.

backing plate A metal plate to which the brake lining is fixed.

backlash The clearance between teeth in mesh with each other.

balancers A device designed to adjust battery voltage to compensate for unequal charges in multiple batteries. Also called *battery equalizers*.

ball hitch Trailer hitching device that consist of a tongue-type tow bar that loops over a ball.

ball hitch A single point connection configuration for a hitch that uses a tongue shaped draw bar, which loops over a ball connected to the tow vehicle.

ball-nut rack A metal block with a threaded hole that is part of the recirculating-ball steering system.

ball-peen (engineer's hammer) A hammer that has a head that is rounded on one end and flat on the other; designed to work with metal items.

banjo A drive axle housing with a removable carrier. Also called a *removable carrier type*.

barrier cream A cream that looks and feels like a moisturizing cream but has a specific formula to provide extra protection from chemicals and oils.

battery A device that converts and stores electrical energy through chemical reactions.

battery charger A device that charges a battery, reversing the discharge process.

battery equalizers A device designed to adjust battery voltage to compensate for unequal charges in multiple batteries. Also called *balancers*.

battery isolator systems A system designed to separate the main starting battery and the auxiliary battery. Also called a *split charge relay*.

battery management system (BMS) A system of electrical devices used to manage battery performance.

baud rate The rate at which serial data is transmitted.

beach mark Semi-circular mark in a fracture indicating repeated overload.

bead breaker A tool used to break the tire bead seal from the rim.

bead seat The edge of the rim that creates a seal between the tire bead and the wheel.

bearing adjuster Threaded wheel used to tighten the side bearing races.

bearing adjuster lock Lock to secure the bearing adjusters.

bearing growth The increase in bearing size as it is pressed on to a shaft.

bearing preload The load applied to a bearing before any vehicle weight or rolling loads are applied.

bellcrank A shaft used in a mechanical linkage with a pivot in the center that reverses the normal direction of motion.

bellows The spring component of an air spring suspension; a tough rubber bag filled with air. Also called *air spring* and *air bag*.

belt routing label A label that lists a diagram of the serpentine belt routing for the engine accessories.

bench grinder (pedestal grinder) A grinder that is fixed to a bench or pedestal.

bench vice A device that securely holds material in jaws while it is being worked on.

bevel gear Gear cut on an angle allowing a power flow to turn a corner.

bevel gears Gears that intersect at an angle—usually 90 degrees.

biased torque differential A differential capable of sending more torque to one wheel than the other when a wheel slip condition is encountered. Also known as a *proportional differential*.

bias-ply tire A tire constructed in a latticed, criss-crossing structure, with alternate plies crossing over each other and laid with the cord angles in opposite directions.

bidirectional communication Two-way multiplex communication.

bimetallic gauge A gauge in which two dissimilar pieces of metal are bonded together and expand at different rates when heated, thereby converting the heating effect of electricity into mechanical movement.

biodiesel A renewable fuel made by chemically combining natural oils from soybeans (or cottonseeds, canola, etc.; animal fats; or even recycled cooking oil) with an alcohol such as methanol (or ethanol).

bipolar transistor A transistor that combines either two P or N materials with a single P or N-type material forming PNP or NPN transistors.

bit The smallest piece of digital information that is either a 1 or 0.

bladder An inflatable bag, or sack, that contains fluids or gas.

blind rivet A rivet that can be installed from its insertion side.

blink code A method of providing fault code data for a specific system that involves counting the number of flashes from a warning lamp and observing longer pauses between the light blinks. Also called *flash code*.

blocking ring A synchronizer part that increases or decreases a gear's speed to match shaft speed, so that the synchronizer sleeve can lock the gear to the shaft.

Bluetooth A short-range wireless technology that can automatically connect a device into a network.

bobtailing A tractor traveling without a trailer.

bobtailing proportioning relay (BPR) valve A specialized relay valve used to reduce delivery pressure to the rear brakes of a tractor when no trailer is towed.

bolt A type of threaded fastener with a thread on one end and a hexagonal head on the other.

bolt cutters Strong cutters available in different sizes, designed to cut through non-hardened bolts and other small-stock material.

bolt pattern The number and spacing of the wheel nuts or wheel studs on the wheel hub on the wheel rim.

bore The inside diameter of a tube.

bottoming tap A thread-cutting tap designed to cut threads to the bottom of a blind hole.

bow A type of frame damage characterized by the upward bending of the frame rails that can be caused by uneven loading of the frame. The opposite of sag.

brake balance The ability of the braking system to apply the correct amount of braking torque to each wheel end at the correct time.

brake band A friction faced metal band that surrounds a planetary component; when applied hydraulically, it holds the component stationary.

brake block Brake friction material that is 0.75 inch (19 mm) thick.

brake drum A short, wide, hollow cylinder that is capped on one end and bolted to a vehicle's wheel; it has an inner friction surface that the brake shoe is forced against.

brake fade The inability of the brakes to maintain its effectiveness.

brake fluid Hydraulic fluid that transfers forces under pressure through the hydraulic lines to the wheel braking units.

brake foundations The braking components found at the wheel ends.

brake lag The time delay between driver brake pedal application and brake actuation due to the slower speed of air pressure transmission through air lines and valves.

brake lines Made of seamless, double-walled steel, and able to transmit more than 6,895 kPa of hydraulic pressure through the hydraulic brake system.

brake lining Brake friction material that is 0.5 inch (13 mm) thick.

brake pull (brake steer) An unintended left or right direction change by a vehicle during a brake application.

brake shoes A steel shoe and brake lining friction material that apply force to the brake drum during braking.

brake stroke length The distance travelled by the brake chamber pushrod.

brake timing imbalance A situation in which some brakes receive air faster than others.

brake torque The force applied to the foundation brakes during braking.

break torque The unloading of the driveline to allow a shift to occur.

Bridge Formula B See Federal Bridge Gross Weight Formula.

British thermal unit (Btu) The amount of energy required to heat or cool one pound of water 1°F.

broken back arrangement A method of angle cancellation in which the U-joint angles will intersect at a point exactly at the middle of the shaft length. Also known as an *intersecting angle arrangement*.

B-train A combination vehicle in which the tractor pulls a semi-trailer and a third, full trailer behind the semi-trailer.

B-type lock A mechanism that uses two swinging jaws and a yoke to lock the jaws securely around the kingpin.

bump steer The undesired condition produced when hitting a bump where the vehicle darts to one side as the steering linkage is pushed or pulled as a result of the travel of the suspension. The steering wheel may also be violently forced from the drivers grip during severe bump steer.

byte A unit of 8 bits.

cab forward (CF) A tractor with the engine located ahead of the cab.

cab harness The harness that connects the shift selector to the electronic control unit.

cab over engine (COE) A tractor with the engine located beneath the cab.

caliper A hydraulic device that uses pressure from the master cylinder to apply the brake pads against the rotor.

calorie The unit of energy that reflects the amount of energy required to raise the temperature of 1 gram of water by 1°C.

cam brakes Brakes that use an "S" shaped cam that twists between two rollers to expand a set of brake shoes.

camber The side-to-side vertical tilt of the wheel. It is viewed from the front of the vehicle and measured in degrees. See also negative camber and positive camber.

cam-opposite A situation when the cam rotates the opposite direction of the drum's rotation to energize the brakes.

cam-over conditions When the linings and or brake camshafts are worn enough to allow the cam to rotate past the rollers.

cam-same A situation when the cam rotates the same direction as the drum's rotation to energize the brakes.

cancellation The act of cancelling the non-uniform velocity in a driveshaft.

capacitance touch screen A display screen that uses two transparent plates, one of which is electrically charged.

capacitor A circuit-control device made up of two plates separated by an insulating material.

carbon dioxide One of the resulting gases produced when burning a hydrocarbon fuel; thought to contribute to global warming.

Cardan joint A joint with four trunnions and four bearing caps. Also known as a *Hooke joint* or a *universal joint*.

cast drums Brake drums made from cast iron.

cast ductile iron Cast iron that is ductile (bendable) not brittle.

cast spoke wheel A type of heavy-duty commercial wheel that uses three, five, or six cast-iron spokes integrated with a bearing hub.

castellated nut A nut with slots, similar to towers on a castle, that is used with split pins; it is used primarily to secure wheel bearings.

caster The angle formed through the wheel pivot points when viewed from the side in comparison to a vertical line through the wheel.

caster adjusting shim An angular shim used at the front leaf spring mount to roll the I-beam axle forward or back to set the caster angle.

caster shimmy The small, rapid, side-to-side movement of the steering wheel resulting from excess positive caster.

cavitation The formation of air bubbles in the transmission fluid as a result of low pressure at the pump inlet.

C-channel C-shaped steel beam that is the most common frame rail in heavy trucks.

C-clamp A clamp shaped like the letter C; it comes in various sizes and can clamp various items.

center bearing A bearing pressed on to a machined surface after the splined area of a driveshaft's slip yoke spline; used to support a multiple piece driveshaft. Also called a *hanger bearing*.

centrifugal force Apparent force by which a rotating mass tries to move outward away from its axis of rotation.

centrifugal switch A switch that is only activated when centrifugal forces are placed on a vehicle.

centrifuge drums Brake drums made with a cast iron core surrounded by a steel band.

ceramic friction facings Friction facings made mostly of man-made materials specifically designed to produce desirable characteristics.

chafing Wear or abrasion due to prolonged or constant friction.

charge The amount of refrigerant present in the system or the process of installing refrigerant in the system.

charge-depleting operating mode (CD) A mode of operation in which the vehicle is powered only—or almost only—by the energy stored in the battery.

charge-sustaining mode (CS) A mode of operation in which the batteries' state of charge (SOC) may rise and fall slightly and energy storage modules are kept at a 40% state of charge.

chassis dynamometer A machine with rollers that allows a vehicle to attain road speed and load while sitting still in the shop.

chassis wiring harness The wiring that connects the transmission, the TPS, and the variable speed sensor to the transmission electronic control unit.

chemical compound Helps prevent fasteners from loosening; it is applied to one thread, then the other fastener is screwed onto it. This creates a strong bond between them, but one that stays plastic, so they can be separated by a wrench.

chemical fade A type of brake fade that takes place when steam or gases from vaporized lining materials form between hot lining and the drum reducing the coefficient of friction.

chlorofluorocarbons (CFCs) A chlorine-based composition of a fluorine hydrocarbon compound.

chrome A bright, shiny corrosion-resistant metal; it is mostly used for decorative purposes, such as on hubcaps.

chuff test A test performed on the antilock braking systems that results in air pressure being exhausted from the modulator and making a short chuffing sound.

circuit (wire) tracer An electronic service tool used to trace a single wire over a distance where multiple wires are bundled, shorted, or open.

circuit breaker A device that trips and opens a circuit, preventing excessive current flow in a circuit. It is resettable to allow for reuse.

clamp force The force squeezing the clutch disc between the pressure plate and the flywheel. Also called *load*.

cleaning gun A device with a nozzle controlled by a trigger fitted to the outlet of pressure cleaners.

clearance sensing ASA A type of automatic slack adjuster that reduces pushrod travel based on torque input to the ASA.

clock spring A special rotary electrical connector located between the steering wheel and the steering column that maintains a constant electrical connection with the wiring system while the vehicle's steering wheel is being turned.

clockwise The clockwise direction of rotation of a gear as you look at it corresponding to the motion of the clock; also known as *forward*.

closed-end wrench A wrench with a closed or ring end to grip bolts and nuts.

closed-loop control The time during a shift in progress on a World Transmission that the transmission ECU is actively adjusting on-coming clutch application pressure using pulse-width modulation to control shift quality.

club hammer The club hammer is like a small mallet, with two square faces made of high-carbon steel. It is the heaviest type of hammer that can be used one-handed.

clutch alignment tool A tool that holds the clutch discs in alignment as the clutch is installed and without which it is impossible to slide the transmission input shaft through the new clutch discs.

clutch bell housing The housing surrounding the clutch that bolts to the flywheel housing.

clutch bell housing pilot A small protrusion on the front of the clutch bell housing that fits into a mating recess in the flywheel housing.

clutch brake A small frictional brake usually mounted on the transmission input shaft; clutch brakes are designed to slow down or stop the inertia of the transmission gearing so shifts into first or reverse can be made without clashing.

clutch brake actuation The point of clutch pedal actuation on a pull-type clutch when the clutch brake is being actuated or squeezed. Also called *squeeze*.

clutch capacity The amount of torque the clutch can safely handle without slipping.

clutch chatter The condition of the clutch alternately engaging and slipping quite rapidly when the driver engages the clutch.

clutch cover The outside part of the clutch that is bolted to the flywheel and which holds all of the clutch components except the clutch disc. Mistakenly, but commonly, called the pressure plate.

clutch jack A tool with a clutch alignment tool that fits into the clutch, used to carry the weight of the clutch for installation or removal.

clutch linkage The mechanical connection between the drivers clutch pedal and the clutch cross shaft.

coefficient of friction (CoF) The amount of friction between two particular objects in contact; calculated by dividing the force required to move the object by the weight of the object.

coil spring A helical metal spring.

coil spring style clutch A clutch that uses coils springs mounted perpendicular to the pressure plate to provide the clamp load.

cold cranking amps (CCA) A measurement of the load, in amps, that a battery can deliver for 30 seconds while maintaining a voltage of 1.2 volts per cell (7.2 volts for a 12-volt battery) or higher at 0°F (–18°C).

cold curing A retreading process that uses a molded, pre-cured tread strip or tread ring which is glued to the casing.

cold operation inhibit Restriction on transmission operation when the temperature is too cold for the transmission fluid to do its job.

collar shift transmission A transmission that uses sliding clutches or sliding collars to select gear ratios.

collision avoidance system A vehicle stability control system that detects objects beside and in front of a vehicle that have the potential to collide with the vehicle.

combination (series-parallel) circuit A circuit that uses elements both of series and parallel circuits.

combination pliers A type of pliers for cutting, gripping, and bending.

combination valve A valve that combines either all or some of the following into one housing—the proportioning valve, the metering valve, and the pressure differential valve.

combination vehicles Two or more combined or coupled vehicle units.

combination wrench A type of wrench that has an open end on one end and a closed-end wrench on the other.

combo stud A mounting stud attached to an air spring that also receives the fitting to fill the spring with air.

Commercial Electronic Control (CEC) The second iteration of Allison's electronically controlled transmission.

Commercial Vehicle Safety Alliance (CVSA) A nonprofit organization dedicated to improve the safe operation of commercial vehicles in North America by establishing a uniform, reciprocal enforcement of commercial vehicle safety standards.

companion flange A splined flange attached to a vehicle component, such as a drive axle pinion shaft, that bolts to a flange yoke on a driveshaft.

complicated fracture A fracture in which the bone has penetrated a vital organ.

compound planetary gear set Planetary gear power flow that utilizes more than one gear set to produce the ratios.

compound ratio Any gear ratio that involves more than one pair of gears.

compound shift A shift where two parts of the transmission are being shifted at once.

compound split operation Blending torque from the motors and engine together.

compression A force that pushes down on the top flange of a frame rail between two support points and which tends to squeeze the flange of the frame rail together.

condensation Moisture that collects on cooler surfaces as a result of hot vapors coming into contact with the cooler surface.

condenser A component of the HVAC system that transfers heat from the system to the atmosphere.

conductance test A type of battery test that determines the battery's ability to conduct current.

conduction The transfer of heat through a solid item, such as a body panel or evaporator.

conductor A material that easily allows electricity to flow through it. It is made up of atoms with very few outer shell electrons, which are loosely held by the nucleus.

connecting drum A device used by Allison to connect some of the planetary gear components.

constant mesh transmission A transmission in which the main and countershaft gears are always in mesh.

constant velocity joint A joint that delivers a uniform speed to the driven shaft.

constant-current charger A battery charger that automatically varies the voltage applied to the battery to maintain a constant amperage flow into the battery.

constant-ratio steering gears Steering gears that use sector shafts with teeth of equal lengths.

constant-voltage charger A direct current (DC) power that is a step-down transformer with a rectifier to provide the DC voltage to charge.

contact patch The area of the tire that is in actual contact with the road.

contact pattern The contact area between two gear teeth in contact.

control valve body The heart of the hydraulic control; it holds the spool valve responsible for shifting.

controlled area networks (CAN) A distributed network control system in which no single central control module is used.

controlled traction differential A differential that will allow the engine to build more torque before the wheels can slip.

convection The transfer of heat through a gas.

conventional current theory The theory that the direction of current flow is positive to negative.

conventional steering system A steering system with a solid axle and a single steering gear.

converter dolly A single or set of dual axle that supports a fifth wheel. Converter dollies convert semi-trailers into full trailers.

convoluted air spring An air spring with a top and bottom mounting plate and one, two, or three girdle hoops. The girdle hoops add lateral stability to the spring.

coolant A fluid that contains special anti-freezing and anti-corrosion chemicals mixed with water.

coolant label A label that lists the type of coolant installed in the cooling system.

copper A non-ferrous, pure metal that can be alloyed (combined) with other metals but is not combined with iron.

counterclockwise The counter-clockwise direction of rotation of a gear as you look at it corresponding to the motion of the clock; also known as *backward*.

counter-electromotive force (CEMF) An electromagnetic force produced by the spinning magnetic field of the armature, which induces current in the opposite direction of battery current through the motor.

countershaft The shaft inside a transmission driven by the input gear.

counts The unit that Allison uses to describe throttle position based on the variable voltage signal from a TPS, Throttle Position Sensor.

coupler Trailer hitching device, similar to pintle hooks, but in which the towing horn pivots and is not fixed.

coupling phase A torque converter operating phase when the turbine and the impeller are at close to the same speed.

coupling shaft A short shaft usually at the front of a drive line. Also known as a *jack shaft*.

crack pressure The air signal pressure required to begin delivery of air pressure from a relay valve.

crank axle A dead axle in which the main beam is lower than the wheel spindles.

cranking amps (CA) A measurement of the load, in amps, that a battery can deliver for 30 seconds while maintaining a voltage of 1.2 volts per cell (7.2 volts for a 12-volt battery) or higher at 32°F (–0°C).

crankshaft A vehicle engine component that transfers the reciprocating movement of pistons into rotary motion.

crimp Join two pieces of material by folding and pinching together.

critical speed The rotational speed at which a driveshaft starts to bow off its center line due to centrifugal force, leading to vibration and shaft failure.

cross members Cross beams that join the two frame rails together to form a ladder type frame.

cross-arm A description for an arm that is set at right angles or 90 degrees to another component.

cross-cut chisel A type of chisel for metal work that cleans out or cuts key ways.

cross-phasing When a coupling shaft is phased at 90 degrees to the second driveshaft.

cross-shaft A rotating shaft that holds the clutch release fork.

crown gear A large bevel gear that is driven by a smaller pinion gear in the bevel gear set. Also known as a *ring gear*.

CSA 2010 basic score Calculated ratings on compliance, safety, and accountability initiated by the Federal Motor Carrier Safety Administration (FMCSA).

C-train A combination vehicle similar to an A-train but using a dolly that has two parallel drawbars.

current clamp A device that claps around a conductor to measure current flow. It is often used in conjunction with a digital volt-ohm meter (DVOM).

current track Another name for a DIN diagram.

curved file A type of file that has a curved surface for filing holes.

cycling clutch orifice tube (CCOT) A fixed-orifice tube with pressure control obtained by cycling the compressor clutch on and off.

cylinder An actuator that converts hydraulic power into linear mechanical force. Also known as *ram*.

D capacity The maximum horizontal pulling force that can be safely applied to the fifth wheel. Also called *draw bar capacity*.

D'Arsonval gauge A type of electromagnetic gauge that moves a pointing needle directly proportional to current flow through an electromagnet attached to the pointer.

dampening disc A disc with a ring of torsional dampening springs around its hub designed to absorb engine torsional vibrations.

data bus The typology forming the communication pathway of modules in a network.

data bus driven gauges The function of the gauge is the same as for the computer-driven gauge, based on data bus messages from the PCM.

data link adapter A device used to translate serial data from the DLC into a format readable by a desktop or laptop computer.

daytime running lights (DRL) Lights designed to improve vehicle visibility in the daytime.

DC-to-AC inverter A device that takes the straight, unchanging wave of DC current and flips, or inverts, the current's polarity to resemble an AC wave signal.

dead axle An axle that supports vehicle weight only.

dead-blow hammer A type of hammer that has a cushioned head to reduce the amount of head bounce.

dedendum The lower, thicker, part of an involute tooth contact area.

deep cycle battery A battery used to deliver a lower, steady level of power for a much longer time.

defrost cycle A situation in which the evaporator releases heat instead of absorbing it, and the condenser absorbs heat instead of transferring it.

defroster A heated component that operates to clear the windows.

Delta windings Stator windings in which the windings are connected in the shape of a triangle.

demountable rim A type of wheel rim that can be removed from the cast-iron spoke hub attached to the axle. Also called an *open-center rim*.

depth micrometers A micrometer that measures the depth of an item such as how far a piston is below the surface of the block.

de-rate Reducing drive torque by reducing engine power; used as strategy to reduce wheel slip, or loss of directional control.

desiccant Silica beads used in the air dryer to trap and hold moisture and oil until the dryer is purged.

detent balls Spring-loaded steel balls that hold the shift rails in position.

Deutsch connector A compact, environmentally sealed electrical connector that uses solid, round metal pins and hollow female sockets.

Deutsche Institute Norm (DIN) diagram A schematic wiring diagram on which symbols, terminal connection numbers, line symbols, and operational status of items such as switches and relays are defined by a DIN standard. Also called *current track*.

diagnostic data link (DDL) connector The location on the vehicle where the technician can plug in diagnostic software.

diagnostic link connector (DLC) The connection point for electronic service tools used to access fault code and other information provided by chassis electronic control modules.

diagnostic trouble code (DTC) A code logged by the electronic control module when electrical faults or system problems occur in commercial vehicle control systems.

diagonal-cutting pliers Cutting pliers for small wire or cable.

dial bore gauge A gauge that is used to measure the inside diameter of bores with a high degree of accuracy and speed.

dial indicators A dial that can also be known as a dial gauge, and as the name suggests, has a dial and needle where measurements are read.

diamond A type of frame damage characterized by one frame rail moving forward or backward in relation to the other.

diaphragm A flexible partition separating two cavities.

diaphragm spring clutch A clutch that uses a single diaphragm spring, also known as a *Belleville spring*, to provide the clamping force.

die A device used to cut threads on a bolt or shaft.

die stock handle A handle for securely holding dies to cut threads.

differential braking Applying the brakes on an individual slipping wheel to transfer torque to a stationary or slowly turning wheel with traction.

differential case The housing that holds the differential gears.

differential cross The mechanism that holds the differential pinion or spider gears. Also known as the *differential spider*.

differential gear A gear arrangement that splits the available torque equally between two wheels while allowing them to turn at different speeds when required.

differential gear set Consists of two side gears, four pinion gears, and a cross; allows for speed difference between the two axle shafts of the drive axle when turning.

differential lock A device that prevents differential action by locking one side gear to the differential case.

differential mode transmission A situation in which network modules detect the voltage difference between two wires to determine if a signal is a 1 or a 0.

differential pinion gear A beveled gear that is a component of the differential gear set; it is fitted to the four legs of the differential cross and rotates with it. Also known as a *spider gear*.

differential spider The mechanism that holds the differential pinion or spider gears. Also known as the *differential cross*.

differential voltage Refers to the voltage difference on a wire pair when one wires voltage is the mirror opposite voltage. A wide separation between the voltage pulses represents a 1 and a narrow separation represents a 0.

digital multimeter A type of multimeter that provides numerical displays of electrical data.

digital signals Electrical signals that represent data in discrete, finite values. Digital signals are considered as binary meaning it is either on or off, yes or no, high or low, 0 or 1.

DIP switches A small slide switch located at the rear of the speedometer head placed in either an on or off (1 or 0) position.

direct current (DC) Movement of current that flows in one direction only.

direct drive A starter motor drive system in which the motor armature directly engages the flywheel through a pinion gear.

direct tire pressure monitoring system (direct TPMS) A type of automated tire pressure monitoring system that measures tire pressure and possibly temperature via a sensor installed inside each wheel.

directional stability control systems A stability control system that assists the driver in maintaining a vehicle's intended driving path by controlling yaw.

disc wheel A steel or aluminum wheel rim that supports a tire and attaches to the hub using wheel studs and nuts.

dislocation The displacement of a joint from its nor- mal position; it is caused by an external force stretching the ligaments beyond their elastic limit.

displacement The volume of fluid that is moved by the pump in one complete revolution.

DIWATM A dedicated bus transmission from Voith.

double check valves A brake valve with two air inlets and one air outlet. Only the higher inlet pressure will leave the single valve outlet.

double clutch A technique drivers use to synchronize gear and shaft speed.

double flare A seal that is made at the end of metal tubing or pipe.

double reduction drive axle A drive axle that uses two gear reductions at all times.

double-insulated Tools or appliances that are designed in such a way that no single failure can result in a dangerous voltage coming into contact with the outer casing of the device.

dowel pins Used to keep components in place where shearing forces are high, such as valve plates on high-pressure pumps.

drag link A connecting linkage that transfers movement of the pitman arm to the upper steering arm.

draw bars Bars used to connect tow vehicles to a tractor or lead towing unit.

draw bar capacity The maximum horizontal pulling force that can be safely applied to the fifth wheel. Also called *"D" capacity*.

drift punch A type of punch used to start pushing roll pins to prevent them from spreading.

drill chuck A device for securely gripping drill bits in a drill.

drill press A device that incorporates a fixed drill with multiple speeds and an adjustable worktable. It can be free-standing or fixed to a bench.

drill vice A tool with jaws that can be attached to a drill press table for holding material that is to be drilled.

drivability items Warning lights such as misfires, rough idle, and check engine.

drive axle The axle that drives the vehicle by turning the power from the driveshaft 90 degrees to deliver it to the wheels and providing the final gear reduction in the drive train. Also known as a *live axle*.

drive axle carrier The component that holds the support bearings for the drive axle gearing.

drive line A series of driveshafts, yokes, and support bearings used to connect a transmission to the rear axle.

drive line angularity Refers to the angles at the universal joints.

drive pin Pin used in a pot-type flywheel to drive the intermediate plate.

drive pins Vertical pins that attach to the frame of a rubber spring equalizing beam suspension. The drive pins pass through the rubber spring elements and locate and align the spring saddles while the suspension articulates.

drive pulley Any belt-driven pulley used to power an accessory such as power steering or the air-conditioning compressor.

Driver Post-Operation Vehicle Inspection Report (DVIR) In the United States, FMCSA legislation requires drivers to prepare a report in writing at the completion of each day's work for each commercial vehicle the driver has operated that day. Specifics of the legislation are contained in FMCVS 49.396.11.

drop arm An arm that transfers the steering box output shaft motion to the steering linkage by converting rotational movement into liner motion. Also called a *pitman arm*.

drop center tubular axle A dead axle used on trailer that drops in the middle.

dropbox A component that is bolted to the back of the transmission and connects the front and rear axles via the driveshaft; allows the output of a transmission to flow to both the rear and the front axles. Also called *transfer case*.

drop-center wheel rim A type of wheel rim that fits over the brake drum and is concave.

dryer integrated module (DRM) An AD-IS type dryer with the addition of an air reservoir used to assist purging of the spin-on dryer desiccant cartridge.

DT-12 A twelve-speed AMT manufactured by Detroit Diesel.

dual circuit integrity test A test performed to verify the functioning of the automatic emergency brake system.

dual mass flywheel A flywheel with two sections separated by torsional springs; one section attaches to the engine crankshaft and the clutch cover is bolted to the other section.

dual power inverter module (DPIM) The module responsible for converting energy from the ESS into AC currents used to power the EZV drive motors.

dual-circuit system A split between the air brake circuits on commercial vehicles for safety purposes. A failure in one circuit does not affect the operation of the second air brake circuit.

dual-clutch transmission A transmission with two separate input shafts controlled by two separate clutches.

dual-mode hybrid drive train A hybrid system that combines both mechanical and electrical propulsion systems.

dump valve A driver operated air valve to release the air from an air suspension system while at the loading dock.

duplex gauge Two air gauges in a single housing.

durapoid gearing A specially designed spiral bevel gear set designed to provide increased strength and load carrying capability.

duty cycle The percentage of time a PWM signal is ON in comparison to OFF time.

ear protection Protective gear worn when the sound levels exceed 85 decibels, when working around operating machinery for any period of time, or when the equipment you are using produces loud noise.

edge code A code representing the CoF of a brake and its composition.

e-fuse A software-controlled fuse that uses field effect transistors for the circuit control device. Also called *virtual fuses*.

elasticity The amount of stretch or give a material has.

electric shift assembly The shift actuation system for an Eaton AutoShift or UltraShift transmission that contains two shift motors, the shift finger, and the shift finger position sensors.

electric vehicle (EV) A vehicle in which only electric motors are used to move a vehicle.

electrical capacity The amount of electrical current a lead-acid battery can supply.

electrical resistance A material's property that reduces voltage and amperage in an electrical current.

electrically erasable read only memory (EEPROM) Non-volatile memory technology that is used to store operating instructions or programming for an ECM.

electro-hydraulic control (electro-hydraulic valve body) The valve body used to control electronically controlled transmissions and consisting of solenoids, spool valves, and, usually, pressure switches.

electrolysis The use of electricity to break down water into hydrogen and oxygen gases.

electrolyte An electrically conductive solution.

electromagnet A conductor wound in a coil that produces a magnetic field when current flows through it.

electromagnetic induction The production of an electrical current in a conductor when it moves through a magnetic field or a magnetic field moves past it.

electron theory of current movement The movement of negatively charged electrons to a positive charge.

Electronic Air Control (EAC) A controlled area network (CAN)-operated air supply system that regulates the air compressor load and unload cycle, plus additional optional air supply system components.

electronic cooling package (ECP) A system of fans and electronic controls that maintains a hybrid ESS within a set temperature range.

electronic stability regulation (ESR) A vehicle control system that minimizes the likelihood of a rollover, loss of vehicle direction, and wheel slip. Also called *automatic traction control (ATC)*.

electronic wear indicators Devices that measure brake pad wear electronically and send signals directly to the driver.

electrostatic theory The idea that like charges repel one another and unlike electrical charges attract.

emergency brake circuit The air circuit responsible for the application and release of power springs in the brake chambers. Also referred to as the spring brake circuit or park brake circuit.

end yoke A splined yoke attached to a component such as a transmission output shaft.

energy storage system (ESS) A system that stores and distributes electrical current to the various components of a hybrid drive system.

engine hoist A small crane used to lift engines.

Engine Synchro Shift (ESS) Meritor's first AMT; limited to synchronizing engine speeds to assist the shifting process.

engine-driven hydraulic pump A power steering pumpdriven by a belt or gear driven by the engine.

Environmental Protection Agency (EPA) Federal government agency that deals with issues related to environmental safety.

EP40/50 System Models of Allison's Electric Propulsion system. Also known as *Allison's Electrically Variable (EV) Drive*.

epicyclical gear Gears that revolve around a common centerline.

equalizer The support for a tandem drive axle, using a standard leaf spring suspension system; it supports the rear of the front spring and the front of the rear spring.

equalizing beam A beam with each end attached to the axles of a tandem axle arrangement and its center attached to the frame directly or through a spring system. The beam reduces the impact of road bumps to the frame by 50% and equalizes the load carried by each of the axles. Also called a *walking beam*.

equalizing beam suspensions Used on tandem suspension systems; two large equalizing beams between the two axles equalize the load between the four wheels.

equalizing bracket A bracket connecting the rear of the front leaf spring to the front of the rear leaf spring on a tandem axle suspension; used to equalize the loading of each axle during suspension articulation.

ethylene glycol A chemical that resists freezing but is very toxic to people and animals.

evaporator The cold surface of the air-conditioning system that absorbs heat from a cab or vehicle interior and transfers that heat to the atmosphere through a condenser.

evaporator freezing A condition in which excess refrigerant floods the evaporator.

external bleeding The loss of blood from an external wound; blood can be seen escaping.

extreme pressure (EP) additive Additives usually found in hypoid gear lube and which should not be used in Fuller Roadranger transmissions and most heavy-duty transmissions because it tends to oxidize at relatively low temperatures.

failsafe operation The minimal transmission function that occurs when electrical power is lost.

false brinelling A condition where lubricant is squeezed out from between the needles and the trunnions of a U-joint leading to wear; caused by too small or no angle at the joint so lubricant is not distributed.

fast adaptive A type of adaptive control used when the transmission is new and makes large changes to bring the shift close to the optimal shift profile quickly.

fast chargers A type of battery charger that charges batteries quickly.

fasteners Devices that securely hold items together, such as screws, cotter pins, rivets, and bolts.

fatigue failure Failure of components due to repeated overload.

fault mode identifier (FMI) The type of failure detected in the SPN, PID, or SID.

feather key Used to prevent the free rotation of gears or pulleys on a shaft; usually attached to levers that have to slide along a shaft to allow engagement of a part. The connection is a positive fitting and serves to transmit torques and revs, for example, on the driveshaft of a belt pulley.

Federal Bridge Formula See Federal Bridge Gross Weight Formula

Federal Bridge Gross Weight Formula Laws that limit the weight-to-length ratio of heavy trucks with the goal of protecting roads and bridges from the damage caused by the concentrated weight of shorter trucks. Also known as *Bridge Formula B* or *Federal Bridge Formula*.

Federal Motor Carrier Safety Administration (FMCSA) All companies that operate commercial vehicles within the United States to move freight, passengers, or transport any cargo interstate, must be registered with the FMCSA.

Federal Motor Carrier Safety Regulation (FMCSR) Regulations issued by the Federal Motor Carrier Safety Administration (FMCSA), published in the U.S. Federal Register, and compiled in the U.S. Code of Federal Regulations (CFR).

Federal Motor Vehicle Safety Standard 121 (FMVSS 121) The legislated performance standard for air brake systems on commercial vehicles.

feedback A sensed output parameter that is compared to the input command.

feeler gauges Flat metal strips used to measure the width of gaps, such as the clearance between valves and rocker arms. Also called *feeler blades*.

ferrous metals Metals that use iron as an alloying agent. Cast iron, steel, and stainless steel are the main categories of iron alloys used in the automotive industry.

field effect transistor (FET) A unipolar transistor that uses an electric field to control the conductivity of a semiconductor material.

fifth wheel A plate-type coupling device designed to support the weight of a semi-trailer.

fillet radius The radius shape between the bottoms of two teeth. Also called *root*.

finished rivet A rivet after the completion of the riveting process.

fire rings Steel rings integrated into the cylinder head gasket nearest the combustion chambers that provide extra sealing to seal in the high combustion pressures.

first aid The immediate care given to an injured or suddenly ill person.

first-degree burns Burns that show reddening of the skin and damage to the outer layer of skin only.

fishplate Flat plate used to re-enforce the frame rail or a plate bolted to the frame rail web to attach components to the frame.

fishtailing A condition when the drive axles of a vehicle push the rear of a vehicle and steering control is lost. Also called *power jackknifing*.

flange The flat surface at the top and bottom of a frame rail.

flange case half The half of the differential case that the crown gear attaches to.

flange yoke A yoke with two ears to hold a U-joint and a flat flange to bolt to a companion flange.

flare-nut wrench A type of closed-end wrench that has a slot in the box section to allow the wrench to slip through a tube or pipe. Also called a *flare tubing wrench*.

flash code A strategy used by ECUs to report fault codes by flashing or blinking fault lamps, using long and short pauses between the light flashes to represent numerical fault codes. Also called *blink code*.

flashback arrestor A spring-loaded valve installed on oxyacetylene torches as a safety device to prevent flame from entering the torch hoses.

flashing Reprogramming or recalibrating the ECM. Information is stored in the ECMs memory.

flat washers Spread the load of bolt heads or nuts as they are tightened and distribute it over a greater area. They are particularly useful in protecting aluminum alloy.

flat-nosed pliers Pliers that are flat and square at the end of the nose.

flat-tip screwdriver A type of screwdriver that fits a straight slot in screws.

flat-type flywheel A flywheel that is predominately flat, with all of its components inside the cover; the clutch cover bolts to it.

flex plate A flexible plate used to connect the torque converter to the engine.

flitch plates Angle iron that is attached to the fifth wheel on one side and is bolted to the frame on another side.

floatation tire Large tire with a low aspect ratio. Also called *wide-base tire*.

floating caliper A disc brake caliper that floats on two pins.

flooded lead-acid battery A lead–acid battery in which the plates are immersed in a water–acid electrolyte solution.

flow How much fluid is being moved in relation to the work that is being done.

flow-control valve A valve used in power steering pumps to regulate the volume of fluid flow out of the power steering pump.

fluid analysis Chemical analysis of the transmission fluid revealing contaminant levels.

fluid coupling A power transfer device that uses fluid to transmit power to the driveline.

fluid head In fluid dynamics, head is the concept that relates the energy in an incompressible fluid to the height of an equivalent static column of that fluid. In the case of a hydraulic pump, because the tank is above the pump and the fluid will run to the pump inlet by gravity, the height of the tank equals the fluid head.

fluorescent bulb A light bulb that uses electrically heated filaments located at each end of a tube filled with a small amount of mercury or a noble gas, such as neon, argon, or xenon.

flywheel A heavy round metal disc attached to the end of the crankshaft to smooth out vibrations from the crankshaft assembly and provide one of the friction surfaces for a clutch disc used on manual transmission/transaxle applications.

flywheel friction surface The flat friction surface of the flywheel face.

flywheel housing The round housing bolted to the rear of the engine to which the clutch bell housing is bolted.

flywheel housing face The part of the flywheel housing that mates to the clutch bell housing.

flywheel housing pilot A small recess in the flywheel housing that receives the clutch bell housing pilot.

foot valve The center of the brake delivery system. Also called the *treadle valve*.

forcing screw The center screw on a gear, bearing, or pulley puller. Also called a *jacking screw*.

forward bias A situation in which a diode conducts current.

forward clutch A clutch that is applied in all forward gears or ranges; it is not found on overdrive transmissions.

frame angle The angle the vehicle's frame makes with regard to horizontal measurement to the ground. See also positive frame angle and negative frame angle.

frame centerline alignment An alignment method that uses the vehicle frame and not its axles as the reference point for making alignment adjustments.

frame rail web The upright section of the frame rail. Also called *web*.

free play Clearance between two components

free stroke measurement The brake pushrod stroke length using a lever to move the slack adjuster.

Freedomline Twelve- and sixteen-speed ZF AMTs released in partnership with Meritor

Freon A refrigerant produced by reacting carbon tetrachloride, commonly used as "carb-cleaner," with fluorine gas.

frequency The number of events or cycles that occur in a period, usually 1 second.

frequency-sensing relay A relay connected to the alternator that detects alternating current only when the alternator is charging.

friction The relative resistance to motion between any two bodies in contact with one another.

friction dampening Controlling torsional vibration by using friction material in between the various plates in a clutch friction disc.

friction modifier Additive in transmission fluid designed to enhance the friction characteristics of certain clutch materials.

friction plates Steel plates faced with friction material and used in a hydraulic clutch. They are splined to a planetary gear set component.

front/rear split system A brake system in which the front brakes operate on one hydraulic circuit and the rear brakes from the other.

fuel (gasoline, diesel) A derivative of crude oil.

fuel cell An electrochemical device that combines hydrogen and oxygen to produce electricity and water.

full fielding Making the alternator produce maximum amperage output.

full floating axle shaft An axle that carries none of the vehicle weight.

full floating bearings The wheel bearings are supported entirely by the axle housing.

full throttle downshift A downshift forced by the driver by pushing on the throttle. Also called *detent downshift* or *kick down* depending on the manufacturer.

full trailer A trailer that is supported at both ends with an axle and does not rest on a fifth wheel.

full-box rail A box-shaped frame rail.

fully oscillating fifth wheel A type of fifth wheel designed to provide front-to-rear and side-to-side movement between the tractor and semi-trailer.

galvanic corrosion Corrosion of the material caused by the electrolytic effect that can occur when two dissimilar metals are in contact.

galvanic reaction A chemical reaction that produces electricity when two dissimilar metals are placed in an electrolyte.

galvanized Coated with zinc, for rust protection.

garter spring A metal spring wrapped circularly around the inside of a lip seal to keep it in constant contact with the moving shaft.

gas pocket Imperfection in the adhesion of molten metal during the casting or forming process.

gas welding goggles Protective gear designed for gas welding; they provide protection against foreign particles entering the eye and are tinted to reduce the glare of the welding flame.

gasket scraper A broad, sharp, flat blade to assist in removing gaskets and glue.

gateway module A module that translates communication between different networks operating using different protocols or speeds.

gear jamming An attempt by the driver to shift without using the clutch; usually causes at least some damage to the transmission sliding clutches. Also called *float shifting*.

gear pullers A tool with two or more legs and a cross-bar with a center forcing screw to remove gears.

gear pump A pump consisting of an internal and external toothed gear.

gear ratio The relationship between two gears in mesh as a comparison to input versus output.

gear reduction Any gear set that reduces output speed while at the same time increases output torque. Also known as *underdrive ratio*.

gear set contact pattern The indication as to where the gears will contact each other during operation.

gear slip out The condition in which a transmission jumps out of gear and to neutral when under load, caused by worn components such as sliding clutches and shift forks. Also called *jump out*.

gel cell battery A type of battery to which silica has been added to the electrolyte solution to turn the solution to a gel-like consistency.

generoid An asymmetrical tooth design similar to the durapoid; it gives added strength to the hypoid and amboid gear sets. Also called *hypoid generoid*.

geometric centerline alignment An alignment method that establishes a vehicle's centerline by placing a line from the midpoint of the front axle and the midpoint of the rear-most axle.

gerotor pump A pump consisting of a rotor turning inside a matching chamber.

Gibb-head key Used to prevent the free rotation of gears or pulleys on a shaft; designed to be pulled out easily and are used when a gear or a pulley has to be attached to a shaft.

gimbals Two or more concentric circles used to support an item; while the circles can move, the supported object will remain stationary.

gladhands The air couplers attached to the trailer hoses connecting the tractor and trailer air systems.

glazing On brake linings, a cause of brake fade characterized by a hard glassy burnt appearance to the lining surface diminishing its coefficient of friction.

glazing On brake drums, a mirror-like finish produced through continuous braking pressure and pressure between lining and brake drums.

global warming potential (GWP) A measure of a refrigerant's contribution to global warming over 100 years for a given mass compared to the same mass of carbon dioxide.

governor An air control valve that regulates the air system cut-in and cut-out pressure. The governor also controls the purging of the air dryer.

governor cut-in pressure The pressure at which the governor loads the compressor.

governor cut-out pressure The pressure at which the governor unloads the compressor.

governor valve A valve that creates a pressure based on road speed.

gradability The capability of a vehicle to maintain forward motion on a specified grade while sustaining a minimum speed.

graphing meter An electrical test instrument used to analyze waveforms and graphically plot an electrical value of a signal over time.

grinding wheels and discs Abrasive wheels or flat discs fitted to bench, pedestal, and portable grinders.

gross combined vehicle weight (GCWR) A specific maximum weight limit determined by the vehicle manufacturer and which takes into account two individual (yet attached) vehicles—the tow vehicle, or tractor, and the trailer.

gross combined weight rating (GCWR) A specific maximum weight limit determined by the vehicle manufacturer.

gross trailer weight (GTW) The maximum carrying capacity of a trailer calculated by measuring the trailer weight and load.

gross vehicle weight (GVW) The maximum design weight of a vehicle including a full tank of fuel, fully loaded to its capacity, and with all passengers.

gross vehicle weight rating (GVWR) The design rating specified by a manufacturer as the recommended maximum weight of a vehicle when fully loaded to capacity, including all passengers and a full tank of fuel.

gross weight limit The maximum legal weight of a vehicle that can travel on roads and bridges.

ground The return path for electrical current in a vehicle chassis, other metal of the vehicle, or dedicated wire.

ground shaft A stationary shaft that holds the inner hub of the stator one-way clutch. Also called *stator support shaft*.

grounded circuit A circuit characterized by an unwanted low resistance connection between battery positive power and chassis ground.

guide studs Long threaded studs that stop a component from falling while the attaching bolts are removed.

Hall effect sensor A sensor commonly used to measure the rotational speed of a shaft; they have the advantage of producing a digital signal square waveform and have strong signal strength at low shaft rotational speeds.

halogen bulb A light bulb produced by adding small quantities of gases from the halogen family, such as iodine or bromine.

halogen infrared discharge (HID) bulb A light bulb that has a special coating on an inside portion of the bulb wall which reflects infrared heat back onto the filament, causing it to burn hotter.

hanger bearing A bearing pressed on to a machined surface after the splined area of a driveshaft's slip yoke spline; used to support a multiple piece driveshaft. Also called a *center bearing*.

hardening A manufacturing process that makes the surface of a gear much harder than its core: typically, the surface is hardened to a depth of not more than 0.050" (1.2 mm).

harmonic vibration An inherent vibration that occurs at precisely 50% of a shaft's critical speed.

hazard Anything that could hurt you or someone else.

hazardous environment A place where hazards exist.

hazardous material Any material that poses an unreasonable risk of damage or injury to persons, property, or the environment if it is not properly controlled during handling, storage, manufacture, processing, packaging, use and disposal, or transportation.

headgear Protective gear that includes items like hairnets, caps, or hard hats.

heat buildup A dangerous condition that occurs when the glove can no longer absorb or reflect heat and heat is transferred to the inside of the glove.

heat fade The loss or reduction in the coefficient of friction as the brake temperature increases.

heater core An in-cab heat exchanger that regulates heating by circulating engine coolant.

heating ventilation and air-conditioning (HVAC) system The system in the vehicle responsible for heating and cooling the air.

heat-treated alloy steel Highly engineered steel with a yield strength of at least 110,000 psi (758 MPa).

heel The end of a crown gear tooth furthest from the center of its axis.

height-control valve An air valve that maintains air spring suspension ride height.

helical double reduction drive axle A double reduction drive axle that uses a helical gear set for the second gear reduction.

helical double reduction two-speed drive axle A double reduction drive axle that uses two selectable sets of helical gears as the second gear reduction.

helical drop gear The set of gears that drive the pinion gear of the front drive axle of a tandem.

helical gear A gear with teeth cut on an angle or spirally to its axis of rotation.

herringbone gear A gear cut with opposite helices on each side of the face.

Hertz (Hz) The unit for electrical frequency measurement, in cycles per second.

high resistance Describes a circuit or components with more resistance than designed.

high-carbon steel Steel alloyed with carbon at levels of 0.9–2.5%.

high-impedance multimeter A meter that samples very little of a circuit's own current to take a measurement.

high-intensity discharge (HID) lamps Lamps that use an electric arc to produce higher light outputs of between 2,800 and 3,800 lumens.

high-voltage interlock loop (HVIL) A device that prevents access to potentially hazardous energized electrical circuits.

historical fault A fault that took place at one time but that is now corrected and no longer active.

hold regulator valve A spool valve that creates a pressure used to prevent upshifts.

hollow punch A punch with a center hollow for cutting circles in thin materials such as gaskets.

Hooke joint A joint with four trunnions and four bearing caps. Also known as a *Cardan joint* or a *universal joint*.

Hooke's law A law of physics that states that force delivered by a spring to an object is directly related to its compression or extension; the greater the spring is compressed, the more force the spring delivers.

horsepower A unit of measure of power that conveys how fast the engine can turn while producing torque.

hose Flexible line used to direct liquids or gases.

hot curing A retreading process in which the casing is covered with uncured rubber and then placed in a mold and heated. Also called *mold curing*.

housing An enclosed case for a mechanism.

hub-piloted disc wheel A type of disc wheel that uses a series of machined pads on the hub to help center the wheel.

Huck® fastener A riveted connection with ridges instead of threads and with the nut swaged onto the bolt, preventing the collar from being tightened after the fastener is installed.

hybrid electric vehicle (HEV) A type of vehicle that combines an internal combustion engine with an electric propulsion system into a new or hybrid powertrain configuration.

HybriDrive Propulsion System A series-type hybrid propulsion system developed by BAE, an aerospace and defense technology company.

hydraulic accumulator A device that stores hydraulic energy and acts as an emergency power source in the event of system pump failure.

hydraulic circuit A pathway connecting one part of the transmission's hydraulic control with another part.

hydraulic clutch A hydraulically actuated power train control device that squeezes friction and reaction plates together to either drive (input) or hold a planetary gear component stationary.

hydraulic cylinder or ram A device that uses hydraulic fluid pressure and convert it to Linear mechanical movement.

hydraulic hoist A type of hoist that the vehicle is driven onto that uses two long, narrow platforms to lift the vehicle.

hydraulic jack A type of vehicle jack that uses oil under pressure to lift vehicles.

hydraulic launch assist (HLA) An alternative to electric hybrid drives in which application of standard friction service brakes is prevented until just before a complete vehicle stop.

hydraulic retarder Retarder systems that pump transmission fluid between a turning cupped rotor and stationary cupped housing, thereby creating fluid pressure and fluid friction that slow the vehicle.

hydrometer An instrument used to measure the specific gravity of liquids.

hygroscopic When brake fluid absorbs water from the atmosphere.

hypoid gearing A type of spiral bevel gear set that mounts the pinion gear below the centerline of the crown gear.

hysteresis This occurs when something is deflected but does not rebound with the same force, usually due to the internal friction inherent in the material as it deflects.

I-beam I-shaped beam used for frame rails on heavier vehicles; can be aluminum or steel.

idle validation switch (IVS) A circuit used for safety reasons that is used to verify throttle position.

idler gear Gear used in transmissions to drive a vehicle backward.

impact driver A tool that is struck with a blow to provide an impact turning force to remove tight fasteners.

impeller The bladed element in a torque converter or fluid coupling that is fixed to the housing and therefore rotates with it.

incandescent bulb A conventional bulb that electrically heats a filament of metal to the temperature at which it produces light.

incipient fault A fault that is the result of system or component deterioration.

inclinometer/accelerometer Sensors included in the transmission control system that allow it to adapt to topography and operating conditions.

included angle The angle of camber added or subtracted to the steering axis inclination angle. This is the angle of the pivot points in relation to the camber angle of the wheel.

indirect tire pressure monitoring system (indirect TPMS) A type of automated tire pressure monitoring system that uses the anti-lock braking system of a vehicle to measure the difference in the rotational speed of the four wheels to determine tire pressure.

inductive amp clamp A device that measures amperage by measuring a conductor's magnetic field strength, which is proportional to amperage.

inertia brake A type of transmission shaft brake geared to one countershaft, which controls gearing rotational speed while shifting.

inertia break A component used to control the speed of the transmission countershaft and main shaft gears.

inertia shift Weight that moves from the rear of the vehicle to the front during braking.

inertial excitation The force caused by the speeding up and slowing down of the shaft driven through an angle. These stem from the operating angles of the U-joint at the drive end of the driveshaft and are caused by the sheer weight of the driveshaft being accelerated and decelerated twice per revolution.

inlet pressure regulating valve Regulates the maximum air intake pressure supplied to the air compressor from a turbocharged engine's intake manifold.

input force The force applied to the input piston, measured in either kilograms (kg), newtons (N), or pounds (lb).

input member The element of the planetary gear set that receives input from the power source.

input shaft The component to which the clutch discs are splined.

insert valve A small valve in the splitter cylinder cover on a Fuller transmission that controls air flow to the front or rear of the splitter cylinder piston.

inside diameter (ID) A precise measurement of line capacity.

inside micrometer Micrometer that measures inside dimensions.

insulated gate bipolar transistor (IGBT) A specialized field effect transistor (FET) that inverts DC current to three-phase, variable-frequency, and variable-voltage AC current.

insulator A material that holds electrons tightly and prevents electron movement.

integral carrier housing A drive axle housing that does

intelligent charger A battery charger that varies its output according to the sensed condition of the battery it is charging.

inter-axle differential A differential gear set that splits the available torque equally between two drive axles. Also called a *power divider*.

interleaf friction Friction caused by the leaves in a multileaf spring pack rubbing together during suspension articulation can be effective in stopping unwanted oscillation.

interlock system A system that prevents the transmission from engaging two main shaft gears at once.

intermediate plate A plate driven by the flywheel or the clutch cover and providing a friction surface for the back of the front friction disc and the front of the rear friction disc in a dual disc clutch assembly.

intermediate tap One of a series of taps designed to cut an internal thread. Also called a *plug tap*.

intermittent circuit A circuit characterized by uneven current flow.

intermittent fault A fault that is not ongoing and can be both active and historical.

internal bleeding The loss of blood into the body cavity from a wound; there is no obvious sign of blood.

intersecting angle arrangement A method of angle cancellation in which the U-joint angles will intersect at a point exactly at the middle of the shaft length. Also known as a *broken back arrangement*.

Intuitive Diagnostic System (IDS) Proprietary software system available on BAE propulsion systems to aid technicians in diagnosing service issues.

inversion valve A normally open valve which requires air pressure to close. Another name often given to a *spring brake relay valve*.

inverter A device that changes direct current into alternating current. Also called a *wave inverter*.

involute A gear design shape that compensates for the changing point of contact between gears as they rotate through mesh.

I-Shift The Volvo AMT; Mack trucks use the same transmission.

ISO 3731 connector A type of connector commonly used in Europe that uses dedicated pins to transmit ABS information between the tractor and trailer.

isometric diagram A wiring diagram used to locate a component within a system and which shows the outline of a vehicle or piece of equipment where the component can be found.

J-1587 Older SAE communication protocol; quite slow in terms of data transmission at 9600 bits per second.

J-1939 Newer SAE communication protocol; data transmission at a rate of at least 250,000 bits per second and up to 500,000 bits/second.

J-560 trailer connector A trailer cord plug and receptacle located at the rear of the tractor.

jack shaft A short shaft usually at the front of a drive line. Also known as a *coupling shaft*.

jack stands Metal stands with adjustable height to hold a vehicle once it has been jacked up.

jackknifing A condition caused by incorrect pneumatic balance between a tractor and trailer. Typically, tractor brakes have applied before the trailer brakes at too high a pressure. When the tractor brakes lock, the trailer will rotate around the kingpin.

jounce The upward motion of the wheels and axles in reaction to road bumps or terrain.

jounce block A rubber (usually) bumper that stops the axle from contacting the vehicle frame during severe suspension articulation. Also called *axle stop*.

jump out The condition in which a transmission jumps out of gear and to neutral when under load, caused by worn components such as sliding clutches and shift forks. Also called *gear slip out*.

keep alive memory (KAM) Memory that is retained by the ECM when the key is off.

key-off electrical loads Unwanted drain on the vehicle battery when the vehicle is off. Also called *parasitic draw*.

kinetic energy The energy of a body in motion.

kinetic friction The friction between two surfaces that are sliding against each other

kingpin A pin that connects each steering knuckle to the solid I-beam axle.

kingpin The pin attached to a trailer's upper coupler, which is used to lock the fifth wheel to the trailer.

kingpin inclination angle (KPI) The angle formed between true vertical and the angle of the kingpin. Also called *steering axis inclination angle*.

Kirchhoff's law A law that states that the sum of the current flowing into a junction is the same as the current flowing out of the junction.

labor guide A guide that provides information to make estimates for repairs.

ladder logic The designed-in logic of a circuit that determines what activates a specific circuit.

ladder-type frame A frame consisting of two rails joined together by a series of cross members.

land The largest diameter in a spool; used to block flow paths.

landing gear Retractable legs attached to the trailer, which support a semi-trailer when it is not resting on a fifth wheel.

latching solenoids Solenoids that need only a short burst of electricity to move to an open or closed position and they remain in that state until they are energized again.

latent heat The quantity of heat required to produce a change of state from a solid to a liquid or a liquid to a gas.

latent heat of fusion The process of removing heat energy to matter to effect a change of state.

latent heat of vaporization The process of adding heat energy to matter to effect a change of state.

lateral stability The vehicle's ability to be stable from side to side.

leading shoes Brake shoes that are installed so that they are applied in the same direction as the forward rotation of the drum and thus are self-energizing.

leading/trailing shoe drum brake arrangement A type of brake shoe arrangement where one shoe is positioned in a leading manner and the other shoe in a trailing manner.

leaf spring A spring formed by elliptical steel leaves; can be single leaf or multileaf.

left- and right-hand camshafts S-cams used on either side of a vehicle that rotate in opposite directions.

lengthwise bearing The contact pattern along the tooth face from the toe toward the heel.

Lepelletier gear set A compound planetary gear set consisting of three interconnected planetary gears capable of producing six forward ratios and one reverse.

lever A simple machine that can allow a large object to be moved with less force.

lift axle A non-drive (dead) axle that can be mechanically raised and lowered to meet requirements regulated for maximum axle weight loads.

light-emitting diode (LED) A diode that produces light in different colors depending on the doping material used in its manufacture.

limiter valve An air pressure proportioning valve used to increase brake application pressure to the front brakes when a trailer is not towed by a tractor. Also known as a *ratio valve*.

linear Extending or moving in one dimension only.

line-haul A truck that spends most of its time in on highway operations under medium to heavy loading.

lines Term used interchangeably with pipes or tubes.

lip-type dynamic oil seal A seal with a precisely shaped dynamic rubber lip that is held in contact with a moving shaft by a garter spring. An example would be a valve seal or camshaft seal.

lithium-ion (Li-ion) battery A type of battery that does not use a galvanic reaction and in which a gel, salt, or solid material replaces the electrolyte solution.

live (drive) axle An axle that is powered and can move the vehicle. Also called a *drive axle*.

live axle The axle that drives the vehicle by turning the power from the driveshaft 90 degrees to deliver it to the wheels and providing the final gear reduction in the drive train. Also known as a *drive axle*.

load The force squeezing the clutch disc/s between the pressure plate and the flywheel. Also called *clamping force*.

load test A battery test that subjects the battery to a high rate of discharge, and the voltage is then measured after a set time to see how well the battery creates that current flow.

load-dumping A feature that allows temporary suppression of high-voltage spikes.

loading The state of the air compressor when it is building system air pressure. The unloader valves are not active.

locking differential A system that actively prevents differential action from occurring when engaged.

locking pliers A type of plier where the jaws can be set and locked into position.

locking tang A small flat piece of metal that stops the large internal adjusting ring from moving when the clutch is operating.

lockout/tagout A safety tag system to ensure that faulty equipment or equipment in the middle of repair is not used.

lock-up clutch The clutch that locks the turbine to the converter shell when conditions are correct for 100% efficiency.

lock–up clutch disc The friction disc used in a lock-up clutch.

lock-up clutch piston The hydraulically actuated piston that applies the lock-up clutch.

lock-up clutch/piston assembly A combination lockup clutch disc and piston assembly; used in light-duty vehicles.

long stroke chambers Brake chambers manufactured with a 3 inch, (76 mm), stroke.

low profile tire A type of tire that has a shorter sidewall height than conventional tires.

low-inertia A new design auxiliary section that momentarily disengages the auxiliary from the main box during compound shifts, making it easier to move the shift lever.

low-voltage burn-out A damaging condition for starter motors in which excess current flows through the starter, causing the motor to burn out prematurely.

low-voltage disconnect (LVD) A device that monitors battery voltage and disconnects non-critical electrical loads when battery voltage level falls below a preset threshold value.

L-plate L-shaped beams that can be bolted to the outside of the C-channel to increase the rails' RBM.

lubrication failure Failure caused by incorrect lubricant, contaminated lubricant, or lack of lubricant.

lumen The units used to measure light intensity.

machine screw A screw with a slot for screwdrivers.

magnetic pickup tools An extending shaft, often flexible, with a magnet fitted to the end for picking up metal objects.

magnetism The force that attracts or repels magnetic charges; or the property of a material to respond to a magnetic field.

main pressure regulator valve (MPRV) A spool valve that produces main or control pressure.

main shaft The shaft that is driven by the countershaft and provides output for the transmission. Also called *output shaft*.

mandrel The shaft of a pop rivet.

mandrel head The head of the pop rivet that connects to the shaft.

manifold gauge set A set of calibrated gauges for high and low pressure that can show pressure and vacuum readings for use with air-conditioning systems.

manual selector valve The spool valve that is moved by the operator's shift linkage to select a gear.

manual slack adjusters A manually adjusted lever between the brake chamber and the S-cam all but obsolete today.

manual-ranging multimeter A multimeter that must be set to the correct range first based on anticipated values measured.

map (pictorial) diagram A wiring diagram that shows the entire vehicle wiring circuit using pictorial symbols.

master disconnect switch A switch located in the battery compartments that enables technicians to disconnect the power circuit for maintenance or emergencies.

match mounting The process of matching up the tire's highest point with the rim's lowest point for the purpose of reducing the tire's radial run-out.

maximum bending moment The point on the frame at which the load force is concentrated.

maximum forward overdrive The highest (fastest) ratio possible in a planetary gear set.

maximum forward reduction The lowest (slowest) ratio possible in a planetary gear set.

measuring tapes A flexible type of ruler and a common measuring tool.

mechanical advantage Anything that allows us to move greater distances or weight with less effort.

mechanical fade Loss of brake effectiveness that occurs when drums expand due to heat.

mechanical fingers Spring-loaded fingers at the end of a flexible shaft that pick up items in tight spaces.

mechanical jacks A type of vehicle jack that uses mechanical leverage to lift a vehicle.

medium-carbon steel Steel alloyed with carbon at levels of 0.25–0.6%.

message identifier (MID) Also called *module identifier*, the electronic control module that has identified a fault. J-1587 protocols use MIDs.

metering valve A valve that delays brake application pressure to the front disk brakes until a certain level of pressure builds in the system.

Metri-Pack connector A pull-to-seat electrical connector with flat terminals instead of round

microcontroller A special-purpose processor with limited capabilities, designed to perform a set of specific tasks.

micrometers Precise measuring tools designed to measure small distances and are available in both millimeter (mm) and inch calibrations.

micron gauge A device designed to measure vacuum very precisely.

minimum forward overdrive The second highest (fastest) ratio possible in a planetary gear set.

minimum forward reduction The second lowest (slowest) ratio possible in a planetary gear set.

miter boxes A gear arrangement which allows sharp angle changes in the steering column.

Mode 1 In split-mode operation, the mode that is for low-speed operation.

Mode 2 In split-mode operation, the mode that is for high-speed operation.

modulated lock-up A lock-up clutch application strategy that is designed for maximum vehicle performance.

modulated main solenoid A pulse-width-modulated solenoid that controls main pressure in fourth generation and later World Transmissions (WT).

modulator cable A mechanical cable connected to the throttle that operates the modulator valve.

modulator valve A valve that produces a pressure based on throttle position. Also called the *throttle valve*.

modulator valves An electrically operated ABS air control valve used to modulate the air pressure supplied to service brake chambers.

momentary engine ignition interrupt relay (MEIIR) A relay controlled by the TCU that cuts the engine ignition or fuelling in the event that a DM clutch will not disengage.

monoleaf spring A leaf spring with a single leaf usually found in front spring applications only.

Morse taper A tapered mounting shaft for drill bits and chucks in larger drills and lathes.

MOSFET A field effect transistor made from metal-oxide semiconductor material.

mount Steel backed rubber support that holds the power train components.

movable cam rings Rings used in self-adjusting clutches that take up the space of the threaded adjusting ring in the clutch cover.

muffler A device to quiet the pipes of the air-conditioning system with baffles placed inside to deaden the sound of refrigerant moving.

multilayer steel (MLS) head gasket A gasket composed of multiple layers of steel and coated with a rubberlike substance that adheres to metal surfaces. They are typically used between the cylinder head and the cylinder block.

multileaf spring A leaf spring with more than one steel plate or leaf stacked together and used for a spring. Also called a *spring pack*.

multi-mesh gearing Main shaft and countershaft gears that have finer cut teeth—meaning more teeth are in mesh for increased strength.

multiple countershaft transmission A transmission with more than one countershaft; used to distribute the torque between more teeth on the main shaft and countershaft speed gears to increase torque capacity of the transmission.

multiplexing Transmission of more than one electrical signal or message takes place over a single wire or pair of wires.

multi-temp unit A reefer configured to control multiple temperatures in different areas of the trailer.

N material A material with a movable negative charge

N-95 mask A face mask that filters out 95% of all airborne particles.

needle-nosed pliers Pliers with long tapered jaws for gripping small items and getting into tight spaces.

negative camber When the top of the tire is closer to the center of the vehicle than the bottom of the tire.

negative frame angle The condition where the vehicle's rear is lower than the front.

negative offset When the hub mounting surface is towards the brake side or back of the wheel's centerline.

negative scrub radius A condition in which the point of center contact between the road surface and the tire and the point where the steering axis centerline contacts the road surface intersect above the road surface.

negative temperature coefficient (NTC) thermistor A thermistor in which resistance decreases as the temperature increases.

network node A point on a network.

neutral axis The area in the middle of a frame rail web where the tension and compression forces cancel each other out. Also called *neutral fiber*.

neutral fiber The area in the middle of a frame rail web where the tension and compression forces cancel each other out. Also called *neutral axis*.

neutral safety switch A switch operated by the transmission shift linkage that prevents the vehicle from being started except when in park or neutral. Also known as the *PRNDL switch* on some transmissions.

neutral with no clutches (NCC) The status of a vehicle in neutral gear when no clutches are applied and an indication of a possible failure mode for Allison World Transmission (WT).

nickel–metal hydride (NiMH) battery A battery in which metal hydroxide forms the negative electrode and nickel oxide forms the positive electrode.

nippers Pliers designed to cut protruding items level with the surface.

nomenclature The meaning of the letters and digits in truck transmission's model numbers.

nominal crack pressure (NCP) The minimum air signal pressure required to begin delivery of air pressure from a relay valve.

nominal diameter A size code figure, for reference purposes only, as indicated in the tire and rim size designation.

nominal shim pack A shim pack that would be used if the pinion had a zero variation.

non-asbestos organic (NAO) lining Brake friction material commonly used in line haul tractors where far less braking takes place.

non-drive (dead) axle An axle that does not supply power to the wheels.

non-ferrous metals Pure metals such as copper; can also be used in alloys.

non-latching solenoid A solenoid that requires constant electric power to remain in the open position.

non-uniform velocity The phenomenon that a shaft driven through an angle will accelerate and decelerate twice per revolution.

non-volatile memory Memory that is not lost when power is removed or lost.

normally closed solenoid A solenoid that blocks the flow of fluid when it is not electrically energized.

normally open solenoid A solenoid that is open when not electrically energized.

North American Standard Out-of-Service Criteria (OOSC) Defects that require a vehicle to be taken out of service until repaired.

no-slack coupler A lock mechanism that uses serrated edges between the locking bar and wedge to ensure no play in the coupling.

NOX sensor A sensor that detects oxygen ions originating from nitric oxide (NOX) from among the other oxygen ions present in the exhaust gas.

NPN transistor A type of bipolar transistor with two blocks of N material and one block of P material.

N-type material Semiconductor material with a small amount of extra electrons.

nut A fastener with a hexagonal head and internal threads for screwing on bolts.

Nylock nut Keeps the nut and bolt done up tightly; can have a plastic or nylon insert. Tightening the bolt squeezes it into the insert, where it resists any movement. The self-locker is highly resistant to being loosened.

OBD manager Software that identifies fault codes and ensures emissions systems are operating correctly.

Occupational Safety and Health Administration (OSHA) Government agency created to provide national leadership in occupational safety and health.

off-board diagnostics Procedures to isolate a fault based on fault code information, including retrieving fault code information, monitoring system operation, performing actuator tests and pinpoint electrical tests, and inspecting components.

off-going ratio test A test performed at the beginning of a shift in progress in the World Transmission (WT) to ensure that the off-going clutch has released.

offset screwdriver A screwdriver with a 90-degree bend in the shaft for working in tight spaces.

offset vice A vice that allows long objects to be gripped vertically.

ohm The unit for measuring electrical resistance.

Ohm's law A law that defines the relationship between amperage, resistance, and voltage.

oil seal Any seal used to seal oil in and dirt, moisture, and debris out.

oil slinger A stamped steel ring used to throw lubricant in a certain direction.

oil weep Very minor oil seepage usually caused by a wicking effect and not usually a reason for a repair.

oiler A device used to add oil to the air-conditioning system.

on-board diagnostics (OBD) Self-diagnostic capabilities of electronic control modules that allow them to evaluate voltage and current levels of circuits to which they are connected and determine if data is in the correct operational range.

on-coming ratio test A test performed near the end of a shift in progress in the World Transmission (WT) to ensure that the on-coming clutch has applied.

one-way check valve A valve with the purpose to protect the air reservoirs and other air system storage units from completely draining if a leak occurs downstream of one reservoir.

one-way clutch A roller or sprag type device that allows rotation in one direction but locks in the opposite direction. Also called *over-running clutch*.

open circuits Describes a circuit that has a break and no current can flow.

open fracture A fracture in which the bone is protruding through the skin or there is severe bleeding.

open-center rim A type of wheel rim that can be removed from the cast-iron spoke hub attached to the axle. Also called a *demountable rim*.

open-end wrench A wrench with open jaws to allow side entry to a nut or bolt.

open-loop ramp rate A predictable increase in clutch apply pressure; the open-loop ramp rate is controlled by the transmission ECU.

operator's manual A document that contains information about a vehicle which is a valuable source of information for both the owner and the technician.

organic facings Friction facings made of various natural materials such as cotton fibers, rubber, aluminum, glass, copper or brass fibers, and carbon material.

organic light-emitting diode (OLED) A light-emitting diode that uses carbon-based semiconductor material.

O-ring Rubber-type rings available in different sizes used to seal pipe fittings.

oscillation The rhythmic up and down motion of the suspension caused by road shock. It must be stopped by dampening or vehicle stability could be lost.

out-of-range monitoring Validating sensor data to verify a system is operating within an expected range for a given operating condition.

output force Force that equals the working pressure multiplied by the surface area of the output piston, expressed as newtons or kilograms.

output member The element of the planetary gear set that is connected to the transmission output shaft.

output shaft The shaft that is driven by the countershaft and provides output for the transmission. Also called *main shaft*.

output shaft The output shaft of an inter-axle differential. The rear side gear is part of or splined to the output shaft. Also known as the *through shaft*.

outrigger brackets A frame-body attachment consisting of brackets welded to the vehicle and then bolted to the frame web.

outside diameter (OD) A general measurement (often a nominal specification, rather than an actual measurement) used in specification of pipe.

outside micrometer Measures the outside dimensions of an item.

overall diameter The diameter of an inflated tire at the outermost surface of the tread.

overcharging Overfilling of the air-conditioning system; may result in poor cooling or mechanical failure of the system.

overcrank protection (OCP) thermostat A thermostat that monitors the temperature of the motor and opens a relay circuit to interrupt the current to the solenoid if prolonged cranking causes the motor temperature to exceed a safe threshold.

overdrive ratio A ratio that provides a speed increase and output torque decrease.

overhung mount pinion A pinion mounted with only two opposed tapered roller bearings.

overrunning alternator decoupler (OAD) A pulley that uses an internal spring and clutch system that allows it to rotate freely in one direction and provide limited, spring-like movement in the other direction.

over-running clutch A roller or sprag type device that allows rotation in one direction but locks in the opposite direction. Also called *one-way clutch*.

overslung A suspension where the leaf spring sits on top of the axle.

oxyacetylene torch A gas welding system that combines oxygen and acetylene.

P material A material with a movable positive charge.

paraffin (mineral oil) Used mainly as a cleaning agent in the commercial vehicle industry.

parallax error A visual error caused by viewing measurement markers at an incorrect angle.

parallel alternators The practice of connecting alternators in parallel to provide higher charging voltage at idle with more available amperage.

parallel circuit A circuit in which all components are connected directly to the voltage supply.

parallel drive A vehicle in which both the engine and electric motor work together, blending motor and engine torque, to propel the vehicle.

parallel joint arrangement Two or more universal joint arrangements where the joint angles form parallel lines; a method of angle cancellation for use with parallel angles. Also known as the *waterfall arrangement*.

parallel keys Used to prevent the free rotation of gears or pulleys on a shaft and can be used to secure a gear wheel on its shaft.

parallel wiring A type of custom-made wiring harness that encloses multiple conductors into a single vinyl insulator covering.

parallelogram A design element in suspension systems to keep the wheels or the axles in alignment throughout suspension articulation.

parameter group number (PGN) A package of serial data transmitted over the CAN network that includes SPN, source addresses, and FMI, as well as commands, data, requests, acknowledgments, negative-acknowledgments, and fault codes.

parameter identifier (PID) A value or identifier of an item being reported with fault data.

parasitic draw Unwanted drain on the vehicle battery when the vehicle is off. Also called *key-off electrical load.*

parasitic loss An unnecessary load on the engine that wastes fuel.

park brake circuit The air circuit responsible for the application and release of power springs in the brake chambers. Also referred to as the *spring brake circuit* or *emergency brake circuit*.

park/emergency braking system The air circuit responsible for the application of the spring brakes for parking. It also has the capability to enable several controlled brake applications if a major air leak occurs in either the primary or secondary air brake circuits.

parts program A computer software program for identifying and ordering replacement vehicle parts.

parts specialist The person who serves customers at the parts counters.

Pascal's law The law of physics that states that pressure applied to a fluid in one part of a closed system will be transmitted equally to all other areas of the system.

passive sensor A sensor that does not use a current supplied by the ECM to operate.

PBS Injection Booster An option for the Bendix EAC system which injects a blast of compressed air into the engine intake manifold to reduce turbocharger lag.

peak torque The maximum torque an engine can produce.

peening A term used to describe the action of flattening a rivet through a hammering action.

performance testing The process of recreating a driving situation to check air-conditioning performance and vent temperature.

personal protective equipment (PPE) Safety equipment designed to protect the technician, such as safety boots, gloves, clothing, protective eyewear, and hearing protection.

phasing Lining up the inboard yoke ears of driveshaft so that the non-uniform velocity cancellation occurs in the proper quadrant of the circle.

Phillips screwdriver A type of screwdriver that fits a head shaped like a cross in screws; also called *Phillips head screwdriver*.

photodiode A diode that will forward bias only when light strikes it.

photometric certification A certification based on testing lamps to evaluate factors such as light color, brightness, and the angle at which the light is effectively observed.

photon A particle of energy and the basic unit of light.

photoresistor A semiconductor-type of resistor in which resistance decreases as light intensity increases.

photovoltaic (PV) effect The conversion of light into electricity.

Piezoelectric effect A type of electricity produced by bending or squeezing a unique type of quartz crystal.

piezoresistive sensor A sensor that uses a piezoresistive crystal arranged with a Wheatstone bridge to measure the change in resistance of the piezo crystal; these sensors are adapted to measuring vibration and dynamic or continuous pressure changes.

pilot bearing A bearing that supports the front of the transmission input shaft; mounted in the flywheel or the rear of the crankshaft.

pilot bearing bore The hole in the center of the flywheel that holds the pilot bearing.

pilot pad The lugs attached to the bearing hub to locate the wheel assembly correctly during assembly.

pin punch A type of punch in various sizes with a straight or parallel shaft.

pinion A gear or cog with a number of small teeth; used with a rack to convert linear to circular motion.

pinion bearing cage A removable casting that holds the two bearing races that support the pinion gear.

pinion depth The mounting position of the pinion in relation to the crown gear center of axis.

pinion gear A small driving gear.

pinion pilot bearing A small bearing that supports the inboard end of the pinion gear when the pinion is straddle mounted. Also called *spigot bearing*.

pinion variation number A dimension to add or remove from the nominal pinion depth dimension.

pintle A bolt or pin forming the pivot of a hinge.

pintle hook Trailer hitching device that uses a fixed towing horn, which connects with a draw bar eye, attached to the towed vehicle.

pipe A rigid tube of metal, plastic, or other substance, used to convey fluids.

piston A solid disk that moves within a tube (or cylinder) under fluid pressure.

pitch The number of teeth per unit of pitch diameter on a gear.

pitch circle The theoretical point on the tooth face halfway between the root and the top land where only rolling motion exists. Also called the *pitch diameter*.

pitch diameter The theoretical point on the tooth face halfway between the root and the top land where only rolling motion exists. Also called the *pitch circle*.

pitman arm A pitman arm converts the steering gear sector shaft movement to a sweeping arc resembling linear movement. Also called a *drop arm*.

plain bevel gear A bevel gear set with straight-cut teeth.

plain case half The half of the differential case that does not bolt to the crown gear.

plan angle An angle where the driveshaft moves toward the side of a vehicle when viewed from above.

planetary carrier The housing that holds the pinion gears of a planetary gear set and their shafts.

planetary double reduction drive axle A planetary drive axle that is permanently fixed in low range.

planetary gear A gear arrangement consisting of a ring gear with internal teeth, a carrier with two or more small pinion gears in constant mesh with the ring gear, and an externally toothed sun gear in the center in constant mesh with the planetary pinions.

planetary gear reduction drive A type of gear reduction system in which a planetary gear set reduces the starter profile to multiply motor torque to the pinion gear.

planetary two-speed drive axle A two-speed drive axle that uses a planetary gear set for the low range.

planned down-time The practice of scheduling major repairs and overhauls before declining performance or system failure makes them urgent (and thus expensive).

pliers A hand tool with gripping jaws.

plug-in hybrid electric vehicle (PHEV) Any type of hybrid electric vehicle containing a battery storage system that uses an external source to recharge the battery when the vehicle is not in operation.

plunger A mechanical device that provides a thrusting motion, such as a piston.

PM service checklist An itemized task list of mechanical safety procedures.

PM service intervals The frequency of a PM schedule.

PM-A PM-A inspections are visual assessments of all safety-related items such as brakes, tires, horn, wipers, steering components, suspension components, and lighting.

PM-B PM-B inspections include all of the checks and adjustments performed in PM-A, as well as an oil change, and oil filter and fuel filter changes. The inspection items include the engine and driveline, as well as greater detail checks of the braking, steering, and other chassis systems.

PM-C PM-C inspections are annual and include all the items in PM-A and B, as well as comprehensive checks of all chassis components. Scheduled fluid changes and component adjustment, repair, or replacement are performed at this time.

pneumatic balance The correct timing of brake application air pressure to each vehicle axle at the correct pressure.

pneumatic imbalance The incorrect timing of brake application air pressure to vehicle axles or brake application at the wrong pressure. Pneumatic imbalance leads to tractor jackknifing or trailer swing-out.

pneumatic jacks A type of vehicle jack that uses compressed gas or air to lift a vehicle.

PNP transistor A type of bipolar transistor with two blocks of P material and one block of N material.

polarity The state of charge, positive or negative.

policy A guiding principle that sets the shop direction.

polyalkylene glycol (PAG) Synthetic oil used in all R-134a systems.

polyalphaolefin (PAO) Synthetic oil used in R-12 systems.

polymeric positive temperature coefficient (PPTC) device (resettable fuse) A thermistor-like electronic device used to protect against circuit overloads. Also called *resettable fuse*.

pop-rivet gun A hand tool for installing pop rivets.

portable lifting hoists A type of vehicle hoist that is portable and can be moved from one location to another.

ports Openings for intake or outlet of a fluid.

positive camber When the tires are closer together at the bottom and farther apart at the top.

positive frame angle The condition where the vehicle's rear is higher than the front.

positive offset When the plane of the hub mounting surface is shifted from the centerline towards the outside or front side of the wheel.

positive scrub radius A condition in which the point of center contact between the road surface and the tire and the point where the steering axis centerline contacts the road surface intersect below the road surface.

positive temperature coefficient (PTC) thermistor A thermistor in which resistance increases as the temperature increases.

potentiometer A variable resistor with three connections— one at each end of a resistive path, and a third sliding contact that moves along the resistive pathway.

pot-type flywheel A flywheel shaped like a deep pot inside which all of the components of the clutch are housed with the exception of the clutch cover.

power divider A differential gear set that splits the available torque equally between two drive axles. Also called an *inter-axle differential*.

power flow The path that power takes from the beginning of an assembly to the end. In a transmission, power flow changes as different gears are selected by the driver.

power jackknife A condition when the drive axles of a vehicle push the rear of a vehicle and steering control is lost. Also called *fishtailing*.

power line carrier (PLC) technology Technology that enables multiplex communication over constantly powered wires.

power line carrier (PLC) technology A data transmission technology enabling data exchange between the tractor and trailer ABS.

power springs Springs in brake actuators used to apply park brakes or internal pushrod lock mechanisms.

power steering pump A hydraulic pump that provides hydraulic pressure to the steering gear, which reduces the force required by the driver to turn the steering wheel.

Power Steering System Analyzer (PSSA) A combination flow meter, shut-off valve, and pressure gauge used to diagnose hydraulic problems in power steering systems.

power take-off device (PTO) A device attached to the transmission that is gear-driven and can be used to run accessories.

power tools Tools powered by electricity or compressed air.

power train control device Device used to input or hold planetary gear components to affect a power flow. These can be hydraulic clutches, brake bands, or oneway sprag or roller clutches.

power unit The hydraulic assist portion of the power steering gear.

pre-dampening A series of small torsional dampening springs designed to prevent gear rattle at idle.

predictive PM A statistical analysis of when equipment and component failures are likely to occur, including replacing parts or equipment before malfunctions happen.

preload Negative endplay, or less than zero clearance.

preset hub A wheel hub that uses a precision spacer and close-tolerance bearings to eliminate the need for manual adjustment.

pressure The force per unit area applied to the surface of an object.

pressure balanced A feature of air control system valves which ensures air application pressure is consistent to the brake chambers even when small leaks drain air from delivery components such as lines and chambers.

pressure bleeder A device that bleeds a hydraulic system by pressurizing the fluid.

pressure control solenoid (PCS) The term to denote clutch control solenoids in an Allison Fourth Generation Electro-Hydraulic Control transmission.

pressure differential valve A valve that detects pressure loss in either of the two hydraulic systems of a split hydraulic brake system.

pressure plate The friction surface of the clutch cover. This is the plate that squeezes the clutch disc against the flywheel.

pressure protection valve A normally closed valve that opens after a preset pressure is reached. Pressure protection valves are used to control the charging of air system reservoirs or circuits draining out of the reservoir.

pressure transients Minor fluctuations on the gauges that may indicate a problem.

pressure washer/cleaner A cleaning machine that boosts low-pressure tap water to a high-pressure output.

pressure-compensating balance valve A feature of air brake valves that ensures a consistent delivery of air pressure is maintained in spite of leaks in the delivery system lines or air chambers.

pressure-compensating relay valve A relay valve having a pressure balanced inlet and exhaust valve to ensure consistent air delivery pressure to the brakes.

prick punch A punch with a sharp point for accurately marking a point on metal.

primary battery A battery in which chemical reactions are not reversible and the battery cannot be recharged.

primary circuit Refers to the split brake circuit system used on commercial vehicles. The primary circuit generally operates the rear brakes while the secondary circuit operates the front brakes.

primary modulation The pulse-modulated signal sent to a solenoid to initiate fluid flow.

primary piston A brake piston in the master cylinder moved directly by the pushrod or the power booster; it generates hydraulic pressure to move the secondary piston.

primary reservoir One of two air reservoirs responsible for holding pressurized air for the dual air brake system.

primary sources People who have direct experience with the same or a similar problem.

primary winding The coil of wire in the low-voltage circuit, which creates the magnetic field in a step-up transformer.

priority valve A check valve that protects the hydraulic controls.

proactive maintenance Reflects the understanding that the cost of repairing an unexpected breakdown is usually much greater than preventive maintenance.

proactive PM Preventative maintenance that is typically based on distance traveled, engine hours, time, or fuel used.

procedure A list of the steps required to get the same result each time a task or activity is performed.

Procision Eaton's dual-clutch seven-speed AMT; introduced in 2014.

profile bearing Contact pattern between the root and the top land of the tooth.

prognostic capability The ability by some transmission ECUs to predict fluid and filter change intervals.

prognostics A self-diagnostic maintenance schedule that informs the driver when the oil, filters, or the transmission itself requires service. Prognostics are offered on the Allison World Transmissions (WTs) since 2009 and can be turned on or off by the vehicle owner if desired.

prognostics Allison transmission's prognostic capability for fluid and filter change intervals; also capable of determining clutch and transmission life.

programmable read only memory (PROM) Memory that stores programming information and cannot be easily written over.

programmable read-only memory (PROM) chip A memory chip particular to the application of the vehicle in which it is found.

programmed lock-up A strategy that applies the lock-up clutch as soon as possible for improved fuel economy. Also called *systematic lock-up*.

proportional differential A differential capable of sending more torque to one wheel than the other when a wheel slip condition is encountered. Also known as a *biased torque differential*.

proportioning valve On air brakes, a valve that functions to change service brake application pressure by reducing service brake application relative to signal pressure from the foot valve.

proportioning valve On hydraulic brakes, a valve that limits brake application pressure to the rear brakes when the vehicle is not heavily loaded.

propulsion control system (PCS) module A microprocessor- based device that supplies electrical output signals based on input data collected from a vehicle's sensors.

Propylene glycol An organic based chemical that resists freezing and, unlike ethylene glycol, is non-toxic.

prove-out sequence A sequence in which the warning lights for several brief seconds with the key on and engine off or during key-on engine cranking.

pry bars (crowbars) A high-strength carbon-steel rod with offsets for levering and prying.

psia The units of pressure, in pounds per square inch, at sea level.

psig The units of pressure, in pounds per square inch, expressed relative to the environment's atmospheric pressure.

PT chart A pressure-temperature chart that shows the relationship between air-conditioning pressures and evaporator temperature.

P-type material Semiconductor material having electron deficiency or a place to hold additional electrons.

pull-down switch A switch connected between the ECM and a negative ground current potential.

pullers A generic term to describe hand tools that mechanically assist the removal of bearings, gears, pulleys, and other parts.

pull-to-seat terminal A terminal installed by inserting the wire through the connector cavity, crimping on a terminal, and then pulling the terminal back into the connector cavity to seat it.

pull-type clutch A clutch with an integral release bearing, which is pulled towards the transmission to disengage the clutch.

pull-up switch A switch connected between the ECM and a battery positive.

pulse charger A battery charger that sends current into the battery in pulses of one-second cycles; used to recover sulfated batteries.

pulse width modulation (PWM) An electrical signal that varies in on and off time.

pump A device that generates a flow of fluid.

punches A generic term to describe a high-strength carbon-steel shaft with a blunt point for driving. Center and prick punches are exceptions and have a sharp point for marking or making an indentation.

purge cycle The time between the closing and opening of the dryer purge valve, or the loading and unloading of the air compressor. Oil and moisture trapped in the dryer desiccant are purged when the air compressor unloads.

purge valve The air dryer valve, located at the dryer outlet, which controls the purge cycle. Opening the purge valve enables trapped oil and moisture to exhaust to the atmosphere through the valve.

pusher axle A rear, non-drive rear mounted axle, ahead of the drive axle.

push-pull park/emergency control valve Hand-operated dash valve used to control the operation of the spring brakes for a straight truck, tractor, and/or trailer.

push-to-seat terminal A terminal inserted into the back of the connector cavity to seat after the terminal is crimped to the wire.

push-type clutch A clutch in which the release bearing is pushed towards the engine to release the clutch.

quick-adjust A small mechanism used to turn the large adjusting ring in the clutch cover when adjustment is required.

quick-release (QR) valve An air valve that is used to speed-up the release of air pressure from air lines. The valve exhaust closes when supplied air and then opens when air pressure drops.

rack A bar with teeth; used with a pinion to convert linear to circular motion.

rack-and-pinion gear A gear consisting of a flat rack with either spur or helically cut teeth on one side and a meshing circular pinion gear.

rack-and-pinion steering system A type of steering gear arrangement that uses two gears. A smaller round pinion gear located at the end of the steering shaft connects to a linear gear called the rack. The pinion gear moves the rack from side-to-side as the pinion rotates. The side-to-side motion of the rack controls the direction of the steer tires.

radial placed belt A tire construction with belts placed at 90 degrees to the tire centerline and wrapped from side to side around the tire beads

radial ply tire A tire with two or more layers of casing plies and cord loops running radially from bead to bead.

radial thrust Thrust that tries to push gears in mesh apart perpendicular to their axis.

radiant heat transfer The transfer of heat through a medium, such as a gas or vacuum, which does not cause the medium itself to heat.

ramp-off rate The specific reduction in clutch apply pressure for the clutch that is being released during a shift in the World Transmission (WT).

random access memory (RAM) A temporary storage place for information that needs to be quickly accessed.

range gear Any speed gear; in Eaton transmissions, it refers to the low-range gear in the auxiliary section.

range shift cylinder The shift cylinder to control range shifts in the auxiliary.

range verification tests Tests constantly being performed by the Allison World Transmission (WT) control system whenever there is no shift in progress the test compares turbine times the gear ratio to the output speed to ensure the transmission is not slipping.

ratchet A generic term to describe a handle for sockets that allows the user to select direction of rotation. It can turn sockets in restricted areas without the user having to remove the socket from the fastener.

ratcheting screwdriver A screwdriver with a selectable ratchet mechanism built into the handle that allows the screwdriver tip to ratchet as it is being used.

ratio step The difference between one ratio and the next available.

ratio test A test performed at the beginning and end of a shift in process.

ratio valve An air pressure proportioning valve used to increase brake application pressure to the front brakes when a trailer is not towed by a tractor. Also known as a *limiter valve*.

rattle gun The most common air tool in a workshop; also called the *air-impact wrench* or *impact gun*.

Ravigneaux gear set A popular compound planetary gear set with two planetary gear sets sharing a common carrier; capable of producing four forward speeds and one reverse.

rawl pins Often used to hold components on rotating shafts. They are a type of shear pin, used when excessive force is used to avoid further damage to a component.

reaction member The element of the planetary gear set that is held stationary.

reaction plates Metal plates in the hydraulic clutch; usually splined to the clutch hub or the transmission case.

reactive maintenance Service is only performed after equipment is broken, temporarily keeping vehicle and fleet operating costs low.

read only memory (ROM) Memory used for permanent storage of instructions and fixed values used by the ECM that control the microprocessor.

rebound The downward motion of the wheel and axle after a road bump or shock has occurred.

receiver-dryer A storage reservoir for refrigerant that also absorbs moisture from the air-conditioning system.

recirculating-ball steering gear A steering gear that uses a worm gear inside a metal ball-nut having a threaded hole for the worm. Gear teeth are cut into one outside edge of the ball-nut, which engages the sector shaft.

reclaim/recycle machine An air-conditioning machine designed to remove and recycle refrigerant for reuse.

reclaiming The process of removing refrigerant from the air-conditioning system by using an air-conditioning machine; also called *recovering*.

recovering *See reclaiming.*

rectification A process of converting alternating current (AC) into direct current (DC).

reduction gear drive A starter motor drive system in which the motor multiplies torque to the starter pinion gear by using an extra gear between the armature and the starter drive mechanism.

reefer A truck-trailer refrigeration temperature-control system.

reference voltage (Vref) A precisely regulated voltage supplied by the ECM to sensors; the value is typically 5 VDC, but some manufacturers use 8 or 12 volts.

refrigerant identifiers Devices used to check for impurities in the air-conditioning system.

refrigerant label A label that lists the type and total capacity of refrigerant that is installed in the A/C system.

regenerative braking A feature of hybrid vehicles by which generators recover energy during braking.

regrooving A process that uses a heated cutting tool to carve new tread or add stripes to a tire.

relay valve Critical devices used to speed up the flow of air during brake application and release.

release bearing A hollow bearing through which the input shaft passes, which allows for the push or pull against rotating clutch release levers to release the clutch.

release bearing free travel The distance the release bearing moves while releasing the clutch in a pull-type clutch.

release bolt A bolt that compresses the power spring of spring brakes and releases the park brake.

release fork (yoke) The actuator that moves the release bearing.

reluctor A toothed wheel used with magnetic sensors, usually to measure shaft speed.

reluctor wheel The toothed wheel mounted on the wheel hub, which is used by the wheel speed sensor to generate wheel speed data. Also called the *exciter ring*.

remote sensing Referencing the battery positive connection through an input terminal that is used for the regulator reference voltage.

remote shift linkage A transmission shift linkage that is not mounted directly above the shift cover and that must be properly maintained and lubricated to prevent hard shifting.

removable carrier type A drive axle housing with a removable carrier. Also called a *banjo*.

repair order A form used by shops to collect information regarding a vehicle coming in for repair, also referred to as a work order.

reserve capacity The time, in minutes, that a new, fully charged battery at 80°F (26.7°C) will supply a constant load of 25 amps without its voltage dropping below 10.5 volts for a 12-volt battery.

residual magnetism The small amount of magnetism left on the rotor after it is initially magnetized by the coil windings' magnetic field.

residual pressure valve (residual check valve) In drum brake systems, a valve that maintains pressure in the wheel cylinders slightly above atmospheric pressure so that air does not enter the system through the seals in the wheel cylinders.

resilient mounts Attachments that are spring loaded or made with rubber or polyurethane elements that accommodate movement.

resist bending moment (RBM) The frame strength calculated using the section modulus of the frame rail and its yield strength.

resistive circuit A circuit in which grounds and power connections cannot properly function due to overly high resistance.

resistive touch screen A display screen composed of two flexible, transparent sheets lightly coated with an electrically conductive yet slightly resistive material.

resistor A component designed to produce electrical resistance.

resolver A special sensor that measures the rotor position and speed for the PCS to properly manage the motor operation by reducing current flow and shutting down the system as needed.

resonance The frequency at which the driveline's vibrations are the most damaging.

resonant frequency The frequency at which the driveline enters into a resonant condition where all the components start to oscillate in unison.

respirator Protective gear used to protect the wearer from inhaling harmful dusts or gases. Respirators range from single-use disposable masks to types that have replaceable cartridges. The correct types of cartridge must be used for the type of contaminant encountered.

retarder Any system used to slow a vehicle's momentum and augment the service brake.

retreading The process of applying new tread to an existing tire casing as a way to extend the service life of the tire.

retrofit kit An aftermarket kit that has the fittings and oil to change an R-12 unit over to an R-134a unit.

return on investment (ROI) The ratio of dollars spent on a vehicle for its purchase and maintenance compared to how much the vehicle earns.

reverse bias A situation in which a diode blocks current flow.

reverse idler shaft Shaft that supports the reverse idler gear.

reverse overdrive A reverse direction overdrive ratio through the planetary gear set.

reverse reduction A reverse direction underdrive ratio through the planetary gear set.

reversing sleeve pistons A type of air spring with a piston that pushes into the air spring bag or bellows as the suspension articulates. Also known as a *rolling lobe piston*.

rheostat A variable resistor constructed of a fixed input terminal and a variable output terminal, which vary current flow by passing current through a long resistive tightly coiled wire.

rigid fifth wheel A type of fifth wheel that does not oscillate about either axis of the vehicle. It does not articulate from side to side or front to back. It is fixed in location.

rim diameter The distance across the center of the rim, from bead seat to bead seat.

rim flange The exterior lip that holds the tire in place.

rim width The distance across the rim flanges at the bead seat.

ring gear On air brakes, an internally toothed gear that surrounds the pinion gears.

ring gear A large bevel gear that is driven by a smaller pinion gear in the bevel gear set. Also known as a *crown gear*.

road feel The force transmitted from the tires back through the steering system to the driver.

Roadranger valve The driver's shift knob that controls range and splitter shifting.

rod The part of a linear actuator that transfers force from the piston to the load.

roll stability control (RSC) A vehicle control system that measures lateral acceleration of a vehicle to minimize the likelihood of a vehicle rollover.

rolling circumference The distance covered by one revolution of the tire.

rolling lobe piston A type of air spring with a piston that pushes into the air spring bag or bellows as the suspension articulates. Also known as a *reversing sleeve piston*.

rolling resistance The tendency of a tire to resist rolling along naturally when under load.

root The radius shape between the bottoms of two teeth. Also called *fillet radius*.

root diameter The smallest circle of the gear measured at the fillet radius (root) of the teeth.

rotary flow Fluid flow inside the torque converter that follows the rotation of the housing.

rotary piston compressors HVAC compressors that use cylindrical-shaped housings and enclose multiple pistons to minimize noise, vibration, and harshness.

rotary valve A valve connected to the input shaft of the steering gear that controls the direction of pressurized fluid through the steering gear. Along with the torsion bar, changes in torque applied to the steering wheel and the direction of torque will alter the direction of fluid flow through the valve. Also called a *spool valve*.

rotating clutch A hydraulic clutch used to input a planetary gear component.

roto-chambers Actuators with a unique diaphragm construction which delivers consistent output force regardless of the pushrod position.

rotor The main rotating part of a disc brake system.

rubber spring A suspension system utilizing rubber as the spring medium commonly found on heavier vehicles.

Rzeppa joint A constant velocity joint invented by Alfred Rzeppa in 1926.

SAE J1128 standard A standard that specifies the dimensions, test methods, and requirements for single-core primary wire intended for use in road vehicle applications.

SAE J-560 standard The SAE standards for the configuration of trailer electrical cables and plugs.

safe working load (SWL) The maximum safe lifting load for lifting equipment.

safety data sheet (SDS) A sheet that provides information about handling, use, and storage of a material that may be hazardous.

safety relief valve A pressure relief valve located in the service–supply or wet tank; used to prevent tank rupture from overpressurization. The valve typically opens at pressures above 150 psi (1,034 kPa).

sag A type of frame damage characterized by the downward bending of the frame rail between two support points. The opposite of bow.

sand or bead blasters A cleaning system that uses high pressure fine particles of glass bead or sand.

S-cam A cam shaft used to force brake shoes onto the brake drum.

scheduled lock-up Torque converter lock-up that occurs at a preset point; this saves fuel.

schematic diagram A line drawing that explains how a system works by using symbols and connecting lines.

screw extractor A tool for removing broken screws or bolts.

screw Usually smaller than bolts and are sometimes referred to as metal threads. They can have a variety of heads and are used on smaller components. The thread often extends from the tip to the head so they can hold together components of variable thickness.

scrub angle The distance between two imaginary points on the road surface—the point of center contact between the road surface and the tire, and the intersecting point where the steering axis centerline and the tire centerline contact the road surface. The difference between the intersection of a point on the tire contact patch between true vertical and the KPI angle.

scrub radius The difference between the intersection of a point on the tire contact patch between true vertical and the KPI angle. Scrub radius forms the pivot point for the tire contact with the road. See also positive scrub radius and negative scrub radius.

sealed lead–acid battery A battery that does not have a liquid electrolyte nor requires the addition of water. Also called a *valve-regulated lead–acid battery (VRLA)* or *recombinant battery*.

sealed release bearing A release bearing with no grease nipple or zerk.

seamless Formed in one piece; lacking seams, and thus smooth and regular.

secondary battery A rechargeable battery.

secondary circuit Refers to the split brake circuit system used on commercial vehicles. The primary circuit generally operates the rear brakes while the secondary circuit operates the front brakes.

secondary couple vibrations A vibration, caused by U-joint angles, that travels the length of the driveshaft.

secondary modulation (sub-modulation) A very high frequency pulse-width modulation of the current flowing through the primary modulated circuit of a World Transmission (WT) solenoid. The secondary modulation occurs at between 12000 and 19000 Htz and is used to fine tune the solenoid function.

secondary piston A piston that is moved by hydraulic pressure generated by the primary piston in the master cylinder.

secondary reservoir One of two air reservoirs responsible for holding pressurized air for the dual air brake system.

secondary safety latch An additional mechanism used as an added step to unlatch or release a fifth wheel locking jaw.

secondary sources Secondhand information compiled from a variety of sources.

secondary winding The coil of wire in which high voltage is induced in a step-up transformer.

second-degree burns Burns that involve blistering and damage to the outer layer of skin.

section break A point where the diameter of a shaft or thickness of a component changes.

section change A point where a component becomes thicker or thinner or more or less rigid forming a weak point where breakage can begin.

section height The height of the sidewalls.

section modulus An engineering calculation used to determine the strength of a frame rail based only on its shape, height, width, and thickness

section width The distance between the outside of the sidewalls on an inflated tire without any load on it.

self-adjusting clutches Clutches with an automatically adjusting system that relies on pressure plate movement to cause an adjustment.

self-dampening The interleaf friction in a leaf spring pack that helps to stop spring oscillation.

self-diagnostic The TCU capability to analyze its own functions.

self-energization A braking effect that causes the shoe-drum friction to rotate the brake shoe into the drum with more force.

self-exciting alternator An alternator that relies on the residual magnetism found in the rotor after operating as a way to switch on the voltage regulator and supply current to the rotor.

self-powered refrigeration units A transport refrigeration system powered by a small horsepower diesel engine.

self-steering axle An axle whose wheel will automatically follow the curve of a turn.

self-tapping screw A screw that cuts down its own thread as it goes. It is made of hard material that cuts a mirror image of itself into the hole as you turn it.

semiconductor A material that can have properties of both conductors and insulators and that can switch back and forth between either state using small electrostatic charges.

semi-floating axle shaft An axle shaft that carries the entire weight of the vehicle on its outer end.

semi-floating bearings Wheel bearings that support the drive axle that transmits torque.

semi-metallic lining Brake friction material heat resistant semi-metallic blends are for higher temperatures and load service ratings.

semi-oscillating fifth wheel Fifth wheels that pivot slightly in both horizontal and vertical directions; the standard type of fifth wheel used in on-highway applications.

semi-trailer A trailer that has some of its load carried by the tractor through a hitching device.

sensible heat Heat that can be sensed or felt.

sensing The voltage reference point the alternator uses for regulation of the output.

SensoTop A system used by Voith that senses topography and adapts the shifting schedule accordingly.

separator plate A plate that separates the control valve body and the transmission case.

sequentially Operating in a series, or in logical order.

serial communication Communication using zeroes and ones to transmit data in a series, one bit after another in sequence.

serial data Pieces of data sent by the master module.

series circuit The simplest type of electrical circuit with multiple loads but only one path for current to flow.

series drive A vehicle in which only an electric traction motor supplies torque to propel the vehicle.

series-parallel drive A more complex system enabling an engine only, an electric motor only, and a combined engine-motor operation. Also called *power-split configuration*.

serrated edge shake-proof washer A washer that is used to anchor smaller screws.

service brake priority A trailer spring brake relay valve which will not allow the park-spring brakes to release until the service air reservoir is filled.

service campaign and recall A corrective measure conducted by manufacturers when a safety issue is discovered with a particular vehicle.

service history A complete list of all the servicing and repairs that have been performed on a vehicle.

service reservoir The first air reservoir to receive air from the air compressor or dryer. Water and oil condense in this tank, which supplies the primary and secondary air reservoirs. Also called the *supply reservoir*.

servo A control system that compares the output feedback signal to the input command signal and makes automatic adjustments to provide the commanded output.

servo action A drum brake design where one brake shoe, when activated, applies an increased activating force to the other brake shoe, in proportion to the initial activating force; further enhances the self-energizing feature of some drum brakes.

setback The distance one wheel is set back from the wheel on the opposite side of the axle.

severe service operating conditions Conditions consist of towing or hauling heavy loads, extensive idling and/or stop-and-go, low-speed driving encountered in inner-city traffic, delivery, off-road dusty conditions, and multiple drivers.

severe-duty service A vehicle that is operated under extreme (maximum) loading most of the time, or one that is operated on heavy grades.

shedding A process that reduces the plate surface area and therefore reduces capacity. Shedding may also produce short circuits between the bottom of positive and negative plates.

shift by wire Shifting controlled completely by the transmission electronic control.

shift cable A mechanical cable connected to the driver's shift lever and the transmission manual valve.

shift cover The cover on the transmission that holds the shift rails and forks.

shift finger A flat-sided piece that sits into the shift gates.

shift forks The forks that move the sliding clutches or collars in the transmission.

shift gate Rectangular notches either formed or attached to the shift rails.

shift lever The shift control the driver uses to change the main box gear position.

shift lever and tower The shift lever and the tower that connects it to the transmission.

shift logic The logical process created by the transmission controller using data gained from the vehicle to determine when and how shifting should occur.

shift modulator valve A valve that is moved by modulator pressure and governor pressure for shifting.

shift point The road speed at which a shift occurs.

shift relay valve The spool valve that directs clutch apply pressure to the correct clutch.

shift signal valve A spool valve that is moved by governor pressure for shifting.

shift solenoid 1 (SS1) The solenoid used in fourth-generation and later World Transmissions (WTs) to control the position of the C-1 and C-2 latch valves.

shift tower A raised section with a pivot into which the shift lever fits.

shipping blocks Wooden blocks that support the release bearing and cage the pressure plate on pull-type clutches.

shipping bolts Bolts used to cage the pressure plate of self-adjusting clutches, such as the Eaton Solo and the SACHs Twin Xtend.

shock Inadequate tissue oxygenation resulting from serious injury or illness.

shock absorber A (usually) hydraulic piston and cylinder arrangement designed to minimize spring oscillation.

shock bracket A bracket, usually part of the spring mounted that the shock absorber bolts to.

shock load failure Fracture caused by one sudden shock.

shop or service manual Manufacturer's or after-market information on the repair and service of vehicles.

short circuit An electrical circuit that is formed between two points, allowing current to flow through an unintended pathway.

short circuits Describe a condition in which the current flows along an unintended route.

shunt truck A tractor designed to move semi-trailers around a warehouse yard or intermodal facility. Also known as a *terminal tractor*.

shunts Internal conductors with small calibrated resistance and that direct current flow into the meter while measuring amperage.

side bearing bore The opening machined into the differential carrier that holds the side bearing races.

side bearing cap The cap that bolts the side bearing races to the side bearing bores.

side gears Part of the differential gear set; the side gears are splined to the axles.

sidesway A type of frame damage characterized by a sideways bending or deformation of the frame.

simple fracture A fracture that involves no open wound or internal or external bleeding.

simple machine The simplest mechanism that allows us to gain mechanical advantage.

Simpson gear set The most common compound planetary gear set; consists of two planetary gears sharing a common sun gear; capable of producing three forward and one reverse ratio.

sine wave A mathematical function that describes a repetitive waveform, such as an alternating current signal.

single countershaft transmissions A transmission with only one countershaft.

single flare A sealing system made on the end of metal tubing.

skew The difference in distance between any axle end and the perpendicular centerline. Also called *axle setback* or *setback*.

skive To pare, or cut thin layers off an object to reduce its thickness.

slack adjuster A mechanical lever between the brake chamber and the foundation brake assembly.

slave air valve The valve on the side of a Fuller transmission that controls air flow to the range shift cylinder.

slave cylinder The hydraulic cylinder used to release the clutch in hydraulically actuated clutch systems.

slider mechanism A plate the fifth wheel is attached to that has a ratchet-like set of plungers that enable the fifth wheel to be repositioned forward or backward along the tractor frame.

sliding clutch A device with splines on the inside and outside used as a gear selection method for manual transmissions.

sliding collar A device with splines on the inside only, used as a gear selection method in manual transmissions.

sliding gear transmission A transmission with a gear that is splined to a transmission main shaft and is slid into and out of mesh with a countershaft gear.

sliding T-handle A handle fitted at 90 degrees to the main body that can be slid from side to side.

slip joint A splined shaft and tube assembly that allows driveshaft length changes.

slip yoke A splined tube that allows for driveshaft length changes.

slow adaptive A type of adaptive control that involves making small changes to the shifts as a way to mitigate the effects of clutch wear and solenoid drive and degradation.

slow charger A battery charger that charges at low current.

smart charger A battery charger with microprocessor controlled charging rates and times.

smart electrification A feature that enables the EP 40/50 system's motors to switch over to generating mode to produce as much as 300 amps at 24 volts at idle.

smoke controls A system on mechanically fuelled engines to limit smoke emissions.

snap ring pliers A pair of pliers for installing and removing internal or external snap rings.

snapshot A snapshot records all the relevant TCU data before and after a diagnostic code is set to ease diagnoses.

snub braking A braking technique that should be used when downhill braking. It requires the truck brakes to be applied hard to slow the truck down to about 5 mph (2 kph), then continued repeatedly until the bottom of the hill is reached.

snubber A shock absorbing insulator used to absorb shock loads transmitted by the trailer when the tow vehicle is accelerating or decelerating.

socket An enclosed metal tube commonly with 6 or 12 points to remove and install bolts and nuts.

soft (slack) brakes A situation in which the brakes are applied but the vehicle is not slowing or stopping effectively.

soft-dampened clutch A clutch with extra-long travel windows for its dampening springs; used to combat resonance in a driveline.

solenoid An electromagnetic switch.

solid I-beam A type of solid steering axle named for its forged I-beam design.

solvent A highly flammable liquid that can dissolve other substances.

solvent tank A tank containing solvents to clean vehicle parts.

source address (SA) The field that designates which control module is sending the message.

specific gravity A measurement of the density of a substance.

specific heat The amount of heat a substance must absorb to undergo a temperature change of 1°F.

speed brace A U-shaped socket wrench that allows highspeed operation. Also called a *speeder handle*.

speed gears The gears on the countershaft and main shaft that create the transmission ratios, also known as *range gears*.

speed nut A nut usually made of thin metal; it does not need to be held when started but it is not as strong as a conventional nut. A fast and convenient way to secure a screw.

spider gear A beveled gear that is a component of the differential gear set; it is fitted to the four legs of the differential cross and rotates with it. Also known as a *differential pinion gear*.

spigot bearing A small bearing that supports the inboard end of the pinion gear when the pinion is straddle mounted. Also called *pinion pilot bearing*.

spinout A low traction situation where one drive wheel or one drive axle spins wildly while the other remains stationary.

spiral bevel gear A bevel gear set with spirally or helically cut gears.

spiral bevel gearing Bevel gears that are cut helically, making the gear set stronger and quieter.

spiral-wound cell battery A type of AGM battery in which the positive and negative electrodes are coiled into a tight spiral cell with an absorbent micro-glass mat placed between the plates.

split ball gauge (small hole gauge) A gauge that is good for measuring small holes where telescoping gauges cannot fit.

split charge relay A system designed to separate the main starting battery and the auxiliary battery. Also called a *battery isolator system*.

split guide ring The split guide ring that is attached to the impeller and the turbine blades and creates a circular fluid passage.

splitter shift cylinder The shift cylinder that controls the splitter sliding clutch.

spool valve A valve that has a series of lands and cutaways in a precise fitting bore.

spool valve A valve connected to the input shaft of the steering gear that controls the direction of pressurized fluid through the steering gear. Along with the torsion bar, changes in torque applied to the steering wheel and the direction of torque will alter the direction of fluid flow through the valve. Also called a *rotary valve*.

sprain An injury in which a joint is forced beyond its natural movement limit.

spray-wash cabinet A cleaning cabinet that sprays solvent under pressure to clean vehicle parts.

spring brake Brakes used on rear drive axles to apply park brakes which are also referred to as "maxi-brakes."

spring brake priority A trailer spring brake relay valve which will allow the park-spring brakes to release with only air supplied by the trailer supply valve.

spring brake relay valve A specialized relay valve that is used to supply air to hold off the spring brakes or release air and apply the spring brakes. Also called an *inversion valve*.

spring pack A leaf spring with more than one steel plate or leaf stacked together and used for a spring. Also called a *multi-leaf spring*.

spring rate The amount of force required to deflect the spring; a low spring rate means a softer spring and therefore ride; a higher spring rate adds more lateral stability but gives a harsher ride.

spring washer A washer that compresses as the nut tightens; the nut is spring loaded against this surface, which makes it unlikely to work loose. The ends of the spring washer also bite into the metal.

sprung weight The portion of the vehicle supported by the springs; includes the frame, the body, the load, and any accessories.

spur gear A gear with teeth cut parallel to its axis of rotation.

square file A type of file with a square cross-section.

square thread A thread type with square shoulders used to translate rotational to lateral movement.

squeeze The point of clutch pedal actuation on a pull-type clutch when the clutch brake is being actuated or squeezed. Also called *clutch brake actuation*.

stabilizer bars Transversely mounted bars that control axle alignment and add lateral stability while the vehicle is turning by transferring some of the load from the side of the vehicle on the outside of a turn to the side on the inside of the turn.

stainless steel A rust-resistant steel alloy containing chromium; normally resistant to stain and tarnish.

stall speed The maximum speed the engine can drive the torque converter impeller with the turbine held stationary.

standard (imperial) system Bolts, nuts, and studs can have either metric or imperial threads. They are designated by their thread diameter, thread pitch, length, and grade. Imperial measures are in feet, inches, and fractions of inches. Most countries use metric.

standard hub A wheel hub that uses manually adjusted wheel bearing end play.

stand-by mode A reefer operating mode during which the engine is not driving the compressor.

start enable relay The start enable relay is controlled by the TCU and interrupts the circuit to the starter solenoid unless the TCU passes a self-check and verifies the transmission is in neutral

startability The capability of a vehicle to commence moving forward on a specified grade.

starting, lighting, and ignition (SLI) battery A battery designed for one, short-duration, deep discharge of up to 50% depth of discharge (DOD) during engine cranking.

state of charge The amount of refrigerant in a system compared to how much should be in it.

state of charge test A test that indicates how charged or discharged a battery is, not how much capacity it has.

static radius The distance from the tire center to ground level.

stationary clutch A hydraulic clutch used to hold a planetary gear component stationary and usually splined to the transmission case.

stator The element inside a torque converter most responsible for torque multiplication.

stator inner hub The inner race of the stator one-way clutch; it splines to the stator ground shaft.

stator support shaft A stationary shaft that holds the inner hub of the stator one-way clutch. Also called *ground shaft.*

steel ruler A ruler that is made from stainless steel. Stainless steel rulers commonly come in various lengths.

steering angle sensor A sensor that measures the rotational angle of the steering wheel.

steering arm An arm that extends from the steering knuckle. The tie-rods connect to these arms in order to steer the wheels.

steering axis inclination angle (SAI) The angle formed by an imaginary line running through the upper and lower steering pivots relative to vertical as viewed from the front. The angle formed between true vertical and the angle of the kingpin. Also called *kingpin inclination angle (KPI).*

steering axle An axle that allows the vehicle to turn.

steering column A column affixed between the steering wheel and the steering box, usually made to collapse during a crash.

steering gear A device that converts the rotary motion of the steering wheel to the linear motion needed to steer the vehicle.

steering geometry A geometric arrangement of linkages in the steering of a vehicle designed to solve the problem of keeping the wheels properly oriented through various positions of the steering and suspension systems

steering knuckle A device that connects the front wheel to the suspension; it pivots on the top and bottom, thus allowing the front wheels to turn.

steering linkage Steel rods that connect the steering box to the steering arms on the steering knuckle.

steering ratio The mechanical advantage produced by the steering gear, which converts large turns of the steering wheel into smaller turns of the tire to ease steering for the driver.

steering shafts The shaft that connects the steering wheel to the steering gear assembly of an vehicle.

steering stops Bolts used to limit the turning angle of the steering knuckle.

steering system A term used to describe all the components and parts involved in steering a vehicle.

step-down transformer A transformer used to reduce voltage in the secondary coil. A battery charger would use a step-down transformer to change 120 volts into 12 to charge a 12-volt battery.

step-up transformer A transformer used to increase the voltage from a lower input voltage to a higher output, such as an ignition coil.

straddle mount pinion A pinion supported by two opposed tapered roller bearings and a small spigot bearing.

straight edges A measuring device generally made of steel to check how flat a surface is.

straight grinder A powered grinder with the wheel set at 90 degrees to the shaft.

strain An injury caused by the overstretching of muscles and tendons.

stress concentration Anything that reduces or changes the integrity or strength of the material. Also called *stress riser*.

stress riser Anything that reduces or changes the integrity or strength of the material. Also called *stress concentration*.

stringer Small inclusion in a cast or formed metal that weaken it.

stroke The range of motion of a cylinder.

stroke sensing ASA A slack adjuster that makes adjustments to slack based on the measured rotation between a brake application and release.

stud A type of threaded fastener with a thread cut on each end, as opposed to having a bolt head on one end.

stud-piloted disc wheel A type of disc wheel that retains the disc using studs attached to the hub and a tapered, or ball-type, wheel nut to center the disc onto the hub.

sulfation A chemical reaction that results in the soft sulfate turning to a hardened crystalline form that cannot be driven from the plates in the battery.

sulfuric acid A type of acid that when mixed with pure water forms the basis of battery acid or electrolyte.

sun gear The small, externally toothed gear at the center of the planetary gear set.

sun gear shaft The shaft that connects the front and center sun gears in the Allison transmission.

super single tire Wide-base low profile tire used to replace two conventional single tires on an axle to save weight and reduce wheel end parts.

superheat The temperature differential between the refrigerant vapor at the evaporator and the refrigerant vapor at the evaporator inlet.

supplemental additive Aftermarket additive available for automatic transmissions but not recommended by manufacturers.

supply reservoir The first air reservoir to receive air from the air compressor or dryer. Water and oil condense in this tank which supplies the primary and secondary air reservoirs. Also called the *service reservoir*.

supporting statement A statement that urges the speaker to elaborate on a particular topic.

SureShift Meritor's first line of fully automated transmissions.

suspect parameter number (SPN) A numerical identifier that defines the data in a fault message and the priority of the fault.

swaged When two metal components are fitted together by deforming the metal of one to fit the other precisely.

swaging A method of joining a fitting to a fluid conductor by deforming either the fitting or the conductor to form a strong joint.

swash plate A displacement unit on which displacement pistons are arranged axially to a driveshaft.

swing clearance The clearance remaining between a trailer and tractor when the combination vehicle is cornering.

swing shackle A spring mounting system consisting of two upright flat bars side-by-side. The top of the bars are pinned to the frame spring bracket and the bottom of the bars are pinned to the rear leaf spring eye. Shackles allow the leaf spring length to change as the suspension oscillates.

synchronized transmission A transmission that uses sliding clutches or collars fitted over synchronizer hubs that are splined to the main shaft to select gear ratios.

synchronizer A device to match shaft and gear speeds for clash-free engagement.

synchronous speed The point at which the on-coming clutch has applied and there is no more slippage. Turbine shaft seed times the gear ratio equals output shaft speed.

Synflex A reinforced nylon material used to make flexible airlines.

synthetic-based lubricant A lubricant that is manufactured rather than refined and so has much longer service life; it can be a blend of natural and synthetic materials.

system identifier (SID) A fault code used by J-1587 protocols that identifies which subsystem has failed.

system manager A transmission control module used with older Gen 1 and Gen 2 Eaton AutoShift transmissions.

systematic lock-up A strategy that applies the lock-up clutch as soon as possible for improved fuel economy. Also called *programmed lock-up*.

tab washer A washer that gets its name from the small tabs that are folded back to secure the washer. After the nut or bolt has been tightened, the washer remains exposed and is folded up to grip the flats and prevent movement.

tachograph A device fitted to a vehicle to record various pieces of information, such as time, speed, rest periods, and distance travelled by each of the vehicle's drivers.

tag axle A rear non-drive axle mounted behind the drive axle.

tandem Two drive axles connected by a power divider.

tandem axle A two-axle tractor or trailer configuration.

tap A term used to generically describe an internal thread-cutting tool.

tap handle A tool designed to securely hold taps for cutting internal threads.

taper key Used to prevent the free rotation of gears or pulleys on a shaft; used to anchor a pulley to a shaft or a disc to a driving shaft.

taper pins Used to position parts on a shaft; for example, gears, pulleys, and collars.

taper tap A tap with a tapper; it is usually the first of three taps used when cutting internal threads.

taper-current charger A battery charger that applies either constant voltage or constant amperage to the battery through a manually adjusted current selection switch.

TC-Tronic A ZF AMT that uses a torque converter for input; for heavy applications.

technical service bulletin (TSB) Information issued by manufacturers to alert technicians of unexpected problems or changes to repair procedures.

telematics A branch of information technology that uses specialized applications for long-distance transmission of information to and from a vehicle.

telescoping gauge Gauge used for measuring distances in awkward spots such as the bottom of a deep cylinder.

tensile strength The amount of force required before a material deforms or breaks.

tension A force that tries to pull apart the bottom flange of a frame rail supported between two points.

terminal tractor A tractor designed to move semi-trailers around a warehouse yard or intermodal facility. Also known as a *shunt truck*.

test certificate A certificate issued when lifting equipment has been checked and deemed safe.

test light The simplest piece of electrical test equipment, which consists of either a 12- or 24-volt incandescent light bulb connected to an insulated lead and a sharpened metal probe.

thermal efficiency A measurement of how much of the fuel used is actually turned into power to drive the vehicle.

thermal fuse A type of fuse opened by heat produced from resistance caused by high amperage flow.

thermistor A temperature-sensitive variable resistor commonly used to measure coolant, oil, fuel, and air temperatures.

thermocouple A thermoelectric device consisting of two dissimilar metals that produce voltage when heated.

thermostatic expansion valve (TXV) An expansion device used in commercial vehicle air-conditioning systems.

third-degree burns Burns that involve white or blackened areas and damage to all skin layers and underlying structures and tissues.

thread chaser A device similar to a die that cleans up rusty or damaged threads.

thread pitch The coarseness or fineness of a thread as measured by the distance from the peak of one thread to the next, in threads per inch.

thread repair A generic term to describe a number of processes that can be used to repair threads.

three Cs Concern (the concern, or problem, with the vehicle); cause (the cause of the concern); and correction (fixing the problem).

three-coil gauge A gauge in which three field coils are wound in series, with a coil at minimum reading, one at maximum reading, and one between the two.

three-quarters floating bearing The wheel bearing is supported by the axle housing but the outer flange of the drive axle rides on the bearing, rarely seen today.

three-way valve A valve that directs hot refrigerant gas to either the condenser (in cool mode) or directly to the evaporator (in heat or defrost modes).

threshold limit value (TLV) The maximum allowable concentration of a given material in the surrounding air.

throttle valve A valve that produces a pressure based on throttle position. Also called the *modulator valve*.

through shaft The output shaft of an inter-axle differential. The rear side gear is part of or splined to the through shaft. Also known as *output shaft*.

thrust angle The relationship between the centerline of the vehicle and the angle of the rear tires.

thrust line The direction in which the rear wheels are pointing.

thrust screw A screw that stops the crown gear from flexing under load.

tie-rod A steering component that transfers linear motion from the steering box to the steering arms at the front wheels.

tie-rod end Articulating ball-and-socket joints attached to each end of the tie-rod.

time division multiplexing A type of multiplexing used in on-board networks and that works by dividing the time available to each network module or device.

time to full apply (TFA) The point after synchronous speed has been detected at which the solenoid controlling the on-coming clutch in a World Transmission (WT) is commanded to full pressure (that is, to fully apply the clutch).

timing chain A steel chain connecting the crankshaft assembly to the camshaft assembly.

timing gear A sprocket attached to the crankshaft assembly and the camshaft assembly.

tin A metal most often used as a corrosion-resistant coating in automotive applications.

tin snips Cutting device for sheet metal; works in a similar fashion to scissors.

tire bead Steel wire wound together to form a cable; when bundled together, they sit at the wheel rim to form an airtight seal between the tire and the rim.

tire casing The foundational body of the tire, consisting of several layers of fabric cord, called plies, encased with a rubber compound; a network of cords that give the tire shape and strength; also known as *casing cords*.

tire flap A piece of rubber that wraps around the rim to protect the inner tube from chafing, pinching, and cracking caused by friction between the valve stem slot in the rim and the edges of the tire bead.

tire inflation pressure The level of air in the tire that provides it with load-carrying capacity and which affects overall vehicle performance.

tire pressure gauge A gauge used to measure the air pressure within a tire.

tire pressure monitoring system (TPMS) A system with in wheel sensors that monitors tire inflation pressure and temperature.

tire tread separation The separation of the tread from the tire casing.

TMC RP 618 A procedure established by The Maintenance Council for obtaining acceptable wheel bearing end play of 0.001" and 0.005" (0.025 mm and 0.127 mm).

toe A measurement of how much the front wheels are turned in or out from a straight-ahead position. The angle is referenced from a position directly above the tires and facing forward.

toe The end of a crown gear tooth closest to the center of its axis.

toe-in A condition that exists when, as seen from above, the wheels are closer together at the front and farther apart at the rear.

toe-out A condition that exists when, as seen from above, the wheels are closer together in the rear and farther apart at the front.

toe-out on turns A geometric steering concept that the inner wheel should have a smaller turning angle than the outside wheel. Also called *Ackermann angle*.

tongue weight (TW) The weight supported by the ball (tongue) in a ball hitch.

tongue weight (TW) The weight supported by the ball (tongue) in a ball hitch.

tooth face The area that actually comes into contact with a mating gear and is parallel to the gear's axis of rotation.

top land The apex of a tooth.

topoid A type of amboid gear set with the pinion gear mounted even higher than a normal amboid set.

torque The twisting force applied to a shaft that may or may not result in motion.

torque angle A method of tightening bolts or nuts based on angles of rotation.

torque balance A situation in which braking torque is uniform for all wheels.

torque converter A type of fluid coupling that is also capable of multiplying torque.

torque converter control (TCC) A control solenoid used in fourth-generation and later World Transmissions (WTs).

torque limiting A reduction in engine power out; used as strategy to reduce wheel slip or loss of directional control.

torque multiplication phase Occurs whenever the impeller is turning significantly faster than the turbine.

torque rise The difference between engine torque produced at rated speed (maximum engine RPM under load) and peak torque. Torque rise is expressed as a percentage of torque at the rated speed.

torque rod A rod that transfers acceleration, braking, and lateral forces from the axle to the frame and also maintains axle alignment. Torque rods can usually be adjusted by one method or another to realign the axles when required.

torque specification Describes the amount of twisting force allowable for a fastener or a specification showing the twisting force from an engine crankshaft; supplied by manufacturers.

torque wrench A tool used to measure the rotational or twisting force applied to fasteners.

torque-to-yield (TTY) A method of tightening bolts close to their yield point or the point at which they will not return to their original length.

torque-to-yield (TTY) bolts Bolts that are tightened using the torque-to-yield method.

Torsen A biased torque differential from General Motors.

torsion bar Bars in a vehicle's suspension system that twist in response to the movement of the wheels and absorb their vertical movement.

torsion rod A thin, spring-like metal rod that connects to one end of the rotary valve to change its position.

torsional excitation Twisting forces caused by inertial excitation.

torsional vibrations Vibrations caused by twisting forces on the driveshaft; these occur twice per revolution.

torsional vibrations Powerful vibrations caused by the firing force, twisting and accelerating the crankshaft every time a cylinder fires.

torus The hollowed-out donut shape of the rear of the converter housing and the turbine.

torx bolt Often found in vehicle engines in places such as cylinder heads to blocks, where particular tightening sequences are required.

total indicated runout (TIR) The difference between the high and low measurement of a flat surface, such as the flywheel friction surface.

total mesh adjustment A setting of the appropriate depth for the sector shaft and nut so as not to bind or have excess free play.

toxic dust Any dust that may contain fine particles that could be harmful to humans or the environment.

track rod Typically, transversely mounted torque rods that counteract lateral forces acting on the vehicle.

tracking The positioning of the tires relative to the vehicle. Also called *wheel alignment*.

traction battery A rechargeable battery used for propulsion in hybrid electric vehicles.

traction control An enhancement to the ABS system that is used to improve vehicle stability when accelerating.

traction motor An electric motor that provides propulsion to a vehicle.

tractor protection valves A valve that controls the supply of air to the trailer from the tractor. The valve automatically isolates the tractor air reservoirs from being completely drained if a trailer breaks away from a tractor.

trailer The cargo carrying portion of a combination vehicle.

trailer axle A non-drive axle used by trailers and which generally has no steering linkage unless it is a self-steering axle.

trailer brake control valve A hand-operated, cabmounted control valve used to manually apply the trailer service brakes.

trailer supply valve A push-pull valve in the cab used to supply air pressure to the trailer air brake reservoirs.

trailer swing-out A condition caused by incorrect pneumatic balance between a tractor and trailer. Typically, trailer brakes are applied at too high a pressure locking the trailer brakes. The trailer tires slide and cause the trailer to swing out into an adjacent lane.

trailing arms Refers to large strong beams attached to the vehicle frame and to the axle, they support the spring medium.

trailing shoes Brake shoes installed so that they are applied in the opposite direction to the forward rotation of the brake drum; not self-energizing and less efficient at developing braking force.

transfer case A component that is bolted to the back of the transmission or connected to it by a short driveshaft; allows the output of a transmission to flow to both the rear and the front axles. Also called *dropbox*.

transient voltage suppression (TVS) diodes Specialized diodes in the rectifier bridge that become resistive rather than conductive at a specific voltage level.

transmission control module (TCM) The electronic controller that issues commands to the solenoids inside the transmission to obtain the desired range. Also known as the *transmission electronic control unit (ECU)*.

transmission control unit (TCU) The unit that controls the shifting in an electronically automated transmission. Also called *transmission electronic control module (ECM)*.

transmission electronic control module (ECM) The unit that controls the shifting in an electronically automated transmission. Also called *transmission control unit (TCU)*.

transmission electronic control unit (ECU) The electronic controller that issues commands to the solenoids inside the transmission to obtain the desired range. Also called the *transmission control unit (TCU)*.

transmission oil cooler A series of oil tubes or passages that are cooled by engine coolant.

transmission vent A vent on the transmission that is open to atmospheric pressure.

transport temperature control Heating or cooling over a wide range of outside temperatures and product storage temperatures.

transverse vibrations Vibrations caused by shaft imbalance; these occur once per revolution.

TranSynd fluid A full synthetic fluid produced by Castrol, to Allison specification; TranSynd is the recommended fluid for all Allison transmissions.

Traxon ZF's latest AMT with five different input modules available.

tread A cap of molded rubber compound attached to the top of a tire's belt system.

treadle valve The center of the brake delivery system. Also called the *foot valve*.

trickle charger A battery charger that charges at a low amperage rate.

tridem Three drive axles connected by power dividers.

trimmer An accumulator used in the ATEC/CEC systems to smoothen out the shift process.

trimmer regulator valve A valve that modulates trimmer valve action.

trimmer valve A valve used to soften a clutch application.

trinary switch A switch with three sets of internal contacts to protect against low pressure, cutout in case of high pressure, and turn the engine fan on and off.

trunnion The smooth ends of the U-joint cross that accepts the bearing caps.

TruTrac A biased torque differential produced by Eaton.

tube yoke A yoke with two ears that accept a U-joint and which is welded to the driveshaft tube.

tube-flaring tool A tool that makes a sealing flare on the end of metal tubing.

tubeless tire A tire in which the air is not sealed in an inner tube.

tube-type tire A tire in which an inner tube containing the air is separate from the casing.

tubing Metal pipe that is intended to be bent and shaped to fit an application.

tubing cutter A hand tool for cutting pipe or tubing squarely.

turbine The torque converter element that is splined to the transmission input shaft.

turbine pull down A decrease in turbine speed as a shift is in progress that results from the on-coming clutch starting to control its gear train component; the signal for the transmission to enter closed-loop control of the shift in progress.

turbocharger cut-off valves An air-operated valve which closes the air inlet to the air dryer to prevent engine intake boost pressure from leaking out the dryer's purge port.

turning radius A measure of how small a circle the vehicle can turn in when the steering wheel is turned to the limit.

twin-leading-shoe drum brake Brake shoe arrangement in which both brake shoes are self-energizing in the forward direction.

twist A type of frame damage that occurs when one rail bends up and the other rail bends down.

twist drill A hardened steel drill bit for making holes in metals, plastics, and wood.

two-height fifth wheel A specialty stationary fifth wheel that can be either air or hydraulically raised or lowered.

Type 1 circuit breaker A cycling circuit breaker that automatically resets.

Type 2 circuit breaker A non-cycling circuit breaker.

Type 3 circuit breaker A circuit breaker that requires manual reset.

Type K thermocouple A low-cost, general-purpose, temperature-sensing element connected to the same meter terminals for measuring DC millivolts.

typology The manner in which modules are connected to one another.

U-bolt A frame-body attachment that goes over a sub-frame attached to the vehicle body and down both sides of the frame rail before being clamped at the bottom flange of the rail.

U-joint A cross-shaped joint with bearings on each leg where one set of parallel legs is connected to the end of one shaft and the other set of parallel legs is connected to the end of a second shaft. This arrangement allows the shafts to operate at shallow angles to each other. Also called a *universal joint*.

ultra capacitor A new generation of high-capacity and high-energy density capacitors.

UltraShift Eaton's two-pedal AMT; completely shift by wire with no clutch pedal.

underdrive ratio Any ratio that decreases output speed while increasing output torque. Also known as a *gear reduction*.

underslung A suspension system where the leaf spring is mounted under the axle.

undertread The depth of the area between the bottom of the original tread grooves and the top of the uppermost breaker.

United States Department of Transport (USDOT) number Any hazardous materials carriers who move enough materials requiring a safety permit must also register for a USDOT number.

universal joint A cross-shaped joint with bearings on each leg where one set of parallel legs is connected to the end of one shaft and the other set of parallel legs is connected to the end of a second shaft. This arrangement allows the shafts to operate at shallow angles to each other. Also called a *U-joint*, a *Cardan joint*, or a *Hooke joint*.

unloader valves Air-operated piston-like valves used to physically hold open the air compressor's intake air check valves.

unloading The state of the air compressor when it is not building air pressure. Unloader valves hold the check valves open.

unsprung weight The vehicle weight not supported by the suspension system, includes the axles, the tires, wheels and the brakes.

untripped rollovers A vehicle rollover condition occurring when a truck strikes a curb and then rolls down an embankment.

upper coupler A steel plate and a kingpin fastened to the underside of the forward portion of a semi-trailer frame and designed to tow and support the weight of the trailer.

V blocks Metal blocks with a V-shaped cutout for holding shafts while working on them. Also referred to as *vee blocks*.

vacuum booster A vacuum operated boost system for hydraulic brakes.

vacuum gauge A gauge designed to read negative pressure or vacuum.

vacuum pump A pump used to evacuate the air-conditioning system and put it into a deep vacuum or low pressure to remove moisture

validating statement A statement that shows common interest in the topic being discussed.

Valley Forge (VF) diagram A schematic wiring diagram that uses SAE-type symbols.

valve adjusting cam Small cam on the end of the shift signal valves that, when turned, increase the shift point.

valve body test stand A special test stand specifically for testing and setting up Allison transmission control valve bodies and shift points.

valve-regulated lead–acid (VRLA) battery A type of sealed lead–acid battery used in heavy-duty equipment. It does not require the addition of water. Also called a *sealed lead–acid battery (SLA)* or *recombinant battery*.

vane pump A hydraulic pump that uses sliding vanes to move the fluid.

variable capacitance pressure sensor An active sensor that measures both dynamic and static pressure.

variable pitch stator A stator with blades that can change the angle to alter the torque converter multiplication factor.

variable reluctance sensor A sensor used to measure rotational speed, including wheel speed, vehicle speed, engine speed, and camshaft and crankshaft position.

variable spring rate A spring or suspension system where more force is required to deflect the spring as load is added, allow a soft rate when unloaded and a much stiffer suspension when loaded.

variable-bleed solenoid (VBS) Hydraulic solenoids used in late-model Allison World Transmissions (WTs), which control application by allowing some of the pressure going to a device to bleed off to exhaust.

variable-ratio steering gears Steering gears that use sector shafts with long and short lengths of teeth.

vehicle emission control information (VECI) label A label used by technicians to identify engine and emission control information for the vehicle.

vehicle hoist A type of vehicle lifting tool designed to lift the entire vehicle.

vehicle identification number (VIN) A unique serial number composed of 17 characters—letters and digits—that is assigned to each vehicle produced.

vehicle safety certification (VSC) label A label certifying that the vehicle meets the Federal Motor Vehicle Safety, Bumper, and Theft Prevention Standards in effect at the time of manufacture.

vehicle speed sensor (VSS) An inductive pick-up sensor that reads the speed of the transmission output shaft.

vehicle-powered refrigeration units A transport refrigeration system that is powered by a compressor located in the vehicle's engine.

vernier caliper An accurate measuring device for internal, external, and depth measurements that incorporates fixed and adjustable jaws.

vertical load The weight supported by a hitching device, which is applied downwards by the weight of the trailer.

vibrasorbers Flexible stainless steel lines that connect the compressor inlet and outlet to the trailer refrigeration system and absorb compressor movement and vibration.

vibration analyzer A device used to identify the root cause of vehicle vibration.

virtual fuse A software-controlled fuse that uses field effect transistors for the circuit control device A circuit protection strategy that monitors circuit amperage with software and shuts off the circuit when amperage exceeds a predetermined threshold. Also called *e-fuses*.

vocation The type of service a vehicle is involved in.

vocational A truck that is subject to primarily off-road operation and typically is heavily loaded.

volatile memory Volatile memory refers to a type of data storage that is lost or erased when the ignition power is switched off.

volatile organic compounds (VOCs) Evaporative emissions that vehicles emit.

volt The unit used to measure potential difference or electrical pressure.

voltage The speed at which electrons travel from atom to atom.

vortex flow The flow of fluid from the impeller, through the turbine, through the stator, and back to the impeller.

wad punch A type of punch that is hollow for cutting circular shapes in soft materials, such as gaskets.

walking beam A beam with each end attached to the axles of a tandem axle arrangement and its center attached to the frame directly or through a spring system. The beam reduces the impact of road bumps to the frame by 50% and equalizes the load carried by each of the axles. Also called an *equalizing beam*.

warding file A type of thin, flat file with a tapered end.

water fade A type of brake fade that occurs when water gets between the friction surfaces and the drum and acts as a lubricant and reduces braking efficiency.

water wicking The movement of water through wiring due to its adhesive and cohesive properties.

waterfall arrangement Two or more universal joint arrangement where the joint angles form parallel lines; a method of angle cancellation for use with parallel angles. Also called *parallel joint arrangement*.

water-pump pliers Adjustable pliers with parallel jaws that allow you to increase or decrease the size of the jaws by selecting a different set of channels.

Watt's law A law that defines the relationship between power, amperage, and voltage.

wave inverter A device that changes the shape of electrical current waves.

Weather-Pack connector An environmentally sealed push-to-seat electrical connection system supplied in one- to six-pin configurations.

web The upright portion of the frame rail. Also called *frame rail web*.

wedge brakes Brakes that use a wedge pushed between two rollers as a lever to apply the brakes.

weight matching The process of matching the tire's lightest point with the rim's heaviest point (generally at the valve stem) for the purpose of reducing the tire's radial imbalance.

welding helmet Protective gear designed for arc welding; it provides protection against foreign articles entering the eye, and the lens is tinted to reduce the glare of the welding arc.

wet load Very damp products.

wet tank Another name for the service or supply reservoir. It is called a wet tank since moisture and vaporized oil condense in this tank.

wheel alignment The positioning of the tires relative to the vehicle. Also called *tracking*.

wheel cylinders A hydraulic cylinder with one or two pistons, seals, dust boots, and a bleeder screw that pushes the brake shoes into contact with the brake drum to slow or stop the vehicle.

wheel end The assembly at the end of the axle.

wheel end play The free movement of the wheel hub assembly along the axle spindle axis.

wheel hop A situation where the wheels literally hop off the ground and lose their contact with the road, caused by excessive suspension wind-up usually due to extreme braking but can occur on acceleration too.

wheel lock-up A condition where the drive or steer tires have stopped rotating when braking.

wheel nuts The nuts that secure the wheel onto the wheel studs.

wheel offset The distance from the hub mounting surface to the centerline of the wheel.

wheel rim The outer circular lip of the metal on which the inside edge of the tire is mounted.

wheel slip A condition in which excess torque from the drivetrain causes the tire to break free from the road surface. Also called *wheel spin*.

wheel spin A condition in which excess torque from the drivetrain causes the tire to break free from the road surface. Also called *wheel slip*.

wheel studs The threaded fasteners that attach the wheel to the vehicle.

wide-base tire Large tire with a low aspect ratio. Also called *floatation tire*.

wide-range planar sensor A type of sensor technology that uses a current pump to calculate relative concentrations of oxygen, nitric oxide, and ammonia in exhaust gases.

Wilson gear set A compound planetary gear set consisting of three planetary gears interconnected; capable of producing five forward and one reverse ratio.

World Transmission Electronic Control (WTEC) Allison's original electronic transmission control system for the World Transmission.

worm and crown Older drive axle gear arrangement capable of very high gear reductions in a compact space. Also known as *worm wheel*.

worm gear A gear with a helical, threaded shaft that is attached to the steering column and meshes with a ball nut that transfers motion from the steering wheel to the steering linkage. Also called the worm shaft.

worm wheel Older drive axle gear arrangement capable of very high gear reductions in a compact space. Also known as *worm and crown*.

wrench A generic term to describe tools that tighten and loosen fasteners with hexagonal heads.

Wye windings Stator windings in which one end of each phase winding is taken to a central point where the ends are connected together.

yaw The rotation of a vehicle around its vertical axis; the difference between the vehicle's intended direction and the actual direction of travel.

yaw control Minimizing the slip or difference between the desired or steered direction of a vehicle and actual direction a vehicle is moving.

yield point The point at which a bolt is stretched so hard that it fails; it is measured in pounds per square inch (psi) or kilopascals (kPa) of bolt cross-section.

yield strength An engineering term used to describe the amount of force required to permanently deform a material. Yield strength occurs at the material's elastic limit—the maximum force a material can withstand and still return to its original configuration.

Zener diode A type of diode that behaves like a typical silicon diode up to a precise voltage threshold called the Zener point. After it reaches the Zener point voltage, the diode conducts in both directions.

Zener point The voltage at which a diode will conduct current in both directions instead of just one

zero offset When the plane of the hub mounting surface is even with the centerline of the wheel.

INDEX

Note: Page numbers followed by *f*, or *t* indicate materials in figures, or tables, respectively.

A

A-frames, 798, 812
A-train, 21, 22*f*, 30, 1106, 1107*f*, 1132
A-type lock, 1118–1119, 1118*f*, 1132
  adjustment, 1126
A type regulators, 441, 442*f*
abnormal noises, performance testing, 1738
abnormal system operation, 631
ABS. *See* anti-lock braking system
absorbed glass mat (AGM) batteries, 345, 347, 356–357, 356*f*, 367, 431, 444
  advantages, 356
  spiral cell Optima battery, 345*f*
abuse failures, 1635–1637, 1639
  transmission failure, 1293
AC-to-DC inverter, 1661, 1665
ACC. *See* adaptive cruise control
accelerated wear, 1554
accelerator position sensor (APS), 558, 565, 565*f*
accident report, 50–51
accidents and injuries
  possibility of, 71, 71*f*
  precautions for avoiding, 71
account system, vehicle, 61–62
accumulators, 1409, 1754, 1765, 1797–1798, 1832
  cycling clutch orifice tub (CCOT), 1717
  functions of, 1824
  hydraulic, 1824–1827
  relay valve, 1497
  removing, inspecting, and instalment of, 1754–1756
  safety precautions for hydraulic, 1826–1827
  types of, 1824–1826
acetylene, 139
acid, 147–148
Ackerman arms, 1573
Ackermann angle, 737, 745, 746*f*, 757
Ackermann principle, 745, 757
Ackermann steering arms, 856, 857*f*
ACLS. *See* automatic chassis lubrication system
ACPU. *See* air-conditioning protection unit
ACTG. *See* alternating current traction generator
active fault, 631, 655
active listener, 41*f*
active plate, 378
active sensors, 563, 593
  electronic control module (ECM), 559*f*
  vs. passive sensors, 558–559
ACTM. *See* alternating current traction motor
actual frame strength, 768–769
actual gear contact patterns, 1624, 1625*f*
actuating rod, 1070
actuation systems, clutch
  air-assisted hydraulic actuation systems, 1156–1158
  automatically actuated clutches, 1158–1160
  hydraulic actuation systems, 1156
  mechanical linkage system, 1155–1156, 1156*f*
actuator stroke, 985*t*
actuators, 1797
  brake, 904, 905*f*
  hydraulic, 1815–1819, 1816*f*
  linear, 1815–1817
  rotary, 1817
AD-IS. *See* Air Dryer Integrated System
adaptive control, 1521, 1526
adaptive cruise control (ACC), 1059–1060, 1059*f*, 1063
adaptive learning, 1307, 1336
adaptive logic control, 1462
ADB. *See* air disc brakes
addendum, 1195, 1207
additives, ATF, 146–147
adequate ventilation, 75
adhesives and sealants, 183–184
adjustable air pressure, 813
adjustable drag links, 855
adjusted pull-type clutch, 1171, 1171*f*
adjusters, types of, 1072
  star wheel-type adjuster, 1073, 1073*f*
  wedge-type adjuster, 1073, 1073*f*
adjusting ring, 1170, 1171*f*, 1172, 1189
adjustment procedures, clutch, 1169–1170
  linkage adjustment, 1169–1170
  pull-type clutch adjustment, 1169
  push-type clutch adjustment, 1169
ADLO. *See* automatic disengagement lockout
adsorbtion, 939, 963
Advanced Battery Technologies, 334, 345
advanced brake testing, 990–995
AED. *See* automated external defibrillator
aeration, 1423, 1441, 1814, 1832
aerodynamic, 17, 17*f*
aftertreatment system monitors, 635, 642*f*
  DPF monitoring, 640–641
  SCR monitoring, 641
AGS. *See* Automatic Gear Shift
air-assisted hydraulic actuation systems, 1156–1158
air bag, 813, 836
air bellows, 813
air booster units, 1082–1083, 1083*f*
  direct operation, 1084, 1085*f*
  indirect operation, 1083–1084, 1083*f*–1085*f*
air brake circuits, 925, 928. *See also* air brake systems
  air delivery and control systems. *See* air delivery and control systems, components of
  air supply systems. *See* air supply systems
  park/emergency brake circuit, 955–956, 955*f*–956*f*
  trailer air circuits. *See* trailer air circuits
air brake foundation systems, 890–892
  air disc brakes, 915–918
  cam brake system. *See* cam brake system
  subcomponents of, 897*f*
  wedge brake systems, 919, 919*f*
air brake pressure balance testing, 993–995
air brake systems, 887–890, 926, 927*f*, 1080. *See also* air-over-hydraulic braking systems
  advantages of, 926–928, 927*f*
  basic principles of, 926
  components, complaints and remedies for, 976*t*–980*t*
  disadvantages of, 928
  full inspection of, 1868, 1869–1870
  subsystems and control circuits, 928–930, 929*f*–930*f*
  testing, 981

air brake valves, inspecting and servicing, 995–1005
air brakes, adjusting, 1021–1029
  automatic slack adjusters, 1024–1029
  inch, 1021–1023
  manual slack adjusters, 1024
air braking problems, troubleshooting, 976–980, 976*t*–980*t*
air breather cap filter, 1797
air buildup time, 1007
air charging systems, 930
air chisel. *See* air hammer
air compressors, 930–931, 931*f*–932*f*, 1006–1007
  discharge line, 932
  operation—loading and unloading, 931–932, 932*f*
air-conditioning components, 1875, 1877–1879
  engine-off engine compartment inspection, conducting, 1877
air-conditioning compressor
  cross-sectional view of, 1703–1706, 1705*f*
  rules for, 1724
  switches to, 1717, 1718*f*
air-conditioning compressor clutch, 1737, 1765
air-conditioning filters, identifying need for, 1750
air-conditioning fittings, removing and inspection of, 1751, 1754, 1755
air-conditioning machine, 1741, 1765
air-conditioning protection and diagnostic system (APADS), 1694, 1722–1725, 1727
  control system, 1721, 1723*f*
  H-type TXV for, 1725*f*
  inputs, 1725
air-conditioning protection unit (ACPU), 1723, 1727
air-conditioning (AC) systems
  adding oil to, 1761, 1762
  additional filters, 1750
  capacity of, 1736
    overcharge, 1737
    state of charge, 1737
    undercharge, 1737
  components of, 1695, 1696*f*, 1703, 1704*f*
  compressor and clutch, 1703, 1705–1706, 1707*f*
  conditions, 1740–1741
  controls, 1721–1722
  diagnosis of, 1737–1738
    cabin air filter, 1740
    condenser, inspecting for airflow restrictions, 1739
    conditions, 1740–1741
    eliminating odors, 1740
    evaporator housing water drain, inspection of, 1739–1740
    performance testing, 1738, 1739
  fundamentals of, 1695–1697
  high and low side of, 1708
  history of, 1694–1695
  identification sticker, 1736*f*
  layout of heavy-duty mobile, 1695, 1695*f*
  maintenance and repair, 1741
    accumulator, removing, inspecting, and installing, 1754–1756
    additional AC filters, identifying need for, 1750
    air-conditioning system, evacuating, 1759–1760
    charging AC system, 1761
    compressor clutch, inspecting, testing and replacing, 1751, 1752–1753
    compressor, removing, inspecting, and reinstalling, 1753–1754
    condenser, removing, inspecting, and reinstalling, 1754, 1756
    drive belt, inspecting and replacing, 1751
    evaporator, removing, inspecting, and installing, 1758–1759
    flush, 1749–1750
    heater control valves, inspecting and testing, 1763
    heater core, removing, inspecting, and reinstalling, 1763
    identifying refrigerant type, 1744, 1745
    leak testing, 1744–1747
    mufflers, hoses, lines, and fittings, removing and inspecting, 1751, 1754, 1755
    oil and capacity, determination of, 1761, 1762
    orifice tube, removing, inspecting, and installing, 1758
    reclaiming and recovering air-conditioning system, 1747–1749
    refrigerant equipment maintenance, 1761, 1762
    tools, 1741–1742, 1741*f*–1743*f*
    TXV, removing, inspecting, and installing, 1755, 1757
  odors eliminating, 1740
  principles, 1697–1703
  problems, 1723–1724
  service process, 1735–1736
    determining refrigerant type, 1736, 1736*f*
  servicing heating and, 1731–1765
air control modules, 609*f*, 610*f*
air-control solenoid valve, 1310, 1336
air control systems, 1243
  FR model transmission shift controls, 1247–1251, 1249*f*–1251*f*
    SynchroSaver, 1250–1251, 1251*f*
    range shift control, 1243–1244, 1243*f*–1245*f*
    splitter shift control, 1245–1247, 1245*f*–1249*f*
air-cushioned pintle hook, 23, 1110*f*
air delivery and control systems, components of, 944, 944*f*
  anti-compounding relay valves, 951–953, 952*f*
  brake proportioning relay valves, 953–954, 953*f*–955*f*
  foot valves. *See* foot valves
  relay valves. *See* relay valves
air disc brakes (ADB), 893, 915–918, 1029*f*
  actuation system—brake, 916
  adjustment, 1031
  advantages of, 915
  auto-adjustment, 916, 917
  brake pad inspection, 1029
  potentiometer-type wear indicator, 1031*f*
  rotor surface inspection, 1029
air drill, 119–120, 120*f*, 156
Air Dryer Integrated System (AD-IS), 940, 940*f*–941*f*, 963
air dryers, 938–939, 939*f*, 1009
  advanced technologies, 940–941, 941*f*–942*f*, 943
  charge and purge cycle, 939–940, 940*f*
air filter/pressure regulator, 1243–1244, 1243*f*, 1256
air hammer, 119, 120*f*, 156
air hoses, 1009–1010
air-impact wrench, 120, 120*f*, 156
air jacks, 189
air leakage test, 981–983
air leaks, 1275, 1275*f*
air lines, 1009–1010
  inspecting, 1864–1865
air loss, inspecting wheel assembly for, 694, 695
air nozzle, 119, 120*f*, 156
air-operated cylinders, 926
air-over-hydraulic braking systems, 1070, 1082, 1099. *See also* hydraulic braking systems
  air booster units, 1082–1084, 1083*f*–1085*f*
  fluid leaks, inspecting for, 1091
  inspecting, 1867–1868
  piston stroke detector, 1084, 1086, 1086*f*
  removing and replacing master cylinder/actuator, 1092
air pressure, 887, 906
air pressure switch, 514*f*
air quality, 75
  running engines, 75–76, 76*f*
air ratchet, 119, 120*f*, 156
air relay, circuit with, 948, 949*f*
air reservoirs, 933–934, 935*f*, 1008

air shift control, 1591–1592
air shift systems, 1591, 1591*f*
air-spring construction, 813–814, 814*f*, 815*f*
air spring control, 816–817, 817*f*
air spring equalizing beam suspensions, 816–817,
air spring suspension systems, 799, 800, 813, 813*f*
  air-spring construction, 813–814, 814*f*, 815*f*
  air spring equalizing beam suspensions, 816–817,
  combination leaf/air spring, 814–815, 815*f*, 816*f*
air spring systems, inspection and maintenance, 827, 828
air springs, 798, 836
air starter motor, 398, 398*f*
air supply systems
  components of, 929*f*, 930
    air compressors, 930–932, 931*f*–932*f*
    air dryers, 938–943, 939*f*–942*f*
    air reservoirs, 933–934, 935*f*
    governor, 933, 933*f*–934*f*
    valves, 934–938, 936*f*–938*f*
  servicing
    air compressor, 1006–1007
    air dryers, 1009
    air lines and hoses, 1009–1010
    air reservoirs, 1008
    alcohol evaporator and injector systems, 1009
    dash pressure gauges, 1009
    governor, 1007–1008
  troubleshooting problems in, 943, 943*f*
air supply valve, inspecting and testing, 1000, 1002
air suspension system, inspection and maintenance, 830
air system
  inspection of, 1278, 1279
  problems, 1274–1277
    air leaks, 1275, 1275*f*
    crossed airlines, 1274–1275
    Roadranger valve, 1275–1277, 1276*f*
air tanks. *See* air reservoirs
air tools, 119–120
  creeper, 120
  grease gun, 120
airbag in SRS, 872
airflow restrictions, inspecting condenser for, 1739
AL factor, 898, 898*f*, 921
alcohol evaporator systems, 1009
alcohol injection system, 1009
algorithms, 298, 550
Alison 2400 series converter, 1355, 1355*f*
Alison World Transmission, 1362*f*, 1365
  to input shaft, 1362*f*
alkalis, 148, 156
Allen head screw, 164, 165*f*, 198
Allen keys. *See* Allen wrenches
Allen wrenches, 125, 126*f*, 156, 164, 165*f*, 198
Allison 4000 series transmissions, fluid and filter change intervals on, 1425*t*
Allison AT 500 series transmission, cutaway view of, 1395, 1396*f*
Allison DOC service tool, 1685, 1687
Allison DOC software, 1504
Allison Electronic Control Information System (ECIS), 1451
Allison EP drive system, 1672*f*
Allison EV Drive Hybrid Systems
  components, 1673–1683
  maintenance, 1684–1685
  operating modes, 1683–1684
  overview of, 1670–1672
Allison EV transmission
  modules of, 1673*f*
  views of, 1674*f*
Allison fifth generation electronic control
  prognostics, 1498–1499
  retarders, 1497–1498
  shift selectors, 1499–1504
Allison fourth generation electronic control, 1488
  electro-hydraulic control valve body, 1488–1497
  fifth range, 1492, 1493*f*
  first range, 1490
  fluid flows, 1490–1494
  fourth range, 1492, 1493*f*
  neutral, 1490
  retarders, 1497
  reverse, 1492, 1494, 1495*f*
  second range, 1490
  sixth range, 1492, 1494*f*
  solenoid application chart, 1489*t*
  third range, 1490, 1492*f*
Allison shift point adjustment, 1430, 1432–1434
Allison-supplied TPS, 1449
Allison TC-10-TS, 1504–1506
  power flows, 1506–1514
Allison Transmission Electronic Control (ATEC), 1395, 1446–1447, 1448*f*, 1471–1472, 1526
  clutch application chart for, 1454*t*
  first range, 1456, 1457*f*
  fourth range, 1457, 1459*f*
  neutral, 1456
  reverse, 1457, 1459*f*
  second range, 1456–1457, 1458*f*
  shift logic, 1454–1459, 1455*f*
  solenoids, 1452–1454
  third range, 1457, 1458*f*
  transmission ECU. *See* transmission electronic control unit
  trimmer operation, 1460–1461
  wiring harnesses, 1452
Allison transmission power flows, 1397, 1397*t*
  first range, 1397, 1398*f*
  fourth range, 1399, 1400*f*, 1401
  neutral, 1397, 1398*f*
  reverse, 1401, 1401*f*
  second range, 1397, 1399, 1399*f*
  third range, 1399, 1400*f*
Allison World Transmission models, 1428
alloy wheels, 707
alternating current (AC), 217–218, 217*f*, 223, 334, 431–433
alternating current (AC) ripple, 288*f*, 439, 440*f*, 457
alternating current traction generator (ACTG), 1656, 1657*f*, 1665
alternating current traction motor (ACTM), 1657–1659, 1658*f*–1659*f*, 1665
alternating electrical current, measurement of, 540
alternator, 430, 433*f*
  "A" circuit, 451
  advantages, 431–432
  "B" circuit, 451
  brushes, 455
    and brushless, 434–435
  cable voltage drop test, 452
  classification, 433
  components, 433–446
  cooling, 444–445, 444*f*
  vs. DC generator, 430
  drive belts, pulleys, and tensioners, inspecting, adjusting, and replacing, 449–450
  dual, 446
  electrical current, 433
  end frames and bearings, 445, 445*f*
  exciting, 435–436
  functions, 431
  heavy vehicle, 430*f*
  oscilloscope, 440*f*
  overhauling, 454–455
  principles, 432–433
  removing, inspecting, and replacing, 453–454
  voltage, 451
  wiring connections, 446–449
alternator ripple, 437, 457
aluminium, 152, 707
aluminum alloy, 769, 789
amber colored, 1050
ambient temperature
  on inflation pressure, effect of, 680, 681*f*
  range, SAE grades, 1607*t*
  switch, 1722
amboid gears, 1577, 1577*f*, 1600
American Chemical Society, 1694
American National Standards Institute (ANSI), 93–94
American Petroleum Institute (API), 1855

American Society of Automotive Engineers (SAE), 1855
American Wire Gage (AWG), 463, 464*f*
ammeter, 373, 384–385
  instrument, 453
  shunts, 311, 311*f*
ammonia sensors, 569, 574, 593
AMP connectors, 468
amp-hour, 341, 347
amperage, 211, 223, 234, 253, 254, 254*f*–256*f*, 257–258, 309, 401, 418, 451. *See also* amperage—ammeters
  in Ohm's law, 257*f*
  reducing, 258
  and voltage, 336
amperage regulation, 442
amperage—ammeters, 316–318, 316*f*–318*f*
  inductive amp clamps, 318–319, 318*f*–319*f*, 318*t*
ampere (amp), 211, 223
amps-volts and resistance (AVR) test, 216*f*
AMT. *See* automated manual transmission
analog meters, 308, 309*f*, 325
analog signals, 539–541, 541*f*, 553
analog to digital conversion, 543, 543*f*–544*f*, 553
anemometer, 1742, 1743*f*, 1765
angle gauge, 174
angle grinders, 118–119, 119*f*, 156
angle of drive, driveshaft systems, 1534
angle of wire movement, 237
angle spring clutch, 1146, 1146*f*, 1162
  adjustment
    with locking tang, 1170, 1170*f*
    with quick-adjust device, 1171, 1171*f*
angular motion, 1815, 1832
anisotropic, 178, 198
ANSI. *See* American National Standards Institute
anti-compounding circuit, inspecting and testing, 998, 1001
anti-compounding valves, 951–953, 952*f*, 963
anti-drain-back check valves, 1354, 1367
anti-fade, 900, 921
anti-freeze, 145–146, 145*f*
anti-lock braking system (ABS), 609, 667, 1088
  configurations of, 1088–1089, 1089*f*
  module, 1089–1090, 1090*f*
anti-rattle springs, 1184, 1184*f*, 1189
anti-seize compound, 170, 170*f*, 198
anti-lock braking system (ABS), 887, 990, 1038, 1039*f*–1041*f*, 1063
  components, 1042
    ABS configuration, 1051–1052
    ABS trailer cords, 1049–1050, 1050*f*
    ECU, 1042–1044
    indicator lights and switches, 1050–1051
    modulator valves, 1046–1049
    wheel speed sensors, 1044–1046
  configurations, 1051–1052
  electronic control modules, 1041*f*
  enhancements to, 1052
    stability and safety enhancement systems, 1055–1060
    traction control, 1052–1055
  fault location and impact on, 1061*t*
  features and benefits, 1038–1040, 1039*t*
  fundamentals of, 1038–1041
  maintaining, 1060–1061
  modulator, 1046–1049
  system requirements, 1040–1041
antimony alloy, 344
APADS. *See* air-conditioning protection and diagnostic system
API. *See* American Petroleum Institute
application chart, 1382, 1382*t*, 1389
applied stroke measurement, 984, 1033
  measuring brake stroke length with, 985
apprenticeship students, 38*f*
APS. *See* accelerator position sensor
arbitration, 616, 623
argon (Ar), 210
armature, 403, 422, 425
  commutator and commutation, 403–406
  components of, 403–406
  damaged, 415
  features of, 404*f*
  magnetic fields, 398–399, 398*f*
  rotation, 407
  shaft and windings, 403
  windings, 399, 400, 403
articulated bus, 13*f*
articulation, 18, 30, 799, 836
Arvin Meritor AutoJust clutch, 1146
Arvin Meritor system, 1670, 1683, 1684*f*
AS-Tronic, 1304, 1323, 1336
ASA. *See* automatic slack adjusters
asbestos, 152, 896
  exposure, 1147–1148
  fibers, 1147
asbestosis, 152, 1147
ASE certification. *See* Automotive Service Excellence certification
aspect ratio, 671, 701
ASR. *See* automatic slip regulation
asynchronous AC motor, 1676, 1676*f*, 1687
ATC. *See* automatic traction control
ATEC. *See* Allison Transmission Electronic Control
ATF. *See* automatic transmission fluid
ATO series, 264
atom
  model of, 209*f*
  parts of, 208*f*
auto range shift valve, 1303, 1303*f*
auto-ranging multimeters, 310, 310*f*, 310*t*, 312*f*, 325
automated external defibrillator (AED), 98
automated manual transmission (AMT), 1300, 1336
  benefits of, 1300–1301
  electronic, types of, 1302
    Detroit Diesel's DT-12, 1305
    Eaton Fuller's automated transmissions, 1302–1304
    Mercedes Benz's AGS, 1305
    Meritor/ZF's automated transmissions, 1304–1305
    Volvo Trucks' I-Shift, 1305
  operation of
    Detroit Diesel's DT-12, 1326
    Eaton Fuller AutoShift and UltraShift operations, 1306–1314
    Eaton Fuller transmission nomenclature, 1314
    Eaton Procision automated transmission, 1314–1322
    Mercedes Benz/Daimler Trucks Automatic Gear Shift (AGS), 1328–1329
    Meritor/ZF, 1323–1326
    Volvo Trucks' I-Shift, 1327–1328
  torque break in shifting, role of, 1301–1302
  troubleshooting, 1329–1334
automated transmission ECUs, 1333, 1334
automatic chassis lubrication system (ACLS), 1855
automatic disengagement lockout (ADLO), 412, 412*f*, 425
automatic downshifting, 1414
  full throttle downshift, 1414–1415, 1414*f*
  reverse hydraulic operation, 1415
  shift point control, 1415, 1415*f*
automatic drain valves, 937–938, 938*f*, 963
automatic emergency brake system, 988, 990
Automatic Gear Shift (AGS), 1328–1329, 1336
automatic neutral at standstill, 1516
automatic slack adjusters (ASAs), 911–915, 921, 1021, 1024–1029, 1026*f*
  types of, 912*f*
automatic slip regulation (ASR), 1052, 1063
automatic steering stops, 864, 866*f*
automatic traction control (ATC), 264, 1043, 1052, 1054*f*, 1055, 1055*f*, 1063

automatic transmission fluid (ATF), 146–147, 146*f*, 1794
automatic transmissions, 1342, 1347, 1351, 1355, 1447. *See also* hydraulically controlled automatic transmissions
  diagnostics, 1427
  electronically controlled, 1394
  fundamentals of, 1422–1426
  maintenance of, 1428–1439
    adjusting shift linkage and neutral safety switch, 1437–1439
    Allison shift point adjustment, 1430, 1432–1434
    checking transmission cooler and lines, 1437
    cooler and lines, 1437, 1438
    general transmission inspection, 1428–1429
    inspecting flex plate and torque converter, 1436–1437
    inspecting/replacing power train mounts, 1430
    oil and filter change procedures for, 1430
    removing and reinstalling the, 1435–1436
    system pressure testing, 1430
  out-of-service (OSS) criteria for, 1428
  performing an oil and filter change, 1430
  pressure testing, 1359–1361, 1432
  recommended, 1426–1427
  shifting, 1412–1414, 1413*f*
  troubleshooting problems with, 1427–1428
  types of, 1426–1427
automatically actuated clutches, 1158
  electric clutch actuator, 1159, 1159*f*
  two-pedal centrifugal clutch actuation system, 1158
  wet clutches, 1159–1160
automotive clutches, 1142
  components of, 1141
automotive engines, 423
Automotive Service Excellence (ASE) certification, 38
AutoSelect, 1302, 1336
AutoShift, 1303, 1336
  transmissions, 1307*f*
auxiliary air-conditioning units, 1699, 1700*f*
auxiliary sections, 1231–1232, 1231*f*, 1256
  air control. *See* air control systems
  disassembling, 1282, 1285
  four-speed, 1241–1243, 1241*f*–1242*f*
  low-inertia, 1239–1243, 1239*f*–1242*f*
  power flows, 1232, 1232*f*
  reassembling and timing of, 1287–1288
  reinstallation of, 1289–1291, 1291*t*
  removing from fuller ten-speed FR model, 1282, 1284
  three-speed, 1235–1239, 1235*f*, 1237*f*–1239*f*
  two-speed, 1232–1235, 1232*f*–1234*f*
auxiliary springs, 805, 805*f*, 836
auxiliary transmissions. *See also* auxiliary sections
  multiple countershaft transmissions and, 1227–1228, 1228*f*
    floating main shaft system, 1228–1229, 1228*f*–721*f*
    main box power flows, 1229–1231, 1230*f*–1231*f*
    power flows, 1229, 1229*f*
available voltage test, 415
aviation snips, 125, 125*f*, 156
AVR test. *See* amps-volts and resistance test
AWG. *See* American Wire Gage
axial piston pumps, 1812
axial starter motors, 403
axial thrust, 1202, 1207
axle alignment, 814
axle flange, 1615
axle lubricants, 1855
axle parallelism, 750–751, 757
axle perpendicularity, 748, 757
axle setback, 746, 746*f*, 757
axle shafts, types of, 1597, 1597*f*
axle shift control, 1588–1592
axle spacing, 19, 20*f*
axle spread, 1108, 1132
axle stops, 799, 799*f*, 836
axle tracking, 746, 750–751
axles, 730, 731*f*, 757
  adjusting and aligning, 829, 831–833
  fundamentals of, 1572–1575
    dead axles, 1574
    drive axles, 1574–1575
    steering axles, 1573–1574

B

"B" circuit alternator, 451
B-train, 21–22, 22*f*, 30, 1106–1107, 1108*f*
B-type lock, 1119, 1119*f*, 1132
  adjustment, 1126–1127
  locking mechanism of, 1127*f*
"B" type regulators, 441–442, 442*f*
back-dazzle, 498
back taper, 1273, 1274*f*, 1295
background color, 74
backing plate, 1073, 1099, 1346, 1346*f*
  look-up clutch bolted to converter housing, 1354*f*
backlash, 1197, 1207
bad headlight, 41
BAE HybriDrive Propulsion Systems, 1652–1653, 1652*f*, 1653*t*, 1654*f*
baffle, internal, 934
balance piston, 1465
balance weights, check shaft for, 1551*f*
balancers, 361–363, 367
ball bearings, 848
ball hitches, 24, 30, 1110–1111, 1132
  pintle hook with, 1109*f*
ball-nut rack, 848, 876
ball-peen (engineer's) hammer, 127, 128*f*, 156
ball ramp, 1312, 1312*f*
band. *See* brake band
banjo housing, 1578, 1578*f*, 1600
bar magnet, 432
barrier cream, 92, 92*f*, 102
barrier voltage, 291
BASIC. *See* Bendix Air System Inspection Cup
batteries, 143, 156, 330–333
  bank configuration, 342*f*
  capacity of, 402
  cases, 338–339
  charging and discharging cycle, 343–344
  checks, 414
  classifications, 330–331
  construction and operation, 335–345
  faulty, 414
  functions, 331–333
  gassing, 344
  inspecting, 1861, 1864
  internal resistance of, 342– 343
  low- and no-maintenance, 344–345
  ratings, 339–341, 341*f*
  selection, 341–342
  in series circuits, connecting, 254*f*
  sizing and terminal configuration, 339
  store electricity in chemical form, 147, 147*f*
  technology, 334
  types and classification of, 333–335
battery bank configuration, 341, 342*f*
battery chargers, 143–145, 144*f*, 156
  safety, 144
battery charging
  and discharging cycle, 343–344
  states of, 444
battery chemistries
  discharge cycle to battery life for, 357*t*
  properties for different, 352, 353*t*
battery configuration, 380
battery control interface module (BCIM) monitors, 1678
Battery Council International (BCI) group number, 339, 341
battery equalizers, 361–363, 362*f*, 363*f*, 367
battery failure, 374–375
battery isolator systems, 360, 361*f*, 367
battery management systems (BMS), 359–360, 367
  battery balancers and equalizers, 361–363
  battery isolators, 360
  battery monitors, 364

hybrid battery management systems, 364–365
low-voltage disconnect (LVD), 360–361
operation of, in hybrid vehicle chassis, 364, 365*f*
transit bus with rooftop battery tubs and, 354*f*
battery modules, condition of good *vs.* defective, 1661*t*
battery monitoring system (BMS), 1660–1661, 1661*t*
battery monitors, 364
battery technologies, 352, 431
application of, 352
battery management systems, 359–365
energy density of, 352, 352*f*
types of, 352–359
lithium-ion battery, 353–355
low-voltage disconnect (LVD), 360–361
nickel–metal hydride (NiMH) battery, 352–353
ultra capacitors, 358–360
valve-regulated lead-acid battery (VRLA), 355–358
battery voltage, 217
baud rate, 543, 553
baulk rings. *See* blocking rings
BCI group number. *See* Battery Council International group number
beach marks, 1634, 1639
gear teeth fatigue fractures, 1634*f*
bead breaker, 690, 701
bead filler, 674
bead seat, 707, 725
beam-style torque wrench, 172
bearing adjuster locks, 1612, 1639
bearing adjusters, 1612, 1639
bearing growth, 1618, 1639
bearing preload, 717, 725
bearings, 434
alternator end frames and, 445
bellcrank, 1222, 1222*f*, 1256
bellows, air, 813, 836
belt plies, 674
belt routing label, 63, 63*f*, 65
belt system, constructions of tire, 673–674, 673*f*–674*f*
bench grinders, 72–73, 118–119, 119*f*
bench vice, 131, 131*f*, 156
bending failures, 1634
Bendix AD-9 dryer, 1009*f*
Bendix AD-IS air dryer, 940, 940*f*–941*f*
Bendix ADB system, 915–917, 917*f*–918*f*
Bendix Air System Inspection Cup (BASIC), 983
oil accumulation chart, 984
Bendix clearance sensing slack, 911, 912*f*
Bendix D2 governor circuit, 933, 934*f*
Bendix's Trailer Remote Diagnostic Unit (TRDU), 1044
bent-axis piston, 1817
pumps, 1811, 1812*f*
bent plates, 1125
Bernoulli principle, 1798
bevel gears, 1203, 1204*f*, 1207, 1575, 1600
bias, 801
bias-belted tires, 673*f*, 674
bias-ply tire, 673, 673*f*, 674, 701
biased torque differential, 1584–1585, 1584*f*, 1600
bidirectional communications, 607, 623
bimetallic gauges, 515, 516*f*, 529
bimetallic strip, 266
binary code, 541, 603
binding, steering-related problems, 865*t*
biodegradable hydraulic fluids, 1794
biodiesel fuel, 149, 156
bipolar stepper motor, 518, 520*f*
bipolar transistors, 294, 301
conventional, 294*f*
bit, 542, 542*f*, 553
bladder-type gas-charged accumulator, 1825, 1825*f*, 1832
blade-type fuses, 264
bleeding, 98, 98*f*
air from steering system, 871
hydraulic clutch system
gravity bleeding method, 1175–1176
manual bleeding method, 1176, 1177
pressure or vacuum bleeding method, 1176, 1177
blind hole, 132
blind rivet, 135, 135*f*, 156
blink codes, 514, 514*f*, 529, 642, 645–646, 645*f*, 655, 1042, 1063
block style tire tread, 675
block-type synchronizer, 1218–1220, 1219*f*
blocking rings, 1218, 1219, 1256
blower motor speed control circuit, 281, 281*f*
Bluetooth technology, 617, 618, 623
BMS. *See* battery management systems; battery monitoring system
bobtailing proportioning relay (BPR) valve, 953, 953*f*, 963
bobtailing valves, 953, 963
body electrical systems
control of, 491*f*
fundamentals of, 490–491
instrumentation. *See* instrumentation
lighting systems. *See* lighting systems
body mountings inspection, performing, 1861, 1863
boiling point of coolant, 1700, 1701*f*
bolt cutters, 125, 125*f*, 156
bolt pattern, 708, 725
bolts, 165, 166*f*, 169*f*, 170, 198, 1184, 1184*f*
bonded ground system, 230*f*
bonded lining, 896
boost pressure control monitoring systems, 635, 640
boost solenoid, 1090
bore, 1818, 1832
Bosch/AMP connectors, 468
bottle jacks, 189
bottoming tap, 132, 156
bow, 778, 778*f*, 789
box-shape carriage, suspension system, 794
BPR. *See* bobtailing proportioning relay valve
braided steel, 673–674
brake actuators, 904, 905*f*, 915
brake adjustment indicators, 1024
brake application (foot) valve, guidelines for inspect and testing, 995, 997
brake balance, 972, 1033
testing, 990–992
brake band, 1379, 1379*f*, 1389
brake block, 896, 897*f*, 921
material, 896, 898
brake caliper, 1074
brake chambers, 904, 907*f*, 926
brake control valve, inspecting and testing, 1000, 1003
brake disc, 1073–1074, 1073*f*. *See also* rotor
brake drums, 902–904, 903*f*, 1012–1015, 1012*f*, 1070, 1099
service guidelines for, 1014*t*
brake dust
hazards, 973–974
safely cleaning, 88
brake fade, 900*f*, 915, 916*f*, 921, 1071, 1074
chemical fade, 902
glazing of brake lining, 902
heat fade, 899–22
mechanical fade, 902
water fade, 900
brake fluid, 148, 149*f*, 1070, 1099
brake foundations, 890, 921
components, 890, 891*f*
brake friction material, 896
brake full function valve, inspecting and testing, 1003, 1005
brake lag, 928, 963
brake lathes, 139*f*, 1029, 1030
brake lines, 1075, 1099
brake lining, 896, 921
glazing of, 902
brake pad, 891, 891*f*, 915–917, 917*f*–918*f*
inspection, 1029
wear, 1030–1031
brake pedal, 1795
brake pressure sensor, 1058, 1662, 1662*f*
brake proportioning relay valves, 953, 953*f*
front axle limiter valves, 953–954, 954*f*
quick-release valves, 954, 954*f*–955*f*
brake pull, 975, 1033
brake running clearance, 1029–1031

brake shoes, 895–896, 1070, 1099
  configurations and actuation mechanisms, 1071
    single-leading- and trailing-shoe configuration, 1071, 1072*f*
    two-leading brake shoes, 1072, 1072*f*
  disassembling, 1017
  edge codes, 899*f*
  inspecting and removing, 1015–1017
  installing, 1017–1018
brake spider plate, 1021
brake steer. *See* brake pull
brake stroke length, 981, 984–986, 1033
brake stroke travel, red zip tie, 985*f*
brake systems
  adjusting air, 1021–1031
  advanced testing, 990–995
  air supply, 1006–1010
  complaints, 974–975
  diagnosing, malfunctions, 974–980
  preliminary testing, 980–990
  service, safety during, 972–974
  servicing foundation, 1010–1021
  testing on, 980–1005
brake test, 48*f*
brake timing imbalance, 992–993, 1033
brake torque, 885, 887, 887*f*, 902, 921, 951
brake valves, 1820
  delivery pressure *vs.* service brake chamber pressure, 953, 953*f*
  hydraulic. *See* hydraulic brake valves
brake wash station, 88
brake washers, 141
braking force, 884–885, 885*f*, 887, 887*f*, 915, 927*f*, 1039
braking noise, 974–975
braking odors, 975
braking power, 885
braking systems
  air and hydraulic, 887–890
  air brake foundation systems. *See* air brake foundation systems
  air-over-hydraulic. *See* air-over-hydraulic braking systems
  anti-lock, 887
  brake torque & inertia shift, 885, 887, 887*f*
  components, 882, 883*f*, 890
  foundation technologies, 886*f*
  hydraulic. *See* hydraulic braking systems
  inspecting, 1866, 1867–1868
  legislative standards for, 884
  power, 885
  tractor and trailer, 889*f*
  types of, 887–890
  vehicle weight and speed, influence of, 884–885, 885*f*, 886*f*
  working of, 884–887
brass, 151–152, 152*f*
break-out box, 320–321, 321*f*
break-out harnesses, 321*f*
break torque, 1301, 1336
breakage, U-joint fractures and, 1554, 1555*f*
breaker bar, 123, 123*f*
breathing devices, 93
  disposable dust mask, 93, 93*f*
  respirator, 93, 93*f*
Bridge Formula B, 19, 19*f*, 30, 1108, 1132
bridges, 619, 1107
brinelling, 1552, 1554*f*
British thermal unit (Btu), 1699, 1699*f*, 1727
broken back arrangement, 1542–1543, 1542*f*, 1567. *See also* intersecting angle arrangement
broken back configuration, 1545
broker brake. *See* trailer brake control valves
brushes alternators, 434–435, 435*f*
brushes rings, alternator components, 433
brushes, starter motor, 415, 421
brushless alternators, 434–435
Btu. *See* British thermal unit
bucking coil, 517, 518*f*
buffers, 543
bump steer, 853, 876
  steering-related problems, 865*t*
burnishing, 1017
burns, 100, 100*f*
bus brake systems, legislation for, 882, 883*f*
bus network, 600
bushings, 146, 733, 733*f*
  starter motor, 415
business letter, effective writing, 49
butt connector, 466*f*
byte, 542, 542*f*, 553

C

C-channel, 764, 765*f*, 771, 789
  frame rail, 770*f*
C-clamp, 131*f*, 132, 157
C-clip. *See* circlips
C-dollies, 1107
C-train, 22, 22*f*, 30, 1106, 1107
C-type fluid, 1427
CA. *See* cranking amps
cab door inspection, performing, 1861, 1862
cab forward (CF), 1105, 1105*f*, 1132
cab harness, 1452, 1526
cab-over-engine (COE), 17, 1105, 1105*f*, 1132
  configuration, 17, 18*f*
  vehicle, 18*f*
cab tilt systems, engine-off engine compartment inspection, conducting, 1878
cabin air, 1697*f*, 1703
  filter, 1740
cable linkage clutch actuation systems, 1156, 1157*f*
"cable-pulling" type, hand brake, 1074
cabs, 17–18, 17*f*
caging bolt. *See* release (caging) bolts
calcium, 344
calibration, 111
calipers, 1071, 1099
calorie, 1699, 1727
cam (hanger) brackets, 804, 804*f*, 807, 807*f*
cam brake system, 891, 921
  brake block material, 896, 897*f*, 898
  brake chambers & actuators, 904, 907*f*
  brake drums, 902–904, 903*f*
  brake fade, 900*f*
    chemical fade, 902
    glazing of brake lining, 902
    heat fade, 899–22
    mechanical fade, 902
    water fade, 900
  brake shoes, 895–896
  brake torque, 902
  coefficient of friction, 896, 897*f*, 898–899
  dual brake chambers, 905–906, 908
  edge codes, 898, 899, 899*f*
  left- and right-hand camshafts, 894, 895*f*
  long stroke chambers, 904–905
  operation, 892–893
  release (caging) bolts, 906, 908, 909*f*
  roto-chambers, 908, 909, 910*f*
  S-cam brackets, 894–895, 895*f*, 896*f*
  self-energization, 893, 893*f*
  slack adjusters, 909–915, 911*f*
cam-opposite camshaft, 894, 894*f*, 921
cam-over conditions, 1011, 1033
cam-same camshaft, 894, 921
camber, 737–739, 738*f*, 739*f*, 739*t*, 757
camshaft sensor, 577
camshafts, 894, 1019–1021
  installing, 1019–1020, 1019*f*–1021*f*
  removing, 1020
  wear points, 1019*f*
CAN. *See* controlled area network
CAN BUS, 1498
CAN-bus network, 644, 645
  defects, 618, 619*f*
  problem, symptoms of, 618*f*
CAN-controlled alternators, 451
CAN-driven gauge, 519, 521*f*
CAN-hi, 613
Canadian Ozone Depletion Prevention, 1734
cancellation of non-uniform velocity, 1542, 1567
  effect, 613
cap screw, 164
capability, inspector qualifications, 1854
capacitance touch screens, 526, 527*f*, 529
capacitors, 287–289, 287*f*, 288*f*, 301, 359

electrolytic, 288*f*
smoothing, 288, 288*f*, 439
testing, 289, 289*f*
capacity, fifth wheel ratings and, 1114–1115
carbon dioxide, 75, 1300, 1336
carbon monoxide, 75
carbon pile tester, 451
carbon resistors, 279, 280, 280*f*
Cardan joint, 1532, 1567. *See also* universal joints
Cardano, Gerolamo, 1532
cargo-handling devices, inspecting, 1879–1880
carrier, 1372, 1373*f*, 1389, 1578, 1600
planetary gears, role of, 1373–1374
cartridge fuses, 264
cartridge mechanism, 1821
cases, battery, 338–339
casing cords. *See* tire casings
cast drums, 902, 921
cast ductile iron, 1207
cast iron, 151
cast spoke hub, 710, 710*f*, 711, 712*f*
cast spoke wheel, 709–712, 710*f*, 725
castellated nut, 167, 167*f*, 198
caster, 739–742, 740*f*, 741*f*, 757
caster adjusting shim, 806, 836
caster shimmy, 741, 757, 855–856
Cat Electronic Technician (ET) software, 1523
catalytic converters, 75–76
catastrophic damage, 1355
caterpillar automatic transmissions, 1521–1523
caution, 74, 74*f*
cavitation, 1423, 1441, 1832
CCA. *See* cold cranking amps
CCM. *See* comprehensive component monitor
CCOT. *See* cycling clutch orifice tube
CCW. *See* counter clockwise
CD. *See* charge-depleting operating mode
CEC. *See* Commercial Electronic Control
CEL. *See* check engine lamp
cell phone technology, 617
cellular-based vehicle communications, 536
CEMF. *See* counter-electromotive force
center bearing, 1537, 1567. *See also* hanger bearing
inspecting and servicing of, 1565
center bolt, 133
center punch, 134, 134*f*
center ring gear, 1399, 1401
center wear on tires, 686
central hub, 1149
central processing unit (CPU), 542
clock, integrated circuit devices, 549, 549*f*
centralized network control, 600–602
centrifugal force, 1347, 1347*f*, 1367, 1533
centrifugal switch, 667, 701
centrifuge drums, 902, 921
ceramic clutch facings, 1148, 1148*f*
ceramic friction facings, 1148, 1148*f*, 1162
ceramic piezoelectric crystals, 232*f*
CF. *See* cab forward
CFCs. *See* chlorofluorocarbons
CFM. *See* cubic feet of air pumped per minute; cubic feet per minute
chafing, 1801, 1832
chain blocks, 187, 187*f*
chain drives from old Cadillac, 1532, 1532*f*
chains, 187, 187*f*, 188*f*
Chalmers rubber spring equalizing beam suspensions, 811–812, 811*f*, 812*f*
Chalmers Suspension International, 811
Chalmers system, 811, 812
channel locks, 124
charge, 1736, 1765
air-conditioning system, 1735, 1761
vs. open circuit voltage, 357*t*
state of, 1737, 1765
charge cycle, air dryers, 939–940, 940*f*
charge-depleting operating mode (CD), 1660, 1665
charge-sustaining mode (CS), 1660, 1665
charging batteries, 381–383
charging circuits, wires of, 453
charging cycle, 343–344, 343*f*
charging system, 431. *See also* alternator
circuit voltage drop, testing, 452
diagnosis, 449–454, 449*t*
heavy vehicle, 431*f*
output test, 450–452
set point, 443–444
vehicle, 450–452
charging system indicator light, 512
chariots, horse-drawn, 794, 794*f*
chassis configuration, 16*f*
chassis dynamometer, 136, 156
chassis equipment, 18
chassis frames, 13, 13*f*
chassis inspection pit, 40*f*
chassis lubrication systems, 1855
chassis parts check, steering system, 864
chassis wiring, 465
chassis wiring harness, 1452, 1526
check engine lamp (CEL), 514
check valves, 1781, 1820, 1821*f*
chemical compounds, 170, 170*f*
chemical fade, 902, 921
chemical gloves, 91, 91*f*
chemistry, electricity from, 241–242
chest compressions, 97, 97*f*
chirps, 1043
chisels, 128, 128*f*
chlorinated polyethylene (CPE) insulation, 465
chlorine-free refrigerant (R404a), 1782
chlorofluorocarbons (CFCs), 1695, 1720, 1727
chrome, 152, 157
chuff test, 990, 1033
circlips, 1535, 1536
circuit, 250
classification
circuit arrangement, 252–259
circuit malfunctions, 260–263
operational state, 252
current flow in, 250–251, 251*f*
elements of, 250*f*
factors affecting resistance in, 213*f*
protection devices, 263–264
circuit breakers, 265–266
inspecting and testing, 267–269
major harness protection, 265
PPT coefficient fuses, 266–267
thermal fuses, 264–265
virtual fuses, 267
circuit arrangement, 252–259
circuit breakers, 265–266
classification of, 267*t*
three types of, 266*f*
circuit control device
complex electronic controls. *See* electronic controls
simple. *See* simple circuit control device
circuit identification, 462
circuit malfunctions, 260–263
circuit monitoring—voltage drop measurement, 580
circuit tracers, 319, 320*f*, 325
city transit bus, 12*f*
CKP sensor. *See* crank position sensor
clamp force (load), 1142, 1143*f*, 1162
clamping force, 708*f*, 709*t*
vs. wheel nut torque, 708–709
clamps tool, 131–132
claws, heavy alternator, 434
cleaning equipment, tools
brake washers, 141
pressure washers/cleaners, 140
sand or bead blasters, 141
solvent tanks, 140–141
spray-wash cabinets, 140
cleaning gun, 140, 157
cleaning solution, 140
clearance sensing, 1026
clearance sensing ASAs, 911, 921
clicker-style torque wrench, 172
clock spring, 843, 876
clockwise, 1197, 1207
closed center position, 1823, 1823*f*
closed-center pump, 1814
closed-end wrench, 121, 121*f*, 157
closed hydraulic system, 250, 251*f*
closed-loop control, 1474, 1526
closed-loop hydraulic system, 1791, 1793*t*
closed switch, 278–279, 279*f*
clothing, care of, 90
club hammer, 127, 128*f*, 157
clutch alignment tool, 1176, 1189

clutch application chart
 for Allison AT, MT, and HT series, 1397, 1397*t*
 for Allison World Transmissions, 1467*t*
 for ATEC/CEC transmission, 1454*t*
clutch bell housing, 1180, 1180*f*, 1189
clutch bell housing pilot, 1180, 1189
clutch brake actuation, 1169, 1189
clutch brake squeeze, 1169–1170
clutch brakes, 1153–1154, 1162
 conventional, 1154
 limiting torque, 1155
 torque-limiting, 1154–1155, 1154*f*
clutch capacity, 1142, 1162
clutch chatter, 1172, 1189
clutch cover, 1141, 1143*f*, 1151*f*, 1162
clutch disc, 1141, 1144*f*, 1147, 1149*f*
clutch fill, 1474
clutch friction discs, 1147, 1177, 1183, 1183*f*
 intermediate plate of, 1184*f*
clutch jack, 1178, 1189
clutch linkage, 1168, 1189
clutch operation, electrical connections for, 1706, 1707*f*
clutch pedal, 1170, 1171
clutch servicing, 1168
clutch switch circuit, 410*f*
clutches
 adjustment of, 1169
 complaints, 1173*t*
 components of, 1147–25
  air-assisted hydraulic actuation systems, 1156–1158
  automatically actuated clutches, 1158
  ceramic clutch facings, 1148, 1148*f*
  clutch actuation systems, 1155
  clutch brakes, 1153–1154
  clutch friction discs, 1147
  conventional clutch brake, 1154
  flywheels, 1150–1151, 1151*f*
  hydraulic actuation systems, 1156, 1157*f*
  intermediate plates, 1151
  limiting torque clutch brake, 1155, 1155*f*
  mechanical linkage, 1155–1156, 1156*f*
  organic facings, 1147–1148, 1147*f*
  pilot bearings and release bearings, 1151–1153, 1152*f*
  rigid and dampened disc styles, 1148, 1148*f*
  torque-limiting clutch brake, 1154–1155, 1154*f*
  vibration control, 1149–1150
 cover, 1143, 1145*f*
 definition of, 1141
 forward, 1382
 fundamentals of, 1140–1142, 1140*f*
  capacity, 1142
  functions, 1142
  modern, 1141, 1141*f*
  role of friction, 1141–1142, 1141*f*
 hub, 1378, 1378*f*
 hydraulic, 1378–1379, 1378*f*–1379*f*, 1389
 inspection of, 1168
 low and reverse, 1382
 maintenance and repair of, 1172–1187
  bleeding hydraulic clutch system. *See* bleeding, hydraulic clutch system
  component inspection with clutch removed, 1180–1182
  hydraulic clutch system, 1174–1175
  installing, 1182–1186
  push-type clutch, checking and adjusting, 1172–1174
  reinstalling transmission, 1186–1187
 one-way. *See* one-way clutches
 preventative maintenance of, 1168–1172
  adjustment procedures, 1169–1170
  release bearing free travel, 1170–1171
  release fork free play, 1171–1172
  self-adjusting clutches, 1172
 purpose of, 1141
 removing, 1176, 1178–1179
 roller-type one-way, 1379–1380, 1380*f*
 rotating, 1378, 1389
 rotating hydraulic, 1372–1373
 sprag-type one-way, 1379–1380, 1380*f*
 stationary, 1379, 1379*f*, 1389
 troubleshooting clutch problems, 1172, 1173*t*
 types and design of, 1142–1146
  angle spring clutch, 1146, 1146*f*
  coil spring style clutch, 1143–1144, 1143*f*
  diaphragm spring clutch, 1144–1146, 1144*f*–1145*f*
  self-adjusting clutches, 1146, 1146*f*
 vehicle, 1142*f*
clutching teeth, 1217
CMVs. *See* commercial motor vehicles
CMVSS 103, 1696
coach market, Allison transmission in, 1394–1395
coarse file, 130
coaxial, 1149
code readers, 323
COE. *See* cab-over-engine
coefficient of friction (Cof), 146, 157, 896, 897*f*, 898–22, 902, 921, 1141–1142, 1141*f*, 1147, 1148, 1162
 edge code, 899*t*
Cof. *See* coefficient of friction
coil of wire, 432
coil spring style clutch, 1143, 1143*f*, 1162
coil springs, 798, 836
cold chisel, 128, 128*f*
cold cranking amps (CCA), 339–340, 347
cold curing process, 675, 677, 677*t*, 701
cold-formed semi-circular retaining strap, 1538, 1538*f*
cold operation inhibits, 1424, 1441
cold-start emissions strategies, 636
cold switch, 1721
collapsed slots, 1555
collar shift transmission, 1214, 1256
collision avoidance systems, 1058–1059, 1059*f*, 1063
 front sensor of, 1060, 1061*f*
collisions, 1651–1652
color codes, 470
combination circuits, 256
combination leaf/air spring suspension systems, 814–815, 815*f*, 816*f*
combination pliers, 124, 124*f*, 157
combination valve, 1079, 1080*f*, 1099
combination vehicles, 21–24, 30, 1104, 1104*f*, 1132
 truck-trailer, 1105–1107
combination wrench, 121, 121*f*, 157
combo stud, 814, 836
combustion theory, 138
Commercial Electronic Control (CEC), 1395, 1446–1447, 1448*f*, 1526. *See also* Allison Transmission Electronic Control
 clutch application chart for, 1454*t*
commercial motor vehicles (CMVs), 1108, 1847
commercial vehicle battery, 372–373
 capacity, 380–381
 causes of battery failure, 374–375
 charging commercial, 383
 conductance testing, 380
 inspecting, testing, and maintenance, 375–383
 jump-starting vehicles, 383–384
 load testing, 381
 measuring parasitic draw, 385
 parasitic draw, measuring, 384–385
 performing, state of charge test, 383
 recycling, 386
 service precautions, 373–374
commercial vehicle electrical systems, 265
commercial vehicle electronics, use of, 598*t*
commercial vehicle industry, careers in, 36–40
 countries' qualifications, 39
 job classifications, 37
 master technicians, 38–39
 service technicians, 37–38
 specialty technicians, 39
 technician duties, 36–37
 working conditions, 39–40
Commercial Vehicle Safety Alliance (CVSA), 777, 820, 1853, 1883
 decal, 1853*f*

commercial vehicle tires
construction of, 673, 673*f*
belt system, 673–674, 673*f*–674*f*
fuel economy, tire construction and, 682–683, 683*f*
inner liner, 675
sidewalls, 674
tire beads, 674, 675*f*
tire casings, 673
tire inflation factors, 678–682, 679*f*, 680*t*, 681*f*–682*f*
tread. *See* tread
diagnosis of. *See* tire diagnosis
fundamentals of, 662
tire differences, 663, 663*f*
tire functions, 663–664, 663*f*–664*f*
introduction of, 662, 662*t*
load ratings for, 680*t*
maintenance and service of, 683
adjusting tire pressure, 685, 686
checking for tire wear patterns, 685–687, 687*t*–688*t*
common issues, 684
dismounting tire, 686, 689, 690
dynamic balancing tire, 693–694
inspecting wheel assembly, 694, 695
mounting tire, 692
replacing valve stem, 689, 692
tools, 683–684
using tire pressure gauge, 684–685, 684*f*
working on heavy-duty wheels and tires, 689, 691
safety of. *See* tire safety
secure during inflation, 665, 665*f*
speed ratings for, 680*t*
types of, 667
tire identification and sizing, 669–671, 669*f*–670*f*, 671*t*
tire profile, 671–672, 672*f*
tubeless and tube-type tires, 667–668, 667*f*–669*f*
commercial vehicles, 6, 7*f*
classification of, 21–24
A-trains, 21
B-trains, 21–22
C-trains, 22
hitching devices, 23–24
design factors for, 13–18
cabs, 17–18
chassis equipment, 18
chassis frames, 13
engines, 13–14
power trains, 14–16
suspensions, 18
operational characteristics, 6–8
off-highway, 8
on-highway, 7, 8
turnpike or interstate, 7
urban, 8
terms and conventions, 25–28, 25*f*
vocational applications of, 8–13
construction, 9
fire service, 9
heavy haul, 10
intercity coach, 10
line-haul trucks, 10
logging trucks, 10–11
mining, 11
pick-up and delivery, 8
refuse collection, 11
rescue vehicles, 12
school bus, 12
urban transit coach, 12–13
weight and length, classification of, 18–21
Federal Bridge Gross Weight Formula, 19–20
vehicle weight ratings, 20–21
communication
multiplexing, 599
in team, 45
commutation, 403
commutator, 403–406
companion flange, 1536, 1536*f*, 1567
compass, electronic, 524
complicated fracture, 99, 102
component mountings inspection, performing, 1863
component serviceability, 319
composite leaf springs, 802–803, 803*f*
out-of-service criteria for, 820*f*
compound drive line angles, 1548–1550, 1549*f*
compound gears, 1200*f*
compound planetary gear sets, 1380, 1382–1383, 1382*f*, 1382*t*, 1383*f*, 1389
power flows. *See* Simpson gear set
compound ratio, 1199, 1207
compound shift, 1240, 1256
compound split operation, 1683, 1687
compound starter motor, 399
comprehensive component monitor (CCM), 579–580, 636
compressed air, 119
compressed air brake systems, 926. *See also* air brake systems
concept of, 926, 927*f*
compression, 765–766, 789
compression forces
frame, 766*f*
tension forces along frame, 766*f*
compressor, 1695
clutches, 1706, 1707*f*
controls, 1721–1722
gas, 1700, 1701*f*
removing, inspecting, and reinstallment of, 1751, 1753–1754
thermostatic switch cycles, 1713, 1714*f*
compressor clutch
air-conditioning, 1737, 1765
inspecting, testing, and replacement of, 1751, 1752–1753
computer-based materials, vehicle, 48
computer-controlled actuator, 1159
computer-controlled air-conditioning systems, 1740–1741
computer databases, 56*f*
computer memory, integrated circuit devices, 549, 550*f*
EEPROM and flash memory, 550
RAM, 550
ROM, 549–550, 551*f*
computerized power train management systems, 541
condensation, 1699, 1703, 1707, 1727
of moisture, 1696, 1697, 1699*f*
condenser, 1695, 1707–1708, 1727, 1780–1781
check valves, 1781
inspecting for airflow restrictions, 1739
removing, inspecting, and reinstallment of, 1754, 1756
conductance test, 378, 380, 389
conduction, 1698, 1727
conductivity, 209–210
conductor, 210*t*, 223
conductor movement, direction of, 237*f*
conductors, 209, 250
number and size of, 238*f*
cone-type clutch, 1140–1141, 1140*f*
connecting drum, 1395, 1417
connectors, inspecting, repairing/replacing, 453
constant-current charger, 381–382, 389
constant-mesh collar shift transmissions, 1217–1218, 1218*f*. *See also* sliding clutch; sliding collar
constant-mesh synchronized transmissions, 1218
block- or insert-type synchronizer, 1218–1220, 1219*f*
disc-and-plate-type synchronizer, 1220–1221, 1221*f*
pin-type synchronizer, 1220, 1220*f*
plain-type synchronizer, 1218, 1219*f*
constant mesh transmissions, 1214, 1256
constant-rate leaf spring assemblies, 803, 803*f*
constant-ratio steering gears, 847–848, 847*f*, 876
constant velocity joints, 1550, 1550*f*, 1567
constant-voltage chargers, 381, 382*f*, 389
construction, vehicles, 9
contact patch, 663, 663*f*, 701, 795, 795*f*, 836
for radial and bias tire, 673, 674*f*
contact patterns, 1610, 1639
contact point of driving tooth, 1196
contact to inflation pressure, ratio of, 663, 664*f*
contaminated lubricant, 1637
contemporary truck electrical system architecture, 207*f*
continuity, 309

continuous duty relays, 285, 286*f*
continuous monitor, 636–641
control air pressure, 1047
control axle torque, 795–796
control circuits, 1411
control devices, 250
control main pressure, 1477
control modules, 1464, 1503
  stability, 1058, 1060
control solenoid, 1591
control valve body, 1402, 1404*f*, 1417
controlled area network (CAN), 611–612, 623, 941
  checking for shorts in, 621
  J-1939 *vs.* J-1708/1587, 612
  multiple networks, 617
  network messages, 615–617
  serial communication, 612–615
controlled traction differentials, 1581, 1582, 1582*f*, 1600
convection, 1698, 1727
conventional batteries, 353
conventional clutch brake, 1154
conventional control systems, 490–491
conventional current theory, 215, 223
conventional hypoid pattern, 1623, 1625*f*
conventional integral steering system, 843, 844*f*
conventional steering system, 843, 844*f*, 876
conventional test light, 260*f*
conventional tractor, 1105*f*
converter dolly, 1106–1107, 1132
converter flow valve, 1496
converter regulator valve, 1494, 1496
converter shell, 1344, 1344*f*, 1345*f*, 1347*f*
converter, torque. *See also* torque converters
  out passageway, 1353, 1353*f*
  in passageway, 1353, 1353*f*
convoluted air spring, 813, 836
convoluted type air spring bellows, 813, 814*f*
coolant, 145, 145*f*, 157
coolant label, 63, 63*f*, 65
coolant temperature, 631, 633
coolers, 1798
  transmission oil, inspection of, 1277–1278
cooling cycle, 1776, 1778, 1778*f*
cooling fan, 444*f*
cooling mechanism (air and oil), 434
cooling system
  alternator, 444–445, 444*f*
  of engine, 241
  engine-off engine compartment inspection, conducting, 1878
  monitor, engine, 636, 640
  operation, 631
cooling system pressure gauge, 137, 137*f*
copper (Cu), 151, 151*f*, 157, 210
conductivity of different metals compared to, 210*t*
corded drills, 117
cordless drills, 117, 118*f*, 734*f*
cordless light, 77
core charge, 386
core plugs, 183, 183*f*
corrosion, 218*f*
corrosion damage, 779, 779*f*
corrosion inhibitors, 145, 146
counter clockwise (CCW), 1019, 1197, 1207
counter-electromotive force (CEMF), 400, 401*f*, 425, 433, 433*f*
counterbalance valves, 1820
countershaft, 1213, 1256
  transmission, 1194*f*
counts, 1449, 1450*f*, 1526
couplers, 23–24, 24*f*, 30, 1109–1110, 1109*f*, 1132
coupling, 230
coupling jaws, 1117–1118
coupling phase, 1349–1351, 1350*f*–1351*f*, 1367
coupling shaft, 1537, 1537*f*, 1567
  measurement of slope, 1546, 1547*f*
CPE insulation. *See* chlorinated polyethylene insulation
CPU. *See* central processing unit
crack pressure, 950–951, 963
crack repair, 784–787
cracked frames, 777–778
crank axles, 1574, 1600
crank position (CKP) sensor, 636–637
crankcase ventilation (CV) systems, 629, 636, 640
cranking amps (CA), 340, 347
cranking speed, 417
cranking system. *See* starting systems
crankshaft, 115, 157, 636, 637*f*, 1142, 1149, 1150
  position, 569, 570*f*, 576, 577
  seals, 181–182
  speed, 639
crash-and-rescue truck, 12*f*
creep torque, 1677
creeper, 120
crescent wrench, 121
crimp, 1805, 1832
crimp-type connectors, 470–471, 471*f*
criteria, inspector qualifications, 1854
critical speed, 1533, 1567
  bow related to, 1539, 1539*f*
  shaft mass and, 1539–1540
  vibrations, 1551
cross-arm, 133, 157
cross-cut chisel, 128, 128*f*, 157
cross members, 766, 770–771, 784*f*, 789
  hat-style, 771*f*
cross-phasing, 1545, 1567
  and incremental phasing adjustments, 1544–1545
cross-sectional view of air-conditioning compressor, 1705, 1705*f*
cross-shaft, 1168, 1189
cross tube, 1573
crossed airlines, 1274–1275
crowbars. *See* pry bars
crown gear, 1203, 1575, 1600
crown gear runout
  checking, 1622
  measuring, 1624
crown gear set, 1616–1617, 1617*f*
cruciform kingpins, 1116
crude oil, 148
CS. *See* charge-sustaining mode
CSA 2010 basic score, 1850, 1883
CSI. *See* customer satisfaction index
cubic feet of air pumped per minute (CFM), 930
cubic feet of displacement, increase in power output, 535*t*
cubic feet per minute (CFM), 1742
Cummins INSITE, programmable engine parameters screen shot from, 537*f*
cup and cone, 1140
cup holders, 231
cupping on tiers, 685
current
  alternating, 433
  amount of, 433
  regulation, 442
current clamp, 385, 389
current flow, 295
  direction of, 215–216
current inverters, 1661, 1661*f*
current movement, electron theory of, 215
current track, 475, 485
curved files, 130, 131*f*, 157
cushion segments, 1147, 1147*f*
customer pickup, vehicle for, 55
customer satisfaction index (CSI), 54
customer service, 53–55, 54*f*
customer's vehicle, 55
cutters, 124
cutting tools, 125
CV systems. *See* crankcase ventilation systems
CVSA. *See* Commercial Vehicle Safety Alliance
CX transmissions, 1522–1523, 1523*f*
CX28 transmissions, 1521–1522, 1521*f*, 1522*f*
CX31 transmissions, 1521–1522, 1522*f*
CX35 transmissions, 1522
cycling clutch orifice tube (CCOT), 1708, 1712*f*, 1717, 1727
  accumulator of, 1713, 1713*f*, 1718*f*
  system, 1714*f*
cylinder identification, 576
cylinders, 1815, 1832
  double-acting, 1817
  hydraulic, 1796

master. *See* master cylinder
range shift, 1244, 1257
single-acting and telescoping, 1816–1817
splitter shift, 1254, 1257
wheel. *See* wheel cylinders

D

"D" capacity, 1114, 1132
D-shackles, 188, 188*f*, 195
DAA. *See* Eaton Drive Line Angle Analyzer
Daimler Trucks Automatic Gear Shift, 1305, 1305*f*, 1328–1329, 1329*f*
model MBT660-6OA, 1329*t*
dampened disc styles, 1148, 1148*f*
dampening discs, 1149, 1149*f*, 1162
DANA model, breakdown of, 1608, 1610
Dana Spicer Life series XS universal joints, 1557
dangers, 71, 74, 74*f*
D'Arsonval gauges, 515–517, 516*f*, 529
dash gauges, 943, 943*f*
dash pressure guage, 1009
data bus, 603, 623
arbitration, 616–617
data link adapters, 323, 323*f*, 325
data link connector (DLC), 607, 607*f*
performing, 620
data mechanical (DM) Autoclutch, 1158, 1158*f*
data mechanical (DM) clutch, 1306, 1308, 1313, 1313*f*
day cab, 17, 1105*f*
daytime running lights (DRL), 499, 507
Dayton Electric Company, 395–396
DC. *See* direct current
DC-to-AC inverter, 1661, 1665
DC-to-DC converter, use of, 1671*f*
DDL connector. *See* diagnostic data link connector
de-rating, 1053, 1063
dead axle, 1572, 1574, 1574*f*, 1600
dead-blow hammer, 128, 128*f*, 157
decoding, VIN, 27–28
dedendum, 1195, 1207
deep cycle batteries, 334–335, 347
vs. SLI battery, 336–337, 336*f*
deep-reduction gear, 1235, 1235*f*
deep socket, 123, 123*f*
DEF. *See* diesel exhaust fluid
defective battery, 361
defective brakes, criteria for, 1868
defective equipment report, 50, 50*f*
defrost cycle, 1772, 1778, 1778*f*, 1783
defroster, 1696, 1727
DELCO™, 396
Delco Remy™, 395, 395*f*
delta configurations, 436, 437*f*
delta pressure (Delta P) sensor, 640
delta windings, 436, 457
delta-wound alternators, 437
demountable rim, 710, 725
dents, vibration, 1552
depletion zone, 290*f*
depth micrometers, 111–112, 111*f*, 157
depth of discharge (DOD), 334
desiccant, 939, 939*f*, 963
detent balls, 1217, 1256
detent downshift. *See* full throttle downshift
Detroit Deisel, 1577, 1577*f*
Detroit Diesel's DT-12, 1305, 1326, 1326*f*
Detroit engine, 39
Deutsch connectors, 468, 469*f*, 485
DT series of, 468
Deutsche Institute Norm (DIN) diagram, 474–481, 476*f*, 485
diagram, 479*f*
relay diagram, 480*f*
symbols, 478*f*
wiring diagram, elements of, 477
device codes, component and, 478
diagnosing failures, process for, 1632–1633
diagnostic blink codes, APADS module from LEDs, 1725, 1725*f*
diagnostic code display, 1684
diagnostic data link (DDL) connector, 1452, 1526
diagnostic equipment, tools
dynamometer, 136, 136*f*
pressure testers/tire inflators, 136–137, 137*f*
scan tool, 137, 138, 138*f*
diagnostic link connector (DLC), 633, 655
diagnostic mode code, 1500
diagnostic optimized connection (DOC) tool, 1685
diagnostic (scan) tool, diagnose transmissions, 1331–1332
diagnostic trouble codes (DTCs), 322, 642, 655, 1359, 1360, 1499, 1523, 1684
diagnostics, automatic transmission, 1427
diagonal-cutting pliers, 124, 124*f*, 157
diagonal split, brake line configuration, 1077–1078, 1078*f*
dial bore gauge, 113–114, 114*f*, 157
dial gauges. *See* dial indicators
dial indicators, 115, 116, 157, 1363, 1552
checks, 1180, 1181
dial torque wrench, 173
dial type, pocket tire pressure gauges, 684–685
diamond, 778, 778*f*, 781, 789
diaphragm spring clutch, 1143*f*, 1144–1146, 1144*f*, 1162
rockwell pull-type, 1145*f*
diaphragm-type gas-charged accumulator, 1825, 1825*f*, 1832
die, 132, 132*f*, 157
die nut, 132, 132*f*
die stock handle, 132, 132*f*, 157
dielectric material, 287
dielectric non-conductive grease, use of, 263*f*
diesel engines, 534, 535*f*
diagnostic monitoring of, 634
efficiently power refrigeration units, 1773*f*
requirements for, 629
diesel exhaust aftertreatment systems, 636
diesel exhaust fluid (DEF), 641, 1854
diesel fuel oil, 148–149, 149*f*
diesel-fueled, OBD emissions thresholds for, 634*t*, 642*t*
diesel misfire detection, threshold for, 636
diesel particulate filters (DPFs), 562*f*, 635
monitoring, 640, 641*f*
differential braking, 1054–1055, 1054*f*, 1063
differential carrier
disassembling and removing, 1610–1614
reassembling, 1621–1627
reinstalling, 1631
differential case, 1575, 1579*f*, 1600
disassembling and removing, 1610–1614
reassembling, 1621–1627
differential cross, 1579, 1579*f*, 1600
differential gear sets, 1578, 1579*f*, 1600
functions of, 1578–1581
types of, 1581
biased torque (proportional) differentials, 1584–1585
controlled traction and locking differentials, 1581–1584
double reduction and multi-speed drive axles, 1585–1592
inter-axle differentials (power dividers), 1592–1596
preventing inter-axle differential spinout, 1596–1597
differential gears, 1575, 1600
differential locks, 1583, 1583*f*, 1600
differential mode transmission, 613, 613*f*, 623
differential pinion gears, 1579, 1600
differential spider, 1579, 1600
differential voltage, 542, 542*f*, 553
DIfferential-WAndler (DIWA) transmission, Voith, 1514
automatic neutral at standstill, 1516
components, 1515–1516
control system, 1521
operation, 1514–1515
power flows, 1516–1519
first gear, 1517, 1517*f*
fourth gear, 1519, 1519*f*
neutral, 1516, 1516*f*
reverse, 1519, 1520*f*
second gear, 1517, 1518
third gear, 1517, 1518*f*, 1519
retarder operation, 1519–1521, 1520*f*
torque converter oil flow, 1515

digital CAN gauges, 518–519, 521*f*
digital communication, 603
digital language electronic modules, 241
digital modules, 603
digital multimeters, 141, 141*f*, 215, 216*f*, 308, 309*f*, 325, 541
digital regulators, 442
digital signals, 541–542, 541*f*–542*f*, 553
 analog to digital conversion, 543, 543*f*–544*f*
 bits and bytes, 542, 542*f*
 serial data, 542–543, 542*f*
digital torque wrench, 173
digital type, pocket tire pressure gauges, 685
digital volt-ohmmeter (DVOM), 372, 385–386, 587, 1741
digital watch, 541
dimmer switch, 499
DIN diagram. *See* Deutsche Institute Norm diagram
diode problems, rectifier, 439
diode rectifier, 455
diode scale, 319, 319*f*
diodes, 284*f*, 285, 289–290, 291*f*
 clamping application of, 293–294
 forward bias, 291–292
 symbol for, 291*f*
 trio, 439*f*
 types of, 292–293, 292*f*
DIP. *See* dual inline package switches
dipstick tube, 1423*f*
direct-acting type, air boosters, 1083, 1084, 1085*f*
direct current (DC), 217–218, 217*f*, 223, 330, 344
 generator, 430, 431
direct current (DC) motors
 principles, 398–399
 types of
  low-voltage burn-out, 401–402, 402*f*
  series motors, 399–401
direct current (DC) Power Link Contactor, 1659
direct-drive starter motor, 396, 396*f*, 397, 407, 425
Direct Shift Gearbox (DSG), 1315–1316
direct TPMS, 666, 701
directional control valves, 1821–1823, 1822*f*
directional stability control (DSC) systems, 1056–1058, 1057*f*, 1063
 sensors in, 1058*t*
dirt moisture, 1697, 1698*f*
disc brakes, 891, 891*f*, 900, 901*f*, 915, 916*f*, 1073–1074, 1073*f*, 1079
disc-type synchronizer, 1220–1221, 1221*f*
disc wheel, 709, 712–716, 713*f*, 725
discharge rates, defective battery, 361
discharge service valves, 1780, 1780*f*
discharge valves, 931, 932*f*, 934
discharging cycle, 343–344, 343*f*
dislocation, 100, 102
displacement, 1832
disposable dust mask, 93, 93*f*
distributed network control, 600–602
distribution block, 1855
DIWA. *See* DIfferential-WAndler
DIWA™, 1395, 1417
DLC. *See* data link connector
dock walk, 818
DOD. *See* depth of discharge
dog teeth, 1214, 1218
DOM tube. *See* drawn-over-mandrel tube
doors, safety equipment, 75
doorway, safety equipment, 75
doped silicon, 289
DOT. *See* US Department of Transportation
dotted line, 481
double-acting cylinders, 1817, 1817*f*, 1818*f*
double-acting shock absorber, 800
double-action wheel cylinder, 1078, 1078*f*
double Cardan joints, 1550, 1550*f*
double check valves, 951, 952*f*, 963
double clutch, 1217, 1256
double decker bus, 13*f*
double flare, 133, 134*f*, 157
double-insulated, 77, 102
double oscillating fifth wheel. *See* fully oscillating fifth wheel
double pole double throw (DPDT), 276, 277*t*
double pole single throw (DPST), 276, 277*t*
double reduction drive axles, 1585, 1585*f*, 1600
 axle shift control, 1588–1592
 helical double reduction drive axles, 1585
 helical double reduction two-speed drive axles, 1585–1586
 planetary two-speed and planetary double reduction axles, 1586–1588
double-walled tubing, 470
double wishbone system, 798
dowel pins, 176, 176*f*, 198
DPDT. *See* double pole double throw switch
DPFs. *See* diesel particulate filters
DPST. *See* double pole single throw
drag links, 735, 735*f*, 757, 842, 854–855, 876, 1573
drain valves, 937–938, 938*f*
draw bar capacity, 1114, 1132
draw bars, 23, 30, 1106, 1109–1111, 1110*f*, 1132
drawn-over-mandrel (DOM) tube, 1535, 1535*f*
drift punch, 134–135, 134*f*, 157
drill bits, 117–118, 118*f*
drill chuck, 117, 157
drill press, 117, 118, 118*f*, 157
drill vice, 131, 131*f*, 157
drills, 117–118
drivability items, 1851, 1883
drive axle gearing and housings, types of, 1575–1578
drive axle housings, 1578, 1578*f*
drive axle leaf spring suspensions, 807, 807*f*, 808*f*
drive axle lubrications, 1606–1607
 guidelines for changing, 1608, 1609
 intervals for, 1608*t*
 SAE grades of, 1607*t*
drive axle slope, 1546, 1547*f*
drive axle systems, diagnosing
 failures in, 1631–1632
 process for diagnosing failures, 1632–1633
drive axles, 1573, 1574–1575, 1574*f*, 1598*f*, 1600
 changing lubricant and filters, 1609
 components, 1616–1617
 failures, types of, 1633–1637
 fundamentals of servicing
  lube change intervals and procedures, 1607–1608
  lubrication, 1606–1607
 with integral pinion support, shim pack thickness for, 1620–1621
 for leaks, inspecting, 1607
 nomenclature, 1610
 overhaul—reassembly
  differential case and differential carrier, reassembling, 1621–1627
  pinion bearing, 1617, 1618*f*
  pinion bearing preload, 1621
  pinion depth, setting, 1618–1621
  pinion gear, 1621
 overhaul—removal and inspection, 1608–1610
  differential carrier and differential case, disassembling, 1610–1614
  drive axle components, 1616–1617
 with removable pinion cage, shim pack thickness for, 1620
 with traction, 1595*f*
drive belt, inspecting and replacement of, 1751
drive belts alternator, 449–450
drive cycle, 444
drive gear, 1197–1199
drive line angularity, 1545, 1567
 compound, 1548–1550, 1549*f*
 examples of, 1546–1548, 1548*f*
 measurement and calculation of, 1545–1546, 1546*f*–1547*f*
drive line vibration diagnostics, 1551, 1551*f*
drive lines, 1535, 1567. *See also* driveshaft systems
drive mechanism, 434, 445–446

drive pinion, removing, 1615–1616
drive pins, 811, 836, 1151, 1162
drive pulley, 1752, 1765
driveshaft hand brake system, 1074, 1074*f*
drive straps, 1144, 1144*f*, 1145*f*
drive train, 1873
  inspecting, 1874–1875
  systems, 1289, 1291
drive wheel, truck classification by, 15*t*
drive–axle alignment, recommended practices for, 749*t*
driven gear, 1808
driven plate, 1149
driver information screens, 524–526
  capacitance touch screens, 526
  LCD, 525
  resistive touch screens, 525–526
Driver Post-operation Vehicle Inspection Report (DVIR), 1851, 1851*f*, 1853, 1883
driver shift control, 1308
driver shift knob. *See* Roadranger valve
Driver Vehicle Inspection Report (DVIR), 59, 59*f*, 61–62, 1851
driver while, 1808
drivers, 299*f*
driver's input, 1448–1449, 1449*f*
driveshaft angle cancellation, 1542
  rule number one, 1542
  rule number three, 1543, 1543*f*
  rule number two, 1542–1543, 1542*f*
driveshaft capacity, 1534
driveshaft failure, 1552
  accelerated wear, 1554
  brinelling, 1552, 1554*f*
  hanger bearing failures, 1555, 1555*f*
  spalling or galling, 1552, 1554, 1554*f*
  twisted tubing, 1554–1555, 1555*f*
  U-joint fractures and breakage, 1554, 1555*f*
driveshaft runout, measurement of, 1552, 1554*f*
driveshaft series, 1534
  recommended limits for, 1534, 1534*t*
driveshaft systems, 1531–1567
  components of, 1535
    coupling shaft, 1537, 1537*f*
    driveshaft tube, 1535, 1535*f*
    driveshaft yokes, 1535–1536, 1535*f*–1536*f*
    fastening systems, 1538, 1538*f*
    slip joint, 1536, 1537*f*
    universal joints, 1537–1538, 1538*f*
  fundamentals of, 1533, 1533*f*
    angle of drive, 1534
    driveshaft series, 1534, 1534*t*
    length changes, 1533–1534
    strength, 1533
  hardware removal of, 1559–1561, 1560*f*–1561*f*
  inspection and maintenance of, 1555–1557, 1556*f*–1557*f*
    inspecting and installing universal joints, 1561–1563
    lubrication, 1557–1558, 1557*t*–1558*t*, 1558*f*–1559*f*
    removing driveshaft, 1559–1561, 1560*f*–1561*f*
    replacing center (hanger) bearings, 1562, 1564–1565
    replacing universal joint, 1559
  introduction of, 1532–1533, 1532*f*–1533*f*
  operation of, 1539
    constant velocity joints, 1550, 1550*f*
    cross and incremental phasing adjustments, 1544–1545
    drive line angularity. *See* drive line angularity
    driveshaft angle cancellation, 1542–1543, 1542*f*–1543*f*, 1543*t*
    non-uniform velocity, 1540–1542, 1540*f*–1541*f*
    phasing, 1543–1544, 1544*f*
    shaft mass and critical speed, 1539–1540, 1539*f*
  removing and reinstalling of, 1564
  troubleshooting vibrations and failures, 1551
    analyzing driveshaft failure, 1552, 1554–1555, 1554*f*–1555*f*
    diagnosing vibrations, 1551–1552, 1553*f*
    drive line vibration diagnostics, 1551, 1551*f*
    measuring driveshaft runout, 1552, 1554*f*
driveshaft tube, 1535, 1535*f*
driveshaft vibrations, 1542
driveshaft yokes, 1535–1536
  end yokes, 1535–1536, 1536*f*
  flange yoke, 1536, 1536*f*
  tube yokes, 1535, 1535*f*
driving tooth, 1196
DRL. *See* daytime running lights
DRM. *See* dryer integrated module
drop arm, 735, 757, 854, 854*f*, 855*f*, 876
drop bed auto hauler, 8*f*
drop boxes, 1251, 1256. *See also* transfer cases
drop-center cross member, 771
drop center tubular axles, 1574, 1600
drop-center wheel rim, 667, 701
drop forward, 770
drop front, 770
drop-front frame, 770*f*
drop-style tie-rod end, 856, 856*f*
droplights, portable, 76–77, 77*f*
drum brake systems, 919*f*
drum brakes, 1071, 1079
  assembly, removing and replacement of, 1094
  single-leading-shoe (SLS). *See* single-leading-shoe drum brake
  types of adjusters used with, 1072
    star wheel-type adjuster, 1073, 1073*f*
    wedge-type adjuster, 1073, 1073*f*
drum disc lathe, 139, 139*f*
drum pilot pads, 1013*f*
drum replacement guide, 1015*t*
drum service guidelines, 1014*t*
dry batteries, 337
dryer integrated module (DRM), 941, 942*f*, 963
DSC systems. *See* directional stability control systems
DSG. *See* direct shift gearbox
DT-12, 1336
  system, 1305, 1305*f*
DTCs. *See* diagnostic trouble codes
dual box systems, 854
  steering box, 855
dual brakes
  chambers, 905–906, 908
  circuits, 890
dual circuit integrity test, 990, 991, 1033
dual-circuit systems, 928, 963
dual-clutch module for ZF Traxon transmissions, 1326*f*
dual-clutch transmissions, 1301, 1315, 1336
dual disc pull-type clutch, 1142
  installing
    14" inch clutch, 1183–1185
    15.5" inch clutch, 1185–1186
dual-drive tractor, 16*f*
dual-gear systems, 870
dual inline package (DIP) switches, 522, 523, 523*f*, 529, 683
dual mass flywheel, 1150, 1150*f*, 1162
dual-mode Allison EP system, configuration of, 1672*f*
dual-mode hybrid drive train, 1683–1684, 1687
dual mode hybrids system, 1672*f*
dual-path throttle position sensors, 565
dual power inverter module (DPIM), 1679*f*
  AC-DC electronic wave inverter, 1679*f*
  DC-AC electronic wave inverter, 1679*f*
  function and construction, 1679–1680
  high voltage interlock loop (HVIL), 1682–1683
  operation, 1680–1682
dual range drive axles, 1586
dual-steering boxes, 871
dump solenoid, 1090
dump truck, 9*f*
  maximum bending moment, 768*f*
dump valve, 816, 836
dumping clutch, abuse failures, 1293
duplex gauge, 993, 993*f*, 994*f*, 1033
duplex wedge brake system, 919, 919*f*
durapoid gearing, 1576, 1576*f*, 1600
durapoid spiral bevel gearing, 1625, 1627*f*

duty cycle, 546–548, 547*f*–548*f*, 553, 1473, 1526
DVIR. *See* Driver Post-operation Vehicle Inspection Report; Driver Vehicle Inspection Report
DVOM. *See* digital volt-ohmeter
dye leak detector, 1742, 1743*f*
dye testing for leaks, 1744–1746
dynamic balancing of tires, 693–694
dynamic oil seals, 721*f*
dynamic pumps, 1807
dynamometer, 39*f*, 136, 136*f*

E

E-fuses, 267
EAC. *See* Electronic Air Control
ear protection, 92–93, 93*f*, 102
ears, 1566
Earth's magnetic field, 524, 524*f*
EAS. *See* Electronic Air System
Easy Pedal Clutch, 1146, 1146*f*
Eaton angle spring clutch, 1146, 1146*f*
Eaton AutoShift, 1303
Eaton Corporation, 1143, 1155, 1159
Eaton Corporation's UltraShift transmission, 1301*f*
Eaton Drive Line Angle Analyzer (DAA), 1545, 1552
Eaton FO-8406-ASW, 1159–1160, 1160*f*
Eaton Fuller AutoShift 10-speed transmission, 1303
Eaton Fuller AutoShift and UltraShift operations, 1306–1314
Eaton Fuller transmission nomenclature, 1314
Eaton Fuller's automated transmissions, 1302–1304
Eaton Fuller's Super Ten Top Two, 1302–1303, 1302*f*–1303*f*
Eaton Gen 3 electronics, 1307*f*
Eaton Procision automated transmission, 1314–1322
Eaton Procision operation, 1316–1317
Eaton Procision transmission, 1316, 1316*f*
Eaton's electronically actuated clutch, 1313*f*
Eaton's Solo clutch, 1146
ECA. *See* electric clutch actuator
ECIS. *See* Allison Electronic Control Information System
ECMs. *See* electronic control modules
EcoLife transmissions, 1521
EcoMat transmissions, 1521
economical electronic version, 747
ECP. *See* electronic cooling package
ECPCs. *See* electronic clutch-pressure control units
ECSI. *See* Emergency Care and Safety Institute
ECU. *See* electronic control units
edge code, 898, 899, 921
  brake shoe, 899*f*
  coefficient of friction, 899*t*
edge wears on tiers, 686
educational requirements, service technicians, 38
EEPROM. *See* electrically erasable programmable read only memory
effective PM program, 1851, 1852*f*
efficiency monitoring, 637
EGR. *See* exhaust gas recirculation
eighteen-speed transmissions with four-speed auxiliary sections, 1241–1243, 1241*f*–1242*f*
elastic limit of material, 768
elastic section modulus, 767
elasticity, 174, 198, 795
electric charge movement, conventional current theory of, 215
electric circuits, 252
electric clutch actuator (ECA), 1159, 1159*f*
electric current, 211
  heating effect of, 219–220
  movement of, 210–214
electric droplights, 76–77, 77*f*
electric modulator system, 1406
electric motors, 258, 259*f*
electric power drill, 119
electric shift assembly, 1309–1310, 1336
  shift finger and shift rail in, 1309*f*
electric shift control, 1588–1591, 1589*f*
electric shock
  effects of, 1649–1650, 1650*t*
  zap of, 228
electric solenoids, 1311, 1311*f*
electric starter motors. *See* starter motors
electric vehicles (EV), 1644, 1665
electric wiring, 462–483
  color coding, 464–465, 465*t*
  connectors, 466–468, 466*f*
  failure and repair, 468–471, 470*t*
  footage of, 463*f*
  number coding, 465, 466*f*
  requirements, 462
  wire sizing, 462–464, 463*f*, 463*t*
electrical capacity, 339, 347
electrical circuits, 260
  continuity monitoring, 633
  vs. electronic circuits, 220–221
electrical components, inspecting, 1866–1867
electrical current, 433
electrical current flow, concepts of, 212*t*
electrical devices, 207, 212, 217
electrical displays, 1333
electrical equipment
  battery chargers, 143–145
  electrical testing equipment, 142–143
    alternator test bench, 143
    jump leads, circuit with, 142
    multimeter to measure voltage, 142
    opens, shorts, grounds, and high resistance, 142–143
    test light, circuit with, 142
  Ohm's law to diagnose circuits, using, 142
electrical exhaust, inspecting, 1866–1867
electrical fault, 414
electrical fundamentals, 207–208
electrical lubrication, inspecting, 1866–1867
electrical measurement
  basic multimeter with, 309, 309*f*
  with multimeters, 312
    amperage—ammeters, 316–319, 316*f*–319*f*, 318*t*
    diode scale, 319, 319*f*
    resistance—ohmmeters, 312–314, 312*f*–314*f*
    temperature, 319
    voltage—voltmeters, 314–315, 314*f*–316*f*, 316*t*
  symbols and meanings for, 310, 310*f*
electrical noise, 613
electrical pathway, 252*f*
electrical resistance, 212, 223
electrical safety, 76, 76*f*
  hybrid drive systems, 1649, 1649*f*
    collisions, 1651–1652
    effects of electric shock, 1649–1650, 1650*t*
    high voltage disconnect, 1650, 1651*f*
    insulated gloves, 1651, 1651*f*
    routine inspection, 1651
  portable electrical equipment, 76, 77*f*
  portable shop lights/droplights, 76–77, 77*f*
electrical switches, 1333
electrical symbol, 472*f*
electrical system
  components, 206
  modern, 599*f*
  software control of, 605–606, 605*f*
electrical system control modules (ECM), 431, 443
  controlled alternator, 443*f*
electrical system controllers (ESCs), 609, 611*f*
electrical terminals, specialized grease for, 243*f*
electrical test instruments, 305. *See also* electrical measurement
  circuit tracers, 319, 320*f*
  electronic service tools—scanners. *See* electronic service tools—scanners
  graphing meters and oscilloscopes, 319–321, 320*f*–321*f*
  introduction of, 306
  multimeters, 308–311, 309*f*–311*f*
    basic electrical measurements, 309, 309*f*
    electrical measurements with. *See* electrical measurement

manual and auto-ranging meters, 310, 310*f*, 310*t*
meter shunts, 311, 311*f*
test lights, 306–307, 306*f*–307*f*
self-powered LED test lights, 308
self-powered test light, 307–308, 308*f*
vibration analyzers, 321
electrical testing equipment, 142–143
electrical, under-vehicle inspections, 1872, 1873
electrically erasable programmable read only memory (EEPROM), 550, 553
electrically operated solenoids, redirect flow of hot refrigerant, 1776*f*
Electrically Variable (EV) Drive, 1670, 1671, 1676
transmission unit, 1673
electricity, 209
from chemistry, 241–242
from friction, 228–230
fuel cells, 242–243
from heat, 230–232
from light, 230
from magnetism, 232–241
electromagnetism, 234–241
induction and twisted pair wires, 241
from pressure, 232
principles of, 206–207
basic electricity, 208–210
electrical fundamentals, 207–208
electrical *vs.* electronic circuits, 220–221
understanding conductivity, 210–220
sources of, 228
from thermocouple, 231*f*
electro-hydraulic control system, 1451, 1526
WTEC II and WTEC III, 1473*f*
electronic control unit, 1471–1472
hydraulic control, 1476–1477
latch valve fluid flows, 1485–1488
latch valves, 1485
solenoid fluid flows, 1477–1484
solenoids and solenoid control, 1472–1476
electro-hydraulic valve body, 1451, 1453, 1454, 1454*f*, 1464, 1526
valves use in, 1494–1497
accumulator relay valve, 1497
converter flow valve, 1496
converter regulator valve, 1494, 1496
exhaust backfill valve, 1497
lube pressure regulator valve, 1496
overdrive knock-down valve, 1496
electrodes, 353, 358, 359
area of, 242*f*
and wires, 785*t*
electrolysis, 344, 347
electrolytes, 210, 241, 331, 337–338, 347, 353, 359
level and condition, 375
technology, 356, 358
electrolytic capacitor, 288*f*
electrolytic effect, 779
electromagnet, 234, 245
electromagnetic coil gauges, 517
electromagnetic coils, 238
relays use, 283
winding, 285
electromagnetic fields, 404
multi-loop motor and, 406*f*
single-loop motor and, 405*f*
electromagnetic induction, 237–238, 245, 432*f*
electromagnetic interference (EMI), 612, 613, 613*f*
electromagnetism, 234–241
electromagnets, 398
electron flow, 237
electron theory, 216
electron theory of current movement, 215, 223
Electronic Air Control (EAC), 941, 942*f*, 963
Electronic Air System (EAS), 942*f*
electronic alignment, 747
electronic circuits, electrical circuits *vs.*, 220–221
electronic clutch-pressure control units (ECPCs), 1522
electronic compass, 524
electronic control, benefits of, 534
increased power and efficiency, 534, 535*f*, 535*t*
information reporting capabilities, 535, 536*f*
programmable vehicle features, 537, 537*f*
safety, 536–537
self-diagnostic capabilities, 538, 538*f*
telematics, 536, 536*f*–537*f*
electronic control modules (ECMs), 206, 265, 278, 278*f*–280*f*, 490, 491*f*, 513, 535, 536, 542, 548–549, 563–567, 570, 574, 577–581, 586, 588, 605*f*, 606–607, 631, 632, 636, 1359, 1360
active *vs.* passive sensors, 558, 559*f*
field effect transistors, 579*f*
pins, 483*f*
pull-down switch, 560, 561*f*
pull-up switch, 560, 561*f*
reference voltage, 559, 559*f*
transistors in, 575, 576*f*
electronic control systems, 628
electronic control units (ECU), 817, 818, 1042–1044, 1055*f*, 1059, 1306, 1310, 1312, 1314, 1333, 1503
configuration, 1042
and on-board network communication, 1043–1044
electronic controls
diodes. *See* diodes
electronic *vs.* electrical control, 289
integrated circuits, 298–299
transistors, 294–298
electronic cooling package (ECP), 1659, 1665
electronic leak detector, 1742, 1743*f*
testing for leaks, 1744, 1746
electronic pressure control (EPC), 1360
electronic service tools, 538, 543
electronic service tools—scanners, 321–322, 322*f*
additional functions, 323
code readers, 323
data link adapters, 323, 323*f*
SAE requirements for OBD scan tools, 322
electronic shift controls, 1503
electronic shift selectors, 1333
electronic shock absorbers, 801–802
electronic signal processing systems, 533
elements of, 538, 539*f*
outputs, 539, 540*f*
processing, 539
sensing functions, 539
functions of, 548–549, 548*f*
computer memory, 549–551, 550*f*–551*f*
CPU clock, 549, 549*f*
introduction of, 534
operating principles of, 533–551
types of, 539, 540*f*
analog signals, 539–541, 541*f*
digital signals, 541–543, 541*f*–544*f*
pulse-width modulation, 544–548, 544*f*–548*f*
electronic stability control systems, 1090
electronic stability regulation (ESR), 1052, 1063
electronic switches, 513
electronic versions, 56
electronic *vs.* electrical control, 289
electronic wear indicators, 1030, 1030*f*, 1031*f*, 1033
electronically automated manual transmissions, types of
Detroit Diesel's DT-12, 1305
Eaton Fuller's automated transmissions, 1302–1304, 1302*f*
Mercedes Benz's AGS, 1305, 1305*f*
Meritor/ZF's automated transmissions, 1304–1305, 1304*f*
Volvo Trucks' I-Shift, 1305, 1305*f*
electronically automated transmissions, 1313–1314
electronically controlled accessories, 607–608
electronically controlled air suspension systems, 817–818, 818*f*, 819*f*
electronically controlled automatic transmissions, 1394

ATEC and CEC
ECU, 1447–1448, 1448*f*
shift logic, 1454–1459, 1455*f*
solenoids, 1452–1454
transmission inputs, 1448–1452
trimmer operation, 1460–1461
wiring harnesses, 1452
electro-hydraulic control—WTEC II and WTEC III
electronic control unit, 1471–1472
hydraulic control, 1476–1477
latch valve fluid flows, 1485–1488
latch valves, 1485
solenoid fluid flows, 1477–1484
solenoids and solenoid control, 1472–1476
World Transmission. *See* World Transmission
electronically controlled range valve, 1310
electronically controlled splitter valve, 1310
electronically controlled transmissions, 1360
electrons, 208, 209, 215, 219, 229, 250, 251
electrons movement, 209*f*, 215
from atom to atom, 211*t*
electrophoretic process, 779
electrostatic charging, 230
electrostatic discharge (ESD), 228
electrostatic forces, 208, 215*f*
of repulsion, 251
electrostatic laws, 208, 208*f*
electrostatic theory, 208, 208*f*, 223
EMD. *See* engine manufacturer diagnostics
emergency brake circuit, 930, 930*f*, 963
Emergency Care and Safety Institute (ECSI), 97
emergency/hand brakes. *See* hand/emergency brakes
emergency showers, 80, 80*f*
EMI. *See* electromagnetic interference
emissions system
deterioration, 643
failure, identify, 632
monitors, 635–636
emitter, 294*f*
of transistor, 294*f*, 295
emitter-collector circuit, 295, 295*f*, 297*f*
empathy, 41
employability skills, 40
listening, 40–42
reading, 45–48
speaking, 42–45
writing, 48–52
end cutting pliers, 124
end frames, 434
end yokes, 1535–1536, 1536*f*, 1567
energy density of battery technologies, 352, 352*f*
energy efficiency, 352
energy storage system (ESS), 1659–1660, 1660*f*, 1665, 1677–1679, 1678*f*, 1687
AC-DC electronic wave inverter, 1679*f*
DC-AC electronic wave inverter, 1679*f*
overview of, 1679*f*
state of charge (SOC), 1660, 1661*f*
engine, 13–14
oil, used, 89, 89*f*
running, 75–76, 76*f*
engine compartment, inspecting, 1873, 1875–1879
engine cooling system monitor, 636, 640
engine-driven air compressor. *See* air compressors
engine-driven hydraulic pump, 858, 876
engine-driven power steering pumps, 860
engine dynamometer, 136
engine fan operation, 1724–1725
engine hoists, 192–193, 193*f*, 198
and stands, using, 194–196
engine management system
electrical signals in stages of, 539*f*
overview of components, 535*f*
engine manufacturer diagnostics (EMD), 577, 579
system, 629
engine-off engine compartments, inspecting, 1875–1878
engine oil, 149–150, 149*f*, 1855
engine-on engine compartment inspection, conducting, 1879–1880
engine-on inspection, performing internal cab, 1860–1861
engine rotation, 423
engine scanner, 138
Engine Synchro Shift (ESS), 1304, 1336
engine temperature, 640
engine test switch, 1663
engine torque, 1213
environment, work, 72
Environmental Protection Agency (EPA), 72, 102, 1353, 1735, 1856
and Occupational Safety and Health Administration (OSHA), 72
EP. *See* extreme pressure; extreme pressure additives
EP40 systems, 1670, 1687
EP50 systems, 1670, 1687
EPA. *See* Environmental Protection Agency
EPC. *See* electronic pressure control
epicyclical gears, 1372, 1389. *See also* planetary gears
equalizer, 807, 836
equalizer beam suspension systems, inspection and maintenance, 823
equalizer beams, 811, 811*f*, 823
equalizer bracket, 807
equalizing beam, 836
equalizing beam (walking beam) suspensions, 808–809, 808*f*, 809*f*, 836
chalmers rubber spring, 811–812, 811*f*, 812*f*
leaf spring, 810
rubber spring, 810–811, 811*f*
solid mount, 809–810, 810*f*
types of, 808
equalizing bracket, 836
ESCs. *See* electrical system controllers
ESR. *See* electronic stability regulation
ESS. *See* energy storage system; Engine Synchro Shift
ET software. *See* Cat Electronic Technician
ethylene glycol, 145, 157, 1426, 1441
EV. *See* electric vehicles
evacuation of air-conditioning system, 1735, 1759
using micron gauge, 1759, 1760
using vacuum gauge, 1759, 1760
evacuation routes, 71, 71*f*
evaporator, 1695, 1696, 1697*f*, 1715–1716, 1727, 1781
housing water drain, inspection of, 1739–1740
removing, inspecting, and reinstallment of, 1758–1759
evaporator freezing, 1710, 1727
evaporator thermostatic switch, 1725
excessive caster, 741, 741*f*
excessive charging system voltage, 263
excessive corrosion, 779*f*
excessive turning radius, steering-related problems, 865*t*
excitation, 1534
inertial, 1551, 1567
torsional, 1534, 1567
exhaust backfill valve, 1497
exhaust gas recirculation (EGR)
rates, 569, 571, 575, 579
system, 629, 638*f*
gas, 637, 638*f*, 639
monitor, 635, 637–639
sensor, 639*f*
exhaust gases, 75
exhaust, under-vehicle inspections, 1872, 1873
exhaust valves, 934, 948–949
expansion device, 1708–1715
expansion valve, 1781, 1782*f*
explosion paths for tire, direction of, 664*f*
extension cord, 76, 77*f*
exterior inspections, performing, 1861–1867
exterior lighting circuits, 492
external bleeding, 98, 102
external gear types, 1817
external power-assist steering system, 843–844, 844*f*
external power-assist system, 843
external snap ring pliers, 124*f*, 125
external voltage regulator, 441, 441*f*
extinguisher, fire, 78
classification, 78

fire blankets, 79–80
operation, 78–79, 79*f*
types, 78, 79*f*
extreme pressure (EP) additives, 1262–1263, 1295
extreme pressure (EP) system, 723
diagnostic warning lights for, 1685*f*
maintenance, 1684–1685
eye injuries, 98–99, 99*f*
eye protection, 93–94
full face shield, 94–95, 95*f*
gas welding goggles, 94, 94*f*
safety glasses, 94, 94*f*
safety goggles, 95, 95*f*
welding helmet, 94, 94*f*
eyewash stations, 80, 80*f*

F

factory manuals, 56
factory scan tool, 1502
failed components, three—inspect, 1632
failsafe operation, 1452, 1485, 1485*f*, 1526
failure mode identifier (FMI), 579, 580*t*, 584, 584*f*
failures, 631
drive axle systems
diagnosing, 1631
driveshaft systems
hanger bearing, 1555, 1555*f*
troubleshooting, 1551–1555. *See also* vibrations
fall hazards, 96
false brinelling, 1542, 1552, 1567
fans. *See* impeller
fast adaptive mode, 1473, 1526
fast chargers, 143, 157
fasteners, 121, 123, 164, 198, 770–772
bolts, studs, and nuts, 165–170, 166*f*, 167*f*
chemical compounds, 170, 170*f*
screws, 164–165, 164*f*, 165*f*
and torque, 170–171, 170*f*
fastening systems, driveshafts components of, 1538, 1538*f*
faster clutch application, 1410
faster-sampling graphing meter, 320
fatigue crack, 784*f*
fatigue failures, 776, 783, 1634–1635, 1639
beach marks, 1634*f*
fault, 631
accommodation, 631
detection, 631
isolation, 631
fault code, 536
diagnostic, 536*f*, 632*f*
fault code of 32, 514
fault detection methods, 279
fault mode identifier (FMI), 647, 648*t*, 649, 649*f*, 650*f*, 650*t*–651*t*, 655
fault mode indicators (FMIs), 579, 586
faults codes, 1663
feather key, 177, 177*f*, 198
feathering, tire, 685
Federal Bridge Formula, 19, 30, 1108, 1132
Federal Bridge Gross Weight Formula, 19–20, 30, 1108, 1132
Federal/Canadian Motor Vehicle Standard 108 (FMVSS 108), 492
Federal Motor Carrier Safety Administration (FMCSA), 1847, 1850, 1883
Federal Motor Carrier Safety Regulation (FMCSR), 1853, 1883
Federal Motor Vehicle Safety Standard (FMVSS) 121, 732
Federal Motor Vehicle Safety Standard 119 (FMVSS 119), 678
Federal Motor Vehicle Safety Standard 121 (FMVSS 121), 889, 892, 904, 921, 928, 930, 933, 948, 956–958, 963
Federal Motor Vehicle Safety Standards (FMVSS), 492, 847, 972, 981
feedback, 1822, 1832
feeler blades. *See* feeler gauges
feeler gauges, 116–117, 157
ferrous metals, 151, 157
FETs. *See* field effect transistors
field coils, 403, 404*f*, 406
damaged, 415
field effect transistors (FETs), 221, 267, 268*f*, 279, 295–297, 296*f*, 297*f*, 505*f*, 575, 579, 609, 623, 633
circuit monitoring of, 588*f*
ECM, 579*f*
field excitation, 441
field method, 752
field winding, 398–401, 398*f*, 422
15.5″ dual disc pull-type clutch, 1185–1186
fifth generation electronic control system, Allison, 1471
of World Transmission, 1497–1504
prognostics, 1498–1499
retarders, 1497–1498
shift selectors, 1499–1504
fifth wheels, 23, 23*f*, 30, 1104, 1111*f*, 1112–1115, 1112*f*, 1132
check, 863, 864
construction of, 1116–1122
coupling mountings, inspecting, 1864–1865
cut-away demo of, 1117*f*
and hitching devices, 1104–1109
layout, 1117*f*
locking and unlocking problems to, 1123*t*
locking mechanisms, 1117–1120
lubricating, 1124
maintenance and service of, and upper couplers, 1122, 1124–1129
mounting, 1120–1121, 1120*f*
proper and improper loading of, 1118*f*
ratings and capacity, 1114–1115
semi-trailer connects to tractor using, 1104*f*
service adjustments, 1126–1129
slider mechanism, 1128
sliders, 1121–1122
top plates, 1117
troubleshooting, 1122
types of, and coupling devices, 1109–1116
upper coupler, lower coupler, and kingpin of, 1115*f*
file brush. *See* file card
file card, 130, 131*f*
files, 129–130
teeth on, 129*f*
fillet radius, 1195, 1207. *See also* root
filter change, oil and, 1430, 1431
filters, 1797, 1797*f*
identifying need for AC, 1750
fingers, 1144
finished rivet, 135, 157
fire
blankets, 79–80
classifications, 78
extinguisher. *See* extinguisher, fire
preventing, 77
draining fuel, 78
spillage risks, 78
using fuel retriever, 78
fire-resistant hydraulic fluids, 1794
fire rings, 178, 198
fire service, 9
fire truck, 9*f*
first aid, 97, 102. *See also* personal protective equipment (PPE); safety
concepts, 97–98, 97*f*
principles, 97
bleeding, 98, 98*f*
burns and scalds, 100, 100*f*
eye injuries, 98–99, 99*f*
fractures, 99
sprains, strains, and dislocations, 99–100
first clutch, ATEC/CEC, 1456
first-degree burns, 100, 100*f*, 102
first driveshaft. *See also* coupling shaft
slope of, 1546, 1547*f*
fishplate, 771, 789
fishplate mounts, 774–775, 775*f*
fishtailing, 1053, 1063
fittings, 1796, 1804–1806
removing and inspection of, 1751, 1754, 1755
fixed-orifice tube (FOT) systems, 1717
fixed ramp rate, 1474
fixed-type resistors, 279–280, 280*f*
flange, 765, 774*f*, 789
repairing a crack in, 787
flange case half, 1613, 1639
flange half, 1579
flange nuts, 715*f*
flange yoke, 1536, 1536*f*, 1567

flare-nut wrench, 121, 121*f*, 157
flare-tubing wrench. *See* flare-nut wrench
flaring tools, 133–134
  components of, 134*f*
flash codes, 645–646, 645*f*, 1042, 1063
flash memory, 550
flash programming. *See* flashing
flashback arrestor, 139, 157
flashing, 550, 553
flat files, 130, 130*f*
flat-nosed pliers, 124, 124*f*, 157
flat-tip screwdriver, 126, 126*f*, 157
flat-type flywheels, 1151, 1151*f*, 1162
flat washers, 167, 168*f*, 198
flatbed truck, 10*f*
fleet operation, 1847, 1850, 1851, 1853
flex plates, 420–421, 1351–1352, 1352*f*, 1367
  and torque converter, 1436–1437
flexible hose guidelines, 1805–1806, 1805*f*–1806*f*
flexible hoses, 1801–1802
flexible joint, steering column with, 846*f*
flexible line, 1801–1802
flitch plates, 1120, 1120*f*, 1132
float-center position, 1823, 1823*f*
floatation tire. *See* wide-base tire
floating caliper, 915, 921
  system, 916, 917*f*
flooded cell batteries, 337
  specific gravity and voltage reading for, 338*t*
  typical sediment chamber in, 339*f*
flooded cell battery, 147
flooded lead–acid batteries, 335–336, 347
floor jacks, 189, 189*f*, 191
flow, 1807, 1832
flow-control valves, 860, 861, 862*f*, 863, 876, 1820–1821
  with steering wheel at full lock, 863, 863*f*
flow rate, 1796
fluid aeration, 1814
fluid analysis, 1426, 1426*t*, 1441
fluid change frequency, 1424–1426
fluid coupling, 1342, 1343*f*, 1367
fluid-filled shock absorbers, 801
fluid handling, 1426
fluid head, 1807, 1832
fluid level, 1423–1424, 1424*f*
  and inspecting fluid loss, 1429
fluid level plug, 1597–1598
fluid loss, fluid level and inspecting, 1429
fluid pressure, 1410, 1477, 1799*f*
fluid sensors
  fluid temperature sensor, 1450
  forward and reverse pressure switches, 1450
  oil pressure switch/sensor, 1451–1452
fluid temperature sensor, 1450
fluidic oil level sensor, 1451, 1452, 1452*f*
fluids
  changing transmission, 1266, 1267
  checking level of manual transmission, 1266, 1267
  and lubricants. *See* lubricants
  used engine oil and, 89, 89*f*
fluorescent bulbs, 494–496, 507
  disadvantage of, 496
  operation of, 496*f*
flush, air-conditioning system, 1749–1750
flushing cooler lines, 1437
  inspecting and, 1438
flux, 233
flux density, 234
flywheel, 396, 1183
  ring gear, 407
flywheel friction surface, 1180, 1189
flywheel housing, 1180, 1189
flywheel housing face, 1181, 1189
flywheel housing pilot, 1180, 1181, 1189
flywheels, 1141, 1144, 1150–1151, 1151*f*, 1162
FMCSA. *See* Federal Motor Carrier Safety Administration
FMCSR. *See* Federal Motor Carrier Safety Regulation
FMIs. *See* fault mode indicators
FMVSS. *See* Federal Motor Vehicle Safety Standards
FMVSS 103, 1696
FMVSS 108. *See* Federal/Canadian Motor Vehicle Standard 108
FMVSS 119. *See* Federal Motor Vehicle Safety Standard 119
FMVSS 121. *See* Federal Motor Vehicle Safety Standard 121
FO-8406-ASW models, 1159, 1160*f*
folded engine hoist, 193*f*
follow-up inspection, 1858
FOM-15D310B-LST, nomenclature for, 1315*t*
Fontaine-style no-slack lock, 1128*f*
foot valves, 944–945, 944*f*–945*f*, 963
  construction, 945–946, 945*f*
  operation, 946, 946*f*–947*f*, 948
  troubleshooting problems with, 948, 948*f*
footwear, 90, 91*f*
force multiplication, 887, 888*f*
forced throttle downshifts, 1414
forces, 1795–1796
  acting on frame, 764–766
forcing screw, 133, 157
forging process, driveshaft tube, 1535
fork, 732
forward bias, 289, 291–292, 301
forward clutch, 1382, 1395, 1399, 1417
forward reverse valve, 1454
forward seating valves, 1780, 1780*f*
FOT systems. *See* fixed-orifice tube systems
foundation brakes, servicing, 1010–1011
  brake drums, 1012–1015
  brake shoes, 1015–1018
  camshafts, 1019–1021
four-channel ABS, 1088–1089, 1089*f*
four-cylinder compressors, 1780
four sensors/four modulators (4S/4M), 1051*f*
4000 series transmission, 1462
four-speed auxiliary sections, eighteen-speed transmission with, 1241–1243, 1241*f*–1242*f*
14″ clutch pot-style flywheel, intermediate plate drive pins, 1182
14″ dual disc pull-type clutch, 1183–1185
fourth clutches, ATEC/CEC, 1457
fourth generation electronic control system, 1471
fourth-generation transmission controls with prognostics, Post-2009, 1502–1503
FR model transmissions, 1263, 1263*f*, 1274, 1275*f*
  removing auxiliary section from, 1282, 1284
  shift controls, 1247–1251, 1249*f*–1250*f*
fractures, 99
frame
  inspecting, 1865
  under-vehicle inspections, 1872, 1873
frame alignment, 779–782
  manually, checking, 780, 786
frame angle, 742, 757
frame centerline alignment, 747, 757
frame design
  actual frame strength, 768–769
  forces acting on frame, 764–766
  frame strength, 766–768
frame hangers, inspection and maintenance, 823
frame material, 769–770
frame rail design, 765*f*
frame rail web, 766, 789
frame reinforcement, 771–772, 783
frame repairs, 779–782
  flux-cored filler wire in, 782
frame slope, 1545, 1546*f*
frame strength, calculating, 766–768
free play, 1169, 1189
  release bearing, 1169
free stroke measurement, 984, 1033
Freedomline, 1336
  of two-pedal automated transmissions, 1304
freewheeling, 1358
freeze-frame data, 633, 644
freight truck, 10*f*
Freightliner's rack-and-pinion steering system, 844, 844*f*, 854
freon, 1694, 1720, 1727
frequency, 548, 548*f*, 553
frequency-sensing relay, 412, 425
friction, 1141, 1162

electricity from, 228–230
role of, 1141–1142
friction dampening, 1150, 1162
friction discs, 1143*f*, 1144, 1149, 1151*f*, 1346, 1346*f*, 1352, 1353*f*, 1397
clutch, 1177, 1183, 1183*f*
friction material, 1140–1141, 1355, 1355*f*
brake, 896
friction modifiers, 1423, 1441
friction plates, 1378, 1378*f*, 1389
friction-surface contact, 991
front axle inspection, 751, 753, 754
front axle limiter valves, 953–954, 954*f*
front axle modulator valves, location and configuration of, 1048*f*
front housing, 1355, 1355*f*
front leaf spring suspension system, 805, 806*f*
front planetary gear set, 1515, 1517
front/rear split system, 1071, 1099
front steering-axle leaf spring suspensions, 805–807, 805*f*, 806*f*
front support/charging pump module, 1465
frosting, 1292
fuel (gasoline, diesel), 157
draining, 78
engine-off engine compartment inspection, conducting, 1878
retriever, using, 78
vapor, 77–78
fuel cells, 242–243, 245
fuel economy, tire construction and, 682–683, 683*f*
fuel gauge, 521, 522
fuel-injection quantity, 639
fuel-injection timing, 639
fuel sensor, water in, 513*f*
fuel system monitor, 635, 639–640
fuel tank sending unit, 521
full air brake systems, inspecting, 1868, 1869–1870
full-box rail, 764, 789
full face shield, 94–95, 95*f*
full fielding, 451, 457
full floating axle shaft, 1597, 1600
full floating bearings, 716, 725
full-thickness burns. *See* third-degree burns
full throttle downshift, 1414–1415, 1414*f*, 1417
full trailer, 21, 30, 1106, 1107*f*, 1132
Fuller, Eaton, 1262–1263, 1263*f*, 1268, 1270, 1273, 1277, 1279, 1291
countershaft ten-speed transmission, components of, 1230, 1230*f*
lube change intervals, recommendations for, 1263, 1264*t*
model FS-5205-A, information plate for, 1229, 1229*f*
ten-speed FR model transmissions, 1274, 1275*f*
removing auxiliary section from, 1282, 1284
vehicle application definitions of, 1263, 1264*t*
fully oscillating fifth wheel, 1113, 1114*f*, 1132
functional monitoring, 632–633, 635
functions, alternator, 431
fuse links, 265
fuses, 264*f*, 265, 265*f*
ratings by wire gauge, 265*t*
fusible metal strip, 268

G

galling. *See* spalling
galvanic batteries, 331
galvanic corrosion, 779, 789
galvanic reaction, 241, 242, 242*f*, 331, 343, 347
galvanized, 1799, 1832
garbage trucks, 11, 12*f*
garter spring, 181, 181*f*, 182, 198
gas-charged accumulators, 1824–1826
gas compression, 1700, 1701*f*, 1703, 1704*f*
gas extraction hoses, 75
gas-loaded accumulators, 1824
gas pockets, 1633, 1639
gas sensors, 569
gas shock absorbers, 801
gas welding goggles, 94, 94*f*, 102
gasket scraper, 129, 129*f*, 157
gaskets and seals, 177, 1464
adhesives and sealants, 183–184
crankshaft seals, 181–182
head gaskets, 177–179, 178*f*
lip-type seals, 178, 181, 181*f*, 182
mechanical seals, 183
ring seals, 181, 182*f*, 183
gasoline engines, 396, 534
gassing, battery, 344, 347
gates, safety equipment, 75
gateway module, 602, 606*f*, 623
gauge operating systems
bimetallic gauges, 515, 516*f*
D'Arsonval gauges, 515–517, 516*f*
two- and three-coil movements, 516–517
digital CAN gauges, 518–519
mechanical gauges, 515
stepper motor gauges, 517–518, 520*f*
bipolar stepper motor, 518, 520*f*
unipolar stepper motor, 517–518, 519*f*, 519*t*
GCWR. *See* gross combined weight rating
gear design, 1195–1197
gear face contact during mesh, 1196
gear nomenclature, 1195
involute tooth shape, 1196–1197
gear-driven pumps, 860
gear interaction, 1197–1198
gear jamming, 1336
technique, 1301
gear oil, 150, 150*f*
gear oil filling, 848
gear power steering pump, 860, 862*f*
gear pullers, 133, 133*f*, 157
gear pumps, 1401, 1402*f*, 1417, 1808, 1808*f*, 1811*f*
operation, 1810–1811
gear ratios, 14, 1198–1200, 1198*f*, 1207
gear rattle, 1268, 1270, 1270*f*
gear reduction, 1198, 1207
gear rotation, 1197, 1197*f*
gear select motor, 1309, 1310
gear set contact patterns, 1622–1625, 1639
gear slip out, 1273–1274, 1273*f*, 1274*f*, 1295
gear teeth, 1817
gear tooth nomenclature, 1622–1625
gearbox fluid, guidelines to change, 1266, 1267
gears
anatomy of, 1195*f*
concept, 1194–1195
deep-reduction, 1235, 1235*f*
epicyclical, 1372, 1389
fundamentals of, 1195–10
helical-cut, 1373
pinion, 1372, 1373*f*, 1389
planetary. *See* planetary gears
range, 1213, 1257
ring, 1372, 1373*f*, 1389
sets
compound planetary, 1380, 1382–1383, 1382*f*, 1382*t*, 1383*f*
Lepelletier, 1381, 1389
Ravigneaux, 1380, 1381, 1381*f*, 1389
Simpson. *See* Simpson gear set
Wilson, 1381, 1389
speed, 1214, 1257
spur-cut, 1373
spur gears, 1201–1202, 1202*f*
spur-type, 1270
sun, 1372, 1373*f*, 1389
types of, 1201–1205
gel cell battery, 358, 367
Gen 1 software, 1308
Gen 2 software, 1308
Gen 3 shift controller from Freightliner, 1308, 1308*f*
Gen 3 software, 1307, 1308
general-purpose cloth gloves, 92, 92*f*
general purpose thermoplastic wire (GPT), 465
generators, 237, 431
generic scan tool, 1502
generoid gear design, 1577–1578, 1578*f*, 1600
generoid gearing contact patterns, 1625, 1627*f*
geometric centerline alignment, 747, 748*f*, 757

performing, 755
gerotor pump, 1401, 1417
Gibb-head keys, 177, 177*f*, 198
gimbals, 1533, 1567
glad hand test unit, 994*f*
gladhands, 957–958, 958*f*, 963
glazing, 975, 1033
of brake lining, 902, 921
Glidecoat, 1536
Global Positioning System (GPS), 1854
displays fuel stop locations, 536
tracking system, 206–207
global warming potential (GWP), 1720, 1727
gloves, hand protection
chemical, 91, 91*f*
general-purpose cloth, 92, 92*f*
leather, 91, 91*f*
light-duty, 91, 92*f*
glycol, 146
goggles
gas welding, 94, 94*f*
safety, 95, 95*f*
goose neck trailers, 1111
gouges, 1559
governor, 933, 933*f*–934*f*, 963
governor cut-in, 1007–1008, 1033
governor pressure, 1407
affected by output shaft speed, 1408, 1408*f*
governor valves, 1407, 1407*f*–1408*f*, 1417
GPS. *See* Global Positioning System
GPT. *See* general purpose thermoplastic wire
gradability, 14, 30
graphing meters, 319–321, 320*f*–321*f*, 325
gravel hauler, 11*f*
gravity bleeding method, 1175–1176
grease gun, 120
green-colored trailer cord, 1050
green LEDs, APADS module, 1725, 1725*f*
Greenhouse Gas Emission Standards (2006), 941
grey iron, 151
grid corrosion, 375, 375*f*
grinding wheels, 119
and discs, 118, 157
gross combined weight rating (GCWR), 21, 30, 1109, 1132
gross trailer weight (GTW), 24, 30, 1110, 1132
gross vehicle weight (GVW), 20–21, 30, 1108, 1132
classification of chassis by, 20*t*, 1108*t*
per axle, 20*f*
gross vehicle weight rating (GVWR), 20–21, 21*f*, 30, 63, 1108–1109, 1133
gross weight limits, 19, 21*t*, 30, 1108, 1109*t*, 1133
ground circuits, 217
ground shaft, 1346, 1346*f*, 1367. *See also* stator support shaft
ground straps, 230
disconnecting, 230*f*
grounded bracelet, 229*f*
grounded circuit fault, 262*f*
grounded circuits, 260, 261–262
grounds, 142, 143, 157, 223
growling noise, 1270
GTW. *See* gross trailer weight
guide studs, 1176, 1183, 1189
guidelines, air leakage test, 981–983
GVW. *See* gross vehicle weight
GVWR. *See* gross vehicle weight rating
GWP. *See* global warming potential
GXL, 465

H

H-series certification, 39
"H" TXV, 1711
H-type TXV, 1711, 1711*f*
for APADS system, 1725*f*
hacksaw, 131, 131*f*
hair containment, 95
half-round yokes, 1536
Hall effect sensors, 319, 570–571, 571*f*, 586, 586*f*, 593, 1310
camshaft reluctor wheel of, 578*f*
operation of camshaft position, 572*f*
signals of, and variable reluctance sensor, 572*f*
testing of, 589–590
throttle position sensor, 566*f*
Hall effect speed sensor, 1676
Hall effect switches, 1449
halogen bulbs, 496–497, 496*f*, 507
cycle, 497*f*
halogen infrared discharge (HID) bulbs, 497, 497*f*, 507
hammers, 127–128
hand/emergency brakes, 1074, 1074*f*
electrically activated, 1074, 1075*f*
mechanical, 1074, 1074*f*
spring brake park brake, 1075, 1075*f*
hand-operated lever, 1821
hand reamer, 733*f*
hand tools, 120–134
Allen wrenches, 125, 126*f*
chisels, 128, 128*f*
clamps, 131–132
cutting tools, 125
files, 129–130, 130*f*, 131*f*
flaring tools, 133–134, 134*f*
gasket scraper, 129, 129*f*
hacksaw, 131, 131*f*
hammers, 127–128, 128*f*
magnetic pickup tools and mechanical fingers, 127, 127*f*
pliers, 123–125, 124*f*, 125*f*
pry bars, 128–129, 129*f*
pullers, 133, 133*f*
screwdrivers, 126–127, 126*f*
sockets, 122–123, 122*f*, 123*f*
taps and dies, 132, 132*f*
thread repair, 132–133
wrenches, 121–122, 121*f*, 122*f*
handrails, 74
hands
cleaning, 92, 92*f*
protection, 90–91
barrier cream, 92, 92*f*
chemical gloves, 91, 91*f*
cleaning your hands, 92, 92*f*
general-purpose cloth gloves, 92, 92*f*
leather gloves, 91, 91*f*
light-duty gloves, 91, 92*f*
hanger bearing, 1537, 1537*f*, 1567
failures, 1555, 1555*f*
inspecting and replacement of, 1562, 1564–1565
hanger brackets, 804
hard braking system, 537
"hard pedal," brake, 899, 902
hard shifting, 1271–1273, 1272*f*
hard steering, steering-related problems, 865*t*
hard tire tread, 682
hard-working shocks, 800
hardening, 1195, 1207
harmonic vibration, 1540, 1567
harness connectors, 467*f*
hat-style cross member, 771*f*
hazard, 72, 102
slip, trip, and fall, 96
hazardous environment, 72, 102
identifying, 72–73
hazardous materials, 80, 102
cleaning toxic dust safely, 88
material safety data sheets (MSDS), 80, 81*f*–87*f*, 87
used engine oil and fluids, 89, 89*f*
HCFCs. *See* hydrochlorofluorocarbons
HD-OBD system. *See* heavy-duty on-board diagnostics system
HDVs. *See* heavy-duty vehicles
head gaskets, 177–179, 178*f*
headgear, 90, 102
headlamp system, 498–499
healing, 1277
heat buildup, 91, 102
heat, electricity from, 230–232
heat fade, 899–22, 921
heat measurement, terminology of, 1698–1700
heat-shrink tubing, 470
heat shrinking, 1351
heat-treated alloy steel, 769, 789
heater control valves, inspecting and testing, 1763
heater core, 1698, 1727
removing, inspecting, and reinstallment of, 1763
heaters, 1798

heating, 230, 1770
and cooling capacities, compares, 1699, 1700*t*
cycle, 1776
principles in transportation refrigeration, 1773, 1773*t*
"heating effect of current," 219
heating, ventilation, and air-conditioning (HVAC) systems, 1695, 1698, 1700, 1719
heavy-duty braking system, 1069
heavy-duty clutches. *See* clutches
heavy-duty commercial batteries groups (12-VOlT), 340*t*
heavy-duty commercial vehicles. *See also* commercial vehicles
springs, 798–799
heavy-duty electrical systems, sophistication of, 206
heavy-duty electromagnetic compressor clutch, construction of, 1706, 1706*f*
heavy-duty locking differential, 1583*f*
heavy-duty on-board diagnostics (HD-OBD) system, 575, 577, 579, 587, 607
definitions, 631
emissions codes, 644–645
fundamentals of, 628–631
development of, 628–629
self-diagnostic capabilities and approaches, 629–631
legislation for diesels, 633–634
maintaining, 641–642
DTCs. *See* diagnostic trouble codes
emissions system deterioration, 643
off-board diagnostics, 642, 643*f*
readiness code, 643
monitors, types of, 631–641
comprehensive component monitor, 636
continuous and non-continuous monitors, 636–641
system monitors, 634–636
thresholds, 637
heavy-duty on-highway truck, 38*f*
heavy-duty steering columns, 845
heavy-duty steering systems components, 842–843
heavy-duty torque converters, 1362
heavy-duty truck drive axles
functions of differential gear sets, 1578–1581
fundamentals of, 1572–1575
lubricating drive axles, 1597–1598
types of axle shafts, 1597
types of differential gear sets, 1581–1597
types of drive axle gearing and housings, 1575–1578
heavy-duty trucks, suspension systems types on, 802
heavy-duty vehicles (HDVs), 207, 630*f*, 630*t*, 1069, 1697, 1698*f*
disc brake system, 1073*f*
parallelogram, 798, 798*f*
technicians, 36
wheel arrangements, 665, 666*f*
heavy-duty wheels and tires, general safety precautions for working, 689, 691
heavy haul, 10
configuration, 10*f*
heavy-vehicle alternator, 430*f*
service life of, 434–435
heavy-vehicle charging system, 431*f*
heel, 1622, 1639
height-control valve, 816, 816*f*, 817*f*, 836
height sensors, 817
Heli-coil, 175, 175*f*
helical-cut gears, 1373
helical double reduction drive axles, 1585, 1600
helical double reduction two-speed drive axles, 1585–1586, 1586*f*, 1600
helical drop gear, 1593, 1600
helical gears, 1202–1203, 1202*f*
helical inserts, 175
helical pinion gear, 1585, 1586
helmet, welding, 94, 94*f*
Hendrickson's AirTek system, 805
Hendrickson's IFS, 805
HEPA. *See* high-efficiency particulate absorbing; high-efficiency particulate assistance
herringbone gears, 1203, 1203*f*, 1207
hertz (Hz), 217, 223, 548, 548*f*, 553
HEVs. *See* hybrid electric vehicles
hex keys. *See* Allen wrenches
hibernation mode, 252
high and reverse clutch, 1382
high beams, headlamp system, 498–499, 499*f*
high-bias sensors, 587
high-carbon steel, 767, 789
high-compression-ratio diesel engines, 395
high-efficiency particulate absorbing (HEPA), 88
high-efficiency particulate assistance (HEPA), 974
high-impedance multimeters, 308, 314*f*, 325
high-intensity discharge (HID) lamps, 497–498, 498*f*, 507
high line pressure, 1360
high-pressure cutout switch, 1722
high-pressure fan switch, 1722
high-pressure switch, H-type TXV for APADS system, 1725*f*
high resistance, 142, 143, 158
high-resistance circuits, 262
high-side driver faults, 588
high stall speed, 1358
high-torque-multiplication torque converter, 1349
high-torque-rise engines, 14, 14*f*
high-viscosity liquid, 150
high-voltage battery packs, 144, 144*f*
high voltage cables, 307, 307*f*
high voltage connection points in ACTG, 1657*f*
high voltage disconnect, 1650, 1651*f*
high voltage interlock loop (HVIL), 1682–1683, 1683*f*, 1687
higher electron voltage, 211
historical fault, 631, 655
hitches, 1109–1111
hitching devices, 23–24, 1111
HLA. *See* hydraulic launch assist
hold regulator valve, 1410, 1417
hollow punches, 135, 158
Hooke joint, 1532, 1567. *See also* Cardan joint
Hooke, Robert, 1532
Hooke's law, 1144, 1162
horse-drawn chariots, 794, 794*f*
horsepower, 13, 30, 884, 884*f*
per centimeter *vs*. load per drive tire, 663*f*
hose end fittings, 1804–1805, 1805*f*
hoses, 1740, 1765, 1801–1802, 1832
removing and inspection of, 1751, 1754, 1755
hot curing process, 675, 677, 677*t*, 701
housekeeping and orderliness, 96
housings, 1344, 1344*f*, 1345*f*, 1818, 1832
starter motor, 403, 403*f*, 422
types of drive axle gearing and, 1575–1578
HT-740/750 transmission, 1394
hub, 904
hub flange run-out, measurement of, 698
hub-piloted disc wheel, 712, 713*f*, 714–716, 725
features of, 715*f*
hub-piloted systems, hardware for, 714*f*
Huck® fastener, 771, 771*f*, 789
hunter alignment system, 747*f*
HVAC systems. *See* heating, ventilation, and air-conditioning systems
hybrid battery management systems, 364–365, 365*f*
hybrid drive systems. *See also* series-type hybrid drives
electrical safety. *See* electrical safety
fundamentals of, 1644–1645, 1645*f*
introduction to, 1644
maintenance and service, 1663
types of, 1645–1648, 1646*f*–1648*f*
comparing parallel and series systems, 1648, 1648*t*
non-electric hybrid drive systems, 1648–1649, 1649*f*, 1649*t*
hybrid electric traction motor for ZF Traxon transmissions, 1326*f*
hybrid electric vehicles (HEVs), 332–334, 1644, 1665

hybrid vehicles, 144, 144*f*
HybriDrive Propulsion Systems, 1665
  BAE systems, 1652–1653, 1652*f*, 1653*t*, 1654*f*
  central control module for, 1655*f*
  generation 1 and 2 of, 1654*f*
  location of, 1655*f*
  overview, 1653
  schematic of, 1656*f*
hydraulic ABS systems. *See also* anti-lock braking system (ABS)
  bleeding, 1097
hydraulic accumulators, 1797–1798, 1824–1827, 1824*f*
  safety precautions for, 1826–1827
  types of, 1824–1826
hydraulic actuators, 1815–1819, 1816*f*
  construction of, 1818–1819
  hydraulic motors, 1818
  linear actuators (hydraulic cylinders), 1815–1817
  rotary actuators, 1817
hydraulic analogy, 213
hydraulic brake valves, 1079
  combination valve, 1079, 1080*f*
  metering valves, 1079
  pressure differential valves, 1079, 1079*f*
  proportioning valves, 1079
hydraulic brakes, inspecting, 1867–1868
hydraulic braking systems, 887–890, 890*f*, 1070–1071, 1070*f*
  air-over, 1082
    air booster units, 1082–1084, 1083*f*–1085*f*
    piston stroke detector, 1084, 1086, 1086*f*
  anti-lock braking system (ABS), 1088–1090, 1089*f*–1090*f*
  bleeding air out of, 1095
  foundation components of, 1071
    adjusters used with drum brakes, 1072–1073, 1073*f*
    brake shoe configurations, 1071–1072, 1072*f*
    disc brakes, 1073–1074, 1073*f*
    drum brakes, 1071
  fundamental configurations for, 1069
    air-over-hydraulic braking systems, 1070
    hydraulic braking systems, 1070–1071, 1070*f*
  hydraulic components of, 1075
    hydraulic brake valves. *See* hydraulic brake valves
    master cylinder, 1075–1078, 1076*f*–1078*f*
    wheel cylinders, 1078–1079, 1078*f*
  inspecting for fluid leaks, 1091
  introduction of, 1069
  maintenance of, 1090–1097
  park brake and emergency circuits, 1086
    arrangement and operation of, 1087, 1087*f*
    park brake off and applied, 1087, 1087*f*–1088*f*
    service brake applied, 1088, 1089*f*
  power-assist system, 1080
    hydroboost systems, 1081–1082, 1081*f*–1082*f*
    vacuum brake booster or servo, 1080–1081, 1080*f*
hydraulic circuits, 1411–1412, 1412*f*, 1417
hydraulic clutch actuation systems, 1156, 1157*f*
hydraulic clutch piston, 1352, 1353*f*
hydraulic clutch system, 1378–1379, 1378*f*, 1379*f*, 1389
  bleeding/flushing, 1175–1177
  checking and adjusting, 1174, 1175
hydraulic clutches, 1462
hydraulic control, 1476–1477, 1478*f*–1484*f*
hydraulic cylinder, 1796, 1815–1817, 1816*f*, 1832
hydraulic filter, 1829–1830
  change, 1830*f*
hydraulic fluids, 148, 1798, 1829–1830
  role of, 1791, 1794
hydraulic hoist, 190, 191*f*, 198
  using, 194
hydraulic jack, 188, 198
hydraulic launch assist (HLA), 1648, 1649*f*, 1665
  specifications of, 1649*t*
hydraulic model of parallel circuit, 256*f*
hydraulic motors, 1818, 1818*f*, 1820*f*
hydraulic multiplication of driver input force, 887, 888*f*
hydraulic piston, 1346, 1346*f*
hydraulic pressure, 1314, 1352, 1430, 1795–1796
hydraulic pumps, 1806–1807, 1806*f*–1807*f*
  calculations, 1809–1810
  cavitation, 1814
  displacement, 1809
  failure, causes of, 1814–1815
  gear pump operation, 1810–1811
  piston pump operation, 1811–1812
  positive-displacement pumps, 1807–1808
  power, 1810
  symbols, 1815
  theoretical flow rate, 1809
  types of, 860–861, 861*f*, 862*f*, 863, 863*f*
  vane pump operation, 1811
  variable-displacement pump operation, 1812–1814
  volumetric efficiency, 1809–1810
hydraulic retarder, 1497–1498, 1498*f*, 1526
hydraulic shock absorbers, 799–801, 800*f*, 801*f*
hydraulic steering dampener, 855, 856*f*
hydraulic systems, 1795*f*
  advantages and disadvantages of, 1792*t*
  closed-loop, 1791, 1793*f*
  in commercial vehicles, 37*f*
  components of, 1796–1798
  fundamentals of, 1791–1794
  maintenance and service of, 867
    bleeding air from steering system, 871
    checking oil aeration, 870–871
    internal leakage, testing for, 870, 871
    PSSA, 867–870, 867*f*, 868*f*
    SRS, removing and replacing, 872–873
  open-loop, 1791, 1793*f*
  preventative maintenance, 1827–1830
  role of, 1791, 1794
  types of, 1791
hydraulically assisted power steering, 858, 858*f*
hydraulically controlled automatic transmissions, 1393–1417
  components of, 1401–1404, 1402*f*–1404*f*
    hydraulic circuits, 1411–1412, 1412*f*
    transmission control valves. *See* transmission control valves
  fundamentals of, 1395
    Allison transmission power flows. *See* Allison transmission power flows
    transmission design, 1395–1397, 1396*f*
  history of, 1394–1395
  introduction of, 1394
  operation of, 1412
    automatic downshifting. *See* automatic downshifting
    automatic transmission shifting, 1412–1414, 1413*f*
hydraulically controlled transmissions, 1359, 1432*f*, 1447, 1449, 1450, 1453, 1456, 1460
  shift point adjustment on, 1434
hydraulics, 1792*t*
  accumulator, 1797–1798
  hoses, 1801, 1801*f*, 1803*f*, 1832
  lines, 1796, 1798, 1798*f*, 1802
    flexible line (hoses), 1801–1802
    rigid lines (pipe and tubing), 1799–1801
    routing of, 1803–1804, 1803*f*
    sizing, 1802
  operating principles, 1794–1796, 1796*f*
  pipes, 1802*f*

tank, 1797, 1797*f*
tubing, 1803*f*
types of, 1798*f*
hydroboost hydraulic systems, 1069, 1081–1082, 1081*f*–1082*f*
dual-circuit master cylinder, removing and replacement of, 1093
hydrocarbon (HC) dosing system, 640
hydrochlorofluorocarbons (HCFCs), 1719, 1782
hydrofluorocarbons (HFCs) refrigerants, 1719, 1719*t*
hydrogen, 144
in fuel cell, process of converting, 243*f*
hydrolysis, 339
hydrometer, 337, 338*f*, 347, 378*f*
hydropneumatic accumulators, 1824
hydrostatic drive motor, 1795*f*
hydrostatic systems, 1795, 1795*f*
hygroscopic, 148, 158
hypoid gearing, 1576–1577, 1577*f*, 1600
hypoid generoid, 1577
hysteresis, 674, 682, 801, 836
Hz. *See* hertz

I

I-beam, 764, 765*f*, 789, 1573, 1573*f*, 1574
I-Shift, 1336
automated transmission series, 1305, 1305*f*
dual-clutch transmission, 1327, 1328*f*
"I" terminal, 447
ibuprofen, 100
IC. *See* integrated circuits
ID. *See* input force
idle validation switch (IVS), 565, 593
throttle position sensor (TPS), 565*f*
idler gears, 1201, 1201*f*, 1207
IDS. *See* Intuitive Diagnostic System
ignition switch, 411
ignition systems, 289
impact driver, 126*f*, 127, 158
impact gun, 120
impedance testing, 378
impeller, 1344–1345, 1345*f*, 1367
in-service wheel alignment, 748, 749*t*
inactive diagnostic trouble codes, 1331
inboard mounted drums, 903*f*, 904
incandescent bulbs, 492–494, 507
failures, types of, 494, 495*f*
incandescent test lights, 308
incipient fault, 631, 655
inclinometer/accelerometer, 1497, 1526
included angle, 744, 744*f*, 757
incremental phasing adjustments, cross phasing and, 1544–1545
Index Sensors, 1722
indicator lights, 1050–1051
indirect-acting type, air boosters, 1082–1084, 1083*f*–1085*f*
indirect TPMS, 667, 701
induction and twisted pair wires, 241
induction motors, 1676
inductive amp clamps, 318–319, 318*f*–319*f*, 318*t*, 325
inductive pick-up, 1450
ineffective PM program, 1851, 1852*f*
inert gas, 493
inertia, 1351
inertia brake, 1155, 1162, 1310–1313, 1311*f*, 1312*f*, 1336
UltraShift transmission, 1312*f*
inertia shift, 885, 887, 921
inertial excitation stem, 1551, 1567
inflation pressure, determination of, 679–680, 680*t*, 681*f*–682*f*
inflation safety, 680–681
information sources, researching and using, 46–48, 46*f*
initial pitting, 1292
injector drive modules, 241, 241*f*
injector voltage, 639–640
injuries, accidents and
possibility of, 71, 71*f*
precautions for avoiding, 71
injury
eye, 98–99, 99*f*
protection practices
housekeeping and orderliness, 96
lifting, 96, 96*f*
proper ventilation, 96
safe attitude, 95–96
slip, trip, and fall hazards, 96
inlet pressure regulating valve, 936, 963
inline axial piston, 1817
pumps, 1811, 1812*f*
inline fuses, 264, 265
inline tire pressure gauge, 665
inner tube, hydraulic shock absorbers, 800
input force, 1796, 1833
input member, 1373, 1389
input module, 605
input shaft, 1141, 1163, 1213, 1256, 1402, 1402*f*
end play, guidelines for, 1627, 1630
replacement of, 1279, 1280–1282
insert-type synchronizer. *See* block-type synchronizer
insert valve, 1245, 1246*f*, 1256
inside diameter (ID), 1799, 1800*f*, 1833
inside micrometers, 111–112, 111*f*, 158
inspections, shop safety, 89
inspector qualifications, 1854–1855
instructions, effective speaking, 44–45
instrument cluster, 536*f*, 609*f*
instrument cluster dimmer switches, 281, 281*f*
instrument voltage regulator (IVR), 515
instrumentation
driver information screens, 524–526
gauge operating systems. *See* gauge operating systems
sending units, 519–522
speedometers, 522–524
troubleshooting gauge problems, 526–527
warning lights, 512–515
insulated gate bipolar transistor (IGBT), 1680, 1687
insulated gloves, 1651, 1651*f*
insulating material, 287
insulation stress test, 437
insulators, 209, 210*t*, 223
intake
engine-off engine compartment inspection, conducting, 1878
manifold, 639
intake stroke, 931, 932*f*, 934
integral carrier housing, 1578, 1600
integral double check valve, 956
integral oil cooler, 1263, 1263*f*
integral steering gear, 852, 853*f*
integrated circuits (IC), 298–299
intelligent charger, 382, 389
inter-axle differentials, 1592–1596, 1596*f*, 1597, 1598, 1601
overhauling, 1627–1631
spline in, 1593*f*
intercity coach, 10
interleaf friction, 797, 836
interlock system, 1216, 1216*f*, 1256
intermediate gear band. *See* second gear band
intermediate plate, 1143*f*, 1151, 1151*f*, 1163, 1183, 1184
on drive pins, 1182, 1182*f*
drive slots on, 1185*f*
intermediate plate drive pins, 14" clutch pot-style flywheel, 1182
intermediate tap, 132, 158
intermittent circuits, 262–263
causes of open and, 260*f*
intermittent duty relays, 285, 286*f*, 409
intermittent fault, 631, 655
internal bleeding, 98, 102
internal cab engine-on inspection, performing, 1860–1861
internal cab inspections, performing, 1858–1861
internal cab key-off inspection, performing, 1859
internal cab key-on inspection, performing, 1860
internal gear types, 1817
internal leakage, testing for, 870, 871
internal resistance of batteries, 342–343
internal snap ring pliers, 124*f*, 125
International Standards Organization (ISO) relays, 283, 284*f*
International System of Units, 169
interrupter switch, 505, 505*f*
intersecting angle arrangement, 1542–1543, 1542*f*, 1567. *See also* broken back arrangement
interstate, 7

Intuitive Diagnostic System (IDS), 1654, 1655, 1661–1662, 1665
inversion valve, 956, 956*f*, 963
  guidelines for inspect and testing, 998, 1000
inverters, 218, 223
  AC-to-DC, 1661, 1665
  current, 1661, 1661*f*
  DC-to-AC, 1661, 1665
  wave, 1661, 1665
involute, 1196, 1207
  tooth during mesh, 1196*f*
ion, 209
ISO 3731 connector, 1050, 1063
ISO 3731 trailer plug, 501, 501*f*
ISO flare, 133, 134*f*
ISO relays. *See* International Standards Organization relays
isolated field alternator, 442, 442*f*
isolation fault detection, 1684
isometric diagram, 472, 474, 485
IVR. *See* instrument voltage regulator
IVs. *See* idle validation switch

J

J-1587, 1337
  communications, 1302
  fault code
    comparing J-1939 and, 649*t*
    construction of, 645, 646–648, 646*f*
    J-1939 fault code, comparison of, 651*t*
  J-1939 network *vs.*, 612
J-1708
  J-1939 fault code, comparison of, 651*t*
  J-1939 network *vs.*, 612
J-1939, 1307, 1337
  fault code
    construction of, 648–652, 649*f*, 649*t*, 650*f*, 652*f*
    FMIs, 650*t*, 651*t*
    J-1587 fault code, compare and, 649*t*
    and J-1708/J-1587 fault codes, 651*t*
  network, 600, 601*f*, 602, 608, 611*f*
    vs. J-1708/1587, 612
    message, 616*f*
    serial data waveform from, 612*f*
    terminating resistor for, 614*f*
J-560 electrical connector, 501, 501*f*, 507
J-24314 tool, 1430, 1432*f*
J-560 trailer connector, 1040, 1041*f*, 1050*t*, 1063
J-560 trailer cord, terminals on, 262–263
J-560-trailer plug, 501, 501*f*, 503*f*
jack shaft, 1537, 1567. *See also* coupling shaft
jack stands, 188–191, 198
jacking bolt, 133
jackknifing, 950, 963, 991
jacks, 188–189, 189*f*
jamb nut, 1171
jewelry, watches and, 95
job card, 48*f*
job classifications, commercial vehicle industry, 37
joints
  Cardan, 1532, 1567
  constant velocity, 1550, 1550*f*, 1567
  double Cardan, 1550, 1550*f*
  Hooke, 1532, 1567. *See also* Cardan joint
  Rzeppa, 1550, 1550*f*, 1567
  slip, 1536, 1537*f*, 1567
Joule's law, 220
jounce, 796–797, 836
jounce blocks, 799, 799*f*, 836
jump leads, circuit with, 142
jump out, 1273, 1295. *See also* gear slip out
jump-starting vehicles, 383–384
just stands. *See* jack stands

K

KAM. *See* keep alive memory
keep alive memory (KAM), 550, 553
Kenworth air spring systems, 818–819, 819*f*
Kenworth's AG 130, 805
key-off electrical loads, 333, 347
key-off inspection, performing internal cab, 1859
key-on inspection, performing internal cab, 1860
kinetic energy, 884, 885, 921
  shock absorber, 797
kinetic friction, 1142, 1163
kingpin inclination angle (KPI), 743–744, 757
  and included angle, checking, 750, 752
kingpins, 732, 733*f*, 757, 856, 857*f*, 1112, 1116*f*, 1133, 1574
  lubricating, 754
  profiles and materials, 732–734
  service tool, 1126*f*
  straightness, length, and wear, 1125–1126
  upper coupler, lower coupler, and, of fifth wheel, 1115*f*
  for wear, inspecting, 753
Kirchhoff's law, 252, 580
knock sensors, 567
knocking noise, 1270, 1270*f*
KPI. *See* kingpin inclination angle

L

L-plate, 771, 789
labeling refrigerant, 1748
labor guide, 58–59, 58*f*, 60, 65
ladder logic, 490–491, 507, 617, 623
ladder rungs, 253
ladder-type frame, 13*f*, 764, 765*f*, 789
landing gear, 1106, 1106*f*, 1128–1129, 1133
  mechanism in, 1129*f*
lands, 1822, 1822*f*, 1833
large-bore diesel engines, 445
large-gauge wire, 447
latch valves, 1485, 1485*f*
latching solenoids, 1452, 1453*f*, 1456–1457, 1459*f*, 1526
late-model equipment, 264
late-model vehicles, 1697, 1698*f*
latent heat, 1698, 1703, 1727
latent heat of condensation, 1699, 1699*f*
latent heat of evaporation, 1703
latent heat of fusion, 1699, 1727
latent heat of vaporization, 1699, 1699*f*, 1727
lateral run-out, 697
lateral stability, 796, 796*f*, 836
LCDs. *See* liquid crystal displays
lead, 151
lead-acid batteries, 242, 1660
lead-acid flooded cell battery, 147
lead dioxide (PbO_2), 335
lead peroxide (PbO_2), 343
lead sulfate ($PbSO_4$), 343
lead–acid batteries, 334
leading shoes, 1071, 1072*f*, 1099
leading/trailing shoe drum brake arrangement, 1071, 1099
leaf spring, 798, 836
leaf spring equalizing beam suspensions, 810
leaf spring mounting systems, 805–807
leaf spring systems, 802
  auxiliary springs, 805, 805*f*
  composite leaf springs, 802–803, 803*f*
  constant-rate leaf spring assemblies, 803, 803*f*
  drive axle leaf spring suspensions, 807, 807*f*, 808*f*
  inspection and maintenance, 821
  multileaf spring packs, 802, 802*f*, 803*f*
  taper leaf and parabolic leaf springs, 804, 804*f*
  variable-rate/progressive-rate leaf springs, 804, 804*f*
leak testing
  air-conditioning system, 1735, 1744
    dye testing, 1744–1746
    electronic leak detection testing, 1744, 1746
    nitrogen testing, 1747
  torque converter, 1360, 1361
  turbine end play and, 1363, 1365, 1365*f*
leaks
  engine-on engine compartment inspection, conducting, 1879–1880
  testing treadle valve for, 1094
leather gloves, 91, 91*f*
LEDs. *See* light-emitting diodes
left-hand camshafts, 894, 895*f*, 921
left hand rule, 235

left-hand-thread adjusting screw, 867
length changes, driveshaft systems, 1533–1534
lengthwise bearing, 1622, 1639
Lepelletier gear set, 1381, 1389
less clutch slippage, 1410
levelling valve, replacement, 830
levels, engine-on engine compartment inspection, 1879–1880
lever principle, equalizing beams, 809, 809*f*
levers, 1197, 1198*f*, 1207
    in clutch design, use of, 1146
Li-ion technology, 355
life and limb system, 842
life cycle of batteries, 357*t*
lift axles, 735–736, 757
lifting, 96, 96*f*
    in shop, 185–186, 185*f*, 186*f*
lifting equipment, 185–186, 186*f*
    safe use of, 186–187
    using, 193–196
light
    alligator clip, 307
    electricity from, 230
light-duty commercial vehicles, springs, 798
light-duty gloves, 91, 92*f*
light-duty torque converters, 1362
light-duty vehicles, parallelogram, 798, 798*f*
light-emitting diodes (LEDs), 292, 293*f*, 301, 308, 499–501, 500*f*, 507
    advantages of, 500, 501
    diagnostic, 1725
    disadvantages of, 501
    self-powered test lights, 308
lighting circuits, 256, 492
lighting control module, 505*f*
lighting systems
    circuits, 492
    technologies
        daytime running lights, 499
        fluorescent bulb, 494–496
        halogen bulbs, 496–497
        halogen infrared discharge bulbs, 497
        headlamp, 498–499
        high-intensity discharge lamps, 497–498
        incandescent bulbs, 492–494
        light-emitting diodes, 499–501
    trailer cords and plug, 501–505
lightweight casings, 673
limiter valve, 953–954, 954*f*, 963
limiting torque clutch brake, 1155, 1155*f*
LIN. *See* local interconnect network
line-haul, 1263, 1295
line-haul trucks, 10
line sizing, 1802–1803
line wrenches, 1742
linear actuators, 1815–1817
linear diagrams, 472
linear motion, 1815
lineman gloves, 1651, 1651*f*
lines, 1740, 1765
    removing and inspection of, 1751, 1754, 1755
lines of force, 234, 236–238, 239*f*
linkage adjustment, 1169–1170
lip-type dynamic oil seal, 181, 198
lip-type seals, 178, 181, 181*f*, 182
LIPE/Haldex adjustment, 1171
liquid, change of heat, 1702, 1702*f*
liquid crystal displays (LCDs), 525, 525*f*
liquid line dryer, 1781
listening, effective, 40–42
lithium batteries, 334
lithium-ion batteries, 353–355, 354*f*, 367, 1660, 1660*f*
live (drive) axles, 730, 731*f*, 757, 1573, 1601
load (clamp force), 250, 1142, 1163
load-dumping, 444, 457
load range, 797–798, 797*f*
load-sensitive valves, 1079
load-sharing type suspension, 807
load test, 380
    battery, 381
loaded *vs.* unloaded alignment, 748
loading valves, 935, 963
local interconnect network (LIN), 601*f*
lock-up clutch, 1344, 1346*f*, 1367, 1515
    apply passage, 1353, 1353*f*
    assembly, 1346, 1346*f*
    backing plate bolted to converter housing, 1354*f*
    complaints, 1356
    engagement and disengagement, 1356
    operation, 1352–1353, 1353*f*
        testing, 1359, 1360
lock-up clutch disc, 1354, 1354*f*, 1367
    with torsional dampening, 1355, 1355*f*
lock-up clutch piston, 1354, 1354*f*, 1367
lock-up clutch/piston assembly, 1355, 1355*f*, 1367
lock-up converter, 1522
locking devices and tools
    fasteners, 164
        bolts, studs, and nuts, 165–170, 166*f*, 167*f*
        chemical compounds, 170, 170*f*
        screws, 164–165, 164*f*, 165*f*
    measuring, torque wrenches, 172–175, 172*f*, 173*f*
locking differentials, 1581, 1583–1584, 1601
locking keys, 176–177, 176*f*
locking pins, 176
locking pliers, 125, 125*f*, 158
locking tang, 1170, 1170*f*, 1189
lockout/tagout, 51–52, 109, 109*f*, 158
logging trucks, 10–11, 11*f*
logical faults. *See* rationality faults
long shaft systems, 1537
long stroke (LS) chambers, 904, 905, 921, 1024
longitudinal split, brake line configuration, 1077, 1077*f*
low-amperage fuses, 265
low-and high-current output stators, 436, 437*f*
low and reverse band, 1382
low and reverse clutch, 1382
low aspect ratio tires, 672
low beams, headlamp system, 498–499, 499*f*
low-bias sensors, 587
low-frequency radio waves, 241
low-inertia, 1239, 1256
low-inertia auxiliary sections, 1239–1241, 1239*f*–1240*f*
    power flows through, 1241–1243, 1241*f*–1242*f*
low line pressure, 1360
low-maintenance batteries, 334*f*, 344–345
low oil level pressure sensor, 1451, 1451*f*
low-pressure cutout switch, 1721–1722
low-pressure switch, H-type TXV for APADS system, 1725*f*
low-pressure warning switch, 943, 943*f*
low profile (LP) tires, 672, 682, 701
low-side driver faults, 588
low stall speed, 1358
low-torque-rise engines, 14, 14*f*
low-viscosity liquid, 150
low-voltage burn-out, 401–402, 402*f*, 425
low-voltage disconnect (LVD) systems, 360–361, 367
    identifying and testing, 385–387
lower flange, 770
lower-stall torque converter, 1349
LP. *See* low profile tires
lube, 1607
lube change intervals, 1607–1608
    Fuller recommendations for, 1263, 1264*t*
lube oil, 1598
lube oil pressure switch, 1451
lube pressure, 1477*t*, 1501*t*
lubricant fill level, even with edge of check hole, 1266, 1266*f*
lubricants, 108. *See also* tools
    fluids and
        acid and alkali, 147–148
        anti-freeze, 145–146, 145*f*
        automatic transmission fluid, 146–147, 146*f*
        biodiesel, 149
        brake fluid, 148, 148*f*
        diesel oil, 148–149, 149*f*
        engine oil, 149–150, 149*f*
        gear oil, 150, 150*f*
        paint, 150, 150*f*
        paraffin, 150
        solvents, 150
        synthetic oils, 150

water, 150
in PMI, 1855
lubricating drive axles, 1597–1598
lubricating oil, 1142
lubrication, 1169, 1262, 1263, 1265, 1557–1558, 1558*f*–1559*f*
drive axle, 1606–1607
guidelines for changing, 1608, 1609
intervals for, 1608*t*
SAE grades of, 1607*t*
extended intervals Spicer Life series driveshafts, 1557, 1558*t*
inspecting, 1866–1867
normal intervals, 1557, 1557*t*
lubrication failures, 1637, 1639
lubrication pressure regulator valve, 1496
lumen, 497–498, 507
lunettes, 23, 1110*f*
LVD systems. *See* low-voltage disconnect systems

M

machine screw, 164, 165*f*, 198
machinery guards, 74
mack trucks, 1595*f*
proportional differentials in, 1594–1596
MAF sensor. *See* mass airflow sensor
magnesium wheels, 707
magnetic field, 238, 241, 398, 398*f*, 404*f*, 430
armature, 398, 398*f*
in commercial vehicles, sources of, 524
of current-carrying conductor, 235
direction of, 237*f*
speed of, 239*f*
strength, 399
magnetic field flux, 234
magnetic field strength, 235*f*
magnetic force, 235
magnetic induction, 232
magnetic lines of force, 232, 233, 233*f*, 234*f*
magnetic pickup tools, 127, 127*f*, 158
magnetic switches, 285–286, 285*f*
magnetism, 245
electricity from, 232–241
magneto ignition systems, 471
magnetoresistive (MR) sensors, 558
main pressure for gear, 1501*t*
main pressure regulator valve (MPRV), 1402, 1404–1405, 1404*f*–1405*f*, 1417, 1477, 1477*t*, 1496, 1496*f*
main shaft, 1213–1214, 1214*f*, 1256, 1395, 1417
floating system, 1228–1229, 1228*f*–1229*f*
main shaft module, 1465
malfunction indicator lamp (MIL), 514, 587, 629
mandrel, 135, 158
mandrel head, 135, 158
manifold gauge set, 1741–1742, 1742*f*, 1765
to service ports on compressor, 1780, 1780*f*
manifold style condenser *vs.* serpentine, construction of, 1707, 1707*f*
manual actuators, 1821
manual bleeding method, 1176, 1177
manual lifting, procedure for, 185
manual-manifold block, 1855
manual-ranging multimeters, 310, 310*f*, 310*t*, 312*f*, 325
manual recirculating-ball steering gears, 848, 849*f*
manual selector valve, 1405–1406, 1417
manual slack adjusters, 911, 914*f*, 921, 1024
manual slide release, 1121, 1121*f*
manual steering gears, 846
manual transmission, checking fluid level of, 1266, 1267
map diagram, 472, 473*f*, 485
Martensite spotting, 1013, 1013*f*
mass airflow (MAF) sensor, 575, 575*f*, 637
diagnostics of, 590
master cylinder, 1075–1077, 1076*f*, 1156, 1175
remove and replace air-over-hydraulic, 1092
removing and replacing dual-circuit, 1093
split braking systems, 1077–1078, 1077*f*–1078*f*
master disconnect switch, 1660, 1661*f*, 1665
master, inspector qualifications, 1854
master module, 601
master-slave networks, 601
master technicians, 38–39
match mounting, 701
materials, 152
for manufacturing seals, 180*t*
used in vehicle industry, 153*t*–154*t*
maxi-brakes, 904, 908, 909*f*
maxi fuses, 265
maxi spring, 908, 909*f*
maximum bending moment, 768, 789
maximum driveshaft low gear torque. *See* wheel slip torque
maximum forward overdrive, 1375, 1375*f*, 1377–1378, 1389
maximum forward reduction, 1374, 1374*f*, 1377, 1389
MBT520-6DA, 1328
MBT660-6OA, 1328
measuring tapes, 110, 110*f*, 158
measuring wheel end play, 719
mechanical advantage, 1194, 1207, 1791, 1833
mechanical fade, 902, 921
mechanical fault, starting system, 414–415
mechanical fingers, 127, 127*f*, 158
mechanical gauges, 515
mechanical jack, 188, 198
mechanical seals, 183
mechanical systems, 606
medium-carbon steel, 768, 789
MEIIR. *See* momentary engine ignition interrupt relay
mental barriers, 41
Mercedes Benz, 1328–1329
AGS, 1305, 1305*f*
Mercedes Benz ECM, integrated circuits used in, 548*f*
Meritor RMX10-165-C2S002, nomenclature for, 1326*t*
Meritor Wabco systems, 1042
Meritor/ZF, 1323–1326
air disc brake system, 917, 918*f*
AutoJust clutch, 1146
automated transmissions, 1304–1305, 1304*f*
mesh, gear face contact, 1196
meshing gears, 1197*f*
mesothelioma, 152, 1148
message format, 615–616
message identifier (MID), 647, 647*f*, 647*t*, 655
metal fuse wire, 264
metal oxide semiconductors, 221
metals, 151–152
meter shunts, 311, 311*f*
metering valves, 1079, 1099
testing, 1096
metri-pack connector, 467, 468*f*, 485
Metric Gauge system, 463
metric micrometer, 112
metric system, 168, 169, 169*f*
metric threads, 169
micro-discharge cycles, 355, 355*f*
microcontrollers, 299, 548, 550, 553
micrometers, 158
common types of, 111
metric, 112
outside, inside, and depth, 111–112, 111*f*
standard, 112
micron gauge, 1742, 1743*f*, 1765
evacuating air-conditioning system using, 1759, 1760
microprocessors, 298, 299*f*, 548
controls operation of output drivers, 546, 547*f*
power train control, 537, 542
MID. *See* message identifier
MIL. *See* malfunction indicator lamp
mineral oil. *See* paraffin
mini-cube relays. *See* International Standards Organization (ISO) relays
Mini ISO relays, 284*f*
minimum forward overdrive, 1375, 1376*f*, 1378, 1389
minimum forward reduction, 1374–1375, 1375*f*, 1377, 1389
mining operation trucks, 11

misfire detection monitor, 635–637
miter boxes, 846, 846*f*, 876
MLS head gasket. *See* multilayer steel head gasket
mobile gantries, 187
mobile repair truck, 40*f*
Mod Main solenoid, 1488, 1490
Mode 1, 1683, 1687
Mode 2, 1683, 1687
model-based diagnostics, 631
modern charging systems, 431
modern electrical system, 599*f*
modulated lock-up, 1352, 1367, 1411, 1417
modulated main solenoid (Mod Main), 1488, 1490, 1526
modulator, 990*f*
modulator cable, 1429, 1441
modulator function, 1049, 1049*f*
modulator pressure, 1406
modulator valves, 1040, 1046–1049, 1047*f*, 1063, 1406–1407, 1406*f*, 1417. *See also* throttle valve
  anti-lock braking, 1048–1049
  construction, 1047
  non-anti-lock braking, 1047
  operation of, 1048*f*
module connector pin assignments, 482–483
moisture, condensation of, 1697, 1697*f*
mold curing. *See* hot curing process
momentary contact switches, 277
momentary engine ignition interrupt relay (MEIIR), 1308–1309, 1337
monitor, 632
  readiness codes, 634*f*
monoleaf springs, 805, 836
Montreal protocol, 1734
Morse code, 603
Morse taper, 158, 188
MOS semiconductors, 221
MOSFET, 221, 221*f*, 223
  field effect transistor, 295–297, 296*f*
motor-center position, 1823
motor effect, 404
motor vehicle air conditioners (MVAC), 1734
motor vehicle battery, 144
motorcycle tire, 663
mountainous highway, 8
mounted drill, 117
mountings
  inspecting, 1861, 1864
  under-vehicle inspections, 1872, 1873
mounts, 1430, 1441
movable cam rings, 1172, 1189
MPMT. *See* multi-pole multi-throw switch
MPRV. *See* main pressure regulator valve
MR sensors. *See* magnetoresistive sensors
MT-640/650 transmission, 1394
MT-25 transmission, 1394
mufflers, 1754, 1765
  removing and inspection of, 1751, 1754, 1755
multi-loop starter motor and electromagnetic fields, 406*f*
multi-mesh gearing, 1229, 1256
multi-piece driveshafts, 1539
multi-pole multi-throw (MPMT), 276
multi-rib serpentine belt, 445*f*
multi-shaft steering columns, 846
multi-speed drive axles. *See* double reduction drive axles
multi-stranded wire, 465
multi-temp unit, 1774, 1774*f*, 1783
multilayer steel (MLS) head gasket, 178, 178*f*, 198
multileaf spring, 798, 836
multileaf spring packs, 802, 802*f*, 803*f*
multimeters, 141, 141*f*, 308, 309*f*
  electrical measurements with, 309, 309*f*, 312–319
  manual and auto-ranging meters, 310, 310*f*, 310*t*
  to measure voltage, 142
  meter shunts, 311, 311*f*
  to protect meter and user, 315, 316*t*
multiple-battery configurations, 341
multiple countershaft transmissions, 1227, 1256
  and auxiliary transmissions. *See* auxiliary transmissions
multiple networks, gateways joining, 617
multiple-path throttle position sensors, 565
multiplex electrical control system, 605*f*
multiplexing, 599, 603, 623
  advantages, 604–609
  communication, 604
  SAE J2497, 618–619
  time division. *See* time division multiplexing (TDM)
mushroom-shaped kingpins, 1116
mutual induction, 238–241, 240*f*
MVAC. *See* motor vehicle air conditioners
Mylar (a type of nylon) gasket, 714

N

N-95 mask, 973, 1033
N/C solenoids. *See* normally closed solenoids
N material, 289–290, 290*f*, 294, 294*f*, 301
N-type material, 221, 223
NAO lining. *See* non-asbestos organic lining
narrow metal strip, 219
National Fire Prevention Association (NFPA), 1428
National Highway Traffic Safety Administration (NHTSA), 677, 1855
National Institute of Occupational Safety and Health (NIOSH), 75, 973, 1148
National Lubricating Grease Institute (NLGI), 1557
Navistar system, 1714, 1715*f*
Navistar's ESCs, 609, 611*f*
Navistar's "On Command" system, 1854, 1854*f*
NC. *See* normally closed
NCC. *See* neutral no clutches
NCP. *See* nominal crack pressure
needle deflection, 516
needle-nosed pliers, 124, 124*f*, 158
needle valves, 1820–1821, 1821*f*
negative camber, 737–738, 738*f*, 757
negative caster, 740*f*
negative frame angle, 742, 742*f*, 757
negative ion, 209
negative offset, 707, 725
negative scrub radius, 744, 757
negative temperature coefficient (NTC) thermistors, 282, 282*f*, 301, 561, 562*f*
neoprene, 76, 77*f*
network
  centralized network control, 600–602
  classification, 599–602
  distributed network control, 600–602
  J-1939, 601*f*
  local interconnect network, 601*f*
  messages, 615–617
  multiple, 617–618
  on-board vehicle. *See* on-board vehicle networks
  outputs and inputs, 609–611
  physical network layer, 600
  problems, 618
  protocol, 600
  signals, 614
  truck chassis, 602*f*
  typology, 600, 600*f*
  wireless network communication, 617–618
network control systems, 490–491
network node, 618, 623
neutral
  ATEC/CEC, 1456, 1456*f*
  fluid flows, WTEC, 1477
  power flows, World Transmission, 1467–1468
neutral axis, 766, 789
neutral fiber, 766, 789
neutral forward regulator circuit (NFRC), 1411
neutral junction, 436
neutral no clutches (NCC), 1486–1488, 1526
neutral-range valve, 1454, 1456, 1457, 1461
neutral safety switch, 1441
  adjusting shift linkage and, 1437–1439
neutrons, 208
NFPA. *See* National Fire Prevention Association

NFRC. *See* neutral forward regulator circuit
NHTSA. *See* National Highway Traffic Safety Administration
nickel–metal hydride (NiMH) battery, 334, 352–353, 353*f*, 367, 1660, 1677, 1678, 1678*f*
90-degree angle, 986, 1021, 1024
NIOSH. *See* National Institute of Occupational Safety and Health
nippers, 124, 124*f*, 158
nitrogen-filled tires, 681–682, 685
nitrogen testing, performing to find leaks, 1747
NLGI. *See* National Lubricating Grease Institute
NO. *See* normally open
no-load test, 417
no-maintenance batteries, 334*f*, 344–345
no-slack coupler, 1119–1120, 1133
no-slack locks, 1128
noise
  steering-related problems, 865*t*
  transmission, 1268
    gear rattle at idle, 1268, 1270, 1270*f*
    growling, 1270
    knocking, 1270, 1270*f*
    whining, 1270
noise, vibration, and harshness (NVH), 1705
nomenclature, 1265, 1295
  of transmission model numbers, 1265, 1265*f*
nominal crack pressure (NCP), 951, 963
nominal diameter, 669, 701
nominal dimension, 1618
nominal shim pack, 1620, 1639
non-asbestos organic (NAO) lining, 896, 921
non-continuous monitor, 636–641
non-drive (dead) axles, 730, 757
  types and functions of, 730–731
    lift, tag, and pusher axles, 735–736
    steering axles, 731–734, 731*f*
    steering stops, 734–735
non-electric hybrid drive systems, 1648–1649, 1649*f*, 1649*t*
non-ferrous metals, 151, 158
non-latching solenoids, 1452, 1453*f*, 1456–1457, 1459*f*, 1460, 1526
non-positive displacement pumps, 1807
non-uniform velocity, 1532, 1540–1542, 1540*f*–1541*f*, 1567
non-volatile memory (NVM), 550, 551*f*, 553, 1655
nonverbal feedback, 41–42
normally closed (N/C) solenoids, 276, 1472, 1473*f*, 1490, 1492, 1526
normally open (N/O) solenoids, 276, 1472, 1473*f*, 1490, 1492, 1526
North American Market, 1303
North American Standard Out-of-Service Criteria (OOSC), 1853, 1883
North American Truck, Allison transmission in, 1391–1395
NO_X sensor, 569, 574, 574*f*, 579, 593, 632, 633*f*, 641
NPN transistor, 294, 301
NTC thermistors. *See* negative temperature coefficient thermistors
number punch set, 135*f*
nuts, 166, 169*f*, 170, 198
NVH. *See* noise, vibration, and harshness
NVM. *See* non-volatile memory
Nylock nut, 166
nylon/brass tip mallet, 128*f*

O

O-rings, 178, 181, 859, 1754, 1765
OAD pulleys. *See* overrunning alternator decoupler pulleys
OBD. *See* on-board diagnostics
OBD manager, 634, 655
OBD standard, 607
OBD system. *See* on-board diagnostics system
OC. *See* occurence count
Occupational Safety and Health Administration (OSHA) regulations, 72, 103, 706, 973
  and Environmental Protection Agency (EPA), 72
occurence count (OC), 649, 650*f*
OCP thermostat. *See* overcrank protection thermostat
OD. *See* outside diameter
odometers, 523–524
OEM. *See* original equipment manufacturer
off-board diagnostics, 588–589, 630, 631, 642, 643*f*, 655
off-going clutch pressure, 1474
off-going ratio test, 1476, 1526
off-line filter, 1797
offset screwdriver, 126, 126*f*, 158
offset vice, 131, 158
ohm-meter, 214, 260, 614–615
ohms, 212, 214*f*, 223, 257*f*
Ohm's law, 213, 214, 218, 223, 251, 256–257, 581*f*
  amperage in, 257*f*
  to diagnose circuits, 142
oil aeration check, 870–871
oil consumption test, 983–984
oil-cooled alternator, 444*f*
oil cooler, 1798*f*
  and filter, inspection of, 1277–1278
  integral, 1263, 1263*f*
oil-filled gauges, 1742
oil filter, 1266, 1268
  and cooler, inspection of, 1277–1278
oil-filter wrench, 122, 122*f*
oil filtration, 1685
oil leaks, 1268, 1269
oil pressure sending units, 521
oil pressure switch/sensor, 1451–1452
oil seals, 178, 198
oil slinger, 1621, 1639
oil weep, 1268, 1295
oiler, 1742, 1765
oils, 1855
  and capacity, determination of, 1761
    adding proper amount, 1761, 1762
  and filter change, 1430, 1431
OLEDs. *See* organic light-emitting diodes
on-board diagnostics (OBD) system, 261, 262*f*, 322, 607, 623, 628–629, 629*f*, 655. *See also* heavy-duty on-board diagnostics (HD-OBD) system
  circuits, 260
  enabling, 606–607
  executive, 632, 635, 644
  SAE requirements for scan tools, 322
on-board diesel monitor, 637
on-board electronic self-diagnostic systems, 1782
on-board navigation system, 206
on-board network communication, ECU and, 1043–1044
on-board vehicle networks
  CAN. *See* controlled area network (CAN)
  network classification, 599–602
  overview of, 598–599
  power line carrier (PLC) communication, 618–621
  TDM. *See* time division multiplexing
  wireless network communication, 617–618
on-coming ratio test, 1476, 1526
on-vehicle wheel balancers, 138, 139*f*, 694
one-way check valve, 931, 932*f*, 934, 963
one-way clutches, 407, 408*f*, 1346, 1367
  roller-type, 1350, 1351*f*, 1379–1380, 1380*f*
  sprag-type, 1350, 1351*f*, 1379–1380, 1380*f*
one-way communication, direct TPMS, 667
OOSC. *See* North American Standard Out-of-Service Criteria
OOSO. *See* out-of-service order
open and intermittent circuits, causes of, 260*f*
open-center position, 1823, 1823*f*
open-center rim, 710, 725
open circuit faults, 260
open-circuit voltage, 376
  vs. charge, 357*t*
open circuits, 142–143, 158, 438*f*
open-end adjustable wrench, 121
open-end wrench, 121–122, 121*f*, 158
open fracture, 99, 103
open-loop hydraulic system, 1791, 1793*t*
open-loop ramp rate, 1474, 1526

open switch, 279, 279*f*
operating instructions, 616
operating temperature, 1424
operating vehicles, life cycle costs of, 535
operation of systems, 1879–1880
operational algorithms, 539
operational phases, torque converter, 1349
  coupling phase, 1349–1351, 1350*f*–1351*f*
  torque multiplication phase, 1349, 1350*f*
operational state, 252
operator's manual, vehicle, 55–56, 55*f*, 65
optimal tread compounds, 682
orderliness, housekeeping and, 96
organic facings, 1147–1148, 1163
organic friction discs, 1147, 1147*f*
organic light-emitting diodes (OLEDs), 293, 301, 500
orifice tube system, 1711–1715, 1737
  evaporator inlet, 1711, 1712*f*, 1713*f*
  removing, inspecting, and installment of, 1758
original equipment manufacturer (OEM), 639, 645, 646, 648, 798–799, 1308, 1329, 1331
  software, 1060, 1060*f*
  wire identification, 466*t*
oscillation, 795, 836
oscilloscopes, 141, 141*f*, 319–321, 320*f*–321*f*
  alternator, 440*f*
OSHA. *See* Occupational Safety and Health Administration
OSS criteria. *See* out-of-service criteria
out-of-range monitoring, 633, 655
out-of-service (OSS) criteria
  for automatic transmissions, 1428
  criteria for truck frames, 777
  suspension system, 820–821, 820*f*
out-of-service order (OOSO), 1853
outboard mounted drums, 903*f*, 904, 904*f*
output circuits, 575
output force, 1796, 1833
output member, 1373, 1389
output shaft, 1213, 1256, 1594, 1601. *See also* main shaft
output speed sensor, 1308
outrigger brackets, 774, 789
outrigger mounts, 774, 774*f*, 776*f*
outside diameter (OD), 1799, 1800*f*, 1833
outside micrometer, 111–112, 111*f*, 113, 158
over-all diameter, 669, 701
over center adjustment, 866–867, 867*f*
over-running clutch, 1346, 1367. *See also* one-way clutches
overcharging, 1737, 1765
overcrank protection (OCP) thermostat, 411, 425
overdrive knock-down valve, 1496
overdrive ratio, 1199, 1207
overhaul, starter motor, 421–423
overhead cranes, 193, 193*f*
overhung mount pinion, 1615, 1639
overrunning alternator decoupler (OAD) pulleys, 446, 457
overrunning clutch. *See* one-way clutches
overslung, 796, 837
oversteer, 848
  steering-related problems, 865*t*
oxyacetylene torches, 139–140, 158
  safety needs to, 140
oxygen cylinder, 140
oxygen in fuel cell, process of converting, 243*f*
oxygen recombination, 356
oxygen sensors, 571, 573, 573*f*
ozone depletion, 1720

P

P-1 planetary gear set, 1469
P-2 planetary gear set, 1468, 1468*f*
P-3 planetary gear set, 1468, 1468*f*, 1470*f*
P-1 ring gear, 1466, 1469–1471
P-2 ring gear, 1466, 1469, 1470
P-3 ring gear, 1466, 1468–1471
P-1 sun gear, 1466, 1469–1471
P-2 sun gear, 1466, 1469–1471
P-3 sun gear, 1466, 1468, 1471
P material, 289–290, 290*f*, 294, 294*f*, 301
P-type material, 221, 223
P-type shoes, 1017
PAG. *See* polyalkylene glycol
paint, 150, 150*f*
painted lines, safety equipment, 74
PAO. *See* polyalphaolefin
parabolic leaf springs, 804, 804*f*
paraffin (mineral oil), 150, 158
parallax error, 115, 158
parallel alternators, 446, 457
parallel, charging battery banks, 382–383
parallel circuits, 253–256, 255*f*
parallel drive, 1645, 1646*f*, 1665
  advantages and disadvantages, 1671–1672
  comparing with series systems, 1648, 1648*t*
parallel hybrids, operating modes of, 1683–1684
parallel joint arrangement, 1542, 1542*f*, 1567. *See also* waterfall arrangement
parallel keys, 176, 176*f*, 198
parallel wiring, 465, 485
parallelogram, 798, 798*f*, 837
parameter group number (PGN), 649, 652*t*, 655
parameter identifier (PID), 647, 648*t*, 655
parasitic drains, 374
parasitic draw, 333, 347
  measuring, 384–385
parasitic loss, 1402, 1417, 1496
park brake circuit, 930, 930*f*, 963
park/emergency braking circuit, 955, 955*f*, 963
  inversion valve, 956, 956*f*
  push-pull control valves, 955–956, 956*f*
parking brake hand (control), guidelines for inspect and testing, 998, 999
parking brake testing, 986
parking brakes, 890, 904. *See also* hand/emergency brakes
  and emergency circuits, 1086
    arrangement and operation of, 1087, 1087*f*
    park brake off and applied, 1087, 1087*f*–1088*f*
    service brake applied, 1088, 1089*f*
  spring brake, 1075, 1075*f*
partial-thickness burns. *See* second-degree burns
parts per million (ppm), 75
parts program, 59, 60, 65
parts specialist, 59, 65
Pascal's law, 1794–1795, 1833
PASS. *See* Pull, Aim, Squeeze, Sweep
passive sensors, 593
  vs. active sensors, 558–559
  electronic control module (ECM), 559*f*
PBS Injection Booster, 941, 942*f*, 943, 963
$PbSO_4$. *See* lead sulfate
PC-based service software, 1685
PCM. *See* powertrain control module
PCS. *See* pressure control solenoids; propulsion control system module
peak torque, 13, 30
pedal free play, 1172
pedestal grinders. *See* bench grinders
peening, 127, 158
PEL. *See* permissible exposure limit
pencil type, pocket tire pressure gauges, 684
pencil-type pressure gauge, 136
Pentium IV processor, 542
performance testing, 1735, 1738, 1739, 1765
  abnormal noises, 1738
permissible exposure limit (PEL), 75
personal protective equipment (PPE), 70, 70*f*, 90, 90*f*, 103, 108. *See also* first aid; safety
breathing devices. *See* breathing devices
  ear protection, 92–93, 93*f*
  eye protection. *See* eye protection
  hair containment, 95
  hand protection. *See* hands
  headgear, 90
  protective clothing, 90
    footwear, 90, 91*f*
    work clothing, 90
  watches and jewelry, 95
personal space, 53
petroleum-based hydraulic fluids, 1794

PGN. *See* parameter group number
PGN 61444, 649
phase winding connections, 436–437
phasing, 1543–1544, 1544*f*, 1551, 1567
  cross and incremental, adjustments of, 1544–1545
PHEV. *See* plug-in hybrid electric vehicle
Phillips screwdriver, 126, 126*f*, 158
phone communication, 44
photodiodes, 292, 293*f*, 301
photometric certification, 492, 492*f*, 507
photons, 492, 499
photoresistors, 282, 283*f*, 301
photovoltaic (PV) effect, 230, 245
physical network layer, 600
pickle fork, 732
pictorial diagrams, 472, 473*f*
pictorial message, 74
PID. *See* parameter identifier
piezo crystals, 232
  newest application for, 232*f*
piezoelectric effect, 232, 245
piezoresistive sensors, 566–567, 567*f*, 568*f*, 593
pilot bearing bore, 1180, 1182–1183, 1182*f*, 1189
pilot bearings, 1151–1153, 1152*f*, 1163
pilot pad, 715, 715*f*, 725
pin punches, 135, 135*f*, 158
pin-type synchronizer, 1220, 1220*f*
pinion, 1817, 1833
  clearance, adjusting, 408
    methods of, 409
  drive gear, 407
  of starter motor, 394–395, 406
pinion bearing cage, 1615, 1639
pinion bearing preload, setting, 1617, 1618, 1621
pinion depth, 1606, 1639
  setting shims, 1619*f*
pinion gears, 1203, 1205, 1205*f*, 1207, 1372, 1373*f*, 1389, 1575, 1601
  installing, 1621
  set, 1616–1617, 1617*f*
pinion pilot bearing, 1615, 1639
pinion spigot bearing, 1617, 1618*f*
pinion variation number, 1619, 1619*f*, 1639
pintle, 1812, 1833
pintle hooks, 23–24, 24*f*, 30, 1109–1111, 1133
  with ball hitch, 1109*f*
pipe, 1799–1802, 1833
pipe wrenches, 122, 122*f*
piston, 1817, 1833
piston axial compressor, operation of, 1705, 1705*f*
piston pumps, 1808, 1808*f*
  operation, 1811–1812
piston stroke detector, 1084, 1086, 1086*f*
piston-type gas-charged accumulator, 1825, 1825*f*
pitch, 1196, 1207
pitch circle, 1196, 1207
pitch diameter, 1196, 1207
pitman (drop) arm, 735, 757, 854, 854*f*, 855*f*, 876
plain bevel gears, 1576, 1576*f*, 1601
plain case half, 1613, 1639
plain-type synchronizer, 1218, 1219*f*
plan angle, 1545, 1567
planetary double reduction drive axle, 1586–1588, 1601
planetary gear reduction drive starter motor, 397–398, 397*f*, 425
planetary gear sets, 1462, 1466, 1468–1469, 1469*f*, 1470*f*
  ring gear of, 1506, 1516
  schematic shows of, 1395, 1396*f*
planetary gears, 1372, 1389
  combinations of, 1380
    Ravigneaux gear set, 1381, 1381*f*
    Simpson gear set, 1380–1381, 1381*f*
    Wilson, Lepelletier, and ZF gear sets, 1381
  compound power flows, 1382–1385, 1382*f*–1387*f*, 1382*t*
  fundamentals of, 1372–1373, 1373*f*
    role of carrier, 1373–1374
    rules of planetary gears, 1373
  introduction of, 1372
  motion, 1374
  power flows, 1374, 1374*t*
    maximum forward overdrive, 1375, 1375*f*
    maximum forward reduction, 1374, 1374*f*
    minimum forward overdrive, 1375, 1376*f*
    minimum forward reduction, 1374–1375, 1375*f*
    reverse overdrive, 1376–1377, 1376*f*, 1377*f*
    reverse reduction, 1376, 1376*f*
  power train control devices. *See* power train control devices
  ratio calculations for, 1377–1378
  roles and results of, 1374, 1374*t*
  rules of, 1373
  versatile and strong, 1373*f*
planetary modules, 1465
planetary two-speed drive axle, 1586–1588, 1587*f*, 1589*f*, 1601
planned down-time, 1829, 1833
plastic section modulus, 767
plate-and-fin evaporator construction, 1714, 1715*f*
plate sulfation, 344, 344*f*
plate technology, VRLAs, 356
plate-type synchronizer, 1220–1221, 1221*f*
plates
  friction, 1378, 1378*f*, 1389
  reaction, 1378, 1378*f*, 1389
plausibility monitoring, 633
PLC communication. *See* power line carrier communication
PLC technology. *See* power line carrier technology
PLC4TRUCKS, 618
pliers, 123–125, 124*f*, 158
plies, 673
plug-in hybrid electric vehicle (PHEV), 1645, 1647–1648, 1648*f*, 1665
plug tap. *See* intermediate tap
plunger, 1822, 1833
PM. *See* preventative maintenance
PM-A inspections, 1847, 1883
PM-B inspection, 1847, 1883
  PM inspection sheet for, 1848*f*
PM-C inspections, 1847, 1883
  PM inspection sheet for, 1848*f*
PM service checklist, 1851, 1853, 1883
PM service intervals, 1851, 1883
PMI. *See* preventative maintenance and inspection
pneumatic balance, 950, 963, 991, 1033
pneumatic imbalance, 951, 964
pneumatic jack, 188, 199
pneumatic starter motor, 398, 398*f*
pneumatic systems in commercial vehicles, 37*f*
pneumatic tire changers, 138, 139*f*
PNP transistor, 294, 301
POE. *See* polyolester oil
point-to-point electrical connection method, 604, 604*f*
point-to-point wiring technique, 604, 604*f*
polarity, 215, 223
polarity forces, 215*f*
pole pieces, 434
poles, 276
policy, 72, 103
polyalkylene glycol (PAG), 1721, 1727, 1761
polyalphaolefin (PAO), 1721, 1727
polymeric positive temperature coefficient device (PPTC), 266–267, 267*f*
polyolester oil (POE), 1782
polyvinyl chloride (PVC), 152
poor lifting and handling techniques, 71, 71*f*
pop-rivet guns, 135, 135*f*, 158
portable drill, 117, 118*f*
portable electrical equipment, 76, 77*f*
portable lifting hoists, 191–192, 192*f*, 199
portable shop lights/droplights, 76–77, 77*f*
portalift mobile hoists, 191, 192*f*
ports, 1817, 1833
position sensors, 1310, 1310*f*
positive camber, 737, 738*f*, 739*f*, 741*f*, 758
positive caster, 740, 740*f*, 741*f*
positive-displacement pumps, 1807*t*
  types of, 1807–1808
positive electrical charges, 208
positive frame angle, 742, 758

positive ion, 209
positive offset, 707, 725
positive scrub radius, 744, 758
positive separator roll pins, 1185, 1186*f*
positive temperature coefficient (PTC) thermistor, 282, 282*f*, 301, 561, 562*f*
post-testing of air-conditioning system, 1735–1736
pot-type flywheels, 1151, 1151*f*, 1163
potential difference, 215
potentiometers, 281, 281*f*, 301, 564, 593
power-assist piston, 854
power-assisted steering systems, 847
  steering ratios, 848
power distribution boxes, 265, 266*f*
power distribution flow, 477–478
power distribution modules, 609*f*
power dividers, 1592–1596, 1592*f*, 1598*f*
  components, 1592–1594, 1593*f*
  disassembling, 1628–1629
  reassembling, 1630
  reinstalling, 1631
power flow, 1215–1216, 1256, 1576, 1595*f*
  eighteen-speed transmission with four-speed auxiliary, 1241–1243, 1241*f*–1242*f*
  main box, 1229–1231, 1230*f*–1231*f*
  multiple countershaft transmission, 1229, 1229*f*
  planetary gears, 1374, 1374*t*
    compound. *See* Simpson gear set
    maximum forward overdrive, 1375, 1375*f*
    maximum forward reduction, 1374, 1374*f*
    minimum forward overdrive, 1375, 1376*f*
    minimum forward reduction, 1374–1375, 1375*f*
    reverse overdrive, 1376–1377, 1376*f*, 1377*f*
    reverse reduction, 1376, 1376*f*
  single countershaft transmissions. *See* single countershaft transmissions
  through deep-reduction three-speed auxiliary section, 1237, 1237*f*–1239*f*, 1239
  in two-speed auxiliary section, 1233, 1233*f*–1234*f*, 1235
power grinders, 118
power jackknifing, 1053, 1063
power line carrier (PLC) communication, 618–621
  multiplexing SAE J2497, 618–619
  smart mode operation, 619–621
power line carrier (PLC) technology, 618, 623, 1043, 1043*f*, 1063
power recirculating-ball steering gears, 849, 849*f*, 850*f*
  rotary valve, 850, 851*f*, 852, 852*f*, 853*f*
  torsion rod, 852–853, 853*f*
power source, 250
power-split configuration, 1645, 1647*f*, 1665, 1670
power springs, 904, 906, 908, 908*f*, 909*f*, 921
power steering box, 1573*f*
power steering coolers, 860
power steering fluid, 858–860, 859*f*, 860*f*
power steering gear systems, 734, 843, 847
power steering hoses, 858–860, 859*f*, 860*f*
power steering pumps, 858, 860, 876
power steering reservoirs, 860, 871
Power Steering System Analyzer (PSSA), 867–870, 867*f*, 868*f*, 876
  measure pump maximum relief pressure, 868, 869
  test flow volume, 868, 870
power steering systems, hydraulic components of, 857–858
  hydraulic pumps, types of, 860–861, 861*f*, 862*f*, 863, 863*f*
  hydraulically assisted power steering, 858, 858*f*
  power steering coolers, 860
  power steering fluid and hoses, 858–860, 859*f*, 860*f*
  power steering pumps, 860
power take-off device (PTO), 1252–1253, 1253*f*, 1256, 1268
  drive lines, 1550
  inspection of, 1279, 1280
  provision, 1464, 1465*f*
power tools, 117–119, 158
  bench and angle grinders, 118–119, 119*f*
  drills and drill bits, 117–118, 118*f*
power train control devices, 1372, 1378, 1389
  brake band and servo, 1379, 1379*f*
  hydraulic clutch, 1378–1379, 1378*f*, 1379*f*
  roller- or sprag-type one-way clutches, 1379–1380, 1380*f*
power train control microprocessor, 542
power train mounts, 1433
  inspecting or replacing, 1430
power trains, 14–16
  in conventional heavy truck, 14*f*
power unit, 858, 876
power flows of World Transmission, 1466–1471, 1466*f*
powertrain control module (PCM), 1359
Pozidriv screwdriver, 126, 126*f*
PPE. *See* personal protective equipment
PPID. *See* proprietary parameter identification
ppm. *See* parts per million
pre-dampening, 1150, 1163, 1270, 1270*f*, 1295
precure. *See* cold curing process
predict, 1829, 1833
predictive PM, 1848, 1883
preload, 708, 717, 725, 1606, 1639
premanufactured exhaust gaskets, 177, 177*f*
preset hub, 716, 717*f*, 720–721, 725
  comparison of standard hub and, 717*t*
  unit, 720*f*
pressure, 1700–1703, 1798, 1833
  in cooling system, increase, 1700, 1701*f*
  electricity from, 232
pressure-balanced devices, 945, 964
pressure bleeding method, 1175–1177, 1189
pressure-compensating balance valve, 949, 964
pressure-compensating relay valve, 946, 964
pressure compression gauge, 137, 137*f*
pressure control solenoids (PCS), 1488, 1526
pressure control valves, 1819–1820
pressure-cycling switch, 1713, 1722
  accumulator of CCOT system, 1713, 1713*f*
  thermostatic switch cycles, 1713, 1714*f*
pressure differential valves, 1079, 1079*f*, 1099
  testing, 1096
pressure filter, 1797
pressure gauges. *See* pressure testers
pressure plate, 1141, 1143, 1143*f*, 1144, 1145*f*, 1163, 1184
pressure protection valves, 816, 817*f*, 937, 937*f*, 964
pressure-reducing valves, 1819–1820
pressure-relief valves, 860, 1819, 1823–1824
pressure-sensitive electrical switch, 948, 948*f*
pressure-sensitive valves, 1079
pressure sensors, 566–569
  testing of, 589
pressure solenoid, 1090
pressure switches, 277, 1451, 1452
pressure testers, 136–137
pressure testing, 1428, 1428*f*
  automatic transmission, 1359–1361, 1432
pressure transients, 1742, 1765
pressure vacuum gauge, 137, 137*f*
pressure washers/cleaners, 140, 158
preventative maintenance (PM), 1846–1847
  costs and resale price, 1846*f*
  costs of, 1849*f*
  inspection sheet for PM-B and PM-C inspections, 1848*f*
  performs, 1850–1851
  program development, 1851–1856

program, effective and ineffective, 1851, 1852*f*
shop and vehicle rules for, 1856
shop setup for functionality, 1856, 1856*f*
preventative maintenance and inspection (PMI), 1846–1847
guidelines in, 1856, 1857*f*
lubricants in, 1855
process, 1856, 1858–1880
record-keeping requirements, 1854
shop and vehicle rules for, 1856
shop setup functionality, 1856, 1856*f*
types of, 1847–1851
prick punch, 134, 134*f*, 158
primary alignment angles, 737
primary battery, 330, 347
primary brake shoe. *See* leading shoes
primary circuit systems, 928, 929*f*, 964
primary modulation control, 1473, 1526
primary piston, 1076, 1099
primary reservoir, 933, 964
primary sources, 47, 47*f*, 65
primary winding, 238, 245
priority fault codes, 651, 652*t*
priority valve, 1408, 1409*f*, 1417
PRO-TORQ® nut system, 719
proactive maintenance, 1847, 1883
reactive maintenance *vs.*, 1848*t*
proactive PM, 1847, 1883
procedure, 72, 103
Procision transmission, 1314, 1337
from Eaton, 1316*f*
fifth gear power flow in, 1321*f*
first gear power flow in, 1318*f*
fourth gear power flow in, 1320*f*
neutral, 1317*f*
power flows, 1317–1322
reverse power flow in, 1318*f*
second gear power flow in, 1319*f*
seventh gear power flow in, 1322*f*
sixth gear power flow in, 1322*f*
third gear power flow in, 1320*f*
production date code, VIN and, 26–27
professional environment, working in, 52–53, 52*f*, 53*f*
professional workplace habits, 52–55
profile bearing, 1622, 1639
prognostic capability, 1424, 1441
prognostics, 1424, 1441, 1498–1499, 1526
programmable electronic controls, 537, 537*f*
programmable read-only memory (PROM) chip, 549, 550*f*, 553, 1448, 1448*f*, 1527
in transmission ECU, 1451
programmable software, 537
programmed lock-up, 1352, 1367
progressive-rate leaf springs, 804, 804*f*
Prolink scanner, 322*f*
PROM chip. *See* programmable read-only memory chip
propeller shaft hand brake system, 1074, 1074*f*
proportional differential, 1584–1585, 1601
proportional solenoid, 1822
proportioning valves, 953, 964, 1079, 1099
testing, 1096
proprietary parameter identification (PPID), 646
proprietary subsystem identification description (PSID), 646
propulsion control system (PCS) module, 1654–1656, 1655*f*–1656*f*, 1665
propylene glycol, 145, 158
protection devices of circuit, 263–264
circuit breakers, 265–266
inspecting and testing, 267–269
major harness protection, 265
PPT coefficient fuses, 266–267
thermal fuses, 264–265
virtual fuses, 267
protective clothing, 90
footwear, 90, 91*f*
work clothing, 90
protons, 208
prove-out sequence, 513–514, 529
proximity switches, 277
pry bars (crowbars), 128–129, 129*f*, 158
psia, 1700, 1727
PSID. *See* proprietary subsystem identification description
psig, 1700, 1727
PSSA. *See* power steering system analyzer
PT chart, 1742, 1743*f*, 1765
PTC thermistor. *See* positive temperature coefficient thermistor
PTO. *See* power take-off device
Pull, Aim, Squeeze, Sweep (PASS), 78–79, 79*f*
pull-down circuit, 283
pull-down resistor, 585, 585*t*, 586*f*
pull-down switch, 560–561, 561*f*, 593
pull-to-seat terminal, 467, 485
pull-type clutch, 1142, 1143*f*, 1163
adjustment, 1169, 1187
release bearing, 1152–1153, 1152*f*
pull-up circuit, 283
pull-up resistors, 580, 584, 584*t*
pull-up switch, 560–561, 561*f*, 593
pullers, 133, 133*f*, 158
pulleys, 445–446
alternator, 449–450
and fan, 455
pulling/wandering, steering-related problems, 865*t*
pulse wheel, 570
pulse-width modulation (PWM), 544–546, 544*f*–547*f*, 553, 1472–1473, 1496*f*, 1497, 1527
duty cycle, 546–548, 547*f*–548*f*
frequency, 548, 548*f*
pulsed charger, 382, 389
pump volumetric efficiency, 1809–1810
pumps, 1344–1345, 1345*f*, 1796, 1807, 1833
cavitation, 1814, 1814*f*
drive hub, 1344, 1344*f*, 1353
failure, causes of, 1814–1815
hydraulic. *See* hydraulic pumps
symbols, 1815, 1815*f*
punches tools, 134–135, 158
punctuality, 53, 53*f*
purge cycle, 939–940, 940*f*, 964
purge valve, 939, 939*f*, 964
push-pull park/emergency control valve, 955–956, 956*f*, 964
push-pull type solenoids, 286, 286*f*
push-to-seat terminal, 467, 485
push-type clutch, 1142, 1163
adjustment, 1169
installing, 1182–1183
release bearing, 1152, 1152*f*
pusher axles, 16, 735–736, 758, 1572, 1601
PVC. *See* polyvinyl chloride
PWM. *See* pulse-width modulation

Q

quartz silica glass, 496, 507
questioning, effective speaking, 43–44
quick-adjust device, 1171, 1171*f*, 1189
quick connect fittings, 934, 935*f*
quick release (QR) brakes, 1017
quick-release (QR) valves, 954, 954*f*–955*f*, 964
guidelines for inspect and testing, 995, 996

R

R-134a, properties of, 1720, 1720*f*
"R" terminal, 436, 448
R404a, chlorine-free refrigerant, 1782
rack, 1817, 1833
rack-and-pinion actuators, 1817, 1819, 1820*f*
rack and pinion gears, 1205, 1205*f*, 1207
rack-and-pinion steering systems, 853–854, 854*f*, 876
rack-and-pinion type steering, 843, 844, 844*f*
rack gears, 1205, 1205*f*, 1207
radial piston, 1817
radial piston pumps, 1811, 1812, 1812*f*
radial placed belts, 673
radial-ply tires, 673, 673*f*, 674, 701
radial run-out, 697, 712
radial thrust, 1202, 1207
radial tires, 665, 682
radiant heat transfer, 1698, 1727
radio receiver, 261*f*
radio transmitter, 260, 261*f*
radio waves, 260

radiosatellite, 536
rail select motor, 1309, 1310
rails, 770–771
    reinforced frame, 771, 772*f*
RAM. *See* random access memory
ram, 1796, 1832
ramp-off rate, 1474, 1527
random access memory (RAM), 550, 553
range cylinder, 1274, 1274*f*
    components of, 1276, 1276*f*
range gears, 1213, 1257
range shift control, 1243–1244, 1243*f*–1245*f*
range shift cylinder, 1244, 1257
range synchronizer, 1273, 1274*f*
    overhauling, 1286
range tests, 1474–1476
range verification test, 1474–1476, 1475*f*, 1527
rat-tail file, 130
ratchet drive, 119
ratcheting closed-end wrench, 121, 121*f*, 122
ratcheting open-end wrench, 121
ratcheting screwdriver, 126, 126*f*, 159
ratchets, 109, 123, 123*f*, 158
ratio gear, 1253
ratio steps, 1213, 1257
ratio tests, 1476, 1527
ratio valve, 964. *See also* limiter valve
rationality faults, 633
rationality monitoring, 633
rattle gun, 120, 159
Ravigneaux, Frenchman Pol, 1381
Ravigneaux gear set, 1380, 1381, 1381*f*, 1389
rawl pins, 176, 199
RBM. *See* resist bending moment
re-circulating ball nuts, 1309, 1309*f*
reaction member, 1373, 1389
    torque converters, 1345–1346, 1346*f*
reaction plates, 1378, 1378*f*, 1389
reactive maintenance, 1847, 1883
    vs. proactive maintenance, 1848*t*
read only memory (ROM), 549–550, 551*f*, 553
readiness code, 634, 643
reading, effective, 45–48
reamers, 734
rear cover module, 1465
rear engine, school bus with, 12*f*
rear main seal, 181, 182*f*
rear planetary ring gear, 1401
rear seals, replacement of, 1282, 1283
rear side gear, 1594*f*
rear-wheel-drive vehicle suspensions, 798
rebound, 797, 797*f*, 837
rebounding hammer, 128
recalibration process, sequence of, 1310, 1311*f*
recap tires. *See* retreading tires
receiver/drier, 1716–1717, 1727
    cross section of, 1715, 1715*f*
    elements of, 1716, 1716*f*
    removing, inspecting, and installment of, 1754–1756
receiver tank, 1781, 1781*f*
receiver tank outlet valve (RTOV), 1781
reciprocating-piston compressors, operation of, 1779, 1779*f*
recirculating-ball steering gears, 876
    manual, 848, 849*f*
    power, 849, 849*f*, 850*f*
        rotary valve, 850, 851*f*, 852, 852*f*, 853*f*
        torsion rod, 852–853, 853*f*
recirculating-ball steering systems, 848
reclaim/recycle machine, 1741, 1741*f*, 1765
reclaiming, 1735, 1747–1748, 1765
    recycling, labeling, and storing refrigerant, 1748, 1749
    removed refrigerant oil, inspecting condition of, 1749
record-keeping requirements, PMI, 1854
recovering, 1747–1748, 1765. *See also* reclaiming
rectification, 437, 457
rectifier, 434, 437–441, 439*f*
    bridge, 444
    diode problems, 439
rectifying diodes, 292
recycling refrigerant, 1748, 1749
red LEDs, APADS module, 1725, 1725*f*
reduction gear drive starter motor, 396, 397, 397*f*, 425
reefers, 1770, 1773, 1783
    cooling or heating capacity of, 1773
reference voltage (Vref), 559, 559*f*, 593
    regulated, 583
    reference voltage sensors—three-wire sensors, 561, 563–564, 563*f*
refractometer, 337, 338*f*, 378*t*
refrigerant, 1717–1721
    check valves, 1781
    color and consistency of, 1716, 1717*f*
    determination types of, 1736, 1736*f*
    equipment maintenance, 1761, 1762
    HFC, 1719*t*
    identifying types, 1744, 1745
    inspecting condition of removed oil, 1748
    labeling, 1748
    properties of, 1719
    recycling, 1748, 1749
    at Sea Level, boiling points of, 1782*t*
    solenoids, operation of, 1777*f*
    special-purpose, 1720
    storing, 1748
    types, 1719–1720
refrigerant identifiers, 1736, 1736*f*, 1741, 1741*f*, 1765
refrigerant label, 63, 63*f*, 65
refrigeration cycle, terms and concepts related to, 1698–1703
refrigeration oil, 1717–1721
refrigeration system, 1703–1721, 1770, 1771*f*
    different from air conditioning, 1771*f*
    for heating and cooling, 1775, 1775*f*
    maintenance, 1782
    principles of, 1703
    removes heat from truck box or trailer body, 1771*f*
refuse vehicles, 11–12
regeneration disable switch, 1662
regenerative braking, 1644, 1665
regrooving, 678, 701
regular battery maintenance, 372
regular wear, 1291–1293
regulators, 441, 455
    "A" type, 441, 442*f*
    voltage, 441–443
relay valves, 948, 949*f*, 964
    anti-compounding, 951–953, 952*f*
    applications, 948–949
    brake proportioning, 953, 953*f*
        front axle limiter valves, 953–954, 954*f*
        quick-release valves, 954, 954*f*–955*f*
    crack pressures, 950–951
    guidelines for inspect and testing, 998
    pneumatic brake balance, 950
    pneumatic brake imbalance, 951
    pressure compensating balance, 949
    release, 949, 950*f*
relays, 282–286
    mini ISO, 284*f*
    operation of, 283*f*
release bearing, 1143, 1145*f*, 1151–1153, 1152*f*, 1163
release bearing free travel, 1169–1171, 1189
    angle spring clutch adjustment
        with locking tang, 1170, 1170*f*
        with quick-adjust device, 7, 7*f*
    LIPE/Haldex adjustment, 1171
release (caging) bolts, 906, 908, 909*f*, 921
release fork (yoke), 1152, 1153, 1153*f*, 1163, 1169
    free play, 1171–1172
reliable pressure gauge set, 1741–1742
reluctance, 233, 233*f*, 569
reluctor, 1282, 1295
reluctor wheel, 1044, 1063
remolding tires. *See* retreading tires
remote power modules, 607, 608*f*, 609
remote sensing, 447, 448*f*, 457
remote shift linkage, 1271, 1295
    inspect and replacement of, 1271
removable carrier type, 1578, 1601
repair order, 49–50, 59, 61–62, 65
repulsion cause electrons, forces of, 213*f*
rescue vehicles, 12

reserve capacity, 340–341, 347
reserve tube, hydraulic shock absorbers, 800
reservoir safety valve, 934, 935f
reservoirs, 1797, 1797f
resettable fuse, 266–267
residual check valve. *See* residual pressure valve
residual magnetism, 435, 457
residual pressure valve, 1076, 1099
resilient mounting systems, 775–776
resilient mounts, 775, 789
resist bending moment (RBM), 767, 768, 789
resistance, 218, 219, 250, 254f, 258, 267, 309
  relationship between amperage and, 257
  of sending unit, 522, 523f
resistance—ohmmeters, measuring, 312–314, 312f–314f
resistive circuits, 262
resistive ground, 263f
resistive ground connections, 262
  identifying, 269
resistive sensors, 559, 561, 563
resistive touch screens, 525–526, 526f, 529
resistive type gauges, 521
resistors, 212, 223, 279–282, 279f, 284f
  carbon, 279, 280, 280f
  fixed, 279–280, 280f
  resistance value of, 278
  stepped, 281, 281f
  surface mount, 280f
  variable, 281–282
  wire-wound (power), 279
resolver, 1659, 1665
resonance, 1149, 1163
resonant frequency, 1149, 1163
respirator, 93, 93f, 103
restrictor cans, 811, 811f, 812
retarder module, 1465
retarders, 945–946, 1497–1498, 1497f, 1499f, 1527
retreading tires, 675, 677–678, 677f–678f, 677t–678t, 701
retrofit kit, 1742, 1743f, 1765
return filter, 1797
return on investment (ROI), 1846, 1883
return springs, 1079
reverse bias, 291, 301
reverse high range, 1512, 1514f
reverse hydraulic operation, automatic downshifting, 1415
reverse idler shaft, 1214, 1257
reverse low range, 1512, 1513f
reverse overdrive, 1376–1377, 1376f, 1377f, 1378, 1389
reverse range
  ATEC/CEC, 1457, 1459f
  hydraulic flow in, 1484f
  power flows in, 1471
reverse reduction, 1376, 1376f, 1389
reversible sleeve air bellows, 813, 814f
reversing sleeve (rolling lobe) pistons, 813, 837
rheostats, 281, 281f, 301, 516f, 521f, 561–563, 562f, 593
rib-type treads, 682
ribbed tires, 675
right-hand camshafts, 894, 895f, 921
rigid disc styles, 1148, 1148f
rigid fifth wheel, 1113–1114, 1114f, 1133
rigid lines, 1799–1801
rim diameter, 707, 725
rim flange, 707, 725
rim width, 707, 725
rims
  fundamentals of, 707–709
  of wheel, 707f
ring gears, 396, 406, 408f, 420–421, 1197, 1372, 1373f, 1389, 1575, 1601
ring network, 600
ring seals, 181, 182, 182f
rippled plates, 1125
river wear, 687
riveting tools, 135–136
RMX10-165-C2S002, nomenclature for Meritor, 1326t
road alligators, 677, 677f
road feel, 842, 852, 876
road grade, 7f
road train, 22f
Roadranger valve, 1240–1241, 1240f, 1243, 1257, 1275–1277, 1276f
roadside service calls, ranking of reasons for, 662t
rod, 1818, 1833
ROI. *See* return on investment
roll bar, 129f
roll stability control (RSC), 1055–1056, 1063
roller power steering pump, 860, 861f
roller-type one-way clutches, 1350, 1351f, 1379–1380, 1380f
rollers, 891, 891f
rolling circumference, 669, 701
rolling lobe piston, 837
rolling resistances, 664, 701
  by tire position, 664f
ROM. *See* read only memory
Roman chariots, 794, 794f
root, 1195, 1207, 1622, 1624f, 1639. *See also* fillet radius
root diameter, 1195, 1207
Rosin-core solder wire, 470
rotary actuators, 1817
rotary-control valve, 850
rotary flow, 1347, 1350f, 1367
  and vortex flow, 1346–1349, 1347f, 1348f
rotary piston compressors, 1705–1706, 1706f, 1727
rotary valve, 849, 850, 850f, 876
  alignments on, 850, 852f
  cross section of, 850, 851f
  hydraulic circuits, 852, 853f
  and torsion bar, 852, 853f
rotary vane power steering pump, 860, 861f
rotating clutch module, 1465, 1465f, 1466
rotating clutches, 1378, 1389, 1397. *See also* hydraulic clutch
rotating hydraulic clutches, 1372–1373
rotating-plate mechanism, 1821
rotating worm wheel, 1590
roto-chambers, 908, 909, 910f, 921
rotor surface inspection, 1029
rotors, 433–436, 435f, 454–455, 890, 891, 1070, 1099, 1497–1498, 1811
routes, evacuation, 71, 71f
routine inspection of hybrid drive system, 1651
RSC. *See* roll stability control
RTOV. *See* receiver tank outlet valve
RTV silicone, 184
rubber axle stops, 799f
rubber bushings, 809, 809f, 812
rubber cushions, 24, 1537
rubber dust, 1556
rubber insulator block, 807
rubber piston cup, 1077
rubber spring equalizing beam suspensions, 808, 808f, 810–811, 811f
rubber springs, 798, 810–811, 811f, 837
"rule of thumb" guideline, 258
run-out, 115
Rzeppa, Alfred, 1550
Rzeppa joint, 1550, 1550f, 1567

S

S-cam, 892, 921
  brackets, 894–895, 895f, 896f
  brake foundation system, 892f, 893f
S-series certification, 39
S-shaped camshaft, 892
SA. *See* source address
SAE. *See* Society of Automotive Engineers
SAE 50 weight engine oil, 1262
SAE-compliant electronic leak detector, uses of, 1744
SAE grade 8 bolts, 1120
SAE J2497, 618–619
SAE J-560 standard, 1049, 1060, 1063
SAE J1128 standard, 464–465, 485
SAE specification for dimension, 1180f
SAE Type I circuit, 297
SAE Type II circuit, 297
safe attitude, 95–96
safe-edge files, 130
safe working load (SWL), 185, 199
safety, 69–102. *See also* first aid; personal protective equipment (PPE)
  equipment, 74–75
  glasses, 94, 94f

goggles, 95, 95*f*
hazardous materials. *See* hazardous materials
inspections for shop, 89
overview, 70–73, 71*f*
standard measures, 74
air quality, 75–76, 76*f*
electrical safety, 76–77, 76*f*, 77*f*
extinguishing fires, 78–80, 79*f*
eyewash stations and emergency showers, 80, 80*f*
preventing fires, 77–78
safety equipment, 74–75
shop layout, 77
signs, 74, 74*f*
use of electronic engine, 536–537
safety/circuit protection devices, 250
safety data sheets (SDS), 80, 81*f*–87*f*, 103
identifying information on, 87
safety enhancement systems, 1055–1060
safety locks, 192
safety relief valve, 933–934, 964
safety switches circuit, 409, 410*f*
sag, 778, 778*f*, 789
SAI. *See* steering axis inclination angle
sand or bead blasters, 141, 159
SAS. *See* steering angle sensors
saturated temperature, 1719
scaffolding, 1650, 1651*f*
scalds, 100, 100*f*
scan tools, 137, 138, 1359
scanners, 137, 138
electronic service tools, 321–322
additional functions, 323
code readers, 323
data link adapters, 323, 323*f*
SAE requirements for OBD scan tools, 322
scheduled lock-up, 1411, 1417
schematic diagram, 474, 475*f*, 485
Deutsche institute norm (DIN) Diagrams, 474–481
Valley Forge diagrams, 481–483
school buses, 12, 430
with rear engine, 12*f*
Schrader valve (circled), governor with, 1008*f*
SCR. *See* selective catalyst reduction
scratches, 1559
screw extractors, 132, 159
screw-in valve stems, 689
replacement of, 692
screwdrivers, 126–127, 126*f*, 164
screws, 164–165, 164*f*, 165*f*, 199
scrub angle, 744, 758
scrub radius, 744–745, 758
SDS. *See* safety data sheets
seal driver, 723*f*
sealant detector, 1741, 1741*f*
sealants, adhesives and, 183–184
sealed lead–acid (SLA) battery, 334, 347
sealed release bearings, 1169, 1189
seamless, 1799, 1833
second clutch, ATEC/CEC, 1457
second-degree burns, 100, 100*f*, 103
second driveshaft, 1546
second gear band, 1382
second planetary ring gear, 1515–1519
second wrench, 1754
secondary angles, 737
secondary battery, 330, 330*f*, 347
secondary circuit systems, 928, 929*f*, 964
secondary couple vibrations, 1551, 1567
secondary modulation, 1473, 1527
secondary piston, 1076, 1099
secondary reservoir, 933, 964
secondary safety latch, 1118, 1133
secondary sources, 47, 47*f*, 65
secondary winding, 238, 245
"secondary," brake shoe. *See* trailing shoes
section break, 1633, 1639
section change, 784, 789
section height, 669, 701
section modulus (SM), 767, 789
section width, 669, 701
sector shaft of steering gear, 854, 855*f*
secure D-shackles, 188, 188*f*
selective catalyst reduction (SCR) systems, 574, 1854
monitor, 641
self-adjusting clutches, 1146, 1146*f*, 1163, 1172
installing, 1186
self-dampening, 799, 802, 837
self-diagnostic, 1337
self-diagnostic capability, 1301
self-diagnostic mode and retrieving codes, 1330
self-diagnostic trouble codes, 1427
self-energization, 893, 893*f*, 921, 1071
self-exciting alternators, 436, 447*f*, 457
self-induction, 238, 239*f*, 240*f*
self-locking nut, 167*f*
self-powered electrical probe, 308*f*
self-powered LED test lights, 308
self-powered refrigeration units, 1773, 1783
cool truck body, 1772*f*
for semi trailer, 1774*f*
for straight truck, 1774*f*
self-powered test light, 307–308, 308*f*
self-powered voltmeters, 308
self-servo effect, 1072
self-steering axle, 736, 736*f*, 1572, 1573*f*, 1601
self-tapping screw, 164, 165*f*, 199
semi-elliptical spring pack, 804
semi-floating axle shafts, 1597, 1601
semi-floating bearing, 716, 725
semi-metallic linings, 896, 921
semi-oscillating fifth wheels, 1113, 1113*f*, 1133
semi-trailers, 21, 30, 1106, 1107*f*, 1133
tractor using fifth wheel, 1104*f*
semiconductors, 210, 210*t*, 220–221, 223, 289
sending units, 519–522
and gauges, 521–522
resistance of, 522, 523*f*
with two-coil gauges, 522*f*
sensible heat, 1698, 1727
sensing, 447, 457
sensitive microelectronic circuits, 228
Sensor Input Voltage High, 261
Sensor Input Voltage Low, 261
sensor signal circuits, 262*f*
sensor wheel, 570
sensors, 1056, 1503
active *vs.* passive, 558–559
air gap, 1060
ammonia, 574
in directional stability control system, 1058*t*
dual- and multiple-path throttle position, 565–566
fault detection principles
circuit monitoring— voltage drop measurement, 580
comprehensive component monitor, 579–580
low- and high-side driver faults, 588
pull-up resistors, 580
regulated reference voltage (Vref), 583
smart-diagnosable switches, 580–582
three-wire sensor circuit monitoring, 585–587
Hall effect, 570–571
high- and low-bias, 587
idle validation switches and throttle position, 565
introduction, 558
maintenance of, 588–590
mass airflow, 575
NO_x sensors, 574
and on-board diagnostics, 577–579
output circuits, 575
oxygen, 571, 573, 573*f*
piezoresistive, 566–567, 567*f*, 568*f*
and position calculations, 575–577
pressure, 566–569
reduction in number of, 609
resistive, 559, 561, 563
soot sensors, 575
switches as, 560–561
three-wire, 563–566
two-wire pull-up circuit monitoring, 583–585
voltage generators, 569–570
SensoTop, 1521, 1527
separator plates, 336, 1220, 1411–1412, 1417
sequencing valves, 1819
sequentially, 1816, 1833
serial communication, 612–615, 623

serial data, 601, 613*f*, 623
digital signals, 542–543, 542*f*
series chargers, 382
series, charging battery banks, 382–383
series circuits, 252–253
connecting batteries in, 254*f*
observations for, 253*f*
series drive, 1645, 1646*f*, 1665
comparing with parallel systems, 1648, 1648*t*
series-parallel Allison EP system, configuration of, 1671, 1672*f*
series-parallel circuits. *See* combination circuits
series-parallel drive, 1645, 1647*f*, 1665, 1670
comparison of, 1648, 1648*t*
Series Parallel Electrical Systems, 412
series starter motor, 399–401, 400*f*
current flow, 400
operational characteristics, 400–401
series-type hybrid drives. *See also* hybrid drive systems
BAE HybriDrive Propulsion Systems, 1652–1653, 1652*f*, 1653*t*, 1654*f*
HybriDrive Series Propulsion System Overview, 1653
major system components of, 1654, 1655*f*
AC traction generator (ACTG), 1656, 1657*f*
AC traction motor (ACTM), 1657–1659, 1658*f*–1659*f*
battery monitoring system, 1660–1661, 1661*t*
brake pressure sensor, 1662, 1662*f*
current inverters, 1661, 1661*f*
energy storage system (ESS), 1659–1660, 1660*f*
engine test switch, 1663
Intuitive Diagnostic System (IDS), 1661–1662
propulsion control system module, 1654–1656, 1655*f*–1656*f*
regeneration disable switch, 1662
state of ESS charge, 1660, 1661*f*
unique system inputs, 1662
series-wound motors, 399, 400
serpentine belt, 445
failure conditions for, 450*f*
replacing, 450
serpentine *vs.* manifold style condenser, construction of, 1707, 1707*f*
serrated edge shake-proof washers, 167, 199
service brake, 1088, 1089*f*
service brake chamber pressure *vs.* brake valve delivery pressure, 953, 953*f*
service brake priority, 960, 961*f*, 964
service campaign and recall, 57–58, 65
service chamber, 905, 906*f*, 908*f*
service history, 62, 62*f*, 65
service information programs, 56–57
service manual, 56, 65
service reservoir, 933, 964
service resources. *See* vehicle resources
service technicians of vehicle, 37–38
service valve, operation of, 1780, 1780*f*
servicing equipment
brake lathes, 139*f*
drum disc lathe, 139, 139*f*
engine scanner, 138
on-vehicle wheel balancer, 138, 139*f*
pneumatic tire changer, 138, 139*f*
wheel alignment machine, 138, 138*f*
servo action, 1072, 1099
servo piston, 1379, 1379*f*
servo system, 1080–1081, 1080*f*, 1822, 1833
set-point test, 451
setback, 746, 758
severe-duty service, 1263, 1295
severe service operating conditions, 1851, 1883
SG. *See* specific gravity
SGR-type wire, 465
shackles, 188
shaft mass, and critical speed, 1539–1540, 1539*f*
shaft runout, 1552, 1554*f*
shaft slope measurements, 1546
shaft speed sensors, 1307–1308
shaft speeds, U-joint operating angles and, 1543, 1543*t*
shaft spline for wear, 1180, 1180*f*
shear stresses, 170
shedding, 375, 389
Sheppard model steering box, pitman arm puller for, 854, 855*f*
shift by wire, 1300, 1337
shift cables, 1437, 1441
shift controls, 1215–1216, 1215*f*–1216*f*, 1448–1449, 1449*f*
shift cover, 1247, 1257
shift finger, 1215, 1215*f*, 1257
shift forks, 1215, 1216*f*, 1257
shift gates, 1215, 1215*f*, 1257
shift lever, 1176, 1189, 1215, 1215*f*, 1257
shift linkage and neutral safety switch, 1437–1439
shift logic, 1454–1459, 1527
ATEC/CEC neutral, 1456
shift modulator valve, 1407, 1417
shift pattern generator (SPG), 1446
shift point, 1430, 1441
shift point control, automatic downshifting, 1415, 1415*f*
shift rail gates, 1309, 1309*f*
shift rail interlock, 1216–1217, 1216*f*
shift rail nut, 1309, 1309*f*
shift relay valves, 1407, 1409*f*, 1417
in ATEC/CEC, 1453–1454
shift selectors, 1499–1504
shift sequence, 1474
shift signal valves, 1407–1408, 1409*f*, 1417
shift solenoid 1 (SS1), 1488, 1527
shift tower, 1176, 1189, 1215, 1257
shifting strategies, 1314
shim pack thickness
for drive axle with integral pinion support, 1620–1621
for drive axle with removable pinion cage, 1620
shimmy, steering-related problems, 865*t*
shipping blocks, 1178, 1189
shipping bolts, 1178, 1189
shock, 99, 103
shock absorber valves, 800, 801*f*
shock absorbers, 741, 741*f*, 797, 799, 837
hydraulic, 799–801, 800*f*, 801*f*
inspection and maintenance, 827, 829
shock bracket, 806, 837
shock load failures, 1633, 1633*f*, 1639
shock loads, 1272*f*, 1554, 1555*f*
failures, 1293
shoe brake systems, 919*f*
shop
layout, 77
policies and procedures, 72
portable lights, 76–77, 77*f*
safety inspections, 89
shop manual, 56, 56*f*
shop rules, for PM and PMI, 1856
shop safety inspection forms, 50
shop setup for PM and PMI functionality, 1856
short circuits, 142–143, 159, 260–261, 261*f*, 438*f*
short-range wireless technology, 536
shorted diode, 439
shunt starter motor, 399, 400*f*
shunt truck, 1105, 1106*f*, 1133
shunts, 315, 325
shutoff valve, 868
SI series Delco alternators, 442
SID. *See* system identifier
side bearing bore, 1612
side bearing cap, 1623, 1639
side bearing preload, setting, 1621–1623
side curtains, 11*f*
side gears, 1579, 1601
sidesway, 778, 778*f*, 789
signal off time *vs.* on time, 547
signal word, 74, 74*f*
signs, 74, 74*f*
silicon, 289
silicon diodes, 437
silicone sealants, 184, 184*f*
silver alloy, 345
simple circuit control device, 276–289
capacitors. *See* capacitors
complex electronic controls
diodes, 289–294
electronic *vs.* electrical control, 289
integrated circuits, 298–299

transistors, 294–298
relays, 282–286, 283*f*, 284*f*
resistors. *See* resistors
solenoids, 286–287, 286*f*
switches, 276–279, 276*f*, 278*f*
assorted, 278*t*
smart, 277–279, 280*f*
types of, 276–277, 278*f*
simple circuits, 252
simple fracture, 99, 103
simple machines, 1197, 1207
simplex wedge brake system, 919, 919*f*
Simpson gear set, 1380–1381, 1381*f*, 1382–1383, 1382*f*–1383*f*, 1382*t*, 1389, 1399
first gear (low) in, 1383–1384, 1384*f*
neutral or park in, 1383
reverse in, 1385, 1387*f*
second gear in, 1385, 1385*f*
third gear (high or direct) in, 1385, 1386*f*
Simpson, Howard, 1380–1381
sine wave, 217, 223
single-acting cylinder, 1816–1817, 1816*f*, 1818*f*
single-axle drive line, 1545
single-channel ABS, 1088, 1089*f*
single-channel graphing meter, 320
single channel modulator, 1047*f*
single countershaft transmissions, 1221, 1221*f*, 1257
overdrive shifting, 1221–1222, 1222*f*
power flows, 1222–1227
fifth gear, 1224, 1226, 1226*f*
first gear, 1224, 1224*f*
five-speed transmission, 1222, 1223*f*
fourth gear, 1224, 1226*f*
information plate from Eaton Fuller transmission, 1227, 1227*f*
reverse, 1223–1224, 1223*f*
second gear, 1224, 1225*f*
third gear, 1224, 1225*f*
single-cylinder compressor, 931, 932*f*
single-disc clutch, 17″ (43.2 cm), 1327*f*
single drive axle, 807, 807*f*
single engine position sensor, 576–577
single flare, 133, 134*f*, 159
single-leading-shoe drum brake (SLS), 1071
and trailing-shoe configuration, 1071, 1072*f*
single-loop starter motor and electromagnetic fields, 405*f*
single park brake valve, 955*f*
single phase, 438*f*
single pole double throw (SPDT) switch, 276, 277*t*
single pole single throw (SPST) switch, 276, 277*t*, 560
single service brake chamber, 906, 907*f*
single steering box systems, 855
sintered bronze air filter, 1266, 1266*f*
six sensors/four modulators (6S/4M), 1051*f*
six sensors/six modulators (6S/6M), 1052*f*
six-speed FO-6406B-DM3, nomenclature for, 1315*t*
skew setback, 746, 758
skiving, 1805, 1833
SLA battery. *See* sealed lead–acid battery
slack adjusters, 909–915, 911*f*, 921
automatic slack adjusters, 911–915
manual slack adjusters, 911, 914*f*
slack brakes, 974
slave air valve, 1244
slave cylinder, 1156, 1163
slave module, 601
sleep mode, 252
SLI batteries
vs. deep cycle battery, 336–337, 336*f*
uses thinner plates, 336, 337*f*
slider mechanism, 1121, 1133
fifth wheel, 1128
sliding-bridge jacks, 189
sliding clutch, 1214, 1214*f*, 1217, 1218*f*, 1257, 1596. *See also* constant-mesh collar shift transmissions
sliding collar, 1214, 1214*f*, 1257. *See also* constant-mesh collar shift transmissions
sliding gear transmissions, 1214, 1217, 1257
sliding mechanism, 845
sliding-plate mechanism, 1821
sliding T-handle, 123, 123*f*, 159
slings, 187–188
slip hazards, 96
slip joint, 1536, 1537*f*, 1567
unscrew before separation of, 1560, 1561*f*
slip rings, alternator components, 433–434
slip yokes, 846, 1176, 1189
slipper plates, 1813
slippery surface, wheel on, 1581*f*
slipping belts, 1738
slipping clutches, 1428
slow adaptive mode, 1473, 1527
slow chargers, 143, 159
SLS. *See* single-leading-shoe drum brake
SM. *See* section modulus
small gauge wire, 447
small hole gauge. *See* split ball gauge
smart chargers, 143, 159, 357, 357*f*, 367
smart-diagnosable switches, 580–582
smart electrification, 1671, 1687
smart mode operation, PLC, 619–621
smarter engines, 534
smoke controls, 1358, 1367
smoothing capacitor, 288, 288*f*
snap ring pliers, 124*f*, 125, 157
snapshot, 1307, 1337
sniffer, 1742, 1743*f*
snub braking, 951, 964
snubber, 1109, 1110*f*, 1133
SOC. *See* state of charge
Society of Automotive Engineers (SAE), 46, 492*f*, 579, 580*t*, 584, 584*f*, 607, 1802*t*
failure mode identifier (FMI), 579, 580*t*, 584, 584*f*
standards of, 501
sockets, 109, 120, 122–123, 159
construction of, 122*f*
soft brakes, 974
soft-dampened clutches, 1149–1150, 1163
with travel damper, 1150*f*
soft-faced hammers, 127
soft iron laminated core, 233*f*
soft tire tread, 682
software-based diagnostics, 538
software-based record keeping, 1853–1854
software control of electrical system, 605–606, 605*f*
software-controlled fuses, 267
solar cells, 230, 230*f*
soldering wires, 470
solenoid control relay, 409–411
solenoid-operated shift mechanism, 406
solenoids, 286–287, 286*f*, 406, 407*f*, 421, 1452–1454, 1454*f*, 1822, 1833
contact disc, 414*f*
control, 1472–1476
control relay, 409–411
fluid flows, 1477–1484, 1484*t*
inspecting and testing relays and, 419–421
plunger, 408*f*
range verification and ratio tests, 1474–1476
shift control logic, 1473–1474
and shift mechanism, 406
shift sequence, 1474
types of, 1452, 1453*f*, 1472, 1473*f*
winding, testing of, 420
solid I-beam, 731, 731*f*, 758
solid I-beam leaf spring suspension, 805, 805*f*
solid mount equalizing beam suspensions, 809–810, 810*f*
SOLO self-adjusting clutch, 1313*f*
solvent, 150, 159
solvent tanks, 140–141, 159
soot sensors, 575
sound deadeners, 1535
soundproof rooms, safety equipment, 74–75
source address (SA), 648, 655
south pole, 437
space, nonverbal message, 53
spacer, 1616, 1616*f*
spade fuses, 264
spade-type fuses, 264
spalling, 1552, 1554, 1554*f*
SPDT. *See* single pole double throw switch
speaking, effective, 42–45

specialty technicians, 39
of vehicle, 39
specific gravity (SG), 337, 338*t*
of battery, 378*f*
of electrolyte, 376
specific heat, 1699, 1727
speed, 1796
speed brace, 123, 124*f*, 159
speed gears, 1214, 1257
speed increase, 1377–1378
speed nut, 167, 167*f*, 199
speed reduction, 1377
speed sensors, 237
speeder handle, 123
speeding system, 537
speedometer adapter, 1591
speedometers, 522–524
electronic compasses, 524
tachographs, 524
tachometers and odometers, 523–524
SPG. *See* shift pattern generator
Spicer 10 series, 1534, 1534*t*
Spicer Anglemaster tool, 1546
Spicer, Clarence, 1532
Spicer Life series driveshaft
extended lubrication intervals for, 1557, 1558*t*
slip yokes, 1536
spider gears, 1579, 1580*f*, 1581*f*, 1601
rotation of, 1594
spigot bearing, 1615, 1618, 1639
spillage risks, 78
spindle washers, 168, 168*f*
spindles, 916–917, 1574
spinout, 1601, 1636, 1636*f*
preventing inter-axle differential, 1596–1597
spiral bevel gearing, 1203, 1204*f*, 1207
spiral bevel gears, 1575, 1575*f*, 1576, 1601
spiral cell Optima battery of AGM-type battery, 345*f*
spiral-wound cell battery, 358, 358*f*, 367
splash lubrication, 1598
splicing frames, 782–784
spline for wear, 1180, 1180*f*
splined hub, 1149, 1149*f*
split ball gauge (small hole gauge), 112, 113, 159
split braking systems, 1077–1078, 1077*f*–1078*f*
split charge relays, 360, 367
split circuit braking system, 1071
split guide ring, 1345, 1345*f*, 1346*f*, 1367
split-mode operation, 1683
split pins, 175–176, 175*f*, 501
splitter gears, 1235
splitter shift control, 1245–1247, 1245*f*–1249*f*
splitter shift cylinder, 1254, 1257
SPN. *See* suspect parameter number
spool-type directional control valves, 1822, 1822*f*
spool-type mechanism, 1821
spool valves, 849, 850*f*, 876, 1402, 1404, 1404*f*, 1417
sprag-type one-way clutches, 1350, 1351*f*, 1379–1380, 1380*f*
sprain, 99, 103
spray-wash cabinets, 140, 159
spreader bar, 194, 195
spring brake chamber, 906, 906*f*, 908*f*
and wheel cylinder, operation of, 1087, 1087*f*
spring brake priority, 960, 961*f*, 964
spring brake relay valve, 956, 956*f*, 965
spring brakes, 904, 921, 972
servicing, 986–988
spring brakes actuator, 989–990
spring-loaded accumulators, 1824, 1826, 1826*f*
spring-loaded torsional damper hub, 1355
spring pack, 798, 837
spring parking brakes, 1075, 1075*f*, 1086
spring rate, 797–798, 797*f*, 837
spring-tab bearing cap retainers, 1538, 1538*f*
spring (lock) washer, 167, 199
springs, 795, 798–799, 1822
sprung weight, 795, 796, 796*f*, 837
SPST switch. *See* single pole single throw switch
spur-cut gears, 1373
spur gears, 1201–1202, 1202*f*
spur-type gears, 1270
SPX Genisys bi-directional scanner, 322*f*
square drive, 123, 123*f*
square file, 130, 130*f*, 159
square threads, 165, 199
squeeze, 1169, 1170, 1189
SRS. *See* supplemental restraint system
SS1. *See* shift solenoid 1
stability, vehicle, 1055–1060
stabilizer bars, 813, 837
stainless steel flex line, 932
stainless steels, 151, 151*f*, 1799, 1833
stall speed, 1349, 1367
stall test, 1356–1357
interpreting results, 1358–1359
performing on engine with smoke controls, 1358
stand-by mode, 1774, 1783
standard hub, 716–719, 717*f*, 725
comparison of preset hub and, 717*t*
standard (imperial) system, 168, 169*f*, 198
standard thread shapes, 166*f*
standard tire identification markings, 669, 670*f*, 671
standard transmission servicing, 1261–1295
failure analysis of, 1289, 1291
abuse failures, 1293
regular wear or maintenance failures, 1291–1293
fundamentals of, 1262–1265, 1263*f*, 1264*t*, 1265*f*
introduction of, 1262
preventative maintenance of, 1265–1268, 1266*f*
problems troubleshooting, 1268
air system problems, 1274–1277, 1275*f*, 1276*f*
gear slip out, 1273–1274, 1273*f*, 1274*f*
hard shifting, 1271–1273, 1272*f*
oil leaks, 1268, 1269
transmission noise, 1268, 1270, 1270*f*
vibration, 1270, 1271*f*
repair and maintenance of, 1277
air system, inspection of, 1278, 1279
auxiliary section, removing and disassemble, 1282, 1284–1285
general precautions and procedures, 1277
input shaft, replacement of, 1279–1282
overhauling range synchronizer, 1286
power take-off, inspection of, 1279, 1280
rear seals, replacement of, 1282, 1283
reassembling and timing auxiliary section, 1287–1288
reinstallation of auxiliary section, 1289–1291, 1291*t*
transmission oil cooler and filter, inspection of, 1277–1278
standard transmissions, 1211–1257, 1342, 1351
air control, auxiliary sections. *See* air control systems
auxiliary sections. *See* auxiliary sections
fundamentals of, 1212–1213, 1213*f*
shift controls, 1215–1216, 1215*f*–1216*f*
shift rail interlock, 1216–1217, 1216*f*
transmission shafts, 1213–1214, 1213*f*–1214*f*
introduction of, 1212, 1212*f*
multiple countershaft and auxiliary transmissions, 1227–1228, 1228*f*
floating main shaft system, 1228–1229, 1228*f*–1229*f*
main box power flows, 1229–1231, 1230*f*–1231*f*
multiple countershaft transmission power flows, 1229, 1229*f*
power take-off device (PTO), 1252–1253, 1253*f*
single countershaft transmissions. *See* single countershaft transmissions
transfer case, 1251–1252, 1251*f*

with power take-off option, 1251, 1252*f*
types of, 1217
constant-mesh collar shift transmissions, 1217–1218, 1218*f*
constant-mesh synchronized transmissions. *See* constant-mesh synchronized transmissions
sliding-gear transmissions, 1217
star network interconnections, 600, 600*f*
star wheel-type adjuster, 1073, 1073*f*
start enable relay, 1308, 1337
startability, 14, 30
starter cable voltage loss test, 253
starter draw test, 417
starter housing, 403
starter motor circuit, 253
starter motors, 394–395, 394*f*
classification, 395–398
components of
armatures, 403–406
solenoid and shift mechanism, 406–407
starter drive mechanisms, 407–408
starter housing and field coils, 403
control circuit, 410*f*
ADLO lockout, 412
inspecting and testing, 419, 420
overcrank protection, 411
series parallel electrical systems, 412
solenoid control relay, 409–411
voltage drop, 418–419
voltage-sensing relay, 412, 413*f*
current draw testing, 417–418
direct drive, 396, 396*f*, 397
electrical circuit of, 418–419
faults, 415
fields, 403*f*
low-voltage burn-out, 401–402
overhauling, 421–423
planetary gear reduction drive, 397–398, 397*f*
reduction gear drive, 396, 397, 397*f*
ring gear/flex plate, 420–422
rotation, 423
series. *See* series starter motor
starter draw, 418
tests, 415–420
starter relay bypass test, 419
starting, lighting, and ignition (SLI) batteries, 332, 334, 347, 358, 360
starting systems
complaint, 417
diagnosis, 416*t*
fundamentals of
DC motor principles, 398–399
demands on, 395
starter motor classification, 395–398
testing
electrical and mechanical problems, difference between, 414–415
starter motor tests, 415–420
state of charge (SOC), 337, 364, 376–378, 389, 1737, 1765
performing a battery, 379
specific gravity and voltage reading, 378*t*
static electricity, 228
static radius, 669, 701
stationary clutch, 1379, 1379*f*, 1389, 1466, 1516
stator, 434, 436–437, 436*f*, 1345–1346, 1346*f*, 1347*f*, 1367
short and open circuit, 438*f*
testing, 437
windings, 436
stator inner hub, 1348, 1367
stator support shaft, 1346, 1346*f*, 1367, 1402, 1402*f*
steel, 151
steel-backed bronze (bimetal) bushings, 733
steel gauges, 116
steel hammer, 127, 128*f*
steel ruler, 110, 110*f*, 159
steel tubing, 1535, 1802
steer axle steering stops, 864, 866*f*
steering angle sensors (SAS), 843, 872, 877, 1060
steering arms, 732, 758, 856, 857*f*, 877
steering axis inclination angle (SAI), 743, 758
steering axles, 731–734, 731*f*, 758, 1572, 1572*f*, 1573–1574, 1601
steering box, 1573, 1573*f*
steering columns, 845–846, 846*f*, 877
steering complaints, 863–864, 865*f*
steering components, 1875, 1877–1879
engine-off engine compartment inspection, conducting, 1877
steering gears, 842, 846–847, 877
hydraulic assist to, 849, 850*f*
manual, 846
manual recirculating-ball steering gears, 848, 849*f*
power, 847
power recirculating-ball steering gears, 849, 849*f*, 850*f*
rotary valve, 850, 851*f*, 852, 852*f*, 853*f*
torsion rod, 852–853, 853*f*
rack-and-pinion steering systems, 853–854, 854*f*
sector shaft of, 854
steering ratio, 847–848, 847*f*
steering geometry, 745–746, 758
steering knuckles, 732, 732*f*, 759, 845, 856–857, 877, 1573
steering linkage, 854–856, 877
drag link, 854–855
kingpins, 856, 857*f*
pitman (drop) arm, 854, 854*f*, 855*f*
steering arms, 856, 857*f*
tie-rod ends, 855–856, 855*f*, 856*f*
steering pull, 853
steering ratio, 847–848, 847*f*, 877
steering-related problems, 864, 865*t*
steering rotary valve, 850, 851*f*
steering shafts, 845–846, 846*f*, 877
steering stops, 734–735, 759, 877
steer axle, 864, 866*f*
steering systems, 842, 877
classifications, 843–844, 843*f*, 844*f*
components of, 844–845
steering columns and shafts, 845–846, 846*f*
steering gears. *See* steering gears
steering knuckle, 856–857
steering linkage, 854–856
steering wheels, 845, 845*f*
diagram of, 843, 844*f*
fundamentals of, 842–843
maintenance and service, 863
centering the steering gear, 864, 866
over center adjustment, 866–867, 867*f*
steer axle steering stops, 864, 866*f*
steering complaints, 863–864, 865*f*
worm gear preload adjustment, 866
power. *See* power steering systems, hydraulic components of
steering wheel-mounted SRS, 872
steering wheel spokes, 845, 845*f*
steering wheels, 845, 845*f*
Stemco® nut system, 719
step-down transformer, 238, 245
step-up transformer, 238, 245
stepped resistors, 281, 281*f*
stepper motor gauges, 517–518, 520*f*
stepper starter motor, 399
sticker, air-conditioning identification, 1736*f*
stop screw, in power piston, 849, 849*f*
stopping distance requirements, 892–893, 892*t*
storing refrigerant, 1748
straddle mount pinion, 1615, 1639
straight edges, 116, 159
straight grinder, 119, 159
straight truck, 8, 8*f*
maximum bending moment, 768*f*
straight wire conductor, 238
strain, 99–100, 103
strain gauge wires, 566, 566*f*
strength, driveshaft systems, 1533
stress concentration, 766, 789
stress riser, 766, 789
stress testing, 437
stresses, frame, 766
caused by frame attachments, 776–777, 776*f*
stringers, 1633, 1639

stripping wires, cutting and, 469
stroke, 1823, 1833
stroke detector
  direct air booster and, operation of, 1084, 1085*f*
  piston, 1084, 1086, 1086*f*
stroke sensing ASAs, 911, 913*f*, 921
stroke-sensing slacks, 1025–1026
stud, 168, 168*f*, 199
stud-piloted disc wheel, 713–714, 713*f*, 714*f*, 725
sub-modulation, 1473, 1527
substantial energy, lost to vehicle braking, 1644, 1645*f*
suction filter, 1797
suction service valves, 1780, 1780*f*
sulfation (three-minute charge) test, 343, 344, 344*f*, 347, 374–375
sulfuric acid, 144, 147, 159, 337
sun gear, 1372, 1373*f*, 1389, 1587, 1588*f*
sun gear shaft, 1395, 1399, 1417
super single tires, 20*f*, 672, 672*f*, 701
Super Ten main shaft, 1303, 1303*f*
Super Ten Top Two shift pattern, 1302, 1302*f*
Super Ten transmission, 1302, 1303
superficial burns. *See* first-degree burns
superheat, 1710, 1715, 1727
supplemental additives, 1427, 1427*f*, 1441
supplemental restraint system (SRS), 513–514
  air bag, steering wheel with, 845, 845*f*
  removing and replacing, 872–873
supply reservoir, 933, 965. *See also* service reservoir
supporting statement, 42, 65
SureShift, 1337
SureShift line of transmissions, 1304
surface fatigue, 1634
surface mount resistors, 280*f*
suspect parameter number (SPN), 648, 649, 649*f*, 650*f*, 650*t*, 655
suspension, inspecting, 1865
suspension ride height, inspecting, 1865
suspension systems
  air spring, 813, 813*f*
    combination leaf/air spring, 814–815, 815*f*, 816*f*
    construction, 813–814, 814*f*, 815*f*
    equalizing beam suspensions, 816–817,
  components of, 798
    axle stops/jounce blocks, 799, 799*f*
    shock absorbers, 799–802
    springs, 798–799
    torque rods, 799, 799*f*
  electronically controlled air suspension systems, 817–818, 818*f*, 819*f*
  equalizing beam (walking beam) suspensions, 808–809, 808*f*, 809*f*
    Chalmers rubber spring, 811–812, 811*f*, 812*f*
    leaf spring, 810
    rubber spring, 810–811, 811*f*
    solid mount, 809–810, 810*f*
    types of, 808
  fundamentals of, 794–795
    basic suspension terms, 796–798, 796*f*–798*f*
    functions of, 795–796, 795*f*, 796*f*
  on heavy-duty trucks, types of, 802
  inspection and maintenance, 819
    adjusting and aligning axles, 829, 831–833
    air spring systems, 827, 828
    air suspension system, 830
    equalizer beam suspension systems, 823
    frame hangers, 823
    in-service inspection, 821, 822
    leaf spring systems, 821
    levelling valve replacement, 830
    out-of-service criteria, 820–821, 820*f*
    play measurement, 823
    rear beam suspension components, 823, 826
    rear spring suspension components, 823, 825
    removing and replacing front spring components, 823, 824
    replacing rubber center bushings, 823, 827
    ride height adjustment, 827, 829–831
    shock absorbers, 827, 829
  leaf spring systems, 802
    auxiliary springs, 805, 805*f*
    composite leaf springs, 802–803, 803*f*
    constant-rate leaf spring assemblies, 803, 803*f*
    drive axle leaf spring suspensions, 807, 807*f*, 808*f*
    leaf spring mounting systems, 805–807
    multileaf spring packs, 802, 802*f*, 803*f*
    taper leaf and parabolic leaf springs, 804, 804*f*
    variable-rate/progressive-rate leaf springs, 804, 804*f*
suspension, vehicle, 18
swaged, 771, 789
swaging, 1805, 1833
swash plate, 1811, 1833
swing clearance, 1121, 1133
swing shackle, 807, 837
switch functions, 610*f*
switches, 276–279, 276*f*, 278*f*, 1050–1051
  assorted, 278*t*
  digital signals, 560, 560*f*
  engine test, 1663
  magnetic, 285, 285*f*
  pull-up and pull-down, 560–561
  regeneration disable, 1662
  smart, 277–279, 280*f*
  smart-diagnosable, 580–582
  types of, 276–277, 278*f*
switching type transistor, 547*f*
SWL. *See* safe working load
SXL, 465
symptom-based diagnoses, 1428
synchronized transmission, 1214, 1257
synchronizer, 1214, 1257
  block- or insert-type, 1218–1220, 1219*f*
  disc-and-plate-type, 1220–1221, 1221*f*
  pin-type, 1220, 1220*f*
  plain-type, 1218, 1219*f*
synchronous speed, 1474, 1476, 1527
SynchroSaver, 1250–1251, 1251*f*
Synflex, 928, 930*f*, 965
synthetic-based lubricants, 1262, 1263*f*, 1295
synthetic hydraulic fluids, 1794
synthetic lubricating oils, 150
synthetic slings, 187
system faults, diagnosis of, 698
system identifier (SID), 647, 647*t*, 655
system manager, 1306, 1337
system monitors, 634–636
system pressure testing, 1430
systematic lock-up, 1352, 1367. *See also* programmed lock-up

T

tab washer, 199
tachographs, 524, 529
tachometers, 523–524
tag axles, 16, 735–736, 759, 1572, 1601
tagout, 51–52, 51*f*, 109, 109*f*, 157
tandem axle spinout, 1596*f*
tandem axles, 1045, 1108, 1133
tandem-center position, 1823, 1823*f*
tandem configurations, 16*f*
tandem drive axle, 1608, 1610
tandem drive leaf spring suspensions, 807, 808*f*
tandem drives, 1573, 1592, 1592*f*, 1601
tandem master cylinders, 1076*f*
tandem suspension systems, 808
tanker, 9*f*
tap, 132, 132*f*, 159
tap handle, 132, 132*f*, 159
taper-current chargers, 382, 382*f*, 389
taper keys, 176, 177*f*, 199
taper leaf, 802, 803*f*
taper leaf springs, 804
taper pins, 176, 199
taper tap, 132, 159
tapered device, 1820, 1833
tapered kingpins, 733, 733*f*
tappets, 916, 917
tapping a thread, 164
TC-10-TS, Allison

clutch application chart, 1506*t*
eighth range, 1509, 1511*f*
fifth range, 1509, 1510*f*
first range, 1506, 1507*f*
fourth range, 1506, 1509, 1509*f*
neutral, 1506, 1507*f*
ninth range, 1512, 1512*f*
power flows, 1506–1514
reverse ranges, 1512, 1513*f*, 1514*f*
second range, 1506, 1508*f*
seventh range, 1509, 1511*f*
sixth range, 1509, 1510*f*
tenth range, 1512, 1513*f*
third range, 1506, 1508*f*
TC-Tronic, 1304, 1337
TCC. *See* torque converter clutch; torque converter control
TCM. *See* transmission control module
TCU. *See* transmission control unit
TDC. *See* top dead center
TDM. *See* time division multiplexing
technical assistance services, 48
technical service bulletin (TSB), 45–46, 57, 65
technology, battery, 334
teeth, 1817, 1833
telematics technology, 536, 536*f*–537*f*, 553, 617*f*, 642, 655
telephone skills, 44
telescoping cylinders, 1816–1817, 1817*f*, 1833
telescoping gauges, 112, 113*f*, 159
temperature, 319
charging system set point, 444
concept of, 1700–1703
temperature sending units, 521
temperature-sensing bulb, 1781
temperature-sensitive switches, 277
temperature-sensitive variable resistor, 282, 282*f*
Tempilstick™, 785, 785*f*
temporary barriers, safety equipment, 75
ten-speed RTO-16910A-DM3, nomenclature for, 1315*t*
tensile strength, 768, 789
of bolt, 169, 169*f*, 170, 199
tension, 765–766, 789
and compression forces along frame, 766*f*
tension flange, 776
tension stresses, 170
tension wrench. *See* torque wrenches
tensioners, 449–450
terminal designation for circuits, 478, 480
terminal tractor, 1105, 1133
terminating resistors, 614–615
for J-1939 network, 614*f*
measuring resistance of, 615
test bench, alternator, 143, 143*f*
test certificate, 186, 186*f*, 199
test lights, 306–308, 325
circuit with, 142
self-powered LED test lights, 308
self-powered test light, 307–308, 308*f*
testing battery capacity, 373, 380–381
testing capacitors, 289
testing stators, 437
TFA. *See* time to full apply
The Maintenance Council (TMC), 827
thermal efficiency, 1300, 1337
thermal expansion valve system (TXV), 1737
removing, inspecting, and installment of, 1755, 1757
thermal fuses, 264–265, 264*f*
thermistors, 282, 282*f*, 561, 593
applications, 561*f*
circuit, 562*f*
circuit monitoring of, 583, 583*f*
inverse relationship between temperature and resistance of, 589*t*
non-linear relationship between temperature and resistance of, 589*t*
testing of, 589
Thermo King compressor, 1779, 1779*f*
thermocouple, 230, 245
electricity from, 231*f*
thermocouple principles, 231
thermocouple pyrometer, 231*f*
thermoelectric device (TED), 231
thermoelectricity, 230
thermometer, 539
in reservoir, 868, 868*f*
thermostat, OCP, 411, 411*f*
thermostatic expansion valve (TXV), 1708–1711, 1727, 1781, 1782*f*
equalization, 1708, 1709*f*
operation, 1708–1710
system, 1708, 1709*f*
use of, 1708, 1710*f*
valve spring, 1710–1711
thermostatic switch, 1721
thicker windings, 236*f*
thimble, 112
third clutch, ATEC/CEC, 1457
third-degree burns, 100, 100*f*, 103
thirteen-speed RTLOM-16913A-DM3, nomenclature for, 1315*t*
32-bit processor, 542, 542*f*
thread chaser, 132, 159
thread files, 130, 131*f*, 132
thread insert, 133
thread pitch, 169, 169*f*, 199
thread repair, 132, 159
types of, 132–133
three-channel ABS, 1088, 1089*f*
three-coil gauge, 516–517, 518*f*, 529
three Cs, 49, 65
3.0-Mhz processor, 542
three phases, AC ripple, 440*f*, 441*f*
three-position directional control valves, 1823
three-quarters floating bearing, 716, 725
3000 series transmissions, 1462
three-speed auxiliary sections, 1235–1237, 1235*f*
power flow through a deep-reduction, 1237–1239, 1237*f*–1239*f*
three-way valve, 1775–1776, 1776*f*–1777*f*, 1783
three-wire sensor
circuit monitoring, 585–587
fault code descriptions for, 589*t*
threshold limit values (TLVs), 87, 103
threshold monitoring, 632
throttle, 1449
throttle pedal position sensors, 282
throttle position sensor (TPS), 540, 541*f*, 564, 564*f*, 1447, 1447*f*, 1449
to calculate pulse width, 546, 546*f*
Hall effect, 566*f*
idle validation switch (IVS), 565, 565*f*
throttle pressure, 1406
throttle valve, 1406, 1417. *See also* modulator valves
through shaft, 1594, 1601
throws, 276
thrust angle, 747, 748*f*, 759
thrust line, 747, 748*f*, 759
thrust screw, 1612, 1639
installing, 1625–1627, 1627*f*
thrust washers, 1580, 1581*f*
tie rod arms, 1573
tie-rod ends, 743, 743*f*, 753, 754, 759, 855–856, 855*f*, 856*f*, 877
tie-rods, 732, 732*f*, 753, 754, 759, 854, 855, 877
Tiger Tool U-Joint puller, 1559, 1560*f*
tiller trucks, 1572
time division multiplexing (TDM), 603–604, 603*f*, 623
advantages of, 604–605
electronically controlled accessories, 607–609
enabling on-board diagnostics, 606–607
reduction in number of sensors, 609
software control of electrical system, 605–606
network outputs and inputs, 609–611
rule of, 603*f*
time, nonverbal message, 53
time to full apply (TFA), 1474, 1527
timing chain, 181, 199
timing gears, 181, 199
Timoney Technology, 819, 819*f*
tin, 152, 159
tin-plated copper wiring, 469
tin snips, 125, 125*f*, 159
tipper truck, 9*f*
TIR. *See* total indicated run out
tire balancing, 693–694
tire beads, 668, 674, 675*f*, 701
tire cages, 665, 665*f*
tire casings, 673, 701
tire changer, pneumatic, 138, 139*f*

tire configuration, 15*f*
tire diagnosis in commercial vehicles
  inspecting and calibrating TPMS, 698, 699
  measurement of run-outs, 695, 697–699
  repair, 694–696
tire dismounting, 686, 689, 690
tire feathering, 685
tire flap, 668, 701
tire identification and sizing, 669–671, 669*f*–670*f*, 671*t*
tire inflation factors, 678–679, 679*f*
  determination of inflation pressure, 679–680, 680*t*, 681*f*–682*f*
  inflation safety, 680–681
  nitrogen fill, 681–682
tire inflation pressure, 665, 701
tire inflators, tools, 136–137
tire life *vs.* inflation pressure, 679*f*
tire mounting, 692
tire pressure, checking and adjustment of, 685, 686
tire pressure gauges, 684–685, 684*f*, 701
  with attached inflation device, 136
  with no inflation device, 136, 137*f*
tire pressure monitoring systems (TPMS), 665–667, 667*f*, 685, 701, 725
  inspection, diagnosis and calibration of, 698, 699
tire profile, 671
  low profile tires, 672
  wide-base or super single tires, 672, 672*f*
tire regrooving, 678
tire repair, 694–696
Tire Retread and Repair Information Bureau, 675
tire rolling resistance, 664*f*
tire run-out, measurement of, 697
tire safety, 664–665, 664*f*–665*f*
  HDV wheel arrangements, 665, 666*f*
  tire pressure monitoring systems, 665–667, 667*f*
tire size, 1045*f*
tire tread separation, 677, 677*f*, 678*t*, 701
tire wear patterns, checking for, 685–687
tires. *See also* commercial vehicle tires
  inspecting, 1868, 1870–1872
  section width, 669
TLVs. *See* threshold limit values
TMC. *See* The Maintenance Council
TMC RP 618, 717, 725
  steps in, procedures, 718
toe, 742–743, 742*t*, 743*f*, 759, 1622, 1639
toe-in, 742, 742*t*, 743*f*, 750, 751, 759
toe-out, 742, 743*f*, 750, 751, 759
toe-out on turns, 737, 759
toggle switches, 277, 278*t*
ton of refrigeration (TR), 1699
tone wheel, 570
tongue weight (TW), 24, 30, 1110, 1111, 1133
tools. *See also* lubricants
  additional
    punches, 134–135, 134*f*, 135*f*
    riveting, 135–136, 135*f*
  air. *See* air tools
  cleaning equipment
    brake washers, 141
    pressure washers/cleaners, 140
    sand or bead blasters, 141
    solvent tanks, 140–141
    spray-wash cabinets, 140
  diagnostic equipment. *See* diagnostic equipment, tools
  electrical equipment. *See* electrical equipment
  and equipment fundamentals, 109–110
    identify metric or imperial designation, 109–110
    lockout/tagout, 109, 109*f*
  hand. *See* hand tools
  maintenance and repairing AC systems, 1741–1742, 1741*f*–1743*f*
  materials, 152–154
  metals, 151–152
  oxyacetylene, 139–140
  power. *See* power tools
  precision measuring, 110–117
    dial bore gauge, 113–114, 114*f*
    dial indicators, 115, 116
    feeler gauges, 116–117
    measuring tapes, 110, 110*f*
    outside, inside, and depth micrometers, 111–112, 111*f*, 113
    split ball gauge, 112, 113
    stainless steel ruler, 110, 110*f*
    straight edges, 116
    telescoping gauge, 112, 113*f*
    vernier calipers, 114–115
  preparation and safety, 108–109
    work safe and stay safe, 108–109
  vehicles, use of, 1856, 1857*t*
tooth face, 1195, 1207, 1622, 1639
top dead center (TDC), 569, 576–577
top land, 1195, 1207, 1622, 1639
top-mount worm gear, 1575, 1575*f*
top two transmission's control module, 1302, 1302*f*
topoid gear, 1577, 1601
torch handle, 140
torque, 168, 199, 518, 708, 1194, 1207
  brake, 885, 887, 887*f*, 902
torque angle, 174
torque angle gauge, 173, 175
torque balance, 991, 1033
torque break in shifting, role of, 1301–1302
torque charts, 170–171, 171*f*, 171*t*–172*t*, 1631*t*
torque converter clutch (TCC), 1359, 1360
torque converter control (TCC), 1488, 1527
torque converter housing module, 1464, 1465, 1465*f*
torque converter hydraulic circuits, 1353*f*–1355*f*
torque converter lock-up control, 1460, 1461*f*
torque converter lock-up cutch control, 1410–1411
torque converter module, 1464
torque converter oil flow, 1515
torque converters, 1342, 1367
  components of, 1344, 1344*f*
    converter shell or housing, 1344, 1344*f*, 1345*f*
    impeller or pump, 1344–1345, 1345*f*
    lock-up clutch assembly, 1346, 1346*f*
    stator or reaction member, 1345–1346, 1346*f*
    turbine, 1345, 1345*f*
  converter shell or housing, 1344*f*
  disassembling of, 1363
  failure troubleshooting, 1355–1356
    engine with smoke controls, 1358
    interpreting stall test results, 1358–1359
    leak testing, 1360, 1361
    pressure testing an automatic transmission, 1359–1361
    stall testing, 1356–1357
    testing lock-up clutch operation, 1359, 1360
  flex plate and, 1436–1437
  fundamentals of, 1342–1344, 1343*f*
  heavy-duty, 1362
  high-torque-multiplication, 1349
  hydraulic circuits, 1353–1355, 1353*f*–1355*f*
  inspecting components of, 1364
  introduction of, 1342
  leak testing, 1360, 1361, 1363–1365, 1365*f*
  light-duty, 1362
  lock-up clutch, 1359. *See also* lock-up clutch
  operation of, 1346
    flex plates, 1351–1352, 1352*f*
    lock-up clutch operation, 1352–1353, 1353*f*
    rotary flow and vortex flow, 1346–1349, 1347*f*–1348*f*
    torque converter hydraulic circuits, 1353–1355, 1353*f*–1355*f*
    torque converter operational phases, 1349–1351, 1350*f*–1351*f*
  reassembling of, 1362–1363, 1365*f*
  servicing of, 1362, 1362*f*, 1363, 1364
    reassembling torque converter, 1362–1364, 1365*f*

turbine end play and torque converter leak checks, 1363, 1365, 1365*f*
torque leaf, 804, 807, 807*f*
torque limiting, 1053–1054, 1053*f*, 1063
torque-limiting clutch brake, 1154–1155, 1154*f*
torque multiplication phase, 1349, 1350*f*, 1367
torque rise, 13, 30
torque rods, 798, 799, 799*f*, 812, 812*f*, 837
longitudinal and transverse, 823
torque sequence, 174, 174*f*
torque specification, 170, 199
torque-to-yield (TTY), 174, 199
torque-to-yield (TTY) bolts, 174, 199
torque wrenches, 172–175, 172*f*, 173*f*, 199
Torsen differential, 1584, 1601
torsion bars, 798, 837, 850, 850*f*
rotary valve and, 852, 853*f*
torsion rod, 852–853, 853*f*, 877
torsional dampening, lock-up clutch disc with, 1355, 1355*f*
torsional dampening springs, 1143*f*
torsional excitation, 1534, 1567
torsional failures, 1634
torsional vibrations, 1142, 1149–1150, 1163, 1551, 1567
torus, 1344, 1367
torx bolts, 166, 167*f*, 199
torx drivers, 166
total indicated run out (TIR), 1180, 1189
total mesh adjustment, 867, 877
tower, 467
toxic dust, 88, 103
cleaning safely, 88
TPMS. *See* tire pressure monitoring systems
TPMS-integrated valve stems, 692
TPS. *See* throttle position sensor
track rods, 798, 799, 837
tracking, 736, 759
traction battery, 334–335, 347
traction control, 1052–1055, 1063
traction motors, 1644, 1665, 1670, 1675–1677, 1687
traction tire treads, 675
tractor-engine, 1105
tractor jackknife, 992*f*
tractor protection valves, 958–960, 959*f*, 965
inspecting and testing, 1003, 1004
tractor valve, 995
tractors, 1105–1106
maximum bending moment, 768*f*
using fifth wheel, semi-trailer connects to, 1104*f*
tradesperson's triangle for calculating power, 257*f*
traditional self-diagnostic strategies, 630
trailer ABS module, 1048*f*
trailer air circuits, 957, 957*f*
gladhands, 957–958, 958*f*
trailer system valves, 958
braking priority valves, 960, 961*f*
tractor protection valves, 958–960, 959*f*
trailer air supply valve, 958
trailer brake control (TC) valve, 958
trailer spring brake valves, 960
trailer air supply valve, inspecting and testing, 1000, 1002
trailer axles, 746, 759
trailer brake control valves, 957*f*, 958, 965
inspecting and testing, 1000, 1003
trailer brake full function valve, inspecting and testing, 1003, 1005
trailer cords, 501–505
turn signal circuits, 502–505, 504*f*, 505*f*
trailer dead axles, 1574*f*
trailer gladhands, 930
trailer hitch classification, 24*t*
trailer lubrication, 1855
trailer plugs, 501–505
trailer refrigeration systems, 1769–1783. *See also* transportation refrigeration systems
components of, 1778
compressors, 1779–1780, 1779*f*–1780*f*
condenser, 1780–1781
evaporator, 1781
expansion valve, 1781, 1782*f*
liquid line drier, 1781
receiver tank, 1781, 1781*f*
fundamentals of, 1770–1772, 1771*f*–1772*f*
heating, cooling, and defrost cycles, 1774–1775, 1775*f*
cooling cycle, 1776, 1778, 1778*f*
defrost cycle, 1778, 1778*f*
heating cycle, 1776
three-way (3-way) valve, 1775–1776, 1776*f*–1777*f*
introduction to, 1770
maintenance, 1782
unique refrigeration fluids, 1781
compressor oils, 1782
refrigerant, 1781–1782, 1782*t*
trailer spring brake valves, 960
trailer supply valve, 955–956, 956*f*, 958, 965
trailer swing-out, 950, 965, 992*f*
trailering tire treads, 675
comparison of drive, steer, and, 676*t*
trailers, 1106, 1133
trailing arms, 798, 814, 837
trailing shoes, 1071, 1072*f*, 1099
transducers, 558
transfer cases, 1251–1252, 1251*f*, 1257
with power take-off option, 1251, 1252*f*
transient voltage suppression (TVS) diodes, 444, 457
transistors, 221, 294
applications, 295
bias, 295
emitter of, 295
gain, 296*f*
MOSFETS, 295–297
transit bus garage, 39*f*
transmission angle, 1546
transmission control, 1306–1307, 1306*f*, 1307*f*
transmission control module (TCM), 1359, 1488, 1488*f*, 1527, 1673, 1675, 1675*f*, 1687
scanning, 1502
transmission control unit (TCU), 1300, 1307, 1329, 1337, 1447
transmission control valves, 1404
governor valve, 1407, 1407*f*–1408*f*
hold regulator valve, 1410
main pressure regulator valve, 1404–1405, 1404*f*–1405*f*
manual selector valve, 1405–1406
modulator valve, 1406–1407, 1406*f*
priority valve, 1408, 1409*f*
shift relay valves, 1407, 1409*f*
shift signal valves, 1407–1408, 1409*f*
torque converter lock-up cutch control, 1410–1411
trimmer valves and trimmer regulator valve, 1408–1410, 1410*f*, 1411*f*
transmission electronic control module (ECM), 1300, 1337
transmission electronic control unit (ECU), 1447–1448, 1471–1472, 1474, 1527
driver's input or shift control, 1448–1449, 1449*f*
fluid sensors. *See* fluid sensors
to on-coming and off-going clutch solenoid, 1475*f*
PROM chip in, 1451
throttle position sensor, 1449
vehicle speed sensor, 1449–1450, 1450*f*
WTEC 11 and 111, 1472–1476
transmission fluid, 1343. *See also* automatic transmissions
aeration of, 1356
fundamentals of, 1422–1426
types of, 1426–1427
transmission inspection, general, 1428–1429
transmission jacks, 189
transmission lubricants, 1855
transmission oil cooler, 1354, 1367
transmission oil temperature, 1472
transmission shaft hand brake system, 1074, 1074*f*
transmission slope, 1546, 1547*f*

transmission train, 1873
  inspecting, 1874–1875
transmission vent, 1423, 1441
transmissions. *See also* automatic transmissions; hydraulically controlled automatic transmissions; standard transmission servicing; standard transmissions
  auxiliary. *See* auxiliary transmissions
  case, 1213
  collar shift, 1214, 1256
  constant mesh, 1214, 1256
  constant-mesh collar shift, 1217–1218, 1218*f*
  constant-mesh synchronized. *See* constant-mesh synchronized transmissions
  cover plates, replacing, 1269
  design, 1395–1397, 1396*f*
  electronically controlled, 1360
  failure analysis of, 1291
  fluid, changing, 1266, 1267
  gearing in truck, 1213, 1213*f*
  hydraulic control system components, 1401–1404, 1402*f*–1404*f*
    control valves. *See* transmission control valves
    hydraulic circuits, 1411–1412, 1413*f*
  hydraulically controlled, 1359
  multiple countershaft, 1227, 1256
  noise. *See* noise, transmission
  oil cooler and filter, inspection of, 1277–1278
  overhaul, 1277
  preventative maintenance of, 1266*f*
  problems troubleshooting
    air system problems, 1275*f*, 1276*f*
    gear slip out, 1273*f*, 1274*f*
    hard shifting, 1272*f*
    oil leaks, 1269
    transmission noise, 1270, 1270*f*
    vibration, 1271*f*
  reinstalling, 1186–1187
  repair and maintenance of
    inspecting air system, 1278, 1279
    inspecting power take-off, 1280
    reinstalling auxiliary section, 1289–1291, 1291*t*
    removing and disassembling auxiliary section, 1284–1285
    replacing input shaft, 1280–1282
    replacing rear seals, 1283
  shafts, 1213, 1213*f*
    main shaft, 1213–1214, 1214*f*
    reverse idler shaft, 1214
  single countershaft. *See* single countershaft transmissions
  standard, 1342, 1351
  synchronized, 1214, 1257
transport temperature control, 1770, 1783
  cooling capacity of, 1773*t*
transportation refrigeration systems
  heating principles in, 1773, 1773*t*
  types of, 1773–1774, 1773*f*–1774*f*
transverse vibrations, 1551, 1567
TranSynd fluid, 1424, 1426, 1426*f*, 1441
trapped air volume, 663, 663*f*
Traxon system, 1304, 1305*f*, 1337
tread, 675, 676*t*, 701
  depth, 678, 679*f*
  retreading tires, 675, 677–678, 677*f*–678*f*, 677*t*–678*t*
  tire regrooving, 678
treadle valve, 965. *See also* foot valves
  and brake application valve, 944, 944*f*
  testing for leakage, 1094
triangular file, 130, 130*f*
triboelectric current, 229*f*
triboelectric series, 228, 229*t*
triboelectricity, 228
trickle charger, 381, 389
tridem axle, 1573, 1601
trimmer operation, 1460–1461, 1460*f*, 1527
  torque converter lock-up control, 1460, 1461*f*
  transmission operation during electrical failure, 1460–1461, 1461*f*
trimmer regulator valve, 1408, 1410, 1411*f*, 1417
trimmer valves, 1408–1410, 1410*f*, 1417
trinary switch, 1722
trip hazards, 96
trip reports, monitoring vehicle operation, 536*f*
troubleshoot engine operation, diagnostic routines to, 536*f*
troubleshooting automated manual transmissions, 1329–1334
troubleshooting instrument gauge problems, 526–527, 527*t*
troubleshooting problems with automatic transmissions, 1427–1428
troubleshooting tooth patterns, 1625, 1626*t*
truck brake systems, legislation for, 882, 883*f*
truck dead axles, 1574
truck frames, 764
  backbone of vehicle, 765*f*
  design and construction of, 769–772
    fasteners, 771–772
    frame material, 769–770
    rails, cross members, and fasteners, 769–771
  frame-supported attachments, 772–777
  fundamentals of frame design, 764–769
  maintenance and service of, 777–787
truck service center, 37*f*
true empathy, 41
trunnions, 1532, 1537, 1567, 1815, 1833
TruTrac, 1584, 1601
TSB. *See* technical service bulletin
TTY. *See* torque-to-yield
tub, 1678
tube fittings, 1804, 1804*t*
tube-flaring tool, 133, 159
tube-type tire, 667, 668*f*, 701
  compared to tubeless tires, 668, 668*f*
  two-and three-piece split rim configurations for, 668, 669*f*
tube yokes, 1535, 1535*f*, 1567
tubeless casings, 673
tubeless tire, 667, 667*f*, 701
  compared to tube-type tires, 668, 668*f*
tubing, 1799–1801, 1801*t*, 1833
tubing cutter, 134, 134*f*, 159
tubular axles, 1574
turbine, 1344, 1345, 1345*f*, 1367
  blade, 1345*f*, 1347
  end play check, 1363, 1365, 1365*f*
  front support bushing, 1354*f*
turbine pull down, 1474, 1527
turbine shaft, 1402, 1402*f*
turbocharger boost pressure, 1007
turbocharger cut-off valves, 936–937, 937*f*, 965
turbulence, 1802, 1833
turning motion, 404
turning radius, 745, 759
turnpike, 7
TVS diodes. *See* transient voltage suppression diodes
TW. *See* tongue weight
12-volt DC systems, power calculations for, 258–259
12-volt electrical system, 430
24-volt DC systems, power calculations for, 258–259
24-volt systems, 259*f*
  advantages of, 258
Twin Extend, 1146
twin-leading-shoe drum brake, 1071, 1099
twist, 778, 778*f*, 789
twist drill, 117, 159
twisted frame, 778
twisted pair wires, induction and, 241
twisted tubing, 1554–1555, 1555*f*
twisted wire pair data buses, 613–614
twisting failures, 1634
twisting voltage-sensitive wiring, 241*f*
two-button module, trailer supply valve, 958
two-channel ABS, 1088, 1089*f*
two-coil gauge, 516–517, 517*f*
  sending units with, 522*f*
two-cylinder compressor, 931, 932*f*
two-cylinder reciprocating-piston design, air compressor, 930
two direct-acting air boosters, 1083*f*
two-height fifth wheels, 1114, 1133
two-leading brake shoes, 1072, 1072*f*
two-position directional control valves, 1822–1823, 1822*f*

two-speed auxiliary sections, 1232, 1232*f*
power flow in, 1233–1235, 1233*f*–1234*f*
two stroke Detroit diesel engine, 398
two-way communication, direct TPMS, 667
two-wire pull-up circuit monitoring, 583–585
two-wire sensor, fault code descriptions for, 589*t*
TXL, 465
TXV. *See* thermal expansion valve system; thermostatic expansion valve
type 1 circuit breakers, 266, 267*t*
type 2 circuit breakers, 266, 267*t*
type 3 circuit breakers, 266, 267*t*
type K thermocouples, 319, 325
typology, 600, 623

U

U-bolt mounts, 773–774, 773*f*, 789
U-joints, 845, 846, 877. *See also* universal joints
ULSD. *See* ultra-low sulfur diesel
ultra capacitors, 358–359, 359*f*, 360*f*, 367, 402, 402*f*
ultra-low sulfur diesel (ULSD), 149
ultra-shift transmissions models, 1155
Eaton two-pedal, 1158
UltraShift operations, Eaton Fuller AutoShift and, 1306–1314, 1337
UltraShift transmissions, 1307*f*
inertia brake in, 1312*f*
under-vehicle drive train, inspecting, 1874–1875
under-vehicle frame, 1873
under-vehicle inspections, performing, 1872–1873
under-vehicle transmission, inspecting, 1874–1875
undercharge, air conditioner capacity, 1737
orifice tube system, 1737
thermal expansion valve system, 1737
undercuts, 1822, 1822*f*, 1833
underdrive. *See* reverse reduction
underdrive ratio, 1198, 1207
underinflation, 666
underslung, 796, 837
understeer, steering-related problems, 865*t*
undertread, 678, 701
unequal charge, defective battery, 361
unipolar stepper motor, 517–518, 519*f*, 519*t*
unique system inputs, series-type hybrid drives, 1662
unique voltage signal, 526
unique voltage value, 526
United States Department of Transport (USDOT) number, 1847, 1883
universal joints (U-joint), 123, 124*f*, 845, 846, 877, 1532, 1533*f*, 1537–1538, 1538*f*, 1567
angles, 1550*f*, 1551
disassembling and inspecting with bolted end, 1561, 1562
in driveshaft, replacement of, 1559
fractures and breakage, 1554, 1555*f*
inspecting and installing of, 1561, 1563
operating angles and shaft speeds, 1543, 1543*t*
University of Michigan Transportation Research Institute, 951
unloaded alignment, loaded *vs.*, 748
unloader valves, 934–936, 936*f*, 965, 1819
unresponsive steering motion, 848
unsprung weight, 796, 796*f*, 837
untripped rollovers, 1056, 1063
upper couplers, 23, 23*f*, 30, 1112, 1115–1116, 1133
of fifth wheel, 1115*f*
service of fifth wheels and, 1122, 1124–1129
upper flanges, 770
urban transit coaches, 12–13
US Department of Transportation (DOT)
brake fluid, 148
new truck tire markings, 671, 671*t*
retreaded truck tires markings, 671, 671*t*
USDOT number. *See* United States Department of Transport number
user-formed gasket, 179–180

V

V-730 ("V") drive series, 1394
V blocks, 115, 159
V-type belts, 445–446
vacuum assist hydraulic systems, 1080–1081, 1080*f*
dual-circuit master cylinder, removing and replacement of, 1093
vacuum bleeding method, 1176, 1177
vacuum booster, 1069, 1099
vacuum brake booster, 1080–1081, 1080*f*
vacuum gauge, 1742, 1743*f*, 1765
evacuating air-conditioning system using, 1759, 1760
vacuum modulator, 1406
vacuum modulator valves, 1429
vacuum pump, 1742, 1743*f*, 1765
changing oil, 1762
validating statement, 42, 65
Valley Forge (VF) diagram, 481–483, 481*f*, 485
valve adjusting cams, 1430, 1441
valve body test stand, 1432, 1441
valve plate, 1813, 1833
valve-regulated lead–acid (VRLA) battery, 334, 334*f*, 347, 355–358
valve spring, thermostatic expansion valve (TXV), 1710–1711
valve stem, replacement of, 689, 692
valves, 934, 1410, 1417, 1819
anti-drain-back check, 1354, 1367
check, 1820
combination, 1079, 1080*f*, 1099
directional control, 1821–1823
double check, 951, 952*f*, 963
drain, 937–938, 938*f*
dump, 816
flow control, 1820–1821
foot. *See* foot valves
front axle limiter, 953–954, 954*f*
governor, 1407, 1407*f*–1408*f*, 1417
height-control, 816*f*
hold regulator, 1410, 1417
hydraulic brake. *See* hydraulic brake valves
inlet pressure regulating, 936, 963
insert, 1245, 1246*f*, 1256
inversion, 956, 956*f*, 963
limiter, 953–954, 954*f*, 963
load-sensitive, 1079
loading, 935, 963
main pressure regulator, 1402, 1404–1405, 1404*f*–1405*f*, 1417
manual selector, 1405–1406, 1417
metering, 1079, 1099
modulator, 1406–1407, 1406*f*, 1417
needle, 1820–1821, 1821*f*
one-way check, 931, 932*f*, 934, 963
pressure-compensating balance, 949, 964
pressure-compensating relay, 946, 964
pressure control, 1819–1820
pressure differential, 1079, 1079*f*, 1099
pressure protection, 937, 937*f*, 964
pressure-relief, 1823–1824
pressure-sensitive, 1079
priority, 1408, 1409*f*, 1417
proportioning, 953, 964, 1079, 1099
purge, 939, 939*f*, 964
push-pull park/emergency control, 955–956, 956*f*, 964
quick-release, 954, 954*f*–955*f*, 964
relay. *See* relay valves
reservoir safety, 934, 935*f*
residual pressure, 1076, 1099
Roadranger, 1240–1241, 1240*f*, 1243, 1257, 1275–1277, 1276*f*
safety relief, 933–934, 964
shift modulator, 1407, 1417
shift relay, 1407, 1409*f*, 1417
shift signal, 1407–1408, 1409*f*, 1417
slave air, 1244, 1257
spool, 1402, 1404, 1404*f*, 1417
spool-type directional control, 1822
three-position directional control, 1823
throttle, 1406, 1417
tractor protection, 958–960, 959*f*, 965
trailer brake control, 957*f*, 958, 965
trailer spring brake, 960
trailer supply, 955–956, 956*f*, 958, 965
transmission control. *See* transmission control valves

trimmer regulator, 1408, 1410, 1411*f*, 1417
turbocharger cut-off, 936–937, 937*f*, 965
two-position directional control, 1822–1823
unloader, 934–936, 936*f*, 965
vane power steering pump, rotary, 860, 861*f*
vane pumps, 1402, 1417, 1808, 1808*f*, 1811, 1811*f*
vane-type actuators, 1817, 1819*f*
vanes, 1808, 1817, 1833
vapor
change of heat, 1702, 1702*f*
fuel, 77–78
variable-bleed solenoids (VBS), 1488, 1489*f*, 1527
variable capacitance pressure sensor, 567–569, 593
cross section of, 568*f*
variable displacement, 1808, 1833
variable-displacement piston pumps, 1813–1814, 1813*f*
variable-displacement pump operation, 1812–1814
variable-displacement vane pumps, 1812–1813, 1813*f*
variable orifice tube (VOV), 1714
variable pitch stators, 1349, 1367
variable-rate leaf springs, 804, 804*f*
variable-ratio steering gears, 847, 847*f*, 848, 877
variable reluctance sensor (VR), 219*f*, 235*f*, 522, 569–570, 570*f*, 593, 1044, 1063
applications of, 569*f*
signals of Hall effect sensor and, 572*f*
testing of, 589
variable reluctance type sensors, 218, 540
variable resistors, 281–282
variable spring rate, 812, 837
Variable Valve Timing (VVT) system, 636
VBS. *See* variable-bleed solenoids
VDC. *See* volts direct current
VE. *See* volumetric efficiency
VECI label. *See* vehicle emission control information label
vehicle
construction, 9
electrical and mechanical systems on
electrical system, 444
history and condition, investigation of, 1632
modular construction techniques of, 474*f*
vehicle accessories, 607–608
vehicle alignment
fundamentals of, 736
alignment angles, 737–745
performing
axle tracking and parallelism, 750–751
front axle inspection, 751, 753, 754
in-service wheel alignment, 748, 749*t*
KPI and included angle, checking, 750, 752
tie-rods and tie-rod ends, inspecting and servicing, 753, 754
toe-in and toe-out, measuring, 750, 751
vehicle application, definitions of, 1263, 1264*t*
vehicle batteries, 151. *See also* batteries
vehicle charging systems, 450–452
vehicle clutch, 1142*f*
vehicle control module (VCM), 1675
vehicle driveshaft, 1593
vehicle emission control information (VECI) label, 63, 63*f*, 65
vehicle frame, conducting exterior inspections of, 777
vehicle hoists, 190–192, 199
vehicle identification number (VIN), 26–28, 26*f*, 27*f*, 30
decoding, 27–28
and production date code, 26–27
vehicle industry, materials used in, 153*t*–154*t*
vehicle information, 47–48
vehicle information labels, 63
vehicle inspection form, 51
vehicle interface module (VIM), 1334, 1449, 1449*f*, 1503
vehicle jack, 188, 189
vehicle network, 598
vehicle-powered refrigeration units, 1773, 1783
vehicle preparation, 973
vehicle resources, 55–63
labor guide, 58–59, 58*f*, 60, 65
parts program, 59, 60, 65
repair order information, 59, 61–62, 65
service campaigns and recalls, 57–58, 65
service history, 62, 62*f*, 65
service information programs, 56–57
shop manual, 56, 56*f*
technical service bulletins (TSBs), 57, 65
vehicle information labels, 63
vehicle operators' manual, 55–56, 55*f*, 65
vehicle rules for PM and PMI, 1856
vehicle safety certification (VSC) label, 63, 63*f*, 65
vehicle servicing, 70
vehicle speed sensor (VSS), 1283, 1447, 1447*f*, 1449–1450, 1450*f*, 1498, 1527
vehicle stability system, 872, 1055–1060
control modules, 1058, 1060
control systems, 1058, 1058*f*
vehicle suspension, 18
vehicle technicians, 36–37
vehicle tires. *See* commercial vehicle tires
vehicle torque, 1597
vehicle weight, 679, 1597
vehicle weight ratings, 20–21, 1108–1109
and capacity, 1107–1108
velocity, 1802, 1833
vent, 1818, 1833
ventilation, 96
verbal feedback, 42
verbal language, 42
vernier calipers, 110, 114–115, 159
vernier micrometers, 111
vertical load, 1114, 1133
VF diagram. *See* Valley Forge diagram
vibrasorbers, 1780, 1783
vibration analyzers, 321, 325
vibration control, 1149–1150
vibrations, 375, 1270, 1271*f*
critical speed, 1551
driveshaft, 1542
driveshaft system troubleshooting, 1551
analyzing driveshaft failure, 1552, 1554–1555, 1554*f*–1555*f*
diagnosing vibrations, 1551–1552, 1553*f*
drive line vibration diagnostics, 1551, 1551*f*
measuring driveshaft runout, 1552, 1554*f*
secondary couple, 1551, 1567
torsional, 1551, 1567
yoke speed, 1540–1541, 1541*f*
vice grips. *See* locking pliers
VIM. *See* vehicle interface module
VIN. *See* vehicle identification number
VIR. *See* Vehicle Inspection Report
virtual fuses, 267, 297–298
viscosity, 150, 1794, 1833
viscosity index improvers, 1855
visual inspection, 1847
visual stroke indicator, 1022*f*
vocation vehicles, 1168, 1189
vocational vehicles, 1263, 1295
VOCs. *See* volatile organic compounds
Voith DIWA transmissions. *See* DIfferential-WAndler (DIWA) transmission, Voith
volatile organic compounds (VOCs), 159
volatile RAM, 550, 553
volt, 212, 223
voltage drop, 253*f*, 254*f*, 280*f*
testing starter circuit, 418–419
wire gauges to minimize, 258*t*
voltage drop test, 258
voltage fluctuation, 439
voltage generators, 569–570
voltage reading, 376
voltage regulators, 282, 434, 435, 441–443
circuit, 431

voltage-sensing relay, 412, 413*f*
voltage spikes, 283, 284*f*, 285, 288, 411, 411*f*
voltages, 211, 223, 309. *See also* voltage—voltmeters
AGM cells, 356
amperage and, 336
Li-ion cells, 354
reading for flooded cell batteries, 338*t*
voltage—voltmeters, 314–315, 314*f*–316*f*, 316*t*
voltaic pile, 331
voltmeter, 417, 417*f*, 418, 448*f*, 451
volts, 257*f*
volts direct current (VDC), 559, 1678
volume ratio, 1474
volumetric efficiency (VE), 1809–1810
Volvo ATO2512C, nomenclature for, 1328*t*
Volvo I-shift clutch, 1144, 1144*f*
Volvo I-Shift nameplate, 1328*f*
Volvo transmission nomenclature, 1328
Volvo Trucks' I-Shift, 1327–1328, 1327*f*
Volvo Trucks' I-Shift automated manual transmission, 1305, 1305*f*
vortex flow, 1347, 1350*f*, 1367
and rotary flow, 1346–1349, 1347*f*, 1348*f*
VOV. *See* variable orifice tube
VR sensor. *See* variable reluctance sensor
Vref. *See* reference voltage
VRLA battery. *See* valve-regulated lead–acid battery
VSC label. *See* vehicle safety certification label
VSS. *See* vehicle speed sensor
VVT system. *See* variable valve timing system

W

wad punches, 135, 135*f*, 159
walk-around inspection, performing, 1858
walking beam, 837
walking beam suspensions. *See* equalizing beam (walking beam) suspensions
warding file, 130, 130*f*, 159
warning, 74, 74*f*
warning lights, 512–515, 512*f*, 514*f*, 645–646
EP system, 1684, 1685*f*
washers, types of, 168*f*
watches and jewelry, 95
water, 150
water fade, 900, 921
water freezes, 145, 145*f*
water-pump pliers, 124, 159
water wicking, 469, 485
waterfall arrangement, 1542, 1542*f*, 1567. *See also* parallel joint arrangement
water–glycol fluids, 1794
wattage, 212
Watt's law, 257–258, 258*f*
wave inverters, 218, 1661, 1665
waveforms, 218*f*
wear bars, 678, 679*f*
wear pads, 812, 812*f*
weather-pack connector, 467, 468*f*, 485
web, 770, 789
repairing a crack in, 787
webbed slings, 187
wedge brake systems, 890, 891, 891*f*, 919*f*, 921
wedge-type adjuster, 1073, 1073*f*
wedge-type coupling, 1119, 1120*f*
weight-loaded accumulators, 1824, 1826, 1826*f*
weight matching, 701
Welch plugs, 183, 1558, 1559*f*
welding, 782
amperage and voltage recommendations for, 785*t*
welding helmet, 94, 94*f*, 103
well-based rims, 686, 689, 690
wet cell battery, typical plate arrangement in, 335*f*
wet clutches, 1159–1160
wet-line, 11
wet load, 1770, 1783
wet tank, 933, 965
Wheatstone bridge electrical circuit, 567*f*
wheel alignment, 736, 759
inspection of, 1868, 1872
machine, 138, 138*f*
types of, 747–748
wheel configuration, 15*f*
wheel cylinders, 1070, 1078–1079, 1078*f*, 1099
spring brake chamber and, 1087, 1087*f*
wheel end, 706–707, 725
dual wheel, 706*f*
of single wheel, 706*f*
wheel end play, 719, 725
wheel hop, 795, 837
wheel hubs, 707*f*, 1597
types of, 716–721
wheel lock-up, 1038, 1048, 1063
wheel nut torque *vs.* clamping force, 708–709
wheel nuts, 707–708, 725
wheel offset, 707, 725
wheel pilot pads, 1013*f*
wheel rim, 707, 711–712, 725
removing and fitting tire from, 689, 691
wheel run-out, measurement of, 698
wheel slip, 1052, 1063
wheel slip torque, 1539
wheel speed sensors, 1044–1046, 1044*f*–1046*f*
wheel speeds, 1053*f*
wheel spin, 1052, 1063
wheel studs, 707–708, 725
wheels
fundamentals of, 707–709
guidelines, 708, 709
hub lubricants, 723
inspecting, 1868, 1870–1872
maintaining and servicing, and hubs, 721–723
seals, 721–723
on slippery surface, 1581*f*
types, 709–716
whining noise, 1270
wide-base tire, 672, 672*f*, 701
wide-range planar sensor, 573, 573*f*, 593
Wilson gear set, 1381, 1389
wind-up, 795–796
winding junction points, 437
windings, 236*f*, 403*f*, 408*f*, 436
armature, 399, 400, 403
field, 398–400, 398*f*
of intermittent duty magnetic switches, 285, 286*f*
primary, 238, 245
secondary, 238, 245
thicker, 236*f*
wire coil, 434
wire gauges
fuses ratings by, 265*t*
to minimize voltage drop, 258*t*
wire rope slings, 187
wire tracers, 319. *See also* circuit tracers
wire-wound (power) resistors, 279
wireless network communication, 617–618
wires
of charging circuits, 453
coil of, 432
electrodes and, 785*t*
wiring. *See* electric wiring
wiring connections, alternator, 446–449
wiring diagrams, 471
isometric, 472, 474
map, 472
schematic, 474–483
wiring harnesses, 1333, 1452, 1503
wooden peg gears, 1195*f*
wooden shipping blocks, 1183*f*, 1185, 1185*f*
work clothing, 90
care of clothing, 90
work environment, 72
work sheet, to record angles, 1545, 1546*f*
working conditions, of bus and truck technicians, 39–40
working pressure, 1796, 1833
World Transmission (WT), 1395, 1462, 1462*f*, 1463*t*
electro-hydraulic control system, 1476–1477
fifth range, 1470, 1470*f*
first range, 1468, 1468*f*
fourth generation control
hydraulic flow for, 1490*f*–1495*f*
valves in, 1495*f*
fourth range, 1469, 1470, 1470*f*
modules, 1464–1465, 1464*f*, 1465*f*
neutral power flow, 1467–1468

power flow of, 1466–1471, 1466*f*
reverse, 1471, 1472*f*
second range, 1468–1469, 1468*f*
sixth range, 1470–1471, 1471*f*
third range, 1469, 1469*f*
3000, 4000, and B series, 1462, 1464
World Transmission Electronic Control (WTEC), 1462, 1471, 1527
electro-hydraulic control. *See* electro-hydraulic control system
fifth range, 1481, 1482*f*
first range, 1477, 1478*f*
failsafe operation, 1486
fourth range, 1480, 1481*f*
neutral fluid flow, 1477
failsafe operation, 1485–1486
reverse, 1483, 1484*f*
failsafe operation, 1487–1488
second range, 1478, 1479*f*
failsafe operation, 1486
sixth range, 1482, 1483*f*
failsafe operation, 1487
third range, 1479, 1480*f*
failsafe operation, 1486–1487
worm and crown, 1575, 1601
worm gear preload adjustment, 866
worm gears, 848, 849*f*, 877, 1204–1205, 1204*f*, 1207
worm shaft, 850
worm tracks, 1412, 1412*f*
worm wheel, 1575, 1601
pin on, 1590*f*
worn gear cylinder, 870
worn gears, 577
worn power-assist piston seals, 870
wrap around probe, 307, 307*f*
wrenches, 121 122, 121*f*, 122*f*, 159, 1199
writing, effective, 48–52, 49*f*
WT. *See* World Transmission
WTEC. *See* World Transmission Electronic Control
WTEC II and III, clearing codes on, 1500–1502, 1500*f*
Wye configurations, 436, 437*f*
Wye windings, 436, 457
Wye-wound stators, 437

X

xenon lamps, 497

Y

yaw, 1056, 1063
rate sensor, 1060
yaw control, 1056, 1063
yield point, 174, 199
yield strength, 767–768, 789
yoke (release fork), 1152
yoke puller tool, 1615, 1615*f*
yoke speed vibrations, 1540–1541, 1541*f*

Z

Zener diodes, 265, 292, 293*f*, 301
Zener point, 292, 293*f*, 301
zero caster, 740*f*
zero offset, 707, 725
zero scrub radius, 745
zero-volt reference (ZVR), 583, 586, 587
zero volt return (ZVR), 563
zeroing. *See* calibration
ZF design, 1324*f*
ZF Friedrichshafen AG, 1521
ZF gear sets, 1381
ZF independent front suspension system, 819, 819*f*
ZF Intarder, 1305*f*
ZF Meritor Transmission Electronic Controller (ZMTEC), 1323
ZF O-16G10C-E18002, nomenclature for, 1326*t*
ZF rack-and-pinion steering gear, 853, 854*f*
ZF Sachs AG self-adjusting clutch, 1146
ZF transmission, 1323–1326
four solenoid-controlled air actuators in, 1325*f*
ZF Traxon transmissions, dual-clutch module and hybrid electric traction motor, 1326*f*
ZF's AS-Tronic transmission, 1323*f*
shaft gears in, 1324*f*
zipper rupture, 678, 678*f*
zirconium-dioxide (ZrO_2), 571, 573, 574
ZMTEC. *See* ZF Meritor Transmission Electronic Controller
ZrO_2. *See* zirconium-dioxide
ZTEC, 1323, 1324
ZVR. *See* zero-volt reference; zero volt return